Chambers
French
Students'
Dictionary

Chambers

CHAMBERS
An imprint of Chambers Harrap Publishers Ltd
7 Hopetoun Crescent, Edinburgh, EH7 4AY

Chambers Harrap is an Hachette UK company

© Chambers Harrap Publishers Ltd 2009

Chambers® is a registered trademark of Chambers Harrap Publishers Ltd

First published by Chambers Harrap Publishers Ltd 2009
Previously published as *Harrap's Compact French Dictionary* in 1997
Second edition published 2002
Third edition published 2007

Database right Chambers Harrap Publishers Ltd (makers)

A CIP catalogue record for this book is available from the British Library.

ISBN 978 0550 10529 5

10 9 8 7 6 5 4 3 2 1

www.chambers.co.uk

Designed by Chambers Harrap Publishers Ltd, Edinburgh
Typeset in Frutiger and Cheltenham by Chambers Harrap Publishers Ltd, Edinburgh
Printed and bound in Italy by La Tipografica Varese S.p.A.

Editor and Project Manager / Éditrice et directrice de projet
Kate Nicholson

Publishing Manager / Direction éditoriale
Anna Stevenson

Prepress / Prépresse
Isla MacLean

Contents

Table des matières

Preface

This dictionary provides the most comprehensive coverage possible of the essential vocabulary of the French and English spoken today, making it the ideal resource for users from beginner to intermediate level, whether in a learning environment, at home or in the workplace.

In addition to its very broad range of everyday vocabulary, it also contains a wide variety of terms that have recently made their way into the language, including **carbon credits, identity theft, metrosexual, billet électronique** and **grippe aviaire**. Further entries include many hundreds of idiomatic expressions and slang terms, and excellent coverage of American English and Canadian, Belgian and Swiss French. Technical terms from many fields, including IT, finance, education, media and business, will all be found alongside encyclopedic information such as proper and geographical names.

The text is enriched with boxed notes focusing on culture-specific topics which require more explanation than a simple translation can provide. There are over two hundred notes of this type in the dictionary, covering subjects as diverse as **ASBO, civil partnership** and **smoking ban** in Britain and the United States, and in the French context **exception française, DROM** and **foulard islamique**.

Finally, the supplement in the middle of the book contains verb tables and a communication guide for each language. This features model letters and advice on how to correspond in the foreign language (showing both British and American conventions on the English side), as well as advice on job applications with model CVs and letters. Last but not least, there are sections on e-mails and small ads which will help non-native speakers decipher a range of common abbreviations.

Préface

Ce dictionnaire propose un panorama très complet de l'anglais et du français d'aujourd'hui. Il constitue l'outil idéal pour tout utilisateur de niveau débutant à intermédiaire, en situation d'apprentissage comme au bureau.

En plus d'un traitement détaillé du vocabulaire de tous les jours, cet ouvrage contient des néologismes tels que **carbon credits, identity theft, metrosexual, billet électronique** et **grippe aviaire**. On y trouvera aussi des centaines d'expressions idiomatiques et des termes familiers et argotiques en abondance. Ce dictionnaire propose également des quantités d'américanismes, des canadianismes, des belgicismes et des helvétismes. Il contient en outre des termes techniques issus de domaines aussi variés que l'informatique, la finance, l'éducation, les médias et le monde des affaires, ainsi que des noms propres et des noms de lieux.

Le texte s'enrichit d'encadrés culturels lorsqu'une simple traduction ne saurait suffire à apporter l'information nécessaire au lecteur. Le dictionnaire comprend plus de deux cent encadrés de ce type qui traitent de thèmes très divers tant du côté anglais-français (**ASBO, civil partnership, smoking ban**) que du côté français-anglais (**exception française, DROM, foulard islamique**).

Le supplément qui se trouve en milieu d'ouvrage contient des tableaux de conjugaison ainsi qu'un guide de communication pour chacune des langues. Ce guide propose des modèles de lettres et des conseils pour correspondre de façon efficace dans l'autre langue (le guide aborde les conventions britanniques et américaines) ainsi que des modèles de lettres de demande d'emploi et de CV. Enfin, le guide comprend une partie sur la correspondance par e-mails et une autre sur les petites annonces, si souvent source de difficultés de compréhension en raison des nombreuses abréviations que l'on y trouve.

Structure of Entries
Structure des entrées

major ['meɪdʒə(r)] **1** *n* (**a**) *Mil (in air force)* ≃ commandant *m*, *Can & Belg* ≃ major *m*; *(in infantry)* chef *m* de bataillon; *(in cavalry)* chef *m* d'escadron; **m. general** général *m* de division (**b**) *Am Univ (subject)* matière *f* principale
2 *adj* (**a**) *(important)* majeur(e); *(most important)* principal(e); *(accident, illness)* très grave; **of m. importance** de la plus haute importance (**b**) *Mus* majeur(e)
3 *vi Am Univ* **to m. in sth** se spécialiser en qch

management ['mænɪdʒmənt] *n* (**a**) *(activity) (of company, project)* gestion *f*, direction *f*; *(of economy, resources, shop, hotel)* gestion; **m. consultant** conseiller(ère) *m,f* en gestion; **m. studies** études *fpl* de gestion (**b**) *(managers, employers)* direction *f*; **under new m.** *(sign)* changement de propriétaire; **m. buyout** = rachat d'une société par la direction; **m. team** équipe *f* dirigeante

managing director ['mænɪdʒɪŋdaɪ'rektə(r)] *n* directeur(trice) *m,f* général(e)

melt [melt] **1** *vt also Fig* faire fondre
2 *vi* fondre; **to m. into thin air** s'évaporer, disparaître; **to m. into the crowd** se fondre dans la foule
▶**melt away** *vi (of snow)* fondre; *(of clouds, vapour)* se dissiper; *(of crowd)* se disperser; *(of objections, opposition)* s'évanouir
▶**melt down** *vt sep (metal)* fondre

minute¹ ['mɪnɪt] **1** *n* (**a**) *(of time)* minute *f*; **ten minutes past/to three** trois heures dix/moins dix; **wait a m.!** attendez une minute!; **go downstairs this m.!** descends immédiatement!; **just a m.** une minute; **the m. my back was turned** dès que j'ai eu le dos tourné; **any m.** d'une minute à l'autre; **in a m.** dans une minute; **at the last m.** à la dernière minute; **m. hand** *(of watch)* grande aiguille *f*; **m. steak** steak *m* minute (**b**) *(note)* note *f*; **minutes** *(of meeting)* compte rendu *m*
2 *vt (make note of)* inscrire au procès-verbal
minute² [maɪ'njuːt] *adj* (**a**) *(small)* infime, minuscule (**b**) *(detailed)* minutieux(euse)

MOD [eməʊ'diː] *n Br Pol (abbr* **Ministry of Defence**) ministère *m* de la Défense

mollusc, *Am* **mollusk** ['mɒləsk] *n* mollusque *m*

académie [akademi] *nf* (**a**) *(des lettres, des sciences, d'art)* academy; **l'A. française** = learned society responsible for promoting the French language and imposing standards (**b**) *(école)* school, academy; **a. de musique/dessin** music/art school (**c**) *(dans l'Éducation nationale)* Br ≃ local education authority, *Am* ≃ school district

académique [akademik] *adj* (**a**) *Scol* = relating to a local education authority (**b**) *Péj (style)* conventional (**c**) *Belg, Suisse & Can* **l'année a.** the academic year

acquiescer [16] [akjese] *vi* to acquiesce (**à** to); **a. d'un signe de tête** to nod in agreement

aider [ede] **1** *vt* to help; *(sujet: gouvernement)* to aid; **que puis-je faire pour vous a.?** how may I help you?; **je me suis fait a.** par un ami I got a friend to help me; **a. qn à faire qch** to help sb to do sth; **a. qn à monter/sortir** to help sb up/out; *Ironique* **tu veux que je t'aide?** stop that!; **elle n'aide jamais** she never helps (out)
2 aider à *vt ind* to contribute towards; **a. à faire qch** to help to do sth
3 s'aider *vpr* (**a**) *(soi-même)* **s'a. de qch** to use sth; **marcher en s'aidant d'une canne/de béquilles** to walk with the aid of a stick/crutches; *Prov* **aide-toi et le ciel t'aidera** God helps those who help themselves (**b**) *(l'un l'autre)* to help each other

amnistier [66] [amnistje] *vt* to grant an amnesty to

arrière-plan (*pl* **arrière-plans**) [arjɛrplɑ̃] *nm aussi Fig* background; **à l'a.** in the background

arrière-saison (*pl* **arrière-saisons**) [arjɛrsezɔ̃] *nf Br* late autumn, *Am* late fall

arrière-train (*pl* **arrière-trains**) [arjɛrtrɛ̃] *nm (d'un animal)* (hind)quarters; *Fam (d'une personne)* rump, rear

artériosclérose [arterjoskleroz] *nf* hardening of the arteries, *Spéc* arteriosclerosis

athlétisme [atletism] *nm* athletics *(singulier);* **épreuves d'a.** athletic events

avril [avril] *nm* April; **le premier a.** *(jour des farces)* April Fools' Day; *Prov* **en a., ne te découvre pas d'un fil** ne'er cast a clout till May is out; *voir aussi* **janvier**

English Phonetic Symbols

Symboles phonétiques de l'anglais

Consonnes/Consonants

[b] but [bʌt]

[d] dab [dæb]

[dʒ] jam [dʒæm]; gem [dʒem]

[f] fat [fæt]

[g] go [gəʊ]

[h] hat [hæt]

[j] yet [jet]

[k] cat [kæt]

[l] lad [læd]

[m] mat [mæt]

[n] no [nəʊ]

[ŋ] bang [bæŋ]

[p] pat [pæt]

[r] rat [ræt]

[(r)] (seulement prononcé en cas de liaison avec le mot suivant) far [fɑː(r)]

[s] sat [sæt]

[ʃ] sham [ʃæm]

[t] tap [tæp]

[tʃ] chat [tʃæt]

[θ] thatch [θætʃ]

[ð] that [ðæt]

[v] vat [væt]

[w] wall [wɔːl]

[z] zinc [zɪŋk]

[ʒ] pleasure [pleʒə(r)]

[χ] loch [lɒχ]

Voyelles/Vowels

[æ] bat [bæt]

[ɑː] art [ɑːt]

[e] bet [bet]

[ɜː] curl [kɜːl]

[ə] amend [ə'mend]

[iː] bee [biː]

[ɪ] bit [bɪt]

[ɒ] wad [wɒd]

[ɔː] all [ɔːl]

[ʊ] put [pʊt]

[uː] shoe [ʃuː]

[ʌ] cut [kʌt]

Diphtongues/Diphthongs

[aɪ] life [laɪf]

[aʊ] house [haʊs]

[eə] there [ðeə(r)]

[eɪ] date [deɪt]

[əʊ] low [ləʊ]

[ɪə] beer [bɪə(r)]

[ɔɪ] boil [bɔɪl]

[ʊə] poor [pʊə(r)]

Symboles phonétiques du français
French Phonetic Symbols

Consonants/Consonnes

[b]	beau [bo]
[d]	donner [dɔne]
[f]	feu [fø]
[g]	garde [gard]
[ʒ]	gilet [ʒilɛ]
[k]	camp [kɑ̃]
[l]	lait [lɛ]
[m]	mon [mɔ̃]
[n]	né [ne]
[ŋ]	parking [parkiŋ]
[ɲ]	campagne [kɑ̃paɲ]
[p]	pain [pɛ̃]
[r]	rare [rar]
[s]	six [sis]
[ʃ]	chose [ʃoz]
[t]	table [tabl]
[v]	vie [vi]
[z]	zéro [zero]

Vowels/Voyelles

[a]	chat [ʃa]
[ɑ]	âge [ɑʒ]
[e]	été [ete]
[ə]	le [lə]; devin [dəvɛ̃]
[ø]	feu [fø]
[œ]	seul [sœl]
[ɛ]	père [pɛr]
[i]	vite [vit]
[ɔ]	donner [dɔne]
[o]	chaud [ʃo]
[u]	tout [tu]
[y]	cru [kry]
[ɑ̃]	enfant [ɑ̃fɑ̃]
[ɛ̃]	vin [vɛ̃]
[ɔ̃]	bon [bɔ̃]
[œ̃]	un [œ̃]

Semi-vowels/Semi-voyelles

[w]	noir [nwar]
[j]	yoga [jɔga]; rail [raj]
[ɥ]	huit [ɥit]

Abbreviations

Abréviations

gloss	=	glose
[introduces an explanation]		[introduit une explanation]
cultural equivalent	≃	équivalent culturel
[introduces a translation		[introduit une traduction
which has a roughly		dont les connotations
equivalent status in the		dans la langue cible sont
target language]		comparables]
abbreviation	*abbr, abrév*	abréviation
adjective	*adj*	adjectif
adverb	*adv*	adverbe
agriculture	*Agr*	agriculture
American English	*Am*	anglais d'Amérique du Nord
anatomy	*Anat*	anatomie
architecture	*Archit*	architecture
article	*art*	article
astrology	*Astrol*	astrologie
astronomy	*Astron*	astronomie
cars	*Aut*	automobile
auxiliary	*aux*	auxiliaire
aviation	*Aviat*	aviation
Belgian French	*Belg*	belgicisme
botany	*Bot*	botanique
British English	*Br*	anglais britannique
Canadian French	*Can*	canadianisme
chemistry	*Chem, Chim*	chimie
cinema	*Cin*	cinéma
commerce	*Com*	commerce
computing	*Comput*	informatique
conjunction	*conj*	conjonction
construction	*Constr*	construction
cooking	*Culin*	cuisine
economics	*Econ, Écon*	économie
electricity, electronics	*Elec, Élec*	électricité, électronique
European Union	*EU*	Union européenne
euphemism	*Euph*	euphémisme

exclamation	*exclam*	exclamation
feminine	*f*	féminin
familiar	*Fam*	familier
figurative	*Fig*	figuré
finance	*Fin*	finance
geography	*Geog, Géog*	géographie
geology	*Geol, Géol*	géologie
grammar	*Gram*	grammaire
history	*Hist*	histoire
humorous	*Hum*	humoristique
industry	*Ind*	industrie
invariable	*inv*	invariable
Irish English	*Ir*	anglais d'Irlande
journalism	*Journ*	journalisme
law	*Jur*	droit
linguistics	*Ling*	linguistique
literary	*Lit, Litt*	littéraire
masculine	*m*	masculin
medicine	*Med, Méd*	médecine
weather	*Met, Météo*	météorologie
military	*Mil*	militaire
music	*Mus*	musique
noun	*n*	nom
shipping	*Naut*	nautisme
feminine noun	*nf*	nom féminin
feminine plural noun	*nfpl*	nom féminin pluriel
masculine noun	*nm*	nom masculin
masculine and feminine noun [same form for both genders]	*nmf*	nom masculin et féminin [formes identiques]
masculine and feminine noun [different form in the feminine]	*nm,f*	nom masculin et féminin [formes différentes]
masculine plural noun	*nmpl*	nom masculin pluriel
plural noun	*npl*	nom pluriel
proper noun	*npr*	nom propre
officially approved term	*Offic*	recommandation officielle
computing	*Ordinat*	informatique
parliament	*Parl*	parlement
pejorative	*Pej, Péj*	péjoratif
photography	*Phot*	photographie
physics	*Phys*	physique
plural	*pl*	pluriel
politics	*Pol*	politique

past participle	*pp*	participe passé
prefix	*pref, préf*	préfixe
preposition	*prep, prép*	préposition
proper noun	*pr n*	nom propre
pronoun	*pron*	pronom
proverb	*Prov*	proverbe
psychology	*Psy*	psychologie, psychiatrie
past tense	*pt*	prétérit
something	*qch*	quelque chose
somebody	*qn*	quelqu'un
registered trademark	®	marque déposée
radio	*Rad*	radio
rail	*Rail*	chemins de fer
religion	*Rel*	religion
somebody	*sb*	quelqu'un
school	*Sch, Scol*	domaine scolaire
Scottish English	*Scot*	anglais d'Écosse
formal	*Sout*	soutenu
specialist term	*Spec, Spéc*	vocabulaire de spécialité
something	*sth*	quelque chose
suffix	*suff*	suffixe
technical term	*Tech*	terme technique
telecommunications	*Tel, Tél*	télécommunications
textiles	*Tex*	textile
theatre	*Theat, Théât*	théâtre
television	*TV*	télévision
typography, printing	*Typ*	typographie, imprimerie
European Union	*UE*	Union européenne
university	*Univ*	domaine universitaire
verb	*v*	verbe
intransitive verb	*vi*	verbe intransitif
reflexive verb	*vpr*	verbe pronominal
transitive verb	*vt*	verbe transitif
transitive verb used with a preposition [e.g. **parvenir** à (to reach); ils sont **parvenus** à un accord (they reached an agreement)]	*vt ind*	verbe transitif indirect [par exemple: **parvenir** à; ils sont **parvenus** à un accord]
inseparable transitive verb [phrasal verb where the verb and the adverb or preposition cannot be separated, e.g. **look after**; he **looked after** the children]	*vt insep*	verbe transitif à particule inséparable [par exemple: **look after** (s'occuper de); he **looked after** the children (il s'occupait des enfants)

separable transitive verb [phrasal verb where the verb and the adverb or preposition can be separated, e.g. **send back**; she **sent** the present **back** *or* she **sent back** the present]	*vt sep*	verbe transitif à particule séparable [par exemple; **send back** (rendre); she **sent** the present **back** *ou* **she** **sent back** the present (elle a rendu le cadeau)]
vulgar	*Vulg*	vulgaire
zoology	*Zool*	zoologie

All other labels are written in full.
Toutes les autres indications d'usage sont données en entier.

English-French
Anglais-Français

A, a¹ [eɪ] n (**a**) (letter) A, a m inv; **to get from A to B** aller d'un point à un autre; **from A to Z** de A à Z; **A bomb** bombe f A; Br Sch **A level** = diplôme de fin d'études secondaires sanctionnant une matière déterminée; Br Sch **A levels** ≃ baccalauréat m; Br **A road** ≃ (route f) nationale f; **A side** (of record) face f A; **A-Z** (street guide) index m des rues; **an A-Z of gardening** le jardinage de A à Z (**b**) Sch (grade) **to get an A** (in exam) avoir mention bien ou très bien; (in homework, essay) ≃ avoir entre 14 et 20 (**c**) Mus la m inv

A levels
Cet examen, qui ouvre l'accès aux études supérieures en Grande-Bretagne, est beaucoup plus spécialisé que le baccalauréat français ; il ne comprend que deux ou trois matières (exceptionellement quatre). D'autre part, les mentions sont très importantes pour pouvoir choisir l'université où l'on souhaite faire ses études. En Écosse l'examen équivalent aux "A levels" s'appelle le "Higher" ou "Higher Grade".

a² [ə, stressed eɪ]

a devient **an** [ən, stressed æn] devant voyelle ou h muet.

indefinite art (**a**) (in general) un (une); **a man** un homme; **a woman** une femme; **an hour** une heure; **he's got a red nose** il a le nez rouge; **I haven't got a car** je n'ai pas de voiture; **what a day!** quelle journée! (**b**) (with professions, nationalities) **he's an Englishman/a father/a lawyer** il est anglais/père/avocat (**c**) (with prices, rates) **30 pence a kilo** 30 pence le kilo; **three times a week** trois fois par semaine; **50 kilometres an hour** 50 kilomètres (à l')heure (**d**) (a certain) **a Mr Watkins phoned** un certain M. Watkins a appelé

AA [eɪ'eɪ] n (**a**) (abbr **Automobile Association**) = club automobile britannique offrant notamment des services de dépannage (**b**) (abbr **Alcoholics Anonymous**) AA mpl

AAA n (**a**) ['θriː'eɪz] Br (abbr **Amateur Athletics Association**) = fédération britannique d'athlétisme (**b**) [trɪpəl'eɪ] Am (abbr **American Automobile Association**) = club automobile américain

A & E [eɪænd'iː] n Br Med (abbr **accident and emergency**) service m des urgences, urgences fpl

A & R [eɪənd'ɑː(r)] n (abbr **artists and repertoire**) = service d'une maison de disque chargé de recruter de nouveaux artistes; **A & R man** = personne qui recrute de nouveaux artistes

AB [eɪ'biː] n Am (abbr **Artium Baccalaureus**) (diploma) ≃ licence f de lettres; (graduate) ≃ licencié(e) m,f ès lettres

abaci ['æbəsaɪ] pl of abacus

aback [ə'bæk] adv taken a. (by) déconcerté(e) (par)

abacus ['æbəkəs] (pl **abaci** ['æbəsaɪ] or **abacuses** ['æbəkəsɪz]) n boulier m

abandon [ə'bændən] **1** n with a. avec abandon; **to drive with reckless a.** conduire avec insouciance **2** vt abandonner; (match) interrompre; **to a. ship** abandonner le navire

abase [ə'beɪs] vt **to a. oneself** s'abaisser, s'humilier

abashed [ə'bæʃt] adj penaud(e); **to be** or **feel a. (at sth)** avoir honte (de qch)

abate [ə'beɪt] vi (of storm, pain) se calmer; (of noise) diminuer

abattoir ['æbətwɑː(r)] n abattoir m

abbess ['æbɪs] n abbesse f

abbey ['æbɪ] (pl **abbeys**) n abbaye f

abbot ['æbət] n abbé m

abbreviate [ə'briːvɪeɪt] vt abréger

abbreviation [əbriːvɪ'eɪʃən] n abréviation f

ABC [eɪbiː'siː] n (**a**) (alphabet) alphabet m; **an ABC of gardening** un ABC du jardinage (**b**) (abbr **American Broadcasting Corporation**) = chaîne de télévision américaine (**c**) (abbr **Australian Broadcasting Corporation**) = chaîne de télévision australienne

abdicate ['æbdɪkeɪt] **1** vt **to a. the throne** abdiquer; **to a. responsibility** abdiquer devant ses responsabilités **2** vi (of monarch) abdiquer

abdication [æbdɪ'keɪʃən] n (of throne) abdication f; (of responsibilities) abandon m

abdomen ['æbdəmən] n Anat & Zool abdomen m

abdominal [æb'dɒmɪnəl] adj Anat abdominal(e)

abdominals [æb'dɒmɪnəlz] npl (muscles, exercises) abdominaux mpl

abduct [əb'dʌkt] vt enlever

abduction [əb'dʌkʃən] n enlèvement m

aberration [æbə'reɪʃən] n aberration f; **in a moment of a.** dans un moment de folie

abet [ə'bet] (pt & pp abetted) vt Law **to aid and a. sb** être le complice de qn

abetting [ə'betɪŋ] n Law aiding and a. complicité f

abeyance [ə'beɪəns] n **in a.** (of law, custom) en désuétude

abhor [əb'hɔː(r)] (pt & pp abhorred) vt détester, avoir horreur de

abhorrence [əb'hɒrəns] n horreur f

abhorrent [əb'hɒrənt] adj odieux(euse)

abide [ə'baɪd] *vt (tolerate)* **I can't a.** **him** je ne peux pas le supporter
▸**abide by** *vt insep (promise)* tenir; *(rule, decision)* se plier à, se soumettre à; **I a.** **by what I said** je maintiens ce que j'ai dit
abiding [ə'baɪdɪŋ] *adj (impression)* durable; **my a. memory of him is his generosity** je garde de lui le souvenir de quelqu'un de très généreux
ability [ə'bɪlɪtɪ] *(pl abilities)* n (**a**) *(talent, skill)* capacités *fpl* (**in** en), compétence *f* (**in** en) (**b**) *(capability)* capacité *f* (**to** à); **to the best of one's a.** de son mieux
abject ['æbdʒekt] *adj (miserable)* malheureux(euse); *(contemptible)* abject(e); **to make an a. apology** s'excuser platement; **a. poverty** misère *f* noire
ablaze [ə'bleɪz] *adj* en feu, en flammes; **to set sth a.** embraser qch; *Fig* **her eyes were a. with anger** ses yeux brillaient de colère
able ['eɪbəl] *adj* (**a**) *(competent) (person, performance)* compétent(e) (**b**) **to be a. to do sth** *(be physically capable)* pouvoir faire qch; *(know how to)* savoir faire qch; **I won't be a. to come** je ne pourrai pas venir; **we waited all afternoon, but we weren't a. to see him** nous avons attendu tout l'après-midi mais nous n'avons pas réussi à le voir
able-bodied ['eɪbəl'bɒdɪd] *adj* robuste; *Naut* **a. seaman** matelot *m* de deuxième classe
ably ['eɪblɪ] *adj* de façon compétente; **a. assisted by** efficacement assisté par
abnormal [æb'nɔːməl] *adj* anormal(e)
abnormality [æbnɔː'mælɪtɪ] *(pl abnormalities)* n *(irregularity)* anomalie *f*; *(physical)* malformation *f*
abnormally [æb'nɔːməlɪ] *adv* anormalement
aboard [ə'bɔːd] **1** *adv (on ship, aeroplane)* à bord; **to go a.** monter à bord
2 *prep (ship, aeroplane)* à bord de; *(bus, train)* dans
abode [ə'bəʊd] n *Lit* demeure *f*; *Law* **of no fixed a.** sans domicile fixe; *Law* **right of a.** droit *m* de séjour
abolish [ə'bɒlɪʃ] *vt* abolir; *(law)* abroger
abolition [æbə'lɪʃən] n abolition *f*; *(of law)* abrogation *f*
abominable [ə'bɒmɪnəbəl] *adj* abominable; **the a. snowman** l'abominable homme *m* des neiges
abomination [əbɒmɪ'neɪʃən] n abomination *f*
aborigine [æbə'rɪdʒɪnɪ] n aborigène *mf*
abort [ə'bɔːt] **1** *vt* (**a**) *Med (woman)* avorter; **the foetus was aborted** la grossesse a été interrompue (**b**) *(project) & Comput* abandonner
2 *vi Med* avorter, faire une fausse couche
abortion [ə'bɔːʃən] n avortement *m*, IVG *f*; **to have an a.** se faire avorter
abortive [ə'bɔːtɪv] *adj (attempt, plan)* avorté(e)
abound [ə'baʊnd] *vi* abonder (**in** or **with** en)
about [ə'baʊt] **1** *prep* (**a**) *(regarding)* **a book a. France** un livre sur la France; **the good/bad thing a....** ce qu'il y a de bien/de mauvais dans...; **what's it a.?** de quoi s'agit-il?; **to talk a. sth** parler de qch; **to argue a. sth** se disputer au sujet de qch; **we must do something a. this problem** il faut faire quelque chose à ce sujet
(**b**) *(in various parts of)* **to walk a. the town** se promener dans la ville; **to look a. the room** parcourir la pièce du regard
2 *adv* (**a**) *(in different directions, places)* **to walk a.** se promener; **to run a.** courir à droite et à gauche; **to be lying a.** traîner
(**b**) *(in the general area)* **is Jack a.?** est-ce que Jack est

dans les environs *ou* parages?; **there was nobody a.** il n'y avait personne
(**c**) *(approximately)* environ, à peu près; **a. thirty** environ trente, une trentaine; **a. ten years** environ dix ans, une dizaine d'années; **at a. one o'clock** vers une heure; **she's a. as tall as you** elle est grande à peu près comme toi; **I've just a. finished** j'ai pratiquement terminé; **a. time!** ce n'est pas trop tôt!
(**d**) *(on the point of)* **to be a. to do sth** aller faire qch, être sur le point de faire qch; **I'm not a. to... (have no intention of)** je n'ai pas l'intention de...
about-face [əbaʊt'feɪs], **about-turn** [əbaʊt'tɜːn] n *(radical change)* volte-face *f inv*
above [ə'bʌv] **1** *prep* (**a**) *(physically)* au-dessus de; **the Seine a. Paris** la Seine en amont de Paris
(**b**) *(with numbers)* plus de; **the temperature didn't rise a. 10°C** la température n'a pas dépassé 10°C
(**c**) *(in rank)* **he is a. me** il est mon supérieur
(**d**) *(not subject to)* **to be a. suspicion** être au-dessus de tout soupçon; **her behaviour is a. criticism** il n'y a rien à redire à son attitude
(**e**) *(superior to)* **he thinks he's a. all that** il se croit au-dessus de tout ça; **she's not a. telling lies** elle est capable de mentir; **to get a. oneself** se donner des airs
(**f**) **a. all** surtout; **they value friendship a. all else** ils font passer l'amitié avant tout le reste
2 *adv* (**a**) *(in general)* au-dessus; **the tenants (of the flat) a.** les locataires du dessus; **from a.** *(from one's superiors)* d'en haut
(**b**) *(in book, document)* ci-dessus
above-board [əbʌv'bɔːd] *adj (honest)* franc (franche), honnête
above-mentioned [əbʌv'menʃənd], **above-named** [əbʌv'neɪmd] *adj* susdit(e), susnommé(e)
abrasion [ə'breɪʒən] n *(on skin)* écorchure *f*
abrasive [ə'breɪsɪv] **1** n *(substance)* abrasif *m*
2 *adj (surface, substance)* abrasif(ive); *(person, manner)* caustique
abreast [ə'brest] *adv* de front; **to come a. of** arriver à la hauteur de; **a. keep a. of** *(events, progress)* se tenir au courant de
abridged [ə'brɪdʒd] *adj* abrégé(e)
abroad [ə'brɔːd] *adv* à l'étranger; **our colleagues from a.** nos collègues étrangers; **to get a.** *(of news)* se répandre
abrupt [ə'brʌpt] *adj* (**a**) *(sudden)* brusque, soudain(e); **the train came to an a. halt** le train s'est brusquement *ou* soudainement arrêté (**b**) *(curt)* abrupt(e), brusque
abruptly [ə'brʌptlɪ] *adv* (**a**) *(suddenly)* brusquement, soudainement (**b**) *(curtly)* de façon abrupte, avec brusquerie
abscess ['æbses] n abcès *m*
abscond [əb'skɒnd] *vi Formal* s'enfuir, prendre la fuite
abseil ['æbseɪl] *vi* descendre en rappel; **to a. down sth** descendre qch en rappel
abseiling ['æbseɪlɪŋ] n rappel *m*, descente *f* en rappel; **to go a.** faire du rappel
absence ['æbsəns] n absence *f*; **in the a. of** *(person)* en l'absence de; *(thing)* faute de; *Law* **sentenced in one's a.** condamné(e) par contumace; *Prov* **a. makes the heart grow fonder** l'éloignement renforce l'affection
absent 1 *adj* ['æbsənt] *(pupil, expression)* absent(e); *Mil* **a. without leave** porté(e) manquant(e)
2 *vt* [æb'sent] **to a. oneself (from)** s'absenter (de)

absentee [æbsən'tiː] *n* absent(e) *m,f*; **a.** landlord propriétaire *mf* absentéiste
absenteeism [æbsən'tiːɪzm] *n* absentéisme *m*
absent-minded [æbsənt'maɪndɪd] *adj* distrait(e)
absent-mindedness [æbsənt'maɪndɪdnɪs] *n* distraction *f*
absolute ['æbsəluːt] *adj* (**a**) *(total)* absolu(e); **a.** majority majorité *f* absolue; **a.** monarch monarque *mf* absolu(e) (**b**) *(emphatic)* he's an a. fool! il est complètement idiot!; **a.** nonsense! n'importe quoi!; **an a.** disgrace/disaster un véritable scandale/désastre
absolutely [æbsə'luːtlɪ] *adv* absolument; you're a. right vous avez absolument *ou* tout à fait raison; do you support him? – a./a. not vous le soutenez? – absolument/absolument pas
absolution [æbsə'luːʃən] *n Rel* absolution *f*
absolve [əb'zɒlv] *vt Rel* absoudre (**from** *or* **of** de); *(from duty)* dispenser (**from** *or* **of** de); to be absolved from blame être innocenté(e)
absorb [əb'zɔːb] *vt (liquid)* absorber; *(losses)* essuyer; to be absorbed in sth être absorbé(e) par qch
absorbent [əb'zɔːbənt] *adj* absorbant(e); *Am* a. cotton coton *m* hydrophile
absorbing [əb'zɔːbɪŋ] *adj (work)* absorbant(e); *(book, question)* passionnant(e)
abstain [əb'steɪn] *vi* s'abstenir (**from** de)
abstemious [əb'stiːmɪəs] *adj* sobre
abstention [əb'stenʃən] *n Pol* abstention *f*
abstinence ['æbstɪnəns] *n* abstinence *f*
abstract ['æbstrækt] **1** *n* (**a**) *(concept)* the a. l'abstrait *m* (**b**) *(of article)* résumé *m*
2 *adj* abstrait(e)
3 *vt* [æb'strækt] *Formal (remove)* extraire (**from** de)
abstraction [æb'strækʃən] *n* abstraction *f*
abstruse [əb'struːs] *adj* obscur(e)
absurd [əb'sɜːd] *adj* absurde
absurdity [əb'sɜːdɪtɪ] *(pl* absurdities) *n* absurdité *f*
ABTA ['æbtə] *n (abbr* Association of British Travel Agents) = association d'agences de voyage britanniques
abundance [ə'bʌndəns] *n* abondance *f*; an a. of talent un grand talent; in a. en abondance
abundant [ə'bʌndənt] *adj* abondant(e); to be a. in sth abonder en qch
abundantly [ə'bʌndəntlɪ] *adv* en abondance; a. clear tout à fait clair(e)
abuse **1** *n* [ə'bjuːs] (**a**) *(of power)* abus *m* (**b**) *(insults)* injures *fpl*, insultes *fpl*; term of a. injure *f*, insulte *f* (**c**) *(cruelty)* mauvais traitements *mpl*, maltraitance *f*; (**sexual**) a. sévices *mpl* sexuels
2 *vt* [ə'bjuːz] (**a**) *(misuse)* abuser de (**b**) *(insult)* injurier, insulter (**c**) *(ill-treat) (physically)* maltraiter; *(sexually)* faire subir des sévices sexuels à
abusive [ə'bjuːsɪv] *adj (person, language)* grossier(ère)
abysmal [ə'bɪzməl] *adj (ignorance)* sans bornes; *(performance, quality)* épouvantable
abyss [ə'bɪs] *n also Fig* abîme *m*, gouffre *m*
AC ['eɪ'siː] *n Elec (abbr* alternating current) courant *m* alternatif
a/c *n (abbr* account) compte *m*
academic [ækə'demɪk] **1** *n (university teacher)* universitaire *mf*; *(intellectual)* intellectuel(elle) *m,f*
2 *adj* (**a**) *(of school)* scolaire; *(of university)* universitaire; her a. achievements are impressive elle a fait de brillantes études; a. year année *f* universitaire (**b**) *(intellectual)* intellectuel(elle) (**c**) *(theoretical)*

théorique; it's entirely a. whether he did it or not qu'il l'ait fait ou non n'a aucune importance
academy [ə'kædəmɪ] *(pl* academies) *n* académie *f*; a. of music conservatoire *m* (de musique)
ACAS ['eɪkæs] *n (abbr* Advisory, Conciliation and Arbitration Service) = organisme britannique indépendant d'arbitrage des conflits du travail
accede [æk'siːd] *vi Formal* (**a**) to a. to *(request, demand)* accéder à; *(agreement, changes)* accepter (**b**) *(of monarch)* to a. to the throne accéder au trône
accelerate [ək'seləreɪt] **1** *vt (progress)* accélérer; *(downfall)* précipiter
2 *vi (of car, driver)* accélérer; *(of pace)* s'accélérer
acceleration [əkselə'reɪʃən] *n* accélération *f*
accelerator [ək'seləreɪtə(r)] *n* accélérateur *m*
accent ['æksənt] *n* accent *m*; to put the a. on sth *(emphasize)* mettre l'accent sur qch
accentuate [æk'sentʃueɪt] *vt* accentuer
accept [ək'sept] *vt* (**a**) *(gift, apology, defeat)* accepter; *(responsibility)* assumer (**for** de); *(concede)* admettre; to a. (that)... admettre que... (**b**) *(into university)* admettre
acceptable [ək'septəbəl] *adj* acceptable; to be a. to sb *(suit)* convenir à qn
acceptance [ək'septəns] *n* (**a**) *(of invitation, apology, defeat)* acceptation *f*; to find a. être reconnu(e) (**b**) *(to university)* admission *f*; a. speech = discours prononcé par le lauréat d'un prix
access ['ækses] **1** *n* accès *m* (**to** à); to have a. to sth avoir accès à qch; to gain a. to *(get inside)* s'introduire dans; *(reach)* accéder à; *Br* a. ramp bretelle *f* d'accès; a. road route *f* d'accès; *Br (of motorway)* bretelle *f* d'accès; *Comput* a. code code *m* d'accès; *Comput* a. provider fournisseur *m* d'accès; *Comput* a. time temps *m* d'accès
2 *vt Comput* accéder à
accessible [ək'sesəbəl] *adj (place, explanation)* accessible; *(person)* joignable
accession [ək'seʃən] *n (to power, throne)* accession *f*; *EU* a. countries pays *mpl* en phase d'adhésion
accessory [ək'sesərɪ] *(pl* accessories) *n* (**a**) *(extra)* accessoire *m* (**b**) *Law* complice *mf* (**to** de)
accident ['æksɪdənt] *n* accident *m*; by a. par accident *ou* hasard; to have an a. avoir un accident; *Br Med* a. and emergency (unit) service *m* des urgences, urgences *fpl*; a. insurance assurance *f* accidents
accidental [æksɪ'dentəl] *adj* accidentel(elle); *Law* a. death mort *f* accidentelle
accidentally [æksɪ'dentəlɪ] *adv* accidentellement
accident-prone ['æksɪdəntprəʊn] *adj* prédisposé(e) aux accidents
acclaim [ə'kleɪm] **1** *n* louanges *fpl*; to meet with great critical a. être salué(e) par la critique
2 *vt (person)* acclamer; *(performance, film)* applaudir
acclamation [æklə'meɪʃən] *n (cheering)* acclamations *fpl*
acclimatize [ə'klaɪmətaɪz] **1** *vt (animal, plant)* acclimater; to become acclimatized to *(person)* s'habituer à, s'accoutumer à
2 *vi* s'acclimater (**to** à)
accolade ['ækəleɪd] *n* honneur *m*
accommodate [ə'kɒmədeɪt] *vt* (**a**) *(provide room for)* loger (**b**) *(satisfy)* satisfaire
accommodating [ə'kɒmədeɪtɪŋ] *adj (helpful)* obligeant(e); *(easy to please)* accommodant(e)

accommodation [əkɒmə'deɪʃən] *n* (**a**) *(lodging)* logement *m*; *(in hotel)* chambre *f* (d'hôtel) (**b**) *Formal (agreement)* compromis *m*

accompaniment [ə'kʌmpənɪmənt] *n Mus* accompagnement *m*; *Culin* garniture *f*

accompany [ə'kʌmpənɪ] *(pt & pp* **accompanied**) *vt* accompagner; **to be accompanied by sth** s'accompagner de qch

accomplice [ə'kʌmplɪs] *n* complice *mf*

accomplish [ə'kʌmplɪʃ] *vt (task)* accomplir; *(aim)* atteindre

accomplished [ə'kʌmplɪʃt] *adj (musician, cook)* accompli(e); *(actor)* doué(e); *(performance)* très au point

accord [ə'kɔːd] **1** *n* accord *m*; **in a. with** en accord avec; **with one a.** d'un commun accord; **of one's own a.** de son plein gré
2 *vt* accorder (**to** à)
▸**accord with** *vt insep* concorder avec

accordance [ə'kɔːdəns] *n* **in a. with** en accord avec; **his statement is not in a. with the facts** sa déclaration ne concorde pas avec les faits

according to [ə'kɔːdɪŋtuː] *prep* (**a**) *(depending on)* selon; **a. whether one is rich or poor** selon que l'on est riche ou pauvre; **a. which method you use** selon la méthode utilisée (**b**) *(in conformity with)* selon; **to go a. plan** se dérouler comme prévu (**c**) *(citing a source)* selon, d'après

accordingly [ə'kɔːdɪŋlɪ] *adv* (**a**) *(appropriately)* en conséquence (**b**) *(therefore)* par conséquent

accordion [ə'kɔːdɪən] *n* accordéon *m*

accost [ə'kɒst] *vt* accoster, aborder

account [ə'kaʊnt] *n* (**a**) *(at bank)* compte *m*; *Com* **accounts department** comptabilité *f* (**b**) *(reckoning)* to **keep (an) a. of sth** tenir un compte de qch; **to take sth into a., to take a. of sth** *(consider)* tenir compte de qch, prendre qch en compte; **taking everything into a.** *(after all)* au bout du compte; **to call sb to a.** demander des comptes à qn; **to be brought to a.** avoir des comptes à rendre (**c**) *(importance)* **of no a.** sans importance (**d**) **on a. of** *(because of)* à cause de; **on no a., not on any a.** en aucun cas, surtout pas; **to set up in business on one's own a.** s'installer à son compte; **don't do it on my a.!** ne le faites surtout pas pour moi! (**e**) *(report)* description *f*; **to give an a. of sth** faire le récit de qch; *Fig* **to give a good a. of oneself** *(in fight, contest)* bien se défendre; **by all accounts** au dire de tous
▸**account for** *vt insep* (**a**) *(explain, justify)* expliquer; **five people have still not been accounted for** *(are still missing)* cinq personnes n'ont toujours pas été retrouvées; **there's no accounting for taste** chacun ses goûts (**b**) *(constitute)* constituer

accountability [əkaʊntə'bɪlɪtɪ] *n* responsabilité *f* (**to** envers)

accountable [ə'kaʊntəbəl] *adj* responsable (**to sb** envers qn; **for sth** de qch); *(for sum of money)* redevable (**for** de); **to hold sb a.** tenir qn pour responsable

accountancy [ə'kaʊntənsɪ] *n* comptabilité *f*

accountant [ə'kaʊntənt] *n* comptable *mf*

accounting [ə'kaʊntɪŋ] *n* comptabilité *f*; **a. period** période *f* comptable

accrue [ə'kruː] *vi Fin (of interest)* s'accumuler; **to a. to sb** *(of interest, benefits)* revenir à qn

accumulate [ə'kjuːmjʊleɪt] **1** *vt* accumuler
2 *vi* s'accumuler

accumulation [əkjuːmjʊ'leɪʃən] *n* accumulation *f*

accuracy ['ækjʊrəsɪ] *n (of calculation, translation)* exactitude *f*, précision *f*; *(of firearm, shot)* précision; *(of portrayal)* fidélité *f*

accurate ['ækjʊrət] *adj (calculation, translation)* exact(e), précis(e); *(firearm, shot)* précis(e); *(portrayal)* fidèle

accurately ['ækjʊrətlɪ] *adv (calculate, translate)* avec exactitude *ou* précision; *(aim)* avec précision; *(portray)* fidèlement

accusation [ækjʊ'zeɪʃən] *n* accusation *f*; **to make an a. (against sb)** porter *ou* lancer une accusation (contre qn)

accuse [ə'kjuːz] *vt* **to a. sb (of sth/of doing sth)** accuser qn (de qch/de faire qch)

accused [ə'kjuːzd] *(pl* **accused**) *n Law* **the a.** l'inculpé(e) *m,f*

accuser [ə'kjuːzə(r)] *n* accusateur(trice) *m,f*

accusing [ə'kjuːzɪŋ] *adj (look, tone)* accusateur(trice)

accustom [ə'kʌstəm] *vt* accoutumer, habituer; **to be accustomed to sth/to doing sth** être habitué à qch/ à faire qch; **to get** *or* **grow accustomed to sth/to doing sth** s'accoutumer *ou* s'habituer à qch/à faire qch

AC/DC ['eɪsiː'diːsiː] **1** *n Elec (abbr* **alternating current/direct current)** courant alternatif/courant continu
2 *adj Fam (bisexual)* **to be A.** marcher à voile et à vapeur

ace [eɪs] **1** *n* (**a**) *(in cards)* as *m*; **a. of spades** as de pique; *Fig* **to have an a. up one's sleeve** avoir un atout en réserve; **to come within an a. of doing sth** être à deux doigts de faire qch (**b**) *(tennis)* ace *m* (**c**) *Fam (expert)* as *m*; **flying a.** as *m* de l'aviation
2 *adj Br Fam (very good)* super *inv*

acerbic [ə'sɜːbɪk] *adj* acerbe

acetate ['æsɪteɪt] *n Chem* acétate *m*

acetic acid [æ'siːtɪk'æsɪd] *n* acide *m* acétique

ache [eɪk] **1** *n* douleur *f*; **aches and pains** douleurs *fpl*
2 *vi (of person)* avoir mal; **my head aches** j'ai mal à la tête; **my leg aches** j'ai mal à la jambe, ma jambe me fait mal; *Fig* **to be aching to do sth** mourir d'envie de faire qch

achieve [ə'tʃiːv] *vt (aim)* atteindre, parvenir à; **to a. success** réussir; **to a. a lot** faire beaucoup de chemin

achievement [ə'tʃiːvmənt] *n (action)* réalisation *f*; *(thing achieved)* réussite *f*

Achilles' heel [əkɪliːz'hiːl] *n* talon *m* d'Achille

acid ['æsɪd] **1** *n* (**a**) *(chemical)* acide *m* (**b**) *Fam (LSD)* acide *m*; **a. house** *(music)* acid house *m*
2 *adj* (**a**) *(chemical, taste)* acide; **a. rain** pluies *fpl* acides; *Fig* **a. test** test *m* décisif (**b**) *(tone, remark)* aigre

acidic [ə'sɪdɪk] *adj* acide; *(tone, remark)* aigre

acidity [ə'sɪdɪtɪ] *n (of chemical, taste)* acidité *f*; *(of tone, remark)* aigreur *f*

acknowledge [ək'nɒlɪdʒ] *vt (mistake, debt, truth)* admettre, reconnaître; **to a. (receipt of) a letter** accuser réception d'une lettre; **this restaurant is acknowledged to be the best in the city** ce restaurant est reconnu comme le meilleur de la ville; **she didn't a. me** *or* **my presence** elle m'a ignoré

acknowledg(e)ment [ək'nɒlɪdʒmənt] *n (of mistake, debt, truth)* reconnaissance *f*; **in a. of** *(service, achievement)* en reconnaissance de; *(letter)* en réponse à); **acknowledg(e)ments** *(in book)* remerciements *mpl*; **a. slip** *(for letter)* accusé *m* de réception

ACLU ['eɪsiːeljuː] n (abbr **American Civil Liberties Union**) = organisme américain qui milite pour les droits civiques
acne ['æknɪ] n acné f
acolyte ['ækəlaɪt] n disciple mf
acorn ['eɪkɔːn] n gland m
acoustic [ə'kuːstɪk] adj acoustique; **a. guitar** guitare f acoustique
acoustics [ə'kuːstɪks] npl acoustique f
acquaint [ə'kweɪnt] vt (**a**) (with person) **to be acquainted with sb** connaître qn; **to become** or **get acquainted (with)** faire ou lier connaissance (avec) (**b**) (with facts, situation) **to be acquainted with sth** connaître qch; **to a. sb with sth** mettre qn au courant de qch; **to a. oneself with sth** se familiariser avec qch
acquaintance [ə'kweɪntəns] n (**a**) (person) connaissance f (**b**) (familiarity) (with person, facts) familiarité f; **to make sb's a.** faire la connaissance de qn
acquiesce [ækwɪ'es] vi consentir (**in/to** à)
acquiescence [ækwɪ'esəns] n consentement m (**in/to** à)
acquiescent [ækwɪ'esənt] adj consentant(e)
acquire [ə'kwaɪə(r)] vt (knowledge, reputation, property) acquérir; (habit, accent, air) prendre; **to a. a taste for sth** prendre goût à qch; **it's an acquired taste** c'est quelque chose que l'on apprend à aimer
acquisition [ækwɪ'zɪʃən] n acquisition f
acquisitive [ə'kwɪzɪtɪv] adj matérialiste
acquit [ə'kwɪt] (pt & pp **acquitted**) vt (**a**) Law acquitter (**b**) **to a. oneself well/badly** s'en sortir ou s'en tirer bien/mal
acquittal [ə'kwɪtəl] n Law acquittement m
acre ['eɪkə(r)] n = 4047 m², ≃ demi-hectare m; **acres of forest** des hectares de forêt; Fam **acres of space** plein de place
acrid ['ækrɪd] adj âcre
acrimonious [ækrɪ'məʊnɪəs] adj (person, remark) hargneux(euse); (discussion) virulent(e)
acrimony ['ækrɪmənɪ] n acrimonie f, hargne f
acrobat ['ækrəbæt] n acrobate mf
acrobatic [ækrə'bætɪk] adj acrobatique
acrobatics [ækrəʊ'bætɪks] **1** n acrobatie f **2** npl Fig mental a. gymnastique f intellectuelle
acronym ['ækrənɪm] n sigle m
across [ə'krɒs] **1** prep (**a**) (from one side to the other of) **to go a. sth** traverser qch; **to run a. the road** traverser la route en courant; **to swim a. a river** traverser une rivière à la nage; **the bridge a. the river** le pont sur la rivière; **she threw it a. the room** elle l'a lancé à l'autre bout de la pièce (**b**) (on the other side of) de l'autre côté de; **she lives a. the road** elle habite en face; **the woman (from) a. the road** la femme d'en face (**c**) (throughout) **a. the country** dans tout le pays; **a. the political spectrum** dans l'ensemble de la classe politique **2** adv (**a**) (from one side to the other) **to run/swim a.** traverser en courant/à la nage; **go a. and see her** traverse et va la voir (**b**) (with distance) **it's 10 cm/2 km a.** ça fait 10 cm/2 km de large (**c**) **a. from me/my house** en face de moi/de chez moi (**d**) (in crosswords) horizontalement
across-the-board [ə'krɒsðə'bɔːd] adj général(e), systématique

acrylic [ə'krɪlɪk] **1** n (fabric) acrylique m **2** adj (paint, fibre) acrylique; (garment) en acrylique
act [ækt] **1** n (**a**) (thing done) acte m; **to be in the a. of doing sth** être en train de faire qch; **to catch sb in the a. of doing sth** surprendre qn en train de faire qch; **to catch sb in the a.** prendre qn sur le fait ou en flagrant délit; Fam **to get in on the a.** (get involved) se mettre dans le coup; **a. of war** acte m de guerre; Law **a. of God** catastrophe f naturelle (**b**) (of play) acte m; (in cabaret, circus) numéro m; Fig **to put on an a.** faire semblant; Fig **to get one's a. together** se secouer; Fig **it's all an a.** c'est du cinéma (**c**) Law **a. (of parliament)** loi f **2** vt (**a**) (character) jouer (le rôle de), tenir le rôle de; (play) jouer; Fig **to a. the part** se conduire comme il convient (**b**) (behave like) **to a. the fool** or Br **the goat** faire l'imbécile; Fam **a. your age!** arrête de faire l'enfant! **3** vi (**a**) (take action) agir; **to a. for sb** (of lawyer) représenter qn; **to a. as secretary/chairperson** remplir les fonctions de secrétaire/président; **to a. as a warning** servir d'avertissement; **to a. as an incentive** être une motivation (**b**) (behave) agir, se comporter; **to a. stupid** faire l'idiot (**c**) (of actor) jouer; **I always wanted to a.** j'ai toujours voulu être acteur
▸**act on** vt insep (advice, suggestion) suivre; **she acted on the information we gave her** elle a suivi les indications que nous lui avons données
▸**act out** vt sep (fantasy) vivre; (scene) jouer
▸**act up** vi (of car, child, injury) faire des siennes
acting ['æktɪŋ] **1** n (performance) jeu m; (profession) métier m d'acteur **2** adj (temporary) par intérim
action ['ækʃən] n (**a**) (individual act) acte m, action f; Prov **actions speak louder than words** les actes en disent plus long que les paroles (**b**) (activity) action f; **to take a.** prendre des mesures; **to go into a.** passer à l'action; **to be out of a.** (machine, car) être en panne; (person) être hors service; Fam **where's the a. round here?** où est-ce que ça bouge par ici?; Com **a. plan** objectifs mpl (**c**) Mil combats mpl; **to see a. combattre**; **missing in a.** porté(e) disparu(e) (**d**) (of film, novel) action f; TV **a. replay** = répétition d'une séquence précédente (**e**) Law action f, procès m; **to bring an a. against sb** intenter un procès à qn
activate ['æktɪveɪt] vt déclencher
active ['æktɪv] adj (**a**) (person, mind, imagination) actif(ive); (interest, dislike) vif (vive); (volcano) en activité; **to be a. in doing sth** s'employer activement à faire qch; Mil **on a. service** en service actif; **the a. population** (working) la population active (**b**) Gram actif(ive)
actively ['æktɪvlɪ] adv activement; **to a. dislike sb** détester cordialement qn
activist ['æktɪvɪst] n Pol militant(e) m,f
activity [æk'tɪvɪtɪ] (pl **activities**) n activité f; (in street) animation f; **a. book** livre jeu m; **a. centre** centre m aéré
actor ['æktə(r)] n acteur m
actress ['æktrɪs] n actrice f
actual ['æktʃʊəl] adj (**a**) (real) réel(elle); (example) concret(ète); **in a. fact** en fait (**b**) (specific) **I can't remember her a. words** je ne me rappelle pas ses

paroles exactes; **although the garden is big, the a. house is small** le jardin est grand, mais la maison elle-même est petite

actually [ˈæktʃʊəlɪ] adv (**a**) (really) réellement, vraiment; **what a. happened?** qu'est-ce qui s'est passé au juste?; **what she a. means is...** en réalité, ce qu'elle veut dire c'est... (**b**) (in fact) en fait; **I'm not sure, a.** en fait, je ne suis pas sûr

actuary [ˈæktʃʊərɪ] (pl **actuaries**) n actuaire mf

acumen [ˈækjʊmən] n flair m; **business a.** sens m des affaires

acupuncture [ˈækjʊpʌŋktʃə(r)] n Med acupuncture f, acupuncture f

acupuncturist [ˈækjʊpʌŋktʃərɪst] n Med acupuncteur(trice) m,f, acuponcteur(trice) m,f

acute [əˈkjuːt] adj (**a**) (pain) aigu(ë); (remorse, embarrassment) vif (vive); (problem, shortage) grave (**b**) (eyesight) perçant(e) (**c**) (accent, angle) aigu(ë)

acutely [əˈkjuːtlɪ] adv (painful, embarrassing) extrêmement; (aware) profondément

AD [eɪˈdiː] adv (abbr **Anno Domini**) apr. J.-C.

ad [æd] n Fam (classified) petite annonce f; (on radio, TV) pub f

Adam [ˈædəm] n Fam **I wouldn't know him from A.** je ne le connais ni d'Ève ni d'Adam; **A.'s apple** pomme f d'Adam

adamant [ˈædəmənt] adj formel(elle), catégorique (about sur); **to be a. that...** soutenir que...

adapt [əˈdæpt] **1** vt adapter; **to a. oneself to sth** s'adapter à qch
2 vi s'adapter

adaptable [əˈdæptəbəl] adj (instrument, tool) adaptable; (person) souple

adaptation [ædæpˈteɪʃən] n (of book, play) adaptation f; (of machine, design) modification f

adapter [əˈdæptə(r)] n (for several plugs) prise f multiple; (for foreign plugs) adaptateur m

ADC [eɪdiːˈsiː] n Mil (abbr **aide-de-camp**) aide m de camp

add [æd] vt ajouter (to à); (figures) additionner; **this book adds little to the debate** ce livre n'apporte pas grand-chose au débat

▶**add up 1** vt sep (figures) additionner
2 vi (give correct total) être juste ou exact(e); (make sense) tenir debout

▶**add up to** vt insep (amount to) **it adds up to £126** ça fait 126 livres au total ou en tout; **it all adds up to an enjoyable day out** tout cela fera de cette excursion un moment bien agréable; **it doesn't a. up to much** ça ne fait pas grand-chose au bout du compte

adder [ˈædə(r)] n (snake) vipère f

addict [ˈædɪkt] n (drug) a. toxicomane mf; **heroin a.** héroïnomane mf; **to be a TV a.** être accro à la télé

addicted [əˈdɪktɪd] adj **to be a. to sth** (drugs) être dépendant(e) de qch; (TV programme) être accro à qch

addiction [əˈdɪkʃən] n (to drugs) dépendance f (to à), accoutumance f (to à); (to chocolate, films) passion f (to pour)

addictive [əˈdɪktɪv] adj (substance) qui crée une dépendance ou accoutumance; **soap operas are very a.** on devient vite accro aux feuilletons

Addis Ababa [ˈædɪsˈæbəbə] n Addis-Abeba

addition [əˈdɪʃən] n (action) addition f; (thing added) ajout m (to à); (person) nouveau venu (nouvelle venue) m,f; **she's the latest a. to the team** c'est la

dernière arrivée dans l'équipe; **in a. (to)** en plus (de)

additional [əˈdɪʃənəl] adj supplémentaire

additive [ˈædɪtɪv] n additif m

addled [ˈædəld] adj (egg) pourri(e); (brain) confus(e)

add-on [ˈædɒn] n Comput produit m supplémentaire ou complémentaire

address [əˈdres] **1** n (a) (of person, letter) adresse f; **a. book** carnet m d'adresses (**b**) (speech) discours m, allocution f
2 vt (**a**) (letter, remarks, criticism) adresser (**to** à) (**b**) (speak to) (person, crowd) s'adresser à; **he addressed her as "Your Majesty"** il l'a appelée "Votre Majesté" (**c**) (question, problem) aborder; **to a. oneself to sth** (problem) aborder qch; (task) entreprendre qch

adenoids [ˈædɪnɔɪdz] npl Anat végétations fpl

adept [əˈdept] adj habile (at à); **to be a. at doing sth** être habile à faire qch

adequate [ˈædɪkwət] adj (enough) suffisant(e); (satisfactory) satisfaisant(e), adéquat(e); **you were given a. warning** on vous a prévenu suffisamment à l'avance

adequately [ˈædɪkwɪtlɪ] adv (sufficiently) suffisamment; (suitably) convenablement

adhere [ədˈhɪə(r)] vi (stick) adhérer (to à); **to a. to** (rule) observer; (belief) adhérer à; (plan) se conformer à

adherence [ədˈhɪərəns] n (to rule) observation f (to de); (to belief, plan) adhésion f (to à)

adherent [ədˈhɪərənt] n adhérent(e) m,f

adhesion [ədˈhiːʒən] n (**a**) (stickiness) adhérence f (**b**) (to belief, plan) adhésion f (to à)

adhesive [ədˈhiːsɪv] **1** n adhésif m, colle f
2 adj adhésif(ive), collant(e); **a. tape** ruban m adhésif

ad hoc [ædˈhɒk] adj (measure) ad hoc inv; (arrangement) temporaire; **a. committee** comité m spécial ou ad hoc; **on an a. basis** au coup par coup

ad infinitum [ˈædɪnfɪˈnaɪtəm] adv à l'infini; **and so on a.** et ainsi de suite à n'en plus finir

adjacent [əˈdʒeɪsənt] adj adjacent(e); (street) voisin(e); (room) contigu(ë)

adjective [ˈædʒɪktɪv] n adjectif m

adjoin [əˈdʒɔɪn] vt être contigu(ë) ou attenant(e) à

adjoining [əˈdʒɔɪnɪŋ] adj attenant(e)

adjourn [əˈdʒɜːn] **1** vt (meeting, trial) ajourner, remettre à plus tard
2 vi (of meeting, trial) être ajourné(e); **to a. to another room** passer dans une autre pièce

adjournment [əˈdʒɜːnmənt] n ajournement m

adjudge [əˈdʒʌdʒ] vt **to a. sb guilty/the winner** déclarer qn coupable/vainqueur

adjudicate [əˈdʒuːdɪkeɪt] vt juger

adjudication [ədʒuːdɪˈkeɪʃən] n jugement m, décision f

adjudicator [əˈdʒuːdɪkeɪtə(r)] n (in dispute) arbitre m; (in competition) juge m

adjunct [ˈædʒʌŋkt] n (thing) accessoire m

adjust [əˈdʒʌst] **1** vt (machine, mechanism) régler, ajuster; (pay, figures) ajuster; (clothes) rajuster; **to a. oneself to sth** s'adapter à qch
2 vi (of person) s'adapter (to à)

adjustable [əˈdʒʌstəbəl] adj ajustable, réglable; **a. spanner** clé f à molette

adjustment [əˈdʒʌstmənt] n (of machine, mechanism) réglage m; (to pay, figures) réajustement m; **to make**

an a. to sth régler qch; **a period of a.** une période d'adaptation

ad-lib ['æd'lɪb] **1** *adv* en improvisant, de manière improvisée **2** *vi* (*pt & pp* **ad-libbed**) improviser

ad-man ['ædmæn] *n Fam* publicitaire *m*

admin ['ædmɪn] *n Fam* (*work*) travail *m* administratif; (*department*) administration *f*

administer [əd'mɪnɪstə(r)] *vt* (**a**) (*estate, funds*) administrer, gérer; (*territory*) administrer (**b**) (*give*) (*punishment, medication*) administrer; (*blow*) donner

administration [ədmɪnɪ'streɪʃən] *n* (**a**) (*work*) administration *f* (**b**) (*government*) gouvernement *m*

administrative [əd'mɪnɪstrətɪv] *adj* administratif(ive)

administrator [əd'mɪnɪstreɪtə(r)] *n* administrateur (trice) *m,f*

admirable ['ædmərəbəl] *adj* admirable

admiral ['ædmərəl] *n* amiral *m*

Admiralty ['ædmərəltɪ] *n* **the A.** ≃ le ministère de la Marine

admiration [ædmə'reɪʃən] *n* admiration *f* (**for** pour)

admire [əd'maɪə(r)] *vt* admirer

admirer [əd'maɪərə(r)] *n* admirateur(trice) *m,f*

admiring [əd'maɪərɪŋ] *adj* (*look, glance*) admiratif(ive)

admissible [əd'mɪsɪbəl] *adj* (*behaviour, error*) admissible, acceptable; *Law* recevable

admission [əd'mɪʃən] *n* (**a**) (*entry*) (*to school, hospital*) admission *f*; (*to museum, exhibition*) entrée *f*; (*price*) (prix *m* d')entrée *f*; **no a.** (*sign*) entrée interdite (**b**) (*acknowledgement*) (*of guilt*) aveu *m*; (*of crime*) confession *f*; **by his own a.** de son propre aveu

admit [əd'mɪt] (*pt & pp* **admitted**) **1** *vt* (**a**) (*allow to enter*) laisser entrer; (*to hospital, college*) admettre; **to be admitted to hospital** être admis(e) à l'hôpital; **children not admitted** (*sign*) les enfants ne sont pas admis; **a. one** (*on ticket*) entrée valable pour une personne (**b**) (*acknowledge*) (*fact, mistake, guilt*) admettre, reconnaître; (*crime*) avouer; **I must a. you're right** je dois reconnaître que vous avez raison; **to a. defeat** s'avouer vaincu(e) **2** *vi* **to a.** (*mistake*) reconnaître; **I a. to being in a bad mood yesterday** je dois admettre que j'étais de mauvaise humeur hier

admittance [əd'mɪtəns] *n* (*entry*) accès *m*; **to gain a.** parvenir à entrer; **to refuse sb a.** refuser de laisser entrer qn; **no a.** (*sign*) entrée interdite

admittedly [əd'mɪtɪdlɪ] *adv* de l'aveu général; **a., it was dark when I saw him** je dois convenir qu'il faisait sombre quand je l'ai vu

admonish [əd'mɒnɪʃ] *vt* (*reprimand*) admonester, faire des remontrances à (**for** pour)

ad nauseam [æd 'nɔːsɪæm] *adv* à n'en plus finir

ado [ə'duː] *n* **without more or further a.** sans plus de cérémonie *ou* de manières; **much a. about nothing** beaucoup de bruit pour rien

adobe [ə'dəʊbɪ] *n* (*clay*) adobe *m*

adolescence [ædə'lesəns] *n* adolescence *f*

adolescent [ædə'lesənt] *n* adolescent(e) *m,f*

adopt [ə'dɒpt] *vt* (*child, custom, approach, measures*) adopter; (*career, candidate*) choisir; (*tone, attitude*) prendre

adopted [ə'dɒptɪd] *adj* (*child*) adopté(e); (*son, daughter*) adoptif(ive); **my a. country** mon pays d'adoption

adoption [ə'dɒpʃən] *n* adoption *f*

adorable [ə'dɔːrəbəl] *adj* adorable

adoration [ædə'reɪʃən] *n* adoration *f*

adore [ə'dɔː(r)] *vt* adorer

adorn [ə'dɔːn] *vt* orner, parer (**with** de)

adornment [ə'dɔːnmənt] *n* (*decorations*) ornements *mpl*, parure *f*

ADP [eɪdiː'piː] *n Comput* (*abbr* **automatic data processing**) traitement *m* automatique des données

adrenalin(e) [ə'drenəlɪn] *n* adrénaline *f*

Adriatic [eɪdrɪ'ætɪk] *n* **the A.** (**Sea**) la mer Adriatique, l'Adriatique *f*

adrift [ə'drɪft] *adj & adv* **to be a.** (*of boat*) aller à la dérive; **to go a.** (*of plan*) tomber à l'eau; **to come a.** (*come apart*) se défaire

adroit [ə'drɔɪt] *adj* habile (**at doing sth** à faire qch)

ADSL [eɪdiːes'el] *n Comput & Tel* (*abbr* **asymmetric digital subscriber line**) ADSL *m*

adulation [ædjʊ'leɪʃən] *n* adulation *f*

adult ['ædʌlt, ə'dʌlt] **1** *n* adulte *mf* **2** *adj* adulte; (*film*) pour adultes; **a. education** enseignement *m* pour adultes

adulterate [ə'dʌltəreɪt] *vt* (*food*) empoisonner; (*wine*) frelater; (*language*) corrompre

adulteration [ədʌltə'reɪʃən] *n* (*of food*) empoisonnement *m*; (*of wine*) frelatage *m*

adulterer [ə'dʌltərə(r)] *n* adultère *mf*

adulterous [ə'dʌltərəs] *adj* adultère

adultery [ə'dʌltərɪ] *n* adultère *m*; **to commit a.** commettre l'adultère

adulthood ['ædʌlthʊd] *n* âge *m* adulte

advance [əd'vɑːns] **1** *n* (**a**) (*forward movement*) avance *f*; (*progress*) progrès *m*; **to make advances to sb** faire des avances à qn; **in a.** (*book, apply, inform*) à l'avance; (*pay*) d'avance; **six weeks in a.** six semaines à l'avance; **a. booking** réservation *f* à l'avance; **a. notice** *or* **warning** préavis *m* (**b**) (*loan*) avance *f* **2** *vt* (**a**) (*move forward*) faire avancer; (*chess piece*) avancer; (*science, knowledge*) faire progresser, faire avancer (**b**) (*idea, opinion*) avancer, mettre en avant (**c**) (*loan*) avancer **3** *vi* (*move forward*) s'avancer; (*towards* vers); (*make progress*) avancer

advanced [əd'vɑːnst] *adj* avancé(e); **she's very a. for her age** elle est très en avance pour son âge

advantage [əd'vɑːntɪdʒ] *n* avantage *m* (**over** sur); **to take a. of** profiter de; **to turn a situation to one's a.** tourner une situation à son avantage; **it would be to your a.** il serait dans votre intérêt de...; **a. Federer** (*in tennis*) avantage Federer

advantageous [ædvən'teɪdʒəs] *adj* avantageux(euse) (**to** pour)

advent ['ædvənt] *n* (*arrival*) arrivée *f*; *Rel* **A.** l'Avent *m*

adventure [əd'ventʃə(r)] *n* aventure *f*; **a. playground** terrain *m* de jeux (*spécialement aménagé*); **a. story** récit *m* d'aventures; (*novel*) roman *m* d'aventure(s)

adventurer [əd'ventʃərə(r)] *n* aventurier(ère) *m,f*

adventurous [əd'ventʃərəs] *adj* (*person*) aventureux (euse); (*plan*) audacieux(euse)

adverb ['ædvɜːb] *n* adverbe *m*

adversary ['ædvəsərɪ] *n* (*pl* **adversaries**) *n* adversaire *mf*

adverse ['ædvɜːs] *adj* défavorable

adversely ['ædvɜːslɪ] *adv* **to influence sb a.** exercer une influence défavorable sur qn; **a. affected** affecté(e)

adversity [əd'vɜːsɪtɪ] *n* adversité *f*; **in a.** dans l'adversité

advert ['ædvɜːt] *n (for product)* pub *f*; *(for job, event)* annonce *f*
advertise ['ædvətaɪz] **1** *vt* (**a**) *(product, service)* faire de la réclame *ou* de la publicité pour; *(job)* mettre une annonce pour; **advertised on TV** vu(e) à la télé (**b**) *(call attention to)* **he didn't want to a. his presence** il ne voulait pas se faire remarquer **2** *vi (for job)* mettre une annonce; *(to sell product)* faire de la publicité *ou* de la réclame; **to a. for sb** passer une annonce pour trouver qn
advertisement [əd'vɜːtɪsmənt] *n (for product, service)* publicité *f*, réclame *f*; *(for job, event)* annonce *f*; *Fig* **you're not a good a. for your school** vous ne faites pas honneur à votre école
advertiser ['ædvətaɪzə(r)] *n* annonceur(euse) *m,f*
advertising ['ædvətaɪzɪŋ] *n* publicité *f*; **a. agency** agence *f* de publicité; **a. campaign** campagne *f* de publicité
advice [əd'vaɪs] *n* conseil(s) *m(pl)* (**on** sur); **a piece of a.** un conseil; **that's good a.** c'est un bon conseil; **to give sb a.** donner des conseils à qn; **to ask sb's a.** demander conseil à qn; **to take sb's a.** suivre le conseil *ou* les conseils de qn
advisable [əd'vaɪzəbəl] *adj* recommandé(e)
advise [əd'vaɪz] *vt* (**a**) *(give advice to)* conseiller; **to a. sb to do sth** conseiller à qn de faire qch; **to a. sb against doing sth** déconseiller à qn de faire qch; **I wouldn't a. it** je ne le conseillerais *ou* recommanderais pas (**b**) *(inform)* **to a. sb that...** aviser qn que...
adviser, advisor [əd'vaɪzə(r)] *n* conseiller(ère) *m,f*
advisory [əd'vaɪzərɪ] *adj* consultatif(ive); **in an a. capacity** en tant que conseiller
advocate 1 *n* ['ædvəkət] (**a**) *Scot Law* avocat(e) *m,f*; **the Lord A.** ≃ le procureur général (**b**) *(of cause, doctrine)* partisan(e) *m,f*
2 *vt* ['ædvəkeɪt] *(policy, plan)* préconiser, conseiller
AEA [eɪɪ'eɪ] *n Br (abbr* **Atomic Energy Authority)** ≃ Commissariat *m* à l'énergie atomique
AEC [eɪɪ'siː] *n Am (abbr* **Atomic Energy Commission)** ≃ Commissariat *m* à l'énergie atomique
Aegean [ɪ'dʒiːən] *n* **the A. (Sea)** la mer Égée
aegis ['iːdʒɪs] *n Formal* **under the a. of...** sous l'égide de...
aeon, *Am* **eon** ['iːən] *n Fig* éternité *f*; **aeons ago** il y a une éternité
AER [eɪɪ'ɑː(r)] *n Fin (abbr* **annual equivalent rate)** taux *m* actuariel annuel
aerate ['eəreɪt] *vt (water)* gazéifier
aerial ['eərɪəl] **1** *n (of radio, TV)* antenne *f*
2 *adj* aérien(enne)
aerobics [eə'rəʊbɪks] *n* aérobic *m*
aerodrome ['eərədrəʊm] *n* aérodrome *m*
aerodynamic [eərəʊdaɪ'næmɪk] *adj* aérodynamique
aerogram(me) ['eərəgræm] *n* aérogramme *m*
aeronautic(al) [eərə'nɔːtɪk(əl)] *adj* aéronautique
aeroplane ['eərəpleɪn] *n* avion *m*
aerosol ['eərəsɒl] *n* aérosol *m*; **a. spray** atomiseur *m*
aerospace ['eərəʊspeɪs] *n Aviat* aérospatiale *f*; **the a. industry** l'aérospatiale *f*
aesthetic, *Am* **esthetic** [ɪs'θetɪk] *adj* esthétique
aesthetics, *Am* **esthetics** [ɪs'θetɪks] *npl* esthétique *f*
afar [ə'fɑː(r)] *adv Lit* **from a.** de loin
affable ['æfəbəl] *adj* affable, courtois(e)
affair [ə'feə(r)] *n* (**a**) *(matter, concern)* affaire *f*; **that's my a.!** c'est mes affaires!; **to put one's affairs in order**

mettre de l'ordre dans ses affaires; **current affairs** les questions *fpl* d'actualité; **foreign affairs** les affaires étrangères; **affairs of state** les affaires de l'État; **in the present state of affairs** dans l'état actuel des choses (**b**) *(sexual)* liaison *f*; **to have an a. with sb** avoir une liaison avec qn (**c**) *(event)* affaire *f*; **the wedding was a quiet a.** le mariage fut célébré dans l'intimité; **what kind of a. was it?** c'était comment?
affect¹ [ə'fekt] *vt* (**a**) *(have effect on) (person, organ, health)* affecter; *(decision)* influencer; *(of issue, law)* concerner (**b**) *(move emotionally)* affecter, toucher; **to be deeply affected by sth** être très affecté(e) par qch
affect² *vt (indifference, interest)* affecter, feindre; **to a. an accent** prendre un accent
affectation [æfek'teɪʃən] *n* affectation *f*
affected [ə'fektɪd] *adj (unnatural)* affecté(e), maniéré(e)
affection [ə'fekʃən] *n* affection *f*
affectionate [ə'fekʃənət] *adj* affectueux(euse) (**towards** avec *ou* envers)
affidavit [æfɪ'deɪvɪt] *n Law* déclaration *f* par écrit et sous serment
affiliate 1 *n* [ə'fɪlɪət] *(person)* affilié(e) *m,f*
2 *vt* [ə'fɪlɪeɪt] affilier (**to** or **with** à); **affiliated company** filiale *f*
affiliation [əfɪlɪ'eɪʃən] *n* affiliation *f*
affinity [ə'fɪnɪtɪ] *(pl* **affinities)** *n* (**a**) *(liking, attraction)* affinité *f* (**for** or **with/between** avec/entre); **to have an a. with sb/sth** avoir des affinités avec qn/qch (**b**) *(relationship, connection)* lien *m* (**between/with** entre/avec)
affirm [ə'fɜːm] *vt* (**a**) *(state)* affirmer (**b**) *(confirm)* confirmer
affirmation [æfə'meɪʃən] *n* (**a**) *(statement)* affirmation *f*, assertion *f* (**b**) *(confirmation)* confirmation *f*
affirmative [ə'fɜːmətɪv] **1** *n* **to answer in the a.** répondre affirmativement *ou* par l'affirmative
2 *adj* affirmatif(ive); *Am* **a. action** mesures *fpl* d'embauche antidiscriminatoires *(en faveur des minorités)*
affix 1 *n* ['æfɪks] *Ling* affixe *m*
2 *vt* [ə'fɪks] attacher (**to** à); *(notice, poster)* fixer (**to** à)
afflict [ə'flɪkt] *vt* affliger; **afflicted with rheumatism** affligé(e) de rhumatismes
affliction [ə'flɪkʃən] *n (illness)* affection *f*; *(misfortune)* malheur *m*
affluent ['æfluənt] *adj* riche; **the a. society** la société d'abondance
afford [ə'fɔːd] *vt* (**a**) *(financially)* **to be able to a. sth** avoir les moyens d'acheter qch; **I can't a. it** mes moyens ne me le permettent pas; **we can't a. a new car** nous ne pouvons pas nous offrir une nouvelle voiture; **she can a. to eat out twice a week** elle peut se permettre d'aller au restaurant deux fois par semaine (**b**) *(non-financial use)* **I can't a. to wait** je ne peux pas attendre; **can you a. the time?** est-ce que vous avez le temps?; **I can't a. not to** je n'ai pas le choix; **we can't a. another mistake** nous ne pouvons pas nous permettre une nouvelle erreur (**c**) *Formal (give)* offrir, procurer
affordable [ə'fɔːdəbəl] *adj (price, purchase)* abordable; *(house)* (d'un prix) abordable
affray [ə'freɪ] *n Law & Formal* rixe *f*

affront [əˈfrʌnt] **1** *n* affront *m*, offense *f*
2 *vt* offenser, faire (un) affront à; **to be/feel affronted** être/se sentir offensé(e)
Afghan [ˈæfgæn] **1** *n* (**a**) *(person)* Afghan(e) *m,f* (**b**) *(dog)* lévrier *m* afghan
2 *adj* afghan(e); **A. hound** lévrier *m* afghan
Afghanistan [æfˈgænɪstɑːn] *n* l'Afghanistan *m*
afield [əˈfiːld] *adv* **further a.** plus loin
AFL/CIO [eɪefˈelsiːaɪ ˈəʊ] *n* (*abbr* **American Federation of Labor and Congress of Industrial Organizations**) = confédération syndicale américaine
afloat [əˈfləʊt] *adj & adv* à flot; **to stay a.** *(of boat, company)* se maintenir à flot
afoot [əˈfʊt] *adv* **there's something a.** il se prépare *ou* se trame quelque chose
aforementioned [əˈfɔːmenʃənd] *adj* susmentionné(e)
afraid [əˈfreɪd] *adj* (**a**) *(scared)* **to be a.** **(of)** avoir peur (de); **that's (exactly) what I was a. of!** c'est bien ce que je craignais!; **I was a. there would be an accident** je craignais un accident (**b**) *(sorry)* **I'm a. so/not** je crains que oui/que non; **I'm a. she's out** je regrette, mais elle est sortie; **I'm a. I can't help you** j'ai bien peur de ne pouvoir vous aider
afresh [əˈfreʃ] *adv* de nouveau, à nouveau; **to start a.** recommencer
Africa [ˈæfrɪkə] *n* l'Afrique *f*
African [ˈæfrɪkən] **1** *n* Africain(e) *m,f*
2 *adj* africain(e)
African-American [ˈæfrɪkənəˈmerɪkən] **1** *n* Noir(e) *m,f* américain(e)
2 *adj* noir(e) américain(e)
Afrikaans [æfrɪˈkɑːnz] *n* afrikaans *m*
aft [ɑːft] *adv* *Naut* à l'arrière
after [ˈɑːftə(r)] **1** *prep* (**a**) *(with time)* après; **a. dinner** après dîner; **a. three days** au bout de trois jours; **the day a. the battle** le lendemain de la bataille; **it's a. five** il est cinq heures passées; *Am* **it's twenty a. six** il est six heures vingt; **a. all** *(all things considered)* après tout; *(despite everything)* finalement (**b**) *(with motion)* après; **to run a. sb** courir après qn; **close the door a. you** fermez la porte derrière vous; **a. you!** après vous!
(**c**) *(in search of)* **to be a. sb/sth** chercher qn/qch
(**d**) *(expressing sequence)* après; **a. her, he is the best** après elle, c'est lui le meilleur
(**e**) *(expressing repetition)* après; **day a. day** jour après jour; **year a. year** d'une année sur l'autre, tous les ans; **time a. time** cent fois; **it's one thing a. another** j'ai/nous avons/*etc* des problèmes à n'en plus finir
(**f**) *(in honour of)* **to name sb/sth a. sb** donner le nom de qn à qn/qch
2 *adv* après; **soon/long a.** peu/longtemps après; **the week a.** la semaine d'après; **the day a.** le lendemain
3 *conj* *(with subject changes)* après que + *indicative* or *Fam subjunctive*; *(when subject stays the same)* après + *infinitive*; **I came a. he left** je suis arrivé après qu'il ou *Fam* soit parti; **I saw him I went out** je suis sorti après l'avoir vu; **a. doing sth** après avoir fait qch
afterbirth [ˈɑːftəbɜːθ] *n* placenta *m*
aftercare [ˈɑːftəkeə(r)] *n* *(after operation)* soins *mpl* postopératoires; *(of convalescent, delinquent)* surveillance *f*

after-effect [ˈɑːftərəfekt] *n* *(of drug)* effet *m* secondaire; *Fig (of event)* répercussion *f*, contrecoup *m*
afterlife [ˈɑːftəlaɪf] *n* vie *f* après la mort
aftermath [ˈɑːftəmæθ] *n* suites *fpl*, conséquences *fpl*
afternoon [ɑːftəˈnuːn] *n* après-midi *m* *inv* or *f* *inv*; **in the a.** (pendant) l'après-midi; **at two o'clock in the a.** à deux heures de l'après-midi; **good a.!** bonjour!
after-party [ˈɑːftəpɑːtɪ] *n* after *m*
aftersales service [ɑːftəˈseɪlzsɜːvɪs] *n* *Com* service *m* après-vente
aftershave [ˈɑːftəʃeɪv] *n* **a. (lotion)** (lotion *f*) après-rasage *m*
aftersun [ˈɑːftəsʌn] *n* *(cream)* crème *f* après-soleil; *(lotion)* lotion *f* après-soleil
aftertaste [ˈɑːftəteɪst] *n* *also Fig* arrière-goût *m*
afterthought [ˈɑːftəθɔːt] *n* réflexion *f* après coup; **as an a.** après coup
afterwards [ˈɑːftəwədz] *adv* après; **I regretted it a.** par la suite, je l'ai regretté
Aga® [ˈɑːgə] *n* = cuisinière en fonte à l'ancienne
again [əˈgen] *adv* (**a**) *(in general)* de nouveau, encore; **to begin a.** recommencer; **he never came back a.** il n'est plus jamais revenu; **don't do it a.!** ne recommence pas!; **not you a.!** encore toi!; **once a.** encore une fois, une fois de plus; **a. and a.** à maintes reprises; **now and a.** de temps en temps, de temps à autre; **half as much a.** moitié plus; **I'd like half as much a.** je voudrais encore la moitié de ça; **what did you say a.?** qu'avez-vous dit déjà? (**b**) *(besides)* en plus; **(then) a.** *(on the other hand)* d'un autre côté; **a., I may have imagined it** cela dit, il se peut aussi que je l'aie imaginé
against [əˈgenst] *prep* (**a**) *(in opposition to)* contre; **to be a. sb/sth** être contre qn/qch, être opposé(e) à qn/qch; **to have something/nothing a. sb/sth** avoir quelque chose/ne rien avoir contre qn/qch; **a. the law** contraire à la loi, illégal(e) (**b**) *(as protection from)* contre; **to warn sb a. sb/sth** mettre qn en garde contre qn/qch (**c**) *(in contact with)* contre; **to lean a. sth** s'appuyer contre qch (**d**) *(in comparison with)* contre; **three deaths this year (as) a. thirty in 2001** trois morts cette année contre trente en 2001; **the pound rose/fell a. the dollar** la livre a augmenté/chuté par rapport au dollar
age [eɪdʒ] **1** *n* (**a**) *(of person)* âge *m*; **to be twenty years of a.** avoir vingt ans, être âgé(e) de vingt ans; **what a. is she?, what's her a.?** quel âge a-t-elle?; **he doesn't look his a.** il ne fait pas son âge; **people of all ages** des gens de tout âge; **a. of consent** = âge légal où on peut avoir des rapports sexuels; **a. group** tranche *f* d'âge; **a. limit** limite *f* d'âge (**b**) **(old) a.** vieillesse *f* (**c**) *(adulthood)* **to come of a.** atteindre sa majorité; **to be under a.** *Law* être mineur(e); *(not old enough to buy alcohol etc)* ne pas avoir l'âge (**d**) *(era)* âge *m*, époque *f* (**e**) *Fam (long time)* **it's ages since I saw him** il y a une éternité que je ne l'ai pas vu; **I've been waiting (for) ages** ça fait une éternité que j'attends
2 *vt & vi (continuous* aging *or* ageing*)* vieillir
aged *adj* (**a**) [eɪdʒd] *(of the age of)* **a. twenty** âgé(e) de vingt ans (**b**) [ˈeɪdʒɪd] *(old)* âgé(e), vieux (vieille)
ageing, aging [ˈeɪdʒɪŋ] **1** *n* *(of person, wine)* vieillissement *m*; **a. process** processus *m* de vieillissement
2 *adj (becoming older)* vieillissant(e); *(old)* vieux (vieille)
ageism, agism [ˈeɪdʒɪzəm] *n* âgisme *m*

agency ['eɪdʒənsɪ] (*pl* **agencies**) *n* (**a**) *Com* agence *f*; **advertising/travel a.** agence *f* de publicité/de voyages (**b**) **through the a.** of par l'entremise *ou* l'intermédiaire de

agenda [ə'dʒendə] *n* (*of meeting*) ordre *m* du jour; *Fig* programme *m*; **what's on today's a.?** (*for meeting*) quel est l'ordre du jour?; *(for activities)* qu'est-ce qu'il y a au programme pour aujourd'hui?; *Fig* **to set the a.** mener le jeu

agent ['eɪdʒənt] *n* (**a**) *(representative, spy)* agent *m* (**b**) *(instrument)* agent *m*; **to be the a.** of sth être l'instrument de qch

age-old ['eɪdʒəʊld] *adj* séculaire

aggravate ['ægrəveɪt] *vt* (**a**) *(worsen)* aggraver (**b**) *Fam (annoy)* agacer, exaspérer

aggravating ['ægrəveɪtɪŋ] *adj* (**a**) *Law* aggravant(e) (**b**) *Fam (annoying)* agaçant(e), exaspérant(e)

aggravation [ægrə'veɪʃən] *n* (**a**) *(worsening)* aggravation *f* (**b**) *Fam (annoyance)* embêtements *mpl*

aggregate ['ægrɪgət] **1** *n* total *m*, ensemble *m*; **on a.** au total
2 *adj* collectif(ive); **a.** **scores** résultats *mpl* globaux

aggression [ə'greʃən] *n* agressivité *f*; **an act of a.** une agression

aggressive [ə'gresɪv] *adj* agressif(ive)

aggressively [ə'gresɪvlɪ] *adv (violently)* d'une manière agressive; *(speak)* d'un ton agressif; *(vigorously)* énergiquement, avec dynamisme

aggressor [ə'gresə(r)] *n* agresseur *m*

aggrieved [ə'gri:vd] *adj (expression, tone)* vexé(e); **to be** *or* **feel a.** se sentir lésé(e)

aggro ['ægrəʊ] *n Br Fam (violence)* bagarre(s) *f(pl)*; *(trouble)* enquiquinement *m*

aghast [ə'gɑːst] *adj* horrifié(e) (**at** par)

agile ['ædʒaɪl] *adj* agile

agility [ə'dʒɪlɪtɪ] *n* agilité *f*

aging, agism = **ageing, ageism**

agitate ['ædʒɪteɪt] **1** *vt (liquid, person)* agiter
2 *vi* **to a.** **for/against sth** mener une campagne en faveur de/contre qch

agitated ['ædʒɪteɪtɪd] *adj (person)* agité(e)

agitation [ædʒɪ'teɪʃən] *n* agitation *f*

agitator ['ædʒɪteɪtə(r)] *n Pol* agitateur(trice) *m,f*

aglow [ə'gləʊ] *adj (sky)* embrasé(e); **to be a. with** *(of person)* rayonner de

AGM [eɪdʒiː'em] *n Com (abbr* **annual general meeting)** AGA *f*

agnostic [æg'nɒstɪk] **1** *n* agnostique *mf*
2 *adj* agnostique

ago [ə'gəʊ] *adv* **ten years a.** il y a dix ans; **long a.** il y a longtemps; **not long a.** il n'y a pas longtemps; **as long a. as 1840** déjà en 1840, dès 1840; **a short time a., a little while a.** il y a peu de temps, tout à l'heure; **how long a. was that?** c'était il y a combien de temps?

agog [ə'gɒg] *adj* en émoi; **he was a. to hear the latest news** il brûlait d'apprendre les dernières nouvelles

agonize ['ægənaɪz] *vi* se ronger les sangs, se tourmenter (**over** à propos de)

agonizing ['ægənaɪzɪŋ] *adj (pain, death)* atroce; *(silence, wait)* angoissant(e); *(decision, dilemma)* pénible, déchirant(e)

agony ['ægənɪ] (*pl* **agonies**) *n (physical pain)* douleur *f* atroce; *(mental pain)* angoisse *f*; **to be in a.** être au supplice *ou* au martyre; **it's a. walking in these shoes!** c'est un véritable supplice de marcher avec ces chaussures!; **a. aunt** *(in newspaper)* = responsable

de la rubrique courrier du cœur; **a.** **column** *(in newspaper)* courrier *m* du cœur

agoraphobia [ægərə'fəʊbɪə] *n* agoraphobie *f*

agrarian [ə'greərɪən] *adj* agraire

agree [ə'griː] **1** *vt* (**a**) *(reach agreement on) (price, time, conditions)* se mettre d'accord sur; **to a. to do sth** convenir de faire qch; **(are we) agreed?** (nous sommes) d'accord?
(**b**) *(concur)* **to a.** **(that)...** s'accorder à dire que...; **I a. that's expensive, but...** c'est cher, j'en conviens, mais...; **everyone agrees (that) he's the best** tout le monde s'accorde à dire qu'il est le meilleur
(**c**) *(consent)* **to a. to do sth** accepter de faire qch, consentir à faire qch; **we'll have to a. to disagree** *or* **to differ on that** je crois qu'ici il va nous falloir accepter nos différences d'opinion; **it is generally agreed that...** il est généralement admis que...
2 *vi* (**a**) *(be of same opinion, concur)* être d'accord (**about/with** sur/avec); *(after discussion)* se mettre d'accord; **I'm afraid I can't a.** j'ai bien peur de ne pas être du même avis; **I couldn't a. more!** ça c'est bien dit!; **I don't a. with all this violence on television** je n'approuve pas toute cette violence à la télévision (**b**) *(match) (of statements, facts, opinions)* concorder, coïncider (**with** avec); *Gram* s'accorder (**with** avec); (**c**) *(accept)* consentir (**to** à); **to a. to a condition/proposal** accepter une condition/une proposition

▸**agree on** *vt insep* être d'accord sur; *(after discussion)* se mettre d'accord sur

▸**agree with** *vt insep (of food)* réussir à

agreeable [ə'griːəbəl] *adj* (**a**) *(pleasant)* agréable; *(person)* aimable (**b**) *(acceptable)* **if that is a. to you** si cela vous convient

agreed [ə'griːd] *adj (price, time)* convenu(e)

agreement [ə'griːmənt] *n* (**a**) *(contract, assent)* & *Gram* accord *m* (**on** *or* **about** sur); **to come to an a.** tomber *ou* se mettre d'accord; **by mutual a.** d'un commun accord; **the proposal met with unanimous a.** la proposition a été reçue à l'unanimité; **to be in a. with sb** être d'accord avec qn; **to be in a. with a decision** approuver une décision (**b**) *(of facts, account)* **to be in a. with** concorder avec

agricultural [ægrɪ'kʌltʃərəl] *adj* agricole; **a. college** = école supérieure d'agriculture et d'agronomie; **a. labourer** ouvrier *m* agricole

agriculture ['ægrɪkʌltʃə(r)] *n* agriculture *f*

agronomy [ə'grɒnəmɪ] *n* agronomie *f*

aground [ə'graʊnd] *adv* **to run a.** *(of ship)* s'échouer; *(of project, government)* échouer

ahead [ə'hed] *adv* (**a**) *(in space)* devant; **to go on a.** partir devant; **the road was clear a.** devant nous/moi/*etc* la route était libre; **a. of** devant (**b**) *(winning)* **to be a.** être en tête; **to get a.** *(in career)* avancer; **to get a. of sb** dépasser qn (**c**) *(in time)* **to plan a.** faire des projets; **in the years a.** dans les années à venir; **a. of** *(prior to)* avant; **a. of schedule** *(flight, train)* en avance sur l'horaire; *(project)* en avance sur les prévisions; **to be a. of one's time** être en avance sur son temps

ahoy [ə'hɔɪ] *exclam* **a. there!** oh(é)!; **ship a.!** ohé du bateau!

AI [eɪ'aɪ] *n* (**a**) *Comput (abbr* **artificial intelligence)** IA *f* (**b**) *Med (abbr* **artificial insemination)** insémination *f* artificielle (**c**) *Pol (abbr* **Amnesty International)** Amnesty International *f*

aid [eɪd] **1** *n* (**a**) *(help, for disaster relief)* aide *f*, secours *m*; **with the a.** of sb avec l'aide de qn; **with the a.** of sth à l'aide de qch; **to go to sb's a.** aller *ou* se porter au secours de qn; **in a. of** *(fund-raising event)* au profit de; *Fam* **what's (all) this in a. of?** c'est en quel honneur?; **a. worker** *(voluntary)* volontaire *mf*; *(paid)* employé(e) *m,f* d'une organisation humanitaire (**b**) *(device)* outil *m*; **teaching aids** matériel *m* pédagogique, supports *mpl* pédagogiques **2** *vt* aider; *Law* **to a. and abet sb** être le complice de qn

aide [eɪd] *n* assistant(e) *m,f*, conseiller(ère) *m,f*
aide-de-camp [ˈeɪddəˈkɒŋ] *(pl* **aides-de-camp**) *n Mil* aide *m* de camp
aiding [ˈeɪdɪŋ] *n Law* **a. and abetting** complicité *f*
AIDS, Aids [eɪdz] *n* sida *m*; **A. clinic** = clinique spécialisée dans le traitement du sida; **A. sufferer** sidéen(enne) *m,f*, malade *mf* du sida; **A. virus** virus *m* du sida
ailing [ˈeɪlɪŋ] *adj (person)* souffrant(e); *(company, economy)* qui bat de l'aile
ailment [ˈeɪlmənt] *n* mal *m*
aim [eɪm] **1** *n* (**a**) *(at target)* **to take a. (at)** viser; **her a. was good** elle visait bien (**b**) *(goal)* but *m*, dessein *m*; **with the a. of doing sth** dans le but *ou* dessein de faire qch **2** *vt (stone)* lancer (**at** à); *(camera)* braquer (**at** sur); **to a. a gun at sb/sth** mettre qn/qch en joue; **to a. a blow at sb** chercher à frapper qn; **to be aimed at sb** *(of remarks, TV programme)* être destiné(e) à qn **3** *vi* **to a. at** *(with gun)* viser; **to a. to do sth** *(intend)* avoir l'intention de faire qch
aimless [ˈeɪmlɪs] *adj (existence, remark)* sans but
ain't [eɪnt] *very Fam* (**a**) = **is not, am not, are not** (**b**) = **has not, have not**
air [eər] **1** *n* (**a**) *(in general)* air *m*; **by a.** par avion; **to be on the a.** *(of person)* être à l'antenne; *(of programme)* être diffusé(e); **to throw sth (up) in the a.** lancer qch en l'air; **our plans are up in the a.** *(undecided)* nos projets n'ont toujours pas de forme précise; **to be in the a.** *(of rumour)* circuler; *(of feeling, idea)* être dans l'air; **a. bag** Air Bag® *m*; **a. bed** matelas *m* pneumatique; **a. filter** filtre *m* à air; **the A. Force** l'Armée *f* de l'air; **a. freight** fret *m* aérien; **a. freshener** désodorisant *m*; **a. hostess** hôtesse *f* de l'air; **a. rage** rage *f* de l'air; **a. raid** raid *m* aérien; **a. rifle** fusil *m* à air comprimé; **a. show** salon *m* de l'aéronautique; **a. steward** steward *m*; **a. stewardess** hôtesse *f* de l'air; **a. terminal** aérogare *f*; **a. traffic control** contrôle *m* aérien; **a. traffic controller** contrôleur *m* aérien, aiguilleur *m* du ciel (**b**) *(melody)* air *m* (**c**) *(look)* air *m*, apparence *f*; **he has a certain a. about him** c'est quelqu'un qui en impose; **to give oneself** *or* **to put on airs** se donner des airs **2** *vt* (**a**) *(room, clothing, bedding)* aérer (**b**) *(opinions, grievances)* exposer
airborne [ˈeəbɔːn] *adj (seeds, particles)* en suspension dans l'air; *(troops)* aéroporté(e); **once we are a.** une fois que nous aurons décollé
aircon [ˈeəkɒn] *n (abbr* **air-conditioning**) clim *f*
air-conditioned [ˈeəkənˈdɪʃənd] *adj* climatisé(e), à air conditionné
air-conditioning [ˈeəkənˈdɪʃənɪŋ] *n* climatisation *f*
air-cooled [ˈeəkuːld] *adj* refroidi(e) par air
aircraft [ˈeəkrɑːft] *(pl* **aircraft**) *n* avion *m*; **a. carrier** porte-avions *m inv*

air-crew [ˈeəkruː] *n Aviat* équipage *m*
airfare [ˈeəfeə(r)] *n* prix *m* du billet (d'avion)
airfield [ˈeəfiːld] *n* champ *m ou* terrain *m* d'aviation
airing [ˈeərɪŋ] *n* **to give sth an a.** *(room, clothes, bedding)* aérer qch; *(opinions, grievances)* exposer; *Br* **a. cupboard** = placard où se trouve le chauffe-eau
airless [ˈeəlɪs] *adj (room)* qui sent le renfermé; *(evening, atmosphere)* lourd(e)
airlift [ˈeəlɪft] **1** *n* pont *m* aérien **2** *vt (supplies, troops)* transporter par avion; *(refugees)* évacuer par avion
airline [ˈeəlaɪn] *n* ligne *f ou* compagnie *f* aérienne; **a. pilot** pilote *m* de ligne
airlock [ˈeəlɒk] *n* (**a**) *(in submarine, spacecraft)* sas *m* (**b**) *(in pipe)* poche *f* d'air
airmail [ˈeəmeɪl] **1** *n (service)* poste *f* aérienne; **a. letter** aérogramme *m* **2** *adv* **to send sth a.** envoyer qch par avion **3** *vt (letter)* envoyer par avion
airplane [ˈeəpleɪn] *n Am* avion *m*
airport [ˈeəpɔːt] *n* aéroport *m*
air-sea rescue [ˈeəsiːˈreskjuː] *n* sauvetage *m* aérien en mer
airship [ˈeəʃɪp] *n* dirigeable *m*
airsick [ˈeəsɪk] *adj* **to be a.** avoir le mal de l'air
airspace [ˈeəspeɪs] *n* espace *m* aérien
airstrip [ˈeəstrɪp] *n* piste *f* d'atterrissage
airtight [ˈeətaɪt] *adj* hermétique
airtime [ˈeətaɪm] *n* (**a**) *Rad & TV* temps *m* d'antenne (**b**) *Tel* communications *fpl*; **a. provider** fournisseur *m* de communications sans fil
airwaves [ˈeəweɪvz] *npl* ondes *fpl* (hertziennes)
airworthy [ˈeəwɜːðɪ] *adj (aircraft)* en état de voler
airy [ˈeərɪ] *adj* (**a**) *(room, house)* clair(e) et spacieux(-euse) (**b**) *(person, attitude)* insouciant(e), désinvolte
airy-fairy [ˈeərɪˈfeərɪ] *adj Fam (idea, scheme)* farfelu(e)
aisle [aɪl] *n (in supermarket, cinema)* allée *f*; *(in church)* *(at side)* bas-côté *m*; *(central)* allée *f*; *(in plane, bus)* couloir *m*; *Fam* **she had them rolling in the aisles** *(of comedian)* elle a fait mourir le public de rire; **a. seat** *(in plane)* place *f* côté couloir
ajar [əˈdʒɑː(r)] *adj & adv* entrouvert(e)
aka [eɪkərˈeɪ] *adv (abbr* **also known as**) alias
akin [əˈkɪn] *adj & adv* **to be a. to** être apparenté(e) à
alabaster [ˈæləbæstə(r)] *n* albâtre *m*
alacrity [əˈlækrɪtɪ] *n* empressement *m*
alarm [əˈlɑːm] **1** *n* (**a**) *(signal, device)* alarme *f*; **to raise** *or* **give the a.** donner l'alarme; **a. clock** réveil *m*, réveille-matin *m inv*; **a. signal** signal *m* d'alarme (**b**) *(fright, anxiety)* alarme *f*, frayeur *f*; **there's no cause for a.** il n'y a aucune raison de s'alarmer **2** *vt* effrayer, alarmer; **to be alarmed at sth** s'alarmer de qch
alarming [əˈlɑːmɪŋ] *adj* alarmant(e), inquiétant(e)
alarmist [əˈlɑːmɪst] **1** *n* alarmiste *mf* **2** *adj* alarmiste
alas [əˈlæs] *exclam* hélas!
Albania [ælˈbeɪnɪə] *n* l'Albanie *f*
Albanian [ælˈbeɪnɪən] **1** *n* (**a**) *(person)* Albanais(e) *m,f* (**b**) *(language)* albanais *m* **2** *adj* albanais(e)
albatross [ˈælbətrɒs] *n* albatros *m*
albeit [ɔːlˈbiːɪt] *conj* quoique, bien que
albino [ælˈbiːnəʊ] *(pl* **albinos**) *n* albinos *mf*
album [ˈælbəm] *n (record, for photos, stamps)* album *m*

albumen ['ælbjʊmɪn] *n* (**a**) *(in egg)* albumen *m* (**b**) *(in blood)* albumine *f*
alchemy ['ælkəmɪ] *n* alchimie *f*
alcohol ['ælkəhɒl] *n* alcool *m*
alcoholic [ælkə'hɒlɪk] **1** *n (person)* alcoolique *mf* **2** *adj* alcoolique; *(drink)* alcoolisé(e)
alcoholism ['ælkəhɒlɪzəm] *n* alcoolisme *m*
alcopop ['ælkəʊpɒp] *n* alcopop *m*
alcove ['ælkəʊv] *n (in wall)* niche *f*; *(larger)* renfoncement *m*
alder ['ɔːldə(r)] *n* au(l)ne *m*
ale [eɪl] *n* = bière anglaise au malt
alert [ə'lɜːt] **1** *n* alerte *f*; **to be on the a.** être en état d'alerte, être sur le qui-vive **2** *adj (watchful)* éveillé(e); *(lively)* vif (vive); **to be a. to sth** *(aware of)* être conscient(e) de qch **3** *vt* alerter; **to a. sb to a danger** alerter *ou* avertir qn d'un danger
Aleutian Islands [ə'luːʃən'aɪləndz] *npl* **the A.** les îles *fpl* Aléoutiennes
Alexandria [ælɪg'zɑːndrɪə] *n* Alexandrie
alfalfa [æl'fælfə] *n Bot* luzerne *f*
alfresco [æl'freskəʊ] *adj & adv* en plein air
algae ['ældʒiː] *npl* algues *fpl*
algebra ['ældʒɪbrə] *n* algèbre *f*
Algeria [æl'dʒɪərɪə] *n* l'Algérie *f*
Algerian [æl'dʒɪərɪən] **1** *n* Algérien(enne) *m,f* **2** *adj* algérien(enne)
Algiers [æl'dʒɪəz] *n* Alger
algorithm ['ælgərɪðəm] *n Comput* algorithme *m*
alias ['eɪlɪəs] *(pl* **aliases**) **1** *n* nom *m* d'emprunt, faux nom *m* **2** *adv* alias
alibi ['ælɪbaɪ] *n Law* alibi *m*
alien ['eɪlɪən] **1** *n* (**a**) *Formal (foreigner)* étranger(ère) *m,f* (**b**) *(from outer space)* extraterrestre *mf* **2** *adj* (**a**) *(strange)* étranger(ère); **violence is completely a. to his nature** il n'est pas du tout d'un naturel violent (**b**) *(from outer space)* extraterrestre
alienate ['eɪlɪəneɪt] *vt (supporters, readers)* s'aliéner; **they feel alienated from society** ils se sentent exclus *ou* mis à l'écart de la société
alight¹ [ə'laɪt] *adj (burning)* en flammes, en feu; **to set sth a.** mettre le feu à qch
alight² *(pt & pp* **alighted** *or* **alit** [ə'lɪt]) *vi* (**a**) *Formal (from train, car)* descendre (**b**) *(of bird, eyes, glance)* se poser (**on** sur)
align [ə'laɪn] *vt* aligner; **to a. oneself with sb** s'aligner sur qn
alignment [ə'laɪnmənt] *n* alignement *m*; **out of a.** désaligné(e); **in a. (with)** aligné(e) (sur)
alike [ə'laɪk] **1** *adj* semblable, pareil(eille); **to look a.** se ressembler **2** *adv (dress, think)* de la même façon; **old and young a.** les vieux comme les jeunes
alimentary canal [ælɪ'mentərɪkə'næl] *n Anat* tube *m* digestif
alimony ['ælɪmənɪ] *n Law* pension *f* alimentaire
A-list ['eɪlɪst] **1** *adj (star, celebrity)* très en vue **2** *n* **the A.** les vedettes les plus en vue
alit [ə'lɪt] *pt & pp of* **alight²**
alive [ə'laɪv] *adj* (**a**) *(living)* **to be a.** être vivant(e); **to keep sb a.** maintenir qn en vie; **to keep a memory/ custom a.** entretenir un souvenir/une tradition; **to stay a.** survivre; **to be a. and well** bien se porter; **the oldest woman a.** la doyenne du monde (**b**) *(aware)* **to be a. to sth** avoir parfaitement conscience

de qch (**c**) *(full of vitality)* **I've never felt so a.** je ne me suis jamais senti aussi bien de ma vie; **to come a.** s'animer (**d**) *(teeming)* **to be a. with sth** grouiller de qch
alkali ['ælkəlaɪ] *n* alcali *m*
alkaline ['ælkəlaɪn] *adj* alcalin(e)
all [ɔːl] **1** *adj* (**a**) *(every one of)* tous (toutes); **a. men** tous les hommes; **a. the girls** toutes les filles; **a. the others** tous les autres; **a. four of them** tous les quatre; **at a. hours** à des heures impossibles (**b**) *(the whole of)* tout(e); **a. the wine** tout le vin; **a. day** toute la journée; **a. her life** tout sa vie; **a. the time** tout le temps (**c**) *(for emphasis)* **a. sorts of things** toutes sortes de choses; **what's a. that noise?** c'est quoi, tout ce bruit?; **in a. honesty** en toute honnêteté; **for a. his wealth...** il a beau être riche...; **a. that easy** ce n'est pas si facile (que ça); *Fam* **she thinks she's a. that** elle ne se prend pas pour n'importe qui; **you, of a. people, should understand** si quelqu'un doit comprendre ça, c'est bien toi; **of a. the stupid things to say!** ce n'est vraiment pas malin de dire un truc pareil!
2 *pron* (**a**) *(everyone)* tous (toutes) *mpl, fpl*; **a. of us** nous tous; **a. of them say that...,** **they a. say that...** ils disent tous que...; **a. together** tous ensemble (**b**) *(everything)* tout *m*; **that's a.** c'est tout; **he ate a. of it, he ate it a.** il a tout mangé; **a. I said was... I did a. I could** j'ai fait tout ce que j'ai pu; **it was a. I could do not to laugh** j'ai bien failli rire; **best/worst of a.,...** le mieux/le pire, c'est que...; **I like this best of a.** c'est ça que je préfère; **most of a.** surtout; **when a. is said and done** au bout du compte; **it's a. the same to me** ça m'est égal; **thirty men in a.** trente hommes en tout *ou* au total; **a. in a.** dans l'ensemble; **it cost £260, a. in a.** ça a coûté 260 livres tout compris; *Ironic* **it cost a. of £2** ça a coûté la coquette somme de 2 livres
3 *adv* (**a**) *(entirely)* tout; **a. alone** tout(e) seul(e); **to be a. in black** être tout en noir; **to be a. for sth** être pour qch; **a. ears/smiles** tout ouïe/sourire; **I forgot a. about it** j'ai complètement oublié; **he's not a. bad** il n'a pas que de mauvais côtés; **a. over Spain/the world** dans toute l'Espagne/le monde entier; **a. over (place)** partout; **a. too soon** trop tôt; **a. along** depuis le début; **a. but** *(almost)* presque, pratiquement; **it's/he's a. yours** il est à vous; *Fam* **a. in** *(exhausted)* crevé(e) (**b**) **a. at** *(in the slightest)* du tout; **do you know her at a.?** tu la connais?; **if it's at a. possible** si c'était possible; **not at a.** pas du tout; *(when thanked)* je t'en prie (**c**) *(with comparatives)* **a. the better/worse** d'autant mieux/plus mal; **the easier/faster** d'autant plus facile/rapide (**d**) *(in games)* **2 a.** 2 partout; **4 (games) a.** *(in tennis)* 4 jeux partout; **15 a.** *(in tennis)* 15 partout
4 to give one's a. se donner à fond
Allah ['ælə] *n* Allah
allay [ə'leɪ] *vt (doubts, suspicions)* dissiper; *(fear, pain)* soulager
all-clear ['ɔːl'klɪə(r)] *n (after air-raid)* (signal *m* de) fin *f* d'alerte; *Fig (for project)* feu *m* vert
allegation [ælɪ'geɪʃən] *n* allégation *f*
allege [ə'ledʒ] *vt* alléguer, prétendre; **it is alleged that...** on prétend que...

alleged [ə'ledʒd] *adj (thief, culprit)* présumé(e)
allegedly [ə'ledʒɪdlɪ] *adv* prétendument; **he a.** stole
£500 il aurait volé 500 livres
allegiance [ə'liːdʒəns] *n (to party, cause)* fidélité *f*; *(to king)* allégeance *f*
allegory ['ælɪgərɪ] *(pl* **allegories)** *n* allégorie *f*
all-embracing [ɔːlɪm'breɪsɪŋ] *adj (term, category)* large
allergenic [ælə'dʒenɪk] *adj Med* allergisant(e)
allergic [ə'lɜːdʒɪk] *adj* allergique (**to** à)
allergy ['ælədʒɪ] *(pl* **allergies)** *n* allergie *f* (**to** à)
alleviate [ə'liːvɪeɪt] *vt* soulager, calmer
alley ['ælɪ] *(pl* **alleys)** *n (street)* ruelle *f*; **a. cat** chat *m* de gouttière
alleyway ['ælɪweɪ] *n (street)* ruelle *f*
alliance [ə'laɪəns] *n* alliance *f*; **to enter into an a.** with **sb** former une alliance avec qn
allied ['ælaɪd] *adj (countries)* allié(e); *(issues, phenomena)* lié(e)
alligator ['ælɪgeɪtə(r)] *n* alligator *m*; **a. shoes/handbag** chaussures *fpl*/sac *m* en crocodile
all-important ['ɔːlɪm'pɔːtənt] *adj* essentiel(elle), capital(e)
all-in ['ɔːlɪn] *adj (price)* tout compris; **a. wrestling** lutte *f* libre, catch *m*
alliteration [əlɪtə'reɪʃən] *n* allitération *f*
all-new [ɔːl'njuː] *adj* tout(e) dernier(ère)
all-night ['ɔːlnaɪt] *adj (party, session)* qui dure toute la nuit
allocate ['æləkeɪt] *vt (resources, money)* affecter, attribuer (**to** à); *(duties)* assigner (**to** à); *(time)* prévoir (**to** pour)
allocation [ælə'keɪʃən] *n (distribution)* affectation *f*; *(share)* part *f*
allot [ə'lɒt] *(pt & pp* **allotted)** *vt (resources, money)* attribuer (**to** à); *(duties, job)* assigner (**to** à); **in the allotted time** dans le temps imparti
allotment [ə'lɒtmənt] *n* (**a**) *(land)* jardin *m* ouvrier (**b**) *(share)* part *f*; *(of money)* affectation *f*
all-out ['ɔːlaʊt] *adj (resistance, effort)* acharné(e); *(strike, war)* total(e)
allow [ə'laʊ] *vt* (**a**) *(permit)* permettre; **to a. sb to do sth** permettre à qn de faire qch; **a. me!** *(offering help)* permettez(-moi)!; **smoking is not allowed** il est interdit de fumer; **I'm not allowed to do it** je n'ai pas l'autorisation de le faire; **to a. oneself to be deceived/persuaded** se laisser abuser/convaincre (**b**) *(allocate, grant)* accorder; *(time)* compter, prévoir
▸**allow for** *vt insep* tenir compte de; **add another hour to a. for delays** il faut prévoir une heure de plus au cas où il y aurait des retards
allowable [ə'laʊəbəl] *adj (error, delay)* admissible
allowance [ə'laʊəns] *n* (**a**) *(money given)* rente *f*, pension *f*; *(pocket money)* argent *m* de poche; **travel a.** indemnité *f* de transport (**b**) **to make a. for sth** tenir compte de qch; **I'm tired of making allowances for him** j'en ai assez de lui trouver des excuses
alloy ['ælɔɪ] *n* alliage *m*
all-powerful ['ɔːl'paʊəfʊl] *adj* tout-puissant (toute-puissante)
all-purpose ['ɔːl'pɜːpəs] *adj* universel(elle); **a. cleaner/adhesive** détachant *m*/colle *f* tous usages
all right, alright [ɔːl'raɪt] **1** *adj* **are you a.?** ça va?; **he was in a car crash but he's a.** il a eu un accident de voiture mais il n'a rien; **it's a.** *(acceptable)* ce n'est pas mal; *(not a problem)* ce n'est pas grave; **to be a. for**

money avoir suffisamment d'argent; **to be a. at maths/French** se débrouiller en maths/français.
2 *adv (yes)* oui; **is it a. if I smoke?** ça ne vous dérange pas si je fume?; **a., let's get started** bon, commençons
all-round ['ɔːl'raʊnd] *adj (education, improvement)* général(e); **an a. athlete** un(e) athlète complet(ète)
all-rounder ['ɔːl'raʊndə(r)] *n* **she's a good a.** elle est bonne en tout
allspice ['ɔːlspaɪs] *n* poivre *m* de la Jamaïque
all-star ['ɔːl'stɑː(r)] *adj* **an a. cast** une distribution prestigieuse
all-time ['ɔːl'taɪm] *adj (record)* absolu(e); **unemployment has reached an a. high/low** le chômage n'a jamais été aussi élevé/bas
allude [ə'luːd] *vi* **to a. to** faire allusion à
allure [ə'lʊə(r)] *n* attrait *m*
allusion [ə'luːʒən] *n* allusion *f*; **to make an a. to sth** faire allusion à qch
ally **1** *n* ['ælaɪ] *(pl* **allies)** allié(e) *m,f*
2 *vt* [ə'laɪ] *(pt & pp* **allied)** **to a. oneself with** s'allier à *ou* avec
almanac ['ɔːlmənæk] *n* almanach *m*
almighty [ɔːl'maɪtɪ] **1** *n* **the A.** le Tout-Puissant
2 *adj Fam (fuss, row)* terrible
almond ['ɑːmənd] *n* amande *f*; **a. tree** amandier *m*
almost ['ɔːlməʊst] *adv* presque; **it's a. six o'clock** il est presque six heures; **we're a. there** *(in journey)* nous sommes presque arrivés; *(in task)* nous avons presque fini; **she a. missed the bus** elle a failli rater l'autobus
alms [ɑːmz] *npl* aumône *f*
aloft [ə'lɒft] *adv* en l'air
alone [ə'ləʊn] *adj & adv* seul(e); **to leave sb a.** laisser qn tranquille; **to leave sth a.** ne pas toucher à qch; **I did it a.** je l'ai fait tout seul; **to go it a.** faire cavalier seul; **we are not a. in thinking that...** nous ne sommes pas les seuls à penser que...; **you a. can help me** vous seul pouvez m'aider; **I can't afford a bicycle, let a. a car!** je n'ai pas assez d'argent pour m'acheter une bicyclette, encore moins une voiture!
along [ə'lɒŋ] **1** *prep* le long de; **to walk a. the shore** marcher le long de la côte; **to sail a. the coast** longer la côte; **I was walking a. the street** je marchais dans la rue; *Fig* **somewhere a. the way** à un moment donné
2 *adv* **to move a.** avancer; **she'll be a. in ten minutes** elle sera là dans dix minutes; **to bring sth a.** apporter qch; **to bring sb a.** amener qn; **he knew all a.** il le savait depuis le début; **a. with** *(as well as)* ainsi que
alongside [ə'lɒŋ'saɪd] *prep (next to)* à côté de; *(along)* le long de; *Naut* **to come a.** accoster un bateau/quai
aloof [ə'luːf] **1** *adj* distant(e)
2 *adv* **to remain a.** *(from sth)* rester à l'écart (de qch)
aloud [ə'laʊd] *adv* à haute voix; **I was thinking a.** je pensais tout haut
alpha ['ælfə] *n* alpha *m*; *Phys* **a. rays** rayons *mpl* alpha
alphabet ['ælfəbet] *n* alphabet *m*
alphabetical [ælfə'betɪkəl] *adj* alphabétique; **in a. order** dans l'ordre alphabétique
alphabetically [ælfə'betɪklɪ] *adv* alphabétiquement
alphasort ['ælfəsɔːt] *vt Comput* trier par ordre alphabétique

Alpine ['ælpaɪn] adj alpin(e); an A. village un village des Alpes

Alps [ælps] npl the A. les Alpes fpl

already [ɔːl'redɪ] adv déjà; have you finished a.? vous avez déjà fini?; Am Fam enough, a.! ça suffit comme ça!

alright = all right

Alsatian [æl'seɪʃən] 1 n (a) (dog) berger m allemand (b) (person from Alsace) Alsacien(enne) m,f 2 adj alsacien(enne)

also ['ɔːlsəʊ] adv aussi; not only... but a.... non seulement... mais en plus...

also-ran ['ɔːlsəʊræn] n (in horse race) cheval m non classé; Fig (person) perdant(e) m,f

altar ['ɔːltə(r)] n autel m; a. boy enfant m de chœur

alter ['ɔːltə(r)] 1 vt changer; (garment) faire des retouches à; he altered his opinion later il a changé d'avis plus tard; that doesn't a. the fact that... cela ne change rien au fait que... 2 vi changer

alteration [ɔːltə'reɪʃən] n (to design, plan) modification f, changement m; (to timetable) changement; (to garment) retouche f

altercation [ɔːltə'keɪʃən] n altercation f

alter ego ['æltər'iːgəʊ] (pl alter egos) n alter ego m

alternate 1 adj [ɔːl'tɜːnət] alterné(e); on a. days un jour sur deux 2 ['ɔːltəneɪt] vt employer tour à tour 3 ['ɔːltəneɪt] vi alterner (with avec)

alternately [ɔːl'tɜːnətlɪ] adv tour à tour, alternativement

alternating ['ɔːltəneɪtɪŋ] adj alterné(e); Elec a. current courant m alternatif

alternative [ɔːl'tɜːnətɪv] 1 n (choice) choix m, solution f; there is no a. il n'y a pas le choix; she had no a. but to obey elle n'a pu faire autrement que d'obéir 2 adj (a) (plan, route) de remplacement; an a. proposal une contre-proposition (b) (music, comedy) alternatif(ive); a. energy énergies fpl de substitution; a. medicine médecine f douce

alternatively [ɔːl'tɜːnətɪvlɪ] adv (a) (on the other hand) sinon; you could travel by train or a. by bus vous pourriez voyager en train ou bien en autobus (b) (in a different way) autrement

alternator ['ɔːltəneɪtə(r)] n alternateur m

although [ɔːl'ðəʊ] conj bien que + subjunctive; a. it's late bien qu'il soit tard

altitude ['æltɪtjuːd] n altitude f

alto ['æltəʊ] (pl altos) n (male voice) haute-contre f; (female voice) contralto m; a. clef clef f d'ut; a. saxophone saxophone m alto

altogether [ɔːltə'geðə(r)] 1 adv (a) (entirely) complètement; I was not a. pleased je n'étais pas ravi (b) (in total) en tout; a. the bill came to £63 en tout l'addition s'élevait à 63 livres 2 n Fam in the a. (naked) nu(e) comme un ver

altruism ['æltrʊɪzəm] n altruisme m

altruistic [æltrʊ'ɪstɪk] adj altruiste

aluminium [ælju'mɪnɪəm], Am **aluminum** [ə'luːmɪnəm] n aluminium m; a. foil papier m d'aluminium

always ['ɔːlweɪz] adv toujours; I can a. try je peux toujours essayer

always-on ['ɔːlweɪz'ɒn] adj Comput (Internet connection) permanent(e)

AM ['eɪ'em] n Rad (abbr amplitude modulation) AM

am [æm] see be

a.m. ['eɪ'em] adv (abbr ante meridiem) du matin; five a.m. cinq heures du matin

amalgam [ə'mælgəm] n amalgame m

amalgamate [ə'mælgəmeɪt] 1 vt (metals, ideas) amalgamer; (companies) fusionner 2 vi (of companies) fusionner

amass [ə'mæs] vt amasser, accumuler

amateur ['æmətə(r)] 1 n amateur m 2 adj (painter, musician) amateur; Pej (work, performance) d'amateur; a. dramatics théâtre m amateur

amateurish [æmə'tɜːrɪʃ] adj Pej d'amateur

amaze [ə'meɪz] vt stupéfier; I was amazed by his courage son courage m'a stupéfié

amazement [ə'meɪzmənt] n stupéfaction f, stupeur f; in a. avec stupéfaction ou stupeur

amazing [ə'meɪzɪŋ] adj (a) (surprising) stupéfiant(e); it's a. that no one helped her il est incroyable que personne ne lui soit venu en aide (b) (excellent) formidable

Amazon ['æməzən] n (a) the A. (river) l'Amazone f; (region) l'Amazonie f (b) (female warrior) Amazone f

ambassador [æm'bæsədə(r)] n ambassadeur(drice) m,f

amber ['æmbə(r)] 1 n (colour, stone) ambre m; (of traffic light) orange m 2 adj (jewellery) d'ambre; (colour) couleur d'ambre, ambré(e)

ambience, ambiance ['æmbɪəns] n ambiance f

ambiguity [æmbɪ'gjuːɪtɪ] (pl ambiguities) n ambiguïté f

ambiguous [æm'bɪgjʊəs] adj ambigu(ë)

ambition [æm'bɪʃən] n ambition f

ambitious [æm'bɪʃəs] adj ambitieux(euse)

ambivalent [æm'bɪvələnt] adj ambivalent(e)

amble ['æmbəl] vi marcher d'un pas tranquille

ambulance ['æmbjʊləns] n ambulance f; a. man ambulancier m; a. woman ambulancière f

ambush ['æmbʊʃ] 1 n also Fig embuscade f 2 vt also Fig tendre une embuscade à; to be ambushed tomber dans une embuscade

ameba Am = amoeba

amen ['ɑː'men] exclam amen!, ainsi soit-il!

amenable [ə'miːnəbəl] adj souple; to prove a. to a suggestion approuver une proposition

amend [ə'mend] vt (text, law) modifier, amender; (error) corriger

amendment [ə'mendmənt] n (to law, proposal) amendement m

amends [ə'mendz] npl to make a. (for sth) faire amende honorable (pour qch); to make a. to sb for sth dédommager qn de qch

amenities [ə'miːnɪtɪz] npl (shops) commerces mpl; (facilities) équipements mpl collectifs

America [ə'merɪkə] n l'Amérique f

American [ə'merɪkən] 1 n Américain(e) m,f 2 adj américain(e); the A. Civil War la guerre de Sécession; A. football football m américain; A. Indian Indien(enne) m,f d'Amérique

amethyst ['æmɪθɪst] n améthyste f

amiable ['eɪmɪəbəl] adj aimable

amicable ['æmɪkəbəl] adj amical(e); an a. agreement un arrangement à l'amiable

amid [ə'mɪd], **amidst** [ə'mɪdst] prep au milieu de

amino acid [æ'miːnəʊ'æsɪd] n acide m aminé

amiss [ə'mɪs] adj & adv there's something a. il y a quelque chose qui ne va pas; to take sth a. prendre

qch de travers, mal prendre qch; **a cup of coffee wouldn't go a.** une tasse de café serait bienvenue
ammeter ['æmi:tə(r)] *n Elec* ampèremètre *m*
ammonia [ə'məʊnɪə] *n* ammoniac *m*
ammunition [æmjʊ'nɪʃən] *n (for guns)* munitions *fpl*; *Fig (in debate, argument)* arguments *mpl*
amnesia [æm'ni:zɪə] *n* amnésie *f*
amnesty ['æmnɪstɪ] *(pl* **amnesties**) *n* amnistie *f*
amoeba, *Am* **ameba** [ə'mi:bə] *n* amibe *f*
amok [ə'mɒk], **amuck** [ə'mʌk] *adv* **to run a.** être pris(e) de folie furieuse
among [ə'mʌŋ], **amongst** [ə'mʌŋst] *prep* parmi; **a. the crowd** au milieu de la foule; **we are a. friends** nous sommes entre amis; **they quarrel a. themselves** ils se disputent entre eux; **the money was divided a. them** l'argent a été divisé entre eux; **a. the best** parmi les meilleurs; **a. other things** entre autres choses
amoral [eɪ'mɒrəl] *adj* amoral(e)
amorphous [ə'mɔːfəs] *adj (mass, lump)* informe; *(ideas, beliefs)* confus(e)
amount [ə'maʊnt] *n* (**a**) *(sum of money)* somme *f* (**b**) *(quantity)* quantité *f*; **a large a. of time/effort** beaucoup de temps/d'énergie; **a certain a. of discomfort** un certain manque de confort; **in large amounts** en grande quantité; **in small amounts** en petites quantités
▸**amount to** *vt insep* (**a**) *(add up to)* s'élever à; **her debts a. to £700** ses dettes s'élèvent à 700 livres (**b**) *(mean)* **it amounts to the same thing** cela revient au même; *Fig* **he'll never a. to much** il n'arrivera jamais à rien
amp [æmp] *n* (**a**) *Elec (unit)* ampère *m*; **a 13-a. plug** une prise de 13 ampères (**b**) *Fam (amplifier)* ampli *m*
ampere ['æmpeə(r)] *n Elec* ampère *m*
ampersand ['æmpəsænd] *n* esperluette *f*
amphetamine [æm'fetəmɪn] *n* amphétamine *f*
amphibian [æm'fɪbɪən] **1** *n* amphibie *m*
  2 *adj* amphibie
amphibious [æm'fɪbɪəs] *adj* amphibie
amphitheatre, *Am* **amphitheater** ['æmfɪθɪətə(r)] *n* amphithéâtre *m*
ample ['æmpəl] *adj* (**a**) *(large) (woman, bosom)* fort(e) (**b**) *(plentiful)* abondant(e); **to have a. time to do sth** avoir largement le temps de faire qch; **to have a. opportunity to do sth** avoir tout loisir de faire qch; **this will be a.** ce sera largement suffisant
amplifier ['æmplɪfaɪə(r)] *n* amplificateur *m*
amplify ['æmplɪfaɪ] *(pt & pp* **amplified**) *vt (essay, remarks)* développer; *(current, volume)* amplifier
amply ['æmplɪ] *adv* amplement, largement
amputate ['æmpjʊteɪt] *vt* amputer
amputation [æmpjʊ'teɪʃən] *n* amputation *f*
Amsterdam [æmstə'dæm] *n* Amsterdam
amuck [ə'mʌk] = amok
amulet ['æmjʊlet] *n* amulette *f*
amuse [ə'mju:z] *vt* (**a**) *(make laugh)* amuser (**b**) *(occupy)* occuper; **to a. oneself by doing sth** se distraire en faisant qch; **to keep sb amused** distraire qn
amusement [ə'mju:zmənt] *n* (**a**) *(enjoyment)* amusement *m*; **much to everyone's a.** au grand amusement de tous (**b**) *(pastime)* distraction *f*; **a. arcade** galerie *f* de jeux; **a. park** parc *m* d'attractions
amusing [ə'mju:zɪŋ] *adj* amusant(e)
an [ən, *stressed* æn] *see* **a²**

anabolic steroid [ænə'bɒlɪk'stɛrɔɪd] *n* stéroïde *m* anabolisant
anachronism [ə'nækrənɪzəm] *n* anachronisme *m*; **to be an a.** faire figure d'anachronisme
anaconda [ænə'kɒndə] *n* anaconda *m*
anaemia, *Am* **anemia** [ə'ni:mɪə] *n* anémie *f*
anaemic, *Am* **anemic** [ə'ni:mɪk] *adj* anémique
anaesthetic, *Am* **anesthetic** [ænəs'θetɪk] *n (substance)* anesthésique *m*; *(process)* anesthésie *f*; **under a.** sous anesthésie; **local/general a.** anesthésie locale/générale
anaesthetist, *Am* **anesthetist** [ə'ni:sθətɪst] *n* anesthésiste *mf*
anaesthetize, *Am* **anesthetize** [ə'ni:sθətaɪz] *vt* anesthésier
anagram ['ænəgræm] *n* anagramme *f*
anal ['eɪnəl] *adj* anal(e)
analgesic [ænəl'dʒi:zɪk] **1** *n* analgésique *m*
  2 *adj* analgésique
analog *Am* = analogue
analogous [ə'næləgəs] *adj* analogue (**to** à)
analogue, ** *Am* **analog ['ænəlɒg] *n* analogue *m*; **a. clock** horloge *f* à affichage analogique
analogy [ə'nælədʒɪ] *(pl* **analogies**) *n* analogie *f*
analyse, *Am* **analyze** ['ænəlaɪz] *vt* analyser; *Psy* psychanalyser
analysis [ə'næləsɪs] *(pl* **analyses** [ə'næləsiːz]) *n* analyse *f*; *Psy* psychanalyse *f*; *Fig* **in the final a.** en fin de compte, au bout du compte
analyst ['ænəlɪst] *n* analyste *mf*; *Psy* (psych)analyste *mf*
analytic(al) [ænə'lɪtɪk(əl)] *adj* analytique
analyze *Am* = analyse
anarchist ['ænəkɪst] *n* anarchiste *mf*
anarchy ['ænəkɪ] *n* anarchie *f*
anathema [ə'næθəmə] *n* (**a**) *Rel* anathème *m* (**b**) *(repellent)* **the very idea was a. to her** l'idée même lui faisait horreur
anatomical [ænə'tɒmɪkəl] *adj* anatomique
anatomy [ə'nætəmɪ] *n* anatomie *f*
ANC [eɪen'si:] *n (abbr* **African National Congress**) ANC *m*
ancestor ['ænsestə(r)] *n* ancêtre *mf*
ancestral [æn'sestrəl] *adj* ancestral(e); **a. home** demeure *f* ancestrale
ancestry ['ænsestrɪ] *n (descent)* ascendance *f*
anchor ['æŋkə(r)] **1** *n* (**a**) *Naut* ancre *f*; *Fig* planche *f* de salut; **at a.** au mouillage; **to drop a.** jeter l'ancre; **to weigh a.** lever l'ancre (**b**) *(of radio, TV programme)* présentateur(trice) *m,f*
  2 *vt* (**a**) *Naut* ancrer (**b**) *(fix securely)* ancrer (**to** à) (**c**) *(radio, TV programme)* présenter
  3 *vi Naut* jeter l'ancre
anchorman ['æŋkəmən] *n (of radio, TV programme)* présentateur *m* principal
anchorwoman ['æŋkəwʊmən] *n (of radio, TV programme)* présentatrice *f* principale
anchovy ['æntʃəvɪ] *(pl* **anchovies**) *n* anchois *m*
ancient ['eɪnʃənt] **1** *adj* ancien(enne); *Fig (person, car)* très vieux (vieille); **a. history** histoire *f* ancienne; **A. Rome** la Rome antique
  2 *n* **the ancients** les anciens *mpl*
ancillary [æn'sɪlərɪ] *adj* auxiliaire
and [ænd, *unstressed* ənd, ən] *conj* (**a**) *(in general)* et; **she can read a. write** elle sait lire et écrire; **my mother a. father** mon père et ma mère; **chicken a. chips** du poulet-frites; **a vodka a. orange** une vodka

orange; **do that again** a. **I'll hit you!** si tu recommences, je te frappe!; **wait** a. **see** tu verras bien; **nice a. warm** bien chaud(e) (**b**) *(to)* **go** a. **look for it** va le chercher; **come** a. **see me** viens me voir; **try** a. **help me** essaie de m'aider (**c**) *(in numbers)* **two hundred** a. **two** deux cent deux; **four** a. **a half** quatre et demi; **an hour** a. **twenty minutes** une heure vingt; **four** a. **five make nine** quatre et *ou* plus cinq font neuf (**d**) *(expressing repetition)* **hours** a. **hours** pendant des heures et des heures; **better** a. **better** de mieux en mieux; **smaller** a. **smaller** de plus en plus petit(e); **she talked** a. **talked** elle n'arrêtait pas de parler (**e**) a. **so on** a. **so forth** et ainsi de suite

Andalusia [ændə'lu:sɪə] *n* l'Andalousie *f*

Andes ['ændi:z] *npl* **the A.** les Andes *fpl*

Andorra [æn'dɔːrə] *n* l'Andorre *f*

Andorran [æn'dɔːrən] **1** *n* Andorran(e) *m,f* **2** *adj* andorran(e)

androgynous [æn'drɒdʒɪnəs] *adj* androgyne

anecdotal [ænɪk'dəʊtəl] *adj* anecdotique

anecdote ['ænɪkdəʊt] *n* anecdote *f*

anemia, anemic *Am* = anaemia, anaemic

anemone [ə'nemənɪ] *n (flower)* anémone *f*; **sea a.** anémone de mer

anesthetic, anesthetist *etc Am* = anaesthetic, anaesthetist *etc*

anew [ə'njuː] *adv* encore, de nouveau; **to start a.** recommencer

angel ['eɪndʒəl] *n* ange *m*; *Fam* **you're an a.!** tu es un ange!

Angeleno [ændʒə'liːnəʊ] *(pl* **Angelenos)** *n* = personne née à ou habitant Los Angeles

angelic [æn'dʒelɪk] *adj* angélique

anger ['æŋɡə(r)] **1** *n* colère *f*; **a fit of a.** un accès de colère; **to speak in a.** parler sous le coup de la colère; **a. management** = thérapie pour aider les gens coléreux à mieux se maîtriser **2** *vt* mettre en colère **3** *vi* **to be slow/quick to a.** ne pas se mettre facilement/se mettre facilement en colère

angina [æn'dʒaɪnə] *n* angine *f* de poitrine

angle ['æŋɡəl] **1** *n* (**a**) *Math* angle *m*; **at an a. of...** formant un angle de...; **the car hit them at an a.** la voiture les a heurtés de biais; **the shop stands at an a. to the street** le magasin fait l'angle (**b**) *(viewpoint)* point *m* de vue; **seen from this a.** vu sous cet angle **2** *vi* (**a**) *(fish)* pêcher à la ligne (**b**) *Fam* **to a. for an invitation** chercher à se faire inviter

angler ['æŋɡlə(r)] *n (person)* pêcheur(euse) *m,f* à la ligne; **a. fish** baudroie *f*, lotte *f* de mer

Anglican ['æŋglɪkən] **1** *n* anglican(e) *m,f* **2** *adj* anglican(e)

angling ['æŋglɪŋ] *n (fishing)* pêche *f* à la ligne

Anglo-American ['æŋgləʊə'merɪkən] *adj* anglo-américain(e)

Anglo-Saxon ['æŋgləʊ'sæksən] **1** *n* (**a**) *(person)* Anglo-Saxon(ne) *m,f* (**b**) *(language)* anglo-saxon *m* **2** *adj* anglo-saxon(ne)

Angola [æŋ'gəʊlə] *n* l'Angola *m*

Angolan [æŋ'gəʊlən] **1** *n* Angolais(e) *m,f* **2** *adj* angolais(e)

angora [æŋ'gɔːrə] *n* angora *m*; **a. jumper** pull *m* en angora; **a. cat/rabbit** chat *m*/lapin *m* angora

angrily ['æŋgrɪlɪ] *adv* avec colère

angry ['æŋgrɪ] *adj (person)* en colère, fâché(e); *(voice, speech, letter)* furieux(euse); **to get a. (with)** se fâcher (contre), se mettre en colère (contre); **to make sb a.** mettre qn en colère

angst [æŋst] *n* angoisse *f*

anguish ['æŋgwɪʃ] *n* angoisse *f*

anguished ['æŋgwɪʃt] *adj (look, cry)* d'angoisse; *(person)* tourmenté(e)

angular ['æŋgjʊlə(r)] *adj* anguleux(euse)

animal ['ænɪməl] *n* animal *m*; **the a. kingdom** le règne animal; **a. lover** = personne qui aime les animaux; **a. rights** les droits *mpl* des animaux; **he's an a.** *(uncivilized person)* c'est une brute

animate 1 *adj* ['ænɪmɪt] animé(e) **2** *vt* ['ænɪmeɪt] animer

animated ['ænɪmeɪtɪd] *adj (expression, discussion)* animé(e); **to become a.** s'animer; **a. cartoon** dessin *m* animé

animation [ænɪ'meɪʃən] *n* animation *f*

animator ['ænɪmeɪtə(r)] *n Cin* animateur(trice) *m,f*

animism ['ænɪmɪzəm] *n* animisme *m*

animosity [ænɪ'mɒsɪtɪ] *n* animosité *f*

aniseed ['ænɪsiːd] *n (flavour)* anis *m*; *(seed)* graine *f* d'anis

Ankara ['æŋkərə] *n* Ankara

ankle ['æŋkəl] *n* cheville *f*; **a. boots** chaussures *fpl* montantes; **a. socks** socquettes *fpl*

anklet ['æŋklət] *n (ankle bracelet)* bracelet *m* de cheville

annals ['ænəlz] *npl* annales *fpl*

annex 1 *vt* [æ'neks] annexer **2** *n* ['æneks] *Am* = annexe

annexation [ænek'seɪʃən] *n* annexion *f*

annexe, *Am* **annex** ['æneks] *n (of building, document)* annexe *f*

annihilate [ə'naɪəleɪt] *vt* anéantir

annihilation [ənaɪə'leɪʃən] *n* anéantissement *m*

anniversary [ænɪ'vɜːsərɪ] *(pl* **anniversaries)** *n* anniversaire *m*; **wedding a.** anniversaire *m* de mariage

anno Domini ['ænəʊ'dɒmɪnaɪ] *adv* en l'an de grâce

annotate ['ænəteɪt] *vt* annoter

announce [ə'naʊns] *vt* annoncer

announcement [ə'naʊnsmənt] *n (of news)* annonce *f*; *(formal statement)* avis *m*

announcer [ə'naʊnsə(r)] *n (on radio, TV programme)* annonceur(euse) *m,f*, speaker (speakerine) *m,f*

annoy [ə'nɔɪ] *vt* agacer; **to get annoyed** se mettre en colère, se fâcher; **to be annoyed with sb** être en colère contre qn

annoyance [ə'nɔɪəns] *n (feeling)* agacement *m*; *(annoying thing)* ennui *m*

annoying [ə'nɔɪɪŋ] *adj* agaçant(e), ennuyeux(euse); **how a.!** comme c'est ennuyeux!

annual ['ænjʊəl] **1** *n* (**a**) *(plant)* plante *f* annuelle (**b**) *(book)* publication *f* annuelle; *(for children)* album *m* *(publié une fois par an)* **2** *adj* annuel(elle); **a. general meeting** assemblée *f* générale annuelle

annually ['ænjʊəlɪ] *adv (every year)* tous les ans; *(per year)* par an

annul [ə'nʌl] *(pt & pp* **annulled)** *vt Law (contract, marriage)* annuler

anode ['ænəʊd] *n* anode *f*

anodyne ['ænədaɪn] *adj (bland)* anodin(e)

anoint [ə'nɔɪnt] *vt* oindre (**with** de); **to a. sb king** sacrer qn roi

anomalous [ə'nɒmələs] *adj* anormal(e)

anomaly [ə'nɒməlɪ] (*pl* **anomalies**) *n* anomalie *f*
anon¹ [ə'nɒn] *adv Lit (soon)* bientôt
anon² *adj (abbr* **anonymous**) anonyme
anonymity [ænə'nɪmɪtɪ] *n* anonymat *m*
anonymous [ə'nɒnɪməs] *adj* anonyme; **to remain a.** garder l'anonymat
anorak ['ænəræk] *n* anorak *m*
anorexia [ænə'reksɪə] *n* anorexie *f*; **a. nervosa** anorexie *f* mentale
anorexic [ænə'reksɪk] *adj* anorexique
another [ə'nʌðə(r)] *adj & pron* (**a**) *(additional)* un (une) autre *m,f*; **a. cup of tea** une autre tasse de thé; **in a. ten years** dans dix ans; **don't say a. word** plus un mot; **a. Picasso/Vietnam** un nouveau Picasso/Viêt Nam (**b**) *(different)* un (une) autre *m,f*; **that's quite a. matter** c'est une toute autre affaire; **a. time, perhaps** *(declining invitation)* une autre fois, peut-être; **what with one thing and a., I forgot** avec tout ce qui s'est passé, j'ai oublié; **one way or a.** d'une façon ou d'une autre (**c**) *(reciprocal)* **they saw one a.** ils se sont vus
answer ['ɑːnsə(r)] **1** *n (to question, letter)* réponse *f*; *(to problem)* solution *f*; **I knocked but there was no a.** j'ai frappé mais personne n'a répondu; **there's no a.** *(on telephone)* ça ne répond pas; **he has an a. to everything** il a réponse à tout; *Formal* **in a. to your letter** en réponse à votre lettre
    2 *vt* répondre à; **"I'll do it tomorrow,"** he answered "je le ferai demain", a-t-il répondu; **to a. the telephone** répondre au téléphone; **to a. the door** ouvrir (la porte)
    3 *vi (of person)* répondre
► **answer back** *vi (be impertinent)* répondre
► **answer for** *vt insep* répondre de; **he has a lot to a. for** il a beaucoup de comptes à rendre
► **answer to** *vt insep* (**a**) *(be accountable to)* **to a. to sb** être responsable devant qn; **she answers to no one** elle n'a de comptes à rendre à personne (**b**) *(correspond to)* répondre à (**c**) **the dog answers to the name of Rover** le chien répond au nom de Rover
answerable ['ɑːnsərəbəl] *adj* **to be a. to sb** être responsable devant qn; **he is a. to nobody** il n'a de comptes à rendre à personne
answering machine ['ɑːnsərɪŋmə∫iːn], **answerphone** ['ɑːnsəfəʊn] *n* répondeur *m* (téléphonique)
ant [ænt] *n* fourmi *f*; **a. hill** fourmilière *f*
antagonism [æn'tægənɪzəm] *n* antagonisme *m*
antagonist [æn'tægənɪst] *n* antagoniste *mf*
antagonize [æn'tægənaɪz] *vt* rendre hostile
Antarctica [æn'tɑːktɪkə] *n* l'Antarctique *m*
ante ['æntɪ] *n Fam* **to up the a.** *(in gambling, conflict)* augmenter la mise
anteater ['æntiːtə(r)] *n* fourmilier *m*
antecedents [æntɪ'siːdənts] *npl* antécédents *mpl*
antelope ['æntɪləʊp] *n* antilope *f*
antenatal [æntɪ'neɪtəl] *adj* prénatal(e); **a. clinic** cours *m* de préparation à l'accouchement
antenna [æn'tenə] *n* (**a**) *(pl* **antennae** [æn'teniː]) *(of insect, snail)* antenne *f* (**b**) *(pl* **antennas**) *(of radio, TV)* antenne *f*
anterior [æn'tɪərɪə(r)] *adj Formal & Anat* antérieur(e) (**to** à)
anteroom ['æntɪruːm] *n* antichambre *f*
anthem ['ænθəm] *n* hymne *m*; **national a.** hymne *m* national; *Fam* **a club a.** un classique parmi les clubbers

anthology [æn'θɒlədʒɪ] (*pl* **anthologies**) *n* anthologie *f*
anthracite ['ænθrəsaɪt] *n* anthracite *m*
anthrax ['ænθræks] *n (disease)* anthrax *m*
anthropologist [ænθrə'pɒlədʒɪst] *n* anthropologue *mf*
anthropology [ænθrə'pɒlədʒɪ] *n* anthropologie *f*
anti- ['æntɪ] *pref* anti-; **a.-American** antiaméricain(e)
anti-ageing, anti-aging [æntɪ'eɪdʒɪŋ] *adj* **a. cream/treatment** crème *f*/traitement *m* antivieillissement
anti-aircraft ['æntɪeəkrɑːft] *adj (gun, defences)* antiaérien(enne)
antibiotic [æntɪbaɪ'ɒtɪk] *n* antibiotique *m*
antibody ['æntɪbɒdɪ] (*pl* **antibodies**) *n Med* anticorps *m*
Antichrist ['æntɪkraɪst] *n* Antéchrist *m*
anticipate [æn'tɪsɪpeɪt] *vt* (**a**) *(expect)* prévoir, s'attendre à; *(foresee)* anticiper; **we hadn't anticipated such stiff resistance** nous ne nous attendions pas à une telle résistance; **as anticipated, there was trouble** comme on s'y attendait, il y eut des problèmes (**b**) *(foreshadow)* préfigurer, annoncer
anticipation [æntɪsɪ'peɪʃən] *n* (**a**) *(foresight)* prévoyance *f*; **in a. of trouble** en prévision de troubles; **thanking you in a.** en vous remerciant d'avance, avec mes remerciements anticipés (**b**) *(eagerness)* impatience *f*
anticlimax [æntɪ'klaɪmæks] *n* déception *f*
anti-clockwise [æntɪ'klɒkwaɪz] **1** *adj* **in an a. direction** dans le sens inverse des aiguilles d'une montre
    2 *adv* dans le sens inverse des aiguilles d'une montre
antics [æntɪks] *npl* bouffonneries *fpl*; **he's been up to his usual a.** il a encore fait des siennes
anticyclone [æntɪ'saɪkləʊn] *n Met* anticyclone *m*
antidepressant [æntɪdɪ'presənt] *n* antidépresseur *m*
antidote ['æntɪdəʊt] *n also Fig* antidote *m* (**to** contre)
anti-dumping [æntɪ'dʌmpɪŋ] *adj (laws, legislation)* anti-dumping *inv*
anti-Establishment [æntɪ'stæblɪʃmənt] *adj Pol* anticonformiste
antifreeze ['æntɪfriːz] *n* antigel *m*
anti-globalization ['æntɪgləʊbəlaɪ'zeɪʃən] **1** *n* antimondialisation *f*
    2 *adj* antimondialiste
Antigua and Barbuda [æn'tiːgənbɑː'bjuːdə] *n* Antigua-et-Barbuda
antihistamine [æntɪ'hɪstəmiːn] *n Pharm* antihistaminique *m*
antipathy [æn'tɪpəθɪ] *n* antipathie *f* (**towards** pour)
antiperspirant [æntɪ'pɜːspɪrənt] *n* déodorant *m*
Antipodes [æn'tɪpədiːz] *npl* **the A.** l'Australie *f* et la Nouvelle-Zélande
antiquarian [æntɪ'kweərɪən] **1** *n (dealer)* antiquaire *mf*; *(collector)* collectionneur(euse) *m,f* d'antiquités
    2 *adj (book)* ancien(enne); **a. bookshop** = librairie spécialisée dans les livres anciens
antiquated ['æntɪkweɪtɪd] *adj (building, installation)* vétuste; *(idea, method)* vieillot(otte)
antique [æn'tiːk] **1** *n* antiquité *f*; **a. dealer** *mf*; **a. shop** magasin *m* d'antiquités
    2 *adj* ancien(enne); **an a. clock** une pendule ancienne *ou* d'époque; **a. furniture** meubles *mpl* anciens

antiquity [æn'tɪkwɪtɪ] *(pl* **antiquities***) n (historical period, ruin)* antiquité *f*
antiracist [æntɪ'reɪsɪst] *adj* antiraciste
anti-Semitic [æntɪsɪ'mɪtɪk] *adj* antisémite
antiseptic [æntɪ'septɪk] **1** *n* antiseptique *m*
2 *adj* (**a**) *(anti-bacterial)* antiseptique (**b**) *Fig (lacking character or warmth) (place)* aseptisé(e); *(person)* froid(e)
antisocial [æntɪ'səʊʃəl] *adj* (**a**) *(disruptive)* asocial(e) (**b**) *(unsociable)* peu sociable
antithesis [æn'tɪθɪsɪs] *(pl* **antitheses** [æn'tɪθɪsiːz]) *n (opposite)* opposé *m*, antithèse *f*
antlers ['æntləz] *npl* bois *mpl*
antonym ['æntənɪm] *n* antonyme *m*
Antwerp ['æntwɜːp] *n* Anvers
anus ['eɪnəs] *n* anus *m*
anvil ['ænvɪl] *n* enclume *f*
anxiety [æŋ'zaɪətɪ] *(pl* **anxieties***) n* (**a**) *(worry, concern)* inquiétude *f*; *(stronger)* anxiété *f*; **my main a. is...** mon principal souci est...; **there is no cause for a.** il n'y a pas de quoi s'inquiéter; **to feel a.** être anxieux(euse) (**b**) *(eagerness)* désir *m*, souci *m*; **in her a. to help** dans son désir *ou* souci de se rendre utile
anxious ['æŋkʃəs] *adj* (**a**) *(worried)* inquiet(ète); *(stronger)* anxieux(euse); **to be a. for sb** être inquiet(ète) *ou* s'inquiéter pour qn; **to be a. about sth** être inquiet(ète) *ou* s'inquiéter pour qch (**b**) *(worrying) (moment)* d'angoisse; *(period)* angoissant(e) (**c**) **to be a. to do sth** *(impatient)* être impatient(e) de faire qch; *(eager)* tenir à faire qch
anxiously ['æŋkʃəslɪ] *adv* (**a**) *(worriedly)* avec inquiétude; *(stronger)* anxieusement (**b**) *(with impatience)* impatiemment, avec impatience
any ['enɪ] **1** *pron* (**a**) *(some)* **have you got a.?** en avez-vous?; **is/are there a. left?** en reste-t-il?; **can a. of them speak English?** y en a-t-il parmi eux qui parlent anglais?
(**b**) *(in negatives)* **I haven't got a.** je n'en ai pas; **there was nothing in a. of the boxes** il n'y avait rien dans aucune des boîtes; **few, if a., can read** aucun, ou presque aucun, ne sait lire
(**c**) *(no particular one)* n'importe lequel (laquelle) *m,f*; **a. of us** n'importe lequel d'entre nous
(**d**) *(every one)* tous ceux (toutes celles) *mpl, fpl*; **keep a. you find** garde tous ceux que tu trouveras
2 *adj* (**a**) *(some) (singular)* du (de la); *(plural)* des; **do you have a. milk/flour/apples?** avez-vous du lait/de la farine/des pommes?
(**b**) *(in negatives)* **he hasn't got a. money** il n'a pas d'argent; **without a. doubt** sans aucun doute; **that won't do a. good** ça ne servira à rien
(**c**) *(no particular)* n'importe quel (quelle); **come a. day** venez n'importe quel jour; **a. minute now** d'une minute à l'autre
(**d**) *(every)* tout(e); **a. pupil who forgets his books will be punished** tout élève qui oubliera ses livres sera puni; **at a. rate, in a. case** en tout cas
3 *adv* (**a**) *(with comparative)* **I'm not a. better** je ne vais pas mieux; **does that make it a. easier?** est-ce que c'est plus facile comme ça?; **we don't see them a. longer** *or* **more** nous ne les voyons plus; **do you want a. more tea?** veux-tu encore du thé?; **I don't like her a. more than you do** je ne l'aime pas plus que toi
(**b**) *Fam* **a. old how** n'importe comment; **that didn't help us a.** ça ne nous a été d'aucun secours

anybody ['enɪbɒdɪ] *pron* (**a**) *(indeterminate)* quelqu'un; **would a. like some more cake?** quelqu'un veut-il encore du gâteau?; **she'll know if a. does** si quelqu'un doit le savoir, c'est bien elle (**b**) *(in negatives)* **not a.** ne... personne; **there isn't a. here** il n'y a personne ici; **there was hardly a.** il n'y avait presque personne (**c**) *(no matter who)* n'importe qui; **a. will tell you so** n'importe qui *ou* tout le monde vous le dira; **bring along a. you like** amenez qui vous voudrez; **a. else** *or* **but her would have refused** tout autre qu'elle aurait refusé; **it's a.'s guess** Dieu seul le sait; **he's not just a.!** ce n'est pas n'importe qui! (**d**) *(person with status)* **he'll never be a.** il ne fera jamais rien dans la vie
anyhow ['enɪhaʊ] *adv* (**a**) *(however)* de toute façon *ou* manière; **a., let's get back to what we were saying** bref, revenons à ce que nous disions; **I don't care, I'm going a.** ça m'est égal, j'y vais quand même (**b**) *Fam (carelessly)* n'importe comment
anyone ['enɪwʌn] = **anybody**
anyplace ['enɪpleɪs] *Am* = **anywhere**
anything ['enɪθɪŋ] **1** *pron* (**a**) *(indeterminate)* quelque chose; **is there a. I can do?** est-ce que je peux faire quelque chose?; **have you a. to write with?** as-tu de quoi écrire?; **will there be a. else?** *(in shop)* et avec ceci?; **have you a. smaller?** avez-vous quelque chose de plus petit?; *(money)* vous n'avez pas plus petit?; **if a. should happen to me** s'il m'arrivait quelque chose *ou* quoi que ce soit; **is (there) a. the matter?** il y a quelque chose qui ne va pas?
(**b**) *(in negatives)* **not a.** ne... rien; **he doesn't do a.** il ne fait rien; **hardly a.** presque rien
(**c**) *(no matter what)* n'importe quoi; **he eats a.** il mange de tout; **I love a. French** j'aime tout ce qui est français; **she would do a. for me** elle ferait n'importe quoi pour moi; **he was a. but friendly** il était tout sauf amical; **are you angry? – a. but** tu es fâché? – non, loin de là
2 *adv* **is it a. like the other one?** est-ce qu'il ressemble un peu à l'autre ou pas du tout?; **she doesn't look a. like her sister** elle ne ressemble pas du tout à sa sœur; **the food wasn't a. like as bad as they said** la nourriture était loin d'être aussi mauvaise que ce qu'on m'avait dit; *Fam* **as funny/strong as a.** drôle/fort(e) comme tout; *Fam* **to work like a.** travailler comme un fou (une folle); *Fam* **it's not that you're wrong or a.** ce n'est pas que tu aies tort
anyway ['enɪweɪ] = **anyhow (a)**
anywhere ['enɪweə(r)] *adv* (**a**) *(in questions)* quelque part; **did you go a. yesterday?** êtes-vous allé quelque part hier?; **can you see it a.?** tu le vois? (**b**) *(in negatives)* **not a.** ne... nulle part; **I can't find it a.** je ne le trouve nulle part; **we're not getting a.** nous n'avançons pas; **he isn't a. near as clever as her** il est loin d'être aussi intelligent qu'elle (**c**) *(no matter where)* n'importe où; **put it a.** mets-le n'importe où; **I'd know her a.** je la reconnaîtrais entre mille; **it's miles from a.** c'est loin de tout; **a. else** n'importe où
AO(C)B [eɪəʊ(siː)'biː] *(abbr* **any other (competent) business)** divers
aorta [eɪ'ɔːtə] *n* aorte *f*
apart [ə'pɑːt] *adv* (**a**) *(at a distance)* à l'écart *(from* de); **to stand a.** *(of person)* se tenir à l'écart; **the garage stands a. from the house** le garage est séparé de la maison (**b**) *(separated)* **they are far a.** ils sont

éloignés l'un de l'autre; **the two towns are 10 kilometres a.** les deux villes sont à 10 kilomètres l'une
de l'autre; **they're never a.** ils ne se séparent jamais;
with one's legs a. les jambes écartées; **two years a.** à
deux ans d'intervalle; **to set sth a.** for sth réserver
qch à qch; **to live a.** vivre séparément; **it's difficult
to tell them a.** il est difficile de les distinguer l'un de
l'autre; **joking a.,** ... blague à part, ... (**c**) *(to pieces)* **to
take sth a.** *(machine)* démonter qch; **to come a.** *(of
garment)* se découdre (**d**) *(excepting)* **a. from** à part;
a. from the fact that... indépendamment du fait
que...
apartheid [ə'pɑːtaɪt] *n* apartheid *m*
apartment [ə'pɑːtmənt] *n esp Am* appartement *m*; **a.
block, a. building** immeuble *m* d'habitation, *Can*
bloc-appartement *m*
apathetic [æpə'θetɪk] *adj* qui manque d'enthousiasme; **to be a. about sth** être indifférent(e) à qch
apathy ['æpəθɪ] *n* manque *m* d'enthousiasme
ape [eɪp] **1** *n (animal)* grand singe *m*; *Fam* **to go a.** piquer une crise
  2 *vt (imitate)* singer
aperitif [əperɪ'tiːf] *n* apéritif *m*
aperture ['æpətjʊə(r)] *n* ouverture *f*
APEX ['eɪpeks] *adj* **A. ticket** APEX *m (tarif préférentiel
sujet à des restrictions de délai d'achat)*
apex ['eɪpeks] *n* sommet *m*
aphasia [ə'feɪzɪə] *n Med* aphasie *f*
aphid ['eɪfɪd] *n* puceron *m*
aphorism ['æfərɪzəm] *n* aphorisme *m*
aphrodisiac [æfrəʊ'dɪzɪæk] **1** *n* aphrodisiaque *m*
  2 *adj* aphrodisiaque
apiece [ə'piːs] *adv* chacun(e); **they cost £3 a.** ils valent 3 livres pièce *ou* chacun
aplenty [ə'plentɪ] *adv* en abondance
aplomb [ə'plɒm] *n* sang-froid *m*
apocalypse [ə'pɒkəlɪps] *n* apocalypse *f*
apocalyptic [əpɒkə'lɪptɪk] *adj* apocalyptique
apocryphal [ə'pɒkrɪfəl] *adj* apocryphe; **the story is
a.** c'est une histoire inventée
apolitical [eɪpə'lɪtɪkəl] *adj* apolitique
apologetic [əpɒlə'dʒetɪk] *adj (tone, smile)* désolé(e);
to be a. about sth s'excuser de qch; **she was quite a.**
about it elle s'est répandue en excuses
apologize [ə'pɒlədʒaɪz] *vi* s'excuser; **to a. to sb** for
sth s'excuser de qch auprès de qn, présenter ses excuses à qn pour qch; **she apologized for being late/
for not telling him earlier** elle s'est excusée d'être en
retard/de ne pas le lui avoir dit plus tôt
apology [ə'pɒlədʒɪ] *(pl* apologies*) n* excuses *fpl*; **to
make/offer an a.** faire/présenter des excuses; **I
owe you an a.** je vous dois des excuses; *Pej* **an a.
for a dinner** un semblant de dîner
apoplectic [æpə'plektɪk] *adj Fig (angry)* furieux(-
euse); **to be a. with rage** s'étrangler de rage
apoplexy ['æpəpleksɪ] *n Med* apoplexie *f*; *Fig (anger)*
rage *f*
apostle [ə'pɒsəl] *n* apôtre *m*
apostolic(al) [æpɒs'tɒlɪk(əl)] *adj* apostolique
apostrophe [ə'pɒstrəfɪ] *n* apostrophe *f*
appal, *Am* **appall** [ə'pɔːl] *(pt & pp* appalled*) vt (shock)*
choquer, scandaliser; *(fill with horror)* horrifier; **to be
appalled at** *or* **by sth** être choqué(e)/horrifié(e) par
qch; **it appals me to think that...** je suis horrifié(e) à
la pensée que...
appalling [ə'pɔːlɪŋ] *adj (behaviour)* scandaleux(-
euse); *(conditions, smell, weather, film)* épouvantable

apparatus [æpə'reɪtəs] *n (machine)* appareil *m*; *(set of
machines, in laboratory)* équipement *m*; *(in gym)*
agrès *mpl*; **a piece of a.** un appareil
apparel [ə'pærəl] *n Formal or Literary* mise *f*
apparent [ə'pærənt] *adj* (**a**) *(obvious)* clair(e), évi-
dent(e); **it soon became a. that...** il est vite devenu
évident que... (**b**) *(seeming)* apparent(e)
apparently [ə'pærəntlɪ] *adv* apparemment; **a. he's
going to Venice** il paraît qu'il va à Venise
apparition [æpə'rɪʃən] *n* apparition *f*
appeal [ə'piːl] **1** *n* (**a**) *(call)* appel *m* (**for** à); **to make
an a. for help** lancer un appel à l'aide; **charity a.** =
appel aux dons lancé par une organisation caritative
  (**b**) *Law* appel *m*; **on a.** en seconde instance; **A.
Court, Court of A.** cour *f* d'appel (**c**) *(attraction)* attrait *m*; **to have great a.** *(of idea)* être très at-
trayant(e); *(of person)* avoir beaucoup de charme;
their music has a wide a. leur musique attire un public très varié
  2 *vt Am Law* **to a. a decision** faire appel d'une décision
  3 *vi* (**a**) *(make a plea)* **to a. (to sb) for help/money**
demander de l'aide/de l'argent (à qn); **to a. to sb's
generosity** faire appel à la générosité de qn (**b**) **to
a. to sb** *(attract)* attirer qn (**c**) *Law* se pourvoir en appel; **to a. against a decision** faire appel d'une
décision
appealing [ə'piːlɪŋ] *adj (idea)* séduisant(e); *(person,
manner)* sympathique
appear [ə'pɪə(r)] *vi* (**a**) *(come into view)* apparaître; *(of
publication)* paraître; **where did you a. from?** d'où
sors-tu?; **to a. from nowhere** sortir de nulle part; **to
a. on TV** passer à la télé (**b**) *Law* comparaître (**c**)
(look, seem) sembler; **to a. to be lost** avoir l'air d'être
perdu(e); **there appears to be a mistake** il semble
qu'il y ait une erreur; **so it would a.** c'est ce qu'on
dirait
appearance [ə'pɪərəns] *n* (**a**) *(arrival)* apparition *f*,
arrivée *f*; **to put in an a.** faire acte de présence (**b**)
(of actor) to **make a television a.** passer à la télévision (**c**) *(of publication)* parution *f* (**d**) *Law (in court)*
comparution *f* (**e**) *(looks, demeanour)* apparence *f*;
it's wrong to judge by appearances il ne faut pas se
fier aux apparences; **appearances can be deceptive**
les apparences peuvent être trompeuses; **to keep up
appearances** sauver les apparences
appease [ə'piːz] *vt (anger, person)* apaiser, calmer;
Pol composer avec
appeasement [ə'piːzmənt] *n (of person, anger)* apaisement *m*; *Pol* conciliation *f*
append [ə'pend] *vt (list, document)* joindre (**to** à);
(one's signature) apposer (**to** à)
appendage [ə'pendɪdʒ] *n* appendice *m*; **she was
tired of being treated as her husband's a.** elle en
avait assez de n'être traitée que comme la femme de
son mari
appendices [ə'pendɪsiːz] *pl of* appendix
appendicitis [əpendɪ'saɪtɪs] *n* appendicite *f*
appendix [ə'pendɪks] *(pl* appendices [ə'pendɪsiːz]*) n*
(**a**) *Anat* appendice *m*; **to have one's a. (taken) out**
se faire opérer de l'appendicite (**b**) *(of book)* appendice *m*
appetite ['æpɪtaɪt] *n* (**a**) *(for food)* appétit *m*; **to have
a good a.** avoir bon appétit; **to spoil sb's a.** couper
l'appétit à qn; **to give sb an a.** donner faim à qn; *(of
fresh air, walk)* creuser qn (**b**) *(enthusiasm)* (for

knowledge, travel) soif f (**for** de); (*for music, cinema*) goût m (**for** pour)

appetizer ['æpɪtaɪzə(r)] n also Fig amuse-gueule m

appetizing ['æpɪtaɪzɪŋ] adj appétissant(e)

applaud [ə'plɔːd] vt & vi applaudir

applause [ə'plɔːz] n (*clapping*) applaudissements mpl; (*approval*) approbation f

apple ['æpəl] n pomme f; **he was the a.** of her eye (*her favourite*) elle tenait à lui comme à la prunelle de ses yeux; **a. core** trognon m de pomme; **a. juice** jus m de pomme; **a. pie** (*without top crust*) tarte f aux pommes; (*with top crust*) tourte f aux pommes; **as American as a. pie** typiquement américain(e); **a. tart** tarte f aux pommes; **a. tree** pommier m

applecart ['æpəlkɑːt] n **to upset the a.** (*spoil plan*) tout chambouler

apple-pie ['æpəlpaɪ] adj **in a. order** parfaitement en ordre

appliance [ə'plaɪəns] n appareil m; **electrical/domestic a.** appareil m électrique/ménager

applicable [ə'plɪkəbəl] adj applicable; **the rule is a. to everybody** la règle s'applique à tous; **delete where not a.** (*on form*) rayer les mentions inutiles

applicant ['æplɪkənt] n (*for job*) candidat(e) m,f (**for** à)

application [æplɪ'keɪʃən] n (**a**) (*for job*) candidature f (**for** à); (*for passport, patent*) demande f (**for** de); **a. form** (*for job*) formulaire m de candidature; (*detailed*) dossier m de candidature; (*for grant, benefits*) formulaire m de demande (**b**) (*of rule, theory, paint*) application f (**c**) (*effort*) application f, assiduité f

applied [ə'plaɪd] adj (*maths, physics*) appliqué(e)

apply [ə'plaɪ] (pt & pp **applied**) **1** vt (**a**) (*put on*) appliquer (**to** sur) (**b**) (*use*) (*system, theory*) appliquer (**to** à); **to a. one's mind to sth** concentrer ses efforts sur qch; **to a. oneself (to one's work)** s'appliquer
2 vi (**a**) **to a. to sb for sth** s'adresser à qn pour obtenir qch; **to a. for a job** poser sa candidature pour un poste; **to a. for a grant** faire une demande de bourse (**b**) (*of law, rule*) s'appliquer (**to** à)

appoint [ə'pɔɪnt] vt (*person*) nommer; (*committee*) constituer; **to a. sb to a post** nommer qn à un poste; **to a. sb (as) manager** nommer qn directeur(trice)

appointed [ə'pɔɪntɪd] adj Formal (*agreed*) (*place, hour*) convenu(e), dit(e)

appointment [ə'pɔɪntmənt] n (**a**) (*meeting, with doctor*) rendez-vous m; **to make an a. with sb** prendre rendez-vous avec qn; (*with dentist, doctor*) prendre rendez-vous chez qn (**b**) (*to job*) nomination f; (*of committee*) constitution f; **to make an a.** pourvoir un poste; Com **by a. to His/Her Majesty** (*sign*) fournisseur de la Couronne; **appointments** (*in newspaper*) offres d'emploi

apportion [ə'pɔːʃən] vt répartir

appraisal [ə'preɪzəl] n (*of standards, personnel*) évaluation f

appraise [ə'preɪz] vt (*performance, situation*) évaluer; (*value*) estimer

appreciable [ə'priːʃɪəbəl] adj (*change, difference*) appréciable, sensible

appreciate [ə'priːʃɪeɪt] **1** vt (**a**) (*be grateful for*) (*help*) être reconnaissant(e) de; (*kindness*) être sensible à; **I a. your helping me** je vous suis reconnaissant de m'avoir aidé (**b**) (*grasp, understand*) être conscient(e) de; **he doesn't a. how lucky he is** il ne se rend pas

compte de la chance qu'il a (**c**) (*acknowledge*) apprécier
2 vi (*of goods, investment*) prendre de la valeur; (*of value*) augmenter

appreciation [əpriːʃɪ'eɪʃən] n (**a**) (*gratitude*) gratitude f, reconnaissance f; **in a. of** en reconnaissance de (**b**) (*understanding*) conscience f; **she has no a. of what is involved** elle ne se rend pas compte de ce que cela implique (**c**) (*review, assessment*) critique f; **a musical/wine a. society** une société d'amateurs de musique/de vin (**d**) Fin **a. of assets** plus-value f d'actif

appreciative [ə'priːʃɪətɪv] adj (**a**) (*grateful*) reconnaissant(e); **to be a. of sb's help/efforts** être reconnaissant(e) à qn de son aide/des ses efforts (**b**) (*review*) élogieux(euse); (*response*) favorable; **the audience were very a.** le public a beaucoup aimé; **to be a. of sth** apprécier qch

apprehend [æprɪ'hend] vt (**a**) Law (*arrest*) appréhender (**b**) Formal (*understand*) comprendre

apprehension [æprɪ'henʃən] n (**a**) (*fear*) appréhension f (**b**) Law (*arrest*) arrestation f

apprehensive [æprɪ'hensɪv] adj inquiet(ète); **to be a. about sth/doing sth** appréhender qch/de faire qch

apprentice [ə'prentɪs] **1** n apprenti(e) m,f
2 vt **to a. sb to sb** placer qn en apprentissage chez qn

apprenticeship [ə'prentɪʃɪp] n also Fig apprentissage m; **to serve one's a.** faire ses premières armes

approach [ə'prəʊtʃ] **1** n (**a**) (*of person, season*) approche f; **to make an a. to sb** (*proposal*) faire une proposition à qn (**b**) (*method*) approche f (**to** de); **let's try a different a.** essayons d'aborder le problème différemment (**c**) (*route of access*) voie f d'accès; **the approaches to a town** les abords mpl d'une ville; **a. road** voie f d'accès
2 vt (**a**) (*get nearer to*) approcher de; **I'm approaching forty-five** je vais sur mes quarante-cinq ans (**b**) (*go up to*) aborder; (*organization*) approcher; **to be easy/difficult to a.** être d'un abord facile/difficile (**c**) (*problem*) aborder
3 vi approcher

approachable [ə'prəʊtʃəbəl] adj (*person*) d'un abord facile

approaching [ə'prəʊtʃɪŋ] adj (*holiday, season*) qui approche; (*car*) qui vient en sens inverse

appropriate¹ [ə'prəʊprɪət] adj (*suitable*) approprié(e) (**to** à); (*moment*) opportun(e)

appropriate² [ə'prəʊprɪeɪt] vt (**a**) (*take, steal*) s'approprier (**b**) (*set aside*) (*money, funds*) affecter (**to** à)

appropriately [ə'prəʊprɪətlɪ] adv (*suitably*) de manière appropriée; (*properly*) convenablement

appropriation [əprəʊprɪ'eɪʃən] n (*of funds*) affectation f

approval [ə'pruːvəl] n approbation f; **to meet with sb's a.** obtenir l'approbation de qn; Com **on a.** à l'essai

approve [ə'pruːv] vt (*action, proposal*) approuver; (*treaty*) ratifier

▸**approve of** vt insep approuver; **I don't a. of your friends** tes amis ne me plaisent pas; **she doesn't a. of them smoking** elle n'approuve pas qu'ils fument

approving [ə'pruːvɪŋ] adj approbateur(trice)

approx (*abbr* **approximately**) env.

approximate 1 adj [ə'prɒksɪmɪt] approximatif(ive)
2 vi [ə'prɒksɪmeɪt] **to a. to sth** se rapprocher de qch

approximately [əˈprɒksɪmətlɪ] *adv* approximativement, environ
approximation [əprɒksɪˈmeɪʃən] *n* approximation
f
APR [eɪpiːˈɑː(r)] *n Fin (abbr* **annual percentage rate)**
TEG *m*
Apr *(abbr* **April**) avril
apricot [ˈeɪprɪkɒt] *n (fruit)* abricot *m*; **a. tree** abricotier
m
April [ˈeɪprɪl] *n* avril *m*; **A. showers** ≃ giboulées *fpl* de
mars; **A. Fool's Day** le premier avril; *see also* **May**

April Fool's Day
En Grande-Bretagne, le premier avril est l'occasion
de farces en tous genres ; en revanche, la tradition
du poisson en papier n'existe pas.

apron [ˈeɪprən] *n* (**a**) *(clothing)* tablier *m*; **he's still tied
to his mother's a.** strings *(dependent on her)* il est
toujours pendu aux jupes de sa mère (**b**) *Aviat* aire *f*
de stationnement
apt [æpt] *adj* (**a**) *(word, description)* juste (**b**) *(likely)*
to be a. to do sth avoir tendance à faire qch
aptitude [ˈæptɪtjuːd] *n* aptitude *f*, don *m*; **to have an a.
for sth** avoir une aptitude *ou* un don pour qch; **a. test**
test *m* d'aptitude
aptly [ˈæptlɪ] *adv (described)* justement; *(chosen)* bien
aquamarine [ækwəməˈriːn] **1** *n (gem)* aigue-marine *f*
2 *adj (colour)* bleu vert *inv*
aquarium [əˈkweərɪəm] *n* aquarium *m*
Aquarius [əˈkweərɪəs] *n* le Verseau; **to be (an) A.** être
(du) Verseau
aquarobics [ækwəˈrəʊbɪks] *n* aquagym *f*
aquatic [əˈkwætɪk] *adj* aquatique
aqueduct [ˈækwɪdʌkt] *n* aqueduc *m*
aquiline [ˈækwɪlaɪn] *adj* aquilin(e)
Arab [ˈærəb] **1** *n* Arabe *mf*
2 *adj* arabe

Arab
En anglais le mot "Arab" désigne l'ensemble des res-
sortissants des pays de culture arabe, et surtout de
l'Arabie Saoudite. Il n'a pas le sens restreint de
"Maghrébin" que l'on rencontre souvent en français : "the firm was bought by a wealthy Arab family".

Arabia [əˈreɪbɪə] *n* l'Arabie *f*
Arabian [əˈreɪbɪən] *adj* arabe; **the A. Sea** la mer d'Oman
Arabic [ˈærəbɪk] **1** *n (language)* arabe *m*
2 *adj* arabe; **A. numerals** chiffres *mpl* arabes
arable [ˈærəbəl] *adj* arable
arachnid [əˈræknɪd] *n Zool* arachnide *m*
arbiter [ˈɑːbɪtə(r)] *n (in dispute)* arbitre *m*; **the a. of
taste** l'arbitre des élégances
arbitrary [ˈɑːbɪtrərɪ] *adj* arbitraire
arbitrate [ˈɑːbɪtreɪt] **1** *vt* arbitrer
2 *vi* servir d'arbitre (**between** entre)
arbitration [ɑːbɪˈtreɪʃən] *n* arbitrage *m*; **to go to a.** *(of
parties)* avoir recours à l'arbitrage
arbitrator [ˈɑːbɪtreɪtə(r)] *n* médiateur(trice) *m,f*
arc [ɑːk] *n* arc *m*; **a. lamp** lampe *f* à arc
arcade [ɑːˈkeɪd] *n* (**a**) *Archit* galerie *f* (**b**) *(for shopping)* galerie *f* marchande (**c**) *(for video games)*
salle *f* de jeux électroniques; **a. game** jeu *m* électronique

arch¹ [ɑːtʃ] **1** *n* (**a**) *Archit* arche *f* (**b**) *(of foot)* voûte
f plantaire; **to have fallen arches** avoir les pieds
plats
2 *vt* **to a. one's back** *(inwards)* se cambrer; *(outwards)* se voûter
arch² *adj* **a. enemy** ennemi(e) *m,f* juré(e)
arch³ *adj (mischievous)* espiègle
archaeological, Am archeological [ɑːkɪəˈlɒdʒɪ-
kəl] *adj* archéologique
archaeologist, Am archeologist [ɑːkɪˈɒlədʒɪst] *n*
archéologue *mf*
archaeology, Am archeology [ɑːkɪˈɒlədʒɪ] *adj* archéologie *f*
archaic [ɑːˈkeɪɪk] *adj* archaïque
archangel [ˈɑːkeɪndʒəl] *n* archange *m*
archbishop [ɑːtʃˈbɪʃəp] *n* archevêque *m*
archduke [ɑːtʃˈdjuːk] *n* archiduc *m*
archeological, archeologist *etc Am* = **archaeological, archaeologist** *etc*
archer [ˈɑːtʃə(r)] *n* archer *m*
archery [ˈɑːtʃərɪ] *n* tir *m* à l'arc
archetypal [ɑːkɪˈtaɪpəl] *adj* **the a. English village**
l'archétype *m* du village anglais
archetype [ˈɑːkɪtaɪp] *n* archétype *m*
Archimedes [ɑːkɪˈmiːdɪz] *n* Archimède *m*
archipelago [ɑːkɪˈpeləgəʊ] *n (pl* **archipelagoes** *or* **ar-
chipelagos**) *n* archipel *m*
architect [ˈɑːkɪtekt] *n* architecte *mf*; **he was the a.
of his own downfall** il a été l'artisan de sa propre
ruine
architecture [ˈɑːkɪtektʃə(r)] *n* architecture *f*
archives [ˈɑːkaɪvz] *npl* archives *fpl*
archway [ˈɑːtʃweɪ] *n* arche *f*
arctic [ˈɑːktɪk] **1** *n* **the A.** l'Arctique *m*; **the A. Circle** le
cercle (polaire) arctique; **the A. Ocean** l'océan *m* Arctique
2 *adj* (**a**) *(climate)* arctique (**b**) *Fam (very cold)* **a.
spell of a. weather** un froid polaire
ardent [ˈɑːdənt] *adj (desire, love)* ardent(e); *(admirer,
believer)* fervent(e)
ardour [ˈɑːdə(r)] *n (of desire, love)* ardeur *f*; *(religious)*
ferveur *f*
arduous [ˈɑːdjʊəs] *adj* ardu(e), pénible
are [ɑː(r)] *see* **be**
area [ˈeərɪə] *n* (**a**) *(surface)* superficie *f*, surface *f*; **the
room is 24 square metres in a.** la pièce a une surface
de 24 mètres carrés (**b**) *(region)* région *f*; *(of countryside, forest)* zone *f*; *(in building)* partie *f*; *(of town, city)*
quartier *m*; *(of knowledge)* domaine *m*; **the London a.**
la région de Londres; **an a. of agreement** un terrain
d'entente; *Am Tel* **a. code** indicatif *m*; *Com* **a. manager**
directeur(trice) *m,f* régional(e)
arena [əˈriːnə] *n* (**a**) *(Roman)* arène *f*, *(stadium)* stade
m (**b**) *(area of activity)(economic, international)*
scène *f*
aren't [ɑːnt] = **are not**
Argentina [ɑːdʒənˈtiːnə] *n* l'Argentine *f*
Argentine [ˈɑːdʒəntaɪn] **1** *n (person)* Argentin(e) *m,f*;
Old-fashioned **the A.** *(country)* l'Argentine *f*
2 *adj* argentin(e)
Argentinian [ɑːdʒənˈtɪnɪən] **1** *n* Argentin(e) *m,f*
2 *adj* argentin(e)
arguable [ˈɑːgjʊəbəl] *adj* (**a**) *(questionable)* discutable; **it is a. whether it would have made any difference** on peut se demander si ça aurait changé quoi
que ce soit (**b**) *(conceivable)* défendable; **it is a.
that...** on pourrait soutenir que...

arguably [ˈɑːgjʊəblɪ] *adv* it's a. the city's best restaurant on peut dire que c'est le meilleur restaurant de la ville

argue [ˈɑːgjuː] **1** *vt (position)* défendre; **to a. the case for sth** plaider en faveur de qch; **to a. that...** soutenir que...
2 *vi (quarrel)* se disputer (**about** à propos de); **to a. for sth** plaider en faveur de qch; **to a. against sb/sth** s'opposer à qn/qch; **don't a.!** ne discute pas!, pas de discussion!

argument [ˈɑːgjʊmənt] *n* (**a**) *(quarrel)* dispute *f*; *(debate)* discussion *f*; **to have an a. about sth** *(quarrel)* se disputer à propos de qch; *(debate)* discuter de qch; **to get into an a.** se disputer; **and I don't want any arguments!** et pas de discussion! (**b**) *(reason)* **an a. for/against doing sth** une raison de faire/de ne pas faire qch (**c**) *(point)* argument *m* (**for/against** en faveur de/contre); **for a.'s sake** à titre d'exemple

argumentative [ɑːgjʊˈmentətɪv] *adj (person)* qui a l'esprit de contradiction; *(tone)* agressif(ive)

aria [ˈɑːrɪə] *n* aria *f*

arid [ˈærɪd] *adj* aride

Aries [ˈeəriːz] *n* le Bélier; **to be (an) A.** être (du) Bélier

arise [eˈraɪz] *(pt* **arose** [əˈrəʊz], *pp* **arisen** [əˈrɪzən]) *vi (of problem, possibility)* surgir; *(of situation)* naître; *(of question)* se poser; *(of storm)* se lever; **if the need arises** si le besoin s'en fait sentir

aristocracy [ærɪsˈtɒkrəsɪ] *n* aristocratie *f*

aristocrat [ˈærɪstəkræt] *n* aristocrate *mf*

aristocratic [ærɪstəˈkrætɪk] *adj* aristocratique

Aristotle [ˈærɪsˈtɒtəl] *n* Aristote

arithmetic [əˈrɪθmətɪk] *n (calculations)* calculs *mpl*; *(subject)* calcul *m*, arithmétique *f*

arithmetical [ærɪθˈmetɪkəl] *adj* arithmétique; **an a. error** une erreur de calcul

ark [ɑːk] *n* arche *f*

arm [ɑːm] **1** *n* (**a**) *(of person, chair, garment)* bras *m*; **to carry sb/sth in one's arms** porter qn/qch dans ses bras; **to take sb's a.** prendre qn par le bras; **a. in a.** bras dessus bras dessous; **to receive sb with open arms** *(warmly welcome)* recevoir qn à bras ouverts; *Fig* **to keep sb at a.'s length** tenir qn à distance (**b**) *(weapons)* armement *m*; **arms race** course *f* aux armements (**c**) *(in heraldry)* **(coat of) arms** armoiries *fpl*
2 *vt (person, country)* armer; **to a. oneself with the facts** s'armer de faits

armadillo [ɑːməˈdɪləʊ] *(pl* **armadillos**) *n* tatou *m*

Armageddon [ɑːməˈgedən] *n* l'Apocalypse *f*; *Fig* apocalypse *f*

armaments [ˈɑːməmənts] *npl* armement *m*, armes *fpl*

armband [ˈɑːmbænd] *n (at funeral, for swimming)* brassard *m*

armchair [ˈɑːmtʃeə(r)] *n* fauteuil *m*; **an a. sportsman** un sportif en chambre

armed [ɑːmd] *adj* armé(e) (**with** de); **a. forces** forces *fpl* armées; **a. robbery** vol *m* à main armée

Armenia [ɑːˈmiːnɪə] *n* l'Arménie *f*

Armenian [ɑːˈmiːnɪən] **1** *n* Arménien(enne) *m,f*
2 *adj* arménien(enne)

armhole [ˈɑːmhəʊl] *n* emmanchure *f*

armistice [ˈɑːmɪstɪs] *n* armistice *m*; **A. day** l'Armistice *m*

armour [ˈɑːmə(r)] *n* (**a**) *(of knight)* armure *f*; **suit of a.** armure *f* complète (**b**) *Mil (of tank)* blindage *m*; *(tanks)* blindés *mpl*

armoured car [ˈɑːmədˈkɑː(r)] *n* voiture *f* blindée

armoury [ˈɑːmərɪ] *(pl* **armouries**) *n (store)* arsenal *m*

armpit [ˈɑːmpɪt] *n* aisselle *f*

army [ˈɑːmɪ] *(pl* **armies**) *n* armée *f*; *(land forces)* armée *f* de terre; **to be in the a.** être dans l'armée, être militaire

aroma [əˈrəʊmə] *n* arôme *m*

aromatic [ærəʊˈmætɪk] *adj* aromatique

arose [əˈrəʊz] *pt of* **arise**

around [əˈraʊnd] **1** *prep* (**a**) *(position)* autour de; **a. the table** autour de la table; **there were hills all a. the town** il y avait des collines tout autour de la ville; **there were posters all a. the walls** il y avait des posters partout sur les murs; **a. here** par ici (**b**) *(motion)* autour de; **to look a. a room** jeter un coup d'œil à une pièce; **to travel a. the world** faire le tour du monde; **to walk a. the town/the streets** se promener en ville/dans les rues
2 *adv* (**a**) *(surrounding)* autour; **a garden with a fence a.** un jardin avec une clôture autour; **all a.** tout autour; **for miles a.** à des kilomètres à la ronde (**b**) *(in different directions)* **to walk a.** se promener; **there were books lying all a.** il y avait des livres qui traînaient partout (**c**) *(in the general area)* dans le coin; **is Jack a.?** est-ce que Jack est dans le coin?; **there was nobody a.** il n'y avait personne (**d**) *(approximately)* environ; **at a. one o'clock** vers une heure

arousal [əˈraʊzəl] *n (sexual)* excitation *f*; *(of interest, suspicion)* éveil *m*

arouse [əˈraʊz] *vt (sleeping person)* réveiller; *(emotion, desire, suspicion)* éveiller; *(enthusiasm, opposition)* soulever; *(sexually)* exciter

arraign [əˈreɪn] *vt Law* traduire en justice

arraignment [əˈreɪnmənt] *n Law* lecture *f* de l'acte d'accusation

arrange [əˈreɪndʒ] **1** *vt* (**a**) *(put in order)* arranger; *(classify)* ranger (**b**) *(organize) (wedding, meeting)* arranger; *(time, date)* fixer; *(accommodation)* s'occuper de; *(outing)* organiser; *(one's affairs)* mettre en ordre; **to a. where to go/what to do** prévoir où aller/quoi faire; **it was arranged that...** il a été prévu que...; **an arranged marriage** un mariage arrangé
2 *vi* **to a. to do sth** s'arranger pour faire qch; *(with someone else)* convenir *ou* prévoir de faire qch; **they arranged for a taxi to meet me** ils se sont arrangés pour qu'un taxi vienne me chercher

arrangement [əˈreɪndʒmənt] *n* (**a**) *(of objects, furniture)* disposition *f* (**b**) *(plan)* arrangement *m*; **to make arrangements** prendre des dispositions, faire le nécessaire; **I've made all the arrangements** j'ai tout arrangé (**c**) *(agreement)* arrangement *m*; **the a. was that...** il avait été convenu que...; **viewing by a.** *(sign)* visites sur rendez-vous; **to come to an a. with sb** parvenir à un arrangement avec qn (**d**) *Mus* arrangement *m*

array [əˈreɪ] *n (collection)* collection *f*, éventail *m*

arrears [əˈrɪəz] *npl* arriéré *m*; **to be two months in a. with the rent** devoir deux mois de loyer; **to be in a. with one's work** avoir du travail en retard; **to be paid monthly in a.** être payé(e) à la fin du mois

arrest [əˈrest] **1** *n* arrestation *f*; **to be under a.** être en état d'arrestation; **to make an a.** procéder à une arrestation
2 *vt (capture, stop)* arrêter; *(attention)* attirer

arresting [əˈrestɪŋ] *adj (striking)* saisissant(e)

arrival [ə'raɪvəl] *n* arrivée *f*; **on a.** à l'arrivée; **a new a.** *(at work, in club)* un nouveau venu (une nouvelle venue); *(baby)* un nouveau-né (une nouveau-née)

arrive [ə'raɪv] *vi* (**a**) *(at place)* arriver; **to a.** *(solution, decision)* arriver à, parvenir à (**b**) *Fam (attain success)* réussir, arriver

arrogance ['ærəɡəns] *n* arrogance *f*

arrogant ['ærəɡənt] *adj* arrogant(e)

arrow ['ærəʊ] *n* flèche *f*

arrowhead ['ærəʊhed] *n* pointe *f* de flèche

arrowroot ['ærəʊruːt] *n Culin* arrow-root *m*

arse [ɑːs] *Br Vulg* **1** *n* (**a**) *(buttocks)* cul *m*; **to get one's a.** in(to) gear se remuer le cul; **to work one's a. off** bosser comme un nègre; **it's a pain in the a.** c'est emmerdant (**b**) *(stupid person)* connard (connasse) *m,f*; **to make an a. of oneself** se couvrir de ridicule

2 *vt* why don't you come with us? – I can't be arsed tu viens avec nous? – non, j'ai trop la flemme

▸**arse about, arse around** *vi Br Vulg* déconner

arsehole ['ɑːshəʊl] *n Br Vulg* (**a**) *(anus)* trou *m* du cul (**b**) *(stupid person)* connard (connasse) *m,f*; **don't be such an a.!** ne fais pas le salaud (la salope)!

arsenal ['ɑːsənəl] *n* arsenal *m*; *(of devices, arguments)* panoplie *f*

arsenic ['ɑːsənɪk] *n* arsenic *m*

arson ['ɑːsən] *n* incendie *m* criminel *ou* volontaire

arsonist ['ɑːsənɪst] *n* incendiaire *mf*

art [ɑːt] *n* (**a**) *(in general)* art *m*; *(school subject)* arts *mpl* plastiques; *(college course)* beaux-arts *mpl*; **the arts in Great Britain** la création artistique en Grande-Bretagne; **arts and crafts** artisanat *m*; **a. gallery** *(museum)* musée *m* d'art; *(shop)* galerie *f* d'art; **a. school** école *f* des beaux-arts, beaux-arts *mpl* (**b**) *Univ* **arts** lettres *fpl* (**c**) *(technique)* art *m*; **there's an a. to making pastry** la pâtisserie, c'est tout un art

artefact ['ɑːtɪfækt] *n (manufactured object)* objet *m*

arteriosclerosis [ɑː'tɪərɪəʊskləˈrəʊsɪs] *n Med* artériosclérose *f*

artery ['ɑːtərɪ] *(pl* **arteries**) *n* artère *f*

artful ['ɑːtfʊl] *adj* (**a**) *(skilful)* (person) habile; *(solution, reply)* astucieux(euse) (**b**) *(cunning)* malin(igne)

arthritic [ɑːˈθrɪtɪk] *adj* arthritique

arthritis [ɑːˈθraɪtɪs] *n* arthrite *f*

arthropod ['ɑːθrəpɒd] *n Zool* arthropode *m*

arthrosis [ɑːˈθrəʊsɪs] *n Med* arthrose *f*

artichoke ['ɑːtɪtʃəʊk] *n* (**globe) a.** artichaut *m*

article ['ɑːtɪkəl] **1** *n* article *m*; **a. of clothing** vêtement *m*; *Gram* **definite/indefinite a.** article *m* défini/indéfini

2 *vt Law* mettre en apprentissage (**to** chez)

articulate 1 *adj* [ɑːˈtɪkjʊlət] *(person)* qui s'exprime avec facilité; *(account)* clair(e)

2 *vt* [ɑːˈtɪkjʊleɪt] (**a**) *(word)* articuler; **to a. one's words** articuler (**b**) *(idea, feeling)* exprimer

articulated lorry [ɑːˈtɪkjʊleɪtɪdˈlɒrɪ] *n Br* semi-remorque *m*

articulation [ɑːtɪkjʊˈleɪʃən] *n* articulation *f*

artificial [ɑːtɪˈfɪʃəl] *adj* artificiel(elle); *Med* **a. insemination** insémination *f* artificielle; *Comput* **a. intelligence** intelligence *f* artificielle; **a. respiration** respiration *f* artificielle; **a. sweetener** édulcorant *m* (de synthèse)

artificially [ɑːtɪˈfɪʃəlɪ] *adv* artificiellement

artillery [ɑːˈtɪlərɪ] *n* artillerie *f*

artisan [ɑːtɪˈzæn] *n* artisan *m*

artist ['ɑːtɪst] *n* artiste *mf*

artistic [ɑːˈtɪstɪk] *adj* artistique; *(temperament, person)* artiste

artistry ['ɑːtɪstrɪ] *n (of painting, game)* qualité *f* artistique; *(of painter, footballer)* art *m*

artless ['ɑːtlɪs] *adj* *(simple)* naturel(elle); *(clumsy)* maladroit(e)

artwork ['ɑːtwɜːk] *n (in book, magazine)* illustrations *fpl*

arty ['ɑːtɪ] *adj Fam (person, job, style)* artistique; *Pej (person)* prétentieux(euse) *(et passionné(e) d'art)*

arum lily ['eərəmˈlɪlɪ] *n Bot* calla *f*

Aryan ['eərɪən] **1** *n* Aryen(enne) *m,f*

2 *adj* aryen(enne)

as [əz, *stressed* æz] **1** *adv* (**a**) *(with manner)* **as promised/planned** comme promis/prévu; **A as in Anne** A comme Anne

(**b**) *(in comparisons)* **as tall as me** aussi grand(e) que moi; **as white as a sheet** blanc (blanche) comme du linge; **twice as big as** deux fois plus grand que; **I came as fast as I could** je suis venu aussi vite que j'ai pu; **as much money/many people** as autant d'argent/de gens que; **as much/many as you want** autant que tu veux; **as soon as possible** dès que possible; **as recently as last week** pas plus tard que la semaine dernière

(**c**) *(as if)* comme si; **it isn't as if** *or* **though it's difficult** ce n'est pourtant pas compliqué; **she looked as if** *or* **though she was angry** elle avait l'air fâché; **it looks as if** *or* **though he's already left** on dirait qu'il est déjà parti

(**d**) *(as well)* aussi, également; **he has two cars as well as a motorbike** il a une moto et aussi deux voitures

(**e**) *(as for)* quant à

2 *conj* (**a**) *(with time)* **he went out as I came in** il sortit au moment où j'entrais; **as the day went on** à mesure que la journée passait; **we'll see as we go along** nous verrons au fur et à mesure; **as you get older** en vieillissant, avec l'âge; **as always** comme toujours

(**b**) *(with manner)* comme; **as I was saying** comme je disais; **do as you're told** fais ce qu'on te dit; **as often happens,...** comme c'est souvent le cas,...; **it's hard/far enough as it is** c'est assez difficile/loin comme ça; **as it were** pour ainsi dire

(**c**) *(concessive)* **late as it was,...** bien qu'il fût tard,...; **try as she might,...** elle avait beau essayer,...; **strange as it may seem,...** aussi étrange que cela puisse paraître,...; **much as I like her,...** je l'aime bien, mais...

(**d**) *(because)* puisque, comme

(**e**) *(in addition)* **mother is well, as are the children** maman va bien, et les enfants aussi

3 *prep* comme; **to work as a team** travailler en équipe; **to regard sb as a friend** considérer qn comme ami; **I meant it as a compliment** c'était un compliment; **she used it as a bandage** elle s'en est servi comme d'un bandage; **as a mother, I think that...** en tant que mère, je pense que...

asap [eɪeseɪˈpiː] *adv (abbr* **as soon as possible)** dès que possible

asbestos [æsˈbestəs] *n* amiante *f*

asbestosis [æsbesˈtəʊsɪs] *n Med* asbestose *f*

ASBO, Asbo ['æzbəʊ] *n Br (abbr* **Antisocial Behaviour Order)** = injonction contre une personne coupable de harcèlement ou de tout autre comportement antisocial à l'encontre d'autres personnes

ASBO
Il s'agit d'un nouveau type de condamnation prononcée par des juges de proximité à la demande d'institutions locales (écoles, organismes HLM, municipalités...) et qui sanctionne des actes du type larcins, tapage nocturne, harcèlement ou vandalisme. Les injonctions sont adaptées au type de comportement antisocial manifesté par le délinquant, et prennent le plus souvent la forme d'interdictions de fréquenter tel ou tel lieu, de se trouver sur la voie publique après une certaine heure, d'écouter de la musique trop fort, etc. Les "ASBO" ne font pas l'unanimité chez les Britanniques ; en effet, certains estiment que les municipalités ont tendance à en abuser et à ne pas toujours les utiliser à bon escient.

ascend [ə'send] **1** vt (mountain) gravir, faire l'ascension de; (throne) accéder à; (stairs) gravir
2 vi monter
ascendancy, ascendency [ə'sendənsɪ] n ascendant m
ascendant, ascendent [ə'sendənt] n **to be in the a.** prospérer
Ascension [ə'senʃən] n Rel l'Ascension f
ascent [ə'sent] n also Fig ascension f
ascertain [æsə'teɪn] vt établir
ascetic [ə'setɪk] **1** n ascète mf
2 adj ascétique
ASCII ['æskɪ] n (abbr American Standard Code for Information Interchange) ASCII m
ascribe [ə'skraɪb] vt attribuer (to à)
ASEAN ['æzɪæn] n (abbr Association of Southeast Asian Nations) ANASE f
aseptic [eɪ'septɪk] adj aseptique
asexual [eɪ'seksjʊəl] adj asexué(e)
ash¹ [æʃ] n (tree) frêne m
ash² n (from fire, cigarette) cendre f; Rel **A. Wednesday** mercredi m des Cendres
ashamed [ə'ʃeɪmd] adj honteux(euse); **to feel a.** avoir honte; **to be a. of** avoir honte de; **I am a. to say that...** j'avoue à ma grande honte que...; **there is nothing to be a. of** il n'y a pas de quoi avoir honte; **you ought to be a. of yourself!** tu devrais avoir honte!
ashen ['æʃən] adj blême
ashore [ə'ʃɔː(r)] adv (on land) à terre; **to go a.** débarquer
ashtray ['æʃtreɪ] n cendrier m
Asia ['eɪʒə] n l'Asie f; **A. Minor** l'Asie mineure
Asian ['eɪʒən] **1** n Asiatique mf; Br (from Indian subcontinent) = personne originaire du sous-continent indien
2 adj asiatique; Br (from Indian sub-continent) du sous-continent indien; Am **A. American** Américain(e) m,f d'origine asiatique

Asian
Pour les Britanniques, "Asian" désigne le plus souvent les habitants de l'Inde et des pays limitrophes : ainsi, l'expression "the Asian community in Edinburgh" fait référence aux personnes d'origine indienne, pakistanaise et bangladaise qui habitent Édimbourg.

Asiatic [eɪʒɪ'ætɪk] **1** n Asiatique mf
2 adj asiatique
aside [ə'saɪd] **1** adv **to stand a.** s'écarter; **to take sb a.** prendre qn à part; **to put** or **set sth a.** (reserve) mettre qch de côté; **politics a.,...** toute question de politique mise à part,...; **a. from** à part
2 n aparté m
asinine ['æsɪnaɪn] adj stupide
ask [ɑːsk] **1** vt (a) (enquire about) demander; **to a. (sb) a question** poser une question (à qn); **to a. sb sth** demander qch à qn; **to a. sb the time** demander l'heure à qn; **to a. sb the way** demander son chemin à qn; **don't a. me!** je n'en ai pas la moindre idée! (**b**) (request) demander; **to a. sb for sth** demander qch à qn; **to a. to do sth** demander à faire qch; **to a. sb to do sth** demander à qn de faire qch; **to a. a favour of sb, to a. sb a favour** demander un service à qn; **if it isn't asking too much** si ce n'est pas trop demander; **to a. sb's permission to do sth** demander à qn la permission de faire qch (**c**) (invite) inviter; **to a. sb to lunch** inviter qn à déjeuner; **to a. sb out** inviter qn à sortir
2 vi (**a**) (enquire) se renseigner (**about** sur) (**b**) (request) demander; **you only have to a.!** il n'y a qu'à demander!; **to a. for sth** demander qch; Fam **he was asking for it** il l'a cherché
▶**ask after** vt insep demander des nouvelles de
askance [ə'skæns] adv **to look a. at sb** regarder qn de travers
askew [ə'skjuː] adv de travers
asking ['ɑːskɪŋ] n **it's yours for the a.** il suffit de le demander pour l'obtenir; **a. price** prix m demandé
ASL [eɪes'el] n (abbr American Sign Language) = langage par signes d'origine américaine
asleep [ə'sliːp] adj **to be a.** dormir; **to fall a.** s'endormir; **to be fast** or **sound a.** dormir profondément
asocial [eɪ'səʊʃəl] adj asocial(e)
asparagus [ə'spærəgəs] n asperge f
aspect ['æspekt] n (a) (of problem, subject) aspect m (**b**) (of building) exposition f
asperity [æ'sperɪtɪ] n (of character, voice) rudesse f
aspersions [ə'spɜːʃənz] npl **to cast a. on sth** dénigrer qch; **to cast a. on sb's honour** porter atteinte à l'honneur de qn
asphalt ['æsfælt] n asphalte m
asphyxiate [æs'fɪksɪeɪt] vt asphyxier
asphyxiation [æsfɪksɪ'eɪʃən] n asphyxie f
aspic ['æspɪk] n Culin gelée f; **it was as if the house had been preserved in a.** la maison donnait l'impression de n'avoir pas subi le passage du temps
aspirate ['æspɪreɪt] adj Ling aspiré(e)
aspiration [æspɪ'reɪʃən] n (ambition) aspiration f
aspire [ə'spaɪə(r)] vi **to a. to do sth** aspirer à faire qch
aspirin ['æsprɪn] n aspirine f
aspiring [ə'spaɪərɪŋ] adj **to be an a. actor/writer** aspirer à devenir acteur/écrivain
ass¹ [æs] n (a) (animal) âne m (**b**) Fam (idiot) imbécile mf; **to make an a. of oneself** se ridiculiser
ass² n Am very Fam (behind) cul m; **to get one's a. in gear** se remuer le cul; **to work one's a. off** bosser comme un nègre; **a kick in the a.** un coup de pied au cul; **to kick a.** être super
assail [ə'seɪl] vt (a) (attack) attaquer (**b**) **to a. sb with questions** assaillir qn de questions; **assailed by doubts** en proie au doute
assailant [ə'seɪlənt] n agresseur m
assassin [ə'sæsɪn] n assassin m

assassinate [ə'sæsɪneɪt] vt assassiner
assassination [əsæsɪ'neɪʃən] n assassinat m
assault [ə'sɔːlt] **1** n Mil assaut m (**on** de); Law agression f (**on** contre); (criticism) attaque f (**on** contre); Mil a. **course** parcours m du combattant; Mil a. **rifle** fusil m d'assaut
   2 vt Law agresser; **to be sexually assaulted** être victime d'une agression sexuelle
assemble [ə'sembəl] **1** vt (people) rassembler, réunir; (facts, objects) rassembler; (machine, furniture) assembler, monter
   2 vi (of people) se rassembler, se réunir
assembly [ə'semblɪ] (pl **assemblies**) n (**a**) (gathering) assemblée f; Br Sch = rassemblement des élèves d'une école avant d'entrer en classe; **a. hall** (in school) = salle où se réunissent les élèves d'une école (**b**) (of machine, furniture) assemblage m, montage m; **a. instructions** instructions fpl de montage; Ind **a. line** chaîne f de montage
assent [ə'sent] **1** n assentiment m
   2 vi donner son assentiment (**to** à)
assert [ə'sɜːt] vt (one's rights, point of view) faire valoir; **to a. one's authority** asseoir son autorité; **to a. oneself** s'imposer; **to a. that...** affirmer que...
assertion [ə'sɜːʃən] n (statement) déclaration f; (of right) revendication f
assertive [ə'sɜːtɪv] adj assuré(e); **he's not a. enough** il ne s'affirme pas assez
assertiveness [ə'sɜːtɪvnɪs] n assurance f; **a. training** stage m d'affirmation de soi
assess [ə'ses] vt (**a**) (value, damage) estimer; **to a. sb's income** (for tax purposes) évaluer les revenus de qn (**b**) (situation, impact) étudier, analyser; (performance, ability, quality) évaluer
assessment [ə'sesmənt] n (**a**) (of value) estimation f; (for insurance or tax purposes) évaluation f (**b**) (of situation) étude f, analyse f; (of performance, ability, quality) évaluation f
assessor [ə'sesə(r)] n Fin contrôleur m
asset ['æset] n (**a**) (advantage) atout m; **she is a great a. to the firm** c'est quelqu'un de très précieux pour l'entreprise (**b**) Fin **assets** actif m, avoir m; (personal) patrimoine m; **assets and liabilities** l'actif et le passif; Fin **a. stripper** = personne qui rachète une société pour profiter de la réalisation de l'actif; Fin **a. stripping** démembrement m (suite au rachat d'une société)
asshole ['æshəʊl] Am = arsehole
assiduous [ə'sɪdjʊəs] adj assidu(e)
assign [ə'saɪn] vt (task) assigner (**to** à); (funds) affecter (**to** à); (importance) attacher (**to** à); **to a. sb to do sth** charger qn de faire qch
assignation [æsɪg'neɪʃən] n Formal or Hum (meeting) rendez-vous m
assignment [ə'saɪnmənt] n (**a**) (of funds) affectation f; (of tasks) distribution f (**b**) (task) Sch devoir m; Journ reportage m; (of soldier, politician) mission f
assimilate [ə'sɪmɪleɪt] **1** vt assimiler
   2 vi (of immigrants) s'assimiler, s'intégrer
assimilation [əsɪmɪ'leɪʃən] n assimilation f
assist [ə'sɪst] **1** vt (person) aider, assister; (process, development) faciliter; **to a. sb in doing** or **to do sth** aider qn à faire qch; Med **assisted conception** aide f médicale à la procréation; **assisted suicide** suicide m assisté
   2 vi aider

assistance [ə'sɪstəns] n aide f, secours m; **to come to sb's a.** venir en aide à qn; **can I be of any a.?** puis-je être utile à quelque chose?
assistant [ə'sɪstənt] n assistant(e) m,f; (**shop**) **a.** vendeur(euse) m,f; **a. manager** sous-directeur(trice) m,f; Sport **a. referee** (in football) juge m de touche
assizes [ə'saɪzɪz] npl Law assises fpl
associate 1 n [ə'səʊsɪət] (in business) associé(e) m,f; (in crime) complice mf
   2 adj [ə'səʊsɪət] (company) associé(e)
   3 vt [ə'səʊsɪeɪt] (**a**) (mentally) associer (**with** à) (**b**) **to be associated with** avoir des liens avec
   4 vi [ə'səʊsɪeɪt] **to a. with sb** fréquenter qn
associated [ə'səʊsɪeɪtɪd] adj associé(e); **a. company** société f affiliée
association [əsəʊsɪ'eɪʃən] n association f; **the name has unfortunate associations for her** ce nom lui évoque des souvenirs désagréables; **in a. with** en association avec
assorted [ə'sɔːtɪd] adj (colours, flavours) varié(e)s; (biscuits, sweets) assorti(e)s
assortment [ə'sɔːtmənt] n assortiment m
assuage [ə'sweɪdʒ] vt Lit apaiser
assume [ə'sjuːm] vt (**a**) (suppose) supposer; **I a. he'll come** je suppose qu'il viendra; **he was assumed to be rich** on le supposait riche; **let us a. that...** supposons ou mettons que... (**b**) (power, control) prendre; (name) adopter; **to a. responsibility for sth** devenir responsable de qch; **an assumed name** un nom d'emprunt (**c**) (appearance, shape) prendre
assumption [ə'sʌmpʃən] n (**a**) (supposition) supposition f; **to work on the a. that...** se fonder sur l'hypothèse que... (**b**) (of power) prise f (**c**) Rel **the A.** l'Assomption f
assurance [ə'ʃʊərəns] n (**a**) (guarantee) assurance f; **he gave me his a.** il me l'a assuré (**b**) (confidence) assurance f (**c**) Br (insurance) assurance f
assure [ə'ʃʊə(r)] vt assurer; **to a. sb of sth** assurer qn de qch
assured [ə'ʃʊəd] adj (victory, success) assuré(e), certain(e); (person, performance) plein(e) d'assurance
assuredly [ə'ʃʊərɪdlɪ] adv assurément
asterisk ['æstərɪsk] n astérisque m
asteroid ['æstərɔɪd] n astéroïde m
asthma ['æsmə] n asthme m
asthmatic [æs'mætɪk] **1** n asthmatique mf
   2 adj asthmatique mf
astonish [ə'stɒnɪʃ] vt étonner; **to be astonished at** or **by sth** être étonné(e) par qch
astonishing [ə'stɒnɪʃɪŋ] adj (amazing) incroyable; (performance) extraordinaire; **I find it a. that...** je m'étonne que... + subjunctive
astonishment [ə'stɒnɪʃmənt] n étonnement m; **to my a.** à mon grand étonnement
astound [ə'staʊnd] vt stupéfier
astounding [ə'staʊndɪŋ] adj stupéfiant(e), incroyable
astral ['æstrəl] adj astral(e)
astray [ə'streɪ] adv **to go a.** (become lost) s'égarer; **to lead sb a.** (morally) détourner qn du droit chemin
astride [ə'straɪd] prep à cheval sur, à califourchon sur
astringent [ə'strɪndʒənt] **1** n Med astringent m
   2 adj Med astringent(e); Fig (person, voice) caustique
astrologer [ə'strɒlədʒə(r)] n astrologue mf
astrological [æstrə'lɒdʒɪkəl] adj astrologique

astrology [əˈstrɒlədʒɪ] *n* astrologie *f*
astronaut [ˈæstrənɔːt] *n* astronaute *mf*
astronomer [əˈstrɒnəmə(r)] *n* astronome *mf*
astronomic(al) [æstrəˈnɒmɪk(əl)] *adj* astronomique
astronomy [əˈstrɒnəmɪ] *n* astronomie *f*
astrophysics [æstrəʊˈfɪzɪks] *n* astrophysique *f*
Astroturf® [ˈæstrəʊtɜːf] *n* gazon *m* artificiel
astute [əˈstjuːt] *adj* astucieux(euse)
astutely [əˈstjuːtlɪ] *adv* astucieusement
asunder [əˈsʌndə(r)] *adv Lit* **to tear sth a.** mettre qch en pièces
asylum [əˈsaɪləm] *n* asile *m*; **(mental) a.** asile d'aliénés
asylum-seeker [əˈsaɪləmˈsiːkə(r)] *n* demandeur(euse) *m,f* d'asile
asymmetric(al) [eɪsɪˈmetrɪk(əl)] *adj* asymétrique
asymmetry [eɪˈsɪmɪtrɪ] *n* asymétrie *f*
at [æt, *unstressed* ət] *prep* (**a**) *(with place)* à; **at the office** au bureau; **at university** à l'université; **at the station** à la gare; **at the top/bottom (of)** en haut/bas (de); **at John's (house)** chez John; **at home** chez soi, à la maison
(**b**) *(with time)* à; **at six o'clock** à six heures; **at night** la nuit; **at Christmas** à Noël; **at the beginning** au début; **at (the age of) twenty** à (l'âge de) vingt ans
(**c**) *(with price, speed)* à; **at 60 mph** ≃ à 90 km/h; **at 50p a pound** à 50 pence la livre
(**d**) *(with direction)* **to look at sb/sth** regarder qn/qch; **to shout at sb** crier après qn; **to throw sth at sb** jeter qch à qn
(**e**) *(with cause)* **to be angry at sb** être fâché(e) contre qn; **to be surprised at sth** être surpris(e) de *ou* par qch; **to be shocked at sth** être choqué(e) par qch
(**f**) *(with activity)* **to be at work/lunch** être en train de travailler/déjeuner; **she's been at it all weekend** elle n'a pas arrêté du week-end; **while you're at it** tant que tu y es; **to be good/bad at sth** *(subject)* être bon (bonne)/mauvais(e) en qch; **to be good/bad at doing sth** être/ne pas être doué(e) pour faire qch
(**g**) *Comput (in e-mail addresses)* arrobas *m*, arobase *f*; **gwilson at transex, dot, co, dot, uk** gwilson, arrobas, transex, transex, point, co, point, uk
atavistic [ætəˈvɪstɪk] *adj* atavique
ate [eɪt] *pt of* eat
atheism [ˈeɪθɪɪzəm] *n* athéisme *m*
atheist [ˈeɪθɪɪst] *n* athée *mf*
Athens [ˈæθənz] *n* Athènes *f*
athlete [ˈæθliːt] *n* athlète *mf*; **a.'s foot** mycose *f*
athletic [æθˈletɪk] *adj (fit)* athlétique
athletics [æθˈletɪks] *npl* athlétisme *m*
Atlantic [ətˈlæntɪk] **1** *n* **the A.** l'Atlantique *m*
2 *adj (coast)* atlantique; *(island)* de l'Atlantique; **the A. Ocean** l'océan Atlantique
atlas [ˈætləs] *n* atlas *m*
ATM [eɪtiːˈem] *n Fin (abbr* **automated teller machine** *or* automatic teller machine) DAB *m*
atmosphere [ˈætməsfɪə(r)] *n* atmosphère *f*; *Fig* atmosphère, ambiance *f*
atmospheric [ætməsˈferɪk] *adj (pressure)* atmosphérique; *Fig (music, lighting)* d'ambiance
atoll [ˈætɒl] *n Geog* atoll *m*
atom [ˈætəm] *n* atome *m*; **a. bomb** bombe *f* atomique
atomic [əˈtɒmɪk] *adj* atomique; **a. bomb** bombe *f* atomique; **a. energy** énergie *f* atomique; **a. warfare** guerre *f* atomique *ou* nucléaire

▶**atone for** [əˈtəʊn] *vt insep (sin, crime)* expier; *(mistake)* racheter, réparer
atonement [əˈtəʊnmənt] *n (for sin, crime)* expiation *f*; *(for mistake, behaviour)* réparation *f*
atrocious [əˈtrəʊʃəs] *adj (crime)* atroce; *(behaviour)* ignoble; *(meal)* infect(e); *(decision, joke)* très mauvais(e); *(weather, conditions, journey)* épouvantable
atrocity [əˈtrɒsɪtɪ] *(pl* **atrocities**) *n* atrocité *f*
atrophy [ˈætrəfɪ] *(pt & pp* **atrophied**) *vi* s'atrophier
attach [əˈtætʃ] *vt (label, importance)* attacher (**to** à); *(blame, responsibility)* imputer (**to** à); *(document)* joindre (**to** à); *(employee)* détacher (**to** à); **to a. oneself to sb** ne pas lâcher qn d'une semelle; **to be attached to** *(like)* être attaché(e) à
attachment [əˈtætʃmənt] *n* (**a**) *(device)* accessoire *m* (**b**) *(secondment)* détachement *m* (**c**) *(fondness)* attachement *m*; **to form an a. to sb** s'attacher à qn (**d**) *Comput (of e-mail)* fichier *m* joint
attack [əˈtæk] **1** *n* attaque *f*; **to be** *or* **come under a.** être attaqué(e); **to launch an a. on** attaquer; **an a. of nerves** une crise de nerfs; **to have an a. of doubt** être assailli(e) par le doute
2 *vt* attaquer; *(rights)* porter atteinte à; *(problem, task)* s'attaquer à; **to be attacked** se faire attaquer
attacker [əˈtækə(r)] *n (assailant)* agresseur *m*; *(in sport)* attaquant(e) *m,f*
attain [əˈteɪn] *vt (goal, ambition)* réaliser; *(rank, age)* atteindre
attainable [əˈteɪnəbəl] *adj (goal, ambition)* réalisable
attainment [əˈteɪnmənt] *n (of goal, ambition)* réalisation *f*
attempt [əˈtempt] **1** *n* tentative *f*; **to make an a. at doing sth** *or* **to do sth** essayer *ou* tâcher de faire qch; **they made no a. to help** ils n'ont pas essayé d'aider; **to make an a. on sb's life** attenter à la vie de qn; **at the first a.** du premier coup
2 *vt* **to do sth** essayer *ou* tenter de faire qch; **to a. a smile** essayer de sourire; *Law* **attempted murder** tentative *f* d'assassinat
attend [əˈtend] **1** *vt (meeting)* assister à; *(school)* aller à; *(of doctor)* suivre
2 *vi (be present)* être présent(e)
▶**attend to** *vt insep (matter, problem, customer)* s'occuper de
attendance [əˈtendəns] *n (presence)* présence *f*; **to be in a. on sb** s'occuper de qn; **there was a good/poor a.** il y avait beaucoup de/peu de monde; **a. register** registre *m* des présences
attendant [əˈtendənt] *n (in museum, car park)* gardien(enne) *m,f*; *(in cloakroom)* préposé(e) *m,f*; *(at petrol pump)* pompiste *mf*
attention [əˈtenʃən] *n* (**a**) *(in general)* attention *f*; **to pay a. to** *(listen to)* écouter attentivement; *(watch)* regarder attentivement; **to pay a. to detail** faire attention aux détails; **to give sb/sth one's full a.** consacrer toute son attention à qn/qch; **to attract** *or* **catch sb's a.** attirer l'attention de qn; **to draw a. to oneself** se faire remarquer; **your a. please, ladies and gentlemen** mesdames et messieurs, votre attention s'il vous plaît; **for the a. of Mr Harvey** *(in letter)* à l'attention de M. Harvey; *Med* **a. deficit disorder** troubles *mpl* de l'attention; **a. span** capacité *f* de concentration (**b**) *(repairs)* **the engine needs some a.** le moteur a besoin d'être réparé (**c**) *Mil* **a.!** garde-à-vous!; **to stand at** *or* **to a.** être au garde-à-vous

attentive [ə'tentɪv] adj (paying attention) attentif(ive); (considerate) attentionné(e) (**to** pour)
attentively [ə'tentɪvlɪ] adv attentivement
attest [ə'test] **1** vt attester
2 vi **to a. to** témoigner de
attic ['ætɪk] n grenier m
attire [ə'taɪə(r)] n tenue f
attitude ['ætɪtjuːd] n (**a**) (behaviour) attitude f (**b**) (opinion) opinion f; **attitudes have changed** les mentalités ont changé; **what's your a. to abortion?** quelle est votre position sur l'avortement?; **to take the a. that...** considérer que...; Com **a. survey** enquête f d'attitudes (**c**) (pose) pose f; **to strike an a.** prendre une pose affectée
attn Com (abbr **for the attention of**) à l'attention de
attorney [ə'tɜːnɪ] (pl **attorneys**) n Am (lawyer) avocat(e) m,f; **A. General** ≃ ministre m de la justice
attract [ə'trækt] vt attirer; **I'm extremely attracted to her** elle me plaît énormément; **the thought of working for him doesn't a. me** la perspective de travailler pour lui ne m'attire guère
attraction [ə'trækʃən] n (**a**) (power) attirance f; **the prospect holds little a. for me** cette perspective ne m'attire guère (**b**) (attractive aspect) attrait m
attractive [ə'træktɪv] adj (person, offer) séduisant(e); (prospect) attrayant(e); **do you find her a.?** est-ce qu'elle te plaît?
attribute 1 n ['ætrɪbjuːt] attribut m
2 vt [ə'trɪbjuːt] attribuer (**to** à)
attrition [ə'trɪʃən] n usure f; **war of a.** guerre f d'usure
attuned [ə'tjuːnd] adj **to be a. to sth** être accoutumé(e) à qch
atypical [eɪ'tɪpɪkəl] adj atypique
aubergine ['əʊbəʒiːn] n Br aubergine f
auburn ['ɔːbən] adj (hair) auburn inv
auction ['ɔːkʃən] **1** n vente f aux enchères; **to put sth up for a.** mettre qch aux enchères; **a. room** salle f des ventes
2 vt vendre aux enchères
►**auction off** vt sep vendre aux enchères
auctioneer [ɔːkʃə'nɪə(r)] n commissaire-priseur m
audacious [ɔː'deɪʃəs] adj audacieux(euse)
audacity [ɔː'dæsɪtɪ] n audace f
audible ['ɔːdɪbəl] adj audible
audience ['ɔːdɪəns] n (**a**) (spectators, listeners) public m; **a. participation** participation f du public (**b**) (meeting with monarch, Pope) audience f; **to grant sb an a.** accorder une audience à qn
audio ['ɔːdɪəʊ] adj **a. cassette** cassette f audio; **a. equipment** équipement m sonore
audiotypist ['ɔːdɪəʊtaɪpɪst] n audiotypiste mf
audiovisual [ɔːdɪəʊ'vɪzjʊəl] adj audiovisuel(elle)
audit ['ɔːdɪt] Fin **1** n audit m
2 vt vérifier
audition [ɔː'dɪʃən] **1** n audition f
2 vt & vi auditionner
auditor ['ɔːdɪtə(r)] n Fin commissaire m aux comptes
auditorium [ɔːdɪ'tɔːrɪəm] n (of theatre, concert hall) salle f; (lecture theatre) amphithéâtre m
auditory ['ɔːdɪtrɪ] adj auditif(ive)
Aug (abbr **August**) août
augment [ɔːg'ment] vt augmenter, accroître
augur ['ɔːgə(r)] vi **to a. well/badly** être de bon/mauvais augure
August ['ɔːgəst] n août m; see also **May**

august [ɔː'gʌst] adj Lit (distinguished) auguste
aunt [ɑːnt] n tante f
auntie, aunty ['ɑːntɪ] (pl **aunties**) n Fam tata f, tantine f
au pair [əʊ'peə(r)] n (jeune fille f) au pair f
aura ['ɔːrə] n aura f; (of place) atmosphère f
aural ['ɔːrəl] adj auditif(ive)
auspices ['ɔːspɪsɪz] npl **under the a. of** sous l'égide de
auspicious [ɔː'spɪʃəs] adj prometteur(euse)
Aussie ['ɒzɪ] Fam **1** n Australien(enne) m,f
2 adj australien(enne)
austere [ɒ'stɪə(r)] adj austère
austerity [ɒ'sterɪtɪ] n austérité f
Australasia [ɒstrə'leɪʒə] n l'Australasie f
Australasian [ɒstrə'leɪʒən] adj d'Australasie
Australia [ɒ'streɪlɪə] n l'Australie f
Australian [ɒ'streɪlɪən] **1** n Australien(enne) m,f
2 adj australien(enne)
Austria ['ɒstrɪə] n l'Autriche f
Austrian ['ɒstrɪən] **1** n Autrichien(enne) m,f
2 adj autrichien(enne)
autarchy ['ɔːtɑːkɪ] n autocratie f
authentic [ɔː'θentɪk] adj authentique
authenticate [ɔː'θentɪkeɪt] vt authentifier
authenticity [ɔːθen'tɪsɪtɪ] n authenticité f
author ['ɔːθə(r)] n auteur m
authoritarian [ɔːθɒrɪ'teərɪən] adj autoritaire
authoritative [ɔː'θɒrɪtətɪv] adj (**a**) (voice, manner) autoritaire (**b**) (work, document) qui fait autorité
authority [ɔː'θɒrɪtɪ] (pl **authorities**) n (**a**) (power) autorité f; **the authorities** les autorités fpl; **I'd like to speak to someone in a.** je voudrais parler à un responsable (**b**) (authorization) autorisation f; **to give sb a.** to do sth autoriser qn à faire qch; **on one's own a.** de son propre chef (**c**) (expert) **to be an a. on sth** faire autorité en matière de qch; **to have sth on good a.** tenir qch de source sûre
authorization [ɔːθəraɪ'zeɪʃən] n autorisation f
authorize ['ɔːθəraɪz] vt autoriser; **to a. sb to do sth** autoriser qn à faire qch
autism ['ɔːtɪzəm] n autisme m
autistic [ɔː'tɪstɪk] adj autiste
auto ['ɔːtəʊ] (pl **autos**) n Am voiture f, auto(mobile) f
auto- [ɔːtəʊ] pref auto-
autobiographical [ɔːtəʊbaɪə'græfɪkəl] adj autobiographique
autobiography [ɔːtəʊbaɪ'ɒgrəfɪ] (pl **autobiographies**) n autobiographie f
autocrat ['ɔːtəkræt] n autocrate m
autocratic [ɔːtə'krætɪk] adj autocratique
Autocue® ['ɔːtəkjuː] n téléprompteur m
autograph ['ɔːtəgrɑːf] **1** n autographe m; **a. album** or **book** album m d'autographes
2 vt signer, dédicacer
automat ['ɔːtəmæt] n Am = cafétéria équipée de distributeurs automatiques
automate ['ɔːtəmeɪt] vt automatiser
automated ['ɔːtəmeɪtɪd] adj automatisé(e); **a. teller machine** distributeur m automatique de billets)
automatic [ɔːtə'mætɪk] **1** n (car) (voiture f) automatique f; (pistol) (pistolet m) automatique m; (washing machine) machine f à laver automatique
2 adj automatique; Comput **a. data processing** traitement m automatique des données; Aviat **a. pilot** pilote m automatique; Fig **to be on a. pilot** marcher au radar; **a. teller machine** distributeur m automatique (de billets)

automatically [ɔːtəˈmætɪklɪ] *adv* automatiquement
automation [ɔːtəˈmeɪʃən] *n* automatisation *f*
automaton [ɔːˈtɒmətən] *n* automate *m*
automobile [ˈɔːtəməʊbiːl] *n Am* voiture *f*, auto(mobile) *f*
autonomous [ɔːˈtɒnəməs] *adj* autonome
autonomy [ɔːˈtɒnəmɪ] *n* autonomie *f*
autopsy [ˈɔːtɒpsɪ] (*pl* **autopsies**) *n* autopsie *f*
autumn [ˈɔːtəm] *n* automne *m*; **in (the) a.** en automne
autumnal [ɔːˈtʌmnəl] *adj* automnal(e)
auxiliary [ɔːgˈzɪlɪərɪ] **1** *n* (*pl* **auxiliaries**) (*person*) auxiliaire *mf*; *Ling* auxiliaire *m* **2** *adj* auxiliaire
avail [əˈveɪl] **1** *n* **of no a.** *(not effective)* inutile; **to no a.** *(in vain)* en vain **2** *vt* **to a. oneself of sth** profiter de qch
availability [əveɪləˈbɪlɪtɪ] *n* disponibilité *f*
available [əˈveɪləbəl] *adj* disponible; **tickets are still a.** il reste des tickets; **this model is a. in black and in green** ce modèle existe en noir et en vert
avalanche [ˈævəlɑːntʃ] *n also Fig* avalanche *f*
avant-garde [ævɒŋˈgɑːd] *adj* d'avant-garde, avant-gardiste
avarice [ˈævərɪs] *n* avarice *f*
Ave (*abbr* **avenue**) av.
avenge [əˈvendʒ] *vt* venger; **to a. oneself on sb** se venger sur qn
avenue [ˈævɪnjuː] *n* avenue *f*; *Fig* possibilité *f*
aver [əˈvɜː(r)] (*pt & pp* **averred**) *vt Lit* déclarer, affirmer
average [ˈævərɪdʒ] **1** *n* moyenne *f*; **on a.** en moyenne; **above/below a.** supérieur(e)/inférieur(e) à la moyenne **2** *adj* moyen(enne) **3** *vt* atteindre la moyenne de; **to a. eight hours' work a day** travailler en moyenne huit heures par jour
▸**average out** *vi* **it'll a. out over a month** sur un mois ça s'équilibrera
▸**average out at** *vt insep* **my expenses. out at £800 per month** mes dépenses s'élèvent en moyenne à 800 livres par mois
averse [əˈvɜːs] *adj* opposé(e) (**to** à) ; **he is not a. to a glass of wine** il prend volontiers un verre de vin
aversion [əˈvɜːʃən] *n* aversion *f*; **to have an a. to sb/sth** avoir qn/qch en aversion
avert [əˈvɜːt] *vt* (**a**) *(turn away)* *(eyes, thoughts)* détourner (**from** de) (**b**) *(prevent)* *(misfortune, accident)* éviter, prévenir
avian flu [ˈeɪvɪənˈfluː] *n Med* grippe *f* aviaire
aviary [ˈeɪvɪərɪ] (*pl* **aviaries**) *n* volière *f*
aviation [eɪvɪˈeɪʃən] *n* aviation *f*
avid [ˈævɪd] *adj* avide (**for** de)
avidly [ˈævɪdlɪ] *adv* avidement, avec avidité
avocado [ævəˈkɑːdəʊ] (*pl* **avocados**) *n* avocat *m*
avoid [əˈvɔɪd] *vt* éviter; *(question)* esquiver; **to a. doing sth** éviter de faire qch; **to a. sb/sth like the plague** fuir qn/qch comme la peste
avoidable [əˈvɔɪdəbəl] *adj* évitable
avowed [əˈvaʊd] *adj* déclaré(e)
AWACS [ˈeɪwæks] *n Mil* (*abbr* **Airborne Warning and Control System**) AWACS *m*
await [əˈweɪt] *vt* attendre; *Law* **to be awaiting trial** être en instance de jugement
awake [əˈweɪk] **1** *adj* éveillé(e); **he lay a. for hours worrying** l'inquiétude l'a tenu éveillé pendant des heures; *Fig* **he was a. to the danger** il avait conscience du danger **2** *vt* (*pt* **awoke** [əˈwəʊk], *pp* **awoken** [əˈwəʊkən]) réveiller **3** *vi* s'éveiller, se réveiller; *Fig* **to a. to a danger** prendre conscience d'un danger
awaken [əˈweɪkən] (*pt* **awakened** [əˈweɪkənd], *pp* **awakened** *or* **awoken** [əˈwəʊkən]) **1** *vt* réveiller **2** *vi* s'éveiller, se réveiller
awakening [əˈweɪkənɪŋ] *n* réveil *m*
award [əˈwɔːd] **1** *n* (*prize*) prix *m*; *Law* dommages-intérêts *mpl* **2** *vt* (*prize, contract*) décerner; (*damages*) accorder; **to a. sb sth** décerner qch à qn
award-winning [əˈwɔːdwɪnɪŋ] *adj* (*film, book*) primé(e); (*writer, author*) lauréat(e)
aware [əˈweə(r)] *adj* **to be a. of sth** avoir conscience de qch; **to be a. that...** savoir que...; **not that I am a. of** pas que je sache; **as far as I'm a.** autant que je sache; **to become a. of sth** se rendre compte de qch; **politically a.** politisé(e)
awareness [əˈweənɪs] *n* conscience *f*
awash [əˈwɒʃ] *adj* (*flooded*) inondé(e)
away [əˈweɪ] *adv* (**a**) (*in space*) **a long way a.** très loin; **far a.** dans le lointain, au loin; **it's 10 kilometres a.** c'est à 10 kilomètres (d'ici); **to keep a. from** ne pas s'approcher de; **to go a.** partir, s'en aller; **go a.!** va-t'en!; **to put sth a.** ranger qch; **to take sth a. from sb** retirer qch à qn; **to stand a. from sth** se tenir à l'écart de qch; **to turn a.** se détourner (**b**) (*not at school, work*) **to be a.** être absent(e) (**c**) (*in time*) **Christmas is only two weeks a.** nous ne sommes qu'à deux semaines de Noël; **right a.** tout de suite
awe [ɔː] *n* crainte *f* mêlée de respect; **to be in a. of sb/sth** éprouver pour qn/qch une crainte mêlée de respect
awe-inspiring [ˈɔːɪnspaɪərɪŋ] *adj* imposant(e)
awesome [ˈɔːsəm] *adj* (**a**) (*incredible*) impressionnant(e) (**b**) *Am Fam* (*wonderful*) super *inv*
awful [ˈɔːfʊl] *adj* horrible, effroyable; **an a. lot of people** plein de monde; **it cost an a. lot** ça a coûté beaucoup d'argent
awfully [ˈɔːflɪ] *adv* (**a**) (*very badly*) terriblement mal (**b**) (*very*) très; **I'm a. sorry** je regrette infiniment *ou* énormément; **I'm a. glad** je suis rudement content
awhile [əˈwaɪl] *adv* **wait a.** attendez un moment *ou* un peu
awkward [ˈɔːkwəd] *adj* (**a**) (*clumsy*) gauche, maladroit(e) (**b**) (*inconvenient*) (*situation*) embarrassant(e); (*silence*) gêné(e), embarrassé(e); (*location*) peu pratique; **don't be so a.** arrête de nous ennuyer; **to arrive at an a. moment** arriver au mauvais moment; *Fam* **he's an a. customer** il n'est pas commode
awl [ɔːl] *n* alène *f*, poinçon *m*
awning [ˈɔːnɪŋ] *n* (*of shop*) store *m*
awoke [əˈwəʊk] *pt of* **awake**
awoken [əˈwəʊkən] *pp of* **awake, awaken**
AWOL [ˈeɪwɒl] *adj* (*abbr* **absent without leave**) *Mil* **to go A.** s'absenter sans permission; *Fig* disparaître
awry [əˈraɪ] *adv* **to go a.** aller de travers
axe, *Am* ax [æks] **1** *n* hache *f*; *Fig* **to have an a. to grind** agir dans un but intéressé; *Fam* **two hospitals have been given the a.** on va fermer deux hôpitaux **2** *vt Fam* (*jobs*) supprimer; (*costs*) réduire
axes [ˈæksɪːz] *pl of* **axis**

axiom ['æksɪəm] *n* axiome *m*
axiomatic [æksɪə'mætɪk] *adj (evident)* évident(e)
axis ['æksɪs] *(pl* **axes** ['æksiːz]) *n Math* axe *m; Hist* **the A.**
  powers les puissances *fpl* de l'Axe
axle ['æksəl] *n (of vehicle)* essieu *m*
azalea [ə'zeɪlɪə] *n* azalée *f*
Azerbaijan [æzəbaɪ'dʒɑːn] *n* l'Azerbaïdjan *m*

Azerbaijani [æzəbaɪ'dʒɑːnɪ], **Azeri** [ə'zeərɪ] **1** *n* Azerbaïdjanais(e) *m,f*, Azéri(e) *m,f*
  2 *adj* azerbaïdjanais(e), azéri(e)
Azores [ə'zɔːz] *npl* **the A.** les Açores *fpl*
Aztec ['æztek] **1** *n* Aztèque *mf*
  2 *adj* aztèque
azure ['æʒə(r)] **1** *n* azur *m*
  2 *adj* d'azur, azuré(e)

B, b¹ [biː] *n* (**a**) *(letter)* B, b *m inv*; **B-movie** (film *m* de) série *f* B; *Br* **B road** route *f* secondaire (**b**) *Mus* si *m* (**c**) *Sch (grade)* **to get a B** *(in exam)* avoir mention assez bien; *(in homework, essay)* ≃ avoir 12 ou 13 sur 20
b² *(abbr* **born)** né(e)
BA [biːˈeɪ] *n (abbr* **Bachelor of Arts) to have a BA in history** ≃ avoir une licence en histoire; **John Smith BA** ≃ John Smith, licencié ès lettres/en histoire/*etc*
baa [baː] **1** *exclam* bêê!
2 *vi (pt & pp* **baaed** *or* **baa'd** [baːd]) bêler
babble ['bæbəl] **1** *vi* (**a**) *(of baby)* babiller; *(of adult)* bafouiller; **what are you babbling on about?** qu'est-ce que tu baragouines? (**b**) *(of water)* murmurer
2 *n* murmure *m*
babe [beɪb] *n* (**a**) *Lit (baby)* **b. (in arms)** bébé *m* (**b**) *Fam (attractive person)* canon *m*; **hey b.!** salut chéri(e)!
baboon [bəˈbuːn] *n* babouin *m*
baby ['beɪbɪ] **1** *n (pl* **babies**) (**a**) *(child)* bébé *m*; **b. brother** petit frère *m*; **b. sister** petite sœur *f*; **b. boom** baby-boom *m*; *Am* **b. carriage** landau *m*; **b. grand** *(piano)* demi-queue *m*; **b. talk** langage *m* enfantin (**b**) *(idioms)* **to throw the b. out with the bathwater** jeter le bébé avec l'eau du bain; **to leave sb holding the b.** refiler le bébé à qn
2 *vt (pt & pp* **babied)** materner
baby-faced ['beɪbɪfeɪst] *adj* au visage poupin
babyhood ['beɪbɪhʊd] *n* petite enfance *f*
babyish ['beɪbɪʃ] *adj Pej* de bébé
baby-minder ['beɪbɪmaɪndə(r)] *n* nourrice *f*
baby-sit ['beɪbɪsɪt] *(pt & pp* **baby-sat** ['beɪbɪsæt]) *vi* faire du baby-sitting; **to b. for sb** garder l'enfant/les enfants de qn
baby-sitter ['beɪbɪsɪtə(r)] *n* baby-sitter *mf*
baby-walker ['beɪbɪwɔːkə(r)] *n* trotteur *m*
bachelor ['bætʃələ(r)] *n* célibataire *m*; **b. flat** garçonnière *f*; *Am* **b. party** enterrement *m* de vie de garçon; *Univ* **B. of Arts** *(qualification)* ≃ licence *f* ès lettres/en histoire/*etc*; *(person)* ≃ licencié(e) *m,f* ès lettres/en histoire/*etc*; *Univ* **B. of Science** *(qualification)* ≃ licence *f* ès sciences; *(person)* ≃ licencié(e) *m,f* ès sciences
bacillus [bəˈsɪləs] *(pl* **bacilli** [bəˈsɪlaɪ]) *n Biol* bacille *m*
back [bæk] **1** *n* (**a**) *(of person, animal)* dos *m*; *also Fig* **to turn one's b. on sb** tourner le dos à qn; **to sit/stand with one's b. to sb** tourner le dos à qn; **b. pain** mal *m* de dos; **to have b. problems** avoir des problèmes de dos; **b. slapping** *(self-congratulatory)* félicitations *fpl* excessives
(**b**) *(of hand, book)* dos *m*; *(of page)* dos *m*, verso *m*; *(of chair)* dossier *m*; *(of car)* arrière *m*; *(of throat)* fond *m*; **at**

the b. (of), *Am* in b. (of) *(behind)* derrière; *(at far end of)* au fond (de); **the dress fastens at the b.** cette robe s'attache dans le dos; **at the b. of the book** à la fin du livre; **the b. of the neck** la nuque; **he knows London like the b. of his hand** il connaît Londres comme sa poche; *Fam* **at** *or* **in the b. of beyond** au diable; **b. to front** devant derrière, à l'envers
(**c**) *(in sport)* arrière *mf*
(**d**) *(idioms)* **to do sth behind sb's b.** faire qch derrière le dos de qn; **I'll be glad to see the b. of him** je serai content d'en être débarrassé; **with one's b. to the wall** *(in desperate situation)* le dos au mur; **put your b. into it!** il faut t'y mettre!; **to break the b. of the work** faire le plus gros du travail; *Fam* **the boss was on my b. all day** j'ai eu le patron sur le dos toute la journée; *Fam* **get off my b.!** fiche-moi la paix!; *Fam* **to put** *or* **get sb's b. up** braquer qn
2 *adj* (**a**) *(in space)* arrière *inv*; *Fig* **to put sth on the b. burner** remettre qch à plus tard; **b. door** porte *f* de derrière; *Fig* **he got it through the b. door** il a magouillé pour l'avoir; **b. garden** jardin *m* de derrière; **the b. page** la dernière page; *Euph* **b. passage** rectum *m*; **b. road** petite route *f*; *Fig* **to take a b. seat** rester discret(ète); **b. yard** *Br (enclosed area)* arrière-cour *f*, *Am (garden)* jardin *m* de derrière
(**b**) *(in time)* **b. issue** *or* **number** *(of magazine, newspaper)* vieux numéro *m*; **b. pay** rappel *m* de salaire; **b. rent** arriéré(s) *m(pl)* de loyer
3 *adv* (**a**) *(in space)* en arrière; **to stand** *or* **step b.** reculer; **to jump b.** faire un bond en arrière; **we passed it 3 kilometres b.** nous l'avons dépassé à 3 kilomètres d'ici
(**b**) *(in return, retaliation)* **to hit sb b.** rendre son coup à qn; **to call sb b.** rappeler qn; **if you kick me I'll kick you b.** si tu me donnes un coup de pied, je te le rendrai; **to get one's own b. (on sb)** prendre sa revanche (sur qn); **to get b. at sb** prendre sa revanche sur qn
(**c**) *(to original starting point)* **to come b.** revenir; **to go b.** retourner; **when will she be b.?** quand sera-t-elle de retour?; **b. in Britain, the situation was getting serious** la situation s'aggravait en Grande-Bretagne; **(once) b. in London he phoned the hospital** de retour à Londres il a téléphoné à l'hôpital; **a few pages b.** quelques pages plus haut
(**d**) *(in time)* **a few years b.** il y a quelques années; **b. when...** à l'époque où...; **b. in 1982** en 1982; **as far b. as 1914** dès 1914
4 *vt* (**a**) *(support)* soutenir, appuyer; *(financially)* financer
(**b**) *(bet on)* parier *ou* miser sur
(**c**) *(move backwards)* **to b. one's car into the garage**

entrer au garage en marche arrière; **to b. one's car into a lamppost** rentrer dans un lampadaire en faisant marche arrière
5 *vi (move backwards)* reculer; *(in car)* faire marche arrière
▸**back away** *vi* reculer (**from** devant)
▸**back down** *vi (in argument)* céder; *(in conflict)* faire marche arrière
▸**back off** *vi* reculer; *Fam* **b. off!** fiche-moi la paix!
▸**back on to** *vt insep* donner sur
▸**back out** *vi* (**a**) *(move backwards)* sortir à reculons; *(in car)* sortir en marche arrière (**b**) *(from agreement)* se dédire
▸**back up 1** *vt sep* (**a**) *(support)* soutenir, appuyer; *(story, account)* étayer (**b**) *Comput (data, file)* sauvegarder
2 *vi* (**a**) *(move backwards)* reculer; *(in car)* faire marche arrière (**b**) *Comput* sauvegarder
backache ['bækeɪk] *n* mal *m* au dos
backbencher ['bæk'bentʃə(r)] *n Br Parl* député *m* de base

Backbencher
Les "backbenchers" sont assis aux derniers rangs de la Chambre des communes, tandis que les rangs de devant sont réservés aux ministres et aux membres du "**shadow cabinet**"(*voir encadré sous* **shadow**).

backbiting ['bækbaɪtɪŋ] *n Fam* médisance *f*
backbone ['bækbəʊn] *n* épine *f* dorsale, colonne *f* vertébrale; *Fig* **he's got no b.** il n'a rien dans le ventre
backbreaking ['bækbreɪkɪŋ] *adj (work)* éreintant(e)
backchat ['bæktʃæt], *Am* **backtalk** ['bæktɔːk] *n Fam* impertinence *f*
backcloth ['bæklɒθ] *Br* = **backdrop**
backdate ['bækdeɪt] *vt* antidater
backdrop ['bækdrɒp] *n Theat* toile *f* de fond; *Fig* **against a b. of continuing violence** avec, comme toile de fond, un climat de violence permanente
backer ['bækə(r)] *n (of political party)* partisan *m*; *(for project)* commanditaire *m*
backfire [bæk'faɪə(r)] *vi (of car)* pétarader; *Fig* **the plan backfired on them** leur plan s'est retourné contre eux
backgammon ['bækgæmən] *n* backgammon *m*
background ['bækgraʊnd] *n* (**a**) *(of scene)* arrière-plan *m*, fond *m*; **in the b.** à l'arrière-plan, dans le fond; *Fig* **to stay in the b.** rester dans l'ombre; **b. music** *(in restaurant)* musique *f* d'ambiance; **she likes b. music when she's working** elle aime travailler avec un fond sonore; **b. noise** bruit *m* de fond (**b**) *(social)* origines *fpl*; *(educational)* formation *f*; *(professional)* expérience *f*; **from a disadvantaged b.** d'un milieu défavorisé; **we need someone with a b. in computers** il nous faut quelqu'un qui s'y connaisse en informatique (**c**) *(circumstances)* contexte *m*; **against a b. of discord** dans un climat de mécontentement; **can you give me some b. information?** pouvez-vous me donner quelques renseignements?; **I need a bit more b.** il me faut plus de données; **b. reading** lectures *fpl* complémentaires
backhand ['bækhænd] *n (in tennis)* revers *m*
backhanded [bæk'hændɪd] *adj (compliment)* équivoque
backhander ['bækhændə(r)] *n Fam (bribe)* pot-de-vin *m*

backing ['bækɪŋ] *n (support)* soutien *m*; **financial b.** financement *m*
backlash ['bæklæʃ] *n (reaction)* contrecoup *m* (**against** à); *(political)* réaction *f* (**against** à)
backlit ['bæklɪt] *adj Comput* rétro-éclairé(e)
backlog ['bæklɒg] *n* retard *m*; **to have a b. of work** avoir du travail en retard
backpack ['bækpæk] **1** *n* sac *m* à dos
2 *vi* faire de la randonnée; **she backpacked around Europe** elle a fait toute l'Europe, sac à dos
backpacker ['bækpækə(r)] *n* routard(e) *m,f*
back-pedal ['bæk'pedəl] *(pt & pp* **back-pedalled**, *Am* **back-pedaled**) *vi Fig* faire marche arrière
backrest ['bækrest] *n* dossier *m*
back-seat ['bæksiːt] *adj Fam* **b. driver** = personne qui donne des conseils au conducteur; **I don't want any b. driving** je n'ai besoin des conseils de personne quand je conduis
backside [bæk'saɪd] *n Fam* derrière *m*, postérieur *m*
backslash ['bækslæʃ] *n Comput* barre *f* oblique inversée
backsliding ['bækslaɪdɪŋ] *n Fam* rechute *f*; **she was on the lookout for any signs of b.** elle nous/les/*etc* surveillait pour voir si nous nous relâchions
backspace ['bækspeɪs] *n Comput* retour *m* en arrière
backstage [bæk'steɪdʒ] *adv also Fig* dans les coulisses
backstairs [bæk'steəz] *n* escalier *m* de service
backstitch ['bækstɪtʃ] *n (in sewing)* point *m* de piqûre
backstreet ['bækstriːt] *n* petite rue *f*; **b. abortion** avortement *m* clandestin
backstroke ['bækstrəʊk] *n (in swimming)* dos *m* crawlé
backtalk ['bæktɔːk] *Am* = **backchat**
back-to-back [bæktə'bæk] **1** *adj (victories, meetings)* consécutifs(ives)
2 *adv* (**a**) *(physically)* dos à dos (**b**) *(consecutively)* de suite
backtrack ['bæktræk] *vi* (**a**) *(retrace one's steps)* revenir sur ses pas (**b**) *(renege)* faire marche arrière; **to b. on a promise/decision** revenir sur une promesse/une décision
backup ['bækʌp] *n (support)* soutien *m*, appui *m*; *Mil* renforts *mpl*; *Comput* **b. copy/file** copie *f*/fichier *m* de sauvegarde; *Comput* **b. system** système *m* de sauvegarde; **b. team** *(providing support)* équipe *f* technique; *(on standby)* équipe *f* de remplacement
backward ['bækwəd] **1** *adj* (**a**) *(direction)* en arrière; **she left without a b. glance** elle est partie sans se retourner (**b**) *(retarded) (child)* retardé(e), attardé(e); *(country)* en retard; *Br Fam* **he isn't b. in coming forward** il n'a pas peur de se mettre en avant
2 *adv* = **backwards**
backwardness ['bækwədnɪs] *n (of child)* arriération *f* mentale; *(of country)* retard *m*
backwards ['bækwədz] *adv* en arrière; *(walk)* à reculons; *(fall)* à la renverse; *(read)* à l'envers; **to walk b. and forwards** aller et venir; *Fig* **to know sth b.** connaître qch à fond
backwash ['bækwɒʃ] *n (of boat)* remous *m*; *Fig* conséquences *fpl* néfastes
backwater ['bækwɔːtə(r)] *n* (**a**) *(of river)* bras *m* mort (**b**) *(isolated place)* trou *m* perdu
bacon ['beɪkən] *n* (**a**) *(food)* bacon *m* (**b**) *(idioms) Fam* **to save sb's b.** sauver la peau de qn; *Fam* **to bring home the b.** *(earn wages)* faire bouillir la marmite; *(succeed)* réussir

bacteria [bæk'tɪərɪə] *npl* bactéries *fpl*
bacterial [bæk'tɪərɪəl] *adj* bactérien(enne)
bacteriological [bæktɪərɪə'lɒdʒɪkəl] *adj* bactériologique
bacteriology [bæktɪərɪ'ɒlədʒɪ] *n* bactériologie *f*
bad [bæd] (*comparative* **worse** [wɜːs], *superlative* **worst** [wɜːst]) *adj* (**a**) *(of poor quality, unpleasant)* mauvais(e); **it's not b.** *(fair)* ce n'est pas mal; *(good)* ce n'est pas mal du tout; **to be b. at maths** être mauvais(e) en maths; **to be b. at cooking** être mauvais(e) cuisinier(ère); **things are going from b. to worse** c'est de pire en pire *ou* de mal en pis; **it was a b. time to leave** ce n'était pas le moment de partir; **to have a b. time** passer un mauvais moment; **there's b. blood between them** il y a de la rancune entre eux; **to get into sb's b. books** se faire prendre en grippe par qn; **b. cheque** chèque *m* sans provision; *Fin* **b. debts** créances *fpl* douteuses; **in b. faith** de mauvaise foi; **b. feeling** animosité *f*; **I gave it up as a b. job** j'ai fini par laisser tomber; **to be a b. loser** être mauvais(e) perdant(e); **b. luck** malchance *f*; **b. manners** mauvaises manières *fpl*; **in a b. mood** de mauvaise humeur; *Fig* **she's b. news** elle ne t'/lui/*etc* apportera que des ennuis
  (**b**) *(unfortunate)* **it's (really) too b.!, that's too b.!** c'est vraiment dommage!; **to have a b. effect on sth** nuire à qch; **he'll come to a b. end** il finira mal
  (**c**) *(not healthy)* **to have a b. back/heart** avoir le dos/cœur fragile; **smoking is b. for you** fumer est mauvais pour la santé; **to be in a b. way** aller mal
  (**d**) *(wicked)* *(person, behaviour)* méchant(e); **to use b. language** dire des gros mots
  (**e**) *(serious)* *(mistake, accident)* grave; *(pain)* fort(e); **I've got a really b. headache** j'ai vraiment très mal à la tête; **to have a b. cold** avoir un gros rhume
  (**f**) *(rotten)* mauvais(e); **to go b.** *(of fruit)* se gâter, pourrir; *(of milk)* tourner; *Fig* **a b. apple** une brebis galeuse
  (**g**) *(guilty)* **to feel b. about sth** s'en vouloir de qch
baddie, baddy ['bædɪ] *(pl* **baddies***) n Fam* méchant(e) *m,f*
bade [bæd, beɪd] *pt of* **bid**²
badge [bædʒ] *n (of company, organization)* badge *m*; *(fashion accessory)* pin's *m*; *Mil* insigne *m*
badger ['bædʒə(r)] **1** *n (animal)* blaireau *m*
  2 *vt* harceler; **to b. sb into doing sth** harceler qn jusqu'à ce qu'il fasse qch
bad-looking [bæd'lʊkɪŋ] *adj* **not b.** pas mal
badly ['bædlɪ] *adv (comparative* **worse** [wɜːs], *superlative* **worst** [wɜːst]) (**a**) *(not well)* mal; **to do b.** *(in exam, competition)* avoir un mauvais résultat; **he didn't do b.** il ne s'en est pas mal tiré; **she took it very b.** elle a très mal pris la chose; **to be b. off for sth** *(lacking)* manquer de qch; **to be b. off for money** avoir des problèmes d'argent; **to get on b. (with sb)** ne pas s'entendre (avec qn) (**b**) *(seriously)* gravement; **to be b. beaten** *(physically)* être roué(e) de coups; *(in match, competition)* être battu(e) à plates coutures; **b. wounded** gravement *ou* grièvement blessé(e) (**c**) *(greatly)* **to want sth b.** avoir très envie de qch; **to be b. in need of sth** avoir grand besoin de qch
bad-mannered [bæd'mænəd] *adj* mal élevé(e)
badminton ['bædmɪntən] *n* badminton *m*
badmouth ['bædmaʊθ] *vt Fam* débiner
badness ['bædnɪs] *n* (**a**) *(poor quality)* mauvaise qualité *f* (**b**) *(wickedness)* méchanceté *f*

bad-tempered [bæd'tempəd] *adj (person)* grincheux(euse); *(remark)* désagréable
BAF [biːeɪ'ef] *n (abbr* **British Athletics Federation**) = fédération britannique d'athlétisme
baffle ['bæfəl] *vt (confuse)* laisser perplexe; **to be baffled** être perplexe; **I'm baffled as to why she did it** je ne comprends vraiment pas pourquoi elle a fait cela
baffling ['bæfəlɪŋ] *adj* déconcertant(e)
BAFTA ['bæftə] *n (abbr* **British Academy of Film and Television Arts**) = organisation qui décerne chaque année des récompenses aux personnalités du cinéma et de la télévision britanniques; **B. (award)** = prix récompensant les meilleurs films et émissions de télévision en Grande-Bretagne

BAFTA

Il s'agit d'une récompense attribuée aux professionnels du cinéma et de la télévision qui se sont distingués pendant l'année. C'est en quelque sorte l'équivalent britannique des César français. Il existe deux cérémonies, l'une pour les professionnels du cinéma (qui a lieu en février), l'autre pour les gens de télévision (au mois d'avril).

bag [bæg] **1** *n* (**a**) *(of paper, plastic)* sac *m*; *(handbag)* sac à main; **bags under the eyes** des poches sous les yeux; *Fam* **to be a b. of bones** être un sac d'os; *Fig* **it's in the b.** *(of deal, victory)* c'est dans la poche (**b**) *Fam* **bags of** *(lots)* des masses de; **we've got bags of time** nous avons tout le temps; **there's bags of room** il y a plein de place (**c**) *Br very Fam Pej (woman)* **old b.** vieille toupie *f*
  2 *vt (pt & pp* **bagged**) (**a**) *(put in bag)* mettre en sac (**b**) *(in hunting)* abattre, tuer (**c**) *Fam (claim)* accaparer
bagel ['beɪgəl] *n* = petite couronne de pain, *Can* bagel *m*
baggage ['bægɪdʒ] *n* bagages *mpl*; *Aviat* **b. allowance** franchise *f* de bagages; *Aviat* **b. handler** bagagiste *mf*; *Aviat* **b. reclaim** retrait *m* des bagages; *Am* **b. room** consigne *f*
baggy ['bægɪ] *adj (garment) (by design)* large; *(out of shape)* déformé(e)
Baghdad [bæg'dæd] *n* Bagdad
bagpipes ['bægpaɪps] *npl* cornemuse *f*
bah [bɑː] *exclam* bah!
Bahamas [bə'hɑːməz] *npl* **the B.** les Bahamas *fpl*
Bahrain [bɑː'reɪn] *n* Bahreïn
Bahraini [bɑː'reɪnɪ] **1** *n* Bahreïni(e) *m,f*
  2 *adj* bahreïni(e)
bail [beɪl] *n Law (guarantee)* caution *f*; **on b.** sous caution; **to grant sb b.** libérer qn sous caution; **to stand b. for sb** se porter garant(e) de qn
▶**bail out** *vt sep* **to b. sb out** *Law* se porter garant(e) de qn; *Fig* tirer qn d'affaire; *Fig* **to b. a company out** renflouer une entreprise
bailiff ['beɪlɪf] *n* (**a**) *Law* huissier *m* (**b**) *(on estate)* régisseur *m*
bait [beɪt] **1** *n also Fig* appât *m*; *Fig* **to rise to the b.** mordre à l'hameçon; *Fig* **to swallow** *or* **take the b.** mordre à l'hameçon
  2 *vt* (**a**) *(torment)* harceler (**b**) *(attach bait to)* mettre l'appât à
baize [beɪz] *n* feutre *m*
bake [beɪk] **1** *vt (food)* (faire) cuire au four; *(clay)* cuire
  2 *vi* (**a**) *(of food)* cuire (**b**) *Fam* **I'm baking** je crève de chaleur

3 *n (baked dish)* **pasta/vegetable b.** gratin *m* de pâtes/de légumes
baked [beɪkt] *adj* **b. beans** haricots *mpl* blancs à la tomate; **b. potato** pomme *f* de terre au four
baker ['beɪkə(r)] *n* boulanger(ère) *m,f*; **b.'s (shop)** boulangerie *f*; **b.'s dozen** treize à la douzaine
bakery ['beɪkərɪ] *(pl* **bakeries)** *n* boulangerie *f*
baking ['beɪkɪŋ] **1** *n* to do some **b.** *(bread)* faire du pain; *(cakes)* faire de la pâtisserie; **b. powder** levure *f* chimique; **b. sheet** *or* **tray** plaque *f* (du four); **b. soda** bicarbonate *m* de soude; **b. tin** *(for meat)* plat *m* à rôtir; *(for cakes)* moule *m* à gâteau
2 *adj Fam* **it's b. (hot)** on crève de chaleur
balaclava [bælə'klɑːvə] *n* passe-montagne *m*
balance ['bæləns] **1** *n* **(a)** *(equilibrium)* équilibre *m*; **to keep/lose one's b.** garder/perdre son équilibre; **to throw sb off b.** faire perdre son équilibre à qn; *Fig* **to catch sb off b.** prendre qn au dépourvu; **the b. of power** l'équilibre des pouvoirs; **on b.** tout compte fait; **to strike a b.** trouver le juste milieu **(b)** *(of bank account)* solde *m*; *(in accounting)* bilan *m*; *Econ* **b. of trade/payments** balance *f* commerciale/des paiements; **b. sheet** bilan *m* **(c)** *(for weighing)* balance *f*; *Fig* **to hang** *or* **be in the b.** *(of decision, result)* être en jeu
2 *vt (object)* maintenir en équilibre; **he sought to b. the claims of the two parties** il a tenté de contenter les deux partis; **they b. each other well** *(of people)* ils sont complémentaires; *Fin* **to b. the books** arrêter les comptes
3 *vi* **(a)** *(physically)* tenir en équilibre **(b)** **she couldn't get the accounts to b.** elle n'arrivait pas à équilibrer les comptes
balanced ['bælənst] *adj (account, reporting)* objectif(ive); *(judgement)* pondéré(e); **b. diet** alimentation *f* équilibrée
balancing act ['bælənsɪŋ'ækt] *n Fig* **to do a b.** faire des acrobaties
balcony ['bælkənɪ] *(pl* **balconies)** *n (in house, theatre)* balcon *m*
bald [bɔːld] *adj* **(a)** *(person)* chauve; *(tyre)* lisse; **to go b.** devenir chauve, perdre ses cheveux; *Fam* **as b. as a coot** chauve comme un œuf; **b. eagle** aigle *m* à tête blanche; **b. patch** tonsure *f* **(b)** *(plain)* **the b. truth** la vérité toute nue; **a b. statement of the facts** une simple exposition des faits
balderdash ['bɔːldədæʃ] *n Fam* bêtises *fpl*, balivernes *fpl*
balding ['bɔːldɪŋ] *adj* qui commence à perdre ses cheveux; **b. man** un homme à la calvitie naissante
baldly ['bɔːldlɪ] *adv (reply)* sèchement
baldness ['bɔːldnɪs] *n* **(a)** *(of person)* calvitie *f* **(b)** *(of statement, demand)* sécheresse *f*
bale [beɪl] *n (of cloth, paper)* balle *f*; *(of hay)* botte *f*
▶**bale out** *vi (of pilot)* s'éjecter; *Fig (from difficult situation)* s'éclipser
Balearic [bælɪ'ærɪk] **1** *n* **the Balearics** les Baléares *fpl*
2 *adj* **the B. Islands** les îles *fpl* Baléares
baleful ['beɪlfʊl] *adj* sinistre, maléfique; **she gave me a b. look** elle m'a lancé un regard noir
Bali ['bɑːlɪ] *n* Bali
Balinese [bɑːlɪ'niːz] *adj* balinais(e)
balk [bɔːlk] **1** *vt (runner, racehorse)* empêcher de passer
2 *vi* reculer **(at** devant)
Balkan ['bɔːlkən] **1** *n* **the Balkans** les Balkans *fpl*
2 *adj* balkanique

ball¹ [bɔːl] *n* **(a)** *(in game) (for football, rugby, basketball)* ballon *m*; *(for cricket, tennis, golf)* balle *f*; *(for billiards)* bille *f*, boule *f*; *(of paper, of fire)* boule *f*; *(of wool)* pelote *f*; **to roll sth (up) into a b.** mettre qch en boule; **b. bearing** *(ball)* bille *f*; *(device)* roulement *m* à billes; **b. boy/girl** *(in tennis)* ramasseur(euse) *m,f* de balles; **b. game** *(in general)* jeu *m* de balle; *Am (baseball match)* match *m* de baseball; *Fig* **that's a whole new b. game** *(irrelevant)* ça n'a rien à voir; *(different situation)* c'est une autre paire de manches **(b)** *(of foot)* plante *f* **(c)** *Vulg* **balls** *(testicles)* couilles *fpl*; *(nonsense)* conneries *fpl*; *Fig* **to have a lot of balls** avoir des couilles **(d)** *(idioms)* **to be on the b.** *(alert)* avoir de la présence d'esprit; *(knowledgeable)* connaître son affaire; **to start the b. rolling** faire démarrer les choses; **the b. is in your court** la balle est dans votre camp; **to play b.** *(co-operate)* jouer le jeu
ball² *n (party)* bal *m*; *Fam* **to have a b.** s'éclater; **b. dress** *or* **gown** robe *f* de bal
ballad ['bæləd] *n* ballade *f*
ball-and-socket joint [bɔːlən'sɒkɪt'dʒɔɪnt] *n Anat* articulation *f* à emboîtement; *Tech* joint *m* à rotule
ballast ['bæləst] *n* **(a)** *Naut* lest *m* **(b)** *Rail* ballast *m*
ballcock ['bɔːlkɒk] *n* soupape *f* à flotteur
ballerina [bælə'riːnə] *n* ballerine *f*; **prima b.** danseuse *f* étoile
ballet ['bæleɪ] *n* danse *f* classique; *(work)* ballet *m*; **b. dancer** danseur(euse) *m,f* classique; **b. shoe** chausson *m* de danse
ballistic [bə'lɪstɪk] *adj (missile)* balistique; *Fam Fig* **to go b.** piquer une crise
ballistics [bə'lɪstɪks] *npl* balistique *f*
balloon [bə'luːn] **1** *n* **(a)** *(for party, travel)* ballon *m*; *Fam Fig* **when the b. goes up** quand il va y avoir du grabuge **(b)** *(in cartoon)* bulle *f*
2 *vi (swell)* gonfler
ballooning [bə'luːnɪŋ] *n* **to go b.** faire du ballon
balloonist [bə'luːnɪst] *n* aérostier *m*
ballot ['bælət] **1** *n (process)* tour *m* de scrutin; *(vote)* scrutin *m*, vote *m*; **to hold a b.** organiser des élections; **to put sth to a b.** soumettre qch à un vote; **box urne** *f*; **this matter should be decided at the b. box** c'est aux urnes que doit se décider cette question; **b. paper** bulletin *m* de vote; **b. rigging** fraude *f* électorale
2 *vt* consulter
ballpark ['bɔːlpɑːk] *Am* **1** *n* terrain *m* de base-ball
2 *adj* **a b. figure** une estimation
ballpoint ['bɔːlpɔɪnt] *n* **b. (pen)** stylo *m* (à) bille
ballroom ['bɔːlruːm] *n* salle *f* de bal; **b. dancing** danses *fpl* de salon
▶**balls up** [bɔːlz] *vt sep Br very Fam* foirer
balls-up ['bɔːlzʌp] *n Br very Fam* merdier *m*; **to make a b. of sth** foirer qch
ballyhoo [bælɪ'huː] *n Fam* battage *m* publicitaire
balm [bɑːm] *n* baume *m*
balmy ['bɑːmɪ] *adj (weather)* doux (douce)
baloney [bə'ləʊnɪ] *n (sausage)* = type de saucisse mangé froide; *Fam (nonsense)* bêtises *fpl*
balsa ['bɔːlsə] *n* balsa *m*
balsam ['bɔːlsəm] *n* balsam *m*
balsamic vinegar [bɔːl'sæmɪk'vɪnɪgə(r)] *n Culin* vinaigre *m* balsamique
balustrade [bælə'streɪd] *n* balustrade *f*

bamboo [bæm'buː] *n* bambou *m*; **b. shoots** pousses *fpl* de bambou

bamboozle [bæm'buːzəl] *vt Fam* embobiner

ban [bæn] **1** *n* interdiction *f*; **to impose a b. on sth** interdire qch
2 *vt (pt & pp* **banned**) interdire; **to b. sb from doing sth** interdire à qn de faire qch

banal [bə'næl] *adj* banal(e)

banality [bə'nælɪtɪ] *(pl* **banalities**) *n* banalité *f*

banana [bə'nɑːnə] *n* banane *f*; **b. tree** bananier *m*; *Fam* **to be/go bananas** *(mad)* être/devenir cinglé(e); *Fam* **b. republic** république *f* bananière; *also Fig* **b. skin** peau *f* de banane; **b. split** banana split *m inv*

band¹ [bænd] *n* (**a**) *(of metal)* bande *f*, bague *f*; *(around hat)* ruban *m*; *(around cigar)* bague *f*; *(of colour)* bande *f*, raie *f* (**b**) *Rad* bande *f* de fréquence (**c**) *(of ages, tax)* tranche *f*; *(of salaries)* catégorie *f*

band² *n* *(of friends)* groupe *m*, cercle *m*; *(of robbers)* bande *f*; *(of musicians) (rock)* groupe *m*; *(jazz)* orchestre *m*, groupe *m*

▶**band together** *vi* se liguer (**against** contre)

bandage ['bændɪdʒ] **1** *n* bandage *m*; *(for support)* bande *f*
2 *vt* bander; **to b. sb's arm** bander le bras à qn

▶**bandage up** *vt sep* bander

Band-Aid® ['bændeɪd] *n Am* sparadrap *m*

B & B [biːən'biː] *n Br (abbr* **bed and breakfast**) *(service)* ≃ chambre *f* avec petit déjeuner; **to stay at a B & B** ≃ prendre une chambre d'hôte

bandit ['bændɪt] *n* bandit *m*

bandmaster ['bændmɑːstə(r)] *n* chef *m* de musique

bandsman ['bændzmən] *n* musicien *m*

bandstand ['bændstænd] *n* kiosque *m* à musique

b & w *n Phot & Cin (abbr* **black and white**) noir et blanc *inv*

bandwagon ['bændwægən] *n Fam* **to jump on the b.** prendre le train en marche

bandwidth ['bændwɪdθ] *n* (**a**) *Comput* bande *f* passante (**b**) *Rad* largeur *f* de bande

bandy¹ ['bændɪ] *adj* **to have b. legs** avoir les jambes arquées

bandy² *(pt & pp* **bandied**) *vt (words, insults)* échanger; **her name was being bandied about as a possible candidate** son nom est revenu plusieurs fois parmi ceux des candidats possibles

bandy-legged ['bændɪ'leg(ɪ)d] *adj* aux jambes arquées

bane [beɪn] *n* plaie *f*; **he's the b. of my life** il m'empoisonne l'existence

bang [bæŋ] **1** *n* (**a**) *(noise)* claquement *m*; *(explosion)* détonation *f*; **the door shut with a b.** la porte s'est refermée en claquant; *Fig* **to go with a b.** *(of party, event)* être un grand succès (**b**) *(blow)* coup *m* violent; **to get a b. on the head** recevoir un coup sur la tête
2 *adv* (**a**) *Fam* **b. went my hopes of a quiet weekend** pour le week-end tranquille, c'était loupé (**b**) *Fam (exactly)* **b. in the middle** en plein milieu; **b. on time** pile à l'heure
3 *exclam (sound of gun)* pan!; *(explosion)* boum!
4 *vt (hit)* frapper (violemment); **to b. one's head** se cogner la tête
5 *vi (of door, window)* claquer, battre; **the door banged shut** la porte se ferma en claquant; **to b. at** *or* **on the door** frapper à la porte à coups violents; **to b. into sth** se cogner à qch

▶**bang about, bang around** *vi (make noise)* faire du potin

▶**bang on** *vi Fam* **he's always banging on about it** il n'arrête pas de bassiner tout le monde avec cela

▶**bang up** *vt sep Br very Fam (imprison)* boucler

banger ['bæŋə(r)] *n Br* (**a**) *Fam (sausage)* saucisse *f* (**b**) *(firework)* pétard *m* (**c**) *Fam (car)* **old b.** vieille guimbarde *f*

Bangkok [bæŋ'kɒk] *n* Bangkok

Bangladesh [bæŋglə'deʃ] *n* le Bangladesh

Bangladeshi [bæŋglə'deʃɪ] **1** *n* Bangladais *mf*, Bangladais(e) *m,f*
2 *adj* bangladeshi, bangladais(e)

bangle ['bæŋgəl] *n* bracelet *m*

bangs [bæŋz] *npl Am* frange *f*

banish ['bænɪʃ] *vt (exile)* bannir (**from** de); *Fig (thought, fear)* chasser

banishment ['bænɪʃmənt] *n* bannissement *m*

banister ['bænɪstə(r)] *n* rampe *f* d'escalier

banjo ['bændʒəʊ] *(pl* **banjos** *or* **banjoes**) *n* banjo *m*

bank¹ [bæŋk] **1** *n* (**a**) *(of river)* berge *f*, bord *m*; *(of earth)* talus *m* (**b**) *(of clouds, fog)* banc *m* (**c**) *(of lights, switches)* rangée *f*
2 *vt* **the road is banked by trees** la route est bordée d'arbres
3 *vi* (**a**) *(of clouds, snow)* s'amonceler (**b**) *(of plane)* virer

bank² **1** *n* (**a**) *(financial institution)* banque *f*; **b. account** compte *m* en banque; **b. balance** solde *m*; **b. charges** frais *mpl* bancaires; **b. clerk** employé(e) *m,f* de banque; **b. draft** traite *f* bancaire; *Br* **b. holiday** jour *m* férié; **b. loan** prêt *m* bancaire; **b. manager** directeur(trice) *m,f* d'agence; *Fin* **b. rate** taux *m* de l'escompte; **b. statement** relevé *m* de banque; *Am* **b. teller** employé(e) *m,f* de banque (**b**) *(in gambling)* banque *f*; **to break the b.** faire sauter la banque; *Fig* **it won't break the b.** ça ne me/te/le/*etc* ruinera pas (**c**) *(store)* **blood b.** banque *f* du sang; **data b.** banque de données
2 *vt (funds)* mettre *ou* déposer à la banque
3 *vi* **to b. with sb** avoir un compte chez qn; **who do you b. with?** à quelle banque êtes-vous?

▶**bank on** *vt insep (outcome, success)* compter sur

bankbook ['bæŋkbʊk] *n* livret *m* *ou* carnet *m* de compte

banker ['bæŋkə(r)] *n Fin* banquier(ère) *m,f*; **b.'s draft** traite *f* bancaire

banking ['bæŋkɪŋ] *n (business)* opérations *fpl* bancaires; **she's in b.** elle travaille dans la banque

banknote ['bæŋknəʊt] *n* billet *m* de banque

bankroll ['bæŋkrəʊl] *vt Am (finance)* financer

bankrupt ['bæŋkrʌpt] **1** *n Fin* failli(e) *m,f*
2 *adj* failli(e); **to be b.** être en faillite; **to go b.** faire faillite; *Fig* **to be morally b.** avoir perdu toute crédibilité
3 *vt Law* mettre en faillite; *Fig (make poor)* ruiner

bankruptcy ['bæŋkrəptsɪ] *n Law* faillite *f*; *Fig (poverty)* ruine *f*

banner ['bænə(r)] *n* (**a**) *(flag)* bannière *f*; **the Star-Spangled B.** la bannière étoilée; **b. headline** manchette *f* (**b**) *Comput (for advertising on the Internet)* bandeau *m*, bannière *f* publicitaire

bannister ['bænɪstə(r)] = **banister**

banns [bænz] *npl* bans *mpl*

banquet ['bæŋkwɪt] *n* banquet *m*

bantam ['bæntəm] *n* = poulet de petite taille

bantamweight ['bæntəmweɪt] *n (in boxing)* poids *m* coq

banter ['bæntə(r)] **1** *n* taquineries *fpl* **2** *vi* plaisanter

bap [bæp] *n* petit pain *m* rond

baptism ['bæptɪzəm] *n* baptême *m*; *Fig* **a b. of fire** un baptême du feu

baptismal [bæp'tɪzməl] *adj (certificate)* de baptême; **b. font** fonts *mpl* baptismaux

Baptist ['bæptɪst] *n* baptiste *mf*

baptize [bæp'taɪz] *vt* baptiser

bar [bɑː(r)] **1** *n* (**a**) *(of metal)* barre *f*; *(of gold)* lingot *m*; *(of chocolate) (large)* tablette *f*; *(smaller)* barre *f*; *(on window)* barreau *m*; *(of electric fire)* résistance *f*; **b. of soap** savonnette *f*, morceau *m* de savon; **to be behind bars** être derrière les barreaux; **b. chart** histogramme *m*; **b. code** code-barres *m* (**b**) *(obstacle)* obstacle *m*; **to be a b. to sth** faire obstacle à qch; **to impose a b. on sth** interdire qch (**c**) *Law* **the B.** ≃ l'Ordre *m* des avocats, le barreau; **to be called to the B.** s'inscrire au barreau; **to read for the B.** faire son droit; **the prisoner at the b.** l'accusé(e) *m,f* (**d**) *(pub, in hotel)* bar *m*; *(pub counter)* comptoir *m*, bar *m*; **b. staff** personnel *m* de bar (**e**) *Mus* mesure *f* **2** *vt (pt & pp barred)* (**a**) *(door)* barrer; **to b. sb's way** barrer le passage à qn (**b**) *(ban) (from club, pub)* exclure; **to b. sb from doing sth** interdire à qn de faire qch **3** *prep* sauf, à l'exception de; **the finest b. none** sans conteste le (la) meilleur(e)

barb [bɑːb] *n* (**a**) *(on hook, arrow)* barbillon *m* (**b**) *(remark)* pique *f*

Barbadian [bɑː'beɪdɪən] **1** *n* = personne née à ou habitant la Barbade **2** *adj* de la Barbade

Barbados [bɑː'beɪdɒs] *n* la Barbade

barbarian [bɑː'beərɪən] **1** *n* barbare *mf* **2** *adj* barbare

barbaric [bɑː'bærɪk] *adj* barbare; *(manners, behaviour)* de barbare

barbarism ['bɑːbərɪzəm] *n* barbarie *f*

barbarity [bɑː'bærɪtɪ] *(pl* **barbarities** *) n (cruelty)* barbarie *f*; *(act)* atrocité *f*

barbarous ['bɑːbərəs] *adj* barbare

barbecue ['bɑːbɪkjuː] **1** *n* barbecue *m*; **to have a b.** faire un barbecue; **b. sauce** sauce *f* barbecue **2** *vt* cuire au barbecue

barbed [bɑːbd] *adj* (**a**) *(hook)* barbelé(e); **b. wire** *(fil m de fer)* barbelé *m* (**b**) *(remark, comment)* acerbe

barber ['bɑːbə(r)] *n* coiffeur *m* pour hommes, *Can* barbier *m*; **to go to the b.'s** aller chez le coiffeur

barbershop ['bɑːbəʃɒp] *n Am* salon *m* de coiffure *(pour hommes)*; **b. quartet** = quatuor chantant en harmonie

barbie ['bɑːbɪ] *n Br Fam (barbecue)* barbecue *m*, barbeuk *m*

barbiturate [bɑː'bɪtjʊreɪt] *n* barbiturique *m*

bard [bɑːd] *n Lit (poet)* barde *m*; **the B.** Shakespeare

bare [beə(r)] **1** *adj* (**a**) *(not covered)* nu(e); *(countryside)* nu, dénudé(e); **in one's feet** (les) pieds nus; **to lay sth b.** mettre qch à nu, exposer qch (**b**) *(empty) (room, cupboard)* vide; **to strip a house b.** tout enlever dans une maison (**c**) *(just sufficient)* **the b. minimum** le strict minimum; **the b. bones of the case** les grandes lignes de l'affaire; **the b. necessities (of life)** le strict nécessaire; **a b. majority** une petite *ou* faible majorité

2 *vt* mettre à nu, découvrir; **to b. one's teeth** montrer les dents; **to b. one's heart** *or* **soul to sb** ouvrir son cœur à qn

bareback ['beəbæk] **1** *adj* **b. rider** cavalier(ère) *m,f* qui monte à cru **2** *adv* **to ride b.** monter à cru

barefaced ['beəfeɪst] *adj (impudence, lie, liar)* éhonté(e)

barefoot(ed) ['beəfʊt(ɪd)] **1** *adj* (aux) pieds nus **2** *adv* nu-pieds, (les) pieds nus

bareheaded [beə'hedɪd] **1** *adj* nu-tête *inv*, à la tête nue **2** *adv* nu-tête, (la) tête nue

bare-legged [beə'leg(ɪ)d] **1** *adj* aux jambes nues **2** *adv* (les) jambes nues

barely ['beəlɪ] *adv* (**a**) *(scarcely)* à peine; **b. enough** tout juste assez (**b**) *(sparsely)* **b. furnished** avec très peu de meubles

barf [bɑːf] *vi Am Fam* vomir

bargain ['bɑːgɪn] **1** *n* (**a**) *(agreement)* marché *m*, affaire *f*; **to make** *or* **strike a b. with sb** conclure un marché avec qn; **you haven't kept your side** *or* **part of the b.** vous n'avez pas tenu votre part du marché; **to drive a hard b.** ne pas faire de cadeaux; **into the b.** *(in addition)* par-dessus le marché, en plus (**b**) *(good buy)* affaire *f*, occasion *f*; **b. basement** rayon *m* des soldes, solderie *f*; **b. hunter** acheteur(euse) *m,f* à la recherche de bonnes affaires; **b. price** prix *m* exceptionnel **2** *vi* **to b. with sb** négocier avec qn

▸ **bargain away** *vt sep (rights, privileges)* brader

▸ **bargain for** *vt insep (reaction, question)* s'attendre à; **I didn't b. for that** je ne m'y attendais pas; **he got more than he bargained for** il ne s'attendait pas à cela

▸ **bargain on** *vt insep* **I didn't b. on that** je ne m'y attendais pas

barge [bɑːdʒ] *n* péniche *f*

▸ **barge in** *vi (enter)* faire irruption

bargepole ['bɑːdʒpəʊl] *n* gaffe *f*; **I wouldn't touch it with a b.** *(it's disgusting)* ça me dégoûte d'y toucher; *(it's risky)* je ne m'en mêlerais pas

baritone ['bærɪtəʊn] *n* baryton *m*

barium ['beərɪəm] *n Chem* baryum *m*; *Med* **b. meal** (bouillie *f* de) sulfate *m* de baryum

bark¹ [bɑːk] **1** *n (of tree)* écorce *f* **2** *vt* **to b. one's shins** s'écorcher les jambes

bark² **1** *n (of dog)* aboiement *m*; *Fig* **his b. is worse than his bite** il n'est pas si méchant qu'il y paraît **2** *vi (order)* aboyer **3** *vi* aboyer (**at** après); *(of person)* crier (**at** sur); *Fam Fig* **you're barking up the wrong tree** tu fais fausse route

barkeeper ['bɑːkiːpə(r)] *n Am* barman *m*

barley ['bɑːlɪ] *n* orge *m*; **b. sugar** sucre *m* d'orge

barmaid ['bɑːmeɪd] *n Br* serveuse *f* (de bar)

barman ['bɑːmən] *n Br* serveur *m*, barman *m*

barmy ['bɑːmɪ] *adj Br Fam* toqué(e), cinglé(e)

barn [bɑːn] *n* grange *f*; *(for cows)* étable *f*; *(for horses)* écurie *f*; **b. dance** bal *m* folklorique; **b. owl** effraie *f*

barnacle ['bɑːnəkəl] *n* bernacle *f*

barnstorming ['bɑːnstɔːmɪŋ] *adj (speech, performance)* plein(e) de brio

barnyard ['bɑːnjɑːd] *n* cour *f* de ferme

barometer [bə'rɒmɪtə(r)] *n* baromètre *m*

baron ['bærən] *n* baron *m*; *Fig* **press/oil b.** magnat *m* de la presse/du pétrole

baroness ['bærənes] *n* baronne *f*
baronet ['bærənet] *n* baronet *m*
baroque [bə'rɒk] **1** *n* baroque *m*
  2 *adj* baroque
barrack ['bærək] *vt (heckle)* chahuter
barracks ['bærəks] *npl* caserne *f*; **to be confined to b.**
  être consigné(e)
barracuda [bærə'kju:də] *n* barracuda *m*
barrage ['bærɑ:ʒ] **1** *n* (**a**) *(dam)* barrage *m* (**b**) *Mil* tir
  m de barrage; *Fig (of questions, abuse)* flot *m*
  2 *vt* **to b. sb with** *(questions)* assaillir qn de; *(criticism)* accabler qn de
barrel ['bærəl] *n* (**a**) *(container)* tonneau *m*, fût *m*; *(of oil)* baril *m*; *Fam* **to have sb over a b.** tenir qn à sa
  merci; *Fam* **the party wasn't exactly a b. of laughs**
  cette soirée, ça n'a pas été une partie de rigolade; **b.**
  organ orgue *m* de Barbarie (**b**) *(of gun)* canon *m*
barren ['bærən] *adj (woman, land, discussion)* stérile;
  (landscape) désolé(e)
barrenness ['bærənnɪs] *n (of land, discussion)* stérilité
  f
barrette [bə'ret] *n Am* barrette *f*
barricade ['bærɪkeɪd] **1** *n* barricade *f*
  2 *vt* barricader; **to b. oneself** se barricader
barrier ['bærɪə(r)] *n also Fig* barrière *f*; **the Great B.**
  Reef la Grande Barrière
barring ['bɑ:rɪŋ] *prep* sauf; **b. accidents** sauf imprévu;
  b. a miracle à moins d'un miracle
barrister ['bærɪstə(r)] *n Br Law* ≃ avocat(e) *m,f*
barrow ['bærəʊ] *n (wheelbarrow)* brouette *f*
bartender ['bɑ:tendə(r)] *n Am* serveur(euse) *m,f* (de
  bar)
barter ['bɑ:tə(r)] **1** *n* troc *m*
  2 *vt* troquer (**for** contre)
  3 *vi* marchander
basalt ['bæsɔ:lt] *n* basalte *m*
base [beɪs] **1** *n* (**a**) *(of cliff, column)* pied *m*; *(of lamp, statue)* socle *m*; *(of spine)* bas *m*; *(of jug)* cul *m*; *(of triangle, structure)* base *f*; *Fin* **b. rate** taux *m* de base (**b**)
  (for expedition, campaign) base *f*; *(for tourism)* point
  m de départ; **b. camp** camp *m* de base (**c**) *(in baseball)* base *f*; *Fig* **we didn't get past first b.** nous ne
  sommes pas arrivés à grand-chose; **to touch b. (with**
  sb) entrer en contact (avec qn)
  2 *adj* (**a**) *Formal (motive, conduct)* bas (basse), vil(e)
  (**b**) **b. metals** métaux *mpl* vils
  3 *vt (hopes, opinion)* fonder (**on** sur); **to be based on**
  (of calculation, film) être basé(e) sur; **to be based in**
  (of job, troops, company) être basé à
baseball ['beɪsbɔ:l] *n* base-ball *m*; **b. cap** casquette *f*;
  b. mitt gant *m* de base-ball
Basel ['bɑ:zəl] *n* Bâle
baseless ['beɪslɪs] *adj* sans fondement
baseline ['beɪslaɪn] *n (in tennis)* ligne *f* de fond
basement ['beɪsmənt] *n* sous-sol *m*; *Br* **b. flat**, *Am* **b.**
  apartment (appartement *m* en) sous-sol *m*
bases ['beɪsi:z] *pl of* basis
bash [bæʃ] *Fam* **1** *n* (**a**) *(blow)* coup *m*; *(with fist)* coup
  de poing; *Br* **to have a b. at sth/doing sth** essayer
  qch/de faire qch (**b**) *(party)* fête *f*
  2 *vt* **to b. one's head** se cogner la tête
▸**bash in** *vt sep Br Fam (door, headlight)* enfoncer; **I'll b.**
  your head in! je vais te défoncer la tête!
▸**bash up** *vt sep Br Fam (person)* tabasser; *(car)*
  esquinter
bashful ['bæʃfʊl] *adj* timide; *(modest)* modeste

bashfulness ['bæʃfʊlnɪs] *n* timidité *f*; *(modesty)* modestie *f*
BASIC ['beɪsɪk] *n Comput (abbr* **Beginners' All-purpose Symbolic Instruction Code)** basic *m*
basic ['beɪsɪk] **1** *n* **the basics** l'essentiel *m*; *(of language, science)* les rudiments *mpl*; **let's get down to basics** venons-en à l'essentiel; **to get back to basics**
  (traditional values) retrouver les vraies valeurs
  2 *adj (principle, problem, vocabulary)* de base; *(accommodation, understanding)* rudimentaire; **I get**
  the b. idea je vois en gros de quoi il s'agit; **to be b.**
  to sth être essentiel(elle) à qch; **b. pay** salaire *m* de
  base
basically ['beɪsɪklɪ] *adv* (**a**) *(on the whole)* en gros; *(in fact)* en fait (**b**) *(fundamentally)* fondamentalement
basil ['bæzəl] *n* basilic *m*
basilica [bə'zɪlɪkə] *n* basilique *f*
basin ['beɪsən] *n* (**a**) *(for cooking)* bol *m*; *(for washing hands)* lavabo *m*; *(plastic, for washing up)* bassine *f*,
  cuvette *f* (**b**) *Geog* bassin *m*
basis ['beɪsɪs] *(pl* **bases** ['beɪsi:z]) *n (for discussion)*
  base *f*; *(for opinion, accusation)* fondement *m*; **to be**
  paid on a weekly/monthly b. être payé à la semaine/au mois; **on an informal b.** à titre non officiel;
  to have a b. in fact être fondé(e); **on the b. of what**
  you've told me d'après ce que tu m'as dit
bask [bɑ:sk] *vi* **to b. in the sun** se chauffer au soleil; **he**
  basked in her approval il se délectait à l'idée qu'il
  avait son approbation
basket ['bɑ:skɪt] *n (of fruit, for washing)* corbeille *f*;
  (for shopping, in basketball) panier *m*; *Fam* **he's a real**
  b. case il est complètement cinglé
basketball ['bɑ:skɪtbɔ:l] *n* basket(-ball) *m*; **b. player**
  basketteur(euse) *m,f*
basketful ['bɑ:skɪtfʊl] *n* (plein) panier *m*
Basle [bɑ:l] *n* Bâle
basmati rice [bæz'mætɪ'raɪs] *n* riz *m* basmati
Basque [bɑ:sk] **1** *n* (**a**) *(person)* Basque *mf* (**b**) *(language)* basque *m*
  2 *adj* basque; **the B. Country** le Pays basque
bas-relief [bɑ:rɪ'li:f] *n* bas-relief *m*
bass¹ [bæs] *n (seawater)* bar *m*; *(freshwater)* perche *f*
bass² [beɪs] **1** *n (voice, singer, guitar)* basse *f*; *(on amplifier)* basses *fpl*; *(double-bass)* contrebasse *f*
  2 *adj (voice)* de basse; *(guitar, clarinet)* bas (basse);
  b. clef clef *f* de fa; **b. drum** grosse caisse *f*
basset ['bæsɪt] *n* **b. (hound)** basset *m*
bassist ['beɪsɪst] *n* bassiste *mf*
bassoon [bə'su:n] *n* basson *m*
bastard ['bɑ:stəd] **1** *n* (**a**) *(illegitimate child)* bâtard(e)
  m,f (**b**) *Vulg (unpleasant man)* salaud *m*; **you lucky b.!**
  sacré veinard!; **a b. of a job** une vraie galère
  2 *adj (child)* bâtard(e)
baste [beɪst] *vt (meat)* arroser de son jus
bastion ['bæstɪən] *n also Fig* bastion *m*
bat¹ [bæt] *n (animal)* chauve-souris *f*; *Fam* **like a b. out**
  of hell comme un fou (une folle)
bat² *n (for cricket, baseball)* batte *f*; *(for table tennis)*
  raquette *f*; *Fam* **to do sth off one's own b.** faire qch
  de sa propre initiative
  2 *vt (pt & pp* **batted)** **she didn't b. an eyelid** elle n'a
  pas sourcillé *ou* bronché
  3 *vi (in cricket, baseball)* manier la batte; *very Fam*
  Fig **to b. for the other side** *or* **team** *(of gay man)*
  en être, être pédé; *(of lesbian)* être gouine; **to b. for**
  both sides *or* **teams** *(of bisexual)* marcher à voile et
  à vapeur

batch [bætʃ] *n* (*of bread*) fournée *f*; (*of people*) groupe *m*; (*of goods*) lot *m*; *Comput* **b. file** fichier *m* séquentiel; *Comput* **b. processing** traitement *m* par lots
bated ['beɪtɪd] *adj* **with b. breath** en retenant son souffle
bath [bɑːθ] **1** *n* (**a**) (*action*) bain *m*; **to take** *or* **have a b.** prendre un bain; **to give sb a b.** baigner qn; *Br* (*swimming*) **baths** piscine *f*; **b. mat** tapis *m* de bain; **b. salts** sels *mpl* de bain; **b. towel** drap *m* de bain (**b**) (*tub*) baignoire *f*, *Can* bain *m*
2 *vt* baigner
3 *vi* se baigner
bathe [beɪð] **1** *n Old-fashioned* **to go for a b.** (aller) se baigner
2 *vt* (*wound*) laver; **bathed in tears/sweat** baigné(e) de larmes/de sueur
3 *vi Old-fashioned* (*swim*) se baigner
bather ['beɪðə(r)] *n* baigneur(euse) *m,f*
bathing ['beɪðɪŋ] *n* **b. is prohibited** (*sign*) la baignade est interdite; **b. cap** bonnet *m* de bain; **b. costume** *or* **suit** maillot *m* de bain; **b. trunks** slip *m* de bain
bathos ['beɪθɒs] *n* chute *f* du sublime au ridicule
bathrobe ['bɑːθrəʊb] *n* peignoir *m* de bain
bathroom ['bɑːθruːm] *n* salle *f* de bains; *Am* (*toilet*) toilettes *fpl*; **b. cabinet** armoire *f* de toilette *ou* de salle de bains; **b. scales** pèse-personne *m*
bathtub ['bɑːθtʌb] *n* baignoire *f*, *Can* bain *m*
batik [bə'tiːk] *n* batik *m*
batman ['bætmən] *n Mil* ordonnance *f*
baton ['bætən] *n* (*in relay race*) témoin *m*; (*of conductor*) baguette *f*; *Br* (*of policeman*) matraque *f*; **b. charge** charge *f* à la matraque
batsman ['bætsmən] *n* batteur *m*
battalion [bə'tæljən] *n* bataillon *m*
▸**batten down** ['bætən] *vt insep* **to b. down the hatches** condamner les panneaux; *Fig* dresser ses batteries
batter¹ ['bætə(r)] *n* (*in baseball*) batteur *m*
batter² *n* (*in cooking*) pâte *f* à frire
batter³ *vt* (*beat*) cogner sur; (*person*) battre
battered ['bætəd] *adj* (**a**) **b. women** femmes *fpl* battues; **b. child** enfant *m* martyr (**b**) (*hat, saucepan, car*) cabossé(e); (*furniture, house*) délabré(e)
battering ram ['bætərɪŋræm] *n* bélier *m*
battery ['bætərɪ] (*pl* **batteries**) *n* (**a**) (*of radio, clock*) pile *f*; (*of car*) batterie *f*; **to be b. operated** *or* **powered** fonctionner sur piles; **b. charger** chargeur *m* de piles/batteries (**b**) *Mil* batterie *f*; *Fig* (*of criticism, complaints*) déluge *m* (**c**) **a b. of tests** une batterie de tests (**d**) **b. farming** élevage *m* en batterie; **b. hen** poule *f* de batterie
battle ['bætəl] **1** *n* bataille *f*; *Fig* combat *m*, lutte *f*; **it was a b. of wits between them** ils ont joué au plus fin; **to do b. with sb** être en conflit avec qn; **that's half the b.** la partie est à moitié gagnée; **b. cry** cri *m* de guerre; **a b. royal** une violente empoignade
2 *vi* se battre, lutter
battleaxe ['bætəlæks] *n* hache *f* d'armes; *Fam Pej* (*woman*) virago *f*
battledress ['bætəldres] *n* tenue *f* de combat
battlefield ['bætəlfiːld], **battleground** ['bætəlgraʊnd] *n also Fig* champ *m* de bataille
battle-hardened ['bætəl'hɑːdənd] *adj* aguerri(e)
battlements ['bætəlmənts] *npl* remparts *mpl*
battle-scarred ['bætəl'skɑːd] *adj* marqué(e) par la guerre
battleship ['bætəlʃɪp] *n* cuirassé *m*

batty ['bætɪ] *adj Fam* dingue
bauble ['bɔːbəl] *n* (*on Christmas tree*) boule *f*; (*worthless thing*) babiole *f*
baud [bɔːd] *n Comput* baud *m*; **b. rate** débit *m* en bauds
baulk ['bɔːlk] = **balk**
bauxite ['bɔːksaɪt] *n* bauxite *f*
Bavaria [bə'veərɪə] *n* la Bavière
Bavarian [bə'veərɪən] **1** *n* Bavarois(e) *m,f*
2 *adj* bavarois(e)
bawdy ['bɔːdɪ] *adj* grivois(e), paillard(e)
bawl [bɔːl] **1** *vt* brailler
2 *vi* brailler; **to b. at sb** hurler après qn
▸**bawl out** *vt sep* (**a**) (*shout*) hurler (**b**) (*reprimand*) passer un savon à
bay¹ [beɪ] *n* (*shrub*) laurier *m*; **b. leaf** feuille *f* de laurier
bay² **1** *n* (**a**) (*on coastline*) baie *f*; **the B. of Bengal** le golfe du Bengale; **the B. of Biscay** le golfe de Gascogne (**b**) *Archit* travée *f*; (*recess*) renfoncement *m*, niche *f*; **b. window** bow-window *m* (**c**) *Br* (*in bus station, car park*) (*parking*) **b.** aire *f* de stationnement; **loading b.** aire *f* de chargement (**d**) **to keep** *or* **hold sb at b.** tenir qn à distance; **to keep** *or* **hold sth at b.** se préserver de qch
2 *vi* (*of dog, wolf*) hurler; **to b. for sb's blood** réclamer la tête de qn
bayonet ['beɪənɪt] **1** *n* baïonnette *f*
2 *vt* **to b. sb** passer qn à la baïonnette
bazaar [bə'zɑː(r)] *n* (**a**) (*in Middle East*) bazar *m* (**b**) (*in aid of charity*) vente *f* de charité
bazooka [bə'zuːkə] *n* bazooka *m*
BBC [biːbiː'siː] *n* (*abbr* **British Broadcasting Corporation**) BBC *f*

BBC

Les principales stations de radio de la "BBC" sont : Radio 1 (musique pop et rock) ; Radio 2 (variétés) ; Radio 3 (musique classique) ; Radio 4 (actualités, reportages, programmes éducatifs) ; Radio 5 Live (sport et actualités). La BBC comprend également de nombreuses stations locales, ainsi que plusieurs stations de radio numériques spécialisées. Les chaînes de télévision principales de la BBC sont BBC1 (divertissements, dramatiques, informations) et BBC2 (émissions éducatives, dramatiques et comédies moins grand public que BBC1). Ce sont des chaînes hertziennes accessibles à tous, mais la BBC propose également des chaînes de télévision numérique spécialisées. La BBC est financée avec l'argent de la redevance télévision – obligatoire pour tout foyer possédant un téléviseur – et ne diffuse pas de messages publicitaires.

BC [biː'siː] *adv* (*abbr* **before Christ**) av. J.-C.
BCG® [biːsiː'dʒiː] *n Med* BCG® *m*
be [biː]

À l'oral et dans un style familier à l'écrit, le verbe **be** peut être contracté : **I am** devient **I'm**, **he/she/it is** deviennent **he's/she's/it's** et **you/we/they are** deviennent **you're/we're/they're**. Les formes négatives **is not/are not/was not** et **were not** se contractent respectivement en **isn't/aren't/wasn't** et **weren't**.

1 *vi* (*present* **I am, you/we/they are, he/she/it is**; *pt* **were** [wɑː(r)]; *1st and 3rd person singular* **was** [wɒz]; *pp* **been** [biːn]) (**a**) (*with state, condition*) être; **she's clever/pretty** elle est intelligente/jolie; **I'm a doctor/**

lawyer je suis médecin/avocat; **they're English/ Spanish** ils sont anglais/espagnols; **to be hungry/ thirsty** avoir faim/soif; **to be cold/hot** *(of person)* avoir froid/chaud; *(of thing)* être froid(e)/chaud(e); **it's cold/hot** *(weather)* il fait froid/chaud; **to be two metres long/wide** faire deux mètres de long/de large; **three and two are five** trois et deux font cinq (**b**) *(with location)* être; **where is the station?** où est *ou* où se trouve la gare?; **here I am** me voici; **there you are!** te voilà!; **where was I?** *(after digression)* où en étais-je?

(**c**) *(with time, date)* **it's six o'clock** il est six heures; **what day is it today?** quel jour sommes-nous?; **today's Friday/the tenth** c'est vendredi/le dix; **when is the concert?** quand a lieu le concert?; **it's a fortnight since I saw him** je l'ai vu il y a quinze jours

(**d**) *(with age)* **to be twenty (years old)** avoir vingt ans; **how old is he?** quel âge a-t-il?

(**e**) *(with cost)* coûter, valoir; **how much is it?** combien ça coûte?; **the tickets are £5 each** les billets valent 5 livres

(**f**) *(with health)* aller; **how are you?** comment vas-tu?; **I'm fine** ça va; **he's better/worse** il va mieux/plus mal

(**g**) *(with imperatives)* **be good!** sois sage!; **don't be stupid!** ne sois pas ridicule!; **let's be reasonable!** soyons raisonnables!

(**h**) *(with question tags)* **she's beautiful, isn't she?** elle est belle, n'est-ce pas *ou* non?; **they're big, aren't they?** ils sont grands, n'est-ce pas *ou* non?; **he isn't English, is he?** il n'est pas anglais, si?

(**i**) *(as past participle of go)* **I've been to London/to the museum** je suis allé à Londres/au musée; **where have you been?** où étais-tu passé?

2 *v aux* (**a**) *(in continuous tenses)* **to be doing sth** faire qch; **I was reading when the phone rang** j'étais en train de lire quand le téléphone a sonné; **she is/ was laughing** elle rit/riait; **I'm leaving tomorrow** je pars demain; **it's raining** il pleut; **I've been waiting for hours** ça fait des heures que j'attends

(**b**) *(with passives)* **he was killed** il a été tué; **he wasn't allowed to go** on ne l'a pas autorisé à y aller

(**c**) *(followed by infinitive)* **the house is to be sold** la maison doit être vendue; **there is to be an election** des élections sont prévues; **she was never to see them again** elle ne devait jamais les revoir; **you are not to mention this to anyone** tu ne dois en parler à personne

beach [biːtʃ] **1** *n* plage *f*; **b. ball** ballon *m* de plage; **b. hut** cabine *f* sur la plage; **b. towel** drap *m* de plage **2** *vt (boat, ship)* échouer

beachcomber [ˈbiːtʃkəʊmə(r)] *n* = personne qui ramasse des objets échoués ou abandonnés sur la plage

beachhead [ˈbiːtʃhed] *n* tête *f* de pont

beacon [ˈbiːkən] *n (signal, buoy)* balise *f*; *(lighthouse)* phare *m*; *(bonfire)* feu *m* d'alarme; *Fig* **a b. of hope** une source d'espoir

bead [biːd] *n* perle *f*; **a string of beads** un collier

beady [ˈbiːdɪ] *adj* **to have one's b. eyes on sb/sth** surveiller qn/qch de près

beady-eyed [ˈbiːdɪˈaɪd] *adj Pej* aux yeux de fouine; *Fig* au regard perçant

beagle [ˈbiːgəl] *n* beagle *m*

beak [biːk] *n* (**a**) *(of bird)* bec *m*; *Fam (nose)* nez *m* crochu (**b**) *Br Fam (magistrate)* juge *m*

beaker [ˈbiːkə(r)] *n* gobelet *m*

be-all and end-all [ˈbiːɔːləˈnendɔːl] *n Fam* **winning isn't the b.** gagner n'est pas tout

beam [biːm] **1** *n* (**a**) *(in building, in gymnastics)* poutre *f* (**b**) *(of sun, moon)* rayon *m*; *(of torch, headlamp)* faisceau *m* lumineux; *Phys* faisceau *m* (**c**) *(idioms) Fam* **to be off b.** être à côté de la plaque; *Fam* **broad in the b.** *(of person)* large de hanches **2** *vt (programme, information)* transmettre **3** *vi (shine) (of sun, moon)* briller; **to b. with pride/ pleasure** rayonner de fierté/de plaisir

bean [biːn] *n* (**a**) *(vegetable)* haricot *m*; *(of coffee)* grain *m*; **b. curd** pâte *f* de soja (**b**) *(idioms) Fam* **to be full of beans** être plein(e) d'énergie; *Fam* **it isn't worth a b.** ça ne vaut pas un radis; *Fam* **he hasn't got a b.** il n'a pas un radis

beanbag [ˈbiːnbæg] *n (for juggling)* balle *f* lestée; *(for sitting on)* fauteuil *m* poire

beanfeast [ˈbiːnfiːst] *n Br Hum* grande fête *f*

beanie [ˈbiːnɪ] *n* **b. (hat)** bonnet *m*

beanpole [ˈbiːnpəʊl] *n* (**a**) *(stick)* rame *f* (**b**) *Fam (thin person)* asperge *f*

beansprout [ˈbiːnspraʊt] *n* germe *m* de soja

beanstalk [ˈbiːnstɔːk] *n* tige *f* de haricot

bear[1] [beə(r)] *n (animal)* ours *m*; *(female)* ourse *f*; **b. cub** ourson *m*; **to give sb a b. hug** serrer qn très fort dans ses bras; *Fin* **b. market** marché *m* à la baisse

bear[2] (*pt* **bore** [bɔː(r)], *pp* **borne** [bɔːn]) **1** *vt* (**a**) *(carry)* porter; *(weight, load)* supporter; *(bring)* apporter; **to b. sth away** emporter qch; **to b. sth in mind** *(remember)* se souvenir de qch; *(take into account)* tenir compte de qch; **it bears no relation to...** cela n'a aucun rapport avec...; **to b. the responsibility for sth** assumer la responsabilité de qch (**b**) *(endure)* supporter; **I can't b. him** je ne peux pas le supporter; **I couldn't b. it any longer** je n'en pouvais plus; **he can't b. losing** il ne supporte pas de perdre; **it doesn't b. thinking about** l'idée même en est insupportable (**c**) *(produce) (child)* donner naissance à; *Fin (interest)* rapporter; **she bore him three children** elle lui a donné trois enfants; **to b. fruit** *(of tree)* porter des fruits; *(of effort, plan)* porter ses fruits

2 *vi (move)* **to b. (to the) right/left** tourner à droite/ gauche

▸**bear down (up)on** *vt insep* foncer sur

▸**bear out** *vt sep* confirmer, corroborer

▸**bear up** *vi* tenir le coup; **b. up!** courage!

▸**bear with** *vt insep* supporter; **if you could b. with me** si vous voulez bien patienter

bearable [ˈbeərəbəl] *adj* supportable

beard [bɪəd] *n* barbe *f*; **to have a b.** porter la barbe

bearded [ˈbɪədɪd] *adj* barbu(e)

bearer [ˈbeərə(r)] *n (of news, cheque)* porteur(euse) *m,f*; *(of passport)* titulaire *mf*

bearing [ˈbeərɪŋ] *n* (**a**) *(comportment)* port *m* (**b**) *(in mechanism, engine)* palier *m* (**c**) *(orientation)* **to take a (compass) b. (on sth)** relever la position (de qch) au compas; **to find** *or* **get one's bearings** s'orienter; *Fig* **to lose one's bearings** être désorienté(e) (**d**) *(relevance)* rapport *m* (**on** avec)

beast [biːst] *n* (**a**) *(animal)* bête *f*; **b. of burden** bête de somme (**b**) *Fam (unpleasant person)* peau *f* de vache; *(cruel person)* brute *f*; **a b. of a job** un travail pénible

beastly [ˈbiːstlɪ] *adj Fam (unpleasant)* horrible

beat [biːt] **1** *n* (**a**) *(of heart)* battement *m*; *(in bar, of music)* temps *m*; *(rhythm)* rythme *m* (**b**) *Br (of policeman)* ronde *f*; **to be on the b.** faire sa ronde

2 *adj Fam (exhausted)* crevé(e); **dead b.** complètement crevé(e)

3 *vt (pt* **beat,** *pp* **beaten** ['biːtən]) (**a**) *(person, eggs)* battre; **to b. a drum** battre du tambour; **to b.** its **wings** *(of bird)* battre des ailes; **to b. a path through the crowd** se frayer un chemin à travers la foule; *Fam* **b.** **it!** dégage! (**b**) *(defeat)* battre; **that will take some beating** c'est difficile de faire mieux; **I left early to b. the traffic** je suis parti tôt pour éviter les embouteillages; **he beat me to it** il a été plus rapide que moi; **you can't b. a good book** rien de tel qu'un bon livre; *Prov* **if you can't b.** **them, join them** il faut savoir hurler avec les loups; *Fam* **that beats everything!** ça c'est la meilleure!; *Fam* **it beats me why he did it** je ne pige vraiment pas pourquoi il a fait ça; *Fam* **it beats me!** ça me dépasse!

4 *vi* (**a**) *(of heart)* battre (**b**) **to b. about** *or* **around the bush** tourner autour du pot

▸**beat back** *vt sep* repousser

▸**beat down 1** *vt sep (price)* faire baisser; **I b.** **her down to £40** je lui ai fait baisser son prix à 40 livres

2 *vi (of rain)* tomber à verse; *(of sun)* taper

▸**beat off** *vt sep* repousser

▸**beat out** *vt sep (fire, flames)* étouffer

▸**beat up** *vt sep (assault)* tabasser; *Fig* **everybody makes mistakes, don't b. yourself up about it!** tout le monde peut faire des erreurs, arrête de culpabiliser!

beaten ['biːtən] **1** *adj* **b. earth** terre *f* battue; *Fig* **off the b. track** à l'écart

2 *pp of* **beat**

beater ['biːtə(r)] *n* (**a**) *(in hunting)* rabatteur *m* (**b**) *(in cookery)* fouet *m*

beatification [biːætɪfɪ'keɪʃən] *n* béatification *f*

beating ['biːtɪŋ] *n (punishment)* correction *f*; *(in fight)* raclée *f*; *(defeat)* défaite *f*; **to give sb a b.** *(as punishment)* donner une correction à qn; *(beat up)* flanquer une raclée à qn

beat-up ['biːtʌp] *adj Fam (car)* tout(e) déglingué(e)

beaut [bjuːt] *n Fam* **what a b.!** quelle merveille!

beautician [bjuː'tɪʃən] *n* esthéticien(enne) *m,f*

beautiful ['bjuːtɪfʊl] *adj (person, weather, music)* (très) beau (belle); *(smell, taste)* très bon (bonne)

beautifully ['bjuːtɪfʊlɪ] *adv* merveilleusement bien

beautify ['bjuːtɪfaɪ] *(pt & pp* **beautified**) *vt* embellir

beauty ['bjuːtɪ] *(pl* **beauties**) *n (attribute, person)* beauté *f*; *(object)* bijou *m*; **that's the b. of it** c'est ça qui est bien; **b. contest** concours *m* de beauté; **b. parlour** *or* **salon** institut *m* de beauté; **b. queen** reine *f* de beauté; **b. spot** *(on face)* grain *m* de beauté; *(in country)* site *m* remarquable

beaver ['biːvə(r)] *n* castor *m*

▸**beaver away** *vi* travailler d'arrache-pied (**at** à)

becalmed [bɪ'kɑːmd] *adj* encalminé(e)

became [bɪ'keɪm] *pt of* **become**

because [bɪ'kɒz] *conj* parce que; **why?** – **(just) b.** pourquoi? – parce que; **b. of** à cause de

beck [bek] *n* **to be at sb's b. and call** être aux ordres de qn

beckon ['bekən] **1** *vt* faire signe à; **to b. sb in** faire signe à qn d'entrer

2 *vi (of prospect)* être attirant(e); **to b. to sb** faire signe à qn; **fame beckons for him** la gloire l'attend

become [bɪ'kʌm] *(pt* **became** [bɪ'keɪm], *pp* **become**) **1** *vt Formal (of behaviour)* être digne de; *(of clothes, colour)* aller bien à

2 *vi* (**a**) *(come to be)* devenir; **to b. old** vieillir; **to b.**

thin maigrir; **to b. known** *(of truth)* être révélé(e) (**b**) **what will b. of him?** que va-t-il devenir?; **I don't know what has become of her** je ne sais pas ce qu'elle est devenue

becoming [bɪ'kʌmɪŋ] *adj (behaviour)* convenable; *(clothes, colour)* seyant(e)

BEd [biː'ed] *n Univ (abbr* **Bachelor of Education**) *(qualification)* = diplôme universitaire d'aptitude à l'enseignement; *(person)* = titulaire d'un BEd

bed [bed] **1** *n* (**a**) *(for sleeping)* lit *m*; **to be in b.** être au lit; **to go to b.** aller au lit; **to put a child to b.** coucher un enfant; **to go to b. with sb** coucher avec qn; *Fam* **to get out of b. on the wrong side** se lever du pied gauche; **b. and breakfast** *(accommodation)* chambre *f* avec petit déjeuner; **to stay in a b. and breakfast** ≃ prendre une chambre d'hôte; **b. linen** draps *mpl* (*et taies d'oreiller etc)* (**b**) *(of river)* lit *m* (**c**) *(of flowers)* parterre *m*; *(of vegetables)* carré *m* (**d**) *Culin* lit *m*; **on a b. of rice** garni(e) de riz (**e**) *Geol* couche *f*

2 *vt (pt & pp* **bedded**) *Fam Old-fashioned* coucher avec

▸**bed down** *vi* **to b. down (for the night)** s'installer (pour la nuit)

bedbug ['bedbʌg] *n* punaise *f*

bedclothes ['bedkləʊðz] *npl* draps *mpl* et couvertures *fpl*

bedding ['bedɪŋ] *n* draps *mpl* et couvertures *fpl*

bedevil [bɪ'devəl] *(pt & pp* **bedevilled,** *Am* **bedeviled**) *vt* **to be bedevilled by sth** *(complaints)* être assailli(e) de qch; *(problems) (of person)* être accablé(e) de qch; *(of project)* être sapé(e) par qch

bedfellow ['bedfeləʊ] *n Fig* **they make strange bedfellows** ils forment une drôle de paire

bedlam ['bedləm] *n (chaos)* bazar *m*

Bedouin ['beduɪn] **1** *n* Bédouin(e) *m,f*

2 *adj* bédouin(e)

bedpan ['bedpæn] *n* bassin *m*

bedpost ['bedpəʊst] *n* colonne *f* de lit

bedraggled [bɪ'drægəld] *adj (person, clothes)* débraillé(e); *(hair)* échevelé(e)

bedridden ['bedrɪdən] *adj* alité(e); *(permanently)* grabataire

bedrock ['bedrɒk] *n Geol* substrat *m* rocheux; *Fig (of beliefs, faith)* fondement *m*

bed-roll ['bedrəʊl] *n* matériel *m* de couchage

bedroom ['bedruːm] *n* chambre *f* (à coucher)

bedside ['bedsaɪd] *n* chevet *m*; **b. lamp** lampe *f* de chevet; **to have a good b. manner** *(of doctor)* savoir s'y prendre avec les malades; **b. table** table *f* de nuit *ou* de chevet

bedsit ['bedsɪt] *n Br* chambre *f* meublée

bedsock ['bedsɒk] *n* chaussette *f* pour le lit

bedsore ['bedsɔː(r)] *n* escarre *f*

bedspread ['bedspred] *n* dessus-de-lit *m inv*

bedstead ['bedsted] *n* châlit *m*

bedtime ['bedtaɪm] *n* **b.!** c'est l'heure d'aller au lit!; **it's past my b.** je devrais déjà être couché; **b. story** histoire *f* (pour endormir un enfant)

bed-wetting ['bedwetɪŋ] *n* énurésie *f* nocturne

bee [biː] *n* abeille *f*; *Fam* **he's got a b. in his bonnet about** c'est son idée fixe; *Br Fam* **she thinks she's the b.'s knees** elle ne se prend pas pour n'importe qui

beech [biːtʃ] *n* hêtre *m*

beechnut ['biːtʃnʌt] *n* faîne *f*

beef [biːf] *n* (**a**) *(meat)* bœuf *m*; **b. stew** ragoût *m* de bœuf (**b**) *Fam (strength)* **to have plenty of b.** avoir du muscle; **give it some b.!** allez, du nerf! (**c**) *Fam*

(complaint) **what's your b.?** c'est quoi ton problème?
 2 *vi Fam (complain)* rouspéter (**about** contre)
▶**beef up** *vt sep Fam (text, resources)* étoffer
beefburger ['biːfbɜːgə(r)] *n* hamburger *m*
beefeater ['biːfiːtə(r)] *n* = garde de la Tour de Londres
beefsteak ['biːfsteɪk] *n* bifteck *m*
beefy ['biːfɪ] *adj Fam (muscular)* costaud(e)
beehive ['biːhaɪv] *n* (**a**) *(for bees)* ruche *f* (**b**) *(hairstyle)* ≃ choucroute *f*
beekeeper ['biːkiːpə(r)] *n* apiculteur(trice) *m,f*
beeline ['biːlaɪn] *n Fam* **to make a b. for** foncer droit sur
been [biːn] *pp of* be
beep [biːp] **1** *n (of computer, alarm clock)* bip *m*; *(of car)* coup *m* de Klaxon®; *(device)* bip *m*
 2 *vt* biper
 3 *vi (of computer, alarm clock)* faire bip; *(of car)* klaxonner
beer [bɪə(r)] *n* bière *f*; **b. garden** = jardin ou terrasse où les clients d'un pub peuvent consommer; **b. glass** verre *m* à bière
beery ['bɪərɪ] *adj (smell, taste)* de bière; *(breath)* qui sent la bière
beeswax ['biːzwæks] *n* cire *f* d'abeille
beet [biːt] *n* betterave *f* (potagère); *Am* betterave *f* (rouge)
beetle ['biːtəl] *n* scarabée *m*
beetroot ['biːtruːt] *n* betterave *f* (rouge); *Fam* **to go b.** devenir rouge comme une tomate
befall [bɪ'fɔːl] *(pt* befell [bɪ'fel], *pp* befallen [bɪ'fɔːlən]) *vt Lit* arriver à
befit [bɪ'fɪt] *(pt & pp* befitted) *vt Formal* convenir à
befitting [bɪ'fɪtɪŋ] *adj* convenable
before [bɪ'fɔː(r)] **1** *prep* (**a**) *(with time)* avant; **I got here b. you** je suis arrivé avant toi; **the day b. the battle** la veille de la bataille; **b. that,...** avant,... (**b**) *(with place)* devant; **b. my very eyes** sous mes propres yeux (**c**) *(in importance)* avant; **she puts her family b. everything** pour elle, la famille passe avant tout le reste
 2 *adv* (**a**) *(with time)* avant; **two days b.** deux jours avant; **the day b.** le jour précédent, la veille; **the year b.** l'année précédente; **I've seen her b.** je l'ai déjà vue; **I've told you b.** je te l'ai déjà dit (**b**) *(in space)* **this page and the one b.** cette page et celle d'avant *ou* et la précédente
 3 *conj* **b. doing sth** avant de faire qch; **come and see me b. you leave** venez me voir avant de partir; **give it to her b. she cries** donne-le-lui avant qu'elle (ne) se mette à pleurer
beforehand [bɪ'fɔːhænd] *adv* à l'avance; **check b.** vérifiez au préalable
befriend [bɪ'frend] *vt* **to b. sb** se prendre d'amitié pour qn
befuddled [bɪ'fʌdld] *adj (person)* perdu(e); *(mind)* embrouillé(e); **b. with drink** abruti(e) par l'alcool
beg [beg] *(pt & pp* begged) **1** *vt* **to b. sb to do sth** supplier qn de faire qch; **he begged a favour of me** il m'a supplié de lui rendre un service; **to b. sb's forgiveness** implorer le pardon de qn; **I b. your pardon** *(I apologize)* (je vous demande) pardon; *(what did you say?)* pardon?; **I b. to differ** je me permets d'être d'un autre avis; **this begs the question why** on peut se demander pourquoi
 2 *vi (for money)* mendier; **I b. of you!** je vous en supplie!; **to b. for sth** *(money)* mendier qch; *(help)* implorer qch; **to b. for mercy** demander grâce; **there**

are still a few tickets going begging il reste encore quelques billets
began [bɪ'gæn] *pt of* begin
beggar ['begə(r)] **1** *n* mendiant(e) *m,f*; *Br Fam* **poor b.!** pauvre diable!; *Br Fam* **lucky b.!** veinard(e)!; *Prov* **beggars can't be choosers** nécessité fait loi
 2 *vt* **to b. belief** être incroyable; **to b. description** être indescriptible
begin [bɪ'gɪn] *(pt* began [bɪ'gæn], *pp* begun [bɪ'gʌn]) **1** *vt* commencer; *(piece of work, new chapter)* commencer, entamer; **to b. to do sth, to b. doing sth** commencer à faire qch; **he began laughing** il s'est mis à rire; **I couldn't (even) b. to explain** je ne peux (vraiment) pas expliquer
 2 *vi* commencer; **to b. by doing sth** commencer par faire qch; **to b. again** recommencer; **to b. with,...** pour commencer,...
beginner [bɪ'gɪnə(r)] *n* débutant(e) *m,f*
beginning [bɪ'gɪnɪŋ] *n* début *m*, commencement *m*; **in** *or* **at the b.** au début, au commencement; **at the b. of the year/month** au début de l'année/du mois; **I knew from the b. something was wrong** j'ai su dès le début que quelque chose n'allait pas; **to start from the b.** commencer au commencement; **from b. to end** *(read)* du début à la fin
begonia [bɪ'gəʊnɪə] *n* bégonia *m*
begrudge [bɪ'grʌdʒ] *vt* (**a**) *(resent)* **to b. doing sth** faire qch à contrecœur, rechigner à faire qch (**b**) *(envy)* **to b. sb sth** envier qch à qn
beguile [bɪ'gaɪl] *vt* (**a**) *(enchant)* envoûter (**b**) *(deceive)* enjôler; **to b. sb into doing sth** faire faire qch à qn en le séduisant
beguiling [bɪ'gaɪlɪŋ] *adj* enjôleur(euse)
begun [bɪ'gʌn] *pp of* begin
behalf [bɪ'hɑːf] *n* **on b. of sb, on sb's b.** *(act, speak, accept award)* au nom de qn; *(come, convey message)* de la part de qn; **don't worry on my b.** ne vous inquiétez pas pour moi
behave [bɪ'heɪv] *vi (of person)* se conduire, se comporter; *(be good)* bien se tenir; *(of car, machine)* marcher, fonctionner; **b. yourself!** tiens-toi bien!; *(to child)* sois sage!
behavior, behavioral *etc Am* = behaviour, behavioural *etc*
behaviour, *Am* **behavior** [bɪ'heɪvjə(r)] *n* comportement *m*, conduite *f*; **to be on one's best b.** se tenir particulièrement bien
behavioural, *Am* **behavioral** [bɪ'heɪvjərəl] *adj* de comportement
behaviourism, *Am* **behaviorism** [bɪ'heɪvjərɪzəm] *n Psy* behaviorisme *m*
behead [bɪ'hed] *vt* décapiter
beheld [bɪ'held] *pt & pp of* behold
behest [bɪ'hest] *n* **at sb's b., at the b. of sb** sur ordre de qn
behind [bɪ'haɪnd] **1** *prep* derrière; **he hid b. it** il s'est caché derrière; **to be b. sb** *(support)* être avec qn; **to be b. schedule** avoir du retard; **to put sth b. one** *(forget)* ne plus penser à qch; **she's ten minutes b. them** elle a dix minutes de retard sur eux; **to be b. the times** *(old-fashioned)* retarder son temps; **the reasons b. sth** les raisons de qch; **what's b. all this?** qu'est-ce que ça cache?
 2 *adv* derrière; **from b.** *(viewed)* de derrière; *(attacked)* par-derrière; **to stay** *or* **remain b.** *(not leave)* rester; **to be b. with one's work** avoir du travail en retard; **to be b. with the rent** être en retard pour

payer le loyer; **they are only three points b.** *(in contest)* ils ne sont qu'à trois points
3 *n Fam (buttocks)* derrière *m*
behindhand [bɪ'haɪndhænd] *adv* en retard; **to be b. with the rent** être en retard pour payer le loyer; **to be b. with one's work** avoir du travail en retard
behind-the-scenes [bɪ'haɪndðə'siːnz] *adj* secret(ète); **a b. look at politics** un regard en coulisse sur la politique
behold [bɪ'həʊld] *(pt & pp* **beheld** [bɪ'held]) *vt Lit* voir; **a sight to b.** un spectacle
beholden [bɪ'həʊldən] *adj Formal* **to be b. to sb** être redevable à qn
beholder [bɪ'həʊldə(r)] *n Prov* **beauty is in the eye of the b.** ce qu'on aime est toujours beau
beige [beɪʒ] **1** *n* beige *m*
2 *adj* beige
Beijing [beɪ'ʒɪŋ] *n* Pékin, Beijing
being ['biːɪŋ] *n* (**a**) *(creature)* être *m* (**b**) *(existence)* **to come into b.** naître; **to be in b.** exister
Beirut [beɪ'ruːt] *n* Beyrouth
Belarus [belə'ruːs] *n* la Biélorussie
belated [bɪ'leɪtɪd] *adj* tardif(ive); **wishing you a b. happy birthday** je te souhaite un bon anniversaire avec un peu de retard
belch [beltʃ] **1** *n (burp)* rot *m*; **to give a (loud) b.** roter (bruyamment)
2 *vt* **to b. smoke/flames** *(of fire, chimney)* cracher de la fumée/des flammes
3 *vi (of person)* roter
beleaguered [bɪ'liːgəd] *adj (city, army)* assiégé(e); *(government)* assailli(e) de toutes parts; *(person)* accablé(e)
Belfast [bel'fɑːst] *n* Belfast
belfry ['belfrɪ] *(pl* **belfries**) *n* beffroi *m*, clocher *m*
Belgian ['beldʒən] **1** *n* Belge *mf*
2 *adj* belge
Belgium ['beldʒəm] *n* la Belgique
Belgrade [bel'greɪd] *n* Belgrade
belie [bɪ'laɪ] *vt (feelings, background)* ne pas refléter
belief [bɪ'liːf] *n* (**a**) *(conviction)* conviction *f*; *(religious)* croyance *f*; **in the b. that...** étant convaincu(e) que...; **it is my b. that...** je suis convaincu(e) que... (**b**) *(confidence)* foi *f* (**in** en)
believable [bɪ'liːvəbəl] *adj* crédible, plausible
believe [bɪ'liːv] **1** *vt* croire; **I b. (that) I'm right** je crois que j'ai raison; **I b. him to be alive** je crois qu'il est vivant; **she is believed to be in hiding** on pense qu'elle se cache; **I don't b. a word of it** je n'en crois pas un mot; **I could scarcely b. my eyes** j'en croyais à peine mes yeux; **I don't b. it!** c'est pas vrai!
2 *vi* (**a**) **to b. in sth** *(have faith in)* croire à qch; **to b. in God** croire en Dieu; **to b. in sb** *(have confidence in)* avoir foi en qn; **to b. in oneself** avoir confiance en soi (**b**) **to believe in sth** *(be in favour of)* croire à qch; **I don't b. in making promises** je n'aime pas faire de promesses (**c**) *(think, suppose)* croire; **I b. not** je ne crois pas, je crois que non; **I b. so** je crois (que oui)
believer [bɪ'liːvə(r)] *n* (**a**) *(religious person)* croyant(e) *m,f*; **to be a b.** être croyant(e) (**b**) *(supporter)* **to be a b. in sth** croire à qch
belittle [bɪ'lɪtəl] *vt* rabaisser; **to b. oneself** se rabaisser
Belize [be'liːz] *n* le Belize
bell [bel] *n (of church)* cloche *f*; *(handbell, on cat)* clochette *f*; *(on door, bicycle)* sonnette *f*; **to ring the b.** *(on door)* sonner; *Br Fam* **to give sb a b.** passer un

coup de fil à qn; **b. jar** cloche *f*; *Am* **b. pepper** poivron *m*; **b. tower** clocher *m*
belladonna [belə'dɒnə] *n* belladone *f*
bell-bottoms ['belbɒtəmz] *npl* pantalon *m* (à) pattes d'éléphant
bell-boy ['belbɔɪ] *n Am Fam* groom *m*
belle [bel] *n* beauté *f*; **the b. of the ball** la reine du bal
bellhop ['belhɒp] *n Am Fam* groom *m*
bellicose ['belɪkəʊs] *adj* belliqueux(euse)
belligerence [be'lɪdʒərəns] *n* agressivité *f*
belligerent [be'lɪdʒərənt] **1** *n (in war)* belligérant(e) *m,f*; *(in dispute)* partie *f*
2 *adj (aggressive)* agressif(ive), belliqueux(euse); *(at war)* belligérant(e)
bellow ['beləʊ] **1** *n (of bull)* beuglement *m*, mugissement *m*; *(of person)* braillement *m*
2 *vi (of bull)* beugler, mugir; *(of person)* brailler
bellows ['beləʊz] *npl (pair of)* **b.** soufflet *m*
bell-ringer ['belrɪŋə(r)] *n* carillonneur(euse) *m,f*
belly ['belɪ] *(pl* **bellies**) *n* ventre *m*; **to have a full/an empty b.** avoir le ventre plein/vide; *Fam Fig* **to go b. up** *(of company)* faire faillite; **b. dance** danse *f* du ventre; **b. dancer** danseuse *f* du ventre *ou* orientale; **b. laugh** gros rire *m*
bellyache ['belɪeɪk] *Fam* **1** *n* mal *m* au ventre
2 *vi (complain)* rouspéter, râler *(about sb/about sth* après qn/au sujet de qch)
belly-button ['belɪbʌtən] *n Fam* nombril *m*
belly-flop ['belɪflɒp] **1** *n* plat *m*
2 *vi (pt & pp* **belly-flopped**) faire un plat
bellyful ['belɪfʊl] *n Fam* **to have had a b. of sb/sth** en avoir marre *ou* ras le bol de qn/qch
belong [bɪ'lɒŋ] *vi* (**a**) **to b. to** *(be property of)* appartenir à; **that book belongs to me** ce livre m'appartient *ou* est à moi (**b**) **to b. to** *(club, party)* être membre de; *(category)* appartenir à (**c**) *(have a proper place)* aller; **to put sth back where it belongs** remettre qch à sa place; **the saucepans don't b. in that cupboard** les casseroles ne vont pas *ou* ne se rangent pas dans ce placard; **I feel I b. here** ici je me sens à ma place
belonging [bɪ'lɒŋɪŋ] *n* **to have a sense of b.** se sentir à sa place
belongings [bɪ'lɒŋɪŋz] *npl* affaires *fpl*
beloved 1 *n* [bɪ'lʌvɪd] *Lit* bien-aimé(e) *m,f*
2 *adj* [bɪ'lʌvɪd, bɪ'lʌvd] bien-aimé(e)
below [bɪ'ləʊ] **1** *prep* (**a**) *(line, age, temperature)* au-dessous de; *(bridge, ground)* sous (**b**) *(with numbers)* moins de
2 *adv* au-dessous, en bas; *(in text)* ci-dessous; **on the floor b.** à l'étage du dessous; **it's 10 degrees b.** il fait moins dix
belt [belt] **1** *n* (**a**) *(for trousers)* ceinture *f*; *Fig* **to tighten one's b.** se serrer la ceinture; *Fig* **to have under one's b.** *(driving licence, degree)* avoir qch en poche; *(experience)* avoir qch à son actif; *Fig* **that was a bit below the b.** *(of remark, criticism)* c'était un coup bas (**b**) *(of machine)* courroie *f* (**c**) *(of land)* région *f*, zone *f* (**d**) *Fam (blow)* coup *m*; **to give sb a b.** flanquer un gnon à qn
2 *vt (hit) (ball)* cogner dans; *(person)* flanquer un gnon à
3 *vi Fam (move quickly)* **to b. along** foncer; **to b. down the stairs** dévaler *ou* descendre les escaliers quatre à quatre
▸**belt out** *vt sep Fam (song)* brailler
▸**belt up** *vi Br very Fam (be quiet)* la fermer; **b. up!** la ferme!

bemoan [bɪ'məʊn] *vt (loss, somebody's death)* pleurer; *(one's fate)* se lamenter sur

bemused [bɪ'mjuːzd] *adj* perplexe

bench [bentʃ] *n (seat) & Pol* banc *m; (worktable)* établi *m; Br Law* **the b.** *(magistrates)* la magistrature; *(court)* la cour; **to be on the b.** *(in sports)* être remplaçant(e)

benchmark ['bentʃmɑːk] *n* repère *m*, (point *m* de) référence *f*

bend [bend] **1** *n* (**a**) *(of road)* virage *m*, tournant *m; (of river)* méandre *m; (of pipe)* coude *m; Fam* **round the b.** dingue (**b**) **the bends** *(decompression sickness)* la maladie des caissons
2 *vt (pt & pp* bent [bent]) *(leg, arm, wire)* plier; *(head)* baisser; *(light)* réfracter; **do not b.** *(on envelope)* ne pas plier; **on bended knee** à genoux; **to b. the rules** faire une entorse au règlement; *Br Fam* **to b. sb's ear** tenir la jambe à qn
3 *vi (of road)* tourner; *(of river)* faire un coude; *(of branch)* plier
▸**bend down** *vi* se pencher
▸**bend over** *vi* se pencher; *Fig* **to b. over backwards to do sth** se décarcasser pour faire qch

bender ['bendə(r)] *n Fam* beuverie *f;* **to go on a b.** prendre une cuite

bendy ['bendɪ] *adj* flexible; *Br* **b. bus** autobus *m* à soufflet

beneath [bɪ'niːθ] **1** *prep* (**a**) *(physically)* sous (**b**) *(unworthy of)* **to marry b. one** faire une mésalliance; **she thinks it's b. her to work** elle pense que travailler est indigne d'elle; **b. contempt** parfaitement méprisable
2 *adv* dessous, au-dessous; **from b.** de dessous

Benedictine [benɪ'dɪktɪn] *adj Rel* bénédictin(e)

benediction [benɪ'dɪkʃən] *n Rel* bénédiction *f*

benefactor ['benɪfæktə(r)] *n* bienfaiteur *m*

benefactress ['benɪfæktrɪs] *n* bienfaitrice *f*

beneficent [bɪ'nefɪsənt] *adj (system)* bienfaisant(e); *(person)* bon (bonne)

beneficial [benɪ'fɪʃəl] *adj* bénéfique (**to** pour)

beneficiary [benɪ'fɪʃərɪ] *(pl* **beneficiaries**) *n* bénéficiaire *mf*

benefit ['benɪfɪt] **1** *n* (**a**) *(advantage)* profit *m;* **to have the b. of sth** pouvoir profiter de qch; **for sb's b., for the b. of sb** à l'intention de qn; **that remark was for my b.** cette remarque m'était destinée; **to give sb the b. of the doubt** accorder à qn le bénéfice du doute (**b**) *(charity event)* spectacle *m* de bienfaisance; **b. match** match *m* de bienfaisance (**c**) *(state payment)* allocation *f;* **to be on b.** toucher une aide de l'État; **social security benefits** prestations *fpl* sociales
2 *vt (person, country)* profiter à; *(trade)* favoriser
3 *vi* **to b. from sth** tirer profit de qch; **you'll b. from a holiday** ça te fera du bien d'aller en vacances; **who stands to b. most?** à qui cela profitera-t-il le plus?

Benelux ['benɪlʌks] *n* Benelux *m;* **the B. countries** les pays du Benelux

benevolence [bɪ'nevələns] *n* bienveillance *f*

benevolent [bɪ'nevələnt] *adj* bienveillant(e); **b. society** association *f* de bienfaisance

Bengal [beŋ'gɔːl] *n* le Bengale

Bengali [beŋ'gɔːlɪ] **1** *n* (**a**) *(person)* Bengali *mf* (**b**) *(language)* bengali *m*
2 *adj* bengali

benign [bɪ'naɪn] *adj (attitude)* bienveillant(e); *(climate)* doux (douce); *(tumour)* bénin(igne)

Benin [be'niːn] *n* le Bénin

bent [bent] **1** *n (taste)* penchant *m*, inclination *f; (aptitude)* dispositions *fpl;* **to have a musical b.** avoir des dispositions pour la musique
2 *adj* (**a**) *(curved)* tordu(e); *(out of shape)* plié(e); *(person, back)* voûté(e) (**b**) *Br Fam (dishonest)* pourri(e); **b. copper** *(flic m)* ripou *m* (**c**) *Br very Fam (homosexual)* pédé, = terme injurieux qualifiant un homosexuel (**d**) **to be b. on doing sth** *(determined)* être résolu(e) à faire qch; **to be b. on sth** vouloir à tout prix qch
3 *pt & pp of* **bend**

benzene ['benziːn] *n Chem* benzène *m*

benzine ['benziːn] *n Chem* benzine *f*

bequeath [bɪ'kwiːð] *vt Formal* léguer (**to** à)

bequest [bɪ'kwest] *n Formal* legs *m*

berate [bɪ'reɪt] *vt* réprimander

Berber ['bɜːbə(r)] **1** *n* Berbère *mf*
2 *adj* berbère

bereaved [bɪ'riːvd] *npl* **the b.** la famille du défunt (de la défunte)
2 *adj* en deuil; **recently b.** qui vient de perdre un être cher

bereavement [bɪ'riːvmənt] *n* deuil *m; Br* **b. counselling** = aide psychologique aux personnes en deuil

bereft [bɪ'reft] *adj* **to be b. of sth** être privé(e) de qch; **to feel b.** se sentir totalement seul(e)

beret ['bereɪ] *n* béret *m*

bergamot ['bɜːgəmɒt] *n* bergamote *f*

berk [bɜːk] *n Br Fam* andouille *f;* **to feel a right b.** se sentir idiot(e)

Berlin [bɜː'lɪn] *n* Berlin; **the B. Wall** le mur de Berlin

Berliner [bɜː'lɪnə(r)] *n* Berlinois(e) *m,f*

Bermuda [bə'mjuːdə] *n* les Bermudes *fpl;* **B. shorts** bermuda *m*

Bern(e) [bɜːn] *n* Berne

berry ['berɪ] *(pl* **berries**) *n* baie *f*

berserk [bə'zɜːk] *adj Fam* **to go b.** devenir fou furieux (folle furieuse)

berth [bɜːθ] **1** *n* (**a**) *(on train, ship)* couchette *f* (**b**) *(in harbour)* poste *m* à quai; *Fig* **to give sb a wide b.** éviter qn
2 *vt (boat)* amarrer à quai
3 *vi (of boat)* aborder *ou* se ranger à quai

beseech [bɪ'siːtʃ] *(pt & pp* besought [bɪ'sɔːt]) *vt Lit* supplier

beseeching [bɪ'siːtʃɪŋ] *adj* suppliant(e)

beset [bɪ'set] *(pt & pp* beset) *vt* assaillir; **to be beset by doubts** être assailli(e) par le doute; **to be beset with dangers/difficulties** être en proie à toutes sortes de dangers/difficultés

beside [bɪ'saɪd] *prep* (**a**) *(next to)* à côté de; *(sea, lake)* au bord de; **that's b. the point** cela n'a rien à voir; **to be b. oneself with joy/anger** être fou (folle) de joie/de colère (**b**) *(compared to)* à côté de, par rapport à

besides [bɪ'saɪdz] **1** *prep* à part; **other people b. ourselves** d'autres gens que nous; **what else can you do b. type?** à part taper, que savez-vous faire?; **b. being an excellent singer, she also plays the violin** non seulement elle chante très bien, mais en plus elle joue du violon; **b. which she was unwell** sans compter qu'elle ne se sentait pas bien
2 *adv* en plus; **many more b.** bien d'autres encore

besiege [bɪ'siːdʒ] *vt (castle, town)* assiéger; *Fig* **to b. sb with complaints/requests** assaillir qn de plaintes/demandes

besmirch [bɪ'smɜːtʃ] *vt Lit* souiller

besotted [bɪˈsɒtɪd] *adj* **to be b.** **with** *(person, car)* s'être entiché(e) de; *(idea)* être obsédé(e) par
besought [bɪˈsɔːt] *pt & pp of* **beseech**
bespatter [bɪˈspætə(r)] *vt* éclabousser (**with** de)
bespectacled [bɪˈspektəkəld] *adj* qui porte des lunettes, à lunettes
bespoke [bɪˈspəʊk] *adj* (fait(e)) sur mesure; **b. tailor** tailleur *m* à façon
best [best] *(superlative of* **good, well**) **1** *n* **the b.** *(the best thing)* ce qu'il y a de mieux; **that's the b. I could find** c'est ce que j'ai trouvé de mieux; **at b.** au mieux; **the b. of it is...** le plus beau, c'est...; **at the b. of times** en temps normal; **to do one's b.** faire de son mieux (**to** pour); **to look one's b.** être à son avantage; **to be at one's b.** être au mieux de sa forme; **to bring out the b. in sb** révéler les qualités de qn; **to get the b. of the bargain** faire une bonne affaire; **to get the b. out of sth** tirer le meilleur parti de qch; **to make the b. of sth** s'accommoder de qch; **we are the b. of friends** nous sommes les meilleurs amis du monde; **to be in the b. of health** se porter à merveille; **to the b. of my knowledge** autant que je sache; **to the b. of one's ability** de son mieux; **he can sing with the b. of them** il chante aussi bien que n'importe qui; **to hope for the b.** avoir espoir; **to have** *or* **get the b. of both worlds** gagner sur les deux tableaux; *Fam* **all the b.!** *(wishing somebody luck)* bonne chance!; *(at end of letter)* amitiés; **my brother sends his b.** mon frère vous fait ses amitiés
2 *adj* meilleur(e); **my b. dress** ma plus belle robe; **she is b. at French** *(of group of people)* c'est la meilleure en français; **to put one's b. foot forward** faire de son mieux; **the b. part of a year** pratiquement un an; **I'm acting in your b. interests** j'agis au mieux de vos intérêts; **it is b. to...** le mieux, c'est de...; *Com* **b. before date** date *f* limite de consommation; **the b. case scenario** le scénario le plus optimiste; **b. man** *(at wedding)* garçon *m* d'honneur; **may the b. man win** *(in contest)* que le meilleur gagne; *Com* **b. practice** pratiques *fpl* d'excellence
3 *adv* le mieux; **as b. I could** du mieux que j'ai pu, de mon mieux; **you know b.** c'est vous qui êtes le mieux placé pour savoir; **do as you think b.** fais comme bon te semblera; **the b. dressed man** l'homme le mieux habillé; **she came off b.** *(in argument)* elle a eu le dessus
4 *vt (in contest, argument)* l'emporter sur

Best man

Dans les pays anglo-saxons, le garçon d'honneur présente l'alliance au marié et prononce un discours lors de la réception de mariage.

bestial [ˈbestɪəl] *adj* bestial(e)
bestiality [bestɪˈælɪtɪ] *n* bestialité *f*
bestow [bɪˈstəʊ] *vt* accorder (**on** à)
bestseller [bestˈselə(r)] *n* bestseller *m*
bestselling [bestˈselɪŋ] *adj (book, author)* à succès
bet [bet] **1** *n* pari *m*; **to make** *or* **place a b.** parier; *Fig* **my b. is that he'll come** je parie qu'il viendra; *Fig* **your best b. would be to...** ce que tu as de mieux à faire, c'est de...; *Fig* **it's a safe b.** il y a gros à parier
2 *vt (pt & pp* **bet** *or* **betted)** *also Fig* parier; *Fam Fig* **I b. you she'll win** je te parie qu'elle va gagner; *Fam Fig* **b. you I will!** chiche (que je le fais)!
3 *vi* parier (**on** sur); **to b. on a horse** miser sur un cheval; *Fig* **I wouldn't b. on it!** je n'y compterais pas

trop!; *Fam* **you b.!** et comment!; *Fam* **John says he's sorry – I b. (he does)!** John dit qu'il regrette – tu parles!
betel [ˈbiːtəl] *n* bétel *m*; **b. nut** noix *f* d'arec
Bethlehem [ˈbeθlɪhem] *n* Bethléem
betide [bɪˈtaɪd] *vt Lit* **woe b. him/you!** malheur à lui/à toi!
betray [bɪˈtreɪ] *vt also Fig* trahir; **to b. sb to the enemy** livrer qn à l'ennemi
betrayal [bɪˈtreɪəl] *n* **(a)** *(of person, country)* trahison *f*; **b. of trust** abus *m* de confiance (**b**) *(of emotion)* indice *m*
betrothal [bɪˈtrəʊðəl] *n Lit* fiançailles *fpl*
betrothed [bɪˈtrəʊðd] *Lit* **1** *n* fiancé(e) *m,f*
2 *adj* fiancé(e)
better [ˈbetə(r)] *(comparative of* **good, well**) **1** *n* **I expected b. of you** j'attendais mieux de ta part; **you should respect your (elders and) betters** il faut respecter ses aînés; **to change for the b.** *(of person)* changer en bien; *(of situation)* s'améliorer; **to get the b. of sb** avoir le dessus sur qn; **her shyness got the b. of her** sa timidité a été trop forte; **the sooner/faster the b.** le plus tôt/vite possible sera le mieux
2 *adj* meilleur(e); **to be b.** *(after illness)* aller mieux; **to get b.** *(of person, wound)* aller mieux; *(of situation, weather)* s'arranger; **he's b. at maths/running than his brother** il est meilleur en maths/à la course que son frère; **it would be b. for you to go** il vaudrait mieux que vous y alliez; **that's b.!** voilà qui est mieux!; **b. luck next time!** tu feras mieux la prochaine fois!; **the b. part of a week** pratiquement une semaine; *Br Fam* **my b. half** ma moitié
3 *adv* mieux; **to look b.** *(of ill person)* avoir meilleure mine; **b. and b.** de mieux en mieux; **so much the b., all the b.** d'autant mieux; **for b. or worse** pour le meilleur et pour le pire; **you had b. not stay** tu ferais mieux de ne pas rester; **to think b. of it** se raviser; **to be b. off** *(financially)* être plus à l'aise; *(in situation)* être mieux
4 *vt (improve)* améliorer; *(surpass)* faire mieux que; **to b. oneself** améliorer sa situation
betterment [ˈbetəmənt] *n* amélioration *f*; *(of mankind)* progrès *m*
betting [ˈbetɪŋ] *n (bets)* paris *mpl*; *Fam Fig* **the b. is that...** il y a fort à parier que...; **what's the b. that...?** combien tu paries que...?; **b. slip** bulletin *m* de pari; **b. shop** ≃ PMU *m*
between [bɪˈtwiːn] **1** *prep* entre; **(in) b. now and Monday** d'ici lundi; **we bought it b. us** nous l'avons acheté à nous deux/trois/*etc*; **this is strictly b. you and me** que cela reste entre nous; **b. you, me and the gatepost** (soit dit) entre nous
2 *adv* **(in) b.** au milieu
bevel [ˈbevəl] **1** *n* biseau *m*
2 *vt (pt & pp* **bevelled**, *Am* **beveled)** biseauter
beverage [ˈbevərɪdʒ] *n* boisson *f*; *Can* **b. room** bar *m*
bevvied [ˈbevɪd] *adj Br Fam (drunk)* bourré *m*
bevvy [ˈbevɪ] *(pl* **bevvies)** *n Br Fam (drink)* alcool *m*
bevy [ˈbevɪ] *(pl* **bevies)** *n (group) (of people)* bande *f*; *(of birds)* volée *f*
bewail [bɪˈweɪl] *vt (loss)* pleurer; *(one's fate)* se lamenter sur
beware [bɪˈweə(r)] *vi* se méfier (**of** de); **b.!** attention!; **b. of the dog** *(sign)* chien méchant
bewilder [bɪˈwɪldə(r)] *vt* dérouter, laisser perplexe
bewildered [bɪˈwɪldəd] *adj* dérouté(e), perplexe
bewildering [bɪˈwɪldərɪŋ] *adj* déroutant(e)

bewilderment [bɪˈwɪldəmənt] *n* perplexité *f*; **to his b.** à son grand étonnement

bewitch [bɪˈwɪtʃ] *vt* ensorceler

bewitching [bɪˈwɪtʃɪŋ] *adj (smile, beauty)* enchanteur(eresse)

beyond [bɪˈjɒnd] **1** *prep* (**a**) *(in space, time)* au-delà de; **the house is b. the church** la maison est après l'église (**b**) *(surpassing)* **to live b. one's means** vivre au-dessus de ses moyens; **it's b. me (how they can do it)** ça me dépasse (qu'ils puissent faire ça); **due to circumstances b. our control** en raison de circonstances indépendantes de notre volonté; **it's b. my power** ça n'est pas en mon pouvoir; **I'm b. caring** ça m'est complètement égal; **it's b. doubt** cela ne fait aucun doute; **it's b. question** c'est incontestable; **it's b. a joke** ce n'est plus drôle; **b. belief** incroyable; **b. reach** hors de portée; **b. repair** irréparable (**c**) *(except)* à part
  2 *adv* au-delà
  3 *n* **the b.** l'au-delà *m*

Bhutan [buːˈtɑːn] *n* le Bhoutan

bias [ˈbaɪəs] **1** *n* (**a**) *(inclination)* préjugé *m*, parti *m* pris (**against/towards** contre/en faveur de) (**b**) *(in sewing)* biais *m*
  2 *vt (pt & pp* **bias(s)ed**) influencer (**against/towards** contre/en faveur de)

bias(s)ed [ˈbaɪəst] *adj (article, account)* partial(e); *(person)* de parti pris; *(opinion)* préconçu(e); **to be b. in sb's favour** avoir un préjugé en faveur de qn

bib [bɪb] *n (for baby)* bavoir *m*, bavette *f*; *(of apron, dungarees)* bavette *f*

bible [ˈbaɪbəl] *n also Fig* bible *f*; **the B.** la Bible; *Fam* **b. basher** grenouille *f* de bénitier; *Am* **the B. Belt** = ensemble des États du sud des États-Unis où le fondamentalisme chrétien est très répandu

biblical [ˈbɪblɪkəl] *adj* biblique; *Fam Hum* **to know sb in the b. sense** connaître qn au sens biblique du terme

bibliography [bɪblɪˈɒɡrəfɪ] *(pl* **bibliographies**) *n* bibliographie *f*

bibliophile [ˈbɪblɪəfaɪl] *n* bibliophile *mf*

bicameral [baɪˈkæmərəl] *adj Pol* bicaméral(e)

bicarbonate [baɪˈkɑːbəneɪt] *n* bicarbonate *m*; **b. of soda** bicarbonate de soude

bicentenary [baɪsenˈtiːnərɪ], *Am* **bicentennial** [baɪsenˈtenɪəl] **1** *n* bicentenaire *m*
  2 *adj* bicentenaire

biceps [ˈbaɪseps] *(pl* **biceps**) *n Anat* biceps *m*

bicker [ˈbɪkə(r)] *vi* se chamailler

bickering [ˈbɪkərɪŋ] *n* chamailleries *fpl*

bicycle [ˈbaɪsɪkəl] *n* bicyclette *f*, vélo *m*; **to ride a b.** faire de la bicyclette *ou* du vélo; **b. clip** pince *f* à vélo; **b. kick** *(in football)* retourné *m* bicyclette

bid¹ [bɪd] **1** *n* (**a**) *(offer)* offre *f*; *(at auction)* enchère *f*; **to make a b. (for sth)** faire une offre (pour qch); *(at auction)* faire une enchère (sur qch) (**b**) *(attempt)* tentative *f* (**for sth/to do sth** de qch/pour faire qch); **a rescue/suicide b.** une tentative de sauvetage/de suicide; **to make a b. for power** *(legally)* viser le pouvoir; *(illegally)* faire une tentative de coup d'État
  2 *vt (pt & pp* **bid**) *(offer)* offrir; *(at auction)* faire une enchère de; **what am I bid for this table?** que m'offrez-vous pour cette table?
  3 *vi* **to b. for sth** faire une offre pour qch; *(at auction)* faire une enchère sur qch

bid² *(pt* **bade** [bæd, beɪd] *or* **bid**, *pp* **bidden** [ˈbɪdən] *or* **bid**) *vt Lit* **to b. sb welcome** souhaiter la bienvenue à qn; **to b. sb goodbye** faire ses adieux à qn

bidder [ˈbɪdə(r)] *n (at auction)* enchérisseur(euse) *m,f*; **the highest b.** le plus offrant

bidding¹ [ˈbɪdɪŋ] *n (at auction)* enchères *fpl*

bidding² *n Lit (command)* **at sb's b.** sur l'ordre de qn

bide [baɪd] *vt* **to b. one's time** attendre le bon moment

bidet [ˈbiːdeɪ] *n* bidet *m*

biennial [baɪˈenɪəl] **1** *n (plant)* plante *f* bisannuelle
  2 *adj* bisannuel(elle)

bier [bɪə(r)] *n* brancards *mpl*

biff [bɪf] *Fam* **1** *n* gnon *m*
  2 *vt* flanquer un gnon à

bifocal [baɪˈfəʊkəl] **1** *n* **bifocals** lunettes *fpl* à double foyer
  2 *adj* bifocal(e), à double foyer

big [bɪɡ] **1** *adj* (**a**) *(tall, large)* grand(e); *(fat)* gros (grosse); *(drop, increase)* fort(e); *(fashionable)* à la mode; **to get big(ger)** *(taller)* grandir; *(fatter)* grossir; **my b. brother** mon grand frère; **a b. problem** un gros problème; **to be a b. eater** être un gros mangeur (une grosse mangeuse); **a b. hand for our guest!** on applaudit bien fort notre invité!; **the B. Apple** = surnom de New York; **b. business** les milieux d'affaires; *Aut* **b. end** tête *f* de bielle; **b. game** *(in hunting)* gros gibier *m*; **b. spender** panier *m* percé; **b. toe** gros orteil *m*; **b. top** *(of circus)* chapiteau *m*; **b. wheel** *(at fair)* grande roue *f* (**b**) *(idioms)* **it's her b. day tomorrow** demain c'est son grand jour; **to have b. ideas** avoir de grands projets; **don't get any b. ideas!** ne t'excite pas trop!; *Fam* **what's the b. idea?** c'est quoi cette histoire?; **to earn b. money** gagner beaucoup d'argent; **to make it b.**, **to hit the b. time** réussir; **to go in for sth b. time** *or* **in a b. way** adorer qch; **did you have fun? – b. time!** vous vous êtes amusés – oui, vachement bien!; *Ironic* **that's b. of you!** tu es trop bon!; **to be too b. for one's boots** ne plus se sentir; **to be b. on sth** tenir à qch; **to have a b. mouth** *(be indiscreet)* parler trop; *Fam* **b. gun** gros bonnet *m*; *Fig* **a b. name** un grand nom; *Fam* **b. shot** *or* **noise** gros bonnet *m*
  2 *adv* **to talk b.** faire l'important; **to think b.** voir grand

Big Ben
Nom de la cloche de la Tour de l'horloge à Westminster, souvent donné à tort à la tour elle-même. Elle est considérée comme un des monuments principaux de Londres.

bigamist [ˈbɪɡəmɪst] *n* bigame *mf*

bigamous [ˈbɪɡəməs] *adj* bigame

bigamy [ˈbɪɡəmɪ] *n* bigamie *f*

biggie, biggy [ˈbɪɡɪ] *(pl* **biggies**) *n Fam* **it's going to be a b.** *(storm, new film)* ça va faire mal; *Am* **no b.!** ce n'est pas de problème!

bighead [ˈbɪɡhed] *n Fam* crâneur(euse) *m,f*

bigheaded [bɪɡˈhedɪd] *adj* crâneur(euse); **to get b.** commencer à avoir la grosse tête

big-hearted [bɪɡˈhɑːtɪd] *adj* **to be b.** avoir le cœur sur la main

bigot [ˈbɪɡət] *n* sectaire *mf*

bigoted [ˈbɪɡətɪd] *adj* sectaire (**against** à l'égard de)

bigotry [ˈbɪɡətrɪ] *n* sectarisme *m*

bigwig [ˈbɪɡwɪɡ] *n Fam* gros bonnet *m*

bike [baɪk] *n* vélo *m*; *(motorcycle)* moto *f*; *Br Fam* **on your b.!** *(go away)* dégage!; *(don't talk nonsense)* à d'autres!; b. **shed** remise *f* à vélo
biker ['baɪkə(r)] *n Fam* motard(e) *m,f*
bikini [bɪ'kiːnɪ] *n* bikini® *m*; b. **bottom** bas *m* de maillot; b. **top** haut *m* de maillot
bilateral [baɪ'lætərəl] *adj* bilatéral(e)
bilberry ['bɪlbərɪ] *(pl bilberries) n* myrtille *f*
bile [baɪl] *n* bile *f*; *Fig (bitterness)* hargne *f*
bilge [bɪldʒ] *n Fam (nonsense)* bêtises *fpl*
bilingual [baɪ'lɪŋgwəl] *adj* bilingue
bilious ['bɪlɪəs] *adj* (a) *(nauseous)* nauséeux(euse); b. **attack** crise *f* de foie; b. **yellow** jaunâtre (b) *(bad-tempered)* hargneux(euse)
Bill [bɪl] *n Br Fam* **the (Old) B.** *(the police)* les flics *mpl*
bill¹ [bɪl] **1** *n (of bird)* bec *m*
2 *vi Fam* **to b. and coo** roucouler
bill² **1** *n* (a) *(in restaurant)* addition *f*; *(for goods, services)* facture *f*; *(in hotel)* note *f*; *Fin* b. **of exchange** lettre *f* de change (b) *Am (banknote)* billet *m* (c) *(notice)* affiche *f*; *Fig* b. **(stick) no bills** *(sign)* défense d'afficher; *Theat* **to head** *or* **top the b.** être en tête d'affiche (d) *(list)* b. **of fare** menu *m*; **to give sb a clean b. of health** trouver qn en parfaite santé; *Fam* **to fit the b.** faire l'affaire (e) *Pol (proposed law)* projet *m* de loi; B. **of Rights** = les dix premiers amendements à la Constitution américaine
2 *vt* (a) *(give invoice to)* envoyer la facture à (b) *(publicize)* annoncer
billboard ['bɪlbɔːd] *n* panneau *m* d'affichage
billet ['bɪlɪt] *Mil* **1** *n* cantonnement *m*
2 *vt* cantonner
billfold ['bɪlfəʊld] *n Am* portefeuille *m*
billiard ['bɪljəd] *n* billiards billard *m*; b. **ball/table** boule *f*/table *f* de billard
billion ['bɪljən] *n* milliard *m*; *Old-fashioned* billion *m*; *Fam* **I've got billions of things to do!** j'ai des tonnes de choses à faire!
billionaire [bɪljə'neə(r)] *n* milliardaire *mf*
billow ['bɪləʊ] **1** *n (of smoke)* nuage *m*
2 *vi* ondoyer
billowy ['bɪləʊɪ] *adj* ondoyant(e); *(sea)* houleux(euse)
billposter ['bɪlpəʊstə] *n* billposters will be prosecuted *(sign)* ≃ défense d'afficher
billy-can ['bɪlɪkæn] *n* gamelle *f*
billy-goat ['bɪlɪgəʊt] *n* bouc *m*
bimbo ['bɪmbəʊ] *(pl bimbos) n Fam Pej* minette *f*
bin [bɪn] **1** *n* poubelle *f*
2 *vt (pt & pp binned) Fam* mettre à la poubelle
binary ['baɪnərɪ] *adj Math & Comput* binaire; b. **code/number** code *m*/nombre *m* binaire
bind [baɪnd] **1** *n Fam* plaie *f*; **to be in a b.** avoir un embêtement
2 *vt (pt & pp bound* [baʊnd]) (a) *(tie)* attacher; **to be bound hand and foot** être pieds et poings liés; **they are bound together by ties of friendship** ils sont unis par les liens de l'amitié (b) *(book)* relier (c) *(book)* relier (d) *(cause to stick)* lier (e) *(oblige)* **to be bound by sth** être lié(e) par qch; **she bound me to secrecy** elle m'a fait jurer de garder le secret; **you are bound to report any change in your income** vous êtes tenu de signaler tout changement dans vos revenus
▸**bind over** *vt sep Law* sommer
▸**bind up** *vt sep* (a) *(cut, wound)* bander (b) **to be bound up with sth** *(involved)* être lié(e) à qch

binder ['baɪndə(r)] *n* (a) *(for papers)* classeur *m* (b) *(bookbinder)* relieur(euse) *m,f* (c) *(farm machinery)* lieuse *f*
binding ['baɪndɪŋ] **1** *n* reliure *f*
2 *adj (contract, promise)* qui engage *ou* lie
binge [bɪndʒ] *Fam* **1** *n (drinking spree)* beuverie *f*; **to go on a b.** prendre une cuite; **to have a chocolate b.** faire une orgie de chocolat; b. **drinking** = fait de boire de grandes quantités d'alcool en une soirée, de façon régulière
2 *vi* **to b. on sth** *(drink)* s'enfiler des litres de qch; *(food)* s'empiffrer de qch
bingo ['bɪŋgəʊ] **1** *n* ≃ loto *m*; b. **hall** = salle où l'on joue au "bingo"
2 *exclam* et voilà!

Bingo

Ce jeu d'argent très populaire en Grande-Bretagne et aux États-Unis est très proche du jeu de loto ; il est souvent pratiqué dans d'anciens cinémas ou des salles municipales. Les participants sont en grande majorité des dames d'un certain âge issues de la classe ouvrière.

binman ['bɪnmæn] *n Br* éboueur *m*
binoculars [bɪ'nɒkjʊləz] *npl* jumelles *fpl*
bint [bɪnt] *n Br very Fam* pétasse *f*
bio ['baɪəʊ] *adj bio inv*; b. **yoghurt** yaourt *m* bio
biochemical [baɪəʊ'kemɪkəl] *adj* biochimique
biochemist [baɪəʊ'kemɪst] *n* biochimiste *mf*
biochemistry [baɪəʊ'kemɪstrɪ] *n* biochimie *f*
biodegradable [baɪəʊdɪ'greɪdəbəl] *adj* biodégradable
biodiversity [baɪəʊdaɪ'vɜːsɪtɪ] *n* biodiversité *f*
biographer [baɪ'ɒgrəfə(r)] *n* biographe *mf*
biographic(al) [baɪə'græfɪk(əl)] *adj* biographique
biography [baɪ'ɒgrəfɪ] *(pl biographies) n* biographie *f*
biological [baɪə'lɒdʒɪkəl] *adj* biologique; b. **clock** horloge *f* interne *ou* biologique; **my b. clock is ticking away** *(of woman)* mon temps est compté si je veux avoir des enfants; b. **warfare** guerre *f* bactériologique; b. **washing powder** lessive *f* aux enzymes; b. **weapons** armes *fpl* biologiques
biologist [baɪ'ɒlədʒɪst] *n* biologiste *mf*
biology [baɪ'ɒlədʒɪ] *n* biologie *f*
biometric [baɪə'metrɪk] *adj* biométrique; b. **identifier** identifiant *m* biométrique
biopsy ['baɪɒpsɪ] *(pl biopsies) n Med* biopsie *f*
biorhythm ['baɪəʊrɪðəm] *n* rythme *m* biologique
biosphere ['baɪəsfɪə(r)] *n* biosphère *f*
biotechnology [baɪəʊtek'nɒlədʒɪ] *n* biotechnologie *f*
bipartisan [baɪ'pɑːtɪzæn] *adj Pol* bipartite
biped ['baɪped] *n* bipède *m*
biplane ['baɪpleɪn] *n* biplan *m*
birch [bɜːtʃ] **1** *n* bouleau *m*; **to give sb the b.** fouetter qn
2 *vt (beat)* fouetter
bird [bɜːd] *n* (a) *(in general)* oiseau *m*; *(poultry)* volaille *f*; b. **of paradise** oiseau *m* de paradis; b. **of prey** oiseau *m* de proie, rapace *m*; *Med* b. **flu** grippe *f* aviaire; b. **sanctuary** réserve *f* ornithologique; b. **table** mangeoire *f* pour oiseaux (b) *Br Fam (woman)* nana *f* (c) *(idioms) Fam* **a little b. told me** on m'en petit doigt qui me l'a dit; **the b. has flown** l'oiseau s'est envolé; *Prov* **a b. in the hand is worth two in the bush** un tiens vaut mieux que deux tu l'auras; *Prov* **birds of a feather flock together** qui se ressemble

s'assemble; **to kill two birds with one stone** faire d'une pierre deux coups; *Euph* **it's time you told him about the birds and the bees** il serait temps de lui expliquer que les bébés ne naissent pas dans les choux

birdbath ['bɜːdbɑːθ] *n* vasque *f* pour les oiseaux

bird-brained ['bɜːdbreɪnd] *adj Fam (idea)* extravagant(e); **to be b.** *(of person)* avoir une cervelle d'oiseau

birdcage ['bɜːdkeɪdʒ] *n* cage *f* à oiseaux; *(in zoo)* volière *f*

birdie ['bɜːdɪ] *n* (**a**) *Fam (bird)* petit oiseau *m; Fig* **watch the b.!** *(when taking photo)* attention, le petit oiseau va sortir! (**b**) *(in golf)* birdie *m*

birdseed ['bɜːdsiːd] *n* graines *fpl* pour oiseaux

bird's-eye view ['bɜːdzaɪ'vjuː] *n* vue *f* d'ensemble

birdwatcher ['bɜːdwɒtʃə(r)] *n* ornithologue *mf* amateur

birdwatching ['bɜːdwɒtʃɪŋ] *n* **to go b.** aller observer les oiseaux

Birmingham ['bɜːmɪŋəm] *n* Birmingham

Biro® ['baɪrəʊ] *(pl* **Biros***) n Br* stylo *m* (à) bille

birth [bɜːθ] *n* naissance *f;* **to give b. (to)** accoucher (de); **at b.** à la naissance; **by b.** de naissance; **from b.** *(blind, deaf)* de naissance; **b. certificate** acte *m* de naissance; **b. control** contrôle *m* des naissances; *Fig* **b. pangs** accouchement *m* douloureux; **b. rate** taux *m* de natalité

birthday ['bɜːθdeɪ] *n* anniversaire *m; Fam* **to be in one's b. suit** *(man)* être en costume d'Adam; *(woman)* être en costume d'Ève; **b. card/present** carte *f*/cadeau *m* d'anniversaire

birthing pool ['bɜːθɪŋ'puːl] *n* piscine *f* d'accouchement

birthmark ['bɜːθmɑːk] *n* tache *f* de naissance, envie *f*

birthplace ['bɜːθpleɪs] *n* lieu *m* de naissance

birthright ['bɜːθraɪt] *n* droit *m* acquis à la naissance; *Fig* droit élémentaire

Biscay ['bɪskeɪ] *n see* **bay²**

biscuit ['bɪskɪt] *n* biscuit *m; Br Fam* **that really takes the b.!** ça, c'est le bouquet!

bisect [baɪ'sekt] *vt* couper en deux

bisexual [baɪ'seksjʊəl] **1** *n* bisexuel(elle) *m,f* **2** *adj* bisexuel(elle)

bishop ['bɪʃəp] *n* évêque *m; (in chess)* fou *m*

bishopric ['bɪʃəprɪk] *n* évêché *m*

bison ['baɪsən] *n* bison *m*

bistro ['biːstrəʊ] *(pl* **bistros***) n* petit restaurant *m*

bit¹ [bɪt] *n* (**a**) *(in horseriding)* mors *m; Fig* **to get the b. between one's teeth** prendre le mors aux dents (**b**) *(for drill)* mèche *f*

bit² *n* (**a**) *(piece)* bout *m; (of film, book)* passage *m;* **a b. of news** une nouvelle; **to take sth to bits** démonter qch; **to tear sth to bits** déchirer qch en petits morceaux; **to smash sth to bits** briser qch en mille morceaux; **he has eaten every b.** il a mangé jusqu'à la dernière miette; **to do one's b.** participer; *Br Fam* **she's a b. of all right** c'est une belle nana; *Fam* **to have a b. on the side** *(have male lover)* avoir un amant; *(have female lover)* avoir une maîtresse; **bits and pieces** *(personal belongings)* affaires *fpl; (small items)* trucs *mpl*

(**b**) **a b. (of)** *(expressing degree)* un peu (de); **a b. late/heavy/tired** un peu en retard/lourd(e)/fatigué(e); **we had a b. of difficulty in finding him** nous avons eu quelque difficulté à le trouver; **he's a b. of a know-all** il a un côté je-sais-tout; **b. by b.** petit à petit;

not a b. of it! pas du tout!; **wait a b.!** attends une minute!; **it takes a b. of getting used to** il faut un moment pour s'y habituer; **a good b. older** nettement plus âgé(e); **a little b. (of)** un tout petit peu (de); **every b. as good/interesting as** tout aussi bon (bonne)/intéressant(e) que; *Fam* **that's a b. much!** ça c'est un peu fort!; **b. part** *(in play, film)* petit rôle *m* (**c**) *Comput* bit *m* (**d**) *Fam (coin)* pièce *f; Am* **two bits** vingt-cinq cents *mpl*

bit³ *pt of* **bite**

bitch [bɪtʃ] **1** *n* (**a**) *(female dog)* chienne *f* (**b**) *very Fam Pej (woman)* garce *f;* **I've had a b. of a day!** j'ai eu une putain de journée!; **life's a b.!** chienne de vie!
2 *vi Fam (complain)* râler, rouspéter *(about* après*); (say nasty things)* déblatérer *(about* contre*)*

bitchy ['bɪtʃɪ] *adj Fam* vache

bite [baɪt] **1** *n* (**a**) *(of person)* coup *m* de dent; *(of dog)* morsure *f; (of insect)* piqûre *f; (of snake)* morsure *f*, piqûre *f* (**b**) *(mouthful)* bouchée *f;* **to take a b. out of sth** mordre dans qch; **I haven't had a b. to eat all day** je n'ai rien mangé de la journée (**c**) *Fig (of speech, article)* mordant *m; (of sauce)* piquant *m*
2 *vt (pt* **bit** [bɪt], *pp* **bitten** ['bɪtən]) (**a**) *(of person, dog)* mordre; *(of insect)* piquer; *(of snake)* mordre, piquer; **the dog bit him in the leg** le chien l'a mordu à la jambe; **to b. one's nails** se ronger les ongles (**b**) *(idioms)* **to b. one's tongue** *(stay silent)* se mordre la langue; **to b. the bullet** faire contre mauvaise fortune bon cœur; *Fam* **to b. the dust** *(of scheme, plan)* tomber à l'eau; **to b. the hand that feeds one** cracher dans la soupe; *Prov* **once bitten twice shy**
3 *vi* (**a**) *(of person, dog)* mordre; *(of insect)* piquer; *(of snake)* mordre, piquer; **to b. into sth** mordre dans qch (**b**) *Fig (be felt)* se faire sentir

▸**bite off** *vt sep* couper d'un coup de dent; *Fig* **to b. off more than one can chew** avoir les yeux plus gros que le ventre; *Fam Fig* **to b. sb's head off** rembarrer qn

biting ['baɪtɪŋ] *adj (wind, satire)* cinglant(e)

bitmap ['bɪtmæp] *n Comput* bitmap *m*

bitmapped ['bɪtmæpt] *adj Comput* pixélisé(e)

bitten ['bɪtən] *pp of* **bite**

bitter ['bɪtə(r)] **1** *n Br (beer)* = bière anglaise brune faite avec beaucoup de houblon
2 *adj* (**a**) *(taste)* amer(ère); *Fig* **it was a b. pill to swallow** la pilule était amère, c'était dur à avaler (**b**) *(harsh) (wind, cold)* glacial(e); *(weather)* rigoureux(-euse); *(opposition, resistance)* âpre; *(struggle)* implacable; *(tears, disappointment)* amer(ère); **to go on to the b. end** aller jusqu'au bout (**c**) *(resentful)* amer(ère); *(words)* acerbe; **to feel** *or* **be b. about sth** éprouver de l'amertume à propos de qch

bitterly ['bɪtəlɪ] *adv* (**a**) *(extremely)* extrêmement; *(opposed)* résolument, farouchement; **b. regret doing sth** regretter amèrement d'avoir fait qch; **it was b. cold** il faisait un froid de canard (**b**) *(resentfully)* avec amertume

bitterness ['bɪtənɪs] *n* amertume *f*

bittersweet ['bɪtəswiːt] *adj also Fig* doux-amer (douce-amère)

bitty ['bɪtɪ] *adj Fam (patchy)* décousu(e)

bitumen ['bɪtjʊmɪn] *n* bitume *m*

bivouac ['bɪvʊæk] **1** *n* bivouac *m*
2 *vi (pt & pp* **bivouacked***)* bivouaquer

bi-weekly [baɪ'wiːklɪ] **1** *adj (fortnightly)* bimensuel(elle); *(twice weekly)* bihebdomadaire

2 *adv (fortnightly)* deux fois par mois; *(twice weekly)* deux fois par semaine

bizarre [bɪ'zɑ:(r)] *adj* bizarre

blab [blæb] *(pt & pp* **blabbed**) *Fam* **1** *vt* dire **2** *vi (chatter)* bavarder; *(betray secret)* vendre la mèche; **don't go blabbing to everybody** ne va pas le dire à tout le monde

black [blæk] **1** *n* (**a**) *(colour)* noir *m*; **b. doesn't suit her** le noir ne lui va pas (**b**) *(person)* Noir(e) *m,f* (**c**) **in the b.** *(person)* solvable; *(account)* créditeur(trice) (**d**) *(idioms)* **it says here in b. and white** c'est écrit noir sur blanc; **he sees everything in b. and white** avec lui, c'est ou tout l'un ou tout l'autre **2** *adj* (**a**) *(colour)* noir(e); **a b. man** un Noir; **a b. woman** une Noire; **to be b.** *(bruised)* être couvert(e) de bleus; **b. belt** *(in martial arts)* ceinture *f* noire; **b. box** *(flight recorder)* boîte *f* noire; **b. coffee** café *m* noir; **b. eye** œil *m* poché; *Astron* **b. hole** trou *m* noir; **b. humour** humour *m* noir; **b. ice** verglas *m*; *Br* **b. pudding** boudin *m* noir; **b. sheep** brebis *f* galeuse (**b**) *(evil, unfavourable)* noir(e); **to give sb a b. look** jeter à qn un regard noir; **the future is looking b.** l'avenir est sombre; **b. magic** magie *f* noire; **it was a b. mark against him** c'était un mauvais point pour lui; **b. spot** *(for accidents)* point *m* noir (**c**) *(unofficial)* **b. economy** économie *f* souterraine; **b. market** marché *m* noir (**d**) *(in proper names)* **the B. Country** = la région de Birmingham *(qui est très industrielle)*; **the B. Death** la peste noire; **the B. Forest** la Forêt-Noire; **B. Forest gateau** forêt-noire *f*; *Br* **B. Maria** panier *m* à salade; **the B. Sea** la mer Noire **3** *vt* (**a**) *(blacken)* noircir; **to b. one's face** se noircir le visage (**b**) *(boycott)* mettre à l'index, boycotter ▸**black out 1** *vt sep* (**a**) *(censor)* rayer *(d'un gros trait noir)* (**b**) *(city)* plonger dans l'obscurité (**c**) *(TV programme)* interrompre **2** *vi (faint)* perdre connaissance, s'évanouir

The Black Country
Le Pays noir désigne, en Grande-Bretagne, la région des West Midlands, autrefois riche en aciéries et en mines de charbon.

black-and-white [blækən'waɪt] *adj (film, photograph)* (en) noir et blanc *inv*; *(TV)* noir et blanc *inv*
blackball ['blækbɔ:l] *vt* blackbouler
blackberry ['blækbərɪ] *(pl* **blackberries**) *n* mûre *f*
blackbird ['blækbɜ:d] *n* merle *m* noir
blackboard ['blækbɔ:d] *n* tableau *m* (noir)
blackcurrant ['blækʌrənt] *n* cassis *m*
blacken ['blækən] *vt* noircir; *Fig* **to b. sb's character** calomnier qn
blackguard ['blæɡɑ:d] *n* Old-fashioned* fripouille *f*
blackhead ['blækhed] *n* point *m* noir
blackjack ['blækdʒæk] *n* (**a**) *Am (truncheon)* nerf *m* de bœuf (**b**) *(card game)* black jack *m*, ≃ vingt-et-un *m*
blackleg ['blækleɡ] *n* Fam (strikebreaker)* jaune *m*
blacklist ['blæklɪst] **1** *n* liste *f* noire **2** *vt* mettre sur la liste noire
blackmail ['blækmeɪl] **1** *n* chantage *m*; **emotional b.** chantage affectif **2** *vt* faire chanter
blackness ['blæknɪs] *n* noirceur *f*
blackout ['blækaʊt] *n* (**a**) *(during air-raid)* black-out *m inv*; *Fig* **to impose a news b.** empêcher la divulgation d'une information (**b**) *(fainting fit)* évanouissement *m*

blacksmith ['blæksmɪθ] *n* forgeron *m*; *(who shoes horses)* maréchal-ferrant *m*
bladder ['blædə(r)] *n* vessie *f*
blade [bleɪd] *n* *(of knife, sword)* lame *f*; *(of propeller, oar)* pale *f*; *(of grass)* brin *m*
blame [bleɪm] **1** *n* responsabilité *f*, faute *f*; **to put the b. (for sth) on sb** faire porter à qn la responsabilité (de qch); **to take the b. for sth** endosser la responsabilité de qch **2** *vt* rendre responsable, faire porter la responsabilité à (**for** de); **to b. sb for doing sth** reprocher à qn d'avoir fait qch; **I am to b.** je suis fautif, c'est de ma faute; **the bad weather was to b.** c'était à cause du mauvais temps; **I b. myself for what happened** je m'en veux pour ce qui est arrivé; **I don't b. you for wanting to leave** je ne te reproche pas de vouloir partir; **she has nobody to b. but herself** elle n'a de reproche à faire qu'à elle-même
blameless ['bleɪmlɪs] *adj* irréprochable
blameworthy ['bleɪmwɜ:ðɪ] *adj (person)* coupable, blâmable; *(conduct)* répréhensible
blanch [blɑ:ntʃ] **1** *vt* Culin* blanchir **2** *vi (go pale)* blêmir, pâlir
blancmange [blə'mɒnʒ] *n* blanc-manger *m*
bland [blænd] *adj (person, appearance)* terne; *(food)* insipide, fade; *(music)* sans intérêt; *(promise)* vain(e); **despite her b. assurances...** malgré ses protestations de politesse...
blandishments ['blændɪʃmənts] *npl* cajoleries *fpl*; **to resist sb's b.** ne pas se laisser amadouer par qn
blandly ['blændlɪ] *adv (speak, reply)* mielleusement
blank [blæŋk] **1** *n* (**a**) *(space)* blanc *m*; **fill in the blanks** remplissez les blancs *ou* les (espaces) vides; *Fig* **to draw a b.** faire chou blanc (**b**) *(rifle cartridge)* cartouche *f* à blanc; **to fire blanks** tirer à blanc; *Fam Fig* être stérile **2** *adj (paper, screen)* blanc (blanche), vierge; *(face)* sans expression; **with a b. expression on his face** le visage sans expression; **to look b.** avoir l'air déconcerté *ou* ahuri; **my mind went b.** j'ai eu un trou; **b. cheque** chèque *m* en blanc; *Fig* **to give sb a b. cheque** donner carte blanche à qn; **b. tape** cassette *f* vierge; **b. verse** *mpl* blancs ▸**blank out** *vt sep also Fig* effacer
blanket ['blæŋkɪt] **1** *n* couverture *f*; *Fig (of fog, cloud)* manteau *m* **2** *adj (general)* général(e), global(e); **the government imposed a b. ban on demonstrations** le gouvernement a interdit toutes les manifestations; **b. term** terme *m* général
blankly ['blæŋklɪ] *adv (without expression)* sans expression; *(without understanding)* l'air déconcerté; **she stared in b. into space** elle avait le regard perdu dans le vide
blare ['bleə(r)] **1** *n* beuglements *mpl* **2** *vi (of TV, radio)* beugler ▸**blare out** *vt sep* beugler **2** *vi* beugler; **the music was blaring out** la musique était à fond
blarney ['blɑ:nɪ] *n* Fam* boniments *mpl*
blasé ['blɑ:zeɪ] *adj* blasé(e); **she was very b. about the accident** l'accident ne lui avait fait ni chaud ni froid
blaspheme [blæs'fi:m] *vi* blasphémer
blasphemous ['blæsfəməs] *adj* blasphématoire
blasphemy ['blæsfəmɪ] *n* blasphème *m*

blast [blɑːst] **1** *n* (**a**) *(of wind)* coup *m*, rafale *f*; *(of heat)* bouffée *f*; *(of steam)* jet *m*; *(of whistle, horn)* coup; **at full b.** *(radio, TV, heater)* à fond; **b. furnace** haut-fourneau *m* (**b**) *(explosion)* explosion *f*; *(shock wave)* souffle *m* d'une explosion; *Fam* **meeting her/ hearing that song was a real b. from the past!** la rencontrer/cette chanson m'a ramené des années en arrière! (**c**) *Fam (good time)* **it was a b.** c'était génial; **we had a b.** on s'est super marrés
2 *vt* (**a**) *(hole, tunnel)* creuser *(en dynamitant)*; **the building had been blasted by a bomb** le bâtiment avait été détruit par une bombe; *Fam* **to b. sb's head off** faire sauter la tête à qn (**b**) *Fam (criticize)* démolir (**c**) *Br Fam* **b. (it)!** zut alors!
▸**blast off** *vi (of space rocket)* décoller
blast-off ['blɑːstɒf] *n (of space rocket)* lancement *m*
blatant ['bleɪtənt] *adj* flagrant(e), manifeste; *(lie)* éhonté(e)
blatantly ['bleɪtəntlɪ] *adv* de façon flagrante; **b. obvious** tout à fait évident(e)
blather ['blæðə(r)] *vi Fam* raconter des bêtises
blaze [bleɪz] **1** *n* (**a**) *(fire)* feu *m*; **many people died in the b.** beaucoup de gens ont péri dans les flammes (**b**) *(of colour, light)* éclat *m*; **the film was released in a b. of publicity** ils ont fait une publicité monstre pour la sortie du film; **to go out in a b. of glory** s'en aller plein(e) de gloire (**c**) *Fam* **what the blazes does he want?** mais qu'est-ce qu'il veut, bon sang?
2 *vt Fig* **to b. a trail** ouvrir la voie
3 *vi (of fire, sun)* flamboyer; *(of light)* être éclatant(e); **the house was blazing with lights** la maison était tout illuminée; **to b. with anger** *(of person)* fulminer; *(of eyes)* lancer des éclairs de colère
blazer ['bleɪzə(r)] *n* blazer *m*
blazing ['bleɪzɪŋ] *adj (burning)* en feu, enflammé(e); *Fig* **a b. row** une violente dispute
bleach [bliːtʃ] **1** *n* (eau *f* de) Javel *f*
2 *vt (clothes)* passer à l'eau de Javel *ou* à la Javel; *(hair)* décolorer
bleak [bliːk] *adj (landscape, weather)* morne, triste; *(outlook)* lugubre; *(prospect)* peu encourageant(e)
bleary ['blɪərɪ] *adj (eyes)* rouge
bleary-eyed [blɪərɪ'aɪd] *adj* **to be b.** *(from lack of sleep)* avoir de petits yeux; *(from hay fever, crying)* avoir les yeux rouges
bleat [bliːt] **1** *n (of sheep)* bêlement *m*
2 *vi (of sheep)* bêler; *Fig (complain)* ronchonner (**about** à propos de)
bleed [bliːd] *(pt & pp* **bled** [bled]) **1** *vt Med* saigner; *(radiator)* purger; *Fig* **to b. sb dry** saigner qn à blanc
2 *vi* saigner; **her nose is bleeding** elle saigne du nez; **to b. to death** saigner à mort
bleeder ['bliːdə(r)] *n Br very Fam* salaud *m*
bleeding ['bliːdɪŋ] **1** *n* saignement *m*; **has the b. stopped?** est-ce que tu saignes/est-ce qu'il saigne/ *etc* toujours?
2 *adj* (**a**) *(wound)* qui saigne (**b**) *Br very Fam (for emphasis)* **you b. liar!** sale menteur!; **you b. idiot!** espèce de con!
3 *adv Br very Fam (for emphasis)* foutrement; **that was b. stupid!** c'était vraiment con!
bleep [bliːp] **1** *n* bip *m*
2 *vi* faire bip
bleeper ['bliːpə(r)] *n (pager)* bip *m*
blemish ['blemɪʃ] **1** *n (mark)* marque *f*; *Fig* **it left a b. on her reputation** cela a entaché sa réputation
2 *vt Fig (reputation)* entacher

blench [blentʃ] *vi* avoir un mouvement de recul
blend [blend] **1** *n* mélange *m*
2 *vt* mélanger (**with** à *ou* avec)
3 *vi* se mélanger, se mêler; **the colours b. together well** ces couleurs se marient bien *ou* vont bien ensemble
▸**blend in** *vi (with surroundings)* se fondre (**with** dans)
▸**blend into** *vt insep (surroundings)* se fondre dans; **to b. into the background** se fondre dans le décor
blender ['blendə(r)] *n* mixer *m*, mixeur *m*
bless [bles] *(pt & pp* **blessed** *or* **blest** [blest]) *vt* (**a**) *(say blessing for)* bénir; **God b. you!** que Dieu te bénisse!; **b. you!** *(when somebody sneezes)* à tes souhaits! (**b**) **to be blessed with sth** *(talent, beauty)* être doté(e) de qch; **they have been blessed with two fine children** ils ont deux beaux enfants
blessed ['blesɪd] *adj* (**a**) *(holy)* béni(e) (**b**) *Fam (for emphasis)* **the whole b. day** toute la sainte journée; **the whole b. lot** tout le bazar, tout le bataclan; **it's a b. nuisance having to...** quelle barbe d'avoir à...; **I can't see a b. thing!** je n'y vois absolument rien!
blessing ['blesɪŋ] *n* (**a**) *(religious)* bénédiction *f*; *Fig* **to give sb/sth one's b.** donner à qn/qch sa bénédiction (**b**) *(benefit, advantage)* bienfait *m*; **it was a b. in disguise** finalement, ça a été une bonne chose; **it was a mixed b.** il y avait du bon et du mauvais; **to count one's blessings** s'estimer heureux de ce qu'on a
blest [blest] *pt & pp of* **bless**
blether ['bleðə(r)] *vi Fam (talk foolishly)* raconter des bêtises; *Scot (chat)* papoter
blew [bluː] *pt of* **blow²**
blight [blaɪt] **1** *n (on cereals)* rouille *f*; *(on potatoes)* brunissure *f*; *Fig* **to cast a b. over sth** jeter un froid sur qch
2 *vt Fig* assombrir; *(hopes)* anéantir
blighter ['blaɪtə(r)] *n Br Fam Old-fashioned* type *m*, gars *m*; **lucky b.** veinard *m*
blimey ['blaɪmɪ] *exclam Br Fam* zut alors!
blind¹ [blaɪnd] **1** *npl* **the b.** les aveugles *mpl*; **school for the b.** école *f* pour aveugles; **they don't know what they're doing, it's like the b. leading the b.** ils ne savent pas ce qu'ils font, ils sont aussi nuls l'un que l'autre
2 *adj* (**a**) *also Fig* aveugle; **a b. man** un aveugle; **a b. woman** une aveugle; **b. in one eye** borgne, aveugle d'un œil; **as b. as a bat** myope comme une taupe; **to be b. to sth** ne pas voir qch; **to turn a b. eye to sth** fermer les yeux sur qch; *also Fig* **b. with fury** aveuglé(e) par la colère; *also Fig* **b. alley** impasse *f*; **b. date** = rencontre arrangée avec quelqu'un que l'on ne connaît pas; **b. man's buff** *(jeu m de)* colin-maillard *m*; **b. spot** *(for driver)* angle *m* mort; *Fig* **to have a b. spot for maths** être nul (nulle) en maths (**b**) *Fam (for emphasis)* **he didn't take a b. bit of notice** il n'y a pas prêté la moindre attention; **it didn't make a b. bit of difference** ça n'a pas fait la moindre différence
3 *adv* **b. drunk** ivre mort(e)
4 *vt* aveugler; *Fig* **love blinded her to his faults** aveuglée par l'amour, elle n'a pas vu ses défauts
blind² *n Br (for windows)* store *m*
blindfold ['blaɪndfəʊld] **1** *n* bandeau *m*
2 *vt* **to b. sb** mettre un bandeau à qn; **to be blindfolded** avoir les yeux bandés
blinding ['blaɪndɪŋ] *adj* (**a**) *(light)* aveuglant(e); *Fig (intensity, realization)* affolant(e) (**b**) *Br Fam (excellent)* génial(e)
blindly ['blaɪndlɪ] *adv Fig* aveuglément

blindness ['blaɪndnɪs] n cécité f; Fig aveuglement m
bling (bling) [blɪŋ('blɪŋ)] Fam **1** n (jewellery) bijoux mpl, quincaillerie f
2 adj (ostentatious) tape-à-l'œil; **that car is so b.!** cette voiture est vraiment tape-à-l'œil!
blink [blɪŋk] **1** n (**a**) (of eyes) clignement m de paupières (**b**) Br Fam **to be on the b.** (of TV, machine) faire des siennes
2 vt **to b.** one's eyes cligner des yeux
3 vi (of person) cligner des yeux; (of light) clignoter
blinkered ['blɪŋkəd] adj (approach, attitude) borné(e); **to be b.** (of person) avoir des œillères
blinkers ['blɪŋkəz] npl (**a**) (for horse) œillères fpl; Fig **to be wearing b.** avoir des œillères (**b**) Fam (indicators) clignotants mpl
blinking ['blɪŋkɪŋ] adj (**a**) (light) clignotant(e) (**b**) Br Fam (for emphasis) sacré(e); **what a b. nuisance!** quelle barbe!; **you b. idiot!** espèce d'imbécile!
blip [blɪp] n (on radar screen) spot m; Fam (temporary problem) hic m inv, os m
bliss [blɪs] n bonheur m, béatitude f; **breakfast in bed, what b.!** le petit déjeuner au lit, quel bonheur!
blissful ['blɪsfʊl] adj (person) (bien)heureux(euse); (holiday) plein(e) de bonheur; **I'd rather remain in b.** ignorance j'aime autant ne pas savoir
blissfully ['blɪsfʊlɪ] adv merveilleusement; **b. happy** au comble du bonheur; **to be b. unaware that...** ne pas se douter le moins du monde que...
blister ['blɪstə(r)] **1** n (on skin) ampoule f, cloque f; (on paint) cloque f
2 vt (skin) provoquer des ampoules sur; (paint) faire des cloques sur
3 vi (of skin) se couvrir d'ampoules; (of paint) cloquer
blistering ['blɪstərɪŋ] adj (sun, heat) brûlant(e); (criticism, attack) virulent(e)
blithe ['blaɪð] adj (attitude, disregard) désinvolte; Lit (person) joyeux(euse), allègre
blithely ['blaɪðlɪ] adv (ignore, disregard) avec une complète désinvolture; Lit (happily) joyeusement, allègrement
blithering ['blɪðərɪŋ] adj **a b. idiot** un(e) sombre idiot(e)
blitz [blɪts] **1** n (air bombardment) blitz m, bombardement m aérien; Hist **the B.** le Blitz; Fam Fig **to have a b. on sth** s'attaquer à qch
2 vt (bomb) bombarder; Fam Fig **to b. sb with letters/complaints** bombarder qn de lettres/plaintes
blizzard ['blɪzəd] n tempête f de neige
bloated ['bləʊtɪd] adj (stomach, face) gonflé(e); (ego) énorme
blob [blɒb] n (**a**) (of cream, jam, paint) tache f; (of ink) pâté m (**b**) (indistinct shape) silhouette f
bloc [blɒk] n Pol bloc m
block [blɒk] **1** n (**a**) (of wood, stone) bloc m; (for execution, of butcher) billot m; Fam **I'll knock your b. off!** je vais te casser la gueule!; **b. and tackle** (for lifting) palan m; **b. capitals** majuscules fpl en caractères d'imprimerie; **b. diagram** (flow chart) schéma m fonctionnel (**b**) Br (building) immeuble m; Am (group of buildings) pâté m de maisons; Br **b. of flats** immeuble m (**c**) (of shares) paquet m; **b. of seats** bloc-sièges m inv; **b. booking** réservation f ou location f de groupe; **b. vote** vote m groupé
2 vt (**a**) (pipe, road, proposal) bloquer; (view) cacher; **to b. sb's way** barrer ou bloquer le passage à

qn; Fin **to b. a cheque** faire opposition à un chèque (**b**) Comput (text) sélectionner
▸**block off** vt sep (road, exit) barrer
▸**block out** vt sep (light) empêcher d'entrer ou de passer; (a memory) refouler; (music, noise) faire abstraction de
▸**block up** vt sep (tunnel, passageway) boucher; (door, window) murer; **to have a blocked-up nose** avoir le nez bouché
blockade [blɒ'keɪd] **1** n blocus m (**on** à)
2 vt bloquer, faire le blocus de
blockage ['blɒkɪdʒ] n obstruction f
blockbuster ['blɒkbʌstə(r)] n (film) superproduction f; (novel) best-seller m
blockhead ['blɒkhed] n Fam lourdaud m
blog [blɒg] n Comput (abbr weblog) blog m
blogger ['blɒgə(r)] n Comput blogueur(euse) m,f
blogging ['blɒgɪŋ] n Comput blogging m, création f de blogs
bloke [bləʊk] n Br Fam type m
blonde [blɒnd] **1** n blond(e) m,f
2 adj blond(e)
blood [blʌd] **1** n (**a**) (substance) sang m; **to give b.** donner du sang; **b. bank** banque f du sang; **b. cell** globule m sanguin; **b. clot** caillot m; **b. count** numération f globulaire; **b. donor** donneur(euse) m,f de sang; **b. group** groupe m sanguin; **b. poisoning** septicémie f, toxémie f; **b. pressure** tension f (artérielle); **to have low/high b. pressure** avoir la tension basse/ de la tension; **b. relation** parent(e) m,f; Am **b. sausage** boudin m noir; **b. sports** la chasse; **b. test** prise f de sang; **b. transfusion** transfusion f sanguine; **b. vessel** vaisseau m sanguin (**b**) (idioms) **to have b. on one's hands** avoir du sang sur les mains; **it makes my b. boil** ça me fait bouillir; **it makes my b. run cold** ça me glace le sang; **in cold b.** de sang-froid; **he's after your b.** il en a après toi; **to have sth in one's b.** avoir qch dans le sang; **it's like trying to get b. out of a stone** c'est comme si on se heurtait à un mur; Prov **b. is thicker than water** la famille passe avant tout
2 vt (initiate) initier
bloodbath ['blʌdbɑːθ] n bain m de sang
bloodcurdling ['blʌdkɜːdlɪŋ] adj à vous tourner les sangs
bloodhound ['blʌdhaʊnd] n limier m
bloodless ['blʌdlɪs] adj (**a**) (without bloodshed) **it was a b. coup** le coup d'État s'est déroulé sans effusion de sang (**b**) (pale) exsangue
bloodletting ['blʌdletɪŋ] n (**a**) Med saignée f (**b**) (slaughter, feud) effusion f de sang
bloodshed ['blʌdʃed] n effusion f de sang; **without b.** sans verser le sang
bloodshot ['blʌdʃɒt] adj (eyes) injecté(e) de sang
bloodstain ['blʌdsteɪn] n tache f de sang
bloodstained ['blʌdsteɪnd] adj taché(e) de sang
bloodstream ['blʌdstriːm] n sang m
bloodsucker ['blʌdsʌkə(r)] n also Fig sangsue f
bloodthirsty ['blʌdθɜːstɪ] adj (person) sanguinaire; (film) sanglant(e)
bloody ['blʌdɪ] **1** adj (**a**) (bleeding, bloodstained) ensanglanté(e); (battle, revolution) sanglant(e); Fig **to give sb a b. nose** mettre une raclée à qn (**b**) Br very Fam foutu(e); **you b. fool!** connard (connasse)!; **b. hell!** merde!
2 adv Br very Fam **it's b. hot!** il fait une putain de chaleur!; **I'm b. tired** putain, qu'est-ce que je suis crevé; **not b. likely!** putain, il n'y a pas de danger!;

he can b. well do it himself! il peut parfaitement se démerder tout seul!

bloody-minded [blʌdɪ'maɪndɪd] adj Br to be b. être un(e) emmerdeur(euse); don't be so b.! arrête d'emmerder le monde!

bloom [bluːm] 1 n fleur f; in (full) b. (tree) en fleur(s); (flower) éclos(e); in the b. of youth à ou dans la fleur de l'âge
2 vi (of garden, flower, talent) fleurir; Fig to be blooming with health être resplendissant(e) ou éclatant(e) de santé

bloomer ['bluːmə(r)] n (a) Fam (mistake) bourde f (b) (bread) ≃ bâtard m court

bloomers ['bluːməz] npl culotte f bouffante

blooming ['bluːmɪŋ] Br Fam 1 adj sacré(e); you b. idiot! espèce d'idiot(e)!
2 adv b. good sacrément bon (bonne); b. awful carrément horrible; he's b. useless! il est totalement nul!

blossom ['blɒsəm] 1 n fleur f; in b. en fleur(s)
2 vi fleurir; Fig s'épanouir; Fig she had blossomed into a charming young woman elle était devenue une charmante jeune femme

blot [blɒt] 1 n (of ink) pâté m; Fig a b. on sb's reputation une tache faite à la réputation de qn; Fig to be a b. on the landscape gâcher le paysage
2 vt (pt & pp blotted) (stain) tacher; (with ink) faire un pâté/des pâtés sur; to b. one's lipstick fixer son rouge à lèvres (en pressant les lèvres sur un mouchoir en papier); Fig to b. one's copybook ternir sa réputation
▸**blot out** vt sep (sun, light) masquer; (memory) effacer

blotch [blɒtʃ] n (on skin) tache f

blotchy ['blɒtʃɪ] adj (skin) couvert(e) de taches

blotter ['blɒtə(r)] n buvard m

blotting paper ['blɒtɪŋpeɪpə(r)] n buvard m; a sheet of b. un buvard

blotto ['blɒtəʊ] adj Br Fam (drunk) bourré(e)

blouse [blaʊz] n chemisier m, corsage m

blow¹ [bləʊ] n (a) (hit) coup m; to come to blows (over sth) en venir aux mains (pour ou au sujet de qch); Fig to strike a b. for sth remporter une victoire pour qch; Fig to soften the b. atténuer le choc (b) (setback) coup m; this news was a b. to us cette nouvelle a été pour nous un coup rude; it was a b. to her pride un coup à son amour-propre et a pris un coup

blow² [bləʊ] (pt blew [bluː], pp blown [bləʊn]) 1 vt (a) (of wind, person) the wind blew down the fence le vent a renversé la barrière; the wind blew the door open le vent a fait s'ouvrir la porte; to b. glass souffler le verre; to b. the horn klaxonner; to b. a whistle donner un coup de sifflet; Fig to b. the whistle on sb/sth dénoncer qn/qch; to b. the dust off sth souffler sur qch pour en enlever la poussière; to b. sb a kiss envoyer un baiser à qn; to b. bubbles faire des bulles; to b. one's nose se moucher; Fig to b. one's own trumpet chanter ses propres louanges (b) Elec to b. a fuse faire sauter un plomb; Fig (of person) disjoncter; Fam Fig the Grand Canyon blew my mind! quel pied, le Grand Canyon!; Fam Fig the prices blew my mind! j'ai été affolé par les prix! (c) Fam (chance) gâcher; that's blown it! ça a tout gâché!, ça a fait tout louper! (d) Fam (money) claquer (on sth pour s'acheter qch)
2 vi (a) (of wind, person) souffler; to b. down ou over (of fence, tree) se renverser; the door blew open/shut le vent a ouvert/fermé la porte; to b. on one's fingers se souffler sur les doigts; Fig to b. hot

and cold souffler le chaud et le froid (b) Elec (of fuse) sauter
▸**blow away 1** vt sep to b. sth away (of wind) faire s'envoler qch; Fam Fig to b. sb away (shoot dead) descendre qn; Fam Fig his last movie blew me away! son dernier film, c'est le pied!
2 vi (of paper, hat) s'envoler
▸**blow off 1** vt sep (of wind) emporter; Fam Fig to b. sb's head off faire sauter la cervelle à qn
2 vi (of hat) s'envoler
▸**blow out** vt sep (of wind) éteindre; (candle, match) souffler
▸**blow over** vi (of storm, argument) se calmer; the scandal soon blew over le scandale fut vite oublié
▸**blow up 1** vt sep (a) (balloon, tyre) gonfler (b) (explode) faire sauter (c) (enlarge) (photograph) agrandir; Fig the incident was blown up out of all proportion on a fait une histoire incroyable autour de ce petit incident
2 vi (of bomb) exploser, sauter; Fig (lose one's temper) piquer une colère; to b. up at sb/sth se mettre en colère contre qn/qch

blow-by-blow ['bləʊbaɪ'bləʊ] adj (account) détaillé(e), minutieux(euse)

blow-dry ['bləʊdraɪ] 1 n brushing m
2 vt to b. sb's hair faire un brushing à qn

blower ['bləʊə(r)] n Br Fam (telephone) bigophone m

blowhole ['bləʊhəʊl] n (of whale) évent m

blowjob ['bləʊdʒɒb] n Vulg pipe f; to give sb a b. tailler une pipe à qn

blowlamp ['bləʊlæmp] = blowtorch

blown [bləʊn] pp of blow²

blow-out ['bləʊaʊt] n (a) (of tyre) éclatement m (b) Fam (big meal) gueuleton m

blowpipe ['bləʊpaɪp] n sarbacane f

blowtorch ['bləʊtɔːtʃ] n (for welding) chalumeau m, lampe f à souder; (for removing paint) brûloir m

blow-up ['bləʊʌp] adj (inflatable) a b. beachball un ballon de plage gonflable; a b. mattress un matelas pneumatique

blowzy ['blaʊzɪ] adj négligé(e)

blub [blʌb] (pt & pp blubbed) vi Fam pleurer comme une madeleine

blubber ['blʌbə(r)] 1 n (fat) graisse f
2 vi Fam (cry) pleurer comme une madeleine

bludgeon ['blʌdʒən] vt matraquer; Fig to b. sb into doing sth obliger brutalement qn à faire qch

blue [bluː] 1 n (a) (colour) bleu m; Fig out of the b. à l'improviste; her resignation came out of the b. sa démission nous a pris par surprise (b) the blues (music) le blues; Fam to have the blues (be depressed) avoir le cafard
2 adj (a) (colour) bleu(e); b. with cold bleu(e) de froid; Fam she can complain until she's b. in the face elle peut se plaindre autant qu'elle veut; once in a b. moon tous les trente-six du mois; Fam to scream b. murder crier comme un putois; b. blood sang bleu; b. cheese bleu m; b. whale baleine f bleue (b) Fam (sad) to feel b. avoir le cafard (c) Fam (obscene) grivois(e), paillard(e); to tell b. jokes/stories en raconter des vertes et des pas mûres; b. movie film m porno

bluebell ['bluːbel] n jacinthe f des bois

blueberry ['bluːbərɪ] (pl blueberries) n airelle f, myrtille f, Can bleuet m

bluebird ['bluːbɜːd] n rouge-gorge m bleu

bluebottle ['bluːbɒtl] n mouche f de la viande

blue-chip [ˈbluːtʃɪp] *adj Fin* **b. shares** valeurs *fpl* de père de famille; **b. company** affaire *f* de premier ordre
blue-collar [ˈbluːˈkɒlə(r)] *adj* **b. worker** col *m* bleu
blue-eyed [ˈbluːaɪd] *adj* aux yeux bleus; *Br Fam* **his mother's b.** boy le petit chéri de sa maman
blueprint [ˈbluːprɪnt] *n Archit & Ind* plan *m*; *Fig* projet *m*; **a b. for success** une garantie de succès
Bluetooth® [ˈbluːtuːθ] *n Tel* (technologie *f*) Bluetooth® *m*
bluff¹ [blʌf] **1** *n (deception)* bluff *m*; **to call sb's b.** *(at cards)* inviter qn à mettre les cartes sur la table; *(in negotiation)* prendre qn au mot
  2 *vt* **you're bluffing me** tu bluffes; **to b. one's way out of a tricky situation** se tirer d'affaire par un coup de bluff
  3 *vi* bluffer
bluff² *n (cliff)* à-pic *m inv*
bluff³ *adj (manner)* direct(e)
blunder [ˈblʌndə(r)] **1** *n* gaffe *f*
  2 *vi (make mistake)* faire une gaffe; **to b. along** *(move clumsily)* avancer d'un pas maladroit; **to b. against** *or* **into sb/sth** heurter qn/à qch
blunderbuss [ˈblʌndəbʌs] *n* tromblon *m*
blunt [blʌnt] **1** *adj* (**a**) *(blade)* émoussé(e); *(pencil)* mal taillé(e) (**b**) *(manner)* brutal(e); *(question, statement)* direct(e); *(refusal)* net (nette); *(person)* brusque; **to be b.,...** pour parler franchement,...
  2 *vt (blade)* émousser; *(pencil)* épointer; *Fig (anger, enthusiasm)* émousser, atténuer
bluntly [ˈblʌntlɪ] *adv (frankly)* franchement; **I told him b. that...** je lui ai dit tout net que...
bluntness [ˈblʌntnɪs] *n* (**a**) *(of blade)* manque *m* de tranchant (**b**) *(of manner, statement)* rudesse *f*; *(of person)* franchise *f*
blur [blɜː(r)] **1** *n (vague shape)* forme *f* vague; *(unclear memory)* vague souvenir *m*; **without my glasses, everything is a b.** sans mes lunettes, je suis complètement dans le brouillard; **to go by in a b.** *(of time)* passer à toute vitesse
  2 *vt (pt & pp blurred)* brouiller, troubler
  3 *vi se* brouiller; *(of memories)* s'estomper
blurb [blɜːb] *n (on book cover)* notice *f* publicitaire
blurred [blɜːd] *adj (ink)* qui a bavé; *(writing)* flou(e); *(vision)* trouble
▸**blurt out** [blɜːt] *vt sep* laisser échapper; **"I love him!"** **she blurted out** "je l'aime!" lâcha-t-elle
blush [blʌʃ] **1** *n* (**a**) *(on face)* rougeur *f*; *Fig* **to spare sb's blushes** éviter à qn un embarras (**b**) *Am (makeup)* fard *m* à joues
  2 *vi* rougir; **to b. with shame** rougir de honte; **to b. at the thought of sth** rougir en pensant à qch; **I b. to admit it** j'ai honte de l'admettre
blusher [ˈblʌʃə(r)] *n* blush *m*, fard *m* à joues
bluster [ˈblʌstə(r)] **1** *n* protestations *fpl* véhémentes
  2 *vi* protester avec véhémence
blustery [ˈblʌstərɪ] *adj (day)* venteux(euse), de grand vent; *(wind)* violent(e)
BMA [biːeˈmeɪ] *n (abbr* **British Medical Association**) ≃ ordre *m* des médecins
BO [biːˈəʊ] *n Fam (abbr* **body odour**) odeur *f* corporelle; **to have BO** sentir mauvais
boa [ˈbəʊə] *n* **b.** (**constrictor**) boa *m* (constricteur); (**feather**) **b.** boa *m*
boar [ˈbɔː(r)] *n (male pig)* verrat *m*; *(wild pig)* sanglier *m*
board [bɔːd] **1** *n* (**a**) *(of wood)* planche *f*; *(for notices)* panneau *m*; *(for chess)* échiquier *m*; *(for draughts)* damier *m*; *(for Monopoly®* etc) tableau *m*; *(blackboard)* tableau; **to go by the b.** *(of plan, system)* être abandonné(e); **across the b.** globalement; **b. game** jeu *m* de société *(avec des pions etc)* (**b**) *(of company)* conseil *m*, comité *m*; **b. (of directors)** conseil d'administration; **b. of enquiry** commission *f* d'enquête; **b. of examiners** jury *m* d'examen; *Br* **B. of Trade** ≃ ministère *m* du Commerce; **b. meeting** réunion *f* du conseil (**c**) *(meals)* **half b.** demi-pension *f*; **full b.** pension *f* complète; **b. and lodging** *(in hotel)* pension complète (**d**) **on b.** à bord; **to go on b.** monter à bord; *Fig* **to take sth on b.** *(idea, proposal)* prendre qch en considération; *(problem)* tenir compte de qch
  2 *vt (ship, plane)* embarquer; *(train, bus)* monter dans
  3 *vi* (**a**) *(lodge)* être en pension (**with** chez); *(at school)* aller en pension (**b**) *Aviat* **flight AB123 is now boarding** l'embarquement du vol AB123 a commencé
▸**board up** *vt sep (house, window)* condamner
boarder [ˈbɔːdə(r)] *n (lodger)* pensionnaire *mf*; *(at school)* interne *mf*, pensionnaire *mf*
boarding [ˈbɔːdɪŋ] *n* (**a**) **b. card** *or* **pass** carte *f* d'embarquement (**b**) **b. house** pension *f* de famille; **b. school** pensionnat *m*

Boarding schools

Les "boarding schools", traditionnellement réservées à la progéniture de la haute bourgeoisie, existent en Grande-Bretagne depuis des siècles et furent pendant très longtemps caractérisées par une discipline stricte et un confort rudimentaire. Aujourd'hui encore, les "boarding schools" prônent des valeurs traditionnelles et sont fréquentées par des enfants issus de milieux aisés du fait de leur coût élevé. Ces établissements sont pourtant dû s'adapter à la société moderne : ils sont maintenant très souvent mixtes et acceptent des pensionnaires d'origine sociale un peu plus variée qu'autrefois.

boardroom [ˈbɔːdruːm] *n* salle *f* de réunion *(du conseil d'administration)*
boardwalk [ˈbɔːdwɔːk] *n Am* = passage en bois sur la plage
boast [bəʊst] **1** *n* vantardise *f*
  2 *vt* **the school boasts a fine library** l'école est fière de posséder une belle bibliothèque
  3 *vi* se vanter (**about** de); **it's nothing to b. about!** il n'y a pas de quoi se vanter!
boastful [ˈbəʊstfʊl] *adj* vantard(e), fanfaron(onne)
boasting [ˈbəʊstɪŋ] *n* vantardise *f*, fanfaronnade *f*
boat [bəʊt] *n* bateau *m*; *(small)* canot *m*, embarcation *f*; **to come by b.** venir en bateau, prendre le bateau; *Fig* **we're all in the same b.** nous sommes tous dans le même cas; *Fig* **to push the b. out** *(celebrate lavishly)* faire des frais; **the B. Race** = course annuelle d'aviron sur la Tamise entre les universités de Cambridge et d'Oxford
boat-builder [ˈbəʊtbɪldə(r)] *n* constructeur *m* de bateaux
boater [ˈbəʊtə(r)] *n (hat)* canotier *m*
boathouse [ˈbəʊthaʊs] *n* hangar *m* pour bateaux
boating [ˈbəʊtɪŋ] *n* canotage *m*; **to go b.** faire du canotage
boat-load [ˈbəʊtləʊd] *n* cargaison *f*; *Fig* **by the b.** par bateaux entiers
boatswain [ˈbəʊsən] *n Naut* maître *m* d'équipage

boatyard ['bəʊtjɑːd] *n* chantier *m* de construction pour canots et bateaux de plaisance
Bob [bɒb] *n Br Fam* **and B.'s your uncle!** et voilà le travail!
bob¹ [bɒb] **1** *n* (**a**) *(curtsey)* petite révérence *f* (**b**) *(hairstyle)* (coupe *f* au) carré *m* (**c**) *(bobsleigh)* bobsleigh *m*
2 *vt (pt & pp* bobbed) (**a**) **to b. one's head** hocher la tête (**b**) **to have one's hair bobbed** se faire faire un carré
3 *vi* **to b. up and down** s'agiter; **to b. about** *(on water)* se balancer
bob² *(pl* bob) *n Br Fam Old-fashioned (shilling)* shilling *m*; **that must cost a few b.** à mon avis, ce n'est pas donné; **he's not short of a b. or two** il a de quoi
bobbin ['bɒbɪn] *n* bobine *f*
bobble ['bɒbəl] *n (on hat)* pompon *m*
bobby ['bɒbɪ] *(pl* bobbies) *n Br Fam (policeman)* flic *m*
bobsled ['bɒbsled], **bobsleigh** ['bɒbsleɪ] *n* bobsleigh *m*
bod [bɒd] *n Fam* (**a**) *Br (man)* type *m*; *(woman)* femme *f* (**b**) *(body)* corps *m*; **he's got a nice b.** il est bien foutu
bode [bəʊd] *vi* **to b. well/ill (for)** être de bon/mauvais augure (pour)
bodice ['bɒdɪs] *n* corsage *m*
bodily ['bɒdɪlɪ] **1** *adj* corporel(elle), physique; **b. functions** fonctions *fpl* corporelles; **b. needs** besoins *mpl* physiques
2 *adv (grab)* à bras-le-corps; **he was carried b. to the door** on l'a saisi à bras-le-corps et puis on l'a transporté jusqu'à la porte
body ['bɒdɪ] *(pl* bodies) *n* (**a**) *(of person, animal)* corps *m*; *(dead)* cadavre *m*, corps; **to have enough to keep b. and soul together** avoir juste de quoi vivre; *Fam* **over my dead b.!** plutôt crever!; **b. bag** sac *m* mortuaire; *Fig* **to deliver a b. blow (to)** porter un coup terrible (à); **b. builder** culturiste *mf*; **b. building** culturisme *m*; **b. count** *(of casualties)* comptage *m* des morts; *(of those present)* comptage *m* des présents; **b. language** *(of performer)* gestuelle *f*; **I could tell by his b. language** je le savais d'après la façon dont il se tenait; **b. odour** odeur *f* corporelle; **b. piercing** piercing *m*; **b. stocking** *(without legs)* body *m*; *(with legs)* combinaison *f* collante; **b. warmer** petit gilet *m* chaud (**b**) *(of wine)* corps *m*; *(of hair)* volume *m* (**c**) *(group)* corps *m*; **a large b. of people** une foule nombreuse; **b. of evidence** ensemble *m* de preuves; **b. of water** masse *f* d'eau; **public b.** organisme *m* public; **the b. politic** le corps politique (**d**) *(main part) (of car)* carrosserie *f*; *(of letter)* corps *m*; *(of argument)* essentiel *m*; **b. shop** atelier *m* de carrosserie (**e**) *(garment)* body *m*
bodyguard ['bɒdɪgɑːd] *n (person)* garde *m* du corps; *(group)* gardes *mpl* du corps
bodywork ['bɒdɪwɜːk] *n (of car)* carrosserie *f*
Boer ['bəʊə(r)] *n* Boer *mf*; **the B. War** la guerre des Boers
boffin ['bɒfɪn] *n Br Fam Hum (scientist)* savant *m*
bog [bɒg] *n* (**a**) *(marsh)* marécage *m* (**b**) *Br very Fam (toilet)* chiottes *fpl*; **b. roll** PQ *m*
▸**bog down** *(pt & pp* bogged) *vt sep* **to get bogged down (in)** *(mud)* s'enliser (dans), s'embourber (dans); *(details)* se perdre (dans)
bogey ['bəʊgɪ] *(pl* bogeys) *n* (**a**) *(cause of fear)* hantise *f* (**b**) *Fam (from nose)* crotte *f* de nez
bogeyman ['bəʊgɪmæn] *n* **the b.** le croque-mitaine, le Père fouettard

boggle ['bɒgəl] *vi Fam* **to b. at doing sth** rechigner à faire qch; **the mind boggles!** ça laisse rêveur!
Bogotá [bɒgə'tɑː] *n* Bogotá
bogus ['bəʊgəs] *adj* faux (fausse); *Fam* **he's completely b.** c'est vraiment un faux jeton
Bohemian [bəʊ'hiːmɪən] **1** *n (native of Bohemia)* Bohémien(enne) *m,f*; *(artistic person)* bohème *mf*
2 *adj (person, lifestyle)* bohème; *(from Bohemia)* bohémien(enne)
boil¹ [bɔɪl] *n (on skin)* furoncle *m*
boil² **1** *n* **to come to the b.** arriver à ébullition; **to bring sth to the b.** amener qch à ébullition; *Fig* **to go off the b.** ne plus marcher très fort
2 *vt* faire bouillir; **to b. the kettle** mettre de l'eau à chauffer
3 *vi* bouillir; **the kettle's boiling** la bouilloire siffle; **the saucepan has boiled dry** l'eau de la casserole s'est complètement évaporée; **to b. with rage** bouillir (de colère)
▸**boil down to** *vt insep Fam* **it all boils down to...** ça revient à...
▸**boil over** *vi (of milk, soup)* déborder; *Fig (of situation)* empirer, s'aggraver
▸**boil up** *vt sep (water, milk)* faire bouillir
boiler ['bɔɪlə(r)] *n* chaudière *f*; **b. maker** chaudronnier *m*; **b. room** salle *f* des chaudières, chaufferie *f*; **b. suit** bleu *m* de chauffe
boiling ['bɔɪlɪŋ] **1** *adj* bouillant(e); *Fam* **I'm b.!** je crève de chaleur!; **b. point** point *m* d'ébullition; *Fig* **the situation has reached b. point** la situation est explosive
2 *adv* **it's b. hot** il fait une chaleur à crever
boisterous ['bɔɪstərəs] *adj* bruyant(e)
bold [bəʊld] *adj* (**a**) *(brave)* hardi(e), intrépide (**b**) *(shameless)* **as b. as brass** culotté(e) (**c**) *(striking) (colour)* vif (vive); *(handwriting)* vigoureux(euse); *Typ* **b. type** caractères *mpl* gras
boldly ['bəʊldlɪ] *adv (bravely)* hardiment
boldness ['bəʊldnɪs] *n (bravery)* hardiesse *f*
Bolivia [bə'lɪvɪə] *n* la Bolivie
Bolivian [bə'lɪvɪən] **1** *n* Bolivien(enne) *m,f*
2 *adj* bolivien(enne)
bollard ['bɒlɑːd, 'bɒləd] *n Naut* bollard *m*; *Br (traffic barrier)* borne *f*
bollocking ['bɒləkɪŋ] *n very Fam* **to give sb a b.** engueuler qn
bollocks ['bɒləks] *npl Br Vulg (testicles)* couilles *fpl*; **b.!** *(nonsense)* c'est des conneries!
Bolshevik ['bɒlʃəvɪk] **1** *n* bolchevique *mf*
2 *adj* bolchevique
Bolshevism ['bɒlʃəvɪzəm] *n* bolchevisme *m*
bolshie, bolshy ['bɒlʃɪ] *adj Fam* râleur(euse)
bolster ['bəʊlstə(r)] **1** *n (pillow)* traversin *m*
2 *vt (confidence, pride)* renforcer, consolider
bolt [bəʊlt] **1** *n* (**a**) *(on door)* verrou *m*; *(metal fastening)* boulon *m*; *Fam* **he has shot his b.** il a échoué après avoir tenté sa dernière carte (**b**) *Fam (dash)* **to make a b. for it** se sauver à toutes jambes; **she made a b. for the door** elle s'est précipitée vers la porte; **b. hole** refuge *m* (**c**) **b. of lightning** foudre *f*; *Fig* **it came like a b. from the blue** ça a été comme un coup de tonnerre
2 *adv* **b. upright** droit(e) comme un i
3 *vt* (**a**) *(lock)* verrouiller; *(fasten with bolts)* boulonner (**b**) *(food)* engloutir
4 *vi (of horse)* s'emballer; *(of person)* décamper, déguerpir
▸**bolt down** *vt sep (food)* engloutir

bomb [bɒm] **1** *n* bombe *f*; *Br Fam* **to go like a b.** foncer; *Fam* **to cost a b.** coûter les yeux de la tête; **b. disposal expert** démineur *m*; **b. scare** alerte *f* à la bombe **2** *vt* bombarder **3** *vi Am (fail)* faire un bide
▸**bomb along** *vi Fam (go quickly)* foncer
bombard [bɒmˈbɑːd] *vt* bombarder; *Fig* **to b. sb with questions** bombarder *ou* assaillir qn de questions
bombardment [bɒmˈbɑːdmənt] *n* bombardement *m*
bombast [ˈbɒmbæst] *n* emphase *f*
bombastic [bɒmˈbæstɪk] *adj* ampoulé(e), emphatique
bomber [ˈbɒmə(r)] *n (aircraft)* bombardier *m*; *(person)* poseur(euse) *m,f* de bombe; **b. jacket** blouson *m* d'aviateur
bombing [ˈbɒmɪŋ] *n (aerial)* bombardement *m*; *(by terrorists)* attentat *m* à la bombe
bombshell [ˈbɒmʃel] *n* obus *m*; *Fig* **to drop a b.** faire une révélation fracassante; *Fam Fig* **a blonde b.** une magnifique blonde
bombsite [ˈbɒmsaɪt] *n* zone *f* bombardée; *Fig* **your bedroom is (like) a b.!** quel capharnaüm, ta chambre!
bona fide [ˈbəʊnəˈfaɪdɪ] *adj* véritable
bonanza [bəˈnænzə] *n* aubaine *f*; **a b. year** une année exceptionnelle
bonbon [ˈbɒnbɒn] *n* bonbon *m*
bonce [bɒns] *n Fam (head)* caboche *f*
bond [bɒnd] **1** *n* (**a**) *(attachment)* lien *m*; **to feel a b. with sb** se sentir lié(e) à qn (**b**) *Fin* obligation *f* (**c**) *Law* caution *f*; *Formal* **my word is my b.** je n'ai qu'une parole (**d**) *Com* **in b.** en dépôt **2** *vt* (**a**) *(stick)* coller (**b**) *Fig (unite)* **to b. together** créer des liens entre **3** *vi* (**a**) *(stick)* adhérer (**b**) *Fig (form attachment)* créer des liens affectifs (**with sb** avec qn)
bondage [ˈbɒndɪdʒ] *n* (**a**) *(slavery)* esclavage *m* (**b**) *(sexual)* = pratique sexuelle où l'un des partenaires est attaché
bonding [ˈbɒndɪŋ] *n (emotional attachment)* liens *mpl* affectifs; **male b.** amitié *f* virile; *Fam Hum* **they're doing some male b. in the pub** ils sont allés au pub entre hommes
bone [bəʊn] **1** *n* (**a**) *(of person, animal)* os *m*; *(of fish)* arête *f*; **b. china** porcelaine *f* tendre; **b. meal** engrais *m* *(de cendre d'os)*; **b. marrow** moëlle *f*; *Med* **b. marrow transplant** greffe *f* de moëlle (**b**) *(idioms)* **to work one's fingers to the b.** se tuer au travail; **b. idle** *or* **lazy** paresseux(euse) comme une couleuvre; **I feel it in my bones** je le sens; **b. of contention** sujet *m* de dispute; *Fam* **to have a b. to pick with sb** avoir un compte à régler avec qn; **she made no bones about it** elle ne l'a pas caché; **close to the b.** *(tactless, risqué)* limite **2** *vt (chicken, meat)* désosser; *(fish)* ôter les arêtes de
▸**bone up on** *vt insep Fam* potasser
bone-dry [ˈbəʊnˈdraɪ] *adj* complètement sec (sèche)
bonfire [ˈbɒnfaɪə(r)] *n (for burning rubbish)* feu *m*; *(for celebration)* feu *m* de joie; *Br* **B. Night** = soirée du 5 novembre, célébration de la tentative de Guy Fawkes de faire sauter le Parlement en 1605
bong [bɒŋ] *n (sound)* bong *m*
bonhomie [ˈbɒnɒmiː] *n* bonhomie *f*
bonk¹ [bɒŋk] *n Fam (hit)* frapper
bonk² *Br very Fam* **1** *n* **to have a b.** s'envoyer en l'air **2** *vt* s'envoyer en l'air avec **3** *vi* s'envoyer en l'air
bonkers [ˈbɒŋkəz] *adj Br Fam* dingue

Bonn [bɒn] *n* Bonn
bonnet [ˈbɒnɪt] *n* (**a**) *(hat)* bonnet *m* (**b**) *Br (of car)* capot *m*
bonny [ˈbɒnɪ] *adj Scot* joli(e)
bonsai [ˈbɒnzaɪ] *n* bonsaï *m*
bonus [ˈbəʊnəs] *n* (**a**) *(money)* prime *f*; **b. scheme** système *m* de primes de rendement (**b**) *(advantage)* avantage *m*; **b. number** *(in lottery)* numéro *m* supplémentaire
bony [ˈbəʊnɪ] *adj (person, limb)* maigre, décharné(e); *(fish)* plein(e) d'arêtes
boo [buː] **1** *n (pl* **boos**) huée *f* **2** *vt (pt & pp* **booed**) huer **3** *exclam* hou!; **he wouldn't s. to a goose** c'est un grand timide
boob [buːb] *Br Fam* **1** *n* (**a**) *(mistake)* gaffe *f*; **to make a b.** faire une gaffe (**b**) *(breast)* nichon *m*; **b. tube** *(garment)* bustier *m* **2** *vi (make mistake)* faire une gaffe
booby-prize [ˈbuːbɪpraɪz] *n* prix *m* décerné au dernier *(en guise de plaisanterie)*
booby-trap [ˈbuːbɪtræp] **1** *n (explosive device)* objet *m* piégé; *(practical joke)* piège *m* **2** *vt (pt & pp* **booby-trapped**) piéger *(en guise de farce)*
book [bʊk] **1** *n* (**a**) *(in general)* livre *m*; *(of stamps)* carnet *m*; *(of matches)* pochette *f*; *Fin* **the books** *(of company)* les comptes *mpl*; **b. club** club *m* du livre; **b. end** serre-livres *m inv*; **b. group** cercle *m* de lecture; **b. review** critique *f* littéraire; *Br* **b. token** chèque-cadeau *m* pour les livres (**b**) *(idioms)* **physics is a closed b. to me** je ne comprends absolument rien à la physique; **in my b.** à mon avis; **to be in sb's good books** être dans les petits papiers de qn, être bien vu(e) par qn; **to be in sb's bad books** être mal vu(e) par qn; **to bring sb to b.** forcer qn à rendre des comptes; **by** *or* **according to the b.** selon la procédure; **to throw the b. at sb** infliger la peine maximale à qn **2** *vt* (**a**) *(seat, room, table, ticket)* réserver; *(performer)* engager; **to b. sb on a flight** réserver une place pour qn sur un vol; **fully booked** *(hotel, flight)* complet(ète) (**b**) *(for traffic offence)* dresser une contravention à; *(in football match)* donner un carton jaune à
▸**book in** **1** *vt sep* **to b. sb in** *(to hotel)* réserver une chambre à qn **2** *vi Br (take a room)* prendre une chambre
▸**book up** **1** *vt sep* **the hotel is fully booked up** l'hôtel est complet; **I'm booked up for this evening** je suis pris toute la semaine **2** *vi (make reservation)* réserver
bookable [ˈbʊkəbəl] *adj (seat, flight)* qui peut être réservé(e)
bookbinder [ˈbʊkbaɪndə(r)] *n* relieur(euse) *m,f*
bookbinding [ˈbʊkbaɪndɪŋ] *n* reliure *f*
bookcase [ˈbʊkkeɪs] *n* bibliothèque *f*
bookie [ˈbʊkɪ] *n Fam (bookmaker)* bookmaker *m*
booking [ˈbʊkɪŋ] *n* (**a**) *(reservation)* réservation *f*; **to make a b.** effectuer une réservation; **b. office** bureau *m* de location (**b**) *(in football)* carton *m* jaune
bookish [ˈbʊkɪʃ] *adj (person)* studieux(euse); *Pej (approach, style)* livresque
bookkeeping [ˈbʊkkiːpɪŋ] *n Fin* comptabilité *f*
booklet [ˈbʊklɪt] *n* brochure *f*
bookmaker [ˈbʊkmeɪkə(r)] *n (in betting)* bookmaker *m*

bookmark ['bʊkmɑːk] **1** n (**a**) (for book) marque-page m inv (**b**) Comput (for Web page) signet m **2** vt Comput (Web page) créer un signet sur

bookmarker ['bʊkmɑːkə(r)] = **bookmark 1** (**a**)

bookseller ['bʊksələ(r)] n libraire mf

bookshelf ['bʊkʃelf] (pl **bookshelves** ['bʊkʃelvz]) n étagère f; **bookshelves** (furniture) bibliothèque f

bookshop ['bʊkʃɒp] n librairie f

bookstall ['bʊkstɔːl] n (in railway station, airport) kiosque m à journaux; (selling second-hand books) étalage m de bouquiniste

bookstore ['bʊkstɔː(r)] n Am librairie f

bookworm ['bʊkwɜːm] n Fig passionné(e) m,f de lecture

boom¹ [buːm] n (**a**) Naut (barrier) estacade f; (for sail) bôme f (**b**) Cin & TV perche f

boom² n (economic) boom m; **b. town** ville f en plein essor économique **2** vi (prosper) prospérer, réussir; **business is booming** les affaires sont en plein essor

boom³ 1 n (sound) détonation f **2** vi (of thunder, gun) gronder; (of person) tonitruer

boomerang ['buːməræŋ] n boomerang m

booming ['buːmɪŋ] adj (voice) tonitruant(e)

boon [buːn] n bénédiction f, aubaine f

boor ['bʊə(r)] n rustaud(e) m,f

boorish ['bʊərɪʃ] adj rustre, grossier(ère)

boost [buːst] **1** n to give sth a b. (production, economy) relancer qch; **to give sb's confidence a b.** redonner confiance à qn; **to give sb's morale a b.** remonter le moral à qn **2** vt (production, economy) relancer; Tel (signal) régénérer; **to b. sb's hopes** redonner espoir à qn

booster ['buːstə(r)] n (**a**) **b.** (**rocket**) fusée f de démarrage (**b**) Elec survolteur m (**c**) Med **b.** (**shot**) piqûre f de rappel (**d**) **b. seat** (for child) réhausseur m

boot [buːt] **1** n (**a**) (footwear) (for walking) brodequin m; (for sport) chaussure f; (ankle-length) bottine f; (knee-length) botte f (**b**) Br (of car) coffre m (**c**) (idioms) **the b. is on the other foot** les rôles sont inversés; Fam **to give sb the b.** mettre qn à la porte; Fam **to get the b.** se faire mettre à la porte; Fam **they put** or **stuck the b. into him** (kicked) ils l'ont roué de coups de pied; (criticized) ils lui ont passé un savon; **he's a liar and a thief to b.** c'est un menteur et par-dessus le marché c'est un voleur **2** vt (**a**) Fam (kick) donner un coup de pied dans; **to b. sb out** mettre qn à la porte (**b**) Comput amorcer **3** vi Comput s'amorcer

▸**boot up** Comput **1** vt sep (computer) amorcer **2** vi (computer) s'amorcer; (person) démarrer

bootee [buːˈtiː] n chausson m (de bébé)

booth [buːð] n (at fair) baraque f, stand m; (for telephone) cabine f; (in voting) isoloir m; (in restaurant) alcôve f

bootlace ['buːtleɪs] n lacet m (de botte)

bootleg ['buːtleg] adj (alcohol) de contrebande; (recording) pirate

bootstrap ['buːtstræp] n (**a**) (part of boot) tirant m de botte; Fig **to pull oneself up by one's bootstraps** se faire tout(e) seul(e) (**b**) Comput routine f d'amorçage

booty ['buːtɪ] n (loot) butin m

booze [buːz] Fam **1** n alcool m **2** vi picoler

boozer ['buːzə(r)] n Fam (person) poivrot(e) m,f; Br (pub) pub m

booze-up ['buːzʌp] n Br Fam beuverie f; **to have a b.** prendre une cuite

boozy ['buːzɪ] adj Fam (voice, breath) aviné(e); (party, evening) bien arrosé(e)

bop¹ [bɒp] Fam **1** n (dance) danse f **2** vi (pt & pp **bopped**) (dance) danser

bop² Fam **1** n (blow) léger coup m **2** vt (pt & pp **bopped**) (hit) donner un léger coup à

boracic [bəˈræsɪk] adj Chem borique

border ['bɔːdə(r)] **1** n (**a**) (edge) bord m; (in garden) plate-bande f (**b**) (frontier) frontière f; **the Borders** = région vallonnée du sud-est de l'Écosse; **b. guard** garde-frontière m; **b. town** ville f frontière ou frontalière **2** vt (country) avoir une frontière commune avec; (road) border

▸**border on** vt insep (of country) avoir une frontière commune avec; **to b. on insanity/the ridiculous** friser la folie/le ridicule

borderland ['bɔːdəlænd] n zone f frontalière

borderline ['bɔːdəlaɪn] n frontière f, ligne f de démarcation; **a b. case** un cas limite

bore¹ ['bɔː(r)] **1** n (person) raseur(euse) m,f; (thing) chose f ennuyeuse; **what a b.!** quelle barbe! **2** vt ennuyer

bore² **1** n (calibre) calibre m **2** vt (with drill) forer; **to b. a hole in sth** percer un trou dans qch

bore³ pt of **bear²**

bored [bɔːd] adj (sigh, look) d'ennui; **to be b.** s'ennuyer; Fam **to be b. stiff** or **to tears** s'ennuyer à mourir

boredom ['bɔːdəm] n ennui m

boring ['bɔːrɪŋ] adj ennuyeux(euse)

born [bɔːn] **1** adj **to be a b. writer/leader** être un écrivain/leader né **2** (pp of bear) **to be b.** naître; **I was b. in London/in 1975** je suis né(e) à Londres/en 1975; Fam **I wasn't b. yesterday** je ne suis pas né(e) de la dernière pluie

born-again ['bɔːnəgen] adj **b. Christian** chrétien(-enne) m,f, régénéré(e)

borne [bɔːn] pp of **bear²**

Borneo ['bɔːnɪəʊ] n Bornéo

borough ['bʌrə] n Br circonscription f électorale urbaine

borrow ['bɒrəʊ] **1** vt emprunter (**from sb** à qn); **to be living on borrowed time** (of ill person, government) ne plus en avoir pour longtemps **2** vi emprunter (**from sb** à qn)

borrower ['bɒrəʊə(r)] n emprunteur(euse) m,f

borstal ['bɔːstəl] n Br Formerly maison f de redressement

Bosnia(-Herzegovina) ['bɒznɪə(hɜːtsəgəˈviːnə)] n la Bosnie(-Herzégovine)

Bosnian ['bɒznɪən] **1** n Bosniaque mf **2** adj bosniaque; **B. Croat/Muslim/Serb** Croate mf/Musulman(e) m,f/Serbe mf de Bosnie

bosom ['bʊzəm] **1** n (of woman) poitrine f; Fig **in the b. of one's family** au sein de sa famille **2** adj **b. friend** ami(e) m,f intime

Bosphorus ['bɒsfərəs] n **the B.** le Bosphore

boss¹ [bɒs] n (on shield) ombon m, ombo m

boss² Fam **1** n (at work) patron(onne) m,f; **to be one's own b.** être son propre patron; **to show sb who's b.** montrer à qn qui commande **2** vt **to b. sb about** or **around** donner des ordres à qn

bossy ['bɒsɪ] *adj* autoritaire; *Fam* a **b. boots** un petit chef, un tyran

bosun ['bəʊsən] *n Naut* maître *m* d'équipage

botanic(al) [bə'tænɪk(əl)] *adj* botanique; **b. garden(s)** jardin *m* botanique

botanist ['bɒtənɪst] *n* botaniste *mf*

botany ['bɒtənɪ] *n* botanique *f*

botch [bɒtʃ] *Fam* **1** *n* travail *m* salopé; **to make a b. of** *sth (job)* saloper qch; *(interview, exam)* rater qch complètement
2 *vt* **to b. sth (up)** *(job)* saloper qch; *(interview, exam)* rater complètement

botched [bɒtʃt] *adj Fam* raté(e); **a b. job** un travail de sagouin

both [bəʊθ] **1** *pron* les deux; **b. (of them) are dead** ils sont morts tous les deux; **b. of us saw it** nous l'avons vu tous les deux
2 *adj* les deux; **b. (the) brothers** les deux frères; **b. my parents** mes deux parents; **on b. sides** des deux côtés; **you can't have it b. ways** on ne peut pas tout avoir
3 *adv* **b. in Britain and in France** aussi bien en Grande-Bretagne qu'en France; **she is b. intelligent and beautiful** elle est à la fois intelligente et belle

bother ['bɒðə(r)] **1** *n (trouble)* ennui *m*; **if it's not too much b.** si cela ne vous dérange pas trop; **to go to the b. of doing sth** prendre la peine de faire qch
2 *vt* (**a**) *(annoy)* déranger; **my back's still bothering me** j'ai toujours des problèmes de dos; **I'm sorry to b. you but...** je suis désolé de vous déranger mais... (**b**) *(care)* **to be bothered about sth** s'inquiéter de qch; *Fam* **I can't be bothered** ça ne me dit rien; *Fam* **I'm not bothered** ça m'est égal
3 *vi (care)* s'inquiéter (**about** de); **he didn't even b. to apologize** il n'a même pas pris la peine de s'excuser; **don't b.!** ce n'est pas la peine!
4 *exclam* zut!

bothersome ['bɒðəsəm] *adj* ennuyeux(euse), gênant(e)

Botox® ['bəʊtɒks] *n Pharm* Botox® *m*; **to have B.** se faire faire des injections de Botox®

Botswana [bɒt'swɑːnə] *n* le Botswana

bottle ['bɒtəl] **1** *n* (**a**) *(container)* bouteille *f*; *(for perfume)* flacon *m*; *(for baby)* biberon *m*; *Fam* **to take to** *or* **hit the b.** se mettre à picoler; **b. bank** conteneur *m* pour la récupération du verre usagé; **b. green** vert bouteille *inv*; **b. opener** ouvre-bouteilles *m inv*, décapsuleur *m*; **b. party** = soirée où chacun apporte une bouteille (**b**) *Br Fam (courage)* cran *m*; **to lose one's b.** se dégonfler
2 *vt* mettre en bouteille

▶**bottle out** *vi Br very Fam* se dégonfler; **he bottled out of the fight** il a eu peur de se battre

▶**bottle up** *vt sep (emotions, anger)* refouler, ravaler

bottled ['bɒtəld] *adj* en bouteille; **b. water** eau *f* minérale

bottle-feed ['bɒtəlfiːd] *(pt & pp* **bottle-fed** ['bɒtəlfed]*) vt* nourrir au biberon

bottleneck ['bɒtəlnek] *n (in road)* rétrécissement *m* de la chaussée; *(in traffic)* embouteillage *m* (dû à un rétrécissement de la chaussée); *(in production)* goulot *m* d'étranglement

bottom ['bɒtəm] **1** *n* (**a**) *(lowest part)* (of well, box, sea) fond *m*; *(of street)* bout *m*; *(of stairs, mountain, page)* bas *m*; *(of ship)* carène *f*, fond *m*; **from the b. of one's heart** du fond du cœur; **to be at the b. of the class** être le (la) dernier(ère) de la classe; **to touch b.**

(of boat) toucher le fond (**b**) *(buttocks)* derrière *m* (**c**) *(idioms)* **to be at the b. of sth** être à l'origine de qch; **to get to the b. of sth** aller au fond des choses; **at b.** au fond; **the b. has fallen out of the market** le marché s'est effondré; *Fam* **bottoms up!** cul sec!
2 *adj* du bas; **b. deck** *(on bus)* niveau *m* inférieur; **b. floor** rez-de-chaussée *m inv*; *Fam* **you can bet your b. dollar that...** vous pouvez être sûr que...; **in b. gear** en première; **the b. line** *(financially)* le solde final; *Fig* **the b. line is that he is unsuited to the job** le fait est qu'il n'est pas fait pour ce travail

▶**bottom out** *vi (of recession, slump)* atteindre son maximum; *(of price)* atteindre son minimum

bottomless ['bɒtəmlɪs] *adj (abyss)* sans fond; *(reserve)* inépuisable; *Fig* **a b. pit** un gouffre

bottommost ['bɒtəmməʊst] *adj* le (la) plus bas (basse)

botulism ['bɒtjʊlɪzəm] *n* botulisme *m*

boudoir ['buːdwɑː(r)] *n* boudoir *m*

bouffant ['buːfɒn] *adj (hair)* bouffant(e)

bough [baʊ] *n* branche *f*

bought [bɔːt] *pt & pp of* **buy**

boulder ['bəʊldə(r)] *n* gros bloc *m* de roche

boulevard ['buːləvɑːd] *n* boulevard *m*

bounce [baʊns] **1** *n* (**a**) *(of ball)* rebond *m* (**b**) *Fig (energy)* entrain *m*
2 *vt* (**a**) *(ball)* faire rebondir; *Fig* **to b. an idea off sb** soumettre une idée à qn *(de manière informelle)* (**b**) *Fam (cheque)* refuser d'honorer
3 *vi* (**a**) *(of ball)* rebondir (**off** contre); **to b. into/out of a room** *(of person)* entrer/sortir d'une pièce en sautillant (**b**) *Fam* **the cheque bounced** le chèque a été refusé *(parce qu'il était sans provision)*

▶**bounce back** *vi (after illness, disappointment)* se remettre rapidement

bouncer ['baʊnsə(r)] *n Fam (doorman)* videur *m*

bouncing ['baʊnsɪŋ] *adj* **a b. baby** un bébé en pleine santé

bouncy ['baʊnsɪ] *adj* (**a**) *(ball)* qui rebondit bien; *(mattress)* élastique; *Br* **b. castle** château *m* gonflable (**b**) *Fig (person)* plein(e) d'entrain

bound¹ [baʊnd] **1** *n (leap)* bond *m*; **at one b.** d'un bond
2 *vi (leap)* bondir

bound² [baʊnd] *adj* (**a**) *(destined)* **b. for** en route pour (**b**) *(in predictions)* **he's b. to come** il ne peut pas manquer de venir; **it was b. to happen** ça devait arriver

bound³ [baʊnd] *pt & pp of* **bind**

boundary ['baʊndərɪ] *(pl* **boundaries**) *n* limite *f*

bounder ['baʊndə(r)] *n Fam Old-fashioned* goujat *m*

boundless ['baʊndlɪs] *adj* illimité(e), sans bornes

bounds [baʊndz] *npl (limit)* limites *fpl*; **out of b.** interdit(e); **it is not beyond the b. of possibility** c'est dans le domaine du possible; **to know no b.** *(of ambition)* être sans bornes

bountiful ['baʊntɪfʊl] *adj* abondant(e)

bounty ['baʊntɪ] *(pl* **bounties**) *n* (**a**) *(reward)* récompense *f*; **b. hunter** chasseur *m* de primes (**b**) *(generosity)* générosité *f*

bouquet [buː'keɪ] *n (of flowers, wine)* bouquet *m*

bourbon ['bɜːbən] *n (whisky)* bourbon *m*

bourgeois ['bʊəʒwɑː] *adj* bourgeois(e)

bourgeoisie [bʊəʒwɑː'ziː] *n* bourgeoisie *f*

bout [baʊt] *n (of illness)* accès *m*; *(of work, activity)* période *f* (**b**) *(boxing match)* combat *m*

boutique [buː'tiːk] *n* boutique *f*

bovine ['bəʊvaɪn] *adj* bovin(e)

bow¹ [bəʊ] *n* (**a**) *(weapon)* arc *m*; *(for violin)* archet *m* (**b**) *(in hair, on dress)* nœud *m*; **b. tie** nœud *m* papillon

bow² [baʊ] *n (of ship)* proue *f*, avant *m*

bow³ 1 *n* salut *m*; **to take a b.** saluer
2 *vt* **to b. one's head** baisser la tête
3 *vi* (**a**) *(as greeting, sign of respect)* saluer; *Fig* **to b. down before sb** s'incliner devant qn (**b**) *Fig (yield)* **to b. to sb/sth** s'incliner devant qn/qch
▸**bow out** *vi (resign)* tirer sa révérence

bowdlerize ['baʊdləraɪz] *vt* expurger

bowed [baʊd] *adj (back)* voûté(e); *(head)* baissé(e); **b. with age** courbé(e) par le fardeau des ans

bowel ['baʊəl] *n* intestin *m*; *Lit* **the bowels of the earth** les entrailles *fpl* de la terre; **b. complaint** affection *f* intestinale; **b. movement** selles *fpl*; **to have a b. movement** aller à la selle

bower ['baʊə(r)] *n* tonnelle *f*

bowl¹ [bəʊl] *n* (**a**) *(small dish)* bol *m*; *(for salad)* saladier *m*; *(for soup)* assiette *f* creuse (**b**) *(of toilet)* cuvette *f*

bowl² 1 *n* bowls *(game)* boules *fpl*
2 *vi (in cricket)* lancer la balle; *(in tenpin bowling)* jouer au bowling
▸**bowl along** *vi (of car, bicycle)* rouler à toute vitesse
▸**bowl over** *vt sep (knock down)* renverser; *Fig (astound)* **to be bowled over by sth** être stupéfié(e) par qch

bow-legged [bəʊ'legɪd] *adj* aux jambes arquées

bowler ['bəʊlə(r)] *n* (**a**) **b. (hat)** chapeau *m* melon (**b**) *(in cricket)* lanceur *m*; *(in tenpin bowling)* joueur(euse) *m,f* de bowling

bowling ['bəʊlɪŋ] *n (game)* jeu *m* de boules; **b. alley** piste *f* de bowling; *(building)* bowling *m*; **b. green** terrain *m* de boules *(gazonné)*

box [bɒks] **1** *n* (**a**) *(container)* boîte *f*; *(larger)* caisse *f*; *(postal)* boîte *f* postale; **b. camera** appareil *m* photo compact (**b**) *(on form)* case *f*; *(containing text)* encadré *m*; **(penalty) b.** *(in football)* surface *f* de réparation (**c**) *Br Fam* **the b.** *(television)* la télé (**d**) *(in theatre)* loge *f*
2 *vt* (**a**) *(place in box)* mettre en boîte/en caisse (**b**) **to b. sb's ears** gifler qn
3 *vi (fight)* boxer

boxer ['bɒksə(r)] *n* (**a**) *(fighter)* boxeur *m*; **b. shorts, boxers** *(underwear)* caleçon *m* (**b**) *(dog)* boxer *m*

boxing ['bɒksɪŋ] *n* boxe *f*; **b. glove/match** gant *m*/ match *m* de boxe; **b. ring** ring *m*

Boxing Day ['bɒksɪŋ'deɪ] *n Br* le lendemain de Noël

box-office ['bɒksɒfɪs] *n* bureau *m* de location; **a b. success** un succès au box-office

boxroom ['bɒksruːm] *n* petite chambre *f*

boy [bɔɪ] *n* garçon *m*; **a night out with the boys** une soirée avec les copains; *Fam* **oh b.!** ça alors!; *Fam* **boys will be boys** il faut bien que jeunesse se passe; **b. band** boys band *m*; *Br Fam* **b. racer** = jeune conducteur *m* imprudent; **B. Scout** scout *m*

boycott ['bɔɪkɒt] **1** *n* boycott *m*
2 *vt* boycotter

boyfriend ['bɔɪfrend] *n* petit ami *m*

boyhood ['bɔɪhʊd] *n* enfance *f*

boyish ['bɔɪɪʃ] *adj (looks)* de garçon; *(behaviour)* (of man) de garçon; *(of woman)* de garçon manqué

BR [biː'ɑː(r)] *n Formerly (abbr* **British Rail***)* ≃ la SNCF

bra [brɑː] *n* soutien-gorge *m*

brace [breɪs] **1** *n* (**a**) *(on teeth)* appareil *m* dentaire *ou* orthodontique (**b**) *Br* **braces** *(for trousers)* bretelles *fpl* (**c**) *(of birds, pistols)* paire *f* (**d**) **b. and bit** *(tool)* vilebrequin *m (avec mèche)*
2 *vt* (**a**) **to b. oneself** *(for impact)* s'accrocher; *Fig* **to b. oneself (for sth)** se préparer (à qch); **the b. position** *(on plane)* la position de sécurité (**b**) *(reinforce)* consolider

bracelet ['breɪslɪt] *n* bracelet *m*

bracing ['breɪsɪŋ] *adj (wind, weather)* vivifiant(e)

bracken ['brækən] *n* fougère *f*

bracket ['brækɪt] **1** *n* (**a**) *(for shelves)* équerre *f* (**b**) *(in writing)* parenthèse *f*; **in brackets** entre parenthèses (**c**) *(category) (of tax)* tranche *f*; *(of salaries)* fourchette *f*; **the fifteen to twenty age b.** les quinze à vingt ans
2 *vt* (**a**) *(word, phrase)* mettre entre parenthèses (**b**) *(classify)* associer; **to b. together** mettre dans la même catégorie

brackish ['brækɪʃ] *adj* saumâtre

brag [bræg] *(pt & pp* **bragged***) vi* se vanter (**about** de)

braggart ['brægət] *n* vantard(e) *m,f*

braid [breɪd] **1** *n (of hair)* tresse *f*, natte *f*; *(of cloth)* galon *m*
2 *vt (hair, thread)* tresser

Braille [breɪl] *n* braille *m*

brain [breɪn] **1** *n* cerveau *m*; **brains** *(as food)* cervelle *f*; *Fam* **to have brains** être intelligent(e); *Fam* **she's the brains of the business** c'est elle le cerveau de l'entreprise; *Fam* **to have money/sex on the b.** être obsédé(e) par l'argent/le sexe; **b. damage** lésions *fpl* cérébrales; **b. dead** dans un coma dépassé; **the b. drain** la fuite des cerveaux; **b. surgeon** neurochirurgien(enne) *m,f*; **b. tumour** tumeur *f* au cerveau; *Fam* **b. wave** *(brilliant idea)* idée *f* de génie
2 *vt Fam (hit)* assommer

brainbox ['breɪnbɒks] *n Fam* cerveau *m*

brainchild ['breɪntʃaɪld] *n (idea, project)* idée *f*, trouvaille *f*; **the scheme is his b.** le projet est son bébé

brainless ['breɪnlɪs] *adj* stupide

brainpower ['breɪnpaʊə(r)] *n* intelligence *f*

brainstorm ['breɪnstɔːm] *Fam* **1** *n* (**a**) *Br (mental confusion)* moment *m* d'égarement (**b**) *Am (brilliant idea)* idée *f* de génie
2 *vi* faire du brainstorming

brainstorming ['breɪnstɔːmɪŋ] *n* brainstorming *m*, remue-méninges *m*; **a b. session** un brainstorming

brainwash ['breɪnwɒʃ] *vt* faire un lavage de cerveau à; **to b. sb into doing sth** faire faire qch à qn à force d'endoctrinement

brainwashing ['breɪnwɒʃɪŋ] *n* lavage *m* de cerveau à

brainy ['breɪnɪ] *adj Fam* intelligent(e)

braise [breɪz] *vt* braiser

brake [breɪk] **1** *n* frein *m*; **to apply the brake(s)** freiner; *Fig* **to put the brakes on a project** ralentir l'exécution d'un projet; **b. fluid** liquide *m* de freins; **b. lights** feux *mpl* de stop; **b. pedal** pédale *f* de frein
2 *vi* freiner

braking distance ['breɪkɪŋ'dɪstəns] *n* distance *f* de freinage

bramble ['bræmbəl] *n* ronce *f*

bran [bræn] *n* son *m*

branch [brɑːntʃ] **1** *n* (**a**) *(of tree, family, subject)* branche *f*; *(of river)* bras *m*; *(of railway, road)* embranchement *m*; **b. line** *(of railway)* ligne *f* secondaire (**b**) *(of shop)* succursale *f*; *(of bank)* agence *f*
2 *vi* bifurquer
▸**branch off** *vi (of discussion)* bifurquer (**into** vers)
▸**branch out** *vi* se diversifier; **to b. out into** étendre ses activités à

brand [brænd] **1** n (**a**) (of product) marque f; Fig she has her own b. of humour elle a un sens de l'humour particulier; **b. image** image f de marque; **b. leader** marque la plus vendue; **b. name** marque f (**b**) (on cattle) marque f (au fer rouge) **2** vt (cattle) marquer au fer rouge; Fig the image was branded on her memory l'image était gravée dans sa mémoire; Fig **to b. sb (as) a liar/coward** coller à qn l'étiquette de menteur(euse)/lâche
branded ['brændɪd] adj (product) logotisé(e), de marque
brandish ['brændɪʃ] vt brandir
brand-new ['bræn(d)'njuː] adj flambant neuf (neuve)
brandy ['brændɪ] (pl brandies) n (cognac) cognac m; (more generally) eau-de-vie f; **cherry b.** cherry m
brash [bræʃ] adj (person, behaviour) effronté(e); (colour, décor) tape-à-l'œil inv
brass [brɑːs] n (**a**) (metal) laiton m; Br Fam **it's not worth a b. farthing** ça ne vaut pas un clou; **to get down to b. tacks** en venir aux faits; Br Fam **it's b. monkeys** or **b. monkey weather** il fait un froid de canard (**b**) Mus (brass instruments) cuivres mpl; **b. band** fanfare f (**c**) Br Fam (money) oseille f, pognon m (**d**) Br Fam (cheek, nerve) culot m; **to have a b. neck** avoir du culot, être culotté(e)
▶**brass off** vt sep Br Fam **to be brassed off (with)** en avoir marre (de)
brassière ['bræzɪə(r)] n soutien-gorge m
brassy ['brɑːsɪ] adj Fam (person, manner) exubérant(e)
brat [bræt] n Pej morveux(euse) m,f
bravado [brə'vɑːdəʊ] n bravade f
brave [breɪv] **1** n (nativeAmerican) brave m **2** adj courageux(euse); **a b. effort** un bel effort; **a b. new world** un paradis; Pej & Ironic un monde utopique; **to put a b. face on it** faire bonne contenance **3** vt braver
bravely ['breɪvlɪ] adv courageusement
bravery ['breɪvərɪ] n courage m
bravo [brɑː'vəʊ] exclam bravo!
brawl [brɔːl] **1** n bagarre f; **a drunken b.** une querelle d'ivrognes **2** vi se bagarrer
brawn [brɔːn] n Fam (strength) muscle m; **he's all b. and no brain** il a du muscle mais rien dans la tête
brawny ['brɔːnɪ] adj musclé(e)
bray [breɪ] **1** n (of donkey) braiment m; Fig (of person) braillement m **2** vi (of donkey) braire; Fig (of person) brailler
brazen ['breɪzən] adj effronté(e), impudent(e); (lie) éhonté(e)
▶**brazen out** vt sep **to b. it out** s'en tirer au culot
brazier ['breɪzɪə(r)] n brasero m
Brazil [brə'zɪl] n le Brésil
brazil [brə'zɪl] n **b. (nut)** noix f du Brésil
Brazilian [brə'zɪlɪən] **1** n (**a**) (person) Brésilien(enne) m,f (**b**) (bikini wax) épilation f maillot brésilienne **2** adj brésilien(enne); **B. wax** épilation f maillot brésilienne
breach [briːtʃ] **1** n (**a**) (in wall) brèche f; Fig **to step into the b.** (in emergency) intervenir au pied levé (**b**) (of agreement, contract) rupture f (**of** de); (of trust) abus m (**of** de); (of discipline) manquement m (**of** à); (of rules) infraction f (**of** à); Law **b. of the peace** atteinte f à l'ordre public (**c**) (in relationship) **it caused a b. in their relationship** cela les a conduits à se brouiller

2 vt (**a**) (defences) ouvrir une brèche dans (**b**) (agreement, contract) rompre; (rules) enfreindre
bread [bred] n (**a**) (food) pain m; **a loaf of b.** un pain; **b. and butter** du pain beurré; Fig gagne-pain m; Fig **he knows which side his b. is buttered on** il sait où est son intérêt; **b. bin** boîte f à pain; **b. knife** couteau m à pain (**b**) very Fam (money) blé m, pognon m
bread-and-butter [bredən'bʌtə(r)] adj Fam **b. issues** questions fpl essentielles; Culin **b. pudding** pudding m au pain
breadbasket ['bredbɑːskɪt] n corbeille f à pain
breadboard ['bredbɔːd] n planche f à pain
breadcrumb ['bredkrʌm] n miette f de pain; **breadcrumbs** (in recipe) chapelure f; **fried in breadcrumbs** pané(e)
breadline ['bredlaɪn] n **on the b.** indigent(e), sans ressources
breadth [bredθ] n (**a**) (width) largeur f (**b**) (of mind, opinions) largeur f; (of outlook, understanding) ampleur f
breadwinner ['bredwɪnə(r)] n **to be the b.** faire bouillir la marmite
break [breɪk] **1** n (**a**) (in bone) fracture f; (in wall, fence) brèche f; (in clouds) trouée f; (in electric circuit) rupture f; **at b. of day** au point du jour; Elec **b. switch** disjoncteur m (**b**) (interval, rest) pause f; (holidays) vacances fpl; (commercial) **b.** (on TV, radio) page f de publicité; **without a b.** sans interruption; **a b. in the weather** un changement de temps; Fam **give me a b.!** fichemoi la paix deux minutes! (**c**) Fam (escape) évasion f; **to make a b. for it** se faire la belle; **to make a b. for the exit** se précipiter vers la sortie (**d**) Fam (chance) chance f; **to have a lucky b.** avoir de la veine; **this could be your big b.** ça pourrait être la chance de ta vie
2 vt (pt **broke** [brəʊk], pp **broken** ['brəʊkən]) (**a**) (in general) casser; **to b. one's arm** se casser le bras; **to b. sth into pieces** mettre qch en morceaux; **to b. the sound barrier** franchir le mur du son; Fig **to b. the ice** briser la glace; **to b. one's journey** s'arrêter en route; Fig **b. a leg!** (good luck!) bonne chance! (**b**) (cushion) (fall, force) amortir (**c**) (destroy) (person, resistance, strike) briser; (health) ruiner; **to b. sb's heart** briser le cœur à qn; **to b. sb's serve** (in tennis) prendre le service de qn (**d**) (infringe) (agreement, promise) rompre; (rule, speed limit) enfreindre (**e**) (news, story) annoncer (**to** à) **3** vi (**a**) (of glass, machine, bone) se casser; (of weather) changer; (of sea) se lever; (of waves) se briser; (of voice) (with emotion) se briser; (at puberty) muer; **to b. in two** se casser en deux; **to b. loose** se détacher (**b**) (of news, story) éclater
▶**break away** vi (move away) se détacher; (escape) s'évader
▶**break away from** vt (**a**) (escape) (person) échapper à; (place) s'évader de (**b**) (cut ties with) (party, country) quitter; (family) couper les ponts avec
▶**break down 1** vt sep (**a**) (destroy) (resistance) briser (**b**) (analyse) décomposer (**into** en) **2** vi (**a**) (of car, machine) tomber en panne; (of talks) échouer; (of argument) s'effondrer; (of person under pressure) craquer; **to b. down (in tears)** fondre en

larmes (**b**) *(change chemically)* se décomposer (**into en**)

▸**break even** *vi* rentrer dans ses frais

▸**break in 1** *vt sep (horse)* dresser; *(new shoes)* faire; *(new recruit)* former; **to b. oneself in to sth** se faire à qch
2 *vi (of burglar)* entrer par effraction

▸**break into** *vt insep* (**a**) *(of burglar)* entrer par effraction dans (**b**) *(begin suddenly)* **to b. into laughter** éclater de rire; **to b. into song/a run** se mettre à chanter/courir (**c**) *(showbusiness)* percer dans; *(market)* percer sur

▸**break off 1** *vt sep* (**a**) *(detach)* casser (**b**) *(terminate) (relations, engagement)* rompre
2 *vi* (**a**) *(become detached)* se casser (**b**) *(stop talking, working)* s'interrompre

▸**break open 1** *vt sep (door)* enfoncer; *(lock, safe)* forcer
2 *vi* s'ouvrir

▸**break out** *vi* (**a**) *(escape)* s'évader (**of** de) (**b**) *(of argument)* éclater; *(of disease)* se déclarer; **to b. out in a sweat** se mettre à transpirer; **to b. out in a rash** avoir une éruption de boutons

▸**break through 1** *vt insep (wall)* faire une brèche dans; *(barrier)* forcer; *Fig (someone's reserve, shyness)* vaincre
2 *vi (of sun)* percer les nuages

▸**break up 1** *vt sep* (**a**) *(reduce to pieces)* couper en morceaux (**b**) *(estate, company)* morceler; *(machine)* démonter (**c**) *(fight, quarrel)* faire cesser
2 *vi* (**a**) *(disintegrate)* se disloquer (**b**) *(end) (of talks)* cesser; *(of meeting, school term)* se terminer; *(of school)* fermer; *(of pupils)* être en vacances; **to b. up with sb** *(end relationship)* rompre avec qn

▸**break with** *vt insep* rompre avec

breakable ['breɪkəbəl] **1** *n* breakables objets *mpl* fragiles
2 *adj* fragile

breakage ['breɪkɪdʒ] *n* **were there any breakages?** est-ce qu'il y a eu de la casse?; **all breakages must be paid for** *(sign)* tout article cassé doit être payé

breakaway ['breɪkəweɪ] *adj* dissident(e)

breakdown ['breɪkdaʊn] *n* (**a**) *(of car, machine, computer)* panne *f*; *(of talks, in communication)* rupture *f*; **to have a b.** *(of motorist)* tomber en panne; **b. truck** dépanneuse *f*, camion *m* de dépannage (**b**) *Psy* (**nervous**) **b.** dépression *f* nerveuse; **to have a b.** faire une dépression nerveuse (**c**) *(analysis)* détail *m*

breaker ['breɪkə(r)] *n (wave)* déferlante *f*

break-even point [breɪk'iːvənpɔɪnt] *n Fin* seuil *m* de rentabilité

breakfast ['brekfəst] **1** *n* petit déjeuner *m*; **to have b.** prendre son petit déjeuner, déjeuner; **b. cereal** céréales *fpl*; **b. television** émissions *fpl* (télévisées) du matin
2 *vi* prendre son petit déjeuner, déjeuner; **to b. on sth** manger qch au petit déjeuner

break-in ['breɪkɪn] *n* cambriolage *m*

breaking ['breɪkɪŋ] *n* (**a**) *Law* **b. and entering** entrée *f* par effraction (**b**) **b. point** *(of patience)* limite *f*; **to reach b. point** *(of person)* être à bout; *(of marriage)* être au bord de la rupture

breakneck ['breɪknek] *adj* **at b. speed** à toute allure

break-out ['breɪkaʊt] *n (from prison)* évasion *f*

breakthrough ['breɪkθruː] *n (discovery)* découverte *f* majeure; **there has been a b. in talks** un pas décisif a

été franchi dans les négociations; **to make a b.** *(discovery)* faire une découverte majeure; *(in talks)* faire un pas décisif

breakwater ['breɪkwɔːtə(r)] *n* brise-lames *m inv*

bream [briːm] *(pl* **bream***)* *n* brème *f*

breast [brest] *n (of woman) & Lit (of man)* sein *m*; *(of chicken)* blanc *m*; **to make a clean b. of it** tout avouer; **b. cancer** cancer *m* du sein; **b. implants** implants *mpl* mammaires; **b. milk** lait *m* maternel; **b. pocket** poche *f* de poitrine

breastbone ['brestbəʊn] *n* sternum *m*

breast-feed ['brestfiːd] *(pt & pp* **breast-fed** ['brestfed]*) vt & vi* allaiter

breastplate ['brestpleɪt] *n* plastron *m (de cuirasse)*

breaststroke ['brest(s)trəʊk] *n* brasse *f*

breath [breθ] *n* souffle *m*; **to take a deep b.** inspirer profondément; **to pause for b.** s'arrêter pour reprendre sa respiration; **bad b.** mauvaise haleine *f*; **they are not to be mentioned in the same b.** on ne saurait les comparer; **in the next b.** aussitôt après; *also Fig* **to hold one's b.** retenir son souffle; *Fam* **don't hold your b.!** ce n'est pas demain la veille!; **to waste one's b.** gaspiller sa salive; **out of b.** à bout de souffle, hors d'haleine; **to get short of b.** s'essouffler; **to get one's b. back** reprendre haleine, reprendre son souffle; **under one's b.** à voix basse; *Fig* **to take sb's b. away** couper le souffle à qn; **a b. of wind/of air** un souffle de vent/d'air; **to go out for a b. of fresh air** sortir prendre l'air; *Fig* **she's a real b. of fresh air** elle apporte une bouffée d'air frais; **b. test** Alcotest® *m*

breathalyse, breathalyze ['breθəlaɪz] *vt* faire passer l'Alcotest® à

Breathalyser, Breathalyzer ['breθəlaɪzə(r)] *n* Alcotest® *m*

breathe [briːð] **1** *vt* (**a**) *(inhale)* respirer (**b**) *(idioms)* **to b. a sigh of relief** pousser un soupir de soulagement; *Lit* **to b. one's last** rendre son dernier soupir; **don't b. a word (of it)!** pas un mot!; **to b. fire** *(in anger)* jeter feu et flammes; **to b. new life into sth** *(project, scheme)* insuffler une force nouvelle à qch
2 *vi* respirer; *(exhale)* souffler; **to b. heavily** *(noisily)* respirer bruyamment; *(with difficulty)* respirer avec difficulté; *Fig* **to b. easily again** respirer; *Fig* **to b. down sb's neck** *(follow)* talonner qn; *(nag)* être tout le temps sur le dos de qn

▸**breathe in 1** *vt* inhaler
2 *vi* inspirer

▸**breathe out** *vi* expirer

breather ['briːðə(r)] *n Fam (rest)* pause *f*; **to take a b.** faire une pause

breathing ['briːðɪŋ] *n* respiration *f*; **b. apparatus** bouteille *f* d'oxygène et masque; *Fig* **to give sb some b. space** laisser respirer qn

breathless ['breθlɪs] *adj (person)* hors d'haleine, essoufflé(e); *(calm)* plat(e); *(silence)* profond(e)

breathtaking ['breθteɪkɪŋ] *adj (beauty, scenery)* à couper le souffle; *(speed)* vertigineux(euse); *(audacity)* sidérant(e)

breathy ['breθɪ] *adj (voice)* haletant(e)

bred [bred] *pt & pp of* **breed**

breech [briːtʃ] *n* (**a**) *Med* **b. delivery** *or* **birth** (accouchement *m* par le) siège *m* (**b**) *(of gun)* culasse *f*

breeches ['brɪtʃɪz] *npl* **(pair of) b.** culotte *f*

breed [briːd] **1** *n also Fig* race *f*
2 *vt (pt & pp* **bred** [bred]*) (animals)* élever; *Fig (discontent)* engendrer
3 *vi* se reproduire

breeder ['briːdə(r)] n (of animals) éleveur(euse) m,f; Phys b. reactor surgénérateur m
breeding ['briːdɪŋ] n (**a**) (of animals) élevage m; b. ground lieu m de reproduction; Fig (of discontent, revolution) foyer m (**b**) (of person) (good) b. éducation f, manières fpl
breeze [briːz] **1** n brise f; Fam it was a b. c'était du gâteau
2 vi to b. in/out (quickly) entrer/sortir en coup de vent; (casually) entrer/sortir avec désinvolture
breeze-block ['briːzblɒk] n Br parpaing m
breezy ['briːzɪ] adj (**a**) (weather) venteux(euse) (**b**) (casual) désinvolte
brethren ['breðrɪn] npl Rel frères mpl
Breton ['bretɒn] **1** n Breton(onne) m,f
2 adj breton(onne)
breviary ['briːvɪərɪ] (pl breviaries) n Rel bréviaire m
brevity ['brevɪtɪ] n brièveté f
brew [bruː] **1** n (beer) bière f; (tea) thé m; Fig (mixture) mélange m
2 vt (beer) brasser; (tea) faire infuser, préparer
3 vi (of beer) fermenter; (of tea) infuser; there's a storm brewing il y a de l'orage dans l'air; Fig there's something brewing il se trame quelque chose; there's trouble brewing il va y avoir du grabuge
▸**brew up** vi Br Fam faire du thé
brewer ['bruːə(r)] n brasseur m
brewery ['bruːərɪ] (pl breweries) n brasserie f (fabrique)
briar ['braɪə(r)] n (plant) bruyère f; (pipe) pipe f de bruyère; b. rose églantine f
bribe [braɪb] **1** n pot-de-vin m
2 vt acheter; to b. sb into doing sth acheter qn pour qu'il fasse qch
bribery ['braɪbərɪ] n corruption f
bric-à-brac ['brɪkəbræk] n bric-à-brac m
brick [brɪk] n (for building) brique f; Fig to drop a b. faire une gaffe; b. wall mur m en briques; you're banging your head against a b. wall tu perds ton temps
▸**brick up** vt sep murer
brickie ['brɪkɪ] n Br Fam maçon m
bricklayer ['brɪkleɪə(r)] n maçon m
brickwork ['brɪkwɜːk] n briquetage m
bridal ['braɪdəl] adj nuptial(e); b. dress or gown robe f de mariée; b. suite suite f nuptiale
bride [braɪd] n mariée f; the b. and groom les mariés mpl
bridegroom ['braɪdgruːm] n marié m
bridesmaid ['braɪdzmeɪd] n demoiselle f d'honneur
bridge¹ [brɪdʒ] **1** n (over river) pont m; (on ship) passerelle f; (on teeth) bridge m; (of nose) arête f; Fig we'll cross that b. when we come to it chaque chose en son temps; Fig b. building réconciliation f
2 vt (river) construire un pont sur; to b. a gap (in knowledge) combler une lacune; to b. the gap between rich and poor combler le fossé entre les riches et les pauvres
bridge² n (card game) bridge m
bridgehead ['brɪdʒhed] n Mil tête f de pont
bridging loan ['brɪdʒɪŋləʊn] n Fin prêt-relais m
bridle ['braɪdəl] **1** n bride f; b. path piste f cavalière
2 vt (horse) brider
3 vi (with anger) s'indigner (at de)
brief [briːf] **1** n Law dossier m; (instructions) consignes fpl

2 adj bref (brève); (garment) court(e); in b.,..., to be b.,... en bref,...
3 vt (inform) mettre au courant (on de)
briefcase ['briːfkeɪs] n serviette f
briefing ['briːfɪŋ] n (meeting) briefing m; (information) instructions fpl
briefly ['briːflɪ] adv brièvement; (hesitate, smile) pendant un court instant; (put) b.,... en bref,...
briefs [briːfs] npl (underwear) slip m
brier = briar
brigade [brɪ'geɪd] n brigade f
brigadier [brɪgə'dɪə(r)] n général m de brigade
brigand ['brɪgənd] n Lit brigand m
bright [braɪt] **1** adj (**a**) (sun, light) brillant(e); (day) clair(e); (colour) vif (vive); to go b. red (blush) devenir rouge comme une tomate (**b**) (hopeful) the future looks b. l'avenir s'annonce bien; the situation is looking a bit brighter la situation commence à s'améliorer; Fig the only b. spot is... la seule chose positive est...; to look on the b. side (of things) prendre les choses du bon côté (**c**) (cheerful) vif (vive) (**d**) (clever) (person) intelligent(e); (idea) lumineux(euse); to be b. at sth être doué(e) en qch
2 adv b. and early de bon matin
brighten ['braɪtən] **1** vt (room, mood) égayer
2 vi (of weather, sky) s'éclaircir; (of face, eyes) s'éclairer; (of prospects) s'améliorer
▸**brighten up** vt sep (room) égayer
2 vi (of person) devenir plus gai(e); (of weather, sky) s'éclaircir; (of face) s'éclairer; (of prospects) s'améliorer
bright-eyed ['braɪtaɪd] adj aux yeux brillants; Fig (eager) enthousiaste; Fam b. and bushy-tailed frais (fraîche) et dispos(e)
brightly ['braɪtlɪ] adv (say) gaiement; (lit, coloured) vivement; the sun was shining b. il faisait un soleil radieux; to smile b. faire un sourire radieux
brightness ['braɪtnɪs] n (of light, sun, colour) éclat m; (of lighting) intensité f; (on TV) luminosité f
brilliance ['brɪljəns] n (**a**) (of light, colour) éclat m (**b**) (of person) intelligence f; (of idea) ingéniosité f
brilliant ['brɪljənt] adj (**a**) (light) éclatant(e); (sun, smile) radieux(euse) (**b**) (scientist, career, pupil) brillant(e) (**c**) (excellent) formidable
brilliantly ['brɪljəntlɪ] adv (**a**) (coloured, lit) vivement (**b**) (acted, played) brillamment
brim [brɪm] **1** n (of cup, glass, hat) bord m; to be full to the b. (with) être plein(e) à ras bord (de)
2 vi (pt & pp brimmed) to be brimming with sth (liquid) être rempli(e) à ras bord de qch; (enthusiasm, ideas) déborder de qch; eyes brimming with tears yeux noyés de larmes
▸**brim over** vi also Fig déborder (with de)
brimful ['brɪmfʊl] adj plein(e) à ras bord; Fig b. of health/life débordant(e) de santé/vie
brimstone ['brɪmstəʊn] n Fig to preach fire and b. menacer les fidèles des feux de l'enfer
brine [braɪn] n saumure f
bring [brɪŋ] (pt & pp brought [brɔːt]) vt (**a**) (cause to come) (object, letter, news) apporter; (person, animal) amener; to b. sth to sb's attention signaler qch à l'attention de qn; what brings you to London? qu'est-ce qui vous amène à Londres?; to b. sth out of sth (box, bag) sortir qch de qch; to b. a child into the world mettre un enfant au monde; Law to b. an action against sb intenter un procès à qn (**b**) (cause) provoquer; it has brought me great happiness cela m'a procuré un grand bonheur; to b. sb (good) luck/bad

luck porter bonheur/malheur à qn; **to b. new hope to sb** redonner de l'espoir à qn; **to b. tears to sb's eyes** faire venir les larmes aux yeux de qn (**c**) *(to a particular condition)* **to b. sth into disrepute** discréditer qch; **to b. sth into question** remettre qch en question; **to b. sth to an end** mettre fin à qch; **to b. sth to light** *(crime, secret)* révéler qch; **to b. sth to mind** faire penser à qch; **I couldn't bring myself to do it** je n'ai pas pu me décider *ou* me résoudre à le faire (**d**) *(be sold for)* rapporter
▸**bring about** *vt sep (cause)* entraîner, provoquer
▸**bring along** *vt sep (person)* amener; *(object)* apporter
▸**bring back** *vt sep* (**a**) *(person)* ramener; *(gift)* rapporter; **to b. sb back to life** ramener qn à la vie; **to b. sb back to health** rendre la santé à qn (**b**) *(memory)* rappeler (**c**) *(law, practice)* rétablir
▸**bring down** *vt sep* (**a**) *(from shelf, attic)* descendre (**b**) *(soldier, plane)* abattre; *(government)* faire tomber, renverser; *Fam* **her performance brought the house down** son interprétation lui a valu des applaudissements enthousiastes (**c**) *(lower) (price, temperature)* faire baisser
▸**bring forward** *vt sep* (**a**) *(proposal)* émettre; *(plan)* proposer; *(reasons, evidence)* avancer (**b**) *(advance time of)* avancer (**c**) *Com (in bookkeeping)* reporter
▸**bring in** *vt sep* (**a**) *(expert, consultant)* faire appel à; **the police brought him in for questioning** la police l'a emmené au poste pour l'interroger (**b**) *(earn) (of person)* gagner; *(of investment, sale)* rapporter (**c**) *(law, act)* introduire (**d**) *Law (verdict)* rendre
▸**bring off** *vt sep (accomplish)* réussir
▸**bring on** *vt sep (cause)* provoquer; **you've brought it on yourself** tu l'as cherché
▸**bring out** *vt sep* (**a**) *(publish)* sortir (**b**) *(cause to appear)* **to b. out the best/the worst in sb** faire ressortir les qualités/les défauts de qn; **strawberries b. her out in a rash** les fraises lui donnent de l'urticaire; **to b. sb out of their shell** faire sortir qn de sa coquille
▸**bring round** *vt sep* (**a**) *(revive)* ranimer, faire revenir à soi (**b**) *(persuade)* convaincre; **she brought him round to her point of view** elle l'a rallié à son point de vue (**c**) *(conversation)* amener (**to** sur)
▸**bring to** *vt sep (revive)* ranimer, faire revenir à soi
▸**bring together** *vt sep* réunir
▸**bring up** *vt sep* (**a**) *(subject)* soulever (**b**) *(child)* élever; **I was brought up to be polite** on m'a appris à être poli (**c**) *(vomit)* vomir
bring-and-buy ['brɪŋən'baɪ] *n Br* **b. (sale)** vente *f* de charité

Bring-and-buy
Ces brocantes sont en général destinées à réunir des fonds pour une œuvre de charité. On y vend des articles d'occasion et des produits faits maison.

brink [brɪŋk] *n also Fig* bord *m*; *Fig* **to be on the b. of sth** *(war, ruin, disaster)* être au bord de qch; *(death, success)* être à deux doigts de qch; **to be on the b. of doing sth** être à deux doigts de faire qch
brinkmanship ['brɪŋkmənʃɪp] *n* politique *f* de la corde raide
brisk [brɪsk] *adj* (**a**) *(weather)* frais (fraîche); *(wind)* vivifiant(e) (**b**) *(person) (efficient)* énergique; *(dismissive)* vif (vive); (**c**) *(rapid)* **at a b. pace** *(work)* rapidement; *(walk)* d'un pas vif; **to go for a b. walk** se

promener d'un pas vif; **business is b.** les affaires marchent bien
briskly ['brɪsklɪ] *adv* (**a**) *(efficiently)* énergiquement; *(dismissively)* vivement (**b**) *(rapidly) (walk)* d'un pas vif
bristle ['brɪsəl] **1** *n (of plant, brush, face)* poil *m*; *(of pig)* soie *f*
2 *vi* (**a**) *(of animal, animal's fur)* se hérisser; **to b. (with anger) (at)** (**b**) **to be bristling with** *(people)* grouiller de; *(difficulties)* être hérissé(e) de
Brit [brɪt] *n Fam* Britannique *mf*
Britain ['brɪtən] *n* la Grande-Bretagne
British ['brɪtɪʃ] **1** *npl* **the B.** les Britanniques *mpl*
2 *adj* britannique; **B. Columbia** la Colombie-Britannique; **B. Council** = organisme chargé de promouvoir la langue et la culture anglaises; **the B. Isles** les îles *fpl* Britanniques; **B. Summer Time** heure *f* d'été *(en Grande-Bretagne)*

British Council
Le British Council est un organisme public chargé de promouvoir la langue et la culture anglaises, et de renforcer les liens culturels avec les autres pays.

Briton ['brɪtən] *n* Britannique *mf*; *Hist* ancient **B.** Breton(onne) *m,f (de la Grande-Bretagne)*
Brittany ['brɪtənɪ] *n* la Bretagne
brittle ['brɪtəl] *adj (object, hair, voice)* cassant(e); *(bones)* friable
broach [brəʊtʃ] *vt (subject)* aborder
broad¹ [brɔːd] *adj (road, smile, sense, mind)* large; *(accent)* fort(e), prononcé(e); *(humour)* grossier(ère); *(hint)* appuyé(e); **in b. daylight** en plein jour; *Fig* au grand jour; **to be in b. agreement** être d'accord sur l'essentiel; *Fig* **to be a b. church** admettre de nombreuses tendances; **a b. outline** les grandes lignes *fpl*; **b. bean** fève *f*
broad² *n Am Fam (woman)* gonzesse *f*
broadband ['brɔːdbænd] *Tel & Comput* **1** *n* connexion *f* à haut débit *ou* à large bande, ADSL *m*; **have you got b.?** est-ce que tu as l'ADSL?
2 *adj* à haut débit, à large bande; **b. network** réseau *m* à haut débit *ou* à large bande, réseau *m* ADSL
broadcast ['brɔːdkɑːst] **1** *n* émission *f*
2 *vt (pt & pp* **broadcast)** diffuser; *Fam* **don't b. it!** ne va pas le crier sur les toits!
3 *vi (of station)* émettre
broadcaster ['brɔːdkɑːstə(r)] *n (person)* présentateur(trice) *m,f*; *(TV station)* chaîne *f* de télévision; *(radio station)* station *f* de radio
broadcasting ['brɔːdkɑːstɪŋ] *n (action)* diffusion *f*; **he works in b.** *(radio)* il travaille à la radio; *(TV)* il travaille à la télé
broaden ['brɔːdən] **1** *vt* élargir; **to b. one's horizons** élargir son horizon
2 *vi* **b. (out)** s'élargir
broadly ['brɔːdlɪ] *adv (generally)* en gros; **to smile b.** faire un large sourire; **b. speaking** en gros
broad-minded [brɔːd'maɪndɪd] *adj (person)* large d'esprit; *(attitude)* ouvert(e)
broadsheet ['brɔːdʃiːt] *n* journal *m* grand format *(synonyme de qualité)*
broad-shouldered [brɔːd'ʃəʊldəd] *adj* large d'épaules; *Fig* **to be b.** *(resilient)* bien encaisser

broadside ['brɔːdsaɪd] *n Naut* **to fire a b.** tirer une bordée; *Fig* **to fire a b. at sb/sth** attaquer violemment qn/qch

brocade [brəʊ'keɪd] *n* brocart *m*

broccoli ['brɒkəlɪ] *n* brocolis *mpl*

brochure ['brəʊʃə(r)] *n* brochure *f*

brogue [brəʊg] *n (accent)* accent *m*

brogues [brəʊgz] *npl (shoes)* = chaussures solides souvent ornées de petits trous

broil [brɔɪl] *vt & vi Am* griller

broke [brəʊk] **1** *adj Fam* fauché(e); **to go for b.** jouer le tout pour le tout
2 *pt of* **break**

broken ['brəʊkən] **1** *adj (object, bone)* cassé(e); *(promise)* rompu(e); *(marriage, heart, person)* brisé(e); *(ground, surface)* irrégulier(ère); **to speak b. English** parler un mauvais anglais; **b. home** famille *f* désunie
2 *pp of* **break**

brokenhearted [brəʊkən'hɑːtɪd] *adj* **to be b.** avoir le cœur brisé

broker ['brəʊkə(r)] *n Fin (for shares, currency)* agent *m* de change; *Com (for goods, insurance)* courtier *m*

brolly ['brɒlɪ] *(pl* **brollies)** *n Br Fam* pépin *m*, pébroc *m*

bromide ['brəʊmaɪd] *n Chem* bromure *m*; *Fig* banalité *f*

bronchial ['brɒŋkɪəl] *adj Anat* bronchique; **b. pneumonia** broncho-pneumonie *f*; **b. tubes** bronches *fpl*

bronchitic [brɒŋ'kɪtɪk] *adj* bronchitique

bronchitis [brɒŋ'kaɪtɪs] *n* bronchite *f*; **to have b.** avoir une bronchite

bronze [brɒnz] **1** *n* bronze *m*; **to win a b.** *(medal)* remporter une médaille de bronze; **the B. Age** l'âge *m* du bronze
2 *adj (material)* de *ou* en bronze; *(colour)* couleur bronze *inv*

bronzed [brɒnzd] *adj* bronzé(e)

bronzer ['brɒnzə(r)] *n* poudre *m* à soleil

brooch [brəʊtʃ] *n* broche *f*

brood [bruːd] **1** *n (of birds)* couvée *f*; *Hum (of children)* progéniture *f*
2 *vi (of hen)* couver; *Fig* **to b. (over or about sth)** ruminer (qch)

broody ['bruːdɪ] *adj (hen)* couveuse; *Fig (woman)* en mal d'enfant

brook¹ [brʊk] *n (stream)* ruisseau *m*

brook² *vt Formal (tolerate)* tolérer

broom [bruːm] *n* **(a)** *(plant)* genêt *m* **(b)** *(for cleaning)* balai *m*; *Fig* **a new b.** = un nouvel arrivant qui veut tout changer

broomstick ['bruːmstɪk] *n* manche *m* à balai

Bros *npl Com (abbr* **Brothers) Richardson B.** Richardson frères

broth [brɒθ] *n (soup) (thin)* bouillon *m*; *(thick)* potage *m*

brothel ['brɒθəl] *n* maison *f* close

brother ['brʌðə(r)] *n* frère *m*

brotherhood ['brʌðəhʊd] *n* fraternité *f*; *Rel* confrérie *f*; **the b. of man** la fraternité humaine

brother-in-law ['brʌðərɪnlɔː] *(pl* **brothers-in-law)** *n* beau-frère *m*

brought [brɔːt] *pt & pp of* **bring**

brow [braʊ] *n* **(a)** *(forehead)* front *m*; *(eyebrow)* sourcil *m* **(b)** *(of hill)* sommet *m*

browbeat ['braʊbiːt] *(pt* **browbeat,** *pp* **browbeaten** ['braʊbiːtən]) *vt* intimider; **to b. sb into doing sth** forcer qn à faire qch en usant d'intimidation

brown [braʊn] **1** *n* marron *m*
2 *adj* marron *inv*; *(hair)* brun(e); *(skin)* mat(e); *(tanned)*

bronzé(e); *(bread, flour, rice)* complet(ète); **b. paper** papier *m* kraft; **b. sugar** sucre *m* roux, cassonade *f*
3 *vi (in cooking)* faire dorer
4 *vi (in cooking)* dorer

browned-off ['braʊnd'ɒf] *adj Br Fam* **to be b. (with)** en avoir marre (de); **to be b. with doing sth** en avoir marre de faire qch

brownfield site ['braʊnfiːld'saɪt] *n* terrain *m* à bâtir *(après démolition de bâtiments préexistants)*

Brownie ['braʊnɪ] *n* ≃ jeannette *f*; *Fig* **to win or get b. points** se faire bien voir

brownie ['braʊnɪ] *n (cake)* brownie *m (petit gâteau au chocolat et aux noix)*

brown-nose ['braʊnnəʊz] *vi Vulg* faire le lèche-cul

browse [braʊz] **1** *n* **to have a b.** *(in shop)* regarder; **to have a b. through sth** *(collection, shelves)* jeter un œil sur qch; *(magazine)* feuilleter qch
2 *vt Comput* **to b. the Web** naviguer sur le Web
3 *vi* **(a)** *(in shop)* regarder; **to b. through sth** *(collection, shelves)* jeter un œil sur qch; *(magazine)* feuilleter qch **(b)** *(of animal)* brouter

browser ['braʊzə(r)] *n Comput* logiciel *m* de navigation, navigateur *m*, *Can* fureteur *m*

bruise [bruːz] **1** *n (on body)* bleu *m*; *(on fruit)* meurtrissure *f*
2 *vt (person)* faire un bleu à; *Fig (feelings, pride)* blesser; **to b. one's arm** se faire un bleu au bras
3 *vi (of person)* se faire des bleus; *(of fruit)* s'abîmer

bruiser ['bruːzə(r)] *n Fam* grosse brute *f*

bruising ['bruːzɪŋ] **1** *n (bruises)* bleus *mpl*
2 *adj (encounter, experience)* douloureux(euse)

Brummie ['brʌmɪ] *n Fam* = personne née à ou habitant Birmingham

brunch [brʌntʃ] *n* brunch *m*

Brunei [bruː'naɪ] *n* le Brunei

brunette [bruː'net] *n* brune *f*

brunt [brʌnt] *n* **to bear or take the b. of sth** *(attack)* essuyer le plus fort de qch; *(anger)* faire les frais de qch

bruschetta [brʌs'ketə] *n Culin* bruschetta *f*

brush [brʌʃ] **1** *n* **(a)** *(for clothes, hair)* brosse *f*; *(for sweeping)* balai *m*; *(for painting)* pinceau *m* **(b)** *(action)* **to give sth a b.** donner un coup de brosse à qch; **to give the floor a b.** donner un coup de balai; **to give one's hair a b.** se donner un coup de brosse **(c)** *(light touch)* effleurement *m*; *Fam* **to have a b. with the law** avoir des démêlés avec la justice **(d)** *(of fox)* queue *f* **(e)** *(undergrowth)* broussailles *fpl*
2 *vt* **(a)** *(clothes, shoes)* brosser; **to b. one's hair/teeth** se brosser les cheveux/les dents; **to b. the floor** balayer **(b)** *(touch lightly)* effleurer
3 *vi* **to b. against sb/sth** effleurer qn/qch; **to brush past sb/sth** effleurer qn/qch en passant

▸ **brush aside** *vt sep (objection, obstacle)* balayer; *(opponent)* écarter

▸ **brush off** *vt sep* **(a)** *(from clothes, shoes)* enlever d'un coup de brosse **(b)** *(person)* envoyer promener; *(insult, incident)* ignorer

▸ **brush up** *vt sep* **(a)** *(leaves, crumbs)* balayer **(b)** *Fam (subject, language)* **to b. up (on)** se remettre (à)

brushed [brʌʃt] *adj (nylon)* gratté(e); **b. cotton** pilou *m*, finette *f*

brush-off ['brʌʃɒf] *n Fam* **to give sb the b.** envoyer promener qn

brush-up ['brʌʃʌp] *n* **to have a wash and b.** faire un brin de toilette

brushwood ['brʌʃwʊd] *n (as fuel)* petit bois *m*; *(undergrowth)* broussailles *fpl*

brushwork ['brʌʃwɜːk] n Art touche f
brusque [bruːsk] adj brusque
brusquely ['bruːsklɪ] adv (behave) avec brusquerie; (say) d'un ton brusque
Brussels ['brʌsəlz] n Bruxelles; **B.** sprout chou m de Bruxelles
brutal ['bruːtəl] adj brutal(e); (attack, crime) sauvage
brutality [bruː'tælɪtɪ] n brutalité f; (of attack, crime) sauvagerie f
brutalize ['bruːtəlaɪz] vt (ill-treat) brutaliser; (make insensitive) rendre insensible
brutally ['bruːtəlɪ] adv avec brutalité; (beat, attack) sauvagement
brute [bruːt] **1** n (animal) bête f; (person) brute f
  2 adj **b. force** or **strength** force f brutale
brutish ['bruːtɪʃ] adj bestial(e)
BS [biː'es] n Am (abbr **Bachelor of Science**) **to have a BS in computer science/physics** avoir une licence d'informatique/de physique; **John Smith BS** John Smith, licencié en chimie/informatique/etc
BSc [biːes'siː] n Br (abbr **Bachelor of Science**) **to have a B. in computer science/physics** avoir une licence d'informatique/de physique; **John Smith B.** John Smith, licencié en chimie/informatique/etc
BSE [biːes'iː] n (abbr **bovine spongiform encephalopathy**) EBS f, maladie f de la vache folle
BSI [biːes'aɪ] n (abbr **British Standards Institution**) = association britannique de normalisation
BST [biːes'tiː] n (abbr **British Summer Time**) heure f d'été (en Grande-Bretagne)
bubble ['bʌbəl] **1** n (of air, soap) bulle f; Fig **the b. has burst** le rêve est terminé; **b. bath** bain m moussant; Comput **b. jet printer** imprimante f à bulles
  2 vi (form bubbles) bouillonner
▸**bubble over** vi (of liquid) déborder; Fig **to b. over with joy** ne plus se tenir de joie
bubblegum ['bʌbəlgʌm] n chewing-gum m
bubbly ['bʌblɪ] **1** n Fam (champagne) champ m
  2 adj (**a**) (liquid) plein(e) de bulles (**b**) (person) débordant(e) de vitalité
bubonic [bjuː'bɒnɪk] adj **b. plague** peste f bubonique
buccaneer [bʌkə'nɪə(r)] n boucanier m
Bucharest [buːkə'rest] n Bucarest
buck [bʌk] **1** n (**a**) Am Fam (dollar) dollar m; **to make a fast** or **quick b.** faire du fric (**b**) (of deer, rabbit) mâle m (**c**) Fam (responsibility) **to pass the b.** refiler le bébé; **the b. stops here** (with me) en dernier ressort, c'est moi le responsable; (with you) en dernier ressort, c'est toi le responsable
  2 vt **to b. the system/a trend** aller à l'encontre de l'ordre établi/d'une tendance
  3 vi (of horse) faire le saut de mouton
▸**buck up** Fam **1** vt sep (encourage) remonter le moral à; **to b. one's ideas up** se prendre en main
  2 vi Fam (cheer up) reprendre courage; (hurry) se grouiller
bucket ['bʌkɪt] **1** n seau m; Br Fam **it's raining buckets** il tombe des cordes; Fam **to cry buckets** pleurer comme une madeleine; Fam **b. shop** (for air tickets) agence f de voyages à prix réduits
  2 vi Br Fam **it's bucketing (down)** il tombe des cordes
buckle ['bʌkəl] **1** n boucle f
  2 vt (**a**) (fasten) boucler (**b**) (deform) déformer; (wheel) voiler
  3 vi (deform) se déformer; (of wheel) se voiler; (of knees) flancher; **she buckled at the knees** ses jambes ont cédé sous elle

▸**buckle down** vi s'y mettre; **to b. down to a task** s'atteler à une tâche
▸**buckle up** vi Am (in car) attacher sa ceinture
buckshot ['bʌkʃɒt] n chevrotine f
buckskin ['bʌkskɪn] n daim m (peau)
buckteeth [bʌk'tiːθ] npl dents fpl de lapin
bucktoothed [bʌk'tuːθt] adj **to be b.** avoir des dents de lapin
buckwheat ['bʌkwiːt] n sarrasin m
bucolic [bjuː'kɒlɪk] adj Lit bucolique
bud [bʌd] **1** n (of leaf, branch) bourgeon m; (of flower) bouton m
  2 vi (pt & pp budded) (of tree) bourgeonner; (of flowers) être en boutons
Budapest ['buːdəpest] n Budapest
Buddha ['bʊdə] n Bouddha
Buddhist ['bʊdɪst] **1** n bouddhiste mf
  2 adj (priest, doctrine) bouddhiste; (art, temple) bouddhique
budding ['bʌdɪŋ] adj (genius, actor) en herbe; (talent) naissant(e)
buddy ['bʌdɪ] (pl **buddies**) n Fam (friend) pote m; **hey, b.!** dis donc, mec!
budge [bʌdʒ] **1** vt (move) bouger; Fig (convince) faire changer d'avis
  2 vi (move) bouger; Fig (yield) céder
budgerigar ['bʌdʒərɪgɑː(r)] n perruche f
budget ['bʌdʒɪt] **1** n budget m; Br Pol **the B.** le budget; **to go over b.** dépasser le budget; **to be within b.** être dans les limites du budget; **b. deficit/surplus** déficit m/excédent m budgétaire
  2 adj (inexpensive) économique; **b. prices** prix mpl avantageux
  3 vt (time, money) gérer
  4 vi **to b. for sth** prévoir qch
budgetary ['bʌdʒɪtərɪ] adj Fin budgétaire
budgie ['bʌdʒɪ] n Fam perruche f
Buenos Aires ['bwenɒs'aɪrɪz] n Buenos Aires
buff [bʌf] **1** n (**a**) (colour) couleur f chamois (**b**) Fam **in the b.** (naked) à poil (**c**) (enthusiast) mordu(e) m,f; **film b.** cinéphile mf
  2 adj (couleur) chamois inv; (envelope) en papier kraft
  3 vt (polish) lustrer
buffalo ['bʌfələʊ] (pl **buffalo** or **buffaloes**) n buffle m
buffer¹ ['bʌfə(r)] n (on railway track) butoir m; Comput mémoire f tampon; **to act as a b.** faire tampon; **b. state** état m tampon; **b. zone** zone f tampon
buffer² n Br Fam **old b.** vieux schnock m
buffet¹ ['bʌfɪt] vt (of wind) secouer; Fig **to be buffeted by the waves/by events** être ballotté(e) par les vagues/par les événements
buffet² ['bʊfeɪ] n (**a**) (sideboard) buffet m (**b**) (meal) buffet m; **b. lunch/dinner** buffet m (**c**) (in station) buffet m; **b. car** (on train) wagon-restaurant m
buffeting ['bʌfɪtɪŋ] n **to take a b.** (of ship) être violemment ballotté(e); Fig (of person) être fortement ébranlé(e)
buffoon [bə'fuːn] n bouffon m; **to play the b.** faire le pitre
bug [bʌg] **1** n (**a**) (insect) insecte m; (bed bug) punaise f (**b**) Fam (illness) virus m, microbe m; **a stomach b.** un embarras gastrique; **there's a b. going round** il y a un virus qui traîne; Fig **the travel b.** le virus des voyages (**c**) Comput bug m, bogue m (**d**) (listening device) micro m
  2 vt (pt & pp bugged) (**a**) (telephone) mettre sur écoute; (building, room) cacher des micros dans (**b**)

Fam (annoy) taper sur les nerfs à; *(nag)* embêter; **stop bugging me about it!** arrête de m'embêter avec ça!

bugbear ['bʌgbeə(r)] *n Fam* cauchemar *m*
bug-eyed [bʌg'aɪd] *adj* aux yeux exorbités
bug-free [bʌg'friː] *adj* (**a**) *Comput (program)* exempt de bogues (**b**) *(without listening devices)* sans micros clandestins
bugger ['bʌgə(r)] **1** *n very Fam (unpleasant person)* connard(asse) *m,f*; **you silly b.!** espèce d'andouille!; **the poor b.!** le pauvre!; **it's a b. of a job** c'est une vraie galère; **b. all** que dalle; **he knows b. all about it** il y connaît que dalle
2 *vt* (**a**) *(sodomize)* sodomiser (**b**) *Br very Fam* **b. (it)!** merde!; **I'll be buggered if I'm going to do it!** tu peux toujours courir pour que je le fasse!; **I'm buggered if I know** j'en sais foutre rien; **that's really buggered it!** ça a tout foutu en l'air!
▸**bugger about, bugger around** *Br very Fam* **1** *vt sep* **to b. sb about** se foutre de la gueule de qn
2 *vi* glander
▸**bugger off** *vi Br very Fam* se casser, foutre le camp
▸**bugger up** *vt sep Br very Fam (plan)* foutre en l'air; *(TV, machine)* bousiller
buggered ['bʌgəd] *adj Br very Fam (broken)* foutu(e); *(exhausted)* nase
buggery ['bʌgərɪ] *n* (**a**) *Law* sodomie *f* (**b**) *Br very Fam* **to run like b.** prendre ses jambes à son cou
buggy ['bʌgɪ] *(pl* **buggies)** *n* (**a**) *Br (pushchair)* poussette *f*; *Am (pram)* landau *m* (**b**) *(carriage)* boghei *m*, buggy *m*
bugle ['bjuːgəl] *n* clairon *m*
bugler ['bjuːglə(r)] *n* (sonneur *m* de) clairon *m*
build [bɪld] **1** *n* carrure *f*
2 *vt (pt & pp* **built** [bɪlt]) construire; **to be built (out) of sth** être construit(e) en qch; **to b. sth into sth** *(include)* inclure qch dans qch; **to b. one's hopes on sth** fonder ses espoirs sur qch
▸**build on 1** *vt sep (add)* ajouter
2 *vt insep (success)* tirer parti de
▸**build up 1** *vt sep* (**a**) *(resources)* accumuler; **to b. up speed/one's strength** prendre de la vitesse/des forces; **don't b. your hopes up** ne te fais pas d'illusions (**b**) *(custom)* se constituer; *(reputation)* se faire; *(company)* développer; **to b. up an immunity (to sth)** s'immuniser (contre qch) (**c**) *(hype)* faire du battage autour de
2 *vi (of clouds)* s'amasser; *(of hurricane, storm)* se préparer; *(of tension, pressure)* s'accumuler
builder ['bɪldə(r)] *n* maçon *m*; *(business owner)* entrepreneur *m* (dans le bâtiment)
building ['bɪldɪŋ] *n* (**a**) *(structure)* bâtiment *m*; immeuble *m* (**b**) *(action)* construction *f*; **the b. trade** le bâtiment; **b. block** cube *m*; *Fig* élément *m* essentiel; **b. site** chantier *m* (de construction); *Br* **b. society** ≃ société *f* de crédit immobilier

Building societies
Les "building societies" fonctionnent comme des banques mais elles n'ont pas de système de compensation. Établissements consentant des prêts immobiliers aux particuliers, elles jouent un rôle important dans la vie en Grande-Bretagne. Au cours des dernières années, de nombreuses "building societies" ont abandonné leur statut de sociétés mutuelles pour devenir des banques cotées en Bourse.

build-up ['bɪldʌp] *n (of tension, forces)* accumulation *f*; *(hype)* battage *m*; **the b. to Christmas/the match** la période précédant Noël/le match
built [bɪlt] *pt & pp of* **build**
built-in ['bɪl'tɪn] *adj (cupboard)* encastré(e); *(included)* compris(e); **b. obsolescence** obsolescence *f* programmée
built-up ['bɪl'tʌp] *adj* **b. area** agglomération *f* urbaine
bulb [bʌlb] *n* (**a**) *(of plant)* bulbe *m* (**b**) *(light bulb)* ampoule *f*
bulbous ['bʌlbəs] *adj* bulbeux(euse); **a b. nose** un gros nez
Bulgaria [bʌl'geərɪə] *n* la Bulgarie
Bulgarian [bʌl'geərɪən] **1** *n* (**a**) *(person)* Bulgare *mf* (**b**) *(language)* bulgare *m*
2 *adj* bulgare
bulge [bʌldʒ] **1** *n* renflement *m*
2 *vi (of stomach)* être gonflé(e); *(of bag, pocket)* être bourré(e) (**with** de)
bulimia [bə'lɪmɪə] *n* boulimie *f*
bulk [bʌlk] **1** *n* (**a**) *(mass)* masse *f*; **the b. (of sth)** la majeure partie (de qch) (**b**) *Com* **in b.** en gros; **b. purchase** achat *m* en gros
2 *vt* **to b. sth out** étoffer qch
3 *vi* **to b. large** *(of problem)* occuper une place importante
bulkhead ['bʌlkhed] *n Naut* cloison *f*
bulky ['bʌlkɪ] *adj* volumineux(euse), encombrant(e)
bull¹ [bʊl] *n* (**a**) *(animal)* taureau *m*; **b. elephant** éléphant *m* mâle; *Fin* **b. market** marché *m* à la hausse (**b**) *very Fam (nonsense)* conneries *fpl* (**c**) *(idioms)* **to take the b. by the horns** prendre le taureau par les cornes; **like a b. in a china shop** comme un éléphant dans un magasin de porcelaine
bull² *n Rel* bulle *f*
bulldog ['bʊldɒg] *n* bouledogue *m*; **b. clip** pince *f* à dessin
bulldoze ['bʊldəʊz] *vt (land)* aplanir au bulldozer; *(building)* démolir au bulldozer; *Fig* **to b. sb into doing sth** forcer qn à faire qch
bulldozer ['bʊldəʊzə(r)] *n* bulldozer *m*
bullet ['bʊlɪt] *n* (**a**) *(for gun)* balle *f*; **b. hole** impact *m* de balle; **b. wound** blessure *f* par balle (**b**) *Comput* **b. point** puce *f*
bulletin ['bʊlɪtɪn] *n* bulletin *m*; **b. board** *Am (noticeboard)* panneau *m* d'affichage; *Comput* serveur *m* télématique; *Can* babillard *m*
bulletproof ['bʊlɪtpruːf] *adj (car, glass)* blindé(e); **b. vest** gilet *m* pare-balles
bullfight ['bʊlfaɪt] *n* corrida *f*, course *f* de taureaux; *(art)* tauromachie *f*
bullfighter ['bʊlfaɪtə(r)] *n* torero *m*
bullfighting ['bʊlfaɪtɪŋ] *n (bullfights)* courses *fpl* de taureaux; *(art)* tauromachie *f*
bullfinch ['bʊlfɪntʃ] *n* bouvreuil *m*
bullfrog ['bʊlfrɒg] *n* grenouille-taureau *f*, *Can* ouaouaron *m*
bullion ['bʊljən] *n* **gold b.** lingots *mpl* d'or
bullish ['bʊlɪʃ] *adj Fin (market)* à la hausse; *Fig (optimistic)* optimiste
bullock ['bʊlək] *n* bœuf *m*
bullring ['bʊlrɪŋ] *n* arène *f*
bull's-eye ['bʊlzaɪ] *n* mille *m*; *also Fig* **to hit the b.** mettre dans le mille
bullshit ['bʊlʃɪt] *Vulg* **1** *n (nonsense)* conneries *fpl*
2 *exclam* c'est des conneries tout ça!
3 *vt (pt & pp* **bullshitted)** **to b. sb** raconter des

conneries à qn; **she bullshitted her way into the job** elle a bluffé pour avoir le poste **4** *vi* *(talk nonsense)* dire des conneries
bully ['bʊlɪ] **1** *n* (*pl* **bullies**) *(child)* petite brute *f*; *(adult)* tyran *m*; **don't be such a b.** ne sois pas si tyrannique **2** *vt* (*pt & pp* **bullied**) maltraiter; **to b. sb into doing sth** forcer qn à faire qch **3** *exclam Ironic* **b. for you!** bravo!
bully-boy ['bʊlɪbɔɪ] *n* voyou *m*; **b. tactics** manœuvres *fpl* d'intimidation
bullying ['bʊlɪɪŋ] **1** *n* brimades *fpl* **2** *adj* brutal(e)
bulrush ['bʊlrʌʃ] *n* jonc *m*
bulwark ['bʊlwɜːk] *n also Fig* rempart *m* (**against** contre)
bum [bʌm] *Fam* **1** *n* (**a**) *Br (buttocks)* derrière *m* (**b**) *Am (tramp)* clochard(e) *m,f* **2** *adj (of poor quality)* minable; **to get a b. deal** se faire avoir **3** *vt* (*pt & pp* **bummed**) **to b. a cigarette from** *or* **off sb** taxer une cigarette à qn; **to b. a ride** se faire prendre en stop
▸**bum around** *vi Fam (be idle)* glander; *(travel)* vadrouiller
bumblebee ['bʌmbəlbiː] *n* bourdon *m*
bumbling ['bʌmbəlɪŋ] *adj* **b. fool** *or* **idiot** imbécile *mf*
bumf [bʌmf] *n Fam* paperasse *f*
bummer ['bʌmə(r)] *n Fam* **what a b.!** quelle poisse!
bump [bʌmp] **1** *n* (**a**) *(jolt)* secousse *f*; **to land with a b.** tomber violemment par terre; *Fig* **to come back down to earth with a b.** redescendre brusquement sur terre (**b**) *(lump)* bosse *f* **2** *vt* cogner; **to b. one's head** se cogner la tête
▸**bump into** *vt insep (collide with)* rentrer dans; *Fam (meet by chance)* tomber sur
▸**bump off** *vt sep Fam (kill)* liquider
▸**bump up** *vt sep Fam (price)* gonfler, augmenter
bumper ['bʌmpə(r)] **1** *Br (of car)* pare-chocs *m inv*; **b. car** *(at fairground)* auto *f* tamponneuse; **b. sticker** autocollant *m (pour voiture)* **2** *adj* **b. crop** récolte *f* exceptionnelle; **b. issue** numéro *m* exceptionnel
bumpkin ['bʌmpkɪn] *n* **(country) b.** péquenaud(e) *m,f*
bump-start ['bʌmpstɑːt] *vt* **to b. a car** pousser une voiture pour la faire démarrer
bumptious ['bʌmpʃəs] *adj* suffisant(e)
bumpy ['bʌmpɪ] *adj (road)* cahoteux(euse); *(journey)* agité(e); *(landing)* violent(e); *Fam Fig* **to give sb/sth a b. ride** malmener qn/qch
bun [bʌn] *n* (**a**) *(sweet)* petit gâteau *m* brioché; *(for burger)* petit pain *m* rond (**b**) *(hairstyle)* chignon *m*
bunch [bʌntʃ] *n* (*of flowers)* bouquet *m*; (*of bananas)* régime *m*; (*of grapes)* grappe *f*; (*of keys)* trousseau *m*; (*of people)* bande *f*; (*of cyclists)* peloton *m*; **bunches** *(hairstyle)* couettes *fpl*; **he's the best of a bad b.** c'est le moins mauvais du lot; **she's the best** *or* **the pick of the b.** c'est la meilleure du lot; **a whole b. of things to do** tout un tas de choses à faire
▸**bunch together** *vi (of people)* se serrer
bundle ['bʌndəl] **1** *n* (*of clothes)* paquet *m*; (*of banknotes, papers)* liasse *f*; (*of straw)* botte *f*; *Fam* **I don't go a b. on horror films** je ne suis pas un fana de films d'horreur; *Fam Ironic* **you're a b. of laughs!** c'est fou ce que tu as l'air gai!; *Fam* **she's a b. of nerves** c'est un paquet de nerfs **2** *vt* **to b. sb out of the door** mettre qn dehors sans

ménagement; **to b. sb into a car** embarquer qn dans une voiture
▸**bundle off** *vt sep (send)* expédier
bung [bʌŋ] **1** *n* (**a**) *(plug)* bonde *f* (**b**) *Br Fam (bribe)* bakchich *m* **2** *vt Br Fam (put)* mettre; *(throw)* balancer; **b. it there** mets-le là; **b. me over an orange** balance-moi une orange
▸**bung up** *vt sep Fam* boucher; **my nose is bunged up** j'ai le nez bouché
bungalow ['bʌŋgələʊ] *n* pavillon *m* de plain-pied
bungee jumping ['bʌndʒiːdʒʌmpɪŋ] *n* saut *m* à l'élastique
bunghole ['bʌŋhəʊl] *n* bonde *f*
bungle ['bʌŋgəl] **1** *vt (attempt)* rater; *(job)* gâcher **2** *vi* se tromper
bunion ['bʌnjən] *n* oignon *m (au pied)*
bunk¹ [bʌŋk] *n (bed)* lit *m*; *(in train, ship)* couchette *f*; **b. beds** lits *mpl* superposés
bunk² *n Br Fam* **to do a b.** *(run away)* se faire la malle
▸**bunk off** *vi Br Fam (from school)* sécher (les cours)
bunker ['bʌŋkə(r)] *n* (**a**) *(for coal)* coffre *m* à charbon (**b**) *Mil* bunker *m*, blockhaus *m*; **nuclear b.** abri *m* antiatomique (**c**) *Br (on golf course)* bunker *m*
bunkum ['bʌŋkəm] *n Fam* âneries *fpl*
bunny ['bʌnɪ] (*pl* **bunnies**) *n Fam* **b. (rabbit)** petit lapin *m*
Bunsen burner ['bʌnsən'bɜːnə(r)] *n* bec *m* Bunsen
bunting ['bʌntɪŋ] *n (decorations)* guirlandes *fpl* de fanions
buoy [bɔɪ] *n* bouée *f*
▸**buoy up** *vt sep (person, prices)* soutenir
buoyancy ['bɔɪənsɪ] *n (in water)* flottabilité *f*; *Fig (of market)* stabilité *f*
buoyant ['bɔɪənt] *adj (in water)* qui flotte; *Fig (economy, prices)* stable; *Fig (person, mood)* plein(e) d'allant
burble ['bɜːbəl] *vi (of stream)* murmurer; *(of person)* marmonner
burden ['bɜːdən] **1** *n also Fig* fardeau *m*; **b. of taxation** pression *f* fiscale; *Law* **b. of proof** charge *f* de la preuve **2** *vt Fig* accabler (**with** de)
burdensome ['bɜːdənsəm] *adj* lourd(e)
bureau ['bjʊərəʊ] (*pl* **bureaux** ['bjʊərəʊz]) *n* (**a**) *(desk)* bureau *m*, secrétaire *m*; *Am (chest of drawers)* commode *f* (**b**) *(office)* bureau *m*; *Am (government department)* service *m*
bureaucracy [bjʊə'rɒkrəsɪ] *n* bureaucratie *f*
bureaucrat ['bjʊərəkræt] *n* bureaucrate *mf*
bureaucratic [bjʊərə'krætɪk] *adj* bureaucratique
bureaux ['bjʊərəʊz] *pl of* **bureau**
burgeon ['bɜːdʒən] *vi (of trade)* se développer; *(of crime)* augmenter; *(of relationship)* s'épanouir; **a burgeoning talent** un talent qui s'affirme
burger ['bɜːgə(r)] *n* hamburger *m*
burglar ['bɜːglə(r)] *n* cambrioleur(euse) *m,f*; **b. alarm** alarme *f* (de sécurité)
burglarize ['bɜːgləraɪz] *vt Am* cambrioler
burglar-proof ['bɜːgləpruːf] *adj* inviolable
burglary ['bɜːglərɪ] (*pl* **burglaries**) *n* cambriolage *m*
burgle ['bɜːgəl] *vt* cambrioler
Burgundy ['bɜːgəndɪ] *n* la Bourgogne
burgundy ['bɜːgəndɪ] *adj (colour)* bordeaux *inv*
burial ['berɪəl] *n* enterrement *m*; **b. ground** cimetière *m*
burka, burkha ['bɜːkə] *n* burka *f*, burqa *f*
Burkina-Faso [bɜː'kiːnə'fæsəʊ] *n* le Burkina

burlesque [bɜːˈlesk] **1** *n (caricature)* parodie *f*; *(style)* burlesque *m*
  2 *adj* burlesque
burly [ˈbɜːlɪ] *adj* bien bâti(e)
Burma [ˈbɜːmə] *n Formerly* la Birmanie
Burmese [bɜːˈmiːz] **1** *npl* **the B.** les Birmans *mpl*
  2 *n* (**a**) *(person)* Birman(e) *m,f* (**b**) *(language)* birman *m*
  3 *adj* birman(e)
burn¹ [bɜːn] **1** *n* brûlure *f*
  2 *vt (pt & pp* burnt [bɜːnt] *or* burned) (**a**) *(fuel, building)* brûler; **to b.** one's hand/one's finger se brûler la main/le doigt; **his cigarette burnt a hole in the carpet** sa cigarette a fait un trou dans la moquette (**b**) *(idioms)* **to have money to b.** avoir de l'argent à ne plus savoir quoi en faire; **to b.** one's boats *or* one's bridges brûler ses vaisseaux; **to b.** the candle at both ends brûler la chandelle par les deux bouts; **to b.** the midnight oil travailler tard
  3 *vi* brûler; *(of light)* briller; **the fire is burning low** le feu baisse; *Fig* **to b.** with desire brûler de désir; **to b.** with anger bouillonner de colère; **to b.** with enthusiasm déborder d'enthousiasme
▸**burn down 1** *vt sep* incendier
  2 *vi* être détruit(e) par le feu
▸**burn out 1** *vt sep* **to b.** itself out *(of fire)* s'éteindre; *Fig* **to b.** oneself out *(become exhausted)* s'épuiser
  2 *vi (of fire)* s'éteindre
▸**burn up 1** *vt sep (energy)* dépenser
  2 *vi (of rocket)* se désintégrer
burn² *n Scot (stream)* ruisseau *m*
burner [ˈbɜːnə(r)] *n* brûleur *m*
burning [ˈbɜːnɪŋ] *adj (on fire)* en feu; *(very hot)* brûlant(e); *(passion, ambition)* dévorant(e); **a b.** issue une question brûlante
burnish [ˈbɜːnɪʃ] *vt* polir, brunir
burnt [bɜːnt] **1** *adj* brûlé(e)
  2 *pt & pp of* burn¹
burnt-out [ˈbɜːntˈaʊt] *adj (building, car)* calciné(e); *Fig (person)* usé(e)
burp [bɜːp] **1** *n* rot *m*
  2 *vi* roter
burqa = burka
burr¹ [bɜː(r)] *n (of plant)* bardane *f*; *(on tree trunk)* broussin *m*
burr² *n* **to speak with a b.** grasseyer
burrow [ˈbʌrəʊ] **1** *n (of animal)* terrier *m*
  2 *vi (of animal)* creuser la terre
bursar [ˈbɜːsə(r)] *n Univ* intendant(e) *m,f*
bursary [ˈbɜːsərɪ] *(pl* bursaries) *n (grant)* bourse *f* (d'études)
burst [bɜːst] **1** *n (of laughter)* éclat *m*; *(of enthusiasm)* élan *m*; **a b.** of activity une poussée d'activité; **a b.** of applause une salve d'applaudissements; **a b.** of gunfire une rafale; **a b.** of speed une pointe de vitesse
  2 *vt (pt & pp* burst) *(balloon, tyre)* faire éclater; **to b.** its banks *(of river)* déborder, sortir de son lit
  3 *vi (of balloon, bubble, tyre, pipe)* éclater; *Fig* **to be bursting with pride** déborder de fierté; **to be bursting with impatience** bouillir d'impatience; **to be bursting to do sth** mourir d'envie de faire qch; **to be bursting (for the toilet)** avoir un besoin pressant; *Fig* **to be bursting at the seams** *(of room)* être plein(e) à craquer
▸**burst into** *vt insep* (**a**) *(enter)* faire irruption dans (**b**) *(suddenly start)* **to b.** into flames prendre feu; **to b.**

into song se mettre à chanter; **to b.** into laughter/tears éclater de rire/en sanglots
▸**burst open** *vi (of door)* s'ouvrir brusquement; *(of packet)* éclater
▸**burst out** *vi* **to b.** out laughing éclater de rire; **to b.** out crying éclater en sanglots
Burundi [bəˈrʊndɪ] *n* le Burundi
bury [ˈberɪ] *(pt & pp* buried) *vt (body, treasure)* enterrer; *(of avalanche, mudslide) & Fig (hide)* ensevelir; **to b.** oneself in one's work se plonger dans son travail; **to b.** one's face in one's hands enfouir son visage dans ses mains; **to b.** the hatchet enterrer la hache de guerre
bus [bʌs] **1** *n (pl* buses *or* busses) (**a**) *(vehicle)* bus *m*, autobus *m*; **by b.** en bus; **b.** conductor/driver receveur(euse) *m,f*/conducteur(trice) *m,f* de bus; **b.** route ligne *f* de bus; **b.** shelter Abribus® *m*; **b.** station gare *f* routière; **b.** stop arrêt *m* d'autobus (**b**) *Comput* bus *m*
  2 *(pt & pp* bused *or* bussed) transporter en autobus
bush [bʊʃ] *n (plant)* buisson *m*; **the b.** *(in Africa, Australia)* la brousse; *Fam* **b.** telegraph téléphone *m* arabe
bushed [bʊʃt] *adj Fam (exhausted)* vanné(e), claqué(e)
bushel [ˈbʊʃəl] *n* boisseau *m*; *Fig* **don't hide your light under a b.** ne cache pas ton talent
bushfire [ˈbʊʃfaɪə(r)] *n* feu *m* de brousse
bushy [ˈbʊʃɪ] *adj* touffu(e)
busily [ˈbɪzɪlɪ] *adv* **to be b.** doing sth être très occupé(e) à faire qch
business [ˈbɪznɪs] *n* (**a**) *(task, concern)* affaire *f*; **it's none of your b.** cela ne te regarde pas, ce ne sont pas tes affaires; **it's/it's not my b. to...** ce n'est/ce n'est pas à moi de...; **mind your own b.!** occupe-toi de tes affaires *ou* de ce qui te regarde!; **to make it one's b. to do sth** prendre sur soi de faire qch; **to go about one's b.** vaquer à ses occupations; **to get down to b.** se mettre au travail; **to mean b.** ne pas plaisanter; **I'm sick of the whole b.** j'en ai assez de toute cette histoire; **he was working like nobody's b.** il travaillait très dur; **she can tell jokes like nobody's b.** elle raconte très bien les histoires drôles; *Br Fam* **it's the b.** *(excellent)* c'est génial
  (**b**) *(individual company)* affaire *f*, entreprise *f*; *(commercial activity)* affaires; **to be in the entertainment b.** être dans le spectacle; **the travel b.** les métiers *ou* le secteur du tourisme; **I'm not in the b. of making compromises** ce n'est pas mon genre de faire des compromis; **to be in b.** être dans les affaires; **to set up in b.** s'établir *ou* s'installer à son compte; **to go into b.** s'installer; **to go into b. with sb** monter une affaire avec qn; **to go out of b.** fermer; **to go to London on b.** aller à Londres pour affaires; **how's b.?** comment vont les affaires?; **it's good/bad for b.** c'est bon/mauvais pour les affaires; **to talk b.** parler affaires; **to do b. with sb** traiter avec qn; *Fin* **b.** account compte *m* professionnel; **b.** card carte *f* de visite; **b.** class *(on plane)* classe *f* affaires; **b.** hours *(of shop)* heures *fpl* d'ouverture; *(of office)* heures de bureau; **b.** lunch déjeuner *m* d'affaires; **b.** management gestion *f* d'entreprise; **b.** park parc *m* d'activités; **b.** school école *f* de commerce; **b.** studies études *fpl* commerciales *ou* de commerce; **b.** trip voyage *m* d'affaires
businesslike [ˈbɪznɪslaɪk] *adj* professionnel(elle)

businessman ['bɪznɪsmæn] *n* homme *m* d'affaires; **to be a good b.** avoir le sens des affaires
businesswoman ['bɪznɪswʊmən] *n* femme *f* d'affaires; **to be a good b.** avoir le sens des affaires
busk [bʌsk] *vi Br* jouer de la musique *(dans les rues ou le métro)*
busker ['bʌskə(r)] *n Br* musicien(enne) *m,f (dans les rues ou le métro)*
busman ['bʌsmən] *n Fam* **a b.'s holiday** = vacances pendant lesquelles on fait la même chose qu'à son travail
bust¹ [bʌst] *n* (**a**) *(of woman)* poitrine *f*; **b. measurement** tour *m* de poitrine (**b**) *(statue)* buste *m*
bust² *Fam* **1** *adj* (**a**) *(broken)* fichu(e) (**b**) **to go b.** *(bankrupt)* faire faillite
  2 *vt (pt & pp busted or bust)* (**a**) *(break)* bousiller (**b**) *(arrest)* coffrer
▶**bust out** *vi Fam (escape)* se tirer (**of** de)
▶**bust up** *vt sep Fam (disrupt) (event)* interrompre; *(relationship)* ficher en l'air
bustle ['bʌsəl] **1** *n (commotion)* animation *f*
  2 *vi* **to b. (about)** s'activer, s'affairer
bust-up ['bʌstʌp] *n Fam (dispute)* engueulade *f*; *(of relationship)* fin *f*; **to have a b.** *(argue)* s'engueuler
busy ['bɪzɪ] **1** *adj* (**a**) *(person)* occupé(e); *(day, week)* chargé(e); *(road)* à grande circulation; **to keep sb b.** occuper qn; **to keep oneself b.** s'occuper; **to be b. doing sth** être occupé(e) à faire qch; **the train was very b.** il y avait beaucoup de monde dans le train (**b**) *Am (telephone line)* occupé(e); **I keep getting the b. signal** ça sonne toujours occupé
  2 *vt (pt & pp busied)* **to b. oneself with sth** s'occuper à qch
busybody ['bɪzɪbɒdɪ] *(pl busybodies)* *n Fam* fouineur(euse) *m,f*
but [bʌt] **1** *prep (except)* sauf, à part; **any day b. tomorrow** n'importe quand sauf demain; **it's nothing b. prejudice** ce ne sont rien que des préjugés; **she is anything b. stupid** elle est loin d'être bête; **b. for** sans; **the last b. one** l'avant-dernier(ère) *m,f*; **the next b. one** le (la) deuxième
  2 *adv Formal* seulement; **he is b. a child** ce n'est qu'un enfant; **had I b. known!** si (seulement) j'avais su!; **one can b. try** on peut toujours essayer
  3 *conj* mais; **not once b. twice** pas une fois, mais deux; **I told her to do it b. she refused** je lui ai dit de le faire mais elle a refusé; **b. I tell you I saw it!** mais puisque je te dis que je l'ai vu!; **I had no choice b. to go** je n'ai pas pu faire autrement que d'y aller; **what could I do b. invite him?** comment pouvais-je faire autrement que de l'inviter?
  4 *n* **no buts!** il n'y a pas de "mais" qui tienne!
butane ['bju:teɪn] *n* butane *m*
butch [bʊtʃ] *adj Fam* hommasse
butcher ['bʊtʃə(r)] **1** *n also Fig* boucher(ère) *m,f*; **b.'s (shop)** boucherie *f*; **to go to the b.'s** aller chez le boucher *ou* à la boucherie
  2 *vt (animal)* abattre; *Fig (person, song)* massacrer
butchery ['bʊtʃərɪ] *n also Fig* boucherie *f*
butler ['bʌtlə(r)] *n* majordome *m*, maître *m* d'hôtel
butt [bʌt] **1** *n* (**a**) *(of rifle)* crosse *f*; *(of cigarette)* mégot *m*; *Fig* **to be the b. of a joke** être la cible d'une plaisanterie (**b**) *Am Fam (buttocks)* fesses *fpl*
  2 *vt (hit with head)* donner un coup de tête à
▶**butt in** *vi (interrupt)* intervenir
butter ['bʌtə(r)] **1** *n* beurre *m*; **she looks as if b. wouldn't melt in her mouth** on lui donnerait le bon Dieu sans confession; **b. bean** = gros haricot blanc;

b. dish beurrier *m*; **b. knife** couteau à beurre; **b. mountain** montagne *f* de beurre
  2 *vt* beurrer
▶**butter up** *vt sep Fam (flatter)* passer de la pommade à
buttercup ['bʌtəkʌp] *n* bouton *m* d'or
butterfingers ['bʌtəfɪŋgəz] *n Fam* empoté(e) *m,f*
butterfly ['bʌtəflaɪ] *(pl butterflies)* *n* papillon *m*; *Fig* **to have butterflies (in one's stomach)** avoir l'estomac noué; **b. (stroke)** *(in swimming)* (brasse *f)* papillon *m*
buttermilk ['bʌtəmɪlk] *n* babeurre *m*
butterscotch ['bʌtəskɒtʃ] *n* caramel *m* dur au beurre
buttock ['bʌtək] *n* fesse *f*
button ['bʌtən] **1** *n* (**a**) *(on shirt, machine)* bouton *m*; **b. mushroom** petit champignon *m* de Paris (**b**) *Am (badge)* badge *m*
  2 *vt (shirt, dress)* boutonner; *Fam* **b. it!** la ferme!
▶**button up** *vt sep (shirt, dress)* boutonner
buttonhole ['bʌtənhəʊl] **1** *n* boutonnière *f*
  2 *vt (detain)* coincer
buttress ['bʌtrɪs] **1** *n Archit* contrefort *m*; *Fig* pilier *m*
  2 *vt Fig (support)* renforcer
buxom ['bʌksəm] *adj (plump)* plantureux(euse); *(full-bosomed)* à la poitrine généreuse
buy [baɪ] **1** *n* **a good/bad b.** une bonne/mauvaise affaire
  2 *vt (pt & pp bought* [bɔːt]*)* (**a**) *(purchase)* acheter; **to b. sb sth, to b. sth for sb** acheter qch à *ou* pour qn; **to b. sth from sb** acheter qch à qn; *Fig* **to b. time** gagner du temps; **he's bought it** *(has died)* il a passé l'arme à gauche (**b**) *Fam (believe)* avaler
▶**buy back** *vt sep (supplies)* faire des stocks de
▶**buy into** *vt insep (company, scheme)* acheter des parts de
▶**buy off** *vt sep Fam* acheter
▶**buy out** *vt sep Com* racheter la part de
▶**buy up** *vt sep (land, shares)* acheter; *(supplies)* faire des stocks de
buyer ['baɪə(r)] *n* acheteur(euse) *m,f*; **b.'s market** marché *m* demandeur
buy-out ['baɪaʊt] *n Com* rachat *m*
buzz [bʌz] **1** *n* (**a**) *(noise)* bourdonnement *m*; *(of plane)* vrombissement *m*; *Fam* **b. word** mot *m* à la mode (**b**) *Fam (phone call)* **to give sb a b.** passer un coup de fil à qn (**c**) *Fam (activity)* **I love the b. of London** j'adore l'animation de Londres (**d**) *Fam (thrill)* **to get a b. out of doing sth** prendre son pied à faire qch
  2 *vt Fam (on intercom)* appeler à l'Interphone®; *(on pager)* biper
  3 *vi (make noise)* bourdonner; *Fig* **to b. with excitement** *(of town)* bourdonner d'excitation; **my head was buzzing** j'avais la tête lourde; *Fam* **the party was really buzzing** la soirée était super animée
▶**buzz off** *vi Br Fam* se tirer
buzzard ['bʌzəd] *n* buse *f*
buzzer ['bʌzə(r)] *n (on intercom)* bouton *m* de l'Interphone®; *(on clock, oven)* sonnerie *f*
buzzing ['bʌzɪŋ] *n* bourdonnement *m*
by [baɪ] **1** *prep* (**a**) *(agent)* par; **he was arrested by the police** il a été arrêté par la police, la police l'a arrêté; **made by hand** fait(e) (à la) main; **a play by Shakespeare** une pièce de Shakespeare
  (**b**) *(with manner, means)* **by train/car/plane** en train/voiture/avion; **by doing sth** en faisant qch; **to pay by credit card** payer par carte de crédit; **to have a child by sb** avoir un enfant de qn; **to take sb by the hand/arm** prendre qn par la main/le bras; **to know sb by name/sight** connaître qn de nom/de vue; **to**

earn one's living by teaching gagner sa vie en enseignant
(**c**) *(close to)* près de; **by the fire** près du feu; **by the sea** au bord de la mer; **by the side of the road** sur le bord de la route
(**d**) *(via)* par; **by land/sea** par terre/mer
(**e**) *(past)* **to walk by sb/sth** passer devant qn/qch; **to drive by sb/sth** passer devant qn/qch (en voiture)
(**f**) *(at or before)* **she should be here by now** elle devrait être ici à l'heure qu'il est; **it'll be ready by tomorrow** ce sera prêt pour demain; **by 1980 they were all dead** en 1980 ils étaient déjà tous morts; **by then it was too late** il était déjà trop tard
(**g**) *(during)* **by day/night** de jour/nuit
(**h**) *(with measurements, quantities, numbers)* **to divide/multiply by three** diviser/multiplier par trois; **3 metres by 2** 3 mètres sur 2; **to sell sth by weight** vendre qch au poids; **one by one** un par un
(**i**) *(according to)* **to go by appearances** se fier aux apparences; **to call sb by their first name** appeler qn par son prénom; **what do you mean by that?** qu'est-ce que tu entends par là?
(**j**) *(with reflexive pronouns)* **by oneself** tout(e) seul(e)
(**k**) *(as a result of)* **by accident/chance/mistake** par accident/hasard/erreur

2 *adv* (**a**) **by and large** dans l'ensemble; **by the way,...** au fait,... (**b**) *(past)* **to go/walk by** passer; **to drive by** passer (en voiture)
bye [baɪ] *exclam Fam* au revoir!, salut!; **b. for now!** à bientôt!
bye-bye ['baɪ'baɪ] *exclam Fam* au revoir!, salut!
by-election ['baɪɪlekʃən] *n Pol* élection *f* partielle
Byelorussia [bɪeləʊ'rʌʃə] = **Belarus**
Byelorussian [bɪeləʊ'rʌʃən] **1** *n* Biélorusse *mf*
2 *adj* biélorusse
bygone ['baɪgɒn] **1** *n* **let bygones be bygones** oublions le passé
2 *adj* révolu(e); **in b. days** autrefois
by-line ['baɪlaɪn] *n (in newspaper)* signature *f*
bypass ['baɪpɑːs] **1** *n* (**a**) *(road)* rocade *f* (**b**) *(heart operation)* pontage *m*
2 *vt (of road) also Fig* contourner; *(middleman)* court-circuiter
by-product ['baɪprɒdʌkt] *n* sous-produit *m*, dérivé *m*;
bystander ['baɪstændə(r)] *n* passant(e) *m,f*
byte [baɪt] *n Comput* octet *m*
byway ['baɪweɪ] *n (road)* petite route *f*
byword ['baɪwɜːd] *n* **to be a b. for** être synonyme de
Byzantine [bɪ'zæntaɪn] *adj also Fig* byzantin(e)

C¹, c¹ [siː] *n* (**a**) *(letter)* C, c *m inv* (**b**) *Mus* do *m*, ut *m* (**c**) *Sch (grade)* **to get a C** *(in exam)* avoir mention passable; *(in homework, essay)* ≃ avoir 10 ou 11 sur 20

C² (**a**) *(abbr* **centigrade)** C (**b**) *(abbr* **century)** s.; **C16** XVIᵉ s.

c², ca *(abbr* **circa)** *(approximately)* env.; *(with dates)* vers

CAB [siːeɪˈbiː] *n (abbr* **Citizens' Advice Bureau)** = organisme bénévole britannique de conseil, notamment en matière juridique et sociale

cab [kæb] *n* (**a**) *(taxi)* taxi *m*; **c. driver** chauffeur(euse) *m,f* de taxi (**b**) *(of train, lorry)* cabine *f*

cabaret [ˈkæbəreɪ] *n* cabaret *m*; **c. artist** artiste *mf* de cabaret

cabbage [ˈkæbɪdʒ] *n* chou *m*; **red c.** chou *m* rouge; **c. white** *(butterfly)* piéride *f* du chou

cabbie, cabby [ˈkæbɪ] *(pl* **cabbies)** *n Fam* (chauffeur *m* de) taxi *m*

cabin [ˈkæbɪn] *n (of ship, plane)* cabine *f*; *(hut)* cabane *f*; **c. boy** *(on ship)* mousse *m*; **c. crew** *(on plane)* équipage *m*

cabinet [ˈkæbɪnɪt] *n* (**a**) *(piece of furniture)* meuble *m* (à tiroirs); *(with glass front)* vitrine *f* (**b**) *Pol* cabinet *m*; **c. meeting** ≃ Conseil *m* des ministres; **c. minister** ministre *m*, membre *m* du cabinet

cabinet-maker [ˈkæbɪnɪtmeɪkə(r)] *n* ébéniste *mf*

cable [ˈkeɪbəl] **1** *n (electrical) & Tel* câble *m*; **c. car** téléphérique *m*; **c. (television)** *(télévision f* par) câble *m*; *Comput* **c. modem** modem-câble *m*
2 *vt (message)* câbler; **to c. sb** envoyer un câble à qn

caboodle [kəˈbuːdəl] *n Fam* **the whole (kit and) c.** tout le bazar *ou* bataclan

cacao [kəˈkɑːəʊ] *n (plant)* cacaotier *m*, cacaoyer *m*; **c. bean** fève *f* de cacao

cache [kæʃ] *n* (**a**) *(of drugs, arms)* cache *f* (**b**) *Comput* antémémoire *f*, mémoire-cache *f*

cack-handed [kækˈhændɪd] *adj Fam* maladroit(e)

cackle [ˈkækəl] **1** *n* (**a**) *(of hen)* caquet *m* (**b**) *Fam (talking)* caquetage *m*; *(laugh)* gloussement *m*
2 *vi* (**a**) *(of hen)* caqueter (**b**) *Fam (laugh)* glousser

cacophonous [kəˈkɒfənəs] *adj* cacophonique

cactus [ˈkæktəs] *(pl* **cacti** [ˈkæktaɪ] *or* **cactuses)** *n* cactus *m*

CAD [kæd] *n Comput (abbr* **computer-aided design, computer-assisted design)** CAO *f*

cad *n Br Fam Old-fashioned* mufle *m*

cadaver [kəˈdævə(r)] *n Formal* cadavre *m*

cadaverous [kəˈdævərəs] *adj* cadavérique

caddie [ˈkædɪ] *n (in golf)* caddie *m*

caddy [ˈkædɪ] *(pl* **caddies)** *n* **(tea) c.** boîte *f* à thé

cadence [ˈkeɪdəns] *n* cadence *f*, rythme *m*

cadet [kəˈdet] *n Mil* élève *m* officier; **c. corps** peloton *m* de préparation militaire

cadge [kædʒ] *vt Fam* quémander (**from** *or* **off** à); **to c. a meal off** *or* **from sb** se faire inviter à manger par qn; **can I c. a lift from you?** tu me déposes?

cadmium [ˈkædmɪəm] *n Chem* cadmium *m*

Caesarean, Caesarian [sɪˈzeərɪən] *n* C. **(section)** césarienne *f*

Caesar salad [ˈsiːsəˈsæləd] *n Culin* = salade à base de romaine, de croûtons et d'une vinaigrette additionnée d'œuf

café, cafe [ˈkæfeɪ] *n* café *m*

Café

En Grande-Bretagne, le mot "café" désigne une sorte de snack où l'on peut prendre un repas léger et boire du thé ou du café.

---

cafeteria [kæfɪˈtɪərɪə] *n* cafétéria *f*

cafetiere [kæfəˈtjeə(r)] *n* cafetière *f* (à piston)

caff [kæf] *n Br Fam* bistro *m*

caffeine [ˈkæfiːn] *n* caféine *f*; **c. free** décaféiné(e)

cage [keɪdʒ] **1** *n (for bird, animal)* cage *f*; *(of lift)* cabine *f*
2 *vt* mettre en cage; **to feel caged in** se sentir prisonnier (ère)

cagey [ˈkeɪdʒɪ] *adj (evasive)* évasif(ive) (**about** sur); *(cautious)* prudent(e)

cagoule [kəˈguːl] *n* K-way® *m inv*

cahoots [kəˈhuːts] *npl Fam* **to be in c. (with sb)** être de mèche (avec qn)

CAI [siːeɪˈaɪ] *n Comput (abbr* **computer-aided instruction, computer-assisted instruction)** EAO *m*

cairn [ˈkeən] *n* cairn *m*

Cairo [ˈkaɪrəʊ] *n* Le Caire

cajole [kəˈdʒəʊl] *vt* enjôler; **to c. sb into doing sth** amadouer qn pour qu'il fasse qch

cake [keɪk] *n* (**a**) *(food)* gâteau *m*; *(pastry)* petit gâteau *m*; **c. shop** pâtisserie *f*; **c. tin** moule *m* à gâteau (**b**) *(of soap)* pain *m* (**c**) *(idioms)* **it's a piece of c.** c'est du gâteau; *Prov* **you can't have your c. and eat it** on ne peut pas avoir le beurre et l'argent du beurre; *Am Fam* **that really takes the c.!** ça, c'est le bouquet!
2 *vt* **her shoes were caked with mud** ses chaussures étaient couvertes de boue

CAL [kæl] *n Comput (abbr* **computer-aided learning, computer-assisted learning)** EAO *m*

calamity [kəˈlæmɪtɪ] *(pl* **calamities)** *n* calamité *f*

calcium [ˈkælsɪəm] *n* calcium *m*

calculate ['kælkjʊleɪt] **1** vt calculer; (consequences, risk) évaluer; **his remark was calculated to shock** sa remarque était destinée à choquer **2** vi **to c. on sth** compter sur qch; **to c. on doing sth** compter faire qch

calculated ['kælkjʊleɪtɪd] adj (risk) calculé(e); (crime) prémédité(e)

calculating ['kælkjʊleɪtɪŋ] adj calculateur(trice)

calculation [kælkjʊ'leɪʃən] n calcul m

calculator ['kælkjʊleɪtə(r)] n calculatrice f

calculus ['kælkjʊləs] n Math calcul m

calendar ['kælɪndə(r)] n calendrier m; **c. month** mois m civil; **c. year** année f civile

calf¹ [kɑːf] (pl **calves** [kɑːvz]) n (animal) veau m; **the cow is in** or **with c.** la vache est pleine; **Fig to kill the fatted c.** tuer le veau gras

calf² (pl **calves** [kɑːvz]) n (of leg) mollet m

calfskin ['kɑːfskɪn] n veau m

caliber Am = **calibre**

calibrate ['kælɪbreɪt] vt étalonner, calibrer

calibre, Am **caliber** ['kælɪbə(r)] n also Fig calibre m

calico ['kælɪkəʊ] n calicot m

California [kælɪ'fɔːnɪə] n la Californie

call [kɔːl] **1** n (**a**) (shout) appel m, cri m (**b**) (appeal) appel m (**for** à); **a c. to arms** un appel aux armes (**c**) (on phone) appel m, coup m de téléphone; **to give sb a c.** passer un coup de téléphone à qn; **to make a c.** passer un coup de téléphone ou de fil; **to return sb's c.** rappeler qn; **c. centre** centre m d'appels; **c. girl** call-girl f (**d**) (visit) visite f; **to pay a c. on sb** rendre visite à qn (**e**) (demand) demande f; **there are a lot of calls on my time** je suis très pris; **there's not much c. for it** il n'y a pas beaucoup de demande; **there's no c. for that kind of language!** inutile d'être impoli!; **to be on c.** (of doctor) être de garde **2** vt (**a**) (shout to) appeler (**b**) (summon) appeler; **he's been called away** il a dû s'absenter; **he called me over to show me something** il m'a appelé pour que je vienne voir quelque chose; **to c. a meeting** décider d'organiser une réunion; **to c. a strike** appeler à la grève; **to c. sb's attention to sth** attirer l'attention de qn sur qch (**c**) (on phone) appeler, téléphoner à; (taxi) appeler (**d**) (name) appeler; **she's called Katy** elle s'appelle Katy; **to c. sb names** injurier qn; **to c. sb a liar/a thief** traiter qn de menteur/de voleur; **c. yourself a computer expert!** et moi qui te croyais bon en informatique!; **let's c. it £10** disons (que ce sera) 10 livres; **do you c. that clean?** tu trouves vraiment que c'est propre?; **let's c. it a day** assez pour aujourd'hui **3** vi (**a**) (shout) appeler; **to c. to sb** appeler qn; **to c. for help** appeler au secours ou à l'aide (**b**) (on phone) appeler, téléphoner; **to c. for an ambulance** appeler une ambulance; **who's calling?** qui est à l'appareil? (**c**) (visit) passer; **this train will c. at York and Peterborough** ce train s'arrêtera à York et Peterborough

►**call back** vt sep & vi rappeler

►**call for** vt insep (**a**) (require) nécessiter; **this calls for a celebration!** il faut fêter ou arroser ça!; **that wasn't called for!** c'était parfaitement déplacé! (**b**) (demand) réclamer (**c**) Br (collect) (person) passer chercher; (object) passer prendre

►**call in 1** vt sep (doctor, police) appeler, faire venir; (expert) faire appel à **2** vi (visit) passer (**on sb** chez qn)

►**call off** vt sep (**a**) (cancel) (match, holiday) annuler; (search, strike) mettre fin à; (engagement) rompre (**b**) (dog, attacker) rappeler

►**call on** vt insep (**a**) (request) **to c. on sb to do sth** (urgently) demander instamment à qn de faire qch; (politely) inviter qn à faire qch (**b**) (visit) rendre visite à

►**call out 1** vt sep (**a**) (doctor, plumber, troops) appeler; **to c. sb out on strike** donner l'ordre de grève à qn (**b**) (shout) appeler **2** vi (shout) crier

►**call up** vt sep (**a**) (on phone) appeler, téléphoner à (**b**) (memory, image) évoquer (**c**) Mil appeler (sous les drapeaux)

callbox ['kɔːlbɒks] n cabine f téléphonique

caller [kɔːlə(r)] n (visitor) visiteur(euse) m,f; (on phone) correspondant(e) m,f; **next c.,** please appel suivant, s'il vous plaît; **c. identification, c. ID** identification f d'appel

calligraphy [kə'lɪɡrəfɪ] n calligraphie f

calling ['kɔːlɪŋ] n (vocation) vocation f

callipers ['kælɪpəz] npl (**a**) (for legs) attelles fpl (**b**) (measuring device) compas m

callisthenics [kælɪs'θenɪks] n gymnastique f rythmique

callous ['kæləs] adj dur(e)

call-up ['kɔːlʌp] n Mil appel m (sous les drapeaux); **c. papers** ordre m d'incorporation

callus ['kæləs] n cal m

calm [kɑːm] **1** n calme m; also Fig **a dead c.** un calme plat; also Fig **the c. before the storm** le calme qui précède la tempête **2** adj calme, tranquille; (sea) calme; **to keep c.** rester calme; **to grow calmer** se calmer **3** vt calmer, apaiser; **to c. one's nerves** se calmer

►**calm down 1** vt sep calmer **2** vi se calmer

calmly ['kɑːmlɪ] adv calmement

Calor Gas® ['kæləˈɡæs] n butane m

calorie ['kælərɪ] n calorie f

calumny ['kæləmnɪ] (pl **calumnies**) n calomnie f

calve [kɑːv] vi (of cow) vêler

calves [kɑːvz] pl of **calf¹, calf²**

calypso [kə'lɪpsəʊ] (pl **calypsos**) n Mus calypso m

CAM [sɪː'eɪ'em] n Comput (abbr computer-aided manufacture, computer-assisted manufacture) FAO f

cam [kæm] n Tech came f

Cambodia [kæm'bəʊdɪə] n le Cambodge

Cambodian [kæm'bəʊdɪən] **1** n Cambodgien(enne) m,f **2** adj cambodgien(enne)

camcorder ['kæmkɔːdə(r)] n Caméscope® m

came [keɪm] pt of **come**

camel ['kæməl] n chameau m; (female) chamelle f; **c. coat** manteau m en poil de chameau; **c. driver** chamelier m

camelhair ['kæməlheə(r)] n poil m de chameau

camellia [kə'miːlɪə] n camélia m

cameo ['kæmɪəʊ] (pl **cameos**) n (**a**) (jewellery) camée m; **c. brooch** camée (**b**) (in film) **c. (role)** brève apparition f (d'un acteur connu)

camera ['kæmərə] n (photographic) appareil photo m; TV & Cin caméra f; **TV off c.** hors champ;

on c. à l'écran; **c. crew** équipe *f* de prise de vue (**b**) *Law* **in c.** à huis clos
cameraman ['kæmərəmən] *n* cameraman *m*
Cameroon [kæmə'ru:n] *n* le Cameroun
camisole ['kæmɪsəʊl] *n* caraco *m*, *Can & Suisse* camisole *f*
camomile ['kæməmaɪl] *n* camomille *f*; **c. tea** camomille *f*
camouflage ['kæməflɑ:ʒ] **1** *n also Fig* camouflage *m* **2** *vt also Fig* camoufler
camp¹ [kæmp] **1** *n* camp *m*, campement *m*; **c. bed** lit *m* de camp; **c. site** *(establishment)* (terrain *m* de) camping *m*; *(in general)* campement *m* **2** *vi* **to c. (out)** camper
camp² *adj* (**a**) *(effeminate)* efféminé(e) (**b**) *(theatrical)* *(person)* cabotin(e); *(behaviour, manner)* théâtral(e) (**c**) *(in dubious taste)* kitsch *inv*
campaign [kæm'peɪn] **1** *n* campagne *f* **2** *vi* faire campagne (**for/against** pour/contre)
campaigner [kæm'peɪnə(r)] *n* militant(e) *m,f*; **to be a c. for/against sth** faire campagne pour/contre qch
camper ['kæmpə(r)] *n (person)* campeur(euse) *m,f*; *(vehicle)* camping-car *m*
campfire ['kæmpfaɪə(r)] *n* feu *m* de camp
camphor ['kæmfə(r)] *n* camphre *m*
camping ['kæmpɪŋ] *n* camping *m*; **to go c.** faire du camping; **c. site** (terrain *m* de) camping *m*
campus ['kæmpəs] *n* campus *m*
camshaft ['kæmʃɑ:ft] *n Aut* arbre *m* à cames
can¹ [kæn] **1** *n* (**a**) *(of food)* boîte *f*; *(of drink)* can-(n)ette *f*; *(for petrol)* bidon *m*; *(of paint)* pot *m*; *Fig* **to open a c. of worms** mettre à jour toutes sortes d'histoires désagréables; **c. opener** ouvre-boîte *m* (**b**) *Am very Fam (toilet)* chiottes *fpl*; *(prison)* taule *f*, tôle *f* **2** *vt (pt & pp canned)* (**a**) *(fruit, meat)* mettre en boîte *ou* en conserve; *Fig* **canned laughter** *(on radio, TV)* rires *mpl* préenregistrés (**b**) *Am Fam* **c. it!** *(keep quiet)* la ferme!
can² [kən, *stressed* kæn]

Le verbe **can** n'a ni infinitif, ni gérondif, ni participe. Pour exprimer l'infinitif ou le participe on aura recours à la forme correspondante de **be able to** (**he wanted to be able to speak English; she has always been able to swim**). La forme négative est **can't**, qui s'écrit **cannot** dans la langue soutenue.

modal aux v (**a**) *(be able to)* pouvoir; **I c. go** je peux y aller; **I c. see/hear them** je les vois/entends; **we can't possibly do it** nous ne pouvons en aucun cas le faire; **he'll do what he c.** il fera ce qu'il pourra; **how c. you tell?** à quoi vois-tu ça?; **it can't be done** c'est impossible à faire (**b**) *(know how to)* savoir; **I c. swim** je sais nager; **c. you speak English?** parles-tu anglais? (**c**) *(indicating possibility)* pouvoir; **it c. get very hot here** il peut faire très chaud ici; **it can't have been easy for her** ça n'a pas dû être facile pour elle; **you CAN'T be serious!** tu n'es pas sérieux!; **what c. it be?** qu'est-ce que ça peut bien être? (**d**) *(with requests, permission)* pouvoir; **c. I ask you something?** je peux vous demander quelque chose?; **you can't smoke in here** on ne peut pas fumer ici
Canada ['kænədə] *n* le Canada
Canadian [kə'neɪdɪən] **1** *n* Canadien(enne) *m,f* **2** *adj* canadien(enne)
canal [kə'næl] *n* canal *m*

Canary [kə'neərɪ] *n* **the C. Islands, the Canaries** les *(îles fpl)* Canaries *fpl*
canary [kə'neərɪ] *(pl* **canaries**) *n* canari *m*; **c. yellow** jaune canari *inv*
cancel ['kænsəl] *(pt & pp cancelled, Am canceled)* **1** *vt* annuler; *(cheque)* faire opposition à **2** *vi* se décommander
►**cancel out** *vt sep* annuler; **to c. each other out** s'annuler
cancellation [kænsə'leɪʃən] *n* annulation *f*; **c. fee** frais *mpl* d'annulation
Cancer ['kænsə(r)] *n (sign of zodiac)* le Cancer; **to be (a) C.** être (du) Cancer; *Geog* **theTropic of C.** le tropique du Cancer
cancer ['kænsə(r)] *n (disease)* cancer *m*; **lung/skin c.** cancer *m* du poumon/de la peau; **c. research** cancérologie *f*
cancerous ['kænsərəs] *adj Med* cancéreux(euse)
candelabra [kændɪ'lɑ:brə] *n* candélabre *m*
candid ['kændɪd] *adj* franc (franche)
candidacy ['kændɪdəsɪ] *n* candidature *f*
candidate ['kændɪdeɪt] *n* candidat(e) *m,f* (**for** à); **to stand as a c.** poser sa candidature, se présenter
candidature ['kændɪdətʃə(r)] = **candidacy**
candidly ['kændɪdlɪ] *adv* franchement
candied ['kændɪd] *adj* glacé(e), confit(e); **c. peel** zeste *m* confit
candle ['kændəl] *n* bougie *f*; **he can't hold a c. to you** il ne t'arrive pas à la cheville; **it's not worth the c.** le jeu n'en vaut pas la chandelle
candlelight ['kændəllaɪt] *n* lumière *f* d'une bougie; **by c.** à la chandelle *ou* bougie
candlelit ['kændəllɪt] *adj* aux chandelles
candlestick ['kændəlstɪk] *n* bougeoir *m*; *(taller)* chandelier *m*
can-do ['kændu:] *adj* dynamique, entreprenant(e); **c. attitude** *or* **spirit** esprit *m* de battant *ou* de gagneur
candour ['kændə(r)] *n* franchise *f*
candy ['kændɪ] *n (pl* **candies**) *n Am (sweet)* bonbon *m*; *(sweets)* bonbons *mpl*; **c. bar** barre *f* chocolatée; **c. store** confiserie *f*
candyfloss ['kændɪflɒs] *n Br* barbe *f* à papa
cane [keɪn] **1** *n (of sugar, bamboo)* canne *f*, tige *f*; *(walking stick)* canne; *(for punishment)* verge *f*, baguette *f*; **to get the c.** recevoir des coups de verge *ou* de baguette; **c. furniture** meubles *mpl* en rotin; **c. sugar** sucre *m* de canne **2** *vt (beat)* frapper avec une verge *ou* une baguette
canine ['keɪnaɪn] **1** *n* (**a**) *(tooth)* canine *f* (**b**) *(animal)* canidé *m* **2** *adj* canin(e)
canister ['kænɪstə(r)] *n* boîte *f* (en métal); *(of gas)* bonbonne *f*
canker ['kæŋkə(r)] *n also Fig* chancre *m*
cannabis ['kænəbɪs] *n* cannabis *m*
cannery ['kænərɪ] *(pl* **canneries**) *n* conserverie *f*
cannibal ['kænɪbəl] *n* cannibale *mf*
cannibalize ['kænɪbəlaɪz] *vt* cannibaliser
cannon ['kænən] *(pl* **cannons** *or* **cannon**) *n* canon *m*; *Fig* **to be a loose c.** n'en faire qu'à sa tête; **c. fodder** chair *f* à canon
cannonball ['kænənbɔ:l] *n* boulet *m* de canon
cannot ['kænɒt] *see* **can**
canny ['kænɪ] *adj* rusé(e)
canoe [kə'nu:] *n* canoë *m*
canoeing [kə'nu:ɪŋ] *n* canoë-kayak *m*; **to go c.** faire du canoë-kayak

canoeist [kə'nuːɪst] n canoéiste mf
canon ['kænən] n (**a**) (religious decree) & Fig canon m;
c. law droit m canon (**b**) (priest) chanoine m
canonize ['kænənaɪz] vt Rel canoniser
canoodle [kə'nuːdəl] vi Hum se faire des mamours
canopy ['kænəpɪ] (pl canopies) n (above bed) baldaquin m; (outside shop) auvent m; (parachute) parachute m; (of tree branches) canopée f
cant [kænt] n (hypocrisy) langage m hypocrite
can't [kɑːnt] = can not
cantaloup(e) ['kæntəluːp] n melon m (cantaloup)
cantankerous [kæn'tæŋkərəs] adj revêche, acariâtre
canteen [kæn'tiːn] n (**a**) (restaurant) cantine f (**b**)
(water bottle) gourde f (**c**) (of cutlery) ménagère f
canter ['kæntə(r)] **1** n (on horse) petit galop m
2 vi (of horse) aller au petit galop; Fig to c. through a
speech expédier un discours; Fig to c. through an
exam réussir un examen haut la main
cantilever ['kæntɪliːvə(r)] n Tech poutre f en porte-à-
faux; c. bridge pont m cantilever
Cantonese [kæntə'niːz] **1** n (language) cantonais m
2 adj cantonais(e)
canvas ['kænvəs] n (**a**) (cloth) (grosse) toile f; under c.
(in tent) sous la tente; Naut sous voiles (**b**) Art toile
f
canvass ['kænvəs] **1** vt (**a**) Pol to c. sb faire campagne
auprès de qn (**b**) Com (consumers) sonder; Fig to c.
opinion sonder l'opinion
2 vi (**a**) Pol faire du porte-à-porte (dans le cadre
d'une campagne électorale) (**b**) Com faire du
démarchage
canvasser ['kænvəsə(r)] n Pol = personne qui fait du
porte-à-porte dans le cadre d'une campagne
électorale
canyon ['kænjən] n canyon m, cañon m
canyoning ['kænjənɪŋ] n Sport canyoning m
CAP [siːeɪ'piː] n (abbr Common Agricultural Policy)
PAC f
cap [kæp] **1** n (**a**) (hat) (without peak) bonnet m; (with
peak) casquette f; Sport to win a c. être sélection-
né(e) dans l'équipe nationale; Fig to go c. in hand
to sb se présenter chapeau bas devant qn; Prov if
the c. fits (wear it) qui se sent morveux se mouche
(**b**) (cover) (of bottle) capsule f; (of pen) capuchon m
(**c**) (for toy gun) amorce f (**d**) (contraceptive) diaphragme m
2 vt (pt & pp capped) (**a**) (cover) recouvrir (with de)
(**b**) to have a tooth capped se faire refaire l'émail
d'une dent (**c**) (surpass, do better than) surpasser;
that caps the lot! c'est le bouquet!; to c. it all,... pour
couronner le tout,.. (**d**) Sport to be capped for England être sélectionné(e) dans l'équipe d'Angleterre
(**e**) (spending) limiter
capability [keɪpə'bɪlɪtɪ] (pl capabilities) n capacité f
(to do sth de faire qch); it is beyond our capabilities
c'est au-dessus de nos moyens
capable ['keɪpəbəl] adj capable; to be c. of doing sth
être capable de faire qch; the business is in c. hands
l'affaire est entre de bonnes mains
capably ['keɪpəblɪ] adv avec compétence
capacious [kə'peɪʃəs] adj Formal vaste, spacieux(euse)
capacitor [kə'pæsɪtə(r)] n Elec condensateur m
capacity [kə'pæsɪtɪ] (pl capacities) n (**a**) (of container,
bus, theatre) & Elec capacité f; the stadium has a c. of
50,000 le stade peut accueillir 50 000 spectateurs;
full to c. plein(e); there was a c. crowd at the match
le stade était bondé pour le match (**b**) (aptitude) to

have a c. for sth être capable de qch; to be beyond
sb's c. dépasser les compétences de qn; to be within
sb's c. être dans les possibilités de qn; c. for work
capacité f de travail (**c**) (output) capacité f; at full c.
à plein (**d**) (role) in my c. as... en ma qualité de...;
they are here in an official c. ils sont ici à titre officiel
cape¹ [keɪp] n (cloak) pèlerine f, cape f
cape² n Geog cap m; the C. of Good Hope le cap de
Bonne-Espérance; C. Town Le Cap
caper¹ ['keɪpə(r)] n Culin câpre f
caper² **1** n (prank) cabriole f; what a c.! (fuss) quel
cirque!
2 vi to c. (about) faire des cabrioles
Cape Verde [keɪp'vɜːd] n le Cap-Vert
capillary [kə'pɪlərɪ] **1** (pl capillaries) n capillaire m
2 adj capillaire
capital ['kæpɪtəl] **1** n (**a**) (letter) majuscule f, capitale f
(**b**) c. (city) capitale f (**c**) Fin capital m; Fig to make c.
out of sth tirer parti de qch; c. assets actif m immobi-
lisé; c. expenditure dépenses fpl en capital; c. gains
tax impôt m sur les plus-values (en capital); c. goods
biens mpl d'équipement; c. investment investissement m de capitaux
2 adj (**a**) (letter) majuscule; c. T T majuscule; he's
rich with a c. R il est vraiment très riche (**b**) Law c.
crime or offence crime m capital ou puni de mort; c.
punishment peine f capitale (**c**) (important) capi-
tal(e); of c. importance d'une importance capitale
(**d**) Br Old-fashioned (splendid) extra inv
capitalism ['kæpɪtəlɪzəm] n capitalisme m
capitalist ['kæpɪtəlɪst] **1** n capitaliste mf
2 adj capitaliste
capitalization [kæpɪtəlaɪ'zeɪʃən] n Fin capitalisation f
capitalize ['kæpɪtəlaɪz] vt (**a**) Fin capitaliser (**b**) (initial letter) écrire avec une majuscule; (whole word)
écrire en majuscules
▶**capitalize on** vt insep profiter de, tirer parti de
Capitol ['kæpɪtəl] n Am Pol the C. le Capitole; C. Hill =
la colline du Capitole, à Washington, où se trouve le
Congrès américain

Capitol Hill

Ce nom désigne, par extension, le Congrès américain. Par exemple, "The proposed bill is in danger of
being rejected on Capitol Hill." ("La proposition de
loi risque d'être rejetée par le Congrès américain.")

capitulate [kə'pɪtjʊleɪt] vi capituler (to devant)
capon ['keɪpən] n Culin chapon m
cappuccino [kæpʊ'tʃiːnəʊ] (pl cappuccinos) n cappuccino m
caprice [kə'priːs] n caprice m
capricious [kə'prɪʃəs] adj capricieux(euse)
Capricorn ['kæprɪkɔːn] n (sign of zodiac) le Capricorne; to be (a) C. être (du) Capricorne; Geog theTropic of C. le tropique du Capricorne
capsicum ['kæpsɪkəm] n Culin poivron m
capsize [kæp'saɪz] **1** vt faire chavirer
2 vi chavirer
capstan ['kæpstən] n Naut cabestan m
capsule ['kæpsjuːl] n (of medicine) gélule f; (space) c.
capsule f spatiale
Capt (abbr Captain) Capt

captain ['kæptɪn] **1** *n* capitaine *m*
2 *vt* être le capitaine de; **he captained them to victory** il les a conduits à la victoire
captaincy ['kæptɪnsɪ] *n (in sport)* **during her c.** pendant qu'elle était capitaine
caption ['kæpʃən] *n* légende *f*
captivate ['kæptɪveɪt] *vt* fasciner
captivating ['kæptɪveɪtɪŋ] *adj* fascinant(e)
captive ['kæptɪv] **1** *n* captif(ive) *m,f*; **to be taken c.** être fait(e) prisonnier(ère)
2 *adj* captif(ive); **he had a c. audience** *(spellbound)* son auditoire était subjugué; *(had no choice but to listen)* son auditoire était forcé de l'écouter
captivity [kæp'tɪvɪtɪ] *n* captivité *f*; **in c.** en captivité
captor ['kæptə(r)] *n* ravisseur(euse) *m,f*
capture ['kæptʃə(r)] **1** *n* capture *f*; *(of town, enemy, position)* prise *f*
2 *vt (person, animal)* capturer; *(town, enemy, position)* prendre (**from** à); *(in chess)* prendre; *Fig (mood)* rendre; **to c. sb's imagination** parler à l'imagination de qn; **to c. the moment** saisir l'instant
car [kɑː(r)] *n* (**a**) *(automobile)* voiture *f*, automobile *f*; **by c.** en voiture; **c. bomb** voiture *f* piégée; **c. boot sale** = vente à la brocante où les vendeurs exposent leurs marchandises à l'arrière de leur voiture; **c. crash** accident *m* de voiture; **c. door** portière *f* de voiture; *Br* **c. hire**, *Am* **c. rental** location *f* de voitures; **c. industry** industrie *f* automobile; *Br* **c. park** parc *m* de stationnement, parking *m*; **c. phone** téléphone *m* de voiture; **c. pool** = groupe de personnes effectuant régulièrement un trajet dans la même voiture; **c. radio** autoradio *m* (**b**) *Am (rail wagon)* voiture *f*, wagon *m*
carafe [kə'ræf] *n* carafe *f*
caramel ['kærəməl] *n* caramel *m*
carat ['kærət] *n* carat *m*; **18-c. gold** or *m* (à) 18 carats
caravan ['kærəvæn] *n* caravane *f*; *(pulled by horse)* roulotte *f*; **c. holiday** vacances *fpl* en caravane; **c. site** camping *m* (pour caravanes)
caraway ['kærəweɪ] *n* carvi *m*, cumin *m* des prés; **c. seeds** graines *fpl* de carvi
carbohydrate [kɑːbəʊ'haɪdreɪt] *n* hydrate *m* de carbone; *(in food)* glucide *m*; **low-/high-c. diet** régime *m* hypoglucidique/hyperglucidique
carbolic [kɑː'bɒlɪk] *adj Chem* **c. acid** phénol *m*; **c. soap** ≃ savon *m* de Marseille
carbon ['kɑːbən] *n* carbone *m*; **c. copy** copie *f* (au carbone); *Fig* **she is a c. copy of her mother** c'est la copie conforme de sa mère; **c. dioxide** dioxyde *m* de carbone, gaz *m* carbonique; **c. credits** crédits *mpl* de carbone; **c. emissions** émissions *fpl* de carbone; **c. fibre** fibre *f* de carbone; **c. monoxide** monoxyde *m* de carbone; **c. paper** (papier *m*) carbone *m*
carbonated ['kɑːbəneɪtɪd] *adj* gazéifié(e); *(naturally)* gazeux(euse)
carbonize ['kɑːbənaɪz] *vt* carboniser
carbuncle ['kɑːbʌŋkəl] *n Med* furoncle *m*
carburettor, *Am* **carburetor** ['kɑːbjʊretə(r)] *n* carburateur *m*
carcase, carcass ['kɑːkəs] *n (of animal)* carcasse *f*
carcinogenic [kɑːsɪnə'dʒenɪk] *adj Med* carcinogène
card [kɑːd] *n* (**a**) *(for card game)* carte *f*; **to play cards** jouer aux cartes; **c. game** jeu *m* de cartes; **c. table** table *f* de jeux; **c. trick** tour *m* de cartes (**b**) *(with printed information)* carte *f*; *(postcard)* carte *f* (postale); *Pol* **c. vote** = scrutin où chaque délégué muni d'une carte vote pour la totalité des membres qu'il représente; **c.**

index *or* **file** fichier *m* (**c**) *(for payment, telephones)* carte *f* (**d**) *(cardboard)* carton *m* (fin) (**e**) *Comput* carte *f* (**f**) *(idioms)* **play your cards right and you could get promoted** si tu mènes bien ton jeu, tu seras peut-être promu; **to put one's cards on the table** jouer cartes sur table; **to have a c. up one's sleeve** avoir un atout dans son jeu; **it is** *Br* **on** *or Am* **in the cards that...** il est bien possible que...; *Br Fam* **to get one's cards** se faire virer
cardamom ['kɑːdəməm] *n* cardamome *f*
cardboard ['kɑːdbɔːd] *n* carton *m*; **c. box** (boîte *f* en) carton *m*; **c. city** = campement où les sans-abri vivent dans des cartons; *Fig & Pej* **c. characters** personnages *mpl* sans aucune profondeur
card-carrying ['kɑːdkærɪŋ] *adj* **c. member** adhérent(e) *m,f*
cardholder ['kɑːdhəʊldə(r)] *n (of credit card)* titulaire *mf*
cardiac ['kɑːdɪæk] *adj* cardiaque; **c. arrest** arrêt *m* cardiaque
cardigan ['kɑːdɪgən] *n* cardigan *m*
cardinal ['kɑːdɪnəl] **1** *n Rel* cardinal *m*
2 *adj* cardinal(e); *Fig* **it's a c. sin** c'est impardonnable
cardiograph ['kɑːdɪəgræf] *n* cardiographe *m*
cardiologist [kɑːdɪ'ɒlədʒɪst] *n* cardiologue *mf*
cardiology [kɑːdɪ'ɒlədʒɪ] *n* cardiologie *f*
cardiovascular [kɑːdɪəʊ'væskjʊlə(r)] *adj* cardiovasculaire
cardphone ['kɑːdfəʊn] *n* téléphone *m* à carte
cardsharp ['kɑːdʃɑːp], **cardsharper** ['kɑːdʃɑːpə(r)] *n* tricheur(euse) *m,f* professionnel(elle)
care [keə(r)] **1** *n* (**a**) *(worry)* souci *m*; **she doesn't have a c. in the world** elle n'a pas le moindre souci
(**b**) *(attention)* soin *m*; *(medical treatment)* soins *mpl* médicaux; **to put a lot of c. into sth** apporter beaucoup de soin à qch; **to drive without due c.** conduire imprudemment; **to take c. of** s'occuper de; **to take c. of oneself** savoir se débrouiller tout(e) seul(e); *(healthwise)* prendre soin de sa santé; **to take c. to do sth** faire bien attention à faire qch; **take c.!** *(goodbye)* à bientôt!; **take good c. of yourself** fais bien attention à toi; *Br* **c. in the community** = système de soins prodigués aux malades mentaux en dehors du milieu hospitalier
(**c**) *(protection)* soins *mpl*; *(of clothes, machine)* entretien *m*; **to put a child in c.** mettre un enfant à l'Assistance publique; **to be in** *or* **under sb's c.** avoir été confié(e) à qn; **write to me c. of Mrs Wallace** écrivez-moi chez Mme Wallace *ou* aux bons soins de Mme Wallace
2 *vt* (**a**) *(mind)* **I don't c. what he says** peu m'importe ce qu'il en dit; **I don't c. whether he likes it or not** peu m'importe que cela lui plaise ou non
(**b**) *(like)* **would you c. to come with me?** aimeriez-vous m'accompagner?
3 *vi* (**a**) *(be concerned)* se préoccuper, se soucier (**about** de); **that's all he cares about** c'est tout ce qui l'intéresse; **to c. about sb** *(be fond of)* aimer qn
(**b**) *(mind)* **I don't c.** ça m'est égal; **who cares?** qu'est-ce que ça peut faire?; **I could be dead for all they c.!** ils se moquent éperdument de ce qui peut m'arriver!; **I couldn't c. less** je m'en moque éperdument
▶**care for** *vt insep* (**a**) *(look after)* soigner (**b**) *(like)* aimer

career [kə'rɪə(r)] **1** n carrière f; **it's a good/bad c. move** c'est bon/mauvais pour ma/ta/etc carrière; **c. break** interruption f de carrière; **c. path** (strategy) plan m de carrière; (prospects) perspectives fpl de carrière; **careers officer** conseiller(ère) m,f d'orientation; **careers service** service m d'orientation professionnelle **2** vi **to c. (along)** aller à vive allure; **the car careered off the road** la voiture a quitté la route à vive allure
careerist [kə'rɪərɪst] n Pej carriériste mf
carefree ['keəfri:] adj insouciant(e)
careful ['keəful] adj (**a**) (cautious) prudent(e); **be c. of that step** fais attention à la marche; **(be) c.!** fais attention!; **to be c. to do sth** faire bien attention à faire qch; **she was c. not to mention his name** elle a bien fait attention à ne pas mentionner son nom; **be c. what you say** fais attention à ce que tu dis; **you can't be too c.** these days on n'est jamais trop prudent de nos jours (**b**) (thorough) (work, inspection) minutieux(euse); **after c. consideration** après mûre réflexion
carefully ['keəfəlɪ] adv (**a**) (cautiously) prudemment (**b**) (thoroughly) soigneusement, avec soin; (listen) attentivement; **c. worded** aux termes choisis (avec soin)
careless ['keəlɪs] adj (**a**) (negligent) négligent(e); (work) négligé(e); **to be c. about one's appearance** être négligé; **a c. mistake** une faute d'inattention, une étourderie; **a c. remark** une remarque inconsidérée (**b**) (unconcerned) insouciant(e)
carelessly ['keəlɪslɪ] adv (negligently) négligemment
carelessness ['keəlɪsnɪs] n (negligence) négligence f
carer ['keərə(r)] n (professional) aide mf à domicile; (relative) = personne s'occupant d'un parent malade ou âgé
caress [kə'res] **1** n caresse f **2** vt caresser
caretaker ['keəteɪkə(r)] n concierge mf, gardien(-enne) m,f; **c. government** gouvernement m intérimaire
careworn ['keəwɔ:n] adj usé(e) par les soucis
cargo ['kɑ:gəʊ] (pl cargoes or cargos) n cargaison f; **c. boat** or **ship** cargo m; **c. plane** avion-cargo m
Caribbean [kærɪ'bi:ən, Am kə'rɪbɪən] **1** n **the C. (Sea)** la mer des Caraïbes; **the C.** (region) la Caraïbe **2** adj caraïbe
caribou ['kærɪbu:] n caribou m
caricature ['kærɪkətjʊə(r)] **1** n caricature f **2** vt caricaturer
caricaturist [kærɪkə'tjʊərɪst] n caricaturiste mf
caries ['keəri:z] n Med carie f
caring ['keərɪŋ] adj (society, personality) humain(e); (parent) aimant(e); (atmosphere) chaleureux(euse); **the c. professions** les professions fpl médicales et paramédicales
carnage ['kɑ:nɪdʒ] n carnage m
carnal ['kɑ:nəl] adj charnel(elle)
carnation [kɑ:'neɪʃən] n œillet m
carnival ['kɑ:nɪvəl] n (celebration) carnaval m; (funfair) fête f foraine
carnivore ['kɑ:nɪvɔ:(r)] n carnivore m
carnivorous [kɑ:'nɪvərəs] adj carnivore
carob ['kærəb] n (fruit) caroube f; (tree) caroubier m
carol ['kærəl] n (Christmas) **c.** chant m de Noël; **c. service** = office religieux qui précède Noël

Carol service
Le "carol service" se tient juste avant Noël et se compose surtout de chants de Noël et de lectures de la Bible.

carouse [kə'raʊz] vi faire la fête
carousel [kærə'sel] n (**a**) Am (at funfair) chevaux mpl de bois, manège m (**b**) (at airport) carrousel m (pour bagages) (**c**) (for slides) magasin m
carp¹ [kɑ:p] (pl carp) n (fish) carpe f
carp² vi se plaindre (**at** de)
Carpathians [kɑ:'peɪθɪənz] npl **the C.** les Carpates fpl
carpenter ['kɑ:pɪntə(r)] n menuisier m; (on building site) charpentier m
carpentry ['kɑ:pɪntrɪ] n menuiserie f; (on building site) charpenterie f
carpet ['kɑ:pɪt] **1** n (**a**) (rug) & Fig (of flowers, snow) tapis m; (fitted) moquette f; **c. bombing** bombardement m intensif; **c. shampoo** shampo(o)ing m pour moquette; **c. slippers** pantoufles fpl (**b**) (idioms) **to pull the c. out from under sb** faire un tour de cochon à qn **2** vt (**a**) (with rug) recouvrir d'un tapis; (with fitted carpet) moquetter; Fig **to be carpeted with snow** être recouvert(e) de neige (**b**) Fam (tell off) sermonner
carpet-sweeper ['kɑ:pɪtswi:pə(r)] n balai m mécanique
car-pooling ['kɑ:pu:lɪŋ] n covoiturage m
carport ['kɑ:pɔ:t] n abri m pour voiture
carriage ['kærɪdʒ] n (**a**) (vehicle) voiture f (**b**) (of train) voiture f, wagon m (**c**) Br (of typewriter) chariot m; **c. return** retour-chariot m (**d**) Com (transport) transport m; (cost) frais mpl de port; **c. forward** (en) port dû; **c. free** franco de port; **c. paid** (en) port m payé (**e**) (bearing) (of person) port m
carriageway ['kærɪdʒweɪ] n chaussée f
carrier ['kærɪə(r)] n (**a**) (of disease, germs) porteur(-euse) m,f (**b**) Com (company, airline) transporteur m (**c**) (on bicycle) porte-bagages m inv (**d**) **c. (bag)** sac m (en papier ou en plastique)
carrion ['kærɪən] n charogne f
carrot ['kærət] n also Fig carotte f; **a c. and stick approach** la carotte et le bâton
carry ['kærɪ] (pt & pp carried) **1** vt (**a**) (transport, convey) porter; (goods, passengers) transporter; (electricity, fuel) acheminer; (gun, money) avoir sur soi; (a scar) avoir; (disease) être porteur(euse) de; **the current carried the raft out to sea** le courant a emporté le radeau au large; **to c. an image in one's head** avoir une image en tête; **to be carrying sb's child** (be pregnant) porter l'enfant de qn; Fig **to c. the can** porter le chapeau; Fig **she refused to c. the can for their mistake** elle refusa qu'ils lui fassent porter la responsabilité de leur erreur (**b**) (involve) (risk) comporter; **to c. a fine/penalty** être passible d'une amende/d'une peine; **to c. weight/authority** avoir du poids/de l'autorité (**c**) (develop) **to c. sth too far** pousser qch trop loin; **to c. an argument to its logical conclusion** aller au bout d'un raisonnement (**d**) (capture, win) **to c. all before one** (be successful) remporter tous les prix; (win support, approval) vaincre toutes les résistances; **his argument carried the day** son argument l'a emporté (**e**) (proposal, motion) voter

(**f**) *(of newspaper, news programme) (story)* faire état de; *(advertisement)* contenir (**g**) *Com (keep in stock)* vendre (**h**) **to c. oneself** *(behave)* se conduire (**i**) *Math* **c. two** et je retiens deux **2** *vi (of sound)* porter; **her voice carries well** elle a une voix qui porte bien
▸**carry away** *vt sep* (**a**) *(take away)* emporter (**b**) **to get carried away** *(excited)* s'emballer
▸**carry forward** *vt sep Fin* reporter; **carried forward** report, à reporter
▸**carry off** *vt sep* (**a**) *(take away)* emporter; *(prize)* remporter (**b**) *(do successfully)* **she carried it off (well)** elle s'en est bien sortie
▸**carry on 1** *vt sep (tradition)* perpétuer; *(business, trade)* exercer; *(correspondence)* entretenir; *(conversation)* poursuivre **2** *vi* (**a**) *(continue)* continuer, poursuivre; **to c. on doing sth** continuer de *ou* à faire qch (**b**) *Fam (behave badly)* mal se conduire; **I don't like the way she carries on** je n'aime pas ses façons (**c**) *Fam (have an affair)* avoir une liaison (**with** avec) (**d**) *(talk)* parler sans cesse (**about** de)
▸**carry out** *vt sep (plan, threat, decision)* mettre à exécution; *(experiment, test)* faire, effectuer; *(instructions)* exécuter

carryall ['kærɔ:l] *n Am* fourre-tout *m inv*
carrycot ['kærɪkɒt] *n* porte-bébé *m inv*
carry-on ['kærɪ'ɒn] **1** *n Fam* ramdam *m*; **what a c.!** quel cirque! **2** *adj* **c. items** *(on plane)* bagages *mpl* à main
carry-out ['kærɪaʊt] *n Am & Scot (meal)* repas *m* à emporter; *(restaurant)* = restaurant qui fait des plats à emporter
carsick ['kɑ:sɪk] *adj* **to be c.** être malade en voiture
cart¹ [kɑ:t] **1** *n (vehicle)* charrette *f*; *(trolley)* chariot *m*; *Fig* **to put the c. before the horse** mettre la charrue avant les bœufs **2** *vt Fam (carry)* trimballer
▸**cart off** *vt sep Fam* **to c. sb off** emmener qn
cart² *n (abbr* **cartridge**) cassette *f*
carte blanche ['kɑːt'blɑ̃ʃ] *n* **to give sb c. (to do sth)** donner carte blanche à qn (pour faire qch)
cartel [kɑ:'tel] *n Econ* cartel *m*
carthorse ['kɑ:thɔ:s] *n* cheval *m* de trait; *Fig* lourdaud(e) *m,f*
cartilage ['kɑ:tɪlɪdʒ] *n* cartilage *m*
cartographer [kɑ:'tɒɡrəfə(r)] *n* cartographe *mf*
cartography [kɑ:'tɒɡrəfɪ] *n* cartographie *f*
carton ['kɑ:tən] *n (of yoghurt, cream)* pot *m*; *(of milk, fruit juice)* brique *f*; *(of cigarettes)* cartouche *f*
cartoon [kɑ:'tu:n] *n (drawing)* dessin *m* humoristique; *(film)* dessin *m* animé; **c. (strip)** bande *f* dessinée
cartoonist [kɑ:'tu:nɪst] *n* dessinateur(trice) *m,f*
cartridge ['kɑ:trɪdʒ] *n* (**a**) *(for gun, pen, of film)* cartouche *f*; **c. belt** cartouchière *f* (**b**) **c. paper** papier *m* à cartouche
cartwheel ['kɑ:twi:l] *n* roue *f* de charrette; **to turn cartwheels** faire la roue
carve [kɑ:v] *vt (wood, stone, statue)* sculpter; *(name)* graver; *(meat)* découper
▸**carve out** *vt sep* **to c. out a career for oneself** faire carrière; **the company carved out a niche for itself** la société s'est taillé une place sur le marché
▸**carve up** *vt sep Fig (territory)* découper

carving ['kɑ:vɪŋ] *n* (**a**) *Art* sculpture *f* (**b**) **c. knife** *(for meat)* couteau *m* à découper
carwash ['kɑ:wɒʃ] *n* portique *m* de lavage automatique (de voitures); *(sign)* lavage automatique
cascade [kæs'keɪd] **1** *n* cascade *f* **2** *vi* tomber en cascade
case¹ [keɪs] *n* (**a**) *(instance, situation) & Med* cas *m*; **a c. in point** un cas d'espèce; **in c. of emergency/accident** en cas d'urgence/d'accident; **in c. he isn't there** au cas où il ne serait pas là; **I'll take it just in c.** je vais le prendre au cas où; **just in c. it rains** au cas où il pleuvrait; **in any c.** *(besides)* de toute façon; **in that c.** dans ce cas; **in such a c.** en pareil cas; **as the c. may be** suivant le cas; **if that's the c.** dans ce cas-(là), s'il en est ainsi; *Med* **c. history** antécédents *mpl*; **c. study** étude *f* de cas (**b**) *Law* affaire *f*; **the c. will be heard on 5 January** l'audience aura lieu le 5 janvier; **the c. for the defence** la défense; **the c. for the prosecution** l'accusation *f*; *Fig* **the c. for sb/sth** les arguments *mpl* en faveur de qn/qch; *Fig* **she has a good c.** elle a de bons arguments; **c. law** droit *m* jurisprudentiel
case² *n* (**a**) *(container) (for spectacles, cigarettes, musical instrument)* étui *m*; *(for jewellery)* écrin *m*; **(packing) c.** caisse *f*; **a c. of wine** une caisse de vin; **(display** *or* **glass) c.** vitrine *f* (**b**) *(suitcase)* valise *f*; *(briefcase)* porte-documents *m inv* (**c**) *Typ* **lower/upper c.** bas *m*/haut *m* de casse
casement ['keɪsmənt] *n* **c. (window)** fenêtre *f* à deux battants
case-sensitive ['keɪs'sensɪtɪv] *adj Comput* qui distingue les majuscules des minuscules
cash [kæʃ] **1** *n (coins, banknotes)* liquide *m*; *Fam (money in general)* sous *mpl*; **to pay (in) c.** payer en liquide *ou* en espèces; **c. on delivery** paiement *m* à la livraison; **c. and carry** *(shop)* magasin *m* de demi-gros; **c. in hand** fonds *m ou* argent *m* en caisse; **c. box** caisse *f*; **c. card** carte *f* de retrait; *Fig* **c. cow** vache *f* à lait; **c. crop** culture *f* commerciale; **c. desk** caisse *f*; **c. dispenser** *or* **machine** distributeur *m* automatique de billets; *Fin* **c. flow** trésorerie *f*; **c. price** prix *m* au comptant; **c. register** caisse *f* enregistreuse **2** *vt (cheque, postal order)* encaisser
▸**cash in on** *vt insep Fam* profiter de, tirer profit de
cashback ['kæʃbæk] *n Br (in supermarket)* = espèces retirées à la caisse d'un supermarché lors d'un paiement par carte de crédit
cash-book ['kæʃbʊk] *n* livre *m ou* journal *m* de caisse
cashew ['kæʃu:] *n* **c. (nut)** noix *f* de cajou
cashier [kæ'ʃɪə(r)] *n* caissier(ère) *m,f*
cashmere ['kæʃmɪə(r)] *n* cachemire *m*
cashpoint ['kæʃpɔɪnt] *n* distributeur *m* automatique de billets
casing ['keɪsɪŋ] *n Tech* boîtier *m*; *(of sausage)* boyau *m*
casino [kə'si:nəʊ] *(pl* **casinos**) *n* casino *m*
cask [kɑ:sk] *n* fût *m*, tonneau *m*
casket ['kɑ:skɪt] *n* (**a**) *(for jewellery)* coffret *m* (**b**) *(coffin)* cercueil *m*
Caspian Sea ['kæspɪən'si:] *n* **the C.** la mer Caspienne
cassava [kə'sɑ:və] *n* manioc *m*
casserole ['kæsərəʊl] *n (pot)* cocotte *f*; *(food)* ragoût *m*
cassette [kæ'set] *n* cassette *f*; **c. player** lecteur *m* de cassettes; **c. recorder** magnétophone *m* à cassettes
cassock ['kæsək] *n* soutane *f*

cast [kɑːst] **1** n (**a**) (of play, film) (actors) acteurs mpl; (list) distribution f; Cin & TV **c. and credits** générique f (**b**) (moulded object) moulage m; Med (plaster) **c.** plâtre m; Fig **c. of mind** tournure f d'esprit (**c**) **to have a c. in one's eye** (squint) avoir une coquetterie dans l'œil **2** vt (pt & pp cast) (**a**) (throw) (stone) jeter, lancer; (shadow, net, line) jeter; **to c. one's eyes over sth** parcourir qch des yeux; **to c. doubt on sth** jeter un doute sur qch, faire planer un doute sur qch; Fig **to c. light on sth** permettre de comprendre qch; **to c. one's mind back to sth** revenir sur qch, se rappeler qch; **to c. its skin** (of reptile) muer; **to c. a spell over sb** envoûter qn (**b**) **to c. one's vote (for)** voter (pour) (**c**) (film, play) faire la distribution de; **she was cast as** or **in the role of Desdemona** on l'a choisie pour le rôle de Desdémone (**d**) (metal, statue) couler; **c. iron** fonte f
▸**cast about, cast around** vi to c. about or around for sth chercher qch
▸**cast aside** vt sep (idea, prejudice) se défaire de
▸**cast away** vt sep **to be cast away** faire naufrage
▸**cast down** vt sep **to be cast down** être abattu(e) ou découragé(e)
▸**cast off 1** vt sep (clothes, chains) rejeter, enlever; (chains) se libérer de **2** (**a**) Naut larguer les amarres (**b**) (in knitting) arrêter les mailles
▸**cast on** vi (in knitting) monter les mailles
castanets [kæstə'nets] npl castagnettes fpl
castaway ['kɑːstəweɪ] n naufragé(e) m,f
caste [kɑːst] n (social rank) caste f
caster sugar ['kɑːstəʃʊgə(r)] n sucre m en poudre
castigate ['kæstɪgeɪt] vt Formal critiquer sévèrement
casting ['kɑːstɪŋ] **1** n (of play, film) distribution f, casting m **2** adj **c. vote** voix f prépondérante
cast-iron ['kɑːstaɪən] adj en ou de fonte; Fig (alibi, guarantee) en béton
castle ['kɑːsəl] **1** n château m; (in chess) tour f; Fig **to build castles in the air** bâtir des châteaux en Espagne **2** vi (in chess) roquer
cast-off ['kɑːstɒf] **1** n (garment) vieux vêtement m; (person) laissé-pour-compte (laissée-pour-compte) m,f **2** adj **c. clothing** vieux vêtements mpl
castor ['kɑːstə(r)] n (on furniture) roulette f
castor oil [kɑːstə'rɔɪl] n huile f de ricin
castrate [kæs'treɪt] vt châtrer, castrer
castration [kæs'treɪʃən] n castration f
casual ['kæʒʊəl] adj (**a**) (remark, glance) en passant (**b**) (relaxed, informal) décontracté(e); (conversation) à bâtons rompus; (clothes) sport inv (**c**) (careless) désinvolte (**d**) (meeting) fortuit(e) (**e**) (employment, worker) temporaire
casualization ['kæʒʊəlaɪ'zeɪʃən] Br **the c. of labour** la précarisation de l'emploi
casually ['kæʒʊəlɪ] adv (**a**) (remark, glance) en passant (**b**) (informally) avec décontraction; (dress) sport (**c**) (carelessly) avec désinvolture (**d**) (meet) par hasard
casualty ['kæʒʊəltɪ] (pl casualties) n victime f; **c. (department)** (service m des) urgences fpl
cat [kæt] n (**a**) (animal) chat m; (female) chatte f; **the big cats** les grands fauves mpl; **c. burglar** monte-en-

l'air m inv; **c.'s eye®** (on road) catadioptre m; **c. flap** chatière f; **c. litter** litière f pour chats (**b**) (idioms) **to play a c.-and-mouse game with sb** jouer au chat et à la souris avec qn; Fam **to be like a c. on a hot tin roof** or **on hot bricks** ne pas tenir en place; **to let the c. out of the bag** vendre la mèche; **to fight like c. and dog** être comme chien et chat; **to set the c. among the pigeons** jeter un pavé dans la mare; Fam **there isn't enough room to swing a c.** il n'y a même pas la place de se retourner; Fam **he thinks he's the cat's whiskers** il se croit sorti de la cuisse de Jupiter
cataclysm ['kætəklɪzəm] n cataclysme m
Catalan ['kætəlæn] **1** n (**a**) (person) Catalan(e) m,f (**b**) (language) catalan m **2** adj catalan(e)
catalogue, Am **catalog** ['kætəlɒg] **1** n catalogue m **2** vt inventorier
Catalonia [kætə'ləʊnɪə] n la Catalogne
catalyst ['kætəlɪst] n also Fig catalyseur m
catamaran [kætəmə'ræn] n catamaran m
catapult ['kætəpʌlt] **1** n (hand-held) fronde f, lance-pierre m; (on aircraft carrier) & Hist (weapon) catapulte f **2** vt catapulter; **to c. sb to stardom** propulser qn vers la gloire
cataract ['kætərækt] n (in river) & Med cataracte f
catarrh [kə'tɑː(r)] n inflammation f des muqueuses respiratoires
catastrophe [kə'tæstrəfɪ] n catastrophe f
catastrophic [kætə'strɒfɪk] adj catastrophique
catatonic [kætə'tɒnɪk] adj Med catatonique
catcall ['kætkɔːl] n sifflet m
catch [kætʃ] **1** n (**a**) (of ball) prise f au vol; **good c.!** bien attrapé! (**b**) (in fishing) prise f; (of a whole day) pêche f (**c**) (fastening) (of door) loquet m; (of window) loqueteau m; (of bracelet) fermoir m (**d**) (disadvantage) **where's the c.?** c'est quoi le truc ou le piège?; **it's a c.-22 situation** c'est un cercle vicieux **2** vt (pt & pp caught [kɔːt]) (**a**) (ball, thief) attraper; (fish) prendre; **caught you!** je t'y prends!; **to c. sb doing sth** surprendre qn en train de ou à faire qch; **you won't c. me doing that again** on ne m'y reprendra plus; **to be caught in a storm** être surpris(e) par un orage; **to c. the sun** (of room, garden) être ensoleillé(e); (of person) prendre des couleurs; Fam **to c. some rays** se dorer la pilule (**b**) (bus, train) prendre; (film) voir (**c**) (hear) saisir (**d**) (manage to find) trouver; **you've caught me at a bad time** tu arrives; mes téléphones au mauvais moment; **I'll c. you later!** on se voit plus tard! (**e**) (clothes) accrocher (on à); **to c. one's fingers in the door** se prendre ou se coincer les doigts dans la porte (**f**) (attention) attirer; **to c. sb's eye** attirer l'attention de qn (**g**) (illness) attraper; **I caught this cold from you** c'est toi qui m'as passé ce rhume; **you'll c. your death out there!** tu vas attraper la mort!; **to c. fire** or **light** prendre feu (**h**) (of blow, missile) atteindre; **the stone caught her on the arm** la pierre l'a atteinte au bras; Fam **you'll c. it!** (get into trouble) ça va être ta fête! **3** vi (**a**) (of fire) prendre

(**b**) *(in door)* se prendre, se coincer; *(on a nail)* s'accrocher
(**c**) *(of person)* **to c. at sth** s'accrocher à qch
▶**catch on** *vi* (**a**) *(of fashion)* prendre (**b**) *Fam (understand)* piger
▶**catch out** *vt sep (of difficult question)* piéger; *(of situation)* surprendre
▶**catch up 1** *vt sep* (**a**) *(reach)* rattraper (**b**) **to get caught up in sth** *(discussion)* être entraîné(e) dans qch; *(book, film)* être absorbé(e) par qch; *(traffic jam)* être pris(e) dans qch
2 *vi (close gap, get closer)* **to c. up with sb** rattraper qn; **to c. up with sth** *(news, gossip)* se mettre au courant de qch; **to c. up with one's work** se mettre à jour dans son travail; **his past caught up with him** son passé a resurgi
catch-all ['kætʃɔːl] *adj Fam* fourre-tout *inv*
catching ['kætʃɪŋ] *adj (disease, habit)* contagieux(euse)
catchment area ['kætʃmənt'eərɪə] *n (of school)* = zone desservie par une école; *(of hospital)* = zone desservie par un hôpital
catchphrase ['kætʃfreɪz] *n (political)* slogan *m*; *(of comedian)* formule *f* favorite
catchy ['kætʃɪ] *adj (tune, slogan)* facile à retenir
catechism ['kætəkɪzəm] *n* catéchisme *m*
categorical [kætɪ'ɡɒrɪkəl] *adj (denial, refusal)* catégorique; *(evidence)* formel(elle)
categorize ['kætɪɡəraɪz] *vt* étiqueter (**as** comme)
category ['kætɪɡərɪ] *(pl* **categories)** *n* catégorie *f*
cater ['keɪtə(r)] *vi* (**a**) *(provide food)* s'occuper de la nourriture; **to c. for** *(guests)* fournir le repas pour; *(event)* fournir le(s) repas de (**b**) **to c. for** *(needs, tastes)* satisfaire; **parties catered for** *(sign in restaurant)* noces et banquets
caterer ['keɪtərə(r)] *n* traiteur *m*
catering ['keɪtərɪŋ] *n (trade)* restauration *f*; **to do the c.** fournir le(s) repas; **c. school** école *f* hôtelière
caterpillar ['kætəpɪlə(r)] *n* chenille *f*; **c. track** *(on tank, tractor)* chenille
catfish ['kætfɪʃ] *n* poisson-chat *m*
cathartic [kə'θɑːtɪk] *adj* cathartique
cathedral [kə'θiːdrəl] *n* cathédrale *f*; **c. city** ville *f* épiscopale, évêché *m*
catheter ['kæθɪtə(r)] *n Med* cathéter *m*
cathode ['kæθəʊd] *n Elec* cathode *f*; **c. ray tube** tube *m* cathodique
Catholic ['kæθlɪk] *Rel* **1** *n* catholique *mf*; **to be a C.** être catholique
2 *adj* catholique
catholic ['kæθlɪk] *adj (wide-ranging)* éclectique
Catholicism [kə'θɒlɪsɪzəm] *n* catholicisme *m*
catkin ['kætkɪn] *n* chaton *m (d'arbre)*
catnap ['kætnæp] *n Fam* petit somme *m*
catsuit ['kætsuːt] *n* combinaison *f* collante
cattle ['kætəl] *npl* bétail *m*; **c. breeding** élevage *m* de bétail; **c. grid** = grille recouvrant une fosse et empêchant le passage du bétail; *also Fig* **c. market** marché *m ou* foire *f* aux bestiaux; **c. truck** bétaillère *f*
catty ['kætɪ] *adj Fam* vache; **c. remark** vacherie *f*
catwalk ['kætwɔːk] *n* podium *m*
Caucasian [kɔː'keɪʒən] **1** *n (white person)* Blanc (Blanche) *m,f (de type européen)*
2 *adj (in ethnology)* blanc (blanche) *(de type européen)*
Caucasus ['kɔːkəsəs] *n* **the C.** le Caucase
caucus ['kɔːkəs] *n Pol Br* = comité à l'intérieur d'un parti politique; *Am* caucus *m*

caught [kɔːt] *pt & pp of* **catch**
cauldron ['kɔːldrən] *n* chaudron *m*
cauliflower ['kɒlɪflaʊə(r)] *n* chou-fleur *m*; **c. cheese** chou-fleur au gratin; *Fam* **c. ear** oreille *f* en chou-fleur
cause [kɔːz] **1** *n* (**a**) *(origin)* cause *f*; **c. and effect** la cause et l'effet (**b**) *(reason)* raison *f*, motif *m*; **to have good c. for doing sth** avoir de bonnes raisons de faire qch; **and with good c.** et pour cause; **to give c. for complaint** donner lieu à des plaintes; **to give c. for concern** être inquiétant(e) (**c**) *(purpose, mission)* cause *f*; **to make common c. (with sb)** faire cause commune (avec qn); **it's all in a good c.** *(for charity)* c'est pour une bonne cause; *Fig* c'est pour la bonne cause
2 *vt* provoquer; *(trouble)* causer; **to c. sb grief** faire de la peine à qn; **to c. sb to do sth** faire faire qch à qn; **he caused the plan to fail** il a fait échouer le plan
causeway ['kɔːzweɪ] *n* chaussée *f (sur un marécage)*
caustic ['kɔːstɪk] *adj also Fig* caustique; **c. soda** soude *f* caustique
cauterize ['kɔːtəraɪz] *vt Med* cautériser
caution ['kɔːʃən] **1** *n* (**a**) *(prudence)* prudence *f*; **c.!** *(sign)* attention!; **to exercise c.** être prudent(e); **to throw c. to the wind(s)** abandonner toute prudence (**b**) *(warning)* avertissement *m*
2 *vt* (**a**) *(warn)* mettre en garde (**against sth** contre qch); **to c. sb against doing sth** déconseiller à qn de faire qch (**b**) *Sport* donner un avertissement à (**c**) *Law* **to c. sb** *(on arrest)* informer qn de ses droits; *(instead of prosecuting)* donner un avertissement à qn
cautionary ['kɔːʃənərɪ] *adj* **a c. tale** une histoire édifiante
cautious ['kɔːʃəs] *adj* prudent(e)
cautiously ['kɔːʃəslɪ] *adv* prudemment, avec prudence
cautiousness ['kɔːʃəsnɪs] *n* prudence *f*
cavalier [kævə'lɪə(r)] *adj* cavalier(ère)
cavalry ['kævəlrɪ] *n* cavalerie *f*
cave [keɪv] *n* grotte *f*; **c. dweller** *(contemporary)* troglodyte *m*; *(prehistoric)* homme *m* des cavernes; **c. paintings** peintures *fpl* rupestres
▶**cave in** *vi (of ground, structure)* s'affaisser; *Fig (stop resisting)* céder (**to** à)
caveman ['keɪvmæn] *n* homme *m* des cavernes
cavern ['kævən] *n* caverne *f*
cavernous ['kævənəs] *adj* immense
caviar(e) ['kævɪɑː(r)] *n* caviar *m*
cavity ['kævɪtɪ] *(pl* **cavities)** *n* cavité *f*; **c. wall insulation** isolation *f* des murs creux
cavort [kə'vɔːt] *vi* faire des cabrioles; *Fig* batifoler
caw [kɔː] **1** *n* croassement *m*
2 *vi* croasser
cayenne ['keɪ'en] *n* **c. (pepper)** (poivre *m* de) Cayenne *m*
CB [siː'biː] *n (abbr* **Citizens' Band**) CB *f*
CBE [siːbiː'iː] *n (abbr* **Commander of the (Order of the) British Empire**) = distinction honorifique britannique
CBI [siːbiː'aɪ] *n Br (abbr* **Confederation of British Industry**) = confédération du patronat britannique
cc [siː'siː] *n (abbr* **cubic centimetre(s)**) cm³
CCTV [siːsiːtiː'viː] *n (abbr* **closed-circuit television**) télévision *f* en circuit fermé
CD [siː'diː] *n (a) (abbr* **compact disc**) CD *m*, compact *m*; **CD burner** graveur *m* de CD; **CD player** lecteur *m* laser

ou de CD; **CD rack** casier *m* de rangement pour CD; **CD writer** graveur *m* de CD (**b**) *(abbr* **Corps Diplomatique**) CD *m*
CDI [si:di:'aɪ] *n Comput (abbr* **compact disc interactive)** CD-I *m inv*
CD-R [si:di:'ɑ:(r)] *n Comput* (**a**) *(abbr* **compact disc recorder)** graveur *m* de disque compact (**b**) *(abbr* **compact disc recordable)** CD-R *m*
Cdr *n (abbr* **Commander)** commandant *m*
Cdre *n (abbr* **Commodore)** contre-amiral *m*
CD-ROM [si:di:'rɒm] *n Comput (abbr* **compact disc read-only memory)** CD-ROM *m inv*
CD-RW [si:di:ɑ:'dʌbəlju:] *n Comput (abbr* **compact disc rewritable)** CD-RW *m*, CD *m* réinscriptible
cease [si:s] **1** *vt* cesser; **to c.** doing sth cesser de faire qch; **to c.** fire cesser le feu
2 *vi* cesser (**from doing sth** *or* **to do sth** de faire qch); **it never ceases to amaze me** ça ne laisse jamais de m'étonner
cease-fire ['si:faɪə(r)] *n* cessez-le-feu *m inv*
ceaseless ['si:slɪs] *adj* incessant(e), continuel(elle)
ceaselessly ['si:slɪslɪ] *adv* sans cesse, continuellement
cedar ['si:də(r)] *n (tree, wood)* cèdre *m*
cede [si:d] *vt Law (territory, property)* céder; **to c. a point** concéder un point
cedilla [sɪ'dɪlə] *n* cédille *f*
Ceefax® ['si:fæks] *n Br* = télétexte de la BBC
ceilidh ['keɪlɪ] *n* = bal folklorique écossais ou irlandais
ceiling ['si:lɪŋ] *n (of room) & Fig (limit)* plafond *m*; *Fig* **to hit the c.** piquer une crise; **c. price** prix *m* plafond
celeb [sə'leb] *n Fam* célébrité *f*; **celebs** les people *mpl*
celebrant ['selɪbrənt] *n Rel* officiant *m*
celebrate ['selɪbreɪt] **1** *vt (anniversary, win, occasion)* célébrer, fêter; *(mass)* célébrer
2 *vi* faire la fête
celebrated ['selɪbreɪtɪd] *adj* célèbre
celebration [selɪ'breɪʃən] *n* célébration *f*; **celebrations** *(festivities)* festivités *fpl*; **in c. of sth** pour célébrer *ou* fêter qch; **this calls for a c.!** il faut fêter *ou* arroser ça!
celebrity [sɪ'lebrɪtɪ] *(pl* **celebrities)** *n (person, fame)* célébrité *f*
celeriac [sɪ'lerɪæk] *n* céleri-rave *m*
celery ['selərɪ] *n* céleri *m*
celestial [sɪ'lestɪəl] *adj* céleste
celibacy ['selɪbəsɪ] *n (chastity)* absence *f* de rapports sexuels; *(by choice)* chasteté *f*; *Rel* célibat *m*
celibate ['selɪbət] *adj* **to be c.** ne pas avoir de rapports sexuels; *(by choice)* être chaste; *Rel* être célibataire
cell [sel] *n* (**a**) *(in prison, monastery) & Pol & Comput* cellule *f* (**b**) *esp Am Fam Tel (cellphone)* portable *m*, *Can* cellulaire *m*
cellar ['selə(r)] *n* cave *f*
cellist ['tʃelɪst] *n* violoncelliste *mf*
cello ['tʃeləʊ] *(pl* **cellos)** *n* violoncelle *m*
cellophane® ['seləfeɪn] *n Br* Cellophane® *f*
cellphone ['selfəʊn] *n esp Am Tel* (téléphone *m*) portable *m*, *Can* cellulaire *m*
cellular ['seljʊlə(r)] *adj* cellulaire; **c. phone** téléphone *m* cellulaire, *Can* cellulaire *m*
cellulite ['seljʊlaɪt] *n* cellulite *f*
celluloid® ['seljʊlɔɪd] *n* Celluloïd® *m*
cellulose ['seljʊləʊs] *n* cellulose *f*

Celsius ['selsɪəs] *adj* Celsius; **10 degrees C.** 10 degrés Celsius
Celt [kelt] *n* Celte *mf*
Celtic ['keltɪk] *adj* celte, celtique
cement [sɪ'ment] **1** *n* ciment *m*; **c. mixer** bétonnière *f*
2 *vt also Fig* cimenter
cemetery ['semətrɪ] *(pl* **cemeteries)** *n* cimetière *m*
cenotaph ['senətɑ:f] *n* cénotaphe *m*
censor ['sensə(r)] **1** *n* censeur *m*; **the censors banned the film** la censure a interdit le film
2 *vt* censurer
censorious [sen'sɔ:rɪəs] *adj* sévère (**of** vis-à-vis de)
censorship ['sensəʃɪp] *n* censure *f*
censure ['senʃə(r)] **1** *n* critique *f*; *Pol* **vote of c.** motion *f* de censure
2 *vt* blâmer; *(officially)* donner un blâme à
census ['sensəs] *n* recensement *m*
cent [sent] *n* cent *m*; *Am Fam* **I haven't got a c.** je n'ai pas un rond
centaur ['sentɔ:(r)] *n* centaure *m*
centenarian [sentɪ'neərɪən] *n* centenaire *mf*
centenary [sen'ti:nərɪ] *(pl* **centenaries)**, *Am* **centennial** [sen'tenɪəl] **1** *n* centenaire *m*
2 *adj* centenaire
center *Am* = **centre**
centigrade ['sentɪɡreɪd] *adj* centigrade; **10 degrees c.** 10 degrés centigrades
centigram(me) ['sentɪɡræm] *n* centigramme *m*
centilitre, *Am* **centiliter** ['sentɪli:tə(r)] *n* centilitre *m*
centime ['sɒnti:m] *n* centime *m*
centimetre, *Am* **centimeter** ['sentɪmi:tə(r)] *n* centimètre *m*
centipede ['sentɪpi:d] *n* mille-pattes *m inv*
central ['sentrəl] *adj* central(e); **C. London** le centre de Londres; **our hotel is quite c.** notre hôtel est dans le centre; **of c. importance** d'une importance capitale; **C. America** l'Amérique *f* centrale; **C. American** d'Amérique centrale; **c. bank** banque *f* centrale; **C. Europe** l'Europe *f* centrale; **C. European** d'Europe centrale; **C. European Time** heure *f* de l'Europe centrale; **c. government** gouvernement *m* central; **c. heating** chauffage *m* central, *Aut* **c. locking** verrouillage *m* centralisé; **c. nervous system** système *m* nerveux central; *Comput* **c. processing unit** unité *f* centrale; **c. reservation** *(on motorway)* terre-plein *m* central; *Am* **C. Standard Time** heure *f* du centre de l'Amérique du Nord
Central African Republic ['sentrəl 'æfrɪkən-rɪ'pʌblɪk] *n* République *f* centrafricaine
centralize ['sentrəlaɪz] *vt* centraliser
centrally ['sentrəlɪ] *adv (funded, administered)* de façon centralisée; **c. located** central(e); **the flat is c. heated** l'appartement a le chauffage central
centre, *Am* **center** ['sentə(r)] **1** *n* centre *m*; **in the c.** au centre; *Pol* **left/right of c.** du centre gauche/droit; **c. of gravity** centre de gravité; **c. of attention** centre d'attraction; **c. forward** *(in football)* avant-centre *m*; *Theat* **c. stage** centre *m* de la scène; *Fig* **his concerns always take c. stage** ses soucis à lui doivent toujours passer avant tout
2 *vt (attention, interest)* concentrer (**on** sur)
▶**centre on,** *Am* **center on** *vt insep* se concentrer sur; *(conversation)* tourner autour de
centrefold, *Am* **centerfold** ['sentəfəʊld] *n (in magazine)* double page *f* centrale détachable; *(nude photo)* photo *f* de pin-up

centrepiece, *Am* **centerpiece** ['sentəpi:s] *n (on table)* centre *m* de table; *(main attraction)* pièce *f* de résistance
centrifugal [sentrɪ'fju:gəl] *adj* centrifuge
century ['sentʃərɪ] *(pl* **centuries)** *n* siècle *m*; **the 19th c.** le 19ᵉ siècle
CEO [si:i:'əʊ] *n Com (abbr* **Chief Executive Officer)** P.-D.G. *m*
ceramic [sə'ræmɪk] **1** *n (material)* céramique *f*; **ceramics** *(art)* céramique *f*; *(objects)* céramiques *fpl*
2 *adj* en céramique
cereal ['sɪərɪəl] *n* céréale *f*; **(breakfast) c.** céréales *fpl*
cerebellum [serɪ'beləm] *n Anat* cervelet *m*
cerebral ['serɪbrəl] *adj (intellectual)* & *Anat* cérébral(e); *Med* **c. palsy** paralysie *f* cérébrale
cerebrum ['serɪbrəm] *n Anat* cerveau *m*
ceremonial [serɪ'məʊnɪəl] **1** *n* cérémonial *m*
2 *adj* de cérémonie
ceremonious [serɪ'məʊnɪəs] *adj* cérémonieux(euse)
ceremony ['serɪmənɪ] *(pl* **ceremonies)** *n* cérémonie *f*; **without c.** sans cérémonies; **to stand on c.** faire des cérémonies
cert [sɜ:t] *n Fam* **it's a (dead) c.** c'est garanti
certain ['sɜ:tən] *adj* (**a**) *(sure) (failure, victory)* certain(e), assuré(e); *(cure, solution)* infaillible; **I can't say for c.** je ne peux pas l'affirmer; **I'll tell you next week for c.** je vous le dirai la semaine prochaine sans faute; **to know sth for c.** être certain(e) de qch; **to be c. of sth** être sûr(e) *ou* certain(e) de qch; **they're c. of winning** ils sont assurés de gagner; **to make c. of sth** *(find out)* s'assurer de qch; *(be sure to get)* s'assurer qch; **he is c. to come** il viendra à coup sûr (**b**) *(particular)* certain(e); **a c. PhilipThomas** un certain Philip Thomas
certainly ['sɜ:tənlɪ] *adv* certainement; **c. not!** certainement pas!; **she's c. very clever, but...** certes elle est très intelligente, mais...
certainty ['sɜ:təntɪ] *(pl* **certainties)** *n (strong likelihood)* certitude *f*; *(conviction)* conviction *f*; **there is no c. that we will win** il n'est pas certain que nous gagnions; **to know sth for a c.** être certain(e) de qch
certifiable ['sɜ:tɪfaɪəbəl] *adj Fam (mad)* bon (bonne) pour l'asile
certificate [sə'tɪfɪkət] *n* certificat *m*; *(in education)* diplôme *m*
certify ['sɜ:tɪfaɪ] *(pt* & *pp* **certified)** *vt* (**a**) *(confirm)* certifier; **this is to c. that...** nous certifions par la présente que...; **to c. sb (insane)** déclarer que l'état de santé de qn nécessite l'internement psychiatrique (**b**) *(give certificate to)* délivrer un certificat à
certitude ['sɜ:tɪtju:d] *n* certitude *f*
cervical ['sɜ:vɪkəl, sə'vaɪkəl] *adj* **c. cancer** cancer *m* du col de l'utérus; **c. smear** frottis *m* vaginal
cervix ['sɜ:vɪks] *(pl* **cervices** ['sɜ:vɪsi:z]) *n Anat* col *m* de l'utérus
cessation [se'seɪʃən] *n* cessation *f*
cesspit ['sespɪt], **cesspool** ['sespu:l] *n* fosse *f* d'aisances; *Fig* cloaque *m*
Ceylon [sɪ'lɒn] *n Formerly* Ceylan
cf [si:'ef] *(abbr* **confer, compare)** cf
CFC [si:ef'si:] *(pl* **CFCs)** *n (abbr* **chlorofluorocarbon)** CFC *m*
CFO [si:ef'əʊ] *n Am Com (abbr* **Chief Financial Officer)** chef *m* comptable
Chad [tʃæd] *n* leTchad

chafe [tʃeɪf] **1** *vt (skin)* irriter; *(of shoes)* blesser
2 *vi (of skin)* être irrité(e); *(of shoes)* frotter (**against** contre); *Fig* **to c. at** *or* **against sth** *(resent)* s'irriter de qch
chaff [tʃɑ:f] **1** *n* balle *f*; *Fig* **to separate the wheat from the c.** séparer le bon grain de l'ivraie
2 *vt (tease)* taquiner
chaffinch ['tʃæfɪntʃ] *n* pinson *m*
chagrin ['ʃægrɪn] *n Formal* dépit *m*
chain [tʃeɪn] **1** *n* chaîne *f*; *(for medallion)* chaînette *f*; **in chains** enchaîné(e); **to pull the c.** *(in toilet)* tirer la chasse (d'eau); **c. gang** chaîne *f* de forçats; **c. letter** = lettre faisant partie d'une chaîne; **c. mail** cotte *f* de mailles; **c. reaction** réaction *f* en chaîne; **c. saw** tronçonneuse *f*; **c. store** magasin *m* à succursales multiples
2 *vt (prisoner)* enchaîner; *(dog, bicycle)* attacher avec une chaîne (**to** à)
▶**chain up** *vt sep (prisoner)* enchaîner; *(dog, bicycle)* attacher avec une chaîne (**to** à)
chain-smoke ['tʃeɪnsməʊk] *vi* fumer cigarette sur cigarette
chair [tʃeə(r)] **1** *n* (**a**) *(seat)* chaise *f*; *(armchair)* fauteuil *m* (**b**) *(chairperson)* président(e) *m,f*; **to be in the c.** présider (**c**) *Univ (of professor)* chaire *f*
2 *vt (meeting)* présider
chairlift ['tʃeəlɪft] *n* télésiège *m*
chairman ['tʃeəmən] *n (of meeting, political party)* président *m*; *(of company)* président-directeur *m* général, P-DG *m*
chairmanship ['tʃeəmənʃɪp] *n* présidence *f*
chairperson ['tʃeəpɜ:sən] *n* président(e) *m,f*
chairwoman ['tʃeəwʊmən] *n* présidente *f*
chalet ['ʃæleɪ] *n* chalet *m*
chalice ['tʃælɪs] *n Rel* calice *m*
chalk [tʃɔ:k] **1** *n* craie *f*; **they are like c. and cheese** c'est le jour et la nuit; *Fam* **not by a long c.** loin s'en faut
2 *vt (mark)* marquer à la craie; *(write)* écrire à la craie
▶**chalk up** *vt sep (victory)* remporter
chalkboard ['tʃɔ:kbɔ:d] *n Am* tableau *m* (noir)
chalky ['tʃɔ:kɪ] *adj (soil, complexion)* crayeux(euse); *(taste, texture)* plâtreux(euse)
challenge ['tʃælɪndʒ] **1** *n* défi *m* (**to** à); **to launch a leadership c.** chercher à conquérir la direction du parti; **the job presents a real c.** ce travail est très stimulant
2 *vt* (**a**) *(of job)* mettre à l'épreuve, être stimulant(e) pour; **to c. sb to do sth** défier qn de faire qch; **he challenged me to a fight** il m'a défié de me battre contre lui (**b**) *(statement, authority)* contester (**c**) *Mil* interpeller
challenger ['tʃælɪndʒə(r)] *n Sport* challenger *m*
challenging ['tʃælɪndʒɪŋ] *adj (job)* stimulant(e)
chamber ['tʃeɪmbə(r)] *n* (**a**) *(hall)* chambre *f*; *Pol* **Lower/Upper C.** Chambre *f* basse/haute; **C. of Commerce** Chambre *f* de commerce; **c. music** musique *f* de chambre; **c. pot** pot *m* de chambre (**b**) *Law* **chambers** *(of barrister, judge)* cabinet *m (au tribunal)* (**c**) *(of heart)* cavité *f*; *(of revolver)* chambre *f*
chambermaid ['tʃeɪmbəmeɪd] *n* femme *f* de chambre
chameleon [kə'mi:lɪən] *n* caméléon *m*
chamois *n* (**a**) ['ʃæmɪ] **c. (leather)** peau *f* de chamois (**b**) ['ʃæmwɑ:] *(deer)* chamois *m*
champ¹ [tʃæmp] *n Fam* champion(onne) *m,f*
champ² *vi Fig* **to c. at the bit** ronger son frein
champagne [ʃæm'peɪn] *n* champagne *m*

champion ['tʃæmpɪən] **1** *n* (*in sport, of cause*) champion(onne) *m,f*; **world/European c.** champion(onne) *m,f* du monde/d'Europe **2** *vt* défendre **championship** ['tʃæmpɪənʃɪp] *n* championnat *m*

chance [tʃɑːns] **1** *n* (**a**) *(luck)* hasard *m*; **by c.** par hasard; **to leave nothing to c.** ne rien laisser au hasard; **by any c.** par hasard; *Fam* **c. would be a fine thing!** ça ne risque pas! (**b**) *(opportunity)* occasion *f*; **to give sb a c.** donner une chance à qn; **she was trying to apologize but you didn't give her a c.** elle essayait de s'excuser mais tu ne lui en as pas laissé l'occasion; **now's your c.!** à toi de jouer!; **it's your last c.** c'est ta dernière chance; **to have an eye to the main c.** chercher à tirer profit de toutes les occasions (**c**) *(likelihood)* chance *f* (**of** de); **to have** *or* **stand a c. of doing sth** avoir des chances de faire qch; **he never stood a c.** *(of escaping, surviving etc)* il n'avait aucune chance de s'en tirer; **there's no c. of that happening** il n'y a aucune chance que cela se produise; **(the) chances are (that)...** il y a fort à parier que... (**d**) *(risk)* risque *m*; **to take a c.** prendre un risque **2** *adj (discovery)* accidentel(elle); *(meeting)* fortuit(e) **3** *vt* **to c. doing sth** prendre le risque de faire qch; *Fam* **to c. one's arm** tenter le coup **4** *vi* **to c. to do sth** faire qch par hasard
►**chance on, chance upon** *vt insep* tomber (par hasard) sur

chancellor ['tʃɑːnsələ(r)] *n* (**a**) *Univ Br* président(e) *m,f* honoraire; *Am* président(e) *m,f* (**b**) *Pol (in Austria, Germany)* chancelier *m*; *Br Pol* **C. (of the Exchequer)** Chancelier *m* de l'Échiquier, ≃ ministre *m* des Finances

chancy ['tʃɑːnsɪ] *adj Fam (risky)* risqué(e)

chandelier [ʃændə'lɪə(r)] *n* lustre *m*

change [tʃeɪndʒ] **1** *n* (**a**) *(alteration)* changement *m*; **a c. for the better/worse** une amélioration/détérioration; **a c. of address** un changement d'adresse; **a c. of clothes** des vêtements *mpl* de rechange; **to have a c. of heart** changer d'avis; **for a c.** pour une fois; *Ironic* **pour changer; that makes a c.** ça change un peu; *Euph* **the c. (of life)** *(menopause)* le retour d'âge (**b**) *(money)* monnaie *f*; **small** *or* **loose c.** petite ou menue monnaie; **have you got c. for a £10 note?** avez-vous la monnaie de 10 livres ou sur un billet de 10 livres? **2** *vt* (**a**) *(alter)* changer; *(transform)* transformer (**into** en); **to c. one's mind** changer d'avis; **to c. the subject** changer de sujet (**b**) *(exchange)* changer (**for** pour ou contre); **to c. hands** *(of money, car)* changer de mains; **to c. trains** changer de train; **to c. places with sb** changer de place avec qn; *Fig* **I wouldn't like to c. places with him** je ne voudrais pas être à sa place (**c**) *(money)* changer; **to c. dollars into euros** changer des dollars en euros (**d**) **to get changed** *(put on other clothes)* se changer **3** *vi* (**a**) *(alter)* changer; **to c. into sth** se transformer en qch (**b**) *(put on other clothes)* se changer (**c**) *(of passenger)* changer
►**change over** *vi* changer; **to c. over from sth to sth** passer de qch à qch; **to c. over to another channel** changer de chaîne

changeable ['tʃeɪndʒəbəl] *adj (person, mood)* changeant(e); *(weather)* variable

changeless ['tʃeɪndʒlɪs] *adj* immuable

changeover ['tʃeɪndʒəʊvə(r)] *n (to new system, currency)* passage *m* (**to** à); *(after election, appointment)* transition *f*

changing ['tʃeɪndʒɪŋ] *adj* changeant(e)
changing room ['tʃeɪndʒɪŋruːm] *n* vestiaire *m*; *(in shop)* cabine *f* d'essayage

channel ['tʃænəl] **1** *n* (**a**) *(waterway)* chenal *m*; *(of communication, distribution)* canal *m*; **to go through the proper channels** suivre la filière officielle (**b**) *TV* chaîne *f*; *Rad* bande *f* de fréquences; **C. 4** = chaîne de télévision privée britannique (**c**) **the (English) C.** la Manche; **the C. Islands** les îles *fpl* Anglo-Normandes; **the C. Tunnel** le tunnel sous la Manche **2** *vt (pt & pp* **channelled,** *Am* **channeled)** canaliser (**to** vers)

channel-hop ['tʃænəlhɒp] *(pt & pp* **channel-hopped)** *vi TV Fam* zapper

chant [tʃɑːnt] **1** *n* (**a**) *(of demonstrators)* slogan *m* (**b**) *Rel* psalmodie *f* **2** *vt* scander **3** *vi* (**a**) *(of demonstrators)* scander des slogans; *Rel* psalmodier

chaos ['keɪɒs] *n* chaos *m*; **our plans were thrown into c.** nos projets ont été bouleversés; **c. theory** théorie *f* du chaos

chaotic [keɪ'ɒtɪk] *adj* chaotique

chap [tʃæp] *n Fam (man)* bonhomme *m*, type *m*; **a good c.** un brave type

chapel ['tʃæpəl] *n* chapelle *f*

chaperone ['ʃæpərəʊn] **1** *n* chaperon *m* **2** *vt* chaperonner

chaplain ['tʃæplɪn] *n Rel* aumônier *m*

chaplaincy ['tʃæplɪnsɪ] *n* aumônerie *f*

chapped [tʃæpt] *adj (lips, skin)* gercé(e)

chapter ['tʃæptə(r)] *n* chapitre *m*; **c. of accidents** une série noire; *Fig* **to quote c. and verse for sth** donner les références exactes de qch

char¹ [tʃɑː(r)] *(pt & pp* **charred)** *vt (burn)* carboniser

char² *Br Fam n (cleaning lady)* femme *f* de ménage **2** *vi (pt & pp* **charred)** *(clean)* faire des ménages

char³ *n Br Fam (tea)* thé *m*

character ['kærɪktə(r)] *n* (**a**) *(in novel, film, play)* personnage *m*; **c. actor/actress** acteur(trice) *m,f* de genre *(qui se spécialise dans les rôles secondaires ou excentriques)* (**b**) *(personality)* caractère *m*; **his remark was in/out of c.** ça lui ressemble bien/ça ne lui ressemble pas d'avoir fait une remarque pareille; **to have/lack c.** avoir du/manquer de caractère; **a person of good c.** une personne honorable; **c. assassination** diffamation *f*; **c. reference** *(when applying for job)* références *fpl*; *Law* **c. witness** témoin *m* de moralité (**c**) *(unusual person)* personnage *m*; **he's quite a c.!** c'est un personnage! (**d**) *(letter)* caractère *m*; *Comput* **c. set** jeu *m* de caractères

characteristic [kærɪktə'rɪstɪk] **1** *n* caractéristique *f* **2** *adj* caractéristique; **it's c. of him** ça lui ressemble bien, c'est bien de lui

characterization [kærɪktəraɪ'zeɪʃən] *n (of problem, situation)* description *f*; *(in novel)* psychologie *f* des personnages

characterize ['kærɪktəraɪz] *vt (describe)* décrire; *(be characteristic of)* caractériser

charade [*Br* ʃə'rɑːd, *Am* ʃə'reɪd] *n (farce)* mascarade *f*; **charades** *(party game)* charades *fpl* mimées

charcoal ['tʃɑːkəʊl] *n* charbon *m* de bois; *Art* fusain *m*; **c. drawing** (dessin *m* au) fusain; **c. grey** anthracite *m* *inv*

charge [tʃɑːdʒ] **1** *n* (**a**) *(cost)* frais *mpl*; **to do sth free of c.** faire qch gratuitement; **it's free of c.** c'est gratuit; **c. account** compte *m* clients; **c. card** carte *f* de paiement *(de grand magasin)* (**b**) *Law* chef *m* d'accusation; **to be arrested on a c. of...** être arrêté(e) pour...; **to bring a c. against sb** accuser qn; **c. sheet** ≃ procès-verbal *m* (**c**) *(responsibility)* **to take c. of sth** prendre qch en charge; **to be in c. of** être responsable de; **I'm in c. here!** c'est moi le chef ici! (**d**) *(of explosive)* charge *f* **2** *vt* (**a**) *(price)* faire payer, demander; **to c. sb £10** faire payer 10 livres à qn; **c. it to my account** mettez ça sur mon compte (**b**) *Law* inculper (**with** de) (**c**) *(attack)* attaquer (**d**) *Elec* charger; *Fig* **a highly charged atmosphere** une atmosphère très tendue **3** *vi* *(rush)* charger; **to c. in/out** entrer/sortir en trombe

chariot ['tʃærɪət] *n* char *m*

charisma [kəˈrɪzmə] *n* charisme *m*

charismatic [kærɪzˈmætɪk] *adj* charismatique

charitable ['tʃærɪtəbəl] *adj* *(person, action)* charitable; *(organization)* caritatif(ive); *(work)* pour une association caritative

charity ['tʃærɪtɪ] *(pl* **charities**) *n* (**a**) *(quality)* charité *f*; *Prov* **c. begins at home** charité bien ordonnée commence par soi-même (**b**) *(organization)* association *f* caritative

charlady ['tʃɑːleɪdɪ] *(pl* **charladies**) *n Br* femme *f* de ménage

charlatan ['ʃɑːlətən] *n* charlatan *m*

Charlie ['tʃɑːlɪ] *n Br Fam* **to feel a right** *or* **proper C.** se sentir vraiment bête

charm [tʃɑːm] **1** *n* (**a**) *(attractiveness)* charme *m*; **to turn on the c.** faire le charmeur/la charmeuse; **c. offensive** offensive *f* de charme (**b**) *(spell)* charme *m*; **it worked like a c.** ça a marché comme sur des roulettes (**c**) *(lucky)* **c.** amulette *f* **2** *vt* charmer; **she charmed the money out of him** elle lui a extorqué son argent en lui faisant du charme; **to lead a charmed life** être né(e) sous une bonne étoile

charmer ['tʃɑːmə(r)] *n* charmeur(euse) *m,f*

charming ['tʃɑːmɪŋ] *adj also Ironic* charmant(e)

charred [tʃɑːd] *adj* carbonisé(e)

chart [tʃɑːt] **1** *n* *(graph)* diagramme *m*, graphique *m*; *(map)* carte *f*; **the charts** *(pop music)* le hit-parade **2** *vt* (**a**) *(on map)* porter sur une carte (**b**) *Fig (progress, rise)* retracer

charter ['tʃɑːtə(r)] **1** *n* *(of town)* charte *f*; *(of university)* statuts *mpl*; **c. flight** (vol *m*) charter *m* **2** *vt* *(plane, ship)* affréter

chartered accountant ['tʃɑːtədəˈkaʊntənt] *n* expert-comptable *m*

charwoman ['tʃɑːwʊmən] *n Br* femme *f* de ménage

chary ['tʃeərɪ] *adj* circonspect(e); **to be c. of doing sth** hésiter à faire qch

chase [tʃeɪs] **1** *n* *(pursuit)* poursuite *f*; **to give c. to sb** donner la chasse à qn **2** *vt* *(pursue)* poursuivre, donner la chasse à; *(sexually)* courir après **3** *vi* **to c. after sb** *(pursue)* poursuivre qn, donner la chasse à qn; *(sexually)* courir après qn

▸**chase up** *vt sep (person)* relancer; *(letter)* retrouver la trace de

chaser ['tʃeɪsə(r)] *n* = alcool bu après une bière ou vice versa

chasm ['kæzəm] *n also Fig* gouffre *m*, abîme *m*

chassis ['ʃæsɪ] *n (of car)* châssis *m*

chaste [tʃeɪst] *adj* chaste

chasten ['tʃeɪsən] *vt* rendre plus humble

chastise [tʃæsˈtaɪz] *vt* châtier; *(criticize)* fustiger

chastisement [tʃæsˈtaɪzmənt] *n* châtiment *m*; *(criticism)* fustigation *f*

chastity ['tʃæstɪtɪ] *n* chasteté *f*; **c. belt** ceinture *f* de chasteté

chat [tʃæt] **1** *n* (**a**) *(conversation)* discussion *f*; **to have a c. (with sb)** discuter *ou* bavarder (avec qn); **c. show** *(on TV)* talk-show *m* (**b**) *Comput (on Internet)* bavardage *m*, chat *m*; **c. room** site *m* de bavardage, salon *m*, *Can* bavardoir *m* **2** *vi (pt & pp* **chatted**) *also Comput* bavarder; **to c. about sth** discuter de qch

▸**chat up** *vt sep Br Fam* draguer

chattel ['tʃætəl] *n Law* bien *m* meuble

chatter ['tʃætə(r)] **1** *n* bavardage *m*, papotage *m* **2** *vi (talk)* bavarder, papoter; **my teeth were chattering** je claquais des dents

chatterbox ['tʃætəbɒks] *n Fam* pie *f*, moulin *m* à paroles

chatty ['tʃætɪ] *adj (person)* bavard(e); *(letter)* plein(e) de détails

chauffeur ['ʃəʊfə(r)] **1** *n* chauffeur *m* **2** *vt* conduire

chauvinism ['ʃəʊvɪnɪzəm] *n (patriotism)* chauvinisme *m*; **(male) c.** machisme *m*

chauvinist ['ʃəʊvɪnɪst] **1** *n (patriot)* chauvin(e) *m,f*; **(male) c.** *(sexist)* macho *m* **2** *adj (patriotic)* chauvin(e); *(sexist)* macho

chauvinistic [ʃəʊvɪˈnɪstɪk] = **chauvinist** *adj*

chav [tʃæv] *n Br Fam Pej* racaille *f*, lascar *m*

cheap [tʃiːp] **1** **to do sth on the c.** faire qch à peu de frais *ou* pour pas cher **2** *adj* (**a**) *(inexpensive)* bon marché *inv*, pas cher (chère); **cheaper** meilleur marché *inv*, moins cher (chère); **c. rate** tarif *m* réduit (**b**) *(of little value)* de peu de valeur; *(vulgar)* de mauvais goût; **to feel c.** *(of person)* se sentir minable; **it's c. and nasty** c'est de la camelote **3** *adv Fam* **it was going c.** c'était bon marché

cheapen ['tʃiːpən] *vt (degrade)* gâcher; **to c. oneself** s'abaisser

cheaply ['tʃiːplɪ] *adv (buy)* (à) bon marché, à bas prix; *(live, travel)* à peu de frais, pour pas cher

cheapskate ['tʃiːpskeɪt] *n Fam* radin(e) *m,f*

cheat [tʃiːt] **1** *n (dishonest person)* escroc *m*; *(at games)* tricheur(euse) *m,f*; *(deception, trick)* tricherie *f*, triche *f* **2** *vt* duper, rouler; *(financially)* escroquer; **to c. sb out of sth** *(money)* escroquer qch à qn; *(chance)* priver qn de qch **3** *vi* tricher

▸**cheat on** *vt insep (be unfaithful to)* tromper

cheating ['tʃiːtɪŋ] *n* tricherie *f*, triche *f*; **that's c.!** c'est de la triche!

Chechnia, Chechnya ['tʃetʃnɪə] *n* la Tchétchénie

check¹ [tʃek] **1** *n* (**a**) *(inspection)* vérification *f*, contrôle *m* (**on** de); **to run a c. on sb** enquêter sur qn (**b**) *(restraint)* **to keep sb in c.** tenir qn en échec; **to keep sth in c.** *(emotion, enemy advance)* contenir qch; *Pol* **checks and balances** équilibre *m* des pouvoirs (**c**) *(in chess)* échec *m*; **in c.** en échec

(**d**) *Am (cheque)* chèque *m*; *(restaurant bill)* addition *f*
2 *vt* (**a**) *(verify, examine) (information, statement)* vérifier; *(passport, ticket)* contrôler; **to c. that...** vérifier *ou* s'assurer que... (**b**) *(restrain) (inflation)* enrayer; *(emotion, impulse, enemy advance)* contenir (**c**) *Am (coat, hat)* mettre au vestiaire; *(bag, luggage)* mettre à la consigne **3** *vi* vérifier; **to c. on sth** vérifier qch; **to c. on sb** surveiller qn; **you'd better c. with her** vous feriez mieux de lui demander
►**check in 1** *vt sep (baggage)* enregistrer
2 *vi (at hotel)* remplir le registre; *(at airport)* se présenter à l'enregistrement
►**check off** *vt sep Am (on list)* cocher
►**check out 1** *vt sep* (**a**) *(investigate) (person)* se renseigner sur; *(information)* vérifier (**b**) *Fam (look at)* mater
2 *vi (leave hotel)* quitter l'hôtel
►**check up** *vi* vérifier; **to c. up on sb** surveiller qn
check² **1** *n (pattern)* carreaux *mpl*
2 *adj* à carreaux, *Can* carreauté(e)
checkers ['tʃekəz] *npl Am* jeu *m* de dames
check-in ['tʃekɪn] *n (at airport)* **c. (desk)** (comptoir *m* d')enregistrement *m*
checking account ['tʃekɪŋəkaʊnt] *n Am Fin* compte *m* courant
checklist ['tʃeklɪst] *n* liste *f* de vérification
checkmate ['tʃekmeɪt] **1** *n (in chess)* échec *m* et mat
2 *vt (in chess)* faire échec et mat à; *Fig (opponent)* faire échec à
checkout ['tʃekaʊt] *n (in supermarket)* caisse *f*
checkpoint ['tʃekpɔɪnt] *n (poste m de)* contrôle *m*
checkroom ['tʃekruːm] *n Am (for coats)* vestiaire *m*; *(for luggage)* consigne *f*
checkup ['tʃekʌp] *n Med* bilan *m* complet
cheek [tʃiːk] **1** *n* (**a**) *(of face)* joue *f*; **to dance c. to c.** danser joue contre joue; **c. by jowl (with sb)** coude à coude (avec qn); *Fig* **to turn the other c.** tendre l'autre joue (**b**) *(buttock)* fesse *f* (**c**) *Fam (impudence)* toupet *m*, culot *m*; **he's got a c.!** il est culotté *ou* gonflé!
2 *vt Fam (be impudent to)* être insolent(e) avec
cheekbone ['tʃiːkbəʊn] *n* pommette *f*
cheeky ['tʃiːkɪ] *adj Fam* effronté(e)
cheep [tʃiːp] *vi (of bird)* piailler
cheer [tʃɪə(r)] **1** *n (shout)* hourra *m*; **cheers** acclamations *fpl*, bravos *mpl*; **three cheers for Mary!** un ban pour Mary! (**b**) *Fam* **cheers!** *(when drinking)* (à votre) santé!; *Br (goodbye)* à bientôt!; *Br (thanks)* merci! (**c**) *Lit (good spirits)* **to be of good c.** être de bonne humeur
2 *vt* (**a**) *(applaud)* acclamer (**b**) *(make happier)* remonter le moral à
3 *vi (shout)* pousser des hourras *ou* des acclamations
►**cheer on** *vt sep (support)* encourager
►**cheer up 1** *vt sep (person)* remonter le moral à; *(room)* égayer
2 *vi (of person)* reprendre courage; **c. up!** courage!
cheerful ['tʃɪəfʊl] *adj (person)* gai(e), de bonne humeur; *(room, music, mood)* gai(e); *(conversation)* enjoué(e)
cheerfully ['tʃɪəfʊlɪ] *adv* gaiement, avec entrain; *Fam* **I could c. strangle him!** je l'étranglerais volontiers!
cheerily ['tʃɪərɪlɪ] *adv* gaiement
cheerio [tʃɪərɪ'əʊ] *exclam* salut! *(au revoir)*

cheerleader ['tʃɪəliːdə(r)] *n* pom-pom girl *f*
cheerless ['tʃɪəlɪs] *adj* morne; *(room)* triste
cheery ['tʃɪərɪ] *adj* joyeux(euse), gai(e)
cheese [tʃiːz] *n* fromage *m*; *Fam (say)* **c.!** *(for photograph)* souriez!; **c. sandwich/omelette** sandwich *m*/omelette *f* au fromage
►**cheese off** *vt sep Fam* **to be cheesed off (with)** en avoir marre (de)
cheeseboard ['tʃiːzbɔːd] *n (selection)* plateau *m* de fromages
cheeseburger ['tʃiːzbɜːgə(r)] *n* cheeseburger *m*
cheesecake ['tʃiːzkeɪk] *n* gâteau *m* au fromage blanc
cheetah ['tʃiːtə] *n* guépard *m*
chef [ʃef] *n* chef *m* (cuisinier)
chemical ['kemɪkəl] **1** *n* produit *m* chimique
2 *adj* chimique; **c. warfare** guerre *f* chimique; **c. weapons** armes *fpl* chimiques
chemist ['kemɪst] *n* (**a**) *Br (pharmacist)* pharmacien(-enne) *m,f*; **c.'s (shop)** pharmacie *f* (**b**) *(scientist)* chimiste *mf*
chemistry ['kemɪstrɪ] *n* chimie *f*; *Fig* **there was a certain c. between them** il y avait une certaine affinité entre eux
chemo ['kiːməʊ] *n Fam Med* chimio *f*
chemotherapy [kiːməʊ'θerəpɪ] *n Med* chimiothérapie *f*
cheque [tʃek] *n Fin* chèque *m*; **to make out** *or* **write a c. (to sb)** faire un chèque (à l'ordre de qn); **a c. for £10** un chèque de 10 livres; **c. card** carte *f* bancaire *(sans laquelle un chéquier n'est pas valable)*
chequebook ['tʃekbʊk] *n* carnet *m* de chèques, chéquier *m*; **c. journalism** = dans les milieux de la presse, pratique qui consiste à payer des sommes importantes pour le témoignage d'une personne impliquée dans une affaire
chequered ['tʃekəd] *adj (patterned)* à carreaux, *Can* carreauté(e); *Fig* **she's had a c. career** elle a eu une carrière en dents de scie
cherish ['tʃerɪʃ] *vt (memory, person)* chérir; *(hopes)* caresser, nourrir
cherry ['tʃerɪ] *(pl cherries)* *n (fruit)* cerise *f*; **c. (tree)** cerisier *m*; **c. orchard** cerisaie *f*
cherub ['tʃerəb] *(pl cherubs* or *cherubim* ['tʃerəbɪm]) *n* chérubin *m*
chess [tʃes] *n* échecs *mpl*; **a game of c.** une partie d'échecs; **c. player** joueur(euse) *m,f* d'échecs
chessboard ['tʃesbɔːd] *n* échiquier *m*
chessman ['tʃesmæn], **chesspiece** ['tʃespiːs] *n* pièce *f* (de jeu d'échecs)
chest [tʃest] *n* (**a**) *(of person)* poitrine *f*; *Fig* **to get it off one's c.** dire ce qui a sur le cœur (**b**) *(box)* coffre *m*, caisse *f*; **c. of drawers** commode *f*
chestnut ['tʃesnʌt] **1** *n (nut)* châtaigne *f*; *(tree, wood)* châtaignier *m*; **(horse) c.** marron *m* d'Inde; *Fam* **an old c.** une plaisanterie usée
2 *adj (hair) (horse)* alezan(e)
chew [tʃuː] *vt* mâcher, mastiquer; *(cigar, end of pen)* mâchonner; **to c. one's nails** se ronger les ongles
►**chew over** *vt sep Fam* réfléchir à, cogiter sur
chewing gum ['tʃuːɪŋgʌm] *n* chewing-gum *m*
chewy ['tʃuːɪ] *adj (meat)* caoutchouteux(euse); *(sweet)* mou (molle)
chic [ʃiːk] *adj* élégant(e), chic *inv*
chick [tʃɪk] *n* (**a**) *(young bird)* oisillon *m*; *(young chicken)* poussin *m* (**b**) *Fam (woman)* nana *f*; **c. flick** = film qui plaît particulièrement aux femmes; **c. lit** = genre

romanesque destiné à un public de jeunes femmes et qui est censé refléter leurs préoccupations

chicken ['tʃɪkɪn] **1** n (**a**) (bird) poulet m; Prov **don't count your chickens (before they are hatched)** il ne faut pas vendre la peau de l'ours avant de l'avoir tué; **c. feed** (food) nourriture f pour volaille; Fam Fig **that's c. feed!** c'est une misère! (**b**) Fam (coward) lâche mf, froussard(e) m,f **2** adj Fam (cowardly) froussard(e)
▸**chicken out** vi Fam se dégonfler
chickenpox ['tʃɪkɪnpɒks] n varicelle f
chickpea ['tʃɪkpi:] n pois m chiche
chicory ['tʃɪkərɪ] (pl chicories) n endive f
chide [tʃaɪd] (pt chided or chid [tʃɪd], pp chided or chidden ['tʃɪdən]) vt Lit réprimander
chief [tʃi:f] **1** n (of tribe) chef m; Fam **the c.** (boss) le patron; Mil **c. of staff** chef d'état-major; (White House) **c. of staff** secrétaire m de la Maison-Blanche **2** adj (most important) principal(e); **c. assistant** principal(e) collaborateur(trice) m,f; Com **c. executive** directeur(trice) m,f général(e); Am **c. executive officer** directeur(trice) m,f général(e); Am **c. financial officer** chef m comptable
chiefly ['tʃi:flɪ] adv principalement, surtout
chieftain ['tʃi:ftən] n (of clan) chef m
chiffon ['ʃɪfɒn] n mousseline f de soie
chilblain ['tʃɪlbleɪn] n engelure f
child [tʃaɪld] (pl children ['tʃɪldrən]) n enfant mf; **it's c.'s play** c'est un jeu d'enfant; **children's literature** littérature f enfantine ou pour enfants; **c. abuse** mauvais traitements mpl à enfant; (sexual) sévices mpl sexuels infligés à un enfant; **c. benefit** ≃ allocations fpl familiales; **c. labour** travail m des enfants; **c. minder** nourrice f; **c. protection** protection f de l'enfance
child-bearing ['tʃaɪldbeərɪŋ] n maternité f; **of c. age** en âge d'avoir des enfants
childbirth ['tʃaɪldbɜ:θ] n accouchement m; **to die in c.** mourir en couches
childcare ['tʃaɪldkeə(r)] n garde f d'enfants
childhood ['tʃaɪldhʊd] n enfance f
childish ['tʃaɪldɪʃ] adj Pej puéril(e); **don't be so c.!** ne fais pas l'enfant!
childless ['tʃaɪldlɪs] adj sans enfant(s)
childlike ['tʃaɪldlaɪk] adj enfantin(e)
childproof ['tʃaɪldpru:f] adj **c. bottle** = bouteille pourvue d'une capsule de sécurité; **c. lock** (in car) serrure f de sécurité pour enfants
children ['tʃɪldrən] pl of child
Chile ['tʃɪlɪ] n le Chili
Chilean ['tʃɪlɪən] **1** n Chilien(enne) m,f **2** adj chilien(enne)
chill [tʃɪl] **1** n coup m de froid; **to catch a c.** prendre froid; **a c. of fear** un frisson de peur; **there's a c. in the air** le fond de l'air est frais **2** adj froid(e), glacé(e) **3** vt (wine, food) mettre au frais; (of wind) glacer; **serve chilled** (on product) servir frais **4** vi Fam se détendre; **c.!** on se calme!
▸**chill out** vi Fam se détendre; **c. out!** on se calme!
chilled [tʃɪld] adj **1** (wine, drink) frais (fraîche); (food) frigorifié(e) **2** Fam (relaxed) cool (inv)
chilli ['tʃɪlɪ] (pl chillis or chillies) n (dish) chili m con carne; **c. (pepper)** piment m (rouge); **c. powder** piment m en poudre
chilling ['tʃɪlɪŋ] adj (frightening) qui donne des frissons

chill-out room ['tʃɪlaʊtru:m] n (in nightclub) espace m chill-out
chilly ['tʃɪlɪ] adj also Fig froid(e)
chime [tʃaɪm] **1** n (of bells) carillon m **2** vt the clock chimed nine o'clock le carillon de l'horloge sonna neuf heures **3** vi (of clock, bells) carillonner
▸**chime in** vi Fam (in conversation) intervenir
chimney ['tʃɪmnɪ] (pl chimneys) n cheminée f; Fam **to smoke like a c.** (of person) fumer comme un pompier; **c. sweep** ramoneur m
chimneypot ['tʃɪmnɪpɒt] n tuyau m de cheminée
chimpanzee [tʃɪmpæn'zi:], Fam **chimp** [tʃɪmp] n chimpanzé m
chin [tʃɪn] n menton m; Fig **to keep one's c. up** tenir bon, tenir le coup
China ['tʃaɪnə] n la Chine
china ['tʃaɪnə] n porcelaine f; **c. clay** kaolin m
Chinese [tʃaɪ'ni:z] **1** npl **the C.** (people) les Chinois mpl **2** n (**a**) (person) Chinois(e) m,f (**b**) (language) chinois m **3** adj chinois(e)
Chink [tʃɪŋk] n Fam Chinetoque mf, = terme raciste désignant un Chinois
chink¹ [tʃɪŋk] n (gap) fente f, lézarde f; Fig **to find a c. in sb's armour** trouver le talon d'Achille de qn
chink² **1** n (sound) tintement m **2** vt (coins, glasses) faire tinter **3** vi tinter
Chinky ['tʃɪŋkɪ] n Fam (**a**) (restaurant) (resto m) chinois m; (meal) repas m chinois (**b**) = Chink
chintz [tʃɪnts] n chintz m
chinwag ['tʃɪnwæg] n Fam **to have a c.** tailler une bavette
chip [tʃɪp] **1** n (**a**) (of wood, glass) éclat m; (in plate, cup) ébréchure f; **this cup has a c. in it** cette tasse est ébréchée (**b**) **chips** Br (French fries) frites fpl; Am (crisps) (pommes fpl) chips mpl, Can croustilles fpl; Br **c. shop** = petite boutique où l'on vend du poisson pané et frit, accompagné de frites (**c**) (in gambling) jeton m (**d**) Comput & (on credit card) puce f (**e**) (idioms) **he's a c. off the old block** c'est son père tout craché; **to have a c. on one's shoulder** en vouloir à tout le monde; Fam **when the chips are down** dans les moments critiques; Fam **he's had his chips** (it's too late for him) il est cuit ou fichu **2** vt (pt & pp chipped) (cut at) (stone, wood) tailler; (damage) (knife, plate) ébrécher; (furniture) écorner; **to c. one's tooth** se casser un petit bout de dent **3** vi (of plate, cup) s'ébrécher
▸**chip in** vi Fam (give money) participer; **to c. in with a suggestion** intervenir pour faire une suggestion
chipboard ['tʃɪpbɔ:d] n aggloméré m
chipmunk ['tʃɪpmʌŋk] n tamia m rayé, Can suisse m
chiropodist [kɪ'rɒpədɪst] n pédicure mf
chiropody [kɪ'rɒpədɪ] n pédicurie f
chirp [tʃɜ:p] **1** n (of birds) gazouillis m, pépiement m; (of grasshopper) chant m **2** vt & vi (of bird) gazouiller, pépier; (of grasshopper) chanter
chirpy ['tʃɜ:pɪ] adj d'humeur joyeuse
chirrup ['tʃɪrəp] = chirp
chisel ['tʃɪzəl] **1** n (tool) ciseau m; (for sculpture) burin m **2** vt (pt & pp chiselled, Am chiseled) (**a**) (in woodwork,

sculpture) ciseler; *Fig* **chiselled features** visage *m* délicatement ciselé (**b**) *very Fam (cheat)* rouler
chit [tʃɪt] *n* (**a**) *(memo, note)* note *f; (voucher)* bon *m* (**b**) *Fam Old-fashioned Pej* **a c.**
chitchat ['tʃɪttʃæt] *n Fam* bavardage *m,* papotage *m*
chivalrous ['ʃɪvəlrəs] *adj* chevaleresque; *(towards women)* galant(e)
chivalry ['ʃɪvəlrɪ] *n (courteous behaviour)* courtoisie *f; (towards women)* galanterie *f; Hist* chevalerie *f*
chives [tʃaɪvz] *npl* ciboulette *f*
chiv(v)y ['tʃɪvɪ] *(pt & pp* **chiv(v)ied**) *vt Br Fam* harceler; **to c. sb into doing sth** harceler qn jusqu'à ce qu'il fasse qch; **to c. sb along** faire se presser qn
chloride ['klɔːraɪd] *n Chem* chlorure *m*
chlorinate ['klɔːrɪneɪt] *vt* chlorer
chlorine ['klɔːriːn] *n Chem* chlore *m*
chloroform ['klɒrəfɔːm] *n Chem* chloroforme *m*
chlorophyl(l) ['klɒrəfɪl] *n Biol* chlorophylle *f*
choc-ice ['tʃɒkaɪs] *n Br* = glace individuelle rectangulaire enrobée de chocolat
chock [tʃɒk] *n (for wheel of car, plane)* cale *f*
chock-a-block ['tʃɒkə'blɒk] *adj Br Fam* plein(e) à craquer
chocolate ['tʃɒklət] **1** *n* chocolat *m;* **hot c.** chocolat chaud
2 *adj (made of chocolate)* en chocolat; *(chocolate-flavoured)* au chocolat; **c. (coloured)** chocolat *inv*
choice [tʃɔɪs] **1** *n* choix *m;* **to make a c.** choisir, faire un choix; **you have no c.** vous n'avez pas le choix; **I had no c. but to leave** je ne pouvais que partir; **there isn't much c.** il n'y a pas grand choix; **available in a wide c. of colours** disponible dans une large gamme de coloris
2 *adj* (**a**) *(well chosen)* choisi(e); **she used some c. language** *(offensive)* elle a juré comme un charretier (**b**) *(food)* de choix; *(wine)* fin(e)
choir ['kwaɪə(r)] *n* chœur *m*
choirboy ['kwaɪəbɔɪ] *n* jeune choriste *m*
choke [tʃəʊk] **1** *n (of car)* starter *m*
2 *vt* (**a**) *(strangle)* étrangler (**b**) *(block) (sink, road)* boucher
3 *vi* s'étrangler; **to c. with anger** s'étrangler de colère; **she choked on a fishbone** elle a failli s'étouffer en avalant une arête
▶**choke back** *vt sep (tears, words, anger)* ravaler
choker ['tʃəʊkə(r)] *n (necklace)* collier *m* (court)
cholera ['kɒlərə] *n* choléra *m*
cholesterol [kə'lestərɒl] *n* cholestérol *m*
choose [tʃuːz] *(pt* **chose** [tʃəʊz], *pp* **chosen** ['tʃəʊzən]) **1** *vt* choisir; **to c. to do sth** choisir de faire qch; **there's not much to c. between them** ils se valent
2 *vi* choisir (**between** entre); **I'll do as I c.** je ferai comme il me plaît
choosy ['tʃuːzɪ] *adj Fam* difficile
chop [tʃɒp] **1** *n* (**a**) *(with axe)* coup *m; Fam* **to get the c.** *(get sacked)* se faire sacquer (**b**) *(of lamb, pork)* côtelette *f* (**c**) **chops** *(of person)* joue *f; (of animal)* bajoues *fpl;* **to lick one's chops** se pourlécher les babines
2 *vt (pt & pp* **chopped**) *(wood)* couper; *(meat, vegetables)* couper en morceaux; *(finely)* hacher
3 *vi* **to c. and change** changer sans cesse; **he's always chopping and changing** il change d'avis comme de chemise
▶**chop down** *vt sep (tree)* abattre
▶**chop off** *vt sep* trancher, couper; **to c. sb's head off** couper la tête à qn

chopper ['tʃɒpə(r)] *n* (**a**) *(cleaver)* couperet *m; (axe)* hachette *f* (**b**) *Fam (helicopter)* hélico *m*
chopping ['tʃɒpɪŋ] *n* **c. block** *(of butcher)* billot *m;* **c. board** planche *f* (à découper)
choppy ['tʃɒpɪ] *adj (sea, lake)* agité(e)
chopsticks ['tʃɒpstɪks] *npl* baguettes *fpl*
choral ['kɔːrəl] *adj* choral(e); **c. society** chorale *f*
chord [kɔːd] *n* (**a**) *Mus* accord *m; Fig* **her speech struck a c. with the electorate** son discours a trouvé un écho auprès des électeurs (**b**) *Math (of arc)* corde *f*
chore [tʃɔː(r)] *n* (**a**) **chores** *(in household)* travaux *mpl* ménagers (**b**) *(unwelcome task)* corvée *f*
choreograph ['kɒrɪəɡrɑːf] *vt* faire la chorégraphie de; *Fig* orchestrer
choreographer [kɒrɪ'ɒɡrəfə(r)] *n* chorégraphe *mf*
choreography [kɒrɪ'ɒɡrəfɪ] *n* chorégraphie *f*
chorister ['kɒrɪstə(r)] *n* choriste *mf*
chortle ['tʃɔːtəl] **1** *n* gloussement *m* (de joie)
2 *vi* glousser (de joie)
chorus ['kɔːrəs] **1** *n* (**a**) *(of song)* refrain *m* (**b**) *(group of singers, actors)* chœur *m; Fig* **a c. of protest** un concert de protestations; **c. girl** danseuse *f* de revue
2 *vt* dire en chœur
chose [tʃəʊz] *pt of* **choose**
chosen ['tʃəʊzən] **1** *adj* choisi(e); **the c. few** les heureux élus *mpl;* **the C. people** le peuple élu
2 *pp of* **choose**
Christ [kraɪst] **1** *n* le Christ *m,* Jésus-Christ *m*
2 *exclam very Fam* bon Dieu!; **C. Almighty!** nom de Dieu!
christen ['krɪsən] *vt (name)* baptiser
christening ['krɪsənɪŋ] *n* baptême *m*
Christian ['krɪstʃən] **1** *n* chrétien(enne) *m,f;* **to be a C.** être chrétien
2 *adj* chrétien(enne); **C. name** prénom *m*
Christianity [krɪstɪ'ænɪtɪ] *n* christianisme *m*
Christmas ['krɪsməs] **1** *n* Noël *m;* **at C.** à Noël; **Merry** or **Happy C.!** joyeux Noël!; **C. cake** gâteau *m* de Noël *(aux fruits secs);* **C. card** carte *f* de Noël; **C. carol** chant *m* de Noël; **C. cracker** = papillote contenant un pétard une surprise traditionnelle au moment des fêtes; **C. Day** jour *m* de Noël; **C. Eve** veille *f* de Noël; **C. pudding** pudding *m* (de Noël); **C. tree** sapin *m* de Noël

Christmas cracker

Si vous êtes invité à un repas de Noël chez des Britanniques, vous trouverez très probablement un "Christmas cracker" à côté de votre assiette. Il s'agit d'une sorte de petit cylindre de carton en forme de papillote qui contient généralement un chapeau en papier, une blague ou une devinette, ainsi qu'un petit jouet ou un colifichet. Une personne tire un chaque côté du "Christmas cracker" qui s'ouvre alors en claquant – chaque "cracker" contenant un petit pétard – et une des deux personnes se retrouve avec la moitié de pétard qui contient les petites surprises.

chrome [krəʊm] *adj* chromé(e)
chromium ['krəʊmɪəm] *n Chem* chrome *m*
chromosome ['krəʊməsəʊm] *n Biol* chromosome *m*
chronic ['krɒnɪk] *adj* (**a**) *(invalid, illness, unemployment)* chronique (**b**) *Fam (bad)* atroce

chronicle ['krɒnɪkəl] **1** n chronique f; Fig (of disasters) suite f
2 vt faire la chronique de
chronological [krɒnə'lɒdʒɪkəl] adj chronologique
chronology [krə'nɒlədʒɪ] n chronologie f
chrysalis ['krɪsəlɪs] n Zool chrysalide f
chrysanthemum [krɪ'sænθəməm] n chrysanthème m
chubby ['tʃʌbɪ] adj potelé(e), dodu(e); (face) jouf-flu(e); **c.-cheeked** joufflu(e)
chuck [tʃʌk] vt Fam (**a**) (throw) lancer, balancer (**b**) (boyfriend, girlfriend) plaquer; **to get chucked** se faire plaquer
▸**chuck away** vt sep Fam balancer; Fig (opportunity) foutre en l'air
▸**chuck out** vt sep Fam (throw away) balancer; (from house, school, club) vider
chuckle ['tʃʌkəl] **1** n petit rire m
2 vi rire tout bas
chuffed [tʃʌft] adj Br Fam tout(e) content(e) (**about** de)
chug [tʃʌg] (pt & pp **chugged**) vi (train) haleter; Fam **he's still chugging along in the same job** il a toujours le même boulot pépère
chum [tʃʌm] n Fam copain (copine) m,f
chummy ['tʃʌmɪ] adj Fam copain (copine); **to be a bit too c.** être un peu trop familier(ère)
chump [tʃʌmp] n Fam (**a**) (foolish person) idiot(e) m,f (**b**) **to be off one's c.** être timbré(e)
chunk [tʃʌŋk] n gros morceau m; (of bread) quignon m; (of time) partie f
chunky ['tʃʌŋkɪ] adj (**a**) (well-built) bien bâti(e); (fat) grassouillet(ette); (sweater) gros (grosse) (**b**) (stew, soup) avec des morceaux
church [tʃɜːtʃ] n (**a**) (building) église f; (French Protes-tant) temple m; **to go to c.** aller à l'église/au temple; **c. hall** salle f paroissiale (**b**) (institution) l'Église f; **the C. of England** l'Église f anglicane; **the C. of Scotland** l'Église f d'Écosse
churchgoer ['tʃɜːtʃgəʊə(r)] n pratiquant(e) m,f
churchyard ['tʃɜːtʃjɑːd] n cimetière m
churlish ['tʃɜːlɪʃ] adj (rude) grossier(ère); (surly) revêche
churn [tʃɜːn] **1** n (for making butter) baratte f; (for milk) bidon m à lait
2 vt (butter) battre; **the propeller churned up the water** l'eau bouillonnait sous l'action des hélices
3 vi **my stomach's churning** (because of nervous-ness) j'ai l'estomac noué
▸**churn out** vt sep Fam (books) pondre (en série); (goods) produire en série
chute [ʃuːt] n (**a**) (for parcels) glissière f; (rubbish) **c.** vide-ordures m inv (**b**) (in swimming pool, play-ground) toboggan m (**c**) Fam (parachute) parachute m
chutney ['tʃʌtnɪ] n (pl **chutneys**) n chutney m
CIA [siːaɪ'eɪ] n Am (abbr **Central Intelligence Agency**) CIA f
cicada [sɪ'kɑːdə] n cigale f
CID [siːaɪ'diː] n Br (abbr **Criminal Investigation Depart-ment**) ≃ P.J.
cider ['saɪdə(r)] n Br (alcoholic) cidre m; Am (juice) jus m de pommes; Am **hard c.** cidre m; **c. vinegar** vinaigre m de cidre
cigar [sɪ'gɑː(r)] n cigare m
cigarette [sɪgə'ret] n cigarette f; **c. ash** cendre f de cigarette; **c. butt** or **end** mégot m; **c. case** étui m à

cigarettes; **c. holder** fume-cigarette m inv; **c. lighter** briquet m; (in car) allume-cigare m; **c. machine** distributeur m automatique de cigarettes; **c. packet** paquet m de cigarettes; **c. paper** papier m à cigarettes
C-in-C [siːɪn'siː] n Mil & Naut (abbr **Commander-in-Chief**) commandant m en chef
cinch [sɪntʃ] n Fam **it's a c.** c'est un jeu d'enfant
cinder ['sɪndə(r)] n cinders cendres fpl; **burnt to a c.** complètement carbonisé(e)
Cinderella [sɪndə'relə] n Cendrillon
cine ['sɪnɪ] pref **c. camera** caméra f; **c. film** pellicule f
cinema ['sɪnəmə] n Br cinéma m; **to go to the c.** aller au cinéma
cinnamon ['sɪnəmən] n cannelle f
cipher ['saɪfə(r)] n (code) chiffre m, code m; Fig **he's a mere c.** c'est un zéro
circa ['sɜːkə] prep (of time) aux alentours de; (of amount) environ
circle ['sɜːkəl] **1** n (**a**) (shape) cercle m; **to sit in a c.** s'asseoir en cercle; Fig **to go round in circles** tourner en rond (**b**) (movement) **to come full c.** revenir à son point de départ (**c**) (in theatre) balcon m; **lower/upper c.** premier/deuxième balcon m; (group) cer-cle m, groupe m; **in certain circles** dans certains mi-lieux
2 vt (**a**) (go round) tourner autour de (**b**) (surround) entourer (**with** de)
3 vi (of plane, birds) tourner, décrire des cercles
circuit ['sɜːkɪt] n (**a**) (electric) circuit m; **c. breaker** dis-joncteur m (**b**) (in motor racing) (course) circuit m; (lap) tour m
circuitous [sə'kjuːɪtəs] adj (route) détourné(e); (rea-soning) alambiqué(e)
circular ['sɜːkjʊlə(r)] **1** n (letter) circulaire f; (advertise-ment) prospectus m
2 adj (movement, argument) circulaire
circulate ['sɜːkjʊleɪt] **1** vt faire circuler
2 vi circuler
circulation [sɜːkjʊ'leɪʃən] n (of air, blood, money) circulation f; (of newspaper) tirage m; **for inter-nal c. only** (document) à usage interne uniquement; Fig **to be out of c.** (of person) disparaître de la circula-tion
circumcise ['sɜːkəmsaɪz] vt (boy) circoncire; (girl) exciser
circumcision [sɜːkəm'sɪʒən] n circoncision f; **female c.** excision f
circumference [sə'kʌmfərəns] n circonférence f
circumflex ['sɜːkəmfleks] n accent m circonflexe
circumlocution [sɜːkəmlə'kjuːʃən] n circonlocution f, périphrase f
circumnavigate [sɜːkəm'nævɪgeɪt] vt **to c. sth** faire le tour de qch en bateau
circumscribe ['sɜːkəmskraɪb] vt (limit) limiter
circumspect ['sɜːkəmspekt] adj circonspect(e)
circumstances ['sɜːkəmstənsɪz] npl circonstances fpl; **in** or **under the c.** étant donné les circonstances; **in** or **under no c.** en aucun cas, sous aucun prétexte; **due to c. beyond our control** en raison de circonstances indépendantes de notre volonté
circumstantial [sɜːkəm'stænʃəl] adj **evidence** preuves fpl indirectes
circumvent [sɜːkəm'vent] vt (law, rule) contourner
circus ['sɜːkəs] n cirque m
cirrhosis [sɪ'rəʊsɪs] n Med cirrhose f

CIS [siːaɪˈes] n (abbr **Commonwealth of Independent States**) CEI f

cissy [ˈsɪsɪ] (pl **cissies**) n Fam poule f mouillée

cistern [ˈsɪstən] n citerne f; (in lavatory) réservoir m de chasse d'eau

citadel [ˈsɪtədel] n citadelle f

citation [saɪˈteɪʃən] n citation f

cite [saɪt] vt citer

citizen [ˈsɪtɪzən] n citoyen(enne) m,f; (of city) habitant(e) m,f; c.'s **band** (radio) citizen band f

citizenship [ˈsɪtɪzənʃɪp] n citoyenneté f

citric acid [ˈsɪtrɪkˈæsɪd] n acide m citrique

citrus fruit [ˈsɪtrəsfruːt] n agrumes mpl; a c. un agrume

city [ˈsɪtɪ] (pl **cities**) n (grande) ville f; Br the C. la City (quartier des affaires de Londres); c. **centre** centre-ville m; c. **hall** (building) mairie f; Am (local government) administration f municipale

City
La "City", quartier financier de la capitale, est une circonscription administrative autonome de Londres ayant sa propre police.

civic [ˈsɪvɪk] adj (duty, pride) civique; (building, authorities) municipal(e); c. **centre** salle f municipale

civil [ˈsɪvəl] adj (a) (of society) civil(e); c. **aviation** aviation f civile; c. **defence** protection f civile; c. **disobedience** résistance f passive; c. **engineering** génie m civil; c. **law** (subject) droit m civil; c. **liberties** libertés fpl civiques; Br Law c. **partnership** = loi qui garantit aux couples homosexuels les mêmes droits qu'aux couples mariés en matière de succession, de retraite, et pour les questions de garde et d'éducation des enfants; Law c. **rights** droits mpl civils; c. **servant** fonctionnaire mf; the c. **service** la fonction publique; c. **war** guerre f civile (b) (polite) poli(e)

Civil Partnership
Le "Civil Partnerships Act" (loi sur le partenariat civil) a été voté par le parlement britannique en 2004, et la loi est entrée en application en décembre 2005. Il garantit aux couples homosexuels les mêmes droits qu'aux couples mariés en matière de succession, de retraite, ainsi que pour ce qui concerne la garde et l'éducation des enfants. Bien que le partenariat civil ne soit pas à proprement parler un mariage, les termes "gay marriage" et "same-sex marriage" (mariage unisexe) s'emploient couramment et de nombreux couples organisent des festivités comme pour un mariage traditionnel. Il faut noter que contrairement au PACS, les "civil partnerships" ne concernent que les couples homosexuels.

civilian [sɪˈvɪljən] **1** n civil m
2 adj civil(e)

civility [sɪˈvɪlɪtɪ] (pl **civilities**) n politesse f

civilization [sɪvɪlaɪˈzeɪʃən] n civilisation f

civilize [ˈsɪvɪlaɪz] vt civiliser

civilized [ˈsɪvɪlaɪzd] adj civilisé(e); their divorce was very c. leur divorce s'est passé sans heurts

CJD [siːdʒeɪˈdiː] n Med (abbr **Creutzfeld-Jakob disease**) MJC f; **new variant CJD** nouveau variant m de MJC

cl (abbr **centilitre**) cl

clad [klæd] **1** adj c. **in** vêtu(e) de
2 pt & pp of **clothe**

claim [kleɪm] **1** n (a) (demand) (for damages, compensation) demande f d'indemnisation; (as a right) revendication f; to lay c. to sth revendiquer qch; I have many claims on my time je suis très pris; it's his only c. to fame c'est la seule façon dont il se soit distingué; the town's only c. to fame la seule chose pour laquelle cette ville soit connue (b) (assertion) déclaration f; she makes no c. to originality elle ne prétend pas être originale
2 vt (a) (as a right) revendiquer; to c. **damages** (from sb) réclamer des dommages et intérêts (à qn); to c. **responsibility for sth** revendiquer qch (b) (assert) to c. that... affirmer que...; he claims to be an expert il prétend être un expert (c) (lost property) réclamer (d) (life) the epidemic has claimed thousands of lives l'épidémie a fait des milliers de victimes

claimant [ˈkleɪmənt] n (to throne) prétendant(e) m,f; Law (for social security, insurance) demandeur(-eresse) m,f

clairvoyant [kleəˈvɔɪənt] **1** n voyant(e) m,f
2 adj extralucide

clam [klæm] n palourde f

▶**clam up** (pt & pp **clammed**) vi Fam se fermer comme une huître

clamber [ˈklæmbə(r)] vi to c. **up sth** escalader qch

clammy [ˈklæmɪ] adj moite

clamorous [ˈklæmərəs] adj bruyant(e)

clamour [ˈklæmə(r)] **1** n (noise) clameur f; (protest) tollé m
2 vi to c. **for sth** réclamer qch à grands cris

clamp [klæmp] **1** n (tool) serre-joint m; (fixed to bench) étau m; Med clamp m; BrAut (wheel) c. sabot m (de Denver)
2 vt (fasten) fixer; (car) mettre un sabot à

▶**clamp down on** vt insep faire la chasse à

clampdown [ˈklæmpdaʊn] n répression f (on de); a c. on crime un plan de lutte contre la criminalité

clan [klæn] n also Fig clan m

clandestine [klænˈdestɪn] adj clandestin(e)

clang [klæŋ] **1** n bruit m métallique
2 vi (of bell) retentir; the gate clanged shut le portail se ferma avec un bruit métallique

clanger [ˈklæŋə(r)] n Fam gaffe f; to drop a c. faire une gaffe

clank [klæŋk] **1** n bruit m métallique
2 vi cliqueter

clap [klæp] **1** n (a) (with hands) to give sb a c. applaudir qn; c. of thunder un coup de tonnerre (b) very Fam the c. la chaude-pisse
2 vt (pt & pp **clapped**) (a) (applaud) applaudir; to c. one's hands applaudir; (once) frapper dans ses mains; to c. sb on the back donner une tape sur le dos à qn (b) (put) he clapped his hat on il enfonça son chapeau sur sa tête; Fam to c. sb in jail coller qn en prison; Fam to c. eyes on sb/sth voir qn/qch; I've never clapped eyes on her before je ne l'ai jamais vue de ma vie
3 vi (applaud) applaudir

clapped-out [ˈklæptˈaʊt] adj Br Fam (car, machine) déglingué(e)

clapper [ˈklæpə(r)] n (of bell) battant m; Br Fam to run like the clappers courir à toutes jambes

clapping [ˈklæpɪŋ] n (applause) applaudissements mpl

claptrap ['klæptræp] *n Fam* bêtises *fpl*
claret ['klærət] *n* bordeaux *m* (rouge)
clarification [klærɪfɪ'keɪʃən] *n* clarification *f*, éclaircissement *m*
clarify ['klærɪfaɪ] (*pt & pp* **clarified**) *vt* clarifier, éclaircir
clarinet [klærɪ'net] *n* clarinette *f*
clarity ['klærɪtɪ] *n* clarté *f*
clash [klæʃ] **1** *n* (**a**) (*of opinions, interests*) conflit *m*; (*between people, armies*) affrontement *m* (**b**) (*of metal objects*) fracas *m*
2 *vi* (**a**) (*come into conflict*) s'affronter; **to c. with sb** affronter qn; **police clashed with protesters** il y a eu des heurts entre la police et les manifestants (**b**) (*of evidence, explanations*) ne pas correspondre; (*of colours*) jurer (**c**) (*of events*) **to c. with** tomber en même temps que (**d**) (*of metal objects*) s'entrechoquer
clasp [klɑːsp] **1** *n* (*on necklace, handbag*) fermoir *m*; **c. knife** canif *m*
2 *vt* (*grip*) serrer; (*embrace*) étreindre; **to c. sb's hand** serrer la main à qn
class [klɑːs] **1** *n* (*in school, category, social group*) classe *f*; **to be in a c. of one's own** être insurpassable; **c. struggle** lutte *f* des classes
2 *vt* (*classify*) classer (**as** parmi)
classic ['klæsɪk] **1** *n* (**a**) (*book, film etc*) classique *m* (**b**) *Sch & Univ* **classics** lettres *fpl* classiques
2 *adj* classique
classical ['klæsɪkəl] *adj* classique; **c. music** musique *f* classique
classification [klæsɪfɪ'keɪʃən] *n* classification *f*; (*of students*) classement *m*
classified ['klæsɪfaɪd] **1** *n* **the classifieds** (*in newspaper*) les petites annonces *fpl*
2 *adj* (**a**) (*secret*) confidentiel(elle) (**b**) **c. advertisements** (*in newspaper*) petites annonces *fpl*
classify ['klæsɪfaɪ] (*pt & pp* **classified**) *vt* classer
classmate ['klɑːsmeɪt] *n* camarade *mf* de classe
classroom ['klɑːsruːm] *n* (salle *f* de) classe *f*
classy ['klɑːsɪ] *adj Fam* qui a de la classe; (*bar*) chic *inv*
clatter ['klætə(r)] **1** *n* (*of shoes*) claquement *m*; (*of dishes*) fracas *m*
2 *vi* **the car clattered along the road** la voiture descendit la rue dans un bruit de ferraille; **to c. about** (*of person*) s'activer bruyamment
clause [klɔːz] *n* (*of contract*) clause *f*; *Gram* proposition *f*
claustrophobia [klɔːstrə'fəʊbɪə] *n* claustrophobie *f*
claustrophobic [klɔːstrə'fəʊbɪk] *adj* (*person*) claustrophobe; (*place, situation*) où l'on se sent claustrophobe
clavicle ['klævɪkəl] *n* clavicule *f*
claw [klɔː] **1** *n* (*of animal*) griffe *f*; (*of bird of prey*) serre *f*; (*of crab, lobster*) pince *f*; **c. hammer** arrache-clou *m*
2 *vt* (*scratch*) griffer; *Fig* **to c. one's way to the top** parvenir au sommet à force de travail
▸**claw back** *vt* (*money*) récupérer
clay [kleɪ] *n* argile *f*, (terre *f*) glaise *f*; **c. court** (*for tennis*) court *m* en terre battue; **c. pigeon** pigeon *m* d'argile; **c. pigeon shooting** ball-trap *m*
clean [kliːn] **1** *n* **to give sth a c.** nettoyer qch
2 *adj* (**a**) (*not dirty*) propre; (*piece of paper*) blanc (blanche), *Fam* **game/fight** un jeu/une bataille dans les règles; **c. living** vie *f* saine; **to have a c. driving licence** avoir tous ses points sur son permis de conduire (**b**) (*not obscene*) décent(e); **it's good c. fun** c'est innocent (**c**) (*shape, outline*) net (nette); **to**

make a c. break (*of couple*) rompre une bonne fois pour toutes
3 *adv* (**a**) (*completely*) **to cut c. through sth** couper qch net; *Fam* **I c. forgot** j'ai complètement oublié (**b**) *Fam* **to come c.** dire la vérité
4 *vt* nettoyer; **to c. one's teeth/hands** se laver les dents/mains
▸**clean out** *vt sep* (**a**) (*cupboard, room*) nettoyer à fond (**b**) *Fam* (*leave without money*) nettoyer, plumer
▸**clean up 1** *vt sep* nettoyer
2 *vi* (**a**) (*tidy up*) nettoyer; (*wash oneself*) se laver (**b**) *Fam* (*win money*) toucher un gros paquet
clean-cut ['kliːn'kʌt] *adj* (*features*) net (nette), bien dessiné(e); (*person*) à l'apparence très soignée
cleaner ['kliːnə(r)] *n* (*person*) agent *m* de service; (*substance*) produit *m* de nettoyage; **c.'s** (*shop*) pressing *m*; *Fam Fig* **to take sb to the c.'s** (*cheat*) nettoyer ou plumer qn
cleaning ['kliːnɪŋ] *n* nettoyage *m*; (*housework*) ménage *m*; **c. lady** femme *f* de ménage
cleanliness ['klenlɪnɪs] *n* (*of place, person*) propreté *f*
cleanly ['kliːnlɪ] *adv* proprement; (*fight*) dans les règles
cleanse [klenz] *vt* nettoyer; (*skin*) démaquiller
cleanser ['klenzə(r)] *n* (*for skin*) démaquillant *m*
clean-shaven ['kliːn'ʃeɪvən] *adj* rasé(e) de près
cleansing lotion ['klenzɪŋləʊʃən] *n* lait *m* démaquillant
clear [klɪə(r)] **1** *n* **to be in the c.** (*not under suspicion*) être lavé(e) de tout soupçon; (*out of danger*) être hors de danger
2 *adj* (**a**) (*liquid, image, directions*) clair(e); (*picture*) net (nette); (*glass*) transparent(e); (*skin*) net (nette); **on a c. day** par temps clair; **all c.!** la voie est libre!; **to have a c. conscience** avoir la conscience tranquille; **as c. as a bell** (*of voice, sound*) cristallin(e); **c. profit** bénéfice *m* net; **c. winner** vainqueur *m* incontesté
(**b**) (*obvious*) clair(e), évident(e); **to make it c. to sb that...** bien faire comprendre à qn que...; **it is c. that...** il est clair *ou* évident que...; **to make oneself c.** se faire comprendre; **I wasn't c. what she meant** je n'étais pas sûr d'avoir parfaitement compris ce qu'elle voulait dire
(**c**) (*space, road, passageway*) libre
(**d**) **to be c. of sth** (*rid of*) être débarrassé(e) de qch
3 *adv* **to steer c. of** éviter; **stand c. of the doors!** attention à la fermeture automatique des portières!
4 *vt* (**a**) (*road, area*) dégager; **the police cleared the square of demonstrators** la police a forcé les manifestants à évacuer la place; **to c. one's throat** se racler la gorge; **to c. the table** débarrasser la table; **to c. a debt** s'acquitter d'une dette; *Fig* **to c. the decks** déblayer le terrain; *Fig* **to c. the way for sth** ouvrir la voie à qch; *Fig* **to c. the air** (*ease tension*) détendre l'atmosphère; (*clarify matters*) mettre les choses au point
(**b**) (*exonerate*) disculper, innocenter; **to c. sb of blame** disculper qn; **to c. sb's name** blanchir (le nom de) qn
(**c**) (*jump over*) sauter, franchir
(**d**) (*authorize*) approuver; **I'll need to c. it with the boss** il faut que j'obtienne la permission du patron
5 *vi* (**a**) (*of weather*) s'éclaircir; (*of sky*) se dégager; (*of fog*) se lever
(**b**) (*of cheque*) **the cheque hasn't cleared yet** le chèque n'a pas encore été viré

▶**clear away** *vt sep (dishes)* ranger; *(obstruction)* enlever

▶**clear off** *vi Br Fam (leave)* filer, se tirer

▶**clear out 1** *vt sep (cupboard)* vider; *(garage, shed)* débarrasser

2 *vi Fam (leave)* filer, se tirer

▶**clear up 1** *vt sep* (**a**) *(room)* ranger (**b**) *(doubt, misunderstanding)* dissiper; **to c. up a matter** tirer une affaire au clair

2 *vi (of weather)* s'éclaircir

clearance ['klɪərəns] *n* (**a**) *Com* **c. sale** liquidation *f* (**b**) *(authorization)* autorisation *f* (**c**) *(space)* espace *m* (libre)

clear-cut ['klɪə'kʌt] *adj (division, outline, feature)* net (nette); *(opinion)* tranché(e); **it's not as c. as that** ce n'est pas aussi simple que ça

clear-headed ['klɪə'hedɪd] *adj* lucide

clearing ['klɪərɪŋ] *n (in forest)* clairière *f*

clearing house ['klɪərɪŋhaʊs] *n Fin* chambre *f* de compensation

clearly ['klɪəlɪ] *adv* (**a**) *(explain, write)* clairement; *(see)* bien (**b**) *(obviously)* évidemment; **he is c. wrong** il est évident qu'il a tort

clearness ['klɪənsɪ] *n* clarté *f*; *(of image)* netteté *f*

clearout ['klɪəraʊt] *n* **to have a c.** faire le nettoyage par le vide

clear-sighted ['klɪə'saɪtɪd] *adj (perceptive)* clairvoyant(e)

cleavage ['kliːvɪdʒ] *n (of woman)* décolleté *m*

cleave [kliːv] *(pt* **cleaved** *or* **cleft** [kleft] *or* **clove** [kləʊv], *pp* **cleaved** *or* **cleft** *or* **cloven** ['kləʊvən]) *vt Lit* fendre

▶**cleave to** *(pt & pp* **cleaved**) *vt insep Formal* être fidèle à

cleaver ['kliːvə(r)] *n* hachoir *m*

clef [klef] *n Mus* clé *f*, clef *f*

cleft [kleft] **1** *n* fissure *f*

2 *adj* fendu(e); **c. palate** division *f* palatine; **to be caught in a c. stick** *(in awkward situation)* être entre le marteau et l'enclume

3 *pt & pp of* **cleave**

clemency ['klemənsɪ] *n* clémence *f*

clementine ['klemənti:n] *n* clémentine *f*

clench [klentʃ] *vt* **to c. one's fist/teeth** serrer le poing/ les dents

Cleopatra [kli:əʊ'pætrə] *n* Cléopâtre

clergy ['klɜːdʒɪ] *n* clergé *m*

clergyman ['klɜːdʒɪmən] *n* ecclésiastique *m*; *(Protestant)* pasteur *m*; *(Catholic)* prêtre *m*

cleric ['klerɪk] *n Rel* ecclésiastique *m*

clerical ['klerɪkəl] *adj* (**a**) *(administrative)* **c. assistant** employé(e) *m,f* de bureau; **c. work** travail *m* de bureau (**b**) *Rel* clérical(e)

clerk [klɑːk, *Am* klɜːrk] *n* (**a**) *(office worker)* employé(e) *m,f* de bureau (**b**) *Am (in shop)* vendeur(euse) *m,f*

clever ['klevə(r)] *adj (intelligent)* intelligent(e); *(plan, idea)* ingénieux(euse); **to be c. with one's hands** être adroit(e) de ses mains; *Br Fam* **to be too c. by half** être trop malin(igne); *Br Fam* **a c. Dick** un petit malin

cleverly ['klevəlɪ] *adv (intelligently)* intelligemment; *(planned)* ingénieusement

cleverness ['klevənɪs] *n (intelligence)* intelligence *f*; *(of plan)* ingéniosité *f*; *(skill)* adresse *f*

cliché ['kli:ʃeɪ] *n* cliché *m*

click [klɪk] **1** *n (sound)* petit bruit *m* sec

2 *vt* (**a**) **to c. one's heels** claquer les talons; **to c.**
one's tongue faire claquer sa langue (**b**) *Comput* cliquer

3 *vi* (**a**) *(make a sound)* faire un petit bruit sec (**b**) *Fam (become obvious)* faire tilt; **it suddenly clicked** tout à coup ça a fait tilt (**c**) *Fam (of people)* **we clicked straight away** ça a accroché tout de suite entre nous (**d**) *Comput* **to c. on** cliquer sur qch

clickable ['klɪkəbəl] *adj Comput* cliquable

client ['klaɪənt] *n* client(e) *m,f*

clientele [kli:ən'tel] *n* clientèle *f*

cliff [klɪf] *n* falaise *f*

cliffhanger ['klɪfhæŋə(r)] *n* **it was a real c.** il y a eu du suspense jusqu'au bout

climactic [klaɪ'mæktɪk] *adj* qui constitue le point culminant

climate ['klaɪmət] *n* climat *m*

climatic [klaɪ'mætɪk] *adj* climatique

climax ['klaɪmæks] **1** *n (of events)* paroxysme *m*; *(of career)* apogée *m*; *(of film, book)* point *m* culminant; *(sexual)* orgasme *m*

2 *vi (of events)* atteindre son paroxysme; *(of career)* atteindre son apogée; *(of film, book)* atteindre son point culminant; *(sexually)* atteindre l'orgasme

climb [klaɪm] **1** *n* montée *f*, ascension *f*

2 *vt (tree)* grimper à; *(mountain)* faire l'ascension de; *(rock face)* escalader; *(stairs)* monter

3 *vi (of road, prices)* grimper; *(of plane)* monter; **to c. over sth** passer par-dessus qch

▶**climb down** **1** *vt insep (descend)* descendre

2 *vi* (**a**) *(descend)* descendre (**b**) *Fig (in argument)* céder, en rabattre

climbdown ['klaɪmdaʊn] *n* dérobade *f*, reculade *f*

climber ['klaɪmə(r)] *n* (**a**) *(mountaineer)* alpiniste *mf* (**b**) *(plant)* plante *f* grimpante

climbing ['klaɪmɪŋ] **1** *n (hill-walking)* randonnée *f* en montagne; *(of rockface)* escalade *f*; *(mountaineering)* alpinisme *m*; **c. frame** cage *f* à poules

2 *adj (plant)* grimpant(e)

clinch [klɪntʃ] **1** *n (of fighters)* corps à corps *m*; *(of lovers)* étreinte *f*

2 *vt (settle) (deal)* conclure; *(argument)* résoudre; **that clinches it!** voilà qui règle le problème une fois pour toutes!

cling [klɪŋ] *(pt & pp* **clung** [klʌŋ]) *vi* **to c. to** *(rope, person)* s'accrocher à; *Fig (opinion)* persister dans; *(faith)* se raccrocher à

clingfilm ['klɪŋfɪlm] *n* film *m* alimentaire

clinic ['klɪnɪk] *n (part of hospital)* service *m*; *Br (private hospital)* clinique *f*

clinical ['klɪnɪkəl] *adj* (**a**) *Med* clinique (**b**) *(unemotional)* froid(e), aseptisé(e)

clink¹ [klɪŋk] **1** *n (sound)* tintement *m*

2 *vt* faire tinter; **to c. glasses with sb** trinquer avec qn

3 *vi (of glasses)* tinter

clink² *n very Fam (prison)* taule *f*

clip¹ [klɪp] **1** *n (for papers)* trombone *m*; *(for hair)* barrette *f*

2 *vt (pt & pp* **clipped**) *(papers)* attacher *(avec un trombone)* (**to** à)

3 *vi* **to c. together** s'emboîter

clip² **1** *n* (**a**) *Fam (blow)* **to give sb a c. round the ear** flanquer une taloche à qn (**b**) *(of film, programme)* extrait *m*; *Comput* **c. art** clipart *m*

2 *(pt & pp* **clipped**) *vt* (**a**) *(hit)* **to c. sb round the ear** flanquer une taloche à qn (**b**) *(hedge)* tailler; *(ticket)* poinçonner; *(dog)* couper les poils à; *(hair, nails)*

couper; *Fig* **to c. sb's wings** réduire la marge de manœuvre de qn
clipboard ['klɪpbɔːd] *n* planchette *f* porte-papiers *(à pince)*
clip-on ['klɪpɒn] *adj* **c. earring** clip *m*; **c. microphone** micro-cravate *m*; **c. sunglasses** = verres teintés que l'on fixe à une autre paire de lunettes
clipped [klɪpt] *adj (speech, tone)* saccadé(e)
clipper ['klɪpə(r)] *n (ship)* clipper *m*
clippers ['klɪpəz] *npl (for hair)* tondeuse *f*; *(for nails)* coupe-ongles *m inv*; *(for hedge)* cisaille *f*
clipping ['klɪpɪŋ] *n (from newspaper)* coupure *f*
clique [kliːk] *n* clique *f*
clitoris ['klɪtərɪs] *n* clitoris *m*
cloak [kləʊk] **1** *n* cape *f*; *Fig* **under the c. of darkness** sous le couvert de la nuit
  2 *vt Fig* **cloaked in secrecy** enveloppé(e) de mystère
cloak-and-dagger [kləʊkən'dægə(r)] *adj (film, book)* d'espionnage; *Fig (mysterious)* mystérieux(euse)
cloakroom ['kləʊkruːm] *n* vestiaire *m*
clobber¹ ['klɒbə(r)] *n Br Fam (clothes)* frusques *fpl*, fringues *fpl*; *(belongings)* barda *m*
clobber² *vt Fam (hit)* tabasser; *(defeat)* battre à plate couture
clock [klɒk] **1** *n* (**a**) *(large)* horloge *f*; *(small)* pendule *f*; **round the c.** vingt-quatre heures sur vingt-quatre; **a race against the c.** une course contre la montre; **to put the clocks forward/back** *(in spring, autumn)* avancer/retarder les pendules; *Fig* **to turn the c. back** revenir en arrière; **c. radio** radio-réveil *m* (**b**) *Fam (mileometer)* compteur *m* kilométrique
  2 *vt (measure speed of)* chronométrer; *(reach speed of)* atteindre
▶**clock in** *vi* pointer *(en arrivant sur son lieu de travail)*
▶**clock off** *vi* pointer *(en quittant son lieu de travail)*
▶**clock on** = clock in
▶**clock out** = clock off
▶**clock up** *vt sep (profits)* réaliser; *(votes)* totaliser; **this car has clocked up 10,000 miles** cette voiture a 10 000 miles au compteur
clockmaker ['klɒkmeɪkə(r)] *n* horloger(ère) *m,f*
clockwise ['klɒkwaɪz] *adv* dans le sens des aiguilles d'une montre
clockwork ['klɒkwɜːk] **1** *n* **to go like c.** *(of interview, ceremony)* marcher comme sur des roulettes; **to run like c.** *(of office, system)* être réglé(e) comme du papier à musique
  2 *adj (toy)* mécanique
clod [klɒd] *n (of earth)* motte *f*
clog [klɒg] **1** *n (shoe)* sabot *m*
  2 *vt (pt & pp* **clogged** *) (block)* boucher
  3 *vi* se boucher
▶**clog up** *vt sep* boucher
  2 *vi* se boucher
cloister ['klɔɪstə(r)] *n* cloître *m*
cloistered ['klɔɪstəd] *adj* **to lead a c. life** mener une vie de reclus(e)
clone [kləʊn] **1** *n also Fig* clone *m*
  2 *vt Biol* cloner
cloning ['kləʊnɪŋ] *n* clonage *m*
close¹ [kləʊs] **1** *adj* (**a**) *(in distance, time, relationship)* proche; **to be in c. contact with sb** être en contact étroit avec qn; **a c. friend** un(e) ami(e) intime; **a c. relative** un proche parent; **that was a c. call** *or* **shave** il s'en est fallu de peu; **at c. quarters** de près; **at c. range** de près; **c. combat** corps à corps *m* (**b**) *(inspection)*

minutieux(euse); *(attention)* soutenu(e); **to keep a c. watch on sb/sth** surveiller qn/qch de près (**c**) *(weather)* lourd(e); *(room)* qui sent le renfermé (**d**) *(contest, election)* serré(e)
  2 *adv (near)* près; **to hold sb c.** serrer qn; **c. to** près de; **c. to tears** au bord des larmes; **c. to victory** proche de la victoire; **to come c. to death** frôler la mort; **to be c. to sb** *(emotionally)* être proche de qn; **c. at hand** à proximité; **to follow c. behind sb** suivre qn de près; **to be c. on fifty** friser la cinquantaine; **c. up** de près
  3 *n (cul-de-sac)* impasse *f*
close² [kləʊz] **1** *n (end)* fin *f*; **to draw to a c.** tirer à sa fin; **to bring sth to a c.** clore qch
  2 *vt* (**a**) *(door, eyes, book, road)* fermer; *Fig* **to c. ranks around sb** faire bloc autour de qn (**b**) *(meeting, debate)* clore; *(account)* fermer; *(deal)* conclure (**c**) *(business, shop)* fermer
  3 *vi (of shop, business)* fermer; *(of door)* se fermer
▶**close down 1** *vt (production, operations)* cesser; *(business, factory)* fermer
  2 *vi (of business, factory)* fermer; **Channel 6 closes down at midnight** les émissions sur Channel 6 se terminent à minuit
▶**close in** *vi (of night)* tomber; **to c. in on sb** se rapprocher de qn
▶**close up 1** *vt sep (shop)* fermer
  2 *vi* (**a**) *(of wound, hole)* se refermer (**b**) *(of shopkeeper)* fermer
close-cropped ['kləʊs'krɒpt] *adj (hair)* coupé(e) ras
closed [kləʊzd] *adj* fermé(e); **c. circuit television** télévision *f* en circuit fermé; **behind c. doors** à huis clos; *Ind* **c. shop** = usine ou société qui n'embauche que des travailleurs syndiqués
close-fitting ['kləʊs'fɪtɪŋ] *adj* bien ajusté(e)
close-knit ['kləʊs'nɪt] *adj (community, group)* très soudé(e); *(family)* très uni(e)
closely ['kləʊslɪ] *adv* (**a**) *(examine, listen, watch)* attentivement; *(resemble)* beaucoup; **to be c. related** *(of concepts)* être étroitement lié(e)s; *(of people)* être proches parents; **c. contested** très serré(e) (**b**) *(populated)* densément; **c. packed** très serré(e)
closeness ['kləʊsnɪs] *n (physical proximity)* proximité *f*; *(of relationship, contact)* intimité *f*
close-run ['kləʊs'rʌn] *adj (election, race)* serré(e)
close-set ['kləʊs'set] *adj (eyes)* rapproché(e)
closet ['klɒzɪt] **1** *n* placard *m*; *Fig* **to come out of the c.** révéler son homosexualité
  2 *adj* **c. homosexual** = personne qui cache son homosexualité; *Hum* **he's a c. Celine Dion fan** il n'ose pas avouer qu'il aime Celine Dion
  3 *vt* enfermer; **to c. oneself away** s'enfermer, s'isoler
close-up ['kləʊsʌp] *n* gros plan *m*; **in c.** en gros plan
closing ['kləʊzɪŋ] *n* fermeture *f*; **c. date** date *f* limite; **c. prices** cours *mpl* de clôture; **c. speech** discours *m* de clôture; **c. time** heure *f* de fermeture
closure ['kləʊʒə(r)] *n (of company, shop)* fermeture *f* *(définitive)*
clot [klɒt] **1** *n* (**a**) *(of blood)* caillot *m* (**b**) *Fam (stupid person)* andouille *f*
  2 *vi (pt & pp* **clotted** *) (of blood)* (se) coaguler
cloth [klɒθ] *n* (**a**) *(material)* tissu *m*; **a man of the c.** un membre du clergé (**b**) *(duster)* chiffon *m*
clothe [kləʊð] *(pt & pp* **clad** [klæd] *or* **clothed** *) vt* vêtir, habiller

clothes [kləʊðz] *npl* vêtements *mpl*; **to put one's c. on** s'habiller; **to take one's c. off** se déshabiller; **c. brush** brosse *f* à habits; **c. hanger** cintre *m*; **c. horse** séchoir *m (à linge)*; **c. line** corde *f* à linge; **c. peg** pince *f* à linge; **c. rack** séchoir *m* (à linge)

clothing [ˈkləʊðɪŋ] *n (clothes)* vêtements *mpl*; **an article of c.** un vêtement; **the c. industry** l'industrie *f* du vêtement

clotted cream [ˈklɒtɪdˈkriːm] *n Br* = crème fraîche très épaisse, typique du sud-ouest de l'Angleterre

cloud [klaʊd] **1** *n* (**a**) *(in sky)* nuage *m; Fig (of insects)* nuée *f* (**b**) *(idioms)* **to be under a c.** être en disgrâce; **to have one's head in the clouds** être dans les nuages; *Fam* **to be on c. nine** être aux anges
2 *vt* (**a**) *(mirror)* embuer (**b**) *(happiness)* jeter une ombre sur; *(judgement)* affecter; **to c. the issue** embrouiller la question
▶**cloud over** *vi (of sky)* se couvrir

cloudburst [ˈklaʊdbɜːst] *n* averse *f*

cloudless [ˈklaʊdlɪs] *adj* sans nuages

cloudy [ˈklaʊdɪ] *adj* (**a**) *(sky, day)* nuageux(euse) (**b**) *(liquid)* trouble

clout [klaʊt] *Fam* **1** *n* (**a**) *(blow)* coup *m*; **to give sb a c. (with sth)** frapper qn (avec qch) (**b**) *(power, influence)* influence *f*; **to have a lot of c.** avoir le bras long
2 *vt (hit)* flanquer une taloche à

clove¹ [kləʊv] *n (of garlic)* gousse *f*

clove² *n (spice)* clou *m* de girofle

clove³ *pt of* **cleave**

cloven [ˈkləʊvən] **1** *adj* **c. hoof** sabot *m* fendu
2 *pp of* **cleave**

clover [ˈkləʊvə(r)] *n* trèfle *m; Fig* **to be in c.** être comme un coq en pâte

clown [klaʊn] **1** *n* clown *m*; **to act the c.** faire le clown
2 *vi* **to c. about** *or* **around** faire le clown

cloying [ˈklɔɪɪŋ] *adj (taste, smell)* écœurant(e)

club [klʌb] **1** *n* (**a**) *(society)* club *m; Fam Fig* **join the c.!** tu n'es pas le seul/la seule!; **c. sandwich** sandwich *m* mixte; *Am* **c. soda** eau *f* de Seltz (**b**) *(nightclub)* boîte *f* (de nuit) (**c**) *(weapon)* massue *f*, gourdin *m; (in golf)* club *m* (**d**) **clubs** *(in cards)* trèfle *m*; **ace of clubs** as *m* de trèfle
2 *vt (pt & pp* **clubbed**) *(hit)* frapper avec une massue
3 *vi* **to go clubbing** aller en boîte
▶**club together** *vi* se cotiser (**to buy** pour acheter)

Clubs

Les "clubs" britanniques sont des lieux de rencontre et de détente très fermés, qui jouent un rôle important dans la vie sociale des milieux aisés en Grande-Bretagne. Traditionnellement ces institutions (notamment les "gentlemen's clubs" londoniens, tels que l'Athenaeum ou le Carlton Club) étaient interdites aux femmes, mais récemment cette tendance a commencé à changer.

clubhouse [ˈklʌbhaʊs] *n* pavillon *m*

cluck [klʌk] **1** *n* gloussement *m*
2 *vi* glousser

clue [kluː] *n (in crime, mystery)* indice *m; (in crossword)* définition *f*; **to give sb a c.** donner un indice à qn, mettre qn sur la voie; **where's Lola? – I haven't a c.!** où est Lola? – je n'en ai pas la moindre idée!; *Fam* **he hasn't a c.** *(is incompetent)* il est vraiment nul
▶**clue up** *vt sep Fam* **to be clued up (on sth)** être très calé(e) (en qch)

clueless [ˈkluːlɪs] *adj Br Fam* nul (nulle)

clump [klʌmp] **1** *n* (**a**) *(of bushes)* massif *m; (of people)* groupe *m* (**b**) *(sound)* bruit *m* bref et sourd
2 *vi* **to c. about** marcher d'un pas lourd

clumsiness [ˈklʌmzɪnɪs] *n (of person, movement)* maladresse *f*

clumsy [ˈklʌmzɪ] *adj (person, movement)* maladroit(e)

clung [klʌŋ] *pt & pp of* **cling**

cluster [ˈklʌstə(r)] **1** *n (of grapes)* grappe *f; (of people, islands, houses)* groupe *m*
2 *vi* **to c. round sb/sth** se grouper autour de qn/qch

clutch¹ [klʌtʃ] **1** *n* (**a**) *(in car)* embrayage *m*; **to let the c. in/out** embrayer/débrayer; **c. pedal** pédale *f* d'embrayage (**b**) *(grasp)* **to fall into sb's clutches** tomber entre les griffes de qn
2 *vt* tenir fermement
3 *vi* **to c. at sth** s'agripper à qch; *Fig* **to c. at straws** se raccrocher à n'importe quoi

clutch² *n (of eggs)* couvée *f*

clutter [ˈklʌtə(r)] **1** *n* désordre *m*; **in a c.** en désordre
2 *vt* encombrer; **to be cluttered (up) with sth** être encombré(e) de qch

cluttered [ˈklʌtəd] *adj* encombré(e)

cm *n (abbr* **centimetre(s)**) cm

CND [siːenˈdiː] *n Br (abbr* **Campaign for Nuclear Disarmament**) = mouvement prônant le désarmement nucléaire

CO [siːˈəʊ] *n Mil (abbr* **Commanding Officer**) chef *m* de corps

Co, co [kəʊ] *n (abbr* **company**) Cie; *Fig* **Jane and co** Jane et compagnie

c/o [siːˈəʊ] *(abbr* **care of**) chez, aux bons soins de

coach [kəʊtʃ] **1** *n* (**a**) *Br (bus)* car *m; (horse-drawn carriage)* carrosse *m; (section of train)* voiture *f*, wagon *m*; **c. party** excursionnistes *mpl (voyageant en car)*; **c. trip** excursion *f* en car (**b**) *Am Aviat* **c. class** classe *f* économique (**c**) *(of athlete, team)* entraîneur(euse) *m,f*
2 *vt (athlete, team)* entraîner; **to c. sb for an exam** donner des leçons particulières à qn en préparation à un examen

coachbuilder [ˈkəʊtʃbɪldə(r)] *n Aut* carrossier *m*

coagulant [kəʊˈægjʊlənt] *n Med* coagulant *m*

coagulate [kəʊˈægjʊleɪt] *vi* coaguler

coal [kəʊl] *n* (**a**) charbon *m*; **c. bunker** coffre *m* à charbon; **c. merchant** négociant *m* en charbon; **c. mine** mine *f* de charbon; **c. miner** mineur *m*; **c. mining** extraction *f* du charbon; **c. tar** goudron *m* de houille (**b**) *(idioms)* **to carry coals to Newcastle** porter de l'eau à la rivière

coalesce [kəʊəˈles] *vi* s'unir

coalfield [ˈkəʊlfiːld] *n* bassin *m* houiller

coalition [kəʊəˈlɪʃən] *n* coalition *f*

coalman [ˈkəʊlmæn] *n* charbonnier *m*

coarse [kɔːs] *adj* (**a**) *(person, language)* grossier(ère), vulgaire (**b**) *(surface, texture)* grossier(ère); **to have c. hair** avoir le cheveu épais et rêche

coarsely [ˈkɔːslɪ] *adv* (**a**) *(vulgarly)* vulgairement (**b**) *(roughly)* **c. chopped/ground** haché(e)/moulu(e) grossièrement

coarseness [ˈkɔːsnɪs] *n* (**a**) *(of person, language)* grossièreté *f*, vulgarité *f* (**b**) *(of surface, texture)* grossièreté *f*

coast [kəʊst] **1** *n* côte *f; Fig* **the c. is clear** la voie est libre
2 *vi (in car, on bicycle)* avancer en roue libre; *Fig* **she**

coasted through her exams elle a eu ses examens haut la main
coastal ['kəʊstəl] *adj* côtier(ère)
coaster ['kəʊstə(r)] *n* (**a**) *(for glass)* dessous *m* de verre (**b**) *(ship)* caboteur *m*
coastguard ['kəʊstgɑːd] *n* garde-côte *m*
coastline ['kəʊstlaɪn] *n* littoral *m*
coat [kəʊt] **1** *n* (**a**) *(garment)* manteau *m*; **c. hanger** cintre *m*; **c. hook** patère *f* (**b**) *(of horse)* robe *f*; *(of dog)* pelage *m* (**c**) *(of snow, paint)* couche *f* (**d**) *(in heraldry)* **c. of arms** armoiries *fpl*
2 *vt (with mud, paint)* couvrir (**with** de); *(with chocolate, sugar)* enrober (**with** de)
coating ['kəʊtɪŋ] *n (of paint, dust)* couche *f*; *(of chocolate)* enrobage *m*
co-author [kəʊˈɔːθə(r)] **1** *n* coauteur *m*
2 *vt* **to c. a book with sb** écrire un livre en collaboration avec qn
coax [kəʊks] *vt* enjôler; **to c. sb to do** *or* **into doing sth** amener qn à faire qch par des cajoleries; **to c. sth out of sb** obtenir qch de qn par des cajoleries
cob [kɒb] *n* (**a**) *(horse)* cob *m* (**b**) *(of corn)* épi *m*
cobalt ['kəʊbɔːlt] *n* cobalt *m*; **c. blue** bleu *m* de cobalt
cobble ['kɒbəl] **1** *n* pavé *m*
2 *vt* paver
▸**cobble together** *vt sep* bricoler
cobbled ['kɒbəld] *adj (path, street)* pavé(e)
cobbler ['kɒblə(r)] *n* cordonnier *m*
cobblers ['kɒbləz] *npl Br* (**a**) *very Fam (nonsense)* conneries *fpl* (**b**) *Vulg (testicles)* couilles *fpl*
COBOL ['kəʊbɒl] *n* Comput *(abbr* **Common Business Oriented Language)** Cobol *m*
cobra ['kəʊbrə] *n* cobra *m*
cobweb ['kɒbweb] *n* toile *f* d'araignée; *Fig* **to brush the cobwebs off sth** ressortir qch
cocaine [kəʊˈkeɪn] *n* cocaïne *f*
cock [kɒk] **1** *n* (**a**) *(male fowl)* coq *m*; **c. sparrow** moineau *m* mâle (**b**) *Vulg (penis)* bite *f*
2 *vt (gun)* armer; **to c. a snook at sb** faire la nique à qn; **to c. its ears** *(of horse, dog)* dresser les oreilles
▸**cock up** *vt sep Br very Fam (plan, arrangement)* faire foirer; *(exam)* se planter à
cockade [kɒˈkeɪd] *n* cocarde *f*
cock-a-doodle-doo ['kɒkəduːdəlˈduː] *exclam* cocorico!
cock-a-hoop ['kɒkəˈhuːp] *adj* enchanté(e)
cockatoo [kɒkəˈtuː] *n* cacatoès *m*
cocked [kɒkt] *adj* **to knock sb into a c. hat** *(outclass)* surpasser qn
cockerel ['kɒkərəl] *n* jeune coq *m*
cocker spaniel [kɒkəˈspænjəl] *n* cocker *m*
cockeyed ['kɒkaɪd] *adj Fam (decision, plan)* farfelu(e)
cockfight ['kɒkfaɪt] *n* combat *m* de coqs
cockle ['kɒkəl] *n* (**a**) *(shellfish)* coque *f* (**b**) *Fam* **it warmed the cockles of his heart** ça lui a réchauffé le cœur
Cockney ['kɒknɪ] **1** *n* (**a**) *(person)* cockney *mf* (**b**) *(dialect)* cockney *m*
2 *adj* cockney
cockpit ['kɒkpɪt] *n* cabine *f* de pilotage, cockpit *m*
cockroach ['kɒkrəʊtʃ] *n* cafard *m*
cocksure ['kɒkˈʃʊə(r)] *adj (person, manner)* présomptueux(euse)
cocktail ['kɒkteɪl] *n also Fig* cocktail *m*; **c. dress** robe *f* de cocktail; **c. lounge** bar *m* confortable *(dans un pub, un hôtel)*; **c. party** cocktail *m*; **c. shaker** shaker *m*; **c. stick** pique *f*

cocky ['kɒkɪ] *adj Fam* culotté(e)
cocoa ['kəʊkəʊ] *n (powder, drink)* cacao *m*; **c. butter** beurre *m* de cacao
coconut ['kəʊkənʌt] *n* noix *f* de coco; **c. milk** lait *m* de coco; **c. palm** cocotier *m*
cocoon [kəˈkuːn] **1** *n also Fig* cocon *m*
2 *vt Fig (protect)* couver
COD [siːəʊˈdiː] *n Com (abbr* **cash on delivery)** paiement *m* à la livraison
cod [kɒd] *(pl* **cod)** *n* morue *f*; **c. liver oil** huile *f* de foie de morue
coddle ['kɒdəl] *vt (child)* dorloter
code [kəʊd] **1** *n* (**a**) *(cipher)* code *m*; **in c.** codé(e); **c. book** code *m*; **c. name** nom *m* de code; **c. number** numéro *m* de code (**b**) *(rules)* **c. of conduct** déontologie *f*, code *m* de conduite
2 *vt (message)* coder
codeine ['kəʊdiːn] *n* codéine *f*
codify ['kəʊdɪfaɪ] *(pt & pp* **codified)** *vt* codifier
codswallop ['kɒdzwɒləp] *n Br Fam* foutaises *fpl*
coeducational [kəʊedjʊˈkeɪʃənəl] *adj (school)* mixte
coefficient [kəʊɪˈfɪʃənt] *n Math* coefficient *m*
coerce [kəʊˈɜːs] *vt* forcer, contraindre; **to c. sb into doing sth** contraindre qn à faire qch
coercion [kəʊˈɜːʃən] *n* coercition *f*
coexist [kəʊɪgˈzɪst] *vi* coexister
coexistence [kəʊɪgˈzɪstəns] *n* coexistence *f*
C of E [siːəvˈiː] *adj Rel (abbr* **Church of England)** anglican(e)
coffee ['kɒfɪ] *n* café *m*; **c. bar** café *m*; **c. bean** grain *m* de café; **c. break** pause-café *f*; **c. cup** tasse *f* à café; **c. grinder** moulin *m* à café; **c. grounds** marc *m* de café; **c. machine** *(in café)* percolateur *m*; *(vending machine)* machine *f* à café; *(in home)* cafetière *f* électrique; **c. mill** moulin *m* à café; **c. pot** cafetière *f*; **c. spoon** cuillère *f* à café; **c. table** table *f* basse; **c. table book** grand livre *m* illustré
coffer ['kɒfə(r)] *n (chest)* coffre *m*; *Fig* **the coffers** *(of company, country)* les caisses *fpl*
coffin ['kɒfɪn] *n* cercueil *m*
cog [kɒg] *n (tooth on gearwheel)* dent *f*; *(gearwheel)* roue *f* dentée, rouage *m*; *Fig* **a c. in the machinery** un rouage dans la machine
cogent ['kəʊdʒənt] *adj* convaincant(e)
cogitate ['kɒdʒɪteɪt] *vi Formal* méditer, réfléchir
cognac ['kɒnjæk] *n* cognac *m*
cognition [kɒgˈnɪʃən] *n* cognition *f*
cohabit [kəʊˈhæbɪt] *vi* vivre en concubinage (**with** avec)
cohabitation [kəʊhæbɪˈteɪʃən] *n* concubinage *m*
coherence [kəʊˈhɪərəns] *n* cohérence *f*
coherent [kəʊˈhɪərənt] *adj* cohérent(e)
cohesion [kəʊˈhiːʒən] *n* cohésion *f*
cohesive [kəʊˈhiːsɪv] *adj* cohésif(ive)
coiffure [kwɑːˈfjʊə(r)] *n* coiffure *f*
coil [kɔɪl] **1** *n* (**a**) *(of rope, wire)* rouleau *m*; *(electrical)* bobine *f*; *(contraceptive device)* stérilet *m* (**b**) *(single loop)* anneau *m*
2 *vt* enrouler (**around** autour de)
▸**coil up** *vt (of snake)* se lover
coin [kɔɪn] **1** *n* (**a**) *(of money)* pièce *f* (de monnaie); *Fig* **the other side of the c.** le revers de la médaille
2 *vt (phrase, word)* inventer; **to c. money** battre monnaie; *Fam* **he's coining it** il se fait un fric fou; *Hum & Ironic* **..., to c. a phrase** ..., comme on dit

coinage ['kɔɪnɪdʒ] n (**a**) (coins) monnaie f (**b**) (word) mot m nouveau, néologisme m; (phrase) expression f nouvelle
coincide [kəʊɪn'saɪd] vi coïncider (**with** avec)
coincidence [kəʊ'ɪnsɪdəns] n coïncidence f
coincidental [kəʊɪnsɪ'dentəl] adj fortuit(e)
coin-operated ['kɔɪnɒpəreɪtɪd] adj (machine) à pièces
coitus ['kɔɪtəs] n Formal coït m; **c. interruptus** coït m interrompu
coke [kəʊk] n (**a**) (fuel) coke m (**b**) Fam (cocaine) coke f
col (abbr **column**) col
colander ['kɒləndə(r)] n passoire f
cold [kəʊld] **1** n (**a**) (low temperature) froid m; **to feel the c.** être frileux(euse); Fig **to be left out in the c.** rester sur la touche (**b**) (illness) rhume m; **to have a c.** avoir un rhume; **to catch a c.** attraper un rhume
 2 adj also Fig froid(e); **I'm c.** j'ai froid; **it's c.** (weather) il fait froid; **to get c.** (of food) refroidir; (of weather) se refroidir; also Fig **to be in a c. sweat** avoir des sueurs froides; Fam **that leaves me c.** ça me laisse froid; **that's c. comfort** c'est une maigre consolation; Fig **to get c. feet (about sth)** hésiter (à faire qch) à la dernière minute; **to give sb the c. shoulder** snober qn; **c. cream** cold-cream m; Met **c. front** front m froid; **c. meats** viandes fpl froides; **c. sore** bouton m de fièvre, Can feu m sauvage; **c. start** (of car) démarrage m à froid; **c. storage** conservation f par le froid; **c. war** guerre f froide
 3 adv **to do sth c.** faire qch à froid; Fam Fig **to be out c.** être sans connaissance
cold-blooded ['kəʊld'blʌdɪd] adj (animal) à sang froid; Fig (person) froid(e), insensible; **c. murder** meurtre m commis de sang-froid
cold-hearted ['kəʊld'hɑːtɪd] adj (person, decision) impitoyable
coldly ['kəʊldlɪ] adv froidement
coldness ['kəʊldnɪs] n froideur f
cold-shoulder ['kəʊld'ʃəʊldə(r)] vt snober
coleslaw ['kəʊlslɔː] n = salade de chou blanc à la mayonnaise
colic ['kɒlɪk] n colique f
collaborate [kə'læbəreɪt] vi also Pej collaborer (**with** avec)
collaboration [kəlæbə'reɪʃən] n also Pej collaboration f
collaborator [kə'læbəreɪtə(r)] n also Pej collaborateur(trice) m,f
collage ['kɒlɑːʒ] n collage m
collapse [kə'læps] **1** n (of building, prices) effondrement m
 2 vi (of person, building, prices) s'effondrer, s'écrouler
collapsible [kə'læpsəbəl] adj (table, bed) pliant(e)
collar ['kɒlə(r)] **1** n (of shirt) col m; (for dog) collier m
 2 vt Fam (seize) pincer
collarbone ['kɒləbəʊn] n clavicule f
collate [kə'leɪt] vt rassembler
collateral [kə'lætərəl] **1** n Fin nantissement m
 2 adj Euph Mil **c. damage** dégâts mpl collatéraux
colleague ['kɒliːg] n collègue mf
collect [kə'lekt] **1** adv Am **to call sb c.** appeler qn en PCV, Can faire un appel à frais virés à qn
 2 vt (**a**) (stamps, paintings) collectionner, faire collection de (**b**) (gather) (belongings) rassembler; (information, news) recueillir; (rubbish) ramasser;

(taxes) lever; **to c. the dust** (of ornament) prendre la poussière; **to c. sb** (pick up) passer prendre qn (**c**) (compose) **to c. one's thoughts** se concentrer; **to c. oneself** se calmer
 3 vi (of people) se rassembler; (of things) s'amasser; (of dust) s'accumuler
collected [kə'lektɪd] adj (**a**) (calm) calme (**b**) **c. works** œuvres fpl complètes
collection [kə'lekʃən] n (**a**) (of stamps, paintings) collection f (**b**) (act of collecting) (of money) recouvrement m; (of rubbish) ramassage m; (of taxes) levée f; **to take a c.** (for charity) faire une collecte; **c. plate** (in church) plat m de quête
collective [kə'lektɪv] **1** n (group) collectif m; (farm) coopérative f agricole
 2 adj collectif(ive); **c. bargaining** = négociations afin d'établir une convention collective; **c. noun** collectif m
collectively [kə'lektɪvlɪ] adv collectivement
collectivize [kə'lektɪvaɪz] vt collectiviser
collector [kə'lektə(r)] n (**a**) (of stamps, paintings) collectionneur(euse) m,f; **c.'s item** pièce f de collection (**b**) **c. of taxes** percepteur m
college ['kɒlɪdʒ] n Br (of further education) établissement m d'enseignement supérieur; Br (part of university) = association d'enseignants et d'étudiants au sein de certaines universités, disposant d'une semi-autonomie administrative; Am (university) université f; **to be at c.** être étudiant(e); **c. of education** ≃ école f normale
collide [kə'laɪd] vi entrer en collision (**with** avec)
collie ['kɒlɪ] n colley m
colliery ['kɒlɪərɪ] n (pl **collieries**) n houillère f, mine f de charbon
collision [kə'lɪʒən] n collision f; Fig **to be on a c. course** aller droit au conflit
colloquial [kə'ləʊkwɪəl] adj familier(ère)
colloquialism [kə'ləʊkwɪəlɪzəm] n expression f familière
collude [kə'luːd] vi être de connivence (**with** avec)
collusion [kə'luːʒən] n collusion f; **to be in c. with sb** être de connivence avec qn
collywobbles ['kɒlɪwɒbəlz] npl Fam **to have the c.** avoir la trouille
cologne [kə'ləʊn] n eau f de Cologne
Colombia [kə'lʌmbɪə] n la Colombie
Colombian [kə'lʌmbɪən] **1** n Colombien(enne) m,f
 2 adj colombien(enne)
colon ['kəʊlən] n (**a**) Anat côlon m (**b**) (punctuation mark) deux-points m
colonel ['kɜːnəl] n colonel m
colonial [kə'ləʊnɪəl] adj colonial(e)
colonialism [kə'ləʊnɪəlɪzəm] n colonialisme m
colonist ['kɒlənɪst] n colon m
colonize ['kɒlənaɪz] vt coloniser
colonnade [kɒlə'neɪd] n Archit colonnade f
colony ['kɒlənɪ] n (pl **colonies**) n colonie f
color, colored etc Am = colour, coloured etc
colossal [kə'lɒsəl] adj colossal(e)
colour, Am color ['kʌlə(r)] **1** n (**a**) (red, blue etc) couleur f; **what c. is it?** de quelle couleur est-ce?; **c. bar** (racial discrimination) discrimination f raciale; **c. blindness** daltonisme m; **c. scheme** coloris mpl, couleurs fpl; **c. supplement** (of newspaper) supplément m en couleurs; **c. television** télévision f couleur (**b**) (idioms) **to be off c.** (of person) ne pas être dans son assiette; **to give c. to a story** rendre un récit plus

vivant; **let's see the c.** of your money voyons la couleur de ton argent; **to pass with flying colours** être reçu(e) brillamment *ou* haut la main; **to show one's true colours** se montrer sous son vrai jour; **to nail one's colours to the mast** afficher ses opinions **2** *vt* (**a**) *(of chemical, dye)* colorer; *(with felt-tips, crayons)* colorier; **to c. one's hair** se faire une couleur (**b**) *Fig (judgement, view)* fausser **3** *vi (blush)* rougir
▸**colour in,** *Am* **color in** *vt sep* colorier
colour-blind, *Am* **color-blind** ['kʌləblaɪnd] *adj* daltonien(enne)
colour-coded, *Am* **color-coded** ['kʌləkəʊdɪd] *adj* différencié(e) par des couleurs
coloured, *Am* **colored** ['kʌləd] *adj* (**a**) *(illustration)* en couleurs; *(pen, ink)* de couleur; **brightly c.** aux couleurs vives; *Fig* **a highly c. narrative** un récit haut en couleurs (**b**) *(person)* de couleur
colourful, *Am* **colorful** ['kʌləfʊl] *adj* coloré(e); *(vivid)* coloré(e), pittoresque; **a c. character** un personnage haut en couleurs
colouring, *Am* **coloring** ['kʌlərɪŋ] *n* (**a**) *(in food)* colorants *mpl* (**b**) *(complexion)* teint *m*; **to have dark/fair c.** avoir le teint mat/clair (**c**) **c. book** album *m* à colorier
colourless, *Am* **colorless** ['kʌləlɪs] *adj* (**a**) *(clear)* incolore (**b**) *Fig (dull)* insipide, fade
colt [kəʊlt] *n* poulain *m*
Columbus ['kə'lʌmbəs] *n* **Christopher C.** Christophe Colomb
column ['kɒləm] *n (of troops, text, in building)* colonne *f*; *(newspaper feature)* rubrique *f*
columnist ['kɒləmɪst] *n (for newspaper, magazine)* chroniqueur(euse) *m,f*
coma ['kəʊmə] *n* coma *m*; **to go into a c.** tomber dans le coma; **to be in a c.** être dans le coma
comatose ['kəʊmətəʊs] *adj also Fig* comateux(euse)
comb [kəʊm] **1** *n* (**a**) *(for hair)* peigne *m*; **to give one's hair a c.** se donner un coup de peigne (**b**) *(of cock)* crête *f* **2** *vt* (**a**) *(hair)* peigner; **to c. one's hair** se peigner (**b**) *(search)* ratisser, passer au peigne fin
combat ['kɒmbæt] **1** *n* combat *m*; **c. jacket** veste *f* de treillis; *Br* **c. trousers,** *Am* **c. pants** battle-dress *m*, pantalon *m* multi-poches; **c. zone** zone *f* de combat **2** *vt (disease, prejudice, crime)* combattre
combatant ['kɒmbətənt] **1** *n* combattant(e) *m,f* **2** *adj* combattant(e)
combination [kɒmbɪ'neɪʃən] *n* combinaison *f*; **a c. of circumstances** un concours de circonstances; **c. lock** serrure *f* à combinaison; **c. skin** peau *f* mixte; *Med* **c. therapy** trithérapie *f*
combine 1 *n* ['kɒmbaɪn] (**a**) **c. (harvester)** moissonneuse-batteuse *f* (**b**) *Econ* cartel *m* **2** *vt* [kəm'baɪn] combiner, allier; **to c. business with pleasure** joindre l'utile à l'agréable **3** *vi* [kəm'baɪn] *(of people)* s'associer; *(of companies)* fusionner; *(of chemical elements)* se combiner
combustible [kəm'bʌstɪbəl] *adj* combustible
combustion [kəm'bʌstʃən] *n* combustion *f*; **c. chamber** chambre *f* de combustion
come [kʌm] *(pt* came [keɪm], *pp* come) *vi* (**a**) *(move)* venir (**from** de); *(arrive)* arriver; **to c. from France/Edinburgh** venir de France/d'Édimbourg; **to c. to the end of sth** arriver à la fin de qch; **here he comes!** le voilà!; **coming!** j'arrive!; **c., c.!** allons, allons!; **she always comes to me for help** elle s'adresse toujours

à moi quand elle a besoin d'aide; **she came running towards us** elle vint vers nous en courant, elle courut vers nous; **the rain came pouring down** il s'est mis à tomber des cordes; **nothing comes between her and her work** son travail passe avant tout; *Fig* **she has come a long way since then** elle a fait du chemin depuis; *Fam* **I don't know whether I'm coming or going!** je ne sais plus où j'en suis! (**b**) *(in time)* **c. January** en janvier; **c. next summer** l'été prochain; **in the days/years to c.** dans les jours/années à venir; **it came as a shock/surprise to me** ça m'a fait un choc/une surprise; *Fam* **he had it coming (to him)** ça lui pendait au nez (**c**) *(happen)* **to c. to do sth** finir par faire qch; **c. to think of it** maintenant que j'y pense; **to take things as they c.** prendre les choses comme elles viennent; **c. what may** quoi qu'il arrive; **how c....?** comment se fait-il que...? + *subjunctive* (**d**) *(in sequence)* **to c. first/last** *(in race, competition)* finir premier/dernier; **October comes before November** octobre vient avant novembre; **what comes next?** qu'est-ce qui vient après? (**e**) *(exist, be available)* **to c. in three sizes/colours** exister en trois tailles/couleurs; **work of that quality doesn't c. cheap** du travail de cette qualité, ça se paie; **he's as tough as they c.** il n'y a pas plus dur que lui (**f**) *(become)* **to c. loose** se défaire; **to c. true** se réaliser; **to c. open** s'ouvrir; **to c. of age** devenir majeur(e) (**g**) *(reach)* **to c. up/down to** arriver (jusqu')à (**h**) *very Fam (reach orgasm)* jouir
▸**come about** *vi* se produire, arriver
▸**come across 1** *vt insep (find)* tomber sur **2** *vi (make an impression)* **to c. across well/badly** bien/mal passer; **he comes across as a nice person** il a l'air gentil
▸**come after** *vt insep (chase)* poursuivre
▸**come along** *vi* (**a**) **c. along!** allons, pressons! (**b**) *(make progress) (of project, work)* avancer; **his French is coming along well** il fait des progrès en français (**c**) *(arrive)* venir
▸**come at** *vt insep (attack)* attaquer
▸**come away** *vi (become detached)* se détacher
▸**come back** *vi* revenir; **it's all coming back to me** ça me revient; **to c. back to what I was saying...** pour revenir à ce que je disais...
▸**come by 1** *vt insep (acquire)* obtenir, trouver **2** *vi (visit)* passer
▸**come down** *vi* (**a**) *(descend)* descendre; *(of temperature, prices)* baisser; *Fig* **to c. down in the world** déchoir; **to c. down with the flu** attraper la grippe (**b**) *(decide)* **to c. down in favour of sb/sth** décider en faveur de qn/qch (**c**) **to c. down to** *(be a matter of)* se ramener à, se résumer à; **it comes down to the fact that...** le fait est que...
▸**come down on** *vt insep (reprimand)* passer un savon à
▸**come forward** *vi* se présenter; **no one has come forward with any suggestions** personne n'a fait de suggestions
▸**come in** *vi* (**a**) *(of person)* entrer; *(of tide)* monter; **c. in!** entrez!; **to c. in first/second** arriver premier/deuxième (**b**) *(have a role)* intervenir; **and where do I c. in?** et moi, qu'est-ce que je fais?; **to c. in useful** être utile

▶**come in for** *vt insep* **to c. in for criticism** faire l'objet de critiques
▶**come into** *vt insep* (**a**) *(room, city)* entrer dans; **to c. into the world** venir au monde; **to c. into existence** être créé(e); **to c. into force** *or* **effect** *(of law, ruling)* entrer en vigueur; **to c. into power** arriver au pouvoir; **luck didn't c. into it** la chance n'a rien à voir làdedans (**b**) *(inherit)* hériter de
▶**come of** *vi (result from)* **no good will c. of it** cela n'amènera rien de bon; **that's what comes of being too ambitious** c'est ce qui arrive lorsqu'on est trop ambitieux
▶**come off 1** *vt insep* (**a**) *(horse, bicycle)* tomber de (**b**) **c. off it!** arrête ton char!
2 *vi* (**a**) *(be removed)* *(of button)* se détacher; *(of paint)* s'écailler; *(of stain)* partir (**b**) *(succeed)* réussir; **to c. off well/badly** *(in contest)* bien/mal s'en tirer
▶**come on** *vi* (**a**) **c. on!** allez! (**b**) *(make progress)* *(of project, work)* avancer; **his chess is coming on** il fait des progrès aux échecs; **I feel a cold coming on** je sens que je suis en train de m'enrhumer (**c**) *(of lights)* s'allumer; *(of heating)* se mettre en route
▶**come out** *vi* (**a**) *(of person, magazine, film)* sortir; *(of sun)* paraître; *(of truth)* se faire jour; **to c. out on strike** se mettre en grève; **to c. out in a rash** se couvrir de boutons; **to c. out in favour of/against sth** se prononcer pour/contre qch; **he came out of the deal well/badly** il a fait une bonne/mauvaise affaire; **to c. out with** *(remark, opinion)* sortir (**b**) *(of tooth, hair)* tomber; *(of screw)* se dévisser; *(of stain)* partir (**c**) *(as gay or lesbian)* déclarer son homosexualité, faire son come-out
▶**come over 1** *vt insep (affect)* **a strange feeling came over me** j'ai eu une sensation étrange; **what's come over you?** qu'est-ce qui te prend?
2 *vi* (**a**) *(visit)* passer (**b**) *(make impression)* **to c. over well/badly** bien/mal passer (**c**) *(feel)* **to c. over all funny** se sentir tout(e) drôle; **to c. over all dizzy** être pris(e) de vertiges
▶**come round** *vi* (**a**) *(visit)* passer (**b**) *(regain consciousness)* reprendre connaissance (**c**) *(accept)* accepter; **to c. round to sb's way of thinking** se rallier à l'opinion de qn
▶**come through 1** *vi (of message, news)* arriver
2 *vt insep (survive)* *(war, crisis, illness)* survivre à
▶**come to 1** *vt insep* (**a**) *(amount to)* s'élever à; **the scheme never came to anything** le projet n'a jamais abouti (**b**) *(reach)* **to c. to the point** en venir au fait; **to c. to a conclusion** arriver à une conclusion; **what is the world coming to?** où va-t-on?; **I never thought it would c. to this** je ne me doutais pas qu'on en arriverait là (**c**) *(be a matter of)* **when it comes to...** pour ce qui est de...; **if it comes to that...** à ce compte-là...
2 *vi (regain consciousness)* reprendre connaissance
▶**come together** *vi (gather)* se rassembler
▶**come up** *vt insep (stairs, hill)* monter
2 *vi* (**a**) *(of sun)* se lever; *(of opportunity, question, problem)* se présenter; **to c. up against a problem** rencontrer un problème; **there are some interesting films coming up on television** il y a quelques films intéressants qui vont bientôt passer à la télévision; **I'll let you know if anything comes up** je te préviendrai si quelque chose se présente; **the case comes up (for trial) tomorrow** le procès commence demain (**b**) **to**

c. up with *(funding, solution)* trouver; *(idea, theory)* proposer
▶**come upon** *vt insep (find)* tomber sur
▶**come up to** *vt insep* (**a**) *(approach)* s'approcher de (**b**) *(equal)* **the film didn't c. up to my expectations** le film n'était pas à la hauteur de mes espérances
comeback ['kʌmbæk] *n* **to make a c.** *(of fashion)* revenir; *(of actor, sportsperson)* faire un come-back
COMECON ['kɒmɪkɒn] *n Formerly (abbr* **Council for Mutual Economic Assistance)** COMECON *m*
comedian [kə'miːdɪən] *n* comique *mf*; *Fig (practical joker)* farceur(euse) *m,f*
comedienne [kəmiːdɪ'en] *n* comique *f*
comedown ['kʌmdaʊn] *n Fam* régression *f*
comedy ['kɒmɪdɪ] *(pl* **comedies)** *n (play, film)* comédie *f*; *(of situation)* comique *m*; *(situation comedy)* sitcom *m*; **c. show** *(on TV)* spectacle *m* comique
come-on ['kʌmɒn] *n Fam (enticement)* appât *m*; **to give sb the c.** *(sexually)* faire du gringue à qn
comer ['kʌmə(r)] *n* **open to all comers** ouvert(e) à tous
comet ['kɒmɪt] *n* comète *f*
comeuppance [kʌm'ʌpəns] *n Fam* **to get one's c.** avoir ce qu'on mérite
comfort ['kʌmfət] **1** *n* (**a**) *(ease)* confort *m*; *(financial)* aisance *f*; **to do sth in the c. of one's own home** faire qch confortablement chez soi; **comforts** *(luxuries)* commodités *fpl*; **I like my home comforts** j'aime mon petit confort; **the bullets were too close for c. food** = chose que l'on mange pour se remonter le moral; *Am* **c. station** toilettes *fpl* publiques; *Fig* **to step out of one's c. zone** s'aventurer en terrain inconnu (**b**) *(consolation)* réconfort *m*, consolation *f*; **if it's any c.,...** si ça peut vous consoler,...; **to take c. from** *or* **in sth** trouver du réconfort dans qch
2 *vt (console)* réconforter, consoler
comfortable ['kʌmftəbəl] *adj* (**a**) *(place, bed, chair)* confortable; *(person)* bien *inv*, à l'aise; **to be c.** *(of patient)* ne pas souffrir; **to make oneself c.** se mettre à l'aise *ou* à son aise; **I wouldn't feel c. accepting that money** ça me mettrait mal à l'aise d'accepter cet argent (**b**) *(majority, income)* confortable; **to be in c. circumstances** mener une vie aisée
comfortably ['kʌmftəblɪ] *adv* (**a**) *(sit)* confortablement; **to be c. off** *(financially)* être à l'aise financièrement; **to live c.** mener une vie aisée facilement; **to win c.** gagner avec une avance confortable
comforter ['kʌmfətə(r)] *n Am (quilt)* édredon *m*, *Can* confortable *m*
comforting ['kʌmfətɪŋ] *adj* réconfortant(e)
comfy ['kʌmfɪ] *adj Br Fam (place, bed, chair)* confortable; *(person)* bien *inv*, à l'aise
comic ['kɒmɪk] **1** *n* (**a**) *(performer)* comique *mf* (**b**) **c. (book)** bande *f* dessinée, BD *f*
2 *adj* comique; **c. opera** opéra-comique *m*; **to provide some c. relief** détendre l'atmosphère; **c. strip** bande *f* dessinée, BD *f*
comical ['kɒmɪkəl] *adj* comique
coming ['kʌmɪŋ] **1** *n (of person)* venue *f*, arrivée *f*; *(of God)* approche *f*; **comings and goings** allées *fpl* et venues; **c. of age** majorité *f*; **on his c. of age** à sa majorité
2 *adj (year, election)* prochain(e); *(elections, difficulties)* à venir

Coming of age
À sa majorité, c'est-à-dire à 18 ans, un(e) jeune Britannique acquiert le droit de voter, de faire partie d'un jury, de boire de l'alcool dans les pubs et de se marier sans le consentement de ses parents.

comma ['kɒmə] n virgule f
command [kə'mɑːnd] **1** n (**a**) (order) ordre m; Comput commande f; Comput **c. language** langage m de commandes (**b**) (authority, control) commandement m; **to be in c.** (of sth) (army, ship) commander (qch); **to be in c. of the situation** maîtriser la situation; **to be at sb's c.** être aux ordres de qn; **to have sth at one's c.** avoir qch à sa disposition; **she has a good c. of English** elle a une bonne maîtrise de l'anglais; **c. economy** économie f planifiée
2 vt (**a**) (give order to) **to c. sb to do sth** ordonner ou commander à qn de faire qch (**b**) (ship, regiment) commander (**c**) (have at one's disposal) avoir à sa disposition (**d**) (respect, admiration, attention) forcer; **to c. a high price** se vendre cher
commandant [kɒmən'dænt] n Mil commandant m
commandeer [kɒmən'dɪə(r)] vt réquisitionner
commander [kə'mɑːndə(r)] n Mil commandant m; Naut capitaine m de frégate; **c.-in-chief** commandant en chef
commanding [kə'mɑːndɪŋ] adj (**a**) Mil **c. officer** chef m de corps (**b**) (voice) impérieux(euse); (appearance) qui en impose; (position) dominant(e); (lead) considérable
commandment [kə'mɑːndmənt] n Rel commandement m
commando [kə'mɑːndəʊ] **1** n (pl **commandos** or **commandoes**) Mil (soldier, unit) commando m
2 adv Fam **to go c.** ne pas porter de slip
commemorate [kə'meməreɪt] vt commémorer
commemoration [kəmemə'reɪʃən] n commémoration f
commemorative [kə'memərətɪv] adj commémoratif(ive)
commence [kə'mens] vt & vi Formal commencer; **to c. doing sth** commencer à faire qch
commencement [kə'mensmənt] n (**a**) Formal (beginning) commencement m, début m (**b**) Am Univ remise f des diplômes
commend [kə'mend] vt (**a**) (praise) louer, féliciter; **to c. sb for bravery** louer qn pour sa bravoure (**b**) (recommend) recommander; **the train journey has little to c. it** je ne vous recommande pas le voyage en train (**c**) Lit (entrust) recommander (**to** à)
commendable [kə'mendəbəl] adj louable
commendation [kɒmen'deɪʃən] n (praise) éloges mpl; (in competition) mention f spéciale; Mil citation f
commensurate [kə'menʃərət] adj Formal proportionnel(elle) (**with** à)
comment ['kɒment] **1** n commentaire m, observation f (**on** sur); **no c.!** je n'ai rien à dire!
2 vt **to c. that...** faire remarquer ou observer que...; **"how interesting,"** he **commented** "comme c'est intéressant", remarqua-t-il ou observa-t-il
3 vi faire des commentaires (**on** sur)
commentary ['kɒməntəri] n (pl **commentaries**) n commentaire m
commentate ['kɒmənteɪt] vi faire le commentaire; **to c. on sth** commenter qch

commentator ['kɒmənteɪtə(r)] n commentateur(-trice) m,f
commerce ['kɒmɜːs] n commerce m
commercial [kə'mɜːʃəl] **1** n (advertisement) publicité f, pub f
2 adj also Pej commercial(e); **c. artist** graphiste mf; Fin **c. bank** banque f commerciale; **c. break** page f de publicité; **c. law** droit m commercial; **c. traveller** voyageur m de commerce; **c. value** valeur f marchande; **c. vehicle** véhicule m de commerce
commercialism [kə'mɜːʃəlɪzəm] n Pej mercantilisme m
commercialized [kə'mɜːʃəlaɪzd] adj Pej commercial(e)
commercially [kə'mɜːʃəlɪ] adv commercialement; **c. available** disponible dans le commerce
commie ['kɒmɪ] Fam Pej **1** n coco mf
2 adj coco
commiserate [kə'mɪzəreɪt] vi **to c. with sb** (show sympathy) témoigner de la sympathie à qn; (feel sympathy) éprouver de la compassion pour qn
commiseration [kəmɪzə'reɪʃən] n commisération f; **you have my commiserations** je suis désolé(e) pour vous
commission [kə'mɪʃən] **1** n (**a**) Com (payment) commission f (**b**) (of work, painting) commande f (**c**) (investigating body) commission f (**d**) Naut **in c.** armé(e); **out of c.** désarmé(e) (**e**) Mil brevet m d'officier
2 vt (**a**) (order) (work, painting) commander; **to c. sb to do sth** charger qn de faire qch (**b**) Mil **to be commissioned** être nommé(e) officier
commissionaire [kəmɪʃə'neə(r)] n portier m
commissioner [kə'mɪʃənə(r)] n membre m d'une commission; **c. of police** ≃ commissaire m de police; Law **c. for oaths** = homme de loi habilité à recevoir des déclarations sous serment
commit [kə'mɪt] (pt & pp **committed**) **1** vt (**a**) (error, crime) commettre; **to c. suicide** se suicider (**b**) **to c. oneself** (promise) s'engager; **to c. oneself to sth/doing sth** s'engager à qch/faire qch; **to c. sth to sth** (resources, troops) engager qch dans qch (**c**) (entrust) confier (**to** à); **to c. sth to writing** coucher qch par écrit; **to c. sth to memory** apprendre qch par cœur (**d**) (confine) **to c. sb (to prison)** incarcérer qn; **to c. sb (to mental institution)** interner qn (**e**) Law **to c. sb for trial** mettre qn en accusation
2 vi (emotionally) s'engager, s'investir
commitment [kə'mɪtmənt] n (**a**) (obligation) engagement m; **family/business commitments** obligations fpl familiales/professionnelles (**b**) (dedication) dévouement m (**to** à); **to make a c.** s'engager; **she lacks c.** elle ne s'investit pas assez
committed [kə'mɪtɪd] adj dévoué(e) (**to** à); (Christian, socialist) convaincu(e); **to be c. (to one's work)** beaucoup s'impliquer (dans son travail)
committee [kə'mɪtɪ] n comité m, commission f
commode [kə'məʊd] n (**a**) (chest of drawers) commode f (**b**) (toilet) chaise f percée
commodious [kə'məʊdɪəs] adj Formal spacieux(euse)
commodity [kə'mɒdɪtɪ] (pl **commodities**) n Econ marchandise f, produit m; Fin matière f première; **to be a rare c.** être une denrée rare; **commodities market** marché m des matières premières
commodore ['kɒmədɔː(r)] n Naut ≃ contre-amiral m

common ['kɒmən] **1** n (**a**) to have sth in c. (with) avoir qch en commun (avec); **in c.** with (similar to) de même que (**b**) (land) terrain m communal **2** adj (**a**) (frequent) commun(e), courant(e); **in c.** use d'usage courant (**b**) (shared) commun(e); **it is** by c. consent the best de l'avis de tous, c'est le meilleur; **C.** Agricultural Policy politique f agricole commune; Fin c. currency monnaie f unique; also Fig c. denominator dénominateur m commun; the c. good le bien commun; Fig c. ground terrain m d'entente; **it's c.** knowledge (that)... tout le monde sait que...; **the C.** Market le Marché commun; Sch c. room (for pupils) salle f commune; (for teachers) salle f des professeurs (**c**) (average) c. or garden ordinaire, standard inv; the c. cold le rhume; the c. man l'homme m de la rue; the c. people les gens mpl ordinaires; c. sense bon sens m (**d**) Pej (vulgar) vulgaire

commoner ['kɒmənə(r)] n roturier(ère) m,f
common-law ['kɒmənlɔ:] adj c. husband concubin m; c. marriage concubinage m; c. wife concubine f

commonly ['kɒmənlɪ] adv communément
commonplace ['kɒmənpleɪs] **1** n lieu m commun **2** adj courant(e)
Commons ['kɒmənz] npl the (House of) C. la Chambre des communes
Commonwealth ['kɒmənwelθ] n the C. le Commonwealth; the C. games les jeux mpl du Commonwealth
commotion [kə'məʊʃən] n (noise) vacarme m; (disruption) agitation f
communal ['kɒmjʊnəl] adj (bathroom, resource) commun(e); (life) communautaire
commune 1 n ['kɒmju:n] (collective) communauté f **2** vi [kə'mju:n] to c. with nature communier avec la nature
communicable [kə'mju:nɪkəbəl] adj (disease) transmissible
communicant [kə'mju:nɪkənt] n Rel communiant(e) m,f
communicate [kə'mju:nɪkeɪt] **1** vt communiquer; (illness) transmettre **2** vi communiquer (with avec)
communication [kəmju:nɪ'keɪʃən] n communication f; to be in c. with sb être en contact avec qn; c. cord sonnette f d'alarme
communicative [kə'mju:nɪkətɪv] adj communicatif(ive)
communion [kə'mju:njən] n Rel communion f; to take C. communier
communism ['kɒmjʊnɪzəm] n communisme m
communist ['kɒmjʊnɪst] **1** n communiste mf **2** adj communiste
community 1 n [kə'mju:nɪtɪ] (pl communities) n communauté f; the business c. le milieu des affaires; c. centre foyer m municipal; c. service travail m d'intérêt général; c. spirit esprit m communautaire
commute [kə'mju:t] **1** vt Law commuer (to en) **2** vi to c. (to work) faire la navette entre son domicile et son travail
commuter [kə'mju:tə(r)] n banlieusard(e) m,f (qui fait la navette entre son domicile et son travail); c. train train m de banlieue
Comoros ['kɒmərɒs] n the C. (Islands) les Comores fpl
compact 1 n ['kɒmpækt] (**a**) (for powder) poudrier m (**b**) (treaty) accord m (**c**) Am (car) petite voiture f

2 adj [kəm'pækt] compact(e); c. disc disque m compact; c. disc player lecteur m de disques compacts **3** vt [kəm'pækt] compacter
companion [kəm'pænjən] n (**a**) (friend) compagnon (compagne) m,f; (of elderly woman) dame f de compagnie; travelling c. compagnon (compagne) m,f de voyage (**b**) (guidebook) guide m
companionable [kəm'pænjənəbəl] adj (person) sociable; (manner) amical(e)
companionship [kəm'pænjənʃɪp] n compagnie f
company ['kʌmpənɪ] (pl companies) n (**a**) (companionship) compagnie f; in his c. en sa compagnie; to keep sb c. tenir compagnie à qn; to be good c. être d'agréable compagnie; the dog is good c. for her le chien lui fait de la compagnie; to part c. with sb (split up) se séparer de qn; (disagree) ne plus être d'accord avec qn; to get into bad c. avoir de mauvaises fréquentations; to do sth in c. (in public) faire qch en public; to be expecting c. (guests) attendre de la visite (**b**) (business) société f; publishing c. maison f d'édition; Hobbs and C. Hobbs et Compagnie; Fam Fig Victor and c. Victor et compagnie; c. car voiture f de fonction; c. policy politique f de la société; Com c. secretary secrétaire mf général(e) (**c**) (army unit, theatre group) compagnie f
comparable ['kɒmpərəbəl] adj comparable (to à)
comparative [kəm'pærətɪv] **1** n Gram comparatif m **2** adj (**a**) (relative) relatif(ive); she's a c. stranger to me je la connais relativement peu (**b**) (study, research) comparatif(ive); (psychology, literature) comparé(e)
compare [kəm'peə(r)] **1** vt comparer (with or to avec ou à); compared with or to par rapport à, à côté de; Fig to c. notes échanger ses impressions **2** vi être comparable (with à); to c. favourably with sth ne le céder en rien à qch **3** n Lit beyond c. sans pareil(eille)
comparison [kəm'pærɪsən] n comparaison f; in or by c. (with) en comparaison (avec); there is no c. il n'y a pas de comparaison; to draw or make a c. between sth and sth faire la comparaison entre qch et qch
compartment [kəm'pɑ:tmənt] n compartiment m
compass ['kʌmpəs] n (**a**) (for finding direction) boussole f; (of boat) compas m (**b**) Math (pair of) compasses compas m (**c**) (scope) (of mind) portée f; (of powers) étendue f
compassion [kəm'pæʃən] n compassion f
compassionate [kəm'pæʃənət] adj (person, attitude) compatissant(e); (by nature) humain(e); to be c. towards sb éprouver de la compassion pour qn; on c. grounds pour raisons personnelles; c. leave congé m exceptionnel pour raisons personnelles
compatibility [kəmpætə'bɪlɪtɪ] n compatibilité f
compatible [kəm'pætəbəl] adj compatible (with avec)
compatriot [kəm'pætrɪət] n compatriote mf
compel [kəm'pel] (pt & pp compelled) vt forcer, obliger; to c. sb to do sth forcer ou obliger qn à faire qch; to c. admiration/respect forcer l'admiration/le respect
compelling [kəm'pelɪŋ] adj (film, performance) captivant(e); (argument) convaincant(e); (urge) irrésistible
compendium [kəm'pendɪəm] n (book) précis m; (of games) sélection f
compensate ['kɒmpenseɪt] **1** vt dédommager (for de) **2** vi to c. for sth compenser qch

compensation [kɒmpen'seɪʃən] *n* compensation *f*; *(money)* dédommagement *m*, indemnité *f*
compensatory [kɒmpen'seɪtərɪ] *adj* compensatoire
compere ['kɒmpeə(r)] **1** *n* animateur(trice) *m,f*, présentateur(trice) *m,f*
2 *vt* animer, présenter
compete [kəm'piːt] *vi* (**a**) *(contend)* rivaliser (**with** avec); *(of company)* être en concurrence (**with** avec); **to c. for sth** se disputer qch (**b**) *(in race, competition)* concourir (**for** pour)
competence ['kɒmpɪtəns] *n* (**a**) *(ability)* compétence *f*, compétences *fpl* (**b**) *Law* compétence *f*
competent ['kɒmpɪtənt] *adj (person)* compétent(e); **a c. piece of work** du bon travail
competition [kɒmpɪ'tɪʃən] *n* (**a**) *(contest)* concours *m*; *(in sport)* compétition *f* (**b**) *(rivalry)* rivalité *f*; *(between companies, candidates)* concurrence *f*; **to be in c. with sb** être en concurrence avec qn; **the c.** *(opponents) (in sport)* les adversaires *mpl*; *(in business)* la concurrence; **there's no c.!** il n'y a aucune comparaison!
competitive [kəm'petɪtɪv] *adj (person)* qui a l'esprit de compétition; *(atmosphere)* de compétition; *(price, company)* compétitif(ive); **c. sports** sports *mpl* de compétition; *Com* **c. tendering** appel *m* d'offres
competitor [kəm'petɪtə(r)] *n* concurrent(e) *m,f*
compilation [kɒmpɪ'leɪʃən] *n* compilation *f*
compile [kəm'paɪl] *vt (list)* dresser; *(dictionary)* rédiger
complacency [kəm'pleɪsənsɪ] *n* autosatisfaction *f*
complacent [kəm'pleɪsənt] *adj* content(e) de soi; **to be c. about sth** faire de l'autosatisfaction à propos de qch
complain [kəm'pleɪn] *vi* se plaindre (**about** de); **to c. of** *(illness)* se plaindre de; **I can't c. about the service** je n'ai pas à me plaindre du service; **how are things? – can't c.** comment ça va? – je n'ai pas à me plaindre
complaint [kəm'pleɪnt] *n* (**a**) *(grievance)* récrimination *f*; *(official)* plainte *f*, réclamation *f*; **to have cause** *or* **grounds for c.** avoir des raisons de se plaindre; **to lodge** *or* **make a c. against sb** porter plainte contre qn (**b**) *(illness)* maladie *f*
complement 1 *n* ['kɒmplɪmənt] (**a**) *Gram* complément *m* (**b**) *Naut & Fig* **the full c.** l'effectif *m* complet
2 *vt* ['kɒmplɪment] compléter
complementary [kɒmplɪ'mentərɪ] *adj* complémentaire; **c. medicine** médecines *fpl* alternatives *ou* parallèles
complete [kəm'pliːt] **1** *adj* (**a**) *(whole)* complet(ète); *(utter)* total(e); **he is a c. fool** il est complètement idiot (**b**) *(finished)* achevé(e)
2 *vt* (**a**) *(finish)* achever; (**b**) *(make whole)* compléter
completely [kəm'pliːtlɪ] *adv* complètement
completion [kəm'pliːʃən] *n* achèvement *m*; **on c.** *(of work)* à l'achèvement; **to near c.** toucher à sa fin
complex ['kɒmpleks] **1** *n* *(of buildings, psychological)* complexe *m*; **to have a c. about sth** être complexé(e) par qch
2 *adj* complexe
complexion [kəm'plekʃən] *n* teint *m*; **to have a fair c.** avoir le teint clair; *Fig* **that puts a different c. on things** voilà qui change tout
complexity [kəm'pleksɪtɪ] *n* (*pl* **complexities**) *n* complexité *f*
compliance [kəm'plaɪəns] *n* observation *f* (**with** de); **in c. with** conformément à
compliant [kəm'plaɪənt] *adj* complaisant(e), accommodant(e)
complicate ['kɒmplɪkeɪt] *vt* compliquer

complicated ['kɒmplɪkeɪtɪd] *adj* compliqué(e)
complication [kɒmplɪ'keɪʃən] *n* complication *f*
complicity [kəm'plɪsɪtɪ] *n* complicité *f* (**in** dans)
compliment 1 *n* ['kɒmplɪmənt] compliment *m*; **to pay sb a c.** faire un compliment à qn; **with compliments** avec nos compliments; **compliments of the season** meilleurs vœux; **compliments slip** papillon *m* à en-tête *(portant la mention "avec les compliments de...")*
2 *vt* ['kɒmplɪment] **to c. sb on sth** *(bravery, command of language)* féliciter qn pour qch; *(dress, haircut)* faire des compliments à qn sur qch
complimentary [kɒmplɪ'mentərɪ] *adj* (**a**) *(praising)* élogieux(euse) (**about** à l'égard de) (**b**) *(free)* gratuit(e); **c. ticket** billet *m* de faveur
comply [kəm'plaɪ] (*pt & pp* **complied**) *vi* **to c. with** *(rule)* se conformer à, se plier à; *(order)* obéir à; *(request)* accéder à
component [kəm'pəʊnənt] **1** *n* *(electrical, chemical)* composant *m*; *Fig* composante *f*
2 *adj* **c. part** pièce *f* détachée; *Fig* composante *f*
compose [kəm'pəʊz] *vt* (**a**) *(music, poetry)* composer (**b**) *(constitute)* **to be composed of** être composé(e) de, se composer de (**c**) *(calm)* **to c. oneself** se ressaisir
composed [kəm'pəʊzd] *adj* calme
composer [kəm'pəʊzə(r)] *n* compositeur(trice) *m,f*
composite ['kɒmpəzɪt] *adj (photograph)* composite
composition [kɒmpə'zɪʃən] *n* composition *f*; *(essay)* rédaction *f*
compositor [kəm'pɒzɪtə(r)] *n Typ* compositeur(trice) *m,f*
compost ['kɒmpɒst] **1** *n* compost *m*; **c. heap** tas *m* de compost
2 *vt (make into compost)* faire du compost à partir de; *(treat with compost)* composter
composure [kəm'pəʊʒə(r)] *n* sang-froid *m*
compound¹ ['kɒmpaʊnd] **1** *n* ['kɒmpaʊnd] *Chem & Gram* composé *m*
2 *adj* ['kɒmpaʊnd] composé(e); *Med* **c. fracture** fracture *f* compliquée; *Fin* **c. interest** intérêts *mpl* composés
3 *vt* [kəm'paʊnd] *(problem, difficulty)* aggraver
compound² ['kɒmpaʊnd] *n (enclosure)* enceinte *f*
comprehend [kɒmprɪ'hend] *vt* comprendre
comprehensible [kɒmprɪ'hensəbəl] *adj* compréhensible
comprehension [kɒmprɪ'henʃən] *n* compréhension *f*; **it is beyond my c.** cela dépasse mon entendement
comprehensive [kɒmprɪ'hensɪv] *adj (answer, programme)* complet(ète); *(study)* exhaustif(ive); *(view)* d'ensemble; *(defeat, victory)* écrasant(e); *Fin* **c. insurance** assurance *f* tous risques; *Br* **c. (school)** établissement *m* secondaire *(n'opérant pas de sélection à l'entrée)*

Comprehensive schools

Les "comprehensive schools" ont été introduites en Grande-Bretagne dans les années 60 dans le but d'assurer l'égalité des chances pour tous les enfants, quel que soit leur origine sociale. Aujourd'hui 90 pour cent des élèves du secondaire fréquentent ce type d'établissement scolaire. Cependant l'insuffisance des crédits alloués à l'éducation ainsi que la persistance d'un système d'enseignement privé dont ne peuvent bénéficier que les classes aisées rendent très aléatoire la réalisation d'un projet de démocratisation de l'enseignement.

compress 1 *n* ['kɒmpres] *Med* compresse *f*
2 *vt* [kəm'pres] *(air, gas)* comprimer; *Fig (text)* condenser
compression [kəm'preʃən] *n (of air, gas)* compression *f*; *Fig* raccourcissement *m*
compressor [kəm'presə(r)] *n* compresseur *m*
comprise [kəm'praɪz] *vt* comprendre, se composer de; **to be comprised of** comprendre, se composer de
compromise ['kɒmprəmaɪz] **1** *n* compromis *m*; **c. solution** solution *f* de compromis
2 *vt (person, security)* compromettre; *(principles)* transiger sur; **to c. oneself** se compromettre
3 *vi* transiger (**on** sur)
compromising ['kɒmprəmaɪzɪŋ] *adj* compromettant(e)
compulsion [kəm'pʌlʃən] *n (urge)* besoin *m*; *(obligation)* contrainte *f*; **under c.** sous la contrainte; **to be under no c. to do sth** ne pas être obligé(e) de faire qch
compulsive [kəm'pʌlsɪv] *adj (smoker, gambler, liar)* invétéré(e); **c. eating** boulimie *f*; **it's c. viewing** c'est captivant
compulsory [kəm'pʌlsərɪ] *adj* obligatoire; **c. redundancy** ≃ licenciement *m* sec; **c. retirement** mise *f* à la retraite d'office
compunction [kəm'pʌŋkʃən] *n* remords *m*, scrupules *mpl*
computation [kɒmpjʊ'teɪʃən] *n* calcul *m*
compute [kəm'pjuːt] *vt* calculer
computer [kəm'pjuːtə(r)] *n* ordinateur *m*; **to be c. literate** avoir des connaissances en informatique; **c. game** jeu *m* électronique; *Fam* **c. geek** allumé(e) *m,f* d'informatique; **c. printout** impression *f*; **c. program** programme *m* informatique; **c. programmer** programmeur(euse) *m,f*; **c. programming** programmation *f*; **c. science** informatique *f*; **c. scientist** informaticien(enne) *m,f*; **c. simulation** simulation *f* par ordinateur
computer-aided [kəm'pjuːtər'eɪdɪd], **computer-assisted** [kəm'pjuːtərə'sɪstɪd] *adj* assisté(e) par ordinateur
computerization [kəmpjuːtəraɪ'zeɪʃən] *n* informatisation *f*
computerize [kəm'pjuːtəraɪz] *vt* informatiser
computing [kəm'pjuːtɪŋ] *n* informatique *f*
comrade ['kɒmreɪd] *n* camarade *mf*
comradeship ['kɒmreɪdʃɪp] *n* camaraderie *f*
con¹ [kɒn] *Fam* **1** *n (swindle)* arnaque *f*; **c. man** arnaqueur *m*
2 *vt (pt & pp* **conned)** *(swindle)* arnaquer; **to c. sth out of sb** arnaquer qn de qch; **to c. sb into doing sth** persuader qn de faire qch par la ruse
con² *n Fam (convict)* taulard(e) *m,f*
con³ *n (disadvantage) see* **pro²**
concave [kɒn'keɪv] *adj* concave
conceal [kən'siːl] *vt* cacher, dissimuler (**from** à)
concealer [kən'siːlə(r)] *n (make-up)* camoufleur *m*
concede [kən'siːd] **1** *vt* concéder; **to c. defeat** s'avouer vaincu(e); **to c. that...** admettre que...
2 *vi* s'incliner
conceit [kən'siːt] *n (vanity)* vanité *f*, suffisance *f*
conceited [kən'siːtɪd] *adj* vaniteux(euse), suffisant(e)
conceivable [kən'siːvəbəl] *adj* concevable, imaginable; **it is c. that...** il est concevable que... + *subjunctive*
conceivably [kən'siːvəblɪ] *adv* **we might c. get there by six** il se peut que nous soyons arrivés pour six

heures; **she couldn't c. have done it** il est inconcevable qu'elle ait fait ça
conceive [kən'siːv] **1** *vt* (**a**) *(child, idea)* concevoir (**b**) *(understand)* concevoir
2 *vi* **to c. of sth** concevoir qch
concentrate ['kɒnsəntreɪt] **1** *n* concentré *m*
2 *vt* concentrer (**on** sur)
3 *vi* se concentrer (**on** sur); **to c. on doing sth** s'appliquer à faire qch
concentration [kɒnsən'treɪʃən] *n* concentration *f*; **c. camp** camp *m* de concentration; **to have a short c. span** ne pas avoir une grande capacité de concentration
concentric [kɒn'sentrɪk] *adj Math* concentrique
concept ['kɒnsept] *n* concept *m*
conception [kən'sepʃən] *n* (**a**) *(of child, idea)* conception *f* (**b**) *(understanding)* **to have no c. of sth** n'avoir aucune idée *ou* notion de qch
conceptual [kən'septjʊəl] *adj* conceptuel(elle)
conceptualize [kən'septjʊəlaɪz] *vt* conceptualiser
concern [kən'sɜːn] **1** *n* (**a**) *(interest)* **it's no c. of mine/yours** cela ne me/vous regarde pas; **this is a matter of public c.** c'est une affaire qui nous concerne tous (**b**) *(worry, compassion)* inquiétude *f*, souci *m*; **to give cause for c.** être un sujet d'inquiétude; **there is no cause for c.** il n'y a pas de raison de s'inquiéter; **to show c.** se montrer inquiet(ète) (**c**) *(company)* entreprise *f*
2 *vt* (**a**) *(affect)* concerner; **to c. oneself with sth** se préoccuper *ou* se soucier de qch; **as far as I'm concerned,...** pour moi,..., ce qui me concerne,...; **to whom it may c.** à qui de droit (**b**) *(worry)* inquiéter (**c**) *(be about)* **it concerns your request for a transfer** c'est au sujet de votre demande de transfert
concerned [kən'sɜːnd] *adj (worried)* inquiet(ète) *(about* au sujet de)
concerning [kən'sɜːnɪŋ] *prep* au sujet de
concert ['kɒnsət] *n* (**a**) *(musical)* concert *m*; **c. hall** salle *f* de concert; **c. pianist** concertiste *mf* (**b**) *(cooperation)* **in c. (with)** de concert (avec)
concerted [kən'sɜːtɪd] *adj* concerté(e)
concertina [kɒnsə'tiːnə] *n* concertina *m*
concerto [kən'tʃɜːtəʊ] *(pl* **concertos)** *n* concerto *m*
concession [kən'seʃən] *n* (**a**) *(compromise, giving up)* concession *f* (**b**) *(discount)* tarif *m* réduit
concessionary [kən'seʃənərɪ] *adj (fare)* réduit(e)
conciliate [kən'sɪlɪeɪt] *vt* apaiser
conciliation [kənsɪlɪ'eɪʃən] *n* conciliation *f*; *(in dispute)* conciliation *f*, arbitrage *m*; **the dispute went to c.** le conflit a été soumis à l'arbitrage
conciliatory [kən'sɪlɪətərɪ] *adj* conciliant(e)
concise [kən'saɪs] *adj* concis(e)
conclude [kən'kluːd] **1** *vt* (**a**) *(speech, book, treaty)* conclure; *(conference, festival)* clore (**b**) *(deduce)* **to c. that...** conclure que...
2 *vi* se conclure (**with** sur); *(of speaker)* conclure (**with** sur); *(of conference, festival)* se clore (**with** sur)
concluding [kən'kluːdɪŋ] *adj* final(e)
conclusion [kən'kluːʒən] *n* (**a**) *(inference)* conclusion *f*; **to come to** *or* **reach a c.** arriver à une conclusion (**b**) *(end)* conclusion *f*; **in c.** pour conclure, en conclusion
conclusive [kən'kluːsɪv] *adj* concluant(e)
concoct [kən'kɒkt] *vt also Fig* concocter
concoction [kən'kɒkʃən] *n (drink, dish)* mixture *f*
concord ['kɒŋkɔːd] *n (harmony)* entente *f*

concordance [kən'kɔːdəns] *n (agreement)* accord *m*; **to be in c. with sth** être en accord avec qch
concourse ['kɒnkɔːs] *n (in airport, railway station)* hall *m*
concrete ['kɒnkriːt] **1** *n* béton *m*; **c. jungle** univers *m* de béton; **c. mixer** bétonnière *f*
2 *adj* en béton; *Fig (definite)* concret(ète)
concubine ['kɒŋkjʊbaɪn] *n* concubine *f*
concur [kən'kɜː(r)] *(pt & pp* **concurred**) *vi (of person)* être d'accord (**with** avec); *(of findings, results)* concorder (**with** avec)
concurrent [kən'kʌrənt] *adj* simultané(e), concordant(e)
concurrently [kən'kʌrəntlɪ] *adv* simultanément
concussed [kən'kʌst] *adj* commotionné(e)
concussion [kən'kʌʃən] *n* commotion *f* cérébrale
condemn [kən'dem] *vt* (**a**) *(disapprove of)* condamner (**b**) *Law (sentence)* condamner (**to** à); **condemned cell** cellule *f* de condamné à mort (**c**) *(building)* déclarer inhabitable
condemnation [kɒndem'neɪʃən] *n* condamnation *f*
condensation [kɒnden'seɪʃən] *n* (**a**) *(moisture) (on glass)* buée *f*; *(on walls)* condensation *f* (**b**) *(process)* condensation *f*
condense [kən'dens] **1** *vt* condenser; **condensed milk** lait *m* condensé
2 *vi* se condenser
condenser [kən'densə(r)] *n Tech* condensateur *m*
condescend [kɒndɪ'send] *vi* **to c. to do sth** condescendre à faire qch; **to c. towards sb** se montrer condescendant(e) envers qn
condescending [kɒndɪ'sendɪŋ] *adj* condescendant(e)
condescension [kɒndɪ'senʃən] *n* condescendance *f*
condiment ['kɒndɪmənt] *n* condiment *m*
condition [kən'dɪʃən] **1** *n* (**a**) *(state)* état *m*; *(of person)* forme *f*; **in good/bad c.** *(of machine, road)* en bon/mauvais état; **you're in no c. to drive** tu n'es pas en état de conduire; **to be in good c./out of c.** *(of person)* être/ne pas être en forme (**b**) *(circumstances)* conditions *fpl*; **working conditions** conditions de travail; **driving conditions** état *m* des routes; *Law* **conditions of employment** contrat *m* de travail (**c**) *(requirement)* condition *f*; **on (the) c. that...** à (la) condition que... + *subjunctive*; **on no c.** sous aucun prétexte, en aucun cas (**d**) *(disease)* maladie *f*; **heart c.** maladie du cœur
2 *vt* (**a**) *(influence)* conditionner; **to be conditioned by** *(depend on)* dépendre de; **we have been conditioned to believe that...** on nous a appris que...; *Psy* **conditioned reflex** réflexe *m* conditionné (**b**) *(hair)* mettre de l'après-shampo(o)ing sur
conditional [kən'dɪʃənəl] **1** *n Gram* **the c.** le conditionnel
2 *adj* conditionnel(elle); **to be c. on** dépendre de; *Law* **c. discharge** liberté *f* conditionnelle
conditionally [kən'dɪʃənəlɪ] *adv (accept, grant)* sous certaines conditions
conditioner [kən'dɪʃənə(r)] *n (for hair)* après-shampo(o)ing *m*
conditioning [kən'dɪʃənɪŋ] *n (psychological)* conditionnement *m*
condo ['kɒndəʊ] *(pl* **condos**) *n Am Fam (abbr* **condominium**) appartement *m* en copropriété
condolences [kən'dəʊlənsɪz] *npl* condoléances *fpl*
condom ['kɒndəm] *n* préservatif *m*

condominium [kɒndə'mɪnɪəm] *n Am (apartment)* appartement *m* en copropriété
condone [kən'dəʊn] *vt* excuser
condor ['kɒndɔː(r)] *n* condor *m*
conducive [kən'djuːsɪv] *adj* **to be c. to** être favorable *ou* propice à
conduct 1 *n* ['kɒndʌkt] *(behaviour)* conduite *f*
2 *vt* [kən'dʌkt] (**a**) *(business, orchestra)* diriger; *(campaign, inquiry, experiment)* mener; **to c. oneself** se conduire (**b**) *(guide)* guider; **we were conducted round the factory** on nous a fait visiter l'usine; **a conducted tour** une visite guidée (**c**) *(heat, electricity)* conduire
3 *vi* [kən'dʌkt] *Mus* diriger
conductivity [kɒndʌk'tɪvɪtɪ] *n Phys* conductivité *f*
conductor [kən'dʌktə(r)] *n* (**a**) *Br (on bus)* receveur *m* (**b**) *(of orchestra)* chef *m* d'orchestre (**c**) *Phys* conducteur *m*
conductress [kən'dʌktrɪs] *n Br (on bus)* receveuse *f*
conduit ['kɒndɪt] *n* conduit *m*
cone [kəʊn] *n* (**a**) *(shape)* cône *m* (**b**) *(of pine)* pomme *f* de pin (**c**) *(for ice cream)* cornet *m* (**d**) *(for traffic)* cône *m* de signalisation
cone-shaped ['kəʊnʃeɪpt] *adj* conique
confab ['kɒnfæb] *n Fam* **to have a c. about sth** discuter de qch
confectioner [kən'fekʃənə(r)] *n* confiseur(euse) *m,f*; *Culin* **c.'s custard** crème *f* pâtissière; **c.'s (shop)** confiserie *f*; *Am* **c.'s sugar** sucre *m* glace
confectionery [kən'fekʃənərɪ] *n (sweets)* confiserie *f*
confederacy [kən'fedərəsɪ] *n* confédération *f*
confederate [kən'fedərət] **1** *n (accomplice)* complice *mf*
2 *adj Pol* confédéré(e)
confederation [kənfedə'reɪʃən] *n* confédération *f*
confer [kən'fɜː(r)] *(pt & pp* **conferred**) **1** *vt (title, degree, powers)* octroyer (**on** à)
2 *vi (discuss) (of several people)* se consulter; **to c. with sb about sth** discuter de qch avec qn
conference ['kɒnfərəns] *n* conférence *f*, congrès *m*; *Com* **to be in c.** être en conférence; *Tel* **c. call** téléconférence *f*
confess [kən'fes] **1** *vt (crime, mistake)* confesser, avouer; *(feeling)* avouer; *Rel* confesser; **to c. that...** confesser *ou* avouer que...
2 *vi* avouer; *Rel* se confesser; **to c. to sth** *(crime, mistake)* confesser *ou* avouer qch; *(feeling)* avouer qch
confession [kən'feʃən] *n* confession *f*, aveu *m*; *Rel* confession; **to go to c.** aller se confesser
confessional [kən'feʃənəl] *n Rel* confessionnal *m*
confessor [kən'fesə(r)] *n Rel* confesseur *m*
confetti [kən'fetɪ] *n* confettis *mpl*
confidante [kɒnfɪ'dænt] *n* confident(e) *m,f*
confide [kən'faɪd] **1** *vt* **to c. sth to sb** confier qch à qn
2 *vi* **to c. in sb** se confier à qn
confidence ['kɒnfɪdəns] *n* (**a**) *(trust)* confiance *f* (**in** en); **I have every c. that...** je ne doute pas un instant que...; **to take sb into one's c.** se confier à qn; **c. trick** escroquerie *f* (**b**) *(self-assurance)* confiance *f* en soi (**c**) *(secret)* confidence *f*; **in c.** en confidence
confident [kən'fɪdənt] *adj* (**a**) *(self-assured) (person)* sûr(e) de soi; *(smile, exterior)* confiant(e) (**b**) *(certain)* certain(e); **to be c. of doing sth** être certaine de faire qch
confidential [kɒnfɪ'denʃəl] *adj* confidentiel(elle)

confidentiality [kɒnfɪdenʃɪ'ælɪtɪ] *n* confidentialité *f*; *Com c.*
agreement accord *m* de confidentialité
confidentially [kɒnfɪ'denʃəlɪ] *adv* confidentiellement, en confidence
confidently ['kɒnfɪdəntlɪ] *adv* (**a**) *(with self-assurance)* avec assurance (**b**) *(with certainty)* avec confiance
configuration [kənfɪgjʊ'reɪʃən] *n* configuration *f*
confine [kən'faɪn] *vt* (**a**) *(imprison)* enfermer; **to be confined to bed** être alité(e); **to be confined to barracks** être consigné(e); **confined space** espace *m* restreint (**b**) *(limit)* **to c. oneself to sth/doing sth** se limiter *ou* s'en tenir à qch/à faire qch
confinement [kən'faɪnmənt] *n* (**a**) *(in prison)* emprisonnement *m* (**b**) *Old-fashioned Med (labour)* couches *fpl*
confines ['kɒnfaɪnz] *npl (of town)* confins *mpl*; *Fig (limits)* limites *fpl*; **within the c. of** dans les limites de
confirm [kən'fɜːm] *vt* confirmer; *(power, position)* consolider, renforcer
confirmation [kɒnfə'meɪʃən] *n also Rel* confirmation *f*
confirmed [kən'fɜːmd] *adj (smoker, liar)* invétéré(e); *(bachelor)* endurci
confiscate ['kɒnfɪskeɪt] *vt* confisquer (**from** à)
confiscation [kɒnfɪs'keɪʃən] *n* confiscation *f*
conflict 1 *n* ['kɒnflɪkt] conflit *m*; **to come into c. with** entrer en conflit avec; **c. diamonds** diamants *mpl* de la guerre
  2 *vi* [kən'flɪkt] être en contradiction (**with** avec)
conflicting [kən'flɪktɪŋ] *adj (opinions)* opposé(e); *(reports, evidence)* contradictoire
confluence ['kɒnfluəns] *n (of rivers)* confluent *m*
conform [kən'fɔːm] *vi* se plier aux règles; **to c. to** *(rules)* obéir à, se plier à; *(standards)* être en conformité avec; **to c. with** être conforme à
conformist [kən'fɔːmɪst] **1** *n* conformiste *mf* **2** *adj* conformiste
conformity [kən'fɔːmɪtɪ] *n* conformité *f*; **in c. with** en conformité *ou* en accord avec
confound [kən'faʊnd] *vt* (**a**) *(puzzle)* laisser perplexe (**b**) *(frustrate) (plans)* faire échouer (**c**) *(surprise)* confondre (**d**) *Fam (damn)* **c. it!** quelle barbe!; **c. him!** le diable l'emporte!
confront [kən'frʌnt] *vt* affronter, faire face à; **to be confronted by sth** être confronté(e) à qch; **to c. sb with sth** confronter qn à qch
confrontation [kɒnfrʌn'teɪʃən] *n* affrontement *m*
confuse [kən'fjuːz] *vt (bewilder)* embrouiller; *(mix up)* confondre (**with** avec)
confused [kən'fjuːzd] *adj (person)* perdu(e); *(instructions, account, mind)* confus(e); **I'm c.** je m'y perds; **to get c.** s'embrouiller
confusing [kən'fjuːzɪŋ] *adj (bewildering)* déroutant(e); *(muddled)* confus(e); **it's very c.** on s'y perd
confusion [kən'fjuːʒən] *n (bewilderment)* perplexité *f*; *(disorder, lack of clarity)* confusion *f*; **to throw sth into c.** chambouler qch
congeal [kən'dʒiːl] *vi (of blood)* (se) coaguler
congenial [kən'dʒiːnɪəl] *adj* agréable
congenital [kən'dʒenɪtəl] *adj* congénital(e); *Fig* **he's a c. liar** il ment tout le temps, c'est congénital
conger ['kɒŋgə(r)] *n* **c. (eel)** congre *m*
congested [kən'dʒestɪd] *adj (road)* encombré(e); *(area, town)* surpeuplé(e); *Med (lungs)* congestionné(e); *(nose)* bouché(e)

congestion [kən'dʒestʃən] *n (of traffic)* encombrements *mpl*; *(of area, town)* surpeuplement *m*; *Med (of lungs)* congestion *f*
conglomerate [kən'glɒmərət] *n* conglomérat *m*
Congo ['kɒŋgəʊ] *n* **the C.** *(country)* le Congo
Congolese [kɒŋgə'liːz] **1** *n* Congolais(e) *m,f*
  2 *adj* congolais(e)
congratulate [kən'grætjʊleɪt] *vt* féliciter (**on** de); **to c. oneself on having done sth** se féliciter d'avoir fait qch
congratulations [kəngrætjʊ'leɪʃənz] *npl* félicitations *fpl*; **c. on your promotion/passing your exams** félicitations pour votre promotion/vos examens
congratulatory [kən'grætjʊleɪtərɪ] *adj* de félicitations
congregate ['kɒŋgrɪgeɪt] *vi* se rassembler, s'assembler
congregation [kɒŋgrɪ'geɪʃən] *n (of church)* assemblée *f* des fidèles
congress ['kɒŋgres] *n (conference)* congrès *m*; *Am Pol* **C.** le Congrès *(assemblée législative américaine)*

Congress

Le "Congress", organe législatif américain, est constitué du "Senate" (voir encadré à ce mot) et de la Chambre des représentants. Une proposition de loi doit obligatoirement être approuvée séparément par ces deux Chambres.

Congressman ['kɒŋgresmən] *n Am Pol* membre *m* du Congrès
Congresswoman ['kɒŋgreswʊmən] *n Am Pol* membre *m* du Congrès
conical ['kɒnɪkəl] *adj* conique
conifer ['kɒnɪfə(r)] *n* conifère *m*
coniferous [kə'nɪfərəs] *adj (forest)* de conifères; **c. tree** conifère *m*
conjecture [kən'dʒektʃə(r)] **1** *n* conjecture *f*; **it's sheer c.** ce ne sont que des suppositions
  2 *vt* supposer
  3 *vi* faire des conjectures
conjugal ['kɒndʒʊgəl] *adj* conjugal(e)
conjugate ['kɒndʒʊgeɪt] *Gram* **1** *vt* conjuguer
  2 *vi* se conjuguer
conjugation [kɒndʒʊ'geɪʃən] *n Gram* conjugaison *f*
conjunction [kən'dʒʌŋkʃən] *n* conjonction *f*; **in c. with** conjointement avec
conjunctivitis [kəndʒʌŋktɪ'vaɪtɪs] *n* conjonctivite *f*
conjure ['kʌndʒə(r)] *vi (do magic)* faire des tours de passe-passe; *Fig* **a name to c. with** un nom prestigieux
► **conjure up** *vt sep* (**a**) *(produce)* faire apparaître; **she conjured up a meal** elle s'est débrouillée pour préparer un repas en un rien de temps; **to c. sth up out of nowhere** faire apparaître qch comme par magie (**b**) *(call to mind)* évoquer
conjurer ['kʌndʒərə(r)] *n* prestidigitateur *m*, illusionniste *mf*
conjuring ['kʌndʒərɪŋ] *n* prestidigitation *f*; **c. trick** tour *m* de prestidigitation *ou* de passe-passe
conjuror = **conjurer**
conk [kɒŋk] *n Fam (nose)* blair *m*, pif *m*
► **conk out** *vi Fam* (**a**) *(stop working)* flancher; **the car conked out on me** la voiture m'a claqué entre les doigts (**b**) *(fall asleep)* se mettre à pioncer
conker ['kɒŋkə(r)] *n Fam (chestnut)* marron *m* d'Inde; *Br* **conkers** *(game)* = jeu qui consiste à faire éclater

le marron que son adversaire tient au bout d'une ficelle

conman ['kɒnmæn] *n* escroc *m*

connect [kə'nekt] **1** *vt* (**a**) *(pipes, wires, circuits)* relier (**to** à); **to c. sth to the mains** brancher qch sur secteur (**b**) *(link, associate)* **to c. sth/sth to sb/sth** établir un lien entre qn/qch et qn/qch; **there is nothing to c. the two crimes** il n'y a aucun lien entre les deux crimes; **to be connected with** avoir un lien *ou* un rapport avec; **the two issues are not connected** les deux questions n'ont aucun rapport; **are they connected?** *(of people)* sont-ils parents?; **to be well connected** *(of person)* avoir des relations (**c**) *Tel* mettre en ligne *ou* en communication (**with** avec); **can you c. me with reservations?** pourriez-vous me passer le service des réservations?

   2 *vi* (**a**) *(of pipes, wires, roads)* être relié(e) (**with** avec); *(of rooms)* communiquer (**with** avec) (**b**) *(of train, plane)* assurer la correspondance (**with** avec) (**c**) *(of blow)* atteindre son but; **the blow connected with his knee** le coup l'a atteint au genou

▸**connect up** *vt sep (pipes, wires)* raccorder

connection [kə'nekʃən] *n* (**a**) *(link, association)* lien *m*, rapport *m*; **in c. with** à propos de; **in this c.** à ce propos (**b**) *(acquaintance)* relation *f*; **to have important connections** avoir des relations en haut lieu (**c**) *(of pipes, wires)* raccordement *m* (**d**) *(train, plane)* correspondance *f*

connivance [kə'naɪvəns] *n* connivence *f*

connive [kə'naɪv] *vi* (**a**) *(conspire)* comploter; **to c. with sb** être de connivence avec qn (**b**) **to c. at sth** *(let happen)* laisser faire qch

conniving [kə'naɪvɪŋ] *adj* intrigant(e)

connoisseur [kɒnə'sɜː(r)] *n* connaisseur(euse) *m,f* (**of** en)

connotation [kɒnə'teɪʃən] *n* connotation *f*

conquer ['kɒŋkə(r)] *vt (country, someone's heart)* conquérir; *(difficulty, fears)* vaincre

conquering ['kɒŋkərɪŋ] *adj* victorieux(euse)

conqueror ['kɒŋkərə(r)] *n* vainqueur *m*

conquest ['kɒŋkwest] *n* conquête *f*; **to make a c. of sb** faire la conquête de qn

conscience ['kɒnʃəns] *n* conscience *f*; **to have a clear c.** avoir la conscience tranquille; **to have a guilty c.** avoir mauvaise conscience; **to have sth on one's c.** avoir qch sur la conscience; **to have no c. about doing sth** ne pas avoir de scrupules à faire qch; **in all c.** raisonnablement

conscientious [kɒnʃɪ'enʃəs] *adj* consciencieux(euse); **c. objector** objecteur *m* de conscience

conscious ['kɒnʃəs] *adj* (**a**) *(awake)* conscient(e) (**b**) *(aware)* **to be c. of sth/that...** être conscient(e) de qch/que...; **to become c. of sth** prendre conscience de qch, s'apercevoir de qch; *Psy* **the c. mind** la conscience (**c**) *(intentional)* conscient(e); **to make a c. effort to do sth** faire un effort particulier pour faire qch; **to make a c. decision to do sth** chercher délibérément à faire qch

consciousness ['kɒnʃəsnɪs] *n* (**a**) *(wakefulness)* conscience *f*; **to lose/regain c.** perdre/reprendre connaissance (**b**) *(awareness)* conscience *f* (**of** de); **to raise people's c. of sth** sensibiliser les gens à qch

conscript 1 *n* ['kɒnskrɪpt] conscrit *m*
   2 *vt* [kən'skrɪpt] enrôler; **to be conscripted** être appelé(e) (sous les drapeaux)

conscription [kən'skrɪpʃən] *n* conscription *f*

consecrate ['kɒnsɪkreɪt] *vt Rel & Fig* consacrer

consecration [kɒnsɪ'kreɪʃən] *n* consécration *f*

consecutive [kən'sekjʊtɪv] *adj* consécutif(ive); **on three c. days** trois jours consécutifs, trois jours de suite

consensus [kən'sensəs] *n* consensus *m*

consent [kən'sent] **1** *n* consentement *m*, assentiment *m*
   2 *vi* **to c. to sth/to do sth** consentir à qch/à faire qch

consequence ['kɒnsɪkwəns] *n* (**a**) *(result)* conséquence *f*; **as a c., in c.** par conséquent; **to take the consequences** subir les conséquences (**b**) *(importance)* importance *f*; **of little c.** de peu d'importance; **of no c.** sans importance

consequent ['kɒnsɪkwənt] *adj* résultant(e); **c. upon sth** qui résulte de qch; **the war and its c. loss of life** la guerre et les pertes en vies humaines qui en résultent

consequently ['kɒnsɪkwəntlɪ] *adv* par conséquent

conservation [kɒnsə'veɪʃən] *n* (*of environment*) protection *f*; *(of energy)* économies *fpl*; **c. area** *(of town, city)* quartier *m* préservé; *(nature reserve)* réserve *f* naturelle

conservationist [kɒnsə'veɪʃənɪst] *n* défenseur *m* de l'environnement

Conservative [kən'sɜːvətɪv] *Br Pol* **1** *n* conservateur(trice) *m,f*
   2 *adj* conservateur(trice); **the C. Party** le Parti conservateur

conservative [kən'sɜːvətɪv] **1** *n* conservateur(trice) *m,f*
   2 *adj* conservateur(trice); *(conventional)* classique; **at a c. estimate** au bas mot

conservatory [kən'sɜːvətərɪ] *(pl* **conservatories***) n* (**a**) *(room)* véranda *f* (**b**) *Mus* conservatoire *m*

conserve 1 *n* ['kɒnsɜːv] *(jam)* confiture *f*
   2 *vt* [kən'sɜːv] *(monument, language, tradition)* préserver; *(water, energy)* faire des économies de

consider [kən'sɪdə(r)] *vt* (**a**) *(think over)* considérer; *(offer, matter)* étudier; **he was considering whether to go out when...** il était en train de se demander s'il allait sortir lorsque...; **to c. doing sth** envisager de faire qch; **to c. sb for a job** envisager qn pour un poste (**b**) *(take into account)* penser, réfléchir à; *(possibility)* envisager; *(person's feelings)* tenir compte de; **all things considered** tout bien considéré (**c**) *(regard)* considérer; **I c. her a friend** je la considère comme une amie; **c. it done** considère que c'est déjà fait; **c. yourself dismissed** considère-toi comme renvoyé

considerable [kən'sɪdərəbəl] *adj* considérable; **after c. difficulty** après bien des difficultés

considerate [kən'sɪdərət] *adj* prévenant(e) (**towards** envers); **that wasn't very c. of you** ce n'était pas très aimable de ta part

consideration [kənsɪdə'reɪʃən] *n* (**a**) *(deliberation)* **to be under c.** être à l'étude; **after due c.** après mûre réflexion; **to take sth into c.** prendre qch en considération (**b**) *(factor)* facteur *m* (**c**) *(respect)* considération *f*; **show some c.!** tu pourrais faire preuve d'un peu de considération!; **out of c. for** par égard pour (**d**) *(payment)* contribution *f*; **for a small c.** en échange d'une modique somme

considering [kən'sɪdərɪŋ] **1** *prep* étant donné, vu
   2 *conj* étant donné que; **c. (that) he is so young** étant donné son jeune âge
   3 *adv (after all)* **not bad c.** pas mal après tout

consign [kən'saɪn] vt (**a**) (dispose of) reléguer (**to** à); she was consigned to a life of loneliness elle fut condamnée à une existence solitaire (**b**) (entrust) confier (**to** à) (**c**) (send) expédier (**to** à)
consignment [kən'saɪnmənt] n (of goods) envoi m, expédition f
▸**consist in** [kən'sɪst] vt insep **to c. in doing sth** consister à faire qch; **to c. in sth** résider dans qch, se résumer à qch
▸**consist of** vt insep consister en, se composer de
consistency [kən'sɪstənsɪ] n (**a**) (of substance, liquid) consistance f (**b**) (of arguments, ideas) cohérence f; (of behaviour, person) logique f; (of performer, results) régularité f
consistent [kən'sɪstənt] adj (arguments, ideas) cohérent(e); (behaviour, person) logique; (quality, standard) constant(e); (performer, results) régulier(ère); (refusal, failure) persistant(e); **to be c. with** concorder avec
consistently [kən'sɪstəntlɪ] adv (play, perform) avec régularité; (fail, deny, oppose) toujours
consolation [kɒnsə'leɪʃən] n consolation f; **if it's any c.** si ça peut te consoler; **c. prize** prix m de consolation
console¹ ['kɒnsəʊl] n (control panel) console f
console² [kən'səʊl] vt consoler (**for** de); (bereaved person) réconforter
consolidate [kən'sɒlɪdeɪt] **1** vt also Fig consolider; (position) renforcer; (power) asseoir
2 vi se consolider
consolidation [kənsɒlɪ'deɪʃən] n also Fig consolidation f; (of position, power) renforcement m
consoling [kən'səʊlɪŋ] adj réconfortant(e)
consonant ['kɒnsənənt] **1** n consonne f
2 adj Formal **c. with** en accord avec
consort ['kɒnsɔːt] n (spouse of monarch) époux (épouse) m,f; (**prince**) **c.** prince m consort
▸**consort with** [kən'sɔːt] vt insep frayer avec, fréquenter
consortium [kən'sɔːtɪəm] (pl consortiums or consortia [kən'sɔːtɪə]) n Com consortium m
conspicuous [kən'spɪkjʊəs] adj (easily visible) bien visible; (bravery) remarquable; **to look c.** ne pas passer inaperçu(e); **to make oneself c.** se faire remarquer; **in a c. position** bien en évidence; **to be c. by one's absence** briller par son absence; **c. consumption** consommation f ostentatoire
conspiracy [kən'spɪrəsɪ] (pl conspiracies) n conspiration f; **c. theory** théorie f du complot
conspirator [kən'spɪrətə(r)] n conspirateur(trice) m,f
conspiratorial [kənspɪrə'tɔːrɪəl] adj de conspirateur; **a c. wink** un coup d'œil complice
conspire [kən'spaɪə(r)] vi (of person) se liguer (**against/with** contre/avec); (for political reasons) conspirer (**against/with** contre/avec); **circumstances conspired against me** les circonstances se sont liguées contre moi
constable ['kʌnstəbəl] n Br agent m de police; (rural) gendarme m; **chief c.** = commissaire m de police divisionnaire
constabulary [kən'stæbjʊlərɪ] (pl constabularies) n police f
constant ['kɒnstənt] **1** n Math & Phys constante f
2 adj (**a**) (unchanging) (price, temperature) constant(e); (friend) fidèle (**b**) (continual) (attention, noise, care) continuel(elle); (questions, complaints) incessant(e); **a c. stream of insults** un flot d'injures ininterrompu

constellation [kɒnstə'leɪʃən] n constellation f
consternation [kɒnstə'neɪʃən] n consternation f
constipated ['kɒnstɪpeɪtɪd] adj also Fig constipé(e)
constipation [kɒnstɪ'peɪʃən] n constipation f
constituency [kən'stɪtjʊənsɪ] (pl constituencies) n circonscription f (électorale)
constituent [kən'stɪtjʊənt] **1** n (**a**) Pol électeur(trice) m,f (**b**) (part) élément m constitutif
2 adj constitutif(ive); **c. part** élément m constitutif
constitute ['kɒnstɪtjuːt] vt constituer
constitution [kɒnstɪ'tjuːʃən] n (**a**) (of state, organization) constitution f (**b**) (of person) constitution f; **to have a strong c.** avoir une santé de fer; **to have a weak c.** être de santé fragile
constitutional [kɒnstɪ'tjuːʃənəl] **1** n (walk) (courte) promenade f
2 adj (reform, decision, monarchy) constitutionnel(elle)
constrain [kən'streɪn] vt contraindre, obliger (**to do** à faire); **to feel constrained to do sth** se sentir obligé(e) de faire qch
constraint [kən'streɪnt] n contrainte f; **to place constraints upon** imposer des contraintes à; **under c.** sous la contrainte
constrict [kən'strɪkt] vt (blood vessel) resserrer; (movement) gêner; **to feel constricted** se sentir à l'étroit
constriction [kən'strɪkʃən] n (of blood vessel) constriction f; (of person) gêne f
construct 1 n ['kɒnstrʌkt] (idea) concept m
2 vt [kən'strʌkt] construire
construction [kən'strʌkʃən] n (**a**) (building) & Gram construction f; **under c.** en construction; **the c. industry** l'industrie f du bâtiment, le bâtiment; **c. site** chantier m (de construction); **c. worker** ouvrier m du bâtiment (**b**) (interpretation) **to put a favourable/an unfavourable c. on sth** bien/mal interpréter qch
constructive [kən'strʌktɪv] adj constructif(ive)
construe [kən'struː] vt interpréter
consul ['kɒnsəl] n consul m
consular ['kɒnsjʊlə(r)] adj consulaire
consulate ['kɒnsjʊlət] n consulat m
consult [kən'sʌlt] **1** vt consulter (**on** sur ou à propos de)
2 vi consulter (**with sb/about sth** qn/à propos de qch)
consultancy [kən'sʌltənsɪ] (pl consultancies) n (**a**) (of doctor) poste m de spécialiste (haut placé dans la hiérarchie hospitalière) (**b**) Com conseil m; **to do c. work** être consultant(e)
consultant [kən'sʌltənt] n (**a**) (doctor) spécialiste mf (pratiquant à l'hôpital) (**b**) (adviser) consultant(e) m,f
consultation [kɒnsəl'teɪʃən] n (**a**) (reference) consultation f; (discussion) délibération f; **to hold a c. with sb** s'entretenir avec qn; **in c. with sb** en consultation avec qn
consume [kən'sjuːm] vt (food, fuel, power) consommer; **to be consumed with jealousy/desire** brûler de jalousie/désir
consumer [kən'sjuːmə(r)] n (of product) consommateur(trice) m,f; **c. durables** biens mpl de consommation durables; **c. goods** biens mpl de consommation; Econ **c. price index** indice m des prix de détails; **c. protection** la défense du consommateur; **c. research**

étude f de marché; **c. society** société f de consommation; **c. spending** dépenses fpl de consommation **consumerism** [kən'sjuːmərızəm] n consumérisme m **consummate 1** adj [kən'sʌmɪt] (linguist, cook) de premier ordre; (snob, hypocrite) parfait(e) **2** vt ['kɒnsəmeɪt] (marriage, relationship) consommer **consumption** [kən'sʌmpʃən] n (**a**) (of goods, resources) consommation f; **unfit for human c.** impropre à la consommation (**b**) Old-fashioned Med (tuberculosis) consomption f **contact** ['kɒntækt] **1** n (**a**) (act of touching) contact m; **to be in/come into c. with** être en/entrer en contact avec; **to make c. with sb** prendre contact avec qn; **to lose c. with sb** perdre contact avec qn; **to get in c. with sb** contacter qn; **c. lenses, Fam contacts** lentilles fpl (de contact) (**b**) (acquaintance) relation f; **he has lots of contacts** il connaît beaucoup de monde **2** vt se mettre en rapport avec, contacter **contagious** [kən'teɪdʒəs] adj (disease) contagieux(euse); (laughter) communicatif(ive) **contain** [kən'teɪn] vt (**a**) (hold) contenir, renfermer; (include) contenir (**b**) (control) contenir; **to c. oneself** se contenir; **he was unable to c. his laughter** il ne put s'empêcher de rire **container** [kən'teɪnə(r)] n (for storage) récipient m; (for transport) conteneur m; **c. lorry** camion m adapté au transport des conteneurs; **c. ship** (navire m) porte-conteneurs m inv **contaminate** [kən'tæmɪneɪt] vt also Fig contaminer **contamination** [kəntæmɪ'neɪʃən] n contamination f **contd** (abbr continued) **c. on page 14** suite (à la) page 14 **contemplate** ['kɒntempleɪt] **1** vt (look at) contempler; (consider) réfléchir à; **to c. doing sth** envisager de ou songer à faire qch **2** vi (consider) méditer **contemplation** [kɒntem'pleɪʃən] n contemplation f **contemplative** [kən'templətɪv] adj contemplatif(ive) **contemporary** [kən'tempərərɪ] (pl contemporaries) **1** n contemporain(e) m,f **2** adj contemporain(e) **contempt** [kən'tempt] n mépris m; **to hold sb/sth in c.** avoir du mépris pour qn/qch, mépriser qn/qch; **to be beneath c.** être des plus méprisables; Law **c. of court** outrage m au tribunal **contemptible** [kən'temptəbəl] adj méprisable **contemptuous** [kən'temptjʊəs] adj méprisant(e); **to be c. of sth** mépriser qch **contend** [kən'tend] **1** vt (maintain) **to c. that...** prétendre ou soutenir que... **2** vi (**a**) (struggle) **to c. with sth** lutter contre qch; (difficulties) affronter qch; **they still had the chairman to c. with** il leur restait à régler le problème du PD-G (**b**) (compete) **to c. for sth** se battre pour qch; (for job, promotion) être en concurrence pour qch **contender** [kən'tendə(r)] n (in sport) concurrent(e) m,f; (in election, for job) candidat(e) m,f **content¹** ['kɒntent] n (**a**) (quantity) teneur f; (of book, speech, essay) fond m; **protein/fibre c.** teneur f en protéines/fibres (**b**) **contents** (of pockets, drawer, house) contenu m; **contents page** (of book) table f des matières **content²** [kən'tent] **1** adj (happy) content(e), satisfait(e) (**with** de); **to be c. with one's lot** se contenter de son sort **2** vt contenter; **to c. oneself with sth/with doing sth** se contenter de qch/de faire qch

contented [kən'tentɪd] adj (person) content(e), satisfait(e) (**with** de); (smile, sigh) de satisfaction **contention** [kən'tenʃən] n (**a**) (dispute) dispute f (**b**) (competition) **to be in c. (for sth)** être en compétition (pour qch) (**c**) (opinion) affirmation f; **it is my c. that...** j'affirme que... **contentious** [kən'tenʃəs] adj (issue, views) controversé(e); (person) querelleur(euse) **contentment** [kən'tentmənt] n contentement m **contest 1** n ['kɒntest] (competition) concours m; (for job, presidency) lutte f; (in boxing) combat m **2** vt [kən'test] (right, ability, will) contester; **to c. a seat** se porter candidat(e); **a fiercely contested election** une élection très disputée **contestant** [kən'testənt] n (in competition, game) concurrent(e) m,f; (in election) candidat(e) m,f **context** ['kɒntekst] n contexte m; **in/out of c.** en/hors contexte; **to put sth into c.** replacer qch dans son contexte **contextualize** [kən'tekstjʊəlaɪz] vt contextualiser **continent¹** ['kɒntɪnənt] n (land mass) continent m; Br **the C.** l'Europe f (continentale) **continent²** adj Med continent(e) **continental** [kɒntɪ'nentəl] adj (**a**) (in geography) continental(e); **c. drift** dérive f des continents; **c. shelf** plate-forme f continentale (**b**) Br (European) européen(enne), d'outre-Manche; **d'Europe continentale; c. breakfast** = petit déjeuner se composant de tartines et d'une boisson chaude; **c. quilt** couette f

Continental breakfast

Ce terme désigne un petit déjeuner léger, par opposition au "English breakfast" (petit déjeuner anglais), beaucoup plus copieux et comportant un plat chaud.

contingency [kən'tɪndʒənsɪ] (pl contingencies) n éventualité f; **to allow for every c.** parer à toute éventualité; **c. fund** caisse f ou fond m de prévoyance; **c. plan** plan m d'urgence **contingent** [kən'tɪndʒənt] adj contingent(e); **to be c. upon sth** dépendre de qch **continual** [kən'tɪnjʊəl] adj continuel(elle), incessant(e) **continuation** [kəntɪnjʊ'eɪʃən] n (of story) suite f; (of action, work) prolongation f; (of road) prolongement m **continue** [kən'tɪnjuː] **1** vt (activity, journey) continuer, poursuivre; (after interruption) reprendre, continuer; (tradition) perpétuer; **to c. to do or doing sth** continuer ou se faire qch; **to be continued à suivre; continued on page 30** suite (à la) page 30 **2** vi continuer; (of situation) se prolonger; **to c. on one's way** continuer ou poursuivre son chemin; **she will c. as director until December** elle continuera d'assumer ses fonctions de directrice jusqu'en décembre; **the situation cannot c.** cette situation ne peut pas durer **continuity** [kɒntɪ'njuːɪtɪ] n continuité f; **c. announcer** (on TV, radio) speaker(ine) m,f; **c. girl** scripte f **continuous** [kən'tɪnjʊəs] adj continu(e); Sch & Univ **c. assessment** contrôle m continu; Comput **c. paper** or **stationery** papier m (en) continu **contort** [kən'tɔːt] **1** vt tordre **2** vi se tordre (**with** de) **contortion** [kən'tɔːʃən] n (of features) crispation f; (of body) contorsion f

contour ['kɒntʊə(r)] *n* contour *m*; **c. (line)** courbe *f* de niveau; **c. map** carte *f* en courbes de niveau
contraband ['kɒntrəbænd] *n* contrebande *f*; **c. goods** marchandises *fpl* de contrebande
contraception [kɒntrə'sepʃən] *n* contraception *f*
contraceptive [kɒntrə'septɪv] **1** *n* contraceptif *m* **2** *adj* **c. pill** pilule *f* contraceptive
contract 1 *n* ['kɒntrækt] contrat *m*; **to be under c.** être sous contrat; **to enter into a c.** passer un contrat; **to take out a c.** on **sb** *(hire assassin)* engager un tueur à gages pour assassiner qn; **c. killer** tueur *m* à gages **2** *vt* [kən'trækt] *(illness, debt)* contracter; **to c. to do sth** s'engager (par contrat) à faire qch **3** *vi* [kən'trækt] *(shrink)* se contracter
►**contract out 1** *vt sep (work)* sous-traiter **2** *vi Com (of insurance policy, pension plan)* arrêter de souscrire (**of** à)
contraction [kən'trækʃən] *n* contraction *f*
contractor [kən'træktə(r)] *n (businessman)* entrepreneur *m* (en bâtiment); *(worker)* ouvrier *m* (en bâtiment)
contractual [kən'træktjʊəl] *adj* contractuel(elle)
contradict [kɒntrə'dɪkt] *vt (disagree with)* contredire; *(deny)* démentir; **to c. oneself** se contredire
contradiction [kɒntrə'dɪkʃən] *n* contradiction *f*; **it's a c. in terms** c'est parfaitement contradictoire
contradictory [kɒntrə'dɪktərɪ] *adj* contradictoire
contraflow ['kɒntrəfləʊ] *n* **c. (system)** *(on motorway)* (système *m* de) circulation *f* à contre-courant
contralto [kən'træltəʊ] *(pl* **contraltos**) *n* contralto *mf*
contraption [kən'træpʃən] *n Fam* machin *m*, truc *m*
contrary ['kɒntrərɪ] **1** *n* contraire *m*; **on the c.** au contraire; **unless you hear to the c.** sauf avis contraire; **there was no evidence to the c.** il n'y avait pas de preuve du contraire **2** *adj* (**a**) *(opposite)* contraire (**to** à); *(ideas, interests)* opposé(e) (**to** à); **c. to my expectations** contre mon attente; **c. to popular belief** contrairement à ce que croient la plupart des gens (**b**) [kən'treərɪ] *(awkward)* contrariant(e)
contrast 1 *n* ['kɒntrɑːst] contraste *m* (**between** entre); **in c. with** *or* **to** par opposition à; **by c.** par contraste **2** *vt* [kən'trɑːst] mettre en contraste (**with** avec) **3** *vi* [kən'trɑːst] faire contraste (**with** avec)
contrasting [kən'trɑːstɪŋ] *adj (attitudes, lifestyles)* qui fait contraste; *(colours)* opposé(e), contrasté(e)
contravene [kɒntrə'viːn] *vt* enfreindre
contravention [kɒntrə'venʃən] *n (of law)* infraction *f* (**of** à); **in c. of a treaty** en violation d'un traité
contribute ['kɒntrɪbjuːt, kən'trɪbjuːt] **1** *vt (money)* verser; *(time, clothes)* donner; **to c. an article to a newspaper** écrire un article pour un journal; **he didn't c. anything to the discussion** il n'a pas pris part à la discussion **2** *vi* (**a**) *(give money, goods etc)* contribuer (**to** à); *(to charity)* donner (**to** à); *(to newspaper)* collaborer (**to** à); **to c. to a discussion** prendre part à une discussion (**b**) *Fin (to pension fund)* cotiser (**to** à)
contribution [kɒntrɪ'bjuːʃən] *n* (**a**) *(of money, goods etc)* contribution *f* (**to** à); **the chocolate mousse was David's c.** c'est David qu'il faut remercier pour la mousse au chocolat (**b**) *Fin (to pension fund)* cotisation *f*

contributor [kən'trɪbjʊtə(r)] *n (to charity)* donateur(trice) *m,f*; *(to newspaper)* collaborateur(trice) *m,f* (**to** de)
contributory [kən'trɪbjʊtərɪ] *adj (cause, factor)* concourant(e); **to be a c. factor in sth** concourir à qch; *Law* **c. negligence** manque *m* de précautions; *Fin* **c. pension scheme** système *m* de retraite par répartition
contrite ['kɒntraɪt] *adj* contrit(e)
contrition [kən'trɪʃən] *n* contrition *f*
contrivance [kən'traɪvəns] *n (device)* appareil *m*; *(scheme, plan)* système *m*
contrive [kən'traɪv] *vt* inventer; **to c. to do sth** trouver le moyen de faire qch
contrived [kən'traɪvd] *adj* forcé(e), qui manque de naturel
control [kən'trəʊl] **1** (**a**) *(power, restriction)* contrôle *m*; **to impose controls on prices** imposer le contrôle des prix; **to take c. (of the situation)** prendre les choses en main; **to have c. over** *(power)* contrôler; *(authority)* avoir de l'autorité sur; **to be in c. of sth** contrôler qch; **to be back in c.** avoir repris le contrôle; **to get out of c.** devenir incontrôlable; **to let sth get out of c.** perdre le contrôle de qch; **to bring a fire under c.** maîtriser un incendie; **to keep one's feelings under c.** maîtriser ses émotions; **everything is under c.** je domine/nous dominons/*etc* la situation; **to lose c. (of oneself)** ne plus être maître de soi; **to regain c. (of oneself)** se ressaisir; *Pej* **c. freak** = personne qui veut tout régenter; **c. group** groupe *m* témoin; **c. tower** *(at airport)* tour *f* de contrôle (**b**) *(device)* **the controls** les commandes *fpl*; **to be at the controls** être aux commandes; **c. panel** tableau *m* de bord **2** *vt (pt & pp* **controlled**) *(production, expenditure, prices)* contrôler; *(business)* diriger; *(child, pupils)* avoir de l'autorité sur; *(disease)* maintenir à un niveau raisonnable; *(vehicle)* garder le contrôle de; **to c. oneself** se maîtriser; **to c. one's anger** maîtriser sa colère
controlled [kən'trəʊld] *adj (person)* maître de soi, posé(e); *(experiment, explosion)* contrôlé(e)
controlling interest [kən'trəʊlɪŋ'ɪntrest] *n Fin* participation *f* majoritaire
controversial [kɒntrə'vɜːʃəl] *adj* **to be c.** *(of film, decision)* être controversé(e); *(of person)* être provocateur(trice)
controversy ['kɒntrəvɜːsɪ, kən'trɒvəsɪ] *(pl* **controversies**) *n* controverse *f*, polémique *f*; **to cause a lot of c.** provoquer une grande controverse *ou* une vive polémique
conundrum [kə'nʌndrəm] *n (riddle)* devinette *f*; *(mystery)* énigme *f*
conurbation [kɒnɜː'beɪʃən] *n* conurbation *f*
convalesce [kɒnvə'les] *vi* être en convalescence
convalescence [kɒnvə'lesəns] *n* convalescence *f*
convalescent [kɒnvə'lesənt] *adj (patient)* convalescent(e); **c. home** maison *f* de repos
convection [kən'vekʃən] *n* convection *f*; **c. heater** convecteur *m*
convene [kən'viːn] **1** *vt (meeting)* convoquer **2** *vi (of meeting, committee)* se réunir
convenience [kən'viːnɪəns] *n* commodité *f*; **at your c.** quand cela vous conviendra; *Formal* **at your earliest c.** dans les meilleurs délais; **(public) c.** *(toilet)* toilettes *fpl* publiques; **c. food** aliments *mpl* tout prêts; *Am* **c.**

store = supérette de quartier qui reste ouverte tard le soir, *Can* dépanneur *m*

convenient [kən'viːnɪənt] *adj (arrangement, method)* commode, pratique; **to be c. (for sb)** *(of arrangement)* être commode *ou* pratique (pour qn); *(of time)* convenir (à qn)

convent ['kɒnvənt] *n Rel* couvent *m*; **c. school** école *f* tenue par des sœurs

convention [kən'venʃən] *n* (**a**) *(conference)* convention *f*, congrès *m* (**b**) *(agreement)* convention *f* (**c**) *(established practice)* usage *m*; **the c. is that...** l'usage veut que...

conventional [kən'venʃənəl] *adj (behaviour, ideas)* conventionnel(elle); *(person)* conformiste; **c. warfare** guerre *f* conventionnelle; **c. weapon** arme *f* conventionnelle; **c. wisdom** sagesse *f* populaire

converge [kən'vɜːdʒ] *vi* converger (**on** sur)

convergence [kən'vɜːdʒəns] *n* convergence *f*; *EU* **c. criteria** critères *mpl* de convergence

conversant [kən'vɜːsənt] *adj* **to be c. with sth** s'y connaître en qch; *(with events, developments)* être au courant de qch

conversation [kɒnvə'seɪʃən] *n* conversation *f*; **to have a c. with sb** avoir une conversation avec qn; **to make c.** faire la conversation; **the vase is quite a c. piece** le vase suscite bien des commentaires; *Fam* **to be a c. stopper** *or* **killer** arrêter net la conversation

conversational [kɒnvə'seɪʃənəl] *adj (style)* de la conversation; *Comput (mode)* dialogue; **c. Spanish** espagnol *m* courant

conversationalist [kɒnvə'seɪʃənəlɪst] *n* **to be a good c.** avoir de la conversation; **I'm not much of a c.** je ne suis pas brillant causeur

converse[1] [kən'vɜːs] *vi (talk)* converser (**about** sur), s'entretenir (**about** de)

converse[2] ['kɒnvɜːs] *n (opposite)* **the c.** le contraire

conversely [kən'vɜːslɪ] *adv* inversement

conversion [kən'vɜːʃən] *n* (**a**) *(transformation)* conversion *f*; *(of building)* aménagement *m*; **c. table** *(for measurements)* table *f* de conversion (**b**) *(in rugby)* transformation *f*

convert 1 *n* ['kɒnvɜːt] *Rel & Fig* converti(e) *m,f* (**to** à)
2 *vt* [kən'vɜːt] (**a**) *Rel & Fig* convertir (**to** à); *(building)* aménager (**into** en) (**b**) *(in rugby)* **to c. a try** transformer un essai
3 *vi* [kən'vɜːt] *Rel & Fig* se convertir (**to** à)

convertible [kən'vɜːtəbəl] **1** *n (car)* décapotable *f*
2 *adj (sofa)* convertible; *(car)* décapotable; **c. currency** monnaie *f ou* devise *f* convertible

convex [kɒn'veks] *adj* convexe

convey [kən'veɪ] *vt* (**a**) *(communicate)* transmettre; **to c. one's meaning** communiquer sa pensée (**b**) *(transport)* transporter

conveyance [kən'veɪəns] *n* (**a**) *(of goods, passengers)* transport *m* (**b**) *Old-fashioned (vehicle)* véhicule *m*

conveyancing [kən'veɪənsɪŋ] *n Law* procédure *f* translative de propriété

conveyor belt [kən'veɪəbelt] *n* convoyeur *m*, tapis *m* roulant

convict 1 *n* ['kɒnvɪkt] détenu(e) *m,f*
2 *vt* [kən'vɪkt] **to c. sb (of)** déclarer qn coupable (de)

conviction [kən'vɪkʃən] *n* (**a**) *Law* condamnation *f*; **to have no previous convictions** n'avoir jamais été condamné(e) (**b**) *(belief)* conviction *f*; **to lack c.** manquer de conviction

convince [kən'vɪns] *vt* convaincre (**of/that** de/que); **I was convinced I was right** j'étais convaincu d'avoir raison

convincing [kən'vɪnsɪŋ] *adj* convaincant(e); *(defeat)* décisif(ive)

convivial [kən'vɪvɪəl] *adj (person)* chaleureux(euse); *(atmosphere)* joyeux(euse)

convoluted ['kɒnvəluːtɪd] *adj (argument, explanation)* compliqué(e)

convoy ['kɒnvɔɪ] *n* convoi *m*

convulse [kən'vʌls] *vt* secouer; **to be convulsed with laughter/pain** se tordre de rire/de douleur

convulsions [kən'vʌlʃənz] *npl Med* convulsions *fpl*; *Fig* **to be in c.** *(of laughter)* se tordre

coo [kuː] (*pt & pp* **cooed**) *vi (of dove)* roucouler; *Fam* **to c. over sb/sth** s'extasier devant qn/qch

cook [kʊk] **1** *n* cuisinier(ère) *m,f*; *Prov* **too many cooks spoil the broth** on n'arrive jamais à rien quand tout le monde met son grain de sel
2 *vt (meal)* préparer; *(food)* (faire) cuire; *Fig* **to c. the books** falsifier les comptes
3 *vi (of food)* cuire; *(of person)* faire la cuisine; *Fam* **what's cooking?** qu'est-ce qui se passe?

▸**cook up** *vt sep (excuse, story)* inventer

cookbook ['kʊkbʊk] *n* livre *m* de cuisine

cooker ['kʊkə(r)] *n (stove)* cuisinière *f*

cookery ['kʊkərɪ] *n* cuisine *f*; *Br* **c. book** livre *m* de cuisine

cookie ['kʊkɪ] *n* (**a**) *Am (biscuit)* biscuit *m*; *Fam* **that's the way the c. crumbles!** c'est la vie(, que veux-tu) (**b**) *(person)* **a tough c.** un(e) dur(e) à cuire; **a smart c.** un(e) malin(igne) (**c**) *Comput* cookie *m*, cafteur *m*, *Can* témoin *m*

cooking ['kʊkɪŋ] *n (process)* cuisson *f*; *(activity)* cuisine *f*; **to do the c.** faire la cuisine; **c. apple** pomme *f* à cuire; **c. chocolate** chocolat *m* à cuire; **c. foil** papier *m* alu; **c. time** temps *m* de cuisson; **c. utensils** ustensiles *mpl* de cuisine

cool [kuːl] **1** *n* (**a**) *(coldness)* fraîcheur *f* (**b**) *(calm)* **to keep/lose one's c.** garder/perdre son sang-froid
2 *adj* (**a**) *(wind, weather, drink)* frais (fraîche); *(coffee, bathwater)* tiède; **it's c. outside** il fait frais dehors; *Fam* **the flat cost a c. million** l'appartement a coûté la coquette somme d'un million de livres/de dollars/*etc* (**b**) *(calm)* calme; *(unfriendly)* froid(e); **c. as a cucumber** parfaitement calme; **keep c.!** ne t'angoisse pas!; **to keep a c. head** garder la tête froide; **to be a c. customer** *(cheeky)* être culotté(e); *(self-possessed)* avoir beaucoup de sang-froid (**c**) *Fam (good)* cool *inv*; *(trendy)* branché(e)
3 *adv Fam* **to play it c.** rester calme
4 *vt* rafraîchir, refroidir; *Fam* **c. it!** on se calme!; *Fam* **to c. one's heels** poireauter
5 *vi (of liquid)* refroidir; *(of anger)* passer; *(of passion, enthusiasm)* se refroidir

▸**cool down 1** *vt sep* (**a**) *(of cold drink)* rafraîchir (**b**) *(make calm)* calmer
2 *vi* (**a**) *(of weather)* se rafraîchir; *(of liquid)* refroidir (**b**) *(become calm)* se calmer

▸**cool off** *vi* (**a**) *(of person)* se rafraîchir (**b**) *(of passion, enthusiasm)* se refroidir; *(of angry person)* se calmer

coolant ['kuːlənt] *n* liquide *m* de refroidissement

cool-headed ['kuːl'hedɪd] *adj* calme; **to remain c.** garder la tête froide

cooling ['kuːlɪŋ] *adj (drink)* rafraîchissant(e); *(agent)* réfrigérant(e); *Ind & Com* **c. off period** période *f* de réflexion; **c. tower** tour *f* de réfrigération

coop [kuːp] *n (for chickens)* poulailler *m*; *Fig* **to fly the c.** se faire la malle
▸**coop up** *vt sep* **to keep sb cooped up** tenir qn enfermé(e); **to feel cooped up** se sentir à l'étroit
co-op [ˈkəʊɒp] *n* coopérative *f*
cooperate [kəʊˈɒpəreɪt] *vi* coopérer (**with** avec)
cooperation [kəʊɒpəˈreɪʃən] *n* coopération *f*
cooperative [kəʊˈɒpərətɪv] **1** *n* coopérative *f*
2 *adj* coopératif(ive)
coopt [kəʊˈɒpt] *vt* coopter (**onto** à)
coordinate 1 *n* [kəʊˈɔːdɪnət] (**a**) *Math* coordonnée *f*
(**b**) **coordinates** *(clothes)* coordonnés *mpl*
2 *vt* [kəʊˈɔːdɪneɪt] coordonner
coordination [kəʊɔːdɪˈneɪʃən] *n* coordination *f*
coordinator [kəʊˈɔːdɪneɪtə(r)] *n* coordinateur(trice) *m,f*
co-owner [ˈkəʊˈəʊnə(r)] *n* copropriétaire *mf*
cop [kɒp] **1** *n Fam* (**a**) *(policeman)* flic *m*; **to play cops and robbers** jouer aux gendarmes et aux voleurs (**b**) *Br* **it's not much c.** ça ne vaut pas grand-chose
2 *vt (pt & pp copped)* **to c. it** *(be punished)* se faire pincer; *(die)* clamser
▸**cop out** *vi Fam (avoid responsibility)* se défiler; *(choose easy solution)* choisir la solution de facilité; **to c. out of doing sth** ne pas avoir le cran de faire qch
cope [kəʊp] *vi* se débrouiller, s'en tirer; **to c. with** *(demand, situation)* faire face à; *(problem, difficulty)* venir à bout de; **I just can't c.** je n'y arrive pas; **he can't c. with his job** il ne s'en sort pas dans son travail
Copenhagen [kəʊpənˈheɪgən] *n* Copenhague
copier [ˈkɒpɪə(r)] *n (photocopier)* (photo)copieuse *f*
copilot [ˈkəʊpaɪlət] *n* copilote *m*
copious [ˈkəʊpɪəs] *adj* copieux(euse); *(tears, notes, amounts)* abondant(e)
cop-out [ˈkɒpaʊt] *n Fam* solution *f* de facilité
copper [ˈkɒpə(r)] **1** *n* (**a**) *(metal)* cuivre *m*; *Fam* **coppers** *(coins)* petite monnaie *f* (**b**) *Fam (policeman)* flic *m*
2 *adj* **c.(-coloured)** *(couleur)* cuivre *inv*, cuivré(e)
copperplate [ˈkɒpəpleɪt] *n* **c. (writing)** écriture *f* moulée
coppice [ˈkɒpɪs] *n* taillis *m*
coproduce [kəʊprəˈdjuːs] *vt Cin & TV* coproduire
coproduction [kəʊprəˈdʌkʃən] *n Cin & TV* coproduction *f*
copse [kɒps] *n* taillis *m*
copublish [kəʊˈpʌblɪʃ] *vt* coéditer
copublishing [kəʊˈpʌblɪʃɪŋ] *n* coédition *f*
copulate [ˈkɒpjʊleɪt] *vi* copuler
copulation [kɒpjʊˈleɪʃən] *n* copulation *f*
copy [ˈkɒpɪ] **1** *(pl* **copies)** *n* (**a**) *(reproduction)* copie *f* (**b**) *(of letter, document)* copie *f*, double *m*; **c. typist** dactylo *mf* (**c**) *(of book)* exemplaire *m*; *(of newspaper)* numéro *m* (**d**) *Journ (written material)* copie *f*; **story made good c.** ça a fait un bon sujet d'article; **c. editor** *(in journalism)* secrétaire *mf* de rédaction; *(in publishing)* réviseur *m* (**e**) *Comput* **c. and paste** copier-coller *m*
2 *vt (pt & pp copied)* *(painting, document, text)* & *Comput* copier; **to c. sth to disk** copier qch sur disquette; **to c. and paste sth** faire un copier-coller sur qch
3 *vi (in exam)* copier
copybook [ˈkɒpɪbʊk] *n* cahier *m* d'écriture; **c. example** exemple *m* classique

copycat [ˈkɒpɪkæt] *Fam* **1** *n* copieur(euse) *m,f*
2 *adj* **c. crime/murder** délit *m*/meurtre *m* inspiré par un autre
copyright [ˈkɒpɪraɪt] **1** *n* droit *m* d'auteur, copyright *m*; **to be out of c.** être tombé(e) dans le domaine public
2 *adj* protégé(e) par le droit d'auteur
copywriter [ˈkɒpɪraɪtə(r)] *n* rédacteur(trice) *m,f* publicitaire
coquette [kɒˈket] *n Lit* coquette *f*
coral [ˈkɒrəl] *n* corail *m*; **c. island** île *f* corallienne; **c. reef** récif *m* corallien; **the C. Sea** la mer de Corail
cord [kɔːd] *n* (**a**) *(string)* grosse ficelle *f*; *(for curtains, pyjamas)* cordon *m* (**b**) *(corduroy)* velours *m* côtelé; **a c. jacket** une veste en velours côtelé; **cords** pantalon *m* en velours côtelé
cordial [ˈkɔːdɪəl] **1** *n (drink)* sirop *m*
2 *adj (friendly)* cordial(e)
cordless [ˈkɔːdlɪs] *adj* sans fil; **c. telephone** (téléphone *m*) sans-fil *m*
cordon [ˈkɔːdən] *n* cordon *m*
▸**cordon off** *vt sep (road)* barrer; *(area)* boucler
corduroy [ˈkɔːdərɔɪ] *n* velours *m* côtelé; **c. trousers** pantalon *m* en velours côtelé
core [kɔː(r)] **1** *n (of apple)* trognon *m*; *(of earth, magnet)* noyau *m*; *(of nuclear reactor)* centre *m*; *(of argument, problem)* cœur *m*; **hard c.** noyau *m* dur; **he's rotten to the c.** il est pourri jusqu'à la moelle; *Sch* **c. curriculum** tronc *m* commun
2 *vt (apple)* évider
Corfu [kɔːˈfuː] *n* Corfou
coriander [kɒrɪˈændə(r)] *n* coriandre *f*
cork [kɔːk] **1** *n (material)* liège *m*; *(stopper)* bouchon *m* (en liège)
2 *vt (bottle)* boucher
corked [kɔːkt] *adj (wine)* bouchonné(e)
corkscrew [ˈkɔːkskruː] *n* tire-bouchon *m*
cormorant [ˈkɔːmərənt] *n* cormoran *m*
corn¹ [kɔːn] *n* (**a**) *Br (wheat)* blé *m* (**b**) *Am (maize)* maïs *m*; **c. on the cob** maïs *m* en épi; **c. bread** pain *m* à la farine de maïs; **c. meal** farine *f* de maïs; **c. oil** huile *f* de maïs
corn² *n (on foot)* cor *m*; **c. plaster** pansement *m* pour cors
cornea [ˈkɔːnɪə] *n Anat* cornée *f*
corned beef [ˈkɔːndˈbiːf] *n* corned-beef *m*
corner [ˈkɔːnə(r)] **1** *n* (**a**) *(of room, street, page, screen)* coin *m*; **out of the c. of one's eye** du coin de l'œil; **it's just round the c.** c'est juste au coin; *Fig* **Christmas is just round the c.** on en est tout près de Noël; **to turn the c.** tourner au coin de la rue; *Fig (of economy, company)* passer la période critique; **c. shop** épicerie *f* du coin, *Can* dépanneur *m* (**b**) *(bend in road)* tournant *m*; *Fig* **to cut corners** *(with time)* faire les choses à la va-vite; *(with materials, money)* faire les choses à l'économie (**c**) *(in football)* **c. (kick)** corner *m*; **to take a c.** tirer un corner
2 *vt* (**a**) *(person, animal)* acculer (**b**) *(market)* accaparer
3 *vi (of car, driver)* prendre un virage
cornerstone [ˈkɔːnəstəʊn] *n also Fig* pierre *f* angulaire
cornet [ˈkɔːnɪt] *n* (**a**) *(musical instrument)* cornet *m* à pistons (**b**) *(ice-cream)* **c.** cornet *m*
cornfield [ˈkɔːnfiːld] *n (of wheat)* champ *m* de blé; *(of maize)* champ *m* de maïs
cornflakes [ˈkɔːnfleɪks] *npl* corn flakes *mpl*

cornflour ['kɔːnflaʊə(r)] n Br farine f de maïs
cornflower ['kɔːnflaʊə(r)] n (plant) bleuet m; **c. blue** bleu barbeau inv
cornstarch ['kɔːnstɑːtʃ] n Am farine f de maïs
cornice ['kɔːnɪs] n corniche f
Cornish ['kɔːnɪʃ] **1** npl **the C.** (people) les Cornouaillais mpl **2** n (language) cornique m **3** adj cornouaillais(e); Br **C. pasty** feuilleté m à la viande
Cornwall ['kɔːnwəl] n Cornouailles f
corny ['kɔːnɪ] adj Fam (joke) nul (nulle); (film, novel) tarte
corollary [kə'rɒlərɪ] (pl **corollaries**) n corollaire m
coronary ['kɒrənərɪ] Med **1** (pl **coronaries**) n infarctus m (du myocarde) **2** adj coronarien(enne); **c. thrombosis** infarctus m du myocarde
coronation [kɒrə'neɪʃən] n couronnement m; Br **c. chicken** = morceaux de poulet préparés avec de la mayonnaise au curry
coroner ['kɒrənə(r)] n Law coroner m
corporal¹ ['kɔːpərəl] adj corporel(elle); **c. punishment** châtiment m corporel
corporal² n Mil (in infantry) caporal m; (in cavalry, artillery) brigadier m
corporate ['kɔːpərət] adj Com (of companies in general) d'entreprise; (of a specific company) d'une société; **c. culture** culture f d'entreprise; **c. image** image f de marque de l'entreprise
corporation [kɔːpə'reɪʃən] n (**a**) Com société f; **c. tax** impôt m sur les sociétés (**b**) (council) conseil m municipal
corps [kɔː(r)] (pl **corps** [kɔːz]) n Mil corps m
corpse [kɔːps] n cadavre m; **a lifeless c.** un corps inerte
corpulent ['kɔːpjʊlənt] adj corpulent(e)
corpuscle ['kɔːpʌsəl] n Anat corpuscule m; **red/white (blood) corpuscles** globules mpl rouges/blancs
corral [kɒ'rɑːl] n Am corral m
correct [kə'rekt] **1** adj (**a**) (accurate) exact(e); **to prove c.** se vérifier, s'avérer juste; **if my memory is c.** si j'ai bonne mémoire; **he is c.** (right) il a raison; **that's c.** c'est exact (**b**) (person, behaviour) correct(e), convenable; **it wasn't the c. thing to say/do** ce n'était pas la chose à dire/faire **2** vt (homework, proofs, error) corriger; (misunderstanding) dissiper; **c. me if I'm wrong, but...** reprenez-moi si je me trompe, mais...; **I stand corrected** j'avais tort
correction [kə'rekʃən] n correction f; **c. fluid** liquide m correcteur
corrective [kə'rektɪv] **1** n correctif m **2** adj (action, measure) rectificatif(ive), correctif(ive); **c. surgery** chirurgie f réparatrice
correlate ['kɒrɪleɪt] **1** vt mettre en rapport ou en corrélation (**with** avec); **they are closely correlated** ils sont étroitement liés **2** vi être en rapport ou en corrélation (**with** avec)
correlation [kɒrɪ'leɪʃən] n corrélation f
correspond [kɒrɪs'pɒnd] vi (**a**) (be in accordance) correspondre (**with** or **to** à) (**b**) (be equivalent) correspondre (**to** à), être l'équivalent (**to** de) (**c**) (write letters) correspondre (**with** avec)
correspondence [kɒrɪs'pɒndəns] n (**a**) (relationship) rapport m (**between** entre) (**b**) (letter-writing) correspondance f; **I don't get much c.** je ne reçois pas

beaucoup de courrier; **c. course** cours m par correspondance
correspondent [kɒrɪs'pɒndənt] n correspondant(e) m,f
corresponding [kɒrɪ'spɒndɪŋ] adj correspondant(e)
corridor ['kɒrɪdɔː(r)] n couloir m, corridor m; Fig **the corridors of power** les hautes sphères fpl du pouvoir
corroborate [kə'rɒbəreɪt] vt corroborer, confirmer
corroboration [kərɒbə'reɪʃən] n corroboration f, confirmation f
corrode [kə'rəʊd] **1** vt (metal) corroder, attaquer; Fig (society) miner; (optimism, friendship) entamer **2** vi (of metal) se corroder
corrosion [kə'rəʊʒən] n corrosion f
corrosive [kə'rəʊsɪv] **1** n corrosif m **2** adj corrosif(ive)
corrugated ['kɒrəgeɪtɪd] adj (cardboard) ondulé(e); **c. iron** tôle f ondulée
corrupt [kə'rʌpt] **1** adj (dishonest) corrompu(e) **2** vt corrompre; Comput altérer; **to c. sb's morals** dépraver qn
corruption [kə'rʌpʃən] n corruption f
corset ['kɔːsɪt] n corset m
Corsica ['kɔːsɪkə] n la Corse
Corsican ['kɔːsɪkən] **1** n Corse mf **2** adj corse
cortege [kɔː'teʒ] n cortège m
cortex ['kɔːteks] (pl **cortices** ['kɔːtɪsiːz]) n cortex m
cortisone ['kɔːtɪzəʊn] n cortisone f
cos¹ [kɒz] conj Br Fam parce que
cos² [kɒs] n **c.** (lettuce) romaine f
cosh [kɒʃ] Br **1** n matraque f **2** vt matraquer
cosmetic [kɒz'metɪk] **1** n cosmétique m, produit m de beauté **2** adj Fig (superficial) superficiel(elle); **c. surgery** chirurgie f esthétique
cosmic ['kɒzmɪk] adj cosmique; Fig prodigieux(euse)
cosmonaut ['kɒzmənɔːt] n cosmonaute mf
cosmopolitan [kɒzmə'pɒlɪtən] adj cosmopolite
cosmos ['kɒzmɒs] n cosmos m
cosset ['kɒsɪt] vt couver, choyer
cost [kɒst] **1** n (**a**) (price) coût m; Law **costs** dépens mpl; also Fig **at little/great c.** à peu de/à grands frais; **at great c. to his health** au prix de sa santé; Econ **c. of living** coût de la vie; Com **c. of production** coût de production; Fin **c. accounting** comptabilité f analytique; Econ **c. benefit analysis** analyse f coûts-bénéfices; Com **c. price** prix m coûtant (**b**) (idioms) **to count the c. of sth** tirer la leçon de qch; **at all costs** à tout prix; **as I found out to my c.** comme je l'ai appris à mes dépens **2** vt (**a**) (pt & pp **cost**) also Fig coûter; **how much does it c.?** combien ça coûte?; **it costs £25** ça coûte ou c'est 25 livres; **whatever it costs** quel qu'en soit le prix; Fam **to c. a fortune** or **the earth** coûter les yeux de la tête; **the attempt cost him his life** cette tentative lui a coûté la vie (**b**) (pt & pp **costed**) Com (budget) évaluer le coût de
co-star ['kəʊstɑː(r)] **1** n (in film) partenaire mf à l'écran **2** vi (pt & pp **co-starred**) **the film co-stars Natalie Portman** Natalie Portman joue aussi dans ce film; **co-starring Ewan McGregor** avec Ewan McGregor **3** vi jouer dans un des rôles principaux
Costa Rica ['kɒstə'riːkə] n le Costa Rica

Costa Rican ['kɒstə'riːkən] **1** *n* Costaricien(enne) *m,f*
2 *adj* costaricien(enne)
cost-effective [kɒstɪ'fektɪv] *adj* rentable
costing ['kɒstɪŋ] *n Com (of job)* évaluation *f* du coût; *(of article)* évaluation *f* du prix de revient
costly ['kɒstlɪ] *adj* cher (chère), coûteux(euse); **it was a c. mistake** c'est une erreur qui a coûté cher
costume ['kɒstjʊm] *n* costume *m*; **(swimming) c.** maillot *m* de bain; **c. drama** film *m*/pièce *f* en costumes d'époque; **c. jewellery** bijoux *mpl* fantaisie
cosy, *Am* **cozy** ['kəʊzɪ] *adj (room, atmosphere)* douillet(ette), confortable; *(armchair, pub)* confortable; **to feel c.** *(in room)* être confortablement installé(e); *Fig & Pej* **they have a c. relationship** ils sont un peu trop copain-copain
cot [kɒt] *n Br (for child)* lit *m* d'enfant, petit lit *m*; *Am (folding bed)* lit *m* pliant; *Br* **c. death** mort *f* subite du nourrisson
cottage ['kɒtɪdʒ] *n* = petite maison, généralement à la campagne; **thatched c.** chaumière *f*; **c. cheese** fromage *m* blanc (égoutté); **c. hospital** = hôpital de médecine générale en zone rurale; **c. industry** industrie *f* artisanale; *(at home)* industrie *f* familiale; **c. pie** hachis *m* Parmentier
cotton ['kɒtən] *n* coton *m*; **a c. shirt** une chemise en coton; *Br* **c. bud** Coton-Tige® *m*; *Am* **c. candy** barbe *f* à papa; *Br* **c. wool** ouate *f*, coton *m* hydrophile
▶**cotton on** *vi Fam* piger; **to c. on to sth** piger qch
couch [kaʊtʃ] **1** *n* divan *m*, canapé *m*; *(at doctor's)* lit *m*; *Fam* **to be a c. potato** passer sa vie devant la télé
2 *vt (express)* formuler
cougar ['kuːgə(r)] *n* couguar *m*, puma *m*
cough [kɒf] **1** *n* toux *f*; **to have a c.** tousser; **c. drop** pastille *f* pour la toux; **c. mixture** sirop *m* pour la toux
2 *vi* tousser
▶**cough up 1** *vt sep (phlegm, blood)* cracher; *Fam (money)* allonger
2 *vi Fam (pay)* allonger
could [kʊd]

> La forme négative est **couldn't**. Dans les contextes où il est nécessaire d'utiliser une langue plus soignée, on écrit **could not**.

modal aux v (**a**) *(was able to)* **we couldn't do it** nous n'avons pas pu le faire; **he did what he c.** il a fait ce qu'il pouvait; **I c. hear them talking** je les entendais parler; **I c. have tried harder** j'aurais pu faire plus d'efforts; **he couldn't have been kinder** il a été on ne peut plus aimable; **how could you!** comment as-tu pu faire ça!; **I c. have hit him!** *(I was so angry)* je l'aurais battu!
(**b**) *(knew how to)* **I c. swim well at that age** à cet âge-là je savais déjà bien nager; **c. you speak French then?** tu parlais français à cette époque-là?
(**c**) *(indicating possibility)* **it c. be weeks before he's better** il pourrait se passer des semaines avant qu'il se rétablisse; **it c. have been worse** ça aurait pu être pire
(**d**) *(with requests)* **c. you get me some water?** est-ce que tu pourrais m'apporter de l'eau?
(**e**) *(in conditional, suggestions)* (it) **c. be** peut-être; **if I had more money I c. buy a new car** si j'avais plus d'argent je pourrais acheter une nouvelle voiture; **we c. always telephone** on pourrait toujours téléphoner

couldn't ['kʊdənt] = **could not**
couldn't-care-less ['kʊdəntkeə'les] *adj* **c. attitude** je-m'en-foutisme *m*
council ['kaʊnsəl] *n* (**a**) *(assembly)* conseil *m*; **C. of Europe** Conseil de l'Europe (**b**) *(local government)* municipalité *f*; **to be on the c.** être au conseil municipal; *Br* **c. house** ≃ habitation *f* à loyer modéré, H.L.M. *f*; **c. tax** = en Grande-Bretagne, impôt regroupant taxe d'habitation et impôts locaux
councillor ['kaʊnsɪlə(r)] *n* conseiller(ère) *m,f*, membre *m* du conseil
counsel ['kaʊnsəl] **1** *n* (**a**) *(advice)* conseil *m*, avis *m*; **to keep one's own c.** *(about plans)* garder ses projets pour soi; *(about opinions)* garder ses opinions pour soi (**b**) *Br (lawyer)* avocat(e) *m,f*; **c. for the defence** avocat *m* de la défense; **c. for the prosecution** procureur *m*; **King's/Queen's C.** = membre haut placé du barreau
2 *vt (pt & pp* **counselled,** *Am* **counseled)** *(caution, patience)* conseiller; **to c. sb** *(advise)* conseiller qn; *(give psychological help to)* apporter une aide psychologique à qn; **to c. sb to do sth** conseiller à qn de faire qch
counselling, *Am* **counseling** ['kaʊnsəlɪŋ] *n* assistance *f* psychosociale
counsellor ['kaʊnsələ(r)] *n* (**a**) *(adviser, therapist)* conseiller(ère) *m,f* (**b**) *Am Law* avocat(e) *m,f*
counselor *Am* = **counsellor** (**a**)
count¹ [kaʊnt] *n (nobleman)* comte *m*
count² **1** *n* (**a**) *(calculation)* compte *m*, comptage *m*; *(of ballot papers)* dépouillement *m*; **at the last c.** au dernier comptage; **to keep c. of sth** tenir le compte de qch; **to lose c.** se perdre dans ses calculs; *Fig* **c. of how many times I've asked you to...** je t'ai demandé je ne sais combien de fois de... (**b**) *(in boxing)* *& Fig* **to be out for the c.** être K.-O. (**c**) *Law* chef *m* d'accusation; *Fig* **on a number of counts** à plusieurs égards
2 *vt* (**a**) *(enumerate)* compter; **there were four of us counting/not counting the dog** nous étions quatre en comptant/sans compter le chien (**b**) *(consider)* considérer (**as** comme); **c. yourself lucky you weren't killed** estime-toi heureux de n'avoir pas été tué
3 *vi* (**a**) *(add up)* compter; **to c. (up) to ten** compter jusqu'à dix (**b**) *(be important, valid)* compter; **that doesn't c.** ça ne compte pas; **it counts as one of my worst experiences** ça a été une de mes pires expériences
▶**count against** *vt insep* jouer contre
▶**count down** *vi* faire le compte à rebours
▶**count in** *vt sep (include)* compter; **c. me in!** j'en suis!
▶**count on** *vt insep* compter sur; **to c. on sb to do sth** compter sur qn pour faire qch
▶**count out** *vt sep* (**a**) *(money)* compter (**b**) *(exclude)* **c. me out!** ne comptez pas sur moi! (**c**) *(in boxing)* **to be counted out** être (mis(e)) K.-O.
▶**count up** *vt sep* compter
countable ['kaʊntəbəl] *adj* comptable
countdown ['kaʊntdaʊn] *n* compte *m* à rebours
countenance ['kaʊntɪnəns] *Formal* **1** *n* (**a**) *(face)* visage *m* (**b**) *(support)* **to give c. to** *(rumours)* accréditer; *(plans)* approuver
2 *vt (support)* approuver
counter¹ ['kaʊntə(r)] *n* (**a**) *(in shop)* comptoir *m*; *(in supermarket)* rayon *m*; *(in bank)* guichet *m*; **available over the c.** *(medicine)* en vente libre; **to buy/sell**

sth under the c. acheter/vendre qch au noir (**b**) *(token in game)* jeton *m* (**c**) *(counting device)* compteur *m*

counter² **1** *adv* **c. to** contrairement à; **to run c. to** aller à l'encontre de **2** *vt* contrer; **to c. that...** riposter que... **3** *vi* riposter

counteract [kaʊntər'ækt] *vt (influence)* contrecarrer; *(rumours, effects)* neutraliser

counterattack ['kaʊntərətæk] **1** *n* contre-attaque *f* **2** *vt & vi* contre-attaquer

counter-clockwise *Am* = **anti-clockwise**

counterfeit ['kaʊntəfɪt] **1** *n* faux *m* **2** *adj* faux (fausse) **3** *vt* contrefaire

counterfoil ['kaʊntəfɔɪl] *n* talon *m*, souche *f*

counterintelligence ['kaʊntərɪn'telɪdʒəns] *n* contre-espionnage *m*

countermand ['kaʊntəmɑ:nd] *vt* annuler

countermeasure ['kaʊntəmeʒə(r)] *n* contre-mesure *f*

counteroffensive ['kaʊntərə'fensɪv] *n* contre-offensive *f*

counterpane ['kaʊntəpeɪn] *n* couvre-lit *m*

counterpart ['kaʊntəpɑ:t] *n (person)* homologue *mf*; *(system)* équivalent *m*

counterpoint ['kaʊntəpɔɪnt] *n Mus* contrepoint *m*

counterproductive ['kaʊntəprə'dʌktɪv] *adj* contre-productif(ive)

counterproposal ['kaʊntəprə'pəʊzəl] *n* contre-proposition *f*

counter-revolution ['kaʊntərevə'lu:ʃən] *n* contre-révolution *f*

counter-revolutionary ['kaʊntərevə'lu:ʃənərɪ] **1** *n* (*pl* **counter-revolutionaries**) contre-révolutionnaire *mf* **2** *adj* contre-révolutionnaire

countersign ['kaʊntəsaɪn] *vt* contresigner, viser

counterweight ['kaʊntəweɪt] *n* contrepoids *m*

countess ['kaʊntɪs] *n* comtesse *f*

countless ['kaʊntlɪs] *adj* innombrable; **on c. occasions** à maintes occasions; **c. times** un nombre incalculable de fois

country ['kʌntrɪ] (*pl* **countries**) *n* (**a**) *(land, nation)* pays *m*; *(homeland)* patrie *f* (**b**) *(as opposed to town)* campagne *f*; **in the c.** à la campagne; **c. (music), c. and western (music)** country *m* ou *f*; **c. club** = club sportif ou de loisirs situé à la campagne; **c. house** = grande maison de campagne, souvent historique

countryside ['kʌntrɪsaɪd] *n* campagne *f*

county ['kaʊntɪ] (*pl* **counties**) *n* comté *m*; **c. council** ≃ conseil *m* général; **c. town** chef-lieu *m* de comté

coup [ku:] *n (surprising achievement)* (beau) coup *m*; *Pol* **c. (d'état)** coup *m* d'État

couple ['kʌpəl] **1** *n* (**a**) *(of things)* **a c. of** *(two)* deux; *(a few)* quelques (**b**) *(people)* couple *m*; **the happy c.** les heureux époux *mpl*; **c. therapy** thérapie *f* de couple **2** *vt* (**a**) *(associate)* associer (**with** à) (**b**) *(combine)* allier (**with** à) **3** *vi* s'accoupler

couplet ['kʌplɪt] *n* distique *m*

coupon ['ku:pɒn] *n (form)* coupon *m*; **(money-off) c.** *(for discount)* bon *m* de réduction

courage ['kʌrɪdʒ] *n* courage *m*; **to have the c. to do sth** avoir le courage de faire qch; **to have the c. of one's convictions** avoir le courage de ses opinions

courageous [kə'reɪdʒəs] *adj* courageux(euse)

courageously [kə'reɪdʒəslɪ] *adv* courageusement, avec courage

courgette [kʊə'ʒət] *n Br* courgette *f*

courier ['kʊrɪə(r)] *n (messenger)* messager *m*, coursier *m*; *(in tourism)* guide *mf*; *(drug smuggler)* passeur(euse) *m,f*

course [kɔ:s] **1** *n* (**a**) *(of river, time, events)* cours *m*; **to be on c.** *Naut* suivre le cap; *Fig* être en bonne voie; *Naut* **to be off c.** dévier de son cap; **in the c. of time** *(gradually)* à la longue; *(eventually)* finalement; **in the c. of the evening** au cours de la soirée; **c. of action** ligne *f* de conduite; **to be in the c. of doing sth** être en train de faire qch; **in the normal c. of events** en temps normal; **to let things take** *or* **run their c.** laisser les choses suivre leur cours normal (**b**) **of c.** naturellement, bien sûr; **of c. not** bien sûr que non (**c**) *(at college, university)* cours *m* (**in** de); **c. of lectures** série *f* de conférences (**d**) *Med* **c. of treatment** traitement *m* (**e**) *(of meal)* plat *m* (**f**) *(for race)* parcours *m*; *(for horseracing)* champ *m* de courses; *(for golf)* terrain *m* **2** *vi (of liquid)* couler

court [kɔ:t] **1** *n* (**a**) *Law* cour *f*, tribunal *m*; **to go to c.** aller en justice; **to take sb to c.** faire un procès à qn; **to settle a case out of c.** arranger une affaire à l'amiable; **c. of appeal** cour *f* d'appel; **c. of inquiry** commission *f* d'enquête; **c. of law** cour *f*, tribunal *m*; **c. appearance** comparution *f* en justice; *Mil* **c. martial** cour *f* martiale (**b**) *(for tennis, squash)* court *m* (**c**) *(royal)* cour *f*; *Fig* **to hold c.** tenir des discours à un entourage admiratif; **c. shoe** escarpin *m* **2** *vt* (**a**) *Old-fashioned (woo)* courtiser (**b**) *(seek) (friendship, favour)* rechercher; *(death)* braver; *(disaster, danger)* aller au-devant de **3** *vi Old-fashioned* **to be courting** *(of couple)* se fréquenter

courteous ['kɜ:tɪəs] *adj* courtois(e), poli(e)

courtesy ['kɜ:təsɪ] (*pl* **courtesies**) *n* courtoisie *f*, politesse *f*; **by c. of...** avec l'aimable autorisation de...; **to exchange courtesies** se faire des politesses; **c. call** visite *f* de politesse; **c. car** = voiture mise à la disposition d'un client par un hôtel ou un garage

courthouse ['kɔ:thaʊs] *n Am* palais *m* de justice, tribunal *m*

courtier ['kɔ:tɪə(r)] *n (man)* courtisan *m*; *(woman)* dame *f* de la cour

court-martial ['kɔ:t'mɑ:ʃəl] (*pt & pp* **court-martialled**, *Am* **court-martialed**) *vt* faire passer en cour martiale; **to be court-martialled** passer en cour martiale

courtroom ['kɔ:tru:m] *n Law* salle *f* d'audience

courtship ['kɔ:tʃɪp] *n (of people)* cour *f*; *(of animals)* période *f* nuptiale; **c. display** parade *f* nuptiale

courtyard ['kɔ:tjɑ:d] *n* cour *f*

cousin ['kʌzən] *n* cousin(e) *m,f*

cove [kəʊv] *n* crique *f*

covenant ['kʌvənənt] *Law* **1** *n* convention *f*, contrat *m* **2** *vt* promettre par contrat

Coventry ['kʌvəntrɪ, 'kɒvəntrɪ] *n Fig* **to send sb to C.** mettre qn en quarantaine

cover ['kʌvə(r)] **1** *n* (**a**) *(lid)* couvercle *m* (**b**) *(for cushion, typewriter, chair)* housse *f* (**c**) *(bedspread)* couvre-lit *m*; **covers** *(blankets)* couvertures *fpl* (**d**) *(of book, magazine)* couverture *f*; **from c. to c. de** la première à la dernière page; **c. price** prix *m* de vente (**e**) *(shelter)* **to take c.** s'abriter; **to break c.** sortir à découvert; *Fig* se manifester publiquement; **under c. of darkness** à la faveur de la nuit (**f**) *Fin (in insurance)* couverture *f* (**g**) *(song)* **c. (version)** reprise *f* (**h**) *Am* c. letter *(for job application)* lettre *f* de motivation; *(sent with other documents)* lettre *f* d'accompagnement **2** *vt* (**a**) *(person, object)* couvrir (**with/in** de); **to c. one's eyes** se couvrir les yeux; **to c. a wall with paint** recouvrir un mur de peinture; **to c. oneself with glory** se couvrir de gloire; **to c. one's costs** couvrir ses frais; **to c. a song** *(of musician)* reprendre une chanson (**b**) *(hide) (embarrassment, confusion)* dissimuler; **to c. one's tracks** brouiller les pistes (**c**) *(travel over)* parcourir; **we covered 100 km in one day** nous avons fait *ou* parcouru 100 km en un jour; *Fig* **to c. a lot of ground** traiter de nombreux problèmes (**d**) *(of book, lecture)* traiter de; **to c. a story** *(of journalist)* couvrir un sujet (**e**) *Fin (with insurance)* couvrir (**for** *or* **against** contre); *Fig* **to c. oneself** *(take precautions)* se couvrir

▸**cover for** *vt insep (replace)* remplacer; *(provide excuses for)* couvrir

▸**cover up 1** *vt sep* (**a**) *(corruption, mistakes)* dissimuler; *(scandal)* étouffer (**b**) *(put cover on)* recouvrir **2** *vi (conceal the truth)* cacher la vérité (**for sb** pour protéger qn)

coverage ['kʌvərɪdʒ] *n (on TV, in newspapers)* couverture *f* médiatique

covering ['kʌvərɪŋ] *n (on furniture)* housse *f*; *(of snow, dust)* couche *f*; *(of chocolate)* nappage *m*; *Br* **c. letter** *(for job application)* lettre *f* de motivation; *(sent with other documents)* lettre *f* d'accompagnement

coverlet ['kʌvəlɪt] *n* dessus-de-lit *m inv*

covert ['kʌvət] *adj (operation)* secret(ète), clandestin(e); *(look)* furtif(ive)

cover-up ['kʌvərʌp] *n* there was a c. l'affaire a été étouffée

covet ['kʌvɪt] *vt Formal* convoiter

covetous ['kʌvɪtəs] *adj Formal* envieux(euse); **to be c. of sth** convoiter qch

cow¹ [kaʊ] *n* (**a**) *(animal)* vache *f*; *(female elephant, whale)* femelle *f*; **till the cows come home** *(wait)* jusqu'à la saint-glinglin; *(argue, talk)* à n'en plus finir (**b**) *Br very Fam Pej (woman)* peau *f* de vache

cow² *vt* intimider; **to look cowed** avoir un air de chien battu

coward ['kaʊəd] *n* lâche *mf*, poltron(onne) *m,f*

cowardice ['kaʊədɪs], **cowardliness** ['kaʊədlɪnəs] *n* lâcheté *f*, poltronnerie *f*

cowardly ['kaʊədlɪ] *adj* lâche

cowboy ['kaʊbɔɪ] *n* (**a**) *(cattle handler, in westerns)* cow-boy *m*; **c. boots** santiags *fpl*; **c. hat** chapeau *m* de cow-boy (**b**) *Br Fam Pej (workman)* filou *m*

cower ['kaʊə(r)] *vi* se tapir; **to c. before sb** trembler devant qn

cowhide ['kaʊhaɪd] *n* peau *f* de vache

cowl [kaʊl] *n (on monk's habit, on chimney)* capuchon *m*; **c. neck** col *m* boule

coworker ['kəʊwɜːkə(r)] *n Am* collègue *mf*

cowshed ['kaʊʃed] *n* étable *f*

cox [kɒks] **1** *n (in rowing)* barreur(euse) *m,f* **2** *vt & vi* barrer

coy [kɔɪ] *adj (shy)* timide; *Pej (affectedly shy)* (faussement) timide (**about** à propos de)

coyote [kɔɪˈəʊtɪ] *n* coyote *m*

cozy *Am* = cosy

CPA [siːpiːˈeɪ] *n Am (abbr* **certified public accountant**) ≃ expert-comptable *m*

CPD [siːpiːˈdiː] *n (abbr* **continuing professional development**) formation *f* permanente *ou* continue

CPU [siːpiːˈjuː] *n Comput (abbr* **central processing unit**) unité *f* centrale

crab [kræb] *n* (**a**) *(crustacean)* crabe *m* (**b**) **c. apple** pomme *f* sauvage (**c**) *very Fam* **crabs** *(pubic lice)* morpions *mpl*

crabbed ['kræbɪd] *adj (writing)* en pattes de mouche

crabby ['kræbɪ] *adj Fam* maussade, grincheux(euse)

crack [kræk] **1** *n* (**a**) *(in glass, porcelain)* fêlure *f*; *(in wood)* fente *f*; *(in wall)* lézarde *f*; *(in ice, rock)* fissure *f*; **at the c. of dawn** à la pointe du jour (**b**) *(sound) (of branches, ice)* craquement *m*; *(of whip)* claquement *m*; *(of gunfire)* détonation *f*; *Fig* **to give sb a fair c. of the whip** donner toutes ses chances à qn; *Fig* **to have a c. at sth** tenter sa chance à qch (**c**) *(blow)* coup *m* (**on** sur) (**d**) *Fam (joke, insult)* plaisanterie *f* (**e**) *(drug)* crack *m*
2 *adj Fam (team, regiment)* d'élite; **c. shot** fin tireur *m*
3 *vt* (**a**) *(glass, porcelain)* fêler; *(wood)* fendre; *(wall)* lézarder; *(ice, rock)* fissurer (**b**) *(make sound with) (whip)* faire claquer; *(fingers)* faire craquer (**c**) *Fam (hit)* **to c. sb over the head** assommer qn; **she cracked her head against the wall** elle s'est cogné la tête contre le mur (**d**) *(solve) (problem)* résoudre; *(code)* décrypter (**e**) *(break into) (safe)* percer; *(nut)* casser (**f**) *Fam (joke)* raconter
4 *vi* (**a**) *(of glass, porcelain)* se fêler; *(of wood)* se fendre; *(of wall)* se lézarder; *(of ice, rock)* se fissurer; *(of paint)* se craqueler (**b**) *(of voice)* se casser (**c**) *(of person under pressure)* craquer (**d**) *(make sound) (of branches, ice)* craquer; *(of whip)* claquer; *(of gunfire)* retentir; *Fam Fig* **to get cracking** se grouiller

▸**crack down** *vi* **to c. down (on)** prendre des mesures énergiques (contre)

▸**crack up** *Fam* **1** *vt sep* **it's not all it's cracked up to be** ce n'est pas aussi bien qu'on le dit **2** *vi (go mad)* craquer

crackbrained ['krækbreɪnd] *adj Fam* dingue

crackdown ['krækdaʊn] *n* mesures *fpl* énergiques (**on** en matière de)

cracked [krækt] *adj Fam (mad)* dingue, cinglé(e)

cracker ['krækə(r)] *n* (**a**) *(biscuit)* biscuit *m* salé, cracker *m* (**b**) *(firework)* pétard *m*; *(at Christmas)* diablotin *m* (**c**) *Br Fam (excellent thing, person)* pure merveille *f*; **she's a c.** *(very attractive)* elle est canon

crackers ['krækəz] *adj Br Fam* dingue, cinglé(e)

crackle ['krækəl] **1** *n (of twigs)* craquement *m*; *(of shots, fire)* crépitement *m*; *(of frying)* grésillement *m*; *(of radio)* crachotement *m* **2** *vi (of twigs)* craquer; *(of shots, fire)* crépiter; *(of frying)* grésiller; *(of radio)* crachoter

crackling ['kræklɪŋ] *n* (**a**) *(of fire)* crépitement *m*; *(on radio)* crachotement *m* (**b**) *(pork skin)* couenne *f* grillée

crackpot ['krækpɒt] *Fam* **1** *n (person)* fêlé(e) *m,f*, cinglé(e) *m,f* **2** *adj (plan)* dingue

cradle ['kreɪdəl] **1** *n* (**a**) *(of child, civilization)* berceau *m*; **from the c. to the grave** du berceau à la tombe (**b**) *(for cleaning windows)* nacelle *f* **2** *vt (baby)* bercer *(dans ses bras)*; *(object)* tenir délicatement

craft¹ [krɑːft] **1** n (**a**) (skill) habileté f; (professional) métier m (**b**) (cunning) ruse f
2 vt (produce) travailler; **beautifully crafted** magnifiquement travaillé(e)
craft² (pl **craft**) n (boat) (petite) embarcation f
craftsman [ˈkrɑːftsmən] n artisan m; **this is the work of a real c.** c'est l'œuvre d'un spécialiste
craftsmanship [ˈkrɑːftsmənʃɪp] n habileté f (manuelle); **a wonderful piece of c.** un pur chef-d'œuvre; **the c. is magnificent** c'est vraiment du beau travail
crafty [ˈkrɑːftɪ] adj malin(igne)
crag [kræg] n rocher m à pic
craggy [ˈkrægɪ] adj (rocky) rocheux(euse); (features) anguleux(euse)
cram [kræm] (pt & pp **crammed**) **1** vt fourrer, entasser (into dans); **to c. food into one's mouth** se gaver, s'empiffrer; **to be crammed (with)** être bourré(e) (de)
2 vi (**a**) (crowd) s'entasser (into dans) (**b**) Fam (study) bûcher
cramp [kræmp] **1** n crampe f
2 vt (restrict) gêner; Fam **to c. sb's style** priver qn de ses moyens
cramped [kræmpt] adj (surroundings) exigu(ë); **to be c. for space** être à l'étroit
cranberry [ˈkrænbərɪ] (pl **cranberries**) n canneberge f; **c. sauce** sauce f à la canneberge
crane [kreɪn] **1** n (lifting device, bird) grue f; **c. fly** (insect) tipule f
2 vt **to c. one's neck** tendre le cou
3 vi **to c. forward** tendre le cou
cranium [ˈkreɪnɪəm] (pl **crania** [ˈkreɪnɪə]) n Anat boîte f crânienne
crank¹ [kræŋk] n (gear mechanism) manivelle f
crank² n Fam (**a**) Br (eccentric) excentrique mf; **a religious c.** un fanatique religieux (**b**) Am & Ir (bad-tempered person) grognon(onne) m,f
crankshaft [ˈkræŋkʃɑːft] n Aut vilebrequin m
cranky [ˈkræŋkɪ] adj Fam (**a**) Br (eccentric) excentrique (**b**) Am & Ir (bad-tempered) grognon(onne)
crap [kræp] **1** n (**a**) Vulg (excrement) merde f; **to have or take a c.** chier (**b**) very Fam (junk) saloperies fpl; (nonsense) conneries fpl; (disgusting substance) saloperie f; **don't talk c.!** ne dis pas de conneries!
2 adj very Fam (bad) nul (nulle)
crash [kræʃ] **1** n (**a**) (noise) fracas m (**b**) (accident) (in car) accident m; (in train, plane) catastrophe f; **c. barrier** glissière f de sécurité; **c. helmet** casque m; **c. landing** atterrissage m en catastrophe (**c**) (financial) krach m
2 adj **c. course** cours m intensif; **c. diet** régime m amaigrissant intensif
3 vt (**a**) **to c. one's car** avoir un accident de voiture (**b**) Fam **to c. a party** = aller à une fête sans y être invité
4 vi (**a**) (make noise) s'écraser avec fracas; **to c. to the ground** s'écrouler avec fracas; **he was crashing around in the kitchen** il s'agitait bruyamment dans la cuisine (**b**) (of cars) se percuter; **to c. into** rentrer dans (**c**) (of business) faire faillite; (of economy) s'effondrer (**d**) Comput tomber en panne (**e**) Fam (spend night) pieuter; (fall sleep) s'écrouler; **can I c. at your place?** je peux pieuter chez toi?
▸**crash out** vi Fam (go to sleep) s'écrouler; **he was crashed out on the sofa** il roupillait sur le divan
crashing [ˈkræʃɪŋ] adj **a c. bore** (person) une personne assommante; (task) une besogne assommante
crash-land [ˈkræʃlænd] vi atterrir en catastrophe

crass [kræs] adj grossier(ère); **c. ignorance** ignorance f crasse; **c. stupidity** immense bêtise f
crate [kreɪt] n (box) caisse f; (for fruit) cageot m; (for bottles) casier m
crater [ˈkreɪtə(r)] n cratère m
cravat [krəˈvæt] n foulard m
crave [kreɪv] **1** vt (cigarette) avoir très envie de; (affection) être en manque de; (opportunity) attendre avec impatience
2 vi **to be craving for sth** (cigarette) avoir très envie de qch; (affection) être en manque de qch; (opportunity) attendre qch avec impatience
craving [ˈkreɪvɪŋ] n envie f irrésistible; **to have a c. for sth** (cigarette) avoir très envie de qch; (affection) être en manque de qch
crawl [krɔːl] **1** n (**a**) (slow pace) **to move at a c.** (of car, driver) rouler au pas; (of person) piétiner sur place (**b**) (swimming stroke) crawl m
2 vi (**a**) (of person) ramper; (of baby) marcher à quatre pattes; (of car) rouler au pas (**b**) Fam (be infested) **to be crawling with** grouiller de; **to make sb's skin c.** flanquer des boutons à qn (**c**) Fam (be obsequious) faire le lèche-bottes; **to c. to sb** lécher les bottes à qn
crawler [ˈkrɔːlə(r)] n Fam (obsequious person) lèchebottes mf inv
crayfish [ˈkreɪfɪʃ] n écrevisse f
crayon [ˈkreɪɒn] n (wax) crayon m gras; (pencil) crayon m de couleur
craze [kreɪz] n engouement m (for pour)
crazed [kreɪzd] adj (look, person) fou (folle)
crazy [ˈkreɪzɪ] adj fou (folle); **to go c.** devenir fou (folle); **to drive sb c.** rendre qn fou (folle); Fam **to be c. about sb/sth** être fou (folle) de qn/qch; Fam **like c.** (run, work) comme un fou (une folle); **c. golf** minigolf m; **c. paving** dallage m irrégulier en pierres plates
creak [kriːk] **1** n (of hinge) grincement m; (of floor, shoes) craquement m
2 vi (of hinge) grincer; (of floor, shoes) craquer
creaky [ˈkriːkɪ] adj (hinge) grinçant(e); (floor) qui craque; Fig (plot, dialogue) boiteux(euse)
cream [kriːm] **1** n (**a**) (of milk) crème f; **c. of tomato/ chicken soup** crème f de tomates/volaille; **c. cake** gâteau m à la crème; **c. cheese** fromage m frais à tartiner (**b**) Fig **the c.** (best part) la crème (de la crème) (**c**) (lotion) crème f (**d**) (colour) crème m
2 adj **c.(-coloured)** (de couleur) crème inv
3 vt Culin (butter) battre en crème
▸**cream off** vt sep Fig (money, profits) écrémer; **the universities c. off the best students** les universités sélectionnent les meilleurs étudiants
creamy [ˈkriːmɪ] adj (taste, consistency) crémeux(euse); (skin) laiteux(euse)
crease [kriːs] **1** n (in skin, fabric) pli m
2 vt (fabric) froisser; **to c. one's brow** plisser le front
3 vi (of fabric) se froisser; (of face, brow) se plisser
▸**crease up** vi Fam (laugh) se tordre (de rire)
create [kriːˈeɪt] **1** vt créer; **to c. a sensation/a good impression** faire sensation/bonne impression
2 vi Fam (get angry) faire une scène
creation [kriːˈeɪʃən] n création f
creative [kriːˈeɪtɪv] adj (person, activity) créatif(ive); (process, imagination) créateur(trice); Fin **c. accounting** manipulations fpl comptables; **c. writing** techniques fpl de l'écriture
creator [kriːˈeɪtə(r)] n créateur(trice) m,f; Rel **the C.** le Créateur

creature ['kri:tʃə(r)] *n (person)* créature *f*, être *m*; *(animal)* bête *f*; **to be a c.** of habit avoir ses petites habitudes; **c. comforts** confort *m* matériel; **to like one's c. comforts** aimer son confort

crèche [kreʃ] *n (nursery)* crèche *f*; *(in shopping centre)* halte-garderie *f*

credence ['kri:dəns] *n* **to give c. to sth** ajouter foi à qch

credentials [krɪ'denʃəlz] *npl* (**a**) *(proof of identity)* pièces *fpl* justificatives d'identité; *(of ambassador)* lettres *fpl* de créance (**b**) *(proof of ability)* références *fpl*; *Fig* **to establish one's c.** faire ses preuves

credibility [kredɪ'bɪlɪtɪ] *n* crédibilité *f*; **c. gap** manque *m* de crédibilité

credible ['kredɪbəl] *adj* crédible; **it is hardly c. that...** il est difficile de croire que...

credit ['kredɪt] **1** *n* (**a**) *(financial)* crédit *m*; **to be in c.** *(of person)* avoir un compte créditeur; *(of account)* être créditeur(trice); **to give sb c.** faire crédit à qn; **to buy/sell sth on c.** acheter/vendre qch à crédit; **c. card** carte *f* de crédit; *Econ* **c. control** encadrement *m* du crédit; **c. limit** plafond *m* de crédit; **c. note** avoir *m*; *Fin* **c. rating** degré *m* de solvabilité; *Econ* **c. squeeze** restrictions *fpl* de crédit; **c. transfer** transfert *m*, virement *m* (**b**) *(belief)* **to give c. to sth** ajouter foi à qch; **to gain c.** *(of theory)* être accepté(e) (**c**) *(recognition)* mérite *m*; **you have to give him c. for his honesty** tu es bien forcé de reconnaître qu'il est honnête; **to take the c. for sth** s'attribuer le mérite de qch; **to do sb c.** faire honneur à qn; **it does you c.** c'est tout à ton honneur; **c. where c.'s due** il faut rendre à César ce qui est à César; **to her c.** she refused elle a refusé, ce qui est tout à son honneur; **she is a c. to the school** elle fait honneur à l'école (**d**) **credits** *(of film)* générique *m*

2 *vt* (**a**) *(money)* virer (**to an account** sur un compte) (**b**) *(attribute)* **to c. sb with sth** attribuer qch à qn (**c**) *(believe)* croire; **would you c. it?** tu te rends compte?

creditable ['kredɪtəbəl] *adj (praiseworthy)* honorable; *(efforts, attempt)* louable

creditor ['kredɪtə(r)] *n Fin* créditeur(trice) *m,f*

credulity [krɪ'dju:lɪtɪ] *n* crédulité *f*

credulous ['kredjʊləs] *adj* crédule

creed [kri:d] *n also Fig* principes *mpl*; **political c.** credo *m* politique

creek [kri:k] *n (small bay)* crique *f*; *(stream)* ruisseau *m*; *Fam Fig* **to be up the c. (without a paddle)** être dans le pétrin

creep [kri:p] **1** *n Fam* (**a**) *(unpleasant man)* type *m* répugnant; *(obsequious person)* lèche-bottes *mf inv* (**b**) **to give sb the creeps** faire froid dans le dos à qn

2 *vi (pt & pp crept* [krept]*) (of animal, person)* ramper; *(of plants)* ramper; *(vertically)* grimper; **to c. in/out** entrer/sortir à pas de loup; **to c. into bed** se glisser sous les draps; **old age has crept up on me** je me fais vieux; *Fam* **it makes my flesh c.** ça me flanque des boutons

creeper ['kri:pə(r)] *n (plant)* plante *f* rampante; *(climbing)* plante *f* grimpante

creeping ['kri:pɪŋ] *adj (gradual)* progressif(ive)

creepy ['kri:pɪ] *adj Fam* sinistre

creepy-crawly ['kri:pɪ'krɔ:lɪ] *(pl creepy-crawlies) n Fam* bestiole *f*, insecte *m*

cremate [krɪ'meɪt] *vt* incinérer

cremation [krɪ'meɪʃən] *n* incinération *f*

crematorium [kremə'tɔ:rɪəm] *(pl crematoria* [kremə-'tɔ:rɪə]*) n* crématorium *m*

creole ['kri:əʊl] **1** *n* (**a**) *(person)* Créole *mf* (**b**) *(language)* créole *m*

2 *adj* créole

creosote ['krɪəsəʊt] *n* créosote *f*

crêpe [kreɪp, krep] *n* (**a**) *(textile)* crêpe *m*; **c. bandage** bande *f* Velpeau®; **c. paper** papier *m* crépon; **c.(-rubber) soles** semelles *fpl* de crêpe (**b**) *(pancake)* crêpe *f*

crept [krept] *pt & pp of* **creep**

crescendo [krɪ'ʃendəʊ] *(pl crescendos) n Mus & Fig* crescendo *m inv*; **to rise to a c.** *(of music, complaints)* aller crescendo

crescent ['kresənt] **1** *n (shape)* croissant *m*; *(street)* rue *f* en croissant

2 *adj* **c.(-shaped)** en forme de croissant *ou* de demi-lune; **c. moon** croissant *m* de lune

cress [kres] *n* cresson *m*

crest [krest] *n (of bird, wave, helmet)* crête *f*; *(of hill)* sommet *m*; *(coat of arms)* armoiries *fpl*; *Fig* **to be on the c. of a wave** être dans une période faste

crestfallen ['krestfɔ:lən] *adj* abattu(e), découragé(e)

Cretan ['kri:tən] **1** *n* Crétois(e) *m,f*

2 *adj* crétois(e)

Crete [kri:t] *n* la Crète

cretin ['kretɪn] *n Fam* crétin(e) *m,f*

crevice ['krevɪs] *n (in rock)* crevasse *f*, fissure *f*; *(in wall)* lézarde *f*

crew [kru:] **1** *n (of ship, plane)* équipage *m*; *(of ambulance)* équipe *f*; *Fam (gang, group)* bande *f*; **c. cut** *(hairstyle)* brosse *f*, cheveux *mpl* (coupés) en brosse; **c. neck** col *m* ras le cou

2 *vt (ship)* **the ship was crewed by...** le bateau avait un équipage de...

crib [krɪb] **1** *n* (**a**) *esp Am (cradle)* berceau *m*; *(Nativity scene)* crèche *f*; *Am* **c. death** mort *f* subite du nourrisson (**b**) *Fam* **c. (sheet)** *(in exam)* antisèche *f*

2 *vt (pt & pp cribbed) Fam (copy)* pomper

crick [krɪk] **1** *n* **to have a c. in one's neck** avoir un torticolis

2 *vt* **to c. one's neck** attraper un torticolis

cricket¹ ['krɪkɪt] *n (insect)* grillon *m*

cricket² *n (sport)* cricket *m*; *Fig* **that's not c.!** ce n'est pas du jeu!; **c. ball** balle *f* de cricket; **c. bat** batte *f* de cricket; **c. pitch** terrain *m* de cricket

crikey ['kraɪkɪ] *exclam Fam* mince alors!

crime [kraɪm] *n (act)* crime *m*; *Law* délit *m*; *(phenomenon)* criminalité *f*; **c. is on the increase** la criminalité augmente; *Fig* **it's a c. to waste money like that** c'est un crime de gaspiller l'argent de cette façon; **c. wave** vague *f* de criminalité; **c. writer** auteur *m* de romans policiers

Crimea [kraɪ'mɪə] *n* la Crimée

Crimean [kraɪ'mɪən] *adj* de Crimée; **the C. War** la guerre de Crimée

criminal ['krɪmɪnəl] **1** *n* criminel(elle) *m,f*

2 *adj* criminel(elle); *Fig* **it's c. to knock down that building** c'est un crime de démolir ce bâtiment; **to go to c. court** être jugé(e) au pénal; **c. law** droit *m* pénal; **c. lawyer** avocat *m* au pénal; **c. offence** délit *m*; *(more serious)* crime *m*; **c. record** casier *m* judiciaire

criminalize ['krɪmɪnəlaɪz] *vt* criminaliser

criminology [krɪmɪ'nɒlədʒɪ] *n* criminologie *f*

crimp [krɪmp] *vt (hair)* friser; *(pastry)* pincer

crimson ['krɪmzən] **1** *n* pourpre *m*

2 *adj* pourpre; **to go c. with rage** devenir rouge de colère

cringe [krɪndʒ] *vi* (**a**) *(show fear)* avoir un mouvement de recul (**b**) *(be embarrassed)* avoir envie de rentrer sous terre; **it makes me c.** ça me donne envie de rentrer sous terre

cringing [ˈkrɪndʒɪŋ] *adj (afraid)* craintif(ive); *(servile)* servile

crinkle [ˈkrɪŋkəl] **1** *n (in paper, fabric)* pli *m*
  2 *vt (paper, fabric)* froisser; **to c. one's nose** froncer le nez
  3 *vi (of brow, nose)* se froncer; *(of face)* se rider

crinkly [ˈkrɪŋklɪ] *adj (skin)* ridé(e); *(paper, fabric)* froissé(e)

cripple [ˈkrɪpəl] **1** *n* estropié(e) *m,f*
  2 *vt* estropier; *Fig (industry, system)* paralyser

crippling [ˈkrɪplɪŋ] *adj* (**a**) *(illness)* invalidant(e) (**b**) *(effect, strike)* paralysant(e); *(taxes)* écrasant(e)

crisis [ˈkraɪsɪs] *(pl* **crises** [ˈkraɪsiːz]*) n* crise *f*; **to be in c.** être en (pleine) crise; **c. management** habileté *f* à gérer les situations de crise; **c. point** point *m* critique

crisp [krɪsp] **1** *n Br* **(potato) crisps** (pommes *fpl*) chips *fpl, Can* croustilles *fpl*; **a c.** une chips, *Can* une croustille
  2 *adj (apple, lettuce)* croquant(e); *(pastry)* croustillant(e); *(bank note)* neuf (neuve); *(sheets)* frais (fraîche); *(snow)* qui crisse sous les pas; *(air, breeze)* vif (vive); *(style)* vif (vive) et précis(e); *(tone)* brusque, tranchant(e)

crispbread [ˈkrɪspbred] *n* pain *m* suédois

crisply [ˈkrɪsplɪ] *adv (say)* d'un ton brusque *ou* tranchant; *(write)* dans un style vif et précis

crispy [ˈkrɪspɪ] *adj* croustillant(e)

criss-cross [ˈkrɪskrɒs] **1** *vt* entrecroiser
  2 *vi* s'entrecroiser

criterion [kraɪˈtɪərɪən] *(pl* **criteria** [kraɪˈtɪərɪə]*) n* critère *m*

critic [ˈkrɪtɪk] *n (reviewer)* critique *mf*; *(opponent)* détracteur(trice) *m,f*

critical [ˈkrɪtɪkəl] *adj* (**a**) *(judgemental)* critique (**of** à l'égard de); **to be c. of sb/sth** critiquer qn/qch (**b**) *(essay, study)* critique; **to be a c. success** être acclamé(e) par la critique (**c**) *(decisive)* critique; **the next few days will be c.** les prochains jours seront décisifs; **in a c. condition** *(of patient)* dans un état critique

criticism [ˈkrɪtɪsɪzəm] *n* critique *f*

criticize [ˈkrɪtɪsaɪz] **1** *vt* critiquer; **to c. sb for sth** reprocher qch à qn; **to c. sb for doing sth** reprocher à qn de faire/d'avoir fait qch
  2 *vi* critiquer

critique [krɪˈtiːk] *n* critique *f*

croak [krəʊk] **1** *n (of frog)* coassement *m*; *(of raven)* croassement *m*
  2 *vi* (**a**) *(of frog)* coasser; *(of raven)* croasser; *(of person)* parler d'une voix rauque (**b**) *Fam (die)* claquer

Croat [ˈkrəʊæt] **1** *n (person)* Croate *mf*
  2 *adj* croate

Croatia [krəʊˈeɪʃə] *n* la Croatie

Croatian [krəʊˈeɪʃən] = **Croat**

crochet [ˈkrəʊʃeɪ] **1** *n* (travail *m* au) crochet *m*; **c. hook** crochet *m*
  2 *vt (shawl, blanket)* faire au crochet
  3 *vi* faire du crochet

crock [krɒk] *n* (**a**) *(pot)* pot *m* de terre (**b**) *Fam* **old c.** *(person)* croulant(e) *m,f*

crockery [ˈkrɒkərɪ] *n* vaisselle *f*

crocodile [ˈkrɒkədaɪl] *n* (**a**) *(animal)* crocodile *m*; **c. tears** larmes *fpl* de crocodile (**b**) *(line of people)* **to walk in a c.** marcher en rangs par deux

crocus [ˈkrəʊkəs] *n* crocus *m*

croft [krɒft] *n* petite ferme *f*

crone [krəʊn] *n Pej* old **c.** vieille bique *f*

crony [ˈkrəʊnɪ] *(pl* **cronies**) *n* copain (copine) *m,f*

crook [krʊk] **1** *n* (**a**) *(criminal)* escroc *m* (**b**) *(of shepherd)* houlette *f*; *(of bishop)* crosse *f* (**c**) *(curve)* coude *m*; **in the c. of one's arm** au creux du bras
  2 *vt (finger, arm)* plier

crooked [ˈkrʊkɪd] *adj* (**a**) *(not straight)* de travers; *(nose)* tordu(e); **a c. smile** un sourire en coin (**b**) *(dishonest, illegal)* malhonnête

croon [kruːn] *vt & vi* chantonner, fredonner

crop [krɒp] **1** *n* (**a**) *(of fruit, vegetables)* récolte *f*; *(of cereals)* moisson *f*; *Fig* **this year's c.** of films la production cinématographique de cette année (**b**) *(handle of whip)* **(riding) c.** cravache *f* (**c**) *(short haircut)* coupe *f* très courte (**d**) **c. top** top *m* court
  2 *vt (pt & pp* **cropped**) (**a**) *(cut)* couper; *(hair)* couper ras; **cropped hair** cheveux *mpl* coupés ras (**b**) *(of cattle)* brouter

▸**crop up** *vi (of issue, question)* surgir; *(of problem, opportunity)* se présenter; *(of name)* être mentionné(e)

cropper [ˈkrɒpə(r)] *n Fam* **to come a c.** se prendre une gamelle

croquet [ˈkrəʊkeɪ] *n* croquet *m*

croquette [krɒˈket] *n Culin* croquette *f*

cross [krɒs] **1** *n* (**a**) *(sign, shape)* croix *f*; **to make the sign of the c.** faire le signe de croix (**b**) *(hybrid)* & *Fig* croisement *m* (**between** entre) (**c**) *(in boxing)* coup *m* croisé; *(in football)* centre *m*
  2 *adj (annoyed)* fâché(e); **to get c. (with sb)** se fâcher (contre qn); **to be c. with oneself** s'en vouloir; **we've never had a c. word** nous n'avons jamais eu un mot plus haut que l'autre
  3 *vt* (**a**) *(river, road)* traverser; **to c. sb's path** se trouver sur le chemin de qn; **it crossed my mind that...** il m'est venu à l'esprit que... (**b**) *(make into shape of cross)* croiser; **to c. oneself** se signer; **to c. one's legs/arms** croiser les jambes/bras; **to keep one's fingers crossed** croiser les doigts; **to c. one's eyes** loucher; *Fig* **to c. swords (with sb)** croiser le fer (avec qn); *Fig* **we must have got our wires crossed** nous avons dû mal nous comprendre; *Fam* **c. my heart (and hope to die)** croix de bois, croix de fer (**c**) *(oppose)* contrecarrer (**d**) *(animals, plants)* croiser (**with** avec); (**e**) *(in writing)* **to c. a cheque** barrer un chèque; **to c. one's t's** mettre une barre à ses t
  4 *vi* (**a**) *(of roads, lines)* se croiser; **our letters crossed in the post** nos lettres se sont croisées (**b**) *(go across)* traverser; **to c. from Dover to Calais** faire la traversée de Douvres à Calais

▸**cross off, cross out** *vt sep* barrer, rayer

crossbar [ˈkrɒsbɑː(r)] *n (on bike)* barre *f*; *(of goalposts)* barre *f* transversale

crossbow [ˈkrɒsbəʊ] *n* arbalète *f*

crossbreed [ˈkrɒsbriːd] *n (of animals)* croisement *m*; *(of plants)* hybride *m*

cross-Channel [ˈkrɒsˈtʃænəl] *adj* transmanche *inv*

crosscheck [ˈkrɒsˈtʃek] **1** *n* vérification *f* (par recoupement)
  2 *vt* vérifier par recoupement

cross-country [ˈkrɒsˈkʌntrɪ] *adj* **c. runner** coureur(euse) *m,f* de fond; **c. running** cross *m*; **c. skier** fondeur(euse) *m,f*; **c. skiing** ski *m* de fond

cross-examination [ˈkrɒsɪgzæmɪˈneɪʃən] *n Law* contre-interrogatoire *m*; *Fig* interrogatoire *m* serré

cross-examine ['krɒsɪg'zæmɪn] *vt Law* soumettre à un contre-interrogatoire; *Fig* soumettre à un interrogatoire serré; **to c. sb about sth** interroger qn en détail sur qch

cross-eyed ['krɒsaɪd] *adj* **to be c.** loucher

crossfire ['krɒsfaɪə(r)] *n* feu *m* croisé; *Fig* **to be caught in the c.** être pris(e) entre deux feux

crossing ['krɒsɪŋ] *n* (**a**) *(of sea, river)* traversée *f* (**b**) *(in street)* passage *m* (pour) piétons, passage *m* clouté

cross-legged ['krɒs'leg(ɪ)d] *adv* **to sit c.** être assis(e) en tailleur

cross-platform [krɒs'plætfɔːm] *adj Comput* multiplateforme

cross-purposes ['krɒs'pɜːpəsɪz] *npl* **to be at c.** ne pas parler de la même chose

cross-reference ['krɒs'refərəns] *n* renvoi *m*

crossroads ['krɒsrəʊdz] *(pl* **crossroads**) *n* carrefour *m*, croisement *m*; *Fig (decisive moment)* point *m* crucial

cross-section ['krɒs'sekʃən] *n* coupe *f ou* section *f* transversale; *Fig (of population)* échantillon *m* représentatif

cross-trainer ['krɒstreɪnə(r)] *n (gym equipment)* cross-trainer *m*

cross-training ['krɒstreɪnɪŋ] *n Sport* cross-training *m*

crosswind ['krɒswɪnd] *n* vent *m* de travers

crossword ['krɒswɜːd] *n* **c. (puzzle)** mots *mpl* croisés

crotch [krɒtʃ] *n* entrejambe *m*

crotchet ['krɒtʃɪt] *n Mus* noire *f*

crotchety ['krɒtʃətɪ] *adj Fam* grognon

crouch [kraʊtʃ] *vi (of animal)* se tapir; *(of person)* s'accroupir

croupier ['kruːpɪə(r)] *n* croupier *m*

crow [krəʊ] **1** *n (bird)* corbeau *m*; **as the c. flies** à vol d'oiseau; **c.'s feet** *(on face)* pattes *fpl* d'oie; **c.'s nest** *(on ship)* nid-de-pie *m*
2 *vi* (**a**) *(of cock)* chanter (**b**) *(exult)* se vanter (**about** de)

crowbar ['krəʊbɑː(r)] *n* levier *m*

crowd [kraʊd] **1** *n* (**a**) *(large number of people)* foule *f*; *(at sporting event)* public *m*; **there was a c. at the cinema** il y avait beaucoup de monde au cinéma; *Fig* **to stand out from the c.** se distinguer de la masse; *Fig* **to follow the c.** suivre le mouvement; **to be a c. puller** attirer les foules (**b**) *Fam (group)* bande *f*
2 *vt (people, objects)* entasser; *(streets, square)* envahir; **don't c. me!** laisse-moi respirer!
3 *vi* **to c. (together)** s'entasser; **to c. round sb** se presser autour de qn

▸**crowd out** *vt sep (of deal, market)* exclure (**of** de)

crowded ['kraʊdɪd] *adj (place)* bondé(e); *(day, schedule)* chargé(e)

crown [kraʊn] **1** *n* (**a**) *(of monarch)* couronne *f*; **the C.** *(the monarchy)* la Couronne; *Br Law* **c. court** ≃ assises *fpl*, Cour *f* d'assises; **c. jewels** joyaux *mpl* de la Couronne; **c. prince** prince *m* héritier (**b**) *(top) (of head)* sommet *m* de la tête; *(of hat)* haut *m*; *(of hill)* sommet; *(of tooth)* couronne *f*
2 *vt also Fig* couronner; *Fam* **I'll c. you!** *(hit on the head)* je vais te flanquer une calotte!; **and to c. it all...** et pour couronner le tout...

crowning ['kraʊnɪŋ] *adj (achievement)* suprême; **c. glory** couronnement *m*

crucial ['kruːʃəl] *adj* (**a**) *(very important)* crucial(e) (**b**) *very Fam (very good)* d'enfer

crucible ['kruːsɪbəl] *n* creuset *m*; *Fig (test)* épreuve *f*

crucifix ['kruːsɪfɪks] *n* crucifix *m*

crucifixion [kruːsɪ'fɪkʃən] *n* crucifixion *f*

crucify ['kruːsɪfaɪ] *(pt & pp* **crucified**) *vt* crucifier; *Fig (criticize)* descendre en flammes; *(defeat)* écraser

crude [kruːd] *adj* (**a**) *(unsophisticated, unrefined)* grossier(ère); **c. (oil)** pétrole *m* brut (**b**) *(rude, vulgar)* vulgaire

cruel ['krʊəl] *adj* cruel(elle); *(winter)* rude; **you have to be c. to be kind** qui aime bien châtie bien

cruelty ['krʊəltɪ] *n* cruauté *f*

cruet ['kruːɪt] *n Culin* **c. (stand** *or* **set)** service *m* à condiments

cruise [kruːz] **1** *n (on ship)* croisière *f*; **to go on a c.** faire une croisière; **c. missile** missile *m* de croisière; **c. ship** bateau *m* de croisière
2 *vi (of passengers)* être en croisière; *(of taxi)* être en maraude; *(of car)* rouler; *Fam (look for sexual partner)* draguer; **cruising speed** *(of ship, plane)* vitesse *f* de croisière

cruiser ['kruːzə(r)] *n (ship)* **(battle) c.** croiseur *m*; **(cabin) c.** yacht *m* de croisière

crumb [krʌm] *n also Fig* miette *f*; **my only c. of comfort is...** mon seul petit réconfort est...

crumble ['krʌmbəl] **1** *n (dessert)* crumble *m (dessert aux fruits recouvert de pâte sablée)*
2 *vt (bread, cake)* émietter
3 *vi (of stone)* s'effriter; *(of bread)* s'émietter; *Fig (of empire, hopes)* s'effondrer

crumbly ['krʌmblɪ] *adj* friable

crumpet ['krʌmpɪt] *n* (**a**) *(teacake)* = petite crêpe épaisse mangée avec du beurre, de la confiture etc (**b**) *very Fam (women)* nanas *fpl*; **a nice bit of c.** une belle nana

crumple ['krʌmpəl] **1** *vt (material, dress)* froisser, chiffonner; **to c. sth into a ball** mettre qch en boule
2 *vi (of material, dress)* se froisser, se chiffonner; *Fig (of face)* se crisper

crunch [krʌntʃ] **1** *n (sound)* craquement *m*; *(of snow, gravel)* crissement *m*; *Fig* **when it comes to the c.** au moment crucial; *Fig* **if it comes to the c.** au pire
2 *vt (with teeth)* croquer (dans)
3 *vi (of snow, gravel)* crisser; **to c. on sth** *(with teeth)* croquer (dans) qch

crunchy ['krʌntʃɪ] *adj* croquant(e); *(snow, gravel)* qui crisse sous les pas

crusade [kruː'seɪd] **1** *n also Fig* croisade *f*
2 *vi* **to c. for/against sth** se battre pour/contre qch

crusader [kruː'seɪdə(r)] *n Hist* croisé *m*; *Fig* militant(e) *m,f* **(for/against** pour/contre)

crush [krʌʃ] **1** *n* (**a**) *(crowd)* foule *f*; *(confusion)* bousculade *f*; **c. barrier** barrière *f* de sécurité (**b**) *Br (drink)* **orange/lemon c.** = boisson gazeuse à l'orange/au citron (**c**) *Fam (infatuation)* béguin *m*; **to have a c. on sb** avoir le béguin pour qn pincer pour qn
2 *vt* écraser; *(grapes)* presser; *(ice)* piler; *(in a drawer, suitcase)* entasser; *Fig (opponent)* écraser; *(revolt)* étouffer, mater; *(hopes, person)* anéantir
3 *vi (be crammed)* s'entasser; *(crease)* se froisser

crushing ['krʌʃɪŋ] *adj Fig (defeat)* écrasant(e); *(blow)* terrible; *(remark)* cinglant(e)

crust [krʌst] *n (of bread, pie, the earth)* croûte *f*; *Fam* **to earn a c.** gagner sa croûte

crustacean [krʌs'teɪʃən] *n* crustacé *m*

crusty ['krʌstɪ] *adj* (**a**) *(bread, roll)* croustillant(e) (**b**) *(person)* acariâtre

crutch [krʌtʃ] n (**a**) (for walking) béquille f; Fig (support) soutien m; **to be on crutches** marcher avec des béquilles (**b**) (crotch) entrejambe m

crux [krʌks] n (of matter, problem) cœur m

cruzado [kruːˈzɑːdəʊ] (pl **cruzados**) n cruzado m

cry [kraɪ] **1** n (pl **cries**) (**a**) (call) (of person, animal) cri m; (in demonstration) slogan m; **to give a c.** pousser un cri; **a c. for help** un appel au secours; **to be a far c. from sth** n'avoir rien à voir avec qch (**b**) (weeping) **to have a good c.** pleurer un bon coup
2 vt (pt & pp **cried** [kraɪd]) (**a**) (exclaim) crier (**b**) (weep) **to c. oneself to sleep** s'endormir en pleurant
3 vi (**a**) (weep) pleurer; **to c. over sth** se lamenter sur qch; Prov **it's no use crying over spilt milk** ce qui est fait est fait (**b**) (shout, call) crier; **to c. for help** appeler à l'aide ou au secours
▸**cry off** vi (from invitation) se décommander
▸**cry out 1** vt sep (**a**) (shout) crier (**b**) (weep) **to c. one's eyes** or **heart out** pleurer toutes les larmes de son corps
2 vi (shout) pousser un cri; Fam **for crying out loud!** mais bon sang!; Fam **that wall is crying out for a coat of paint** ce mur aurait grand besoin d'une couche de peinture

crybaby [ˈkraɪbeɪbɪ] (pl **crybabies**) n Fam pleurnicheur(euse) m,f

crying [ˈkraɪɪŋ] **1** n (weeping) pleurs mpl
2 adj (need) urgent(e); **it's a c. shame that...** il est scandaleux que... + subjunctive

crypt [krɪpt] n crypte f

cryptic [ˈkrɪptɪk] adj énigmatique; **c. crossword** = mots croisés dont les définitions sont des énigmes

crystal [ˈkrɪstəl] **1** n cristal m; **c. ball** boule f de cristal; **c. vase** vase m de ou en cristal
2 adj (clear) cristallin(e), limpide

crystal-clear [ˈkrɪstəlˈklɪə(r)] adj (water) limpide; (explanation) clair(e) comme de l'eau de roche

crystallize [ˈkrɪstəlaɪz] **1** vt Chem cristalliser; **crystallized fruit** fruits mpl confits
2 vi Chem & Fig se cristalliser

CSA [siːesˈeɪ] n Br (abbr **Child Support Agency**) = organisme gouvernemental qui décide du montant des pensions alimentaires et les prélève au besoin

CSE [siːesˈiː] n Br Formerly (abbr **Certificate of Secondary Education**) = diplôme de fin d'études du premier cycle de l'enseignement secondaire

CST [siːesˈtiː] n Am (abbr **Central Standard Time**) = heure du centre de l'Amérique du Nord

cub [kʌb] n (of fox) renardeau m; (of bear) ourson m; (of lion) lionceau m; (of wolf) louveteau m; **C. (Scout)** louveteau m

Cuba [ˈkjuːbə] n Cuba

Cuban [ˈkjuːbən] **1** n Cubain(e) m,f
2 adj cubain(e)

cubbyhole [ˈkʌbɪhəʊl] n cagibi m

cube [kjuːb] **1** n (shape) cube m; (of sugar) morceau m; Math **c. root** racine f cubique
2 vt Math élever au cube

cubic [ˈkjuːbɪk] adj cubique; **c. capacity** volume m; **c. metre** mètre m cube

cubicle [ˈkjuːbɪkəl] n (**a**) (in hospital, dormitory) box m; (in swimming pool) cabine f; (in public toilet) W.-C. m (**b**) Am (for office worker) box m

cubism [ˈkjuːbɪzəm] n Art cubisme m

cuckold [ˈkʌkəld] **1** n cocu m
2 vt cocufier, faire cocu

cuckoo [ˈkʊkuː] **1** n (pl **cuckoos**) (bird) coucou m; **c. clock** coucou m
2 adj Fam (mad) dingue

cucumber [ˈkjuːkʌmbə(r)] n concombre m

cud [kʌd] n **to chew the c.** ruminer

cuddle [ˈkʌdəl] **1** n câlin m; **to give sb a c.** faire un câlin à qn
2 vt câliner, faire des câlins à
3 vi se câliner, se faire des câlins; **to c. up to sb** se pelotonner ou se blottir contre qn

cuddly [ˈkʌdlɪ] adj Fam (child, animal) mignon(onne) à croquer; Euph (plump) rond(e); **c. toy** peluche f

cudgel [ˈkʌdʒəl] **1** n gourdin m, trique f; Fig **to take up the cudgels on sb's behalf** prendre fait et cause pour qn
2 vt (pt & pp **cudgelled**, Am **cudgeled**) donner des coups de gourdin ou de trique à; **to c. one's brains** se creuser la cervelle

cue¹ [kjuː] n (of actor) réplique f; Fig (signal) signal m; **on c.** au bon moment; Fig **to take one's c. from sb** prendre exemple sur qn; **c. card** (for public speaker) aide-mémoire m inv

cue² n (in billiards, pool) queue f; **c. ball** boule f blanche

cuff¹ [kʌf] n (of shirt) poignet m; Fam **cuffs** (handcuffs) menottes fpl; Fam **off the c.** au pied levé; **c. links** boutons mpl de manchette

cuff² Fam **1** n (blow) calotte f
2 vt (hit) donner une calotte à

cuisine [kwɪˈziːn] n cuisine f

cul-de-sac [ˈkʌldəsæk] n also Fig impasse f

culinary [ˈkʌlɪnərɪ] adj culinaire

cull [kʌl] **1** n (of seals, deer) abattage m
2 vt (**a**) (herd) réduire la taille de; (animal) abattre (**b**) (select) sélectionner (**from** parmi)

culminate [ˈkʌlmɪneɪt] vi **to c. in sth** aboutir à qch

culmination [kʌlmɪˈneɪʃən] n point m culminant

culottes [kuːˈlɒts] npl jupe-culotte f

culpable [ˈkʌlpəbəl] adj coupable (**of** de); Scot Law **c. homicide** homicide m involontaire

culprit [ˈkʌlprɪt] n coupable mf

cult [kʌlt] n culte m; (sect) secte f; **c. figure** personnage m culte; **c. film** film m culte

cultivate [ˈkʌltɪveɪt] vt also Fig cultiver

cultivated [ˈkʌltɪveɪtɪd] adj cultivé(e)

cultivation [kʌltɪˈveɪʃən] n culture f

cultivator [ˈkʌltɪveɪtə(r)] n (for farm) cultivateur m; (for garden) motoculteur m; (person) cultivateur(-trice) m,f

cultural [ˈkʌltʃərəl] adj culturel(elle)

culture [ˈkʌltʃə(r)] n (**a**) (artistic activity, refinement) culture f; Hum **c. vulture** fou (folle) m,f de culture (**b**) (society) culture f; **c. shock** choc m culturel (**c**) Biol culture f

cultured [ˈkʌltʃəd] adj (educated) cultivé(e); **c. pearl** perle f de culture

cumbersome [ˈkʌmbəsəm] adj (luggage, furniture) encombrant(e); (procedure, style) lourd(e)

cumin [ˈkʌmɪn] n cumin m

cumulative [ˈkjuːmjʊlətɪv] adj cumulatif(ive)

cunning [ˈkʌnɪŋ] **1** n (deviousness) ruse f; (ingenuity) astuce f, ingéniosité f
2 adj (devious) rusé(e); (ingenious) astucieux(euse), ingénieux(euse)

cunt [kʌnt] n Vulg (vagina) chatte f; (as insult) enculé(e) m,f

cup [kʌp] **1** *n* (**a**) *(for drinking, measurement)* tasse *f*; *(plastic, paper)* gobelet *m*; *Fam Fig* it's not my **c.** of tea ce n'est pas ma tasse de thé; **it's not everyone's c.** of tea tout le monde n'aime pas (**b**) *(trophy)* coupe *f*; **c. final** finale *f* de coupe; **c. tie** match *m* éliminatoire de coupe (**c**) *(of bra)* bonnet *m* **2** *vt* *(pt & pp* **cupped**) **to c. one's hands round one's mouth** mettre ses mains en porte-voix; **to c. one's hand behind one's ear** mettre sa main en cornet
cupboard [ˈkʌbəd] *n* placard *m*; *Fam* **c. love** amour *m* intéressé; **c. space** rangements *mpl*
cupcake [ˈkʌpkeɪk] *n* = sorte de madeleine
Cupid [ˈkjuːpɪd] *n* Cupidon
cuppa [ˈkʌpə] *n Br Fam* tasse *f* de thé
curable [ˈkjʊərəbəl] *adj* guérissable
curate [ˈkjʊərət] *n Rel* vicaire *m*; **this book is a bit of a c.'s egg** il y a du bon et du mauvais dans ce livre
curator [kjʊəˈreɪtə(r)] *n* conservateur(trice) *m,f*
curb [kɜːb] **1** *n* (**a**) *(limit)* **to put a c.** on sth mettre un frein à qch (**b**) *Am (of road)* bordure *f* de trottoir **2** *vt (spending)* réduire; *(emotions)* réfréner
curd [kɜːd] *n* **curd(s)** lait *m* caillé; **c. cheese** fromage *m* blanc battu
curdle [ˈkɜːdəl] **1** *vt* cailler **2** *vi* (se) cailler
cure [ˈkjʊə(r)] **1** *n* remède *m* (**for** contre); **there is no known c.** on n'a pas encore trouvé de remède; **beyond c.** *(person)* incurable; *(situation)* irrémédiable **2** *vt* (**a**) *(person)* guérir (**of** de) (**b**) *(preserve) (by salting)* saler; *(by smoking)* fumer; *(by drying)* sécher; *(hides)* traiter
cure-all [ˈkjʊərɔːl] *n* panacée *f*
curfew [ˈkɜːfjuː] *n* couvre-feu *m*
curio [ˈkjʊərɪəʊ] *(pl* **curios**) *n* curiosité *f*
curiosity [kjʊərɪˈɒsɪtɪ] *(pl* **curiosities**) *n* curiosité *f*; *Prov* **c. killed the cat** la curiosité est un vilain défaut
curious [ˈkjʊərɪəs] *adj (inquisitive, strange)* curieux(-euse); **to be c. to see/know** vouloir voir/savoir par curiosité
curl [kɜːl] **1** *n (of hair)* boucle *f*; *(of smoke)* volute *f* **2** *vt (hair)* boucler; *(tightly)* friser; **to c. one's lip** faire une moue dédaigneuse; **to c. oneself into a ball** se rouler en boule **3** *vi (of hair)* boucler; *(tightly)* friser; *(of paper, leaves)* se recroqueviller; *(of smoke)* s'élever en volutes
▸**curl up** *vi* (**a**) *(make oneself comfortable)* se pelotonner (**b**) *(protect oneself)* se rouler en boule (**c**) *(of paper, leaves)* se recroqueviller
curler [ˈkɜːlə(r)] *n (for hair)* bigoudi *m*
curlew [ˈkɜːljuː] *n* courlis *m*
curling [ˈkɜːlɪŋ] *n* (**a**) *(sport)* curling *m* (**b**) **c. tongs** fer *m* à friser
curly [ˈkɜːlɪ] *adj (hair)* bouclé(e); *(tightly)* frisé(e)
currant [ˈkʌrənt] *n* raisin *m* de Corinthe; **c. bun** petit pain *m* aux raisins
currency [ˈkʌrənsɪ] *(pl* **currencies**) *n* (**a**) *(money)* monnaie *f*; *(foreign)* devise *f*; **c. converter** convertisseur *m* de monnaie; **c. market** marché *m* monétaire (**b**) *(acceptance)* **to gain c.** *(of theory)* être accrédité(e); *(of idea, belief)* se répandre; **to give c. to a rumour** faire courir un bruit
current [ˈkʌrənt] **1** *n (of river, electricity) & Fig (trend)* courant *m*; *Fig* **to swim against the c.** aller à contre-courant **2** *adj* (**a**) *(existing, present)* actuel(le); **c. affairs** actualité *f*; **c. issue** *(of magazine)* dernier numéro *m* (**b**) *Br Fin* **c. account** compte *m* courant; **c. assets**

actif *m* de roulement; **c. expenditure** dépenses *fpl* courantes; **c. liabilities** passif *m* exigible (**c**) *(common)* courant(e)
currently [ˈkʌrəntlɪ] *adv* actuellement
curriculum [kəˈrɪkjʊləm] *(pl* **curricula** [kəˈrɪkjʊlə]) *n Sch* programme *m*; **c. vitae** curriculum vitae *m inv*
curry¹ [ˈkʌrɪ] **1** *n (pl* **curries**) curry *m*; **chicken c.** curry *m* de poulet; **c. powder** curry *m* **2** *vt* *(pt & pp* **curried**) **curried lamb** agneau *m* au curry
curry² *vt* **to c. favour with sb** s'insinuer dans les bonnes grâces de qn
curse [kɜːs] **1** *n* (**a**) *(jinx, affliction)* malédiction *f*, mauvais sort *m*; *(swearword)* juron *m*; **to put a c. on sb** jeter un sort à qn (**b**) *(scourge)* fléau *m* **2** *vt* maudire; **to be cursed with sth** être affligé(e) de qch **3** *vi* jurer
cursor [ˈkɜːsə(r)] *n Comput* curseur *m*
cursory [ˈkɜːsərɪ] *adj* superficiel(elle)
curt [kɜːt] *adj* sec (sèche)
curtail [kɜːˈteɪl] *vt (shorten)* abréger, écourter; *(limit)* réduire
curtain [ˈkɜːtən] *n* rideau *m*; **to draw the curtains** *(open)* ouvrir les rideaux; *(close)* fermer *ou* tirer les rideaux; *Fam Fig* **it's curtains for her** elle est fichue; *Theat* **c. call** rappel *m*; **c. raiser** *Theat* lever *m* de rideau; *Fig* prélude *m* (**to** à); **c. ring** anneau *m* de rideau; **c. rail** *ou* **rod** tringle *f* à rideau
▸**curtain off** *vt sep* séparer par un rideau
curts(e)y [ˈkɜːtsɪ] **1** *n (pl* **curtsies** *or* **curtseys**) révérence *f* **2** *vi* *(pt & pp* **curtsied** *or* **curtseyed**) faire la révérence (**to** à)
curvaceous [kɜːˈveɪʃəs] *adj* pulpeux(euse)
curvature [ˈkɜːvətʃə(r)] *n* courbure *f*; **c. of the spine** scoliose *f*
curve [kɜːv] **1** *n* courbe *f*; *(in road)* tournant *m*, virage *m*; *(in river)* méandre *m* **2** *vi (of spine)* se courber; *(of road)* faire une courbe; *(of river)* serpenter
curved [kɜːvd] *adj (line)* courbe; *(spine)* courbé(e)
curvy [ˈkɜːvɪ] *adj* **1** *(road, line)* sinueux(euse) **2** *Fam (woman)* bien roulée
cushion [ˈkʊʃən] **1** *n (on chair, sofa)* coussin *m*; *(on billiard table)* bande *f* **2** *vt (blow, impact)* amortir; **to c. sb against sth** protéger qn contre qch
cushy [ˈkʊʃɪ] *adj Fam* pépère (*e*); **a c. number** une bonne planque
custard [ˈkʌstəd] *n* crème *f* anglaise; **c. pie** *(in slapstick comedy)* tarte *f* à la crème; **c. powder** préparation *f* instantanée pour crème anglaise
custodial [kʌsˈtəʊdɪəl] *adj Law* **c. sentence** peine *f* de prison
custodian [kʌsˈtəʊdɪən] *n* gardien(enne) *m,f*
custody [ˈkʌstədɪ] *n* (**a**) *(of children, important papers)* garde *f*; **to have c. of sb** avoir la garde de qn; **in safe c.** sous bonne garde (**b**) *Law* garde *f* à vue; **to take sb into c.** placer qn en garde à vue
custom [ˈkʌstəm] *n* (**a**) *(tradition, practice)* coutume *f*; *(habit)* habitude *f* (**b**) *(of individual)* habitude *f*; **to rise early** il avait l'habitude de se lever tôt (**b**) *Com* clientèle *f*; **to take one's c. elsewhere** aller se fournir ailleurs
customary [ˈkʌstəmərɪ] *adj (usual)* habituel(le); *(traditional)* traditionnel(le); **it is c. to...** il est d'usage de...

custom-built ['kʌstəmbɪlt] *adj (car, offices)* construit(e) sur mesure; *(kitchen units)* fabriqué(e) sur mesure
customer ['kʌstəmə(r)] *n* client(e) *m,f*; *Fam Fig* he's an awkward c. c'est un type pas commode; *Com* c. services (department) service *m* clientèle
customize ['kʌstəmaɪz] *vt (vehicle)* customiser; *(kitchen, computer)* personnaliser
custom-made ['kʌstəm'meɪd] *adj* (fait(e)) sur mesure
customs ['kʌstəmz] *npl* douane *f*; to go through c. passer la douane; c. declaration déclaration *f* en douane; c. duty droits *mpl* de douane; c. officer douanier(ère) *m,f*
cut [kʌt] 1 *n* (a) *(in flesh, text, film)* coupure *f*; *(in wood, cloth)* entaille *f*; c. of meat morceau *m* (de viande); *Fam* to be a c. above sb/sth être un cran au-dessus de qn/qch (b) *(in wages, prices)* réduction *f* (c) *(blow)* coup *m*; the c. and thrust of debate les joutes *fpl* oratoires (d) *Fam (share)* part *f* (e) *(of clothes, hair)* coupe *f*
   2 *adj Fig* c. and dried *(clear)* simple; *(decided)* décidé(e); c. flowers fleurs *fpl* coupées; c. glass cristal *m* taillé
   3 *vt (pt & pp cut)* (a) *(in general)* couper; *(into slices)* trancher, découper; to c. one's finger/nails se couper le doigt/les ongles; to c. sb's hair couper les cheveux à qn; to have one's hair cut se faire couper les cheveux; to c. sth in two *or* in half couper qch en deux; to c. sth to pieces couper qch en morceaux; to c. oneself loose *or* free se dégager, se libérer; to c. a record enregistrer un disque; *Comput* to c. and paste sth faire un couper-coller sur qch (b) *(wages, prices)* réduire (c) *(idioms)* to c. one's losses limiter les dégâts; to c. one's teeth on sth se faire les dents sur qch; to c. sb (dead) faire semblant de ne pas voir qn; it's cutting it *or* things (a bit) fine ça fait (un peu) juste; to c. sb short couper la parole à qn; to c. sth short écourter qch; to c. a long story short... bref...
   4 *vi* (a) *(of knife, scissors)* couper; *(of wind)* être cinglant(e); *Cin* c.! coupez! (b) *(idioms)* that's an argument that cuts both ways c'est un argument à double tranchant; *Fam* to c. and run décamper
▸**cut across** *vt insep* (a) *(field)* couper à travers (b) *(transcend)* transcender
▸**cut back 1** *vt sep* (a) *(bush, tree)* tailler (b) *(costs, production)* réduire
   2 to c. back on sth *(spending, time)* réduire qch; to c. back on smoking/drinking fumer/boire moins
▸**cut down 1** *vt sep* (a) *(tree, soldier)* abattre; to be c. down in one's prime être fauché(e) à la fleur de l'âge (b) *(speech, text)* abréger; *(spending, time)* réduire; *Fig* to c. sb down to size rabattre son caquet à qn
   2 *vi* = cut back
▸**cut in** *vi* (a) *(interrupt conversation)* intervenir (b) *(in car)* to c. in in front of sb faire une queue de poisson à qn
▸**cut into** *vt insep (with knife)* entamer; *(of rope, handle)* blesser
▸**cut off** *vt sep* (a) *(remove)* couper; to c. off sb's head trancher la tête à qn, décapiter qn; *Fig* that would be cutting off your nose to spite your face ça va te retomber sur le nez (b) *(disconnect)* couper; we've been c. off *(had electricity disconnected)* on nous a coupé l'électricité; I've been c. off *(during phone conversation)* j'ai été coupé (c) *(isolate)* isoler; to be c. off from être coupé(e) de

▸**cut out 1** *vt sep* (a) *(picture, article)* découper; *(tumour)* enlever; *Fam* to have one's work c. out avoir du pain sur la planche; to be c. out for sth être fait(e) pour qch (b) *(stop)* supprimer; to c. out smoking/desserts arrêter de fumer/de manger des desserts; *Fam* c. it out! ça va maintenant! (c) *(exclude)* to c. sb out of one's will déshériter qn; to c. sb out of a deal évincer qn
   2 *vi (of engine)* caler; *(of machine)* s'arrêter
▸**cut up 1** *vt sep* (a) *(food, paper)* couper; *(into slices)* découper (b) *Fam (upset)* to be c. up (about sth) être complètement chamboulé(e) (par qch)
   2 *vi Fam* to c. up rough *(of person)* devenir agressif(ive)
cut-and-paste ['kʌtənd'peɪst] *n Comput* couper-coller *m*
cutback ['kʌtbæk] *n* réduction *f*
cute [kjuːt] *adj* mignon(onne)
cuticle ['kjuːtɪkəl] *n* cuticule *f*
cutlery ['kʌtləri] *n* couverts *mpl*; *Com* argenterie *f*
cutlet ['kʌtlɪt] *n* côtelette *f*
cutoff ['kʌtɒf] *n* c. date date *f* limite; c. point limite *f*; *(for tax)* seuil *m*
cutout ['kʌtaʊt] *n* (a) *(shape)* silhouette *f* (b) *Elec* disjoncteur *m*
cut-price ['kʌt'praɪs] *adj (goods)* à prix réduit; *(rate)* réduit(e)
cutthroat ['kʌtθrəʊt] 1 *n* assassin *m*
   2 *adj (competition)* acharné(e); c. razor coupe-choux *m inv*
cutting ['kʌtɪŋ] 1 *n* (a) *(of plant)* bouture *f* (b) **(newspaper)** c. coupure *f* de journal *ou* de presse (c) **(railway)** c. voie *f* en déblai
   2 *adj (wind, remark)* cinglant(e); c. edge tranchant *m*; *Fig* to be at the c. edge of technology être à la pointe du progrès
cuttlefish ['kʌtəlfɪʃ] *n* seiche *f*
CV [siː'viː] *n (abbr* curriculum vitae) CV *m*
cyanide ['saɪənaɪd] *n Chem* cyanure *m*
cybercafé [saɪbə'kæfeɪ] *n* cybercafé *m*
cybernetics [saɪbə'netɪks] *n* Comput cybernétique *f*
cybersex ['saɪbəseks] *n Comput* cybersexe *m*
cyberspace ['saɪbəspeɪs] *n Comput* cyberespace *m*
cybersquatting ['saɪbəskwɒtɪŋ] *n Comput* cybersquatting *m*, *Offic* cybersquattage *m*
cyberstalking ['saɪbəstɔːkɪŋ] *n Comput* cybertraque *f*, *Offic* cyberharcèlement *m*
cyberterrorism [saɪbə'terərɪzəm] *n Comput* cyberterrorisme *m*
cyberterrorist [saɪbə'terərɪst] *n Comput* cyberterroriste *mf*
cyclamen ['sɪkləmən] *(pl* cyclamen) *n* cyclamen *m*
cycle ['saɪkəl] 1 *n* (a) *(pattern)* cycle *m* (b) *(bicycle)* bicyclette *f*, vélo *m*; c. lane voie *f* réservée aux vélos; c. path piste *f* cyclable; c. racing course *f* cycliste
   2 *vi* aller à bicyclette *ou* à vélo
cyclic(al) ['saɪklɪk(əl)] *adj* cyclique
cycling ['saɪklɪŋ] *n* cyclisme *m*; to go on a c. holiday faire du cyclotourisme; c. shorts cuissard *m*; c. track piste *f* cycliste
cyclist ['saɪklɪst] *n* cycliste *mf*
cyclone ['saɪkləʊn] *n Met* cyclone *m*
cygnet ['sɪgnɪt] *n* jeune cygne *m*
cylinder ['sɪlɪndə(r)] *n (shape)* cylindre *m*; *(gas container)* bouteille *f*; four-/eight-c. engine moteur *m* à quatre/huit cylindres; c. block bloc-cylindres *m*; c. head culasse *f*

cylindrical [sɪ'lɪndrɪkəl] *adj* cylindrique
cymbal ['sɪmbəl] *n* cymbale *f*
cynic ['sɪnɪk] *n* cynique *mf*
cynical ['sɪnɪkəl] *adj* cynique (**about** sur)
cypress ['saɪprəs] *n* cyprès *m*
Cypriot ['sɪprɪət] **1** *n* Chypriote *mf*, Cypriote *mf*
2 *adj* chypriote, cypriote
Cyprus ['saɪprəs] *n* Chypre

cyst [sɪst] *n Med* kyste *m*
cystitis [sɪs'taɪtɪs] *n Med* cystite *f*
czar [zɑ:(r)] *n* tsar *m*, czar *m*
Czech [tʃek] **1** *n* (**a**) *(person)* Tchèque *mf* (**b**) *(language)* tchèque *m*
2 *adj* tchèque; **the C. Republic** la République tchèque
Czechoslovakia [tʃekəʊslə'vækɪə] *n Formerly* la Tchécoslovaquie

D¹, d [diː] *n* (**a**) *(letter)* D, d *m inv* (**b**) *Mus* ré *m* (**c**) *Sch* *(grade)* **to get a D** ≃ avoir entre 8 et 10 sur 20

D² *Am Pol* (*abbr* **Democrat**) démocrate

DA [diːˈeɪ] *n Am Law* (*abbr* **district attorney**) ≃ procureur *m* de la République

DAB [diːeɪˈbiː] *n* (*abbr* **digital audio broadcasting**) diffusion *f* audionumérique

dab [dæb] **1** *n (of paint)* petit coup *m*; *(of glue)* point *m*; *(of perfume)* goutte *f*; *Br Fam* **dabs** *(fingerprints)* empreintes *fpl* (digitales)
2 *adj* **to be a d. hand at sth** être doué(e) pour qch
3 *vt* (*pt & pp* **dabbed**) *(paint)* passer; *(eyes, wound)* tamponner

dabble [ˈdæbəl] **1** *vt* **to d. one's feet in the water** balancer ses pieds dans l'eau
2 *vi* **d. in politics/journalism** faire vaguement de la politique/du journalisme

dabbler [ˈdæblə(r)] *n* amateur(trice) *m,f*

dachshund [ˈdækshʊnd] *n* teckel *m*

dad [dæd] *n Fam* papa *m*

daddy [ˈdædɪ] (*pl* **daddies**) *n Fam* papa *m*

daddy-longlegs [ˈdædɪˈlɒŋlegz] (*pl* **daddy-longlegs**) *n Fam* tipule *f*

daffodil [ˈdæfədɪl] *n* jonquille *f*

daft [dɑːft] *adj Br* idiot(e); **to be d. about sb/sth** être fou (folle) de qn/qch

dagger [ˈdægə(r)] *n* (**a**) *(weapon)* dague *f* (**b**) *(idioms)* **to be at daggers drawn (with sb)** être à couteaux tirés (avec qn); **to look daggers at sb** foudroyer qn du regard

dago [ˈdeɪgəʊ] (*pl* **dagoes** *or* **dagos**) *n very Fam* = terme injurieux désignant un Espagnol, un Portugais, un Italien ou un Latino-Américain

dahlia [ˈdeɪlɪə] *n* dahlia *m*

daily [ˈdeɪlɪ] **1** *n* (*pl* **dailies**) (**a**) *(newspaper)* quotidien *m* (**b**) *Br Fam (maid)* femme *f* de ménage *(qui vient tous les jours)*
2 *adj* quotidien(enne); **on a d. basis** *(paid, calculated)* à la journée; *(used)* quotidiennement; *Fam* **the d. grind** le train-train quotidien; **d. paper** quotidien *m*
3 *adv* tous les jours, quotidiennement; **twice d.** deux fois par jour

dainty [ˈdeɪntɪ] *adj* délicat(e)

dairy [ˈdeərɪ] (*pl* **dairies**) *n (shop)* crémerie *f*; *(factory)* laiterie *f*; **d. cow** vache *f* laitière; **d. farm** = ferme spécialisée dans la production laitière; **d. farming** élevage *m* de vaches laitières; **d. produce** produits *mpl* laitiers

dais [ˈdeɪɪs] *n* estrade *f*

daisy [ˈdeɪzɪ] (*pl* **daisies**) *n* pâquerette *f*; *(bigger)* marguerite *f*; *Fam* **to push up the daisies** manger les pissenlits par la racine; **d. chain** guirlande *f* de pâquerettes

daisywheel [ˈdeɪzɪwiːl] *n (on printer)* marguerite *f*

dale [deɪl] *n* vallée *f*

dalliance [ˈdælɪəns] *n Lit* badinage *m*

dally [ˈdælɪ] (*pt & pp* **dallied**) *vi (dawdle)* traîner, lambiner; **to d. over a decision** mettre du temps à se décider; **to d. with sb** flirter avec qn

Dalmatian [dælˈmeɪʃən] *n (dog)* dalmatien *m*

dam [dæm] **1** *n* barrage *m*
2 *vt* (*pt & pp* **dammed**) *(river, lake)* construire un barrage sur
▶**dam up** *vt sep (river, lake)* construire un barrage sur

damage [ˈdæmɪdʒ] **1** *n* (**a**) *(to machine, building)* dégâts *mpl*; *(to health, reputation)* mal *m*; **to do** *or* **cause d. to** *(building)* faire des dégâts dans; *(health, reputation)* nuire à; *Fig* **the d. is done** le mal est fait; *Br Fam* **what's the d.?** ça fait combien?; **we have to do some d. limitation** il faut limiter les dégâts (**b**) **damages** *(compensation)* dommages-intérêts *mpl*
2 *vt (machine, building)* abîmer, endommager; *(health, reputation)* nuire à; *(chances)* compromettre; *(person)* faire du tort à

damaging [ˈdæmɪdʒɪŋ] *adj* préjudiciable (**to** à)

Damascus [dəˈmæskəs] *n* Damas

damask [ˈdæməsk] *n* damas *m*

dame [deɪm] *n* (**a**) *Am Fam (woman)* pépée *f*; *Br (in pantomime)* = dans la "pantomime", personnage comique de vieille dame tenu par un homme (**b**) *Br (title)* = titre donné à une femme ayant reçu une distinction honorifique

damn [dæm] **1** *n very Fam* **I don't give a d.** j'en ai rien à fiche; **it's not worth a d.** ça ne vaut pas un clou
2 *adj very Fam* **d.** fichu(e); **you d. fool!** espèce d'idiot(e)!; **he's a d. nuisance** qu'est-ce qu'il peut être casse-pieds!
3 *adv very Fam* sacrément; **d. all** que dalle; **you know d. well what I mean!** tu sais fichtrement bien ce que je veux dire!
4 *exclam very Fam* **d.!** zut!, mince!
5 *vt* (**a**) *(criticize severely)* éreinter; **to d. sb with faint praise** éreinter qn sous couleur d'éloge (**b**) *very Fam* **d. the expense!** au diable l'avarice!; **d. it!** zut!, mince!; **well I'll be damned!** ben mince alors!

damnation [dæmˈneɪʃən] **1** *n Rel* damnation *f*
2 *exclam Fam* **d.!** bon sang!

damned [dæmd] **1** *npl Rel* **the d.** les damnés *mpl*
2 *adj & adv very Fam* = **damn**

damning ['dæmɪŋ] *adj (admission, revelation)* accablant(e)

damp [dæmp] **1** *n* humidité *f*
2 *adj* humide; *(skin)* moite; **d. course** isolant *m* contre l'humidité; *Fig* **d. squib** déception *f*
3 *vt (make wet)* humecter; **to d. down a fire** couvrir un feu

dampen [dæmpən] *vt (make wet)* humecter; *Fig* **to d. sb's spirits** décourager qn

damper ['dæmpə(r)] *n Mus* étouffoir *m*; *Fig* **to put a d. on sth** jeter un froid sur qch

damsel ['dæmzəl] *n Lit* damoiselle *f*; *Hum* **a d. in distress** une belle éplorée

damson ['dæmzən] *n (fruit)* prune *f* de Damas; *(tree)* prunier *m* de Damas

dance [dɑːns] **1** *n* danse *f*; *(event)* soirée *f* dansante; *(for young people)* boum *f*; *(formal)* bal *m*; *Fam* **to lead sb a (merry) d.** donner du fil à retordre à qn; **d. band** orchestre *m* de danse; **d. floor** piste *f* de danse; **d. hall** salle *f* de bal; **d. music** *(in clubs)* dance (music) *f*
2 *vt (waltz, tango)* danser
3 *vi* danser; **they danced down the road** ils ont descendu la rue en dansant

dancer ['dɑːnsə(r)] *n* danseur(euse) *m,f*

dancing ['dɑːnsɪŋ] *n* danse *f*; **d. shoes** chaussons *mpl* de danse

dandelion ['dændɪlaɪən] *n* pissenlit *m*

dander ['dændə(r)] *n Fam* **to get sb's d. up** hérisser qn

dandruff ['dændrəf] *n* pellicules *fpl*

dandy ['dændɪ] **1** *n (pl dandies)* dandy *m*
2 *adj Fam* génial(e); **everything's just (fine and) d.** tout marche comme sur des roulettes

Dane [deɪn] *n* Danois(e) *m,f*

danger ['deɪndʒə(r)] *n* danger *m*; **in d.** en danger; **out of d.** hors de danger; **to be in d. of doing sth** risquer de faire qch; **there's no d. that...** il n'y a pas de danger que... + *subjunctive*; **to be on the d. list** *(of patient)* être dans un état critique; **to be off the d. list** *(of patient)* être hors de danger; **d. money** prime *f* de risque; *Fig* **d. sign** signal *m* d'alarme

dangerous ['deɪndʒərəs] *adj* dangereux(euse)

dangerously ['deɪndʒərəslɪ] *adv* dangereusement; **they came d. close to losing** ils ont bien failli perdre

dangle ['dæŋɡəl] **1** *vt* balancer; *Fig* **to d. sth in front of sb** faire miroiter qch à qn
2 *vi (of legs)* pendre; *(from rope, chain)* se balancer; *Fig* **to keep sb dangling** laisser qn dans l'incertitude

Danish ['deɪnɪʃ] **1** *n (a) (language)* danois *m* (**b**) *(pastry)* = sorte de chausson fourré
2 *adj* danois(e); **D. pastry** = sorte de chausson fourré

dank [dæŋk] *adj* humide et froid(e)

Danube ['dænjuːb] *n* **the D.** le Danube

dapper ['dæpə(r)] *adj* soigné(e)

dappled ['dæpəld] *adj* tacheté(e); *(horse)* pommelé(e)

dare ['deə(r)] **1** *n* défi *m*; **to do sth for a d.** faire qch par défi
2 *vt* **to d. to do sth** oser faire qch; **to d. sb to do sth** défier qn de faire qch; **I d. you!** chiche!; **don't you d. (do that)!** ne t'avise pas de faire ça!; **how d. you!** comment oses-tu!; **I d. say** sans doute, c'est bien possible

daredevil ['deədevəl] **1** *n* casse-cou *mf inv*
2 *adj (person)* casse-cou *inv*; *(stunt, escape)* audacieux(euse)

daring ['deərɪŋ] **1** *n* audace *f*
2 *adj* audacieux(euse)

dark [dɑːk] **1** *n* (**a**) *(darkness)* obscurité *f*; **before/after d.** avant/après la tombée de la nuit; **in the d.** dans le noir (**b**) *(idioms)* **to be in the d. (about)** ne pas être au courant (de)
2 *adj* (**a**) *(not light)* sombre; *(skin, hair)* foncé(e); **it's d. by six o'clock** il fait nuit à six heures; **it's getting d.** il commence à faire nuit; **d. glasses** lunettes *fpl* noires; *Fig* **d. horse** *(competitor)* outsider *m*; *(in politics)* candidat(e) *m,f* surprise; *(secretive person)* personne *f* pleine de mystère (**b**) *Fig (thought)* sombre, morose; *(period)* sombre; *(look)* noir(e); *Hist* **the D. Ages** le Haut Moyen Âge; *Fig* **to be in the D. Ages** être encore au Moyen Âge

darken ['dɑːkən] **1** *vt (sky, colour)* assombrir; **never d. my door again!** ne remettez plus les pieds chez moi!
2 *vi (of sky, colour, thoughts)* s'assombrir

darkness ['dɑːknɪs] *n* obscurité *f*; **in d.** dans l'obscurité

darkroom ['dɑːkruːm] *n* chambre *f* noire

dark-skinned ['dɑːk'skɪnd] *adj* à la peau mate

darling ['dɑːlɪŋ] **1** *n (term of address) (to woman)* chérie *f*; *(to man)* chéri *m*; **she's the d. of the press** c'est la coqueluche des journaux
2 *adj (dear)* cher (chère); *(charming)* adorable

darn¹ [dɑːn] *vt (mend)* repriser

darn² *Fam* **1** *adj* sacré(e); **it's a d. nuisance!** c'est vachement embêtant!
2 *exclam* **d. (it)!** zut!

darning ['dɑːnɪŋ] *n* reprisage *m*; **d. needle** aiguille *f* à repriser

dart [dɑːt] **1** *n* (**a**) *(missile)* flèche *f*; **darts** *(game)* fléchettes *fpl* (**b**) *(movement)* **to make a d. for sth** se ruer vers qch
2 *vt* **to d. a glance at sb** jeter un regard à qn
3 *vi* **to d. in/out** entrer/sortir comme une flèche

dartboard ['dɑːtbɔːd] *n* cible *f (de jeu de fléchettes)*

dash [dæʃ] **1** *n* (**a**) *(of liquid)* goutte *f*; *(of humour, colour)* touche *f* (**b**) *(hyphen, in Morse code)* tiret *m* (**c**) *(run)* course *f* effrénée; **to make a d. for sth** se ruer vers qch; **to make a d. for it** s'enfuir (**d**) *(style)* panache *m*; **to cut a d.** avoir fière allure (**e**) *(of car)* tableau *m* de bord
2 *vt* (**a**) *(throw)* jeter; **to d. sth to the ground** jeter qch par terre (**b**) *(destroy) (hopes)* réduire à néant; *Fam* **d. (it)!** zut!
3 *vi* **to d. in/out** entrer/sortir comme une flèche; **I dashed about** *or* **around all day** j'ai couru toute la journée; *Fam* **I must d.** il faut que je file
▸**dash off 1** *vt sep (letter)* écrire en vitesse
2 *vi (leave)* filer

dashboard ['dæʃbɔːd] *n (of car)* tableau *m* de bord

dashing ['dæʃɪŋ] *adj (person)* fringant(e); *(appearance)* élégant(e)

DAT [diːˈtiː] *n (abbr digital audio tape)* DAT *m*

data ['deɪtə] *n* informations *fpl*; *Comput* données *fpl*; **an item** *or* **a piece of d.** une information/donnée; **bank d.** banque *f* de données; **d. entry, d. input** entrée *f* de données; *Comput* **d. processing** traitement *m* de l'information; **d. protection** protection *f* de l'information; *Law* **D. Protection Act** loi *f* sur la protection de l'information *(en Grande-Bretagne)*

database ['deɪtəbeɪs] *n Comput* base *f* de données

date¹ [deɪt] *n (fruit)* datte *f*; **d. palm** palmier *m* dattier

date² **1** *n* (**a**) *(day)* date *f*; **d. of birth** date *f* de naissance; **what's the d. (today)?** le combien sommes-nous (aujourd'hui)?; **to d.** à ce jour; **up to d.** *(with work)* à jour; *(with events, news)* au courant; *(in*

fashion) à la mode; **out of d.** périmé(e); **d. stamp** tampon *m ou* timbre *m* à date (**b**) *(with girlfriend, boyfriend)* rendez-vous *m*; **d. rape** = viol commis par une connaissance, un ami etc (**c**) *Am (girlfriend, boyfriend)* ami(e) *m,f*
2 *vt* (**a**) *(letter, ticket)* dater (**b**) *Am (go out with)* sortir avec
3 *vi* (**a**) **to d. from** *or* **back to** *(of custom, practice)* remonter à; *(of building)* dater de (**b**) *(go out of fashion)* dater

Date

Pour donner une date en anglais, on n'emploie pas l'article à l'écrit. En anglais britannique, on écrira donc "Monday 25th December 2007" ou, de plus en plus souvent, "Monday 25 December 2007", et, en abrégé, "25.12.07". Notez cependant qu'à l'oral, on prononce "Monday the twenty-fifth of December…". En anglais américain, le mois est indiqué avant le jour. On écrira ainsi "Monday December 25 2007" et, en abrégé, "12.25.07", et on prononcera "December twenty-five".

datebook ['deɪtbʊk] *n Am* agenda *f*
dateline ['deɪtlaɪn] *n Geog* ligne *f* de changement de date
dating agency ['deɪtɪŋeɪdʒənsɪ] *n* agence *f* matrimoniale
dative ['deɪtɪv] *n Gram* datif *m*
daub [dɔːb] *vt* barbouiller (**with** de)
daughter ['dɔːtə(r)] *n* fille *f*
daughter-in-law ['dɔːtərɪnlɔː] *(pl* daughters-in-law) *n* belle-fille *f*
daunt [dɔːnt] *vt* intimider; **nothing daunted** nullement decouragé(e)
daunting ['dɔːntɪŋ] *adj* intimidant(e)
dawdle ['dɔːdəl] *vi* traînasser, lambiner
dawn [dɔːn] **1** *n also Fig* aube *f*; **at d.** à l'aube; **from d. to dusk** du lever au coucher du soleil; **the d. chorus** le chant des oiseaux à l'aube
2 *vi (of day)* se lever; *Fig (of life, civilization)* naître
▶**dawn on** *vt insep* **the truth finally dawned on her** la vérité a fini par lui apparaître; **it dawned on me that…** je me suis rendu compte que…
day [deɪ] *n* (**a**) *(period of daylight, twenty-four hours)* jour *m*; *(referring to duration)* journée *f*; **once/twice a d.** une fois/deux fois par jour; **the d. before yesterday** avant-hier; **the d. after tomorrow** après-demain; **all d.** toute la journée; **d. after d.** jour après jour; **to change from d. to d.** changer d'un jour sur l'autre; **to live from d. to d.** vivre au jour le jour; **one d., one of these days** un de ces jours; **any d. now** d'un jour à l'autre; **the other d.** l'autre jour; **every other d.** tous les deux jours, un jour sur deux; **a year ago to the d.** il y a un an jour pour jour; **from d. one** dès le début; **to take a d. off** prendre un jour de congé; **to be paid by the d.** être payé(e) à la journée; **to work d. and night** travailler jour et nuit; *Fam* **he's sixty if he's a d.** il a soixante ans bien sonnés; **d. nursery** crèche *f*; **d. pupil** externe *mf*; **d. release** formation *f* continue en alternance; **d. return** *(train ticket)* aller et retour *m* valable pour la journée; **d. school** externat *m*; **d. shift** *(in factory)* équipe *f* de jour; **d. trip** excursion *f* d'une journée
(**b**) *(era)* **in my d.** de mon temps; **in this d. and age** à notre époque; **this government/TV has had its d.** ce gouvernement/cette télé a fait son temps; **in the days**

of… du temps de…; **these days** de nos jours; **in those days** en ce temps-là; **those were the days!** c'était le bon temps!; **in days to come** à l'avenir
(**c**) *(idioms)* **it's all in a d.'s work** c'est la routine; **to make sb's d.** mettre qn de bonne humeur; *Fam* **let's call it a d.** ça suffit pour aujourd'hui; *Fam* **that'll be the d.!** c'est pas demain la veille!; **to name the d.** *(of wedding)* choisir la date de son mariage; **to carry** *or* **win the d.** l'emporter
daybreak ['deɪbreɪk] *n* lever *m* du jour; **at d.** au lever du jour
daydream ['deɪdriːm] **1** *n* rêverie *f*; *Pej* rêvasserie *f*
2 *vi* rêver (**about** à); *Pej* rêvasser
daylight ['deɪlaɪt] *n* jour *m*, lumière *f*; **it was still d.** il faisait encore jour; *Fig* **it's d. robbery!** c'est du vol pur et simple!; **d. saving time** heure *f* d'été
daytime ['deɪtaɪm] *n* jour *m*, journée *f*; **in the d.** pendant la journée; **d. television** = émissions de télévision diffusées pendant la journée
day-to-day ['deɪtə'deɪ] *adj* courant(e), quotidien(-enne); **on a d. basis** au jour le jour
daze [deɪz] **1** *n* **in a d.** *(from news)* abasourdi(e); *(from drug, blow)* étourdi(e)
2 *vt (of news)* abasourdir; *(of drug, blow)* étourdir
dazed [deɪzd] *adj (by news)* abasourdi(e); *(by drug, blow)* étourdi(e)
dazzle ['dæzəl] *vt also Fig* éblouir
dazzling ['dæzlɪŋ] *adj also Fig* éblouissant(e)
DC [diː'siː] *n* (**a**) *Elec (abbr* direct current) courant *m* continu (**b**) *(abbr* District of Columbia) DC
deacon ['diːkən] *n Rel* diacre *m*
deaconess [diːkə'nes] *n Rel* diaconesse *f*
dead [ded] **1** *adj* (**a**) *(not alive)* mort(e); **a d. man** un mort; **a d. woman** une morte; *Fig* **to be d. to the world** dormir d'un sommeil profond; *Fam* **over my d. body!** moi vivant, jamais!; *Fam* **I wouldn't be seen d. in that dress!** je ne porterais cette robe pour rien au monde!; *Fam* **as d. as a doornail** *or* **a dodo** mort(e) et bien mort(e); *Fig* **d. and buried** mort(e) et enterré(e); *Fam* **if Dad finds out, you're d.** si Papa l'apprend, il va te tuer; **the D. Sea** la mer Morte
(**b**) *(numb) (limb)* engourdi(e); **to go d.** s'engourdir
(**c**) *(voice, eyes)* éteint(e); *(phone)* sans tonalité; *(battery)* mort(e); **this place is d. in winter** cet endroit est mort en hiver; **a d. ball** *(in football)* ballon *m* mort; *also Fig* **d. end** cul-de-sac *m*; *Fig* **d. weight** poids *m* mort; *Fig Pej* **d. wood** personnel *m* inutile
(**d**) *(absolute)* **d. calm** calme *m* plat; **d. heat** *(in race)* arrivée *f* ex aequo; *Fam* **it was a d. loss** ça n'a servi à rien; **he's a d. loss** c'est un bon à rien; *Fam* **to be a d. ringer for sb** être le sosie de qn
2 *adv* (**a**) *(completely)* **to be d. set against sth** être totalement opposé(e) à qch; **to stop d.** s'arrêter net; *Br Fam* **you're d. right** tu as entièrement raison; *Fam* **d. beat** *or* **tired** crevé(e); **d. slow** *(sign)* roulez au pas
(**b**) *Fam (very)* vachement
(**c**) *(exactly)* **d. on six o'clock** à six heures précises; **d. on time** exactement à l'heure
3 *n* **a d. of night** au plus profond de la nuit; **in the d. of winter** au cœur de l'hiver
4 *npl* **the d.** les morts *mpl*; **to rise from the d.** ressusciter d'entre les morts; **the living d.** les morts-vivants *mpl*
deadbeat ['dedbiːt] *n Fam* feignant(e) *m,f*
deaden ['dedən] *vt (blow, sound)* amortir; *(pain)* calmer; **to become deadened to sth** devenir insensible à qch

deadline ['dedlaɪn] *n (day)* date *f* limite; *(time)* heure *f* limite; **to work to a d.** avoir un délai à respecter

deadlock ['dedlɒk] **1** *n* impasse *f*
2 *vt* **to be deadlocked** *(of talks, negotiations)* être au point mort

deadly ['dedlɪ] **1** *adj* (**a**) *(poison, blow, enemy)* mortel(elle); *(weapon)* meurtrier(ère); *(silence)* de mort; **d. nightshade** belladone *f* (**b**) *Fam (boring)* mortel(elle)
2 *adv (very)* **d. accurate** extrêmement précis(e); **d. boring** d'un ennui mortel; **to be d. serious** être on ne peut plus sérieux(euse)

deadpan ['dedpæn] *adj (expression)* figé(e); *(humour)* pince-sans-rire *inv*

deaf [def] **1** *adj* sourd(e); **d. and dumb** sourd-muet (sourde-muette); **to go d.** devenir sourd; **as d. as a post** sourd comme un pot; **to turn a d. ear to sb/ sth** faire la sourde oreille à qn/qch; **the appeal fell on d. ears** l'appel n'a pas été entendu
2 *npl* **the d.** les sourds *mpl*

deaf-aid ['defeɪd] *n* appareil *m* acoustique

deafen ['defən] *vt (make deaf)* rendre sourd(e); *(temporarily)* assourdir

deafening ['defənɪŋ] *adj* assourdissant(e)

deafness ['defnəs] *n* surdité *f*

deal¹ [diːl] *n (wood)* planche *f*

deal² **1** *n* (**a**) *(agreement)* affaire *f*, marché *m*; **to do a d.** conclure un marché; **it's a d.!** marché conclu!; **to get a good/bad d.** faire une bonne/mauvaise affaire; **he's had a raw d.** on ne lui a jamais fait de cadeaux; *Fam Ironic* **big d.!** la belle affaire! **it's no big d.** ce n'est pas bien grave (**b**) *(amount)* **a good** *or* **great d.** beaucoup; **not a great d.** peu; **to have a great d. to do** avoir beaucoup à faire; **a good** *or* **great d. of my time** une grande partie de mon temps; **a good d. quicker/easier** beaucoup plus rapide/facile (**c**) *(in cards)* **whose d. is it?** c'est à qui de donner?; **your d.!** à vous de donner!
2 *vt (pt & pp dealt* [delt]*)* (**a**) *(cards)* donner, distribuer (**b**) **to d. sb/sth a blow** donner un coup à qn/ qch (**c**) *(drugs)* vendre
3 *vi* (**a**) *(in card game)* donner, distribuer (**b**) *(trade)* **to d. in leather** faire le commerce des cuirs

▸**deal out** *vt sep (cards)* distribuer; **to d. out justice** rendre la justice

▸**deal with** *vt insep (subject)* traiter de; *(problem)* s'occuper de; **I know how to d. with him** je sais m'y prendre avec lui

dealbreaker ['diːlbreɪkə(r)] *n Com & Fig* = événement ou décision qui rend impossible toute poursuite des négociations

dealer ['diːlə(r)] *n* (**a**) *(in card game)* donneur(euse) *m,f* (**b**) *Com* marchand(e) *m,f; (in cars)* concessionnaire *m; (in drugs)* dealer *m*, revendeur(euse) *m,f*

dealings ['diːlɪŋz] *npl* rapports *mpl*, relations *fpl;* **to have d. with sb** traiter avec qn

dealt [delt] *pt & pp of* deal²

dean [diːn] *n Rel & Univ* doyen *m*

dear [dɪə(r)] **1** *n* **my d.** *(to man)* chéri; *(to woman)* chérie; **poor d.** mon pauvre/ma pauvre; **be a d. and...** sois un amour et...; *Fam* **an old d.** une grand-mère
2 *adj* (**a**) *(loved)* cher (chère); **to hold sb/sth d.** tenir à qn/qch; **a d. friend** un bon ami/une bonne amie; **a place d. to the hearts of...** un endroit cher à...; *Fam* **to hang on for d. life** s'accrocher désespérément (**b**) *(in letter)* **D. Sir** Monsieur; **D. Madam** Madame; **D. Sir or Madam, D. Sir/Madam** Monsieur, Madame; **D. Mr**

Thomas Cher M. Thomas; **D. Andrew** Cher Andrew; **My dearest Gertrude** Ma chère Gertrude (**c**) *(expensive)* cher (chère)
3 *adv (buy, sell)* cher; *Fig* **it cost me d.** ça m'a coûté cher
4 *exclam* **oh d.!** mon Dieu!

dearly ['dɪəlɪ] *adv (very much)* **to love sb d.** aimer qn de tout son cœur; **I would d. love to know** j'aimerais vraiment savoir; *Fig* **she paid d. for her mistake** elle a payé très cher son erreur

dearth [dɜːθ] *n* pénurie *f* (**of** de)

death [deθ] *n* (**a**) *(end of life)* mort *f;* **to put sb to d.** mettre qn à mort, exécuter qn; **a fight to the d.** une lutte à mort; **d. camp** camp *m* de la mort; **d. certificate** acte *m* de décès; **d. mask** masque *m* mortuaire; **d. penalty** peine *f* de mort; **d. rate** taux *m* de mortalité; *Am* **d. row** quartier *m* des condamnés à mort; **d. sentence** condamnation *f* à mort; **d. squad** escadron *m* de la mort; **d. throes** agonie *f;* **d. toll** nombre *m* de morts; **D. Valley** la Vallée de la Mort; **d. warrant** ordre *m* d'exécution (**b**) *(idioms)* **to look like d. (warmed up)** avoir l'air d'un(e) déterré(e); **to be sick to d. of** sth en avoir marre de qch; **to be scared to d.** être mort(e) de peur; **those children will be the d. of me!** ces enfants finiront par me tuer!; **you'll catch your d. (of cold)!** tu vas attraper la crève!; **to be at d.'s door** être à l'article de la mort; **to sound the d. knell for sth** sonner le glas de qch

deathbed ['deθbed] *n* lit *m* de mort

deathly ['deθlɪ] *adj (pallor)* mortel(elle); *(silence)* de mort

deathtrap ['deθtræp] *n* **this house/car is a d.** cette maison/voiture est très dangereuse

deathwatch beetle ['deθwɒtʃ'biːtəl] *n* vrillette *f*

debacle [deɪ'bɑːkəl] *n* débâcle *f*

debar [diː'bɑː(r)] *(pt & pp debarred) vt (from club)* exclure; **to d. sb from doing sth** interdire à qn de faire qch

debase [dɪ'beɪs] *vt (person)* rabaisser; *(reputation)* ternir; *(currency)* déprécier; **to d. oneself** se déprécier

debasement [dɪ'beɪsmənt] *n (of person)* rabaissement *m; (of currency)* dépréciation *f*

debatable [dɪ'beɪtəbəl] *adj* discutable

debate [dɪ'beɪt] **1** *n* discussion *f; (organized)* débat *m;* **after much d.** après bien des discussions
2 *vt (issue)* débattre de, discuter de; **he debated whether to do it** il se demandait s'il le ferait ou non
3 *vi* participer à des débats

debating society [dɪ'beɪtɪŋsəsaɪətɪ] *n* = société qui organise des débats

debauched [dɪ'bɔːtʃt] *adj* débauché(e)

debauchery [dɪ'bɔːtʃərɪ] *n* débauche *f*

debilitate [dɪ'bɪlɪteɪt] *vt* débiliter

debilitating [dɪ'bɪlɪteɪtɪŋ] *adj* débilitant(e)

debility [dɪ'bɪlɪtɪ] *n* débilité *f*

debit ['debɪt] *Fin* **1** *n* (**a**) *(on account)* débit *m; Fig* **on the d. side,...** l'inconvénient, c'est que...; **d. card** = carte de paiement à débit immédiat, ≃ carte *f* Bleue®
2 *vt (person, account)* débiter (**with** de)

debonair [debə'neə(r)] *adj* élégant(e) et raffiné(e)

debrief [diː'briːf] *vt* faire faire un compte rendu de fin de mission à

debriefing [diː'briːfɪŋ] *n* compte *m* rendu de fin de mission

debris ['debriː] *n (of building)* décombres *mpl; (of plane, car)* débris *mpl*

debt [det] *n* dette *f*; **to be in d.** avoir des dettes; *Fig* **I shall always be in your d.** je vous serai toujours redevable; **to owe sb a d.** of gratitude être redevable à qn; **d. collector** agent *m* de recouvrement
debtor ['detə(r)] *n* débiteur(trice) *m,f*
debug [di:'bʌg] (*pt & pp* **debugged**) *vt Comput (program)* déboguer
debunk [di:'bʌŋk] *vt Fam (theory)* discréditer; *(myth)* détruire
debut ['deɪbju:] *n* début *m*; **to make one's d.** faire ses débuts
Dec (*abbr* **December**) décembre
decade ['dekeɪd] *n* décennie *f*
decadence ['dekədəns] *n* décadence *f*
decadent ['dekədənt] *adj* décadent(e)
decaf ['di:kæf] *n Fam (coffee)* déca *m*
decaffeinated [di:'kæfɪneɪtɪd] *adj* décaféiné(e)
decant [dɪ'kænt] *vt* décanter
decanter [dɪ'kæntə(r)] *n* carafe *f*
decapitate [dɪ'kæpɪteɪt] *vt* décapiter
decathlon [dɪ'kæθlɒn] *n* décathlon *m*
decay [dɪ'keɪ] **1** *n* (**a**) *(of wood)* pourriture *f*; *(of teeth)* carie *f* (**b**) *(of civilization)* déclin *m*; *(of building)* délabrement *m*
  2 *vi* (**a**) *(of wood)* pourrir; *(of teeth)* se carier (**b**) *(of civilization)* péricliter; *(of building)* se délabrer
decayed [dɪ'keɪd] *adj (food)* pourri(e); *(tooth)* carié(e); *(corpse)* décomposé(e)
decease [dɪ'si:s] *n Formal* décès *m*
deceased [dɪ'si:st] *Formal* **1** *n* **the d.** le défunt (la défunte)
  2 *adj* décédé(e)
deceit [dɪ'si:t] *n* tromperie *f*, supercherie *f*
deceitful [dɪ'si:tfʊl] *adj (person)* fourbe; *(behaviour)* malhonnête
deceive [dɪ'si:v] *vt* tromper, abuser; **to be deceived by appearances** se laisser abuser par les apparences; **to d. oneself** se mentir à soi-même; **to d. sb into doing sth** faire faire qch à qn en le manipulant; **I thought my eyes were deceiving me** je n'en croyais pas mes yeux
decelerate [di:'seləreɪt] *vi* ralentir
December [dɪ'sembə(r)] *n* décembre *m*; *see also* **May**
decency ['di:sənsɪ] *n (respectability)* décence *f*; **to have the common d. to do sth** avoir la décence de faire qch; **he didn't even have the d. to tell us first** il n'a même pas eu la politesse de nous avertir avant
decent ['di:sənt] *adj* (**a**) *(respectable)* respectable; *Fam* **are you d.?** es-tu visible? (**b**) *(of acceptable quality, size)* convenable, correct(e) (**c**) *(kind)* gentil(ille)
decently ['di:səntlɪ] *adv* (**a**) *(respectably)* convenablement; **to dress d.** s'habiller décemment (**b**) *(to an acceptable degree)* convenablement, correctement (**c**) *(kindly)* gentiment
decentralization [di:sentrəlaɪ'zeɪʃən] *n* décentralisation *f*
decentralize [di:'sentrəlaɪz] *vt* décentraliser
deception [dɪ'sepʃən] *n* tromperie *f*, supercherie *f*
deceptive [dɪ'septɪv] *adj* trompeur(euse)
deceptively [dɪ'septɪvlɪ] *adv* **it looks d. easy** c'est moins facile que ça en a l'air; **she looks d. shy** c'est une fausse timide
decibel ['desɪbel] *n* décibel *m*
decide [dɪ'saɪd] **1** *vt (outcome, match, future)* décider de; **to d. to do sth** décider de faire qch; **it was decided to wait for her reply** il fut décidé d'attendre sa réponse; **that was what decided me** c'est ce qui

m'a décidé; **that decides the matter** ça règle la question
  2 *vi* décider; **to d. on sth** choisir qch; **to d. against doing sth** décider de ne pas faire qch; **they decided against going out** ils décidèrent de ne pas sortir; **to d. in favour of doing sth** décider de faire qch
decided [dɪ'saɪdɪd] *adj* (**a**) *(person)* décidé(e); *(opinion)* ferme (**b**) *(difference, preference, improvement)* net (nette)
decidedly [dɪ'saɪdɪdlɪ] *adv* (**a**) *(answer, say)* d'un ton résolu (**b**) *(very)* franchement; **he was d. unhelpful** il n'a pas été serviable du tout
decider [dɪ'saɪdə(r)] *n (goal)* but *m* décisif; *(match)* match *m* décisif
deciding [dɪ'saɪdɪŋ] *adj* décisif(ive)
deciduous [dɪ'sɪdjʊəs] *adj* à feuilles caduques
decimal ['desɪməl] **1** *n* décimale *f*
  2 *adj* décimal(e); **d. point** virgule *f*; **correct to five d. places** exact(e) jusqu'à la cinquième décimale
decimalization [desɪməlaɪ'zeɪʃən] *n* décimalisation *f*
decimate ['desɪmeɪt] *vt* décimer
decipher [dɪ'saɪfə(r)] *vt* déchiffrer
decision [dɪ'sɪʒən] *n* (**a**) *(of question)* décision *f* (**b**) *(resolve)* fermeté *f*, résolution *f*
decision-making [dɪ'sɪʒənmeɪkɪŋ] *n* prise *f* de décision
decisive [dɪ'saɪsɪv] *adj* (**a**) *(person, manner)* résolu(e) (**b**) *(action, event)* décisif(ive)
deck [dek] **1** *n* (**a**) *(of ship)* pont *m*; *(of bus)* niveau *m*, étage *m*; **on d.** sur le pont; **d. chair** transat *m* (**b**) **d. (of cards)** jeu *m* (de cartes) (**c**) **decks** *(for DJ)* platines *fpl*
  2 *vt* **to d. oneself out in one's Sunday best** se mettre sur son trente et un
decking ['dekɪŋ] *n* plancher *m*
declaim [dɪ'kleɪm] *vt & vi* déclamer
declamatory [dɪ'klæmətərɪ] *adj* déclamatoire
declaration [deklə'reɪʃən] *n* déclaration *f*; **the D. of Independence** la Déclaration d'indépendance
declare [dɪ'kleə(r)] **1** *vt* déclarer; **to d. war (on)** déclarer la guerre (à); **have you anything to d.?** *(at customs)* avez-vous quelque chose à déclarer?
  2 *vi* **to d. for/against sth** se déclarer en faveur de/contre qch; *Old-fashioned* **I do d.!** ça alors!
declassify [di:'klæsɪfaɪ] (*pt & pp* **declassified**) *vt (document)* ne plus considérer comme confidentiel
declension [dɪ'klenʃən] *n Gram* déclinaison *f*
decline [dɪ'klaɪn] **1** *n* déclin *m*; **to go into d.** *(of person, company, industry)* dépérir; *(of economy)* perdre de sa vigueur; *(of health)* se détériorer; **to be on the d.** *(of inflation, crime)* être en baisse
  2 *vt* (**a**) *(offer, invitation)* décliner; **to d. to do sth** refuser de faire qch (**b**) *Gram* décliner
  3 *vi* (**a**) *(refuse)* refuser (**b**) *(of health, influence)* décliner, baisser; **to d. in importance** perdre de son importance
declining [dɪ'klaɪnɪŋ] *adj (decreasing)* en baisse; *(deteriorating)* déclinant(e)
decode [di:'kəʊd] *vt* décoder
decoder [di:'kəʊdə(r)] *n* décodeur *m*
decompose [di:kəm'pəʊz] *vi* se décomposer
decomposition [di:kɒmpə'zɪʃən] *n* décomposition *f*
decompression [di:kəm'preʃən] *n* décompression *f*; **d. chamber** chambre *f* de décompression; **d. sickness** maladie *f* des caissons
decongestant [di:kən'dʒestənt] *n Med* décongestionnant *m*
decontaminate [di:kən'tæmɪneɪt] *vt* décontaminer

decor ['deɪkɔː(r)] *n* décor *m*
decorate ['dekəreɪt] *vt* (**a**) *(with decorations)* décorer (**with de**) (**b**) *(with paint)* peindre; *(with wallpaper)* tapisser (**c**) *(with medal)* décorer
decoration [dekə'reɪʃən] *n* (**a**) *(of room, cake)* décoration *f* (**b**) *(medal)* décoration *f*, médaille *f*
decorative ['dekərətɪv] *adj* décoratif(ive)
decorator ['dekəreɪtə(r)] *n* (**painter and**) **d.** (peintre *m*) décorateur *m*
decorous ['dekərəs] *adj Formal* bienséant(e)
decorum [dɪ'kɔːrəm] *n* convenances *fpl*, décorum *m*
decoy 1 *n* ['diːkɔɪ] *also Fig* leurre *m*
2 *vt* [dɪ'kɔɪ] leurrer
decrease 1 *n* ['diːkriːs] diminution *f*, baisse *f* (**in de**); **to be on the d.** être en diminution
2 *vt* [dɪ'kriːs] réduire, baisser
3 *vi* [dɪ'kriːs] diminuer, baisser
decreasing [dɪ'kriːsɪŋ] *adj* décroissant(e), en baisse
decree [dɪ'kriː] **1** *n* décret *m*; *Law* **d. absolute** jugement *m* irrévocable; **d. nisi** jugement *m* provisoire
2 *vt* décréter
decrepit [dɪ'krepɪt] *adj (person)* décrépit(e); *(thing)* délabré(e)
decriminalize [diː'krɪmɪnəlaɪz] *vt* dépénaliser
decry [dɪ'kraɪ] *(pt & pp* **decried**) *vt* décrier
dedicate ['dedɪkeɪt] *vt (book, song)* dédier (**to** à); **to d. oneself to sth** se consacrer à qch; **she dedicated her life to helping the poor** elle a consacré sa vie aux pauvres
dedicated ['dedɪkeɪtɪd] *adj* (**a**) *(committed)* dévoué(e); **to be d. to sth** se consacrer à qch; **she is d. to helping the poor** elle se consacre aux pauvres; **he is d. to his family** il est entièrement dévoué à sa famille (**b**) *Comput* spécialisé(e); **d. word processor** machine *f* servant uniquement au traitement de texte
dedication [dedɪ'keɪʃən] *n* (**a**) *(of book, song)* dédicace *f* (**b**) *(devotion)* dévouement *m*
deduce [dɪ'djuːs] *vt* déduire (**from** de)
deduct [dɪ'dʌkt] *vt* déduire (**from** de)
deductible [dɪ'dʌktəbəl] *adj* déductible; *Fin* **d. for tax purposes** déductible des impôts
deduction [dɪ'dʌkʃən] *n* (**a**) *(subtraction)* déduction *f*; **after deductions** une fois les prélèvements effectués (**b**) *(conclusion)* déduction *f*; **by a process of d.** par déduction
deed [diːd] *n* (**a**) *(action)* acte *m*, action *f*; **to do one's good d. for the day** faire sa bonne action de la journée (**b**) *Law (document)* acte *m* notarié; **d. of covenant** = document par lequel on s'engage à verser régulièrement une somme à un organisme; **to change one's name by d. poll** changer légalement son nom
deem [diːm] *vt Formal* juger, estimer
deep [diːp] **1** *n Lit* **the d.** l'océan *m*
2 *adj* (**a**) *(water, sleep, thinker, cut)* profond(e); **to be 10 metres d.** faire 10 mètres de profondeur; **two/four d.** sur deux/quatre rangs; *Fig* **to be in d. water** être dans le pétrin; **d. in debt** criblé(e) de dettes; **d. in thought** plongé(e) dans ses pensées; **d. end** *(of swimming pool)* côté *m* le plus profond; *Fig* **to go off the d. end (at sb)** s'emporter (contre qn); *Fig* **to be thrown in at the d. end** être mis(e) dans le bain; **the D. South** *(of United States)* le Sud profond (**b**) *(colour)* foncé(e), sombre; *(sound)* grave
3 *adv* profondément; **to walk d. into the forest** pénétrer profondément dans la forêt; **to look d. into**

sb's **eyes** pénétrer qn du regard; **to work d. into the night** travailler tard dans la nuit; **d. down he's very kind** au fond il est très gentil; **to run d.** *(of emotions, prejudice, mistrust)* être profond(e)
deepen ['diːpən] **1** *vt (well, ditch)* approfondir; *(sorrow, interest)* augmenter; **to d. sb's understanding of sth** permettre à qn de mieux comprendre qch
2 *vi* (**a**) *(of river, silence)* devenir plus profond(e); *(of conviction, belief)* augmenter; *(of mystery)* s'épaissir (**b**) *(of sound, voice)* devenir plus grave
deep-freeze ['diːp'friːz] *n* congélateur *m*
deep-fry ['diːp'fraɪ] *vt* faire cuire dans la friture
deep-fryer ['diːp'fraɪə(r)] *n* friteuse *f*
deep-rooted [diːp'ruːtɪd] *adj* profondément enraciné(e)
deep-sea ['diːp'siː] *adj* **d. diver** plongeur *m* sous-marin; **d. fishing** pêche *f* hauturière
deep-seated ['diːp'siːtɪd] *adj (dislike)* profond(e); *(belief, prejudice)* profondément enraciné(e)
deer ['dɪə(r)] *(pl* **deer**) *n (male)* daim *m*; *(female)* biche *f*
deerstalker ['dɪəstɔːkə(r)] *n (hat)* chapeau *m* de chasse *(à la Sherlock Holmes)*
deface [dɪ'feɪs] *vt (monument, statue)* dégrader; *(poster, wall)* barbouiller
de facto [deɪ'fæktəʊ] *adj & adv* de facto
defamation [defə'meɪʃən] *n* diffamation *f*
defamatory [dɪ'fæmətərɪ] *adj* diffamatoire
defame [dɪ'feɪm] *vt* diffamer
default [dɪ'fɔːlt] **1** *n* (**a**) *Law (failure to appear in court)* défaut *m*; *Fig* **by d.** par défaut (**b**) *Comput* **d. drive** lecteur *m* par défaut; **d. font** police *f* par défaut
2 *vi Law* (**a**) *(fail to appear in court)* ne pas comparaître (**b**) *(fail to pay)* **to d. on alimony payments** manquer au versement de la pension alimentaire
defaulter [dɪ'fɔːltə(r)] *n Law* contumace *mf*; *(debtor)* débiteur(trice) *m*,*f* défaillant(e)
defeat [dɪ'fiːt] **1** *n* défaite *f*
2 *vt (army, opponent)* vaincre; *(government)* mettre en minorité; **that defeats the object** *or* **purpose** ça va à l'encontre du but recherché
defeatism [dɪ'fiːtɪzəm] *n* défaitisme *m*
defeatist [dɪ'fiːtɪst] **1** *n* défaitiste *mf*
2 *adj* défaitiste
defecate ['defəkeɪt] *vi* déféquer
defect 1 *n* ['diːfekt] défaut *m*
2 *vi* [dɪ'fekt] **to d. to the enemy** passer à l'ennemi
defection [dɪ'fekʃən] *n* défection *f*
defective [dɪ'fektɪv] *adj (machine, reasoning)* défectueux(euse); *(hearing)* déficient(e)
defector [dɪ'fektə(r)] *n* transfuge *mf*
defence, *Am* **defense** [dɪ'fens] *n* défense *f*; **to come to sb's d.** venir à l'aide de qn; **she said in her d. that...** elle a dit à sa décharge que...; *Law* **d. counsel** avocat *m* de la défense; **d. mechanism** *(psychological)* mécanisme *m* de défense; *Law* **witness for the d.** témoin *m* à décharge
defenceless, *Am* **defenseless** [dɪ'fensləs] *adj* sans défense
defend [dɪ'fend] **1** *vt* défendre (**from** *or* **against** contre)
2 *vi (in sport)* défendre
defendant [dɪ'fendənt] *n Law* défendeur(eresse) *m*,*f*
defender [dɪ'fendə(r)] *n* défenseur *m*
defending [dɪ'fendɪŋ] *adj* **d. champion** champion(onne) *m*,*f* en titre
defense, defenseless *Am* = **defence, defenceless**
defensible [dɪ'fensəbəl] *adj* défendable

defensive [dɪ'fensɪv] **1** *n* on the d. sur la défensive **2** *adj* défensif(ive); **to be/get d.** être/se mettre sur la défensive
defer [dɪ'fɜː(r)] (*pt & pp* **deferred**) **1** *vt (postpone)* différer, remettre **2** *vi* **to d. to s.o** s'en remettre à
deference ['defərəns] *n* déférence *f*; **out of** *or* **in d.** to par déférence pour
deferential [defə'renʃəl] *adj (person)* déférent(e); *(air, tone)* de déférence, respectueux(euse)
deferment [dɪ'fɜːmənt] *n* ajournement *m*, report *m*
defiance [dɪ'faɪəns] *n* défi *m*; **in d. of** au mépris de
defiant [dɪ'faɪənt] *adj (gesture, look)* de défi; *(person)* provocant(e)
deficiency [dɪ'fɪʃənsɪ] (*pl* **deficiencies**) *n* (**a**) *(lack) (of resources)* manque *m*; *(of vitamins, minerals)* carence *f* (**b**) *(flaw)* défaut *m*
deficient [dɪ'fɪʃənt] *adj* insuffisant(e); **to be d. in** manquer de
deficit ['defɪsɪt] *n Fin* déficit *m*
defile [dɪ'faɪl] *vt (memory)* salir; *(sacred place, tomb)* profaner
definable [dɪ'faɪnəbəl] *adj* définissable
define [dɪ'faɪn] *vt* définir
definite ['defɪnɪt] *adj* (**a**) *(precise)* précis(e); *(decision)* définitif(ive) (**b**) *(noticeable)* net (nette) (**c**) *(certain)* certain(e); *(insistent)* catégorique; **I can't be d.** je n'en suis pas sûr (**d**) *Gram* **d. article** article *m* défini
definitely ['defɪnɪtlɪ] *adv* (**a**) *(certainly)* sans aucun doute; **I'll d. be there** c'est sûr que j'y serai; **are you going? – d.!** est-ce que vous y allez? – absolument!; **d. not!** certainement pas! **he told me very d. that he didn't want to go** il m'a dit très clairement qu'il ne voulait pas y aller (**b**) *(noticeably)* nettement
definition [defɪ'nɪʃən] *n* (**a**) *(of word)* définition *f*; **by d.** par définition (**b**) *(of image)* définition *f*; *(of binoculars)* netteté *f*
definitive [dɪ'fɪnɪtɪv] *adj (book)* qui fait autorité; *(version)* définitif(ive); **she was the d. Juliet** elle était la Juliette idéale
deflate [diː'fleɪt] **1** *vt* (**a**) *(ball, tyre)* dégonfler (**b**) *Econ* **to d. the economy** pratiquer une politique déflationniste (**c**) *(person)* démonter **2** *vi (of tyre)* se dégonfler
deflated [diː'fleɪtɪd] *adj (person)* déprimé(e)
deflation [diː'fleɪʃən] *n Econ* déflation *f*
deflationary [diː'fleɪʃənərɪ] *adj Econ* déflationniste
deflect [dɪ'flekt] **1** *vt (ball, bullet)* (faire) dévier; *(sound)* renvoyer; *(criticism)* détourner; *Fig (person)* détourner (**from** de) **2** *vi (of ball, bullet)* dévier
deflection [dɪ'flekʃən] *n (of ball, bullet)* déviation *f*
deforestation [diːfɒrɪs'teɪʃən] *n* déboisement *m*
deform [dɪ'fɔːm] *vt* déformer
deformation [diːfɔː'meɪʃən] *n* déformation *f*
deformity [dɪ'fɔːmɪtɪ] (*pl* **deformities**) *n* difformité *f*
defraud [dɪ'frɔːd] *vt (tax office)* frauder; *(employer)* escroquer; **to d. sb of sth** escroquer qch à qn
defray [dɪ'freɪ] *vt Formal* **to d. sb's expenses** défrayer qn; **to d. the cost of sth** rembourser les frais de qch
defrost [diː'frɒst] *vt (fridge)* dégivrer; *(food)* décongeler **2** *vi (of fridge)* se dégivrer; *(of food)* se décongeler
deft [deft] *adj* adroit(e), habile
defunct [dɪ'fʌŋkt] *adj (person)* défunt(e); *(organization)* dissous(oute); *(law)* abandonné(e)
defuse [diː'fjuːz] *vt also Fig* désamorcer

defy [dɪ'faɪ] (*pt & pp* **defied**) *vt (authority, law)* braver; *(logic, analysis)* défier; **to d. description** défier toute description; **to d. sb to do sth** mettre qn au défi de faire qch
degenerate 1 *n* [dɪ'dʒenərət] dégénéré(e) *m,f* **2** *adj* [dɪ'dʒenərət] dégénéré(e) **3** *vi* [dɪ'dʒenəreɪt] dégénérer (**into** en)
degeneration [dɪdʒenə'reɪʃən] *n* dégénérescence *f*
degradation [degrə'deɪʃən] *n* avilissement *m*; *(squalor)* misère *f*
degrade [dɪ'greɪd] *vt* avilir; **I won't d. myself by answering that** je ne m'abaisserai pas à répondre à cela
degrading [dɪ'greɪdɪŋ] *adj* avilissant(e), dégradant(e)
degree [dɪ'griː] *n* (**a**) *(extent)* degré *m*, point *m*; **to a d., to some d.** jusqu'à un certain point; **to such a d. that...** à (un) tel point que...; **by degrees** petit à petit; **a d. of risk** un certain risque; **a d. of truth** une part de vérité; (**b**) *(of temperature, in geometry)* degré *m*; **it's 25 degrees** *(temperature)* il fait 25 degrés (**c**) *(at university)* diplôme *m* universitaire; *(bachelor's)* ≃ licence *f*; *(master's)* ≃ maîtrise *f*; *(PhD)* doctorat *m*; **to take** *or* **do a d.** préparer un diplôme
dehumanize [diː'hjuːmənaɪz] *vt* déshumaniser
dehumidifier [diːhjuː'mɪdɪfaɪə(r)] *n* déshumidificateur *m*
dehydrated [diːhaɪ'dreɪtɪd] *adj* déshydraté(e); **to get d.** se déshydrater
dehydration [diːhaɪ'dreɪʃən] *n* déshydratation *f*
de-icer [diː'aɪsə(r)] *n* dégivreur *m*
deify ['diːɪfaɪ] (*pt & pp* **deified**) *vt* déifier
deign [deɪn] *vt* **to d. to do sth** condescendre à *ou* daigner faire qch
deindustrialization [diːɪndʌstrɪəlaɪ'zeɪʃən] *n* désindustrialisation *f*
deity ['diːɪtɪ] (*pl* **deities**) *n* divinité *f*, dieu (déesse) *m,f*
dejected [dɪ'dʒektɪd] *adj* abattu(e), découragé(e)
dejection [dɪ'dʒekʃən] *n* abattement *m*, découragement *m*
delay [dɪ'leɪ] **1** *n* retard *m*; **without d.** sans délai; **an hour's d.** une heure de retard; **all flights are subject to d.** tous les vols risquent d'avoir du retard **2** *vt* (**a**) *(hold up) (project, decision, act)* retarder; *(traffic)* ralentir; **to be delayed** *(of train, plane)* avoir du retard; **delaying tactics** manœuvres *fpl* dilatoires (**b**) *(put off) (decision, publication)* différer; **we can't d. telling her any longer** on ne peut plus attendre davantage, nous devons le lui dire **3** *vi* tarder; **don't d.!** faites vite!
delayed-action [dɪleɪd'ækʃən] *adj (drug, fuse, shutter)* à retardement
delectable [dɪ'lektəbəl] *adj* délicieux(euse)
delegate 1 *n* ['delɪgət] délégué(e) *m,f* **2** *vt* ['delɪgeɪt] *(power, responsibility)* déléguer (**to** à); **to d. sb to do sth** déléguer qn pour faire qch **3** *vi* ['delɪgeɪt] déléguer
delegation [delɪ'geɪʃən] *n* délégation *f*
delete [dɪ'liːt] *vt* supprimer; **d. where inapplicable** rayer les mentions inutiles
deleterious [delɪ'tɪərɪəs] *adj Formal* délétère
deletion [dɪ'liːʃən] *n* suppression *f*
deli ['delɪ] *n Fam (shop)* épicerie *f* fine; *(café)* restaurant-traiteur *m*
deliberate 1 *adj* [dɪ'lɪbərət] (**a**) *(intentional)* délibéré(e); **it wasn't d.** ça n'était pas voulu (**b**) *(unhurried) (movement)* mesuré(e); *(person)* méticuleux(euse) **2** *vi* [dɪ'lɪbəreɪt] *(think)* réfléchir (**on** sur); *(discuss)* délibérer (**on** sur)

deliberately [dɪˈlɪbərətlɪ] adv (**a**) (intentionally) délibérément; **she did it d.** elle l'a fait exprès (**b**) (unhurriedly) de façon mesurée

deliberation [dɪlɪbəˈreɪʃən] n (**a**) (thought) réflexion f; (discussion) délibération f, débat m (**b**) (unhurriedness) mesure f; **with d.** posément

delicacy [ˈdelɪkəsɪ] (pl **delicacies**) n (**a**) (quality) délicatesse f (**b**) (food) mets m délicat

delicate [ˈdelɪkət] adj délicat(e)

delicately [ˈdelɪkətlɪ] adv (**a**) (finely) délicatement (**b**) (tactfully) avec délicatesse

delicatessen [delɪkəˈtesən] n (shop) épicerie f fine; (café) restaurant-traiteur m

delicious [dɪˈlɪʃəs] adj délicieux(euse)

delight [dɪˈlaɪt] **1** n plaisir m, joie f; **to my/her d.** à mon/son grand plaisir; **to take d. in sth** se réjouir de qch; **the car is a d. to drive** conduire cette voiture est un plaisir; **the delights of camping** les joies du camping; **the delights of Blackpool** les charmes de Blackpool
2 vt ravir, réjouir
3 vi **to d. in doing sth** prendre plaisir à faire qch; Hum **he delights in the name of Fergus Fotherington** il répond au joli nom de Fergus Fotherington

delighted [dɪˈlaɪtɪd] adj ravi(e), enchanté(e) (**with** de)

delightful [dɪˈlaɪtfʊl] adj (person, smile) charmant(e); (meal, evening) délicieux(euse)

delightfully [dɪˈlaɪtfʊlɪ] adv (sing, write) merveilleusement

delimit [diːˈlɪmɪt] vt délimiter

delineate [dɪˈlɪnɪeɪt] vt (plan, proposal) définir

delinquency [dɪˈlɪŋkwənsɪ] n délinquance f

delinquent [dɪˈlɪŋkwənt] **1** n délinquant(e) m,f
2 adj délinquant(e)

delirious [dɪˈlɪrɪəs] adj also Fig délirant(e); **to be d.** délirer

deliriously [dɪˈlɪrɪəslɪ] adv follement; **d. happy** fou (folle) de joie

delirium [dɪˈlɪrɪəm] n also Fig délire m; Med **d. tremens** delirium tremens m

deliver [dɪˈlɪvə(r)] **1** vt (**a**) (letter, parcel) remettre, distribuer (**to** à); (water, electricity, gas) distribuer; (goods) livrer; **to have sth delivered** faire livrer qch; Fig **to d. the goods** tenir ses engagements (**b**) (blow) donner; Sport (pass) faire; (speech, verdict) prononcer; (ultimatum) poser; **to d. a service** proposer un service (**c**) (baby) mettre au monde
2 vi livrer; Fig (keep one's promise) tenir ses engagements; Com **we d.** nous livrons à domicile; Fig **he just doesn't d.** il n'est pas à la hauteur

deliverance [dɪˈlɪvərəns] n Formal délivrance f (**from** de)

delivery [dɪˈlɪvərɪ] (pl **deliveries**) n (**a**) (of letter, parcel) distribution f, remise f; (of goods) livraison f; **to take d. of sth** prendre livraison de qch; **d. date** date f de livraison; **d. man** livreur m; **d. van** camion m de livraison (**b**) (way of speaking) diction f (**c**) (of baby) accouchement m

delta [ˈdeltə] n (of river, Greek letter) delta m inv; **d. wing** (of plane) aile f delta

delude [dɪˈluːd] vt tromper; **to d. oneself** se faire des illusions

deluge [ˈdeljuːdʒ] **1** n also Fig déluge m
2 vt inonder (**with** de)

delusion [dɪˈluːʒən] n illusion f; **to be under a d.** se faire des illusions; **delusions of grandeur** mégalomanie f

de luxe [dɪˈlʌks] adj de luxe, haut de gamme inv

delve [delv] vi also Fig **to d. into** fouiller dans

demagogue [ˈdeməgɒg] n démagogue mf

demand [dɪˈmɑːnd] **1** n (**a**) (request) demande f, exigence f; **to make demands on sb** exiger beaucoup de qn (**b**) (for goods) demande f (**for** de); **to be in d.** être demandé(e) ou recherché(e)
2 vt exiger, réclamer

demanding [dɪˈmɑːndɪŋ] adj (person) exigeant(e); (job) astreignant(e)

demarcation [diːmɑːˈkeɪʃən] n démarcation f; Ind **d. dispute** conflit m d'attributions; **d. line** ligne f de démarcation

demean [dɪˈmiːn] vt humilier; **to d. oneself** s'abaisser

demeanour, Am **demeanor** [dɪˈmiːnə(r)] n comportement m

demented [dɪˈmentɪd] adj fou (folle)

dementia [dɪˈmenʃɪə] n démence f

demerara sugar [deməˈreərəˈʃʊgə(r)] n cassonade f

demigod [ˈdemɪgɒd] n demi-dieu m

demilitarize [diːˈmɪlɪtəraɪz] vt démilitariser

demise [dɪˈmaɪz] n also Fig disparition f

demister [diːˈmɪstə(r)] n BrAut dispositif m antibuée

demo [ˈdeməʊ] (pl **demos**) n Fam (**a**) (protest) manif f (**b**) **d. (tape)** maquette f

demob [diːˈmɒb] (pt & pp **demobbed**) vt Br Fam démobiliser

demobilize [diːˈməʊbɪlaɪz] vt démobiliser

democracy [dɪˈmɒkrəsɪ] (pl **democracies**) n démocratie f

Democrat [ˈdeməkræt] n (US politician) démocrate mf

democrat [ˈdeməkræt] n démocrate mf

democratic [deməˈkrætɪk] adj démocratique

democratically [deməˈkrætɪklɪ] adv démocratiquement

demographic [deməˈgræfɪk] adj démographique

demolish [dɪˈmɒlɪʃ] vt (building, theory) démolir; Fam (eat) engloutir; (in game) écraser

demolition [deməˈlɪʃən] n démolition f

demon [ˈdiːmən] n démon m; Fam **he's a d. tennis player** c'est un as du tennis

demonic [dɪˈmɒnɪk] adj démoniaque

demonstrable [dɪˈmɒnstrəbəl] adj démontrable

demonstrate [ˈdemənstreɪt] **1** vt (fact, theory) démontrer; **to d. how sth works** montrer comment qch fonctionne
2 vi (protest) manifester (**for/against** pour/contre)

demonstration [demənˈstreɪʃən] n (**a**) (of fact, theory) démonstration f (**b**) (political) manifestation f

demonstrative [dɪˈmɒnstrətɪv] adj also Gram démonstratif(ive)

demonstrator [ˈdemənstreɪtə(r)] n (**a**) (protester) manifestant(e) m,f (**b**) (of machine) démonstrateur(trice) m,f

demoralize [dɪˈmɒrəlaɪz] vt démoraliser

demoralizing [dɪˈmɒrəlaɪzɪŋ] adj démoralisant(e)

demote [dɪˈməʊt] vt rétrograder

demotion [dɪˈməʊʃən] n rétrogradation f

demur [dɪˈmɜː(r)] (pt & pp **demurred**) vi soulever une objection

demure [dɪˈmjʊə(r)] adj réservé(e)

demystify [diːˈmɪstɪfaɪ] (pt & pp **demystified**) vt démystifier

den [den] n (**a**) (of lion, fox, bear) antre m, tanière f; Fig **a d. of iniquity** un lieu de perdition; **a d. of thieves** un repaire de voleurs (**b**) (room) ≃ bureau m

denationalize [diːˈnæʃənəlaɪz] vt dénationaliser

denature [diːˈneɪtʃə(r)] vt dénaturer

denial [dɪˈnaɪəl] n (**a**) (of request) refus m; (of right) atteinte f; **d. of justice** déni m de justice (**b**) (of accusation, rumour, guilt) démenti m (**c**) (psychological) dénégation f; **to be in d.** refuser de se rendre à l'évidence

denigrate [ˈdenɪɡreɪt] vt dénigrer

denim [ˈdenɪm] n (toile f de) jean m, denim m; **denims** (jeans) un jean; **d. skirt/shirt** jupe f/chemise f en jean

Denmark [ˈdenmɑːk] n le Danemark

denomination [dɪnɒmɪˈneɪʃən] n (**a**) (religious) confession f (**b**) Fin valeur f

denominator [dɪˈnɒmɪneɪtə(r)] n Math dénominateur m

denote [dɪˈnəʊt] vt indiquer

dénouement [deɪˈnuːmɒŋ] n dénouement m

denounce [dɪˈnaʊns] vt dénoncer

dense [dens] adj (**a**) (smoke, fog, jungle, crowd) dense (**b**) Fam (stupid) bouché(e)

densely [ˈdenslɪ] adv **d. populated** fortement peuplé(e); **d. wooded** très boisé(e)

density [ˈdensɪtɪ] n densité f

dent [dent] **1** n bosse f; Fig **the wedding put a d. in his savings** le mariage a fait un trou dans ses économies **2** vt cabosser; Fig (confidence) entamer

dental [ˈdentəl] adj dentaire; **d. appointment** rendez-vous m chez le dentiste; **d. floss** fil m dentaire; **d. hygiene** hygiène f dentaire; **d. nurse** assistant(e) m,f dentaire; **d. surgeon** chirurgien-dentiste (chirurgienne-dentiste) m,f

dentist [ˈdentɪst] n dentiste mf; **to go to the d.'s** aller chez le dentiste

dentistry [ˈdentɪstrɪ] n dentisterie f

dentures [ˈdentʃəz] npl (set of) d. dentier m

denude [dɪˈnjuːd] vt dénuder; **to be denuded of sth** être dépourvu(e) de qch

denunciation [dɪnʌnsɪˈeɪʃən] n dénonciation f

Denver boot [ˈdenvəbuːt] n Am Aut sabot m de Denver

deny [dɪˈnaɪ] (pt & pp denied) vt (**a**) (request) refuser; **to d. sb his rights** priver qn de ses droits; **to d. oneself sth** se priver de qch (**b**) (fact) nier; (rumour) démentir; **to d. responsibility** nier avoir été responsable de qch; **to d. doing sth** nier avoir fait qch; **there's no denying that...** il est indéniable que...; **to d. all knowledge of sth** nier avoir connaissance de qch

deodorant [diːˈəʊdərənt] n déodorant m; (for room) désodorisant m

depart [dɪˈpɑːt] vi (leave) partir (**from** de); **to d. from** (tradition, subject, truth) s'écarter de

department [dɪˈpɑːtmənt] n (in company) service m; (in shop) rayon m; Univ département m; (of government) ministère m; Fig **that's my d.** c'est mon rayon; **d. store** grand magasin m

departmental [diːpɑːtˈmentəl] adj (manager) de service; Univ **d. head** chef m de département

departure [dɪˈpɑːtʃə(r)] n (from place) départ m; (from tradition) écart m; (from plan) modification f; Fig **a new d.** un nouveau départ; **d. lounge** (in airport) salle f d'embarquement; **d. time** heure f de départ

depend [dɪˈpend] vi **to d. on** dépendre de; **that depends, it all depends** ça dépend; **to d. on sb** (rely on) compter sur qn; (financially) être à la charge de qn; **you can d. on it** tu peux compter là-dessus; **it depends on how much money I have** cela dépend de l'argent que j'ai; Ironic **you can d. on him to be late** tu peux compter sur lui pour être en retard

dependable [dɪˈpendəbəl] adj (person, machine) fiable; (information) sûr(e)

dependant [dɪˈpendənt] n personne f à charge

dependence [dɪˈpendəns] n (reliance) dépendance f (**on** à)

dependency [dɪˈpendənsɪ] (pl **dependencies**) n dépendance f; **d. culture** = situation d'une société dont les membres ont une mentalité d'assistés

dependent [dɪˈpendənt] adj (child) à charge; **to be d. on** dépendre de; **to be d. on sb** (financially) être à la charge de qn

depict [dɪˈpɪkt] vt (of painting) représenter; (of film, book) décrire

depiction [dɪˈpɪkʃən] n (in painting) représentation f; (in film, book) description f

depilatory [dɪˈpɪlətərɪ] adj dépilatoire

deplete [dɪˈpliːt] vt réduire, diminuer

depleted uranium [dɪˈpliːtɪdjʊˈreɪnjəm] n uranium m appauvri

depletion [dɪˈpliːʃən] n réduction f, diminution f

deplorable [dɪˈplɔːrəbəl] adj déplorable

deplore [dɪˈplɔː(r)] vt déplorer

deploy [dɪˈplɔɪ] vt déployer

deployment [dɪˈplɔɪmənt] n déploiement m

depopulate [diːˈpɒpjʊleɪt] vt dépeupler

depopulation [diːpɒpjʊˈleɪʃən] n dépeuplement m

deport [dɪˈpɔːt] vt (criminal) déporter; (immigrant) expulser

deportation [diːpɔːˈteɪʃən] n (of criminal) déportation f; (of immigrant) expulsion f

deportment [dɪˈpɔːtmənt] n (**a**) (posture) maintien m (**b**) (behaviour) comportement m

depose [dɪˈpəʊz] vt déposer

deposit [dɪˈpɒzɪt] **1** n (**a**) (in bank) dépôt m; Br **d. account** compte m de dépôt (**b**) (returnable) caution f; (first payment) acompte m, arrhes fpl; **to put down a d. on sth** verser un acompte pour qch (**c**) (of minerals) gisement m; (of wine) dépôt m (**d**) Br Pol **to lose one's d.** perdre son cautionnement **2** vt déposer

deposition [diːpəˈzɪʃən] n Law déposition f

depositor [dɪˈpɒzɪtə(r)] n Fin déposant(e) m,f

depot [ˈdepəʊ] n Mil & Com dépôt m; Am (bus station) gare f routière

depravation [deprəˈveɪʃən] n dépravation f

depraved [dɪˈpreɪvd] adj dépravé(e)

depravity [dɪˈprævɪtɪ] n dépravation f

deprecate [ˈdeprɪkeɪt] vt dévaloriser

deprecating [ˈdeprɪkeɪtɪŋ], **deprecatory** [ˈdeprɪkeɪtərɪ] adj désapprobateur(trice); **to be d. about sb/sth** dévaloriser qn/qch

depreciate [dɪˈpriːʃɪeɪt] vi (in value) se déprécier

depreciation [dɪpriːʃɪˈeɪʃən] n (in value) dépréciation f

depress [dɪˈpres] vt (**a**) (person) déprimer; Fig (prices) faire baisser; (economy, market) affaiblir (**b**) (button, lever) appuyer sur

depressed [dɪˈprest] adj (person) déprimé(e); Fig (economy, market, region) touché(e) par la crise; **to make sb d.** déprimer qn

depressing [dɪ'presɪŋ] *adj* déprimant(e)
depression [dɪ'preʃən] *n* (**a**) *(of person, economy)* dépression *f* (**b**) *Met* dépression *f* (**c**) *(hollow)* creux *m*; *(in landscape)* dépression *f*
deprivation [deprɪ'veɪʃən] *n (hardship)* privations *fpl*; **emotional d.** carence *f* affective
deprive [dɪ'praɪv] *vt* **to d. sb of sth** priver qn de qch
deprived [dɪ'praɪvd] *adj* défavorisé(e); *(childhood)* malheureux(euse)
dept *(abbr* **department)** dép.
depth [depθ] *n* profondeur *f*; **in d.** *(investigate, discuss)* en profondeur; **to be out of one's d.** *(of swimmer)* ne plus avoir pied; *Fig* ne pas être à la hauteur; **in the depths of winter** au cœur de l'hiver; **in the depths of despair** au plus profond du désespoir; *Naut* **d. charge** grenade *f* sous-marine; *Phot* **d. of field** profondeur *f* de champ
deputation [depjʊ'teɪʃən] *n* délégation *f*
depute [dɪ'pjuːt] *vt* **to d. sb to do sth** charger qn de faire qch
deputize ['depjʊtaɪz] *vi* **to d. for sb** remplacer qn
deputy ['depjʊtɪ] *(pl* **deputies)** *n (second-in-command)* adjoint(e) *m,f*; *(replacement)* remplaçant(e) *m,f*; *(political representative)* député *m*; *Am (policeman)* shérif *m* adjoint; **d. head** *(of school)* directeur(-trice) *m,f* adjoint(e); **d. manager** directeur(trice) *m,f* adjoint(e); **d. prime minister** vice-Premier ministre *m*
derail [dɪ'reɪl] **1** *vt Fig (project, plan)* faire avorter; **to be derailed** *(of train)* dérailler
 2 *vi (of train)* dérailler
derailment [dɪ'reɪlmənt] *n* déraillement *m*
deranged [dɪ'reɪndʒd] *adj* dérangé(e)
derby ['dɑːbɪ] *(pl* **derbies)** *n* (**a**) *(football match)* derby *m* (**b**) *Am (hat)* chapeau *m* melon
deregulate [diː'regjʊleɪt] *vt (economy, market)* déréguler; *(prices)* libérer; *(industry)* déréglementer
deregulation [diːregjʊ'leɪʃən] *n (of economy, market)* dérégulation *f*; *(of industry)* déréglementation *f*
derelict ['derəlɪkt] *adj* abandonné(e); *(ruined)* en ruines
dereliction [derɪ'lɪkʃən] *n* abandon *m*; **d. of duty** manquement *m* au devoir
deride [dɪ'raɪd] *vt* ridiculiser
derision [dɪ'rɪʒən] *n* dérision *f*
derisive [dɪ'raɪsɪv] *adj* moqueur(euse)
derisory [dɪ'raɪsərɪ] *adj* dérisoire
derivation [derɪ'veɪʃən] *n (source)* origine *f*
derivative [dɪ'rɪvətɪv] **1** *n Chem & Gram* dérivé *m*
 2 *adj* banal(e), sans originalité
derive [dɪ'raɪv] **1** *vt* dériver, provenir (**from** de); **to d. pleasure from sth** prendre plaisir à qch; **to be derived from** provenir de
 2 *vi* **to d. from** provenir de
dermatitis [dɜːmə'taɪtɪs] *n Med* dermite *f*, dermatite *f*
dermatologist [dɜːmə'tɒlədʒɪst] *n Med* dermatologiste *mf*, dermatologue *mf*
dermatology [dɜːmə'tɒlədʒɪ] *n Med* dermatologie *f*
derogatory [dɪ'rɒgətərɪ] *adj* désobligeant(e)
derrick ['derɪk] *n* derrick *m*
derv [dɜːv] *n Br (fuel)* gas-oil *m*, gazole *m*
desalination [diːsælɪ'neɪʃən] *n* dessalement *m*
descend [dɪ'send] **1** *vt (hill, stairs)* descendre
 2 *vi* (**a**) *(go down)* descendre; *(of darkness, dusk)* tomber; **in descending order** en ordre décroissant; **every summer tourists d. on the town** chaque été les touristes débarquent en ville; *Fig* **to d. to sb's level**

s'abaisser au niveau de qn (**b**) **to d.** *or* **be descended from sb** *(be related to)* descendre de qn
descent [dɪ'sent] *n* (**a**) *(of plane, from mountain)* descente *f* (**b**) *(ancestry)* **to be of Norman d.** être d'origine normande
describe [dɪs'kraɪb] *vt* décrire
description [dɪs'krɪpʃən] *n* description *f*; *(issued by police)* signalement *m*; **to answer** *or* **fit the d.** répondre au signalement; **beyond d.** indescriptible; **birds of all descriptions** des oiseaux de toutes sortes; **he's a journalist of some d.** il travaille dans le journalisme
descriptive [dɪs'krɪptɪv] *adj* descriptif(ive)
desecrate ['desɪkreɪt] *vt* profaner
desecration [desɪ'kreɪʃən] *n* profanation *f*
desegregation [diːsegrɪ'geɪʃən] *n* déségrégation *f*
desert[1] ['dezət] *n* désert *m*; **d. island** île *f* déserte
desert[2] [dɪ'zɜːt] **1** *vt* abandonner; **to d. one's post** *(of soldier)* déserter son poste
 2 *vi (from army)* déserter
deserted [dɪ'zɜːtɪd] *adj* désert(e)
deserter [dɪ'zɜːtə(r)] *n* déserteur *m*
desertion [dɪ'zɜːʃən] *n Law* abandon *m* du domicile conjugal; *Mil* désertion *f*
deserts [dɪ'zɜːts] *npl* **he got his just d.** il a eu ce qu'il méritait
deserve [dɪ'zɜːv] *vt* mériter; **to d. to do sth** mériter de faire qch; **she deserves to be punished** elle mérite une punition
deserving [dɪ'zɜːvɪŋ] *adj (person)* méritant(e); *(action, cause)* méritoire; **to be d. of praise** être digne d'éloge
design [dɪ'zaɪn] **1** *n* (**a**) *(pattern)* motif *m* (**b**) *(style) (furniture)* modèle *m*; *(of clothes)* coupe *f* (**c**) *(drawing) (of building, machine)* plan *m* (**d**) *(subject)* design *m*, stylisme *m* (**e**) *(planning) (of product, machine, website)* conception *f* (**f**) *(intention)* dessein *m*; **by d.** à dessein; **to have designs on** avoir des vues sur
 2 *vt (building, vehicle, website)* concevoir; *(clothes, furniture)* créer; **to be designed for sth/to do sth** *(intended)* être destiné(e) à qch/à faire qch
designate ['dezɪgneɪt] **1** *vt* désigner; qch; **this area has been designated a national park** cette zone a été classée parc national
 2 *adj* désigné(e)
designation [dezɪg'neɪʃən] *n* (**a**) *(appointment)* nomination *f*; *(of funds)* affectation *f* (**b**) *(title)* désignation *f*
designer [dɪ'zaɪnə(r)] *n* concepteur(trice) *m,f*; *(of building)* architecte *mf*; *(of clothes)* styliste *mf* (de mode); *(of theatre set)* décorateur(trice) *m,f*; **d. clothes** vêtements *mpl* de marque; **d. drugs** drogues *fpl* de synthèse; **d. label** griffe *f* de grande marque
desirable [dɪ'zaɪərəbəl] *adj* souhaitable; *(job, location)* attrayant(e); *(sexually)* désirable; **a d. residence** une belle résidence
desire [dɪ'zaɪə(r)] **1** *n* désir *m*, envie *f*; **I have no d. to go** je n'ai aucune envie d'y aller
 2 *vt* désirer; **to d. to do sth** désirer faire qch, avoir envie de faire qch; **it leaves a lot to be desired** ça laisse beaucoup à désirer
desirous [dɪ'zaɪərəs] *adj Formal* désireux(euse) (**of** de)
desist [dɪ'zɪst] *vi Formal* cesser; **to d. from doing sth** cesser de faire qch

desk [desk] *n (in school)* table *f*; *(with lid)* pupitre *m*; *(in office, home)* bureau *m*; *(hotel reception)* réception *f*; **d. diary** agenda *m*; **a d. job** un travail de bureau; **d. lamp** lampe *f* de bureau

desktop ['desktɒp] *n Comput (screen area)* bureau *m*; **d. computer** ordinateur *m* de bureau; **d. publishing** publication *f* assistée par ordinateur

desolate ['desələt] *adj (place)* désolé(e); *(future, prospect)* sombre; *(person)* abattu(c), affligé(e)

desolation [desə'leɪʃən] *n* désolation *f*; *(of person)* affliction *f*

despair [dɪs'peə(r)] **1** *n* désespoir *m*; **to be in d.** être désespéré(e); **to drive sb to d.** désespérer qn
2 *vi* désespérer; **I d. of you** tu me désespères

despairing [dɪ'speərɪŋ] *adj* désespéré(e)

despatch = dispatch

desperate ['despərət] *adj* désespéré(e); **to be in d. need of sth** avoir désespérément besoin de qch; **to be d. to do sth** vouloir à tout prix faire qch; **to be d. for sth** avoir désespérément besoin de qch

desperately ['despərətlɪ] *adv* désespérément; *(ill)* très gravement; **to be d. in love** être éperdument amoureux(euse); **to be d. sorry about sth** être affreusement désolé(e) de qch

desperation [despə'reɪʃən] *n* désespoir *m*; **in d.** par désespoir

despicable [dɪ'spɪkəbəl] *adj* méprisable

despise [dɪ'spaɪz] *vt* mépriser

despite [dɪs'paɪt] *prep* malgré

despondency [dɪs'pɒndənsɪ] *n* abattement *m*

despondent [dɪ'spɒndənt] *adj* abattu(e)

despot ['despɒt] *n* despote *m*

despotic [dɪs'pɒtɪk] *adj* despotique

despotism ['despətɪzəm] *n* despotisme *m*

dessert [dɪ'zɜːt] *n* dessert *m*; **d. wine** vin *m* doux

dessertspoon [dɪ'zɜːtspuːn] *n* cuillère *f* à dessert

destabilize [diː'steɪbəlaɪz] *vt* déstabiliser

destination [destɪ'neɪʃən] *n* destination *f*; **to reach one's d.** arriver à destination; *Comput* **d. disk/drive** disquette *f*/lecteur *m* cible

destine ['destɪn] *vt* destiner

destined ['destɪnd] *adj* **(a)** *(meant)* destiné(e); **to be d. to do sth** être destiné à faire qch; **he was d. to become famous** *(by fate)* il était destiné à devenir célèbre; *(reporting a fact)* il devait plus tard devenir célèbre **(b)** *(of plane, ship)* **d. for** à destination de

destiny ['destɪnɪ] *(pl* **destinies***) n* destin *m*, destinée *f*

destitute ['destɪtjuːt] *adj* sans ressources; **to be utterly d.** être dans la misère

destress [diː'stres] **1** *vt* **to d. oneself/one's life** se déstresser
2 *vi* **massage is a good way to d.** le massage est un bon moyen de déstresser

destroy [dɪs'trɔɪ] *vt* **(a)** *(damage, ruin)* détruire **(b)** *(animal)* abattre; *(vermin)* éliminer

destroyer [dɪs'trɔɪə(r)] *n (ship)* contre-torpilleur *m*

destruction [dɪs'trʌkʃən] *n* destruction *f*; *(damage)* ravages *mpl*

destructive [dɪs'trʌktɪv] *adj* destructeur(trice)

desultory ['desəltərɪ] *adj (conversation)* décousu(e); *(attempt)* peu convaincant(e)

detach [dɪ'tætʃ] *vt* détacher (**from** de); **to d. oneself (from)** s'éloigner (de)

detachable [dɪ'tætʃəbəl] *adj* amovible

detached [dɪ'tætʃt] *adj* **(a)** *(separate)* détaché(e), séparé(e); **to become** *ou* **get d. from sth** se détacher de qch; **d. house** maison *f* individuelle, pavillon *m*; *Med*

d. retina décollement *m* de la rétine **(b)** *(disinterested) (tone)* détaché(e); **he's rather d.** il sait garder ses distances

detachment [dɪ'tætʃmənt] *n* **(a)** *(military unit)* détachement *m* **(b)** *(objectivity)* détachement *m*

detail ['diːteɪl] **1** *n* **(a)** *(item of information)* détail *m*; **to pay attention to d.** être minutieux(euse); **to go into detail(s)** entrer dans les détails; **in d.** en détail; **details** *(information)* renseignements *mpl*; *(address and phone number)* coordonnées *fpl* **(b)** *Mil* détachement *m*
2 *vt* **(a)** *(describe)* détailler **(b)** *Mil* **to d. sb to do sth** donner l'ordre à qn de faire qch

detailed ['diːteɪld] *adj (account, description)* détaillé(e); *(work)* minutieux(euse)

detain [dɪ'teɪn] *vt (in prison)* placer en détention; *(in hospital)* garder; *(delay)* retenir; **such details need not d. us** ne nous laissons pas arrêter par de tels détails

detainee [diːteɪ'niː] *n* détenu(e) *m,f*

detangle [diː'tæŋgəl] *vt (hair)* démêler

detect [dɪ'tekt] *vt (change, emotion, trace of substance)* déceler; *(error, pattern)* découvrir; *Med (disease)* dépister; *Mil (mines etc)* détecter

detection [dɪ'tekʃən] *n (of error)* découverte *f*; *Med (of disease)* dépistage *m*; *Mil (of mines etc)* détection *f*; **to escape d.** *(of mistake, change)* passer inaperçu(e); *(of burglar)* **d.** ne pas être découvert(e); **crime d.** le travail de détective

detective [dɪ'tektɪv] *n (private)* détective *m*; *(police officer)* ≃ inspecteur(trice) *m,f* de police; **d. story** roman *m* policier; **d. work** enquêtes *fpl*

detector [dɪ'tektə(r)] *n* détecteur *m*

détente [deɪ'tɒnt] *n* détente *f*

detention [dɪ'tenʃən] *n* **(a)** *Law* détention *f*; *Law* **d. centre** ≃ centre de détention pour mineurs **(b)** *Sch* retenue *f*

deter [dɪ'tɜː(r)] *(pt & pp* **deterred***) vt* dissuader; **to d. sb from doing sth** dissuader qn de faire qch

detergent [dɪ'tɜːdʒənt] *n (for cleaning)* produit *m* de nettoyage

deteriorate [dɪ'tɪərɪəreɪt] *vi* se détériorer

deterioration [dɪtɪərɪə'reɪʃən] *n* détérioration *f*

determination [dɪtɜːmɪ'neɪʃən] *n* détermination *f*

determine [dɪ'tɜːmɪn] *vt* **(a)** *(decide)* **to d. to do sth** décider de faire qch; **to d. that...** décider que... **(b)** *(cause, date)* déterminer

determined [dɪ'tɜːmɪnd] *adj* déterminé(e), résolu(e); **to be d. to do sth** être déterminé(e) *ou* résolu(e) à faire qch; **I'm d. that we'll succeed** je suis déterminé à ce que nous réussissions

deterrent [dɪ'terənt] **1** *n* moyen *m* de dissuasion; **to act as a d.** avoir un effet dissuasif
2 *adj (effect)* dissuasif(ive)

detest [dɪ'test] *vt* détester

dethrone [dɪ'θrəʊn] *vt* détrôner

detonate ['detəneɪt] **1** *vt* faire exploser
2 *vi* exploser

detonation [detə'neɪʃən] *n* explosion *f*, détonation *f*

detonator ['detəneɪtə(r)] *n* détonateur *m*

detour [diː'tʊə(r)] *n* détour *m*

detoxification [diːtɒksɪfɪ'keɪʃən], *Fam* **detox** ['diːtɒks] *n* désintoxication *f*; **d. centre/programme** centre *m*/cure *f* de désintoxication

►**detract from** [dɪ'trækt] *vt insep* diminuer; **I don't want to d. from her achievement, but...** je ne veux pas minimiser ce qu'elle a accompli, mais...

detractor [dɪˈtræktə(r)] n détracteur(trice) m,f
detriment [ˈdetrɪmənt] n to the d. of au détriment de;
without d. to sans porter préjudice à
detrimental [detrɪˈmentəl] adj préjudiciable (to à);
to have a d. effect on nuire à
detritus [dɪˈtraɪtəs] n détritus mpl
Dettol® [ˈdetɒl] n = solution antiseptique
deuce [djuːs] n (in tennis) égalité f
Deutschmark [ˈdɔɪtʃmɑːk] n Formerly (deutsche) mark m
devaluation [diːvæljʊˈeɪʃən] n (a) (of currency) dévaluation f (b) (of person, achievement) dévalorisation f
devalue [diːˈvæljuː] vt (a) (currency) dévaluer (b) (person, achievement) dévaloriser
devastate [ˈdevəsteɪt] vt (crops, village) dévaster; (person) anéantir; **I was devastated by the news** la nouvelle m'a anéanti
devastating [ˈdevəsteɪtɪŋ] adj (storm, bombardment) dévastateur(trice); (news, findings, argument) accablant(e); (criticism) cinglant(e); (charm, beauty) irrésistible
devastation [devəsˈteɪʃən] n dévastation f
develop [dɪˈveləp] **1** vt (a) (skills, theory, argument) développer; (product) mettre au point (b) (region) développer; (site) aménager; **developed countries** pays mpl développés (c) (acquire) (infection, illness) attraper; (habit) prendre; **to d. a liking** or **taste for sth** se mettre à aimer qch (d) (film) développer
2 vi (a) (grow) se développer; **to d. into** devenir (b) (become apparent) apparaître
developer [dɪˈveləpə(r)] n (a) (of land) promoteur m (b) Phot révélateur m
developing [dɪˈveləpɪŋ] adj (region, country) en (voie de) développement; (crisis) en évolution
development [dɪˈveləpmənt] n (a) (growth) développement m; (of idea) évolution f; **d. aid** aide f au développement; Br **d. area** = zone à fort taux de chômage où l'État incite les industries à venir s'installer; **d. studies** études fpl du développement (b) (progress, change) développement m; **there have been some interesting developments** il y a eu quelques faits nouveaux intéressants; **the latest developments in medical research** les dernières découvertes médicales
deviant [ˈdiːvɪənt] adj déviant(e)
deviate [ˈdiːvɪeɪt] vi dévier (from de); Fig s'écarter (from de)
deviation [diːvɪˈeɪʃən] n déviation f (from par rapport à); Fig écart m (from par rapport à)
device [dɪˈvaɪs] n (a) (mechanism) dispositif m; (gadget) appareil m; (explosive) **d.** engin m explosif (b) (method, scheme) stratagème m; **to leave sb to their own devices** laisser qn se débrouiller
devil [ˈdevəl] n (a) (evil spirit) diable m; **the D.** le Diable (b) Fam (person) **poor d.!** pauvre diable!; **you little d.!** (to child) petit diable!; **you lucky d.!** veinard(e)! (c) (for emphasis) **what the d. are you doing?** mais qu'est-ce que tu fabriques?; **how the d....?** comment diable...?; **we had a d. of a job moving it** nous avons eu un mal de chien à le déplacer (d) (idioms) **he's a bit of a d.** c'est un sacré numéro; **go on, be a d.!** allez, laisse-toi tenter!; **to work like the d.** travailler comme un fou (une folle); **to be (caught) between the d. and the deep blue sea** avoir à choisir entre la peste et le choléra; **speak of the d.!** quand on parle du loup!; Prov **better the d. you know (than the d. you don't)** on sait ce qu'on

perd, on ne sait pas ce qu'on trouve; **to play d.'s advocate** se faire l'avocat du diable
devilish [ˈdevəlɪʃ] adj diabolique
devil-may-care [ˈdevəlmeɪˈkeə(r)] adj insouciant(e)
devious [ˈdiːvɪəs] adj (person, mind) retors(e); (plan, route) tortueux(euse); (means) détourné(e)
devise [dɪˈvaɪz] vt imaginer, élaborer
devoid [dɪˈvɔɪd] adj dénué(e), dépourvu(e) (of de)
devolution [diːvəˈluːʃən] n Pol décentralisation f

Devolution

Ce terme désigne la décentralisation parlementaire au sein du Royaume Uni, processus engagé depuis l'élection du gouvernement travailliste de Tony Blair en 1997. Après cette victoire, le nouveau gouvernement organisa des référendums en Écosse et au Pays de Galles, à la suite de quoi un parlement écossais fut instauré à Édimbourg et une assemblée nationale galloise à Cardiff, répondant ainsi aux attentes des nombreux Écossais et Gallois qui revendiquaient depuis longtemps un plus grand degré d'autonomie. (Voir aussi encadrés sous **Scottish Parliament** et **Welsh Assembly**.)

devolve [dɪˈvɒlv] **1** vt déléguer
2 vi **to d. on** incomber à; **power devolves on the regional assembly** le pouvoir appartient à l'assemblée régionale
devote [dɪˈvəʊt] vt consacrer (to à); **to d. oneself to** se consacrer à
devoted [dɪˈvəʊtɪd] adj (parent) dévoué(e); (admirer) fervent(e); **years of d. service** des années de bons et loyaux services; **they are d. to each other** ils sont très attachés l'un à l'autre
devotee [devəʊˈtiː] n (of writer, artist) admirateur(trice) m,f; (of idea) partisan m,f; (of sport, music) passionné(e) m,f
devotion [dɪˈvəʊʃən] n (to cause, friend, family) dévouement m; (to god, saint) dévotion f; **devotions** (prayers) prières fpl
devour [dɪˈvaʊə(r)] vt also Fig dévorer
devout [dɪˈvaʊt] adj (person) dévot(e); (wish) fervent(e)
dew [djuː] n rosée f
dewy-eyed [djuːˈaɪd] adj (loving) ému(e); (naive) ingénu(e)
dexterity [deksˈterɪtɪ] n dextérité f
dext(e)rous [ˈdekstrəs] adj adroit(e), habile
diabetes [daɪəˈbiːtiːz] n diabète m
diabetic [daɪəˈbetɪk] **1** n diabétique mf; **d. chocolate** chocolat m pour diabétiques
2 adj diabétique
diabolical [daɪəˈbɒlɪkəl] adj (a) (evil) diabolique (b) Fam (very bad) épouvantable
diadem [ˈdaɪədem] n diadème m
diagnose [ˈdaɪəgnəʊz] vt also Fig diagnostiquer
diagnosis [daɪəgˈnəʊsɪs] n (pl diagnoses [daɪəgˈnəʊsiːz]) n also Fig diagnostic m
diagnostic [daɪəgˈnɒstɪk] adj diagnostique
diagonal [daɪˈægənəl] **1** n diagonale f
2 adj diagonal(e)
diagram [ˈdaɪəgræm] n schéma m
dial [ˈdaɪəl] **1** n (of clock, phone) cadran m; (control knob) bouton m; Am **d. tone** tonalité f
2 vt (pt & pp dialled, Am dialed) (phone number) composer; (operator, country) appeler
dialect [ˈdaɪəlekt] n dialecte m

dialectic(al) [daɪə'lektɪk(əl)] *adj* dialectique
dialling ['daɪəlɪŋ] *n Br* **d. code** indicatif *m*; **d. tone** tonalité *f*
dialogue, *Am* **dialog** ['daɪəlɒg] *n* dialogue *m*; *Comput* **d. box** boîte *f* de dialogue
dialysis [daɪ'ælɪsɪs] *n Med* dialyse *f*
diameter [daɪ'æmɪtə(r)] *n* diamètre *m*; **the wheel is 60 cm in d.** la roue a un diamètre de 60 cm
diametrically [daɪə'metrɪklɪ] *adv* diamétralement
diamond ['daɪəmənd] *n (gem)* diamant *m*; *(shape)* losange *m*; **diamonds** *(card suit)* carreau *m*; **d.** jubilee soixantième anniversaire *m*; **d. necklace/ring** collier *m*/bague *f* de *ou* en diamants
diaper ['daɪəpə(r)] *n Am* couche *f*
diaphanous [daɪ'æfənəs] *adj* diaphane
diaphragm ['daɪəfræm] *n Anat & (contraceptive)* diaphragme *m*
diarrhoea, *Am* **diarrhea** [daɪə'rɪə] *n* diarrhée *f*
diary ['daɪərɪ] *(pl* **diaries)** *n (personal)* journal *m* (intime); *(for appointments)* agenda *m*
diatribe ['daɪətraɪb] *n* diatribe *f* (**against** contre)
dice [daɪs] **1** *n (pl* **dice)** dé *m*; **to play d.** jouer aux dés
  2 *vt (food)* couper en dés
  3 *vi* **to d. with death** jouer avec sa vie
dicey ['daɪsɪ] *adj Fam* risqué(e)
dichotomy [daɪ'kɒtəmɪ] *(pl* **dichotomies)** *n* dichotomie *f*
dick [dɪk] *n* (**a**) *Vulg (penis)* bite *f* (**b**) *Am Fam (detective)* privé *m*
dickens ['dɪkɪnz] *n Br Fam* **who/what/why the d....?** qui/que/pourquoi diable...?
dickhead ['dɪkhed] *n Vulg* tête *f* de nœud
dicky ['dɪkɪ] *adj Br Fam* **to have a d. heart** avoir le cœur fragile
dictate 1 *n* ['dɪkteɪt] ordre *m*; **she followed the dictates of her conscience** elle fit ce que lui dictait sa conscience
  2 *vt* [dɪk'teɪt] (**a**) *(letter, passage, conditions)* dicter (**b**) *(determine)* imposer; *(choice)* dicter
  3 *vi* [dɪk'teɪt] (**a**) *(dictate text)* dicter (**b**) *(give orders)* **to d. to sb** donner des ordres à qn; **I won't be dictated to!** je n'ai pas d'ordres à recevoir!
dictation [dɪk'teɪʃən] *n* dictée *f*; **to take d.** écrire sous la dictée
dictator [dɪk'teɪtə(r)] *n* dictateur *m*
dictatorial [dɪktə'tɔːrɪəl] *adj (power, regime)* dictatorial(e); *(manner, tone)* autoritaire
dictatorship [dɪk'teɪtəʃɪp] *n* dictature *f*
diction ['dɪkʃən] *n (pronunciation)* diction *f*; *(choice of words)* style *m*
dictionary ['dɪkʃənərɪ] *(pl* **dictionaries)** *n* dictionnaire *m*
did [dɪd] *pt of* **do²**
didactic [dɪ'dæktɪk] *adj* didactique
diddle ['dɪdəl] *vt Fam* rouler; **he diddled me out of £500** il m'a escroqué 500 livres
didn't ['dɪdənt] = **did not**
die¹ [daɪ] *n* (**a**) *(pl* **dice** [daɪs]) *(in games)* dé *m*; **the d. is cast** les dés sont jetés (**b**) *(pl* **dies** [daɪz]) *(mould)* matrice *f*
die² *(pt & pp* **died,** *continuous* **dying) 1** *vi* mourir *(* **from** *or* **of** de); **she is dying** elle est mourante; **to d. hard** *(of habit, rumour)* avoir la vie dure; *Fam* **never say d.!** il ne faut jamais désespérer!; *Fam* **I nearly died (of shame)** j'ai cru mourir de honte; *Fam* **to be dying to do sth** mourir d'envie de faire qch; *Fam* **I'm dying for a cigarette** je meurs d'envie de fumer une

cigarette; **the engine died on me/us/etc** le moteur a calé
  2 *vt* **to d. a natural/violent death** mourir de mort naturelle/violente; *Fig* **to d. a death** *(of proposal)* tomber à l'eau; *(of performer)* faire un bide
▸**die away** *vi (of sound, voice)* s'affaiblir
▸**die down** *vi (of fire)* baisser; *(of wind)* tomber; *(of sound)* s'affaiblir; *(of excitement, scandal)* se calmer
▸**die off** *vi* mourir
▸**die out** *vi (of family, species)* s'éteindre
diehard ['daɪhɑːd] **1** *n* réactionnaire *mf*
  2 *adj* pur(e) et dur(e)
diesel ['diːzəl] **1** *n (fuel)* gas-oil *m*, gazole *m*; *(car, railway engine)* diesel *m*
  2 *adj (engine, train)* diesel; **d. oil** *or* **fuel** gas-oil *m*, gazole *m*
diet ['daɪət] **1** *n (usual food)* alimentation *f*; *(restricted food)* régime *m*; **a balanced d.** un régime équilibré; **to be/go on a d.** être/se mettre au régime; **d. foods** aliments *mpl* allégés
  2 *vi* être au régime
dietary ['daɪətərɪ] *adj* alimentaire; **d. fibre** fibres *fpl* (alimentaires)
dietician [daɪə'tɪʃən] *n* diététicien(enne) *m,f*
differ ['dɪfə(r)] *vi* (**a**) *(be different)* différer (**from** de); **to d. in size/colour** être de taille/couleur différente (**b**) *(disagree)* ne pas être d'accord; **to d. with sb** ne pas être d'accord avec qn; **I beg to d.** permettez-moi d'être d'un autre avis; **to agree to d.** garder chacun son opinion
difference ['dɪfərəns] *n* (**a**) *(disparity)* différence *f* (**between/in** entre/de); **that doesn't make any d.** ça ne fait aucune différence; **it makes no d. to me** cela m'est égal; **that makes all the d.** voilà qui change tout; **a car with a d.** une voiture pas comme les autres (**b**) *(disagreement)* désaccord *m*, différend *m*; **d. of opinion** divergence *f* d'opinion; **we have to settle our differences** il faut nous mettre d'accord
different ['dɪfərənt] *adj* (**a**) *(not the same)* différent(e) (**from** de); **that's quite a d. matter** ça, c'est une autre affaire; **she feels a d. person** elle ne se sent plus la même; **he just wants to be d.** il veut se singulariser (**b**) *(various)* différents(es), divers(es)
differential [dɪfə'renʃəl] **1** *n (in wages, prices)* écart *m*; *Math* **d. calculus** calcul *m* différentiel; *Aut* **d. (gear)** différentiel *m*
  2 *adj* différentiel(elle)
differentiate [dɪfə'renʃɪeɪt] **1** *vt* différencier (**from** de)
  2 *vi* faire la différence (**between** entre)
differently ['dɪfərəntlɪ] *adv* différemment
difficult ['dɪfɪkəlt] *adj* difficile; **to find it d. to do sth** avoir du mal à faire qch; **he's d. to get on with** il n'est pas commode; **you're just being d.** tu le fais exprès pour embêter le monde; **to make life d. for sb** compliquer la vie à qn
difficulty ['dɪfɪkəltɪ] *(pl* **difficulties)** *n* difficulté *f*; **to have d. in doing sth** avoir du mal à faire qch; **to make difficulties for sb** créer des difficultés à qn
diffidence ['dɪfɪdəns] *n* manque *m* de confiance en soi
diffident ['dɪfɪdənt] *adj* peu sûr(e) de soi; **to be d. about doing sth** hésiter à faire qch
diffuse 1 *adj* [dɪ'fjuːs] diffus(e)
  2 *vt* [dɪ'fjuːz] diffuser, répandre
  3 *vi* [dɪ'fjuːz] se diffuser, se répandre

dig [dɪg] **1** *n* (**a**) *(in archaeology)* fouilles *fpl* (**b**) *(poke)* **a d.** in the ribs un coup de coude dans les côtes (**c**) *(remark)* pique *f*; **to have a d.** at sb lancer une pique à qn
2 *vt* (*pt & pp* **dug** [dʌg]) (**a**) *(hole, grave, ditch)* creuser; *(garden)* bêcher; *Fig* **she is digging her own grave** elle est en train de creuser sa propre tombe (**b**) *(thrust)* **to d. sth into sth** planter qch dans qch (**c**) *Fam Old-fashioned (like)* **she really digs that kind of music** ce genre de musique, ça la botte (**d**) *Fam Old-fashioned (look at)* mater; **d. that guy over there** mate un peu le mec, là-bas (**e**) *Fam Old-fashioned (understand)* piger; **you d.?** tu piges?
3 *vi (of person, animal)* creuser; *(in archaeology)* faire des fouilles; **to d. for sth** creuser pour trouver qch
▶**dig in 1** *vt sep Fig* **to d. one's heels in** s'entêter
2 *vi* (**a**) *(of soldiers)* se retrancher (**b**) *Fam (eat)* attaquer
▶**dig out** *vt sep* (**a**) *(bullet, splinter)* extraire; *(person from ruins, snow drift)* dégager (**b**) *Fam (information)* dénicher
▶**dig up** *vt sep* (**a**) *(plant)* arracher; *(treasure, body)* déterrer; *(road)* excaver (**b**) *Fam (information, person)* dénicher
digest 1 *n* ['daɪdʒest] *(summary)* condensé *m*
2 *vt* [dɪ'dʒest] *also Fig* digérer
digestible [dɪ'dʒestəbəl] *adj* digeste
digestion [dɪ'dʒestʃən] *n* digestion *f*
digestive [dɪ'dʒestɪv] *adj* digestif(ive); **d. (biscuit)** = sorte de sablé; **d. system/tract** système *m*/tube *m* digestif
digger ['dɪgə(r)] *n (machine)* excavateur *m*
digibox ['dɪdʒɪbɒks] *n TV* décodeur *m* numérique
digicam ['dɪdʒɪkæm] *n* caméra *f* numérique
digit ['dɪdʒɪt] *n* (**a**) *(finger)* doigt *m*; *(toe)* orteil *m* (**b**) *(number)* chiffre *m*
digital ['dɪdʒɪtəl] *adj* numérique; **d. camera** appareil *m* photo numérique; **d. recording** enregistrement *m* numérique; **d. signature** signature *f* numérique *ou* électronique; **d. television** *(technique)* télévision *f* numérique; *(appliance)* téléviseur *m* numérique
digitally ['dɪdʒɪtəlɪ] *adv* numériquement, sous forme digitale; *Mus* **d. recorded** enregistré en numérique
digitize ['dɪdʒɪtaɪz] *vt Comput* numériser
dignified ['dɪgnɪfaɪd] *adj* digne
dignify ['dɪgnɪfaɪ] (*pt & pp* **dignified**) *vt* donner de la dignité à; **I won't d. that remark with a response!** je ne m'abaisserai pas à répondre à cette remarque!
dignitary ['dɪgnɪtərɪ] (*pl* **dignitaries**) *n* dignitaire *m*
dignity ['dɪgnɪtɪ] *n* dignité *f*; **she considered it beneath her d. to respond** elle estimait indigne d'elle de répondre
digress [daɪ'gres] *vi* faire une digression; **to d. from** s'écarter de; ..., **but I d.** ..., mais je m'égare
digression [daɪ'greʃən] *n* digression *f*
digs [dɪgz] *npl Br Fam Old-fashioned* chambre *f* meublée
dike = dyke
dilapidated [dɪ'læpɪdeɪtɪd] *adj* délabré(e)
dilapidation [dɪlæpɪ'deɪʃən] *n* délabrement *m*
dilate [daɪ'leɪt] **1** *vt* dilater
2 *vi* se dilater
dilation [daɪ'leɪʃən] *n* dilatation *f*
dilatory ['dɪlətərɪ] *adj Formal (reply)* dilatoire; **to be d. in doing sth** tarder à faire qch

dilemma [daɪ'lemə] *n* dilemme *m*; **to be in a d.** être placé(e) devant un dilemme
dilettante [dɪlɪ'tɑːntɪ] *n* dilettante *mf*
diligence ['dɪlɪdʒəns] *n* application *f*, zèle *m*
diligent ['dɪlɪdʒənt] *adj* consciencieux(euse)
dill [dɪl] *n* aneth *m*
dilly-dally ['dɪlɪ'dælɪ] (*pt & pp* **dilly-dallied**) *vi Fam (loiter)* traînasser; *(hesitate)* tergiverser
dilute [daɪ'luːt] **1** *adj* dilué(e)
2 *vt (liquid)* diluer; *Fig (policy, proposal)* édulcorer
dilution [daɪ'luːʃən] *n Fig (of policy, proposal)* édulcoration *f*
dim [dɪm] **1** *adj* (**a**) *(light, chance, hope)* faible; *(outline, memory)* vague; *(eyesight)* faible, trouble; *(future)* sombre; **to take a d. view of sth** avoir une piètre opinion de qch (**b**) *(stupid)* bête
2 *vt* (*pt & pp* **dimmed**) *(light)* baisser, atténuer
3 *vi (of light)* baisser
dime [daɪm] *n Am (pièce f de)* 10 cents *mpl*; *Fam* **they're not worth a d.** ça ne vaut pas un clou; *Fam* **a d. a dozen** il y en a à la pelle
dimension [daɪ'menʃən] *n also Fig* dimension *f*
diminish [dɪ'mɪnɪʃ] *vt & vi* diminuer; *Law* **diminished responsibility** responsabilité *f* atténuée
diminishing [dɪ'mɪnɪʃɪŋ] *adj* décroissant(e); **the law of d. returns** la loi des rendements décroissants
diminutive [dɪ'mɪnjʊtɪv] **1** *n Gram* diminutif *m*
2 *adj* minuscule
dimly ['dɪmlɪ] *adv (lit)* faiblement; *(remember, see)* vaguement
dimmer ['dɪmə(r)] *n* (**a**) **d. (switch)** variateur *m* (**b**) *Am Aut* **dimmers** phares *mpl* code
dimple ['dɪmpəl] *n* fossette *f*
dimwit ['dɪmwɪt] *n Fam* andouille *f*
din [dɪn] *n Fam* vacarme *m*
dine [daɪn] *vi* dîner, *Belg, Can & Suisse* souper
▶**dine out** *vi* dîner dehors; **to d. out on a story** rabâcher une histoire
diner ['daɪnə(r)] *n* (**a**) *(person)* dîneur(euse) *m,f* (**b**) *Am (restaurant)* petit restaurant *m*
ding-dong ['dɪŋ'dɒŋ] *n* (**a**) *(sound)* ding dong *m* (**b**) *Fam (fight)* bagarre *f*
dinghy ['dɪŋ(g)ɪ] (*pl* **dinghies**) *n* (**rubber**) **d.** canot *m* pneumatique; *(sailing)* **d.** dériveur *m*
dingo ['dɪŋgəʊ] (*pl* **dingoes**) *n* dingo *m*
dingy ['dɪndʒɪ] *adj (room, street)* miteux(euse); *(colour)* terne
dining ['daɪnɪŋ] *n* **d. car** *(on train)* wagon-restaurant *m*; **d. hall** *(in school)* réfectoire *m*; **d. room** salle *f* à manger; **d. table** table *f* de salle à manger
dinner ['dɪnə(r)] *n (evening meal)* dîner *m*, *Belg, Can & Suisse* souper *m*; *(lunch)* déjeuner *m*; **what's for d.?** qu'est-ce qu'on mange?; **to have d.** *(in evening)* dîner; *(at midday)* déjeuner; **d. hour** *(at school)* heure *f* du déjeuner; **d. jacket** smoking *m*; **d. lady** = femme de service aux cantines scolaire; **d. party** dîner; **d. service** service *m* de table; **d. time** *(in evening)* heure *f* du dîner; *(lunchtime)* heure *f* du déjeuner
dinosaur ['daɪnəsɔː(r)] *n also Fig* dinosaure *m*
dint [dɪnt] *n Formal* **by d. of** à force de; **by d. of her efforts** grâce à ses efforts
diocese ['daɪəsɪs] *n Rel* diocèse *m*
diode ['daɪəʊd] *n Elec* diode *f*
dioxide [daɪ'ɒksaɪd] *n Chem* dioxyde *m*
dip [dɪp] **1** *n* (**a**) *(slope)* descente *f*; *(hollow)* dépression *f*; *(in prices, figures)* baisse *f* (**b**) *Fam (swim)* baignade *f*; **to go for a d.** faire trempette (**c**) *(sauce)*

= sauce dans laquelle on trempe des crudités, des biscuits salés etc **2** *vt (pt & pp* **dipped**) (**a**) *(immerse)* plonger (**b**) *(lower)* baisser; *Br* **to d.** one's headlights se mettre en codes *(quand on est en pleins phares)* **3** *vi (of ground)* descendre; *(of prices, temperature)* baisser; **the sun dipped below the horizon** le soleil descendit derrière l'horizon
►**dip into** *vt insep (savings, capital)* puiser dans; *(book)* feuilleter
DipEd [dɪp'ed] *n Br (abbr* **Diploma in Education**) ≃ CAPES *m*
diphtheria [dɪf'θɪərɪə] *n Med* diphtérie *f*
diphthong ['dɪfθɒŋ] *n Ling* diphtongue *f*
diploma [dɪ'pləʊmə] *n* diplôme *m*
diplomacy [dɪ'pləʊməsɪ] *n also Fig* diplomatie *f*
diplomat ['dɪpləmæt] *n* diplomate *mf*
diplomatic [dɪplə'mætɪk] *adj* diplomatique; *Fig (person)* diplomate; *Br* **d. bag**, *Am* **d. pouch** valise *f* diplomatique; **d. corps** corps *m* diplomatique; **d. immunity** immunité *f* diplomatique
dipper ['dɪpə(r)] *n (ladle)* louche *f*; **the Big D.** *(constellation)* la Grande Ourse; **big d.** *(at fairground)* montagnes *fpl* russes
dipsomaniac [dɪpsə'meɪnɪæk] *n* dipsomane *mf*
dipstick ['dɪpstɪk] *n* (**a**) *Aut* jauge *f* de niveau d'huile (**b**) *Fam (idiot)* abruti(e) *m,f*
dire ['daɪə(r)] *adj (consequences)* tragique; *Fam (bad)* épouvantable; **d. poverty** misère *f* noire; **to be in d. need of sth** avoir un besoin urgent de qch; **to be in d. straits** être dans une mauvaise passe
direct [dɪ'rekt] **1** *adj* direct(e); *(refusal, denial)* catégorique; **the d. opposite** l'exact opposé; **to be a d. descendant of sb** descendre de qn en ligne directe; *Elec* **d. current** courant *m* continu; *Fin* **d. debit** prélèvement *m* automatique; **d. hit** coup *m* au but; **d. mail** publipostage *m*; *Gram* **d. object** complément *m* d'objet direct; *Pol* **d. rule** administration *f* centrale; *Com* **d. selling** vente *f* directe; *Gram* **d. speech** discours *m* direct; *Fin* **d. taxation** contributions *fpl* directes
2 *adv* directement; *(broadcast)* en direct *(* **from** de)
3 *vt* (**a**) *(remark)* adresser (**at** à); *(gaze, light)* diriger (**at** sur); *(funds, effort)* consacrer (**towards** à); **can you d. me to the station?** pouvez-vous m'indiquer le chemin de la gare? (**b**) *(company, actors)* diriger; *(traffic)* régler; *(play)* mettre en scène; *(film)* réaliser (**c**) *(instruct)* **to d. sb to do sth** ordonner à qn de faire qch; **as directed** selon les instructions
direction [dɪ'rek∫ən] *n* (**a**) *(way)* direction *f*, sens *m*; **in the d. of** en direction de; **they ran off in all directions** ils sont partis en courant dans toutes les directions; **the town was surrounded by hills in all directions** la ville était entourée de tous côtés par des collines (**b**) *(management) (of project)* direction *f*; *(of play)* mise *f* en scène; *(of film)* réalisation *f*; **under the d. of** *(orchestra)* sous la direction de (**c**) **directions** *(to place)* indications *fpl*; *(for use)* instructions *fpl*; **to ask for directions** demander son chemin
directive [dɪ'rektɪv] *n* directive *f*, instruction *f*
directly [dɪ'rektlɪ] **1** *adv* (**a**) *(go, write)* directement; **to be d. descended from sb** descendre de qn en ligne directe (**b**) *(exactly)* juste; **d. opposite** juste en face de (**c**) *(frankly) (answer, speak)* ouvertement (**d**) *(soon)* immédiatement; **I'll be there d.** j'arrive tout de suite

2 *conj* aussitôt que, dès que; **I'll come d. I've finished** je viendrai dès que j'aurai fini
director [dɪ'rektə(r)] *n (manager)* directeur(trice) *m,f*; *(board member)* administrateur(trice) *m,f*; *(of film)* réalisateur(trice) *m,f*; *(of play)* metteur *m* en scène; *Br Law* **D. of Public Prosecutions** = magistrat dont le rôle recouvre à la fois celui du procureur général et celui du procureur de la République
directorate [dɪ'rektər(e)ɪt] *n (board)* conseil *m* d'administration
directorship [dɪ'rektə∫ɪp] *n* direction *f*
directory [dɪ'rektərɪ] *(pl* **directories**) *n (of phone numbers)* annuaire *m*; *Comput* répertoire *m*; **(street) d.** index *m* (des rues); *Br Tel* **d. enquiries** renseignements *mpl* (téléphoniques)
dirge [dɜːdʒ] *n* chant *m* funèbre; *Fam Fig* chanson *f* lugubre
dirham [dɪ'ræm] *n* dirham *m*
dirt [dɜːt] *n* (**a**) *(on clothes, body)* saleté *f*; *(mud)* boue *f*; *(soil)* terre *f*; **to treat sb like d.** traiter qn comme un chien; *Fam* **dog d.** crotte *f* de chien; **d. road** *or* **track** chemin *m* de terre (**b**) *Fam (scandal)* cancans *mpl*, ragots *mpl*; **to dish the d. on sb** colporter des ragots sur qn
dirt-cheap ['dɜːt't∫iːp] *Fam* **1** *adj* donné(e)
2 *adv* pour trois fois rien
dirty ['dɜːtɪ] **1** *adj* (**a**) *(unclean) (person, hands, clothes)* sale; *(with mud)* crotté(e); **to get d.** se salir; *also Fig* **to get one's hands d.** se salir les mains; *Fig* **to wash one's d. linen in public** laver son linge sale en public (**b**) *Fig (unpleasant, unsavoury)* **it's a d. business** c'est une activité peu reluisante; **to give sb a d. look** regarder qn d'un sale œil; **d. work** sale boulot *m* (**c**) *(book, film, joke)* cochon(onne); *(language, word)* grossier(ère); **d. old man** vieux cochon *m*; **d. weekend** week-end *m* coquin; **"communism" is a d. word nowadays** "communisme" est un mot tabou de nos jours
2 *adv* (**a**) *(fight)* déloyalement (**b**) *(obscenely)* **to talk d.** dire des cochonneries (**c**) *Fam (for emphasis)* vachement; **a d. great hole** un sacré grand trou
3 *vt (pt & pp* **dirtied**) salir
4 *n Br Fam* **to do the d. on sb** jouer un sale tour à qn
disability [dɪsə'bɪlɪtɪ] *(pl* **disabilities**) *n* handicap *m*, infirmité *f*; **d. allowance** pension *f* d'invalidité
disable [dɪs'eɪbəl] *vt (person)* rendre infirme; *(ship)* désemparer; *(alarm system)* désactiver
disabled [dɪs'eɪbəld] **1** *npl* **the d.** les handicapés *mpl*
2 *adj* handicapé(e); **d. toilet** toilettes *fpl* pour handicapés
disabuse [dɪsə'bjuːz] *vt Formal* **to d. sb (of an idea)** détromper qn
disadvantage [dɪsəd'vɑːntɪdʒ] **1** *n* désavantage *m*, inconvénient *m*; **to be at a d.** être désavantagé(e); **to put sb at a d.** désavantager qn
2 *vt* désavantager
disadvantaged [dɪsəd'vɑːntɪdʒd] *adj* défavorisé(e)
disaffected [dɪsə'fektɪd] *adj* mécontent(e); *(stronger)* révolté(e)
disaffection [dɪsə'fek∫ən] *n* désaffection *f*
disagree [dɪsə'griː] *vi* (**a**) *(quarrel)* ne pas être d'accord; **to d. with sb (about)** ne pas être d'accord avec qn (sur) (**b**) *(of reports, figures)* ne pas concorder (**c**) *(of climate, food)* **to d. with sb** ne pas réussir à qn
disagreeable [dɪsə'griːəbəl] *adj* désagréable
disagreement [dɪsə'griːmənt] *n* (**a**) *(failure to agree)* désaccord *m*; **to be in d. with sb** être en désaccord

avec qn (**b**) *(quarrel)* différend *m* (**c**) *(discrepancy)* différence *f*
disallow [dɪsə'laʊ] *vt Formal (objection, claim)* rejeter; *(goal, try)* refuser
disappear [dɪsə'pɪə(r)] *vi* disparaître
disappearance [dɪsə'pɪərəns] *n* disparition *f*
disappoint [dɪsə'pɔɪnt] *vt* décevoir
disappointed [dɪsə'pɔɪntɪd] *adj* déçu(e) (**in** *or* **with** par)
disappointing [dɪsə'pɔɪntɪŋ] *adj* décevant(e)
disappointment [dɪsə'pɔɪntmənt] *n* déception *f*; **to be a d.** être décevant(e)
disapproval [dɪsə'pruːvəl] *n* désapprobation *f*
disapprove [dɪsə'pruːv] *vi* désapprouver; **to d. of sth** désapprouver qch; **he disapproves of them** ils ne lui plaisent pas
disapproving [dɪsə'pruːvɪŋ] *adj (tone, look)* désapprobateur(trice); **to be d. of sth** désapprouver qch
disarm [dɪs'ɑːm] *vt & vi* désarmer
disarmament [dɪs'ɑːməmənt] *n* désarmement *m*; **d. talks** conférence *f* sur le désarmement
disarming [dɪs'ɑːmɪŋ] *adj (smile, honesty)* désarmant(e)
disarray [dɪsə'reɪ] *n* désordre *m*; **in d.** en désordre
disaster [dɪ'zɑːstə(r)] *n* désastre *m*; *(earthquake, fire, crash)* catastrophe *f*; **d. area** région *f* sinistrée; *Fam Fig (person)* maladroit(e) *m,f*; **d. movie** film *m* catastrophe
disastrous [dɪ'zɑːstrəs] *adj* désastreux(euse)
disband [dɪs'bænd] **1** *vt (regiment)* supprimer; *(organization)* dissoudre
2 *vi (of organization)* se dissoudre; *(of regiment)* être supprimé(e)
disbelief [dɪsbɪ'liːf] *n* incrédulité *f*; **in d.** *(listen, watch)* avec incrédulité
disbelieve [dɪsbɪ'liːv] *vt* ne pas croire
disburse [dɪs'bɜːs] *vt Formal* débourser
disc, *Am* **disk** [dɪsk] *n* disque *m*; *Aut* **d. brake** frein *m* à disque; **d. jockey** disc-jockey *m*
discard [dɪs'kɑːd] *vt (person)* laisser tomber; *(plan, proposal)* abandonner; *(object)* se débarrasser de
discern [dɪ'sɜːn] *vt (shape, object)* discerner; *(sound, difference)* percevoir
discernible [dɪ'sɜːnɪbəl] *adj (shape, object)* discernable; *(sound, difference)* perceptible
discerning [dɪ'sɜːnɪŋ] *adj (person)* perspicace; *(taste)* fin(e)
discharge 1 *n* ['dɪstʃɑːdʒ] (**a**) *(of patient)* sortie *f*; *(authorization)* autorisation *f* de sortie; *(of prisoner)* mise *f* en liberté, libération *f*; *(of soldier)* libération; *(for unfitness)* réforme *f* (**b**) *(of firearm)* décharge *f* (**c**) *(of gas, chemical)* dégagement *m*; *(of pus, fluid)* écoulement *m*
2 *vt* [dɪs'tʃɑːdʒ] (**a**) *(patient)* laisser sortir; *(prisoner)* libérer; *(employee)* congédier, renvoyer; *(soldier)* libérer; *(for unfitness)* réformer (**b**) *(firearm)* décharger (**c**) *(gas, chemical)* dégager; *(fluid)* déverser; **to d. pus** suppurer (**d**) *(duty, debt)* s'acquitter de; *(fine)* payer
disciple [dɪ'saɪpəl] *n* disciple *mf*
disciplinarian [dɪsɪplɪ'neərɪən] *n* **to be a strict d.** être stricte en matière de discipline
disciplinary ['dɪsɪplɪnərɪ] *adj* disciplinaire
discipline ['dɪsɪplɪn] **1** *n* discipline *f*
2 *vt (punish)* punir; **to d. oneself** se discipliner
disclaim [dɪs'kleɪm] *vt (renounce)* renoncer à; *(deny)* démentir

disclaimer [dɪs'kleɪmə(r)] *n* démenti *m*
disclose [dɪs'kləʊz] *vt* révéler
disclosure [dɪs'kləʊʒə(r)] *n* révélation *f*
disco ['dɪskəʊ] *(pl* **discos)** *n (place)* discothèque *f*, boîte *f* (de nuit); *(music)* disco *m* ou *f*
discolour, *Am* **discolor** [dɪs'kʌlə(r)] *vt (fade)* décolorer; *(stain) (with age)* jaunir; *(with smoke)* noircir; **to become discoloured** se décolorer
discomfiture [dɪs'kʌmfɪtʃə(r)] *n* embarras *m*
discomfort [dɪs'kʌmfət] *n (lack of comfort)* inconfort *m*; *(pain)* légère douleur *f*; **to be in some d.** éprouver une légère douleur
disconcert [dɪskən'sɜːt] *vt* déconcerter, décontenancer
disconcerted [dɪskən'sɜːtɪd] *adj* déconcerté
disconcerting [dɪskən'sɜːtɪŋ] *adj* déconcertant(e)
disconnect [dɪskə'nekt] *vt (gas, electricity, phone)* couper; *(machine, appliance)* débrancher
disconsolate [dɪs'kɒnsələt] *adj* désespéré(e) (**at** par)
discontent [dɪskən'tent] *n* mécontentement *m*
discontented [dɪskən'tentɪd] *adj* mécontent(e) (**with** de)
discontinue [dɪskən'tɪnjuː] *vt* interrompre; *Com* **discontinued line** fin *f* de série
discord ['dɪskɔːd] *n* discorde *f*
discordant [dɪs'kɔːdənt] *adj (opinions, sound)* discordant(e)
discotheque ['dɪskətek] *n* discothèque *f*, boîte *f* (de nuit)
discount 1 *n* ['dɪskaʊnt] remise *f*; **at a d.** au rabais
2 *adj* ['dɪskaʊnt] *(goods, prices)* discount
3 *vt* (**a**) ['dɪskaʊnt] *(price)* baisser; *(goods)* solder (**b**) [dɪs'kaʊnt] *(suggestion, rumours)* ignorer, ne pas tenir compte de; *(possibility, fact)* écarter
discourage [dɪs'kʌrɪdʒ] *vt* (**a**) *(dishearten)* décourager (**b**) *(dissuade)* **to d. sb from doing sth** dissuader qn de faire qch
discouragement [dɪs'kʌrɪdʒmənt] *n* (**a**) *(loss of enthusiasm)* découragement *m* (**b**) *(dissuasion)* **to act as** *or* **be a d. (to sth)** avoir un effet dissuasif (sur qch)
discouraging [dɪs'kʌrɪdʒɪŋ] *adj* décourageant(e)
discourse *Formal* **1** *n* ['dɪskɔːs] *(speech)* discours *m*; *(conversation)* conversation *f*
2 *vi* [dɪs'kɔːs] **to d. (up)on sth** discourir sur qch
discourteous [dɪs'kɜːtɪəs] *adj* discourtois(e)
discourtesy [dɪs'kɜːtəsɪ] *n* impolitesse *f*
discover [dɪs'kʌvə(r)] *vt* découvrir
discovery [dɪs'kʌvərɪ] *(pl* **discoveries)** *n* découverte *f*
discredit [dɪs'kredɪt] **1** *n* discrédit *m*; **to be a d. to sb/ sth** déshonorer qn/qch; **much to their d., they didn't even apologize** ils ne se sont même pas excusés, ce qui ne leur fait pas honneur
2 *vt (person, theory)* discréditer
discreet [dɪs'kriːt] *adj* discret(ète)
discrepancy [dɪs'krepənsɪ] *(pl* **discrepancies)** *n* décalage *m* (**between** entre)
discretion [dɪs'kreʃən] *n* (**a**) *(tact)* discrétion *f* (**b**) *(judgement)* jugement *m*; **at the manager's d.** à la discrétion du directeur; **to use one's own d.** juger par soi-même
discretionary [dɪs'kreʃənərɪ] *adj* discrétionnaire
discriminate [dɪs'krɪmɪneɪt] **1** *vt* distinguer (**from** de)
2 *vi* **to d. between** faire la différence entre; **to d. against** faire de la discrimination envers; **to be discriminated against** être victime de discrimination; **to d. in favour of** favoriser

discriminating [dɪsˈkrɪmɪneɪtɪŋ] *adj* perspicace
discrimination [dɪskrɪmɪˈneɪʃən] *n* (**a**) *(bias)* discrimination *f* (**b**) *(taste)* discernement *m* (**c**) *(differentiation)* différenciation *f*
discriminatory [dɪsˈkrɪmɪnətərɪ] *adj* discriminatoire
discursive [dɪsˈkɜːsɪv] *adj* discursif(ive)
discus [ˈdɪskəs] *n* disque *m*
discuss [dɪsˈkʌs] *vt (issue, problem)* discuter de; *(author, book, report)* examiner, parler de; **I don't wish to d. it** je ne veux pas en parler
discussion [dɪsˈkʌʃən] *n* discussion *f*; **under d.** en discussion
disdain [dɪsˈdeɪn] **1** *n* dédain *m*
 2 *vt* dédaigner; **to d. to do sth** dédaigner de faire qch
disdainful [dɪsˈdeɪnful] *adj* dédaigneux(euse)
disease [dɪˈziːz] *n* maladie *f*
diseased [dɪˈziːzd] *adj* malade
disembark [dɪsemˈbɑːk] *vt & vi* débarquer
disembodied [dɪsɪmˈbɒdɪd] *adj* désincarné(e)
disenchanted [dɪsɪnˈtʃɑːntɪd] *adj* désenchanté(e); **to be d. with sth** être déçu(e) par qch
disenchantment [dɪsɪnˈtʃɑːntmənt] *n* désenchantement *m*
disengage [dɪsɪnˈgeɪdʒ] **1** *vt* dégager (**from** de); **to d. oneself from sth** se retirer de qch
 2 *vi* se retirer (**from** de); *Mil* cesser le combat
disentangle [dɪsɪnˈtæŋgəl] *vt* démêler
disfavour, *Am* **disfavor** [dɪsˈfeɪvə(r)] *n* **to be in d.** être en défaveur; **to fall into d. (with sb)** tomber en disgrâce (auprès de qn)
disfigure [dɪsˈfɪgə(r)] *vt* défigurer
disfigurement [dɪsˈfɪgəmənt] *n* défigurement *m*
disgrace [dɪsˈgreɪs] **1** *n (shame)* honte *f*; **to be in d. (with sb)** être en disgrâce (auprès de qn); **to be a d. to one's family/country** déshonorer sa famille/son pays; **it's a d.!** c'est une honte!
 2 *vt* déshonorer, couvrir de honte; **to d. oneself** se déshonorer
disgraceful [dɪsˈgreɪsful] *adj* honteux(euse); **it's d.!** c'est honteux *ou* scandaleux!
disgracefully [dɪsˈgreɪsfulɪ] *adv* scandaleusement, honteusement
disgruntled [dɪsˈgrʌntəld] *adj* mécontent(e)
disguise [dɪsˈgaɪz] **1** *n (costume)* déguisement *m*; **in d.** déguisé(e)
 2 *vt* déguiser; **to d. oneself as** se déguiser en; **there is no disguising the fact that...** on ne peut pas cacher le fait que...
disgust [dɪsˈgʌst] **1** *n* dégoût *m*; **to fill sb with d.** remplir qn de dégoût, écœurer qn; **in d.** dégoûté(e), écœuré(e)
 2 *vt* dégoûter; **to be disgusted with oneself** se dégoûter
disgusting [dɪsˈgʌstɪŋ] *adj* répugnant(e)
dish [dɪʃ] **1** *n (bowl, food)* plat *m*; **d. of the day** plat *m* du jour; **dishes** *(crockery)* vaisselle *f*; **to do the dishes** faire la vaisselle
 2 *vt Fam* **to d. the dirt** tout raconter
▸**dish out** *vt sep (food)* servir; *(money, advice)* distribuer
▸**dish up** *vt sep (meal)* servir
disharmony [dɪsˈhɑːmənɪ] *n* désaccord *m*
dishcloth [ˈdɪʃklɒθ] *n (for washing)* lavette *f*; *(for drying)* torchon *m*
disheartening [dɪsˈhɑːtənɪŋ] *adj* décourageant(e)

dishevelled [dɪˈʃevəld] *adj (person, appearance)* débraillé(e); *(hair)* ébouriffé(e); *(clothes)* en désordre
dishonest [dɪsˈɒnɪst] *adj* malhonnête
dishonesty [dɪsˈɒnɪstɪ] *n* malhonnêteté *f*
dishonour, *Am* **dishonor** [dɪsˈɒnə(r)] **1** *n* déshonneur *m*
 2 *vt* déshonorer
dishonourable, *Am* **dishonorable** [dɪsˈɒnərəbəl] *adj* déshonorant(e)
dishtowel [ˈdɪʃtaʊəl] *n* torchon *m*
dishwasher [ˈdɪʃwɒʃə(r)] *n (person)* plongeur(euse) *m,f*; *(machine)* lave-vaisselle *m inv*
dishwater [ˈdɪʃwɔːtə(r)] *n also Fig* eau *f* de vaisselle
dishy [ˈdɪʃɪ] *adj Br Fam Old-fashioned* mignon(onne)
disillusioned [dɪsɪˈluːʒənd] *adj* désillusionné(e); **to be d. with sb/sth** être déçu(e) par qn/qch; **to become d.** perdre ses illusions
disincentive [dɪsɪnˈsentɪv] *n* **to be a d. (to sth)** avoir un effet dissuasif (sur qch)
disinclination [dɪsɪnklɪˈneɪʃən] *n* manque *m* d'enthousiasme (**to do sth** à faire qch)
disinclined [dɪsɪnˈklaɪnd] *adj* **to be d. to do sth** être peu disposé(e) à faire qch
disinfect [dɪsɪnˈfekt] *vt* désinfecter
disinfectant [dɪsɪnˈfektənt] *n* désinfectant *m*
disinformation [dɪsɪnfəˈmeɪʃən] *n* désinformation *f*
disingenuous [dɪsɪnˈdʒenjʊəs] *adj (person, answer)* peu sincère; *(manner, smile)* faux (fausse)
disinherit [dɪsɪnˈherɪt] *vt* déshériter
disintegrate [dɪsˈɪntɪgreɪt] *vi* se désintégrer; *(of confidence)* s'effriter; *(of marriage, relationship)* se désagréger
disintegration [dɪsɪntɪˈgreɪʃən] *n* désintégration *f*; *(of marriage, relationship)* désagrégation *f*
disinterest [dɪsˈɪntərɪst] *n (impartiality)* impartialité *f*; *(lack of interest)* désintérêt *m*, indifférence *f*
disinterested [dɪsˈɪntərɪstɪd] *adj (unbiased)* impartial(e); *(uninterested)* indifférent(e)
disinvestment [dɪsɪnˈvestmənt] *n Fin* désinvestissement *m*
disjointed [dɪsˈdʒɔɪntɪd] *adj (style, speech)* décousu(e); *(movements)* saccadé(e)
disk [dɪsk] *n* (**a**) *Comput (hard)* disque *m*; *(floppy)* disquette *f*; **d. drive** unité *f* de disques (**b**) *Am* = **disc**
diskette [dɪsˈket] *n Comput* disquette *f*
dislike [dɪsˈlaɪk] **1** *n* aversion *f* (**of** *or* **for** pour); **we have the same likes and dislikes** nous avons les mêmes goûts; **to take a d. to sb/sth** prendre qn/qch en grippe
 2 *vt* ne pas aimer; **I don't d. him** il ne me déplaît pas
dislocate [ˈdɪsləkeɪt] *vt* (**a**) *(shoulder, hip)* déboîter; **to d. one's shoulder** se déboîter l'épaule (**b**) *(plan, timetable)* perturber
dislocation [dɪsləˈkeɪʃən] *n* (**a**) *(of shoulder, hip)* déboîtement *m* (**b**) *(of plan, timetable)* perturbation *f*
dislodge [dɪsˈlɒdʒ] *vt (opponent, leader)* déloger (**from** de); *(brick, slate)* arracher; *(obstacle)* déplacer; *(something stuck)* décoincer
disloyal [dɪsˈlɔɪəl] *adj* déloyal(e)
disloyalty [dɪsˈlɔɪəltɪ] *n* déloyauté *f*
dismal [ˈdɪzməl] *adj (face, countryside)* lugubre; *(failure, performance)* lamentable; *(future)* sombre
dismantle [dɪsˈmæntəl] *vt (empire, network)* démanteler; *(machine)* démonter
dismay [dɪsˈmeɪ] **1** *n* consternation *f*; **in d.** consterné(e); **(much) to my d.** à ma grande consternation
 2 *vt* consterner

dismember [dɪs'membə(r)] *vt also Fig* démembrer
dismiss [dɪs'mɪs] *vt* (**a**) *(from job)* renvoyer (**b**) *(send away)* congédier; *(pupils)* libérer; *Mil* **d.!** rompez! (**c**) *(thought, theory)* rejeter; *(proposal, suggestion)* écarter; *(danger, threat)* ignorer; **she is dismissed as an airhead** elle est considérée comme une évaporée (**d**) *Law (case)* classer; *(appeal, charge)* rejeter
dismissal [dɪs'mɪsəl] *n* (**a**) *(of employee)* renvoi *m*, licenciement *m* (**b**) *Law (of case)* fin *f* de non-recevoir; *(of appeal, charge)* rejet *m*
dismissive [dɪs'mɪsɪv] *adj* dédaigneux(euse); **to be d. of sb/sth** faire peu de cas de qn/qch
dismount [dɪs'maʊnt] *vi (from horse, bicycle)* descendre, mettre pied à terre
disobedience [dɪsə'biːdɪəns] *n* désobéissance *f*
disobedient [dɪsə'biːdɪənt] *adj* désobéissant(e); **to be d. to sb** désobéir à qn
disobey [dɪsə'beɪ] *vt (person, order)* désobéir à; *(law)* enfreindre
disorder [dɪs'ɔːdə(r)] *n* (**a**) *(confusion, unrest)* désordre *m*; **in d.** en désordre (**b**) *Med* troubles *mpl*; **a nervous d.** des troubles nerveux
disordered [dɪs'ɔːdəd] *adj* désordonné(e)
disorderly [dɪs'ɔːdəlɪ] *adj (untidy, unruly)* désordonné(e); *(crowd)* agité(e); *Law* **d. conduct** atteinte *f* à l'ordre public
disorganization [dɪsɔːgənaɪ'zeɪʃən] *n* désorganisation *f*
disorganized [dɪs'ɔːgənaɪzd] *adj* désorganisé(e)
disorientate [dɪs'ɔːrɪənteɪt], **disorient** [dɪs'ɔːrɪənt] *vt* désorienter
disorienting [dɪs'ɔːrɪəntɪŋ] *adj* déroutant(e)
disown [dɪs'əʊn] *vt* désavouer, renier
disparage [dɪs'pærɪdʒ] *vt* dénigrer
disparaging [dɪs'pærɪdʒɪŋ] *adj* désobligeant(e)
disparate ['dɪspərɪt] *adj* disparate
disparity [dɪs'pærɪtɪ] *(pl* **disparities**) *n* disparité *f*
dispassionate [dɪs'pæʃənət] *adj (calm)* calme; *(impartial)* impartial(e)
dispatch [dɪs'pætʃ] **1** *n* (**a**) *(of letter, parcel)* expédition *f*, envoi *m* (**b**) *(message)* dépêche *f*; *Mil* **to be mentioned in dispatches** être cité(e) à l'ordre du jour; **d. rider** *Mil* estafette *f*; *(courier)* coursier(ère) *m,f* (**c**) *Formal (promptness)* promptitude *f*; **with d.** promptement
2 *vt* (**a**) *(send)* envoyer (**b**) *(kill)* liquider
dispel [dɪs'pel] *(pt & pp* **dispelled**) *vt* dissiper
dispensable [dɪs'pensəbəl] *adj* dont on peut se passer
dispensary [dɪs'pensərɪ] *(pl* **dispensaries**) *n Med (in pharmacy)* officine *f*; *(in hospital)* pharmacie *f*
dispensation [dɪspen'seɪʃən] *n Law & Rel (exemption)* dispense *f* (**from** de)
dispense [dɪs'pens] *vt (justice)* rendre; *(advice)* prodiguer; *(medication)* préparer; *(of vending machine)* distribuer
▶**dispense with** *vt insep* se passer de; **to d. with the need for sth** rendre qch superflu(e)
dispensing chemist [dɪs'pensɪŋ'kemɪst] *n* pharmacien(enne) *m,f*
dispersal [dɪs'pɜːsəl] *n* dispersion *f*
disperse [dɪs'pɜːs] **1** *vt (seeds, people)* disperser; *(knowledge, information)* propager
2 *vi (of crowd)* se disperser; *(of darkness, mist, clouds)* se dissiper
dispirited [dɪs'pɪrɪtɪd] *adj* découragé(e), abattu(e)

displace [dɪs'pleɪs] *vt* (**a**) *(shift)* déplacer; **displaced persons** personnes *fpl* déplacées (**b**) *(supplant)* remplacer, supplanter
displacement [dɪs'pleɪsmənt] *n* (**a**) *(of water, people)* déplacement *m* (**b**) *(substitution)* remplacement *m*
display [dɪs'pleɪ] **1** *n* (**a**) *(of goods)* étalage *m*; *(of crafts, paintings)* exposition *f*; **on d.** à l'étalage; *(sign, notice)* affiché(e); **d. cabinet** vitrine *f*; **d. copy** *(of book)* exemplaire *m* de démonstration; **d. window** vitrine *f* (**b**) *(demonstration)* démonstration *f* (**c**) *Comput* écran *m*
2 *vt* (**a**) *(goods)* exposer; *(sign, notice)* afficher (**b**) *(emotion)* manifester; *(talent, concern, ignorance)* faire preuve de (**c**) *(on screen)* afficher
displease [dɪs'pliːz] *vt* mécontenter, contrarier; **to be displeased with sb/sth** ne pas être satisfait(e) de qn/qch
displeasure [dɪs'pleʒə(r)] *n* déplaisir *m*, mécontentement *m*
disposable [dɪs'pəʊzəbəl] *adj* (**a**) *(nappy, lighter)* jetable (**b**) *(funds, income)* disponible
disposal [dɪs'pəʊzəl] *n* (**a**) *(getting rid)* enlèvement *m*, élimination *f* (**b**) *(of property)* cession *f*, vente *f* (**c**) *(availability)* **to have sth at one's d.** avoir qch à sa disposition
dispose [dɪs'pəʊz] *vt Formal (arrange)* disposer
▶**dispose of** *vt insep* (**a**) *(rubbish)* jeter, se débarrasser de; *(problem)* régler (**b**) *(kill)* se débarrasser de
disposed [dɪs'pəʊzd] *adj (willing)* **to be d. to do sth** être disposé(e) à faire qch
disposition [dɪspə'zɪʃən] *n* (**a**) *(temperament)* tempérament *m*, nature *f* (**b**) *(inclination)* tendance *f*; **to have a d. to sth** avoir tendance à faire qch (**c**) *Formal (arrangement)* disposition *f*
dispossess [dɪspə'zes] *vt* déposséder (**of** de)
Disprin® [dɪsprɪn] *n* = marque d'analgésique
disproportionate [dɪsprə'pɔːʃənət] *adj* disproportionné(e) (**to** à)
disprove [dɪs'pruːv] *(pp* **disproved**, *Law* **disproven** [dɪs'prəʊvən]) *vt* réfuter
dispute [dɪs'pjuːt] **1** *n* (**a**) *(debate)* controverse *f*; *(argument)* dispute *f*; **the matter in d.** l'objet de la controverse; **it's beyond d.** c'est incontestable; **it's open to d.** c'est contestable; **(industrial) d.** conflit *m* social
2 *vt (discuss)* discuter; *(call into question)* contester
3 *vi* se quereller (**with/about** avec/à propos de)
disqualification [dɪskwɒlɪfɪ'keɪʃən] *n (from competition)* disqualification *f*; **d. from driving** retrait *m* de permis
disqualify [dɪs'kwɒlɪfaɪ] *(pt & pp* **disqualified**) *vt (from competition)* disqualifier (**from** de); **to d. sb from driving** retirer le permis de conduire à qn
disquiet [dɪs'kwaɪət] *n Formal* inquiétude *f*
disregard [dɪsrɪ'gɑːd] **1** *n* mépris *m*
2 *vt* ignorer, ne tenir aucun compte de
disrepair [dɪsrɪ'peə(r)] *n* délabrement *m*; **in (a state of) d.** délabré(e); **to fall into d.** se délabrer
disreputable [dɪs'repjʊtəbəl] *adj (person)* peu recommandable; *(behaviour)* peu honorable; *(neighbourhood, pub)* mal famé(e)
disrepute [dɪsrɪ'pjuːt] *n* discrédit *m*; **to bring sb/sth into d.** discréditer qn/qch; **to fall into d.** tomber en discrédit
disrespect [dɪsrɪ'spekt] *n* irrespect *m*; **to treat sb with d.** manquer de respect à qn; **I meant no d.** je ne voulais pas être irrespectueux

disrespectful [dɪsrɪ'spektfʊl] *adj* irrespectueux(-euse); **to be d.** to sb manquer de respect à qn
disrupt [dɪs'rʌpt] *vt* perturber
disruption [dɪs'rʌpʃən] *n (of traffic, life, routine)* perturbation *f*; *(of meeting)* interruption *f*
disruptive [dɪs'rʌptɪv] *adj* perturbateur(trice); **to be d.** faire du chahut
dissatisfaction [dɪsætɪs'fækʃən] *n* mécontentement *m* (**with** envers)
dissatisfied [dɪ'sætɪsfaɪd] *adj* mécontent(e) (**with** de)
dissect [dɪ'sekt] *vt also Fig* disséquer
dissemble [dɪ'sembəl] *vt & vi* dissimuler
disseminate [dɪ'semɪneɪt] **1** *vt* propager, répandre **2** *vi* se propager, se répandre
dissension [dɪ'senʃən] *n* dissension *f*
dissent [dɪ'sent] **1** *n* désaccord *m* **2** *vi* être en désaccord (**from** avec)
dissenter [dɪ'sentə(r)] *n Pol* dissident(e) *m,f*
dissenting [dɪ'sentɪŋ] *adj* dissident(e)
dissertation [dɪsə'teɪʃən] *n* mémoire *m*
disservice [dɪ'sɜːvɪs] *n* **to do sb/sth a d.** rendre un mauvais service à qn/qch
dissident ['dɪsɪdənt] **1** *n* dissident(e) *m,f* **2** *adj* dissident(e)
dissimilar [dɪ'sɪmɪlə(r)] *adj* différent(e) (**to** de)
dissipate ['dɪsɪpeɪt] **1** *vt (fears, doubts)* dissiper; *(money, energy)* gaspiller **2** *vi (of mist, doubts)* se dissiper
dissipation [dɪsɪ'peɪʃən] *n (debauchery)* débauche *f*
dissociate [dɪ'səʊsɪeɪt] *vt* dissocier (**from** de); **to d. oneself from sb/sth** se dissocier *ou* se désolidariser de qn/qch
dissolute ['dɪsəluːt] *adj* dissolu(e)
dissolve [dɪ'zɒlv] **1** *vt* dissoudre **2** *vi* se dissoudre; **to d. into tears** fondre en larmes
dissuade [dɪ'sweɪd] *vt* **to d. sb from doing sth** dissuader qn de faire qch
distance ['dɪstəns] **1** *n* distance *f*; **from a d.** de loin; **in the d.** au loin; **within five minutes' walking d.** à cinq minutes de marche; **a short d. away** tout près; **some d. away** assez loin; **to keep one's d.** garder ses distances; **to keep sb at a d.** tenir qn à distance; *Sport & Fig* **to go the d.** tenir la distance; **d. learning** enseignement *m* à distance **2** *vt* **to d. oneself from sb/sth** prendre ses distances vis-à-vis de qn/qch
distant ['dɪstənt] *adj* (**a**) *(far-off)* lointain(e); **in the d. past** il y a très longtemps; **in the d. future** dans un avenir lointain; **3 kilometres d.** à 3 kilomètres de distance (**b**) *(reserved)* distant(e) (**c**) *(distracted)* distrait(e); **she had a d. look** son regard était perdu dans le vague
distantly ['dɪstəntlɪ] *adv* (**a**) **to be d. related to sb** être un parent éloigné de qn (**b**) *(distractedly)* distraitement
distaste [dɪs'teɪst] *n* dégoût *m* (**for** pour)
distasteful [dɪs'teɪstfʊl] *adj* déplaisant(e)
distemper¹ [dɪs'tempə(r)] *n (animal disease)* maladie *f* de Carré
distemper² *n (paint)* détrempe *f*
distend [dɪs'tend] **1** *vt* distendre **2** *vi* se distendre
distil, *Am* **distill** [dɪs'tɪl] *(pt & pp* **distilled)** *vt* distiller
distillery [dɪs'tɪlərɪ] *(pl* **distilleries)** *n* distillerie *f*
distinct [dɪs'tɪŋkt] *adj* (**a**) *(different)* distinct(e) (**from** de); **as d. from** par opposition à (**b**) *(clear)* clair(e);

(preference, improvement, difference) net (nette); **it's a d. possibility** c'est fort possible
distinction [dɪs'tɪŋkʃən] *n* (**a**) *(difference)* distinction *f*; **to draw a d. between** faire une distinction entre (**b**) *(honour, excellence)* distinction *f*; *Ironic* **I had the d. of coming last** j'ai eu l'honneur de venir en dernier; **a writer/scientist of d.** un écrivain/scientifique réputé; **with d.** *(perform, serve)* brillamment (**c**) *(in exam)* mention *f* bien
distinctive [dɪs'tɪŋktɪv] *adj* distinctif(ive)
distinctly [dɪs'tɪŋktlɪ] *adv* (**a**) *(clearly) (speak, hear)* distinctement; *(remember)* très bien; **I d. told you not to do it** je t'ai clairement dit de ne pas le faire (**b**) *(decidedly) (better, easier)* nettement; *(stupid, ill-mannered)* vraiment
distinguish [dɪs'tɪŋgwɪʃ] **1** *vt* (**a**) *(recognize)* distinguer (**b**) *(characterize, differentiate)* distinguer (**from** de); **distinguishing marks** *(on passport)* signes *mpl* particuliers (**c**) **to d. oneself (by sth/by doing sth)** se distinguer (par qch/en faisant qch) **2** *vi* **to d. between** faire la distinction entre
distinguished [dɪs'tɪŋgwɪʃd] *adj (performance, career)* brillant(e); *(person, air)* distingué(e)
distort [dɪs'tɔːt] *vt also Fig* déformer
distorted [dɪs'tɔːtɪd] *adj also Fig* déformé(e)
distortion [dɪs'tɔːʃən] *n also Fig* distorsion *f*, déformation *f*
distract [dɪs'trækt] *vt* distraire; **to d. sb's attention** détourner l'attention de qn; **to be easily distracted** se laisser facilement distraire
distracted [dɪs'træktɪd] *adj* (**a**) *(with thoughts elsewhere)* distrait(e) (**b**) *(distraught)* affolé(e)
distracting [dɪs'træktɪŋ] *adj* gênant(e), qui distrait
distraction [dɪs'trækʃən] *n* (**a**) *(interruption, amusement)* distraction *f* (**b**) *(madness)* **to drive sb to d.** rendre qn fou (folle)
distraught [dɪs'trɔːt] *adj* angoissé(e); **d. with grief** fou (folle) de douleur
distress [dɪs'tres] **1** *n (mental)* désarroi *m*; *(physical)* douleur *f*; **to be in d.** *(mentally)* être bouleversé(e); *(physically)* souffrir; *(of ship)* être en détresse; **d. signal** signal *m* de détresse **2** *vt (upset)* bouleverser
distressed [dɪs'trest] *adj* bouleversé(e)
distressing [dɪs'tresɪŋ] *adj* bouleversant(e)
distribute [dɪs'trɪbjuːt] *vt (give out) & Com (supply)* distribuer; *(spread out)* répartir
distribution [dɪstrɪ'bjuːʃən] *n (giving out) & Com (supplying)* distribution *f*; *(spreading out)* répartition *f*; **d. of wealth** distribution des richesses; *Com* **d. cost** coût *m* de distribution; **d. rights** droits *mpl* de distribution
distributor [dɪs'trɪbjʊtə(r)] *n* (**a**) *(person, company)* distributeur(trice) *m,f*; *(of cars)* concessionnaire *mf* (**b**) *Aut* distributeur *m*
district ['dɪstrɪkt] *n (of country)* région *f*; *(of town, city)* quartier *m*; *(administrative)* district *m*; *Am* **d. attorney** ≃ procureur *m* de la République; *Br* **d. council** conseil *m* municipal; **d. nurse** infirmière *f* visiteuse
distrust [dɪs'trʌst] **1** *n* méfiance *f* (**of** à l'égard de) **2** *vt* se méfier de
distrustful [dɪs'trʌstfʊl] *adj* méfiant(e); **to be d. of** se méfier de
disturb [dɪs'tɜːb] *vt* (**a**) *(interrupt)* déranger; *(criminal)* surprendre; *(someone's sleep)* troubler; *Law* **to d. the peace** troubler l'ordre public (**b**) *(worry)* perturber

(**c**) *(disarrange)* *(papers, room)* déranger; *(surface of water)* agiter; *(ground)* remuer

disturbance [dɪs'tɜːbəns] *n* (**a**) *(nuisance)* dérangement *m* (**b**) *(atmospheric, emotional)* perturbation *f* (**c**) *(fight)* bagarre *f*; *(riot)* émeute *f*; **to cause** *or* **create a d.** semer le désordre; *Law* troubler l'ordre public

disturbed [dɪs'tɜːbd] *adj (night, sleep)* agité(e); *(mentally, emotionally)* perturbé(e)

disturbing [dɪs'tɜːbɪŋ] *adj* perturbant(e), troublant(e)

disunity [dɪs'juːnɪtɪ] *n* désunion *f*

disuse [dɪs'juːs] *n* **to fall into d.** tomber en désuétude

ditch [dɪtʃ] **1** *n (at roadside)* fossé *m*; *(as defence)* douve *f*; *(for drainage)* rigole *f*
2 *vt Fam (get rid of)* (*thing*) se débarrasser de; *(plan, idea)* abandonner; *(boyfriend, girlfriend)* plaquer

dither ['dɪðə(r)] *Fam* **1** *n* **to be in a d.** être dans tous ses états
2 *vi* hésiter, tergiverser; **stop dithering!** décide-toi!

ditto ['dɪtəʊ] *adv* idem; *Fam* **I'm hungry – d.** j'ai faim – itou *ou* moi aussi

ditty ['dɪtɪ] *(pl* **ditties**) *n Fam* chansonnette *f*

ditzy ['dɪtsɪ] *adj esp Am Fam* étourdi(e)

diva ['diːvə] *n* diva *f*; *Fig* **she's a bit of a d.** elle est un peu comédienne

divan [dɪ'væn] *n* divan *m*; **d. bed** divan-lit *m*

dive [daɪv] **1** *n* (**a**) *(of swimmer)* plongeon *m*; *(of marine, diver)* plongée *f*; **to make a d. for sth** *(rush)* se précipiter vers qch; **to go into a d.** *(of plane)* piquer du nez (**b**) *Fam Pej (place)* bouge *m*
2 *vi (Am pt* **dove** [dəʊv]) plonger; *(of plane)* piquer; **to d. for cover** plonger à couvert; **to d. for the exit / into the pub** se précipiter vers la sortie/au pub

diver ['daɪvə(r)] *n* plongeur(euse) *m,f*; *(deep sea)* scaphandrier *m*

diverge [daɪ'vɜːdʒ] *vi (of rays, opinions)* diverger; *(of roads)* se séparer; *(of people)* avoir des opinions divergentes

divergence [daɪ'vɜːdʒəns] *n* divergence *f*

divergent [daɪ'vɜːdʒənt], **diverging** [daɪ'vɜːdʒɪŋ] *adj* divergent(e)

diverse [daɪ'vɜːs] *adj* divers(e)

diversification [daɪvɜːsɪfɪ'keɪʃən] *n* diversification *f*

diversify [daɪ'vɜːsɪfaɪ] *(pt & pp* **diversified**) **1** *vt* diversifier
2 *vi* se diversifier

diversion [daɪ'vɜːʃən] *n* (**a**) *(of traffic)* déviation *f*; *(of plane, funds)* détournement *m*; **to create a d.** faire diversion (**b**) *(amusement)* distraction *f*

diversity [daɪ'vɜːsɪtɪ] *n* diversité *f*

divert [daɪ'vɜːt, dɪ'vɜːt] *vt* (**a**) *(traffic)* dévier; *(plane, funds, attention)* détourner (**b**) *(amuse)* **to d. oneself** se distraire

divest [daɪ'vest] *vt Formal* **to d. sb of sth** *(authority)* priver qn de qch; *(possession)* débarrasser qn de qch

divide [dɪ'vaɪd] **1** *vt* (**a**) *(money, food)* partager (**between/among** entre); **to d. sth in two/three** diviser qch en deux/trois (**b**) *Math* diviser (**by** par) (**c**) *(separate)* séparer (**from** de)
2 *vi (of road)* bifurquer; *(of group)* se diviser; **to d. and rule** diviser pour régner
3 *n* fossé *m*

▶**divide up** *vt sep* partager

divided [dɪ'vaɪdɪd] *adj* divisé(e)

dividend ['dɪvɪdend] *n* dividende *m*; *Fig* **to pay dividends** porter ses fruits

dividers [dɪ'vaɪdəz] *npl (mathematical instrument)* compas *m* à pointe sèche

dividing [dɪ'vaɪdɪŋ] *adj* **d. line** ligne *f* de démarcation; **d. wall** mur *m* de séparation

divine [dɪ'vaɪn] **1** *adj also Fig* divin(e)
2 *vt* deviner

diving ['daɪvɪŋ] *n (in swimming pool)* plongeon *m*; *(sub-aqua)* plongée *f*; **d. bell** cloche *f* à plongeur; **d. board** plongeoir *m*; **d. suit** scaphandre *m*

divinity [dɪ'vɪnɪtɪ] *(pl* **divinities**) *n* (**a**) *(divine nature, god)* divinité *f* (**b**) *(subject)* théologie *f*; *(in school)* instruction *f* religieuse

divisible [dɪ'vɪzəbəl] *adj* divisible

division [dɪ'vɪʒən] *n* (**a**) *(separation)* partage *m* (**b**) *(distribution)* répartition *f*, partage *m*; **d.** division *f* du travail (**c**) *(discord)* division *f* (**d**) *(unit)* division *f*; **first/second d.** *(in sporting league)* première/deuxième division *f*

divisive [dɪ'vaɪsɪv] *adj* qui crée des divisions

divorce [dɪ'vɔːs] **1** *n* divorce *m*; **d. proceedings** procédure *f* de divorce
2 *vt* (**a**) *(husband, wife)* divorcer de; **to get divorced (from sb)** divorcer (de qn) (**b**) *Fig* séparer (**from** de)
3 *vi* divorcer

divorcee [dɪvɔː'siː] *n* divorcé(e) *m,f*

divulge [daɪ'vʌldʒ] *vt* divulguer

DIY [diːaɪ'waɪ] *n (abbr* **do-it-yourself**) bricolage *m*

dizzy ['dɪzɪ] *adj* (**a**) *(unsteady)* étourdi(e); **to feel d.** avoir le vertige; *Fig* **to reach the d. heights of...** atteindre les hauteurs vertigineuses de...; **d. spell** étourdissement *m* (**b**) *Fam (frivolous)* écervelé(e); **a d. blonde** une blonde évaporée

DJ ['diːdʒeɪ] *n* (**a**) *(abbr* **disc jockey**) DJ *m* (**b**) *Fam (abbr* **dinner jacket**) smoking *m*

Djibouti [dʒɪ'buːtɪ] *n* Djibouti

DNA [diːen'eɪ] *n (abbr* **deoxyribonucleic acid**) ADN *m*

do¹ [dəʊ] *n Mus* do *m*

do² [duː]

Les formes négatives sont **don't/doesn't** et **didn't**, qui deviennent **do not/does not** et **did not** à l'écrit, dans un style plus soutenu.

1 *v aux (3rd person singular* **does** [dʌz], *pt* **did** [dɪd], *pp* **done** [dʌn]) (**a**) *(in negatives)* **I don't speak French** je ne parle pas français; **I didn't see him** je ne l'ai pas vu (**b**) *(in questions)* **do you speak French?** (est-ce que) tu parles français?; **did you see him?** (est-ce que) tu l'as vu?; **don't you speak French?** tu ne parles pas français?; **didn't you see him?** tu ne l'as pas vu? (**c**) *(for emphasis)* **he DOES speak French!** mais oui, il parle français!; **I DIDN'T see him!** mais non, je ne l'ai pas vu!; **it doesn't matter – it DOES matter!** pas grave – si, c'est grave! (**d**) *(as substitute for main verb)* **she writes better than I do** elle écrit mieux que moi; **if you want to speak to her, do it now** si tu veux lui parler, fais-le tout de suite; **do you speak French? – yes, I do/no, I don't** parlez-vous français? – oui/non; **I like Paris – so do I** j'aime Paris – moi aussi; **you left the door unlocked – so I did** tu as laissé la porte ouverte – effectivement; **you said you would go – no, I didn't** tu as dit que tu irais – non, ce n'est pas vrai (**e**) *(in tag questions)* **you speak French, don't you?** vous parlez français, n'est-ce pas *ou* non?; **John doesn't live there, does he?** John n'habite pas là, si?; **they said they'd come, didn't they?** ils ont bien dit qu'ils viendraient, non?; **you didn't see her, did you?** est-ce que tu l'as vue ou pas?

2 *vt* (**a**) *(in general)* faire; **what do you do?** *(what's your job?)* que faites-vous dans la vie?; **don't do that**

again! ne refais jamais ça!; **what are you going to do about it?** qu'est-ce que tu vas faire?

(**b**) *(activity)* faire; **to do the housework/the dishes** faire le ménage/la vaisselle; **to do one's hair** se coiffer; **to do one's teeth** se brosser les dents; *Fam* **to do drugs** se droguer; **they do good food here** ils font de la bonne cuisine ici; **it just isn't done!** ça ne se fait pas, c'est tout!; *Fam* **let's do lunch!** on se fait une bouffe?

(**c**) *(have effect on)* **to do sb good** faire du bien à qn; **that hairstyle does nothing/does a lot for her** cette coiffure ne la flatte pas/la flatte; **this music does nothing for me** cette musique ne me plaît pas tellement

(**d**) *(be enough for)* **will £10 do you?** est-ce que 10 livres te suffiront?; **that'll do me** ça m'ira

(**e**) *(study)* faire; **to do French/physics** faire du français/de la physique

(**f**) *(with speed, distance)* **the car was doing 100 (miles per hour)** ≃ la voiture faisait du 160 (à l'heure); **we did 500 km on the first day** nous avons fait 500 km le premier jour

(**g**) *Fam (cheat)* avoir; **I've been done!** je me suis fait avoir!

(**h**) *Fam (prosecute)* pincer; **to get done for speeding** se faire pincer pour excès de vitesse

3 *vi* (**a**) *(act)* **to do well/badly** bien/mal se débrouiller; **do as you're told** fais ce qu'on te dit; **you would do well to accept** tu ferais bien d'accepter; **how do you do?** enchanté(e); **how are you doing?** (comment) ça va?

(**b**) *(be enough)* **two bottles of wine will do** deux bouteilles de vin suffiront; **that'll do** *(is satisfactory)* ça ira; *(stop it)* ça suffit maintenant!

4 *n* (**a**) **the do's and don'ts** les choses *fpl* à faire et à ne pas faire

(**b**) *(pl* **dos**) *Fam (party)* fête *f*

▸**do away with** *vt insep* (**a**) *(abolish)* supprimer (**b**) *Fam (kill)* zigouiller

▸**do down** *vt sep* rabaisser; **to do oneself down** se rabaisser

▸**do for** *vt insep Fam* **to be done for** être fichu(e)

▸**do in** *vt sep Fam* (**a**) *(kill)* zigouiller (**b**) *(exhaust)* **to be done in** être complètement crevé(e) (**c**) *(injure)* **to do one's back/knee in** se bousiller le dos/genou

▸**do out of** *vt sep Fam* **to do sb out of sth** *(job)* priver qn de qch; *(money)* faire perdre qch à qn

▸**do over** *vt sep Fam (beat up)* **to d. sb over** tabasser qn

▸**do up** **1** *vt sep* (**a**) *(fasten)* fermer; *(shoelaces)* attacher (**b**) *(wrap)* envelopper (**c**) *(improve appearance of)* restaurer; *(room, house)* rénover; *Fam* **to do oneself up** *(dress smartly)* se faire beau (belle)

2 *vi (of clothes)* se fermer

▸**do with** *vt insep* (**a**) *(benefit from)* **I could do with a cup of tea** je prendrais bien une tasse de thé; **you could do with a haircut** tu aurais bien besoin de te faire couper les cheveux (**b**) *(be connected with)* **to have nothing to do with sb/sth** *(be unconnected to)* n'avoir rien à voir avec qn/qch; *(not get involved with)* n'avoir rien à faire avec qn/qch; **I had nothing to do with it** je n'ai rien à voir là-dedans; **it's nothing to do with you** *(not your business)* ça ne te regarde pas (**c**) *(finish using)* **to have done with sth** avoir fini avec qch; **have you done with the scissors yet?** est-ce que tu as fini avec les ciseaux?; **it's all over and done with** c'est du passé

▸**do without 1** *vt insep* se passer de

2 *vi* se priver

doc [dɒk] *n Fam (doctor)* toubib *m*

docile ['dəʊsaɪl] *adj* docile

dock¹ [dɒk] **1** *n (for ships)* dock *m*; **d. workers** dockers *mpl*

2 *vi (of ship)* accoster; *(of two spacecraft)* s'arrimer

dock² *n Law* banc *m* des accusés; *Fig* **to be in the d.** être sur la sellette

dock³ *vt* (**a**) *(tail)* couper (**b**) *(wages)* faire une retenue sur

docker ['dɒkə(r)] *n* docker *m*

dockyard ['dɒkjɑːd] *n* chantier *m* naval

doctor ['dɒktə(r)] **1** *n* (**a**) *(medical)* docteur *m*, médecin *m*; **to go to the d.('s)** aller chez le médecin; *Fam Fig* **just what the d. ordered** exactement ce qu'il me fallait (**b**) *Univ* docteur *m*; **D. of Science** docteur ès sciences

2 *vt* (**a**) *Fam (accounts, evidence)* falsifier (**b**) *(cat)* castrer

doctorate ['dɒktərɪt] *n Univ* doctorat *m* (**in** en)

doctrinaire [dɒktrɪ'neə(r)] *adj* doctrinaire

doctrinal [dɒk'traɪnəl] *adj* doctrinal(e)

doctrine ['dɒktrɪn] *n* doctrine *f*

document 1 *n* ['dɒkjʊmənt] document *m*; *Comput* **d. reader** lecteur *m* de documents

2 *vt* ['dɒkjʊment] (**a**) *(show in detail)* présenter (**b**) *(support)* étayer; **the first documented case** le premier cas établi

documentary [dɒkjʊ'mentərɪ] **1** *n* (*pl* **documentaries**) *(TV programme)* documentaire *m*

2 *adj (film)* documentaire; *(proof)* littéral(e)

documentation [dɒkjʊmen'teɪʃən] *n* documentation *f*

docusoap ['dɒkjʊsəʊp] *n TV* docu-soap *m*

dodder ['dɒdə(r)] *vi* marcher d'un pas hésitant

doddering ['dɒdərɪŋ] *adj (walk)* hésitant(e); **a d. old fool** un vieux gâteux (une vieille gâteuse)

doddle ['dɒdəl] *n Br Fam* **it's a d.** c'est simple comme bonjour

dodge [dɒdʒ] **1** *n* (**a**) *Fam (trick)* truc *m*, combine *f*; **tax d.** combine pour payer moins d'impôts (**b**) *(movement)* écart *m*

2 *vt (blow, responsibility, question)* esquiver; *(person)* éviter; *(police)* échapper à

3 *vi* **to d. (out of the way)** faire un bond de côté

dodgems ['dɒdʒəmz] *npl* autos *fpl* tamponneuses

dodgy ['dɒdʒɪ] *adj Br Fam (suspect)* louche; *(not working properly)* en mauvais état; *(risky)* risqué(e); *(food, weather)* douteux(euse)

dodo ['dəʊdəʊ] *(pl* **dodoes** *or* **dodos**) *n* dodo *m*, dronte *m*; (**as**) **dead as a d.** mort(e) et enterré(e)

DOE [diːəʊ'iː] *n Br (abbr* **Department of the Environment**) ≃ ministère *m* de l'Environnement

doe [dəʊ] *n (deer)* biche *f*; *(rabbit)* lapine *f*

does [dʌz] *see* **do²**

doesn't ['dʌzənt] = **does not**

doff [dɒf] *vt* **to d. one's cap to sb** se découvrir devant qn

dog [dɒg] **1** *n* (**a**) *(animal)* chien *m*; **d. biscuit** biscuit *m* pour chien; **d. collar** collier *m* de chien; *Fam (of cleric)* col *m* blanc *(d'un religieux)*; **d. food** nourriture *f* pour chien; **d. handler** maître-chien *m*; *Br* **d. licence** = permis nécessaire pour posséder un chien; **to do the d. paddle** nager comme un petit chien; **d. racing** courses *fpl* de lévriers; **d. show** exposition *f* canine; **d. tag** plaque *f* d'identité (**b**) *Fam (person)* **you lucky**

d.! sacré(e) veinard(e)!; **dirty d.** sale type *m* (**c**) *Fam Pej (ugly woman)* cageot *m* (**d**) *Am (hot dog)* hot dog *m* (**e**) *(idioms) Fam* **to lead a d.'s life** avoir une vie de chien; *Fam* **to make a d.'s breakfast** *or* **dinner of sth** gâcher qch; *Fam* **it's a d.-eat-d. world** c'est un monde sans pitié; *Fam* **to go to the dogs** *(of place)* aller à vau-l'eau; *(of person)* filer un mauvais coton; *Fam* **to be a d. in the manger** être un empêcheur de tourner en rond; *Prov* **you can't teach an old d. new tricks** les vieilles habitudes ont la vie dure; *Prov* **every d. has his day** tout le monde a son heure de gloire **2** *vt (pt & pp* **dogged**) *(follow)* suivre de près; **to d. sb's footsteps** être sur les talons de qn; **to be dogged by scandal/misfortune** être poursuivi(e) par le scandale/la malchance

dog-eared ['dɒgɪəd] *adj (page)* corné(e); *(book)* aux pages cornées
dogfight ['dɒgfaɪt] *n (between planes)* combat *m* aérien; *(between people)* bagarre *f*
dogfish ['dɒgfɪʃ] *n* roussette *f*
dogged ['dɒgɪd] *adj* tenace
doggerel ['dɒgərəl] *n (comical)* poésie *f* burlesque; *(bad)* vers *mpl* de mirliton
doggy ['dɒgɪ] *(pl* **doggies**) *n Fam* toutou *m*; **d. bag** = petit sac fourni par certains restaurants pour que les clients puissent emporter les restes
doghouse ['dɒghaʊs] *n* (**a**) *Am* niche *f*, chenil *m* (**b**) *Fam* **to be in the d.** (**with sb**) ne pas être en odeur de sainteté (auprès de qn)
dogma ['dɒgmə] *n* dogme *m*
dogmatic [dɒg'mætɪk] *adj* dogmatique
do-gooder ['duː'gʊdə(r)] *n Fam Pej* âme *f* charitable
dogsbody ['dɒgzbɒdɪ] *(pl* **dogsbodies**) *n Br Fam* factotum *m*
dog-tired ['dɒg'taɪəd] *adj Fam* claqué(e), crevé(e)
dogwood ['dɒgwʊd] *n* cornouiller *m*
doh¹ [dəʊ] *n Mus* do *m*
doh² *exclam* que je suis bête!
doily ['dɔɪlɪ] *(pl* **doilies**) *n* napperon *m*
doing ['duːɪŋ] *n* (**a**) **this is his d.** c'est son œuvre; **it was none of my d.** je n'y étais pour rien; **that takes some d.** il faut le faire (**b**) **doings** faits *mpl* et gestes *mpl*
do-it-yourself [duːɪtjɔː'self] *n* bricolage *m*; **a d. enthusiast** un(e) adepte du bricolage
doldrums ['dɒldrəmz] *npl* **to be in the d.** *(of person)* broyer du noir; *(of economy)* être en plein marasme
dole [dəʊl] *n Br Fam* (indemnités *fpl* de) chômage *m*; **to be on the d.** être au chômage; *Fig* **to join the d. queue** se retrouver au chômage
▸**dole out** *vt sep Fam* distribuer
doleful ['dəʊlfʊl] *adj* triste
doll [dɒl] *n* poupée *f*; **d.'s house** maison *f* de poupée
▸**doll up** *vt sep Fam* **to d. oneself up** se pomponner
dollar ['dɒlə(r)] *n* dollar *m*; **d. bill** billet *m* de un dollar
dollop ['dɒləp] *n Fam (of cream, mashed potato)* bonne cuillerée *f*; *(of mud, clay)* tas *m*
dolly ['dɒlɪ] *(pl* **dollies**) *n* (**a**) *Fam (toy)* poupée *f* (**b**) *(for camera)* chariot *m*
dolphin ['dɒlfɪn] *n* dauphin *m*
dolt [dəʊlt] *n Fam* andouille *f*
domain [də'meɪn] *n also Fig* domaine *m*; *Comput* **d. name** nom *m* de domaine
dome [dəʊm] *n* dôme *m*
domestic [də'mestɪk] **1** *adj* (**a**) *(appliance, use, tasks)* ménager(ère); *(animal)* domestique; **d. bliss** bonheur *m* familial; *Br* **d. science** *(school subject)* cours *mpl* de

couture et de cuisine; **d. servant** domestique *mf*; **d. violence** violence *f* domestique *ou* familiale (**b**) *(policy, flight, affairs)* intérieur(e); *(economy, currency)* national(e)
2 *n Br* (**a**) *(cleaner)* domestique *mf* (**b**) *Fam (fight)* querelle *f* domestique
domesticate [də'mestɪkeɪt] *vt (animal)* domestiquer; *Hum* **to be domesticated** *(of person)* se débrouiller plutôt bien avec les travaux ménagers
domicile ['dɒmɪsaɪl] *n Law* domicile *m*
dominance ['dɒmɪnəns] *n (of disease, gene)* dominance *f*; *(of race, political party)* prédominance *f*; *(of person)* supériorité *f*
dominant ['dɒmɪnənt] *adj* dominant(e); *(person, character)* dominateur(trice)
dominate ['dɒmɪneɪt] *vt & vi* dominer
domination [dɒmɪ'neɪʃən] *n* domination *f*
domineering [dɒmɪ'nɪərɪŋ] *adj* dominateur(trice)
Dominica [də'mɪnɪkə] *n* la Dominique
Dominican [də'mɪnɪkən] **1** *n* Dominicain(e) *m,f*
2 *adj* dominicain(e); **the D. Republic** la République Dominicaine
dominion [də'mɪnjən] *n* domination *f*; *Can* **D. day** Fête *f* du Canada *(anniversaire de l'indépendance canadienne, le 1er juillet)*
domino ['dɒmɪnəʊ] *(pl* **dominoes**) *n* domino *m*; *Pol & Fig* **d. effect** effet *m* d'entraînement
don¹ [dɒn] *n Br Univ* professeur *m* d'université *(surtout à Oxford et Cambridge)*
don² *(pt & pp* **donned**) *vt Formal (clothing)* mettre, revêtir
donate [də'neɪt] *vt* faire don de; **to d. blood** donner son sang
donation [də'neɪʃən] *n* donation *f*; don *m*
done [dʌn] *pp of* **do²**
donkey ['dɒŋkɪ] *(pl* **donkeys**) *n (animal) & Fam (person)* âne *m*; *Fam* **I haven't seen her for d.'s years** je ne l'ai pas vue depuis une éternité; *Fam* **to talk the hind legs off a d.** avoir la langue bien pendue; **d. jacket** ≃ caban *m*; *Fam* **d. work** travail *m* pénible
donor ['dəʊnə(r)] *n* donneur(euse) *m,f*; **d. card** carte *f* de donneur d'organe
don't [dəʊnt] = **do not**
donut *Am* = **doughnut**
doodle ['duːdəl] **1** *n* gribouillis *m*, gribouillage *m*
2 *vi* gribouiller
doom [duːm] **1** *n* destin *m (funeste)*; **to be all d. and gloom** voir tout en noir
2 *vt* **to be doomed** *(of person) (unlucky)* être marqué(e) par le destin; *(about to die)* être perdu(e); **to be doomed (to failure)** *(of project)* être voué(e) à l'échec; **to be doomed to do sth** être condamné(e) à faire qch
doom-laden ['duːmleɪdən] *adj* funeste, sinistre
doomsday ['duːmzdeɪ] *n* jour *m* du Jugement dernier; *Fig* **till d.** indéfiniment
door [dɔː(r)] *n* porte *f*; *(of train, car)* portière *f*; **to answer the d.** aller ouvrir (la porte); **to see sb to the d.** raccompagner qn à la porte; **to show sb the d.** mettre qn à la porte; **to shut the d. in sb's face** fermer la porte au nez de qn; **she lives two doors away** elle habite deux portes plus loin; *Fig* **to lay sth at sb's d.** imputer qch à qn; **out of doors** dehors, en plein air; **d. handle** poignée *f* de porte; **d. knocker** heurtoir *m*
doorbell ['dɔːbel] *n* sonnette *f*
doorkeeper ['dɔːkiːpə(r)] *n* portier *m*
doorknob ['dɔːnɒb] *n* bouton *m* de porte

doorman ['dɔːmən] *n (in hotel)* portier *m*; *(in block of flats)* concierge *m*
doormat ['dɔːmæt] *n* paillasson *m*; *Fig* **to treat sb like a d.** traiter qn comme un moins que rien
doorpost ['dɔːpəʊst] *n* montant *m* de porte
doorstep ['dɔːstep] *n* pas *m* de la porte, seuil *m*; *Fig* **on one's d.** à deux pas
doorstop ['dɔːstɒp] *n (fixed)* butoir *m*; *(wedge)* cale-porte *m*
door-to-door ['dɔːtə'dɔː(r)] *adj* **d. canvassing** porte-à-porte *m* électoral; **d. salesman** démarcheur *m*
doorway ['dɔːweɪ] *n* porte *f*; **in the d.** dans l'embrasure de la porte
dopamine ['dəʊpəmɪn] dopamine *f*
dope [dəʊp] **1** *n* (**a**) *very Fam (cannabis)* shit *m*; *Fam* **d. test** *(for athlete)* contrôle *m* antidopage (**b**) *Fam (idiot)* andouille *f*
2 *vt (person, horse) (to make faster)* doper; *(to make slower)* droguer; *(food, drink)* mettre une drogue dans
dopey ['dəʊpɪ] *adj Fam* idiot(e)
dorm [dɔːm] *n Fam (dormitory)* dortoir *m*
dormant ['dɔːmənt] **1** *adj (volcano)* en sommeil; *(conflict, emotion)* latent(e); *(idea)* qui sommeille **2** *adv* **to lie d.** être en sommeil
dormer window ['dɔːmə'wɪndəʊ] *n* lucarne *f*
dormitory ['dɔːmɪtərɪ] *(pl* **dormitories)** *n* (**a**) dortoir *m*; **d. town** cité-dortoir *f* (**b**) *Am Univ* résidence *f* universitaire
dormouse ['dɔːmaʊs] *(pl* **dormice** ['dɔːmaɪs]*)* *n* loir *m*
dorsal ['dɔːsəl] *adj* dorsal(e)
DOS [dɒs] *n Comput (abbr* **disk operating system)** DOS *m*
dose [dəʊs] **1** *n (amount)* dose *f*; **a bad d. of (the) flu** une bonne grippe; **to have a d. of measles** avoir la rougeole **2** *vt Fam* bourrer (**with** de); **to d. oneself (up) with pills** se bourrer de médicaments
dosh [dɒʃ] *n Br Fam (money)* fric *m*
doss [dɒs] *vi Fam* **to d. (down)** crécher
dosser ['dɒsə(r)] *n Br very Fam (tramp)* clodo *mf*
doss-house ['dɒshaʊs] *n Br Fam* asile *m* de nuit
dossier ['dɒsɪeɪ] *n* dossier *m*
dot [dɒt] **1** *n* point *m*; **on the d.** à l'heure pile; **at three o'clock on the d.** à trois heures pile; *Com* **d. com (company)** start-up *f*, jeune pousse *f*; *Comput* **d. matrix printer** imprimante *f* matricielle **2** *vt (pt & pp* **dotted)** parsemer (**with** de); **to d. an i/ a j** mettre un point sur un i/un j; **dotted line** pointillé *m*; **to sign on the dotted line** ≃ signer à l'endroit indiqué; *Fig* donner son consentement; *Fig* **to d. the i's (and cross the t's)** peaufiner les détails
dotage ['dəʊtɪdʒ] *n* **to be in one's d.** être gâteux(euse)
dot-com [dɒt'kɒm] *adj Comput* qui a trait à la netéconomie; **d. millionnaire** = personne qui a fait fortune en montant une start-up
dot-commer [dɒt'kɒmə(r)] *n* = personne qui travaille dans le secteur de la netéconomie
▸**dote on, dote upon** [dəʊt] *vt insep* adorer
doting ['dəʊtɪŋ] *adj* **he has a d. mother** sa mère l'aime à la folie
dotty ['dɒtɪ] *adj Fam (person, idea)* toqué(e); **to be d. about sb** être fou (folle) de qn
double ['dʌbəl] **1** *n* (**a**) *(of person)* double *m*, sosie *m* (**b**) *(hotel room)* chambre *f* pour deux personnes (**c**) **doubles** *(in tennis)* double *m*; **a doubles match** un

double (**d**) **at** *or* **on the d.** à l'instant (**e**) *(measure of drink)* double *m*
2 *adj* double; **d. m** *(when spelling)* deux m; **d. five two one** *(figure)* deux fois cinq deux un; *(phone number)* cinquante-cinq, vingt et un; **d. agent** agent *m* double; **d. bass** contrebasse *f*; **d. bed** grand lit *m*, lit *f* à deux personnes; **d. bill** *Cin* double programme *m*; *TV (two films)* = programmation de deux longs métrages à la suite; *(two episodes of series)* = programmation de deux épisodes d'une série télévisée à la suite; **d. chin** double menton *m*; *Br* **d. cream** ≃ crème *f* fraîche épaisse; *Br* **to talk d. Dutch** parler chinois; **d. fault** *(in tennis)* double faute *f*; **to be in d. figures** *(of statistic)* avoir atteint plus de dix; **inflation is now in d. figures** l'inflation a passé la barre des 10 pour cent; **to lead a d. life** mener une double vie; **d. meaning** double sens *m*; **d. room** chambre *f* pour deux personnes; **to have d. standards** faire deux poids, deux mesures; **to do a d. take** marquer un temps d'arrêt *(par surprise)*; **a d. whisky** un double whisky; *Br* **d. yellow line** = double ligne jaune indiquant une zone de stationnement interdit
3 *adv* **to see d.** voir double; **to fold sth d.** plier qch en deux; **to be bent d.** être plié(e) en deux
4 *vt* (**a**) *(multiply by two)* doubler (**b**) *(fold)* plier en deux
5 *vi* (**a**) *(increase twofold)* doubler (**b**) **to d. as sth** servir aussi de qch
▸**double back** *vi* rebrousser chemin
▸**double up** *vi (bend)* se plier en deux (**with** de)
double-barrelled ['dʌbəl'bærəld] *adj (shotgun)* à deux coups; *(surname)* à rallonge
double-breasted ['dʌbəl'brestɪd] *adj (jacket, suit)* croisé(e)
double-check ['dʌbəl'tʃek] *vt & vi* bien vérifier
double-click ['dʌbəl'klɪk] *Comput* **1** *n* double-clic *m* **2** *vt* cliquer deux fois sur, double-cliquer **3** *vi* cliquer deux fois, faire un double-clic (**on** sur)
double-cross ['dʌbəl'krɒs] *vt* trahir, doubler
double-dealing ['dʌbəl'diːlɪŋ] *n* fourberie *f*
double-decker ['dʌbəl'dekə(r)] *n Br (bus)* autobus *m* à impériale *ou* à étage
double-edged ['dʌbəl'edʒd] *adj also Fig* à double tranchant
double-glazing ['dʌbəl'gleɪzɪŋ] *n* double vitrage *m*
double-jointed [dʌbəl'dʒɔɪntəd] *adj* désarticulé(e)
double-lock ['dʌbəl'lɒk] *vt* fermer à double tour
double-park ['dʌbəl'pɑːk] *vi* se garer en double file
double-quick ['dʌbəl'kwɪk] *adv* en vitesse
doubly ['dʌbəlɪ] *adv* doublement; **to make d. sure of sth** bien vérifier qch; **d. difficult** deux fois plus difficile; **to be d. careful** redoubler de prudence
doubt [daʊt] **1** *n* doute *m*; **to have doubts about sth** avoir des doutes sur qch; **to be in d.** *(of person)* douter (**about** de); *(of outcome)* être incertain(e); **when in d.** en cas de doute, dans le doute; **beyond d.** sans le moindre doute; **no d.** sans doute; **there is no d. that...** il ne fait aucun doute que...; **there's no d. about her guilt** sa culpabilité ne fait aucun doute; **there is some d. about...** il y a des doutes quant à...
2 *vt* douter de; **I d. it** j'en doute; **I d. if it makes him happy** je doute que cela le rende heureux
doubtful ['daʊtfʊl] *adj* (**a**) *(uncertain) (person)* dubitatif(ive); *(outcome)* incertain(e); **to be d. about sth** avoir des doutes sur qch (**b**) *(questionable)* douteux(euse)

dough [dəʊ] n (**a**) (for bread) pâte f (**b**) Fam (money) fric m
doughnut, Am donut ['dəʊnʌt] n beignet m, Can beigne m
dour [dʊə(r)] adj austère
douse [daʊs] vt (**a**) (soak) arroser (**b**) (extinguish) éteindre
dove¹ [dʌv] n colombe f
dove² [dəʊv] Am pt of **dive**
dovecot(e) ['dʌvkɒt] n colombier m
Dover ['dəʊvər] n Douvres
dovetail ['dʌvteɪl] vi (fit closely) concorder, cadrer (with avec)
dowager ['daʊədʒə(r)] n douairière f
dowdy ['daʊdɪ] adj (person) inélégant(e); (clothes, image) démodé(e)
dowel ['daʊəl] n cheville f
down¹ [daʊn] n (feathers) duvet m
down² 1 prep **to go d. the stairs/the street** descendre les escaliers/la rue; **to run d. the stairs/the street** descendre les escaliers/la rue en courant; **to fall d. the stairs** dégringoler les escaliers; **the tears ran d. her cheeks** les larmes coulaient sur ses joues
2 adv (**a**) (with motion) **to come/go d.** descendre; **to fall d.** tomber; **to bend d.** se pencher; **petrol has come** or **gone d. in price** le prix de l'essence a baissé; **I'll be d. in a minute** je descends tout de suite; **d. with traitors!** à bas les traîtres!
(**b**) (with position) en bas; **d. here/there** ici/là en bas; **further d.** plus bas; **petrol is d. in price** le prix de l'essence a baissé; **one d., two to go!** et d'un! encore deux et c'est fini!; **everyone from the boss d.** tout le monde, même le chef
(**c**) (in crosswords) verticalement
(**d**) (idioms) **to be d. on sb/sth** avoir une dent contre qn/qch; **it's a d. to her** (her decision) c'est à elle de décider; (her achievement) c'est grâce à elle; **I'm d. to my last pound/cigarette** il ne me reste plus qu'une livre/une cigarette
3 n Fam **to have a d. on sb/sth** avoir une dent contre qn/qch
4 adj (**a**) (depressed) déprimé(e)
(**b**) **to be d.** (of computer, telephones) être en panne
5 adj (**a**) (aircraft) abattre
(**b**) (drink) descendre; **to d. tools** (of workers) se mettre en grève
down-and-out ['daʊnən'aʊt] Fam 1 n (tramp) clochard(e) m,f
2 adj sans le sou
downbeat ['daʊnbiːt] adj (**a**) (gloomy, pessimistic) triste, pessimiste (**b**) (restrained) réservé(e) (about sur)
downcast ['daʊnkɑːst] adj (eyes) baissé(e); (person) abattu(e), découragé(e)
downer ['daʊnə(r)] n Fam (**a**) (drug) tranquillisant m (**b**) (depressing situation) situation f déprimante; (depressing event) événement m déprimant
downfall ['daʊnfɔːl] n (of government) chute f; (of person) ruine f
downgrade ['daʊngreɪd] 1 vt (job, hotel) déclasser; (employee) rétrograder
2 n descente f
downhearted [daʊn'hɑːtɪd] adj découragé(e)
downhill ['daʊn'hɪl] 1 adj (slope) en pente; **d. skiing** ski m alpin ou de descente
2 adv **to go d.** (of road, car) descendre; Fig (of person, career) être sur le déclin; (of business) péricliter

Downing Street ['daʊnɪŋ'striːt] n Downing Street, = rue de Londres où se trouve la résidence officielle du Premier ministre britannique

Downing Street

C'est à Downing Street à Londres que se trouvent les résidences officielles du Premier ministre, au n° 10, et du ministre des Finances, au n° 11. Le terme "Downing Street" est souvent employé pour désigner le gouvernement.

download Comput 1 n ['daʊnləʊd] téléchargement m
2 vt [daʊn'ləʊd] télécharger
3 vt [daʊn'ləʊd] effectuer un téléchargement; **graphic files take a long time to d.** le téléchargement de fichiers graphiques est très lent
downmarket [daʊn'mɑːkɪt] adj (product) bas de gamme inv; (area, place) populaire
down payment [daʊn'peɪmənt] n acompte m
downpour ['daʊnpɔː(r)] n averse f
downright ['daʊnraɪt] 1 adj (stupidity, dishonesty) véritable; **it's a d. lie!** c'est un mensonge flagrant!
2 adv (stupid, untrue) carrément
downsizing ['daʊnsaɪzɪŋ] n réduction f d'effectifs
Down's syndrome ['daʊnz'sɪndrəʊm] n trisomie f 21
downstairs 1 adj ['daʊnsteəz] (on a lower floor) de l'étage du dessous; (on ground floor) du rez-de-chaussée; **the d. flat** l'appartement du dessous; **the d. bathroom** la salle de bains du bas
2 adv [daʊn'steəz] en bas; **to come/go d.** descendre; **he lives d.** il habite à l'étage au-dessous
downstream [daʊn'striːm] adv en aval; (with movement) vers l'aval
downswing ['daʊnswɪŋ] n Econ tendance f à la baisse
down-to-earth [daʊntə'ɜːθ] adj terre à terre inv
downtown ['daʊn'taʊn] Am 1 n (city centre) centre-ville m
2 adj du centre-ville; **d. LA** le centre de Los Angeles
3 adv au centre-ville
downtrodden ['daʊntrɒdən] adj opprimé(e)
downturn ['daʊntɜːn] n (in inflation) baisse f; (in economy) ralentissement m
down under [daʊn'ʌndə(r)] adv Br Fam (in Australia) en Australie; (in New Zealand) en Nouvelle-Zélande
downward ['daʊnwəd] adj vers le bas; **a d. trend** tendance à la baisse
downwards ['daʊnwədz] adv vers le bas
dowry ['daʊrɪ] (pl dowries) n dot f
doze [dəʊz] 1 n somme m; **to have a d.** faire un somme
2 vi somnoler
▶**doze off** vi s'assoupir
dozen ['dʌzən] n douzaine f; **half a d./a d. eggs** une demi-douzaine/une douzaine d'œufs; Fam **dozens of times/people** des dizaines de fois/gens
dozy ['dəʊzɪ] adj (**a**) (sleepy) **to feel d.** avoir envie de dormir (**b**) Fam (stupid) abruti(e)
Dr (abbr Doctor) Dr
drab [dræb] adj (person, colour) terne; (atmosphere, city) morne
drachma ['drækmə] n drachme f
draconian [drə'kəʊnɪən] adj draconien(enne)
draft¹ [drɑːft] 1 n (**a**) (of letter) brouillon m; (of law, proposal) avant-projet m; (of novel) jet m (**b**) Fin traite f (**c**) Am (conscription) conscription f; **d. dodger** insoumis m

2 vt (**a**) (letter) faire le brouillon de; (proposal) rédiger; (law, bill) préparer (**b**) (recruit) **to d. sb in** détacher qn

draft² Am = **draught**

draftsman Am = **draughtsman**

drafty Am = **draughty**

drag [dræg] **1** n (**a**) (air resistance) traînée f; **d. racing** courses fpl de dragsters (**b**) Fam (person) raseur(-euse) m,f; (task) corvée f; **the party was a real d.** la soirée était vraiment rasante (**c**) Fam (on cigarette) taffe f; **to take** or **have a d. on a cigarette** tirer une taffe sur une cigarette (**d**) Fam (women's clothing worn by man) **to be in d.** être travesti; **d. artist** travesti m; **d. queen** travelo m (**e**) Am Fam (street) **the main d.** la rue principale
2 vt (pt & pp **dragged**) (**a**) (pull) traîner; **to d. sb out of bed** tirer qn de son lit; Fig **to d. one's feet over doing sth** tarder à faire qch; Fig **to d. oneself away from sth** s'arracher à qch; **don't d. me into this!** ne me mêlez pas à vos histoires!; **to d. sb's name through the mud** traîner qn dans la boue (**b**) (pond, canal) draguer
3 vi (of film, day) traîner en longueur; (of conversation) languir

▶**drag on** vi (of meeting, film) traîner en longueur, s'éterniser

▶**drag out** vt sep (meeting, speech) faire traîner

▶**drag up** vt sep (refer to) ressortir

drag-and-drop ['drægən'drɒp] n Comput glisser-lâcher m

dragnet ['drægnet] n (in deep-sea fishing) seine f, senne f; Fig (to catch criminals) rafle f

dragon ['drægən] n also Fig dragon m

dragonfly ['drægənflaɪ] (pl **dragonflies**) n libellule f

dragoon [drə'gu:n] **1** n (soldier) dragon m
2 vt **to d. sb into doing sth** forcer qn à faire qch

drain [dreɪn] **1** n (**a**) (for water, sewage) égout m; Fig **to throw money down the d.** jeter l'argent par les fenêtres; **that's five years' work down the d.** voilà cinq années de travail perdues; **that's my holiday down the d.** ce sont mes vacances qui tombent à l'eau (**b**) (on resources) ponction f (**on** sur); (on strength) perte f (**on** de)
2 vt (liquid) vider; (vegetables) égoutter; **to d. one's glass** finir son verre; Fig **to feel drained** être épuisé(e) ou vidé(e)
3 vi (of liquid) s'écouler; (of dishes) égoutter; (of sink, washing machine) se vider; (of river) se jeter; **the colour drained from her face** elle est devenue blême

▶**drain away** vi (of liquid) s'écouler; Fig (of strength, enthusiasm) s'épuiser; (of fear, tension) s'apaiser

drainage ['dreɪnɪdʒ] n drainage m

drainpipe ['dreɪnpaɪp] n tuyau m d'écoulement; **d. trousers, drainpipes** pantalon m cigarette

drake [dreɪk] n canard m (mâle)

dram [dræm] n (of whisky) goutte f

drama ['drɑːmə] n (**a**) (art form) théâtre m; (play) drame m; Fig **to make a d. out of sth** faire un drame de qch; **d. school** école f d'art dramatique; Fam Pej **d. queen** comédien(enne) m,f (**b**) (excitement) action f

dramatic [drə'mætɪk] adj (**a**) (work) dramatique; (actor) de théâtre (**b**) (significant) spectaculaire (**c**) (theatrical) théâtral(e)

dramatically [drə'mætɪklɪ] adv (**a**) (change, increase, drop) de manière spectaculaire (**b**) (theatrically) de façon théâtrale

dramatist ['dræmətɪst] n auteur m dramatique, dramaturge mf

dramatize ['dræmətaɪz] vt (**a**) (adapt) (for stage) adapter pour la scène; (for screen) adapter pour l'écran (**b**) (exaggerate) dramatiser

drank [dræŋk] pt of **drink**

drape [dreɪp] **1** npl Am **drapes** (curtains) rideaux mpl
2 vt (table, coffin) draper (**with** de); **to d. sth over sth** draper qch sur qch

drastic ['dræstɪk] adj (solution, change) radical(e); (improvement, decline) spectaculaire; (action) énergique; (shortage, difficulty) dramatique

drat [dræt] exclam Fam **d. (it)!** nom de nom!

draught, Am **draft** [drɑːft] n (**a**) (wind) courant m d'air; **d. excluder** bourrelet m (**b**) (of drink) gorgée f; (of air) bouffée f (**c**) **on d.** (beer) à la pression; **d. beer** bière f pression

draughtboard ['drɑːftbɔːd] n Br damier m

draughts ['drɑːfts] n Br (game) (jeu m de) dames fpl

draughtsman, Am **draftsman** ['drɑːftsmən] n dessinateur(trice) m,f

draughty, Am **drafty** ['drɑːftɪ] adj plein(e) de courants d'air

draw [drɔː] **1** n (**a**) (in match, argument) match m nul (**b**) (lottery) loterie f, tombola f; (for sporting competition) tirage m au sort (**c**) (attraction) attraction f
2 vt (pt **drew** [druː], pp **drawn** [drɔːn]) (**a**) (picture, diagram, map) dessiner; (circle, line) tracer; **to d. sb's picture** faire le portrait de qn (**b**) (pull) (cart) tirer; (person) attirer (**towards** vers); **to d. the curtains** (open or shut) tirer les rideaux; **to d. breath** souffler (**c**) (extract) retirer; (pistol, sword) dégainer; (water, wine) tirer; Fig (strength, comfort) retirer, puiser (**from** de); **to d. a knife on sb** menacer qn d'un couteau; **to d. a salary** toucher un salaire; **to d. blood** (of dog) mordre jusqu'au sang; (of cat) griffer jusqu'au sang; **to d. lots for sth** tirer qch au sort; **to d. straws** tirer à la courte paille; Fig **to d. the short straw** ne pas avoir de chance; **to d. a conclusion from sth** tirer une conclusion de qch; **she refused to be drawn on the issue** elle refusa de se laisser entraîner sur ce sujet; **they were drawn against the champions** (in competition) le tirage au sort a décidé qu'ils joueraient contre les champions (**d**) (attract) attirer; **to d. a crowd** (of incident) créer un attroupement; (of play) attirer le public; **to feel drawn to sb/sth** se sentir attiré(e) par qn/qch; Fig **to d. sb's fire** s'attirer les foudres de qn
3 vi (**a**) (make picture) dessiner (**b**) (in game) faire match nul (**with** avec) (**c**) (move) **to d. ahead of sb** devancer qn; **to d. level with sb** rattraper qn; **to d. to an end** or **a close** tirer ou toucher à sa fin; **to d. near** (s')approcher; **to d. to a halt** s'arrêter

▶**draw back 1** vt sep (sheet, veil) retirer
2 vi reculer; **to d. back from doing sth** hésiter à faire qch

▶**draw in** vi (of night) raccourcir

▶**draw on 1** vt insep (resources, savings) tirer sur; (experience) se servir de
2 vi (of evening) approcher

▸**draw out** *vt sep* (**a**) *(encourage to talk)* faire parler (**b**) *(prolong)* faire durer

▸**draw up 1** *vt sep* (**a**) *(chair)* approcher; **she drew herself up to her full height** elle s'est dressée de toute sa hauteur (**b**) *(plan, list)* dresser; *(will)* rédiger
2 *vi (of vehicle)* s'arrêter

drawback ['drɔːbæk] *n* inconvénient *m*
drawbridge ['drɔːbrɪdʒ] *n* pont-levis *m*
drawer [drɔː(r)] *n* tiroir *m*
drawers [drɔːəz] *npl* *Old-fashioned (for women)* culotte *f*; *(for men)* caleçon *m*
drawing ['drɔːɪŋ] *n* dessin *m*; **d. board** planche *f* à dessin; *Fig* **it's back to the d. board!** retour à la case départ!; **d. paper** papier *m* à dessin; **d. pin** punaise *f*; **d. room** salon *m*
drawl [drɔːl] **1** *n* voix *f* traînante
2 *vi* parler d'une voix traînante
drawn [drɔːn] **1** *adj (face)* blême; *(features)* tiré(e); **to look d.** avoir les traits tirés
2 *pp of* **draw**
drawstring ['drɔːstrɪŋ] *n* cordon *m*
dread [dred] **1** *n* terreur *f*; **to have a d. of sth** avoir la hantise de qch
2 *vt* **to d. sth/doing sth** appréhender *ou* redouter qch/de faire qch; **I d. to think!** je n'ose pas imaginer!
dreaded ['dredɪd] *adj* redouté(e)
dreadful ['dredfʊl] *adj* (**a**) *(terrible)* épouvantable, affreux(euse); **to feel d.** se sentir vraiment mal; **I feel really d. about it!** quand j'y pense, je suis horriblement gêné! (**b**) *Fam (for emphasis)* terrible; **it's a d. bore/shame!** c'est vraiment rasant/dommage!
dreadfully ['dredfʊlɪ] *adv* (**a**) *(very badly)* affreusement (**b**) *Fam (extremely)* terriblement, horriblement
dreadlocks ['dredlɒks] *npl* dreadlocks *mpl*
dream [driːm] **1** *n* rêve *m*; **to have a d. (about)** rêver (de); **to have a bad d.** faire un mauvais rêve; **a d. come true** un rêve devenu réalité; **it worked like a d.** ça a marché à merveille
2 *adj* de rêve; **my d. house** la maison de mes rêves; **d. team** dream team *f*; **d. world** monde *m* imaginaire; *Fig* **to live in a d. world** vivre en pleine utopie
3 *vt (pt & pp* dreamt [dremt] *or* dreamed) **to d. that...** rêver que...; *Fig* **I never dreamt you would take me seriously** je n'aurais jamais pensé que tu me prendrais au sérieux
4 *vi* rêver (**of** *or* **about** de); *Fig* **I wouldn't d. of it!** je n'y songerais même pas!
▸**dream up** *vt sep (scheme, excuse)* imaginer, inventer
dreamcatcher ['driːmkætʃə(r)] *n* attrapeur *m* de rêves
dreamer ['driːmə(r)] *n* rêveur(euse) *m,f*
dreamt [dremt] *pt & pp of* **dream**
dreamy ['driːmɪ] *adj* (**a**) *(person, expression)* rêveur(euse) (**b**) *Fam (wonderful)* magnifique, ravissant
dreary ['drɪərɪ] *adj* morne
dredge [dredʒ] *vt (canal, harbour)* draguer; *Fig* **to d. one's memory** fouiller dans ses souvenirs
▸**dredge up** *vt sep (body, object)* repêcher; *Fig (scandal, memory)* déterrer
dredger ['dredʒə(r)] *n (boat)* dragueur *m*
dregs [dregz] *npl (of wine)* lie *f*; *(of coffee)* marc *m*; *(in cup)* fond *m* de tasse; *Fig* **the d. of society** les bas-fonds *mpl* de la société

drench [drentʃ] *vt* tremper (**with** *or* in de); **drenched to the skin** trempé(e) jusqu'aux os
dress [dres] **1** *n* (**a**) *(for woman)* robe *f* (**b**) *(clothing)* tenue *f*; **to have good d. sense/no d. sense** savoir/ne pas savoir s'habiller; **d. circle** premier balcon *m*; **d. rehearsal** *(répétition f)* générale *f*; **d. shirt** chemise *f* de soirée
2 *vt* (**a**) *(person)* habiller, vêtir; **to d. oneself, to get dressed** s'habiller; **to be dressed in black/in rags** être vêtu(e) de noir/de haillons; **well/badly dressed** bien/mal habillé(e) (**b**) *(wound)* panser (**c**) *(salad)* assaisonner; **dressed crab** chair *f* de crabe
3 *vi* s'habiller
▸**dress down** *vi* s'habiller simplement
▸**dress up** *vi (elegantly)* se faire beau (belle), s'habiller; *(in fancy dress)* se déguiser (**as** en)
dress-down Friday ['dresdaʊn'fraɪdeɪ] *n* = journée du vendredi, où, contrairement au reste de la semaine, les employés sont libres de s'habiller comme ils le souhaitent
dresser ['dresə(r)] *n* (**a**) *(in kitchen)* vaisselier *m* (**b**) *Am (dressing table)* coiffeuse *f* (**c**) *Theat (person)* habilleur(euse) *m,f*
dressing ['dresɪŋ] *n* (**a**) **d. gown** robe *f* de chambre; **d. room** *(in theatre)* loge *f*; *(in gym, sports centre)* vestiaire *m*; *(in home)* cabinet *m* de toilette; **d. table** coiffeuse *f* (**b**) *(for wound)* pansement *m* (**c**) *(for salad)* assaisonnement *m*
dressing-down ['dresɪŋ'daʊn] *n Fam* savon *m*; **to give sb a d.** passer un savon à qn
dressmaker ['dresmeɪkə(r)] *n* couturière *f*
dressmaking ['dresmeɪkɪŋ] *n* couture *f*
dressy ['dresɪ] *adj (clothes, party)* habillé(e), élégant(e)
drew [druː] *pt of* **draw**
drib [drɪb] *n* **in dribs and drabs** au compte-gouttes
dribble ['drɪbəl] **1** *n (saliva)* bave *f*; *(of blood, oil)* filet *m*
2 *vi* (**a**) *(of person)* baver (**b**) *(of liquid)* dégouliner; *Fig* **to d. in/out** *(of people)* entrer/sortir au compte-gouttes (**c**) *(of footballer)* dribbler
drier ['draɪə(r)] *n (for clothes)* séchoir *m*; *(for hair) (on stand)* casque *m*; *(hand-held)* sèche-cheveux *m inv*
drift [drɪft] **1** *n* (**a**) *(of current)* direction *f*, sens *m*; *(of events)* cours *m*; **the d. towards home ownership** la tendance actuelle à l'accession à la propriété; **the d. from the land** l'exode *m* rural; **d. net** *(for fishing)* filet *m* dérivant (**b**) *(meaning)* sens *m* général; *Fam* **I get the/your d.** je pige (**c**) *(of snow)* congère *f*; *(of leaves)* amoncellement *m*; *(of fog, mist)* traînée *f*
2 *vi* (**a**) *(of boat)* dériver, aller à la dérive; *(of smoke)* flotter; *(of events)* tendre (**towards** vers); *(of person)* se laisser porter par les événements; **people drifted in and out** les gens entraient et sortaient nonchalamment; **to d. apart** *(of friends)* se perdre de vue; *(of couple)* devenir des étrangers l'un pour l'autre; **to d. into crime** sombrer peu à peu dans la délinquance (**b**) *(of sand, snow)* s'amonceler, s'entasser
drifter ['drɪftə(r)] *n (person)* **she's a bit of a d.** elle n'a pas vraiment de but dans la vie
driftwood ['drɪftwʊd] *n (in sea)* bois *m* flottant *ou* flotté; *(on shore)* bois *m* rejeté par la mer
drill [drɪl] **1** *n* (**a**) *(tool)* foret *m*, mèche *f*; *(electric)* perceuse *f*; *(of dentist)* fraise *f*, roulette *f*; *(pneumatic)* marteau *m* piqueur; **d. bit** foret *m* (**b**) *(training)* exercice *m*

2 *vt* (**a**) *(well)* forer; *(hole)* percer (**b**) *(soldiers)* entraîner; *Fam* **to d.** sth **into sb** enfoncer qch dans la tête de qn
3 *vi* (**a**) *(for oil)* forer (**for** pour trouver); *(in wall, rock)* percer (**into** dans) (**b**) *(of troops)* faire l'exercice
drink [drɪŋk] **1** *n* boisson *f*; **to have a d.** prendre un verre, boire quelque chose; **to go for a d.** aller prendre un verre; **to pay for the drinks** payer les consommations; *Fam* **the d.** *(sea)* la baille; **to take to d.** se mettre à boire; **to have a d.** problem (trop) boire; **drinks machine** distributeur *m* automatique de boissons
2 *vt* (*pt* **drank** [dræŋk], *pp* **drunk** [drʌŋk]) boire; **she drank us all under the table** nous avions tous roulé sous la table depuis longtemps qu'elle était encore debout
3 *vi* boire; **to d. like a fish** boire comme un trou; **to d. to sb** *or* **to sb's health** boire à la santé de qn; *Fig* **to d. to sth** arroser qch; **to d. in the atmosphere** se pénétrer de l'atmosphère
▸**drink up 1** *vt sep* finir (de boire)
2 *vi* vider son verre
drinkable ['drɪŋkəbəl] *adj (water)* potable; *(wine, beer)* buvable
drink-driver ['drɪŋk'draɪvə(r)] *n Br* conducteur(trice) *m,f* ivre
drink-driving ['drɪŋk'draɪvɪŋ] *n Br* conduite *f* en état d'ivresse
drinker ['drɪŋkə(r)] *n* buveur(euse) *m,f*; **to be a heavy d.** boire beaucoup
drinking ['drɪŋkɪŋ] *n* **d. is bad for you** l'alcool est mauvais pour la santé; **d. chocolate** chocolat *m* en poudre; **d. fountain** fontaine *f* publique; **d. straw** paille *f*; **d. water** eau *f* potable
drip [drɪp] **1** *n* (**a**) *(drop)* goutte *f*; *(sound)* bruit *m* de l'eau qui goutte (**b**) *(in hospital)* goutte-à-goutte *m inv*; **to be on a d.** être sous perfusion (**c**) *Fam Pej (weak person)* mou (molle) *m,f*
2 *vt* (*pt & pp* **dripped**) laisser tomber goutte à goutte; **you're dripping water everywhere!** tu mets de l'eau partout!; **to be dripping with sweat/blood** ruisseler de sueur/sang; *Fig* **to be dripping with jewels** être couvert(e) de bijoux
3 *vi (of liquid)* tomber goutte à goutte, goutter; *(of tap)* fuire
drip-dry ['drɪp'draɪ] *adj (shirt, fabric)* ne nécessitant aucun repassage
dripping ['drɪpɪŋ] **1** *n* graisse *f* de rôti
2 *adj (tap)* qui fuit
3 *adv* **d. wet** trempé(e)
drive [draɪv] **1** *n* (**a**) *(trip)* promenade *f* en voiture; **it's an hour's d. away** c'est à une heure en voiture; **to go for a d.** aller faire une promenade en voiture (**b**) *(of car)* **left-/right-hand d.** conduite *f* à gauche/à droite; **four-wheel d.** *(car)* quatre-quatre *m inv*; *(system)* propulsion *f* à quatre roues motrices; **front-/rear-wheel d.** *(car, system)* traction *f* avant/arrière; (**c**) *Comput* lecteur *m*, unité *f* (**d**) *(in golf, tennis)* drive *m* (**e**) *(initiative)* énergie *f*, dynamisme *m* (**f**) *(of house)* allée *f* (**g**) *(campaign)* **sales/membership d.** campagne *f* pour attirer les acheteurs/de nouveaux membres
2 *vt* (*pt* **drove** [drəʊv], *pp* **driven** ['drɪvən]) (**a**) *(car, train)* conduire; **to d. sb somewhere** conduire qn en voiture quelque part; **could you d. me home?** pourriez-vous me reconduire chez moi? (**b**) *(direct, guide)* *(cattle)* mener, conduire; *(people)* chasser (**c**) *(push)*

to d. sb to sth/to do sth pousser qn à qch/à faire qch; **to d. sb mad** rendre qn fou (folle); **to d. oneself too hard** trop exiger de soi-même; **to d. a hard bargain** ne pas faire de cadeau; **to d. prices up/down** faire monter/baisser les prix (**d**) *(machine)* actionner, faire marcher; **to be driven by electricity** marcher à l'électricité
3 *vi (in car)* conduire; **can you d.?** savez-vous conduire?; **I don't d.** je n'ai pas mon permis; **to d. to work** aller au travail en voiture
▸**drive at** *vt insep* **what are you driving at?** où voulez-vous en venir?
▸**drive away 1** *vt sep* (**a**) *(in car)* emmener en voiture (**b**) *(repel)* chasser
2 *vi (in car)* s'en aller en voiture
▸**drive off 1** *vt sep (repel)* chasser
2 *vi (in car)* s'en aller en voiture
▸**drive on** *vi (in car)* continuer (sa route)
drive-by shooting ['draɪvbaɪ'ʃuːtɪŋ] *n* = fusillade exécutée d'une voiture en marche
drive-in ['draɪvɪn] *n (cinema)* drive-in *m, Can* ciné-parc *m*; *(restaurant)* = restaurant où on est servi dans sa voiture
drivel ['drɪvəl] *n Fam* bêtises *fpl*, balivernes *fpl*; **to talk (a load of) d.** dire n'importe quoi
driven ['drɪvən] *pp of* **drive**
driver ['draɪvə(r)] *n* (**a**) *(of car, bus)* conducteur(trice) *m,f*; *(of lorry, taxi)* chauffeur(euse) *m,f*; *(of train)* mécanicien(enne) *m,f*; *Am* **d.'s license** permis *m* de conduire (**b**) *(golf club)* driver *m*
driveway ['draɪvweɪ] *n* allée *f*
driving ['draɪvɪŋ] **1** *n (in car)* conduite *f*; *Fig* **to be in the d. seat** être aux commandes; **d. instructor** moniteur(trice) *m,f* d'auto-école; **d. lessons** leçons *fpl* de conduite; *Br* **d. licence** permis *m* de conduire; **d. school** auto-école *f*; **d. test** (examen *m* du) permis *m* de conduire
2 *adj (rain)* battant(e); *Fig* **d. force** moteur *m*
drizzle ['drɪzəl] **1** *n* crachin *m*
2 *vi* bruiner
droll [drəʊl] *adj* drôle, comique; *Ironic* **oh, very d.!** très drôle!
dromedary ['drɒmədərɪ] *(pl* **dromedaries**) *n* dromadaire *m*
drone [drəʊn] **1** *n* (**a**) *(bee)* faux-bourdon *m* (**b**) *(of conversation, traffic, plane)* bourdonnement *m*
2 *vi* (**a**) *(of bee)* bourdonner (**b**) *(of person)* parler d'un ton monotone
▸**drone on** *vi* parler ad nauseam *(d'une voix monotone)* (**about** de)
drool [druːl] *vi (dribble)* baver; *Fig* **to d. over sb/sth** baver d'admiration devant qn/qch; *Fig* **she was drooling at the idea** elle en salivait d'avance
droop [druːp] *vi (of head)* pencher; *(of shoulders)* tomber; *(of flower)* pencher la tête; *Fig (of person)* perdre ses forces
drop [drɒp] **1** *n* (**a**) *(of liquid)* goutte *f*; **drops** *(for eyes, nose)* gouttes; **you've had a d. too much** *(to drink)* tu as bu un coup de trop; *Fig* **it's only a d. in the ocean** ce n'est qu'une goutte d'eau dans l'océan (**b**) *(fall) (in prices, numbers)* chute *f*, baisse *f* (**in** de); *(by parachute)* parachutage *m*; **a d. of 10 metres** un à-pic ou escarpement de 10 mètres; *Fig* **at the d. of a hat** sans la moindre hésitation
2 *vt* (*pt & pp* **dropped**) (**a**) *(allow to fall)* laisser tomber; *(bomb)* lâcher; **to d. sb a line/a card** envoyer ou écrire un mot/une carte à qn; **I'll d. you at the station**

(in car) je te déposerai à la gare (**b**) *(lower) (prices, one's eyes)* baisser (**c**) *(abandon) (subject, idea, plan)* abandonner; **to d. sb** *(as friend)* laisser tomber qn; *(from team)* écarter qn; **to d. maths/French** *(of student)* arrêter les maths/le français; *Law* **to d. the charges** abandonner les poursuites (**d**) *(omit) (letter, syllable)* omettre, supprimer; *(when speaking)* ne pas prononcer (**e**) *(lose) (points)* perdre **3** *vi* (**a**) *(of object)* tomber; *(of ground)* s'affaisser; **he dropped to sixth place** il est descendu à la sixième place; *Fam* **I'm ready to d.** *(with fatigue)* je tombe de fatigue; *Fam* **people are dropping like flies** les gens tombent comme des mouches; **to d. dead** tomber raide mort(e); *Fam* **d. dead!** va te faire voir!; *Fam* **let it d.!** laisse tomber! (**b**) *(of prices, temperature, voice)* baisser; *(of wind)* tomber; *(of speed)* diminuer
▸**drop by** *vi (visit)* passer
▸**drop in** *vi* passer (**on sb** chez qn)
▸**drop off 1** *vt sep (person from car)* déposer **2** *vi* (**a**) **to d. off (to sleep)** s'assoupir, s'endormir (**b**) *(of membership, attendance)* diminuer
▸**drop out** *vi* (**a**) *(of object) (from pocket, bag)* tomber (**b**) *(of person) (from contest)* se retirer; *(from society)* devenir un(e) marginal(e); *(from university)* abandonner ses études
▸**drop round 1** *vt sep (deliver)* déposer **2** *vi (visit)* passer

drop-kick ['drɒpkɪk] *vt* **to d. the ball** donner un coup de pied tombé (au ballon)

droplet ['drɒplɪt] *n* gouttelette *f*

dropout ['drɒpaʊt] *n Fam (from society)* marginal(e) *m,f*; *(from university)* étudiant(e) *m,f* qui abandonne ses études

dropper ['drɒpə(r)] *n (for medicine)* compte-gouttes *m inv*

droppings ['drɒpɪŋz] *npl (of birds)* fiente *f*; *(of animals)* crottes *fpl*

dross [drɒs] *n Fam (rubbish)* rebut *m*; **I've never heard such d. in all my life** je n'ai jamais entendu de telles bêtises

drought [draʊt] *n* sécheresse *f*

drove [drəʊv] **1** *n* **to arrive in droves** arriver en foule **2** *pt of* **drive**

drown [draʊn] **1** *vt* (**a**) *(in water)* noyer; **to d. oneself** se noyer; **to d. one's sorrows** noyer son chagrin dans l'alcool (**b**) *(sound)* couvrir **2** *vi (die)* se noyer
▸**drown out** *vt sep (sound)* couvrir; *(person)* couvrir la voix de

drowse [draʊz] *vi* somnoler

drowsiness ['draʊzɪnɪs] *n* somnolence *f*

drowsy ['draʊzɪ] *adj* **to be** *or* **feel d.** avoir envie de dormir

drudge [drʌdʒ] *n (man)* homme *m* de peine; *(woman)* bonne *f* à tout faire

drudgery ['drʌdʒərɪ] *n* travail *m* pénible *ou* ingrat

drug [drʌg] **1** *n (medicine)* médicament *m*; *(narcotic)* drogue *f*; **hard/soft drugs** drogues dures/douces; **to take drugs** se droguer; **d. abuse** usage *m* de stupéfiants; **d. addict** drogué(e) *m,f*; **d. dealer** *(large-scale)* trafiquant *m* de drogue; *(small-scale)* dealer *m*; **d. pusher** dealer *m*; **d. squad** brigade *f* des stupéfiants **2** *vt (pt & pp* **drugged***)* droguer

druggie ['drʌgɪ] **1** *adj (relating to drugs)* **he hangs out with a d. crowd** il traîne avec une bande de junkies;

it's a bit of a d. area il y a pas mal de junkies qui traînent par là-bas **2** *n* camé(e) *m,f*

druggist ['drʌgɪst] *n Am* pharmacien(enne) *m,f*

drugstore ['drʌgstɔː(r)] *n Am* drugstore *m*

druid ['druːɪd] *n* druide *m*

drum [drʌm] **1** *n* (**a**) *(musical instrument)* tambour *m*; **d. kit, drums** batterie *f* (**b**) *(container)* fût *m*; *(for oil)* bidon *m* **2** *vt (pt & pp* **drummed***)* **to d. one's fingers** tambouriner de ses doigts; **to d. sth into sb** enfoncer qch dans la tête de qn **3** *vi (play drums)* jouer de la batterie; **the rain was drumming on the window panes** la pluie tambourinait contre les vitres
▸**drum up** *vt (support, enthusiasm)* chercher à susciter

drummer ['drʌmə(r)] *n (in pop band)* batteur(euse) *m,f*; *(in military band)* tambour *m*

drumstick ['drʌmstɪk] *n* (**a**) *(for playing drums)* baguette *f* de tambour (**b**) *(chicken leg)* pilon *m*

drunk [drʌŋk] **1** *n (man)* homme *m* soûl; *(woman)* femme *f* soûle; *(habitual)* ivrogne *mf* **2** *adj* ivre, soûl(e); **to get d.** se soûler; *Law* **d. and disorderly** en état d'ivresse sur la voie publique; *Fig* **d. with joy/power** ivre de joie/puissance **3** *pp of* **drink**

drunkard ['drʌŋkəd] *n* ivrogne *mf*

drunk-driver ['drʌŋk'draɪvə(r)] *Am* = **drink-driver**

drunk-driving ['drʌŋk'draɪvɪŋ] *Am* = **drink-driving**

drunken ['drʌŋkən] *adj (person)* ivre; *(party)* bien arrosé(e); **in a d. stupor** hébété(e) par l'alcool; **d. brawl** querelle *f* d'ivrognes

dry [draɪ] **1** *adj* (**a**) *(weather, clothing, skin, hair, wine)* sec (sèche); *(day)* sans pluie; **to run** *or* **go d.** *(of river)* s'assécher; *(of spring)* (se) tarir, s'épuiser; **d. as a bone** complètement sec; *Naut* **d. dock** cale *f* sèche; **d. ice** neige *f* carbonique; **d. land** terre *f* ferme; **d. rot** pourriture *f* sèche; **d. run** coup *m* d'essai, test *m* (**b**) *(boring) (style, person)* ennuyeux(euse) (**c**) *(humour)* pince-sans-rire *inv* **2** *vt (pt & pp* **dried***)* sécher; *(clothes)* faire sécher; *(skin)* dessécher; *(dishes)* essuyer; **to d. oneself** se sécher; **to d. one's hair** se sécher les cheveux **3** *vi* sécher
▸**dry out** *vi* (**a**) *(of alcoholic)* se faire désintoxiquer (**b**) *(of wood, ground)* sécher; *(of skin)* se dessécher
▸**dry up** *vi* (**a**) *(of well, pool)* se dessécher, tarir (**b**) *(of funds, conversation)* tarir; *(of inspiration)* se tarir (**c**) *(forget one's lines)* oublier son texte; *(have nothing more to say)* ne plus rien avoir à dire

dry-clean ['draɪ'kliːn] *vt* nettoyer à sec

dry-cleaner's ['draɪ'kliːnəz] *n* teinturerie *f*, pressing *m*

dry-cleaning [draɪ'kliːnɪŋ] *n* (**a**) *(process)* nettoyage *m* à sec (**b**) *(clothes)* vêtements *mpl* laissés chez le teinturier

dryer = **drier**

DSS [diːes'es] *n Br (abbr* **Department of Social Security***)* ≃ Sécurité *f* sociale

DTI [diːtiː'aɪ] *n Br (abbr* **Department of Trade and Industry***)* ≃ ministère *m* du Commerce et de l'Industrie

DTP [diːtiː'piː] *n Comput (abbr* **desktop publishing***)* PAO *f*

DTs [diː'tiːz] *npl (abbr* **delirium tremens***)* **the D.** le delirium tremens

dual ['dju:əl] *adj* double; **d. carriageway** *(road)* route *f* à deux chaussées; **d. nationality** double nationalité *f*; **d. ownership** copropriété *f*

dual-band ['dju:əl'bænd] *adj Tel* dual-band, bibande

dual-purpose ['dju:əl'pɜ:pəs] *adj* à double emploi

dub [dʌb] *(pt & pp dubbed) vt* (**a**) *(film)* doubler (**into** en) (**b**) *(nickname)* surnommer

dubbing ['dʌbɪŋ] *n (of film)* doublage *m*

dubious ['dju:bɪəs] *adj* (**a**) *(uncertain)* incertain(e); **to be d. (about)** avoir quelques doutes (au sujet de) (**b**) *(questionable)* douteux(euse)

Dublin ['dʌblɪn] *n* Dublin

Dubliner ['dʌblɪnə(r)] *n* Dublinois(e) *m,f*

duchess ['dʌtʃɪs] *n* duchesse *f*

duchy ['dʌtʃɪ] (pl **duchies**) *n* duché *m*

duck [dʌk] **1** *n* canard *m*; *(female)* cane *f*; **to take to sth like a d. to water** faire qch comme si on l'avait fait toute sa vie; **criticism runs off him like water off a d.'s back** les critiques glissent sur lui; **d. pond** mare *f* aux canards
  2 *vt* (**a**) *(head)* baisser subitement; **to d. sb** *(under water)* faire faire le plongeon à qn (**b**) *(avoid)* se dérober à; **to d. the issue/question** se dérober
  3 *vi (lower head)* baisser la tête, se baisser; *(under water)* plonger sous l'eau; **to d. behind a tree** se cacher derrière un arbre

▶**duck out of** *vt insep* **to d. out of doing sth** éviter de faire qch; **he ducked out of the meeting** il s'est débrouillé pour ne pas assister à la réunion

duck-billed platypus ['dʌkbɪld'plætɪpəs] *n* ornithorynque *m*

duckling ['dʌklɪŋ] *n (male)* caneton *m*; *(female)* canette *f*

duct [dʌkt] *n* conduit *m*

dud [dʌd] *Fam* **1** *n (person)* incapable *mf*; *(shell)* obus *m* qui n'a pas éclaté; *(banknote)* faux *m*
  2 *adj (shell)* qui n'a pas éclaté; *(banknote)* faux (fausse); *(cheque)* en bois

dude [du:d] *n Am* type *m*

due [dju:] **1** *n* (**a**) *(what is owed)* dû *m*; **to give her her d.**, she did apologize pour lui rendre justice, il faut reconnaître qu'elle s'est excusée (**b**) **dues** *(membership fees)* cotisation *f*
  2 *adj* (**a**) *(owed)* dû (due); **to fall d.** échoir, arriver à échéance; **are you d. any money from her?** vous doit-elle de l'argent?; **you're d. an apology** je vous dois/il vous doit/etc une excuse; **d. to** par suite de, en raison de; **what is it d. to?** c'est dû à quoi?; *Fin* **d. date** échéance *f* (**b**) *(merited, proper)* dû (due), mérité(e); **to give sb d. warning** avertir qn dans les formes; **after d. consideration** après mûre réflexion; **with all d. respect,...** avec tout le respect que je vous dois,...; **in d. course** *(when appropriate)* en temps voulu; *(eventually)* le moment venu (**c**) *(expected)* **the train is d. (in** *or* **to arrive)** le train doit arriver d'un moment à l'autre; **when is he due (in** *or* **to arrive)?** quand doit-il arriver?; **when is the baby d.?** pour quand la naissance est-elle prévue?; **she's d. back any minute** elle doit revenir d'un moment à l'autre; **the film/book is d. out soon** le film/livre va sortir sous peu
  3 *adv* **d. north/south** plein nord/sud

duel ['djuəl] **1** *n* duel *m*; **to fight a d.** se battre en duel
  2 *vi (pt & pp duelled, Am dueled)* se battre en duel

duet [dju:'et] *n* duo *m*; *(for piano)* morceau *m* à quatre mains

duff [dʌf] *Fam* **1** *adj* nul (nulle)
  2 *n Br* **to be up the d.** *(pregnant)* être en cloque
▶**duff up** *vt sep Fam* rosser, tabasser

duffel = **duffle**

duffer ['dʌfə(r)] *n Br Fam* (**a**) *(incompetent person)* nul (nulle) *m,f* (**b**) *(old man)* vieux bonhomme *m*

duffle ['dʌfəl] *n* **d. (coat)** duffle-coat *m*; **d. bag** sac *m* (de) marin

dug [dʌg] *pt & pp of* **dig**

dugout ['dʌgaʊt] *n* (**a**) *(canoe)* pirogue *f* (**b**) *(shelter)* *Mil* tranchée-abri *f*; *Sport* banc *m* de touche

duke [dju:k] *n* duc *m*

dull [dʌl] **1** *adj* (**a**) *(boring)* ennuyeux(euse), terne; **as d. as ditchwater** ennuyeux(euse) comme la pluie (**b**) *(unintelligent)* lent(e) (**c**) *(not sharp) (pain, sound)* sourd(e); *(blade, senses)* émoussé(e) (**d**) *(not bright) (colour, surface)* terne; *(eyes)* sans éclat; *(weather, sky)* sombre, maussade
  2 *vt* (**a**) *(pleasure)* rendre moins vif (vive); *(pain)* endormir, calmer; *(sound)* amortir, assourdir; *(blade, senses)* émousser (**b**) *(make less bright)* ternir

duly ['dju:lɪ] *adv* (**a**) *(properly)* dûment (**b**) *(as expected)* comme prévu

dumb [dʌm] *adj* (**a**) *(unable to speak)* muet(ette); **to be struck d.** *(with astonishment)* en rester muet(ette); **d. animal** bête *f*; **d. insolence** silence *m* insolent (**b**) *Fam (stupid)* bête; **d. blonde** blonde *f* évaporée

▶**dumb down** *vt sep (population, electorate)* infantiliser; *(media, programme)* faire baisser le niveau de

dumbbell ['dʌmbel] *n* haltère *m*

dumbfounded [dʌm'faʊndɪd] *adj* abasourdi(e), ébahi(e)

dumbing down ['dʌmɪŋ'daʊn] *n (of population, electorate)* infantilisation *f*; *(of media, programme)* baisse *f* de niveau

dumbstruck ['dʌmstrʌk] = **dumbfounded**

dumbwaiter ['dʌmweɪtə(r)] *n (lift)* monte-plats *m inv*

dummy ['dʌmɪ] **1** *n (pl dummies)* (**a**) *(in shop window)* mannequin *m*; *(of ventriloquist)* marionnette *f*; *(model, fake)* objet *m* factice (**b**) *Br (for baby)* tétine *f* (**c**) *Fam (idiot)* abruti(e) *m,f*
  2 *adj (fake)* factice; **d. run** coup *m* d'essai

dump [dʌmp] **1** *n* (**a**) *(for refuse)* décharge *f*; *Fam Pej (town)* bled *m* paumé; *(house)* dépotoir *m*; **d. truck** tombereau *m*, dumper *m* (**b**) *Mil (store)* dépôt *m* (**c**) *Comput* vidage *m*
  2 *vt* (**a**) *(put down)* déposer (**b**) *(dispose of)* se débarrasser de; *(waste)* déverser; *Fam (boyfriend, girlfriend)* plaquer (**c**) *Comput (memory)* vider

dumper ['dʌmpə(r)] *n* **d. (truck)** tombereau *m*, dumper *m*

dumping ['dʌmpɪŋ] *n* (**a**) **no d.** *(sign)* décharge interdite; **d. ground** décharge *f*; *Fig* dépotoir *m* (**b**) *Econ* dumping *m*

dumpling ['dʌmplɪŋ] *n (in stew)* boulette *f* de pâte; *Scot* = sorte de plum-pudding écossais

dumps [dʌmps] *npl Fam* **to be down in the d.** broyer du noir, avoir le cafard

dumpy ['dʌmpɪ] *adj Fam (person, appearance)* boulot(otte)

dunce [dʌns] *n (at school)* âne *m*, cancre *m*; **d.'s cap** bonnet *m* d'âne

dune [dju:n] *n* dune *f*

dung [dʌŋ] *n (of cow)* bouse *f*; *(of horse)* crottin *m*; *(of wild animal)* fumées *fpl*

dungarees [dʌŋgə'ri:z] *npl* **(a pair of) d.** une salopette *f*; *(of workman)* un bleu de travail

dungeon ['dʌndʒən] *n* (*underground*) cachot *m*; *Hist* (*tower*) donjon *m*

dunghill ['dʌŋhɪl] *n* tas *m* de fumier

dunk [dʌŋk] *vt* tremper

Dunkirk [dʌn'kɜːk] *n* Dunkerque

duo ['djuːəʊ] (*pl* **duos**) *n* (*in music*) duo *m*; (*two people*) couple *m*

duodenal [djuːəʊ'diːnəl] *adj* (*ulcer*) duodénal(e)

dupe [djuːp] **1** *n* dupe *f*
2 *vt* duper, tromper; **to d. sb into doing sth** faire faire qch à qn en le dupant

duplicate 1 *n* ['djuːplɪkət] (*of key*) double *m*; (*of letter, receipt*) double, duplicata *m*; **in d.** en double, en deux exemplaires
2 *adj* ['djuːplɪkət] **a d. key** un double de la clé; **a d. copy** un duplicata
3 *vt* ['djuːplɪkeɪt] (**a**) (*copy*) faire un double/duplicata de; (*on photocopier*) faire une photocopie de (**b**) (*do again*) refaire

duplication [djuːplɪ'keɪʃən] *n* (**a**) (*copying*) reproduction *f* (**b**) (*repetition*) répétition *f*

duplicitous [djuː'plɪsɪtəs] *adj* fourbe, faux (fausse)

duplicity [djuː'plɪsɪtɪ] *n* duplicité *f*

durability [djʊərə'bɪlɪtɪ] *n* (*of material*) résistance *f*; (*of friendship*) durabilité *f*

durable ['djʊərəbəl] **1** *n* (**consumer) durables** biens *mpl* durables
2 *adj* (*material*) résistant(e); (*friendship*) durable

duration [djʊ'reɪʃən] *n* durée *f*; **for the d.** pour longtemps

duress [djʊ'res] *n* **under d.** sous la contrainte

during ['djʊərɪŋ] *prep* pendant, durant; (*in the course of*) au cours de

dusk [dʌsk] *n* crépuscule *m*; **at d.** au crépuscule, à la tombée de la nuit

dust [dʌst] **1** *n* (**a**) (*dirt, powder*) poussière *f*; **d. cover** (*for furniture*) housse *f*; **d. cover** *or* **jacket** (*for book*) chemise *f*, jaquette *f* (**b**) (*action*) **to give sth a d.** passer un coup de chiffon sur qch (**c**) (*idioms*) **once the d. has settled** une fois que les choses se seront calmées; *Fam* **you won't see me for d.!** vous ne me reverrez pas de sitôt!
2 *vt* (**a**) (*clean*) dépoussiérer, épousseter (**b**) (*sprinkle*) (*with flour, sugar*) saupoudrer (**with** de)
3 *vi* (*clean*) épousseter

▶**dust down, dust off** *vt sep* (*furniture*) épousseter; *Fig* (*legislation*) dépoussiérer; (*one's French*) se remettre à

dustbin ['dʌstbɪn] *n Br* poubelle *f*

dustcart ['dʌstkɑːt] *n* benne *f* à ordures

duster ['dʌstə(r)] *n* (*cloth*) chiffon *m* (à poussière); (*for blackboard*) brosse *f*

dustman ['dʌstmən] *n Br* éboueur *m*

dustpan ['dʌstpæn] *n* pelle *f* (à poussière)

dustsheet ['dʌstʃiːt] *n* housse *f*

dust-up ['dʌstʌp] *n Fam* (*brawl*) bagarre *f*; **to have a d. with sb** se bagarrer avec qn

dusty ['dʌstɪ] *adj* poussiéreux(euse), couvert(e) de poussière; **to get d.** se couvrir de poussière

Dutch [dʌtʃ] **1** *npl* **the D.** (*people*) les Hollandais *mpl*
2 *n* (*language*) hollandais *m*
3 *adj* hollandais(e); *Fam* **I need some D. courage** j'ai besoin d'un verre pour me donner du courage; **D. cap** (*contraceptive*) diaphragme *m*
4 *adv Fam* **to go D.** payer chacun sa part

Dutchman ['dʌtʃmən] *n* Hollandais *m*, Néerlandais *m*; *Fam* **if that's a real diamond, (then) I'm a D.** si ça c'est un vrai diamant, alors je mange mon chapeau

Dutchwoman ['dʌtʃwʊmən] *n* Hollandaise *f*, Néerlandaise *f*

dutiful ['djuːtɪfʊl] *adj* (*obedient*) obéissant(e)

duty ['djuːtɪ] (*pl* **duties**) *n* (**a**) (*obligation*) devoir *m* (**to** envers); **to do one's d.** faire son devoir; **to fail in one's d.** manquer à son devoir; **to make it one's d. to...** se faire un devoir de...; **it's your d. to...** il est de votre devoir de... (**b**) (*task*) **duties** fonctions *fpl*; **to take up** *or* **assume one's duties** entrer en fonctions; **to carry out** *or* **perform one's duties** exercer ses fonctions (**c**) (*of soldier, employee*) **to be on/off d.** être/ne pas être de service; **d. roster** tableau *m* de service (**d**) *Fin* (*tax*) droit *m*; **to pay d. on sth** payer une taxe sur qch

duty-free ['djuːtɪ'friː] **1** *n* marchandises *fpl* hors taxe
2 *adj* (*cigarettes, wine, perfume*) hors taxe; **d. shop** magasin *m* hors taxe

duvet ['duːveɪ] *n* couette *f*; **d. cover** housse *f* de couette; **d. day** = journée de congé supplémentaire pouvant être prise de façon impromptue

DVD [diːviː'diː] *n Comput* (*abbr* **Digital Versatile Disk, Digital Video Disk**) DVD *m*, disque *m* vidéo numérique

DVD-ROM [diːviːdiː'rɒm] *n Comput* (*abbr* **Digital Versatile Disk read-only memory**) DVD-ROM *m*, DVD-Rom *m*

dwarf [dwɔːf] (*pl* **dwarfs** *or* **dwarves** [dwɔːvz]) **1** *n* nain(e) *m,f*
2 *adj* nain(e)
3 *vt* (*be taller than*) écraser; *Fig* (*achievement, success*) éclipser

dwell [dwel] (*pt & pp* **dwelled** *or* dwelt [dwelt]) *vi Lit* (*live*) demeurer

▶**dwell on, dwell upon** *vt insep* remâcher, ressasser; **let's not d. on it** n'y pensons plus

dwelling ['dwelɪŋ] *n Lit* **d. (place)** demeure *f*, résidence *f*; **d. house** maison *f* d'habitation

dwelt [dwelt] *pt & pp of* dwell

dwindle ['dwɪndəl] *vi* diminuer; **to d. (away) to nothing** se réduire à rien

dwindling ['dwɪndəlɪŋ] *adj* (*funds, membership*) en baisse; (*enthusiasm*) faiblissant(e)

DWP [diːdʌbəljuː'piː] *n Br Pol* (*abbr* **Department for Work and Pensions**) ≃ ministère *m* du Travail

dye [daɪ] **1** *n* (*for clothes, hair*) teinture *f*
2 *vt* teindre; **to d. sth black/red** teindre qch en noir/rouge; **to d. one's hair** se teindre les cheveux

dyed-in-the-wool ['daɪdɪnðə'wʊl] *adj* (*conservative, Englishman*) bon teint *inv*

dying ['daɪɪŋ] **1** *npl* **the d.** les mourants *mpl*, les moribonds *mpl*
2 *adj* (*person*) mourant(e), agonisant(e); (*industry, tradition*) moribond(e); **to my d. day** jusqu'à ma mort; **d. wish** dernières volontés *fpl*; **d. words** dernières paroles *fpl*

dyke [daɪk] *n* (**a**) (*barrier*) digue *f* (**b**) *very Fam* (*lesbian*) gouine *f*, = terme injurieux désignant une lesbienne

dynamic [daɪ'næmɪk] **1** *n* (*driving force*) dynamique *f*
2 *adj also Fig* dynamique

dynamics [daɪ'næmɪks] *npl* dynamique *f*

dynamism ['daɪnəmɪzəm] *n* (*of person, society*) dynamisme *m*

dynamite ['daɪnəmaɪt] **1** *n also Fig* dynamite *f*; *Fam* **it's d.!** *(marvellous)* c'est du tonnerre!
2 *vt* dynamiter
dynamo ['daɪnəməʊ] *(pl* **dynamos**) *n* dynamo *f*
dynastic [dɪ'næstɪk] *adj* dynastique
dynasty ['dɪnəstɪ] *(pl* **dynasties**) *n* dynastie *f*

dysentery ['dɪsəntrɪ] *n* dysenterie *f*
dysfunctional [dɪs'fʌŋkʃənəl] *adj* **a d. family** une famille à problèmes
dyslexia [dɪs'leksɪə] *n* dyslexie *f*
dyslexic [dɪs'leksɪk] *adj* dyslexique
dystrophy ['dɪstrəfɪ] *n Med* dystrophie *f*

E, e [iː] *n* (**a**) *(letter)* E, e *m inv* (**b**) *Mus* mi *m* (**c**) *(abbr east)* E (**d**) *(abbr ecstasy)* X *f*, ecsta *f*

each [iːtʃ] **1** *adj* chaque; **e. one of us** chacun(e) de nous *ou* d'entre nous **2** *pron* (**a**) *(both, all)* chacun(e) *m,f*; **e. of us** chacun(e) de nous *ou* d'entre nous; **we e. earn £300** nous gagnons chacun 300 livres; **peaches at 25 pence e.** pêches à 25 pence chacune *ou* 25 pence pièce; **a little of e.** un peu de chaque (**b**) *(reciprocal)* **e. other** *(two)* l'un l'autre (l'une l'autre); *(more than two)* les uns les autres (les unes les autres); **separated from e. other** séparé(e) l'un(e) de l'autre; **they hate e. other** ils se haïssent; **we write to e. other** nous nous écrivons

eager ['iːgə(r)] *adj (look, voice)* avide; *(supporter)* fervent(e); *(desire, hope)* ardent(e), vif (vive); **to be e. for sth/to do sth** désirer vivement qch/faire qch; **to be e. to please** être désireux(euse) de plaire; *Fam* **to be an e. beaver** être zélé(e)

eagerly ['iːgəlɪ] *adv (listen)* avidement; *(work, talk)* avec enthousiasme; **e. awaited** attendu(e) avec impatience

eagerness ['iːgənɪs] *n* impatience *f*; *(to learn, please)* vif désir *m*; **to show e. in doing sth** montrer un intérêt très vif à faire qch

eagle ['iːgəl] *n* aigle *m*

eagle-eyed [iːgə'laɪd] *adj* aux yeux d'aigle

ear ['ɪə(r)] *n* (**a**) *(part of body)* oreille *f*; **to have an e. for music** avoir l'oreille musicale; **to have an e. for languages** avoir une bonne oreille pour les langues; *Med* **e., nose and throat specialist** oto-rhino(-laryngologiste) *mf*; **e. lobe** lobe *m* de l'oreille (**b**) *(of wheat)* épi *m* (**c**) *(idioms)* **to play it by e.** *(improvise)* improviser; **to have sb's e.** avoir l'oreille de qn; **to keep one's e. to the ground** être sur le qui-vive; **to go in one e. and out the other** *(of words, information)* entrer par une oreille et sortir par l'autre; *Fam* **to be up to one's ears in debt** être endetté(e) jusqu'au cou; *Fam* **to be up to one's ears in work** être accablé(e) de travail; *Fam* **to be thrown out on one's e.** se faire jeter dehors *ou* sur le pavé; **I'm all ears** je suis tout ouïe; **my ears were burning** j'avais les oreilles qui sifflaient; **the house was falling down around their ears** la maison s'écroulait tout autour d'eux

earache ['ɪəreɪk] *n* mal *m* d'oreille(s); **to have (an) e.** avoir mal à l'oreille/aux oreilles

eardrum ['ɪədrʌm] *n* tympan *m*

earful ['ɪəfʊl] *n Fam* **to give sb an e.** passer un savon à qn; **to get an e.** se faire passer un savon

earl [ɜːl] *n* comte *m*

earlier ['ɜːlɪə(r)] **1** *adj (previous)* plus ancien(enne); **I caught an e. train** j'ai pris un train qui partait plus tôt; **her e. novels** ses romans précédents **2** *adv* **e. (on)** avant; **a few days e.** quelques jours plus tôt; **no e. than tomorrow** pas avant demain; **as we saw e.** comme nous l'avons vu auparavant

earliest ['ɜːlɪəst] **1** *n* **at the e.** au plus tôt; **the e. I can be there is four o'clock** je pourrai être là à quatre heures au plus tôt **2** *adj (opportunity, memory)* premier(ère); **from the e. times** depuis les temps les plus reculés; **at the e. possible moment** le plus tôt possible, dans les plus brefs délais

early ['ɜːlɪ] **1** *adj* (**a**) *(in the day)* matinal(e); **to have an e. night** se coucher tôt; **to have an e. breakfast** déjeuner de bonne heure; **to be an e. riser** être matinal, se lever de bon matin; *Prov* **the e. bird catches the worm** l'avenir appartient à ceux qui se lèvent tôt (**b**) *(at beginning of period of time)* **in (the) e. summer** au début de l'été; **at an e. age** tout(e) jeune; **he's in his e. thirties** il a la trentaine; **in the e. 1980s** au début des années 80; **an e. example of...** un des premiers exemples de... (**c**) *(ahead of time)* en avance; **half an hour e.** en avance d'une demi-heure (**d**) *(premature) (death)* prématuré(e); **e. retirement** préretraite *f*; *Mil* **e. warning system** système *m* radar de préalerte (**e**) *(in future)* **at an e. date** prochainement **2** *adv* (**a**) *(in the day)* de bonne heure, tôt; **e. in the morning** le matin de bonne heure; **e. in the evening** tôt dans la soirée; **as e. as possible** le plus tôt possible (**b**) *(at beginning of period of time)* **e. in the year** au début de l'année; **e. on** dès l'abord; **e. in one's life** dans sa jeunesse; **e. in one's career** au début de sa carrière (**c**) *(ahead of time)* en avance; **too e.** trop tôt (**d**) *(prematurely) (die)* prématurément; **to retire e.** prendre une retraite anticipée

earmark ['ɪəmɑːk] *vt (funds)* assigner, affecter (**for** à); **the building is earmarked for closure** il est prévu que ce bâtiment soit fermé

earn [ɜːn] *vt (money)* gagner; *(rest, respect)* mériter; **to e. sb's love** gagner le cœur de qn; **to e. sb's praise** valoir des éloges à qn; **to e. one's living** gagner sa vie

earner ['ɜːnə(r)] *n* **(wage)** salarié(e) *m,f*; **to be a big/small e.** gagner beaucoup/peu; *Br Fam* **a nice little e.** une bonne petite affaire

earnest ['ɜːnɪst] **1** *n* **in e.** sérieusement; **things have started in e.** les choses ont vraiment commencé **2** *adj (person, effort, discussion)* sérieux(euse); *(expression)* pénétré(e), grave; *(voice)* pressant(e); *(desire)* profond(e)

earnestly ['ɜːnɪstlɪ] *adv* sérieusement; *(desire)* profondément; *(hope, believe)* sincèrement
earning power ['ɜːnɪŋ'paʊə(r)] *n* revenu *m* potentiel
earnings ['ɜːnɪŋz] *npl (of person)* salaire *m*; *(of company)* bénéfices *mpl*; **e. related** *(pensions, benefits)* proportionnel(elle) au salaire
earphones ['ɪəfəʊnz] *npl* écouteurs *mpl*
earpiece ['ɪəpiːs] *n (of telephone)* écouteur *m*
earplug ['ɪəplʌg] *n* boule *f* Quiès®
earring ['ɪərɪŋ] *n* boucle *f* d'oreille
earshot ['ɪəʃɒt] *n* **within/out of e.** à portée/hors de portée de voix
ear-splitting ['ɪəsplɪtɪŋ] *adj* à vous déchirer *ou* crever les tympans
earth [ɜːθ] **1** *n* (**a**) *(planet)* **the E.** la Terre; *Fam* **where/ why on e....?** où/pourquoi diable...?; **to cost the e.** coûter les yeux de la tête; **to promise sb the e.** promettre la lune à qn; **e. mother** *(in mythology)* déesse *f* de la terre; *Fam Fig* mère *f* nourricière; *Br* **e. tremor** secousse *f* sismique (**b**) *(ground)* sol *m*; *(soil)* terre *f*; *Fig* **to come back to e. (with a bump)** revenir (brutalement) sur terre; *Fig* **to go to e.** *(of fugitive)* se terrer (**c**) *Br Elec* terre *f*, masse *f*
2 *vt Br Elec* mettre à la terre
earthenware ['ɜːθənweə(r)] **1** *n* poterie *f* (de terre)
2 *adj* en ou de terre cuite
earthling ['ɜːθlɪŋ] *n* terrien(enne) *m,f*
earthly ['ɜːθlɪ] *adj* (**a**) *(life, existence)* terrestre (**b**) *Fam (for emphasis)* **there's no e. reason why...** il n'y a absolument aucune raison pour que...; **she hasn't got an e. (chance)** elle n'a pas la moindre chance
earthquake ['ɜːθkweɪk] *n* tremblement *m* de terre, séisme *m*
earth-shattering ['ɜːθʃætərɪŋ] *adj Fam* stupéfiant(e)
earthworks ['ɜːθwɜːks] *n* travaux *mpl* de terrassement; *Mil* fortifications *fpl* en terre
earthworm ['ɜːθwɜːm] *n* ver *m* de terre
earthy ['ɜːθɪ] *adj* (**a**) *(of or like earth)* terreux(euse); **to have an e. smell** sentir la terre (**b**) *(coarse)* truculent(e); *(uninhibited)* direct(e)
earwax ['ɪəwæks] *n* cérumen *m*, cire *f*
earwig ['ɪəwɪg] *n (insect)* perce-oreille *m*
ease [iːz] **1** *n* (**a**) *(facility)* facilité *f*, aisance *f*; **with e.** avec facilité *ou* aisance (**b**) *(comfort)* tranquillité *f*, bien-être *m*; **at e.** à l'aise; **to put sb at (their) e.** mettre qn à l'aise; **to put** *or* **set sb's mind at e.** rassurer qn; **a life of e.** une vie d'oisiveté
2 *vt* (**a**) *(alleviate) (pain)* calmer, soulager; **to e. sb's mind** rassurer qn (**b**) *(relax) (pressure)* soulager; *(tension)* réduire; *(restrictions)* assouplir (**c**) *(move carefully, slowly)* déplacer doucement
3 *vi (of pain, pressure)* s'atténuer; *(of wind, rain)* se calmer; *(of situation)* se détendre
▸**ease off, ease up** *vi (of pain, rain)* se calmer
easel ['iːzəl] *n* chevalet *m*
easily ['iːzɪlɪ] *adv* (**a**) *(without difficulty)* facilement, sans difficulté; **that's e. said** c'est facile à dire (**b**) *(undoubtedly)* **e. the best** de loin le meilleur/la meilleure; **he is e. forty** il a au moins quarante ans (**c**) *(comfortably)* à son aise
easiness ['iːzɪnɪs] *n* (**a**) *(of task)* facilité *f* (**b**) *(of manner)* décontraction *f*
east [iːst] **1** *n* est *m*; **to the e. (of)** à l'est (de); **the E.** *(the Orient)* l'Orient *m*; *(Eastern Europe)* l'Est
2 *adj (coast, side)* est *inv*; *(wind)* d'est; **E. Africa** l'Afrique *f* orientale; **the E. End** = les quartiers pauvres et

populeux de l'est de Londres ou Glasgow; *Formerly* **E. Germany** l'Allemagne *f* de l'Est; *Old-fashioned* **the E. Indies** les Indes *fpl* orientales; **the E. Side** = les quartiers est de New York
3 *adv* à l'est; *(travel)* vers l'est; **e. of the Rhine** à l'est du Rhin; **to face e.** être orienté(e) à l'est
eastbound ['iːstbaʊnd] *adj (train, traffic)* en direction de l'est
Easter ['iːstə(r)] *n* Pâques *fpl*; **at E.** à Pâques; **E. egg** œuf *m* de Pâques; **E. Island** l'île *f* de Pâques; **E. Sunday** dimanche *m* ou jour *m* de Pâques; **E. week** *(following Easter)* semaine *f* de Pâques; *(Holy Week)* semaine *f* sainte
easterly ['iːstəlɪ] **1** *n (wind)* vent *m* d'est
2 *adj (point)* à l'est; *(wind)* d'est, qui vient de l'est; **in an e. direction** vers l'est
eastern ['iːstən] *adj* est *inv*; *(of Far East)* oriental(e); **e. France** l'est de la France; **E. Europe** l'Europe *f* de l'est; *Am* **E. Standard Time** heure *f* de la côte est de l'Amérique du Nord
eastward ['iːstwəd] **1** *adj (in the east)* à l'est, dans l'est
2 *adv* = **eastwards**
eastwards ['iːstwədz] *adv (face, point)* à l'est; *(go, travel)* vers l'est
easy ['iːzɪ] **1** *adj* (**a**) *(not difficult)* facile; *(solution)* simple; **to be e. to please** ne pas être difficile; **e. to get on with** facile à vivre; *Fam* **e. as ABC** *or* **as pie** facile comme tout, simple comme bonjour; **the e. way out** la solution de facilité; *Fam* **e. money** argent *m* facile; *Fam* **e. on the eye** agréable à regarder; *Com* **by e. payments, on e. terms** avec facilités de paiement; *Fam* **I'm e.** *(I don't mind)* ça m'est égal; *very Fam* **she's e.** *(sexually)* elle couche avec tout le monde (**b**) *(comfortable, relaxed) (pace, time)* tranquille; *(manners)* libre, dégagé(e); *(style)* facile, naturel(elle); *Fam* **to be on e. street** ne pas avoir de problèmes financiers; **to have an e. time (of it)** avoir la vie facile; **e. chair** fauteuil *m*; *Mus* **e. listening** variété *f*
2 *adv* vas-y ou on sb/sth y aller doucement avec qn/qch; **to take things** *or* **it e.** *(lead a life of ease)* mener une vie tranquille; *(not overdo things)* ralentir; **take it e.!** *(calm down)* t'en fais pas!; **that's easier said than done** c'est plus facile à dire qu'à faire; **e. come, e. go** ça va, ça vient
easy-going ['iːzɪ'gəʊɪŋ] *adj (tolerant)* coulant(e), accommodant(e); *(calm)* décontracté(e)
eat [iːt] *(pt ate* [et, eɪt], *pp eaten* ['iːtən]) **1** *vt* (**a**) *(food)* manger; **to e. one's breakfast** prendre son petit déjeuner (**b**) *(idioms)* **to e. sb out of house and home** ruiner qn en nourriture; *Fam* **I could e. a horse!** j'ai une faim de loup!; *Fam* **he won't e. you!** il ne va pas te manger!; *Fam* **what's eating you?** qu'est-ce qui te tracasse?; **to e. one's words** se rétracter; *Fam* **if it works, I'll e. my hat** si ça réussit, je mange mon chapeau
2 *vi* manger; *Fig* **you'll have them eating out of your hand** ils te mangeront dans la main
▸**eat away at** *vt insep (erode) (rocks, self-confidence)* éroder, miner; *(foundations)* saper
▸**eat into** *vt insep (erode) (time, savings)* entamer
▸**eat out** *vi* manger au restaurant
▸**eat up 1** *vt sep* (**a**) *(food)* manger jusqu'à la dernière miette, finir (**b**) *(petrol, money)* consommer beaucoup de
2 *vi* finir son assiette; **e. up!** mange!
eaten ['iːtən] *pp of* **eat**

eater ['i:tə(r)] *n* mangeur(euse) *m,f*; **to be a fussy e.** être difficile (sur la nourriture)

eatery ['i:tərɪ] (*pl* **eateries**) *n Am* (café-)restaurant *m*

eats [i:ts] *npl Fam* bouffe *f*

eau de Cologne ['əʊdəkə'ləʊn] *n* eau *f* de Cologne

eaves [i:vz] *npl* avant-toit *m*

eavesdrop ['i:vzdrɒp] (*pt & pp* **eavesdropped**) *vi* **to e.** (**on sb/sth**) écouter (qn/qch) avec indiscrétion; **she was eavesdropping outside the door** elle écoutait à la porte

ebb [eb] **1** *n (of tide)* reflux *m*; **e. tide** marée *f* descendante; *Fig* **the e. and flow** *(of events)* les fluctuations *fpl*; *Fig* **to be at a low e.** *(of person)* ne pas avoir le moral; *(of spirits)* être bien bas; *(of finances, relations)* aller mal
   2 *vi (of tide)* baisser
▸**ebb away** *vi (of water)* s'écouler; *(of strength, enthusiasm)* faiblir, baisser

ebony ['ebənɪ] *n* ébène *f*

EBRD [i:bi:ɑ:'di:] *n (abbr* **European Bank for Reconstruction and Development**) BERD *f*

ebullience [ɪ'bʌlɪəns] *n* bouillonnement *m*, effervescence *f*

ebullient [ɪ'bʌlɪənt] *adj* bouillant(e), exubérant(e)

EC [i:'si:] *n (abbr* **European Community**) CE *f*

e-card ['i:kɑ:d] *n* carte *f* électronique

e-cash ['i:kæʃ] *n* argent *m* électronique, argent virtuel, e-cash *m*

eccentric [ek'sentrɪk] **1** *n* excentrique *mf*
   2 *adj* excentrique

eccentricity [eksen'trɪsɪtɪ] *n* excentricité *f*

ecclesiastic [ɪkli:zɪ'æstɪk] **1** *n* ecclésiastique *m*
   2 *adj* ecclésiastique

ECG [i:si:'dʒi:] *n Med (abbr* **electrocardiograph**) électrocardiographe *m*

echelon ['eʃəlɒn] *n* échelon *m*

echinacea [ekɪ'neɪʃə] *n Bot & Med* échinacée *f*

echo ['ekəʊ] **1** *n (pl* **echoes**) *also Fig* écho *m*
   2 *vt (pt & pp* **echoed**) *(words)* répéter; *(opinion)* se faire l'écho de
   3 *vi* résonner (**with** de)

eclair [eɪ'kleə(r)] *n (pastry)* éclair *m*; **chocolate e.** éclair *m* au chocolat

eclectic [ə'klektɪk] *adj (tastes, style)* éclectique; *(blend)* hétérogène

eclipse [ɪ'klɪps] *also Fig* **1** *n* éclipse *f*
   2 *vt* éclipser

eco-friendly ['i:kəʊfrendlɪ] *adj (product)* écologique, vert(e); *(lifestyle, person)* qui respecte l'environnement

ecological [i:kə'lɒdʒɪkəl] *adj (damage, balance)* écologique; *(campaign, activist)* écologiste

ecologist [ɪ'kɒlədʒɪst] *n* écologiste *mf*

ecology [ɪ'kɒlədʒɪ] *n* écologie *f*

e-commerce ['i:kɒmɜ:s] *n* commerce *m* électronique

economic [i:kə'nɒmɪk] *adj* (**a**) *Econ* économique (**b**) *(profitable)* rentable; **to make sth e.** rentabiliser qch

economical [i:kə'nɒmɪkəl] *adj (cost-effective)* économique; *(style)* concis(e); **to be e. with the truth** ne dire la vérité qu'à moitié

economically [i:kə'nɒmɪklɪ] *adv* économiquement; *(written)* dans un style concis

economics [i:kə'nɒmɪks] **1** *n* économie *f*
   2 *npl (financial aspects)* aspects *mpl* financiers

economist [ɪ'kɒnəmɪst] *n* économiste *mf*

economize [ɪ'kɒnəmaɪz] *vi* économiser (**on** sur)

economy [ɪ'kɒnəmɪ] *(pl* **economies**) *n* économie *f*; **economies of scale** économies *f* d'échelle; *Aviat* **e.**

class classe *f* économique; **e. drive** politique *f* de réduction des dépenses; **e. measure** mesure *f* d'économie; **e. size** *(of packet)* taille *f* économique

ecotax ['i:kəʊtæks] *n* taxe *f* écologique, écotaxe *f*

ecoterrorist ['i:kəʊterərɪst] *n* = militant écologiste ayant recours à des actions violentes

ecotourism ['i:kəʊtʊərɪzəm] *n* écotourisme *m*

ecowarrior ['i:kəʊwɒrɪə(r)] *n* écoguerrier(ère) *m,f*

ecstasy ['ekstəsɪ] *(pl* **ecstasies**) *n* (**a**) *(emotional state)* extase *f*; **to go into ecstasies over sth** s'extasier devant qch (**b**) *(drug)* ecstasy *f*

ecstatic [ek'stætɪk] *adj* fou (folle) de joie; **he was e. about** *or* **over the news** la nouvelle l'a rendu fou de joie

ECT [i:si:'ti:] *n Med (abbr* **electroconvulsive therapy**) traitement *m* par électrochocs

ECU, ecu ['ekju:, 'i:kju:] *n (abbr* **European Currency Unit**) ÉCU *m*, écu *m*

Ecuador ['ekwədɔ:(r)] *n* l'Équateur *m*

ecumenical [i:kjʊ'menɪkəl] *adj Rel* œcuménique

eczema ['eksɪmə] *n* eczéma *m*; **to have e.** avoir de l'eczéma

ed [ed] (**a**) *(abbr* **edition**) éd(it) (**b**) *(abbr* **editor**) éd., édit

eddy ['edɪ] **1** *n (pl* **eddies**) tourbillon *m*
   2 *vi (pt & pp* **eddied**) *(of water)* faire des remous; *(of wind, snow)* tourbillonner

Eden ['i:dən] *n* l'Éden *m*

edge [edʒ] **1** *n* (**a**) *(of table, road, river)* bord *m*; *(of wood)* lisière *f*; *(of book)* tranche *f*; **at the water's e.** au bord de l'eau; **to be on the e. of** *(new age)* être au seuil de; *(war)* être au bord de; *Fig* **to be on the e. of one's seat** retenir son souffle (**b**) *(of blade, tool)* tranchant *m*; *(of stone)* arête *f*; **to take the e. off** *(blade, appetite)* émousser; *(enjoyment)* gâter; *Fig* **to be on e.** être énervé(e); *Fig* **to set sb on e.** énerver qn (**c**) *(advantage)* **to have the e. (over sb)** être avantagé(e) (par rapport à qn)
   2 *vt (in sewing)* border (**with** de)
   3 *vi (move slowly)* **to e. past sb** passer lentement devant qn; **to e. towards** avancer lentement vers
▸**edge out** *vt sep (supplant)* évincer (**of** de)

edgeways ['edʒweɪz], **edgewise** ['edʒwaɪz] *adv (on its edge)* de chant; *(from side)* de côté; *Fam* **I can't get a word in e.** je ne peux pas en placer une

edgy ['edʒɪ] *adj* nerveux(euse); **to get e.** s'énerver

edible ['edɪbəl] *adj (safe to eat)* comestible; *(fit to eat)* mangeable

edict ['i:dɪkt] *n Formal* édit *m*

edification [edɪfɪ'keɪʃən] *n* édification *f*

edifice ['edɪfɪs] *n also Fig* édifice *m*

edify ['edɪfaɪ] *(pt & pp* **edified**) *vt* édifier

edifying ['edɪfaɪɪŋ] *adj* édifiant(e)

Edinburgh ['edɪnbrə] *n* Édimbourg

Edinburgh Festival

Le festival international d'arts d'Édimbourg, créé en 1947, est aujourd'hui l'un des plus grands événements culturels du monde ; il se tient chaque année dans la capitale écossaise au mois d'août. Le festival "off" ("the Fringe") est une grande rencontre du théâtre expérimental et un lieu très important pour les acteurs et les comiques qui veulent se faire connaître. Des centaines de représentations sont données chaque jour et toutes sortes de lieux sont transformés en salles de spectacle le temps du festival.

edit ['edɪt] vt (**a**) (correct) réviser; (prepare for publication) préparer pour la publication; **edited by** (coordinated by) sous la direction de (**b**) (film) monter (**c**) (manage) (newspaper, magazine) diriger (**d**) Comput éditer
▶**edit out** vt sep (scene) couper
editing ['edɪtɪŋ] n Cin montage m
edition [ɪ'dɪʃən] n (of book, newspaper) édition f; **in Tuesday's e.** of the programme dans l'émission de mardi
editor ['edɪtə(r)] n (**a**) (of published work) (author) rédacteur(trice) m,f; (in charge) directeur(trice) m,f (**b**) (of film) monteur(euse) m,f (**c**) (of newspaper, magazine) rédacteur(trice) m,f en chef; (of section) rédacteur(trice) (**d**) Comput (software) éditeur m
editorial [edɪ'tɔ:rɪəl] **1** n éditorial m
2 adj de rédaction
EDP [i:di:'pi:] n Comput (abbr **electronic data processing**) traitement m électronique de l'information
educate ['edjʊkeɪt] vt éduquer, instruire; **he was educated at Oxford** il a fait ses études à Oxford
educated ['edjʊkeɪtɪd] adj instruit(e); **I made an e. guess** j'ai émis une hypothèse, mais je ne risquais guère de me tromper
education [edjʊ'keɪʃən] n (process of learning, knowledge) éducation f; (process of teaching) enseignement m; **to get (oneself) an e.** faire des études; **to complete one's e.** terminer ses études; Fig **it was an e. working over there** c'était instructif de travailler là-bas
educational [edjʊ'keɪʃənəl] adj (system) éducatif(-ive); (establishment, publisher) scolaire; (qualification) d'enseignement; (experience, visit) instructif(ive)
Edwardian [ed'wɔ:dɪən] adj (architecture, furniture) de l'époque d'Édouard VII; **the E. era** ≃ la Belle Époque
EEC [i:i:'si:] n Formerly (abbr **European Economic Community**) CEE f
eel [i:l] n anguille f
eerie ['ɪərɪ] adj (atmosphere, cry) sinistre; (silence) de mort; (feeling) étrange
eerily ['ɪərɪlɪ] adv étrangement
eff [ef] vi Fam Euph **to e. and blind** débiter des grossièretés
efface [ɪ'feɪs] vt effacer
effect [ɪ'fekt] **1** n (**a**) (result) effet m (**on** sur); **to take e.** (of drug, medicine) faire effet, agir; (of law) prendre effet; **to put sth into e.** mettre qch en application; **in e.** en fait; **or words to that e.** ou quelque chose d'approchant (**b**) (impression) effet m; **for e.** pour faire de l'effet (**c**) Formal **personal effects** effets mpl personnels
2 vt Formal (cause) (change, rescue) effectuer; (saving, wish) réaliser; (solution) apporter (**to** à)
effective [ɪ'fektɪv] adj (**a**) (efficient, successful) efficace; (argument, speech) convaincant(e) (**b**) (actual, real) (profit, value) réel(elle); **she will assume e. control of the business** c'est elle qui dirigera concrètement l'entreprise (**c**) Law (in force) **to be e.** prendre effet
effectively [ɪ'fektɪvlɪ] adv (**a**) (efficiently) avec efficacité; (speak) de façon convaincante (**b**) (really) en fait, en réalité; **they are e. the same** en fait, ils sont identiques
effectiveness [ɪ'fektɪvnɪs] n efficacité f
effeminate [ɪ'femɪnət] adj efféminé(e)
effervescent [efə'vesənt] adj also Fig effervescent(e)
effete [ɪ'fi:t] adj (person) veule; (gesture) efféminé(e)

efficacious [efɪ'keɪʃəs] adj Formal efficace
efficacy ['efɪkəsɪ] n Formal efficacité f
efficiency [ɪ'fɪʃənsɪ] n efficacité f; (output, productivity) rendement m
efficient [ɪ'fɪʃənt] adj efficace; (productive) performant(e); **to be e. at sth** faire qch avec compétence
efficiently [ɪ'fɪʃəntlɪ] adv efficacement
effigy ['efɪdʒɪ] (pl **effigies**) n effigie f
effing ['efɪŋ] Fam Euph **1** adj fichu(e)
2 n **there was a lot of e. and blinding** on a eu droit à un chapelet de jurons
effluent ['eflʊənt] n effluents mpl
effort ['efət] n (**a**) (exertion) effort m; **to make an e. (to do sth)** faire un effort (pour faire qch); **put some e. into it!** fais un effort!; **to be worth the e.** valoir la peine (**b**) (attempt) tentative f (**at doing sth** pour faire qch); **a good e.** un bel effort; **a poor e.** un effort insuffisant
effortless ['efətlɪs] adj (victory, success) facile; (skill, grace) naturel(elle)
effortlessly ['efətlɪslɪ] adv facilement, sans effort
effrontery [ɪ'frʌntərɪ] n effronterie f
effusive [ɪ'fju:sɪv] adj (person) démonstratif(ive), expansif(ive); (welcome, speech) enthousiaste
effusively [ɪ'fju:sɪvlɪ] adv (praise, welcome) avec un enthousiasme débordant; (thank) avec effusion
EFL [i:e'fel] n (abbr **English as a Foreign Language**) anglais m langue étrangère
EFT [i:ef'ti:] n Comput (abbr **electronic funds transfer**) transfert m de fonds électronique
EFTA ['eftə] n (abbr **European Free Trade Association**) AELE f
EFTPOS ['eftpɒs] n Comput (abbr **electronic funds transfer at point of sale**) transfert m de fonds électronique sur point de vente
eg [i:'dʒi:] adv (abbr **exempli gratia**) p. ex.
egalitarian [ɪgælɪ'teərɪən] **1** n égalitariste mf
2 adj (society) égalitaire
egalitarianism [ɪgælɪ'teərɪənɪzəm] n égalitarisme m
egg [eg] n (**a**) (of bird, fish etc) œuf m; **e. cup** coquetier m; **e. flip** (with milk) lait m de poule; (with alcohol) lait m de poule alcoolisé; Am Culin **e. roll** pâté m impérial; **e. timer** sablier m; **e. white** blanc m d'œuf; **e. yolk** jaune m d'œuf (**b**) (idioms) **a good e.** (man) un brave type; (woman) une brave fille; **a bad e.** (man) un sale type; (woman) une sale bonne femme; **to have e. on one's face** être ridicule; Prov **don't put all your eggs in one basket** il ne faut pas mettre tous ses œufs dans le même panier
▶**egg on** vt sep encourager (**to do sth** à faire qch)
egghead ['eghed] n Hum or Pej intello mf
eggplant ['egplænt] n Am aubergine f
eggshell ['egʃel] n coquille f d'œuf
eggwhisk ['egwɪsk] n fouet m
egis Am = aegis
ego ['i:gəʊ] (pl **egos**) n ego m; **to have a big e.** être très imbu(e) de soi-même; **to give sb's e. a boost** flatter l'ego de qn; Fam **he's on an e. trip** il fait ça uniquement parce que ça flatte son ego
egocentric [i:gəʊ'sentrɪk] adj égocentrique
egoist ['i:gəʊɪst] n égoïste mf
egotism ['i:gəʊtɪzəm] n égocentrisme m
egotist ['i:gəʊtɪst] n égocentrique mf
egotistic(al) [i:gəʊ'tɪstɪk(əl)] adj égocentrique
e-government ['i:gʌvəmənt] n administration f électronique
Egypt ['i:dʒɪpt] n l'Égypte f

Egyptian 153 elector

Egyptian [ɪ'dʒɪpʃən] **1** n Égyptien(enne) m,f **2** adj égyptien(enne)
EHIC ['iːhɪk] n (abbr **European Health Insurance Card**)
E. **(card)** CEAM f, carte f européenne d'assurance maladie
eiderdown ['aɪdədaʊn] n édredon m
eight [eɪt] **1** n huit m inv; **come at e.** venez à huit heures; **e. and e. are sixteen** huit et huit font seize; **there were e. of us** nous étions huit; **all e. of them left** tous les huit sont partis, ils sont partis tous les huit; **the e. of hearts** (in cards) le huit de cœur **2** adj huit; **e. cars** huit voitures; **e. pounds** huit livres; **on page e.** (à la) page huit; **to be e.** (years old) avoir huit ans; **they live at number e.** ils habitent au numéro huit; **e. o'clock** huit heures; **it's e. minutes to five** il est cinq heures moins huit; Am Tel **e. hundred number** ≃ numéro m vert
eighteen [eɪ'tiːn] **1** n dix-huit m inv **2** adj dix-huit; see also **eight**
eighteenth [eɪ'tiːnθ] **1** n (a) (fraction) dix-huitième m; (in series) dix-huitième mf (b) (of month) dix-huit m inv **2** adj dix-huitième; see also **eighth**
eighth [eɪtθ] **1** n (a) (fraction) huitième m; (in series) huitième mf; **Edward the E.** Édouard Huit (b) (of month) huit m inv; **(on) the e. of May** le huit mai; **we're leaving on the e.** nous partons le huit **2** adj huitième
eightieth ['eɪtɪɪθ] **1** n (fraction) quatre-vingtième m; (in series) quatre-vingtième mf **2** adj quatre-vingtième
eighty ['eɪtɪ] **1** n quatre-vingts m inv; **he was doing e.** (in car) il faisait du quatre-vingt (à l'heure); **in the eighties** (decade) dans les années quatre-vingt; **to be in one's eighties** avoir quatre-vingts ans passés; **the temperature was in the eighties** il faisait dans les vingt-cinq degrés **2** adj quatre-vingts; **e. cars/passengers** quatre-vingts voitures/passagers; **e. percent** quatre-vingt pour cent; **she's about e.** (years old) elle a dans les quatre-vingts ans
Eire ['eərə] n l'Eire f
either ['aɪðə(r), 'iːðə(r)] **1** adj (a) (one or the other) l'un (l'une) ou l'autre; **I didn't like e. book** je n'ai aimé ni l'un ni l'autre de ces livres; **e. candidate may win** les deux candidats ont des chances de gagner (b) (both) les deux; **on e. side** des deux côtés; **in e. case** dans les deux cas **2** pron (one or the other) l'un (l'une) m,f ou l'autre; **e. (of them) will do** l'un ou l'autre fera l'affaire; **I don't want e. (of them)** je ne veux ni l'un ni l'autre; **I don't believe e. of you** je ne vous crois ni l'un ni l'autre **3** conj **e.... or...** ou... ou..., soit... soit...; **e. you or your brother** ou toi ou ton frère, soit toi soit ton frère; **she doesn't eat e. meat or fish** elle ne mange ni viande ni poisson; **e. come in or go out!** ou tu rentres ou tu sors! **4** adv if you don't go, I won't go e. si tu n'y vas pas, moi non plus; **I don't like him – I don't e.** je ne l'aime pas – moi non plus
either-or ['aɪðərɔː(r)] adj **it's an e. situation** c'est soit l'un soit l'autre
ejaculate [ɪ'dʒækjʊleɪt] vi (a) (of man) éjaculer (b) Old-fashioned (exclaim) s'exclamer
ejaculation [ɪdʒækjʊ'leɪʃən] n (a) (of semen) éjaculation f (b) Old-fashioned (exclamation) exclamation f

eject [ɪ'dʒekt] **1** vt (cassette) éjecter; (troublemaker) expulser **2** vi (from plane) s'éjecter
ejection [ɪ'dʒekʃən] n (of cassette, from plane) éjection f; (of troublemaker) expulsion f
ejector seat [ɪ'dʒektə(r)siːt] n siège m éjectable
►**eke out** [iːk] vt sep (money) dépenser avec parcimonie; (rations, supplies) consommer avec parcimonie; **to e. out a living** gagner péniblement sa vie
elaborate 1 adj [ɪ'læbərət] (meal) élaboré(e); (drawing, description) détaillé(e); (excuse, scheme) compliqué(e) **2** vt [ɪ'læbəreɪt] (formulate) élaborer; (flesh out) développer **3** vi [ɪ'læbəreɪt] être plus précis; **to e. on sth** donner plus de détails sur qch
elan [eɪ'lɑːn] n Lit impétuosité f
elapse [ɪ'læps] vi s'écouler
elastic [ɪ'læstɪk] **1** n élastique m **2** adj also Fig élastique; **e. band** élastique m, bracelet m en caoutchouc
elasticated [ɪ'læstɪkeɪtɪd] adj (garment, material) extensible; (waist) élastique
elasticity [iːlæs'tɪsɪtɪ] n also Fig élasticité f
Elastoplast® [ɪ'læstəplɑːst] n Élastoplast® m
elated [ɪ'leɪtɪd] adj transporté(e) (de joie)
elation [ɪ'leɪʃən] n exaltation f
elbow ['elbəʊ] **1** n coude m; **out at the elbows** (of pullover, jacket) troué(e) aux coudes; Fig **to give sb the e.** (employee) se débarrasser de qn; (lover) plaquer qn; Fig **to use some e. grease** mettre de l'huile de coude **2** vt **to e. sb (in the ribs)** donner un coup de coude (dans les côtes) à qn; **to e. sb aside** écarter qn d'un coup de coude; Fig jouer des coudes pour évincer qn; **to e. one's way through** se frayer un passage en jouant des coudes
elbowroom ['elbəʊrʊm] n Fam Fig **to have enough e.** avoir assez de liberté
elder¹ ['eldə(r)] **1** n (a) (older person) aîné(e) m,f; **young people should respect their elders** les jeunes doivent le respect à leurs aînés (b) (of tribe) ancien(enne) m,f; (of church) = membre d'une congrégation protestante chargé de seconder le ministre dans certaines tâches **2** adj (brother, sister) aîné(e); **e. statesman** grand homme m politique
elder² n (tree) sureau m
elderberry ['eldəberɪ] n (pl **elderberries**) n baie f de sureau
elderly ['eldəlɪ] **1** npl **the e.** les personnes fpl âgées **2** adj âgé(e)
eldest ['eldɪst] **1** n **the e.** l'aîné(e) m,f **2** adj aîné(e)
elect [ɪ'lekt] **1** adj élu(e) **2** vt (a) (councillor, MP) élire (b) Formal (choose) **to e. to do sth** choisir de faire qch
election [ɪ'lekʃən] n élection f; **to hold an e.** procéder à une élection; **to stand for e.** se présenter aux élections; **e. campaign** campagne f électorale
electioneering [ɪlekʃə'nɪərɪŋ] n propagande f électorale
elective [ɪ'lektɪv] **1** n Univ (course) option f **2** adj (assembly) électoral(e); Univ (course) optionnel(elle); Med **e. surgery** chirurgie f de confort
elector [ɪ'lektə(r)] n électeur(trice) m,f

electoral [ɪˈlektərəl] *adj* électoral(e); **e. reform** réforme *f* du mode de scrutin; **e. roll** liste *f* électorale
electorate [ɪˈlektərət] *n* électorat *m*
electric [ɪˈlektrɪk] *adj* électrique; *Fig (atmosphere)* chargé(e) d'électricité; *Br* **e. blanket** couverture *f* chauffante; **e. blue** bleu *m* électrique; **e. chair** chaise *f* électrique; **e. cooker** cuisinière *f* électrique; **e. light** *(appliance)* lumière *f* électrique; *(lighting)* éclairage *m ou* lumière *f* électrique; **e. shock** décharge *f* électrique; *Med* électrochoc *m*
electrical [ɪˈlektrɪkəl] *adj* électrique; **e. engineering** électrotechnique *f*
electrically [ɪˈlektrɪkəlɪ] *adv* **e. powered/operated** qui fonctionne à l'électricité; **e. charged** chargé(e) d'électricité
electrician [ɪlekˈtrɪʃən] *n* électricien(enne) *m,f*
electricity [ɪlekˈtrɪsɪtɪ] *n* électricité *f*
electrification [ɪlektrɪfɪˈkeɪʃən] *n* électrification *f*
electrify [ɪˈlektrɪfaɪ] *(pt & pp* **electrified)** *vt* électrifier; *Fig (excite)* électriser
electrifying [ɪˈlektrɪfaɪɪŋ] *adj Fig* électrisant(e)
electrocardiogram [ɪlektrəʊˈkɑːdɪəʊɡræm] *n Med* électrocardiogramme *m*
electrocardiograph [ɪlektrəʊˈkɑːdɪəʊɡræf] *n Med* électrocardiographe *m*
electrocute [ɪˈlektrəkjuːt] *vt* électrocuter; **to e. oneself** s'électrocuter
electrocution [ɪlektrəˈkjuːʃən] *n* électrocution *f*
electrode [ɪˈlektrəʊd] *n* électrode *f*
electrolysis [ɪlekˈtrɒlɪsɪs] *n* électrolyse *f*
electromagnet [ɪlektrəʊˈmæɡnɪt] *n* électroaimant *m*
electron [ɪˈlektrɒn] *n* électron *m*; **e. microscope** microscope *m* électronique
electronic [ɪlekˈtrɒnɪk] *adj* électronique; *Fin* **e. banking** bancatique *f*; *Comput* **e. mail** courrier *m* électronique; **e. media** médias *mpl* électroniques; *Comput* **e. office** bureau *m* informatisé; **e. tag** *(for criminal)* bracelet *m* électronique *ou* de cheville
electronically [ɪlekˈtrɒnɪklɪ] *adv* électroniquement
electronics [ɪlekˈtrɒnɪks] **1** *n (subject)* électronique *f*; **e. company** société *f* d'électronique; **the e. industry** l'industrie *f* (de l')électronique
  2 *npl* **the e.** *(of machine)* le système électronique
electroplated [ɪˈlektrəpleɪtɪd] *adj* plaqué(e) *(par électrodéposition)*
electroshock [ɪlektrəʊˈʃɒk] *adj* **e. therapy** *or* **treatment** traitement *m* par électrochocs
elegance [ˈelɪɡəns] *n* élégance *f*
elegant [ˈelɪɡənt] *adj (person, appearance, movement)* élégant(e); *(reasoning)* clair(e) et simple
elegantly [ˈelɪɡəntlɪ] *adv* avec élégance; **e. proportioned** aux proportions élégantes
elegy [ˈelɪdʒɪ] *(pl* **elegies)** *n* élégie *f*
element [ˈelɪmənt] *n* (**a**) *(constituent part)* part *f*; **an e. of danger/chance** une part de danger/chance; **this film has all the elements of a hit movie** ce film réunit tous les ingrédients d'un grand succès (**b**) *(factor)* **the e. of surprise** l'effet *m* de surprise; **the human/time e.** le facteur humain/temps (**c**) *(in society)* **element** *m*; **undesirable elements** éléments *mpl* indésirables; **the hooligan e.** la frange constituée par les hooligans (**d**) *Chem* élément *m* (**e**) *(of kettle, electric fire)* résistance *f* (**f**) *(force of nature)* **the four elements** les quatre éléments *mpl*; *Fig* **to brave the elements** braver les éléments; **to be in one's e.** être dans son élément

elemental [elɪˈmentəl] *adj* (**a**) *(basic)* fondamental(e) (**b**) *(primitive)* élémentaire, primitif(ive)
elementary [elɪˈmentərɪ] *adj* élémentaire; *Am (education)* primaire; **my Arabic is rather e.** je parle un arabe assez rudimentaire; *Am* **e. school** école *f* primaire
elephant [ˈelɪfənt] *n* éléphant *m*
elephantine [elɪˈfæntaɪn] *adj (movements)* lourd(e) et gauche; *(proportions)* éléphantesque
elevate [ˈelɪveɪt] *vt* élever (**to** à); **to e. sb to the peerage** élever qn à la pairie
elevated [ˈelɪveɪtɪd] *adj (position, rank)* élevé(e); *(thoughts, discussion)* qui vole haut; *(language)* soutenu(e); **e. railway** métro *m* aérien
elevation [elɪˈveɪʃən] *n* (**a**) *(height)* altitude *f* (**b**) *(promotion)* élévation *f* (**to** à) (**c**) *Archit* élévation *f*
elevator [ˈelɪveɪtə(r)] *n* (**a**) *Am (lift)* ascenseur *m* (**b**) *(for goods)* élévateur *m* (**c**) *(on aeroplane wing)* gouvernail *m* de profondeur
eleven [ɪˈlevən] **1** *n* onze *m inv*; **the French e.** *(football team)* le onze de France
  2 *adj* onze; *see also* **eight**
eleven-plus [ɪˈlevənˈplʌs] *n Br Sch* = examen de sélection pour l'entrée dans le secondaire en Grande-Bretagne
elevenses [ɪˈlevənzɪz] *npl Br Fam* casse-croûte *m inv* *(vers onze heures du matin)*
eleventh [ɪˈlevənθ] **1** *n* (**a**) *(fraction)* onzième *m*; *(in series)* onzième *mf* (**b**) *(of month)* onze *m inv*
  2 *adj* onzième; **at the e. hour** à la dernière minute; *see also* **eighth**
elf [elf] *(pl* **elves** [elvz]) *n* elfe *m*
elicit [ɪˈlɪsɪt] *vt (information, smile)* tirer (**from** de); *(reaction, response)* susciter (**from** de la part de)
eligibility [elɪdʒɪˈbɪlɪtɪ] *n (for grant, benefit)* droit *m* (**for** à); *(for job)* admissibilité *f*; *(to vote)* éligibilité *f*
eligible [ˈelɪdʒɪbəl] *adj (for job)* admissible; *(to vote)* éligible; **to be e. for a grant** avoir droit à une subvention; **e. bachelor** bon parti *m*
eliminate [ɪˈlɪmɪneɪt] *vt* éliminer
elimination [ɪlɪmɪˈneɪʃən] *n* élimination *f*; **by a process of e.** (en procédant) par élimination
elite [eɪˈliːt] **1** *n* élite *f*
  2 *adj* d'élite
elitism [eɪˈliːtɪzəm] *n* élitisme *m*
elitist [eɪˈliːtɪst] **1** *n* élitiste *mf*
  2 *adj* élitiste
elixir [ɪˈlɪksə(r)] *n Lit* élixir *m*
Elizabethan [ɪlɪzəˈbiːθən] **1** *n* = Anglais vivant sous le règne d'Élisabeth 1ère
  2 *adj* élisabéthain(e)
elk [elk] *n* élan *m*
ellipse [ɪˈlɪps] *n Math* ellipse *f*
ellipsis [ɪˈlɪpsɪs] *(pl* **ellipses** [ɪˈlɪpsiːz]) *n Gram* ellipse *f*
elliptical [ɪˈlɪptɪkəl] *adj* elliptique
elm [elm] *n* orme *m*
elocution [eləˈkjuːʃən] *n* élocution *f*, diction *f*
elongate [ˈiːlɒŋɡeɪt] *vt* allonger
elope [ɪˈləʊp] *vi* s'enfuir (pour se marier)
eloquence [ˈeləkwəns] *n* éloquence *f*
eloquent [ˈeləkwənt] *adj* éloquent(e)
else [els] *adv* **anyone e.** n'importe qui; *(in negative sentences)* personne d'autre; **is anyone e. interested?** quelqu'un d'autre est-il intéressé?; **someone e.** quelqu'un d'autre; **everyone e.** tous les autres; **no one e.** personne d'autre; **anything e.** n'importe quoi d'autre; *(in negative sentences)* rien d'autre; **do you have**

anything e. to do? as-tu autre chose à faire?; **something e.** autre chose, quelque chose d'autre; **everything e.** tout le reste; **nothing e.** rien d'autre; **somewhere e.** autre part, ailleurs; **anywhere e.** (n'importe où) ailleurs; *(in negative sentences)* nulle part ailleurs; **everywhere e.** partout ailleurs; **nowhere e.** nulle part ailleurs; **who e.** was there? qui d'autre était là?; **who broke it?** – Peter, **who e.?** qui l'a cassé? – Peter, qui d'autre veux-tu que ce soit!; **what e.?** quoi d'autre?; **when e.?** à quel autre moment/quelle autre date?; **where e.** did you go? où êtes-vous allés encore?; **how e.?** de quelle autre manière?; **why e.?** pour quelle autre raison?; **little e.** pas grand-chose d'autre; **there isn't much e.** we can do nous ne pouvons pas faire grand-chose d'autre; **or e.** *(otherwise)* sinon; **do what I tell you or e.!** fais ce que je te dis ou sinon...!
elsewhere ['elswea(r)] *adv* ailleurs, autre part
ELT [i:el'ti:] *n (abbr* English Language Teaching*)* anglais *m* langue étrangère
elucidate [ɪ'lu:sɪdeɪt] *vt (mystery)* élucider; *(reasons)* expliquer
elude [ɪ'lu:d] *vt* échapper à
elusive [ɪ'lu:sɪv] *adj (person)* insaisissable; *(concept)* difficile à saisir
elver ['elvə(r)] *n* civelle *f*
elves [elvz] *pl of* elf
emaciated [ɪ'meɪsɪeɪtɪd] *adj* émacié(e)
e-mail ['i:meɪl] **1** *n* courrier *m* électronique, e-mail *m*, Can courriel *m*; **e. address** adresse *f* électronique, adresse *f* e-mail
2 *vt (person)* envoyer un courrier électronique *ou* un e-mail à; *(file, message)* envoyer par courrier électronique *ou* par e-mail
emanate ['emaneɪt] **1** *vt* dégager
2 *vi* émaner (**from** de)
emancipate [ɪ'mænsɪpeɪt] *vt* émanciper
emancipated [ɪ'mænsɪpeɪtɪd] *adj* émancipé(e)
emancipation [ɪmænsɪ'peɪʃən] *n* émancipation *f*
e-marketing ['i:mɑ:kɪtɪŋ] *n* e-marketing *m*, webmarketing *m*
emasculate [ɪ'mæskjʊleɪt] *vt Fig* amputer
embalm [ɪm'bɑ:m] *vt* embaumer
embankment [ɪm'bæŋkmənt] *n (beside railway)* talus *m*; *(beside river)* berge *f*, quai *m*
embargo [em'bɑ:gəʊ] *(pl* embargoes*)* **1** *n* embargo *m*; **to put an e. on** mettre un embargo sur
2 *vt* mettre un embargo sur
embark [ɪm'bɑ:k] *vi* embarquer; *Fig* **to e. up on sth** s'embarquer dans qch
embarrass [ɪm'bærəs] *vt* embarrasser, gêner; *(make ashamed)* faire honte à
embarrassed [ɪm'bærəst] *adj (ashamed, uncomfortable)* embarrassé(e), gêné(e); *(financially)* gêné(e) (financièrement)
embarrassing [ɪm'bærəsɪŋ] *adj* embarrassant(e), gênant(e); **how e.!** comme ça a dû être/c'est embarrassant!
embarrassment [ɪm'bærəsmənt] *n* embarras *m*, gêne *f*; **much to my e.** à mon grand embarras; **to be an e. to sb** être une source d'embarras pour qn
embassy ['embəsɪ] *(pl* embassies*)* *n* ambassade *f*; **the French E.** l'ambassade *f* de France
embattled [ɪm'bætəld] *adj* assiégé(e) de toutes parts
embed [ɪm'bed] *(pt & pp* embedded*)* *vt* (**a**) **to be embedded in sth** être fiché(e) dans qch; *(with cement)* être scellé(e) dans qch; *Fig* **to be embedded in sb's**

memory être gravé(e) dans la mémoire de qn; **embedded journalist** reporter *m* embarqué *ou* incorporé (**b**) *Comput* intégrer
embellish [ɪm'belɪʃ] *vt (room)* embellir (**with** de); *(account)* enjoliver
embers ['embəz] *npl* braises *fpl*
embezzle [ɪm'bezəl] *vt* détourner (**from** de)
embezzlement [ɪm'bezəlmənt] *n* **e. (of funds)** détournement *m* de fonds
embezzler [ɪm'bezlə(r)] *n* escroc *m*
embitter [ɪm'bɪtə(r)] *vt (person)* aigrir, remplir d'amertume
embittered [ɪm'bɪtəd] *adj (person)* aigri(e)
emblazon [ɪm'bleɪzən] *vt (shield)* orner (**with** de); *Fig (name, headline)* étaler
emblem ['embləm] *n* emblème *m*
embodiment [ɪm'bɒdɪmənt] *n* incarnation *f*
embody [ɪm'bɒdɪ] *(pt & pp* embodied*)* *vt* incarner
embolden [ɪm'bəʊldən] *vt* enhardir; **to e. sb to do sth** donner le courage de faire qch
embolism ['embəlɪzəm] *n Med* embolie *f*
embossed [ɪm'bɒst] *adj (metal, leather)* repoussé(e); *(letter, wallpaper, design)* en relief
embrace [ɪm'breɪs] **1** *n* étreinte *f*
2 *vt* (**a**) *(person)* étreindre; *Fig (belief, religion)* embrasser (**b**) *(include)* couvrir
3 *vi* s'étreindre
embroider [ɪm'brɔɪdə(r)] *vt (cloth)* broder; *Fig (account, report)* enjoliver
embroidery [ɪm'brɔɪdərɪ] *n* broderie *f*
embroil [ɪm'brɔɪl] *vt* entraîner (**in** dans); **to get embroiled in sth** se laisser entraîner dans qch
embryo ['embrɪəʊ] *(pl* embryos*)* *n* embryon *m*; *Fig* **in e.** *(plan, idea)* à l'état embryonnaire
embryonic [embrɪ'ɒnɪk] *adj Biol* embryonnaire; *(plan, idea)* à l'état embryonnaire
emend [ɪ'mend] *vt* corriger
emendation [i:men'deɪʃən] *n* correction *f*
emerald ['emərəld] *n* émeraude *f*; **an e. necklace** collier d'émeraudes; **e. (green)** (vert *m*) émeraude *m*; **the E. Isle** la verte Érin
emerge [ɪ'mɜ:dʒ] *vi (of person, truth)* émerger (**from** de); **it later emerged that...** il est apparu par la suite que...
emergence [ɪ'mɜ:dʒəns] *n (from hiding)* apparition *f*; *(of truth)* révélation *f*; *(of new state, new leader)* émergence *f*
emergency [ɪ'mɜ:dʒənsɪ] *(pl* emergencies*)* *n* urgence *f*; **in an e., in case of e.** en cas d'urgence; *Med* **e. contraception** contraception *f* d'urgence; **e. exit** sortie *f* de secours; **e. landing** atterrissage *m* forcé; *Pol* **e. powers** pouvoirs *mpl* extraordinaires; *Am Med* **e. room** salle *f* des urgences; **e. services** services *mpl* d'urgence; **e. stop** arrêt *m* d'urgence; *Fin* **e. tax** impôt *m* extraordinaire
emergent [ɪ'mɜ:dʒənt] *adj (talent, ability)* naissant(e); *(nation)* en voie de développement
emery ['emərɪ] *n* émeri *m*; **e. board** lime *f* à ongles *(en papier émeri)*; **e. paper** papier *m* émeri
emetic [ɪ'metɪk] **1** *n* émétique *m*
2 *adj* émétique
emigrant ['emɪgrənt] **1** *n* émigrant(e) *m,f*; *(when settled)* émigré(e) *m,f*
2 *adj* migrant(e); *(when settled)* émigré(e)
emigrate ['emɪgreɪt] *vi* émigrer
emigration [emɪ'greɪʃən] *n* émigration *f*
émigré ['emɪgreɪ] *n* émigré(e) *m,f*

eminence ['emɪnəns] n (**a**) (importance) position f éminente; (of post) distinction f (**b**) (title of cardinal) **Your E.** Votre Éminence
eminent ['emɪnənt] adj éminent(e)
eminently ['emɪnəntlɪ] adv éminemment
emirate ['emɪreɪt] n émirat m
emissary ['emɪsərɪ] (pl **emissaries**) n émissaire m
emission [ɪ'mɪʃən] n (of gas, light, bank notes) émission f
emit [ɪ'mɪt] (pt & pp **emitted**) vt (heat, signal, sound) émettre; (smell) dégager; (sigh, cry) pousser
emoticon [ɪ'məʊtɪkɒn] n Comput émoticon m, Can binette f
emotion [ɪ'məʊʃən] n (strength of feeling) émotion f; (individual feeling) sentiment m; **full of e.** ému(e)
emotional [ɪ'məʊʃənəl] adj (person, reaction) émotif(ive); (problem, shock) émotionnel(elle); (film, farewell) émouvant(e); **to get e.** être ému(e)
emotionally [ɪ'məʊʃənəlɪ] adv (thank, welcome) avec effusion; **to be e. involved with sb** avoir une relation intime avec qn; **to get e. involved (with sb)** s'attacher (à qn); **e. deprived** en manque d'affection
emotive [ɪ'məʊtɪv] adj (issue) sensible; (argument, words) qui fait vibrer la corde sensible
empathize ['empəθaɪz] vi **to e. with** (person) comprendre; (plight, problems) compatir à
empathy ['empəθɪ] n affinité(s) f(pl); (power, ability) capacité f à s'identifier à autrui
emperor ['empərə(r)] n empereur m
emphasis ['emfəsɪs] (pl **emphases** ['emfəsɪːz]) n accent m; **to lay or place e. on sth** (point, fact) mettre l'accent sur qch; (word, syllable) appuyer sur qch
emphasize ['emfəsaɪz] vt (point, fact) insister sur; (word, syllable) appuyer sur
emphatic [ɪm'fætɪk] adj (denial, response, person) catégorique; (gesture, tone) énergique
emphatically [ɪm'fætɪkəlɪ] adv (say) énergiquement; (refuse, deny) catégoriquement; **most e.!** absolument!
empire ['empaɪə(r)] n also Fig empire m
empirical [em'pɪrɪkəl] adj empirique
empiricism [em'pɪrɪsɪzəm] n empirisme m
employ [ɪm'plɔɪ] 1 n Formal **to be in sb's e.** être employé(e) par qn
2 vt (workers, force, skills) employer; (tool, means) utiliser
employable [ɪm'plɔɪəbəl] adj (person) susceptible d'être employé; (tool, means) utilisable; **a degree makes you more e.** une licence donne plus de chances de trouver du travail
employee [em'plɔɪiː] n employé(e) m,f; **employees** (staff) personnel m, salariés mpl
employer [ɪm'plɔɪə(r)] n employeur(euse) m,f
employment [ɪm'plɔɪmənt] n (**a**) (work) emploi m; **to be in e.** avoir un emploi; **to be without e.** être sans emploi; **to give e. to sb** employer qn; **e. agency** or **bureau** bureau m ou agence f de placement (**b**) (use) (of money, force) emploi m; (of tool) utilisation f
empower [ɪm'paʊə(r)] vt **to e. sb to do sth** habiliter qn à faire qch
empowering [ɪm'paʊərɪŋ] adj (role, effect) émancipateur(trice)
empress ['empris] n impératrice f
emptiness ['emptɪnɪs] n vide m
empty ['emptɪ] 1 n (bottle) bouteille f vide
2 adj (container, existence) vide; (promise, threat,

words) en l'air; **on an e. stomach** l'estomac vide, à jeun
3 vt vider
4 vi se vider
▸**empty out** vt sep (pockets) vider
empty-handed ['emptɪ'hændɪd] adv les mains vides, bredouille
empty-headed ['emptɪ'hedɪd] adj sans cervelle; **to be e.** n'avoir rien dans la tête
EMS [iːem'es] n (abbr **European Monetary System**) SME m
EMU [iːem'juː] n (abbr **Economic and Monetary Union**) union f économique et monétaire
emu ['iːmjuː] n émeu m
emulate ['emjʊleɪt] vt imiter
emulsion [ɪ'mʌlʃən] n émulsion f
enable [ɪ'neɪbəl] vt (**a**) (allow) **to e. sb to do sth** permettre à qn de faire qch (**b**) Comput (function, device) mettre en service
enact [ɪ'nækt] vt (tragedy, play) jouer; (law) promulguer
enamel [ɪ'næməl] **1** n émail m
2 vt (pt & pp **enamelled,** Am **enameled**) émailler
enamoured, Am **enamored** [ɪ'næməd] adj **to be e. of** être entiché(e) de; **I'm not exactly e. of the idea** je ne peux pas dire que cette idée me ravisse
encampment [ɪn'kæmpmənt] n Mil camp m, campement m
encapsulate [ɪn'kæpsjʊleɪt] vt résumer
encase [ɪn'keɪs] vt envelopper; (in concrete) noyer
enchant [ɪn'tʃɑːnt] vt (**a**) (charm) enchanter, ravir (**b**) (put under a spell) ensorceler
enchanting [ɪn'tʃɑːntɪŋ] adj (idea) très séduisant(e); (voice, person, smile) charmant(e), ravissant(e)
enchantment [ɪn'tʃɑːntmənt] n enchantement m
enchantress [ɪn'tʃɑːntrɪs] n enchanteresse f
encircle [ɪn'sɜːkəl] vt (of road, walls) entourer; (of army, police) encercler, cerner
enclave ['enkleɪv] n enclave f
enclose [ɪn'kləʊz] vt (**a**) (surround) entourer; **an enclosed space** un espace clos (**b**) (include in letter) joindre (**in** à); **enclosed please find..., please find enclosed...** veuillez trouver ci-joint ou ci-inclus...
enclosure [ɪn'kləʊʒə(r)] n (**a**) (area) enceinte f; (for animals) enclos m; (in horseracing) paddock m (**b**) (in letter) pièce f jointe
encode [en'kəʊd] vt coder, chiffrer; Comput encoder
encompass [ɪn'kʌmpəs] vt englober, couvrir
encore ['ɒŋkɔː(r)] n = chanson, morceau etc exécutés à la suite d'un rappel; **to call for an e.** bisser; **e.! bis!**
encounter [ɪn'kaʊntə(r)] **1** n rencontre f
2 vt (person, difficulty) rencontrer; (enemy) affronter
encourage [ɪn'kʌrɪdʒ] vt encourager; **to e. sb to do sth** encourager qn à faire qch
encouragement [ɪn'kʌrɪdʒmənt] n encouragement m; **to give sb e.** encourager qn
encouraging [ɪn'kʌrɪdʒɪŋ] adj encourageant(e); (smile) d'encouragement
▸**encroach on, encroach upon** [ɪn'krəʊtʃ] vt insep empiéter sur; **the sea is encroaching on the land** la mer gagne du terrain
encrusted [ɪn'krʌstɪd] adj **e. with** (jewels) incrusté(e) de; (mud) couvert(e) de
encrypt [en'krɪpt] vt Comput crypter, chiffrer
encumber [ɪn'kʌmbə(r)] vt Formal **to be encumbered with** être encombré(e) par

encumbrance [ɪn'kʌmbrəns] *n Formal* gêne *f*, embarras *m* (**to** pour)
encyclical [ɪn'sɪklɪkəl] *n Rel* encyclique *f*
encyclop(a)edia [ɪnsaɪklə'piːdɪə] *n* encyclopédie *f*
encyclop(a)edic [ɪnsaɪklə'piːdɪk] *adj* encyclopédique
end [end] **1** *n* (**a**) *(extremity)* bout *m*, extrémité *f*; **from one e. to the other** d'un bout à l'autre; **e. to e.** bout à bout; **to stand sth on e.** mettre qch debout; **his hair was standing on e.** ses cheveux se dressaient sur sa tête; *Fig* **to come to the e. of the road** *or* **line** être en fin de parcours (**b**) *(of month, book, meeting)* fin *f*; **for days on e.** pendant des jours entiers; **to put an e. to sth** mettre fin à qch; **to come to an e.** prendre fin; *Fig* **at the e. of the day** au bout du compte; **in the e.** finalement; **she gave me the money back in the e.** elle a fini par me rembourser; **it's not the e. of the world** ce n'est pas la fin du monde; *Fam* **no e. of** énormément de; **e. product** produit *m* fini; *Fig* résultat *m* (**c**) *(aim, purpose)* fin *f*, but *m*; **an e. in itself** une fin en soi; **to what e.?** à quelle fin?, dans quel but?; **with this e. in view** dans ce but, à cette fin; **the e. justifies the means** la fin justifie les moyens (**d**) *(idioms)* *Fam* **to keep one's e. up** ne pas se laisser abattre; *Fam* **to make ends meet** joindre les deux bouts; *Fam* **this job will be the e. of me!** ce boulot, j'y laisserai ma peau!; *Fam* **to get (hold of) the wrong e. of the stick** mal comprendre; **we shall never hear the e. of it!** on n'a pas fini d'en entendre parler!
2 *vt* finir, terminer; *(argument, uncertainty)* mettre fin à; *Fam* **to e. it all** *(commit suicide)* en finir
3 *vi* finir, se terminer; *(of road, path)* s'arrêter; **it ended in a fight/a divorce** ça a fini en bagarre/par un divorce
▸**end up** *vi* finir; *(in particular place)* se retrouver; **to e. up doing sth** finir par faire qch
endanger [ɪn'deɪndʒə(r)] *vt (person, life)* mettre en danger; *(chances, future, health)* compromettre; **an endangered species** une espèce menacée
endear [ɪn'dɪə(r)] *vt* **to e. oneself to sb** se rendre sympathique aux yeux de qn; **these remarks did not e. her to the voters** ces réflexions ne lui ont pas gagné la faveur des électeurs
endearing [ɪn'dɪərɪŋ] *adj (person, personality)* attachant(e); *(smile, habit)* charmant(e)
endearment [ɪn'dɪəmənt] *n* **terms of e.** mots *mpl* tendres
endeavour, *Am* **endeavor** [ɪn'devə(r)] *Formal* **1** *n* effort *m*
2 *vt* **to e. to do sth** s'efforcer de faire qch
endemic [en'demɪk] *adj* endémique; *Fig* **e. to** propre à
ending ['endɪŋ] *n (of story)* fin *f*; *(of word)* terminaison *f*
endive ['endaɪv] *n* (**a**) **(curly) e.** (chicorée *f*) frisée *f* (**b**) *Am (chicory)* endive *f*
endless ['endlɪs] *adj (desert, number, possibilities)* infini(e); *(list, wait, task)* interminable
endocrine ['endəʊkraɪn] *adj Med* **e. gland** glande *f* endocrine
endocrinology [endəʊkraɪ'nɒlədʒɪ] *n* endocrinologie *f*
endorse [ɪn'dɔːs] *vt* (**a**) *(document, cheque)* endosser; *Br (driving licence)* décompter des points sur (**b**) *(approve) (action)* approuver; *(opinion)* souscrire *ou* adhérer à; *(candidature)* appuyer (**c**) *(product)* faire de la publicité pour; **sportswear endorsed by top athletes** des vêtements de sport recommandés par des sportifs de haut niveau

endorsement [ɪn'dɔːsmənt] *n* (**a**) *(on document, cheque)* endos *m*; *Br (on driving licence)* = mention portée sur le permis de conduire à la suite d'une infraction (**b**) *(approval) (of action)* approbation *f* (**of** de); *(of opinion)* adhésion *f* (**of** à); *(of candidature)* appui *m* (**of** à) (**c**) **the singer has made a fortune from her e. of cosmetic products** cette chanteuse a gagné une fortune en faisant de la publicité pour des cosmétiques
endow [ɪn'daʊ] *vt* doter (**with** de)
endowment [ɪn'daʊmənt] *n* (**a**) *Fin* dotation *f*; **e. mortgage** prêt-logement *m* lié à une assurance-vie (**b**) *(talent)* don *m*, talent *m*
endurable [ɪn'djʊərəbəl] *adj* supportable
endurance [ɪn'djʊərəns] *n* endurance *f*; **beyond e.** au-delà des limites du supportable; **e. test** épreuve *f* d'endurance; *Fig* **this is a real e. test** ma patience est mise à rude épreuve
endure [ɪn'djʊə(r)] **1** *vt (violence, hardship)* endurer; *(person, insults)* supporter
2 *vi (last)* survivre
enduring [ɪn'djʊərɪŋ] *adj* durable
enema ['enəmə] *n* lavement *m*
enemy ['enəmɪ] **1** *n (pl* **enemies**) ennemi(e) *m,f*; **to make enemies** se faire des ennemis; **to be one's own worst e.** se desservir soi-même
2 *adj (army, ship)* ennemi(e)
energetic [enə'dʒetɪk] *adj* énergique
energetically [enə'dʒetɪklɪ] *adv* énergiquement
energy ['enədʒɪ] *n* énergie *f*; **to save e.** faire des économies d'énergie; **e. crisis** crise *f* de l'énergie
energy-saving ['enədʒɪseɪvɪŋ] *adj* qui économise l'énergie
enervating ['enəveɪtɪŋ] *adj* débilitant(e)
enfeeble [ɪn'fiːbəl] *vt* affaiblir
enfold [ɪn'fəʊld] *vt* envelopper (**in** dans); **to e. sb in one's arms** serrer qn dans ses bras
enforce [ɪn'fɔːs] *vt (regulation)* mettre en vigueur; *(rights)* faire valoir; **to e. the law** faire respecter la loi
enforcement [ɪn'fɔːsmənt] *n (of a law)* mise *f* en vigueur
enfranchise [ɪn'fræntʃaɪz] *vt* accorder le droit de vote à
engage [ɪn'geɪdʒ] **1** *vt* (**a**) *(employ)* engager; *(workmen)* embaucher (**b**) *(occupy) (person)* occuper; *(attention)* fixer; **to e. sb in conversation** engager la conversation avec qn; **to be engaged in doing sth** être occupé(e) à faire qch (**c**) *Mil (enemy)* attaquer (**d**) *(cog, gear)* mettre en prise; **to e. the clutch** embrayer
2 *vi* (**a**) **to e. in** *(activity, sport)* s'adonner à (**b**) *(of cog wheel)* (s')engager
engaged [ɪn'geɪdʒd] *adj* (**a**) *(to be married)* fiancé(e) (**b**) *(busy)* occupé(e) (**in** à); *Br (phone, public toilet)* occupé; **to be otherwise e.** avoir d'autres engagements
engagement [ɪn'geɪdʒmənt] *n* (**a**) *(to be married)* fiançailles *fpl*; **e. ring** bague *f* de fiançailles (**b**) *(appointment)* rendez-vous *m* (**c**) *(military action)* combat *m*, engagement *m*
engaging [ɪn'geɪdʒɪŋ] *adj* engageant(e), attrayant(e)
engender [ɪn'dʒendə(r)] *vt* faire naître, engendrer
engine ['endʒɪn] *n* (**a**) *(of car, plane, ship)* moteur *m*; **e. room** salle *f* des machines; **e. trouble** panne *f* de moteur (**b**) *(of train)* locomotive *f*; **e. driver** conducteur(trice) *m,f*, mécanicien(enne) *m,f*

engineer [endʒɪ'nɪə(r)] **1** *n (technical specialist)* ingénieur *m*; *(mechanic)* dépanneur *m*; *(on ship)* mécanicien *m*
2 *vt (cause) (plan, downfall, defeat)* machiner, manigancer; *(situation)* manigancer
engineering [endʒɪ'nɪərɪŋ] *n* ingénierie *f*
England ['ɪŋglənd] *n* l'Angleterre *f*
English ['ɪŋglɪʃ] **1** *n (language)* anglais *m*; **E. breakfast** petit déjeuner *m* anglais; **E. class/teacher** cours *m*/ professeur *m* d'anglais
2 *npl* **the E.** les Anglais *mpl*
3 *adj* anglais(e); **the E. Channel** la Manche

English Breakfast

Le petit déjeuner traditionnel anglais se compose d'un plat chaud (des œufs au bacon, par exemple), de céréales ou de porridge, et de toasts à la marmelade d'oranges, le tout accompagné de café ou de thé ; aujourd'hui il est généralement remplacé par une collation plus légère.

Englishman ['ɪŋglɪʃmən] *n* Anglais *m*
Englishwoman ['ɪŋglɪʃwomən] *n* Anglaise *f*
engrave [ɪn'greɪv] *vt* graver
engraver [ɪn'greɪvə(r)] *n* graveur *m*
engraving [ɪn'greɪvɪŋ] *n* gravure *f*
engrossed [ɪn'grəʊst] *adj* plongé(e) (**in** dans), absorbé(e) (**in** par)
engrossing [ɪn'grəʊsɪŋ] *adj* absorbant(e), captivant(e)
engulf [ɪn'gʌlf] *vt (of waves, flames)* engloutir; *(of feeling)* s'emparer de
enhance [ɪn'hɑːns] *vt (quality of life, chances)* améliorer; *(beauty, colour)* rehausser, mettre en valeur; *(ability, effect)* renforcer; *(reputation, pleasure)* accroître; *(value)* augmenter
enigma [ɪ'nɪgmə] *n* énigme *f*
enigmatic [enɪg'mætɪk] *adj* énigmatique
enjoy [ɪn'dʒɔɪ] *vt* (**a**) *(take pleasure from)* prendre plaisir à; *(film, book, concert)* aimer; *(food, drink)* savourer; **to e. doing sth** aimer faire qch; **to e. oneself** s'amuser (**b**) *(benefit from)* jouir de
enjoyable [ɪn'dʒɔɪəbəl] *adj* agréable
enjoyment [ɪn'dʒɔɪmənt] *n* plaisir *m*; **to get e. out of sth** retirer du plaisir de qch; **to get e. out of doing sth** prendre plaisir à faire qch
enlarge [ɪn'lɑːdʒ] **1** *vt* agrandir; *(hole)* élargir
2 *vi* s'agrandir; **to e. (up) on sth** s'étendre sur qch
enlargement [ɪn'lɑːdʒmənt] *n* agrandissement *m*; *(of hole)* élargissement *m*
enlighten [ɪn'laɪtən] *vt* éclairer (**on** sur)
enlightened [ɪn'laɪtənd] *adj* éclairé(e)
enlightenment [ɪn'laɪtənmənt] *n (clarification)* éclaircissement *m*; **for your e.** pour votre édification; *Hist* **the E.** le Siècle des Lumières
enlist [ɪn'lɪst] **1** *vt (support, help)* s'assurer; *(soldier)* enrôler, engager
2 *vi (of soldier)* s'engager
enliven [ɪn'laɪvən] *vt* animer; *(party)* égayer, animer
en masse ['ɒn'mæs] *adv* en masse, tous ensemble
enmesh [ɪn'meʃ] *vt* **to be enmeshed in sth** être empêtré(e) dans qch
enmity ['enmɪtɪ] *n* inimitié *f*, hostilité *f*
enormity [ɪ'nɔːmɪtɪ] *n* énormité *f*
enormous [ɪ'nɔːməs] *adj (in physical size)* énorme; *(patience, gratitude, power, intelligence)* immense; *(strength)* colossal(e)
enormously [ɪ'nɔːməslɪ] *adv* énormément

enough [ɪ'nʌf] **1** *adj* assez de; **e. money/wine** assez d'argent/de vin; **more than e. food** plus de nourriture qu'il n'en faut
2 *pron* assez; **to be e.** suffire; **more than e.** plus qu'il n'en faut; **that's e.!** ça suffit!; **e. is e.** il ne faut pas exagérer; **to have e.** to live on avoir de quoi vivre; **e. said!** je vois!; **to have had e. of sb/sth** en avoir assez de qn/qch
3 *adv* (**a**) *(sufficiently)* assez; **good e.** assez bon (bonne); **he didn't try hard e.** il n'a pas vraiment essayé (**b**) *(reasonably)* assez; **she's a nice e. girl** c'est une fille assez sympa; **oddly** *or* **strangely e.,...** chose curieuse,...
enquire = **inquire**
enquiry = **inquiry**
enrage [ɪn'reɪdʒ] *vt* rendre furieux(euse)
enrapture [ɪn'ræptʃə(r)] *vt* éblouir, émerveiller
enraptured [ɪn'ræptʃəd] *adj* ébloui(e), émerveillé(e)
enrich [ɪn'rɪtʃ] *vt* enrichir
enrol, *Am* **enroll** [ɪn'rəʊl] *(pt & pp* **enrolled**) **1** *vt (soldier)* enrôler; *(student)* immatriculer; *(worker)* embaucher
2 *vi (of soldier)* s'enrôler; *(of students)* s'inscrire
enrolment, *Am* **enrollment** [ɪn'rəʊlmənt] *n (of soldier)* enrôlement *m*; *(of student)* immatriculation *f*; *(of worker)* embauche *f*
ensconce [ɪn'skɒns] *vt* **to e. oneself** s'installer confortablement (**in** dans)
ensemble [ɒn'sɒmbəl] *n* ensemble *m*
enshrine [ɪn'ʃraɪn] *vt* **to be enshrined in sth** *(of belief, principle)* être enraciné(e) dans qch
ensign ['ensaɪn] *n* (**a**) *(flag)* drapeau *m*; *Naut* pavillon *m* national (**b**) *Am (naval officer)* enseigne *m (de vaisseau de deuxième classe)*
enslave [ɪn'sleɪv] *vt* réduire à l'esclavage, asservir
ensnare [ɪn'sneə(r)] *vt (animal, criminal)* prendre au piège; *Fig (lover)* attirer dans ses filets
ensue [ɪn'sjuː] *vi* s'ensuivre
ensuing [ɪn'sjuːɪŋ] *adj (in the past)* qui a suivi; *(in the future)* qui suivra
en suite ['ɒn'swiːt] *adj* **e. bathroom** *(in hotel)* salle *f* de bains particulière; *(in house)* salle *f* de bains attenante
ensure [ɪn'ʃʊə(r)] *vt* assurer; **to e. that...** faire en sorte que... + *subjunctive*
ENT [iːen'tiː] *n (abbr* **Ear, Nose and Throat)** ORL *f*; **E. specialist** ORL *mf*
entail [ɪn'teɪl] *vt* (**a**) *(involve)* entraîner, occasionner; *(difficulties)* comporter; **what does the job e.?** en quoi le travail consiste-t-il? (**b**) *Law* **to e. an estate** substituer un bien
entangle [ɪn'tæŋgəl] *vt* **to get** *or* **become entangled in sth** *(of person, animal)* s'empêtrer dans qch; *(of hair, string, wires)* s'emmêler dans qch; *Fig* **he got entangled in the dispute** il s'est retrouvé impliqué dans la dispute
entanglement [ɪn'tæŋgəlmənt] *n* enchevêtrement *m*; **emotional entanglements** complications *fpl* sentimentales
enter ['entə(r)] **1** *vt* (**a**) *(house, country, army)* entrer dans; *(university)* entrer à; *(race, exam, competition)* participer à; **to e. sb for an exam** inscrire qn à un examen; **to e. sb for a race** inscrire qn au nombre des participants d'une course; **it never entered my head that...** il ne m'est jamais venu à l'esprit que...; **to e. a protest** protester formellement (**b**) *Comput (data)* entrer, introduire

2 *vi (go in)* entrer; **to e. for a race** se faire inscrire pour une course

▶**enter into** *vt insep* (**a**) *(begin) (service, relationship)* entrer en; *(dispute)* entrer dans; *(negotiations)* entamer, engager; **to e. into partnership with sb** s'associer avec qn; **to e. into conversation with sb** engager une conversation avec qn (**b**) *(have a part in)* **money doesn't e. into it** l'argent n'entre pas en ligne de compte

enterprise ['entəpraız] *n* (**a**) *(undertaking, company)* entreprise *f* (**b**) *(initiative)* initiative *f*

enterprising ['entəpraızıŋ] *adj* entreprenant(e); *(imaginative)* plein(e) d'imagination; *(solution)* ingénieux(euse)

entertain [entə'teın] **1** *vt* (**a**) *(amuse)* divertir, amuser; **to e. guests** recevoir (des invités) (**b**) *(consider) (idea)* considérer; *(hope)* nourrir; *(fear, suspicion)* éprouver
2 *vi (receive guests)* recevoir

entertainer [entə'teınə(r)] *n* fantaisiste *mf*; *(comedian)* comique *mf*

entertaining [entə'teınıŋ] **1** *n (of guests)* **to do a lot of e.** recevoir beaucoup
2 *adj (amusing)* divertissant(e), amusant(e)

entertainment [entə'teınmənt] *n* (**a**) *(amusement)* divertissement *m*, amusement *m*; *Com* **e. allowance** indemnité *f* de représentation (**b**) *(performances)* spectacle *m*, divertissement *m*; **the e. business** l'industrie *f* du spectacle; **entertainments guide** guide *m* des spectacles

enthral, *Am* **enthrall** [ın'θrɔːl] *(pt & pp* **enthralled)** *vt* captiver, passionner; *(of object, beauty)* fasciner; *(of prospect, idea)* enthousiasmer

enthralling [ın'θrɔːlıŋ] *adj* captivant(e), passionnant(e); *(object, beauty)* fascinant(e); *(prospect, idea)* enthousiasmant(e)

enthuse [ın'θjuːz] **1** *vt* enthousiasmer
2 *vi* s'enthousiasmer (**about** *or* **over** pour)

enthusiasm [ın'θjuːzıæzəm] *n* enthousiasme *m*

enthusiast [ın'θjuːzıæst] *n* passionné(e) *m,f*; **a golf e.** un(e) passionné(e) de golf

enthusiastic [ınθjuːzı'æstık] *adj* enthousiaste

enthusiastically [ınθjuːzı'æstıklı] *adv* avec enthousiasme

entice [ın'taıs] *vt* attirer, séduire; **to e. sb to do sth** inciter qn à faire qch; **to e. sb away from sb/sth** appâter qn pour qu'il quitte qn/qch

enticing [ın'taısıŋ] *adj (offer, idea)* séduisant(e), tentant(e); *(dish)* alléchant(e); *(smile)* charmeur(euse)

entire [ın'taıə(r)] *adj* (**a**) *(whole)* entier(ère), tout(e); **the e. day** toute la journée, la journée entière (**b**) *(intact)* intact(e)

entirely [ın'taıəlı] *adv* entièrement, complètement

entirety [ın'taıərətı] *n* intégralité *f*; **in its e.** dans son intégralité, intégralement

entitle [ın'taıtəl] *vt* (**a**) *(allow)* **to e. sb to sth** donner à qn droit à qch; **to e. sb to do sth** permettre à qn de faire qch; **to be entitled to sth** avoir droit à qch; **to be entitled to do sth** avoir le droit de faire qch (**b**) *(book, chapter, song)* intituler

entitlement [ın'taıtəlmənt] *n* droit *m* (**to** à); **holiday e.** congé *m* annuel *(auquel on a droit)*

entity ['entıtı] *(pl* **entities)** *n* entité *f*

entomologist [entə'mɒlədʒıst] *n* entomologiste *mf*

entomology [entə'mɒlədʒı] *n* entomologie *f*

entourage ['ɒntuːrɑːʒ] *n* entourage *m*

entrails ['entreılz] *npl* entrailles *fpl*

entrance¹ ['entrəns] *n* (**a**) *(way in, act of entering)* entrée *f*; **to make one's e. to gain e. to** s'introduire *ou* pénétrer dans (**b**) *(admission) (to club)* admission *f*; *(to cinema)* entrée *f*; **e. examination** examen *m* d'entrée; **e. hall** *(in house)* vestibule *m*; *(in hotel)* hall *m*

entrance² [ın'trɑːns] *vt (charm)* ravir, transporter

entrancing [ın'trɑːnsıŋ] *adj* ravissant(e), enchanteur(eresse)

entrant ['entrənt] *n (in race, competition)* inscrit(e) *m,f*; *(in examination)* candidat(e) *m,f*

entreat [ın'triːt] *vt* **to e. sb to do sth** implorer qn de faire qch

entreaty [ın'triːtı] *(pl* **entreaties)** *n* prière *f*, supplication *f*

entrée ['ɒntreı] *n (dish before main course)* entrée *f*; *Am (main course)* plat *m* de résistance

entrenched [ın'trentʃd] *adj (views, ideas)* arrêté(e); *(customs)* enraciné(e)

entrepreneur [ɒntrəprə'nɜː(r)] *n* entrepreneur *m*

entrepreneurial [ɒntrəprə'nɜːrıəl] *adj (person)* qui a l'esprit d'entreprise; *(skill, talents)* d'entrepreneur

entrust [ın'trʌst] *vt* **to e. sb with sth, to e. sth to sb** confier qch à qn

entry ['entrı] *(pl* **entries)** *n* (**a**) *(way in, act of entering)* entrée *f*; **to make one's e.** faire son entrée; **to gain e. to** s'introduire *ou* pénétrer dans (**b**) *(of competitor)* inscription *f*; **e. form** feuille *f* d'inscription (**c**) *(in encyclopedia)* article *m*; *(in dictionary)* entrée *f*; *(in diary)* note *f*

entry-level ['entrılevəl] *adj* (**a**) *(bottom-of-the-range)* bas de gamme, d'entrée de gamme (**b**) *(job)* au bas de l'échelle; *(salary)* de début de carrière

entryphone ['entrıfəʊn] *n* Interphone® *m*

entwine [ın'twaın] **1** *vt* entrelacer
2 *vi* s'entrelacer

enumerate [ı'njuːməreıt] *vt* énumérer, détailler

enunciate [ı'nʌnsıeıt] *vt (sound, word)* prononcer, articuler; *(opinion, view)* énoncer

envelop [ın'veləp] *vt (envelop* **(in** dans)

envelope ['envələʊp, 'ɒnvələʊp] *n* enveloppe *f*

enviable ['envıəbəl] *adj* enviable

envious ['envıəs] *adj* envieux(euse); **to be e. of sb** envier qn

enviously ['envıəslı] *adv* avec envie

environment [ın'vaırənmənt] *n* (**a**) *(surroundings)* milieu *m*; **a pleasant working e.** des conditions *fpl* de travail agréables; **a hostile e.** un climat d'hostilité, une ambiance hostile (**b**) *(nature)* **the e.** l'environnement *m*; **Department** *or* **Ministry of the E.** ministère *m* de l'Environnement

environmental [ınvaırən'mentəl] *adj* **e. damage** dégâts *mpl* causés à l'environnement; **e. disaster** désastre *m* écologique; **e. policy** politique *f* de l'environnement

environmentalist [ınvaırən'mentəlıst] *n* écologiste *mf*

environment-friendly [ın'vaırənmənt'frendlı], **environmentally-friendly** [ınvaırən'mentəlı'frendlı] *adj (policy)* respectueux(euse) de l'environnement; *(technology, product)* non polluant(e)

environs [ın'vaırənz] *npl* environs *mpl*, alentours *mpl*

envisage [ın'vızıdʒ], *Am* **envision** [en'vıʒən] *vt* envisager

envoy ['envɔı] *n* envoyé(e) *m,f*

envy ['envı] **1** *n* envie *f*, jalousie *f*; **to be the e. of sb** être un objet d'envie pour qn

2 *vt (pt & pp* **envied***)* envier; **to e. sb sth** envier qch à qn

enzyme ['enzaɪm] *n* enzyme *f*

EOC [iːəʊ'siː] *Br (abbr* **Equal Opportunities Commission***)* = organisme gouvernemental qui veille à l'égalité des chances sur le lieu de travail

eon *Am* = aeon

epaulette, *Am* **epaulet** ['epəlet] *n* épaulette *f*

ephemeral [ɪ'femərəl] *adj* éphémère

e-petition ['iːpətɪʃən] *n* e-pétition *f*

epic ['epɪk] **1** *n (poem, novel)* épopée *f; (film)* film *m* à grand spectacle
2 *adj* épique

epicentre, *Am* **epicenter** ['epɪsentə(r)] *n* épicentre *m*

epicurean [epɪkjʊ'rɪən] **1** *n* épicurien(enne) *m,f*
2 *adj* épicurien(enne)

epidemic [epɪ'demɪk] *also Fig* **1** *n* épidémie *f*
2 *adj* épidémique

epidermis [epɪ'dɜːmɪs] *n Anat* épiderme *m*

epidural [epɪ'djuːrəl] *n Med* péridurale *f*

epigram ['epɪgræm] *n* épigramme *f*

epilepsy ['epɪlepsɪ] *n* épilepsie *f*

epileptic [epɪ'leptɪk] **1** *n* épileptique *mf*
2 *adj* épileptique; **e. fit** crise *f* d'épilepsie

epilogue ['epɪlɒg] *n* épilogue *m*

Epiphany [ɪ'pɪfənɪ] *n* Épiphanie *f*

episcopal [ɪ'pɪskəpəl] *adj* épiscopal(e); **e. palace** évêché *m*

episcopalian [ɪpɪskə'peɪlɪən] **1** *n* épiscopalien(enne) *m,f*
2 *adj* épiscopalien(enne)

episode ['epɪsəʊd] *n (part of story)* épisode *m; (incident)* incident *m*

epistle [ɪ'pɪsəl] *n also Hum* épître *f*

epitaph ['epɪtɑːf] *n* épitaphe *f*

epithet ['epɪθet] *n* épithète *f*

epitome [ɪ'pɪtəmɪ] *n* **to be the e. of sth** être l'exemple même de qch

epitomize [ɪ'pɪtəmaɪz] *vt* incarner

epoch ['iːpɒk] *n* époque *f*

epoch-making ['iːpɒkmeɪkɪŋ] *adj* qui fait date

eponymous [ɪ'pɒnɪməs] *adj* éponyme

EPS [iːpiː'es] *n (abbr* **earnings per share***)* BPA *m*

equable ['ekwəbəl] *adj* constant(e); *(person)* à l'humeur égale

equal ['iːkwəl] **1** *adj* égal(e) *m,f;* **to treat sb as an e.** traiter qn d'égal à égal
2 *adj* (**a**) *(identical)* égal(e) (**to** à); **all things being e.** en principe; **in e. measure** en quantité égale; **on e. terms** sur un pied d'égalité; **e. opportunities** égalité *f* des chances; **e. pay** égalité *f* des salaires; **e. rights** égalité *f* des droits (**b**) *(good enough)* **to be e. to sth** être à la hauteur de qch
3 *vt (pt & pp* **equalled,** *Am* **equaled***)* égaler

equality [ɪ'kwɒlɪtɪ] *n* égalité *f*

equalize ['iːkwəlaɪz] **1** *vt* égaliser; *(chances, forces)* équilibrer
2 *vi (in sport)* égaliser

equalizer ['iːkwəlaɪzə(r)] *n* (**a**) *(in sport)* but *m* égalisateur (**b**) *Elec* égaliseur *m* de potentiel

equally ['iːkwəlɪ] *adv* (**a**) *(to an equal degree)* tout aussi (**b**) *(in equal amounts) (share, divide)* en parts égales (**c**) *(likewise)* tout aussi bien, de la même manière

equanimity [ekwə'nɪmɪtɪ] *n* sérénité *f*

equate [ɪ'kweɪt] *vt* assimiler (**with** avec)

equation [ɪ'kweɪʒən] *n* équation *f; Fig* **money doesn't even enter the e.** les questions d'argent n'entrent même pas en ligne de compte

equator [ɪ'kweɪtə(r)] *n* équateur *m*

equatorial [ekwə'tɔːrɪəl] *adj* équatorial(e); **E. Guinea** la Guinée équatoriale

equestrian [ɪ'kwestrɪən] **1** *n* cavalier(ère) *m,f; (in circus)* écuyer(ère) *m,f*
2 *adj (sport, ability)* équestre

equidistant [ekwɪ'dɪstənt] *adj* équidistant(e)

equilateral [ekwɪ'lætərəl] *adj* équilatéral(e)

equilibrium [ekwɪ'lɪbrɪəm] *n* équilibre *m*

equinox ['ekwɪnɒks] *n* équinoxe *m*

equip [ɪ'kwɪp] *(pt & pp* **equipped***)* *vt* (**a**) *(provide with equipment)* équiper (**with** de); **the plane is equipped with the latest technology** l'avion est doté des équipements les plus modernes (**b**) *(prepare)* préparer (**for** pour)

equipment [ɪ'kwɪpmənt] *n* équipement *m; (in factory)* installations *fpl,* matériel *m;* **e. allowance** subvention *f* pour l'achat de matériel

equitable ['ekwɪtəbəl] *adj* équitable

Equity ['ekwɪtɪ] *n* = syndicat britannique des artistes de théâtre et de télévision

equity ['ekwɪtɪ] *(pl* **equities***) n* (**a**) *(fairness)* équité *f* (**b**) *Fin (of shareholders)* fonds *mpl* ou capitaux *mpl* propres; *(of company)* capital *m* actions; **equities** actions *fpl* ordinaires

equivalent [ɪ'kwɪvələnt] **1** *n* équivalent *m*
2 *adj* équivalent(e) (**to** à)

equivocal [ɪ'kwɪvəkəl] *adj* équivoque, ambigu(ë)

equivocate [ɪ'kwɪvəkeɪt] *vi* user d'équivoques *ou* de faux-fuyants

equivocation [ɪkwɪvə'keɪʃən] *n* paroles *fpl* équivoques, faux-fuyants *mpl*

ER [iː'ɑː(r)] *n* (**a**) *Br (abbr* **Elizabeth Regina***)* la Reine Elizabeth (**b**) *Am (abbr* **Emergency Room***)* urgences *fpl*

era ['ɪərə] *n* ère *f*

eradicate [ɪ'rædɪkeɪt] *vt* éradiquer

erase [ɪ'reɪz] *vt* effacer; *(with eraser)* gommer

eraser [ɪ'reɪzə(r)] *n* gomme *f*

erect [ɪ'rekt] **1** *adj* droit(e), debout; *(penis, nipples)* en érection
2 *vt (building)* ériger; *(statue)* élever, ériger; *(scaffolding)* dresser

erection [ɪ'rekʃən] *n* (**a**) *(of building, statue)* construction *f,* érection *f* (**b**) *(erect penis)* érection *f*

ergonomic [ɜːgə'nɒmɪk] *adj* ergonomique

ergonomics [ɜːgə'nɒmɪks] *n* ergonomie *f*

Eritrea [erɪ'treɪə] *n* l'Érythrée *f*

Eritrean [erɪ'treɪən] **1** *n* Érythréen(enne) *m,f*
2 *adj* érythréen(enne)

ERM [iːɑː'rem] *n (abbr* **Exchange Rate Mechanism***)* mécanisme *m* de change *(du SME)*

ermine ['ɜːmɪn] *n* hermine *f*

erode [ɪ'rəʊd] **1** *vt (rock, soil)* éroder; *(metal)* corroder, ronger; *Fig (confidence, power)* miner
2 *vi (of rock, soil)* s'éroder; *(of metal)* se corroder; *Fig (of confidence, power)* s'éroder peu à peu

erogenous [ɪ'rɒdʒɪnəs] *adj* érogène; **e. zone** zone *f* érogène

Eros ['ɪərɒs] *n* Éros

erosion [ɪ'rəʊʒən] *n (of rock, soil) & Fig (of confidence, power)* érosion *f; (of metal)* corrosion *f*

erotic [ɪ'rɒtɪk] *adj* érotique

eroticism [ɪ'rɒtɪsɪzəm] *n* érotisme *f*

err [ɜ:(r)] *vi (make mistake)* faire erreur; **to e. on the side of caution** pécher par excès de prudence; *Prov* **to e. is human** l'erreur est humaine

errand ['erənd] *n* commission *f*, course *f*; **to run errands for sb** (aller) faire des commissions *ou* des courses pour qn; *Old-fashioned* **e. boy** garçon *m* de courses

erratic [ɪ'rætɪk] *adj (service, results, pulse)* irrégulier(ère); *(playing, performance)* inégal(e); *(behaviour)* imprévisible; *(person)* lunatique; *(driving)* mal assuré(e)

erroneous [ɪ'rəʊnɪəs] *adj* erroné(e)

error ['erə(r)] *n (mistake)* erreur *f*, faute *f*; **to make an e.** faire une erreur; **in e.** par erreur; **an e. of judgement** une erreur de jugement; **to see the e. of one's ways** reconnaître ses erreurs

ersatz ['ɜ:zæts] *adj* **e. coffee** un succédané de café

erstwhile ['ɜ:stwaɪl] *adj Lit* ancien(enne)

erudite ['erʊdaɪt] *adj* érudit(e)

erudition [erʊ'dɪʃən] *n* érudition *f*

erupt [ɪ'rʌpt] *vi (of volcano)* entrer en éruption; *(of person)* exploser; *(of anger, violence)* éclater; *(of spot)* sortir

eruption [ɪ'rʌpʃən] *n* éruption *f*

escalate ['eskəleɪt] *vi (of prices)* monter en flèche; *(of conflict)* s'intensifier, s'aggraver

escalation [eskə'leɪʃən] *n (of prices)* montée *f* en flèche; *(of conflict)* escalade *f*

escalator ['eskəleɪtə(r)] *n* escalier *m* roulant, Escalator® *m*

escalope ['eskəlɒp] *n* escalope *f*

escapade ['eskəpeɪd] *n* fredaine *f*, frasque *f*

escape [ɪs'keɪp] **1** *n (of person)* évasion *f*; *(of gas, water)* fuite *f*; **to make one's e.** s'échapper; *Com* **e. clause** clause *f* échappatoire; **e. route** *(from fire)* itinéraire *m* de sortie de secours; *(of criminal)* itinéraire *m* emprunté pour s'échapper
2 *vt (danger, punishment)* échapper à; **to e. sb's notice** échapper à l'attention de qn; **her name escapes me** son nom m'échappe
3 *vi (of person, gas, water)* s'échapper (**from** de); *(from prison)* s'évader (**from** de); **to e. unhurt** s'en tirer indemne; **he escaped to Italy** il s'est enfui en Italie; **to e. from reality** s'évader de la réalité

escapee [eskeɪ'pi:] *n* évadé(e) *m,f*

escapism [ɪs'keɪpɪzəm] *n* évasion *f* (hors de la réalité)

escapist [ɪs'keɪpɪst] **1** *n* personne *f* qui cherche à s'évader de la réalité
2 *adj* d'évasion

escapologist [eskə'pɒlədʒɪst] *n* prestidigitateur *m* spécialiste de l'évasion

escarpment [ɪs'kɑ:pmənt] *n* escarpement *m*

eschew [ɪs'tʃu:] *vt* éviter; **to e. sb's company** fuir *ou* éviter qn

escort 1 *n* ['eskɔ:t] *(a) (for convoy)* escorte *f*; *(for tourists)* guide *m*; *(ship)* bâtiment *m* d'escorte; **under e.** sous escorte; *Mil* **e. duty** service *m* d'escorte (**b**) *(from agency) (woman)* hôtesse *f*; *(man)* call boy *m*; **e. agency** agence *f* d'hôtesses
2 *vt* [ɪs'kɔ:t] escorter; *(prisoner)* conduire sous escorte

escudo [e'sku:dəʊ] *(pl escudos) n* escudo *m*

e-signature ['i:sɪgnətʃə(r)] *n Comput* signature *f* électronique, e-signature *f*

Eskimo ['eskɪməʊ] **1** *n (pl Eskimos)* Esquimau(aude) *m,f*
2 *adj* esquimau(aude), eskimo *inv*

Eskimo

Aux États-Unis et au Canada le terme "Eskimo" est souvent considéré comme injurieux ; on préfère le terme "Inuit". Les Canadiens utilisent aussi les termes "First Nations" et "First Peoples" pour parler de leur communautés autochtones.

esophagus *Am* = **oesophagus**

esoteric [esəʊ'terɪk] *adj* ésotérique

ESP [i:es'pi:] *n (abbr* **extrasensory perception**) perception *f* extra-sensorielle

especially [ɪs'peʃəlɪ] *adv* (**a**) *(in particular)* surtout (**b**) *(more than normally)* particulièrement; **we were e. lucky with the weather** le temps nous a été particulièrement favorable (**c**) *(expressly)* (tout) spécialement, exprès; **I did it e. for you** je l'ai fait spécialement *ou* exprès pour vous

Esperanto [espə'ræntəʊ] *n* l'Espéranto *m*

espionage ['espɪɒnɑ:ʒ] *n* espionnage *m*

esplanade [esplə'neɪd] *n* esplanade *f*

espouse [ɪs'paʊz] *vt* épouser

espresso [es'presəʊ] *(pl espressos) n* expresso *m*

Esq *(abbr* **Esquire**) **Derek Wilson, E.** = Monsieur Derek Wilson

essay ['eseɪ] *n (at school)* composition *f*; *(for younger pupils)* rédaction *f*; *(at university)* dissertation *f*

essayist ['eseɪɪst] *n* essayiste *mf*

essence ['esəns] *n* (**a**) *(most important part or quality)* essence *f*; *(of speech)* essentiel *m*; *(of question)* fond *m*; **in e.** essentiellement, surtout; **the very e. of bravery** le courage même; **time is of the e.** le temps est le facteur prioritaire (**b**) *Culin (extract)* extrait *m*

essential [ɪ'senʃəl] **1** *n* **essentials** *(basic foodstuffs)* produits *mpl* de première nécessité; *(basic issues)* essentiel *m*; **just pack a few essentials** ne prends que l'essentiel
2 *adj* (**a**) *(basic)* essentiel(elle); **e. oil** huile *f* essentielle (**b**) *(indispensable)* essentiel(elle), indispensable (**to** *or* **for** à); **it is e. that...** il est essentiel que... + *subjunctive*

essentially [ɪ'senʃəlɪ] *adv* essentiellement

Essex ['esɪks] *n* l'Essex *m*, = comté dans le sud-est de l'Angleterre; *Br Fam Pej* **E. girl** ≃ minette *f*; *Br Fam Pej* **E. man** = stéréotype du réactionnaire bête et vulgaire, originaire de l'Essex

Essex

Il s'agit de stéréotypes sociaux apparus au cours des années 80. L'"Essex Girl" (originaire de l'Essex, comté situé à l'est de Londres) est censée être une jeune femme d'origine modeste aux mœurs légères, vulgaire, bruyante, et peu intelligente. L'"Essex Man" est lui aussi vulgaire et bruyant ; de plus, il est réactionnaire et inculte.

EST [i:es'ti:] *n Am (abbr* **Eastern Standard Time**) heure *f* de la côte est de l'Amérique du Nord

establish [ɪs'tæblɪʃ] *vt* (**a**) *(set up) (company)* fonder; *(custom)* instaurer; *(system, organization)* établir; **to e. oneself in business** s'établir dans les affaires; **to e. a reputation** se faire une réputation; **the film established her as an important director** avec ce film, elle s'est affirmée comme un metteur en scène important (**b**) *(prove)* établir

established [ɪs'tæblɪʃt] *adj* établi(e); *(fact)* acquis(e)

establishment [ɪs'tæblɪʃmənt] *n* (**a**) **the E.** *(dominant group)* l'establishment *m*; *(prevailing values)* l'ordre *m* établi (**b**) *(hotel, restaurant)* établissement *m* (**c**) *(of company, organization)* constitution *f*; *(of fact)* constatation *f*

estate [ɪs'teɪt] *n* (**a**) *Law (possessions)* biens *mpl* (**b**) *(land)* terre *f*, propriété *f*; *Br* (**housing**) **e.** lotissement *m*; *(with council houses)* cité *f* HLM.; *Br* **e. agency** agence *f* immobilière; *Br* **e. agent** agent *m* immobilier (**c**) *Br* **e. (car)** break *m*

esteem [ɪs'tiːm] **1** *n* estime *f*, considération *f*; **to hold sb in high e.** avoir qn en haute estime; **to hold sb in low e.** avoir peu d'estime pour qn
  2 *vt* (**a**) *(person)* estimer; *(thing)* priser (**b**) *Formal (consider)* considérer; **she esteemed it a great honour to be invited** elle se sentit fort honorée d'avoir été invitée

esthetic *Am* = **aesthetic**

estimate 1 *n* ['estɪmət] *(calculation)* évaluation *f*, calcul *m*; *Com* devis *m*; **at a rough e.** à vue de nez
  2 *vt* ['estɪmeɪt] estimer, évaluer; *(value)* estimer

estimation [estɪ'meɪʃən] *n* (**a**) *(calculation)* estimation *f*, évaluation *f* (**b**) *(judgement)* jugement *m*, opinion *f*; **in my e.** à mon avis; **to go up/down in sb's e.** monter/descendre dans l'estime de qn

Estonia [es'təʊnɪə] *n* l'Estonie *f*

Estonian [es'təʊnɪən] **1** *n* (**a**) *(person)* Estonien(enne) *m,f* (**b**) *(language)* estonien *m*
  2 *adj* estonien(enne)

estranged [ɪs'treɪndʒd] *adj (couple)* séparé(e); **her e. husband** son mari, dont elle est séparée; **their e. son** leur fils, avec qui ils sont brouillés

estrogen *Am* = **oestrogen**

estuary ['estjʊərɪ] *(pl* **estuaries**) *n* estuaire *m*

ETA 1 [ˌiːtiː'eɪ] *(abbr* **estimated time of arrival**) HPA *f*
  2 ['etə] *(abbr* **Euskadi Ta Askatasuna**) ETA *f*

e-tail ['iːteɪl] *n* vente *f* en ligne

et al [et'æl] *(abbr* **et alii**) et autres

etc [et'setrə] *(abbr* **et cetera**) etc

etch [etʃ] *vt* graver à l'eau-forte; *Fig* **to be etched in sb's memory** être gravé(e) dans la mémoire de qn

etching ['etʃɪŋ] *n (gravure f* à l') eau-forte *f*

eternal [ɪ'tɜːnəl] *adj* éternel(elle); *Fig (continual)* continuel(elle), sans fin

eternally [ɪ'tɜːnəlɪ] *adv* éternellement

eternity [ɪ'tɜːnɪtɪ] *n* éternité *f*; *Fam* **to wait/last an e.** attendre/durer une éternité; **e. ring** = bague entièrement sertie de pierres symbolisant l'éternité du mariage

ether ['iːθə(r)] *n* éther *m*

ethereal [ɪ'θɪərɪəl] *adj* éthéré(e); *(fragile)* léger(ère), impalpable

ethical ['eθɪkəl] *adj* éthique, moral(e)

ethically ['eθɪklɪ] *adv* sur le plan éthique; **to behave e.** suivre la déontologie

ethics ['eθɪks] *npl* éthique *f*, morale *f*; *(of profession)* déontologie *f*

Ethiopia [iːθɪ'əʊpɪə] *n* l'Éthiopie *f*

Ethiopian [iːθɪ'əʊpɪən] **1** *n (person)* Éthiopien(enne) *m,f*
  2 *adj* éthiopien(enne)

ethnic ['eθnɪk] *adj* ethnique; **e. cleansing** purification *f* ethnique; **e. minority** minorité *f* ethnique

ethnically ['eθnɪklɪ] *adv* du point de vue ethnique

ethnocentric [eθnəʊ'sentrɪk] *adj* ethnocentrique

ethnography [eθ'nɒɡrəfɪ] *n* ethnographie *f*

ethnology [eθ'nɒlədʒɪ] *n* ethnologie *f*

ethos ['iːθɒs] *n (of people)* génie *m*; *(of class)* culture *f*

e-ticket ['iːtɪkɪt] *n (for travel)* billet *m* électronique

etiquette ['etɪket] *n* étiquette *f*; **professional e.** usages *mpl* professionnels

Etruscan [ɪ'trʌskən] **1** *n* (**a**) *(person)* Étrusque *mf* (**b**) *(language)* étrusque *m*
  2 *adj* étrusque

etymological [etɪmə'lɒdʒɪkəl] *adj* étymologique

etymology [etɪ'mɒlədʒɪ] *n* étymologie *f*

EU [iː'juː] *n (abbr* **European Union**) UE *f*

eucalyptus [juːkə'lɪptəs] *n* eucalyptus *m*

Eucharist ['juːkərɪst] *n* **the E.** l'eucharistie *f*

eulogize ['juːlədʒaɪz] *vt* faire l'éloge de

eulogy ['juːlədʒɪ] *(pl* **eulogies**) *n* éloge *m*

eunuch ['juːnək] *n* eunuque *m*

euphemism ['juːfɪmɪzəm] *n* euphémisme *m*

euphemistic [juːfɪ'mɪstɪk] *adj* euphémique

euphoria [juː'fɔːrɪə] *n* euphorie *f*

euphoric [juː'fɔːrɪk] *adj* euphorique

Eurasian [jʊə'reɪʒən] **1** *n* Eurasien(enne) *m,f*
  2 *adj* eurasien(enne); *(continent)* eurasiatique

EURATOM [jʊə'rætəm] *n (abbr* **European Atomic Energy Community**) CEEA *f*, EURATOM *f*

eureka [jʊə'riːkə] *exclam* eureka!

euro ['jʊərəʊ] *(pl* **euros**) *n (European currency)* euro *m*; **e. area, e. zone** zone *f* euro

Eurocrat ['jʊərəʊkræt] *n* eurocrate *mf*

Eurodollar ['jʊərəʊdɒlə(r)] *n* eurodollar *m*

Euro-election ['jʊərəʊ'lekʃən] *n* **the Euro-elections** les élections *fpl* européennes

Euroland ['jʊərəʊlænd] *n* Eurolande *f*

Euro-MP ['jʊərəʊempiː] *n* député(e) *m,f*, européen(enne)

Europe ['jʊərəp] *n* l'Europe *f*

European [jʊərə'piːən] **1** *n* Européen(enne) *m,f*
  2 *adj* européen(enne); **E. Commission** Commission *f* européenne; **E. Community** Communauté *f* européenne; **E. Court of Human Rights** Cour *f* européenne des droits de l'homme; **E. Court of Justice** Cour de justice européenne; **E. Currency Unit** unité *f* monétaire européenne; **E. Economic Community** Communauté *f* économique européenne; **E. Free Trade Association** Association *f* européenne de libre-échange; **E. Monetary System** Système *m* monétaire européen; **E. Parliament** Parlement *m* européen; **E. Union** Union *f* européenne

Europhile ['jʊərəʊfaɪl] *n* europhile *mf*, partisan *m* de l'Europe unie

Eurosceptic [jʊərəʊ'skeptɪk] *n* eurosceptique *mf*

Eurostar® ['jʊərəʊstɑː(r)] *n* Eurostar® *m*

Eustachian tube [juːs'teɪʃən'tjuːb] *n Anat* trompe *f* d'Eustache

euthanasia [juːθə'neɪzɪə] *n* euthanasie *f*

evacuate [ɪ'vækjʊeɪt] *vt* évacuer

evacuation [ɪvækjʊ'eɪʃən] *n* évacuation *f*

evacuee [ɪvækjʊ'iː] *n* évacué(e) *m,f*

evade [ɪ'veɪd] *vt (blow)* esquiver, éviter; *(question)* éluder; *(pursuer)* échapper à; *(responsibilities)* se soustraire à, se dérober à; **to e. tax** frauder le fisc

evaluate [ɪ'væljʊeɪt] *vt* évaluer

evaluation [ɪvæljʊ'eɪʃən] *n* évaluation *f*

evangelical [iːvæn'dʒelɪkəl] **1** *n* protestant(e) *m,f*, évangélique
  2 *adj* évangélique

evangelism [ɪ'vændʒɪlɪzəm] *n* évangélisme *m*

evangelist [ɪ'vændʒɪlɪst] *n* évangéliste *mf*

evangelize [ɪ'vændʒɪlaɪz] **1** *vt* évangéliser; *(person)* prêcher l'Évangile à **2** *vi* prêcher l'Évangile

evaporate [ɪ'væpəreɪt] **1** *vt* faire évaporer; **evaporated milk** lait *m* condensé **2** *vi (of liquid)* s'évaporer; *Fig (of enthusiasm, hope)* s'envoler

evaporation [ɪvæpə'reɪʃən] *n* évaporation *f*

evasion [ɪ'veɪʒən] *n (escape)* évasion *f*, fuite *f*; *(of pursuer, responsibilities, question)* dérobade *f*; **(tax) e.** fraude *f* fiscale

evasive [ɪ'veɪsɪv] *adj (person, reply)* évasif(ive); **to take e. action** faire une manœuvre d'évitement

eve [iːv] *n (day before)* veille *f*; **on the e. of** à la veille de

even ['iːvən] **1** *adj* (**a**) *(flat)* égal(e); *(smooth)* uni(e) (**b**) *(regular) (breathing, pace)* régulier(ère), égal(e); *(temperature)* constant(e); **to have an e. temper** être d'humeur égale; **e. number** nombre *m* pair (**c**) *(equal)* **to have an e. chance (of doing sth) with sb** prendre sa revanche sur qn **2** *adv* (**a**) même; *(with comparatives)* encore; **without e. speaking** sans même dire un mot; **I never e. saw it** je ne l'ai même pas vu; **e. bigger/more interesting** encore plus gros (grosse)/intéressant(e); **e. as I speak** au moment même où je parle (**b**) *(in phrases)* **e. if** même si; **e. now** même maintenant, aujourd'hui encore; **e. so** cependant, quand même; **e. then** *(already)* déjà (à cette époque); *(all the same)* même dans ces conditions; **e. though** bien que + *subjunctive* **3** *vt (make equal)* rendre égal(e); **to e. the odds** égaliser les chances

▶**even out 1** *vt sep (differences)* niveler; *(workload)* répartir plus également; *(inequalities)* réduire; **to e. things out** rendre les choses équitables **2** *vi (of differences)* se niveler; *(of workload)* être réparti(e) plus également; *(of inequalities)* se réduire

▶**even up** *vt sep* égaliser; **to e. things up** équilibrer les choses

even-handed ['iːvən'hændɪd] *adj* juste, équitable

evening ['iːvnɪŋ] *n* soir *m*; *(referring to duration)* soirée *f*; **tomorrow e.** demain soir; **yesterday e.** hier soir; **good e.!**, *Fam* **e.!** bonsoir!; **in the e.** le soir; **a musical/cultural e.** une soirée musicale/culturelle; **e. class** cours *m* du soir; **e. dress** *(for men)* tenue *f* de soirée; *(for women)* robe *f* du soir; **e. paper** journal *m* du soir; **e. performance** *(of play)* représentation *f* en soirée

evenly ['iːvənlɪ] *adv* (**a**) *(uniformly)* uniformément (**b**) *(regularly) (breathe)* régulièrement, de façon régulière; *(speak)* calmement (**c**) *(equally) (divide, distribute)* également, de façon égale; **e. matched** *(in size)* de grandeur égale; *(in strength)* de force égale

evensong ['iːvənsɒŋ] *n Rel* office *m* du soir

event [ɪ'vent] *n* (**a**) *(occurrence)* événement *m*; **in any e.** en tout cas; **in the e. of fire** en cas d'incendie; **in the e. of her refusing** au cas où elle refuserait; **after the e.** après coup; **e. or events coordinator** *or* **manager** organisateur(trice) *m,f* d'événements (**b**) *(in athletics)* épreuve *f*

even-tempered ['iːvən'tempəd] *adj* d'humeur égale

eventful [ɪ'ventfʊl] *adj (day, life)* mouvementé(e), riche en événements

eventual [ɪ'ventʃʊəl] *adj* final(e), définitif(ive)

eventuality [ɪventjʊ'ælɪtɪ] *(pl* **eventualities)** *n* éventualité *f*; **in that e.** dans cette éventualité

eventually [ɪ'ventjʊəlɪ] *adv (in the end)* finalement, en fin de compte; *(at a future date)* par la suite; **they e. reached the castle** ils ont fini par arriver au château; **he'll do it e.** il le fera tôt ou tard

ever ['evə(r)] *adv* (**a**) *(at any time)* **have you e. been to Spain?** es-tu déjà allé en Espagne?; **do you e. see Alan these days?** ça t'arrive de voir Alan?; **the worst/best e.** le pire/meilleur qui soit; **more than e.** plus que jamais; **she's a liar/fool if e. there was one** c'est une menteuse/idiote de première (**b**) *(always)* **e. since (then)/1960** depuis (lors)/1960; **all she e. does is criticize** elle ne fait que critiquer; **she was as friendly as e.** elle était toujours aussi aimable; **e. the gentleman, he opened the door for her** toujours galant, il lui ouvrit la porte; **e. so pretty** si joli(e); **e. so much** *or* **such a lot of money** tant d'argent; **e. so slightly** très légèrement; **e. such a nice girl** une fille si sympathique

evergreen ['evəɡriːn] **1** *n (tree)* arbre *m* à feuilles persistantes; *(bush)* arbuste *m* à feuilles persistantes **2** *adj* à feuilles persistantes; *Fig* **e. topic** question *f* toujours d'actualité

everlasting [evə'lɑːstɪŋ] *adj (eternal)* éternel(elle); *(continual)* continuel(elle), sans fin

evermore [evə'mɔː(r)] *adv Formal* toujours; **for e.** à jamais

every ['evrɪ] *adj* (**a**) *(each)* chaque; **children of e. age** des enfants de tous âges; **at e. opportunity** à la moindre occasion; **from e. side** de tous côtés; **e. one of us** chacun(e) d'entre nous; **e. man for himself!** chacun pour soi! (**b**) *(indicating regular occurrence)* **e. week** chaque semaine, toutes les semaines; **e. ten years** tous les dix ans; **e. other** *or* **second line** une ligne sur deux; **e. so often, e. now and again** de temps en temps (**c**) *(for emphasis)* **you have e. right to be angry** vous avez tout lieu d'être mécontent; **e. bit as good/intelligent as...** tout aussi bon (bonne)/intelligent(e) que...; **she has e. chance of winning** elle a de très fortes chances de gagner

everybody ['evrɪbɒdɪ] *pron* tout le monde, chacun(e) *m,f*; **e. I know** tous ceux que je connais se trouvaient là; **e. else** tous les autres; **e. who is anybody** les gens qui comptent

everyday ['evrɪdeɪ] *adj* (**a**) *(daily)* journalier(ère), quotidien(enne); **it's an e. occurrence** ça se produit tous les jours (**b**) *(used every day)* de tous les jours; **for e. wear/use** à porter/utiliser tous les jours

everyone ['evrɪwʌn] = **everybody**

everything ['evrɪθɪŋ] *pron* tout; **e. I did seemed to go wrong** tout ce que je faisais semblait vouer à l'échec; **he did e. possible** il a fait tout son possible; **money isn't e.** l'argent n'est pas tout

everywhere ['evrɪweə(r)] *adv* partout; **to look e.** regarder partout; **e. you go** où que vous alliez, partout où vous allez; **e. you look there is poverty** de quelque côté que l'on se tourne, on voit la misère

evict [ɪ'vɪkt] *vt* expulser

eviction [ɪ'vɪkʃən] *n* expulsion *f*; **e. order** avis *m* d'expulsion

evidence [' evɪdəns] **1** *n* (**a**) *(reason for belief)* évidence *f*; *(indication)* marque *f*, signe *m*; **to be in e.** être en évidence; **to show e.** **of** donner des signes de; **there was no e.** **of his stay in the house** rien ne montrait qu'il eût séjourné dans la maison (**b**) *(in court case)* preuve *f*; *(testimony)* témoignage *m*; **to give e.** témoigner; **to call sb in e.** appeler qn à la barre des témoins; **to turn** *Br* **King's/Queen's** *or Am* **State's e.** témoigner contre ses complices *(sous promesse de pardon)*
2 *vt Formal* **as evidenced by...** comme en témoigne...
evident ['evɪdənt] *adj* évident(e), manifeste
evidently ['evɪdəntlɪ] *adv* (**a**) *(clearly)* manifestement, à l'évidence; **there have e.** **been some problems** il est clair *ou* évident qu'il y a eu des problèmes (**b**) *(apparently)* apparemment; **so she won't be coming? – e.** **not** alors elle ne vient pas? – il semble bien que non
evil ['iːvəl] **1** *n* mal *m*
2 *adj (person, look)* mauvais(e), malveillant(e); *(influence, effect)* maléfique; *(spirit)* malfaisant(e), malin(igne); *(temper)* coléreux(euse)
evildoer ['iːvəlduːə(r)] *n Lit* homme méchant (femme méchante) *m,f*
evil-looking ['iːvəlʊkɪŋ] *adj* à l'aspect malfaisant
evil-minded ['iːvəl'maɪndɪd] *adj* malintentionné(e)
evil-smelling ['iːvəl'smelɪŋ] *adj* nauséabond(e)
evince [ɪ'vɪns] *vt Formal* faire montre de
evocation [evə'keɪʃən] *n* évocation *f*
evocative [ɪ'vɒkətɪv] *adj* évocateur(trice) (**of** de)
evoke [ɪ'vəʊk] *vt* (**a**) *(conjure up)* évoquer (**b**) *(provoke)* provoquer, susciter
evolution [iːvə'luːʃən] *n* évolution *f*, développement *m*
evolutionary [iːvə'luːʃənərɪ] *adj* évolutif(ive)
evolve [ɪ'vɒlv] **1** *vt (theory, plan)* élaborer, mettre au point
2 *vi (of species, situation)* évoluer, se développer
ewe [juː] *n* brebis *f*
ex [eks] *n Fam (former husband, wife, girlfriend, boyfriend)* ex *mf*
ex- [eks] *pref (former)* ex-; **ex-minister/teacher** ancien ministre *m*/professeur *m*
exacerbate [eg'zæsəbeɪt] *vt* aggraver
exact [ɪg'zækt] **1** *adj* exact(e), précis(e); **at the e. moment when...** juste au moment où..., au moment précis où...; **those were her e. words** c'est ce qu'elle a dit mot pour mot; **the e. opposite** exactement le contraire; **on 5 January, to be e.** le 5 janvier, pour être précis
2 *vt (obedience, tax)* exiger (**from** de); *(promise)* extorquer (**from** à)
exacting [ɪg'zæktɪŋ] *adj* exigeant(e)
exactitude [ɪg'zæktɪtjuːd] *n Formal* exactitude *f*
exactly [ɪg'zæktlɪ] *adv* exactement; **not e.** pas tout à fait; *Ironic* pas vraiment
exaggerate [ɪg'zædʒəreɪt] *vt & vi* exagérer
exaggerated [ɪg'zædʒəreɪtɪd] *adj* exagéré(e)
exaggeration [ɪgzædʒə'reɪʃən] *n* exagération *f*
exalt [ɪg'zɔːlt] *vt Formal* exalter
exalted [ɪg'zɔːltɪd] *adj* (**a**) *(high) (rank)* élevé(e); *(person)* haut placé(e) (**b**) *Formal (joyful)* exalté(e)
exam [ɪg'zæm] *n* examen *m*; **to take** *or* **sit an e.** passer un examen; **e. result** résultat *m* d'examen
examination [ɪgzæmɪ'neɪʃən] *n* examen *m*; *Med* examen *m* médical; **to take** *or* **sit an e.** passer un exa-

men; **e. board** ≃ académie *f (division administrative de l'enseignement)*; **e. result** résultat *m* d'examen
examine [ɪg'zæmɪn] *vt (evidence, patient, question)* examiner; *(student)* faire passer un examen à; **to e. one's conscience** faire son examen de conscience
examinee [ɪgzæmɪ'niː] *n* candidat(e) *m,f*
examiner [ɪg'zæmɪnə(r)] *n* examinateur(trice) *m,f*
example [ɪg'zɑːmpəl] *n* exemple *m*; **for e.** par exemple; **to set an e. (to sb)** donner l'exemple (à qn); **to make an e. of sb** faire un exemple de qn; **to follow sb's e.** suivre l'exemple de qn; **to lead by e.** montrer l'exemple
exasperate [ɪg'zɑːspəreɪt] *vt* exaspérer; **to get exasperated** s'irriter
exasperating [ɪg'zɑːspəreɪtɪŋ] *adj* exaspérant(e)
exasperation [ɪgzɑːspə'reɪʃən] *n* exaspération *f*
excavate ['ekskəveɪt] *vt (hole, tunnel)* creuser; *(remains)* déterrer, exhumer; *(site)* faire des fouilles dans
excavation [ekskə'veɪʃən] *n* excavation *f*
excavator ['ekskəveɪtə(r)] *n (machine)* excavatrice *f*
exceed [ɪk'siːd] *vt* (**a**) *(limits)* excéder, dépasser; *(hopes, fears)* dépasser; *(one's authority)* outrepasser (**b**) *(number, amount)* dépasser
exceedingly [ɪk'siːdɪŋlɪ] *adv* extrêmement
excel [ɪk'sel] *(pt & pp* excelled*)* **1** *vt also Ironic* **excel oneself** se surpasser
2 *vi* exceller (**at** *or* **in** à *ou* en)
excellence ['eksələns] *n* excellence *f*
excellency ['eksələnsɪ] *n* **Your/His E.** Votre/Son Excellence *f*
excellent ['eksələnt] *adj* excellent(e)
except [ɪk'sept] **1** *prep* sauf, à l'exception de; **nobody e. him** personne excepté *ou* sauf lui; **I would go, e.** **I'm busy** j'irais bien, mais je suis occupé(e); **e. for** à part...; **e. that** excepté que, si ce n'est que; **e. when** sauf *ou* à part quand
2 *vt* excepter, exclure (**from** de); **present company excepted** les personnes présentes exceptées; **not excepting...** sans excepter...
exception [ɪk'sepʃən] *n* (**a**) *(thing excepted)* exception *f*; **to make an e. of sth/for sb** faire une exception pour qch/qn; **with the e. of...** à l'exception de..., exception faite de...; **without e.** sans exception; **the e. proves the rule** c'est l'exception qui confirme la règle (**b**) **to take e. to sth** *(be offended)* se formaliser de qch; *(object)* trouver à redire à qch
exceptionable [ɪk'sepʃənəbəl] *adj Formal* critiquable; *(offensive)* offensant(e)
exceptional [ɪk'sepʃənəl] *adj* exceptionnel(elle)
exceptionally [ɪk'sepʃənəlɪ] *adv* exceptionnellement; *(in exceptional cases)* à titre exceptionnel
excerpt ['eksɜːpt] *n* extrait *m* (**from** de)
excess [ɪk'ses] *n* excès *m*; **to do sth to e.** faire qch à l'excès; **to pay the e.** *(on ticket)* payer un supplément; **e. baggage** excédent *m* de bagages
excessive [ɪk'sesɪv] *adj* excessif(ive)
excessively [ɪk'sesɪvlɪ] *adv* extrêmement; *(eat, drink)* à l'excès
exchange [ɪks'tʃeɪndʒ] **1** *n* (**a**) *(of prisoners, ideas)* échange *m*; **in e. (for)** en échange (de); **a heated e.** un échange de paroles assez vives; **e. visit** échange *m*; **e. controls** contrôle *m* des changes; **e. rate** taux *m* de change; **e. rate mechanism** mécanisme *m* de change (**c**) **(Stock) E.** Bourse *f (des valeurs)* (**d**) **(telephone) e.** central *m* téléphonique

2 *vt* échanger; **to e. sth for sth** échanger qch contre qch
exchangeable [ɪks'tʃeɪndʒəbəl] *adj* échangeable (**for** contre)
exchequer [eks'tʃekə(r)] *n Br* **the E.** ≃ le Trésor Public; **the Chancellor of the E.** le Ministre des Finances
excise 1 *n* ['eksaɪz] **e. (duties)** *(tax)* droits *mpl* d'accise
2 *vt* [ɪk'saɪz] *(remove) (tumour)* exciser; *(piece of text)* couper
excitable [ɪk'saɪtəbəl] *adj* nerveux(euse)
excite [ɪk'saɪt] *vt* (**a**) *(get worked up)* énerver, surexciter; *(arouse enthusiasm in)* enthousiasmer; *(stimulate)* exciter (**b**) *(give rise to) (admiration, desire)* provoquer; *(envy, interest)* susciter; *(curiosity)* piquer
excited [ɪk'saɪtɪd] *adj (worked up)* énervé(e), excité(e); *(enthusiastic)* enthousiaste; **to get e. (about)** s'exciter (pour); *(angry)* s'énerver (contre)
excitedly [ɪk'saɪtɪdlɪ] *adv (speak, laugh)* avec animation; *(wait)* avec une impatience fébrile
excitement [ɪk'saɪtmənt] *n (agitation)* agitation *f*; *(enthusiasm)* animation *f*, enthousiasme *m*; **to cause great e.** faire sensation
exciting [ɪk'saɪtɪŋ] *adj* passionnant(e); *(idea, prospect)* enthousiasmant(e)
exclaim [ɪks'kleɪm] **1** *vt* **"leave me alone!" he exclaimed** "laissez-moi!" s'est-il écrié
2 *vi* s'exclamer, s'écrier
exclamation [ekskla'meɪʃən] *n* exclamation *f*; *Br* **e. mark,** *Am* **e. point** point *m* d'exclamation
exclamatory [eks'klæmətərɪ] *adj* exclamatif(ive)
exclude [ɪks'kluːd] *vt* exclure (**from** de); *(doubt, suspicion)* écarter; **excluding...** à l'exclusion de...
exclusion [ɪks'kluːʒən] *n* exclusion *f* (**from** de); **to the e. of...** à l'exclusion de...
exclusive [ɪks'kluːsɪv] **1** *n (in newspaper, on TV)* exclusivité *f*
2 *adj* (**a**) *(right, article, interview)* exclusif(ive) (**b**) *(chic)* huppé(e); *(club, social circle)* très fermé(e); *(clothing, jewellery)* de grande marque (**c**) *(only)* seul(e), unique
3 *adv* **e. of delivery** frais de livraison non compris; **e. of tax** hors taxes
exclusively [ɪks'kluːsɪvlɪ] *adv* exclusivement; *(in newspaper, on TV)* en exclusivité
excommunicate [ekskə'mjuːnɪkeɪt] *vt* excommunier
excommunication [ekskəmjuːnɪ'keɪʃən] *n* excommunication *f*
excrement ['ekskrɪmənt] *n* excrément *m*
excrescence [eks'kresəns] *n* excroissance *f*
excrete [ɪks'kriːt] *vt Formal* excréter
excruciating [ɪks'kruːʃɪeɪtɪŋ] *adj (pain, embarrassment)* atroce; **the whole evening was e.** *(embarrassing)* on a été gênés toute la soirée; *(boring)* on s'est horriblement ennuyés toute la soirée
excruciatingly [ɪks'kruːʃɪeɪtɪŋlɪ] *adv (painful, embarrassing)* atrocement; *Fam* **e. funny** tordant(e)
excursion [ɪks'kɜːʃən] *n* excursion *f*
excuse 1 *n* [ɪks'kjuːs] excuse *f*; **that's no e.** ce n'est pas une excuse *ou* une raison; **a poor e. for a father/bus service** un père/un service d'autobus lamentable
2 *vt* [ɪks'kjuːz] (**a**) *(forgive)* excuser, pardonner; **e. me!** pardon!, excusez-moi!; **e. me?** *(what did you say?)* pardon? (**b**) *(exempt)* exempter, dispenser (**from** de) (**c**) **to e. oneself** s'excuser
ex-directory [eksdɪ'rektərɪ] *adj Br* **to be e.** *(of person, number)* être sur la liste rouge
execrable ['eksɪkrəbəl] *adj* exécrable, abominable

execute ['eksɪkjuːt] *vt (prisoner, order)* exécuter; *(plan, operation)* mettre à exécution
execution [eksɪ'kjuːʃən] *n (of prisoner, order)* exécution *f*; **in the e. of one's duty** dans l'exercice de ses fonctions
executioner [eksɪ'kjuːʃənə(r)] *n* bourreau *m*
executive [ɪg'zekjʊtɪv] **1** *n (businessman)* cadre *m*; *(committee)* bureau *m*, comité *m* central
2 *adj (post)* de cadre; *(car, suite)* de luxe; *Br* **e. director** directeur(trice) *m,f* administratif(ive)
executor [ɪg'zekjʊtə(r)] *n Law* exécuteur(trice) *m,f* testamentaire
exemplary [ɪg'zemplərɪ] *adj* exemplaire
exemplify [ɪg'zemplɪfaɪ] *(pt & pp* **exemplified)** *vt* illustrer
exempt [ɪg'zempt] **1** *adj* exempté(e), dispensé(e) (**from** de)
2 *vt* exempter, dispenser (**from** de)
exemption [ɪg'zem(p)ʃən] *n* exemption *f*, dispense *f* (**from** de)
exercise ['eksəsaɪz] **1** *n* exercice *m*; **to take e.** faire de l'exercice; **e. bike** vélo *m* d'appartement; **e. book** cahier *m*
2 *vt* (**a**) *(body, mind)* exercer (**b**) *(right, influence)* exercer; *(caution, restraint)* user de
3 *vi* faire de l'exercice; *(train)* s'entraîner
exert [ɪg'zɜːt] *vt (pressure, influence)* exercer; *(force)* faire usage de; **to e. oneself** se remuer, se donner du mal
exertion [ɪg'zɜːʃən] *n (of force)* usage *m*, emploi *m*; *(effort)* effort *m*
exfoliant [eks'fəʊlɪənt] *n* exfoliant *m*
exfoliate [eks'fəʊlɪeɪt] **1** *vt* exfolier
2 *vi* s'exfolier
exhale [eks'heɪl] *vi* expirer
exhaust [ɪg'zɔːst] **1** *n (on car)* échappement *m*; **e. (fumes)** gaz *mpl* d'échappement; **e. pipe** tuyau *m* d'échappement
2 *vt (person, resources)* épuiser
exhausted [ɪg'zɔːstɪd] *adj* épuisé(e)
exhausting [ɪg'zɔːstɪŋ] *adj* épuisant(e)
exhaustion [ɪg'zɔːstʃən] *n* épuisement *m*
exhaustive [ɪg'zɔːstɪv] *adj (list)* exhaustif(ive); *(analysis, description)* détaillé(e), minutieux(euse); *(enquiry, search)* approfondi(e)
exhibit [ɪg'zɪbɪt] **1** *n (in art exhibition)* objet *m* exposé; *(in court case)* pièce *f* à conviction
2 *vt (object, goods)* exhiber, montrer (**b**) *(painting in exhibition)* exposer (**c**) *(show) (courage, judgement)* faire preuve de; **to e. signs of stress/wear** donner des signes de tension/d'usure
exhibition [eksɪ'bɪʃən] *n* (**a**) *(of paintings)* exposition *f*; *Fam Fig* **to make an e. of oneself** se donner en spectacle (**b**) *(of courage, bad manners)* démonstration *f*; **it was a disgraceful e.** ce fut un spectacle honteux
exhibitionist [eksɪ'bɪʃənɪst] *n* (**a**) *(show-off)* = personne qui aime se faire remarquer (**b**) *Psy* exhibitionniste *mf*
exhibitor [ɪg'zɪbɪtə(r)] *n* exposant(e) *m,f*
exhilarated [ɪg'zɪləreɪtɪd] *adj* grisé(e)
exhilarating [ɪg'zɪləreɪtɪŋ] *adj (air, walk)* vivifiant(e); *(experience)* exaltant(e), grisant(e); *(news)* enthousiasmant(e)
exhort [ɪg'zɔːt] *vt* exhorter, encourager (**to do sth** à faire qch)
exhortation [ɪgzɔː'teɪʃən] *n* exhortation *f*

exhume [eks'hju:m] *vt* exhumer, déterrer
exigent ['eksɪdʒənt] *adj Formal* (**a**) *(urgent)* urgent(e), pressant(e) (**b**) *(demanding)* exigeant(e)
exile ['eksaɪl] **1** *n* (**a**) *(banishment)* exil *m*, bannissement *m*; **in e.** en exil (**b**) *(exiled person)* exilé(e) *m,f*
2 *vt* exiler
exist [ɪg'zɪst] *vi* (**a**) *(be in existence)* exister; *(of conditions)* régner (**b**) *(survive)* se maintenir en vie, survivre (**on** avec)
existence [ɪg'zɪstəns] *n* existence *f*; **in e.** existant(e), qui existe; **to come into e.** naître; **to go out of e.** disparaître, cesser d'exister
existential [egzɪs'tenʃəl] *adj* existentiel(elle)
existentialism [egzɪs'tenʃəlɪzəm] *n* existentialisme *m*
existentialist [egzɪs'tenʃəlɪst] **1** *n* existentialiste *mf*
2 *adj* existentialiste
existing [ɪg'zɪstɪŋ] *adj* existant(e), actuel(elle)
exit ['eksɪt] **1** *n* sortie *f*; **to make an e.** sortir; *Pol* **e. poll** = sondage effectué auprès des électeurs immédiatement après qu'ils ont voté; **e. visa** visa *m* de sortie
2 *vi (leave)* & *Comput* sortir
exodus ['eksədəs] *n* exode *m*
ex officio ['eksəʊ'fɪʃɪəʊ] *adj (member)* de droit
exonerate [ɪg'zɒnəreɪt] *vt (absolve)* disculper, innocenter (**from** *or* **of** de)
exorbitant [ɪg'zɔ:bɪtənt] *adj* exorbitant(e)
exorcism ['eksɔ:sɪzəm] *n* exorcisme *m*
exorcist ['eksɔ:sɪst] *n* exorciste *mf*
exorcize ['eksɔ:saɪz] *vt* exorciser
exotic [ɪg'zɒtɪk] *adj* exotique
expand [ɪks'pænd] **1** *vt (production, output)* accroître; *(empire, company)* agrandir; *(mind, circle of friends)* élargir; *(range, idea)* développer
2 *vi (of solid, gas)* se dilater; *(of company)* s'agrandir
▸**expand on, expand upon** *vt insep* développer
expanded [ɪks'pændɪd] *adj* étendu(e); *Comput (memory)* expansé(e); **e. polystyrene** polystyrène *m* expansé
expanding [ɪks'pændɪŋ] *adj (market, company)* en expansion, qui se développe; *(universe)* en expansion
expanse [eks'pæns] *n* étendue *f*
expansion [ɪks'pænʃən] *n* expansion *f*; *(of gas)* dilatation *f*; *Comput* **e. card** carte *f* d'extension
expansive [ɪks'pænsɪv] *adj (gas)* dilatable; *(person)* expansif(ive); **in an e. mood** d'humeur expansive
expat [eks'pæt] **1** *n Br Fam* expatrié(e) *m,f*
2 *adj Br Fam* expatrié(e)
expatriate 1 *n* [eks'pætrɪət] expatrié(e) *m,f*
2 *adj* [eks'pætrɪət] expatrié(e)
3 *vt* [eks'pætrɪeɪt] expatrier
expect [ɪks'pekt] **1** *vt* (**a**) *(anticipate)* s'attendre à; **to e. to do sth** compter *ou* espérer faire qch; **to e. sb to do sth** s'attendre à ce que qn fasse qch; **I expected as much** je m'y attendais; **to e. the worst** s'attendre au pire; **to be expecting a baby** attendre un bébé (**b**) *(require)* **to e. sb to do sth** attendre de qn qu'il/elle fasse qch; **to e. sth from sb** attendre qch de qn; **I know what is expected of me** je sais ce qu'on attend de moi; **to e. too much from sb/sth** trop attendre de qn/qch (**c**) *(suppose)* **to e. (that)...** penser que...; **I e. so/not** je crois bien que oui/non
2 *vi (be pregnant)* **to be expecting** attendre un bébé
expectancy [ɪks'pektənsɪ] *n* attente *f*; **an air of e.** l'air d'attendre quelque chose
expectant [ɪks'pektənt] *adj* impatient(e); **e. mother** future maman *f*

expectation [ekspek'teɪʃən] *n* espérance *f*; **in (the) e. of sth** dans l'attente de qch; **to have high expectations of sb/sth** attendre beaucoup de qn/qch; **to come up to expectations** se montrer à la hauteur; **to fall short of (sb's) expectations** décevoir (qn); **contrary to all expectations** contre toute attente
expected [ɪks'pektɪd] *adj* attendu(e); *(hoped for)* espéré(e)
expectorant [ɪks'pektərənt] **1** *n Med* expectorant *m*
2 *adj* expectorant(e)
expediency [ɪks'pi:dɪənsɪ] *n* opportunité *f*; *Pej (opportunism)* opportunisme *m*
expedient [ɪks'pi:dɪənt] **1** *n* expédient *m*
2 *adj* opportun(e), expédient(e)
expedite ['ekspɪdaɪt] *vt Formal* activer, accélérer
expedition [ekspə'dɪʃən] *n* expédition *f*; *Fam* **a shopping e.** une séance de shopping
expeditionary [ekspə'dɪʃənərɪ] *adj Mil* **e. force/corps** force *f*/corps *m* expéditionnaire
expel [ɪks'pel] *(pt & pp* **expelled**) *vt* expulser; *(from school)* renvoyer
expendable [ɪks'pendəbəl] *adj (person)* qui n'est pas irremplaçable; *(troops)* que l'on peut sacrifier
expenditure [ɪks'pendɪtʃə(r)] *n (of money, energy)* dépense *f*
expense [ɪks'pens] *n* (**a**) *(cost)* dépense *f*, frais *mpl*; **to go to great e. (to do sth)** faire de grosses dépenses (pour faire qch); **no e. was spared** on n'a pas regardé à la dépense; **at the e. of one's health/sanity** aux dépens de sa santé/santé mentale; **to make a joke at sb's e.** faire une plaisanterie aux dépens de qn (**b**) *Com* **expenses** frais *mpl*, dépenses *fpl*; **it's on expenses** ça va sur la note de frais; **all expenses paid** tous frais payés; **e. account** note *f* de frais
expensive [ɪks'pensɪv] *adj (object, shop, restaurant)* cher (chère); *(procedure, habit)* couteux(euse); *(tastes)* de luxe; *(mistake)* qui coûte cher
experience [ɪks'pɪərɪəns] **1** *n* expérience *f*; **to learn from e.** tirer les leçons d'une expérience; **in my e.** d'après mon expérience
2 *vt (emotions, pain)* ressentir; *(hunger, success)* connaître, faire l'expérience de; *(difficulties, problems)* avoir; *(ill-treatment)* subir
experienced [ɪks'pɪərɪənst] *adj* expérimenté(e); **to be e. in sth** avoir de l'expérience en qch; *(observer)* averti(e)
experiment [ɪks'perɪmənt] **1** *n* expérience *f*; **as an e.** à titre d'essai
2 *vi* expérimenter (**on** sur); **to e. with** *(technique, drugs)* essayer
experimental [ɪksperɪ'mentəl] *adj* expérimental(e)
expert ['ekspɜ:t] **1** *n* expert *m*, spécialiste *mf*
2 *adj* expert(e), habile; *(advice, opinion)* d'un(e) expert(e); **to be e. in *or* at sth** être expert(e) en qch; *Comput* **e. system** système *m* expert; *Law* **e. witness** expert(e) *m,f* cité comme témoin
expertise [ekspɜ:'ti:z] *n (technical, financial)* compétence *f*, connaissances *fpl*; *(as cook, carpenter)* savoir-faire *m*
expertly ['ekspɜ:tlɪ] *adv* de manière experte
expiate ['ekspɪeɪt] *vt Formal* expier
expire [ɪks'paɪə(r)] *vi* (**a**) *(of law, deadline, passport)* expirer (**b**) *Lit (die)* expirer
expiry [ɪks'paɪərɪ] *n* expiration *f*, fin *f*; **e. date** (date *f* d')échéance *f*, date *f* d'expiration
explain [ɪks'pleɪn] **1** *vt* expliquer; **to e. oneself** *(make oneself clear)* s'expliquer; *(justify oneself)* se justifier

2 *vi* donner des explications, expliquer; *(make one-self clear)* s'expliquer

▸**explain away** *vt sep (give explanation for)* donner une explication satisfaisante à; *(justify)* justifier

explanation [eksplə'neɪʃən] *n* explication *f*; **to give an e. of sth** *(make clear)* expliquer; *(justify)* justifier qch

explanatory [ɪks'plænətərɪ] *adj* explicatif(ive)

expletive [ɪks'pliːtɪv] *n* juron *m*

explicable [eks'plɪkəbəl] *adj* explicable

explicit [eks'plɪsɪt] *adj* explicite

explicitly [eks'plɪsɪtlɪ] *adv* de manière explicite

explode [ɪks'pləʊd] **1** *vt (bomb)* faire exploser; *Fig (idea, theory)* démontrer la fausseté de
　2 *vi (of bomb)* & *Fig (with anger)* exploser; *(of mine)* sauter; **to e. with laughter** éclater de rire

exploit 1 *n* ['eksplɔɪt] exploit *m*
　2 *vt* [eks'plɔɪt] (**a**) *(take unfair advantage of)* exploiter (**b**) *(use) (resources, scandal)* exploiter; *(talents)* mettre à profit

exploitation [eksplɔɪ'teɪʃən] *n* exploitation *f*

exploration [eksplə'reɪʃən] *n* exploration *f*

exploratory [ɪks'plɒrətərɪ] *adj (trip)* d'exploration; *(surgery, discussions, talks)* exploratoire

explore [ɪks'plɔː(r)] **1** *vt (area, countryside)* explorer; *(possibility, idea)* étudier
　2 *vi* partir en exploration

explorer [ɪks'plɔrə(r)] *n* explorateur(trice) *m,f*

explosion [ɪks'pləʊʒən] *n also Fig* explosion *f*

explosive [ɪks'pləʊsɪv] **1** *n* explosif *m*
　2 *adj also Fig* explosif(ive)

exponent [ɪks'pəʊnənt] *n* (**a**) *(of theory, idea)* avocat(e) *m,f*; *(of piece of music)* interprète *mf* (**b**) *Math* exposant *m*

exponential [ekspəʊ'nenʃəl] *adj* exponentiel(elle)

export 1 *n* ['ekspɔːt] (**a**) *(product)* article *m* d'exportation; **exports** *(of country)* exportations *fpl* (**b**) *(activity)* exportation *f*; **e. duty** droit(s) *m(pl)* de sortie; **e. licence** licence *f* d'exportation; **e. trade** exportations *fpl*
　2 *vt* [eks'pɔːt] *also Comput* exporter

exportation [ekspɔː'teɪʃən] *n* exportation *f*

exporter [eks'pɔːtə(r)] *n* exportateur(trice) *m,f*

expose [ɪks'pəʊz] *vt* (**a**) *(to air, cold, danger)* & *Phot* exposer (**to** à); *(wire)* mettre à jour; **to e. oneself to danger** s'exposer au danger (**b**) *(reveal) (secret)* éventer; *(crime)* dévoiler; *(criminal)* démasquer; *(feelings)* afficher; **to e. sb as a traitor/criminal** révéler que qn est un traître/criminel; **to e. oneself** *(of flasher)* s'exhiber

exposé [eks'pəʊzeɪ] *n (article, book)* exposé *m*; *(of scandal, corruption)* révélations *fpl*

exposed [ɪks'pəʊzd] *adj* exposé(e) (**to** à)

exposition [ekspə'zɪʃən] *n (explanation)* exposition *f*, exposé *m*

expostulate [ɪks'pɒstjʊleɪt] *vi Formal* vitupérer

exposure [ɪks'pəʊʒə(r)] *n* (**a**) *(to air, cold, danger)* exposition *f*; **to die of e.** mourir de froid (**b**) *(publicity)* couverture *f*; **to get a lot of e.** faire l'objet d'une importante couverture médiatique (**c**) *(of crime)* révélation *f*; *(of criminal, scandal)* dénonciation *f* (**d**) *Phot* pose *f*; **e. meter** posemètre *m*

expound [ɪks'paʊnd] *vt Formal* exposer

express [ɪks'pres] **1** *n (train)* express *m*, rapide *m*
　2 *adj* (**a**) *(clear) (purpose, instruction)* exprès(esse) *(order)* formel(elle) (**b**) *(rapid) (letter, delivery)* exprès *inv*; *(train)* express *inv*
　3 *adv* **to send sth e.** envoyer qch en exprès
　4 *vt* exprimer; **to e. oneself** s'exprimer

expression [ɪks'preʃən] *n* expression *f*

expressionism [ɪks'preʃənɪzəm] *n* expressionnisme *m*

expressionist [ɪks'preʃənɪst] **1** *n* expressionniste *mf*
　2 *adj* expressionniste

expressionless [ɪks'preʃənlɪs] *adj* sans expression

expressive [ɪks'presɪv] *adj* expressif(ive); *(gesture, silence)* éloquent(e)

expressly [ɪks'preslɪ] *adv* expressément

expropriate [eks'prəʊprɪeɪt] *vt* exproprier

expropriation [eksprəʊprɪ'eɪʃən] *n* expropriation *f*

expulsion [ɪks'pʌlʃən] *n* expulsion *f*; *(from school)* renvoi *m*

expunge [ɪks'pʌndʒ] *vt* effacer

expurgate ['ekspɜːgeɪt] *vt* expurger

exquisite ['ekskwɪzɪt] *adj* exquis(e); *(pleasure)* vif (vive)

exquisitely [eks'kwɪzɪtlɪ] *adv* d'une manière exquise

extant [eks'tænt] *adj* qui existe encore

extempore [ɪks'tempərɪ] **1** *adj (speech)* impromptu(e)
　2 *adv* **to speak e.** improviser

extemporize [ɪks'tempəraɪz] *vi* improviser

extend [ɪks'tend] **1** *vt* (**a**) *(in space)* étendre, allonger; *(knowledge)* accroître; *(frontiers)* faire reculer; *(house)* agrandir (**b**) *(in time)* prolonger (**c**) *(give, offer) (one's hand)* tendre; *(thanks)* présenter; *(support)* offrir; *Fin* **to e. credit to sb** accorder un crédit à qn
　2 *vi* (**a**) *(in space)* s'étendre (**b**) *(in time)* se prolonger, continuer

extended family [ɪks'tendɪd'fæmɪlɪ] *n* famille *f* élargie

extension [ɪks'tenʃən] *n* (**a**) *(to building)* annexe *f* (**b**) *(in time)* prolongation *f*; *(for essay)* délai *m* supplémentaire (**c**) *(for telephone)* poste *m* (**d**) **e. (cable)** rallonge *f* (**e**) **(hair) extensions** rajouts *mpl*

extensive [ɪks'tensɪv] *adj (area, knowledge)* vaste, étendu(e); *(damage, repairs)* important(e); **to make e. use of sth** faire un usage considérable de qch

extensively [ɪks'tensɪvlɪ] *adv (travel, read)* énormément; *(revised, rewritten)* entièrement (**damaged**) gravement; **to use sth e.** se servir beaucoup de qch

extent [ɪks'tent] *n* (**a**) *(of land, damage, knowledge)* étendue *f* (**b**) *(degree)* **to an e.** to a certain e. dans une certaine mesure; **to a large e.** en grande partie, dans une large mesure; **to such an e. that...** à tel point que...; **to what e.?** jusqu'à quel point?

extenuating circumstances [ɪks'tenjʊeɪtɪŋ'sɜːkəmstænsɪz] *npl* circonstances *fpl* atténuantes

exterior [ɪks'tɪərɪə(r)] **1** *n (of building, car)* extérieur *m*; *(of person)* dehors *mpl*
　2 *adj* extérieur(e)

exterminate [ɪks'tɜːmɪneɪt] *vt* exterminer; *(disease)* éradiquer

extermination [ɪkstɜːmɪ'neɪʃən] *n* extermination *f*; *(of disease)* éradication *f*

external [ɪks'tɜːnəl] *adj (events, trade, debt)* extérieur(e); *(angle, damage, wall)* externe; *Univ (examiner)* de l'extérieur; *Pol* **e. affairs** affaires *fpl* étrangères ou extérieures; **e. use** *(on medicine)* à usage externe

extinct [ɪks'tɪŋkt] *adj (animal, species)* disparu(e), qui n'existe plus; *(volcano)* éteint(e)

extinction [ɪks'tɪŋkʃən] *n* extinction *f*; **to be threatened with e.** être en voie de disparition

extinguish [ɪks'tɪŋgwɪʃ] *vt (fire)* éteindre; *(hope)* anéantir

extinguisher [ɪks'tɪŋgwɪʃə(r)] *n* extincteur *m*

extirpate ['ekstɜːpeɪt] *vt Formal* extirper

extol, *Am* **extoll** [ɪks'təʊl] *(pt & pp* extolled*) vt (virtues, merits)* exalter, vanter; *(beauty)* célébrer, chanter

extort [ɪks'tɔːt] *vt (money)* extorquer (**from** à); *(promise)* arracher (**from** à)

extortion [ɪks'tɔːʃən] *n* extorsion *f*

extortionate [ɪks'tɔːʃənɪt] *adj* exorbitant(e)

extra ['ekstrə] **1** *n (in film)* figurant(e) *m,f; (on bill)* supplément *m*
2 *adj* (**a**) *(additional)* supplémentaire, de plus; **no e. charge** sans supplément de prix; **e. time** *(in sporting contest)* prolongation *f* (**b**) *(spare)* de réserve, de rechange
3 *adv* (**a**) *(more than usual)* extrêmement; **to be e. careful** faire particulièrement attention; **e. large** *(clothing)* grand patron; **e. special** très spécial(e) (**b**) *(charge, pay)* en plus, en sus

extract 1 *n* ['ekstrækt] (**a**) *(concentrate)* extrait *m*, concentré *m* (**b**) *(from book, film)* extrait *m*
2 *vt* [ɪks'trækt] *(tooth, raw material)* extraire (**from** de); *(confession, information)* soutirer (**from** à)

extraction [ɪks'trækʃən] *n* (**a**) *(removal)* extraction *f* (**b**) *(origin) (social)* extraction *f*; *(geographical)* origine *f*; **she is of Danish e.** elle est d'origine danoise

extractor fan [ɪks'træktəfæn] *n* aérateur *m*

extracurricular ['ekstrəkə'rɪkjʊlə(r)] *adj Sch* extra-scolaire

extradite ['ekstrədaɪt] *vt* extrader

extradition [ekstrə'dɪʃən] *n* extradition *f*

extrajudicial ['ekstrədʒuː'dɪʃəl] *adj* extrajudiciaire

extramarital ['ekstrə'mærɪtəl] *adj* extraconjugal(e)

extramural ['ekstrə'mjʊərəl] *adj Univ* de formation continue

extraneous [ɪks'treɪnɪəs] *adj Formal (details)* sans rapport; *(considerations)* en dehors de la question

Extranet ['extrənet] *n Comput* Extranet *m*

extraordinarily [ɪks'trɔːdənərɪli] *adv* extra-ordinairement

extraordinary [ɪks'trɔːdənrɪ] *adj* extraordinaire; **e. general meeting** assemblée *f* générale extraordinaire; **e. powers** pouvoirs *mpl* extraordinaires

extrapolate [ɪk'stræpəleɪt] *vt & vi* extrapoler (**from** à partir de)

extrapolation [ɪkstræpə'leɪʃən] *n* extrapolation *f*

extrasensory perception ['ekstrə'sensərɪpə'sepʃən] *n* perception *f* extrasensorielle

extraterrestrial ['ekstrətɪ'restrɪəl] **1** *n* extra-terrestre *mf*
2 *adj* extra-terrestre

extravagance [ɪks'trævəgəns] *n* (**a**) *(excessive spending)* gaspillage *m* (**b**) *(extravagant purchase)* folie *f*

extravagant [ɪks'trævəgənt] *adj (person)* dépensier(ère); *(tastes)* dispendieux(euse); *(object)* hors de prix

extravaganza [ekstrævə'gænzə] *n (lavish production)* grand spectacle *m*

extreme [ɪks'triːm] **1** *n* extrême *m*; **in the e.** à l'extrême; **to go from one e. to the other** passer d'un extrême à l'autre; **to go to extremes** pousser les choses à l'extrême
2 *adj* extrême; *Pol* **the e. left/right** l'extrême gauche *f*/droite *f*; **e. sports** sports *mpl* extrêmes

extremely [ɪks'triːmlɪ] *adv* extrêmement

extremism [ɪks'triːmɪzəm] *n* extrémisme *m*

extremist [ɪks'triːmɪst] **1** *n* extrémiste *mf*
2 *adj* extrémiste

extremity [ɪks'tremɪtɪ] *(pl* extremities*) n* (**a**) *(end)* extrémité *f* (**b**) **extremities** *(of body)* extrémités *fpl* (**c**) *(extreme situation)* situation *f* extrême; *(extreme measure)* mesure *f* extrême

extricate ['ekstrɪkeɪt] *vt* dégager, tirer; **to e. oneself from** *(danger, difficulties)* se tirer de

extrovert ['ekstrəvɜːt] **1** *n* extraverti(e) *m,f*
2 *adj* extraverti(e)

exuberance [ɪg'zjuːbərəns] *n* exubérance *f*

exuberant [ɪg'zjuːbərənt] *adj* exubérant(e)

exude [ɪg'zjuːd] *vt (sweat, odour)* exsuder; *(health, confidence)* déborder de

exult [ɪg'zʌlt] *vi* exulter, se réjouir (**in** de)

exultant [ɪg'zʌltənt] *adj (mood)* joyeux(euse); *(cry)* de triomphe

eye [aɪ] **1** *n* (**a**) *(of person, storm)* œil *m*; *(of needle)* chas *m*; **to open/close one's eyes** ouvrir/fermer les yeux; **to look sb straight in the e.** regarder qn droit dans les yeux; **as far as the e. can see** à perte de vue; **to make e. contact with sb** regarder qn (droit) dans les yeux; *Fam Hum* **e. candy** *(men)* beaux mecs *mpl*; *(women)* belles nanas *fpl*; **e. drops** *(medicine)* gouttes *fpl* pour les yeux; **at e. level** à la hauteur des yeux; **e. shadow** ombre *f* à paupières; **e. test** examen *m* de la vue
(**b**) *(idioms)* **in the eye(s) of the law** aux yeux de la loi; **to be in the public e.** occuper une position en vue; **to have an e. for a bargain** savoir reconnaître une bonne affaire; **to have an e. for detail/colour** avoir l'œil pour les détails/les couleurs; **to look at sth with a critical e.** regarder qch d'un œil critique; **to see e. to e. with sb** voir les choses du même œil que qn; **for your eyes only** confidentiel(elle); **to keep one's eyes and ears open** rester en éveil; **to keep one's eyes peeled** *or* **skinned** ouvrir l'œil; **to open sb's eyes to sth** ouvrir *ou* dessiller les yeux à qn sur qch; **to shut** *ou* **close one's eyes to sth** fermer les yeux sur qch; **to do sth with one's eyes open** faire qch en connaissance de cause; **to catch sb's e.** attirer l'attention de qn; **to have eyes in** *or* **at the back of one's head** avoir des yeux derrière la tête; **he only has eyes for her** il n'a d'yeux que pour elle; **to set** *or* **lay eyes on sth** poser les yeux sur qch; **I saw it with my own eyes** je l'ai vu de mes propres yeux; **to run** *or* **cast one's e. over sth** jeter un coup d'œil sur qch; **to keep an e. on sb/sth** surveiller qn/qch; **to keep an e. out for sb/sth** être à l'affût de qch; **to have one's e. on sb/sth** *(be watching)* avoir qn/qch à l'œil; *(have in mind)* avoir l'œil sur qn/qch; **to make eyes at sb** faire de l'œil à qn; **with an e. to...** en vue de...; **to be up to one's eyes in work** avoir du travail par-dessus la tête; **to be up to one's eyes in debt** être endetté(e) jusqu'au cou; *Fam* **that's one in the e. for him!** ça lui fera les pieds!; **an e. for an e., a tooth for a tooth** œil pour œil, dent pour dent
2 *vt* regarder, observer

▸**eye up** *vt sep* reluquer

eyeball ['aɪbɔːl] *n* globe *m* oculaire

eyebrow ['aɪbraʊ] *n* sourcil *m*; *Fig* **to raise one's eyebrows** *(in surprise)* lever les sourcils

eye-catching ['aɪkætʃɪŋ] *adj* accrocheur(euse)

eyeful ['aɪfʊl] *n Fam* **to get an e. of sb/sth** *(look at)* reluquer qn/qch

eyeglass ['aɪglɑːs] *n* monocle *m*

eyeglasses ['aɪglɑːsɪz] *npl Am (spectacles)* lunettes *fpl*

eyelash [ˈaɪlæʃ] n cil m
eyelid [ˈaɪlɪd] n paupière f; Fig **she didn't bat an e.** elle n'a pas sourcillé
eyeliner [ˈaɪlaɪnə(r)] n eye-liner m
eye-opener [ˈaɪəʊpənə(r)] n révélation f; **it was an e. for him** ça lui a ouvert les yeux
eyepatch [ˈaɪpætʃ] n cache m (sur l'œil)
eyeshade [ˈaɪʃeɪd] n visière f
eyesight [ˈaɪsaɪt] n vue f
eyesore [ˈaɪsɔː(r)] n horreur f

eyestrain [ˈaɪstreɪn] n fatigue f oculaire
eyetooth [ˈaɪtuːθ] (pl **eyeteeth** [ˈaɪtiːθ]) n canine f; **I'd give my eyeteeth to go with them** je donnerais n'importe quoi pour aller avec eux
eyewash [ˈaɪwɒʃ] n (for eye) collyre m; Fig (nonsense) boniment m, poudre f aux yeux
eyewitness [ˈaɪwɪtnɪs] n témoin m oculaire
eyrie [ˈɪərɪ] n aire f
e-zine, ezine [ˈiːziːn] n ezine m, e-zine m, magazine m électronique

F, f [ef] *n* (**a**) *(letter)* F, f *m inv*; *Br Euph* **the F word** = euphémisme désignant le mot "fuck" (**b**) *Mus* fa *m*

fa [faː] *n Mus* fa *m*

FA [eˈfeɪ] *n* *(abbr* **Football Association**) = fédération anglaise de football

fab [fæb] *adj Br Fam* sensass

fable [ˈfeɪbəl] *n* fable *f*

fabled [ˈfeɪbəld] *adj* légendaire; *Fig* fabuleux(euse)

fabric [ˈfæbrɪk] *n (cloth)* tissu *m*, étoffe *f*; *(of building)* structure *f*; *Fig* **the f. of society** le tissu social; **f. conditioner** (produit *m*) assouplissant *m*

fabricate [ˈfæbrɪkeɪt] *vt (news, story, alibi)* forger, fabriquer; *(make)* fabriquer

fabulous [ˈfæbjʊləs] *adj* fabuleux(euse)

fabulously [ˈfæbjʊləslɪ] *adv (rich)* fabuleusement

façade [fæˈsɑːd] *n also Fig* façade *f*

face [feɪs] **1** *n* (**a**) *(of person)* visage *m*, figure *f*; *very Fam* **shut your f.!** ferme-la!, la ferme!; **I know that f!** je connais cette tête-là!; **I told him to his f.** je le lui ai dit en face; **I shall never be able to look her in the f. again** je ne pourrai plus jamais la regarder en face; **to show one's f.** se montrer; **to set one's f. against sth** se braquer contre qch; **in the f. of** *(danger, threat, enemy)* devant, face à; *Br* **f. cloth** ≃ gant *m* de toilette; **f. cream** crème *f* pour le visage; **f. pack** masque *m*; **f. powder** poudre *f*

(**b**) *(expression)* mine *f*; **to make** *or* **pull faces** faire des grimaces; **to keep a straight f.** garder son sérieux; **to put a good f. on it** garder le sourire

(**c**) *(appearance)* **on the f. of it** à première vue; **to save f.** sauver la face; **to lose f.** perdre la face; **the changing f. of Britain** le visage changeant de la Grande-Bretagne; **to take sth at f. value** prendre qch au pied de la lettre

(**d**) *(surface) (of the earth)* surface *f*; *(of clock)* cadran *m*; *(of coin, cliff)* face *f*; *Fig* **to disappear off the f. of the earth** se volatiliser; **f. down** *(person)* sur le ventre; *(document)* face imprimée dessous; *(playing card)* à l'envers; **f. up** *(person)* sur le dos; *(document)* face imprimée dessus; *(playing card)* à l'endroit

2 *vt* (**a**) *(confront) (difficulty, danger)* affronter, faire face à; **to be faced with sth** être confronté(e) à qch; **to f. facts** regarder les choses en face; **he faces six months in prison** il risque six mois de prison; **I can't f. going to work today** je n'ai pas le courage d'aller travailler aujourd'hui; **let's f. it** soyons réalistes; *Fig* **to f. the music** *(deal with situation)* faire front; *(accept consequences)* assumer ses responsabilités

(**b**) *(look towards)* faire face à; **to f. the front** regarder devant soi

3 *vi* **to f. north/south** *(of house)* être orienté(e) au nord/sud; **to f. towards** *(of person)* se tourner vers

▸ **face up to** *vt insep (person)* tenir tête à; *(reality, fears)* affronter

faceless [ˈfeɪslɪs] *adj* anonyme

face-lift [ˈfeɪslɪft] *n (plastic surgery)* lifting *m*; *Fig (of building)* restauration *f*; **to have a f.** se faire faire un lifting

face-saving [ˈfeɪsseɪvɪŋ] *adj* qui permet de sauver la face

facet [ˈfæsɪt] *n (of gem, character)* facette *f*; *(of problem, situation)* dimension *f*

facetious [fəˈsiːʃəs] *adj* facétieux(euse); **don't be f.!** ne plaisante pas!

face-to-face [ˈfeɪstəˈfeɪs] **1** *adj* **a f. meeting** un face à face

2 *adv (meet)* face à face

facial [ˈfeɪʃəl] **1** *n* soin *m* du visage; **to have a f.** se faire faire un soin du visage

2 *adj* facial(e); *(expression, hair)* du visage

facile [ˈfæsaɪl] *adj Pej* facile

facilitate [fəˈsɪlɪteɪt] *vt* faciliter

facility [fəˈsɪlɪtɪ] *(pl* **facilities**) *n* (**a**) *(ease)* facilité *f* (**b**) *(skill)* **to have a f. for sth** avoir un don pour qch (**c**) **facilities** *(equipment)* équipement *m*; *(place, building)* installations *fpl*; **shopping facilities** magasins *mpl*; **transport facilities** moyens *mpl* de transport (**d**) *(building)* **a detention f.** un établissement pénitentiaire (**e**) *(feature) (of computer, stereo)* fonction *f*

facsimile [fækˈsɪmɪlɪ] *n (copy)* fac-similé *m*; *(fax)* télécopie *f*

fact [fækt] *n* fait *m*; **in f.** en fait; **to distinguish f. from fiction** discerner la fiction de la réalité; **the f. is (that)...** le fait est que...; **it's a f. that...** c'est un fait que...; **to know for a f. (that)...** savoir pertinemment que...; **it's a f. of life** c'est une réalité; **to tell sb the facts of life** expliquer à qn comment on fait les enfants

fact-finding [ˈfæktfaɪndɪŋ] *adj* d'enquête; **f. mission** mission *f* d'information

faction [ˈfækʃən] *n* faction *f*

factor [ˈfæktə(r)] *n (aspect, in maths)* facteur *m*

factory [ˈfæktərɪ] *(pl* **factories**) *n* usine *f*; *(small)* fabrique *f*; **f. farming** élevage *m* industriel

factual [ˈfæktʃʊəl] *adj* basé(e) sur les faits

faculty [ˈfækəltɪ] *(pl* **faculties**) *n (of mind, in university)* faculté *f*; *Am* **the f.** *(teaching staff)* le personnel enseignant

fad [fæd] *n* mode *f* (**for** de)

fade [feɪd] 1 *vt* faner
2 *vi (of flower, material, colour)* se faner; *(of light)* baisser; *(of memory)* s'éteindre; *(of hope)* s'amenuiser; **to f.** from memory s'effacer de la mémoire
▸**fade away** *vi (of sound)* s'éteindre; *Fig (of person)* s'éteindre peu à peu
▸**fade out** 1 *vt sep Cin* fermer en fondu; *(music)* terminer par un fondu
2 *vi* se terminer en fondu
faded ['feɪdɪd] *adj (flower, colour)* fané(e); *(photograph, garment)* décoloré(e)
fading ['feɪdɪŋ] *adj (light)* pâlissant(e)
faeces ['fiːsiːz] *npl* fèces *fpl*
▸**faff about, faff around** [fæf] *vi Br Fam (waste time)* glander; *(potter)* bricoler
fag [fæg] *n* (**a**) *Br Fam (cigarette)* clope *m or f* (**b**) *Br Fam (unpleasant job)* corvée *f* (**c**) *Am very Fam (homosexual)* pédé *m,* = terme injurieux désignant un homosexuel
faggot ['fægət] *n* (**a**) *(firewood)* fagot *m* (**b**) *Br (meatball)* boulette *f* de viande (**c**) *Am very Fam (homosexual)* pédé *m,* = terme injurieux désignant un homosexuel
Fahrenheit ['færənhaɪt] *adj* Fahrenheit *inv*
fail [feɪl] 1 *n* (**a**) *(in exam)* échec *m* (**b**) **without f.** sans faute
2 *vt (exam, test)* échouer à, rater; *(candidate)* recaler; **to f. a drugs test** être positif(ive) au contrôle anti-dopage; **words f. me** les mots me manquent; **his nerve failed him** le courage lui a fait défaut; **I won't f. you** vous pouvez compter sur moi
3 *vi (of person, plan)* échouer; *(of business)* faire faillite; *(of engine)* caler; *(of memory, eyesight, light)* baisser; *(of brakes)* lâcher; **to f. to do sth** *(not succeed)* ne pas arriver à faire qch; *(forget)* négliger de faire qch; **I f. to see what the problem is** je ne vois pas où est le problème; **if all else fails** en désespoir de cause; **to f. in one's duty** manquer à son devoir; **it never fails** *(of strategy, excuse)* ça marche à tous les coups
failed [feɪld] *adj (artist, politician)* raté(e)
failing ['feɪlɪŋ] 1 *n (fault)* faiblesse *f*, défaut *m*
2 *adj (sight, strength)* qui baisse; **to be in f. health** avoir une santé défaillante
3 *prep* à défaut de; **f. that** à défaut; **f. all else** en désespoir de cause
fail-safe ['feɪlseɪf] *adj (mechanism)* à sûreté intégrée
failure ['feɪljə(r)] *n* (**a**) *(of plan, attempt)* échec *m*; *(of machine)* panne *f*; *(of company)* faillite *f*; **to be a f.** *(of show, film)* faire un bide; **f. to keep a promise** manquement *m* à une promesse; **f. to pay a bill** défaut *m* de paiement d'une facture (**b**) *(person)* raté(e) *m,f*
faint [feɪnt] 1 *n* **to fall down in a f.** s'évanouir
2 *adj* (**a**) *(hope, light, sound)* faible; *(mark, writing)* à peine visible; *(colour)* pâle; *(idea)* vague; **I haven't got the faintest idea** je n'ai pas la moindre idée (**b**) *(weak, unwell)* **to feel** *or* **be f.** *(of person)* se sentir mal
3 *vi (lose consciousness)* s'évanouir
faint-hearted ['feɪnt'hɑːtɪd] *adj* timoré(e); **not for the f.** à déconseiller aux âmes sensibles
faintly ['feɪntlɪ] *adv* (**a**) *(remember, hear, see)* vaguement; *(shine)* faiblement (**b**) *(slightly) (uneasy, ridiculous)* légèrement
fair¹ ['feə(r)] *n* (**a**) *Br (funfair)* fête *f* foraine (**b**) *(trade fair)* foire *f*

fair² 1 *adj* (**a**) *(just)* juste, équitable; *(price)* raisonnable; *(fight)* loyal(e); **it's not f.** ce n'est pas juste; **fair's f.!** ce n'est que justice!; **f. enough!** *(OK)* d'accord!; *(rightly so)* ça se comprend!; **it is f. to say (that)...** on peut dire que...; **to be f.,...** pour être honnête,...; **by f. means or foul** par tous les moyens; *Prov* **all's f. in love and war** tous les moyens sont bons; *Fam* **to give sb a f. crack of the whip** donner sa chance à qn; **to be f. game** être une proie facile; **f. play** fair-play *m*, *Offic* franc-jeu *m*; **to get one's f. share** recevoir son dû; **we've had our f. share of problems** nous avons eu notre lot de problèmes; **f. trade** commerce *m* équitable (**b**) *(quite good)* assez bon (bonne); **a f. idea** une assez bonne idée; **at a f. pace** à une allure assez rapide; **a f. amount of** pas mal de; **f. to middling** comme ci comme ça (**c**) *(weather)* beau (belle) (**d**) *(light-coloured) (hair)* blond(e); *(skin)* pâle (**e**) *(attractive)* beau (belle); *Old-fashioned* **the f.** *or* **fairer sex** le beau sexe
2 *adv (act, fight)* loyalement; *(play)* jouer franc jeu; **you can't say fairer than that** il n'y a pas plus équitable; **to beat sb f. and square** battre qn à plates coutures
fairground ['feəgraʊnd] *n* parc *m* d'attractions
fair-haired ['feə'heəd] *adj* blond(e)
fairly ['feəlɪ] *adv* (**a**) *(quite)* assez; **it is f. certain (that)...** il est à peu près certain que... (**b**) *(justly)* équitablement; *(play, fight)* loyalement; *(describe)* objectivement (**c**) *(for emphasis)* **we f. raced home** nous sommes rentrés ventre à terre
fair-minded ['feə'maɪndɪd] *adj* équitable
fairness ['feənɪs] *n* (**a**) *(of person, decision)* impartialité *f*; **in all f.** en toute justice (**b**) *(of hair)* blondeur *f*; *(of skin)* pâleur *f*
fair-sized ['feə'saɪzd] *adj* assez grand(e)
fairway ['feəweɪ] *n* fairway *m*
fair-weather friend ['feəweðə'frend] *n* ami(e) *m,f* des beaux *ou* bons jours
fairy ['feərɪ] *(pl* fairies) *n* (**a**) *(magical being)* fée *f*; **f. godmother** bonne fée *f*; **f. lights** guirlande *f* lumineuse *(pour sapin de Noël)* (**b**) *very Fam (homosexual)* tapette *f,* = terme injurieux désignant un homosexuel
fairytale ['feərɪteɪl] *n* conte *m* de fées; **a f. ending** une fin digne d'un conte de fées
faith [feɪθ] *n* foi *f*; **to have f. in sb** avoir foi en qn; **to be of the Catholic/Jewish f.** être de religion catholique/juive; **to keep f. with sb** tenir ses engagements envers qn; **in good f.** en toute bonne foi; **f. healer** guérisseur(euse) *m,f*
faithful ['feɪθfʊl] 1 *npl* **the f.** les fidèles *mpl*
2 *adj* fidèle
faithfully ['feɪθfʊlɪ] *adv* fidèlement; **yours f.** *(in formal letter)* recevez l'expression de mes/nos sentiments distingués
fake [feɪk] 1 *n (object)* faux *m*; *(person)* bluffeur *m*
2 *adj* faux (fausse); **f. tan** *(product)* autobronzant *m*
3 *vt (signature)* contrefaire; *(result)* truquer; **to f. an illness** feindre d'être malade
falafel [fə'læfəl] *n Culin* falafels *mpl*
falcon ['fɔːlkən] *n* faucon *m*
falconry ['fɔːlkənrɪ] *n* fauconnerie *f*
Falkland ['fɔːklənd] *n* **the F. Islands, the Falklands** les Malouines *fpl*, the Falkland *fpl*
fall [fɔːl] 1 *n* (**a**) *(of person, prices, besieged city, snow)* chute *f*; **to have a f.** tomber, faire une chute; *Fig* **to be**

heading for a f. courir à sa perte; *Am Fam* **f. guy** *(sca-pegoat)* bouc *m* émissaire
(**b**) *Am (autumn)* automne *m*
(**c**) *falls (waterfall)* chutes *fpl*
2 *vi (pt* **fell** [fel]*, pp* **fallen** ['fɔːlən]) (**a**) *(drop, fall over)* tomber; **to f. down a hole** tomber dans un trou; **to f. off a bicycle/chair** tomber d'un vélo/d'une chaise; *Fig* **to f. into a trap** tomber dans un piège; *also Fig* **to f. flat** tomber à plat; **to f. to pieces** *(of object)* tomber en morceaux; *Fig (of person)* craquer; **to f. short of doing sth** ne pas réussir à faire qch
(**b**) *(decrease) (of price, temperature, standards)* chuter, baisser
(**c**) *(of government, city, soldier)* tomber
(**d**) *(of silence, darkness, light)* tomber; **the responsibility fallacious falls on you** c'est à vous qu'en incombe la responsabilité; *Formal* **it falls to me to introduce...** j'ai l'honneur de vous présenter...
(**e**) *(become)* **to f. asleep** s'endormir; **to f. ill** tomber malade; **to f. in love (with)** tomber amoureux(euse) (de); **to f. silent** se taire; **to f. victim to an epidemic** être victime d'une épidémie; **the match fell victim to the weather** le match a dû être annulé en raison du mauvais temps
(**f**) *(be classified)* se classer; **to f. into two categories** se diviser en deux catégories; **suddenly everything fell into place** soudain tout est devenu clair
(**g**) *(occur)* **Christmas Day falls on a Thursday** Noël tombe un jeudi
▸**fall away** *vi (of ground)* descendre; *(of attendance)* diminuer
▸**fall back on** *vt insep (resort to)* se rabattre sur
▸**fall behind** *vi (in race)* se faire distancer; **to f. behind with the rent** être en retard pour payer son loyer
▸**fall down** *vi (of person)* tomber; *(of building)* s'écrouler, s'effondrer; **that's where your argument falls down** c'est par là que pèche ton raisonnement
▸**fall for** *vt insep Fam* (**a**) *(fall in love with)* tomber amoureux(euse) de (**b**) *(trick)* se laisser prendre à; **to f. for it** s'y laisser prendre
▸**fall in** *vi* (**a**) *(of roof)* s'écrouler, s'effondrer (**b**) *Mil (of troops)* former les rangs
▸**fall off** *vi* (**a**) *(of object)* tomber (**b**) *(of profits, attendance)* diminuer
▸**fall out** *vi* (**a**) *(quarrel)* se brouiller, se fâcher (**with** avec) (**b**) *Mil* rompre les rangs
▸**fall over 1** *vi* tomber (par terre)
2 *vt insep (stumble on)* trébucher sur; *Fig* **to be falling over oneself to do sth** *(be very keen)* se mettre en quatre pour faire qch
▸**fall through** *vi (of plan, deal)* tomber à l'eau
fallacious [fə'leɪʃəs] *adj* erroné(e)
fallacy ['fæləsɪ] *(pl* **fallacies**) *n* erreur *f*
fallen ['fɔːlən] **1** *npl* **the f.** les soldats *mpl* tombés au combat
2 *adj (angel)* déchu(e); *(woman)* perdu(e)
3 *pp of* **fall**
fallible ['fælɪbəl] *adj* faillible
Fallopian tube [fə'ləʊpɪən'tjuːb] *n Anat* trompe *f* de Fallope
fallout ['fɔːlaʊt] *n (nuclear)* retombées *fpl* radioactives; *Fig (from scandal)* retombées *fpl*; **f. shelter** abri *m* antiatomique
fallow ['fæləʊ] *adj* en jachère; **to lie f.** être en jachère; *Fig* **a f. period** un passage à vide

false [fɔːls] *adj* faux (fausse); **f. alarm** fausse alerte *f*; *Fig* **f. dawn** faux espoir *m*; **f. economy** fausse économie *f*; **f. friend** *(in foreign language)* faux ami *m*; *Psy* **f. memory syndrome** syndrome *m* des faux souvenirs; **f. modesty** fausse modestie *f*; *Fig* **to strike a f. note** *(in film)* sonner faux; *(of person)* faire une gaffe; **f. pregnancy** grossesse *f* nerveuse; **under f. pretences** *(illegally)* par des moyens frauduleux; *(by lying)* sous des prétextes fallacieux; **f. start** *(in race)* faux départ *m*; **f. teeth** dentier *m*; **to bear f. witness** faire un faux témoignage
falsehood ['fɔːlshʊd] *n* mensonge *m*
falsely ['fɔːlslɪ] *adv (described)* faussement; *(accused)* à tort; *(smile)* avec fausseté
falsetto [fɔːl'setəʊ] *(pl* **falsettos**) *n Mus* voix *f* de fausset
falsify ['fɔːlsɪfaɪ] *(pt & pp* **falsified**) *vt* (**a**) *(forge) (records, document)* falsifier (**b**) *(disprove) (theory)* prouver la fausseté de
falter ['fɔːltə(r)] *vi also Fig* vaciller; *(of voice)* hésiter
fame [feɪm] *n* renom *m*, renommée *f*; **to seek f. and fortune** rechercher la gloire et la fortune
famed [feɪmd] *adj* célèbre (**for** pour)
familiar [fə'mɪlɪə(r)] *adj* (**a**) *(well-known)* familier(ère) (**to** à) (**b**) *(intimate)* familier(ère), intime; **to be on f. terms with sb** avoir des rapports amicaux avec qn; **to get too f. with sb** se permettre trop de familiarités avec qn (**c**) *(acquainted)* **to be f. with sb/sth** bien connaître qn/qch
familiarity [fəmɪlɪ'ærɪtɪ] *n* (**a**) *(intimacy)* familiarité *f*; **f. breeds contempt** avec l'habitude vient la lassitude (**b**) *(acquaintance)* connaissance *f* (**with** de)
familiarize [fə'mɪlɪəraɪz] *vt* **to f. sb with sth** familiariser qn avec qch; **to f. oneself with sth** se familiariser avec qch
family ['fæmɪlɪ] *(pl* **families**) *n* famille *f*; **it runs in the f.** c'est de famille, ça tient de famille; **to start a f.** fonder une famille; **to treat sb as one of the f.** traiter qn comme un membre de la famille; *Fam* **to be in the f. way** être enceinte; **f. allowance** allocations *fpl* familiales; **f. business** entreprise *f* familiale; **f. doctor/life** docteur *m*/vie *f* de famille; **f. man** bon père *m* de famille; **f. planning** planning *m* familial; **f. planning clinic** (centre *m* de) planning *m* familial; **f. resemblance** air *m* de famille; **f. room** *(in hotel)* chambre *f* familiale; *Am (in house)* salle *f* de séjour; *Br (in pub)* salle réservée aux familles; **f. tree** arbre *m* généalogique
famine ['fæmɪn] *n* famine *f*; **f. relief** aide *f* aux victimes d'une famine
famished ['fæmɪʃd] *adj* affamé(e)
famous ['feɪməs] *adj* célèbre (**for** pour)
famously ['feɪməslɪ] *adv Fam* **to get on f. (with sb)** s'entendre à merveille (avec qn)
fan¹ [fæn] **1** *n (cooling device) (hand-held)* éventail *m*; *(mechanical)* ventilateur *m*; **f. belt** *(of car)* courroie *f* de ventilateur; **f. heater** radiateur *m* soufflant
2 *vt (pt & pp* **fanned**) (**a**) *(face, person)* éventer; **to f. oneself** s'éventer (**b**) *(fire, passions)* attiser
▸**fan out** *vi* se déployer en éventail
fan² *n (enthusiast)* fan *mf*; *(of sports team)* supporter *m*; *Fig* **I'm not a f. of electric cookers** je n'aime pas trop les cuisinières électriques; **f. club** fan-club *m*; **f. mail** courrier *m* des admirateurs
fanatic [fə'nætɪk] **1** *n* fanatique *mf*
2 *adj* fanatique
fanatical [fə'nætɪkəl] *adj* fanatique

fanciful ['fænsɪfʊl] *adj* (**a**) *(unrealistic) (idea, project)* chimérique; *(person)* qui se fait des idées (**b**) *(design, style)* plein(e) de fantaisie
fancy ['fænsɪ] **1** *(pl* **fancies**) *n* (**a**) *(imagination)* imagination *f* (**b**) *(whim)* fantaisie *f*, caprice *m* (**c**) *(liking)* to take a f. to sb prendre qn en affection; *(sexually)* s'enticher de qn; **to take a f.** to sth s'enticher de qch; the house didn't take her f. la maison ne lui a pas plu **2** *adj (jewels, gadget, hat)* fantaisie *inv*; *(party, hotel)* chic *inv*; *(food, decoration)* recherché(e); **f. dress** déguisement *m*; **f. dress party** soirée *f* déguisée **3** *vt (pt & pp* fancied) (**a**) *Fam (want)* I didn't f. the idea ça ne me tentait pas; do you f. a drink? ça te dit de boire un verre? (**b**) *Br Fam (be attracted to)* he fancies her elle lui plaît (**c**) *(imagine)* to f. (that)... croire *ou* penser que...; I f. I've seen her before j'ai l'impression de l'avoir déjà vue; *Fam* f. that! ça alors!; f. meeting you here! si je m'attendais à te/vous rencontrer ici! (**d**) *(have good opinion of)* to f. sb to win penser que qn va gagner; *Pej* he fancies himself il ne se prend pas pour n'importe qui; to f. oneself as a writer/musician se prendre pour un écrivain/musicien; I don't f. his chances of getting the job je crois qu'il a peu de chances d'obtenir le poste
fanfare ['fænfeə(r)] *n* fanfare *f*
fanfic ['fænfɪk] *n Fam* fanfic *f*, fanfiction *f*
fang [fæŋ] *n (of dog)* croc *m*; *(of snake)* crochet *m*
fanny ['fænɪ] *(pl* fannies) *n* (**a**) *Br Vulg (vagina)* chatte *f* (**b**) *Am Fam (buttocks)* derrière *m*, fesses *fpl*; **f. pack** banane *f*
fantasize ['fæntəsaɪz] *vi* fantasmer (about sur)
fantastic [fæn'tæstɪk] *adj* (**a**) *Fam (excellent)* formidable, fantastique (**b**) *(enormous) (price)* astronomique; *(wealth, size)* prodigieux(euse) (**c**) *(unbelievable) (claim, story)* grotesque, absurde (**d**) *(strange) (creature)* fantastique
fantasy ['fæntəzɪ] *(pl* fantasies) *n* (**a**) *(unrealistic idea)* chimère *f*; *(sexual)* fantasme *m* (**b**) *(imagination)* fantaisie *f* (**c**) *(literature)* littérature *f* fantastique
FAO [efeɪ'əʊ] *n (abbr* Food and Agriculture Organization) FAO *f*
FAQ [efeɪ'kjuː] *n Comput (abbr* frequently asked questions) FAQ
far [fɑː(r)] *(comparative* farther ['fɑːðə(r)] *or* further ['fɜːðə(r)], *superlative* farthest ['fɑːðɪst] *or* furthest ['fɜːðɪst]) **1** *adj* in the f. distance au loin, dans le lointain; the f. end l'autre bout; *Pol* the f. left/right l'extrême gauche *f*/droite *f*; the F. East l'Extrême-Orient *m*; it's a f. cry from ça n'a rien à voir avec **2** *adv* (**a**) *(in distance)* loin; how f. is it to Toulouse? combien y a-t-il jusqu'à Toulouse?; f. away (from) loin (de); as f. as jusqu'à; *also Fig* to go f. aller loin; *Fig* to go so f. as to do sth aller jusqu'à faire qch; *Fig* to go too f. aller trop loin; *also Fig* f. from... loin de...; *Fig* f. from it loin de là; *Fig* f. be it from me to... loin de moi l'idée de...; f. and wide partout; *Fig* as f. as I can see pour autant que je puisse en juger; as f. as I know (pour) autant que je sache; as f. as I'm concerned en ce qui me concerne; *Fig* as f. as possible autant que possible
(**b**) *(in time)* so f. jusqu'ici, jusqu'à présent; so f. so good jusqu'ici tout va bien; for as f. back as I can remember d'aussi loin que je me souvienne; to work f. into the night travailler jusqu'à une heure avancée de la nuit
(**c**) *(much)* beaucoup; f. better/bigger beaucoup

mieux/plus grand; by f. de loin; f. and away the best de loin le meilleur/la meilleure
faraway ['fɑːrəweɪ] *adj* lointain(e); *(look)* perdu(e) dans le vague
farce [fɑːs] *n* farce *f*; *Fig* it's a f.! c'est grotesque!
farcical ['fɑːsɪkəl] *adj* grotesque
fare [feə(r)] **1** *n* (**a**) *(for journey)* tarif *m*; to pay one's f. acheter son billet (**b**) *(taxi passenger)* client(e) *m,f* (**c**) *Formal (food)* chère *f* **2** *vi* se débrouiller
farewell [feə'wel] *n* adieu *m*; to say *or* make one's farewells faire ses adieux; **f. dinner** dîner *m* d'adieu
far-fetched ['fɑː'fetʃt] *adj (idea, plan)* tiré(e) par les cheveux
far-flung ['fɑːflʌŋ] *adj* lointain(e)
farm [fɑːm] **1** *n* ferme *f*; **f. animals** animaux *mpl* de ferme; **f. labourer** ouvrier *m* agricole **2** *vt (land)* cultiver, exploiter **3** *vi* être cultivateur(trice)
▶**farm out** *vt sep (work)* confier en sous-traitance (to à); *(child)* confier (to à)
farmer ['fɑːmə(r)] *n* fermier(ère) *m,f*, agriculteur(trice) *m,f*; **farmers' market** *m* fermier
farmhouse ['fɑːmhaʊs] *n* (corps *m* de) ferme *f*
farming ['fɑːmɪŋ] *n (business)* agriculture *f*
farmland ['fɑːmlænd] *n* terres *fpl* arables
farmyard ['fɑːmjɑːd] *n* cour *f* de ferme
Faroe ['feərəʊ] *n* the F. Islands, the Faroes les îles *fpl* Féroé
far-off ['fɑːrɒf] *adj (country, time)* lointain(e); *(place)* éloigné(e)
far-out ['fɑːraʊt] *adj Fam (strange)* farfelu(e); *Old-fashioned* f.! *(fantastic)* génial!
far-reaching ['fɑːˈriːtʃɪŋ] *adj (decision, change)* de grande envergure; *(consequences)* d'une grande portée
Farsi ['fɑːsiː] *n* farsi *m*
far-sighted ['fɑːsaɪtɪd] *adj* (**a**) *(forward-looking) (person)* prévoyant(e); *(decision)* avisé(e) (**b**) *Am (longsighted)* presbyte
fart [fɑːt] *Fam* **1** *n* pet *m* **2** *vi* péter
▶**fart about, fart around** *vi Fam (waste time)* glander
farther ['fɑːðə(r)] *comparative of* far
farthest ['fɑːðɪst] *superlative of* far
farthing ['fɑːðɪŋ] *n Br Hist* quart *m* de penny; *Fam* hasn't got a (brass) f. il n'a pas le sou
fascinate ['fæsɪneɪt] *vt* fasciner
fascinating ['fæsɪneɪtɪŋ] *adj* fascinant(e)
fascination [fæsɪ'neɪʃən] *n* fascination *f*
fascism ['fæʃɪzəm] *n* fascisme *m*
fascist ['fæʃɪst] **1** *n* fasciste *mf* **2** *adj* fasciste
fashion ['fæʃən] **1** *n* (**a**) *(in clothes)* mode *f*; in f. à la mode; out of f. démodé(e), passé(e) de mode; **f. designer** styliste *mf*; *(big name)* couturier(ère) *m,f*; **f. house** maison *f* de couture; **f. plate** gravure *f* de mode; *Fig* élégant(e) *m,f*; **f. show** défilé *m* de mode; *Pej* **f. victim** esclave *mf* de la mode (**b**) *(manner)* manière *f*; **after a f.** tant bien que mal **2** *vt (form)* façonner; *(make)* confectionner
fashionable ['fæʃənəbəl] *adj* à la mode
fashionista [fæʃə'niːstə] *n* modeux(euse) *m,f*
fast¹ [fɑːst] **1** *adj* (**a**) *(rapid)* rapide; *Fam* he pulled a f. one on me il m'a joué un mauvais tour; **f. food** restauration *f* rapide; **f. food restaurant** fast-food *m*; the f.

lane *(of motorway)* la voie rapide; *Fig* **to live life in the f. lane** vivre à cent à l'heure (**b**) *(clock, watch)* **my watch is (five minutes) f.** ma montre avance (de cinq minutes) (**c**) *(secure) (grip)* ferme, solide; *(door, lid)* bien fermé(e); *(colour)* résistant(e)

   2 *adv* (**a**) *(rapidly)* vite, rapidement; **not so f.!** pas si vite!; **to play f. and loose with the facts** truquer les faits; **to play f. and loose with sb's emotions** jouer avec les sentiments de qn (**b**) *(securely)* solidement; **to hold f.** tenir bon; **f. asleep** profondément endormi(e)

fast² **1** *n (lack of food)* jeûne *m*; *Rel* **f. day** jour *m* de jeûne

   2 *vi* jeûner; *Med* être à la diète

fasten ['fɑːsən] **1** *vt (door, window)* fermer; *(belt, buttons)* attacher; *Fig* **to f. one's eyes on sth** fixer son regard sur qch

   2 *vi (garment)* s'attacher

fastener ['fɑːsənə(r)] *n (of garment) (hook)* agrafe *f*; *(press stud)* bouton-pression *m*; *(of bag, jewellery)* fermoir *m*

fast-forward [fɑːst'fɔːwəd] **1** *n* avance *f* rapide

   2 *vt (cassette)* mettre en avance rapide

fastidious [fæ'stɪdɪəs] *adj* difficile; *(about manners, hygiene, details)* pointilleux(euse) (**about** sur)

fast-moving ['fɑːst'muːvɪŋ] *adj* rapide

fat [fæt] **1** *n* (**a**) *(flesh)* graisse *f*; *(of cooked meat)* gras *m*; *(for cooking)* matière *f* grasse; **f. content** teneur *f* en graisse ou en lipides (**b**) *(idioms)* Fam **the f.'s in the fire!** ça va chauffer!; **to live off the f. of the land** vivre comme un coq en pâte; **to chew the f.** (**with sb**) tailler le bout de gras (avec qn)

   2 *adj (person)* gros (grosse); *Fam (cheque, profit, salary)* gros (grosse); **to get f.** grossir; *Fig* **to grow f. at the expense of others** *(become rich)* s'engraisser aux dépens des autres; *Fam* **a f. lot of good that'll do you!** ça te fera une belle jambe!; *Fig* **f. cat** = personne touchant un salaire extrêmement élevé de façon injustifiée; *Fam* **f. chance!** tu parles!

fatal ['feɪtəl] *adj* mortel(elle)

fatalistic [feɪtə'lɪstɪk] *adj* fataliste

fatality [fə'tælɪtɪ] *(pl* **fatalities**) *n* (**a**) *(person killed)* mort *m* (**b**) *(fate)* fatalité *f*

fatally ['feɪtəlɪ] *adv (wounded)* mortellement; **f. ill** condamné(e); **to be f. damaging to sth** causer un tort irréparable à qch

fate [feɪt] *n* destin *m*, sort *m*; **to suffer** *or* **share the same f.** avoir le même sort; **it's a f. worse than death** c'est ce qu'on peut imaginer de pire

fated ['feɪtɪd] *adj* **to be f. to do sth** être destiné(e) à faire qch

fateful ['feɪtfʊl] *adj (words, day)* fatidique

father ['fɑːðə(r)] **1** *n (parent, priest)* père *m*; **from f. to son** de père en fils; **he was like a f. to me** il était comme un père pour moi; **like f., like son** tel père, tel fils; **Our F.** *(God)* Notre Père; **F. Christmas** le Père Noël; **F.'s Day** la fête des pères; **to be a f. figure to sb** jouer le rôle du père pour qn

   2 *vt (child)* engendrer

fatherhood ['fɑːðəhʊd] *n* paternité *f*

father-in-law ['fɑːðərɪnlɔː] *n* beau-père *m*

fatherly ['fɑːðəlɪ] *adj* paternel(elle)

fathom ['fæðəm] **1** *n (unit of measurement)* = 1,8 m, brasse *f*

   2 *vt (understand)* comprendre

▸**fathom out** *vt sep (understand)* comprendre

fatigue [fə'tiːg] **1** *n* (**a**) *(tiredness)* fatigue *f*; **metal f.** fatigue *f* des métaux (**b**) *Mil* **f. (duty)** corvée *f*; **fatigues** *(clothes)* treillis *m*

   2 *vt (person)* fatiguer

fatso ['fætsəʊ] *(pl* **fatsos** *or* fatsoes) *n Fam (man)* gros lard *m*; *(woman)* grosse vache *f*

▸**fatten up** ['fætən] *vt sep* faire grossir, engraisser

fatty ['fætɪ] **1** *n (pl* **fatties**) *Fam* gros (grosse) *m,f*; **hey f.!** eh, bouboule!

   2 *adj (food, meat)* gras (grasse); *(tissue)* adipeux(-euse); **f. acid** acide *m* gras

fatuous ['fætjʊəs] *adj* idiot(e)

faucet ['fɔːsɪt] *n Am* robinet *m*

fault [fɔːlt] **1** *n* (**a**) *(flaw)* défaut *m*; *(in mechanism, on phone line)* problème *m*; **to find f. with** trouver à redire à; **to be generous to a f.** être généreux(euse) à l'excès (**b**) *(guilt)* faute *f*; **to be at f.** être en faute; **whose f. is it?** à qui la faute?; **it's my f.** c'est (de) ma faute; **through no f. of mine** sans que ce soit de ma faute (**c**) *(in tennis, squash)* faute *f* (**d**) *(geological)* faille *f*

   2 *vt (person)* prendre en défaut; *(logic)* trouver une faille dans; **her attitude can't be faulted** il n'y a rien à redire à sa conduite

faultless ['fɔːltlɪs] *adj* impeccable

faulty ['fɔːltɪ] *adj* défectueux(euse)

faun [fɔːn] *n* faune *m*

fauna ['fɔːnə] *n* faune *f*

favor, favorable *etc Am* = **favour, favourable** *etc*

favour, *Am* **favor** ['feɪvə(r)] **1** *n* (**a**) *(approval)* **to be in/out of f.** *(of person)* être bien/mal vu(e); *(of method)* être/ne plus être en faveur; **to look on sb/sth with f.** être bien disposé(e) envers qn/qch; **to find f. with sb** trouver grâce aux yeux de qn (**b**) *(act of kindness)* service *m*; **to do sb a f.** rendre service à qn; *Fam* **do me a f. and shut up!** ferme-la, tu veux!; **to ask sb a f.,** **to ask a f. of sb** demander un service à qn (**c**) *(advantage)* **that's a point in her f.** c'est un élément en sa faveur; *Fin* **balance in your f.** solde *m* en votre faveur (**d**) **in f. of** *(in preference to)* en faveur de; **to be in f. of sth** être partisan(e) de qch/être favorable à qch

   2 *vt* (**a**) *(prefer)* être pour, être partisan(e) de; **to f. sb** *(be biased towards)* favoriser qn (**b**) *(honour)* **to f. sb with sth** gratifier qn de qch

favourable, *Am* **favorable** ['feɪvərəbəl] *adj* favorable; *(terms)* avantageux(euse); **f. light** sous un jour favorable

favourite, *Am* **favorite** ['feɪvərɪt] **1** *n* favori(ite) *m,f*, préféré(e) *m,f*; *(in betting)* favori(ite)

   2 *adj* favori(ite), préféré(e)

favouritism, *Am* **favoritism** ['feɪvərɪtɪzəm] *n* favoritisme *m*

fawn¹ [fɔːn] **1** *n* (**a**) *(deer)* faon *m* (**b**) *(colour)* fauve *m*

   2 *adj (colour)* fauve

fawn² *vi* **to f. on sb** *(of person)* ramper devant qn; *(of dog)* faire fête à qn

fax [fæks] **1** *n (machine)* fax *m*, *Offic* télécopieur *m*; *(message)* fax *m*, *Offic* télécopie *f*; **f. modem** modem-fax *m*; **f. number** numéro *m* de fax

   2 *vt (message, document)* faxer, envoyer par fax; *(person)* envoyer un fax à

faze [feɪz] *vt Fam* déconcerter

FBI [efbiː'aɪ] *n Am (abbr* **Federal Bureau of Investigation)** FBI *m*

fear [fɪə(r)] **1** *n* peur *f*; *(worry)* crainte *f*; **to be** *or* **go in f. of** avoir peur de, redouter; **to go in f. of one's life**

craindre pour sa vie; *Fam* **to put the f.** of God into sb faire une peur bleue à qn; **he didn't tell her for f.** of her reaction il ne lui a rien dit par peur de sa réaction; **for f.** of doing sth de peur de faire qch; **I didn't tell him, for f.** that he'd be angry je ne lui ai rien dit, de peur qu'il ne se mette en colère; *Fam* **no f.!** pas de danger!
 2 *vt* craindre, redouter; **I f. there's been a misunderstanding** je crains qu'il (n')y ait eu un malentendu; **I f. so/not** je crains que oui/non; **to f. the worst** craindre le pire
 3 *vi* **to f. for** craindre pour; **never f.!** ne crains rien!
fearful ['fɪəfʊl] *adj* (**a**) *(pain, consequence, noise)* épouvantable (**b**) *(person)* apeuré(e); **to be f.** of doing sth avoir peur de faire qch
fearless ['fɪəlɪs] *adj* intrépide
fearlessly ['fɪəlɪslɪ] *adv* avec intrépidité
fearsome ['fɪəsəm] *adj* effrayant(e)
feasibility [fiːzə'bɪlɪtɪ] *n* possibilité *f*; *(of plan)* faisabilité *f*; **f. study** étude *f* de faisabilité
feasible ['fiːzəbəl] *adj* faisable
feast [fiːst] **1** *n* festin *m*, banquet *m*; *Rel* **f. day** (jour *m* de) fête *f*
 2 *vt* **to f. one's eyes on sth** repaître ses yeux de qch
 3 *vi* **to f. on** se régaler de
feat [fiːt] *n* exploit *m*; **a f. of skill** un tour de force
feather ['feðə(r)] **1** *n* plume *f*; **you could have knocked me down with a f.** je n'en revenais pas; *Fig* **that's a f. in her cap** elle peut en être fière; **f. bed** lit *m* de plumes
 2 *vt Fig* **to f. one's nest** faire son beurre
featherweight ['feðəweɪt] *n* (*in boxing*) poids *m* plume
feathery ['feðərɪ] *adj* doux (douce) et léger(ère) comme de la plume
feature ['fiːtʃə(r)] **1** *n* (**a**) *(of face)* trait *m* (**b**) *(characteristic)* caractéristique *f* (**c**) **f.** (**film**) long métrage *m* (**d**) *(in newspaper)* article *m* de fond; *(on television, radio)* reportage *m*; **f. writer** éditorialiste *mf*
 2 *vt (of magazine, exhibition)* présenter; **a film featuring...** un film ayant pour vedette...
 3 *vi (appear)* figurer
featureless ['fiːtʃəlɪs] *adj* sans caractéristiques marquées
Feb (*abbr* **February**) février
febrile ['fiːbraɪl] *adj* fébrile
February ['febrʊərɪ] *n* février *m*; *see also* **May**
feckless ['feklɪs] *adj* (**a**) *(irresponsible)* irresponsable (**b**) *(ineffectual)* incapable
Fed [fed] *n Am* (**a**) (*abbr* **Federal Reserve Board**) banque *f* centrale (des États-Unis) (**b**) (*abbr* **Federal Reserve (System)**) (système *m* de) Réserve *f* fédérale
fed [fed] *pt & pp of* **feed**
federal ['fedərəl] *adj* fédéral(e)
federalism ['fedərəlɪzəm] *n* fédéralisme *m*
federalist ['fedərəlɪst] **1** *n* fédéraliste *mf*
 2 *adj* fédéraliste
federation [fedə'reɪʃən] *n* fédération *f*
fed up [fed'ʌp] *adj Fam* **to be f. (with)** en avoir ras le bol (de), en avoir marre (de)
fee [fiː] *n (of lawyer, doctor)* honoraires *mpl*; *(for entrance)* droit *m* d'entrée; *(for membership)* cotisation *f*; **school fees** droits *mpl* d'inscription; **a f.-paying school** une école privée
feeble ['fiːbəl] *adj* faible; *(attempt)* peu convaincant(e)
feeble-minded ['fiːbəl'maɪndɪd] *adj* faible d'esprit

feebly ['fiːblɪ] *adv* faiblement; *(protest, reprimand)* mollement
feed [fiːd] **1** *n* (**a**) *(animal food)* nourriture *f* (**b**) *(for baby) (from breast)* tétée *f*; *(from bottle)* biberon *m*
 2 *vt* (*pt & pp* **fed** [fed]) (**a**) *(give food to)* donner à manger à; *(baby) (from breast)* donner la tétée à; *(from bottle)* donner son biberon à; *(plant)* mettre de l'engrais à; **we were well fed** nous étions bien nourris; **to f. one's family** nourrir sa famille (**b**) *(supply)* **to f. a fire** alimenter un feu; **to f. coins into a machine** mettre des pièces dans une machine; **to f. sb with information** fournir des informations à qn
 3 *vi (survive)* **to f. on** se nourrir de
feedback ['fiːdbæk] *n Elec* effet *m* Larsen; *Fig (response)* écho *m*, réactions *fpl*
feel [fiːl] **1** *n* (**a**) *(sensation)* toucher *m*; **the f. of silk against her skin** le contact de la soie contre sa peau; **the film has an authentic f. to it** le film dégage une impression d'authenticité
 (**b**) *(knack)* **to have a f. for translation/music** avoir un sens inné de la traduction/musique; **to get the f. of sth** s'habituer à qch
 2 *vt* (*pt & pp* **felt** [felt]) (**a**) *(touch)* toucher; *(investigate)* tâter; **to f. one's way** *(in darkness)* avancer à tâtons; *Fig (in new situation)* essayer de s'habituer (**b**) *(be physically aware of)* sentir; **I felt the floor tremble or trembling** j'ai senti le sol trembler (**c**) *(experience) (relief, pain, despair)* ressentir; **I f. it in my bones** *(have intuition)* je le sens (**d**) *(believe)* **to f. (that)...** penser que...
 3 *vi* (**a**) *(physically)* **to f. tired** se sentir fatigué(e); **to f. ill** ne se sentir bien; **to f. hot/cold/hungry/thirsty** avoir chaud/froid/faim/soif; **my foot feels better** j'ai moins mal au pied; **how are you feeling?** comment ça va *ou* te sens-tu?; **I don't f. myself** je ne suis pas dans mon assiette; **to f. up to doing sth** *(well enough)* se sentir assez bien pour faire qch; *(competent enough)* se sentir de taille à faire qch; **to f. (like) a new man/woman** se sentir comme neuf/neuve
 (**b**) *(emotionally)* se sentir; **to f. strongly about sth** avoir des idées très arrêtées sur qch; **I f. bad about leaving her** cela m'ennuie de la quitter; **how would you f. if...?** comment est-ce que tu te sentirais si...?; **it feels strange** c'est étrange; **I felt as if I'd seen him before** j'avais l'impression de l'avoir déjà vu; **to f. like doing sth** avoir envie de faire qch; **I f. like a cup of tea** *(would like)* j'ai envie d'une tasse de thé
 (**c**) *(have sympathy)* **to f. for sb** plaindre qn
 (**d**) *(of things)* **to f. hard/hot** être dur(e)/chaud(e); **it feels like (it's going to) rain** on dirait qu'il va pleuvoir (**e**) *(search)* **to f. in one's pockets for sth** chercher qch dans ses poches; **he felt on the ground for the key** il chercha sa clé à tâtons sur le sol
feeler ['fiːlə(r)] *n (of insect)* antenne *f*; *(of snail)* corne *f*; *Fig* **to put out feelers** tâter le terrain
feelgood ['fiːlgʊd] *adj Fam* **a f. film** un film qui donne la pêche; **the f. factor** l'optimisme *m* ambiant
feeling ['fiːlɪŋ] *n* (**a**) *(sense of)* **f.** toucher *m*; **to have no f. in one's arm** avoir le bras mort (**b**) *(sensation) (of cold, pain)* sensation *f* (**c**) *(emotion, impression)* sentiment *m*; **a f. of joy/anger** de la joie/colère; **to speak with f.** *(emotionally)* parler avec émotion; *(warmly)* parler avec chaleur; **I know the f.!** je sais ce que c'est!; **I had a f. I might find you here** je

pensais bien vous trouver ici; **to hurt sb's feelings** blesser qn; **to have no feelings** n'avoir aucun cœur; **feelings were running high** les esprits étaient très échauffés; **no hard feelings!** sans rancune! (**d**) *(sensitivity)* sensibilité *f*; **to have a f. for sth** *(music, art)* être sensible à qch
feet [fiːt] *pl of* **foot**
feign [feɪn] *vt (anger, surprise)* feindre; **to f. illness/ sleep** feindre d'être malade/de dormir
feint [feɪnt] **1** *n (in combat sports)* feinte *f*
  2 *vi (in combat sports)* faire une feinte
feisty ['faɪstɪ] *adj (lively)* plein(e) d'entrain; *(combative)* qui a du cran
felicitous [fɪ'lɪsɪtəs] *adj* heureux(euse)
feline ['fiːlaɪn] **1** *n* félin *m*
  2 *adj* félin(e)
fell¹ [fel] *pt of* **fall**
fell² *vt (tree)* abattre, couper; *(opponent)* terrasser
fell³ *adj* **at one f. swoop** d'un seul coup
fell⁴ *n (hill)* colline *f*
fellow ['feləʊ] *n* (**a**) *(comrade)* camarade *mf*; **f. citizen** concitoyen(enne) *m,f*; **f. countryman/country-woman** compatriote *mf*; **f. passenger** compagnon (compagne) *m,f* de voyage; **f. worker** collègue *mf*; **f. student** camarade *mf* d'études; **f. feeling** sympathie *f*; *Fig* **f. traveller** *(in politics)* compagnon (compagne) *mf* de route (**b**) *(teacher)* professeur *m* titulaire; *(student)* boursier(ère) *m,f*; *(of academy, society)* membre *m* (**c**) *Fam (man)* gars *m*
fellowship ['feləʊʃɪp] *n* (**a**) *(friendship)* camaraderie *f* (**b**) *(association)* association *f*, corporation *f* (**c**) *(at university)* bourse *f* de recherche
felon ['felən] *n Law* criminel(elle) *m,f*
felony ['felənɪ] *(pl* **felonies***) n Law* crime *m*
felt¹ [felt] *n (fabric)* feutre *m*; *(thinner)* feutrine *f*
felt² *pt & pp of* **feel**
felt-tip ['felt'tɪp] *n* **f. (pen)** *(crayon m)* feutre *m*
female ['fiːmeɪl] **1** *n (person)* femme *f*; *(animal, plant)* femelle *f*
  2 *adj (person)* féminin(e); *(animal, plant)* femelle
feminine ['femɪnɪn] **1** *n Gram* féminin *m*; **in the f.** au féminin
  2 *adj* féminin(e)
femininity [femɪ'nɪnɪtɪ] *n* féminité *f*
feminism ['femɪnɪzəm] *n* féminisme *m*
feminist ['femɪnɪst] **1** *n* féministe *mf*
  2 *adj* féministe
femur ['fiːmə(r)] *n Anat* fémur *m*
fen [fen] *n (marshy land)* marais *m*; **the Fens** = plaines marécageuses à l'est de l'Angleterre
fence [fens] **1** *n* (**a**) *(barrier)* clôture *f*; *(more solid)* barrière *f*; *Fig* **to sit on the f.** ménager la chèvre et le chou; *Fig* **to get off the f.** se prononcer (**b**) *Fam (receiver of stolen property)* receleur(euse) *m,f*
  2 *vi (as sport)* faire de l'escrime
▶**fence off** *vt sep* séparer par une clôture
fencing ['fensɪŋ] *n (sport)* escrime *f*
fend [fend] *vi* **to f. for oneself** se débrouiller (tout(e) seul(e))
▶**fend off** *vt sep (attack, blow)* parer; *(question)* éluder
fender ['fendə(r)] *n* (**a**) *Am (of car)* aile *f* (**b**) *(for fireplace)* garde-feu *m inv*
fennel ['fenəl] *n* fenouil *m*
ferment 1 *n* ['fɜːment] *(commotion)* agitation *f*; **in a (state of) f.** en effervescence
  2 *vi* [fə'ment] *(of alcoholic drink)* fermenter
fermentation [fɜːmen'teɪʃən] *n* fermentation *f*

fern [fɜːn] *n* fougère *f*
ferocious [fə'rəʊʃəs] *adj* féroce
ferocity [fə'rɒsɪtɪ] *n* férocité *f*
ferret ['ferɪt] **1** *n* furet *m*
  2 *vi* **to f. (about) for sth** fouiller à la recherche de qch
▶**ferret out** *vt sep (object, information)* dénicher
ferris wheel ['ferɪs'wiːl] *n* grande roue *f*
ferrous ['ferəs] *adj* ferreux(euse)
ferry ['ferɪ] **1** *n (pl* **ferries***)* bac *m*; *(larger)* ferry *m*
  2 *vt (pt & pp* **ferried***)* transporter
  3 *vi* **to f. back and forth** faire la navette
ferryman ['ferɪmən] *n* passeur *m*
fertile ['fɜːtaɪl] *adj also Fig* fertile
fertility [fɜː'tɪlɪtɪ] *n also Fig* fertilité *f*; **f. treatment** traitement *m* de la stérilité
fertilize ['fɜːtɪlaɪz] *vt (egg, plant)* féconder; *(soil)* fertiliser
fertilizer ['fɜːtɪlaɪzə(r)] *n* engrais *m*
fervent ['fɜːvənt] *adj (admirer, nationalist)* fervent(e); *(belief, desire)* ardent(e)
fervour, *Am* **fervor** ['fɜːvə(r)] *n* ferveur *f*
fester ['festə(r)] *vi (of wound)* s'infecter; *Fig (of situation)* s'envenimer; *(of dislike, resentment)* s'aviver
festival ['festɪvəl] *n* festival *m*; *(religious)* fête *f*
festive ['festɪv] *adj* de fête; **in f. mood** d'humeur festive; **the f. season** *(Christmas)* les fêtes *fpl* (de fin d'année)
festivity [fes'tɪvɪtɪ] *(pl* **festivities***) n (merriness)* gaieté *f*; **the festivities** *(celebrations)* les festivités *fpl*
festoon [fes'tuːn] *vt* orner (**with** de)
fetal *Am* = **foetal**
fetch [fetʃ] *vt* (**a**) *(bring)* aller chercher (**b**) *(be sold for)* rapporter
▶**fetch up** *vi (end up) (of people)* se retrouver
fetching ['fetʃɪŋ] *adj (person, hat, smile)* ravissant(e)
fête [feɪt] **1** *n* fête *f*
  2 *vt* fêter

Fête
En Grande-Bretagne, les "village fêtes" sont des manifestations en plein air où l'on vend des produits faits maison et où l'on organise des manifestations sportives et des jeux pour enfants ; elles sont généralement destinées à réunir des fonds pour une œuvre de charité.

fetid ['fetɪd] *adj* fétide
fetish ['fetɪʃ] *n (object)* fétiche *m*; **to have a f. for sth** faire une fixation sur qch
fetter ['fetə(r)] **1** *n* **fetters** *(on slave, prisoner)* fers *mpl*; *Fig (on rights, freedom)* entraves *fpl*
  2 *vt (slave, prisoner)* enchaîner; *Fig (union, women)* entraver la liberté de
fettle ['fetəl] *n* **in good** *or* **fine f.** en condition
fetus *Am* = **foetus**
feud [fjuːd] **1** *n* querelle *f*
  2 *vi* se quereller (**with** avec)
feudal ['fjuːdəl] *adj* féodal(e); *Fig (approach, attitude)* moyenâgeux(euse)
feudalism ['fjuːdəlɪzəm] *n* le système féodal
fever ['fiːvə(r)] *n also Fig* fièvre *f*; **to have a f.** avoir de la fièvre; **excitement had risen to f. pitch** l'excitation était à son comble
feverish ['fiːvərɪʃ] *adj* fiévreux(euse); *Fig (atmosphere)* de fièvre

few [fjuː] **1** adj (**a**) (not many) peu de; **f. friends** peu d'amis; **too f. people/opportunities** trop peu de gens/d'occasions; **f. and far between** rarissime; **every f. minutes** toutes les deux ou trois minutes; **as f. as a dozen finished the race** seuls une douzaine d'entre eux ont terminé la course (**b**) (some) **a f.** quelques; **a f. friends** quelques amis; **a good f., quite a f.** pas mal de; **in the next f. days** dans les jours qui suivent/suivirent **2** pron (**a**) (not many) peu; **there are too f. of us** nous sommes trop peu nombreux; **f. of them** peu d'entre eux; **f., if any children** aucun enfant ou presque (**b**) (some) **a f.** quelques-uns (quelques-unes) mpl,fpl; **a f. of the survivors** quelques-uns des survivants; **a f. of them** quelques-uns d'entre eux **3** n **the f. who came** les rares personnes qui sont venues

fewer ['fjuːə(r)] (comparative of few) **1** adj moins de; **f. friends** moins d'amis; **no f. than thirty** pas moins de trente; **the houses became f.** les maisons devenaient plus rares; **f. and f. people** de moins en moins de gens **2** pron moins; **there are f. (of them) than I thought** il y en a moins que je ne pensais

fewest ['fjuːɪst] (superlative of few) **1** adj le moins de **2** pron le moins

fiasco [fɪ'æskəʊ] (pl fiascos) n fiasco m

fib [fɪb] Fam **1** n bobard m **2** vi (pt & pp fibbed) raconter des bobards

fibber ['fɪbə(r)] n Fam menteur(euse) m,f

fibre, Am **fiber** ['faɪbə(r)] n fibre f; (in diet) fibres fpl; **f. optics** technologie f des fibres optiques

fibreglass, Am **fiberglass** ['faɪbəɡlɑːs] n fibre f de verre

fibrous ['faɪbrəs] adj fibreux(euse)

fickle ['fɪkəl] adj (friend, fan) inconstant(e); (lover) inconstant, volage; (weather) changeant(e)

fiction ['fɪkʃən] n (genre) fiction f; (books) livres mpl de fiction; (lie) invention f

fictional ['fɪkʃənəl] adj fictif(ive)

fictitious [fɪk'tɪʃəs] adj fictif(ive)

fiddle ['fɪdəl] **1** n (**a**) (violin) violon m (**b**) Br Fam (swindle) combine f; **to be on the f.** traficoter **2** vt Br Fam (cheat) combiner; **to f. the accounts** truquer les comptes **3** vi (**a**) (play violin) jouer du violon (**b**) (fidget) **to f. (about or around) with sth** tripoter qch

fiddler ['fɪdlə(r)] n violoniste mf

fiddlesticks ['fɪdəlstɪks] exclam Old-fashioned (nonsense) balivernes fpl!; (expressing annoyance) zut de zut!

fiddly ['fɪdlɪ] adj Fam minutieux(euse)

fidelity [fɪ'delɪtɪ] n fidélité f

fidget ['fɪdʒɪt] **1** n **to be a f.** ne pas tenir en place **2** vi gigoter; **stop fidgeting!** arrête de gigoter!

fidgety ['fɪdʒɪtɪ] adj agité(e)

field [fiːld] **1** n (**a**) (of farm) & Comput champ m; (for sport) terrain m; (of oil, coal) gisement m; **to work in the f.** (not in office) travailler sur le terrain; **f. of vision** champ visuel; **f. events** (in athletics) le saut et le lancer; Am **f. hockey** hockey m sur gazon; **f. study** étude f sur le terrain; Sch & Univ **f. trip** voyage m d'étude; **f. work** (scientific) recherches fpl sur le terrain (**b**) Mil **in the f.** en campagne; Fig **to have a f. day** s'en donner à cœur joie; **f. glasses** jumelles fpl; **f. gun** canon m (de campagne); **f. hospital** antenne f chirurgicale; **f. marshal** ≃ maréchal m de France (**c**) (of knowledge)

domaine m (**d**) (in race, contest) partants mpl; **to lead the f.** Sport mener le peloton; Fig occuper la première place **2** vt (**a**) (team) composer; (candidates) présenter (**b**) (question) répondre à

fieldmouse ['fiːldmaʊs] (pl fieldmice ['fiːldmaɪs]) n mulot m

fiend [fiːnd] n (cruel person) monstre m; (demon) démon m; **sex f.** obsédé(e) m,f sexuel(elle); **jazz f.** fanatique mf de jazz

fiendish ['fiːndɪʃ] adj (scheme, question) diabolique; (weather, temper) abominable

fiendishly ['fiːndɪʃlɪ] adv (difficult) horriblement

fierce ['fɪəs] adj (animal, look) féroce; (appearance, person) redoutable; (wind, storm, criticism) violent(e); (contest) acharné(e)

fiercely ['fɪəslɪ] adv (look) d'un œil féroce; (fight) avec acharnement; (criticize) violemment

fiery ['faɪərɪ] adj (red) ardent(e); (sky) enflammé(e); (food) très épicé(e); (person, temper) fougueux(euse)

FIFA ['fiːfə] n (abbr **Fédération Internationale de Football Association**) FIFA f

fifteen [fɪf'tiːn] **1** n (**a**) (number) quinze m inv (**b**) Sport (rugby team) quinze m **2** adj quinze; see also **eight**

fifteenth [fɪf'tiːnθ] **1** n (**a**) (fraction) quinzième m (**b**) (in series) quinzième mf (**c**) (of month) quinze m inv **2** adj quinzième; see also **eighth**

fifth [fɪfθ] **1** n (**a**) (fraction) cinquième m (**c**) (of month) cinq m inv (**b**) (in series) cinquième mf **2** adj cinquième; Pol **f. column** cinquième colonne f; Am Fig **to be the f. wheel** tenir la chandelle; see also **eighth**

fiftieth ['fɪftɪəθ] **1** n (**a**) (fraction) cinquantième m (**b**) (in series) cinquantième mf **2** adj cinquantième

fifty ['fɪftɪ] **1** n cinquante m inv **2** adj cinquante; see also **eighty**

fig¹ [fɪɡ] n (fruit) figue f; Fam **she doesn't give** or **care a f.** elle s'en fiche éperdument; **f. leaf** feuille f de figuier; (in paintings) feuille f de vigne; Fig **it's just a f. leaf** ce n'est qu'une couverture; **f. tree** figuier m

fig² (abbr **figure**) fig

fight [faɪt] **1** n (**a**) (physical) bagarre f; (verbal) dispute f; (boxing match) combat m; **to get into a f. with sb** (physical) se battre avec qn; (verbal) se disputer avec qn; **to start a f. (with sb)** provoquer une bagarre (avec qn); **to put up a good f.** bien se défendre (**b**) (spirit) **to show some f.** résister; **there was no f. left in him** il n'avait plus le cœur à se battre (**c**) (struggle) lutte f (**for/against** pour/contre) **2** vt (pt & pp fought [fɔːt]) (person) se battre contre; (decision, enemy) combattre; (disease, fire, temptation) lutter contre; (election) participer à; **to f. a war** être en guerre; Law **to f. a case** (of lawyer) défendre une cause; (of defendant) être en procès; Fig **I'm not going to f. your battles for you** c'est à vous de vous débrouiller; **to f. one's way through a crowd** se frayer un chemin à travers une foule **3** vi (**a**) (physically) se battre (**against** contre); (verbally) se disputer; **to f. shy of doing sth** éviter à tout prix de faire qch (**b**) (struggle) lutter (**for/against** pour/contre); **to f. for breath** suffoquer
► **fight back 1** vt sep (tears) retenir; (anger) réprimer **2** vi (retaliate) se défendre

▸**fight off** *vt sep (attacker)* repousser; *(illness)* combattre

▸**fight out** *vt sep* **f. it out amongst yourselves** réglez ça entre vous

fighter ['faɪtə(r)] *n (in fight)* combattant(e) *m,f; (for cause)* lutteur(euse) *m,f;* **she's a real f.** *(determined)* c'est une battante; **f. (plane)** avion *m* de chasse; **f. squadron/pilot** escadron *m*/pilote *m* de chasse

fighting ['faɪtɪŋ] **1** *n (scuffles)* bagarres *fpl; Mil* combat *m*
2 *adj* **to have a f. chance** avoir encore de bonnes chances; **to be f. fit** être dans une forme éblouissante

figment ['fɪgmənt] *n* **it's a f. of your imagination** c'est le fruit de ton imagination

figurative ['fɪgərətɪv] *adj (sense)* figuré(e); *(art)* figuratif(ive)

figuratively ['fɪgərətɪvlɪ] *adv* **f. speaking** métaphoriquement parlant

figure ['fɪgə(r)] **1** *n* (**a**) *(number)* chiffre *m;* **to be good at figures** être bon (bonne) en calcul; **to reach double figures** *(of score)* atteindre la dizaine; *(of inflation, unemployment)* dépasser la barre des dix pour cent (**b**) *(body shape)* silhouette *f;* **to have a good f.** *(of woman)* avoir une jolie silhouette; **a fine f. of a man** un bel homme; **to cut a sorry f.** avoir l'air pitoyable (**c**) *(person, character)* personnage *m;* **a distinguished f.** une personnalité (**d**) *(illustration, geometric shape)* figure *f* (**e**) *(expression)* **f. of speech** figure *f* de rhétorique; **it's just a f. of speech** c'est une façon de parler
2 *vt* **to f. (that)...** *(think)* penser que...; *(estimate)* supposer que...
3 *vi* (**a**) *(appear) (in list, book)* figurer (**b**) *Fam (make sense)* **that figures!** ça se tient!

▸**figure on** *vt insep* **to f. on doing sth** compter faire qch

▸**figure out** *vt sep (amount)* calculer; *(solution)* trouver; *(problem, person)* arriver à comprendre

figurehead ['fɪgəhed] *n (on ship)* figure *f* de proue; *Fig (of country, party)* représentant(e) *m,f* nominal(e), *Pej* homme *m* de paille

Fiji ['fiːdʒiː] *n* les (îles *fpl*) Fidji *fpl*

Fijian [fiː'dʒiːən] **1** *n* Fidjien(enne) *m,f*
2 *adj* fidjien(enne)

filament ['fɪləmənt] *n Elec* filament *m*

filch [fɪltʃ] *vt Fam* faucher (**from sb** à qn)

file¹ [faɪl] **1** *n (tool)* lime *f*
2 *vt (metal)* limer; **to f. one's nails** se limer les ongles

file² [faɪl] *n* (**a**) *(folder)* chemise *f; (ring-bound)* classeur *m; (documents)* dossier *m* (**on** sur); **to have sth on f.** avoir qch dans ses dossiers (**b**) *Comput* fichier *m;* **f. manager** gestionnaire *m* de fichiers; **f. server** serveur *m* de fichiers
2 *vt* (**a**) *(documents, letters)* classer (**b**) *(complaint, claim, request)* déposer
3 *vi* **to f. for divorce** demander le divorce

file³ [faɪl] **1** *n (line)* file *f;* **in single f.** en file indienne
2 *vi* **to f. past sb/sth** défiler devant qn/qch; **to f. in/out** entrer/sortir l'un(e) après l'autre

filial ['fɪlɪəl] *adj* filial(e)

filigree ['fɪlɪgriː] *n* filigrane *m*

Filipino [fɪlɪ'piːnəʊ] **1** *n (pl* **Filipinos)** Philippin(e) *m,f*
2 *adj* philippin(e)

fill [fɪl] **1** *n* **to eat one's f.** manger à sa faim; *Fig* **to have had one's f. of sth** en avoir assez de qch
2 *vt* (**a**) *(container)* remplir (**with** de); **to be filled

with admiration/hope être plein(e) d'admiration/ d'espoir; **to have a tooth filled** se faire plomber une dent (**b**) *(occupy) (time)* occuper; **to f. a vacancy** *(of employer)* pourvoir à un poste vacant
3 *vi* se remplir (**with** de)

▸**fill in** **1** *vt sep* (**a**) *(hole)* combler, boucher; *(form)* remplir; **to f. in time** occuper son temps (**b**) *Fam (inform)* **to f. sb in (on sth)** mettre qn au courant (de qch)
2 *vi* **to f. in for sb** remplacer qn

▸**fill out** **1** *vt sep (form, application)* remplir
2 *vi (get fatter)* grossir

▸**fill up** **1** *vt sep (glass)* remplir jusqu'au bord; *Fam* **f. her up!** *(with petrol)* le plein!
2 *vi* (**a**) *(of tank, container)* se remplir (**b**) *(buy petrol)* faire le plein

fillet ['fɪlɪt] **1** *n (of fish, beef)* filet *m;* **f. steak** filet *m* de bœuf
2 *vt (fish)* découper en filets

filling ['fɪlɪŋ] **1** *n* (**a**) *(in tooth)* plombage *m; (in sandwich, pie)* garniture *f* (**b**) **f. station** station-service *f*
2 *adj (food, meal)* bourratif(ive); **it was very f.** cela m'a rassasié

filly ['fɪlɪ] *(pl* **fillies)** *n (horse)* pouliche *f*

film [fɪlm] **1** *n (movie)* film *m; (layer, for camera)* pellicule *f;* **a (roll of) f.** une pellicule, un rouleau de pellicule; **f. actor/actress** acteur *m*/actrice *f* de cinéma; **f. critic** critique *mf* de cinéma; **f. director** réalisateur(trice) *m,f;* **f. festival** festival *m* du cinéma; **the f. industry** l'industrie *f* cinématographique; **f. library** cinémathèque *f;* **f. maker** cinéaste *mf;* **f. script** scénario *m,* script *m;* **f. star** vedette *f* de cinéma, star *f;* **f. studio** studio *m* de cinéma
2 *vt & vi* filmer

Filofax® ['faɪləʊfæks] *n* Filofax® *m*

filter ['fɪltə(r)] **1** *n* filtre *m;* **f. coffee** café *m* filtre; **f. paper** papier *m* filtre; *Aut* **f. lane** voie *f* de dégagement; *Aut* **f. signal** *(on traffic light)* flèche *f* de dégagement
2 *vt* filtrer
3 *vi* (**a**) *(move slowly)* **to f. in/out** entrer/sortir lentement (**b**) *Aut (of traffic)* **to f. to the right/left** dégager à droite/gauche pour tourner

▸**filter out** *vt sep also Fig* éliminer

▸**filter through** **1** *vt insep (of liquid, light)* passer à travers
2 *vi (of information)* filtrer

filth [fɪlθ] *n (dirt)* crasse *f; (in street)* immondices *fpl; (obscene words)* obscénités *fpl;* **it's f.** *(of book, film)* c'est dégoûtant

filthy ['fɪlθɪ] **1** *adj* (**a**) *(very dirty)* dégoûtant(e) (**b**) *(very bad)* **in a f. temper** d'une humeur massacrante; **to give sb a f. look** regarder qn d'un sale œil; *Br* **f. weather** temps *m* de chien (**c**) *(obscene)* obscène
2 *adv Fam* **f. rich** pourri(e) de fric

fin [fɪn] *n (of fish)* nageoire *f; (of aeroplane)* empennage *m; Am (of swimmer)* palme *f*

final ['faɪnəl] **1** *n* (**a**) *(of competition)* **the f.** la finale (**b**) *Univ* **finals** *Br* examens *mpl* de dernière année; *Am* examens *mpl* finaux
2 *adj* (**a**) *(last)* dernier(ère); **f. demand** dernier avis *m;* **f. warning** dernier avertissement *m* (**b**) *(definitive)* final(e); **the umpire's decision is f.** la décision de l'arbitre est sans appel; **and that's f.!** un point, c'est tout!

finale [fɪ'nɑːlɪ] *n* finale *m*

finalist ['faɪnəlɪst] *n* finaliste *mf*

finalize ['faɪnəlaɪz] *vt (details, plans)* mettre au point; *(deal)* conclure
finally ['faɪnəlɪ] *adv* (**a**) *(lastly)* finalement (**b**) *(at last)* enfin; **she had f.** met him elle l'avait enfin rencontré (**c**) *(irrevocably)* définitivement; **it hasn't been f. decided yet** aucune décision définitive n'a encore été prise
finance [faɪ'næns, fɪ'næns] **1** *n* (**a**) *(subject)* finance *f*; **f. company** *or* **house** société *f* financière (**b**) **finances** *(funds)* finances *fpl* **2** *vt* financer
financial [faɪ'nænʃəl, fɪ'nænʃəl] *adj* financier(ère); **it was not a f. success** cela n'a pas rapporté beaucoup d'argent; **f. adviser** conseiller *m* financier; **f. market** marché *m* financier; **f. statement** bilan *m* financier; *Br* **f. year** exercice *m* comptable

Financial year
Pour les impôts sur le revenu en Grande-Bretagne, l'année fiscale commence le 6 avril.

financially [faɪ'nænʃəlɪ, fɪ'nænʃəlɪ] *adv* financièrement
financier [faɪ'nænsɪə(r)] *n* financier *m*
finch [fɪntʃ] *n* fringillidé *m*
find [faɪnd] **1** *n* découverte *f*; **it's quite a f.** c'est une fameuse trouvaille
2 *vt (pt & pp* **found** [faʊnd]) (**a**) *(discover)* trouver; **to try to f. sth** chercher qch; **she was nowhere to be found** elle était introuvable; **I found her waiting in the hall** je l'ai trouvée qui attendait dans le vestibule; **this flower is commonly found in England** on trouve couramment cette fleur en Angleterre; **I found myself back where I'd started** je me suis retrouvé à mon point de départ; **you will f. that I'm right** tu verras que j'ai raison; **I was surprised to f. that…** j'ai découvert avec surprise que…; **he couldn't f. it in his heart to tell her** il n'avait pas le cœur à le lui dire; **to f. one's way** trouver son chemin; **to f. a way to do sth** trouver moyen de faire qch; **to f. oneself** *(spiritually)* se trouver (**b**) *(experience)* trouver; **they will f. it easy/difficult** cela leur sera facile/difficile; **to f. it necessary to do sth** se trouver dans la nécessité de faire qch; **she found it impossible to understand him** elle avait beaucoup de mal à le comprendre; **how did you f. the meal?** le repas vous a-t-il plu?; **I found myself agreeing with her** il s'est trouvé que j'étais d'accord avec elle (**c**) *Law* **to f. sb guilty/not guilty** déclarer qn coupable/non coupable
3 *vi Law* **to f. for/against sb** rendre un verdict en faveur de/contre qn
▸**find out 1** *vt sep* (**a**) *(discover)* découvrir (**b**) *(person)* prendre en défaut
2 *vi* **to f. out about sth** apprendre qch
finder ['faɪndə(r)] *n* **the f. of the money** la personne qui trouva/trouvera l'argent; *Fam* **finders keepers (losers weepers)** celui qui le trouve le garde
findings ['faɪndɪŋz] *npl* conclusions *fpl*; *Law (of jury, court)* verdict *m*
fine¹ [faɪn] **1** *n (penalty)* amende *f*
2 *vt* condamner à une amende; **to f. sb £10** infliger une amende de 10 livres à qn
fine² **1** *adj* (**a**) *(excellent)* excellent(e); *(foods, wine)* fin(e); *(weather)* beau; **to appeal to sb's finer feelings** faire appel aux bons sentiments de qn; **she's a f. woman** c'est une femme admirable; **f. art, the f.**

arts les beaux-arts *mpl*; **she's got it down to a f. art** elle fait ça à la perfection (**b**) *(satisfactory)* bien *inv*; **she's/everything's f.** elle/tout va bien; **that's f. by me** je n'y vois aucune objection (**c**) *Ironic* **you're a f. one to talk!** tu peux bien parler!; **this is another f. mess you've got us into!** tu nous a encore mis dans un beau pétrin! (**d**) *(thin) (hair, rain, line)* fin(e) (**e**) *(subtle) (distinction)* subtil(e); **not to put too f. a point on it** pour parler carrément; **there's a f. line between eccentricity and madness** il n'y a qu'un pas de l'excentricité à la folie
2 *adv* très bien; **they get on f.** ils s'entendent (très) bien
finely ['faɪnlɪ] *adv* (**a**) *(judged)* soigneusement; *(written, painted)* admirablement; *Fig* **f. balanced** équilibré(e) (**b**) *(chopped, ground, grated)* finement
finery ['faɪnərɪ] *n* parure *f*; **she was dressed in all her f.** elle était habillée avec élégance
finesse [fɪ'nes] *n* finesse *f*
finger ['fɪŋɡə(r)] **1** *n* (**a**) *(of hand, glove)* doigt *m*; **to keep one's fingers crossed** croiser les doigts; **f. bowl** rince-doigts *m inv*; **f. food** *(snacks)* amuse-gueule *mpl* (**b**) *(measure)* **a f. of brandy** un doigt de cognac (**c**) *Aviat* passerelle *f* (**d**) *(idioms)* **he's got them (wrapped) round his little f.** il fait d'eux ce qu'il veut; **to have a f. in every pie** être mêlé(e) à tout; **don't you dare lay a f. on him** je vous défends de le toucher; **she never lifts a f.** elle ne lève jamais le petit doigt pour m'aider; **I can't quite put my f. on it** je n'arrive pas à mettre le doigt dessus; **to get one's fingers burnt** se brûler les doigts; *Br very Fam* **get** *or* **pull your f. out!** remue-toi!
2 *vt* (**a**) *(feel)* tâter (**b**) *very Fam (inform on)* balancer
fingernail ['fɪŋɡəneɪl] *n* ongle *m*
fingerprint ['fɪŋɡəprɪnt] *n* empreinte *f* digitale
fingertip ['fɪŋɡətɪp] *n* bout *m* du doigt; **to have sth at one's fingertips** savoir qch sur le bout des doigts
finicky ['fɪnɪkɪ] *adj (person)* tatillon(onne); *(job, device)* compliqué(e)
finish ['fɪnɪʃ] **1** *n* (**a**) *(end) (of day, meeting)* fin *f*; *(of race)* arrivée *f* (**b**) *(surface) (of fabric, leather)* apprêt *m*; **paint with a gloss/matt f.** peinture *f* vernie/mate (**c**) *(workmanship)* finition *f*
2 *vt* (**a**) *(end)* finir, terminer; **to f. doing sth** finir *ou* terminer de faire qch (**b**) *(kill) (person)* achever; *Fam* **he's finished!** il est fini!
3 *vi* finir, se terminer; **to f. fourth** *(in race, contest)* finir *ou* terminer quatrième
▸**finish off 1** *vt sep* (**a**) *(complete, use up)* finir, terminer (**b**) *(kill)* achever; *(ruin) (chances, hopes)* anéantir
2 *vi* finir, terminer
▸**finish up** *vt sep (use up)* finir
2 *vi (end up)* se retrouver; **to f. up doing sth** finir par faire qch
▸**finish with** *vt insep* (**a**) *(stop using)* **to f. with sth** finir de se servir de qch (**b**) *(boyfriend, girlfriend)* laisser tomber
finished ['fɪnɪʃt] *adj* (**a**) *(completed)* fini(e); *(supplies)* épuisé(e) (**b**) *(performance)* soigné(e)
finishing ['fɪnɪʃɪŋ] *adj* **to put the f. touches to sth** mettre la dernière main à qch; **f. line** ligne *f* d'arrivée; **f. school** = école d'arts d'agrément pour les jeunes filles
finite ['faɪnaɪt] *adj* limité(e); *Gram (verb)* conjugué(e)
Finland ['fɪnlənd] *n* la Finlande
Finn [fɪn] *n (person)* Finlandais(e) *m,f*, Finnois(e) *m,f*

Finnish ['fɪnɪʃ] **1** *n (language)* finlandais *m*, finnois *m* **2** *adj* finlandais(e), finnois(e)

fir [fɜː(r)] *n* **f. (tree)** sapin *m*; **f. cone** pomme *f* de pin

fire ['faɪə(r)] **1** *n* (**a**) *(in hearth)* feu *m*; *(large, destructive)* incendie *m*; *(heater)* appareil *m* de chauffage; **electric/gas f.** radiateur *m* électrique/au gaz; **on f. en feu; to catch f.** prendre feu; **to set f. to sth, to set sth on f.** mettre le feu à qch; **f.! au feu!;** *Fig* **to play with f.** jouer avec le feu; *Fig* **to fight f. with f.** combattre le feu par le feu; **f. alarm** sirène *f* d'incendie; *Br* **f. brigade,** *Am* **f. department** sapeurs-pompiers *mpl*, pompiers *mpl*; **f. door** porte *f* coupe-feu; **f. drill** exercice *m* d'évacuation en cas d'incendie; **f. engine** voiture *f* de pompiers; **f. escape** escalier *m* de secours; **f. extinguisher** extincteur *m*; **f. fighter** pompier *m*; **to be a f. hazard** constituer un risque d'incendie; **f. hydrant** bouche *f* d'incendie; **f. insurance** assurance *f* contre l'incendie; **f. regulations** *(laws)* normes *fpl* de protection contre les incendies; *(instructions)* consignes *fpl* en cas d'incendie; **f. sale** = vente d'objets endommagés dans une incendie; **f. station** caserne *f* de pompiers

(**b**) *(of artillery)* tirs *mpl*; **to open f.** ouvrir le feu; **to hold one's f.** ne pas tirer; **to come under f.** être exposé(e) aux tirs; *Fig (be criticized)* être exposé à de sévères critiques; **f. power** puissance *f* de tir

(**c**) *Fig (enthusiasm)* fougue *f*, ardeur *f*

2 *vt* (**a**) *(shoot) (missile, flare)* lancer; **to f. a gun (at)** tirer un coup de fusil (sur); *Fig* **to f. a question at sb** poser une question à qn à brûle-pourpoint

(**b**) *(dismiss)* virer

(**c**) oil-/gas-fired central heating chauffage *m* central au mazout/au gaz; *Fig* **to f. sb's imagination** enflammer l'imagination de qn

(**d**) *(pottery)* cuire

3 *vi* (**a**) *(with gun)* tirer (**at** sur); *Fam Fig* **f. away!** *(to questioner)* allez-y!

(**b**) *(of engine)* tourner

firearm ['faɪərɑːm] *n* arme *f* à feu

firebrand ['faɪəbrænd] *n (torch)* tison *m*, brandon *m*; *Fig (person)* brandon *m* de discorde

firecracker ['faɪəkrækə(r)] *n* pétard *m*

firefly ['faɪəflaɪ] *(pl* fireflies*)* *n* luciole *f*

fireguard ['faɪəɡɑːd] *n* garde-feu *m inv*

firelight ['faɪəlaɪt] *n* lumière *f* du feu

firelighter ['faɪəlaɪtə(r)] *n* allume-feu *m inv*

fireman ['faɪəmən] *n* pompier *m*

fireplace ['faɪəpleɪs] *n* cheminée *f*

fireproof ['faɪə'pruːf] *adj* ignifugé(e)

fireside ['faɪəsaɪd] *n* **by the f.** au coin du feu

firewall ['faɪəwɔːl] *n Comput* firewall *m*, contrôle *m* d'accès

firewood ['faɪəwʊd] *n* bois *m* de chauffage

firework ['faɪəwɜːk] *n* pièce *f* d'artifice; **fireworks, f. display** feu *m* d'artifice; *Fig* **there'll be fireworks** il va y avoir du grabuge

firing ['faɪərɪŋ] *n* tir *m*; *Fig* **to be in the f. line** être l'objet de violentes critiques; **f. squad** peloton *m* d'exécution

firm¹ [fɜːm] *n (company)* entreprise *f*, firme *f*

firm² **1** *adj* (**a**) *(fruit, body, mattress, handshake)* ferme; *Fig (foundations, friendship)* solide; **the f. favourite** le/la grand(e) favori(ite); **it's my f. belief (that)...** j'ai la ferme conviction que... (**b**) *(strict)* ferme (**c**) *(definite) (decision)* ferme; *(date)* précis(e); *(evidence)* sérieux(euse)

2 *adv* **to stand f.** tenir bon *ou* ferme; **to hold f. to**

one's principles/beliefs être fidèle à ses principes/croyances

firmly ['fɜːmlɪ] *adv* (**a**) *(securely)* solidement; **I f. believe (that)...** j'ai la ferme conviction que... (**b**) *(strictly)* fermement

first [fɜːst] **1** *n* (**a**) *(in series)* premier(ère) *m,f*; **we were the f. to arrive** nous étions les premiers arrivés; **it's the f. I've heard of it** c'est la première fois que j'en entends parler, première nouvelle; **Edward the F.** Edward Premier

(**b**) *(of month)* premier *m*; **we're leaving on the f.** nous partons le premier

(**c**) *(beginning)* **from f. to last** du début jusqu'à la fin; **from the f.** dès le début; **at f.** d'abord

(**d**) *Br Univ* **to get a f.** *(in degree)* ≃ avoir sa licence avec mention très bien

(**e**) *(first gear)* première *f*

(**f**) *(unique event)* première *f*

2 *adj* premier(ère); **for the f. time** pour la première fois; **at f. hand** de première main; **f. things f.!** commençons par le commencement!; **I don't know the f. thing about motorbikes** je ne connais absolument rien aux motos; **f. thing (in the morning)** dès le matin; **at f. light** aux premières lueurs du jour; **at f. sight** à première vue; **in the f. place** d'abord; **f. aid** *(skill)* secourisme *m*; *(treatment)* premiers soins *mpl*; **f. cousin** cousin(e) *m,f* germain(e); **f. edition** édition *f* originale; **f. gear** première *f* (vitesse *f*); *Am* **the f. lady** première dame des États-Unis *(épouse du président)*; *Naut* **f. mate** second *m*; **f. name** prénom *m*; **f. night** *(of play)* première *f*; *Law* **f. offender** = personne qui commet un délit pour la première fois; **the F. World War** la Première Guerre mondiale

3 *adv* (**a**) *(firstly)* d'abord; **f. and foremost** avant toute chose; **f. of all** en premier lieu, d'abord

(**b**) *(for the first time)* pour la première fois; **I f. met her in London** je l'ai rencontrée pour la première fois à Londres

(**c**) *(before others)* le premier (la première); **you go f.!** *(in queue)* passez devant!; **to come f.** *(in race)* arriver premier(ère); *(in exam)* être reçu(e) premier(-ère); **my family comes f.** ma famille passe avant le reste; **f. come, f. served** les premiers arrivés sont les premiers servis; **ladies f.!** les femmes d'abord!; **I won't do it, I'd resign f.** plutôt démissionner que de faire ça

first-aid [fɜːst'eɪd] *adj* **f. certificate** brevet *m* de secourisme; **f. kit** trousse *f* de secours

first-born ['fɜːstbɔːn] *n Lit* premier-né (première-née) *m,f*

first-class ['fɜːstklɑːs] **1** *adj* (**a**) *(compartment, ticket)* de première classe (**b**) **f. stamp** timbre *m* au tarif normal (**c**) *Univ* **f. honours (degree)** ≃ licence *f* avec mention bien ou très bien (**d**) *(excellent)* excellent(e)

2 *adv* (**a**) *(travel)* en première classe (**b**) *(post)* au tarif normal

first-degree ['fɜːstdɪ'ɡriː] *adj* (**a**) *Med (burns)* au premier degré (**b**) *Am Law* **f. murder** assassinat *m*

first-hand ['fɜːsthænd] *adj & adv* de première main

firstly ['fɜːstlɪ] *adv* premièrement, en premier lieu

first-past-the-post ['fɜːstpɑːstðə'pəʊst] *adj Pol* **f. system** scrutin *m* à un tour

first-rate ['fɜːstreɪt] *adj* excellent(e)

first-time buyer ['fɜːsttaɪm'baɪə(r)] *n (of property)* primo-accédant *m*

fiscal ['fɪskəl] *adj* fiscal(e); **f. policy** politique *f* budgétaire; **f. year** année *f* fiscale

Fiscal year
En Grande-Bretagne, l'année fiscale commence le 1er avril pour les entreprises et le 6 avril pour les particuliers. Aux États-Unis, l'année fiscale correspond à l'année civile pour les particuliers.

fish [fɪʃ] **1** *n* (*pl* **fish** *or* **fishes**) (**a**) (*animal*) poisson *m*; *Br* **f. and chips** poisson *m* frit avec des frites; **f.-and-chip shop** = magasin où l'on vend du poisson frit et des frites ainsi que d'autres produits cuits dans la friture; **f. cake** croquette *f* de poisson; **f. farm** établissement *m* piscicole; *Br* **f. fingers,** *Am* **f. sticks** bâtonnets *mpl* de poisson; **f. knife** couteau *m* à poisson; **f. slice** pelle *f* à poisson; **f. tank** aquarium *m* (**b**) (*idioms*) **there are plenty more f. in the sea** un de perdu, dix de retrouvés; **to have other f. to fry** avoir d'autres chats à fouetter; **to feel like a f. out of water** ne pas se sentir dans son élément; **to be neither f. nor fowl** n'être ni chair ni poisson
2 *vt* (**a**) (*river*) pêcher (**b**) (*remove*) **to f. sb/sth from somewhere** sortir qn/qch de quelque part
3 *vi* pêcher; *Fig* **to f. for compliments** rechercher les compliments; **she fished around in her pocket for some change** elle a fouillé dans sa poche pour trouver de la monnaie

fisherman ['fɪʃəmən] *n* pêcheur *m*
fish-hook ['fɪʃhʊk] *n* hameçon *m*
fishing ['fɪʃɪŋ] *n* pêche *f*; **to go f.** aller à la pêche; **f. boat** bateau *m* de pêche; **f. grounds** lieux *mpl* de pêche; **f. line** ligne *f*; **f. net** filet *m* de pêche; **f. port** port *m* de pêche; **f. rod** canne *f* à pêche
fishmonger ['fɪʃmʌŋɡə(r)] *n* poissonnier(ère) *m,f*; **f.'s (shop)** poissonnerie *f*
fishnet ['fɪʃnet] *adj* (*stockings, tights*) résille *inv*
fishy ['fɪʃɪ] *adj* (**a**) (*smell, taste*) de poisson (**b**) *Fam* (*suspicious*) louche
fission ['fɪʃən] *n* fission *f*
fissure ['fɪʃə(r)] *n* (*in mountain, rock*) fissure *f*; *Med* scissure *f*
fist [fɪst] *n* poing *m*; *Fig* **she made a good f. of it** elle s'en est plutôt bien sortie
fistful ['fɪstfʊl] *n* poignée *f*
fistfight ['fɪstfaɪt] *n* bagarre *f* aux poings
fisticuffs ['fɪstɪkʌfs] *npl* *Hum* coups *mpl* de poing
fit¹ [fɪt] *n* (*seizure*) attaque *f*; **to have a f.** avoir une attaque; *Fam Fig* **to have** *or* **throw a f.** piquer une crise; **in a f. of temper** dans un accès de colère; **a f. of coughing** une quinte de toux; **a f. of crying** une crise de larmes; **to be in fits (of laughter)** se tordre de rire; **in fits and starts** par à-coups
fit² **1** *n* **the jacket is a good f.** cette veste me/te/*etc* va bien; **comfortable/tight f.** coupe *f* confortable/ajustée; **these trousers are a bit of a tight f.** ce pantalon est un peu juste
2 *adj* (**a**) (*appropriate*) **f. to eat** mangeable; **f. to drink** buvable; **f. for the bin** bon (bonne) à jeter; **f. for human consumption** propre à la consommation; **a meal f. for a king** un repas digne d'un *ou* de roi; **do as you see** *or* **think f.** faites comme bon vous semblera; **to see f. to do sth** juger bon de faire qch; **that's all he's f. for** il n'est bon qu'à cela; **to be f. to do sth** (*worthy of*) être digne de faire qch; **to be f. to drop** tomber de fatigue
(**b**) (*healthy*) en forme; **to retrouve the form**; **to keep f.** se maintenir en forme; **to be f. to do sth** (*healthy enough*) être en état de faire qch; *Fam* **to be as f. as a fiddle** péter la forme
(**c**) *Br Fam* (*attractive*) canon *inv*
3 *vt* (*pt* & *pp* **fitted**) (**a**) (*match*) correspondre à; **to make the punishment f. the crime** proportionner la peine au délit
(**b**) (*be the right size for*) **to f. sb** aller à qn; **this key fits the lock** cette clé rentre dans la serrure
(**c**) (*install*) adapter (**to/on** à/sur); **to f. a carpet** poser de la moquette; **to f. sth with** équiper *ou* pourvoir qch de qch
(**d**) (*insert*) **to f. sth into/onto sth** faire rentrer qch dans/sur qch; **we can f. another two people inside** il y a encore de la place pour deux personnes
4 *vi* (**a**) (*be the right size*) (*of lid, key, plug*) aller; **to f. together** s'adapter; **to f. into sth** rentrer dans qch
(**b**) (*of clothes*) **it fits perfectly** ça me/te/*etc* va parfaitement
▸ **fit in 1** *vt sep* (*in timetable*) caser
2 *vi* (**a**) (*go into place*) aller (**b**) (*of person*) (*in company, group*) s'intégrer; **you don't f. in here** tu n'es pas à ta place ici
▸ **fit up** *vt sep very Fam* (*frame*) **to be fitted up** être victime d'un coup monté
fitful ['fɪtfʊl] *adj* (*sleep*) agité(e); **to make f. progress** progresser par à-coups
fitness ['fɪtnɪs] *n* (**a**) (*health*) forme *f*; *Br* **f. centre** club *m* de gym; **f. room** salle *f* de musculation (**b**) (*suitability*) aptitude *f* (**for** à)
fitted ['fɪtɪd] *adj* (**a**) (*jacket, dress*) ajusté(e); **f. carpet** moquette *f*; **f. sheet** drap-housse *m* (**b**) (*kitchen*) intégré(e); (*wardrobe*) encastré(e)
fitting ['fɪtɪŋ] **1** *n* (**a**) (*of clothes*) essayage *m*; **f. room** cabine *f* d'essayage (**b**) **fittings** (*in office*) installations *fpl*; (*in house*) accessoires *mpl*
2 *adj* approprié(e) (**to** à)
five [faɪv] **1** *n* cinq *m inv*
2 *adj* cinq; **f. o'clock shadow** barbe *f* d'un jour; *see also* **eight**
fiver ['faɪvə(r)] *n* *Br Fam* (*sum*) cinq livres *fpl*; (*note*) billet *m* de cinq livres
fix [fɪks] **1** *n* (**a**) *Fam* (*difficulty*) **to be in a f.** être dans le pétrin; **to get into a f.** se fourrer dans le pétrin (**b**) *Fam* (*of drug*) dose *f*; *Fig* **she needs her daily f. of chocolate** il lui faut sa dose quotidienne de chocolat
(**c**) *Fam* **to be a f.** (*of election, contest*) être truqué(e)
2 *vt* (**a**) (*attach securely*) fixer (**to** à); **to f. sth in one's memory** graver qch dans sa mémoire; **to f. sth's attention on sth** fixer son attention sur qch; **to f. one's eyes on sb/sth** fixer qn/qch (**b**) (*decide*) (*limit, price*) fixer (**c**) (*repair*) arranger, réparer (**d**) (*arrange*) (*meeting*) arranger; **to f. one's hair** se coiffer; *Fam* **I'll f. him!** je vais lui faire son affaire! (**e**) *Fam* (*election, contest*) truquer
▸ **fix up** *vt sep* (**a**) (*arrange*) arranger (**b**) (*provide*) **to f. sb up with a job/flat** trouver un emploi/appartement à qn; **I've fixed you up with a date** je t'ai arrangé un rendez-vous galant
fixation [fɪk'seɪʃən] *n* fixation *f*; **to have a f. about sth** faire une fixation sur qch
fixed [fɪkst] *adj* (**a**) (*price, costs, income*) fixe; **f. assets** immobilisations *fpl* (**b**) (*definite*) (*ideas*) bien arrêté(e); (*plans*) précis(e) (**c**) *Fam* **how are you f. for money/time?** tu as de l'argent/le temps? (**d**) *Fam* (*election, contest*) truqué(e)
fixer ['fɪksə(r)] *n* *Fam* combinard(e) *m,f*

fixture ['fɪkstʃə(r)] n (**a**) **fixtures (and fittings)** (in house, office) installations fpl fixes; **bathroom fixtures** sanitaires mpl; Fam **to be a f.** (of person) faire partie des meubles (**b**) Br (in sport) rencontre f

fizz [fɪz] **1** n (**a**) (sound) pétillement m; (bubbles) gaz m (**b**) Fam (soft drink) boisson f gazeuse; (champagne) champ m
2 vi (of champagne) pétiller

▸**fizzle out** ['fɪzəl] vi Fam (of plan) tomber à l'eau; (of enthusiasm, interest) retomber; (of relationship) partir en eau de boudin

fizzy ['fɪzɪ] adj (wine) mousseux(euse); (soft drink) gazeux(euse)

fjord [fjɔːd] n fjord m

flab [flæb] n Fam (fat) graisse f

flabbergasted ['flæbəgɑːstɪd] adj Fam abasourdi(e)

flabby ['flæbɪ] adj (person, features) bouffi(e); (limbs) mou (molle); Fig (argument, reasoning) qui manque de rigueur

flaccid ['flæsɪd] adj flasque

flag [flæg] **1** n drapeau m; Naut pavillon m; **F. Day** (in United States) = le 14 juin, fête commémorant l'adoption du drapeau américain; **f. day** (for charity) = jour où une association caritative organise une collecte en vendant des macarons, des insignes etc
2 vt (pt & pp **flagged**) marquer; (mark) signaler; **to f. (down) a taxi** héler un taxi
3 vi (of person, conversation, interest) faiblir; (of strength, spirits) baisser

Flag day

Les "flag days" britanniques, durant lesquels on sollicite des dons auprès des passants, ont généralement lieu le samedi. Les donateurs reçoivent un papillon en papier qu'ils portent tout au long de la journée.

flagellate ['flædʒəleɪt] vt flageller

flagpole ['flægpəʊl] n mât m (de drapeau)

flagrant ['fleɪɡrənt] adj flagrant(e)

flagrantly ['fleɪɡrəntlɪ] adv de façon flagrante; **f. dishonest** d'une malhonnêteté flagrante

flagship ['flægʃɪp] n (of fleet) navire m amiral; Fig (of range of products, party) fleuron m

flagstone ['flægstəʊn] n dalle f

flail [fleɪl] **1** n (tool) fléau m
2 vt agiter
3 vi (of rope, cable) se balancer; (of arms, legs) s'agiter dans tous les sens

▸**flail about, flail around** vi (of arms, legs) s'agiter dans tous les sens; (of person) se débattre

flair ['fleə(r)] n don m (for pour); **to do sth with f.** faire qch avec style; **to have a f. for business** avoir le sens des affaires; **to have a f. for doing sth** avoir le don de faire qch

flak [flæk] n tir m antiaérien ou de DCA; Fig critiques fpl; **she got a lot of f. for her decision** sa décision a été très critiquée; **f. jacket** gilet m pare-balles

flake [fleɪk] **1** n (of snow, cereal) flocon m; (of paint) écaille f; (of soap) paillette f; **a f. of skin** un bout de peau morte
2 vi (of paint) s'écailler; **my skin is flaking** je pèle

▸**flake out** vi Fam s'effondrer de fatigue

flaky ['fleɪkɪ] adj (**a**) (paint) écaillé(e); (pastry) feuilleté(e) (**b**) Am (eccentric) loufoque

flamboyant [flæm'bɔɪənt] adj (person, behaviour) extravagant(e); (gesture) théâtral(e); (clothes, colours) voyant(e)

flame [fleɪm] **1** n flamme f; **to go up in flames** prendre feu; Fig (of hopes, chances) partir en fumée; **to burst into flames** s'enflammer; Fam **old f.** ancien(enne) amoureux(euse) m,f
2 vt Comput descendre en flammes
3 vi (**a**) (of fire) flamber (**b**) Comput rédiger un message injurieux

flamenco [flə'meŋkəʊ] n flamenco m

flameproof ['fleɪmpruːf] adj ignifugé(e); (dish) qui va sur le feu

flamethrower ['fleɪmθrəʊə(r)] n lance-flammes m inv

flaming ['fleɪmɪŋ] **1** adj (**a**) (burning) enflammé(e); Fig (sunset) flamboyant(e); **a f. temper** une colère noire (**b**) Br Fam (for emphasis) sacré(e)
2 adv Br Fam vachement; **don't be so f. stupid!** ne sois pas si bête, merde!
3 n Comput envoi de messages injurieux

flamingo [flə'mɪŋɡəʊ] (pl **flamingos**) n flamant m

flammable ['flæməbəl] adj inflammable

flan [flæn] n tarte f

Flanders ['flɑːndəz] n les Flandres fpl, la Flandre

flank [flæŋk] **1** n flanc m; (of beef, mutton) flanchet m
2 vt flanquer (with or by de)

flannel ['flænəl] n (**a**) (fabric) flanelle f; **(pair of) flannels** pantalon m en flanelle (**b**) Br (face cloth) ≃ gant m de toilette (**c**) Br Fam (evasive words, flattery) blabla m

flap [flæp] **1** n (**a**) (of envelope, book cover, tent) rabat m; (of aeroplane) volet m (**b**) Fam (panic) **to be in a f.** être affolé(e), paniquer
2 vt (pt & pp **flapped**) **to f. its wings** (of bird) battre des ailes; **to f. one's arms** agiter les bras
3 vi (**a**) (of wings, flag) battre (**b**) Fam (panic) s'affoler, paniquer

flapjack ['flæpdʒæk] n (**a**) Br (biscuit) = biscuit épais à l'avoine (**b**) Am (pancake) = petite crêpe épaisse

flare ['fleə(r)] **1** n (**a**) (signal) signal m lumineux; (rocket) fusée f éclairante (**b**) **(pair of) flares** pantalon m (à) pattes d'éléphant
2 vt (nostrils) dilater
3 vi (of fire) flamboyer; **tempers flared at the meeting** le ton est monté à la réunion

▸**flare up** vi (of fire) s'embraser; (of medical condition) se déclencher; (of anger, trouble) éclater

flash [flæʃ] **1** n (**a**) (of light) éclair m; **a f. of lightning** un éclair; **f. of wit** trait m d'esprit; **f. of inspiration** éclair m de génie; **in a f.** (very quickly) en un clin d'œil; Fig **a f. in the pan** un feu de paille; **f. flood** crue f subite; Fig **a f. point** point m de rupture; (region) point m chaud (**b**) (in photography) flash m; **f. photography** photographie f au flash (**c**) Comput **f. drive** clé f USB
2 adj Br Fam (showy) (clothes, car, jewellery) tape-à-l'œil inv; (person) aux goûts tapageurs
3 vt (smile, look) lancer (**at** à); (card, badge) montrer rapidement (**at** à); **to f. one's headlights at sb** faire un appel de phares à qn
4 vi (**a**) (of diamond) briller; (of light) clignoter (**b**) (move quickly) **to f. past** passer comme un éclair; **my life flashed before me** ma vie a défilé devant mes yeux (**c**) Fam (expose oneself) s'exhiber (**at** devant)

flashback ['flæʃbæk] n (in novel, film) flash-back m inv; retour m en arrière

flasher ['flæʃə(r)] n Br Fam (a) (man exposing himself) exhibitionniste m (b) (car indicator) clignotant m

flashing ['flæʃɪŋ] adj (light) clignotant(e)

flashlight ['flæʃlaɪt] n torche f électrique

flashy ['flæʃɪ] adj Fam (clothes, car, jewellery) tape-à-l'œil inv; (person) aux goûts tapageurs

flask [flɑːsk] n (for alcohol) flasque f; (in chemistry) fiole f; **(Thermos®) f**. (bouteille f) Thermos® f

flat [flæt] **1** n (**a**) Br (apartment) appartement m (**b**) Fam (flat tyre) pneu m à plat; (punctured) pneu m crevé
2 adj (**a**) (surface) plat(e); (nose) camus; **as f. as a pancake** plat(e) comme une galette; Fam (flat-chested) plate comme une limande; **f. cap** casquette f; **f. racing** plat m; **f. rate** tarif m unique; Comput & TV **f. screen** écran m plat; **f. tyre** pneu m à plat; (punctured) pneu crevé (**b**) (refusal) **to give a f. refusal** ser net (**c**) (existence) monotone; (voice) terne; (battery) à plat; (drink) éventé(e) (**d**) (in music) (a semitone lower) bémol; (out of tune) en dessous du ton; **B f.** si m inv bémol
3 adv (**a**) (level) à plat; **to fall f. on one's face** tomber à plat ventre; Fig se casser le nez; Fig **to fall f.** (of joke) tomber à plat; **he pressed himself f. against the wall** il s'est plaqué contre le mur (**b**) (completely) **to turn sb down f.** opposer un refus catégorique à qn; **in twenty seconds f.** en vingt secondes pile; **to work f. out** travailler d'arrache-pied; Fam **to be f. broke** être complètement fauché(e)

flat-chested ['flæt'tʃestɪd] adj **to be f.** avoir peu de poitrine

flatfish ['flætfɪʃ] n poisson m plat

flat-footed ['flæt'fʊtɪd] adj **to be f.** avoir les pieds plats

flatly ['flætlɪ] adv (refuse, deny) catégoriquement

flatmate ['flætmeɪt] n Br colocataire mf; **we used to be flatmates** nous partagions un appartement

flatten ['flætən] vt aplatir; **to f. oneself against a wall** s'aplatir contre un mur; Fam **to f. sb** casser la tête à qn

flatter ['flætə(r)] vt (of person, clothes) flatter; Fam **don't f. yourself!** ne te fais pas trop d'illusions!

flattering ['flætərɪŋ] adj (words, photo) flatteur(-euse); (clothes, colour) qui avantage

flattery ['flætərɪ] n flatterie f

flatulence ['flætjʊləns] n Med flatulence f

flaunt [flɔːnt] vt (knowledge, wealth) étaler; (jewels) exhiber; Fig (ignorance, bad manners) étaler sans complexes

flavour, Am **flavor** ['fleɪvə(r)] **1** n (**a**) (of food) goût m; (of ice cream, yoghurt) parfum m (**b**) (characteristic) note f; **her stories have a Provençal f.** ses histoires fleurent bon la Provence
2 vt (savoury food) relever (**with** de); (sweet food) parfumer (**with** à); **vanilla flavoured** parfumé(e) à la vanille

flavouring, Am **flavoring** ['fleɪvərɪŋ] n parfum m; **artificial f.** arôme m artificiel

flavourless, Am **flavorless** ['fleɪvəlɪs] adj Br sans saveur, insipide

flaw [flɔː] n défaut m; (in plan, argument) faille f

flawed [flɔːd] adj qui a un défaut/des défauts; (plan, argument) bancal(e)

flawless ['flɔːlɪs] adj parfait(e)

flax [flæks] n lin m

flay [fleɪ] vt (flog) fouetter; Fig (criticize) éreinter

flea [fliː] n puce f; Fam **to send sb away with a f. in his/her ear** envoyer promener qn; **f. market** (marché m aux) puces fpl

fleabite ['fliːbaɪt] n piqûre f de puce

flea-bitten ['fliːbɪtən] adj (person, animal) plein(e) de puces; Fam (shabby) miteux(euse)

fleck [flek] **1** n (of colour, light) petite tache f; (of dust) grain m
2 vt tacheter (**with** de); **hair flecked with grey** cheveux mpl grisonnants

fled [fled] pt & pp of **flee**

fledgling ['fledʒlɪŋ] **1** n (young bird) oisillon m
2 adj Fig (person) novice, débutant(e); (company, state) naissant(e)

flee [fliː] (pt & pp **fled** [fled]) vi fuir, s'enfuir; **to f. from persecution** fuir la persécution

fleece [fliːs] **1** n (**a**) (of sheep) toison f (**b**) (garment) fourrure f polaire
2 vt Fam (cheat) estamper

fleecy ['fliːsɪ] adj duveteux(euse)

fleet [fliːt] n (of ships) flotte f; (of taxis, buses) parc m; Fig (convoy) file f; **F. Street** = rue de Londres, dont le nom sert à désigner les grands journaux britanniques

Fleet Street

Traditionnellement, cette rue de la City était celle des journaux. Aujourd'hui, beaucoup de journaux ont établi leur siège dans d'autres quartiers, notamment dans les Docklands. Cependant, le terme "Fleet Street" est encore employé pour désigner la presse et le monde du journalisme.

fleet-footed ['fliːt'fʊtɪd] adj Lit au pied léger

fleeting ['fliːtɪŋ] adj (moment, happiness, glance) fugace; (beauty) éphémère; (visit) court(e), rapide; **to catch a f. glimpse of sb/sth** entrevoir qn/qch

Flemish ['flemɪʃ] **1** n (language) flamand m
2 adj flamand(e)

flesh [fleʃ] n (of man, animal) chair f; **in the f.** en chair et en os; **to make sb's f. creep** or **crawl** donner la chair de poule à qn; **his own f. and blood** (children) la chair de sa chair; (close family) les siens mpl; **f. wound** blessure f superficielle

▶**flesh out** vt sep (plan, remarks) étoffer

fleshy ['fleʃɪ] adj charnu(e)

flew [fluː] pt of **fly⁴**

flex [fleks] **1** n Br (cable) cordon m
2 vt (arms, knees) fléchir; (muscles) faire jouer; **they're just flexing their muscles** ce n'est qu'une démonstration d'autorité de leur part

flexible ['fleksɪbəl] adj (material, approach, timetable) flexible; (person's character) souple

flexitime ['fleksɪtaɪm], Am **flextime** [flekstaɪm] n horaires mpl flexibles ou à la carte

flick [flɪk] **1** n (**a**) (with finger) pichenette f; (of whip, tail) petit coup m; **at the f. of a switch** en appuyant juste sur un bouton; **f. knife** couteau m à cran d'arrêt (**b**) Br Fam Old-fashioned **the flicks** (cinema) le ciné, le cinoche
2 vt (with finger) donner une chiquenaude à; **he flicked the cigarette ash onto the carpet** il fit tomber la cendre de sa cigarette sur le tapis; **to f. the hair out of one's eyes** écarter les cheveux de ses yeux

▶**flick through** vt insep (book, magazine) feuilleter; (photographs) passer rapidement en revue

flicker ['flɪkə(r)] **1** *n (of flame)* vacillement *m*; *Fig (of hope)* lueur *f*; *(of interest, annoyance)* pointe *f*; **a f. of light** une lueur vacillante **2** *vi (of flame, light)* vaciller

flier ['flaɪə(r)] *n* (**a**) *(passenger)* = personne qui voyage en avion (**b**) *(leaflet)* prospectus *m*

flight [flaɪt] *n* (**a**) *(act of flying, specific trip)* vol *m*; **it's a two-hour f. from Edinburgh** c'est à deux heures de vol d'Édimbourg; *Fig* **f. of fancy** lubie *f*; **f. attendant** *(male)* steward *m*; *(female)* hôtesse *f* de l'air; **f. deck** *(of aircraft)* poste *m* ou cabine *f* de pilotage; **f. path** trajectoire *f* de vol; **f. recorder** enregistreur *m* de vol; **f. simulator** simulateur *m* de vol (**b**) *(group of birds)* vol *m*, volée *f*; *Fig* **in the top f.** parmi les tout premiers (**c**) **f. (of stairs)** escalier *m*; **two flights up from me** deux étages au-dessus de chez moi (**d**) *(escape)* fuite *f*; **to put sb to f.** mettre qn en fuite

flightless ['flaɪtlɪs] *adj* coureur(euse)

flighty ['flaɪtɪ] *adj (fickle)* volage

flimsy ['flɪmzɪ] *adj (structure, fence)* peu solide; *(dress, excuse, plot)* léger(ère); *(evidence)* ténu(e)

flinch [flɪntʃ] *vi (with pain)* tressaillir; *(at an idea)* frémir; **to do sth without flinching** faire qch sans broncher; **to f. from doing sth** hésiter à faire qch

fling [flɪŋ] **1** *n Fam (affair)* aventure *f* **2** *vt (pt & pp flung* [flʌŋ]) jeter; *(ball)* lancer; **to f. oneself into an armchair** se jeter dans un fauteuil; **to f. one's arms around sb** prendre qn dans ses bras; *Fig* **to f. oneself into a task** se lancer dans une tâche

▶**fling out** *vt sep (object)* jeter; *(person)* mettre à la porte; *(proposal, case)* rejeter

flint [flɪnt] *n (stone)* silex *m*; *(of lighter)* pierre *f* (à briquet)

flip [flɪp] **1** *n Fam* **the f. side** *(of record)* la face B; *Fig (of situation)* le revers de la médaille **2** *vt (pt & pp flipped) (record, pancake, card)* retourner; **to f. the switch** appuyer sur l'interrupteur; **to f. a coin** jouer à pile ou face; *Fam* **to f. one's lid** *(get angry)* piquer une crise; *(go mad)* perdre la boule **3** *vi Fam (get angry)* piquer une crise; *(go mad)* perdre la boule

▶**flip through** *vt insep (book, magazine)* feuilleter; *(photos, samples)* jeter un coup d'œil à

flipboard ['flɪpbɔːd], **flipchart** ['flɪptʃɑːt] *n* tableau *m* à feuilles (mobiles)

flip-flops ['flɪpflɒps] *npl* (**a pair of**) f. des tongs *fpl*

flippant ['flɪpənt] *adj* désinvolte, cavalier(ère)

flipper ['flɪpə(r)] *n (of animal)* nageoire *f*; *(of diver)* palme *f*

flip-top ['flɪptɒp] *adj (carton, pack)* à rabat; *(mobile phone)* à clapet

flirt [flɜːt] **1** *n* charmeur(euse) *m,f* **2** *vi* flirter (**with** avec); *Fig* **to f. with an idea** caresser une idée

flirtatious [flɜː'teɪʃəs] *adj (look, smile)* charmeur(euse); **to be f.** aimer flirter; **to be f. with sb** flirter avec qn

flit [flɪt] **1** *n Br Fam* **to do a moonlight f.** déménager à la cloche de bois **2** *vi (pt & pp flitted)* **to f. about** *(of bird)* voleter; *Fig* **to f. from one thing to another** *(of person)* s'éparpiller

float [fləʊt] **1** *n* (**a**) *(on fishing line)* bouchon *m*; *(for swimming, on net)* flotteur *m* (**b**) *(in procession)* char *m* (**c**) *(money)* fonds *m* de caisse **2** *vt* (**a**) *(ship)* mettre à flot (**b**) *(idea, proposal)* émettre; *(company)* introduire en Bourse

3 *vi* flotter; **to f. to the surface** remonter à la surface; **to f. on one's back** *(of swimmer)* faire la planche; **the bottle floated out to sea** la bouteille a été emportée vers le large; *Fam Fig* **he's floating around somewhere** il traîne par là

floating ['fləʊtɪŋ] *adj* flottant(e); *(population)* fluctuant(e); **f. voter** électeur(trice) *m,f* indécis(e)

flock [flɒk] **1** *n (of sheep)* troupeau *m*; *(of birds)* vol *m*, volée *f*; *Rel (congregation)* ouailles *fpl*; *Fig (of people)* foule *f* **2** *vi (gather)* **to f. around sb** s'attrouper autour de qn; **people are flocking to the exhibition** les gens vont en masse *ou* en foule voir l'exposition

flog [flɒg] *(pt & pp flogged) vt* (**a**) *(beat)* fouetter; *Fam* **to be flogging a dead horse** se dépenser en pure perte; *Fam* **to f. a subject to death** s'étendre indéfiniment sur un sujet (**b**) *Br Fam (sell)* vendre

flood [flʌd] **1** *n* inondation *f*; *(of light)* flot *m*; **the F.** *(in the Bible)* le Déluge; **to be in floods (of tears)** verser des torrents de larmes **2** *vt (land, bathroom)* inonder; **to be flooded with light** être inondé(e) de lumière; **the river flooded its banks** la rivière a débordé *ou* est sortie de son lit; **to f. the market (with sth)** inonder le marché (de qch); **to be flooded with complaints/telephone calls** être submergé(e) de réclamations/de coups de fil **3** *vi (of river)* déborder; **the sun's rays came flooding through the window** les rayons du soleil entraient à flots par la fenêtre; **letters came flooding in** nous avons/ils ont/*etc* été submergés de lettres; **it all came flooding back** tout m'/lui/*etc* est revenu d'un coup

floodgate ['flʌdgeɪt] *n Fig* **to open the floodgates to sth** laisser la porte ouverte à qch

flooding ['flʌdɪŋ] *n* inondation(s) *f(pl)*

floodlight ['flʌdlaɪt] *n* projecteur *m*; **by f.** à la lumière des projecteurs

floodlit ['flʌdlɪt] *adj (stadium, match)* éclairé(e) aux projecteurs; *(building)* illuminé(e)

floor [flɔː(r)] **1** *n* (**a**) *(of room, forest)* sol *m*; *(of Stock Exchange)* parquet *m*; *(of ocean)* fond *m*; **f. show** spectacle *m* de cabaret (**b**) *(at meeting, debate)* **to give sb the f.** donner la parole à qn; **to take the f.** prendre la parole; **questions from the f.** questions *fpl* du public (**c**) *(storey)* étage *m*; **to live ten floors up** habiter au dixième étage **2** *vt (knock down)* envoyer au tapis; *Fig (of question, criticism)* désarçonner

floorboard ['flɔːbɔːd] *n* latte *f* de plancher

floozie, floozy ['fluːzɪ] *(pl floozies) n very Fam Pej* pouffiasse *f*

flop [flɒp] **1** *n (failure)* fiasco *m*, bide *m*; **to be a f.** *(of film)* faire un bide *m*; *(of party)* être un bide **2** *vi (pt & pp flopped)* (**a**) *(fall) (into water)* tomber; *(onto seat)* s'affaler (**b**) *(fail)* échouer; *(of film)* faire un bide; *(of party)* être un bide

floppy ['flɒpɪ] **1** *n (pl floppies) Comput* disquette *f* **2** *adj (ears)* pendant(e); *(garment)* flottant(e); *(hat)* mou (molle); *Comput* **f. disk** disquette *f*

flora ['flɔːrə] *n (plant life)* flore *f*

floral ['flɔːrəl] *adj* floral(e); **f. tribute** *(at funeral)* couronne *f* de fleurs

Florence ['flɒrəns] *n* Florence

florid ['flɒrɪd] *adj (style)* fleuri(e); *(complexion)* rubicond(e)

Florida ['flɒrɪdə] *n* la Floride

florist ['flɒrɪst] n fleuriste mf; **f.'s (shop)** fleuriste m
floss [flɒs] **1** n **(dental) f.** fil m dentaire
2 vt nettoyer avec du fil dentaire
flotation [fləʊ'teɪʃən] n Com (of company) lancement m
flotsam ['flɒtsəm] n **f. (and jetsam)** débris mpl refoulés par la mer; Fig **the f. of society** les laissés-pour-compte mpl de la société
flounce [flaʊns] **1** n (in sewing) volant m
2 vi **to f. in/out** entrer/sortir de façon théâtrale
flounder ['flaʊndə(r)] **1** n (fish) flet m
2 vi (in water, mud) patauger; (in job, course, speech) perdre pied
flour ['flaʊə(r)] **1** n farine f
2 vt fariner
flourish ['flʌrɪʃ] **1** n (gesture) grand geste m théâtral; (musical, in writing) fioriture f
2 vt (brandish) brandir
3 vi (of plant, person) prospérer; (of business, arts) être florissant(e)
flourishing ['flʌrɪʃɪŋ] adj (plant) qui prospère; (business) florissant(e)
flout [flaʊt] vt (rule, instruction) faire fi de; (person) défier l'autorité de; (authority) défier
flow [fləʊ] **1** n (of liquid) écoulement m; (of electrical current, information) circulation f; (of tide, capital) flux m; **f. of traffic** circulation f; Fig **in full f.** en plein discours; Fig **to follow the f.** of an argument suivre (le fil d')un raisonnement; Fig **to go with the f.** suivre le mouvement; **f. chart** organigramme m
2 vi (a) (of liquid) couler; (of electrical current) circuler; (of traffic) s'écouler; Fig (of writing) couler bien; (of ideas) affluer; **to f. into the sea** (of river) se jeter dans la mer (b) **to f. from** (result from) découler de
flower ['flaʊə(r)] **1** n fleur f; **to be in f.** être en fleur(s); Fig **in the first f. of youth** dans la fleur de l'âge; **f. arranging** art m floral; **f. garden** jardin m d'agrément; **f. girl** = jeune demoiselle d'honneur; **f. show** exposition f florale
2 vi fleurir
flowerbed ['flaʊəbed] n parterre m de fleurs
flowerpot ['flaʊəpɒt] n pot m de fleurs
flowing ['fləʊɪŋ] adj (hair) flottant(e); (movement, style) fluide
flown [fləʊn] pp of **fly⁴**
flu [flu:] n grippe f; **a dose** or **bout of (the) f.** une grippe; **to have (the) f.** avoir la grippe
fluctuate ['flʌktjʊeɪt] vi (of prices) fluctuer; (of pulse, temperature) varier
fluctuation [flʌktjʊ'eɪʃən] n (of prices) fluctuation f; (of pulse, temperature) variation f
flue [flu:] n (of heater, chimney) tuyau m
fluency ['flu:ənsɪ] n aisance f (of/in de/en)
fluent ['flu:ənt] adj (speech, style) fluide; **he is f. in French, he speaks f. French** il parle couramment français
fluently ['flu:əntlɪ] adv (express oneself) avec facilité ou aisance; (speak language) couramment
fluff [flʌf] **1** n peluche f; **a bit of f.** une peluche; Br Fam (pretty girl) nana f, gonzesse f
2 vt (a) **to f. sth (up)** (pillow, duvet) remettre qch en forme (en le secouant) (b) Fam (botch) rater
fluffy ['flʌfɪ] adj duveteux(euse); (clouds) cotonneux(euse)
fluid ['flu:ɪd] **1** n fluide m, liquide m; **bodily fluids** sécrétions fpl

2 adj (substance) fluide, liquide; (style, movement) fluide; (situation, plans) mal défini(e); **f. ounce** = 0,03 l
fluidity [flu:'ɪdɪtɪ] n (of style, movement) fluidité f; (of situation, plans) imprécision f
fluke [flu:k] n Fam (stroke of luck) coup m de veine ou de bol; **by a f.** par hasard; **his success was a pure f.** c'est un hasard qu'il ait réussi
fluk(e)y ['flu:kɪ] adj Fam (person) veinard(e)
flummox ['flʌməks] vt Fam scier
flung [flʌŋ] pt & pp of **fling**
flunk [flʌŋk] Fam **1** vt (exam) rater; (student) recaler, coller
2 vi (in exam) être recalé(e) ou collé(e)
flunkey ['flʌŋkɪ] (pl flunkeys) n Fam Pej larbin m
fluorescent [flʊə'resənt] adj fluorescent(e)
fluoride ['flʊəraɪd] n fluorure m; **f. toothpaste** dentifrice m au fluor
flurry ['flʌrɪ] (pl flurries) n (of snow) bourrasque f; **a f. of activity/excitement** une soudaine activité/excitation
flush [flʌʃ] **1** n (a) (beginning) **in the first f. of youth** dans tout l'éclat de sa jeunesse (b) (in cards) flush m (c) (in toilet) chasse f (d'eau)
2 adj (even) de niveau, flush; (b) Fam (rich) plein(e) aux as
3 vt **to f. the toilet** tirer la chasse (d'eau)
4 vi (a) (of person) rougir (with de) (b) (of toilet) **the toilet flushed isn't flushing properly** la chasse d'eau ne fonctionne pas bien
▸**flush out** vt sep (force to emerge) déloger
flushed [flʌʃd] adj (person, face) rouge (with de)
fluster ['flʌstə(r)] vt démonter; **to get flustered** se démonter
flute [flu:t] n (a) Mus flûte f traversière (b) (glass) flûte f
flutter ['flʌtə(r)] **1** n (a) (of wings, eyelashes, heart) battement m; Fig **to be in a f.** (of excitement) être en émoi (b) Br Fam (bet) petit pari m; **to have a f.** parier ou jouer une petite somme (on sur)
2 vt **to f. its wings** (of bird) battre des ailes; **to f. one's eyelashes at sb** regarder qn en battant des cils
3 vi (of birds, insects) voleter; (of heart) battre; (of flag) flotter
flux [flʌks] n **to be in a state of f.** changer perpétuellement
fly¹ [flaɪ] n (a) **f., flies** (of trousers) braguette f (b) **f. sheet** (of tent) auvent m
fly² Br Fam **1** n **to do sth on the f.** (spontaneously) faire qch sur le coup
2 adj (cunning) malin(igne)
fly³ (pl flies) n (insect) mouche f; **he wouldn't hurt a f.** il ne ferait de mal à une mouche; **they were dropping like flies** ils tombaient comme des mouches; Fig **a f. in the ointment** un os; Fam Fig **there are no flies on her** elle est loin d'être bête; **I wish I could be a f. on the wall** (at interview, meeting) si je pouvais être une petite souris
fly⁴ (pt flew [flu:], pp flown [fləʊn]) **1** vt (a) (plane) piloter; (goods) transporter en avion; (route) emprunter; **to f. Air India** voyager avec Air India (b) (kite) faire voler; **to f. a flag** (of ship) arborer un pavillon; Fig **to f. the flag (for one's country)** défendre les couleurs de son pays (c) (flee) s'enfuir de; Fig **to f. the nest** (of child) quitter le foyer familial
2 vi (a) (of bird, plane) voler; (of passenger) voyager en avion, prendre l'avion; **to f. over London** survoler

Londres; **to f. across the Atlantic** traverser l'Atlantique en avion (**b**) *(of flag, hair)* flotter (**c**) *(move quickly)* **I must f.** il faut que je file; **to f. to sb's help** voler au secours de qn; **how time flies!** comme le temps passe!; **the door flew open** la porte s'est ouverte brusquement; **to f. into a rage** sortir de ses gonds; *Fam* **to send sb/sth flying** envoyer rouler qn/qch; **to f. in the face of reason/logic** défier la raison/toute logique

▸**fly away** *vi (of bird, papers)* s'envoler

▸**fly in 1** *vt sep (troops, rescuers)* transporter en avion
   2 *vi (of passenger)* arriver en avion

▸**fly out 1** *vt sep (survivors)* transporter en avion
   2 *vi (of passenger)* partir en avion

fly-by-night ['flaɪbəmaɪt] *adj Fam Pej (company)* véreux(euse)

flyer = flier

flying ['flaɪɪŋ] **1** *n (as pilot)* pilotage *m*; *(as passenger)* voyages *mpl* en avion; **she loves f.** *(as pilot)* elle adore piloter; *(as passenger)* elle adore prendre l'avion; **f. club** aéro-club *m*; **f. lessons** leçons *fpl* de pilotage; **f. time** heures *fpl* de vol
   2 *adj* (**a**) *(bird, fish)* volant(e); **they were hurt by f. glass** ils ont été blessés par des éclats de verre; **to pass with f. colours** réussir haut la main; **f. boat** hydravion *m*; **f. doctor** médecin *m* volant; **f. saucer** soucoupe *f* volante (**b**) *(rapid)* **a f. visit** une visite éclair; **to get off to a f. start** très bien démarrer

flyleaf ['flaɪliːf] *(pl* flyleaves ['flaɪliːvz]*) n* page *f* de garde

Flymo® ['flaɪməʊ] *n* = tondeuse à gazon sur coussin d'air

flyover ['flaɪəʊvə(r)] *n BrAut* pont *m* routier

flypaper ['flaɪpeɪpə(r)] *n* papier *m* tue-mouches, *Can* collant *m* à mouches

fly-past ['flaɪpɑːst] *n Aviat* défilé *m* aérien

flyweight ['flaɪweɪt] *n (in boxing)* poids *m* mouche

FM [e'fem] *n Rad (abbr* **frequency modulation**) FM *f*

FO [ef'əʊ] *n Br (abbr* **Foreign Office**) (ministère *m* des) Affaires *fpl* étrangères

foal [fəʊl] **1** *n (horse)* poulain *m*; *(female)* pouliche *f*
   2 *vi* pouliner

foam [fəʊm] **1** *n (on sea)* écume *f*; *(on beer, bath)* mousse *f*; **f. rubber** caoutchouc *m* Mousse®
   2 *vi (of sea)* écumer; *(of beer, bath)* mousser; **to f. at the mouth** baver; *Fig* écumer de rage

foamy ['fəʊmɪ] *adj (sea)* écumeux(euse); *(beer)* moussant(e)

fob [fɒb] *n* chaîne *f* (de montre); **f. watch** montre *f* de gousset

▸**fob off** *(pt & pp* fobbed*) vt sep Fam* **to f. sb off with an excuse** se débarrasser de qn en lui racontant des salades; **to f. sth off on sb** refiler *ou* fourguer qch à qn

focal ['fəʊkəl] *adj* focal(e); **f. point** foyer *m*; *Fig (of discussion)* point *m* central

focus ['fəʊkəs] **1** *n (pl* focuses *or* foci ['fəʊkaɪ]*) (of lens)* foyer *m*; *Fig (of discontent)* cible *f*; *(of interest, attention)* centre *m*; *Com & Pol* **f. group** *(of customers)* groupe *m* témoin; **to be in f.** être au point; **to be out of f.** ne pas être au point
   2 *vt (lens, camera)* mettre au point; *(rays, attention, energy)* concentrer (**on** sur); **all eyes were focused on him** tous les regards étaient tournés vers lui
   3 *vi* **to f. on sth** *(with camera)* faire la mise au point

sur qch; *(with eyes)* fixer qch; *Fig (of debate, speaker)* se concentrer sur qch

fodder ['fɒdə(r)] *n* fourrage *m*

foe [fəʊ] *n* ennemi *m*

foetal, *Am* **fetal** ['fiːtəl] *adj* fœtal(e); **in the f. position** en position fœtale

foetus, *Am* **fetus** ['fiːtəs] *n* fœtus *m*

fog [fɒg] *n* brouillard *m*; *Fig* **to be in a f.** *(confused)* être dans le brouillard; **f. lamp** *or* **light** *(on car)* (phare *m*) antibrouillard *m*

▸**fog up** *(pt & pp* fogged*) vi (of windows, glasses)* s'embuer

fogbound ['fɒgbaʊnd] *adj (port, airport)* bloqué(e) en raison du brouillard

fogey ['fəʊgɪ] *(pl* fogeys*) n Fam* **old f.** vieux (vieille) schnock *m,f*

foggy ['fɒgɪ] *adj* brumeux(euse); **it's f.** il y a du brouillard; *Fam* **I haven't (got) the foggiest (idea)!** je n'en ai pas la moindre idée!

foghorn ['fɒghɔːn] *n (on ship)* corne *f* de brume; *Fam* **a voice like a f.** une voix de stentor

fogy *(pl* fogies*)* = fogey

foible ['fɔɪbəl] *n (habit)* manie *f*; *(weakness)* point *m* faible

foil [fɔɪl] **1** *n* (**a**) *(metal sheet)* feuille *f*; **(cooking** *or* **kitchen) f.** papier *m* alu(minium) (**b**) *(complement)* **to act as a f. (to** *or* **for)** servir de repoussoir (à) (**c**) *(sword)* fleuret *m*
   2 *vt (plan, ambitions)* contrecarrer; *(attempt, coup)* faire échouer

foist [fɔɪst] *vt* refiler (**on** à); *(ideas)* imposer (**on** à)

fold¹ [fəʊld] *n (sheep)* **f.** parc *m* à moutons

fold² **1** *n* pli *m*; *(of fat)* bourrelet *m*
   2 *vt* (**a**) *(bend)* plier; **to f. sth in two** *or* **in half** plier qch en deux; **to f. one's arms** croiser les bras (**b**) *(in cooking)* mélanger délicatement
   3 *vi* (**a**) *(of chair, table)* se plier, se replier (**b**) *Fam (of business)* plier boutique

▸**fold up 1** *vt sep* plier, replier
   2 *vi (of map, chair)* se plier, se replier

foldaway ['fəʊldəweɪ] *adj (table, bed)* pliant(e)

folder ['fəʊldə(r)] *n (file, document wallet)* chemise *f*; *(ring binder)* classeur *m*; *Comput* répertoire *m*

folding ['fəʊldɪŋ] *adj (chair, table)* pliant(e); **f. doors** porte *f* en accordéon

foliage ['fəʊlɪdʒ] *n* feuillage *m*

folio ['fəʊlɪəʊ] *(pl* folios*) n* folio *m*

folk [fəʊk] **1** *npl Fam (people)* gens *mpl*; **my/your folks** *(family)* ma/ta famille
   2 *adj (traditional)* folklorique; **f. (music)** (musique *f*) folk *m*; **f. singer** chanteur(euse) *m,f* folk; **f. song** chanson *f* folk

folklore ['fəʊklɔː(r)] *n* folklore *m*

follow ['fɒləʊ] **1** *vt (act, performance)* passer après; *(career)* poursuivre; **the road follows the coast** la route longe la côte; **to f. one's nose** *(go straight ahead)* aller tout droit; *(act instinctively)* y aller à l'instinct
   2 *vi* (**a**) *(come after)* suivre; **proceed as follows** procéder comme suit (**b**) *(result)* s'ensuivre; **it follows that...** il s'ensuit que... (**c**) *(understand)* suivre

▸**follow on** *vi* (**a**) *(go after)* **you go ahead, we'll f. on** pars devant, nous te suivons (**b**) *(continue)* **to f. on from sth** découler de qch

▸**follow through 1** *vt sep (project, plan)* mener à son terme
   2 *vi* **he's full of ideas but he seldom follows**

through il a beaucoup d'idées, mais il les met rarement à exécution
▸**follow up** *vt sep (advantage, success)* exploiter; *(opportunity)* saisir; *(contact)* garder; *(clue)* suivre
follower ['fɒləʊə(r)] *n (of team)* supporter *m*; *(of ideas, politician)* partisan(e) *m,f*; *(of philosopher)* disciple *m*
following ['fɒləʊɪŋ] **1** *n (supporters) (of team)* supporters *mpl*; *(of ideas, politician)* partisans *mpl*; *(of programme)* public *m*
2 *pron* **the f.** *(things, points)* ce qui suit; *(people)* les personnes *fpl* suivantes
3 *adj* suivant(e); **(on) the f.** day le jour suivant, le lendemain
4 *prep* après
follow-up ['fɒləʊʌp] *n Com (of orders)* suivi *m*
folly ['fɒlɪ] *n* folie *f*; **an act of f.** une folie
foment [fə'ment] *vt Lit* fomenter
fond [fɒnd] *adj* (**a**) **to be f.** of sb/sth aimer bien qn/qch; **to become f.** of sb s'attacher à qn; **to become f.** of sth prendre goût à qch; **to be f.** of doing sth aimer bien faire qch (**b**) *(loving)* tendre, affectueux(euse); **f. memories (of)** de bons souvenirs (de) (**c**) *(hope)* naïf(ïve)
fondle ['fɒndəl] *vt* caresser
fondly ['fɒndlɪ] *adv* (**a**) *(lovingly)* tendrement, affectueusement (**b**) *(naively)* naïvement
fondness ['fɒndnɪs] *n* (**a**) *(affection)* tendresse *f*, affection *f* (**for** pour) (**b**) *(liking)* penchant *m* (**for** pour)
font [fɒnt] *n* (**a**) *Rel* fonts *mpl* baptismaux (**b**) *Typ & Comput* police *f* de caractères, fonte *f*
food [fuːd] *n* nourriture *f*; **Chinese/Mexican f.** la cuisine chinoise/mexicaine; **to be off one's f.** ne pas avoir d'appétit; **to give sb f. for thought** donner à penser *ou* à réfléchir à qn; *Biol* **f. chain** chaîne *f* alimentaire; **f. industry** industrie *f* alimentaire; **f. poisoning** intoxication *f* alimentaire; **f. processor** robot *m* de cuisine
foodstuffs ['fuːdstʌfs] *npl* produits *mpl* alimentaires
fool [fuːl] **1** *n (stupid person)* imbécile *mf*, idiot(e) *m,f*; *(jester)* fou *m*; **you'd be a f. to buy it** tu serais bien bête de l'acheter; **any f. knows that** le premier imbécile venu sait ça; **a f. of a doctor** un imbécile de docteur; **to play** *or* **act the f.** faire l'idiot; **to make a f. of** sb *(make look ridiculous)* ridiculiser qn; *(tease)* se moquer de qn; **to make a f. of oneself** se couvrir de ridicule; **the more f. you!** tu es vraiment bête!; **I felt such a f.** je me suis senti vraiment bête; **she's no** *or* **nobody's f.** on ne la lui fait pas, elle est maligne; **to live in a f.'s paradise** se bercer d'illusions; *Fam* **there's no f. like an old f.** il n'y a pire fou qu'un vieux fou
2 *vt (deceive)* avoir, duper; **you can't f. me** on ne m'a pas comme ça; **to let oneself be fooled by sth** se laisser avoir par qch; **you could have fooled me!** je ne l'aurais pas cru!
▸**fool about, fool around** *vi* (**a**) *(act foolishly)* faire l'imbécile; **to f. about** *or* **around with sth** *(clumsily, for fun)* jouer avec qch; *(fiddle)* tripoter qch (**b**) *(waste time)* perdre son temps (**c**) *(have affair(s))* avoir une aventure/des aventures
foolhardy ['fuːlhɑːdɪ] *adj* téméraire, imprudent(e)
foolish ['fuːlɪʃ] *adj (stupid)* idiot(e); *(imprudent)* insensé(e); **to make sb look f.** ridiculiser qn
foolishly ['fuːlɪʃlɪ] *adv (stupidly)* bêtement; *(imprudently)* imprudemment

foolproof ['fuːlpruːf] *adj (method, plan)* infaillible; *(device)* indétraquable
foot [fʊt] *(pl* **feet** [fiːt]) **1** *n* (**a**) *(of person, horse, chair)* pied *m*; *(of other animal)* patte *f*; **to put one's feet up** *(have a rest)* se reposer; **to set f.** on poser le pied sur; **I shall never set f.** in his house again je ne remettrai jamais les pieds chez lui; **to be on one's feet all day** être debout du matin au soir; **to be on one's feet again** *(after illness)* être de nouveau sur pied; **on f.** à pied; **under f.** sous les pieds; *Mil* **f. patrol** patrouille *f* à pied; **f. pump** pompe *f* à pied; **f. soldier** fantassin *m*, soldat *m* d'infanterie (**b**) *(of mountain, stairs)* pied *m*; *(of page)* bas *m*; *(of bed, table)* bout *m* (**c**) *(in poetry)* pied *m* (**d**) *(unit of measurement)* = 0,3048 m, pied *m* (anglais); **three f.** *or* **feet six (inches)** trois pieds six pouces (**e**) *(idioms)* **to have one's feet firmly on the ground** avoir les pieds sur terre; **to have one f. in the grave** avoir un pied dans la tombe; **to have a f. in both camps** avoir un pied dans chaque camp; **she hasn't put a f. wrong** elle n'a pas commis la moindre erreur; **to put one's f. down** *(be firm)* faire preuve de fermeté; *(refuse)* mettre le holà; *Fam* **to put one's f. in it** mettre les pieds dans le plat, faire une gaffe; **to find one's feet** s'adapter; **to get a f. in the door** avoir un pied dans la place; *Fam* **my f.!** mon œil!
2 *vt* **to f. the bill** payer la note
footage ['fʊtɪdʒ] *n Cin* séquences *fpl*, images *fpl*
foot-and-mouth disease [fʊtən'maʊθdɪ'ziːz] *n* fièvre *f* aphteuse
football ['fʊtbɔːl] *n (soccer)* football *m*; *(American)* football américain *m*; *(ball)* ballon *m* (de football); **f. club** club *m* de foot(ball); **f. fan** supporter *m* d'une équipe de football; **f. ground** terrain *m* de football; **f. hooligan** hooligan *m*; **f. pitch** terrain *m* de football; **f. player** footballeur(euse) *m,f*; *Br* **f. pools** ≃ loto *m* sportif; **f. supporter** supporter *m* d'une équipe de football
footballer ['fʊtbɔːlə(r)] *n* footballeur(euse) *m,f*
footbridge ['fʊtbrɪdʒ] *n* passerelle *f*
foothills ['fʊthɪlz] *npl* contreforts *mpl*
foothold ['fʊthəʊld] *n* prise *f* (pour le pied); *Fig* **to gain a f.** *(of theory, feeling)* se propager
footing ['fʊtɪŋ] *n* (**a**) *(balance)* **to lose one's f.** perdre l'équilibre (**b**) *(level)* **on an equal f.** sur un pied d'égalité; **to be on a friendly f. with sb** avoir des rapports amicaux avec qn
footlights ['fʊtlaɪts] *npl Theat* rampe *f*
footloose ['fʊtluːs] *adj* libre; **to be f. and fancy-free** être libre comme l'air
footman ['fʊtmən] *n* valet *m* de pied
footnote ['fʊtnəʊt] *n* note *f* de bas de page; *Fig* détail *m*
footpath ['fʊtpɑːθ] *n* sentier *m*
footprint ['fʊtprɪnt] *n* trace *f* de pas; *(of bare foot)* empreinte *f* de pied
footrest ['fʊtrest] *n* repose-pieds *m inv*
footsie ['fʊtsɪ] *n Fam* **to play f. with sb** faire du pied à qn
footsore ['fʊtsɔː(r)] *adj* **to be f.** avoir mal aux pieds
footstep ['fʊtstep] *n* pas *m*; *Fig* **to follow in sb's footsteps** suivre les traces de qn
footwear ['fʊtweə(r)] *n* chaussures *fpl*
footwork ['fʊtwɜːk] *n* jeu *m* de jambes; *Fig* **it required some rather fancy f.** il a fallu faire des pieds et des mains
fop [fɒp] *n* dandy *m*

foppish ['fɒpɪʃ] *adj* de dandy

for [fɔː(r), *unstressed* fə(r)] **1** *prep* (**a**) *(expressing purpose, destination)* pour; **to leave f.** **France** partir pour la France; **there's no time f.** **that** il n'y a pas de temps pour ça; **what's it f.?** c'est pour quoi faire?; **can you give me something f. the pain?** pouvez-vous me donner quelque chose contre la douleur?

(**b**) *(because of)* pour, en raison de; **she couldn't sleep f. the pain** elle ne pouvait pas dormir à cause de la douleur

(**c**) *(expressing cost, amount)* **I bought it f. £10** je l'ai acheté 10 livres; **a cheque f. £50** un chèque de 50 livres

(**d**) *(considering)* pour; **he is big f. his age** il est grand pour son âge; **f. all the good it will do** pour ce que ça changera; **f. all his wealth, he was still unhappy** en dépit de toutes ses richesses, il était toujours malheureux

(**e**) *(representing)* **A f.** **Anne** A comme Anne; **what's the French f.** "**book**"? comment dit-on "book" en français?

(**f**) *(duration)* **I was there f. a month** je suis resté là-bas (pendant) un mois; **I've been here f. a month** il y a un mois que je suis ici, je suis ici depuis un mois; **I will be here f. a month** je serai ici pendant un mois; **I haven't been there f. a month** je n'y suis pas allé depuis un mois; **I'm going away f. a fortnight** je pars pour quinze jours; **we have enough food f. two days** nous avons suffisamment à manger pour deux jours

(**g**) *(with point in time)* **f. the first/last time** pour la première/dernière fois; **I need it f. Friday** j'en ai besoin pour vendredi

(**h**) *(as compared to)* pour; **they sell ten red bikes f. every black one** ils vendent dix vélos rouges pour un noir

(**i**) *(in favour of)* **to be f. sth** être pour qch, être favorable à qch; *Fam* **I'm all f. it!** je suis tout à fait pour!

(**j**) *(introducing an infinitive clause)* **it is too early f. me to decide** il est trop tôt pour que je prenne une décision; **it will be difficult f. her to come** il lui sera difficile de venir; **it took an hour f. us to get there** il nous a fallu une heure pour arriver là-bas

(**k**) *(idioms)* **f. all I know** pour ce que j'en sais; **that's men f. you!** c'est bien les hommes!; *Fam* **he's f. it!** qu'est-ce qu'il va prendre!

2 *conj Lit (because)* car

forage ['fɒrɪdʒ] **1** *n (animal food)* fourrage *m*; *Mil* **f. cap** calot *m*

2 *vi* **to f. for sth** fouiller pour trouver qch

foray ['fɒreɪ] *n* incursion *f* (**into** dans)

forbear [fɔː'beə(r)] *(pt* forbore [fɔː'bɔː(r)], *pp* forborne [fɔː'bɔːn]) *vi Formal* **to f. to do sth** s'abstenir de faire qch

forbearance [fɔː'beərəns] *n Formal* patience *f*

forbid [fə'bɪd] *(pt* forbade [fə'bæd, fə'beɪd], *pp* **forbidden** [fə'bɪdən]) *vt* interdire; **to f. sb to do sth** interdire à qn de faire qch; **smoking is forbidden** il est interdit de fumer; **God f.!** Dieu m'en/nous en préserve!

forbidding [fə'bɪdɪŋ] *adj (appearance, look, landscape)* sinistre; *(task)* rébarbatif(ive)

force [fɔːs] **1** *n* (**a**) *(strength, power, influence)* force *f*; **by sheer** *or* **brute f.** par la force; **by f. of circumstance(s)** par la force des circonstances; **f. of habit** la force de l'habitude; **several forces conspired to**

bring about his downfall plusieurs facteurs ont contribué à provoquer sa chute; **to join forces (to do sth)** joindre ses efforts (pour faire qch) (**b**) *Mil* **the (armed) forces** les forces *fpl* armées; **to join forces (to do sth)** joindre ses efforts (pour faire qch); **they turned out in (full) f.** ils sont venus en masse (**c**) *(effect)* **to come into f.** entrer en vigueur

2 *vt* (**a**) *(compel)* **to f. sb to do sth** *or* **into doing sth** forcer *ou* obliger qn à faire qch; **to f. sth on qn** imposer qch à qn; **they forced the enemy back** ils ont repoussé l'ennemi (**b**) *(obtain by effort)* **to f. the issue** précipiter les choses; **to f. sb's hand** forcer la main à qn; **to f. one's way through a crowd** se frayer un passage à travers la foule; **to f. oneself on sb** *(sexually)* essayer d'abuser de qn physiquement

▸**force down** *vt sep* (**a**) *(aircraft)* obliger à atterrir (**b**) *(food)* se forcer à avaler

▸**force open** *vt sep (door, window, lock)* forcer

forced [fɔːst] *adj (manner, laugh)* forcé(e), artificiel(elle); **f. labour** travail *m* forcé; *Aviat* **f. landing** atterrissage *m* forcé; *Mil* **f. march** marche *f* forcée

force-feed ['fɔːsfiːd] *(pt & pp* force-fed ['fɔːsfed]) *vt (person)* nourrir de force; *(livestock)* gaver

forceful ['fɔːsfʊl] *adj (person, language)* énergique; *(argument)* puissant(e)

forceps ['fɔːseps] *npl* forceps *mpl*; **f. delivery** accouchement *m* aux forceps

forcible ['fɔːsɪbəl] *adj* (**a**) *Law* **f. entry** entrée *f* par effraction (**b**) *(argument)* puissant(e); *(reminder)* brutal(e)

forcibly ['fɔːsɪblɪ] *adv* (**a**) *(by force)* de force (**b**) *(argue)* vigoureusement

ford [fɔːd] **1** *n* gué *m*

2 *vt* traverser à gué

fore [fɔː(r)] **1** *n* **to come to the f.** *(of person)* commencer à être connu(e); *(of issue)* être mis(e) en évidence

2 *adj Naut* à l'avant

forearm ['fɔːrɑːm] *n* avant-bras *m inv*

forebear ['fɔːbeə(r)] *n* ancêtre *mf*

foreboding [fɔː'bəʊdɪŋ] *n* (mauvais) pressentiment *m*

forecast ['fɔːkɑːst] **1** *n* prévisions *fpl*; *(in horseracing)* pronostics *mpl* (des courses); **(weather) f.** prévisions *fpl* météorologiques, météo *f*

2 *vt (pt & pp* forecast(ed)) prévoir; *(in horseracing)* pronostiquer

foreclose [fɔː'kləʊz] *vt Fin* **to f. a mortgage** saisir un immeuble hypothéqué

forecourt ['fɔːkɔːt] *n (of petrol station)* devant *m*

forefathers ['fɔːfɑːðəz] *npl* aïeux *mpl*

forefinger ['fɔːfɪŋgə(r)] *n* index *m*

forefront ['fɔːfrʌnt] *n* **to be in the f. of** être au premier plan de

forego [fɔː'gəʊ] *(pt* forewent [fɔː'went], *pp* foregone [fɔː'gɒn]) *vt* renoncer à

foregone ['fɔːgɒn] *n* **to be a f. conclusion** être couru(e) d'avance

foreground ['fɔːgraʊnd] **1** *n* premier plan *m*; **in the f.** au premier plan

2 *vt* mettre au premier plan

forehand ['fɔːhænd] *n (in tennis)* coup *m* droit; **f. volley** volée *f* de face

forehead ['fɒrɪd, 'fɔːhed] *n* front *m*

foreign ['fɒrɪn] *adj* étranger(ère); **f. affairs** les affaires *fpl* étrangères; **f. aid** aide *f* aux pays étrangers; *(from point of view of recipient)* aide *f* de l'étranger;

Med **f. body** corps *m* étranger; *Journ* **f. correspondent** correspondant(e) *m,f* à l'étranger; **f. currency** devises *fpl* étrangères; **f. legion** légion *f* étrangère; *Pol* **F. Minister,** *Br* **F. Secretary** ministre *m* des Affaires étrangères; *Br Pol* **F. Office** ministère *m* des Affaires étrangères; **f. trade** commerce *m* extérieur

foreigner ['fɒrɪnə(r)] *n* étranger(ère) *m,f*

foreleg ['fɔːleg] *n* patte *f* de devant; *(of horse)* membre *m* antérieur

foreman ['fɔːmən] *n (of workers)* contremaître *m*; *(of jury)* président *m*

foremost ['fɔːməʊst] *adj* le (la) plus important(e)

forename ['fɔːneɪm] *n* prénom *m*

forensic [fə'rensɪk] *adj Law* légal(e); **f. evidence** résultats *mpl* des expertises médico-légales; **f. medicine** médecine *f* légale; **f. scientist** médecin *m* légiste

foreplay ['fɔːpleɪ] *n* préliminaires *mpl* amoureux

forerunner ['fɔːrʌnə(r)] *n* (**a**) *(person)* précurseur *m* (**of** de) (**b**) *(sign)* signe *m* précurseur (**of** de)

foresee [fɔː'siː] *(pt* **foresaw** [fɔː'sɔː], *pp* **foreseen** [fɔː'siːn]) *vt* prévoir

foreseeable [fɔː'siːəbəl] *adj* prévisible; **in the f. future** dans un avenir proche; **for the f. future** dans l'immédiat

foreshadow [fɔː'ʃædəʊ] *vt* annoncer

foresight ['fɔːsaɪt] *n* prévoyance *f*

foreskin ['fɔːskɪn] *n Anat* prépuce *m*

forest ['fɒrɪst] *n* forêt *f*; **f. fire** incendie *m* de forêt; *Am* **f. ranger** garde *m* forestier

forestall [fɔː'stɔːl] *vt* devancer

forester ['fɒrɪstə(r)] *n* (garde *m*) forestier *m*

forestry ['fɒrɪstrɪ] *n* sylviculture *f*; **the F. Commission** ≃ Les Eaux et Forêts *fpl*; **f. worker** *(forester)* forestier *m*; *(lumberjack)* bûcheron *m*

foretaste ['fɔːteɪst] *n* avant-goût *m* (**of** de)

foretell [fɔː'tel] *(pt & pp* **foretold** [fɔː'təʊld]) *vt* prédire

forethought ['fɔːθɔːt] *n* prévoyance *f*

forever [fə'revə(r)] *adv* (**a**) *(eternally)* pour toujours; **nothing lasts f.** tout a une fin; **the journey seemed to last f.** il semblait que le voyage ne finirait jamais (**b**) *(repeatedly)* sans cesse; **he was f. changing his mind** il changeait sans cesse *ou* constamment d'avis (**c**) *Fam (a long time)* une éternité; **to take f. (to do sth)** mettre un temps infini (à faire qch)

forewarn [fɔː'wɔːn] *vt* prévenir, avertir; *Prov* **forewarned is forearmed** un homme averti en vaut deux

forewent [fɔː'went] *pt of* **forego**

foreword ['fɔːwɜːd] *n* avant-propos *m inv*, préface *f*

forfeit ['fɔːfɪt] **1** *n (in game)* gage *m*; *Law* amende *f* **2** *vt (rights)* être déchu(e) de; *(property)* se faire confisquer; *(someone's respect)* perdre

forgave [fə'geɪv] *pt of* **forgive**

forge [fɔːdʒ] **1** *n* forge *f* **2** *vt* (**a**) *(metal, alliance)* forger (**b**) *(cheque, signature, banknote)* contrefaire; **to f. a document/passport** faire un faux document/passeport

▸**forge ahead** *vi* (**a**) *(make progress)* faire des progrès; *(of company)* aller de l'avant (**b**) *(outstrip competitors)* prendre de l'avance (**of** sur)

forged [fɔːdʒd] *adj* faux (fausse)

forgery ['fɔːdʒərɪ] *(pl* **forgeries**) *n* (**a**) *(activity)* contrefaçon *f*; *(of document, banknote)* falsification *f* (**b**) *(thing forged)* faux *m*

forget [fə'get] *(pt* **forgot** [fə'gɒt], *pp* **forgotten** [fə'gɒtən]) **1** *vt* oublier; **to f. to do sth** oublier de faire qch; **to f. how to do sth** oublier comment on fait qch,

ne plus savoir faire qch; **to be forgotten** tomber dans l'oubli; **f. it!** *(in reply to apology, thanks)* il n'y a pas de quoi!; *(stop talking about it)* laisse tomber! **2** *vi* oublier; **to f. about sb/sth** oublier qn/qch; **you can f. about going to London!** tu peux faire une croix sur ton voyage à Londres!; **let's f. about it** n'y pensons plus

forgetful [fə'getfʊl] *adj* **to be f.** avoir mauvaise mémoire

forget-me-not [fə'getmiːnɒt] *n* myosotis *m*

forgivable [fə'gɪvəbəl] *adj* excusable, pardonnable

forgive [fə'gɪv] *(pt* **forgave** [fə'geɪv], *pp* **forgiven** [fə'gɪvən]) **1** *vt* pardonner; **to f. sb for sth** pardonner qch à qn; **if you'll f. the pun** pardonnez-moi ce jeu de mots; **f. me for interrupting** pardonnez-moi de vous interrompre **2** *vi* pardonner; **to f. and forget** oublier sa rancune

forgiveness [fə'gɪvnɪs] *n* pardon *m*

forgiving [fə'gɪvɪŋ] *adj* indulgent(e)

forgo = **forego**

forgot [fə'gɒt] *pt of* **forget**

forgotten [fə'gɒtən] *pp of* **forget**

fork [fɔːk] **1** (**a**) *(for food)* fourchette *f* (**b**) *(for gardening)* fourche *f* (**c**) *(in road, path)* bifurcation *f* **2** *vi (of road, path)* bifurquer

▸**fork out** *Fam* **1** *vt sep* allonger **2** *vi* casquer (**for** pour)

forked [fɔːkt] *adj (stick, tongue)* fourchu(e); **f. lightning** éclairs *mpl*

fork-lift truck ['fɔːklɪft'trʌk] *n* chariot *m* (élévateur) à fourche

forlorn [fə'lɔːn] *adj (person, look)* triste, malheureux(euse); *(hope, attempt)* désespéré(e)

form [fɔːm] *n* (**a**) *(shape) (of object, animal)* forme *f*; *(of person)* silhouette *f*; **to take the f. of sth** prendre la forme de qch (**b**) *(type)* forme *f*; **in the f. of** sous forme de qch; **f. of address** titre *m* de politesse (**c**) *(politeness)* **as a matter of f., for f.'s sake** pour la forme, par pure formalité; **it's good/bad f. to...** cela se fait/ne se fait pas de... (**d**) *(for applications, orders)* formulaire *m* (**e**) *(condition, performance)* forme *f*; *(in horseracing)* performances *fpl*; **to be in** *or* **on good f.** être en forme; **on present f.** si l'on en juge par la situation actuelle (**f**) *Br Sch (class, year)* classe *f*

2 *vt (government, character)* former; *(idea)* avoir; *(opinion)* se faire; *(relationship, friendship)* nouer; *(organization, obstacle)* constituer; **to f. a plan** projeter de faire qch; **to f. part of sth** faire partie de qch

3 *vi* se former

formal ['fɔːməl] *adj (manner)* cérémonieux(euse); *(offer, occasion, invitation)* officiel(elle); *(language)* soutenu(e); **f. dress** tenue *f* de soirée

formality [fɔː'mælɪtɪ] *(pl* **formalities**) *n (procedure)* formalité *f*

formalize ['fɔːməlaɪz] *vt* officialiser

formally ['fɔːməlɪ] *adv (behave)* de façon cérémonieuse; *(invite, announce)* officiellement; **to dress f.** *(for evening reception)* porter une tenue de soirée

format ['fɔːmæt] **1** *n* format *m* **2** *vt (pt & pp* **formatted**) *Comput* formater

formation [fɔː'meɪʃən] *n (act, arrangement)* formation *f*; *(of idea, plan)* élaboration *f*; **f. flying** vol *m* en groupe

formative ['fɔːmətɪv] *adj* formateur(trice); **the f. years** les années *fpl* de formation

former ['fɔːmə(r)] **1** *pron* **the f.** le premier (la première), celui-là (celle-là); *(plural)* les premiers (les premières), ceux-là (celles-là)
2 *adj (pupil, colleague, job)* ancien(enne) *(before noun)*; **in f. times** autrefois; **in a f. life** dans une vie antérieure

formerly ['fɔːməlɪ] *adv* autrefois; **Mrs Connelly, f. Miss Paton** Mme Connelly, née Paton; **Zambia, f. Northern Rhodesia** la Zambie, ancienne Rhodésie du Nord

formidable ['fɔːmɪdəbəl] *adj (opponent, difficulty)* redoutable; *(performance, talent)* formidable

formula ['fɔːmjʊlə] (*pl* **formulas** *or* **formulae** ['fɔːmjʊliː]) *n* (**a**) *(scheme, in maths, chemistry)* formule *f*; **the f. for success** la clé de la réussite; **a peace f.** une solution en faveur de la paix; *Aut* **F. 1** formule 1 (**b**) *Am (baby food)* lait *m* en poudre

formulate ['fɔːmjʊleɪt] *vt (plan, proposal)* élaborer; *(thought, opinion)* formuler

fornication [fɔːnɪ'keɪʃən] *n Formal* fornication *f*

forsake [fə'seɪk] (*pt* **forsook** [fə'sʊk], *pp* **forsaken** [fə'seɪkən]) *vt Lit* (**a**) *(abandon)* abandonner (**b**) *(renounce)* renoncer à

forswear [fɔː'sweə(r)] (*pt* **forswore** [fɔː'swɔː(r)], *pp* **forsworn** [fɔː'swɔːn]) *vt Lit* renoncer à

fort [fɔːt] *n* fort *m*, forteresse *f*; *Fig* **to hold the f.** monter la garde

forte ['fɔːtɪ] *n* fort *m*

forth [fɔːθ] *adv* en avant; **to go f.** avancer; **to walk back and f.** marcher de long en large, faire les cent pas; **from that day f.** à dater de ce jour; **and so f.** et cetera, et ainsi de suite

forthcoming [fɔːθ'kʌmɪŋ] *adj* (**a**) *(election)* prochain(e); *(book, film)* qui sortira bientôt (**b**) *(available)* **no money was f.** l'argent n'est pas arrivé (**c**) *(informative)* expansif(ive) *(about* sur)

forthright ['fɔːθraɪt] *adj* franc (franche)

forthwith [fɔːθ'wɪθ] *adv Formal* immédiatement, sur-le-champ

fortieth ['fɔːtɪəθ] **1** *n* (**a**) *(fraction)* quarantième *m* (**b**) *(in series)* quarantième *mf*
2 *adj* quarantième

fortification [fɔːtɪfɪ'keɪʃən] *n* fortification *f*

fortified ['fɔːtɪfaɪd] *adj (town)* fortifié(e) (**b**) **f. wine** vin *m* doux (naturel), vin *m* de liqueur

fortify ['fɔːtɪfaɪ] (*pt & pp* **fortified**) *vt Mil* fortifier; **to f. oneself** se prémunir

fortitude ['fɔːtɪtjuːd] *n* force *f* morale

fortnight ['fɔːtnaɪt] *n Br* quinzaine *f*, quinze jours *mpl*; **a f. today** aujourd'hui en quinze; **a f.'s holiday** quinze jours *ou* deux semaines *fpl* de vacances

fortnightly ['fɔːtnaɪtlɪ] *Br* **1** *adj* bimensuel(elle)
2 *adv* tous les quinze jours, bimensuellement

fortress ['fɔːtrɪs] *n* forteresse *f*

fortuitous [fɔː'tjuːɪtəs] *adj Formal* fortuit(e)

fortunate ['fɔːtʃənət] *adj* heureux(euse); **to be f.** avoir de la chance; **to be f. enough to do sth** avoir la chance de faire qch

fortunately ['fɔːtʃənətlɪ] *adv* heureusement, par bonheur

fortune ['fɔːtʃən] *n* (**a**) *(riches)* fortune *f*; **to make a** *or* **one's f.** faire fortune; *Fam* **to cost a (small) f.** coûter une fortune *ou* les yeux de la tête (**b**) *(luck)* chance *f*; **good f.** chance *f*; **bad f.** malchance *f*; **to tell sb's f.** dire la bonne aventure à qn

fortune-teller ['fɔːtʃəntelə(r)] *n* diseur(euse) *m,f* de bonne aventure

forty ['fɔːtɪ] **1** *n* quarante *m inv*
2 *adj* quarante; *Fam* **to have f. winks** piquer *ou* faire un petit somme; *see also* **eighty**

forum ['fɔːrəm] *n* forum *m*; *Comput (on Internet)* groupe *m* de discussion; **a f. for debate** un lieu de débat

forward ['fɔːwəd] **1** *n (in sport)* avant *m*
2 *adj* (**a**) *(position)* avant *inv*; *(movement)* en avant, vers l'avant; **f. planning** planification *f*; *Fin* **f. market** marché *m* à terme (**b**) *(impudent, bold)* effronté(e), hardi(e)
3 *adv* (**a**) *(of time)* **from this/that day f.** à partir d'aujourd'hui/de ce jour-là; **to put the clocks f.** avancer les pendules (**b**) *(of direction)* en avant; **to walk f.** avancer (**c**) *(of position)* à l'avant; **we're sitting too far f.** *(in cinema, theatre)* nous sommes assis trop près; **the seat is too far f.** le siège est trop avancé
4 *vt* (**a**) *(letter)* faire suivre; *(complaint, query)* faire passer (**to** à) (**b**) *(one's career, interests)* favoriser

forwarding agent ['fɔːwədɪŋ'eɪdʒənt] *n Com* (agent *m*) transitaire *m*

forward-looking ['fɔːwədlʊkɪŋ] *adj* progressiste

forwards ['fɔːwədz] *adv* = **forward**

fossil ['fɒsəl] *n* fossile *m*; *Fam* **an old f.** *(man)* un vieux croûton; *(woman)* une vieille bique; **f. fuel** combustible *m* fossile

fossilized ['fɒsɪlaɪzd] *adj* fossilisé(e); *Fig* sclérosé(e)

foster ['fɒstə(r)] **1** *adj* **f. child** = enfant placé dans une famille d'accueil; **f. parents** famille *f* d'accueil, parents *mpl* nourriciers
2 *vt* (**a**) *(child)* prendre en famille d'accueil (**b**) *(idea, hope)* nourrir, entretenir; *(friendship)* stimuler

fought [fɔːt] *pt & pp of* **fight**

foul [faʊl] **1** *n (in sport)* faute *f*
2 *adj* (**a**) *(disgusting) (smell, taste)* infect(e), nauséabond(e); *(weather)* sale; *(air)* vicié(e); *(language)* ordurier(ère); **to be in a f. mood** être d'une humeur massacrante (**b**) *(illegal)* **f. play** *Sport* jeu *m* irrégulier; *Law* acte *m* criminel; **f. play is not suspected** on ne croit pas à un meurtre
3 *adv* (**a**) **to smell f.** puer; **to taste f.** avoir un goût infect (**b**) **to fall f. of the law** avoir des démêlés avec la justice
4 *vt* (**a**) *(pollute)* salir (**b**) *(entangle)* s'enchevêtrer autour de (**c**) *(in sport)* commettre une faute contre

▸ **foul up** *vt sep Fam (ruin)* gâcher

foul-mouthed ['faʊlmaʊðd] *adj* grossier(ère), mal embouché(e)

found[1] [faʊnd] *vt* (**a**) *(city, organization)* fonder; *(company)* créer; *(empire)* établir (**b**) *(base)* baser, fonder (**on** sur)

found[2] *pt & pp of* **find**

foundation [faʊn'deɪʃən] *n* (**a**) *(of city, organization)* fondation *f*; *(of company)* création *f* (**b**) *(basis)* fondement *m*, base *f*; **to be without f.** être dénué(e) de fondement (**c**) **foundations** *(of building, society)* fondations *fpl* (**d**) *(make-up)* **f. (cream)** fond *m* de teint

founder[1] ['faʊndə(r)] *n (of hospital, school)* fondateur(trice) *m,f*; **f. member** membre *m* fondateur

founder[2] *vi (of ship)* s'échouer; *Fig (of project, talks)* avorter

founding father ['faʊndɪŋ'fɑːðə(r)] *n* père *m* fondateur

foundling ['faʊndlɪŋ] *n Old-fashioned* enfant *mf* trouvé(e)

foundry ['faʊndrɪ] *(pl* **foundries**) *n* fonderie *f*

fount [faʊnt] *n Lit & Fig* source *f*
fountain ['faʊntɪn] *n* fontaine *f*; **f. pen** stylo *m* (à) plume
four [fɔː(r)] **1** *n* quatre *m inv*; **on all fours** à quatre pattes **2** *adj* quatre; **to the f. corners of the earth** aux quatre coins du monde; *see also* **eight**
four-eyes ['fɔːraɪz] *n Fam* binoclard(e) *m,f*
four-figure ['fɔːˈfɪgə(r)] *adj* **a f. sum** un montant de quatre chiffres
fourfold ['fɔːfəʊld] **1** *adj* **a f. increase** une augmentation au quadruple **2** *adv* **to increase f.** quadrupler
four-legged ['fɔːˈlegɪd] *adj* quadrupède; *Hum* **f. friend** ami *m* à quatre pattes
four-letter word ['fɔːletəˈwɜːd] *n* gros mot *m*
four-poster ['fɔːˈpəʊstə(r)] *n* **f. (bed)** lit *m* à baldaquin
foursome ['fɔːsəm] *n* groupe *m* de quatre personnes
fourteen ['fɔːtiːn] **1** *n* quatorze *m inv* **2** *adj* quatorze; *see also* **eight**
fourteenth [fɔːˈtiːnθ] **1** *n* (**a**) *(fraction)* quatorzième *m* (**b**) *(in series)* quatorzième *mf* (**c**) *(of month)* quatorze *m inv* **2** *adj* quatorzième; *see also* **eighth**
fourth [fɔːθ] **1** *n* (**a**) *(fraction)* quatrième *m* (**b**) *(in series)* quatrième *mf* (**c**) *(of month)* quatre *m inv* **2** *adj* quatrième; *see also* **eighth**
fourthly ['fɔːθlɪ] *adv* quatrièmement
fowl [faʊl] *(pl* **fowl)** *n* volaille *f*
fox [fɒks] **1** *n* renard *m*; *Fig* **a sly old f.** *(cunning person)* un vieux renard; **f. cub** renardeau *m*; **f. hunt** chasse *f* au renard **2** *vt (perplex)* laisser perplexe; *(deceive)* duper
foxglove ['fɒksglʌv] *n* digitale *f* (pourprée)
fox-hunting ['fɒkshʌntɪŋ] *n* chasse *f* au renard
foxtrot ['fɒkstrɒt] *n* fox-trot *m inv*
foxy ['fɒksɪ] *adj Fam* (**a**) *(sly)* rusé(e) (**b**) *Am (sexy)* sexy *inv*
foyer ['fɔɪeɪ] *n (in theatre)* foyer *m*; *(in cinema, hotel)* hall *m*
fraction ['frækʃən] *n (in maths)* fraction *f*; *Fig (small part)* petite partie *f*; **a f. too small/large** un tout petit peu trop petit(e)/grand(e)
fractional ['frækʃənəl] *adj (very small)* infime
fractious ['frækʃəs] *adj (adult)* de mauvaise humeur; *(baby)* pleurnicheur(euse); *(tone, expression)* irrité(e)
fracture ['fræktʃə(r)] **1** *n* fracture *f* **2** *vt (bone)* fracturer; *(pipe)* fendre **3** *vi (of bone)* se fracturer; *(of pipe)* se fendre
fragile ['frædʒaɪl] *adj* fragile; *Fam* **I'm feeling a bit f. this morning** *(after drinking)* j'ai un peu la gueule de bois ce matin
fragility [frəˈdʒɪlɪtɪ] *n* fragilité *f*
fragment 1 *n* ['frægmənt] fragment *m*; **I only heard a f. of what was said** je n'ai entendu que des bribes de la conversation **2** *vi* [fræg'ment] *(of object)* se fragmenter; *(of organization)* éclater
fragrance ['freɪgrəns] *n* parfum *m*
fragrant ['freɪgrənt] *adj* odorant(e), parfumé(e)
frail [freɪl] *adj (person)* frêle; *(object)* fragile
frailty ['freɪltɪ] *n* faiblesse *f*
frame [freɪm] **1** *n* (**a**) *(of picture)* cadre *m*, encadrement *m*; *(of door, window)* encadrement *m* (**b**) *(of person, animal)* ossature *f*; *(of building, bridge)* charpente *f*; *(of bicycle)* cadre *m*; *(of glasses)* monture *f* (**c**) **f. of mind** état *m* d'esprit; **f. of reference** système *m* de référence

2 *vt* (**a**) *(surround)* encadrer (**b**) *(compose) (answer)* formuler; *(law)* rédiger (**c**) *Fam (falsely incriminate)* monter un coup contre
framework ['freɪmwɜːk] *n (structure)* cadre *m*, structure *f*; *(of building, construction)* charpente *f*; *Fig* **within the f. of** dans le cadre de
franc [fræŋk] *n (currency)* franc *m*; *Formerly* **Belgian/ French f.** franc *m* suisse; **Swiss f.** franc *m* suisse
France [frɑːns] *n* la France
franchise ['fræntʃaɪz] **1** *n* (**a**) *Com* franchise *f* (**b**) *Pol* droit *m* de vote **2** *vt Com* franchiser
francophile ['fræŋkəʊfaɪl] **1** *n* francophile *mf* **2** *adj* francophile
francophone ['fræŋkəʊfəʊn] **1** *n* francophone *mf* **2** *adj* francophone
frank [fræŋk] **1** *adj* franc (franche); **to be f....** pour être franc... **2** *vt (letter)* affranchir
Frankfurt ['fræŋkfɜːt] *n* Francfort
frankfurter ['fræŋkfɜːtə(r)] *n* saucisse *f* de Francfort
frankincense ['fræŋkɪnsens] *n* encens *m*
frankly ['fræŋklɪ] *adv* franchement
frantic ['fræntɪk] *adj (rush, pace)* frénétique; *(attempt, effort)* désespéré(e); **f. with worry** fou (folle) d'inquiétude
frantically ['fræntɪklɪ] *adv* frénétiquement; *(work, write)* avec frénésie; *(try)* désespérément
fraternal [frəˈtɜːnəl] *adj* fraternel(elle)
fraternity [frəˈtɜːnɪtɪ] *(pl* **fraternities)** *n* (**a**) *(brotherliness)* fraternité *f* (**b**) *(group)* confrérie *f*; **the banking/medical f.** la confrérie des banquiers/médecins (**c**) *Am Univ* = organisation d'étudiants; **f. house** = maison communautaire (d'étudiants d'une même organisation)
fraternize ['frætənaɪz] *vi* fraterniser (**with** avec)
fraud [frɔːd] *n* (**a**) *(person)* imposteur *m* (**b**) *(deception)* supercherie *f*; *(crime)* fraude *f*; **the F. Squad** ≃ (le service de) la Répression des Fraudes
fraudulent ['frɔːdjʊlənt] *adj (charge, accusation, feelings)* faux (fausse); *(claim, transaction)* frauduleux(euse)
fraught [frɔːt] *adj (person, situation)* tendu(e); *(day)* éprouvant(e); **f. with danger** rempli(e) d'embûches; **f. with emotion** chargé(e) d'émotion
fray¹ [freɪ] *n (brawl)* bagarre *f*; **to enter the f.** entrer dans l'arène
fray² **1** *vt (material)* user **2** *vi (of material)* s'user; *(of tempers)* s'échauffer; *(of nerves)* craquer
frazzle ['fræzəl] *n* **to be burnt to a f.** *(of food)* être carbonisé(e); *Fam (of person)* être brûlé(e) par le soleil
frazzled ['fræzəld] *adj Fam (person)* lessivé(e), épuisé(e); *(nerves)* à plat
freak [friːk] **1** *n* (**a**) *(strange being)* monstre *m*, phénomène *m*; **f. show** exhibition *f* de monstres (**b**) *(strange event)* **by a f. of fortune** par un coup de chance; **f. accident** accident *m* imprévisible; **f. storm** orage *m* inattendu (**c**) *(enthusiast)* fana *mf*; **jazz/film f.** fana *mf* de jazz/cinéma **2** *vi* = **freak out** *vi*
freak out *Fam* **1** *vt sep (shock, scare)* faire flipper **2** *vi (panic)* paniquer; *(become angry)* piquer une crise
freckle ['frekəl] *n* tache *f* de rousseur
free [friː] **1** *adj* (**a**) *(unrestricted)* libre (**from** or **of** de); *(movement)* dégagé(e); **to be f. of sb** être débarrassé(e)

de qn; **f. from worry** sans souci; **to be f. to do sth** être libre de faire qch; **to set sb f.** rendre sa liberté à qn; **f. and easy** décontracté(e); *Fam* **feel f.** to borrow the car n'hésitez pas à emprunter la voiture; **(as) f. as a bird** libre comme l'air; **to be a f. agent** être libre (de ses mouvements); *Fig* **to have a f. hand** avoir pleine liberté d'action; *Econ* **f. enterprise** libre entreprise *f*; **f. fall** *(of parachutist, economy)* chute *f* libre; **f. kick** *(in football)* coup *m* franc; *Econ* **f. market** économie *f* de marché; **f. speech** liberté *f* d'expression; **f. throw** *(in basketball)* lancer *m* franc; **f. trade** libre-échange *m*; **f. verse** vers *mpl* libres; **f. will** libre arbitre *m*; **to do sth of one's own f. will** faire qch de son plein gré

(b) *(unoccupied) (person, seat, table, time)* libre **(c)** *(without charge)* gratuit(e); **f. gift** cadeau *m* **(d)** *(generous)* **to be f. with one's advice** être prodigue en conseils

2 *adv* *(without charge)* gratuitement; **to do sth for f.** faire qch gratuitement

3 *vt (pt & pp* **freed** [fri:d]*) (prisoner, time, place)* libérer (**from** de); *(something stuck)* dégager (**from** de); **to f. oneself from** *or* **of sth** se libérer de qch

freedom ['fri:dəm] *n* liberté *f*; **to have the f. to do sth** être libre de faire qch; **f. of information** libre accès *m* à l'information; **f. of speech/worship** liberté *f* d'expression/de culte; **to give sb the f. of the city** nommer qn citoyen(enne) d'honneur de la ville; **f. fighter** guérillero *m*, révolutionnaire *mf*

free-for-all ['fri:fərɔ:l] *n Fam* bagarre *f*

freehold ['fri:həʊld] *n Law* propriété *f* foncière perpétuelle et libre

freeholder ['fri:həʊldə(r)] *n* propriétaire (à perpétuité)

freelance ['fri:lɑ:ns] **1** *n* travailleur(euse) *m,f* indépendant(e)

2 *adj* indépendant(e), free-lance *inv*

3 *adv* **to work f.** travailler en indépendant(e) *ou* en free-lance

4 *vi* travailler en indépendant(e) *ou* en free-lance

freelancer ['fri:lɑ:nsə(r)] *n* travailleur(euse) *m,f* indépendant(e), free-lance *mf*

freeloader ['fri:ləʊdə(r)] *n Fam* pique-assiette *mf inv,* parasite *m*

freely ['fri:lɪ] *adv (give)* sans compter; *(speak)* en toute liberté; *(spend)* libéralement; **f. available** *(for sale)* en vente libre; *(easy to get hold of)* qu'on peut se procurer facilement

freemason ['fri:meɪsən] *n* franc-maçon *m*

freemasonry ['fri:meɪsənrɪ] *n* franc-maçonnerie *f*

Freepost® ['fri:pəʊst] *n Br* ≃ correspondance-réponse *f*

free-range ['fri:'reɪndʒ] *adj (chicken)* fermier(ère); **f. eggs** œufs *mpl* de poules élevées en plein air

freestyle ['fri:staɪl] **1** *n (in swimming)* nage *f* libre; *(skateboarding, skiing, snowboarding, rap music)* freestyle *m*

2 *adj (skateboarding, skiing, snowboarding, rap music)* freestyle

freethinker ['fri:θɪŋkə(r)] *n* libre-penseur(euse) *m,f*

free-to-air ['fri:tu:'eə(r)] *adj TV (channel)* en clair

freeware ['fri:weə(r)] *n Comput* logiciel *m* (du domaine) public, gratuiciel *m*

freeway ['fri:weɪ] *n Am* autoroute *f*

freewheel ['fri:wi:l] *vi (on bicycle)* être en roue libre; *(in car)* rouler au point mort

freeze [fri:z] **1** *n (in weather)* gel *m*, gelée *f*; **price/ wage f.** gel *m* des prix/salaires

2 *vt (pt* **froze** [frəʊz]*, pp* **frozen** ['frəʊzən]*) (food)* congeler; *(prices, assets)* geler; **to be frozen to death** être mort(e) de froid

3 *vi* **(a)** *(of weather)* **it's freezing** *(below zero)* il gèle; *Fig (very cold)* on gèle **(b)** *(of liquid, food)* geler; **to f. to death** mourir de froid; *Fam* **I'm freezing** je suis gelé **(c)** *(stand still)* s'arrêter net, se figer; **f.!** ne bougez plus!

▶**freeze out** *vt sep Fam* **to f. sb out** *(of conversation, deal)* exclure qn; *Com* **to f. out the competition** évincer les concurrents

▶**freeze over** *vi (of pond, river)* geler

▶**freeze up** *vi (of pond, mechanism)* geler

freeze-dried ['fri:z'draɪd] *adj (coffee, herbs)* lyophilisé(e)

freeze-frame ['fri:z'freɪm] *n Cin* arrêt *m* sur image

freezer ['fri:zə(r)] *n* congélateur *m*; *(ice-box)* freezer *m*

freezing ['fri:zɪŋ] *adj* **f. (cold)** *(room, weather, temperature)* glacial(e); *(water)* glacé(e); **it's f. cold in here** on meurt de froid ici; **f. fog** brouillard *m* givrant

freight [freɪt] *Com* **1** *n (transport)* fret *m*, transport *m* de marchandises; *(goods)* cargaison *f*; *(price)* prix *m* de transport; **f. train** train *m* de marchandises

2 *vt (goods)* transporter

freighter ['freɪtə(r)] *n (ship)* cargo *m*

French [frentʃ] **1** *n (language)* français *m*; *Hum* **pardon my F.** *(after swearing)* excusez mon langage; **F. class/teacher** classe *f*/professeur *m* de français

2 *npl* **the F.** *(people)* les Français *mpl*

3 *adj* français(e); **F. Canadian** *(person)* Canadien(-enne) *m,f* français(e); **F. fries** frites *fpl*; **F. horn** cor *m* d'harmonie; **F. kiss** baiser *m* avec la langue; *Br Old-fashioned* **F. letter** capote *f* anglaise; **F. loaf** *or* **stick** baguette *f*; **F. Polynesia** la Polynésie Française; **F. window** porte-fenêtre *f*

French-Canadian ['frentʃkə'neɪdjən] *n* canadien(-enne) français(e)

Frenchman ['frentʃmən] *n* Français *m*

French-speaking ['frentʃ'spi:kɪŋ] *adj* francophone

Frenchwoman ['frentʃwʊmən] *n* Française *f*

frenetic [frə'netɪk] *adj* frénétique

frenzied ['frenzɪd] *adj (person)* affolé(e); *(attack)* déchaîné(e); *(activity)* frénétique; **f. with rage/worry** fou (folle) de rage/d'inquiétude

frenzy ['frenzɪ] *(pl* **frenzies**) *n* frénésie *f*, folie *f*; **to work oneself into a f.** se mettre dans tous ses états

frequency ['fri:kwənsɪ] *(pl* **frequencies**) *n* fréquence *f*; **f. band** bande *f* de fréquences

frequent 1 *adj* ['fri:kwənt] fréquent(e); **it's a f. occurrence** cela se produit souvent

2 *vt* [frɪ'kwent] fréquenter

frequently ['fri:kwəntlɪ] *adv* fréquemment, souvent

fresco ['freskəʊ] *(pl* **frescos** *or* **frescoes**) *n* fresque *f*

fresh [freʃ] **1** *adj* **(a)** *(food, news)* frais (fraîche); **to smell f.** sentir bon le frais; **to get some f. air** s'aérer; **f. water** *(not salty)* eau *f* douce; **it's still f. in my mind** c'est encore frais dans ma mémoire; **as f. as a daisy** frais et dispos *inv* **(b)** *(page, attempt, drink)* nouveau(elle) *(before noun)*; **to make a f. start** recommencer à zéro **(c)** *(original) (approach, writing)* nouveau (nouvelle), original(e) **(d)** *Am Fam (cheeky)* insolent(e); **to get f. with sb** *(sexually)* faire des avances à qn

2 *adv* f. **from** *(school, university)* frais émoulu(e) de; **we're** f.

out of lemons nous n'avons plus de citrons

freshen ['freʃən] *vi (of wind, weather)* rafraîchir

▶**freshen up** *vi (wash)* faire un brin de toilette

fresher ['freʃər] *n Br Univ* étudiant(e) *m,f* de première année; **freshers' week** = semaine d'orientation précédant la rentrée universitaire pour les nouveaux étudiants

Freshers' week

Dans les universités britanniques, les étudiants de première année arrivent généralement une semaine avant le début des cours afin de se familiariser avec leur nouvel environnement et achever les formalités administratives. Durant cette semaine, baptisée "freshers' week", les nouveaux étudiants ont l'occasion de faire connaissance lors de rencontres organisées par leur université. Il y a également ment une "freshers' fair" durant laquelle les étudiants sont invités à s'inscrire à toutes sortes de clubs proposant des activités sportives ou culturelles et où ils peuvent obtenir des informations sur les services qui leur sont proposés. Dans la plupart des universités, la semaine se termine par une grande soirée, le "freshers' ball".

freshly ['freʃlɪ] *adv* fraîchement; **f. baked** sortant du four; **f. made** qui vient d'être fait

freshman ['freʃmən] *n Am Univ* étudiant(e) *m,f* de première année

freshness ['freʃnɪs] *n* (**a**) *(of food)* fraîcheur *f* (**b**) *(originality)* nouveauté *f*, originalité *f*

freshwater ['freʃwɔːtə(r)] *adj (fish)* d'eau douce

fret [fret] *(pt & pp* **fretted**) *vi (worry)* s'inquiéter, se tourmenter

fretful ['fretfʊl] *adj* inquiet(ète)

Freudian ['frɔɪdɪən] *adj* freudien(enne); **F. slip** lapsus *m*

FRG [efɑː'dʒiː] *n (abbr* **Federal Republic of Germany**) RFA *f*

Fri *(abbr* **Friday**) vendredi

friar ['fraɪə(r)] *n* religieux *m*, moine *m*

fricassee [frɪkə'siː] *n* fricassée *f*

friction ['frɪkʃən] *n also Fig* friction *f*

Friday ['fraɪdɪ] *n* vendredi *m*; *see also* **Saturday**

fridge [frɪdʒ] *n* frigo *m*

fridge-freezer ['frɪdʒ'friːzə(r)] *n* frigo *m* avec congélateur

fried [fraɪd] *adj* frit(e)

friend [frend] *n* ami(e) *m,f*; **to be friends with sb** être ami(e) avec qn; **to make friends with sb** devenir ami(e) avec qn; **that's what friends are for** c'est à ça que servent les amis; **we're just good friends** nous sommes bons amis, c'est tout; **he's no f. of mine** ce n'est pas un ami; **to have friends in high places** avoir des amis bien placés; **to be a f. of the arts** être un défenseur des beaux-arts; *Prov* **a f. in need is a f. indeed** c'est dans le besoin que l'on connaît ses amis

friendless ['frendlɪs] *adj (person)* sans amis; *(childhood)* solitaire

friendly ['frendlɪ] **1** *n Sport* match *m* amical
2 *adj* amical(e); **f. advice** conseils *mpl* d'ami; **a f. nation** un pays ami; **to be f. with sb** être ami(e) avec qn; **to be on f. terms with sb** être en bons termes

avec qn; *Mil* **f. fire** tirs *mpl* provenant de son propre camp

friendship ['frendʃɪp] *n* amitié *f*

fries [fraɪz] *npl* **(French) f.** frites *fpl*

frieze [friːz] *n Art & Archit* frise *f*

frigate ['frɪgət] *n* frégate *f*

fright [fraɪt] *n* peur *f*, effroi *m*; **to take f.** prendre peur; **to get a f.** avoir peur; **to give sb a f.** faire peur à qn; *Fam* **to look a f.** être à faire peur

frighten ['fraɪtən] **1** *vt* effrayer, faire peur à; **to f. sb into doing sth** faire peur à qn jusqu'à ce qu'il fasse qch; *Fam* **to f. the life** *or* **the wits out of sb** rendre qn fou (folle) de peur
2 *vi* **I don't f. easily** je ne me laisse pas effrayer facilement

frightened ['fraɪtənd] *adj* apeuré(e); **to be f. (of)** avoir peur (de); **to be f. to do sth** avoir peur de faire qch

frightening ['fraɪtənɪŋ] *adj* effrayant(e)

frightful ['fraɪtfʊl] *adj* épouvantable, affreux(euse)

frightfully ['fraɪtfʊlɪ] *adv* terriblement

frigid ['frɪdʒɪd] *adj (sexually)* frigide; *(smile, atmosphere)* glacial(e)

frill [frɪl] *n* volant *m*; *Fig* **no frills** *(ceremony)* sans chichis; *(holiday)* rudimentaire

frilly ['frɪlɪ] *adj* à volants

fringe [frɪndʒ] *n* (**a**) *(on clothes, lampshade) & Br (of hair)* frange *f* (**b**) *(edge) (of forest)* lisière *f*; *(of town)* abords *mpl*; **on the fringes of society** en marge de la société; **f. benefits** avantages *mpl* divers; *Br Theat* **f. festival** festival *m* off; *Pol* **f. group** groupuscule *m*; **f. theatre** théâtre *m* alternatif

frisk [frɪsk] **1** *vt (search)* fouiller
2 *vi* **to f. about** gambader

frisky ['frɪskɪ] *adj (person)* plein(e) d'entrain; *(horse)* nerveux(euse)

fritter ['frɪtə(r)] *n Culin* beignet *m*

▶**fritter away** *vt sep* gaspiller

frivolity [frɪ'vɒlɪtɪ] *n (pl* **frivolities**) *n* frivolité *f*

frivolous ['frɪvələs] *adj* frivole; *(remark)* futile

frizzy ['frɪzɪ] *adj* crépu(e)

fro [frəʊ] *adv* **to go to and f.** aller et venir

frock [frɒk] *n (dress)* robe *f*; **f. coat** redingote *f*

frog [frɒg] *n* (**a**) *(animal)* grenouille *f*; *Fam* **to have a f. in one's throat** avoir un chat dans la gorge (**b**) *Br Fam (French person)* = terme xénophobe, souvent humoristique, désignant un Français

frogman ['frɒgmən] *n* homme-grenouille *m*

frogmarch ['frɒgmɑːtʃ] *vt* emmener de force

frogspawn ['frɒgspɔːn] *n* œufs *mpl* de grenouille

frolic ['frɒlɪk] *(pt & pp* **frolicked**) *vi* s'ébattre

from [frɒm, *unstressed* frəm] *prep* (**a**) *(expressing place of origin)* de; **where are you f.?, where do you come f.?** d'où êtes-vous?, d'où venez-vous?; **she's f. Portugal** elle vient du Portugal; **f. Edinburgh to Paris** d'Édimbourg à Paris; **the train f. Manchester** le train de Manchester; **10 km f. Paris** à 10 km de Paris (**b**) *(expressing time)* à partir de; **f. tomorrow** à partir de demain; **f. then (on)** depuis ce jour-là; **f. the beginning** dès le début; **f. six to seven o'clock** de six heures à sept heures; **f. morning to** *or* **till night** du matin au soir; **five years f. now** dans cinq ans; **blind f. birth** aveugle de naissance (**c**) *(expressing range, change)* **f.... to...** de... à...; **children f. seven to nine years** les enfants de sept à neuf ans; **wine f. £6 a bottle** du vin à partir de 6 livres la bouteille

(**d**) *(expressing source)* de; **to buy sth f. sb** acheter qch à qn; **to drink f. a cup** boire dans une tasse; **a quotation f. the Bible** une citation tirée de la Bible; **made f. rubber** en caoutchouc
(**e**) *(expressing removal)* de; **to take sth f. sb** prendre qch à qn; **he was banned f. the club** il a été exclu du club
(**f**) *(on the basis of)* **f. what I heard/saw…** d'après ce que j'ai entendu/vu…

frond [frɒnd] *n (of fern)* fronde *f*; *(of palm)* feuille *f*

front [frʌnt] **1** *n* (**a**) *(not back)* devant *m*; *(of car, plane, boat)* avant *m*; *(of building)* façade *f*; **on the f. of the book** sur la couverture du livre; **at the f. of the book** au début du livre; **I sat in (the) f.** *(of car)* j'étais assis devant; *Br* **the f.** *(at seaside)* le front de mer, la promenade
(**b**) *(outward appearance)* **his kindness is only a f.** sa gentillesse n'est qu'une façade; **the company is a f. for their arms dealing** l'entreprise sert de couverture à leur trafic d'armes; **f. man** *(of TV, radio programme)* présentateur *m*; *(of pop group, organization)* leader *m*
(**c**) *Mil, Pol & Met* front *m*; *Fig* **on all fronts** sur tous les fronts; *Met* **warm/cold f.** front chaud/froid
(**d**) **in f.** devant; *(in race, contest)* en tête; **in f. of** devant
(**e**) *Fam* **to pay up f.** payer d'avance; **to be up f. about sth** être franc (franche) au sujet de qch
2 *adj* de devant; *Br Pol* **f. bench** = le banc des ministres et celui du cabinet fantôme; **f. door** porte *f* d'entrée; *Mil* **f. line** front *m*; **f. cover** couverture *f*; **f. page** *(of newspaper)* première page *f*; **f. room** *(lounge)* salon *m*; **f. row** premier rang *m*; **to have a f.-row seat** *(in theatre)* être (assis(e)) au premier rang; *Fig* être aux premières loges; **f. seat** *(in car)* siège *m* avant; **f. teeth** dents *fpl* de devant; **f. view** vue *f* de face
3 *vt (organization, pop group)* être à la tête de; *(government)* diriger; *(TV programme)* présenter
4 *vi (of building)* **the house fronts onto the river** la maison donne sur le fleuve

frontage ['frʌntɪdʒ] *n (of building)* façade *f*; *(of shop)* devanture *f*

frontal ['frʌntəl] *adj Anat* frontal(e); *Mil (attack)* de front

frontier ['frʌntɪə(r)] *n* frontière *f*; **the frontiers** *(of knowledge, science)* les limites *fpl*; **f. guard** garde-frontière *m*; **f. town** ville *f* frontalière

frontispiece ['frʌntɪspiːs] *n* frontispice *m*

frontrunner ['frʌntrʌnə(r)] *n* favori(ite) *m,f*

frost [frɒst] *n* gel *m*; **there was a f.** il a gelé

▸**frost over, frost up** *vi (of window)* se couvrir de givre

frostbite ['frɒstbaɪt] *n* gelure *f*

frostbitten ['frɒstbɪtən] *adj* gelé(e)

frosted ['frɒstɪd] *adj (glass)* dépoli(e)

frosting ['frɒstɪŋ] *n Am (on cake)* glaçage *m*

frosty ['frɒstɪ] *adj (night, air)* glacé(e); *Fig (welcome, smile)* glacial(e)

froth [frɒθ] **1** *n (on beer, cappuccino)* mousse *f*; *(on waves)* écume *f*
2 *vi (of liquid)* mousser; **he was frothing at the mouth** il bavait; *(with anger)* il écumait de rage

frothy ['frɒθɪ] *adj (beer, cappuccino)* mousseux(euse)

frown [fraʊn] **1** *n* froncement *m* de sourcils
2 *vi* froncer les sourcils; **to f. at sb** regarder qn en fronçant les sourcils

▸**frown on, frown upon** *vt insep (disapprove of)* désapprouver

froze [frəʊz] *pt of* freeze

frozen ['frəʊzən] **1** *adj (food)* congelé(e), surgelé(e); *(lake, hands)* gelé(e)
2 *pp of* freeze

fructose ['frʌktəʊs] *n* fructose *m*

frugal ['fruːgəl] *adj* frugal(e)

fruit [fruːt] *n* fruit *m*; **some f.** *(several pieces)* des fruits *mpl*; *(one piece)* un fruit; *Fig* **to bear f.** *(of plan, investment)* porter ses fruits; **fruits of the forest** fruits *mpl* des bois; **f. bowl** coupe *f* à fruits; **f. juice** jus *m* de fruit; *Br* **f. machine** machine *f* à sous; **f. salad** salade *f* de fruits; **f. tree** arbre *m* fruitier

fruitcake ['fruːtkeɪk] *n* cake *m*; *Fam (mad person)* fou (folle) *m,f*

fruitful ['fruːtfʊl] *adj (discussion)* fructueux(euse)

fruition [fruːˈɪʃən] *n* **to come to f.** *(of plan, effort)* porter ses fruits

fruitless ['fruːtlɪs] *adj (attempt, search, trip)* infructueux(euse)

fruity ['fruːtɪ] *adj (taste)* fruité(e); *Fam (voice)* étoffé(e)

frump [frʌmp] *n Fam* **she's a f.** elle fait mémère

frumpish ['frʌmpɪʃ], **frumpy** ['frʌmpɪ] *adj Fam* **to be f.** faire mémère

frustrate [frʌsˈtreɪt] *vt (person)* décevoir, frustrer; *(plan)* contrarier

frustrated [frʌsˈtreɪtɪd] *adj* frustré(e)

frustrating [frʌsˈtreɪtɪŋ] *adj* frustrant(e)

frustration [frʌsˈtreɪʃən] *n* frustration *f*

fry [fraɪ] *(pt & pp* fried) **1** *vt* faire frire
2 *vi* frire

frying pan ['fraɪŋpæn] *n* poêle *f* (à frire); **to jump out of the f. into the fire** tomber de Charybde en Scylla

ft *(abbr* foot *or* feet) p., pd.

FTP [eftiːˈpiː] *n Comput (abbr* **File Transfer Protocol)** FTP

fuchsia ['fjuːʃə] *n* fuchsia *m*

fuck [fʌk] *Vulg* **1** *n (intercourse)* baise *f*; **to have a f.** baiser; **I don't give a f.** j'en ai rien à foutre; **what the f. do you think you're doing?** putain, mais qu'est-ce que tu fous?; **f. knows why he came!** mais pourquoi il est venu, bordel!; **f.! bordel!, merde!**
2 *vt* baiser; **f. it!** et merde!; **f. you!** va te faire foutre!
3 *vi* baiser

▸**fuck about, fuck around** *vi Vulg (play the fool)* déconner; *(waste time)* glander

▸**fuck off** *vi Vulg (go away)* se casser; **f. off!** va te faire foutre!

fuck-all ['fʌkˈɔːl] *n Vulg* **he's done f. this week** il a fait que dalle cette semaine; **she knows f. about it** elle en sait que dalle

fucked ['fʌkt] *adj Vulg (broken, ruined)* foutu(e)

fucking ['fʌkɪŋ] *Vulg* **1** *adj* **he's a f. idiot!** c'est un connard!; **where's the f. car?** où est cette putain de voiture?
2 *adv (cold, brilliant, stupid)* foutrement

fuddy-duddy ['fʌdɪdʌdɪ] *(pl* **fuddy-duddies)** *n* **an old f.** *(man)* un vieux schnock; *(woman)* une vieille mémère

fudge [fʌdʒ] **1** *n (sweet)* caramel *m* mou
2 *vt* **to f. the issue** éluder la question

fuel ['fjʊəl] **1** *n* combustible *m*; *(for engine)* carburant *m*; *Fig* **to add f. to the flames** jeter de l'huile sur le feu; **f. consumption** *(of car)* consommation *f* (d'essence); **f. gauge** jauge *f* de carburant; **f. injection**

injection f de carburant; **f. pump** pompe f d'alimentation; **f. tank** réservoir m
2 vt (pt & pp **fuelled**, Am **fueled**) Fig (hatred) attiser; (speculation) nourrir
fug [fʌg] n Br Fam odeur f de renfermé; (in smoke-filled room) atmosphère f enfumée
fugitive ['fjuːdʒɪtɪv] n fugitif(ive) m,f
fugue [fjuːg] n Mus fugue f
fulcrum ['fʌlkrəm] n pivot m
fulfil, Am **fulfill** [fʊl'fɪl] (pt & pp **fulfilled**) vt (plan, ambition) réaliser; (condition, duty) remplir; (need) répondre à; **to feel fulfilled** (of person) se sentir épanoui(e)
fulfilment, Am **fulfillment** [fʊl'fɪlmənt] n (of plan, condition) réalisation f; (satisfaction) épanouissement m; **to find** or **achieve f.** s'épanouir
full [fʊl] **1** adj (**a**) (container) plein(e) (**of** de); (hotel, bus, car park) complet(ète); (day) chargé(e); **to be f. of praise for sb** ne pas tarir d'éloges sur qn; **to be f. of oneself** être imbu(e) de soi-même; **f. to the brim** plein à ras bords; **don't speak with your mouth f.!** ne parle pas la bouche pleine!; **to be f. (up)** (of person) être rassasié(e); **on a f. stomach** le ventre plein
(**b**) (complete) (amount) intégral(e); (explanation, recovery) complet(ète); (support) total(e); **to take f. responsibility for sth** assumer l'entière responsabilité de qch; **she gave me the f. story** elle m'a raconté toute l'histoire; **the f. horror** toute l'horreur; **to lead a f. life** avoir une vie bien remplie; **I waited two f. hours** or **a f. two hours** j'ai attendu deux bonnes heures; **in f. flow** (speaker) en plein discours; **to be in f. swing** (of party, sales) battre son plein; **in f. view of** sous les yeux de; **f. board** pension f complète; Phot **in f. colour** en couleur; **f. fare** plein tarif m; **f. house** (in theatre) salle f comble; (in cards) main f pleine; **f. moon** pleine lune f; **f. name** nom m et prénom m; **f. price** plein tarif m; **f. stop** (punctuation) point m final; **f. time** (in sport) fin f de match
(**c**) (maximum) **at f. speed** à toute vitesse; **at f. stretch** (work) à plein rendement; **to get f. marks** (in exam) avoir tous les points
(**d**) (skirt, sleeve) bouffant(e); **a f. figure** (of woman) un corps épanoui; **f. lips** lèvres fpl charnues ou pleines
2 adv **you know f. well that...** tu sais parfaitement que...; **it hit him f. in the face** il a reçu le coup en pleine figure
3 n **to pay in f.** payer intégralement; **name in f.** nom et prénoms; **to live life to the f.** vivre pleinement
fullback ['fʊlbæk] n (in football, rugby) arrière m
full-blown ['fʊl'bləʊn] adj (row) vrai(e); (crisis) de grande envergure; **to have f. Aids** avoir le sida
full-bodied ['fʊl'bɒdɪd] adj (wine) corsé(e)
full-fledged ['fʊl'fledʒd] Am = **fully-fledged**
full-grown ['fʊl'grəʊn] adj adulte
full-length ['fʊl'leŋθ] adj (portrait, mirror) en pied; (dress) long (longue); **f. film** long métrage m
fullness ['fʊlnɪs] n **in the f. of time** avec le temps
full-page ['fʊl'peɪdʒ] adj (advert, illustration) pleine page
full-scale ['fʊl'skeɪl] adj (**a**) (model) grandeur nature inv (**b**) (search) de grande envergure; **f. war** guerre f généralisée

full-time ['fʊl'taɪm] adj & adv à temps complet, à plein temps; Fig **looking after the twins is a f. job** s'occuper des jumeaux ne laisse pas une minute de libre; **to be in f. employment** travailler à plein temps
full-timer ['fʊl'taɪmər] n travailleur(euse) m,f à temps complet ou à plein temps
fully ['fʊlɪ] adv (**a**) (completely) complètement, entièrement; (understand, be aware) parfaitement, tout à fait; **f. booked** complet(ète); **f. grown** adulte (**b**) (at least) **it takes f. two hours** cela prend au moins deux heures
fully-fledged ['fʊlɪ'fledʒd] adj Br Fig qualifié(e)
fulminate ['fʌlmɪneɪt] vi fulminer (**against** contre)
fulness = **fullness**
fulsome ['fʊlsəm] adj enthousiaste; **to be f. in one's praise of sb/sth** porter qn/qch aux nues
fumble ['fʌmbəl] **1** vt (ball) mal attraper
2 vi fouiller; **to f. for sth** fouiller pour trouver qch; (in dark) tâtonner pour trouver qch; **to f. for words** chercher ses mots; **he fumbled with the switch** il a essayé maladroitement de faire fonctionner l'interrupteur
fume [fjuːm] n **fumes** émanations fpl; (from car exhaust) gaz mpl d'échappement; **petrol fumes** vapeurs fpl d'essence
2 vi (**a**) (give off fumes) fumer (**b**) (be angry) **to be fuming** rager, être furieux(euse)
fumigate ['fjuːmɪgeɪt] vt désinfecter par fumigation
fun [fʌn] n plaisir m; **to have f.** s'amuser; **it's/he's great** c'est/il est très amusant; **there'll be f. and games** (trouble) il va y avoir du grabuge; **it's no f. having to stay at home** ce n'est pas drôle de devoir rester à la maison; **to make f. of** se moquer de; **to be a figure of f.** être la risée de tous; **to say sth in f.** dire qch pour rire ou en plaisantant; **to do sth for f.** or **for the f. of it** faire qch pour s'amuser; Ironic **what f.!** c'est drôle!; **f. fur** fourrure f synthétique
function ['fʌŋkʃən] **1** n (**a**) (role) & Math fonction f; Comput **f. key** touche f de fonction (**b**) (party) réception f; (public) cérémonie f
2 vi fonctionner; **to f. as** jouer le rôle de, faire fonction de
functional ['fʌŋkʃənəl] adj (**a**) (practical) fonctionnel(elle) (**b**) (operational) opérationnel(elle)
functionary ['fʌŋkʃənərɪ] (pl **functionaries**) n fonctionnaire mf
fund [fʌnd] **1** n (**a**) (of money) fonds m; **funds** fonds mpl, capitaux mpl; **to be in funds** être en fonds; Fin **f. manager** gestionnaire mf de fonds (**b**) (of information) mine f
2 vt financer
fundamental [fʌndə'mentəl] **1** n **fundamentals** principes mpl, fondements mpl
2 adj fondamental(e), essentiel(elle); **her f. honesty** sa profonde honnêteté
fundamentalist [fʌndə'mentəlɪst] **1** n (religious) intégriste mf, fondamentaliste mf
2 adj (religious) intégriste, fondamentaliste
fundamentally [fʌndə'mentəlɪ] adv fondamentalement
funding ['fʌndɪŋ] n financement m
fundraiser ['fʌndreɪzə(r)] n (person) collecteur(trice) m,f de fonds; (event) = manifestation organisée au profit d'une œuvre de bienfaisance
fundraising ['fʌndreɪzɪŋ] n collecte f de fonds
funeral ['fjuːnərəl] n enterrement m; (formal) funérailles fpl, obsèques fpl; Fam **that's your f.!** c'est ton

problème!; **f. director** entrepreneur *m* de pompes funèbres; *Mus* **f. march** marche *f* funèbre; **f. parlour** établissement *m* de pompes funèbres; **f. procession** cortège *m* funèbre; **f. service** service *m* funèbre

funfair ['fʌn'feə(r)] *n* fête *f* foraine

fungal ['fʌŋgəl] *adj* **f. infection** mycose *f*

fungus ['fʌŋgəs] (*pl* **fungi** ['fʌŋgaɪ]) *n* (*mushroom, toadstool*) champignon *m*; (*on walls*) moisissure *f*; *Med* fongus *m*

funk [fʌŋk] *n* (**a**) *Mus* funk *m* (**b**) *Fam Old-fashioned* (*fright*) **to be in a f.** avoir une peur bleue

funky ['fʌŋkɪ] *adj Fam* funky *inv*

funnel ['fʌnəl] **1** *n* (**a**) (*of locomotive, steamship*) cheminée *f* (**b**) (*for filling*) entonnoir *m*
2 *vt* (*pt & pp* **funnelled**, *Am* **funneled**) (*direct*) (*funds*) acheminer (**to** vers); **to f. liquid into sth** verser un liquide dans qch

funnies ['fʌnɪz] *npl Am* **the f.** les bandes *fpl* dessinées (*dans un journal*)

funnily ['fʌnɪlɪ] *adv* (*strangely*) bizarrement; **f. enough,...** bizarrement,...

funny ['fʌnɪ] *adj* (**a**) (*amusing*) drôle, amusant(e); **are you trying to be f.?** tu te crois drôle?; *Ironic* **very f.!** très drôle!; *Fam* **f. bone** petit juif *m* (**b**) (*strange*) bizarre, drôle; **I feel a bit f.** (*ill*) je me sens un peu bizarre; **to taste/smell f.** avoir un drôle de goût/une drôle d'odeur; **f., I thought I'd locked the door** c'est curieux, je croyais avoir fermé la porte à clé; (**it's**) **f. you should say that** c'est drôle que tu dises ça; *Fam* **he's a bit f. in the head** il est un peu bizarre; *Fam* **I don't want any f. business!** et pas de blagues!; *Fam* **f. farm** maison *f* de fous

fur [fɜː(r)] *n* (**a**) (*hair*) poils *mpl*; (*animal skin*) fourrure *f*; *Fig* **the f. was flying** ça chauffait; **f. coat** manteau *m* de fourrure; **f. trade** commerce *m* de fourrures (**b**) (*in kettle, boiler*) tartre *m*

furious ['fjʊərɪəs] *adj* (*person*) furieux(euse) (**with** contre); (*quarrel, storm*) violent(e); **to be f. with oneself** être en colère contre soi-même; **at a f. speed** à une vitesse folle

furiously ['fjʊərɪəslɪ] *adv* furieusement; (*work, write*) frénétiquement

furlong ['fɜːlɒŋ] *n* = 201 m, furlong *m*

furnace ['fɜːnɪs] *n* fourneau *m*; *Fig* **it's like a f. in here!** quelle fournaise!

furnish ['fɜːnɪʃ] *vt* (**a**) (*house, flat*) meubler (**b**) *Formal* (*provide*) fournir; **to f. sb with sth** fournir qch à qn

furnished ['fɜːnɪʃd] *adj* (*flat, room*) meublé(e); **f. accommodation** (*logement m*) meublé *m*

furnishings ['fɜːnɪʃɪŋz] *npl* ameublement *m*

furniture ['fɜːnɪtʃə(r)] *n* meubles *mpl*, mobilier *m*; **a piece of f.** un meuble; **f. polish** encaustique *f* pour les meubles; **f. remover** déménageur *m*; **f. shop** magasin *m* de meubles *ou* d'ameublement; **f. van** camion *m* de déménagement

furore [fjʊ'rɔːrɪ], *Am* **furor** ['fjʊrɔː(r)] *n* (*uproar*) scandale *m*

furrow ['fʌrəʊ] **1** *n* (*in field*) sillon *m*; (*on face*) ride *f* profonde
2 *vt Lit* **his brow was furrowed with worry** son front était plissé par l'inquiétude

furry ['fɜːrɪ] *adj* (*animal*) à poil; **f. toy** peluche *f*; **to have a f. tongue** avoir la langue chargée

further ['fɜːðə(r)] (*comparative of* **far**) **1** *adj* (**a**) (*more distant*) plus loin
(**b**) (*additional*) supplémentaire; **upon f. consideration** après plus ample réflexion; **until f. notice** jusqu'à nouvel ordre; **without f. delay** sans plus attendre; *Br* **f. education** = enseignement supérieur dispensé par un établissement autre qu'une université
2 *adv* (**a**) (*in general*) plus loin; **this mustn't go any f.** (*don't tell anyone else*) il faut que cela reste entre nous; **I didn't question him any f.** je ne l'ai pas interrogé davantage; **that doesn't get us much f.** ça ne nous avance pas beaucoup; **f. back** (*in space*) plus loin en arrière; (*in time*) plus loin dans le temps; **f. on** (*in space*) plus loin; (*in time*) plus tard
(**b**) *Formal* (*moreover*) de plus; **f. to your letter...** suite à votre lettre...
3 *vt* (*cause, career*) faire avancer

furthermore [fɜːðə'mɔː(r)] *adv Formal* en outre, de plus

furthermost ['fɜːðəməʊst] *adj Lit* le (la) plus reculé(e)

furthest ['fɜːðɪst] (*superlative of* **far**) **1** *adj* le (la) plus éloigné(e)
2 *adv* le plus loin

furtive ['fɜːtɪv] *adj* sournois(e)

fury ['fjʊərɪ] *n* (*of person, storm*) fureur *f*; **to be in a f.** (*of person*) être furieux(euse); *Fam* **to work like f.** travailler avec acharnement

fuse, *Am* **fuze** [fjuːz] **1** *n* (**a**) (*for plug*) fusible *m*; **f. box** boîte *f* à fusibles; **f. wire** fusible *m* (**b**) (*for dynamite*) détonateur *m*; (*in bomb*) amorce *f*; *Fam Fig* **to have a short f.** (*be short-tempered*) se mettre facilement en colère
2 *vt* (*melt*) fondre; (*join*) fusionner
3 *vi* (**a**) (*of metals*) fondre; **to f. together** fusionner (**b**) (*of organizations, parties*) fusionner (**c**) *Br Elec* **the lights have fused** les plombs ont sauté

fused [fjuːzd] *adj Elec* (*plug, appliance*) muni(e) d'un fusible

fuselage ['fjuːzəlɑːʒ] *n* fuselage *m*

fusillade [fjuːzɪ'leɪd] *n* (*of bullets*) fusillade *f*; *Fig* (*of criticism, questions*) avalanche *f*

fusion ['fjuːʒən] *n* fusion *f*

fuss [fʌs] **1** *n* histoires *fpl*; **what's all the f. about?** qu'est-ce que c'est que toutes ces histoires?; **I don't want any f.** pas de cérémonie; **a lot of f. about** *or* **over nothing** beaucoup d'histoires pour pas grandchose; **I don't see what all the f. is about** je ne vois pas pourquoi on en fait un tel cas; **to kick up** *or* **make a f.** faire des histoires; **to make a f. of sb** être aux petits soins pour qn
2 *vt Fam* **I'm not fussed** ça m'est égal
3 *vi* faire des histoires; **to f. about** s'activer

fusspot ['fʌspɒt], *Am* **fussbudget** ['fʌsbʌdʒɪt] *n Fam* chichiteux(euse) *m,f*

fussy ['fʌsɪ] *adj* (**a**) (*person*) difficile, exigeant(e); **I'm not f.** (*don't mind*) ça m'est égal (**b**) (*dress, décor*) surchargé(e)

futile ['fjuːtaɪl] *adj* (*attempt, protest*) vain(e); (*remark, suggestion*) futile

futility [fjuː'tɪlɪtɪ] *n* futilité *f*

futon ['fuːtɒn] *n* futon *m*

future ['fjuːtʃə(r)] **1** *n* (**a**) (*in time*) avenir *m*; **in (the) f.** à l'avenir; **in the near/distant f.** dans un avenir proche/lointain; **she's got a job with a (good) f.** elle a une situation pleine d'avenir (**b**) *Fin* **futures** opérations *fpl* à terme; **futures market** marché *m* à terme (**c**) *Gram* futur *m*; **the f. perfect** le futur antérieur **2** *adj* futur(e); **at some f. date** à une date ultérieure; **for f. reference** à titre d'information

futuristic [ˈfjuːtʃəˈrɪstɪk] *adj* futuriste

fuze *Am* = **fuse**

fuzz [fʌz] *n* (**a**) *(on fabric)* peluches *fpl*; *(on peach, skin)* duvet *m* (**b**) *Fam* **the f.** *(police)* les flics *mpl*

fuzzy [ˈfʌzɪ] *adj (outline, photo)* flou(e); *(idea)* vague; *(hair)* crépu(e); **f. logic** logique *f* floue

FYI *(written abbr* **for your information***)* à titre indicatif

G

G, g¹ [dʒiː] n (**a**) (letter) G, g m inv (**b**) Mus sol m
g² (abbr **gramme**) gr
gab [gæb] (pt & pp **gabbed**) vi Fam (talk) papoter; (gossip) jaser
gabardine [gæbə'diːn] n gabardine f
gabble ['gæbəl] **1** n a g. of conversation un bruit de conversation
  2 vi (incoherently) bredouiller; **to g. on** papoter
gable ['geɪbəl] n pignon m; **g. end** (wall) pignon m
Gabon ['gæbən] n le Gabon
Gabonese [gæbə'niːz] **1** n Gabonais(e) m,f
  2 adj gabonais(e)
▸**gad about** [gæd] (pt & pp **gadded**) vi Fam être en vadrouille
gadfly ['gædflaɪ] (pl **gadflies**) n (insect) taon m; Fig (person) casse-pieds mf inv
gadget ['gædʒɪt] n gadget m
Gaelic ['geɪlɪk, Scot 'gælɪk] **1** n gaélique m
  2 adj gaélique; **G. football** = jeu de balle irlandais à quinze où il est autorisé de taper dans le ballon avec la main
Gaels [geɪlz] npl the G. les Gaëls mpl
gaff [gæf] n (**a**) (in fishing) gaffe f (**b**) Br Fam (home) piaule f (**c**) Fam **to blow the g. (on)** vendre la mèche (à propos de)
gaffe [gæf] n (blunder) gaffe f
gaffer ['gæfə(r)] n (**a**) Br Fam (boss) chef m (**b**) Fam (old man) **an old g.** un vieux bonhomme (**c**) Cin chef m électricien, gaffer m (**d**) **g. tape** ruban m adhésif en toile
gag [gæg] **1** n (**a**) (on mouth) bâillon m (**b**) Fam (joke) blague f
  2 vt (pt & pp **gagged**) (person) bâillonner; Fig (media, opposition) museler
  3 vi (retch) avoir des haut-le-cœur
gaga ['gɑːgɑː] adj Fam gâteux(euse), gaga inv
gage Am = gauge
gaggle ['gægəl] n also Fig troupeau m
gaiety ['geɪətɪ] n gaieté f
gaily ['geɪlɪ] adv (happily) joyeusement; (laugh) de bon cœur; **g. coloured** aux couleurs gaies
gain [geɪn] **1** n (**a**) (profit) gain m, profit m; **for personal g.** par intérêt personnel (**b**) (increase) augmentation f (**in** de); Fin (on stock market) hausse f; **to make gains** (progress) progresser; Fin (of shares) augmenter
  2 vt (**a**) (advantage, degree) obtenir; (victory, prize) remporter; (reputation, experience) acquérir; (sympathy, respect) gagner; **to g. entrance (to)** entrer (dans); (of burglar) s'introduire (dans) (**b**) (increase) **to g. weight/speed** prendre du poids/de la vitesse; also

Fig **to g. ground on** gagner du terrain sur; **to g. time** gagner du temps
  3 vi (**a**) (benefit) **to g. by sth** bénéficier de qch (**b**) (increase) **to g. in confidence** gagner de l'assurance; **to g. in popularity** devenir populaire (**c**) (of clock) avancer
▸**gain on** vt insep also Fig gagner du terrain sur
gainful ['geɪnfʊl] adj **g. employment** un emploi rémunéré
gainfully ['geɪnfʊlɪ] adv **to be g. employed** avoir un emploi rémunéré
gainsay [geɪn'seɪ] (pt & pp **gainsaid** [geɪn'sed]) vt Formal contredire; **there's no gainsaying her ability** son talent est indéniable
gait [geɪt] n démarche f
gal [gæl] n Fam Old-fashioned fille f
gala ['gɑːlə] n gala m; **swimming g.** compétition f de natation; **g. evening/performance** soirée f/représentation f de gala
galactic [gə'læktɪk] adj galactique
Galapagos [gə'læpəgəs] npl **the G. (Islands)** les (îles fpl) Galapagos fpl
galaxy ['gæləksɪ] (pl **galaxies**) n galaxie f; Fig **a g. of stars** une pléiade de vedettes
gale [geɪl] n (strong wind) vent m violent; Fig **a g. of laughter** un éclat de rire
gall [gɔːl] **1** n (**a**) Med bile f; **g. bladder** vésicule f biliaire (**b**) (impudence) culot m
  2 vt (annoy) irriter, exaspérer
gallant ['gælənt] adj (brave) brave, vaillant(e); (polite) galant(e)
gallantry ['gæləntrɪ] n (bravery) bravoure f; (politeness) galanterie f
galleon ['gælɪən] n galion m
gallery ['gælərɪ] (pl **galleries**) n (**a**) (art) g. (for sale) galerie f (d'art); (for exhibition) musée m (**b**) (in theatre) galerie f; Fig **to play to the g.** (of politician) chercher à épater la galerie
galley ['gælɪ] (pl **galleys**) n (**a**) (ship) galère f; **g. slave** galérien m (**b**) (ship's kitchen) cuisine f (**c**) Typ **g. (proof)** placard m
Gallic ['gælɪk] adj (French) français(e); Hist (of Gaul) gaulois(e)
galling ['gɔːlɪŋ] adj humiliant(e)
▸**gallivant about, gallivant around** ['gælɪvænt] vi être en vadrouille
gallon ['gælən] n (in UK) = 4,54 l, gallon m; (in US) = 3,78 l, gallon m
gallop ['gæləp] **1** n galop m; **at a g.** au galop
  2 vi galoper; Fig **to g. through one's work** expédier son travail

gallows ['gæləʊz] *n* potence *f*, gibet *m*; **g. humour** humour *m* noir
gallstone ['gɔːlstəʊn] *n* calcul *m* biliaire
galore [gə'lɔː(r)] *adv Fam* à profusion, à gogo
galvanize ['gælvənaɪz] *vt also Fig* galvaniser; **to g. sb into action** pousser qn à agir
galvanized ['gælvənaɪzd] *adj* galvanisé(e)
Gambia ['gæmbɪə] *n* **the G.** la Gambie
Gambian ['gæmbɪən] **1** *n* Gambien(enne) *m,f* **2** *adj* gambien(enne)
gambit ['gæmbɪt] *n* (*in chess*) gambit *m*; (*in negotiation, diplomacy*) tactique *f*; **opening g.** (*in negotiation, diplomacy*) manœuvre *f* d'approche
gamble ['gæmbəl] **1** *n* (*risk*) risque *m*; **to take a g.** prendre un risque **2** *vt* (*money*) jouer, parier **3** *vi* jouer (de l'argent); **to g. on the horses** jouer aux courses; **she gambled on nobody noticing** elle comptait sur le fait que personne ne s'en apercevrait
gambler ['gæmblə(r)] *n* joueur(euse) *m,f*
gambling ['gæmblɪŋ] *n* jeux *mpl* d'argent; **g. debts** dettes *fpl* de jeu; **g. den** tripot *m*
gambol ['gæmbəl] (*pt & pp* **gambolled**, *Am* **gamboled**) *vi* gambader
game [geɪm] **1** *n* (**a**) (*activity, sport*) jeu *m*; (*of cards, pool, chess*) partie *f*; (*match*) match *m*; **to have a g. of tennis/football** faire une partie de tennis/foot(ball); **g., set and match** (*in tennis*) jeu, set et match; **politics is just a g. to them** pour eux, la politique n'est qu'un jeu; **g. show** jeu *m* télévisé; **g. over** (*in computer game*) game over, fin *f* de partie; *Fam Fig* c'est foutu (**b**) *Br* **games** (*at school*) sports *mpl* de plein air; (*sporting event*) jeux *mpl* (**c**) (*animals, food*) gibier *m*; **g. reserve** réserve *f* de gibier (**d**) (*idioms*) **to play the g.** jouer le jeu; **two can play at that g.** on peut jouer à deux à ce petit jeu-là; **to beat sb at his own g.** battre qn à sa propre jeu; **to play games with sb** jouer avec qn; **to give the g. away** vendre la mèche; **what's his g.?** où veut-il en venir?; **I know what your g. is!** je sais bien où vous voulez en venir!; **the g.'s up for him** c'est fichu pour lui; **I've been in this g. a long time** ça fait longtemps que je suis de la partie; *Br Fam* **to be on the g.** (*of prostitute*) faire le trottoir **2** *adj* (**a**) (*brave*) courageux(euse); **to be g.** (**to do sth**) être partant(e) (pour faire qch) (**b**) *Fam* **a g. leg** une patte folle
gamekeeper ['geɪmkiːpə(r)] *n* garde-chasse *m*
gamely ['geɪmlɪ] *adv* courageusement
gamer ['geɪmə(r)] *n Comput* = amateur de jeux vidéo
gaming ['geɪmɪŋ] *n Comput* (*pratique f des*) jeux *mpl* électroniques
gamma ['gæmə] *n* gamma *m*; *Phys* **g. rays** rayons *mpl* gamma
gammon ['gæmən] *n* jambon *m*; **g. steak** = tranche épaisse de jambon (servie grillée)
gammy ['gæmɪ] *adj Fam* **a g. leg** une patte folle
gamut ['gæmət] *n* gamme *f*; **to run the g. of emotions** passer par toute la gamme des émotions
gamy ['geɪmɪ] *adj* (*flavour*) faisandé(e)
gander ['gændə(r)] *n* (**a**) (*male goose*) jars *m* (**b**) *Br very Fam* **to take a g. (at)** (*look*) jeter un coup d'œil (à)
gang [gæŋ] *n* (*of criminals, children, friends*) bande *f*; (*of workers*) équipe *f*; **g. rape** viol *m* collectif
▸**gang up** *vi* **to g. up on sb** se liguer contre qn; **to g. up with sb** s'allier avec qn

gangbang ['gæŋbæŋ] *n very Fam* (*group rape*) viol *m* collectif
Ganges ['gændʒiːz] *n* **the G.** le Gange
gangland ['gæŋlænd] *n* (*underworld*) milieu *m*, pègre *f*; **g. boss/killer** caïd *m*/tueur *m* du milieu; **g. killing** règlement *m* de compte (*entre gangsters*)
gangling ['gæŋglɪŋ] *adj* dégingandé(e)
ganglion ['gæŋglɪən] (*pl* **ganglia** ['gæŋglɪə]) *n* ganglion *m*
gangplank ['gæŋplæŋk] *n* passerelle *f*
gang-rape ['gæŋreɪp] *vt* commettre un viol collectif sur
gangrene ['gæŋgriːn] *n* gangrène *f*; **to have g.** avoir la gangrène
gangrenous ['gæŋgrɪnəs] *adj* gangreneux(euse)
gangster ['gæŋstə(r)] *n* gangster *m*; **g. film** film *m* de gangsters
gangway ['gæŋweɪ] *n* (*in theatre*) allée *f*; (*in plane, train*) couloir *m*; (*on ship*) passerelle *f*; **g.!** dégagez, s'il vous plaît!
gannet ['gænɪt] *n* (*bird*) fou *m* de Bassan; *Fig* (*greedy person*) goinfre *mf*
gantry ['gæntrɪ] (*pl* **gantries**) *n* (*for crane, over railway*) portique *m*; (*for rocket*) tour *f* de lancement
gaol *Br* = **jail**
gap [gæp] *n* (**a**) (*space*) espace *m*; (*narrower*) interstice *m*; (*in wall*) brèche *f*; (*in text*) blanc *m* (**b**) (*difference*) (*in age, ability*) écart *m*; **the g. between rich and poor** le fossé entre les riches et les pauvres (**c**) (*in knowledge*) lacune *f*; **his death leaves a g. in all our lives** sa mort nous laisse un vide; *Com* **a g. in the market** un créneau (**d**) (*in time*) intervalle *m* (**e**) (*mountain pass*) col *m*
gape [geɪp] *vi* (**a**) (*stare*) rester bouche bée; **to g. at sb/sth** regarder qn/qch bouche bée (**b**) (*open*) (*of door, blouse*) s'ouvrir tout(e) grand(e); (*of wound, hole*) être béant(e)
gaping ['geɪpɪŋ] *adj* béant(e)
garage ['gærɑːʒ, 'gærɪdʒ] *n* (*for storing or repairing cars*) garage *m*; (*petrol station*) station-service *f*
garb ['gɑːb] *n Lit* costume *m*
garbage ['gɑːbɪdʒ] *n* (**a**) *Am* (*rubbish*) ordures *fpl*; **g. bag** sac-poubelle *m*; **g. can** poubelle *f*; **g. heap** tas *m* d'ordures; **g. man** éboueur *m* (**b**) (*nonsense*) âneries *fpl*; **to talk g.** dire n'importe quoi
garbled ['gɑːbəld] *adj* confus(e)
garden ['gɑːdən] **1** *n* jardin *m*; *Fig* **to lead sb up the g. path** faire marcher qn; **g. centre** jardinerie *f*; *Br* **g. flat** appartement *m* en rez-de-chaussée avec jardin; **g. furniture** meubles *mpl* de jardin; **g. gnome** nain *m* de jardin; **g. party** réception *f* en plein air, garden-party *f*; **g. shed** resserre *f* **2** *vi* jardiner, faire du jardinage
gardener ['gɑːdnə(r)] *n* jardinier(ère) *m,f*
gardening ['gɑːdnɪŋ] *n* jardinage *m*; **to do the g.** s'occuper du jardin
gargantuan [gɑː'gæntjʊən] *adj* gargantuesque
gargle ['gɑːgəl] *vi* se gargariser (**with** avec)
gargoyle ['gɑːgɔɪl] *n* gargouille *f*
garish ['geərɪʃ] *adj* (*clothes*) voyant(e); (*taste*) vulgaire; (*colours*) criard(e); (*light*) cru(e)
garland ['gɑːlənd] **1** *n* guirlande *f* **2** *vt* enguirlander (**with** de)
garlic ['gɑːlɪk] *n* ail *m*; **g. bread** = pain chaud au beurre d'ail; **g. butter** beurre *m* d'ail; **g. sausage** saucisson *m* à l'ail
garment ['gɑːmənt] *n* vêtement *m*

garnet ['gɑːnɪt] *n* grenat *m*
garnish ['gɑːnɪʃ] **1** *n* garniture *f*
2 *vt* garnir (**with** avec)
garret ['gærət] *n* mansarde *f*
garrison ['gærɪsən] **1** *n* garnison *f*; **g. duty** service *m* de garnison; **g. town** ville *f* de garnison
2 *vt (troops)* mettre en garnison
garrotte [gə'rɒt] **1** *n* garrot *m*
2 *vt* exécuter au garrot
garrulous ['gærʊləs] *adj (person)* loquace, bavard(e); *(account, letter)* verbeux(euse)
garter ['gɑːtə(r)] *n* jarretière *f*; *Br* **the Order of the G.** l'Ordre *m* de la Jarretière; *Am* **g. belt** porte-jarretelles *m inv*; **g. snake** couleuvre *f*
gas [gæs] **1** *n* (**a**) *(substance, fuel)* gaz *m inv*; *Med* (gaz) anesthétique *m*; **g. bill** note *f* de gaz; **g. chamber** chambre *f* à gaz; **g. cooker** cuisinière *f* à gaz; **g. cylinder** bouteille *f* de gaz; **g. fire** radiateur *m* à gaz; **g. lamp** lampe *f* à gaz; **g. mask** masque *m* à gaz (**b**) *Am (gasoline)* essence *f*; *Fam* **to step on the g.** appuyer sur le champignon; **g. station** station-service *f*; **g. tank** réservoir *m* (**c**) *Am Fam (amusing situation)* **to have a g.** rigoler; **what a g.!** quelle rigolade!
2 *vt (pt & pp* **gassed**) *(person)* asphyxier; *(deliberately)* gazer; **to g. oneself** se suicider au gaz
3 *vi Fam (chat)* jacasser
gasbag ['gæsbæg] *n Fam (chatterbox)* bavard(e) *m,f*; *(boaster)* vantard(e) *m,f*
gaseous ['gæsɪəs, 'geɪsɪəs] *adj* gazeux(euse)
gash [gæʃ] **1** *n (in skin, wood)* entaille *f*; *(in metal)* fente *f*
2 *vt* entailler
gasket ['gæskɪt] *n (in engine)* joint *m* de culasse; *Fam* **to blow a g.** piquer une colère
gasoline ['gæsəliːn] *n Am* essence *f*
gasometer [gæ'sɒmɪtə(r)] *n* gazomètre *m*
gasp [gɑːsp] **1** *n (of surprise)* sursaut *m*; **to be at one's last g.** être sur le point de rendre son dernier soupir
2 *vi* avoir le souffle coupé (**with** *or* in de); **to make sb g.** couper le souffle à qn; **to g. for breath** *or* **for air** haleter, suffoquer; *Fam* **to be gasping for a cigarette/a drink** mourir d'envie de fumer une cigarette/de boire un verre
gassy ['gæsɪ] *adj* trop gazeux(euse)
gastric ['gæstrɪk] *adj* gastrique; **g. flu** grippe *f* gastro-intestinale; **g. juices** sucs *mpl* gastriques; **g. ulcer** ulcère *m* à l'estomac
gastritis [gæs'traɪtɪs] *n* gastrite *f*; **to have g.** avoir une gastrite
gastro-enteritis [gæstrəʊəntə'raɪtɪs] *n* gastro-entérite *f*; **to have g.** avoir une gastro-entérite
gastronomic [gæstrə'nɒmɪk] *adj* gastronomique
gastronomy [gæs'trɒnəmɪ] *n* gastronomie *f*
gasworks ['gæswɜːks] *n* usine *f* à gaz
gate [geɪt] *n* (**a**) *(in garden, field)* barrière *f*; *(of city, in airport)* porte *f* (**b**) *Sport (spectators)* nombre *m* de spectateurs; *(takings)* recette *f*
gâteau ['gætəʊ] *(pl* **gâteaux** ['gætəʊz]) *n* gros gâteau *m* à la crème
gatecrash ['geɪtkræʃ] *vt Fam* **to g. a party** aller à une fête sans y être invité(e)
gatecrasher ['geɪtkræʃə(r)] *n Fam* intrus(e) *m,f*
gatehouse ['geɪthaʊs] *n* loge *f*
gatekeeper ['geɪtkiːpə(r)] *n* gardien(enne) *m,f*
gatepost ['geɪtpəʊst] *n* montant *m* (de porte); *Fam* **between you, me and the g.** entre nous

gateway ['geɪtweɪ] *n* entrée *f*; *Fig* **the g. to the East** la porte de l'Orient; **the g. to success** la voie de la réussite
gather ['gæðə(r)] *vt* (**a**) *(collect) (people, belongings)* rassembler; *(information)* recueillir; *(wood, papers)* ramasser; *(fruit, flowers)* cueillir; *(harvest)* rentrer; **to g. one's thoughts** rassembler ses idées; **to g. sb in one's arms** serrer qn dans ses bras (**b**) *(accumulate)* **to g. dirt** s'encrasser; *also Fig* **to g. dust** ramasser de la poussière; **to g. speed** prendre de la vitesse (**c**) *(conclude, understand)* **to g. that...** croire comprendre que...; **as you may have already gathered,...** comme vous avez déjà dû le deviner,...
2 *vi (of people)* se rassembler; *(of things)* s'accumuler; *(of storm)* se préparer
▸**gather round 1** *vt insep* se rassembler autour de
2 *vi* se rassembler
▸**gather together 1** *vt sep (belongings)* rassembler; *(evidence)* recueillir
2 *vi (of people)* se rassembler
▸**gather up** *vt sep* ramasser
gathering ['gæðərɪŋ] **1** *n (group)* attroupement *m*; *(meeting)* réunion *f*
2 *adj (darkness, speed)* croissant(e); *also Fig* **the g. storm** l'orage qui se prépare
GATT [gæt] *n (abbr* **General Agreement on Tariffs and Trade**) GATT *m*
gauche [gəʊʃ] *adj* gauche, maladroit(e)
gaudily ['gɔːdɪlɪ] *adv* de façon criarde
gaudy ['gɔːdɪ] *adj* tape-à-l'œil *inv*; *(colours)* criard(e)
gauge [geɪdʒ] **1** *n* (**a**) *(size) (of screw, wire, gun)* calibre *m*; *(of railway track)* écartement *m* (**b**) *(measuring device)* jauge *f* (**c**) *Fig (indicator)* signe *m*, indicateur *m* (**of** de)
2 *vt* évaluer
Gaul [gɔːl] *n Hist (region)* la Gaule; *(inhabitant)* Gaulois(e) *m,f*
gaunt [gɔːnt] *adj* décharné(e)
gauntlet ['gɔːntlɪt] *n (glove)* gant *m* à manchette; *Hist* gantelet *m*; *Fig* **to throw** *or* **fling down the g. (to sb)** jeter le gant (à qn); *Fig* **to take up the g.** relever le gant; *Fig* **to run the g. of sth** s'exposer à qch
gauze [gɔːz] *n* gaze *f*
gave [geɪv] *pt of* **give**
gavel ['gævəl] *n* marteau *m*
gawk [gɔːk] *vi Fam* rester bouche bée; **to g. at sb/sth** rester bouche bée à regarder qn/qch
gawky ['gɔːkɪ] *adj Fam* gauche, empoté(e)
gawp [gɔːp] *vi Fam* rester bouche bée; **to g. at sb/sth** rester bouche bée à regarder qn/qch
gay [geɪ] **1** *n (homosexual)* homosexuel(elle) *m,f*
2 *adj* (**a**) *(homosexual)* homosexuel(elle), gay *inv*; **g. marriage** mariage *m* homosexuel; **g. parenting** homoparentalité *f*; **g. pride** = revendication par les homosexuels de leur orientation sexuelle; **g. rights** les droits *mpl* des homosexuels (**b**) *Old-fashioned (happy)* gai(e); with **g. abandon** avec insouciance
Gaza ['gɑːzə] *n* Gaza; **the G. Strip** la Bande de Gaza
gaze [geɪz] **1** *n* regard *m*; **to meet** *or* **return sb's g.** regarder qn dans les yeux
2 *vi* **to g. at sb/sth** regarder fixement qn/qch; **to g. into space** regarder dans le vague
gazelle [gə'zel] *n* gazelle *f*
gazette [gə'zet] *n* journal *m* officiel
gazetteer [gæzɪ'tɪə(r)] *n* index *m* géographique

gazump [gə'zʌmp] *vt Br Fam* = revenir sur une promesse de vente de maison pour accepter l'offre plus élevée d'une tierce personne
GB ['dʒiː'biː] *n (abbr* **Great Britain)** GB
GBH [dʒiːbiː'eɪtʃ] *n Law (abbr* **grievous bodily harm)** coups *mpl* et blessures *fpl*
GCE [dʒiːsiː'iː] *n Br Formerly (abbr* **General Certificate of Education)** = diplôme de fin d'études secondaires
GCHQ [dʒiːsiːeɪtʃ'kjuː] *n Br (abbr* **Government Communications Headquarters)** = service de renseignement et d'écoute du gouvernement britannique
GCSE [dʒiːsiːes'iː] *n Br (abbr* **General Certificate of Secondary Education)** = diplôme de fin de premier cycle de l'enseignement secondaire, sanctionnant une matière déterminée

---

GCSE
Cet examen a remplacé les "O levels", ou le "GCE O level", et le "CSE". On le passe après cinq ans de scolarité dans l'enseignement secondaire. Chaque élève choisit les matières dans lesquelles il veut se présenter (généralement entre cinq et dix) selon un système d'unités de valeur. Le nombre d'unités et les notes obtenues déterminent le passage dans la classe supérieure. Les élèves qui sont admis au GCSE peuvent ensuite préparer les "**A levels**" (*voir encadré à ce mot*). En Écosse, l'examen équivalent au GCSE s'appelle le "Standard Grade".

GDP [dʒiːdiː'piː] *n Econ (abbr* **gross domestic product)** PIB *m*
GDR [dʒiːdiː'ɑː(r)] *n Formerly (abbr* **German Democratic Republic) the G.** la RDA
gear [gɪə(r)] *n* (**a**) *(on car, bicycle)* vitesse *f; Fig* **to put sb's plans out of g.** perturber les projets de qn; **first/ second g.** première *f*/seconde *f* (vitesse); *Br* **g. lever** changement *m* de vitesse (**b**) *Fam (equipment)* attirail *m; (belongings)* affaires *fpl* (**c**) *Br Fam (clothes)* fringues *fpl*
▸**gear to** *vt sep* **to g. sth to sth** adapter qch à qch
▸**gear towards** *vt sep* **to be geared towards sb/sth** s'adresser à qn/qch
gearbox ['gɪəbɒks] *n* boîte *f* (de changement) de vitesses
gearstick ['gɪəstɪk] *n* changement *m* de vitesses
gee [dʒiː] *exclam* (**a**) *(to horse)* **g. up!** hue! (**b**) *Am* **g. (whizz)!** ça alors!
gee-gee ['dʒiːdʒiː] *n Fam (in children's language)* dada *m*
geek [giːk] *n Fam* ringard(e) *m,f*
geeky ['giːkɪ] *adj Fam* ringard(e)
geese [giːs] *pl of* **goose**
geezer ['giːzə(r)] *n Fam* (**a**) *Br* type *m;* **old g.** vieux bonhomme *m* (**b**) *Am (old man)* vioc *m*
Geiger counter ['gaɪgə'kaʊntə(r)] *n* compteur *m* Geiger
gel [dʒel] **1** *n* gel *m*
2 *vi (of liquid)* se gélifier; *Fig (of ideas, plans)* prendre forme; *(of team)* se souder
gelatine ['dʒelətiːn] *n* gélatine *f*
gelatinous [dʒɪ'lætɪnəs] *adj* gélatineux(euse)
gelding ['geldɪŋ] *n* hongre *m*
gelignite ['dʒelɪgnaɪt] *n* gélignite *f*
gem [dʒem] *n (precious stone)* pierre *f* précieuse; *Fig (person)* perle *f; (film, joke, goal)* pure merveille *f*
Gemini ['dʒemɪnaɪ] *n (sign of zodiac)* les Gémeaux *mpl;* **to be (a) G.** être (des) Gémeaux

gemstone ['dʒemstəʊn] *n* pierre *f* gemme
gen [dʒen] *n Br Fam (information)* tuyaux *mpl*
gender ['dʒendə(r)] *n* (**a**) *Gram* genre *m* (**b**) *(sex)* sexe *m*
gene [dʒiːn] *n Biol* gène *m; Fig* **it's in his genes** *(of talent, characteristic)* c'est héréditaire; **g. pool** patrimoine *m* génétique; **g. therapy** thérapie *f* génétique
genealogy [dʒiːnɪ'ælədʒɪ] *n* généalogie *f*
genera ['dʒenərə] *pl of* **genus**
general ['dʒenərəl] **1** *n* (**a**) **in g.** en général (**b**) *Mil* général *m*
2 *adj* général(e); **as a g.** rule en règle générale; **in g. terms** en termes généraux; **g. anaesthetic** anesthésie *f* générale; **G. Assembly** *(of United Nations)* Assemblée *f* générale; **g. election** élections *fpl* législatives; *Mil* **G. Headquarters** (grand) quartier *m* général; **g. knowledge** culture *f* générale; **g. manager** directeur(trice) *m,f* général(e); **g. meeting** assemblée *f* générale; **g. practice** *(in medicine)* médecine *f* générale; **g. practitioner** *(doctor)* médecin *m* généraliste; **the g. public** le grand public; **g. store** bazar *m;* **g. strike** grève *f* générale
generality [dʒenə'rælɪtɪ] *(pl* **generalities)** *n* généralité *f*
generalization [dʒenərəlaɪ'zeɪʃən] *n* généralisation *f*
generalize ['dʒenərəlaɪz] **1** *vt* **to become generalized** *(of practice, belief)* se généraliser
2 *vi* généraliser
generally ['dʒenrəlɪ] *adv (taken overall)* dans l'ensemble; *(as a general rule)* généralement, en général; **g. speaking** d'une manière générale
generate ['dʒenəreɪt] *vt (electricity, heat)* produire; *(income)* créer; *(reaction, response)* provoquer; *(interest, ideas)* faire naître
generation [dʒenə'reɪʃən] *n* (**a**) *(of people, products)* génération *f;* **from g. to g.** de génération en génération; **the younger/older g.** la jeune/l'ancienne génération; **the g. gap** le fossé entre les générations; **G. X/Y** génération *f* X/Y (**b**) *(of electricity)* production *f*
generator ['dʒenəreɪtə(r)] *n Elec* générateur *m*
generic [dʒɪ'nerɪk] *adj* générique
generosity [dʒenə'rɒsɪtɪ] *n* générosité *f*
generous ['dʒenərəs] *adj* généreux(euse)
generously ['dʒenərəslɪ] *adv* généreusement
genesis ['dʒenɪsɪs] *n* genèse *f;* **(the Book of) G.** la Genèse
genetic [dʒɪ'netɪk] *adj* génétique; **g. code** *m* génétique; **g. engineering** génie *m* génétique; **g. fingerprinting** empreinte *f* génétique
genetically [dʒɪ'netɪklɪ] *adv* génétiquement; **g. modified** génétiquement modifié(e)
genetics [dʒɪ'netɪks] *n* génétique *f*
Geneva [dʒɪ'niːvə] *n* Genève; **Lake G.** le Lac de Genève, le Lac Léman; **the G. Convention** la Convention de Genève
genial ['dʒiːnɪəl] *adj* cordial(e)
geniality [dʒiːnɪ'ælɪtɪ] *n* cordialité *f*
genially ['dʒiːnɪəlɪ] *adv* cordialement
genie ['dʒiːnɪ] *(pl* **genii** ['dʒiːnɪaɪ]) *n* génie *m*
genital ['dʒenɪtəl] **1** *npl* **genitals** organes *mpl* génitaux
2 *adj* génital(e)
genitive ['dʒenɪtɪv] *Gram* **1** *n* génitif *m;* **in the g.** au génitif
2 *adj* génitif(ive)

genius ['dʒiːnɪəs] *n* génie *m*; *Ironic* **to have a g. for sth/doing sth** avoir le génie de qch/de faire qch; **man/work of g.** homme *m*/œuvre *f* de génie

Genoa ['dʒenəʊə] *n* Gênes

genocide ['dʒenəsaɪd] *n* génocide *m*

genre ['ʒɒnrə] *n* (*of film, novel*) genre *m*

gent [dʒent] *n Br Fam* (**a**) (*well-bred man*) gentleman *m* (**b**) (*man*) homme *m*; **gents' footwear** chaussures *fpl* pour hommes; **gents** (*toilets*) toilettes *fpl* des hommes; (*sign*) messieurs

genteel [dʒen'tiːl] *adj* (*refined*) distingué(e); (*respectable*) comme il faut; *Pej* (*affected*) maniéré(e)

Gentile ['dʒentaɪl] *n* gentil *m*

gentle ['dʒentəl] *adj* (*person, manner*) doux (douce); (*push, breeze, rise, slope*) léger(ère); (*hint*) discret(ète); (*exercise*) modéré(e); **to be g. with sb** être doux (douce) avec qn; **to be g. with sth** faire attention à qch; *Fam* **a g. giant** un agneau sous des airs de brute

gentleman ['dʒentəlmən] *n* (**a**) (*well-bred man*) gentleman *m*; **g.'s agreement** gentleman's agreement (**b**) (*man*) homme *m*; **Ladies and Gentlemen!** mesdames et messieurs!

gentlemanly ['dʒentəlmənlɪ] *adj* bien élevé(e)

gentleness ['dʒentəlnɪs] *n* douceur *f*

gently ['dʒentlɪ] *adv* (*speak, remind*) gentiment; (*slope*) en pente douce; **g. (does it)!** allez-y doucement!

gentrification [dʒentrɪfɪ'keɪʃən] *n Br* (*of area, street*) embourgeoisement *m*

gentrified ['dʒentrɪfaɪd] *adj Br* (*area, street*) qui s'est embourgeoisé(e)

gentry ['dʒentrɪ] *n* petite noblesse *f*

genuflect ['dʒenjʊflekt] *vi Formal* faire une génuflexion

genuine ['dʒenjʊɪn] *adj* (**a**) (*manuscript, painting*) authentique; (*gold, leather*) véritable; (*excuse*) valable; (*offer*) sérieux(euse) (**b**) (*sincere*) sincère; **it was a g. mistake** ce n'était pas intentionnel

genuinely ['dʒenjʊɪnlɪ] *adv* (*sincerely*) sincèrement, vraiment

genus ['dʒiːnəs] (*pl* **genera** ['dʒenərə]) *n Biol* genre *m*

geo- ['dʒiːəʊ] *pref* géo-

geographer [dʒɪ'ɒgrəfə(r)] *n* géographe *mf*

geographic(al) [dʒɪə'græfɪk(əl)] *adj* géographique

geography [dʒɪ'ɒgrəfɪ] *n* géographie *f*

geologic(al) [dʒɪə'lɒdʒɪk(əl)] *adj* géologique

geologist [dʒɪ'ɒlədʒɪst] *n* géologue *mf*

geology [dʒɪ'ɒlədʒɪ] *n* géologie *f*

geometric(al) [dʒɪə'metrɪk(əl)] *adj* géométrique

geometry [dʒɪ'ɒmɪtrɪ] *n* géométrie *f*

geophysics [dʒɪəʊ'fɪzɪks] *n* géophysique *f*

geopolitics [dʒɪəʊ'pɒlɪtɪks] *n* géopolitique *f*

Geordie ['dʒɔːdɪ] *n Br Fam* = personne née à ou habitant Tyneside

Georgia ['dʒɔːdʒə] *n* (*country, US state*) la Géorgie

Georgian ['dʒɔːdʒən] **1** *n* (**a**) (*person*) Géorgien(enne) *m,f* (**b**) (*language*) géorgien *m*
2 *adj* géorgien(enne)

geothermal [dʒiːəʊ'θɜːməl] *adj* géothermique

geranium [dʒə'reɪnɪəm] *n* géranium *m*

gerbil ['dʒɜːbɪl] *n* gerbille *f*

geriatric [dʒerɪ'ætrɪk] **1** *n* malade *mf* gériatrique; *Fam Pej* (*old person*) gâteux(euse) *m,f*
2 *adj* (*hospital*) gériatrique; (*care*) aux vieillards; **g. medicine** gériatrie *f*

geriatrics [dʒerɪ'ætrɪks] *n* gériatrie *f*

germ [dʒɜːm] *n* (**a**) (*causing disease*) microbe *m*; **g. warfare** guerre *f* bactériologique (**b**) (*of seed*) & *Fig* (*of idea*) germe *m*

German ['dʒɜːmən] **1** *n* (**a**) (*person*) Allemand(e) *m,f* (**b**) (*language*) allemand *m*; **G. class/teacher** cours *m*/professeur *m* d'allemand
2 *adj* allemand(e); **G. measles** rubéole *f*; **G. shepherd** berger *m* allemand

germane [dʒɜː'meɪn] *adj Formal* approprié(e); **to be g. to sth** avoir rapport à qch

Germanic [dʒɜː'mænɪk] *adj* germanique

Germany ['dʒɜːmənɪ] *n* l'Allemagne *f*

germinate ['dʒɜːmɪneɪt] *vi* germer

germination [dʒɜːmɪ'neɪʃən] *n* germination *f*

gerrymandering ['dʒerɪmændərɪŋ] *n Pol* charcutage *m* électoral

gerund ['dʒerənd] *n Gram* gérondif *m*

gestation [dʒes'teɪʃən] *n also Fig* gestation *f*; **g. period** période *f* de gestation

gesticulate [dʒes'tɪkjʊleɪt] *vi* gesticuler

gesture ['dʒestʃə(r)] **1** *n also Fig* geste *m*; *Fig* **as a g. of friendship** en témoignage d'amitié
2 *vi* (*single action*) faire un geste; (*repeatedly*) faire des gestes; **to g. to sb** faire signe à qn; **to g. towards sb/sth** désigner qn/qch d'un geste

get [get] (*pt & pp* **got** [gɒt], *Am pp* **gotten** ['gɒtən]) **1** *vt* (**a**) (*obtain*) obtenir; (*job*) trouver; **to g. sth for sb** obtenir qch pour qn; **I got the idea from a book** j'ai trouvé l'idée dans un livre; **to g. the right answer** trouver la solution; **to g. the wrong answer** se tromper

(**b**) (*buy*) acheter; **to g. sth for sb** acheter qch à qn
(**c**) (*receive*) (*present, reply*) recevoir; (*surprise, shock*) avoir; **we can't g. Radio 4 here** on ne reçoit pas Radio 4 ici; **to g. £20,000 a year** gagner 20 000 livres par an; **we don't g. many visitors here** nous ne recevons pas beaucoup de visites ici
(**d**) (*catch*) (*person, disease*) attraper; (*train, bus*) prendre; *Fam* **I'll g. you for that** je t'aurai
(**e**) (*fetch*) aller chercher; **to g. sth for sb** aller chercher qch pour qn; **can I g. you anything?** je te rapporte quelque chose?
(**f**) *Fam* (*annoy*) énerver
(**g**) *Fam* (*understand*) piger; **do you g. my meaning?** tu vois ce que je veux dire?; **to g. the point** piger; **to g. a joke** saisir une blague
(**h**) (*send*) **to g. sth to sb** faire parvenir qch à qn
(**i**) (*cause to be in a certain state*) **to g. sth dry/wet** sécher/mouiller qch; **to g. sth clean/dirty** nettoyer/ salir qch; **you've got him worried** tu l'as fait s'inquiéter; **to g. sb pregnant** mettre qn enceinte; **to g. the children to bed** envoyer les enfants au lit
(**j**) (*cause to be done*) **to g. sth done** faire faire qch; **to g. the house painted** faire peindre la maison; **she got her work finished** elle a terminé son travail
(**k**) (*cause to do*) **to g. sb to do sth** faire faire qch à qn; **she got me to help her** elle m'a persuadé de l'aider; **you can g. them to wrap it for you** tu peux leur demander de te l'emballer
(**l**) (*do gradually*) **to g. to know sb** apprendre à connaître qn; **you'll g. to like him** tu finiras par l'apprécier; **she soon got to thinking that...** elle se mit bientôt à penser que...
(**m**) (*have opportunity*) **to g. to do sth** avoir l'occasion de faire qch
(**n**) (*possess*) (*with* **have**) **she hasn't got a car** elle n'a pas de voiture; **she's got measles/Aids** elle a la

rougeole/le sida; **what's that got to do with it?** qu'est-ce que ça a à voir?

(**o**) *(must) (with* have) **I've got to go** il faut que j'y aille; **it's got to be done** il faut que ce soit fait

2 *vi* (**a**) *(arrive)* arriver; **to g. home** arriver chez soi; **to g. back** arriver; **how do you g. there?** comment fait-on pour y aller?; **he got as far as chapter five** il est allé jusqu'au chapitre cinq; **it got to the point where...** ça en est arrivé à un point où...

(**b**) *(move) also Fig* **to g. in sb's way** se mettre sur le chemin de qn; **where has he got to?** où est-il passé?; **we're getting nowhere** on n'avance pas

(**c**) *(become)* **to g. angry** se mettre en colère; **to g. better** s'améliorer; **to g. drunk** se soûler; **to g. old** vieillir

(**d**) *(with past participle)* **to g. broken** être cassé(e); **to g. stolen** être volé(e); **to g. killed** se faire tuer; **to g. dressed** s'habiller; **to g. married** se marier

(**e**) *(start)* **to g. going** *(leave)* se mettre en route; *(start get working)* se mettre au travail; **to g. talking with sb** entrer en conversation avec qn

▶**get about** *vi (of person)* se déplacer; *(of news, rumour)* circuler

▶**get across** *vt sep (ideas, message)* faire passer

▶**get ahead** *vi* avancer

▶**get along** *vi* (**a**) *(leave)* s'en aller, partir (**b**) *(progress)* **how are you getting along in your new job?** comment ça va, votre nouveau travail?; **we can g. along without them** nous pouvons très bien nous passer d'eux (**c**) *(have good relationship)* s'entendre

▶**get around 1** *vt insep (problem, difficulty)* contourner; **there's no getting around it, we'll have to tell her** on n'a pas le choix, il va falloir lui dire

2 *vi* = **get about**

▶**get around to** *vt insep* **to g. around to doing sth** trouver le temps de faire qch

▶**get at** *vt insep* (**a**) *(have access to)* accéder à; *(reach)* atteindre; **to g. at the truth** découvrir la vérité (**b**) *(imply)* **what are you getting at?** où veux-tu en venir? (**c**) *Fam (criticize)* s'en prendre à

▶**get away** *vi (escape, leave)* se sauver; *(have a holiday)* s'échapper; *Fam* **g. away!** *(expressing disbelief)* sans blague!

▶**get away with** *vt insep* (**a**) *(fine, warning)* s'en tirer avec (**b**) *(crime)* **he stole the money and got away with it** il a volé l'argent et il ne s'est pas fait prendre; *Fig* **that child gets away with murder** on lui passe tout à ce gosse

▶**get back 1** *vt sep (recover)* récupérer; *(strength)* reprendre

2 *vi (return)* revenir

▶**get back at** *vt insep* **to g. back at sb (for sth)** se venger de qn (pour qch)

▶**get behind 1** *vt insep (support)* soutenir

2 *vi (become delayed)* prendre du retard (**with** *or* **in** dans)

▶**get by** *vi (manage)* se débrouiller, s'en tirer (**on/in** avec/en)

▶**get down 1** *vt sep* (**a**) *(reduce) (weight)* perdre; *(costs, temperature)* faire baisser (**b**) *(depress)* déprimer (**c**) *(fetch)* descendre

2 *vi (descend)* descendre (**from** de)

▶**get down to** *vt insep* se mettre à; **to g. down to the facts** en venir aux faits

▶**get in 1** *vt sep* (**a**) *(bring inside)* rentrer (**b**) *(insert)* **I couldn't g. a word in** je n'ai pas pu en placer une (**c**) *(stock up with)* faire provision de

2 *vi* (**a**) *(gain entrance)* entrer (**b**) *(arrive)* arriver (**c**) *(be elected)* être élu(e)

▶**get into** *vt insep* (**a**) *(house)* entrer dans; *(car)* monter dans; **to g. into Parliament** être élu(e) député; **to g. into trouble** s'attirer des ennuis; *Fam* **I don't know what's got into her** je ne sais pas ce qui lui prend (**b**) *(clothes, boots)* enfiler; **I can't g. into my dress any more** je n'entre plus dans ma robe (**c**) *Fam (become interested in) (activity)* commencer à s'intéresser à; *(book)* rentrer dans

▶**get in with** *vt insep (group of people)* se mettre bien avec

▶**get off 1** *vt sep* (**a**) **to g. sb off** *(save from punishment)* tirer qn de là (**b**) *(send)* **to g. the children off to school** envoyer les enfants à l'école

2 *vt insep (train, bus)* descendre de

3 *vi* (**a**) *(from train, bus)* descendre; *Fig* **I told him where to g. off** (**b**) *(go unpunished)* s'en tirer (**c**) *(begin)* **to g. off to sleep** s'endormir; **to g. off to a good/bad start** commencer bien/mal

▶**get off on** *vt insep very Fam* **to g. off on sth** être excité(e) par qch; **to g. off on doing sth** prendre son pied à faire qch

▶**get off with** *vt insep Br Fam* lever

▶**get on 1** *vt sep (clothes)* mettre, enfiler

2 *vt insep (train, bus, plane)* monter dans

3 *vi* (**a**) *(enter train, bus)* monter (**b**) *(progress)* réussir; **to g. on in life** *or* **in the world** réussir dans la vie; **how are you getting on?** *(how are you?)* comment ça va?; **how did you g. on?** *(in exam, at meeting)* comment ça s'est passé? (**c**) *(have good relationship)* s'entendre; **to g. on well/badly with sb** s'entendre bien/mal avec qn (**d**) *(age)* **to be getting on (in years)** se faire vieux (vieille)

▶**get on for** *vt insep (approach)* **he must be getting on for fifty** il doit approcher la cinquantaine; **it was getting on for midnight** il était presque minuit; **there were getting on for 200 people there** on approchait les 200 personnes

▶**get onto** *vt insep* (**a**) *(contact)* se mettre en rapport avec (**b**) *(move onto subject of)* en arriver à; **they eventually got onto (the subject of) money** ils en vinrent finalement à parler d'argent

▶**get out 1** *vt sep* (**a**) *(bring out)* sortir (**b**) *(remove)* (**nail, splinter)* retirer; *(stain)* faire partir

2 *vi* (**a**) *(leave)* sortir (**b**) *(of secret, news)* transpirer

▶**get out of** *vt insep (vehicle)* sortir de; **to g. out of the way** s'écarter; **g. out of here!** *(go away)* va-t-en!; *Fam (I don't believe you)* arrête de dire des bêtises!; **to g. out of doing sth** s'arranger pour ne pas faire qch

▶**get over 1** *vt sep (idea, information)* faire passer; *(facts)* expliquer

2 *vt insep* (**a**) *(road, river)* traverser, franchir; *(wall, fence)* passer par-dessus (**b**) *(illness, trauma)* se remettre de

▶**get over with** *vt sep* **to g. sth over with** en finir avec qch

▶**get round 1** *vt insep* = **get around**

2 *vi* = **get about**

▶**get round to** *vt insep* = **get around to**

▶**get through 1** *vt sep (communicate)* **to g. sth through to sb** faire comprendre qch à qn

2 *vt insep* (**a**) *(pass through)* passer à travers (**b**) *(survive) (test, interview)* survivre à; *(period of time)*

tenir (**c**) *(finish)* achever (**d**) *(consume) (food, drink)* consommer; *(money)* dépenser **3** *vi* (**a**) *(arrive) (of news)* parvenir; *(of messenger)* arriver (**b**) **to g. through to sb** *(on telephone)* obtenir la communication avec qn; *Fig (make understand)* se faire comprendre par qn

▶**get together 1** *vt sep (money)* réunir; *(belongings, ideas)* rassembler **2** *vi (of people)* se réunir

▶**get up 1** *vt sep* (**a**) *(out of bed)* faire lever (**b**) *(dress up)* **he got himself up in his best clothes** il a mis ses plus beaux vêtements (**c**) *very Fam (achieve erection)* **he couldn't g. it up** il n'a pas réussi à bander **2** *vt insep Fig* **to g. up sb's nose** taper sur les nerfs à qn **3** *vi (rise)* se lever

▶**get up to** *vt insep (do)* **what have you been getting up to recently?** qu'est-ce que tu as fait ces derniers temps?; **to g. up to mischief** faire des bêtises; **he's been getting up to his old tricks** il a encore fait des siennes

getaway ['getəweɪ] *n* fuite *f*; **to make one's g.** prendre la fuite; **g. car** = voiture utilisée pour prendre la fuite **get-rich-quick** ['get'rɪtʃ'kwɪk] *adj Fam* **a g. scheme** un moyen de devenir riche rapidement **get-together** ['gettəgeðə(r)] *n Fam* réunion *f* (entre amis) **get-up** ['getʌp] *n Fam (clothes)* accoutrement *m*; *(fancy dress)* déguisement *m* **get-up-and-go** ['getʌpənd'gəʊ] *n Fam* énergie *f* **get-well card** ['get'wel'kɑːd] *n* carte *f* de prompt rétablissement

geyser ['giːzə(r)] *n* (**a**) *(spring)* geyser *m* (**b**) *Br (water heater)* chauffe-eau *m inv* **Ghana** ['gɑːnə] *n* le Ghana **Ghanaian** [gɑː'neɪən] **1** *n* Ghanéen(enne) *m,f* **2** *adj* ghanéen(enne) **ghastly** ['gɑːstlɪ] *adj (terrible)* horrible, épouvantable; *(mistake)* monstrueux(euse) **Ghent** [gent] *n* Gand **gherkin** ['gɜːkɪn] *n* cornichon *m* **ghetto** ['getəʊ] *(pl* **ghettoes** *or* **ghettos)** *n* ghetto *m*; *Fam* **g. blaster** grand radiocassette *m* portatif **ghost** [gəʊst] **1** *n* fantôme *m*; **you look as though you've seen a g.** on dirait que tu as vu un revenant; **not the g. of a chance** pas la moindre chance; **to give up the g.** *(of person, machine)* rendre l'âme; **g. story** histoire *f* de fantôme; **g. town** ville *f* fantôme **2** *vt* **to g. a book** servir de nègre pour un livre **ghostly** ['gəʊstlɪ] *adj* spectral(e) **ghostwrite** ['gəʊstraɪt] *vt* **to g. a book** servir de nègre pour un livre **ghostwriter** ['gəʊstraɪtə(r)] *n* nègre *m* **ghoul** [guːl] *n (evil spirit)* goule *f*; *Fig (morbid person)* personne *f* morbide **ghoulish** ['guːlɪʃ] *adj (humour, remark)* morbide; *(scene)* macabre **GHQ** [dʒiːeɪtʃ'kjuː] *n Mil (abbr* **General Headquarters)** QG *m inv* **GI** [dʒiː'aɪ] *n Am Fam* GI *m inv* **giant** ['dʒaɪənt] **1** *n* géant(e) *m,f*; **g. killer** *(in sport)* vainqueur *m* surprise **2** *adj* géant(e) **gibber** ['dʒɪbə(r)] *vi* baragouiner **gibbering** ['dʒɪbərɪŋ] *adj* au discours incohérent; *Fam* **a g. idiot** un(e) pauvre idiot(e)

gibberish ['dʒɪbərɪʃ] *n* charabia *m*; **to talk g.** dire n'importe quoi **gibbet** ['dʒɪbɪt] *n* gibet *m*, potence *f* **gibbon** ['gɪbən] *n* gibbon *m* **gibe** [dʒaɪb] **1** *n* moquerie *f* **2** *vi* **to g. at sb** se moquer de qn **giblets** ['dʒɪblɪts] *npl* abats *mpl* **Gibraltar** [dʒɪ'brɔːltə(r)] *n* Gibraltar **giddiness** ['gɪdɪnɪs] *n* étourdissement *m*, vertige *m* **giddy** ['gɪdɪ] *adj* **to be** *or* **feel g.** avoir le vertige; **it makes me (feel) g.** ça me donne le vertige; *Fig* **the g. heights** les hautes sphères *fpl* **GIF** [dʒɪf] *n Comput (abbr* **Graphic Information Format)** GIF *m* **gift** [gɪft] *n* (**a**) *(present)* cadeau *m*; *Prov* **never look a g. horse in the mouth** à cheval donné on ne regarde pas la bouche; **g. shop** boutique *f* de cadeaux; **g. token** chèque-cadeau *m*; **g. wrap** papier *m* cadeau (**b**) *(talent)* don *m*; **to have a g. for sth** être doué(e) pour qch; **to have the g. of the gab** *(be talkative)* avoir la langue bien pendue; *(speak persuasively)* avoir du bagout **gifted** ['gɪftɪd] *adj* doué(e); *(artist, musician)* de talent **gift-wrapped** ['gɪftræpt] *adj* sous paquet-cadeau **gig** [gɪg] *n* (**a**) *Fam (pop concert)* concert *m* (**b**) *Old-fashioned (carriage)* cabriolet *m* **gigabyte** ['dʒɪgəbaɪt] *n Comput* gigaoctet *m* **gigantic** [dʒaɪ'gæntɪk] *adj* colossal(e), gigantesque **giggle** ['gɪgəl] **1** *n* (**a**) *(laugh)* petit rire *m* idiot; **to have (a fit of) the giggles** avoir le fou rire (**b**) *Fam (amusement)* **what a g.!** quelle rigolade!; **to do sth for a g.** faire qch pour rigoler **2** *vi* rire (nerveusement) **giggly** ['gɪgəlɪ] *adj* **to be g.** pouffer de rire **gigolo** ['dʒɪgələʊ] *(pl* **gigolos)** *n* gigolo *m* **gild** [gɪld] *(pt & pp* **gilded** *or* gilt [gɪlt]) *vt* dorer; *Fig* **to g. the lily** surcharger **gill** [dʒɪl] *n (liquid measure)* = 0,142 l, quart *m* de pinte **gills** [gɪlz] *npl (of fish)* ouïes *fpl*, branchies *fpl*; *Fig* **to be green about the g.** avoir le teint verdâtre **gilt** [gɪlt] **1** *n* dorure *f*; *Fin* **gilts** titres *mpl ou* fonds *mpl* d'État **2** *adj* doré(e) **3** *pt & pp of* **gild** **gilt-edged** ['gɪltedʒd] *adj Fin* **g. securities** *or* **stocks** titres *mpl ou* fonds *mpl* d'État **gimlet** ['gɪmlɪt] *n (tool)* vrille *f*; *Fig* **g. eyes** yeux *mpl* perçants **gimme** ['gɪmiː] *Fam* = **give me** **gimmick** ['gɪmɪk] *n* truc *m*, astuce *f* **gimmicky** ['gɪmɪkɪ] *adj* artificiel(elle), qui relève du procédé **gin** [dʒɪn] *n* gin *m*; **a g. and tonic** un gin tonic **ginger** ['dʒɪndʒə(r)] **1** *n* gingembre *m*; **g. ale** = boisson gazeuse au gingembre pouvant servir à couper un alcool; **g. beer** limonade *f* au gingembre **2** *adj (hair)* roux (rousse) ▶**ginger up** *vt sep Fam (person, group)* stimuler; *(film, story)* donner du punch à **gingerbread** ['dʒɪndʒəbred] *n* pain *m* d'épice; **g. man** = bonhomme en biscuit parfumé au gingembre **gingerly** ['dʒɪndʒəlɪ] *adv* avec précaution **gingham** ['gɪŋəm] *n* vichy *m* **gingivitis** [dʒɪndʒɪ'vaɪtɪs] *n Med* gingivite *f* **ginormous** [dʒaɪ'nɔːməs] *adj Fam* gigantesque, énorme **ginseng** ['dʒɪnseŋ] *n* ginseng *m*

gipsy ['dʒɪpsɪ] (*pl* **gipsies**) *n* (*Eastern European*) tzigane *mf*; (*Spanish*) gitan(e) *m,f*; **g. caravan** roulotte *f*
giraffe [dʒɪ'rɑːf] *n* girafe *f*
gird [gɜːd] (*pt & pp* **girded** *or* **girt** [gɜːt]) *vt Lit* **to g. one's loins** se ceindre les reins
girder ['gɜːdə(r)] *n* poutre *f* (métallique)
girdle ['gɜːdəl] **1** *n* (*corset*) gaine *f*
2 *vt Lit* (*surround*) ceindre, entourer
girl [gɜːl] *n* fille *f*; **a French g.** une (jeune) Française; **g. band** girls band *m*; *Br* **G. Guide,** *Am* **G. Scout** éclaireuse *f*
girlfriend ['gɜːlfrend] *n* (*lover*) petite amie *f*; (*friend*) amie *f*
girlhood ['gɜːlhʊd] *n* enfance *f*, jeunesse *f*
girlie ['gɜːlɪ] *n Fam* **to have a g. chat** bavarder entre filles; **g. mag** magazine *m* érotique
girlish ['gɜːlɪʃ] *adj* (*of girl*) de fille; (*of woman, effeminate man*) de jeune fille; **g. laughter** rire *m* de jeune fille
giro ['dʒaɪrəʊ] (*pl* **giros**) *n Br* (**a**) *Fin* **g. account** compte *m* chèque postal, CCP *m* (**b**) *Fam* (*unemployment cheque*) allocation *f* (de) chômage
Girobank ['dʒaɪrəʊbæŋk] *n* = service bancaire de la Poste britannique, ≃ service *m* de chèques postaux
girt [gɜːt] *pt & pp* of **gird**
girth [gɜːθ] *n* (*of tree*) circonférence *f*; (*of person*) corpulence *f*
gist [dʒɪst] *n* essentiel *m*; **to get the g.** saisir l'essentiel
git [gɪt] *n Br very Fam* con (conne) *m,f*
give [gɪv] **1** *vt* (*pt* **gave** [geɪv], *pp* **given** ['gɪvən]) (**a**) (*in general*) donner; (*as present*) offrir; **to g. sth to sb, to g. sb sth** donner qch à qn; (*as present*) offrir qch à qn; **to g. sb a dirty look** lancer un regard noir à qn; **he was given ten years/a fine** il a été condamné à dix ans de prison/à une amende; **g. her my love** embrasse-la pour moi; **she gave her age as twenty** elle a déclaré qu'elle avait vingt ans; **she gave me to understand that...** elle m'a fait comprendre que...; **g. or take a few minutes/pence** à quelques minutes/pence près (**b**) (*with noun to form verbal expressions*) **to g. a laugh** partir d'un éclat de rire; **to g. a sigh** pousser un soupir; **to g. sb a smile** sourire à qn; **to g. sb a fright** faire peur à qn; **to g. sb a kiss** embrasser qn; **he gave his face a wash** il s'est lavé le visage; **she gave the soup a stir** elle a remué la soupe
2 *vi* (**a**) (*donate*) donner; **please g. generously** soyez généreux, s'il vous plaît; **to g. of one's time** donner de son temps (**b**) (*yield, break*) (*of cloth, shoes*) se faire; (*of rope*) lâcher; (*of support, door*) céder
3 *n* (*of fabric*) élasticité *f*
►**give away** *vt sep* (**a**) (*give for nothing*) donner (**b**) (*prize*) distribuer; **to g. the bride away** conduire la mariée à l'autel (**c**) (*reveal*) trahir
►**give back** *vt sep* rendre
►**give in 1** *vt sep* (*hand over*) remettre
2 *vi* (*surrender*) céder (**to** à); (*admit defeat*) abandonner
►**give off** *vt sep* (*smell, heat*) dégager
►**give onto** *vt insep* **the house gives directly onto the street** la maison donne directement sur la rue
►**give out 1** *vt sep* (**a**) (*money, food*) distribuer; (*information*) donner (**b**) (*noise*) émettre; (*heat*) répandre
2 *vi* (*of supplies, patience*) s'épuiser; (*of luck*) tourner
►**give over 1** *vt sep* (*money, objects*) remettre; (*devote*) consacrer (**to** à)
2 *vi Fam* (*stop*) **g. over, will you?** arrête, d'accord?

►**give up 1** *vt sep* (*possessions*) renoncer à; (*activity, hope*) abandonner; **to g. up smoking** arrêter de fumer; **to g. up one's job** quitter son emploi; **to g. sb up for dead** considérer qn comme mort(e)
2 *vi* abandonner; **to g. up on sb** perdre tout espoir en qn; (*of doctors*) perdre tout espoir en ce qui concerne qn; **to g. up on sth** laisser tomber qch
►**give way** *vi* (**a**) (*collapse*) (*of support*) céder; (*of floor, ceiling*) s'effondrer; (*of rope, legs*) lâcher; (*of ground*) se dérober (**b**) (*yield*) (*in argument*) céder (**to** à); (*in car*) céder le passage (**to** à); **her tears gave way to laughter** ses larmes ont cédé la place au rire
give-and-take ['gɪvən'teɪk] *n* concessions *fpl* (mutuelles); **there has to be some g.** il faut que chacun y mette du sien
giveaway ['gɪvəweɪ] *n Fam* (**a**) (*revelation*) **what she said about the night before was the g.** ce qu'elle a dit sur la soirée précédente la trahie; **it was a dead g.** cela en disait long (**b**) (*free gift*) cadeau *m*; **g. price** prix *m* imbattable
given ['gɪvən] **1** *adj* (**a**) (*specific*) (*time, place*) donné(e); **at a g. point** à un moment donné; **g. name** prénom *m* (**b**) (*apt, likely*) **to be g. to doing sth** avoir tendance à faire qch
2 *conj* (**a**) (*considering*) étant donné; **g. that...** étant donné que...; **g. the nature of the case** étant donné la nature de l'affaire (**b**) **g. the chance again** si l'occasion se représentait
3 *pp* of **give**
gizmo ['gɪzməʊ] (*pl* **gizmos**) *n Fam* truc *m*, machin *m*
gizzard ['gɪzəd] *n* gésier *m*
glacé cherry ['glæseɪ'tʃerɪ] *n* cerise *f* confite
glacial ['gleɪsɪəl] *adj* glaciaire; *Fig* glacial(e)
glacier ['glæsɪə(r)] *n* glacier *m*
glad [glæd] *adj* heureux(euse), content(e) (**about** de); **I would be g. to assist you** je serais ravi de pouvoir vous aider; **to be g. of sth** (*grateful for*) être heureux(euse) d'avoir qch; *Fig* **to give sb the g. eye** faire de l'œil à qn; *Fam* **to put on one's g. rags** se mettre sur son trente et un
gladden ['glædən] *vt* réjouir
glade [gleɪd] *n Lit* clairière *f*
gladiator ['glædɪeɪtə(r)] *n* gladiateur *m*
gladiolus [glædɪ'əʊləs] (*pl* **gladioli** [glædɪ'əʊlaɪ]) *n* glaïeul *m*
gladly ['glædlɪ] *adv* avec plaisir, volontiers
glamorize ['glæməraɪz] *vt* (*lifestyle*) rendre séduisant(e); (*violence*) esthétiser; (*person*) idéaliser
glamorous ['glæmərəs] *adj* (*person*) élégant(e); (*job, image, lifestyle*) prestigieux(euse); (*place*) chic *inv*, élégant(e); (*dress*) magnifique
glamour, *Am* **glamor** ['glæmə(r)] *n* (*of person*) élégance *f*; (*of job, image, lifestyle*) prestige *m*; (*of place*) chic *m inv*, élégance *f*; *Fam* **g. girl** belle fille *f*, pin-up *f*; **g. model** mannequin *m* de charme
glance [glɑːns] **1** *n* coup *m* d'œil; **to have a g. at sth** jeter un coup d'œil à qch; **at a g.** d'un coup d'œil; **at first g.** au premier coup d'œil
2 *vi* **to g. at** regarder brièvement, jeter un coup d'œil à; **to g. through sth** parcourir qch rapidement
►**glance off** *vt insep* (*of blow, missile*) ricocher sur
glancing ['glɑːnsɪŋ] *adj* (*blow*) oblique
gland [glænd] *n* glande *f*
glandular ['glændjʊlə(r)] *adj* glandulaire; **g. fever** mononucléose *f* infectieuse
glare [gleə(r)] **1** *n* (**a**) (*angry stare*) regard *m* furieux (**b**) (*bright light*) éclat *m*, lumière *f* éblouissante; *Fig*

in the full g. of publicity sous les feux des médias
2 *vi (stare angrily)* **to g. at sb/sth** fixer qn/qch d'un air furieux
glaringly ['gleərɪŋlɪ] *adv* **it's g. obvious** ça saute aux yeux
Glasgow ['glɑːzgəʊ] *n* Glasgow
glass [glɑːs] *n* verre *m*; *(glassware)* verrerie *f*; **a g. of wine** un verre de vin; **g. bottle** bouteille *f* en verre; **g. case** vitrine *f*; **g. door** porte *f* vitrée; **g. eye** œil *m* de verre; **g. wool** laine *f* de verre
glass-blowing ['glɑːsbləʊɪŋ] *n* soufflage *m* du verre
glasses ['glɑːsɪz] *npl (spectacles)* lunettes *fpl*
glassful ['glɑːsfʊl] *n* verre *m*
glasshouse ['glɑːshaʊs] *n Br* serre *f*; *Prov* **people who live in glasshouses shouldn't throw stones** il faut être sans défauts pour critiquer autrui
glasspaper ['glɑːspeɪpə(r)] *n* papier *m* de verre
glassware ['glɑːsweə(r)] *n* verrerie *f*
glassworks ['glɑːswɜːks] *n* verrerie *f*; *(for crystal)* crystallerie *f*
glassy ['glɑːsɪ] *adj (eyes, look)* vitreux(euse); *(water)* immobile
Glaswegian [glæz'wiːdʒən] **1** *n* = personne née à ou habitant Glasgow
2 *adj* de Glasgow
glaucoma [glɔː'kəʊmə] *n* glaucome *m*; **to have g.** avoir un glaucome
glaze [gleɪz] **1** *n (on pottery)* vernis *m*; *(on pastry)* glaçage *m*
2 *vt* (**a**) *(window)* vitrer (**b**) *(pottery)* vernisser; *(pastry)* glacer
▶**glaze over** *vi (of eyes)* devenir vitreux(euse)
glazed [gleɪzd] *adj* (**a**) *(roof, door)* vitré(e) (**b**) *(pottery)* vernissé(e) (**c**) *(eyes, look)* vitreux(euse), terne
glazier ['gleɪzɪə(r)] *n* vitrier *m*
gleam [gliːm] **1** *n (of light)* rayon *m*; *Fig* **a g. of hope** une lueur d'espoir
2 *vi* luire, briller; *(of water)* miroiter
gleaming ['gliːmɪŋ] *adj* étincelant(e)
glean [gliːn] *vt* glaner
glee [gliː] *n (delight)* joie *f*; *(malicious pleasure)* jubilation *f*
gleeful ['gliːfʊl] *adj (happy)* joyeux(euse); **to be g.** *(maliciously happy)* jubiler
glen [glen] *n Ir & Scot* vallée *f*
glib [glɪb] *adj (person, excuse)* désinvolte; *(reply)* spécieux(euse)
glibly ['glɪblɪ] *adv (reply)* de façon désinvolte; *(speak)* avec aisance
glide [glaɪd] *vi (move smoothly)* glisser; *(of aircraft, bird)* planer
glider ['glaɪdə(r)] *n (aircraft)* planeur *m*
gliding ['glaɪdɪŋ] *n (sport)* vol *m* à voile
glimmer ['glɪmə(r)] **1** *n* faible lueur *f*; *(of water)* reflet *m*; *Fig* **a g. of hope** une lueur d'espoir
2 *vi (of light)* luire; *(of water)* miroiter; *(of metal)* étinceler
glimpse [glɪmps] **1** *n* **to catch a g. of** entrevoir; **a g. of the future** un aperçu de (ce que sera) l'avenir
2 *vt* entrevoir
glint [glɪnt] **1** *n (of light) (flash)* éclat *m*; *(continuous)* scintillement *m*; *(of water)* reflet *m*; **with a g. in her eye** avec une lueur dans le regard
2 *vi (of light, eye)* briller; *(of water, metal)* scintiller
glisten ['glɪsən] *vi (of water, metal)* scintiller; **his forehead glistened with sweat** la sueur perlait sur son front

glitter ['glɪtə(r)] **1** *n* (**a**) *(sparkle)* scintillement *m*; *Fig (of occasion)* éclat *m*, faste *m* (**b**) *(decoration, makeup)* paillettes *fpl*
2 *vi* scintiller; *Prov* **all that glitters is not gold** tout ce qui brille n'est pas d'or
glittering ['glɪtərɪŋ] *adj (jewels)* scintillant(e); *Fig (occasion, career)* brillant(e)
glitz [glɪts] *n* clinquant *m*, tape-à-l'œil *m*
glitzy ['glɪtsɪ] *adj Fam* tape-à-l'œil *inv*
gloat [gləʊt] *vi (at one's own success)* jubiler (**at** à l'idée de); *(about somebody else's misfortune)* se réjouir (**about** *or* **over** de); **I don't like to g., but...** ce n'est pas que ça me réjouisse, mais...
global ['gləʊbəl] *adj (comprehensive)* global(e); *(worldwide)* mondial(e); **g. village** village *m* planétaire; **g. warming** réchauffement *m* de la planète
globalization ['gləʊbəlaɪ'zeɪʃən] *n Econ* mondialisation *f*
globally ['gləʊbəlɪ] *adv (comprehensively)* globalement; *(worldwide)* mondialement
globe [gləʊb] *n (sphere)* globe *m*; *(with map)* globe *m* terrestre; **the g.** *(the earth)* le globe terrestre; **to travel the g.** voyager dans le monde entier
globetrotter ['gləʊbtrɒtə(r)] *n Fam* globe-trotter *mf*
globule ['glɒbjuːl] *n* gouttelette *f*
gloom [gluːm] *n* (**a**) *(darkness)* obscurité *f* (**b**) *(sadness)* morosité *f*
gloomily ['gluːmɪlɪ] *adv (sadly)* sombrement
gloomy ['gluːmɪ] *adj* (**a**) *(dark)* sombre; *(weather)* morose (**b**) *(sad)* triste (**c**) *(pessimistic)* pessimiste; **g. thoughts** idées *fpl* noires
glorified ['glɔːrɪfaɪd] *adj* **she's just a g. secretary** elle n'est rien de plus qu'une secrétaire; **it's just a g. motor scooter** ce n'est pas qu'un scooter amélioré
glorify ['glɔːrɪfaɪ] *(pt & pp glorified) vt* (**a**) *(extol)* célébrer; *Rel* **to g. God** rendre gloire à Dieu (**b**) *(war, violence)* glorifier
glorious ['glɔːrɪəs] *adj* (**a**) *(reign, victory)* glorieux(-euse) (**b**) *(view, sunshine)* magnifique
gloriously ['glɔːrɪəslɪ] *adv* (**a**) *(die, reign)* avec gloire (**b**) *(beautifully)* superbement; **it was g. sunny** il faisait un soleil splendide
glory ['glɔːrɪ] *n* (**a**) *(honour)* gloire *f* (**b**) *(splendour)* splendeur *f*
▶**glory in** *vt insep* se glorifier de
gloss¹ [glɒs] *n (in text)* glose *f*
gloss² *n (shine)* lustre *m*; *Fig* vernis *m*; *Fig* **to take the g. off sth** gâcher qch; **g. paint** peinture *f* brillante
▶**gloss over** *vt insep* passer sur
glossary ['glɒsərɪ] *(pl glossaries) n* glossaire *m*
glossy ['glɒsɪ] *adj (hair)* brillant(e); *(fur, leather)* luisant(e), lustré(e); *(surface)* brillant(e), poli(e); **g. brochure** brochure *f* luxueuse; **g. magazine** magazine *m* de luxe; **g. paper** papier *m* glacé
glottal stop ['glɒtəl'stɒp] *n Ling* coup *m* de glotte
glove [glʌv] *n* gant *m*; *Fig* **the gloves are off** tous les coups sont permis; **g. box** *or* **compartment** *(in car)* boîte *f* à gants; **g. puppet** marionnette *f* à gaine
glow [gləʊ] **1** *n (light)* lueur *f*; *(on cheeks)* couleurs *fpl*; **the g. of the setting sun** l'embrasement du couchant; *Fig* **a g. of pride/satisfaction** un vif sentiment de fierté/satisfaction
2 *vi (of light, fire)* rougeoyer; *Fig* **to be glowing with health** être resplendissant(e) de santé; *Fig* **to g. with pride/pleasure** rayonner de fierté/plaisir
glower ['glaʊə(r)] *vi* **to g. at sb** lancer des regards noirs à qn

glowing ['glɘʊɪŋ] *adj (cigarette, coal)* incandescent(e); *(metal)* chauffé(e) au rouge; *Fig (praise, words)* chaleureux(euse); *(description, report)* enthousiaste; *Fig* **to paint sth in g. colours** présenter qch sous un jour très favorable

glow-worm ['glɘʊwɜ:m] *n* ver *m* luisant

glucose ['glu:kɘʊs] *n* glucose *m*

glue [glu:] **1** *n* colle *f*
2 *vt* coller (**to** à); *Fig* **to be glued to the television** être cloué(e) devant la télévision

glue-sniffing ['glu:snɪfɪŋ] *n* inhalation *f* de colle

glum [glʌm] *adj* triste, morose

glut [glʌt] **1** *n (of goods)* encombrement *m*
2 *vt (pt & pp* **glutted)** (**a**) *(market, economy)* encombrer, inonder (**b**) **to g. oneself (on)** se gaver (de)

glutinous ['glu:tɪnɘs] *adj* gluant(e)

glutton ['glʌtɘn] *n (greedy person)* goinfre *mf*, glouton(onne) *m,f*; *Fig* **to be a g. for punishment** être masochiste

gluttony ['glʌtɘnɪ] *n* goinfrerie *f*, gloutonnerie *f*

glycaemic index, *Am* **glycemic index** [glaɪ'si:mɪk'ɪndeks] *n* index *m* glycémique

glycerin ['glɪsɘrɪn], **glycerine** ['glɪsɘri:n], **glycerol** ['glɪsɘrɒl] *n* glycérine *f*

GM [dʒi:'em] *adj* (**a**) *(abbr* **genetically modified)** génétiquement modifié(e) (**b**) *Br (abbr* **grant maintained)** subventionné(e) *(par l'État)*

GMO [dʒi:em'ɘʊ] *n (abbr* **genetically modified organism)** OGM *m*

GMT [dʒi:em'ti:] *n (abbr* **Greenwich Mean Time)** GMT *m*

gnarled [nɑ:ld] *adj* noueux(euse)

gnash [næʃ] *vt* **to g. one's teeth** grincer des dents

gnat [næt] *n* moucheron *m*

gnaw [nɔ:] **1** *vt (of rodent)* ronger
2 *vi* (**a**) *(of rodent)* ronger **b. through sth** ronger qch (**b**) *Fig (of doubt, guilt)* **to g. away at sb** ronger qn

gnome [nɘʊm] *n* gnome *m*

GNP [dʒi:en'pi:] *n Econ (abbr* **Gross National Product)** PNB *m*

gnu [nu:] *n* gnou *m*

go [gɘʊ] **1** *vi (3rd person singular* **goes** [gɘʊz], *pt* **went** [went], *pp* **gone** [gɒn]) (**a**) *(move)* aller; **to go to France** aller en France; **to go to the doctor('s)** aller chez le docteur; **to go home** rentrer chez soi; **to go swimming/skiing** (aller) nager/skier; **the proceeds will go to charity** l'argent recueilli sera versé à des œuvres de charité; *Fig* **where do we go from here?** et maintenant, qu'est-ce qu'on fait?
(**b**) *(leave)* partir, s'en aller; **I've got to go** il faut que j'y aille; **let's go!** allons-y!
(**c**) *(function)* marcher; *(of bell)* sonner; **to keep the conversation going** entretenir la conversation
(**d**) *(progress)* aller; **to go well/badly** bien/mal se passer; *Fam* **how's it going?** comment ça va?; **how does the tune/story go?** c'est quoi, l'air/l'histoire, déjà?
(**e**) *(of time)* passer; **the time went quickly/slowly** le temps a passé vite/lentement; **it has just gone eight** il est huit heures à peine passées; **there are only five minutes to go** il ne reste que cinq minutes
(**f**) *(disappear, deteriorate)* disparaître; *(of light bulb)* griller; *(of fuse)* sauter; *(of batteries)* s'user; **her sight/voice is going** elle est en train de perdre la vue/la voix; **most of my money goes on food** l'essentiel de mon argent passe dans la nourriture
(**g**) *(forming future)* **to be going to do sth** aller faire

qch; **I was going to walk** j'allais y aller à pied; **it's going to rain** il va pleuvoir
(**h**) *(match)* aller (**with** avec); **these colours go/don't go** ces couleurs vont bien/ne vont pas ensemble
(**i**) *(be available)* **there's a job going at the factory** il y a une place à l'usine; **is there any wine going?** est-ce qu'il y a du vin?; **it went for £12** on l'a vendu 12 livres
(**j**) *(fit)* entrer; **the piano won't go through the door** le piano ne passera pas par la porte; **four into three won't go** trois n'est pas divisible par quatre
(**k**) *(belong)* aller; **the cups go on that shelf** les tasses vont sur cette étagère
(**l**) *(become)* devenir; **to go crazy** devenir fou (folle); **to go red** rougir; **to go cold** refroidir
(**m**) *(be the rule)* **what she says goes** c'est elle qui commande
(**n**) *Fam (urinate)* aller aux toilettes
(**o**) *Am* **two burgers to go** *(to take away)* deux hamburgers à emporter
2 *vt* (**a**) *(make sound)* & *Fam (say)* faire; **cows go moo** la vache fait meuh; **to go bang/plop** faire paf/plouf
(**b**) *(idioms)* **to go it alone** se lancer en solo; **to go one better than sb** faire mieux que qn, surenchérir sur qn; *Fam* **I could really go a beer!** je me ferais bien une bière!
3 *n (pl* **goes)** (**a**) *(expressing activity)* **to be on the go** ne pas s'arrêter; **she had three boyfriends on the go at the same time** elle avait trois copains en même temps; **it's all go** ça n'arrête pas; **from the word go** dès le début
(**b**) *(energy)* **to be full of go** être très dynamique
(**c**) *(success)* **to make a go of sth** réussir qch
(**d**) *(turn)* tour *m*; **(it's) your go!** *(in game)* c'est ton tour!, c'est à toi!; **to have a go at doing sth** essayer de faire qch; *Fam* **let's have a go!** allons-y!; *(let me try)* laisse-moi essayer!; **at one go** d'un coup; **£1 a go** *(at fair)* 1 livre le tour
(**e**) *(idioms)* **to have a go at sb** incendier qn

▸**go about 1** *vi (circulate) (of person)* se promener; *(of rumour)* circuler; **you can't go about saying things like that!** il ne faut pas raconter des choses pareilles!; **there's a bug going about** il y a un microbe qui se promène
2 *vt insep* (**a**) *(travel) (country)* parcourir (**b**) *(tackle) (task)* vaquer à; **to go about doing sth** s'y prendre pour faire qch; **how do I go about getting a licence?** que dois-je faire pour obtenir un permis?

▸**go across** *vt insep & vi* traverser

▸**go after** *vt insep (pursue)* **to go after sb** courir après qn; **to go after sth** essayer d'obtenir qch

▸**go against** *vt insep* (**a**) *(contradict) (principles, instincts)* aller à l'encontre de (**b**) *(be unfavourable to)* **the decision went against him** la décision lui a été défavorable

▸**go ahead** *vi* (**a**) *(take place)* avoir lieu; **to go ahead with sth** commencer *ou* entreprendre qch; **may I say something?** – **go ahead** puis-je dire quelque chose? – allez-y (**b**) *(go in front)* passer devant; **to go ahead of sb** devancer qn

▸**go along** *vi (proceed)* se dérouler; **as we go along en** chemin; **to do sth as one goes along** faire qch au fur et à mesure

▸**go along with** *vt insep (suggestion, plan)* approuver, être d'accord avec

▸**go at** *vt insep (person, task)* s'attaquer à

▸**go away** *vi (leave)* partir; *(disappear)* disparaître; **go away!** allez-vous-en!; **to go away on business/for the weekend** partir en voyage d'affaires/en weekend

▸**go back** *vi* (**a**) *(return)* revenir; **to go back to doing sth** se remettre à faire qch; **to go back to sleep** se rendormir; **to go back to one's old ways** reprendre ses anciennes habitudes (**b**) *(in time)* **to go back to** remonter à; *Fam* **we go back a long way** ça fait longtemps qu'on se connaît

▸**go back on** *vt insep (promise)* revenir sur

▸**go before 1** *vi (precede)* précéder
    2 *vt insep* **to go before the court** *(of defendant, case)* passer au tribunal

▸**go by** *vi* (**a**) *(pass)* passer; **to watch the world go by** regarder passer les gens (**b**) *(of time)* s'écouler
    2 *vt insep* (**a**) *(be guided by)* **to go by appearances** juger d'après les apparences; **to go by the rules** respecter les règles (**b**) *(be known by)* **to go by the name of** être go connu(e) sous le nom de go

▸**go down 1** *vt insep (descend)* descendre
    2 *vi* (**a**) *(descend)* descendre; *(of sun)* se coucher; *(of ship)* sombrer; **to go down on one's knees** s'agenouiller; *Fig* se mettre à genoux; **to go down with an illness** tomber malade (**b**) *(be defeated)* être vaincu(e); **I'm not going to go down without a fight** je me battrai jusqu'au bout (**c**) *(of level, temperature, prices)* baisser; *(of tyre, balloon)* se dégonfler (**d**) *(be received)* **to go down well/badly** être bien/mal reçu(e); **he has gone down in history as a tyrant** l'histoire a retenu de lui l'image d'un tyran

▸**go for** *vt insep* (**a**) *(attack)* attaquer; **if you really want the job, go for it!** si tu veux vraiment le poste, bats-toi!; *Fam* **go for it!** vas-y! (**b**) *(like)* avoir un faible pour (**c**) *(choose)* prendre (**d**) **he has got a lot going for him** il a bien des atouts (**e**) *(apply to)* s'appliquer à; **the same goes for you** ça vaut aussi pour toi

▸**go in** *vi (enter)* entrer; *(fit)* rentrer; *(of sun)* se cacher

▸**go in for** *vt insep* (**a**) *(competition)* s'inscrire à (**b**) *(like)* **she doesn't go in for cooking/sports** elle n'est pas très portée sur la cuisine/les sports

▸**go into** *vt insep* (**a**) *(enter)* entrer dans (**b**) *(examine)* examiner

▸**go off 1** *vi* (**a**) *(leave)* partir (**with** avec) (**b**) *(of meat, fish)* s'avarier; *(of milk)* tourner (**c**) *(of bomb)* exploser; *(of alarm)* se déclencher; **the gun went off** le coup est parti (**d**) *(of event)* **to go off well** *or* **smoothly** se dérouler bien (**e**) *(stop working)* **the power went off** l'électricité a été coupée; **the light went off** la lumière s'est éteinte
    2 *vt insep (lose liking for)* ne plus aimer, se lasser de; **I've gone off the idea** l'idée ne me séduit plus

▸**go on 1** *vi* (**a**) *(continue)* continuer; **to go on doing sth** continuer à faire qch; **as time wears on** avec le temps (**b**) *(proceed)* **to go on to sth** passer à qch; **to go on to do sth** poursuivre en faisant qch (**c**) *(talk excessively)* **don't go on about it!** arrête de parler de ça!; **he does go on a bit** il est un peu soûlant; **to go on at sb** s'en prendre à qn (**d**) *(happen)* se passer; **what's going on here?** qu'est-ce qui se passe ici? (**e**) *(of electricity, light, heating)* s'allumer
    2 *vt insep* (**a**) *(be guided by)* se fonder sur; **the police have nothing to go on** la police n'a rien sur quoi se fonder (**b**) *(approach)* **she's two going on three** elle

va sur ses trois ans; *Hum* **he's nine going on nineteen** il a neuf ans mais il est déjà très mûr

▸**go out** *vi* (**a**) *(leave)* sortir; **to go out for a meal** aller au restaurant; **to go out on strike** se mettre en grève (**b**) *(date)* sortir ensemble; **to go out with sb** sortir avec qn (**c**) *(of fire, light)* s'éteindre (**d**) *(become unfashionable)* passer de mode (**e**) *(be eliminated)* être éliminé(e) (**f**) *(of TV, radio programme)* être diffusé(e)

▸**go over 1** *vi* (**a**) *(cross)* **to go over to sb** aller vers qn (**b**) *(switch)* **to go over to sth** passer à qch (**c**) *(of suggestion, joke)* **to go over well/badly** être bien/mal reçu(e)
    2 *vt insep* (**a**) *(bridge)* passer; *(road)* traverser; **the ball went over the wall** la balle est passée par-dessus le mur (**b**) *(examine)* passer en revue; *(figures, accounts)* vérifier; **to go over sth in one's mind** repasser qch dans son esprit

▸**go round 1** *vt insep* **to go round town** faire un tour en ville; **to go round the shops** faire les magasins
    2 *vi* (**a**) *(visit)* **I said I'd go round (and see her)** j'ai dit que j'irai la voir; **she's gone round to a friend's** elle est allée voir un ami (**b**) *(circulate)* *(of rumour)* circuler; *(of cold, flu)* se promener (**c**) *(be enough)* **there was enough food/drink to go round** il y avait assez à manger/boire pour tout le monde

▸**go through 1** *vt insep* (**a**) *(penetrate)* traverser (**b**) *(suffer)* subir (**c**) *(complete)* *(formalities)* accomplir (**d**) *(examine)* passer en revue; *(one's notes, speech)* revoir; *(suitcase, house)* fouiller; **to go through sb's pockets** fouiller les poches de qn (**e**) *(use up)* *(money)* dépenser; *(food)* consommer; **we've gone through six bottles of milk** nous avons bu six bouteilles de lait
    2 *vi (be completed)* *(of deal)* être conclu(e); *(of bill)* passer; *(of divorce)* être prononcé(e)

▸**go through with** *vt insep* aller jusqu'au bout de; **I can't go through with the wedding** finalement, je ne me marie plus; **I can't go through with it** je ne peux pas le faire

▸**go under** *vi (of ship)* couler; *Fig (of firm)* faire faillite

▸**go up 1** *vt insep* monter
    2 *vi* (**a**) *(climb, rise)* monter; *(of theatre curtain)* se lever; **to go up to bed** monter se coucher; **a shout went up from the crowd** un cri s'éleva de la foule; *Fig* **to go up in the world** *(socially)* monter son chemin (**b**) *(of prices, temperature)* monter, grimper; **to go up in sb's estimation** monter dans l'estime de qn (**c**) *(explode)* sauter

▸**go up to** *vt insep* (**a**) *(approach)* se diriger vers (**b**) *(reach)* aller jusqu'à

▸**go with** *vt insep* (**a**) *(accompany)* aller (de pair) avec; **a company car goes with the job** le poste donne droit à une voiture de fonction (**b**) *(harmonize with)* aller avec

▸**go without 1** *vi* se priver; **I'd rather go without** je préfère m'en passer
    2 *vt insep* se passer de

goad [gəʊd] **1** *n Fig (remark, criticism)* aiguillon *m*
    2 *vt Fig (person)* provoquer; **to g. sb into doing sth** harceler qn jusqu'à ce qu'il fasse qch

▸**goad on** *vt sep* aiguillonner

go-ahead ['gəʊəhed] **1** *n* **to give sb/sth the g.** donner le feu vert à qn/qch
    2 *adj (enterprising)* entreprenant(e), dynamique

goal [gəʊl] n (**a**) (aim) but m, objectif m (**b**) (in football, hockey) but m; **g. kick** coup m de pied de but; **g. line** ligne f de but; **g. scorer** buteur(euse) m,f **goalkeeper** ['gəʊlkiːpə(r)], Fam **goalie** ['gəʊlɪ] n gardien m de but, goal m

goalless ['gəʊllɪs] adj **g. draw** match m nul

goalmouth ['gəʊlmaʊθ] n (in football) (entrée f du) but m

goalpost ['gəʊlpəʊst] n poteau m de but; **the goalposts** les buts mpl; Fig **to move** or **shift the goalposts** changer les règles du jeu

goat [gəʊt] n chèvre f; **g.'s milk** lait m de chèvre; Fam **it really gets my g.!** ça me tape vraiment sur les nerfs!; Fam **to act** or **play the g.** faire l'idiot(e)

goatherd ['gəʊthɜːd] n chevrier(ère) m,f

goatskin ['gəʊtskɪn] n peau f de chèvre

gob [gɒb] Br very Fam **1** n (mouth) gueule f; **shut your g.!** (ferme) ta gueule!

2 vi (pt & pp **gobbed**) (spit) mollarder

gobble ['gɒbəl] **1** vt (eat) engloutir

2 vi (of turkey) glouglouter

▸**gobble up** vt sep also Fig engloutir

gobbledygook ['gɒbəldɪguːk] n Fam charabia m

go-between ['gəʊbɪtwiːn] n intermédiaire mf

goblet ['gɒblɪt] n verre m à pied; (in medieval times) coupe f

goblin ['gɒblɪn] n lutin m

gobsmacked ['gɒbsmækt] adj Br Fam **to be g.** en rester estomaqué(e)

go-cart = go-kart

god [gɒd] n (**a**) (divine being) dieu m; **G.** Dieu m; **G. forbid!** Dieu m'en garde!; **G. willing** si Dieu le veut; **I wish to G. I hadn't told him** si seulement je ne lui avais rien dit; **in G.'s name** au nom du Ciel; Fam **(oh) my G.!** mon Dieu!; Fam **for G.'s sake!** pour l'amour du ciel!; Fam **G. knows** Dieu seul le sait; Fam **he thinks he's G.'s gift to women** il s'imagine que toutes les femmes sont folles de lui (**b**) Fam **the gods** (in theatre) le poulailler

godchild ['gɒdtʃaɪld] n filleul(e) m,f

goddam(n) ['gɒdæm] Am very Fam **1** adj sacré(e), fichu(e); **that g. dog!** ce sacré chien!

2 adv vachement

3 exclam nom de Dieu!

goddaughter ['gɒddɔːtə(r)] n filleule f

goddess ['gɒdɪs] n déesse f

godfather ['gɒdfɑːðə(r)] n parrain m

god-fearing ['gɒdfɪːrɪŋ] adj pieux(euse)

godforsaken ['gɒdfəseɪkən] adj perdu(e)

godless ['gɒdlɪs] adj impie

godmother ['gɒdmʌðə(r)] n marraine f

godparent ['gɒdpeərənt] n (godfather) parrain m; (godmother) marraine f; **my godparents** mon parrain et ma marraine

godsend ['gɒdsend] n aubaine f

godson ['gɒdsʌn] n filleul m

go-getter ['gəʊgetə(r)] n Fam battant(e) m,f

goggle ['gɒgəl] vi ouvrir des yeux ronds; **to g. at sb/ sth** regarder qn/qch avec des yeux ronds

goggle-eyed ['gɒgəlaɪd] adv Fam avec des yeux ronds

goggles ['gɒgəlz] npl (for swimming) lunettes fpl de plongée; (for skiing) lunettes fpl de ski; (for worker) lunettes fpl protectrices

go-go dancer ['gəʊgəʊ'dɑːnsə(r)] n danseuse f de boîte de nuit

going ['gəʊɪŋ] **1** n (**a**) (progress) **that's very good g.!** voilà qui n'est pas mal du tout!; **it's slow g.** (at work) ça n'avance pas vite (**b**) (condition of ground) terrain m; Fig **the book/film was pretty heavy g.** le livre/film était plutôt indigeste; Fig **to get out while the g. is good** se retirer tant que la chance nous/leur/etc est favorable

2 adj (**a**) (successful) **a g. concern** une affaire qui tourne (**b**) (current) (price, rate) courant(e), actuel(elle)

going-away ['gəʊɪŋə'weɪ] adj **g. party/present** fête f/cadeau m d'adieu

going-over ['gəʊɪŋ'əʊvə(r)] n Fam **to give sb a g.** (beating) tabasser qn; (criticism) sonner les cloches à qn

goings-on ['gəʊɪŋzɒn] npl Fam (activities) activités fpl; (events) événements mpl

goitre, Am **goiter** ['gɔɪtə(r)] n goitre m

go-kart ['gəʊkɑːt] n (child's toy) petit chariot m; (with engine) kart m; **g. racing** karting m

gold [gəʊld] **1** n or m; **g. bullion** or m en barre; **g. dust** poussière f d'or; **tickets are like g. dust** les billets valent de l'or; **g. leaf** or **foil** feuille f d'or; **g. medal** médaille f d'or; also Fig **g. mine** mine f d'or; **g. plate** orfèvrerie f; Fin **g. reserves** réserves fpl d'or; Am Hist **the G. Rush** la ruée vers l'or

2 adj (made of gold) en or; (gold-coloured) doré(e)

gold-digger ['gəʊld'dɪgə(r)] n Fam Pej (woman) croqueuse f de diamants

golden ['gəʊldən] adj (made of gold) en or; (gold-coloured) doré(e); **a g. opportunity** une occasion en or; **the g. age** l'âge m d'or; **g. boy** enfant m chéri; **g. eagle** aigle m royal; **g. girl** enfant f chérie; **g. handshake** (retirement bonus) indemnité f de départ; **g. jubilee** jubilé m; **g. rule** règle f d'or; Fin **g. share** action f privilégiée; **g. wedding** noces fpl d'or

goldfinch ['gəʊldfɪntʃ] n chardonneret m

goldfish ['gəʊldfɪʃ] (pl **goldfish**) n poisson m rouge; **g. bowl** bocal m à poissons rouges; **it's like living in a g. bowl** c'est comme vivre en vitrine

gold-plated [gəʊld'pleɪtɪd] adj plaqué(e) or

goldsmith ['gəʊldsmɪθ] n orfèvre m

golf [gɒlf] n golf m; **g. ball** balle f de golf; **g. club** (stick, association) club m de golf; **g. course** terrain m de golf

golfer ['gɒlfə(r)] n joueur(euse) m,f de golf

golfing ['gɒlfɪŋ] n golf m; **g. umbrella** grand parapluie m (de golf)

golly ['gɒlɪ] exclam Fam Old-fashioned fichtre!

gondola ['gɒndələ] n (**a**) (boat) gondole f (**b**) (cable car) cabine f de téléphérique

gondolier [gɒndə'lɪə(r)] n gondolier m

gone [gɒn] **1** adj (**a**) (past) **it's g. nine o'clock** il est neuf heures passées (**b**) Fam **to be six months g.** (pregnant) être enceinte de six mois; **to be pretty far g.** (drunk) être complètement bourré(e); **to be g. on sb** (infatuated) avoir le béguin pour qn

2 pp of **go**

goner ['gɒnə(r)] n Fam **I thought she was a g.** (would die) j'ai cru qu'elle allait y passer; **I'm a g. if she finds out** si elle l'apprend, je suis mort

gong [gɒŋ] n gong m; Br Fam (medal) breloque f

gonna ['gɒnə] Fam = **going to**

gonorrhoea, Am **gonorrhea** [gɒnə'rɪə] n blennorragie f; **to have g.** avoir une blennorragie

goo [guː] n Fam (**a**) (sticky substance) substance f visqueuse (**b**) (sentimentality) guimauve f

good [gʊd] **1** *n* (**a**) bien *m*; **to do g.** faire le bien; **he's up to no g.** il prépare un mauvais coup; **to see the g. in sb/sth** voir les bons côtés de qn/qch (**b**) *(benefit)* **I did it for your own g.** je l'ai fait pour ton bien; **it was all to the g.** c'était tout bénéfice; **we were £100 to the g.** nous avons fait 100 livres de bénéfice; **for the g.** of one's health pour sa santé; **for the common g.** dans l'intérêt général; **it will do you g.** cela te fera du bien; **it won't do any g.** cela ne servira à rien; **what's the g. of that?** à quoi bon?; **it's no g.** ça ne sert à rien; **it's no g. complaining** cela ne sert à rien de se plaindre; **he's no g.** *(incompetent)* il est nul; *(morally bad)* il ne vaut pas grand-chose (**c**) **for g.** *(permanently)* pour toujours; **she is gone for g.** elle est partie pour de bon **2** *adj (comparative* **better** ['betə(r)], *superlative* **best** [best]) (**a**) *(in quality)* bon (bonne); *(weather, handwriting)* beau (belle); **she looks g. in that hat** ce chapeau lui va bien, elle est bien avec ce chapeau; **to taste g.** avoir bon goût; **(that) sounds g.!** bonne idée!; **g. to eat** comestible; **it's g. to see you** ça fait plaisir de vous voir; *Fam* **that's a g. one!** *(of story, joke)* elle est bien bonne!; **he thinks he's too g. for us** il se croit trop bien pour nous; **to earn g. money** bien gagner sa vie; **you've got a g. chance** tu as tes chances; **to be on to a g. thing** être sur un bon filon; **to have a g. time** s'amuser; **to show sb a g. time** faire passer un bon moment à qn; **all in g. time** chaque chose en son temps; **too g. to be true** trop beau pour être vrai; **as g. as new** comme neuf (neuve); **he as g. as called me a liar** pour un peu, il m'aurait traité de menteur; **the g. old days** le bon vieux temps; **g. afternoon!** bonjour!; **the G. Book** la sainte Bible; **he's a g. friend** c'est un ami; **G. Friday** le Vendredi Saint; *Fam* **g. grief!** fichtre!; **the g. life** la belle vie; *Fam* **g. Lord!, g. heavens!, g. gracious!** bon sang!; **g. morning!** bonjour!; **g. night!** bonne nuit!; **the G. Samaritan** le bon Samaritain (**b**) *(advantageous)* **a g. opportunity** une bonne occasion; **to be in a g. position to do sth** être bien placé(e) pour faire qch; **it's looking g.** ça se présente bien (**c**) *(beneficial)* bon (bonne); **he doesn't know what's g. for him** il n'a pas un sou de bon sens; **to be g. for business** être bon pour les affaires; **it's a g. thing we were here** heureusement que nous étions là; **g. riddance!** bon débarras! (**d**) *(skilful)* bon (bonne) (**at** en); **to be g. with one's hands** être habile de ses mains; **to be g. with children** savoir y faire avec les enfants; **to be g. in bed** bien faire l'amour (**e**) *(well-behaved)* sage; **be g.!** *(to child)* sois sage!; **to be as g. as gold** être sage comme une image; **to lead a g. life** mener une vie respectable; **g. conduct** *or* **behaviour** bonne conduite *f* (**f**) *(kind)* gentil(ille); **that's very g. of you** c'est bien aimable *ou* très gentil de votre part; **he was very g. about it** il s'est montré très compréhensif; **to do sb a g. turn** rendre un service à qn (**g**) *(valid)* **a g. reason** une bonne raison, une raison valable; **he's g. for £25,000** *(has in credit)* il dispose de 25 000 livres (**h**) *(for emphasis)* bon (bonne); **a g. two hours** deux bonnes heures; **a g. deal of, a g. many** beaucoup de; **to have a g. look at sb/sth** bien regarder qn/qch; **to have a g. cry** pleurer un bon coup; **a g. long time** un bien long moment

(**i**) **to make g.** *(of person)* faire son chemin; **to make g. one's losses** compenser ses pertes; **to make g. one's promise** tenir sa promesse; **he made g. his escape** il a réussi son évasion **3** *adv* (**a**) **I'll do it when I'm g. and ready** je le ferai quand ça me chantera (**b**) *(as comment, answer)* bien; **I feel better today** – **g.** je me sens mieux aujourd'hui – tant mieux

Good Friday

En Grande-Bretagne, il est traditionnel, le jour du Vendredi Saint, de manger des "hot cross buns" (petits pains ronds aux fruits secs, marqués d'une croix).

The Good Friday Agreement

Le processus de paix en Irlande du Nord, qui a été amorcé par les cessez-le-feu des groupes paramilitaires républicains et unionistes en 1994, a abouti au "Good Friday Agreement", l'accord de paix signé à Belfast en avril 1998. Cet accord a mis en place la "Northern Ireland Assembly", un parlement en partie autonome avec un partage démocratique du pouvoir entre les communautés protestante et catholique. Depuis son instauration, cependant, le parlement a été suspendu à plusieurs reprises, notamment à cause d'une polémique sur le désarmement de l'IRA et dissensions continuelles entre unionistes et républicains. Cependant, la décision de l'IRA – rendue publique en juillet 2005 – de renoncer à la lutte armée de façon permanente puis l'annonce de la destruction de son arsenal laisse espérer une évolution vers des relations plus harmonieuses entre les deux communautés.

goodbye [gʊd'baɪ] *n* au revoir *m*; **g.!** au revoir!; **to say g. to sb** dire au revoir à qn; **he can say g. to his hopes of winning** il peut dire adieu à ses espoirs de victoire

good-for-nothing ['gʊdfənʌθɪŋ] *n* bon (bonne) *m,f* à rien

good-humoured, *Am* **good-humored** [gʊd'hjuːməd] *adj (debate, meeting)* détendu(e); **to be g.** *(of person)* avoir un caractère enjoué

good-looking ['gʊdlʊkɪŋ] *adj* beau (belle)

good-natured [gʊd'neɪtʃəd] *adj (person)* d'un caractère agréable; *(remarks, laugh)* bon enfant *inv*

goodness ['gʊdnɪs] *n* (**a**) *(of person)* bonté *f* (**b**) *(of food)* qualités *fpl* nutritives (**c**) *(in exclamations)* **g. (me)!** mon Dieu!; **thank g.!** Dieu merci!; **for g. sake!** pour l'amour de Dieu!

goods [gʊdz] *npl* (**a**) *Law* biens *mpl* (**b**) *(articles)* articles *mpl*, marchandises *fpl*; *Fig* **to deliver the g.** remplir ses engagements; *Fig* **to come up with the g.** faire le nécessaire; **g. train/depot** train *m*/dépôt *m* de marchandises

good-tempered [gʊd'tempəd] *adj (person)* d'un caractère facile; *(discussion)* aimable

goodwill [gʊd'wɪl] *n* (**a**) *(benevolence)* bienveillance *f*; *(willingness)* bonne volonté *f* (**b**) *Com* fonds *m* de commerce

goody ['gʊdɪ] *Fam* **1** *n (pl* **goodies**) (**a**) *(person)* bon *m*; **the goodies and the baddies** *(in film, game)* les bons *mpl* et les méchants *mpl* (**b**) **goodies** *(nice food)* bonnes choses *fpl*; *(nice things)* petits cadeaux *mpl* **2** *exclam* chouette!

goody-goody ['gʊdɪgʊdɪ] *Fam Pej* **1** *n (pl* **goody-goodies**) fayot *m*
2 *adj* fayot
gooey ['guːɪ] *adj Fam* (**a**) *(sticky)* gluant(e) (**b**) *(sentimental)* à la guimauve
goof [guːf] *Am Fam* **1** *n* (**a**) *(blunder)* gaffe *f*, bourde *f* (**b**) *(idiot)* cave *m*
2 *vi* faire une gaffe *ou* une bourde
▸**goof about, goof around** *vi Am Fam* faire l'idiot(e)
▸**goof off** *Am Fam* **1** *vt insep* **to g. off work** ne pas aller bosser
2 *vi* flemmarder, glandouiller
▸**goof up** *Fam* **1** *vt sep* bousiller, saloper
2 *vi* merder
goofy ['guːfɪ] *adj Fam* (**a**) *(stupid)* loufoque (**b**) *Br* **to have g. teeth** avoir les dents qui courent après le bifteck
google ['guːgəl] *Fam* **1** *vt* **to g. sb/sth** faire une recherche sur qn/qch sur Internet
2 *vi* **to g. (for sb/sth)** faire une recherche (sur qn/qch) sur Internet
goolies ['guːlɪz] *npl Br very Fam (testicles)* couilles *fpl*
goon [guːn] *n Fam* (**a**) *Br (stupid person)* imbécile *mf* (**b**) *Am (thug)* gorille *m*
goose [guːs] *(pl* **geese** [giːs]) *n* oie *f*; *Fig* **his g. is cooked** il est fichu; **to kill the g. that lays the golden egg** tuer la poule aux œufs d'or; *Br* **g. pimples,** *Am* **g. bumps** chair *f* de poule
gooseberry ['gʊzbərɪ] *(pl* **gooseberries**) *n* groseille *f* à maquereau; *Br Fam* **to play g.** tenir la chandelle; **g. bush** groseillier *m*
gooseflesh ['guːsfleʃ] *n* chair *f* de poule
goose-step ['guːsstep] **1** *n* pas *m* de l'oie
2 *vi (pt & pp* **goose-stepped**) marcher au pas de l'oie
gopher ['gəʊfə(r)] *n (animal)* spermophile *m*
gore [gɔː(r)] **1** *n (blood)* sang *m* (versé)
2 *vt (of bull)* encorner; **to be gored to death** être tué(e) à coups de corne
gorge [gɔːdʒ] **1** *n (valley)* gorge *f*, défilé *m*
2 *vt* **to g. oneself** se gorger, se gaver (**on** de)
3 *vi* se gorger, se gaver (**on** de)
gorgeous ['gɔːdʒəs] *adj* magnifique; *(meal, food)* excellent(e)
gorilla [gə'rɪlə] *n* gorille *m*
gormless ['gɔːmlɪs] *adj Br Fam* balourd(e)
gorse [gɔːs] *n* ajoncs *mpl*
gory ['gɔːrɪ] *adj (film, crime, war)* sanglant(e); *(covered in blood)* ensanglanté(e); *Fig & Hum* **in g. detail** avec tous les détails
gosh [gɒʃ] *exclam Fam* ça alors!
goshawk ['gɒshɔːk] *n* autour *m*
gosling ['gɒzlɪŋ] *n* oison *m*
go-slow [gəʊ'sləʊ] *n Br* grève *f* du zèle
gospel ['gɒspəl] *n* évangile *m*; **to take sth as g.** accepter qch comme parole d'évangile; **g. (music)** gospel *m*; **g. singer** chanteur(euse) *m,f* de gospel
gossamer ['gɒsəmə(r)] *n* (**a**) *(spider's web)* fils *mpl* de la Vierge (**b**) *(fabric)* gaze *f* légère
gossip ['gɒsɪp] **1** *n* (**a**) *(person)* bavard(e) *m,f*; *(ill-natured)* commère *f* (**b**) *(talk)* bavardages *mpl*; *(ill-natured)* commérage(s) *m(pl)*; **have you heard the latest g.?** tu sais la nouvelle?; **to have a g. (about)** bavarder (à propos de); **g. column** *(in newspaper)* chronique *f* mondaine; **g. columnist** échotier(ère) *m,f*

2 *vi* bavarder; *(ill-naturedly)* colporter des commérages
gossipy ['gɒsɪpɪ] *adj (person)* bavard(e); *(ill-natured)* cancanier(ère); *(letter, conversation)* plein(e) de petits potins
got [gɒt] *pt & pp of* **get**
Gothic ['gɒθɪk] **1** *n (artistic style, language)* gothique *m*
2 *adj* gothique
gotta ['gɒtə] *Fam* = **got to**
gotten ['gɒtən] *Am pp of* **get**
▸**gouge out** [gaʊdʒ] *vt sep (hole, path)* creuser; **to g. sb's eye out** arracher l'œil à qn
goulash ['guːlæʃ] *n* goulasch *m*
gourd ['gʊəd] *n* gourde *f*
gourmet ['gʊəmeɪ] *n* gourmet *m*, gastronome *mf*; **g. restaurant** restaurant *m* gastronomique
gout [gaʊt] *n (disease)* goutte *f*
Gov (**a**) *(abbr* **government**) gouvernement *m* (**b**) *(abbr* **governor**) gouverneur *m*
govern ['gʌvən] *vt* (**a**) *(state, country)* gouverner (**b**) *(of scientific law)* régir (**c**) *(emotions)* maîtriser, contenir
governess ['gʌvənɪs] *n* gouvernante *f*
governing ['gʌvənɪŋ] *adj (party, coalition)* au pouvoir; *(concept, principle)* directeur(trice); **g. body** conseil *m* d'administration
government ['gʌvənmənt] *n* gouvernement *m*; **g. intervention** intervention *f* du gouvernement
governmental [gʌvən'mentəl] *adj* gouvernemental(e)
governor ['gʌvənə(r)] *n (of colony, bank, US state)* gouverneur *m*; *(of prison)* directeur *m*; *(of school)* = fonctionnaire gestionnaire d'une école; *Br Fam* **the g.** *(boss)* le patron; **g. general** gouverneur *m* général
governorship ['gʌvənəʃɪp] *n (post)* poste *m* de gouverneur; *(function)* fonctions *fpl* de gouverneur
Govt *(abbr* **government**) gouvernement *m*
gown [gaʊn] *n (of woman)* robe *f*; *(of magistrate, academic)* robe *f*, toge *f*; *(of surgeon)* blouse *f*
GP [dʒiː'piː] *n Br (abbr* **general practitioner**) *(médecin m)* généraliste *mf*
GPO [dʒiːpiː'əʊ] *n Br Formerly (abbr* **General Post Office**) ≃ PTT *fpl*
gr *(abbr* **gramme(s)**) g
grab [græb] **1** *n* **to make a g. at** *or* **for sth** essayer d'attraper qch; **to be up for grabs** être à qui veut le prendre; *(be for sale)* être à qui veut l'acheter
2 *vt (pt & pp* **grabbed**) (**a**) *(seize)* **to g. (hold of) sb/sth** saisir qn/qch; *(more tightly)* empoigner qn/qch; **I'll g. a sandwich later** j'avalerai un sandwich plus tard (**b**) *Fam (attract)* **the idea doesn't g. me** ça ne me dit rien; **how does that g. you?** ça te dit?
3 *vi* **to g. at sth** essayer de s'agripper à qn; **to g. at sth** essayer d'attraper qch
grace [greɪs] **1** *n* (**a**) *(of movement, dancer, manners)* grâce *f*; **to do sth with (a) good/bad g.** faire qch de bonne/mauvaise grâce; **to have the (good) g. to do sth** avoir la grâce de faire qch (**b**) *(favour)* **to be in sb's good graces** être dans les bonnes grâces de qn (**c**) *Rel* **in a state of g.** en état de grâce; **to fall from g.** perdre la grâce; *Fig* tomber en disgrâce; **there, but for the g. of God, go I** je remercie le ciel de m'avoir épargné (**d**) *(for payment of a bill)* **seven days' g.** sept jours de délai *ou* de grâce (**e**) *(prayer before meal)* bénédicité *m* (**f**) *(form of address)* **Your G.** *(to bishop)* Monseigneur; *(to duke)* Monsieur le duc; *(to duchess)* Madame la duchesse

2 *vt* (**a**) *(honour)* honorer (**with** de) (**b**) *(decorate)* embellir, enjoliver
graceful ['greɪsfʊl] *adj (person, movement)* gracieux(euse); *(speech, style)* élégant(e)
gracefully ['greɪsfʊlɪ] *adv* avec grâce, gracieusement
graceless ['greɪslɪs] *adj* (**a**) *(inelegant)* disgracieux(-euse) (**b**) *(rude)* effronté(e)
gracious ['greɪʃəs] **1** *adj* (**a**) *(kind, polite)* poli(e), affable; *(in victory)* courtois(e) (**b**) *(elegant)* pleine(e) de raffinement
2 *exclam* **g. (me)!, goodness g.!** mon Dieu!
graciously ['greɪʃəslɪ] *adv* avec grâce; *(accept, invite)* de bonne grâce
gradation [grə'deɪʃən] *n (of colours)* gradation *f*; *(on thermometer)* degré *m*; *(of meaning)* nuance *f*
grade [greɪd] **1** *n* (**a**) *(rank)* grade *m*, rang *m*; *(in profession)* échelon *m* (**b**) *(quality)* qualité *f*; *(of vegetable, fruit)* calibre *m*; *Fig* **to make the g.** se montrer à la hauteur (**c**) *Am Sch (mark)* note *f* (**d**) *Am (year at school)* classe *f*; **g. school** ≃ école *f* primaire
2 *vt* (**a**) *(classify)* classer; *(fruit, vegetables)* calibrer (**b**) *Am (essay, exercise)* noter
gradient ['greɪdɪənt] *n* (**a**) *(of slope)* dénivellation *f* (**b**) *(of temperature)* gradient *m*
gradual ['grædjʊəl] *adj* progressif(ive), graduel(elle)
gradualism ['grædjʊəlɪzm] *n* gradualisme *m*
gradually ['grædjʊəlɪ] *adv* progressivement, peu à peu
graduate 1 *n* ['grædjʊət] *Br (from university)* ≃ licencié(e) *m,f*; *Am (from high school)* bachelier(ère) *m,f*
2 *adj* ['grædjʊət] *Am (postgraduate)* **g. studies** études *fpl* de troisième cycle
3 *vi* ['grædjʊeɪt] (**a**) *Br (from university)* obtenir sa licence; *Am (from high school)* avoir son bac (**b**) *(progress)* **to g. from sth to sth** passer de qch à qch
graduated ['grædjʊeɪtɪd] *adj (thermometer)* gradué(e); *(pay rise)* progressif(ive)
graduation [grædjʊ'eɪʃən] *n (from school, university)* remise *f* des diplômes; **g. ceremony** cérémonie *f* de remise des diplômes

Graduation
Dans les pays anglo-saxons, la "graduation" est la cérémonie officielle au cours de laquelle les étudiants reçoivent leur diplôme des mains du président de l'université. La cérémonie de remise des diplômes est une occasion solennelle – dans certaines universités elle se fait en latin – et les étudiants doivent porter la toge traditionnelle avec capuchon et mortier. Le diplôme ainsi que la photo prise le jour de la cérémonie sont ensuite gardés précieusement par la famille. Aux États-Unis, le terme "graduation" désigne également la cérémonie organisée en l'honneur des élèves qui achèvent leurs études secondaires.

graffiti [græ'fiːtiː] *n* graffiti *mpl*; **a piece of g.** un graffiti
graft¹ [grɑːft] **1** *n (technique)* greffe *f*; *(thing grafted)* greffon *m*
2 *vt* greffer (**onto** sur)
graft² *Fam* **1** *n* (**a**) *Am (bribe)* pot-de-vin *m* (**b**) *Br (work)* **(hard) g.** boulot *m*
2 *vi Br (work hard)!*, bosser dur
grafter ['grɑːftə(r)] *n Br Fam* bosseur(euse) *m,f*
grain [greɪn] *n* (**a**) *(of wheat, salt, sand)* grain *m*; **a g. of truth** une once de vérité (**b**) *(in photo, wood)*

grain *m*; *(in meat, material)* fil *m*; *Fig* **it goes against the g. for me to do it** ce n'est pas dans ma nature de le faire (**c**) *(cereals)* céréales *fpl*
grainy ['greɪnɪ] *adj* granuleux(euse)
gram [græm] *n* gramme *m*
grammar ['græmə(r)] *n* grammaire *f*; **g. (book)** (livre *m* de) grammaire *f*; *Br* **g. school** ≃ lycée *m*

Grammar school
En Grande-Bretagne, ce terme désigne une école secondaire recevant une aide de l'État mais pouvant être privée, réputée dispenser un enseignement de qualité de type traditionnel et préparant aux études supérieures. L'admission se fait sur concours ("eleven-plus") ou sur dossier. Moins de cinq pour cent des élèves britanniques fréquentent ce type d'école, qui existe en Angleterre, au pays de Galles et en Irlande du Nord.

grammarian [grə'meərɪən] *n* grammarien(enne) *m,f*
grammatical [grə'mætɪkəl] *adj* grammatical(e)
grammatically [grə'mætɪklɪ] *adv* grammaticalement
gramme [græm] *n* gramme *m*
gramophone ['græməfəʊn] *n Br Old-fashioned* gramophone *m*
gran [græn] *n Br Fam (grandmother)* grand-mère *f*; *(term of address)* mamie *f*, mémé *f*
granary ['grænərɪ] *n (pl granaries)* grenier *m*; *Br* **g. bread** = sorte de pain complet
grand [grænd] **1** *adj* (**a**) *(imposing)* grandiose, imposant(e); **to do things on a g. scale** faire les choses en grand; *Mus & Fig* **g. finale** apothéose *f*; *Am* **g. jury** = jury qui décide si une affaire doit être portée ou non devant les tribunaux; **g. master** *(in chess)* grand maître *m*; **the G. National** = steeple-chase le plus célèbre d'Angleterre; **g. piano** piano *m* à queue; **g. slam** grand chelem *m*; **g. total** somme *f* totale (**b**) *Fam (excellent)* excellent(e)
2 *n (pl grand) Fam (thousand pounds)* mille livres *fpl*; *(thousand dollars)* mille dollars *mpl*
grandchild ['græntʃaɪld] *(pl grandchildren* ['græntʃɪldrən]) *n (boy)* petit-fils *m*; *(girl)* petite fille *f*; **grandchildren** petits-enfants *mpl*
grandad ['grændæd] *n Fam* (**a**) *(grandfather)* grand-père *m*; *(term of address)* papy *m*, pépé *m* (**b**) *Pej (old man)* pépé *m*
grand-dad ['grændæd], **grandaddy** ['grændædɪ] *(pl grandaddies) n Fam* grand-père *m*; *(term of address)* papy *m*, pépé *m*
granddaughter ['grændɔːtə(r)] *n* petite fille *f*
grandeur ['grændjə(r)] *n (of person)* grandeur *f*, noblesse *f*; *(of building, surroundings)* splendeur *f*, magnificence *f*
grandfather ['grænfɑːðə(r)] *n* grand-père *m*; **g. clock** horloge *f* (de parquet)
grandiloquent [græn'dɪləkwənt] *adj* grandiloquent(e)
grandiose ['grændɪəʊs] *adj (building)* monumental(e); *(term, title)* pompeux(euse); *(idea, scheme)* démesuré(e)
grandly ['grændlɪ] *adv (impressively)* de façon grandiose; *(pompously)* de façon pompeuse
grandma ['grænmɑː] *n Fam* grand-mère *f*; *(term of address)* mamie *f*, mémé *f*
grandmother ['grænmʌðə(r)] *n* grand-mère *f*
grandpa ['grænpɑː] *n Fam* grand-père *m*; *(term of address)* papy *m*, pépé *m*

grandparent ['grænpeərənt] *n* grand-parent *m*
grandson ['grænsʌn] *n* petit-fils *m*
grandstand ['grænstænd] *n* tribune *f* d'honneur; *Fig* **to have a g.** view of sth être bien placé(e) pour voir qch
granite ['grænɪt] *n* granit *m*
granny ['grænɪ] (*pl* **grannies**) *n Fam* grand-mère *f*; *(term of address)* mamie *f*, mémé *f*; **g. flat** = partie d'une maison aménagée indépendamment pour héberger un parent âgé; **g. knot** double nœud *m*
grant [grɑːnt] **1** *n (financial aid)* subvention *f*; *(for student)* bourse *f* (d'études)
2 *vt* (**a**) *(allow) (permission)* donner; *(interview, request)* accorder; **to take sth for granted** considérer qch comme allant de soi ou comme étant dû; **to take sb for granted** croire que qn sera toujours là (**b**) *(award) (money, subsidy)* accorder, allouer (**c**) *(admit)* admettre; **I g. that he's talented** je reconnais qu'il a du talent
granular ['grænjʊlə(r)] *adj* granuleux(euse)
granulated sugar ['grænjʊleɪtɪd'ʃʊɡə(r)] *n* sucre *m* semoule
granule ['grænjʊl] *n (of salt, sand)* grain *m*; *(of coffee)* granule *m*
grape [greɪp] *n* grain *m* de raisin; **some grapes** du raisin; **g. harvest** vendange(s) *f(pl)*; **g. juice** jus *m* de raisin; **g. picker** vendangeur(euse) *m,f*
grapefruit ['greɪpfruːt] *n* pamplemousse *m*; **g. juice** jus *m* de pamplemousse
grapevine ['greɪpvaɪn] *n* vigne *f*; *(climbing)* treille *f*; *Fam* **I heard on the g. that...** j'ai entendu par le téléphone arabe que...
graph [grɑːf] *n* graphique *m*, diagramme *m*; **g. paper** papier *m* millimétré
graphic ['græfɪk] *adj* (**a**) *(vivid)* très détaillé(e); *(language)* cru(e); **in g. detail** de façon très détaillée (**b**) **g. artist** graphiste *mf*; **g. arts** arts *mpl* graphiques; **g. design** conception *f* graphique; **g. designer** graphiste *mf*; **g. equalizer** égalisateur *m* graphique; **g. novel** bande *f* dessinée (pour adultes)
graphically ['græfɪklɪ] *adv (describe)* de façon très détaillée
graphics ['græfɪks] **1** *n (art)* arts *mpl* graphiques
2 *npl Comput* graphismes *mpl*, graphiques *mpl*
graphite ['græfaɪt] *n* graphite *m*, mine *f* de plomb
graphology [græ'fɒlədʒɪ] *n* graphologie *f*
grapnel ['græpnəl] *n Naut* grappin *m*
grapple ['græpəl] *vi (fight)* lutter corps à corps (**with** avec); *Fig (with problem)* se débattre (**with** avec)
grappling hook ['græplɪŋ'hʊk], **grappling iron** ['græplɪŋ'aɪən] *n Naut* grappin *m*
grasp [grɑːsp] **1** *n* (**a**) *(hold)* prise *f*; *Fig* **to have sth within one's g.** avoir qch à sa portée (**b**) *(understanding)* compréhension *f* (**of** de)
2 *vt* (**a**) *(hold firmly)* saisir; *(more tightly)* empoigner; **to g. sb's arm** saisir qn par le bras; *Fig* **to g. the opportunity** saisir l'occasion (**b**) *(understand)* saisir, comprendre
grasping ['grɑːspɪŋ] *adj (mean)* avide, cupide
grass [grɑːs] **1** *n* (**a**) *(plant)* herbe *f*; *Fig* **she doesn't let the g. grow under her feet** elle ne perd pas de temps; **the g. is always greener (on the other side of the fence)** c'est toujours mieux ailleurs; *Fig* **g. roots** *(of organization)* base *f*; **g. roots support/opposition** soutien *m*/opposition *f* de la base; **g. snake** couleuvre *f* (à collier); **g. widow** = femme dont le mari est souvent en déplacement (**b**) *(lawn)* pelouse

f, gazon *m*; **keep off the g.** *(sign)* pelouse interdite; **g. court** *(in tennis)* court *m* en gazon (**c**) *(pasture)* herbage *m*; *Fig* **to put sb out to g.** mettre qn à la retraite
(**d**) *Fam (marijuana)* herbe *f* (**e**) *Br Fam (informer)* balance *f*, indic *m*
2 *vi Br Fam (inform)* moucharder; **to g. on sb** balancer qn
grass-green ['grɑːs'griːn] *adj* vert gazon *inv*
grasshopper ['grɑːshɒpə(r)] *n* sauterelle *f*
grassland ['grɑːslænd] *n* prairie *f*, pré *m*
grassy ['grɑːsɪ] *adj* herbu(e), herbeux(euse)
grate[1] [greɪt] *n (of hearth)* grille *f*; *(fireplace)* foyer *m*
grate[2] **1** *vt (cheese, nutmeg)* râper
2 *vi (of machinery)* grincer; **to g. on the ear** *(of voice)* écorcher les oreilles; *(of sound)* faire mal aux oreilles; **it really grates on me** *or* **on my nerves** ça me tape vraiment sur les nerfs
grateful ['greɪtfʊl] *adj* reconnaissant(e) (**for** de); **I would be g. if you could let me know** je vous serais reconnaissant de m'en informer
gratefully ['greɪtfʊlɪ] *adv* avec reconnaissance
grater ['greɪtə(r)] *n* râpe *f*
gratification [grætɪfɪ'keɪʃən] *n* satisfaction *f*
gratified ['grætɪfaɪd] *adj* satisfait(e), content(e)
gratify ['grætɪfaɪ] *(pt & pp* **gratified**) *vt (person)* faire plaisir à; *(wish, desire)* satisfaire
gratifying ['grætɪfaɪɪŋ] *adj* satisfaisant(e)
grating[1] ['greɪtɪŋ] *adj (noise)* grinçant(e); *(voice)* éraillé(e)
grating[2] *n (grille)* grille *f*
gratis ['grɑːtɪs] *adv* gratis
gratitude ['grætɪtjuːd] *n* gratitude *f*, reconnaissance *f*
gratuitous [grə'tjuːɪtəs] *adj* gratuit(e)
gratuitously [grə'tjuːɪtəslɪ] *adv* gratuitement, sans raison
gratuity [grə'tjuːɪtɪ] *(pl* **gratuities**) *n Formal (tip)* pourboire *m*
grave [greɪv] **1** *n* tombe *f*; *Fig* **it would make him turn in his g.** ça le ferait se retourner dans sa tombe; **to have one foot in the g.** avoir un pied dans la tombe
2 *adj (manner, voice)* solennel(elle); *(situation)* grave; **to make a g. mistake** se tromper lourdement
gravedigger ['greɪvdɪɡə(r)] *n* fossoyeur *m*
gravel ['grævəl] *n* gravier *m*; **g. path** allée *f* de gravier; **g. pit** carrière *f* de gravier
gravelly ['grævəlɪ] *adj (sand, soil)* graveleux(euse); *(voice)* râpeux(euse)
gravely ['greɪvlɪ] *adv* gravement
graven ['greɪvən] *adj* **g. image** idole *f*
graveside ['greɪvsaɪd] *n* **at the g.** près de la tombe
gravestone ['greɪvstəʊn] *n* pierre *f* tombale
graveyard ['greɪvjɑːd] *n* cimetière *m*
gravitate ['grævɪteɪt] *vi* **to g. towards sth** *(of person)* être attiré(e) par qch; **most of the guests had gravitated towards the bar** la plupart des invités s'étaient rapprochés du bar
gravitational [grævɪ'teɪʃənəl] *adj* gravitationnel(elle); **g. pull** gravitation *f*
gravity ['grævɪtɪ] *n* (**a**) *(physical force)* gravité *f*, pesanteur *f* (**b**) *(seriousness)* gravité *f*
gravy ['greɪvɪ] *n* = sauce à base de jus de viande; **g. boat** saucière *f*; *Fam* **g. train** assiette *f* au beurre; **to get on the g. train** trouver un filon
gray *Am* = **grey**
graze[1] [greɪz] **1** *vt (of farmer) (cattle)* faire paître
2 *vi (of cattle)* paître

graze² **1** *n* écorchure *f*; *(less serious)* égratignure *f*
2 *vt* écorcher; *(less seriously)* égratigner
grease [griːs] **1** *n* graisse *f*; **g. gun** pistolet *m* graisseur **2** *vt (machine)* graisser, lubrifier; *(cake tin)* beurrer; **to back one's hair** se gominer les cheveux; *Fam Fig* **to g. sb's palm** graisser la patte à qn; *Fam* **like greased lightning** en quatrième vitesse
greasepaint [ˈgriːspeɪnt] *n* maquillage *m* de théâtre
greaseproof paper [ˈgriːspruːfˈpeɪpə(r)] *n* papier *m* sulfurisé
greasy [ˈgriːsɪ] *adj* (**a**) *(covered in grease)* graisseux(euse); *(hair, skin, food)* gras (grasse) (**b**) *Fam Pej (manner)* mielleux(euse)
great [greɪt] **1** *n* grand nom *m*
2 *adj* (**a**) *(large, important)* grand(e); **a g. many people** beaucoup de monde; **to reach a g. age** parvenir à un âge avancé; **to take g. care (of)** prendre grand soin (de); **they are g. friends** ce sont de grands amis (**b**) *(in proper names)* **G. Britain** la Grande-Bretagne; **G. Dane** danois *m*; **the G. Lakes** les Grands Lacs *mpl*; **Greater London** Londres et son agglomération; *Hist* **the G. War** la Grande Guerre (**c**) *Fam (very good)* formidable, génial(e); **to have a g. time** bien s'amuser (**d**) *(enthusiastic)* **to be a g. knitter/reader** adorer tricoter/la lecture; **to be a g. believer in doing sth** être partisan(e) de faire qch; *Fam* **she's a g. one for having everything planned in advance** avec elle, on peut être sûr que tout sera préparé à l'avance
3 *adv Fam* (**a**) *(well)* très bien; **to feel g.** se sentir en super forme (**b**) *(for emphasis)* **a. big dog** un chien énorme; **you g. fat slob!** espèce de gros tas!
great-aunt [ˈgreɪtɑːnt] *n* grand-tante *f*
greatcoat [ˈgreɪtkəʊt] *n* pardessus *m*
great-grandchild [ˈgreɪtˈgrænt∫aɪld] *(pl* **great-grandchildren** [ˈgreɪtˈgrænt∫ɪldrən]*) n (boy)* arrière-petit-fils *m*; *(girl)* arrière-petite-fille *f*; **great-grandchildren** arrière-petits-enfants *mpl*
great-granddaughter [ˈgreɪtˈgrændɔːtə(r)] *n* arrière-petite-fille *f*
great-grandfather [ˈgreɪtˈgrænfɑːðə(r)] *n* arrière-grand-père *m*
great-grandmother [ˈgreɪtˈgrænmʌðə(r)] *n* arrière-grand-mère *f*
great-grandparents [ˈgreɪtˈgrænpeərənts] *npl* arrière-grands-parents *mpl*
great-grandson [ˈgreɪtˈgrænsʌn] *n* arrière-petit-fils *m*
greatly [ˈgreɪtlɪ] *adv* très
greatness [ˈgreɪtnɪs] *n* (**a**) *(of person, action)* grandeur *f*; **to achieve g.** rejoindre les plus grands (**b**) *(of thing, problem)* importance *f*
great-uncle [ˈgreɪtʌŋkəl] *n* grand-oncle *m*
grebe [griːb] *n* grèbe *m*
Grecian [ˈgriː∫ən] *adj* grec (grecque)
Greece [griːs] *n* la Grèce
greed [griːd] *n (for food)* gourmandise *f*; *(for money)* avidité *f*, cupidité *f*; *(for fame, power)* recherche *f* avide (**for** de)
greedily [ˈgriːdɪlɪ] *adv (eat)* goulûment; *(look, say)* avec gourmandise
greediness [ˈgriːdɪnɪs] = **greed**
greedy [ˈgriːdɪ] *adj (for food)* gourmand(e); *(for money, fame, power)* avide; *Fam* **g. guts** goinfre *mf*
Greek [griːk] **1** *n* (**a**) *(person)* Grec (Grecque) *m,f* (**b**) *(language)* grec *m*; **modern G.** le grec moderne; *Fam* **it's all G. to me** c'est de l'hébreu pour moi
2 *adj* grec (grecque); **G. salad** salade *f* grecque

green [griːn] **1** *n* (**a**) *(colour)* vert *m* (**b**) **greens** *(vegetables)* légumes *mpl* verts (**c**) *(grassy area)* pelouse *f*, gazon *m*; *(in golf)* green *m* (**d**) *(environmentalist)* écologiste *mf*; **the Greens** les Verts
2 *adj* (**a**) *(colour)* vert(e); **to go** *or* **turn g.** *(of traffic lights)* passer au vert; *(of person, fields)* verdir; **to be g. with envy** être vert de jalousie; *Fig* **to give sb the g. light (to do sth)** donner le feu vert à qn (pour faire qch); **to have** *Br* **g. fingers** *or Am* **a g. thumb** avoir la main verte; **g. beans** haricots *mpl* verts; **g. belt** zone *f* verte; *Am* **g. card** ≃ permis *m* de travail; **g. salad** salade *f* verte (**b**) *(young, inexperienced)* jeune, inexpérimenté(e); *(naive)* naïf (naïve) (**c**) *(environmentalist)* écologiste; **the G. Party** le parti écologiste, les Verts *mpl*
greenback [ˈgriːnbæk] *n Am Fam* billet *m* vert
greenery [ˈgriːnərɪ] *n* verdure *f*
green-eyed [ˈgriːnaɪd] *adj* aux yeux verts; *Fig* **the g. monster** la jalousie
greenfield [ˈgriːnfiːld] *n* **g. site** terrain *m* non-bâti *(à l'extérieur d'une ville)*
greenfly [ˈgriːnflaɪ] *n (pl* **greenflies**) *n* puceron *m*
greengage [ˈgriːngeɪdʒ] *n* reine-claude *f*
greengrocer [ˈgriːngrəʊsə(r)] *n Br* marchand(e) *m,f* de fruits et légumes; **g.'s (shop)** magasin *m* de fruits et légumes
greenhouse [ˈgriːnhaʊs] *n* serre *f*; **g. effect** effet *m* de serre
Greenland [ˈgriːnlənd] *n* le Groenland
Greenlander [ˈgriːnləndə(r)] *n* Groenlandais(e) *m,f*
Greenwich Mean Time [ˈgrenɪtʃˈmiːntaɪm] *n* temps *m* universel
greet [griːt] *vt (say hello to)* saluer; *(welcome) (person, idea)* accueillir
greeting [ˈgriːtɪŋ] *n* salut *m*; *(more formal)* salutation *f*; **New Year greetings** vœux *mpl* de bonne année; *Br* **greetings card**, *Am* **g. card** carte *f* de vœux

Greetings cards

Le terme "greetings card" (ou "greeting card", sans 's', en anglais américain) s'emploie pour désigner toute carte pré-imprimée célébrant toute une gamme d'occasions telles qu'anniversaires, naissances, mariages, Noël, la Saint-Valentin, pour féliciter quelqu'un pour son nouveau travail, pour lui souhaiter un prompt rétablissement, etc.... Il faut noter que contrairement aux Français, qui envoient leurs cartes de vœux en janvier, les Britanniques envoient les leurs avant Noël. Le plus souvent, on donne les cartes aux gens que l'on côtoie quotidiennement en mains propres. Par ailleurs, on ne saurait se contenter de souhaiter "bon anniversaire!" à quelqu'un : la carte est de rigueur. Elle accompagne également tout cadeau.

gregarious [grɪˈgeərɪəs] *adj* sociable
gremlin [ˈgremlɪn] *n Fam* diablotin *m*
Grenada [grəˈneɪdə] *n* la Grenade
grenade [grəˈneɪd] *n* grenade *f*
grenadier [grenəˈdɪə(r)] *n* grenadier *m*
grenadine [ˈgrenədiːn] *n* grenadine *f*
grew [gruː] *pt of* **grow**
grey, *Am* **gray** [greɪ] **1** *n (colour)* gris *m*
2 *adj* gris(e); *Fig (dull)* morne; **to go g.** *(grey-haired)* grisonner; *Fig* **g. area** une zone d'ombre; **g. matter** *(brain)* matière *f* grise
3 *vi (of hair)* grisonner

grey-haired ['greɪheəd] *adj* aux cheveux gris
greyhound ['greɪhaʊnd] *n* lévrier *m*; **g. racing** courses *fpl* de lévriers; **g. stadium** cynodrome *m*
greying ['greɪɪŋ] *adj (hair)* grisonnant(e)
grid [grɪd] *n* (**a**) *(bars)* grille *f*, grillage *m* (**b**) *(on map)* quadrillage *m*; **g. layout** *(of town)* quadrillage, damier *m*; **g. reference** coordonnées *fpl* (**c**) *Br (for electricity)* réseau *m* électrique
griddle ['grɪdəl] *n (for cooking)* tôle *f*
gridiron ['grɪdaɪən] *n* (**a**) *(for cooking)* gril *m* (**b**) *Am (American football)* football *m* américain; *(playing field)* terrain *m* de football
gridlock ['grɪdlɒk] *n* embouteillage *m* monstre
gridlocked ['grɪdlɒkt] *adj (road, negotiations)* bloqué(e)
grief [griːf] *n* (**a**) *(pain)* chagrin *m*; **to come to g.** échouer; *Fam* **good g.!** mon Dieu!; *Am* **g. counseling** = aide psychologique aux personnes en deuil (**b**) *Fam (hassle)* **to give sb g.** embêter qn
grief-stricken ['griːfstrɪkən] *adj* accablé(e) de douleur *ou* de chagrin
grievance ['griːvəns] *n* (**a**) *(resentment)* grief *m* (**b**) *(complaint)* doléance *f*; **to air one's grievances** exprimer ses doléances; *Ind* **g. procedure** procédure *f* pour porter plainte
grieve [griːv] **1** *vt* chagriner, affliger
2 *vi* **to g. for sb/over sth** pleurer qn/qch
grieving ['griːvɪŋ] *adj* éploré(e)
grievous ['griːvəs] *adj Formal* grave; *Law* **g. bodily harm** coups *mpl* et blessures *fpl*
grievously ['griːvəslɪ] *adv (seriously)* gravement; **you are g. mistaken** vous commettez une grave erreur
griffin ['grɪfɪn] *n* griffon *m*
grill [grɪl] **1** *n Br (for cooking)* gril *m*; *(food)* grillade *f*; **a mixed g.** un assortiment de grillades
2 *vt* (**a**) *Br (cook)* griller (**b**) *Fam (interrogate)* cuisiner
grille [grɪl] *n (bars)* grille *f*; **(radiator) g.** *(on car)* calandre *f*
grilling ['grɪlɪŋ] *n Fam (interrogation)* **to give sb a g.** cuisiner qn
grim [grɪm] *adj* (**a**) *(stern)* sévère; *(gloomy) (place)* sinistre; *(news, report)* sombre; **to hang on like g. death** se cramponner; **to look g.** *(of person) (serious)* avoir l'air sombre; *(ill)* avoir très mauvaise mine (**b**) *Fam (bad)* lamentable; **how do you feel? – pretty g.!** comment te sens-tu? – pas terrible!
grimace ['grɪməs] **1** *n* grimace *f*
2 *vi* grimacer, faire la grimace
grime [graɪm] *n* saleté *f*
grimly ['grɪmlɪ] *adv (fight, hold on)* avec acharnement
grimy ['graɪmɪ] *adj* encrassé(e)
grin [grɪn] **1** *n* grand sourire *m*
2 *vi (pt & pp* **grinned)** faire un grand sourire (**at** à); *Fig* **to g. and bear it** tâcher de garder le sourire
grind [graɪnd] **1** *n Fam (work)* corvée *f*; **the daily g.** le train-train quotidien
2 *vt (pt & pp* **ground** [graʊnd]) (**a**) *(grain, coffee)* moudre; **to g. one's teeth** grincer des dents (**b**) *(glass, gems)* dépolir
3 *vi (of wheels, gears)* grisser; **to g. to a halt** *(of car, machine)* s'immobiliser; *(of project, economy)* s'arrêter
▶**grind down** *vt sep Fig* venir à bout de
▶**grind on** *vi (proceed relentlessly)* ne pas en finir
▶**grind out** *vt sep (article, novel)* pondre

grinder ['graɪndə(r)] *n (for coffee, pepper)* moulin *m*; *(for polishing)* polissoire *f*; *(for sharpening)* meule *f*
grinding ['graɪndɪŋ] *adj (poverty)* extrême; **to come to a g. halt** *(of car, machine)* s'immobiliser; *(of project, economy)* s'arrêter
grindstone ['graɪndstəʊn] *n* meule *f*; *Fig* **to keep one's nose to the g.** travailler dur
gringo ['grɪŋgəʊ] *(pl* **gringos)** *n Am Fam* gringo *m*
grip [grɪp] *n* (**a**) *(hold, grasp)* prise *f*; **to have a strong g.** avoir une bonne poigne; **to get a g. on sth** avoir prise sur qch; *Fig* **to get to grips with sth** s'attaquer à qch; *Fig* **to get a g. on oneself** se ressaisir; *Fig* **get a g.!** reprends-toi!, ressaisis-toi!; *Fig* **to have a firm g. on a situation** avoir la situation bien en main; **to lose one's g.** lâcher prise; **to lose one's g. on sth** lâcher qch; *Fig* **to lose one's g. on reality** perdre pied avec la réalité; *Fig* **to be in the g. of a disease/a crisis** être en proie à une maladie/une crise (**b**) *(handle)* poignée *f* (**c**) **(hair) g.** pince *f* (à cheveux) (**d**) *Am (bag)* mallette *f*
2 *vt (pt & pp* **gripped)** *(seize)* saisir, prendre; *(hold)* empoigner, agripper; *(of tyres)* adhérer à; *Fig* **to be gripped by panic** être pris(e) de panique; *Fig* **the audience was gripped by the play** la pièce a captivé les spectateurs
3 *vi (of tyre)* adhérer
gripe [graɪp] **1** *n* (**a**) *Fam (complaint)* **to have a g. about sth** avoir à se plaindre de qch; **what's your g.?** de quoi te plains-tu? (**b**) *(pain)* **gripes** coliques *fpl*; **g. water** = médicament pour coliques infantiles
2 *vi Fam (complain)* ronchonner, râler (**about** à propos de)
gripping ['grɪpɪŋ] *adj* passionnant(e), palpitant(e)
grisly ['grɪzlɪ] *adj* macabre, sinistre
grist [grɪst] *n* **it's all g. to the mill** cela apporte de l'eau à mon/ton/*etc* moulin
gristle ['grɪsəl] *n* nerfs *mpl*
gristly ['grɪslɪ] *adj* nerveux(euse)
grit [grɪt] **1** *n* (**a**) *(gravel)* gravillons *mpl*; *(in eye)* poussière *f*; *(for icy roads)* sable *m* (**b**) *(courage, determination)* cran *m*
2 *vt (pt & pp* **gritted)** (**a**) *(road)* sabler (**b**) *(clench)* **to g. one's teeth** grincer des dents; *Fig* serrer les dents
gritter ['grɪtə(r)] *n Br* camion *m* de sablage
gritty ['grɪtɪ] *adj* (**a**) *(soil, road)* plein(e) de gravillons (**b**) *(determined)* qui a du cran, résolu(e) (**c**) **g. realism** réalisme *m* cru
grizzle ['grɪzəl] *vi (complain)* ronchonner, râler (**about** à propos de)
grizzled ['grɪzəld] *adj (hair, person)* grisonnant(e)
grizzly ['grɪzlɪ] **1** *n (pl* **grizzlies) g. (bear)** grizzly *m*
2 *adj (hair, person)* grisonnant(e)
groan [grəʊn] **1** *n (of pain)* gémissement *m*; *(of disappointment, dismay)* grognement *m*; *(of chair, floor)* grincement *m*
2 *vi (in pain)* gémir, pousser un gémissement; *(in disappointment, dismay)* grogner, pousser un grognement; **to g. under the weight of sth** *(of shelf, chair)* se creuser sous le poids de qch
grocer ['grəʊsə(r)] *n* épicier(ère) *m,f*; **g.'s (shop)** épicerie *f*
groceries ['grəʊsərɪz] *npl (provisions)* provisions *fpl*
grocery ['grəʊsərɪ] *(pl* **groceries)** *n (shop)* épicerie *f*
grog [grɒg] *n Fam* grog *m*
groggy ['grɒgɪ] *adj Fam* groggy *inv*
groin [grɔɪn] *n* aine *f*

groom [gru:m] **1** n (**a**) (of horse) palefrenier m (**b**) (at wedding) marié m
2 vt (horse) panser; (dog) toiletter; Fig (candidate) préparer
groomed [gru:md] adj soigné(e); **to be well-g.** (person) être soigné(e) de sa personne; (horse) être bien entretenu(e)
groove [gru:v] n (in wood, metal) rainure f; (in record) sillon m; Fig **to get stuck in a g.** s'encroûter
groovy ['gru:vɪ] adj Fam chouette
grope [grəʊp] **1** vt (**a**) **to g. one's way forward** avancer à tâtons (**b**) Fam (sexually) peloter, tripoter
2 vi **to g. (about) for sth** chercher qch à tâtons
gross [grəʊs] **1** n (pl **gross**) (quantity) grosse f, douze douzaines fpl
2 adj (**a**) (blatant) (error) grossier(ère); (ignorance) crasse; (abuse) choquant(e); (injustice) flagrant(e); Law **g. negligence** négligence f coupable (**b**) (vulgar) grossier(ère) (**c**) (profit, income, weight) brut(e); Econ **g. domestic product** produit m intérieur brut; **g. national product** produit m national brut (**d**) Fam (disgusting) répugnant(e)
3 vt (profit) gagner brut; **to g. £40,000 a year** gagner brut 40 000 livres par an
▸**gross out** vt sep Am Fam dégoûter, débecter
grossly ['grəʊslɪ] adv (exaggerated) grossièrement; (negligent) extrêmement; (unfair) vraiment; **g. overweight** obèse
grotesque [grəʊˈtesk] adj grotesque
grotto ['grɒtəʊ] (pl **grottoes** or **grottos**) n grotte f
grotty ['grɒtɪ] adj Br Fam minable; **to feel g.** se sentir vaseux(euse)
grouch [graʊtʃ] Fam **1** n (**a**) (person) râleur(euse) m,f (**b**) (complaint) plainte f
2 vi râler, ronchonner (**about** à propos de)
grouchy ['graʊtʃɪ] adj Fam râleur(euse), ronchon(onne)
ground [graʊnd] **1** n (**a**) (earth) sol m, terre f; **to sit on the g.** s'asseoir par terre; **above g.** en surface; **below g.** sous terre; **burnt to the g.** entièrement brûlé(e); Fig **to get off the g.** (of project) démarrer; Fig **to work oneself into the g.** se tuer au travail; **to go to g.** se cacher; **to run sb to g.** traquer qn; **g. control** contrôle m au sol; **g. crew** personnel m au sol; Br **g. floor** rez-de chaussée m; Mil **g. forces** forces fpl au sol; **g. frost** gelée f blanche; **at g. level** au rez-de-chaussée; **g. rules** règles fpl de base; **g. staff** (at sports ground) = personnel responsable de l'entretien d'un terrain de sport; Br (at airport) personnel m au sol
(**b**) (land) terrain m; Fig **to find common g. for negotiations** trouver un terrain d'entente en vue de négociations; **to be sure of one's g.** être sûr(e) de son fait; Fig **to be on shaky g.** être en terrain miné; Fig **to change** or **shift one's g.** changer de tactique; Fig **to break new g.** faire œuvre de pionnier; Fig **to cover a lot of g.** (of book, lecture) couvrir de très nombreux domaines; Fig **to gain g. on sb** gagner du terrain sur qn; Fig **to lose g. to sb** perdre du terrain sur qn; Fig **to stand** or **hold one's g.** tenir bon
(**c**) **grounds** (of school, hospital, country house) parc m
(**d**) **grounds** (reasons) raisons fpl, motifs mpl; **to have (good) grounds for doing sth** avoir de bonnes raisons de faire qch; **on grounds of ill-health** pour raisons de santé; Law **grounds for divorce** motif m de divorce

2 adj (coffee, pepper) moulu(e); Am **g. meat** viande f hachée
3 vt (**a**) (base) baser, appuyer (**on** sur)
(**b**) (educate) **to g. sb in sth** former qn à qch
(**c**) Am (electrical current) mettre à la masse
(**d**) (aeroplane) interdire de vol
(**e**) (prevent from going out) priver de sortie
4 pt & pp of **grind**
ground-breaking ['graʊndbreɪkɪŋ] adj révolutionnaire
groundhog ['graʊndhɒg] n marmotte f d'Amérique
grounding ['graʊndɪŋ] n (**a**) (basis) fondement m (**b**) (basic knowledge) bases fpl (**in** de ou en)
groundless ['graʊndlɪs] adj sans fondement
groundnut ['graʊndnʌt] n Br arachide f; **g. oil** huile f d'arachide
groundsheet ['graʊndʃi:t] n tapis m de sol
groundsman ['graʊndzmən] n = responsable de l'entretien d'un terrain de sport
groundswell ['graʊndswel] n **a g. of support** un raz-de-marée
groundwork ['graʊndwɜ:k] n travail m préparatoire; **to do** or **lay the g. (for sth)** préparer le terrain (pour qch)
group [gru:p] **1** n groupe m; **g. booking** réservation f de groupe; **g. decision** décision f collective; **g. dynamics** dynamique f de groupe; **g. photograph** photographie f de groupe; **g. therapy** thérapie f de groupe
2 vt grouper
3 vi se grouper
groupie ['gru:pɪ] n Fam groupie f
grouping ['gru:pɪŋ] n (of people) groupe m
grouse¹ [graʊs] (pl **grouse**) n (bird) tétras m, grouse f
grouse² Fam **1** n (complaint) **to have a g. (about sth)** avoir des raisons de se plaindre (de qch)
2 vi ronchonner, grogner (**about** au sujet de)
grout [graʊt] n mastic m
grove [grəʊv] n bosquet m
grovel ['grɒvəl] (pt & pp **grovelled**, Am **groveled**) vi (on ground) être à quatre pattes; **to g. to sb** ramper ou s'aplatir devant qn
grovelling, Am **groveling** ['grɒvəlɪŋ] adj obséquieux(euse)
grow [grəʊ] (pt **grew** [gru:], pp **grown** [grəʊn]) **1** vt (**a**) (vegetables) cultiver; (flowers) faire pousser; **to g. a beard** se laisser pousser la barbe; **to g. one's hair** se laisser pousser les cheveux (**b**) Com (company) développer
2 vi (**a**) (plant) pousser; (person, animal) grandir; (problem) s'aggraver; (economy, feeling) croître; Fam **it'll g. on you** (of music, book) tu finiras par t'y intéresser (**b**) (become) devenir; **to g. old** vieillir; **to g. angry** se fâcher (**c**) (come eventually) **to g. to like sth** finir par aimer qch
▸**grow apart** vi (of people) s'éloigner
▸**grow out of** vt insep (**a**) (become too big for) **he's grown out of his shoes** ses chaussures sont maintenant trop petites pour lui (**b**) (become too old for) **she grew out of her dolls** elle a passé l'âge de jouer à la poupée; **most children g. out of such behaviour** la plupart des enfants cessent de se conduire ainsi en grandissant
▸**grow up** vi (become adult) grandir; **when I g. up** quand je serai grand; **when I was growing up** quand j'étais petit; Fam **g. up!** ne fais pas l'enfant!

grower ['grəʊə(r)] n (person) cultivateur(trice) m,f; (of trees, flowers) horticulteur(trice) m,f
growing ['grəʊɪŋ] adj (child) en pleine croissance; (town, population) en pleine expansion; (debt) qui augmente, qui va croissant; (discontent) croissant(e); **there was a g. fear that...** on craignait de plus en plus que...; **g. pains** (of child) douleurs fpl de croissance; Fig (of firm, country) difficultés fpl de croissance
growl [graʊl] 1 n (of dog) grondement m 2 vi (of dog) gronder; (of person) grogner, grommeler (**at** contre)
growling ['graʊlɪŋ] n (of dog) grondement m
grown [grəʊn] 1 adj grand(e); **a g. woman** une adulte; **to be fully g.** avoir atteint sa taille adulte 2 pp of **grow**
grown-up 1 n ['grəʊnʌp] grand(e) m,f, grande personne f; **the grown-ups** les grands mpl, les grandes personnes fpl 2 adj [grəʊn'ʌp] (person, topic) adulte; **he was very g. about it** il a fait preuve de beaucoup de maturité
growth [grəʊθ] n (a) (of person, plant, economy) croissance f; (of population, demand) augmentation f; **a week's g. of beard** une barbe d'une semaine; **g. area** secteur m en expansion; **g. industry** industrie f en expansion (b) (tumour) grosseur f
grub [grʌb] n (a) (larva) larve f (b) Fam (food) bouffe f; **g.'s up!** à la bouffe!
▶**grub about, grub around** (pt & pp grubbed) vi Fam farfouiller (**for sth** pour trouver qch)
grubby ['grʌbɪ] adj crasseux(euse)
grudge [grʌdʒ] 1 n rancune f; **to bear sb a g.** en vouloir à qn 2 vt (a) (give unwillingly) **to g. sb sth** donner qch à qn à contrecœur (b) (resent) **to g. doing sth** faire qch à contrecœur; **she grudges him his success** elle lui en veut parce qu'il a réussi
grudging ['grʌdʒɪŋ] adj accordé(e) à contrecœur; **to be g. in one's praise** être avare de compliments
grudgingly ['grʌdʒɪŋlɪ] adv à contrecœur
gruel ['gruːəl] n gruau m
gruelling, Am **grueling** ['gruːəlɪŋ] adj (journey, experience) épuisant(e)
gruesome ['gruːsəm] adj abominable, horrible; **to relate sth in g. detail** raconter qch jusqu'aux détails les plus horribles
gruesomely ['gruːsəmlɪ] adv abominablement
gruff [grʌf] adj (tone, manner) bourru(e); (voice) gros (grosse)
gruffly ['grʌflɪ] adv d'un ton bourru
grumble ['grʌmbəl] 1 n grommellement m, grognement m; **she obeyed without so much as a g.** elle a obéi sans la moindre protestation 2 vi (of person) grommeler; (of stomach) gargouiller; **to g. about sth** rouspéter contre qch; **(I) mustn't g.** il ne faut pas se plaindre
grumbler ['grʌmblə(r)] n grincheux(euse) m,f
grumbling ['grʌmblɪŋ] 1 n ronchonnements mpl 2 adj grognon(onne); **g. appendix** appendicite f chronique
grump [grʌmp] n Fam grincheux(euse) m,f
grumpily ['grʌmpɪlɪ] adv en ronchonnant
grumpy ['grʌmpɪ] adj grognon(onne)
grunge [grʌndʒ] n (music, fashion) grunge m
grunt [grʌnt] 1 n (of pig, person) grognement m; **to give a g.** pousser un grognement 2 vi (of pig, person) grogner

GSM [dʒiːes'em] n Tel (abbr global system for mobile communication) GSM m
Guadeloupe [gwɑːdə'luːp] n la Guadeloupe
guarantee [gærən'tiː] 1 n (spoken, written) garantie f; **she gave me her g.** that it wouldn't happen again elle m'a assuré que cela ne se reproduirait plus; **there's no g. that she'll come** ce n'est pas sûr qu'elle vienne; Com **under g.** sous garantie 2 vt garantir; **I can't g. that she'll come** je ne garantis pas qu'elle viendra; **the watch is guaranteed for two years** cette montre est garantie deux ans; Fin **to g. sb against loss** garantir qn contre les pertes
guaranteed [gærən'tiːd] adj garanti(e)
guarantor [gærən'tɔː(r)] n garant(e) m,f
guard [gɑːd] 1 n (a) (defences) **to be on one's g.** être sur ses gardes; **to put sb on his g.** mettre qn en garde; **to put sb off his g.** déjouer la vigilance de qn; **to catch sb off his g.** prendre qn au dépourvu; **his g. was down** il ne se méfiait pas (b) (supervision) garde f; **to keep sb under g.** garder qn sous surveillance; **to be on g. duty** être de garde; **g. dog** chien m de garde (c) (sentry) garde m; (on train) chef m de train; Am (in prison) gardien m; Mil (group of sentries) garde f; **g. of honour** garde f d'honneur; Br **g.'s van** (on train) fourgon m du chef de train (d) (device) (on machine) protection f (e) (in basketball) défenseur m 2 vt garder; **to g. sb from danger** protéger qn d'un danger
▶**guard against** vt insep se prémunir contre; **he was keen to g. against any further mistakes** il prenait garde de ne pas commettre de nouvelles erreurs
guarded ['gɑːdɪd] adj circonspect(e), prudent(e)
guardedly ['gɑːdɪdlɪ] adv avec circonspection, avec prudence
guardhouse ['gɑːdhaʊs] n Mil poste m de garde; (prison) prison f
guardian ['gɑːdɪən] n (of standards) gardien(enne) m,f; Law (of minor) tuteur(trice) m,f; **g. angel** ange m gardien
guardianship ['gɑːdɪənʃɪp] n Law (of minor) tutelle f
guardrail ['gɑːdreɪl] n garde-fou m, parapet m; (on ship) bastingage m
guardroom ['gɑːdruːm] n corps m de garde
guardsman ['gɑːdzmən] n garde m (de la garde royale)
Guatemala [gwætɪ'mɑːlə] n le Guatemala
Guatemalan [gwætɪ'mɑːlən] 1 n Guatémaltèque mf 2 adj guatémaltèque
guava ['gwɑːvə] n goyave f; **g. tree** goyavier m
guerrilla [gə'rɪlə] n guérillero m; **g. warfare** guérilla f
guess [ges] 1 n estimation f; **to have** or **make a g.** deviner; Ironic **I'll give you three guesses!** devine!; **at a g., (I'd say) three hundred** je dirais environ trois cents; **your g. is as good as mine** j'en ai pas la moindre idée; **it's anybody's g.** qui sait? 2 vt (a) (attempt to answer) deviner; **g. who I saw!** devine qui j'ai vu!; **g. what!** tu sais quoi?; **you've guessed it!** tu as deviné! (b) (suppose) supposer, croire; **I g. you're right** tu dois avoir raison 3 vi deviner; **to g. right** deviner juste; **to g. wrong** se tromper; **to keep sb guessing** laisser qn dans l'ignorance; **to g. at sth** essayer de deviner qch
guessing game ['gesɪŋgeɪm] n jeu m de devinettes; Fig **it's a bit of a g.** on ne peut que spéculer
guesstimate ['gestɪmɪt] n Fam calcul m au pif
guesswork ['gesweːk] n conjecture f; **it's pure** or **sheer g.** c'est de la pure conjecture

guest [gest] n *(at home, party, on TV programme)* invité(e) m,f; *(at hotel)* client(e) m,f; **be my g.!** je t'en prie!; **to make a g. appearance** *(on TV programme)* passer en invité vedette; *(in film)* participer à titre exceptionnel; **g. artist** invité(e) m,f vedette; **g. room** chambre f d'amis; **g. speaker** conférencier(ère) m,f *(invité par une organisation ou une association)*; **g. star** invité(e) m,f vedette; **g. worker** travailleur(euse) m,f immigré(e)

guesthouse ['gesthaʊs] n pension f de famille

guff [gʌf] n Fam âneries fpl

guffaw [gʌ'fɔː] **1** n gros rire m
 2 vi s'esclaffer

GUI ['guːɪ] n Comput *(abbr* **Graphical User Interface)** interface f utilisateur graphique

Guiana [gaɪ'ɑːnə] n la Guyane

guidance ['gaɪdəns] n direction f; **under the g. of** sous la direction de; **for your g.** à titre d'information; Am **g. counselor** conseiller(ère) m,f d'orientation

guide [gaɪd] **1** n (**a**) *(person)* guide m; **(Girl) G.** éclaireuse f; **g. dog** chien m d'aveugle (**b**) *(book)* guide m (**to** de) (**c**) *(indication)* indication f (**to** sur); **as a g.** à titre indicatif
 2 vt guider; **to be guided by sth** suivre qch

guidebook ['gaɪdbʊk] n guide m

guided ['gaɪdɪd] adj **g. missile** missile m guidé; **g. tour** visite f guidée

guideline ['gaɪdlaɪn] n *(indication)* indication f; **guidelines** directives fpl; **as a general g.** en règle générale

guiding ['gaɪdɪŋ] adj *(principle, concept)* directeur(trice)

guild [gɪld] n *(association)* association f

guilder ['gɪldə] n florin m

guile [gaɪl] n ruse f

guileless ['gaɪllɪs] adj candide

guillemot ['gɪlɪmɒt] n guillemot m

guillotine ['gɪlətiːn] **1** n *(for execution)* guillotine f; *(for cutting paper)* massicot m; Br Pol **to put a g. on a bill** = imposer une limite de temps aux débats précédant un vote
 2 vt *(execute)* guillotiner

guilt [gɪlt] n culpabilité f; **to feel g.** se sentir coupable; **g. complex** complexe m de culpabilité; **to be on a g. trip** culpabiliser

guiltily ['gɪltɪlɪ] adv d'un air coupable

guiltless ['gɪltlɪs] adj innocent(e)

guilty ['gɪltɪ] adj coupable; **to find sb g./not g.** déclarer qn coupable/non coupable; **to feel g.** se sentir coupable; **to have a g. conscience** avoir mauvaise conscience; **g. secret** secret m inavouable

Guinea ['gɪnɪ] n la Guinée

guinea ['gɪnɪ] n (**a**) Br *(coin)* guinée f (**b**) **g. fowl** pintade f; **g. pig** cobaye m, cochon m d'Inde; Fig **to be a g. pig** servir de cobaye

Guinea-Bissau ['gɪnɪbɪ'saʊ] n la Guinée-Bissau

Guinean [gɪ'neɪən] **1** n Guinéen(enne) m,f
 2 adj guinéen(enne)

guise [gaɪz] n apparence f; **in** or **under the g. of** sous l'apparence de; **in a different g.** sous une autre forme

guitar [gɪ'tɑː(r)] n guitare f

guitarist [gɪ'tɑːrɪst] n guitariste mf

gulch [gʌltʃ] n Am ravin m

gulf [gʌlf] n (**a**) *(bay)* golfe m; **the (Persian) G.** le golfe Persique; **the G. of Mexico** le golfe du Mexique; **the G. Stream** le Gulf Stream; **the G. War** la guerre du Golfe; **G. War syndrome** syndrôme m de la guerre du

Golfe (**b**) *(between people, ideas)* abîme m, gouffre m (**between** entre)

gull [gʌl] n mouette f, goéland m

gullet ['gʌlɪt] n gosier m

gullibility [gʌlɪ'bɪlɪtɪ] n crédulité f

gullible ['gʌlɪbəl] adj crédule

gully ['gʌlɪ] *(pl* **gullies)** n petit ravin m

gulp [gʌlp] **1** n (**a**) *(of food)* bouchée f; *(of drink)* gorgée f; *(of surprise)* serrement m de gorge
 2 vt *(food, drink)* engloutir
 3 vi *(with surprise)* avoir un serrement de gorge
▸**gulp down** vt sep *(food, drink)* engloutir

gum [gʌm] **1** n (**a**) *(in mouth)* gencive f; **g. disease** gingivite f (**b**) *(adhesive)* colle f (**c**) **(chewing) g.** chewing gum m (**d**) *(resin)* **g. arabic** gomme f arabique; **g. tree** gommier m; Fam Fig **to be up a g. tree** être dans le pétrin
 2 vt *(pt & pp* **gummed)** *(stick)* coller
▸**gum up** vt sep *(mechanism)* enrayer; *(eyes)* coller

gumboot ['gʌmbuːt] n botte f de caoutchouc

gummed [gʌmd] adj gommé(e)

gummy ['gʌmɪ] adj collant(e)

gumption ['gʌmpʃən] n Fam *(common sense)* jugeote f; *(courage)* cran m

gumshield ['gʌmʃiːld] n protège-dents m inv

gun [gʌn] **1** n (**a**) *(pistol)* pistolet m; *(rifle)* fusil m; *(artillery piece)* canon m; **g. carriage** affût m de canon; **g. dog** chien m d'arrêt; **g. laws** législation f sur les armes à feu; **g. licence** permis m de port d'armes (**b**) *(idioms)* Fam **big g.** huile f; Fam **to be going great guns** marcher très fort; **to stick to one's guns** tenir bon; **to jump the g.** s'emballer
 2 vt *(pt & pp* **gunned)** *(engine)* accélérer
▸**gun down** vt sep abattre
▸**gun for** vt insep **to be gunning for sb** en avoir après qn; **she's gunning for his job** elle fait tout ce qu'elle peut pour lui prendre son poste

gunboat ['gʌnbəʊt] n cannonière f; **g. diplomacy** politique f de la cannonière

gunfight ['gʌnfaɪt] n fusillade f

gunfire ['gʌnfaɪə(r)] n *(of artillery)* tirs mpl d'artillerie; *(of smaller guns)* coups mpl de feu

gunge [gʌndʒ] n Fam matière f gluante

gung-ho [gʌŋ'həʊ] adj (**a**) *(overly enthusiastic)* d'un enthousiasme irritant (**b**) *(keen for war)* va-t-en-guerre inv

gunk [gʌŋk] n Fam matière f gluante

gunman ['gʌnmən] n homme m armé

gunner ['gʌnə(r)] n artilleur m

gunpoint ['gʌnpɔɪnt] n **at g.** sous la menace d'une arme à feu

gunpowder ['gʌnpaʊdə(r)] n poudre f (à canon); Br Hist **the G. Plot** la conspiration des poudres

The Gunpowder Plot

Les catholiques, menés par Guy Fawkes, organisèrent ce complot pour faire sauter le Parlement britannique et tuer le roi Jacques Ier et sa famille, le 5 novembre 1605, en réaction au refus royal d'instaurer la liberté de culte. Le complot fut déjoué. On commémore cet événement, appelé **"Guy Fawkes' Night"** *(voir encadré à ce mot)*, par des feux d'artifice et des feux de joie.

gunrunner ['gʌnrʌnə(r)] n trafiquant(e) m,f d'armes

gunrunning ['gʌnrʌnɪŋ] n trafic m d'armes

gunship ['gʌnʃɪp] *n* **(helicopter)** g. hélicoptère *m* de combat
gunshot ['gʌnʃɒt] *n* coup *m* de feu; g. **wound** blessure *f* par balle
gunsmith ['gʌnsmɪθ] *n* armurier *m*
gunwale ['gʌnəl] *n Naut* plat-bord *m*
gurgle ['gɜːgəl] **1** *n (of liquid)* gargouillement *m; (of baby)* gazouillis *m*
2 *vi (of liquid)* gargouiller; *(of baby)* gazouiller
gurney ['gɜːnɪ] *n Am* chariot *m* d'hôpital
guru ['guru:] *n* gourou *m*
gush [gʌʃ] **1** *n (of water)* jaillissement *m; Fig (of words)* flot *m*
2 *vi* (**a**) *(of water)* jaillir; **tears gushed from her eyes** elle pleurait à chaudes larmes (**b**) *Pej (talk effusively)* s'extasier (**over** or **about** devant)
gushing ['gʌʃɪŋ] *adj Pej (person, praise)* exubérant(e)
gusset ['gʌsɪt] *n* soufflet *m*
gust [gʌst] **1** *n (of wind)* rafale *f; (of hot air)* bouffée *f*
2 *vi (of wind)* souffler par rafales
gusto ['gʌstəʊ] *n* enthousiasme *m;* **with (great)** g. avec (beaucoup d')enthousiasme
gusty ['gʌstɪ] *adj (wind)* qui souffle par rafales; *(day, weather)* de grand vent
gut [gʌt] **1** *n* (**a**) *(intestine)* intestin *m; Fam* **guts** *(of person, machine)* entrailles *fpl; Fam* **to sweat** or **work one's guts out** se tuer à la tâche; *Fam* **to hate sb's guts** ne pas pouvoir sentir qn; *Fam* **I'll have his guts for garters** je vais le massacrer; **a g. feeling** une intuition; **g. reaction** réaction *f* viscérale (**b**) *Fam (stomach)* bide *m* (**c**) *Fam* **guts** *(courage)* cran *m;* **I didn't have the guts to tell them** je n'ai pas eu le courage de le leur dire
2 *vt (pt & pp* **gutted)** (**a**) *(fish)* vider (**b**) *(building) (of fire)* ravager; *(of builder)* vider entièrement
gutless ['gʌtlɪs] *adj Fam* lâche
gutsy ['gʌtsɪ] *adj Fam* courageux(euse), qui a du cran
gutted ['gʌtɪd] *adj Br Fam (disappointed)* effondré(e)
gutter ['gʌtə(r)] **1** *n (in street)* caniveau *m; (on roof)* gouttière *f; Fig* **to end up in the g.** finir sous les ponts; *Fig* **to drag oneself out of the g.** se sortir de la misère; *Fam Pej* **g. press** presse *f* à scandales
2 *vi (of candle)* vasciller

guttural ['gʌtərəl] *adj* guttural(e)
guy¹ [gaɪ] *n Fam* (**a**) *(man)* type *m*, mec *m;* **a tough g.** un dur (**b**) *(person)* **hi guys!** salut la compagnie!
guy² *n* g. **(rope)** *(for tent)* tendeur *m*
Guyana [gaɪˈænə] *n* le Guyana
Guyanese [gaɪəˈniːz] **1** *n* Guyanais(e) *m,f*
2 *adj* guyanais(e)
Guy Fawkes Night ['gaɪˈfɔːksˈnaɪt] *n Br* = soirée du 5 novembre, célébration de la tentative de Guy Fawkes de faire sauter le Parlement en 1605

Guy Fawkes Night

Cette fête se déroule en plein air autour d'un grand feu de joie sur lequel on est censé brûler une effigie ("the Guy") de Guy Fawkes, l'instigateur de la conspiration des poudres *(voir encadré* **The Gunpowder Plot**). Des feux d'artifice sont également organisés.

guzzle ['gʌzəl] *vt Fam (food)* engloutir; *(drink)* siffler
gym [dʒɪm] *n (gymnasium)* gymnase *m; (gymnastics)* gym *f;* g. **shoes** chaussures *fpl* de gym
gymkhana [dʒɪmˈkɑːnə] *n* concours *m* hippique
gymnasium [dʒɪmˈneɪzɪəm] *n* gymnase *m*
gymnast ['dʒɪmnæst] *n* gymnaste *mf*
gymnastic [dʒɪmˈnæstɪk] *adj* gymnastique
gymnastics [dʒɪmˈnæstɪks] **1** *n* gymnastique *f*
2 *npl Fig* **mental/verbal** g. gymnastique *f* intellectuelle/verbale
gynaecological, *Am* **gynecological** [gaɪnɪkəˈlɒdʒɪkəl] *adj* gynécologique
gynaecologist, *Am* **gynecologist** [gaɪnɪˈkɒlədʒɪst] *n* gynécologue *mf*
gynaecology, *Am* **gynecology** [gaɪnɪˈkɒlədʒɪ] *n* gynécologie *f*
gyp [dʒɪp] *n Br Fam* **to give sb g.** faire souffrir qn
gypsum ['dʒɪpsəm] *n* gypse *m*
gypsy = **gipsy**
gyrate [dʒaɪˈreɪt] *vi (of planet, sphere)* tourner; *(of dancer)* tournoyer
gyration [dʒaɪˈreɪʃən] *n* giration *f*
gyroscope ['dʒaɪrəskəʊp] *n* gyroscope *m*

H, h [eɪtʃ] *n (letter)* H, h *m inv*; **H bomb** bombe *f* H
haberdashery [ˈhæbədæʃərɪ] *(pl haberdasheries) n*
(**a**) *Br (sewing items, shop)* mercerie *f* (**b**) *Am (men's clothes, shop)* chemiserie *f*
habit [ˈhæbɪt] *n* (**a**) *(custom, practice)* habitude *f*; **to be in the h. of doing sth** avoir l'habitude de faire qch; **to get into the h. of doing sth** prendre l'habitude de faire qch; **to get out of the h.** de doing sth perdre l'habitude de faire qch; **don't make a h. of it!** que cela ne devienne pas une habitude!; **from force of h.** par habitude (**b**) *Fam (addiction to drugs)* accoutumance *f*; **to kick the h.** décrocher (**c**) *(of monk, nun)* habit *m*
habitable [ˈhæbɪtəbəl] *adj* habitable
habitat [ˈhæbɪtæt] *n* habitat *m*
habitation [hæbɪˈteɪʃən] *n* habitation *f*; **there were no signs of h.** l'endroit semblait inhabité; **fit for h.** habitable; **unfit for h.** inhabitable
habitual [həˈbɪtjʊəl] *adj (generosity, rudeness)* habituel(elle); *(liar, drunk)* invétéré(e)
habitually [həˈbɪtjʊəlɪ] *adv* habituellement
habituate [həˈbɪtjʊeɪt] *vt Formal* habituer (**to** à); **become habituated to sth** s'habituer à qch
hacienda [hæsɪˈendə] *n* ranch *m*, hacienda *f*
hack¹ [hæk] **1** *vt* (**a**) *(cut)* tailler, taillader; **to h. sb/sth to pieces** tailler qn/qch en pièces; **to h. one's way through the jungle** se frayer un chemin dans la jungle à la machette (**b**) *very Fam (cope with)* **he can't h. it** il ne s'en sort pas
2 *vi* (**a**) *(cut)* **to h. at sth** taillader qch (**b**) *(cough)* tousser d'une toux sèche (**c**) *Comput* **to h. into sth** entrer dans qch par effraction
▸**hack down** *vt sep* abattre
▸**hack off** *vt sep* (**a**) *(branch, limb)* couper (**b**) *Fam* **to be hacked off (with sb/sth)** en avoir marre (de qn/qch)
hack² *n* (**a**) *Fam Pej (journalist)* journaliste *mf* besogneux(euse); *(political activist)* militant(e) *m,f* (**b**) *(horseride)* **to go for a h.** aller faire une promenade à cheval (**c**) *Am Fam (taxi)* taxi *m*
hacker [ˈhækə(r)] *n Comput* pirate *m* informatique
hacking jacket [ˈhækɪŋˈdʒækɪt] *n* veste *f* d'équitation
hackles [ˈhækəlz] *npl (of dog)* poils *mpl* du cou; *(of bird)* plumes *fpl* du cou; *Fig* **to make sb's h. rise** hérisser qn
hackney cab [ˈhæknɪkæb], **hackney carriage** [ˈhæknɪˈkærɪdʒ] *n Formal (taxi)* fiacre *m*
hackneyed [ˈhæknɪd] *adj (argument)* rebattu(e); *(language)* banal(e); **h. expression** lieu *m* commun
hacksaw [ˈhæksɔː] *n* scie *f* à métaux
had [hæd] *pt & pp of* **have**

haddock [ˈhædək] *(pl haddock or haddocks) n* églefin *m*
hadn't [ˈhædənt] = **had not**
haemoglobin, *Am* **hemoglobin** [hiːməʊˈgləʊbɪn] *n* hémoglobine *f*
haemophilia, *Am* **hemophilia** [hiːməʊˈfɪlɪə] *n* hémophilie *f*
haemophiliac, *Am* **hemophiliac** [hiːməʊˈfɪlɪæk] *n* hémophile *mf*
haemorrhage, *Am* **hemorrhage** [ˈhemərɪdʒ] **1** *n also Fig* hémorragie *f*
2 *vi Med* faire une hémorragie; *Fig (of support, funds)* diminuer
haemorrhoids, *Am* **hemorrhoids** [ˈhemərɔɪdz] *npl Med* hémorroïdes *fpl*
hag [hæg] *n Pej* vieille taupe *f*
haggard [ˈhægəd] *adj* hâve
haggis [ˈhægɪs] *n* = panse de brebis farcie *(plat national écossais)*
haggle [ˈhægəl] *vi* marchander (**with sb** avec qn); **to h. over sth** marchander qch; **to h. about** *or* **over the price of sth** chicaner sur le prix de qch
hagiography [hægɪˈɒgrəfɪ] *n* hagiographie *f*
Hague [heɪg] *n* **the H.** La Haye
hail¹ [heɪl] **1** *n* grêle *f*; *Fig* **a h. of bullets/insults** une pluie de balles/d'injures; **a h. of blows** une volée de coups
2 *vi* **it's hailing** il grêle
hail² *vt* (**a**) *(attract attention of)* héler (**b**) *(acclaim)* saluer (**as** comme)
▸**hail from** *vt insep* être originaire de
hailstone [ˈheɪlstəʊn] *n* grêlon *m*
hailstorm [ˈheɪlstɔːm] *n* averse *f* de grêle
hair [heə(r)] *n (on head)* cheveux *mpl*; *(on body, animal)* poils *mpl*; *(single hair) (on head)* cheveu *m*; *(on body, animal)* poil *m*; **to have fair/long h.** avoir les cheveux clairs/longs; **to do one's h.** se coiffer; **to comb one's h.** se peigner; **to brush one's h.** se brosser les cheveux; **to have** *or* **get one's h. cut** se faire couper les cheveux; **if you harm** *or* **touch a h. on that child's head...** si tu touches à un cheveu de la tête de cet enfant...; **to make sb's h. stand on end** faire dresser les cheveux sur la tête à qn; **keep your h. on!** calmez-vous!; *Fam* **to get in sb's h.** enquiquiner qn; *Fig* **to let one's h. down** se laisser aller; *Fam Hum* **that'll put hairs on your chest!** ça va te donner du poil de la bête!; *Fam* **h. of the dog** *(for hangover)* = verre d'alcool pris pour calmer la gueule de bois; **h. gel** gel *m* pour les cheveux; *Br* **h. slide** barrette *f*; **h. straighteners** défriseur *m*
hairband [ˈheəbænd] *n* bandeau *m*

hairbrush ['heəbrʌʃ] n brosse f à cheveux
haircut ['heəkʌt] n coupe f de cheveux; **to have a h.** se
faire couper les cheveux
hairdo ['heədu:] (pl **hairdos**) n Fam coiffure f
hairdresser ['heədresə(r)] n coiffeur(euse) m,f; **to go
to the h.'s** aller chez le coiffeur
hairdressing ['heədresɪŋ] n coiffure f; **h. salon** salon
m de coiffure
hairdryer ['heədraɪə(r)] n sèche-cheveux m inv
hairgrip ['heəgrɪp] n pince f à cheveux
hairless ['heəlɪs] adj (face) glabre; (puppy) sans poils
hairline ['heəlaɪn] n (**a**) (of person) naissance f des
cheveux; **to have a receding h.** avoir le front qui se
dégarnit (**b**) **h. crack** (in pipe, wall) légère fêlure f; **h.
fracture** (of bone) fêlure f
hairnet ['heənet] n résille f, filet m à cheveux
hairpiece ['heəpi:s] n postiche m
hairpin ['heəpɪn] n épingle f à cheveux; **h. bend** (on
road) virage m en épingle à cheveux
hair-raising ['heəreɪzɪŋ] adj à faire dresser les cheveux sur la tête
hair's-breadth ['heəzbredθ] n **by a h.** (win, lose) de
justesse; **the car missed him by a h.** la voiture l'a
frôlé; **to be within a h. of** être à deux doigts de
hairspray ['heəspreɪ] n laque f
hairstyle ['heəstaɪl] n coiffure f
hairy ['heərɪ] adj (**a**) (covered in hair) velu(e), poilu(e)
(**b**) Fam (scary) effrayant(e)
Haiti ['heɪtɪ] n Haïti
Haitian ['heɪʃən] **1** n Haïtien(enne) m,f
 2 adj haïtien(enne)
hake [heɪk] (pl **hake** or hakes) n merlu m, colin m
halcyon days ['hælsɪən'deɪz] npl Lit jours mpl heureux
hale [heɪl] adj vigoureux(euse); **to be h. and hearty**
être en pleine forme
half [ha:f] **1** n (pl **halves** [ha:vz]) (**a**) (in general) moitié f; **h. an hour** une demi-heure; **h. past ten** dix
heures et demie; **it's h. past** il est la demie; **to fold/
cut sth in h.** plier/couper qch en deux; **h. a dozen**
une demi-douzaine; **h. of them** la moitié d'entre
eux; **to have h. a mind to do sth** avoir bien envie de
faire qch; Hum **my better** or **other h.** ma moitié; Br
she is too clever by h. elle est beaucoup trop maligne; **she doesn't do things by halves** elle ne fait
pas les choses à moitié; **to go halves with sb** partager avec qn; Fam **you don't know the h. of it!** tu ne
sais pas tout! (**b**) (fraction) demie f, moitié f; **three
and a h.** trois et demi (**c**) first/second h. (in match)
première/deuxième mi-temps f (**d**) (ticket) billet m
demi-tarif (**e**) Br (half pint) demi m
 2 adj demi(e); **h. board** demi-pension f; **h. day** demi-
journée f; **h. hour** demi-heure f; **every h. hour** toutes
les demi-heures; **h. price** demi-tarif m; **at h. price** à
moitié prix
 3 adv à moitié; **to h. do sth** faire qch à moitié; **h. full/
empty** à moitié plein(e)/vide; **you're h. right** tu n'as
pas tout à fait tort; Br Fam **not h.!** plutôt!; Br Fam **it
isn't h. cold!** il fait rudement froid!
half- [ha:f] pref **h.-asleep** à moitié endormi(e); **h.-dead**
à moitié mort(e); **h.-naked** à moitié nu(e)
half-baked [ha:f'beɪkt] adj Fam bancal(e)
halfbreed ['ha:fbri:d] n métis(isse) m,f
half-brother ['ha:fbrʌðə(r)] n demi-frère m
half-caste ['ha:fka:st] n métis(isse) m,f
half-cock [ha:f'kɒk] n Fam Fig **to go off at h.** (of
plan, event) avorter, échouer

half-hearted ['ha:f'ha:tɪd] adj (effort, performance)
timide, hésitant(e); (belief, support) peu enthousiaste
half-heartedly ['ha:f'ha:tɪdlɪ] adv sans grand enthousiasme, sans conviction
half-hourly [ha:f'aʊəlɪ] adv toutes les demi-heures
half-life ['ha:flaɪf] n Phys demi-vie f
half-mast ['ha:f'ma:st] n Br **at h.** (flag) en berne; Fam
(socks) en accordéon
half-sister ['ha:f'sɪstə(r)] n demi-sœur f
half-size ['ha:f'saɪz] n (in shoes) demi-pointure f
half-term ['ha:f'tɜ:m] n Br **h. (holiday)** = congé de
milieu de trimestre
half-timbered [ha:f'tɪmbəd] adj Archit & Constr à
colombages
half time ['ha:f'taɪm] n (in match) mi-temps f
half-truth ['ha:f'tru:θ] n demi-vérité f
halfway [ha:f'weɪ] **1** adj **at the h. point** (in space) à
mi-chemin; (in time) à la moitié; **h. house** (for rehabilitation) centre m de réadaptation (pour anciens déte-
nus, malades mentaux, drogués etc); Fig compromis
m; **h. line** (on sports pitch) ligne f médiane
 2 adv à mi-chemin; Fig **to meet sb h.** faire un compromis avec qn
halfwit ['ha:fwɪt] n simple mf d'esprit
halfwitted [ha:f'wɪtɪd] adj stupide
half-yearly ['ha:f'jɪəlɪ] adj semestriel(elle)
halibut ['hælɪbət] (pl halibut or halibuts) n flétan m
halitosis [hælɪ'təʊsɪs] n mauvaise haleine f
hall [hɔ:l] n (**a**) (entrance room) entrée f; (corridor)
couloir m (**b**) (for concerts, meetings) salle f (**c**) Br
Univ **h. of residence** résidence f universitaire
hallmark ['hɔ:lma:k] n (on metal) poinçon m; Fig (typical quality) signe m
hallo = hello
hallowed ['hæləʊd] adj saint(e), béni(e)
Hallowe'en [hæləʊ'i:n] n = veille de la Toussaint

Hallowe'en

Il s'agit d'une fête d'origine païenne célébrée dans
les pays anglo-saxons la veille de la Toussaint, à
l'époque de l'année où les morts étaient censés
rendre visite aux vivants. Aujourd'hui la tradition
demeure : on évide des citrouilles pour les
transformer en lanternes en forme de crâne, et les
enfants vont de maison en maison déguisés en sorcières ou en fantômes. De nos jours, la coutume
britannique a adopté la tradition américaine du
"trick or treat", consistant pour les enfants à demander un petit cadeau aux habitants des maisons
visitées et à les menacer d'un mauvais tour s'ils re-
fusent.

hallucinate [hə'lu:sɪneɪt] vi avoir des hallucinations
hallucination [həlu:sɪ'neɪʃən] n hallucination f
hallucinatory [hə'lu:sɪnətərɪ] adj hallucinatoire
hallucinogenic [həlu:sɪnəʊ'dʒenɪk] adj hallucinogène
hallway ['hɔ:lweɪ] n (entrance room) entrée f; (corridor) couloir m
halo ['heɪləʊ] (pl haloes or halos) n auréole f
halt [hɒlt] **1** n halte f, arrêt m; **to come to a h.** s'arrêter;
to bring sth to a h. interrompre ou faire cesser qch;
to call a h. to sth mettre fin à qch
 2 vt interrompre
 3 vi s'arrêter
halter ['hɔ:ltə(r)] n (**a**) (for horse) licou m (**b**) **h. top**
bain m de soleil

halterneck ['hɔːltənek] *adj (dress, top)* dos-nu *inv*
halting ['hɔːltɪŋ] *adj (voice, progress)* hésitant(e)
halve [hɑːv] *vt* (**a**) *(divide in two)* diviser en deux; *(cake, fruit)* couper en deux (**b**) *(reduce by half)* réduire de moitié
halves [hɑːvz] *pl of* **half**
ham [hæm] **1** *n* (**a**) *(meat)* jambon *m* (**b**) *Fam (actor)* cabotin(e) *m,f*; **h. acting** cabotinage *m*
　2 *vt (pt & pp* **hammed**) *Fam (of actor)* **to h. it up** en faire trop
Hamburg ['hæmbɜːg] *n* Hambourg
hamburger ['hæmbɜːgə(r)] *n* hamburger *m*
ham-fisted ['hæm'fɪstɪd] *adj Fam* maladroit(e)
hamlet ['hæmlɪt] *n* hameau *m*
hammer ['hæmə(r)] **1** *n* marteau *m*; **to come under the h.** *(be auctioned)* être mis(e) aux enchères; *Fam* **to go at it h. and tongs** mettre le paquet; **the h. and sickle** la faucille et le marteau
　2 *vt* (**a**) *(hit with hammer) (nail)* enfoncer (**into** dans); *(wall)* taper à coups de marteau; *Fig* **to h. one's point home** insister lourdement (**b**) *(hit with fist) (object)* frapper du poing; *(person)* frapper à coups de poing (**c**) *Fam (defeat)* écraser
▸**hammer away at** *vt insep Fig (problem)* travailler avec acharnement sur
▸**hammer out** *vt sep Fig (plan, compromise)* mettre au point
hammering ['hæmərɪŋ] *n* (**a**) *(noise)* martèlement *m* (**b**) *Fam (defeat)* raclée *f*; **they gave us a real h.** ils nous ont mis une vraie raclée
hammock ['hæmək] *n* hamac *m*
hamper ['hæmpə(r)] **1** *n (for food)* panier *m*; (**Christmas**) **h.** = panier garni de gourmandises offert à Noël
　2 *vt (hinder)* gêner, entraver
hamster ['hæmstə(r)] *n* hamster *m*
hamstring ['hæmstrɪŋ] **1** *n* tendon *m* du jarret
　2 *vt (pt & pp* **hamstrung** ['hæmstrʌŋ]) *(incapacitate)* paralyser
hand [hænd] **1** *n* (**a**) *(part of body)* main *f*; *(of clock, watch)* aiguille *f*; **to hold hands** se tenir par la main; **h. in h.** la main dans la main; **to hold sth in one's h.** tenir qch à la main; **to take sb by the h.** prendre qn par la main; **on one's hands and knees** à quatre pattes; **by h.** *(make, wash)* à la main; *(on envelope)* en ville, E.V.; **hands off!** pas touche!; **hands up!** haut les mains!; **h. basin** lavabo *m*; **h. cream** crème *f* pour les mains; **h. grenade** grenade *f*; **h. luggage** bagages *mpl* à main
　(**b**) *(worker)* ouvrier(ère) *m,f*; *(sailor)* matelot *m*; **to be an old h. at sth** avoir une expérience considérable de qch
　(**c**) *(handwriting)* **in his own h.** de sa main
　(**d**) *(in cards)* main *f*, jeu *m*; *Fig* **to show one's h.** dévoiler son jeu
　(**e**) *(idioms)* **at** or **on h.** disponible; **to have sth to h.** avoir qch sous la main; **to ask for sb's h. (in marriage)** demander la main de qn; **to be in good hands** être en de bonnes mains; **to fall into the wrong hands** tomber en de mauvaises mains; **it's out of my hands** ça ne dépend plus de moi; **to change hands** *(of money, car)* changer de mains; **to have a h. in sth** être impliqué(e) dans qch; **to go h. in h. with sth** aller de pair avec qch; **to try one's h. at sth** s'essayer à qch; **to turn one's h. to sth** s'essayer à qch; **to give** or **lend sb a h.** donner un coup de main à qn; **to give sb a big h.** *(applaud)* applaudir qn bien fort; **to suffer at sb's hands** souffrir aux mains de qn; **on**

(the) one h. d'une part; **on the other h.** d'autre part; **to have time on one's hands** avoir du temps à soi; **to have a situation in h.** maîtriser une situation; **to take sb in h.** prendre qn en main; **to get out of h.** devenir incontrôlable; **to dismiss a suggestion out of h.** rejeter une proposition sur-le-champ; **to have one's hands full** être débordé(e); **to have one's hands tied** avoir les mains liées; **to be h. in glove with sb** être de mèche avec qn; **to live from h. to mouth** mener une existence précaire; **to lose money h.** over fist perdre des sommes considérables; **to make money h. over fist** gagner une fortune; **to win hands down** gagner haut la main
　2 *vt* donner, passer; **he handed her the letter to read** il lui a passé la lettre pour qu'elle la lise; *Fig* **to h. sth to sb on a plate** apporter qch à qn sur un plateau; *Fig* **you've got to h. it to him** c'est une qualité qu'il faut lui reconnaître
▸**hand back** *vt sep* rendre, repasser
▸**hand down** *vt sep* (**a**) *(jewellery, tradition, skill)* transmettre (**b**) *(give)* passer
▸**hand in** *vt sep* remettre; **to h. in one's resignation** donner sa démission
▸**hand on** *vt sep* transmettre
▸**hand out** *vt sep* distribuer
▸**hand over** *vt sep* donner
▸**hand round** *vt sep* faire circuler
handbag ['hændbæg] *n* sac *m* à main
handball ['hændbɔːl] *n* (**a**) *(game)* handball *m* (**b**) *(offence)* main *f*
handbook ['hændbʊk] *n* guide *m*, manuel *m*
handbrake ['hændbreɪk] *n* frein *m* à main
handclap ['hændklæp] *n* **to give sb the slow h.** = applaudir quelqu'un très lentement pour signifier son dédain
handcuff ['hændkʌf] *vt* passer les menottes à
handcuffs ['hændkʌfs] *npl* menottes *fpl*
handful ['hændfʊl] *n (of sand, rice, people)* poignée *f*; *Fig* **that child is a real h.** cet enfant n'est pas facile
handgun ['hændgʌn] *n* revolver *m*, pistolet *m*
handicap ['hændɪkæp] **1** *n* handicap *m*
　2 *vt (pt & pp* **handicapped**) handicaper
handicapped ['hændɪkæpt] **1** *npl* **the h.** les handicapés *mpl*
　2 *adj* handicapé(e)
handicraft ['hændɪkrɑːft] *n (skill)* artisanat *m*; *(object)* objet *m* artisanal
handiwork ['hændɪwɜːk] *n* travail *m* manuel; *Hum* **this looks like Jane's h.!** ça, c'est signé Jane!
handkerchief ['hæŋkətʃɪf] *n* mouchoir *m*
handle ['hændəl] **1** *n (of broom, knife, saucepan)* manche *m*; *(of suitcase, door)* poignée *f*; *(of cup)* anse *f*; *Fig* **to fly off the h.** piquer une colère; *Fig* **to get a h. on sth** piger qch
　2 *vt* (**a**) *(touch, hold)* manipuler, toucher à; **h. with care** *(on parcel)* ≃ fragile; **to h. the ball** *(in football)* toucher le ballon avec la main (**b**) *Fam (cope with) (situation, crisis)* faire face à (**c**) *Com (business, contract, client)* s'occuper de
　3 *vi (of car, boat)* **to h. well** être maniable
handlebars ['hændəlbɑːz] *npl* guidon *m*
handmade ['hænd'meɪd] *adj* fait(e) à la main
hand-me-downs ['hændmɪdaʊnz] *npl Fam* **I wear my brother's h.** je mets les vieilles frusques de mon frère
handout ['hændaʊt] *n* (**a**) *(donation)* don *m* (**b**) *(leaflet)* prospectus *m*

hand-picked ['hænd'pɪkd] *adj (person, team)* trié(e) sur le volet
handrail ['hændreɪl] *n* rampe *f*
handset ['hændset] *n (of telephone)* combiné *m*
hands-free ['hændz'friː] *adj Tel* mains libres
handshake ['hændʃeɪk] *n* poignée *f* de main
hands-off ['hæn'zɒf] *adj (approach, style)* non-interventionniste
handsome ['hænsəm] *adj* (**a**) *(physically attractive)* beau (belle) (**b**) *(praise)* sincère; *(price, profit)* considérable; *(reward)* beau (belle)
handsomely ['hænsəmlɪ] *adv* (**a**) *(dressed, furnished)* élégamment (**b**) *(rewarded, paid)* généreusement
hands-on ['hæn'zɒn] *adj* **the director has a h.** style of management le directeur n'a pas peur de mettre la main à la pâte; **h. training** formation *f* pratique
handstand ['hændstænd] *n* **to do a h.** faire un équilibre sur les mains
hand-to-hand ['hæntə'hænd] *adj (combat)* au corps à corps
hand-to-mouth ['hæntə'maʊθ] **1** *adj (existence)* précaire
2 *adv* **to live h.** tirer le diable par la queue
handwriting ['hændraɪtɪŋ] *n* écriture *f*
handwritten ['hændrɪtən] *adj* manuscrit(e)
handy ['hændɪ] *adj* (**a**) *(useful)* pratique; **to come in h.** être utile (**b**) *(convenient)* commode; **the flat is very h. for the shops** l'appartement est tout près des commerces (**c**) *(within reach)* à portée de la main; **have you got a pen h.?** est-ce que tu as un stylo à portée de la main? (**d**) *(skilful)* bricoleur(euse); **he's very h. in the kitchen** il est bon cuisinier
handyman ['hændɪmæn] *n* homme *m* à tout faire
hang [hæŋ] **1** *n Fam* **to get the h. of sth** piger qch
2 *vt (pt & pp hung* [hʌŋ]) (**a**) *(suspend) (from ceiling)* pendre, suspendre; *(on wall)* accrocher (**b**) **to h. one's head** baisser la tête; **he hung his head in shame** il baissa la tête sous l'effet de la honte (**c**) *(pt & pp hanged) (criminal)* pendre
3 *vi* (**a**) *(be suspended) (from ceiling)* être suspendu(e); *(on wall)* être accroché(e); *Fig* **she hung on his every word** elle était pendue à ses lèvres (**b**) *(be executed)* être pendu(e) (**c**) *(of clothes)* tomber
▸**hang about, hang around** *vi Fam (wait)* poireauter; **to keep sb hanging about** *or* **around** faire poireauter qn
▸**hang back** *vi* hésiter
▸**hang in** *vi Fam* **h. in there!** accroche-toi!, tiens bon!
▸**hang on 1** *vi* (**a**) *Fam (wait)* patienter, attendre (**b**) *(survive)* tenir le coup
2 *vt insep (depend on)* dépendre de
▸**hang on to** *vt insep* garder
▸**hang out 1** *vt sep (washing)* étendre
2 *vi* (**a**) *(from pocket, box)* dépasser (**b**) *Fam (spend time)* traîner
▸**hang together** *vi (of argument, statements)* se tenir
▸**hang up 1** *vt sep (hat, picture)* accrocher
2 *vi (on telephone)* raccrocher; **to h. up on sb** raccrocher au nez de qn
hangar ['hæŋə(r)] *n* hangar *m*
hangdog ['hæŋdɒg] *adj (look, expression)* de chien battu
hanger ['hæŋə(r)] *n (for clothes)* cintre *m*
hanger-on [hæŋə'rɒn] *(pl* hangers-on) *n* parasite *m*, pique-assiette *m inv*
hang-glider ['hæŋglaɪdə(r)] *n (aircraft)* deltaplane *m*; *(person)* deltiste *mf*

hang-gliding ['hæŋglaɪdɪŋ] *n* deltaplane *m*; **to go h.** faire du deltaplane
hanging ['hæŋɪŋ] *n (execution)* pendaison *f*
hangman ['hæŋmən] *n* bourreau *m*
hangnail ['hæŋneɪl] *n* envie *f*
hang-out ['hæŋaʊt] *n Fam* repaire *m*
hangover ['hæŋəʊvə(r)] *n* (**a**) *(from drinking)* gueule *f* de bois (**b**) *(practice, belief)* reste *m*, vestige *m*
hang-up ['hæŋʌp] *n Fam* complexe *m*; **to have a h. about sth** être complexé(e) à propos de qch
hanker ['hæŋkə(r)] *vi* **to h. after** *or* **for sth** avoir très envie de qch
hankering ['hæŋkərɪŋ] *n* **to have a h. for sth** avoir très envie de qch
hankie, hanky ['hæŋkɪ] *(pl* hankies) *n Fam* mouchoir *m*
hanky-panky ['hæŋkɪ'pæŋkɪ] *n Fam* (**a**) *(sexual activity)* galipettes *fpl* (**b**) *(underhand behaviour)* entourloupettes *fpl*
Hanover ['hænəʊvə(r)] *n* Hanovre
haphazard [hæp'hæzəd] *adj (choice, decision)* pris(e) au hasard; *(attempt)* mal organisé(e)
haphazardly [hæp'hæzədlɪ] *adv* n'importe comment
hapless ['hæplɪs] *adj Formal* infortuné(e)
happen ['hæpən] *vi* arriver, se produire; **it happened ten years ago** c'est arrivé il y a dix ans; **what happened?** que s'est-il passé?; **to h. again** se reproduire; **it so happens (that)...** il se trouve justement que...; **as if nothing had happened** comme si de rien n'était; **as it happens,...** justement...; **what has happened to him?** que lui est-il arrivé?; **to h. to meet sb** rencontrer qn par hasard; **I h. to know (that)...** il se trouve que je sais que...; **do you h. to know whether...?** savez-vous par hasard si...?
▸**happen on, happen upon** *vt insep* tomber sur
happening ['hæpənɪŋ] **1** *n* événement *m*
2 *adj Fam (town) (lively)* dynamique; *(trendy)* branché(e), dans le coup
happily ['hæpɪlɪ] *adv* (**a**) *(play)* gentiment; *(chat)* tranquillement; **a h. married couple** un ménage heureux; **they lived h. ever after** ≃ ils vécurent heureux et eurent beaucoup d'enfants (**b**) *(fortunately)* heureusement, par bonheur (**c**) *(willingly)* volontiers
happiness ['hæpɪnɪs] *n* bonheur *m*
happy ['hæpɪ] *adj* (**a**) *(content, cheerful)* heureux(euse); **to be h. with sth** être satisfait(e) de qch; **to make sb h.** rendre qn heureux(eurse); **to keep sb h.** satisfaire qn; **a story with a h. ending** une histoire qui finit bien; **a h. medium** le juste milieu; **h. birthday/Christmas!** joyeux anniversaire/Noël!; **h. New Year!** bonne année! (**b**) *(fortunate) (choice, phrase)* heureux(euse) (**c**) *(willing)* **to be h. to do sth** être heureux(euse) de faire qch
happy-clappy ['hæpɪ'klæpɪ] *adj Br Fam Pej* agaçant(e) de par sa joie exubérante *(appliqué aux chrétiens évangéliques)*
happy-go-lucky ['hæpɪgəʊ'lʌkɪ] *adj* insouciant(e)
harangue [hə'ræŋ] **1** *n* harangue *f*
2 *vt* haranguer (**about** au sujet de)
harass [hə'ræs, 'hærəs] *vt* harceler
harassed [hə'ræst, 'hærəst] *adj* stressé(e)
harassment ['hærəsmənt, hə'ræsmənt] *n* harcèlement *m*; **police h.** harcèlement policier
harbour, Am harbor ['hɑːbə(r)] **1** *n* port *m*
2 *vt (fugitive)* cacher; *(hope, suspicion)* nourrir; **to h. a grudge against sb** garder rancune à qn

hard [hɑːd] **1** *adj* (**a**) *(substance)* dur(e); *(fact, evidence)* tangible; **in h.** as nails être un(e) dur(e) à cuire; **in h.** cash en liquide; *Comput* **h.** copy copie *f* sur papier; **h.** core *(of group)* noyau *m* dur; **h.** court *(for tennis)* court *m* en dur; *Comput* **h.** disk disque *m* dur; **h.** drugs drogues *fpl* dures; *Pol* **h.** left/right extrême gauche *f*/droite *f*; *Comput* **h.** return retour *m* chariot obligatoire; *Br* **h.** shoulder *(on motorway)* bande *f* d'arrêt d'urgence

(**b**) *(difficult)* difficile; *(strenuous)* pénible; **it was h.** work persuading him to come ça n'a pas été facile de le convaincre de venir; **it's h. to say...** il est difficile de dire...; **to be h. to please** être difficile (à satisfaire); **to learn sth the h. way** apprendre qch à ses dépens; **to do things the h. way** se compliquer la vie; **h. of hearing** dur(e) d'oreille

(**c**) *(harsh) (person, conditions, life)* dur(e); **to be h. on sb** être dur(e) avec qn; **to have a h. time (of it)** en baver; **to give sb a h. time** mener la vie dure à qn; **a h. winter** un hiver rigoureux; **no h. feelings?** sans rancune?; **to take a h. line on sth** prendre une position très ferme sur qch; **h. luck!**, *Fam* **h. cheese!** pas de chance!

(**d**) *(intense)* **to be a h. worker** travailler dur; *Law* **h. labour** travaux *mpl* forcés; *Com* **to give sb the h. sell** essayer de convaincre qn d'acheter à toute force

(**e**) *(water)* calcaire

2 *adv* (**a**) *(work)* dur; *(push, hit)* fort; **to try h.** faire de son mieux; **to look h. at sb/sth** regarder qn/qch fixement; **to think h.** bien réfléchir; **to be h. at work** être en plein travail; **it's raining h.** il pleut à verse; **to feel h. done by** se sentir brimé(e)

(**b**) *(near)* **h. by** tout près de; **to follow h. upon sb/sth** suivre qn/qch de près

hard-and-fast [ˈhɑːdənˈfɑːst] *adj (rule)* absolu(e)

hardback [ˈhɑːdbæk] **1** *n* livre *m* cartonné

2 *adj* cartonné(e)

hardball [ˈhɑːdbɔːl] *n Am* base-ball *m*; *Fam Fig* **to play h.** employer les grands moyens

hard-bitten [ˈhɑːdˈbɪtən] *adj* endurci(e)

hardboard [ˈhɑːdbɔːd] *n* aggloméré *m*

hard-boiled [hɑːdˈbɔɪld] *adj (egg)* dur(e); *Fig (person)* dur(e) à cuire

hard-core [ˈhɑːdkɔː(r)] *adj (supporter)* inconditionnel(elle); *(pornography)* hard *inv*; *(punk)* hard-core *inv*

hard-earned [hɑːdˈɜːnd] *adj* durement gagné(e)

harden [ˈhɑːdən] **1** *vt* endurcir; **to h. oneself to sth** s'endurcir à qch

2 *vi (of substance, attitude)* durcir

hardened [ˈhɑːdənd] *adj (steel)* trempé(e); *(drinker)* invétéré(e); *(criminal)* endurci(e)

hard-fought [ˈhɑːdˈfɔːt] *adj (election, contest)* âprement disputé(e)

hard-headed [hɑːdˈhedɪd] *adj (attitude, person)* réaliste

hard-hearted [ˈhɑːdˈhɑːtɪd] *adj* dur(e)

hard-hitting [hɑːdˈhɪtɪŋ] *adj (criticism, report)* sans indulgence

hardliner [hɑːdˈlaɪnə(r)] *n (politician, activist)* jusqu'au-boutiste *mf*

hardly [ˈhɑːdlɪ] *adv (scarcely)* à peine; **h. had I arrived when...** j'étais à peine arrivé que...; **you can h. expect me to do that** vous ne vous attendez tout de même pas à ce que je fasse ça; **I can h. believe it** j'ai du mal à y croire; *also Ironic* **I can h. wait** j'ai hâte d'y être; **h. ever** presque jamais; **h. anyone/anything** presque personne/rien

hardness [ˈhɑːdnɪs] *n* (**a**) *(of substance)* dureté *f* (**b**) *(of problem)* difficulté *f*

hard-on [ˈhɑːdɒn] *n Vulg* **to have/get a h.** bander

hard-pressed [hɑːdˈprest], **hard-pushed** [hɑːdˈpʊʃt] *adj* en difficulté; **to be h. for time/money** manquer de temps/d'argent; **to be h. to do sth** avoir du mal à faire qch

hardship [ˈhɑːdʃɪp] *n* épreuve *f*; **to live in h.** vivre dans la misère

hard-up [hɑːdˈʌp] *adj Fam* fauché(e), raide, sans un rond

hardware [ˈhɑːdweə(r)] *n* (**a**) *(tools)* matériel *m*; **(military)** **h.** *(weapons)* matériel *m* militaire, armement *m*; **h. store** quincaillerie *f* (**b**) *Comput* matériel *m*, hardware *m*

hard-wearing [hɑːdˈweərɪŋ] *adj* résistant(e)

hard-won [hɑːdˈwʌn] *adj* durement acquis(e)

hard-working [ˈhɑːdˈwɜːkɪŋ] *adj* travailleur(euse)

hardy [ˈhɑːdɪ] *adj* résistant(e), robuste

hare [heə(r)] *n* lièvre *m*; **to run with the hares and hunt with the hounds** manger à tous les râteliers

▸ **hare off** *vi Br Fam* partir en trombe

harebrained [ˈheəbreɪnd] *adj* écervelé(e)

harelip [ˈheəlɪp] *n* bec-de-lièvre *m*

harem [hɑːˈriːm] *n* harem *m*

haricot [ˈhærɪkəʊ] *n* **h. (bean)** haricot *m* blanc

hark [hɑːk] *exclam Lit* écoutez!; *Fam* **h. at him!** comme il y va!

▸ **hark back** *vi* **to h. back to sth** évoquer qch; **he's always harking back to that mistake I made** il revient toujours sur l'erreur que j'ai faite

harlot [ˈhɑːlət] *n Lit* prostituée *f*

harm [hɑːm] **1** *n* mal *m*; *(to reputation)* tort *m*; **to do sb h.** faire du mal à qn; **to do oneself h.** se faire du tort; **it will do more h. than good** cela va faire plus de mal que de bien; **I can't see any h. in it** je ne vois pas de mal à ça; **there's no h. in trying** ça ne coûte rien d'essayer; **you will come to no h.** il ne t'arrivera rien (de mal); **out of h.'s way** en sûreté, en lieu sûr

2 *vt (physically)* faire du mal à; *(health, reputation, cause)* nuire à; *(skin, fabric)* abîmer

harmful [ˈhɑːmfʊl] *adj (influence, activity)* néfaste; *(substance, ray)* nocif(ive)

harmless [ˈhɑːmlɪs] *adj (person, animal)* inoffensif(ive); *(joke)* innocent(e); **it's just a bit of h. fun** ça ne fait de mal à personne

harmonica [hɑːˈmɒnɪkə] *n* harmonica *m*

harmonious [hɑːˈməʊnɪəs] *adj* harmonieux(euse)

harmonization [hɑːmənaɪˈzeɪʃən] *n* harmonisation *f*

harmonize [ˈhɑːmənaɪz] **1** *vt* harmoniser

2 *vi* s'harmoniser (**with** avec)

harmony [ˈhɑːmənɪ] *(pl* **harmonies)** *n also Fig* harmonie *f*; **in h. with** en harmonie ou en accord avec; **to live in h. (with)** vivre en harmonie (avec)

harness [ˈhɑːnɪs] **1** *n* (**a**) *(for horse, baby, of parachute)* harnais *m*; *(for climber)* baudrier *m* (**b**) *(idioms)* **to work in h. (with)** travailler en équipe (avec); **to die in h.** mourir à la tâche

2 *vt (horse)* harnacher; *(to a cart)* atteler; *(resources)* exploiter

harp [hɑːp] *n* harpe *f*

▸ **harp on** *vi* **to h. on about sth** revenir sans arrêt sur qch

harpist [ˈhɑːpɪst] *n* harpiste *mf*

harpoon [hɑːˈpuːn] **1** *n* harpon *m*

2 *vt* harponner

harpsichord [ˈhɑːpsɪkɔːd] *n* clavecin *m*

harpy ['hɑːpɪ] (*pl* **harpies**) *n* harpie *f*
harrow ['hærəʊ] *n* herse *f*
harrowing ['hærəʊɪŋ] *adj* (*experience, sight*) pénible; (*account, image*) déchirant(e)
harry ['hærɪ] (*pt & pp* **harried**) *vt* harceler
harsh [hɑːʃ] *adj* (*voice, sound*) strident(e); (*climate*) rude; (*treatment, person*) dur(e)
harshly ['hɑːʃlɪ] *adv* (*answer, speak, treat*) durement
harvest ['hɑːvɪst] **1** *n* (*of fruit*) récolte *f*; (*of crops*) moisson *f*; (*of grapes*) vendange *f*; **h. festival** = fête religieuse pour célébrer la fin de la moisson
2 *vt* (*fruit*) récolter; (*crops*) moissonner; (*grapes*) vendanger; *Fig* (*information*) récolter
has [hæz] *see* **have**
has-been ['hæzbiːn] *n Fam Pej* has been *mf inv*
hash [hæʃ] *n* (**a**) (*stew*) hachis *m*; **h. browns** = pommes de terre rapées et sautées (*présentees parfois sous forme de galette*) (**b**) *very Fam* (*hashish*) hasch *m* (**c**) (*symbol*) **h. mark, h. sign** dièse *m* (**d**) (*idioms*) *Fam* **to make a h. of sth** faire un beau gâchis de qch
hashish ['hæʃiːʃ] *n* haschich *m*
hasn't ['hæznt] = **has not**
hassle ['hæsəl] *Fam* **1** *n* embêtements *mpl*; **it's too much h.** c'est trop de tintouin; **it's a real h. buying a house** l'achat d'une maison est un vrai casse-tête; **to give sb h.** faire des histoires à qn
2 *vt* embêter, harceler; **don't h. me!** arrête de m'embêter!
haste [heɪst] *n* hâte *f*; **in h.** en hâte, à la hâte; **to make h.** se dépêcher, se hâter; *Prov* **more h. less speed** hâtez-vous lentement
hasten ['heɪsən] **1** *vt* (*accelerate*) précipiter; **to h. sb's departure** avancer *ou* hâter le départ de qn
2 *vi* se presser; **I h. to add...** je m'empresse d'ajouter...
hastily ['heɪstɪlɪ] *adv* (*write, prepare*) hâtivement; (*say, eat*) précipitamment; **too h.** trop vite
hasty ['heɪstɪ] *adj* (*departure, removal*) précipité(e); (*meal*) rapide; (*reply, decision*) irréfléchi(e); **to jump to a h. conclusion** conclure à la légère
hat [hæt] *n* chapeau *m*; *also Fig* **to take one's h. off to sb** tirer son chapeau à qn; *Fig* **to pass the h. round** (*collect money*) faire la quête; *Fig* **to throw one's h. in the ring** (*enter contest*) se porter candidat(e); *Fam Fig* **to keep sth under one's h.** garder qch pour soi; *Fig* **I'm speaking with my lawyer's h. on** je parle en ma qualité de juriste; **h. stand** portemanteau *m*; **h. trick** (*of goals*) = trois buts marqués par le même joueur; (*of victories*) triplé *m*
hatch¹ [hætʃ] *n* (*of ship*) écoutille *f*; *Fam* **down the h.!** cul sec!; (*serving*) **h.** passe-plat *m*
hatch² **1** *vt* (*egg*) faire éclore; *Fig* (*scheme, plot*) tramer
2 *vi* (*of egg*) éclore
hatchback ['hætʃbæk] *n* (*car*) (*three-door*) voiture *f* à trois portes, trois-portes *f inv*; (*five-door*) voiture *f* à cinq portes, cinq-portes *f inv*
hatchet ['hætʃɪt] *n* hachette *f*; *Fam* **to do a h. job on sb/sth** (*of critic, reviewer*) démolir qn/qch; *Fam* **h. man** homme *m* de main
hate [heɪt] **1** *n* haine *f*; **h. mail** lettres *fpl* d'injures
2 *vt* détester, haïr; **to h. doing sth** détester faire qch, avoir horreur de faire qch; **she hates to be contradicted** elle a horreur qu'on la contredise; *Fam* **I h. to tell you, but I think you've missed your train** ça

m'ennuie de te le dire, mais je pense que tu as raté ton train
hateful ['heɪtful] *adj* odieux(euse)
hatpin ['hætpɪn] *n* épingle *f* à chapeau
hatred ['heɪtrɪd] *n* haine *f* (**of/for** de/pour)
haughty ['hɔːtɪ] *adj* hautain(e)
haul [hɔːl] **1** *n* (**a**) (*fish caught*) prise *f*; (*loot*) butin *m*; (*of drugs, stolen goods*) saisie *f* (**b**) *Fam* (*journey*) parcours *m*, trajet *m*; **it's a long h.** la route est longue; *Fig* **2** *vt* (**a**) (*pull*) tirer; (*tow*) remorquer; *Fam* **he was hauled in for questioning** on l'a emmené pour l'interroger; *Fam Fig* **to h. sb over the coals** (*reprimand*) passer un savon à qn; **she was hauled up before the headmaster** elle a été convoquée chez le proviseur
(**b**) (*transport*) transporter par camion
haulage ['hɔːlɪdʒ] *n* (*transportation*) transport *m* (*routier*); (*costs*) (*frais mpl de*) transport *m*; **h. firm** entreprise *f* de transports routiers
haulier [hɔːlɪə(r)], *Am* **hauler** ['hɔːlə(r)] *n* (*company*) entreprise *f* de transports routiers
haunch [hɔːntʃ] *n* (*of person*) hanche *f*; (*of venison*) cuissot *m*; **to sit** *or* **squat on one's haunches** être accroupi(e)
haunt [hɔːnt] **1** *n* (*of criminals*) repaire *m*; (*of group of people*) (*lieu m de*) rendez-vous *m*; **it's one of his favourite haunts** (*favourite places*) c'est un des endroits qu'il fréquente habituellement
2 *vt also Fig* hanter
haunted ['hɔːntɪd] *adj* (*castle, room*) hanté(e); *Fig* **he has a h. look** il a l'air égaré
haunting ['hɔːntɪŋ] *adj* obsédant(e)
Havana [hə'vænə] *n* la Havane; **H. (cigar)** havane *m*
have [hæv]

1 *vt* (*pt & pp* **had**) (**a**) (*own*) avoir; **they've (got) a big house** ils ont une grande maison; **she doesn't h.** *or* **hasn't got a car** elle n'a pas de voiture; **I've (got) things to do** j'ai des choses à faire; **you can h. it back tomorrow** je te le rendrai demain; **to h. sb in one's power** tenir qn à sa merci; **to h. it on good authority that...** tenir de source sûre que...
(**b**) (*with noun to denote activity*) **to h. a swim** se baigner; **to h. a shave** se raser; **to h. a bath** prendre un bain; **to h. lunch** déjeuner; **to h. a cigarette** fumer une cigarette; **to h. a drink** prendre un verre; **to h. a good/bad time** passer un bon/mauvais moment
(**c**) (*with illnesses*) **to h. a cold** être enrhumé(e); **to h. flu/cancer** avoir la grippe/un cancer
(**d**) (*cause to do, to be done*) **to h. sb do sth** faire faire qch à qn; **to h. sth done** faire faire qch; **to h. one's hair cut** se faire couper les cheveux; **h. him call me** dis-lui de m'appeler; **I'll h. you know that...!** je vous signale que...!
(**e**) (*in passive constructions*) **I had my watch stolen** on m'a volé ma montre; **three houses had their windows broken** trois des fenêtres brisées dans trois maisons
(**f**) (*allow*) **I won't h. it!** je n'accepte pas ça!; **I won't h. you causing trouble!** pas question que tu fasses des histoires!
(**g**) (*be compelled*) **to h. (got) to do sth** devoir faire qch; **I h.** *or* **I've got to go** je dois y aller; **you don't h. to come with me** tu n'es pas obligé de venir avec moi; **do you h.** *or* **h. you got to work?** est-ce qu'il faut

vraiment que tu travailles?; **it has** or **it's got to be done** il faut que ce soit fait (**h**) Fam (idioms) **to be had** (cheated) se faire avoir; **to h. had it** être fichu(e); **to h. had it with sb/sth** en avoir marre de qn/qch; **he had it coming** ça lui pendait au nez

2 v aux avoir/être

> Most French verbs will conjugate with **avoir** to form the perfect tense. However, all reflexive verbs and many intransitive verbs – mainly of motion – will conjugate with **être**.

to h. seen avoir vu; **to h. left** être parti(e); **to h. hurt oneself** s'être blessé(e); **I've worked here for three years** je travaille ici depuis trois ans; **we've seen this film before – no we haven't!** nous avons déjà vu ce film – mais non!; **you haven't done the dishes – yes, I h.!** tu n'as pas fait la vaisselle – si, je l'ai faite!; **you h. told him, haven't you?** tu le lui as dit, n'est-ce pas ou non?; **you haven't forgotten, h. you?** tu n'as pas oublié, n'est-ce have pas ou hein?

3 n **the haves and the have-nots** les riches mpl et les pauvres mpl

▸**have in** vt sep Fam **to h. it in for sb** en avoir après qn

▸**have off** vt sep Br very Fam **to h. it off (with sb)** (have sexual intercourse) s'envoyer en l'air (avec qn)

▸**have on** vt sep (**a**) (be wearing) porter; **to h. nothing on** être nu(e) (**b**) Fam (fool) **to h. sb on** faire marcher qn (**c**) (have arranged) **to h. a lot on** avoir beaucoup à faire; **to h. nothing on** n'avoir rien de prévu

▸**have out** vt sep (**a**) (have removed) **to h. a tooth out** se faire arracher une dent; **to h. one's appendix out** se faire opérer de l'appendicite (**b**) (resolve) **to h. it out with sb** s'expliquer avec qn

▸**have up** vt sep **to be had up (for sth)** être jugé(e) (pour qch)

haven ['heɪvən] n refuge m

haven't ['hævənt] = have not

haversack ['hævəsæk] n sac m à dos

havoc ['hævək] n (**a**) (damage) ravages mpl, dégâts mpl; **to cause** or **wreak h.** faire des ravages (**b**) (confusion) pagaille f; **to play h. with sth** (plans) chambouler qch

Hawaii [hə'waɪiː] n Hawaii

Hawaiian [hə'waɪən] **1** n Hawaiien(enne) m,f **2** adj hawaiien(enne)

hawk¹ [hɔːk] n also Pol faucon m; **to watch sb/sth like a h.** ne pas quitter qn/qch du regard

hawk² vt **to h. one's wares** (in market, street) vendre ses marchandises à la criée; (from door to door) faire du porte-à-porte

hawk-eyed ['hɔːkaɪd] adj **to be h.** avoir des yeux de lynx

hawkish ['hɔːkɪʃ] adj Pol belliciste

hawser ['hɔːzə(r)] n aussière f

hawthorn ['hɔːθɔːn] n aubépine f

hay [heɪ] n foin m; **to make h.** faire les foins; Fig **to make h. while the sun shines** en profiter tant que ça dure

hayfever ['heɪfiːvə(r)] n rhume m des foins

hayloft ['heɪlɒft] n fenil m

haystack ['heɪstæk] n meule f de foin

haywire ['heɪwaɪə(r)] adv Fam **to go h.** (of plan) mal tourner; (of mechanism) se détraquer

hazard ['hæzəd] **1** n (danger) danger m, risque m; **a fire h.** un risque d'incendie; **a health h.** un danger pour la santé; **h. lights** feux mpl de détresse **2** vt (one's life, fortune) risquer; (opinion) hasarder; **to h. a guess** essayer de deviner

hazardous ['hæzədəs] adj dangereux(euse); (financial venture) hasardeux(euse)

haze [heɪz] n (mist) brume f; (of doubt, confusion) atmosphère f; **my mind was in a h.** j'avais l'esprit embrouillé

hazel ['heɪzəl] **1** n (colour) (couleur f) noisette f; **h. (tree)** noisetier m **2** adj (colour) noisette inv; **h. eyes** yeux mpl (couleur) noisette

hazelnut ['heɪzəlnʌt] n noisette f

hazily ['heɪzɪlɪ] adv vaguement

hazy ['heɪzɪ] adj (weather) brumeux(euse); (image, memory) flou(e), vague; **to be h. about sth** (remember vaguely) n'avoir qu'un vague souvenir de qch

HDTV [eɪtʃdiːtiː'viː] n TV (abbr high-definition television) TVHD f

he [hiː] **1** pron il; **he's Scottish** il est écossais; **he hasn't got it!** ce n'est pas lui qui l'a! **2** n **it's a he** (of animal) c'est un mâle

head [hed] **1** n (**a**) (part of body) tête f; **a fine h. of hair** une belle chevelure; **from h. to foot** or **toe** de la tête aux pieds; **to stand on one's h.** faire le poirier; Fig **to stand sth on its h.** retourner qch; **to win by a h.** (of horse) gagner d'une tête; Fig **she's h. and shoulders above the other candidates** les autres candidats ne lui arrivent pas à la cheville; **h. cold** rhume m de cerveau; **h. start** (advantage) avantage m; (in race) avance f (**b**) (intellect, mind) tête f; **to do sums in one's h.** calculer de tête; **to have a good h. on one's shoulders** avoir la tête sur les épaules; **to have a good h. for business** avoir le sens des affaires; **to have a good h. for figures** être à l'aise avec les chiffres; **to have a (good) h. for heights** ne pas avoir le vertige; **to take it into one's h.** se mettre en tête de faire qch; **to take it into one's h. that...** se mettre dans la tête que...; **it never entered my h. that...** il ne m'est jamais venu à l'esprit que...; **to put ideas into sb's h.** donner des idées à qn; Fam **he's not right in the h.** il a un grain (**c**) (of pin, hammer, list, bed) tête f; (of arrow) pointe f; (of page, stairs) haut m; (of table) bout m; (on beer) mousse f; (on tape recorder) tête f; **a h. of lettuce/cabbage** un pied de laitue/chou; **heads or tails?** (when tossing coin) pile ou face?; **to build up a h. of steam** (of campaign) s'intensifier; (of person) progresser rapidement; **to come to a h.** (of conflict, crisis) atteindre un paroxysme (**d**) (person in charge) (of family, the Church, business) chef m; **h. of state** chef m d'État; Br Sch **h. (teacher)** directeur(trice) m,f; Br Sch **h. boy/girl** = élève choisi parmi les grands pour maintenir la discipline et représenter son école; **h. office** siège m (social); **h. waiter** maître m d'hôtel (**e**) (unit) **£10 per h.** or **a h.** 10 livres par personne; **six h. of cattle** six têtes de bétail (**f**) (idioms) **we put our heads together** nous nous y sommes tous mis; **they'll have your h. (on a plate) for this** cela te coûtera ta tête; **to bury** or **have one's h. in the sand** pratiquer la politique de l'autruche; **to give sb his h.** lâcher la bride à qn; **on your own h. be it** à tes risques et périls; **to go over sb's h.** (appeal to higher authority) ne pas consulter qn (en suivant la voie hiérarchique); Fam **to shout one's h. off** crier à tue-tête; **the wine/praise went to his h.** le

vin/compliment lui est monté à la tête; *Prov* **two heads are better than** deux avis valent mieux qu'un; **off the top of one's h.** au hasard; **it was** *or* **went over my h.** ça m'a dépassé; **I can't make h.** nor **tail of this** ça n'a ni queue ni tête; *Fam* **to lose one's h.** *(panic)* perdre la tête; *(get angry)* perdre son calme; *Fam* **to keep one's h.** garder son calme; *Fam* **to be off one's h.** avoir perdu la boule; **to fall h.** over heels **in love with sb** tomber éperdument amoureux de qn **2** *vt* (**a**) *(lead)* *(organization, campaign)* diriger; *(list)* venir en tête de
(**b**) *(steer)* diriger; **one of the locals headed me in the right direction** un des habitants m'a indiqué la bonne direction
(**c**) *(put a title on)* *(page, chapter)* intituler
(**d**) *(in football)* **to h. the ball** faire une tête
3 *vi* *(move)* se diriger; **they were heading out of town** ils sortaient de la ville
▸**head for** *vt insep* se diriger vers; **you're heading for disaster** tu vas droit au désastre; **you're heading for trouble** tu vas avoir des ennuis
▸**head off 1** *vt sep* *(divert)* éviter
2 *vi* *(depart)* partir
headache ['hedeɪk] *n* mal *m* de tête; *Fig* *(problem)* casse-tête *m inv*; **to have a h.** avoir mal à la tête
headband ['hedbænd] *n* bandeau *m*
headboard ['hedbɔːd] *n* tête *f* de lit
headbutt ['hedbʌt] *vt* donner un coup de tête à
headcase ['hedkeɪs] *n Fam* cinglé(e) *m,f*
headdress ['heddres] *n* coiffure *f*
headed ['hedɪd] *adj* **h. (note)paper** papier *m* à en-tête
header ['hedə(r)] *n* (**a**) *Typ* en-tête *m* (**b**) *(in football)* *(coup m de)* tête *f*
headfirst ['hedfɜːst] *adv* la tête la première
headgear ['hedɡɪə(r)] *n* couvre-chef *m*
head-hunt ['hedhʌnt] *vt Com* **to be head-hunted** être recruté(e) par un chasseur de têtes
head-hunter ['hedhʌntə(r)] *n Com* chasseur *m* de têtes
heading ['hedɪŋ] *n* *(of chapter, article)* titre *m*; *(of letter)* en-tête *m*; **it comes** *or* **falls under the h. of...** c'est à mettre sous la rubrique de...
headlamp ['hedlæmp] *n* *(on car)* phare *m*
headland ['hedlənd] *n* cap *m*, pointe *f*
headlight ['hedlaɪt] *n* *(on car)* phare *m*
headline ['hedlaɪn] **1** *n* *(of TV news)* titre *m*; *(of newspaper)* *(gros)* titre *m*; **to hit the headlines** faire la une des journaux; **to be h. news** faire la une des journaux
2 *vt* *(article, story)* intituler
headlong ['hedlɒŋ] **1** *adj* **there was a h. rush for the bar** tout le monde s'est rué vers le bar
2 *adv* *(fall)* la tête la première; *(rush)* tête baissée
headmaster [hed'mɑːstə(r)] *n Br Sch* directeur *m*
headmistress [hed'mɪstrɪs] *n Br Sch* directrice *f*
head-on ['he'dɒn] *adj & adv* de front; **to meet sb h.** aborder qn de front; **a h. collision** une collision frontale
headphones ['hedfəʊnz] *npl* écouteurs *mpl*
headquarters [hed'kwɔːtəz] *npl* *(of organization)* siège *m* *(social)*; *Mil* quartier *m* général
headrest ['hedrest] *n* appui-tête *m inv*
headroom ['hedruːm] *n* *(under bridge, inside car)* hauteur *f*
headscarf ['hedskɑːf] *(pl* **headscarves** ['hedskɑːvz]*) n* foulard *m*
headset ['hedset] *n* écouteurs *mpl*
headstone ['hedstəʊn] *n* *(on grave)* pierre *f* tombale

headstrong ['hedstrɒŋ] *adj* têtu(e), entêté(e)
headway ['hedweɪ] *n* **to make h.** avancer, faire des progrès
headwind ['hedwɪnd] *n* vent *m* contraire; *Naut* vent *m* debout
heady ['hedɪ] *adj* *(atmosphere)* enivrant(e); *(wine, perfume)* capiteux(euse); *(heights, days)* grisant(e)
heal [hiːl] **1** *vt* *(wound, person)* guérir; *(disagreement)* régler; *Fig* **wounds which only time would h.** des blessures que seul le temps cicatriserait
2 *vi* *(of wound)* **to h. (up** *or* **over)** cicatriser
health [helθ] *n* santé *f*; **to be in good/poor h.** être en bonne/mauvaise santé; *Fig* **the economy is in good h.** l'économie se porte bien; **the Department of H.** ≃ le ministère de la Santé; **to drink (to) sb's h.** boire à la santé de qn; **h. care** soins *mpl* médicaux; *Br* **h. centre** dispensaire *m*; **h. club** club *m* de remise en forme; **h. cover** *(insurance)* assurance *f* médicale; **h. farm** centre *m* de remise en forme; **h. food** produits *mpl* biologiques; **h. hazard** *or* **risk** risque *m* pour la santé; **h. insurance** assurance *f* maladie; **h. resort** station *f* climatique; *(by sea)* station *f* balnéaire; **the H. Service** ≃ la Sécurité *f* sociale; **h. visitor** = infirmière effectuant des visites de contrôle à domicile
healthy ['helθɪ] *adj* *(person)* en bonne santé; *(climate)* salubre; *(food, habit, economy)* sain(e); **a h. appetite** un bon appétit; **it is a h. sign that...** c'est bon signe que...; **he has a h. respect for his opponents** il apprécie ses adversaires à leur juste valeur
heap [hiːp] **1** *n* tas *m*; *Fig* **people at the top/bottom of the h.** ceux qui sont en haut/bas de l'échelle sociale; *Fam* **she's got heaps of money** elle a plein d'argent; *Fam* **we've got heaps of time** on a largement le temps
2 *vt* entasser; **his plate was heaped with food** son assiette était remplie de nourriture; **to h. sth with** remplir qch de; **a heaped spoonful** *(in recipe)* une cuillerée bien pleine; **to h. riches/praise on sb** couvrir qn de richesses/d'éloges; **to h. insults on sb** abreuver qn d'injures
hear [hɪə(r)] *(pt & pp heard [hɜːd]*) **1** *vt* (**a**) *(perceive)* entendre; **to h. sb speak** entendre qn parler; **I can hardly h. myself think!** on ne s'entend plus ici!; **to make oneself heard** se faire entendre; **let's h. it for...** applaudissons bien fort...; **have you heard the one about...?** est-ce que tu connais celle de...? (**b**) *(listen to)* écouter; **h., h.!** *(at meeting)* bravo!; *Law* **to h. a case** juger une affaire (**c**) *(find out)* entendre *(dire)*, apprendre; **have you heard the news?** tu connais la nouvelle?; **I h. you're getting married** j'ai entendu dire que tu te mariais
2 *vi* entendre; **I can't h. properly** je n'entends pas bien; **to h. from sb** avoir des nouvelles de qn; **you'll be hearing from my lawyer!** vous allez entendre parler de mon avocat!; **to h. of** *or* **about sth** entendre parler de qch; **I won't h. of it!** je ne veux pas en entendre parler!
▸**hear out** *vt sep* **to h. sb out** écouter qn jusqu'au bout
hearing ['hɪərɪŋ] *n* (**a**) *(sense)* ouïe *f*, audition *f*; **h. aid** audiophone *m* (**b**) *(earshot)* **to be within/out of h.** être à portée/hors de portée de voix (**c**) *(chance to explain)* **to give sb a fair h.** laisser parler qn, laisser qn s'expliquer (**d**) *Law* *(inquiry)* audition *f*
hearsay ['hɪəseɪ] *n* ouï-dire *m inv*, on-dit *m inv*; *Law* **h. evidence** déposition *f* sur la foi d'autrui
hearse [hɜːs] *n* corbillard *m*

heart [hɑːt] *n* (**a**) *(organ)* cœur *m*; **to have h. trouble, to have a weak** *or* **bad h.** être cardiaque; **h. attack** crise *f* cardiaque; **h. disease** maladie *f* cardiaque; **h. failure** arrêt *m* cardiaque; **h. surgeon** chirurgien(enne) *m,f* cardiologique; **h. surgery** chirurgie *f* cardiaque; **h. transplant** transplantation *f* cardiaque (**b**) *(seat of the emotions)* cœur *m*; **to have a big h.** avoir bon cœur; **a h. of gold** un cœur d'or; **a h. of stone** un cœur de pierre; **have a h.!** ayez un peu de cœur!; **her h.'s in the right place** elle a bon cœur; **with a heavy h.** le cœur gros; **my h. sank** j'ai été très déçu; **to have one's h. in one's mouth** être terrorisé(e); **to break sb's h.** briser le cœur à qn; **to wear one's h. on one's sleeve** ne pas cacher ses sentiments; **affairs** *or* **matters of the h.** affaires *fpl* de cœur; *Ironic* **my h. bleeds for you** ça me fait de la peine pour toi; **in my h. of hearts** au fond de mon cœur; **from the bottom of one's h.** du fond du cœur; **he loved her with all his h.** il l'aimait de toute son âme; **at h.** au fond; **to have sb's welfare/interests at h.** avoir le bien-être/les intérêts de qn à cœur; **to take sth to h.** prendre qch à cœur; **to set one's h. on sth** vouloir qch à tout prix; **he's a man after my own h.** il est comme moi; **to one's h.'s content** tout son soûl (**c**) *(enthusiasm, courage)* **to take h.** reprendre courage; **to lose h.** se décourager; **he tried to convince them but his h. wasn't in it** il a essayé de les convaincre mais le cœur n'y était pas; **I didn't have the h. to tell him** je n'ai pas eu le cœur de lui dire (**d**) **by h.** *(know, learn)* par cœur (**e**) *(centre) (of city, forest)* cœur *m*; **the h. of the matter** le fond du problème (**f**) *(in cards)* **hearts** cœur *m*

heartache ['hɑːteɪk] *n* chagrin *m*, peine *f*

heartbeat ['hɑːbiːt] *n (rhythm)* pouls *m*; *(single beat)* battement *m* de cœur

heartbreaking ['hɑːbreɪkɪŋ] *adj* déchirant(e), navrant(e)

heartbroken ['hɑːbrəʊkən] *adj* **to be h.** avoir le cœur brisé

heartburn ['hɑːbɜːn] *n (indigestion)* brûlures *fpl* d'estomac

hearten ['hɑːtən] *vt* encourager

heartening ['hɑːtənɪŋ] *adj* encourageant(e)

heartfelt ['hɑːtfelt] *adj* sincère, qui vient du cœur

hearth [hɑːθ] *n (fireplace, home)* foyer *m*

hearthrug ['hɑːθrʌg] *n* devant *m* de foyer

heartily ['hɑːtɪlɪ] *adv (welcome, applaud)* chaleureusement; *(agree)* de tout cœur; *(eat)* avec appétit; **to be h. sick of sth** être profondément dégoûté(e) de qch

heartlands ['hɑːtlændz] *npl* centre *m*, cœur *m*

heartless ['hɑːtlɪs] *adj* sans cœur, cruel(elle)

heartrending ['hɑːtrendɪŋ] *adj* déchirant(e), navrant(e)

heart-searching ['hɑːtsɜːtʃɪŋ] *n* **after much h.** après avoir longuement réfléchi

heartstrings ['hɑːtstrɪŋz] *npl* **to tug at sb's h.** jouer sur la corde sensible de qn

heart-throb ['hɑːtθrɒb] *n Fam* idole *f*

heart-to-heart ['hɑːtə'hɑːt] *n* **to have a h. with sb** avoir une conversation à cœur ouvert avec qn

heart-warming ['hɑːtwɔːmɪŋ] *adj* réconfortant(e), qui réchauffe le cœur

hearty ['hɑːtɪ] *adj* (**a**) *(person, laugh)* jovial(e); *(approval, welcome)* chaleureux(euse); **to have a h. dislike of sth** avoir une sainte horreur de qch; **my heartiest congratulations** mes plus sincères félicitations (**b**) *(substantial) (meal, appetite)* solide

heat [hiːt] **1** *n* (**a**) *(high temperature)* chaleur *f*; **to give out h.** dégager de la chaleur; **to cook at a moderate/low h.** faire cuire à feu moyen/doux; **h. exhaustion** coup *m* de chaleur; **h. haze** brume *f* de chaleur; **h. loss** déperdition *f* de chaleur; **h. rash** boutons *mpl* de chaleur; *Med* **h. treatment** thermothérapie *f* (**b**) *(passion)* feu *m*; **in the h. of the moment/argument** dans le feu de l'action/de la discussion (**c**) *Fam (pressure)* **to turn up the h.** mettre la pression; **the h. is on** la tension est à son comble (**d**) *(of female animal)* **in** *or* **on h.** en chaleur (**e**) *(in sport)* éliminatoire *f* **2** *vt (food, water)* faire chauffer; *(room, building)* chauffer

▸**heat up** *vt sep* réchauffer **2** *vi (of water)* chauffer; *(of room)* se réchauffer; *Fig (of argument, contest)* s'animer

heated ['hiːtɪd] *adj* (**a**) *(room, building, swimming pool)* chauffé(e) (**b**) *(argument)* animé(e); **to become h.** *(of person)* s'échauffer

heater ['hiːtə(r)] *n* radiateur *m*

heath [hiːθ] *n (land)* lande *f*

heathen ['hiːðən] *n Rel* païen(enne) *m,f*; *Hum* barbare *mf*

heather ['heðə(r)] *n* bruyère *f*

heating ['hiːtɪŋ] *n* chauffage *m*

heatproof ['hiːtpruːf] *adj* résistant(e) à la chaleur; *(clothing)* isolant(e)

heatstroke ['hiːtstrəʊk] *n* coup *m* de chaleur

heatwave ['hiːtweɪv] *n* vague *f* de chaleur

heave [hiːv] **1** *n* effort *m* **2** *vt* (**a**) *(pull)* tirer fort; *(push)* pousser fortement; *(lift)* soulever avec effort; **she heaved herself out of her chair** elle s'extirpa de sa chaise; **to h. a sigh of relief** pousser un soupir de soulagement (**b**) *Fam (throw)* balancer **3** *vi* (**a**) *(pull)* **they heaved on the rope** ils tirèrent sur la corde fortement (**b**) *(of deck, ground)* tanguer, se soulever; *(of bosom)* se soulever (**c**) *(retch)* avoir des haut-le-cœur; *(vomit)* vomir (**d**) *(pt & pp* **hove** [həʊv]) *also Fig* **to h. into view** paraître à l'horizon

▸**heave to** *(pt & pp* **hove** [həʊv]) *vi Naut* se mettre en panne

heaven ['hevən] *n* paradis *m*, ciel *m*; **in h.** au paradis, au ciel; *Fig (overjoyed)* aux anges; **this is h.!** c'est le paradis!; **to move h. and earth to do sth** remuer ciel et terre pour faire qch; **the heavens opened** il s'est mis à pleuvoir à torrents; *Fam* **it stinks to high h.** ça pue; **(good) heavens!, heavens above!** juste ciel!, mon Dieu!; **thank h. (for that)!** Dieu merci!; **h. knows why...** Dieu seul sait pourquoi...; **for h.'s sake!** pour l'amour du ciel!; **h. forbid!** que le ciel nous en préserve!

heavenly ['hevənlɪ] *adj* (**a**) **h. body** corps *m* céleste (**b**) *Fam (weather, food)* divin(e)

heaven-sent ['hevənsent] *adj* providentiel(elle)

heavily ['hevɪlɪ] *adv (fall, walk, tax)* lourdement; *(sleep)* profondément; *(breathe)* bruyamment; **to drink/smoke h.** boire/fumer beaucoup; **it was raining h.** il pleuvait à torrents; **to rely** *or* **depend h. on** dépendre beaucoup de; **h. built** solidement charpenté(e); **to be h. defeated** subir une lourde défaite

heaving ['hiːvɪŋ] *adj Br Fam (very busy)* hyper animé(e)

heavy ['hevɪ] **1** *n (pl* **heavies**) *Fam (tough guy)* dur *m* **2** *adj* (**a**) *(in weight, food)* lourd(e); **how h. is it?** combien est-ce que ça pèse?; **a h. blow** un coup violent; *Fig* un coup rude; **h. goods vehicle** poids lourd; **h. industry** industrie *f* lourde; **h. metal** *Chem* métal *m* lourd; *(music)* heavy metal *m* (**b**) *(large, thick) (coat, shoes)* gros (grosse); **h. losses** lourdes pertes *fpl* (**c**) *(intense) (fighting)* violent(e); *(rain, showers)* fort(e); *(drinker, smoker)* gros (grosse); **a h. cold** un gros rhume; **there was h. traffic** il y avait beaucoup de circulation; **to be a h. sleeper** avoir le sommeil lourd; **to come under h. fire** essuyer un feu nourri (**d**) *(oppressive) (smell)* fort(e); *(sky, fine, sentence)* lourd(e); **h. responsibility** lourde responsabilité *f* (**e**) *(hard) (work, day, breathing)* pénible; **it was h. going** c'était difficile *ou* ardu; **h. seas** grosse mer *f* (**f**) *Fam (threatening) (situation)* difficile, pénible; **to get h. with sb** être agressif(ive) avec qn (**g**) *Fam (serious) (book, article)* intello

heavy-duty [hevɪˈdjuːtɪ] *adj (machine)* à usage industriel; *(clothing, boots)* résistant(e)

heavy-handed [hevɪˈhændɪd] *adj (clumsy)* maladroit(e); *(government, policy)* autoritaire; **the police responded in a h. way** la police est intervenue de façon très agressive

heavyweight [ˈhevɪweɪt] *n (in boxing)* poids *m* lourd; *Fig* **a political h.** un grand ponte de la politique; **an intellectual h.** un(e) grand(e) intellectuel(elle)

Hebrew [ˈhiːbruː] **1** *n (language)* hébreu *m* **2** *adj* hébraïque

Hebrides [ˈhebrɪdiːz] *npl* **the H.** les (îles *fpl*) Hébrides *fpl*

heck [hek] *n Fam* **h.!** zut!; **what the h. are you doing here?** qu'est-ce que tu fiches là?; **what the h.!** et puis flûte!; **a h. of a lot** des masses

heckle [ˈhekəl] **1** *vt* interpeller, interrompre **2** *vi* chahuter

heckler [ˈheklə(r)] *n* chahuteur(euse) *m,f*

heckling [ˈheklɪŋ] *n* chahut *m*

hectare [ˈhektɑː(r)] *n* hectare *m*

hectic [ˈhektɪk] *adj (busy)* agité(e); *(eventful)* mouvementé(e); **a h. life** une vie trépidante

hector [ˈhektə(r)] *vt* rudoyer

hectoring [ˈhektərɪŋ] *adj* autoritaire

he'd [hiːd] = **he had, he would**

hedge [hedʒ] **1** *n* (**a**) *(in field, garden)* haie *f* (**b**) *(barrier)* **a h. against inflation** une protection contre l'inflation **2** *vt* (**a**) *(field)* entourer d'une haie (**b**) **to h. one's bets** se couvrir **3** *vi (in discussion)* ne pas se mouiller

hedgehog [ˈhedʒhɒg] *n* hérisson *m*

hedgerow [ˈhedʒrəʊ] *n* haie *f*

hedonism [ˈhedənɪzəm, ˈhiːdənɪzəm] *n* hédonisme *m*

hedonist [ˈhedənɪst, ˈhiːdənɪst] **1** *n* hédoniste *mf* **2** *adj* hédoniste

heed [hiːd] **1** *n* **to pay (no) h. to, to take (no) h. of** (ne pas) tenir compte de **2** *vt (warning, advice)* tenir compte de

heedless [ˈhiːdlɪs] *adj* **to be h. of** ne pas tenir compte de

heel [hiːl] **1** *n (of foot, shoe, sock)* talon *m*; **high heels** talons *mpl* hauts; **he had the police at his heels** il avait la police sur les talons *ou* à ses trousses; **to take to one's heels** prendre ses jambes à son cou; **to turn on one's h.** tourner les talons; *Fam* **to cool** *or* **kick one's heels** *(wait)* poireauter; *Fig* **to bring sb to h.** *(bring under control)* mettre qn au pas **2** *vt (shoe)* réparer le talon de

hefty [ˈheftɪ] *adj Fam (person)* costaud(e); *(suitcase, box)* lourd(e); *(blow)* puissant(e); *(bill, fine)* gros (grosse)

heifer [ˈhefə(r)] *n* génisse *f*

height [haɪt] *n (of building, tree)* hauteur *f*; *(of mountain)* altitude *f*; *(of person)* taille *f*; **what h. are you?** combien mesurez-vous?; **to gain/lose h.** *(of plane)* prendre/perdre de l'altitude; **to be afraid of heights** avoir le vertige; **she's at the h. of her powers** elle est au maximum de ses capacités; **she's at the h. of her career** elle est à l'apogée de sa carrière; **the h. of fashion** la dernière mode; **it's the h. of madness!** c'est de la folie pure!; **at the h. of the storm** au plus fort de l'orage; **the season is at its h.** la saison bat son plein

heighten [ˈhaɪtən] *vt (sensation)* intensifier; *(tension)* augmenter; **to h. public awareness** sensibiliser l'opinion

heinous [ˈheɪnəs] *adj Formal (crime)* abominable, atroce

heir [eə(r)] *n* héritier(ère) *m,f*; **to be h. to sth** être l'héritier(ère) *m,f* de qch; **h. apparent** héritier(ère) *m,f* présomptif(ive)

heiress [ˈeərɪs] *n* héritière *f*

heirloom [ˈeəluːm] *n* **a family h.** un objet de famille

held [held] *pt & pp of* **hold**

helicopter [ˈhelɪkɒptə(r)] *n* hélicoptère *m*

heliport [ˈhelɪpɔːt] *n* héliport *m*

helium [ˈhiːlɪəm] *n* hélium *m*

hell [hel] *n* (**a**) *Rel* enfer *m*; *Fam* **h.!** zut alors! (**b**) *Fam (for emphasis)* **a h. of a price** un prix salé; **what the h. do you think you're doing?** qu'est-ce que tu fous?; **who the h. are you?** qui diable êtes-vous?; **she put up a h. of a fight** elle s'est bien défendue; **to have a h. of a time** *(good)* s'éclater; *(bad)* en baver; **a h. of a lot of...** énormément de...; **he's one** *or* **a h. of a guy** c'est un brave type (**c**) *Fam (idioms)* **it was h.** c'était l'enfer; **to feel like h.** se sentir horriblement mal; **to make sb's life h.** faire de la vie de qn un enfer; **these shoes are giving me h.** ces chaussures me font un mal de chien; **all h. broke loose** ce fut le chaos; **there'll be h. to pay if...** ça va barder si...; **go to h.!** va te faire voir!; **to run like h.** courir comme un dératé; **like h. (I will)!** certainement pas!; **until h. freezes over** jusqu'à la saint-glinglin; **come h. or high water** quoi qu'il arrive; **to run h. for leather** courir ventre à terre; **to do sth for the h. of it** faire qch sans raison particulière

he'll [hiːl] = **he will, he shall**

hellbent [ˈhelbent] *adj Fam* **to be h. on doing sth** vouloir à tout prix faire qch

hellhole [ˈhelhəʊl] *n Fam (bar, club)* bouge *m*; *(prison)* enfer *m*

hellish [ˈhelɪʃ] *adj Fam* infernal(e)

hello [heˈləʊ] *exclam* bonjour!; *(on phone)* allô!; **to say h. to sb** dire bonjour à qn; **h., what's this?** *(indicating surprise)* tiens, qu'est-ce que c'est que ça?

hell-raiser [ˈhelreɪzə(r)] *n Fam* perturbateur(trice) *m,f*

helm [helm] *n (of ship)* barre *f*; *also Fig* **to be at the h.** être à la barre

helmet [ˈhelmɪt] *n* casque *m*

helmsman [ˈhelmzmən] *n* timonier *m*

help [help] **1** *n* (**a**) *(aid)* aide *f*; **to shout for h.** crier à l'aide; **h.!** à l'aide!, au secours!; **to be of h. to sb** aider qn; **thank you, you've been a great h.** merci beaucoup de votre aide; **there was no h. for it** il n'y avait rien à faire; **with the h. of sth** *(implement)* à l'aide de qch; **with the h. of sb** *(person)* avec l'aide de qn; **h. desk** service *m* d'assistance téléphonique; *Comput* **h. file** fichier *m* d'aide (**b**) *(cleaning woman)* femme *f* de ménage **2** *vt* (**a**) *(aid)* aider; **to h. sb (to) do sth** aider qn à

faire qch; **to h. sb to their feet** aider qn à se mettre debout; **to h. sb on/off with his coat** aider qn à mettre/enlever son manteau; **to h. one another** s'entraider; **to h. oneself to sth** se servir en *ou* de qch; **h. yourself!** servez-vous! (**b**) *(prevent)* **I can't h. it** je ne peux pas m'en empêcher; **it can't be helped** on n'y peut rien; **I couldn't h.** laughing/overhearing je ne pouvais pas m'empêcher de rire/d'écouter; **he can't h.** being bald ce n'est pas de sa faute s'il est chauve; **not if I can h. it!** pas si je peux l'éviter!
3 *vi* aider; **can I h.?** puis-je vous aider?; **that doesn't h.** very much cela ne nous avance pas beaucoup
▸**help out** *vt sep & vi* aider
helper ['helpə(r)] *n* aide *mf*, assistant(e) *m,f*
helpful ['helpfʊl] *adj (person)* serviable; *(advice, device, book)* utile; **to be h.** *(of person)* se rendre utile, aider
helpfully ['helpfʊlɪ] *adv* obligeamment
helping ['helpɪŋ] **1** *n (portion)* part *f*, portion *f*; **I had a second h. of spaghetti** je me suis resservi des spaghettis
2 *adj* **to lend a h. hand** donner un coup de main
helpless ['helplɪs] *adj (powerless)* impuissant(e); *(invalid)* impotent(e); **we were h. to prevent it** nous n'avons pas pu l'empêcher; **to be h. with laughter** être plié(e) de rire
helplessly ['helplɪslɪ] *adv (watch)* sans pouvoir agir; *(struggle)* en vain
helpline [helplaɪn] *n* service *m* d'assistance téléphonique
Helsinki [hel'sɪŋkɪ] *n* Helsinki
helter-skelter ['heltə'skeltə(r)] **1** *n (at fairground)* toboggan *m*
2 *adv* **to run h.** courir comme un fou (une folle); **to fall h.** faire une chute spectaculaire
hem [hem] **1** *n* ourlet *m*
2 *vt (pt & pp* hemmed*)* ourler
▸**hem in** *vt sep (surround)* cerner
he-man ['hiːmæn] *n Fam* homme *m* viril
hemisphere ['hemɪsfɪə(r)] *n* hémisphère *m*
hemline ['hemlaɪn] *n* ourlet *m*
hemlock ['hemlɒk] *n* ciguë *f*
hemoglobin, hemophilia *etc Am* = **haemoglobin, haemophilia** *etc*
hemorrhage, hemorrhoids *Am* = **haemorrhage, haemorrhoids**
hemp [hemp] *n* chanvre *m*
hen [hen] *n* poule *f*; *Br Fam* **h. night, h. party** = soirée organisée entre amies avant le mariage de l'une d'entre elles; **she's having her h. night** elle enterre sa vie de célibataire

Hen night

En Grande-Bretagne, le phénomène des "hen nights" est une tradition bien établie. Il s'agit d'une sorte de rite de passage pour enterrer sa vie de jeune fille. La future mariée part en virée nocturne avec ses amies ; souvent toutes portent des déguisements identiques. Généralement abondamment arrosées, ces soirées se prolongent jusqu'au petit matin dans une ambiance de fête et peuvent comporter des strip-teaseurs et d'autres divertissements. Parfois les "hen nights" prennent la forme d'un week-end dépaysant passé entre copines dans une autre ville ou même à l'étranger. L'équivalent masculin de la "hen night" est la "**stag party**" *(voir l'entrée* **stag***)*.

hence [hens] *adv* (**a**) *(thus)* d'où; **h. his anger** d'où sa colère (**b**) *(from now)* d'ici; **five years h.** d'ici cinq ans
henceforth [hens'fɔːθ] *adv Formal* dès lors, désormais
henchman ['henʃmən] *n Pej* acolyte *m*
hencoop ['henkuːp] *n* cage *f* à poules
henhouse ['henhaʊs] *n* poulailler *m*
henna ['henə] *n* henné *m*
henpecked ['henpekt] *adj* mené(e) par le bout du nez
hepatitis [hepə'taɪtɪs] *n* hépatite *f*
her [*unstressed* hə(r), *stressed* hɜː(r)] **1** *pron* (**a**) *(direct object)* la; **I hate h.** je la déteste; **I love h.** je l'aime; **I can understand her son but not** HER je comprends son fils, mais elle, je ne la comprends pas (**b**) *(indirect object)* lui; **I gave h. the book** je lui ai donné le livre; **I gave it to h.** je le lui ai donné (**c**) *(after preposition)* elle; **I'm thinking of h.** je pense à elle (**d**) *(as complement of verb* **to be***)* elle; **it's h.!** c'est elle!; **it was h. who did it** c'est elle qui l'a fait
2 *possessive adj* (**a**) *(singular)* son (sa); *(plural)* ses; **h. husband** son mari; **h. family** sa famille; **h. parents** ses parents; **it wasn't** HER **idea!** ce n'est pas elle qui en a eu l'idée! (**b**) *(for parts of body)* **she hit h. head** elle s'est cogné la tête
herald ['herəld] **1** *n (messenger)* héraut *m*; *Fig (sign)* signe *m* avant-coureur
2 *vt* annoncer
heraldry ['herəldrɪ] *n* héraldique *f*
herb [hɜːb] *n* herbe *f* aromatique
herbal ['hɜːbəl] *adj* à base de plantes; **h. tea** tisane *f*
herbalist ['hɜːbəlɪst] *n* herboriste *mf*
herbicide ['hɜːbɪsaɪd] *n* herbicide *m*
herbivorous [hɜː'bɪvərəs] *adj* herbivore
herd [hɜːd] **1** *n (of cattle, sheep, elephants)* troupeau *m*; *(of horses)* troupe *f*; *(of people)* groupe *m*; *Pej* troupeau *m*; **the h. instinct** l'instinct *m* grégaire
2 *vt (cattle, people)* rassembler
herdsman ['hɜːdzmən] *n* gardien *m* de troupeau
here [hɪə(r)] **1** *adv* ici; **over h.** par ici; **h. it/he is** le voilà; **h.!** *(at roll call)* présent!; **come h.!** viens ici!; **h., come and look at this!** eh! viens voir ça!; **she's not h.** elle n'est pas là; **h. she comes** la voilà; **h. and now** immédiatement; **h. and there** çà et là; *Fig* **that's neither h. nor there** ça n'a aucun rapport; **what have we h.?** qu'est-ce que c'est que ça?; **h.'s what you have to do** voilà ce que tu as à faire; **h. goes!** allons-y!; **h.'s to the future!** à l'avenir!
2 *n* **the h. and now** le présent
hereafter [hɪər'ɑːftə(r)] **1** *n Lit* **the h.** l'au-delà *m*
2 *adv Formal (below)* ci-après; *(in the future)* dorénavant
hereby [hɪə'baɪ] *adv Formal (in writing)* par la présente; *(in speech)* solennellement
hereditary [hɪ'redɪtərɪ] *adj* héréditaire
heredity [hɪ'redɪtɪ] *n* hérédité *f*
heresy ['herəsɪ] *(pl* heresies*)* *n* hérésie *f*
heretic ['herətɪk] *n* hérétique *mf*
heretical [hɪ'retɪkəl] *adj* hérétique
heritage ['herɪtɪdʒ] *n* patrimoine *m*
hermaphrodite [hɜː'mæfrədaɪt] **1** *n* hermaphrodite *mf*
2 *adj* hermaphrodite
hermetic [hɜː'metɪk] *adj* hermétique
hermetically [hɜː'metɪklɪ] *adv* hermétiquement

hermit ['hɜːmɪt] n ermite m; **h. crab** bernard-l'ermite m inv

hernia ['hɜːnɪə] n hernie f

hero ['hɪərəʊ] (pl **heroes**) n héros m; **h. worship** adulation f, idolâtrie f

heroic [hɪ'rəʊɪk] adj héroïque

heroically [hɪ'rəʊɪklɪ] adv héroïquement

heroics [hɪ'rəʊɪks] npl coup m d'éclat

heroin ['herəʊɪn] n (drug) héroïne f; **h. addict** héroïnomane mf

heroine ['herəʊɪn] n (female hero) héroïne f

heroism ['herəʊɪzəm] n héroïsme m

heron ['herən] n héron m

hero-worship ['hɪərəʊwɜːʃɪp] (pt & pp **hero-worshipped**) vt idolâtrer

herpes ['hɜːpiːz] n herpès m

herring ['herɪŋ] (pl **herring** or **herrings**) n hareng m

hers [hɜːz] possessive pron (**a**) (singular) le sien (la sienne) m,f; (plural) les siens (les siennes) mpl, fpl; **my house is big, but h. is bigger** j'ai une grande maison, mais la sienne est plus grande encore (**b**) (used attributively) **this book is h.** ce livre est à elle; **a friend of h.** un de ses amis; **where's that brother of h.?** où son frère a-t-il bien pu passer?

herself [hɜː'self] pron (**a**) (reflexive) **she spoils h.** elle se gâte; **she hurt h.** elle s'est blessée (**b**) (emphatic) elle-même; **she h. has never...** elle-même n'a jamais...; **she told me h.** elle me l'a dit elle-même; **she's not h. today** elle n'est pas dans son état normal aujourd'hui (**c**) (after preposition) **she lives by h.** elle vit seule; **she bought it for h.** elle se l'est acheté; **she talks to h.** elle parle toute seule

he's [hiːz] = he is, he has

hesitancy ['hezɪtənsɪ] n hésitation f

hesitant ['hezɪtənt] adj hésitant(e); **to be h. about doing sth** hésiter à faire qch

hesitate ['hezɪteɪt] vi hésiter

hesitation [hezɪ'teɪʃən] n hésitation f; **without h.** sans hésitation, sans hésiter

heterogeneous [hetərə'dʒiːnɪəs] adj hétérogène

heterosexual [hetərəʊ'seksjʊəl] **1** n hétérosexuel(elle) m,f

2 adj hétérosexuel(elle)

heterosexuality [hetərəʊseksjʊ'ælɪtɪ] n hétérosexualité

het up ['hetʌp] adj Br Fam énervé(e); **to get h. (about sth)** se mettre dans tous ses états (pour qch)

heuristics [hjuː'rɪstɪks] npl heuristique f

hew [hjuː] (pp **hewn** [hjuːn] or **hewed**) vt (wood) couper; (rock) tailler

hexagon ['heksəgən] n hexagone m

hexagonal [hek'sægənəl] adj hexagonal(e)

hey [heɪ] exclam eh!; **h. presto!** le tour est joué!

heyday ['heɪdeɪ] n apogée m; **in its h.** à son apogée; **in his h.** au sommet de sa gloire

HGV [eɪtʃdʒiː'viː] n Br (abbr **heavy goods vehicle**) PL m; **H. licence** permis m PL

hi [haɪ] exclam Fam salut!

hiatus [haɪ'eɪtəs] n (interruption) interruption f; (in conversation) silence m; (in manuscript, records) lacune f

hibernate ['haɪbəneɪt] vi hiberner

hibernation [haɪbə'neɪʃən] n hibernation f; **to go into h.** entrer en hibernation

hiccup ['hɪkʌp] **1** n hoquet m; Fig (in plan) accroc m; **to have (the) hiccups** avoir le hoquet

2 vi avoir le hoquet; (once) avoir un hoquet

hick [hɪk] n Am Fam péquenaud(e) m,f

hickory ['hɪkərɪ] (pl **hickories**) n (tree, wood) hickory m, noyer m blanc d'Amérique

hid [hɪd] pt of **hide¹**

hidden ['hɪdən] **1** adj caché(e); **h. agenda** programme m secret

2 pp of **hide¹**

hide¹ [haɪd] **1** n (for birdwatching) affût m

2 vt (pt **hid** [hɪd], pp **hidden** ['hɪdən]) cacher (**from** à); **to have nothing to h.** n'avoir rien à cacher; **to be hidden from sight** être caché(e); **to h. oneself** se cacher

3 vi se cacher (**from** de)

hide² n (skin) peau f; Fig **to save one's h.** sauver sa peau; **I haven't seen h. nor hair of her** je ne l'ai pas vue du tout

hide-and-seek [haɪdən'siːk] n cache-cache m; **to play h.** jouer à cache-cache

hidebound ['haɪdbaʊnd] adj rigide, borné(e)

hideous ['hɪdɪəs] adj (ugly) hideux(euse); (horrific) horrible

hideously ['hɪdɪəslɪ] adv horriblement, affreusement

hide-out ['haɪdaʊt] n cachette f

hiding¹ ['haɪdɪŋ] n (concealment) **to be in h.** se cacher; **to go into h.** se cacher; **to come out of h.** sortir de sa cachette; (after war) sortir de la clandestinité; **h. place** cachette f

hiding² n Fam (beating) raclée f; **to give sb a h.** donner une raclée à qn; Fig **to be on a h. to nothing** n'avoir aucune chance

hierarchical [haɪə'rɑːkɪkəl] adj hiérarchique

hierarchy ['haɪərɑːkɪ] (pl **hierarchies**) n hiérarchie f

hieroglyphics [haɪərə'glɪfɪks] npl hiéroglyphes mpl

hi-fi ['haɪfaɪ] n hi-fi f inv; (stereo system) chaîne f (hi-fi)

higgledy-piggledy ['hɪgəldɪ'pɪgəldɪ] Fam **1** adj en désordre

2 adv pêle-mêle

high [haɪ] **1** n (**a**) (peak) (in career, performance) sommet m; (in quantity, degree) maximum m; **unemployment has reached a new h.** le chômage a atteint un nouveau record; **to be on a h.** (from drugs) planer; (from success) être sur un petit nuage; **the highs and lows** les hauts mpl et les bas mpl (**b**) (weather front) anticyclone m

2 adj (**a**) (mountain, building) haut(e), élevé(e); **to be 2 metres h.** faire 2 mètres de haut; Fam **to be left h. and dry** être laissé(e) en plan; **h. jump** saut m en hauteur; Fam Fig **you'll be for the h. jump** tu vas te faire engueuler; **h. jumper** sauteur(euse) m,f en hauteur; **h. tide** marée f haute; **h. wire** corde f raide (**b**) (price, speed, standards) élevé(e); (quality) premier(-ère); **to have a h. opinion of sb** avoir une haute opinion de qn; Am **h. beams** feux mpl de route; **h. explosive** explosif m puissant; **h. point** point m culminant; **in h. spirits** plein(e) d'entrain; Law **h. treason** haute trahison f; **h. winds** vents mpl forts (**c**) (rank, position) haut(e); **to act all h. and mighty** agir avec beaucoup d'arrogance; **h. command** haut commandement m; **H. Commission** haut-commissariat m; **H. Court** ≃ tribunal m de grande instance; **H. Mass** grand-messe f; **h. school** = école secondaire qui accueille les élèves de 15 à 18 ans; **h. society** haute société f (**d**) (in tone, pitch) aigu(ë); Fig **h. note** (of career, performance) point m culminant (**e**) (with time) **it's h. time you got yourself a job** il est grand temps que tu trouves un travail; **h. noon** plein midi m; **h. summer** plein été m; Br **h. tea** = dîner pris assez tôt

dans la soirée (**f**) *(meat)* avancé(e) (**g**) *Fam* **to be h.**
(on drugs) planer; *Fig (on success, excitement)* être euphorique
3 *adv (aim, jump)* haut; **to hunt h.** **and low for sth**
remuer ciel et terre pour trouver qch; **feelings were**
running h. la tension montait
highbrow ['haɪbraʊ] *adj* intellectuel(elle)
highchair ['haɪtʃeə(r)] *n* chaise *f* haute
Higher ['haɪər] *n Scot* = diplôme de fin d'études secondaires sanctionnant une matière déterminée
higher education ['haɪəredjʊ'keɪʃən] *n* enseignement *m* supérieur
high-flier, high-flyer ['haɪ'flaɪə(r)] *n (person)* bat-
tant(e) *m,f; (company)* société *f* qui va de l'avant
high-flying ['haɪ'flaɪɪŋ] *adj* ambitieux(euse)
high-frequency [haɪ'fri:kwənsɪ] *adj* (à) haute fréquence *inv*
high-handed [haɪ'hændɪd] *adj* autoritaire, despotique
high-heeled ['haɪ'hi:ld] *adj* à talons hauts
Highland ['haɪlənd] *adj (from Scottish Highlands)* des
Highlands; **H. cattle** vaches *fpl* des Highlands; **H.**
games jeux *mpl* écossais

Highland games
En Écosse, il s'agit d'une sorte de kermesse locale
en plein air où se déroulent simultanément toutes
sortes de concours (danse, cornemuse) et
d'épreuves sportives (courses, lancer du marteau,
mais aussi "tossing the caber", "tug o' war", etc.).

Highlander ['haɪləndə(r)] *n (of Scotland)* habitant(e)
m,f des Highlands
Highlands ['haɪləndz] *npl* **the H.** *(of Scotland)* les
Highlands *fpl*
high-level ['haɪlevəl] *adj (talks)* à haut niveau; *(dele-*
gation) de haut niveau
highlight ['haɪlaɪt] **1** *n* (**a**) *(of performance, career)*
point *m* culminant; **highlights** *(of match, event)* moments *mpl* forts (**b**) **highlights** *(in hair) (artificial)*
mèches *fpl; (natural)* reflets *mpl*
2 *vt* (**a**) *(problem, difference)* mettre en évidence,
souligner (**b**) *(with highlighter)* surligner; *Comput*
(block of text) sélectionner
highlighter ['haɪlaɪtə(r)] *n (pen)* surligneur *m*
highly ['haɪlɪ] *adv* (**a**) *(very)* très, extrêmement; **h.**
paid très bien payé(e); **h. seasoned** fortement assai-
sonné(e); **h. strung** hypersensible (**b**) *(favourably)*
to think h. of sb avoir une haute opinion de qn; **to**
speak h. of sb parler de qn en termes élogieux
high-minded ['haɪ'maɪndɪd] *adj (sentiments, beha-*
viour) noble; *(person)* qui a des principes
Highness ['haɪnɪs] *n* **His/Her Royal H.** Son Altesse *f*
high-pitched ['haɪpɪtʃt] *adj* aigu(ë)
high-powered ['haɪ'paʊəd] *adj (engine, car, tele-*
scope) très puissant(e); *(job)* à hautes responsabilités; *(person)* qui occupe un poste à hautes
responsabilités
high-pressure ['haɪ'preʃə(r)] *adj* (**a**) *(cylinder, gas,*
machine) à haute pression (**b**) *(salesman)* agres-
sif(ive)
high-profile ['haɪ'prəʊfaɪl] *adj (person)* très en vue;
(campaign) de grande envergure
high-resolution ['haɪrezə'lu:ʃən] *adj* *Comput*
(screen, graphics) à haute résolution
high-rise ['haɪ'raɪz] **1** *n (block of flats)* tour *f*
2 *adj* **h. building** tour *f*

high-risk ['haɪrɪsk] *adj (strategy, investment)* à haut
risque
highroad ['haɪrəʊd] *n Old-fashioned* grand-route *f;*
Fig **the h. to success** la voie du succès
high-speed ['haɪ'spi:d] *adj* ultra-rapide; *(train)* à
grande vitesse; **h. chase** course-poursuite *f* infernale
high-spirited [haɪ'spɪrɪtɪd] *adj* plein(e) d'entrain
high-tech ['haɪ'tek] *adj (appliance)* perfectionné(e);
(industry) de pointe; *(approach, solution)* qui a recours à une technologie de pointe
high-up ['haɪʌp] *adj Fam (important)* haut placé(e)
highway ['haɪweɪ] *n (main road)* (route *f*) nationale *f;*
(motorway) autoroute *f; Fam Fig* **that's h. robbery!**
c'est du vol!; **H. Code** code *m* de la route
highwayman ['haɪweɪmən] *n* bandit *m* de grand
chemin
hijack ['haɪdʒæk] *vt (plane)* détourner; *(car, lorry)* s'emparer de force de; *(idea)* s'approprier
hijacker ['haɪdʒækə(r)] *n (of plane)* pirate *m* de l'air
hike [haɪk] **1** *n* (**a**) *(walk)* randonnée *f;* **to go on** *or* **for**
a h. faire une randonnée; *Fam Fig* **go take a h.!**
lâche-moi les baskets! (**b**) *(in prices)* hausse *f*
2 *vt (prices)* augmenter
3 *vi (walk)* faire de la randonnée
hiker ['haɪkə(r)] *n* randonneur(euse) *m,f*
hiking ['haɪkɪŋ] *n* randonnée *f;* **to go h.** faire de la randonnée; **h. boots** chaussures *fpl* de marche
hilarious [hɪ'leərɪəs] *adj* hilarant(e)
hilariously [hɪ'leərɪəslɪ] *adv* **h. funny** à se tordre de
rire; **to laugh h.** se tordre de rire
hilarity [hɪ'lærɪtɪ] *n* hilarité *f;* **his suggestion was**
greeted with much h. sa suggestion déclencha l'hilarité générale
hill [hɪl] *n* (**a**) *(small mountain)* colline *f; Fig* **to be over**
the h. commencer à se faire vieux (vieille) (**b**) *(slope)*
côte *f*, pente *f;* **to go down/up the h.** descendre/
monter la côte
hillbilly ['hɪlbɪlɪ] *n (pl* **hillbillies**) *n Am* péquenaud(e)
m,f
hillock ['hɪlək] *n* butte *f*
hillside ['hɪlsaɪd] *n* coteau *m*
hilltop ['hɪltɒp] *n* sommet *m* de la colline
hillwalker ['hɪlwɔːkə(r)] *n* randonneur(euse) *m,f*
hillwalking ['hɪlwɔːkɪŋ] *n* randonnée *f* en basse
montagne
hilly ['hɪlɪ] *adj* vallonné(e)
hilt [hɪlt] *n (of sword)* poignée *f; (of knife, dagger)* manche *m; Fig* **to back sb to the h.** soutenir qn sans
réserve
him [hɪm] *pron* (**a**) *(direct object)* le; **I hate h.** je le déteste; **I love h.** je l'aime; **I can understand his son but**
not HIM je comprends son fils, mais lui, je ne le comprends pas (**b**) *(indirect object)* lui; **I gave h. the book**
je lui ai donné le livre; **I gave it to h.** je le lui ai donné
(**c**) *(after preposition)* lui; **I'm thinking of h.** je pense à
lui (**d**) *(as complement of verb to be)* lui; **it's h.!** c'est
lui!; **it was h. who did it** c'est lui qui l'a fait
Himalayan [hɪmə'leɪən] *adj* himalayen(enne)
Himalayas [hɪmə'leɪəz] *npl* **the H.** l'Himalaya *m*
himself [hɪm'self] *pron* (**a**) *(reflexive)* **he spoils h.** il se
gâte; **he hurt h.** il s'est blessé (**b**) *(emphatic)* lui-
même; **he has never...** lui-même n'a jamais...;
he told me h. il me l'a dit lui-même; **he's not h.**
today il n'est pas dans son état normal aujourd'hui
(**c**) *(after preposition)* **he lives by h.** il vit seul; **he**
bought it for h. il se l'est acheté; **he talks to h.** il parle
tout seul

hind¹ [haɪnd] *adj (back)* de derrière; **h. legs** pattes *fpl* de derrière
hind² *n (female deer)* daim *m* femelle
hinder ['hɪndə(r)] *vt (impede)* gêner; *(delay)* retarder; **to h. sb from doing sth** empêcher qn de faire qch
Hindi ['hɪndɪ] *n (language)* hindi *m*
hindquarters ['haɪndkwɔːtəz] *npl* arrière-train *m*
hindrance ['hɪndrəns] *n* entrave *f*, obstacle *m*
hindsight ['haɪndsaɪt] *n* recul *m*; **with (the benefit of) h.** avec le recul
Hindu ['hɪnduː] **1** *n* Hindou(e) *m,f*
 2 *adj* hindou(e)
Hinduism ['hɪnduːɪzəm] *n* hindouisme *m*
hinge [hɪndʒ] *n* charnière *f*, gond *m*; **to come off its hinges** sortir de ses gonds
▶**hinge on, hinge upon** *vt insep (depend on)* dépendre de
hint [hɪnt] **1** *n* (**a**) *(allusion)* allusion *f*; *(clue)* indice *m*; **to drop sb a h.** faire une allusion à l'intention de qn; **to take the h.** comprendre l'allusion; **he can't take a h.** il faut lui mettre les points sur les i (**b**) *(sign)* signe *m* (**c**) *(small amount)* soupçon *m* (**d**) *(piece of advice)* truc *m*, conseil *m*
 2 *vt* **to h. that...** insinuer *ou* laisser entendre que...
▶**hint at** *vt insep* faire allusion à
hinterland ['hɪntəlænd] *n* arrière-pays *m inv*
hip¹ [hɪp] *n (part of body)* hanche *f*; **to break one's h.** se casser le col du fémur; **h. flask** flasque *f*; **h. joint** articulation *f* de la hanche; **h. pocket** poche *f* revolver
hip² *adj Fam (fashionable)* branché(e)
hip-hop ['hɪphɒp] *n (music)* hip-hop *m inv*
hippo ['hɪpəʊ] *(pl* **hippos**) *n Fam* hippopotame *m*
hippopotamus [hɪpə'pɒtəməs] *(pl* **hippopotami** [hɪpə'pɒtəmaɪ]) *n* hippopotame *m*
hippy ['hɪpɪ] *(pl* **hippies**) *n* hippie *mf*
hire [haɪə(r)] **1** *n* (**a**) *(of car, cycle)* location *f*; **for h.** à louer; *(taxi)* libre; **h. car** voiture *f* de location; *Com* **h. purchase** achat *m* à crédit; **h. purchase agreement** contrat *m* de vente à tempérament
 2 *vt* (**a**) *(car, equipment)* louer (**b**) *(lawyer, worker)* engager
▶**hire out** *vt sep Br (boat, bicycle)* louer; *(one's services)* offrir
hired ['haɪəd] *adj (car, suit)* de location; **h. hand** *(on farm)* ouvrier(ère) *m,f* agricole
hirsute ['hɜːsjuːt] *adj Lit* velu(e)
his [hɪz] **1** *possessive adj* (**a**) *(singular)* son (sa); *(plural)* ses; **h. job** son travail; **h. wife** sa femme; **h. parents** ses parents; **it wasn't HIS idea!** ce n'est pas lui qui en a eu l'idée! (**b**) *(for parts of body)* **he hit h. head** il s'est cogné la tête
 2 *possessive pron* (**a**) *(singular)* le sien (la sienne) *m,f*, *(plural)* les siens (les siennes) *mpl, fpl*; **my house is big, but h. is bigger** j'ai une grande maison, mais la sienne est plus grande encore (**b**) *(used attributively)* **this book is h.** ce livre est à lui; **a friend of h.** un de ses amis; **where's that brother of h.?** où son frère a-t-il bien pu passer?
Hispanic [hɪs'pænɪk] **1** *n Am* Latino-Américain(e) *m,f*
 2 *adj* hispanique
hiss [hɪs] **1** *n (sound)* sifflement *m*; *(to express disapproval)* sifflet *m*
 2 *vt & vi* siffler
histogram ['hɪstəgræm] *n* histogramme *m*
historian [hɪs'tɔːrɪən] *n* historien(enne) *m,f*
historic [hɪs'tɒrɪk] *adj* historique
historical [hɪs'tɒrɪkəl] *adj* historique

historically [hɪs'tɒrɪklɪ] *adv* historiquement
history ['hɪstərɪ] *(pl* **histories**) *n* (**a**) *(the past)* histoire *f*; **to go down in h.** *(of event)* faire date; *(of person)* entrer dans l'histoire; *Fig* **that's (ancient) h.** c'est de l'histoire ancienne; **h. book/teacher** livre *m*/professeur *m* d'histoire (**b**) *(medical record)* antécédents *mpl*; **there is a h. of diabetes in his family** il y a des cas de diabète dans sa famille
histrionic [hɪstrɪ'ɒnɪk] *adj Pej* théâtral(e)
histrionics [hɪstrɪ'ɒnɪks] *npl Pej* comédie *f*, cinéma *m*; **to have h.** faire une scène *ou* du cinéma
hit [hɪt] **1** *n* (**a**) *(blow)* coup *m*; *(in shooting)* tir *m* réussi; **to score a direct h.** taper dans le mille; **h. list** *(of targets)* liste *f* noire; **h. man** tueur *m* à gages (**b**) *(success)* succès *m*; **to be a h.** avoir beaucoup de succès auprès de qn; **h. (record)** hit *m* (**c**) *Comput (visit to website)* hit *m*, accès *m*; **this website counted 5,000 hits last week** ce site Web a été consulté 5 000 fois la semaine dernière
 2 *adj (film, play)* à succès
 3 *vt (pt & pp* **hit**) (**a**) *(of person)* frapper; *(of bullet)* atteindre; *(of car)* percuter; *Comput (key)* frapper, appuyer sur; **to h. one's head (on sth)** se cogner la tête (contre qch); **Fig it suddenly hit me that...** j'ai réalisé tout d'un coup que...; *Fig* **he didn't know what had hit him** il n'a pas eu le temps de se rendre compte de ce qui lui arrivait (**b**) *(reach) (barrier, difficulty)* heurter à; **to h. a note** atteindre une note; **to h. 90 (miles an hour)** ≃ faire du 140 (à l'heure); **to h. an all-time low** *(of investment, relationship)* être au plus bas; **the circus hits town tomorrow** le cirque arrive en ville demain; **it hits the shops next week** c'est en vente la semaine prochaine; *Fam* **to h. the hay** *or* **the sack** se pieuter; *Fam* **to h. the road** *(leave)* se mettre en route; *Fam* **to h. the** *Br* **roof** *or Am* **ceiling** sortir de ses gonds (**c**) *(affect)* toucher; **to be hard hit by sth** être durement touché(e) par qch
 4 *vi* frapper
▶**hit back 1** *vt sep* **to h. sb back** rendre un coup à qn
 2 *vi also Fig* riposter (**at** à)
▶**hit off** *vt sep Fam* **to h. it off** accrocher
▶**hit on** *vt insep (idea, solution)* trouver
▶**hit out** *vi* **to h. out at sb** *(physically)* frapper qn; *(verbally)* s'en prendre à qn
▶**hit upon** = hit on
hit-and-run ['hɪtən'rʌn] *adj* **h. accident** accident *m* avec délit de fuite
hitch [hɪtʃ] **1** *n* (**a**) *(difficulty)* problème *m*; **without a h.** sans anicroche (**b**) *(knot)* nœud *m*
 2 *vt* (**a**) *(attach)* attacher (**to** à); *Fam Fig* **to get hitched** *(married)* passer devant Monsieur le Maire (**b**) *Fam* **to h. a lift** faire du stop
 3 *vi Fam* faire du stop; **to h. to Paris** aller à Paris en stop
▶**hitch up** *vt sep (trousers, skirt)* remonter
hitchhike ['hɪtʃhaɪk] *vi* faire de l'auto-stop; **to h. to Paris** aller à Paris en auto-stop
hitchhiker ['hɪtʃhaɪkə(r)] *n* auto-stoppeur(euse) *m,f*
hi-tech = high-tech
hither ['hɪðə(r)] *adv Lit* ici; **h. and thither** çà et là
hitherto ['hɪðə'tuː] *adv* jusqu'ici, jusqu'à présent
hit-or-miss ['hɪtɔː'mɪs] *adj* aléatoire, approximatif(ive)
HIV [eɪtʃaɪ'viː] *n (abbr* **human immunodeficiency virus)** VIH *m*; **to be H. positive/negative** être séropositif(ive)/séronégatif(ive)

hive [haɪv] *n* ruche *f*; *Fig* **a h. of activity** une véritable ruche

▸**hive off** *vt sep (money, profits)* séparer

HMG [eɪtʃem'dʒiː] *n Br (abbr* **Her/His Majesty's Government**) = le gouvernement de sa majesté *(expression utilisée sur les documents officiels)*

HMI [eɪtʃem'aɪ] *n Br (* **a**) *(abbr* **Her/His Majesty's Inspectorate**) ≃ Inspection *f* académique (**b**) *(abbr* **Her/His Majesty's Inspector**) ≃ inspecteur(trice) *m,f* de l'éducation nationale

HMS [eɪtʃem'es] *n (abbr* **Her/His Majesty's Ship**) = abréviation précédant le nom des navires de la marine britannique

HMSO [eɪtʃemes'əʊ] *n (abbr* **Her/His Majesty's Stationery Office**) ≃ Imprimerie *f* nationale

HNC [eɪtʃen'siː] *n Br (abbr* **Higher National Certificate**) = brevet de technicien en Grande-Bretagne, ≃ BTS *m*

HND [eɪtʃen'diː] *n Br (abbr* **Higher National Diploma**) = brevet de technicien supérieur en Grande-Bretagne, ≃ DUT *m*

hoard [hɔːd] **1** *n (of food)* réserve *f*, provisions *fpl*; *(of money)* trésor *m*
2 *vt (food)* amasser, stocker; *(money)* amasser, thésauriser

hoarder ['hɔːdə(r)] *n* personne *f* qui fait des réserves; **she's a real h.** elle ne jette rien

hoarding ['hɔːdɪŋ] *n (* **a**) *(of food)* stockage *m* (**b**) *(for poster)* panneau *m* d'affichage

hoarfrost ['hɔːfrɒst] *n* givre *m*, gelée *f* blanche

hoarse [hɔːs] *adj* enroué(e); **to shout oneself h.** s'enrouer à force de crier

hoary ['hɔːrɪ] *adj (story)* vieux (vieille); *(joke)* éculé(e)

hoax [həʊks] **1** *n* canular *m*; **to play a h.** on sb faire un canular à qn; **(bomb)** fausse alerte *f* à la bombe; **h. caller** auteur *m* de canular(s) téléphonique(s)
2 *vt* faire un canular à

hob [hɒb] *n (on electric cooker)* table *f* de cuisson; *(on hearth)* plaque *f*

hobble ['hɒbəl] *vi* boitiller

hobby ['hɒbɪ] *(pl* **hobbies**) *n* passe-temps *m inv*, hobby *m*

hobbyhorse ['hɒbɪhɔːs] *n (toy)* cheval *m* de bois *(tête emmanchée sur un bâton)*; *Fig (favourite subject)* dada *m*

hobnail boot ['hɒbneɪl'buːt] *n* chaussure *f* ferrée

hobnob ['hɒbnɒb] *(pt & pp* **hobnobbed**) *vi Fam* **to h. with sb** frayer avec qn

hock[1] [hɒk] *n (wine)* vin *m* du Rhin

hock[2] *Fam* **1** *n* **to be in h.** *(of object)* être au clou; *(of person)* être endetté(e)
2 *vt* mettre au clou

hockey ['hɒkɪ] *n Br (on grass)* hockey *m* (sur gazon); *Am (on ice)* hockey *m* (sur glace); **h. stick** crosse *f* de hockey

hocus-pocus ['həʊkəs'pəʊkəs] *n (trickery)* tromperie *f*, supercherie *f*; *(talk)* paroles *fpl* trompeuses

hoe [həʊ] **1** *n* houe *f*, binette *f*
2 *vt (pt & pp* **hoed**) biner, sarcler

hog [hɒg] **1** *n (* **a**) *(pig)* porc *m* châtré; *Fam* **to go the whole h.** aller jusqu'au bout (**b**) *(glutton)* glouton(onne) *m,f*, goinfre *mf*
2 *vt (pt & pp* **hogged**) *Fam (monopolize)* monopoliser; **to h. the limelight** monopoliser l'attention

Hogmanay [hɒgmə'neɪ] *n Scot* la Saint-Sylvestre

Hogmanay

Ce mot désigne les fêtes de la veille du nouvel an célébrées en Écosse. Traditionnellement, les Écossais préféraient célébrer la nouvelle année plutôt que Noël et jusqu'au XVIIIème siècle, la tradition était d'offrir des cadeaux le jour de l'an. Les coutumes écossaises sont aussi anciennes que diverses : des coups de canon sont tirés à minuit ; à ce moment les gens vont rendre visite à leurs voisins avec un morceau de charbon en guise de cadeau, et tout le monde boit une petite goutte de whisky pour fêter la nouvelle année.

hogwash ['hɒgwɒʃ] *n Fam* âneries *fpl*

hoist [hɔɪst] **1** *n (device)* appareil *m* de levage
2 *vt* hisser; **he hoisted himself on to the wall** il s'est hissé sur le mur; *Fig* **to be hoist with one's own petard** se faire prendre à son propre piège

hoity-toity ['hɔɪtɪ'tɔɪtɪ] *adj* **to be h.** se donner de grands airs

hold [həʊld] **1** *n (* **a**) *(grip)* prise *f*; **to have h. of sb/sth** tenir qn/qch; **to catch** *or* **take h. of sth** saisir qch; *Fig* **to get h. of sth** *(find)* trouver qn; *(on phone)* joindre qn; *Fig* **to get h. of sth** se procurer qch; **to let go one's h.** relâcher son étreinte, lâcher prise; **to lose one's h. on reality** perdre le sens des réalités; *Fig* **to have a h. on** *or* **over sb** avoir de l'emprise sur qn
(**b**) *(in wrestling)* prise *f*; *Fig* **no holds barred** tous les coups sont permis
(**c**) **to be on h.** *(of project)* être en suspens; *(of telephone caller)* être en attente; **to put sth on h.** mettre qch en suspens; **to put sb on h.** *(on telephone)* mettre qn en attente
(**d**) *(of ship)* cale *f*; *(of plane)* soute *f*
2 *vt (pt & pp* **held** [held]) (**a**) *(grip)* tenir; **to h. sb/sth tight** tenir qn/qch serré(e), serrer qn/qch; **to h. hands** se tenir (par) la main; **to h. sth in position** maintenir qch en place; **to h. sb prisoner** retenir qn prisonnier(ère); **the police are holding him for questioning** il a été placé en garde à vue; **to h. sb's interest/attention** retenir l'intérêt/l'attention de qn; **to h. sb to his promise** obliger qn à tenir sa promesse; **to h. one's breath** retenir sa respiration *ou* son souffle; *Fig* **don't h. your breath!** ce n'est pas pour demain! **there's no holding her** il n'y a pas moyen de l'arrêter; **h. your tongue!** tais-toi!; *Fam* **h. it!**, **h. your horses!** attendez!; **to h. a note** *(of singer)* tenir une note; **h. the line!** *(on telephone)* ne quittez pas!
(**b**) *(keep) (town, position)* tenir; *(ticket, room)* réserver; **to h. one's ground** tenir bon; **to h. one's own** se défendre
(**c**) *(carry)* **to h. one's head high** garder la tête haute; **to h. oneself well** se tenir bien
(**d**) *(contain)* contenir; *Fig* **to h. water** *(of theory, story)* tenir la route; **nobody knows what the future holds** personne ne sait ce que l'avenir nous réserve; **it holds no interest for me** ça ne présente aucun intérêt pour moi
(**e**) *(conduct) (negotiations)* mener; *(meeting)* organiser; *(conversation)* avoir
(**f**) *(possess) (title, rank, opinion)* avoir; *(job, position)* occuper; *(record)* détenir; **to h. office** être en fonction
(**g**) *(consider)* **to h. sb responsible** tenir qn pour responsable; **to h. sb in respect** respecter qn; **to h. that...** soutenir que...

3 *vi* (**a**) *(of rope)* tenir; **h. tight!** tiens bon!; **please h.!** *(on telephone)* ne quittez pas!

(**b**) *(of agreement, weather)* durer; *(of luck)* persister; **the same holds (true) for you** cela vaut aussi pour toi

▸**hold against** *vt sep* **to h. sth against sb** reprocher qch à qn

▸**hold back 1** *vt sep* (**a**) *(restrain)* *(person, emotion)* retenir; *(progress, project)* ralentir, freiner (**b**) *(conceal)* cacher
2 *vi* *(refrain)* se retenir (**from doing** de faire)

▸**hold down** *vt sep* (**a**) *(restrain)* *(person)* immobiliser; *(taxes, prices)* bloquer (**b**) *(job)* *(occupy)* avoir; *(keep)* garder

▸**hold forth** *vi* disserter, pérorer (**about** *or* **on** sur)

▸**hold off 1** *vt sep* (**a**) *(keep at bay)* tenir à distance (**b**) *(delay)* remettre à plus tard, repousser; **to h. off making a decision** remettre une décision à plus tard
2 *vi* *(delay)* attendre

▸**hold on** *vi* (**a**) *(last)* tenir (**b**) *(wait)* patienter; **h. on!** attendez!; *(on telephone)* ne quittez pas! (**c**) *(not let go)* s'accrocher

▸**hold on to** *vt insep* (**a**) *(rope, handle)* s'agripper à; *Fig (idea, hope)* s'accrocher à (**b**) *(keep)* garder

▸**hold out 1** *vt sep* *(one's hand)* tendre; *(hope, opportunity)* offrir
2 *vi* (**a**) *(resist)* tenir (le coup) (**b**) *(wait)* **to h. out for a better offer** attendre une meilleure offre (**c**) *(last)* durer

▸**hold over** *vt sep* remettre, reporter

▸**hold together 1** *vt sep* **to h. sth together** faire tenir qch; **to be held together with sth** tenir avec qch
2 *vi* *(of party, group of people)* rester uni(e); *(of marriage, relationship)* tenir

▸**hold up 1** *vt sep* (**a**) *(support)* soutenir (**b**) *(raise)* lever; *Fig* **to h. sb/sth up as an example** montrer *ou* citer qn/qch en exemple; *Fig* **to h. sb/sth up to ridicule** tourner qn/qch en ridicule (**c**) *(delay)* retarder (**d**) *(rob)* attaquer
2 *vi* *(of theory, alibi)* (se) tenir; *(of good weather)* se maintenir; **she's holding up well under the pressure** elle tient bien le coup

▸**hold with** *vt insep* *(agree with)* être d'accord avec; *(approve of)* approuver

holdall ['həʊldɔːl] *n* fourre-tout *m inv*

holder ['həʊldə(r)] *n* (**a**) *(of licence, ticket, record, trophy)* détenteur(trice) *m,f*; *(of passport, degree)* titulaire *mf*; *(of belief, opinion)* tenant *m* (**b**) *(device)* support *m*

holding ['həʊldɪŋ] *n* (**a**) *(property)* propriété *f* (**b**) *(of shares)* participation *f*; *Com* **h. company** holding *m* (**c**) *Fig* **h. operation** opération *f* destinée à gagner du temps

hold-up ['həʊldʌp] *n* (**a**) *(delay)* *(in plan)* retard *m*; *(of traffic)* ralentissement *m* (**b**) *(armed robbery)* hold-up *m inv*; attaque *f* à main armée (**c**) **hold-ups** *(stockings)* bas *mpl* jarretière

hole [həʊl] **1** *n* (**a**) *(opening)* trou *m*; *(of rabbit, fox)* terrier *m*; *also Fig* **to make a h. in sth** faire un trou dans qch; *Fig* **to pick holes in sth** relever les failles de qch; *Fig* **a h. in the law** un vide juridique; **to get a h. in one** *(in golf)* faire un trou en un; *Fam Fig* **to be in a h.** *(in difficulty)* être dans le pétrin (**b**) *Fam Pej* *(room, house)* taudis *m*; *(town)* trou *m*

2 *vt* *(ship)* faire une brèche dans; *(in golf)* **to h. a putt** faire le trou

▸**hole up** *vi Fam (hide)* se terrer

holiday ['hɒlɪdeɪ] **1** *n* (**a**) *Br (vacation)* vacances *fpl*; **a month's h.** un mois de vacances; **to be on h.** être en vacances; **to go on h.** aller *ou* partir en vacances; **h. camp** camp *m* de vacances; *Fig* **it was no h.** camp ce n'était pas une partie de plaisir; **h. home** résidence *f* secondaire; **h. season** saison *f* touristique (**b**) *(day off)* (jour *m* de) congé *m* (**c**) *(public)* jour *m* férié
2 *vi Br* passer les vacances; *(in summer)* passer les vacances d'été

holidaymaker ['hɒlɪdeɪmeɪkə(r)] *n Br* vacancier(ère) *m,f*; *(in summer)* estivant(e) *m,f*

holiness ['həʊlɪnɪs] *n* sainteté *f*; **Your H.** Votre Sainteté

holistic [həʊ'lɪstɪk] *adj* holistique

Holland ['hɒlənd] *n* la Hollande

holler ['hɒlə(r)] *vi Fam* brailler

hollow ['hɒləʊ] **1** *n* creux *m*
2 *adj* (**a**) *(container, cheeks)* creux(euse); *(eyes)* cave (**b**) *(sound)* creux(euse); *(voice)* blanc (blanche); *(laugh)* forcé(e) (**c**) *(promise, guarantee)* vain(e); *(victory)* sans signification
3 *adv* (**a**) **to sound h.** sonner creux (**b**) *Fam* **to beat sb h.** battre qn à plate(s) couture(s)

▸**hollow out** *vt sep* évider

holly ['hɒlɪ] *n* houx *m*

hollyhock ['hɒlɪhɒk] *n* rose *f* trémière

holocaust ['hɒləkɔːst] *n* holocauste *m*

hologram ['hɒləgræm] *n* hologramme *m*

holster ['həʊlstə(r)] *n* étui *m* de revolver

holy ['həʊlɪ] *adj* saint(e); *Fam* **h. cow** *or* **smoke!** ça alors!; **the H. Bible** la Sainte Bible; **H. Communion** communion *f*; **the H. Father** le Saint-Père; **the H. Ghost** *or* **Spirit** le Saint-Esprit; *Fam Pej* **H. Joe** grenouille *f* de bénitier; **the H. Land** la Terre Sainte; **h. orders** ordres *mpl*; **h. war** guerre *f* sainte; **h. water** eau *f* bénite; **H. Week** la semaine sainte

homage ['hɒmɪdʒ] *n* hommage *m*; **to pay h. to sb** rendre hommage à qn

home [həʊm] **1** *n* (**a**) *(house)* maison *f*; *(of animal, plant)* habitat *m*; **at h.** à la maison, chez soi; **to feel at h.** se sentir chez soi; **make yourself at h.** faites comme chez vous; **to leave h.** *(in the morning)* partir de chez soi; *(one's parents' home)* partir de chez ses parents; **to be away from h.** être en déplacement; **to work at** *or* **from h.** travailler à domicile; **to be a h. from h.** être un second chez-soi; **to make one's h. in France** s'établir en France; **old people's h.** maison *f* de retraite; **children's h.** foyer *m* pour enfants; **h. address** adresse *f* personnelle, domicile *m*; **h. banking** banque *f* à domicile; **h. brew** bière *f* maison; **h. cooking** cuisine *f* familiale; *Br* **the H. Counties** = les comtés limitrophes de Londres; **h. economics** *(school subject)* arts *mpl* ménagers; **h. help** aide *f* ménagère; **h. improvements** travaux *mpl* de rénovation; **h. life** vie *f* de famille; *Fin* **h. loan** prêt *m* immobilier; **h. movie** film *m* amateur; **h. owner** propriétaire *mf*; *Am Sch* **h. room** = salle où l'on fait l'appel; **h. run** *(in baseball)* tour *m* complet; **the h. straight** *(in athletics)* la dernière ligne droite; **to tell sb a few h. truths** dire ses quatre vérités à qn (**b**) *(country, region)* patrie *f*; **at h. and abroad** dans notre pays et à l'étranger; **an example nearer h.** un exemple qui nous concerne plus; **Milan, the h. of fashion** Milan, capitale de la mode; **h. front** arrière *m*; **h. news** nouvelles *fpl* nationales; *Br Pol* **H. Office** ≃ ministère *m* de l'Intérieur; **h. owner** propiétaire *f*; *Pol* **h. rule** régime *m* d'autonomie politique; *Br Pol* **the H. Secretary** ≃ le ministre de l'Intérieur **2** *adv* (**a**) *(to or at one's house)* à la maison, chez soi; *Fig* **to bring sth h. to sb** faire comprendre qch à qn; **to send sb h.** *(to house)* renvoyer qn chez soi; *(to home country)* rapatrier qn (**b**) *(all the way)* **he hammered the nail h.** il enfonça complètement le clou; **the bolt slid h.** le verrou se ferma

►**home in on** *vt insep (target)* se diriger vers; *(mistake, evidence)* relever

homecoming ['həʊmkʌmɪŋ] *n (to one's house)* retour *m* (au foyer); *(to one's country)* retour *m* au pays

home-grown ['həʊm'grəʊn] *adj (vegetables)* du jardin; *Fig (not imported)* national(e)

homeland ['həʊmlænd] *n* patrie *f*, pays *m* (d'origine)

homeless ['həʊmlɪs] **1** *npl* **the h.** les sans-abri *mpl* **2** *adj* sans abri

homely ['həʊmlɪ] *adj* (**a**) *Br (person, atmosphere, decor)* agréable et sans prétention (**b**) *Am (plain)* sans charme

home-made ['həʊm'meɪd] *adj* fait(e) maison

homemaker ['həʊmmeɪkər] *n esp Am* femme *f* au foyer

homeopath ['həʊmɪəʊpæθ] *n* homéopathe *mf*

homeopathic [həʊmɪəʊ'pæθɪk] *adj* homéopathique

homeopathy [həʊmɪ'ɒpəθɪ] *n* homéopathie *f*

homesick ['həʊmsɪk] *adj* **to be** *or* **feel h.** avoir le mal du pays; *(of child)* s'ennuyer de ses parents; **to be h. for sth** avoir la nostalgie de qch

homesickness ['həʊmsɪknɪs] *n* mal *m* du pays

homespun ['həʊmspʌn] *adj Fig (wisdom, advice)* simple

homestead ['həʊmsted] *n* propriété *f*; *(farm)* ferme *f*

homeward ['həʊmwəd] **1** *adj* de retour **2** *adv (to one's house)* vers sa maison; *(to one's country)* vers son pays; **to be h.-bound** être sur le chemin du retour

homewards ['həʊmwədz] *adv* = **homeward**

homework ['həʊmwɜːk] *n Sch* devoirs *mpl*; **to do one's h.** faire ses devoirs; *Fig* faire des recherches

homicidal [hɒmɪ'saɪdəl] *adj* meurtrier(ère)

homicide ['hɒmɪsaɪd] *n* homicide *m*

homily ['hɒmɪlɪ] *(pl* **homilies**) *n* homélie *f*, sermon *m*

homing ['həʊmɪŋ] *adj* **h. device** mécanisme *m* d'autoguidage; **h. pigeon** pigeon *m* voyageur

homogeneous [hɒmə'dʒiːnɪəs, hə'mɒdʒɪnəs] *adj* homogène

homogenize [hɒ'mɒdʒənaɪz] *vt* homogénéiser

homonym ['hɒmənɪm] *n* homonyme *m*

homophobia [hɒmə'fəʊbɪə] *n* homophobie *f*

homophobic [hɒmə'fəʊbɪk] *adj* homophobique

homosexual [hɒmə'seksjʊəl] **1** *n* homosexuel(elle) *m,f* **2** *adj* homosexuel(elle)

homosexuality [hɒməseksjʊ'ælɪtɪ] *n* homosexualité *f*

Hon *adj Br Parl (abbr* **Honourable)** **the H. member for** Monsieur/Madame le député de

honcho ['hɒntʃəʊ] *(pl* **honchos**) *n Fam* **the head h.** le boss

Honduras [hɒn'djʊərəs] *n* le Honduras

hone [həʊn] *vt (skill)* peaufiner

honest ['ɒnɪst] *adj* honnête (**with** avec); **she has an h. face** elle a un visage franc; **the h. truth** la vérité

vraie; **to be h., I don't know** honnêtement *ou* à dire vrai, je ne sais pas; **to earn an h. living** gagner honnêtement sa vie; *Hum* **to make an h. woman of sb** *(marry)* faire de qn une honnête femme

honestly ['ɒnɪstlɪ] *adv* (**a**) *(legitimately, sincerely)* honnêtement; **to obtain sth h.** obtenir qch par des moyens honnêtes; **I can h. say that...** honnêtement, je peux dire que... (**b**) *(expressing indignation)* **well h.!** franchement!; **h.! some people!** il y a des gens, je te jure!

honesty ['ɒnɪstɪ] *n* honnêteté *f*; **in all h.** en toute honnêteté; *Prov* **h. is the best policy** l'honnêteté est toujours récompensée

honey ['hʌnɪ] *n* (**a**) *(food)* miel *m* (**b**) *Fam (term of endearment)* chéri(e) *m,f*

honeycomb ['hʌnɪkəʊm] **1** *n* rayon *m* de miel **2** *vt* **the mountain is honeycombed with tunnels** la montagne est truffée de tunnels

honeymoon ['hʌnɪmuːn] *n* voyage *m* de noces; *Fig* **the h. is over** l'état de grâce est terminé **2** *vi* partir en voyage de noces

honeysuckle ['hʌnɪsʌkəl] *n* chèvrefeuille *m*

Hong Kong ['hɒŋ'kɒŋ] *n* Hongkong

honk [hɒŋk] **1** *n (of goose)* cri *m*; *(of car horn)* coup *m* de Klaxon® **2** *vi (of goose)* cacarder; *(of car driver)* klaxonner

honor, honorable *etc Am* = **honour, honourable** *etc*

honorary ['ɒnərərɪ] *adj (member)* honoraire; *(title)* honorifique; *Univ* **h. degree** grade *m* honoris causa

honour, *Am* **honor** ['ɒnə(r)] **1** *n* (**a**) *(respect)* honneur *m*; **in h. of** en l'honneur de; **in h. of the occasion** pour l'occasion; **to have the h. of doing sth** avoir l'honneur de faire qch; *Hum* **to what do I owe this h.?** qu'est-ce qui me vaut cet honneur?; **Your H.** *(judge)* Votre Honneur (**b**) *(good name)* honneur *m*; **to feel h. bound to do sth** se sentir tenu(e) par l'honneur de faire qch; **on my (word of) h.!** parole d'honneur!; *Prov* **(there is) h. among thieves** les loups ne se mangent pas entre eux (**c**) *(award, distinction)* **honours list** = liste de distinctions honorifiques accordées par le souverain britannique; **honours degree** = diplôme universitaire obtenu avec mention; **he was buried with full military honours** il a été enterré avec tous les honneurs militaires; *Hum* **to do the honours** *(serve food or drink)* faire les honneurs; *(make introductions)* faire les présentations **2** *vt* honorer; **I felt honoured that they had invited me** je me suis senti honoré par leur invitation

honourable, *Am* **honorable** ['ɒnərəbəl] *adj* honorable; *Br Parl* **the H. member for** Monsieur/Madame le député de; **h. mention** mention *f* spéciale

honourably, *Am* **honorably** ['ɒnərəblɪ] *adv* honorablement

hooch [huːtʃ] *n Am Fam (liquor)* gnôle *f*

hood [hʊd] *n* (**a**) *(of coat, cloak)* capuche *f*; *(with eyeholes)* cagoule *f*; *Br (of car, pram)* capote *f*; *Am (car bonnet)* capot *m*; *(over cooker, fireplace)* hotte *f* (**b**) *Am Fam (gangster)* truand *m*

hoodie ['hʊdɪ] *n Fam* sweat *m* à capuche

hoodlum ['huːdləm] *n Fam* voyou *m*

hoodwink ['hʊdwɪŋk] *vt Fam* embobiner; **to h. sb into doing sth** embobiner qn pour qu'il fasse qch

hoof [huːf] **1** *n (pl* **hooves** [huːvz]) sabot *m* **2** *vt Fam* **to h. it** aller à pinces

hoo-ha ['huːhɑː] *n Fam (fuss)* tintouin *m*

hook [hʊk] **1** *n* (**a**) *(for hanging)* *(in general)* crochet *m*; *(for coats)* patère *f*; *(for meat)* croc *m*; *(on clothes)* agrafe *f*; *(for fishing)* hameçon *m*; **to leave the phone off the h.** *(on purpose)* laisser le téléphone décroché; *(accidentally)* mal raccrocher son téléphone; *Fam Fig* **to get** *or* **let sb off the h.** tirer qn d'affaire; *Fam* **he swallowed it h., line and sinker** *(believed it)* il a tout gobé; *Fam* **by h.** **or by crook** coûte que coûte (**b**) *(in boxing)* crochet *m*
2 *vt* accrocher; **to h. a fish** attraper un poisson
▸**hook up 1** *vt sep Comput* connecter (**to** à)
2 *vi* (**a**) *(of dress)* s'agrafer (**b**) *Comput* se connecter; *TV* **to h. up with** faire une émission en duplex avec

hooked [hʊkt] *adj* (**a**) **h. nose** nez *m* crochu (**b**) *Fam (addicted)* **to be h.** (**on**) être accro (à); *(on cinema, jazz)* être mordu(e) (de)

hooker [hʊkər] *n* (**a**) *Br (in rugby)* talonneur *m* (**b**) *Am Fam (prostitute)* pute *f*

hook(e)y ['hʊkɪ] *n Am Fam* **to play h.** sécher les cours

hooligan ['huːlɪgən] *n* hooligan *m*, vandale *m*

hooliganism ['huːlɪgənɪzəm] *n* hooliganisme *m*, vandalisme *m*

hoop [huːp] *n* cerceau *m*; *(in croquet)* arceau *m*; *Fig* **to put sb through the hoops** mettre qn à l'épreuve

hooray [hoˈreɪ] *exclam* hourra!

hoot [huːt] **1** *n* (**a**) *(of owl)* hululement *m*; *(of horn)* coup *m* de Klaxon®; *(of ship, factory whistle)* mugissement *m*; **hoots of laughter** éclats *mpl* de rire; *Fam Fig* **I don't give a h.** *or* **two hoots** je m'en fiche comme de l'an quarante (**b**) *Fam* **she's a h.!** elle est tordante!; **it was a h.!** c'était tordant!
2 *vt (person)* huer; **he was hooted off the stage** il a quitté la scène sous les huées
3 *vi (of owl)* hululer; *(of train)* siffler; *(of car)* klaxonner; **to h. with laughter** hurler de rire

hooter ['huːtə(r)] *n Br* (**a**) *(of ship, factory)* sirène *f*; *(of car)* Klaxon® *m* (**b**) *Fam (nose)* pif *m*

hoover® ['huːvə(r)] **1** *n* aspirateur *m*
2 *vt (room)* passer l'aspirateur dans; *(carpet)* passer l'aspirateur sur

hooves [huːvz] *pl of* **hoof**

hop [hɒp] **1** *n (jump)* saut *m*; *Fam (dance)* bal *m*; **a short h.** *(journey)* un petit voyage; *Fam Fig* **to catch sb on the h.** prendre qn de court *ou* au dépourvu
2 *vt (pt & pp hopped)* *Fam* **h. it!** fiche le camp!
3 *vi (jump)* sauter; *(on one leg)* sauter à cloche-pied; *Fam* **h. in!** *(to car)* allez, grimpe!; **he hopped onto the first train** il a sauté dans le premier train
▸**hop off** *vi Fam* ficher le camp

hope [həʊp] **1** *n* espoir *m*; **in the h. of doing sth** dans l'espoir de faire qch; **in the h. that...** dans l'espoir que...; **to have little h. of doing sth** avoir peu de chances de faire qch; **to have hopes of doing sth** avoir l'espoir de faire qch; **don't get your hopes up** n'espère pas trop; **to raise hopes of sth** faire naître l'espoir de qch; **she hasn't got a h. of winning** elle n'a aucun espoir de gagner; *Ironic* **some h.!** tu peux toujours rêver!; *Fam* **we live in h.!** l'espoir fait vivre!
2 *vt* **to h. to do sth** espérer faire qch; **to h. (that)...** espérer que...; **I h. you're right** j'espère que tu as raison; **I h. and pray that...** je prie le ciel que...; **I h. so** j'espère (bien); **I h. not** j'espère que non
3 *vi* espérer; **to h. for sth** espérer qch; **don't h. for too much** n'en attends pas trop; **we'll just have to h.**

for the best espérons que tout se passe bien; **to h. against h.** espérer malgré tout

hopeful ['həʊpfʊl] **1** *n Fam* **a young h.** un jeune espoir
2 *adj (situation)* encourageant(e); *(person)* optimiste; **to be h. that...** avoir bon espoir que...

hopefully ['həʊpfʊlɪ] *adv* (**a**) *(with luck)* avec un peu de chance; **h. not** espérons que non (**b**) *(in a hopeful manner)* **to do sth h.** faire qch plein(e) d'espoir

hopeless ['həʊplɪs] *adj* (**a**) *(without hope) (person, cause, situation)* désespéré(e); **it's h.!** ça ne sert à rien! (**b**) *Fam (very bad)* nul (nulle) (**at** en)

hopelessly ['həʊplɪslɪ] *adv* (**a**) *(inconsolably)* avec désespoir (**b**) *(completely)* complètement; **he was h. in love with her** il était éperdument amoureux d'elle

hopping ['hɒpɪŋ] *adv Fam* **to be h. mad** être fou (folle) de rage

hops [hɒps] *npl (for making beer)* houblon *m*

hopscotch ['hɒpskɒtʃ] *n* marelle *f*

horde [hɔːd] *n* horde *f*

horizon [həˈraɪzən] *n* horizon *m*; **on the h.** à l'horizon; *Fig* en vue

horizontal [hɒrɪˈzɒntəl] **1** *n* horizontale *f*
2 *adj* horizontal(e)

horizontally [hɒrɪˈzɒntəlɪ] *adv* horizontalement

hormonal [hɔːˈməʊnəl] *adj* hormonal(e)

hormone ['hɔːməʊn] *n* hormone *f*; **h. replacement therapy** monothérapie *f* de substitution

horn [hɔːn] *n* (**a**) *(of animal)* corne *f*; *(of insect)* antenne *f* (**b**) *(musical instrument)* cor *m*; *(on car)* Klaxon® *m*; **to sound one's h.** klaxonner (**c**) *(idioms)* **to be on the horns of a dilemma** être en proie à un dilemme

horned [hɔːnd] *adj* à cornes

hornet ['hɔːnɪt] *n* frelon *m*; *Fig* **to stir up a h.'s nest** mettre le feu aux poudres

hornpipe ['hɔːnpaɪp] *n* matelote *f*

horn-rimmed ['hɔːnrɪmd] *adj* **h. spectacles** *or* **glasses** lunettes *fpl* à monture d'écaille

horny ['hɔːnɪ] *adj* (**a**) *(hands)* calleux(euse) (**b**) *very Fam (sexually aroused)* excité(e); *(sexually attractive)* bandant(e)

horoscope ['hɒrəskəʊp] *n* horoscope *m*

horrendous [hɒˈrendəs] *adj* horrible, affreux(euse)

horrendously [hɒˈrendəslɪ] *adv* horriblement, affreusement

horrible ['hɒrəbəl] *adj* (**a**) *(unpleasant)* horrible, affreux(euse); **how h.!** quelle horreur! (**b**) *(unkind)* méchant(e) (**to** avec)

horribly ['hɒrɪblɪ] *adv* horriblement; **to behave h.** se conduire horriblement mal

horrid ['hɒrɪd] *adj* (**a**) *(unpleasant)* affreux(euse) (**b**) *(unkind)* méchant(e) (**to** avec)

horrific [hɒˈrɪfɪk] *adj* horrible

horrify ['hɒrɪfaɪ] *(pt & pp horrified)* *vt* horrifier

horrifying ['hɒrɪfaɪɪŋ] *adj* horrifiant(e)

horror ['hɒrə(r)] *n* horreur *f*; **to my h.,...** à ma grande horreur,...; **to have a h. of sth** avoir horreur de qch; **it gives me the horrors** ça me donne le frisson; *Fam* **that child's a little h.** cet enfant est un petit monstre; **h. film** film *m* d'horreur; *Fig* **h. story** histoire *f* épouvantable

horror-stricken ['hɒrəstrɪkən], **horror-struck** ['hɒrəstrʌk] *adj* frappé(e) d'horreur

horse [hɔːs] *n* (**a**) *(animal)* cheval *m*; **h. chestnut** *(tree)* marronnier *m*; *(fruit)* marron *m*; **h. racing** courses *fpl* de chevaux; *Br* **h. riding** équitation *f*; **h. show** concours *m* hippique; **h. trading** *(in negotiation)* maquignonnage *m* (**b**) *(in gymnastics)* cheval *m* d'arçons (**c**) *(idioms)* **to get on one's high h.** monter sur ses grands chevaux; *Fam* **I could eat a h!** j'ai une faim de loup!; **to eat like a h.** manger comme quatre; **to hear sth straight from the h.'s mouth** entendre qch de la bouche de l'intéressé

▸**horse about, horse around** *vi* chahuter

horseback ['hɔːsbæk] *n* **on h.** à cheval; *Am* **h.-riding** équitation *f*

horsebox ['hɔːsbɒks] *n* van *m*

horse-drawn ['hɔːsdrɔːn] *adj* tiré(e) par des chevaux

horsefly ['hɔːsflaɪ] *(pl* **horseflies**) *n* taon *m*

horsehair ['hɔːsheə(r)] *n* crin *m* (de cheval)

horseman ['hɔːsmən] *n* cavalier *m*

horsemanship ['hɔːsmənʃɪp] *n (skill)* talent *m* de cavalier

horseplay ['hɔːspleɪ] *n* chahut *m*

horsepower ['hɔːspaʊə(r)] *n* puissance *f* (en chevaux); *(unit)* cheval-vapeur *m*

horseradish ['hɔːsrædɪʃ] *n* raifort *m*

horseshoe ['hɔːsʃuː] *n* fer *m* à cheval

horsewhip ['hɔːswɪp] **1** *n* cravache *f*
2 *vt (pt & pp* **horsewhipped**) cravacher

horsewoman ['hɔːswʊmən] *n* cavalière *f*

hors(e)y ['hɔːsɪ] *adj* (**a**) *(horse-like)* chevalin(e) (**b**) *(keen on horses)* passionné(e) de chevaux (**c**) *Br Fam (upper-class)* = typique de la noblesse de campagne britannique, élégant et féru d'équitation

horticultural [hɔːtɪˈkʌltʃərəl] *adj* horticole

horticulture ['hɔːtɪkʌltʃə(r)] *n* horticulture *f*

hose [həʊz] **1** *n (pipe)* tuyau *m*
2 *vt* arroser (au jet d'eau)

▸**hose down** *vt sep* laver au jet

hosepipe ['həʊzpaɪp] *n* tuyau *m* d'arrosage

hosiery ['həʊzɪərɪ] *n* bonneterie *f*

hospice ['hɒspɪs] *n (hospital)* = établissement pour malades en phase terminale

hospitable [hɒsˈpɪtəbəl] *adj* hospitalier(ère)

hospitably [hɒsˈpɪtəblɪ] *adv* avec hospitalité

hospital ['hɒspɪtəl] *n* hôpital *m*; **in h.** à l'hôpital; **h. bed/food** lit *m*/nourriture *f* d'hôpital; **h. care** soins *mpl* hospitaliers; *Br* **h. trolley** chariot *m* d'hôpital

hospitality [hɒspɪˈtælɪtɪ] *n* hospitalité *f*

hospitalize ['hɒspɪtəlaɪz] *vt* **to be hospitalized** être hospitalisé(e)

host¹ [həʊst] **1** *n* (**a**) *(at home, party)* hôte *m*; *(on TV, radio)* animateur(trice) *m,f*; **h. city/country** ville *f*/pays *m* d'accueil (**b**) *Biol (of parasite)* hôte *m* (**c**) *Comput* ordinateur *m* principal; *(in network)* serveur *m*
2 *vt* (**a**) *(party)* donner, organiser; *(TV, radio show)* animer (**b**) *Comput (website)* héberger

host² *n (great number)* **a (whole) h. of** (toute) une foule de

host³ *n Rel* hostie *f*

hostage ['hɒstɪdʒ] *n* otage *m*; **to take/hold sb h.** prendre/garder qn en otage; **to offer a h. to fortune** hypothéquer l'avenir

hostel ['hɒstəl] *n (for homeless people, students)* foyer *m*; *(youth hostel)* auberge *f* de jeunesse

hostess ['həʊstɪs] *n (at home, party)* hôtesse *f*; *(on TV, radio)* animatrice *f*; *(on plane)* hôtesse *f* (de l'air); **h. trolley** desserte *f*

hostile ['hɒstaɪl, *Am* 'hɒstəl] *adj* hostile (**to** à); *Com* **h. takeover bid** OPA *f* hostile

hostility [hɒsˈtɪlɪtɪ] *(pl* **hostilities**) *n* hostilité *f* (**towards** envers); **hostilities** *(fighting)* hostilités *fpl*

hot [hɒt] *adj* (**a**) *(having high temperature)* chaud(e); **to get h.** *(of person)* commencer à avoir chaud; *(of thing)* être chaud; **it's h.** *(of person)* avoir chaud; *(of thing)* être chaud; **it's h.** *(of weather)* il fait chaud; *Med* **h. flushes** bouffées *fpl* de chaleur; *Am* **h. tub** = sorte de Jacuzzi® que l'on installe dehors (**b**) *(spicy) (food)* épicé(e); *(pepper, mustard)* fort(e) (**c**) *(close)* **you're getting h.** *(in guessing game)* tu brûles; **to be h. on sb's trail** être aux trousses de qn (**d**) *Fam (good)* **to be h. on sth** *(be knowledgeable about)* être calé(e) en qch; *(attach importance to)* être très à cheval sur qch; **it wasn't such a h. idea** l'idée n'était pas si géniale; **how are you? – not so h.** comment ça va? – pas terrible; **to be h. stuff (at)** être un as (en) (**e**) *Fam (sexy)* sexy *inv* (**f**) *Fam (stolen)* chouré(e) (**g**) *(idioms)* **h. off the press** *(of news)* de dernière minute; *(of book)* qui vient juste de paraître; **too h. to handle** *(issue)* brûlant(e); **to have a h. temper** s'emporter facilement; **to get h. under the collar** se mettre en colère; *Fam* **it's all just h. air** tout ça, c'est du vent; **they're selling like h. cakes** ils se vendent comme des petits pains; **h. desking** = pratique qui consiste à ne pas assigner de bureaux individuels aux employés, ces derniers étant libres de s'installer à n'importe quel poste de travail inoccupé; **h. favourite** *(in race)* grand(e) favori(te) *m,f*; **the h. gossip** les derniers potins *mpl*; **h. line** *(telephone number)* permanence *f* téléphonique; **h. news** les toutes dernières nouvelles; *Fam* **h. potato** *(controversial issue)* sujet *m* brûlant; **to be in the h. seat** *(of politician, manager)* avoir toutes les responsabilités; **h. spot** *(trouble spot)* point *m* chaud; *Fam* **to get into h. water** *(in difficult situation)* s'attirer des ennuis

▸**hot up** *(pt & pp* **hotted**) *vi Fam (of situation, conflict)* s'envenimer; *(of race, debate, contest)* s'animer

hot-air balloon ['hɒteəbə'luːn] *n* montgolfière *f*

hotbed ['hɒtbed] *n* **a h. of rebellion/intrigue** un foyer de rébellion/d'intrigue

hot-blooded ['hɒt'blʌdɪd] *adj* au sang chaud, passionné(e)

hotchpotch ['hɒtʃpɒtʃ] *n Fam* mélange *m*

hotdog ['hɒtdɒg] *n* hot dog *m*

hotel [həʊ'tel] *n* hôtel *m*; **h. room/manager** chambre *f*/gérant(e) *m,f* d'hôtel; **the h. trade** l'industrie *f* hôtelière

hotelier [həʊ'teljeɪ] *n* hôtelier(ère) *m,f*

hotfoot ['hɒt'fʊt] *Fam* **1** *adv* en vitesse
2 *vt* **to h. it** aller à toute vitesse

hothead ['hɒthed] *n* tête *f* brûlée

hotheaded ['hɒt'hedɪd] *adj* exalté(e)

hothouse ['hɒthaʊs] *n* serre *f* (chaude)

hotly ['hɒtlɪ] *adv* *(reply, protest)* vivement; **h. contested** âprement disputé(e)

hotplate ['hɒtpleɪt] *n* (on cooker) plaque *f* (chauffante); *(for keeping food warm)* chauffe-plat *m*

hotpot ['hɒtpɒt] *n (stew)* ragoût *m*

hots ['hɒts] *npl very Fam* **to have the h. for sb** craquer pour qn

hotshot ['hɒtʃɒt] *n Fam (expert)* as *m*, crack *m*

hotspot ['hɒtspɒt] *n Comput (for WiFi® access)* point *m* chaud

hot-tempered ['hɒt'tempəd] *adj* colérique, coléreux(euse)

hot-water [hɒt'wɔːtə(r)] *adj* d'eau chaude; **h. bottle** bouillotte *f*

hound [haʊnd] **1** *n (dog)* chien *m* de chasse **2** *vt (persecute)* traquer, pourchasser

hour ['aʊə(r)] *n* heure *f*; **an h. and a half** une heure et demie; **half an h.** une demi-heure; **to pay sb by the h.** payer qn à l'heure; **to take hours over sth** mettre des heures à faire qch; **we've been waiting for hours** ça fait des heures que nous attendons; **to work long hours** faire de longues journées (de travail); **to keep late hours** *(of person)* se coucher tard; **till all hours** jusqu'à très tard; **where were you in my h. of need?** où étais-tu quand j'avais besoin de toi?; **h. hand** *(of watch, clock)* petite aiguille *f*

hourglass ['aʊəglɑːs] *n* sablier *m*; **an h. figure** une taille de guêpe

hourly ['aʊəlɪ] **1** *adj* **at h. intervals** toutes les heures; **h. rate** taux *m* horaire **2** *adv (every hour)* toutes les heures; *(at any time)* d'un moment à l'autre

house 1 *n* [haʊs] (**a**) *(dwelling)* maison *f*; **to stay at sb's h.** loger chez qn; **from h. to h.** de porte à porte; **they keep open h.** leur maison est toujours ouverte; *Fig* **to put one's h. in order** balayer devant sa porte; **to get on like a h. on fire** *(very well)* s'entendre comme larrons en foire; **the H. of Commons/Lords** la Chambre des communes/lords; **the Houses of Parliament** le Parlement; **the H. of Representatives** la Chambre des représentants; *Law* **to be under h. arrest** être assigné(e) à résidence; **h. guest** invité(e) *m,f*; **h. martin** hirondelle *f* de fenêtre; **h. painter** peintre *m* en bâtiment; **h. party** partie *f* de campagne; **h. plant** plante *f* d'intérieur *ou* d'appartement; **h. spider** araignée *f* commune (**b**) *Com (company)* maison *f*; **h. style** style *m* maison (**c**) *(restaurant)* **on the h.** aux frais de la maison; **h. wine** vin *m* de la maison (**d**) *Theat* **an empty/good h.** une salle vide/pleine (**e**) **h. (music)** house music *f* (**f**) *Br Sch* = groupe d'élèves d'une école secondaire qui disputent ensemble des compétitions sportives etc **2** *vt* [haʊz] *(person)* loger; *(collection, mechanism)* contenir, recevoir

House of Commons
La Chambre des communes britannique est composée de 659 députés ("MPs") élus pour cinq ans et qui siègent environ 175 jours par an. Les députés du parti majoritaire s'assoient d'un côté de la Chambre (les "government benches"), tandis que les députés de l'opposition s'assoient de l'autre côté (sur les "opposition benches"). Si un projet de loi n'obtient pas l'approbation de la majorité des députés dans la Chambre des communes, il est renvoyé à la Chambre des lords, et doit par ailleurs obtenir l'assentiment du souverain avant de devenir loi.

House of Lords
La Chambre des lords est composée de pairs et d'hommes d'Église. Il s'agit de la plus haute cour au Royaume-Uni (en excluant l'Écosse). Elle a le pouvoir d'amender certains projets de loi qui ont été votés par la Chambre des communes. Le gouvernement travailliste de Tony Blair, élu en 1997, a entrepris des réformes visant à réduire les pouvoirs de la Chambre des lords de façon radicale.

House of Representatives
La Chambre des représentants constitue, avec le Sénat, l'organe législatif américain ; ses membres sont élus par le peuple, en proportion de la population de chaque État. Tous les projets de loi concernant les dépenses du gouvernement doivent venir de la Chambre des représentants.

houseboat ['haʊsbəʊt] *n* péniche *f* aménagée
housebound ['haʊsbaʊnd] *adj* confiné(e) chez soi
housebreaker ['haʊsbreɪkə(r)] *n* cambrioleur(euse) *m,f*
housebreaking ['haʊsbreɪkɪŋ] *n* cambriolage *m*
housecoat ['haʊskəʊt] *n* robe *f* d'intérieur
housefly ['haʊsflaɪ] *(pl* **houseflies**) *n* mouche *f* domestique
household ['haʊshəʊld] *n* ménage *m*; **h. appliance** appareil *m* électroménager; **h. chores** tâches *fpl* ménagères; **he's a h. name** tout le monde connaît son nom
householder ['haʊshəʊldə(r)] *n (owner)* propriétaire *mf*; *(tenant)* locataire *mf*
househusband ['haʊshʌzbənd] *n* homme *m* au foyer
housekeeper ['haʊskiːpə(r)] *n (private)* gouvernante *f*; *(in institution)* intendante *f*
housekeeping ['haʊskiːpɪŋ] *n* **h. (money)** argent *m* du ménage
housemaid ['haʊsmeɪd] *n* bonne *f*, femme *f* de chambre; **h.'s knee** *(inflammation)* inflammation *f* du genou
houseman ['haʊsmən] *n Br Med* interne *mf*
housemaster ['haʊsmɑːstə(r)] *n Br Sch* = dans une école secondaire, professeur chargé d'une "house"
housemistress ['haʊsmɪstrɪs] *n Br Sch* = dans une école secondaire, professeur chargé d'une "house"
houseproud ['haʊspraʊd] *adj* **she's very h.** elle prend grand soin de son intérieur
houseroom ['haʊsruːm] *n* **I wouldn't give it h.** *(theory, suggestion)* je ne perdrais pas mon temps avec ça; **I wouldn't give that table h.!** je ne voudrais pas de cette table chez moi!
house-sitter ['haʊssɪtə(r)] *n* = personne qui garde la maison en l'absence de ses occupants
house-to-house ['haʊstə'haʊs] *adj* **to make a h. search** fouiller chaque maison
house-trained ['haʊstreɪnd] *adj (dog)* propre; *Hum (husband, partner)* bien dressé(e)
housewarming ['haʊswɔːmɪŋ] *n* **h. (party)** pendaison *f* de crémaillère; **to have a h. party** pendre la crémaillère
housewife ['haʊswaɪf] *(pl* **housewives** ['haʊswaɪvz]) *n* femme *f* au foyer
housework ['haʊswɜːk] *n* ménage *m*
housing ['haʊzɪŋ] *n* logement *m*; *Br* **h. association** = organisme *m* d'aide au logement; *Br* **h. benefit** ≃ allocation *f* logement; *Br* **h. estate** *(council-owned)* cité *f* HLM; *(private)* lotissement *m*; **the h. market** le marché de l'immobilier; *Am* **h. project** cité *f* HLM
hove [həʊv] *pt & pp of* **heave**
hovel ['hɒvəl] *n* taudis *m*
hover ['hɒvə(r)] *vi* (**a**) *(of bird)* planer; *(of helicopter)* effectuer un vol stationnaire (**b**) *(of person)* **to h. near sb** être derrière le dos de qn
hovercraft ['hɒvəkrɑːft] *n* hovercraft *m*, aéroglisseur *m*
how [haʊ] *adv* (**a**) *(in what way, by what means)* comment; **h. did they find out?** comment l'ont-ils

appris?; **h. do you spell it?** comment ça s'écrit?; *Fam* **h. come?** comment ça se fait?; *Fam and* **h.!** et comment! (**b**) *(to what extent)* **h. much money?** combien d'argent?; **h. many people?** combien de gens?; **h. old are you?** quel âge as-tu?; **h. big is it?** c'est grand comment?; **h. long have you been here?** depuis combien de temps êtes-vous ici?; **h. often do you see him?** tu le vois tous les combien?; **you know h.** difficult it is tu sais à quel point c'est difficile; **h. useful will it be?** est-ce que ce sera très utile? (**c**) *(greetings, enquiries after health)* **h. are you?** comment vas-tu?; *Fam* **h. are things?, how's it going?** ça va?; **h.'s business?** comment vont les affaires? (**d**) *(in exclamations)* que, comme; **h. pretty she is!** qu'elle est jolie!, comme elle est jolie!; **h. disgusting!** c'est vraiment dégoûtant!; **h. true!** c'est bien vrai!; **h. she's changed!** comme elle a changé! (**e**) *(in suggestions)* **h. about a game of cards?** et si on faisait une partie de cartes?; **h. about going out for a meal?** et si on allait manger quelque part?; **h. about it?** ça te dirait?; **h. about you?** et toi?

howdy ['haʊdɪ] *exclam Am Fam* salut!

however [haʊ'evə(r)] **1** *adv* (**a**) *(in whatever degree)* si... que + *subjunctive*; **h. clever she is** si intelligente qu'elle soit; **h. hard she tried, she couldn't do it** elle avait beau essayer, elle n'y arrivait pas (**b**) *(in whatever way)* **h. you look at it...** de quelque façon qu'on envisage la chose... (**c**) *(in what way)* comment; **h. did she find out?** comment a-t-elle bien pu l'apprendre?

2 *conj* pourtant, cependant; **h., this does not explain why she...** ceci n'explique pourtant pas pourquoi elle...

howl [haʊl] **1** *n (of animal, person)* hurlement *m*; **howls of derision** des huées *fpl*

2 *vi (of animal, person)* hurler; **to h. with laughter** hurler de rire

▸**howl down** *vt sep* huer

howler ['haʊlə(r)] *n Fam (mistake)* bourde *f*

howling ['haʊlɪŋ] **1** *n (of wind, wolf)* hurlement *m*; *(of baby)* hurlements *mpl*

2 *adj (wolf)* qui hurle; *(gale, wind)* furieux(euse); *Fam* **it wasn't exactly a h. success** ça n'a pas vraiment eu un succès fou

HP, hp [eɪtʃ'piː] *n* (**a**) *(abbr* horsepower) CV *m* (**b**) *(abbr* hire purchase) achat *m* à crédit

HQ [eɪtʃ'kjuː] *n (abbr* headquarters) QG *m*

hr *(abbr* hour) h

HRH [eɪtʃɑː'reɪtʃ] *n Br (abbr* Her/His Royal Highness) SAR

HRM [eɪtʃɑː'rem] *n (abbr* human resource management) GRH *f*

HRT [eɪtʃɑː'tiː] *n Med (abbr* hormone replacement therapy) hormonothérapie *f* de substitution

HTML [eɪtʃtiːem'el] *n Comput (abbr* HyperText Markup Language) HTML

HTTP [eɪtʃtiːtiː'piː] *n Comput (abbr* HyperText Transfer Protocol) HTTP

hub [hʌb] *n* (**a**) *(of wheel)* moyeu *m* (**b**) *(of community)* centre *m*; **h. airport** aéroport *m* important *(qui sert de plaque tournante)*

hubbub ['hʌbʌb] *n* brouhaha *m*

hubby ['hʌbɪ] *(pl* hubbies) *n Fam* petit mari *m*

hubcap ['hʌbkæp] *n (of wheel)* enjoliveur *m*

huddle ['hʌdəl] **1** *n (of people)* petit groupe *m*; *(of things)* tas *m*

2 *vi* se blottir

▸**huddle together** *vi* se blottir les uns contre les autres

▸**huddle up** *vi* se blottir

Hudson Bay [hʌdsən'beɪ] *n* la baie d'Hudson

hue¹ [hjuː] *n (colour)* teinte *f*

hue² *n* **h. and cry** tollé *m*; **to raise a h. and cry about** sth crier haro sur qch

huff [hʌf] **1** *n Fam* **to be in a h.** faire la tête

2 *vi* **to h. and puff** *(blow)* souffler; *Fig (show annoyance)* maugréer

huffy ['hʌfɪ] *adj Fam (sulky)* susceptible

hug [hʌg] **1** *n* étreinte *f*; **to give sb a h.** serrer qn (dans ses bras)

2 *vt (pt & pp* hugged) (**a**) *(embrace)* serrer (dans ses bras) (**b**) *Fig (shore, kerb)* serrer; *(ground)* raser

huge [hjuːdʒ] *adj (very big)* énorme; *(very tall, long)* immense

hugely ['hjuːdʒlɪ] *adv* énormément, extrêmement

hulk [hʌlk] *n* (**a**) *(of ship)* épave *f* (**b**) *Fam (person)* mastodonte *m*

hulking ['hʌlkɪŋ] *adj Fam* **a h. great man** une armoire à glace

hull [hʌl] **1** *n* (**a**) *(of ship)* coque *f* (**b**) *(of pea)* cosse *f*

2 *vt (peas)* écosser

hullabaloo [hʌləbə'luː] *(pl* hullabaloos) *n Fam* raffut *m*

hullo = hello

hum [hʌm] **1** *n* bourdonnement *m*

2 *vt (pt & pp* hummed) *(tune)* fredonner

3 *vi* (**a**) *(of person)* fredonner; *(of insect, computer)* bourdonner; *(of engine, fridge)* ronronner; **to h. and haw** hésiter; **to h. with activity** bourdonner d'activité (**b**) *Fam (smell)* chlinguer

human ['hjuːmən] **1** *n* (être *m*) humain *m*

2 *adj* humain(e); **h. being** être *m* humain; **h. cloning** clonage *m* humain; **h. error** erreur *f* humaine; **h. nature** la nature humaine; **h. resources** ressources *fpl* humaines; **h. rights** droits *mpl* de l'homme; **h. shield** bouclier *m* humain

humane [hjʊ'meɪn] *adj* humain(e)

humanely [hjʊ'meɪnlɪ] *adv* humainement

humanism ['hjuːmənɪzəm] *n* humanisme *m*

humanistic [hjuːmə'nɪstɪk] *adj* humaniste

humanitarian [hjʊmænɪ'teərɪən] **1** *n* philanthrope *mf*

2 *adj* humanitaire

humanity [hjʊ'mænɪtɪ] *(pl* humanities) *n* humanité *f*; *Univ* **humanities** lettres *fpl*

humanize ['hjuːmənaɪz] *vt* humaniser

humankind [hjuːmən'kaɪnd] *n* humanité *f*

humanly ['hjuːmənlɪ] *adv* **to do everything h. possible** faire tout ce qui est humainement possible

humble ['hʌmbəl] **1** *adj (meek)* humble; *(unpretentious)* modeste; **in my h. opinion** à mon humble avis; *Fig* **to eat h. pie** reconnaître qu'on a tort

2 *vt* humilier

humbling ['hʌmbəlɪŋ] *adj* humiliant(e)

humbly ['hʌmbəlɪ] *adv (meekly)* humblement; *(modestly)* modestement

humbug ['hʌmbʌg] *n* (**a**) *(nonsense)* balivernes *fpl* (**b**) *(hypocrite)* charlatan *m* (**c**) *Br (sweet)* berlingot *m*

humdinger ['hʌmdɪŋə(r)] *n Fam* **a h. of a film/book** un film/livre extra

humdrum ['hʌmdrʌm] *adj* monotone

humerus ['hjuːmərəs] *(pl* humeri ['hjuːməraɪ]) *n Anat* humérus *m*

humid ['hju:mɪd] *adj* humide
humidifier [hjʊ'mɪdɪfaɪə(r)] *n* humidificateur *m*
humidity [hjʊ'mɪdɪtɪ] *n* humidité *f*
humiliate [hjʊ'mɪlɪeɪt] *vt* humilier
humiliating [hjʊ'mɪlɪeɪtɪŋ] *adj* humiliant(e)
humiliation [hjʊmɪlɪ'eɪʃən] *n* humiliation *f*
humility [hjʊ'mɪlɪtɪ] *n* humilité *f*
hummingbird ['hʌmɪŋbɜːd] *n* colibri *m*
hummus ['hʊmʊs, 'hʌməs] *n* houmous *m*
humor, humorless *Am* = humour, humourless
humorous ['hju:mərəs] *adj (situation)* drôle, comique; *(writer, drawing, remark)* humoristique
humorously ['hju:mərəslɪ] *adv* avec humour
humour, *Am* **humor** ['hju:mə(r)] **1** *n* (**a**) *(fun)* humour *m* (**b**) *Formal (mood)* humeur *f*
  2 *vt (indulge)* faire plaisir à
humourless, *Am* **humorless** ['hju:məlɪs] *adj* dépourvu(e) d'humour
hump [hʌmp] **1** *n (on back, road)* bosse *f*
  2 *vt* (**a**) *Fam (carry)* trimbaler (**b**) *Vulg (have sex with)* sauter
humpback ['hʌmpbæk] *n* **h. bridge** pont *m* en dos d'âne; **h. whale** baleine *f* à bosse
humus ['hju:məs] *n* humus *m*
hunch [hʌntʃ] **1** *n (intuition)* intuition *f*; **to have a h. that...** avoir l'intuition que...
  2 *vt* **to h. one's shoulders** rentrer les épaules
hunchback ['hʌntʃbæk] *n* bossu(e) *m,f*
hundred ['hʌndrəd] **1** *n* cent *m*; **one** *or* **a h.** cent *m*; **a h. and twenty-five pages** cent vingt-cinq pages; **two h. pages** deux cents pages; **I've told you hundreds of times** je te l'ai dit des centaines de fois; **to live to be a h.** vivre jusqu'à cent ans
  2 *adj* cent; **a h. kilometres an hour** cent kilomètres à l'heure; **one** *or* **a h. per cent** cent pour cent; **to be a h. per cent certain** être sûr(e) à cent pour cent; **I'm not feeling a h. per cent** je ne me sens pas au mieux de ma forme; **the h. metres** *(in athletics)* le cent mètres
hundredfold ['hʌndrədfəʊld] *adv* **to increase a h.** centupler
hundredth ['hʌndrədθ] **1** *n* (**a**) *(fraction)* centième *m* (**b**) *(in series)* centième *mf*
  2 *adj* centième; *Fam* **for the h. time, no!** pour la centième fois, non!; *see also* **eighth**
hundredweight ['hʌndrədweɪt] *n Br* = 50,8 kg, (poids *m* de) 112 livres *fpl*; *Am* = 45,36 kg, (poids *m* de) 100 livres *fpl*
hung [hʌŋ] **1** *adj* **h. jury/parliament** jury *m*/parlement *m* sans majorité
  2 *pt & pp of* **hang**
Hungarian [hʌŋ'geərɪən] **1** *n* (**a**) *(person)* Hongrois(e) *m,f* (**b**) *(language)* hongrois *m*
  2 *adj* hongrois(e)
Hungary ['hʌŋgərɪ] *n* la Hongrie
hunger ['hʌŋgə(r)] *n* faim *f*; *Fig (for power)* soif *f* (**for** de); **h. strike** grève *f* de la faim
▸**hunger after, hunger for** *vt insep Fig* avoir soif de
hungrily ['hʌŋgrɪlɪ] *adv also Fig* avidement
hungry ['hʌŋgrɪ] *adj* **to be h.** avoir faim; **to be h. for knowledge** être avide de connaissances
hunk [hʌŋk] *n* (**a**) *(of bread, meat)* gros morceau *m* (**b**) *Fam (attractive man)* beau mec *m*
hunky ['hʌŋkɪ] *adj Fam (man)* bien foutu
hunt [hʌnt] **1** *n (for animals)* chasse *f*; *(for person, work)* recherche *f*

  2 *vt (animal)* chasser; *(criminal)* pourchasser
  3 *vi* (**a**) *(search)* **to h. for** rechercher (**b**) *(kill animals)* chasser
▸**hunt down** *vt sep (animal, person)* traquer; *(information)* dénicher
▸**hunt out** *vt sep (find) (person)* retrouver; *(thing)* dénicher
hunted ['hʌntɪd] *adj (look)* hagard(e)
hunter ['hʌntə(r)] *n* chasseur *m*
hunting ['hʌntɪŋ] *n* chasse *f*; **to go h.** aller à la chasse; **h. ground** terrain *m* de chasse; **h. lodge** pavillon *m* de chasse

Hunting

Depuis plusieurs années, la chasse à courre au renard constitue pour le gouvernement britannique un dossier controversé. En effet, une partie de plus en plus importante de la population s'oppose à ce type de chasse, considéré comme barbare ; mais il existe également en face un groupe de pression pro-chasse très actif qui s'oppose à toute réforme et qui met l'accent sur les conséquences néfastes qu'une interdiction de la chasse au renard aurait sur le mode de vie rural et sur l'emploi dans les campagnes. En 2005 une loi fut finalement votée, interdisant ce type de chasse. Cependant certains irréductibles continuent à s'opposer à cette décision.

huntsman ['hʌntsmən] *n* chasseur *m*
hurdle ['hɜːdəl] **1** *n (in race)* haie *f*; *Fig (obstacle)* obstacle *m*
  2 *vt (jump over)* sauter, franchir
hurdler ['hɜːdlə(r)] *n Sport* coureur(euse) *m,f* de haies
hurdling ['hɜːdəlɪŋ] *n Sport* course *f* de haies
hurl [hɜːl] **1** *vt* jeter, lancer (**at** sur); *(insults)* lancer (**at** à); **to h. oneself at sb** se jeter *ou* se ruer sur qn
  2 *vi Fam (vomit)* dégobiller
hurling ['hɜːlɪŋ] *n* = jeu irlandais voisin du hockey sur gazon qui oppose deux équipes de quinze joueurs
hurly-burly ['hɜːlɪ'bɜːlɪ] *n Fam* tohu-bohu *m inv*
hurrah [hʊ'rɑː], **hurray** [hʊ'reɪ] *exclam* hourra!
hurricane ['hʌrɪkən, *Am* 'hʌrɪkeɪn] *n* ouragan *m*; **h. lamp** lampe *f* tempête
hurried ['hʌrɪd] *adj (gesture, conversation, meal)* rapide; *(departure)* précipité(e); *(work)* fait(e) à la hâte; *(decision, choice)* pris(e) à la hâte
hurriedly ['hʌrɪdlɪ] *adv* précipitamment
hurry ['hʌrɪ] **1** *n* hâte *f*; **to be in a h. (to do sth)** être pressé(e) (de faire qch); **to do sth in a h.** faire qch à la hâte; **to leave in a h.** partir à la hâte; **I won't do that again in a h.** je ne suis pas prêt(e) de recommencer; **there's no h.** rien ne presse; **what's the h.?** qu'est-ce qui presse?
  2 *vt (pt & pp* **hurried**) *(person)* presser; *(work)* hâter; **he was hurried to hospital** on l'a transporté d'urgence à l'hôpital
  3 *vi* se dépêcher, se presser; **to h. to do sth** se dépêcher *ou* se presser de faire qch; **to h. into/out of a room** se précipiter dans/hors d'une pièce
▸**hurry along 1** *vt sep (person)* faire se dépêcher; *(work)* accélérer
  2 *vi* se presser
▸**hurry back** *vi* se dépêcher de revenir

▶**hurry on 1** *vt sep (person)* faire circuler; *(work)* faire accélérer
2 *vi (leave)* partir en hâte
▶**hurry up 1** *vt sep* faire accélérer
2 *vi* se dépêcher; **h. up!** vite!, dépêche-toi!
hurt [hɜːt] **1** *n (emotional)* blessure *f*
2 *adj* blessé(e)
3 *vt (pt & pp* **hurt**) (**a**) *(physically)* faire mal à; *(reputation, chances)* nuire à; **to h. oneself** se faire mal; **to h. one's foot** se faire mal au pied; **to get h.** se blesser; *Fig* **it won't h. him to have to wait** ça ne lui fera pas de mal d'attendre un peu (**b**) *(emotionally)* faire du mal *ou* de la peine à; **to h. sb's feelings** blesser qn
4 *vi* (**a**) *(cause pain)* faire mal; **where does it h.?** où est-ce que ça fait mal?; **my foot hurts** j'ai mal au pied, mon pied me fait mal (**b**) *(emotionally)* faire mal
hurtful ['hɜːtfʊl] *adj* blessant(e)
hurtle ['hɜːtəl] *vi* **to h. along** avancer à toute vitesse; **to h. down the street** dévaler la rue; **to h. towards** foncer sur
husband ['hʌzbənd] **1** *n* mari *m*
2 *vt Formal (one's resources)* ménager
husbandry ['hʌzbəndrɪ] *n* agriculture *f*; **animal h.** élevage *m*
hush [hʌʃ] **1** *n (quiet)* silence *m*; **h.!** chut!
2 *vt* calmer
▶**hush up** *vt sep (scandal)* étouffer
hushed [hʌʃt] *adj (conversation)* étouffé(e); *(silence)* profond(e); **to talk in h. tones** parler à voix basse
hush-hush ['hʌʃhʌʃ] *adj Fam* top secret *inv*
husk [hʌsk] **1** *n (of seed)* enveloppe *f*; *(of pea)* cosse *f*; *(of nut)* brou *m*
2 *vt (grain)* décortiquer
husky¹ ['hʌskɪ] *adj (voice)* rauque
husky² *(pl* **huskies**) *n (dog)* husky *m*
hussar [hʊ'zɑː(r)] *n Mil* hussard *m*
hussy ['hʌsɪ] *(pl* **hussies**) *n Old-fashioned or Hum* gourgandine *f*
hustings ['hʌstɪŋz] *npl* **on the h.** en campagne
hustle ['hʌsəl] **1** *n* **h. (and bustle)** effervescence *f*
2 *vt (shove, push)* **to h. sb away** emmener qn de force; **I was hustled into a small room** on m'a poussé dans une petite pièce
hustler ['hʌslə(r)] *n Am Fam (swindler)* arnaqueur(euse) *m,f*; *(prostitute)* prostitué(e) *m,f*
hut [hʌt] *n (shed)* cabane *f*; *(dwelling)* hutte *f*
hutch [hʌtʃ] *n (for rabbit)* clapier *m*
hyacinth ['haɪəsɪnθ] *n* jacinthe *f*
hybrid ['haɪbrɪd] **1** *n* hybride *m*
2 *adj* hybride
hydrangea [haɪ'dreɪndʒə] *n* hortensia *m*
hydrant ['haɪdrənt] *n* prise *f* d'eau; **fire h.** bouche *f* d'incendie
hydraulic [haɪ'drɔːlɪk] *adj* hydraulique; **h. engineering** hydraulique *f*
hydraulics [haɪ'drɔːlɪks] *n* hydraulique *f*
hydrocarbon [haɪdrəʊ'kɑːbən] *n* hydrocarbure *m*
hydrochloric acid [haɪdrəʊ'klɒrɪk'æsɪd] *n* acide *m* chlorhydrique
hydroelectric [haɪdrəʊɪ'lektrɪk] *adj* hydroélectrique
hydroelectricity [haɪdrəʊɪlek'trɪsɪtɪ] *n* hydroélectricité *f*
hydrofoil ['haɪdrəfɔɪl] *n* hydrofoil *m*, hydroptère *m*
hydrogen ['haɪdrədʒən] *n* hydrogène *m*; **h. bomb** bombe *f* à hydrogène

hydrolysis [haɪ'drɒlɪsɪs] *n* hydrolyse *f*
hydrophobia [haɪdrə'fəʊbɪə] *n Med (rabies)* rage *f*
hydroplane ['haɪdrəpleɪn] *n (boat)* hydroglisseur *m*; *(seaplane)* hydravion *m*
hydroxide [haɪ'drɒksaɪd] *n* hydroxyde *m*
hyena [haɪ'iːnə] *n* hyène *f*
hygiene ['haɪdʒiːn] *n* hygiène *f*
hygienic [haɪ'dʒiːnɪk] *adj* hygiénique
hymen ['haɪmen] *n* hymen *m*
hymn [hɪm] *n* cantique *m*; **h. book** livre *m* de cantiques
hymnal ['hɪmnəl] *n* livre *m* de cantiques
hype [haɪp] *Fam* **1** *n (publicity)* battage *m* (publicitaire)
2 *vt (publicize)* faire du battage (publicitaire) pour
hype up *vt sep Fam* (**a**) *(publicize)* faire du battage (publicitaire) pour (**b**) **to be hyped up** *(excited)* être surexcité(e)
hyper ['haɪpə(r)] *adj Fam (overexcited)* surexcité(e); **she's very h.** elle est très speed
hyperactive [haɪpə'ræktɪv] *adj* hyperactif(ive)
hyperbola [haɪ'pɜːbələ] *n Math* hyperbole *f*
hyperbole [haɪ'pɜːbəlɪ] *n* hyperbole *f*
hypercritical [haɪpə'krɪtɪkəl] *adj* hypercritique
hyperinflation [haɪpərɪn'fleɪʃən] *n Econ* hyperinflation *f*
hyperlink ['haɪpəlɪŋk] *n Comput* hyperlien *m*
hypermarket ['haɪpəmɑːkɪt] *n* hypermarché *m*
hypersensitive [haɪpə'sensɪtɪv] *adj* hypersensible
hypertension [haɪpə'tenʃən] *n Med* hypertension *f*
hypertext ['haɪpətekst] *n Comput* hypertexte *m*; **h. link** lien *m* hypertexte
hyphen ['haɪfən] *n* trait *m* d'union
hyphenate ['haɪfəneɪt] *vt (word)* mettre un trait d'union à; **a hyphenated word** un mot à trait d'union
hypnosis [hɪp'nəʊsɪs] *n* hypnose *f*
hypnotic [hɪp'nɒtɪk] *adj* hypnotique
hypnotism ['hɪpnətɪzəm] *n* hypnotisme *m*
hypnotist ['hɪpnətɪst] *n* hypnotiseur(euse) *m,f*
hypnotize ['hɪpnətaɪz] *vt* hypnotiser
hypoallergenic [haɪpəʊælə'dʒenɪk] *adj* hypoallergénique
hypochondria [haɪpə'kɒndrɪə] *n* hypocondrie *f*
hypochondriac [haɪpə'kɒndrɪæk] *n* hypocondriaque *mf*
hypocrisy [hɪ'pɒkrɪsɪ] *n* hypocrisie *f*
hypocrite ['hɪpəkrɪt] *n* hypocrite *mf*
hypocritical [hɪpə'krɪtɪkəl] *adj* hypocrite
hypodermic [haɪpə'dɜːmɪk] **1** *n* seringue *f* hypodermique
2 *adj* hypodermique
hypotenuse [haɪ'pɒtənjuːz] *n Math* hypoténuse *f*
hypothermia [haɪpəʊ'θɜːmɪə] *n* hypothermie *f*; **to have h.** faire de l'hypothermie
hypothesis [haɪ'pɒθəsɪs] *(pl* **hypotheses** [haɪ'pɒθəsiːz]) *n* hypothèse *f*
hypothesize [haɪ'pɒθəsaɪz] **1** *vt* **to h. that...** émettre l'hypothèse que...
2 *vi* faire des hypothèses
hypothetical [haɪpə'θetɪkəl] *adj* hypothétique
hysterectomy [hɪstə'rektəmɪ] *(pl* **hysterectomies**) *n* hystérectomie *f*; **to have a h.** subir une hystérectomie
hysteria [hɪs'tɪərɪə] *n* (**a**) *(panic)* hystérie *f* (**b**) *(laughter)* fou rire *m*
hysterical [hɪs'terɪkəl] *adj* (**a**) *(uncontrolled)* hystérique; **to be h.** faire une crise de nerfs; **h. laughter** fou rire *m* (**b**) *(very funny)* tordant(e)

hysterically [hɪsˈterɪklɪ] *adv* (**a**) *(uncontrolledly)* sans pouvoir se contrôler; **to laugh h.** avoir le fou rire (**b**) **h. funny** tordant(e)

hysterics [hɪsˈterɪks] *npl* (**a**) *(panic)* crise *f* de nerfs; **to go into** *or* **have h.** avoir une crise de nerfs (**b**) *(laughter)* fou rire *m*; **to be in h.** avoir le fou rire

I¹, i [aɪ] *n (letter)* I, i *m inv*
I² *pron* je; **I'm Scottish** je suis écossais; **I haven't got it!** ce n'est pas moi qui l'ai!
IAEA [aɪeɪiːˈeɪ] *n (abbr* **International Atomic Energy Agency**) AIEA *f*
IAP [aɪeɪˈpi] *n Comput (abbr* **Internet Access Provider**) fournisseur *m* d'accès à l'Internet
IBA [aɪbiːˈeɪ] *n (abbr* **Independent Broadcasting Authority**) ≃ CSA *m (organisme qui contrôle les chaînes de télévision et de stations de radio privées britanniques)*
Iberian [aɪˈbiːrɪən] *adj* ibérique; **the I. Peninsula** la péninsule Ibérique
ibex [ˈaɪbeks] *n* bouquetin *m*
ibid [ˈɪbɪd] *adv (abbr* **ibidem**) ibid
IBM [aɪbiːˈem] *n (abbr* **intercontinental ballistic missile**) MBI *m*
IBRD [aɪbiːɑːˈdiː] *n (abbr* **International Bank for Reconstruction and Development**) BIRD *f*
IBS [aɪbiːˈes] *n (abbr* **irritable bowel syndrome**) colopathie *f* fonctionnelle
ice [aɪs] **1** *n* (**a**) *(frozen water, ice-cream)* glace *f*; *(on road)* verglas *m*; **i. age** période *f* glaciaire; **i. bucket** seau *m* à glace; **i. cube** glaçon *m*; **i. floe** banquise *f*; **i. hockey** hockey *m* sur glace; **i. lolly** glace *f* à l'eau; **i. pack** sachet *m* de glace; **i. pick** pic *m* à glace; **i. rink** patinoire *f* (**b**) *(idioms)* **to put a project on i.** geler un projet; **to break the i.** rompre la glace; **to be skating on thin i.** avancer sur un terrain glissant; **that cuts no i. with me** ça ne marche pas avec moi
2 *vt (cake)* glacer
▸**ice over** *vi* geler
▸**ice up** *vi* se givrer
iceberg [ˈaɪsbɜːg] *n* iceberg *m*; *Fig* **that's just the tip of the i.** ce n'est que la partie visible de l'iceberg; **i. lettuce** = variété croquante de laitue de serre
icebound [ˈaɪsbaʊnd] *adj* bloqué(e) par les glaces
icebox [ˈaɪsbɒks] *n Br (in fridge)* freezer *m*; *Am (fridge)* réfrigérateur *m*
icebreaker [ˈaɪsbreɪkə(r)] *n (ship)* brise-glace *m inv*; *Fig (at party, in conversation)* **it's a good i.** c'est un bon moyen de briser la glace
icecap [ˈaɪskæp] *n* calotte *f* glaciaire
ice-cold [ˈaɪsˈkəʊld] *adj* glacé(e); *(wind)* glacial(e)
ice-cream [aɪsˈkriːm] *n* glace *f*; **i. cone** cornet *m* de glace; **i. maker** sorbetière *f*; **i. parlour** salon *m* de dégustation de glaces; **i. van** camionnette *f* de vendeur de glaces
iced [aɪst] *adj* (**a**) *(water)* avec des glaçons (**b**) *(cake)* glacé(e)
Iceland [ˈaɪslənd] *n* l'Islande *f*

Icelander [ˈaɪsləndə(r)] *n* Islandais(e) *m,f*
Icelandic [aɪsˈlændɪk] **1** *n (language)* islandais *m*
2 *adj* islandais(e)
ice-skate [ˈaɪsˈskeɪt] **1** *n* patin *m* à glace
2 *vi* faire du patin à glace
ice-skating [ˈaɪsˈskeɪtɪŋ] *n* patinage *m* (sur glace)
icicle [ˈaɪsɪkəl] *n* glaçon *m (qui pend d'une gouttière etc)*
icing [ˈaɪsɪŋ] *n (on cake)* glaçage *m*; *Fig* **the i. on the cake** la cerise sur le gâteau; **i. sugar** sucre *m* glace
icon [ˈaɪkɒn] *n Rel & Comput* icône *f*; *Fig* **gay i.** idole *f* gay
iconoclastic [aɪkɒnəʊˈklæstɪk] *adj* iconoclaste
icy [ˈaɪsɪ] *adj* (**a**) *(road)* verglacé(e); *(ground)* gelé(e); *(water, hands)* glacé(e); *(wind)* glacial(e) (**b**) *Fig (expression, reply)* glacial(e)
ID [ˈaɪˈdiː] *n (abbr* **identification**) papiers *mpl* (d'identité); **ID card** carte *f* d'identité
I'd [aɪd] = I had, I would
idea [aɪˈdiːə] *n* (**a**) *(individual notion)* idée *f*; **to put an i. into sb's head** mettre une idée dans la tête de qn; **the very i.!** quelle idée!; *Fam* **what's the big i.?** qu'est-ce qui te prend? (**b**) *(concept)* conception *f*; **to have an i. that...** avoir l'impression que...; **that's not my i. of fun** ce n'est pas vraiment comme ça que je m'amuserais; **it's her i. of a joke** elle trouve ça drôle; **I have no i.** je n'ai aucune idée; **I had no i. that...** je ne savais pas que...; **I thought the i. was for them to come here** je croyais qu'il était prévu qu'ils viennent ici; **the general i. is to...** l'idée est de...
ideal [aɪˈdiːəl] **1** *n* idéal *m*
2 *adj* idéal(e) (**for** pour)
idealism [aɪˈdɪəlɪzəm] *n* idéalisme *m*
idealist [aɪˈdɪəlɪst] *n* idéaliste *mf*
idealistic [aɪdɪəˈlɪstɪk] *adj* idéaliste
idealize [aɪˈdɪəlaɪz] *vt* idéaliser
ideally [aɪˈdiːəlɪ] *adv* (**a**) *(extremely well)* idéalement; **they're i. matched** ils vont parfaitement bien ensemble (**b**) *(in an ideal situation)* dans l'idéal
identical [aɪˈdentɪkəl] *adj* identique; **i. twins** *(boys)* vrais jumeaux *mpl*; *(girls)* vraies jumelles *fpl*
identification [aɪdentɪfɪˈkeɪʃən] *n* (**a**) *(of body, criminal)* identification *f* (**b**) *(documents)* papiers *mpl* (d'identité)
identifier [aɪˈdentɪfaɪə(r)] *n Comput* identificateur *m*, identifieur *m*
identify [aɪˈdentɪfaɪ] *(pt & pp* **identified**) **1** *vt* (**a**) *(recognize)* identifier (**b**) *(associate)* **to i. sth with sth** identifier qch à qch
2 *vi* s'identifier (**with sb** à qn); **I can't i. with his problems** j'ai du mal à comprendre ses problèmes

identifying mark [aɪˈdentɪfaɪɪŋˈmɑːk] n signe m particulier
Identikit® [aɪˈdentɪkɪt] n I. (picture) portrait-robot m
identity [aɪˈdentɪtɪ] (pl **identities**) n identité f; **it was a case of mistaken i.** il y a eu erreur sur la personne; **i. card** carte f d'identité; **i. crisis** crise f d'identité; **i. parade** séance f d'identification; Comput **i. theft** vol m d'identité
ideological [aɪdɪəˈlɒdʒɪkəl] adj idéologique
ideology [aɪdɪˈɒlədʒɪ] (pl **ideologies**) n idéologie f
idiocy [ˈɪdɪəsɪ] n idiotie f
idiom [ˈɪdɪəm] n (expression) expression f, locution f; (dialect) idiome m
idiomatic [ɪdɪəˈmætɪk] adj idiomatique
idiosyncrasy [ɪdɪəʊˈsɪŋkrəsɪ] (pl **ideosyncracies**) n particularité f; (foible) petite manie f
idiosyncratic [ɪdɪəʊsɪŋˈkrætɪk] adj particulier(ère)
idiot [ˈɪdɪət] n idiot(e) m,f
idiotic [ɪdɪˈɒtɪk] adj idiot(e)
idle [ˈaɪdəl] **1** adj (a) (unoccupied) (factory, machine) arrêté(e); (person) désœuvré(e); **an i. moment** un moment libre (b) (lazy) oisif(ive) (c) (futile) (threat, boast) vain(e); (gossip, rumour) pour passer le temps; (curiosity) simple
2 vi (of engine) tourner au ralenti
▸**idle away** vt sep (time) passer à ne rien faire; **we idled the afternoon away chatting** nous avons passé l'après-midi à bavarder
idleness [ˈaɪdəlnɪs] n (a) (inaction) inactivité f (b) (laziness) oisiveté f
idler [ˈaɪdlə(r)] n (lazy person) paresseux(euse) m,f
idly [ˈaɪdlɪ] adv (a) (inactively) sans rien faire (b) (casually) négligemment
idol [ˈaɪdəl] n idole f
idolatry [aɪˈdɒlətrɪ] n idolâtrie f
idolize [ˈaɪdəlaɪz] vt idolâtrer
idyll [ˈɪdɪl] n (situation) situation f idyllique; (place) endroit m idyllique
idyllic [ˈɪdɪlɪk] adj idyllique
ie [ˈaɪˈiː] (abbr id est) c.-à-d.
if [ɪf] **1** conj (a) (conditional) si; **if I were rich...** si j'étais riche...; **if I were you...** si j'étais toi..., à ta place... (b) (conceding) **the film was good, if rather long** le film était un peu long, mais bien; **if anything it's better** c'est presque mieux (c) (whether) si; **I asked if it was true** j'ai demandé si c'était vrai (d) (in phrases) **if not** sinon; **there were hundreds, if not thousands, of people** il y avait des centaines de gens, voire des milliers; **if so** si c'est le cas; **if only I had more money...** si seulement j'avais plus d'argent...; **if and when they arrive...** quand ils arriveront, s'ils arrivent...; **she sees them rarely, if at all** or **if ever** elle ne les voit jamais, ou alors très rarement
2 n **ifs and buts** restrictions fpl; **it's a big if** c'est un grand point d'interrogation
IFA [aɪefˈeɪ] n Fin (abbr **independent financial adviser**) conseiller(ère) m,f financier(ère) indépendant(e)
iffy [ˈɪfɪ] adj Fam (doubtful) incertain(e); (suspect) louche
igloo [ˈɪgluː] (pl **igloos**) n igloo m
ignite [ɪgˈnaɪt] **1** vt (fire) allumer; (paper) enflammer; Fig (conflict) déclencher
2 vi (of fire) prendre; (of paper) s'enflammer; Fig (of conflict) se déclencher
ignition [ɪgˈnɪʃən] n (of car) allumage m; **to switch on/off the i.** mettre/couper le contact; **i. key** clé f de contact

ignoble [ɪgˈnəʊbəl] adj ignoble
ignominious [ɪgnəˈmɪnɪəs] adj ignominieux(euse)
ignoramus [ɪgnəˈreɪməs] n ignorant(e) m,f, ignare mf
ignorance [ˈɪgnərəns] n (a) (lack of knowledge) ignorance f; **out of** or **through i.** par ignorance (b) (ill manners) manque m d'éducation
ignorant [ˈɪgnərənt] adj (a) (lacking knowledge) (person) ignorant(e); (remark) d'ignorant; **to be i. of sth** ignorer qch (b) (ill-mannered) mal élevé(e)
ignore [ɪgˈnɔː(r)] vt ignorer; **just i. him!** ne fais pas attention à lui!
iguana [ɪgˈwɑːnə] n iguane m
ilk [ɪlk] n **of that i.** de ce genre
ill¹ [ɪl] n pl **ills** maux mpl
2 adj (a) (unwell) malade; **to feel i.** ne pas se sentir bien; **to fall** or **be taken i.** tomber malade (b) (bad, poor) **i. effects** effets mpl néfastes; **i. feeling** animosité f; **i. fortune** malchance f; **to be in i. health** être en mauvaise santé; **i. at ease** mal à l'aise; **of i. repute** mal famé(e); **i. will** malveillance f
3 adv mal; **I can i. afford it** je peux difficilement me le permettre; **to speak/think i. of sb** dire/penser du mal de qn
ill² (abbr **illustration**) ill
I'll [aɪl] = **I will, I shall**
ill-advised [ˈɪlədˈvaɪzd] adj (person) malavisé(e); (decision, comment) peu judicieux(euse); **to be i. to do sth** être malavisé de faire qch
ill-bred [ˈɪlˈbred] adj mal élevé(e)
ill-concealed [ˈɪlkənˈsiːld] adj mal dissimulé(e)
ill-considered [ˈɪlkənˈsɪdəd] adj irréfléchi(e)
ill-disposed [ˈɪldɪsˈpəʊzd] adj **to be i. towards sb/sth** être mal disposé(e) envers qn/qch
illegal [ɪˈliːgəl] adj illégal(e); (immigrant) clandestin(e)
illegality [ɪlɪˈgælɪtɪ] n illégalité f
illegible [ɪˈledʒɪbəl] adj illisible
illegitimate [ɪlɪˈdʒɪtɪmət] adj illégitime
ill-equipped [ˈɪlɪˈkwɪpd] adj mal équipé(e); Fig **to be i. to do sth** ne pas être apte à faire qch
ill-fated [ˈɪlˈfeɪtɪd] adj (day, occasion) fatal(e); (person, enterprise) malheureux(euse)
ill-founded [ˈɪlˈfaʊndɪd] adj sans fondement
ill-gotten gains [ˈɪlgɒtənˈgaɪnz] npl biens mpl mal acquis
illiberal [ɪˈlɪbərəl] adj (person) intolérant(e); (measure) restrictif(ive)
illicit [ɪˈlɪsɪt] adj illicite
ill-informed [ˈɪlɪnˈfɔːmd] adj mal informé(e); (idea) inexact(e)
ill-intentioned [ˈɪlɪnˈtenʃənd] adj malintentionné(e)
illiteracy [ɪˈlɪtərəsɪ] n analphabétisme m
illiterate [ɪˈlɪtərət] **1** n analphabète mf
2 adj analphabète
ill-mannered [ˈɪlˈmænəd] adj grossier(ère)
ill-natured [ˈɪlˈneɪtʃəd] adj désagréable
illness [ˈɪlnɪs] n maladie f
illogical [ɪˈlɒdʒɪkəl] adj illogique
ill-suited [ˈɪlˈsuːtɪd] adj inapproprié(e) (**to** à); (person) inapte (**to** à)
ill-tempered [ˈɪlˈtempəd] adj (person) qui a un mauvais caractère; (remark) désagréable
ill-timed [ˈɪlˈtaɪmd] adj inopportun(e)
ill-treat [ˈɪlˈtriːt] vt maltraiter
illuminate [ɪˈluːmɪneɪt] vt (a) (light up) (room) éclairer; (building) illuminer (b) (clarify) éclairer
illuminating [ɪˈluːmɪneɪtɪŋ] adj éclairant(e)

illumination [ɪlu:mɪ'neɪʃən] *n* (**a**) *(lighting)* éclairage *m*; **illuminations** *(decorative lights)* illuminations *fpl* (**b**) *(clarification)* éclaircissements *mpl*
ill-use 1 *n* ['ɪl'ju:s] mauvais traitement *m*
2 *vt* ['ɪl'ju:z] maltraiter
illusion [ɪ'lu:ʒən] *n* illusion *f*; **to be under the i. that…** s'imaginer que…; **to be under** *or* **have no illusions about sb/sth** ne se faire aucune illusion sur qn/qch
illusory [ɪ'lu:sərɪ] *adj* illusoire
illustrate ['ɪləstreɪt] *vt* illustrer
illustration [ɪləs'treɪʃən] *n* illustration *f*
illustrator ['ɪləstreɪtə(r)] *n* illustrateur(trice) *m,f*
illustrious [ɪ'lʌstrɪəs] *adj* illustre
ILO [aɪe'ləʊ] *n* (*abbr* **International Labour Organization**) OIT *f*
I'm [aɪm] = **I am**
image ['ɪmɪdʒ] *n* image *f*; **to be the i. of sb** être le portrait de qn
imagery ['ɪmɪdʒərɪ] *n* imagerie *f*, images *fpl*
imaginary [ɪ'mædʒɪnərɪ] *adj* imaginaire
imagination [ɪmædʒɪ'neɪʃən] *n* imagination *f*; **it's (all in) your i.** tu te fais des idées; **use your i!** fais preuve d'un peu d'imagination!
imaginative [ɪ'mædʒɪnətɪv] *adj (person)* imaginatif(ive); *(excuse, solution)* original(e)
imagine [ɪ'mædʒɪn] *vt* imaginer; **to i. doing sth** s'imaginer faire qch; **to i. sb doing sth** imaginer qn faisant qch; **I can't i. why…** je n'arrive pas à comprendre pourquoi…; **you're imagining things** tu te fais des idées; **you must have imagined it** tu as dû rêver
imbalance [ɪm'bæləns] *n* déséquilibre *m*
imbecile ['ɪmbɪsi:l] *n* imbécile *mf*
imbibe [ɪm'baɪb] *vt* *Formal (drink)* absorber; *Fig (knowledge, ideas)* absorber, assimiler
imbue [ɪm'bju:] *vt Formal* **to i. sb with sth** imprégner qn de qch; **to be imbued with scorn/fervour** *(of speech, book)* être empreint(e) de mépris/ferveur
IMF [aɪe'mef] *n* (*abbr* **International Monetary Fund**) FMI *m*
imitate ['ɪmɪteɪt] *vt* imiter
imitation [ɪmɪ'teɪʃən] *n (action, copy)* imitation *f*; **in i. of** à l'imitation de; **i. jewellery** faux bijoux *mpl*; **i. leather** similicuir *m*, imitation *f* cuir
imitative ['ɪmɪtətɪv] *adj* imitatif(ive)
imitator ['ɪmɪteɪtə(r)] *n* imitateur(trice) *m,f*
immaculate [ɪ'mækjʊlət] *adj* impeccable; *Rel* **the I. Conception** l'Immaculée Conception *f*
immaterial [ɪmə'tɪərɪəl] *adj* sans importance
immature [ɪmə'tjʊə(r)] *adj* immature
immaturity [ɪmə'tjʊərɪtɪ] *n* immaturité *f*
immeasurable [ɪ'meʒərəbəl] *adj* incommensurable
immediacy [ɪ'mi:dɪəsɪ] *n* immédiateté *f*; *(of danger, disaster)* imminence *f*
immediate [ɪ'mi:dɪət] *adj* (**a**) *(instant)* immédiat(e); *(danger)* imminent(e) (**b**) *(nearest) (vicinity)* proche; *(future)* immédiat(e); **the i. family** les proches parents *mpl*
immediately [ɪ'mi:dɪətlɪ] **1** *adv* immédiatement, tout de suite
2 *conj* dès que
immemorial [ɪmɪ'mɔ:rɪəl] *adj* **from time i.** depuis des temps immémoriaux
immense [ɪ'mens] *adj* immense
immensely [ɪ'menslɪ] *adv (interesting, painful)* extrêmement; *(rich)* immensément; *(enjoy oneself)* énormément

immensity [ɪ'mensɪtɪ] *n* immensité *f*; *(of problem, task)* énormité *f*
immerse [ɪ'mɜ:s] *vt also Fig* plonger (**in** dans); **to i. oneself in sth** se plonger dans qch
immigrant ['ɪmɪgrənt] **1** *n* immigré(e) *m,f*
2 *adj* immigré(e)
immigrate ['ɪmɪgreɪt] *vi* immigrer
immigration [ɪmɪ'greɪʃən] *n* immigration *f*; **to go through i.** passer (à) l'immigration; **i. control** services *mpl* de l'immigration; **i. officer** agent *m* des services de l'immigration
imminent ['ɪmɪnənt] *adj* imminent(e)
immobile [ɪ'məʊbaɪl] *adj* immobile
immobilize [ɪ'məʊbɪlaɪz] *vt* immobiliser
immoderate [ɪ'mɒdərət] *adj* immodéré(e)
immodest [ɪ'mɒdɪst] *adj (vain)* présomptueux(euse); *(indecent)* impudique
immoral [ɪ'mɒrəl] *adj* immoral(e); **i. earnings** gains *mpl* du proxénétisme
immorality [ɪmə'rælɪtɪ] *n* immoralité *f*
immortal [ɪ'mɔ:təl] **1** *adj* immortel(elle) *m,f*
2 *adj* immortel(elle); *(memory)* impérissable
immortality [ɪmɔ:'tælɪtɪ] *n* immortalité *f*
immovable [ɪ'mu:vəbəl] *adj (object)* fixe; *Fig (person, opposition)* inébranlable
immune [ɪ'mju:n] *adj (to disease)* immunisé(e) (**to** contre); *Fig (to criticism)* imperméable (**to** à); **i. from taxation** exonéré(e) d'impôts; *Med* **i. deficiency** immunodéficience *f*; *Med* **i. system** système *m* immunitaire
immunity [ɪ'mju:nɪtɪ] *n (to disease)* immunité *f*; *(from taxation)* exonération *f*; *Law* **i. (from prosecution)** immunité
immunization [ɪmjʊnaɪ'zeɪʃən] *n* immunisation *f*
immunize ['ɪmjʊnaɪz] *vt* immuniser (**against** contre)
immunosuppression ['ɪmjʊ:nəʊsə'preʃən] *n Med* immunosuppression *f*
immutable [ɪ'mju:təbəl] *adj* immuable
imp [ɪmp] *n (sprite)* lutin *m*; *Fig (mischievous child)* coquin(e) *m,f*
impact 1 [ɪ'ɪmpækt] impact *m*; **to make an i. on sb/sth** avoir un impact sur qn/qch; **on i.** au moment de l'impact
2 *vt* [ɪm'pækt] *(collide with)* heurter; *(influence)* avoir un impact sur
impacted [ɪm'pæktɪd] *adj (tooth)* inclus(e)
impair [ɪm'peə(r)] *vt (sight, hearing)* affaiblir; *(relations, chances)* compromettre
impale [ɪm'peɪl] *vt* empaler (**on** sur)
impart [ɪm'pa:t] *vt Formal (heat, light, quality)* donner; *(knowledge, news)* transmettre
impartial [ɪm'pa:ʃəl] *adj* impartial(e)
impartiality [ɪmpa:ʃɪ'ælɪtɪ] *n* impartialité *f*
impassable [ɪm'pa:səbəl] *adj (river, barrier)* infranchissable; *(road)* impraticable
impasse ['æmpa:s] *n* impasse *f*; **to have reached an i.** être dans une impasse
impassioned [ɪm'pæʃənd] *adj* passionné(e)
impassive [ɪm'pæsɪv] *adj* impassible
impassively [ɪm'pæsɪvlɪ] *adv* impassiblement
impatience [ɪm'peɪʃəns] *n* impatience *f*
impatient [ɪm'peɪʃənt] *adj* impatient(e); **to be i. to do sth** être impatient(e) de faire qch; **to be i. for sth** avoir soif de qch; **to get i. (with sb)** s'impatienter (contre qn)
impatiently [ɪm'peɪʃəntlɪ] *adv* avec impatience

impeach [ɪmˈpiːtʃ] *vt Am Law* mettre en accusation *(selon la procédure qui vise les hauts fonctionnaires américains)*
impeccable [ɪmˈpekəbəl] *adj* impeccable
impede [ɪmˈpiːd] *vt* gêner
impediment [ɪmˈpedɪmənt] *n* (**a**) *(obstacle)* obstacle *m* (**b**) *(disability)* handicap *m*
impel [ɪmˈpel] *(pt & pp* **impelled**) *vt* (**a**) *(oblige)* obliger; *(incite)* pousser (**b**) *(push)* propulser
impending [ɪmˈpendɪŋ] *adj* imminent(e)
impenetrable [ɪmˈpenɪtrəbəl] *adj (defences, mystery)* impénétrable; *(jargon)* incompréhensible
imperative [ɪmˈperətɪv] **1** *n Gram* impératif *m*; **in the i.** à l'impératif
2 *adj* impératif(ive); **it is i. that he should come** il faut impérativement qu'il vienne
imperceptible [ɪmpəˈseptɪbəl] *adj* imperceptible
imperfect [ɪmˈpɜːfɪkt] **1** *n Gram* **the i.** l'imparfait *m*; **in the i.** à l'imparfait
2 *adj (not perfect)* imparfait(e); *Gram* de l'imparfait; **i. tense** imparfait *m*
imperfection [ɪmpəˈfekʃən] *n* imperfection *f*
imperial [ɪmˈpɪərɪəl] *adj* (**a**) *(of empire)* impérial(e) (**b**) *(weights and measures)* = relatif au système de mesure anglo-saxon utilisant les miles, les pints etc
imperialism [ɪmˈpɪərɪəlɪzəm] *n* impérialisme *m*
imperialist [ɪmˈpɪərɪəlɪst] **1** *n* impérialiste *mf*
2 *adj* impérialiste
imperil [ɪmˈperɪl] *(pt & pp* **imperilled**, *Am* **imperiled**) *vt* mettre en péril
imperious [ɪmˈpɪərɪəs] *adj* impérieux(euse)
impermanent [ɪmˈpɜːmənənt] *adj* temporaire
impersonal [ɪmˈpɜːsənəl] *adj* impersonnel(elle)
impersonate [ɪmˈpɜːsəneɪt] *vt (pretend to be)* se faire passer pour; *(imitate)* imiter
impersonation [ɪmpɜːsəˈneɪʃən] *n (pretence of being)* usurpation *f* d'identité; *(imitation)* imitation *f*
impersonator [ɪmˈpɜːsəneɪtə(r)] *n (impostor)* imposteur *m*; *(mimic)* imitateur(trice) *m,f*
impertinence [ɪmˈpɜːtɪnəns] *n* impertinence *f*
impertinent [ɪmˈpɜːtɪnənt] *adj* impertinent(e)
imperturbable [ɪmpəˈtɜːbəbəl] *adj* imperturbable
impervious [ɪmˈpɜːvɪəs] *adj also Fig* imperméable (**to** à)
impetuous [ɪmˈpetjʊəs] *adj* impétueux(euse)
impetus [ˈɪmpɪtəs] *n* élan *m*
▸**impinge on** [ɪmˈpɪndʒ] *vt insep* affecter, avoir un effet sur
impious [ˈɪmpɪəs] *adj* impie
impish [ˈɪmpɪʃ] *adj* espiègle
implacable [ɪmˈplækəbəl] *adj* implacable
implant 1 *n* [ˈɪmplɑːnt] *Med* implant *m*
2 *vt* [ɪmˈplɑːnt] (**a**) *Med* implanter (**b**) *(opinion, belief)* inculquer
implausible [ɪmˈplɔːzəbəl] *adj* peu plausible, invraisemblable
implement 1 *n* [ˈɪmplɪmənt] instrument *m*; *(for cooking)* ustensile *m*; *(for gardening, DIY)* outil *m*
2 *vt* [ˈɪmplɪment] *(plan, agreement)* mettre en application
implementation [ɪmplɪmenˈteɪʃən] *n (of plan, agreement)* mise *f* en œuvre, application *f*
implicate [ˈɪmplɪkeɪt] *vt* impliquer
implication [ɪmplɪˈkeɪʃən] *n* implication *f*; **by i.** implicitement

implicit [ɪmˈplɪsɪt] *adj* (**a**) *(implied)* implicite; **it was i. in her remarks** c'était impliqué dans ses remarques (**b**) *(absolute)* absolu(e); **i. faith** confiance *f* aveugle
implied [ɪmˈplaɪd] *adj* implicite
implore [ɪmˈplɔː(r)] *vt* implorer; **to i. sb to do sth** implorer qn de faire qch
imploring [ɪmˈplɔːrɪŋ] *adj* implorant(e)
imply [ɪmˈplaɪ] *(pt & pp* **implied**) *vt* (**a**) *(insinuate)* insinuer, sous-entendre (**b**) *(involve)* impliquer; *(presuppose)* supposer
impolite [ɪmpəˈlaɪt] *adj* impoli(e)
impoliteness [ɪmpəˈlaɪtnɪs] *n* impolitesse *f*
imponderable [ɪmˈpɒndərəbəl] **1** *n* impondérable *m*
2 *adj* impondérable
import 1 *n* [ˈɪmpɔːt] (**a**) *(item, activity)* importation *f*; **i. duty** droit *m* de douane à l'importation (**b**) *Formal (importance)* importance *f*
2 *vt* [ɪmˈpɔːt] *also Comput* importer
importance [ɪmˈpɔːtəns] *n* importance *f*; **of the utmost i.** de la plus haute importance; **it is of no great i.** ça n'a pas grande importance; **to attach i. to sth** attacher de l'importance à qch; **to be full of one's own i.** être imbu(e) de sa personne
important [ɪmˈpɔːtənt] *adj* important(e); **to be i. to sb** être important(e) pour qn; **to become more i.** prendre de l'importance; **it's not i.** c'est sans importance
importantly [ɪmˈpɔːtəntlɪ] *adv (speak)* d'un air important; **but, more i....** mais, plus important...
importation [ɪmpɔːˈteɪʃən] *n* importation *f*
importer [ɪmˈpɔːtə(r)] *n* importateur(trice) *m,f*
import-export [ˈɪmpɔːtˈekspɔːt] *n* **i. (trade)** import-export *m*
importune [ɪmˈpɔːtjuːn] *vt Formal* importuner
impose [ɪmˈpəʊz] **1** *vt (silence, one's will, restrictions)* imposer (**on** à); **to i. a tax on sth** taxer qch; **to i. a fine on sb** condamner qn à (payer) une amende
2 *vi (take advantage)* s'imposer
▸**impose on, impose upon** *vt insep (take advantage of)* abuser de; **to i. on** *or* **upon sb** abuser de la gentillesse de qn
imposing [ɪmˈpəʊzɪŋ] *adj* imposant(e)
imposition [ɪmpəˈzɪʃən] *n* (**a**) *(of tax, fine)* imposition *f* (**b**) *(unfair demand)* **it was a bit of an i.** il y avait de l'abus
impossibility [ɪmpɒsɪˈbɪlɪtɪ] *(pl* **impossibilities**) *n* impossibilité *f*; **it's a physical i.** c'est matériellement impossible
impossible [ɪmˈpɒsɪbəl] **1** *n* **the i.** l'impossible *m*; **to do/achieve the i.** faire/réussir l'impossible
2 *adj* impossible; **to make it i. for sb to do sth** mettre qn dans l'impossibilité de faire qch
impossibly [ɪmˈpɒsɪblɪ] *adv (extremely)* incroyablement
impostor [ɪmˈpɒstə(r)] *n* imposteur *m*
impotence [ˈɪmpətəns] *n* impuissance *f*
impotent [ˈɪmpətənt] *adj* impuissant(e)
impound [ɪmˈpaʊnd] *vt Law* saisir; *(car)* mettre à la fourrière
impoverish [ɪmˈpɒvərɪʃ] *vt* appauvrir
impoverished [ɪmˈpɒvərɪʃd] *adj* appauvri(e)
impracticable [ɪmˈpræktɪkəbəl] *adj* impraticable, irréalisable
impractical [ɪmˈpræktɪkəl] *adj (suggestion)* irréaliste; *(person)* qui manque de sens pratique
imprecise [ɪmprɪˈsaɪs] *adj* imprécis(e)
imprecision [ɪmprɪˈsɪʒən] *n* imprécision *f*

impregnable [ɪmˈpregnəbəl] *adj (fortress)* imprenable; *Fig (argument)* irréfutable, inattaquable
impregnate [ˈɪmpregneɪt] *vt* (**a**) *(fertilize)* féconder
(**b**) *(soak)* imprégner (**with** de)
impresario [ɪmprəˈsɑːrɪəʊ] *(pl* **impresarios**) *n* imprésario *m*
impress [ɪmˈpres] *vt* (**a**) *(make an impression on)* impressionner; **to be impressed with** *or* **by sb/sth** être
impressionné(e) par qn/qch; **to i. sb favourably/un-
favourably** faire une impression favorable/défavo-
rable à qn (**b**) *(emphasize)* **to i. sth on sb** faire
comprendre qch à qn (**c**) *(imprint)* **to i. sth on sth** imprimer qch sur qch
impression [ɪmˈpreʃən] *n* (**a**) *(effect)* impression *f*; **to
make an i. on sb** marquer qn; **to make an i.** on sth
avoir un impact sur qch; **to make a good/bad i.** (**on
sb**) faire bonne/mauvaise impression (à qn); **to create a false i.** donner une fausse impression; **to be
under the i. that...** avoir l'impression que...; **to give
the i. that...** donner l'impression que... (**b**) *(imprint)*
(in wax, snow) empreinte *f* (**c**) *(of book)* réimpression
f (**d**) *(imitation)* imitation *f*; **to do impressions** faire
des imitations; **to do an i. of sb** imiter qn
impressionable [ɪmˈpreʃənəbəl] *adj* impressionnable
impressionism [ɪmˈpreʃənɪzəm] *n Art* impressionnisme *m*
impressionist [ɪmˈpreʃənɪst] **1** *n* (**a**) *Art* impressionniste *mf* (**b**) *(mimic)* imitateur(trice) *m,f*
2 *adj Art* impressionniste
impressionistic [ɪmpreʃəˈnɪstɪk] *adj* vague
impressive [ɪmˈpresɪv] *adj* impressionnant(e)
imprint 1 *n* [ˈɪmprɪnt] empreinte *f*
2 *vt* [ɪmˈprɪnt] imprimer (**on** sur); **her words are im-
printed on my memory** ses mots restent gravés dans
ma mémoire
imprison [ɪmˈprɪzən] *vt* emprisonner
imprisonment [ɪmˈprɪzənmənt] *n* emprisonnement
m
improbability [ɪmprɒbəˈbɪlɪtɪ] *(pl* **improbabilities**) *n*
improbabilité *f*
improbable [ɪmˈprɒbəbəl] *adj (unlikely)* improbable;
(unbelievable) invraisemblable
impromptu [ɪmˈprɒmptjuː] **1** *adj (speech, party)* im-
provisé(e)
2 *adv (unexpectedly)* à l'improviste; *(ad lib)* au pied
levé
improper [ɪmˈprɒpə(r)] *adj* (**a**) *(use, purpose)* mau-
vais(e); *(behaviour)* déplacé(e); *Law* **i. practices** pratiques *fpl* malhonnêtes (**b**) *(lewd)* indécent(e)
impropriety [ɪmprəˈpraɪətɪ] *n* inconvenance *f*; *(of
language)* impropriété *f*
improve [ɪmˈpruːv] **1** *vt* améliorer; *(invention, technique)* perfectionner; **to i. one's mind** se cultiver
2 *vi* s'améliorer; *(of business)* reprendre
▸**improve on, improve upon** *vt insep* améliorer; **to
i. on a bid** surenchérir
improved [ɪmˈpruːvd] *adj (system, design)* perfec-
tionné(e)
improvement [ɪmˈpruːvmənt] *n* amélioration *f* (**in**
de); *(of invention, technique)* perfectionnement *m*;
to be an i. on être meilleur(e) que; **there's room for
i.** on peut faire mieux; **to make improvements (to a
house)** faire des travaux d'aménagement (dans une
maison)
improvident [ɪmˈprɒvɪdənt] *adj Formal (person)*
imprévoyant(e)

improvisation [ɪmprəvaɪˈzeɪʃən] *n* improvisation
f
improvise [ˈɪmprəvaɪz] *vt & vi* improviser
imprudent [ɪmˈpruːdənt] *adj* imprudent(e)
impudence [ˈɪmpjʊdəns] *n* impudence *f*, insolence
f
impudent [ˈɪmpjʊdənt] *adj* impudent(e), insolent(e)
impugn [ɪmˈpjuːn] *vt Formal* mettre en doute
impulse [ˈɪmpʌls] *n* impulsion *f*; **to feel an i.** **to do sth**
avoir une soudaine envie de faire qch; **on i.** sur un
coup de tête; **i. buying** achat *m* d'impulsion
impulsive [ɪmˈpʌlsɪv] *adj* impulsif(ive)
impunity [ɪmˈpjuːnɪtɪ] *n* impunité *f*; **with i.** en toute
impunité
impure [ɪmˈpjʊə(r)] *adj* impur(e)
impurity [ɪmˈpjʊərətɪ] *(pl* **impurities**) *n* impureté *f*
impute [ɪmˈpjuːt] *vt Formal* **to i. sth to sb** imputer *ou*
attribuer qch à qn
in [ɪn] **1** *prep* (**a**) *(with place)* dans; **in the garden** dans
le jardin; **in France** en France; **in Japan** au Japon; **in
the USA** aux États-Unis; **in Paris** à Paris; **in hospital** à
l'hôpital; **in town** en ville; **in bed** au lit; **in here** ici; **in
there** là; *Fig* **I didn't think she had it in her to...** je ne
l'aurais pas crue capable de...
(**b**) *(with expressions of time)* **in 1927/April** en 1927/
avril; **in (the) spring** au printemps; **in (the) summer**
en été; **in the afternoon** l'après-midi; **in the 70s** dans
les années 70
(**c**) *(expressing manner)* **in French** en français; **to
write in pen** écrire au stylo; **in a loud voice** d'une
voix forte; **in this way** ainsi, de cette façon
(**d**) *(within, during)* **she did it in three hours** elle l'a
fait en trois heures; **he'll be here in three hours** il
sera ici dans trois heures; **I haven't seen him in years**
ça fait des années que je ne l'ai pas vu
(**e**) *(with situation, arrangement)* **in the rain** sous la
pluie; **in the sun** au soleil; **dressed in white** habil-
lé(e) en blanc; **in danger** en danger; **in twos** deux
par deux; **in a circle/line** en rond/rang
(**f**) *(with numbers, quantities, ratios)* **one in ten** un
sur dix; **in small/large quantities** en petite/grande
quantité; **2 metres in length/height/width** 2 mètres
de long/de haut/de large; **she's in her sixties** elle a la
soixantaine; **the temperature was in the nineties** ≃
il faisait dans les trente degrés
(**g**) *(with gerund)* **to have no difficulty in doing sth**
ne pas avoir de mal à faire qch; **in saying this...** en
disant cela...
(**h**) *(with field of activity)* **to be in insurance/pub-
lishing** être dans les assurances/l'édition
2 *adv* (**a**) *(inside)* dedans; **to go in** entrer, rentrer
(**b**) *(not out)* là; **is your mother in?** est-ce que ta
mère est là?; **to stay in** *(at home)* rester à la maison
(**c**) **to be in** *(of plane, train)* être arrivé(e)
(**d**) *(fashionable)* à la mode
(**e**) **in that...** puisque..., vu que...
(**f**) *(idioms)* **to have it in for sb** en vouloir à qn; **she's
in for a shock/surprise** elle va avoir un choc/une surprise; **to be in on a plan/secret** être dans le coup;
he's in for it ça va être sa fête
3 *adj* **the in crowd** les branchés *mpl*
4 *n* **the ins and outs** *(of question)* les tenants *mpl* et
les aboutissants *mpl*; *(of plot)* les subtilités *fpl*
inability [ɪnəˈbɪlɪtɪ] *n* incapacité *f* (**to do sth** à faire
qch)
inaccessibility [ɪnæksesɪˈbɪlɪtɪ] *n* inaccessibilité *f*
inaccessible [ɪnækˈsesɪbəl] *adj* inaccessible (**to** à)

inaccuracy [ɪn'ækjʊrəsɪ] (*pl* **inaccuracies**) *n (of estimate, translation, report)* inexactitude *f*; *(of rifle, instrument)* manque *m* de précision
inaccurate [ɪn'ækjʊrət] *adj (estimate, translation, report)* inexact(e); *(rifle, instrument)* qui manque de précision
inaction [ɪn'ækʃən] *n* inaction *f*
inactive [ɪn'æktɪv] *adj* inactif(ive)
inactivity [ɪnæk'tɪvɪtɪ] *n* inactivité *f*
inadequacy [ɪn'ædɪkwəsɪ] (*pl* **inadequacies**) *n* insuffisance *f*; **a feeling of i.** un complexe d'infériorité
inadequate [ɪn'ædɪkwət] *adj* insuffisant(e); **to feel i.** ne pas se sentir à la hauteur
inadmissible [ɪnəd'mɪsɪbəl] *adj Law (evidence)* irrecevable
inadvertent [ɪnəd'vɜːtənt] *adj* involontaire
inadvertently [ɪnəd'vɜːtəntlɪ] *adv* par inadvertance
inadvisable [ɪnəd'vaɪzəbəl] *adj* déconseillé(e)
inalienable [ɪn'eɪlɪənəbəl] *adj Formal* inaliénable
inane [ɪ'neɪn] *adj* idiot(e), stupide
inanimate [ɪn'ænɪmət] *adj* inanimé(e)
inanity [ɪ'nænɪtɪ] *n* ineptie *f*
inapplicable [ɪn'æplɪkəbəl] *adj* inapplicable (**to** à); **delete where i.** *(sign)* rayer la mention inutile
inappropriate [ɪnə'prəʊprɪət] *adj (behaviour, remark)* déplacé(e); *(dress)* peu approprié(e) (**to** à); *(time)* inopportun(e)
inapt [ɪn'æpt] *adj* peu approprié(e)
inarticulate [ɪnɑː'tɪkjʊlɪt] *adj (sound)* inarticulé(e); **to be i.** *(of person)* avoir du mal à s'exprimer; **to be i. with rage** bégayer de rage
inasmuch as [ɪnəz'mʌtʃəz] *conj Formal* dans la mesure où
inattention [ɪnə'tenʃən] *n* inattention *f*
inattentive [ɪnə'tentɪv] *adj* inattentif(ive) (**to** à)
inaudible [ɪn'ɔːdɪbəl] *adj* inaudible
inaugural [ɪ'nɔːgjʊrəl] *adj* inaugural(e)
inaugurate [ɪ'nɔːgjʊreɪt] *vt (building, exhibition)* inaugurer; *(president)* investir
inauguration [ɪnɔːgjʊ'reɪʃən] *n (of building, exhibition)* inauguration *f*; *(of president)* cérémonie *f* de prise de fonctions
inauspicious [ɪnɔːs'pɪʃəs] *adj* peu propice; **to get off to an i. start** mal commencer
inauthentic [ɪnɔː'θentɪk] *adj* inauthentique
in-between [ɪnbɪ'twiːn] *adj* intermédiaire
inborn ['ɪnbɔːn] *adj* inné(e)
inbound ['ɪnbaʊnd] *adj (flight, passenger)* à l'arrivée
inbox ['ɪnbɒks] *n Comput (for e-mail)* boîte *f* de réception, corbeille *f* d'arrivée
inbred ['ɪnbred] *adj (person)* de parents consanguins; *(distrust, confidence)* inné(e)
in-built ['ɪnbɪlt] *adj (trait)* inhérent(e); **his height gives him an i. advantage** sa taille lui donne un avantage dès le départ
Inc [ɪŋk] *adj (abbr* **Incorporated**) ≃ SARL
Inca ['ɪŋkə] **1** *n* Inca *mf*
2 *adj* inca
incalculable [ɪn'kælkjʊləbəl] *adj (consequences, damage)* incalculable; *(help, value)* inestimable
incandescent [ɪnkæn'desənt] *adj* incandescent(e); *Fig* **i. with rage** fou (folle) de rage
incantation [ɪnkæn'teɪʃən] *n* incantation *f*
incapable [ɪn'keɪpəbəl] *adj* incapable (**of** de); *(through illness)* impotent(e); *(through drink)* ivre mort(e); **to be i. of doing sth** être incapable de faire qch

incapacitate [ɪnkə'pæsɪteɪt] *vt* rendre impotent(e); **to be incapacitated for work** être inapte au travail
incapacity [ɪnkə'pæsɪtɪ] *n* incapacité *f*; **i. to do sth** incapacité à faire qch
incarcerate [ɪn'kɑːsəreɪt] *vt Formal* incarcérer
incarceration [ɪnkɑːsə'reɪʃən] *n Formal* incarcération *f*
incarnate [ɪn'kɑːneɪt] *adj* incarné(e)
incarnation [ɪnkɑː'neɪʃən] *n* incarnation *f*; **in a previous i.** dans une vie antérieure
incautious [ɪn'kɔːʃəs] *adj* imprudent(e)
incendiary [ɪn'sendɪərɪ] **1** *n (pl* **incendiaries**) *(arsonist)* incendiaire *mf*; *(bomb)* bombe *f* incendiaire
2 *adj also Fig* incendiaire
incense¹ ['ɪnsens] *n* encens *m*
incense² [ɪn'sens] *vt (anger)* rendre furieux(euse)
incentive [ɪn'sentɪv] *n (stimulus)* motivation *f*; *(payment)* prime *f*; **there is no i. for students to work hard** il n'y a rien qui encourage les étudiants à travailler dur; **i. bonus** *or* **payment** prime *f* de rendement; **i. scheme** *(for workers)* système *m* de primes
inception [ɪn'sepʃən] *n* début *m*
incessant [ɪn'sesənt] *adj* incessant(e)
incest ['ɪnsest] *n* inceste *m*
incestuous [ɪn'sestjʊəs] *adj* incestueux(euse); *Fig (environment, group)* très fermé(e)
inch [ɪntʃ] *n (***a**) *(unit of measurement)* = 2,54 cm, pouce *m*; **i. by i.** petit à petit, peu à peu (**b**) *(idioms)* **I know every i. of this town** je connais cette ville comme ma poche; **he's every i. the gentleman** c'est le parfait gentleman; **to miss sth by inches** manquer qch d'un cheveu; **to be within an i. of doing sth** être à deux doigts de faire qch; **she won't give an i.** elle ne cédera pas d'un pouce; **give her an i. and she'll take a mile** tu lui en donnes jusqu'au coude, elle en prendra long comme le bras
▸**inch along, inch forward** *vi* avancer tout doucement
incidence ['ɪnsɪdəns] *n (frequency)* taux *m*; *(of disease)* incidence *f*
incident ['ɪnsɪdənt] *n* incident *m*; *(in book, film)* scène *f*; **full of i.** riche en incidents; *Br* **i. room** *(in police station)* salle *f* des opérations
incidental [ɪnsɪ'dentəl] *adj (minor)* accessoire (**to** par rapport à); **i. expenses** faux frais *mpl*; **i. music** *(in film)* musique *f*
incidentally [ɪnsɪ'dentəlɪ] *adv (by the way)* au fait
incinerate [ɪn'sɪnəreɪt] *vt* incinérer; *Fig* carboniser
incineration [ɪnsɪnə'reɪʃən] *n* incinération *f*
incinerator [ɪn'sɪnəreɪtə(r)] *n* incinérateur *m*
incipient [ɪn'sɪpɪənt] *adj Formal* naissant(e)
incision [ɪn'sɪʒən] *n* incision *f*
incisive [ɪn'saɪsɪv] *adj* incisif(ive)
incisor [ɪn'saɪzə(r)] *n* incisive *f*
incite [ɪn'saɪt] *vt (violence, unrest)* inciter à; **to i. sb to do sth** inciter qn à faire qch
incitement [ɪn'saɪtmənt] *n* incitation *f* (**to** à)
incivility [ɪnsɪ'vɪlɪtɪ] *(pl* **incivilities**) *n Formal* incivilité *f*
inclement [ɪn'klemənt] *adj Formal (weather)* inclément(e)
inclination [ɪnklɪ'neɪʃən] *n (***a**) *(liking)* inclination *f*, penchant *m* (**for** pour); *(desire)* envie *f*; **to have an i. to do sth** avoir envie de faire qch (**b**) *(tendency)* tendance *f* (**towards** à); **to have an i. to do sth** avoir tendance à faire qch; **by i.** de *ou* par nature (**c**) *(angle)* inclinaison *f*

incline 1 *n* ['ɪnklaɪn] *(slope)* pente *f*
2 *vt* [ɪn'klaɪn] (**a**) *(cause)* **to i. sb to do sth** inciter qn
à faire qch (**b**) *(lean)* incliner; **to i. one's head** incliner la tête (**c**) **to be inclined to do sth** *(tend)* avoir
tendance à faire qch; **I'm inclined to agree** j'aurais
tendance à être d'accord
3 *vi* [ɪn'klaɪn] *(lean)* s'incliner; *(tend)* **to i. to** *or* **towards** pencher pour; **to i. to the belief that...** être
porté(e) à croire que...
include [ɪn'klu:d] *vt* inclure, comprendre; *(in letter)*
joindre; **the price does not i. accommodation** le logement n'est pas compris dans le prix
including [ɪn'klu:dɪŋ] *prep* y compris; **seven not i. the
children** sept sans compter les enfants; **up to and i.
page 40** jusqu'à la page 40 incluse
inclusion [ɪn'klʊʒən] *n* inclusion *f*
inclusive [ɪn'klu:sɪv] *adj (price, sum)* net (nette); **to be
i. of** comprendre; **i. of VAT** TVA comprise; **from 4 to
12 February i.** du 4 au 12 février inclus
incognito [ɪnkɒg'ni:təʊ] *adv* incognito
incoherence [ɪnkəʊ'hɪərəns] *n* incohérence *f*
incoherent [ɪnkəʊ'hɪərənt] *adj* incohérent(e)
income ['ɪnkəm] *n* revenu *m*; *Br* **i. support** ≃ RMI *m*; **i.
tax** impôt *m* sur le revenu
incoming ['ɪnkʌmɪŋ] *adj (government, president)*
nouveau(elle); *(plane, train)* à l'arrivée; *(phone call)*
de l'extérieur; *(tide)* montant(e) **i. mail** courrier *m*
(du jour)
incommensurate [ɪnkə'menʃərɪt] *adj* **to be i. with**
ne pas être proportionné(e) à
incommunicado [ɪnkəmju:nɪ'kɑ:dəʊ] *adj (uncontactable)* injoignable
in-company ['ɪnkʌmpənɪ] *adj* **i. training** formation *f*
sur le lieu de travail
incomparable [ɪn'kɒmpərəbəl] *adj* incomparable
incompatible [ɪnkəm'pætɪbəl] *adj* incompatible
(**with** avec)
incompetence [ɪn'kɒmpɪtəns] *n* incompétence *f*
incompetent [ɪn'kɒmpɪtənt] *adj* incompétent(e)
incomplete [ɪnkəm'pli:t] *adj* (**a**) *(not whole)* incomplet(ète) (**b**) *(not finished)* inachevé(e)
incomprehensible [ɪnkɒmprɪ'hensɪbəl] *adj* incompréhensible
incomprehension [ɪnkɒmprɪ'henʃən] *n* incompréhension *f*
inconceivable [ɪnkən'si:vəbəl] *adj* inconcevable
inconclusive [ɪnkən'klu:sɪv] *adj (evidence, results)*
peu concluant(e); **the meeting/investigation was i.**
la réunion/l'enquête n'a abouti à rien
incongruity [ɪnkɒŋ'gru:ɪtɪ] *(pl* **incongruities)** *n* incongruité *f*
incongruous [ɪn'kɒŋgrʊəs] *adj* incongru(e)
inconsequential [ɪnkɒnsɪ'kwenʃəl] *adj* insignifiant(e), sans importance
inconsiderate [ɪnkən'sɪdərɪt] *adj (person)* sans
égards pour les autres; *(remark)* déplacé(e); **it was i.
of you not to invite her** ce n'est pas gentil de ta part
de ne pas l'avoir invitée
inconsistency [ɪnkən'sɪstənsɪ] *(pl* **inconsistencies)** *n*
(in argument) incohérence *f*; *(between reports, descriptions)* contradiction *f*; *(uneven quality)* irrégularité *f*
inconsistent [ɪnkən'sɪstənt] *adj (person)* incohérent(e); *(uneven)* irrégulier(ère); **to be i. with** ne pas
concorder *ou* cadrer avec
inconsolable [ɪnkən'səʊləbəl] *adj* inconsolable

inconspicuous [ɪnkən'spɪkjʊəs] *adj* qui passe
inaperçu(e)
incontestable [ɪnkən'testəbəl] *adj* incontestable
incontinence [ɪn'kɒntɪnəns] *n* incontinence *f*
incontinent [ɪn'kɒntɪnənt] *adj* incontinent(e)
incontrovertible [ɪnkɒntrə'vɜ:tɪbəl] *adj Formal*
incontestable
inconvenience [ɪnkən'vi:njəns] **1** *n* désagrément *m*;
to be an i. to sb déranger qn
2 *vt* déranger
inconvenient [ɪnkən'vi:njənt] *adj (time)* mauvais(e);
(place, arrangement) peu commode; **if it's not i.** si
cela ne vous dérange pas; **it's a bit i. just now** ça ne
tombe pas très bien en ce moment
incorporate [ɪn'kɔ:pəreɪt] *vt* incorporer; *(have as
quality)* comprendre
incorrect [ɪnkə'rekt] *adj* incorrect(e)
incorrigible [ɪn'kɒrɪdʒɪbəl] *adj* incorrigible
incorruptible [ɪnkə'rʌptɪbəl] *adj* incorruptible
increase 1 *n* ['ɪnkri:s] *(in price, rate, sales)* augmentation *f*, hausse *f* (**in** de); *(in salary)* augmentation (de
salaire); *(in pain, population)* accroissement *m* (**in**
de); **to be on the i.** être en hausse
2 *vt* [ɪn'kri:s] augmenter; **to i. one's efforts** redoubler d'efforts; **to i. one's speed** accélérer
3 *vi* [ɪn'kri:s] augmenter; **to i. in price** augmenter; **to
i. in value** prendre de la valeur
increasing [ɪn'kri:sɪŋ] *adj* croissant(e)
increasingly [ɪn'kri:sɪŋlɪ] *adv* de plus en plus
incredible [ɪn'kredɪbəl] *adj* (**a**) *(unbelievable)* incroyable (**b**) *Fam (excellent)* génial(e)
incredibly [ɪn'kredɪblɪ] *adv* (**a**) *(extremely)* incroyablement; *Fam* **i. good** génial(e) (**b**) *(unbelievably)* **i.,
no one was hurt** aussi incroyable que cela puisse
paraître, personne n'a été blessé
incredulous [ɪn'kredjʊləs] *adj* incrédule
increment ['ɪnkrɪmənt] *n* augmentation *f*
incremental [ɪnkrɪ'mentəl] *adj (increasing)* croissant(e); **i. increases** augmentations *fpl* régulières
incriminate [ɪn'krɪmɪneɪt] *vt* incriminer, mettre en
cause
incriminating [ɪn'krɪmɪneɪtɪŋ] *adj* compromettant(e)
incubate ['ɪnkjʊbeɪt] *vt (of bird)* couver; *(baby)* mettre
en couveuse
incubation [ɪnkjʊ'beɪʃən] *n* incubation *f*; *Med* **i. period** *(of infection)* durée *f* d'incubation
incubator ['ɪnkjʊbeɪtə(r)] *n (for eggs)* incubateur *m*;
(for babies) couveuse *f*
inculcate ['ɪnkʌlkeɪt] *vt Formal* **to i. sth in sb, to i. sb
with sth** inculquer qch à qn
incumbent [ɪn'kʌmbənt] *Formal* **1** *n* **the present i.**
(of the presidency) le président en exercice
2 *adj* **it is i. on sb to do sth** il incombe *ou* appartient
à qn de faire qch
incur [ɪn'kɜ:(r)] *(pt & pp* **incurred)** *vt (blame, expense)*
encourir; *(loss)* subir; *(risk)* courir; *(person's anger)*
s'attirer; *(debt)* contracter
incurable [ɪn'kjʊərəbəl] *adj also Fig* incurable
incurious [ɪn'kjʊərɪəs] *adj* peu curieux(euse)
incursion [ɪn'kɜ:ʃən] *n Formal* incursion *f*
indebted [ɪn'detɪd] *adj (financially)* endetté(e); *(for
help, advice)* redevable (**to** à); **I am i. to my family
for all their support** je suis reconnaissant à ma famille pour son soutien
indebtedness [ɪn'detɪdnɪs] *n (financial)* endettement *m*; *(for help, advice)* dette *f* (**to** envers)

indecency [ɪn'diːsənsɪ] *n* indécence *f*; *Law* attentat *m* à la pudeur

indecent [ɪn'diːsənt] *adj* indécent(e); **to do sth with i.** haste mettre un empressement déplacé à faire qch; *Law* **i.** assault attentat *m* à la pudeur; *Law* **i.** exposure outrage *m* public à la pudeur

indecipherable [ɪndɪ'saɪfərəbəl] *adj* indéchiffrable

indecision [ɪndɪ'sɪʒən] *n* indécision *f*

indecisive [ɪndɪ'saɪsɪv] *adj (person)* indécis(e); *(battle, election)* à l'issue peu claire

indecorous [ɪn'dekərəs] *adj Formal* peu digne

indeed [ɪn'diːd] *adv* (**a**) *(used with 'very')* vraiment; **very big i.** vraiment très grand(e); **thank you very much i.** merci mille fois (**b**) *(in confirmation)* en effet, effectivement; *(certainly)* certainement (**c**) *(what's more)* en fait, et même; **I think so, i. I'm sure of it** je pense que oui, en fait j'en suis sûr (**d**) *(expressing ironic surprise)* **have you i.?** vraiment?

indefatigable [ɪndɪ'fætɪgəbəl] *adj Formal* infatigable

indefensible [ɪndɪ'fensɪbəl] *adj (behaviour, attitude)* injustifiable, impardonnable; *(theory)* indéfendable

indefinable [ɪndɪ'faɪnəbəl] *adj* indéfinissable

indefinite [ɪn'defɪnɪt] *adj* (**a**) *(period of time, number)* indéterminé(e) (**b**) *(idea, plan)* mal défini(e) (**c**) *Gram* indéfini(e)

indefinitely [ɪn'defɪnɪtlɪ] *adv* indéfiniment

indelible [ɪn'delɪbəl] *adj also Fig* indélébile

indelicate [ɪn'delɪkət] *adj* indélicat(e)

indemnify [ɪn'demnɪfaɪ] *(pt & pp* indemnified*) vt* **to i. sb for sth** *(compensate)* indemniser *ou* dédommager qn de qch; **to i. sb against sth** *(give security)* assurer qn contre qch

indemnity [ɪn'demnɪtɪ] *(pl* indemnities*) n (guarantee)* garantie *f*, assurance *f*; *(money)* indemnité *f*, dédommagement *m*

indent *Typ* **1** *n* ['ɪndent] alinéa *m*
2 *vt* [ɪn'dent] mettre en retrait

indentation [ɪnden'teɪʃən] *n (mark)* trace *f*, empreinte *f*; *(in coastline)* découpure *f*; *Typ* alinéa *m*

independence [ɪndɪ'pendəns] *n* indépendance *f* (**from** par rapport à); **I. Day** *(in America)* fête *f* nationale de l'Indépendance *(aux États-Unis)*

independent [ɪndɪ'pendənt] *adj* indépendant(e) (**of** de); *Fin* **i. financial adviser** conseiller(ère) *m,f* financier(ère) indépendant(e); *Br* **i. school** école *f* privée

independently [ɪndɪ'pendəntlɪ] *adv* indépendamment; **i. of** indépendamment de; **to live i.** être indépendant(e)

in-depth ['ɪndepθ] *adj* approfondi(e), en profondeur

indescribable [ɪndɪ'skraɪbəbəl] *adj* indescriptible

indestructible [ɪndɪs'trʌktəbəl] *adj* indestructible

indeterminate [ɪndɪ'tɜːmɪnət] *adj* indéterminé(e)

index ['ɪndeks] **1** *n (of book)* index *m*; *(in library)* fichier *m*; **i. finger** index; *Fin* **i. fund** fonds *m* indiciel
2 *vt* (**a**) *(book)* dresser l'index de (**b**) *Fin (wages)* indexer (**to** sur)

index-linked ['ɪndeks'lɪŋkt] *adj Fin* indexé(e)

India ['ɪndɪə] *n* l'Inde *f*

Indian ['ɪndɪən] **1** *n* Indien(enne) *m,f*
2 *adj* indien(enne); **I. elephant** éléphant *m* d'Asie; **in I. file** en file indienne; **the I. Ocean** l'océan *m* Indien; **I. summer** été *m* indien

indicate ['ɪndɪkeɪt] **1** *vt* (**a**) *(point to, show)* indiquer (**b**) *(intention, opposition, willingness)* signaler
2 *vi (of car driver)* mettre son clignotant

indication [ɪndɪ'keɪʃən] *n (sign)* signe *m*; *(information)* indication *f*; **she gave no i. of her feelings** elle n'a

rien laissé voir de ses sentiments; **there is every i. that..., all the indications are that...** tout porte à croire que...

indicative [ɪn'dɪkətɪv] **1** *n Gram* indicatif *m*; **in the i.** à l'indicatif
2 *adj* **to be i. of** être symptomatique de

indicator ['ɪndɪkeɪtə(r)] *n* (**a**) *(sign)* indice *m*; **economic indicators** indicateurs *mpl* économiques (**b**) *Br (of car)* clignotant *m*, *Belg* clignoteur *m*, *Suisse* signofil(e) *m*

indict [ɪn'daɪt] *vt Law* inculper (**for** de)

indictable [ɪn'daɪtəbəl] *adj Law* **i. offence** délit *m*

indictment [ɪn'daɪtmənt] *n Law* inculpation *f*; *Fig* **it is an i. of our society** c'est une preuve accablante de l'état de notre société

indie ['ɪndɪ] *adj Br (music, band)* indépendant(e)

indifference [ɪn'dɪfərəns] *n* indifférence *f* (**to** pour); **it's a matter of complete i. to me** cela m'est complètement indifférent

indifferent [ɪn'dɪfərənt] *adj* (**a**) *(not interested)* indifférent(e) (**to** à); **I am** *or* **feel i. about him** ça m'est indifférent (**b**) *(mediocre)* médiocre

indigenous [ɪn'dɪdʒɪnəs] *adj* indigène

indigestible [ɪndɪ'dʒestɪbəl] *adj also Fig* indigeste

indigestion [ɪndɪ'dʒestʃən] *n* troubles *mpl* digestifs; **to have an attack of i.** avoir des troubles digestifs

indignant [ɪn'dɪgnənt] *adj* indigné(e); **to get i. about sth** s'indigner de qch

indignation [ɪndɪg'neɪʃən] *n* indignation *f*

indignity [ɪn'dɪgnɪtɪ] *n* indignité *f*

indigo ['ɪndɪɡəʊ] **1** *n* indigo *m*
2 *adj* indigo *inv*

indirect [ɪndɪ'rekt] *adj* indirect(e); *(person)* pas direct(e); *Com* **i. costs** frais *mpl* indirects; *Gram* **i. object** complément *m* d'objet indirect; *Gram* **i. speech** discours *m* indirect

indirectly [ɪndɪ'rektlɪ] *adv* indirectement

indiscernible [ɪndɪ'sɜːnɪbəl] *adj (reason)* obscur(e); *(difference)* imperceptible

indiscipline [ɪn'dɪsɪplɪn] *n* indiscipline *f*

indiscreet [ɪndɪs'kriːt] *adj* indiscret(ète)

indiscretion [ɪndɪs'kreʃən] *n* indiscrétion *f*

indiscriminate [ɪndɪs'krɪmɪnɪt] *adj* **i. killing** tuerie *f* générale; **to be i. in one's praise** distribuer des compliments à tort et à travers

indispensable [ɪndɪs'pensəbəl] *adj* indispensable

indisposed [ɪndɪs'pəʊzd] *adj Formal (ill)* indisposé(e)

indisputable [ɪndɪs'pjuːtəbəl] *adj (evidence, argument)* incontestable; *(leader)* incontesté(e)

indissoluble [ɪndɪ'sɒljʊbəl] *adj Formal* indissoluble

indistinct [ɪndɪs'tɪŋkt] *adj* indistinct(e)

indistinguishable [ɪndɪs'tɪŋgwɪʃəbəl] *adj* impossible à distinguer (**from** de)

individual [ɪndɪ'vɪdjʊəl] **1** *n (person)* individu *m*; **a private i.** un particulier
2 *adj* (**a**) *(of or for one person)* individuel(elle); *(bathroom)* privé(e); **i. tuition** cours *mpl* particuliers (**b**) *(characteristic)* personnel(elle)

individualist [ɪndɪ'vɪdjʊəlɪst] *n* individualiste *mf*

individuality [ɪndɪvɪdjʊ'ælɪtɪ] *n* individualité *f*

individually [ɪndɪ'vɪdjʊəlɪ] *adv* individuellement

indivisible [ɪndɪ'vɪzəbəl] *adj* indivisible

Indochina [ɪndəʊ'tʃaɪnə] *n* l'Indochine *f*

indoctrinate [ɪn'dɒktrɪneɪt] *vt* endoctriner; **to i. sb with an idea** inculquer une idée à qn

indoctrination [ɪndɒktrɪ'neɪʃən] *n* endoctrinement *m*

indolent ['ɪndələnt] *adj Formal* paresseux(euse)

indomitable [ɪn'dɒmɪtəbəl] *adj* indomptable
Indonesia [ɪndəʊ'niːʒə] *n* l'Indonésie *f*
Indonesian [ɪndəʊ'niːʒən] **1** *n* (**a**) *(person)* Indoné-
sien(enne) *m,f* (**b**) *(language)* indonésien *m*
2 *adj* indonésien(enne)
indoor ['ɪndɔː(r)] *adj (swimming pool, tennis court)*
couvert(e); *(plant)* d'appartement; *(photography)*
d'intérieur; **i. athletics** athlétisme *m* en salle
indoors [ɪn'dɔːz] *adv* à l'intérieur; **to go i.** rentrer; **I've**
been i. all day je suis resté(e) enfermé(e) toute la
journée
induce [ɪn'djuːs] *vt* (**a**) *(persuade)* **to i. sb to do sth**
persuader qn de faire qch (**b**) *(cause)* provoquer (**c**)
Med **to i.** labour provoquer l'accouchement; **she's**
had to be induced il a fallu provoquer l'accouchement
inducement [ɪn'djuːsmənt] *n (incentive)* incitation *f*;
(financial) avantage *m* financier
induction [ɪn'dʌkʃən] *n* (**a**) *(into job)* période *f* d'introduction; **i. course** stage *m* de formation (**b**) *Med*
(of labour) déclenchement *m* (**c**) *Elec* induction *f*
inductive [ɪn'dʌktɪv] *adj (reasoning)* inductif(ive)
indulge [ɪn'dʌldʒ] **1** *vt (child)* gâter; *(passion)* donner
libre cours à; **they indulged his every whim** ils lui
passaient tous ses caprices; **to i. oneself** se faire plaisir; **go on, i. me!** allez, fais-moi plaisir!
2 *vi* **to i. in sth** *(as a habit)* se livrer à qch; *(as a treat)*
s'offrir qch
indulgence [ɪn'dʌldʒəns] *n* (**a**) *(leniency)* indulgence
f (**b**) *(treat)* gâterie *f*
indulgent [ɪn'dʌldʒənt] *adj* indulgent(e) (**to** avec)
industrial [ɪn'dʌstrɪəl] *adj* industriel(elle); **i. action**
grève *f*; **to take i. action** faire grève; **i. disease** maladie *f* professionnelle; **i. dispute** conflit *m* entre la direction et les travailleurs; **i. espionage** espionnage *m*
industriel; *Br* **i. estate** zone *f* industrielle; **i. injury** accident *m* du travail; **i. park** zone *f* industrielle; **i. rela-**
tions relations *fpl* entre les travailleurs et le patronat;
the I. Revolution la révolution industrielle; **i. tribunal**
≃ conseil *m* de prud'hommes; **i. unrest** conflits *mpl*
sociaux; **i. waste** déchets *mpl* industriels
industrialist [ɪn'dʌstrɪəlɪst] *n* industriel *m*
industrialize [ɪn'dʌstrɪəlaɪz] *vt* industrialiser
industrious [ɪn'dʌstrɪəs] *adj* travailleur(euse)
industry ['ɪndʌstrɪ] *(pl* **industries)** *n* (**a**) *(economic*
sector) industrie *f*; **heavy/light i.** l'industrie *f* lourde/
légère; **the aircraft/mining i.** l'industrie *f* aéronau-
tique/minière; **the tourist/entertainment i.** l'industrie *f* du tourisme/du spectacle (**b**) *(hard work)*
assiduité *f*
inebriated [ɪn'iːbrɪeɪtɪd] *adj Formal or Hum* ivre
inedible [ɪn'edɪbəl] *adj (plant, mushroom)* non comestible; *(food)* immangeable
ineffable [ɪn'efəbəl] *adj Formal* ineffable
ineffective [ɪnɪ'fektɪv] *adj* inefficace
ineffectual [ɪnɪ'fektjʊəl] *adj* inefficace
inefficiency [ɪnɪ'fɪʃənsɪ] *n* inefficacité *f*, manque *m*
d'efficacité
inefficient [ɪnɪ'fɪʃənt] *adj* inefficace
inelegant [ɪn'elɪgənt] *adj* inélégant(e)
ineligible [ɪn'elɪdʒɪbəl] *adj* **to be i. for sth** ne pas
avoir droit à qch; **to be i. to do sth** ne pas avoir le
droit de faire qch
inept [ɪn'ept] *adj (person)* incompétent(e); *(remark)*
inepte
ineptitude [ɪn'eptɪtjuːd] *n* incompétence *f*
inequality [ɪnɪ'kwɒlɪtɪ] *(pl* **inequalities)** *n* inégalité *f*

inequitable [ɪn'ekwɪtəbəl] *adj Formal* inéquitable
inert [ɪ'nɜːt] *adj* inerte
inertia [ɪ'nɜːʃɪə] *n* inertie *f*
inescapable [ɪnɪ'skeɪpəbəl] *adj (conclusion)* incontournable; *(resemblance)* indéniable; **it's an i. fact**
that... il est indéniable que...
inessential [ɪnɪ'senʃəl] *adj* non essentiel(elle)
inestimable [ɪn'estɪməbəl] *adj* inestimable
inevitability [ɪnevɪtə'bɪlɪtɪ] *n* caractère *m* inévitable
inevitable [ɪn'evɪtəbəl] **1** *n* **the i.** l'inévitable *m*
2 *adj* inévitable; *(conclusion)* incontournable
inevitably [ɪn'evɪtəblɪ] *adv* inévitablement
inexact [ɪnɪg'zækt] *adj (memory, estimate)* imprécis(e)
inexcusable [ɪnɪks'kjuːzəbəl] *adj* inexcusable
inexhaustible [ɪnɪg'zɔːstɪbəl] *adj* inépuisable
inexorable [ɪn'eksərəbəl] *adj* inexorable
inexpensive [ɪnɪks'pensɪv] *adj* pas cher (chère), bon
marché *inv*
inexperience [ɪnɪks'pɪərɪəns] *n* inexpérience *f*
inexperienced [ɪnɪks'pɪərɪənst] *adj* (**a**) *(person)* in-
expérimenté(e); **to be i. in doing sth** ne pas avoir
l'habitude de faire qch (**b**) *(ear, eye)* inexercé(e)
inexplicable [ɪnɪks'plɪkəbəl] *adj* inexplicable
inexpressible [ɪnɪks'presɪbəl] *adj* inexprimable
inexpressive [ɪnɪks'presɪv] *adj* inexpressif(ive)
inextricably [ɪneks'trɪkəblɪ] *adv* inextricablement
infallibility [ɪnfælɪ'bɪlɪtɪ] *n* infaillibilité *f*
infallible [ɪn'fælɪbəl] *adj* infaillible
infamous ['ɪnfəməs] *adj (well-known)* tristement
célèbre; *(crime, rumour)* infâme
infamy ['ɪnfəmɪ] *n Formal* infamie *f*
infancy ['ɪnfənsɪ] *n (childhood)* petite enfance *f*; *Fig*
when medicine was still in its i. alors que la médecine en était encore à ses balbutiements
infant ['ɪnfənt] *n* bébé *m*; **i. mortality** mortalité *f* infantile; **i. school** = école primaire pour enfants de 5 à 7
ans
infanticide [ɪn'fæntɪsaɪd] *n* infanticide *m*
infantile ['ɪnfəntaɪl] *adj Pej* infantile, puéril(e)
infantry ['ɪnfəntrɪ] *n* infanterie *f*
infantryman ['ɪnfəntrɪmən] *n* soldat *m* d'infanterie,
fantassin *m*
infatuated [ɪn'fætjʊeɪtɪd] *adj* **to be i. with sb** être en-
tiché(e) de qn
infatuation [ɪnfætjʊ'eɪʃən] *n (with person)* tocade *f*,
passade *f* (**with** pour)
infect [ɪn'fekt] *vt (water, food)* contaminer; *(with pre-*
judice) corrompre; **to become infected** *(of wound)*
s'infecter; **to i. sb with sth** transmettre qch à qn; **her**
enthusiasm infected us all elle nous a communiqué
son enthousiasme
infection [ɪn'fekʃən] *n* infection *f*
infectious [ɪn'fekʃəs] *adj* (**a**) *(disease)* infectieux(-
euse); *(person)* contagieux(euse) (**b**) *(laughter, en-*
thusiasm) communicatif(ive)
infer [ɪn'fɜː(r)] *(pt & pp* **inferred)** *vt* déduire (**from** de)
inference ['ɪnfərəns] *n* conclusion *f*; **by i.** par déduction
inferior [ɪn'fɪərɪə(r)] **1** *n* inférieur(e) *m,f*; **to be sb's i.**
être inférieur à qn
2 *adj* inférieur(e) (**to** à)
inferiority [ɪnfɪərɪ'ɒrɪtɪ] *n* infériorité *f*; **i. complex**
complexe *m* d'infériorité
infernal [ɪn'fɜːnəl] *adj* (**a**) *(diabolical)* infernal(e), diabolique (**b**) *Fam (for emphasis)* **it's an i. nuisance** c'est
diablement embêtant; **that i. idiot!** cette espèce d'idiot!

inferno [ɪnˈfɜːnəʊ] (*pl* **infernos**) *n* (*hell*) enfer *m*; (*blaze*) brasier *m*
infertile [ɪnˈfɜːtaɪl] *adj* stérile
infertility [ɪnfɜːˈtɪlɪtɪ] *n* stérilité *f*
infest [ɪnˈfest] *vt* **to be infested with** *or* **by sth** être infesté(e) de qch
infidelity [ɪnfɪˈdelɪtɪ] *n* infidélité *f*
infighting [ˈɪnfaɪtɪŋ] *n* querelles *fpl* intestines
infiltrate [ˈɪnfɪltreɪt] **1** *vt* infiltrer
2 *vi* s'infiltrer
infiltration [ɪnfɪlˈtreɪʃən] *n* infiltration *f*
infinite [ˈɪnfɪnɪt] **1** *n* **the i.** l'infini *m*
2 *adj* infini(e); *Rel & Hum* **in her i. wisdom** dans son infinie sagesse
infinitely [ˈɪnfɪnɪtlɪ] *adv* infiniment
infinitesimal [ɪnfɪnɪˈtesɪməl] *adj* infinitésimal(e)
infinitive [ɪnˈfɪnɪtɪv] *n* *Gram* infinitif *m*; **in the i.** à l'infinitif
infinity [ɪnˈfɪnɪtɪ] *n* infinité *f*; *Math* infini *m*
infirm [ɪnˈfɜːm] *adj* infirme
infirmary [ɪnˈfɜːmərɪ] (*pl* **infirmaries**) *n* (*hospital*) hôpital *m*; (*in school, prison*) infirmerie *f*
infirmity [ɪnˈfɜːmɪtɪ] (*pl* **infirmities**) *n* (*weakness*) infirmité *f*
inflame [ɪnˈfleɪm] *vt* (**a**) (*desire*) allumer; (*curiosity*) attiser; (*crowd*) enflammer (**b**) **to become inflamed** (*of wound*) s'enflammer
inflammable [ɪnˈflæməbəl] *adj* (*substance*) inflammable; *Fig* (*situation*) explosif(ive)
inflammation [ɪnfləˈmeɪʃən] *n* inflammation *f*
inflammatory [ɪnˈflæmətrɪ] *adj* incendiaire
inflatable [ɪnˈfleɪtəbəl] **1** *n* (*rubber dinghy*) canot *m* pneumatique
2 *adj* gonflable
inflate [ɪnˈfleɪt] **1** *vt* (**a**) (*tyre, lifejacket*) gonfler (**b**) (*prices*) faire monter
2 *vi* se gonfler
inflated [ɪnˈfleɪtɪd] *adj* (*tyre, lifejacket*) gonflé(e); **to have an i. opinion of oneself** avoir une opinion trop flatteuse de soi-même
inflation [ɪnˈfleɪʃən] *n* *Econ* inflation *f*
inflationary [ɪnˈfleɪʃənrɪ] *adj* *Econ* inflationniste
inflect [ɪnˈflekt] **1** *vt* (**a**) (*voice*) moduler (**b**) *Gram* ajouter la désinence de
2 *vi* *Gram* prendre une désinence
inflexibility [ɪnfleksɪˈbɪlɪtɪ] *n* rigidité *f*
inflexible [ɪnˈfleksɪbəl] *adj* rigide
inflict [ɪnˈflɪkt] *vt* (*suffering, punishment, defeat*) infliger (**on** à); (*damage*) causer (**on** à); **to i. oneself on sb** infliger sa présence à qn
in-flight [ˈɪnflaɪt] *adj* **i. entertainment** distractions *fpl* en vol; **i. magazine** magazine *f* de bord; **i. meal** repas *m* servi pendant le vol
influence [ˈɪnflʊəns] **1** *n* influence *f* (**on** sur); **to be a good/bad i. (on sb)** avoir une bonne/mauvaise influence (sur qn); **to have i. over sb** avoir de l'influence sur qn; **under the i. of drink** sous l'empire de la boisson
2 *vt* influencer; **to be easily influenced** être influençable
influential [ɪnflʊˈenʃəl] *adj* influent(e)
influenza [ɪnflʊˈenzə] *n* grippe *f*
influx [ˈɪnflʌks] *n* afflux *m*
info [ˈɪnfəʊ] *n* *Fam* renseignements *mpl*
infomercial [ɪnfəʊˈmɜːʃəl] *n* infomercial *m*

inform [ɪnˈfɔːm] **1** *vt* informer (**of** *or* **about** de); **to keep sb informed of sth** tenir qn au courant de qch
2 *vi* **to i. on sb** dénoncer qn
informal [ɪnˈfɔːməl] *adj* (**a**) (*unaffected*) simple (**b**) (*casual*) décontracté(e); (*word, language*) familier(-ère) (**c**) (*unofficial*) (*meeting, talks*) officieux(euse)
informality [ɪnfɔːˈmælɪtɪ] *n* (**a**) (*unaffectedness*) simplicité *f* (**b**) (*casualness*) décontraction *f* (**c**) (*of talks*) caractère *m* officieux
informally [ɪnˈfɔːməlɪ] *adv* (**a**) (*unaffectedly*) avec simplicité (**b**) (*casually*) avec décontraction (**c**) (*hold talks*) officieusement
informant [ɪnˈfɔːmənt] *n* informateur(trice) *m,f*
information [ɪnfəˈmeɪʃən] *n* (**a**) (*news, facts*) renseignements *mpl*; **a piece of i.** un renseignement; **for further i.** pour de plus amples renseignements; **i. bureau** bureau *m* des renseignements; **i. officer** (*press officer*) responsable *mf* de la communication; (*archivist*) documentaliste *mf*; **i. pack** dossier *m* d'information (**b**) *Comput* **i. processing** traitement *m* de l'information; **i. retrieval** recherche *f* documentaire; **i. science** informatique *f*; **the i. superhighway** l'autoroute *f* de l'information, *Can* l'inforoute *f*; **i. technology** informatique *f* (**c**) *AmTel* renseignements *mpl*
informative [ɪnˈfɔːmətɪv] *adj* instructif(ive); **she was very i.** elle nous a appris beaucoup de choses
informed [ɪnˈfɔːmd] *adj* (*person*) bien renseigné(e), bien informé(e); **my i. guess is that...** en me basant sur ce que je sais, je dirais que...; **an i. decision** une décision prise en connaissance de cause
informer [ɪnˈfɔːmə(r)] *n* indicateur *m*
infra dig [ˈɪnfrəˈdɪg] *adj* *Fam* rabaissant(e), dégradant(e)
infrared [ɪnfrəˈred] *adj* infrarouge; **i. camera** caméra *f* infrarouge; *Comput* **i. mouse** souris *f* à infrarouge
infrastructure [ˈɪnfrəstrʌktʃə(r)] *n* infrastructure *f*
infrequent [ɪnˈfriːkwənt] *adj* rare, peu fréquent(e)
infringe [ɪnˈfrɪndʒ] *vt* (*rule, law*) enfreindre; (*right*) empiéter sur
▸**infringe on** *vt insep* empiéter sur
infringement [ɪnˈfrɪndʒmənt] *n* (*of rule, law*) infraction *f* (**of** à); (*of right*) atteinte *f* (**of** à)
infuriate [ɪnˈfjʊərɪeɪt] *vt* exaspérer
infuriating [ɪnˈfjʊərɪeɪtɪŋ] *adj* exaspérant(e)
infuse [ɪnˈfjuːz] **1** *vt* (**a**) (*energy, hope*) insuffler (**into** à) (**b**) (*tea*) faire infuser
2 *vi* (*of tea*) infuser
infusion [ɪnˈfjuːʒən] *n* (*drink*) infusion *f*
ingenious [ɪnˈdʒiːnɪəs] *adj* ingénieux(euse)
ingenuity [ɪndʒɪˈnjuːɪtɪ] *n* ingéniosité *f*
ingenuous [ɪnˈdʒenʊəs] *adj* (*naive*) ingénu(e); (*frank*) franc (franche)
inglorious [ɪnˈglɔːrɪəs] *adj* déshonorant(e), honteux(euse)
ingot [ˈɪŋgət] *n* lingot *m*
ingrained [ɪnˈgreɪnd] *adj* (*prejudice, habit*) enraciné(e); **i. dirt** crasse *f*
ingratiate [ɪnˈgreɪʃɪeɪt] *vt* **to i. oneself (with sb)** se faire bien voir (de *ou* par qn)
ingratiating [ɪnˈgreɪʃɪeɪtɪŋ] *adj* doucereux(euse)
ingratitude [ɪnˈgrætɪtjuːd] *n* ingratitude *f*
ingredient [ɪnˈgriːdɪənt] *n* *also Fig* ingrédient *m*; *Fig* **the missing i.** l'élément *m* manquant
ingrowing [ˈɪngrəʊɪŋ], **ingrown** [ˈɪngrəʊn] *adj* **i. toenail** ongle *m* incarné
inhabit [ɪnˈhæbɪt] *vt* habiter
inhabitable [ɪnˈhæbɪtəbəl] *adj* habitable

inhabitant [ɪnˈhæbɪtənt] n habitant(e) m,f
inhabited [ɪnˈhæbɪtɪd] adj habité(e) (**by** par)
inhale [ɪnˈheɪl] **1** vt (gas, fumes) inhaler; (cigarette smoke) avaler
  2 vi inspirer; (in smoking) avaler la fumée
inhaler [ɪnˈheɪlə(r)] n (for asthmatics) inhalateur m
inherent [ɪnˈherənt] adj inhérent(e) (**in** à)
inherit [ɪnˈherɪt] vt hériter (**from** de)
inheritance [ɪnˈherɪtəns] n héritage m; **i. tax** droits mpl de succession
inhibit [ɪnˈhɪbɪt] vt (progress, growth) entraver; (person) inhiber
inhibited [ɪnˈhɪbɪtɪd] adj (person) inhibé(e)
inhibition [ɪnɪˈbɪʃən] n inhibition f; **to have no inhibitions about doing sth** n'avoir aucune honte à faire qch
inhospitable [ɪnhɒˈspɪtəbəl] adj inhospitalier(ère)
in-house [ˈɪnˈhaʊs] **1** adj (training) interne; (staff) qui travaille sur place
  2 adv sur place
inhuman [ɪnˈhjuːmən] adj inhumain(e)
inhumane [ɪnhjuːˈmeɪn] adj inhumain(e)
inhumanity [ɪnhjuːˈmænɪtɪ] n inhumanité f, cruauté f
inimical [ɪˈnɪmɪkəl] adj Formal (people) ennemi(e), hostile; (conditions) contraire (**to** à)
inimitable [ɪˈnɪmɪtəbəl] adj inimitable
iniquitous [ɪˈnɪkwɪtəs] adj inique
iniquity [ɪˈnɪkwɪtɪ] (pl **iniquities**) n iniquité f
initial [ɪˈnɪʃəl] **1** n initiale f; **initials** (signature) paraphe m
  2 adj initial(e), premier(ère); **in the i. stages of sth** au stade initial de qch
  3 vt (pt & pp **initialled**, Am **initialed**) parapher
initially [ɪˈnɪʃəlɪ] adv au début
initiate [ɪˈnɪʃɪeɪt] vt (**a**) (negotiations) amorcer; (rumour, project) lancer; Law **to i. proceedings (against sb)** entamer des poursuites (contre qn) (**b**) **to i. sb into a secret society/gang** faire subir à qn les épreuves initiatiques d'une société secrète/d'un gang
initiation [ɪnɪʃɪˈeɪʃən] n (**a**) (beginning) commencement m, début(s) m(pl) (**b**) (induction) initiation f; **i. ceremony** rite m d'initiation
initiative [ɪˈnɪʃətɪv] n initiative f; **to take the i. (in doing sth)** prendre l'initiative (de faire qch); **to use one's i.** faire preuve d'initiative; **on one's own i.** de sa propre initiative
inject [ɪnˈdʒekt] vt (drug, money) injecter; (enthusiasm) communiquer; **to i. new life into sth** donner un nouvel essor à qch
injection [ɪnˈdʒekʃən] n injection f, piqûre f; Fig injection; **polio i.** vaccin m contre la polio; **to give sb an i.** faire une piqûre à qn
injudicious [ɪndʒʊˈdɪʃəs] adj peu judicieux(euse), malavisé(e)
injunction [ɪnˈdʒʌŋkʃən] n Law arrêt m, jugement m; **to take out an i. against sb** mettre qn en demeure
injure [ˈɪndʒə(r)] vt (person) blesser; (reputation, interests) nuire à; **to i. oneself** se blesser; **to i. one's leg** se blesser à la jambe; **her pride is injured** elle est blessée dans son orgueil
injured [ˈɪndʒəd] **1** n **the i.** les blessés mpl
  2 adj blessé(e); (look, voice) offensé(e); Law **the i. party** la partie lésée
injurious [ɪnˈdʒʊrɪəs] adj nuisible, préjudiciable (**to** à)

injury [ˈɪndʒərɪ] (pl **injuries**) n (physical) blessure f; **to do oneself an i.** se blesser; **i. time** (in football match) arrêts mpl de jeu
injustice [ɪnˈdʒʌstɪs] n injustice f; **to do sb an i.** être injuste envers qn
ink [ɪŋk] n encre f; **i. pad** tampon m (encreur)
ink-jet [ˈɪŋkdʒet] adj Comput **i. (printer)** imprimante f à jet d'encre
inkling [ˈɪŋklɪŋ] n soupçon m; **to have an i. of sth** se douter de qch
inkwell [ˈɪŋkwel] n encrier m (de pupitre)
inky [ˈɪŋkɪ] adj (**a**) (stained with ink) taché(e) d'encre (**b**) **i. (black)** noir(e) comme (de) l'encre
inlaid [ɪnˈleɪd] adj (with wood) marqueté(e); (with jewels) incrusté(e) (**with** de)
inland 1 adj [ˈɪnlənd] intérieur(e); **the I. Revenue** ≃ le fisc
  2 adv [ɪnˈlænd] (travel) vers l'intérieur; (live) dans les terres
in-laws [ˈɪnlɔːz] npl (spouse's parents) beaux-parents mpl; (spouse's family) belle-famille f
inlet [ˈɪnlet] n (**a**) (of sea) petit bras m de mer (**b**) (of pipe, machine) (orifice m d')entrée f
in-line [ˈɪnlaɪn] adj **i. skates** rollers mpl; **to go i. skating** faire du roller m
inmate [ˈɪnmeɪt] n (in prison) détenu(e) m,f; (in mental hospital) interné(e) m,f
inn [ɪn] n auberge f
innards [ˈɪnədz] npl entrailles fpl
innate [ɪˈneɪt] adj inné(e)
inner [ˈɪnə(r)] adj (**a**) (chamber, lining) intérieur(e); **i. circle** (of party, association) initiés mpl; **i. city** quartiers mpl déshérités du centre-ville; **i. ear** oreille f interne; **i. tube** chambre f à air (**b**) (thought, feeling) intime; (peace) intérieur(e)
innermost [ˈɪnəməʊst] adj (part) le (la) plus profond(e); (thoughts, feelings) le (la) plus secret(ète)
innings [ˈɪnɪŋz] n (in cricket) tournée f, tour m de batte; Fig **she had a good i.** elle a bien profité de la vie
innkeeper [ˈɪnkiːpə(r)] n aubergiste mf
innocence [ˈɪnəsəns] n innocence f
innocent [ˈɪnəsənt] **1** adj innocent(e) m,f; **to act the i.** faire l'innocent
  2 adj innocent(e)
innocuous [ɪˈnɒkjʊəs] adj inoffensif(ive); (remark) anodin(e)
innovate [ˈɪnəveɪt] vi innover
innovation [ɪnəˈveɪʃən] n innovation f
innovative [ˈɪnəveɪtɪv] adj (in)novateur(trice)
innovator [ˈɪnəveɪtə(r)] n (in)novateur(trice) m,f
innuendo [ɪnjʊˈendəʊ] (pl **innuendos** or **innuendoes**) n (insinuation) insinuation f; (in jokes) allusion f grivoise
innumerable [ɪˈnjuːmərəbəl] adj innombrable
inoculate [ɪˈnɒkjʊleɪt] vt vacciner; **to i. sb with sth** inoculer qch à qn; **to i. sb against sth** vacciner qn contre qch
inoculation [ɪnɒkjʊˈleɪʃən] n inoculation f
inoffensive [ɪnəˈfensɪv] adj (animal, person) inoffensif(ive); (remark, humour) qui n'a rien d'offensant; (odour) qui n'a rien de désagréable
inoperable [ɪnˈɒpərəbəl] adj inopérable
inoperative [ɪnˈɒpərətɪv] adj (rule) inopérant(e); (machine) arrêté(e)
inopportune [ɪnˈɒpətjuːn] adj inopportun(e)
inordinate [ɪnˈɔːdɪnət] adj démesuré(e)
inorganic [ɪnɔːˈgænɪk] adj inorganique

in-patient ['ɪnpeɪʃənt] *n* patient(e) *m,f* hospitalisé(e)
input ['ɪnpʊt] **1** *n* (**a**) *Elec* puissance *f* d'alimentation; *(terminal)* entrée *f*; *Comput* entrée *f*, introduction *f* (**b**) *(contribution)* contribution *f*
2 *vt (pt & pp* **input**) *Comput (data)* entrer
inquest ['ɪnkwest] *n Law* enquête *f*; *Fig (in politics, business)* analyse *f*; **to hold an i.** *Law (of coroner)* mener une enquête (**into** sur); *(in politics, business)* faire une analyse (**into** de)
inquire [ɪn'kwaɪə(r)] **1** *vt* demander
2 *vi* se renseigner (**about** sur); **i. within** *(sign)* s'adresser ici
▸**inquire after** *vt insep* demander des nouvelles de
▸**inquire into** *vt insep* faire des recherches sur
inquiring [ɪn'kwaɪrɪŋ] *adj (mind)* curieux(euse); *(look, voice)* interrogateur(trice)
inquiry [ɪn'kwaɪrɪ] *(pl* **inquiries**) *n* (**a**) *(official investigation)* enquête *f*; **to hold an i.** (**into sth**) faire une enquête (sur qch) (**b**) *(request for information)* demande *f* de renseignements; **to make inquiries (about sth)** se renseigner (sur qch); **i. desk** bureau *m* de(s) renseignements
Inquisition [ɪnkwɪ'zɪʃən] *n* **the I.** l'Inquisition *f*
inquisitive [ɪn'kwɪzɪtɪv] *adj (person, mind)* curieux(euse); *(look)* interrogateur(trice)
inroads ['ɪnrəʊdz] *npl* **to make i. into** *(capital, savings)* entamer; *(market)* pénétrer
insane [ɪn'seɪn] *adj (person)* dément(e); *Fam (desire, scheme)* fou (folle); **to go i.** devenir fou, perdre la raison; **to be i. with grief/jealousy** être fou de douleur/jalousie
insanely [ɪn'seɪnlɪ] *adv* comme un fou (une folle); **i. jealous** d'une jalousie maladive
insanitary [ɪn'sænɪtrɪ] *adj* insalubre, malsain(e)
insanity [ɪn'sænɪtɪ] *n (of person)* démence *f*; *Fam (of desire, scheme)* folie *f*
insatiable [ɪn'seɪʃəbəl] *adj* insatiable
inscribe [ɪn'skraɪb] *vt (write)* écrire; *(engrave)* inscrire, graver
inscription [ɪn'skrɪpʃən] *n (on stone, coin)* inscription *f*; *(in book)* dédicace *f*
inscrutable [ɪn'skruːtəbəl] *adj (look, face)* impénétrable; *(remark)* énigmatique
insect ['ɪnsekt] *n* insecte *m*; **i. bite** piqûre *f* d'insecte; **i. repellent** anti-moustiques *m inv*
insecticide [ɪn'sektɪsaɪd] *n* insecticide *m*
insecure [ɪnsɪ'kjʊə(r)] *adj* (**a**) *(person) (generally)* pas sûr(e) de soi, qui manque d'assurance; *(temporarily)* angoissé(e) (**b**) *(government)* fragile; *(job, future)* précaire; **to be financially i.** être dans une situation financière précaire
insecurity [ɪnsɪ'kjʊərɪtɪ] *n* (**a**) *(of person) (lack of confidence)* manque *m* d'assurance; *(anxiety)* angoisse *f* (**b**) *(of job, future)* précarité *f*
insemination [ɪnsemɪ'neɪʃən] *n* insémination *f*
insensible [ɪn'sensɪbəl] *adj Formal (unaware, unconscious)* inconscient(e) (**to** de)
insensitive [ɪn'sensɪtɪv] *adj (person)* insensible (**to** à); *(remark)* indélicat(e)
insensitivity [ɪnsensɪ'tɪvɪtɪ] *n* insensibilité *f*
inseparable [ɪn'sepərəbəl] *adj* inséparable
insert 1 *n* ['ɪnsɜːt] *(in magazine)* encart *m*
2 *vt* [ɪn'sɜːt] *(key, finger)* introduire (**into** dans); *(clause)* insérer (**in** dans); *(advertisement)* mettre (**in** dans)
insertion [ɪn'sɜːʃən] *n* insertion *f*
inset ['ɪnset] *n (in map, picture)* médaillon *m*

inshore [ɪn'ʃɔː(r)] **1** *adj (navigation, fishing)* côtier(ère)
2 *adv (be situated)* sur la côte; *(travel)* vers la côte, vers les terres
inside 1 *n* [ɪn'saɪd] (**a**) *(of house)* intérieur *m*; **on/from the i.** à/de l'intérieur; **to overtake on the i.** *(in Britain)* doubler par la gauche; *(in Europe, USA)* doubler par la droite (**b**) *Fam* **insides** *(internal organs)* entrailles *fpl* (**c**) *(in phrases)* **i. out** *(clothes)* à l'envers; *Fig* **to know sth i. out** connaître qch comme sa poche
2 *adj* ['ɪnsaɪd] intérieur(e); **to have i. information** avoir des informations de première main; *Fam* **it's an i. job** c'est quelqu'un de la maison qui a fait ça; **i. lane** *(in Britain)* voie *f* de gauche; *(in Europe, USA)* voie de droite; **i. left** *(in football)* intérieur *m* gauche; **to know the i. story** connaître les dessous de l'affaire
3 *adv* [ɪn'saɪd] (**a**) *(indoors)* à l'intérieur; **come i.!** entrez! (**b**) *(within oneself)* en son for intérieur (**c**) *Fam (in prison)* en taule
4 *prep* [ɪn'saɪd] (**a**) *(place)* à l'intérieur de, dans (**b**) *(with time)* **i. (of) a week/an hour** en moins d'une semaine/heure
insider [ɪn'saɪdə(r)] *n* initié(e) *m,f*; *Fin* **i. dealing, i. trading** délit *m* d'initié
insidious [ɪn'sɪdɪəs] *adj* insidieux(euse)
insight ['ɪnsaɪt] *n* (**a**) *(perspicacity)* perspicacité *f* (**b**) *(understanding)* aperçu *m*; **to get an i. into sth** avoir un aperçu de qch
insignia [ɪn'sɪgnɪə] *n* insigne *m*
insignificance [ɪnsɪg'nɪfɪkəns] *n* insignifiance *f*; **to pale into i. (beside sth)** sembler totalement insignifiant(e) (à côté de qch)
insignificant [ɪnsɪg'nɪfɪkənt] *adj* insignifiant(e)
insincere [ɪnsɪn'sɪə(r)] *adj* peu sincère, faux (fausse)
insincerity [ɪnsɪn'serɪtɪ] *n* manque *m* de sincérité, fausseté *f*
insinuate [ɪn'sɪnjʊeɪt] *vt* insinuer; **to i. oneself into sb's favour** s'insinuer dans les bonnes grâces de qn
insinuation [ɪnsɪnjʊ'eɪʃən] *n* insinuation *f*
insipid [ɪn'sɪpɪd] *adj* insipide
insist [ɪn'sɪst] **1** *vt* (**a**) *(maintain)* **to i. that...** soutenir *ou* maintenir que... (**b**) *(demand)* **to i. (that) sb does sth** insister pour que qn fasse qch
2 *vi* insister; **to i. on sth** exiger qch; **to i. on doing sth** tenir à faire qch
insistence [ɪn'sɪstəns] *n* insistance *f* (**on** à); **I stayed at her i.** elle insista, et je restai
insistent [ɪn'sɪstənt] *adj (person, demand)* pressant(e); **to be i.** se montrer pressant; **to be i. about sth** insister pour qch
insofar as ['ɪnsəʊ'fɑːrəz] *adv* dans la mesure où
insole ['ɪnsəʊl] *n* semelle *f* intérieure
insolence ['ɪnsələns] *n* insolence *f* (**to** envers)
insolent ['ɪnsələnt] *adj* insolent(e) (**to** envers)
insoluble [ɪn'sɒljʊbəl] *adj* insoluble
insolvency [ɪn'sɒlvənsɪ] *n Fin (of person)* insolvabilité *f*; *(of company)* faillite *f*
insolvent [ɪn'sɒlvənt] *adj Fin (person)* insolvable; *(company)* en faillite
insomnia [ɪn'sɒmnɪə] *n* insomnie *f*
insomniac [ɪn'sɒmnɪæk] *n* insomniaque *mf*
inspect [ɪn'spekt] *vt (passport, luggage, picture)* examiner; *(school, factory)* inspecter; *(troops)* passer en revue
inspection [ɪn'spekʃən] *n (of passport, luggage, picture)* examen *m*; *(of school, factory)* (visite *f* d')inspection *f*;

(of troops) revue *f*; **on closer i.** en y regardant de plus près
inspector [ɪnˈspektə(r)] *n (of schools, factories)* inspecteur(trice) *m,f*; *Br (on train, bus)* contrôleur(euse) *m,f*; *Br* **(police) i.** inspecteur *m* de police
inspiration [ɪnspɪˈreɪʃən] *n* inspiration *f*; **to be an i. to sb** inspirer qn
inspire [ɪnˈspaɪə(r)] *vt* inspirer; **to i. sb to do sth** pousser qn à faire qch; **to i. sth in sb, to i. sb with sth** inspirer qch à qn
inspired [ɪnˈspaɪəd] *adj* inspiré(e)
inspiring [ɪnˈspaɪərɪŋ] *adj (music, speech)* exaltant(e); *(leader)* enthousiasmant(e); **the menu wasn't very i.** le menu n'avait rien de bien tentant
instability [ɪnstəˈbɪlɪtɪ] *n* instabilité *f*
install, *Am* **instal** [ɪnˈstɔːl] *vt* installer; **to i. sb in a post** mettre qn à un poste; **to i. oneself in an armchair** s'installer dans un fauteuil
installation [ɪnstəˈleɪʃən] *n* installation *f*
instalment, *Am* **installment** [ɪnˈstɔːlmənt] *n* (**a**) *(part payment)* versement *m*; **to pay by instalments** payer par versements échelonnés (**b**) *(of radio, TV programme)* épisode *m*
instance [ˈɪnstəns] *n (example)* cas *m*; **for i.** par exemple; **in the first i.** en (tout) premier lieu
instant [ˈɪnstənt] **1** *n (moment)* instant *m*, moment *m*; **this i.** immédiatement; **not an i. too soon** juste à temps; **the i. I saw her** dès que je l'ai vue
2 *adj* (**a**) *(reply, success, dislike)* immédiat(e); *(solution)* instantané(e); *Comput* **i. message** message *m* instantané; *Comput* **i. messaging** messagerie *f* instantanée; *TV* **i. replay** reprise *f* de l'action (**b**) *(coffee, soup)* instantané(e)
instant-access [ɪnstəntˈækses] *adj (bank account)* à accès immédiat
instantaneous [ɪnstənˈteɪnɪəs] *adj* instantané(e)
instantly [ˈɪnstəntlɪ] *adv* instantanément
instead [ɪnˈsted] *adv (in place of something)* à la place; *(in place of somebody)* à ma/sa/etc place; **i. of** *(thing)* au lieu de; *(person)* à la place de; **i. of doing sth** au lieu de faire qch
instep [ˈɪnstep] *n (of foot)* cou-de-pied *m*; *(of shoe)* cambrure *f*
instigate [ˈɪnstɪgeɪt] *vt* être à l'origine de
instigation [ˈɪnstɪgeɪʃən] *n* instigation *f*; **at sb's i.** à l'instigation de qn
instigator [ˈɪnstɪgeɪtə(r)] *n* instigateur(trice) *m,f*
instil, *Am* **instill** [ɪnˈstɪl] *(pt & pp* **instilled)** *vt (courage, pride)* inspirer (**in** à); *(doubt, jealousy)* instiller (**in** à); *(idea)* inculquer (**into** à)
instinct [ˈɪnstɪŋkt] *n* instinct *m*; **he has an i. for the game** ce jeu, chez lui, c'est instinctif
instinctive [ɪnˈstɪŋktɪv] *adj* instinctif(ive)
institute [ˈɪnstɪtjuːt] **1** *n* institut *m*
2 *vt (system, procedure)* établir, instituer; *(search)* lancer; *Law (enquiry)* ordonner; **to i. proceedings (against sb)** entamer *ou* engager des poursuites (contre qn)
institution [ɪnstɪˈtjuːʃən] *n (organization)* institution *f*; *(public, financial)* établissement *m*; *(for old people)* hospice *m*; *(for mental patients)* asile *m*; *Fig* **to become a national i.** *(of event, TV programme)* devenir une institution nationale
institutional [ɪnstɪˈtjuːʃənəl] *adj* institutionnel(elle)
institutionalize [ɪnstɪˈtjuːʃənəlaɪz] *vt* (**a**) *(put in a home)* placer dans un établissement spécialisé; **to become institutionalized** *(of prisoner, patient)* devenir

complètement dépendant(e) (**b**) *(turn into an institution)* institutionnaliser
instruct [ɪnˈstrʌkt] *vt* (**a**) *(teach)* enseigner; **to i. sb in sth** enseigner qch à qn (**b**) *(command)* ordonner; **to i. sb to do sth** ordonner à qn de faire qch
instruction [ɪnˈstrʌkʃən] *n* (**a**) *(training)* instruction *f*, enseignement *m* (**b**) **instructions** *(orders)* instructions *fpl*, directives *fpl* (**c**) **instructions (for use)** notice *f* (d'emploi); **i. manual** manuel *m* d'entretien
instructive [ɪnˈstrʌktɪv] *adj* instructif(ive)
instructor [ɪnˈstrʌktə(r)] *n* (**a**) *(of sporting activity, driving)* moniteur(trice) *m,f* (**b**) *Am (university lecturer)* professeur *m*
instrument [ˈɪnstrəmənt] *n* instrument *m*; **i. board** *or* **panel** *(in plane, car)* tableau *m* de bord
instrumental [ɪnstrʊˈmentəl] **1** *n (music without words)* instrumental *m*
2 *adj* (**a**) *(contributory)* **to be i. in sth** jouer un rôle décisif dans qch (**b**) *(in music)* instrumental(e)
instrumentalist [ɪnstrʊˈmentəlɪst] *n* instrumentiste *mf*
instrumentation [ɪnstrʊmenˈteɪʃən] *n* instrumentation *f*
insubordinate [ɪnsəˈbɔːdɪnət] *adj* insubordonné(e)
insubordination [ɪnsəbɔːdɪˈneɪʃən] *n* insubordination *f*
insubstantial [ɪnsəbˈstænʃəl] *adj (structure, argument)* peu solide; *(meal)* frugal(e); *(book)* creux(-euse), qui manque de substance
insufferable [ɪnˈsʌfrəbəl] *adj* insupportable, intolérable
insufficient [ˈɪnsəfɪʃənt] *adj* insuffisant(e)
insular [ˈɪnsjʊlə(r)] *adj* borné(e); *(climate)* insulaire
insulate [ˈɪnsjʊleɪt] *vt* isoler; *Fig* **to be insulated from sth** être protégé(e) de qch
insulating tape [ɪnsjʊleɪtɪŋˈteɪp] *n* chatterton *m*
insulation [ɪnsjʊˈleɪʃən] *n* isolation *f*
insulin [ˈɪnsjʊlɪn] *n* insuline *f*
insult 1 *n* [ˈɪnsʌlt] *(words, action)* insulte *f*; **to add i. to injury** aggraver les choses
2 *vt* [ɪnˈsʌlt] insulter
insulting [ɪnˈsʌltɪŋ] *adj* insultant(e)
insuperable [ɪnˈsuːpərəbəl] *adj* insurmontable
insurance [ɪnˈʃʊərəns] *n* assurance *f*; *Fig (protection)* garantie *f*; **to take out i.** prendre une assurance; **i. broker** courtier *m* en assurances; **i. claim** demande *f* d'indemnité; *(for more serious damage)* déclaration *f* de sinistre; **i. company** companie *f* d'assurances; **i. policy** police *f* d'assurance; **i. premium** prime *f* d'assurance
insure [ɪnˈʃʊə(r)] *vt* assurer (**against** contre); **to i. one's life** s'assurer sur la vie
insured [ɪnˈʃʊəd] *adj* assuré(e) (**against** contre); **i. value** valeur *f* assurée
insurer [ɪnˈʃʊərə(r)] *n* assureur *m*
insurgent [ɪnˈsɜːdʒənt] *n* insurgé(e) *m,f*
insurmountable [ɪnsəˈmaʊntəbəl] *adj* insurmontable
insurrection [ɪnsəˈrekʃən] *n* insurrection *f*
intact [ɪnˈtækt] *adj* intact(e)
intake [ˈɪnteɪk] *n* (**a**) *(of alcohol, food)* consommation *f*; *(of calories)* absorption *f* (**b**) *(pupils)* élèves *mpl*; *(recruits)* contingent *m* (**c**) *Tech* admission *f*
intangible [ɪnˈtændʒɪbəl] *adj* impalpable
integer [ˈɪntɪdʒə(r)] *n Math* nombre *m* entier

integral ['ɪntɪɡrəl] *adj (essential)* indispensable; **to be an i. part of sth** faire partie intégrante de qch; *Math* **i.** calculus calcul *m* intégral

integrate ['ɪntɪɡreɪt] **1** *vt* intégrer (**into** à) **2** *vi* s'intégrer (**into** à)

integrated ['ɪntɪɡreɪtɪd] *adj* intégré(e); *(school)* qui pratique la déségrégation raciale

integration [ɪntɪ'ɡreɪʃən] *n* intégration *f*

integrity [ɪn'teɡrɪtɪ] *n* intégrité *f*

intellect ['ɪntɪlekt] *n* intellect *m*, intelligence *f*

intellectual [ɪntɪ'lektjʊəl] **1** *n* intellectuel(elle) *m,f* **2** *adj* intellectuel(elle)

intelligence [ɪn'telɪdʒəns] *n* (**a**) *(faculty)* intelligence *f*; *Psy* **i.** quotient quotient *m* intellectuel; **i. test** test *m* d'intelligence (**b**) *(secret service)* services *mpl* secrets; **i. officer** agent *m* de renseignements; **i. service** services *mpl* secrets

intelligent [ɪn'telɪdʒənt] *adj* intelligent(e)

intelligentsia [ɪntelɪ'dʒensɪə] *n* intelligentsia *f*

intelligible [ɪn'telɪdʒɪbəl] *adj* intelligible

intemperate [ɪn'tempərət] *adj Formal (climate)* rude; *(person, behaviour)* intempérant(e)

intend [ɪn'tend] *vt* **to i. to do sth** avoir l'intention de faire qch; **to i. sth for sb** destiner qch à qn; **was that intended?** était-ce intentionnel?; **it was intended as a compliment/a joke** c'était un compliment/pour plaisanter; **I didn't i.** her to see it yet il n'était pas dans mes intentions qu'elle le voie si tôt

intended [ɪn'tendɪd] **1** *n Old-fashioned or Hum (future spouse)* futur(e) *m,f* **2** *adj (consequence, outcome)* prévu(e); *(effect)* escompté(e); *(insult, mistake)* voulu(e)

intense [ɪn'tens] *adj* intense; *(interest, anger)* vif (vive); *(person)* passionné(e)

intensely [ɪn'tenslɪ] *adv* (**a**) *(amusing, boring)* extrêmement (**b**) *(look at, speak)* intensément, avec intensité

intensify [ɪn'tensɪfaɪ] (*pt & pp* **intensified**) **1** *vt (search, effort)* intensifier; *(pressure)* augmenter **2** *vi* s'intensifier

intensity [ɪn'tensɪtɪ] *n* intensité *f*

intensive [ɪn'tensɪv] *adj* intensif(ive); *Med* **i.** care soins *mpl* intensifs; *Med* **i. care unit** unité *f* de soins intensifs

intent [ɪn'tent] **1** *n* intention *f*; **to all intents and purposes** quasiment **2** *adj (look)* intense; **to be i. on doing sth** être résolu(e) *ou* déterminé(e) à faire qch

intention [ɪn'tenʃən] *n* intention *f*; **to have every i. of doing sth** avoir la ferme intention de faire qch; **to have no i. of doing sth** n'avoir nullement l'intention de faire qch

intentional [ɪn'tenʃənəl] *adj* intentionnel(elle), voulu(e)

intentionally [ɪn'tenʃənəlɪ] *adv* intentionnellement; **I didn't do it i.** je ne l'ai pas fait exprès

intently [ɪn'tentlɪ] *adv (listen, look at)* attentivement

inter [ɪn'tɜː(r)] (*pt & pp* **interred**) *vt* inhumer, enterrer

interact [ɪntə'rækt] *vi* (**a**) *(of person)* communiquer (**with** avec); *(of two or more people)* communiquer entre eux (elles) (**b**) *(of chemical)* réagir (**with** avec); *(of two or more chemicals)* réagir entre eux (elles)

interaction [ɪntə'rækʃən] *n* interaction *f*

interactive [ɪntə'ræktɪv] *adj* interactif(ive); **i. whiteboard** tableau *m* interactif

intercede [ɪntə'siːd] *vi* intercéder (**with/for** auprès de/en faveur de)

intercept [ɪntə'sept] *vt* intercepter

interception [ɪntə'sepʃən] *n* interception *f*

intercession [ɪntə'seʃən] *n* intercession *f*

interchange 1 *n* ['ɪntətʃeɪndʒ] *(exchange)* échange *m*; *(on motorway)* échangeur *m* **2** *vt* [ɪntə'tʃeɪndʒ] *(exchange)* échanger; *(transpose)* intervertir

interchangeable [ɪntə'tʃeɪndʒəbəl] *adj* interchangeable

intercom ['ɪntəkɒm] *n* Interphone® *m*

interconnect [ɪntəkə'nekt] *vt* interconnecter

intercontinental [ɪntəkɒntɪ'nentəl] *adj* intercontinental(e); **i. ballistic missile** missile *m* balistique intercontinental

intercourse ['ɪntəkɔːs] *n* (**a**) **(sexual) i.** rapports *mpl* (sexuels) (**b**) *Formal (dealings)* commerce *m*, relations *fpl*

interdependent ['ɪntədɪ'pendənt] *adj* interdépendant(e)

interest ['ɪntrest] **1** *n* (**a**) *(curiosity)* intérêt *m*; *(hobby)* centre *m* d'intérêt; **of i.** intéressant(e); **of historical i.** intéressant du point de vue historique; **to be of i. to sb** intéresser qn; **to take an i. in sth** s'intéresser à qch; **to lose i. (in sth)** se désintéresser (de qch) (**b**) *(stake)* intérêt *m*; **to have a financial i. in sth** avoir investi financièrement dans qch (**c**) *(benefit)* intérêt *m*; **to act in sb's interests** agir dans l'intérêt de qn; **the public i.** l'intérêt *m* public; **it's in my i. to do it** j'ai tout intérêt à le faire; **in the interests of...** dans l'intérêt de... (**d**) *(on loan, investment)* intérêt(s) *m(pl)* **2** *vt* intéresser; **to i. sb in sth** intéresser qn à qch; **can I i. you in a drink?** je peux vous offrir un verre?

interested ['ɪntrestɪd] *adj* intéressé(e); **to be interested in sth** s'intéresser à qch; **he seemed i. in the proposal** il a semblé intéressé par cette proposition

interest-free ['ɪntrest'friː] *adj (loan)* sans intérêt; *(credit)* gratuit(e)

interesting ['ɪntrestɪŋ] *adj* intéressant(e)

interface ['ɪntəfeɪs] *n Comput* interface *f*

interfere [ɪntə'fɪə(r)] *vi* (**a**) *(meddle)* se mêler (**in** de); **he's always interfering** il est toujours à se mêler de ce qui ne le regarde pas; **don't i. with my papers** ne touche pas à mes papiers; *Euph* **to i. with sb** *(sexually)* abuser de qn (**b**) **to i. with sth** *(hinder)* gêner qch

interference [ɪntə'fɪərəns] *n* (**a**) *(meddling)* ingérence *f* (**b**) *Rad & TV* interférences *fpl*

interfering [ɪntə'fɪərɪŋ] *adj* importun(e)

interim ['ɪntərɪm] **1** *n* **in the i.** entre-temps **2** *adj (agreement, report)* provisoire

interior [ɪn'tɪərɪə(r)] **1** *n* intérieur *m* **2** *adj* intérieur(e); **i. decorator** décorateur(trice) *m,f* (d'intérieurs); **i. designer** architecte *mf* d'intérieur

interject [ɪntə'dʒekt] *vt (remark)* lancer; *(protest)* émettre

interjection [ɪntə'dʒekʃən] *n* interjection *f*

interlocking [ɪntə'lɒkɪŋ] *adj (parts)* emboîtable; *(gears)* qui s'enclenchent

interlocutor [ɪntə'lɒkjuːtə(r)] *n Formal* interlocuteur (trice) *m,f*

interloper ['ɪntələʊpə(r)] *n* intrus(e) *m,f*

interlude ['ɪntəluːd] *n also Fig* intermède *m*

intermarriage [ɪntə'mærɪdʒ] *n (within a family)* mariage *m* consanguin; *(with member of another group)* mariage *m*

intermarry [ɪntə'mærɪ] (*pt & pp* **intermarried**) *vi* se marier *(au sein de la même famille)*

intermediary [ɪntə'miːdɪərɪ] (pl **intermediaries**) n intermédiaire mf

intermediate [ɪntə'miːdɪət] adj intermédiaire; (student) de niveau moyen

interminable [ɪn'tɜːmɪnəbəl] adj interminable

intermingle [ɪntə'mɪŋgəl] **1** vt mélanger (**with** avec) **2** vi se mêler (**with** à), se mélanger (**with** avec)

intermission [ɪntə'mɪʃən] n entracte m

intermittent [ɪntə'mɪtənt] adj intermittent(e)

intern 1 n ['ɪntɜːn] Am Med interne mf **2** vt [ɪn'tɜːn] interner

internal [ɪn'tɜːnəl] adj interne; (flight) intérieur(e); **i. combustion engine** moteur m à combustion interne

internalize [ɪn'tɜːnəlaɪz] vt intérioriser

internally [ɪn'tɜːnəlɪ] adv intérieurement; **not to be taken i.** (on medicine container) à usage externe

international [ɪntə'næʃənəl] **1** n (in sport) (player) international(e) m,f; (match) match m international **2** adj international(e); **i. reply coupon** coupon-réponse m international; **I. date line** ligne f de changement de date; Fin **I. Monetary Fund** Fonds m monétaire international

internee [ɪntɜː'niː] n interné(e) m,f

Internet ['ɪntənet] n Comput the **I.** l'Internet m; **I. access** accès m (à l')Internet; **I. banking** opérations fpl bancaires par l'Internet; **I. café** cybercafé m; **I. connection** connexion f à l'Internet; **I. dating** rencontres fpl sur Internet; **I. protocol** protocole m Internet; **I. relay chat** service m de bavardage; **I. service provider** fournisseur m d'accès à l'Internet; **I. user** internaute mf

internment [ɪn'tɜːnmənt] n internement m

internship ['ntɜːnʃɪp] n (with company) stage m en entreprise

interpersonal [ɪntə'pɜːsənəl] adj interpersonnel(elle); **i. skills** qualités fpl relationnelles

interplay ['ɪntəpleɪ] n interaction f (**of** or **between** entre)

Interpol ['ɪntəpɒl] n Interpol

interpolate [ɪn'tɜːpəleɪt] vt Formal (remark, question) glisser; (word, passage) intercaler

interpose [ɪntə'pəʊz] vt interposer (**between** entre)

interpret [ɪn'tɜːprɪt] **1** vt interpréter **2** vi faire l'interprète

interpretation [ɪntɜːprɪ'teɪʃən] n interprétation f

interpreter [ɪn'tɜːprɪtə(r)] n interprète mf

interracial [ɪntə'reɪʃəl] adj interracial(e)

interrelated [ɪntərɪ'leɪtɪd] adj lié(e)

interrogate [ɪn'terəgeɪt] vt interroger

interrogation [ɪnterə'geɪʃən] n interrogatoire m

interrogative [ɪntə'rɒgətɪv] **1** n Gram interrogatif m; (question mark) point m d'interrogation **2** adj (look, tone) interrogateur(trice); Gram interrogatif(ive)

interrogator [ɪn'terəgeɪtə(r)] n interrogateur(trice) m,f

interrupt [ɪntə'rʌpt] **1** vt interrompre **2** vi it's rude to i. ce n'est pas poli d'interrompre les gens; I'm sorry to i. je suis désolé de vous interrompre

interruption [ɪntə'rʌpʃən] n interruption f

intersect [ɪntə'sekt] **1** vt couper **2** vi se couper

intersection [ɪntə'sekʃən] n (**a**) (of roads) carrefour m (**b**) Math intersection f

intersperse [ɪntə'spɜːs] vt **to be interspersed with sth** être parsemé(e) de qch; **sunshine interspersed with showers** temps ensoleillé entrecoupé d'averses

intertwine [ɪntə'twaɪn] **1** vt entremêler (**with** de); **to be intertwined** (of two things) être entrelacé(e)s **2** vi s'entrelacer

interval ['ɪntəvəl] n intervalle m; (at theatre) entracte m; **at regular intervals** à intervalles réguliers; **at weekly intervals** toutes les semaines; **sunny intervals** éclaircies fpl; Sport **i. training** entraînement m par intervalles, interval training m

intervene [ɪntə'viːn] vi (of person) intervenir (**in** dans); (of event) survenir

intervening [ɪntə'viːnɪŋ] adj intermédiaire; **in the i. period** entre-temps, dans l'intervalle

intervention [ɪntə'venʃən] n intervention f

interview ['ɪntəvjuː] **1** n (for job) entretien m; TV & Journ interview f **2** vt (for job) faire passer un entretien à; TV & Journ interviewer

interviewee [ɪntəvjuː'iː] n (for job) candidat(e) m,f (à qui l'on fait passer un entretien); TV & Journ personne f interviewée

interviewer ['ɪntəvjuːə(r)] n (for job) = personne qui fait passer un entretien; TV & Journ intervieweur(-euse) m,f

intestate [ɪn'testeɪt] adj Law **to die i.** mourir intestat

intestinal [ɪntes'taɪnəl] adj intestinal(e)

intestine [ɪn'testɪn] n intestin m; **large i.** gros intestin; **small i.** intestin grêle

intimacy ['ɪntɪməsɪ] n (of relationship, atmosphere) intimité f; Euph (sexual) relations fpl intimes

intimate 1 n ['ɪntɪmət] intime mf **2** adj ['ɪntɪmət] (friend, restaurant) intime; (knowledge) approfondi(e); Euph **to be i. with sb** (sexually) avoir des relations intimes avec qn **3** vt ['ɪntɪmeɪt] Formal (hint at) faire comprendre; (make known) signifier

intimately ['ɪntɪmətlɪ] adv intimement

intimidate [ɪn'tɪmɪdeɪt] vt intimider; **to i. sb into doing sth** forcer qn à faire qch en usant d'intimidation

intimidation [ɪntɪmɪ'deɪʃən] n intimidation f

into ['ɪntʊ] prep (**a**) (with motion, direction) dans; **to go i. a house** entrer dans une maison; **to get i. bed** se mettre au lit; **to crash i. sth** rentrer dans qch (**b**) (expressing change) en; **to change i. sth** se changer en qch; **to translate sth i. English** traduire qch en anglais; **to break sth i. pieces** mettre qch en morceaux (**c**) (in division) **three i. six goes twice** six divisé par trois donne deux (**d**) Fam (keen on) **to be i. jazz** être branché(e) jazz; **he's really i. my sister** il en pince vraiment pour ma sœur

intolerable [ɪn'tɒlərəbəl] adj intolérable

intolerance [ɪn'tɒlərəns] n intolérance f

intolerant [ɪn'tɒlərənt] adj **to be i. of sb** être intolérant(e) à l'égard de qn; **to be i. of sth** ne pas tolérer qch

intonation [ɪntə'neɪʃən] n intonation f

intone [ɪn'təʊn] vt (speak) débiter; (of preacher) psalmodier

intoxicated [ɪn'tɒksɪkeɪtɪd] adj (drunk) ivre; Fig **i. with power/fame** ivre de puissance/gloire

intoxication [ɪntɒksɪ'keɪʃən] n also Fig ivresse f

intractable [ɪn'træktəbəl] adj (person) intraitable; (problem) très délicat(e)

Intranet ['ɪntrənet] n Comput Intranet m

intransigence [ɪn'trænzɪdʒəns] *n Formal* intransigeance *f* (**over** sur)
intransigent [ɪn'trænzɪdʒənt] *adj Formal* intransigeant(e) (**over** sur)
intransitive [ɪn'trænzɪtɪv] *adj Gram* intransitif(ive)
intrauterine device ['ɪntrə'juːtəraɪndɪ'vaɪs] *n Med* stérilet *m*
intravenous ['ɪntrə'viːnəs] *adj Med (drip)* veineux(-euse); **i. injection** intraveineuse *f*
intravenously ['ɪntrə'viːnəslɪ] *adv Med* par voie intraveineuse
in-tray ['ɪntreɪ] *n* bac *m* du courrier à traiter
intrepid [ɪn'trepɪd] *adj* intrépide
intricacy ['ɪntrɪkəsɪ] *(pl* **intricacies)** *n* complexité *f*; **the intricacies of the law** les subtilités du droit
intricate ['ɪntrɪkət] *adj* compliqué(e)
intrigue 1 *n* ['ɪntriːg] intrigue *f*
    2 *vt* [ɪn'triːg] *(interest)* intriguer
intrinsic [ɪn'trɪnsɪk] *adj* intrinsèque
introduce [ɪntrə'djuːs] *vt* (**a**) *(person)* présenter (**to** à); **to i. oneself** se présenter; **to i. sb to sth** initier qn à qch (**b**) *(reform, practice)* introduire
introduction [ɪntrə'dʌkʃən] *n* (**a**) *(of person)* présentation *f*; **to make the introductions** faire les présentations (**b**) *(to book)* avant-propos *m inv*, introduction *f* (**c**) *(of reform, practice)* introduction *f* (**d**) *(first experience)* initiation *f* (**to** à)
introductory [ɪntrə'dʌktərɪ] *adj* d'introduction; *(price, offer)* de lancement
introspection [ɪntrə'spekʃən] *n* introspection *f*
introspective [ɪntrə'spektɪv] *adj (person)* introverti(e); *(mood)* introspectif(ive)
introvert ['ɪntrəvɜːt] *n* introverti(e) *m,f*
introverted [ɪntrə'vɜːtɪd] *adj* introverti(e)
intrude [ɪn'truːd] *vi* (**a**) *(impose oneself)* déranger (**b**) *(interfere)* **her work intrudes on her family life** son travail empiète sur sa vie de famille; **to i. on sb's privacy** s'immiscer dans la vie privée de qn
intruder [ɪn'truːdə(r)] *n* intrus(e) *m,f*
intrusion [ɪn'truːʒən] *n* intrusion *f*
intrusive [ɪn'truːsɪv] *adj* importun(e)
intuition [ɪntjuː'ɪʃən] *n* intuition *f*
intuitive [ɪn'tjuːɪtɪv] *adj* intuitif(ive)
Inuit ['ɪnʊɪt] **1** *n* Inuit *mf*
    2 *adj* inuit
inundate ['mʌndeɪt] *vt* inonder (**with** de); *Fig (with phone calls, letters)* submerger (**with** de)
invade [ɪn'veɪd] *vt* envahir; **to i. sb's privacy** s'immiscer dans la vie privée de qn
invader [ɪn'veɪdə(r)] *n* envahisseur(euse) *m,f*
invalid¹ [ɪn'vælɪd] *adj (document, argument)* non valable; *(marriage)* non valide
invalid² ['ɪnvəlɪd] *n (disabled person)* invalide *mf*, infirme *mf*; *(sick person)* malade *mf*
invalidate [ɪn'vælɪdeɪt] *vt (theory)* infirmer; *(document, contract)* invalider
invaluable [ɪn'væljʊəbəl] *adj* précieux(euse)
invariable [ɪn'veərɪəbəl] *adj* invariable
invariably [ɪn'veərɪəblɪ] *adv* invariablement
invasion [ɪn'veɪʒən] *n* invasion *f*
invasive [ɪn'veɪsɪv] *adj Med (treatment, surgery)* invasif(ive)
invective [ɪn'vektɪv] *n* invectives *fpl*
inveigh [ɪn'veɪ] *vi Formal* **to i. against** invectiver contre
inveigle [ɪn'veɪgəl] *vt* **to i. sb into doing sth** entortiller qn pour qu'il fasse qch

invent [ɪn'vent] *vt* inventer
invention [ɪn'venʃən] *n* (**a**) *(action, thing invented)* invention *f* (**b**) *(creativity)* inventivité *f*
inventive [ɪn'ventɪv] *adj* inventif(ive)
inventiveness [ɪn'ventɪvnəs] *n* inventivité *f*
inventor [ɪn'ventə(r)] *n* inventeur(trice) *m,f*
inventory ['ɪnventərɪ] *(pl* **inventories)** *n (list)* inventaire *m*; *(stock)* stock(s) *m(pl)*
inverse ['ɪnvɜːs] *adj* inverse
invert [ɪn'vɜːt] *vt (turn upside down)* renverser; *(reverse)* inverser, intervertir
invertebrate [ɪn'vɜːtɪbrɪt] **1** *n* invertébré *m*
    2 *adj* invertébré(e)
inverted [ɪn'vɜːtɪd] *adj (upside down)* renversé(e); *(reversed)* inversé(e); **(in)** **i. commas** (entre) guillemets *mpl*; **to be an i. snob** faire du snobisme à l'envers
invest [ɪn'vest] **1** *vt* (**a**) *(money, time)* investir (**in** dans) (**b**) *(right, power)* investir (**with** de)
    2 *vi* investir (**in** dans)
investigate [ɪn'vestɪgeɪt] *vt (crime)* enquêter sur; *(question)* examiner
investigation [ɪnvestɪ'geɪʃən] *n* enquête *f*
investigative [ɪn'vestɪgətɪv] *adj (journalism)* d'investigation
investigator [ɪn'vestɪgeɪtə(r)] *n* enquêteur(euse) *m,f*
investment [ɪn'vestmənt] *n* investissement *m*; **i. account** compte *m* d'investissement; **i. analyst** analyste *mf* en placements; **i. bank** banque *f* d'affaires; **i. fund** fonds *m* commun de placement, fonds *m* d'investissement; **i. income** revenu *m* provenant d'investissements; **i. trust** société *f* de placement
investor [ɪn'vestə(r)] *n* investisseur *m*
inveterate [ɪn'vetərɪt] *adj (gambler, drunkard, liar)* invétéré(e); *(critic)* acharné(e)
invidious [ɪn'vɪdɪəs] *adj (choice, comparison)* inéquitable; *(position, task)* peu enviable
invigilate [ɪn'vɪdʒɪleɪt] *Br* **1** *vt (exam)* surveiller
    2 *vi* surveiller les candidats *(à un examen)*
invigilator [ɪn'vɪdʒɪleɪtə(r)] *n Br (in exam)* surveillant(e) *m,f (des candidats à un examen)*
invigorating [ɪn'vɪgəreɪtɪŋ] *adj* vivifiant(e)
invincible [ɪn'vɪnsɪbəl] *adj* invincible
inviolable [ɪn'vaɪələbəl] *adj Formal* inviolable
inviolate [ɪn'vaɪələt] *adj Formal* inviolé(e)
invisible [ɪn'vɪzɪbəl] *adj* invisible (**to** à); **i. earnings** invisibles *mpl*; **i. ink** encre *f* sympathique
invitation [ɪnvɪ'teɪʃən] *n* invitation *f*
invite 1 *n* ['ɪnvaɪt] *Fam* invit' *f*
    2 *vt* [ɪn'vaɪt] (**a**) *(guest)* inviter; **to i. sb in/up** inviter qn à entrer/monter; **to i. sb to do sth** inviter qn à faire qch; **applications are invited for the post of...** ≃ nous recrutons un... (**b**) *(trouble, criticism) (of person)* aller au-devant de
inviting [ɪn'vaɪtɪŋ] *adj* attrayant(e); *(food)* appétissant(e)
in vitro fertilization [ɪn'viːtrəʊfertɪlaɪ'zeɪʃən] *n* fécondation *f* in vitro
invoice ['ɪnvɔɪs] *Com* **1** *n* facture *f*; **to make out an i.** établir une facture
    2 *vt (goods)* facturer; *(person, company)* envoyer la facture à
invoke [ɪn'vəʊk] *vt Formal (God, law)* invoquer; *(spirit, feeling)* évoquer; **to i. sb's aid** appeler qn à son secours
involuntary [ɪn'vɒlʌntərɪ] *adj* involontaire

involve [ɪn'vɒlv] *vt* (**a**) *(implicate)* **to i. sb in sth** impliquer qn dans qch; **this doesn't i. you** ça ne te concerne pas (**b**) *(entail) (work, expense)* impliquer, entraîner; **his job involves a lot of travel** il est amené à voyager pour mon travail
involved [ɪn'vɒlvd] *adj* (**a**) *(implicated)* **to be/get i. in sth** *(crime, affair)* être impliqué(e) dans qch; **to be i. in an accident** avoir un accident; **to be i. in teaching/ banking** être dans l'enseignement/la banque; **50 people were i. in the project** 50 personnes ont pris part au projet; **the police became i.** la police est intervenue; **don't get i.!** ne te mêle pas de ça!; **how much money is i.?** de combien d'argent s'agit-il? (**b**) *(emotionally)* **to be/get i. with sb** sortir avec qn; **I don't want to get i.** je ne veux pas m'engager (**c**) *(engrossed)* **to get i. in a book/film** s'absorber dans un livre/film; **I'm getting really i. in this job** je commence à trouver ce travail vraiment intéressant (**d**) *(complicated)* compliqué(e)
involvement [ɪn'vɒlvmənt] *n* (**a**) *(participation)* participation *f* (**in** à) (**b**) *(commitment)* engagement *m* (**in** dans)
invulnerable [ɪn'vʌlnərəbəl] *adj* invulnérable (**to** à)
inward ['ɪnwəd] *adj* (**a**) *(thoughts, feelings)* intime (**b**) *(movement)* vers l'intérieur; *Econ* **i. investment** investissements *mpl* étrangers
inward-looking [ɪnwəd'lʊkɪŋ] *adj* replié(e) sur soi-même
inwards ['ɪnwədz] *adv* vers l'intérieur
in-your-face ['ɪnjɔː'feɪs] *adj Fam (film, advertisement)* cru(e); *(attitude, personality)* agressif(ive)
iodine ['aɪədiːn] *n Chem* iode *m*; *(antiseptic)* teinture *f* d'iode
ion ['aɪən] *n* ion *m*
Ionian [aɪ'əʊnɪən] *n* **the I. (Sea)** la mer Ionienne
ionize ['aɪənaɪz] *vt* ioniser
iota [aɪ'əʊtə] *n* iota *m*; **she hadn't changed one i.** elle n'avait pas du tout changé; **not an i. of truth** pas une once de vérité
IOU [aɪəʊ'juː] *n* (= *I owe you*) reconnaissance *f* de dette
IP [aɪ'piː] *n Comput* (*abbr* **Internet Protocol**) IP **address** adresse *f* IP
IPA [aɪpiː'eɪ] *n* (*abbr* **International Phonetic Alphabet**) API *m*
iPod® ['aɪpɒd] *n* iPod® *m*
IQ [aɪ'kjuː] *n* (*abbr* **intelligence quotient**) QI *m*
IRA [aɪɑː'reɪ] *n* (*abbr* **Irish Republican Army**) IRA *f*

IRA

L'IRA est une organisation qui lutte pour la réunification de l'Irlande. En 1969, elle s'est scindée en deux factions : la "Provisional IRA", qui a recours à la violence, et la "Official IRA", qui privilégiait un règlement politique du conflit en Irlande du Nord. En 1995, au début du processus de paix a abouti à l'accord de 1998 (le "Good Friday Agreement", *voir encadré* à **good**) la "Provisional IRA" a déclaré un cessez-le-feu. Le processus de paix a néanmoins longtemps buté sur la question du refus de l'IRA de renoncer à son arsenal. Finalement, en juillet 2005, l'IRA a rendu publique sa décision de renoncer définitivement à la lutte armée dans son combat pour la réunification de l'Irlande. En septembre 2005, la destruction des stocks d'armes de l'IRA fut annoncée.

Iran [ɪ'rɑːn] *n* l'Iran *m*
Iranian [ɪ'reɪnɪən] **1** *n* (**a**) *(person)* Iranien(enne) *m,f* (**b**) *(language)* iranien *m* **2** *adj* iranien(enne)
Iraq [ɪ'rɑːk] *n* l'Irak *m*
Iraqi [ɪ'rɑːkɪ] **1** *n* Irakien(enne) *m,f*, Iraquien(enne) *m,f* **2** *adj* irakien(enne), iraquien(enne)
irascible [ɪ'ræsɪbəl] *adj (person)* irascible; *(temperament)* colérique
irate [aɪ'reɪt] *adj* furieux(euse)
IRC [aɪɑː'siː] *n Comput* (*abbr* **Internet Relay Chat**) IRC, service *m* de bavardage Internet
ire ['aɪə(r)] *n Lit* courroux *m*
Ireland ['aɪələnd] *n* l'Irlande *f*
iris ['aɪrɪs] *n* iris *m*
Irish ['aɪrɪʃ] **1** *npl (people)* **the I.** les Irlandais *mpl* **2** *n (language)* irlandais *m* **3** *adj* irlandais(e); **I. coffee** Irish coffee *m*; **the I. Sea** la mer d'Irlande; **I. stew** = ragoût de mouton, aux pommes de terre et aux oignons
Irishman ['aɪrɪʃmən] *n* Irlandais *m*
Irishwoman ['aɪrɪʃwʊmən] *n* Irlandaise *f*
irk [ɜːk] *vt* agacer
irksome ['ɜːksəm] *adj* agaçant(e)
iron ['aɪən] **1** *n* (**a**) *(metal, golf club)* fer *m*; **made of i.** en fer; **to have an i. constitution** avoir une santé de fer; **an i. will** une volonté de fer; **i. discipline** discipline *f* de fer; **the I. Age** l'âge *m* de fer; **the I. Curtain** le rideau de fer; **i. lung** poumon *m* d'acier; **i. ore** minerai *m* de fer (**b**) *(for clothes)* fer *m* (à repasser); *Fig* **to have several irons in the fire** avoir plusieurs fers au feu **2** *vt & vi (clothes)* repasser
▸**iron out** *vt sep (difficulty)* aplanir; *(problem)* résoudre
ironic(al) [aɪ'rɒnɪk(əl)] *adj* ironique
ironing ['aɪənɪŋ] *n* repassage *m*; **to do the i.** repasser, faire le repassage; **i. board** planche *f ou* table *f* à repasser
ironmonger ['aɪənmʌŋgə(r)] *n Br* quincaillier(ère) *m,f*; **i.'s (shop)** quincaillerie *f*
irony ['aɪrənɪ] *(pl* **ironies**) *n* ironie *f*; **the i. is that...** ce qu'il y a d'ironique, c'est que...
irrational [ɪ'ræʃənəl] *adj* irrationnel(elle)
irreconcilable [ɪrekən'saɪləbəl] *adj (enemy)* irréconciliable; *(hatred)* implacable; *(belief, idea)* incompatible, inconciliable
irredeemable [ɪrɪ'diːməbəl] *adj (fault)* irréparable; *(situation)* irrémédiable
irrefutable [ɪrɪ'fjuːtəbəl] *adj* irréfutable
irregular [ɪ'regjələ(r)] *adj* irrégulier(ère)
irregularity [ɪregjʊ'lærɪtɪ] *(pl* **irregularities**) *n* irrégularité *f*
irrelevance [ɪ'reləvəns], **irrelevancy** [ɪ'reləvənsɪ] *n (of remark, advice)* manque *m* d'à-propos
irrelevant [ɪ'reləvənt] *adj (remark, advice)* hors de propos; **that's i.** cela n'a rien à voir (avec la question)
irreligious [ɪrɪ'lɪdʒəs] *adj* irréligieux(euse)
irremediable [ɪrɪ'miːdɪəbəl] *adj Formal (situation, loss)* irrémédiable; *(mistake)* irréparable
irreparable [ɪ'repərəbəl] *adj* irréparable
irreplaceable [ɪrɪ'pleɪsəbəl] *adj* irremplaçable
irrepressible [ɪrɪ'presɪbəl] *adj (urge)* irrépressible; *(good humour)* à toute épreuve; **he's i.** rien n'entame sa bonne humeur
irreproachable [ɪrɪ'prəʊtʃəbəl] *adj* irréprochable

irresistible [ɪrɪ'zɪstɪbəl] *adj* irrésistible
irresolute [ɪ'rezəluːt] *adj* irrésolu(e), indécis(e)
irrespective of [ɪrɪ'spektɪvəv] *prep* indépendamment de, sans tenir compte de
irresponsible [ɪrɪ'spɒnsɪbəl] *adj* irresponsable
irretrievable [ɪrɪ'triːvəbəl] *adj (loss)* irrémédiable; *(money)* irrécupérable; *(mistake, situation)* irréparable
irreverent [ɪ'revərənt] *adj* irrévérencieux(euse)
irreversible [ɪrɪ'vɜːsɪbəl] *adj (decision, process)* irréversible
irrevocable [ɪ'revəkəbəl] *adj* irrévocable
irrigate ['ɪrɪgeɪt] *vt* irriguer
irrigation [ɪrɪ'geɪʃən] *n* irrigation *f*; **i. canal** *or* **ditch** canal *m* d'irrigation
irritable ['ɪrɪtəbəl] *adj* irritable; **i. bowel syndrome** colopathie *f* fonctionnelle
irritant ['ɪrɪtənt] *n (to eyes, skin)* irritant *m*; *(to person, government)* empêcheur(euse) *m,f* de tourner en rond
irritate ['ɪrɪteɪt] *vt (annoy)* agacer, irriter; *Med* irriter
irritating ['ɪrɪteɪtɪŋ] *adj* agaçant(e), irritant(e)
irritation [ɪrɪ'teɪʃən] *n* agacement *m*, irritation *f*; *Med* irritation *f*
IRS [aɪɑː'res] *n Am (abbr* **Internal Revenue Service)** the I. le fisc
IS [aɪ'es] *n (abbr* **information system)** système *m* informatique
is [ɪz] *see* **be**
ISA ['aɪsə] *n Br Fin (abbr* **individual savings account)** ≃ PEA *m*, plan *m* d'épargne en actions
ISBN [aɪesbiː'en] *n (abbr* **International Standard Book Number)** ISBN *m*
ISIC ['aɪsɪk] *n (abbr* **International Student Identity Card)** **i. (card)** carte *f* ISIC
Islam ['ɪzlɑːm] *n* l'Islam *m*
Islamic [ɪz'læmɪk] *adj* islamique
Islamophobia [ɪzlæmə'fəʊbɪə] *n* islamophobie *f*
Islamophobic [ɪzlæmə'fəʊbɪk] *adj* islamophobe
island ['aɪlənd] *n* île *f*; *(small)* îlot *m*; *(in road)* refuge *m*
islander ['aɪləndə(r)] *n (in general)* insulaire *mf*; *(of specific island)* habitant(e) *m,f* de l'île
isle [aɪl] *n* île *f*; **the I. of Man** l'île *f* de Man; **the I. of Wight** l'île *f* de Wight
isn't ['ɪzənt] = **is not**
ISO [aɪes'əʊ] *n (abbr* **International Standards Organization)** ISO *f*
isobar ['aɪsəʊbɑː(r)] *n* isobare *f*
isolate ['aɪsəleɪt] *vt* isoler *(***from** de)
isolated ['aɪsəleɪtɪd] *adj* isolé(e)
isolation [aɪsə'leɪʃən] *n* isolement *m*; **in i. (from)** isolément (de); **i. ward** salle *f* des contagieux
isotope ['aɪsəʊtəʊp] *n Phys* isotope *m*
ISP [aɪes'piː] *n Comput (abbr* **Internet Service Provider)** fournisseur *m* d'accès à l'Internet
Israel ['ɪzreɪəl] *n* Israël *m*
Israeli [ɪz'reɪlɪ] **1** *n* Israélien(enne) *m,f*
  2 *adj* israélien(enne)
Israelite ['ɪzrəlaɪt] *n Hist* Israélite *mf*
issue ['ɪsjuː, 'ɪʃuː] **1** *n* **(a)** *(topic)* problème *m*, question *f*; **the issues of the day** les questions *fpl* du jour; **that's not the i.** ce n'est pas (là) le problème; **to avoid the i.** esquiver le problème; **to confuse the i.** compliquer les choses; **to make an i. of sth** faire toute une affaire de qch; **at i.** en cause; **to take i.**

with sb exprimer son désaccord avec qn **(b)** *(of banknotes, stamps)* émission *f* **(c)** *(of magazine)* numéro *m*
  2 *vt (banknote, stamp)* émettre; *(order)* donner; **to i. sb with sth** délivrer qch à qn; **to i. a statement** faire une déclaration; *Law* **to i. a summons** notifier une citation
  3 *vi Formal (of blood, smoke, water)* s'échapper *(***from** de); *(of noise)* provenir *(***from** de)
Istanbul [ɪstæn'bʊl] *n* Istanbul
isthmus ['ɪsməs] *n* isthme *m*
IT [aɪ'tiː] *n Comput (abbr* **information technology)** l'informatique *f*
it [ɪt] *pron* **(a)** *(subject)* il (elle) *m,f*; **where's the book?**
  – it's on the shelf où est le livre? – il est sur l'étagère; **put the TV on – it's not working** allume la télé – elle est en panne; **it's a big house** c'est une grande maison; **it's the best film I've ever seen** c'est le meilleur film que j'aie jamais vu **(b)** *(direct object)* le (la) *m,f*; **I can do it** je peux le/la faire; **I saw it** je l'ai vu **(c)** *(indirect object)* lui; **give it something to eat** *(animal)* donne-lui à manger **(d)** *(prepositional object)* **on it** dessus; **under it** dessous; **beside it** à côté; **I forgot about it** j'ai oublié **(e)** *(as impersonal subject)* **it's raining** il pleut; **it's ten o'clock** il est dix heures; **it's cold today** il fait froid aujourd'hui; **it's impossible to work in this heat** il est impossible de travailler avec cette chaleur; **it's me** c'est moi **(f)** *(as complement of verb* **to be)** **that's it** *(that's all)* c'est tout
Italian [ɪ'tæljən] **1** *n* **(a)** *(person)* Italien(enne) *m,f* **(b)** *(language)* italien *m*; **I. class/teacher** classe *f*/professeur *m* d'italien
  2 *adj* italien(enne)
italic [ɪ'tælɪk] *Typ* **1** *n* italic(s) italique *m*
  2 *adj* italique
Italy ['ɪtəlɪ] *n* l'Italie *f*
itch [ɪtʃ] **1** *n* démangeaison *f*; *Fig* **to have an i. to do sth** brûler d'envie de faire qch
  2 *vi (of person)* éprouver des démangeaisons; **my hand itches** j'ai la main qui me démange; *Fig* **to be itching to do sth** brûler d'envie de faire qch
itchy ['ɪtʃɪ] *adj* **I've got an i. hand, my hand's i.** j'ai la main qui me démange; *Fig* **to have i. feet** avoir la bougeotte
it'd ['ɪtəd] = **it would, it had**
item ['aɪtəm] *n (in collection, list)* article *m*; *(in news)* entrefilet *m*; *(longer)* article *m*; **an i. of clothing** un vêtement; **personal items** objets *mpl* personnels; *Fam* **they're an i.** ils sortent ensemble
itemize ['aɪtəmaɪz] *vt* détailler
iterative ['ɪtərətɪv] *adj Comput* itératif(ive)
itinerant [ɪ'tɪnərənt] *adj (preacher)* itinérant(e); *(salesman, musician)* ambulant(e)
itinerary [aɪ'tɪnərərɪ] *(pl* **itineraries)** *n* itinéraire *m*
it'll ['ɪtəl] = **it will**
ITN [aɪtiː'en] *n Br (abbr* **Independent Television News)** = service produisant le journal télévisé d'ITV
its [ɪts] *possessive adj* **(a)** *(singular)* son (sa); *(plural)* ses; **i. bone** son os; **i. litter** sa litière; **i. kittens** ses chatons **(b)** *(for parts of body)* **the bear hurt i. paw** l'ours s'est blessé à la patte
it's [ɪts] = **it is, it has**
itself [ɪt'self] *pron* **(a)** *(reflexive)* **the dog hurt i.** le chien s'est blessé **(b)** *(emphatic)* **this method is simplicity i.** cette méthode est la simplicité même; **the**

town i. isn't very interesting la ville (elle-)même n'est pas d'un grand intérêt (**c**) *(after preposition)* **by i.** tout(e) seul(e); **in i.** en soi

ITV [aɪti:'vi:] *n Br (abbr* **Independent Television**) = chaîne de télévision privée britannique

IUD [aɪju:'di:] *n Med (abbr* **intra-uterine device**) stérilet *m*

I've [aɪv] = **I have**

IVF [aɪvi:'ef] *n Med (abbr* **in vitro fertilization**) FIV *f*

ivory ['aɪvərɪ] *n* ivoire *m*; **the I. Coast** la Côte d'Ivoire; *Fig* **i. tower** tour *f* d'ivoire

ivy ['aɪvɪ] *n (plant)* lierre *m*; *Am* **I. League** = ensemble des huit universités les plus prestigieuses du nord-est des États-Unis

Ivy League
On désigne ainsi un groupe de huit universités du nord-est des États-Unis : Brown, Columbia, Cornell, Dartmouth, Harvard, l'Université de Pennsylvanie, Princeton et Yale. Ces universités (que l'on appelle plus familièrement The Ivies) se caractérisent par une forte proportion d'étudiants de troisième cycle, des moyens financiers importants et la réputation d'excellence de leurs universitaires. Si à l'origine, l'"Ivy League" servait à promouvoir les rencontres sportives entre les universités qui la composaient, elle est depuis devenue synonyme d'un enseignement prestigieux très compétitif, réservé à l'élite.

J, j [dʒeɪ] *n (letter)* J, j *m inv*
jab [dʒæb] **1** *n* (**a**) *(with elbow, finger)* coup *m*; *(in boxing)* direct *m* (**b**) *Br Fam (injection)* piqûre *f*
2 *vt (pt & pp* **jabbed**) he jabbed her in the leg with a pencil il lui a enfoncé un crayon dans la jambe; **to j. a finger at sb** agiter son doigt sous le nez de qn
jabber ['dʒæbə(r)] *vi Fam (talk unclearly)* marmonner; *(chatter)* jacasser
Jack [dʒæk] *pr n* **J. Frost** le Bonhomme Hiver; *Br Fam* **I'm all right, J.** moi, ça va, merci; *Br Fam* **before you could say J. Robinson** avant d'avoir pu dire "ouf"
jack [dʒæk] *n* (**a**) *(person)* **every man j. of them** absolument tout le monde; **j. of all trades** touche-à-tout *mf* (**b**) *(for car)* cric *m* (**c**) *(in cards)* valet *m* (**d**) *(electric plug)* prise *f ou* fiche *f* mâle
▶**jack in** *vt sep Br Fam* plaquer
▶**jack off** *vi Vulg* se branler
▶**jack up** *vt sep Fam (price, salaries)* augmenter
jackal ['dʒækəl] *n* chacal *m*
jackass ['dʒækæs] *n also Fig* âne *m*
jackboot ['dʒækbuːt] *n* botte *f* de cavalier; *Fig* **under the j.** of sous la botte de
jackdaw ['dʒækdɔː] *n* choucas *m*
jacket ['dʒækɪt] *n (coat)* veste *f*; *(of book)* jaquette *f*; *(of boiler)* chemise *f*, enveloppe *f*; **j. potatoes** pommes de terre *fpl* en robe des champs *ou* en robe de chambre
jackhammer ['dʒækhæmə(r)] *n* marteau-piqueur *m*
jack-in-the-box ['dʒækɪnðəbɒks] *n* diable *m* à ressort
jackknife ['dʒæknaɪf] **1** *n (pl* **jackknives**) couteau *m* de poche
2 *vi (of articulated lorry)* **the lorry jackknifed** la remorque du camion s'est soudain mise en travers de la route
jack-o'-lantern ['dʒækə'læntən] *n Am* = lanterne faite dans une citrouille sur laquelle on a creusé un visage
jackpot ['dʒækpɒt] *n (in lottery)* gros lot *m*; **to hit** *or* **win the j.** gagner le gros lot
jack rabbit *n* = gros lièvre commun en Amérique du Nord
Jacobean [dʒækə'bɪən] *adj* = de l'époque de Jacques 1er (1603–1625)
Jacobite ['dʒækəbaɪt] **1** *n* Jacobite *mf*
2 *adj* jacobite
Jacuzzi® [dʒə'kuːzɪ] *n* Jacuzzi® *m*
jade [dʒeɪd] **1** *n (stone, colour)* jade *m*
2 *adj (colour)* **j.(-green)** vert jade *inv*
jaded ['dʒeɪdɪd] *adj (tired)* las (lasse); *(bored)* blasé(e); **to be j. with sth** être las de qch; **to have a j. palate** avoir le palais blasé

Jag [dʒæg] *n Fam (car)* Jaguar® *m*
jag [dʒæg] *n Fam* **to go on a (drinking) j.** prendre une cuite; **to have a crying j.** avoir une crise de larmes
jagged ['dʒægɪd] *adj (coastline, mountain top)* déchiqueté(e), découpé(e); *(blade)* ébréché(e)
jaguar ['dʒægjʊə(r), *Am* 'dʒægwɑː(r)] *n Zool* jaguar *m*
jail [dʒeɪl] **1** *n* prison *f*; **to be in j.** être en prison; **to go to j.** aller en prison
2 *vt* emprisonner, mettre en prison
jailbait ['dʒeɪlbeɪt] *n Am Fam* **she's j.** c'est un coup à se retrouver en taule *(pour détournement de mineur)*
jailbird ['dʒeɪlbɜːd] *n Fam (in prison)* taulard(e) *m,f*; *(recidivist)* cheval *m* de retour
jailbreak ['dʒeɪlbreɪk] *n* évasion *f*
jailer ['dʒeɪlə(r)] *n* geôlier(ère) *m,f*
jailhouse ['dʒeɪlhaʊs] *n Am* prison *f*
jailor = **jailer**
Jakarta [dʒə'kɑːtə] *n* Djakarta
jalopy [dʒə'lɒpɪ] *n (pl* **jalopies**) *Fam* vieille guimbarde *f*, vieux tacot *m*
jam¹ [dʒæm] **1** *n* (**a**) *(crowd) (of people)* foule *f*; *(of traffic)* encombrement *m*, embouteillage *m* (**b**) *(difficult situation)* **to be in/get into a (bit of a) j.** être/se fourrer dans le pétrin (**c**) *(improvised performance)* **j. (session)** jam-session *f*, bœuf *m*
2 *vt (pt & pp* **jammed**) (**a**) *(pack tightly) (objects)* entasser (**into** dans); *(container)* bourrer (**with** de); **people/cars jammed the street** la rue était noire de monde/embouteillée (**b**) *(immobilize) (drawer, mechanism)* coincer, bloquer; *(radio broadcast, station)* brouiller; *(switchboard)* saturer
3 *vi* (**a**) *(of drawer, mechanism)* se coincer, se bloquer (**b**) *(of crowd)* s'entasser (**into** dans) (**c**) *(of musicians)* improviser
▶**jam** *on vt sep* **to j. on the brakes** écraser la pédale de frein
jam² *n (fruit preserve)* confiture *f*; **j. tart** tarte *f* à la confiture
Jamaica [dʒə'meɪkə] *n* la Jamaïque
Jamaican [dʒə'meɪkən] **1** *n* Jamaïcain(e) *m,f*
2 *adj* jamaïcain(e)
jamb [dʒæm] *n* montant *m*
jamboree [dʒæmbə'riː] *n (scouts' meeting)* jamboree *m*; *Fam (celebration)* fête *f*
jamming ['dʒæmɪŋ] *n (of radio broadcast, station)* brouillage *m*
jammy ['dʒæmɪ] *adj* (**a**) *(covered with jam)* plein(e) de confiture (**b**) *Br Fam (lucky)* verni(e)
jam-packed ['dʒæm'pækd] *adj* plein(e) à craquer; *(street)* noir(e) de monde, bondé(e)
Jan *(abbr* **January**) janvier

jangle [ˈdʒæŋgəl] **1** n cliquetis m
 2 vt faire cliqueter
 3 vi cliqueter; Fig her voice made his nerves j. sa voix lui mettait les nerfs en pelote
janitor [ˈdʒænɪtə(r)] n Am & Scot (caretaker) concierge mf
January [ˈdʒænjʊərɪ] n janvier m; see also May
Jap [dʒæp] n very Fam Jap mf, = terme raciste désignant un Japonais
Japan [dʒəˈpæn] n le Japon
Japanese [dʒæpəˈniːz] **1** npl (people) the J. les Japonais mpl
 2 n (a) (person) Japonais(e) m,f (b) (language) japonais m; J. class/teacher classe f/professeur m de japonais
 3 adj japonais(e)
jape [dʒeɪp] n blague f
jar¹ [dʒɑː(r)] **1** n (jolt) choc m, secousse f
 2 vt (pt & pp jarred) also Fig secouer; someone jarred my elbow quelqu'un m'a cogné le coude
 3 vi (a) (make unpleasant sound) rendre un son discordant; to j. on the ears écorcher les oreilles; to j. on the nerves taper sur les nerfs (b) (of colours) jurer; (of ideas) être en contradiction
jar² n (container) pot m; (earthenware) jarre f; Br Fam to have a j. prendre un pot
jargon [ˈdʒɑːgən] n Pej jargon m
jarring [ˈdʒɑːrɪŋ] adj (noise, voice) discordant(e); (blow) qui ébranle tout le corps
jasmine [ˈdʒæzmɪn] n jasmin m
jaundice [ˈdʒɔːndɪs] n jaunisse f
jaundiced [ˈdʒɔːndɪst] adj Fig (attitude, view) aigu(ë), amer(ère); to take a j. view of sth voir qch d'un mauvais œil
jaunt [dʒɔːnt] n excursion f, sortie f
jauntiness [ˈdʒɔːntɪnɪs] n (cheerfulness) enjouement m; (carefreeness) insouciance f
jaunty [ˈdʒɔːntɪ] adj (cheerful) enjoué(e); (carefree) insouciant(e)
Java¹ [ˈdʒɑːvə] n Geog Java
Java²® n Comput Java® m; J. script (langage m) Javascript® m
javelin [ˈdʒævlɪn] n javelot m
jaw [dʒɔː] **1** n mâchoire f; jaws (of animal) gueule f; the jaws of death les griffes fpl de la mort
 2 vi Fam (chat) papoter
jawbone [ˈdʒɔːbəʊn] n maxillaire m
jawbreaker [ˈdʒɔːbreɪkə(r)] n (a) Fam (word) mot m imprononçable; (name) nom m à coucher dehors (b) Am (sweet) = sorte de gros bonbon dur
jay [dʒeɪ] n geai m
jaywalker [ˈdʒeɪwɔːkə(r)] n = piéton qui traverse en dehors des passages cloutés
jaywalking [ˈdʒeɪwɔːkɪŋ] n = fait de traverser en dehors des passages cloutés
jazz [dʒæz] n jazz m; Fam and all that j. et tout le tremblement ou le bazar
▸**jazz up** vt sep Fam (enliven) (clothes, room, style) égayer; (party) animer; (taste) relever
jazzy [ˈdʒæzɪ] adj (tune) jazzy inv; (clothes, pattern) aux couleurs vives
jealous [ˈdʒeləs] adj jaloux(ouse); to be j. of sb être jaloux de qn
jealously [ˈdʒeləslɪ] adv jalousement; to guard sth j. veiller jalousement sur qch
jealousy [ˈdʒeləsɪ] n jalousie f
jeans [dʒiːnz] npl jeans m

Jeep® [dʒiːp] n Jeep® f
jeer [dʒɪə(r)] **1** n (mocking) moquerie f; the jeers of the crowd (booing) les huées fpl de la foule
 2 vt (boo) huer; (mock) se moquer de
 3 vi to j. at sb/sth (boo) huer qn/qch; (mock) se moquer de qn/qch
jeering [ˈdʒɪərɪŋ] **1** n (booing) huées fpl; (mocking) moqueries fpl
 2 adj railleur(euse), moqueur(euse)
jeez [dʒiːz] exclam Fam mince alors!
Jehovah [dʒɪˈhəʊvə] pr n Jéhovah; J.'s Witness témoin m de Jéhovah
jell [dʒel] vi (of liquid) se gélifier; Fig (of ideas, plans) prendre forme; Fig (of team) se souder
jelly [ˈdʒelɪ] (pl jellies) n (dessert, jam) gelée f; Br j. baby = bonbon gélifié en forme de petit bonhomme
jellybean [ˈdʒelɪbiːn] n = bonbon couvert de sucre, en forme de haricot
jellyfish [ˈdʒelɪfɪʃ] n méduse f
jemmy [ˈdʒemɪ] (pl jemmies) n Br pince-monseigneur f
jeopardize [ˈdʒepədaɪz] vt compromettre; (life) mettre en danger
jeopardy [ˈdʒepədɪ] n in j. en danger, en péril; to put sb/sth in j. mettre qn/qch en danger ou en péril
jerk¹ [dʒɜːk] **1** n (sudden pull) secousse f, coup m sec; to give sth a j. tirer sur qch d'un coup sec
 2 vt (pull) tirer brusquement; (in order to move) déplacer par à-coups
 3 vi to j. forward (of car) faire un bond en avant; (of head) partir en avant; to j. to a halt s'arrêter avec des soubresauts
jerk² n Fam (person) abruti(e) m,f
▸**jerk off** vi Vulg (masturbate) se branler
jerkily [ˈdʒɜːkɪlɪ] adv de manière saccadée
jerky [ˈdʒɜːkɪ] adj (movement) saccadé(e); (style) hâché(e)
jerrican [ˈdʒerɪkæn] n jerrican m
jerry-built [ˈdʒerɪbɪlt] adj construit(e) à la va-vite
Jersey [ˈdʒɜːzɪ] n (island) Jersey; J. (cow) jersiaise f
jersey [ˈdʒɜːzɪ] (pl jerseys) n Br (garment) pull(-over) m, tricot m
Jerusalem [dʒəˈruːsələm] n Jérusalem; J. artichoke topinambour m
jest [dʒest] **1** n plaisanterie f; in j. pour plaisanter
 2 vi plaisanter
jester [ˈdʒestə(r)] n farceur(euse) m,f; Hist (court) j. fou m (du roi)
jesting [ˈdʒestɪŋ] adj (remark) pour rire; (tone) de la plaisanterie
Jesuit [ˈdʒezjʊɪt] n jésuite m
Jesuitical [dʒezjʊˈɪtɪkəl] adj Pej (argument, reasoning) de jésuite
Jesus [ˈdʒiːzəs] **1** pr n Jésus; J. Christ Jésus-Christ
 2 exclam Fam J. (Christ)! nom de Dieu!
jet¹ [dʒet] **1** n (a) (plane) jet m, avion m à réaction; j. engine réacteur m, moteur m à réaction; j. fighter chasseur m à réaction; j. lag fatigue f due au décalage horaire; j. propulsion propulsion f par réaction; the j. set la jet-set; j. ski scooter m des mers, jet-ski m (b) (nozzle, of liquid) jet m
 2 vi (pt & pp jetted) Fam (travel by plane) to j. in venir en avion; to j. off s'envoler; to j. around the world passer son temps dans les avions
jet² **1** n (stone) jais m
 2 adj j. (black) de jais

jet-lagged ['dʒetlægd] adj fatigué(e) par le décalage horaire

jet-powered [dʒet'paʊəd], **jet-propelled** [dʒetprə-'peld] adj à réaction

jettison ['dʒetɪsən] vt (cargo) jeter à la mer ou par-dessus bord; (plan, tradition) abandonner

jetty ['dʒetɪ] (pl jetties) n jetée f; (for landing) embarcadère m

Jew [dʒuː] n Juif (Juive) m,f

jewel ['dʒuːəl] n (gem, piece of jewellery) bijou m; Fig (person) perle f

jeweller, Am **jeweler** ['dʒuːələ(r)] n bijoutier(ère) m,f; **j.'s (shop)** bijouterie f

jewellery, Am **jewelry** ['dʒuːəlrɪ] n bijoux mpl; **a piece of j.** un bijou

Jewess ['dʒuːɪs] n Old-fashioned Juive f

Jewish ['dʒuːɪʃ] adj juif (juive)

Jewry ['dʒuːərɪ] n communauté f juive

jib¹ [dʒɪb] n (**a**) (sail) foc m (**b**) (of crane) flèche f (**b**) (idioms) **I don't like the cut of his j.** je n'aime pas son allure

jib² (pt & pp jibbed) vi **to j. at sth/at doing sth** rechigner à qch/à faire qch

jibe [dʒaɪb] **1** n moquerie f
2 vi **to j. at sb** se moquer de qn

jiffy ['dʒɪfɪ] n Fam **in a j.** dans un instant, tout de suite

Jiffy bag® ['dʒɪfɪbæg] n Br enveloppe f matelassée

jig [dʒɪg] **1** n (dance, music) gigue f
2 vi (pt & pp jigged) (dance) danser la gigue

jigger ['dʒɪgə(r)] vt Fam (TV, microwave) bousiller; **to j. one's back/knee** s'esquinter le dos/genou

jiggered ['dʒɪgəd] adj Fam (TV, microwave) bousillé(e); (back, knee) esquinté(e)

jiggery-pokery ['dʒɪgərɪ'pəʊkərɪ] n Br Fam micmac m

jiggle ['dʒɪgəl] **1** vt secouer rapidement
2 vi remuer dans tous les sens

►**jiggle about, jiggle around** vt sep & vi = jiggle

jigsaw ['dʒɪgsɔː] n (**a**) (saw) scie f sauteuse (**b**) (game) **j. (puzzle)** puzzle m

jihad [dʒɪ'hæd] n djihad m

jilt [dʒɪlt] vt (lover) plaquer

jingle ['dʒɪŋgəl] **1** n (**a**) (of bells, coins) tintement m; (of keys) cliquetis m (**b**) (catchy tune) jingle m; Rad & TV (in advertisement) jingle m, Offic sonal m
2 vt (bells, coins) faire tinter; (keys) faire cliqueter
3 vi (of bells, coins) tinter; (keys) cliqueter

jingoism ['dʒɪŋgəʊɪzəm] n Pej chauvinisme m

jingoistic ['dʒɪŋgəʊ'ɪstɪk] adj Pej chauvin(e)

jinx [dʒɪŋks] Fam **1** n (spell, curse) (mauvais) sort m; **to put a j. on sb/sth** jeter un sort à qn/qch
2 vt **to be jinxed** avoir la poisse

JIT [dʒɪt] adj Com (abbr just in time) juste à temps

jitters ['dʒɪtəz] npl Fam **to have** or **get the j.** être à cran

jittery ['dʒɪtərɪ] adj Fam à cran

jive [dʒaɪv] **1** n (music, dance) swing m
2 vi (dance) danser le swing

Jnr (abbr **Junior**) **Thomas Smith, J.** Thomas Smith fils

job [dʒɒb] n (**a**) (employment, post) travail m, emploi m; **to be out of a j.** être sans travail ou emploi; Br Fam **it's jobs for the boys** on place d'abord les petits copains; **j. application** demande f d'emploi; **j. creation** création f d'emplois; **j. description** description f de poste; **to go j. hunting** chercher du travail; **j. losses** suppressions fpl d'emplois; **j. offer** offre f d'emploi; **j. opportunities** débouchés mpl; **j. satisfaction** satisfaction f dans le travail; **j. security** sécurité f de

l'emploi; **j. sharing** partage m de poste; **j. title** fonction f; **j. vacancy** poste m à pourvoir (**b**) (piece of work, task) tâche f; **to do a good j.** faire du beau travail; Fig **to do the j.** (serve purpose) convenir, faire l'affaire; **it was quite a j. getting her to come** la convaincre de venir n'a pas été une mince affaire; Com **j. lot** lot m (**c**) (responsibility, duty) travail m; **to have the j. of doing sth** être chargé(e) de faire qch (**d**) Fam (crime) coup m (**e**) (idioms) Br **it's a good j. (that)...!** heureusement que...!; **that's just the j.!** c'est juste ce qu'il faut!

jobbing ['dʒɒbɪŋ] adj Br (carpenter, electrician) à la tâche ou pièce

Jobcentre ['dʒɒbsentə(r)] n Br ≃ agence f nationale pour l'emploi, ANPE f

job-hopping ['dʒɒbhɒpɪŋ] n = fait de changer d'emploi très fréquemment

jobless ['dʒɒblɪs] **1** npl **the j.** les sans-emploi mpl
2 adj sans emploi

jobseeker ['dʒɒbsiːkə(r)] n Br demandeur m d'emploi

job-share ['dʒɒbʃeə(r)] **1** n poste m partagé
2 vi partager un poste

jockey ['dʒɒkɪ] **1** n (pl jockeys) jockey m; Am **J. shorts** slip m kangourou
2 vi **to j. for position** jouer des coudes

jockstrap ['dʒɒkstræp] n slip m à coquille

jocular ['dʒɒkjʊlə(r)] adj enjoué(e)

jodhpurs ['dʒɒdpəz] npl jodhpurs mpl

Joe [dʒəʊ] pr n Am Fam **he's an ordinary J.** c'est un mec ordinaire; Br **J. Bloggs, J. Public** Monsieur Tout-le-monde

jog [dʒɒg] **1** n (**a**) (push) secousse f; (with elbow) coup m de coude; **to give sb's memory a j.** rafraîchir la mémoire de qn (**b**) (run) course f (à petites foulées); **to break into a j.** se mettre à courir (à petites foulées); **to go for a j.** aller faire un jogging
2 vt (pt & pp jogged) (push) pousser; **to j. sb's elbow** donner un coup de coude à qn; **to j. sb's memory** rafraîchir la mémoire à qn
3 vi (run) faire du jogging; **to go jogging** aller faire un jogging

►**jog along** vi (run) courir à petites foulées; Fig (in job, life) aller petit bonhomme de chemin

jogger ['dʒɒgə(r)] n joggeur(euse) m,f

jogging ['dʒɒgɪŋ] n jogging m; **j. bottoms** pantalon m de jogging; **j. suit** tenue f de jogging

joggle ['dʒɒgəl] vt secouer légèrement

Johannesburg [dʒəʊ'hænɪzbɜːg] n Johannesburg m

john [dʒɒn] n Am Fam (lavatory) petit coin m

John Bull ['dʒɒn'bʊl] pr n (Englishman) l'Anglais m moyen; (England) l'Angleterre f

join [dʒɔɪn] **1** n raccord m; (in fabric) couture f
2 vt (unite, connect) relier; (planks) joindre; **to j. two things together** relier une chose à une autre; **to j. battle** engager le combat; **to j. forces (with sb)** s'unir (à qn) (**b**) (club, political party) adhérer à; (army) s'engager dans; (discussion, game) se joindre à; **to j. a union** se syndiquer; **to j. the queue** se mettre dans la queue; Fam Fig **j. the club!** tu n'es pas le seul (la seule)! (**c**) (meet with) rejoindre; **may I j. you?** (to somebody at table) puis-je me joindre à vous? (**d**) (of river, road) rejoindre; **where the river joins the sea** où le fleuve se jette dans la mer
3 vi (**a**) (of pipes, roads, rivers) se rejoindre (**b**) (in club, political party) adhérer; (in union) devenir membre

►**join in 1** vt insep participer à, prendre part à
2 vi participer

▸**join up** *vi Mil* s'engager

joiner ['dʒɔɪnə(r)] *n Br (carpenter)* menuisier *m*

joint [dʒɔɪnt] **1** *n* (**a**) *(in body)* articulation *f*; **out of j.** déboîté(e); *Br Fig* **to put sb's nose out of j.** dépiter qn (**b**) *(in woodwork)* assemblage *m*; *(in metalwork)* joint *m* (**c**) *(of beef)* rôti *m*; *(of lamb)* gigot *m* (**d**) *Fam (nightclub)* boîte *f*; *(restaurant)* resto *m* (**e**) *Fam (cannabis cigarette)* joint *m*
2 *adj* commun(e); *(effort)* conjugué(e); **j. account** compte *m* joint; **j. custody** garde *f* conjointe; **j. ownership** copropriété *f*; **j. stock company** société *f* par actions; **j. venture** *(undertaking)* entreprise *f* commune; *(company)* société *f* commune *ou* en participation
3 *vt (chicken)* découper

jointly ['dʒɔɪntlɪ] *adv* conjointement

joist [dʒɔɪst] *n* solive *f*

joke [dʒəʊk] **1** *n* (**a**) *(remark, story)* plaisanterie *f*, blague *f*; *(prank, trick)* tour *m*, farce *f*; **to tell** *or* **crack a j. (about sth)** raconter une blague (sur qch); **to make a j. (about sth)** faire une plaisanterie (sur qch); **to make a j. of sth** rire de qch; **to say/do sth for a j.** dire/faire qch pour rire; **the j. was on him** la plaisanterie s'est retournée contre lui; **she can't take a j.** elle n'aime pas la plaisanterie; **it's no j.!** ce n'est pas une mince affaire!; **it's no j. waiting for hours** ce n'est pas drôle d'attendre pendant des heures; **it's getting beyond a j.** ça n'est plus drôle, la plaisanterie a assez duré; **to play a j. on sb** jouer un tour à qn (**b**) *Fam* **to be a j.** *(ridiculous)* être lamentable
2 *vi* plaisanter; **to j. about sth** plaisanter sur qch; **I was only joking** je plaisantais; **you're joking!, you must be joking!** tu plaisantes!, tu veux rire!; **joking apart...** blague à part...

joker ['dʒəʊkə(r)] *n* (**a**) *(clown)* farceur(euse) *m,f*; *(incompetent person)* plaisantin *m* (**b**) *(in cards)* joker *m*; *Fig* **the j. in the pack** la grande inconnue

jokily ['dʒəʊkɪlɪ] *adv* en plaisantant

jokingly ['dʒəʊkɪŋlɪ] *adv* en plaisantant

joky ['dʒəʊkɪ] *adj (person)* blagueur(euse); *(mood, conversation)* jovial(e); *(remark, comment)* moqueur(euse)

jolly ['dʒɒlɪ] **1** *adj (cheerful)* joyeux(euse), gai(e); **the J. Roger** le pavillon noir
2 *adv Br Fam (very)* rudement, drôlement; **j. good!** super!; **it serves him j. well right!** c'est vraiment bien fait pour lui!
3 *vt (pt & pp* **jollied**) **to j. sb into doing sth** amadouer qn pour qu'il fasse qch; **to j. sb along** amadouer qn

jolt [dʒəʊlt] **1** *n* (**a**) *(shake)* secousse *f* (**b**) *(shock, surprise)* choc *m*, coup *m*; **to give sb a j.** faire un choc *ou* un coup à qn
2 *vt (shake)* secouer; *(shock, surprise)* ébranler; **to j. sb into action** secouer les puces à qn; **to j. sb out of a depression** faire sortir qn de son état dépressif
3 *vi (shake)* secouer; **to j. along** *(of vehicle)* cahoter; **to j. to a stop** *(of vehicle)* s'arrêter avec des à-coups; **his head jolted forward/back** sa tête est partie en avant/en arrière

Jordan ['dʒɔːdən] *n (country)* la Jordanie; **the (River) J.** le Jourdain

Jordanian [dʒɔːˈdeɪnɪən] **1** *n* Jordanien(enne) *m,f*
2 *adj* jordanien(enne)

josh [dʒɒʃ] *vt Fam* mettre en boîte

joss stick ['dʒɒsstɪk] *n* bâton *m* d'encens

jostle ['dʒɒsəl] **1** *vt* bousculer; **to j. sb out of the way** écarter qn en jouant des coudes
2 *vi (push)* se bousculer; **to j. for position** *(in contest, job)* jouer des coudes

jot [dʒɒt] *n* **he doesn't care a j.** il s'en fiche complètement; **there isn't a j. of truth in what you say** il n'y a pas une once de vérité dans ce que vous dites; **it doesn't make a j. of difference** ça ne fait pas la moindre différence
▸**jot down** *(pt & pp* **jotted**) *vt sep* noter

jotter ['dʒɒtə(r)] *n* cahier *m*

jottings ['dʒɒtɪŋz] *npl* notes *fpl*

joule [dʒuːl] *n Phys* joule *m*

journal ['dʒɜːnəl] *n (publication)* revue *f*; *(diary)* journal *m*; **to keep a j.** tenir un journal

journalese [dʒɜːnəˈliːz] *n Fam Pej* jargon *m* journalistique

journalism ['dʒɜːnəlɪzəm] *n* journalisme *m*

journalist ['dʒɜːnəlɪst] *n* journaliste *mf*

journalistic [dʒɜːnəˈlɪstɪk] *adj* journalistique

journey ['dʒɜːnɪ] **1** *n (pl* **journeys**) voyage *m*; *(short)* trajet *m*; **a train j.** un voyage en train; **to make a j.** faire un voyage; **to go (away) on a j.** partir en voyage; **to get to** *or* **reach the end of one's j.** arriver à destination; **j. time** durée *f* du voyage; *(shorter distance)* durée *f* du trajet
2 *vi* voyager

joust [dʒaʊst] *vi Hist* jouter; *Fig (compete)* se chamailler

jovial ['dʒəʊvɪəl] *adj* jovial(e), enjoué(e)

jovially ['dʒəʊvɪəlɪ] *adv* jovialement

jowl [dʒaʊl] *n (jaw)* mâchoire *f*; *(cheek)* bajoue *f*

joy [dʒɔɪ] *n* (**a**) *(happiness)* joie *f* (**b**) *(pleasure)* plaisir *m*; **she's a j. to be with** c'est un plaisir d'être avec elle (**c**) *Br Fam (success)* **(did you have** *or* **get) any j.?** ça a marché?

joyful ['dʒɔɪfʊl] *adj (occasion, news)* heureux(euse); *(person, party)* joyeux(euse)

joyfully ['dʒɔɪfʊlɪ] *adv* joyeusement

joyless ['dʒɔɪlɪs] *adj* triste

joyous ['dʒɔɪəs] *adj (occasion, news)* heureux(euse); *(person, party)* joyeux(euse)

joyride ['dʒɔɪraɪd] *n (in stolen car)* = virée dans une voiture volée

joyrider ['dʒɔɪraɪdə(r)] *n* = chauffard qui conduit une voiture volée

joystick ['dʒɔɪstɪk] *n (in aircraft)* manche *m* à balai; *(for computer)* manette *f*

JP [dʒeɪˈpiː] *n Law (abbr* **Justice of the Peace**) juge *m* de paix

Jr *(abbr* **Junior**) **Thomas Smith, Jr** Thomas Smith fils

jubilant ['dʒuːbɪlənt] *adj (shouts)* de joie; *(expression)* réjoui(e); *(person)* exultant(e); *(celebration)* joyeux(euse); **to be j. (at** *or* **about sth)** être transporté(e) de joie (par qch)

jubilation [dʒuːbɪˈleɪʃən] *n* (grande) joie *f*, jubilation *f*

jubilee ['dʒuːbɪliː] *n* **(golden) j.** cinquantième anniversaire *m*, jubilé *m*; **silver/diamond j.** vingt-cinquième/soixantième anniversaire

Judaic [dʒuːˈdeɪɪk] *adj* judaïque

Judaism ['dʒuːdeɪɪzəm] *n* judaïsme *m*

Judas ['dʒuːdəs] *n (traitor)* Judas *m*

judder ['dʒʌdə(r)] *vi Br* être agité(e) de secousses; **to j. to a halt** s'arrêter avec des secousses

judge [dʒʌdʒ] *n* (**a**) *(in law, sport)* juge *m*; *(in competition)* membre *m* du jury (**b**) *(expert)* **to be a good /poor j. of sth** s'y connaître/ne pas s'y connaître en qch; **I'll be the j.** of that c'est moi qui (en) jugerai **2** *vt* (**a**) *(in law, sport)* juger (**b**) *(assess critically)* juger; **to j. sb by** *or* **on sth** juger qn sur *ou* d'après qch; **to j. sth a success/failure** considérer que qn/qch a réussi/échoué; **to j. it necessary to do sth** estimer *ou* juger nécessaire de faire qch; **don't j. a book by its cover** l'habit ne fait pas le moine (**c**) *(estimate)* estimer, évaluer **3** *vi* juger; **to j. by appearances** juger d'après les apparences; **to j. for oneself** juger par soi-même; **judging by...** à en juger par...

judg(e)ment, *Am* **judgment** ['dʒʌdʒmənt] *n* (**a**) *(decision)* jugement *m*; **to sit in j.** *(of judge, court)* siéger; **to pass j.** *(of judge, court)* rendre un jugement; *Fig* **to sit in** *or* **pass j. on sb** porter des jugements sur qn, juger qn; *Rel* **J. Day** le (jour du) Jugement dernier (**b**) *(opinion)* avis *m*, opinion *f*; **to form a j.** se faire un avis *ou* une opinion (**c**) *(discernment)* jugement *m*; **to have good j.** faire preuve de jugement; **to have poor j.** manquer de jugement; **to trust sb's j.** s'en remettre au jugement de qn; **in my j.** à mon sens; **against my better j.** en sachant que c'est/c'était une erreur

judg(e)mental, *Am* **judgmental** [dʒʌdʒ'mentəl] *adj* critique

judicial [dʒuː'dɪʃəl] *adj* judiciaire

judiciary [dʒuː'dɪʃɪərɪ] *n* (*judges*) magistrature *f*; *(branch of government)* pouvoir *m* judiciaire

judicious [dʒuː'dɪʃəs] *adj* judicieux(euse)

judiciously [dʒuː'dɪʃəslɪ] *adv* judicieusement

judiciousness [dʒuː'dɪʃəsnɪs] *n* bon sens *m*

judo ['dʒuːdəʊ] *n* judo *m*

jug [dʒʌg] *n* (**a**) *(for wine, water)* pichet *m*; *(for cream, milk)* pot *m* (**b**) *very Fam (prison)* **in the j.** en taule

juggernaut ['dʒʌgənɔːt] *n Br* poids *m* lourd

juggle ['dʒʌgəl] **1** *vt also Fig* jongler avec **2** *vi also Fig* jongler (**with** avec)

juggler ['dʒʌglə(r)] *n* jongleur(euse) *m,f*

juggling ['dʒʌglɪŋ] *n also Fig* jonglerie *f*

jugular ['dʒʌgjʊlə(r)] **1** *n* jugulaire *f*; *Fig* **to go for the j.** frapper au point sensible **2** *adj* jugulaire

juice [dʒuːs] *n* (**a**) *(of fruit, meat)* jus *m*; *(of plant)* suc *m*; **j. bar** = bar où l'on sert des jus de fruit; **j. extractor** centrifugeuse *f* (**b**) *Fam (electricity, petrol)* jus *m*

juicer ['dʒuːsə(r)] *n* centrifugeuse *f*

juicy ['dʒuːsɪ] *adj* (**a**) *(fruit)* juteux(euse); *(meat)* qui rend du jus (**b**) *Fig (contract, deal)* juteux(euse); *(story)* croustillant(e)

jukebox ['dʒuːkbɒks] *n* juke-box *m*

Jul *(abbr* **July**) juillet

July [dʒuː'laɪ] *n* juillet *m*; *see also* **May**

jumble ['dʒʌmbəl] **1** *n* (*of things*) tas *m*; *(of ideas, words)* fatras *m*; **in a j.** *(things)* en désordre, en pagaille; *(ideas, words)* embrouillé(e); *Br* **j. sale** vente *f* de charité **2** *vt (things)* mélanger; *(ideas, words)* embrouiller

jumbo ['dʒʌmbəʊ] *adj* **j.** (*sized*) énorme, géant(e); **j. jet** jumbo jet *m*, gros-porteur *m*

jump [dʒʌmp] **1** *n* (**a**) *(leap)* saut *m*; *Fig* **go take a j.!** va te faire voir ailleurs!; *Fig* **to be one j. ahead** avoir une longueur d'avance; *Br* **j. leads** câbles *mpl* de démarrage; **j. suit** combinaison *f* (**b**) *(rise)* hausse *f* soudaine (**in** de) (**c**) *(on racecourse)* obstacle *m* **2** *vt (hedge, ditch)* sauter; *Fam* **to j. sb** attaquer qn; **to j. bail** se dérober à la justice *(alors qu'on est en liberté*

provisoire); **to j. the gun** *(in race)* faire un faux départ; *Fig* anticiper, agir prématurément; **to j. the lights** *(in car)* brûler un feu rouge; *Br* **to j. the queue** passer avant son tour; **to j. ship** déserter le navire **3** *vi* (**a**) *(leap)* sauter; **to j. to one's feet** se lever d'un bond; **to j. for joy** sauter de joie; **to j. onto a train** sauter dans un train; **to j. out of the window** sauter par la fenêtre; **to j. to conclusions** tirer des conclusions hâtives; *Fig* **let's wait and see which way she jumps** attendons de voir ce qu'elle va faire; *Fam* **to j. down sb's throat** rabrouer qn; *Fig* **to j. out at sb** *(of mistake, surprising detail)* sauter aux yeux de qn (**b**) *(go directly)* **to j. from one subject to another** *or* **to the next** sauter d'un sujet à l'autre; **the film then jumps to the present** le film passe d'un seul coup au présent (**c**) *(of unemployment, inflation)* faire un bond (**d**) *(make a sudden movement)* *(of person)* sursauter; *(of heart)* faire un bond; *(of record player needle)* sauter; **we nearly jumped out of our skins** ça nous a fichu un coup

▶**jump at** *vt insep (offer, chance)* sauter sur

▶**jump on** *vt insep Fam (reprimand)* sauter sur (**for doing** d'avoir fait)

jumped-up [dʒʌmp'tʌp] *adj Br Fam Pej* prétentieux(euse)

jumper ['dʒʌmpə(r)] *n Br (sweater)* pull(-over) *m*; *Am (sleeveless dress)* robe-chasuble *f*

jumping-off place ['dʒʌmpɪŋ'ɒf pleɪs], **jumping-off point** ['dʒʌmpɪŋ'ɒf pɔɪnt] *n* point *m* de départ; *Fig* tremplin *m*

jump-start ['dʒʌmpstɑːt] *vt* faire démarrer avec des câbles de démarrage

jumpy ['dʒʌmpɪ] *adj* nerveux(euse)

Jun *(abbr* **June**) juin

junction ['dʒʌŋkʃən] *n (of roads, railway lines)* embranchement *m*; *Elec* **j. box** boîte *f* de dérivation

juncture ['dʒʌŋktʃə(r)] *n Formal* **at this j.** à ce moment(-là)

June [dʒuːn] *n* juin *m*; *see also* **May**

jungle ['dʒʌŋgəl] *n also Fig* jungle *f*

junior ['dʒuːnjə(r)] **1** *n* (**a**) *(in age)* **to be sb's j.** être plus jeune que qn; **he's three years my j.** il a trois ans de moins que moi (**b**) *(in rank)* subalterne *mf* (**c**) *Br Sch* écolier(ère) *m,f (entre 7 et 11 ans)*; *Am Sch* élève *mf* de troisième année; *Am Univ* étudiant(e) *m,f* de troisième année **2** *adj* (**a**) *(in age)* **to be j. to sb** être plus jeune que qn; **Thomas Smith, J.** Thomas Smith fils; *Am* **j. high (school)** *(between 11 and 15)* ≃ collège *m* d'enseignement secondaire; *Br* **j. school** *(between 7 and 11)* = classes primaires du cours élémentaire au cours moyen; *Am Sch & Univ* **j. year** avant-dernière année *f* (**b**) *(in rank)* subalterne; **to be j. to sb** être au-dessous de qn; **j. teacher/executive** jeune professeur *m*/cadre *m*; *Br Univ* **j. common room** salle *f* des étudiants du premier cycle de licence; **j. doctor** interne *mf*; *Br Parl* **j. minister** secrétaire *mf* d'État

juniper ['dʒuːnɪpə(r)] *n* (**a**) *(tree)* genévrier *m*; **j. berry** baie *f* de genièvre

junk[1] [dʒʌŋk] *n* (**a**) *(unwanted objects)* bric-à-brac *m*; *(inferior goods)* camelote *f*; *Fin* **j. bond** obligation *f*; **j. food** cochonneries *fpl*; **j. mail** prospectus *mpl*; **j. shop** brocante *f* **2** *vt Fam (discard) (objects)* bazarder; *(plan)* laisser tomber

junk[2] *n (boat)* jonque *f*

junket ['dʒʌŋkɪt] *n* (**a**) *(food)* lait *m* caillé (**b**) *Pej (trip by public official)* voyage *m* aux frais du contribuable
junkie, junky ['dʒʌŋkɪ] *(pl* junkies) *n Fam (drug addict)* drogué(e) *m,f;* **a fast-food/game-show j.** un(e) accro des fast-food/jeux télévisés
junkyard ['dʒʌŋkjɑːd] *n (for metal)* férraille *f*
junta ['dʒʌntə] *n* junte *f*
Jupiter ['dʒuːpɪtə(r)] *n (planet)* Jupiter
jurisdiction [dʒʊərɪs'dɪkʃən] *n* juridiction *f;* **to have j. over sb** avoir autorité sur qn; **to come within** *or* **under the j. of...** être sous la juridiction de...
jurisprudence [dʒʊərɪs'pruːdəns] *n* jurisprudence *f*
jurist ['dʒʊərɪst] *n (legal expert)* juriste *mf*
juror ['dʒʊərə(r)] *n Law* juré(e) *m,f*
jury ['dʒʊərɪ] *(pl* juries) *n Law* jury *m;* **to be** *or* **serve on the j.** être membre *ou* faire partie du jury; **to be on j. duty** *or* **service** être convoqué(e) pour faire partie d'un jury; *Fig* **the j. is still out on that one** ça reste à voir; **j. box** banc *m* des jurés
just [dʒʌst] **1** *adj (fair)* juste; **it's only j. that...** c'est normal que... *+ subjunctive;* **to get one's j. deserts** n'avoir que ce que l'on mérite
2 *adv* (**a**) *(exactly)* exactement; **that's j. what I told her** c'est exactement ce que je lui ai dit; **j. how many are there?** combien y en a-t-il au juste?; **that's j. the point!** justement!, précisément!; **j. my luck!** c'est bien ma chance!; **it's j. as good/difficult as...** c'est tout aussi bon/difficile que...; **j. then** juste à ce moment-là; **j. now** en ce moment; **j. as I was leaving...** juste au moment où je partais...; **I can j. see her as a doctor** je la vois très bien médecin (**b**) *(only)* juste; **she's j. a baby** ce n'est qu'un bébé; **it costs j. $10** ça coûte juste 10 dollars (**c**) *(barely)* juste; **j. before/after** juste avant/après; **j. over/under £50** à peine plus/moins de 50 livres; **it's only j. big enough** c'est tout juste assez grand; **they j. caught the train** ils ont eu le train de justesse; **they j. missed the train** ils ont raté le train d'un cheveu (**d**) *(recently)* **to have j. done sth** venir de faire qch; **j. yesterday/last year** pas plus tard qu'hier/que l'année dernière (**e**) *(simply)* **it was j. wonderful/dreadful!**

c'était tout simplement merveilleux/affreux!; **he j. refuses to listen!** il refuse carrément d'écouter!; **j. ask if you need money** si tu as besoin d'argent, tu n'as qu'à demander (**f**) *(in threats, exhortations)* **j. (you) try/wait!** essaie/attends un peu pour voir!; **(that's) j. as well!** heureusement! (**g**) **j. about** *(almost)* à peu près; **they're j. about the same** ils se valent; **I can j. about manage** j'y arrive tout juste; **to be j. about to do sth** être sur le point de faire qch
justice ['dʒʌstɪs] *n* (**a**) *(power of law)* justice *f;* **to bring sb to j.** traduire qn en justice (**b**) *(fairness)* légitimité *f;* **this photograph doesn't do him j.** cette photo ne le met pas en valeur; **to do j. to a meal** faire honneur à un repas; **to do oneself j.** se montrer sous son meilleur jour (**c**) *(judge)* juge *m; Br* **J. of the Peace** juge de paix
justifiable ['dʒʌstɪfaɪəbəl] *adj* justifié(e), légitime; **j. homicide** légitime défense *f*
justifiably ['dʒʌstɪfaɪəblɪ] *adv* à juste titre
justification [dʒʌstɪfɪ'keɪʃən] *n* justification *f;* **in j. of sth** pour justifier qch
justify ['dʒʌstɪfaɪ] *(pt & pp* justified) *vt* (**a**) *(act, behaviour)* justifier; **to be justified in doing sth** avoir de bonnes raisons de faire qch (**b**) *Comput & Typ (text)* justifier
justly ['dʒʌstlɪ] *adv (fairly)* avec justice; *(deservedly)* à juste titre
▸**jut out** [dʒʌt] *(pt & pp* jutted) **1** *vt sep (chin)* avancer
2 *vi (of balcony, rock)* faire saillie; **to j. out over sth** surplomber qch; **to j. out into the sea** s'avancer dans la mer
jute [dʒuːt] *n* jute *m*
juvenile ['dʒuːvɪnaɪl, *Am* 'dʒuːvɪnəl] **1** *n Law* mineur(e) *m,f*
2 *adj* (**a**) *Law (crime, delinquency)* juvénile; **j. court** tribunal *m* pour enfants; **j. delinquent** jeune délinquant(e) *m,f* (**b**) *Pej (childish)* puéril(e)
juxtapose [dʒʌkstə'pəʊz] *vt* mettre en juxtaposition (**with** avec)
juxtaposition [dʒʌkstəpə'zɪʃən] *n* juxtaposition *f*

K, k [keɪ] *n* (**a**) *(letter)* K, k *m inv* (**b**) *(abbr* **thousand, thousand pounds**) **he earns 30K** il gagne 30 000 livres sterling (**c**) *Comput (abbr* **kilobyte**) KO
Kabul [ˈkɑːbʊl] *n* Kaboul
kaftan [ˈkæftæn] *n* caf(e)tan *m*
kalashnikov [kəˈlæʃnɪkɒv] *n* kalachnikov *m ou f*
kale [keɪl] *n* chou *m* frisé
kaleidoscope [kəˈlaɪdəskəʊp] *n* kaléidoscope *m*
kamikaze [kæmɪˈkɑːzɪ] **1** *n also Fig* kamikaze *m* **2** *adj* kamikaze
Kampuchea [kæmpʊˈtʃɪə] *n Formerly* le Kampuchéa
kangaroo [kæŋɡəˈruː] *n* kangourou *m*; **k. court** tribunal *m* irrégulier
kaput [kəˈpʊt] *adj Fam* kaput *inv*
karaoke [kærɪˈəʊkɪ] *n* karaoké *m*
karate [kəˈrɑːtɪ] *n* karaté *m*; **k. chop** coup *m* de karaté
Kashmir [kæʃˈmɪə(r)] *n* Cachemire
Kashmiri [kæʃˈmɪərɪ] **1** *n* (**a**) *(person)* Cachemirien (enne) *m,f* (**b**) *(language)* cachemirien *m* **2** *adj* cachemirien(enne)
Katmandu [kætmænˈduː] *n* Katmandou
kayak [ˈkaɪæk] *n* kayak *m*
Kazak(h)stan [kæzækˈstɑːn] *n* Kazakhstan *m*
KB [keɪˈbiː] *n Comput (abbr* **kilobyte**) Ko *m*
kebab [kəˈbæb] *n* brochette *f*; **shish k.** chiche-kébab *m*; **doner k.** sandwich *m* grec
kedgeree [kedʒəˈriː] *n* = riz pilaf au poisson fumé et aux œufs durs
keel [kiːl] *n (of ship)* quille *f*; *Fig* **to be on an even k.** être stable
▸**keel over** *vi (of boat)* chavirer; *Fam (of person)* s'écrouler
keen [kiːn] *adj* (**a**) *(enthusiastic)* enthousiaste; *(student)* assidu(e); **to be k. on sb** avoir un faible pour qn; **to be k. on doing sth** *(habitually)* adorer faire qch; *(want to do)* avoir très envie de faire qch; **to be k. to do sth** avoir très envie de faire qch; **to be k. for sth to happen** tenir beaucoup à ce que qch arrive; *Fam* **to be as k. as mustard** déborder d'enthousiasme; **to take a k. interest in sth** s'intéresser de très près à qch (**b**) *(eye, mind, look)* vif (vive); *(price)* compétitif(ive); **to have a k. eye for detail** remarquer jusqu'au moindre détail (**c**) *(intense)* vif (vive); *(remorse)* cuisant(e); *(competition)* intense
keenly [ˈkiːnlɪ] *adv* (**a**) *(enthusiastically)* avec enthousiasme (**b**) *(intensely)* profondément; **to be k. aware of sth** avoir une conscience aiguë de qch; **k. contested** âprement disputé(e)
keep [kiːp] **1** *n* (**a**) **to pay for one's k.** payer sa pension; **to earn one's k.** *(make a living)* gagner sa vie; *(pay one's way)* payer sa pension (**b**) *(of castle)* donjon *m* (**c**) *Fam* **for keeps** pour de bon
2 *vt (pt & pp* **kept** [kept]) (**a**) *(retain)* garder; *(store)* ranger; **to k. sth from sb** dissimuler qch à qn; **to k. its shape/colour** *(of garment)* ne pas se déformer/déteindre; **to k. sb's attention** retenir l'attention de qn; **k. the change** gardez la monnaie (**b**) *(maintain)* **to k. a diary** tenir un journal; **to k. order** maintenir l'ordre; **to k. a record of sth** garder une trace écrite de qch; **to k. a secret** garder un secret (**c**) *(maintain in a certain condition)* **to k. sth secret** garder qch secret; **to k. sb awake** empêcher qn de (s'en)dormir; **to k. sb waiting** faire attendre qn; **she keeps her flat clean** son appartement est toujours bien tenu (**d**) *(look after)* *(poultry, cows)* élever; *(shop)* tenir; *(family, mistress)* entretenir; **a kept woman** une femme entretenue (**e**) *(detain)* retenir; **what kept you?** pourquoi ce retard? (**f**) *(observe)* respecter; *(promise)* tenir; **to k. late hours** se coucher tard; **to k. one's word** tenir parole
3 *vi* (**a**) *(remain)* rester; **to k. well** rester en bonne santé; **to k. quiet** se tenir tranquille; **how are you keeping?** comment allez-vous? (**b**) *(continue)* **to k. straight on** continuer tout droit; **k. (to the) left/right** serrez à gauche/à droite; **to k. doing sth** ne pas arrêter de faire qch; **to k. smiling** garder le sourire; **to k. going** tenir le coup (**c**) *(of food)* se conserver; *Fig* **it will k.** *(of problem)* ça peut attendre
▸**keep away 1** *vt sep* **to k. sb away (from sb/sth)** empêcher qn de s'approcher (de qn/qch)
2 *vi* **to k. away from sb/sth** ne pas s'approcher de qn/qch
▸**keep back 1** *vt sep* (**a**) *(crowd, tears)* retenir; **to k. sth back from sb** cacher qch à qn (**b**) *(delay)* retarder
2 *vi (not approach)* ne pas s'approcher
▸**keep down 1** *vt sep* (**a**) *(head)* baisser; **to k. one's voice down** parler moins fort; **to k. the noise down** faire moins de bruit; *Fig* **to k. one's head down** ne pas se faire remarquer; **I can't k. my food down** je vomis tout ce que je mange (**b**) *(repress) (people)* opprimer; *(prices)* empêcher d'augmenter
2 *vi (not stand up)* se tapir
▸**keep from** *vt sep* **to k. sb from doing sth** empêcher qn de faire qch; **to k. sb from his work** empêcher qn de travailler
▸**keep in** *vt sep (pupil)* garder en retenue; **to k. sb in overnight** *(in hospital)* garder qn pour la nuit
▸**keep in with** *vt insep Fam* **to k. in with sb** rester en bons termes avec qn
▸**keep off 1** *vt sep* **to k. one's hands off sb/sth** ne pas toucher à qn/qch

2 keeper *vt insep* **k. off the grass** *(sign)* Pelouse interdite

3 *vi (stay away)* ne pas intervenir

▸**keep on 1** *vt sep (clothing, employee)* garder; *(lights, TV)* laisser allumé(e); *Fam* **k. your hair on!** on se calme!

2 *vi* continuer; **to k. on doing sth** continuer de faire qch; **to k. on about sth** insister constamment sur qch

▸**keep on at** *vt insep Fam* **to k. on at sb (to do sth)** être toujours sur le dos de qn (pour qu'il fasse qch)

▸**keep out 1** *vt sep (not allow to enter)* empêcher d'entrer

2 *vi (stay away from)* **to k. out of sth** éviter qch; **to k. out of sb's way** éviter qn; **to k. out of danger** rester à l'abri du danger; **to k. out of trouble** ne pas s'attirer d'ennuis; **to k. out of an argument** rester en dehors d'une dispute; **k. out** *(sign)* défense d'entrer

▸**keep to 1** *vt sep* (**a**) *(hold)* **to k. sb to a promise** faire tenir une promesse à qn; **to k. sth to a minimum** minimiser qch (**b**) *(not reveal)* **to k. sth to oneself** garder qch pour soi; **to k. oneself to oneself** rester à l'écart

2 *vt insep (promise)* tenir; *(contract, agreement)* respecter; *(subject)* s'en tenir à; **to k. to one's bed** garder le lit

▸**keep up 1** *vt sep* (**a**) *(custom)* conserver; **to k. up the payments** continuer à payer; **to k. it up** *(continue to do well)* continuer comme ça; **k. up the good work!** continuez à bien travailler!; **to k. up appearances** sauver les apparences (**b**) *(keep awake)* empêcher de dormir

2 *vi* (**a**) *(of rain, snow)* continuer (**b**) *(remain level)* tenir le rythme; **to k. up with sb** aller à la même allure que qn; **to k. up with the Joneses** rivaliser de standing avec ses voisins; **to k. up with events** se tenir informé(e) de l'actualité; **to k. up with the times** être à la page

keeper ['kiːpə(r)] *n (in zoo, park, museum)* gardien(enne) *m,f*; *(gamekeeper)* garde-chasse *m*; *Fam (goalkeeper)* goal *m*

keep-fit ['kiːpˈfɪt] *n* gymnastique *f*; **to do k.** faire de la gymnastique; **k. class** cours *m* de gymnastique

keeping ['kiːpɪŋ] *n* (**a**) *(care)* garde *f*; **to have sb/sth in one's k.** avoir qn/qch sous sa garde (**b**) *(conformity)* **in k. with** conformément à; **out of k. with** en désaccord avec

keepsake ['kiːpseɪk] *n* souvenir *m*

keg [keg] *n* baril *m*

ken [ken] *n* **to be beyond sb's k.** être en dehors des compétences de qn

kennel ['kenəl] *n (for guard dog)* niche *f*; *(for hunting dogs)* chenil *m*; **to put a dog into kennels** mettre un chien en pension

Kenya ['kenjə, 'kiːnjə] *n* Kenya *m*

Kenyan ['kenjən] **1** *n* Kenyan(e) *m,f*

2 *adj* kenyan(e)

kept [kept] *pt & pp of* **keep**

kerb [kɜːb] *n Br* bordure *f* de trottoir

kerbcrawler ['kɜːbkrɔːlə(r)] *n* = personne au volant qui accoste les prostituées

kerbcrawling ['kɜːbkrɔːlɪŋ] *n* = fait d'accoster des prostituées tout en restant dans sa voiture

kerbstone ['kɜːbstəʊn] *n Br* bordure *f* de trottoir

kerfuffle [kəˈfʌfəl] *n Fam (fuss)* histoires *fpl*; *(noise, excitement)* remue-ménage *m*

kernel ['kɜːnəl] *n (of nut)* amande *f*; *(of grain)* grain *m*; *Fig (of problem)* fond *m*, essentiel *m*

kerosene ['kerəsiːn] *n* (**a**) *Am* pétrole *m* (lampant); **k. lamp** lampe *f* à pétrole (**b**) *(aircraft fuel)* kérosène *m*

kestrel ['kestrəl] *n* faucon *m* crécerelle

ketchup ['ketʃəp] *n (tomato)* **k.** ketchup *m*

kettle ['ketəl] *n* bouilloire *f*; **to put the k. on** mettre l'eau à chauffer; *Fam* **that's a different k. of fish** c'est une autre paire de manches

kettledrum ['ketəldrʌm] *n* timbale *f*

key [kiː] **1** *n* (**a**) *(of door, clock, toy)* clé *f*; *(of piano, typewriter)* touche *f*; *Fig* **the k. to happiness/success** la clé du bonheur/de la réussite (**b**) *(to map)* légende *f*; *(to exercise)* solutions *fpl* (**c**) *(in music)* ton *m*; **in the k. of C** en ut; **to be off k.** *(of singer)* chanter faux; *(of musician)* jouer faux

2 *adj (role, factor, figure)* clé; *(influence, consideration)* capital(e); **k. person** pivot *m*; *Br Sch* **k. stage** étape *f* clé de la scolarité

▸**key in** *vt sep (data)* saisir

keyboard ['kiːbɔːd] *n (of piano, computer)* clavier *m*

keyboarder ['kiːbɔːdə(r)] *n* claviste *mf*, opérateur(-trice) *m,f* de saisie

keycard ['kiːkɑːd] *n* carte *f* magnétique *(servant à ouvrir la porte d'une chambre d'hôtel)*

keyhole ['kiːhəʊl] *n* trou *m* de serrure; **k. surgery** chirurgie *f* à incision minimale

keynote ['kiːnəʊt] **1** *n* tonique *f*; *Fig (of speech, approach)* point *m* essentiel

2 *adj (speech)* programme; *(speaker)* principal(e)

keypad ['kiːpæd] *n Comput* pavé *m*

keyring ['kiːrɪŋ] *n* porte-clés *m inv*

keystone ['kiːstəʊn] *n also Fig* clef *f* de voûte

keystroke ['kiːstrəʊk] *n Comput* touche *f*

kg *(abbr* **kilogram)** kg

KGB [keɪdʒiːˈbiː] *n Formerly* KGB *m*

khaki ['kɑːkɪ] **1** *n* (**a**) *(colour)* kaki *m* (**b**) *Am* **khakis** *(trousers)* pantalon *m* de treillis

2 *adj* kaki *inv*

Khartoum [kɑːˈtuːm] *n* Khartoum

kHz *(abbr* **kilohertz)** kHz

kibbutz [kɪˈbʊts] *(pl* **kibbutzim** [kɪbʊtˈsiːm]) *n* kibboutz *m*

kibosh ['kaɪbɒʃ] *n Fam* **to put the k. on sth** faire tomber qch à l'eau

kick [kɪk] **1** *n* (**a**) *(with foot)* coup *m* de pied; *(of horse)* ruade *f*; *(of gun)* recul *m*; **to give sb/sth a k.** donner un coup de pied à qn/dans qch; *Fam Fig* **she needs a k. up the backside** elle a besoin d'un bon coup de pied au derrière; *Fig* **that was a k. in the teeth for him** ça lui a fait un sacré coup; **that drink has a real k. to it!** cette boisson est vraiment traître!; **k. boxing** boxe *f* française (**b**) *Fam (thrill)* **to get a k. out of doing sth** prendre son pied à faire qch; **to do sth for kicks** faire qch pour s'amuser

2 *vt* donner un coup/des coups de pied à; *(football)* taper dans; *Fam Fig* **to k. the bucket** casser sa pipe; *Fig* **to k. a man when he's down** s'acharner sur qn qui a perdu ses moyens; **I could have kicked myself** je me serais donné des gifles; **to k. the habit** *(stop taking drugs)* arrêter (la drogue)

3 *vi* donner un coup/des coups de pied; *(of horse)* ruer; *(of gun)* reculer; *Fam Fig* **to k. against sth** regimber contre qch

▸**kick about, kick around 1** *vt sep (ball)* taper dans; *Fam (idea)* tester; **don't let them k. you around** tu ne devrais pas les laisser te traiter comme ça

2 *vi Fam (hang around)* traîner; **there are plenty of**

people like that kicking around des gens comme ça, ce n'est pas ce qui manque
►**kick in 1** *vt sep (door)* enfoncer à coups de pied; *Fam* **to k. sb's head in** casser la tête à qn **2** *vi Fam* entrer en action; **the painkillers haven't kicked in yet** les analgésiques n'ont pas encore fait effet
►**kick off** *vi (in football)* donner le coup d'envoi; *Fam Fig (in meeting, debate)* démarrer
►**kick out** *vt sep Fam* mettre à la porte
►**kick up** *vt sep Fam* **to k. up a fuss** faire tout un plat *ou* toute une histoire; **to k. up a row** *or* **a racket** faire du boucan

kickback ['kɪkbæk] *n Fam (payment)* pot-de-vin *m*
kickoff ['kɪkɒf] *n (in football)* coup *m* d'envoi; *Fam Fig* **for a k.** *(to start with)* pour commencer
kick-start ['kɪkstɑːt] **1** *n (on motorbike)* kick *m* **2** *vt (motorbike)* démarrer au kick; *Fig (economy)* donner un sérieux coup de pouce à
kid [kɪd] **1** *n* (**a**) *Fam (child)* gamin(e) *m,f*, gosse *mf*; **my k. brother** mon petit frère; **it's k.'s stuff** *(easy)* c'est un jeu d'enfant; *(childish)* c'est bon pour les gosses (**b**) *(young goat)* chevreau *m*; *(female)* chevrette *f*; *(skin)* chevreau *m*; **k. gloves** gants *mpl* en chevreau; *Fig* **to handle sb with k. gloves** prendre des gants avec qn **2** *vt (pt & pp* **kidded**) *Fam (fool)* faire marcher; **to k. oneself** se faire des illusions; **who do you think you're kidding?** tu te fous de moi? **3** *vi* **to be kidding** plaisanter; **no kidding!** sans blague!
kidnap ['kɪdnæp] *(pt & pp* **kidnapped,** *Am* **kidnaped)** *vt* kidnapper, enlever
kidnapper ['kɪdnæpə(r)] *n* ravisseur(euse) *m,f*, kidnappeur(euse) *m,f*
kidnapping ['kɪdnæpɪŋ] *n* enlèvement *m*, kidnapping *m*
kidney ['kɪdnɪ] *(pl* **kidneys)** *n (of person)* rein *m*; *(offal)* rognon *m*; **k. bean** haricot *m* rouge; **k. donor** donneur(euse) *m,f* de rein; **k. machine** rein *m* artificiel
kill [kɪl] **1** *n (in hunting) (action)* mise *f* à mort; *(animals killed)* tableau *m* de chasse; **to be in at the k.** assister à la mise à mort; *Fig* assister au dénouement **2** *vt* (**a**) *(person, animal)* tuer; **to k. oneself** se tuer; *Fam* **to k. oneself laughing** mourir de rire; *Ironic* **don't k. yourself!** surtout, ne te surmène pas!; *Fam* **this one'll k. you** *(of joke)* ça va te faire mourir de rire; **to k. two birds with one stone** faire d'une pierre deux coups; *Fam* **my feet/these shoes are killing me** mes pieds/ces chaussures me font un mal de chien (**b**) *Fig (friendship)* détruire; *(sound)* amortir; *(pain)* calmer; *(chances)* anéantir; *Journ* **to k. a story** retirer une information; **to k. time** tuer le temps **3** *vi* **to shoot to k.** tirer dans l'intention de tuer; *Rel* **thou shalt not k.** tu ne tueras point
►**kill off** *vt sep (people)* tuer; *(character in film, novel)* faire mourir; *Fig (hope)* anéantir
killer ['kɪlə(r)] *n* tueur(euse) *m,f*; **he knew his k.** il connaissait son meurtrier; *Fam Fig* **those steps were a k.!** ces escaliers m'ont tué!; *Fam Fig* **this one's a k.** *(joke)* celle-ci est à mourir de rire; **k. (disease)** maladie *f* meurtrière; *Fam* **k. heels** talons *mpl* vertigineux; *Fig* **to have the k. instinct** être impitoyable; **k. whale** épaulard *m*
killing ['kɪlɪŋ] **1** *n (of person)* meurtre *m*; *(of animals)* destruction *f*; *Fam* **to make a k.** faire un bénéfice énorme

2 *adj Fam (exhausting)* tuant(e); *(very amusing)* tordant(e)
killjoy ['kɪldʒɔɪ] *n* rabat-joie *m inv*
kiln [kɪln] *n* four *m*
kilo ['kiːləʊ] *(pl* **kilos)** *n* kilo *m*
kilobyte ['kɪləbaɪt] *n Comput* kilo-octet *m*
kilogram(me) ['kɪləgræm] *n* kilogramme *m*
kilohertz ['kɪləʊhɜːts] *(pl* **kilohertz)** *n* kilohertz *m*
kilometre, *Am* **kilometer** ['kɪləmiːtə(r), kɪ'lɒmɪtə(r)] *n* kilomètre *m*
kilowatt ['kɪləwɒt] *n* kilowatt *m*; **k.-hour** kilowattheure *m*
kilt [kɪlt] *n* kilt *m*
kilter ['kɪltə(r)] *n Fam* **out of k.** *(of machine part)* déréglé(e) **(with** par rapport à); *(of budget)* déséquilibré(e)
kimono [kɪ'məʊnəʊ] *(pl* **kimonos)** *n* kimono *m*
kin [kɪn] *n Formal* parents *mpl*
kind¹ [kaɪnd] *n* (**a**) *(sort)* genre *m*, espèce *f*; **all kinds of...** toutes sortes de...; **something of the k.** quelque chose comme ça, quelque chose de ce genre; **I said nothing of the k.!** je n'ai jamais dit ça!; **she's really boring – she's nothing of the k.!** elle est vraiment ennuyeuse – mais pas du tout!; **in a k. of way** d'une certaine manière; **well, it's coffee of a k. I suppose** je suppose qu'on peut appeler ça du café; **we're two of a k.** nous sommes pareils; **it's the only one of its k.** c'est le seul de son genre; **he's that k. of person** il est comme ça; **this is my k. of party!** voilà le genre de soirée que j'aime!; **this k. of thing** ce genre de chose (**b**) **in k.** *(payment)* en nature (**c**) *Fam* **you look k. of tired** tu as l'air un peu fatigué; **I k. of expected this** je m'y attendais un peu; **do you like it? – k. of** ça te plaît? – oui, plus ou moins; **it was a k. of saucer-shaped thing** c'était quelque chose qui ressemblait à une soucoupe
kind² *adj* gentil(ille); **to be k. to sb** être gentil avec qn; *Formal* **would you be k. enough to** *or* **so k. as to...?** auriez-vous la bonté de...?; **you are really too k.** vous êtes vraiment trop aimable; **k. to the skin** *(of detergent, soap)* qui n'irrite pas la peau; **by k. permission of...** avec l'aimable autorisation de...
kinda ['kaɪndə] *Fam* = **kind of**
kindergarten ['kɪndəɡɑːtən] *n* jardin *m* d'enfants
kind-hearted [kaɪnd'hɑːtɪd] *adj (person)* qui a bon cœur; *(action)* généreux(euse)
kindle ['kɪndəl] *vt (flame)* allumer; *Fig (emotions)* éveiller
kindling ['kɪndlɪŋ] *n* petit bois *m*
kindly ['kaɪndlɪ] **1** *adv* gentiment; **to speak k. of sb** dire du bien de qn; *Formal* **(would you) k. be quiet!** voudriez-vous avoir la bonté de vous taire!; **she didn't take k. to being criticized** elle a peu apprécié qu'on la critique **2** *adj (person)* gentil(ille); *(tone, advice)* bienveillant(e)
kindness ['kaɪndnɪs] *n* gentillesse *f*; **to do sth out of the k. of one's heart** faire qch par bonté d'âme; **to do sb a k.** rendre service à qn
kindred ['kɪndrɪd] *adj* du même genre, de la même nature; **we are k. spirits** c'est mon alter ego
kinetic [kɪ'netɪk] *adj* cinétique
king [kɪŋ] *n* roi *m*; **K. Charles the First** le roi Charles Ier; **the three kings** *(in the Bible)* les Rois mages; **the k. of the beasts** le roi des animaux; *Fig* **to live like a k.** vivre en grand seigneur

kingdom ['kɪŋdəm] *n* royaume *m*; **the k. of heaven** le royaume des cieux; **the animal/plant k.** le règne animal/végétal; *Fam* **until** *or* **till k. come** jusqu'à la saint-glinglin; *Fam* **to send sb to k. come** envoyer qn ad patres

kingfisher ['kɪŋfɪʃə(r)] *n* martin-pêcheur *m*

kingpin ['kɪŋpɪn] *n Fig (of organization, company)* cheville *f* ouvrière

king-size(d) ['kɪŋsaɪz(d)] *adj* (**a**) *(cigarette)* long (longue); **k. bed** lit *m* très grand format (**b**) *Fam (headache, problem)* sacré(e)

kink [kɪŋk] *n (in wire, rope)* boucle *f*; *(in hair)* frisette *f*; *(in character)* bizarrerie *f*

kinky ['kɪŋkɪ] *adj* (**a**) *(hair)* frisotté(e) (**b**) *Fam (person) (sexually)* qui a des goûts spéciaux; *(eccentric)* extravagant(e); *(garment)* sexy *inv*; *(behaviour, practice)* pervers(e)

kinship ['kɪnʃɪp] *n* parenté *f*

kinsman ['kɪnzmən] *n Lit* parent *m*

kinswoman ['kɪnzwumən] *n Lit* parente *f*

kiosk ['kiːɒsk] *n* kiosque *m*

kip [kɪp] *Br Fam* **1** *n (sleep)* **to have a k.** piquer un roupillon; **to get some k.** roupiller
2 *vi (pt & pp* **kipped)** *(sleep)* roupiller

kipper ['kɪpə(r)] *n* hareng *m* salé et fumé

Kirg(h)izia [kɜːˈgiːzɪə], **Kirg(h)izstan** [kɜːgɪzˈstæn] *n* le Kirghizistan

kirk [kɜːk] *n Scot* église *f*; **the K.** l'Église *f* (presbytérienne) d'Écosse

kiss [kɪs] **1** *n* baiser *m*; **to give sb a k.** donner un baiser à qn; **to give sb the k. of life** faire du bouche-à-bouche à qn; *Fig* **to be the k. of death for sth** porter un coup fatal à qch; *Br* **k. curl** accroche-cœur *m*
2 *vt* embrasser; **to k. sb goodbye** dire au revoir à qn en l'embrassant; **he kissed her on the mouth/hand** il l'a embrassée sur la bouche/lui a baisé la main; *Fig* **you can k. your promotion goodbye** tu peux dire adieu à ta promotion
3 *vi* s'embrasser; **to k. and make up** se réconcilier; **to k. and tell** dévoiler à la presse ses secrets d'alcôve *(impliquant généralement une personne célèbre)*

kiss-and-tell *n Journ* = article où une personne dévoile les détails de sa liaison avec une personne connue

kissogram ['kɪsəgræm] *n* = service permettant de faire délivrer un message, un poème, une chanson etc, souvent grivois, accompagnés d'un baiser, pour une occasion particulière

kit [kɪt] *n* (**a**) *(equipment)* équipement *m*, matériel *m* (**b**) *(clothes)* tenue *f*; *Br Fam* **to get one's k. off** se mettre à poil (**c**) *(for assembly)* **(model) k.** maquette *f*; **to make sth from a k.** faire qch à partir de pièces détachées; **in k. form** en kit *m*
▸**kit out** *(pt & pp* **kitted)** *vt sep* équiper (**with** de)

kitbag ['kɪtbæg] *n* sac *m* de marin; *Mil* sac *m* à paquetage

kitchen ['kɪtʃɪn] *n* cuisine *f*; **k. knife** couteau *m* de cuisine; *Br* **k. paper**, **k. roll** essuie-tout *m inv*, Sopalin® *m*; **k. sink** évier *m*; *Fam* **to take everything but the k. sink** emporter des tonnes de choses; *(of thief)* ne laisser que les murs; **k. unit** élément *m* de cuisine

kitchenette [kɪtʃɪˈnet] *n* coin-cuisine *m*, kitchenette *f*, *Offic* cuisinette *f*

kitchenware ['kɪtʃɪnweə(r)] *n* vaisselle *f* et ustensiles *mpl* de cuisine

kite [kaɪt] *n* (**a**) *(toy)* cerf-volant *m*; **to fly a k.** faire voler un cerf-volant; *Fig* lancer un ballon d'essai; *Fam* **as**

high as a k. excité(e) comme une puce (**b**) *(bird)* milan *m*

kith [kɪθ] *n Lit* **k. and kin** parents *mpl* et amis *mpl*

kitsch [kɪtʃ] *n* kitsch *m*

kitten ['kɪtən] *n* chaton *m*; *Fig* **to have kittens** être dans tous ses états

kitty ['kɪtɪ] *(pl* **kitties)** *n* (**a**) *Fam (cat)* minou *m* (**b**) *(for bills, in cards)* cagnotte *f*

kiwi ['kiːwiː] *n* (**a**) *(bird)* kiwi *m*; **k. fruit** kiwi *m* (**b**) *Fam* **K.** *(New Zealander)* Néo-Zélandais(e) *m,f*

kleptomania [kleptəˈmeɪnɪə] *n* kleptomanie *f*

kleptomaniac [kleptəˈmeɪnɪæk] *n* kleptomane *mf*

km *(abbr* **kilometre)** km

kmph *(abbr* **kilometres per hour)** km/h

knack [næk] *n* talent *m*; *(for manual activity)* tour *m* de main; **to have the k. of** *or* **a k. for doing sth** avoir un don pour faire qch; *Ironic* avoir le don de faire qch; **to get the k. (of doing sth)** attraper le tour de main (pour faire qch)

knacker ['nækə(r)] *n* équarrisseur *m*; **k.'s yard** chantier *m* d'équarrissage

knackered ['nækəd] *adj Br very Fam (tired)* crevé(e); *(broken, damaged)* foutu(e)

knapsack ['næpsæk] *n* sac *m* à dos

knave [neɪv] *n* (**a**) *(in cards)* valet *m* (**b**) *Lit (scoundrel)* coquin *m*, fripon *m*

knead [niːd] *vt (dough)* pétrir; *(muscles)* masser

knee [niː] **1** *n* genou *m*; **to go down on one's knees** s'agenouiller; *Fig* **to bring sb to his knees** obliger qn à capituler
2 *vt (hit with knee)* donner un coup de genou à

kneecap ['niːkæp] **1** *n* rotule *f*
2 *vt (pt & pp* **kneecapped)** tirer dans les rotules à

knee-deep ['niːˈdiːp] *adj* **to be k. in sth** *(in water, snow)* être enfoncé(e) jusqu'aux genoux dans qch; *Fig (in problems)* avoir qch jusqu'au cou; *(in work)* être débordé(e) de qch

knee-high ['niːˈhaɪ] *adj* **to be k.** *(of water, snow)* arriver à hauteur du genou; *Fam* **when I was k. to a grasshopper** quand j'étais haut comme trois pommes; **k. boots/socks** bottes *fpl*/chaussettes *fpl* montantes

kneejerk ['niːdʒɜːk] *adj (reaction, response)* instinctif(ive)

kneel [niːl] *(pt & pp* **knelt** [nelt]) *vi* s'agenouiller, se mettre à genoux (**before/to** devant)

knee-length ['niːleŋθ] *adj (skirt)* qui descend jusqu'aux genoux; *(boots, socks)* qui monte jusqu'aux genoux

knees-up ['niːzʌp] *n Br Fam* **to have a k.** faire la fête

knell [nel] *n Lit* glas *m*; **to toll the k. for sb** signer l'arrêt de mort de qn; **to toll the k. for sth** sonner le glas de qch

knelt [nelt] *pt & pp of* **kneel**

knew [njuː] *pt of* **know**

knickerbocker glory ['nɪkəbɒkəˈglɔːrɪ] *n* = coupe de glace avec fruits et crème Chantilly

knickerbockers ['nɪkəbɒkəz] *npl* knickers *mpl*

knickers ['nɪkəz] *npl* (**a**) *(underwear)* culotte *f*, slip *m*; *Br Fam* **to get one's k. in a twist** perdre les pédales (**b**) *Am (breeches)* knickers *mpl*

knick-knack ['nɪknæk] *n Fam* babiole *f*

knife [naɪf] **1** *n (pl* **knives** [naɪvz]) couteau *m*; **k. and fork** couvert *m*; *Fig* **to get** *or* **have one's k. into sb** en vouloir à qn; *Fig* **the knives are out** ils sont/nous sommes/*etc* à couteaux tirés *ou* en guerre ouverte; **k. sharpener** aiguisoir *m*
2 *vt (stab)* donner un coup de couteau à, poignarder

knife-edge ['naɪfedʒ] *n Fig* **to be on a k.** *(of person)* être sur les nerfs; **to be balanced on a k.** *(of situation, game)* ne tenir qu'à un fil

knife-point ['naɪfpɔɪnt] *n* **at k.** sous la menace d'un couteau

knifing ['naɪfɪŋ] *n* agression *f* au couteau

knight [naɪt] **1** *n* chevalier *m*; *(in chess)* cavalier *m*
2 *vt* faire chevalier

knighthood ['naɪthʊd] *n (title)* **to be given a k.** être fait chevalier

knit [nɪt] *(pt & pp* **knitted** *or* **knit**) **1** *vt (sweater)* tricoter; **to k. one's brows** froncer les sourcils
2 *vi* tricoter, faire du tricot
▸**knit together** *vi (of broken bones)* se ressouder

knitted ['nɪtəd] *adj* tricoté(e)

knitting ['nɪtɪŋ] *n (item produced)* tricot *m*; **to do some k.** tricoter; **k. machine** machine *f* à tricoter; **k. needle** aiguille *f* à tricoter

knitwear ['nɪtweə(r)] *n* lainages *mpl*

knives [naɪvz] *pl of* **knife**

knob [nɒb] *n (on cane)* pommeau *m*; *(on banisters)* pomme *f*; *(on drawer, door)* poignée *f*; *(on radio)* bouton *m*; **a k. of butter** une noix de beurre

knobbly ['nɒblɪ] *adj* couvert(e) de bosses; *(tree)* noueux(euse); **k. knees** genoux *mpl* cagneux

knock [nɒk] **1** *n (blow)* coup *m*; **there was a k. at the door** on frappa à la porte
2 *vt* (**a**) *(hit)* frapper, heurter; **to k. sb to the ground** faire tomber qn en le frappant; **to k. sb unconscious** assommer qn; **to k. one's head against sth** se cogner la tête contre qch; **to k. a hole in sth** faire un trou dans qch; **to k. holes in an argument** démolir un argument; **to k. some sense into sb** apprendre à vivre à qn; *Fig* **to k. sth into shape** mettre qn au pas (**b**) *Fam (criticize)* débiner; **don't k. it until you've tried it** il faut essayer avant de critiquer
3 *vi* (**a**) *(hit)* frapper; **to k. at the door** frapper à la porte; **to k. against sth** heurter qch; **his knees were knocking** ses genoux s'entrechoquaient (**b**) *(of engine)* cogner
▸**knock about, knock around 1** *vt sep* (**a**) *(mistreat)* malmener; *(beat up)* battre (**b**) *Fam (idea, suggestion)* discuter de
2 *vi Fam (hang around)* traîner; **to k. about with sb** fréquenter qn
3 *vt insep Fam (spend time in)* **to k. about the world** rouler sa bosse; **she's been knocking about Glasgow for years** elle traîne à Glasgow depuis des lustres
▸**knock back** *vt sep Fam* (**a**) *(drink)* s'envoyer (**b**) *(reject)* envoyer bouler
▸**knock down** *vt sep* (**a**) *(pedestrian)* renverser (**b**) *(building)* abattre (**c**) *(price)* baisser
▸**knock off 1** *vt sep* (**a**) *(cause to fall off)* faire tomber; **he was knocked off his bike by a car** une voiture a heurté son vélo et il est tombé; *Fam* **to k. sb's head** *or* **block off** casser la figure à qn; *Fam* **to k. sth off the price** baisser un peu le prix (**b**) *Br very Fam (steal)* piquer, faucher (**c**) *Fam (kill)* zigouiller (**d**) *Fam* **k. it off!** *(stop it)* ça suffit!, arrête! (**e**) *Fam (produce quickly)* expédier
2 *vi Fam (finish work)* cesser le travail, finir
▸**knock out** *vt sep* (**a**) *(make unconscious)* mettre K.-O.; *Fam* **to k. sb's brains** *or* **teeth out** arranger le portrait à qn (**b**) *(eliminate from competition)* éliminer
▸**knock over** *vt sep* faire tomber

▸**knock up** *vt sep* (**a**) *(make hastily)* construire en vitesse; *(meal)* préparer en vitesse (**b**) *very Fam (make pregnant)* mettre en cloque

knockdown price ['nɒkdaʊn'praɪs] *n Fam* **at a k.** à très bas prix

knocker ['nɒkə(r)] *n* (**a**) *(on door)* heurtoir *m* (**b**) *very Fam* **knockers** *(breasts)* nichons *mpl*

knocking ['nɒkɪŋ] *n (at door)* coups *mpl*; *(of engine)* cognement *m*

knock-kneed ['nɒk'niːd] *adj* **to be k.** avoir les genoux en dedans

knock-on effect ['nɒkɒnɪ'fekt] *n* répercussions *fpl* en chaîne

knockout ['nɒkaʊt] **1** *n* (**a**) *(in boxing)* knock-out *m inv*; *Fig* coup *m* de grâce (**b**) *Fam* **he's/she's a k.** *(attractive)* il/elle est canon
2 *adj* (**a**) **k. blow** *(in boxing)* coup *m* qui provoque un K.-O.; *Fig* coup *m* de grâce; *Fig* **to deliver the k. blow** donner le coup de grâce (**b**) **k. competition** compétition *f* avec épreuves éliminatoires

knot [nɒt] **1** *n* (**a**) *(in general)* nœud *m*; **to tie/untie a k.** faire/défaire un nœud; *Fam Fig* **to tie the k.** *(get married)* se marier (**b**) *Naut (unit of speed)* nœud *m*; *Fam Fig* **at a rate of knots** à toute allure (**c**) *(group of people)* petit groupe *m*
2 *vt (pt & pp* **knotted**) *(rope, string)* nouer

knotty ['nɒtɪ] *adj (problem)* épineux(euse)

know [nəʊ] **1** *Fam* **to be in the k.** être au courant
2 *vt (pt* **knew** [njuː], *pp* **known** [nəʊn]) (**a**) *(be acquainted with)* connaître; **to get to k. sb** apprendre à connaître qn; **when I first knew her** quand j'ai fait sa connaissance; **I've never known anything like it** je n'ai jamais rien vu de tel; **I k. her to say hello to** nous nous saluons, c'est tout; **knowing him...** le connaissant... (**b**) *(have knowledge of)* savoir; **she thinks she knows all the answers** elle croit avoir réponse à tout; **to k. Spanish** connaître l'espagnol; **to k. a lot/a little about sth** bien s'y connaître/s'y connaître un peu en qch; **she knows what she's talking about** elle sait de quoi elle parle; **to k. how to do sth** savoir faire qch; *Fam* **to k. a thing or two** être malin(igne); **to k. one's own mind** savoir ce que l'on veut; **heaven** *or* **God knows!** Dieu seul le sait! (**c**) *(recognize)* reconnaître (**by** à); *(distinguish)* distinguer (**from** de); **to k. right from wrong** savoir faire la distinction entre le bien et le mal
3 *vi* savoir; **to k. about sth** être au courant de qch; **to get to k. of sth** apprendre qch; **as far as I k.** (pour) autant que je sache; **how should I k.?** comment le saurais-je?; **you never k.** on ne sait jamais; **not that I k. of** pas que je sache; **to k. better than to do sth** savoir qu'il ne faut pas faire qch; **you k....** tu sais...

know-all ['nəʊɔːl] *n Fam* monsieur *m*/madame *f* je-sais-tout

know-how ['nəʊhaʊ] *n Fam* savoir-faire *m*; *(technical)* know-how *m*

knowing ['nəʊɪŋ] **1** *n* **there's no k.** c'est impossible à savoir
2 *adj (look, smile)* entendu(e), complice

know-it-all ['nəʊɪtɔːl] = **know-all**

knowledge ['nɒlɪdʒ] *n* (**a**) *(of fact)* connaissance *f*; **(not) to my k.** (pas) à ma connaissance; **to have no k. of sth** ignorer qch; **to have full k. of sth** avoir pleine connaissance de qch; **it is common k. that...** c'est un fait notoire que...; *Formal* **it has recently come to our k. that...** il a été récemment porté à notre connaissance que... (**b**) *(learning)* savoir *m*,

connaissances *fpl*; **k. is power** savoir c'est pouvoir; *Comput* **k.-based system** système *m* basé sur les connaissances
knowledgeable [ˈnɒlɪdʒəbəl] *adj* savant(e); **to be k. about sth** bien s'y connaître en qch
known [nəʊn] **1** *adj* connu(e); *(notorious)* notoire
  2 *pp of* **know**
knuckle [ˈnʌkəl] *n* articulation *f ou* jointure *f* (du doigt)
▸ **knuckle down** *vi Fam* se mettre au boulot; **to k. down to sth** se mettre à qch
▸ **knuckle under** *vi Fam* mettre les pouces
  knuckle-duster [ˈnʌkəldʌstə(r)] *n* coup-de-poing *m* américain
KO [ˈkeɪˈəʊ] *Fam* **1** *n (pl* **KO's** [ˈkeɪˈəʊz]) *(in boxing)* K.-O. *m*
  2 *vt (pt & pp* **KO'd** [ˈkeɪˈəʊd]) *(in boxing)* mettre K.-O.
koala [kəʊˈɑːlə] *n* **k. (bear)** koala *m*
kopeck [ˈkəʊpek] *n* kopeck *m*
Koran [kəˈrɑːn] *n* **the K.** le Coran
Koranic [kəˈrænɪk] *adj* coranique
Korea [kəˈrɪə] *n* la Corée; **North/South K.** la Corée du Nord/du Sud
Korean [kəˈrɪən] **1** *n* (**a**) *(person)* Coréen(enne) *m,f*
  (**b**) *(language)* coréen *m*
  2 *adj* coréen(enne); **the K. War** la guerre de Corée

kosher [ˈkəʊʃə(r)] *adj* (**a**) *(in Judaism)* casher *inv*; kasher *inv* (**b**) *Fam (legitimate)* réglo *inv*
Kosovan [ˈkɒsəvən] **1** *n* Kosovar *mf*
  2 *adj* kosovar(e)
Kosovo [ˈkɒsəvəʊ] *n* le Kosovo
kowtow [ˈkaʊˈtaʊ] *vi* **to k. to sb** faire des courbettes devant qn
Kraut [kraʊt] *n very Fam* Kraut, Boche *mf*, = terme injurieux désignant un Allemand
Kremlin [ˈkremlɪn] *n* **the K.** le Kremlin
krona [ˈkrəʊnə] *(pl* **kronor** [ˈkrəʊnɔː(r)]) *n* couronne *f*
krone [ˈkrəʊnə] *(pl* **kroner** [ˈkrəʊnə(r)]) *n* couronne *f*
kudos [ˈkjuːdɒs] *n (prestige)* prestige *m*; *(fame)* célébrité *f*
Kurd [kɜːd] **1** *n* Kurde *mf*
  2 *adj* kurde
Kurdish [ˈkɜːdɪʃ] **1** *n (language)* kurde *m*
  2 *adj* kurde
Kurdistan [kɜːdɪˈstæn] *n* le Kurdistan
Kuwait [kʊˈweɪt] *n* le Koweït
Kuwaiti [kʊˈweɪtɪ] **1** *n* Koweïtien(enne) *m,f*
  2 *adj* koweïtien(enne)
kW *(abbr* **kilowatt**) kW

L, l [el] *n* (**a**) *(letter)* L, l *m inv* (**b**) *Br* **L-driver** = personne qui apprend à conduire; **L-plate** = plaque apposée sur une voiture pour signaler que le conducteur est en conduite accompagnée

L-plates
En Grande-Bretagne, la lettre "L" apposée sur l'arrière d'un véhicule indique que le conducteur n'a pas encore son permis mais qu'il est en conduite accompagnée.

LA [el'eɪ] *n (abbr* **Los Angeles**) Los Angeles
Lab *Br Pol (abbr* **Labour**) le parti travailliste, les travaillistes *mpl*
lab [læb] *n Fam (abbr* **laboratory**) labo *m*
label ['leɪbəl] **1** *n* (**a**) *also Fig* étiquette *f* (**b**) *(of record company)* label *m*
2 *vt (pt & pp* **labelled**, *Am* **labeled**) *also Fig* étiqueter; *Fig* **to l. sb a liar** qualifier qn de menteur(euse)
labor, labored *etc Am* = **labour, laboured** *etc*
laboratory [lə'bɒrətrɪ] *(pl* **laboratories**) *n* laboratoire *m*; **l. assistant** laborantin(e) *m,f*
laborious [lə'bɔːrɪəs] *adj (work)* pénible, fatigant(e); *(explanation)* laborieux(euse)
laboriously [lə'bɔːrɪəslɪ] *adv* laborieusement
labour, *Am* **labor** ['leɪbə(r)] **1** *n* (**a**) *(work)* labeur *m*; **l. camp** camp *m* de travail (**b**) *(workers)* main-d'œuvre *f*; **l. costs** coût *m* de la main-d'œuvre; *Am* **L. Day** fête *f* du travail *(aux États-Unis, célébrée le premier lundi de septembre)*; **l. dispute** conflit *m* du travail; *Br Formerly* **L. Exchange** bureau *m* de placement; **l. force** effectifs *mpl*; **l. market** marché *m* du travail; **l. shortage** pénurie *f* de main-d'œuvre (**c**) *Br Pol* **L., the L. Party** le parti travailliste, les travaillistes *mpl* (**d**) *(task)* effort *m*; **to do sth as a l. of love** faire qch pour le plaisir (**e**) *(childbirth)* travail *m*; **to be in l.** être en travail; **l. pains** douleurs *fpl* de l'accouchement
2 *vt* **to l. a point** s'étendre sur un sujet
3 *vi* (**a**) *(of person)* peiner (**over** sur); **to l. in vain** s'éreinter en vain; **to be labouring under a misapprehension** être dans l'erreur (**b**) *(of engine)* peiner
laboured, *Am* **labored** ['leɪbəd] *adj* laborieux(euse); *(breathing)* pénible, difficile
labourer, *Am* **laborer** ['leɪbərə(r)] *n* manœuvre *m*; *(on farm)* ouvrier(ère) *m,f* agricole
labouring, *Am* **laboring** ['leɪbərɪŋ] *adj* **a l. job** du travail *m* de manœuvre
labour-intensive, *Am* **labor-intensive** [leɪbərɪn'tensɪv] *adj* qui demande une main-d'œuvre importante
labour-saving, *Am* **labor-saving** ['leɪbəseɪvɪŋ] *adj* qui simplifie la tâche

labrador ['læbrədɔː(r)] *n* labrador *m*
laburnum [lə'bɜːnəm] *n* cytise *m*
labyrinth ['læbərɪnθ] *n* labyrinthe *m*
labyrinthine [læbə'rɪnθaɪn] *adj Archit* en labyrinthe; *Fig* labyrinthique
lace [leɪs] **1** *n* (**a**) *(cloth)* dentelle *f*; **l. curtain** rideau *m* en *ou* de dentelle (**b**) *(of shoe)* lacet *m*
2 *vt* (**a**) *(shoes)* **to l.** (**up**) lacer (**b**) *(drink)* ajouter de l'alcool à; *Fig (story)* entremêler (**with** de); **to l. a drink with sth** ajouter qch dans une boisson
lacerate ['læsəreɪt] *vt* lacérer
laceration [læsə'reɪʃən] *n* lacération *f*
lace-up ['leɪsʌp] **1** *n (shoe)* chaussure *f* à lacets
2 *adj (shoe)* à lacets
lachrymose ['lækrɪməʊs] *adj Lit* larmoyant(e)
lack [læk] **1** *n* manque *m* (**of** de); **for l. of...** faute de...; **there's no l. of volunteers** ce ne sont pas les volontaires qui manquent
2 *vt* manquer de
3 *vi* **to be lacking in sth** manquer de qch
lackadaisical [lækə'deɪzɪkəl] *adj* désinvolte
lackey ['lækɪ] *(pl* **lackeys**) *n Pej* larbin *m*
lacklustre, *Am* **lackluster** ['læklʌstə(r)] *adj* terne
laconic [lə'kɒnɪk] *adj* laconique
lacquer ['lækə(r)] **1** *n* laque *f*
2 *vt* laquer
lacrosse [lə'krɒs] *n Sport* crosse *f*
lacuna [lə'kjuːnə] *(pl* **lacunae** [lə'kjuːniː] *or* **lacunas**) *n* lacune *f*
lad [læd] *n Fam* (**a**) *(young man)* jeune gars *m*; *(boy)* garçon *m*; **he's a big l.** c'est un grand gaillard; **he's a bit of a l.** c'est un sacré fêtard (**b**) **lads** *(friends)* copains *mpl*, potes *mpl*; **he's gone out with the lads** il est sorti avec les copains; **come on, lads!** allez les mecs!
ladder ['lædə(r)] **1** *n (for climbing, in tights)* échelle *f*; **the social l.** l'échelle sociale; *Fig* **to get one's foot on the l.** mettre un pied à l'étrier; *Fig* **to reach the top of the l.** atteindre le sommet de l'échelle
2 *vt (tights)* filer
3 *vi (of tights)* filer
laden ['leɪdən] *adj* chargé(e) (**with** de)
ladle ['leɪdəl] **1** *n* louche *f*
2 *vt (soup)* servir (à la louche)
▶**ladle out** *vt sep (soup)* servir (à la louche); *Fig* **to l. out advice/praise** distribuer les conseils/les compliments
lady ['leɪdɪ] *(pl* **ladies**) *n* (**a**) *(woman)* dame *f*; **a young l.** *(unmarried)* une jeune fille; *(married)* une jeune dame; **the l. of the house** la maîtresse de maison; *Euph* **a l. of the night** une belle de nuit; **she's no l.** elle

n'a aucune classe; **ladies and gentlemen!** mesdames et messieurs!; **ladies' man** homme *m* à femmes; **ladies' (room)** toilettes *fpl* (des dames); **l. friend** amie *f* (**b**) **Our L.** Notre-Dame *f* (**c**) *(title)* **L. Browne** lady Browne *(titre de noblesse féminin)*; **l. of the manor** châtelaine *f*; **my L.** Madame la Marquise/la Baronne/*etc*; **L. Luck** la chance; *Fam* **to act like L. Muck** jouer à la grande dame

ladybird ['leɪdɪbɜːd] *n* coccinelle *f*

lady-in-waiting ['leɪdɪɪn'weɪtɪŋ] *(pl* **ladies-in-waiting**) *n* dame *f* d'honneur

lady-killer ['leɪdɪkɪlə(r)] *n Fam* bourreau *m* des cœurs

ladylike ['leɪdɪlaɪk] *adj (woman)* comme il faut; *(air, behaviour)* distingué(e)

ladyship ['leɪdɪʃɪp] *n also Ironic* **Her/Your L.** madame *f*

lag [læg] **1** *n* (**a**) *(gap)* décalage *m* (**b**) *very Fam (prisoner)* **old l.** repris *m* de justice

2 *vt (pt & pp* **lagged**) *(pipes, boiler)* isoler

3 *vi (of person, economy)* **to l. behind** être à la traîne; **to l. behind sb/sth** être à la traîne derrière qn/qch

lager ['lɑːgə(r)] *n* bière *f* blonde; *Fam* **l. lout** = voyou imbibé de bière

laggard ['lægəd] *n* traînard(e) *m,f*

lagoon [lə'guːn] *n* lagune *f*; *(of atoll)* lagon *m*

laid [leɪd] *pt & pp of* **lay²**

laid-back [leɪd'bæk] *adj Fam* cool *inv*, relax *inv*

lain [leɪn] *pp of* **lie²**

lair [leə(r)] *n* repaire *m*

laird [leəd] *n Scot* propriétaire *m* foncier

laisser-faire [leseɪ'feə(r)] **1** *n* laisser-faire *m*

2 *adj* de laisser-faire

laity ['leɪtɪ] *n* **the l.** les laïques *mpl*

lake [leɪk] *n* lac *m*; **L. Geneva** le lac de Genève, le lac Léman; **the L. District, the Lakes** la région des lacs *(dans le nord-ouest de l'Angleterre)*

lamb [læm] *n* agneau *m*; **poor l.!** pauvre biquet!; **like lambs to the slaughter** comme des veaux que l'on mène à l'abattoir; **l. chop** côtelette *f* d'agneau

lambast [læm'bæst] *vt* fustiger

lambing ['læmɪŋ] *n* agnelage *m*

lambskin ['læmskɪn] *n* peau *f* d'agneau

lambswool ['læmswʊl] **1** *n* lambswool *m*

2 *adj* en lambswool

lame [leɪm] **1** *adj* (**a**) *(person, horse)* boiteux(euse); *Fig (excuse)* bancal(e); *(plot, argument)* boiteux; **to be l.** boiter; **to go l.** se mettre à boiter; *Fig* **l. duck** canard *m* boiteux (**b**) *Fam (stupid)* nul (nulle)

2 *vt* rendre boiteux(euse)

lamé ['lɑːmeɪ] *n* lamé *m*; **a l. dress** une robe en lamé

lamely ['leɪmlɪ] *adv* maladroitement

lament [lə'ment] **1** *n* lamentation *f*; *Mus* complainte *f*

2 *vt* se lamenter sur; **the late lamented Mr Jones** le regretté M. Jones

3 *vi* se lamenter *(over* sur)

lamentable ['læməntəbəl] *adj* lamentable; *(decision, loss)* déplorable

lamentably ['læməntəblɪ] *adv* lamentablement

lamentation [læmən'teɪʃən] *n* lamentation *f*

laminate 1 *n* ['læmɪnət] stratifié *m*; **l. flooring** revêtement *m* de sol stratifié

2 *vt* ['læmɪneɪt] *(glass)* feuilliter; *(wood, plastic)* stratifier; *(paper, card)* plastifier

laminated ['læmɪneɪtəd] *adj* (**a**) *(glass)* feuilleté(e); *(wood, plastic)* stratifié(e) (**b**) *(paper, card)* plastifié(e)

lamp [læmp] *n* lampe *f*

lamplight ['læmplaɪt] *n* **by l.** à la lumière d'une lampe

lampoon [læm'puːn] **1** *n* pamphlet *m*

2 *vt* brocarder

lamppost ['læmppəʊst] *n* réverbère *m*

lamprey ['læmprɪ] *(pl* **lampreys**) *n* lamproie *f*

lampshade ['læmpʃeɪd] *n* abat-jour *m inv*

lampstand ['læmpstænd] *n* pied *m* de lampe

LAN [eleɪ'en] *n Comput (abbr* **local area network**) réseau *m* local

lance [lɑːns] **1** *n (weapon)* lance *f*

2 *vt (abscess)* percer, inciser

lance corporal ['lɑːns'kɔːpərəl] *n* ≃ caporal *m*

lancer ['lɑːnsə(r)] *n (soldier)* lancier *m*

lancet ['lɑːnsɪt] *n* lancette *f*

land [lænd] **1** *n* (**a**) *(ground, earth)* terre *f*; **on l.** sur terre; **to live off the l.** vivre du produit de la terre; **to be in the l. of the living** être toujours de ce monde; *Mil* **l. forces** armée *f* de terre; **l. reclamation** mise *f* en valeur des sols; **l. reform** réforme *f* agraire (**b**) *(property)* terres *fpl*; **a piece of l.** *(for farming)* un lopin de terre; *(for building)* un terrain (à bâtir) (**c**) *Lit or Formal (nation)* pays *m*; **distant lands** pays *mpl* lointains

2 *vt* (**a**) *(passengers, cargo)* débarquer (**b**) *(plane)* poser (**c**) *(fish)* sortir de l'eau (**d**) *Fam (job, prize)* décrocher (**e**) *Fam (put)* **to l. sb in prison/court** mener qn en prison/au tribunal; **to l. sb in trouble** attirer des ennuis à qn (**f**) *Fam* **to be landed with sth** rester avec qch sur les bras; **I got landed with doing the dishes** c'est moi qui ai dû me taper à la vaisselle (**g**) *Fam (hit)* **to l. sb one** en coller une à qn

3 *vi (of plane)* atterrir; *(of gymnast)* se réceptionner; *Fig* **to l. on one's feet** retomber sur ses pieds

▶**land up** *vi* atterrir

landed ['lændəd] *adj* **l. gentry** noblesse *f* terrienne; **l. proprietor** propriétaire *mf* terrien(enne)

landfall ['lændfɔːl] *n Naut* **to make l.** arriver en vue des côtes

landfill site ['lændfɪl'saɪt] *n* décharge *f* publique

landing ['lændɪŋ] *n* (**a**) *(of cargo, troops)* débarquement *m*; **l. card** carte *f* de débarquement; **l. craft** navire *m* de débarquement; **l. stage** débarcadère *m* (**b**) *(of aircraft)* atterrissage *m*; **l. gear** train *m* d'atterrissage; **l. lights** phares *mpl* d'atterrissage; **l. strip** piste *f* d'atterrissage (**c**) *(of staircase)* palier *m*

landlady ['lændleɪdɪ] *(pl* **landladies**) *n* (**a**) *(of rented accommodation)* propriétaire *f* (**b**) *(of small hotel)* logeuse *f*; *(of pub)* patronne *f*

landlocked ['lændlɒkt] *adj* sans accès à la mer

landlord ['lændlɔːd] *n* (**a**) *(of rented accommodation)* propriétaire *m* (**b**) *(of pub)* patron *m*

landmark ['lændmɑːk] *n (distinctive feature)* point *m* de repère; *Fig (important event)* événement *m* marquant

landmass ['lændmæs] *n* masse *f* continentale

landmine ['lændmaɪn] *n* mine *f* terrestre

landowner ['lændəʊnə(r)] *n* propriétaire *mf* foncier(ère)

landowning ['lændəʊnɪŋ] *adj* **the l. classes** la propriété foncière

landscape ['lændskeɪp] **1** *n* paysage *m*; **l. design** aménagement *m* d'espaces verts; **l. gardener** jardinier(ère) *m,f* paysagiste; *Comput* **l. (orientation)** format *m* paysage; **l. painter** paysagiste *mf*

2 *vt* aménager en espaces verts

landslide ['lændslaɪd] *n* (**a**) *(of earth, rocks)* glissement *m* de terrain (**b**) *(election victory)* raz *m inv* de marée électoral; **to win by a l.** gagner avec une majorité écrasante

landslip ['lændslɪp] *n* glissement *m* de terrain

landward ['lændwəd] **1** *adj (wind)* marin(e); **on the l.**
side du côté des terres
2 *adv* vers la terre
lane [leɪn] *n* (**a**) *(in country)* chemin *m*; *(in town)* ruelle
f, passage *m* (**b**) *(on road)* voie *f*, file *f*; **get in l.**
(sign) mettez-vous sur la bonne file (**c**) *(for runner, swimmer)* couloir *m*
language ['læŋgwɪdʒ] *n* (**a**) *(of a people)* langue *f*; *Fam
Fig* **we don't speak the same l.** nous ne parlons pas
la même langue; **l. laboratory** laboratoire *m* de langues; **l. learning/teaching** apprentissage *m*/enseigne-
ment *m* des langues (**b**) *(style of speech or writing)*
langage *m*
languid ['læŋgwɪd] *adj* alangui(e)
languidly ['læŋgwɪdlɪ] *adv* paresseusement
languish ['læŋgwɪʃ] *vi* languir (**for** après); **to l. in prison** moisir en prison
languor ['læŋgə(r)] *n* langueur *f*
languorous ['læŋgərəs] *adj* alangui(e)
lank [læŋk] *adj (hair)* terne
lanky ['læŋkɪ] *adj* dégingandé(e)
lanolin(e) ['lænəlɪn] *n* lanoline *f*
lantern ['læntən] *n* lanterne *f*
Laos [laʊs] *n* le Laos
Laotian ['laʊʃən] **1** *n* Laotien(enne) *m,f*
2 *adj* laotien(enne)
lap¹ [læp] *n* (**a**) *(part of body)* genoux *mpl*; **to sit on sb's
l.** s'asseoir sur les genoux de qn; **l. dancer** = entraîneuse qui danse nue pour un client (**b**) *(idioms)* **it's
in the l. of the gods** on ne peut que s'en remettre au
sort; **she expects everything to fall into her l.** elle
s'attend à ce que tout lui tombe tout cuit dans le bec;
to live in the l. of luxury vivre dans le luxe
lap² **1** *n (in race)* tour *m*; **l. of honour** tour d'honneur
2 *vt* *(pt & pp lapped)* *(overtake)* prendre un tour
d'avance sur
lap³ *(pt & pp lapped)* *vi (of animal)* laper; **to l. against
sth** *(of waves)* clapoter contre qch
▸**lap up** *vt sep (drink)* laper; *Fam Fig (enjoy indiscriminately)* se délecter de; *(believe)* gober, avaler
laparotomy [læpə'rɒtəmɪ] *(pl laparotomies)* *n Med*
laparotomie *f*
lapdog ['læpdɒg] *n* chien *m* d'appartement; *Fig* toutou *m*
lapel [lə'pel] *n* revers *m*
Lapland ['læplænd] *n* la Laponie
Laplander ['læplændə(r)] *n* Lapon(one) *m,f*
Lapp [læp] **1** *n* (**a**) *(person)* Lapon(one) *m,f* (**b**) *(language)* lapon *m*
2 *adj* lapon(one)
lapse [læps] **1** *n* (**a**) *(of time)* laps *m* de temps (**b**) *(in
standards, concentration)* baisse *f* (**in** de); *(in behaviour)* écart *m* (**in** de)
2 *vi (of concentration, standards)* baisser; *(of person)* retomber dans un travers; **to l. into silence**
taire (**b**) *(of permit, membership)* expirer
lapsed [læpst] *adj (Catholic)* qui ne pratique plus
laptop ['læptɒp] *n Comput* portable *m*
lapwing ['læpwɪŋ] *n* vanneau *m*
larceny ['lɑːsənɪ] *n Law* vol *m*
larch [lɑːtʃ] *n* mélèze *m*
lard [lɑːd] **1** *n (fat)* saindoux *m*
2 *vt Fam Fig* **to l. one's writings with quotations**
truffer ses écrits de citations
larder ['lɑːdə(r)] *n* garde-manger *m inv*
large [lɑːdʒ] **1** *n* **to be at l.** être en liberté; **people at l.,
the public at l.** le grand public

2 *adj* (**a**) *(big)* grand(e); *(fat, bulky)* gros (grosse);
(audience) nombreux(euse); **to grow** *or* **get larger**
s'agrandir; *(of person)* grossir; **to make sth larger**
agrandir qch; **as l. as life** en chair et en os; **larger
than life** haut(e) en couleur (**b**) *(extensive, significant)* **to a l. extent** en grande partie; **a l. part of** une
grande partie de
3 *adv* **by and l.** dans l'ensemble
largely ['lɑːdʒlɪ] *adv* en grande partie
large-scale ['lɑːdʒskeɪl] *adj (map)* à grande échelle;
(undertaking) ambitieux(euse); *(disaster)* immense
largesse [lɑː'ʒes] *n* largesse *f*
lark¹ [lɑːk] *n (bird)* alouette *f*; **to rise with the l.** se lever au chant du coq
lark² *n (joke)* rigolade *f*; **to do sth for a l.** faire qch
pour rire; **I don't like this fancy dress l.** je n'aime pas
du tout cette histoire de bal masqué
▸**lark about, lark around** *vi* faire le fou (la folle)
larva ['lɑːvə] *(pl larvae* ['lɑːviː]*) n* larve *f*
laryngitis [lærɪn'dʒaɪtɪs] *n* laryngite *f*; **to have l.** avoir
une laryngite
larynx ['lærɪŋks] *n* larynx *m*
lasagne [lə'sænjə] *n* lasagnes *fpl*
lascivious [lə'sɪvɪəs] *adj* lascif(ive)
laser ['leɪzə(r)] *n* laser *m*; **l. beam** rayon *m* laser; **l. disc**
disque *m* laser; **l. printer** imprimante *f* laser; **l. surgery** chirurgie *f* au laser
lash [læʃ] **1** *n* (**a**) *(eyelash)* cil *m* (**b**) *(of whip)* coup *m*
de fouet
2 *vt* (**a**) *(with whip)* cingler; *(of rain, waves)* fouetter
(**b**) *(tie)* lier, attacher
3 *vi* **the rain** *or* **it was lashing down** il pleuvait dru
▸**lash out** *vi* (**a**) *(attack)* **to l. out at sb** *(physically)* donner un coup/des coups à qn; *(verbally)* s'en prendre
violemment à qn (**b**) *Fam (spend extravagantly)* claquer un fric fou (**on** pour)
lashings ['læʃɪŋz] *npl Fam (lots)* des tas; **l. of cream/
jam** une tonne de crème/confiture
lass [læs] *n* jeune fille *f*
lassitude ['læsɪtjuːd] *n (weariness)* lassitude *f*; *(laziness)* paresse *f*
lasso [læ'suː] **1** *n (pl lassoes* or **lassos***)* lasso *m*
2 *vt (pt & pp lassoed)* attraper au lasso
last¹ [lɑːst] **1** *n* **the l.** le dernier (la dernière) *m,f*; **the l.
but one** l'avant-dernier(ère) *m,f*; **we'll never hear the
l. of it** on n'a pas fini d'en entendre parler; **I don't
think we've heard the l. of him** je crois que nous n'en
sommes pas encore débarrassés; **that's the l. I saw
of her** je ne l'ai pas revue depuis; **that's the l. of the
wine** on a fini le vin; **to** *or* **till the l.** jusqu'à la fin; **at
(long) l.** enfin
2 *adj* (**a**) *(final)* dernier(ère); **you are my l. hope**
vous êtes mon dernier espoir; **to have the l. word**
avoir le dernier mot; **the l. word in comfort/style** le
summum du confort/de l'élégance; **at the l. moment**
or **minute** au dernier moment, à la dernière minute; **l.
thing at night** avant de se coucher; **to be on one's l.
legs** être au bout du rouleau; **he's the l. person I'd ask
to help me** c'est (bien) la dernière personne à qui je
demanderais de m'aider; **that's the l. thing I'd do** c'est
(bien) la dernière chose que je ferais; **as a l. resort** en
dernier recours; **the L. Judgment** le Jugement dernier; **l. name** nom de famille; **l. rites** derniers sacrements *mpl*; *Fig* **the l. straw** la goutte d'eau qui a fait
déborder le vase (**b**) *(most recent)* dernier(ère); **the
l. time I saw him** la dernière fois que je l'ai vu; **l. January** en janvier (dernier); **l. night** *(during the night)* la

nuit dernière; *(in the evening)* hier (au) soir; **l. Tuesday** mardi *m* dernier; **l. week** la semaine dernière **3** *adv* **to arrive/finish l.** arriver/finir dernier; **when l l. saw him** la dernière fois que je l'ai vu; **l. but not least** enfin

last² *n (for shoe)* forme *f* (à chaussure)

last³ 1 *vt* **that watch will l. you a lifetime** vous pourrez garder cette montre toute votre vie; **it has lasted him well** ça lui a fait de l'usage; **have we got enough to l. us until tomorrow?** en avons-nous assez pour tenir jusqu'à demain?
2 *vi* durer; **it's too good to l.** c'est trop beau pour durer; **the supplies won't l. two months** les provisions ne seront pas suffisantes pour deux mois; **he won't l. long in that job** il ne tiendra pas très longtemps à ce poste; **she won't l. the night** elle ne passera pas la nuit
►**last out 1** *vt sep* **to l. the year out** *(of person)* survivre jusqu'à la fin de l'année; *(of supplies)* suffire pour l'année
2 *vi (of person)* tenir le coup; *(of supplies)* suffire
last-ditch [lɑːst'dɪtʃ] *adj* ultime; **a l. attempt** un ultime effort
lasting ['lɑːstɪŋ] *adj* durable
lastly ['lɑːstlɪ] *adv* pour finir, en dernier lieu
last-minute [lɑːst'mɪnɪt] *adj* de dernière minute
latch [lætʃ] *n* loquet *m*
►**latch onto** *vt insep Fam* (**a**) *(attach oneself to)* **to l. onto sb/sth** s'accrocher à qn/qch (**b**) *(understand)* **to l. onto sth** piger qch
latchkey ['lætʃkiː] *(pl* **latchkeys**) *n* clef *f* de la porte d'entrée; **l. child** = enfant dont les parents travaillent et qui doit rentrer seul après l'école
late [leɪt] **1** *adj* (**a**) *(not on time)* en retard; **to be l. (for sth)** être en retard (pour qch); **to be ten minutes l.** avoir dix minutes de retard (**b**) *(far on in time)* tard; **it's getting l.** il se fait tard; **to keep l. hours** se coucher tard; **in the l. afternoon** en fin d'après-midi; **in l. summer** vers la fin de l'été; **to be in one's l. thirties** approcher de la quarantaine; **in the l. eighties** vers la fin des années 80; *Fig* **it's a bit l. in the day to...** il est un peu tard pour...; **l. booking** réservation *f* de dernière minute (**c**) *(dead)* feu(e); **my l. husband** feu mon mari
2 *adv* (**a**) *(in general)* tard; **to work l.** travailler tard; **l. into the night** jusqu'à une heure avancée de la nuit; **l. in the year** vers la fin de l'année; **l. in life** sur le tard; *Prov* **better l. than never** mieux vaut tard que jamais (**b**) *(recently)* **as l. as last week** pas plus tard que la semaine dernière; **of l.** récemment
latecomer ['leɪtkʌmə(r)] *n* retardataire *mf*
lately ['leɪtlɪ] *adv* dernièrement, récemment; **until l.** jusqu'à ces derniers temps
lateness ['leɪtnɪs] *n (of person, train)* retard *m*; **the l. of the hour** l'heure *f* tardive
latent ['leɪtənt] *adj (disease, tendency)* latent(e); *(period)* de latence
later ['leɪtə(r)] **1** *adj* ultérieur(e); **I caught a l. train** j'ai pris un train qui partait plus tard; **l. events proved that...** la suite des événements a prouvé que...; **her l. novels** ses derniers romans; **in l. life** avec l'âge
2 *adv* **l. (on)** plus tard; **a few days l.** quelques jours plus tard; **no l. than tomorrow** demain au plus tard; **as we shall see l.** comme nous le verrons par la suite; *Fam* **see you l.!** à plus tard!
lateral ['lætərəl] *adj* latéral(e); **l. thinking** approche *f* originale
latest ['leɪtɪst] **1** *n* **at the l.** au plus tard; **the l. I can stay is four o'clock** je peux rester jusqu'à quatre heures au

plus tard; **have you heard the l.?** vous savez la dernière?
2 *adj (most recent)* dernier(ère)
latex ['leɪteks] *n* latex *m*
lathe [leɪð] *n* tour *m*
lather ['læðə(r)] **1** *n* mousse *f*; *Fam* **to work oneself or get into a l. (about sth)** se mettre dans tous ses états (à propos de qch)
2 *vt* savonner
Latin ['lætɪn] **1** *n* (**a**) *(person) (European)* Latin(e) *m,f*; *(Latin American)* Latino-Américain(e) *m,f* (**b**) *(language)* latin *m*
2 *adj* latin(e); **L. America** l'Amérique *f* latine; **L. American** latino-américain(e)
latitude ['lætɪtjuːd] *n also Fig* latitude *f*
latrine [lə'triːn] *n* latrines *fpl*
latte ['lætei] *n* café *m* au lait
latter ['lætə(r)] **1** *n (of two)* **the l.** le second (la seconde)
2 *adj* (**a**) *(of two)* second(e) (**b**) *(last)* dernier(ère); **the l. half or part of June** la deuxième moitié de juin
latter-day ['lætə'dei] *adj* moderne; *Rel* **the L. Saints** les mormons *mpl*
latterly ['lætəlɪ] *adv (recently)* dernièrement, récemment; *(towards the end of a period)* vers la fin
lattice ['lætɪs] *n* treillis *m*; **l. window** fenêtre *f* à croisillons de plomb
latticework ['lætɪswɜːk] *n* treillis *m*
Latvia ['lætvɪə] *n* la Lettonie
Latvian ['lætvɪən] **1** *n* (**a**) *(person)* Letton(onne) *m,f* (**b**) *(language)* letton *m*
2 *adj* letton(onne)
laudable ['lɔːdəbəl] *adj* louable, digne de louanges
laudanum ['lɔːdənəm] *n* laudanum *m*
laugh [lɑːf] **1** *n* rire *m*; *Fam* **to have a good l.** bien se marrer; *Fam* **to do sth for a l.** faire qch pour rire; *Ironic* **that's a l.!** la bonne blague!; *Fam* **he's a good l.** on se marre avec lui; **to have the last l.** être bien vengé(e)
2 *vi* rire (**at** de); **Fam don't make me l.!** laisse-moi rire!; *Fam* **to l. one's head off** être mort(e) de rire; *Fam* **if you get that job, you'll be laughing** si tu obtiens le poste, ça sera super; **he'll be laughing on the other side of his face when...** il rira jaune quand...; *Fam* **to l. all the way to the bank** s'en mettre plein les poches; *Prov* **he who laughs last laughs longest** rira bien qui rira le dernier
3 *vt* **to l. oneself silly** se tordre de rire; **you'll be laughed out of court** vous vous couvrirez de ridicule
►**laugh off** *vt sep* tourner en plaisanterie
laughable ['lɑːfəbəl] *adj* ridicule
laughing ['lɑːfɪŋ] **1** *n* rires *mpl*
2 *adj* rieur(euse); **it's no l. matter** ce n'est pas à prendre à la légère; **she was in no l. mood** elle n'était pas d'humeur à rire; **l. gas** gaz *m* hilarant; **l. stock** risée *f*; **to make sb a l. stock** faire de qn un sujet de plaisanterie
laughter ['lɑːftə(r)] *n* rires *mpl*
launch [lɔːntʃ] **1** *n* (**a**) *(boat)* chaloupe *f*; **(motor) l.** vedette *f* (**b**) *(of ship, rocket, product)* lancement *m*; **l. pad** plate-forme *f* de lancement
2 *vt (ship, rocket, product)* lancer; *(enquiry)* ouvrir; **to l. sb on a career** *(of event)* marquer le début de la carrière de qn
►**launch into** *vt insep (attack, story, complaint)* se lancer dans
launching ['lɔːntʃɪŋ] *n (of ship, rocket, product)* lancement *m*; *(of enquiry)* ouverture *f*; **l. pad** plate-forme *f* de lancement

launder ['lɔːndə(r)] *vt also Fig* blanchir
laundrette [lɔːn'dret], *Am* **Laundromat**®
['lɔːndrəʊmæt], *n* laverie *f* automatique
laundry ['lɔːndrɪ] *n* linge *m*; **to do the l.** faire la lessive;
l. basket panier *m* à linge
laurel ['lɒrəl] *n* laurier *m*; *Fig* **to rest on one's laurels**
se reposer sur ses lauriers; **l. wreath** couronne *f* de
lauriers
lava ['lɑːvə] *n* lave *f*
lavatory ['lævətrɪ] (*pl* **lavatories**) *n* toilettes *fpl*; **to go to
the l.** aller aux toilettes; **l. paper** papier *m* hygiénique
lavender ['lævɪndə(r)] **1** *n (shrub)* lavande *f*; **l. water**
(eau *f* de Cologne à la) lavande *f*
  2 *adj (colour)* bleu lavande *inv*
lavish ['lævɪʃ] **1** *adj* (**a**) *(person)* prodigue (**with**/**in**
de) (**b**) *(gift, meal, décor)* somptueux(euse); *(spending)* extravagant(e); *(portion)* généreux(euse)
  2 *vt* **to l. sth on sb** couvrir qn de qch
lavishly ['lævɪʃlɪ] *adv* somptueusement; **to spend l.**
dépenser sans compter; **to praise sb l.** couvrir qn
d'éloges
law [lɔː] *n* (**a**) *(rule)* loi *f*; **there's no l.** against it aucune
loi ne l'interdit; **the laws of gravity** les lois de la pesanteur; **to be a l.** unto oneself n'en faire qu'à sa tête
(**b**) *(set of rules)* loi *f*; **to be against the l.** être illé-
gal(e); **to break the l.** enfreindre la loi; **to be above
the l.** être au-dessus des lois; **to take the l. into one's
own hands** se faire justice soi-même; **l. and order**
l'ordre *m* public; **l. enforcement** le respect de la loi; **l.
firm** cabinet *m* d'avocats (**c**) *(system of justice, subject)*
droit *m*; **to practise l.** exercer une profession juridique;
l. school faculté *f* de droit; **l. student** étudiant(e) *m,f* en
droit (**d**) *Br Fam* **the l.** *(police)* les flics *mpl*
law-abiding ['lɔːəbaɪdɪŋ] *adj* respectueux(euse) des
lois
lawbreaker ['lɔːbreɪkə(r)] *n* personne *f* qui trans-
gresse la loi
lawcourt ['lɔːkɔːt] *n* cour *f* de justice
lawful ['lɔːfʊl] *adj (legal)* légal(e); *(rightful)* légitime
lawless ['lɔːlɪs] *adj (country, society)* livré(e) à
l'anarchie; *(mob)* sans foi ni loi
lawlessness ['lɔːlɪsnɪs] *n* anarchie *f*
lawmaker ['lɔːmeɪkə(r)] *n* législateur(trice) *m,f*
lawn [lɔːn] *n* pelouse *f*, gazon *m*; **l. tennis** tennis *m*
lawnmower ['lɔːnməʊə(r)] *n* tondeuse *f* (à gazon)
lawsuit ['lɔːsuːt] *n* action *f* en justice; **to bring a l.
against sb** intenter une action en justice contre qn
lawyer ['lɔːjə(r)] *n* avocat(e) *m,f*; *(for wills, conveyancing)*
notaire *m*; *(in company)* conseiller(ère) *m,f* juridique
lax [læks] *adj (discipline, principles, conduct)* relâ-
ché(e); *(person)* laxiste
laxative ['læksətɪv] **1** *n* laxatif *m*
  2 *adj* laxatif(ive)
laxity ['læksɪtɪ], **laxness** ['læksnɪs] *n (of discipline,
principles, conduct)* relâchement *m*; *(of person)* laxisme *m*
lay¹ [leɪ] *adj Rel* laïque; **l. preacher** prédicateur *m*
laïque
lay² (*pt & pp* **laid** [leɪd]) **1** *vt* (**a**) *(place)* mettre, poser;
to l. sb flat coucher *ou* étendre qn; **to l. sth flat** poser
ou coucher qch à plat; **to l. sb to rest** inhumer qn; **to
l. one's hands on sth** mettre la main sur qch; **she
reads everything she can l. her hands on** elle lit tout
ce qui lui tombe sous la main; **if you l. a finger on
her...** si tu touches à un seul cheveu de sa tête...; **to
have nowhere to l. one's head** n'avoir nulle part où
dormir; **to l. eyes on sb/sth** poser les yeux sur qn/

qch; **to l. emphasis on sth** insister sur qch; **to l. the
facts before sb** exposer les faits à qn; **to l. claim to
sth** prétendre à qch; **to l. the blame on sb** faire porter
la responsabilité à qn; **to l. sth bare** mettre qch à nu;
to l. oneself open to criticism s'exposer à la critique;
to l. sb's fears to rest apaiser les craintes de qn (**b**)
(foundations, carpet, trap) poser; *Br* **to l. the table**
mettre la table (**c**) *(egg)* pondre (**d**) **to l. a bet (on)**
parier (sur) (**e**) *very Fam* **to get laid** s'envoyer en l'air
  2 *vi (of bird)* pondre
  3 *pt of* **lie²**
▸ **lay aside** *vt sep* (**a**) *(money)* mettre de côté (**b**) *(pre-
judices, doubt)* oublier
▸ **lay by** *vt sep (money)* mettre de côté
▸ **lay down** *vt sep* (**a**) **to l. down one's arms** rendre *ou*
déposer les armes; **to l. down one's life** sacrifier sa
vie (**b**) *(principle, rule)* établir, poser; **to l. down the
law** dicter sa loi
▸ **lay in** *vt sep (supplies, food)* stocker
▸ **lay into** *vt insep Fam (physically)* rosser; *(verbally)* voler dans les plumes à
▸ **lay off 1** *vt sep (make redundant)* licencier; *(temporarily)* mettre en chômage technique
  2 *vt insep Fam* (**a**) *(abstain from)* arrêter; **to l. off
drink** arrêter de boire (**b**) *(leave alone)* ficher la paix
à
  3 *vi Fam (desist)* arrêter
▸ **lay on** *vt sep (food, drink)* fournir; *(party, entertainment)* organiser
▸ **lay out** *vt sep* (**a**) *(arrange, display)* arranger, disposer; *(dead body)* faire la toilette de (**b**) *(house, town)*
concevoir
layabout ['leɪəbaʊt] *n Fam* bon (bonne) *m,f* à rien
lay-by ['leɪbaɪ] (*pl* **lay-bys**) *n* aire *f* de stationnement
layer ['leɪə(r)] **1** *n* couche *f*
  2 *vt (hair)* dégrader; **to have one's hair layered**
faire faire un dégradé
layman ['leɪmən] *n Rel* laïque *mf*; *(non-specialist)* profane *mf*, non-initié(e) *m,f*
lay-off ['leɪɒf] *n* licenciement *m*; *(temporary)* mise *f* en
chômage technique
layout ['leɪaʊt] *n (of town)* plan *m*; *(of building)* agencement *m*; *(of text)* mise *f* en page
laywoman ['leɪwʊmən] *n Rel* laïque *f*; *(non-specialist)*
profane *f*, non-initiée *f*
laze [leɪz] *vi* **to l. (about** or **around)** paresser,
fainéanter
laziness ['leɪzɪnɪs] *n* paresse *f*, fainéantise *f*
lazy ['leɪzɪ] *adj (person)* paresseux(euse), fainéant(e);
(afternoon) passé(e) à ne rien faire
lazybones ['leɪzɪbəʊnz] (*pl* **lazybones**) *n Fam* flem-
mard(e) *m,f*
lb *(abbr* **pound**) livre *f*
LCD [elsiː'diː] *n (abbr* **liquid crystal display**) affichage
m à cristaux liquides
LDC [eldiː'siː] *n Econ (abbr* **less developed country**)
PVD *m*
LEA [eliː'eɪ] *n (abbr* **local education authority**) = organisme chargé de l'enseignement au niveau régional
lead¹ [led] *n* (**a**) *(metal)* plomb *m*; **l. poisoning** satur-
nisme *m* (**b**) *(for pencil)* mine *f* (**c**) *(idioms)* **to go
down like a l. balloon** tomber à plat; *Fam* **to fill sb
full of l.** truffer qn de plomb
lead² [liːd] *n* (**a**) *(advantage)* avance *f*; **to be in the l.**
être en tête; **to take** *or* **go into the l.** *(in race)* prendre
la tête; *(in match)* mener; **to have a 10-point l.** avoir 10
points d'avance; *Ind* **l. time** *(for production)* délai *m* de

production; *(for delivery)* délai *m* de livraison (**b**) *(example)* exemple *m*; **to give sb the l.** donner l'exemple à qn; **to follow sb's l.** suivre l'exemple de qn (**c**) *(clue)* indice *m* (**d**) *(in card game)* **it's your l.** à vous de jouer (**e**) *(in film, play)* premier rôle *m*, rôle *m* principal (**f**) *(for dog)* laisse *f* (**g**) *(cable)* câble *m ou* fil *m* (électrique)

2 *vt (pt & pp led* [led]) (**a**) *(guide)* mener, conduire; **you l. the way** montre-nous le chemin; **to l. the conversation away from a subject** détourner la conversation; **to be easily led** être très influençable; **that leads me to believe that...** cela m'amène à penser que... (**b**) **to l. a happy/sad life** mener une vie heureuse/triste (**c**) *(be leader of)* mener (**d**) *(be ahead of)* **to l. the field** mener; *Fig* **to l. the field in sth** être en tête dans le domaine de qch; **to l. sb by 8 points** avoir une avance de 8 points sur qn

3 *vi* (**a**) *(of road)* mener, conduire (**to** à) (**b**) **to l. to sth** *(cause)* mener à qch (**c**) *(in competition, race)* mener; *(in card game)* jouer le premier; **you l. and I'll follow** vas-y, je te suis

▸**lead away** *vt sep* emmener
▸**lead off** *vi* (**a**) *(road, corridor)* partir (**from** de) (**b**) *(in discussion)* commencer
▸**lead on** *vt sep (deceive)* tromper, duper
▸**lead up to** *vt insep (of person)* en venir à; *(of event)* précéder; **what are you leading up to?** où veux-tu en venir?

leaded ['ledɪd] *adj* **l. window** fenêtre *f* à croisillons de plomb; **l. petrol** essence *f* au plomb

leaden ['ledən] *adj (heavy)* lourd(e)

leader ['liːdə(r)] *n* (**a**) *(of group)* chef *m*; *Pol* chef *m*, leader *m*, dirigeant(e) *m,f*; *(of riot)* meneur(euse) *m,f*; *(in race)* premier(ère) *m,f*; **to be a born l.** être fait(e) pour commander (**b**) *(in newspaper)* éditorial *m*

leadership ['liːdəʃɪp] *n (people in charge)* dirigeants *mpl*; *(position)* direction *f*; *(quality)* qualités *fpl* d'encadrement; **she has good l. skills** elle a de grandes qualités de leader

lead-free [led'friː] *adj (petrol, paint)* sans plomb
lead-in ['liːdɪn] *n TV & Rad* introduction *f*
leading ['liːdɪŋ] *adj* (**a**) *(best, most important)* principal(e); **l. article** *(in newspaper)* éditorial *m*; **l. lady** *(in film, play)* premier rôle *m* féminin; *Fig* **l. light** personnalité *m* de premier plan; **l. man** *(in film, play)* premier rôle *f* masculin; **l. role** *(in film, play)* premier rôle *m* (**b**) *(team, runner)* de tête (**c**) **l. question** question *f* tendancieuse

leaf [liːf] *(pl leaves* [liːvz]) *n* (**a**) *(of plant)* feuille *f*; *(of book)* feuillet *m*; **to turn over a new l.** s'acheter une conduite; *Fig* **to take a l. out of sb's book** prendre exemple sur qn (**b**) *(of table) (inserted)* rallonge *f*; *(hinged)* battant *m*
▸**leaf through** *vt insep (book, magazine)* feuilleter

leaflet ['liːflɪt] **1** *n* prospectus *m*; *(political)* tract *m*; *(folded)* dépliant *m*
2 *vt (area)* distribuer des prospectus dans

leafy ['liːfɪ] *adj (tree)* feuillu(e); *(street)* ombragé(e); **a l. suburb** une banlieue verte

league [liːg] *n* ligue *f*; *(in sport)* championnat *m*; **to be in l. with sb** être de mèche avec qn; *Fig* **to be in a different l.** être hors classe; *Fig* **they're not in the same l.** ils ne sont pas du même niveau; **l. champions** vainqueurs *mpl* du championnat

leak [liːk] **1** *n also Fig* fuite *f*; *(in boat)* voie *f* d'eau; *Fam* **to take** *or* **have a l.** pisser un coup
2 *vt (information)* divulguer (**to** à); **the pipe was**

leaking gas/water du gaz/de l'eau fuyait du tuyau
3 *vi* fuir; *(of shoe)* prendre l'eau; *(of boat)* faire eau; **the roof is leaking** il y a une fuite dans le toit

leakage ['liːkɪdʒ] *n* fuite *f*
leaky ['liːkɪ] *adj (bucket, pipe, tap)* qui fuit; *(roof)* qui a une fuite; *(shoe)* qui prend l'eau; *(boat)* qui fait eau

lean¹ [liːn] *adj* (**a**) *(person, face)* mince; *(meat)* maigre (**b**) *(harvest)* maigre; *(year)* de vaches maigres

lean² *(pt & pp leant* [lent] *or* **leaned**) **1** *vt* **to l. sth on/against sth** appuyer qch sur/contre qch
2 *vi (of building)* pencher; **to l. on/against sth** s'appuyer sur/contre qch; *Fig* **to l. on sb** *(rely on)* s'appuyer sur qn; *(pressurize)* faire pression sur qn; **the Leaning Tower of Pisa** la tour de Pise; **to l. out of the window** se pencher à la fenêtre
▸**lean back** *vi* se pencher en arrière
▸**lean over 1** *vt insep* **to l. over sb/sth** se pencher par-dessus qn/qch
2 *vi* se pencher

leaning ['liːnɪŋ] *n (tendency)* inclination *f*, penchant *m* (**towards** pour); **to have artistic leanings** avoir des dispositions artistiques

leant [lent] *pt & pp of* **lean²**
lean-to ['liːntuː] *(pl lean-tos) n* appentis *m*
leap [liːp] **1** *n* saut *m*, bond *m*; *Fig* **to take a l. in the dark** faire un saut dans l'inconnu; *Fig* **to advance by leaps and bounds** avancer à pas de géant; **l. year** année *f* bissextile
2 *vt (pt & pp* **leapt** [lept] *or* **leaped**) franchir d'un bond *ou* d'un saut
3 *vi* sauter, bondir; **to l. to one's feet** se lever d'un bond; **to l. at the chance** sauter sur l'occasion; **to l. for joy** sauter de joie

leapfrog ['liːpfrɒg] **1** *n* saute-mouton *m*; **to play l.** jouer à saute-mouton
2 *vt (pt & pp* **leapfrogged**) *Fig* passer avant

leapt [lept] *pt & pp of* **leap**
learn [lɜːn] *(pt & pp* **learnt** [lɜːnt] *or* **learned**) **1** *vt* apprendre
2 *vi* apprendre; **to l. of** *or* **about sth** apprendre qch; **to l. from one's mistakes** tirer un enseignement de ses erreurs

learned ['lɜːnɪd] *adj* savant(e), érudit(e); *Br Law* **my l. friend** mon éminent confrère

learner ['lɜːnə(r)] *n (beginner)* débutant(e) *m,f*; *(student)* étudiant(e) *m,f*; **to be a quick/slow l.** apprendre vite/lentement; **l. (driver)** apprenti(e) *m,f* conducteur(trice)

learning ['lɜːnɪŋ] *n (act of learning)* apprentissage *m*; *(knowledge)* savoir *m*, connaissances *fpl*; **l. curve** courbe *f* d'assimilation; **it was a steep l. curve** l'apprentissage a été difficile

learnt [lɜːnt] *pt & pp of* **learn**
lease [liːs] **1** *n* bail *m*; *Fig* **to give sb a new l. of life** redonner à qn du goût à la vie; **to take on a new l. of life** *(of person)* renaître à la vie; *(of industry, town)* retrouver un nouveau souffle
2 *vt* louer (**from/to** à)

leasehold ['liːshəʊld] *n (contract)* bail *m*; *(property)* location *f* à bail
leaseholder ['liːshəʊldə(r)] *n* locataire *mf*
leash [liːʃ] *n (for dog)* laisse *f*; *Fig* **to keep sb on a tight l.** tenir la bride haute à qn
leasing ['liːsɪŋ] *n Com* location-vente *f*
least [liːst] **1** *n* **the l.** le moins; **..., to say the l.** le moins qu'on puisse dire, c'est que...; **it's the l. I can do** c'est la moindre des choses; **that's the l. of my worries** c'est

le cadet de mes soucis; **at l.** au moins; **he's leaving, at l. that's what I've heard** il part, du moins c'est ce que j'ai entendu dire; **at l. as old as...** au moins aussi vieux que...; **at the very l. they should pay your expenses** ce serait vraiment la moindre des choses qu'ils te remboursent tes frais; **not in the l.** pas du tout; **it doesn't matter in the l.** cela n'a pas la moindre importance
  2 *adj* (*superlative of* **little**) (*smallest*) moindre; **the l. thing annoys her** un rien l'agace
  3 *adv* **the l.** difficile le (la) moins difficile; **l. of all her** elle encore moins que les autres; **when I was l. expecting it** au moment où je m'y attendais le moins

leather ['leðə(r)] **1** *n* cuir *m*
  2 *vt Fam* (*beat*) tanner le cuir à

leather-bound ['leðəbaʊnd] *adj* (*book*) relié(e) en cuir

leathery ['leðərɪ] *adj* (*face, skin*) tanné(e); (*meat*) coriace

leave [liːv] **1** *n* (**a**) (*permission*) permission *f*, autorisation *f*; **to ask l. to do sth** demander la permission *ou* l'autorisation de faire qch; **to grant** *or* **give sb l. to do sth** accorder *ou* donner à qn l'autorisation de faire qch (**b**) (*holiday*) congé *m*; **to be on l.** (*from work*) être en congé; (*from army*) être en permission; **l. of absence** (*from work*) congé *m* exceptionnel; (*from army*) permission *f* exceptionnelle (**c**) (*farewell*) **to take one's l.** (*of sb*) prendre congé (de qn); **to take l. of one's senses** perdre l'esprit
  2 *vt* (*pt & pp* **left** [left]) (**a**) (*depart from*) quitter; **to l. the table** se lever de table; **the car left the road** la voiture a quitté la route (**b**) (*put, deposit*) **to l. sth somewhere** (*on purpose*) laisser qch quelque part; (*accidentally*) oublier qch quelque part; **take it or l. it** (*of offer*) c'est à prendre ou à laisser; **to l. a message for sb** laisser un message pour qn (**c**) (*allow to remain*) laisser; **to l. the door open** laisser la porte ouverte; **to l. oneself open to criticism** laisser la porte ouverte aux critiques; **to l. sth unfinished** laisser qch inachevé(e); **to l. sb to do sth** laisser qn faire qch; **l. it to me** laisse-moi faire; **to l. much** *or* **a lot to be desired** laisser beaucoup à désirer; **let's l. it at that** restons-en là; **to l. well alone** ne pas s'en mêler; **l. me alone!** fiche-moi la paix! (**d**) (*bequeath*) laisser (**to** à); **he leaves a wife and three children** (*after dying*) il laisse une femme et trois enfants (**e**) **to be left** (*remain*) rester; **there are a few chocolates left** il reste quelques chocolats; **three from seven leaves four** sept moins trois égale quatre
  3 *vi* (*depart*) partir

▸**leave behind** *vt sep* **to l. sth behind** (*on purpose*) laisser qch; (*accidentally*) oublier qch; **to l. sb behind** partir sans qn

▸**leave off 1** *vt insep Fam* **to l. off doing sth** arrêter de faire qch; **to l. off work** cesser le travail
  2 *vi* s'arrêter

▸**leave on** *vt sep* (*light, TV*) laisser allumé(e)

▸**leave out** *vt sep* (**a**) (*omit*) omettre (**b**) (*not involve*) **to l. sb out of sth** laisser qn en dehors de qch; **to feel left out** se sentir exclu(e) (**c**) (*leave ready, available*) **I'll l. your dinner out on the table for you** je laisserai ton dîner sur la table; **l. the disks out where I can see them** laisse les disquettes en évidence (**d**) (*leave outside*) laisser dehors; **who left the milk out?** qui a oublié de mettre le lait au frigo? (**e**) *Br Fam* **l. it out!** (*stop it*) arrête!

▸**leave over** *vt sep* **to be left over** (*of food, money*) rester; **there's some lasagne left over** il reste des lasagnes

leaven ['levən] *n* levain *m*

leaves [liːvz] *pl of* **leaf**

leave-taking ['liːvteɪkɪŋ] *n* adieux *mpl*

Lebanese [lebə'niːz] **1** *npl* (*people*) **the L.** les Libanais *mpl*
  2 *n* (*pl* **Lebanese**) (*person*) Libanais(e) *m,f*
  3 *adj* libanais(e)

Lebanon ['lebənən] *n* le Liban

lecher ['letʃə(r)] *n* obsédé *m*

lecherous ['letʃərəs] *adj* lubrique

lechery ['letʃərɪ] *n* lubricité *f*

lectern ['lektən] *n* lutrin *m*

lecture ['lektʃə(r)] **1** *n* (**a**) (*talk*) conférence *f*; (*at university*) cours *m* magistral; **l. theatre** amphithéâtre *m* (**b**) *Fam* (*reprimand*) sermon *m*; **to give sb a l.** faire la morale à qn
  2 *vt Fam* (*reprimand*) faire la morale à
  3 *vi* (*give public speeches*) donner une conférence/des conférences; (*at university*) donner un cours magistral/des cours magistraux

lecturer ['lektʃərə(r)] *n Univ* enseignant(e) *m,f* (*d'université*)

LED [eliː'diː] *n Elec* (*abbr* **light-emitting diode**) LED *f*

led [led] *pt & pp of* **lead²**

ledge [ledʒ] *n* (*on cliff*) corniche *f*; (*of window, on building*) rebord *m*

ledger ['ledʒə(r)] *n* grand livre *m*

leech [liːtʃ] *n also Fig* sangsue *f*; **to cling to sb like a l.** se cramponner à qn comme une sangsue

leek [liːk] *n* poireau *m*

leer [lɪə(r)] **1** *n* (*lustful*) regard *m* lubrique; (*cruel*) regard *m* sadique
  2 *vi* **to l. at sb** (*lustfully*) regarder qn d'un air lubrique; (*cruelly*) regarder qn d'un air sadique

lees [liːz] *npl* (*of wine*) lie *f*

leeward ['liːwəd] **1** *n* côté *m* sous le vent
  2 *adj* sous le vent; **the L. Islands** les îles *fpl* Sous-le-Vent

leeway ['liːweɪ] *n* marge *f* de manœuvre

left¹ [left] **1** *n* gauche *f*; **on** *or* **to the l.** à gauche; **on my l.** à ma gauche
  2 *adj* gauche; **the l. wing** (*of party*) l'aile *f* gauche
  3 *adv* à gauche

left² *pt & pp of* **leave**

left-field ['left'fiːld] *adj Am Fam* (*bizarre*) bizarroïde

left-hand ['left'hænd] *adj* de gauche; (*corner, side*) gauche; **l. drive** conduite *f* à gauche; **on the l. side** à gauche

left-handed [left'hændɪd] **1** *adj* gaucher(ère)
  2 *adv* de la main gauche

left-hander [left'hændə(r)] *n* (*person*) gaucher(ère) *m,f*

left luggage (office) ['left'lʌgɪdʒ('ɒfɪs)] *n Br* consigne *f*

leftover ['leftəʊvə(r)] **1** *adj* **l. food/paint** un reste de nourriture/de peinture
  2 *n* **leftovers** restes *mpl*

left-wing ['leftwɪŋ] *adj* de gauche

left-winger ['left'wɪŋə(r)] *n* homme (femme) *m,f* de gauche

leg [leg] **1** *n* (**a**) (*of person, trousers*) jambe *f*; (*of animal*) patte *f*; (*of table, chair*) pied *m* (**b**) *Culin* (*of lamb*) gigot *m*; (*of chicken*) cuisse *f*; (*of pork*) rôti *m* (**c**) (*of journey, race*) étape *f* (**d**) (*idioms*) **to pull sb's l.** faire

marcher qn; **to show a l.** se lever; **to shake a l.** se remuer; **you don't have a l.** to **stand on** tu n'as rien sur quoi t'appuyer; **to give sb a l. up** donner un coup de pouce à qn; *very Fam* **to get one's l. over** s'envoyer en l'air
2 *vt* (*pt & pp* **legged**) *Fam* **to l. it** jouer des gambettes
legacy ['legəsɪ] (*pl* **legacies**) *n also Fig* legs *m*; **to come into a l.** faire un héritage
legal ['li:gəl] *adj* légal(e); **to take l. action (against sb)** intenter une action (contre qn); **to take l. advice** consulter un avocat; **l. aid** aide *f* juridique; *Am* **l. holiday** jour *m* férié; **the l. profession** les professions *fpl* juridiques; **to be l. tender** avoir cours (légal)
legality [lɪ'gælɪtɪ] *n* légalité *f*
legalization [li:gəlaɪ'zeɪʃən] *n* légalisation *f*
legalize ['li:gəlaɪz] *vt* légaliser
legally ['li:gəlɪ] *adv* légalement
legate ['legɪt] *n Rel* légat *m*
legation [lɪ'geɪʃən] *n* légation *f*
legend ['ledʒənd] *n* légende *f*; **to be a l. in one's own lifetime** être une légende vivante
legendary ['ledʒəndərɪ] *adj* légendaire
leggings ['legɪŋz] *npl* (*of woman*) caleçon *m*; (*of cowboy*) jambières *fpl*
leggy ['legɪ] *adj* (*person*) tout en jambes
legible ['ledʒɪbəl] *adj* lisible
legion ['li:dʒən] *n* légion *f*
legionary ['li:dʒənərɪ] (*pl* **legionaries**) *n* légionnaire *m*
legionnaire [li:dʒə'neə(r)] *n* légionnaire *m*; **l.'s disease** maladie *f* du légionnaire
legislate ['ledʒɪsleɪt] *vi* légiférer (**against** contre)
legislation [ledʒɪs'leɪʃən] *n* (*laws*) législation *f*; (*action*) élaboration *f* des lois
legislative ['ledʒɪslətɪv] *adj* législatif(ive)
legislator ['ledʒɪsleɪtə(r)] *n* législateur(trice) *m,f*
legislature ['ledʒɪslətʃə(r)] *n* corps *m* législatif
legitimacy [lɪ'dʒɪtɪməsɪ] *n* légitimité *f*
legitimate 1 *adj* [lɪ'dʒɪtɪmət] légitime
2 *vt* [lɪ'dʒɪtɪmeɪt] légitimer
legitimately [lɪ'dʒɪtɪmətlɪ] *adv* légitimement
legless ['leglɪs] *adj Br Fam* (*drunk*) complètement bourré(e)
legroom ['legrʊm] *n* place *f* pour les jambes
legume ['legju:m] *n Bot* légumineuse *f*
legwarmers ['legwɔ:məz] *npl* jambières *fpl*
leisure ['leʒə(r), *Am* 'li:ʒər] *n* loisirs *mpl*; **to do sth at one's l.** faire qch à son rythme; **a life of l.** une vie de loisirs; **l. activities** activités *fpl* de loisirs; **l. centre** centre *m* de loisirs; **l. club** club *m* de loisirs; **l. industry** industrie *f* des loisirs; **l. time** temps *m* libre
leisurely ['leʒəlɪ, *Am* 'li:ʒərlɪ] *adj* (*weekend*) relax *inv*; **at a l. pace** sans se presser; **to make l. progress** avancer à son rythme; **to go for a l. stroll** se promener tranquillement
lemming ['lemɪŋ] *n* lemming *m*; **to follow sb like lemmings** suivre qn comme des moutons
lemon ['lemən] **1** *n* (*fruit, colour*) citron *m*; *Fam* **I felt like a real l.** j'ai vraiment eu l'air malin; **l. curd** = pâte à tartiner au citron; **l. sole** limande-sole *f*; **l. squeezer** presse-citron *m*; **l. tea** thé *m* au citron; **l. tree** citronnier *m*
2 *adj* **l. (coloured)** jaune citron *inv*
lemonade [lemə'neɪd] *n* (*carbonated*) limonade *f*; (*freshly squeezed*) citronnade *f*
lemur ['li:mə(r)] *n* maki *m*

lend [lend] (*pt & pp* **lent** [lent]) *vt* (*money, book, pen*) prêter; (*support*) apporter (**to** à); **to l. credibility to sth** rendre qch crédible; **to l. sb a (helping) hand** donner un coup de main à qn; **to l. an ear** *or* **one's ear to...** prêter l'oreille à...; **her work doesn't l. itself to dramatization** son œuvre ne se prête pas à une adaptation théâtrale
lender ['lendə(r)] *n* prêteur(euse) *m,f*
lending ['lendɪŋ] *n* prêt *m*; **l. library** bibliothèque *f* de prêt; **l. rate** taux *m* (*d'un prêt*)
length [leŋθ] *n* (**a**) (*in space*) longueur *f*; **it's 4.50 m in l.** ça fait 4,50 m de long; **the l. and breadth of the country** dans tout le pays (**b**) (*in time*) durée *f*; **at (great) l.** longuement; **a great l. of time** longtemps; **l. of service** ancienneté *f* (**c**) **to go to the l. of doing sth** aller jusqu'à faire qch; **to go to great lengths to do sth** se donner beaucoup de mal pour faire qch; **he would go to any lengths (to do sth)** il ne reculerait devant rien (pour faire qch) (**d**) (*of wood, string*) morceau *m*
lengthen ['leŋθən] **1** *vt* allonger, rallonger
2 *vi* (*of days*) allonger, rallonger; (*of shadows*) s'allonger
lengthily ['leŋθɪlɪ] *adv* longuement
lengthways ['leŋθweɪz], **lengthwise** ['leŋθwaɪz] *adv* dans le sens de la longueur
lengthy ['leŋθɪ] *adj* long (longue)
lenient ['li:nɪənt] *adj* indulgent(e)
Leningrad ['lenɪngræd] *n Formerly* Leningrad
lens [lenz] (*pl* **lenses**) *n* (*of spectacles*) verre *m*; (*of camera*) objectif *m*; (*of eye*) cristallin *m*; (**contact**) **l.** lentille *f* (de contact); **l. cap** capuchon *m* d'objectif
Lent [lent] *n Rel* carême *m*; **to keep L.** faire carême
lent [lent] *pt & pp of* **lend**
lentil ['lentɪl] *n* lentille *f*
Leo ['li:əʊ] (*pl* **Leos**) *n* (*sign of zodiac*) le Lion; **to be (a) L.** être (du) Lion
leopard ['lepəd] *n* léopard *m*
leotard ['li:ətɑ:d] *n* justaucorps *m*
leper ['lepə(r)] *n* lépreux(euse) *m,f*; **l. colony** léproserie *f*
leprechaun ['leprəkɔ:n] *n* lutin *m*, farfadet *m*
leprosy ['leprəsɪ] *n* lèpre *f*; **to have l.** avoir la lèpre
lesbian ['lezbɪən] **1** *n* lesbienne *f*
2 *adj* lesbien(enne)
lesion ['li:ʒən] *n* lésion *f*
Lesotho [lɪ'su:tu:] *n* le Lesotho
less [les] **1** *adj* (*comparative of* **little**) moins de; **it's l. than a week's work** cela représente moins d'une semaine de travail; **the distance is l. than I thought** c'est moins loin que je ne pensais
2 *prep* moins; **a year l. two days** un an moins deux jours; **I've got £50, l. what I spent on the train ticket** j'ai 50 livres, moins ce que j'ai dépensé pour le billet de train
3 *pron* moins; **I don't think any (the) l. of you** tu n'as pas baissé dans mon estime; **I see l. of her nowadays** je la vois moins ces temps-ci; **in l. than an hour** en moins d'une heure; **the l. said about it the better** moins on en parle mieux c'est; *Fam* **l. of that!** ça suffit!
4 *adv* moins; **l. and l.** de moins en moins; **no more, no l.** ni plus ni moins; **still l., even l.** encore moins; **nothing l. than total obedience** rien moins qu'une obéissance totale; **she was driving a Rolls, no l.!** elle conduisait une Rolls-Royce®, rien que ça!; **I expected no l. from you** je n'en attendais pas moins

de vous; **they haven't got a fridge, much l.** a freezer ils n'ont pas de réfrigérateur et encore moins de congélateur

lessen ['lesən] **1** *vt (importance, cost)* diminuer, réduire; *(noise)* atténuer; *(enthusiasm, pain)* calmer **2** *vi (of pain, anger)* se calmer; *(of noise)* s'atténuer

lesser ['lesə(r)] *adj (in size)* plus petit(e); *(in importance)* moindre; **the l. of two evils** un moindre mal; **to a l. extent** *or* **degree** dans une moindre mesure

lesson ['lesən] *n* leçon *f*; **to give English lessons** donner des cours d'anglais; *Fig* **he has learnt his l.** ça lui a servi de leçon; *Fig* **to teach sb a l.** *(of person)* donner une bonne leçon à qn; *(of event, experience)* servir de leçon à qn

lest [lest] *conj Formal* de peur *ou* de crainte que + *subjunctive*; **l. we forget** *(on war memorial)* pour ne pas oublier

let¹ [let] *n (in tennis)* let *m*

let² **1** *n (of property)* location *f*; **short/long l.** location *f* de courte/longue durée **2** *vt (pt & pp* **let)** *(rent out)* louer; **(house) to l.** (maison) à louer

let³ *(pt & pp* **let)** *vt* (**a**) *(allow)* **to l. sb do sth** laisser qn faire qch, permettre à qn de faire qch; **l. me see** voyons un peu; *(show me)* fais(-moi) voir; **to l. sb know sth** faire savoir qch à qn; **to l. sth pass** laisser passer qch; **to l. sth go** lâcher qch; **to l. oneself go** se laisser aller; **to l. sb go** laisser partir qn; *(make redundant)* se séparer de qn; **don't l. it get you down/get to you** ne te laisse pas abattre/affecter par ça; **don't l. me see you here again!** que je ne vous retrouve plus ici!; **can you l. me have it back tomorrow?** pouvez-vous me le rendre demain?; *Math* **l. AB be equal to CD** soit AB égal à CD (**b**) *(with suggestions)* **l.'s go!** allons-y!; **l.'s hurry!** dépêchons-nous!; **l.'s not have an argument about it!** on ne va pas se disputer pour ça!; **now, don't l.'s have any nonsense!** allons, pas de bêtises!

▶**let by** *vt sep (allow to pass)* laisser passer

▶**let down** *vt sep* (**a**) *(hem)* rallonger; *(tyre)* dégonfler; *Fig* **to l. one's hair down** se défouler (**b**) *Fam (disappoint, fail)* décevoir; **the car l. us down again** la voiture nous a encore lâchés

▶**let in** *vt sep* (**a**) *(allow to enter)* laisser entrer; **to l. oneself in** *(to house)* entrer; **to l. in the light** laisser entrer *ou* passer la lumière; (**b**) **to l. in water** *(of shoes)* prendre l'eau (**c**) **to l. sb in on a plan** mettre qn au courant d'un projet; **to l. sb in on a secret** mettre qn dans le secret (**c**) *Fam* **to l. oneself in for a hard time** aller au-devant de grandes difficultés; **what are you letting yourself in for?** est-ce que tu sais à quoi tu t'exposes?

▶**let into** *vt sep* **to l. sb into the house** faire entrer qn; **to l. sb into a secret** mettre qn dans le secret

▶**let off** *vt sep* (**a**) *(bomb)* lâcher; *(firework)* tirer; *Fig* **to l. off steam** se défouler (**b**) *(excuse)* ne pas sanctionner; **I'll l. you off this time** ça va pour cette fois; **they l. him off with a fine** ils s'en sont tiré avec une amende

▶**let on** *vt sep Fam* (**a**) *(tell)* dire; **don't l. on that I was there** n'allez pas dire que j'y étais (**b**) *(claim)* prétendre; **he wasn't as ill as he l. on** il n'était pas aussi malade qu'il le prétendait

▶**let out** *vt sep* (**a**) *(release)* *(person)* laisser sortir; *(prisoner)* libérer; *(air, yell)* laisser échapper; *(secret)* divulguer (**b**) *(jacket, trousers)* élargir (**c**) *(rent out)* louer

▶**let up** *vi (lessen)* diminuer; *(stop)* cesser; **once he's started, he never lets up** une fois lancé, il ne s'arrête plus

let-down ['letdaʊn] *n Fam* déception *f*

lethal ['li:θəl] *adj* mortel(elle); *Fam* **that vodka's l.!** elle est mortelle, cette vodka!; **l. dose** dose *f* létale *ou* mortelle; **l. weapon** arme *f* meurtrière

lethargic [lɪ'θɑ:dʒɪk] *adj* mou (molle)

lethargy ['leθədʒɪ] *n* mollesse *f*

let-out ['letaʊt] *n Fam (from obligation)* excuse *f*, prétexte *m*

letter ['letə(r)] *n* lettre *f*; **the l. of the law** la lettre de la loi; **to do sth to the l.** faire qch à la lettre; **to publish a writer's letters** publier la correspondance d'un écrivain; *Com* **l. of credit/exchange** lettre *f* de crédit/de change; **l. of acknowledgement** accusé *m* de réception; **l. bomb** lettre *f* piégée; **l. box** boîte *f* aux lettres; **l. opener** coupe-papier *m inv*

letterhead ['letəhed] *n* en-tête *m*; *(paper)* papier *m* à en-tête

lettuce ['letɪs] *n* salade *f* (verte)

let-up ['letʌp] *n Fam (in conflict)* trêve *f*; *(in weather)* accalmie *f*; *(in pressure)* relâchement *m*; **to work fifteen hours without a l.** travailler quinze heures sans répit

leukaemia, *Am* **leukemia** [lu:'ki:mɪə] *n* leucémie *f*

level ['levəl] **1** *n* niveau *m*; **at eye l.** à (la) hauteur des yeux; **to be on a l. with sb** être sur un pied d'égalité avec qn; *Fam* **on the l.** régulier(ère); **to come down to sb's l.** se mettre à la portée de qn; **to sink to sb's l.** tomber au niveau de qn; **at ministerial/international l.** à l'échelon ministériel/international **2** *adj* (**a**) *(not sloping)* plat(e); *Fig* **a l. playing field** une situation qui ne défavorise personne (**b**) **to be l. with sb/sth** *(physically)* être au niveau de qn/qch; *(in race, ability, progress)* être au même niveau que qn/qch; **to draw l. with** *(in race, match)* rattraper; **to do one's l. best** faire tout son possible; **l. crossing** passage *m* à niveau; **l. pegging** à égalité; **l. spoonful** cuillerée *f* rase (**c**) *(voice, tone)* égal(e); **to keep a l. head** garder son sang-froid **3** *vt (pt & pp* **levelled,** *Am* **leveled)** (**a**) *(make level)* niveler, égaliser; *(building)* raser (**b**) *(aim)* (blow) porter (**at** à); *(criticism)* adresser (**at** à); *(accusation)* porter (**at** contre) **4** *vi Fam* **to l. with sb** parler franchement à qn

▶**level off, level out** *vi (of ground)* s'aplanir; *(of prices, demand)* se stabiliser; *(of aircraft)* se redresser

level-headed ['levəl'hedɪd] *adj* pondéré(e)

lever ['li:və(r),* Am* 'levə(r)] **1** *n also Fig* levier *m* **2** *vt* **to l. sth open** ouvrir qch au moyen d'un levier

leverage ['li:vərɪdʒ] *n (power)* effet *m* de levier; *Fig (influence)* pression *f*

leveraged buyout ['li:vərɪdʒd'baɪaʊt] *n Fin* OPA *f* à crédit

levitate ['levɪteɪt] *vi* léviter

levitation [levɪ'teɪʃən] *n* lévitation *f*

levity ['levɪtɪ] *n* légèreté *f*

levy ['levɪ] **1** *n (pl* **levies)** taxe *f* (**on** sur) **2** *vt (pt & pp* **levied)** lever, percevoir (**on** sur)

lewd [lu:d] *adj* obscène

lexical ['leksɪkəl] *adj* lexical(e)

lexicographer [leksɪ'kɒgrəfə(r)] *n* lexicographe *mf*

liability [laɪə'bɪlɪtɪ] *n (pl* **liabilities)** (**a**) *Law (responsibility)* responsabilité *f* (**for** de); *Fin* **liabilities** passif *m* (**b**) *(disadvantage)* handicap *m* (**to** pour)

liable ['laɪəbəl] *adj* (**a**) *Law (responsible)* responsable (**for** de) (**b**) *(to tax)* assujetti(e) (**to** à); *(to fine)* passible (**to** de) (**c**) *(likely)* **to be l. to do sth** risquer de faire qch

liaise [li:'eɪz] *vi* to l. with sb *(be in contact with)* assurer la liaison avec qn; *(work together with)* collaborer avec qn

liaison [lɪ'eɪzɒn] *n* (**a**) *(contact)* liaison *f*; *(co-operation)* collaboration *f*; *Mil* **l. officer** officier *m* de liaison (**b**) *(love affair)* liaison *f*

liar ['laɪə(r)] *n* menteur(euse) *m,f*

Lib Dem [lɪb'dem] *Br Pol* **1** *n* = membre du parti libéral démocrate
   2 *adj* libéral(e) démocrat(e)

libel ['laɪbəl] *Law* **1** *n* diffamation *f*; **l. action** procès *m* en diffamation; **l. laws** lois *fpl* contre la diffamation
   2 *vt* (*pt & pp* **libelled,** *Am* **libeled**) diffamer (par écrit)

libellous, *Am* **libelous** ['laɪbələs] *adj* diffamatoire

liberal ['lɪbərəl] **1** *n Pol* **L.** libéral(e) *m,f*
   2 *adj* (**a**) *(tolerant)* libéral(e) (**b**) *(generous, abundant)* généreux(euse); **to be l. with one's praise/advice** ne pas être avare de compliments/de conseils (**c**) *Pol* **L.** libéral(e); *Br* **the L. Democrats** parti *m* libéral démocrate *(parti politique britannique de tendance centriste)*

liberalism ['lɪbərəlɪzəm] *n* libéralisme *m*

liberalize ['lɪbərəlaɪz] *vt* libéraliser; *(law)* assouplir

liberally ['lɪbərəlɪ] *adv* libéralement, généreusement

liberate ['lɪbəreɪt] *vt* libérer

liberated ['lɪbəreɪtɪd] *adj (person)* libéré(e); *(views, ideas)* progressiste

liberating ['lɪbəreɪtɪŋ] *adj* libérateur(trice)

liberation [lɪbə'reɪʃən] *n* libération *f*; **l. movement** mouvement *m* de libération

liberator ['lɪbəreɪtə(r)] *n* libérateur(trice) *m,f*

Liberia [laɪ'bɪərɪə] *n* le Liberia

Liberian [laɪ'bɪərɪən] **1** *n* Libérien(enne) *m,f*
   2 *adj* libérien(enne)

libertarian [lɪbə'teərɪən] **1** *n* libertaire *mf*
   2 *adj* libertaire

liberty ['lɪbətɪ] *(pl* **liberties)** *n* liberté *f*; **at l.** en liberté; **to be at l. to do sth** être libre de faire qch; **to take the l. of doing sth** prendre la liberté de faire qch; **to take liberties with sb/sth** prendre des libertés avec qn/qch; *Fam* **what a l.!** quel culot!

libido [lɪ'bi:dəʊ] *n* libido *f*

Libra ['li:brə] *n (sign of zodiac)* la Balance; **to be (a) L.** être (de la) Balance

librarian [laɪ'breərɪən] *n* bibliothécaire *mf*

library ['laɪbrərɪ] *(pl* **libraries)** *n* bibliothèque *f*; **l. book** livre *m* de bibliothèque; **l. card** carte *f* de bibliothèque

libretto [lɪ'bretəʊ] *(pl* **librettos** *or* **libretti** [lɪ'breti:]) *n Mus* livret *m*

Libya ['lɪbɪə] *n* la Libye

Libyan ['lɪbɪən] **1** *n* Libyen(enne) *m,f*
   2 *adj* libyen(enne)

lice [laɪs] *pl of* **louse**

licence, *Am* **license¹** ['laɪsəns] *n* (**a**) *(permit)* permis *m*; *(for trade, bar)* licence *f*; *Com* **under l.** sous licence; **(driving) l.** permis *m* de conduire; **(TV) l.** redevance *f* (télé); *Br* **l. fee** redevance *f* télévisuelle; **l. number** *(of car)* numéro *m* d'immatriculation; **l. plate** plaque *f* d'immatriculation (**b**) *(freedom)* liberté *f*; *(excessive freedom)* licence *f*

license² *vt Com* accorder une licence à; **to be licensed to carry a gun** avoir un permis de port d'armes

licensed ['laɪsənst] *adj* **l. premises** débit *m* de boissons; **l. restaurant** = restaurant possédant une licence de débit de boissons

licensing ['laɪsənsɪŋ] *n* **l. hours** *(of pub)* heures *fpl* d'ouverture; **l. laws** lois *fpl* relatives aux débits de boissons

Licensing hours

Traditionnellement, les heures d'ouverture des pubs répondent à une réglementation très stricte (liée à la législation sur la vente des boissons alcoolisées), mais celle-ci a été assouplie en 1988. Les pubs d'Angleterre et du pays de Galles peuvent désormais rester ouverts de 11h à 23h. En Écosse, en revanche, la réglementation est moins stricte et les pubs qui en font la demande peuvent rester ouverts beaucoup plus tard certains soirs. Depuis 2005, les pubs d'Angleterre et du pays de Galles ont également la possibilité de faire une demande de licence spéciale les autorisant à ouvrir 24 heures sur 24 mais peu d'établissements se sont montrés intéressés.

licentious [laɪ'senʃəs] *adj* licencieux(euse)

lichen ['laɪkən] *n* lichen *m*

lick [lɪk] **1** *n* (**a**) *(with tongue)* coup *m* de langue; *Fam* **a l. of paint** un petit coup de peinture (**b**) *Fam* **at a great l.,** **at full l.** à toute allure
   2 *vt* (**a**) *(with tongue)* lécher; **to l. one's lips** se lécher les lèvres; *Fig* se (pour)lécher les babines; *Fig* **to l. one's wounds** panser ses blessures; *Fam Fig* **to l. sb's boots** lécher les bottes à qn; *Vulg* **to l. sb's arse** faire du lèche-cul à qn; *Fam* **to l. sb into shape** dresser qn (**b**) *Fam (defeat)* mettre une raclée à

licorice = **liquorice**

lid [lɪd] *n* (**a**) *(of pot, jar)* couvercle *m* (**b**) *(idioms)* **to take the l. off sth** exposer qch au grand jour; **to keep the l. on sth** étouffer qch

lie¹ [laɪ] **1** *n* mensonge *m*; **to tell a l.** dire un mensonge; **to give the l. to sth** démentir qch; **l. detector** détecteur *m* de mensonges
   2 *vi* mentir; **to l. through one's teeth** mentir effrontément

lie² **1** *n* **to find out the l. of the land** *(in politics, business)* tâter le terrain
   2 *vi (pt* **lay** [leɪ], *pp* **lain** [leɪn]) (**a**) *(of person, animal)* *(be in a lying position)* être couché(e) *ou* allongé(e); *(get down)* se coucher, s'allonger; **here lies...** *(on gravestone)* ci-gît...; **to l. in bed** rester au lit; **I lay awake all night** je n'ai pas dormi de la nuit; *Fig* **to l. low** garder un profil bas; *Fig* **to l. in wait for sb** guetter l'arrivée de qn (**b**) *(of object)* être, se trouver; **snow lay on the hills** il y avait de la neige sur les collines; **to l. in ruins** *(of building)* être en ruines; *(of career, hopes)* être détruit(e) (**c**) *(of abstract thing)* **the responsibility lies with the author** la responsabilité incombe à l'auteur; **to know where one's interests l.** savoir où se trouve son intérêt; **the difference lies in that...** la différence réside dans le fait que...; **a brilliant future lies before her** un brillant avenir s'ouvre devant elle; **what lies behind this uncharacteristic generosity?** que cache cette générosité inhabituelle?

▸**lie about, lie around** *vi* traîner

▸**lie back** *vi* s'allonger

▸**lie down** *vi* se coucher, s'étendre; *Fig* **to take criticism/an insult lying down** se laisser critiquer/insulter sans réagir; **I'm not going to take this lying down** je ne vais pas me laisser faire

▸**lie in** *vi* faire la grasse matinée

Liechtenstein ['lɪktenstaɪn] *n* le Liechtenstein
lie-down ['laɪ'daʊn] *n* **to have a l.** faire une sieste
lie-in ['laɪ'ɪn] *n* **to have a l.** faire la grasse matinée
lieu [lju:, lu:] *n in* **l.** à la place; **in l. of** au lieu de
lieutenant [*Br* lef'tenənt, *Am* lu:'tenənt] *n Mil* lieutenant *m*; *Naut* lieutenant *m* de vaisseau; *Am (police officer)* inspecteur *m* de police; *Fig (helper)* lieutenant *m*; **l. colonel** lieutenant-colonel *m*
life [laɪf] (*pl* **lives** [laɪvz]) *n* (**a**) *(existence)* vie *f*; **to take sb's l.** tuer qn; **to take one's own l.** se suicider; **to bring sb back to l.** ramener qn à la vie; **a matter of l. and death** une question de vie ou de mort; **l. after death** la vie après la mort; **to risk one's l., to risk l. and limb** risquer sa vie *ou* sa peau; **to escape with one's l.** avoir la vie sauve; **to lose one's l.** perdre la vie; **no lives were lost** on ne déplore aucune victime; **he held on to the rope for dear l.** il s'accrochait au cordage avec l'énergie du désespoir; **run for your lives!** sauve qui peut!; *Fam* **not on your l.!** jamais de la vie!; *Fam* **l couldn't for the l. of me remember** je n'arrivais absolument pas à me rappeler; **from l.** *(to draw, paint)* d'après nature; **bird l.** oiseaux *mpl*; **plant l.** végétaux *mpl*; **l. belt** ceinture *f* de sauvetage; **l. cycle** cycle *m* de vie; **l. drawing** dessin *m* d'après modèle; **l. force** force *f* vitale; **l. form** forme *f* de vie; **l. jacket** gilet *m* de sauvetage; **l. sciences** sciences *fpl* de la vie
(**b**) *(period of existence)* vie *f*; **she had worked all her l.** elle avait travaillé toute sa vie; **never in (all) my l.** jamais de ma vie; **a l. of Tolstoy** une biographie de Tolstoï; *Fam* **to get l.** en prendre pour perpète; **l. annuity** rente *f* viagère; **l. expectancy** espérance *f* de vie; **l. imprisonment** emprisonnement *m* à vie; **l. insurance** assurance-vie *f*; **l. member** membre *m* à vie; *Br* **l. peer** pair *m* à vie; **l. pension** pension *f* à vie; **l. sentence** condamnation *f* à perpétuité; **l. span** *(of person, animal)* espérance *f* de vie; *(of machine)* durée *f* de vie; **to write one's l. story** écrire son autobiographie
(**c**) *(mode of existence)* vie *f*; *Fam* **to live** *or* **lead the l. of Riley** se la couler douce; **to make a new l. for oneself** refaire sa vie; **way of l.** style *m* de vie; **he makes her l. a misery** il lui rend la vie insupportable; **to make l. worth living** donner un sens à l'existence; *Fam* **how's l.?** comment ça va?; **what a l.!** quelle vie!; **such is** *or* **that's l.!** c'est la vie!; **this is the l.!** voilà ce que j'appelle vivre!; *Fam* **get a l.!** t'es vraiment nul!; **l. coach** coach *m* personnel
(**d**) *(liveliness)* **to come to l.** s'animer; **to bring sb to l.** *(of book, author)* donner vie à qn; **the l. and soul of the party** le boute-en-train de la soirée; **there's l. in the old dog yet** il n'a pas encore dit son dernier mot, le vieux
lifeblood ['laɪfblʌd] *n (of person)* souffle *m* vital; *Fig (of economy, society)* moteur *m*
lifeboat ['laɪfbəʊt] *n* canot *m* de sauvetage
life-giving ['laɪfgɪvɪŋ] *adj (sun, water)* nourricier(-ère); *(aid)* vital(e)
lifeguard ['laɪfgɑːd] *n (at the seaside)* surveillant(e) *m,f* de baignade; *(at swimming pool)* maître *m* nageur
lifeless ['laɪflɪs] *adj* sans vie; *(performance, style)* qui manque de vie
lifelessly ['laɪflɪslɪ] *adv* sans vie
lifelike ['laɪflaɪk] *adj (portrait)* très ressemblant(e)
lifeline ['laɪflaɪn] *n Fig* planche *f* (de salut); **to throw sb a l.** offrir *ou* tendre à qn une planche (de salut)
lifelong ['laɪflɒŋ] *adj* de toujours

lifer ['laɪfə(r)] *n Fam (prisoner)* condamné(e) *m,f* à perpète
life-saver ['laɪfseɪvə(r)] *n Fam* **seatbelts can be life-savers** le port de la ceinture de sécurité peut sauver des vies; *Fig* **you're a l.!** tu me sauves la vie!
life-saving ['laɪfseɪvɪŋ] *adj* salvateur(trice); *(equipment)* de réanimation; **she needed a l. operation** elle devait se faire opérer, c'était une question de vie ou de mort
life-size(d) ['laɪfsaɪz(d)] *adj* grandeur nature *inv*
lifestyle ['laɪfstaɪl] *n* style *m* *ou* mode *m* de vie
life-support ['laɪfsəpɔːt] *adj* **l. system** *or* **machine** respirateur *m* artificiel
life-threatening ['laɪfθretnɪŋ] *adj (disease)* potentiellement mortel(elle); **to be in a l. situation** être en danger de mort
lifetime ['laɪftaɪm] *n (of person)* vie *f*; **in my l.** de mon vivant; **it's the chance of a l.** une telle chance ne se présente qu'une fois dans la vie; **the holiday of a l.** des vacances exceptionnelles
lift [lɪft] **1** *n* (**a**) *(elevator)* ascenseur *m*; **(goods) l.** monte-charge *m inv*; **l. attendant** garçon *m* d'ascenseur; **l. shaft** cage *f* d'ascenseur (**b**) *(car ride)* **to give sb a l.** prendre *ou* emmener qn en voiture; **could you give me a l. to the station?** est-ce que tu peux m'emmener à la gare? (**c**) *Fam* **to give sb a l.** *(cheer up)* remonter le moral à qn
2 *vt* (**a**) *(one's head, eyes, arm)* lever; **he won't l. a finger to help** il ne lèvera pas le petit doigt; **to l. sb (up)** *(after fall)* aider qn à se relever; **to l. a child up** prendre un enfant dans ses bras (**b**) *Fam (take, steal)* piquer; *(arrest)* choper (**c**) *(restrictions, siege)* lever
3 *vi (of mist, fog)* se lever, se dissiper
▶**lift off** *vi (of rocket)* décoller
liftoff ['lɪftɒf] *n (of rocket)* décollage *m*
ligament ['lɪgəmənt] *n* ligament *m*
light¹ [laɪt] **1** *n* (**a**) *(illumination)* lumière *f*; **by the l. of the moon** à la clarté de la lune; **things will look different in the cold l. of day** demain vous verrez les choses sous un autre jour; **to be in sb's l.** faire de l'ombre à qn; *Comput* **l. pen** crayon *m* optique; **l. year** année-lumière *f* (**b**) *(lamp)* lumière *f*; *Fam* **to go out like a l.** s'endormir aussitôt couché(e); **(traffic) lights** feux *mpl* de circulation; **l. bulb** ampoule *f* (**c**) *(fire)* **to set l. to sth** mettre le feu à qch; **have you got a l.?** vous avez du feu? (**d**) *(idioms)* **the l. at the end of the tunnel** le bout du tunnel; **to throw** *or* **cast l. on sth** faire la lumière sur qch; **to bring sth to l.** mettre qch en lumière; **to come to l.** être découvert(e); **to see sb/sth in a new/different l.** voir qn/qch sous un jour nouveau/différent; **in (the) l. of...** *(considering)* à la lumière de...
2 *adj (not dark)* clair(e); **it will soon be l.** il fera bientôt jour
3 *vt (pt & pp* **lit** [lɪt]) (**a**) *(fire, cigarette)* allumer (**b**) *(room, street)* éclairer, illuminer
light² [laɪt] **1** *adj* (**a**) *(not heavy)* léger(ère); **to be l. on one's feet** avoir le pas léger; **to be a l. sleeper** avoir le sommeil léger; **to have a l. touch** avoir la main légère; **l. aircraft** avion *m* petit porteur; **l. artillery** artillerie *f* légère; **l. industry** industrie *f* légère; **l. infantry** infanterie *f* légère (**b**) *(not severe) (job, exercise)* facile, peu fatigant(e); *(rain)* fin(e); *(prison sentence)* léger(ère) (**c**) *(not serious)* léger(ère); **to make l. of sth** prendre qch à la légère; **l. entertainment** variétés *fpl*; **l. reading** lectures *fpl* récréatives; **l. verse** poésie *f* facile
2 *adv* **to travel l.** voyager léger

▸**light on** (pt & pp **lighted**) vt insep tomber sur
▸**light up 1** vt sep (house, room) éclairer; (cigarette) allumer
   2 vi s'éclairer; Fam (of smoker) allumer une cigarette
lighten¹ ['laɪtən] **1** vt (make less dark) éclaircir
   2 vi (of sky) s'éclaircir
lighten² vt (make less heavy) alléger; Fig **to l. sb's load** soulager qn
▸**lighten up** vi Fam se détendre
lighter ['laɪtə(r)] n briquet m; **l. fluid** or **fuel** essence f à briquet
light-fingered [laɪt'fɪŋɡəd] adj Fam **to be l.** être chapardeur(euse)
light-headed [laɪt'hedɪd] adj étourdi(e)
light-hearted [laɪt'hɑːtɪd] adj (person, discussion) enjoué(e); (remark) badin(e); **to take a l. look at sth** poser un regard amusé sur qch
lighthouse ['laɪthaʊs] n phare m; **l. keeper** gardien m de phare
lighting ['laɪtɪŋ] n (act, system) éclairage m
lighting-up time ['laɪtɪŋ'ʌptaɪm] n = heure à laquelle les automobilistes sont tenus d'allumer leurs phares
lightly ['laɪtlɪ] adv légèrement; **to sleep l.** avoir le sommeil léger; **to get off l.** s'en tirer à bon compte; **to speak l. of sth** parler de qch à la légère; **to speak l. of sb** parler de qn sur un ton léger; **to take a decision l.** prendre une décision à la légère
lightness ['laɪtnɪs] n (**a**) (brightness) clarté f (**b**) (in weight) légèreté f
lightning ['laɪtnɪŋ] n (**a**) (bolt) éclairs mpl, foudre f; **l. conductor** paratonnerre m (**b**) (idioms) **as quick as l.**, **with l. speed** rapide comme l'éclair; **l. attack** attaque f éclair; **l. strike** grève f surprise; **l. visit** visite f éclair
lightweight ['laɪtweɪt] **1** n (in boxing) poids m léger; Fig & Pej (in character, intellect) personne f qui manque d'envergure
   2 adj (garment, fabric) léger(ère)
lignite ['lɪɡnaɪt] n lignite m
like¹ [laɪk] **1** n **he and his l.** lui et ses semblables; **it's not for the likes of me** ce n'est pas pour des gens comme moi; **music, painting and the l.** la musique, la peinture et autres choses du même genre; **I've never seen the l. of it** je n'ai jamais vu une chose pareille
   2 adj semblable, pareil(eille); **they are as l. as two peas (in a pod)** ils se ressemblent comme deux gouttes d'eau
   3 prep (**a**) (similar to) **to be l. sb/sth** être semblable à qn/qch, ressembler à qn/qch; **to taste l. sth** avoir le même goût que qch; **to look l. sb/sth** ressembler à qn/qch; **what's the weather l.?** comment est le temps?; **people l. you** des gens comme vous; **you know what she's l.** tu sais comment elle est; **it costs something l. £10** cela coûte dans les 10 livres; **that's more l. it** voilà qui est mieux; **we don't have anything l. as many as that** on est loin d'en avoir autant; **there's nothing l. it!** il n'y a rien de tel!; **she is nothing l. as intelligent as you** elle n'est d'être aussi intelligente que vous; **that's not l. her** cela ne lui ressemble pas; **that's just l. him!** c'est bien de lui!; Prov **l. father, l. son** tel père, tel fils (**b**) (in the manner of) comme; **just l. anybody else** comme tout le monde; Fam **don't be l. that!** ne fais pas l'idiot! (**c**) (such as) tel (telle) que; **take more exercise, l. jogging** fais plus d'exercice, du jogging par exemple
   4 adv Fam **as l. as not** à coup sûr
   5 conj Fam **do it l. I said** fais comme je t'ai dit; **he**

looked **l. he'd seen a ghost** on aurait dit qu'il avait vu un fantôme; **it's not l. he's ill or anything** ce n'est pas comme s'il était malade ou quoi que ce soit
like² **1** n **likes** goûts mpl, préférences fpl; **likes and dislikes** préférences fpl
   2 vt (**a**) (person) bien aimer; **she is well liked** elle est très appréciée (**b**) (enjoy) aimer; **whether she likes it or not,...** que ça lui plaise ou non,...; **l l. to think my father would have agreed** j'aime à penser que mon père aurait approuvé; Fam Ironic **well, I l. that!** elle est bien bonne, celle-là! (**c**) (want) **would you l. a cigarette?** est-ce que tu aimerais une cigarette?; **I would very much l. to go** j'aimerais beaucoup y aller; **I would l. nothing better than...** rien ne me ferait plus plaisir que...; **he doesn't l. people to talk about it** il n'aime pas que l'on en parle; **he thinks he can do anything he likes** il se croit tout permis; **if/when you l.** si/quand vous voulez; **as much as you l.** tant que vous voulez; **as often as you l.** aussi souvent que vous voulez; **I didn't l. to mention it** j'ai préféré ne pas le mentionner
likeable ['laɪkəbəl] adj sympathique
likelihood ['laɪklɪhʊd] n probabilité f; **in all l.** selon toute vraisemblance ou probabilité; **there is little l. of finding it** il y a peu de chance pour qu'on le trouve; **the l. is that...** il est probable que...
likely ['laɪklɪ] **1** adj (**a**) (probable) probable; **it's more than l.** c'est plus que probable; **it's l. to rain** il est probable qu'il pleuve, il pleuvra probablement; Ironic **a l. story!** à d'autres! (**b**) (suitable) approprié(e)
   2 adv **very l.** très probablement; **as l. as not** sûrement; Fam **Not l.!** tu plaisantes?
like-minded [laɪk'maɪndɪd] adj de même avis; (having same tastes) qui ont les mêmes goûts
liken ['laɪkən] vt comparer (**to** à)
likeness ['laɪknɪs] n (**a**) (similarity) ressemblance f; **family l.** air m de famille (**b**) (portrait) portrait m
likewise ['laɪkwaɪz] adv (similarly) de même, aussi; **to do l.** en faire autant
liking ['laɪkɪŋ] n goût m, penchant m; **is it to your l.?** cela est-il à votre goût?; **to have a l. for sth** avoir du goût pour qch, aimer qch; **to take a l. to sth** prendre goût à qch; **to take a l. to sb** se prendre d'amitié pour qn
lilac ['laɪlək] **1** n lilas m
   2 adj lilas inv
Lilo® ['laɪləʊ] (pl **Lilos**) n matelas m pneumatique
lilt [lɪlt] n (of voice) inflexions fpl
lilting ['lɪltɪŋ] adj chantant(e)
lily ['lɪlɪ] (pl **lilies**) n lis m; **l. of the valley** muguet m
lily-livered ['lɪlɪlɪvəd] adj Fam froussard(e)
lima bean ['liːmə'biːn] n haricot m de Lima
limb [lɪm] n (**a**) (of body) membre m; **to tear sb l. from l.** déchiqueter qn, mettre qn en pièces (**b**) (of tree) grosse branche f; Fig **to be out on a l.** (be in dangerous position) être dans une situation délicate; (be alone) être en plan; **to go out on a l.** prendre des risques
limber ['lɪmbə(r)] adj souple
▸**limber up** vi s'échauffer
limbo ['lɪmbəʊ] (pl **limbos**) n (**a**) Rel les limbes mpl; Fig **to be in l.** être dans les limbes (**b**) (dance) limbo m
lime¹ [laɪm] n (fruit) citron m vert; (citrus tree) limettier m; (linden tree) tilleul m; **l. green** vert m jaune; **l. juice** jus m de citron vert
lime² n Chem chaux f
limelight ['laɪmlaɪt] n **to be in the l.** être sous les projecteurs; **to steal the l.** voler la vedette
limerick ['lɪmərɪk] n = poème burlesque en cinq vers

limestone ['laɪmstəʊn] n calcaire m
limey ['laɪmɪ] (pl **limeys**) n Am Fam (British person) Rosbif m
limit ['lɪmɪt] **1** n limite f; **within limits** jusqu'à un certain point; **off limits (to)** inaccessible (à); (forbidden) interdit(e) (à); **to know no limits** être sans limites; **that's the l.!** ce n'est plus possible!; **he's the l.!** il est impossible!
2 vt limiter; **to l. oneself to sth/to doing sth** se limiter à qch/à faire qch
limitation [lɪmɪ'teɪʃən] n limitation f; **to know one's limitations** connaître ses limites
limited ['lɪmɪtəd] adj limité(e); **l. company** société f à responsabilité limitée; **l. edition** édition f à tirage limité; Law **l. liability** responsabilité f limitée
limitless ['lɪmɪtlɪs] adj (wealth, amount, supply) illimité(e); (generosity) sans bornes
limo ['lɪməʊ] (pl **limos**) n Fam limousine f
limousine [lɪmə'ziːn] n limousine f
limp¹ [lɪmp] **1** n boitement m; **to have a l.** boiter
2 vi boiter
limp² adj mou (molle); **to go l.** s'affaisser
limpet ['lɪmpɪt] n bernique f, patelle f; Fig **to stick to sb like a l.** ne pas lâcher qn
limpid ['lɪmpɪd] adj limpide
limply ['lɪmplɪ] adv mollement
linchpin ['lɪntʃpɪn] n Fig (person) cheville f ouvrière; (thing) clé f de voûte
linctus ['lɪŋktəs] n sirop m
linden ['lɪndən] n **l. (tree)** tilleul m
line¹ [laɪn] **1** n (**a**) (mark) ligne f; (drawn) trait m; (on face) ride f; Fig **to draw the l.** se refuser à faire qch; **l. drawing** dessin m au trait (**b**) (row) ligne f, rangée f; (one behind the other) file f; Am (queue) queue f; **to stand in a l.** être en rang; (one behind the other) être en file; Am **to stand or wait in l.** (queue) faire la queue; Fig **to be out of l.** dépasser les bornes; **to be in l. with sth** être conforme à qch; Fig **to be in l. for promotion** être sur la liste des promotions; Fig **to be on the l.** (of one's job, reputation) être en jeu; **l. dancing** = danse de style country effectuée en rangs; Com & Ind **l. manager** chef m d'équipe (**c**) (rope) ligne f; (for clothes) fil m à linge (**d**) (railway track) voie f; (railway route) ligne f (**e**) (direction) **l. of argument** raisonnement m; **l. of attack** plan m d'attaque; **to be in the l. of fire** être dans la ligne de tir; Fig être en butte aux critiques; **to be on the right/wrong lines** être sur la bonne/mauvaise voie; **something along the lines of...** quelque chose dans le genre de... (**f**) (policy) ligne f; **the party l.** la ligne du parti; **to take a firm l. with sb** se montrer ferme avec qn (**g**) (of text) ligne f; (of poem) vers m; **to drop sb a l.** écrire un mot à qn; **to learn one's lines** apprendre son rôle; Fig **to read between the lines** lire entre les lignes (**h**) (family) lignée f; **in a direct l.** en ligne directe (**i**) (telephone connection) ligne f (**j**) Fam (job) **what l. (of business) are you in?** vous travaillez dans quelle branche? (**k**) Com (of goods) ligne f
2 vt (road, river) border; **the crowd lined the street** la foule s'alignait le long du trottoir
▸**line up 1** vt sep (**a**) (form into a line) mettre en ligne, aligner (**b**) (prepare) **to have sb lined up for sth** avoir qn en vue pour qch; **have you got anything lined up for this evening?** avez-vous quelque chose de prévu pour ce soir?
2 vi (form a line) se mettre en rang

line² vt (coat, curtain) doubler (**with** de); (box, drawer) tapisser (**with** de); Fig **to l. one's pockets** se remplir les poches
lineage ['lɪnɪdʒ] n lignée f
linear ['lɪnɪə(r)] adj linéaire; Math **l. equation** équation f linéaire; Comput **l. programming** programmation f linéaire
lined¹ [laɪnd] adj (paper) réglé(e); (face) ridé(e)
lined² adj (coat, curtain) doublé(e) (**with** de)
linen ['lɪnɪn] n (**a**) (fabric) lin m; **a l. dress** une robe en lin (**b**) (clothes) linge m; (sheets, tablecloths etc) linge (de maison); Fig **don't wash your dirty l. in public** il faut laver son linge sale en famille; **l. basket** panier m à linge
liner ['laɪnə(r)] n (ship) (paquebot m) transatlantique m
linesman ['laɪnzmən] n (in tennis) juge m de ligne; (in football) juge de touche
line-up ['laɪnʌp] n (**a**) (of team) composition f; (on TV show) plateau m (**b**) (identity parade) séance f d'identification
linger ['lɪŋgə(r)] vi (of person) s'attarder; (of smell, custom) subsister, persister; **to l. behind** rester en arrière; **to l. over doing sth** prendre son temps pour faire qch
lingerie ['lɑːnʒərɪ] n lingerie f
lingering ['lɪŋgərɪŋ] adj (look) long (longue); (doubt) persistant(e); (death) lent(e)
lingo ['lɪŋgəʊ] (pl **lingoes**) n Fam (language) langue f; (jargon) charabia m
lingua franca ['lɪŋgwə'fræŋkə] n langue f véhiculaire
linguist ['lɪŋgwɪst] n (**a**) (specialist in linguistics) linguiste mf (**b**) (polyglot) **to be a l.** être doué(e) pour les langues
linguistic [lɪŋ'gwɪstɪk] adj linguistique
linguistics [lɪŋ'gwɪstɪks] n linguistique f
lining ['laɪnɪŋ] n (of coat, curtain) doublure f; (of brakes) garniture f; (of stomach) paroi f
link [lɪŋk] **1** n (**a**) (of chain) chaînon m, maillon m; Fig **the weak l.** (in argument) le point faible; (in team) l'élément m faible (**b**) (connection) lien m (**between** entre); (**c**) Comput lien m (**to** avec)
2 vt (physically) relier; (by association) lier; **to l. hands** se donner la main
▸**link up 1** vt relier
2 vi (of roads, travellers) se rejoindre
lino ['laɪnəʊ] n Fam lino m
linoleum [lɪ'nəʊlɪəm] n linoléum m
linseed ['lɪnsiːd] n graine f de lin; **l. oil** huile f de lin
lintel ['lɪntəl] n linteau m
lion ['laɪən] n lion m; Fig **the l.'s share** la part du lion; **l. cub** lionceau m; **l. tamer** dresseur m de lions
lioness ['laɪənes] n lionne f
lion-hearted ['laɪən'hɑːtɪd] adj courageux(euse) comme un lion
lip [lɪp] n (**a**) (of person) lèvre f; (of animal) babine f; **to read sb's lips** lire sur les lèvres de qn; **to pay l. service to sth** faire semblant de s'intéresser à qch; **l. balm** baume m pour les lèvres; **l. gloss** brillant m à lèvres (**b**) (of jug) bec m (**c**) Fam (impudence) insolence f; **less of your l.!** sois un peu moins insolent(e)!
liposuction ['lɪpəʊsʌkʃən] n liposuccion f
lip-read ['lɪpriːd] (pt & pp **lip-read** ['lɪpred]) **1** vt lire sur les lèvres de
2 vi lire sur les lèvres
lipstick ['lɪpstɪk] n rouge m à lèvres
liquefy ['lɪkwɪfaɪ] (pt & pp **liquefied**) **1** vt liquéfier
2 vi se liquéfier

liqueur [lɪ'kjʊə(r)] n liqueur f
liquid ['lɪkwɪd] **1** n liquide m
  2 adj liquide; Fin **l. assets** liquidités fpl; **l. crystal display** affichage m à cristaux liquides
liquidate ['lɪkwɪdeɪt] vt (**a**) Fin (company, debt) liquider; (capital) mobiliser (**b**) Fam (kill) liquider
liquidation [lɪkwɪ'deɪʃən] n Fin (of company, debt) liquidation f; (of capital) mobilisation f; **to go into l.** entrer en liquidation
liquidity [lɪ'kwɪdɪtɪ] n Fin liquidité f; **l. ratio** ratio m de liquidité
liquidize ['lɪkwɪdaɪz] vt (**a**) (gas, solid) liquéfier (**b**) (food) passer au mixeur
liquidizer ['lɪkwɪdaɪzə(r)] n mixeur m
liquor ['lɪkə(r)] n Am alcool m; **l. store** magasin m de vins et spiritueux
liquorice ['lɪkərɪs] n réglisse f
lira ['lɪərə] (pl lire ['lɪərə]) n lire f
Lisbon ['lɪzbən] n Lisbonne
lisp [lɪsp] **1** n zézaiement m; **to have a l.** avoir un cheveu sur la langue
  2 vi avoir un cheveu sur la langue, zézayer
list¹ [lɪst] **1** n liste f
  2 vt (enter in list) faire une liste de; **her phone number isn't listed in the directory** son numéro de téléphone ne figure pas dans l'annuaire; **to be listed on the Stock Exchange** être coté(e) en Bourse; **listed building** immeuble m classé
list² **1** n (of ship) bande f, gîte f
  2 vi (of ship) donner de la bande ou de la gîte
listen ['lɪsən] vi écouter; **to l. to sb/sth** écouter qn/qch; **to l. for sth** tendre l'oreille afin d'entendre qch; **to l. (out) for the phone** guetter la sonnerie du téléphone; **to l. to reason** entendre raison; **he wouldn't l.** il n'a rien voulu savoir
▶**listen in** vi **to l. in (on sth)** écouter (qch)
listener ['lɪsnə(r)] n (**a**) **to be a good l.** savoir écouter (**b**) (to radio programme) auditeur(trice) m,f
listing ['lɪstɪŋ] n (list) liste f; **listings** (in newspaper) rubrique f des spectacles; **listings magazine** programme m de spectacles
listless ['lɪstlɪs] adj apathique
lit [lɪt] pt & pp of **light¹**
litany ['lɪtənɪ] (pl litanies) n litanie f
liter Am = litre
literacy ['lɪtərəsɪ] n alphabétisation f; **l. rate** taux m d'alphabétisation
literal ['lɪtərəl] adj littéral(e)
literally ['lɪtərəlɪ] adv littéralement; **to take sth l.** prendre qch au pied de la lettre
literary ['lɪtərərɪ] adj littéraire
literate ['lɪtərɪt] adj **to be l.** (able to read and write) savoir lire et écrire; (educated) être cultivé(e)
literature ['lɪtərɪtʃə(r)] n (**a**) (fiction, poetry) littérature f (**b**) (information) documentation f
lithe [laɪð] adj agile
lithium ['lɪθɪəm] n lithium m
lithograph ['lɪθəgræf] n lithographie f
Lithuania [lɪθjʊ'emɪə] n la Lituanie
Lithuanian [lɪθjʊ'emɪən] **1** n (**a**) (person) Lituanien(-enne) m,f (**b**) (language) lituanien m
  2 adj lituanien(enne)
litigant ['lɪtɪgənt] n Law partie f
litigate ['lɪtɪgeɪt] vi Law intenter une action en justice
litigation [lɪtɪ'geɪʃən] n Law action f en justice

litigious [lɪ'tɪdʒəs] adj (**a**) Law (contentious) litigieux, contentieux (**b**) Formal Pej (fond of lawsuits) procédurier(ère)
litmus ['lɪtməs] n **l. paper** papier m (de) tournesol; Fig **l. test** test m décisif
litre, Am **liter** ['liːtə(r)] n litre m
litter ['lɪtə(r)] **1** n (**a**) (rubbish) détritus mpl, ordures fpl; **l. bin** poubelle f; **l. lout** = personne qui jette des détritus n'importe où (**b**) (of animal) portée f (**c**) (for cat) litière f; **l. tray** caisse f (pour litière) (**d**) Hist (conveyance) litière f
  2 vt **to be littered with** être couvert(e) ou jonché(e) de
litterbug ['lɪtəbʌg] n Fam = personne qui jette des détritus n'importe où
little ['lɪtəl] **1** n peu m; **to eat l. or nothing** manger peu ou pas du tout; **he knows very l.** il ne sait pas grand-chose; **a l. more** un peu plus; **a l. hot/slow** un peu chaud(e)/lent(e); **every l. helps** les petits ruisseaux font les grandes rivières
  2 adj (**a**) (small) petit(e); **a l. while** un petit moment; **l. finger** petit doigt m (**b**) (comparative **less**, superlative **least**) (not much) peu de; **l. money** peu d'argent; **a l. money** un peu d'argent; **it makes l. sense** ça n'a pas beaucoup de sens
  3 adv (comparative **less**, superlative **least**) peu; **l. by l.** peu à peu; **l. more than an hour ago** il y a à peine une heure; **that's l. short of bribery** ça frise la corruption; **l. did I think that...** j'étais loin de penser que...
littoral ['lɪtərəl] **1** n littoral m
  2 adj littoral(e)
liturgy ['lɪtədʒɪ] (pl liturgies) n liturgie f
live¹ [laɪv] **1** adj (**a**) (person, animal) vivant(e), en vie; Fam **a real l. film star** une vedette de cinéma en chair et en os; **a l. issue** un sujet brûlant (**b**) (performance, broadcast) en direct (**c**) (bomb) non explosé(e); **l. ammunition** balles fpl réelles; **l. wire** fil m sous tension; Fig **to be a l. wire** déborder de vie (**d**) (volcano) actif(ive)
  2 adv (broadcast) en direct; **to perform l.** (of comedian, dancer) être sur scène; (of band) jouer en concert
live² [lɪv] **1** vt vivre; **to l. a long life** vivre longtemps; **to l. a happy life** mener une vie heureuse; **to l. a lie** vivre dans le mensonge; **it makes life worth living** cela donne un sens à la vie
  2 vi vivre; (reside) habiter, vivre; **to l. with sb** vivre avec qn; **as long as I l.** tant que je vivrai; **to l. a little** profiter un peu de la vie; **l. and let l.!** un peu de tolérance!; **you l. and learn** on en apprend tous les jours
▶**live down** vt sep (mistake, one's past) faire oublier; **I'll never l. it down!** je n'ai pas fini d'en entendre parler!
▶**live off** vt insep **to l. off sth** vivre de qch; **to l. off sb** vivre aux crochets de qn
▶**live on 1** vt insep (food) se nourrir de; (capital) vivre sur; **it's not enough to l. on** ce n'est pas suffisant pour vivre
  2 vi (of person) continuer à vivre; (of memory) survivre
▶**live out** vt sep **to l. out one's life** or **days** passer ses jours; **to l. out a fantasy** réaliser un fantasme
▶**live through** vt insep connaître, vivre
▶**live together** vi vivre ensemble
▶**live up** vt sep Fam **to l. it up** faire la fête
▶**live up to** vt insep **to l. up to sb's expectations** répondre aux attentes de qn; **to fail to l. up to expectations** ne pas tenir ses promesses; **to l. up to one's reputation** être à la hauteur de sa réputation
live-in ['lɪvɪn] adj (chauffeur, nanny) logé(e) et nourri(e); **l. lover** compagnon (compagne) m,f
livelihood ['laɪvlɪhʊd] n gagne-pain m inv; **to earn one's l.** gagner sa vie

liveliness ['laɪvlɪnɪs] n vivacité f
lively ['laɪvlɪ] adj (person) plein(e) de vie; (place, party, conversation) animé(e); (music) entraînant(e); (imagination) fertile; **to take a l. interest in sth** s'intéresser vivement à qch; Br Fam **look l.!** grouillez-vous!
▶**liven up** ['laɪvən] **1** vt sep (person) égayer; (place, party, conversation) animer; (proceedings) activer
  2 vi (of person) s'égayer; (of place, party, conversation) s'animer
liver ['lɪvə(r)] n foie m; **l. spot** tache f de vieillesse
Liverpool ['lɪvəpuːl] n Liverpool
Liverpudlian [lɪvə'pʌdlɪən] **1** n = personne née ou habitant à Liverpool
  2 adj de Liverpool
livery ['lɪvərɪ] n livrée f
lives [laɪvz] pl of **life**
livestock ['laɪvstɒk] n bétail m
livid ['lɪvɪd] adj (**a**) (angry) furieux(euse) (**b**) (bluish-grey) livide, blême
living ['lɪvɪŋ] **1** n vie f; **to earn one's l.** gagner sa vie; **what does she do for a l.?** qu'est-ce qu'elle fait dans la vie?; **l. conditions** conditions fpl de vie; **l. expenses** faux frais mpl; **l. room** (salle f de) séjour m, salon m; **l. standards** niveau m de vie
  2 adj vivant(e); **there is not a l. soul to be seen** il n'y a pas âme qui vive; **within l. memory** de mémoire d'homme
lizard ['lɪzəd] n lézard m
llama ['lɑːmə] n lama m
lo [ləʊ] exclam Lit or Hum **lo and behold...** ô surprise...
load [ləʊd] **1** n (**a**) (burden) fardeau m, charge f; **to share** or **spread the l.** répartir le travail; **that's a l. off my mind!** cela m'enlève un poids! (**b**) Fam (lot) **a l. of, loads of** plein de; **it's just a l. of rubbish!** c'est n'importe quoi!; **we've got loads of time** on a largement le temps
  2 vt (lorry, gun, camera) charger; (software) installer; (washing machine) remplir
  3 vi (of lorry) prendre un chargement
▶**load up 1** vt sep charger
  2 vi prendre un chargement
loaded ['ləʊdɪd] adj (**a**) (lorry, gun, camera) chargé(e) (**b**) (dice) pipé(e); (question) insidieux(euse) (**c**) Fam (rich) plein(e) aux as
loading ['ləʊdɪŋ] n chargement m; **l. bay** aire f de chargement
loaf [ləʊf] (pl **loaves** [ləʊvz]) n **a l. (of bread)** un pain; Br Fam Fig **to use one's l.** faire marcher son ciboulot
▶**loaf about, loaf around** vi traîner
loafer ['ləʊfə(r)] n (**a**) (person) fainéant(e) m,f (**b**) (shoe) mocassin m
loam [ləʊm] n terreau m
loan [ləʊn] **1** n (from lender's point of view) prêt m; (from borrower's point of view) emprunt m; **to give sb a l. of sth** prêter qch à qn; **to take out a l.** faire un emprunt; Fam **l. shark** usurier(ère) m,f
  2 vt (money) prêter
loath [ləʊθ] adj **to be l. to do sth** répugner à faire qch
loathe [ləʊð] vt détester; **to l. doing sth** détester faire qch
loathing ['ləʊðɪŋ] n dégoût m, répugnance f
loathsome ['ləʊðsəm] adj répugnant(e)
loaves [ləʊvz] pl of **loaf**
lob [lɒb] **1** n (in tennis) lob m
  2 vt (pt & pp **lobbed**) (**a**) (in tennis) lober (**b**) Fam (throw) balancer

lobby ['lɒbɪ] **1** n (pl **lobbies**) (**a**) (of hotel) hall m; (of theatre) foyer m (**b**) (pressure group) groupe m de pression, lobby m
  2 vt (pt & pp **lobbied**) faire pression sur
  3 vi **to l. for/against sth** faire pression en faveur de/contre qch
lobbyist ['lɒbɪɪst] n membre m d'un groupe de pression
lobe [ləʊb] n lobe m
lobotomy [lə'bɒtəmɪ] (pl **lobotomies**) n lobotomie f
lobster ['lɒbstə(r)] n homard m; **as red as a l.** (sunburnt) rouge comme une écrevisse; **l. pot** casier m à homards
local ['ləʊkəl] **1** n (**a**) (person) **the locals** les gens mpl du coin (**b**) Br Fam (pub) = pub du voisinage
  2 adj local(e); **l. anaesthetic** anesthésie f locale; **l. colour** couleur f locale; **l. government** ≃ administration f municipale; **l. time** heure f locale
locale [ləʊ'kɑːl] n (of events) lieu m; (for a film) lieu m de tournage
locality [ləʊ'kælɪtɪ] (pl **localities**) n voisinage m, environs mpl
localization [ləʊkəlaɪ'zeɪʃən] n localisation f
locally ['ləʊkəlɪ] adv (in neighbourhood) dans le quartier; (in region) dans la région
locate [ləʊ'keɪt] **1** vt (find) localiser; (situate) situer
  2 vi (of company) s'installer
location [ləʊ'keɪʃən] n (**a**) (place) emplacement m; Cin **on l.** en extérieur; Cin **l. shot** plan m en extérieur (**b**) (act of finding) localisation f
loch [lɒχ] n Scot (lake) loch m, lac m
lock[1] [lɒk] **1** n (**a**) (on door) serrure f; **under l. and key** (object) sous clef; (person) sous les verrous; Fig **l., stock and barrel** en entier (**b**) (in wrestling) clef f (**c**) (on canal) écluse f
  2 vt (door, padlock) fermer à clef; **to be locked in each other's arms** être tendrement enlacés(ées); Fig **to l. horns with sb** livrer bataille à qn
  3 vi (of door) se fermer; (of car wheels) se bloquer
▶**lock in** vt sep enfermer à clef
▶**lock out** vt sep enfermer dehors; **I locked myself out of my flat** je me suis enfermé dehors
▶**lock up 1** vt sep (person, valuables) enfermer; (house) fermer à clef
  2 vi fermer
lock[2] n (of hair) mèche f
locker ['lɒkə(r)] n casier m; Am **l. room** vestiaire m
locket ['lɒkɪt] n médaillon m
lockjaw ['lɒkdʒɔː] n Old-fashioned tétanos m
lock-out ['lɒkaʊt] n lock-out m inv
locksmith ['lɒksmɪθ] n serrurier m
lockup ['lɒkʌp] n (**a**) Br (for storage) garage m (**b**) Fam (police cells) violon m, bloc m
locomotion [ləʊkə'məʊʃən] n locomotion f
locomotive [ləʊkə'məʊtɪv] **1** n (train) locomotive f
  2 adj locomotif(ive)
locum ['ləʊkəm] n Br remplaçant(e) m,f
locust ['ləʊkəst] n sauterelle f
locution [ləʊ'kjuːʃən] n locution f
lodge [lɒdʒ] **1** n (of porter, caretaker, masons) loge f; (small house) pavillon m
  2 vt (**a**) (accommodate) loger, héberger (**b**) Law **to l. an appeal** faire appel; **to l. a complaint** porter plainte
  3 vi (a) (live) loger (**b**) (become fixed) se loger; **to be lodged in sb's memory** être gravé(e) dans la mémoire de qn
lodger ['lɒdʒə(r)] n locataire mf (en meublé); (who has meals provided) pensionnaire mf

lodging ['lɒdʒɪŋ] *n* logement *m*; **lodgings** chambre *f* meublée; *Old-fashioned* **l. house** (hôtel *m*) garni *m*

loft [lɒft] *n* grenier *m*

lofty ['lɒftɪ] *adj* (**a**) *(aim, desire)* noble (**b**) *Lit (high)* haut(e)

log [lɒg] **1** *n* (**a**) *(of wood)* bûche *f*; **to sleep like a l.** dormir comme une souche; **l. cabin** hutte *f* en rondins; **l. fire** feu *m* de bois (**b**) *(record)* registre *m*; *(of ship, traveller)* journal *m* de bord; *(of plane)* carnet *m* de vol **2** *vt (pt & pp* **logged**) *(record)* enregistrer; *(in ship's, traveller's log)* noter dans le journal de bord; *(in plane's log)* noter dans le carnet de vol

▸**log in** *vi Comput* entrer

▸**log off** *vi Comput* sortir

▸**log on** *vi Comput* entrer

▸**log out** *vi Comput* sortir

logarithm ['lɒgərɪθəm] *n* logarithme *m*

logbook ['lɒgbʊk] *n* (**a**) *(of ship, traveller)* journal *m* de bord; *(of plane)* carnet *m* de vol (**b**) *Br (for car)* ≃ carte *f* grise

loggerheads ['lɒgəhedz] *n Fam* **to be at l. with sb** être en conflit avec qn

logic ['lɒdʒɪk] *n* logique *f*

logical ['lɒdʒɪkəl] *adj* logique

logically ['lɒdʒɪklɪ] *adv* logiquement

logistic(al) [lə'dʒɪstɪk(əl)] *adj* logistique

logistics [lə'dʒɪstɪks] *npl* logistique *f*; **the l. of the situation** les données *fpl* logistiques de la situation

logjam ['lɒgdʒæm] *n* impasse *f*

logo ['ləʊgəʊ] *(pl* **logos**) *n* sigle *m*, logo *m*

loin [lɔɪn] *n* (**a**) *(of beef)* aloyau *m*; *(of mutton, pork)* filet *m*; *(of veal)* longe *f*; **l. chop** côtes *fpl* premières (**b**) **loins** *(of person)* reins *mpl*

loincloth ['lɔɪnklɒθ] *n* pagne *m*

loiter ['lɔɪtə(r)] *vi* traîner; *(suspiciously)* rôder; *Law* **to l. with intent** = rôder d'une manière suspecte

loll [lɒl] *vi (of person)* se prélasser; *(of head)* tomber en avant; *(of tongue)* pendre

lollipop ['lɒlɪpɒp] *n* sucette *f*; *Br Fam* **l. man/lady** = contractuel qui aide les écoliers à traverser la rue

lollop ['lɒləp] *vi Fam* **to l. along** courir lourdement

lolly ['lɒlɪ] *(pl* **lollies**) *n Fam* (**a**) **(ice) l.** glace *f* à l'eau (**b**) *(lollipop)* sucette *f* (**c**) *Br (money)* fric *m*, flouze *m*

London ['lʌndən] *n* Londres

Londoner ['lʌndənə(r)] *n* Londonien(enne) *m,f*

lone [ləʊn] *adj (single, solitary)* solitaire; *Fig* **a l. wolf** un(e) solitaire

loneliness ['ləʊnlɪnɪs] *n (feeling)* solitude *f*; *(of place)* isolement *m*

lonely ['ləʊnlɪ] *adj (person)* seul(e); *(life, job)* solitaire; *(place)* isolé(e); **to feel l.** se sentir seul; **l. hearts club** club *m* de rencontres; **l. hearts column** rubrique *f* rencontres

loner ['ləʊnə(r)] *n* solitaire *mf*

lonesome ['ləʊnsəm] **1** *n Fam* **to be on one's l.** être abandonné(e) à son triste sort **2** *adj Am* solitaire, seul(e)

long¹ [lɒŋ] **1** *n* **the l. and the short of it is that...** bref,...

2 *adj* (**a**) *(in size)* long (longue); **how l. is the table?** quelle est la longueur de la table?; **to be 4 metres l.** faire 4 mètres de long; **to go the l. way (round)** prendre le chemin le plus long; *Fig* **the best by a l. way** de loin le meilleur (la meilleure); *Fig* **she'll go a l. way** elle ira loin; *Fig* **to go a l. way towards doing sth** beaucoup contribuer à faire qch; *Fam* **to be l. on charm/good ideas** être plein(e) de charme/de bonnes idées; **the l. arm of the law** (le bras de) la

justice; *Fig* **to have a l. face** faire une tête de six pieds de long; **it's a l. shot** ça n'a pas beaucoup de chances de réussir; **not by a l. shot** *or* **chalk** loin s'en faut; **l. johns** caleçon *m* long; *Sport* **l. jump** saut *m* en longueur; *Rad* **l. wave** grandes ondes *fpl*

(**b**) *(in time)* long (longue); **a l. time ago** il y a longtemps; **it's been a l. day** ça a été une longue journée; **the days are getting longer** les jours rallongent; **to take a l. look at sth** regarder longuement qch; **in the l. term** *or* **run** à long terme, à longue échéance; **to have a l. memory** avoir bonne mémoire; **to take the l. view** envisager les choses à long terme; **l. weekend** long week-end *m*, week-end prolongé

3 *adv* (**a**) *(for a long period)* longtemps; **l. live the King/Queen!** vive le roi/la reine!; **as l. as** *(providing)* du moment que, tant que; *(while)* tant que; **to think l. and hard (about sth)** réfléchir longuement (à qch); **she won't be l.** elle ne tardera pas; *(will soon have finished)* elle n'en a pas pour longtemps; **I have l. been convinced of it** j'en suis convaincu depuis longtemps; **how l. have you known her?** depuis combien de temps la connais-tu?; *Fam* **so l.!** au revoir!, à bientôt!; **l. before/after** longtemps avant/après; **l. ago** il y a longtemps

(**b**) *(for the duration of)* **all day l.** toute la journée

(**c**) **I could no longer hear him** je ne l'entendais plus; **I couldn't wait any longer** je ne pouvais plus attendre; **five minutes longer** cinq minutes de plus

long² *vi* **to l. to do sth** rêver de faire qch; **to l. for sth** rêver de qch; *(look forward to)* attendre qch avec impatience; **we're longing for them to leave** il nous tarde qu'ils partent; **a longed-for holiday** des vacances *fpl* très attendues

long³ *(abbr* **longitude)** long

longboat ['lɒŋbəʊt] *n* chaloupe *f*

longbow ['lɒŋbəʊ] *n* arc *m*

long-distance ['lɒŋ'dɪstəns] **1** *adj (runner, race)* de fond; *(telephone call)* longue distance; *Br* **l. lorry driver** conducteur(trice) *m,f* de poids lourd **2** *adv* **to telephone l.** faire un appel longue distance

longevity [lɒn'dʒevɪtɪ] *n* longévité *f*

long-forgotten ['lɒŋfə'gɒtən] *adj* depuis longtemps oublié(e)

longhaired ['lɒŋ'heəd] *adj (cat, dog)* à poil(s) long(s); *(person)* aux cheveux longs

long-haul ['lɒŋ'hɔːl] *adj* long-courrier

longing ['lɒŋɪŋ] *n* profond désir *m*, grande envie *f* (**for de**)

longingly ['lɒŋɪŋlɪ] *adv* avec envie

longitude ['lɒndʒɪtjuːd] *n* longitude *f*

longitudinal [lɒndʒɪ'tjuːdɪnəl] *adj* longitudinal(e)

long-lasting ['lɒŋ'lɑːstɪŋ] *adj* durable, qui dure longtemps

long-life ['lɒŋ'laɪf] *adj (juice, milk)* longue conservation *inv*; *(battery)* longue durée *inv*

long-lost ['lɒŋ'lɒst] *adj (relative)* perdu de vue depuis longtemps

long-range ['lɒŋ'reɪndʒ] *adj (missile)* longue portée; *(forecast)* à long terme; *(plane)* à long rayon d'action

longshoreman [lɒŋ'ʃɔːmən] *n Am* docker *m*

long-sighted [lɒŋ'saɪtɪd] *adj (from birth)* hypermétrope; *(from adulthood)* presbyte

long-sleeved [lɒŋ'sliːvd] *adj* à manches longues

long-standing [lɒŋ'stændɪŋ] *adj (arrangement, friendship)* de longue date

long-suffering [lɒŋ'sʌfərɪŋ] *adj* patient(e)

long-term ['lɒŋtɜːm] *adj (prisoner)* condamné(e) à une longue peine; *(loan, planning)* à long terme; **the l.** unemployed les chômeurs *mpl* de longue durée
long-winded [lɒŋ'wɪndɪd] *adj* verbeux(euse)
loo [luː] *(pl loos) n Br Fam* cabinets *mpl;* **l. roll** *or* **paper** papier *m* toilette
loofah ['luːfə] *n* loofa *m*, luffa *m*
look [lʊk] **1** *n* (**a**) *(act of looking)* **to have** *or* **take a l. at sth** regarder qch; *(quickly)* jeter un coup d'œil à *ou* sur qch; **to have a l. for sth** chercher qch; **let me have a l.** fais(-moi) voir; **to have a l. round the town** faire un tour dans la ville; **to have a l. through some magazines** jeter un coup d'œil à des magazines (**b**) *(glance)* regard *m;* **to give sb. a dirty l.** jeter un regard noir à qn; **if looks could kill** il y a des regards qui tuent (**c**) *(appearance)* air *m;* **I don't like the l. of this** cela ne me look dit rien qui vaille; **I don't like the l. of him** sa tête ne me revient pas; **by the l. of it,...** on dirait bien que... (**d**) **(good) looks** beauté *f;* **to have lost one's looks** être moins beau (belle); **looks don't matter** le physique n'a pas d'importance **2** *vt* **to l. sb in the face** regarder qn en face *ou* dans les yeux; **to l. sb up and down** toiser qn; **l. what you've done!** regarde ce que tu as fait!; **l. where you're going!** vous ne pouvez pas faire attention, non? **3** *vi* (**a**) *(in general)* regarder; **to l. at sb/sth** regarder qn/qch; **he's not much to l. at** il n'est pas très beau; *Fig* **to l. the other way** fermer les yeux; **I'm just looking, thank you** *(in shop)* je ne fais que regarder, merci; **to l. on the bright side** voir les choses du bon côté; **l. here!** dites donc!; **I don't l. at it that way** je ne vois pas les choses comme ça; *Prov* **l. before you leap** il faut réfléchir avant d'agir (**b**) *(search)* **to l. for sb/sth** chercher qn/qch; **we've looked everywhere** nous avons cherché partout (**c**) *(seem, appear)* avoir l'air, paraître; **to l. old** avoir l'air vieux (vieille); **things are looking bad** les choses prennent une mauvaise tournure; **things are looking good** ça a l'air de bien se passer; **to l. one's age** faire son âge; **to l. the part** avoir l'allure qui convient; **what does she l. like?** comment est-elle?; **to l. like sb** ressembler à qn; **it looks like** *or* **as if...** on dirait que...; **it looks like rain** on dirait qu'il va pleuvoir; **you l. as if you've slept badly** vous avez l'air d'avoir mal dormi
▸**look after** *vt insep (take care of)* s'occuper de; **to l. after oneself** se débrouiller tout(e) seul(e); **to l. after sb's house/bag** surveiller la maison/le sac de qn; **can you l. after the children tomorrow?** tu peux garder les enfants demain?
▸**look around 1** *vt insep (town, shops)* faire un tour dans **2** *vi (in town)* faire un tour; *(in shop)* jeter un coup d'œil; **to l. around for sth** essayer de trouver qch
▸**look back** *vi* (**a**) *(in space)* regarder en arrière *ou* derrière soi (**b**) *(in time)* **to l. back on sth** revenir sur qch; **she has never looked back since that day** depuis ce jour sa situation n'a cessé de s'améliorer
▸**look down** *vi (from above)* regarder en bas *ou* vers le bas; *(lower one's eyes)* baisser les yeux; *Fig* **to l. down on sb** regarder qn de haut
▸**look forward to** *vt insep* **to l. forward to sth** attendre qch avec impatience; **I'm looking forward to seeing her again** il me tarde de la revoir; **I l. forward to hearing from you** *(in letter)* dans l'attente de vous lire
▸**look in** *vi* **to l. in (on sb)** passer (voir qn)

▸**look into** *vt insep* examiner
▸**look on 1** *vt insep (consider)* **to l. on sb/sth as...** considérer qn/qch comme... **2** *vi (watch)* regarder
▸**look out 1** *vt sep (find)* trouver, dénicher **2** *vi* (**a**) *(from indoors)* regarder dehors; **to l. out of the window** regarder par la fenêtre (**b**) *(be careful)* faire attention; **l. out!** attention!
▸**look out for** *vt insep* (**a**) *(look for) (person)* guetter; *(thing)* chercher (**b**) *(be on guard for)* faire attention à
▸**look over** *vt insep* jeter un coup d'œil sur
▸**look round** = look around
▸**look through** *vt insep* (**a**) *(inspect) (written material)* parcourir; *(clothes, CDs)* passer en revue (**b**) *(not see)* **to l. straight through sb** regarder qn sans le voir; *(deliberately)* ignorer qn
▸**look to** *vt insep* (**a**) *(rely on)* **to l. to sb (for sth)** compter sur qn (pour qch) (**b**) **to l. to the future** se tourner vers l'avenir
▸**look up 1** *vt sep (word, address)* chercher; *(person)* passer voir **2** *vi (from below)* regarder vers le haut; *(raise one's eyes)* lever les yeux; *Fig* **things are looking up** la situation s'améliore
▸**look upon** *vt insep (consider)* **to l. upon sb/sth as** considérer qn/qch comme
▸**look up to** *vt insep* respecter, estimer
lookalike ['lʊkəlaɪk] *n* sosie *m*
look-in ['lʊkɪn] *n Fam (chance)* **he won't have** *or* **get a l.** il n'a pas la moindre chance; *(in conversation)* il ne pourra pas en placer une
looking-glass ['lʊkɪŋglɑːs] *n Old-fashioned* miroir *m*
lookout ['lʊkaʊt] *n (person)* guetteur *m;* *(on ship)* vigie *f;* **to keep a l. for sb/sth** guetter qn/qch; **to be on the l. for sb/sth** être à la recherche de qn/qch; *Fam* **that's your l.!** ça c'est ton affaire!; **l. post/tower** poste *m*/tour *f* de guet
loom¹ [luːm] *n (for making cloth)* métier *m* à tisser
loom² [luːm] *vi (of person, building)* se dresser; *(of danger, event)* être imminent(e); **to l. large** être très présent(e)
loony ['luːnɪ] *Fam* **1** *n (pl loonies)* dingue *mf;* **l. bin** maison *f* de fous **2** *adj* dingue
loop [luːp] **1** *n* boucle *f* **2** *vt* faire une boucle/des boucles à; **to l. sth around sth** enrouler qch autour de qch; **to l. the loop** *(in plane)* faire un looping
loophole ['luːphəʊl] *n (in law, regulations etc)* point *m* faible; **to find a l.** trouver une échappatoire; **legal l.** vide *m* juridique
loopy ['luːpɪ] *adj Fam* barjo(t)
loose [luːs] **1** *n* **to be on the l.** *(of prisoner)* être en cavale; *(of animal)* être en liberté **2** *adj (animal)* qui s'est échappé(e); *(tooth, plank)* qui bouge; *(piece of clothing)* large, ample; *(skin)* flasque; *(alliance, network)* peu structuré(e); *(translation)* approximatif(ive); *(morals, lifestyle)* dissolu(e); **to come l.** *(of knot)* se défaire; *(of screw)* se desserrer; **to let sb l.** relâcher qn; **to let sb l. on sth** laisser qn toucher à qch; **don't let him l. in the kitchen!** ne le laisse pas faire la cuisine tout seul!; **to let l. a torrent of abuse** lâcher des torrents d'injures; **to buy sth l.** acheter qch en vrac; **l. change** petite *ou* menue monnaie *f;* **l. connection** *(in appliance)* faux contact *m;* **to be at a l. end** ne pas savoir quoi faire; *Fig* **to tie up the l. ends** régler les derniers détails; **l. talk** propos *mpl*

irréfléchis; **to have a l. tongue** ne pas savoir tenir sa langue; **a l. woman** une femme de mauvaise vie **3** *vt Lit (arrow)* décocher; *(bullet)* tirer
▶**loose off** *vt sep (arrow)* décocher; *(bullet)* tirer
loose-fitting ['luːsfɪtɪŋ] *adj* ample, large
loose-leaf ['luːsliːf] *adj* à feuilles mobiles; **l. binder** classeur *m*
loose-limbed ['luːslɪmd] *adj* souple
loosely ['luːslɪ] *adv* (**a**) *(attached)* de façon lâche; **l. packed** *(snow)* poudreux(euse) (**b**) *(roughly)* de façon approximative; **to be l. connected** avoir un lointain rapport; **l. speaking** en gros; **l. translated** traduit librement
loosen ['luːsən] **1** *vt (screw, knot, belt)* desserrer; *(restrictions)* assouplir; **to l. one's grip** relâcher son étreinte; **to l. sb's tongue** délier la langue à qn **2** *vi* se desserrer
▶**loosen up** *vi (relax)* se détendre
loot [luːt] **1** *n (booty)* butin *m*; *Fam (money)* oseille *f* **2** *vt* piller
looter ['luːtə(r)] *n* pillard(e) *m,f*
looting ['luːtɪŋ] *n* pillage *m*
lopsided [lɒpˈsaɪdɪd] *adj (face)* asymétrique; *(picture)* de guingois, de travers; *(grin)* en coin
loquacious [lɒˈkweɪʃəs] *adj Formal* loquace
lord [lɔːd] **1** *n* (**a**) *(aristocrat)* noble *m*; *(feudal)* seigneur *m*; **L. Browne** lord Browne *(titre de noblesse masculin)*; **l. of the manor** châtelain *m*; *Br* **the (House of) Lords** la Chambre des Lords; **the L. Mayor** le lord-maire; **my L.** *(to noble)* Monsieur le Marquis/le Baron/ *etc*; *(to judge)* Monsieur le juge (**b**) *Rel* **the L.** le Seigneur; **the L.'s Prayer** le Notre Père; *Fam* **good L.!** mon Dieu!; *Fam* **L. knows** Dieu seul le sait **2** *vt* **to l. it over sb** traiter qn de haut
lordly ['lɔːdlɪ] *adj (noble)* altier(ère); *Pej (arrogant)* hautain(e)
lordship ['lɔːdʃɪp] *n* autorité *f*; *also Ironic* **His/Your L.** monsieur; *(to judge)* son/votre Honneur
lore [lɔː(r)] *n* tradition *f* orale
lorry ['lɒrɪ] *(pl* **lorries***) n Br* camion *m*; *Fam Euph* **it fell off the back of a l.** *(was stolen)* c'est de la marchandise volée; **l. driver** chauffeur *m* de poids lourd
Los Angeles [lɒsˈændʒəliːz] *n* Los Angeles
lose [luːz] *(pt & pp* **lost** [lɒst]*)* **1** *vt* perdre; **to have nothing to l.** n'avoir rien à perdre; **he had lost interest in his work** son travail ne l'intéressait plus; **it loses something in translation** ça perd à la traduction; **to be lost at sea** périr en mer; **the joke was lost on him** il n'a pas saisi la plaisanterie; **that clock loses five minutes a day** cette pendule retarde de cinq minutes par jour; **that mistake lost her the match** cette erreur lui a coûté le match; **to l. one's way, to get lost** se perdre; *Fam* **get lost!** va te faire voir!; **to l. one's balance** perdre l'équilibre; **to l. sight of sb/sth** perdre qn/qch de vue; *Fam Fig* **you've lost me!** je ne vous suis plus!; **to l. weight** perdre du poids; **we lost him in the crowd** nous avons été séparés dans la cohue; **to l. oneself in a book/one's work** se plonger dans un livre/son travail **2** *vi (in contest)* perdre
▶**lose out** *vi* être perdant(e) (**to sb** par rapport à qn); **to l. out on a deal** être perdant(e) dans une affaire
loser ['luːzə(r)] *n* (**a**) *(in contest)* perdant(e) *m,f*; **to be a bad l.** être mauvais(e) perdant(e) (**b**) *Fam (unsuccessful person)* raté(e) *m,f*, minable *mf*; **a born l.** un(e) vrai(e) raté(e)

losing ['luːzɪŋ] *adj* **to fight a l. battle** être battu(e) d'avance; **the l. side** *(in war)* les vaincus *mpl*; *(in contest)* l'équipe *f* perdante
loss [lɒs] *n* (**a**) *(in contest, war)* perte *f*; **there was a great l. of life** il y a eu de grosses pertes en vies humaines; **to suffer heavy losses** subir de grosses pertes; **it's no great l.** ce n'est pas une grosse perte; *Fam* **it's your l.!** tu ne sais pas ce que tu perds!; **without l. of face** sans perdre la face; **to be at a l. to do sth** être incapable de faire qch; **she's never at a l. for an answer** elle a toujours réponse à tout (**b**) *(financial)* **to make a l.** perdre de l'argent, être déficitaire; **to sell at a l.** vendre à perte; *Fig* **to cut one's losses** sauver les meubles; **l. leader** article *m* ou produit *m* d'appel
loss-making ['lɒsmeɪkɪŋ] *adj* déficitaire
lost [lɒst] **1** *adj* perdu(e); **to give sb/sth up for l.** abandonner tout espoir de retrouver qn/qch; **l. cause** cause *f* perdue; *Br* **l. property (office)** (bureau *m* des) objets *mpl* trouvés; **l. soul** âme *f* en peine **2** *pt & pp of* **lose**
lost-and-found [lɒstənˈfaʊnd] *Am n* **l. (office)** (bureau *m* des) objets *mpl* trouvés
lot [lɒt] **1** *n* (**a**) *(large quantity)* **a l., lots** beaucoup; **the l.** tout; **I bought the l.** j'ai tout acheté; **a l. of** *or* **lots of people** beaucoup de monde; **I see quite a l. of her** je la vois assez souvent; **we had a l. of** *or* **lots of fun** nous nous sommes bien amusés; *Fam* **listen, you l.!** écoutez, vous tous!; *Fam* **that l. next door** la bande d'à côté; *Fam* **he's a bad l.** c'est un bon à rien (**b**) *(destiny)* sort *m*, destin *m*; **to draw** *or* **cast lots for sth** tirer qch au sort; **to throw in one's l. with sb** partager le sort de qn (**c**) *(piece of land)* (lot *m* de) terrain *m*; *(at auction)* lot *m* **2** *adv* **a l.** beaucoup; **a l. bigger** beaucoup *ou* bien plus grand(e); **thanks a l.** merci beaucoup
lotion ['ləʊʃən] *n* lotion *f*
lottery ['lɒtərɪ] *(pl* **lotteries***) n also Fig* loterie *f*
lotto ['lɒtəʊ] *n* loto *m*
lotus ['ləʊtəs] *n* lotus *m*; **l. position** (position *f* du) lotus *m*
loud [laʊd] **1** *adj* (**a**) *(noise)* bruyant(e); *(voice, music)* fort(e); *Pej (person)* fort(e) en gueule; **to be l. in one's praise/condemnation of sth** louer/condamner qch avec force (**b**) *(colour, clothes)* voyant(e) **2** *adv* fort; **to think out l.** penser tout haut; **l. and clear** parfaitement
loudhailer [laʊdˈheɪlə(r)] *n* porte-voix *m* inv
loudly ['laʊdlɪ] *adv* fort; *(complain)* bruyamment
loudmouth ['laʊdmaʊθ] *n Fam* **to be a l.** être *ou* avoir une grande gueule
loudmouthed ['laʊdmaʊðd] *adj Fam* gueulard(e)
loudness ['laʊdnɪs] *n (of noise, voice)* volume *m*
loudspeaker [laʊdˈspiːkə(r)] *n* haut-parleur *m*
Louisiana [luːiːziˈænə] *n* la Louisiane
lounge [laʊndʒ] **1** *n (in house, hotel)* salon *m*; **l. bar** = dans un pub, salle plus confortable où les prix sont légèrement plus élevés; **l. suit** costume *m* de ville; *(on invitation)* tenue *f* de ville **2** *vi* fainéanter
▶**lounge about, lounge around** *vi* traîner
louse [laʊs] *n* (**a**) *(pl* **lice** [laɪs]*) (insect)* pou *m* (**b**) *Fam (pl* **louses***) (person)* salaud *m*
lousy ['laʊzɪ] *adj Fam* nul (nulle); *(weather)* dégueulasse; *(trick)* sale; **to feel l.** se sentir vraiment mal; **we had a l. time on holiday** nous avons passé des vacances nulles
lout [laʊt] *n* voyou *m*
loutish ['laʊtɪʃ] *adj* de voyou

louvre door [ˈluːvəˈdɔː(r)] *adj* porte *f* à persiennes

lovable [ˈlʌvəbəl] *adj* attachant(e)

love [lʌv] **1** *n* (**a**) *(for family, country)* amour *m* (**of** *or* **for** de *ou* pour); **give my l. to your parents** embrasse tes parents pour moi; **with l. from...** *(at end of letter)* affectueusement,...; **Bill sends (you) his l.** Bill t'embrasse; **there's no l. lost between them** ils ne peuvent pas se sentir; **I wouldn't do it for l.** or **money** je ne le ferais pour rien au monde; **to do sth for the l. of it** faire qch pour le plaisir (**b**) *(between lovers)* amour *m*; **to be/fall in l. with sb** être/tomber amoureux(euse) de qn; **to make l. with** *or* **to sb** faire l'amour avec qn; **the l. of my life** l'homme (la femme) de ma vie; **it was l. at first sight** ce fut le coup de foudre; **(my) l.** *(term of endearment)* mon amour; **a l.-hate relationship** une relation faite à la fois d'amour et de haine; **l. affair** liaison *f* (amoureuse); *Fig* passion *f*; **his l. affair with Paris** sa passion pour Paris; *Euph* **l. child** enfant *mf* de l'amour; **l. letter** lettre *f* d'amour; **l. life** vie *f* amoureuse; **l. match** mariage *m* d'amour; **l. nest** nid *m* d'amour; **l. triangle** ménage *m* à trois (**c**) *(in tennis)* **15 l.** 15 à rien; **l. game** jeu *m* blanc **2** *vt (person)* aimer; *(thing)* adorer; **I l. Chinese food** j'adore manger chinois; **to do** *or* **doing sth** adorer faire qch; **I'd l. to come** j'aimerais beaucoup venir

lovebird [ˈlʌvbɜːd] *n Fam Fig* **a pair of lovebirds** un couple de tourtereaux

lovebite [ˈlʌvbaɪt] *n* suçon *m*

loved-up [lʌvdˈʌp] *adj Br Fam* (**a**) *(in love)* amoureux(euse) (**b**) *(after taking ecstasy)* tout(e) gentil(ille) *(sous l'effet de l'ecstasy)*

loveless [ˈlʌvlɪs] *adj* sans amour

lovely [ˈlʌvlɪ] *adj (idea, smell)* très bon (bonne); *(weather)* beau (belle); *(person)* charmant(e); **to have a l. time** passer un bon moment; *Fam* **it's l. and warm** il fait bon

lovemaking [ˈlʌvmeɪkɪŋ] *n (sexual intercourse)* ébats *mpl* amoureux

lover [ˈlʌvə(r)] *n (of person) (man)* amant *m*; *(woman)* maîtresse *f*; *(of nature, good food)* amoureux(euse) *m,f*

lovesick [ˈlʌvsɪk] *adj* qui languit d'amour

lovey-dovey [ˈlʌvɪˈdʌvɪ] *adj Fam (talk)* mièvre, à la guimauve; *(person)* roucoulant(e)

loving [ˈlʌvɪŋ] *adj* affectueux(euse), tendre

low[1] [ləʊ] **1** *n* (**a**) **to reach a new** *or* **an all-time l.** atteindre son niveau le plus bas (**b**) *(weather front)* zone *f* de basse pression **2** *adj* (**a**) *(not high, not loud)* bas (basse); *(neckline)* profond(e); **fuel is getting l.** on n'a plus beaucoup d'essence; **to cook sth over a l. heat** cuire qch à feu doux; **of l. birth** de basse extraction; **the lower classes** les classes les moins aisées; **lower ranks** *(in army)* rangs *mpl* inférieurs; **to have a l. opinion of sb** avoir une mauvaise opinion de qn; *Am Aut* **l. beams** phares *mpl* codes; *Fig* **a l. blow** un coup bas; **the L. Countries** les Pays-Bas *mpl*; **l. tide** marée *f* basse (**b**) *(depressed)* déprimé(e) (**c**) *(ignoble)* **the lowest of the l.** le dernier des derniers (la dernière des dernières); **that's a l. trick!** c'est vraiment un coup vache! **3** *adv* bas; **the l. paid** *mpl*; **turn the music/the lights down l.** baisse la musique/la lumière; **to be running l. on sth** être presque à court de qch

low[2] *vi (of cattle)* meugler

lowbrow [ˈləʊbraʊ] *adj Pej (tastes, interests)* peu intellectuel(elle)

low-budget [ləʊˈbʌdʒɪt] *adj (film)* à petit budget; *(holiday)* bon marché *inv*

low-calorie [ləʊˈkælərɪ] *adj* basses calories, hypocalorique

low-cost [ləʊˈkɒst] *adj* économique; *(housing)* à loyer modéré; *Aviat* **l. airline** low-cost *m*

low-cut [ləʊˈkʌt] *adj* décolleté(e)

low-down [ˈləʊdaʊn] *n Fam* **to give sb the l. on sth** tuyauter qn sur qch; **what's the l. on Peter's resignation?** tu as des tuyaux sur la démission de Peter?

lower[1] [ˈləʊə(r)] *vt* (**a**) *(eyes, blind, head, window)* baisser; *(sail)* amener; *also Fig* **to l. one's guard** baisser sa garde; **to l. one's voice** baisser la voix; **to l. oneself into/onto sth** se laisser glisser dans/sur qch (**b**) *(morally)* **to l. oneself (to do sth)** s'abaisser (à faire qch)

lower[2] [ˈlaʊə(r)] *vi (of sky)* se couvrir; **to l. at sb** *(of person)* lancer des regards noirs à qn

low-fat [ləʊˈfæt] *adj* allégé(e), pauvre en matières grasses

low-flying [ˈləʊˈflaɪɪŋ] *adj* volant à basse altitude

low-grade [ˈləʊˈɡreɪd] *adj* de qualité inférieure

low-key [ləʊˈkiː] *adj (approach, debate)* modéré(e); *(film, style)* sobre, dépouillé(e); *(person)* réservé(e)

lowlands [ˈləʊləndz] *npl* basses terres *fpl*; **the L.** *(of Scotland)* les BassesTerres de l'Écosse

low-level [ˈləʊˈlevəl] *adj* (**a**) *(discussion)* à niveau (**b**) *(radiation)* de faible intensité

lowly [ˈləʊlɪ] *adj* humble, modeste

low-lying [ˈləʊˈlaɪŋ] *adj* de basse altitude

low-rise [ˈləʊraɪz] *adj* (**a**) *(building)* de faible hauteur, bas (basse) (**b**) *(jeans, trousers)* taille basse *inv*

low-salt [ləʊˈsɒlt] *adj* à faible teneur en sel

low-spirited [ləʊˈspɪrɪtɪd] *adj* abattu(e)

low-tech [ˈləʊtek] *adj* rudimentaire

loyal [ˈlɔɪəl] *adj (friend)* loyal(e), dévoué(e); **to be l. to sb/sth** être fidèle à qn/qch

loyalist [ˈlɔɪəlɪst] **1** *n* loyaliste *mf* **2** *adj* loyaliste

Loyalist
Dans le contexte britannique, le mot "loyalist" désigne un protestant d'Irlande du Nord souhaitant rester au sein du Royaume-Uni.

loyally [ˈlɔɪəlɪ] *adv* loyalement

loyalty [ˈlɔɪəltɪ] *(pl* **loyalties***) n* loyauté *f*; **you'll have to decide where your loyalties lie** il faudra que vous décidiez de quel côté vous êtes; **to have divided loyalties** être partagé(e); *Com* **l. card** carte *f* de fidélité

lozenge [ˈlɒzɪndʒ] *n (shape)* losange *m*; *(cough sweet)* pastille *f*

LP [el'piː] *n (abbr* **long player**) 33 tours *m*

LSD [eles'diː] *n (abbr* **lysergic acid diethylamide**) LSD *m*

Lt *(abbr* **Lieutenant**) lt

Ltd *Br (abbr* **limited**) ≃ SARL, *Can* limité

lubricant [ˈluːbrɪkənt] *n* lubrifiant *m*

lubricate [ˈluːbrɪkeɪt] *vt* lubrifier

lubrication [luːbrɪˈkeɪʃən] *n* lubrification *f*

lucid [ˈluːsɪd] *adj* lucide; *(explanation)* clair(e)

luck [lʌk] *n* chance *f*; **(good) l.** bonheur *m*, chance *f*; **good l.!** bonne chance!; **bad l.** malchance *f*; **bad l.!** pas de chance!; **to wish sb l.** souhaiter bonne chance à qn; **to be in l.** avoir de la chance; **to be out of l.** ne pas avoir de chance; **to be down on one's l.** être sur la paille; **to try one's l.** tenter sa chance; **don't push your l.!** ne pousse pas le bouchon trop loin!; **some people have all the l.** il y a vraiment des gens qui ont de la veine; **just my l.!** c'est bien ma chance!; **no such l.!** je n'ai pas (eu) cette chance!; **with any l.** avec un peu de chance

luckily ['lʌkɪlɪ] *adv* par bonheur, heureusement

lucky ['lʌkɪ] *adj (person)* **to be l.** avoir de la chance; **to make a l. guess** tomber juste; **to have a l. escape** l'échapper belle; *Fam* **l. devil, l. beggar** sacré(e) veinard(e) *m,f*; *Ironic* **you'll be l.!** tu peux toujours courir!; **it's l. you came when you did** c'est une chance que tu sois arrivé à ce moment-là; **she's l. to be alive** elle a de la chance d'être encore en vie; **my l. number** mon chiffre porte-bonheur; **it's not my l. day** ce n'est pas mon jour de chance; **that was l.** ça a été un coup de chance; **to strike it l.** décrocher le gros lot; **l. charm** porte-bonheur *m inv*; *Br* **l. dip** = jeu consistant à chercher des cadeaux enfouis dans une caisse remplie de sciure ou dans un sac; **you can thank your l. stars she didn't see you!** tu peux t'estimer heureux qu'elle ne t'ait pas vu!

lucrative ['lu:krətɪv] *adj* lucratif(ive)

lucre ['lu:kə(r)] *n Pej or Hum* lucre *m*

ludicrous ['lu:dɪkrəs] *adj* risible, ridicule

lug [lʌg] *(pt & pp lugged) vt Fam* trimbaler

luggage ['lʌgɪdʒ] *n* bagages *mpl*; **l. label** étiquette *f* à bagages; **l. locker** consigne *f* automatique; **l. rack** *(in train)* porte-bagages *m inv*; *(on car)* galerie *f*; *Br* **l. van** *(on train)* fourgon *m*

lughole ['lʌghəʊl] *n Br Fam* esgourde *f*

lugubrious [lu:'gu:brɪəs] *adj* lugubre

lukewarm ['lu:kwɔ:m] *adj also Fig* tiède; **she was rather l. about my suggestion** ma suggestion ne l'a pas enthousiasmée

lull [lʌl] **1** *n (in fighting)* accalmie *f*; *(in conversation)* pause *f*; *Fig* **the l. before the storm** le calme avant la tempête

2 *vt* **to l. sb to sleep** endormir qn en le berçant; **they were lulled into a false sense of security** ils se sont laissés aller à un sentiment de sécurité illusoire

lullaby ['lʌləbaɪ] *(pl lullabies) n* berceuse *f*

lumbago [lʌm'beɪgəʊ] *n* lumbago *m*

lumbar ['lʌmbə(r)] *adj Anat* lombaire

lumber ['lʌmbə(r)] **1** *n* (**a**) *Br (junk)* bric-à-brac *m*; **l. room** débarras *m* (**b**) *Am (wood)* bois *m* de charpente *ou* de construction

2 *vt* **to get lumbered with sth** se taper *ou* se coltiner qch; **I got lumbered with a huge bill** je me suis retrouvé avec une facture gratinée

3 *vi* **to l. about** *or* **around** avancer d'un pas lourd

lumbering ['lʌmbərɪŋ] *adj (walk)* lourd(e), pesant(e)

lumberjack ['lʌmbədʒæk] *n* bûcheron *m*

luminary ['lu:mɪnərɪ] *(pl luminaries) n Lit* sommité *f*

luminescent [lu:mɪ'nesənt] *adj* luminescent(e)

luminous ['lu:mɪnəs] *adj (paint, road sign, colour)* fluorescent(e)

lump [lʌmp] **1** *n* (**a**) *(of earth)* motte *f*; *(of stone, coal)* morceau *m*; *(in sauce)* grumeau *m*; *(on body)* grosseur *f*; **a l. of sugar** un sucre; *Fig* **it brought a l. to my throat** *(made me sad)* ma gorge se serra; *Fin* **l. sum** somme *f* forfaitaire; **to pay in a l. sum** payer en une seule fois (**b**) *Fam Pej (person)* empoté(e) *m,f*

2 *vt* (**a**) *(group)* **to l. (together)** regrouper; *Pej* mettre dans le même sac (**b**) *Fam (endure)* **you'll just have to (like it or) l. it!** il faudra que tu fasses avec!

lumpy ['lʌmpɪ] *adj (sauce)* grumeleux(euse); *(mattress)* bosselé(e)

lunacy ['lu:nəsɪ] *n* folie *f*

lunar ['lu:nə(r)] *adj* lunaire; **l. eclipse** éclipse *f* de lune; **l. landing** alunissage *m*

lunatic ['lu:nətɪk] **1** *n* fou (folle) *m,f*; **l. asylum** asile *m* d'aliénés

2 *adj (idea, behaviour)* dément(e); **l. fringe** extrémistes *mpl* fanatiques

lunch [lʌntʃ] **1** *n* déjeuner *m*, *Can* dîner *m*; **to have l.** prendre son déjeuner, déjeuner; *Fam Fig* **to be out to l.** *(be crazy)* débloquer; **l. hour** heure *f* du déjeuner

2 *vi* déjeuner, *Can* dîner (**on** de)

luncheon ['lʌntʃən] *n* (**a**) *Formal* déjeuner *m* (**b**) **l. meat** = viande à base de porc présentée en tranches; **l. voucher** chèque-restaurant *m*

lunchtime ['lʌntʃtaɪm] *n* heure *f* du déjeuner

lung [lʌŋ] *n* poumon *m*; **l. cancer** cancer *m* des poumons

lunge [lʌndʒ] **1** *n* mouvement *m* brusque en avant; **to make a l. for** se ruer vers

2 *vi* se ruer (**at** vers)

lupin ['lu:pɪn] *n* lupin *m*

lupus ['lu:pəs] *n Med* lupus *m*

lurch [lɜ:tʃ] **1** *n (of ship, car)* embardée *f*; **a l. to the left/right** *(of politician, party)* un virage à gauche/droite; *Fam* **to leave sb in the l.** laisser qn dans le pétrin

2 *vi (of ship, car)* faire une embardée; *(of person)* tituber; **to l. to the left/right** *(of politician, party)* virer à gauche/droite

lure ['lʊə(r)] **1** *n (attraction)* attrait *m*

2 *vt (into trap, ambush)* attirer; **nothing could l. her away from her computer** rien ne pouvait l'éloigner de son ordinateur

lurid ['lʊərɪd] *adj* (**a**) *(story, description)* cru(e); *(headline)* sensationnel(elle); **she described it in l. detail** elle en a fait une description qui ne laissait rien à l'imagination (**b**) *(gaudy)* criard(e)

lurk [lɜ:k] *vi* être tapi(e); *(of doubt, fear)* subsister

luscious ['lʌʃəs] *adj (woman)* appétissant(e); *(lips)* pulpeux(euse); *(fruit)* succulent(e)

lush [lʌʃ] *adj (plant, vegetation)* luxuriant(e); *Fig (surroundings)* luxueux(euse)

lust [lʌst] *n (sexual)* désir *m* (charnel); *Fig (for power, knowledge)* soif *f* (**for** de)

▸**lust after** *vt insep* convoiter

luster *Am* = **lustre**

lustful ['lʌstfʊl] *adj* lubrique

lustre, lustre *Am* **luster** ['lʌstə(r)] *n* lustre *m*, éclat *m*

lustrous ['lʌstrəs] *adj* brillant(e)

lusty ['lʌstɪ] *adj (person)* vigoureux(euse); *(cry, blow)* puissant(e)

lute [lu:t] *n* luth *m*

Luxembourg ['lʌksəmbɜ:g] *n* le Luxembourg

Luxembourger ['lʌksəmbɜ:gə(r)] *n* Luxembourgeois(e) *m,f*

luxuriant [lʌg'zjʊərɪənt] *adj* luxuriant(e)

luxuriate [lʌg'zjʊərɪeɪt] *vi* se prélasser (**in** dans)

luxurious [lʌg'zjʊərɪəs] *adj* somptueux(euse)

luxury ['lʌkʃərɪ] **1** *n (pl luxuries)* luxe *m*; **to lead a life of l.** vivre dans le luxe

2 *adj* de luxe

lychee [laɪ'tʃi:] *n* litchi *m*

lying ['laɪŋ] **1** *n* mensonges *mpl*

2 *adj (person)* menteur(euse)

lymph [lɪmf] *n Anat* lymphe *f*; **l. node** ganglion *m* lymphatique
lymphatic [lɪmˈfætɪk] *adj* lymphatique
lymphoma [lɪmˈfəʊmə] *n Med* lymphone *m*
lynch [lɪntʃ] *vt* lyncher
lynching [ˈlɪntʃɪŋ] *n* lynchage *m*
lynx [lɪŋks] *n* lynx *m*

Lyons [ˈliːɒn] *n* Lyon
lyre [ˈlaɪə(r)] *n* lyre *f*
lyric [ˈlɪrɪk] *adj* lyrique
lyrical [ˈlɪrɪkəl] *adj* lyrique
lyricism [ˈlɪrɪsɪzəm] *n* lyrisme *m*
lyricist [ˈlɪrɪsɪst] *n* parolier(ère) *m,f*
lyrics [ˈlɪrɪks] *npl (of song)* paroles *fpl*

M¹, m¹ [em] *n (letter)* M, m *m inv*
M² *Br Aut (abbr* **motorway**) autoroute *f*
m² (**a**) (*abbr* **metre(s)**) m (**b**) (*abbr* **mile(s)**) mile(s)
MA [em'eɪ] *n Univ (abbr* **Master of Arts**) **to have an
MA in linguistics** ≃ avoir une maîtrise de linguistique; **John Smith MA** John Smith, titulaire d'une
maîtrise de lettres/droit/*etc*
ma [mɑ:] *n Fam* maman *f*
ma'am [mɑ:m] *n Old-fashioned* madame *f*
mac [mæk] *n Br Fam (raincoat)* imper *m*
macabre [mə'kɑ:bə(r)] *adj* macabre
macaque [mə'kɑ:k] *n Zool* macaque *m*
macaroni [mækə'rəʊnɪ] *n* macaronis *mpl*; **m. cheese**
gratin *m* de macaronis
macaroon [mækə'ru:n] *n* macaron *m*
macaw [mə'kɔ:] *n* ara *m*
Mace® [meɪs] **1** *n (spray)* gaz *m* lacrymogène
  2 *vt Am Fam* bombarder au gaz lacrymogène
mace¹ [meɪs] *n (weapon, symbol of office)* masse *f*
mace² *n (spice)* macis *m*
Macedonia [mæsə'dəʊnɪə] *n* la Macédoine
Macedonian [mæsə'dəʊnɪən] **1** *n* (**a**) *(person)* Macé-
donien(enne) *m,f* (**b**) *(language)* macédonien *m*
  2 *adj* macédonien(enne)
Mach [mæk] *n Phys* **M. (number)** (nombre *m* de) Mach
machete [mə'ʃetɪ] *n* machette *f*
Machiavellian [mækɪə'velɪən] *adj* machiavélique
machinations [mæʃɪ'neɪʃənz] *npl* machinations *fpl*,
manœuvres *fpl*
machine [mə'ʃi:n] **1** *n* machine *f*; *Fig (person)* robot
m; **party/propaganda m.** appareil *m* du parti/de la
propagande; *Comput* **m. code** code *m* machine; **m.
gun** mitrailleuse *f*; *Comput* **m. language** langage *m*
machine; **m. shop** atelier *m* d'usinage; **m. tool** machine-outil *f*; **m. translation** traduction *f* assistée par
ordinateur
  2 *vt* (**a**) *Ind* usiner (**b**) *(with sewing machine)* coudre
ou piquer à la machine
machine-gun [mə'ʃi:ngʌn] *vt* mitrailler
machine-readable [mə'ʃi:n'ri:dəbəl] *adj Comput* lisible par ordinateur
machinery [mə'ʃi:nərɪ] *n (machines)* machines *fpl*,
machinerie *f*; *Fig (of organization)* rouages *mpl*
machinist [mə'ʃi:nɪst] *n (on sewing machine)* mécani-
cien(enne) *m,f*; *(on machine tool)* ouvrier(ère) *m,f*
machismo [mæ'tʃɪzməʊ] *n* machisme *m*
macho ['mætʃəʊ] *adj* macho *inv*
macintosh = mackintosh
mackerel ['mækrəl] *n* maquereau *m*
mackintosh ['mækɪntɒʃ] *n* imperméable *m*

macro ['mækrəʊ] (*pl* **macros**) *n Comput* macro *f*,
macrocommande *f*
macrobiotics ['mækrəʊbaɪ'ɒtɪks] *n* macrobiotique *f*
macrocosm ['mækrəʊkɒzəm] *n* macrocosme *m*
macroeconomics ['mækrəʊi:kə'nɒmɪks] *n* macroéconomie *f*
mad [mæd] *adj* (**a**) *(insane) (person)* fou (folle); *(idea,
plan)* insensé(e); *(dog)* enragé(e); **to go m.** devenir
fou; **as m. as a hatter** fou à lier; **m. with fear** mort(e)
de peur; **there was a m. rush for the door** les gens se
ruèrent vers la porte; *Fam* **to run/work like m.** courir/
travailler comme un fou (une folle); *Fam* **m. cow disease** maladie *f* de la vache folle (**b**) *Fam (enthusiastic)*
to be m. about sth être fou (folle) de qch; **the crowd
went m.** ce fut le délire parmi les spectateurs (**c**) *Fam
(angry)* furieux(euse) *(with or* at contre); **to go m.**
piquer une colère
Madagascan [mædə'gæskən] **1** *n* Malgache *mf*
  2 *adj* malgache
Madagascar [mædə'gæskə(r)] *n* Madagascar *m*
madam ['mædəm] *n (as form of address)* madame *f*; *Br
Fam* **she's a proper little m.** *(of child)* c'est une vraie
petite pimbêche
madcap ['mædkæp] *adj* insensé(e)
madden ['mædən] *vt* exaspérer
maddening ['mædənɪŋ] *adj* exaspérant(e)
made [meɪd] *pt & pp of* **make**
Madeira [mə'dɪərə] *n (island)* Madère *f*; *(wine)* madère *m*
made-up [meɪ'dʌp] *adj* (**a**) *(story, excuse)* inventé(e)
de toutes pièces (**b**) *(wearing make-up)* maquillé(e)
madhouse ['mædhaʊs] *n Fam* maison *f* de fous
madly ['mædlɪ] *adv* (**a**) *(insanely, desperately)* comme
un fou (une folle) (**b**) *Fam (exciting, interested, jealous)* follement; **m. in love** follement *ou* éperdument
amoureux(euse)
madman ['mædmən] *n* fou *m*, dément *m*
madness ['mædnɪs] *n* folie *f*, démence *f*; **it's sheer m.!**
c'est de la folie pure!
madonna [mə'dɒnə] *n* madone *f*
Madrid [mə'drɪd] *n* Madrid
madwoman ['mædwʊmən] *n* folle *f*, démente *f*
maelstrom ['meɪlstrəm] *n (confusion)* tourbillon *m*
maestro ['maɪstrəʊ] *(pl* **maestros**) *n* maestro *m*
Mafia ['mæfɪə] *n* **the M.** la Mafia
mag [mæg] *n Fam* magazine *m*, revue *f*
magazine [mægə'zi:n] *n* (**a**) *(publication)* magazine
m, revue *f* (**b**) *(on radio, TV)* **m. (show)** magazine *m*
(**c**) *(for gun)* magasin *m*; *(ammunition store)* dépôt *m*
de munitions

magenta [məˈdʒentə] **1** n magenta m
2 adj magenta inv
maggot [ˈmæɡət] n asticot m
Maghreb [mæˈɡreb] n the M. le Maghreb
Magi [ˈmeɪdʒaɪ] npl the M. les Rois mpl mages
magic [ˈmædʒɪk] **1** n magie f; as if by m. comme par enchantement; **black/white** m. magie f noire/blanche
2 adj (**a**) (supernatural) magique; **m. carpet** tapis m volant; Fam **m. mushrooms** champignons mpl (hallucinogènes); **m. wand** baguette f magique (**b**) Br Fam (excellent) génial(e)
▶**magic away** (pt & pp **magicked**) vt sep faire disparaître comme par enchantement
magical [ˈmædʒɪkəl] adj magique
magician [məˈdʒɪʃən] n magicien(enne) m,f
magisterial [mædʒɪsˈtɪərɪəl] adj magistral(e); Law de magistrat
magistrate [ˈmædʒɪstreɪt] n Law magistrat m; **magistrates' court** ≃ tribunal m d'instance
magnanimity [mæɡnəˈnɪmɪtɪ] n magnanimité f
magnanimous [mæɡˈnænɪməs] adj magnanime
magnate [ˈmæɡneɪt] n magnat m
magnesium [mæɡˈniːzɪəm] n Chem magnésium m
magnet [ˈmæɡnɪt] n aimant m; Fig (for tourists, investors) pôle m d'attraction
magnetic [mæɡˈnetɪk] adj also Fig magnétique; **m. card** carte f magnétique; **m. compass** boussole f; **m. tape** bande f magnétique
magnetism [ˈmæɡnɪtɪzəm] n also Fig magnétisme m
magnification [mæɡnɪfɪˈkeɪʃən] n grossissement m; (of sound) amplification f
magnificence [mæɡˈnɪfɪsəns] n magnificence f
magnificent [mæɡˈnɪfɪsənt] adj magnifique; (meal, wine) excellent(e)
magnify [ˈmæɡnɪfaɪ] (pt & pp **magnified**) vt (image) grossir, agrandir; (sound) amplifier; Fig (importance, problem) exagérer
magnifying glass [ˈmæɡnɪfaɪɪŋˈɡlɑːs] n loupe f
magnitude [ˈmæɡnɪtjuːd] n ampleur f; **a problem of the first m.** un problème majeur
magnolia [mæɡˈnəʊlɪə] **1** n (tree) magnolia m
2 adj couleur magnolia (inv), blanc rosé (inv)
magnum [ˈmæɡnəm] n (of champagne) magnum m
magpie [ˈmæɡpaɪ] n pie f; Fig **he's a bit of a m.** il a quelque chose du collectionneur fou
mahogany [məˈhɒɡənɪ] **1** n (wood, colour) acajou m
2 adj en acajou
maid [meɪd] n (servant) bonne f, domestique f; **m. of honour** (to queen) demoiselle f d'honneur; Am (at wedding) première demoiselle f d'honneur
maiden [ˈmeɪdən] **1** n Lit (girl) jeune fille f
2 adj (flight, voyage) inaugural(e); **m. aunt** tante f célibataire; **m. name** nom m de jeune fille; Parl **m. speech** premier discours m
mail¹ [meɪl] **1** n (**a**) (letters, parcels) courrier m; **it came in the m.** c'est arrivé au courrier; Am **m. bomb** = lettre ou colis piégé(e) (b) (system) poste f; **by m.** par la poste; Comput **m. bomb** = messages envoyés en masse pour bloquer une boîte aux lettres; Comput **m. merge** publipostage m; Com **m. order catalogue/company** catalogue m/entreprise f de vente par correspondance; **by m. order** par correspondance; **m. train** train m postal (**c**) Comput courrier m électronique, mél m, Can courriel m
2 vt (**a**) (letter) poster; (parcel) envoyer ou expédier par la poste (**b**) Comput (message, document) envoyer

par courrier électronique; (person) envoyer un courrier électronique à
mail² n (armour) mailles fpl
mailbag [ˈmeɪlbæɡ] n sac m postal; **she gets a huge m.** (of celebrity, politician) elle reçoit énormément de courrier
mailbox [ˈmeɪlbɒks] n Am & Comput boîte f aux lettres
mailing [ˈmeɪlɪŋ] n (mailshot) publipostage m, mailing m; **m. list** fichier m d'adresses
mailman [ˈmeɪlmæn] n Am facteur m
mailshot [ˈmeɪlʃɒt] n publipostage m, mailing m
maim [meɪm] vt mutiler, estropier
main [meɪn] **1** n (**a**) (pipe) conduite f (principale); **the mains** (electricity) le secteur; **to turn the water off at the mains** couper l'arrivée d'eau; **gas from the mains** gaz de ville (**b**) **in the m.** (generally) en général, en gros
2 adj principal(e); **the m. thing is to...** l'essentiel est de...; Gram **m. clause** proposition f principale; **m. course** plat m de résistance; **m. entrance** entrée f principale; Rail **m. line** grande ligne f; **m. road** grande route f; Fam **m. squeeze** petit(e) ami(e) m,f; **m. street** rue f principale
mainframe [ˈmeɪnfreɪm] n Comput ordinateur m central
mainland [ˈmeɪnlænd] n continent m; **m. Europe** l'Europe continentale
mainline [ˈmeɪnlaɪn] vi Fam (inject drugs) se piquer
mainly [ˈmeɪnlɪ] adv principalement; **the passengers were m. Spanish** la plupart des passagers étaient espagnols
mainspring [ˈmeɪnsprɪŋ] n Fig (of change, revolution) moteur m
mainstay [ˈmeɪnsteɪ] n (of economy, philosophy) pilier m, base f
mainstream [ˈmeɪnstriːm] **1** n courant m principal
2 adj ordinaire
maintain [meɪnˈteɪn] vt (**a**) (preserve) (order, reputation) maintenir; (silence, attitude) garder; **to m. one's enthusiasm** rester enthousiaste (**b**) (building, machine, road) entretenir (**c**) (family) subvenir aux besoins de (**d**) (state) **to m. that...** soutenir que...
maintenance [ˈmeɪntɪnəns] n (**a**) (of car, building, roads) entretien m; **m. costs** frais mpl d'entretien (**b**) Law (alimony) pension f alimentaire
maisonette [meɪzəˈnet] n (appartement m) duplex m
maize [meɪz] n maïs m
Maj (**a**) Mil (abbr Major) Cdt (**b**) Mus (abbr Major) M
majestic [məˈdʒestɪk] adj majestueux(euse)
majesty [ˈmædʒəstɪ] n majesté f; **His/Her M.** Sa Majesté le Roi/la Reine
major [ˈmeɪdʒə(r)] **1** n (**a**) Mil (in air force) ≃ commandant m, Can & Belg ≃ major m; (in infantry) chef m de bataillon; (in cavalry) chef m d'escadron; **m. general** général m de division (**b**) Am Univ (subject) matière f principale
2 adj (**a**) (important) majeur(e); (most important) principal(e); (accident, illness) très grave; **of m. importance** de la plus haute importance (**b**) Mus majeur(e)
3 vi Am Univ **to m. in sth** se spécialiser en qch
Majorca [məˈjɔːkə] n Majorque f
Majorcan [məˈjɔːkən] **1** n Majorquin(e) m,f
2 adj majorquin(e)
majority [məˈdʒɒrɪtɪ] (pl **majorities**) n (**a**) (in vote) majorité f; **to be in a** or **the m.** être majoritaire; **m. decision** décision f prise à la majorité; Pol **m. rule**

système *m* majoritaire; *Law* **m. verdict** verdict *m* de la majorité; *Pol* **there was a m. vote in favour of...** on a voté à la majorité pour... (**b**) *Law (age)* majorité *f*
make [meɪk] **1** *vt (pt & pp made* [meɪd]) (**a**) *(produce, perform)* faire; *(payment)* effectuer; *(decision)* prendre; **made in Spain** fabriqué(e) en Espagne; **made from** *or* **of stone/wood** en pierre/bois; **I'll show them what I'm made of!** je vais leur montrer de quel bois je me chauffe!; **I'm not made of money!** je ne suis pas millionnaire!; **to m. something of oneself** faire quelque chose de sa vie; **two and two m. four** deux et deux font quatre; **to m. a choice** prendre une décision; **it doesn't m. any difference** cela ne change rien; **to m. a noise** faire du bruit
(**b**) *(earn)* gagner; **to m. a living** gagner sa vie; **to m. a name for oneself** se faire un nom
(**c**) *(make successful)* **this is the book that made her** ce livre l'a rendue célèbre; *Fam* **to m. it** *(be successful)* réussir; **you've got it made** tu as la belle vie; **it's m. or break** ça passe ou ça casse; **it made my day** il m'a fait très plaisir
(**d**) *(cause to be)* **to m. sb happy/sad** rendre qn heureux(euse)/triste; **to m. sb hungry** donner faim à qn; **to m. sb tired** fatiguer qn
(**e**) *(compel)* **to m. sb do sth** faire faire qch à qn; **don't m. me laugh!** tu me fais rire!
(**f**) *(estimate, calculate)* **what time do you m. it?** quelle heure avez-vous?; **I m. it £50 in total** j'arrive à 50 livres en tout
(**g**) *(reach)* **to m. it** *(arrive in time)* arriver à temps; *(finish in time)* finir à temps; **to m. the final** *(of team, competitor)* arriver en finale; **to m. the first team** être sélectionné(e) pour jouer dans la première équipe
(**h**) *(become, be)* **she'll m. a good doctor/singer** elle fera un bon médecin/une bonne chanteuse; **the report makes interesting reading** le rapport est intéressant à lire
(**i**) *(manage to attend)* *(show, meeting)* assister à; **I can m. two o'clock** je peux être là à deux heures
2 *vi* (**a**) **to m. as if** *or* **as though to do sth** *(get ready to)* s'apprêter à faire qch; *(pretend)* faire semblant de faire qch
(**b**) **to m. do** *(cope)* se débrouiller; **to m. do with** se contenter de; **to m. believe (that)...** imaginer que...
(**c**) **to m. sure** *or* **certain of** s'assurer de
3 *n* (**a**) *(brand)* marque *f*
(**b**) *Fam* **to be on the m.** *(financially)* chercher à s'en mettre plein les poches; *(sexually)* draguer
▸**make after** *vt insep (chase)* se lancer à la poursuite de
▸**make for** *vt insep* (**a**) *(head towards)* se diriger vers (**b**) *(contribute to)* contribuer à
▸**make of** *vt sep* **what do you m. of the new manager?** que pensez-vous du nouveau directeur?; **I don't know what to m. of that remark** je ne sais pas comment interpréter cette remarque
▸**make off** *vi Fam (leave)* filer, décamper
▸**make off with** *vt insep Fam (steal)* filer avec
▸**make out 1** *vt sep* (**a**) *(understand, decipher)* comprendre; *(see, hear)* distinguer; *(handwriting)* déchiffrer (**b**) *(write)* *(list, cheque)* faire (**c**) *Fam (claim)* **to m. out (that)...** prétendre que...
2 *vi Am Fam (sexually)* se peloter
▸**make over** *vt sep (transfer)* céder (**to** à)
▸**make up 1** *vt sep* (**a**) *(story, excuses)* inventer (**b**) *(deficit, loss)* combler; **I'll m. it up to you later, I promise** je te le revaudrai, je te le promets (**c**) *(complete)*

(team, amount) compléter (**d**) *(form)* constituer, composer; **to m. up one's mind** se décider (**e**) *(put together) (list)* faire; *(parcel, bed)* faire; **to m. up a prescription** préparer les médicaments prescrits sur une ordonnance (**f**) *(apply make-up to)* maquiller; **to m. oneself up** se maquiller
2 *vi (end quarrel)* se réconcilier
▸**make up for** *vt insep* compenser; *(lost time)* rattraper
make-believe ['meɪkbɪliːv] **1** *n* fantaisie *f*; **to live in a land of m.** ne pas avoir le sens des réalités
2 *adj* imaginaire
makeover ['meɪkəʊvə(r)] *n (of appearance)* séance *f* de maquillage; *Fig* transformation *f*
maker ['meɪkə(r)] *n* (**a**) *(manufacturer)* fabricant *m*; *(of planes, cars)* constructeur *m* (**b**) **to meet one's M.** monter au ciel
makeshift ['meɪkʃɪft] *adj* de fortune
make-up ['meɪkʌp] *n* (**a**) *(cosmetics)* maquillage *m*; **m. artist** maquilleur(euse) *m,f*; **m. bag** trousse *f* à maquillage; **m. remover** démaquillant *m* (**b**) *(composition) (of team, group)* composition *f*; *(of person)* caractère *m*
making ['meɪkɪŋ] *n (of goods)* fabrication *f*; **the film was three years in the m.** le tournage du film a duré trois ans; **history in the m.** l'histoire en train de se faire; **a poet in the m.** un poète en herbe; **the problem is of her own m.** c'est un problème qu'elle s'est elle-même créé; **he has the makings of an actor** il a tout ce qu'il faut pour devenir acteur
maladjusted [mælə'dʒʌstɪd] *adj* inadapté(e)
maladroit [mælə'drɔɪt] *adj* maladroit(e)
malady ['mælədɪ] *(pl* **maladies** *) n Fig* mal *m*
Malagasy ['mæləgæsɪ] **1** *n (language)* malgache *m*
2 *adj* malgache
malaise [mæ'leɪz] *n* malaise *m*
malaria [mə'leərɪə] *n* malaria *f*, paludisme *m*
Malawi [mə'lɑːwɪ] *n* le Malawi
Malawian [mə'lɑːwɪən] **1** *n* Malawien(enne) *m,f*
2 *adj* malawien(enne)
Malay [mə'leɪ] **1** *n* (**a**) *(person)* Malais(e) *m,f* (**b**) *(language)* malais *m*
2 *adj* malais(e)
Malaysia [mə'leɪzɪə] *n* la Malaisie
Malaysian [mə'leɪən] **1** *n* Malais(e) *m,f*
2 *adj* malais(e)
Maldives ['mɔːldiːvz] *npl* **the M.** les (îles *fpl)* Maldives *fpl*
male [meɪl] **1** *n (person)* homme *m*; *(animal)* mâle *m*
2 *adj* mâle; *(sex, attitude, public)* masculin(e); **m. chauvinist pig** phallocrate *m*; **m. nurse** infirmier *m*
malefactor ['mælɪfæktə(r)] *n Lit* malfaiteur(trice) *m, f*
malevolence [mə'levələns] *n* malveillance *f*
malevolent [mə'levələnt] *adj* malveillant(e)
malformed [mæl'fɔːmd] *adj* difforme
malfunction [mæl'fʌŋkʃən] **1** *n* mauvais fonctionnement *m*
2 *vi* mal fonctionner
Mali ['mɑːlɪ] *n* le Mali
malice ['mælɪs] *n* méchanceté *f*; *Law* **with m. aforethought** avec préméditation
malicious [mə'lɪʃəs] *adj* méchant(e), malveillant(e)
maliciously [mə'lɪʃəslɪ] *adv* méchamment, avec malveillance
malign [mə'laɪn] **1** *adj* pernicieux(euse)
2 *vt* calomnier, diffamer

malignant [mə'lɪgnənt] *adj (person)* malveillant(e), méchant(e); *(tumour)* malin(igne)
malinger [mə'lɪŋgə(r)] *vi* faire semblant d'être malade
malingerer [mə'lɪŋgərə(r)] *n* simulateur(trice) *m,f*
mall [mɔːl] *n Am* **(shopping) m.** centre *m* commercial
mallard ['mælɑːd] *n* colvert *m*
malleable ['mælɪəbəl] *adj also Fig* malléable
mallet ['mælɪt] *n* maillet *m*
malnourished [mæl'nʌrɪʃt] *adj* sous-alimenté(e)
malnutrition [mælnjuː'trɪʃən] *n* malnutrition *f*
malpractice [mæl'præktɪs] *n* faute *f* professionnelle
malt [mɔːlt] *n* malt *m*; **m. vinegar** vinaigre *m* de malt; **m. whisky** whisky *m* de malt
Malta ['mɔːltə] *n* Malte *f*
Maltese [mɔːl'tiːz] **1** *n* (**a**) *(person)* Maltais(e) *m,f*; **the M.** les Maltais *mpl* (**b**) *(language)* maltais *m*
2 *adj* maltais(e); **the M. cross** la croix de Malte
maltreat [mæl'triːt] *vt* maltraiter
maltreatment [mæl'triːtmənt] *n* mauvais traitements *mpl*
malware ['mælweə(r)] *n Comput* code *m* malicieux, malware *m*
mammal ['mæməl] *n* mammifère *m*
mammary ['mæmərɪ] *adj Anat* mammaire; **m. glands** glandes *fpl* mammaires
mammography [mæ'mɒgrəfɪ] *(pl* **mammographies**) *n Med* mammographie *f*
mammoth ['mæməθ] **1** *n (animal)* mammouth *m*
2 *adj (huge)* gigantesque
mammy ['mæmɪ] *(pl* **mammies**) *n Fam* maman *f*
man [mæn] **1** *n (pl* **men** [men]) (**a**) *(adult male)* homme *m*; *Fam* **hey, m.!** eh toi!; *Fam* **how you doing, m.?** comment ça va, vieux?; **a m.'s jacket/bicycle** une veste/bicyclette d'homme; **the army will make a m. of him** l'armée en fera un homme; **he took it like a m.** il a pris ça courageusement; **this will separate the men from the boys** c'est là qu'on verra les vrais hommes; **to be m. enough to do sth** être assez courageux pour faire qch; **he's just the m. for the job** c'est l'homme qu'il nous faut; **to be one's own m.** être son (propre) maître; **he's a m.'s m.** il aime bien être avec ses copains; **the m. in the street** l'homme de la rue; **a m. of God** un homme d'église; **a m. of the world** un homme d'expérience (**b**) *(individual, person)* homme *m*; **any m.** n'importe qui; **few men** peu d'hommes; **to reply as one m.** répondre d'une seule voix; **they were patriots to a m.** ils étaient tous patriotes (**c**) *(husband, partner)* **my m.** mon homme (**d**) *(humanity)* l'homme *m* (**e**) *(employee) (in factory)* homme *m*, ouvrier *m*; *(servant)* valet *m*, domestique *m*; *(soldier)* homme *m*, soldat *m*; **our m. in Rome** *(diplomat)* notre envoyé à Rome; *(spy)* notre agent à Rome; *(reporter)* notre correspondant à Rome (**f**) *(in chess)* pièce *f*; *(in draughts)* pion *m*
2 *vt (pt & pp* **manned**) *(machine)* assurer le fonctionnement de; *(plane, boat)* être membre de l'équipage de; **to m. the phone** répondre au téléphone; **a manned flight** un vol habité
manacles ['mænəkəlz] *npl* menottes *fpl*
manage ['mænɪdʒ] **1** *vt* (**a**) *(company, project)* diriger; *(shop, hotel)* être le gérant de; *(economy, resources, money, time)* gérer (**b**) *(situation)* gérer; **to know how to m. sb** savoir (comment) prendre qn; **to m. to do sth** *(succeed)* réussir *ou* arriver à faire qch; **I can't m. three suitcases** je ne peux pas porter trois valises; **£100 is the most that I can m.** *(to pay)* je ne peux pas aller au-delà de 100 livres; **can you m.**

dinner on Thursday? est-ce que vous pouvez venir dîner jeudi?
2 *vi (cope)* se débrouiller (**with** avec); **to m. without sb/sth** pouvoir se passer de qn/qch; **he'll never m. on his own** il n'y arrivera pas tout seul
manageable ['mænɪdʒəbəl] *adj (object, size, vehicle)* maniable; *(hair)* facile à coiffer
management ['mænɪdʒmənt] *n* (**a**) *(activity) (of company, project)* gestion *f*, direction *f*; *(of economy, resources, shop, hotel)* gestion *f*; **m. consultant** conseiller(ère) *m,f* en gestion; **m. studies** études *fpl* de gestion (**b**) *(managers, employers)* direction *f*; **under new m.** *(sign)* changement de propriétaire; **m. buyout** rachat *m* d'une société par la direction; **m. team** équipe *f* dirigeante
manager ['mænɪdʒə(r)] *n (of bank, company)* directeur(trice) *m,f*; *(of shop, hotel, bar)* gérant(e) *m,f*; *(of boxer, singer, football team)* manager *m*
manageress [mænɪdʒə'res] *n (of bank, company)* directrice *f*; *(of shop, hotel, bar)* gérante *f*
managerial [mænɪ'dʒɪərɪəl] *adj* directorial(e); **m. staff** cadres *mpl*; **m. skills** qualités *fpl* de gestionnaire
managing director ['mænɪdʒɪŋdaɪ'rektə(r)] *n* directeur(trice) *m,f* général(e)
Manchester ['mæntʃestə(r)] *n* Manchester
Mancunian [mæŋ'kjuːnɪən] **1** *n* = personne née à ou habitant Manchester
2 *adj* de Manchester
Mandarin ['mændərɪn] *n (language)* mandarin *m*
mandarin ['mændərɪn] *n* (**a**) *(fruit)* mandarine *f* (**b**) *(official)* mandarin *m*
mandate ['mændeɪt] *n* mandat *m*
mandatory ['mændətərɪ] *adj* obligatoire
mandible ['mændɪbəl] *n (of insect)* mandibule *f*; *(of vertebrate)* mâchoire *f* inférieure
mandolin ['mændəlɪn] *n* mandoline *f*
mane [meɪn] *n* crinière *f*
man-eater ['mæniːtə(r)] *n* (**a**) *(animal)* mangeur *m* d'hommes (**b**) *Hum (woman)* mangeuse *f* d'hommes
man-eating ['mæniːtɪŋ] *adj* mangeur(euse) d'hommes
maneuver, maneuverable *Am* = manoeuvre, manoeuvrable
manfully ['mænfʊlɪ] *adv* courageusement, vaillamment
manganese [mæŋgə'niːz] *n Chem* manganèse *m*
mange [meɪndʒ] *n* gale *f*
manger ['meɪndʒə(r)] *n* mangeoire *f*
mangle ['mæŋgəl] **1** *n (for clothes)* essoreuse *f* (à rouleaux)
2 *vt (body)* mutiler; *(car)* broyer; *(text)* massacrer
mango ['mæŋgəʊ] *(pl* **mangoes**) *n* mangue *f*
mangrove ['mæŋgrəʊv] *n* palétuvier *m*; **m. swamp** mangrove *f*
mangy ['meɪndʒɪ] *adj (animal)* galeux(euse); *(carpet, coat)* miteux, miteux(euse)
manhandle ['mænhændəl] *vt (person)* malmener; *(large object)* transporter à la force des bras
manhole ['mænhəʊl] *n (in road)* bouche *f* d'égout; **m. cover** plaque *f* d'égout
manhood ['mænhʊd] *n* (**a**) *(maturity)* âge *m* d'homme; **to reach m.** devenir un homme (**b**) *(masculinity)* virilité *f* (**c**) *(men collectively)* **Scottish m.** les hommes *mpl* écossais
man-hour ['mænaʊə(r)] *n Econ* heure *f* de travail
manhunt ['mænhʌnt] *n* chasse *f* à l'homme

mania ['meɪnɪə] n *(liking)* passion f (**for** pour); *(psychological)* manie f; **to have a m. for doing sth** avoir la manie de faire qch

maniac ['meɪnɪæk] n fou (folle) m,f; **to drive like a m.** conduire comme un fou (une folle)

manic ['mænɪk] adj *Fig (person)* stressé(e); *(activity)* frénétique

manic-depressive ['mænɪkdɪ'presɪv] *Psy* **1** n maniaco-dépressif(ive) m,f
2 adj maniaco-dépressif(ive)

manicure ['mænɪkjʊə(r)] **1** n manucure f; **to have a m.** se faire faire les ongles
2 vt **to m. one's nails** se faire les ongles

manifest ['mænɪfest] **1** n *(of ship, aircraft)* manifeste m
2 adj manifeste, évident(e)
3 vt manifester

manifestation [mænɪfes'teɪʃən] n manifestation f

manifestly ['mænɪfestlɪ] adv manifestement

manifesto [mænɪ'festəʊ] *(pl* **manifestos)** n *Pol* manifeste m

manifold ['mænɪfəʊld] **1** n *Aut* collecteur m
2 adj *Lit (numerous)* multiple, nombreux(euse)

Manila [mə'nɪlə] n Manille

mani(l)la envelope [mə'nɪlə'envələʊp] n enveloppe f en papier kraft

manipulate [mə'nɪpjʊleɪt] vt *also Fig* manipuler

manipulation [mənɪpju'leɪʃən] n *also Fig* manipulation f

manipulative [mə'nɪpjʊlətɪv] adj *Pej* manipulateur (trice)

mankind [mæn'kaɪnd] n l'humanité f

manky ['mæŋkɪ] adj *Br Fam (dirty)* miteux(euse); *(worthless)* nul (nulle)

manliness ['mænlɪnɪs] n virilité f

manly ['mænlɪ] adj viril(e)

man-made ['mænmeɪd] adj *(fabric, product)* synthétique; *(lake, beach)* artificiel(elle); **a m. disaster** un désastre provoqué par l'homme

mannequin ['mænɪkɪn] n *(person)* mannequin m

manner ['mænə(r)] n (**a**) *(way, method, style)* manière f, façon f; **the m. in which...** la manière ou façon dont...; **in a m. of speaking** pour ainsi dire, en quelque sorte (**b**) **manners** *(etiquette)* manières fpl; **it's bad manners to stare** il est mal élevé de dévisager les gens; **he's got no manners** il ne sait pas se tenir (**c**) *(type)* **all m. of people/things** toutes sortes de gens/choses; (**d**) *(attitude, behaviour)* **I don't like his m.** je n'aime pas sa façon d'être; **she's got a very abrasive m.** elle est très acerbe (**e**) **manners** *(social usages)* mœurs fpl

mannered ['mænəd] adj maniéré(e)

mannerism ['mænərɪzəm] n manie f, tic m

manoeuvrable, *Am* **maneuverable** [mə'nu:vrəbəl] adj maniable

manoeuvre, *Am* **maneuver** [mə'nu:və(r)] **1** n *also Fig* manœuvre f; *Fig* **there wasn't much room for m.** la marge de manœuvre était assez limitée; **to be on manoeuvres** *(of soldiers)* être en manœuvre(s)
2 vt manœuvrer; **she manoeuvred the car into the space** elle a garé la voiture dans l'emplacement
3 vi manœuvrer

manor ['mænə(r)] n **m. (house)** manoir m

manpower ['mænpaʊə(r)] n main-d'œuvre f

mansion ['mænʃən] n *(in country)* château m; *(in town)* hôtel m particulier

manslaughter ['mænslɔ:tə(r)] n *Law* homicide m involontaire

mantelpiece ['mæntəlpi:s] n dessus m de cheminée; **on the m.** sur la cheminée

mantis ['mæntɪs] n *Am* mante f religieuse

mantle ['mæntəl] n (**a**) *Lit (of snow)* manteau m; *Fig* **to take on the m. of office** assumer les responsabilités qui incombent au poste (**b**) *(of gas lamp)* manchon m (**c**) *Geol* manteau m

man-to-man [mæntʊ'mæn] adj & adv d'homme à homme

manual ['mænjʊəl] **1** n *(handbook)* manuel m
2 adj *(work, worker)* manuel(elle); **m. dexterity** dextérité f

manually ['mænjʊəlɪ] adv manuellement

manufacture [mænjʊ'fæktʃə(r)] **1** n fabrication f; *(of vehicles)* construction f
2 vt fabriquer; *(vehicles)* construire; *(clothes)* confectionner; *Fig (evidence)* fabriquer (de toutes pièces)

manufacturer [mænjʊ'fæktʃərə(r)] n *Ind* fabricant m; *(of vehicles)* constructeur m

manufacturing [mænjʊ'fæktʃərɪŋ] *Ind* **1** n l'industrie f (manufacturière)
2 adj *(centre, sector)* industriel(elle); **m. capacity** capacité f de production; **m. industries** industries fpl manufacturières

manure [mə'njʊə(r)] **1** n fumier m; **liquid m.** purin m
2 vt engraisser

manuscript ['mænjʊskrɪpt] n manuscrit m

many ['menɪ] *(comparative* **more** [mɔ:(r)]*, superlative* **most** [məʊst]*)* **1** pron beaucoup; **m. of us/them** beaucoup d'entre nous/eux; **not m.** pas beaucoup; **too m.** trop; **as m. as you like** autant que vous voulez; **there were as m. as 100 people there** il y avait bien jusqu'à 100 personnes; *Fam* **to have had one too m.** avoir bu un coup de trop
2 adj beaucoup de; **m. people** beaucoup de gens; **m. times** souvent, bien des fois; **not m.** pas beaucoup de; **in m. ways** de bien des façons; **not in so m. words** pas aussi explicitement; **there were so m. people that...** il y avait tant de gens que...; **a good m. people** un bon nombre de gens; **too m.** trop de; **as m.... as** autant de... que; **m.'s the time I've done that** j'ai fait ça bien des fois; *Prov* **m. hands make light work** à plusieurs, l'ouvrage avance vite

many-coloured ['menɪ'kʌləd] adj multicolore

Maori ['maʊrɪ] **1** n Maori(e) m,f
2 adj maori(e)

map [mæp] **1** n carte f; *(of underground, town)* plan m; *Fig* **this will put Stonybridge on the m.** cela va faire parler de Stonybridge; **m. reference** coordonnées fpl
2 vt *(pt & pp* **mapped)** *(region)* dresser une carte de

▶**map out** vt sep *(route)* tracer; *(plan, programme)* élaborer; **she had her career all mapped out** sa carrière était toute tracée

maple ['meɪpəl] n érable m; **m. leaf** feuille f d'érable; **m. syrup** sirop m d'érable

mar [mɑ:(r)] *(pt & pp* **marred)** vt gâcher

Mar *(abbr* **March)** mars

maracas [mə'rækəz] npl *Mus* maracas fpl

marathon ['mærəθən] n *also Fig* marathon m; **a m. speech** un discours-marathon; **m. runner** marathonien(enne) m,f

marauder [mə'rɔ:də(r)] n maraudeur(euse) m,f

marauding [mə'rɔ:dɪŋ] adj en maraude

marble ['mɑːbəl] *n* (**a**) *(stone)* marbre *m* (**b**) *(glass ball)* bille *f*; *to play* **marbles** jouer aux billes; *Fam Fig* **to lose one's marbles** *(go mad)* perdre la boule

marbled ['mɑːbəld] *adj* marbré(e)

March [mɑːtʃ] *n* mars *m*; *see also* **May**

march [mɑːtʃ] **1** *n* marche *f*; *Fig* **the m. of time** la marche du temps; **on the m.** en marche; **m.** **past** défilé *m*
2 *vt (soldiers)* faire défiler; **he was marched off to prison** il a été emmené en prison
3 *vi (of soldiers)* marcher au pas; *(of soldiers on parade, demonstrators)* défiler; **to m. off** partir; **to m. by** *or* **past (sb/sth)** défiler (devant qn/qch)

marcher ['mɑːtʃə(r)] *n (demonstrator)* manifestant(e) *m,f*

marching orders ['mɑːtʃɪŋ'ɔːdəz] *npl Fam* **to give sb his m.** mettre qn à la porte

mare [meə(r)] *n* jument *f*

margarine [mɑːdʒə'riːn], *Fam* **marge** [mɑːdʒ] *n* margarine *f*

margin ['mɑːdʒɪn] *n* (**a**) *(on page)* marge *f*; **in the m.** dans la marge (**b**) *(edge) (of forest)* orée *f*; **on the margin(s) of society** en marge de la société (**c**) *(gap)* **to win by a narrow m.** gagner de justesse; **to win by an enormous m.** gagner haut la main; **a m. of error** une marge d'erreur (**d**) *Com* marge *f* bénéficiaire

marginal ['mɑːdʒɪnəl] **1** *n Br Pol* siège *m* à majorité précaire
2 *adj* (**a**) *(improvement, increase)* léger(ère) (**b**) *(note)* en marge (**c**) *Br Pol (seat)* à majorité précaire

marginalize ['mɑːdʒɪnəlaɪz] *vt* marginaliser

marginally ['mɑːdʒɪnəlɪ] *adv* légèrement

marigold ['mærɪɡəʊld] *n* souci *m*

marihuana, marijuana [mærɪ'wɑːnə] *n* marijuana *f*

marina [mə'riːnə] *n* port *m* de plaisance

marinade ['mærɪneɪd] *Culin* **1** *n* marinade *f*
2 *vt* (faire) mariner

marinate ['mærɪneɪt] *vt Culin* (faire) mariner

marine [mə'riːn] **1** *n (soldier)* fusilier *m* marin; *Am Fam* **(go) tell it to the marines!** (allez dire ça) à d'autres!
2 *adj (life, biology)* marin(e); **m. engineering** génie *m* maritime

mariner ['mærɪnə(r)] *n Lit* marin *m*

marionette [mærɪə'net] *n* marionnette *f* à fils

marital ['mærɪtəl] *adj* conjugal(e); **m. status** situation *f* de famille

maritime ['mærɪtaɪm] *adj* maritime

marjoram ['mɑːdʒərəm] *n* marjolaine *f*

mark¹ [mɑːk] *n Formerly (German currency)* mark *m*

mark² **1** *n* (**a**) *(scratch, stain)* tache *f*, marque *f* (**b**) *(symbol)* marque *f* (**c**) *(sign, proof)* signe *m*; **as a m. of respect** en signe de respect; **years of imprisonment had left their m. on him** ses années de captivité l'avaient marqué; **to make one's m.** *(succeed)* faire ses preuves (**d**) *(target)* **his comments hit the m.** ses remarques ont touché en plein dans le mille; **unemployment has passed the three million m.** le nombre des chômeurs a dépassé la barre des trois millions; **her accusation was wide of the m.** son accusation était complètement à côté de la plaque; **he's not up to the m.** il n'est pas à la hauteur (**e**) *(in test, exam)* note *f*; **full marks** la note maximale (**f**) *(in race)* **on your marks! get set! go!** à vos marques! prêts! partez!; **to be quick off the m.** démarrer vite; *Fig* avoir l'esprit vif; **to be slow off the m.** prendre un mauvais départ; *Fig* être long à la détente (**g**) *(model,*

of machine) **m. II/III** série *f* II/III (**h**) *(on cooker)* **(gas) m. 4** thermostat *m* 4
2 *vt* (**a**) *(put mark on)* marquer (**b**) *(homework, exam)* noter; **to m. sth right/wrong** compter qch comme juste/faux (**c**) *(indicate)* indiquer; *(anniversary, end, occasion)* marquer; **this decision marks a change in policy** cette décision est le signe d'un changement de politique; *Fig* **to m. time** *(wait)* piétiner (**d**) *(characterize)* caractériser; **his comments were marked by their sarcasm** ses commentaires étaient empreints de sarcasme (**e**) *(in sport) (opponent)* marquer (**f**) *(pay attention to)* **m. my words** notez bien ce que je vais dire
▸ **mark down** *vt sep* (**a**) *(make note of)* noter; **they had him marked down as a troublemaker** ils l'avaient étiqueté comme fauteur de troubles (**b**) *Com (price)* baisser; *(goods)* démarquer
▸ **mark off** *vt sep* (**a**) *(area)* délimiter (**b**) *(tick off)* cocher
▸ **mark out** *vt sep* **to m. sb out** distinguer qn
▸ **mark up** *vt sep (price)* augmenter, majorer; **to be marked up** *(of goods)* avoir augmenté

marked [mɑːkt] *adj* (**a**) *(difference, improvement)* marqué(e), sensible (**b**) *(bearing a mark)* **m. cards** cartes truquées *ou* marquées; **to be a m. man** être surveillé

markedly ['mɑːkɪdlɪ] *adv* nettement

marker ['mɑːkə(r)] *n* (**a**) *(of essay, exam)* correcteur(-trice) *m,f*; **he's a hard m.** il note sévèrement (**b**) **m. (pen)** marqueur *m* (**c**) *(flag, post)* balise *f*; **m. buoy** bouée *f* de balisage

market ['mɑːkɪt] **1** *n* marché *m*; **to put sth on the m.** mettre qch en vente; *Fin* **m. analyst** analyste *mf* du marché; **m. day** jour *m* de marché; *Econ* **(free) m. economy** économie *f* de marché; *Econ* **m. forces** tendances *fpl* du marché; *Br* **m. garden** jardin *m* maraîcher; *Com* **m. leader** leader *m* du marché; *Econ* **m. price** prix *m* du marché; *Com* **m. research** étude *f* de marché; *Com* **m. share** part *f* de marché; *Com* **m. survey** étude *f* de marché; **m. town** ville *f* de marché
2 *vt* commercialiser

marketable ['mɑːkɪtəbəl] *adj* commercialisable

marketing ['mɑːkɪtɪŋ] *n Com (study, theory)* marketing *m*, mercatique *f*; *(of product)* commercialisation *f*; **m. campaign** campagne *f* de marketing; **m. department** service *m* de marketing; **m. manager** responsable *mf ou* directeur(trice) *m,f* du marketing; **m. strategy** stratégie *f* marketing

marketplace ['mɑːkɪtpleɪs] *n* (**a**) *(in village, town)* place *f* du marché (**b**) *Econ* marché *m*; **in the m.** sur le marché

marking ['mɑːkɪŋ] *n* (**a**) **markings** *(on animal) (spots)* taches *fpl*; *(stripes)* rayures *fpl*; *(on plane)* insignes *mpl* (**b**) *(of essay, exam)* correction *f*; **I've got a lot of m. to do** j'ai beaucoup de copies à corriger

markka ['mɑːkə] *n Formerly* mark *m* finlandais

marksman ['mɑːksmən] *n* tireur *m* d'élite

mark-up ['mɑːkʌp] *n (on price)* majoration *f*

marmalade ['mɑːməleɪd] *n* confiture *f* d'oranges

maroon¹ [mə'ruːn] *n* (**a**) *(colour)* bordeaux *m* (**b**) *(firework)* fusée *f* de détresse

maroon² *vt* abandonner; **we were marooned by the floods** nous étions isolés à cause des inondations

marquee [mɑː'kiː] *n* grande tente *f*; *(at circus)* chapiteau *m*

marquis ['mɑːkwɪs] *n* marquis *m*

Marrakesh ['mærəkeʃ] *n* Marrakech *m*

marriage ['mærɪdʒ] *n also Fig* mariage *m*; **a happy m.** un ménage heureux; **she's my aunt by m.** c'est ma tante par alliance; **m. of convenience** mariage *m* de convenance; *Fig* **it was a m. of minds** c'était la rencontre de deux esprits; **m. certificate** certificat *m* de mariage; **m. guidance counsellor** conseiller(ère) *m,f* conjugal(e); **m. vows** vœux *mpl* du mariage

marriageable ['mærɪdʒəbəl] *adj* **a girl of m. age** une fille en âge de se marier

married ['mærɪd] *adj* marié(e); **to get m. (to)** se marier (avec); **m. life** la vie maritale; **m. name** nom *m* de femme mariée; *Mil* **m. quarters** logements *mpl* pour familles

marrow ['mærəʊ] *n* (**a**) *(of bone)* moelle *f* (**b**) *(vegetable)* courge *f*

marrowbone ['mærəʊbəʊn] *n* os *m* à moelle

marrowfat pea ['mærəʊfæt'piː] *n* pois *m* carré

marry ['mærɪ] *(pt & pp* **married**) *vt* (**a**) *(get married to)* épouser, se marier avec; *(of priest, parent)* marier; **will you m. me?** veux-tu m'épouser?; *Fig* **he's married to his job** il n'y a que son travail qui compte (**b**) *(combine)* marier
2 *vi* se marier

►**marry off** *vt sep* marier

Mars [mɑːz] *n (planet)* Mars *f*

Marseilles [mɑːˈseɪ] *n* Marseille

marsh [mɑːʃ] *n* marais *m*, marécage *m*

marshal ['mɑːʃəl] **1** *n* (**a**) *(army officer)* maréchal *m* (**b**) *(at race, demonstration)* membre *m* du service d'ordre
2 *vt (pt & pp* **marshalled,** *Am* **marshaled)** *(vehicles, troops)* rassembler; *(crowd)* canaliser; *(arguments, thoughts)* mettre en ordre

marshland ['mɑːʃlænd] *n* région *f* marécageuse

marshmallow [mɑːʃˈmæləʊ] *n* guimauve *f*

marshy ['mɑːʃɪ] *adj* marécageux(euse)

marsupial [mɑːˈsuːpɪəl] *n* marsupial *m*

martial ['mɑːʃəl] *adj* martial(e); **m. arts** arts *mpl* martiaux; **to declare m. law** proclamer la loi martiale

Martian ['mɑːʃən] *n* Martien(enne) *m,f*

martyr ['mɑːtə(r)] **1** *n* martyr(e) *m,f; Fig* **to be a m. to rheumatism** souffrir le martyre à cause de rhumatismes
2 *vt* martyriser

martyrdom ['mɑːtədəm] *n* martyre *m*

marvel ['mɑːvəl] **1** *n* merveille *f*; **to work marvels** faire des merveilles; **it's a m. they survived** c'est un miracle qu'ils soient encore vivants; *Fam* **you're a m.!** tu es un as!
2 *vi (pt & pp* **marvelled,** *Am* **marveled)** s'émerveiller (**at de**)

marvellous, *Am* **marvelous** ['mɑːvələs] *adj* merveilleux(euse); *Ironic* **(isn't it) m.!** ça, c'est le bouquet *ou* le comble!

Marxism ['mɑːksɪzəm] *n* marxisme *m*

Marxist ['mɑːksɪst] **1** *n* marxiste *mf*
2 *adj* marxiste

marzipan ['mɑːzɪpæn] *n* pâte *f* d'amandes

mascara [mæsˈkɑːrə] *n* mascara *m*

mascot ['mæskət] *n* mascotte *f*

masculine ['mæskjʊlɪn] **1** *n Gram* masculin *m*; **in the m.** au masculin
2 *adj* masculin(e)

masculinity [mæskjʊˈlɪnɪtɪ] *n* masculinité *f*

mash [mæʃ] **1** *n* (**a**) *Fam (mashed potato)* purée *f* (**b**) *(for pigs, poultry)* pâtée *f*
2 *vt* **to m. (up)** broyer; *(vegetables)* écraser

mashed potato [mæʃtpəˈteɪtəʊ] *n* purée *f* de pommes de terre

mask [mɑːsk] **1** *n* masque *m*; *(for eyes only)* loup *m*
2 *vt (conceal)* dissimuler

masked [mɑːskt] *adj* masqué(e)

masking tape ['mɑːskɪnteɪp] *n* ruban *m* de papier adhésif

masochism ['mæsəkɪzəm] *n* masochisme *m*

masochist ['mæsəkɪst] *n* masochiste *mf*

masochistic [mæsəˈkɪstɪk] *adj* masochiste

mason ['meɪsən] *n (builder)* maçon *m*; *(freemason)* franc-maçon *m*

masonry ['meɪsənrɪ] *n (stonework)* maçonnerie *f*

masquerade [mæskəˈreɪd] **1** *n* (**a**) *Fig (disguise)* mascarade *f* (**b**) *(dance)* bal *m* masqué
2 *vi* **to m. as sb** se faire passer pour qn

mass¹ [mæs] **1** *n* (**a**) *(large number)* foule *f*, multitude *f*; *Fam* **I've got masses (of things) to do** j'ai des tas de choses à faire; *Fam* **there's masses of room** il y a plein de place; **m. culture** culture *f* de masse; **m. demonstration** grande manifestation *f*; **m. grave** charnier *m*; **m. hysteria** hystérie *f* collective; **m. media** (mass) médias *mpl*; **m. meeting** grand rassemblement *m*; **m. murderer** tueur *m* fou; **m. production** fabrication *f* en série; **m. protest** protestation *f* en masse; **m. unemployment** chômage *m* sur une grande échelle (**b**) *(shapeless substance)* masse *f* (**c**) *Pol* **the masses** le peuple *m* (**d**) *Phys* masse *f*
2 *vi (of troops, people, clouds)* se masser

mass² *n Rel* messe *f*; **to go to m.** aller à la messe

massacre ['mæsəkə(r)] **1** *n* massacre *m*; *Fam Fig* **it was a m.** *(in sport, election)* ça a été le massacre
2 *vt also Fig* massacrer

massage ['mæsɑːʒ] **1** *n* massage *m*; **m. parlour** salon *m* de massage; **m. therapist** masseur(euse) *m,f*
2 *vt (body)* masser; *Fig* **to m. the figures** manipuler les chiffres

masseur [mæˈsɜː(r)] *n* masseur *m*

masseuse [mæˈsɜːz, *Am* mæˈsuːs] *n* masseuse *f*

massive ['mæsɪv] *adj (increase, scale, dose)* massif(ive); *(amount, building, obstacle)* énorme; *(room)* immense; *(heart attack, stroke)* foudroyant(e)

mass-market [mæsˈmɑːkɪt] *adj (produits)* de grande consommation

mass-produce [mæsprəˈdjuːs] *vt* fabriquer en série

mast [mɑːst] *n (of ship)* mât *m*; *(of radio, TV transmitter)* pylône *m*

mastectomy [mæsˈtektəmɪ] *(pl* **mastectomies**) *n Med* mastectomie *f*

master ['mɑːstə(r)] **1** *n* (**a**) *(man in charge)* maître *m*; *(of ship)* capitaine *m*; **the m. of the house** le maître de maison; **to be one's own m.** être son propre maître; **to be m. of the situation** être maître de la situation; **m. of ceremonies** maître *m* des cérémonies; *(for TV programme)* présentateur *m*; **m. bedroom** chambre *f* principale; **m. copy** original *m*; **m. key** passepartout *m*; **m. plan** plan *m* d'ensemble; **m. race** race *f* supérieure (**b**) *(skilled person)* maître *m*, expert(e) *m,f; Univ* **M. of Arts** *(qualification)* ≃ maîtrise *f* ès lettres; *(person)* ≃ maître *m* ès lettres; *Univ* **M. of Science** *(qualification)* ≃ maîtrise *f* ès sciences; *(person)* ≃ maître *m* ès sciences; **m. mason/builder** maître *m* maçon/d'œuvre; *Mus* **m. class** cours *m* de maître; *Univ* **Masters (degree)** ≃ maîtrise *f* (**in** de) (**c**) *(teacher)* professeur *m*; **fencing/dancing m.** maître *m* d'escrime/de ballet (**d**) *(young boy)* **M. David**

Thomas Monsieur David Thomas (**e**) *Art* an old **m**. une œuvre de maître

2 *vt* maîtriser; *(situation)* dominer

masterful ['mɑːstəfʊl] *adj* autoritaire

masterly ['mɑːstəlɪ] *adj* magistral(e)

mastermind ['mɑːstəmaɪnd] **1** *n* cerveau *m* **2** *vt (project)* diriger, organiser; *(plot, crime)* échafauder

masterpiece ['mɑːstəpiːs] *n* chef-d'œuvre *m*

masterstroke ['mɑːstəstrəʊk] *n* coup *m* de maître

mastery ['mɑːstərɪ] *n* maîtrise *f*

mastiff ['mæstɪf] *n* mastiff *m*

mastitis [mæs'taɪtəs] *n Med* mastite *f*

masturbate ['mæstəbeɪt] *vi* se masturber

masturbation [mæstə'beɪʃən] *n* masturbation *f*

mat [mæt] *n (on floor)* tapis *m; (of straw)* natte *f; (at door)* paillasson *m;* (**table**) **m.** *(for plates)* set *m* de table; *(for dishes)* dessous-de-plat *m inv*

match¹ [mætʃ] *n (for lighting fire, cigarette)* allumette *f*

match² **1** *n* (**a**) *(in sport)* match *m;* **m. point** *(in tennis)* balle *f* de match (**b**) **they're a good m.** *(of clothes)* ils vont bien ensemble; **to meet one's m.** trouver son maître; **to be no m. for sb** ne pas être à l'hauteur par rapport à qn

2 *vt* (**a**) *(equal)* égaler (**b**) *(of colours, clothes)* être assorti(e) à; *(of description, account)* concorder avec (**c**) *(marriage)* **to make a good m.** faire un bon mariage; **we can't m.** their prices nous ne pouvons pas rivaliser avec leurs prix; **to m. sb against sb** opposer qn à qn; **to be well matched** *(of teams, players)* être de même niveau; **a well-matched couple** un couple bien assorti

3 *vi (of colours, clothes)* être assorti(e)s; *(of descriptions, accounts)* concorder

▸**match up** *vt sep (colours, clothes)* assortir

2 *vi (of clothes, colours)* être assorti(e)s; *(of explanations)* concorder; **to m. up to sb's expectations** répondre à l'attente de qn

matchbox ['mætʃbɒks] *n* boîte *f* d'allumettes

matching ['mætʃɪŋ] *adj* assorti(e)

matchless ['mætʃlɪs] *adj* sans pareil

matchmaker ['mætʃmeɪkə(r)] *n* marieur(euse) *m,f*

matchstick ['mætʃstɪk] *n* allumette *f;* **m. man** *or* **figure** bonhomme *m* dessiné de simples traits

mate¹ [meɪt] **1** *n* (**a**) *(sexual partner) (male animal)* mâle *m; (female animal)* femelle *f; (person)* partenaire *mf* (**b**) *Br Fam (friend)* copain (copine) *m,f;* **thanks, m.** merci mon vieux (**c**) *(assistant)* assistant(e) *m,f* (**d**) *(on ship)* officier *m;* (**first**) **m.** second *m*

2 *vt (animals)* accoupler

3 *vi (of animals)* s'accoupler

mate² *(in chess)* **1** *n* mat *m*

2 *vt* mettre mat

material [mə'tɪərɪəl] **1** *n* (**a**) *(substance)* matériau *m*, matière *f; Fig* **he isn't officer m.** il n'a pas l'étoffe d'un officier (**b**) *(for book, article)* matériaux *mpl;* **reading m.** de quoi lire; **she writes all her own m.** *(of singer)* elle écrit ses chansons elle-même (**c**) *(cloth)* tissu *m* (**d**) **materials** *(equipment)* matériel *m*

2 *adj* (**a**) *(needs, possessions)* matériel(elle) (**b**) *(important, relevant)* essentiel(elle); *(fact)* pertinent(e); **the point is m. to my argument** c'est un point essentiel de mon argumentation

materialism [mə'tɪərɪəlɪzəm] *n* matérialisme *m*

materialistic [mətɪərɪə'lɪstɪk] *adj* matérialiste

materialize [mə'tɪərɪəlaɪz] *vi (of hope, threat)* se réaliser; *(of event)* avoir lieu; *(of spirit)* apparaître

materially [mə'tɪərɪəlɪ] *adv* (**a**) *(in money, goods)* matériellement (**b**) *(appreciably)* sensiblement

maternal [mə'tɜːnəl] *adj* maternel(elle)

maternity [mə'tɜːnɪtɪ] *n* maternité *f;* **m. benefit** allocation *f* de maternité; **m. dress** robe *f* de grossesse; **m. hospital** maternité *f;* **m. leave** congé *m* de maternité; **m. ward** maternité *f*

matey ['meɪtɪ] *Br Fam* **1** *n* listen, **m.** écoute, mon pote **2** *adj* pote (**with** avec)

math [mæθ] *n Am* maths *fpl*

mathematical [mæθə'mætɪkəl] *adj* mathématique

mathematician [mæθəmə'tɪʃən] *n* mathématicien(enne) *m,f*

mathematics [mæθə'mætɪks] *n (subject)* mathématiques *fpl; (calculations)* calculs *mpl*

maths [mæθs] *n Br* maths *fpl*

matinée ['mætɪneɪ] *n (of play, film)* matinée *f*

mating ['meɪtɪŋ] *n* accouplement *m;* **m. call** appel *m* du mâle; **m. ritual** parade *f* nuptiale; **m. season** saison *f* des amours

matriarch ['meɪtrɪɑːk] *n* = femme ayant le statut de chef de famille

matriarchal ['meɪtrɪɑːkəl] *adj* matriarcal(e)

matrices ['meɪtrɪsiːz] *pl of* **matrix**

matriculate [mə'trɪkjʊleɪt] *vi* s'inscrire

matriculation [mətrɪkjʊ'leɪʃən] *n* inscription *f*

matrimonial [matrɪ'məʊnɪəl] *adj* matrimonial(e)

matrimony ['mætrɪmənɪ] *n* mariage *m*

matrix ['meɪtrɪks] *n (pl* **matrixes** ['meɪtrɪksɪz] *or* **matrices** ['meɪtrɪsiːz]) *n Math & Tech* matrice *f*

matron ['meɪtrən] *n* (**a**) *Br (in hospital)* infirmière *f* en chef; *(in school)* = intendante et infirmière (**b**) *(older woman)* matrone *f* (**c**) **m. of honour** *(at wedding)* première demoiselle *f* d'honneur

matt [mæt] *adj* mat(e)

matted ['mætɪd] *adj (hair)* emmêlé(e)

matter ['mætə(r)] **1** *n* (**a**) *(affair, issue)* question *f*, problème *m;* **that's a m. of opinion/taste** c'est une question d'opinion/de goût; **it's no easy m.** ce n'est pas simple; **that's quite another m.** ce n'est pas du tout la même chose; **within a m. of hours** en quelques heures; **for that m.** d'ailleurs; **as a m. of course** bien évidemment; **as a m. of fact** en fait; **as matters stand** au point où en sont les choses; **and to make matters worse...** et pour aggraver les choses...; **military matters** questions *fpl* militaires; **business matters** affaires *fpl* (**b**) *(problem)* **what's the m.?** qu'est-ce qu'il y a?; **what's the m. with you?** qu'est-ce que tu as?; **there's something the m. with the car/my foot** j'ai un problème avec la voiture/mon pied (**c**) *(substance)* matière *f* (**d**) *(with "no")* **no m.!** peu importe!; **no m. who/where** qui/où que ce soit; **no m. how hard I try...** j'ai beau essayer...; **no m. what!** do quoi que je fasse

2 *vi* avoir de l'importance (**to** pour); **it doesn't m.** cela n'a pas d'importance, ce n'est rien; **nothing else matters** le reste sans importance; **it doesn't m. to me** ça m'est égal

Matterhorn ['mætəhɔːn] *n* the **M.** le mont Cervin

matter-of-fact ['mætərə'fækt] *adj (person, statement)* terre à terre; *(tone, voice)* neutre; **he was very m. about it** il avait l'air très détaché

matting ['mætɪŋ] *n* tapis *m* de sol tressé

mattress ['mætrɪs] *n* matelas *m*

mature [mə'tjʊə(r)] **1** *adj (person, fruit)* mûr(e); *(hard cheese)* fort(e); **m. garden** jardin *m* planté depuis

plusieurs années; *Br Univ* **m. student** = adulte qui reprend des études
2 *vt (wine)* faire vieillir
3 *vi (of person, fruit)* mûrir; *(of wine)* vieillir; *Fin (of investment)* arriver à échéance
maturity [məˈtjʊərɪtɪ] *n* maturité *f*; *Fin* **on m.** à l'échéance
maudlin [ˈmɔːdlɪn] *adj* larmoyant(e)
maul [mɔːl] *vt (of lion, tiger)* mutiler; *Fig (criticize)* tailler en pièces
Mauritania [mɒrɪˈteɪnɪə] *n* la Mauritanie
Mauritanian [mɒrɪˈteɪnɪən] **1** *n* Mauritanien(enne) *m,f*
2 *adj* mauritanien(enne)
Mauritian [məˈrɪʃən] **1** *n* Mauricien(enne) *m,f*
2 *adj* mauricien(enne)
Mauritius [məˈrɪʃəs] *n* l'île *f* Maurice
mausoleum [mɔːsəˈliːəm] *n* mausolée *m*
mauve [məʊv] **1** *n* mauve *m*
2 *adj* mauve
maverick [ˈmævərɪk] *n* franc-tireur *m*, non-conformiste *mf*
mawkish [ˈmɔːkɪʃ] *adj Pej* mièvre
max [mæks] *(abbr* **maximum)** **1** *n* max *m*
2 *adv Fam* maximum; **it'll take three days m.** ça prendra trois jours maximum
▸**max out** *Fam* **1** *vt sep* **to m. out one's credit card** = dépenser le maximum autorisé avec sa carte de crédit
2 *vi* **to m. out on chocolate** se gaver de chocolat; **to m. out on booze** picoler un max
maxim [ˈmæksɪm] *n* maxime *f*
maxima [ˈmæksɪmə] *pl of* **maximum**
maximize [ˈmæksɪmaɪz] *vt* maximaliser
maximum [ˈmæksɪməm] **1** *n (pl* **maximums** *or* **maxima** [ˈmæksɪmə]) maximum *m*; **to the m.** au maximum
2 *adj* maximum *inv*, maximal(e)
May [meɪ] *n* mai *m*; **in M.** en mai, au mois de mai; **at the beginning/end of M.** début/fin mai; **during M.** en mai; **each** *or* **every M.** chaque année en mai; **in the middle of M.** mi-mai; **last/next M.** en mai dernier/prochain; **on the sixteenth of M.** le seize mai; **she was born on 22 M. 1953** elle est née le 22 mai 1953; **M. Day** le Premier Mai
may [meɪ] *v aux (3rd person singular* **may,** *pt* **might** [maɪt])

may et **might** peuvent s'utiliser indifféremment ou presque dans les expressions de la catégorie **(a)**.

(a) *(expressing possibility)* **he m. return at any moment** il pourrait rentrer à tout moment; **he m. have lost it** il se peut *ou* se pourrait qu'il l'ait perdu; **it m. be that...** il se peut *ou* se pourrait que... + *subjunctive*; **you m. be wondering why...** vous vous demandez peut-être pourquoi...; **you m. well ask!** bonne question!; **we m. as well go** autant y aller; **you m. as well tell them the truth** autant que tu leur dises la vérité **(b)** *Formal (asking for or giving permission)* **m. I come in?** puis-je entrer?; **if I m. say so** si je peux me permettre; **m. I?** *(when borrowing)* vous permettez? **(c)** *Formal (expressing wish, purpose)* **m. she rest in peace!** paix à son âme!; **m. the best man win!** que le meilleur gagne! **(d)** *(with concessions)* **he m. be very talented but I still don't like him** il est peut-être très doué, mais il me déplaît quand même; **be that as it m., that's as m. be** quoi qu'il en soit

Mayan [ˈmaɪən] **1** *n* Maya *mf*
2 *adj* maya
maybe [ˈmeɪbiː] *adv* peut-être; **m. she won't accept** elle n'acceptera peut-être pas
Mayday [ˈmeɪdeɪ] *n (distress signal)* signal *m* de détresse, SOS *m*; **M.!** mayday!
mayhem [ˈmeɪhem] *n* **it was m.** c'était la pagaille
mayonnaise [meɪəˈneɪz] *n* mayonnaise *f*
mayor [ˈmeə(r)] *n* maire *m*
mayoress [ˈmeərəs] *n* mairesse *f*; *(mayor's wife)* femme *f* du maire
maypole [ˈmeɪpəʊl] *n* = mât autour duquel on danse pour célébrer le Premier Mai
maze [meɪz] *n* labyrinthe *m*; *Fig* dédale *m*
MBA [embiːˈeɪ] *n Univ (abbr* **Master of Business Administration)** MBA *m*
MBE [embiːˈiː] *n Br (abbr* **Member of the Order of the British Empire)** = titre honorifique britannique
MBO [embiːˈəʊ] *n Com (abbr* **management buyout)** rachat *m* d'une entreprise par ses cadres
MC [emˈsiː] *n (abbr* **Master of Ceremonies)** maître *m* des cérémonies; *(for TV programme)* présentateur *m*; *(rap artist)* rappeur(euse) *m,f*
Mcjob [məkˈdʒɒb] *n esp Am Fam* boulot *m* à la con *(ennuyeux et mal payé)*
MD [emˈdiː] *n* **(a)** *Com (abbr* **Managing Director)** directeur(trice) *m,f* général(e) **(b)** *Med (abbr* **Doctor of Medicine)** docteur *m* en médecine
ME [eˈmiː] *n Med (abbr* **myalgic encephalomyelitis)** encéphalomyélite *f* myalgique
me¹ [*unstressed* mɪ, *stressed* miː] *pron* **(a)** *(direct object)* me; **she hates me** elle me déteste; **she loves me** elle m'aime; **she can understand my son but not ME** elle comprend mon fils, mais moi, elle ne me comprend pas **(b)** *(indirect object)* **she gave me the book** elle m'a donné le livre; **she gave it to me** elle me l'a donné **(c)** *(after preposition)* moi; **she's thinking of me** elle pense à moi **(d)** *(as complement of verb to be)* moi; **it's me!** c'est moi!; **it was me who did it** c'est moi qui l'ai fait **(e)** *(with interjections)* **silly me!** que je suis bête!; **poor me!** pauvre de moi!
me² [miː] *n Mus* mi *m*
meadow [ˈmedəʊ] *n* prairie *f*, pré *m*
meagre, *Am* **meager** [ˈmiːgə(r)] *adj* maigre
meal¹ [miːl] *n* repas *m*; *Fig* **to make a m. of sth** faire tout un plat de qch
meal² *n (flour)* farine *f*
mealtime [ˈmiːltaɪm] *n* heure *f* du repas
mealy [ˈmiːlɪ] *adj* farineux(euse)
mealy-mouthed [miːlɪˈmaʊðd] *adj Pej* mielleux(euse)
mean¹ [miːn] **1** *n (average)* moyenne *f*
2 *adj (average)* moyen(enne)
mean² *adj* **(a)** *(miserly)* mesquin(e), avare **(b)** *(nasty)* méchant(e); **she has a m. streak** elle peut être méchante quand elle veut; **that was a m. thing to do/say** ce n'est pas chic d'avoir dit ça/fait ça **(c)** *(poor)* **she's no m. photographer** c'est une sacrée photographe; **it was no m. feat** ce n'est pas un mince exploit **(d)** *Fam (good)* **he plays a m. game of pool** c'est un as du billard
mean³ *(pt & pp* **meant** [ment]) *vt* **(a)** *(signify) (of word, event)* signifier; *(of person)* vouloir dire; **what does the word "tacky" m.?** que signifie le mot "tacky"?; **this is Tim, I m. Tom** je vous présente Tim, je veux dire Tom; **I know what you m.** je comprends; **what do you m.?** qu'est-ce que tu veux dire?; **it doesn't m. anything** ça ne veut rien dire **(b)** *(be serious about)*

do you think he meant what he said? pensez-vous qu'il l'ait dit sérieusement?; **I didn't m.** that ce n'est pas ce que je voulais dire; **I m.** it je parle sérieusement; **you don't m.** **it!** tu plaisantes! (**c**) *(be of importance)* **the price means nothing to him** le prix importe peu pour lui; **it means a lot to me** c'est très important pour moi (**d**) *(intend)* **to m.** **to do sth** avoir l'intention de faire qch; **I didn't m.** **to do it** je ne l'ai pas fait exprès; **I m.** him **no harm** je ne lui veux pas de mal; **she means well** ses intentions sont bonnes; **I m.** to succeed je veux réussir; **she meant you to have this ring** elle voulait que tu aies cette bague; **it was meant as a joke/compliment** c'était une blague/un compliment; **this portrait is meant to be of the duke** ce portrait est censé représenter le duc; **you were meant to be here at eight** vous étiez censé arriver à huit heures; **it's meant to be a good film** il paraît que c'est un bon film; **they were meant for each other** ils sont faits l'un pour l'autre

meander [mɪ'ændə(r)] **1** *n* méandre *m* **2** *vi (of river, road)* serpenter; *(of person)* flâner

meaning ['miːnɪŋ] *n* sens *m*, signification *f*; *Fam* **if you get my m.** si tu vois ce que je veux dire; **what's the m. of this?** *(expressing indignation)* qu'est-ce que ça signifie?; **the m.** **of life** le sens de la vie

meaningful ['miːnɪŋfʊl] *adj* significatif(ive); *(relationship)* sérieux(euse)

meaningless ['miːnɪŋlɪs] *adj* vide de sens, sans signification

meanness ['miːnnɪs] *n* (**a**) *(miserliness)* avarice *f* (**b**) *(nastiness)* mesquinerie *f*

means [miːnz] **1** *n (pl* **means***) (method)* moyen *m*; **by m.** of... au moyen de..., à l'aide de...; **there is no m.** of escape il n'y a aucun moyen de s'échapper; **by some m.** or other d'une manière ou d'une autre; **a m.** to an end un moyen (d'arriver à ses fins); **by all m.** *(certainly)* je vous en prie; **by no m.** pas du tout, nullement; **she is by no m.** stupid elle est loin d'être bête; **m.** of communication moyen de communication; **m.** of production moyens de production; **m.** of transport moyen de transport **2** *npl (income, wealth)* moyens *mpl*, ressources *fpl*; **a man of m.** un homme fortuné; **to live beyond/within one's m.** vivre au-dessus de/selon ses moyens; **m.** **test** *(for state benefit)* enquête *f* sur les revenus

meant [ment] *pt & pp of* **mean³**

meantime ['miːntaɪm], **meanwhile** ['miːnwaɪl] **1** *n* **in the m.** *(at the same time)* pendant ce temps; *(between two events)* entre-temps **2** *adv (at the same time)* pendant ce temps; *(between two events)* entre-temps

measles ['miːzəlz] *n* rougeole *f*; **to have (the) m.** avoir la rougeole

measly ['miːzlɪ] *adj Fam* minable

measurable ['meʒərəbəl] *adj* mesurable; *Fig (difference, improvement)* notable, sensible

measure ['meʒə(r)] **1** *n* (**a**) *(measurement, quantity)* mesure *f*; **this was a m.** **of how serious the situation was** cela montrait à quel point la situation était sérieuse; **they allowed her a m.** **of freedom** on lui accordait une certaine liberté; **to get the m.** **of sb** jauger qn; **then he called me a liar for good m.** pardessus le marché, il m'a traité de menteur (**b**) *(degree)* **in some m.** dans une certaine mesure (**c**) *(action, step)* mesure *f*; **to take measures to do sth** prendre des mesures pour faire qch **2** *vt & vi* mesurer

▸**measure up** *vi* être à la hauteur (**to** de)

measured ['meʒəd] *adj* mesuré(e)

measurement ['meʒəmənt] *n* mesure *f*

measuring ['meʒərɪŋ] *n* **m.** **jug** verre *m* gradué; **m.** **spoon** cuillère-mesure *f*; **m.** **tape** mètre *m* ruban

meat [miːt] *n* (**a**) *(food)* viande *f*; *Fig* **to be m.** **and drink to sb** être une aubaine pour qn; **m.** **loaf** pain *m* de viande; *Br Fam Pej* **m.** **market** = boîte réputée pour être un lieu de drague (**b**) *Fig (substantial content)* substance *f*

meatball ['miːtbɔːl] *n* boulette *f* de viande

meaty ['miːtɪ] *adj (taste, smell)* de viande; *Fig (book, film)* riche

Mecca ['mekə] *n* La Mecque; *Fig* paradis *m*

mechanic [mɪ'kænɪk] *n* mécanicien(enne) *m,f*

mechanical [mɪ'kænɪkəl] *adj also Fig* mécanique; **m.** **engineer** ingénieur *m* mécanicien; **m.** **engineering** construction *f* mécanique

mechanics [mɪ'kænɪks] **1** *n* (**a**) *(science)* mécanique *f* (**b**) *(working parts)* mécanisme *m* **2** *npl Fig (processes)* mécanisme *m*

mechanism ['mekənɪzəm] *n* mécanisme *m*

mechanize ['mekənaɪz] *vt* mécaniser

mechanized ['mekənaɪzd] *adj* **m.** **industry** industrie *f* mécanisée; **m.** **troops** troupes *fpl* motorisées

MEd [e'med] *n Univ (abbr* **Master of Education**) maîtrise *f* en sciences de l'éducation

medal ['medəl] *n* médaille *f*

medalist *Am* = **medallist**

medallion [mɪ'dæljən] *n* médaillon *m*

medallist, *Am* **medalist** ['medəlɪst] *n* médaillé(e) *m,f*

meddle ['medəl] *vi (interfere)* se mêler (**in** de); *(tamper)* toucher (**with** à)

meddler ['medlə(r)] *n* indiscret(ète) *m,f*

meddlesome ['medəlsəm] *adj* indiscret(ète)

media ['miːdɪə] *n* (**a**) *(TV, press)* médias *mpl*; **m.** **circus** cirque *m* médiatique; **m.** **coverage** couverture *f* médiatique; **m.** **studies** études *fpl* de communication (**b**) *pl of* **medium**

mediaeval = **medieval**

median ['miːdɪən] *Math* **1** *n* médiane *f* **2** *adj* médian(e)

mediate ['miːdɪeɪt] *vi* servir de médiateur (**for/between** pour/entre)

mediation [miːdɪ'eɪʃən] *n* médiation *f*; **to go to m.** recourir à une médiation

mediator ['miːdɪeɪtə(r)] *n* médiateur(trice) *m,f*

medic ['medɪk] *n Fam (student)* étudiant(e) *m,f* en médecine; *(doctor)* médecin *m*

medical ['medɪkəl] **1** *adj (record, treatment, profession)* médical(e); *(book)* de médecine; *(student)* en médecine; **to seek m.** **advice** consulter un médecin; **m.** **board** commission *f* médicale; **m.** **care** soins *mpl* médicaux; **m.** **certificate** certificat *m* médical; **m.** **examination** visite *f* médicale; **m.** **insurance** assurance *f* maladie; **m.** **practitioner** (médecin *m*) généraliste *mf*; **m.** **records** dossier *m* médical **2** *n (physical examination)* visite *f* médicale; **to pass/fail a m.** être déclaré(e) apte/inapte à la visite médicale

medicated ['medɪkeɪtɪd] *adj (soap)* médical(e); *(shampoo)* traitant(e)

medication [medɪ'keɪʃən] *n* médicaments *mpl*; **to be on m.** être sous traitement

medicinal [me'dɪsɪnəl] *adj* médicinal(e)

medicine ['medɪsɪn] *n* (**a**) *(science)* médecine *f*; **to practise m.** exercer la médecine; **to study m.** faire des études de médecine (**b**) *(drugs)* médicament *m*; *Fig* **to give sb a taste of his own m.** rendre à qn la monnaie de sa pièce; **m. chest** *or* **cabinet** (armoire *f* à) pharmacie *f*; **m. man** *(traditional healer)* sorcier *m*, guérisseur *m*

medieval [medɪ'iːvəl] *adj* médiéval(e)

mediocre [miːdɪ'əʊkə(r)] *adj* médiocre

mediocrity [miːdɪ'ɒkrɪtɪ] *n* médiocrité *f*

meditate ['medɪteɪt] *vi* méditer (**on** sur)

meditation [medɪ'teɪʃən] *n* méditation *f*

Mediterranean [medɪtə'reɪnɪən] **1** *n* **the M.** la (mer) Méditerranée
2 *adj* méditerranéen(enne); **the M. Sea** la mer Méditerranée

medium ['miːdɪəm] **1** *n* (**a**) *(pl* **media** ['miːdɪə] *or* **mediums**) *(means of communication)* moyen *m* de communication; *(means of expression)* moyen *m* d'expression; **through the m. of the press** par voie de presse (**b**) *(in spiritualism)* médium *mf*
2 *adj* moyen(enne); **of m. height** de taille moyenne; **in the m. term** à moyen terme; **m. dry** demi-sec; **m. rare** à point; **m. wave** ondes *fpl* moyennes

medley ['medlɪ] *(pl* **medleys**) *n (mixture)* mélange *m*; *(in music)* pot-pourri *m*; **the 400 metres m.** *(in swimming)* le 400 mètres quatre nages

meek [miːk] *adj* docile; **m. and mild** doux (douce) comme un agneau

meekly [miːklɪ] *adv* docilement

meet [miːt] *(pt & pp* **met** [met]) **1** *vt* (**a**) *(accidentally)* rencontrer; *(by arrangement)* rejoindre, retrouver; *(collect)* attendre, aller chercher; **his eyes met mine** nos regards se sont croisés; **a remarkable sight met our eyes** un spectacle extraordinaire s'offrait à nos yeux; **there's more to this than meets the eye** on ne connaît pas les dessous de cette affaire; **there's more to her than meets the eye** elle cache bien son jeu (**b**) *(become acquainted with)* rencontrer, faire la connaissance de; **have you met my husband?** connaissez-vous mon mari?; **m. Mr Ford** je vous présente M. Ford (**c**) *(join with) (river)* se jeter dans; *(road)* rejoindre (**d**) *(satisfy) (demand, order)* satisfaire; *(condition, requirement)* satisfaire à; *(objection, criticism)* répondre à; *(cost, expense)* prendre en charge, payer (**e**) *(danger)* affronter; *(difficulties)* rencontrer; **to m. one's death** trouver la mort; **to m. one's match** trouver son maître
2 *vi* (**a**) *(accidentally)* se rencontrer; *(by arrangement)* se retrouver; **our eyes met** nos regards se sont croisés (**b**) *(become acquainted)* se rencontrer (**c**) *(of society, assembly)* se réunir (**d**) *(join)* se rencontrer; *(of rivers, roads)* se rejoindre

▸**meet up** *vi (by accident)* se rencontrer; *(by arrangement)* se retrouver; **to m. up with sb** *(by accident)* rencontrer qn; *(by arrangement)* retrouver qn

▸**meet with** *vt insep (difficulty, refusal)* se heurter à; *(danger)* affronter; **to m. with disaster** se solder par un désastre; **to m. with failure** échouer; **to m. with an accident** avoir un accident; **to m. with sb's approval** recevoir l'accord de qn

meeting ['miːtɪŋ] *n* (**a**) *(accidental)* rencontre *f*; *(arranged)* rendez-vous *m*; **m. place** (lieu *m* de) rendez-vous *m*; **m. room** salle *f* de réunion (**b**) *(for business, discussion)* réunion *f*; *(of shareholders)* assemblée *f*; **to be in a m.** être en réunion; **to hold a m.** se réunir

meet-up ['miːtʌp] *n Comput* rencontre *f* organisée sur Internet

megabyte ['megəbaɪt] *n Comput* méga-octet *m*

megahertz ['megəhɜːts] *(pl* **megahertz**) *n Elec* mégahertz *m*

megalomania [megələʊ'meɪnɪə] *n* mégalomanie *f*

megalomaniac [megələʊ'meɪnɪæk] *n* mégalomane *mf*

megaphone ['megəfəʊn] *n* mégaphone *m*, porte-voix *m inv*

megaton ['megətʌn] *n* mégatonne *f*

megawatt ['megəwɒt] *n Elec* mégawatt *m*

melancholy ['melənkəlɪ] **1** *n* mélancolie *f*
2 *adj (person)* mélancolique; *(atmosphere, news)* triste

melanin ['melənɪn] *n* mélanine *f*

melanoma [melə'nəʊmə] *n Med* mélanome *m*

melee ['meleɪ] *n* mêlée *f*

mellifluous [mə'lɪflʊəs] *adj* mélodieux(euse)

mellow ['meləʊ] **1** *adj (flavour)* suave; *(voice, colour)* chaud(e); *(wine)* moelleux(euse); *(light)* doux (douce); *(person)* détendu(e), serein(e)
2 *vi* s'adoucir

melodic [mɪ'lɒdɪk] *adj* mélodique

melodious [mɪ'ləʊdɪəs] *adj* mélodieux(euse)

melodrama ['melədrɑːmə] *n* mélodrame *m*

melodramatic [melədrə'mætɪk] *adj* mélodramatique

melody ['melədɪ] *(pl* **melodies**) *n* mélodie *f*

melon ['melən] *n* melon *m*

melt [melt] **1** *vt also Fig* faire fondre
2 *vi* fondre; **to m. into thin air** s'évaporer, disparaître; **to m. into the crowd** se fondre dans la foule

▸**melt away** *vi (of snow)* fondre; *(of clouds, vapour)* se dissiper; *(of crowd)* se disperser; *(of objections, opposition)* s'évanouir

▸**melt down** *vt sep (metal)* fondre

meltdown ['meltdaʊn] *n Phys* fusion *f*

melting ['meltɪŋ] *n* **m. point** point *m* de fusion; *Fig* **m. pot** melting-pot *m*

member ['membə(r)] *n* membre *m*; *Br & Can Pol* **M. of Parliament** député(e) *m,f*
2 *adj* **m. country/state** pays *m*/État *m* membre

membership ['membəʃɪp] *n* (**a**) *(state)* adhésion *f*; **m. card** carte *f* de membre ou d'adhérent; **m. fee** cotisation *f* (**b**) *(members)* membres *mpl*, adhérents *mpl*; **a large/small m.** une forte/faible adhésion

membrane ['membreɪn] *n* membrane *f*

memento [mɪ'mentəʊ] *(pl* **mementos** *or* **mementoes**) *n* souvenir *m*

memo ['meməʊ] *(pl* **memos**) *n* note *f* de service; **m. pad** bloc-notes *m*

memoir ['memwɑː(r)] *n (essay)* mémoire *m*; *(biography)* biographie *f*; **memoirs** *(autobiography)* mémoires *mpl*

memorable ['memərəbəl] *adj* mémorable

memorandum [memə'rændəm] *(pl* **memoranda** [memə'rændə] *or* **memorandums**) *n* note *f* de service

memorial [mɪ'mɔːrɪəl] **1** *n (monument)* mémorial *m*
2 *adj* commémoratif(ive)

memorize ['meməraɪz] *vt* mémoriser

memory ['memərɪ] *(pl* **memories**) *n* (**a**) *(faculty)* & *Comput* mémoire *f*; **to have a good/bad m.** avoir (une) bonne/mauvaise mémoire; **if my m. serves me right** si ma mémoire est bonne; **from m.** de mémoire; **to lose one's m.** perdre la mémoire; **to commit sth to m.** apprendre qch par cœur; **within living m.** de mémoire d'homme; *Comput* **m. stick** clé *f* USB (**b**) *(thing remembered)* souvenir *m*; **in m. of...** en souvenir de..., à la mémoire de...; **to take a trip down m. lane** se remémorer le passé

men [men] *pl of* **man**

menace ['menɪs] **1** *n (threat)* menace *f*; *(danger)* danger *m*; *Fam Fig (pest)* plaie *f*
2 *vt* menacer

menacing ['menəsɪŋ] *adj* menaçant(e)

menagerie [mɪ'nædʒərɪ] *n* ménagerie *f*

mend [mend] **1** *vt (repair)* réparer; *(clothing)* raccommoder; **to m. one's ways** s'amender
2 *vi (of broken bone)* se ressouder
3 *n Fam* **to be on the m.** aller mieux

menfolk ['menfəʊk] *npl* **the m.** les hommes *mpl*

menial ['miːnɪəl] **1** *n Pej* laquais *m*
2 *adj (job)* subalterne; **m. tasks** corvées *fpl*

meningitis [menɪn'dʒaɪtɪs] *n* méningite *f*; **to have m.** avoir la méningite

menopause ['menəpɔːz] *n* ménopause *f*

menstrual ['menstrʊəl] *adj* menstruel(elle)

menstruate ['menstrʊeɪt] *vi* avoir ses règles

menstruation [menstrʊ'eɪʃən] *n* menstruation *f*

menswear ['menzweə(r)] *n* vêtements *mpl* pour hommes

mental ['mentəl] *adj* (**a**) *(state, age)* mental(e); **to make a m. note of sth/to do sth** essayer de se souvenir de qch/de faire qch; **to have a m. block about sth** faire un blocage sur qch; **m. arithmetic** calcul *m* mental; **m. breakdown** dépression *f* (nerveuse); **m. health** santé *f* mentale; **m. hospital** hôpital *m* psychiatrique; **m. illness** maladie *f* mentale; **m. patient** malade *mf* mental(e) (**b**) *very Fam (mad)* malade, dingue; **to go m.** *(lose one's temper)* devenir dingue

mentality [men'tælɪtɪ] *(pl* **mentalities)** *n* mentalité *f*

mentally ['mentəlɪ] *adv* mentalement; **to be m. handicapped** être handicapé(e) mental(e); **to be m. ill** avoir une maladie mentale

menthol ['menθɒl] *n* menthol *m*; **m. cigarettes** cigarettes *fpl* mentholées

mention ['menʃən] **1** *n* mention *f*; **he gets a brief m. in her autobiography** elle le mentionne brièvement dans son autobiographie; **to make no m. of sth** ne pas faire référence à qch
2 *vt* parler de; *(allude to)* mentionner; **to m. that...** dire que...; **to m. sb in one's will** coucher qn sur son testament; **to be mentioned in dispatches** être cité(e) à l'ordre du jour; **not to m....** sans parler de...; **now (that) you m. it** maintenant que tu le dis; **don't m. it!** il n'y a pas de quoi!

mentor ['mentɔː(r)] **1** *n* mentor *m*
2 *vt* jouer les mentors auprès de

mentoring ['mentɔːrɪŋ] *n* mentoring *m*; **m. scheme** programme *m* de mentoring

menu ['menjuː] *n* (**a**) *(in restaurant) (set)* menu *m*; *(à la carte)* carte *f* (**b**) *Comput* menu *m*; **m. bar** barre *f* de menu

MEP [emiː'piː] *n Br Pol (abbr* **Member of the European Parliament)** député *m* au Parlement européen

mercantile ['mɜːkəntaɪl] *adj* commercial(e)

mercenary ['mɜːsɪnərɪ] **1** *n (pl* **mercenaries)** mercenaire *m*
2 *adj Pej* intéressé(e)

merchandise ['mɜːtʃəndaɪz] **1** *n* marchandises *fpl*
2 *vt* marchandiser

merchandising ['mɜːtʃəndaɪzɪŋ] *n* merchandising *m*, marchandisage *m*

merchant ['mɜːtʃənt] *n (retail)* marchand(e) *m,f*; *(wholesale)* négociant(e) *m,f*; **m. bank** banque *f* d'affaires; **m.**

navy marine *f* marchande; **m. seaman** marin *m* de la marine marchande; **m. ship** navire *m* marchand

merchantman ['mɜːtʃəntmən] *n (ship)* navire *m* marchand

merciful ['mɜːsɪfʊl] *adj (person)* clément(e); *(act)* charitable

mercifully ['mɜːsɪfʊlɪ] *adv* (**a**) *(showing mercy)* avec clémence (**b**) *(fortunately)* heureusement

merciless ['mɜːsɪlɪs] *adj* sans pitié, impitoyable

mercurial [mɜː'kjʊərɪəl] *adj (lively)* vif (vive); *(changeable)* changeant(e), lunatique

Mercury ['mɜːkjʊrɪ] *n (planet)* Mercure *f*

mercury ['mɜːkjʊrɪ] *n (metal)* mercure *m*

mercy ['mɜːsɪ] *n (pl* **mercies)** *n* (**a**) *(clemency)* pitié *f*, clémence *f*; **to have m. on sb** avoir pitié de qn; **to beg for m.** demander grâce; **at the m. of** à la merci de; **m. killing** acte *m* d'euthanasie (**b**) *(blessing)* bonheur *m*, chance *f*; **it's a m. that...** c'est une chance que...; **to be thankful or grateful for small mercies** apprécier ce dont on dispose

mere [mɪə(r)] *adj* simple; **he's a m. child** ce n'est qu'un enfant

merely ['mɪəlɪ] *adv* simplement, seulement

merge [mɜːdʒ] **1** *vt (companies) & Comput* fusionner
2 *vi (of colours, sounds)* se fondre, se confondre; *(of companies)* fusionner; **to m. into the background** se fondre dans le décor

merger ['mɜːdʒə(r)] *n* fusion *f*

meridian [mə'rɪdɪən] *n* méridien *m*

meringue [mə'ræŋ] *n* meringue *f*

merit ['merɪt] **1** *n (advantage, worth)* mérite *m*; **of little/great m.** de peu de/grande valeur; **to judge sth on its merits** juger qch pour ce qu'il vaut; **in order of m.** par ordre de mérite
2 *vt* mériter

meritocracy [merɪ'tɒkrəsɪ] *(pl* **meritocracies)** *n* méritocratie *f*

meritorious [merɪ'tɔːrɪəs] *adj Formal* méritoire, louable

mermaid ['mɜːmeɪd] *n* sirène *f*

merrily ['merɪlɪ] *adv* joyeusement, gaiement

merriment ['merɪmənt] *n* gaieté *f*

merry ['merɪ] *adj* (**a**) *(happy)* joyeux(euse), gai(e); **to make m.** s'amuser; **M. Christmas!** Joyeux Noël!; **the more the merrier** plus on est de fous, plus on rit (**b**) *(slightly drunk)* gai(e)

merry-go-round ['merɪɡəʊraʊnd] *n* manège *m*, *Can, Belg & Suisse* carrousel *m*

mesh [meʃ] **1** *n (of net, sieve)* mailles *fpl*
2 *vi (of gears)* s'engrener

mesmerize ['mezməraɪz] *vt* hypnotiser

mess [mes] **1** *n* (**a**) *(disorder)* désordre *m*; **you look a m.!** tu es dans un triste état!; **to be (in) a m.** *(of room)* être en désordre; *Fig (of person)* être dans le pétrin; *(of one's life)* être un désastre; **he's a m.** il est dans un triste état; *Fig* **to make a m. of sth** *(essay, job)* saloper qch (**b**) *(dirt)* saletés *fpl*; **to make a m. of sth** salir qch; **the dog's done a m. on the carpet** le chien a fait ses besoins sur le tapis (**c**) *Mil (for officers)* mess *m*; *(for soldiers)* réfectoire *m*; **m. tin** gamelle *f*
2 *vi Fam (of dog, cat)* faire ses besoins

▸**mess about, mess around 1** *vt sep (treat badly)* se moquer de
2 *vi* (**a**) *(fool about)* faire l'imbécile; *(waste time)* traîner (**b**) *(tinker)* **to m. about or around with sth** tripoter qch

▶**mess up** *vt sep (hair, room, papers)* mettre en désordre; *(plans)* ficher en l'air

message ['mesɪdʒ] *n* message *m*; **to leave a m. for sb** laisser un message pour qn; *Fam Fig* **to get the m.** piger

messenger ['mesɪndʒə(r)] *n* messager(ère) *m,f*; **m. boy** garçon *m* de courses, coursier *m*

Messiah [mɪ'saɪə] *n Rel* Messie *m*

messianic [mesɪ'ænɪk] *adj* messianique

messily ['mesɪlɪ] *adv* salement; *Fig* **to end m.** *(of relationship)* mal terminer

Messrs ['mesəz] *(abbr* **Messieurs**) MM

messy ['mesɪ] *adj* (**a**) *(dirty)* sale; **it's a m. job** c'est salissant; **to be a m. eater** manger salement (**b**) *(untidy) (room, hair)* en désordre; *(handwriting)* peu soigné(e); *(appearance)* négligé(e) (**c**) *(unpleasantly complex) (affair, situation)* embrouillé(e); *(private life)* troublé(e)

met [met] *pt & pp of* **meet**

metabolic [metə'bɒlɪk] *adj* métabolique

metabolism [mɪ'tæbəlɪzəm] *n* métabolisme *m*

metal ['metəl] **1** *n* métal *m*; **m. detector** détecteur *m* de métaux
2 *adj* en métal

metalled road ['metəld'rəʊd] *n* route *f* empierrée

metallic [mɪ'tælɪk] *adj (sound, voice)* métallique; *(paint)* métallisé(e); *(taste)* de métal

metallurgy [me'tælədʒɪ] *n* métallurgie *f*

metalwork ['metəlwɜːk] *n* ferronnerie *f*

metamorphosis [metə'mɔːfəsɪs] *(pl* **metamorphoses** [metə'mɔːfəsiːz]) *n* métamorphose *f*

metaphor ['metəfə(r)] *n* métaphore *f*

metaphoric(al) [metə'fɒrɪk(əl)] *adj* métaphorique

metaphysical [metə'fɪzɪkəl] *adj* métaphysique

metaphysics [metə'fɪzɪks] *n* métaphysique *f*

▶**mete out** [miːt] *vt sep (punishment)* infliger (**to** à); *(justice)* rendre

meteor ['miːtɪə(r)] *n* météore *m*

meteoric [miːtɪ'ɒrɪk] *adj* météorique; *Fig* **a m. rise** une ascension fulgurante

meteorite ['miːtɪəraɪt] *n* météorite *f*

meteorological [miːtɪərə'lɒdʒɪkəl] *adj* météorologique

meteorology [miːtɪə'rɒlədʒɪ] *n* météorologie *f*

meter¹ ['miːtə(r)] *n* compteur *m*; **to read the m.** relever le compteur; **(parking) m.** parcmètre *m*

meter² *Am* = **metre**¹, **metre**²

methane ['miːθeɪn] *n* méthane *m*

method ['meθəd] *n* méthode *f*; **there's m. in his madness** il n'est pas aussi fou qu'il en a l'air; **m. acting** méthode *f* de Stanislavski

methodical [mɪ'θɒdɪkəl] *adj* méthodique

Methodism ['meθədɪzəm] *n Rel* méthodisme *m*

Methodist ['meθədɪst] *n Rel* méthodiste *mf*

methodology [meθə'dɒlədʒɪ] *n* méthodologie *f*

meths [meθs] *n Br Fam (methylated spirits)* alcool *m* à brûler

methylated spirits ['meθɪleɪtɪd'spɪrɪts] *n Br* alcool *m* à brûler

meticulous [mɪ'tɪkjʊləs] *adj* méticuleux(euse)

metre¹, *Am* **meter** ['miːtə(r)] *n (measurement)* mètre *m*

metre², *Am* **meter** *n (of poetry)* mètre *m*

metric ['metrɪk] *adj* métrique

metronome ['metrənəʊm] *n* métronome *m*

metropolis [mɪ'trɒpəlɪs] *n* métropole *f*

metropolitan [metrə'pɒlɪtən] *adj* urbain(e); **M. France** la France métropolitaine; **the M. Police** la police de Londres

metrosexual [metrəʊ'sekʃuːəl] **1** *n* métrosexuel *m*
2 *adj* métrosexuel(elle)

mettle ['metəl] *n (courage)* courage *m*; **to be on one's m.** être fin prêt(e); **to show one's m.** montrer de quoi on est capable

mew [mjuː] **1** *n* miaulement *m*
2 *vi* miauler

mews [mjuːz] *(pl* **mews**) *n Br* ruelle *f*; **m. cottage** = maison luxueuse aménagée dans une ancienne écurie

Mexican ['meksɪkən] **1** *n* Mexicain(e) *m,f*
2 *adj* mexicain(e); **M. wave** *(at match)* ola *f*

Mexico ['meksɪkəʊ] *n* le Mexique; **M. City** Mexico

mezzanine ['metsəniːn] *n* **m. (floor)** mezzanine *f*

mg [em'dʒiː] *n (abbr* **milligram(s)**) mg

Mgr *(abbr* **Monsignor**) Mgr

MHz *(abbr* **megahertz**) MHz

mi [miː] *n Mus* mi *m*

MI5 [emaɪ'faɪv] *n Br (abbr* **Military Intelligence Section 5**) ≃ DST *f*

MI6 [emaɪ'sɪks] *n Br (abbr* **Military Intelligence Section 6**) ≃ DGSE *f*

miaow [mɪ'aʊ] **1** *n* miaulement *m*; **m.!** miaou!
2 *vi* miauler

mica ['maɪkə] *n* mica *m*

mice [maɪs] *pl of* **mouse**

Michelangelo ['maɪkəl'ændʒələʊ] *pr n* Michel-Ange

mickey ['mɪkɪ] *n Br Fam* **to take the m. (out of sb)** se moquer (de qn)

Mickey Mouse ['mɪkɪ'maʊs] **1** *pr n* Mickey
2 *adj Fam Pej (job, qualification)* à la noix

micro ['maɪkrəʊ] *(pl* **micros**) *n* micro *m*

microbe ['maɪkrəʊb] *n* microbe *m*

microbiology [maɪkrəʊbaɪ'ɒlədʒɪ] *n* microbiologie *f*

microchip ['maɪkrəʊtʃɪp] *n* microprocesseur *m*

microcomputer ['maɪkrəʊkəm'pjuːtə(r)] *n* micro-ordinateur *m*

microcomputing ['maɪkrəʊkəm'pjuːtɪŋ] *n* micro-informatique *f*

microcosm ['maɪkrəʊkɒzəm] *n* microcosme *m*

microfiche ['maɪkrəʊfiːʃ] *n* microfiche *f*

microfilm ['maɪkrəʊfɪlm] **1** *n* microfilm *m*
2 *vt* microfilmer

micrometer [maɪ'krɒmɪtə(r)] *n* micromètre *m*

microphone ['maɪkrəfəʊn] *n* microphone *m*

microprocessor ['maɪkrəʊ'prəʊsesə(r)] *n* micro-processeur *m*

microscope ['maɪkrəskəʊp] *n* microscope *m*

microscopic [maɪkrə'skɒpɪk] *adj* microscopique

microsite ['maɪkrəʊsaɪt] *n Comput* microsite *m*

microsurgery [maɪkrəʊ'sɜːdʒərɪ] *n* microchirurgie *f*

microwave ['maɪkrəʊweɪv] **1** *n Phys* micro-onde *f*; **m. (oven)** (four *m* à) micro-ondes *m inv*
2 *vt* faire cuire au micro-ondes

mid [mɪd] *adj* **in m. ocean** au milieu de l'océan; **m. June** mi-juin; **he stopped in m. sentence** il s'est arrêté au milieu d'une phrase

midair [mɪd'eə(r)] **1** *n* **in m.** en plein ciel
2 *adj (collision)* en plein ciel

mid-Atlantic accent [mɪdət'læntɪk'æksent] *n* accent *m* mi-américain mi-britannique

midday ['mɪd'deɪ] *n* midi *m*; **m. meal** déjeuner *m*

middle ['mɪdəl] **1** *n* (**a**) *(centre)* milieu *m*; **to be in the m. of doing sth** être en train de faire qch; **in the m. of**

the night en pleine nuit; **in the m.** of nowhere dans un coin perdu; *Fig* **to split sth down the m.** partager qch en deux (**b**) *(waist)* taille *f*
2 *adj* du milieu; **m.** age l'âge *m* mûr; *Hist* **the M. Ages** le Moyen Âge; *Mus* **m. C** do *m* du milieu du clavier; **the m. class(es)** les classes *mpl* moyennes; *Fig* **to steer a m. course** adopter une solution intermédiaire; **in the m. distance** au second plan; **the M. East** le Moyen-Orient; **M. Eastern** du Moyen-Orient; *Pol* **the m. ground** le centre; **m. management** cadres *mpl* moyens; **m. name** deuxième prénom *m*; *Fam* **laziness is his m. name!** c'est un incorrigible paresseux!
middle-aged [mɪdəl'eɪdʒd] *adj* d'âge mûr; **he was already m. when...** il avait déjà un certain âge quand...
middlebrow ['mɪdəlbraʊ] *adj* moyen(enne); **a m. novelist** un romancier sans prétentions
middle-class [mɪdəl'klɑːs] *adj* bourgeois(e)
middleman ['mɪdəlmæn] *n* intermédiaire *mf*
middle-of-the-road ['mɪdləvðə'rəʊd] *adj (policy)* modéré(e); *(music)* grand public *inv*
middle-sized ['mɪdəl'saɪzd] *adj* de taille moyenne
middleweight ['mɪdəlweɪt] *n (in boxing)* poids *m* moyen
middling ['mɪdlɪŋ] *adj (fairly good)* moyen(enne); *(mediocre)* médiocre
midfield [mɪd'fiːld] *n (in football)* milieu *m* de terrain; **m. player** milieu *m* de terrain
midfielder [mɪd'fiːldə(r)] *n (in football)* milieu *m* de terrain
midge [mɪdʒ] *n* moucheron *m*
midget ['mɪdʒɪt] **1** *n (small person)* nain(e) *m,f*
2 *adj (miniature)* miniature
midi system ['mɪdɪsɪstəm] *n (stereo)* chaîne *f* midi
Midlands ['mɪdləndz] *npl* **the M.** les Midlands *fpl*
midlife crisis ['mɪdlaɪf'kraɪsɪs] *n* crise *f* aux alentours de la cinquantaine
midmorning [mɪd'mɔːnɪŋ] *n* milieu *m* de matinée
midnight ['mɪdnaɪt] *n* minuit *m*; **to burn the m. oil** travailler tard dans la nuit
midriff ['mɪdrɪf] *n* ventre *m*
midshipman ['mɪdʃɪpmən] *n* aspirant *m* de marine
midst [mɪdst] *n* milieu *m*, cœur *m*; **in the m. of** au milieu de; **in our/their m.** parmi nous/eux
midstream [mɪd'striːm] *n* **in m.** au milieu du courant; *Fig (when speaking)* en plein milieu d'une phrase
midsummer ['mɪdsʌmə(r)] *n* milieu *m* de l'été; **M.'s Day** la Saint-Jean
midterm ['mɪdtɜːm] *n* (**a**) *Pol Br* **m. by-election** = élection législative en milieu de mandat; *Am* **m. elections** = élections qui ont lieu au milieu du mandat présidentiel (**b**) *Sch & Univ* milieu *m* du trimestre; **m. break** vacances *fpl* de milieu de trimestre
midway ['mɪdweɪ] **1** *adj* **at the m. point** *(in space)* à la mi-chemin; *(in time)* à la moitié
2 *adv* à mi-chemin
midweek [mɪd'wiːk] *adv* en milieu de semaine
Mid-West ['mɪd'west] *n* Midwest *m*
Mid-Western [mɪd'westən] *adj* du Midwest
midwife ['mɪdwaɪf] *(pl* **midwives** [mɪdwaɪvz]) *n* sage-femme *f*
midwifery [mɪd'wɪfərɪ] *n* profession *f* de sage-femme
midwinter ['mɪd'wɪntə(r)] *n* milieu *m* de l'hiver
might¹ [maɪt] *n (strength)* force *f*; **with all one's m.** de toutes ses forces; *Prov* **m. is right** la raison du plus fort est toujours la meilleure
might² *v aux*

La forme négative **mightn't** s'écrit **might not** dans un style plus soutenu. **Might** et **may** peuvent s'utiliser indifféremment ou presque dans les expressions de la catégorie **(a)**.

(**a**) *(expressing possibility)* **it m.** be difficult il se peut *ou* se pourrait que ce soit difficile; **it m. be better to phone first** il vaudrait peut-être mieux téléphoner d'abord; **it m. be that...** il se peut *ou* se pourrait que... + *subjunctive*; **you m. want to...** tu pourrais peut-être...; **we m. as well go home** autant rentrer; **you m. as well stay here** autant que vous restiez ici; **I m. as well be talking to myself!** autant parler à un mur! (**b**) *(as past form of may)* **I knew he m. be angry** je me doutais qu'il pourrait se fâcher; **he said he m. be late** il a dit qu'il se pourrait qu'il soit en retard (**c**) *Formal (asking for permission)* **m. I have a word with you?** pourrais-je vous parler un instant? (**d**) *(with concessions)* **it might not be the fastest car in the world, but...** ce n'est peut-être pas la voiture la plus rapide du monde, mais...
mightily ['maɪtɪlɪ] *adv* (**a**) *(powerfully)* avec force, vigoureusement (**b**) *Am Fam (for emphasis)* drôlement
mightn't ['maɪtənt] = **might not**
might've ['maɪtəv] = **might have**
mighty ['maɪtɪ] **1** *adj* (**a**) *(powerful) (nation, army)* puissant(e); *(blow)* grand(e) (**b**) *(large, imposing)* majestueux(euse)
2 *adv Am Fam (for emphasis)* drôlement
migraine ['maɪgreɪn, 'miːgreɪn] *n* migraine *f*; **to have a m.** avoir la migraine
migrant ['maɪgrənt] **1** *n (person)* migrant(e) *m,f*; *(bird)* (oiseau *m*) migrateur *m*
2 *adj (bird)* migrateur(trice); **m. worker** travailleur(-euse) *m,f* immigré(e)
migrate [maɪ'greɪt] *vi (of bird)* migrer; *(of person)* émigrer
migration [maɪ'greɪʃən] *n (of birds)* migration *f*; *(of people)* émigration *f*
migratory ['maɪgrətrɪ] *adj* migratoire; *(bird)* migrateur(trice)
mike [maɪk] *n Fam (microphone)* micro *m*
mild [maɪld] **1** *adj (person, climate, soap, cheese)* (douce); *(curry)* peu épicé(e); *(punishment, annoyance, amusement, criticism)* léger(ère); *(illness)* bénin(igne)
2 *n Br (beer)* = bière brune à faible teneur en houblon
mildew ['mɪldjuː] *n* moisissure *f*
mildly ['maɪldlɪ] *adv* (**a**) *(say)* doucement; ..., **to put it m.** ..., pour ne pas dire plus (**b**) *(moderately)* légèrement
mildness ['maɪldnɪs] *n (of person, weather, punishment)* douceur *f*; *(of criticism)* modération *f*
mile [maɪl] *n (distance)* = 1609 m, mile *m*; **a 200-m. journey** ≃ un voyage de 320 km; **to see for miles** voir à des kilomètres; **it's miles from anywhere** c'est loin de tout; **miles per hour** ≃ kilomètres à l'heure; **he lives miles away** il habite très loin d'ici; *Fam Fig* **to be miles away** être dans la lune; *Fam* **miles better** cent fois mieux; *Fam* **it sticks** *or* **stands out a m.** ça crève les yeux
mileage ['maɪlɪdʒ] *n* (**a**) *(distance travelled)* ≃ kilométrage *m*; **m. allowance** ≃ indemnité *f* kilométrique (**b**) *(rate of fuel consumption)* consommation *f*; *Fig* **to get a lot of m. out of sth** tirer le maximum de qch

milestone ['maɪlstəʊn] *n (on road)* ≃ borne *f* kilométrique; *Fig (in career, history)* étape *f* importante
milieu ['miːljɜː] *n* milieu *m*
militant ['mɪlɪtənt] **1** *n* militant(e) *m,f*
  2 *adj* militant(e)
militarism ['mɪlɪtərɪzəm] *n* militarisme *m*
military ['mɪlɪtərɪ] **1** *adj* militaire; **m. academy** école *f* militaire; **m. man** militaire *m*; **m. police** police *f* militaire; **m. service** service *m* militaire
  2 *npl* **the m.** les militaires *mpl,* l'armée *f*
militate ['mɪlɪteɪt] *vi* **to m. against sth** compromettre qch
militia [mɪ'lɪʃə] *n* milice *f*
milk [mɪlk] **1** *n* lait *m*; **m. of magnesia** lait *m* de magnésie; **m. bottle** bouteille *f* de lait; **m. chocolate** chocolat *m* au lait; **m. churn** bidon *m* à lait; **m. float** camionnette *f* de laitier; **m. jug** pot *m* à lait; **m. round** tournée *f* du laitier; **m. tooth** dent *f* de lait; **m. train** premier train *m* (du matin)
  2 *vt (cow)* traire; *Fam Fig* **to m. sb dry** dépouiller qn; *Fig* **they milked the story for all it was worth** ils ont tiré tout ce qu'ils ont pu de l'histoire
milking ['mɪlkɪŋ] *n* traite *f*; **m. machine** trayeuse *f*; **m. parlour** salle *f* de traite
milkman ['mɪlkmən] *n* = homme qui livre le lait à domicile
milkshake ['mɪlkʃeɪk] *n* milk-shake *m*
milky ['mɪlkɪ] *adj (drink)* avec du lait; *(taste)* de lait; *(colour)* laiteux(euse); **the M. Way** la Voie lactée
mill [mɪl] **1** *n* (**a**) *(grinder)* moulin *m*; *Fam* **to put sb through the m.** en faire baver à qn (**b**) *(textile factory)* filature *f*
  2 *vt (grain)* moudre
▸**mill about, mill around** *vi (of crowd)* grouiller; *(of thoughts, ideas)* se bousculer
millennium [mɪ'lenɪəm] *n* millénaire *m*; *Comput* **m. bug** bogue *m* de l'an deux mille; **M. Dome** = centre d'expositions en forme de dôme construit à Londres à l'occasion de l'an 2000
miller ['mɪlə(r)] *n* meunier(ère) *m,f*
millet ['mɪlɪt] *n* millet *m*
milligram(me) ['mɪlɪgræm] *n* milligramme *m*
millilitre, *Am* **milliliter** ['mɪlɪliːtə(r)] *n* millilitre *m*
millimetre, *Am* **millimeter** ['mɪlɪmiːtə(r)] *n* millimètre *m*
milliner ['mɪlɪnə(r)] *n* modiste *mf*
million ['mɪljən] *n* million *m*; **two m. men** deux millions d'hommes; *Fam* **I've told him a m. times** je le lui ai dit mille fois; *Fam* **thanks a m.!** merci mille fois!; *Fam* **she's one in a m.** elle est unique
millionaire [mɪljə'neə(r)] *n* millionnaire *m*
millionairess [mɪljə'neərɪs] *n* millionnaire *f*
millionth ['mɪljənθ] **1** *n* (**a**) *(fraction)* millionième *m* (**b**) *(in series)* millionième *mf*
  2 *adj* millionième; *see also* **eighth**
millipede ['mɪlɪpiːd] *n* mille-pattes *m inv*
millpond ['mɪlpɒnd] *n* **as calm as a m.** *(of sea)* d'huile
millstone ['mɪlstəʊn] *n* meule *f*; *Fig* **it's a m. round my neck** c'est un boulet que je traîne
milometer [maɪ'lɒmɪtə(r)] *n (in car)* ≃ compteur *m* (kilométrique)
mime [maɪm] **1** *n* mime *m*; **m. (artist)** mime *mf*
  2 *vt* mimer
  3 *vi* mimer; *(of singer)* chanter en play-back
mimic ['mɪmɪk] **1** *n* imitateur(trice) *m,f*
  2 *vt (pt & pp* **mimicked**) imiter
mimicry ['mɪmɪkrɪ] *n* imitation *f*

Min *Mus (abbr* **Minor**) m
min (**a**) *(abbr* **minute(s)**) min (**b**) *(abbr* **minimum**) min
minaret [mɪnə'ret] *n* minaret *m*
mince [mɪns] **1** *n Br* viande *f* hachée; **m. pie** *(containing meat)* tourte *f* à la viande hachée; *(containing fruit)* = tartelette fourrée aux fruits secs et aux épices
  2 *vt (chop up)* hacher; *Fig* **she doesn't m. her words** elle ne mâche pas ses mots
  3 *vi (walk)* marcher à petits pas
mincemeat ['mɪnsmiːt] *n* = mélange de fruits secs et d'épices utilisé en pâtisserie; *Fam Fig* **to make m. of sb** faire de la chair à pâté de qn
mincer ['mɪnsə(r)] *n* hachoir *m*
mincing ['mɪnsɪŋ] *adj (walk, voice)* affecté(e)
mind [maɪnd] **1** (**a**) *(thoughts)* esprit *m*; **in one's m.'s eye** en imagination; **to put** *or* **set sb's m. at rest** rassurer qn; **to bear** *or* **keep sth in m.** garder qch à l'esprit *ou* en tête; **it went completely** *or* **clean out of my m.** ça m'est complètement sorti de l'esprit *ou* de la tête; **to have sth on one's m.** être préoccupé(e) par qch; **to take sb's m. off sth** distraire qn de qch; **I couldn't get it off my m.** je ne pouvais pas m'empêcher d'y penser; **it puts me in m. of sb/sth** ça me rappelle qn/qch
  (**b**) *(opinion)* **to my m.** à mon avis; **to speak one's m.** dire ce qu'on pense; **to change one's m. (about sth)** changer d'avis (au sujet de qch); *Fam* **to give sb a piece of one's m.** dire à qn sa façon de penser; **to be of one m.,** to be of the same m. être du même avis
  (**c**) *(will)* **to know one's own m.** savoir ce qu'on veut; **to have a m. of one's own** savoir penser par soi-même; **to make up one's m.** se décider; **to be in two minds (about sth/about doing sth)** hésiter (sur qch/à faire qch); **to have a good m./half a m. to do sth** avoir bien envie/presque envie de faire qch; **this shopping trolley has a m. of its own** ce caddie n'en fait qu'à sa tête; **to have sb in m.** avoir qn en vue; **to have sth in m.** avoir qch en tête
  (**d**) *(attention)* **to keep one's m. on sth** se concentrer sur qch; **my m. isn't on the job** je n'ai pas la tête à ce que je fais; **if you put your m. to it you could do it** si tu t'y mettais, tu pourrais le faire
  (**e**) *(reason)* raison *f*; **her m. is going** elle perd la raison; *Fam* **to be out of one's m.** avoir perdu la tête; **to be bored out of one's m.** s'ennuyer à mourir; **to be out of one's m. with worry** être fou (folle) d'inquiétude; **no one in his right m. would do that** aucune personne saine d'esprit ne ferait ça
  (**f**) *(person)* esprit *m*; *Prov* **great minds think alike** les grands esprits se rencontrent
  2 *vt* (**a**) *(pay attention to)* faire attention à; **m. you don't fall** fais attention à ne pas tomber; **m. you're not late!** fais en sorte de ne pas être en retard!; **m. the step!** attention à la marche!; **to m. one's language/manners** surveiller son langage/ses manières
  (**b**) *(concern oneself with)* **never m. the car/money** ne t'inquiète pas pour la voiture/l'argent; **m. you,...** remarque,...
  (**c**) *(object to)* **what I m. is...** ce qui me gêne, c'est...; **I don't m. the cold** le froid ne me gêne pas; **I don't m. trying** je veux bien essayer; **if you don't m. my asking,...** si je peux me permettre,...; **would you m. not doing that?** pourrais-tu arrêter ça?; **I wouldn't m. a cup of tea** je prendrais bien une tasse de thé
  (**d**) *(look after)* s'occuper de, garder

3 *vi* (**a**) *(object)* **I don't m.** ça m'est égal; **do you m.!** dites donc!; **do you m. if I smoke?** ça vous dérange si je fume?; **I don't m. if I do!** *(accepting offer)* ce n'est pas de refus!
(**b**) *(concern oneself)* **never m.!** ça ne fait rien!; **never m. about that now** ne t'inquiète pas de ça maintenant; *Fam* **never you m.!** occupe-toi de tes oignons!
▸**mind out** *vi Br* **m. out!** attention!

mind-boggling ['maɪndbɒglɪŋ], **mind-blowing** ['maɪndbləʊɪŋ] *adj Fam* époustouflant(e)

minded ['maɪndɪd] *adj* **to be m. to do sth** vouloir faire qch; **to be mechanically m.** avoir le sens de la mécanique; **to be scientifically m.** avoir l'esprit scientifique

minder ['maɪndə(r)] *n Fam (bodyguard)* gorille *m*

mindful ['maɪndfʊl] *adj* **to be m. of sth** être soucieux(euse) de qch

mindless ['maɪndlɪs] *adj (destruction, violence)* gratuit(e); *(task, job)* abrutissant(e)

mind-numbing ['maɪndnʌmɪŋ] *adj* abêtissant(e)

mind-reader ['maɪndriːdə(r)] *n Fam Hum* **I'm not a m.!** je ne suis pas devin!

mine¹ [maɪn] **1** *n* (**a**) *(for coal, tin, diamonds)* mine *f*; *Fig* **a m. of information** une mine d'informations; **m. shaft** puits *m* de mine (**b**) *(bomb)* **(land) m.** mine *f*; **m. detector** détecteur *m* de mines
2 *vt* (**a**) *(coal, gold)* extraire; *(seam)* exploiter (**b**) *(place mines in)* miner
3 *vi* **to m. for coal/gold** extraire du charbon/de l'or

mine² *possessive pron* (**a**) *(singular)* le mien (la mienne) *m,f*; *(plural)* les miens (les miennes) *mpl,fpl*; **her house is big but m. is bigger** elle a une grande maison, mais la mienne est plus grande encore (**b**) *(used attributively)* **this book is m.** c'est livre est à moi; **a friend of m.** un de mes amis; **where's that brother of m.?** où mon frère a-t-il bien pu passer?

minefield ['maɪnfiːld] *n* champ *m* de mines; *Fig* terrain *m* miné

miner ['maɪnə(r)] *n* mineur *m*

mineral ['mɪnərəl] *n* minéral *m*; *(extracted)* minerai *m*; **m. water** eau *m* minérale

minesweeper ['maɪnswiːpə(r)] *n* dragueur *m* de mines

mingle ['mɪŋɡəl] **1** *vt* mélanger, mêler
2 *vi (of things)* se mélanger, se mêler; *(of person)* parler un peu à tout le monde; **to m. with the crowd** se mêler à la foule

mini ['mɪnɪ] *n (miniskirt)* minijupe *f*

miniature ['mɪnɪtʃə(r)] **1** *n* miniature *f*
2 *adj* miniature

miniaturize ['mɪnɪtʃəraɪz] *vt* miniaturiser

minibus ['mɪnɪbʌs] *n* minibus *m*

minicab ['mɪnɪkæb] *n* radio-taxi *m*

MiniDisc® ['mɪnɪdɪsk] *n* MiniDisc® *m*

minidish ['mɪnɪdɪʃ] *n* mini antenne *f* parabolique

minidisk ['mɪnɪdɪsk] *n* mini-disquette *f*

minigolf ['mɪnɪɡɒlf] *n* minigolf *m*

minim ['mɪnɪm] *n Mus* blanche *f*

minimal ['mɪnɪməl] *adj* minime

minimize ['mɪnɪmaɪz] *vt (importance)* minimiser; *(noise, risk)* réduire au minimum

minimum ['mɪnɪməm] **1** *n* minimum *m*; **to keep sth to a m.** réduire qch au minimum
2 *adj* minimum *inv*, minimal(e); *Fin* **m. lending rate** taux *m* de base; **m. wage** salaire *m* minimum

mining ['maɪnɪŋ] *n* exploitation *f* minière; **m. engineer** ingénieur *m* des mines; **m. industry** industrie *f* minière

minion ['mɪnjən] *n* esclave *mf*

miniskirt ['mɪnɪskɜːt] *n* minijupe *f*

minister ['mɪnɪstə(r)] **1** *n* (**a**) *Pol* ministre *m*; *Br* **M. of Defence/Health** ministre *m* de la Défense/de la Santé (**b**) *Rel* pasteur *m*
2 *vi* **to m. to sb** s'occuper de qn; **to m. to sb's needs** pourvoir aux besoins de qn

ministerial [mɪnɪ'stɪərɪəl] *adj Pol* ministériel(elle)

ministry ['mɪnɪstrɪ] *(pl* **ministries***)* *n* (**a**) *Pol* ministère *m*; *Br* **the M. of Defence/Transport** le ministère de la Défense/des Transports (**b**) *Rel* **the m.** le sacerdoce

mink [mɪŋk] *n* vison *m*; **m. (coat)** (manteau *m* de) vison *m*

minnow ['mɪnəʊ] *n (fish)* vairon *m*; *Fig* (menu) fretin *m*

minor ['maɪnə(r)] **1** *adj* (**a**) *(unimportant)* mineur(e); *(operation)* bénin(igne); *(road)* secondaire (**b**) *Mus* mineur(e)
2 *n Law* mineur(e) *m,f*

Minorca [mɪ'nɔːkə] *n* Minorque

Minorcan [mɪ'nɔːkən] **1** *n* Minorquin(e) *m,f*
2 *adj* minorquin(e)

minority [maɪ'nɒrɪtɪ] *(pl* **minorities***)* *n* minorité *f*; **to be in a** *or* **the m.** être en minorité; **m. party/government** parti *m*/gouvernement *m* minoritaire

minstrel ['mɪnstrəl] *n* ménestrel *m*

mint¹ [mɪnt] *n (plant)* menthe *f*; *(sweet)* bonbon *m* à la menthe; **m. sauce** sauce *f* à la menthe; **m. tea** infusion *f* de menthe

mint² **1** *n* **the (Royal) M.** ≃ (l'hôtel *m* de) la Monnaie; *Fam* **to make a m.** gagner une fortune; **in m. condition** à l'état neuf
2 *vt (coins)* frapper

minuet [mɪnjʊ'et] *n Mus* menuet *m*

minus ['maɪnəs] **1** *n (sign)* moins *m*; *(negative aspect)* inconvénient *m*
2 *adj (quantity, number)* négatif(ive); *B* **m.** *(grade)* B moins; **on the m. side** quant aux inconvénients; **m. sign** signe *m* moins
3 *prep* moins; **ten m. eight leaves two** dix moins huit égale deux; **it's m. 12 (degrees)** il fait moins 12; **he managed to escape, but m. his luggage** il a réussi à s'enfuir, mais sans ses bagages

minuscule ['mɪnəskjuːl] *adj* minuscule

minute¹ ['mɪnɪt] **1** *n* (**a**) *(of time)* minute *f*; **ten minutes past/to three** trois heures dix/moins dix; **wait a m.!** attendez une minute!; **go downstairs this m.!** descends immédiatement!; **just a m.** une minute; **the m. my back was turned** dès que j'ai eu le dos tourné; **any m.** d'une minute à l'autre; **in a m.** dans une minute; **at the last m.** à la dernière minute; **m. hand** *(of watch)* grande aiguille *f*; **m. steak** steak *m* minute (**b**) *(note)* note *f*; **minutes** *(of meeting)* compte rendu *m*
2 *vt (make note of)* inscrire au procès-verbal

minute² [maɪ'njuːt] *adj* (**a**) *(small)* infime, minuscule (**b**) *(detailed)* minutieux(euse)

minutely [maɪ'njuːtlɪ] *adv* minutieusement

mips *Comput (abbr* **million instructions per second***)* MIPS *m*

miracle ['mɪrəkəl] *n also Fig* miracle *m*; **to perform** *or* **work miracles** faire des miracles; **by a** *or* **some m.** par miracle; **m. worker** faiseur(euse) *m,f* de miracles

miraculous [mɪ'rækjʊləs] *adj also Fig* miraculeux(euse)

mirage [mɪ'rɑːʒ] *n* mirage *m*

mire [maɪə(r)] n (mud) boue f; Fig bourbier m
mirror ['mɪrə(r)] **1** n miroir m, glace f; Fig **to hold a m.**
to sth refléter qch; **m. image** (reversed image) image f
inversée; (exact copy) copie f conforme
2 vt also Fig refléter
mirth [mɜːθ] n gaieté f, joie f
misadventure [mɪsəd'ventʃə(r)] n mésaventure f;
Law **death by m.** mort f accidentelle
misanthropic [mɪsən'θrɒpɪk] adj misanthrope
misanthropist [mɪ'sænθrəpɪst] n misanthrope mf
misapprehension [mɪsæprɪ'henʃən] n malentendu
m; **to be (labouring) under a m.** se méprendre
misappropriation ['mɪsəprəuprɪ'eɪʃən] n détournement m
misbehave [mɪsbɪ'heɪv] vi se conduire mal
misbehaviour, Am **misbehavior** [mɪsbɪ'heɪvjə(r)] n
mauvaise conduite f
misc (abbr **miscellaneous**) divers
miscalculate [mɪs'kælkjʊleɪt] **1** vt mal calculer; Fig
mal évaluer
2 vi faire une erreur de calcul; Fig faire un mauvais
calcul
miscalculation [mɪskælkjʊ'leɪʃən] n erreur f de calcul; Fig mauvais calcul m
miscarriage [mɪs'kærɪdʒ] n (**a**) Med fausse couche f;
to have a m. faire une fausse couche (**b**) Law **m. of
justice** erreur f judiciaire
miscarry [mɪs'kærɪ] (pt & pp **miscarried**) vi (**a**) (of woman) faire une fausse couche (**b**) Fig (of plan) avorter
miscast [mɪs'kɑːst] (pt & pp **miscast**) vt **to m. an actor**
donner à un acteur un rôle qui ne lui convient pas
miscellaneous [mɪsə'leɪnɪəs] adj divers(es)
miscellany [mɪ'selənɪ] (pl **miscellanies**) n mélange m
mischief ['mɪstʃɪf] n (**a**) (naughtiness) espièglerie f; **to
get up to m.** faire des bêtises; Hum **to keep sb out of
m.** occuper qn (**b**) (trouble) problèmes mpl; **to make
m. (for sb)** créer des problèmes (à qn) (**c**) Fam (injury) **to do oneself a m.** se faire mal
mischievous ['mɪstʃɪvəs] adj (naughty) espiègle;
(malicious) malveillant(e)
misconception [mɪskən'sepʃən] n idée f fausse
misconduct [mɪs'kɒndʌkt] n inconduite f
misconstrue [mɪskən'struː] vt mal interpréter
misdemeanour, Am **misdemeanor** [mɪsdɪ'miːnə(r)]
n Law délit m
misdiagnose [mɪsdaɪəg'nəuz] vt mal diagnostiquer
misdirect [mɪsdɪ'rekt] vt (**a**) (person) mal orienter (**b**)
(letter) mal adresser
miser ['maɪzə(r)] n avare mf
miserable ['mɪzərəbəl] adj (**a**) (unhappy) malheu-
reux(euse), triste; **to make sb's life m.** faire de la vie
de qn un enfer (**b**) (unpleasant) déplorable; (weather)
épouvantable (**c**) (wretched) misérable; **I only got a
m. £20** je n'ai eu que 20 malheureuses livres
miserably ['mɪzərəblɪ] adv (**a**) (unhappily) tristement
(**b**) (wretchedly) misérablement (**c**) (very badly)
lamentablement
miserly ['maɪzəlɪ] adj avare
misery ['mɪzərɪ] (pt **miseries**) n (**a**) (unhappiness) détresse f; (suffering) malheur m; **to make sb's life a m.**
faire de la vie de qn un enfer; **to put an animal out of
its m.** achever un animal; Hum **to put sb out of his
m.** (tell secret) mettre fin au supplice de qn (**b**) Br Fam
(person) grincheux(euse) m,f
misery-guts ['mɪzərɪgʌts] n Fam grincheux(euse) m,f
misfire [mɪs'faɪə(r)] vi (of gun) faire long feu; Fig (of
plan) rater

misfit ['mɪsfɪt] n inadapté(e) m,f
misfortune [mɪs'fɔːtʃən] n malheur m, malchance f
misgiving [mɪs'gɪvɪŋ] n doute m; **to have misgivings
(about sth)** avoir des doutes (sur qch)
misgovern [mɪs'gʌvən] vt mal gouverner
misguided [mɪs'gaɪdɪd] adj (person, decision) mal in-
spiré(e); (attempt) malencontreux(euse); (energy,
idealism) mal placé(e)
mishandle [mɪs'hændəl] vt (device) mal utiliser; (situation) mal gérer; (person) malmener
mishap ['mɪshæp] n incident m; **without m.** sans
encombre
mishear [mɪs'hɪə(r)] (pt & pp **misheard** [mɪs'hɜːd]) vt &
vi mal comprendre
mishmash ['mɪʃmæʃ] n Fam méli-mélo m
misinterpret [mɪsɪn'tɜːprɪt] vt (words) mal interpréter; (person) mal interpréter les paroles de
misjudge [mɪs'dʒʌdʒ] vt (person) mal juger; (distance,
situation) mal évaluer
misjudg(e)ment [mɪs'dʒʌdʒmənt] n erreur f de
jugement
mislay [mɪs'leɪ] (pt & pp **mislaid** [mɪs'leɪd]) vt égarer
mislead [mɪs'liːd] (pt & pp **misled** [mɪs'led]) vt induire
en erreur, tromper
misleading [mɪs'liːdɪŋ] adj trompeur(euse)
misled [mɪs'led] pt & pp of **mislead**
mismanage [mɪs'mænɪdʒ] vt mal gérer
mismanagement [mɪs'mænɪdʒmənt] n mauvaise
gestion f
misnomer [mɪs'nəumə(r)] n terme m mal approprié
miso ['miːsəu] n Culin miso m
misogynist [mɪ'sɒdʒɪnɪst] n misogyne mf
misplace [mɪs'pleɪs] vt (**a**) (mislay) égarer (**b**) (trust,
confidence) mal placer
misprint ['mɪsprɪnt] n faute f d'impression, coquille f
mispronounce [mɪsprə'naʊns] vt mal prononcer
mispronunciation [mɪsprənʌnsɪ'eɪʃən] n mauvaise
prononciation f
misquote [mɪs'kwəʊt] vt citer incorrectement
misread [mɪs'riːd] (pt & pp **misread** [mɪs'red]) vt (**a**)
(notice, timetable) mal lire (**b**) (misinterpret) mal
interpréter
misrepresent [mɪsreprɪ'zent] vt (facts, theory) dénaturer, déformer; (person) présenter sous un faux jour
misrepresentation [mɪsreprɪzen'teɪʃən] n déformation f
misrule [mɪs'ruːl] n mauvais gouvernement m
Miss [mɪs] n Mademoiselle f; **M. World** Miss Monde
miss [mɪs] **1** n coup m manqué; Fam **to give sth a m.**
(event) s'abstenir d'aller à
2 vt (**a**) (target, bus, chance) manquer, rater; Fig **to
m. the boat** louper le coche; **you're missing the
point** ce n'est pas le problème; **you've just missed
him** tu l'as loupé de peu (**b**) (not hear) ne pas entendre; **she doesn't m. a thing** rien ne lui échappe
(**c**) (feel lack of) **I m. you** tu me manques; **do you m.
me?** est-ce que je te manque? (**d**) (avoid) **the car just
missed me** la voiture m'a évité de peu; **she just
missed being killed** elle a failli ou manqué être tuée
(**e**) (word, line) sauter (**f**) (lack) **the table is missing
one of its legs** il manque un pied à la table
3 vi (miss target) rater ou manquer son coup
▸**miss out 1** vt sep (accidentally) oublier; (intentionally)
omettre
2 vi (not benefit) **to m. out on sth** rater qch; **you
missed out there** tu as raté quelque chose
missal ['mɪsəl] n Rel missel m

misshapen [mɪs'ʃeɪpən] *adj* difforme
missile ['mɪsaɪl, *Am* 'mɪsəl] *n (rocket)* missile *m*; *(object thrown)* projectile *m*; **m. launcher** lance-missiles *m inv*
missing ['mɪsɪŋ] *adj (person) (lost)* disparu(e); *(absent)* absent(e); *(object)* manquant(e); **nothing is m.** il ne manque rien; **m. link** chaînon *m* manquant; **m. person** personne *f* disparue
mission ['mɪʃən] *n* mission *f*
missionary ['mɪʃənərɪ] *(pl* **missionaries)** *n Rel* missionnaire *mf*; **the m. position** la position du missionnaire
missive ['mɪsɪv] *n Formal* missive *f*
misspell ['mɪs'spel] *(pt & pp* **misspelt** ['mɪs'spelt]) *vt* mal écrire
misspent ['mɪs'spent] *adj (time, money)* gaspillé(e); **m. youth** jeunesse *f* dissipée
missus ['mɪsɪz] *n Br Fam (wife)* **the m.** la patronne
mist [mɪst] *n (fog)* brume *f*; *(condensation)* buée *f*
▸**mist over, mist up** *vi (of mirror, glasses)* s'embuer
mistakable [mɪs'teɪkəbəl] *adj* facile à confondre (**for** avec)
mistake [mɪs'teɪk] **1** *n* erreur *f*; *(in grammar, spelling)* faute *f*; **to make a m.** faire *ou* commettre une erreur; **by m.** par erreur; *Fam* **he's a big guy and no m.!** pour être costaud, il est costaud!
2 *vt (pt* **mistook** [mɪs'tʊk], *pp* **mistaken** [mɪs'teɪkən]) (**a**) *(misunderstand)* se tromper sur (**b**) *(confuse)* **to m. sb for** prendre qn pour; **there's no mistaking a voice like that!** avec une voix pareille, on ne peut pas se tromper!
mistakeable = **mistakable**
mistaken [mɪs'teɪkən] **1** *adj (belief, impression)* erroné(e), faux (fausse); **to be m.** se tromper
2 *pp of* **mistake**
Mister ['mɪstə(r)] *n* Monsieur *m*
mistime [mɪs'taɪm] *vt* mal calculer
mistletoe ['mɪsəltəʊ] *n* gui *m*
mistook [mɪs'tʊk] *pt of* **mistake**
mistranslation [mɪstrænz'leɪʃən] *n* erreur *f* de traduction
mistreat [mɪs'triːt] *vt* maltraiter
mistress ['mɪstrɪs] *n* maîtresse *f*; *(in secondary school)* professeur *m*
mistrial [mɪs'traɪəl] *n Law Br* jugement *m* entaché d'un vice de procédure; *Am* = procès dans lequel le jury ne parvient pas à prendre de décision
mistrust [mɪs'trʌst] **1** *n* méfiance *f* (**of** à l'égard de)
2 *vt* se méfier de, ne pas avoir confiance en
mistrustful [mɪs'trʌstfʊl] *adj* méfiant(e); **to be m. of** se méfier de
misty ['mɪstɪ] *adj (place, weather)* brumeux(euse); *(outline, shape)* flou(e)
misunderstand [mɪsʌndə'stænd] *(pt & pp* **misunderstood** [mɪsʌndə'stʊd]) *vt & vi* mal comprendre
misunderstanding [mɪsʌndə'stændɪŋ] *n* (**a**) *(misconception)* malentendu *m* (**about** sur) (**b**) *(disagreement)* mésentente *f*
misuse 1 *n* [mɪs'juːs] *(of equipment, resources)* mauvais emploi *m*; *(of authority)* abus *m*; *(of funds)* détournement *m*
2 *vt* [mɪs'juːz] *(equipment, resources)* mal employer; *(authority)* abuser de; *(funds)* détourner
mite [maɪt] *n* (**a**) *(bug)* acarien *m* (**b**) *Fam (child)* **poor little m.!** pauvre petit(e) *m,f*! (**c**) *Fam (little bit)* **a m. expensive/tired** un tantinet cher (chère)/fatigué(e)
miter *Am* = **mitre**

mitigate ['mɪtɪgeɪt] *vt* atténuer; *Law* **mitigating circumstances** circonstances *fpl* atténuantes
mitigation [mɪtɪ'geɪʃən] *n* atténuation *f*; *Law* **to say sth in m.** dire qch pour sa défense
mitre, *Am* **miter** ['maɪtə(r)] *n Rel* mitre *f*
mitt [mɪt] *n* (**a**) *(mitten)* moufle *f*; *Am* **baseball m.** gant *m* de baseball (**b**) *Fam (hand)* patte *f*
mitten ['mɪtən] *n (glove)* moufle *f*
mix [mɪks] **1** *vt* mélanger; *(drink)* préparer; **to m. business with pleasure** mélanger les affaires et le plaisir
2 *vi* (**a**) *(blend)* se mélanger (**with** avec) (**b**) *(socially)* **to m. with** fréquenter
3 *n* mélange *m*; *(in music)* remix *m*
▸**mix up** *vt sep* (**a**) *(ingredients, papers)* mélanger (**b**) *(people, dates)* confondre (**c**) *Fam* **to be mixed up in sth** *(involved)* être mêlé(e) à qch, être impliqué(e) dans qch; **to get mixed up with sb** se mettre à fréquenter qn
mixed ['mɪkst] *adj* mélangé(e); *Fam* **it was a m. bag** il y avait de tout; **to have m. feelings (about sth)** avoir des sentiments mitigés (envers qch); **m. doubles** *(in tennis)* double *m* mixte; **m. grill** assortiment *m* de grillades; **m. marriage** mariage *m* mixte; **m. school** école *f* mixte
mixed-up [mɪkst'ʌp] *adj Fam (person)* déboussolé(e)
mixer ['mɪksə(r)] *n* (**a**) *(for cooking)* mixe(u)r *m*; *Br* **m. tap** (robinet *m*) mélangeur *m* (**b**) *(socially)* **to be a good m.** être très sociable (**c**) *(drink)* = boisson servant à allonger un alcool
mixing bowl ['mɪksɪŋ'bəʊl] *n* saladier *m*
mixture ['mɪkstʃə(r)] *n* mélange *m*
mix-up ['mɪksʌp] *n* confusion *f* (**over** *or* **with** dans)
mktg *Com (abbr* **marketing)** marketing *m*
ml *(abbr* **millilitre(s))** ml
MLR [emel'ɑː(r)] *n Fin (abbr* **minimum lending rate)** taux *m* de base
mm *(abbr* **millimetre(s))** mm
MMS [emem'es] *n Tel (abbr* **multimedia message service)** MMS *m*
mnemonic [nɪ'mɒnɪk] *n* moyen *m* mnémotechnique
moan [məʊn] **1** *n* (**a**) *(sound)* gémissement *m* (**b**) *(complaint)* plainte *f*
2 *vi* (**a**) *(make sound)* gémir (**b**) *(complain)* ronchonner; **to m. about sth** se plaindre de qch
moat [məʊt] *n* douve *f*
mob [mɒb] **1** *n (crowd)* foule *f*; *Fam* **the M.** la Mafia; **m. rule** loi *f* de la rue
2 *vt (pt & pp* **mobbed)** prendre d'assaut
mobile ['məʊbaɪl] **1** *adj* mobile; **m. home** mobile home *m*; *Br* **m. phone** téléphone *m* portable *ou* mobile, *Can* cellulaire *m*
2 *n* (**a**) *(hanging ornament)* mobile *m* (**b**) *Br Fam (mobile phone)* (téléphone *m*) portable *m* *ou* mobile *m*, *Can* cellulaire *m*
mobility [məʊ'bɪlɪtɪ] *n* mobilité *f*
mobilize ['məʊbɪlaɪz] *vt* mobiliser
mobster ['mɒbstə(r)] *n Am Fam* gangster *m*
moccasin ['mɒkəsɪn] *n* mocassin *m*
mock [mɒk] **1** *adj* faux (fausse), factice; *Br Sch* **m. exam** examen *m* blanc
2 *vt (ridicule)* se moquer de
mockery ['mɒkərɪ] *n* (**a**) *(ridicule)* moqueries *fpl* (**b**) *(travesty)* parodie *f*; **to make a m. of sb** ridiculiser qn; **to make a m. of sth** faire perdre toute crédibilité à qch
mockingbird ['mɒkɪŋbɜːd] *n* moqueur *m*
mock-up ['mɒkʌp] *n* maquette *f*

MOD [eməʊ'diː] *n Br Pol (abbr* **Ministry of Defence**) ministère *m* de la Défense

mod cons ['mɒd'kɒnz] *npl Br Fam* **with all m.** *(house)* tout confort; *(car)* avec toutes les options

mode [məʊd] *n* mode *m*

model ['mɒdəl] **1** *n* (**a**) *(small version)* maquette *f*, modèle *m* réduit; **m.** **aircraft** maquette *f* d'avion (**b**) *(example, paragon)* modèle *m*; **m.** **pupil** élève *mf* modèle (**c**) *(fashion model)* mannequin *m*; *(for artist)* modèle *m*
   2 *vt (pt & pp* **modelled**, *Am* **modeled**) (**a**) to **m.** oneself on sb prendre exemple sur qn (**b**) to **m.** clothes être mannequin (**c**) *Comput* modéliser
   3 *vi (on catwalk, for photographer)* travailler comme mannequin; *(for artist)* poser

modelling, *Am* **modeling** ['mɒdəlɪŋ] *n (career)* mannequinat *m*

modem ['məʊdem] *n Comput* modem *m*; **m.** **cable** câble *m* modem; **m.** **card** carte *f* modem

moderate 1 *n* ['mɒdərɪt] *Pol* modéré(e) *m,f*
   2 *adj* ['mɒdərɪt] modéré(e)
   3 *vt* ['mɒdəreɪt] modérer
   4 *vi* ['mɒdəreɪt] *Formal* présider

moderately ['mɒdərɪtlɪ] *adv* (**a**) *(in moderation)* modérément (**b**) *(quite)* assez

moderation [mɒdə'reɪʃən] *n* modération *f*; **in m.** avec modération

modern ['mɒdən] *adj* moderne; **m.** **art** art *m* moderne; **m.** **languages** langues *fpl* vivantes

modernism ['mɒdənɪzəm] *n* modernisme *m*

modernization [mɒdənaɪ'zeɪʃən] *n* modernisation *f*

modernize ['mɒdənaɪz] **1** *vt* moderniser
   2 *vi* se moderniser

modest ['mɒdɪst] *adj* (**a**) *(unassuming, moderate)* modeste (**b**) *(chaste)* pudique

modestly ['mɒdɪstlɪ] *adv* (**a**) *(unassumingly)* modestement (**b**) *(moderately)* assez, moyennement

modesty ['mɒdɪstɪ] *n* modestie *f*

modicum ['mɒdɪkəm] *n* **a m. of** un minimum de

modification [mɒdɪfɪ'keɪʃən] *n* modification *f*; **to make modifications to sth** apporter des modifications à qch

modify ['mɒdɪfaɪ] *(pt & pp* **modified**) *vt* modifier

modular ['mɒdjʊlə(r)] *adj* modulaire

modulate ['mɒdjʊleɪt] *vt* moduler

modulation [mɒdjʊ'leɪʃən] *n* modulation *f*

module ['mɒdjuːl] *n* module *m*

mogul ['məʊgəl] *n Fig* magnat *m*

mohair ['məʊheə(r)] *n* mohair *m*; **m.** **sweater** pull *m* en mohair

Mohammed [məʊ'hæmɪd] *n* Mahomet

moist [mɔɪst] *adj* humide; *(skin, hand)* moite; *(cake)* moelleux(euse)

moisten ['mɔɪsən] *vt* humecter

moisture ['mɔɪstʃə(r)] *n* humidité *f*

moisturize ['mɔɪstʃəraɪz] *vt* hydrater

moisturizer ['mɔɪstʃəraɪzə(r)] *n* crème *f* hydratante

mojito [məʊ'hiːtəʊ] *(pl* **mojitos**) *n (cocktail)* mojito *m*

molar ['məʊlə(r)] *n* molaire *f*

molasses [mə'læsɪz] *n* mélasse *f*

mold, molder *etc Am* = **mould, moulder** *etc*

Moldavia [mɒl'deɪvɪə], **Moldova** [mɒl'dəʊvə] *n* la Moldavie

Moldavian [mɒl'deɪvɪən], **Moldovan** [mɒl'dəʊvən]
   1 *n* Moldave *mf*
   2 *adj* moldave

mole¹ [məʊl] *n (birthmark)* grain *m* de beauté

mole² *n (animal, spy)* taupe *f*

molecular [mə'lekjʊlə(r)] *adj* moléculaire

molecule ['mɒlɪkjuːl] *n* molécule *f*

molehill ['məʊlhɪl] *n* taupinière *f*

molest [mə'lest] *vt (pester)* importuner; *(sexually)* agresser (sexuellement)

mollify ['mɒlɪfaɪ] *(pt & pp* **mollified**) *vt* calmer, apaiser

mollusc, *Am* **mollusk** ['mɒləsk] *n* mollusque *m*

mollycoddle ['mɒlɪkɒdəl] *vt Fam* dorloter

molt *Am* = **moult**

molten ['məʊltən] *adj* en fusion

mom [mɒm] *n Am Fam* maman *f*

moment ['məʊmənt] *n* moment *m*, instant *m*; **at the m.** en ce moment; **at the last m.** au dernier moment; **for the m.** pour le moment *ou* l'instant; **in a m.** dans un instant; **any m.** d'un instant à l'autre; **wait a m.!**, **one m.!** un moment!, un instant!; **the m. he arrives** dès qu'il arrive; **without a m.'s hesitation** sans une seconde d'hésitation; **to live for the m.** profiter du moment présent; **the man of the m.** l'homme du moment; **the m. of truth** le moment de vérité; **he's not a genius, but he has his moments** ce n'est pas un génie, mais il a parfois des moments d'inspiration

momentary ['məʊməntərɪ] *adj* momentané(e)

momentous [məʊ'mentəs] *adj* capital(e)

momentum [məʊ'mentəm] *n Phys* moment *m*; **to gather m.** *(of campaign)* prendre de l'ampleur; **to lose m.** *(of campaign)* s'essouffler

Mon *(abbr* **Monday**) lundi

Monaco ['mɒnəkəʊ] *n* Monaco

monarch ['mɒnək] *n* monarque *m*

monarchist ['mɒnəkɪst] *n* monarchiste *mf*

monarchy ['mɒnəkɪ] *(pl* **monarchies**) *n* monarchie *f*

monastery ['mɒnəstrɪ] *(pl* **monasteries**) *n* monastère *m*

monastic [mə'næstɪk] *adj* monastique, monacal(e)

Monday ['mʌndɪ] *n* lundi *m*; *see also* **Saturday**

monetarism ['mʌnɪtərɪzm] *n* monétarisme *m*

monetarist ['mʌnɪtərɪst] **1** *n* monétariste *mf*
   2 *adj* monétariste

monetary ['mʌnɪtərɪ] *adj* monétaire

money ['mʌnɪ] *n* argent *m*; **to do sth for the m.** faire qch pour l'argent; **to make m.** *(of person)* gagner de l'argent; *(of business)* rapporter de l'argent; **to be worth a lot of m.** *(of thing)* valoir cher; *(of person)* être très riche; **there's no m. in it** ça ne paie pas; *Fam* **to be in the m.** être plein(e) aux as; **to get one's m.'s worth** en avoir pour son argent; *Fam* **it was m. for old rope** c'était de l'argent facilement gagné; **to put one's m. where one's mouth is** joindre le geste à la parole; *Fam* **to spend m. like water** dépenser sans compter; *Fam* **m. doesn't grow on trees!** l'argent ne se trouve pas sous le sabot d'un cheval!; **for my m.,...** à mon avis,...; **m. laundering** blanchiment *m* d'argent; *Fin* **m. market** marché *m* monétaire; *Econ* **m. supply** masse *f* monétaire

moneybags ['mʌnɪbægz] *n Fam (person)* richard *m,f*

moneybox ['mʌnɪbɒks] *n* tirelire *f*

moneyed ['mʌnɪd] *adj* fortuné(e)

moneylender ['mʌnɪlendə(r)] *n* prêteur(euse) *m,f*; *(usurer)* usurier(ère) *m,f*

moneymaker ['mʌnɪmeɪkə(r)] *n* **to be a m.** *(of shop, business, product)* rapporter

moneymaking ['mʌnɪmeɪkɪŋ] *adj* qui rapporte

Mongol ['mɒŋgəl] *Hist* **1** *n* Mongol(e) *m,f*
   2 *adj* mongol(e)

mongol ['mɒŋgəl] *n Old-fashioned* mongolien(enne) *m,f,* = terme injurieux désignant un trisomique
Mongolia [mɒŋ'gəʊliə] *n* la Mongolie
Mongolian [mɒŋ'gəʊliən] **1** *n* Mongol(e) *m,f*
2 *adj* mongol(e)
mongoose ['mɒŋguːs] *n* mangouste *f*
mongrel ['mʌŋgrəl] *n* bâtard *m*
monitor ['mɒnitə(r)] **1** *n* (**a**) *(supervisor)* superviseur *m* (**b**) *TV & Comput (screen)* moniteur *m*
2 *vt (broadcast, conversation)* écouter; *(patient's condition, operation, results)* surveiller; *(performance)* suivre
monk [mʌŋk] *n* moine *m*
monkey ['mʌŋki] *(pl* **monkeys**) *n (animal)* singe *m*; *Fam Fig* **you little m.!** *(to naughty child)* petit(e) polisson(onne) *m,f*; *Fam* **to make a m. out of sb** se payer la tête de qn; *Br very Fam* **I don't give a m.'s** je m'en fous complètement; *Fam* **m. business** *(dishonest behaviour)* magouilles *fpl; (mischief)* bêtises *fpl;* **m. nut** cacah(o)uète *f;* **m. puzzle (tree)** désespoir *m* des singes; **m. wrench** clef *f* anglaise *ou* à molette
▸**monkey about, monkey around** *vi Fam (fool around)* faire l'imbécile
monkfish ['mʌŋkfiʃ] *n* lotte *f*
mono ['mɒnəʊ] *n* mono *f*
monochrome ['mɒnəkrəʊm] *adj* monochrome; *(photo)* en noir et blanc
monocle ['mɒnəkəl] *n* monocle *m*
monogamous [mɒ'nɒgəməs] *adj* monogame
monogamy [mɒ'nɒgəmi] *n* monogamie *f*
monogram ['mɒnəgræm] *n* monogramme *m*
monograph ['mɒnəgræf] *n* monographie *f*
monolingual [mɒnəʊ'lɪŋgwəl] *adj* monolingue
monolithic [mɒnə'lɪθɪk] *adj* monolithique
monologue ['mɒnəlɒg] *n* monologue *m*
monopolize [mə'nɒpəlaɪz] *vt also Fig* monopoliser
monopoly [mə'nɒpəli] *(pl* **monopolies**) *n also Fig* monopole *m;* **to have a m. on sth** avoir le monopole de qch
monorail ['mɒnəʊreɪl] *n* monorail *m*
monoski ['mɒnəʊskiː] *n* monoski *m*
monosyllabic [mɒnəʊsɪ'læbɪk] *adj (word)* monosyllabique; *(reply)* laconique
monosyllable [mɒnəʊ'sɪləbəl] *n* monosyllabe *m*
monotone ['mɒnətəʊn] *n* ton *m* monotone; **to speak in a m.** parler d'une voix monotone
monotonous [mə'nɒtənəs] *adj* monotone
monotony [mə'nɒtəni] *n* monotonie *f*
Monsignor [mɒn'siːnjə(r)] *n* Monseigneur *m*
monsoon [mɒn'suːn] *n* mousson *f*
monster ['mɒnstə(r)] **1** *n* monstre *m*
2 *adj Fam (enormous)* monstre, colossal(e)
monstrosity [mɒn'strɒsɪti] *(pl* **monstrosities**) *n* monstruosité *f*
monstrous ['mɒnstrəs] *adj* monstrueux(euse)
montage ['mɒntɑːʒ] *n* montage *m*
month [mʌnθ] *n* mois *m;* **in the m. of August** au mois d'août; *Fam* **never in a m. of Sundays** jamais de la vie
monthly ['mʌnθli] **1** *n (pl* **monthlies**) *(magazine)* mensuel *m*
2 *adj* mensuel(elle); **m. payment** *or* **instalment** mensualité *f*
3 *adv* tous les mois; **to be paid m.** être payé au mois *ou* mensuellement
monument ['mɒnjʊmənt] *n also Fig* monument *m* (**to** à)

monumental [mɒnjʊ'mentəl] *adj* monumental(e); *(importance)* capital(e)
moo [muː] **1** *n (pl* **moos**) meuglement *m*, beuglement *m;* **m.!** meuh!
2 *vi (pt & pp* **mooed**) meugler, beugler
▸**mooch about, mooch around** [muːtʃ] *vi Br Fam* traîner
mood [muːd] *n* (**a**) *(state of mind)* humeur *f;* **to be in a good/bad m.** être de bonne/mauvaise humeur; **she's in one of her moods** elle est de mauvaise humeur; **to be in the m. for sth** avoir envie de qch; **to be in the m. for doing sth** être d'humeur à faire qch (**b**) *Gram* mode *m*
moodily ['muːdɪli] *adv (answer, speak)* d'un ton maussade
moody ['muːdi] *adj* (**a**) *(sulky)* maussade (**b**) *(changeable)* lunatique
moon [muːn] *n* **1** lune *f;* **the M.** la Lune; *Fam* **to ask for the m.** demander la lune; *Fam* **to promise sb the m.** promettre la lune à qn; *Fam* **to be over the m.** être aux anges; **m. landing** alunissage *m*
2 *vi Fam (expose one's buttocks)* montrer ses fesses
▸**moon about, moon around** *vi* musarder, flâner
moonbeam ['muːnbiːm] *n* rayon *m* de lune
moonlight ['muːnlaɪt] **1** *n* clair *m* de lune; **in the m., by m.** au clair de lune; *Fam* **to do a m. flit** partir à la cloche de bois
2 *vi Fam (work illegally)* travailler au noir
moonlighting ['muːnlaɪtɪŋ] *n Fam* travail *m* au noir
moonlit ['muːnlɪt] *adj* éclairé(e) par la lune
moonshine ['muːnʃaɪn] *n Fam* (**a**) *(nonsense)* balivernes *fpl*, bêtises *fpl* (**b**) *Am (illegal alcohol)* alcool *m* de contrebande
Moor [mʊə(r)] *n* Maure *mf*
moor[1] [mʊə(r)] *n (heath)* lande *f*
moor[2] *vt (ship)* amarrer
mooring ['mʊərɪŋ] *n* (**a**) *(place)* mouillage *m* (**b**) **moorings** *(chains, ropes)* amarres *fpl*
Moorish ['mʊərɪʃ] *adj* maure, mauresque
moorland ['mʊələnd] *n* lande *f*
moose [muːs] *(pl* **moose**) *n* orignal *m*
moot [muːt] **1** *adj* **it's a m. point** c'est difficile à dire
2 *vt (suggest)* suggérer
mop [mɒp] **1** *n (for floor)* balai *m* à franges; *(with sponge)* balai-éponge *m; Fam* **m. (of hair)** tignasse *f*
2 *vt (pt & pp* **mopped**) **to m. the floor** laver par terre; **to m. one's brow** s'éponger le front
▸**mop up** *vt sep (liquid)* éponger; *Fig (enemy forces)* liquider
▸**mope about, mope around** [məʊp] *vi* broyer du noir
moped ['məʊped] *n (motorbike)* Mobylette® *f*
moral ['mɒrəl] **1** *n* (**a**) *(of story)* morale *f* (**b**) **morals** *(principles)* moralité *f*
2 *adj* moral(e); **m. fibre** force *f* de caractère; **the m. majority** les néo-conservateurs *mpl (surtout aux États-Unis)*; **m. support** soutien *m* moral; **m. victory** victoire *f* morale
morale [mɒ'rɑːl] *n* moral *m;* **to be good/bad for the m.** être bon (bonne)/mauvais(e) pour le moral
moralistic [mɒrə'lɪstɪk] *adj* moraliste
morality [mə'rælɪti] *n* moralité *f*
moralize ['mɒrəlaɪz] *vi* faire la morale, moraliser
morally ['mɒrəli] *adv* moralement; **m. right** moralement correct(e); **m. wrong** contraire à la morale
morass [mə'ræs] *n (marsh)* marais *m; Fig (of detail, despair)* bourbier *m*

moratorium [ˌmɒrə'tɔːrɪəm] (*pl* **moratoria** [ˌmɒrə'tɔːrɪə] *or* **moratoriums**) *n* moratoire *m* (**on** sur)
morbid ['mɔːbɪd] *adj* morbide
morbidly ['mɔːbɪdlɪ] *adv* de façon morbide
mordant ['mɔːdənt] *adj Formal (sarcasm, wit)* mordant(e)
more [mɔː(r)] (*comparative of* **many, much**) **1** *pron* plus; **there are m. of us** nous sommes plus nombreux; **have (some) m.** reprenez-en; **there's no m.** il n'y en a plus; **let's say no m.** about it n'en parlons plus; **she knows m. than you** elle en sait plus long que toi; **we should see m. of each other** nous devrions nous voir plus souvent; **it's just m. of the same** c'est encore et toujours la même chose; **the m. I see her, the m. I like her** plus je la vois, plus elle me plaît; **what's m.,...** qui plus est,...; **what m. can I say?** que puis-je dire de plus?
2 *adj* (**a**) *(larger quantity or number of)* plus de; **m. water/children** plus d'eau/d'enfants; **m. than a hundred people were there** il y avait plus de cent personnes; **he has m. patience than I have** il a plus de patience que moi; **there are m. and m. accidents every year** chaque année, il y a de plus en plus d'accidents (**b**) *(additional quantity or number of)* **one m. month** un mois de plus; **is there any m. bread?** est-ce qu'il y a encore du pain?; **I've no m. money** je n'ai plus d'argent; **I need m. time** il me faut plus de temps
3 *adv* (**a**) *(to form comparative of adjectives and adverbs)* plus (**than** que); **m. interesting** plus intéressant(e); **m. easily** plus facilement; **things are getting m. and m. difficult** les choses deviennent de plus en plus difficiles (**b**) *(to a greater extent)* plus; **you should eat m.** tu devrais manger plus; **I'm m. than satisfied** je suis plus que satisfait; **he was m. surprised than annoyed** il était plus surpris que fâché; **I like her m. than I used to** je l'aime plus qu'avant; **that's m. like it!** voilà qui est mieux!; **m. or less** plus ou moins (**c**) *(with time)* **once/twice m.** une/deux fois de plus; **he doesn't drink any m.** il ne boit plus; **I can't see you any m.** nous ne pouvons plus nous voir
moreover [mɔː'rəʊvə(r)] *adv* de plus
mores ['mɔːreɪz] *npl Formal* mœurs *fpl*
morgue [mɔːg] *n* morgue *f*; *Fig* **this place is like a m.** c'est complètement mort ici
moribund ['mɒrɪbʌnd] *adj* moribond(e)
Mormon ['mɔːmən] *n Rel* mormon(e) *m,f*
morning ['mɔːnɪŋ] *n* matin *m*; *(referring to duration)* matinée *f*; **good m.!, Fam m.!** bonjour!; **tomorrow m.** demain matin; **yesterday m.** hier matin; **the next m., the m. after** le lendemain matin; **the m. before** la veille au matin; *Fam* **it's the m. after (the night before)** c'est un lendemain de cuite; **m., noon and night** du matin au soir; **in the m.** le matin; **on Wednesday m.** mercredi matin; **m. sickness** nausées *fpl* matinales; **m. star** étoile *f* du matin
morning-after pill ['mɔːnɪŋ'ɑːftəpɪl] *n* pilule *f* du lendemain
Moroccan [mə'rɒkən] **1** *n* Marocain(e) *m,f*
2 *adj* marocain(e)
Morocco [mə'rɒkəʊ] *n* le Maroc
moron ['mɔːrɒn] *n* crétin(e) *m,f*
moronic [mə'rɒnɪk] *adj* débile
morose [mə'rəʊs] *adj* morose
morph [mɔːf] *Comput* **1** *vt (image)* transformer par morphing
2 *vi* **to m. into sth** se transformer en qch

morphing ['mɔːfɪŋ] *n Comput* morphing *m*
Morse [mɔːs] *n* **M. (code)** morse *m*
morsel ['mɔːsəl] *n* morceau *m*
mortal ['mɔːtəl] **1** *n* mortel(elle) *m,f*; *Fig & Ironic* **mere mortals** de simples mortels
2 *adj* mortel(elle); **m. enemy** ennemi *m* mortel; **m. remains** dépouille *f* mortelle; **m. sin** péché *m* mortel; **m. wound** blessure *f* mortelle
mortality [mɔː'tælɪtɪ] *n* mortalité *f*
mortally ['mɔːtəlɪ] *adv* mortellement
mortar ['mɔːtə(r)] *n* mortier *m*
mortgage ['mɔːgɪdʒ] **1** *n (from lender's point of view)* prêt *m* immobilier; *(from borrower's point of view)* emprunt *m* immobilier; *(from buyer's point of view)* hypothécaires; **m. (re)payments** remboursements *mpl* d'emprunt; **m. rate** taux *m* de crédit immobilier
2 *vt (property, one's future)* hypothéquer
mortician [mɔː'tɪʃən] *n Am (undertaker)* entrepreneur *m* de pompes funèbres
mortification [mɔːtɪfɪ'keɪʃən] *n Rel* mortification *f*; *Fig (embarrassment)* honte *f*
mortify ['mɔːtɪfaɪ] *(pt & pp* **mortified**) *vt Rel* mortifier; *Fig* **to be mortified** être mort(e) de honte
mortise ['mɔːtɪs] *n* mortaise *f*; **m. lock** serrure *f* encastrée
mortuary ['mɔːtjʊərɪ] *(pl* **mortuaries**) *n* morgue *f*
mosaic [məʊ'zeɪɪk] *n also Fig* mosaïque *f*
Moscow ['mɒskəʊ] *n* Moscou
Moses ['məʊzɪz] *n* Moïse
Moslem ['mɒzləm] = **Muslim**
mosque [mɒsk] *n* mosquée *f*
mosquito [məs'kiːtəʊ] *(pl* **mosquitos** *or* **mosquitoes**) *n* moustique *m*; **m. bite** piqûre *f* de moustique; **m. net** moustiquaire *f*
moss [mɒs] *n* mousse *f*
most [məʊst] *(superlative of* **many, much**) **1** *pron* (**a**) *(the majority)* la plupart; **m. of the people/time** la plupart des gens/du temps; **m. of us/them** la plupart d'entre nous/eux; **he is more interesting than m.** il est plus intéressant que la plupart des gens (**b**) *(greatest amount)* **the m.** le plus; **he earns the m.** c'est lui qui gagne le plus; **at the (very) m.** au maximum; **to make the m. of sth** *(situation, talents)* tirer le meilleur parti de qch; *(time, holiday)* profiter au maximum de qch
2 *adj* (**a**) *(the majority of)* la plupart de; **m. women** la plupart des femmes (**b**) *(greatest amount of)* **the m.** le plus de; **he has the m. money** c'est lui qui a le plus d'argent; **for the m. part** dans l'ensemble
3 *adv* (**a**) *(to form superlative of adjectives and adverbs)* plus; **the m. interesting book** le livre le plus intéressant; **the m. beautiful woman** la plus belle femme; **these are the m. expensive** ce sont les plus chers; **those who answered m. honestly** ceux qui ont répondu le plus franchement (**b**) *(to the greatest extent)* le plus; **the one who works (the) m. is...** celui qui travaille le plus est...; **that's what worries me (the) m.** c'est ce qui m'inquiète le plus; **who do you like m.?** qui préfères-tu?; **what I want m.** ce que je veux par-dessus tout (**c**) *(very)* extrêmement; **m. unhappy** extrêmement malheureux(euse)
mostly ['məʊstlɪ] *adv* (**a**) *(in the main)* principalement, surtout (**b**) *(most often)* le plus souvent, la plupart du temps
MOT [eməʊ'tiː] *n Br* ≃ contrôle *m* technique des véhicules
motel [məʊ'tel] *n* motel *m*

moth [mɒθ] *n* papillon *m* de nuit; *(in clothes)* mite *f*
mothball ['mɒθbɔːl] *n* boule *f* de naphtaline; *Fig* **to put a project in mothballs** mettre un projet au placard
moth-eaten ['mɒθiːtən] *adj* mité(e); *Fam (in poor condition)* miteux(euse)
mother ['mʌðə(r)] **1** *n* mère *f*; **M.'s Day** la fête des Mères; **m. country** patrie *f*; **M. Nature** Dame Nature *f*; *Rel* **M. Superior** Mère *f* supérieure; **m. tongue** langue *f* maternelle
2 *vt* materner
motherboard ['mʌðəbɔːd] *n Comput* carte *f* mère
motherhood ['mʌðəhʊd] *n* maternité *f*
mother-in-law ['mʌðərɪnlɔː] *(pl* **mothers-in-law)** *n* belle-mère *f*
motherland ['mʌðəlænd] *n* patrie *f*
mother-of-pearl ['mʌðərəv'pɜːl] *n* nacre *f*
mother-to-be ['mʌðətə'biː] *(pl* **mothers-to-be)** *n* future mère *f*
motif [məʊ'tiːf] *n* motif *m*
motion ['məʊʃən] **1** *n* (**a**) *(movement)* mouvement *m*; **to set sth in m.** *(machine)* mettre qch en marche; *(process)* déclencher qch; *Fig* **to go through the motions** agir machinalement; *Am* **m. picture** film *m* (**b**) *(in meeting, debate)* motion *f*; **to propose/second a m.** présenter/appuyer une motion (**c**) *(faeces)* selles *fpl*
2 *vt* **to m. sb to do sth** faire signe à qn de faire qch
3 *vi* **to m. to sb to do sth** faire signe à qn de faire qch
motionless ['məʊʃənlɪs] *adj* immobile
motivate ['məʊtɪveɪt] *vt* motiver
motivation [məʊtɪ'veɪʃən] *n* motivation *f*
motive ['məʊtɪv] **1** *n (reason)* motif *m*; *Law (for crime)* mobile *m*
2 *adj* **m. force** *or* **power** force *f* motrice
motley ['mɒtlɪ] *adj* hétéroclite; **m. crew** groupe *m* hétéroclite
motor ['məʊtə(r)] **1** *n (engine)* moteur *m*; *Br Fam (car)* bagnole *f*; **m. industry** industrie *f* automobile; **m. insurance** assurance *f* automobile; *Med* **m. neurone disease** maladie *f* de Charcot; **m. racing** courses *fpl* automobiles; **m. show** salon *m* de l'automobile; **m. vehicle** véhicule *m* automobile
2 *vi* voyager en voiture
motorbike ['məʊtəbaɪk] *n* moto *f*
motorboat ['məʊtəbəʊt] *n* canot *m* à moteur
motorcade ['məʊtəkeɪd] *n* cortège *m* de voitures
motorcar ['məʊtəkɑː(r)] *n Br* voiture *f*
motorcycle ['məʊtəsaɪkəl] *n* moto *f*
motorcyclist ['məʊtəsaɪklɪst] *n* motocycliste *mf*
motoring ['məʊtərɪŋ] *n* conduite *f*; **school of m.** auto-école *f*; **m. offence** infraction *f* au Code de la route
motorist ['məʊtərɪst] *n* automobiliste *mf*
motorize ['məʊtəraɪz] *vt* motoriser
motorized ['məʊtəraɪzd] *adj* motorisé(e)
motorway ['məʊtəweɪ] *n Br* autoroute *f*; **m. services** services *mpl* autoroutiers
mottled ['mɒtəld] *adj (skin)* marbré(e); *(coat, surface)* tacheté(e), moucheté(e)
motto ['mɒtəʊ] *(pl* **mottoes)** *n* devise *f*
mould¹, *Am* **mold** [məʊld] *n (fungus)* moisissure *f*
mould², *Am* **mold 1** *n (in art, cooking)* moule *m*; *Fig* **cast in the same m.** fait(e) dans le même moule; *Fig* **a star in the John Wayne m.** une star dans le style John Wayne; *Fig* **to break the m.** rompre avec la tradition
2 *vt (plastic, person's character)* modeler, façonner

moulder, *Am* **molder** ['məʊldə(r)] *vi (of food)* moisir; *(of building)* se délabrer
moulding, *Am* **molding** ['məʊldɪŋ] *n Archit* moulure *f*
mouldy, *Am* **moldy** ['məʊldɪ] *adj* moisi(e)
moult, *Am* **molt** [məʊlt] *vi (of bird)* muer; *(of cat, dog)* perdre ses poils
mound [maʊnd] *n (hill)* butte *f*; *(of earth, sand)* tas *m*
mount¹ [maʊnt] *n (mountain)* mont *m*; **M. Vesuvius** le Vésuve
mount² **1** *n* (**a**) *(for painting)* carton *m* de montage; *(for slide)* cadre *m* (**b**) *(horse)* monture *f*
2 *vt* (**a**) *(bicycle, horse)* monter sur, enfourcher; *(stairs)* monter; *(ladder)* monter à (**b**) *(photograph, exhibition)* monter; *(machine gun)* installer; *(offensive)* lancer; **to m. guard** monter la garde
3 *vi* (**a**) *(get onto horse)* se mettre en selle (**b**) *(increase)* monter, augmenter
▸**mount up** *vi (of cost, debts)* monter, augmenter
mountain ['maʊntɪn] *n also Fig* montagne *f*; **to make a m. out of a molehill** faire une montagne d'un rien; **m. bike** vélo *m* tout terrain; **m. climbing** alpinisme *m*; **m. lion** puma *m*; **m. range** chaîne *f* de montagnes; **m. rescue team** équipe *f* de secours en montagne; *Am* **M. Standard Time** heure *f* des montagnes Rocheuses
mountaineer [maʊntɪ'nɪə(r)] *n* alpiniste *mf*
mountaineering [maʊntɪ'nɪərɪŋ] *n* alpinisme *m*
mountainous ['maʊntɪnəs] *adj* montagneux(euse)
mounted ['maʊntɪd] *adj* monté(e), à cheval; **the m. police** la police montée
mounting ['maʊntɪŋ] **1** *n (for engine, gun)* support *m*
2 *adj (increasing)* croissant(e)
mourn [mɔːn] *vt* pleurer
2 *vi* **to m. for sb/sth** pleurer qn/qch
mourner ['mɔːnə(r)] *n =* personne assistant aux obsèques
mournful ['mɔːnfʊl] *adj* triste
mourning ['mɔːnɪŋ] *n* deuil *m*; **to be in m. (for sb)** être en deuil (de qn); **to go into m.** prendre le deuil
mouse [maʊs] *(pl* **mice** [maɪs]) *n also Comput* souris *f*; **m. mat,** *Am* **m. pad** tapis *m* de souris
mousetrap ['maʊstræp] *n* tapette *f*, souricière *f*
mousse [muːs] *n* mousse *f*; **chocolate m.** mousse *f* au chocolat
moustache [mə'stæʃ], *Am* **mustache** ['mʌstæʃ] *n* moustache *f*
mousy ['maʊsɪ] *adj* (**a**) *(hair)* châtain terne *inv* (**b**) *(person, manner)* timide, effacé(e)
mouth 1 *n* [maʊθ] *(pl* [maʊðz]) *(of person, horse)* bouche *f*; *(of other animal)* gueule *f*; *(of tunnel)* entrée *f*; *(of river)* embouchure *f*; **we have seven mouths to feed** nous avons sept bouches à nourrir; *Fam* **keep your m.** shut about this garde ça pour toi; *Fam Fig* **to have a big m.** avoir une grande gueule; *Fam* **he's all m.** c'est une grande gueule; **don't put words into my m.** ne me fais pas dire ce que je n'ai pas dit; **m. organ** harmonica *m*
2 *vt* [maʊð] *(insincerely)* débiter; *(silently)* articuler silencieusement
▸**mouth off** *vi (brag)* crâner; *(be rude)* se montrer insolent(e)
mouthful ['maʊθfʊl] *n (of food)* bouchée *f*; *(of drink)* gorgée *f*; *Fam Fig (long word) =* mot long et difficile à prononcer; *(long name)* nom *m* à coucher dehors; *Fam* **to give sb a m.** engueuler qn

mouthpiece ['maʊθpi:s] n (**a**) (of musical instrument) embouchure f; (of telephone) microphone m (**b**) (of government, political party) porte-parole m inv
mouth-to-mouth resuscitation ['maʊθtə'maʊθ-rɪsʌsɪ'teɪʃən] n bouche-à-bouche m inv
mouthwash ['maʊθwɒʃ] n bain m de bouche
mouthwatering ['maʊθwɔ:tərɪŋ] adj (smell) appétissant(e); (prospect) alléchant(e)
movable ['mu:vəbəl] adj mobile; Rel m. feast fête f mobile
move [mu:v] 1 n (**a**) (motion) mouvement m; to make a m. (leave) partir; to make a m. towards sb/sth se diriger vers qn/qch; on the m. en mouvement; Fam to get a m. on se grouiller, se magner (**b**) (action, step) pas m, démarche f; to make the first m. faire le premier pas (**c**) (from home) déménagement m; (from job) changement m de poste (**d**) (in games) coup m; (it's) your m. (c'est) à toi de jouer
2 vt (**a**) (change position of) déplacer; (set in motion) remuer; (employee) muter; to m. house/premises déménager; to m. jobs (within company, sector) changer de poste; Fam to m. oneself se remuer (**b**) Fig (sway) faire changer d'avis; to feel moved to do sth se sentir obligé(e) de faire qch (**c**) (affect emotionally) émouvoir; to m. sb to anger provoquer la colère de qn; to m. sb to tears émouvoir qn jusqu'aux larmes (**d**) (in debate) proposer
3 vi (**a**) (change position) se déplacer; (stir) bouger; (progress, advance) avancer; (leave) partir; to get things moving faire avancer les choses; could you m., please? pourriez-vous vous pousser, s'il vous plaît?; Fam come on, m.! allez, remue-toi! (**b**) (act) agir (**c**) (to new home, office) emménager; to m. to another job changer de travail; to m. to the country s'installer à la campagne (**d**) Fig (be swayed) céder (**e**) (in games) (of player) jouer; (of piece) avancer
▸**move about, move around 1** vt sep (furniture) déplacer; (employee) muter, transférer
2 vi (change position) se déplacer; (stir) bouger; he moves around a lot (in job) il est souvent en déplacement
▸**move along** = move on
▸**move away 1** vt sep éloigner, écarter (from de)
2 vi (from window, person) s'éloigner, s'écarter (from de); (move house) déménager
▸**move back 1** vt sep (further away) reculer; (to former position) remettre en place
2 vi (retreat) s'écarter, (se) reculer; (to former position) retourner (to à)
▸**move forward 1** vt sep (object, date, meeting) avancer; (troops) faire avancer
2 vi (of person, car) (s')avancer
▸**move in** vi (take up residence) emménager
▸**move off** vi (go away) partir, s'éloigner; (start journey) se mettre en marche; (of car) démarrer
▸**move on 1** vt sep (crowd) faire circuler
2 vi (**a**) time's moving on il se fait tard; it's time we were moving on il est temps de partir (**b**) (change subject) passer à autre chose; to m. on to sth passer à qch (**c**) (progress, develop) changer
▸**move out** vi (leave home) déménager
▸**move over** vi (make room) se pousser
▸**move up** vi (**a**) (make room) se pousser (**b**) (be promoted) avoir de l'avancement
moveable = movable

movement ['mu:vmənt] n mouvement m; to watch sb's movements surveiller les faits et gestes de qn; (bowel) m. selles fpl
mover ['mu:və(r)] n (in debate) auteur m d'une motion; the movers and shakers les grands pontes mpl
movie ['mu:vɪ] n Am film m; to go to the movies aller au cinéma; to be in the movies faire du cinéma; m. actor/actress acteur m/actrice f de cinéma; m. camera caméra f; m. industry industrie f cinématographique; m. star vedette f de cinéma; m. theater cinéma m
moviegoer ['mu:vɪɡəʊə(r)] n Am spectateur(trice) m,f de cinéma
moving ['mu:vɪŋ] adj (**a**) (in motion) en mouvement; (train, vehicle) en marche; (parts) mobile; m. staircase escalier m mécanique (**b**) (touching) émouvant(e)
mow [məʊ] (pp mown [məʊn]) vt (lawn) tondre; (hay) faucher
▸**mow down** vt sep (slaughter) faucher
Mozambican [məʊzæm'bi:kən] 1 n Mozambicain(e) m,f
2 adj mozambicain(e)
Mozambique [məʊzæm'bi:k] n le Mozambique
MP [em'pi:] n (**a**) Br & Can Pol (abbr Member of Parliament) député(e) m,f (**b**) Mil (abbr Military Police) police f militaire
MP3 [empi:'θri:] n Comput MP3 m; MP3 player lecteur m MP3
mpg [empi:'dʒi:] n (abbr miles per gallon) ≃ litre m aux cent (kilomètres)
mph [empi:'eɪtʃ] n (abbr miles per hour) ≃ km/h
Mr ['mɪstə(r)] (abbr Mister) Mr McLean M. McLean; Mr Right (ideal husband) l'homme m idéal
Mrs ['mɪsɪz] (abbr Mistress) M. Sole Mme Sole
Ms [mɪz] ≃ Mme (ne donne pas d'indications sur le statut de famille)
MS¹ ['em'es] (abbr multiple sclerosis) sclérose f en plaques
MS² (abbr manuscript) manuscrit m
ms (abbr millisecond) millième m de seconde
MSc [emes'si:] n Univ (abbr Master of Science) to have an M. in chemistry ≃ avoir une maîtrise de chimie; John Smith M. John Smith, titulaire d'une maîtrise de sciences
MSG [emes'dʒi:] n Culin (abbr monosodium glutamate) glutamate m de sodium
MSP [emes'pi:] n (abbr Member of the Scottish Parliament) député(e) m,f du parlement écossais
MST [emes'ti:] n Am (abbr Mountain Standard Time) heure f d'hiver des montagnes Rocheuses
Mt (abbr Mount) Mt.
much [mʌtʃ] (comparative more [mɔ:(r)], superlative most [məʊst]) 1 pron beaucoup; there isn't m. left il n'en reste pas beaucoup; it's not worth m. ça ne vaut pas grand-chose; Formal m. has happened since you left il s'est passé beaucoup de choses depuis ton départ; I'll say this m. for him, he's very polite je dois reconnaître une chose, c'est qu'il est très poli; I don't think m. of him je n'ai pas grande estime pour lui; it didn't come as m. of a surprise ça n'a pas été une grande surprise; she isn't m. of a singer comme chanteuse, elle n'est pas très bonne; twice as m. deux fois plus; I thought as m. c'est ce que je pensais; as m. as possible autant que possible; it was as m. as we could do to stay upright nous avions déjà assez de mal à rester debout; he left without so m. as saying goodbye il est parti sans même dire au revoir; he has drunk so m. that... il a tellement bu que...; so m.

the better tant mieux; **so m. so that...** à tel point que...; **so m. for her promises of help!** c'était bien la peine de promettre qu'elle m'/nous/*etc* aiderait!; *Fam* **that's a bit m.! c'est un peu fort!**

2 *adj*

Hormis dans la langue soutenue et dans certaines expressions, **much** ne s'utilise que dans des structures négatives ou interrogatives.

how m. money? combien d'argent?; **there isn't m. traffic** il n'y a pas beaucoup de circulation; **too m. work** trop de travail; **so m. time** tant de temps; **as m. food as** autant de nourriture que; *Formal* **m. work still needs to be done** il reste encore beaucoup de travail à faire **3** *adv* beaucoup; **I don't like it m.** ça ne me plaît pas beaucoup; **m. better** bien meilleur(e); **m. more difficult** beaucoup plus difficile; **m. the best** de loin le meilleur (la meilleure); **m. the most interesting** de loin le (la) plus intéressant(e); **thank you very m.** merci beaucoup; **m. the same** presque pareil(eille); **m. to my astonishment** à mon grand étonnement; **m. as I like him, I don't really trust him** j'ai beau l'apprécier, je ne lui fais pas vraiment confiance; **the result was m. as I expected** le résultat correspondait assez à mes attentes; **so m.** autant; **I love him so m.** je l'aime tellement; **too m.** trop; **£10 too m.** 10 livres de trop; **this is (really) too m.!** trop c'est trop!

muchness ['mʌtʃnɪs] *n Fam* **they're much of a m.** ils se valent

muck [mʌk] *n Fam (dirt)* saleté *f; (manure)* fumier *m; (bad food)* cochonneries *fpl; (bad quality book, TV programme)* idioties *fpl*

▸**muck about, muck around** *Br Fam* **1** *vt sep (treat badly)* se moquer de **2** *vi* (**a**) *(fool about)* faire l'imbécile; *(waste time)* traîner (**b**) *(tinker)* **to m. about** *or* **around with sth** tripoter qch

▸**muck in** *vi Br Fam (help)* s'y mettre
▸**muck out** *vt sep (stables)* nettoyer
▸**muck up** *vt sep Fam* (**a**) *(make dirty)* cochonner (**b**) *(task)* bâcler; *(plans)* chambouler; *(interview, exam)* rater

muckraking ['mʌkreɪkɪŋ] *n Fam (in journalism)* = pratique consistant à révéler et exploiter à fond des scandales

mucky ['mʌkɪ] *adj Br Fam* sale
mucous ['mjuːkəs] *adj* muqueux(euse)
mucus ['mjuːkəs] *n* mucus *m*, mucosités *fpl*
mud [mʌd] *n* boue *f; Fig* **to throw m. at sb** couvrir qn de boue; *Fam* **his name is m.** il n'a pas la cote; **m. hut** hutte *f* en terre; **m. wrestling** catch *m* dans la boue
mudbank ['mʌdbæŋk] *n* banc *m* de vase
mudflat ['mʌdflæt] *n* banc *m* de boue
muddle ['mʌdəl] **1** *n* confusion *f;* **to be in a m.** *(of things)* être en désordre; *(of person)* ne plus s'y retrouver; **to get into a m.** *(of things)* se mélanger; *(of person)* s'embrouiller
2 *vt* (**a**) *(put in disorder)* mélanger (**b**) *(bewilder)* embrouiller; **to get muddled** s'embrouiller
▸**muddle along** *vi* se débrouiller tant bien que mal
▸**muddle through** *vi* se débrouiller
▸**muddle up** *vt sep* (**a**) *(put in disorder)* mélanger (**b**) *(confuse)* embrouiller; **to get muddled up** s'embrouiller
muddleheaded [mʌdəl'hedɪd] *adj (person)* brouillon(onne); *(thinking)* confus(e)

muddy ['mʌdɪ] **1** *adj (path, water)* boueux(euse); *(clothing, hands)* couvert(e) de boue; *(complexion)* terreux(euse); *(colour)* sale **2** *vt (pt & pp* **muddied**) salir; *Fig* **to m. the waters** brouiller les pistes
mudguard ['mʌdgɑːd] *n* garde-boue *m inv*
mudpack ['mʌdpæk] *n* masque *m* à l'argile
mudslinging ['mʌdslɪŋɪŋ] *n Fam* = fait de dénigrer systématiquement ses adversaires
muesli ['mjuːzlɪ] *n* muesli *m*
muff¹ [mʌf] *vt Br Fam (bungle)* rater, louper
muff² *n (for hands)* manchon *m*
muffin ['mʌfɪn] *n* muffin *m*
muffle ['mʌfəl] *vt* (**a**) *(sound)* assourdir, étouffer (**b**) **to m. oneself up** s'emmitoufler
muffled ['mʌfəld] *adj (sound, footstep)* assourdi(e), étouffé(e)
muffler ['mʌflə(r)] *n* (**a**) *(scarf)* cache-nez *m inv* (**b**) *Am (of car)* silencieux *m*
mufti ['mʌftɪ] *n Fam* **in m.** *(soldier)* en civil
mug [mʌg] **1** *n* (**a**) *(cup)* grande tasse *f* (**b**) *Fam (face)* gueule *f;* **m. shot** photo *f* d'identité judiciaire (**c**) *Br Fam (gullible person)* poire *f;* **it's a m.'s game** on est toujours perdant à ce jeu-là **2** *vt (pt & pp* **mugged**) *(attack)* agresser
▸**mug up** *vi Br Fam (study)* bûcher; **to m. up on sth** potasser qch
mugger ['mʌgə(r)] *n* agresseur *m*
mugging ['mʌgɪŋ] *n* agression *f*
muggins ['mʌgɪnz] *n Br Fam* mézigue *f*
muggy ['mʌgɪ] *adj* lourd(e), étouffant(e)
mulatto [mjuː'lætəʊ] *(pl* **mulattos** *or* **mulattoes**) *n* mulâtre *mf*
mulberry ['mʌlbərɪ] *(pl* **mulberries**) *n (fruit)* mûre *f; (tree)* mûrier *m*
mule [mjuːl] *n* mulet *m; (female)* mule *f*
▸**mull over** [mʌl] *vt sep (consider)* **to m. sth over** retourner qch dans sa tête
mulled wine ['mʌld'waɪn] *n* vin *m* chaud épicé
mullet ['mʌlɪt] *n* (**a**) *(fish)* **grey m.** mulet *m* gris; **red m.** rouget *m* (**b**) *Fam (hairstyle)* = coupe de cheveux longue sur la nuque, courte sur les côtés et en brosse longue sur le dessus
multi-access ['mʌltɪ'ækses] *adj Comput* à accès multiple
multicoloured ['mʌltɪkʌləd] *adj* multicolore
multicultural [mʌltɪ'kʌltʃərəl] *adj* multiculturel(elle)
multidisciplinary ['mʌltɪdɪsɪ'plɪnərɪ] *adj Br* pluridisciplinaire
multifarious [mʌltɪ'feərɪəs] *adj* varié(e), divers(e)
multi-functional [mʌltɪ'fʌŋkʃənəl] *adj* multifonctions *inv*
multilateral [mʌltɪ'lætərəl] *adj* multilatéral(e)
multilingual [mʌltɪ'lɪŋgwəl] *adj* multilingue
multimedia [mʌltɪ'miːdɪə] *adj* multimédia
multimillionaire [mʌltɪmɪlɪə'neə(r)] *n* multimillionnaire *mf*
multinational [mʌltɪ'næʃənəl] **1** *n* multinationale *f* **2** *adj* multinational(e)
multiparty [mʌltɪ'pɑːtɪ] *adj* **m. system** pluripartisme *m*
multiple ['mʌltɪpəl] **1** *n* (**a**) *Math* multiple *m* (**b**) *Com (chain store)* chaîne *f* de magasins **2** *adj* multiple; **m. sclerosis** sclérose *f* en plaques
multiple-choice ['mʌltɪpl'tʃɔɪs] *adj* à choix multiples
multiplex ['mʌltɪpleks] *n Cin* multiplexe *m*, complexe *m* multisalles

multiplication [mʌltɪplɪˈkeɪʃən] n multiplication f; **m. table** table f de multiplication
multiplicity [mʌltɪˈplɪsɪtɪ] n multiplicité f
multiply [ˈmʌltɪplaɪ] (pt & pp **multiplied**) 1 vt multiplier (**by** par) 2 vi (reproduce) se multiplier
multipurpose [mʌltɪˈpɜːpəs] adj polyvalent(e)
multiracial [mʌltɪˈreɪʃəl] adj multiracial(e)
multistorey, Am **multistory** [mʌltɪˈstɔːrɪ] adj à étages; m. (car park) parking m à plusieurs niveaux
multitude [ˈmʌltɪtjuːd] n multitude f
multivitamin [mʌltɪˈvɪtəmɪn, Am mʌltɪˈvaɪtəmɪn] n multivitamine f
mum [mʌm] Fam 1 n Br (mother) maman f 2 adj to keep m. (about sth) ne pas souffler mot (de qch); m.'s the word! motus et bouche cousue!
mumble [ˈmʌmbəl] 1 n marmonnement m 2 vt & vi marmonner
mumbo jumbo [ˈmʌmbəʊˈdʒʌmbəʊ] n (nonsense) âneries fpl; (jargon) charabia m
mummify [ˈmʌmɪfaɪ] (pt & pp **mummified**) vt momifier
mummy¹ [ˈmʌmɪ] (pl **mummies**) n (embalmed body) momie f
mummy² (pl **mummies**) n Br Fam (mother) maman f; a m.'s boy un petit garçon à sa maman
mumps [mʌmps] n (illness) oreillons mpl; to have m. avoir les oreillons
munch [mʌntʃ] vt mâcher
munchies [ˈmʌntʃɪz] npl Fam (**a**) (snacks) amuse-gueule mpl (**b**) (desire to eat) to have the m. avoir la fringale
mundane [mʌnˈdeɪn] adj banal(e), ordinaire
municipal [mjuːˈnɪsɪpəl] adj municipal(e)
municipality [mjuːnɪsɪˈpælɪtɪ] (pl **municipalities**) n municipalité f
munitions [mjuːˈnɪʃənz] npl munitions fpl
mural [ˈmjʊərəl] n peinture f murale
murder [ˈmɜːdə(r)] 1 n (**a**) (killing) meurtre m; Fig she gets away with m. elle peut tout se permettre; m. case affaire f de meurtre; m. inquiry enquête f sur une affaire de meurtre (**b**) Fam Fig (difficult task) cauchemar m, enfer m; finding a parking place on a Saturday is m. c'est l'enfer pour trouver à se garer le samedi 2 vt (**a**) (kill) assassiner; Fam Fig I'll m. you! je vais te tuer!; Fam I could m. a beer/pizza je me taperais bien une bière/une pizza (**b**) Fig (song, tune) massacrer
murderer [ˈmɜːdərə(r)] n meurtrier(ère) m,f, assassin m
murky [ˈmɜːkɪ] adj (weather, sky) sombre; (details, past) trouble
murmur [ˈmɜːmə(r)] 1 n murmure m; to do sth without a m. faire qch sans broncher 2 vi also Fig murmurer
muscle [ˈmʌsəl] n muscle m; Fig (power) poids m; not to move a m. rester immobile
▸**muscle in** vi intervenir (**on** dans)
muscleman [ˈmʌsəlmæn] n Monsieur m muscle
Muscovite [ˈmʌskəvaɪt] 1 n Moscovite mf 2 adj moscovite
muscular [ˈmʌskjʊlə(r)] adj (tissue, pain) musculaire; (person) musclé(e); m. dystrophy myopathie f
Muse [mjuːz] n (in mythology) Muse f; (of poet) muse f
muse [mjuːz] vi rêvasser, songer (**on** or **about** à)
museum [mjuːˈzɪəm] n musée m

mush [mʌʃ] n (**a**) (pulp) bouillie f (**b**) Fig (sentimentality) mièvrerie f
mushroom [ˈmʌʃrʊm] 1 n champignon m; m. cloud champignon atomique 2 vi (of costs, prices) grimper (en flèche); (of town) se développer; (of houses, factories) pousser comme des champignons
mushy [ˈmʌʃɪ] adj (**a**) (food) en bouillie; (ground) détrempé(e); Br m. peas purée f de petits pois (**b**) Fam Fig Pej (sentimental) à l'eau de rose, mièvre
music [ˈmjuːzɪk] n musique f; Fig those words were m. to her ears elle était ravie d'entendre ces mots; m. box boîte f à musique; m. hall music-hall m; m. stand pupitre m (à musique); m. teacher professeur m de musique
musical [ˈmjuːzɪkəl] 1 n (show, film) comédie f musicale 2 adj (tuneful) musical(e); (musically gifted) musicien(enne); m. box boîte f à musique; m. chairs (jeu m des) chaises fpl musicales; also Fig to play m. chairs jouer aux chaises musicales; m. comedy comédie f musicale; m. instrument instrument m de musique
musician [mjuːˈzɪʃən] n musicien(enne) m,f
musicologist [mjuːzɪˈkɒlədʒɪst] n musicologue mf
musings [ˈmjuːzɪŋz] npl rêverie(s) f(pl)
musk [mʌsk] n musc m
musket [ˈmʌskɪt] n mousquet m
musketeer [mʌskəˈtɪə(r)] n mousquetaire m
muskrat [ˈmʌskræt] n rat m musqué
Muslim [ˈmʊzlɪm] 1 n musulman(e) m,f 2 adj musulman(e)
muslin [ˈmʌzlɪn] n mousseline f
mussel [ˈmʌsəl] n moule f; m. bed parc m à moules
must [mʌst] 1 modal aux v (**a**) (expressing obligation) devoir; you m. do it tu dois le faire, il faut que tu le fasses; they mustn't find out il ne faut pas qu'ils l'apprennent; you mustn't tell anyone surtout, n'en parle à personne; this plant m. be watered daily cette plante doit être arrosée chaque jour; I m. say I thought it was quite good je dois avouer que j'ai trouvé ça plutôt bon; will you come with me? – if I m. tu viens avec moi? – s'il le faut; take it if you m. prends-le, si tu le veux vraiment; m. you be so silly? tu te sens obligé d'être aussi bête? (**b**) (suggesting, inviting) you m. come and visit us il faut vraiment que vous nous rendiez visite; we m. go out for a drink sometime il faudrait que nous allions prendre un verre, un de ces jours (**c**) (expressing probability) devoir; you m. be hungry vous devez avoir faim; I m. have made a mistake j'ai dû faire une erreur; you m. be joking! tu veux rire! 2 n Fam (**a**) (necessity) to be a m. être une nécessité; sunglasses/hiking boots are a m. il faut absolument emporter des lunettes de soleil/des chaussures de marche (**b**) (thing not to be missed) this film's a m. ce film est un must
mustache [ˈmʌstæʃ] Am = moustache
mustard [ˈmʌstəd] n moutarde f; Fam Fig he couldn't cut the m. il n'a pas été à la hauteur; m. gas gaz m moutarde; m. powder farine f de moutarde
muster [ˈmʌstə(r)] 1 n Fig to pass m. être acceptable 2 vt (gather) rassembler; to m. one's strength/courage rassembler ses forces/son courage
musty [ˈmʌstɪ] adj (smell) de moisi; to have a m. smell (of room) sentir le renfermé

mutant ['mju:tənt] **1** *n* mutant(e) *m,f*
  2 *adj* mutant(e)
mutate [mju:'teɪt] *vi* muter
mutation [mju:'teɪʃən] *n* mutation *f*
mute [mju:t] **1** *n* (**a**) *(dumb person)* muet(ette) *m,f* (**b**)
  Mus sourdine *f*
  2 *adj* muet(ette)
muted ['mju:tɪd] *adj (sound)* assourdi(e); *(applause)*
  faible; *(protest, criticism)* voilé(e); *(colour)* sourd(e)
mutilate ['mju:tɪleɪt] *vt also Fig* mutiler
mutilation [mju:tɪ'leɪʃən] *n* mutilation *f*
mutineer [mju:tɪ'nɪə(r)] *n* mutiné(e) *m,f*
mutinous ['mju:tɪnəs] *adj* rebelle
mutiny ['mju:tɪnɪ] **1** *n* (*pl* **mutinies**) *(on ship)* mutinerie *f*; *(of workers)* révolte *f*
  2 *vi* (*pt & pp* **mutinied**) *(of crew, soldiers)* se mutiner;
  (of workers) se révolter
mutt [mʌt] *n Fam (dog)* clébard *m*
mutter ['mʌtə(r)] **1** *n* murmure *m*
  2 *vt & vi* marmonner
mutton ['mʌtən] *n* mouton *m*; *Fam* **to look like m.**
  dressed as lamb être habillé(e) trop jeune pour son
  âge
mutual ['mju:tʃʊəl] *adj (reciprocal)* mutuel(elle), réciproque; *(shared)* commun(e); **the feeling is m.** c'est
  réciproque
mutually ['mju:tʃʊəlɪ] *adv* mutuellement, réciproquement; **to be m. exclusive** s'exclure mutuellement
Muzak® ['mju:zæk] *n* musique *f* de fond, fond *m*
  sonore
muzzle ['mʌzəl] **1** *n* (**a**) *(dog's nose)* museau *m*;
  (guard) muselière *f* (**b**) *(of gun)* canon *m*
  2 *vt also Fig* museler
MW (**a**) *Rad (abbr* **Medium Wave)** OM (**b**) *Elec (abbr*
  Megawatts) MW
my [maɪ] **1** *possessive adj* (**a**) *(singular)* mon (ma);
  (plural) mes; **my job** mon travail; **my wife** ma femme;
  my parents mes parents; **it wasn't MY idea!** ce n'est

pas moi qui en ai eu l'idée! (**b**) *(with parts of body)* **I**
  hit my head je me suis cogné la tête
  2 *exclam* oh là là!
Myanmar [maɪæn'mɑ:(r)] *n* le Myanmar
mynah ['maɪnə] *n* **m. (bird)** mainate *m*
myopia [maɪ'əʊpɪə] *n* myopie *f*; *Fig* manque *m* de
  perspicacité
myopic [maɪ'ɒpɪk] *adj* myope; *Fig* à courte vue
myriad ['mɪrɪəd] *adj Lit* innombrable
myrrh [mɜ:(r)] *n* myrrhe *f*
myrtle ['mɜ:təl] *n* myrte *m*
myself [maɪ'self] *pron* (**a**) *(reflexive)* **I hurt m.** je me
  suis blessé (**b**) *(emphatic)* moi-même; **I m. have**
  never... moi-même n'ai jamais...; **I told her m.** je lui
  ai dit moi-même; **I'm not m. today** je ne suis pas dans
  mon état normal aujourd'hui (**c**) *(after preposition)*
  moi; **I live by m.** je vis seul; **I bought it for m.** je me
  le suis acheté; **I talk to m.** je parle tout seul
mysterious [mɪs'tɪərɪəs] *adj* mystérieux(euse)
mysteriously [mɪs'tɪərɪəslɪ] *adv* mystérieusement
mystery ['mɪstərɪ] **1** *n* (*pl* **mysteries**) mystère *m*; **m.**
  tour voyage *m* surprise
  2 *adj (guest, prize)* surprise *inv*; *(benefactor, witness)*
  mystérieux(euse)
mystic ['mɪstɪk] **1** *n* mystique *mf*
  2 *adj* mystique
mystical ['mɪstɪkəl] *adj (person)* mystique; *(power,*
  ceremony) occulte
mysticism ['mɪstɪsɪzəm] *n* mysticisme *m*
mystify ['mɪstɪfaɪ] *(pt & pp* **mystified**) *vt* déconcerter
mystique [mɪs'ti:k] *n* mystère *m*
myth [mɪθ] *n* mythe *m*
mythical ['mɪθɪkəl] *adj* mythique
mythological [mɪθə'lɒdʒɪkəl] *adj* mythologique
mythology [mɪ'θɒlədʒɪ] *(pl* **mythologies**) *n* mythologie *f*
myxomatosis [mɪksəmə'təʊsɪs] *n* myxomatose *f*

N, n [en] *n* (**a**) *(letter)* N, n *m inv* (**b**) *(abbr* north) N

NAACP [eneɪeɪsiːˈpiː] *n Am Pol (abbr* **National Association for the Advancement of Colored People**) = association pour la défense des droits des personnes de couleur

naan [nɑːn] *n* **n. (bread)** = sorte de pain indien servi comme accompagnement

nab [næb] *(pt & pp* **nabbed**) *vt Fam* (**a**) *(catch, arrest)* choper (**b**) *(steal)* piquer, faucher

nadir [ˈneɪdɪə(r)] *n Astron* nadir *m; Fig* **to reach a n.** atteindre son niveau le plus bas

naff [næf] *adj Br Fam (of poor quality)* nul (nulle); *(of poor taste)* ringard(e)

▸**naff off** *vi Br Fam* **n. off!** dégage!

NAFTA [ˈnæftə] *n (abbr* **North American Free Trade Agreement**) ALENA *m*

nag¹ [næg] *n Fam (horse)* carne *f*

nag² **1** *n (person)* enquiquineur(euse) *m,f*
 2 *vt (pt & pp* **nagged**) *(of person)* être sur le dos de; *(of doubt, conscience)* tourmenter; **to n. sb into doing sth** harceler qn pour qu'il fasse qch
 3 *vi* **he's always nagging** il est tout le temps sur mon dos

nagging [ˈnægɪŋ] **1** *n* harcèlement *m*; **I've had enough of your n.** arrête de me harceler
 2 *adj (pain, doubt, worry)* tenace

nail [neɪl] **1** *n* (**a**) *(in carpentry)* clou *m; Fig* **it was another n. in his coffin** c'était un pas de plus vers la fin; *Fig* **the final n. in the coffin** la goutte d'eau qui fait déborder le vase; *Fig* **to hit the n. on the head** mettre le doigt dessus (**b**) *(of person)* ongle *m*; **n. file** lime *f* à ongles; **n. scissors** ciseaux *mpl* à ongles; **n. varnish** *or* **polish** vernis *m* à ongles; **n. varnish** *or* **polish remover** dissolvant *m*
 2 *vt* (**a**) *(fasten)* clouer; **to n. sth shut** clouer qch; *Fig* **to stand nailed to the spot** rester cloué(e) sur place (**b**) *(idioms) Fam* **to n. sb** *(for crime)* coincer qn; *Fam* **to n. a lie** dénoncer un mensonge

▸**nail down** *vt sep (fasten)* clouer, fixer avec des clous; *Fam Fig* **to n. sb down to a date/price** obtenir de qn qu'il fixe une date/un prix

nail-biting [ˈneɪlbaɪtɪŋ] *adj Fam (contest, finish)* palpitant(e); *(wait)* angoissant(e)

nailbrush [ˈneɪlbrʌʃ] *n* brosse *f* à ongles

naive [naɪˈiːv] *adj* naïf(ïve)

naively [naɪˈiːvlɪ] *adv* naïvement

naivety [naɪˈiːvətɪ] *n* naïveté *f*

naked [ˈneɪkɪd] *adj (body, flame)* nu(e); *Fig (aggression, exploitation)* délibéré(e); **visible to the n. eye** visible à l'œil nu

namby-pamby [ˈnæmbɪˈpæmbɪ] *Pej* **1** *n (pl* **namby-pambies**) mollasson(onne) *m,f*
 2 *adj* gnangnan *inv*

name [neɪm] **1** *n* (**a**) *(in general)* nom *m*; **my n. is...** je m'appelle...; **what's your n.?** comment t'appelles-tu?; **to mention sb by n.** désigner nommément qn; **a big n. in the theatre** un grand nom du théâtre; **to put one's n. down (for sth)** s'inscrire (pour qch); **to go by** *or* **under the n. of...** être connu(e) sous le nom de...; **in the n. of...** au nom de...; **in the n. of God** *or* **Heaven!** au nom du Ciel!; **he was President in all but n.** c'était lui le président, même s'il n'en avait pas le titre; **to call sb names** insulter qn; **he hasn't got a penny to his n.** il n'a pas un sou (**b**) *(reputation)* réputation *f*; **to have a good/bad n.** avoir (une) bonne/mauvaise réputation; **to have a n. for** être réputé(e) pour; **to make a n. for oneself** se faire un nom
 2 *vt* (**a**) *(give name to, appoint)* nommer; **to n. sb** *Br* **after** *or Am* **for sb** donner à qn le nom de qn (**b**) *(designate, identify)* citer; **to n. names** donner des noms; **n. your price** dites votre prix

name-calling [ˈneɪmkɔːlɪŋ] *n* insultes *fpl*

name-dropper [ˈneɪmdrɒpə(r)] *n Fam* = personne qui se vante de connaître des gens célèbres

name-dropping [ˈneɪmdrɒpɪŋ] *n Fam* = fait de se vanter de connaître des gens célèbres

nameless [ˈneɪmlɪs] *adj (person)* anonyme; **someone who shall remain n.** quelqu'un que je ne nommerai pas

namely [ˈneɪmlɪ] *adv* c'est-à-dire, à savoir

nameplate [ˈneɪmpleɪt] *n* plaque *f*

namesake [ˈneɪmseɪk] *n* homonyme *mf*

Namibia [nəˈmɪbɪə] *n* la Namibie

Namibian [nəˈmɪbɪən] **1** *n* Namibien(enne) *m,f*
 2 *adj* namibien(enne)

nancy [ˈnænsɪ] *(pl* **nancies**) *n very Fam* **n. (boy)** *(homosexual)* tapette *f*, pédale *f*; *(effeminate man)* chochotte *f*

nanny [ˈnænɪ] *(pl* **nannies**) *n* (**a**) *(for children)* jeune fille *f* au pair (**b**) **n. goat** chèvre *f*

nanosecond [ˈnænəʊsekənd] *n Phys* nanoseconde *f*

nanotechnology [ˌnænəʊtekˈnɒlədʒɪ] *n* nanotechnologie *f*

nap¹ [næp] **1** *n (sleep)* (petit) somme *m*; **to take** *or* **have a n.** faire un (petit) somme
 2 *vi (pt & pp* **napped**) faire un (petit) somme; *Fig* **to be caught napping** être pris(e) au dépourvu

nap² *n (of cloth)* poil *m*

napalm [ˈneɪpɑːm] *n* napalm *m*

nape [neɪp] *n* **n. (of the neck)** nuque *f*

naphthalene [ˈnæfθəliːn] *n* naphtaline *f*

napkin ['næpkɪn] *n* (**a**) (**table**) **n.** serviette *f* (de table);
n. ring rond *m* de serviette (**b**) *Am* (*sanitary towel*)
serviette *f* hygiénique
Naples ['neɪpəlz] *n* Naples
Napoleonic [nəpəʊlɪ'ɒnɪk] *adj* napoléonien(enne)
nappy ['næpɪ] (*pl* **nappies**) *n Br* couche *f*; **n. rash** érythème *m* fessier
narc [nɑːk] *n Am Fam* agent *m* de la brigade des stups
narcissus [nɑː'sɪsəs] (*pl* **narcissi** [nɑː'sɪsaɪ]) *n* narcisse
m
narcosis [nɑː'kəʊsɪs] *n* narcose *f*
narcotic [nɑː'kɒtɪk] **1** *n* (*medicine*) narcotique *m*; (*illegal drug*) stupéfiant *m*; *Am* **narcotics agent** agent *m*
de la brigade des stupéfiants; *Am* **narcotics squad**
brigade *f* des stupéfiants
2 *adj* narcotique
nark [nɑːk] *n Br Fam* (**a**) (*informer*) indic *m* (**b**) (*irritable person*) râleur(euse) *m,f*
narky ['nɑːkɪ] *adj Br Fam* grognon
narrate [nə'reɪt] *vt* raconter
narrative ['nærətɪv] **1** *n* récit *m*
2 *adj* narratif(ive)
narrator [nə'reɪtə(r)] *n* narrateur(trice) *m,f*
narrow ['nærəʊ] **1** *adj* étroit(e); (*majority*) faible; **to
grow** *or* **become n.** se rétrécir; **to have a n. mind**
avoir l'esprit étroit; **to have a n. escape** l'échapper
belle; **to win/lose by a n. margin** gagner/perdre de
justesse; **to take a n. view of sth** adopter un point de
vue étroit sur qch
2 *vt* **to n. one's eyes** (*in suspicion, anger*) froncer les
sourcils
3 *vi* (*of road*) se rétrécir, se resserrer
▸**narrow down** *vt sep* limiter, réduire
narrowly ['nærəʊlɪ] *adv* (*only just*) de peu; **she n.
missed being run over** elle a failli se faire écraser
narrow-minded [nærəʊ'maɪndɪd] *adj* étroit(e)
d'esprit, borné(e)
NASA ['næsə] *n* (*abbr* **National Aeronautics and Space
Administration**) NASA *f*
nasal ['neɪzəl] *adj* nasal(e); **to have a n. voice** parler
du nez
nastily ['nɑːstɪlɪ] *adv* méchamment
nastiness ['nɑːstɪnɪs] *n* (*of person, remark*) méchanceté *f*
nasturtium [nə'stɜːʃəm] *n* capucine *f*
nasty ['nɑːstɪ] *adj* mauvais(e); (*crime*) ignoble; (*shock,
business*) sale; (*accident*) grave; **to be n. to sb** être
méchant(e) avec qn; **to have a n. mind** penser toujours à mal; **to turn n.** (*of situation, weather*) se dégrader, se gâter; **that was a really n. thing to do** c'était
vraiment ignoble de sa/ta/*etc* part; *Fig* **it left a n.
taste in my mouth** ça m'a laissé un arrière-goût désagréable; **a n. piece of work** (*man*) un sale type;
(*woman*) une vraie peste
nation ['neɪʃən] *n* nation *f*
national ['næʃənəl] **1** (**a**) (*person*) ressortissant(e)
m,f (**b**) (*newspaper*) journal *m* national
2 *adj* national(e); **n. anthem** hymne *m* national; *Br*
n. curriculum programme *m* scolaire; **n. debt** dette *f*
publique; **N. Front** = parti britannique d'extrême
droite; **n. grid** réseau *m* national (d'électricité); *Br* **N.
Health Service** = système de santé britannique; *Br* **N.
Heritage** = organisme ayant pour mission la conservation du patrimoine; *Br* **N. Insurance** contributions
fpl sociales; **n. park** parc *m* national; **n. service** service *m* militaire; **N. Trust** = organisme britannique
de conservation du patrimoine historique et naturel

National Health Service

Le "National Health Service" ou "NHS" fut créé par le
gouvernement travailliste en 1948, donnant accès à
chacun aux soins médicaux gratuits. Cependant,
suite notamment aux coupes budgétaires réalisées
dans les années 80, le système de santé britannique est aujourd'hui en crise. Au cours des dernières années, la polémique autour du "National
Health Service" s'est intensifiée et est devenu un enjeu majeur lors des élections en Grande-Bretagne.

nationalism ['næʃənəlɪzəm] *n* nationalisme *m*
nationalist ['næʃənəlɪst] **1** *n* nationaliste *mf*
2 *adj* nationaliste
nationalistic [næʃənə'lɪstɪk] *adj* nationaliste
nationality [næʃə'nælɪtɪ] (*pl* **nationalities**) *n* nationalité *f*
nationalization [næʃənəlaɪ'zeɪʃən] *n* nationalisation
f
nationalize ['næʃənəlaɪz] *vt* nationaliser
nationally ['næʃənəlɪ] *adv* nationalement
nationwide ['neɪʃənwaɪd] **1** *adj* national(e)
2 *adv* dans tout le pays
native ['neɪtɪv] **1** *n* (*person*) natif(ive) *m,f*; (*plant*)
plante *f* indigène; (*animal*) animal *m* indigène; **to be
a n. of** être originaire de; **she speaks English like a n.**
elle parle anglais comme si c'était sa langue maternelle
2 *adj* natal(e); **he returned to his n. London** il est
retourné à Londres, sa ville natale; **n. American** Indien(enne) *m,f* d'Amérique; **n. land** pays *m* natal; **n.
language** langue *f* maternelle; **I'm not a n. speaker
of Spanish** ma langue maternelle n'est pas l'espagnol
Nativity [nə'tɪvɪtɪ] *n Rel* **the N.** la Nativité *f*; **N. play**
mystère *m* de la Nativité
NATO ['neɪtəʊ] *n Mil* (*abbr* **North Atlantic Treaty Organization**) l'OTAN *f*
natter ['nætə(r)] *Br Fam* **1** *n* **to have a n.** bavarder, papoter (**about** sur)
2 *vi* bavarder, papoter (**about** sur)
natty ['nætɪ] *adj Fam* chic *inv*
natural ['nætʃərəl] **1** *adj* (**a**) (*colour, taste*) naturel(elle); (*gift, talent*) inné(e); **to die from n. causes**
mourir de mort naturelle; **n. childbirth** accouchement *m* naturel; **n. disaster** catastrophe *f* naturelle;
n. gas gaz *m* naturel; **n. history** histoire *f* naturelle;
n. mother mère *f* naturelle; **n. resources** ressources
fpl naturelles; **n. sciences** sciences *fpl* naturelles; **n.
yoghurt** yaourt *m* nature (**b**) (*normal*) naturel(elle);
it's only n. c'est tout à fait naturel; *Ind* **n. wastage** départs *mpl* volontaires et en retraite (**c**) (*unaffected*)
naturel(elle)
2 *n* **he's a n. as an actor** c'est un acteur né
naturalism ['nætʃərəlɪzəm] *n* naturalisme *m*
naturalist ['nætʃərəlɪst] *n* naturaliste *mf*
naturalistic ['nætʃərəlɪstɪk] *adj* naturaliste
naturalization [nætʃərəlaɪ'zeɪʃən] *n* naturalisation *f*
naturalize ['nætʃərəlaɪz] *vt* naturaliser
naturally ['nætʃərəlɪ] *adv* (**a**) (*unaffectedly*) naturellement; (*by nature*) de nature; **to come n. to sb** être un
don chez qn (**b**) (*of course*) naturellement
nature ['neɪtʃə(r)] *n* (**a**) (*the natural world*) nature *f*;
let n. take its course laisser faire la nature; **n. reserve**
réserve *f* naturelle; *Sch* **n. study** sciences *fpl* naturelles; **n. trail** = sentier aménagé doté d'explications
concernant la faune et la flore (**b**) (*character*) nature *f*;

to have a jealous n. être d'une nature jalouse; **it's not in her n.** ça n'est pas dans sa nature; **to be shy by n.** être timide de nature (**c**) *(sort)* nature *f*, genre *m*; **problems of this n.** des problèmes de cette nature; *Formal* **what is the n. of your complaint?** quelle est la nature de votre réclamation?

naturist ['neɪtʃərɪst] **1** *n* naturiste *mf*
  2 *adj* naturiste
naught [nɔːt] *n* (**a**) *Lit (nothing)* néant *m*; **to come to n.** se réduire à néant (**b**) *Am* = **nought**
naughtily ['nɔːtɪlɪ] *adv* **to behave n.** être vilain(e)
naughty ['nɔːtɪ] *adj (child)* méchant(e), vilain(e); *(book, picture)* coquin(e)
nausea ['nɔːzɪə] *n* nausée *f*
nauseate ['nɔːzɪeɪt] *vt* donner la nausée à; *Fig* écœurer
nauseating ['nɔːzɪeɪtɪŋ] *adj also Fig* écœurant(e)
nauseous ['nɔːzɪəs] *adj (disgusting)* écœurant(e); **to feel n.** avoir envie de vomir
nautical ['nɔːtɪkəl] *adj* nautique; **n. mile** mille *m* marin *ou* nautique
naval ['neɪvəl] *adj* naval(e); **n. battle** bataille *f* navale; **the N. College** ≃ l'École *f* navale; **n. officer** officier *m* de marine
nave [neɪv] *n (of church)* nef *f*
navel ['neɪvəl] *n* nombril *m*
navel-gazing ['neɪvəlgeɪzɪŋ] *n* nombrilisme *m*
navigable ['nævɪgəbəl] *adj* navigable
navigate ['nævɪgeɪt] **1** *vt* (**a**) *(seas)* naviguer sur; *(ship, plane)* piloter (**b**) *Comput (website)* naviguer sur
  2 *vi (in ship, plane)* naviguer; *(in car)* faire le pilote
navigation [nævɪ'geɪʃən] *n* navigation *f*
navigational [nævɪ'geɪʃənəl] *adj* de navigation
navigator ['nævɪgeɪtə(r)] *n (in ship, plane)* navigateur(trice) *m,f*; *(in car)* copilote *mf*
navvy ['nævɪ] *(pl navvies)* *n Br* terrassier *m*
navy ['neɪvɪ] *(pl navies)* *n* marine *f*; **n. (blue)** bleu marine *m inv*
Nazi ['nɑːtsɪ] **1** *n* Nazi(e) *m,f*
  2 *adj* nazi(e)
Nazism ['nɑːtsɪzəm] *n* nazisme *m*
NB [en'biː] *(abbr* **nota bene**) NB
NBA [enbiː'eɪ] *n Am (abbr* **National Basketball Association**) = fédération américaine de basket-ball
NCO [ensiː'əʊ] *n Mil (abbr* **non-commissioned officer**) sous-officier *m*
NE *(abbr* **northeast**) N-E
Neanderthal [nɪ'ændətɑːl] **1** *n* (**a**) *(during Stone Age)* homme *m* de Neandertal (**b**) *Fig (uncivilized man)* homme *m* des cavernes
  2 *adj* (**a**) *(during Stone Age)* **N. man** homme *m* de Neandertal (**b**) *Fig (attitude, behaviour)* d'homme des cavernes
Neapolitan [nɪːə'pɒlɪtən] **1** *n* Napolitain(e) *m,f*
  2 *adj* napolitain(e)
near [nɪə(r)] **1** *adj* proche; **to the nearest metre** au mètre près; **in the n. future** dans un avenir proche; **it was a n. thing** il s'en est fallu de peu; **the N. East** le Proche-Orient
  2 *adv* près; **to be n. to sth** *(in space)* être près de qch; *(in time)* être proche de qch; **n. at hand** *(of thing)* tout près; *(of event)* tout proche; **to be n. to doing sth** être sur le point de faire qch; **n. to tears/despair** au bord des larmes/du désespoir; **she's nowhere n. finished** elle est loin d'avoir fini; **a n. total failure** un échec presque total
  3 *prep* près de; **he came n. to being run over** il a failli se faire écraser; **nobody comes anywhere n. her**

(in skill, performance) il n'y a personne à son niveau
  4 *n Fam* **my nearest and dearest** mes plus proches parents *mpl*
  5 *vt* (s')approcher de; **to be nearing completion** être presque terminé(e)
nearby 1 *adj* ['nɪəbaɪ] proche
  2 *adv* [nɪə'baɪ] tout près
nearly ['nɪəlɪ] *adv* presque; **we're n. there** *(finished)* nous y sommes presque; *(at destination)* nous sommes presque arrivés; **he n. died** il a failli mourir; **not n. enough money/time** vraiment pas assez d'argent/ de temps; **not n. so beautiful** bien moins beau (belle)
nearly-new [nɪəlɪ'njuː] *adj* = d'occasion mais en parfait état
nearside ['nɪəsaɪd] **1** *n (on right)* côté *m* droit; *(on left)* côté *m* gauche
  2 *adj (on right)* droit(e); *(on left)* gauche
near-sighted [nɪə'saɪtɪd] *adj Am* myope
neat [niːt] *adj* (**a**) *(in habits)* ordonné(e); *(in appearance)* soigné(e); *(work, handwriting)* soigné(e); *(room, house)* bien rangé(e); **to make a n. job of doing sth** faire qch très bien (**b**) *(undiluted)* pur(e) (**c**) *Am Fam (good)* super *inv*
▸**neaten up** [niːtən] *vt sep (hair, garden)* arranger; *(piece of work)* peaufiner
neatly ['niːtlɪ] *adv* (**a**) *(carefully)* soigneusement (**b**) *(skilfully)* habilement, adroitement
neatness ['niːtnɪs] *n (of appearance)* aspect *m* soigné; *(of work)* soin *m*; *(of handwriting)* netteté *f*; *(of room, house)* ordre *m*
nebula ['nebjʊlə] *(pl nebulas or nebulae* ['nebjʊlaɪ]*) n Astron* nébuleuse *f*
nebulous ['nebjʊləs] *adj (vague)* nébuleux(euse)
necessarily [nesɪ'serəlɪ] *adv* nécessairement, forcément
necessary ['nesɪsərɪ] **1** *adj* nécessaire; **it is n. to remind them** il faut le leur rappeler; **to do what is n.** faire le nécessaire; **when(ever) n.** si nécessaire, si besoin est; **a n. evil** un mal nécessaire
  2 *n Fam* **the n.** *(thing, action)* le nécessaire; *(money)* l'argent *m*
necessitate [nɪ'sesɪteɪt] *vt Formal* nécessiter, rendre nécessaire
necessity [nɪ'sesɪtɪ] *(pl necessities) n* nécessité *f*; **out of n.** par nécessité; **the necessities** *(things needed)* le nécessaire; *Prov* **n. is the mother of invention** en cas de besoin, on trouve toujours une solution
neck [nek] **1** *n* (**a**) *(of person, animal)* cou *m*; *(of dress)* encolure *f*, col *m*; *(of bottle)* goulot *m*; *(of guitar, violin)* manche *m*; *(of land)* langue *f*; *(of lamb, beef)* collier *m* (**b**) *(idioms) Fam* **to risk one's n.** risquer sa peau; *Fam* **he got it in the n.** il s'est pris un savon; *Fam* **he's in it up to his n.** il est impliqué là-dedans jusqu'au cou; **to finish n. and n.** finir au coude à coude; *Fam* **to stick one's n. out** se lancer; *Fam* **in this n. of the woods** dans le coin
  2 *vi Fam (of couple)* se peloter
necklace ['neklɪs] *n* collier *m*
neckline ['neklaɪn] *n* encolure *f*
necromancy ['nekrəʊmænsɪ] *n Formal* nécromancie *f*
nectar ['nektə(r)] *n* nectar *m*
nectarine ['nektəriːn] *n* nectarine *f*, brugnon *m*
née [neɪ] *adj* née; **Mrs Richardson, n. Johnston** Mme Richardson, née Johnston
need [niːd] **1** *n* besoin *m* (**for** de); **there is no n. to shout/worry** inutile de crier/de t'inquiéter; **if n. be** en cas de besoin; **to be in n.** *(poor)* être dans le

besoin; **to be in n. of** sth avoir besoin de qch; **in time of n.** dans les moments difficiles; **their n. is greater than mine** ils en ont plus besoin que moi **2** *vt* **to n.** sth/**to do** sth avoir besoin de qch/de faire qch; **I n. more time** il me faut plus de temps; **you'll n. to take more money** il te faudra prendre plus d'argent, il faudra que tu prennes plus d'argent; **I didn't n. to be reminded of it** je n'avais pas besoin qu'on me le rappelle, il était inutile de me le rappeler; **his hair needs cutting** il a besoin d'une coupe de cheveux; **the torch needs a new battery** la lampe a besoin d'une nouvelle pile; **this work needs a lot of patience** ce travail demande beaucoup de patience; *Ironic* **that's all I n.!** il ne (me) manquait plus que ça! **3** *modal aux v*

La forme modale de **need** est la même à toutes les personnes, et s'utilise sans **do/does** (**he need only worry about himself**; **need she go?**; **it needn't matter**).

you needn't worry inutile de t'inquiéter; **you needn't wait** tu n'as pas besoin d'attendre; **n. I say more?** ai-je besoin d'en dire plus?
needful ['niːdfʊl] *n Fam* **to do the n.** faire le nécessaire
needle ['niːdəl] **1** *n* aiguille *f*; **it's like looking for a n. in a haystack** c'est comme chercher une aiguille dans une botte de foin; **n. bank, n. exchange** distributeur-échangeur *m* de seringues; *Fam* **n. match** (*in football*) match *m* acharné **2** *vt Fam* asticoter
needlecraft ['niːdəlkrɑːft] *n* travaux *mpl* d'aiguille
needless ['niːdlɪs] *adj* (*waste, suffering, worry*) inutile; (*remark*) déplacé(e); **n. to say...** il va de soi que...
needlessly ['niːdlɪslɪ] *adv* inutilement
needlework ['niːdəlwɜːk] *n* (*sewing*) couture *f*; (*embroidery*) broderie *f*
need-to-know [niːdtə'nəʊ] *adj* **information is given on a n. basis** les renseignements ne sont donnés qu'aux personnes concernées
needy ['niːdɪ] **1** *npl* **the n.** les nécessiteux *mpl*
2 *adj* (*person*) nécessiteux(euse), dans le besoin
nefarious [nɪ'feərɪəs] *adj* infâme, ignoble
negate [nɪ'geɪt] *vt* (*effect*) annuler; (*work, efforts*) anéantir
negation [nɪ'geɪʃən] *n* (*of work, efforts*) anéantissement *m*
negative ['negətɪv] **1** *n* (**a**) *Gram* **the n.** la forme négative; **to answer in the n.** répondre par la négative; (**b**) (*of photo*) négatif *m*
2 *adj* négatif(ive); **don't be so n.** ne sois pas si négatif; *Fin* **n. equity** plus-value *f* immobilière négative, = situation où l'acquéreur d'un bien immobilier reste redevable de l'emprunt contracté alors que son logement enregistre une moins-value; **n. feedback** réaction *f* négative
negatively ['negətɪvlɪ] *adv* négativement
negativity [negə'tɪvɪtɪ] *n* négativité *f*
neglect [nɪ'glekt] **1** *n* (*of person*) négligence *f*; (*of machine, garden*) manque *m* d'entretien; (*of duties, responsibilities*) manquement *m*; **from** *or* **through n.** par négligence
2 *vt* (**a**) (*not care for*) négliger; **to n.** oneself se négliger (**b**) (*ignore*) (*duties, responsibilities*) manquer à; (*post*) abandonner; **to n. to do** sth négliger de faire qch
neglectful [nɪ'glektfʊl] *adj* négligent(e); **to be n. of** sb/sth négliger qn/qch

negligée, negligee ['neglɪʒeɪ] *n* négligé *m*, déshabillé *m*
negligence ['neglɪdʒəns] *n* négligence *f*; (*of duties, responsibilities*) manquement *m* (**of** à)
negligent ['neglɪdʒənt] *adj* négligent(e)
negligently ['neglɪdʒəntlɪ] *adv* négligemment
negligible ['neglɪdʒɪbəl] *adj* négligeable
negotiable [nɪ'gəʊʃəbəl] *adj* (*demand, salary*) négociable; (*price*) à débattre; (*obstacle*) franchissable; (*road*) praticable
negotiate [nɪ'gəʊʃɪeɪt] **1** *vt* (**a**) (*price, treaty, salary, contract*) négocier (**b**) (*obstacle*) franchir; (*difficulty*) surmonter; (*bend*) négocier
2 *vi* négocier
negotiation [nɪgəʊʃɪ'eɪʃən] *n* négociation *f*; **under n.** en négociation
negotiator [nɪ'gəʊʃɪeɪtə(r)] *n* négociateur(trice) *m,f*
Negress ['niːgrɪs] *n Old-fashioned* négresse *f*
Negro ['niːgrəʊ] *Old-fashioned* **1** *n* (*pl* **Negroes**) nègre *m*
2 *adj* nègre; **N. spiritual** (*song*) Negro spiritual *m*
neigh [neɪ] **1** *n* hennissement *m*
2 *vi* hennir
neighbor, neighborhood *etc Am* = **neighbour, neighbourhood** *etc*
neighbour, *Am* **neighbor** ['neɪbə(r)] *n* voisin(e) *m,f*; **to be a good n.** être bon voisin
neighbourhood, *Am* **neighborhood** ['neɪbəhʊd] *n* (**a**) (*district*) quartier *m*; (*people*) voisinage *m*; *Br* **n. watch** = système de surveillance mis en œuvre par les habitants d'un quartier (**b**) (*vicinity*) voisinage *m*, environs *mpl*; **in the n.** dans les environs; **a figure in the n. of £2,000** un chiffre avoisinant les 2000 livres
neighbouring, *Am* **neighboring** ['neɪbərɪŋ] *adj* voisin(e)
neighbourliness, *Am* **neighborliness** ['neɪbəlɪnɪs] *n* (*relations fpl* de) bon voisinage *m*
neighbourly, *Am* **neighborly** ['neɪbəlɪ] *adj* **they're very n.** ce sont de très bons voisins
neither ['naɪðə(r), 'niːðə(r)] **1** *conj* **n.**... **nor.**.. ni... ni...; **n. you nor your brother** ni toi ni ton frère; **he n. drinks nor smokes** il ne boit pas et ne fume pas non plus; *Fig* **that's n. here nor there** là n'est pas la question **2** *adv* **n. do I** moi non plus; **if you don't go n. shall I** si tu n'y vas pas, moi non plus; **the workers aren't happy and n. is the management** les ouvriers ne sont pas contents et la direction non plus
3 *adj* **n. driver was injured** aucun des deux conducteurs n'a été blessé
4 *pron* **n. (of them) will do** aucun (des deux) ne fera l'affaire; **n. of my two brothers can come** aucun de mes deux frères ne peut venir
neo- ['niːəʊ] *pref* néo-
neoclassical [niːəʊ'klæsɪkəl] *adj* néoclassique
neofascist [niːəʊ'fæʃɪst] **1** *n* néofasciste *mf*
2 *adj* néofasciste
neolithic [niːəʊ'lɪθɪk] *adj* néolithique
neon ['niːɒn] *n* néon *m*; **n. light** lumière *f* au néon; **n. sign** enseigne *f* au néon
Nepal [nɪ'pɔːl] *n* le Népal
Nepalese [nepə'liːz], **Nepali** [ne'pɔːlɪ] **1** *n* (*pl* **Nepalese** *or* **Nepalis**) (**a**) (*person*) Népalais(e) *m,f* (**b**) (*language*) népalais *m*
2 *adj* népalais(e)
nephew ['nefjuː] *n* neveu *m*
nepotism ['nepətɪzəm] *n* népotisme *m*
Neptune ['neptjuːn] *n* (*planet*) Neptune *f*

nerd [nɜ:d] *n Fam Pej (stupid person)* crétin(e) *m,f; (unfashionable person)* ringard(e) *m,f*

nerdy ['nɜ:dɪ] *adj Fam Pej* ringard(e)

nerve [nɜ:v] **1** *n* (**a**) *(in body)* nerf *m*; *Fam* **to get on sb's nerves** taper sur les nerfs à qn; **her nerves were in a terrible state** elle était à bout de nerfs; *Anat* **n. cell** cellule *f* nerveuse; *Fig* **n. centre** *(of organization)* centre *m* nerveux; **n. gas** gaz *m* neurotoxique (**b**) *(courage)* courage *m*; **to have nerves of steel** avoir des nerfs d'acier; **to keep/lose one's n.** garder/perdre son sang-froid (**c**) *Fam (cheek)* culot *m*; **to have the n.** **to do sth** avoir le culot de faire qch

2 *vt* **to n. oneself to do sth** s'armer de courage pour faire qch

nerve-(w)racking ['nɜ:vrækɪŋ] *adj* éprouvant(e)

nervous ['nɜ:vəs] *adj* (**a**) *(apprehensive)* nerveux(euse), anxieux(euse); **to be n. about sth/doing sth** être nerveux *ou* anxieux à l'idée de qch/de faire qch (**b**) *(energy, exhaustion)* nerveux(euse); **n. breakdown** dépression *f* nerveuse; **n. system** système *m* nerveux

nervously ['nɜ:vəslɪ] *adv* nerveusement

nervousness ['nɜ:vəsnɪs] *n* nervosité *f*

nervy ['nɜ:vɪ] *adj Fam (tense)* nerveux(euse)

nest [nest] **1** *n (of bird, insects)* nid *m*; *Fig (of criminals)* repaire *m*; *Fig* **to fly the n.** quitter le nid; **n. of tables** tables *fpl* gigognes; *Fig* **n. egg** pécule *m*

2 *vi (of bird)* faire son nid

nestle ['nesəl] *vi* se pelotonner, se blottir; **to n. up to sb** se blottir contre qn

nestling ['neslɪŋ] *n* oisillon *m*

Net [net] *n Fam Comput* **the N.** le Net; **N. surfer, N. user** internaute *mf*

net¹ [net] **1** *n* filet *m*; *Fig* **to slip through the n.** passer à travers les mailles du filet; **n. curtain** voilage *m*

2 *vt (pt & pp* **netted)** *(animals, fish)* prendre au filet; *Fig (drugs, criminals)* mettre la main sur; *(donations, contracts)* récolter

net² [net] **1** *adj (weight, price, profit)* net (nette)

2 *vt (earn)* **to n. £2,000** gagner 2000 livres net

netball ['netbɔ:l] *n* = sport féminin proche du basketball

nethead ['nethed] *n Fam Comput* accro *mf* de l'Internet

Netherlands ['neðələndz] *npl* **the N.** les Pays-Bas *mpl*

netiquette ['netɪket] *n Fam Comput* netiquette *f*

netting ['netɪŋ] *n* filet *m*

nettle ['netəl] **1** *n (plant)* ortie *f*

2 *vt (irritate)* irriter, énerver

network ['netwɜ:k] **1** *n* réseau *m*

2 *vi (make contacts)* établir un réseau de contacts

networking ['netwɜ:kɪŋ] *n (making contacts)* établissement *m* d'un réseau de contacts

neural ['njʊərəl] *adj Anat* neural(e)

neuralgia [njʊ'rældʒə] *n* névralgie *f*

neurologist [njʊə'rɒlədʒɪst] *n* neurologue *mf*

neurology [njʊə'rɒlədʒɪ] *n* neurologie *f*

neuron ['njʊərɒn], **neurone** ['njʊərəʊn] *n Anat* neurone *m*

neurosis [njʊ'rəʊsɪs] *(pl* **neuroses** [njʊ'rəʊsi:z]*) n* névrose *f*

neurosurgery ['njʊərəʊ'sɜ:dʒərɪ] *n* neurochirurgie *f*

neurotic [njʊ'rɒtɪk] **1** *n* névrosé(e) *m,f*

2 *adj* névrosé(e); **to be n. about sth** être obsédé(e) par qch

neuter ['nju:tə(r)] **1** *n Gram* neutre *m*

2 *adj Gram* neutre

3 *vt (animal)* castrer, châtrer

neutral ['nju:trəl] **1** *n* (**a**) *(country)* pays *m* neutre; *(person)* personne *f* neutre (**b**) *(of car)* point *m* mort; **in n.** au point mort

2 *adj (country, colour)* neutre

neutrality [nju:'trælɪtɪ] *n* neutralité *f*

neutralize ['nju:trəlaɪz] *vt* neutraliser

neutrino [nju'tri:nəʊ] *(pl* **neutrinos**) *n Phys* neutrino *m*

neutron ['nju:trɒn] *n Phys* neutron *m*; **n. bomb** bombe *f* à neutrons

never ['nevə(r)] *adv* (**a**) *(not once)* jamais; **I've n. met him** je ne l'ai jamais rencontré; **n. again!** plus jamais!; **he's n. yet been beaten** il n'a encore jamais été battu; **I've n. yet understood why** je n'ai jamais compris pourquoi (**b**) *(emphatic negative)* **she n. said a word** elle n'a pas dit un mot; **I n. expected this** je ne m'attendais vraiment pas à ça; **he n. even congratulated me** il ne m'a même pas félicité; *Br Fam* **well I n.!** ça alors!

never-ending [nevər'endɪŋ] *adj* interminable

never-never ['nevə'nevə(r)] *n Br Fam* **to buy sth on the n.** acheter qch à crédit

nevertheless [nevəðə'les] *adv* néanmoins, cependant

new [nju:] *adj* nouveau(elle); *(not used)* neuf (neuve); **what's n.?** quoi de neuf?; **that's nothing n.!** ça n'est pas nouveau!; **she's n. to this work** elle débute dans ce travail; **to be n. to a town** être nouveau dans une ville; **N. Age** *(music, thinking)* new age *inv*; **N. Brunswick** le Nouveau-Brunswick; **N. Caledonia** la Nouvelle-Calédonie; **N. Delhi** New Delhi; **N. England** la Nouvelle-Angleterre; **N. Guinea** la Nouvelle-Guinée; *Br Pol* **N. Labour** = nouveau nom donné au parti travailliste vers le milieu des années 90 dans le souci de moderniser l'image; **N. Man** homme *m* de la nouvelle génération *(qui participe équitablement à l'éducation des enfants et aux tâches ménagères)*; **N. Mexico** le Nouveau-Mexique; **n. moon** nouvelle lune *f*; **N. Orleans** la Nouvelle-Orléans; **N. South Wales** la Nouvelle-Galles du Sud; **the N. Testament** le Nouveau Testament; **n. town** ville *f* nouvelle; **n. wave** *(trend)* Nouvelle Vague *f*; **the N. World** le Nouveau Monde; **N. Year** Nouvel An *m*; **N. Year's Day** le jour de l'an; **N. Year's Eve** la Saint-Sylvestre; **N. Year's resolution** résolution *f* du jour de l'an; **N. York** New York; **N. Yorker** New-Yorkais(e) *m,f*

newbie ['nju:bɪ] *n Fam* (**a**) *Am (new recruit)* bleu(e) *m,f* (**b**) *Comput (Internet user)* internaute *mf* novice

newborn ['nju:bɔ:n] **1** *adj* nouveau-né(e); **n. baby** nouveau-né(e) *m,f*

2 *n* nouveau-né(e) *m,f*

newcomer ['nju:kʌmə(r)] *n* nouveau venu (nouvelle venue) *m,f* (**to** dans)

newfangled [nju:'fæŋgəld] *adj Pej (idea)* nouveau(elle); *(gadget)* dernier cri *inv*

Newfoundland ['nju:fəndlænd] *n* Terre-Neuve *f*

newly ['nju:lɪ] *adv* nouvellement, récemment

newlyweds ['nju:lɪwedz] *npl* jeunes mariés *mpl*

newness ['nju:nɪs] *n (of design)* nouveauté *f*; *(of clothing)* état *m* neuf

news [nju:z] *n* nouvelles *fpl*; *(on TV, radio)* informations *fpl*; **a piece of n.** une nouvelle; **in the n.** sous les feux de l'actualité; *Fam* **he's bad n.** il n'est pas fréquentable; *Fam* **that's n. to me!** première nouvelle!; *Prov* **no n. is good n.** pas de nouvelles, bonnes nouvelles; **n. agency** agence *f* de presse; **n. bulletin** bulletin *m* d'informations; **n. conference** conférence *f* de presse; **n. item** information *f*, nouvelle *f*; **n. summary** rappel *m* des titres

newsagent ['nju:zeɪdʒənt] *n Br* marchand(e) *m,f* de journaux; **n.'s (shop)** marchand *m* de journaux

newscaster ['nju:zkɑ:stə(r)] *n* présentateur(trice) *m,f* du journal

newsdealer ['nju:zdi:lə(r)] *n Am* marchand(e) *m,f* de journaux

newsflash ['nju:zflæʃ] *n* flash *m* d'informations

newsgroup ['nju:zgru:p] *n Comput* newsgroup *m*, forum *m* de discussion

newsletter ['nju:zletə(r)] *n* bulletin *m*

newspaper ['nju:zpeɪpə(r)] *n* journal *m*; **n. report** reportage *m*

newspaperman ['nju:zpeɪpəmæn] *n (reporter)* journaliste *m*; *(proprietor)* propriétaire *m* d'un journal

newsprint ['nju:zprɪnt] *n* papier *m* journal

newsreader ['nju:zri:də(r)] *n* présentateur(trice) *m,f* du journal

newsreel ['nju:zri:l] *n* actualités *fpl*

newsroom ['nju:zru:m] *n* (salle *f* de) rédaction *f*

newsstand ['nju:zstænd] *n* kiosque *m* à journaux

newsworthy ['nju:zwɜ:ðɪ] *adj* d'un intérêt médiatique

newt [nju:t] *n* triton *m*

New Zealand [nju:'zi:lənd] *n* la Nouvelle-Zélande

New Zealander [nju:'zi:ləndə(r)] *n* Néo-Zélandais(e) *m,f*

next [nekst] **1** *adj* (**a**) *(in space)* d'à côté; **n. door** à côté (**b**) *(in time, order)* prochain(e); *(subsequent)* suivant(e), d'après; **n. week** la semaine prochaine; **the n. week** la semaine suivante *ou* d'après; **the year after n.** dans deux ans; **the n. time** la prochaine fois; **your name is n. on the list** votre nom est le suivant sur la liste; **the n. but one** pas le prochain, mais celui d'après; **(the) n. to arrive was Carmen** Carmen est arrivée ensuite; **who's n.?** c'est à qui?; **n. please!** au suivant!; **the n. size up/down** la taille au-dessus/au-dessous

2 *adv* (**a**) *(in space)* **n. to** à côté de (**b**) *(in time, order)* ensuite, après; *Fam* **what will they think of n.?** qu'est-ce qu'ils vont encore inventer?; **n. to Paris I like Madrid best** après Paris, la ville que je préfère, c'est Madrid; **when shall we meet n.?** quand nous reverrons-nous?; **the n. best thing would be to...** à défaut, le mieux serait de...; **the n. fastest after the Ferrari was...** la voiture la plus rapide après la Ferrari était...; **who is the n. oldest/youngest after Mark?** qui est le plus âgé/le plus jeune après Mark?; **n. to nothing** quasiment rien; **there is n. to no evidence** il n'y a pratiquement aucune preuve; **in n. to no time** en un rien de temps

next-door ['neks'dɔ:(r)] *adj* d'à côté; **n. neighbour** voisin(e) *m,f* d'à côté

next-of-kin [nekstəv'kɪn] *n* plus proche parent *m*

NFL [enef'el] *n Am (abbr* **National Football League***)* = fédération nationale de football américain

NGO [endʒi:'əʊ] *n (abbr* **non-governmental organization***)* ONG *f*

NHS [eneɪtʃ'es] *n Br (abbr* **National Health Service***)* = système de santé britannique

NI [en'aɪ] *n Br (abbr* **National Insurance***)* contributions *fpl* sociales

nib [nɪb] *n* plume *f*

nibble ['nɪbəl] **1** *n* **to have a n. at sth** grignoter qch; **nibbles** *(snacks)* amuse-gueule *mpl*
2 *vt* grignoter

Nicaragua [nɪkə'ræɡjʊə] *n* le Nicaragua

Nicaraguan [nɪkə'ræɡjʊən] **1** *n* Nicaraguayen(enne) *m,f*
2 *adj* nicaraguayen(enne)

nice [naɪs] *adj* (**a**) *(pleasant)* agréable; *(physically attractive)* beau (belle); *(tasty)* bon (bonne); **a n. idea** une bonne idée; **to be n. to sb** se montrer aimable avec qn; **to have a n. time** bien s'amuser; **have a n. day!** bonne journée!; **it was n. of her to...** c'était gentil de sa part de...; *Ironic* **that's a n. way to behave!** en voilà des manières! (**b**) *(intensive)* **n. and easy** très facile; **n. and handy** bien commode; **a n. warm bath** un bain bien chaud

nice-looking ['naɪslʊkɪŋ] *adj* beau (belle)

nicely ['naɪslɪ] *adv (ask)* gentiment; *(behave, sit)* bien; **to be doing n.** aller bien; **to do n. for oneself** bien se débrouiller

niceties ['naɪsɪtɪz] *npl* subtilités *fpl*

niche [ni:ʃ] *n (in wall)* niche *f*; *(in market)* créneau *m*; **to find one's n. (in life)** trouver sa voie

nick [nɪk] **1** *n* (**a**) *(in wood, on face)* entaille *f* (**b**) **in the n. of time** juste à temps (**c**) *Fam (condition)* **in good/bad n.** en bon/mauvais état (**d**) *Br Fam (prison)* taule *f*; *(police station)* poste *m*
2 *vt* (**a**) *(cut)* entailler (**b**) *Br Fam (arrest)* pincer, épingler (**c**) *Br Fam (steal)* piquer, faucher

nickel ['nɪkəl] *n* (**a**) *(metal)* nickel *m* (**b**) *Am (coin)* pièce *f* de cinq cents

nickname ['nɪkneɪm] **1** *n* surnom *m*
2 *vt* surnommer

nicotine ['nɪkəti:n] *n* nicotine *f*; **n. patch** patch *m* antitabac

niece [ni:s] *n* nièce *f*

niff [nɪf] *Br Fam* **1** *n (bad smell)* puanteur *f*
2 *vi (smell bad)* puer

nifty ['nɪftɪ] *adj Fam* (**a**) *(idea, device)* génial(e) (**b**) *(agile)* vif (vive)

Niger [ni:'ʒeə(r)] *n* le Niger

Nigeria [naɪ'dʒɪərɪə] *n* le Nigéria

Nigerian [naɪ'dʒɪərɪən] **1** *n* Nigérian(e) *m,f*
2 *adj* nigérian(e)

niggardly ['nɪɡədlɪ] *adj (person)* avare, pingre; *(sum, portion)* maigre

nigger ['nɪɡə(r)] *n very Fam* nègre (négresse) *m,f*, = terme raciste désignant un Noir

niggle ['nɪɡ(ə)l] **1** *vt (worry)* tracasser
2 *vi (be overfussy)* couper les cheveux en quatre; **to n. (away) at sb** *(worry)* tracasser qn; *(hassle)* enquiquiner qn

niggling ['nɪɡəlɪŋ] *adj (detail)* insignifiant(e); *(pain, doubt)* persistant(e); **I have a n. feeling that...** je ne peux pas m'empêcher de penser que...

nigh [naɪ] *adv Lit (near)* près, proche; **the end is n.!** la fin est proche! (**b**) **well n.** *(almost)* presque

night [naɪt] *n* nuit *f*; *(evening)* soir *m*; **at n.** la nuit; *(in the evening)* le soir; **late at n.** tard dans la nuit; **all n.** toute la nuit; **last n.** la nuit dernière; *(evening)* hier soir; **tomorrow n.** demain soir; **on Thursday n.** jeudi soir; **good n.!** *(when going to bed)* bonne nuit!, bonsoir!; *(when leaving)* bonsoir!; **to work nights** travailler la nuit; **to have a n. out** sortir; **let's make a n. of it** et si on continuait la soirée?; **n. flight** vol *m* de nuit; **n. owl** oiseau *m* de nuit; **n. school** cours *m* du soir; *Am* **n. table** table *f* de chevet; **n. watchman** veilleur *m* de nuit

nightcap ['naɪtkæp] *n* (**a**) *(hat)* bonnet *m* de nuit (**b**) *(drink)* petit verre *m* (*avant d'aller se coucher*)

nightclub ['naɪtklʌb] *n* boîte *f* de nuit, *Can* club *m* de nuit

nightdress ['naɪtdres] *n* chemise *f* de nuit

nightfall ['naɪtfɔːl] *n* tombée *f* de la nuit; **at n.** à la nuit tombante

nightgown ['naɪtgaʊn] *n* chemise *f* de nuit

nightie ['naɪtɪ] *n Fam* chemise *f* de nuit

nightingale ['naɪtɪŋgeɪl] *n* rossignol *m*

nightjar ['naɪtdʒɑː(r)] *n* engoulevent *m* (d'Europe)

nightlife ['naɪtlaɪf] *n* vie *f* nocturne; **there's not much n.** il n'y a pas grand-chose à faire le soir

nightlong ['naɪtlɒŋ] *adj* qui dure toute la nuit

nightly ['naɪtlɪ] **1** *adj* de toutes les nuits; *(in the evening)* du soir
2 *adv* toutes les nuits; *(in the evening)* tous les soirs

nightmare ['naɪtmeə(r)] *n also Fig* cauchemar *m*

nightmarish ['naɪtmeərɪʃ] *adj* cauchemardesque

nightshirt ['naɪtʃɜːt] *n* chemise *f* de nuit

night-time ['naɪttaɪm] **1** *n* nuit *f*; **at n.** la nuit
2 *adj* nocturne

nihilistic [naɪ(h)ɪ'lɪstɪk] *adj* nihiliste

nil [nɪl] *n* néant *m*; *(in sport)* zéro *m*; **two n.** deux à zéro

Nile [naɪl] *n* **the N.** le Nil

nimble ['nɪmbəl] *adj (person)* souple; *(leap, movement)* leste; *(fingers)* preste; *(mind)* vif (vive)

nimbly ['nɪmbəlɪ] *adv* avec souplesse

nincompoop ['nɪŋkəmpuːp] *n Fam* nigaud(e) *m,f*

nine [naɪn] **1** *n* neuf *m inv*; *Fam* **dressed up to the nines** sur son trente et un; *esp Am* **n. eleven** = le onze septembre; **ever since n. eleven I've been afraid to fly** depuis les attentats du onze septembre, j'ai peur de prendre l'avion
2 *adj* neuf; **n. times out of ten** neuf fois sur dix; **a n.-to-five job** un travail de bureau; **to have n. lives** *(of person)* avoir l'âme chevillée au corps; *see also* **eight**

nineteen [naɪn'tiːn] **1** *n* dix-neuf *m inv*; *Br Fam* **to talk n. to the dozen** bavarder comme une pie
2 *adj* dix-neuf; *see also* **eight**

nineteenth [naɪn'tiːnθ] **1** *n* (**a**) *(fraction)* dix-neuvième *m* (**b**) *(in series)* dix-neuvième *mf* (**c**) *(of month)* dix-neuf *m inv*
2 *adj* dix-neuvième; *Fam Hum* **the n. hole** *(of golf course)* le bar du golf; *see also* **eighth**

ninetieth ['naɪntɪɪθ] **1** *n* (**a**) *(fraction)* quatre-vingt-dixième *m* (**b**) *(in series)* quatre-vingt-dixième *mf*
2 *adj* quatre-vingt-dixième; *see also* **eighth**

ninety ['naɪntɪ] **1** *n* quatre-vingt-dix *m inv*
2 *adj* quatre-vingt-dix; **n. nine times out of a hundred** quatre-vingt-dix-neuf fois sur cent; *see also* **eighty**

ninth [naɪnθ] **1** *n* (**a**) *(fraction)* neuvième *m* (**b**) *(in series)* neuvième *mf* (**c**) *(of month)* neuf *m inv*
2 *adj* neuvième; *see also* **eighth**

nip [nɪp] **1** *n* (**a**) *(pinch)* pincement *m*; *(bite)* morsure *f* légère (**b**) *(of cold, frost)* **there's a n. in the air** il fait frisquet (**c**) *Fam (of drink)* petit verre *m*
2 *(pt & pp* **nipped***) vt* (**a**) *(pinch)* pincer; *(bite)* mordre légèrement; *Fam Fig* **to n. sth in the bud** étouffer qch dans l'œuf (**b**) *(of cold, frost)* pincer, piquer
3 *vi (sting)* piquer

▸**nip out** *vi Br Fam* sortir quelques instants; **to n. out to the supermarket/pub** faire un saut au supermarché/au pub

nipper ['nɪpə(r)] *n Br Fam (child)* gamin(e) *m,f*

nipple ['nɪp(ə)l] *n* mamelon *m*; *(on baby's bottle)* tétine *f*

nippy ['nɪpɪ] *adj Fam* (**a**) *(person, car)* rapide (**b**) *(cold)* vif (vive); **it's a bit n. today** il fait plutôt frisquet aujourd'hui

nit [nɪt] *n* (**a**) *(in hair)* lente *f*; **to have nits** avoir des poux (**b**) *Br Fam (person)* nigaud(e) *m,f*

nit-picker ['nɪtpɪkə(r)] *n Fam* chipoteur(euse) *m,f*

nit-picking ['nɪtpɪkɪŋ] *Fam* **1** *n* chipotage *m*
2 *adj* chipoteur(euse)

nitrate ['naɪtreɪt] *n* nitrate *m*

nitric ['naɪtrɪk] *adj* nitrique

nitrogen ['naɪtrədʒən] *n* azote *m*

nitroglycerine ['naɪtrəʊ'glɪsəriːn] *n* nitroglycérine *f*

nitrous ['naɪtrəs] *adj* nitreux(euse)

nitty-gritty ['nɪtɪ'grɪtɪ] *n Fam* **to get down to the n.** entrer dans le vif du sujet

nitwit ['nɪtwɪt] *n Fam* crétin(e) *m,f*

NNE *(abbr* north-northeast) NNE

NNW *(abbr* north-northwest) NNO

No, no¹ *(abbr* number) n°

no² [nəʊ] **1** *n (pl* **noes** *or* **nos**) non *m*; **she won't take no for an answer** elle n'accepte pas qu'on lui dise non
2 *adj* (**a**) *(not any)* pas de; **there's no bread** il n'y a pas de pain; **of no importance** sans importance; **he's no friend of mine** je ne le compte certainement pas au nombre de mes amis; **I am in no way surprised** je ne suis pas du tout surpris; *Fam* **no way!** pas question! (**b**) *(with gerund)* **there's no denying it** on ne peut pas le nier; **there's no pleasing him** il n'est jamais satisfait; **no smoking** *(sign)* interdiction de fumer
3 *adv* (**a**) *(interjection)* non (**b**) *(not any)* **no richer/poorer** pas plus riche/pauvre; **no more/less than £100** pas plus/moins de 100 livres; **he no longer lives there** il n'habite plus là

Noah ['nəʊə] *pr n* Noé; **N.'s ark** l'arche *f* de Noé

nobble ['nɒbəl] *vt Br Fam* (**a**) *(bribe)* payer (**b**) *(waylay)* coincer

Nobel Prize ['nəʊbel'praɪz] *n* prix *m* Nobel

nobility [nəʊ'bɪlɪtɪ] *n* noblesse *f*

noble ['nəʊbəl] **1** *n* noble *mf*
2 *adj* noble; *Fig (building)* majestueux(euse)

nobleman ['nəʊbəlmən] *n* noble *m*

nobleminded [nəʊbəl'maɪndɪd] *adj (person)* au cœur noble, magnanime; *(sentiment, action)* noble

noblewoman ['nəʊbəlwʊmən] *n* noble *f*

nobly ['nəʊbəlɪ] *adv* avec noblesse

nobody ['nəʊbədɪ] **1** *pron* personne; **n. spoke to me** personne ne m'a parlé; **n. else** personne d'autre; **she's n.'s fool** elle n'est pas née de la dernière pluie; **if you don't have money, you're n.** si on n'a pas d'argent on est un moins que rien
2 *n (pl* **nobodies***) a* **n.** un(e) moins que rien

no-claims bonus ['nəʊ'kleɪmz'bəʊnəs] *n* bonus *m*

nocturnal [nɒk'tɜːnəl] *adj* nocturne

nod [nɒd] **1** *n (in greeting, as signal)* signe *m* de tête; *(in agreement)* signe de tête affirmatif; *Fig* **to give sb/sth the n.** donner le feu vert à qn/qch;
2 *vt (pt & pp* **nodded***)* **to n. one's head** *(in greeting, as signal)* faire un signe de tête; *(in agreement)* faire oui de la tête; **to n. one's agreement/approval** consentir/approuver d'un signe de tête
3 *vi* **to n. in agreement/approval** consentir/approuver d'un signe de tête

▸**nod off** *vi Fam* s'assoupir

node [nəʊd] *n (of curve, plant)* nœud *m*; *Med* ganglion *m*; *Comput* noyau *m*

nodule ['nɒdjuːl] *n* nodule *m*
no-fly zone [nəʊ'flaɪzəʊn] *n Mil* zone *f* d'exclusion aérienne
no-frills [nəʊ'frɪlz] *adj (wedding, event)* tout(e) simple; *(travel)* sans prestation de services; *(car, bicycle)* sans gadgets; **n. airline** low-cost *m*
no-go area [nəʊ'gəʊeərɪə] *adj* zone *f* interdite
no-good ['nəʊgʊd] *adj Fam* **a n. idiot** un(e) imbécile propre à rien; **that n. husband of hers** son bon à rien de mari
no-hoper [nəʊ'həʊpə(r)] *n* tocard(e) *m,f*
noise [nɔɪz] *n* bruit *m*; *Fig* **to make noises about doing sth** parler de faire qch; *Fig* **a big n.** une huile
noiselessly ['nɔɪzlɪslɪ] *adv* sans bruit, silencieusement
noisily ['nɔɪzɪlɪ] *adv* bruyamment
noisy ['nɔɪzɪ] *adj* bruyant(e)
nomad ['nəʊmæd] **1** *n* nomade *mf* **2** *adj* nomade
nomadic [nəʊ'mædɪk] *adj* nomade
no man's land ['nəʊmænz'lænd] *n Fig* no man's land *m*
nomenclature [nəʊ'menklətʃə(r)] *n* nomenclature *f*
nominal ['nɒmɪnəl] *adj* nominal(e); *(damages)* symbolique; *(rent)* insignifiant(e)
nominally ['nɒmɪnəlɪ] *adv* nominalement
nominate ['nɒmɪneɪt] *vt (propose)* proposer (**for/as** pour/comme); *(appoint)* nommer (**to/as** à/comme)
nomination [nɒmɪ'neɪʃən] *n* (**a**) *(proposal)* candidature *f*; *(for film, TV awards)* nomination *f* (**b**) *(appointment)* nomination *f*
nominee [nɒmɪ'niː] *n (proposed)* candidat(e) *m,f*; *(appointed)* personne *f* nommée
non- [nɒn] *pref* non(-)
non-aggression pact [nɒnə'greʃən'pækt] *n Pol* pacte *m* de non-agression
nonalcoholic [nɒnælkə'hɒlɪk] *adj* sans alcool
nonaligned [nɒnə'laɪnd] *adj Pol* non-aligné(e)
nonattendance [nɒnə'tendəns] *n* absence *f*
nonchalance ['nɒnʃələns] *n* désinvolture *f*
nonchalant ['nɒnʃələnt] *adj* désinvolte
nonchalantly [nɒnʃə'ləntlɪ] *adv* avec désinvolture
noncombatant [nɒn'kɒmbətənt] **1** *n Mil* non-combattant(e) *m,f* **2** *adj* non-combattant(e)
noncommissioned officer [nɒnkə'mɪʃənd'ɒfɪsə(r)] *n Mil* sous-officier *m*
noncommittal [nɒnkə'mɪtəl] *adj (answer)* de Normand; **to be n.** ne pas s'engager
nonconformist [nɒnkən'fɔːmɪst] **1** *n* non-conformiste *mf* **2** *adj* non-conformiste
non-denominational [nɒndɪ'nɒmɪ'neɪʃənəl] *adj (school, education)* non confessionel(elle)
nondescript ['nɒndɪskrɪpt] *adj* banal(e); *(colour)* fade
none [nʌn] **1** *pron* aucun(e) *m,f*; **n. of you/us** aucun d'entre vous/nous; **n. of my friends** aucun de mes amis; **n. of this concerns me** rien de tout cela ne me concerne; **it was n. other than the President** c'était le Président, rien de moins; **there was/were n. left** il n'en restait plus; *Fam* **we'll have n. of that!** pas de ça! **2** *adv* **his answer left me n. the wiser** sa réponse ne m'a pas avancé; **n. too happy** pas très satisfait(e); **n. too soon** pas trop tôt
nonentity [nɒ'nentɪtɪ] *(pl* **nonentities***) n* personne *f* sans intérêt

nonessential [nɒnɪ'senʃəl] *adj* qui n'est pas essentiel(elle)
nonetheless [nʌnðə'les] *adv* néanmoins, cependant
nonevent [nɒnɪ'vent] *n* **to be a n.** être décevant(e)
nonexecutive director [nɒnɪg'zekjʊtɪvdaɪ'rektə(r)] *n* = administrateur à titre consultatif
nonexistent [nɒnɪg'zɪstənt] *adj* inexistant(e)
non-fiction [nɒn'fɪkʃən] *n* ouvrages *mpl* généraux
nonflammable [nɒn'flæməbəl] *adj* ininflammable
non-linear [nɒn'lɪnɪə(r)] *adj Comput* non linéaire
non-negotiable [nɒnnɪ'gəʊʃɪəbəl] *adj* non négociable
non-nuclear [nɒn'njuːklɪə(r)] *adj (country)* non nucléarisé(e); *(war, defence)* non nucléaire
no-no ['nəʊnəʊ] *(pl* **no-nos** *or* **no-noes***) n Fam* **that's a n.** c'est à ne pas faire
no-nonsense [nəʊ'nɒnsəns] *adj* direct(e)
non-partisan [nɒn'pɑːtɪzæn] *adj* impartial(e)
non-payment [nɒn'peɪmənt] *n* non-paiement *m*
non-person ['nɒn'pɜːsən] *n* proscrit(e) *m,f*
nonplussed [nɒn'plʌst] *adj* interloqué(e)
non-profit-making [nɒn'prɒfɪtmeɪkɪŋ] *adj* à but non lucratif
non-racist [nɒn'reɪsɪst] *adj* non raciste
nonresident [nɒn'rezɪdənt] *n (of country)* non-résident(e) *m,f*; *(of hotel)* client(e) *m,f*
nonreturnable [nɒnrɪ'tɜːnəbəl] *adj (bottle)* non consigné(e); *(deposit)* non remboursable
nonsense ['nɒnsəns] *n* bêtises *fpl*, idioties *fpl*; **n.!** n'importe quoi!; **to talk (a lot of) n.** dire des bêtises; **to make a n. of sth** ôter tout sens à qch
nonsensical [nɒn'sensɪkəl] *adj* absurde, qui n'a pas de sens
non sequitur [nɒn'sekwɪtə(r)] *n* absurdité *f*
non-sexist [nɒn'seksɪst] *adj* non sexiste
non-smoker [nɒn'sməʊkə(r)] *n* non-fumeur(euse) *m,f*; *(train compartment)* compartiment *m* non-fumeurs
non-specialist [nɒn'speʃəlɪst] **1** *n* non-spécialiste *mf* **2** *adj* non spécialisé(e)
nonstarter [nɒn'stɑːtə(r)] *n* **to be a n.** *(of plan)* être fichu(e) d'avance
nonstick ['nɒn'stɪk] *adj (surface)* anti-adhésif(ive); *(frying pan)* qui n'attache pas
non-stop ['nɒn'stɒp] **1** *adj (journey)* sans arrêt; *(flight)* sans escale **2** *adv* sans arrêt; *(fly)* sans escale
non-tariff barrier ['nɒn'tærɪf'bærɪə(r)] *n Econ* barrière *f* non tarifaire
nontransferable ['nɒntræns'fɜːrəbəl] *adj (ticket, membership)* nominatif(ive); *(property, right)* incessible
nonverbal [nɒn'vɜːbəl] *adj* non-verbal(e)
nonviolent [nɒn'vaɪələnt] *adj* non-violent(e)
noodles ['nuːdəlz] *npl* nouilles *fpl*
nook [nʊk] *n (corner)* recoin *m*; *(retreat)* coin *m*; **every n. and cranny** le moindre recoin
nookie, nooky ['nʊkɪ] *n Fam* crac-crac *m*; **to have a bit of n.** faire une partie de jambes en l'air
noon [nuːn] *n* midi *m*; **at n.** à midi
noonday ['nuːndeɪ] *n Lit* midi *m*; **the n. sun** le soleil de midi
no-one ['nəʊwʌn] = **nobody**
noose [nuːs] *n* nœud *m* coulant; *Fig* **to put one's head in a n.** signer son arrêt de mort
nope [nəʊp] *adv Fam* non
nor [nɔː(r)] **1** *conj* neither... **n.** ni... ni; **neither you n. your brother** ni toi ni ton frère; **he neither drinks n. smokes** il ne boit pas et ne fume pas non plus

2 *adv* n. do I moi non plus; **if you don't go n. shall I** si tu n'y vas pas, moi non plus

Nordic ['nɔːdɪk] *adj* nordique

norm [nɔːm] *n* norme *f*

normal ['nɔːməl] **1** *n* **above/below n.** *(temperature, rate)* au-dessus/au-dessous de la normale; **to get back to n.** redevenir normal(e)
2 *adj* normal(e)

normality [nɔːˈmælɪtɪ], *Am* **normalcy** ['nɔːməlsɪ] *n* normalité *f*; **a return to n.** un retour à la normale

normalization [nɔːməlaɪˈzeɪʃən] *n* normalisation *f*

normalize ['nɔːməlaɪz] **1** *vt* normaliser
2 *vi* redevenir normal(e)

normally ['nɔːməlɪ] *adv* normalement

Norman ['nɔːmən] **1** *n* Normand(e) *m,f*
2 *adj* normand(e)

Normandy ['nɔːməndɪ] *n* la Normandie

north [nɔːθ] **1** *n* nord *m*; **to the n. (of)** au nord (de)
2 *adj (coast, side)* nord; *(wind)* du nord; **N. Africa** Afrique *f* du Nord; **N. African** nord-africain(e); *(person)* Nord-Africain(e) *m,f*; **N. America** Amérique *f* du Nord; **N. American** nord-américain(e); *(person)* Nord-Américain(e) *m,f*; **N. Carolina** la Caroline du Nord; **N. Dakota** le Dakota du Nord; **N. Korea** Corée *f* du Nord; **N. Korean** nord-coréen(enne); *(person)* Nord-Coréen(enne) *m,f*; **the N. Pole** le Pôle Nord; **the N. Sea** la mer du Nord
3 *adv* au nord; *(travel)* vers le nord; **to face n.** *(of house)* être exposé(e) au nord

northbound ['nɔːθbaʊnd] *adj (train, traffic)* en direction du nord; **n. carriageway** voie *f* nord

northeast [nɔːθˈiːst] **1** *n* nord-est *m*
2 *adj (side)* nord-est; *(wind)* du nord-est
3 *adv* au nord-est; *(travel)* vers le nord-est

northeasterly [nɔːθˈiːstəlɪ] **1** *n (wind)* vent *m* du nord-est
2 *adj (direction)* vers le nord-est; *(wind)* du nord-est

northeastern [nɔːθˈiːstən] *adj (region)* (du) nord-est

northerly ['nɔːðəlɪ] **1** *n (pl* **northerlies)** *(wind)* vent *m* du nord
2 *adj (direction)* vers le nord; *(wind)* du nord; **the most n. point** le point le plus au nord

northern ['nɔːðən] *adj (region, accent)* du nord; **n. France** le nord de la France; **n. hemisphere** hémisphère *m* nord; **N. Ireland** l'Irlande *f* du Nord; **N. Ireland Assembly** Assemblée *f* legislative de l'Irlande du Nord; **N. Irish** de l'Irlande du Nord; **the N. Irish** les Irlandais *mpl* du Nord; **N. Lights** aurore *f* boréale

Northern Ireland

L'Irlande du Nord désigne la partie de l'Irlande à majorité protestante restée rattachée à la Grande-Bretagne lors de la partition du pays, en 1921. Les émeutes sanglantes qui ont éclaté en 1969 à la suite de manifestations revendiquant l'égalité des droits pour la minorité catholique ont marqué le début de trente ans de conflit entre catholiques et protestants. Ce conflit vit s'affronter les nationalistes de l'**IRA** (*voir encadré à ce mot*), favorables à un rattachement avec la République d'Irlande, différents groupes paramilitaires protestants anti-catholiques, et l'armée et la police, sous contrôle britannique. Le processus de paix, amorcé en 1994 et qui aboutit au **Good Friday Agreement** (*voir encadré à* **good**) de 1998 marqua une nouvelle étape dans l'histoire de l'Irlande du Nord.

northerner ['nɔːðənə(r)] *n* habitant(e) *m,f* du Nord *(de l'Angleterre)*

north-facing ['nɔːθˈfeɪsɪŋ] *adj* exposé(e) au nord

north-northeast [nɔːθnɔːθˈiːst] *adv* au nord-nord-est; *(travel)* vers le nord-nord-est

north-northwest [nɔːθnɔːθˈwest] *adv* au nord-nord-ouest; *(travel)* vers le nord-nord-ouest

northward ['nɔːθwəd] **1** *adj* au nord
2 *adv* vers le nord

northwards ['nɔːθwədz] *adv* vers le nord

northwest [nɔːθˈwest] **1** *n* nord-ouest *m*
2 *adj (side)* nord-ouest; *(wind)* du nord-ouest
3 *adv* au nord-ouest; *(travel)* vers le nord-ouest

northwesterly [nɔːθˈwestəlɪ] **1** *n (pl* **north-westerlies)** *(wind)* vent *m* du nord-ouest
2 *adj (direction)* vers le nord-ouest; *(wind)* du nord-ouest

northwestern [nɔːθˈwestən] *adj (region)* (du) nord-ouest

North-West Territories ['nɔːθˈwestˈterɪtrɪz] *npl* les Territoires *mpl* du Nord-Ouest

Norway ['nɔːweɪ] *n* la Norvège

Norwegian [nɔːˈwiːdʒən] **1** *n* (**a**) *(person)* Norvégien(enne) *m,f* (**b**) *(language)* norvégien *m*
2 *adj* norvégien(enne)

nose [nəʊz] *n* (**a**) *(of person, animal, aeroplane)* nez *m*; **her n. is bleeding** elle saigne du nez; **to blow one's n.** se moucher (le nez); **to hold one's n.** se boucher le nez; *Fam* **to have a n. job** se faire refaire le nez; **the traffic was n. to tail** les voitures se suivaient pare-chocs contre pare-chocs (**b**) *(idioms)* **it's under your n.** vous l'avez sous le nez; **to turn one's n. up at sth** dédaigner qch; **she walked by with her n. in the air** elle passa, l'air dédaigneux; **to look down one's n. at sb** prendre qn de haut; **to pay through the n. for sth** payer qch une fortune; **to get up sb's n.** taper sur les nerfs à qn; **to lead sb by the n.** mener qn par le bout du nez; **to keep one's n. clean** se tenir à carreau; **to have a n. for sth** savoir flairer qch; **to poke one's n. into other people's business** fourrer son nez dans les affaires des autres

▸**nose about, nose around** *vi Fam* fouiner

nosebleed ['nəʊzbliːd] *n* **to have a n.** saigner du nez

nose-dive ['nəʊzdaɪv] **1** *n (of plane)* (vol *m* en) piqué *m*; *Fig (of prices)* chute *f* rapide
2 *vi (of plane)* piquer du nez; *Fig (of prices)* chuter fortement

nosey ['nəʊzɪ] *adj Fam* fouineur(euse); *(questions)* indiscret(ète); *Br* **n. parker** fouineur(euse) *m,f*

nosh [nɒʃ] *Fam* **1** *n (food)* bouffe *f*
2 *vi (eat)* bouffer

no-show [nəʊˈʃəʊ] *n* défection *f*

nosiness ['nəʊzɪnəs] *n* curiosité *f*

no-smoking [nəʊˈsməʊkɪŋ] *adj (carriage, area)* non-fumeurs; *(seat)* non-fumeur

nostalgia [nɒsˈtældʒɪə] *n* nostalgie *f*

nostalgic [nɒsˈtældʒɪk] *adj* nostalgique

nostalgically [nɒsˈtældʒɪklɪ] *adv* avec nostalgie

nostril ['nɒstrɪl] *n* narine *f*

nosy = nosey

not [nɒt] *adv*

> À l'oral, et à l'écrit dans un style familier, on utilise généralement **not** à la forme contractée lorsqu'il suit un modal ou un auxiliaire (**don't go!; she wasn't there; he couldn't see me**).

n. me/him pas moi/lui; **I don't know** je ne sais pas; **don't move!** ne bouge pas!; **whether she likes it or**

n. que ça lui plaise ou non; **I think/hope n.** je pense/ j'espère que non; **she asked me n.** to tell him elle m'a demandé de ne pas le lui dire; **n. wishing to cause an argument, he said nothing** ne voulant pas provoquer de dispute, il s'est tu; **you understand, don't you?** tu comprends, n'est-ce pas?; **n. at all** pas du tout; *(you're welcome)* je vous en prie; **n. any more** plus maintenant; **n. even** pas même, même pas; **n. only..., but also...** non seulement..., mais encore...; **n. yet** pas encore; **n. that I minded** non pas que ça me dérangeait; **n. that it matters** non pas que ça ait de l'importance; **n. that I know of** pas que je sache

notable ['nəʊtəbəl] *adj (person, thing)* notable; *(achievement, success)* remarquable; **with a few n. exceptions** à quelques exceptions près, et non des moindres

notably ['nəʊtəblɪ] *adv* notamment

notary ['nəʊtərɪ] *(pl* **notaries**) *n Law* **n. (public)** notaire *m*

notation [nəʊ'teɪʃən] *n* notation *f*

notch [nɒtʃ] **1** *n* (**a**) *(in stick)* encoche *f*; *(in belt)* cran *m* (**b**) *(grade, level)* cran *m*
2 *vt* encocher

▸**notch up** *vt sep (victory, sale)* remporter; *(points)* marquer

note [nəʊt] **1** *n* (**a**) *(information, reminder)* note *f*; *(short letter)* mot *m*; **(lecture) notes** notes *fpl* (de cours); **to take** *ou* **make a n. of sth** prendre note de qch; **to take n. of sb/sth** remarquer qn/qch (**b**) *(musical)* note *f*; *Fig (of impatience, anger)* pointe *f*; **on a lighter/more serious n.** pour en venir à un sujet moins/plus sérieux (**c**) *(banknote)* billet *m* (**d**) *(significance)* **of n.** *(event)* remarquable; *(person)* éminent(e)
2 *vt* noter, remarquer; *(error)* relever; *(fact)* constater

▸**note down** *vt sep* prendre note de, noter

notebook ['nəʊtbʊk] *n* carnet *m*; *(larger)* cahier *m*; *Comput* **n. (computer)** portable *m*, ordinateur *m* bloc-notes

noted ['nəʊtɪd] *adj* éminent(e); **to be n. for sth** être réputé(e) pour qch

notepad ['nəʊtpæd] *n* bloc-notes *m*

notepaper ['nəʊtpeɪpə(r)] *n* papier *m* à lettres

noteworthy ['nəʊtwɜːðɪ] *adj* remarquable

nothing ['nʌθɪŋ] **1** *pron* rien; **n. happened** il ne s'est rien passé; **I have n. to do** je n'ai rien à faire; **to have n. to do with sb/sth** *(be unconnected to)* n'avoir rien à voir avec qn/qch; *(not get involved with)* n'avoir rien à faire avec qn/qch; **to say n. of...** sans parler de...; **she was n. if not discreet** elle a été très discrète; **n. new/ remarkable** rien de nouveau/d'exceptionnel; **n. but** rien que; **n. else** rien d'autre; **n. much** pas grandchose; **there is n. more to be said** il n'y a plus rien à dire; **there's n. like a nice steak!** rien de tel qu'un bon steak!; **as a pianist, he has n. on his brother** en tant que pianiste, son frère n'a rien à lui envier; **there's n. in it** *(it's untrue)* il n'y a rien de vrai dans tout ça; **to think n. of doing sth** trouver normal de faire qch; *Fam* **there's n. to it** ce n'est pas sorcier; **£1,000 is n. to her** 1000 livres, ce n'est rien pour elle; **to get angry/worried for** *or* **about n.** se fâcher/s'inquiéter pour un rien; **to do sth for n.** *(in vain, free of charge)* faire qch pour rien
2 *n* **to come to n.** être anéanti(e); **a hundred pounds? – a mere n.!** cent livres? – une bagatelle!
3 *adv* **she looks n. like her sister** elle ne ressemble

n. que ça lui plaise ou non; **I think/hope n.** je pense/

pas du tout à sa sœur; **it was n. like as difficult as they said** c'était loin d'être aussi difficile qu'on le disait

notice ['nəʊtɪs] **1** *n* (**a**) *(warning)* avertissement *m*; *(of resignation, redundancy)* préavis *m*; **to give sb n. (of sth)** avertir qn (de qch); *(of resignation, redundancy)* donner un préavis à qn (pour qch); **until further n.** jusqu'à nouvel ordre; **at short n.** au pied levé; **at a moment's n.** sur-le-champ; **to give in one's n.** *(resign)* donner sa démission, démissionner; **to give sb n.** *(of employer)* licencier qn (**b**) *(attention)* **to take n. of sb/sth** faire *ou* prêter attention à qn/qch; **to take no n. of sb/sth** ne pas prêter la moindre attention à qn/qch; **the fact escaped everyone's n.** ce fait a échappé à tout le monde; **it has come to my n. that...** *(I was told)* on m'a signalé que...; *(I read it)* je me suis rendu compte que... (**c**) *(sign)* écriteau *m*, pancarte *f*; *(poster)* affiche *f* (**d**) *(criticism of play, film)* critique *f*
2 *vt* remarquer, s'apercevoir de; **to be noticed, to get oneself noticed** se faire remarquer
3 *vi* remarquer

noticeable ['nəʊtɪsəbəl] *adj (change, difference)* sensible, perceptible; **it was n. that...** il était évident que...

noticeably ['nəʊtɪsəblɪ] *adv* sensiblement

noticeboard ['nəʊtɪsbɔːd] *n* panneau *m* d'affichage

notification [nəʊtɪfɪ'keɪʃən] *n* avis *m*, notification *f*; **to give sb n. of sth** avertir qn de qch

notify ['nəʊtɪfaɪ] *(pt & pp* **notified**) *vt* annoncer, notifier; **to n. sb of sth** avertir qn de qch

notion ['nəʊʃən] *n* notion *f*; **to have a n. that...** avoir dans l'idée que...; **to have a n. to do sth** avoir envie de faire qch

notoriety [nəʊtə'raɪətɪ] *n* notoriété *f*; **to achieve** *or* **gain n.** se rendre célèbre

notorious [nəʊ'tɔːrɪəs] *adj* tristement célèbre; *(criminal)* notoire; *(place)* mal famé(e); *(liar)* fieffé(e)

notoriously [nəʊ'tɔːrɪəslɪ] *adv* **to be n. tactless/rude** être bien connu(e) pour son manque de tact/son impolitesse; **Scottish weather is n. unpredictable** il est bien connu qu'en Écosse, le temps est très changeant

notwithstanding [nɒtwɪθ'stændɪŋ] *Formal* **1** *prep* en dépit de, malgré
2 *adv* néanmoins; **difficulties n.,...** ces difficultés mises à part,...

nougat ['nuːgɑː] *n* nougat *m*

nought [nɔːt] *n* zéro *m*; **noughts and crosses** ≃ morpion *m (jeu)*

noughties ['nɔːtɪz] *npl Fam* années *fpl* deux mille à deux mille dix

noun [naʊn] *n* nom *m*

nourish ['nʌrɪʃ] *vt* nourrir

nourishing ['nʌrɪʃɪŋ] *adj* nourrissant(e)

nourishment ['nʌrɪʃmənt] *n* nourriture *f*; *(nourishing quality)* richesse *f* nutritive

nous [naʊs] *n Br Fam (common sense)* sens commun, bon sens

Nov *(abbr* **November**) novembre

Nova Scotia ['nəʊvə'skəʊʃə] *n* la Nouvelle-Écosse

novel ['nɒvəl] **1** *n* roman *m*
2 *adj (original)* nouveau(elle), original(e)

novelist ['nɒvəlɪst] *n* romancier(ère) *m,f*

novelty ['nɒvəltɪ] *(pl* **novelties**) *n (newness)* nouveauté *f*; *(cheap object)* bricole *f*; **the n. will soon wear off** l'attrait de la nouveauté ne tardera pas à s'estomper; **n. value** attrait *m* de la nouveauté

November [nəʊ'vembə(r)] *n* novembre *m*; *see also* **May**

novice ['nɒvɪs] *n (beginner)* débutant(e) *m,f* (**at** en); *Rel* novice *mf*

now [naʊ] **1** *adv* (**a**) *(at this moment, these days)* maintenant; **it's n.** *or* **never** c'est maintenant ou jamais; **that'll do for n.** ça suffit pour le moment; **it's two years n.** **since his mother died** ça fait maintenant deux ans que sa mère est morte; **she won't be long n.** elle ne va plus tarder; **any minute/day n.** d'une minute/d'un jour à l'autre; **n. is the time to...** c'est le moment de...; **right n.** *(immediately)* tout de suite; *(at the moment)* pour le moment; **(every) n.** **and then, (every) n.** **and again** de temps en temps, de temps à autre; **up to** *or* **until n.** jusqu'à présent ou maintenant; **from n. on** dorénavant; **in three days from n.** dans trois jours; **she ought to be here by n.** elle devrait déjà être ici; **and n. for some music** et maintenant, un peu de musique (**b**) *(before statement, argument)* bon; **n., there are two ways of interpreting this** bon, il y a deux interprétations possibles; **come n.!** allons!; **n., n.!** **stop quarrelling!** allons, allons! arrêtez de vous disputer! **2** *conj* **n. (that)...** maintenant que...; **n. (that) you mention it,...** maintenant que tu le dis,...

nowadays ['naʊədeɪz] *adv* de nos jours

nowhere ['nəʊweə(r)] **1** *adv* nulle part; **n. else** nulle part ailleurs; **she was n. to be found** elle était introuvable; **qualifications alone will get you n.** les diplômes seuls ne servent à rien; **to be n. near as nice/stupid (as)** être loin d'être aussi agréable/stupide (que); **it's n. near the shopping centre** c'est à des kilomètres du centre commercial; **to finish n.** *(in contest)* finir loin derrière les autres; *Fam* **we're getting n. fast** on perd notre temps **2** *n* **in the middle of n.** dans un coin paumé; **he came from n. to win the race** il a gagné la course après une remontée spectaculaire

noxious ['nɒkʃəs] *adj* nocif(ive)

nozzle ['nɒzəl] *n (of petrol pump)* pistolet *m*; *(of vacuum cleaner)* suceur *m*; *(of pipe)* jet *m*; *(for icing)* douille *f*

nr *(abbr* **near)** près de

NRA [enɑː'reɪ] *n Am (abbr* **National Rifle Association)** = association américaine favorable à la généralisation des armes à feu

NSPCC [enespiːsiː'siː] *n Br (abbr* **National Society for the Prevention of Cruelty to Children)** = comité britannique pour la protection des enfants maltraités

nth [enθ] *adj Fam* énième

nuance ['njuːɒns] *n* nuance *f*

nub [nʌb] *n (of question, argument)* cœur *m*

nubile ['njuːbaɪl] *adj* désirable

nuclear ['njuːklɪə(r)] *adj* nucléaire; **n. bomb** bombe *f* atomique; **n. disarmament** désarmement *m* nucléaire; **n. energy** énergie *f* nucléaire *ou* atomique; **n. family** famille *f* nucléaire; **n. physics** physique *f* nucléaire; **n. power** énergie *f* nucléaire; **n. power station** centrale *f* atomique *ou* nucléaire; **n. reactor** réacteur *m* nucléaire; **n. war** guerre *f* atomique *ou* nucléaire; **n. waste** déchets *mpl* nucléaires; **n. weapon** arme *f* atomique *ou* nucléaire; **n. winter** hiver *m* nucléaire

nuclear-free zone ['njuːklɪəfriː'zəʊn] *n* zone *f* dénucléarisée

nucleus ['njuːklɪəs] *(pl* **nuclei** ['njuːklɪaɪ]) *n also Fig* noyau *m*

nude [njuːd] **1** *n* nu *m*; **in the n.** tout(e) nu(e) **2** *adj* nu(e)

nudge [nʌdʒ] **1** *n* coup *m* de coude **2** *vt* donner un coup de coude à

nudist ['njuːdɪst] *n* nudiste *mf*; **n. camp** *or* **colony** camp *m* de nudistes

nudity ['njuːdɪtɪ] *n* nudité *f*

nugatory ['njuːgətɒrɪ] *adj* sans valeur

nugget ['nʌgɪt] *n (of gold)* pépite *f*; *Fig* **a n. of information** un renseignement précieux

nuisance ['njuːsəns] *n* **to be a n.** *(of person, situation)* être embêtant(e); **to make a n. of oneself** embêter le monde; **n. call** *(on telephone)* appel *m* anonyme

nuke [njuːk] *vt Fam* lâcher la bombe sur

null [nʌl] *adj* nul (nulle); **n. and void** nul et non avenu

nullify ['nʌlɪfaɪ] *(pt & pp* **nullified)** *vt* annuler; *(decree)* invalider

NUM [enjuː'em] *n Br (abbr* **National Union of Mineworkers)** = syndicat britannique de mineurs

numb [nʌm] **1** *adj* engourdi(e); **to go n.** s'engourdir; **n. with cold** engourdi par le froid; **n. with fear** paralysé(e) par la peur **2** *vt (of cold)* engourdir; *(of fear)* paralyser

number ['nʌmbə(r)] **1** *n* (**a**) *(numeral)* nombre *m*; *(when written)* chiffre *m*; *Comput* **n. crunching** calculs *mpl* (rapides) (**b**) *(of house, page, telephone)* numéro *m*; **I live at n. 40** j'habite au (numéro) 40; **(telephone) n.** numéro de téléphone; *Fam* **to look after n. one** s'occuper de sa petite personne; *Br* **N. Ten** le dix Downing Street *(résidence du premier ministre britannique)* (**c**) *(quantity)* nombre *m*; **a large n. of** un grand nombre de; **in small/great numbers** en petit/grand nombre (**d**) *(song)* chanson *f* (**e**) *(idioms)* **he's my n. two** *(subordinate)* c'est mon adjoint; *Fam* **I've got your n.!** je sais ce que tu as en tête!; *Fam* **his n.'s up** son compte est bon; *Fam* **that car/dress is a nice little n.** c'est une jolie petite voiture/robe; *Fam* **she's got a nice little n. there** *(situation)* elle s'est dégoté un bon plan **2** *vt* (**a**) *(assign number to)* numéroter (**b**) *(count)* compter; **his days are numbered** ses jours sont comptés; **to n. sb among one's friends** compter qn parmi ou au nombre de ses amis

number-cruncher ['nʌmbəkrʌntʃə(r)] *n Fam* (**a**) *(person)* comptable *mf* (**b**) *(computer)* ordinateur *m* puissant *(pour le traitement de données numériques)*

numberplate ['nʌmbəpleɪt] *n Br* plaque *f* d'immatriculation *ou* minéralogique

numbly ['nʌmlɪ] *adv (say, react)* mollement; *(stare)* d'un air hébété

numbness ['nʌmnɪs] *n (in body)* engourdissement *m*; *(of emotions)* torpeur *f*

numbskull ['nʌmskʌl] *n Fam* bêta(asse) *m,f*

numeracy ['njuːmərəsɪ] *n* degré *m* d'aptitude en calcul

numeral ['njuːmərəl] *n* chiffre *m*

numerate ['njuːmərət] *adj* **to be n.** savoir compter

numerator ['njuːməreɪtə(r)] *n Math* numérateur *m*

numerical [njuː'merɪkəl] *adj* numérique

numerically [njuː'merɪklɪ] *adv* numériquement

numerous ['njuːmərəs] *adj* nombreux(euse); **on n. occasions** en de nombreuses occasions

nun [nʌn] *n* religieuse *f*, nonne *f*; **to become a n.** prendre la voile

nunnery ['nʌnərɪ] *(pl* **nunneries)** *n* couvent *m*

nuptial ['nʌpʃəl] **1** *n Hum ou Lit* **nuptials** noces *fpl* **2** *adj Lit* nuptial(e)

nurse [nɜːs] **1** n (**a**) (medical) infirmière f; (**male**) n. infirmier m (**b**) (childminder) nurse f **2** vt (look after) soigner; (suckle) allaiter; Fig (feeling, hope) nourrir; (grievance) entretenir; **to n. sb back to health** faire recouvrer la santé à qn
nursery ['nɜːsərɪ] (pl **nurseries**) n (**a**) (for children) (establishment) garderie f; (room in house) chambre f d'enfants; **n. education** enseignement m en maternelle; **n. rhyme** comptine f; **n.** (**school**) maternelle f; **n. slopes** (in skiing) pistes fpl pour débutants (**b**) (for plants) pépinière f
nursing ['nɜːsɪŋ] n (profession) profession f d'infirmière; (care) soins mpl; **n. home** (for old people) maison f de retraite; (for convalescents) maison f de repos; **n. mother** mère f qui allaite; **n. staff** personnel m soignant
nurture ['nɜːtʃə(r)] vt (**a**) (feed) (children, plants) nourrir; (plan, idea) élaborer (**b**) (bring up) faire l'éducation de
NUS [enjuːˈes] n Br (abbr **National Union of Students**) = syndicat britannique d'étudiants
NUT [enjuːˈtiː] n Br (abbr **National Union of Teachers**) = syndicat britannique d'enseignants
nut [nʌt] n (**a**) (food) = noix, noisette, cacahuète, pistache ou autre fruit sec de cette nature; Fig **he's a hard** or **tough n.** c'est un dur; Fig **a tough** or **hard n. to crack** (problem) un problème difficile à résoudre (**b**) Fam (head) caboche f; **to do one's n.** piquer une crise (**c**) Fam (mad person) dingue mf; **a tennis n.** un dingue de tennis (**d**) (for fastening bolt) écrou m; Fig **the nuts and bolts** les notions fpl de base (**e**) very Fam **nuts** (testicles) couilles fpl

nutcase ['nʌtkeɪs] n Fam cinglé(e) m,f
nutcrackers ['nʌtkrækəz] npl (**pair of**) n. casse-noisettes m inv, casse-noix m inv
nuthouse ['nʌthaʊs] n Fam maison f de fous
nutmeg ['nʌtmeg] n (noix f de) muscade f
nutrient ['njuːtrɪənt] **1** n élément m nutritif **2** adj nutritif(ive)
nutrition [njuːˈtrɪʃən] n nutrition f
nutritional [njuːˈtrɪʃənəl] adj nutritionnel(elle); (value) nutritif(ive)
nutritious [njuːˈtrɪʃəs] adj nutritif(ive)
nuts [nʌts] adj Fam (mad) dingue; **to be n. about sb/sth** être dingue de qn/qch
nutshell ['nʌtʃel] n coquille f de noix/noisette/etc; Fig **in a n.,...** bref,...
nutter ['nʌtə(r)] n Br Fam (mad person) dingue mf
nutty ['nʌtɪ] adj (**a**) (in taste) au goût de noisette/noix/etc; (containing nuts) aux noisettes/noix/etc (**b**) Fam (mad) dingue
nuzzle ['nʌzəl] **1** vt renifler **2** vi **to n. against sb** renifler qn
NVQ [enviːˈkjuː] n Br (abbr **National Vocational Qualification**) = diplôme professionnel destiné notamment aux personnes travaillant déjà
NW (abbr **northwest**) N-O
NY [enˈweɪ] n Am (abbr **New York**) NewYork
nylon ['naɪlɒn] n Nylon® m; **nylons** (stockings) bas mpl Nylon®
nymph [nɪmf] n nymphe f
nymphomania [nɪmfəʊˈmeɪnɪə] n nymphomanie f
nymphomaniac [nɪmfəʊˈmeɪnɪæk] n nymphomane f
NZ (abbr **New Zealand**) la Nouvelle-Zélande

O, o [əʊ] *n* (**a**) *(letter)* O, o *m inv*; *Br Formerly Sch* O
level = diplôme de fin de premier cycle de l'enseignement secondaire, sanctionnant une matière déterminée; *Br Formerly Sch* **O levels** ≃ brevet *m* des
collèges (**b**) *(zero)* zéro *m*

oaf [əʊf] *n* lourdaud *m*

oak [əʊk] *n* chêne *m*; **o. apple** noix *f* de galle

OAP [əʊeɪˈpiː] *n Br (abbr* **old age pensioner)** retraité(e)
m,f

oar [ɔː(r)] *n* aviron *m*, rame *f*; *Fig* **to put** *or* **stick one's o.
in** mettre son grain de sel

oarsman [ˈɔːzmən] *n* rameur *m*

oarswoman [ˈɔːzwʊmən] *n* rameuse *f*

OAS [əʊeɪˈes] *n (abbr* **Organization of American
States)** OEA *f*

oasis [əʊˈeɪsɪs] *(pl* **oases** [əʊˈeɪsiːz]) *n also Fig* oasis *f*

oatcake [ˈəʊtkeɪk] *n* galette *f* d'avoine

oath [əʊθ] *n* (**a**) *(pledge)* serment *m*; **o. of allegiance**
serment *m* d'allégeance; **to take** *or* **swear an o.** prêter serment; **on** *or* **under o.** sous serment (**b**) *(swear
word)* juron *m*

oatmeal [ˈəʊtmiːl] *n* farine *f* d'avoine; *(colour)* beige *m*

oats [əʊts] *npl (plant)* avoine *f*; **(porridge) o.** *(food)* flocons *mpl* d'avoine; *Br very Fam* **to get one's o.** s'envoyer en l'air

OAU [əʊeɪˈjuː] *n (abbr* **Organization of African Unity)**
OUA *f*

obdurate [ˈɒbdjʊrɪt] *adj* obstiné(e)

OBE [əʊbiːˈiː] *n Br (abbr* **Officer of the Order of the
British Empire)** = titre honorifique britannique

obedience [əˈbiːdɪəns] *n* obéissance *f*

obedient [əˈbiːdɪənt] *adj* obéissant(e)

obelisk [ˈɒbəlɪsk] *n* obélisque *m*

obese [əʊˈbiːs] *adj* obèse

obesity [əʊˈbiːsɪtɪ] *n* obésité *f*

obey [əˈbeɪ] **1** *vt* obéir à
  2 *vi* obéir

obfuscation [ɒbfʌˈskeɪʃən] *n* obscurcissement *m*

obituary [əˈbɪtjʊərɪ] *(pl* **obituaries)** *n* nécrologie *f*; **o.
column** rubrique *f* nécrologique; **o. notice** nécrologie
f

object 1 *n* [ˈɒbdʒɪkt] (**a**) *(thing, recipient)* objet *m*; **an
o. of contempt/desire** un objet de mépris/de désir;
an o. lesson in un parfait exemple de (**b**) *(aim)* objet
m, but *m*; **the o. of the exercise is to...** cet exercice a
pour objet *ou* but de... (**c**) *(obstacle)* **money/distance
is no o.** le prix/la distance importe peu (**d**) *Gram*
complément *m* d'objet
  2 *vi* [əbˈdʒekt] émettre une objection; **to o. to sth/
to doing sth** ne pas être d'accord avec qch/pour
faire qch

objectify [əbˈdʒektɪfaɪ] *vt* objectiver

objection [əbˈdʒekʃən] *n* (**a**) *(protest)* objection *f*; **to
have no o. to sth** ne voir aucune objection à qch; **I
have no o. to going** ça ne me dérange pas d'y aller
(**b**) *(reason for objecting)* inconvénient *m* (**to** de)

objectionable [əbˈdʒekʃənəbəl] *adj (unpleasant)*
déplaisant(e)

objective [əbˈdʒektɪv] **1** *n (aim, goal)* objectif *m*
  2 *adj (impartial)* objectif(ive)

objectively [ɒbˈdʒektɪvlɪ] *adv* objectivement

objectivity [ɒbdʒekˈtɪvɪtɪ] *n* objectivité *f*

obligation [ɒblɪˈɡeɪʃən] *n* obligation *f*; **to be under an
o. to sb** avoir une dette envers qn; **to be under an o.
to do sth** être dans l'obligation de faire qch

obligatory [ɒˈblɪɡətərɪ] *adj* obligatoire

oblige [əˈblaɪdʒ] *vt* (**a**) *(compel)* obliger; **to be obliged
to do sth** être obligé(e) de faire qch (**b**) *(do a favour
for)* rendre service à (**c**) *(be grateful)* **to be obliged to
sb** être reconnaissant(e) à qn; **I'd be obliged if
you'd...** ça me rendrait service si vous pouviez...;
much obliged merci infiniment

obliging [əˈblaɪdʒɪŋ] *adj* serviable; **it was very o. of
her** c'était très aimable de sa part

oblique [əˈbliːk] *adj (line, angle)* oblique; *(reference,
hint)* indirect(e)

obliterate [əˈblɪtəreɪt] *vt* (**a**) *also Fig (erase)* effacer
(**b**) *(destroy)* détruire; *(town)* rayer de la carte

oblivion [əˈblɪvɪən] *n* oubli *m*; **to sink into o.** sombrer
dans l'oubli

oblivious [əˈblɪvɪəs] *adj* **to be o. to sth** ne pas avoir
conscience de qch

oblong [ˈɒblɒŋ] **1** *n* rectangle *m*
  2 *adj* rectangulaire

obnoxious [əbˈnɒkʃəs] *adj (person, action)* odieux(-
euse); *(smell)* repoussant(e)

oboe [ˈəʊbəʊ] *n* hautbois *m*

oboist [ˈəʊbəʊɪst] *n* hautboïste *mf*

obscene [əbˈsiːn] *adj* obscène; *Fig (profits, prices)*
scandaleux(euse)

obscenely [əbˈsiːnlɪ] *adv* d'une manière obscène; *Fig
(rich)* scandaleusement

obscenity [əbˈsenɪtɪ] *(pl* **obscenities)** *n* obscénité *f*

obscure [əbˈskjʊə(r)] **1** *adj* obscur(e)
  2 *vt* (**a**) *(hide from view)* cacher (**b**) *(make unclear)*
obscurcir

obscurity [əbˈskjʊərɪtɪ] *n* obscurité *f*; **to fall into o.**
tomber dans l'oubli

obsequious [əbˈsiːkwɪəs] *adj Formal* obsé-
quieux(euse)

observable [əbˈzɜːvəbəl] *adj* observable; *(change,
difference)* perceptible

observance [əbˈzɜːvəns] *n (of law, custom)* observation *f*

observant [əbˈzɜːvənt] *adj* observateur(trice)

observation [ɒbzəˈveɪʃən] *n* observation *f; (by police)* surveillance *f;* **to keep sb under o.** surveiller qn; *(in hospital)* garder qn en observation; **to escape o.** passer inaperçu(e); **to make an o.** faire une observation; *Mil* **o. post** poste *m* d'observation

observatory [əbˈzɜːvətərɪ] *(pl* **observatories)** *n* observatoire *m*

observe [əbˈzɜːv] *vt* observer

observer [əbˈzɜːvə(r)] *n* observateur(trice) *m,f*

obsess [əbˈses] *vt* obséder; **to be obsessed with** *or* **by sb** faire une fixation sur qn; **to be obsessed with** *or* **by sth** être obsédé(e) par qch

obsession [əbˈseʃən] *n* obsession *f;* **to become an o.** tourner à l'obsession

obsessive [əbˈsesɪv] *adj (person)* à tendances obsessionnelles; *(fear, hatred, behaviour)* obsessionnel(elle)

obsolescence [ɒbsəˈlesəns] *n* obsolescence *f*

obsolete [ˈɒbsəliːt] *adj* obsolète; *(design, model)* dépassé(e), démodé(e)

obstacle [ˈɒbstəkəl] *n* obstacle *m;* **to put obstacles in sb's way** mettre des bâtons dans les roues à qn; *also Fig* **o. course** course *f* d'obstacles

obstetrician [ɒbsteˈtrɪʃən] *n* obstétricien(enne) *m,f*

obstetrics [ɒbˈstetrɪks] *n* obstétrique *f*

obstinacy [ˈɒbstɪnəsɪ] *n* obstination *f*

obstinate [ˈɒbstɪnət] *adj* obstiné(e); **to be o. about doing sth** s'obstiner à vouloir faire qch

obstreperous [əbˈstrepərəs] *adj Formal* tapageur(euse); **to get o. (about sth)** faire un scandale (à propos de qch)

obstruct [əbˈstrʌkt] *vt* (**a**) *(block) (road, pipe)* obstruer; *(view)* boucher, cacher (**b**) *(hinder)* gêner; *(in sport)* faire obstruction à; *Pol* **to o. a bill** faire de l'obstruction; *Law* **to o. the course of justice** entraver le cours de la justice

obstruction [əbˈstrʌkʃən] *n* (**a**) *(action)* obstruction *f* (**b**) *(blockage) (in road)* encombrement *m; (in pipe)* engorgement *m; Med* obstruction *f;* **to cause an o.** *(on road)* entraver la circulation

obstructive [əbˈstrʌktɪv] *adj* **to be o.** faire de l'obstruction

obtain [əbˈteɪn] **1** *vt* obtenir
2 *vi Formal (of practice)* avoir cours; *(of rule)* être en vigueur

obtainable [əbˈteɪnəbəl] *adj* que l'on peut se procurer; **easily o.** facile à obtenir

obtrusive [əbˈtruːsɪv] *adj (person, behaviour)* importun(e); *(smell)* pénétrant(e)

obtuse [əbˈtjuːs] *adj* obtus(e)

obverse [ˈɒbvɜːs] **1** *n* (**a**) *(of medal)* avers *m* (**b**) *(opposite)* contraire *m*
2 *adj* **o. side** *(of medal)* avers *m*

obviate [ˈɒbvɪeɪt] *vt Formal (difficulty, danger)* parer à

obvious [ˈɒbvɪəs] **1** *n* **to state the o.** enfoncer une porte ouverte
2 *adj* évident(e)

obviously [ˈɒbvɪəslɪ] *adv* (**a**) *(in an obvious way)* manifestement (**b**) *(of course)* évidemment; **o. not** certainement pas

occasion [əˈkeɪʒən] **1** *n* (**a**) *(time)* occasion *f;* **on one o.** une fois; **on several occasions** plusieurs fois, à plusieurs reprises; **on o.** parfois, de temps en temps (**b**) *(event)* occasion *f*, événement *m;* **on the o. of...** à l'occasion de...; **to have a sense of o.** savoir marquer le

coup (**c**) *(opportunity)* occasion *f;* **I'd like to take this o. to...** j'aimerais profiter de cette occasion pour... (**d**) *Formal (cause)* sujet *m*, cause *f;* **to have o. for complaint** avoir des raisons de se plaindre; **to have o. to do sth** avoir lieu de faire qch
2 *vt Formal (cause)* occasionner, causer

occasional [əˈkeɪʒənəl] *adj* occasionnel(elle); *(showers)* intermittent(e); **I have the o. cigar** il m'arrive de fumer un cigare de temps en temps; **o. table** table *f* d'appoint

occasionally [əˈkeɪʒənəlɪ] *adv* occasionnellement, de temps en temps

occidental [ɒksɪˈdentəl] *adj* occidental(e)

occult [ɒˈkʌlt] **1** *n* **the o.** l'occulte *m*
2 *adj* occulte

occupant [ˈɒkjupənt] *n (of house, car)* occupant(e) *m,f; (of bus, plane)* passager(ère) *m,f*

occupation [ɒkjuˈpeɪʃən] *n* (**a**) *(profession)* métier *m*, profession *f; (pastime)* occupation *f* (**b**) *(of house, land)* occupation *f*

occupational [ɒkjuˈpeɪʃənəl] *adj* **o. disease** maladie *f* professionnelle; **o. hazard** risque *m* du métier; **o. therapist** ergothérapeute *mf;* **o. therapy** ergothérapie *f*

occupied [ˈɒkjupaɪd] *adj* occupé(e); **to be o. with sth** être occupé à qch; **to keep sb o.** occuper qn

occupier [ˈɒkjupaɪə(r)] *n (of house)* occupant(e) *m,f*

occupy [ˈɒkjupaɪ] *(pt & pp* **occupied)** *vt (house, attention)* occuper; **to o. one's time (in doing sth)** occuper son temps (à faire qch)

occur [əˈkɜː(r)] *(pt & pp* **occurred)** *vi* (**a**) *(happen) (of event)* avoir lieu; *(of opportunity)* se présenter; *(of problem)* surgir (**b**) *(be present)* apparaître (**c**) *(of idea)* **to o. to sb** venir à l'esprit de qn

occurrence [əˈkʌrəns] *n* (**a**) *(event)* événement *m* (**b**) *(of disease)* incidence *f;* **to be a regular o.** se produire régulièrement

OCD [əʊsiːˈdiː] *n Psy (abbr* **obsessive compulsive disorder)** TOC *m*

ocean [ˈəʊʃən] *n* océan *m; Am* **the o.** *(the sea)* la mer; *Fam* **oceans of** plein de; **o. liner** paquebot *m*

ocean-going [ˈəʊʃəngəʊɪŋ] *adj* de haute mer

Oceania [əʊʃɪˈeɪnɪə] *n* l'Océanie *f*

oceanic [əʊʃɪˈænɪk] *adj* océanique

ocelot [ˈɒsəlɒt] *n* ocelot *m*

ochre, *Am* **ocher** [ˈəʊkə(r)] **1** *n* ocre *m*
2 *adj* ocre *inv*

o'clock [əˈklɒk] *adv* **(it's) one o.** (il est) une heure; **two o.** deux heures

OCR [əʊsiːˈɑː(r)] *n Comput* (**a**) *(abbr* **optical character reader)** lecteur *m* optique (**b**) *(abbr* **optical character recognition)** ROC *f*

Oct *(abbr* **October)** octobre

octagon [ˈɒktəgən] *n* octogone *m*

octagonal [ɒkˈtægənəl] *adj* octogonal(e)

octane [ˈɒkteɪn] *n Chem* octane *m;* **o. number** indice *m* d'octane

octave [ˈɒktɪv] *n* octave *f*

October [ɒkˈtəʊbə(r)] *n* octobre *m; see also* **May**

octogenarian [ɒktədʒɪˈneərɪən] **1** *n* octogénaire *mf*
2 *adj* octogénaire

octopus [ˈɒktəpəs] *n* pieuvre *f*, poulpe *m*

OD [əʊˈdiː] *(pt & pp* **OD'd, OD'ed)** *vi Fam (abbr* **overdose)** faire une overdose (**on** de); *Fig* **I think I've rather OD'd on pizzas** je crois que j'y suis allé un peu fort sur les pizzas

odd [ɒd] **1** *adj* (**a**) *(strange)* bizarre, curieux(euse) (**b**) *(number)* impair(e); **to be the o.** man out être à part; **I felt the o. one out** je ne me suis pas senti à ma place (**c**) *(one of a pair)* dépareillé(e) (**d**) *(occasional)* **I smoke the o. cigarette** il m'arrive de fumer une cigarette de temps en temps; **you've made the o. mistake** tu as fait deux ou trois fautes; **o. jobs** petits travaux *mpl*
2 *adv* **a hundred o. sheep** cent et quelques moutons; **she must be thirty o.** elle doit avoir trente ans ou plus
oddball ['ɒdbɔːl] *n Fam* excentrique *mf*
oddity ['ɒdɪtɪ] (*pl* **oddities**) *n* (**a**) *(strangeness)* bizarrerie *f* (**b**) *(person) (strange)* excentrique *mf*; *(exceptional)* cas *m* à part; *(thing)* curiosité *f*
oddly ['ɒdlɪ] *adv* bizarrement, curieusement; **o. enough,...** chose curieuse,...
oddness ['ɒdnɪs] *n* bizarrerie *f*
odds [ɒdz] *npl* (**a**) *(probability)* chances *fpl*; *(in betting)* cote *f*; **the o. are that...** il y a de grandes chances pour que... + *subjunctive*; **the o. are against her/in her favour** il y a peu de chance(s)/de grosses chances qu'elle réussisse; **against the o.** contre toute attente; **to pay over the o. (for sth)** payer (qch) plus cher que le tarif normal; *Fam* **it makes no o.** ça n'a pas d'importance (**b**) **to be at o. (with sb)** *(of person)* être en désaccord (avec qn); **to be at o. with sth** *(of thing)* contredire qch (**c**) *Fam* **o. and ends, o. and sods** bricoles *fpl*
odds-on [ɒdz'ɒn] *adj* (*horse*) **o. favourite** grand favori *m*; *Fam* **it's o. that...** il y a gros à parier que...
ode [əʊd] *n* ode *f*
odious ['əʊdɪəs] *adj* odieux(euse)
odour, *Am* **odor** ['əʊdə(r)] *n* odeur *f*
odourless, *Am* **odorless** ['əʊdəlɪs] *adj* inodore
odyssey ['ɒdɪsɪ] (*pl* **odysseys**) *n* odyssée *f*
OECD [əʊiːsiː'diː] *n* (*abbr* **Organization for Economic Co-operation and Development**) OCDE *f*
Oedipal ['iːdɪpəl] *adj* oedipien(enne)
oesophagus, *Am* **esophagus** [iː'sɒfəgəs] (*pl* **oesophagi**, *Am* **esophagi** [iː'sɒfəgaɪ]) *n* œsophage *m*
oestrogen, *Am* **estrogen** ['iːstrədʒən] *n* œstrogène *m*
of [ɒv, *unstressed* əv] *prep* (**a**) *(belonging to)* de; **a friend of mine** un de mes amis; **a car of her own** une voiture à elle; **the University of Manchester** l'université de Manchester (**b**) *(with amount, quantity)* **a litre of milk** un litre de lait; **a bottle of wine** une bouteille de vin; **a year of her life** un an de sa vie; **many of us** beaucoup d'entre nous; **there are six of us** nous sommes six; **hundreds of people** des centaines de gens; **a girl of ten** une fille de dix ans; **you of all people should know that** si quelqu'un doit le savoir, c'est bien toi (**c**) *(indicating agency)* **it was nice/clever of you to...** c'était gentil/intelligent de ta part de... (**d**) *(with material)* **made of wood/glass** en bois/verre (**e**) *(with dates, time)* **the 4th of October** le 4 octobre; *Am* **a quarter of one** une heure moins le quart
off [ɒf] **1** *adj* (**a**) *(not functioning) (light, TV)* éteint(e); *(water, electricity)* coupé(e); **the rain is o.** il ne pleut plus; **o. and on, on and o.** *(intermittently)* par intermittence
(**b**) *(cancelled)* annulé(e); **the deal is o.** l'affaire ne se fera pas
(**c**) *(absent from work, school)* absent(e)
(**d**) *(food)* abîmé(e); *(milk)* tourné(e)

(**e**) *(unsuccessful)* **I'm having an o. day** c'est un jour sans; **the o. season** *(in tourism)* la morte-saison
(**f**) **to be well/badly o.** être aisé(e)/pauvre; **you'd be better o. staying where you are** tu ferais mieux de rester où tu es
2 *adv* (**a**) *(away)* **two weeks o.** dans deux semaines; **5 miles o.** ≃ à 8 kilomètres; **to be o.** *(leave)* s'en aller; **I'm o. to London** je pars pour Londres; **o. you go!** allez, file maintenant!
(**b**) *(indicating removal)* **to take o. one's coat** enlever son manteau; **the handle has come o.** la poignée est partie
(**c**) *(with prices)* **20 percent/£5 o.** 20 pour cent/5 livres de réduction
(**d**) *(away from work, school)* **to have a day/week o.** avoir un jour/une semaine de congé; **to take some time o.** prendre des vacances
3 *prep* (**a**) *(away from)* **o. the coast** au large de la côte; **the main road** qui donne dans la rue principale; **o. the record** officieusement
(**b**) *(indicating removal from)* **to fall/jump o. sth** tomber/sauter de qch; **the handle has come o. the saucepan** la poignée s'est détachée de la casserole
(**c**) *(with prices)* **20 percent/£5 o. the price** 20 pour cent/5 livres de réduction sur le prix
(**d**) *(absent from)* **to be o. work/school** être absent(e) de son travail/de l'école
(**e**) *(not liking)* **to be o. one's food** ne pas avoir d'appétit; **to go o. sb/sth** ne plus aimer qn/qch
(**f**) *Fam (from)* **to buy/borrow sth o. sb** acheter/emprunter qch à qn; **to get a cold o. sb** attraper le rhume de qn
offal ['ɒfəl] *n* abats *mpl*
offbeat ['ɒfbiːt] *adj Fam* original(e)
off-chance ['ɒftʃɑːns] *n* **on the o.** à tout hasard; **on the o. that...** en espérant que...
off-colour, *Am* **off-color** [ɒf'kʌlə(r)] *adj* (**a**) *Br (unwell)* **to be o.** ne pas se sentir dans son assiette (**b**) *(joke)* d'un goût douteux
offcut ['ɒfkʌt] *n* chute *f*
off-duty ['ɒf'djuːtɪ] *adj* qui n'est pas de service
offence, *Am* **offense** [ə'fens] *n* (**a**) *Law* infraction *f*; *(more serious)* délit *m* (**b**) *(displeasure)* **to cause sb o.** *(of person, remark)* vexer qn; *(of film, book)* choquer qn; **to take o.** se vexer; **to take o. at sth** mal prendre qch; **no o., but...** ne le prends pas mal, mais...
offend [ə'fend] **1** *vt (of person, remark)* vexer; *(of book, film)* choquer; **to be offended at** *or* **by sth** mal prendre qch
2 *vi Law* commettre une infraction; *(more serious)* commettre un délit; **to o. against good taste** être une insulte au bon goût
offended [ə'fendɪd] *adj* vexé(e)
offender [ə'fendə(r)] *n Law* délinquant(e) *m,f*
offending [ə'fendɪŋ] *adj* fautif(ive)
offense *Am* = **offence**
offensive [ə'fensɪv] **1** *n also Fig* offensive *f*; **to be on/to take the o.** être passé(e)/passer à l'attaque
2 *adj* choquant(e); *(smell)* repoussant(e); **to be o. to sb** se montrer blessant(e) envers qn; **o. weapon** arme *f* offensive
offer ['ɒfə(r)] **1** *n* offre *f*, proposition *f*; **to make sb an o.** faire une offre *ou* une proposition à qn; **on special o.** en promotion; **o. of marriage** demande *f* en mariage
2 *vt* offrir; *(explanation)* donner; *(apologies)* présenter;

to o. sb sth, to o. sth to sb offrir qch à qn; **to o. to do sth** offrir *ou* proposer de faire qch
▸**offer up** *vt sep* offrir
offering [ˈɒfərɪŋ] *n* offre *f*; *(in church)* offrande *f*
offhand [ɒfˈhænd] **1** *adj (nonchalant)* désinvolte; *(abrupt)* brusque, abrupt(e) **2** *adv (immediately)* au pied levé; *(at a rough guess)* à première vue
office [ˈɒfɪs] *n* (**a**) *(place)* bureau *m*; **o. boy** garçon *m* de bureau; **o. building** immeuble *m* de bureaux; **o. hours** heures *fpl* de bureau; **o. junior** = employé de bureau chargé de tâches mineures; **o. worker** employé(e) *m,f* de bureau (**b**) *(position)* charge *f*, fonctions *fpl*; **to hold o.** être au pouvoir; **to be out of o.** ne plus être au pouvoir; **to run for** *or* **to seek o.** se présenter aux élections
officeholder [ˈɒfɪshəʊldə(r)] *n* responsable *mf*
officer [ˈɒfɪsə(r)] *n (in army)* officier *m*; *(in police)* agent *m* de police; *(in local government)* fonctionnaire *mf* municipal(e)
official [əˈfɪʃəl] **1** *n (in public sector)* fonctionnaire *mf*; *(of political party)* responsable *mf* **2** *adj* officiel(elle); *Br* **O. Secrets Act** = document relatif au secret-défense, signé par tous les fonctionnaires
officialdom [əˈfɪʃəldəm] *n Pej* bureaucratie *f*
officialese [əfɪʃəˈliːz] *n Pej* jargon *m* administratif
officially [əˈfɪʃəlɪ] *adv* officiellement
officiate [əˈfɪʃɪeɪt] *vi Rel* officier
officious [əˈfɪʃəs] *adj* trop zélé(e)
officiously [əˈfɪʃəslɪ] *adv* avec trop de zèle
offie [ˈɒfɪ] *n Br Fam (abbr* **off-licence)** ≃ magasin *m* de vins et spiritueux
offing [ˈɒfɪŋ] *n* **in the o.** en perspective, en vue
off-key [ɒfˈkiː] **1** *adj* faux (fausse); *Fig (remark)* déplacé(e) **2** *adv* faux
off-licence [ˈɒflaɪsəns] *n Br* ≃ magasin *m* de vins et spiritueux
offline, off-line [ˈɒflaɪn] *adj Comput (processing)* en différé; *(printer)* déconnecté(e)
off-load [ˈɒfləʊd] *vt (surplus goods)* écouler; **to o. sth onto sb** *(task)* se décharger de qch sur qn; *(blame, responsibility)* rejeter qch sur qn; **to o. sb on sb** refiler qn à qn
off-peak [ˈɒfpiːk] *adj (electricity)* consommé(e) pendant les heures creuses; *(holidays)* en basse saison; *(telephone call, travel)* en dehors des heures de pointe
offprint [ˈɒfprɪnt] *n Typ* tirage *m* à part
off-putting [ˈɒfpʊtɪŋ] *adj* peu engageant(e)
off-sales [ˈɒfseɪlz] *n Br* = vente de boissons alcoolisées à emporter
off-season [ˈɒfsiːzən] *adj* hors saison, en basse saison
offset [ˈɒfset] **1** *n Typ* offset *m* **2** *vt (pt & pp* **offset**) compenser
offshoot [ˈɒfʃʊt] *n (of tree)* rejeton *m*; *(of family)* branche *f*; *(of political party, artistic movement)* ramification *f*
offshore 1 *adj* [ˈɒfʃɔː(r)] *(island)* proche de la côte; *(oil rig)* off shore *inv*; *Fin* **o. investment** placement *m* off-shore **2** *adv* [ɒfˈʃɔː(r)] au large, en mer **3** *vt* [ɒfˈʃɔː(r)] *(work, jobs)* délocaliser
offside 1 *n* [ˈɒfsaɪd] côté *m* du conducteur **2** *adj* (**a**) [ˈɒfsaɪd] *(of car)* côté conducteur (**b**) [ɒfˈsaɪd] *(in sport)* hors jeu

offspring [ˈɒfsprɪŋ] *n* progéniture *f*
offstage [ɒfˈsteɪdʒ] *adj & adv* dans les coulisses
off-the-cuff [ɒfðəˈkʌf] **1** *adj* impromptu(e) **2** *adv* au pied levé
off-the-record [ɒfðəˈrekɔːd] *adj* officieux(euse)
off-the-wall [ɒfðəˈwɔːl] *adj Fam* loufoque
off-white [ˈɒfˈwaɪt] **1** *n* blanc *m* cassé **2** *adj* blanc cassé *inv*
Ofgem [ˈɒfdʒem] *n Br (abbr* **Office of the Gas and Electricity Markets)** = organisme chargé de contrôler les activités des sociétés de distribution de gaz et d'électricité en Grande-Bretagne
OFSTED [ˈɒfsted] *n Br (abbr* **Office for Standards in Education)** = organisme chargé de veiller au maintien du niveau des élèves dans l'enseignement public en Grande-Bretagne
OFT [əʊefˈtiː] *n Br (abbr* **Office of FairTrading)** = organisme britannique de défense des consommateurs et de régulation des pratiques commerciales
OFTEL [ˈɒftel] *n Br (abbr* **Office of Telecommunications)** = organisme chargé de contrôler les activités des sociétés de télécommunications en Grande-Bretagne
often [ˈɒfən, ˈɒftən] *adv* souvent; **how o.?** *(how many times?)* combien de fois?; *(how frequently?)* tous les combien?; **as o. as not** très souvent; **more o. than not** le plus souvent; **every so o.** de temps en temps, de temps à autre
OFWAT [ˈɒfwɒt] *n Br (abbr* **Office of Water Services)** = organisme chargé de contrôler les activités des sociétés de distribution d'eau en Grande-Bretagne
ogle [ˈəʊgəl] *vt* lorgner, reluquer
ogre [ˈəʊgə(r)] *n* ogre *m*
ogress [ˈəʊgrɪs] *n* ogresse *f*
oh [əʊ] *exclam* oh!
ohm [əʊm] *n* ohm *m*
OHMS [əʊetʃem'es] *Br (abbr* **On Her/His Majesty's Service)** = formule apposée sur le courrier émis par les services gouvernementaux
oho [əʊˈhəʊ] *exclam* ah ah!
OHP [əʊetʃˈpiː] *n (abbr* **overhead projector)** rétroprojecteur *m*; **O. slide** transparent *m*
oil [ɔɪl] **1** *n (for cooking, lubricating)* huile *f*; *(petroleum)* pétrole *m*; *(for heating)* mazout *m*; *Fig* **to pour o. on troubled waters** apaiser les esprits; **o. company** compagnie *f* pétrolière; **o. crisis** choc *m* pétrolier; **o. drum** bidon *m* à pétrole; **o. lamp** lampe *f* à pétrole; **o. painting** peinture *f* à l'huile; *Fig Hum* **she's no o. painting** ce n'est pas une beauté; **o. refinery** raffinerie *f* de pétrole; **o. rig** *(on land)* derrick *m*; *(offshore)* plate-forme *f* pétrolière ou de forage; **o. slick** *(on sea)* nappe *f* de pétrole; *(on shore)* marée *f* noire; **o. spill** *(event)* marée *f* noire; *(result)* nappe *f* de pétrole; **o. tanker** pétrolier *m*; **o. well** puits *m* de pétrole **2** *vt* huiler, lubrifier; *Fig* **to o. the wheels** faciliter les choses
oilcan [ˈɔɪlkæn] *n (for applying oil)* burette *f*; *(large container)* bidon *m* à huile
oilfield [ˈɔɪlfiːld] *n* gisement *m* de pétrole
oil-fired [ˈɔɪlfaɪəd] *adj (heating)* au mazout
oilskin [ˈɔɪlskɪn] *n (fabric)* toile *f* cirée; **oilskins** *(garment)* ciré *m*
oily [ˈɔɪlɪ] *adj* (**a**) *(hands, rag)* graisseux(euse); *(skin, hair)* gras (grasse); *(food)* huileux(euse) (**b**) *Pej (manner)* onctueux(euse)
oink [ɔɪŋk] *vi* grogner
ointment [ˈɔɪntmənt] *n* pommade *f*

OK, okay ['əʊ'keɪ] *Fam* **1** *adj (in order)* correct(e), exact(e); *(acceptable)* pas mal; **that's OK by** *or* **with me** ça me va; **is it OK to wear jeans?** ça va si on vient en jean?; **no, it is NOT OK** (il n'en est) pas question; **she was OK about it** elle n'a pas fait d'histoires; **he's an OK sort of guy** c'est un type plutôt bien; **are we OK for time?** est-ce qu'on a assez de temps?
2 *exclam* OK!; **OK, OK! I'll do it now** OK, ça va, je vais le faire
3 *n* **to give (sb) the OK** donner le feu vert (à qn)
4 *vt (pt & pp* **OK'd** *or* **okayed**) donner le feu vert à

okra ['ɒkrə] *n* gombo *m*, okra *m*

old [əʊld] **1** *adj* (**a**) *(aged) (person)* vieux (vieille), âgé(e); *(car)* vieux; **to grow** *or* **get older** vieillir; **o. people** personnes *fpl* âgées; **o. people's home** maison *f* de retraite; **o. age pension** (pension *f* de) retraite *f*; **o. age pensioner** retraité(e) *m,f*; **to go over o. ground** revenir sur des choses qui ont déjà été dites; **to be an o. hand at sth** être rompu(e) à qch; **o. maid** vieille fille *f*; **to be o. hat** être démodé(e); *Fig* **to be one of the o. school** être de la vieille école; **the O. Testament** l'Ancien Testament *m*; **o. wives' tale** conte *m* de bonne femme (**b**) *(with specific age)* **how o. are you?** quel âge avez-vous?; **to be five years o.** avoir cinq ans; **when you're older** *(to child)* quand tu seras plus grand; **at six years o.** à (l'âge de) six ans; **a two-year-o. (child)** un enfant (âgé) de deux ans; **you're o. enough to do that yourself** tu es assez grand pour le faire toi-même (**c**) *(former)* ancien(enne); **in the o. days** autrefois; *Br* **o. boy/girl** *(of school)* ancien(enne) élève *mf*; *Br* **the o. boy network** = la franc-maçonnerie des écoles privées et des universités; **an o. flame** un(e) ancien(-enne) amoureux(euse) (**d**) *(longstanding)* **an o. friend** un(e) vieil (vieille) ami(e); **o. habits die hard** il n'est pas facile de se défaire de ses habitudes (**e**) *Fam (intensifier)* **any o. how** n'importe comment; **any o. thing** n'importe quoi (**f**) *Fam (affectionate)* **o. Fred** ce vieux Fred; **the poor o. thing** le (la) pauvre vieux (vieille); **my** *or* **the o. man** *(father)* le pater; *(husband)* mon homme; **my** *or* **the o. woman** *(mother)* la mater; *(wife)* la bourgeoise
2 *npl* **the o.** les personnes *fpl* âgées

old-fashioned [əʊld'fæʃənd] *adj* (**a**) *(outdated)* démodé(e); *(person)* vieux jeu *inv* (**b**) *(traditional)* à l'ancienne

old-timer [əʊld'taɪmə(r)] *n Fam* (**a**) *(old person)* ancien(enne) *m,f* (**b**) *Am (form of address)* vieux *m*

old-world ['əʊld'wɜːld] *adj (atmosphere, elegance)* suranné(e); *(furnishings)* à l'ancienne

oleander [əʊlɪ'ændə(r)] *n* laurier-rose *m*

olfactory [ɒl'fæktərɪ] *adj* olfactif(ive)

oligarchy ['ɒlɪgɑːkɪ] *(pl* **oligarchies**) *n* oligarchie *f*

olive ['ɒlɪv] **1** *n* olive *f*; *Fig* **to hold out the o. branch** proposer la paix; **o. grove** oliveraie *f*; **o. oil** huile *f* d'olive; **o. tree** olivier *m*
2 *adj (skin)* olivâtre; **o. (green)** (vert) olive *inv*

Olympic [ə'lɪmpɪk] **1** *n* **the Olympics** les Jeux *mpl* olympiques
2 *adj* olympique; **the O. Games** les Jeux *mpl* olympiques

Oman [əʊ'mæn] *n* Oman *m*

Omani [əʊ'mænɪ] **1** *n* Omanais(e) *m,f*
2 *adj* omanais(e)

ombudsman ['ɒmbʊdzmən] *n* ≃ médiateur *m* de la République

omelette, *Am* **omelet** ['ɒmlɪt] *n* omelette *f*; **ham o.** omelette *f* au jambon

omen ['əʊmən] *n* présage *m*, augure *m*

ominous ['ɒmɪnəs] *adj* inquiétant(e); *(event)* de mauvais augure; **an o.-looking sky** un ciel menaçant; **an emergency meeting? – that sounds o.** une réunion d'urgence? – ça ne présage rien de bon

ominously ['ɒmɪnəslɪ] *adv* **she spoke o.** ce qu'elle a dit ne présage rien de bon; **it was o. quiet** il régnait un silence inquiétant

omission [əʊ'mɪʃən] *n* omission *f*

omit [əʊ'mɪt] *(pt & pp* **omitted**) *vt* omettre; **to o. to do sth** omettre de faire qch

omnibus ['ɒmnɪbəs] **1** *n* (**a**) *(book)* recueil *m* (**b**) *Old-fashioned (bus)* omnibus *m*
2 *adj* **o. edition** *(of stories, poems)* recueil *m*; *(on TV, radio)* rediffusion *f* de plusieurs épisodes en continu

omnipotence [ɒm'nɪpətəns] *n* omnipotence *f*, toute-puissance *f*

omnipotent [ɒm'nɪpətənt] *adj* omnipotent(e), tout-puissant (toute-puissante)

omnipresent [ɒmnɪ'prezənt] *adj* omniprésent(e)

omniscient [ɒm'nɪsɪənt] *adj* omniscient(e)

omnivorous [ɒm'nɪvərəs] *adj* omnivore; *Fig (reader)* qui lit de tout

on [ɒn] **1** *adv* (**a**) *(in operation) (light, television)* allumé(e); *(engine)* en marche; **the "on" position** la position marche
(**b**) *(taking place)* **what's on?** *(on TV)* qu'est-ce qu'il y a à la télé?; *(at cinema)* qu'est-ce qui passe au cinéma?; **is the meeting still on?** la réunion doit-elle toujours avoir lieu?; **I've got a lot on** j'ai beaucoup de choses à faire; **on and off, off and on** *(intermittently)* par intermittence
(**c**) *(on duty) (in hospital, surgery)* de garde; *(in shop)* de service
(**d**) *(with clothing)* **to have sth on** porter qch; **to put sth on** mettre qch; **to have nothing on** être nu(e)
(**e**) *(in time)* **earlier on** plus tôt; **later on** plus tard; **from that day on** à dater *ou* à partir de ce jour
(**f**) *(expressing continuation)* **to read/talk/work on** continuer à lire/bavarder/travailler; **he went on and on about it** il n'en finissait pas
(**g**) *(in phrases) Fam* **it's not on!** c'est inadmissible!
2 *prep* (**a**) *(expressing position)* sur; **on the table** sur la table; **on the second floor** au deuxième étage; **on the wall** sur le mur; *(hanging)* au mur; **on page 4** à la page 4; **on the right/left** à droite/gauche; **on foot** à pied; **on horseback** à cheval; **on (the) television** à la télévision; **to be on a committee** faire partie d'un comité; **I haven't got any money on me** je n'ai pas d'argent sur moi
(**b**) *(with time)* **on the 15th** le 15; **on Sunday** dimanche; **on the hour** à l'heure pile; **on that occasion** à cette occasion
(**c**) *(about)* sur; **a book on France** un livre sur la France; **to have sth on sb** disposer d'informations compromettantes pour qn
(**d**) *(introducing a gerund)* **on completing the test, you should...** une fois l'examen terminé, les candidats devront...; **on discovering the corpse, she screamed** elle hurla lorsqu'elle découvrit le corps
(**e**) *(expressing use, support)* **to live on £200 a week** vivre avec 200 livres par semaine; **the drinks are on me** c'est ma tournée; **to be on antibiotics** prendre des antibiotiques; **to be on drugs** se droguer

once [wʌns] **1** *adv* (**a**) *(on one occasion)* une fois; **not o.** jamais; **o. a week** une fois par semaine; **o. or twice** une ou deux fois, une fois ou deux; **o. in a while** une fois de temps en temps; **o. more, o. again** encore une fois; **o. too often** une fois de trop; **o. and for all** une fois pour toutes; **a o.-in-a-lifetime opportunity** une occasion qui ne se présente qu'une fois (**b**) *(formerly)* autrefois; **o. upon a time there was a princess** il était une fois une princesse (**c**) **at o.** *(immediately)* immédiatement, tout de suite; *(at the same time)* à la fois, en même temps **2** *conj* **o. he reached home, he collapsed** une fois arrivé chez lui, il s'effondra; **o. he finishes, we can leave** une fois qu'il aura terminé, nous pourrons partir

once-over ['wʌnsəʊvə(r)] *n Fam* **to give sb/sth the o.** jeter un coup d'œil à qn/qch

oncoming ['ɒnkʌmɪŋ] *adj (traffic)* venant en sens inverse

one [wʌn] **1** *n (number)* un (une) *m,f*; **in ones and twos** par petits groupes; *Fam* **to get o. up on sb** prendre l'avantage sur qn **2** *pron* (**a**) *(identifying)* **this o.** celui-ci (celle-ci); **that o.** celui-là (celle-là); **these ones** ceux-ci (celles-ci); **those ones** ceux-là (celles-là); **which o. do you want?** lequel (laquelle) veux-tu?; **the o. I told you about** celui (celle) dont je t'ai parlé; **the big o.** le (la) grand(e); **the ones with the long sleeves** ceux (celles) qui ont les manches longues; **that's a difficult o.!** *(question)* c'est une question difficile! (**b**) *(indefinite)* un (une); **have you got o.?** tu en as un(e)?; **any o. of us** n'importe lequel d'entre nous; **o. of my friends** un(e) de mes amis; **she's o. of the family** elle fait partie de la famille; **o. of these days** un de ces jours; **it was just o. of those things** on n'y peut rien; **o. after the other** l'un(e) après l'autre; **o. at a time** un(e) à la fois; **o. by o.** un(e) par un(e); **to have had o. too many** *(drinks)* avoir bu un coup de trop (**c**) *(particular person)* **to act like o. possessed** se conduire comme un (une) possédé(e); **I, for o., do not believe it** quant à moi, je n'y crois pas; **I'm not o. to complain** je ne suis pas du genre à me plaindre; **she's not a great o. for parties** les soirées, ce n'est pas son fort (**d**) *(people in general) (subject)* on; *(object)* vous; **o. never knows** on ne sait jamais; **it can make o. unhappy** cela peut vous rendre malheureux; **to do o.'s best** faire de son mieux **3** *adj* (**a**) *(number)* un(e); **page/number o.** page/numéro un; **o. o'clock** une heure; **to be o.** *(year old)* avoir un an; **o. day/evening** un jour/soir; **o. or two people** une ou deux personnes; **for o. thing...** d'abord...; **o. American in two thinks that...** un Américain sur deux pense que... (**b**) *(single)* un(e) seul(e); **I have just o. thing to say** je n'ai qu'une seule chose à dire; **my o. regret** mon seul regret; **the o. person who...** la seule personne qui...; **my o. and only suit** mon seul et unique costume (**c**) *(same)* le même (la même); **they all live in the o. house** ils habitent dans la même maison; **they are o. and the same thing/person** ils ne font qu'un; *Fam* **it's all o. to me** ça m'est égal

one-armed ['wʌnɑːmd] *adj (person)* manchot(e); *Br Fam* **o. bandit** machine *f* à sous

one-eyed ['wʌnaɪd] *adj* borgne

one-horse town ['wʌnhɔːs'taʊn] *n Fam* trou *m* perdu

one-legged [wʌn'legɪd] *adj* unijambiste

one-liner [wʌn'laɪnə(r)] *n Fam* bon mot *m*

one-man ['wʌnmæn] *adj (job)* pour un seul homme; **o. band** homme-orchestre *m*; **o. show** *(by performer)* spectacle *m* solo, one-man-show *m inv*; *(by artist)* exposition *f* individuelle

one-night stand [wʌn'naɪt'stænd] *n Fam (sexual encounter)* rencontre *f* sans lendemain *ou* d'un soir

one-off ['wʌnɒf] *Br Fam* **1** *n (object)* objet *m* unique; *(event)* événement *m* unique; **it was a o.** *(mistake, success)* ça ne se reproduira pas **2** *adj* unique

one-on-one ['wʌnɒn'wʌn] *Am* = **one-to-one**

one-parent family ['wʌnpeərənt'fæmɪlɪ] *n* famille *f* monoparentale

one-party ['wʌn'pɑːtɪ] *adj* à parti unique

one-piece swimsuit ['wʌnpiːs'swɪmsuːt] *n* maillot *m* de bain une pièce

onerous ['əʊnərəs] *adj Formal* lourd(e)

oneself [wʌn'self] *pron* (**a**) *(reflexive)* se; **to look after o.** *(when ill)* se soigner; *(generally)* s'occuper de soi; **to feel o. again** se sentir complètement rétabli(e) (**b**) *(emphatic)* soi-même; **to do sth all by o.** faire qch tout(e) seul(e); **to see for o.** regarder soi-même

one-sided [wʌn'saɪdɪd] *adj* (**a**) *(unequal) (contest)* inégal(e); *(relationship)* à sens unique (**b**) *(biased)* partial(e)

one-time ['wʌntaɪm] *adj* ancien(enne)

one-to-one ['wʌntə'wʌn] *adj (talk, meeting)* seul à seul, en tête-à-tête; **o. tuition** cours *mpl* particuliers

one-track ['wʌntræk] *adj* **to have a o. mind** *(be obsessed with one thing)* avoir une idée fixe; *(be obsessed with sex)* être obsédé(e), ne penser qu'à ça

one-trick pony ['wʌntrɪk'pəʊnɪ] *n Fig* = personne qui n'a qu'une seule corde à son arc

one-upmanship [wʌn'ʌpmənʃɪp] *n Fam* = tendance à s'affirmer supérieur aux autres

one-way ['wʌnweɪ] *adj (street, traffic)* à sens unique; **o. ticket** aller *m* (simple)

ongoing ['ɒngəʊɪŋ] *adj* en cours; *(situation, problem)* qui dure

onion ['ʌnjən] *n* oignon *m*; *Br Fam* **to know one's onions** connaître son affaire

online, on-line [ɒn'laɪn] *adj & adv Comput* en ligne; **o. banking** transactions *fpl* bancaires en ligne; **o. dating** rencontres *fpl* en ligne; **o. help** aide *f* en ligne; **o. shopping** achats *mpl* par Internet

onlooker ['ɒnlʊkə(r)] *n* spectateur(trice) *m,f*; *(at accident)* badaud *m*

only ['əʊnlɪ] **1** *adj* seul(e), unique; **o. child** *(boy)* fils *m* unique; *(girl)* fille *f* unique; **you're not the o. one** tu n'es pas le seul (la seule) **2** *adv* seulement, ne... que; **I was o. joking** c'était (uniquement) pour rire; **permit holders o.** *(sign)* stationnement réservé; **an expert could advise us** seul un expert pourrait nous conseiller; **I o. touched it** je n'ai fait que le toucher; **I shall be o. too pleased to come** je serais ravi de venir; **if o. they knew!, if o. they knew!** s'ils savaient!; **not o...., but also...** non seulement..., mais encore...; **I saw her o. yesterday** je l'ai vue pas plus tard qu'hier; **o. just** de justesse; **it's o. me** ce n'est que moi **3** *conj* mais

ono [əʊen'əʊ] *adv Com (abbr* or nearest offer*)* à débattre

on-off switch ['ɒn'ɒfswɪtʃ] *n* interrupteur *m* marche-arrêt

onomatopoeic [ɒnəmætə'piːɪk] *adj* onomatopéique

onrush ['ɒnrʌʃ] *n (of emotions)* vague *f; (of people)* ruée *f*

onset ['ɒnset] *n* début *m*, commencement *m*

on-site ['ɒnsaɪt] *adj & adv* sur place

onslaught ['ɒnslɔːt] *n* assaut *m*, attaque *f* (**on** contre)

onto ['ɒntʊ, *unstressed* 'ɒntə] *prep* (**a**) *(with direction)* sur (**b**) *(idioms)* **to be o. sb** être sur la piste de qn; **to get o. sb** contacter qn; **to be o. a good thing** avoir tiré le gros lot

onus ['əʊnəs] *n* responsabilité *f*, obligation *f*; **the o. is on the government to resolve the problem** il incombe au gouvernement de résoudre ce problème; *Law* **o. of proof** charge *f* de la preuve

onward ['ɒnwəd] **1** *adj* en avant
2 *adv* = **onwards**

onwards ['ɒnwədz] *adv* **from tomorrow o.** à partir de demain; **from now o.** désormais, dorénavant; **from then o.** à partir de ce moment-là

onyx ['ɒnɪks] *n* onyx *m*

oodles ['uːdəlz] *npl Fam* **o. of** des tonnes de; **to have o. of time** avoir largement le temps

oomph [ʊmf] *n Fam (energy)* punch *m*; **to have plenty of o.** avoir du punch

oops [uːps] *exclam* houp-là!

ooze [uːz] **1** *n* (**a**) *(mud)* vase *f* (**b**) *(flow)* suintement *m*
2 *vt (liquid)* laisser suinter; *Fig (confidence)* déborder de; **to o. charm** avoir un charme fou
3 *vi (of liquid)* suinter (**from** de); *Fig* **to o. with confidence** déborder d'assurance

op [ɒp] *n Fam (medical operation)* opération *f*

opal ['əʊpəl] *n* opale *f*

opaque [əʊ'peɪk] *adj* opaque; *Fig (difficult to understand)* obscur(e)

OPEC ['əʊpek] *n (abbr* **Organization of Petroleum-Exporting Countries)** OPEP *f*

open ['əʊpən] **1** *n* (**a**) **in the o.** *(outside)* dehors; *(not hidden)* sur la place publique; **to bring sth out into the o.** étaler qch au grand jour; **to come out into the o.** révéler qch
(**b**) *(sporting competition)* open *m*
2 *adj* (**a**) *(not shut)* ouvert(e); **o. to the public** ouvert au public; **o. late** *(on sign)* ouvert en nocturne; **to be o. to sb/sth** *(accessible to)* être ouvert(e) à qn/qch; **to be o. to doubt** être sujet(ette) à caution; **to be o. to ridicule** s'exposer à être ridiculisé(e); **to be o. to suggestions** être ouvert à toute suggestion; **in the o. air** au grand air; **to welcome sb with o. arms** accueillir qn à bras ouverts; **o. country** rase campagne *f*; *Law* **in o. court** en audience publique; *Br* **o. day,** *Am* **o. house** journée *f* portes ouvertes; **o. invitation** invitation *f* permanente; *Fig (to thieves)* invitation *f*; *Econ* **o. market** marché *m* libre; **to keep an o. mind (on sth)** réserver son jugement (sur qch); **o. prison** prison *f* ouverte; **o. sandwich** canapé *m*; **the o. sea** le large, la haute mer; **o. season** *(for hunting)* saison *f* de la chasse; *Fig* **to declare o. season on sb/sth** partir en guerre contre qn/qch; **o. spaces** *(parks)* espaces *mpl* verts; **o. ticket** billet *m* open; *Br* **O. University** = organisme d'enseignement universitaire par correspondance doublé d'émissions de télévision et de radio; *Law* **o. verdict** verdict *m* de décès sans cause déterminée; **o. wound** plaie *f* béante
(**b**) *(person, manner)* ouvert(e), franc (franche); *(conflict)* ouvert(e); **to be o. with sb** être franc

(franche) avec qn; **to be o. about sth** être franc (franche) sur qch; **o. letter** *(in newspaper)* lettre *f* ouverte; **o. secret** secret *m* de Polichinelle
3 *adv* **to cut/break sth o.** couper/casser qch; **the door flew o.** la porte s'ouvrit brusquement
4 *vt* ouvrir; *(legs, arms)* écarter; *(negotiations, conversation)* entamer; **to o. fire (on sb)** ouvrir le feu (sur qn); **to o. one's heart to sb** ouvrir son cœur à qn, s'ouvrir à qn
5 *vi (of door, window, flower)* s'ouvrir; *(of shop, bank)* ouvrir; *(of film)* sortir; *(of meeting, negotiations)* commencer; **to o. late** *(of shop)* ouvrir en nocturne; **to o. onto sth** donner sur qch; **the play opens with a death scene** la pièce s'ouvre sur une scène de mort

►**open out 1** *vt sep (paper, map)* ouvrir, déplier
2 *vi (of flower)* s'ouvrir; *(of wings)* se déployer; *(of view)* s'étendre; *(of road, valley)* s'élargir

►**open up 1** *vt sep (shop, business, area)* ouvrir (**to** à); *(possibility, opportunity)* offrir
2 *vi (of shopkeeper, new shop)* ouvrir; *(of flower)* s'ouvrir; *Fig (of person)* s'ouvrir, s'épancher

open-air [əʊpə'neə(r)] *adj (restaurant, market)* en plein air; *(swimming pool)* découvert(e)

open-and-shut case [əʊpənən'ʃʌt'keɪs] *n* **to be an o.** ne pas faire l'ombre d'un doute

opencast ['əʊpənkɑːst] *adj* à ciel ouvert

open-door policy ['əʊpən'dɔːpɒlɪsɪ] *n (for immigrants)* politique *f* d'ouverture des frontières; *(for university)* politique non sélective

open-ended ['əʊpən'endɪd] *adj (contract)* à durée indéterminée; *(question)* ouvert(e); *(discussion)* sans cadre strict

open-heart surgery ['əʊpən'hɑːt'sɜːdʒərɪ] *n* opération *f* à cœur ouvert

opening ['əʊpənɪŋ] **1** *n* (**a**) *(of play, new era)* commencement *m; (of negotiations, Parliament)* ouverture *f* (**b**) *(gap)* ouverture *f*, trou *m* (**c**) *(of cave, tunnel)* entrée *f* (**d**) *(opportunity)* occasion *f* favorable; *(job)* débouché *m*
2 *adj* **o. address** *or* **speech** *(in court case)* déclaration *f* préliminaire; **o. batsman** *(in cricket)* premier batteur *m*; **o. ceremony** cérémonie *f* d'ouverture, inauguration *f*; **o. gambit** *(in chess)* gambit *m; (in conversation, negotiation)* manœuvre *f* d'approche; **o. hours** heures *fpl* d'ouverture; *Theat* **o. night** première *f*; *Br* **o. time** *(of pub)* heure *f* d'ouverture

openly ['əʊpənlɪ] *adv* ouvertement; **she wept o.** elle a pleuré sans retenue

open-minded [əʊpən'maɪndɪd] *adj* **to be o.** avoir l'esprit ouvert

open-mouthed [əʊpən'maʊðd] *adj & adv* bouche bée *inv*

openness ['əʊpənnɪs] *n* franchise *f*

open-plan ['əʊpənplæn] *adj (office)* paysager(ère); *(house)* sans cloisons; **o. kitchen** coin-cuisine *m*

opera ['ɒpərə] *n* opéra *m*; **o. glasses** jumelles *fpl* de théâtre; **o. house** opéra *m*; **o. singer** chanteur(euse) *m,f* d'opéra

operable ['ɒpərəbəl] *adj* opérable

operate ['ɒpəreɪt] **1** *vt (machine)* faire fonctionner; *(bus service)* assurer; **to be operated by electricity** fonctionner à l'électricité
2 *vi* (**a**) *(of machine)* fonctionner; *(of company)* opérer, travailler (**b**) *(of surgeon)* opérer; **to o. on sb (for)** opérer qn (de); **to be operated on** se faire opérer

operatic [ɒpə'rætɪk] *adj* d'opéra

operating [ˈɒpəreɪtɪŋ] *adj* **o. costs** coûts *mpl ou* frais *mpl* d'exploitation; *Comput* **o. system** système *m* d'exploitation; **o. table** table *f* d'opération; *Br* **o. theatre,** *Am* **o. room** salle *f* d'opération

operation [ɒpəˈreɪʃən] *n* (**a**) *(of machine)* fonctionnement *m*; **to be in o.** *(of machine)* être en service; *(of law)* être en vigueur; **to come into o.** *(of law)* entrer en vigueur (**b**) *(process)* opération *f* (**c**) *(of company)* activité *f* (**d**) *(military, surgical)* opération *f*; **to have an o. (for sth)** se faire opérer (de qch); *Mil* **operations room** salle *f* d'opérations *(d'un état-major)*

operational [ɒpəˈreɪʃənəl] *adj (system, factory)* opérationnel(elle)

operative [ˈɒpərətɪv] **1** *n (manual worker)* ouvrier(-ère) *m,f*; *(of machine)* opérateur(trice) *m,f*; *Am (spy)* agent *m* **2** *adj (law, rule)* en vigueur; **to become o.** entrer en vigueur; **the o. word** le mot-clé

operator [ˈɒpəreɪtə(r)] *n* (**a**) *(of machine)* opérateur(-trice) *m,f* (**b**) *Tel* opérateur(trice) *m,f*; **(switchboard) o.** standardiste *mf* (**c**) *Fam* **a smooth o.** un petit finaud

operetta [ɒpəˈretə] *n* opérette *f*

ophthalmology [ɒfθælˈmɒlədʒɪ] *n* ophtalmologie *f*

opinion [əˈpɪnjən] *n* opinion *f*; **in my o.** à mon avis; **to be of the o. that...** être d'avis *ou* estimer que...; **to ask sb's o.** demander l'avis *ou* l'opinion de qn; **to form an o. of sb/sth** se faire une opinion sur qn/qch; **to have a high/low o. of sb** avoir une haute/mauvaise opinion de qn; **o. poll** sondage *m* (d'opinion)

opinionated [əˈpɪnjəneɪtɪd] *adj* dogmatique

opium [ˈəʊpɪəm] *n* opium *m*; **o. addict** opiomane *mf*; **o. den** fumerie *f* d'opium

opossum [ɒˈpɒsəm] *n* opossum *m*

opp *(abbr* **opposite)** ci-contre

opponent [əˈpəʊnənt] *n* adversaire *mf*; *(of government)* opposant(e) *m,f* (**of** à)

opportune [ˈɒpətjuːn] *adj* opportun(e)

opportunism [ɒpəˈtjuːnɪzəm] *n* opportunisme *m*

opportunist [ɒpəˈtjuːnɪst] **1** *n* opportuniste *mf* **2** *adj* opportuniste

opportunity [ɒpəˈtjuːnɪtɪ] *(pl* **opportunities)** *n* occasion *f*; **to have the o.** of doing *or* **to do sth** avoir l'occasion de faire qch; **at every o.** à la moindre occasion; **at the first** *or* **earliest o.** à la première occasion; **if you get an o.** si tu en as l'occasion; **the o.** of a lifetime la chance de sa/ta/*etc* vie; **a job with opportunities** un emploi qui offre des perspectives

oppose [əˈpəʊz] *vt* s'opposer à; **to be opposed to sth** être opposé(e) à qch; **as opposed to...** par opposition à...

opposing [əˈpəʊzɪŋ] *adj (characters, viewpoints)* opposé(e); *(armies)* ennemi(e); *(team)* adverse

opposite [ˈɒpəzɪt] **1** *n* **the o.** le contraire **2** *adj* (**a**) *(side, shore)* opposé(e); *(page)* d'en face; **on the o. side of the street** de l'autre côté de la rue (**b**) *(opinion)* contraire; **in the o. direction** en sens inverse, dans le sens opposé; **the o. sex** l'autre sexe **3** *adv* en face; **the house o.** la maison d'en face **4** *prep* en face de

opposition [ɒpəˈzɪʃən] *n* (**a**) *(resistance)* opposition *f* (**to** à); **to meet with o.** *(of idea, plan)* être contesté(e) (**b**) *(contrast)* **in o. to** contre (**c**) *(opponents)* **the o.** le

camp adverse; *Br Pol* **the O.** l'opposition *f*; *Br Pol* **to be in o.** être dans l'opposition

oppress [əˈpres] *vt* opprimer

oppressed [əˈprest] **1** *npl* **the o.** les opprimés *mpl* **2** *adj* opprimé(e)

oppression [əˈpreʃən] *n* oppression *f*

oppressive [əˈpresɪv] *adj* (**a**) *(law, regime)* oppressif(ive) (**b**) *(atmosphere, heat)* oppressant(e), étouffant(e)

opt [ɒpt] **1** *vt* **to o. to do sth** choisir de faire qch **2** *vi* **to o. for sth** opter pour qch
▸**opt in** *vi* choisir de participer
▸**opt out** *vi* se désengager

optic [ˈɒptɪk] *adj* optique; **o. nerve** nerf *m* optique

optical [ˈɒptɪkəl] *adj* optique; *(instrument)* d'optique; *Comput* **o. character reader** lecteur *m* optique de caractères; *Comput* **o. character recognition** reconnaissance *f* optique de caractères; *Comput* **o. disk** disque *m* optique; **o. fibre** fibre *f* optique; **o. illusion** illusion *f* d'optique

optician [ɒpˈtɪʃən] *n (prescribing)* ophtalmologue *mf*; *(dispensing)* opticien(enne) *m,f*

optics [ˈɒptɪks] *n* optique *f*

optimism [ˈɒptɪmɪzəm] *n* optimisme *m*

optimist [ˈɒptɪmɪst] *n* optimiste *mf*

optimistic [ɒptɪˈmɪstɪk] *adj* optimiste (**about** quant à)

optimize [ˈɒptɪmaɪz] *vt* optimiser

optimum [ˈɒptɪməm] **1** *n* optimum *m* **2** *adj* optimum *inv,* optimal(e)

option [ˈɒpʃən] *n* (**a**) *(choice)* option *f*, choix *m*; **to have the o. of doing sth** avoir la possibilité de faire qch; **to have no o. (but to do sth)** ne pas pouvoir faire autrement (que de faire qch); **a soft** *or* **easy o.** une solution de facilité; **to leave** *or* **keep one's options open** ne pas prendre de décision tout de suite (**b**) *Fin* option *f* (**c**) *(school or university subject)* option *f*

optional [ˈɒpʃənəl] *adj* facultatif(ive); **o. extra** (accessoire *m* en) option *f*; **o. subject** *(at school, university)* matière *f* à option

opt-out [ˈɒptaʊt] **1** *n* désengagement *m* **2** *adj* de désengagement

opulent [ˈɒpjʊlənt] *adj* opulent(e)

OR [əʊˈɑː(r)] *n Am (abbr* **operating room)** salle *f* d'opération

or [ɔː(r), *unstressed* ə(r)] *conj* (**a**) *(in general)* ou; **an hour or so** une heure environ; **in a day or two** dans un jour ou deux; **did she do it or not?** est-ce qu'elle l'a fait ou pas?; **snow or no snow, I'm going!** qu'il neige ou pas, j'y vais! (**b**) *(otherwise)* sinon; **stop it or I'll tell mum!** arrête, sinon je vais le dire à maman! (**c**) *(with negative)* ni; **she didn't write or phone** elle n'a ni écrit ni téléphoné

oracle [ˈɒrəkəl] *n* oracle *m*

oral [ˈɔːrəl] **1** *n (in exam)* oral *m* **2** *adj (tradition, contraception)* oral(e); *(medication)* par voie orale; *(hygiene)* buccal(e); **o. examination** (examen *m*) oral *m*; **o. sex** rapports *mpl* buccogénitaux

orally [ˈɔːrəlɪ] *adv* oralement, de vive voix; *(take medicine)* par voie orale

Orange [ˈɒrɪndʒ] *adj (in Northern Ireland)* orangiste *(protestant)*; **O. march, O. parade** défilé *m* des Orangistes; **O. Order** Ordre *m* des Orangistes

Orange marches

Depuis des siècles, les Orangistes défilent dans les villes d'Irlande du Nord et dans de nombreuses villes de l'ouest de l'Écosse pour commémorer les dates clés de l'histoire du protestantisme en Irlande. L'événement le plus important fut la bataille de la Boyne en 1690 où le protestant Guillaume d'Orange l'emporta sur Jacques II, roi catholique déposé. Les Orangistes sont farouchement attachés à la Couronne britannique et s'opposent à tout rapprochement avec la République d'Irlande. Leurs défilés annuels donnent souvent lieu à de violents affrontements, notamment quand ils traversent les quartiers catholiques.

orange ['ɒrɪndʒ] **1** *n (fruit)* orange *f; (colour)* orange *m;* **o. blossom** fleurs *fpl* d'oranger; **o. grove** orangeraie *f;* **o. juice** jus *m* d'orange; **o. peel** peau *f ou* écorce *f* d'orange; **o. squash** ≃ orangeade *f;* **o. tree** oranger *m*
2 *adj (colour)* orange *inv*
orang-outan(g) [ɔː'ræŋuːtæn, ɔː'ræŋuːtæŋ] *n* orang-outan(g) *m*
oration [ɔː'reɪʃən] *n* allocution *f*
orator ['ɒrətə(r)] *n* orateur(trice) *m,f*
oratory ['ɒrətərɪ] *(pl* **oratories)** *n* (**a**) *(art of speaking)* art *m* oratoire, éloquence *f* (**b**) *Rel (chapel)* oratoire *m*
orb [ɔːb] *n (of regalia)* globe *m; Lit (sphere)* orbe *m*
orbit ['ɔːbɪt] **1** *n* (**a**) *(of planet)* orbite *f;* **in o.** en orbite; **to go into o.** se mettre en orbite (**b**) *(scope)* domaine *m*
2 *vt* être en orbite *ou* décrire une orbite autour de
3 *vi* être en orbite, décrire une orbite
orchard ['ɔːtʃəd] *n* verger *m*
orchestra ['ɔːkɪstrə] *n* orchestre *m;* **o. pit** fosse *f* d'orchestre
orchestral [ɔː'kestrəl] *adj* orchestral(e)
orchestrate ['ɔːkɪstreɪt] *vt also Fig* orchestrer
orchid ['ɔːkɪd] *n* orchidée *f*
ordain [ɔː'deɪn] *vt* (**a**) *Formal (decree)* ordonner; *(measure)* décréter; *Fig* **fate ordained that we should meet** il était écrit que nous devions nous rencontrer (**b**) *(priest)* ordonner
ordeal [ɔː'diːl] *n* épreuve *f;* **it was a bit of an o.** ça a été éprouvant
order ['ɔːdə(r)] **1** *n* (**a**) *(instruction)* ordre *m;* **to give sb an o.** donner un ordre à qn; **to be under orders (to do sth)** avoir reçu des ordres (pour faire qch); **to take orders from sb** recevoir des ordres de qn; *Fin* **pay to the o. of S. Fraser** payer à l'ordre de S. Fraser (**b**) *Com* commande *f;* **to place an o. (with sb)** passer (une) commande (à qn); **to make sth to o.** faire qch sur commande; **o. book** carnet *m* de commandes; **o. form** bon *m* de commande (**c**) *(peace, tidiness)* ordre *m; Fig* **to put one's own house in o.** faire le ménage chez soi (**d**) *(condition)* **out of o.** *(lift, toilets, machine)* hors service; *(telephone)* en dérangement; **in (good) working** *ou* **running o.** en (bon) état de fonctionnement (**e**) *(in meeting)* **o. of the day** ordre *m* du jour; **to call sb to o.** rappeler qn à l'ordre; *Fig* **I think a celebration is in o.** je pense que ça mérite d'être fêté; *Fam* **that's out of o.!** ça ne se fait vraiment pas!; *Rel* **o. of service** office *m; Pol* **o. paper** (copie *f* de l')ordre *m* du jour (**f**) *(system)* ordre *m;* **the new world o.** le nouvel ordre mondial (**g**) *(sequence)* ordre *m;* **in the right/wrong o.** dans le bon ordre/le désordre; **in o.** en ordre; **out of o.** en désordre; **in o. of age/size** par

ordre d'âge/de taille (**h**) *(degree)* ordre *m;* **of the highest o.** de premier ordre; **the higher/lower orders** *(social classes)* les classes *fpl* supérieures/inférieures (**i**) *Rel* ordre *m;* **to take holy orders** entrer dans les ordres (**j**) **in o. to do sth** afin de *ou* pour faire qch; **in o. that...** afin *ou* pour que... + *subjunctive*
2 *vt* (**a**) *(instruct)* **to o. sb to do sth** ordonner à qn de faire qch; **to be ordered to do sth** recevoir l'ordre de faire qch; *Law* **to be ordered to pay costs** être condamné(e) aux dépens (**b**) *Com & (in restaurant)* commander (**c**) *(arrange) (papers, books)* classer, ranger; *(one's thoughts)* mettre de l'ordre dans; **to o. sth according to size** classer *ou* ranger qch par taille
3 *vi (in restaurant)* commander; **are you ready to o.?** vous avez choisi?
▸**order about, order around** *vt sep (person)* commander
▸**order in** *vt sep (supplies)* commander; *(troops)* faire venir
ordered ['ɔːdəd] *adj (organized)* ordonné(e); *(life)* régulier(ère)
orderly ['ɔːdəlɪ] **1** *n (pl* **orderlies)** *(in army)* planton *m; (in hospital)* aide-soignant(e) *m,f*
2 *adj* (**a**) *(tidy)* méthodique; *(life, room)* rangé(e) (**b**) *(well-behaved)* discipliné(e); **in an o. fashion** avec calme
ordinal ['ɔːdɪnəl] **1** *n (nombre m)* ordinal *m*
2 *adj* ordinal(e)
ordinance ['ɔːdɪnəns] *n Formal (decree)* ordonnance *f*
ordinarily ['ɔːdɪnərɪlɪ] *adv* normalement
ordinary ['ɔːdɪnərɪ] **1** *n* **out of the o.** qui sort de l'ordinaire, exceptionnel(elle)
2 *adj* ordinaire; **she was just an o. tourist** c'était une touriste comme une autre; *Br Naut* **o. seaman** ≃ matelot *m; Br Fin* **o. share** action *f* ordinaire
ordination [ɔːdɪ'neɪʃən] *n Rel* ordination *f*
ordnance ['ɔːdnəns] *n Mil (supplies)* matériel *m; (guns)* artillerie *f;* **o. factory** manufacture *f* d'artillerie; *Br* **O. Survey** ≃ Institut *m* Géographique National
ore [ɔː(r)] *n* minerai *m*
oregano [ɒrɪ'gɑːnəʊ] *n* origan *m*
organ ['ɔːgən] *n* (**a**) *(part of body, newspaper)* organe *m;* **o. donor** donneur(euse) *m,f* d'organe; **o. transplant** greffe *f* d'organe (**b**) *(musical instrument)* orgue *m*
organ-grinder ['ɔːgəngraɪndə(r)] *n* joueur(euse) *m,f* d'orgue de Barbarie
organic [ɔː'gænɪk] *adj (disease, chemistry)* organique; *(food, farming)* biologique; **an o. whole** un tout
organism ['ɔːgənɪzəm] *n* organisme *m*
organist ['ɔːgənɪst] *n* organiste *mf*
organization [ɔːgənaɪ'zeɪʃən] *n* organisation *f*
organize ['ɔːgənaɪz] **1** *vt* (**a**) *(put into order)* organiser; **to o. one's time** s'organiser (**b**) *(take care of)* s'occuper de
2 *vi (of workers)* se syndiquer
organized ['ɔːgənaɪzd] *adj (trip)* organisé(e); **o. crime** le crime organisé, le grand banditisme; **o. labour** main-d'œuvre *f* syndiquée
organizer ['ɔːgənaɪzə(r)] *n (person)* organisateur(trice) *m,f; (diary)* agenda *m*
orgasm ['ɔːgæzəm] *n* orgasme *m;* **to have an o.** avoir un orgasme
orgy ['ɔːdʒɪ] *(pl* **orgies)** *n* orgie *f; Fig* **an o. of violence** un déchaînement de violence
orient ['ɔːrɪənt] **1** *n* **the O.** l'Orient *m*
2 *vt* = orientate

oriental [ɔːrɪ'entəl] **1** *n Old-fashioned* O. Oriental(e) *m,f*
2 *adj* oriental(e)
orientate ['ɔːrɪənteɪt] *vt* orienter (**to** *or* **towards** vers); **to o.** oneself s'orienter; **to be orientated towards sb/sth** *(aimed at)* être destiné(e) à qn/qch
orientation [ɔːrɪən'teɪʃən] *n* orientation *f*; **o. course** stage *m* d'initiation
orienteering [ɔːrɪən'tɪərɪŋ] *n* course *f* d'orientation
orifice ['ɒrɪfɪs] *n* orifice *m*
origin ['ɒrɪdʒɪn] *n* origine *f*; **country of o.** pays *m* d'origine; **of Greek o.** d'origine grecque
original [ə'rɪdʒɪnəl] **1** *n (painting, document)* original *m*
2 *adj* (**a**) *(not copied, innovative)* original(e) (**b**) *(first)* d'origine; *Rel* **o. sin** péché *m* originel
originality [ərɪdʒɪ'nælɪtɪ] *n* originalité *f*
originally [ə'rɪdʒɪnəlɪ] *adv* (**a**) *(initially)* à l'origine, au départ; **where do you come from o.?** d'où êtes-vous originaire? (**b**) *(in an innovative way)* d'une façon originale
originate [ə'rɪdʒɪneɪt] **1** *vt* être à l'origine de
2 *vi (of fire)* prendre naissance; **to o. from** *(of person)* être originaire de; **to o. in** *(of custom)* être originaire de
Orkney ['ɔːknɪ] *n* **the O. Islands, the Orkneys** les Orcades *fpl*
ornament 1 *n* ['ɔːnəmənt] ornement *m*
2 *vt* ['ɔːnəment] orner
ornamental [ɔːnə'mentəl] *adj* ornemental(e), décoratif(ive); **o. lake** pièce *f* d'eau
ornate [ɔː'neɪt] *adj (building, surroundings)* orné(e), ornementé(e); *(style)* fleuri(e)
ornithology [ɔːnɪ'θɒlədʒɪ] *n* ornithologie *f*
orphan ['ɔːfən] **1** *n* orphelin(e) *m,f*; **to be left an o.** devenir orphelin(e)
2 *adj* **an o. child** un (une) orphelin(e)
3 *vt* **to be orphaned** devenir orphelin(e)
orphanage ['ɔːfənɪdʒ] *n* orphelinat *m*
orthodontist [ɔːθəʊ'dɒntɪst] *n* orthodontiste *mf*
orthodox ['ɔːθədɒks] *adj* orthodoxe
orthodoxy ['ɔːθədɒksɪ] *n* orthodoxie *f*
orthopaedic, *Am* **orthopedic** [ɔːθə'piːdɪk] *adj* orthopédique; **o. surgeon** (chirurgien *m*) orthopédiste *mf*
orthopaedics, *Am* **orthopedics** [ɔːθə'piːdɪks] *n* orthopédie *f*
Oscar® ['ɒskə(r)] *n Cin* oscar *m*; **the Oscars** *(ceremony)* la cérémonie des oscars, les oscars *mpl*
Oscar-winning ['ɒskəwɪnɪŋ] *adj* **an O. film** un film oscarisé *ou* primé aux oscars; **in her O. role** dans le rôle qui lui a valu l'oscar
oscillate ['ɒsɪleɪt] *vi* osciller
osmosis [ɒz'məʊsɪs] *n also Fig* osmose *f*
osprey ['ɒspreɪ] *(pl* **ospreys)** *n* balbuzard *m*, *Can* aigle *m* pêcheur
ossify ['ɒsɪfaɪ] *(pt & pp* **ossified)** *vi Anat* s'ossifier; *Fig (of person)* se fossiliser; *(of system, organization)* se scléroser
ostensible [ɒs'tensɪbəl] *adj* soi-disant *inv*
ostensibly [ɒs'tensɪblɪ] *adv* soi-disant
ostentation [ɒsten'teɪʃən] *n* ostentation *f*
ostentatious [ɒsten'teɪʃəs] *adj (person)* m'as-tu-vu *inv*; *(thing)* prétentieux(euse)
osteoarthritis [ɒstɪəʊɑː'θraɪtɪs] *n* ostéoarthrite *f*
osteopath ['ɒstɪəpæθ] *n* ostéopathe *mf*
osteoplasty ['ɒstɪəʊplæstɪ] *n Med* ostéoplastie *f*

osteoporosis [ɒstɪəʊpə'rəʊsɪs] *n Med* ostéoporose *f*
ostracism ['ɒstrəsɪzəm] *n* ostracisme *m*
ostracize ['ɒstrəsaɪz] *vt* mettre en quarantaine
ostrich ['ɒstrɪtʃ] *n* autruche *f*
OTC [əʊtiː'siː] *n Br Mil (abbr* **Officers' Training Corps)** = centre de formation pour ceux qui envisagent de devenir officier dans l'armée
other ['ʌðə(r)] **1** *adj* autre; **the o. one** l'autre *mf*; **every o. day/week** un jour/une semaine sur deux; **the o. day/week** l'autre jour/semaine; **the o. four** les quatre autres; **o. people like it** d'autres l'aiment bien; **any o. book** n'importe quel autre livre; **somebody o. than me** quelqu'un d'autre que moi
2 *pron* autre; **others** d'autres *mfpl*; **the others** les autres *mfpl*; **one after the o.** l'un(e) après l'autre; **one or o. of us** l'un d'entre nous; **somewhere or o.** quelque part; **somebody o.** quelqu'un; **some woman or o.** une femme
3 *adv* **the colour's odd, but o. than that, it's perfect** la couleur est bizarre mais à part cela, il est très bien; **she never speaks of him o. than admiringly** elle ne parle jamais de lui autrement qu'avec admiration
otherwise ['ʌðəwaɪz] **1** *adv* autrement; **to be o. engaged** avoir d'autres engagements; **except where o. stated** sauf indication contraire
2 *conj* autrement, sinon
other-worldly [ʌðə'wɜːldlɪ] *adj (person)* détaché(e) de ce monde
OTT [əʊtiː'tiː] *adj Br Fam (abbr* **over the top)** trop *inv*; **that's a bit O.!** c'est un peu exagéré!
Ottawa ['ɒtəwə] *n* Ottawa
otter ['ɒtə(r)] *n* loutre *f*
Ottoman ['ɒtəmən] *Hist* **1** *n* Ottoman(e) *m,f*
2 *adj* ottoman(e)
ottoman ['ɒtəmən] *n (furniture)* ottomane *f*
OU [əʊ'juː] *n Br (abbr* **Open University)** = organisme d'enseignement universitaire par correspondance doublé d'émissions de télévision et de radio
ouch [aʊtʃ] *exclam (expressing pain)* aïe!, ouïe!
ought [ɔːt] *v aux*

La forme négative **ought not** s'écrit **oughtn't** en forme contractée.

(**a**) *(expressing obligation, desirability)* **I o. to be going** je devrais m'en aller; **you oughtn't to worry so much** vous ne devriez pas vous inquiéter autant; **he had drunk more than he o. to** il n'aurait pas dû boire autant; **this o. to have been done before** on aurait dû le faire avant; **they o. not to have waited** ils n'auraient pas dû attendre (**b**) *(expressing probability)* **they o. to be in Paris by now** ils ont dû arriver à Paris maintenant; **you o. to be able to get £150 for the painting** vous devriez pouvoir tirer 150 livres de ce tableau
oughtn't ['ɔːtənt] = **ought not**
ounce [aʊns] *n (unit of weight)* = 28,35 g, once *f*; *Fig* **an o. of** une once de
our ['aʊə(r)] *possessive adj* (**a**) *(singular)* notre; *(plural)* nos; **o. job** notre travail; **o. wives** nos femmes; **it wasn't our idea!** ce n'est pas nous qui en avons eu l'idée! (**b**) *(for parts of body)* **we hit o. heads** nous nous sommes cogné la tête
ours ['aʊəz] *possessive pron* (**a**) *(singular)* le nôtre *m*, la nôtre *f*; *(plural)* les nôtres; **their house is big but o. is bigger** leur maison est grande, mais la nôtre est plus grande encore (**b**) *(used attributively)* **this book is o.** ce livre est à nous; **a friend of o.** un de nos amis;

where's that brother of o.? où notre frère a-t-il bien pu passer?

ourselves [aʊəˈselvz] *pron* (**a**) *(reflexive)* we hurt o. nous nous sommes blessés (**b**) *(emphatic)* nous-mêmes; **we o. have never...** nous-mêmes n'avons jamais...; **we told you o.** nous vous l'avons dit nous-mêmes; **we're not o. today** nous ne sommes pas dans notre état normal aujourd'hui (**c**) *(after preposition)* **we live by o.** nous vivons seuls; **we bought it for o.** nous nous le sommes acheté; **we talk to o.** nous parlons tout seuls

oust [aʊst] *vt* évincer (**from** de)

out [aʊt] **1** *adv* (**a**) *(outside)* dehors; **to go o.** sortir; **o. here** ici; **o. there** dehors; **o.!** *(in tennis)* faute! (**b**) *(not at home, not in)* **to be o.** être sorti(e); **to stay o. late** rentrer tard (**c**) *(not concealed)* **the secret is o.** on a révélé le secret; **he's o.** *(openly gay)* il a révélé son homosexualité; **the sun is o.** il y a du soleil; **the moon is o.** la lune est levée (**d**) *(published)* sorti(e) (**e**) *(not in fashion)* passé(e) de mode (**f**) *(indicating aim)* **to be o. to do sth** chercher à faire qch; **to be o. for money** vouloir à tout prix de l'argent; *Fam* **to be o. to get sb** chercher la perte de qn (**g**) *(unconscious, asleep)* **to be o. cold** *or* **for the count** être K-O; *Fam* **to go o. like a light** s'endormir comme une masse (**h**) *(extinguished)* éteint(e) (**i**) **to be o. (on strike)** faire grève (**j**) *(inaccurate)* faux (fausse); **I was £25 o.** *(over)* j'avais 25 livres de trop; *(under)* il me manquait 25 livres (**k**) *(indicating completion)* **before the week is o.** avant la fin de la semaine (**l**) *(in phrases with "of")* **o. of** *(outside)* hors de; **to go o. of the office** sortir du bureau; **to look o. of the window** regarder par la fenêtre; **to be o. of the country** être en voyage à l'étranger; **o. of reach/danger** hors de portée/danger; **to be o. of cash/ideas** ne plus avoir de liquide/d'idées; **to do sth o. of friendship/curiosity** faire qch par amitié/curiosité; **she paid for it o. of her own money** elle l'a payé de ses propres deniers; **20 o. of 20** 20 sur 20; **three days o. of four** trois jours sur quatre; *Fam* **to be o. of it** *(drunk, on drugs)* être raide; *Fam* **to feel o. of it** ne pas se sentir dans le coup

2 *prep (through)* **to look o. the window** regarder par la fenêtre

out-and-out [aʊtənˈaʊt] *adj (villain, liar)* fieffé(e); *(failure)* total(e); *(disgrace, scandal)* véritable

outback [ˈaʊtbæk] *n* **the o.** l'intérieur *m*

outbid [aʊtˈbɪd] *(pt & pp* **outbid**) *vt* enchérir avec succès sur

outboard [ˈaʊtbɔːd] **1** *n (motor)* moteur *m* hors-bord **2** *adj* **o. motor** moteur *m* hors-bord

outbox [ˈaʊtbɒks] *n Comput (for e-mail)* corbeille *f* de départ

outbreak [ˈaʊtbreɪk] *n (of hostilities, war)* déclenchement *m*; *(of rioting, violence)* flambée *f*; *(of disease)* épidémie *f*

outbuilding [ˈaʊtbɪldɪŋ] *n* dépendance *f*

outburst [ˈaʊtbɜːst] *n* éclat *m*; *(of activity, temper)* accès *m*; *(of hatred, violence)* explosion *f*; *(of enthusiasm)* élan *m*

outcast [ˈaʊtkɑːst] *n* paria *m*

outclass [aʊtˈklɑːs] *vt* surclasser

outcome [ˈaʊtkʌm] *n* résultat *m*, issue *f*

outcrop [ˈaʊtkrɒp] *n* affleurement *m*

outcry [ˈaʊtkraɪ] *(pl* **outcries**) *n (protest)* tollé *m*; **public o.** tollé *m* général

outdated [aʊtˈdeɪtɪd] *adj* démodé(e)

outdid [aʊtˈdɪd] *pt of* **outdo**

outdistance [aʊtˈdɪstəns] *vt* distancer, dépasser

outdo [aʊtˈduː] *(pt* **outdid** [aʊtˈdɪd], *pp* **outdone** [aʊtˈdʌn]) *vt* surpasser; **not to be outdone,...** pour ne pas être en reste,...

outdoor [ˈaʊtdɔː(r)] *adj (life)* au grand air; *(activities, games)* de plein air; *(swimming pool)* découvert(e); **she's an o. person** elle aime le grand air

outdoors [aʊtˈdɔːz] **1** *n* **the great o.** les grands espaces *mpl* **2** *adv* dehors

outer [ˈaʊtə(r)] *adj* extérieur(e); **O. London** la grande banlieue de Londres; **o. space** espace *m* intersidéral

outermost [ˈaʊtəməʊst] *adj (nearest the outside)* le (la) plus à l'extérieur; *(most remote)* le (la) plus reculé(e)

outfit [ˈaʊtfɪt] *n* (**a**) *(clothes)* ensemble *m*, tenue *f* (**b**) *Fam (organization)* boîte *f*

outflank [aʊtˈflæŋk] *vt Mil* déborder; *Fig* prendre par surprise

outflow [ˈaʊtfləʊ] *n (of liquid)* écoulement *m*; *(of capital)* fuite *f*

outgoing [ˈaʊtɡəʊɪŋ] *adj* (**a**) *(departing)* sortant(e) (**b**) *(sociable)* extraverti(e)

outgoings [ˈaʊtɡəʊɪŋz] *npl* dépenses *fpl*

outgrow [aʊtˈɡrəʊ] *(pt* **outgrew** [aʊtˈɡruː], *pp* **outgrown** [aʊtˈɡrəʊn]) *vt (habit, behaviour, toys)* passer l'âge de; **she's outgrown her jacket** son blouson est devenu trop petit pour elle

outhouse [ˈaʊthaʊs] *n* dépendance *f*

outing [ˈaʊtɪŋ] *n* (**a**) *(excursion)* excursion *f*, sortie *f* (**b**) *(of homosexual)* = fait de rendre publique l'homosexualité d'une personne connue

outlandish [aʊtˈlændɪʃ] *adj* incongru(e), bizarre

outlast [aʊtˈlɑːst] *vt (object)* durer plus longtemps que; *(person)* survivre à

outlaw [ˈaʊtlɔː] **1** *n* hors-la-loi *m inv* **2** *vt (practice)* rendre illégal(e); *(person)* mettre hors la loi

outlay [ˈaʊtleɪ] *n (expense)* frais *mpl*, dépenses *fpl*

outlet [ˈaʊtlet] *n* (**a**) *(for water, steam)* orifice *m* de sortie; *(for emotions, energy)* exutoire *m* (**b**) *(shop)* point *m* de vente

outline [ˈaʊtlaɪn] **1** *n* (**a**) *(shape)* silhouette *f*; *(drawing)* tracé *m* (**b**) *(summary) (of play, novel)* résumé *m*; *(of plan, policy)* grandes lignes *fpl*; **in o.** en gros, dans les grandes lignes **2** *vt* (**a**) *(shape)* repasser les contours de; **her figure was outlined against the sky** sa silhouette se découpait sur le ciel (**b**) *(plot of novel)* résumer; *(plan, policy)* donner les grandes lignes de

outlive [aʊtˈlɪv] *vt* survivre à; **she will o. us all** elle nous enterrera tous; **to have outlived its usefulness** *(of machine, theory)* ne plus servir (à rien)

outlook [ˈaʊtlʊk] *n* (**a**) *(prospect)* perspectives *fpl*; *(of weather)* prévisions *fpl* (**b**) *(attitude)* façon *f* de voir les choses; **o. on life** conception *f* de la vie (**c**) *(view)* vue *f* (**over** sur)

outlying [ˈaʊtlaɪɪŋ] *adj* éloigné(e), isolé(e)

outmanoeuvre, *Am* **outmaneuver** [aʊtmə-ˈnuːvə(r)] *vt Mil* l'emporter tactiquement sur; *(in politics, sport)* déjouer les tactiques de

outmoded [aʊtˈməʊdɪd] *adj* démodé(e)

outnumber [aʊtˈnʌmbə(r)] *vt* l'emporter en nombre sur; **we were outnumbered** ils étaient plus nombreux (que nous)

out-of-date [aʊtəvˈdeɪt] *adj (idea, attitude, clothes)* démodé(e); *(passport)* périmé(e)

out-of-doors [aʊtəvˈdɔːz] *adv* = **outdoors**

out-of-pocket expenses [aʊtəv'pɒkɪtɪk'spensɪz] *npl* menues dépenses *fpl*

out-of-the-way [aʊtəvðə'weɪ] *adj (remote)* écarté(e), loin de tout; *(unusual)* insolite, qui sort de l'ordinaire

outpatient ['aʊtpeɪʃənt] *n* malade *mf* en consultation externe; **outpatients' (department)** service *m* des consultations externes

outplacement ['aʊtpleɪsmənt] *n* outplacement *m*, = aide à la recherche d'un nouvel emploi, fournie par l'employeur lors d'un licenciement

outpost ['aʊtpəʊst] *n Mil* poste *m* avancé; *Fig* bastion *m*

output ['aʊtpʊt] **1** *n (of goods)* production *f; (of data, information)* sortie *f; (of generator, machine)* débit *m*
  2 *vt (pt & pp* **output**) produire; *(data, information)* sortir

outrage ['aʊtreɪdʒ] **1** *n* (**a**) *(act)* atrocité *f;* **it's an o.!** c'est un scandale! (**b**) *(indignation)* indignation *f* (**at** face à)
  2 *vt (make indignant)* scandaliser, outrer

outrageous [aʊt'reɪdʒəs] *adj (shocking)* scandaleux(euse); *(clothes, haircut)* extravagant(e)

outrageously [aʊt'reɪdʒəslɪ] *adv (expensive)* scandaleusement; *(behave)* de façon scandaleuse; *(dress)* de façon extravagante

outran [aʊt'ræn] *pt of* **outrun**

outreach worker ['aʊtriːtʃwɜːkə(r)] *n* = employé d'une association travaillant sur le terrain

outrider ['aʊtraɪdə(r)] *n Br (motorcyclist)* motard *m* (d'escorte)

outright 1 *adj* ['aʊtraɪt] *(refusal)* catégorique; *(failure)* total(e); *(winner)* incontesté(e)
  2 *adv* [aʊt'raɪt] (**a**) *(completely)* **to buy sth o.** acheter qch au comptant; **he was killed o.** il fut tué sur le coup (**b**) *(ask, tell)* franchement; *(refuse)* catégoriquement

outrun [aʊt'rʌn] *(pt* **outran** [aʊt'ræn], *pp* **outrun**) *vt* courir plus vite que

outsell [aʊt'sel] *(pt & pp* **outsold** [aʊt'səʊld]) *vt* se vendre mieux que

outset ['aʊtset] *n* **at the o.** au départ; **from the o.** dès le départ

outshine [aʊt'ʃaɪn] *(pt & pp* **outshone** [aʊt'ʃɒn]) *vt (surpass)* éclipser

outside 1 *n* ['aʊtsaɪd] extérieur *m*, dehors *m*; **on the o.** à l'extérieur; *Fig* extérieurement; **from the o.** du dehors, de l'extérieur; **at the o.** *(of estimate)* tout au plus
  2 *adj* ['aʊtsaɪd] *(influence)* extérieur(e); *Rad & TV* **o. broadcast** reportage *m*; **o. lane** *(when driving on left)* file *f* de droite; *(when driving on right)* file *f* de gauche; **the o. world** le monde extérieur; **an o. chance** une petite chance
  3 *adv* [aʊt'saɪd] dehors, à l'extérieur; **to go o.** sortir
  4 *prep* [aʊt'saɪd] (**a**) *(physically)* en dehors de, à l'extérieur de; *(in front of)* devant; **o. office hours** en dehors des heures de bureau (**b**) *(apart from)* en dehors de; (**c**) **(of) a few friends** en dehors de quelques amis

outsider [aʊt'saɪdə(r)] *n* (**a**) *(socially)* étranger(ère) *m,f* (**b**) *(in race, election)* outsider *m*

outsize ['aʊtsaɪz] *adj (clothes)* très grande taille; *(appetite, ego)* démesuré(e)

outskirts ['aʊtskɜːts] *npl* **the o.** la banlieue

outsmart [aʊt'smɑːt] *vt* se montrer plus fin(e) que

outsold [aʊt'səʊld] *pt & pp of* **outsell**

outsource ['aʊtsɔːs] *vt Com* externaliser

outsourcing ['aʊtsɔːsɪŋ] *n Com* externalisation *f*

outspoken [aʊt'spəʊkən] *adj* franc (franche)

outstanding [aʊt'stændɪŋ] *adj* (**a**) *(remarkable)* exceptionnel(elle) (**b**) *(unresolved) (business)* en suspens (**c**) *(unpaid) (amount, debt)* impayé(e); *(payment)* en retard; *(interest)* échu(e)

outstay [aʊt'steɪ] *vt* **I hope I haven't outstayed my welcome** j'espère ne pas avoir abusé de votre hospitalité

outstretched ['aʊtstretʃt] *adj (leg, arm)* tendu(e)

outstrip [aʊt'strɪp] *(pt & pp* **outstripped**) *vt* dépasser

outtake ['aʊtteɪk] *n Cin & TV* coupure *f*

out-tray ['aʊttreɪ] *n* courrier *m* à expédier

outward ['aʊtwəd] **1** *adj* (**a**) *(external)* extérieur(e) (**b**) **o. voyage** *or* **journey** voyage *m* aller
  2 *adv* = **outwards**

outwardly ['aʊtwədlɪ] *adv* en apparence

outwards ['aʊtwədz] *adv* vers l'extérieur

outweigh [aʊt'weɪ] *vt (be more important than)* l'emporter sur

outwit [aʊt'wɪt] *(pt & pp* **outwitted**) *vt* se montrer plus malin(igne) que

outworker ['aʊtwɜːkə(r)] *n* travailleur(euse) *m,f* à domicile

outworn [aʊt'wɔːn] *adj (theory, idea)* périmé(e)

ova ['əʊvə] *pl of* **ovum**

oval ['əʊvəl] **1** *n* ovale *m*
  2 *adj* ovale

ovarian [əʊ'veərɪən] *adj Anat* ovarien(enne)

ovary ['əʊvərɪ] *(pl* **ovaries**) *n Anat* ovaire *m*

ovation [əʊ'veɪʃən] *n* ovation *f;* **to give sb a standing o.** se lever pour applaudir qn

oven ['ʌvən] *n* four *m;* **o. glove** gant *m* isolant

oven-proof ['ʌvənpruːf] *adj* qui va au four

oven-ready ['ʌvənredɪ] *adj* prêt(e) à rôtir

ovenware ['ʌvənweə(r)] *n* vaisselle *f* allant au four

over ['əʊvə(r)] **1** *prep* (**a**) *(above)* au-dessus de; **the plane flew o. our heads** l'avion est passé au-dessus de nos têtes; **I couldn't hear her o. the noise** impossible de l'entendre avec tout ce bruit; *Fig* **her talk was way o. my head** son exposé m'est passé complètement au-dessus de la tête
  (**b**) *(on top of)* sur; **to put a blanket o. sb** mettre une couverture sur qn
  (**c**) *(from one side to the other of)* par-dessus; **to throw sth o. the wall** jeter qch par-dessus le mur; **to read o. sb's shoulder** lire par-dessus l'épaule de qn
  (**d**) *(across)* **to go o. the road** traverser la rue; **to live o. the road** habiter en face; **o. the border** de l'autre côté de la frontière; **the bridge o. the river** le pont qui traverse la rivière
  (**e**) *(about)* **to laugh o. sth** rire de qch; **to fight o. sth** se battre pour qch
  (**f**) *(more than)* plus de; **he's o. fifty** il a plus de cinquante ans; **children o. five** les enfants de plus de cinq ans; **o. and above** en plus de
  (**g**) *(during)* pendant; **o. the last three years** trois dernières années; **o. lunch** en déjeunant
  (**h**) *(recovered from)* **to be o. sth** *(illness, disappointment)* s'être remis(e) de qch; **to be o. sb** *(ex)* ne plus penser à qn
  2 *adv* (**a**) *(across)* **o. here** ici; **o. there** là-bas; **to cross o.** *(the street)* traverser; **to ask** *or* **invite sb o.** **(to one's house)** inviter qn (chez soi)
  (**b**) *(down)* **to fall o.** tomber; **to bend o.** se pencher; **to push sb/sth o.** faire tomber qn/qch
  (**c**) *(everywhere)* **famous the world o.** célèbre dans le monde entier

(**d**) *(expressing repetition)* **three times o.** trois fois de suite; **o. and o. again** encore et encore; **to do sth all o. again** refaire qch

(**e**) *(in excess)* **children of five and o.** les enfants de cinq ans et plus; **there was £5 left o.** il restait 5 livres (**f**) *(on radio)* **o.!** à vous!; **o. and out!** terminé!

3 *adj* **to be (all) o.** être fini(e); **to get sth o. (and done) with** en finir avec qch

4 *n (in cricket)* = série de six balles

overabundant [əʊvərə'bʌndənt] *adj* surabondant(e)

overactive [əʊvər'æktɪv] *adj (imagination)* débridé(e)

overall ['əʊvərɔːl] **1** *adj* global(e); *(size, area)* total(e); **she has o. responsibility for sales** elle est responsable de l'ensemble du service des ventes

2 *adv* dans l'ensemble; **£10 o.** 10 livres en tout; **third o.** troisième au classement général

overalls ['əʊvərɔːlz] *npl* (**a**) *(work garment)* bleu *m* de travail (**b**) *Am (dungarees)* salopette *f*

overanxious [əʊvər'æŋkʃəs] *adj* trop inquiet(ète)

overate [əʊvər'eɪt] *pt of* **overeat**

overawe [əʊvə'rɔː] *vt* **to be overawed by sb/sth** se laisser impressionner par qn/qch

overbalance [əʊvə'bæləns] *vi (of person)* perdre l'équilibre; *(of pile, load)* se renverser

overbearing [əʊvə'beərɪŋ] *adj* autoritaire

overblown [əʊvə'bləʊn] *adj (style)* ampoulé(e)

overboard ['əʊvəbɔːd] *adv* par-dessus bord; **man o.!** un homme à la mer!; *Fig* **to go o. (about)** s'emballer (pour)

overbook [əʊvə'bʊk] **1** *vt (hotel, flight)* surbooker, surréserver

2 *vi (airline, hotel)* surbooker, surréserver

overbooking [əʊvə'bʊkɪŋ] *n* surbooking *m*

overcame [əʊvə'keɪm] *pt* **overcome**

overcapacity ['əʊvəkə'pæsɪti] *n Ind* surcapacité *f*

overcast ['əʊvəkɑːst] *adj (sky, day)* nuageux(euse)

overcautious [əʊvə'kɔːʃəs] *adj* trop prudent(e)

overcharge [əʊvə'tʃɑːdʒ] *vt* **to o. sb for sth** faire payer qch trop cher à qn; **he overcharged me by a pound** il m'a fait payer une livre en trop

overcoat ['əʊvəkəʊt] *n* pardessus *m*

overcome [əʊvə'kʌm] *vt* **overcame** [əʊvə'keɪm], *pp* **overcome**) *vt (opponent, one's fears)* vaincre; *(problem, obstacle)* surmonter; **to be overcome with** *or* **by grief** être accablé(e) de chagrin; **I was quite overcome** j'ai été bouleversé

overcompensate [əʊvə'kɒmpenseɪt] *vi* **to o. for sth** surcompenser qch

overconfident [əʊvə'kɒnfɪdənt] *adj* trop confiant(e)

overcook [əʊvə'kʊk] *vt* (faire) trop cuire; **the vegetables are overcooked** les légumes sont trop cuits

overcrowded [əʊvə'kraʊdəd] *adj* bondé(e)

overcrowding [əʊvə'kraʊdɪŋ] *n* surpeuplement *m*

overdeveloped [əʊvədɪ'veləpt] *adj* trop développé(e)

overdo [əʊvə'duː] *(pt* **overdid** [əʊvə'dɪd], *pp* **overdone** [əʊvə'dʌn]) *vt* exagérer; **to o. it** *(work too hard)* se surmener; **to o. the salt/make-up** forcer sur le sel/le maquillage

overdone [əʊvə'dʌn] **1** *adj (food)* trop cuit(e)

2 *pp of* **overdo**

overdose ['əʊvədəʊs] **1** *n* overdose *f*

2 *vi* faire une overdose (**on** de); *Fig* **to o. on chocolate** exagérer avec le chocolat

overdraft ['əʊvədrɑːft] *n Fin* découvert *m*

overdrawn [əʊvə'drɔːn] *adj* à découvert

overdressed [əʊvə'drest] *adj* trop habillé(e)

overdrive ['əʊvədraɪv] *n Fig* **to go into o.** passer à la vitesse supérieure

overdue [əʊvə'djuː] *adj (person, train)* en retard; *(bill)* impayé(e); *(library book)* qui n'a pas été rendu(e); **this measure is long o.** cette mesure aurait dû être prise il y a longtemps

overeat [əʊvər'iːt] *(pt* **overate** [əʊvər'eɪt], *pp* **overeaten** [əʊvər'iːtən]) *vi* trop manger

overemphasize [əʊvər'emfəsaɪz] *vt* trop mettre l'accent sur

overenthusiastic ['əʊvərenθjuːzɪ'æstɪk] *adj* trop enthousiaste

overestimate [əʊvər'estɪmeɪt] *vt* surestimer; *(danger)* exagérer

overexcited [əʊvərek'saɪtɪd] *adj* surexcité(e)

overexpose [əʊvəreks'pəʊz] *vt Phot* surexposer

overexposed [əʊvərek'spəʊzd] *adj Phot* surexposé(e); *Fig (in the media)* surmédiatisé(e)

overextended [əʊvərek'stendɪd] *adj Fin* incapable de faire face à ses engagements

overfishing [əʊvə'fɪʃɪŋ] *n* surpêche *f*

overflow 1 *n* ['əʊvəfləʊ] *(liquid)* trop-plein *m*; **(pipe)** trop-plein *m*

2 *vi* [əʊvə'fləʊ] déborder; **his desk was overflowing with papers** son bureau disparaissait sous la paperasse

overgrown [əʊvə'grəʊn] *adj (garden)* envahi(e) par les mauvaises herbes; **he's like an o. schoolboy** il se conduit comme un collégien

overhang 1 *n* ['əʊvəhæŋ] *(of roof, cliff)* surplomb *m*

2 *vt* [əʊvə'hæŋ] *(pt & pp* **overhung** [əʊvə'hʌŋ]) surplomber

overhaul 1 *n* ['əʊvəhɔːl] *also Fig* révision *f*

2 *vt* [əʊvə'hɔːl] (**a**) *(machine, policy)* réviser (**b**) *(overtake)* dépasser

overhead 1 *n* ['əʊvəhed] *Com Am* **o.**, *Br* **overheads** frais *mpl* généraux

2 *adj* ['əʊvəhed] *(cable)* aérien(enne); **o. projector** rétroprojecteur *m*

3 *adv* [əʊvə'hed] au-dessus; **a plane flew o.** un avion passa au-dessus de nos têtes

overhear [əʊvə'hɪə(r)] *(pt & pp* **overheard** [əʊvə'hɜːd]) *vt (person)* entendre (par hasard); *(words)* surprendre

overheat [əʊvə'hiːt] *vi (of engine)* chauffer; *(of economy)* être en surchauffe

overhung [əʊvə'hʌŋ] *pp & pt of* **overhang**

overindulge [əʊvərɪn'dʌldʒ] **1** *vt (child)* trop gâter; **to o. oneself** *(drink, eat to excess)* faire des excès

2 *vi* faire des excès

overjoyed [əʊvə'dʒɔɪd] *adj* absolument ravi(e) (**at** de)

overkill ['əʊvəkɪl] *n* **it's o.** c'est exagéré, c'est trop; **media o.** matraquage *m*

overland ['əʊvəlænd] *adj & adv* par voie de terre

overlap 1 *n* ['əʊvəlæp] *(between planks, tiles)* chevauchement *m*

2 *vi* [əʊvə'læp] *(pt & pp* **overlapped**) *(of planks, tiles, periods)* se chevaucher; *(of theories)* avoir des points communs (**with** avec); **to o. with** *(in time)* empiéter sur

overleaf [əʊvə'liːf] *adv* au verso; **see o.** voir au verso

overload 1 *n* ['əʊvələʊd] *Elec* surcharge *f*

2 *vt* [əʊvə'ləʊd] *also Fig* surcharger (**with** de)

overlong [əʊvə'lɒŋ] *adj* trop long (longue)

overlook [əʊvə'lʊk] *vt* (**a**) *(of building, window)* donner sur; **the town is overlooked by the castle** le château surplombe la ville (**b**) *(fail to notice)* oublier (**c**) *(disregard)* fermer les yeux sur

overly ['əʊvəlɪ] *adv* excessivement, trop

overmanning [əʊvə'mænɪŋ] *n* sureffectifs *mpl*

overmuch [əʊvə'mʌtʃ] *adv* outre mesure, trop

overnight [əʊvə'naɪt] **1** *adj* (**a**) *(for one night)* **o. train/flight** train *m*/vol *m* de nuit; **o. bag** petit sac *m* de voyage; **o. stay** séjour *m* d'une nuit; *(in hotel)* nuit *f* (**b**) *(sudden)* soudain(e) **2** *adv* (**a**) *(during the night)* (pendant) la nuit; **to stay o.** passer la nuit; **leave to soak o.** laisser tremper toute la nuit (**b**) *(suddenly)* du jour au lendemain

overoptimistic [əʊvərɒptɪ'mɪstɪk] *adj* trop optimiste (**about** quant à)

overpaid [əʊvə'peɪd] *adj* trop payé(e)

overpass ['əʊvəpɑːs] *n (road)* pont *m*; *(for pedestrians)* passerelle *f*

overpayment [əʊvə'peɪmənt] *n (of taxes)* trop-perçu *m*; *(of employee)* rémunération *f* excessive

overpopulation [əʊvəpɒpjʊ'leɪʃən] *n* surpopulation *f*, surpeuplement *m*

overpower [əʊvə'paʊə(r)] *vt* maîtriser

overpowering [əʊvə'paʊərɪŋ] *adj (heat, smell)* suffocant(e); *(taste)* qui prend à la gorge; *(desire)* irrépressible

overpriced [əʊvə'praɪst] *adj* trop cher(ère)

overproduction [əʊvəprə'dʌkʃən] *n Econ* sur-production *f*

overran [əʊvə'ræn] *pt of* overrun

overrated [əʊvə'reɪtɪd] *adj* surfait(e)

overreach [əʊvə'riːtʃ] *vt* **to o. oneself** trop présumer de ses forces

overreact [əʊvərɪ'ækt] *vi* réagir de façon excessive

override [əʊvə'raɪd] *vt (pt* **overrode** [əʊvə'rəʊd], *pp* **overridden** [əʊvə'rɪdən]) (**a**) *(objections, wishes, regulations)* passer outre à; *(decision)* annuler (**b**) *(take precedence over)* avoir la priorité sur; *Tech (device)* annuler

overriding [əʊvə'raɪdɪŋ] *adj (importance)* capital(e); *(factor)* prépondérant(e)

overrode [əʊvə'rəʊd] *pt of* override

overrule [əʊvə'ruːl] *vt (opinion)* rejeter; *(decision)* annuler; **she was overruled by her boss** son patron a rejeté sa proposition

overrun 1 *vt* [əʊvə'rʌn] *(pt* **overran** [əʊvə'ræn], *pp* **overrun**) (**a**) *(country)* envahir; **the house was overrun with mice** la maison était infestée de souris (**b**) *(allotted time)* dépasser **2** *vi* [əʊvə'rʌn] *(of TV, radio programme)* déborder sur l'horaire **3** *n* ['əʊvərʌn] *Com* (**cost**) **o.** dépassement *m* du budget

oversaw [əʊvə'sɔː] *pt of* oversee

overseas 1 *adj* ['əʊvəsiːz] d'outre-mer; *(trade, debt)* extérieur(e) **2** *adv* [əʊvə'siːz] à l'étranger

oversee [əʊvə'siː] *(pt* **oversaw** [əʊvə'sɔː], *pp* **overseen** [əʊvə'siːn]) *vt* superviser

overseer ['əʊvəsɪə(r)] *n Old-fashioned* contremaître *m*

oversensitive [əʊvə'sensɪtɪv] *adj* hypersensible

oversexed [əʊvə'sekst] *adj* qui a une libido démesurée

overshadow [əʊvə'ʃædəʊ] *vt Fig (of atmosphere, threat)* planer sur; *(of person)* éclipser

overshoe ['əʊvəʃuː] *n Am* caoutchouc *m*

overshoot [əʊvə'ʃuːt] *(pt & pp* **overshot** [əʊvə'ʃɒt]) *vt* dépasser

oversight ['əʊvəsaɪt] *n* oubli *m*, omission *f*

oversimplify [əʊvə'sɪmplɪfaɪ] *(pt & pp* **oversimplified**) *vt* simplifier à outrance

oversized ['əʊvəsaɪzd] *adj (very big)* énorme; *(clothes)* trop grand(e)

oversleep [əʊvə'sliːp] *(pt & pp* **overslept** [əʊvə'slept]) *vi* ne pas se réveiller à temps

overspend [əʊvə'spend] *(pt & pp* **overspent** [əʊvə'spent]) **1** *vt* **to o. one's budget** dépasser son budget **2** *vi* trop dépenser

overspill ['əʊvəspɪl] *n (of population)* excédent *m*; *(from meeting, party)* trop-plein *m*

overstaffing [əʊvə'stɑːfɪŋ] *n* sureffectifs *mpl*

overstate [əʊvə'steɪt] *vt* exagérer

overstay [əʊvə'steɪ] = outstay

overstep [əʊvə'step] *(pt & pp* **overstepped**) *vt* outrepasser; *Fig* **to o. the mark** dépasser les bornes

oversubscribed [əʊvəsəb'skraɪbd] *adj Fin* sursouscrit(e)

overt [əʊ'vɜːt] *adj* manifeste

overtake [əʊvə'teɪk] *(pt* **overtook** [əʊvə'tʊk], *pp* **overtaken** [əʊvə'teɪkən]) *vt & vi* dépasser, doubler; **to be overtaken by events** être dépassé(e) par les événements

over-the-top [əʊvəðə'tɒp] *adj Br Fam* excessif(ive); **that's a bit o.!** c'est un peu exagéré!

overthrow 1 *n* ['əʊvəθrəʊ] renversement *m* **2** *vt* [əʊvə'θrəʊ] *(pt* **overthrew** [əʊvə'θruː], *pp* **overthrown** [əʊvə'θrəʊn]) renverser

overtime ['əʊvətaɪm] **1** *n* heures *fpl* supplémentaires **2** *adv* **to work o.** faire des heures supplémentaires; *Fig (of imagination)* s'emballer

overtly [əʊ'vɜːtlɪ] *adv* ouvertement

overtone ['əʊvətəʊn] *n (of sadness, bitterness)* pointe *f*; *(of violence, racism)* relent *m*; **his speech was full of racist overtones** son discours était truffé de sous-entendus racistes

overtook [əʊvə'tʊk] *pt of* overtake

overture ['əʊvətjʊə(r)] *n Mus* ouverture *f*; *Fig* **to make overtures to sb** *(sexually)* faire des avances à qn; *(in business, politics)* faire des démarches auprès de qn

overturn [əʊvə'tɜːn] **1** *vt (table, government)* renverser; *(boat)* faire chavirer; *(decision)* annuler **2** *vi* se renverser; *(of boat)* chavirer

overuse 1 *n* [əʊvə'juːs] emploi *m* excessif **2** *vt* [əʊvə'juːz] abuser de

overvalue [əʊvə'væljuː] *vt (currency)* surévaluer; *(ability)* surestimer

overview ['əʊvəvjuː] *n* vue *f* d'ensemble

overweight [əʊvə'weɪt] *adj* trop gros (grosse); **to be 10 kilos o.** avoir 10 kilos de trop

overwhelm [əʊvə'welm] *vt (enemy, opponent)* écraser; **overwhelmed with joy** au comble de la joie; **overwhelmed by grief/with work** accablé(e) de chagrin/de travail

overwhelming [əʊvə'welmɪŋ] *adj (need, desire)* irrépressible; *(pressure, defeat, majority)* écrasant(e)

overwhelmingly [əʊvə'welmɪŋlɪ] *adv* massivement

overwork 1 *n* ['əʊvəwɜːk] surmenage *m* **2** *vt* [əʊvə'wɜːk] *(person)* surcharger de travail **3** *vi* [əʊvə'wɜːk] se surmener

overwrite [əʊvə'raɪt] *(pt* **overwrote** [əʊvə'rəʊt], *pp* **overwritten** [əʊvə'rɪtən]) *vt Comput (file)* écraser; **o. mode** mode *m* de superposition

overwrought [əʊvə'rɔːt] *adj* à bout; **to get o. (about sth)** se mettre dans tous ses états (à propos de qch)

ovulate ['ɒvjʊleɪt] *vi Biol* ovuler

ovulation [ɒvjʊˈleɪʃən] *n Biol* ovulation *f*
ovum [ˈəʊvəm] (*pl* **ova** [ˈəʊvə]) *n Biol* ovule *m*
ow [aʊ] *exclam* aïe!, ouïe!
owe [əʊ] *vt also Fig* devoir; **to o. sb sth, to o. sth to sb** devoir qch à qn; **to o. sb an apology** devoir des excuses à qn; **to o. it to oneself to do sth** se devoir de faire qch
owing [ˈəʊɪŋ] *adj* (**a**) **the money o. to me** l'argent qui m'est dû (**b**) **o. to** *(because of)* en raison de, à cause de
owl [aʊl] *n* hibou *m*, chouette *f*
own [əʊn] **1** *adj* propre; **her o. money** son propre argent; **I saw it with my o. eyes** je l'ai vu de mes propres yeux; **I do my o. accounts** je fais mes comptes moi-même; **she's famous in her o. right** elle est célèbre elle aussi; **o. goal** *(in football)* but *m* marqué contre son propre camp, *Suisse* autogoal *m*; *Fig* **to score an o. goal** apporter de l'eau au moulin de l'adversaire
2 *pron* (**a**) **my o.** le mien (la mienne); **the house is my o.** la maison est à moi; **I have money of my o.** j'ai de l'argent à moi; **to make sth one's o.** s'approprier qch; **for reasons of her o.** pour des raisons qui ne regardent qu'elle (**b**) **to do sth on one's o.** *(without company)* faire qch tout(e) seul(e); **I am (all) on my o.** je suis seul(e); **you're on your o.!** *(I won't support you)* débrouille-toi tout(e) seul(e)! (**c**) *(idioms)* **to come into one's o.** montrer ce dont on est capable; **to get one's o. back (on sb)** se venger (de qn); **to hold one's o.** se maintenir
3 *vt* (**a**) *(property)* posséder, être propriétaire de; **who owns this jumper?** à qui est ce pull?; **he behaves as if he owns the place** il se conduit comme en pays conquis (**b**) *Old-fashioned (admit)* avouer
▸**own up** *vi (confess)* avouer; **to o. up to sth** avouer qch
own-brand [ˈəʊnbrænd] *adj Com* vendu(e) sous la marque du distributeur
owner [ˈəʊnə(r)] *n* propriétaire *mf*
owner-occupier [ˈəʊnərˈɒkjʊpaɪə(r)] *n* propriétaire *mf* occupant(e)
ownership [ˈəʊnəʃɪp] *n* propriété *f*; **under new o.** *(sign)* changement de propriétaire; **to be in private/public o.** appartenir au secteur privé/public

ox [ɒks] (*pl* **oxen** [ˈɒksən]) *n* bœuf *m*
Oxbridge [ˈɒksbrɪdʒ] *n* les universités *fpl* d'Oxford et de Cambridge

Oxbridge

"Oxbridge" désigne conjointement les universités d'Oxford et de Cambridge, les plus anciennes et les plus prestigieuses d'Angleterre. Celles-ci se distinguent des autres établissements d'enseignement supérieur, notamment par leur structure collégiale et leurs conditions d'admission très rigoureuses. De nos jours, "Oxbridge" est toujours synonyme d'élitisme en dépit des efforts entrepris pour élargir le recrutement des deux universités. Jusqu'à une époque très récente, un diplôme d'Oxbridge était considéré comme indispensable pour accéder à des postes importants dans le monde de la politique ou de la diplomatie.

oxen [ˈɒksən] *pl of* **ox**
oxide [ˈɒksaɪd] *n Chem* oxyde *m*
oxidize [ˈɒksɪdaɪz] *Chem* **1** *vt* oxyder **2** *vi* s'oxyder
oxtail [ˈɒksteɪl] *n* queue *f* de bœuf
oxygen [ˈɒksɪdʒən] *n* oxygène *m*; **o. bottle** *or* **cylinder** bouteille *f* d'oxygène; **o. mask** masque *m* à oxygène
oxymoron [ɒksɪˈmɔːrɒn] (*pl* **oxymora** [ɒksɪˈmɔːrə]) *n* oxymore *m*, oxymoron *m*
oyster [ˈɔɪstə(r)] *n* huître *f*; *Fig* **the world's your o.** le monde t'appartient; **o. bed** parc *m* à huîtres; **o. farming** ostréiculture *f*
oystercatcher [ˈɔɪstəkætʃə(r)] *n* huîtrier *m*
Oz [ɒz] *n Fam* l'Australie *f*
oz (*abbr* **ounce(s)**) once *f*
ozone [ˈəʊzəʊn] *n Chem* ozone *m*; **o. depletion** diminution *f* de la couche d'ozone; **the o. layer** la couche d'ozone
ozone-friendly [ˈəʊzəʊnˈfrendlɪ] *adj* qui préserve la couche d'ozone

P, p¹ [piː] *n (letter)* P, p *m inv*; *Fam* **to mind one's P's and Q's** bien se tenir; *Br* **P45** = document administratif donné à tout employé lorsqu'il quitte un emploi et devant être présenté à tout nouvel employeur, où figurent le total de ses rémunérations, cotisations et impôts; *Fig* **to be handed one's P45** se faire licencier

p² [piː] *Br* (**a**) *(abbr* **penny**) penny *m* (**b**) *(abbr* **pence**) pence *mpl*

P2P [piːtuːˈpiː] *adj Comput (abbr* **peer-to-peer**) P2P

PA [ˈpiːˈeɪ] *n* (**a**) *(abbr* **public address**) **PA (system)** (système *m* de) sonorisation *f* (**b**) *Com (abbr* **personal assistant**) secrétaire *mf* de direction

pa [pɑː] *n Fam (dad)* papa *m*

p.a. *(abbr* **per annum**) par an

pace [peɪs] **1** *n* (**a**) *(step)* pas *m*; *Fig* **to put sb through his/her paces** mettre qn à l'épreuve (**b**) *(speed)* vitesse *f*, allure *f*; **at a slow/fast p.** à petite/vive allure; **to set the p.** donner l'allure; *Fig* montrer la voie; **to keep p. with sb** suivre qn; *Fig (in activity)* suivre le rythme de qn; **the slower p. of country life** le rythme plus paisible de la vie à la campagne
2 *vt (room, street)* arpenter; **to p. oneself** *(in race, work)* trouver son rythme
3 *vi* **to p. up and down** faire les cent pas

pacemaker [ˈpeɪsmeɪkə(r)] *n* (**a**) *(in race)* meneur(euse) *m,f* de train (**b**) *(for heart)* stimulateur *m* cardiaque

Pacific [pəˈsɪfɪk] *adj* **the P. (Ocean)** le Pacifique, l'océan *m* Pacifique; **the P. Rim** les pays *mpl* de l'Asie-Pacifique; *Am* **P. Standard Time** heure *f* de la côte ouest de l'Amérique du Nord

pacifier [ˈpæsɪfaɪə(r)] *n Am* tétine *f*

pacifism [ˈpæsɪfɪzəm] *n* pacifisme *m*

pacifist [ˈpæsɪfɪst] **1** *n* pacifiste *mf*
2 *adj* pacifiste

pacify [ˈpæsɪfaɪ] *(pt & pp* **pacified**) *vt (country)* pacifier; *(person)* apaiser, calmer

pack [pæk] **1** *n* (**a**) *(rucksack)* sac *m* à dos (**b**) *(of cigarettes, washing powder)* paquet *m*; *(of beer)* pack *m*; *(of playing cards)* jeu *m* (**c**) *(of thieves)* bande *f*; *(of runners, cyclists)* peloton *m*; *(in rugby)* pack *m*; *(of wolves)* meute *f*; **a p. of lies** un tissu de mensonges; **p. animal** animal *m* de bât; **p. ice** banquise *f*
2 *vt* (**a**) *(in box, suitcase)* mettre (dans sa valise/son sac/sa malle/*etc*) (**b**) *(cram) (earth into hole)* tasser; *(passengers into bus, train)* entasser (**c**) *(fill) (hole, box)* bourrer (**with** de); *also Fig* **to p. one's bags** faire ses valises (**d**) **to p. a punch** *(of fighter)* cogner dur; *(of drink)* être costaud
3 *vi* (**a**) *(prepare luggage)* faire ses valises *ou* bagages; *Fam Fig* **to send sb packing** envoyer promener qn

(**b**) *(cram)* **to p. into a room/bus** s'entasser dans une pièce/un bus

► **pack in** *Fam* **1** *vt (job, course)* laisser tomber; **p. it in!** arrête!, ça suffit!
2 *vi (of car, machine)* tomber en rade

► **pack off** *vt sep Fam (send away)* expédier

► **pack up 1** *vt sep (tidy away)* ranger
2 *vi Fam* (**a**) *(of car, machine)* tomber en rade (**b**) *(finish work)* arrêter

package [ˈpækɪdʒ] **1** *n (parcel)* paquet *m*, colis *m*; *(of measures, laws)* ensemble *m*; *(contract)* contrat *m* global; **p. deal** *or* **holiday** forfait *m (comprenant au moins transport et logement)*
2 *vt* emballer, conditionner; *Fig* **to p. sb** *(pop star, politician)* créer l'image de marque de qn

packaging [ˈpækɪdʒɪŋ] *n* emballage *m*

packed [pækt] *adj* (**a**) *(crowded)* bondé(e) (**b**) **p. lunch** panier-repas *m*, casse-croûte *m inv*

packer [ˈpækə(r)] *n (person)* emballeur(euse) *m,f*

packet [ˈpækɪt] *n* (**a**) *(of food, washing powder, cigarettes)* paquet *m*; **p. soup** soupe *f* en sachet (**b**) *Fam (lot of money)* **to make a p.** se faire un fric fou; **that'll cost a p.** ça va coûter bonbon

packhorse [ˈpækhɔːs] *n* cheval *m* de bât

packing [ˈpækɪŋ] *n* (**a**) *(packing material)* emballage *m*; **p. case** caisse *f* d'emballage (**b**) *(for trip)* **to do one's p.** faire ses valises *ou* bagages

pact [pækt] *n* pacte *m*

pad [pæd] **1** *n* (**a**) *(for protection)* protection *f*; *(of dog's, cat's paw)* coussinet *m*; *(of cotton wool)* tampon *m*; *(for helicopters)* aire *f* d'atterrissage; **(writing) p.** bloc *m* (**b**) *Fam (home)* piaule *f*
2 *vt (pt & pp* **padded**) *(furniture)* capitonner (**with** avec)
3 *vi* **to p. about** aller et venir à pas feutrés

► **pad out** *vt sep (speech, essay)* étoffer

padded [ˈpædɪd] *adj (furniture, wall, cell)* capitonné(e); *(jacket)* matelassé(e); **p. shoulders** épaulettes *fpl*

padding [ˈpædɪŋ] *n (for clothes)* ouate *f*; *Fig (in speech, essay)* remplissage *m*

paddle [ˈpædəl] **1** *n* (**a**) *(for canoe)* pagaie *f*; *(of paddle boat)* aube *f*; **p. boat** bateau *m* à aubes (**b**) *(walk in water)* **to have a p.** patauger
2 *vi* **to p. a canoe** pagayer
3 *vi* (**a**) *(in canoe)* pagayer; *(of duck)* nager (**b**) *(walk in water)* patauger

paddling pool [ˈpædlɪŋˈpuːl] *n Br* pataugeoire *f*, *Can* barboteuse *f*

paddock [ˈpædək] *n* paddock *m*

Paddy ['pædɪ] (*pl* **Paddies**) *n Br Fam (Irishman)* = terme injurieux désignant un Irlandais

paddy ['pædɪ] (*pl* **paddies**) *n* **p. (field)** rizière *f*

padlock ['pædlɒk] **1** *n* cadenas *m*
2 *vt* cadenasser

padre ['pɑːdreɪ] *n* aumônier *m* (militaire)

paediatric, *Am* **pediatric** [piːdɪ'ætrɪk] *adj Med (ward)* de pédiatrie; *(specialist, nurse)* en pédiatrie

paediatrician, *Am* **pediatrician** [piːdɪə'trɪʃən] *n Med* pédiatre *mf*

paediatrics, *Am* **pediatrics** [piːdɪ'ætrɪks] *n Med* pédiatrie *f*

paedophile, *Am* **pedophile** ['piːdəʊfaɪl] *n* pédophile *mf*

pagan ['peɪgən] **1** *n* païen(enne) *m,f*
2 *adj* païen(enne)

paganism ['peɪgənɪzəm] *n* paganisme *m*

page¹ [peɪdʒ] *n (of book, on Internet)* page *f*; **on p. 6** (à la) page 6

page² **1** *n (servant, at wedding)* page *m*
2 *vt (call) (by loudspeaker)* appeler par haut-parleur; *(by electronic device)* biper

pageant ['pædʒənt] *n (procession)* spectacle *m* grandiose; *(historical)* spectacle *m* historique

pageantry ['pædʒəntrɪ] *n* pompe *f*, apparat *m*

pageboy ['peɪdʒbɔɪ] *n* page *m*; **p. (haircut)** coiffure *f* à la Jeanne d'Arc

pager ['peɪdʒə(r)] *n* récepteur *m* d'appel

pagination [pædʒɪ'neɪʃən] *n Typ* pagination *f*

pagoda [pə'gəʊdə] *n* pagode *f*

paid [peɪd] **1** *adj* (**a**) *(person, work)* rémunéré(e), payé(e) (**b**) **to put p. to sb's chances/hopes** réduire les chances/espoirs de qn à néant
2 *pt & pp of* **pay**

paid-up ['peɪdʌp] *adj (member)* qui a payé sa cotisation

pail [peɪl] *n* seau *m*

pain [peɪn] **1** *n* (**a**) *(physical)* douleur *f*; *(emotional)* peine *f*; **to cause sb p.** *(physical)* faire souffrir qn; *(emotional)* faire de la peine à qn; **to be in p.** souffrir; **I have a p. in my leg** j'ai une douleur à la jambe (**b**) *(trouble)* **to take pains** *or* **be at great pains to do sth** se donner du mal pour faire qch; **for my pains** pour ma peine (**c**) *Formal* **under p. of death** sous peine de mort (**d**) *(idioms) Fam* **he's a p. (in the neck)** il est casse-pieds; *Vulg* **it's a p. in the arse** c'est chiant; *Fam* **cooking is such a p.!** c'est tellement casse-pieds de faire la cuisine!
2 *vt* peiner

pained [peɪnd] *adj (look, expression)* peiné(e), affligé(e)

painful ['peɪnfʊl] *adj (physically)* douloureux(euse); *(emotionally)* pénible; **it's p. to watch** c'est un spectacle pénible

painfully ['peɪnfʊlɪ] *adv (walk)* avec difficulté; **she fell p.** elle s'est fait mal en tombant; *Fig* **p. shy** d'une timidité maladive

painkiller ['peɪnkɪlə(r)] *n* analgésique *m*

painless ['peɪnlɪs] *adj (not painful)* indolore; *Fig (easy)* facile

painstaking ['peɪnzteɪkɪŋ] *adj* minutieux(euse)

paint [peɪnt] **1** *n* peinture *f*; **wet p.** *(sign)* peinture fraîche; **p. gun** pistolet *m* à peinture; **p. remover** décapant *m*
2 *vt* peindre; *Fam* **to p. one's face** *(put on make-up)* se maquiller; **to p. one's nails** se faire les ongles; *Fig* **to p. a favourable picture of a situation** brosser un tableau favorable d'une situation; *Fig* **to p. the town red** faire la noce
3 *vi* peindre

paintball ['peɪntbɔːl] *n (game)* paintball *m*

paintballing ['peɪntbɔːlɪŋ] *n* **to go p.** faire du paintball

paintbox ['peɪntbɒks] *n* boîte *f* de couleurs

paintbrush ['peɪntbrʌʃ] *n* pinceau *m*

painter ['peɪntə(r)] *n* peintre *m*; **p. and decorator** peintre-tapissier *m*

painting ['peɪntɪŋ] *n (picture)* tableau *m*, peinture *f*; *(activity)* la peinture

paintwork ['peɪntwɜːk] *n* peinture *f*

pair [peə(r)] **1** *n* paire *f*; **in pairs** deux par deux; **a p. of glasses** une paire de lunettes; **a p. of scissors** une paire de ciseaux; **a p. of trousers** un pantalon
2 *vt* **to p. sb with sb** mettre qn avec qn
▸ **pair off 1** *vt sep (people)* mettre deux par deux
2 *vi (of people)* se mettre deux par deux
▸ **pair up** *vi* se mettre ensemble

pajamas *Am* = **pyjamas**

Pakistan [pɑːkɪ'stɑːn] *n* le Pakistan

Pakistani [pɑːkɪ'stɑːnɪ] **1** *n* Pakistanais(e) *m,f*
2 *adj* pakistanais(e)

PAL [pæl] *n (abbr* **phase alternation line)** PAL *m*

pal [pæl] *n Fam* copain (copine) *m,f*; **listen, p.!** fais gaffe, mon vieux!

palace ['pælɪs] *n* palais *m*

palatable ['pælətəbəl] *adj (food)* agréable au palais; *Fig (suggestion)* acceptable

palate ['pælɪt] *n (in mouth)* palais *m*

palatial [pə'leɪʃəl] *adj (impressive)* grandiose; *(luxurious)* luxueux(euse)

palaver [pə'lɑːvə(r)] *n Fam (fuss)* histoire *f*

pale¹ [peɪl] **1** *adj* pâle; **to turn p.** pâlir; **p. with fright** blanc de peur; *Br* **p. ale** = bière brune de couleur claire
2 *vi (of person)* pâlir; **to p. into insignificance** être insignifiant(e)

pale² *n* **beyond the p.** *(behaviour)* inacceptable; *(person)* infréquentable

paleness ['peɪlnɪs] *n* pâleur *f*

Palestine ['pælɪstaɪn] *n* la Palestine

Palestinian [pælɪ'stɪnɪən] **1** *n* Palestinien(enne) *m,f*
2 *adj* palestinien(enne)

palette ['pælɪt] *n Art* palette *f*; **p. knife** couteau *m* à palette

palings ['peɪlɪŋz] *npl (fence)* palissade *f*

palisade [pælɪ'seɪd] *n* palissade *f*

pall¹ [pɔːl] *n* (**a**) *(of smoke)* voile *m* (**b**) *(coffin)* cercueil *m*

pall² *vi (become uninteresting)* perdre son attrait

pallbearer ['pɔːlbeərə(r)] *n* porteur *m* (du cercueil)

pallet ['pælɪt] *n* palette *f*

palliative ['pælɪətɪv] *n* palliatif *m*

pallid ['pælɪd] *adj (face)* blême, blafard(e)

pally ['pælɪ] *adj Br Fam* **to be p. with sb** être copain (copine) avec qn

palm¹ [pɑːm] *n* **p. (tree)** palmier *m*; **p. (leaf)** palme *f*; **P. Sunday** Dimanche *m* des Rameaux

palm² *n (of hand)* paume *f*; *Fig* **to have sb in the p. of one's hand** avoir qn dans sa poche
▸ **palm off** *vt sep* **to p. sth off on sb** refiler qch à qn

palmistry ['pɑːmɪstrɪ] *n* chiromancie *f*

palmtop ['pɑːmtɒp] *n Comput* **p. (computer)** ordinateur *m* de poche

palomino [pælə'miːnəʊ] (*pl* **palominos**) *n (horse)* palomino *m*

palpable ['pælpəbəl] *adj (atmosphere)* palpable; *(lie)* manifeste; *(difference)* sensible

palpate ['pælpeɪt] *vt Med* palper

palpitate ['pælpɪteɪt] *vi also Fig* palpiter

palpitations [pælpɪ'teɪʃənz] *npl* palpitations *fpl*

paltry ['pɔːltrɪ] *adj (amount, sum)* dérisoire; *(excuse)* piètre

pamper ['pæmpə(r)] *vt (person)* dorloter; **to p. oneself** se faire plaisir

pamphlet ['pæmflɪt] *n (informative)* brochure *f*; *(political)* pamphlet *m*

pan¹ [pæn] **1** *n (saucepan)* casserole *f*; *(frying pan)* poêle *f*; *(of scales)* plateau *m*; *(of lavatory)* cuvette *f*; *Fam Fig* **to go down the p.** s'en aller en fumée
2 *vi (pt & pp* **panned**) **to p. for gold** faire de l'orpaillage

pan² *(pt & pp* **panned**) *vt Fam (criticize)* descendre en flammes

▸**pan out** *vi Fam (turn out)* marcher, se dérouler; **it depends how things p. out** ça dépend de comment les choses vont s'arranger

panacea [pænə'sɪə] *n* panacée *f*

panache [pə'næʃ] *n* panache *m*

Pan-African [pæn'æfrɪkən] *adj* panafricain(e)

Panama ['pænəmɑː] *n* le Panama; **the P. Canal** le canal de Panama; **P. (hat)** panama *m*

Panamanian [pænə'meɪnɪən] **1** *n* Panaméen(enne) *m,f*
2 *adj* panaméen(enne)

Pan-American [pænə'merɪkən] *adj* panaméricain(e)

pancake ['pænkeɪk] *n* crêpe *f*; **P. Day** *or* **Tuesday** Mardi *m* gras

pancreas ['pæŋkrɪəs] *n Anat* pancréas *m*

panda ['pændə] *n* panda *m*; *Br* **p. car** voiture *f* de police

pandemonium [pændɪ'məʊnɪəm] *n (confusion)* chaos *m*; *(uproar)* vacarme *m* assourdissant

pander ['pændə(r)] *vi* **to p. to sb/sth** flatter qn/qch

p & p [piːən'piː] *n Br (abbr* **postage and packing**) frais *mpl* de port et d'emballage

pane [peɪn] *n* **p. (of glass)** vitre *f*

panel ['pænəl] *n* **(a)** *(of wood, metal)* panneau *m* **(b)** *(of switches, lights)* tableau *m* de bord; **p. beater** carrossier *m* **(c)** *(of experts)* comité *m*; **p. discussion** table *f* ronde; *(on radio, TV programme)* invités *mpl*

panelling, *Am* **paneling** ['pænəlɪŋ] *n* lambris *m*

panellist, *Am* **panelist** ['pænəlɪst] *n (on radio, TV programme)* invité(e) *m,f*

pang [pæŋ] *n (of guilt, jealousy)* accès *m*; **pangs of hunger** tiraillements *mpl* d'estomac

panhandle ['pænhændəl] *Am* **1** *n* langue *f* de terre
2 *vt Fam* **to p. money from sb** taper qn
3 *vi Fam* faire la manche

panic ['pænɪk] **1** *n* panique *f*, affolement *m*; **in a p.** paniqué(e), affolé(e); **to get into a p.** paniquer, s'affoler; **p. attack** crise *f* d'angoisse; **p. button** bouton *m* déclencheur du signal d'alarme; *Fin* **p. buying/selling** achat *m*/vente *f* sous le coup de la panique; *Fam* **it was p. stations** c'était l'affolement général
2 *vt (pt & pp* **panicked**) affoler
3 *vi* paniquer, s'affoler

panicky ['pænɪkɪ] *adj Fam* **to be/get p.** paniquer, s'affoler

panic-stricken ['pænɪkstrɪkən] *adj* pris(e) de panique, affolé(e)

pannier ['pænɪə(r)] *n (on bicycle)* sacoche *f*; *(on animal)* panier *m* de bât

panoply ['pænəplɪ] *n* panoplie *f*

panorama [pænə'rɑːmə] *n* panorama *m*

panoramic [pænə'ræmɪk] *adj* panoramique

panpipes ['pænpaɪps] *npl Mus* flûte *f* de Pan

pansy ['pænzɪ] *(pl* **pansies**) *n* **(a)** *(flower)* pensée *f* **(b)** *Fam (effeminate man)* tante *f*

pant [pænt] *vi* haleter; **to p. for breath** chercher son souffle

panther ['pænθə(r)] *n* panthère *f*

pantihose = **pantyhose**

panties ['pæntɪz] *npl* (petite) culotte *f*, slip *m*

pantomime ['pæntəmaɪm] *n* **(a)** *Br (show)* = spectacle de Noël inspiré d'un conte de fée **(b)** *(mime)* mime *m*

Pantomime

Le genre typiquement britannique de la "pantomime" est très conventionnel ; certains personnages-types ("pantomime dame", "principal boy") et certaines rengaines ("Behind you!", "Oh yes he is! – Oh no he isn't!") apparaissent dans toutes les pièces. Ces pièces, qui se jouent au moment des fêtes de fin d'année, sont généralement inspirées d'un conte de fées.

pantry ['pæntrɪ] *(pl* **pantries**) *n* garde-manger *m inv*

pants [pænts] *npl* **(a)** *Br (underwear)* slip *m* **(b)** *Am (trousers)* pantalon *m*; *Fam* **to scare the p. off sb** flanquer la trouille à qn

pantyhose ['pæntɪhəʊz] *n Am* collant *m*

pap [pæp] *n Fam Pej (nonsense)* idioties *fpl*

papa [pə'pɑː] *n Old-fashioned* papa *m*

papacy ['peɪpəsɪ] *n* papauté *f*

papal ['peɪpəl] *adj* papal(e)

paper ['peɪpə(r)] **1** *n* **(a)** *(material)* papier *m*; **a piece of p.** un bout ou un morceau de papier; *Fig* **on p.** *(in theory)* sur le papier; **p. aeroplane** avion *m* en papier; **p. bag** sac *m* en papier; **p. cup** gobelet *m* en carton; *Comput* **p. feed** alimentation *f* en papier; **p. mill** papeterie *f* en papier; **p. money** papier-monnaie *m*; **p. plate** assiette *f* en carton; **p. towel** essuie-tout *m inv*; *Comput* **p. tray** chariot *m* d'alimentation en papier **(b)** **papers** *(documents)* papiers *mpl* **(c)** *(examination)* épreuve *f* écrite **(d)** *(scholarly study, report)* article *m*; **to read** *or* **give a p.** faire un exposé **(e)** *(newspaper)* journal *m*; **p. boy/girl** livreur *m*/livreuse *f* de journaux; **p. round** tournée *f* de distribution des journaux; **p. shop** marchand *m* de journaux
2 *vt (wall, room)* tapisser

▸**paper over** *vt sep Fig* **to p. over the cracks** masquer les problèmes

paperback ['peɪpəbæk] *n* livre *m* de poche

paperclip ['peɪpəklɪp] *n* trombone *m*

paperknife ['peɪpənaɪf] *(pl* **paperknives**) *n* coupe-papier *m*

paperweight ['peɪpəweɪt] *n* presse-papiers *m inv*

paperwork ['peɪpəwɜːk] *n* travail *m* administratif, paperasserie *f*; *(documentation)* documents *mpl*

papery ['peɪpərɪ] *adj (skin)* parcheminé(e)

papier-mâché ['pæpjeɪ'mæʃeɪ] *n* papier *m* mâché

paprika ['pæprɪkə] *n* paprika *m*

Papuan ['pæpjʊən] **1** *n* Papou(e) *m,f*
2 *adj* papou(e)

Papua New Guinea ['pæpjʊənjuː'gɪnɪ] *n* Papouasie-Nouvelle-Guinée *f*

papyrus [pə'paɪrəs] n papyrus m
par [pɑː(r)] n (**a**) (equality) égalité f, pair m; **to be on a p. with sb/sth** être au même niveau que qn/qch (**b**) (in golf) par m; **a p.-three (hole)** un par trois; Fig **to be p. for the course** n'avoir rien de surprenant (**c**) Fin (of bills, shares) pair m; **above/below p.** au-dessus/au-dessous du pair; Fig **to feel below p.** ne pas être dans son assiette
parable ['pærəbəl] n parabole f
parabolic [pærə'bɒlɪk] adj parabolique
paracetamol [pærə'siːtəmɒl] n paracétamol m
parachute ['pærəʃuːt] **1** n parachute m; **p. jump** saut m en parachute; **to make a p. jump** sauter en parachute
 2 vt parachuter
 3 vi sauter en parachute
parachuting ['pærəʃuːtɪŋ] n parachutisme m; **to go p.** faire du parachutisme
parachutist ['pærəʃuːtɪst] n parachutiste mf
parade [pə'reɪd] **1** n (procession) défilé m; **on p.** (troops) à l'exercice; **a p. of shops** une rangée de magasins; **p. ground** terrain m de manœuvres
 2 vt (troops) faire défiler; Fig (wealth, knowledge) faire étalage de
 3 vi (of troops) défiler; **to p. about** or **around** (of person) se pavaner
paradigm ['pærədaɪm] n paradigme m
paradise ['pærədaɪs] n paradis m
paradox ['pærədɒks] n paradoxe m
paradoxical [pærə'dɒksɪkəl] adj paradoxal(e)
paraffin ['pærəfɪn] n paraffine f; **p. heater** chauffage m à pétrole; **p. lamp** lampe f à pétrole; **p. wax** paraffine f
paragliding ['pærəglaɪdɪŋ] n parapente m; **to go p.** faire du parapente
paragon ['pærəgən] n modèle m; **a p. of virtue** un modèle de vertu
paragraph ['pærəgræf] n paragraphe m
Paraguay ['pærəgwaɪ] n le Paraguay
Paraguayan [pærə'gwaɪən] **1** n Paraguayen(enne) m,f
 2 adj paraguayen(enne)
parakeet ['pærəkiːt] n perruche f
parallel ['pærəlel] **1** n Math parallèle f; Fig (analogy) parallèle m; **to draw a p. between two things** établir un parallèle entre deux choses; **without p.** sans égal, sans pareil
 2 adj Math parallèle; Fig (analogous) pareil(eille), semblable; **to be** or **run p. to sth** être parallèle à qch; **p. bars** barres fpl parallèles; **p. lines** lignes fpl parallèles; Comput **p. processing** traitement m en simultanéité
 3 vt (be similar to) être analogue à; (be equal to) égaler
parallelogram [pærə'leləgræm] n parallélogramme m
paralyse, Am **paralyze** ['pærəlaɪz] vt also Fig paralyser
paralysis [pə'ræləsɪs] (pl paralyses) n paralysie f
paralytic [pærə'lɪtɪk] **1** n paralytique mf
 2 adj paralytique; Br Fam (very drunk) complètement bourré(e)
paralyze Am = paralyse
paramedic [pærə'medɪk] n auxiliaire mf médical(e)
parameter [pə'ræmɪtə(r)] n paramètre m

paramilitary [pærə'mɪlɪtrɪ] (pl paramilitaries) **1** adj paramilitaire
 2 n paramilitaire mf
paramount ['pærəmaʊnt] adj primordial(e); **of p. importance** d'une importance capitale
paranoia [pærə'nɔɪə] n paranoïa f
paranoid ['pærənɔɪd] adj paranoïaque; **to be p. about sth** être obsédé(e) par qch
paranormal [pærə'nɔːməl] **1** n **the p.** le paranormal
 2 adj paranormal(e)
parapet ['pærəpet] n parapet m
paraphernalia [pærəfə'neɪlɪə] n (equipment) attirail m; (things) affaires fpl; (clutter) bazar m
paraphrase ['pærəfreɪz] **1** n paraphrase f
 2 vt paraphraser
paraplegic [pærə'pliːdʒɪk] **1** n paraplégique mf
 2 adj paraplégique
parascending ['pærəsendɪŋ] n parachute m ascensionnel
parasite ['pærəsaɪt] n also Fig parasite m
parasitic [pærə'sɪtɪk] adj also Fig parasite; (existence) de parasite
parasol ['pærəsɒl] n ombrelle f
paratrooper ['pærətruːpə(r)] n parachutiste m
parboil ['pɑːbɔɪl] vt faire cuire à demi
parcel ['pɑːsəl] n (**a**) (package) colis m, paquet m; **bomb** colis m piégé; **p. post** service m de colis postaux (**b**) (of land) parcelle f
▶**parcel out** (pt & pp parcelled, Am parceled) vt sep répartir
▶**parcel up** vt sep empaqueter, emballer
parchment ['pɑːtʃmənt] n parchemin m; **p. paper** papier m parchemin
pardon ['pɑːdən] **1** n (forgiveness) pardon m; Law grâce f; (**I beg your) p.?** (what did you say?) pardon?, comment?; **I beg your p.!** (in apology) je vous demande pardon!
 2 vt (action, person) pardonner; Law gracier; **to p. sb for sth** pardonner qch à qn; **p. me?** (what did you say?) (je vous demande) pardon?; **p. me!** (in apology) pardonnez-moi!
pardonable ['pɑːdənəbəl] adj pardonnable, excusable
pare [peə(r)] vt (vegetable) éplucher; (apple) peler; (nails) rogner; (expenses) réduire
▶**pare down** vt sep (expenses) réduire
parent ['peərənt] n (father) père m; (mother) mère f; **parents** parents mpl; **p. company** société f ou maison f mère; **p.-teacher association** = association des parents d'élèves et des professeurs
parentage ['peərəntɪdʒ] n origine f
parental [pə'rentəl] adj parental(e)
parenthesis [pə'renθəsɪs] (pl parentheses [pə'renθəsiːz]) n parenthèse f; **in parentheses** entre parenthèses
parenthood ['peərənthʊd] n (fatherhood) paternité f; (motherhood) maternité f; **the joys of p.** le bonheur d'être parent
parenting ['peərəntɪŋ] n art m d'être parent; **p. skills** capacité f à élever des enfants
pariah [pə'raɪə] n paria m
Paris ['pærɪs] n Paris
parish ['pærɪʃ] n paroisse f; **p. church** église f paroissiale; **p. council** conseil m municipal; **p. priest** (Catholic) curé m; (Protestant) pasteur m
parishioner [pə'rɪʃənə(r)] n paroissien(enne) m,f

Parisian [pəˈrɪzɪən] **1** n Parisien(enne) m,f
2 adj parisien(enne)
parity [ˈpærɪtɪ] n égalité f; **to achieve p.** (of pay) obtenir l'égalité
park [pɑːk] **1** n jardin m public, parc m; **p. keeper** gardien(enne) m,f de parc
2 vt (car) garer; Fam **to p. oneself in a chair/in front of the TV** s'installer dans un fauteuil/devant la télé
parka [ˈpɑːkə] n parka f
parking [ˈpɑːkɪŋ] n stationnement m; **no p.** (sign) défense de stationner; **p. attendant** gardien(enne) m,f de parking; Am **p. brake** frein m à main; **p. bay** place f de stationnement; **p. lights** (on car) feux mpl de position; Am **p. lot** parking m; **p. meter** parcmètre m, Can compteur m de stationnement; **p. space** place f (de parking); **p. ticket** contravention f
Parkinson's disease [ˈpɑːkɪnsənzdɪˈziːz] n la maladie de Parkinson
parkland [ˈpɑːklænd] n espace(s) m(pl) vert(s)
parkway [ˈpɑːkweɪ] n Am route f bordée d'arbres et de verdure
parlance [ˈpɑːləns] n langage m; **in legal/political p.** en termes juridiques/politiques; **in common p.** en langage ordinaire
parley [ˈpɑːlɪ] vi parlementer (**with** avec); (more officially) être en pourparlers (**with** avec)
parliament [ˈpɑːləmənt] n parlement m
parliamentarian [pɑːləmənˈteərɪən] n parlementaire mf
parliamentary [pɑːləˈmentərɪ] adj parlementaire; **p. privilege** immunité f parlementaire
parlour, Am **parlor** [ˈpɑːlə(r)] n salon m
Parmesan [pɑːmɪˈzæn] n **P. (cheese)** parmesan m
parochial [pəˈrəʊkɪəl] adj Rel paroissial(e); Fig Pej de clocher; **to be p.** (of person) avoir l'esprit de clocher
parody [ˈpærədɪ] **1** n (pl **parodies**) parodie f (**of** de)
2 vt (pt & pp **parodied**) parodier
parole [pəˈrəʊl] **1** n liberté f conditionnelle; **to be (out) on p.** être en liberté conditionnelle; **p. officer** contrôleur m judiciaire
2 vt mettre en liberté conditionnelle
paroxysm [ˈpærəksɪzəm] n (of anger, guilt, jealousy) crise f; **to be in paroxysms of laughter** avoir le fou rire
parquet [ˈpɑːkeɪ] n **p. (floor)** parquet m
parrot [ˈpærət] **1** n also Fig perroquet m
2 vt répéter comme un perroquet
parrot-fashion [ˈpærətfæʃən] adv comme un perroquet
parry [ˈpærɪ] (pt & pp **parried**) vt (blow) parer; (question) éluder
parsimonious [pɑːsɪˈməʊnɪəs] adj parcimonieux(euse)
parsley [ˈpɑːslɪ] n persil m
parsnip [ˈpɑːsnɪp] n panais m
parson [ˈpɑːsən] n pasteur m
parsonage [ˈpɑːsənɪdʒ] n presbytère m
part [pɑːt] **1** n (**a**) (portion, component) partie f; **p. of the body** partie f du corps; **p. of speech** partie f du discours; **(spare) parts** pièces fpl détachées; **p. two** (of TV series, story) deuxième partie f; **in that p. of the world** dans cette région du monde; **in these parts** dans ces régions; **good in parts** bon (bonne) en partie; **the best/worst p. was when...** le meilleur/le pire ça a été quand...; **the difficult p. is remembering** ce qui est difficile, c'est de se souvenir; **for the best** or **greater p. of five years** pendant presque cinq ans; **the greater p. of the population** la plus

grande partie de la population; **to be p. of sth** faire partie de qch; **it's all p. of growing up** c'est ce qui arrive quand on grandit; **it is p. and parcel of...** c'est partie intégrante de...; **in p.** en partie; **for the most p.** pour la plupart; **p. exchange** reprise f (en compte); **p. owner** copropriétaire mf (**b**) (role) rôle m; **to take p. (in sth)** prendre part (à qch); **to have** or **play a p. in sth** jouer un rôle dans qch; **I want no p. in it** je ne veux rien avoir à faire là-dedans (**c**) (side) **to take sb's p.** prendre le parti de qn; **on the p. of...** de la part de...; **for my p.** pour ma part (**d**) Am (in hair) raie f
2 adv **she's p. French** elle est en partie française; **p. silk p. cotton** soie et coton
3 (of fighters, lovers) séparer; **to p. one's hair** se faire une raie; **to p. company** se séparer
4 vi (**a**) (leave one another) se quitter; (split up) se rompre; **to p. (as) friends** se séparer (en) bons amis; **to p. with sth** se défaire de qch (**b**) (of curtains, lips) s'entrouvrir; (of crowd) s'ouvrir
partake [pɑːˈteɪk] (pt **partook** [pɑːˈtʊk], pp **partaken** [pɑːˈteɪkən]) vi Formal (**a**) **to p. of** (eat, drink) prendre (**b**) (have quality) **to p. of** relever de
partial [ˈpɑːʃəl] adj (**a**) (incomplete) partiel(elle) (**b**) (biased) partial(e) (**c**) (fond) **to be p. to sb/sth** avoir un faible pour qn/qch
partially [ˈpɑːʃəlɪ] adv (**a**) (in part) en partie, partiellement (**b**) (with bias) avec partialité
participant [pɑːˈtɪsɪpənt] n participant(e) m,f
participate [pɑːˈtɪsɪpeɪt] vi participer (**in** à)
participation [pɑːtɪsɪˈpeɪʃən] n participation (**in** à)
participle [ˈpɑːtɪsɪpəl] n Gram participe m
particle [ˈpɑːtɪkəl] n (of matter) particule f; (of dust, sand) grain m; Fig (of truth) once f
particular [pəˈtɪkjʊlə(r)] **1** n détail m; **in p.** en particulier; **I didn't see anything in p.** je n'ai rien vu de particulier; **to go into particulars** entrer dans les détails; **to take down sb's particulars** noter les coordonnées de qn
2 adj (**a**) (specific) particulier(ère); (reason, case, example) précis(e); **which p. thing/person did you have in mind?** à quoi/à qui précisez-vous en particulier?; **on that p. day** ce jour-là (**b**) (special) particulier(ère); **a p. favourite of mine** un (une) de mes favoris (favorites); **she is a p. friend of mine** c'est une de mes meilleures amies; **to take p. care over sth** mettre un soin particulier à qch (**c**) (exacting) méticuleux(euse); **to be p. about sth** être exigeant(e) pour qch; **I'm not p.** ça m'est égal
particularly [pəˈtɪkjʊləlɪ] adv (especially) particulièrement, spécialement
parting [ˈpɑːtɪŋ] n (**a**) (separation) séparation f; **the p. of the ways** la croisée des chemins; **p. shot** pique f (lancée en partant); **p. words** mots mpl d'adieu (**b**) Br (in hair) raie f
partisan [pɑːtɪˈzæn] **1** n partisan(e) m,f
2 adj partisan(e)
partition [pɑːˈtɪʃən] **1** n (in room) cloison f
2 vt (country) partager
▸**partition off** vt sep (room) cloisonner
partly [ˈpɑːtlɪ] adv partiellement, en partie
partner [ˈpɑːtnə(r)] **1** n (in games) partenaire mf; (in business) associé(e) m,f; (in dancing) cavalier(ère) m,f; (in relationship) compagnon (compagne) m,f; **p. in crime** complice mf
2 vt (in games) faire équipe avec; (in dancing) être le (la) cavalier(ère) de

partnership ['pɑ:tnəʃɪp] n association f; **to enter** or **go into p.** (**with sb**) s'associer (avec qn)
partook [pɑ:'tʊk] pt of **partake**
partridge ['pɑ:trɪdʒ] n perdrix f
part-time [pɑ:t'taɪm] adj & adv à temps partiel
part-timer [pɑ:t'taɪmə(r)] n travailleur(euse) m,f à temps partiel
partway ['pɑ:tweɪ] adv **to be p. through sth** ne pas avoir complètement terminé qch; **this will go p. towards covering the costs** cela couvrira en partie les dépenses
party ['pɑ:tɪ] **1** n (pl **parties**) (**a**) (political) parti m; **to follow** or **toe the p. line** suivre la ligne du parti; **p. member** membre m du parti; **p. political broadcast** émission f réservée à un parti politique; **p. politics** politique f de parti; Pej politique f politicienne (**b**) (celebration) fête f; **to have** or **give** or **throw a p.** organiser ou faire une fête; Fig **the p.'s over** la fête est finie; Fam **p. animal** fêtard(e) m,f; Hum **p. piece** numéro m favori (**c**) (group) groupe m; (of workers) équipe f; **p. wall** mur m mitoyen (**d**) Law (participant) partie f; **to be (a) p. to sth** se faire complice de qch
2 vi (pt & pp **partied**) Fam (celebrate) faire la fête
pass¹ [pɑ:s] n (over mountains) col m
pass² **1** n (**a**) (permit) laissez-passer m inv; Mil sauf-conduit m; (for travel) carte f d'abonnement (**b**) (in examination) **to get a p.** avoir la moyenne; **p. mark** moyenne f (**c**) (in sport) passe f (**d**) Fam **to make a p. at sb** faire des avances à qn
2 vt (**a**) (go past) (person) croiser; (destination) dépasser; (frontier) traverser; (car, runner) dépasser, doubler (**b**) (exam, test) réussir (**c**) (bill, resolution) voter (**d**) (give) passer; **p. (me) the salt, please** passe-moi le sel, s'il te plaît (**e**) **to p. the time** (of person) passer le temps; **it passes the time** ça fait passer le temps (**f**) Law **to p. sentence** prononcer le verdict; **to p. judgement on sb** porter un jugement sur qn (**g**) **to p. water** uriner; **to p. wind** avoir des vents
3 vi (**a**) (go past) passer; (overtake) dépasser, doubler; **to p. unobserved** passer inaperçu(e); **to let sth p.** laisser tomber qch; also Fig **p.!** je passe!; **I think I'll p. on the onions** je crois que je ne prendrai pas d'oignons (**b**) (of time) s'écouler, (se) passer; **the weekend passed uneventfully** le week-end s'est passé sans surprises (**c**) (go away) passer (**d**) (in exam) avoir la moyenne (**e**) Lit (take place) **it came to p. that...** c'est alors qu'il arriva que...
▶**pass away** vi Euph décéder
▶**pass down** vt sep (knowledge, tradition) transmettre
▶**pass for** vt insep passer pour; **she'd p. for 25** on pourrait lui donner 25 ans
▶**pass off 1** vt sep **to p. oneself off as sb** se faire passer pour qn; **to p. sth off as sth** faire passer qch pour qch; **she passed it off as a joke** elle a prétendu que c'était une plaisanterie
2 vi (take place) se passer
▶**pass on 1** vt sep (object) faire passer; (news, information) faire circuler; (disease) passer
2 vi Euph décéder
▶**pass out** vi (**a**) (faint) perdre connaissance (**b**) (of military cadet) sortir avec ses diplômes
▶**pass over** vt sep **to p. sb over (for promotion)** ignorer qn au moment d'une promotion
▶**pass through 1** vt insep traverser
2 vi passer
▶**pass up** vt sep (opportunity) laisser passer

passable ['pɑ:səbəl] adj (**a**) (of acceptable quality) passable (**b**) (road, bridge) praticable; (river) franchissable
passage ['pæsɪdʒ] n (**a**) (journey) passage m; **with the p. of time** avec le temps; **to work one's p.** (on ship) travailler pour payer sa traversée (**b**) (corridor) couloir m, corridor m; (alley) passage m (**c**) (extract) passage m
passageway ['pæsɪdʒweɪ] n (corridor) couloir m, corridor m; (alley) passage m
passé [pæ'seɪ] adj dépassé(e)
passenger ['pæsəndʒə(r)] n passager(ère) m,f; **p. seat** place f du passager
passer-by ['pɑ:sə'baɪ] (pl **passers-by**) n passant(e) m,f
passing ['pɑ:sɪŋ] **1** n (**a**) (going past) passage m; **to say sth in p.** dire qch en passant; **p. place** (on road) aire f de croisement (**b**) (of time) écoulement m (**c**) (death) décès m
2 adj (car, motorist) qui passe; (remark) en passant; (whim, attraction) passager(ère)
passion ['pæʃən] n (desire) passion f; (anger, vehemence) emportement m, colère f; **to have a p. for sth** adorer qch; **in a fit of p.** sous le coup de la passion; **she hates him with a p.** elle le hait de toute son âme; **crime of p.** crime m passionnel; Rel **the P. (of Christ)** la Passion (du Christ); **p. fruit** fruit m de la passion
passionate ['pæʃənɪt] adj (lover, embrace) passionné(e); (plea, speech) véhément(e); (believer, defender) fervent(e); **to make p. love** faire l'amour avec passion
passive ['pæsɪv] **1** n Gram **the p.** le passif; **in the p.** au passif
2 adj passif(ive); **p. resistance** résistance f passive; **p. smoking** tabagisme m passif
passive-aggressive ['pæsɪvə'gresɪv] adj Psy passif-agressif (passive-agressive)
passively ['pæsɪvlɪ] adv passivement, avec passivité
passkey ['pɑ:ski:] (pl **passkeys**) n passe-partout m
Passover ['pɑ:səʊvə(r)] n Rel la Pâque (Juive)
passport ['pɑ:spɔ:t] n passeport m; **p. control** contrôle m des passeports; **p. number** numéro m de passeport; **p. photo** photo f d'identité
password ['pɑ:swɜ:d] n mot m de passe
past [pɑ:st] **1** n passé m; **in the p.** autrefois; **a thing of the p.** une chose qui appartient au passé; **to live in the p.** vivre dans le passé
2 adj (a) passé(e); **those days are p.** ces jours sont révolus; **in times p.** autrefois; **to be a p. master at sth** être passé(e) maître dans l'art de qch; **the p. week** la semaine dernière; **the p. few days** ces derniers jours; Gram **p. participle** participe m passé; **in the p. tense** au passé
3 prep (beyond) au-delà de; **to walk p. the house** passer devant la maison; **it's p. four (o'clock)** il est quatre heures passées; **ten p. four** quatre heures dix; **I'm p. caring** je n'en ai plus rien à faire; Fam **to be p. it** avoir fait son temps; Fam **I wouldn't put it p. her** elle en est bien capable
4 adv **to walk** or **go p.** passer; **to run p.** passer en courant
pasta ['pæstə] n pâtes fpl
paste [peɪst] **1** n (**a**) (substance) pâte f (**b**) (pâté) mousse f (**c**) (glue) colle f
2 vt (glue) coller
pastel ['pæstəl] **1** n pastel m
2 adj pastel inv; **p. shades** tons mpl pastel

pasteurize ['pæstjʊraɪz] vt pasteuriser; **pasteurized milk** lait m pasteurisé
pastiche [pæ'stiːʃ] n pastiche m
pastille ['pæstɪl] n pastille f
pastime ['pɑːstaɪm] n passe-temps m inv
pasting ['peɪstɪŋ] n Fam (beating) raclée f; **to give sb a p.** flanquer une raclée à qn
pastor ['pɑːstə(r)] n Rel pasteur m
pastoral ['pɑːstərəl] adj (**a**) (rural) pastoral(e) (**b**) (work, activities) de conseiller(ère)
pastry ['peɪstrɪ] (pl **pastries**) n (dough) pâte f; (cake) pâtisserie f; **p. chef** pâtissier(ère) m,f
pasture ['pɑːstʃə(r)] n pâture f, pré m; **to be put out to p.** (of animals) être mis(e) au pré; Fig (of person) être mis(e) au vert; Fig **to move on to pastures new** aller vers de nouveaux horizons
pasty¹ ['pæstɪ] (pl **pasties**) n (savoury) ≃ feuilleté m
pasty² ['peɪstɪ] adj (face, complexion) terreux(euse); **p.-faced** au teint terreux
pat [pæt] **1** n (**a**) (tap) petite tape f; (on animal) caresse f; Fig **to give sb a p. on the back** féliciter qn (**b**) (of butter) médaillon m
2 adj (answer, explanation) tout(e) prêt(e)
3 adv **to know** or **have sth off p.** savoir qch par cœur
4 vt (pt & pp **patted**) (tap) tapoter; (animal) caresser; **to p. sb on the head/shoulder** donner une tape sur la tête/l'épaule de qn; Fig **to p. sb on the back** féliciter qn
Patagonia [pætə'gəʊnɪə] n la Patagonie
patch [pætʃ] **1** n (**a**) (of cloth) pièce f; (eye) **p.** bandeau m; Fam **his last novel isn't a p. on the others** son dernier roman est loin de valoir les autres (**b**) (of colour, light) tache f; (of fog, mist) nappe f; (of ice) plaque f; **a p. of blue sky** un coin de ciel bleu; Fam Fig **to be going through a bad p.** traverser une mauvaise passe (**c**) (of land) lopin m; (of prostitute, salesperson) secteur m; Fam **keep off my p.!** hors de mon territoire!
2 vt (hole, garment) rapiécer
▸**patch up** vt sep Fam (wounded person) donner les premiers soins à; (marriage, friendship) raccommoder; **to p. things up** (after argument) se raccommoder
patchwork ['pætʃwɜːk] n also Fig patchwork m; **p. quilt** couvre-lit m en patchwork
patchy ['pætʃɪ] adj inégal(e)
pâté ['pæteɪ] n pâté m
patent ['peɪtənt] **1** n (licence) brevet m d'invention; **to take out a p. on sth** faire breveter qch; Com **p. applied for, p. pending** demande de brevet déposée
2 adj (**a**) (patented) breveté(e); **p. medicine** spécialité f pharmaceutique (**b**) (evident) manifeste (**c**) **p. leather** cuir m verni
3 vt (of authorities) breveter; (of inventor) faire breveter
patently ['peɪtəntlɪ] adv manifestement
paternal [pə'tɜːnəl] adj (feelings) paternel(elle); (duty, responsibilities) de père
paternally [pə'tɜːnəlɪ] adv paternellement
paternity [pə'tɜːnɪtɪ] n paternité f; **p. leave** congé m de paternité; Law **p. suit** action f en recherche de paternité; **p. test** test m de recherche de paternité
path [pɑːθ] n (**a**) (track) chemin m; (narrow) sentier m; (in garden) allée f; **their paths had crossed before** leurs chemins s'étaient croisés auparavant (**b**) (of rocket, planet) trajectoire f; (of inquiry, to success) voie f; **the storm destroyed everything in its p.** la tem-

pête a tout détruit sur son passage (**c**) Comput chemin m
pathetic [pə'θetɪk] adj (useless) lamentable; (touching) attendrissant(e)
pathetically [pə'θetɪklɪ] adv (uselessly) lamentablement; (touchingly) de manière attendrissante
pathological [pæθə'lɒdʒɪkəl] adj pathologique
pathologist [pə'θɒlədʒɪst] n pathologiste mf
pathology [pə'θɒlədʒɪ] n pathologie f
pathos ['peɪθɒs] n pathétique m
pathway ['pɑːθweɪ] n sentier m
patience ['peɪʃəns] n (**a**) (quality) patience f; **to try** or **tax sb's p.** mettre la patience de qn à l'épreuve; **to exhaust sb's p.** abuser de la patience de qn; **to lose one's p. (with sb)** perdre patience (avec qn); **I've no p. with him** il m'énerve (**b**) (card game) réussite f; **to play p.** faire une réussite
patient ['peɪʃənt] **1** n patient(e) m,f
2 adj patient(e)
patiently ['peɪʃəntlɪ] adv patiemment
patio ['pætɪəʊ] (pl **patios**) n patio m
patriarch ['peɪtrɪɑːk] n patriarche m
patriarchal [peɪtrɪ'ɑːkəl] adj patriarcal(e)
patriarchy ['peɪtrɪɑːkɪ] (pl **patriarchies**) n patriarcat m
patrimony ['pætrɪmənɪ] n patrimoine m, héritage m
patriot ['pætrɪət, 'peɪtrɪət] n patriote mf
patriotic [pætrɪ'ɒtɪk, peɪtrɪ'ɒtɪk] adj patriotique
patriotism ['pætrɪətɪzəm, 'peɪtrɪətɪzəm] n patriotisme m
patrol [pə'trəʊl] **1** n patrouille f; **to be on p.** être de patrouille; **p. car** voiture f de police
2 vt (pt & pp **patrolled**) patrouiller dans
3 vi patrouiller; **to p. up and down** faire les cent pas
patrolman [pə'trəʊlmæn] n Am agent m de police
patron ['peɪtrən] n (**a**) (of arts) protecteur(trice) m,f, mécène m; (of charity) patron(onne) m,f; **p. saint** (saint(e) m,f) patron(onne) m,f (**b**) (of shop) client(e) m,f
patronage ['pætrənɪdʒ] n (**a**) (of arts, charity) patronage m; **under the p. of** sous le patronage de (**b**) Pej (in politics) copinage m
patronize ['pætrənaɪz] vt (**a**) (arts) protéger; (shop, restaurant) fréquenter (**b**) (treat condescendingly) traiter avec condescendance
patronizing ['pætrənaɪzɪŋ] adj condescendant(e)
patter¹ ['pætə(r)] **1** n (of footsteps) petit bruit m; (of rain) crépitement m
2 vi (of rain) crépiter; **she pattered along the corridor** elle trottinait le long du couloir
patter² ['pætə(r)] n Br Fam (talk) boniment m, baratin m
pattern ['pætən] **1** n (**a**) (design) dessin m, motif m; **p. book** catalogue m d'échantillons (**b**) **p. of behaviour** comportement m type; **a normal p. of events** une suite typique d'événements; **the evening followed the usual p.** la soirée s'est déroulée comme d'habitude; **some clear patterns emerge from the statistics** des tendances nettes ressortent des statistiques (**c**) (in sewing) patron m; (in knitting) modèle m (**d**) (norm) modèle m; **to set a p.** créer un modèle
2 vt (model) **to p. sth on sth** modeler qch sur qch
patterned ['pætənd] adj à motifs
paunch [pɔːntʃ] n ventre m; **to have a p.** avoir du ventre
pauper ['pɔːpə(r)] n indigent(e) m,f; **p.'s grave** fosse f commune

pause [pɔːz] **1** *n (in conversation)* silence *m*; *(rest)* pause *f*; *(in music)* point *m* d'orgue
2 *vi* faire une pause; **to p. for breath** reprendre son souffle
pave [peɪv] *vt (road)* paver (**with** de); *Fig* **to p. the way for sth** ouvrir la voie à qch
pavement ['peɪvmənt] *n Br (beside road)* trottoir *m*; *Am (roadway)* chaussée *f*; **p. artist** artiste *mf* qui dessine sur les trottoirs; **p. café** café *m* avec terrasse
pavilion [pə'vɪlɪən] *n* pavillon *m*
paving ['peɪvɪŋ] *n (with tiles)* carrelage *m*; *(with slabs)* dallage *m*; **p. stone** pavé *m*
paw [pɔː] **1** *n* patte *f*; *Fam* **paws off!** bas les pattes!
2 *vt (of animal)* donner un coup/des coups de patte à; **to p. the ground** frapper le sol du sabot
pawn[1] [pɔːn] *vt* mettre au mont-de-piété *ou* en gage
pawn[2] *n (in chess) & Fig* pion *m*
pawnbroker ['pɔːnbrəʊkə(r)] *n* prêteur(euse) *m,f* sur gage
pawnshop ['pɔːnʃɒp] *n* mont-de-piété *m*, bureau *m* de prêt sur gage
pay [peɪ] **1** *n* paie *f*, salaire *m*; **the p.'s good/bad** ça paie bien/mal; **to be in sb's p.** être à la solde de qn; **p. cheque** chèque *m* de paie; **p. packet** enveloppe *f* de paie; **p. rise** augmentation *f* de salaire; **p. slip** bulletin *m* de salaire; **p. talks** négociations *fpl* salariales
2 *vt (pt & pp paid* [peɪd]*)* (**a**) *(person, money, bill)* payer; **I paid £5 for it** je l'ai payé 5 livres; **to be well/badly paid** être bien/mal payé(e); **I wouldn't do it if you paid me** je ne le ferais pas même si on me payait; **to p. one's way** payer son écot; **to p. cash** payer (argent) comptant; **to p. money into sb's account** verser de l'argent sur le compte de qn (**b**) *(give)* **to p. sb a compliment** faire un compliment à qn; **to p. sb a visit** rendre visite à qn; **to p. tribute to sb** rendre hommage à qn; **to p. one's respects to sb** présenter ses respects à qn (**c**) *(profit)* **it will p. you to do it** c'est dans votre intérêt de le faire
3 *vi* (**a**) *(give payment)* payer; **to p. by cheque** payer par chèque; **to p. through the nose** payer le prix fort (**b**) *(be profitable)* être rentable; **crime doesn't p.** le crime ne paie pas; **it pays to be honest** l'honnêteté est toujours récompensée
▸**pay back** *vt sep (loan, person)* rembourser; *Fig* **I'll p. you back for this!** tu me le paieras!
▸**pay in** *vt sep (cheque, money)* verser sur un compte
▸**pay off 1** *vt sep* (**a**) *(debt)* régler; *(mortgage)* purger; *Fam* **to p. sb off** *(bribe)* soudoyer qn (**b**) *(make redundant)* licencier
2 *vi (of work, efforts)* porter ses fruits
▸**pay out 1** *vt sep* (**a**) *(money)* débourser, dépenser (**b**) *(rope)* laisser filer
2 *vi* payer
▸**pay up** *vi* payer
payable ['peɪəbəl] *adj* payable; **to make a cheque p. to sb** libeller un chèque à l'ordre de qn
pay-as-you-earn [peɪæzjuː'ɜːn] *n Br* prélèvement *m* de l'impôt à la source
pay-as-you-go [peɪæzjuː'gəʊ] *n* (**a**) *Br Tel* paiement *m* par carte prépayée (**b**) *Am Fin* prélèvement *m* de l'impôt à la source
pay-as-you-talk [peɪæzjuː'tɔːk] *n Tel* paiement *m* par carte prépayée
payday ['peɪdeɪ] *n* jour *m* de paie
PAYE [piːeɪwaɪ'iː] *n Br (abbr* **pay-as-you-earn***)* prélèvement *m* de l'impôt à la source
payee [peɪ'iː] *n* bénéficiaire *mf*

paying ['peɪɪŋ] *adj* payant(e); **p. guest** hôte *m* payant
payload ['peɪləʊd] *n* charge *f* utile
paymaster ['peɪmɑːstə(r)] *n* caissier *m*
payment ['peɪmənt] *n* paiement *m*; **to make a p.** effectuer un versement; **to stop p. (on a cheque)** faire opposition sur un chèque; **on p. of £100** contre paiement de 100 livres; **p. by instalments** paiement *m* par acomptes; **p. in full** paiement *m* intégral
payoff ['peɪɒf] *n Fam* (**a**) *(bribe)* pot-de-vin *m* (**b**) *(reward)* récompense *f*
pay-per-view [peɪpə'vjuː] **1** *n* système *m* de télévision à la carte
2 *adj (television)* à la carte
payphone ['peɪfəʊn] *n* téléphone *m* public
payroll ['peɪrəʊl] *n Com* liste *f* du personnel; **to be on the p.** faire partie du personnel
PC ['piːsiː] **1** *n* (**a**) *Br (abbr* **Police Constable***)* = agent de police (**b**) *(abbr* **personal computer***)* PC *m*
2 *adj (abbr* **politically correct***)* politiquement correct(e)
pc *(abbr* **postcard***)* carte *f* postale
PDA [piːdiː'eɪ] *n Comput (abbr* **personal digital assistant***)* PDA *m*, assistant *m* numérique personnel
PDQ *adv Fam (abbr* **pretty damn quick***)* illico
PE ['piː'iː] *n Br (abbr* **physical education***)* EPS *f*
pea [piː] *n* pois *m*; **like two peas in a pod** comme deux gouttes d'eau
peace [piːs] *n* paix *f*; **at p.** en paix; **to make (one's) p. with sb** faire la paix avec qn; **p. of mind** tranquillité *f* d'esprit; *Law* **to disturb the p.** troubler l'ordre public; **p. campaigner** militant(e) *m,f* pour la paix; **P. Corps** = organisation américaine d'aide aux pays du tiers-monde, composée de bénévoles intervenant sur le terrain; **p. movement** mouvement *m* pour la paix; **p. offering** cadeau *m* de réconciliation; **p. process** processus *m* de paix; **p. talks** pourparlers *mpl* de paix; **p. treaty** traité *m* de paix
peaceable ['piːsəbəl] *adj* pacifique
peaceful ['piːsfʊl] *adj (calm)* paisible; *(non-violent)* pacifique
peacekeeping ['piːskiːpɪŋ] *n* maintien *m* de la paix; **p. force** force *f* de maintien de la paix
peace-loving ['piːslʌvɪŋ] *adj* pacifique
peacetime ['piːstaɪm] *n* temps *m* de paix
peach [piːtʃ] *n (fruit)* pêche *f*; *Fam* **she's a p.** elle est canon; *Fam* **a p. of a goal** un but de toute beauté; **p. Melba** pêche *f* Melba; **p. tree** pêcher *m*
peacock ['piːkɒk] *n* paon *m*
peak [piːk] *n* (**a**) *(summit of mountain)* sommet *m*; *(mountain)* pic *m*; *Fig (of success, career)* apogée *m* (**b**) *(of price, inflation, fitness)* maximum *m*; **in p. condition** dans une forme excellente; **p. period** *(for traffic)* heures *fpl* de pointe; *(in shop)* heures *fpl* d'affluence; **p. season** haute saison *f*; *Br TV & Rad* **p. time** prime time *m* (**c**) *(of cap)* visière *f*
2 *vi* culminer (**at** à)
peaky ['piːkɪ] *adj Fam* patraque
peal [piːl] *n (of bells)* sonnerie *f*; *(of thunder)* coup *m*; **peals of laughter** éclats *mpl* de rire
▸**peal out** *vi (of bells)* sonner à toute volée
peanut ['piːnʌt] *n* cacah(o)uète *f*; *Fam Fig* **peanuts** *(small sum of money)* clopinettes *fpl*; **p. butter** beurre *m* de cacah(o)uètes; **p. oil** huile *f* d'arachide
pear [peə(r)] *n* poire *f*; **p. tree** poirier *m*
pearl [pɜːl] *n* (**a**) *(jewel)* perle *f*; **p. diver** pêcheur(euse) *m,f* de perles; **p. necklace** collier *m* de perles (**b**) *(idioms)* **pearls of wisdom** paroles *fpl* pleines de

sagesse; **to cast pearls before swine** jeter des perles aux cochons

pearly ['pɜːlɪ] adj nacré(e); **the P.** Gates les portes fpl du paradis

pear-shaped ['peəʃeɪpt] adj en forme de poire; (female figure) plus fort(e) au niveau des hanches; Br Fam Fig **to go p.** partir en eau de boudin

peasant ['pezənt] n paysan(anne) m,f; Pej (ignorant person) péquenaud(e) m,f

peashooter ['piːʃuːtə(r)] n petite sarbacane f

peat [piːt] n tourbe f; **p. bog** tourbière f

pebble ['pebəl] n caillou m; (on beach) galet m; **p. beach** plage f de galets

pebbledash ['pebəldæʃ] n crépi m

pebbly ['peblɪ] adj caillouteux(euse); (beach) de galets

pecan ['piːkən] n **p.** (nut) noix f de pecan

peccary ['pekərɪ] (pl peccaries) n pécari m

peck [pek] **1** n (a) (of bird) coup m de bec (b) (kiss) bise f; **to give sb a p.** on the cheek faire une bise à qn **2** vt (a) (of bird) (grain) picorer; (person) donner un coup/des coups de bec à (b) (kiss) **to p.** **sb on the cheek** faire une bise à qn

peckish ['pekɪʃ] adj Fam **to be p.** avoir un creux

pecs [peks] npl Fam (pectoral muscles) pectoraux mpl

pectin ['pektɪn] n Chem pectine f

pectoral ['pektərəl] **1** n pectorals pectoraux mpl **2** adj pectoral(e)

peculiar [pɪ'kjuːlɪə(r)] adj (a) (strange) curieux(euse), bizarre (b) (particular) **p. to** particulier(ère) à, propre à; **this species is p. to** France cette espèce n'existe qu'en France

peculiarity [pɪkjuːlɪ'ærɪtɪ] (pl peculiarities) n (strangeness) singularité f, bizarrerie f; (unusual characteristic) particularité f

peculiarly [pɪ'kjuːlɪəlɪ] adv (a) (strangely) singulièrement (b) (especially) particulièrement

pecuniary [pɪ'kjuːnɪərɪ] adj Formal pécuniaire

pedagogic(al) [pedə'gɒdʒɪk(əl)] adj pédagogique

pedagogy ['pedəgɒdʒɪ] n pédagogie f

pedal ['pedəl] **1** n pédale f; **p. bin** poubelle f à pédale **2** vt (pt & pp pedalled, Am pedaled) **to p. a bicycle** être à bicyclette **3** vi pédaler

pedalo ['pedələʊ] (pl pedaloes or pedalos) n Pédalo® m

pedant ['pedənt] n pédant(e) m,f

pedantic [pɪ'dæntɪk] adj pédant(e)

pedantry ['pedəntrɪ] n pédantisme m, pédanterie f

peddle ['pedəl] vt (goods, ideas, theories) colporter; (drugs) faire du trafic de

peddler ['pedlə(r)] n (of goods, ideas, theories) colporteur(euse) m,f; (of drugs) trafiquant(e) m,f

pederast ['pedəræst] n Formal pédéraste m

pedestal ['pedɪstəl] n piédestal m; Fig **to put sb on a p.** mettre qn sur un piédestal; **p. lamp** lampe f sur piédestal

pedestrian [pɪ'destrɪən] **1** n piéton(onne) m,f; **p. crossing** passage m pour piétons, passage m clouté; **p. precinct** zone f piétonnière **2** adj (unimaginative) banal(e)

pedestrianize [pɪ'destrɪənaɪz] vt transformer en zone piétonnière

pediatric, pediatrician etc Am = paediatric, paediatrician etc

pedicure ['pedɪkjʊə(r)] n **to have a p.** se faire soigner les pieds

pedigree ['pedɪgriː] **1** n (a) (of animal) pedigree m (b) (of person) ascendance f, généalogie f; Fig (background) passé m, antécédents mpl **2** adj (animal) de race

pedlar ['pedlə(r)] n colporteur(euse) m,f

pedometer [pɪ'dɒmɪtə(r)] n pédomètre m, podomètre m

pedophile Am = paedophile

pee [piː] Fam **1** n pipi m; **to have a p.** faire pipi **2** vi faire pipi

peek [piːk] **1** n coup m d'œil furtif; **to take** or **have a p.** (at) jeter un coup d'œil furtif (à) **2** vi jeter un coup d'œil furtif (at à)

peel [piːl] **1** n (of apple, vegetable) peau f; (of orange, lemon) écorce f **2** vt (fruit) peler; (vegetable) éplucher; Fam **to keep one's eyes peeled** ouvrir l'œil **3** vi (of paint) s'écailler; (of skin, person) peler

▸**peel off 1** vt sep enlever **2** vi (of paint) s'écailler; (of skin) peler; (of label) s'enlever

peelings ['piːlɪŋz] npl (of potato, carrot) épluchures fpl

peep¹ [piːp] **1** n (furtive glance) coup m d'œil furtif; **to have** or **take a p. (at)** jeter un coup d'œil furtif (à) **2** vi **to p. at sb/sth** jeter un coup d'œil furtif à qn/qch; **to p. through the keyhole** regarder par le trou de la serrure

peep² n (sound) (of bird) pépiement m; (of mouse) cri m; Fam **I don't want to hear another p. out of you** je ne veux plus entendre un mot

peephole ['piːphəʊl] n judas m

Peeping Tom ['piːpɪŋ'tɒm] n Fam voyeur m

peer¹ [pɪə(r)] n (a) (equal) pair m; **p. group** pairs mpl; **p. pressure** influence f du groupe (b) Br (nobleman) pair m

peer² vi **to p. at sb/sth** scruter qn/qch du regard; **to p. over sth** jeter un coup d'œil par-dessus qch

peerage ['pɪərɪdʒ] n Br (rank) pairie f; **the p.** les pairs mpl

peeress [pɪə'res] n Br pairesse f

peerless ['pɪəlɪs] adj sans pareil(eille), hors pair

peer-to-peer [pɪətə'pɪə(r)] adj Comput peer-to-peer

peeve [piːv] vt Fam mettre en rogne; **to be peeved (at)** être en rogne (à cause de)

peevish ['piːvɪʃ] adj irritable, maussade

peewit ['piːwɪt] n vanneau m (huppé)

peg [peg] **1** n (wooden) cheville f; (metal) fiche f; (for coat, hat) patère f; (clothes) **p.** pince f à linge; (tent) **p.** piquet m de tente; **to buy clothes off the p.** acheter du prêt-à-porter; Fig **to take sb down a p. (or two)** remettre qn à sa place **2** vt (pt & pp pegged) (a) **to p. sth in place** fixer qch avec des piquets; **to p. the washing on the line** étendre le linge (en utilisant des pinces à linge) (b) (prices) fixer; (currency) indexer; **to p. sth to the rate of inflation** indexer qch sur le taux de l'inflation

▸**peg out** vi Fam (die) casser sa pipe

pejorative [pɪ'dʒɒrətɪv] adj péjoratif(ive)

Pekinese [piːkɪ'niːz] n (dog) pékinois m

Peking [piː'kɪŋ] n Pékin

pelican ['pelɪkən] n pélican m; Br **p. crossing** feux mpl (à commande manuelle)

pellet ['pelɪt] n (of paper, bread, clay) boulette f; (for gun) plomb m

pell-mell ['pel'mel] adv (run) de façon désordonnée

pelmet ['pelmɪt] *n* cantonnière *f*
pelt¹ [pelt] *n (animal skin)* peau *f*, fourrure *f*
pelt² **1** *vt* bombarder (**with** de)
2 *vi Fam* (**a**) *(rain)* **it was pelting down** il pleuvait à verse (**b**) *(go fast)* aller à toute allure; **to p. upstairs** grimper l'escalier quatre à quatre; **she came pelting along the corridor** elle a déboulé du fond du couloir
pelvic ['pelvɪk] *adj* pelvien(enne)
pelvis ['pelvɪs] *n* pelvis *m*
pen¹ [pen] **1** *n (for writing)* stylo *m*; **to put p. to paper** prendre la plume; *Comput* **p. drive** clé *f* USB; **p. friend** *or* **pal** correspondant(e) *m,f*; **p. name** nom *m* de plume
2 *vt (pt & pp* **penned**) écrire, rédiger
pen² *n (for sheep, cattle)* enclos *m*
pen³ *n Am Fam (prison)* taule *f*
▸**pen in** *vt sep (animals, people)* parquer
penal ['piːnəl] *adj* pénal(e); **p. code** code *m* pénal; **p. colony** colonie *f* pénitentiaire; **p. servitude** travaux *mpl* forcés
penalize ['piːnəlaɪz] *vt* pénaliser
penalty ['penəltɪ] *(pl* **penalties**) *n* (**a**) *(punishment)* peine *f*; **to impose a p. (on sb)** prendre une sanction (contre qn); **on** *or* **under p. of death** sous peine de mort; *Fig* **to pay the p. for sth** subir les conséquences de qch; *Com* **p. clause** clause *f* pénale (**b**) *(in football)* penalty *m*; *(in rugby)* pénalité *f*; **p. area** surface *f* de réparation; **p. kick** penalty *m*
penance ['penəns] *n also Fig* pénitence *f*; **to do p. (for sth)** faire pénitence (pour qch)
pence [pens] *pl of* **penny**
pencil ['pensəl] **1** *n* crayon *m*; **p. case** trousse *f*; **p. drawing** dessin *m* au crayon; **p. sharpener** taille-crayon *m*
2 *vt (pt & pp* **pencilled**, *Am* **penciled**) *(draw)* dessiner au crayon; *(write)* écrire au crayon
▸**pencil in** *vt sep (date)* fixer provisoirement; **to p. sb in** fixer provisoirement un rendez-vous à qn
pencil-pusher ['pensəlpʊʃə(r)] *Am* = **pen-pusher**
pendant ['pendənt] *n* pendentif *m*
pending ['pendɪŋ] **1** *adj (trial)* en instance; *(negotiations)* en cours; *(documents)* en souffrance, en attente
2 *prep* en attendant
pendulum ['pendjʊləm] *n* pendule *m*
penetrate ['penɪtreɪt] *vt & vi* pénétrer
penetrating ['penɪtreɪtɪŋ] *adj (sound, wind, cold)* pénétrant(e); *(voice, scream, stare)* perçant(e)
penetration [penɪ'treɪʃən] *n* pénétration *f*
penguin ['peŋgwɪn] *n* manchot *m*
penicillin [penɪ'sɪlɪn] *n* pénicilline *f*
peninsula [pɪ'nɪnsjʊlə] *n* péninsule *f*; *(smaller)* presqu'île *f*
peninsular [pɪ'nɪnsjʊlə(r)] *adj* péninsulaire
penis ['piːnɪs] *n* pénis *m*
penitence ['penɪtəns] *n* pénitence *f*, repentir *m*
penitent ['penɪtənt] **1** *n* pénitent(e) *m,f*
2 *adj* pénitent(e)
penitentiary [penɪ'tenʃərɪ] *(pl* **penitentiaries**) *n Am* pénitencier *m*
penknife ['pennaɪf] *(pl* **penknives** ['pennaɪvz]) *n* canif *m*
pennant ['penənt] *n* flamme *f*
penne ['peneɪ] *npl (pasta)* penne *mpl*
penniless ['penɪlɪs] *adj* sans le sou
Pennsylvania [pensɪl'veɪnɪə] *n* la Pennsylvanie
penny ['penɪ] *n (pl* **pennies**) (**a**) *Br (coin) (pl* **pence** [pens]) penny *m*; **a 10/50 pence piece** une pièce de

10/50 pence; **it was worth every p.** ça valait le coup; **it didn't cost them a p.** cela ne leur a pas coûté un sou; **p. farthing** vélocipède *m*; **p. pinching** économies *fpl* de bouts de chandelle; **p. whistle** flûtiau *m* (**b**) *Am (cent)* cent *m* (**c**) *(idioms)* **they haven't a p. to their name** il n'ont pas un sou vaillant; **the p.'s dropped** ça a fait tilt; **they're ten a p.** il y en a à la pelle; **a p. for your thoughts** à quoi penses-tu?; **a bad p.** un(e) bon (bonne) à rien
penny-pinching ['penɪpɪntʃɪŋ] *adj (person)* pingre; *(ways, habits)* de radin
pen-pusher ['penpʊʃə(r)] *n Br Fam* gratte-papier *m inv*
pension ['penʃən] *n* pension *f*; *(after retirement)* (pension *f* de) retraite *f*; **to be on a p.** recevoir une pension; *(after retirement)* recevoir une retraite; **p. fund** caisse *f* de retraite; **p. scheme** plan *m* de retraite
▸**pension off** *vt sep* mettre à la retraite
pensionable ['penʃənəbəl] *adj* **p. age** âge *m* de départ en retraite
pensioner ['penʃənə(r)] *n* **(old-age) p.** retraité(e) *m,f*
pensive ['pensɪv] *adj* pensif(ive), songeur(euse)
pensively ['pensɪvlɪ] *adv* pensivement
pentagon ['pentəgən] *n* pentagone *m*; **the P.** *(building)* le Pentagone
pentathlon [pen'tæθlən] *n* pentathlon *m*
Pentecost ['pentɪkɒst] *n* la Pentecôte
penthouse ['penthaʊs] *n* = appartement de standing au dernier étage d'un immeuble
pent-up [pent'ʌp] *adj (desire)* refoulé(e); *(rage, energy)* contenu(e)
penultimate [pe'nʌltɪmɪt] *adj* pénultième, avant-dernier(ère)
penury ['penjʊrɪ] *n* indigence *f*
peony ['piːənɪ] *(pl* **peonies**) *n* pivoine *f*
people ['piːpəl] **1** *pl of* **person** (**a**) *(as group)* gens *mpl*; *(as individuals)* personnes *fpl*; **most p.** la plupart des gens; **old p.** les personnes âgées; **he's one of those p. who think (that)...** c'est le genre de type qui pense que...; **p. say (that)...** les gens disent que...; *Aut* **p. carrier, p. mover** monospace *m*; **p. power** pouvoir *m* populaire; **p. skills** aptitudes *fpl* relationnelles (**b**) *(citizens)* peuple *m*; **the common p.** le peuple; **a man of the p.** un homme du peuple; **p. power** pouvoir *m* populaire; **P.'s Republic** République *f* populaire (**c**) *Fam (family)* **my/his p.** ma/sa famille
2 *n (nation)* peuple *m*; **the Scottish p.** les Écossais *mpl*
3 *vt* peupler
PEP [pep] *n Formerly Fin (abbr* **personal equity plan**) ≃ PEA *m*
pep [pep] *n Fam* entrain *m*, allant *m*; **p. pill** excitant *m*; **p. talk** petit discours *m* d'encouragement
▸**pep up** *(pt & pp* **pepped**) *vt sep Fam (person)* ragaillardir, revigorer; *(event)* animer; *(dish)* relever
pepper ['pepə(r)] **1** *n (spice)* poivre *m*; *(vegetable)* poivron *m*; **p. mill** moulin *m* à poivre; **p. pot** poivrière *f*
2 *vt* (**a**) *(in cooking)* poivrer (**b**) *Fig (speech, essay)* parsemer (**with** de); **to p. sb with bullets** cribler qn de balles
peppercorn ['pepəkɔːn] *n* grain *m* de poivre
peppermint ['pepəmɪnt] *n (plant)* menthe *f* poivrée; *(sweet)* bonbon *m* à la menthe; **p. tea** thé *m* à la menthe
peppery ['pepərɪ] *adj* (**a**) *(dish)* poivré(e) (**b**) *(irritable)* irascible, colérique

peptic ulcer ['peptɪk'ʌlsə(r)] *n* ulcère *m* gastro-duodénal

per [pɜː(r)] *prep* par; **p. day** par jour; **100 km p. hour** 100 km à l'heure; *Formal* **as p.** your instructions conformément à vos instructions; **as p.** usual comme d'habitude; **p.** annum par an; **p.** capita par habitant; **p.** se en soi

perceive [pə'siːv] *vt* percevoir

percent [pə'sent] **1** *n* pourcentage *m*
2 *adv* pour cent

percentage [pə'sentɪdʒ] *n* pourcentage *m*

perceptible [pə'septɪbəl] *adj* perceptible

perceptibly [pə'septɪblɪ] *adv* sensiblement

perception [pə'sepʃən] *n* perception *f*

perceptive [pə'septɪv] *adj (person, remark)* perspicace; *(analysis, article)* pertinent(e)

perch¹ [pɜːtʃ] **1** *n (for bird) & Fig* perchoir *m*; *Fam Fig* **to knock sb off his/her p.** détrôner qn
2 *vi* se percher

perch² *n (fish)* perche *f*

percolate ['pɜːkəleɪt] **1** *vt (coffee)* passer; **percolated coffee** = café préparé dans une cafetière à pression
2 *vi (of liquid)* passer; *Fig (of information)* filtrer

percolator ['pɜːkəleɪtə(r)] *n* cafetière *f* à pression

percussion [pə'kʌʃən] *n* percussion *f*; **p.** instrument instrument *m* à percussion

percussionist [pə'kʌʃənɪst] *n* percussionniste *mf*

peregrine falcon ['perɪgrɪn'fɔːlkən] *n* faucon *m* pèlerin

peremptory [pə'remptərɪ] *adj* péremptoire; *(refusal)* absolu(e)

perennial [pə'renɪəl] **1** *n (plant)* plante *f* vivace
2 *adj (plant)* vivace; *(problem, beauty)* éternel(elle); *(worry)* perpétuel(elle)

perfect 1 *adj* ['pɜːfɪkt] (**a**) *(ideal)* parfait(e); **nobody's p.** personne n'est parfait; **Tuesday would be p.** mardi me conviendrait parfaitement; **to have p.** pitch avoir l'oreille absolue (**b**) *(complete)* **it makes p. sense** c'est parfaitement logique; **she's a p.** stranger je ne la connais pas du tout; **he's a p.** gentleman/fool c'est un parfait homme du monde/imbécile (**c**) *Gram* **the p. (tense)** le passé composé
2 *vt* [pə'fekt] parfaire

perfection [pə'fekʃən] *n* perfection *f*

perfectionist [pə'fekʃənɪst] *n* perfectionniste *mf*

perfectly ['pɜːfɪktlɪ] *adv (faultlessly)* à la perfection; *(completely)* parfaitement

perfidious [pə'fɪdɪəs] *adj Lit* perfide

perforate ['pɜːfəreɪt] *vt* perforer

perforated ['pɜːfəreɪtɪd] *adj* perforé(e); **p. eardrum** tympan *m* perforé; **p. ulcer** perforation *f* ulcéreuse

perforation [pɜːfə'reɪʃən] *n (hole)* perforation *f*; *(on stamp)* dentelure *f*

perform [pə'fɔːm] **1** *vt (play, role, piece of music)* jouer; *(miracle)* faire; *(one's duty)* remplir; **to p. an operation on sb** opérer qn
2 *vi (of machine, car)* marcher; *(of actor)* jouer; *(of singer)* chanter

performance [pə'fɔːməns] *n* (**a**) *(of task, duty)* accomplissement *m*; **p. appraisal** appréciation *f*, évaluation *f* (**b**) *(of sportsperson)* performance *f*; *(of actor)* interprétation *f*; *(of pupil, economy)* résultats *mpl*, performance *f*; *(of machine, car)* performances *fpl* (**c**) *(of play)* représentation *f*; *Fig* **to make a p.** faire toute une histoire; **p. art** performance *f*, action *f*; **p. artist** = artiste spécialisé dans la performance

performance-enhancing drug [pə'fɔːmənsenhɑːnsɪŋ'drʌg] *n* drogue *f* qui améliore les performances

performance-related [pə'fɔːmənsrɪ'leɪtɪd] *adj* en fonction du mérite *ou* résultat; **p. pay** salaire *m* au mérite

performer [pə'fɔːmə(r)] *n* artiste *mf (des arts du spectacle)*

performing [pə'fɔːmɪŋ] *adj (dog, seal)* savant(e); **p. arts** arts *mpl* du spectacle

perfume 1 *n* ['pɜːfjuːm] parfum *m*; **p. counter** rayon *m* parfumerie
2 *vt* [pə'fjuːm] parfumer

perfumed [pə'fjuːmd] *adj* parfumé(e)

perfunctory [pə'fʌŋktərɪ] *adj (examination, glance)* rapide; *(smile)* mécanique; *(letter, instructions)* sommaire

perhaps [pə'hæps] *adv* peut-être; **p. so/not** peut-être que oui/non; **p. she'll come** elle viendra peut-être, peut-être qu'elle viendra

peril ['perəl] *n* péril *m*, danger *m*; **at one's p.** à ses risques et périls

perilous ['perɪləs] *adj* dangereux(euse)

perilously ['perɪləslɪ] *adv* dangereusement

perimeter [pə'rɪmɪtə(r)] *n* périmètre *m*; **p. fence** clôture *f*

period ['pɪərɪəd] *n* (**a**) *(stretch of time)* période *f*; **within the agreed p.** dans les délais convenus; **sunny periods** intervalles *mpl* ensoleillés (**b**) *(in school)* heure *f* de cours; **a French/maths p.** un cours de français/maths (**c**) *(menstruation)* règles *fpl*; **to have one's p.** avoir ses règles; **p. pains** règles *fpl* douloureuses (**d**) *(historical age)* époque *f*; **p. drama** *(on TV)* drame *m* historique; **p. dress** costume(s) *m(pl)* d'époque; **p. furniture** meubles *mpl* d'époque (**e**) *Am (full stop)* point *m*

periodic [pɪərɪ'ɒdɪk] *adj* périodique; *Chem* **p. table** classification *f* périodique

periodical [pɪərɪ'ɒdɪkəl] *n* périodique *m*

periodically [pɪərɪ'ɒdɪklɪ] *adv* périodiquement

peripheral [pə'rɪfərəl] **1** *n Comput* périphérique *m*
2 *adj (area, vision)* périphérique; *(issue, importance)* accessoire

periphery [pə'rɪfərɪ] *(pl* **peripheries**) *n* périphérie *f*

periscope ['perɪskəʊp] *n* périscope *m*

perish ['perɪʃ] *vi* (**a**) *(of person)* périr; **p. the thought!** loin de moi cette pensée! (**b**) *(of rubber, leather)* se détériorer; *(of food)* s'avarier

perishable ['perɪʃəbəl] **1** *n* **perishables** denrées *fpl*
2 *adj* périssable

perishing ['perɪʃɪŋ] *adj Fam (very cold)* **it's p.** il fait un froid de canard

peritonitis [perɪtə'naɪtɪs] *n* péritonite *f*

perjure ['pɜːdʒə(r)] *vt Law* **to p. oneself** faire un faux témoignage

perjury ['pɜːdʒərɪ] *n Law* faux témoignage *m*; **to commit p.** faire un faux témoignage

perk [pɜːk] *n Br Fam* avantage *m*, à-côté *m*

▶**perk up** *Fam* **1** *vt sep (revive)* requinquer, ragaillardir; *(cheer up)* remonter le moral à
2 *vi (revive)* se requinquer, se ragaillardir; *(cheer up)* retrouver sa bonne humeur

perky ['pɜːkɪ] *adj Fam (lively)* plein(e) d'entrain; *(cheerful)* guilleret(ette)

perm [pɜːm] **1** *n* permanente *f*; **to have a p.** se faire faire une permanente

2 *vt* **to have one's hair permed** se faire faire une permanente

permanence ['pɜːmənəns] *n* permanence *f*

permanent ['pɜːmənənt] *adj* permanent(e); *(ink, stain)* indélébile; *(residence, address)* fixe; **p. wave** permanente *f*

permeate ['pɜːmɪeɪt] **1** *vt* **to be permeated with sth** *(liquid)* être saturé(e) de qch; *(smell)* être rempli(e) de qch; *Fig (feeling)* être imprégné(e) de qch **2** *vi* **to p. through sth** *(of liquid)* passer à travers qch; *(of smell)* se répandre dans qch; *Fig (of feeling)* imprégner qch

permissible [pə'mɪsɪbəl] *adj* admissible, acceptable

permission [pə'mɪʃən] *n* permission *f*, autorisation *f*; **to ask for p. to do sth** demander la permission de faire qch; **to give sb p. to do sth** donner à qn la permission de faire qch, autoriser qn à faire qch

permissive [pə'mɪsɪv] *adj* permissif(ive)

permit 1 *n* ['pɜːmɪt] permis *m*; **p. holders only** *(sign)* réservé aux personnes autorisées **2** *vt* [pə'mɪt] *(pt & pp permitted)* permettre; **to p. sb to do sth** permettre à qn de faire qch, autoriser qn à faire qch **3** *vi* [pə'mɪt] **weather permitting** si le temps le permet

permutation [pɜːmjʊ'teɪʃən] *n* permutation *f*

pernicious [pə'nɪʃəs] *adj* pernicieux(euse)

pernickety [pə'nɪkɪtɪ] *adj Fam (person)* tatillon(onne), pointilleux(euse); *(task)* minutieux(euse), délicat(e)

peroxide [pə'rɒksaɪd] *n Chem* peroxyde *m*; **p. blonde** blonde *f* décolorée

perpendicular [pɜːpən'dɪkjʊlə(r)] **1** *n* perpendiculaire *f* **2** *adj* perpendiculaire

perpetrate ['pɜːpɪtreɪt] *vt (crime)* perpétrer; *(fraud, error)* commettre

perpetrator ['pɜːpɪtreɪtə(r)] *n* auteur *m*

perpetual [pə'petjʊəl] *adj (eternal)* perpétuel(elle), éternel(elle); *(constant)* incessant(e), continuel(elle); *Phys* **p. motion** mouvement *m* perpétuel

perpetually [pə'petjʊəlɪ] *adv* perpétuellement

perpetuate [pə'petjʊeɪt] *vt* perpétuer

perpetuity [pɜːpɪ'tjuːɪtɪ] *n Formal* perpétuité *f*; **in p.** à perpétuité

perplex [pə'pleks] *vt* rendre *ou* laisser perplexe

perplexing [pə'pleksɪŋ] *adj* difficile; *(person)* déconcertant(e)

perplexity [pə'pleksɪtɪ] *n* perplexité *f*

persecute ['pɜːsɪkjuːt] *vt* persécuter

persecution [pɜːsɪ'kjuːʃən] *n* persécution *f*; *Psy* **p. complex** délire *m* de persécution

persecutor ['pɜːsɪkjuːtə(r)] *n* persécuteur(trice) *m,f*

perseverance [pɜːsɪ'vɪərəns] *n* persévérance *f*

persevere [pɜːsɪ'vɪə(r)] *vi* persévérer (**with** dans); **to p. in doing sth** persister à faire qch

Persia ['pɜːʒə] *n Hist* la Perse

Persian ['pɜːʒən] **1** (**a**) *(person) Hist* Perse *mf*; *(after 7th century)* Persan(e) *m,f* (**b**) *(language)* persan *m* **2** *adj Hist* perse; *(after 7th century)* persan(e); **P. carpet** tapis *m* persan; **P. cat** chat *m* persan; **the P. Gulf** le golfe Persique

persimmon [pɜː'sɪmən] *n (arbre)* plaqueminier *m*; *(fruit)* kaki *m*

persist [pə'sɪst] *vi* persister; **to p. in doing sth** s'obstiner à faire qch; **to p. in one's belief that...** persister à croire que...

persistence [pə'sɪstəns] *n (of person)* ténacité *f*, obstination *f*; *(of fog, belief)* persistance *f*

persistent [pə'sɪstənt] *adj (person)* tenace; *(problems, pain)* incessant(e), continuel(elle); *(rumours)* persistant(e); **p. offender** récidiviste *mf*; *Med* **p. vegetative state** état *m* végétatif chronique

persistently [pə'sɪstəntlɪ] *adv* continuellement

person ['pɜːsən] *(pl* people ['piːpəl], *Formal* persons) *n* personne *f*; **in p.** en personne; **on one's p.** sur soi; *Gram* in the **first/second/third p.** à la première/deuxième/troisième personne; *Law* **by a p. or persons unknown** par un ou plusieurs inconnus

personable ['pɜːsənəbəl] *adj* charmant(e)

personage ['pɜːsənɪdʒ] *n* personnage *m*

personal ['pɜːsənəl] *adj* personnel(elle); **to make a p. appearance** venir *ou* apparaître en personne; **for p. reasons** pour des raisons personnelles; **don't be p.** ne parle pas des choses aussi personnelles; **it's nothing p., but...** ça n'a rien de personnel, mais...; **p. friend** ami(e) *m,f* personnel(elle); **p. ad** petite annonce *f (pour rencontres)*; **p. assistant** secrétaire *mf* de direction; **p. best** *(in sport)* record *m* personnel; **p. column** petites annonces *fpl (pour rencontres)*; **p. computer** ordinateur *m* individuel; **p. effects** effets *mpl* personnels; **p. growth** développement *m* personnel; **p. hygiene** hygiène *f*; **p. loan** prêt *m* personnel; **p. organizer** *(book)* agenda *m*; *(electronic)* agenda *m* électronique; *Gram* **p. pronoun** pronom *m* personnel; **p. stereo** baladeur *m*

personality [pɜːsə'nælɪtɪ] *(pl* **personalities**) *n* personnalité *f*; **p. cult** culte *m* de la personnalité; *Psy* **p. disorder** trouble *m* de la personnalité

personally ['pɜːsənəlɪ] *adv* personnellement; **don't take it p.** n'en faites pas une affaire personnelle

personification [pɜːsɒnɪfɪ'keɪʃən] *n* incarnation *f*; **to be the p. of meanness** être l'avarice incarnée

personify [pɜː'sɒnɪfaɪ] *(pt & pp* **personified**) *vt* personnifier

personnel [pɜːsə'nel] *n* personnel *m*; **p. department** service *m* du personnel; **p. manager** directeur(trice) *m,f* du personnel

perspective [pə'spektɪv] *n* perspective *f*; **to see things in p.** relativiser les choses; **to put sth in(to) p.** relativiser qch

perspicacious [pɜːspɪ'keɪʃəs] *adj Formal* perspicace

perspiration [pɜːspə'reɪʃən] *n* transpiration *f*

perspire [pə'spaɪə(r)] *vi* transpirer

persuade [pə'sweɪd] *vt* persuader, convaincre; **to p. sb to do sth** persuader *ou* convaincre qn de faire qch; **to p. sb not to do sth** dissuader qn de faire qch

persuasion [pə'sweɪʒən] *n* (**a**) *(act, ability)* persuasion *f*; **powers of p.** pouvoir *m* de persuasion (**b**) *(beliefs)* **political p.** opinions *fpl* politiques; **religious p.** religion *f*, confession *f*

persuasive [pə'sweɪzɪv] *adj (person)* persuasif(ive); *(argument)* convaincant(e)

persuasively [pə'sweɪzɪvlɪ] *adv (say)* d'un ton persuasif; *(argue)* de façon convaincante

pert [pɜːt] *adj* (**a**) *(cheeky)* espiègle; *(reply)* direct(e) (**b**) *(nose, breasts)* pointu(e); *(bottom)* petit(e) et ferme

pertain [pə'teɪn] *vi Formal* **to p. to** *(belong to)* appartenir à; *(be relevant to)* se rapporter à

pertinent ['pɜːtɪnənt] *adj* pertinent(e); **to be p. to** avoir rapport à

perturb [pə'tɜːb] *vt* inquiéter, troubler

Peru [pə'ruː] *n* le Pérou

perusal [pə'ruːzəl] *n Formal* lecture *f*

peruse [pə'ruːz] *vt Formal (read carefully)* lire attentivement; *(read quickly)* feuilleter; *(article)* survoler

Peruvian [pə'ruːvɪən] **1** *n* Péruvien(enne) *m,f*
2 *adj* péruvien(enne)

pervade [pɜː'veɪd] *vt* imprégner

pervasive [pɜː'veɪsɪv] *adj (feeling)* général(e); *(smell)* envahissant(e)

perverse [pə'vɜːs] *adj* (**a**) *(contrary)* contrariant(e); he's just being p. il fait ça pour contrarier; **to take a p. pleasure in doing sth** prendre un malin plaisir à faire qch (**b**) *(sexually deviant)* pervers(e)

perversely [pə'vɜːslɪ] *adv (contrarily)* par pur esprit de contradiction

perversion [pə'vɜːʃən] *n (sexual)* perversion *f*; *(of truth, justice)* travestissement *m*

pervert 1 *n* ['pɜːvɜːt] *(sexual deviant)* pervers(e) *m,f*
2 *vt* [pə'vɜːt] *(corrupt)* pervertir; *(distort)* altérer, dénaturer; *Law* **to p. the course of justice** entraver le bon fonctionnement de la justice

pescatarian [peskə'teɪrɪən] *n* pesco-végétarien(-enne) *m,f*

peseta [pə'seɪtə] *n Formerly* peseta *f*

pesky ['peskɪ] *adj Am Fam* embêtant(e), empoisonnant(e)

peso ['peɪsəʊ] *(pl* **pesos**) *n* peso *m*

pessary ['pesərɪ] *(pl* **pessaries**) *n* ovule *m*

pessimism ['pesɪmɪzəm] *n* pessimisme *m*

pessimist ['pesɪmɪst] *n* pessimiste *mf*

pessimistic [pesɪ'mɪstɪk] *adj* pessimiste

pest [pest] *n* (**a**) *(animal)* animal *m* nuisible; *(insect)* insecte *m* nuisible; **p. control** *(of rats)* dératisation *f*; *(of insects)* déinsectisation *f* (**b**) *Fam (nuisance)* poison *m*, plaie *f*

pester ['pestə(r)] *vt* tourmenter, importuner; **to p. sb to do sth** harceler qn pour qu'il fasse qch; **to p. sb into doing sth** harceler qn jusqu'à ce qu'il fasse qch

pesticide ['pestɪsaɪd] *n* pesticide *m*

pestilence ['pestɪləns] *n Lit* peste *f*

pestle ['pesəl] *n* pilon *m*; **p. and mortar** pilon *m* et mortier *m*

pet [pet] **1** *n* (**a**) *(animal)* animal *m* familier *ou* domestique; **p. food** nourriture *f* pour animaux familiers; **p. shop** animalerie *f* (**b**) *(favourite)* **the teacher's p.** le chouchou (la chouchoute) du professeur; **p. hate** bête *f* noire; **p. name** surnom *m*; **p. subject** dada *m* (**c**) *(term of address)* mon chou
2 *vt (pt & pp* **petted**) *(person, dog)* caresser, câliner

petal ['petəl] *n* pétale *m*; *Br Fam (as term of affection)* mon chou

▸**peter out** ['piːtə(r)] *vi (of conversation, enthusiasm)* tarir; *(of scheme)* n'aboutir à rien; *(of path, stream)* disparaître

petite [pə'tiːt] *adj* menu(e)

petition [pɪ'tɪʃən] **1** *n* pétition *f*
2 *vt (court, sovereign)* adresser *ou* présenter une pétition à
3 *vi* **to p. for sth** faire une pétition pour qch; *Law* **to p. for divorce** faire une demande de divorce

petitioner [pɪ'tɪʃənə(r)] *n Law (for divorce)* pétitionnaire *mf*, requérant(e) *m,f*

petrify ['petrɪfaɪ] *(pt & pp* **petrified**) *vt* pétrifier

petrochemical [petrəʊ'kemɪkəl] **1** *n* produit *m* pétrochimique
2 *adj* pétrochimique

petrol ['petrəl] *n Br* essence *f*; **p. bomb** cocktail *m* Molotov; **p. can** bidon *m* d'essence; **p. pump** pompe *f* à essence; **p. station** station *f* d'essence, station-service *f*; **p. tank** réservoir *m* d'essence

petroleum [pə'trəʊlɪəm] *n* pétrole *m*; **p. jelly** vaseline *f*

petticoat ['petɪkəʊt] *n (from waist)* jupon *m*; *(full-length)* combinaison *f*

petty ['petɪ] *adj* (**a**) *(insignificant)* insignifiant(e); **p. cash** petite caisse *f*; **p. crime** petite délinquance *f*; *Naut* **p. officer** second maître *m* (**b**) *(small-minded)* mesquin(e)

petulance ['petjʊləns] *n* irascibilité *f*

petulant ['petjʊlənt] *adj* irascible

petunia [pɪ'tjuːnɪə] *n* pétunia *m*

pew [pjuː] *n* banc *m* d'église; *Fam* **take a p.!** assieds-toi!

pewter ['pjuːtə(r)] *n* étain *m*

PG [piː'dʒiː] *adj Br Cin (abbr* **Parental Guidance**) = qui exige une autorisation parentale

pH [piː'eɪtʃ] *n Chem* pH *m*

phalanx ['fælæŋks] *n Mil Hist* phalange *f*; *Fig (of officials, journalists)* armée *f*

phallic ['fælɪk] *adj* phallique; **p. symbol** symbole *m* phallique

phallus ['fæləs] *n* phallus *m*

phantom ['fæntəm] *n* fantôme *m*, spectre *m*; **p. pregnancy** grossesse *f* nerveuse

Pharaoh ['feərəʊ] *n* pharaon *m*

pharmaceutical [fɑːmə'sjuːtɪkəl] **1** *n* **pharmaceuticals** produits *mpl* pharmaceutiques
2 *adj* pharmaceutique

pharmacist ['fɑːməsɪst] *n* pharmacien(enne) *m,f*

pharmacology [fɑːmə'kɒlədʒɪ] *n* pharmacologie *f*

pharmacy ['fɑːməsɪ] *(pl* **pharmacies**) *n* pharmacie *f*

phase [feɪz] *n* phase *f*; it's just a p. (he's going through) ça lui passera; *Fig* **out of p.** déphasé(e)

▸**phase in** *vt sep* mettre en place progressivement

▸**phase out** *vt sep* éliminer progressivement

phased [feɪzd] *adj* progressif(ive)

PhD [piːeɪtʃ'diː] *n Univ (abbr* **Doctor of Philosophy**) *(person)* docteur *m*; *(degree)* doctorat *m* (**in** de)

pheasant ['fezənt] *n* faisan *m*

phenomena [fɪn'ɒmɪnə] *pl of* **phenomenon**

phenomenal [fɪ'nɒmɪnəl] *adj* phénoménal(e)

phenomenally [fɪ'nɒmɪnəlɪ] *adv* prodigieusement

phenomenon [fɪ'nɒmɪnən] *(pl* **phenomena** [fɪ'nɒmɪnə]) *n* phénomène *m*

phew [fjuː] *exclam (when hot)* pfff!; *(in relief)* ouf!

phial ['faɪəl] *n* fiole *f*

Philadelphia [fɪlə'delfɪə] *n* Philadelphie

philanderer [fɪ'lændərə(r)] *n Pej* coureur *m* de jupons

philanthropic [fɪlən'θrɒpɪk] *adj* philanthropique; *(person)* philanthrope

philanthropist [fɪ'lænθrəpɪst] *n* philanthrope *mf*

philanthropy [fɪ'lænθrəpɪ] *n* philanthropie *f*

philately [fɪ'lætəlɪ] *n* philatélie *f*

philharmonic [fɪlə'mɒnɪk] *Mus* **1** *n* (orchestre *m*) philharmonique *m*
2 *adj* philharmonique

Philippines ['fɪlɪpiːnz] *npl* **the P.** les Philippines *fpl*

philology [fɪ'lɒlədʒɪ] *n* philologie *f*

philosopher [fɪ'lɒsəfə(r)] *n* philosophe *mf*

philosophic(al) [fɪlə'sɒfɪk(əl)] *adj* philosophique; *(person, attitude)* philosophe

philosophize [fɪ'lɒsəfaɪz] *vi* philosopher

philosophy [fɪ'lɒsəfɪ] *(pl* **philosophies**) *n* philosophie *f*

phishing ['fɪʃɪŋ] *n Fam Comput* phishing *m*, = extorsion de données confidentielles par e-mail

phlegm [flem] *n* flegme *m*

phlegmatic [fleg'mætɪk] *adj* flegmatique

phobia ['fəʊbɪə] *n* phobie *f*; **to have a p. about sth** avoir la phobie de qch

phoenix ['fi:nɪks] *n* phénix *m*; **to rise like a p.** renaître tel un phénix

phone [fəʊn] **1** *n* téléphone *m*; **to be on the p.** *(talking)* être au téléphone; *(have a telephone)* avoir le téléphone; **to give sb a p.** donner un coup de téléphone à qn; **p. bill** facture *f* de téléphone; **p. book** annuaire *m* (du téléphone); **p. box** *or* **booth** cabine *f* téléphonique; **p. call** coup *m* de téléphone; **p. number** numéro *m* de téléphone
  2 *vt* téléphoner à
  3 *vi* téléphoner

phonecard ['fəʊnkɑːd] *n* carte *f* de téléphone

phone-in ['fəʊnɪn] *n* **p. (programme)** = émission au cours de laquelle les téléspectateurs ou les auditeurs peuvent intervenir par téléphone

phoneme ['fəʊniːm] *n* phonème *m*

phonetic [fə'netɪk] *adj* phonétique

phonetics [fə'netɪks] **1** *n (science)* phonétique *f*
  2 *npl (symbols)* symboles *mpl* phonétiques

phoney, *Am* **phony** ['fəʊnɪ] *(pl* **phonies)** *Fam* **1** *n (impostor)* imposteur *m*; *(insincere person)* faux jeton *m*; *(thing)* faux *m*
  2 *adj* bidon

phosphate ['fɒsfeɪt] *n* phosphate *m*

phosphorescent [fɒsfə'resənt] *adj* phosphorescent(e)

phosphorus ['fɒsfərəs] *n* phosphore *m*

photo ['fəʊtəʊ] *(pl* **photos)** *n* photo *f*; **to take sb's p.** prendre qn en photo; **p. album** album *m* (de) photos; **p. booth** Photomaton® *m*; **p. finish** photo-finish *f*; **it's just another p. opportunity** ce n'est qu'un nouveau prétexte pour se faire photographier

photocopier ['fəʊtəʊkɒpɪə(r)] *n* photocopieuse *f*

photocopy ['fəʊtəʊkɒpɪ] **1** *n (pl* **photocopies)** photocopie *f*
  2 *vt (pt & pp* **photocopied)** photocopier

photoelectric [fəʊtəʊɪ'lektrɪk] *adj* photoélectrique; **p. cell** cellule *f* photoélectrique

photogenic [fəʊtəʊ'dʒenɪk] *adj* photogénique

photograph ['fəʊtəɡræf] **1** *n* photographie *f*; **to take sb's p.** prendre qn en photo; **p. album** album *m* de photographies
  2 *vt* photographier, prendre en photo

photographer [fə'tɒɡrəfə(r)] *n* photographe *mf*

photographic [fəʊtə'ɡræfɪk] *adj* photographique; **to have a p. memory** avoir une mémoire photographique

photography [fə'tɒɡrəfɪ] *n* photographie *f*

photosensitive [fəʊtəʊ'sensɪtɪv] *adj* photosensible

Photostat® ['fəʊtəʊstæt] *n* photostat *m*

photosynthesis [fəʊtəʊ'sɪnθɪsɪs] *n Bot* photosynthèse *f*

photosynthesize [fəʊtəʊ'sɪnθɪsaɪz] *vt Bot* fabriquer par photosynthèse

phrasal verb ['freɪzəl'vɜːb] *n Gram* verbe *m* à particule

phrase [freɪz] **1** *n* phrase *f*; **p. book** manuel *m ou* guide *m* de conversation
  2 *vt* (**a**) *(verbally)* exprimer; *(in writing)* tourner (**b**) *Mus* phraser

phraseology [freɪzɪ'ɒlədʒɪ] *n* phraséologie *f*

Phys. Ed. [fɪz'ed] *n Am* EPS *f*

physical ['fɪzɪkəl] **1** *n (examination)* visite *f* médicale
  2 *adj* physique; **p. education** éducation *f* physique; **p. exercise** *or* **training** (exercices *mpl* de) gymnastique *f*; **p. fitness** forme *f* physique; **p. geography** géographie *f* physique; **p. impossibility** impossibilité *f* physique *ou* matérielle; **p. sciences** sciences *fpl* physiques

physically ['fɪzɪklɪ] *adv* physiquement; **p. fit** en bonne forme physique; **p. handicapped** handicapé(e) physique

physician [fɪ'zɪʃən] *n* médecin *m*

physicist ['fɪzɪsɪst] *n* physicien(enne) *m,f*

physics ['fɪzɪks] *n* physique *f*

physiognomy [fɪzɪ'ɒnəmɪ] *n Formal* physionomie *f*

physiological [fɪzɪə'lɒdʒɪkəl] *adj* physiologique

physiology [fɪzɪ'ɒlədʒɪ] *n* physiologie *f*

physiotherapist [fɪzɪəʊ'θerəpɪst] *n* kinésithérapeute *mf*

physiotherapy [fɪzɪəʊ'θerəpɪ] *n* kinésithérapie *f*

physique [fɪ'ziːk] *n* physique *m*

pianist ['pɪənɪst] *n* pianiste *mf*

piano [pɪ'ænəʊ] *(pl* **pianos)** *n* piano *m*; **p. concerto** concerto *m* pour piano; **p. stool** tabouret *m* de piano; **p. tuner** accordeur *m* de pianos

piccolo ['pɪkələʊ] *(pl* **piccolos)** *n* piccolo *m*

piccy ['pɪkɪ] *(pl* **piccies)** *n Br Fam (photograph)* photo *f*

pick [pɪk] **1** *n* (**a**) *(tool)* pic *m*, pioche *f* (**b**) *(choice)* **to take one's p.** choisir; **the p. of the bunch** le (la) meilleur(e) du lot
  2 *vt* (**a**) *(choose)* choisir; **to p. a fight (with sb)** chercher la bagarre (avec qn) (**b**) *(flowers, fruit)* cueillir (**c**) *(other uses)* **to p. a lock** crocheter une serrure; **to p. a guitar** pincer la guitare; **to p. one's nose** mettre les doigts dans le nez; **to p. one's teeth** se curer les dents; **to p. a spot** tripoter un bouton; **to p. sb's pocket** voler dans les poches de qn; **to p. a hole in sth** faire un trou à qch en tirant dessus; *Fig* **to p. holes in sth** trouver des failles dans qch; **to p. sb's brains** soumettre quelque chose à la sagacité de qn
  3 *vi* **to p. and choose** se permettre de choisir

▸**pick off** *vt sep (remove)* enlever, ôter; *(of gunman, sniper)* éliminer

▸**pick on** *vt insep* utiliser comme souffre-douleur

▸**pick out** *vt sep* (**a**) *(remove)* retirer (**b**) *(select)* choisir (**c**) *(recognize)* repérer

▸**pick up** **1** *vt sep* (**a**) *(lift up)* ramasser; *(to upright position)* relever; **to p. up the phone** décrocher (le téléphone); *Fig* **to p. oneself up** se remettre, se reprendre; *Fig* **to p. up the pieces** ramasser les morceaux; *Fig* **to p. up the bill** payer l'addition (**b**) *(collect)* prendre; *(arrest)* arrêter; **to p. up survivors** recueillir des survivants (**c**) *Fam (sexually)* ramasser (**d**) *(learn)* apprendre; *(acquire)* acquérir; **to p. up speed** prendre de la vitesse (**e**) *(radio station, message)* capter (**f**) *(notice)* relever (**g**) *(discussion)* reprendre (**h**) *(make better)* remonter
  2 *vi* (**a**) *(improve)* s'améliorer; *(after illness)* se remettre; *(of match, party)* s'animer; **business is picking up** les affaires reprennent (**b**) *(continue)* **let's p. up where we left off** reprenons (là où nous en étions restés)

pickaxe ['pɪkæks] *n* pioche *f*, pic *m*

picket ['pɪkɪt] **1** *n* (**a**) *(in strike)* piquet *m* de grève; **p. line** piquet *m* de grève (**b**) *(stake)* piquet *m*, pieu *m*; **p. fence** palissade *f*

2 *vt (during strike)* former un piquet de grève aux portes de
pickings ['pɪkɪŋz] *npl* bénéfices *mpl*; **rich p.** gros bénéfices *mpl*
pickle ['pɪkəl] **1** *n* = condiment à base de légumes conservés dans du vinaigre; **pickles** conserves *fpl* au vinaigre; *Fam Fig* **to be in a p.** être dans le pétrin
2 *vt* conserver dans du vinaigre; **pickled cabbage/onions** chou *m* /oignons *mpl* au vinaigre
pick-me-up ['pɪkmiʌp] *n Fam* remontant *m*
pickpocket ['pɪkpɒkɪt] *n* pickpocket *m*, voleur(euse) *m,f* à la tire
pick-up ['pɪkʌp] *n* (**a**) **p. (arm)** *(on record player)* lecteur *m* (phonographique); **p. (truck)** pick-up *m inv (petite camionnette à plateau)*; **p. point** *(for goods, passengers)* point *m* de ramassage (**b**) *Am Fam* **p. line** = formule d'entrée en matière pour commencer à draguer quelqu'un; (**b**) *Fam (improvement)* amélioration *f*; *(of business)* reprise *f*
picky ['pɪkɪ] *adj Fam* difficile (**about** sur)
picnic ['pɪknɪk] **1** *n* pique-nique *m*; **to go on a p.** aller faire un pique-nique, aller pique-niquer; *Fam Fig* **it was no p.** ça n'a pas été une partie de plaisir; **p. basket** *or* **hamper** panier *m* à pique-nique
2 *vi (pt & pp* **picnicked**) pique-niquer, faire un pique-nique
picnicker ['pɪknɪkə(r)] *n* pique-niqueur(euse) *m,f*
Pict [pɪkt] *n Hist* Picte *mf*
pictorial [pɪk'tɔːrɪəl] *adj (magazine)* illustré(e); *(representation)* en images
picture ['pɪktʃə(r)] **1** *n* (**a**) *(painting)* tableau *m*; *(drawing)* dessin *m*; *(in book, on TV)* image *f*; *(photograph)* photo *f*; *Fig (situation)* situation *f*; **to be the p. of health** respirer la santé; **her face was a p.** elle a fait une de ces têtes; *Fig* **to put sb in the p.** mettre qn au courant; *Fam Fig* **I get the p.** je pige; **p. book** livre *m* d'images; **p. frame** cadre *m*; **p. gallery** galerie *f* de peintures; **p. library** banque *f* d'images; *Tel* **p. messaging** = prise et envoi de photos par téléphone portable; **p. postcard** carte *f* postale illustrée; **p. window** baie *f* vitrée (**b**) *Br Fam Old-fashioned (film)* film *m*; **the pictures** le cinéma
2 *vt* (**a**) *(imagine)* **to p. sth (to oneself)** s'imaginer qch; **to p. sb/sth as sth** s'imaginer qn/qch en qch; **to p. sb doing sth** s'imaginer qn en train de faire qch (**b**) *(in photo, painting)* représenter; *Fig (in words)* dépeindre, décrire
picturesque [pɪktʃə'resk] *adj* pittoresque
pidgin ['pɪdʒɪn] *n* pidgin *m*; **p. English/French** ≃ petit nègre *m*
pie [paɪ] *n* tourte *f*; *Fam* **p. in the sky** des châteaux en Espagne; **p. chart** camembert *m*
piece [piːs] *n* (**a**) *(in general)* morceau *m*; *(smaller)* bout *m*; *(of cake)* part *f*; *(newspaper article)* article *m*; **p. of land** *(parcelle f de)* terrain *m*; **a p. of furniture** un meuble; **p. of luggage** *(suitcase)* une valise; *(bag)* un sac; **a p. of advice** un conseil; **a p. of luck** un coup de chance; **a p. of news** une nouvelle; **p. rate** *(pay)* salaire *m* à la pièce (**b**) *(in chess, of jigsaw puzzle)* pièce *f*; *(in dominoes)* domino *m*; *(in draughts)* pion *m* (**c**) *(coin)* pièce *f* (**d**) *(of music)* morceau *m* (**e**) *(of artillery)* pièce *f*; *(firearm)* arme *f* (**f**) *(idioms)* **to be still in one p.** être encore entier(ère); **to give sb a p. of one's mind** dire ses quatre vérités à qn; **to say one's p.** dire ce qu'on a à dire; **p. by p.** par morceaux; *Fig* **to go to pieces** s'effondrer (complètement); **to fall to pieces** tomber en morceaux; *(of house)* se

délabrer, crouler; *(of garment)* partir en morceaux; **to take sth to pieces** démonter qch; **to be a p. of cake** être facile comme tout; *Br Fam* **he's a nasty p. of work** c'est un sale type
►**piece together** *vt sep (parts)* assembler les morceaux de; *(something broken)* recoller les morceaux de; *(facts)* reconstituer
piecemeal ['piːsmiːl] **1** *adj* fragmentaire, parcellaire; *(work)* fait(e) petit à petit
2 *adv* petit à petit
piecework ['piːswɜːk] *n* travail *m* à la tâche *ou* à la pièce
Piedmont ['piːdmɒnt] *n* le Piémont
pier [pɪə(r)] *n (landing stage)* embarcadère *m*; *(at seaside resort)* jetée *f*; *(of bridge)* pilier *m*
pierce [pɪəs] *vt* percer, transpercer; **to have pierced ears** avoir les oreilles percées
piercing ['pɪəsɪŋ] **1** *adj (cry, look)* perçant(e); *(cold)* vif (vive)
2 *n (on face, body)* piercing *m*
piety ['paɪətɪ] *n* piété *f*
pig [pɪg] *n* (**a**) *(animal)* cochon *m*, porc *m* (**b**) *Fam (greedy person)* goinfre *m*, glouton(onne) *m,f*; *(unpleasant man)* salaud *m*; *(unpleasant woman)* salope *f* (**c**) *Fam (policeman)* poulet *m* (**d**) *Fam (idioms)* **to buy a p. in a poke** acheter chat en poche; **pigs might fly!** on peut toujours rêver!; **to make a p.'s ear of sth** bousiller qch, saloper qch; **to make a p. of oneself** s'en mettre plein la lampe
2 *vt (pt & pp* **pigged**) *Fam* **to p. oneself** s'en mettre plein la lampe
►**pig out** *vi Fam* s'en mettre plein la lampe
pigeon ['pɪdʒɪn] *n* pigeon *m*
pigeonhole ['pɪdʒɪnhəʊl] **1** *n* casier *m*
2 *vt (person)* étiqueter, mettre une étiquette à
piggy ['pɪgɪ] *Fam* **1** *n (pl* **piggies**) petit cochon *m*; **p. bank** tirelire *f*, *Can* cochon *m*
2 *adj (eyes)* de cochon
piggyback ['pɪgɪbæk] *n* **to give sb a p.** porter qn sur son dos
pig-headed [pɪg'hedɪd] *adj* entêté(e), têtu(e)
piglet ['pɪglɪt] *n* porcelet *m*
pigment ['pɪgmənt] *n* pigment *m*
pigmentation [pɪgmən'teɪʃən] *n* pigmentation *f*
Pigmy ['pɪgmɪ] *(pl* **Pigmies**) *n* Pygmée *mf*; *Fig* **p.** nain(e) *m,f*
pigsty ['pɪgstaɪ] *(pl* **pigsties**) *n also Fig* porcherie *f*
pigtail ['pɪgteɪl] *n* natte *f*
pike¹ [paɪk] *n (weapon)* pique *f*
pike² *n (fish)* brochet *m*
pilchard ['pɪltʃəd] *n* pilchard *m*
pile [paɪl] *n* (**a**) *(heap)* tas *m*; *(stack)* pile *f*; **to put things in(to) a p.** *(heap)* mettre des choses en tas; *(stack)* empiler des choses; *Fam* **to have piles of** *or* **a p. of things/work to do** avoir un tas de choses/des tonnes de travail à faire; *Fam Fig* **to be at the top/bottom of the p.** être favorisé(e)/défavorisé(e) (**b**) *(large building)* édifice *m* (**c**) *(of carpet)* poils *mpl*
2 *vt* entasser; *(stack)* empiler; **to p. food onto one's plate** bien remplir son assiette
3 *vi Fam* **to p. into a car** s'entasser dans une voiture
►**pile in** *vi* s'entasser
►**pile on** *vt sep* **to p. on the pressure** faire monter la pression; **to p. on the agony** dramatiser; *Fam* **to p. it on** en rajouter; *Fam* **to p. on the pounds** grossir
►**pile out** *vi* sortir en masse
►**pile up** *vi* s'accumuler

pile-driver ['paɪldraɪvə(r)] n sonnette f
piles [paɪlz] npl (haemorrhoids) hémorroïdes fpl; **to have p.** avoir des hémorroïdes
pile-up ['paɪlʌp] n Fam carambolage m
pilfer ['pɪlfə(r)] vt & vi chaparder
pilgrim ['pɪlgrɪm] n pèlerin(e) m,f
pilgrimage ['pɪlgrɪmɪdʒ] n pèlerinage m; **to go on** or **make a p.** aller en pèlerinage, faire un pèlerinage
pill [pɪl] n pilule f; **the p.** (contraceptive) la pilule; **to be on the p.** prendre la pilule
pillage ['pɪlɪdʒ] **1** n pillage m **2** vt & vi piller
pillar ['pɪlə(r)] n also Fig pilier m; **to go from p. to post** courir à droite et à gauche; **a p. of society** un pilier de la société; **to be a p. of strength** être d'un grand soutien; **p. box** bôite f aux lettres
pillion ['pɪljən] **1** n **p. (seat)** siège m arrière **2** adv **to ride p.** monter derrière
pillory ['pɪlərɪ] **1** n (pl **pillories**) pilori m **2** vt (pt & pp **pilloried**) mettre au pilori
pillow ['pɪləʊ] n oreiller m
pillowcase ['pɪləʊkeɪs], **pillowslip** ['pɪləʊslɪp] n taie f d'oreiller
pilot ['paɪlət] **1** n (of plane, ship) pilote m; **p. (programme)** (on TV) émission f pilote; **p. light** veilleuse f; **p. scheme** projet-pilote m; **p. study** étude-pilote f **2** vt (plane, ship) piloter
pimp [pɪmp] n souteneur m, proxénète m
pimple ['pɪmpəl] n bouton m
pimply ['pɪmplɪ] adj boutonneux(euse)
PIN [pɪn] n (abbr **personal identification number**) code m confidentiel
pin [pɪn] **1** n (for sewing) épingle f; (for surgery) broche f; (in grenade) goupille f; **three-p. plug** prise f à trois broches; **(firing) p.** percuteur m; **(safety) p.** épingle f à nourrice; Fam **to have pins and needles** avoir des fourmis; **you could have heard a p. drop** on aurait entendu une mouche voler; **p. money** argent m de poche **2** vt (pt & pp **pinned**) (fasten) (with pin) épingler; (with drawing pin, safety pin) attacher; **to p. sb against** or **to a wall** plaquer qn contre un mur; **to p. the blame on sb** rejeter la responsabilité sur qn; **to p. one's hopes on sb/sth** mettre tous ses espoirs en qn/qch
►**pin down** vt sep (**a**) (trap) coincer (**b**) (identify) mettre le doigt sur (**c**) (force to be definite) **to p. sb down** obliger qn à s'engager; **to p. sb down to a date** obliger qn à donner une date
►**pin up** vt sep (notice) fixer ou accrocher au mur; (hair) relever; (hem) rabattre avec des épingles
pinafore ['pɪnəfɔː(r)] n (apron) tablier m; **p. (dress)** robe f chasuble
pinball ['pɪnbɔːl] n flipper m
pincer ['pɪnsə(r)] n (of crab, insect) pince f; Mil **p. movement** mouvement m en tenailles
pincers ['pɪnsəz] npl (tool) tenailles fpl, pince f
pinch [pɪntʃ] **1** n (**a**) (action) pincement m; **to give sb a p.** pincer qn; Fam Fig **to feel the p.** être gêné(e); **at a p.** à la rigueur (**b**) (of salt, herbs) pincée f; Fig **to take sth with a p. of salt** ne pas prendre qch pour argent comptant **2** vt (**a**) (nip) pincer; **these shoes p. my feet** ces chaussures me serrent (**b**) Fam (steal) piquer, faucher **3** vi (of shoes) serrer
pincushion ['pɪnkʊʃən] n pelote f à épingles

pine¹ [paɪn] n (tree, wood) pin m; **p. cone** pomme f de pin, Can cocotte f; **p. forest** pinède f; **p. needle** aiguille f de pin; **p. nut** pignon m
pine² vi **to p. for sb/sth** se languir de qn/qch
►**pine away** vi languir
pineapple ['paɪnæpəl] n ananas m
ping [pɪŋ] **1** n tintement m **2** vi tinter
ping-pong ['pɪŋpɒŋ] n ping-pong m
pinion ['pɪnjən] **1** n pignon m **2** vt (restrain) **to p. sb (to/against)** clouer ou plaquer qn (à/contre)
pink [pɪŋk] **1** n (**a**) (colour) rose m; Fam **to be in the p.** être en parfaite santé (**b**) (flower) œillet m **2** adj rose; **to turn p.** rosir; **p. gin** = cocktail à base de gin et d'angusture; Br **the p. pound,** Am **the p. dollar** = le pouvoir d'achat des homosexuels; Am Fam **p. slip** lettre f ou avis m de licenciement
pinkeye ['pɪŋkaɪ] n Am conjonctivite f infectieuse
pinkie ['pɪŋkɪ] n Am & Scot petit doigt m
pinnacle ['pɪnəkəl] n sommet m; Fig (of fame, career) apogée m
pinpoint ['pɪnpɔɪnt] vt déterminer, identifier; (place) localiser exactement
pinprick ['pɪnprɪk] n piqûre f d'aiguille
pinstripe ['pɪnstraɪp] n rayures fpl fines; **p. suit** costume m rayé
pint [paɪnt] n (unit of measurement) Br = 0,568l, pinte f; Am = 0,473l, pinte f; Br **a p.** (of beer) ≃ un demi-litre de bière; **I'm going for a p.** je vais prendre une bière
pinto bean ['pɪntəʊ'biːn] n haricot m pinto
pint-size(d) ['paɪntsaɪz(d)] adj Fam tout(e) petit(e)
pin-up ['pɪnʌp] n Fam pin-up f inv
pioneer [paɪə'nɪə(r)] **1** n also Fig pionnier(ère) m,f **2** vt **to p. sth** être le (la) premier(ère) à mettre au point qch
pioneering [paɪə'nɪərɪŋ] adj (work) innovateur(trice); (person) qui fait œuvre de pionnier
pious ['paɪəs] adj pieux(euse)
piously ['paɪəslɪ] adv pieusement, avec piété
pip [pɪp] **1** n (**a**) (of fruit) pépin m (**b**) (on card, die) point m (**c**) (sound) **the pips** (on radio) les bips mpl sonores; (on public telephone) = la tonalité indiquant que le crédit est épuisé **2** vt (pt & pp **pipped**) Br Fam **to be pipped at the post** être coiffé(e) sur le poteau
pipe [paɪp] **1** n (**a**) (tube) tuyau m, canalisation f; (musical instrument) chalumeau m; **the pipes** la cornemuse; **p. band** orchestre m de cornemuses (**b**) (for smoking) pipe f; **to smoke a p.** fumer la pipe; Fam Fig **put that in your p. and smoke it!** mettez ça dans votre poche et votre mouchoir par-dessus!; **p. cleaner** cure-pipe m; **p. dream** chimère f **2** vt (water, oil) canaliser; Fam **piped music** musiquette f
►**pipe down** vi Fam (make less noise) faire moins de bruit; (not talk so much) se taire
►**pipe up** vi (of person) risquer un commentaire; (of voice) se faire entendre
pipeline ['paɪplaɪn] n (for oil) pipeline m, oléoduc m; (for gas) gazoduc m; Fig **to be in the p.** être en préparation
piper ['paɪpə(r)] n (bagpipe player) joueur(euse) m,f de cornemuse; Prov **he who pays the p. calls the tune** est normal que celui qui paie ait le droit de choisir
pipette [pɪ'pet] n pipette f

piping ['paɪpɪŋ] **1** *n* (**a**) (*pipes*) tuyauterie *f*, canalisations *fpl* (**b**) (*sound of bagpipes*) son *m* de la cornemuse (**c**) (*on uniform*) passepoil *m* **2** *adj* (*sound, voice*) flûté(e) **3** *adv* **p. hot** tout(e) chaud(e)

pipsqueak ['pɪpskwiːk] *n Fam* minus *m*

piquant ['piːkənt] *adj* piquant(e)

pique [piːk] **1** *n* dépit *m*; **in a fit of p.** dans un accès de dépit **2** *vt* piquer

piracy ['paɪrəsɪ] *n* (**a**) (*of ships*) piraterie *f* (**b**) (*of videos, software*) piratage *m*

piranha [pɪ'rɑːnə] *n* piranha *m*

pirate ['paɪrət] *n* pirate *m*; **p. edition** édition *f* pirate; **p. radio** radio *f* pirate

pirouette [pɪrʊ'et] **1** *n* pirouette *f* **2** *vi* pirouetter

Pisa ['piːzə] *n* Pise

Pisces ['paɪsiːz] *n* les Poissons *mpl*; **to be (a) P.** être Poissons

piss [pɪs] *very Fam* **1** *n* (*urine*) pisse *f*; **to have a p.** pisser; *Br Fig* **to take the p. out of sb/sth** se foutre de qn/qch; *Br* **p. artist** soûlard(e) *m,f* **2** *vt* **to p. oneself, to p. one's pants** pisser dans son froc **3** *vi* pisser

►**piss about, piss around** *vi Br very Fam* (*behave foolishly*) déconner; (*waste time*) glandouiller

►**piss off** *very Fam* **1** *vt sep* (*annoy*) faire chier; **to be pissed off** en avoir plein le cul **2** *vi* (*go away*) foutre le camp

pissed [pɪst] *adj very Fam* (**a**) *Br* (*drunk*) bourré(e); **to get p.** se soûler la gueule (**b**) *Am* (*angry*) en rogne

piss-up ['pɪsʌp] *n Br very Fam* beuverie *f*

pistachio [pɪ'stɑːʃɪəʊ] (*pl* **pistachios**) *n* (*nut*) pistache *f*; (*tree*) pistachier *m*

pistol ['pɪstəl] *n* pistolet *m*; **p. shot** coup *m* de pistolet

piston ['pɪstən] *n* piston *m*

pit¹ [pɪt] *n* (**a**) (*hole in ground*) fosse *f*; (*coal mine*) mine *f*; **in the p. of one's stomach** au creux de l'estomac; *Fam* **to be the pits** être nul (nulle) (**b**) (*in theatre*) parterre *m*; **the pits** (*in motor racing*) les stands *mpl* de ravitaillement; **p. stop** (*in motor racing*) arrêt m au stand (**c**) (*on metal, glass*) piqûre *f*; (*on skin*) marque *f*, cicatrice *f*

pit² *n* (*of cherry, olive*) noyau *m*

pit³ (*pt & pp* **pitted**) *vt* **to p. sb against sb** mettre qn aux prises avec qn, opposer qn à qn; **to p. oneself against sb** se mesurer à qn; **to p. one's wits against sb** se mesurer intellectuellement à qn

pit-a-pat ['pɪtə'pæt] **1** *n* (*of rain*) crépitement *m*; (*of feet*) trottinement *m*; (*of heart*) battement *m* **2** *adv* **to go p.** (*of rain*) crépiter; (*of feet*) trottiner; (*of heart*) palpiter

pitch¹ [pɪtʃ] **1** *n* (**a**) *Br* (*for market stall*) place *f*, emplacement *m* (**b**) (*for sport*) terrain *m* (**c**) (*in music*) hauteur *f*; *Fig* **to reach such a p. that...** atteindre un tel point que... (**d**) (*talk*) (**sales**) **p.** baratin *m* publicitaire (**e**) (*slope*) inclinaison *f* **2** *vt* (**a**) (*throw*) lancer (**b**) (*aim*) adapter (**at** à) (**c**) (*tent*) monter, dresser **3** *vi* (*of ship, plane*) tanguer

►**pitch in** *vi* mettre du sien

pitch² *n* (*tar*) poix *f*

pitch-black [pɪtʃ'blæk] *adj* noir(e) comme dans un four; **it's p. outside** il fait nuit noire

pitched [pɪtʃt] *adj* (**a**) (*sloping*) en pente (**b**) **p. battle** bataille *f* rangée

pitcher¹ ['pɪtʃə(r)] *n Am* (*jug*) cruche *f*, pichet *m*

pitcher² *n Am* (*in baseball*) lanceur *m*

pitchfork ['pɪtʃfɔːk] *n* fourche *f*

piteous ['pɪtɪəs] *adj* pitoyable

pitfall ['pɪtfɔːl] *n* piège *m*

pith [pɪθ] *n* (*of orange*) peau *f* blanche; (*of argument, idea*) essence *f*; **p. helmet** casque *m* colonial (en sola)

pithy ['pɪθɪ] *adj* concis(e)

pitiable ['pɪtɪəbəl] *adj* pitoyable

pitiful ['pɪtɪfʊl] *adj* pitoyable

pitifully ['pɪtɪfʊlɪ] *adv* pitoyablement

pitiless ['pɪtɪlɪs] *adj* impitoyable

pitta bread ['pɪtəbred] *n* pita *m*

pittance ['pɪtəns] *n* salaire *m* de misère

pituitary gland [pɪ'tjuːɪtərɪ'glænd] *n* hypophyse *f*

pity ['pɪtɪ] **1** *n* (**a**) (*compassion*) pitié *f*; **to take** *or* **have p. on sb** prendre qn en pitié; **for p.'s sake!** par pitié! (**b**) (*misfortune*) **it's a p. (that...)** c'est dommage (que... + *subjunctive*); **what a p.!** quel dommage!; **more's the p.** c'est bien dommage **2** *vt* (*pt & pp* **pitied**) plaindre, avoir pitié de

pitying ['pɪtɪɪŋ] *adj* compatissant(e)

pivot ['pɪvət] **1** *n also Fig* pivot *m* **2** *vi* pivoter (**on** sur); *Fig* (*of plan*) reposer (**on** *or* **around** sur)

pivotal ['pɪvətəl] *adj* (*position*) clef; (*importance*) capital(e)

pixel ['pɪksəl] *n Comput* pixel *m*

pixelize ['pɪksəlaɪz] *vt TV* (*to hide identity*) mosaïquer

pixellated ['pɪksəleɪtɪd] *adj Comput* (*image*) pixélisé(e)

pixie ['pɪksɪ] *n* lutin *m*

pizza ['piːtsə] *n* pizza *f*; **p. parlour** pizzeria *f*

Pk *abbr* **Park**

pkt (*abbr* **packet**) paquet *m*

Pl *abbr* **Place**

placard ['plækɑːd] *n* pancarte *f*

placate [plə'keɪt] *vt* apaiser, calmer

place [pleɪs] **1** *n* (**a**) (*location*) endroit *m*, lieu *m*; (*in street names*) rue *f*; **a p. to live/eat** un logement/un restaurant; **I can't be in two places at once** je ne peux pas être à deux endroits à la fois; *Fam* **all over the p.** (*everywhere*) un peu partout; **my hair was all over the p.** j'étais coiffé n'importe comment; **at the interview he was all over the p.** il a raconté n'importe quoi; *Fam Fig* **to go places** réussir (dans la vie); **p. of birth/business** lieu *m* de naissance/travail; **p. of residence** domicile *m*; **p. of worship** lieu *m* de culte; **p. name** nom *m* de lieu (**b**) (*assigned to person, thing*) place *f*; **to find a p. for sb** (*job*) trouver une place pour qn; **to get a p. at university** être admis(e) à l'université; **there's a time and a p. for everything** il y a un temps pour tout; **to hold sth in p.** tenir qch en place; **to lose one's p.** (*in book*) perdre sa page; **to take p.** avoir lieu; **to take sb's p.** remplacer qn; (*oust*) prendre la place de qn; *Fig* **out of p.** (*remark*) déplacé(e); **to feel out of p.** ne pas se sentir à sa place (**c**) *Fam* (*residence*) chez soi; **my parents' p.** chez mes parents; **your p. or mine?** on va chez toi ou chez moi? (**d**) (*seat, position in queue*) place *f*; **to set** *or* **lay an extra p. at the table** mettre un couvert de plus; **to change places with sb** changer de place avec qn;

Fig être à la place de qn; *Fig* **put yourself in my p.** mettez-vous à ma place; **p. mat** set *m* de table (**e**) *(in competition, society)* place *f*, rang *m*; **in first/ second p.** à la première/seconde place; **in the first p....**, **in the second p....** *(parts of an argument)* en premier lieu..., en second lieu...; **you shouldn't have said it in the first p.** d'abord, tu n'aurais pas dû le dire; **to know one's p.** savoir où est sa place; **to put sb in his p.** remettre qn à sa place (**f**) *Math* **to three decimal places** à trois décimales **2** *vt* (**a**) *(put)* placer, mettre; **the house is well placed** la maison est bien située; **to be well placed to do sth** être bien placé(e) pour faire qch; **I know her face but I can't p. her** je l'ai déjà vue mais je ne sais pas où (**b**) *Com & Fin (order)* passer (**with** à); *(contract)* adjuger (**with** à); **to p. a bet (on sth)** parier (sur qch) (**c**) *(find a job for)* placer (**d**) *(classify)* classer; **to be placed third** se classer troisième

placebo [plæ'si:bəʊ] *(pl* placebos) *n also Fig* placebo *m*; **p. effect** effet *m* placebo

placement ['pleɪsmənt] *n* stage *m*

placenta [plə'sentə] *n* placenta *m*

placid ['plæsɪd] *adj* placide, calme

plagiarism ['pleɪdʒərɪzəm] *n* plagiat *m*

plagiarize ['pleɪdʒəraɪz] *vt* plagier

plague [pleɪg] **1** *n (disease)* peste *f*; *(of insects, frogs)* invasion *f*; **to avoid sb/sth like the p.** éviter qn/qch comme la peste **2** *vt (of person)* harceler; *(of problem)* tourmenter; **to p. sb with questions** harceler qn de questions

plaice [pleɪs] *n* carrelet *m*

plaid [plæd] *n (fabric)* tissu *m* écossais; *(garment)* plaid *m*

plain [pleɪn] **1** *n* plaine *f* **2** *adj* (**a**) *(clear, unambiguous)* clair(e), évident(e); **to make sth p. to sb** faire comprendre qch à qn; **I'll be quite p. with you** je vais être franc avec vous; *Fam* **it's as p. as the nose on your face** ça se voit comme le nez au milieu de la figure; **in p. English** clairement; *Fig* **to be p. sailing** aller tout seul; **p. speaking** franc-parler *m* (**b**) *(simple)* simple; *Fam* **that's just p. foolishness/ignorance** c'est de la pure bêtise/ignorance; **one p., one purl** *(in knitting)* une maille à l'endroit, une maille à l'envers; **p. chocolate** chocolat *m* noir; **a p. clothes policeman** un agent en civil; **p. flour** farine *f (sans levure)* (**c**) *(not beautiful)* quelconque; **a p. Jane** une jeune fille plutôt quelconque

plainly ['pleɪnlɪ] *adv* (**a**) *(clearly)* clairement, nettement; **to speak p.** parler franchement *ou* sans détours (**b**) *(simply)* simplement

plain-spoken [pleɪn'spəʊkən] *adj* franc (franche)

plaintiff ['pleɪntɪf] *n Law* plaignant(e) *m,f*

plaintive ['pleɪntɪv] *adj* plaintif(ive)

plaintively ['pleɪntɪvlɪ] *adv* d'un ton plaintif

plait [plæt] **1** *n* natte *f*, tresse *f* **2** *vt* natter, tresser

plan [plæn] **1** *n* (**a**) *(proposal, intention)* projet *m*; **to go according to p.** marcher comme prévu; **the best p. would be to...** le mieux serait de... (**b**) *(of building, town, essay)* plan *m* **2** *vt (pt & pp* planned) (**a**) *(arrange)* projeter; *(crime)* comploter, tramer; **to p. to do sth** projeter de faire qch; **to go as planned** marcher comme prévu (**b**) *(building, town)* faire le plan de; *(economy)* planifier

3 *vi* faire des projets; **to p. for the future** faire des projets d'avenir

▸**plan out** *vt sep* prévoir (en détail)

plane¹ [pleɪn] *n (surface)* plan *m*

plane² *n (aeroplane)* avion *m*; **by p.** en avion; **p. ticket** billet *m* d'avion

plane³ 1 *n (tool)* rabot *m* **2** *vt* raboter, aplanir

plane⁴ *n* **p. (tree)** platane *m*

planet ['plænɪt] *n* planète *f*

planetarium [plænɪ'teərɪəm] *(pl* planetariums *or* planetaria [plænɪ'teərɪə]) *n* planétarium *m*

planetary ['plænɪtərɪ] *adj* planétaire

plank [plæŋk] *n (of wood)* planche *f*; *Fig (policy)* point *m*

plankton ['plæŋktən] *n* plancton *m*

planner ['plænə(r)] *n* planificateur(trice) *m,f*; *(for towns)* urbaniste *mf*

planning ['plænɪŋ] *n* conception *f*, élaboration *f*; **it's still at the p. stage** c'est encore à l'état de projet; **p. permission** permis *m* de construire

plant [plɑ:nt] **1** *n* (**a**) *(living thing)* plante *f*; **p. life** flore *f* (**b**) *Ind (equipment)* matériel *m*; *(factory)* usine *f*; **p. hire** location *f* de matériel industriel; **p. maintenance** entretien *m* du matériel **2** *vt (tree, flower)* planter; *(crops, field)* semer; *(bomb)* poser; **to p. an idea in sb's mind** mettre une idée dans l'esprit de qn; *Fam* **to p. sth on sb** cacher qch dans les affaires de qn *(pour le/la compromettre en cas de découverte)*

plantain ['plæntɪn] *n* (**a**) *(wild plant)* plantain *m* (**b**) *(fruit)* banane *f* des Antilles; *(tree)* bananier *m* du paradis

plantation [plæn'teɪʃən] *n* plantation *f*

planter ['plɑ:ntə(r)] *n (person)* planteur(euse) *m,f*; *(machine)* planteuse *f*

plaque [plɑ:k] *n* (**a**) *(sign)* plaque *f* (commémorative) (**b**) *(on teeth)* plaque *f* dentaire

plasma ['plæzmə] *n* plasma *m*; **p. screen** écran *m* (à) plasma; **p. TV** télévision *f* à plasma

plaster ['plɑ:stə(r)] **1** *n* (**a**) *(on wall)* plâtre *m*; **p. of Paris** plâtre *m* de Paris; **to put sb's leg in p.** mettre la jambe de qn dans le plâtre; **p. cast** *(for broken bone)* plâtre *m*; *(in art)* moulage *m* en plâtre (**b**) *Br* **(sticking) p.** pansement *m* adhésif **2** *vt* (**a**) *(wall)* plâtrer (**b**) *(cover)* tapisser (**with** de); **plastered with mud** couvert(e) de boue; **her name was plastered over the front pages** son nom s'étalait en première page (**c**) *(make stick)* coller; **the rain had plastered his shirt to his back** la pluie lui avait plaqué la chemise sur le dos

plasterboard ['plɑ:stəbɔ:d] *n* placoplâtre® *m*

plastered ['plɑ:stəd] *adj Fam (drunk)* beurré(e)

plasterer ['plɑ:stərə(r)] *n* plâtrier *m*

plastic ['plæstɪk] **1** *n* (**a**) *(material)* plastique *m* (**b**) *Fam (credit cards)* cartes *fpl* de crédit; **do they take p.?** est-ce qu'ils acceptent les cartes de crédit? **2** *adj (cup, bag)* en plastique; *(bullet)* de plastique; **p. explosive** plastic *m*; **p. surgeon** chirurgien(enne) *m,f* esthétique; **p. surgery** *(cosmetic)* chirurgie *f* esthétique; *(after accident)* chirurgie *f* réparatrice; **p. wrap** film *m* alimentaire

plate [pleɪt] **1** *n* (**a**) *(for food)* assiette *f*; *(for church offering)* plateau *m* de quête; *Fam Fig* **to have a lot on one's p.** avoir du pain sur la planche; *Fam Fig* **to hand sth to sb on a p.** apporter qch à qn sur un plateau; **p. rack** égouttoir *m* (**b**) *(sheet of glass, plastic)* lamelle *f*;

(sheet of metal) plaque *f*; p. **glass** vitrage *m* très épais **2** *vt (with gold)* plaquer en or; *(with silver)* plaquer en argent

plateau ['plætəʊ] *(pl* **plateaux** ['plætəʊz] *or* **plateaus)** *n Geog* plateau *m*; *Fig* **to reach a p.** *(of career, economy)* atteindre un palier

platform ['plætfɔːm] *n* (**a**) *(raised flat surface)* plate-forme *f*; *(in train station) (where passengers stand)* quai *m*; *(where train stops)* voie *f*; **p. 4** *(in train station)* quai n° 4; **p. shoes** chaussures *fpl* à semelles compensées (**b**) *(at meeting)* estrade *f*, tribune *f*; *(political programme)* programme *m* (**c**) *Comput* plate-forme *f*

platform-independent ['plætfɔːmɪndɪ'pendənt] *adj Comput* indépendant(e) de la plate-forme

platinum ['plætɪnəm] *n Chem* platine *m*; **p. blond hair** cheveux blond platine

platitude ['plætɪtjuːd] *n* platitude *f*

platonic [plə'tɒnɪk] *adj* platonique

platoon [plə'tuːn] *n Mil* section *f*, peloton *m*

platter ['plætə(r)] *n (serving plate)* plat *m*

platypus ['plætɪpəs] *n* ornithorynque *m*

plausible ['plɔːzəbəl] *adj (excuse, argument)* plausible; *(person)* convaincant(e)

play [pleɪ] **1** *n* (**a**) *(drama)* pièce *f* (de théâtre) (**b**) *(of children)* at **p.** en train de jouer; **to make great p. of** sth beaucoup insister sur qch; **p. on words** jeu *m* de mots (**c**) *(in sport)* jeu *m*; **in p.** en jeu; **out of p.** hors jeu; *Fig* **to come into p.** entrer en jeu; *Fig* **to make a p. for** sth tenter sa chance à qch (**d**) *Tech* jeu *m* **2** *vt* (**a**) *(game, sport)* jouer à; *(opponent)* affronter; *(shot, card, position)* jouer; **to p. football/chess** jouer au football/aux échecs; *Fig* **stop playing games!** arrête de te moquer de moi/nous/*etc*!; *Fig* **to p. ball** *(cooperate)* coopérer; *Fig* **to p. the Stock Exchange** jouer à la Bourse; **to p. a joke** *or* **a trick on sb** jouer un tour à qn (**b**) *(in play, film)* jouer; **to p. Macbeth** jouer le rôle de Macbeth; *Fig* **to p. an important part in** sth jouer un rôle important dans qch; *Fig* **to p. no part in** sth ne pas intervenir dans qch; *Fig* **to p. the fool** faire l'idiot (**c**) *(musical instrument)* jouer de; *(piece, tune)* jouer; *(CD, tape, record)* mettre; **to p. the piano/the flute** jouer du piano/de la flûte **3** *vi* (**a**) *(of children)* jouer; *(of animals)* folâtrer; **to p. with** sth *(pen, hair)* tripoter qch; *Fig* **to p. with fire** jouer avec le feu; *Fam Fig* **what's she playing at?** à quoi elle joue? (**b**) *(of sportsperson)* jouer; **to p. fair/dirty** jouer franc jeu/en traître; *Fig* **to p. for time** essayer de gagner du temps; *Fig* **to p. into sb's hands** faire le jeu de qn; *Fig* **to p. safe** ne pas prendre de risques (**c**) *(of musician)* jouer; (**d**) *(of actor)* jouer; *(of film, play)* être à l'affiche

▸**play about, play around** *vi* jouer, s'amuser

▸**play along** *vi* coopérer

▸**play back** *vt sep (tape, recording) (for first time)* écouter; *(replay)* réécouter

▸**play down** *vt sep* minimiser

▸**play off** *vt sep* **to p. sb off against sb** monter qn contre qn

▸**play on 1** *vt insep (feelings, fears)* jouer sur **2** *vi (of musician, sportsperson)* continuer à jouer

▸**play out** *vt sep* **the drama being played out before them** le drame qui se déroule sous leurs yeux

▸**play up** *vi Br Fam (of car, child, injury)* faire des siennes

play-acting ['pleɪæktɪŋ] *n* comédie *f*

playboy ['pleɪbɔɪ] *n* play-boy *m*

player ['pleɪə(r)] *n (of game, instrument)* joueur(euse) *m,f*; *(actor)* acteur(trice) *m,f*; *Fig* **the key players** les acteurs principaux

playful ['pleɪfʊl] *adj (person, animal)* joueur(euse); *(mood, tone)* enjoué(e); *(remark)* espiègle

playground ['pleɪgraʊnd] *n (at school)* cour *f* de récréation; *(in park)* aire *f* de jeu

playgroup ['pleɪgruːp] *n* garderie *f*

playhouse ['pleɪhaʊs] *n* (**a**) *(theatre)* théâtre *m* (**b**) *(children's)* maison *f* de poupée

playing ['pleɪɪŋ] *n* **p. card** carte *f* à jouer; **p. field** terrain *m* de jeu

playmate ['pleɪmeɪt] *n* camarade *mf* de jeu

play-off ['pleɪɒf] *n Sport* match *m* de barrage

playpen ['pleɪpen] *n* parc *m (pour bébé)*

playroom ['pleɪruːm] *n* salle *f* de jeu

playschool ['pleɪskuːl] *n* garderie *f*

plaything ['pleɪθɪŋ] *n* jouet *m*

playtime ['pleɪtaɪm] *n (at school)* récréation *f*

playwright ['pleɪraɪt] *n* auteur *m* dramatique

plaza ['plɑːzə] *n Am (shopping centre)* centre *m* commercial

PLC, plc [piːel'siː] *n Br Com (abbr* **public limited company)** ≃ SA *f*

plea [pliː] *n* (**a**) *(appeal)* appel *m* (**for** à) (**b**) *(excuse)* excuse *f* (**c**) *Law* **to enter a p.** of guilty/not guilty plaider coupable/non coupable; *Am* **p. bargaining** = possibilité donnée à l'accusé de voir ses charges réduites s'il plaide coupable

plead [pliːd] **1** *vt Law* **to p. sb's case** *(of lawyer)* plaider la cause de qn; *Law* **to p. insanity** plaider la démence; **to p. ignorance** faire l'ignorant(e) **2** *vi* **to p. with sb (to do sth)** supplier qn (de faire qch); *Law* **to p. guilty/not guilty** plaider coupable/non coupable

pleasant ['plezənt] *adj* agréable

pleasantly ['plezəntlɪ] *adv (smile, behave)* aimablement; *(surprised)* agréablement

pleasantry ['plezəntrɪ] *(pl* **pleasantries)** *n (joke)* plaisanterie *f*; **to exchange pleasantries** *(polite remarks)* échanger des politesses

please [pliːz] **1** *adv* s'il vous/te plaît; **come in, p.** entrez, je vous prie; **p. don't cry** s'il te plaît, ne pleure pas; **p. tell me the truth** dis-moi la vérité(, je t'en prie); **may I? – p. do** puis-je? – je vous en prie; **p. sit down** asseyez-vous, je vous prie; **yes, p.** oui, s'il te plaît **2** *vt* faire plaisir à; **you can't p. everybody** on ne peut pas contenter tout le monde; **p. yourself!** fais comme tu voudras!; **to be easy/hard to p.** être facile/difficile à contenter; **p. God!** plaise à Dieu! **3** *vi* (**a**) *(like)* to **do as one pleases** faire ce que l'on veut; **this way, if you p.** par ici, s'il vous plaît; **and then, if you p., he blamed me for it!** et le comble, c'est qu'il a dit que c'était de ma faute! (**b**) *(give pleasure)* to be pleasing to plaire à; vouloir plaire

pleased [pliːzd] *adj* content(e) (**with** de); **to be p. to do sth** faire qch avec plaisir; **to be p. for sb** être content pour qn; **to be as p. as Punch** être très content comme tout; **he's very p. with himself** il est très content de lui; **to meet you!** enchanté(e)!; **I'm p. to say that...** je suis heureux de vous dire que...

pleasurable ['pleʒərəbəl] *adj* agréable

pleasure ['pleʒə(r)] *n* (**a**) *(contentment, enjoyment)* plaisir *m*; **to take p. in doing sth** prendre plaisir à faire qch; **with p.** avec plaisir; **my p.!** je vous en prie!; *Formal* **I have p. in informing you that...** j'ai le plaisir de vous informer que...; **p. boat** bateau *m* de plaisance; **p. trip** excursion *f* (**b**) *(will)* **at your p.** à votre gré; *Law* **to be detained at** *or* **during Her Majesty's p.** être emprisonné(e)

pleat [pliːt] *n* pli *m*

pleated ['pliːtɪd] *adj* plissé(e)

plebeian [plə'biːən] **1** *n* plébéien(enne) *m,f*
  2 *adj* plébéien(enne)

plebiscite ['plebɪsɪt] *n* plébiscite *m*

plectrum ['plektrəm] *n Mus* médiator *m*

pledge [pledʒ] **1** *n* (**a**) *(promise)* promesse *f* (**b**) *(object)* gage *m*
  2 *vt (promise)* **to p. to do sth** s'engager à faire qch; **to p. one's loyalty/support** accorder sa loyauté/son soutien; **to p. money** *(in radio, television appeal)* faire une promesse de don

plenary ['pliːnərɪ] *adj* plénier(ère); **p. session** séance *f* plénière

plentiful ['plentɪfʊl] *adj* abondant(e)

plenty ['plentɪ] **1** *n* abondance *f*; **a land of p.** un pays d'abondance
  2 *pron* **p. of** beaucoup de; **you've got p. of time** tu as largement le temps; **that's p.** *(of food)* merci, j'en ai assez
  3 *adv Fam* **it's p. big enough** c'est bien assez grand

plethora ['pleθərə] *n* pléthore *f*

pleurisy ['plʊərɪsɪ] *n* pleurésie *f*

pliable ['plaɪəbəl] *adj (wood, plastic)* souple; *(person)* malléable

pliers ['plaɪəz] *npl* pince *f*, tenaille *f*; **a pair of p.** une pince, une tenaille

plight [plaɪt] *n* situation *f* critique; *(of refugees)* détresse *f*

plimsolls ['plɪmsəlz] *npl* tennis *mpl*

plinth [plɪnθ] *n* socle *m*

PLO [piːe'ləʊ] *n (abbr* **Palestine Liberation Organization**) OLP *f*

plod [plɒd] *(pt & pp* **plodded**) *vi* (**a**) *(walk)* marcher péniblement (**b**) *(work)* **to p. (away)** trimer

plonk¹ [plɒŋk] **1** *n (sound)* bruit *m* sourd
  2 *vt Fam* **just p. it down there** tu n'as qu'à le poser là; **to p. oneself down in an armchair** s'affaler dans un fauteuil

plonk² *n Br Fam (wine)* vin *m* ordinaire

plop [plɒp] **1** *n* plouf *m*
  2 *vi (pt & pp* **plopped**) faire plouf

plot [plɒt] **1** *n* (**a**) *(conspiracy)* complot *m* (**b**) *(of play, novel)* intrigue *f*; *Fig* **the p. thickens** l'affaire se corse (**c**) *(land)* parcelle *f*; **(vegetable) p.** potager *m*
  2 *vt (pt & pp* **plotted**) (**a**) *(plan)* comploter; **to p. to do sth** comploter de faire qch (**b**) *(position, course)* déterminer; *(progress, development)* suivre de près (**c**) *Math* tracer

plotter ['plɒtə(r)] *n (conspirator)* conspirateur(trice) *m,f*

plough, Am plow [plaʊ] **1** *n* charrue *f*; **the P.** *(constellation)* le Grand Chariot
  2 *vt (field)* labourer; *Fig (profits)* réinvestir
  3 *vi* labourer; *Fig* **to p. through sth** *(work, reading)* avancer péniblement dans qch; *Fig* **to p. into sth** *(of vehicle)* rentrer dans qch
▸ **plough on with** *vt insep* poursuivre laborieusement
▸ **plough up** *vt sep (field)* labourer

ploughman ['plaʊmən] *n* laboureur *m*; **p.'s lunch** = assiette de fromage ou jambon avec du pain, de la salade et des condiments

plover ['plʌvə(r)] *n* pluvier *m*

plow *Am* = **plough**

ploy [plɔɪ] *n* stratagème *m*, ruse *f*

pluck [plʌk] **1** *n (courage)* courage *m*
  2 *vt (hair, feathers)* arracher; *(flower)* cueillir; *(chicken, turkey)* plumer; *(string of guitar)* pincer; **to p. one's eyebrows** s'épiler les sourcils; **they were plucked from danger by a helicopter** un hélicoptère les a sauvés du danger
  3 *vi* **to p. at sb's sleeve** tirer qn par la manche
▸ **pluck up** *vt sep* **to p. up the courage to do sth** trouver le courage de faire qch

plucky ['plʌkɪ] *adj* courageux(euse)

plug [plʌg] **1** *n* (**a**) *(for sink)* bonde *f* (**b**) *(electrical) (on device)* fiche *f*; *(socket)* prise *f* (de courant); *Fam Fig* **to pull the p. on sth** *(put a stop to)* mettre le holà à qch; *(stop funding)* arrêter de financer qch (**c**) *Aut* **(spark) p.** bougie *f* (**d**) *Fam (publicity)* pub *f*
  2 *vt (pt & pp* **plugged**) (**a**) *(gap, hole)* boucher; *(leak)* colmater (**b**) *Fam (promote)* faire de la pub pour
▸ **plug away** *vi Fam* s'acharner (**at** sur)
▸ **plug in** *vt sep* brancher

plughole ['plʌghəʊl] *n* trou *m* d'écoulement; *Fam Fig* **that's £300 down the p.!** c'est 300 livres foutues en l'air!

plug-in ['plʌgɪn] *n Comput* module *m* externe, *Can* plugiciel *m*

plum [plʌm] **1** *n (fruit)* prune *f*; **p. pudding** plum-pudding *m*; **p. tomato** olivette *f*; **p. tree** prunier *m*
  2 *adj* (**a**) *(colour)* prune *inv* (**b**) *Fam (very good)* **a p. job** un boulot en or

plumage ['pluːmɪdʒ] *n* plumage *m*

plumb [plʌm] **1** *n* **p. (line)** fil *m* à plomb; **to be out of p.** ne pas être d'aplomb
  2 *adv (exactly)* **p. in the centre** en plein centre
  3 *vt Fig* **to p. the depths** toucher le fond; **that's really plumbing the depths!** c'est vraiment le comble du mauvais goût!
▸ **plumb in** *vt sep (washing machine)* brancher

plumber ['plʌmə(r)] *n* plombier *m*

plumbing ['plʌmɪŋ] *n (job, system)* plomberie *f*

plume [pluːm] *n (feather)* plume *f*; *(on hat)* aigrette *f*; *Fig (of smoke)* volute *f*

plummet ['plʌmɪt] *vi (of morale, standards)* chuter; *(of prices)* s'effondrer; **the plane plummeted to the ground** l'avion a piqué et s'est écrasé au sol

plummy ['plʌmɪ] *adj Fam (voice, accent)* snob *inv*

plump [plʌmp] *adj* dodu(e); *(cheeks, face)* rond(e)
▸ **plump for** *vt insep Fam (choose)* se décider pour

plunder ['plʌndə(r)] **1** *n (action)* pillage *m*; *(loot)* butin *m*
  2 *vt* piller

plunge [plʌndʒ] **1** *n (dive)* plongeon *m*; *Fig (decrease)* chute *f*; *Fam Fig* **to take the p.** se jeter à l'eau
  2 *vt* plonger (**into** dans)
  3 *vi (fall)* plonger; *Fig (decrease)* chuter; **she plunged to her death** elle a fait une chute mortelle

plunger ['plʌndʒə(r)] *n (of cafetière, syringe)* piston *m*; *(for clearing sink)* ventouse *f*

plunging ['plʌndʒɪŋ] *adj (prices)* en chute libre; **p. neckline** décolleté *m* plongeant

pluperfect ['pluː'pɜːfɪkt] *n Gram* **the p.** le plus-que-parfait

plural ['plʊərəl] *Gram* **1** *adj* pluriel(elle)
  2 *n* pluriel *m*

pluralism ['plʊərəlɪzəm] *n* pluralisme *m*

plurality [plʊə'rælɪtɪ] *n* pluralité *f*

plus [plʌs] **1** *n* (*pl* **plusses** [ˈplʌsɪz]) (**a**) *p.* **(sign)** (signe *m*) plus *m* (**b**) *(advantage)* plus *m* **2** *adj* but on the p. side... mais d'un autre côté...; **fifteen p.** plus de quinze **3** *prep* plus; **seven p. nine** sept plus neuf

plush [plʌʃ] **1** *n Tex* peluche *f* **2** *adj Fam* luxueux(euse)

Pluto [ˈpluːtəʊ] *n (planet)* Pluton *f*

plutonium [pluːˈtəʊnɪəm] *n Chem* plutonium *m*

ply[1] [plaɪ] *n* **three-p.** *(wood, paper handkerchief)* triple épaisseur; *(wool)* à trois fils

ply[2] *(pt & pp* **plied**) **1** *vt (trade)* exercer; **to p. sb with questions** assaillir qn de questions; **to p. sb with drink** ne pas arrêter de verser à boire à qn **2** *vi (of ship, bus)* **to p. between** faire la navette entre

plywood [ˈplaɪwʊd] *n* contreplaqué *m*

PM [piːˈem] *n (abbr* **Prime Minister)** Premier ministre *m*

p.m. [ˈpiːem] *adv (abbr* **post meridiem)** 6 p.m. 18 h

PMS [piːemˈes] *n (abbr* **premenstrual syndrome)** syndrome *m* prémenstruel

PMT [piːemˈtiː] *n Br (abbr* **premenstrual tension)** syndrome *m* prémenstruel

pneumatic [njuːˈmætɪk] *adj* pneumatique; **p. drill** marteau *m* piqueur

pneumonia [njuːˈməʊnɪə] *n* pneumonie *f*

PO [piːˈəʊ] *n* (**a**) *(abbr* **Post Office)** poste *f*; **PO Box** BP (**b**) *(abbr* **postal order)** mandat *m* postal

poach[1] [pəʊtʃ] *vt Culin (eggs, fish)* pocher

poach[2] *vt* (**a**) *(catch illegally) (fish)* pêcher sans permis; *(game)* chasser sans permis (**b**) *(employee)* débaucher

poacher [ˈpəʊtʃə(r)] *n (of fish, game)* braconnier *m*

pocket [ˈpɒkɪt] **1** *n* (**a**) *(of clothes, bag)* poche *f*; **to go through sb's pockets** faire les poches à qn; **prices to suit every p.** des prix pour toutes les bourses; **to be out of p.** en être de sa poche; **how much are you out of p.?** tu en as eu pour combien?; **to pay for sth out of one's own p.** payer qch de sa poche; *Fig* **to line one's pockets** se remplir les poches; *Fig* **to have sb in one's p.** avoir qn dans sa poche; **p. calculator** calculette *f*; **p. money** argent *m* de poche (**b**) *(in snooker, pool)* poche *f*, blouse *f* (**c**) *(of gas, air, resistance)* poche *f* **2** *vt (put in pocket)* empocher; *Fam (steal)* rafler

pocketbook [ˈpɒkɪtbʊk] *n Am (wallet)* portefeuille *m*; *(handbag)* sac *m* à main

pocketknife [ˈpɒkɪtnaɪf] *(pl* **pocketknives** [ˈpɒkɪtnaɪvz]*)* *n* couteau *m* de poche

pockmarked [ˈpɒkmɑːkt] *adj* grêlé(e)

pod [pɒd] *n (of plant)* gousse *f*

podcast [ˈpɒdkɑːst] *n Comput* podcast *m*

podgy [ˈpɒdʒɪ] *adj* grassouillet(ette)

podiatrist [pəˈdaɪətrɪst] *n* pédicure *mf*

podium [ˈpəʊdɪəm] *n (for speaker, conductor)* estrade *f*; *(for winner)* podium *m*

poem [ˈpəʊɪm] *n* poème *m*

poet [ˈpəʊɪt] *n* poète *m*

poetic [pəʊˈetɪk] *adj* poétique; **it's p. justice that...** ça n'est que justice que...; **p. licence** licence *f* poétique

poetical [pəʊˈetɪkəl] *adj* poétique

poetry [ˈpəʊɪtrɪ] *n* poésie *f*; **p. in motion** un véritable plaisir; **p. reading** lecture *f* de textes poétiques

poignancy [ˈpɔɪnjənsɪ] *n* caractère *m* poignant

poignant [ˈpɔɪnjənt] *adj* poignant(e)

point [pɔɪnt] **1** *n* (**a**) *(location)* endroit *m*; **the highest p.** le point le plus haut; **p. of sale** point *m* de vente; **p.**

of view point *m* de vue (**b**) *(in time)* moment *m*; **at this p. in time** actuellement; **at this p. the phone rang** à ce moment le téléphone a sonné; **to be on the p. of doing sth** être sur le point de faire qch; **to reach the p. of no return** arriver au point de non-retour; **outspoken to the p. of rudeness** d'une franchise qui frise l'impolitesse (**c**) *(of argument, discussion)* point *m*; **the p. is that...** le fait est que...; **I take your p.** je vois ce que tu veux dire; **she has a p.** elle a raison; **to make a p.** faire une remarque; **to get to the p.** en arriver au fait; **that's beside the p.** ça n'a rien à voir; **that's not the p.** il ne s'agit pas de cela; **what's the p.?** à quoi bon?; **to make a p. of doing sth** mettre un point d'honneur à faire qch; **there is no p. in waiting any longer** cela ne sert à rien d'attendre plus longtemps; **in p. of fact** en fait; **to the p.** *(relevant)* pertinent(e); **it has its good points** ça a ses avantages; **up to a p.** jusqu'à un certain point; **not to put too fine a p. on it...** pour parler franchement...; **p. of grammar/of law** question *f* de grammaire/de droit; **p. of order** question *f* de procédure (**d**) *(punctuation mark)* point *m*; *Math* **(decimal) p.** virgule *f* (décimale); **three p. five** trois virgule cinq (**e**) *(in game, exam, on scale)* point *m*; **to win on points** gagner aux points (**f**) *(on compass)* point *m* (**g**) *(of needle, pencil, sword)* pointe *f*; **to end in a p.** avoir un bout pointu (**h**) *(plug socket)* prise *f* (de courant) (**i**) *(of land)* pointe *f* (**j**) *Rail* **points** aiguillage *m* **2** *vt (camera, gun)* braquer (**at** sur); *Fig* **to p. the finger at sb** montrer qn du doigt; **can you p. me in the right direction?** pouvez-vous me dire quelle direction je dois prendre?; **to p. the way (to)** montrer le chemin (à); *Fig* **to p. north** *(of arrow, compass needle)* indiquer le nord; **to be pointing towards sth** *(of car, chair)* être face à qch; **this points to the fact that...** ceci montre *ou* indique que...; **all the evidence points to suicide** tout laisse penser à un suicide

▸**point out** *vt sep (with finger)* montrer; *(error, fact)* signaler

▸**point up** *vt sep (highlight)* mettre en évidence

point-blank [ˈpɔɪntˈblæŋk] **1** *adj (refusal, denial)* catégorique; **at p. range** à bout portant **2** *adv (fire)* à bout portant; *(ask)* de but en blanc; *(refuse, deny)* catégoriquement

pointed [ˈpɔɪntɪd] *adj* (**a**) *(sharp)* pointu(e) (**b**) *(remark)* mordant(e)

pointedly [ˈpɔɪntɪdlɪ] *adv* ostensiblement

pointer [ˈpɔɪntə(r)] *n* (**a**) *(indicator)* aiguille *f*; *(stick)* baguette *f* (**b**) *Fam (advice)* tuyau *m* (**c**) *(dog)* pointer *m*

pointless [ˈpɔɪntlɪs] *adj* inutile; *(life)* absurde; **it would be p.** ça ne servirait à rien

poise [pɔɪz] *n (composure)* assurance *f*; *(balance)* équilibre *m*

poised [pɔɪzd] *adj* (**a**) *(composed)* posé(e) (**b**) *(ready)* **to be p. to do sth** être prêt(e) à faire qch (**c**) *(suspended)* suspendu(e)

poison [ˈpɔɪzən] **1** *n* poison *m*; *Fam* **what's your p.?** qu'est-ce que tu veux boire?; **p. gas** gaz *m* toxique; **p. ivy** sumac *m* vénéneux; **p. pen letter** lettre *f* anonyme malfaisante

2 *vt* (**a**) *(person, food)* empoisonner; **to p. sb's mind against sb** monter qn contre qn (**b**) *(pollute)* contaminer

poisoning ['pɔɪzənɪŋ] *n* (**a**) *(of person, food)* empoisonnement *m*; **to die of p.** mourir empoisonné(e) (**b**) *(pollution)* contamination *f*

poisonous ['pɔɪzənəs] *adj (snake, remark)* venimeux(euse); *(chemical, fumes)* toxique; *(plant, mushroom)* vénéneux(euse); *Fig (rumour)* pernicieux(euse)

poke [pəʊk] **1** *n* coup *m* léger
  2 *vt (person)* donner un coup à; *(object)* tâter; *(fire)* attiser; **to p. sb in the eye** mettre le doigt dans l'œil à qn; **to p. sb in the ribs** *(with elbow)* donner un coup de coude à qn; **to p. a hole in sth** faire un trou dans qch; **to p. one's nose into other people's business** mettre son nez dans les affaires des autres; **to p. one's head out of the window** passer la tête par la fenêtre; **to p. fun at** se moquer de
  3 *vi* **to p. at sth (with one's finger/a stick)** tâter qch (du doigt/avec le bout d'un bâton)

▸**poke about, poke around** *vi (search)* fouiller; *(be nosy)* fourrer son nez partout

▸**poke out 1** *vt sep* **you nearly poked my eye out!** un peu plus et tu me crevais l'œil!
  2 *vi (protrude)* sortir, dépasser

poker¹ ['pəʊkə(r)] *n (for fire)* tisonnier *m*

poker² *n (card game)* poker *m*

poker-faced ['pəʊkəfeɪst] *adj* au visage impassible

poky ['pəʊkɪ] *adj* **a p. little flat** un appartement exigu

Poland ['pəʊlənd] *n* la Pologne

polar ['pəʊlə(r)] *adj* polaire; **p. bear** ours *m* polaire *ou* blanc

polarity [pəʊ'lærɪtɪ] *n* polarité *f*

polarization [pəʊləraɪ'zeɪʃən] *n (of opinion, country)* division *f*

polarize ['pəʊləraɪz] *vt (opinion, country)* diviser

Polaroid® ['pəʊlərɔɪd] *n (camera, photo)* polaroid® *m*

Pole [pəʊl] *n* Polonais(e) *m,f*

pole¹ [pəʊl] *n (post, stick)* perche *f*; *(for flag)* hampe *f*; **p. dancing** = style de danse de strip-tease qui s'exécute autour d'une barre verticale; **the p. vault** le saut à la perche

pole² *n Elec & Geog* pôle *m*; *Fig* **to be poles apart** être diamétralement opposés; **the P. Star** l'étoile *f* polaire

poleaxe, *Am* poleax ['pəʊlæks] *vt (physically)* assommer; *(emotionally)* abasourdir

polecat ['pəʊlkæt] *n* putois *m*

polemic [pə'lemɪk] *n* polémique *f*

polemical [pə'lemɪkəl] *adj* polémique

police [pə'liːs] **1** *npl* **the p.** la police; **two hundred p.** deux cents policiers; **p. car** voiture *f* de police; **p. constable** agent *m* de police; *Am* **p. department** service *m* de police; **p. dog** chien *m* policier; **p. force** police *f*; **p. officer** policier *m*; **p. record** casier *m* judiciaire; **p. state** État *m* policier; **p. station** poste *m* de police
  2 *vt (area, city)* maintenir l'ordre dans; *Fig* réglementer

policeman [pə'liːsmən] *n* agent *m* de police

policewoman [pə'liːswʊmən] *n* femme *f* agent de police

policy ['pɒlɪsɪ] *(pl policies) n* (**a**) *(of government, personal)* politique *f*; **it's a matter of p.** c'est une question de principe; **a good/bad p.** une bonne/mauvaise idée (**b**) *Fin (insurance)* **p.** police *f* (d'assurance); *Fin* **p. holder** assuré(e) *m,f*

polio ['pəʊlɪəʊ] *n* polio *f*

Polish ['pəʊlɪʃ] **1** *n (language)* polonais *m*
  2 *adj* polonais(e)

polish ['pɒlɪʃ] **1** *n* (**a**) *(for shoes)* cirage *m*; *(for furniture, floors)* cire *f*; *(for metal)* pâte *f* à polir; *(for nails)* vernis *m* à ongles (**b**) *(finish, shine)* éclat *m*, brillant *m*; **to give sth a p.** faire briller qch (**c**) *(refinement)* raffinement *m*
  2 *vt (silver, brass)* astiquer; *(shoes, furniture, floor)* cirer; *(stone, metal)* polir

▸**polish off** *vt sep Fam (food)* avaler; *(drink)* descendre; *(work)* expédier; *(opponent)* liquider

▸**polish up** *vt sep (improve)* perfectionner

polished ['pɒlɪʃt] *adj (shoes, furniture, floor)* ciré(e); *(metal, stone, glass)* poli(e); *Fig (manners, style)* raffiné(e)

polite [pə'laɪt] *adj* poli(e) (**to** avec); **in p. society** chez les gens bien

politely [pə'laɪtlɪ] *adv* poliment

politeness [pə'laɪtnɪs] *n* politesse *f*

politic ['pɒlɪtɪk] *adj Formal* sage; **it would not be p. to refuse** ce ne serait pas prudent de refuser

political [pə'lɪtɪkəl] *adj* politique; **she isn't very p.** elle ne s'intéresse pas beaucoup à la politique; **p. asylum** asile *m* politique; **p. correctness** le politiquement correct; **p. prisoner** prisonnier(ère) *m,f* politique; **p. science** sciences *fpl* politiques

politically [pə'lɪtɪklɪ] *adv* politiquement; **p. correct** politiquement correct(e)

politician [pɒlɪ'tɪʃən] *n* homme *m*/femme *f* politique

politicize [pə'lɪtɪsaɪz] *vt* politiser

politics ['pɒlɪtɪks] **1** *n* politique *f*
  2 *npl* (**a**) *(views)* opinions *fpl* politiques (**b**) *(office p.* intrigues *fpl* de bureau

polka ['pɒlkə] *n* polka *f*; **a p. dot tie** une cravate à pois

poll [pəʊl] **1** *n (votes cast)* scrutin *m*; **(opinion) p.** *(survey)* sondage *m*; **to go to the polls** aller aux urnes; *Formerly* **the p. tax** = en Grande-Bretagne, anciens impôts locaux à payer à titre individuel
  2 *vt (votes)* obtenir; *(people)* sonder

pollen ['pɒlən] *n* pollen *m*; **p. count** taux *m* de pollen dans l'atmosphère

pollinate ['pɒlɪneɪt] *vt* polliniser

polling ['pəʊlɪŋ] *n* élections *fpl*, scrutin *m*; **p. booth** isoloir *m*; **p. day** jour *m* du scrutin; **p. station** bureau *m* de vote

pollutant [pə'luːtənt] *n* polluant *m*

pollute [pə'luːt] *vt* polluer

polluter [pə'luːtə(r)] *n* pollueur(euse) *m,f*

pollution [pə'luːʃən] *n* pollution *f*

polo ['pəʊləʊ] *n* (**a**) *Sport* polo *m* (**b**) *Br* **p. neck (sweater)** (pull *m* à) col *m* roulé

poltergeist ['pɒltəgaɪst] *n* esprit *m* frappeur

poly ['pɒlɪ] *(pl polys) n Br Fam Formerly (polytechnic)* établissement *m* d'enseignement supérieur

poly bag ['pɒlɪbæg] *n Fam* sac *m* en plastique

polyester [pɒlɪ'estə(r)] *n* polyester *m*

polygamy [pə'lɪgəmɪ] *n* polygamie *f*

polyglot ['pɒlɪglɒt] **1** *n* polyglotte *mf*
  2 *adj* polyglotte

polygon ['pɒlɪgən] *n* polygone *m*

polymer ['pɒlɪmə(r)] *n Chem* polymère *m*

Polynesia [pɒlɪ'niːzɪə] *n* la Polynésie

Polynesian [pɒlɪ'niːzɪən] **1** *n* Polynésien(enne) *m,f*
  2 *adj* polynésien(enne)

polyp ['pɒlɪp] *n Med* polype *m*

polyphonic [pɒlɪ'fɒnɪk] *adj Mus* polyphonique; *Tel* **p. ringtone** sonnerie *f* polyphonique

polystyrene [pɒlɪ'staɪriːn] *n* polystyrène *m*

polytechnic [pɒlɪ'teknɪk] *n Br Formerly* établissement *m* d'enseignement supérieur

polythene ['pɒlɪθiːn] *n* polyéthylène *m*; **p. bag** sac *m* en plastique

polyunsaturated [pɒlɪʌn'sætjʊreɪtɪd] *adj* poly-insaturé(e)

polyurethane [pɒlɪ'jʊərɪθeɪn] *n* polyuréthane *m*

pom [pɒm] = **pommie**

pomegranate ['pɒmɪɡrænɪt] *n (fruit)* grenade *f*; **p. (tree)** grenadier *m*

pommie, pommy ['pɒmɪ] *(pl* **pommies)** *n Fam* Anglais(e) *m,f*

pomp [pɒmp] *n* pompe *f*; **p. and circumstance** grand apparat *m*

pompom ['pɒmpɒm] *n* pompon *m*

pomposity [pɒm'pɒsɪtɪ] *n* suffisance *f*

pompous ['pɒmpəs] *adj* pompeux(euse)

ponce [pɒns] *n very Fam* (**a**) *(effeminate man)* tapette *f* (**b**) *(pimp)* maquereau *m*

▸**ponce about, ponce around** *vi Fam* (**a**) *(waste time)* traîner (**b**) *(of effeminate man)* se pavaner

poncho ['pɒntʃəʊ] *(pl* **ponchos)** *n* poncho *m*

pond [pɒnd] *n* étang *m*; *(smaller)* mare *f*

ponder ['pɒndə(r)] **1** *vt* réfléchir à, considérer **2** *vi* réfléchir (**on** *or* **over** à)

ponderous ['pɒndərəs] *adj (movement, person)* lourd(e); *(progress, piece of writing)* laborieux(euse)

pong [pɒŋ] *Br Fam* **1** *n (smell)* puanteur *f* **2** *vi* puer

pontiff ['pɒntɪf] *n* pontife *m*

pontificate [pɒn'tɪfɪkeɪt] *vi* pontifier (**about** sur)

pontoon¹ [pɒn'tuːn] *n (float)* ponton *m*; **p. bridge** pont *m* flottant

pontoon² *n (card game)* vingt-et-un *m*

pony ['pəʊnɪ] *(pl* **ponies)** *n* poney *m*; **p. trekking** randonnée *f* à dos de poney

ponytail ['pəʊnɪteɪl] *n* queue *f* de cheval

poo [puː] *n Fam* caca *m*; **to do** *or* **have a p.** faire caca

poodle ['puːdəl] *n* caniche *m*

poof [pʊf], **poofter** ['pʊftə(r)] *n very Fam* pédé *m*, = terme injurieux désignant un homosexuel

pooh¹ [puː] *exclam* bah!

pooh² = **poo**

pooh-pooh ['puː'puː] *vt* rejeter

pool¹ [puːl] *n (pond, of blood)* mare *f*; *(puddle)* flaque *f*; **(swimming) p.** piscine *f*

pool² **1** *n* (**a**) *(of money, helpers)* réserve *f*; *(of knowledge)* mine *f*; **car p.** parc *m* de voitures (**b**) **the (football) pools** = concours de pronostics des matchs de football **2** *vt (ideas, resources)* mettre en commun, grouper

pool³ *n (game)* billard *m* américain; **p. table** (table *f* de) billard *m*

pooped [puːpt] *adj Am Fam* vanné(e)

poor [pʊə(r)] **1** *adj* (**a**) *(not rich)* pauvre; **the p. man's** champagne le champagne du pauvre (**b**) *(bad)* mauvais(e); *(chances)* faible; *(harvest, reward)* maigre; **to be in p. health** ne pas être en bonne santé; **to have a p. memory** ne pas avoir une bonne mémoire; **to be p. at maths** être faible en maths; **p. loser** mauvais(e) perdant(e) *m,f*; **in p. taste** de mauvais goût (**c**) *(expressing sympathy)* **you p. thing!** pauvre petit(e)!; **p. (old) Simon** le pauvre Simon **2** *npl* **the p.** les pauvres *mpl*

poorly ['pʊəlɪ] **1** *adv* mal; *(dressed)* pauvrement; **to be p. off** être pauvre **2** *adj Br* malade, souffrant(e)

pop¹ [pɒp] **1** *n (music)* pop *f* **2** *adj* **p. art** pop art *m*; **p. group** groupe *m* de pop; **p. music** musique *f* pop; **p. singer** chanteur(euse) *m,f* pop; **p. song** chanson *f* pop

pop² *n Am (father)* papa *m*

pop³ **1** *n* (**a**) *(sound)* bruit *m* sec (**b**) *Fam (fizzy drink)* soda *m* **2** *vt (pt & pp* **popped**) (**a**) *(burst)* faire éclater (**b**) *Fam (put quickly)* mettre; **to p. one's head out of the window** passer la tête par la fenêtre; *Fam* **to p. the question** faire sa demande en mariage; **to p. pills** se bourrer de comprimés **3** *vi* (**a**) *(burst)* éclater; *(of cork)* sauter; *(of ears)* se déboucher (**b**) *Fam (go quickly)* **I'm just popping next door** je fais juste un saut chez les voisins; **we popped over to France for the weekend** nous avons fait un saut en France pour le week-end

▸**pop in** *vi Fam* passer

▸**pop off** *vi very Fam (die)* claquer

▸**pop out** *vi Fam (go out)* sortir

pop. *(abbr* **population**) population *f*

popcorn ['pɒpkɔːn] *n* pop-corn *m*

pope [pəʊp] *n* pape *m*

popgun ['pɒpɡʌn] *n* pistolet *m* à bouchon

poplar ['pɒplə(r)] *n* peuplier *m*

poplin ['pɒplɪn] *n* popeline *f*

popper ['pɒpə(r)] *n Br Fam (fastener)* bouton-pression *m*

poppet ['pɒpɪt] *n Fam Old-fashioned* **she's a p.** elle est charmante; **my p.!** ma puce!

poppy ['pɒpɪ] *(pl* **poppies)** *n* coquelicot *m*; **p. seed** graine *f* de pavot

Poppies

Les Britanniques marquent généralement l'armistice de la Première Guerre mondiale en observant deux minutes de silence le 11 novembre à 11 heures du matin. Les cérémonies religieuses liées à l'Armistice ont lieu le deuxième dimanche de novembre ("**Remembrance Sunday**"). A cette occasion l'on dépose des couronnes de coquelicots ("poppies") au pied des monuments aux morts ; par ailleurs nombreux sont ceux et celles qui portent un coquelicot artificiel à la boutonnière dans les jours qui précèdent les commémorations. L'on associe les coquelicots à la Première Guerre mondiale parce qu'ils étaient nombreux dans les champs de Belgique et du nord de la France, où tant de combats se sont déroulés.

poppycock ['pɒpɪkɒk] *n Fam (nonsense)* bêtises *fpl*

Popsicle® ['pɒpsɪkəl] *n Am* glace *f* à l'eau

popstrel ['pɒpstrəl] *n Br Fam* jeune chanteuse *f* pop

populace ['pɒpjʊləs] *n Formal* **the p.** la population

popular ['pɒpjʊlə(r)] *adj* populaire; *(fashionable)* à la mode; *(restaurant, film)* qui a beaucoup de succès; **to make oneself p.** se faire bien voir; **she is p. with her colleagues** elle est appréciée par ses collègues; **by p. demand** à la demande générale; **contrary to p. belief** contrairement à ce que les gens croient

popularity [pɒpjʊ'lærɪtɪ] *n* popularité *f*; **p. rating** cote *f* de popularité

popularize ['pɒpjʊləraɪz] *vt* populariser

popularly ['pɒpjʊləlɪ] *adv* communément; **it is p. believed that...** les gens croient généralement que...
populate ['pɒpjʊleɪt] *vt* peupler
population [pɒpjʊ'leɪʃən] *n* population *f*; **p. explosion** explosion *f* démographique
populous ['pɒpjʊləs] *adj* populeux(euse)
pop-up ['pɒpʌp] **1** *Comput* pop-up *m ou f*
2 *adj (book)* en relief; *(toaster)* automatique; *Comput* **p. menu** menu *m* local
porcelain ['pɔːslɪn] *n* porcelaine *f*; **p. ware** porcelaine *f*
porch [pɔːtʃ] *n Br (entrance)* porche *m*; *Am (veranda)* véranda *f*
porcupine ['pɔːkjʊpaɪn] *n* porc-épic *m*
pore [pɔːr] *n* pore *m*
▸**pore over** *vt insep (examine closely)* étudier soigneusement
pork [pɔːk] *n* porc *m*; **p. chop** côte *f* de porc; **p. pie** ≃ pâté *m* en croûte
porn [pɔːn] *Fam* **1** *n* porno *m*
2 *adj* porno
pornographic [pɔːnə'græfɪk] *adj* pornographique
pornography [pɔː'nɒgrəfɪ] *n* pornographie *f*
porous ['pɔːrəs] *adj* poreux(euse)
porpoise ['pɔːpəs] *n* marsouin *m*
porridge ['pɒrɪdʒ] *n* porridge *m*; **p. oats** flocons *mpl* d'avoine
port¹ [pɔːt] *n* (**a**) *(harbour, town)* port *m*; **in p.** au port; *also Fig* **p. of call** escale *f*; *Prov* **any p. in a storm** nécessité fait loi (**b**) *Comput* port *m*
port² *n Naut (left-hand side)* bâbord *m*
port³ *n (drink)* porto *m*
portable ['pɔːtəbəl] *adj* portable; **p. jukebox** lecteur *m* audio portable
portal ['pɔːtəl] *n Archit & Comput* portail *m*
Port-au-Prince [pɔːtəʊ'prɛs] *n* Port-au-Prince
portcullis [pɔːt'kʌlɪs] *n* sarrasine *f*
portend [pɔː'tend] *vt Formal* présager
portent ['pɔːtent] *n Formal* présage *m*
portentous [pɔː'tentəs] *adj Formal* majeur(e)
porter ['pɔːtə(r)] *n (for carrying luggage)* porteur *m*; *(door attendant)* chasseur *m*; *(in hospital)* brancardier *m*
portfolio [pɔːt'fəʊliəʊ] *(pl* **portfolios***) n (for documents)* porte-documents *m*; *(for drawings)* carton *m*; *(of shares, government minister)* portefeuille *m*; *(of model, artist)* portfolio *m*
porthole ['pɔːthəʊl] *n* hublot *m*
portion ['pɔːʃən] *n* part *f*, partie *f*; *(of food)* portion *f*
▸**portion out** *vt sep* partager
portly ['pɔːtlɪ] *adj* corpulent(e)
portrait ['pɔːtreɪt] *n also Fig* portrait *m*; **to have one's p. painted** faire faire son portrait; **p. gallery** galerie *f* de portraits; *Comput* **p. (orientation)** (orientation *f*) portrait *m*; **p. painter** portraitiste *mf*
portray [pɔː'treɪ] *vt (describe)* dépeindre; *(of actor)* interpréter
portrayal [pɔː'treɪəl] *n (description)* tableau *m*; *(by actor)* interprétation *f*
Portugal ['pɔːtjʊgəl] *n* le Portugal
Portuguese [pɔːtjʊ'giːz] **1** *npl* **the P.** *(people)* les Portugais *mpl*
2 *n* (**a**) *(person)* Portugais(e) *m,f* (**b**) *(language)* portugais *m*
3 *adj* portugais(e)
POS [piːəʊ'es] *n Com (abbr* **point of sale)** PDV *m*
pose [pəʊz] **1** *n* (**a**) *(position)* pose *f* (**b**) *Pej (affectation)* **it's just a p.** c'est pour épater la galerie

2 *vt (problem, question)* poser; *(danger, threat)* représenter
3 *vi also Pej* poser; **to p. as** *(pretend to be)* se faire passer pour
poser ['pəʊzə(r)] *n Fam* (**a**) *Pej (affected person)* poseur(euse) *m,f* (**b**) *(difficult question)* colle *f*
posh [pɒʃ] *Br* **1** *adj (person)* huppé(e); *(accent)* snob *inv*; *(restaurant, area, clothes)* chic *inv*
2 *adv* **to talk p.** parler d'une manière snob
position [pə'zɪʃən] **1** *n* (**a**) *(posture, opinion)* position *f* (**b**) *(of object)* emplacement *m*; *(of enemy, plane, in team sport)* position *f*; **in the on/off p.** *(of switch, lever)* en position marche/arrêt; **in p.** en place; **out of p.** déplacé(e) (**c**) *(situation)* situation *f*; **to be in a strong p.** être dans une position forte; **put yourself in my p.** mets-toi à ma place; **to be in a p. to do sth** être en mesure de faire qch; **to be in no p. to do sth** être mal placé(e) pour faire qch (**d**) *(job)* poste *m*; **a p. of responsibility** un poste à responsabilité
2 *vt (object)* placer; *(town)* situer; *(troops)* poster; **to p. oneself** se placer; **to be well/poorly positioned to do sth** être bien/mal placé(e) pour faire qch
positioning [pə'zɪʃənɪŋ] *n Com* positionnement *m*
positive ['pɒzɪtɪv] *adj* (**a**) *(person, answer, test)* positif(ive); *(evidence, proof)* formel(elle); **to be p. about sth** être optimiste à propos de qch; **on the p. side,...** le bon côté des choses, c'est que...; **p. discrimination** = mesures antidiscriminatoires favorisant les groupes minoritaires (**b**) *(certain)* certain(e), sûr(e) (**about** de); (**c**) *Fam (for emphasis)* véritable (**d**) *Math & Elec* positif(ive)
positively ['pɒzɪtɪvlɪ] *adv* (**a**) *(identify)* formellement (**b**) *(think, react)* de façon positive (**c**) *(for emphasis)* absolument
posse ['pɒsɪ] *n (to catch criminal)* = dans le Far West, groupe d'hommes commandé par un shérif, lancé à la poursuite d'un criminel; *Fam (of friends)* bande *f*
possess [pə'zes] *vt* (**a**) *(property)* posséder; *(quality, faculty)* avoir (**b**) *(of evil spirit)* posséder; **possessed by fear** pris(e) de terreur; **what possessed you to do that?** qu'est-ce qui t'a pris de faire ça?
possession [pə'zeʃən] *n (ownership)* possession *f*; *(thing possessed)* bien *m*; **to be in p. of sth** être en possession de qch; **in full p. of one's faculties** en pleine possession de ses facultés
possessive [pə'zesɪv] **1** *n Gram* **the p.** le possessif
2 *adj* possessif(ive); **she's very p. about or of her children** c'est une mère possessive
possessor [pə'zesə(r)] *n* possesseur *m*
possibility [pɒsɪ'bɪlɪtɪ] *(pl* **possibilities***) n* possibilité *f*; **to be within/outside the bounds of p.** être dans la limite du possible/au delà des limites du possible; **it's a distinct p.** c'est bien possible
possible ['pɒsɪbəl] **1** *adj* possible; **it's p. that...** il est possible que... + *subjunctive*; **as soon as p.** dès que possible; **as much as p.** autant que possible; **anything's p.** tout est possible
2 *n (person)* candidat(e) possible *m,f*; *(thing)* option *f*
possibly ['pɒsɪblɪ] *adv* (**a**) *(perhaps)* peut-être; **p. not** peut-être pas (**b**) *(for emphasis)* that je ne peux vraiment pas l'accepter; **I'll do all I p. can** je ferai tout mon possible
post¹ [pəʊst] **1** *n* (**a**) *(wooden stake)* piquet *m*; *(of goal)* poteau *m* (**b**) *(job, military position)* poste *m*
2 *vt (assign)* affecter
post² *vt (affix)* afficher; **p. no bills** *(sign)* défense d'afficher

post³ *Br* **1** *n (mail)* courrier *m*; **the first p.** la première distribution; **to miss the p.** manquer la levée; **it's in the p.** c'est parti au courrier; **p. office** (bureau *m* de) poste *f*; **the P. Office** *(government department)* ≃ la Poste **2** *vt (letter)* poster; *Fam Fig* **to keep sb posted** tenir qn au courant

postage ['pəʊstɪdʒ] *n* affranchissement *m*; **p. and packing** frais *mpl* de port et d'emballage; **p. paid** port *m* payé; **p. stamp** timbre-poste *m*

postal ['pəʊstəl] *adj* postal(e); **p. order** mandat *m* postal; **p. vote** vote *m* par correspondance

postbag ['pəʊstbæg] *n Br* sac *m* postal

postbox ['pəʊstbɒks] *n Br* boîte *f* aux lettres

postcard ['pəʊstkɑːd] *n* carte *f* postale

postcode ['pəʊstkəʊd] *n Br* code *m* postal

postdate [pəʊst'deɪt] *vt* postdater

post-doc ['pəʊstdɒk] *n Fam Univ* (**a**) *(person)* post-doctorant *m* (**b**) *(position)* poste *m* de chercheur qui a obtenu son doctorat

post-doctorate [pəʊst'dɒtərət] *Univ* **1** *n* post-doctorat *m* **2** *adj* post-doctoral(e)

poster ['pəʊstə(r)] *n (for advertising)* affiche *f*; *(for decoration)* poster *m*; **p. advertising** publicité *f* par affichage; **p. paint** gouache *f*

posterior [pɒs'tɪərɪə(r)] *n Hum (buttocks)* postérieur *m*

posterity [pɒs'terɪtɪ] *n* postérité *f*

postgraduate [pəʊst'grædjʊɪt] **1** *n* étudiant(e) *m,f* de troisième cycle **2** *adj* de troisième cycle

posthaste ['pəʊst'heɪst] *adv* en toute hâte

posthumous ['pɒstjʊməs] *adj* posthume

posthumously ['pɒstjʊməslɪ] *adv* à titre posthume

posting ['pəʊstɪŋ] *n (assignment)* affectation *f*

postman ['pəʊstmən] *n Br* facteur *m*

postmark ['pəʊstmɑːk] *n* cachet *m* de la poste

postmaster ['pəʊstmɑːstə(r)] *n* (**a**) *(in post office)* receveur *m* des postes (**b**) *Comput (for e-mail)* maître *m* de poste

postmistress ['pəʊstmɪstrɪs] *n* receveuse *f* des postes

postmortem [pəʊst'mɔːtəm] *n* autopsie *f*

postnatal [pəʊst'neɪtəl] *adj* postnatal(e)

postoperative [pəʊst'ɒpərətɪv] *adj* postopératoire

postpone [pəʊst'pəʊn] *vt* reporter

postponement [pəʊst'pəʊnmənt] *n* report *m*

postscript ['pəʊsskrɪpt] *n* post-scriptum *m*

postulate ['pɒstjʊleɪt] *vt* poser comme hypothèse

posture ['pɒstʃə(r)] **1** *n* (**a**) *(physical)* posture *f*; **to have good/bad p.** se tenir bien/mal (**b**) *Fig (attitude)* position *f* **2** *vi* prendre des poses

postwar ['pəʊst'wɔː(r)] *adj* d'après-guerre; **the p. period** l'après-guerre *m*

posy ['pəʊzɪ] *(pl posies)* *n* petit bouquet *m*

pot [pɒt] **1** *n* (**a**) *(container)* pot *m*; *(saucepan)* casserole *f*; *(for tea)* théière *f*; *(for coffee)* cafetière *f*; **pots and pans** casseroles *fpl*; **a p. of tea** un thé; *Fam* **to have pots of money** avoir plein de fric; *Fam* **to go to p.** aller à la ruine; **to take a p. shot at sth** tirer à vue sur qch; *Br Prov* **it's a case of the p. calling the kettle black** c'est l'hôpital qui se moque de la charité; **p. plant** plante *f* en pot (**b**) *Fam (marijuana)* hasch *m* **2** *vt (pt & pp potted)* (**a**) *(butter, meat)* mettre en pot; *(plant)* empoter (**b**) *(in snooker, pool)* blouser

potash ['pɒtæʃ] *n* potasse *f*

potassium [pə'tæsɪəm] *n* potassium *m*

potato [pə'teɪtəʊ] *(pl potatoes)* *n* pomme *f* de terre; *Br* **p. crisps,** *Am* **p. chips** chips *mpl*; **p. peeler** épluche-légumes *m*; **p. salad** salade *f* de pommes de terre

potbellied [pɒt'belɪd] *adj (from over-eating)* bedonnant(e); *(from malnourishment)* au ventre ballonné; **p. stove** poêle *m*

potency ['pəʊtənsɪ] *n* puissance *f*; *(virility)* virilité *f*

potent ['pəʊtənt] *adj* puissant(e); *(drink)* fort(e)

potentate ['pəʊtənteɪt] *n* potentat *m*

potential [pə'tenʃəl] **1** *n* potentiel *m*; **to have p.** avoir du potentiel; **to fulfil one's p.** aller au maximum de ses capacités **2** *adj* potentiel(elle)

potentially [pə'tenʃəlɪ] *adv* potentiellement

pothole ['pɒthəʊl] *n (cave)* marmite *f* torrentielle; *(in road)* nid *m* de poule

potholer ['pɒthəʊlə(r)] *n* spéléologue *mf*

potholing ['pɒthəʊlɪŋ] *n* spéléologie *f*; **to go p.** faire de la spéléologie

potion ['pəʊʃən] *n* potion *f*

potluck ['pɒt'lʌk] *n Fam* **to take p.** prendre ce que l'on trouve; **p. supper** dîner *m* où chacun apporte un plat

potpourri [pəʊ'pʊərɪ] *n (of flowers, music)* pot-pourri *m*

potted ['pɒtɪd] *adj* (**a**) *(food)* en terrine (**b**) *(description, history)* condensé(e)

potter ['pɒtə(r)] *n* potier(ère) *m,f*; **p.'s wheel** tour *m* de potier

▶**potter about, potter around** *vi Br (do odd jobs)* bricoler; *(spend time leisurely)* traîner

pottery ['pɒtərɪ] *(pl potteries)* *n* poterie *f*

potty¹ ['pɒtɪ] *(pl potties)* *n* pot *m*; **p. training** apprentissage *m* de la propreté

potty² *adj Br Fam (crazy)* dingue (**about** de)

potty-trained ['pɒtɪtreɪnd] *adj* propre

pouch [paʊtʃ] *n* (**a**) *(for money)* bourse *f*; *(for tobacco)* blague *f*; *(for ammunition)* étui *m* (**b**) *(of marsupial)* poche *f*

pouf(fe) [puːf] *n* pouf *m*

poulterer ['pəʊltərə(r)] *n* volailler(ère) *m,f*

poultice ['pəʊltɪs] *n* cataplasme *m*

poultry ['pəʊltrɪ] *n* volaille *f*; **p. farm** élevage *m* de volaille; **p. farmer** éleveur(euse) *m,f* de volaille

pounce [paʊns] *vi* **to p. on** *(of animal)* bondir sur; *(of person)* se précipiter sur

pound¹ [paʊnd] *n* (**a**) *(unit of weight)* = 453,6 g, livre *f* (**b**) *(British currency)* livre *f*; **p. sign** symbole *m* de la livre sterling; **p. sterling** livre *f* sterling

pound² *n (for dogs, cars)* fourrière *f*

pound³ *vt (crush) (spices, garlic)* piler; *(meat)* attendrir; *(with artillery)* pilonner; **to p. sth to pieces** réduire qch en miettes **2** *vi (of heart)* battre à tout rompre; **to p. on the door** cogner à la porte; **my head is pounding** j'ai des élancements dans la tête

pour [pɔː(r)] **1** *vt* verser (**into/down** dans); **to p. sb a drink** verser à boire à qn; **to p. money into sth** investir beaucoup d'argent dans qch **2** *vi* couler; **it's pouring (with rain)** il pleut à verse; **sweat was pouring off him** il ruisselait de sueur; **tourists were pouring into the palace** les touristes entraient en masse dans le palais

▶**pour in 1** *vt sep (liquid)* verser **2** *vi (of liquid)* couler; *Fig (of people, letters)* affluer

▶**pour out 1** *vt sep (tea, coffee)* verser; *Fig (anger, grief)* déverser; *(emotions)* déballer
2 *vi (of liquid)* se déverser; *Fig (of people)* sortir en masse
pouring ['pɔːrɪŋ] *adj (rain)* torrentiel(elle)
pout [paʊt] **1** *n* moue *f*
2 *vi* faire la moue
poverty ['pɒvətɪ] *n* pauvreté *f*; *Fig (of ideas, resources)* pénurie *f*; **to live in p.** vivre dans la misère; **p. line** seuil *m* de pauvreté
poverty-stricken ['pɒvətɪstrɪkən] *adj* très pauvre
POW [piːəʊ'dʌbəljuː] *n (abbr* **prisoner of war***)* prisonnier(ère) *m,f* de guerre
powder ['paʊdə(r)] **1** *n* poudre *f*; **p. blue** bleu *m* pastel; *Fig* **p. keg** poudrière *f*; **p. puff** houppe *f*; **p. room** toilettes *fpl* pour dames
2 *vt* saupoudrer (**with** de); **to p. one's face** se poudrer le visage; *Euph* **to p. one's nose** aller se laver les mains
powdered ['paʊdəd] *adj (milk, eggs)* en poudre
powdery ['paʊdərɪ] *adj* poudreux(euse)
power ['paʊə(r)] **1** *n* (**a**) *(authority, capacity)* pouvoir *m*; **to come to/be in p.** arriver/être au pouvoir; **to have sb in one's p.** tenir qn à sa merci; **to have the p. to do sth** avoir le pouvoir de faire qch; **to do everything in one's p. (to do sth)** faire tout ce qui est en son pouvoir (pour faire qch); **to be at the height** *or* **peak of one's powers** être au sommet de ses capacités; **it is beyond my p.** je ne peux pas t'aider, cela dépasse mes capacités; *Fam* **to do sb a p. of good** faire énormément de bien à qn; **powers of concentration/persuasion** force *f* de concentration/ persuasion; **p. of speech** usage *m* de la parole; **p. base** base *f* politique; **p. struggle** lutte *f* pour le pouvoir (**b**) *(physical strength)* force *f*, puissance *f*; **p. steering** *(in car)* direction *f* assistée (**c**) *(powerful person, group, nation)* puissance *f*; *Fig* **the p. behind the throne** l'éminence *f* grise; **the powers that be** les autorités *fpl* (**d**) *Law* pouvoir *m*; **p. of attorney** procuration *f* (**e**) *(electricity)* courant *m*; **p. cut** coupure *f* de courant; **p. pack** bloc *m* d'alimentation; **p. plant** centrale *f* électrique; **p. point** prise *f* de courant; **p. shower** douche *f* à jet puissant; **p. station** centrale *f* électrique; (**f**) *Math* puissance *f*; **three to the p. of ten** trois (à la) puissance dix
2 *vt (provide with power)* actionner; **powered by two engines** propulsé(e) par deux moteurs
power-assisted steering ['paʊərəsɪstɪd'stɪərɪŋ] *n Aut* direction *f* assistée
powerbroker ['paʊəbrəʊkə(r)] *n* décideur *m*, décisionnaire *mf*
powerful ['paʊəfʊl] *adj (muscles, engine, voice, country)* puissant(e); *(politician)* influent(e); *(drug, smell)* fort(e); *(speech, image)* impressionnant(e)
powerhouse ['paʊəhaʊs] *n Fam (person)* moteur *m*; *(company)* entreprise *f* très dynamique
powerless ['paʊəlɪs] *adj* impuissant(e); **to be p. to do sth** être impuissant(e) à faire qch
PPP [piːpiː'piː] *n (abbr* **public-private partnership***)* partenariat *m* public-privé
PR [piː'ɑ(r)] *n* (**a**) *(abbr* **public relations***)* RP *fpl* (**b**) *Pol (abbr* **proportional representation***)* représentation *f* proportionnelle
practicable ['præktɪkəbəl] *adj* réalisable
practical ['præktɪkəl] **1** *n (lesson)* travaux *mpl* pratiques; *(exam)* épreuve *f* pratique
2 *adj* (**a**) *(mind, solution)* pratique; **she's very p.** elle

a l'esprit pratique; **for all p. purposes** dans la pratique; **p. joke** farce *f* (**b**) *(virtual)* **it's a p. certainty** c'est pratiquement certain
practicality [præktɪ'kælɪtɪ] *(pl* **practicalities***)* n (of suggestion, plan)* aspect *m* pratique; **practicalities** détails *mpl* pratiques
practically ['præktɪklɪ] *adv* (**a**) *(in a practical manner)* de façon pratique (**b**) *(almost)* pratiquement, presque
practice ['præktɪs] **1** *n* (**a**) *(action, exercise)* pratique *f*; *(in sport)* entraînement *m*; **in p.** dans la *ou* en pratique; **to put sth into p.** mettre qch en pratique; **to be out of p.** avoir perdu l'habitude; *Prov* **p. makes perfect** c'est en forgeant qu'on devient forgeron; **p. match** *(in football, rugby)* match *m* d'entraînement (**b**) *(of medicine, law)* exercice *m* (**c**) *(surgery)* centre *m* médical; *(lawyer's office)* cabinet *m* d'avocat (**d**) *(custom)* pratique *f*; **to make a p. of doing sth** se faire une règle de faire qch; **to be good/bad p.** être conseillé(e)/déconseillé(e)
2 *vt & vi Am* = **practise**
practiced, practicing *Am* = **practised, practising**
practise, *Am* **practice** ['præktɪs] **1** *vt* (**a**) *(musical instrument)* travailler; *(language, sport)* pratiquer; (**b**) *(medicine, law)* exercer (**c**) *(religion, custom)* pratiquer; **to p. what one preaches** mettre en pratique ce que l'on prêche
2 *vi* (**a**) *(of musician)* s'exercer; *(of sportsperson)* s'entraîner (**b**) *(of doctor, lawyer)* exercer
practised, *Am* **practiced** ['præktɪst] *adj (teacher, nurse, speaker)* expérimenté(e); *(liar)* professionnel(elle); *(eye, ear)* exercé(e); *(charm)* étudié(e)
practising, *Am* **practicing** ['præktɪsɪŋ] *adj (doctor, lawyer)* en exercice; *(Christian)* pratiquant(e)
pragmatic [præg'mætɪk] *adj* pragmatique
pragmatism ['prægmətɪzəm] *n* pragmatisme *m*
pragmatist ['prægmətɪst] *n* pragmatiste *mf*
Prague [prɑːg] *n* Prague
prairie ['preərɪ] *n* prairie *f*; **p. dog** chien *m* de prairie; *Am* **p. schooner** chariot *m* bâché
praise [preɪz] **1** *n* éloges *mpl*; **to sing the praises of** faire l'éloge de
2 *vt* faire l'éloge de; *(God)* louer; **to p. sb to the skies** porter qn aux nues
praiseworthy ['preɪzwɜːðɪ] *adj* digne d'éloges
pram [præm] *n Br* landau *m*
prance [prɑːns] *vi (of horse)* caracoler; *(of person)* sautiller; **to p. in/out** entrer/sortir en sautillant
prank [præŋk] *n* farce *f*; **to play a p. on sb** faire une farce à qn
prat [præt] *n Br Fam* andouille *f*
prattle ['prætəl] **1** *n* papotage *m*
2 *vi* papoter (**about** de)
prawn [prɔːn] *n* crevette *f* rose; **p. cocktail** cocktail *m* de crevettes; **p. cracker** beignet *m* de crevette
pray [preɪ] *vi* prier (**for** pour); **to p. to God** prier Dieu; *Fig* **to p. for good weather/rain** prier pour qu'il fasse beau/qu'il pleuve
prayer [preə(r)] *n* prière *f*; **to say one's prayers** dire ses prières; *Fam Fig* **he doesn't have a p.** il n'a aucune chance; **p. beads** chapelet *m*; **p. book** livre *m* de prières; **p. mat** tapis *m* de prière; **p. meeting** réunion *f* de prière
preach [priːtʃ] **1** *vt* prêcher
2 *vi* prêcher; *Fig (moralize)* faire la morale; *Fig* **to p. to the converted** prêcher un converti
preacher ['priːtʃə(r)] *n* prédicateur(trice) *m,f*

preamble ['pri:æmbəl] n Formal préambule m
prearranged [pri:ə'reɪndʒd] adj convenu(e)
precarious [prɪ'keərɪəs] adj précaire
precariously [prɪ'keərɪəslɪ] adv de façon précaire; **p. balanced** en équilibre précaire
precaution [prɪ'kɔ:ʃən] n précaution f; **to take precautions** prendre des précautions; **as a p.** par précaution
precautionary [prɪ'kɔ:ʃənərɪ] adj préventif(ive)
precede [prɪ'si:d] vt précéder
precedence ['presɪdəns] n priorité f; **in order of p.** par ordre de préséance; **to take p.** over sb avoir la préséance sur qn; **to take p.** over sth passer avant qch
precedent ['presɪdənt] n précédent m
preceding [prɪ'si:dɪŋ] adj précédent(e)
precept ['pri:sept] n précepte m
precinct ['pri:sɪŋkt] n (**a**) Br (area) (shopping) **p.** quartier m commerçant piétonnier; **within the precincts of** dans l'enceinte de (**b**) Am (administrative district) circonscription f; (police division) quartier m
precious ['preʃəs] **1** n (term of endearment) **my p.** mon trésor
2 adj also Pej précieux(euse); **that photo is very p. to me** cette photo m'est très chère; Ironic **you and your p. books!** toi et tes sacrés bouquins!
3 adv Fam (for emphasis) **p. little** très peu; **p. little money** très peu d'argent
precipice ['presɪpɪs] n précipice m
precipitate 1 n [prɪ'sɪpɪtɪt] Chem précipité m
2 adj [prɪ'sɪpɪtət] Formal précipité(e)
3 vt [prɪ'sɪpɪteɪt] Formal précipiter
precipitately [prɪ'sɪpɪtətlɪ] adv précipitamment
precipitation [prɪsɪpɪ'teɪʃən] n précipitation f; **annual p.** précipitations annuelles
precipitous [prɪ'sɪpɪtəs] adj (descent) à pic; (steps) raide
précis ['preɪsi:] (pl précis ['preɪsi:z]) n résumé m
precise [prɪ'saɪs] adj (**a**) (exact) précis(e); ..., **to be p.** ..., pour être précis (**b**) (meticulous) méticuleux(euse)
precisely [prɪ'saɪslɪ] adv exactement, précisément; **at six (o'clock) p.** à six heures précises; **p.!** exactement!
precision [prɪ'sɪʒən] n précision f; Mil **p. bombing** bombardement m de précision; **p. instrument** instrument m de précision
preclude [prɪ'klu:d] vt Formal empêcher; **to p. sb from doing sth** empêcher qn de faire qch
precocious [prɪ'kəʊʃəs] adj précoce
precociousness [prɪ'kəʊʃəsnɪs], **precocity** [prɪ'kɒsɪtɪ] n précocité f
preconceived [pri:kən'si:vd] adj préconçu(e)
preconception [pri:kən'sepʃən] n idée f préconçue; (prejudice) préjugé m
precondition [pri:kɒn'dɪʃən] n condition f préalable
precooked [pri:'kʊkt] adj précuit(e)
precursor [prɪ'kɜ:sə(r)] n précurseur m
predate [pri:'deɪt] vt (**a**) (precede) précéder (**b**) (put earlier date on) antidater
predator ['predətə(r)] n prédateur m
predatory ['predətərɪ] adj prédateur(trice); Fig avide
predecessor ['pri:dɪsesə(r)] n (person) prédécesseur m; (object) précédent(e) m,f
predestination [pri:destɪ'neɪʃən] n prédestination f

predestine [pri:'destɪn] vt **to be predestined to do sth** être prédestiné(e) à faire qch
predetermine [pri:dɪ'tɜ:mɪn] vt prédéterminer
predicament [prɪ'dɪkəmənt] n situation f difficile; **to be in a p.** être dans le pétrin
predicate 1 n ['predɪkət] Gram prédicat m
2 vt ['predɪkeɪt] **to be predicated on sth** être fondé(e) sur qch
predict [prɪ'dɪkt] vt (from instinct) prédire; (from information) prévoir
predictable [prɪ'dɪktəbəl] adj prévisible; Fam **you're so p.!** j'aurais pu le deviner!
predictably [prɪ'dɪktəblɪ] adv de manière prévisible; **p., he arrived an hour late** comme on pouvait s'y attendre, il est arrivé une heure en retard
prediction [prɪ'dɪkʃən] n (from instinct) prédiction f; (from information) prévision f
predictive text [prɪ'dɪktɪv'tekst] n Tel écriture f prédictive, T9 m
predispose [pri:dɪs'pəʊz] vt prédisposer; **to be predisposed to do sth** être prédisposé(e) à faire qch
predisposition [pri:dɪspə'zɪʃən] n prédisposition f (to or towards envers)
predominance [prɪ'dɒmɪnəns] n prédominance f
predominant [prɪ'dɒmɪnənt] adj prédominant(e)
predominantly [prɪ'dɒmɪnəntlɪ] adv en majorité, principalement
predominate [prɪ'dɒmɪneɪt] vi prédominer
pre-eminence [prɪ'emɪnəns] n prééminence f
pre-eminent [prɪ'emɪnənt] adj prééminent(e)
pre-empt [prɪ'empt] vt devancer
pre-emptive [prɪ'emptɪv] adj préventif(ive)
preen [pri:n] vt **to p. itself** (of bird) se lisser les plumes; **to p. oneself** (of person) se faire beau (belle), se pomponner; Fig **to p. oneself on one's success** s'enorgueillir de son succès
pre-established [prɪ:ɪs'tæblɪʃt] adj préétabli(e)
prefab ['pri:fæb] n Fam (house) préfabriqué m
prefabricated [pri:'fæbrɪkeɪtɪd] adj préfabriqué(e)
preface ['prefɪs] **1** n (of book) préface f; (to speech) préambule m
2 vt commencer (**with** par)
prefect ['pri:fekt] n Sch = élève des grandes classes chargé de la surveillance
prefer [prɪ'fɜ:(r)] (pt & pp preferred) vt (**a**) (favour) préférer (**to** à); **to p. to do sth** préférer faire qch (**b**) Law **to p. charges** porter plainte
preferable ['prefərəbəl] adj préférable
preferably ['prefərəblɪ] adv de préférence
preference ['prefərəns] n préférence f; **to give sth p.**, **to give p. to sth** donner la préférence à qch; **in p. to** plutôt que; **in order of p.** par ordre de préférence
preferential [prefə'renʃəl] adj (treatment) de faveur; (tariff) préférentiel(elle)
preferred [prɪ'fɜ:d] adj préféré(e)
prefigure [pri:'fɪgə(r)] vt préfigurer
prefix ['pri:fɪks] n préfixe m
pregnancy ['pregnənsɪ] (pl pregnancies) n grossesse f; **p. test** test m de grossesse
pregnant ['pregnənt] adj (**a**) (woman) enceinte; (animal) pleine; **to be three months p.** être enceinte de trois mois (**b**) Fig (pause, silence) éloquent(e)
preheat [pri:'hi:t] vt préchauffer
prehensile [prɪ'hensaɪl] adj préhensile
prehistoric [pri:hɪs'tɒrɪk] adj préhistorique
prehistory [pri:'hɪstərɪ] n préhistoire f

prejudge [pri:'dʒʌdʒ] *vt (actions, motives)* préjuger de; *(person)* juger sans connaître
prejudice ['predʒʊdɪs] **1** *n* (**a**) *(bias)* préjugé *m* (**against/in favour of** contre/en faveur de) (**b**) *Law* **without p. to** sans préjudice de
2 *vt* (**a**) *(bias)* prévenir (**against/in favour of** contre/en faveur de) (**b**) *(harm)* nuire à, faire du tort à
prejudiced ['predʒʊdɪst] *adj* **to be p.** avoir des préjugés (**against/in favour of** contre/en faveur de)
prejudicial [predʒʊ'dɪʃəl] *adj* préjudiciable (**to** à)
preliminary [prɪ'lɪmɪnərɪ] **1** *(pl* **preliminaries**) *n* préliminaire *m*; **preliminaries** *(to investigation, meeting)* préliminaires
2 *adj* préliminaire
prelude ['prelju:d] *n* prélude *m*
premarital [pri:'mærɪtəl] *adj* avant le mariage
premature ['premətjʊə(r)] *adj (baby, action, comment)* prématuré(e); *(baldness, senility, ejaculation)* précoce; *Fam* **you're being a bit p.!** tu vas un peu vite!
prematurely ['premətjʊəlɪ] *adv* prématurément
premeditated [pri:'medɪteɪtɪd] *adj* prémédité(e)
premenstrual [pri:'menstrʊəl] *adj* prémenstruel(-elle); **p. syndrome,** *Br* **p. tension** syndrome *m* prémenstruel
premier ['premɪə(r)] **1** *n (prime minister)* Premier ministre *m*
2 *adj* premier(ère)
premiere ['premɪeə(r)] *n (of play, film)* première *f*
premise ['premɪs] **1** *n (of argument, theory)* prémisse *f*
2 *vt* **to be premised on sth** être fondé(e) sur qch
premises ['premɪsɪz] *npl* locaux *mpl*; **business p.** locaux *mpl* commerciaux; **on the p.** sur place; **off the p.** en dehors de l'établissement; **to see sb off the p.** accompagner qn jusqu'au dehors
premium ['pri:mɪəm] *n* (**a**) *Fin (for insurance)* prime *f*; *(additional sum)* supplément *m*; **at a p.** au prix fort; *Br* **p. bonds** ≃ obligations *fpl* à lots (**b**) *(idioms)* **to be at a p.** être très recherché(e); **to put a p. on sth** accorder de l'importance à qch
premium-rate ['pri:mɪəm'reɪt] *adj Tel (call)* vers un numéro surtaxé; **p. number** numéro *m* surtaxé
premonition [pri:mə'nɪʃən] *n* prémonition *f*; **to have a p. that...** avoir le préssentiment que...
prenatal [pri:'neɪtəl] *adj* prénatal(e)
prenuptial agreement [pri:nʌpʃələ'gri:mənt], *Fam* **prenup** ['pri:nʌp] *n* contrat *m* de mariage
preoccupation [pri:ɒkjʊ'peɪʃən] *n* préoccupation *f* (**with** pour); **to have a p. with sth** être préoccupé(e) par qch
preoccupied [pri:'ɒkjʊpaɪd] *adj* préoccupé(e) (**with** par)
preoccupy [pri:'ɒkjʊpaɪ] *(pt & pp* **preoccupied**) *vt* préoccuper au plus haut point
prep [prep] *n Br Fam (homework)* devoirs *mpl*; **p. school** *Br* école *f* primaire privée; *Am* = école privée qui prépare à l'enseignement supérieur
prepaid [pri:'peɪd] *adj* prépayé(e)
preparation [prepə'reɪʃən] *n* préparation *f*; **preparations** *(for ceremony, party)* préparatifs *mpl*
preparatory [prɪ'pærətərɪ] *adj* préparatoire; **p. school** *Br* école *f* primaire privée; *Am* = école privée qui prépare à l'enseignement supérieur
prepare [prɪ'peə(r)] **1** *vt* préparer
2 *vi* se préparer (**for** à); **to p. to do sth** se préparer à faire qch

prepared [prɪ'peəd] *adj* (**a**) *(willing)* **to be p. to do sth** être prêt(e) à faire qch (**b**) *(ready)* **to be p. for sth** s'attendre à qch (**c**) *(made in advance)* préparé(e) à l'avance; *(excuse, explanation)* tout(e) prêt(e)
prepayment [pri:'peɪmənt] *n* paiement *m* d'avance
preponderance [prɪ'pɒndərəns] *n* prépondérance *f*
preposition [prepə'zɪʃən] *n* préposition *f*
prepositional [prepə'zɪʃənəl] *adj* prépositif(ive)
prepossessing [pri:pə'zesɪŋ] *adj* avenant(e), engageant(e)
preposterous [prɪ'pɒstərəs] *adj* ridicule
preppy ['prepɪ] *adj Am Fam* ≃ BCBG *inv*
preprogrammed [pri:'prəʊɡræmd] *adj Comput* préprogrammé(e)
prequel ['pri:kwəl] *n Cin* = film qui reprend les thèmes et les personnages d'un film réalisé précédemment, mais dont l'action est antérieure
prerecorded [pri:rɪ'kɔ:dɪd] *adj* préenregistré(e)
prerequisite [pri:'rekwɪzɪt] *n* (condition *f*) préalable *m*
prerogative [prɪ'rɒgətɪv] *n* prérogative *f*
presage ['presɪdʒ] *Lit* **1** *n* présage *m*
2 *vt* présager
Presbyterian [prezbɪ'tɪərɪən] **1** *n* presbytérien(enne) *m,f*
2 *adj* presbytérien(enne)
preschool [pri:'sku:l] **1** *n Am* école *f* maternelle
2 *adj* préscolaire
prescribe [prɪ'skraɪb] *vt (medicine, punishment)* prescrire; *(solution)* préconiser; *(task, rule)* exiger
prescription [prɪ'skrɪpʃən] *n* ordonnance *f*; **available on p. only** délivré(e) seulement sur ordonnance; **p. charge** = prix fixe payé sur chaque médicament prescrit sur ordonnance
presence ['prezəns] *n* présence *f*; **in the p. of** en présence de; **to have p.** avoir de la présence; **to make one's p. felt** ne pas passer inaperçu(e); **p. of mind** présence d'esprit
present¹ ['prezənt] **1** *n* **the p.** le présent; **at p.** en ce moment; **for the p.** pour l'instant
2 *adj* (**a**) *(in attendance)* présent(e) (**at** à) (**b**) *(current)* actuel(elle); **at the p. time** *or* **moment** actuellement; *Gram* **the p. tense** le présent; **p. participle** participe *m* présent
present² **1** *n* ['prezənt] *(gift)* cadeau *m*; **to give sb a p.** offrir un cadeau à qn
2 *vt* [prɪ'zent] (**a**) *(introduce, put forward)* présenter; **if the opportunity presents itself** si l'occasion se présente (**b**) *(give) (gift)* donner; *(award, certificate)* remettre; **to p. sth to sb, to p. sb with sth** *(gift)* donner qch à qn; *(award, certificate)* remettre qch à qn
presentable [prɪ'zentəbəl] *adj* présentable; **to make oneself p.** s'arranger
presentation [prezən'teɪʃən] *n* (**a**) *(of person)* présentation *f* (**b**) *(of gift, award)* remise *f*; **to make a p. to sb** *(give present)* offrir un cadeau à qn; *(give award)* remettre un prix à qn (**c**) *(formal talk)* présentation *f*; *(by student)* exposé *m* (**d**) **on p. of** *(passport, coupon)* sur présentation de
present-day [prezənt'deɪ] *adj* actuel(elle)
presenter [prɪ'zentə(r)] *n (on radio, TV)* présentateur(trice) *m,f*
presentiment [prɪ'zentɪmənt] *n* pressentiment *m*
presently ['prezntlɪ] *adv* (**a**) *(soon)* bientôt; *(soon afterwards)* peu de temps après (**b**) *Am (now)* actuellement

preservation [prezə'veɪʃən] n (**a**) (maintenance) maintien m (**b**) (protection) (of species) protection f; (of building) conservation f; **to put a p. order on a building** classer un bâtiment monument historique

preservative [prɪ'zɜːvətɪv] n conservateur m

preserve [prɪ'zɜːv] **1** n (**a**) (jam) confiture f (**b**) (in hunting) réserve f (**c**) (area of dominance) domaine m; **engineering is no longer a male p.** le métier d'ingénieur n'est plus réservé aux hommes **2** vt (**a**) (custom, belief) préserver; (calm, sense of humour) garder; (dignity, self-respect) conserver (**b**) (leather, wood) entretenir (**c**) (fruit) mettre en conserve (**d**) (protect) préserver (**from** de); **saints p. us!** le ciel nous préserve!

preshrunk [priː'ʃrʌŋk] adj lavé(e)

preside [prɪ'zaɪd] vi présider; **to p. over a meeting** présider une réunion

presidency ['prezɪdənsɪ] (pl **presidencies**) n présidence f

president ['prezɪdənt] n (of country) président m; Am (of company) P-DG m

presidential [prezɪ'denʃəl] adj présidentiel(elle)

press [pres] **1** n (**a**) (act of pushing) pression f; **at the p. of a button** en appuyant sur le bouton; **p. stud** bouton-pression m (**b**) (newspapers) **the p.** la presse; **to get a good/bad p.** avoir bonne/mauvaise presse; **p. agency** agence f de presse; **p. box** tribune f de la presse; **p. conference** conférence f de presse; **p. cutting** coupure f de presse; **p. photographer** photographe mf de presse; **p. release** communiqué m de presse (**c**) (machine) (printing) **p.** presse f (typographique); **to go to p.** (of newspaper) partir à l'impression **2** vt (**a**) (button, switch) appuyer sur; (into clay, cement) enfoncer; **she pressed the note into my hand** elle m'a glissé le billet dans la main (**b**) (squeeze) serrer (**c**) (grapes, olives, flowers) presser (**d**) (iron) repasser (**e**) (pressurize) faire pression sur; **to p. sb to do sth** presser qn de faire qch; **to be pressed for time/money** être pressé(e) par le temps/l'argent (**f**) (force) **to p. sth on sb** forcer qn à accepter qch; **to p. home one's advantage** profiter de son avantage; **to p. one's attentions on sb** faire des avances à qn (**g**) (insist on) Law **to p. charges (against sb)** porter plainte (contre qn); **I didn't p. the point** je n'ai pas insisté **3** vi (push) appuyer; (of crowd) se presser
▸**press ahead** = press on
▸**press for** vt insep (demand) exiger
▸**press on** vi continuer; **to p. on with one's work** continuer de travailler

press-gang ['presgæŋ] vt **to p. sb into doing sth** forcer qn à faire qch

pressie ['prezɪ] n Br Fam cadeau m

pressing ['presɪŋ] adj (urgent) pressant(e)

pressman ['presmən] n Br journaliste m

press-up ['presʌp] n Br (exercise) pompe f

pressure ['preʃə(r)] **1** n pression f; **to put p. on sb (to do sth)** faire pression sur qn (pour qu'il fasse qch); **to be under p.** être stressé(e); **p. of work** stress m lié au travail; **p. cooker** Cocotte-Minute® f, autocuiseur m; **p. gauge** manomètre m; **p. group** groupe m de pression; Med **p. point** point m de compression **2** vt **to p. sb to do sth or into doing sth** faire pression sur qn pour qu'il/elle fasse qch

pressurize ['preʃəraɪz] vt (**a**) Tech (container) pressuriser (**b**) (person) **to p. sb (into doing sth)** faire pression sur qn (pour qu'il fasse qch)

prestige [pres'tiːʒ] n prestige m

prestigious [pres'tɪdʒəs] adj prestigieux(euse)

presumably [prɪ'zjuːməblɪ] adv sans doute; **p. she'll come** je suppose qu'elle viendra

presume [prɪ'zjuːm] **1** vt présumer, supposer; **to p. to do sth** se permettre de faire qch; **I p. so** je suppose que oui **2** vi abuser; **I don't want to p. on you** je ne voudrais pas abuser

presumption [prɪ'zʌmpʃən] n présomption f

presumptuous [prɪ'zʌmptjʊəs] adj présomptueux(euse)

presuppose [priːsə'pəʊz] vt présupposer, supposer

presupposition [priːsʌpə'zɪʃən] n présupposition f

pretence [prɪ'tens] n simulation f; **he says he doesn't mind, but it's all a p.** il dit que ça lui est égal, mais il fait semblant; **to make a p. of doing sth** faire semblant de faire qch

pretend [prɪ'tend] vt (**a**) (feign) feindre, simuler; **to p. to do sth** faire semblant de faire qch; **they pretended that nothing had happened** ils ont fait comme si de rien n'était (**b**) (claim) prétendre **2** vi (put on an act) faire semblant **3** adj Fam **p. money** de l'argent pour faire semblant; **a. p. slap** une gifle pour rire

pretension [prɪ'tenʃən] n prétention f

pretentious [prɪ'tenʃəs] adj prétentieux(euse)

pretentiousness [prɪ'tenʃəsnəs] n prétention f

preterite ['pretərɪt] n Gram **the p.** le prétérit

pretext ['priːtekst] n prétexte m; **under** or **on the p. of doing sth** sous prétexte de faire qch

Pretoria [prɪ'tɔːrɪə] n Prétoria

pretty ['prɪtɪ] **1** adj joli(e); **it's not a p. sight** ce n'est pas beau à voir; **to cost a p. penny** coûter la peau des fesses **2** adv (**a**) (fairly) plutôt; **p. certain** pratiquement sûr(e); **they're p. much the same** ils sont pratiquement pareils (**b**) Fam **to be sitting p.** ne pas avoir à s'en faire

pretzel ['pretzəl] n bretzel m

prevail [prɪ'veɪl] vi (**a**) (be successful) l'emporter (**over** sur) (**b**) (persuade) **to p. (up)on sb to do sth** amener qn à faire qch (**c**) (predominate) prédominer

prevailing [prɪ'veɪlɪŋ] adj prédominant(e); (wind) dominant(e)

prevalent ['prevələnt] adj très répandu(e)

prevaricate [prɪ'værɪkeɪt] vi tergiverser

prevarication [prɪværɪ'keɪʃən] n tergiversation f

prevent [prɪ'vent] vt empêcher, éviter; **to p. sb from doing sth** empêcher qn de faire qch; **to p. sth from happening** empêcher que qch n'arrive

preventable [prɪ'ventəbəl] adj évitable

preventative [prɪ'ventətɪv] = preventive

prevention [prɪ'venʃən] n prévention f; Prov **p. is better than cure** mieux vaut prévenir que guérir

preventive [prɪ'ventɪv] adj préventif(ive)

preview ['priːvjuː] **1** n (of play, film) avant-première f; (of new product) aperçu m **2** vt (of film) sortir en avant-première

previous ['priːvɪəs] **1** adj précédent(e); **to have a p. engagement** être déjà pris(e); Law **p. conviction** condamnation f antérieure **2** adv **p. to** avant

previously ['priːvɪəslɪ] adv auparavant

prewar ['priː'wɔː(r)] adj d'avant-guerre

prey [preɪ] *n* proie *f*; *Fig* **to be a p. to** être la proie de; **to fall p. to** devenir la proie de

▸**prey on, prey upon** *vt insep (person)* prendre pour cible; *(fears, doubts)* exploiter; **to p. on sb's mind** tourmenter qn

price [praɪs] **1** *n* prix *m*; **to rise** *or* **increase in p.** augmenter; **at any p.** à tout prix; **not at any p.** à aucun prix; *Fig* **to pay the p. (for sth)** faire les frais (de qch); *Fig* **it's too high a p. (to pay)** c'est trop cher payé; **to put** *or* **set a p. on sb's head** mettre la tête de qn à prix; *Fig* **everyone has his p.** il n'y a pas d'homme qu'on ne puisse acheter; *Fam* **what p. patriotism now?** que vaut le patriotisme maintenant?; **p. cut** baisse *f* des prix; **p. freeze** gel *m* des prix; **p. increase** hausse *f* des prix; **p. index** indice *m* des prix; **p. list** liste *f* de prix; **p. range** gamme *f* de prix; *(budget)* budget *m*; **p. tag** étiquette *f* de prix; **p. war** guerre *f* des prix
2 *vt (decide cost of)* fixer le prix de; *(indicate cost of)* mettre le prix sur; **the toy is priced at £10** le prix du jouet est 10 livres; **to p. oneself out of the market** perdre ses clients en pratiquant des prix trop élevés

price-cutting ['praɪsˌkʌtɪŋ] *n Com* baisse *f* des prix
price-fixing ['praɪsˌfɪksɪŋ] *n Com* alignement *m* des prix
priceless ['praɪslɪs] *adj* (**a**) *(invaluable)* qui n'a pas de prix (**b**) *Fam (funny)* impayable
pricey ['praɪsɪ] *adj Fam* cher(ère)
prick [prɪk] **1** *n* (**a**) *(of needle)* piqûre *f*; *Fig (of conscience)* remords *m* (**b**) *Vulg (penis)* bite *f*; *(man)* con *m*
2 *vt (sausage, potato)* piquer; *(balloon)* percer; **to p. one's finger** se piquer le doigt; **to p. a hole in sth** percer qch

▸**prick up** *vt sep* **to p. up one's ears** *(of animal)* dresser les oreilles; *(of person)* tendre l'oreille

prickle ['prɪkəl] **1** *n* (**a**) *(of hedgehog)* piquant *m*; *(of plant)* épine *f* (**b**) *(sensation)* picotement *m*
2 *vi (of skin)* picoter
prickly ['prɪklɪ] *adj* (**a**) *(animal)* couvert(e) de piquants; *(plant)* à épines; *Fig (person)* susceptible; **p. pear** *(tree)* figuier *m* de Barbarie; *(fruit)* figue *f* de Barbarie (**b**) *(sensation)* de picotement; **p. heat** miliaire *f*
pride [praɪd] **1** *n* (**a**) *(satisfaction)* fierté *f*; *(self-esteem)* amour-propre *m*; *Pej (vanity)* orgueil *m*; **to take p. in sth** mettre sa fierté dans qch (**b**) *(person, thing)* **she is the p. of the family** elle fait la fierté de la famille; **the p. of my collection** le clou de ma collection; **she's his p. and joy** elle fait son bonheur; **to have p. of place** trôner (**c**) *(of lions)* troupe *f*
2 *vt* **to p. oneself on sth** être fier(ère) de qch
priest [priːst] *n* prêtre *m*
priestess ['priːstɪs] *n* prêtresse *f*
priesthood ['priːsthʊd] *n* prêtrise *f*; **to enter the p.** entrer dans les ordres
prig [prɪg] *n* prêcheur(euse) *m,f*
priggish ['prɪgɪʃ] *adj* prêcheur(euse)
prim [prɪm] *adj* **p. (and proper)** *(person, expression)* collet monté *inv*; *(manner)* guindé(e)
primacy ['praɪməsɪ] *n* primauté *f*
prima facie ['praɪmə'feɪʃɪ] **1** *adj Law* **p. case** = affaire qui, au premier abord, paraît légitime
2 *adv* de prime abord
primarily [praɪ'mərɪlɪ] *adv* principalement
primary ['praɪmərɪ] **1** *n (pl* **primaries)** *(election)* primaire *f*
2 *adj* (**a**) *(main)* principal(e); **p. colours** couleurs *fpl* fondamentales (**b**) *(initial)* primaire; **p. education**

enseignement *m* primaire; **p. election** (élection) *f* primaire *f*; **p. school** école *f* primaire

Primary elections

Les élections primaires américaines (directes ou indirectes selon les États) aboutissent à la sélection des candidats qui seront en lice pour représenter les deux grands partis nationaux à l'élection présidentielle. Ces élections ont lieu entre les mois de février et de mai chaque année d'élections présidentielles. Certains États tiennent des meetings électoraux appelés "caucuses" au lieu des élections primaires.

primate ['praɪmeɪt] *n* (**a**) *(animal)* primate *m* (**b**) *Rel* primat *m*
prime [praɪm] **1** *n (best time)* **the p. of life** la fleur de l'âge; **to be in one's p.** être à la fleur de l'âge; **to be past one's p.** ne plus être de première jeunesse
2 *adj* (**a**) *(principal)* principal(e); *(importance)* capital(e); **p. minister** premier ministre *m*; *Math* **p. number** nombre *m* premier; *(TV & Rad)* **p. time** prime time *m* (**b**) *(excellent)* excellent(e); **a p. example (of)** un exemple typique (de); **p. quality** de premier choix
3 *vt* (**a**) *(engine, pump)* amorcer; *(surface)* apprêter (**b**) *(provide with information)* **to p. sb for an interview/an exam** préparer qn à un entretien/un examen
primer[1] ['praɪmə(r)] *n (paint)* apprêt *m*
primer[2] *n (textbook)* manuel *m* élémentaire
primeval [praɪ'miːvəl] *adj* primitif(ive)
primitive ['prɪmɪtɪv] *adj* *(original)* primitif(ive); *(basic)* primitif(ive), rudimentaire
primly ['prɪmlɪ] *adv* d'une manière guindée
primordial [praɪ'mɔːdɪəl] *adj* primordial(e); **p. soup** soupe *f* primitive
primrose ['prɪmrəʊz] *n (plant)* primevère *f*; **p. yellow** jaune pâle *inv*
primula ['prɪmjʊlə] *n* primula *f*
primus (stove)® ['praɪməs('stəʊv)] *n* réchaud *m* portatif
prince [prɪns] *n* prince *m*; **the P. of Wales** le prince de Galles; **P. Charming** le prince charmant
princely ['prɪnslɪ] *adj also Fig* princier(ère)
princess [prɪn'ses] *n* princesse *f*; **the P. Royal** la princesse royale *(fille aînée du souverain)*
principal ['prɪnsɪpəl] **1** *n* (**a**) *Am & Ir (of school)* directeur(trice) *m,f* (**b**) *(of university)* ≃ président *m*
2 *adj* principal(e)
principality [prɪnsɪ'pælɪtɪ] *(pl* **principalities)** *n* principauté *f*
principle ['prɪnsɪpəl] *n* principe *m*; **in p.** en principe; **on p.** par principe
principled ['prɪnsɪpəld] *adj (person)* de principes; *(behaviour)* dicté(e) par des principes; **to be p.** avoir des principes
print [prɪnt] **1** *n* (**a**) *(of fingers)* empreinte *f* (**b**) *(printed matter)* texte *m*; **in p.** disponible en librairie; **out of p.** épuisé(e); **to appear in p.** être publié(e) (**c**) *(characters)* caractères *mpl*; *Fig* **to read the small p.** *(in contract)* lire ce qu'il y a d'écrit en petits caractères (**d**) *(engraving)* estampe *f*; *(photograph)* épreuve *f*; *(textile)* imprimé *m*
2 *vt* (**a**) *(book, newspaper)* imprimer (**b**) *(write clearly)* écrire en script (**c**) *(in photography)* **to p. a negative** tirer une épreuve d'un négatif
3 *vi (write clearly)* écrire en script

▶ **print out** *vt sep Comput* imprimer
printed ['prɪntɪd] *adj* imprimé(e); **p. circuit** circuit *m* imprimé; **p. matter** imprimés *mpl*
printer ['prɪntə(r)] *n (person)* imprimeur *m*; *(machine)* imprimante *f*
printing ['prɪntɪŋ] *n (process, industry)* imprimerie *f*; *(action)* tirage *m*; **p. error** faute *f* d'impression; **p. press** presse *f*
printout ['prɪntaʊt] *n Comput* sortie *f* papier
prior¹ ['praɪə(r)] **1** *adj* antérieur(e); **to have p. knowledge (of sth)** avoir une connaissance préalable (de qch)
2 *adv* **p. to** avant
prior² *n Rel* prieur *m*
prioritize [praɪˈɒrɪtaɪz] **1** *vt* donner la priorité à
2 *vi* établir ses priorités
priority [praɪˈɒrɪtɪ] *(pl* **priorities)** *n* priorité *f*; **to have** *or* **take p. over sb/sth** avoir la priorité sur qn/qch; **to get one's priorities right/wrong** savoir/ne pas savoir ce qui est important
priory ['praɪərɪ] *(pl* **priories)** *n Rel* prieuré *m*
prise [praɪz] *vt* **p. sth off/open** retirer/ouvrir qch en forçant; *Fig* **to p. sth out of sb** *(secret, truth)* soutirer qch à qn
prism ['prɪzəm] *n* prisme *m*
prison ['prɪzən] *n* prison *f*; **p. camp** camp *m* de prisonniers; **p. officer** gardien(enne) *m,f* de prison
prisoner ['prɪzənə(r)] *n* prisonnier(ère) *m,f*; **to take/hold sb p.** faire/retenir qn prisonnier; *Fig* **to take no prisoners** être impitoyable; **p. of conscience** prisonnier(ère) *m,f* d'opinion; **p. of war** prisonnier(ère) *m,f* de guerre
prissy ['prɪsɪ] *adj Fam* collet monté *inv*
pristine ['prɪstiːn] *adj* impeccable
privacy ['prɪvəsɪ, 'praɪvəsɪ] *n* intimité *f*; **in the p. of one's own home** dans l'intimité de son foyer
private ['praɪvɪt] **1** *adj* **(a)** *(personal)* personnel(elle); **can we go somewhere p.?** est-ce qu'on peut se voir en privé?; **p. life** vie *f* privée; *Parl* **p. member** simple député *m*; *Fam* **p. parts** parties *fpl* (génitales) **(b)** *(secret)* confidentiel(elle); **p. and confidential** *(on letter)* confidentiel **(c)** *(for personal use)* privé(e); **p. house** maison *f* particulière; **p. lessons** leçons *fpl* particulières; **p. line** ligne *f* privée; **p. office** bureau *m* personnel; **p. secretary** secrétaire *mf* particulier(ère) **(d)** *(not state-run)* privé(e); **p. detective** *or* **investigator** détective *m* privé; **p. education** enseignement *m* privé; **p. enterprise** entreprise *f* privée; **p. health insurance** assurance *f* maladie privée; **p. school** école *f* privée; **p. sector** secteur *m* privé **(e)** *(not for the public)* privé(e); **p. party** soirée *f* privée; **p. property** propriété *f* privée; **p. road** voie *f* privée
2 *n* **(a)** **in p.** en privé **(b)** *(soldier)* simple soldat *m* **(c)** *Fam* **privates** parties *fpl* (génitales)
privately ['praɪvɪtlɪ] *adv (in private)* en privé; **to be p. educated** faire sa scolarité dans le privé; **p. owned** *(company)* privé(e); *(hotel)* familial(e)
privation [praɪˈveɪʃən] *n* privation *f*
privatization [praɪvɪtaɪˈzeɪʃən] *n* privatisation *f*
privatize ['praɪvɪtaɪz] *vt* privatiser
privet ['prɪvɪt] *n* troène *m*
privilege ['prɪvɪlɪdʒ] **1** *n* privilège *m*; **to have the p. of doing sth** avoir le privilège de faire qch
2 *vt* **to be privileged to do sth** avoir le privilège de faire qch
privy ['prɪvɪ] **1** *n (pl* **privies)** *Old-fashioned (toilet)* cabinets *mpl*

2 *adj* **(a)** *Formal* **to be p. to sth** avoir connaissance de qch **(b)** *Br Pol* **the P. Council** le Conseil privé du souverain
prize¹ [praɪz] **1** *n (award)* prix *m*; **to win a p.** remporter un prix; *Fig* **no prizes for guessing** ce n'est pas difficile de deviner; **p. day** jour *m* de distribution des prix; **p. draw** tombola *f*; **p. money** argent *m* du prix
2 *vt (value)* attacher de la valeur à
prize² = **prise**
prizefight ['praɪzfaɪt] *n* combat *m* professionnel
prizefighter ['praɪzfaɪtə(r)] *n* boxeur *m* professionnel
prizegiving ['praɪzgɪvɪŋ] *n* distribution *f* des prix
prizewinner ['praɪzwɪnə(r)] *n* gagnant(e) *m,f*
pro¹ [prəʊ] *(pl* **pros)** *n Fam (professional)* pro *mf*
pro² **1** *n (advantage)* **the pros and cons** le pour et le contre
2 *prep (in favour of)* pour
proactive [prəʊˈæktɪv] *adj* qui fait preuve d'initiative
pro-am ['prəʊˈæm] *n Sport* tournoi *m* professionnel-amateur
probability [prɒbəˈbɪlɪtɪ] *(pl* **probabilities)** *n* probabilité *f*; **in all p....** il y a de fortes chances que...
probable ['prɒbəbəl] *adj* probable
probably ['prɒbəblɪ] *adv* probablement
probation [prəˈbeɪʃən] *n (in job)* période *f* d'essai; **on p.** *(in job)* à l'essai; *Law* mise *f* en liberté surveillée; **on p.** *(in job)* à l'essai; *Law* en liberté surveillée; **p. officer** agent *m* de probation
probationary [prəˈbeɪʃənərɪ] *adj* d'essai
probationer [prəˈbeɪʃənə(r)] *n (in job)* personne *f* à l'essai
probe [prəʊb] **1** *n* **(a)** *(instrument)* sonde *f*; **(space) p.** sonde *f* spatiale **(b)** *Fam (enquiry)* enquête *f*
2 *vt* **(a)** *(prod)* sonder **(b)** *(enquire into)* enquêter sur
3 *vi* **to p. into sth** *(past, private life)* fouiller dans qch
probity ['prəʊbɪtɪ] *n Formal* probité *f*
problem ['prɒbləm] *n* problème *m*; *Fam* **no p.!** pas de problème!; **p. area** *(in town)* quartier *m* à problèmes; *(in project)* source *f* de problèmes; **p. child** enfant *mf* à problèmes; **p. page** courrier *m* du cœur
problematic(al) [prɒblɪˈmætɪk(əl)] *adj* problématique
procedure [prəˈsiːdʒə(r)] *n* procédure *f*
proceed [prəˈsiːd] **1** *vt* **to p. to do sth** se mettre à faire qch
2 *vi* **(a)** *(go on)* se poursuivre; **to p. to sth** passer à qch; **to p. with sth** poursuivre qch; **how shall we p.?** comment allons-nous procéder? **(b)** *(result)* **to p. from** provenir de
proceedings [prəˈsiːdɪŋz] *npl* **(a)** *(events)* opérations *fpl* **(b)** *Law* poursuites *fpl*; **to take p. (against sb)** engager des poursuites (contre qn)
proceeds ['prəʊsiːdz] *npl* recette *f*
process ['prəʊses] **1** *n* processus *m*; **by a p. of elimination** en procédant par élimination; **she fell down the stairs, breaking her leg in the p.** elle est tombée dans les escaliers, et s'est cassée la jambe; **to be in the p. of doing sth** être en train de faire qch
2 *vt (raw material, information, application)* traiter; *(film)* développer; **processed food** aliments *mpl* conditionnés
processing ['prəʊsesɪŋ] *n (of raw material, information)* traitement *m*; *(of photographs)* développement *m*; *Comput* **p. language** langage *m* de traitement; *Comput* **p. speed** vitesse *f* de traitement
procession [prəˈseʃən] *n* défilé *m*; **in p.** en cortège

processor ['prəʊsesə(r)] n Comput processeur m
pro-choice ['prəʊ'tʃɔɪs] adj partisan(e) de l'avortement
proclaim [prə'kleɪm] vt proclamer
proclamation [proklə'meɪʃən] n proclamation f
proclivity [prəʊ'klɪvɪtɪ] (pl **proclivities**) n Formal tendance f (**for** à)
procrastinate [prəʊ'kræstɪneɪt] vi atermoyer
procrastination [prəʊkræstɪ'neɪʃən] n atermoiements mpl
procreate ['prəʊkrɪeɪt] vi procréer
procreation [prəʊkrɪ'eɪʃən] n procréation f
procure [prə'kjʊə(r)] vt procurer (**for sb** à qn); **to p. sth (for oneself)** se procurer qch
procurement [prə'kjʊəmənt] n acquisition f
prod [prod] 1 n **to give sb a p.** donner un petit coup à qn; Fig pousser qn; **to give sth a p.** donner un petit coup à qch
 2 vt (pt & pp **prodded**) (poke) donner un petit coup dans; Fig **to p. sb (into doing sth)** pousser qn (à faire qch)
prodigal ['prodɪgəl] adj prodigue
prodigious [prə'dɪdʒəs] adj prodigieux(euse)
prodigy ['prodɪdʒɪ] (pl **prodigies**) n prodige m; **child p.** enfant mf prodige
produce 1 n ['prodju:s] (products) produits mpl
 2 vt [prə'dju:s] (**a**) (create) produire; (machine, car) fabriquer; (reaction, feeling) entraîner (**b**) (present) (ticket, passport) présenter; (documents, alibi) fournir; (from pocket, bag) sortir (**c**) (film, play, radio/TV programme) produire
producer [prə'dju:sə(r)] n (**a**) (of crops, goods) producteur(trice) m,f (**b**) (of film, play, radio/TV programme) producteur(trice) m,f
product ['prodʌkt] n produit m; Com **p. development** mise f au point de produit
production [prə'dʌkʃən] n (**a**) (manufacture) production f, fabrication f; **to go into/out of p.** être/ne plus être fabriqué(e); **p. costs** coûts mpl de production; **p. line** chaîne f de fabrication; **p. manager** directeur(trice) m,f de production; **p. process** procédé m de fabrication; **p. target** cible f de production (**b**) (of document, ticket) présentation f; **on p. of** sur présentation de (**c**) (play) mise f en scène; (film, radio/TV programme) production f
productive [prə'dʌktɪv] adj productif(ive)
productivity [prodʌk'tɪvɪtɪ] n Ind productivité f; **p. agreement** accord m de productivité; **p. bonus** prime f de rendement
Prof (abbr **Professor**) (**a**) (title) Professeur (**b**) Fam prof mf
profane [prə'feɪn] 1 adj (**a**) (language) grossier(ère) (**b**) Rel (secular) profane
 2 vt profaner
profanity [prə'fænɪtɪ] (pl **profanities**) n grossièreté f
profess [prə'fes] vt (**a**) (declare) professer (**b**) (claim) prétendre
professed [prə'fest] adj (**a**) (self-declared) avoué(e) (**b**) (pretended) prétendu(e)
profession [prə'feʃən] n (**a**) (occupation) profession f; **the medical/teaching p.** le corps médical/enseignant, by **p.** de profession (**b**) (declaration) déclaration f
professional [prə'feʃənəl] 1 n professionnel(elle) m,f
 2 adj (paid, competent) professionnel(elle); (soldier) de carrière; (army) de métier; **he made a very p. job**

of it il a fait du bon travail; **to turn** or **go p.** (of sportsperson) passer en catégorie professionnelle; **to take p. advice on sth** demander l'avis d'un professionnel sur qch; **p. misconduct** faute f professionnelle; **p. training** formation f professionnelle
professionalism [prə'feʃənəlɪzəm] n professionnalisme m
professor [prə'fesə(r)] n Univ Br ≃ professeur m; Am enseignant(e) m,f d'université
proffer ['profə(r)] vt Formal (advice) offrir; (opinion) avancer; (thanks) présenter; (hand, object) tendre
proficiency [prə'fɪʃənsɪ] n compétence f (**in** or **at** en ou dans); (in language) maîtrise f (**in** en)
proficient [prə'fɪʃənt] adj compétent(e) (**in** or **at** en ou dans)
profile ['prəʊfaɪl] 1 n (**a**) (side view, outline) profil m; **to keep a low p.** garder un profil bas (**b**) (description) portrait m
 2 vt (describe) faire le portrait de
profiling ['prəʊfaɪlɪŋ] n Psy profilage m
profit ['profɪt] 1 n (**a**) (of company, on deal) bénéfice m, profit m; **at a p.** à profit; **to make a p.** réaliser un bénéfice; **p. and loss account** compte m de pertes et profits; **p. margin** marge f bénéficiaire (**b**) (advantage) avantage m
 2 vi **to p. by** or **from** tirer profit de
profitability [profɪtə'bɪlɪtɪ] n rentabilité f
profitable ['profɪtəbəl] adj (company, deal) rentable; (experience) profitable
profitably ['profɪtəblɪ] adv (trade, operate) à profit; (use one's time) profitablement
profiteer [profɪ'tɪə(r)] Pej 1 n profiteur(euse) m,f
 2 vi profiter d'une situation pour faire des bénéfices
profit-making ['profɪtmeɪkɪŋ] adj rentable
profit-sharing ['profɪtʃeərɪŋ] n Com intéressement m
profligate ['proflɪgət] adj Formal prodigue
profound [prə'faʊnd] adj profond(e)
profundity [prə'fʌndɪtɪ] (pl **profundities**) n profondeur f
profuse [prə'fju:s] adj abondant(e)
profusely [prə'fju:slɪ] adv (sweat, bleed) abondamment; **to apologize p.** se confondre en excuses; **to thank sb p.** remercier qn avec effusion
profusion [prə'fju:ʒən] n profusion f
progeny ['prodʒɪnɪ] (pl **progenies**) n Formal progéniture f
prognosis [prog'nəʊsɪs] (pl **prognoses** [prog'nəʊsi:z]) n Med pronostic m; Fig pronostics mpl
program[1] ['prəʊgræm] Comput 1 n programme m
 2 vt & vi programmer
program[2] Am = programme
programmable [prəʊ'græməbəl] adj programmable
programme, Am program ['prəʊgræm] 1 n (for play, concert, political party) programme m; (on TV, radio) émission f; **p. seller** vendeur(euse) m,f de programmes
 2 vt (machine) programmer; **to p. sth to do sth** programmer qch pour faire qch
programmed ['prəʊgræmd] adj Educ **p. instruction** or **learning** enseignement m programmé
programmer ['prəʊgræmə(r)] n Comput programmeur(euse) m,f
progress 1 n ['prəʊgres] (**a**) (improvement) progrès m; **to make p.** faire des progrès (**b**) (movement) marche f; **in p.** en cours; **to make p. (in sth)** progresser (dans qch); **p. report** rapport m

2 *vi* [prəˈgres] (**a**) *(improve)* progresser (**b**) *(advance)* avancer; *(of meeting)* progresser
progression [prəˈgreʃən] *n* progression *f*
progressive [prəˈgresɪv] **1** *adj* (**a**) *(increasing)* progressif(ive); **p. disease** maladie *f* évolutive (**b**) *(radical)* progressiste
2 *n (radical)* progressiste *mf*
progressively [prəˈgresɪvlɪ] *adv* progressivement
prohibit [prəˈhɪbɪt] *vt* interdire; **to p. sb from doing sth** interdire à qn de faire qch
prohibition [prəʊɪˈbɪʃən] *n* interdiction *f*; *Am Hist* **P.** la Prohibition
prohibitive [prəˈhɪbɪtɪv] *adj* prohibitif(ive)
prohibitively [prəˈhɪbɪtɪvlɪ] *adv* **p. expensive** à un prix prohibitif
project 1 *n* [ˈprɒdʒekt] *(undertaking, plan)* projet *m*; *(at school)* dossier *m*; *(at university)* mémoire *m*; *Com* **p. manager** directeur(trice) *m,f* de projet
2 *vt* [prəˈdʒekt] (**a**) *(plan)* prévoir (**b**) *(propel)* projeter; **to p. one's voice** projeter sa voix
3 *vi* [prəˈdʒekt] *(protrude)* dépasser
projectile [prəˈdʒektaɪl] *n* projectile *m*
projection [prəˈdʒekʃən] *n* (**a**) *(in general)* projection *f*; **p. room** *(in cinema)* salle *f* de projection (**b**) *(protruding part)* saillie *f*
projectionist [prəˈdʒekʃənɪst] *n* projectionniste *mf*
projector [prəˈdʒektə(r)] *n* projecteur *m*
prolapse [ˈprəʊlæps] *n Med* prolapsus *m*
proletarian [prəʊlɪˈteərɪən] **1** *n* prolétaire *mf*
2 *adj* prolétarien(enne)
proletariat [prəʊlɪˈteərɪət] *n* prolétariat *m*
pro-life [ˈprəʊˈlaɪf] *adj* contre l'avortement
proliferate [prəˈlɪfəreɪt] *vi* proliférer
proliferation [prəlɪfəˈreɪʃən] *n* prolifération *f*
prolific [prəˈlɪfɪk] *adj* prolifique
prolix [ˈprəʊlɪks] *adj Formal* prolixe
prologue [ˈprəʊlɒg] *n* prologue *m*
prolong [prəˈlɒŋ] *vt* prolonger
prom [prɒm] *n* (**a**) *Br Fam (at seaside)* front *m* de mer (**b**) *Br Fam (concert)* concert *m* (**c**) *Am (school dance)* soirée *f* dansante

Prom

Aux États-Unis, on célèbre la fin des études secondaires par un grand bal formel appelé le "senior prom". Ce bal a lieu à la fin des examens de dernière année et c'est un événement important auquel assistent élèves et professeurs. Les étudiantes et leurs cavaliers sont en tenue de soirée et, au cours de la fête, on élit un roi et une reine du bal ("prom king" et "prom queen").

promenade [ˈprɒmənɑːd] **1** *n Br (at seaside)* front *m* de mer; **p. deck** *(on ship)* pont *m* promenade
2 *vi* se promener
prominence [ˈprɒmɪnəns] *n* (**a**) *(of land)* saillie *f*; *(of physical feature)* proéminence *f* (**b**) *(importance)* importance *f*; **to give sth p.** donner de l'importance à qch; **to come to p.** devenir célèbre
prominent [ˈprɒmɪnənt] *adj* (**a**) *(peak, landscape)* en saillie; *(physical feature)* proéminent(e); **to be in a p. position** être en évidence (**b**) *(important)* important(e)
prominently [ˈprɒmɪnəntlɪ] *adv* bien en vue; **to figure p. in sth** figurer en bonne place dans qch
promiscuity [prɒmɪsˈkjuːɪtɪ] *n* promiscuité *f* sexuelle

promiscuous [prəˈmɪskjʊəs] *adj* qui a des partenaires multiples
promise [ˈprɒmɪs] **1** *n* (**a**) *(pledge)* promesse *f*; **to make a p.** faire une promesse; **to keep/break one's p.** tenir/ne pas tenir sa promesse (**b**) *(potential)* **to show p.** promettre; **she never fulfilled her early p.** *(as a writer, musician)* elle n'a jamais eu le succès qu'elle promettait d'avoir
2 *vt* promettre (**to do** de faire); **to p. sth to sb, to p. sb sth** promettre qch à qn; **it promises to be hot** le temps promet d'être chaud
promising [ˈprɒmɪsɪŋ] *adj* prometteur(euse)
promontory [ˈprɒməntərɪ] (*pl* **promontories**) *n* promontoire *m*
promote [prəˈməʊt] *vt* (**a**) *(raise in rank, encourage)* promouvoir; **to be promoted** *(of employee)* être promu(e); *(of football team)* passer dans la division supérieure; **to p. sb's interests** servir les intérêts de qn (**b**) *Com* faire la publicité de
promoter [prəˈməʊtə(r)] *n* (**of theory, cause**) défenseur(euse) *m,f*; (**of match, concert**) organisateur(trice) *m,f*; *(of show)* impresario *m*
promotion [prəˈməʊʃən] *n* promotion *f*
promotional [prəˈməʊʃənəl] *adj* promotionnel(elle)
prompt [prɒmpt] **1** *adj* (**a**) *(swift)* rapide; **p. payment** paiement *m* dans les plus brefs délais (**b**) *(punctual)* ponctuel(elle)
2 *adv* **at three o'clock p.** à trois heures précises
3 *vt* (**a**) *(cause)* provoquer; **to p. sb to do sth** pousser qn à faire qch (**b**) **to p. sb** *(encourage to speak)* = aider quelqu'un à répondre en lui suggérant quelque chose; **"was he tall?" the policeman prompted** "est-ce qu'il était grand?" suggéra le policier (**c**) *(in theatre)* souffler à
4 *n* (**a**) **to give an actor a p.** souffler sa réplique à un acteur (**b**) *Comput* invite *f*
prompter [ˈprɒmptə(r)] *n Theat* souffleur(euse) *m,f*
promptly [ˈprɒmptlɪ] *adv* (**rapidly, punctually**) rapidement; *(immediately)* immédiatement
prone [prəʊn] *adj* (**a**) *(inclined)* **to be p. to sth** être sujet(ette) à qch; **to be p. to do sth** avoir tendance à faire qch (**b**) *Formal (lying face down)* couché(e) sur le ventre
prong [prɒŋ] *n (of fork)* dent *f*
pronoun [ˈprəʊnaʊn] *n Gram* pronom *m*
pronounce [prəˈnaʊns] **1** *vt* (**a**) *(word)* prononcer (**b**) *(declare) (opinion)* émettre; **to p. that...** déclarer que...; **to p. oneself for/against sth** se prononcer en faveur de/contre qch; **he was pronounced dead/innocent** il a été déclaré mort/innocent; *Law* **to p. sentence** rendre le verdict
2 *vi* **to p. on** se prononcer sur
pronounced [prəˈnaʊnst] *adj* prononcé(e)
pronouncement [prəˈnaʊnsmənt] *n Formal* déclaration *f*
pronto [ˈprɒntəʊ] *adv Fam* illico
pronunciation [prənʌnsɪˈeɪʃən] *n* prononciation *f*
proof [pruːf] **1** *n* (**a**) *(evidence)* preuve *f*; **to give p. of sth** prouver qch; **p. of identity** pièce *f* d'identité; **p. of purchase** preuve *f* d'achat; **to put sth to the p.** mettre qch à l'épreuve; *Prov* **the p. of the pudding is in the eating** il faut juger les choses à l'usage (**b**) *Typ* épreuve *f* (**c**) *(of alcohol)* teneur *f* en alcool; **to be 40 percent p.** faire 40 degrés
2 *adj (resistant)* **to be p. against sth** être résistant(e) à qch

proofread ['pruːfriːd] (*pt & pp* **proofread** ['pruːfred]) *vt Typ* relire, corriger

proofreader ['pruːfriːdə(r)] *n Typ* correcteur(trice) *m,f*

proofreading ['pruːfriːdɪŋ] *n* correction *f* (d'épreuves), relecture *f* (d'épreuves)

prop [prɒp] **1** *n* (**a**) *(physical support)* support *m*; *(emotional support)* soutien *m* (**b**) *(in theatre)* accessoire *m*
2 *vt (pt & pp* **propped**) **to p. sth against sth** appuyer qch contre qch
▸**prop up** *vt sep (building, tunnel)* étayer; *Fig (economy, regime)* soutenir; **to p. sth up against sth** appuyer qch contre qch

propaganda [prɒpə'gændə] *n* propagande *f*

propagate ['prɒpəgeɪt] **1** *vt* propager
2 *vi* se propager

propagation [prɒpə'geɪʃən] *n* propagation *f*

propane ['prəʊpeɪn] *n Chem* propane *m*

propel [prə'pel] (*pt & pp* **propelled**) *vt* propulser; *Fig* pousser

propellant, propellent [prə'pelənt] *n (for rocket)* propergol *m*; *(for aerosol)* gaz *m* propulseur

propeller [prə'pelə(r)] *n* hélice *f*

propelling pencil [prə'pelɪŋ'pensəl] *n* porte-mine *m inv*

propensity [prə'pensɪtɪ] (*pl* **propensities**) *n* propension *f* (**for** à)

proper ['prɒpə(r)] *adj* (**a**) *(correct, real)* vrai(e); *(word)* correct(e); *Gram* **p. noun** nom *m* propre (**b**) *(appropriate)* bon (bonne); *(equipment, clothing)* adéquat(e); *(behaviour)* convenable (**c**) *(characteristic)* **p. to** propre à (**d**) *Br Fam (for emphasis)* **it was a p. disaster** c'était une véritable catastrophe; **we're in a p. mess** nous voilà propres; **he's a p. fool** c'est vraiment un imbécile

properly ['prɒpəlɪ] *adv* (**a**) *(correctly)* correctement (**b**) *(suitably)* convenablement

property ['prɒpətɪ] (*pl* **properties**) *n* (**a**) *(possessions)* biens *mpl*; *(land, house)* propriété *f*; **p. developer** promoteur(trice) *m,f* (immobilier(ère)); **p. market** marché *m* immobilier; **p. tax** impôt *m* foncier (**b**) *(quality)* propriété *f*

prophecy ['prɒfɪsɪ] (*pl* **prophecies**) *n* prophétie *f*

prophesy ['prɒfɪsaɪ] (*pt & pp* **prophesied**) *vt* prédire

prophet ['prɒfɪt] *n* prophète *m*

prophetic [prə'fetɪk] *adj* prophétique

prophylactic [prɒfɪ'læktɪk] *Med* **1** *n* prophylactique *m*; *(condom)* préservatif *m*
2 *adj* prophylactique

propitiate [prə'pɪʃɪeɪt] *vt Formal* gagner les faveurs de

propitious [prə'pɪʃəs] *adj Formal* favorable

proportion [prə'pɔːʃən] **1** *n* (**a**) *(relationship)* proportion *f*; **in p.** proportionné(e); **out of p.** disproportionné(e); **the payment is out of all p. to the work involved** la rétribution n'est pas du tout proportionnelle au travail requis (**b**) *(part, amount)* proportion *f*; **to get sth out of p.** exagérer qch; **try to keep things in p.** essaie de ne pas dramatiser (**c**) **proportions** *(dimensions)* proportions *fpl*
2 *vt* proportionner

proportional [prə'pɔːʃənəl] *adj* proportionnel(elle) (**to** à); *Pol* **p. representation** (représentation *f*) proportionnelle *f*

proportionate [prə'pɔːʃənɪt] *adj* proportionnel(elle) (**to** à)

proposal [prə'pəʊzəl] *n (offer)* proposition *f*; *(plan)* projet *m*; **p. (of marriage)** demande *f* en mariage

propose [prə'pəʊz] **1** *vt* proposer; **to p. a toast** porter un toast; **to p. to do sth, to p. doing sth** *(suggest)* suggérer de faire qch; *(intend)* avoir l'intention de faire qch
2 *vi* **to p. to sb** demander qn en mariage

proposition [prɒpə'zɪʃən] **1** *n* proposition *f*
2 *vt* faire des avances à

propound [prə'paʊnd] *vt Formal* exposer

proprietary [prə'praɪɪtərɪ] *adj (air, attitude)* possessif(ive); *Com* **p. brand** marque *f* déposée

proprietor [prə'praɪətə(r)] *n* propriétaire *mf*

propriety [prə'praɪɪtɪ] *n* bienséance *f*

propulsion [prə'pʌlʃən] *n* propulsion *f*

pro rata ['prəʊ'rɑːtə] *adj & adv* au prorata

prosaic [prəʊ'zeɪk] *adj* prosaïque

proscribe [prəʊ'skraɪb] *vt* proscrire

prose [prəʊz] *n* prose *f*; *(translation in exam)* thème *m*

prosecute ['prɒsɪkjuːt] *Law* **1** *vt* poursuivre en justice
2 *vi (of lawyer)* représenter le ministère public

prosecution [prɒsɪ'kjuːʃən] *n Law (proceedings)* poursuites *fpl* judiciaires; **the p.** *(in trial)* les plaignants *mpl*; *(in crown case)* ≃ le ministère public

prosecutor ['prɒsɪkjuːtə(r)] *n Law* procureur *m*

prospect 1 *n* ['prɒspekt] (**a**) *(expectation, thought)* perspective *f* (**b**) *(chance, likelihood)* perspectives *fpl*; **there is no p. of success** il n'y a aucune chance de réussite; **future prospects** perspectives *fpl* d'avenir; **a job with prospects** un travail qui offre des perspectives d'avenir (**c**) *(view)* vue *f*
2 *vi* [prə'spekt] **to p. for gold** chercher de l'or

prospective [prə'spektɪv] *adj (future)* futur(e); *(potential)* potentiel(elle)

prospector [prə'spektə(r)] *n* prospecteur(trice) *m,f*; *(for gold)* chercheur(euse) *m,f*

prospectus [prə'spektəs] *n* prospectus *m*

prosper ['prɒspə(r)] *vi* prospérer

prosperity [prɒs'perɪtɪ] *n* prospérité *f*

prosperous ['prɒspərəs] *adj* prospère

prostate ['prɒsteɪt] *n Anat* **p. (gland)** prostate *f*

prosthesis [prɒs'θiːsɪs] (*pl* **prostheses** [prɒs'θiːsiːz]) *n* prothèse *f*

prostitute ['prɒstɪtjuːt] **1** *n* prostituée *f*; **male p.** prostitué *m*
2 *vt also Fig* **to p. oneself** se prostituer

prostitution [prɒstɪ'tjuːʃən] *n* prostitution *f*

prostrate 1 *adj* ['prɒstreɪt] *(lying down)* couché(e); *Fig* **p. with grief** terrassé(e) par le chagrin
2 *vt* [prə'streɪt] **to p. oneself** se prosterner

protagonist [prə'tægənɪst] *n* protagoniste *mf*; *(of idea, theory)* partisan(e) *m,f*

protease ['prəʊtɪeɪz] *n* protéase *f*; **p. inhibitor** antiprotéase *f*, inhibiteur *m* de protéase

protect [prə'tekt] *vt* protéger (**from** *or* **against** de)

protection [prə'tekʃən] *n* protection *f*; **p. money** = argent versé à un racketteur; **p. racket** racket *m*

protectionism [prə'tekʃənɪzəm] *n Econ* protectionnisme *m*

protective [prə'tektɪv] *adj* protecteur(trice); **to put sb in p. custody** mettre qn en lieu sûr

protector [prə'tektə(r)] *n (device)* protecteur *m*; *(person)* protecteur(trice) *m,f*

protégé ['prɒtəʒeɪ] *n* protégé(e) *m,f*

protein ['prəʊtiːn] *n* protéine *f*

protest 1 *n* ['prəʊtest] protestation *f*; **to do sth under p.** faire qch contre son gré; **to do sth in p.** faire qch en signe de protestation; **p. song** chanson f engagée; **p. vote** vote m de protestation **2** vt [prə'test] (**a**) (protest against) protester contre (**b**) (one's innocence, love) protester de; **to p. that...** protester en disant que... **3** vi [prə'test] protester (**about/against** à propos de/contre)

Protestant ['prɒtɪstənt] **1** n protestant(e) m,f **2** adj protestant(e)

Protestantism ['prɒtɪstəntɪzəm] n protestantisme m

protestation [prɒtes'teɪʃən] n protestation f

protester [prə'testə(r)] n protestataire mf

protocol ['prəʊtəkɒl] n protocole m; Ecol & Pol **the Kyoto P.** le Protocole de Kyoto

proton ['prəʊtɒn] n Phys proton m

prototype ['prəʊtətaɪp] n prototype m

protracted [prə'træktɪd] adj prolongé(e)

protractor [prə'træktə(r)] n rapporteur m

protrude [prə'truːd] vi dépasser (**from** de); (of jaw, teeth) avancer

protruding [prə'truːdɪŋ] adj en saillie; (jaw, teeth) qui avance

protuberance [prə'tjuːbərəns] n protubérance f

proud [praʊd] **1** adj (person) fier(ère) (**of** de); (moment) grand(e); **as p. as a peacock** fier(ère) comme un paon **2** adv **to do sb p.** faire honneur à qn; **to do oneself p.** se distinguer

proudly ['praʊdlɪ] adv fièrement

prove [pruːv] (pp **proven** ['pruːvən, 'prəʊvən] or **proved**) **1** vt (demonstrate) prouver; **to p. sb wrong/guilty** prouver que qn a tort/est coupable; **to p. oneself** se prouver quelque chose **2** vi **to p. (to be) correct** se révéler correct(e)

proverb ['prɒvɜːb] n proverbe m

proverbial [prə'vɜːbɪəl] adj proverbial(e)

provide [prə'vaɪd] vt (**a**) (supply) fournir; (service, support) offrir; **to p. sb with sth** fournir qch à qn (**b**) (stipulate) stipuler

▸**provide against** vt insep (danger, possibility) parer à

▸**provide for** vt insep (**a**) (support) pourvoir aux besoins de; **he left his family well provided for** il a laissé sa famille à l'abri du besoin (**b**) Formal (allow for) parer à

provided [prə'vaɪdɪd] conj **p. (that)** à condition que + subjunctive

providence ['prɒvɪdəns] n providence f

providential [prɒvɪ'denʃəl] adj providentiel(elle)

provider [prə'vaɪdə(r)] n pourvoyeur(euse) m,f

providing [prə'vaɪdɪŋ] conj **p. (that)** à condition que + subjunctive

province ['prɒvɪns] n (**a**) (of country) province f; **in the provinces** en province (**b**) Fig (domain) domaine m

provincial [prə'vɪnʃəl] adj de province; Pej (parochial) provincial(e)

provision [prə'vɪʒən] n (**a**) **provisions** (supplies) provisions fpl (**b**) (supplying) approvisionnement m (**of** en); (of services) prestation f (**of** de); (**c**) (allowance) **to make p. for sth** prévoir qch (**d**) (in treaty) disposition f; (in contract) clause f

provisional [prə'vɪʒənəl] adj provisoire

provisionally [prə'vɪʒənəlɪ] adv provisoirement

proviso [prə'vaɪzəʊ] (pl **provisos** or **provisoes**) n condition f; **with the p. that** à condition que + subjunctive

provocation [prɒvə'keɪʃən] n provocation f; **at the slightest p.** pour un rien

provocative [prə'vɒkətɪv] adj provocateur(trice)

provoke [prə'vəʊk] vt provoquer; **to p. sb into doing sth** pousser qn à faire qch

provoking [prə'vəʊkɪŋ] adj (irritating) agaçant(e)

provost ['prɒvəst] n (**a**) Br Univ (head of college) doyen m (**b**) Scot (mayor) maire m

prow [praʊ] n (of ship) proue f

prowess ['praʊɪs] n (skill) prouesses fpl

prowl [praʊl] **1** n **to be on the p.** (of person, animal) être en chasse; **to be on the p. for sth** être à l'affût de qch **2** vt (streets, area) rôder dans **3** vi rôder

prowler ['praʊlə(r)] n rôdeur(euse) m,f

proximity [prɒk'sɪmɪtɪ] n proximité f; **in p. to** à proximité de

proxy ['prɒksɪ] (pl **proxies**) n (power) procuration f; (person) mandataire mf; **by p.** par procuration; Comput **p. server** serveur m proxy; Pol **p. vote** vote m par procuration

Prozac® ['prəʊzæk] n Prozac m

prude [pruːd] n prude f

prudence ['pruːdəns] n prudence f

prudent ['pruːdənt] adj prudent(e)

prudish ['pruːdɪʃ] adj pudibond(e)

prune¹ [pruːn] n (fruit) pruneau m

prune² vt (bush, tree) tailler; Fig (article) élaguer

prurient ['prʊərɪənt] adj malsain(e)

Prussia ['prʌʃə] n la Prusse

Prussian ['prʌʃən] **1** n Prussien(enne) m,f **2** adj prussien(enne)

pry [praɪ] (pt & pp **pried**) vi être indiscret(ète); **to p. into sth** mettre son nez dans qch

prying ['praɪɪŋ] adj indiscret(ète)

PS ['piː'es] n (abbr postscript) PS m

psalm [sɑːm] n psaume m

pseud [sjuːd] n Fam prétentieux(euse) m,f

pseudo- ['sjuːdəʊ] pref Fam pseudo-

pseudonym ['sjuːdənɪm] n pseudonyme m

PST [piːes'tiː] n Am (abbr **Pacific Standard Time**) heure f Pacifique

psyche ['saɪkɪ] n psychisme m

▸**psyche out** [saɪk] vt sep Fam (unnerve) déstabiliser

▸**psyche up** [saɪk] vt sep Fam **to p. sb up (for sth)** préparer qn psychologiquement (à qch); **to p. oneself up (for sth)** se préparer psychologiquement (à qch)

psyched [saɪkt] adj Am Fam surexcité(e)

psychedelic [saɪkə'delɪk] adj psychédélique

psychiatric [saɪkɪ'ætrɪk] adj psychiatrique

psychiatrist [saɪ'kaɪətrɪst] n psychiatre mf

psychiatry [saɪ'kaɪətrɪ] n psychiatrie f

psychic ['saɪkɪk] **1** n médium m **2** adj (**a**) (paranormal) paranormal(e) (**b**) (clairvoyant) **to be p., to have p. powers** être médium; Fam **I'm not p.!** je ne suis pas médium!

psycho ['saɪkəʊ] (pl **psychos**) n Fam dingue mf

psychoanalysis [saɪkəʊə'nælɪsɪs] n psychanalyse f

psychoanalyst [saɪkəʊ'ænəlɪst] n psychanalyste mf

psychoanalyze [saɪkəʊ'ænəlaɪz] vt psychanalyser

psychobabble ['saɪkəʊbæbəl] n Fam Pej jargon m des psychologues

psychological [saɪkə'lɒdʒɪkəl] *adj* psychologique; **p. warfare** guerre *f* psychologique

psychologist [saɪ'kɒlədʒɪst] *n* psychologue *mf*

psychology [saɪ'kɒlədʒɪ] *n* psychologie *f*

psychometric [saɪkə'metrɪk] *adj* psychométrique

psychopath ['saɪkəʊpæθ] *n* psychopathe *mf*

psychosis [saɪ'kəʊsɪs] (*pl* **psychoses** [saɪ'kəʊsi:z]) *n* psychose *f*

psychosomatic [saɪkəʊsə'mætɪk] *adj* psychosomatique

psychotherapist [saɪkəʊ'θerəpɪst] *n* psychothérapeute *mf*

psychotherapy [saɪkəʊ'θerəpɪ] *n* psychothérapie *f*

psychotic [saɪ'kɒtɪk] *adj* psychotique

PT [pi:'ti:] *n* (*abbr* **physical training**) EPS *f*

PTA [pi:ti:'eɪ] *n* Sch (*abbr* **Parent-Teacher Association**) ≃ APE *f*

ptarmigan ['tɑːmɪgən] *n* lagopède *m*

Pte *Mil* (*abbr* **private**) p. **Robbie McLean** = Soldat Robbie McLean

PTO [pi:ti:'əʊ] (*abbr* **please turn over**) TSVP

pub [pʌb] *n Br* pub *m*; **p. crawl** tournée *f* des bars; **p. quiz** jeu *m* de culture générale dans un pub

Pubs

Les Britanniques aiment aller prendre quelques verres entre amis, que ce soit dans un pub traditionnel ou dans un "wine bar" (bar à vin moderne), plus branché. La coutume est pour chacun de payer une tournée ("to buy a round"). On commande et on règle les consommations directement au bar – cependant de nombreux pubs servent désormais des repas le midi, qui eux sont le plus souvent apportés à sa table. De nombreux établissements proposent régulièrement des "pub quizzes" au cours desquels des équipes d'habitués se retrouvent pour répondre à des questions portant sur la culture générale posées par un animateur. L'équipe gagnante reçoit un prix d'une valeur modique, ou bien des consommations gratuites.

puberty ['pju:bətɪ] *n* puberté *f*

pubic ['pju:bɪk] *adj* pubien(enne), du pubis

public ['pʌblɪk] **1** *n* **the (general) p.** le grand public; **in p.** en public

2 *adj* public(ique); (*library, swimming pool*) municipal(e); **to go p. with** sth (*reveal information*) révéler qch (*à la presse*); **the company's going p.** la compagnie va être cotée en Bourse; **to make** sth **p.** rendre qch public; **to make a p. appearance** faire une apparition en public; **to be in the p. domain** être dans le domaine public; **at p. expense** aux frais du contribuable; **to be in the p. eye** être très en vue; **a p. figure** une personnalité en vue; **in the p. interest** dans l'intérêt du public; **p. address system** sonorisation *f*; **p. call box** cabine *f* téléphonique; **p. convenience** toilettes *fpl* publiques; *Com* **p. enterprise** entreprise *f* publique; **p. holiday** jour *m* férié; **p. house** pub *m*; *Am* **p. housing** logements *mpl* sociaux, ≃ HLM *f inv*; **p. library** bibliothèque *f* municipale; **p. limited company** ≃ société *f* anonyme; **p. opinion** l'opinion *f* publique; **p. ownership** nationalisation *f*, étatisation *f*; **to be under p. ownership** appartenir à l'état; *Law* **p. prosecutor** procureur *m*; **p. relations** relations *fpl* publiques; **p. school** *Br* école *f* privée, *Am* école *f*

publique; **p. sector** secteur *m* public; **p. spending** dépenses *fpl* publiques; **p. transport** transports *mpl* en commun; *Com* **p. utility** service *m* public

Public schools

En Angleterre et au pays de Galles, le terme "public school" désigne une école privée de type traditionnel. Certaines de ces écoles (Eton et Harrow, par exemple) sont très prestigieuses et élitistes. Les "public schools" sont censées former l'élite de la nation. Aux États-Unis et parfois en Écosse, le terme désigne une école publique.

publican ['pʌblɪkən] *n* patron(onne) *m,f* d'un pub

publication [pʌblɪ'keɪʃən] *n* publication *f*

publicity [pʌb'lɪsɪtɪ] *n* publicité *f*; **p. campaign** campagne *f* publicitaire; **p. stunt** coup *m* de pub

publicize ['pʌblɪsaɪz] *vt* faire connaître au public

publicly ['pʌblɪklɪ] *adv* publiquement; **p. owned** à capitaux publics

public-private partnership ['pʌblɪk'praɪvət'pɑːtnəʃɪp] *n* partenariat *m* public-privé

public-spirited ['pʌblɪk'spɪrɪtɪd] *adj (person)* qui a le sens civique; *(gesture, response)* dicté(e) par le sens civique

publish ['pʌblɪʃ] *vt* publier

publisher ['pʌblɪʃə(r)] *n (person)* éditeur(trice) *m,f*; *(company)* maison *f* d'édition

publishing ['pʌblɪʃɪŋ] *n* édition *f*; **p. house** maison *f* d'édition

pucker ['pʌkə(r)] **1** *vt (brow)* froncer; *(lips)* pincer

2 *vi (of face)* se rider; *(lips)* se plisser

pudding ['pʊdɪŋ] *n* (**a**) *(dessert)* dessert *m* (**b**) *(dish)* pudding *m*; **p. basin** *or* **bowl** jatte *f*

puddle ['pʌdəl] *n* flaque *f*

pudgy ['pʌdʒɪ] *adj* rondelet(ette)

puerile ['pjʊəraɪl] *adj Pej* puéril(e)

Puerto Rican [pweətəʊ'riːkən] **1** *n* Portoricain(e) *m,f*

2 *adj* portoricain(e)

Puerto Rico [pweətəʊ'riːkəʊ] *n* Porto Rico

puff [pʌf] **1** *n (of breath, air)* souffle *m*; *(of smoke, cigarette)* bouffée *f*; *Fam* **to be out of p.** être essoufflé(e); **p. pastry** pâte *f* feuilletée

2 *vt* **to p. smoke into sb's face** envoyer de la fumée à la figure de qn

3 *vi (of person)* souffler; *(of steam engine)* lancer des bouffées de vapeur; **to p. on a cigarette** fumer une cigarette

▶ **puff out** *vt sep (cheeks, chest)* gonfler

▶ **puff up** *vt sep (cheeks)* gonfler; **to be puffed up with pride** être gonflé(e) d'orgueil

Puffa jacket® ['pʌfədʒækɪt] *n* blouson *m* de rappeur

puffin ['pʌfɪn] *n* macareux *m*

puffy ['pʌfɪ] *adj* gonflé(e)

pug [pʌg] *n (dog)* carlin *m*; **p.-nosed** au nez camus

pugnacious [pʌg'neɪʃəs] *adj* pugnace

puke [pju:k] *Fam* **1** *n* dégueulis *m*

2 *vt & vi* dégueuler

pull [pʊl] **1** *n* (**a**) *(act of pulling)* traction *f*; *(of water current)* force *f*; **to give** sth **a p.** tirer qch; **to take a p. at a bottle** boire une gorgée d'une bouteille (**b**) *Fam (influence)* influence *f*; **to have a lot of p.** avoir le bras long

2 *vt* (**a**) *(tug)* tirer; **to p.** sth **open/shut** ouvrir/fermer qch; **to p. a muscle** se froisser un muscle; **to p. a pint** servir une bière; **to p. the trigger** appuyer sur

la gâchette; *Fig* **to p. sth to pieces** démolir qch; *Fam Fig* **to p. sb's leg** faire marcher qn; *Fam Fig* **p. the other one(, it's got bells on)!** à d'autres! (**b**) *(attract)* attirer (**c**) *(extract) (cork)* retirer, enlever; *(tooth)* arracher; **to p. a gun on sb** braquer un pistolet sur qn; *Fam Fig* **it's like pulling teeth** il faut t'/lui/*etc* arracher les vers du nez (**d**) *Br Fam (sexually)* **to p. sb** lever qn, emballer qn (**e**) *(idioms)* **to p. a face** faire la grimace; *Fam* **to p. a bank job** se faire une banque; *Fam* **to p. a fast one on sb** rouler qn
3 *vi* (**a**) *(tug)* tirer (**on** sur); **to p. clear of sth** s'éloigner de qch (**b**) *Fam (sexually)* **did you p. last night?** t'as levé une nana/un mec hier soir?
▸**pull about** *vt sep (handle roughly)* malmener
▸**pull ahead** *vi (in race, election)* prendre la tête (**of** de)
▸**pull apart** *vt sep (break up)* séparer; *Fig (criticize)* massacrer
▸**pull away** *vi (of car, train)* partir; *(from embrace)* s'écarter
▸**pull back 1** *vt sep (curtains)* ouvrir
2 *vi (of person)* se retirer
▸**pull down** *vt sep (demolish)* démolir
▸**pull in 1** *vt sep* (**a**) *(rope, fishing line)* ramener (**b**) *(money)* gagner; *(of deal)* rapporter; **to p. sb in for questioning** arrêter qn pour l'interroger (**c**) *(attract)* attirer
2 *vi (of car)* s'arrêter; *(of train, bus)* arriver
▸**pull off** *vt sep* (**a**) *(clothes)* retirer (**b**) *(task, deal)* réaliser; *(bank raid, burglary)* réussir; **to p. it off** réussir
▸**pull on** *vt sep (clothes)* enfiler, mettre
▸**pull out 1** *vt sep (tooth)* arracher; *Fam Fig* **to p. out all the stops** faire tout son possible
2 *vi* (**a**) *(of car)* déboîter; *(of train)* partir (**b**) *(from race, agreement, deal)* se retirer (**of** de)
▸**pull over** *vi (of driver)* s'arrêter
▸**pull through** *vi (recover)* s'en sortir
▸**pull together 1** *vt sep* **to p. oneself together** se ressaisir
2 *vi* agir de concert
▸**pull up 1** *vt sep Fig* **to p. one's socks up** se ressaisir; **to p. sb up (short)** couper qn dans son élan
2 *vi (of car)* s'arrêter
pull-down menu ['pʊldaʊn'menju:] *n Comput* menu *m* déroulant
pullet ['pʊlɪt] *n* poulette *f*
pulley ['pʊlɪ] *(pl* **pulleys)** *n* poulie *f*
pull-out ['pʊlaʊt] *n (in newspaper, magazine)* supplément *m* détachable
pullover ['pʊləʊvə(r)] *n* pull-over *m*
pulmonary ['pʌlmənərɪ] *adj* pulmonaire
pulp [pʌlp] **1** *n (of fruit)* pulpe *f*; **to reduce sth to (a) p.** écraser qch; *Fam* **to beat sb to a p.** mettre qn en bouillie; **p. fiction** romans *mpl* de gare
2 *vt* écraser
pulpit ['pʊlpɪt] *n* chaire *f*
pulsate [pʌl'seɪt] *vi (of vein)* palpiter; *(of room, music)* vibrer; *(of heart)* battre
pulse¹ [pʌls] *n (of blood)* pouls *m*; *(of light, sound)* vibration *f*; **to feel** *or* **take sb's p.** prendre le pouls de qn
pulse² *n (seed)* légumineuse *f*
pulverize ['pʌlvəraɪz] *vt also Fam Fig* pulvériser
puma ['pju:mə] *n* puma *m*
pumice ['pʌmɪs] *n* **p. (stone)** pierre *f* ponce

pummel ['pʌməl] *(pt & pp* **pummelled,** *Am* **pummeled)** *vt* marteler
pump¹ [pʌmp] *n (ballet shoe)* ballerine *f*; *(plimsoll)* tennis *m ou f*
pump² **1** *n (machine)* pompe *f*
2 *vt* pomper; **to p. sb's stomach** faire un lavage d'estomac à qn; *Fig* **to p. money into sth** injecter des capitaux dans qch; *Fam* **to p. sb for information** tirer les vers du nez à qn; **to p. sb's hand** *(shake vigorously)* donner une poignée de main vigoureuse à qn; *Fam* **to p. iron** *(do weightlifting)* faire de la gonflette
3 *vi (of heart)* battre; *(of machine)* pomper
▸**pump out** *vt sep* pomper
▸**pump up** *vt sep* gonfler
pumpkin ['pʌmpkɪn] *n* potiron *m*, citrouille *f*
pun [pʌn] *n* jeu *m* de mots
punch¹ [pʌntʃ] **1** *n (tool)* poinçon *m*; *(for tickets)* poinçonneuse *f*
2 *vt (metal)* percer; *(ticket)* poinçonner
punch² **1** *n* (**a**) *(blow)* coup *m* (de poing); *Fig* **she didn't pull her punches** elle n'y est pas allée de main morte (**b**) *(energy)* punch *m*; **p. line** *(of joke, story)* chute *f*
2 *vt (hit)* donner un coup de poing à; **to p. sb in the face/on the nose** donner un coup de poing à qn dans la figure/dans le nez
punch³ *n (drink)* punch *m*
Punch and Judy show ['pʌntʃən'dʒu:dɪʃəʊ] *n* ≃ spectacle *m* de Guignol

Punch and Judy

En Grande-Bretagne, le "Punch and Judy show" est un spectacle pour enfants semblable aux Guignols en France. Il est souvent présenté dans un jardin public ou sur une plage. On y retrouve Punch le bossu, sa femme Judy avec laquelle il se querelle constamment, et leur chien Toby.

punchbag ['pʌntʃbæg] *n* sac *m* de sable
punchball ['pʌntʃbɔːl] *n* punching-ball *m*
punch-drunk ['pʌntʃdrʌŋk] *adj* assommé(e)
punch-up ['pʌntʃʌp] *n Fam* bagarre *f*
punchy ['pʌntʃɪ] *adj Fam* plein(e) de punch
punctilious [pʌŋk'tɪlɪəs] *adj* pointilleux(euse)
punctual ['pʌŋktjʊəl] *adj* ponctuel(elle)
punctuality [pʌŋktjʊ'ælɪtɪ] *n* ponctualité *f*
punctually ['pʌŋktjʊəlɪ] *adv* à l'heure
punctuate ['pʌŋktjʊeɪt] *vt* ponctuer (**with** de)
punctuation [pʌŋktjʊ'eɪʃən] *n* ponctuation *f*; **p. mark** signe *m* de ponctuation
puncture ['pʌŋktʃə(r)] **1** *n (in tyre)* crevaison *f*; *(in skin, metal)* perforation *f*; **to have a p.** *(of cyclist, driver)* crever; *(of bicycle, car)* avoir un pneu crevé
2 *vt (tyre)* crever; *(metal, lung)* perforer; *(blister, abscess)* percer
pundit ['pʌndɪt] *n* expert(e) *m,f*
pungent ['pʌndʒənt] *adj (smell, taste)* âcre; *(style, wit)* mordant(e)
punish ['pʌnɪʃ] *vt* punir; **to p. sb for doing sth** punir qn pour avoir fait qch
punishment ['pʌnɪʃmənt] *n* punition *f*; *Law* peine *f*; **to make the p. fit the crime** adapter la punition à la faute; **to take a lot of p.** être mis(e) à rude épreuve
punitive ['pju:nɪtɪv] *adj* punitif(ive)
punk [pʌŋk] *n* punk *mf*; **p. (rock)** punk *m*

punnet ['pʌnɪt] *n* barquette *f*
punt¹ [pʌnt] **1** *n (boat)* barque *f* à fond plat
   2 *vi* **to go punting** faire de la barque
punt² [pʊnt] *n Formerly (Irish currency)* livre *f* irlandaise
punter ['pʌntə(r)] *n (gambler)* parieur(euse) *m,f; Fam (customer)* client(e) *m,f*
puny ['pju:nɪ] *adj* chétif(ive)
pup [pʌp] *n (of dog)* chiot *m; (of seal)* bébé-phoque *m*
pupil¹ ['pju:pəl] *n (student)* élève *mf*
pupil² *n (of eye)* pupille *f*
puppet ['pʌpɪt] *n also Fig* marionnette *f; Fig* **p. government** gouvernement *m* fantoche; **p. show** (spectacle *m* de) marionnettes *fpl*
puppy ['pʌpɪ] *(pl* **puppies)** *n* chiot *m;* **p. fat** rondeurs *fpl* préadolescentes; **p. love** amour *m* d'adolescence
purchase ['pɜːtʃɪs] **1** *n* (**a**) *(action, thing bought)* achat *m;* **p. price** prix *m* d'achat (**b**) *(grip)* prise *f;* **to get a p. on sth** trouver une prise sur qch
   2 *vt* acheter
purchaser ['pɜːtʃəsə(r)] *n* acheteur(euse) *m,f*
purchasing ['pɜːtʃəsɪŋ] *n* **p. manager** directeur(trice) *m,f* des achats; **p. power** pouvoir *m* d'achat
pure [pjʊə(r)] *adj* pur(e); **by p. chance** par pur hasard; **p. mathematics** mathématiques *fpl* pures
purebred ['pjʊəbred] *adj (dog)* de race pure; *(horse)* pur-sang *inv*
purée ['pjʊəreɪ] **1** *n* purée *f*
   2 *vt* réduire en purée
purely ['pjʊəlɪ] *adv* purement; **p. and simply** purement et simplement
purgatory ['pɜːgətərɪ] *n Rel* purgatoire *m; Fig* enfer *m*
purge [pɜːdʒ] **1** *n* purge *f*
   2 *vt* purger
purification [pjʊərɪfɪ'keɪʃən] *n* purification *f*
purify ['pjʊərɪfaɪ] *(pt & pp* **purified)** *vt* purifier
purist ['pjʊərɪst] *n* puriste *mf*
puritan ['pjʊərɪtən] *n* puritain(e) *m,f*
puritanical [pjʊərɪ'tænɪkəl] *adj* puritain(e)
purity ['pjʊərɪtɪ] *n* pureté *f*
purl [pɜːl] **1** *n* maille *f* à l'envers
   2 *vt* tricoter à l'envers
purloin [pɜː'lɔɪn] *vt Formal or Hum* dérober
purple ['pɜːpəl] **1** *n* violet *m*
   2 *adj* violet(ette); **to turn or go p.** *(of person)* devenir cramoisi(e); **pages of p. prose** des pages d'un style ampoulé
purport *Formal* **1** *n* ['pɜːpɔːt] teneur *f*
   2 *vt* [pɜː'pɔːt] **to p. to be sth** prétendre être qch
purpose ['pɜːpəs] *n* (**a**) *(object, aim)* but *m,* objectif *m;* **on p.** exprès; **what is the p. of your visit?** quel est l'objet de votre visite?; **to have a sense of p.** savoir ce que l'on veut; **to be to no p.** ne servir à rien (**b**) *(use)* utilité *f;* **to serve a p.** servir à quelque chose; **to serve no p.** ne servir à rien; **to serve sb's purpose(s)** faire l'affaire de qn; **for all practical purposes** à toutes fins utiles; **for the purposes of** pour les besoins de
purpose-built ['pɜːpəs'bɪlt] *adj* spécialement construit(e)
purposeful ['pɜːpəsfʊl] *adj* résolu(e)
purposely ['pɜːpəslɪ] *adv* délibérément; **to be p. rude** faire exprès d'être grossier(ère)
purr [pɜː(r)] **1** *n* ronron *m,* ronronnement *m*
   2 *vi* ronronner

purse [pɜːs] **1** *n Br (wallet)* porte-monnaie *m inv; Am (handbag)* sac *m* à main; **the public p.** le Trésor public; *Fig* **to hold the p. strings** tenir les cordons de la bourse
   2 *vt* **to p. one's lips** pincer les lèvres
pursue [pə'sju:] *vt* poursuivre; *(pleasure, happiness)* rechercher; *(profession)* exercer
pursuer [pə'sju:ə(r)] *n* poursuivant(e) *m,f*
pursuit [pə'sju:t] *n* (**a**) *(of person, animal)* poursuite *f; (of pleasure, knowledge, happiness)* quête *f;* **to be in p. of** être à la poursuite de; **in hot p.** à ses trousses (**b**) *(activity)* activité *f*
purveyor [pə'veɪə(r)] *n Formal* fournisseur(euse) *m,f*
pus [pʌs] *n* pus *m*
push [pʊʃ] **1** *n* (**a**) *(act of pushing)* poussée *f;* **to give sb/sth a p.** pousser qn/qch; *Fam* **to give sb the p.** *(of employer)* virer qn; *(of lover)* plaquer qn; **at a p.** à la rigueur; **when p. comes to shove, if it comes to the p.** dans le pire des cas (**b**) *Mil (attack)* poussée *f;* **sales p.** campagne *f* de vente; **to make a p. for sth** lutter pour qch
   2 *vt* (**a**) *(in general)* pousser; *(button)* appuyer sur; **to p. the door shut/open** fermer/ouvrir la porte; *(sign)* poussez; **to p. sb out of the way** écarter qn; **to p. one's way through the crowd** se frayer un chemin à travers la foule; *Fig* **don't p. yourself too hard** ne force pas trop; *Fig* **to p. sb into doing sth** pousser qn à faire qch; **to p. one's luck** y aller un peu fort; **to be pushed for time** être très pressé(e) (**b**) *(promote)* faire la promotion de; *(theory)* promouvoir (**c**) *Fam (drugs)* vendre (**d**) *Fam* **to be pushing sixty** approcher de la soixantaine
   3 *vi (in general)* pousser; *(move forward)* avancer; **to p. past sb** passer devant qn en le bousculant; **to p. forward** pousser en avant
▸**push about, push around** *vt sep Fam Fig (bully)* **to p. sb about** faire de qn ce que l'on veut
▸**push ahead** *vi* continuer; **to p. ahead with sth** continuer qch
▸**push aside** *vt sep also Fig* écarter
▸**push in** *vi (in queue)* resquiller
▸**push off** *vi Fam* ficher le camp
▸**push on** *vi (continue)* continuer; **to p. on with sth** continuer qch
▸**push over** *vt sep* faire tomber
▸**push through** *vt sep (reform, law)* faire passer
push-bike ['pʊʃbaɪk] *n Fam* vélo *m*
push-button ['pʊʃ'bʌtən] *adj* à touches
pushchair ['pʊʃtʃeə(r)] *n Br (for baby)* poussette *f*
pusher ['pʊʃə(r)] *n Fam* **(drug) p.** dealer *m*
pushover ['pʊʃəʊvə(r)] *n Fam* **it's a p.** c'est un jeu d'enfant; **she's no p.** elle ne se laisse pas avoir facilement
push-up ['pʊʃʌp] *n Am (exercise)* pompe *f*
pushy ['pʊʃɪ] *adj Fam* bataileur(euse)
puss [pʊs] *n Fam (cat)* minou *m*
pussy ['pʊsɪ] *(pl* **pussies)** *n Fam* **p. (cat)** minou *m;* **p. willow** saule *m* blanc
pussyfoot ['pʊsɪfʊt] *vi Fam* **to p. (around or about)** *(when speaking)* tourner autour du pot; *(in one's actions)* toujours remettre les choses à plus tard
pustule ['pʌstjuːl] *n* pustule *f*
put [pʊt] *(pt & pp* **put) 1** *vt* (**a**) *(place)* mettre; *(on flat surface)* poser; **to p. one's arms around sb** prendre qn dans ses bras; **to p. a man on the moon** envoyer un homme sur la lune; **to p. a limit on sth** mettre une limite à qch; *Fam* **p. it there!** *(shake hands)* tope là!;

Fig **to p.** oneself in sb's hands s'en remettre à qn; *Fig* **to p. sb in his place** remettre qn à sa place; *Fig* **p. yourself in my position** mets-toi à ma place; **to p. a matter right** mettre les choses au point; **to p. money on a horse** parier sur un cheval; **to p. a lot of work into sth** beaucoup travailler à qch; **to p. a stop to sth** mettre fin à qch; **to p. a child to bed** mettre un enfant au lit; **to p. sb to the test** mettre qn à l'épreuve; *Fam Fig* **I didn't know where to p.** myself je ne savais pas où me mettre (**b**) *(present)* **to p. a question to sb** poser une question à qn; **to p. a proposal to sb** soumettre une proposition à qn; **I p. it to you that...** *(in court)* n'est-il pas vrai que...? (**c**) *(express)* **to p. sth well** bien tourner qch; **I couldn't have put it better myself** je n'aurais pas mieux dit; **to p. it bluntly** pour parler franchement; **how shall I p. it...?** comment dire...? (**d**) *(estimate)* estimer (at à); **I'd p. her age at forty** je dirais qu'elle a quarante ans
2 *vi* **to p. to sea** prendre la mer
▸**put about** *vt sep (rumour)* faire courir; **to p. it about that...** faire courir le bruit que...
▸**put across** *vt sep (message, idea)* faire comprendre (to à); **to p. oneself across well/badly** *(at interview)* se mettre/ne pas se mettre en valeur
▸**put aside** *vt sep* (**a**) *(goods, money)* mettre de côté (**b**) *(problem, fact)* laisser de côté
▸**put away** *vt sep* (**a**) *(tidy away)* ranger (**b**) *Fam (prisoner)* enfermer (**c**) *Fam (eat, drink)* s'enfiler, ingurgiter
▸**put back** *vt sep* (**a**) *(replace)* remettre (**b**) *(postpone)* reporter; *(clock, schedule)* retarder; *Fig* **that puts the clock back ten years** cela nous ramène dix ans en arrière
▸**put by** *vt sep (save)* mettre de côté
▸**put down** *vt sep* (**a**) *(set down)* poser; **I couldn't put it down** *(book)* je ne pouvais pas m'arrêter de (le) lire (**b**) *(revolt, opposition)* réprimer (**c**) *(write)* écrire, mettre par écrit; **to p. sth down in writing** mettre qch par écrit; **to p. one's name down for sth** s'inscrire à qch (**d**) *(attribute)* **to p. sth down to sb/sth** attribuer qch à qn/qch (**e**) *(animal)* piquer; **to have a cat/dog put down** faire piquer un chat/un chien (**f**) *(criticize)* rabaisser; **to p. oneself down** se rabaisser
▸**put forward** *vt sep* (**a**) *(plan, theory, candidate)* proposer; *(proposal)* faire (**b**) *(clock, time of meeting)* avancer
▸**put in 1** *vt sep* (**a**) *(install)* installer (**b**) *(claim, application)* soumettre; **to p. in a (good) word for sb** dire un mot en faveur de qn (**c**) *(time)* passer; **they've p. in a lot of work** ils ont énormément travaillé
2 *vi (of ship)* faire escale
▸**put off** *vt sep* (**a**) *(postpone)* remettre à plus tard; **to p. off doing sth** retarder le moment de faire qch (**b**) *(cause to dislike)* **to p. sb off sth** dégoûter qn de qch (**c**) *(disturb)* gêner (**d**) *(discourage)* **to p. sb off doing sth** enlever à qn l'envie de faire qch (**e**) *(make wait)* faire patienter
▸**put on** *vt sep* (**a**) *(clothes)* mettre; **to p. on one's make-up** se maquiller; **to p. on an act** jouer la comédie; **to p. on an accent** prendre un accent; *Fam* **she's just putting it on!** elle fait semblant!; **to p. on weight** grossir, prendre du poids (**b**) *(light, TV, heating)* allumer; *(music, video)* mettre; **to p. the**

kettle on mettre l'eau à chauffer (**c**) *(play, show)* monter
▸**put out** *vt sep* (**a**) *(fire, light)* éteindre (**b**) *(place outside)* mettre dehors (**c**) *(extend)* **to p. out one's hand** tendre la main (**d**) *(arrange for use)* sortir (**e**) *(report, statement)* publier (**f**) *(annoy)* **to be put out** être contrarié(e) (**g**) *(inconvenience)* déranger; **to p. oneself out (for sb)** se donner du mal (pour qn) (**h**) *(dislocate)* **to p. one's shoulder/knee out** se démettre l'épaule/le genou
▸**put through** *vt sep* (**a**) *(on phone)* **to p. sb through to sb** passer qn à qn (**b**) *(subject to)* **to p. sb through sth** faire subir qch à qn; **to p. sb through hell** faire souffrir le martyre à qn
▸**put together** *vt sep (assemble)* assembler; *(file, report)* préparer; *(meal, team)* composer; **she's more intelligent than the rest of them put together** elle est cent fois plus intelligente qu'eux; *Fig* **to p. two and two together** tirer ses conclusions
▸**put up** *vt sep* (**a**) *(tent, fence)* monter; *(ladder)* dresser; *(building)* construire; *(statue)* ériger; *(notice)* afficher; *(painting)* accrocher; *(umbrella)* ouvrir; **to p. up one's hand** lever la main; **to p. one's hair up** relever ses cheveux (**b**) *(increase)* *(price, fee, rent)* augmenter (**c**) *(provide accommodation for)* loger, héberger (**d**) *(provide)* *(money)* verser, fournir; *(candidate)* présenter; **to p. sth up for sale** mettre qch en vente; **to p. up a fight** *or* **a struggle** se défendre
▸**put upon** *vt insep* **to feel put upon** se sentir exploité(e)
▸**put up to** *vt sep* **to p. sb up to doing sth** pousser qn à faire qch; **he put me up to it** c'est lui qui m'a poussé à le faire
▸**put up with** *vt insep* supporter
putative ['pjuːtətɪv] *adj Formal* putatif(ive)
put-down ['pʊtdaʊn] *n Fam* remarque *f* humiliante
putrefy ['pjuːtrɪfaɪ] *(pt & pp* **putrefied**) *vi* se putréfier
putrid ['pjuːtrɪd] *adj* putride
putsch [pʊtʃ] *n* putsch *m*
putt [pʌt] **1** *n (in golf)* putt *m*
2 *vi (in golf)* putter
putter ['pʌtə(r)] *n (golf club)* putter *m*
putty ['pʌtɪ] *n* mastic *m*; *Fig* **he's p. in her hands** elle en fait ce qu'elle veut
put-up job ['pʊtʌp'dʒɒb] *n Fam* coup *m* monté
puzzle ['pʌzl] **1** *n* (**a**) *(game)* casse-tête *m*; *(mental)* devinette *f*; *(jigsaw)* puzzle *m*; **p. book** livre *m* de devinettes et de jeux (**b**) *(mystery)* énigme *f*
2 *vt (person)* rendre perplexe
▸**puzzle out** *vt sep (solution, meaning)* trouver; *(action, motive)* essayer de comprendre
▸**puzzle over** *vt insep* essayer de comprendre
puzzled ['pʌzld] *adj* perplexe
puzzling ['pʌzlɪŋ] *adj* perplexe
PVC [piːviː'siː] *n (abbr* **polyvinyl chloride)** PVC *m*
Pygmy *(pl* **pygmies)** = Pygmy
pyjamas, *Am* **pajamas** [pə'dʒɑːməz] *npl* pyjama *m*; **a pair of p.** un pyjama
pylon ['paɪlən] *n* pylône *m*
pyramid ['pɪrəmɪd] *n* pyramide *f*; *Com* **p. scheme** plan *m* commercial en cascade
pyre ['paɪə(r)] *n* bûcher *m (funéraire)*
Pyrenean [pɪrə'nɪən] *adj* pyrénéen(enne)
Pyrenees [pɪrə'niːz] *npl* **the P.** les Pyrénées *fpl*
Pyrex® ['paɪreks] *n* pyrex® *m*

pyromaniac [paɪrəʊ'meɪnɪæk] n pyromane mf
pyrotechnics [paɪrəʊ'teknɪks] **1** n (science) pyro-
technie f

2 npl (fireworks display) feu m d'artifice; Fig (in
speech, writing) prouesses fpl
python ['paɪθən] n python m

Q, q [kjuː] *n (letter)* Q, q *m inv*
Qatar [kæˈtɑː(r)] *n* le Qatar
Qatari [kæˈtɑːrɪ] **1** *n* habitant(e) *m,f* du Qatar
   2 *adj* du Qatar
QC [kjuːˈsiː] *n Br Law (abbr* **Queen's Counsel**) = membre haut placé du barreau
QED [kjuːiːˈdiː] *(abbr* **quod erat demonstrandum**) CQFD
Q-tip® [ˈkjuːtɪp] *n Am* coton-tige *m*
qty *Com (abbr* **quantity**) qté
quack¹ [kwæk] **1** *n (of duck)* coin-coin *m*
   2 *vi (of duck)* faire coin-coin
quack² *n (doctor) Pej* charlatan *m; Hum* toubib *m*
quad [kwɒd] *n Fam (of school, college)* cour *f*
quad bike [ˈkwɒdbaɪk] *n* quad *m*
quadrangle [ˈkwɒdræŋgəl] *n* (**a**) *(shape)* quadrilatère *m* (**b**) *(of school, college)* cour *f*
quadrant [ˈkwɒdrənt] *n* quart *m* de cercle
quadraphonic [kwɒdrəˈfɒnɪk] *adj* quadriphonique
quadratic equation [kwɒˈdrætɪkɪˈkweɪʒən] *n Math* équation *f* du second degré
quadrilateral [kwɒdrɪˈlætərəl] **1** *n* quadrilatère *m*
   2 *adj* quadrilatéral(e)
quadriplegic [kwɒdrɪˈpliːdʒɪk] **1** *n* tétraplégique *mf*
   2 *adj* tétraplégique
quadruped [ˈkwɒdrʊped] *n* quadrupède *m*
quadruple [kwɒˈdrʊpəl] **1** *adj* quadruple
   2 *vt & vi* quadrupler
quadruplet [ˈkwɒdrʊplet] *n* quadruplé(e) *m,f*
quaff [kwɒf] *vt Lit* boire
quagmire [ˈkwægmaɪə(r)] *n also Fig* bourbier *m*
quail¹ [kweɪl] *(pl* quail) *n (bird)* caille *f*
quail² *vi (of person)* avoir un mouvement de recul
quaint [kweɪnt] *adj (picturesque)* pittoresque; *(old-fashioned)* vieillot(otte)
quake [kweɪk] **1** *n Fam (earthquake)* tremblement *m* de terre
   2 *vi* trembler; **to q. in one's boots** trembler de peur
Quaker [ˈkweɪkə(r)] *n Rel* quaker(eresse) *m,f*
qualification [kwɒlɪfɪˈkeɪʃən] *n* (**a**) *(diploma)* diplôme *m; (skill)* compétence *f* (**b**) *(completion of studies)* **on/after q.** une fois le diplôme obtenu (**c**) *(modification)* précision *f* (**d**) *(for competition)* qualification *f*
qualified [ˈkwɒlɪfaɪd] *adj* (**a**) *(having diploma)* diplômé(e); *(competent)* compétent(e); **to be q. to do sth** *(have diploma)* avoir les diplômes requis pour faire qch; *(be competent)* avoir les compétences requises pour faire qch (**b**) *(modified)* mitigé(e); **a q. success** un demi-succès

qualifier [ˈkwɒlɪfaɪə(r)] *n* (**a**) *(person, team)* qualifié(e) *m,f; (match)* match *m* de qualification (**b**) *Gram* qualificatif *m*
qualify [ˈkwɒlɪfaɪ] *(pt & pp* qualified) **1** *vt* (**a**) *(make competent)* **to q. sb to do sth** donner les compétences nécessaires à qn pour faire qch (**b**) *(modify)* nuancer
   2 *vi* (**a**) *(in competition)* se qualifier; **to q. as a doctor/teacher** obtenir son diplôme de médecin/professeur (**b**) *(be eligible)* **to q. for sth** avoir droit à qch
qualifying [ˈkwɒlɪfaɪŋ] *adj* (**a**) *(round, match)* éliminatoire (**b**) *(exam)* d'entrée
qualitative [ˈkwɒlɪtətɪv] *adj* qualitatif(ive)
quality [ˈkwɒlɪtɪ] *(pl* qualities) *n* qualité *f;* **of good/poor q.** de bonne/mauvaise qualité; **q. of life** qualité *f* de la vie; **q. circle** cercle *m* de qualité; **q. control** contrôle *m* (de) qualité; **q. goods** marchandises *fpl* de qualité; *Br* **q. newspaper** journal *m* sérieux; **she wants to spend more q. time with her children** elle veut passer davantage de temps avec ses enfants
qualm [kwaːm] *n* doute *m;* **to have no qualms about doing sth** *(doubts)* ne pas hésiter une seconde avant de faire qch; *(scruples)* n'avoir aucun scrupule à faire qch
quandary [ˈkwɒndərɪ] *(pl* quandaries) *n* dilemme *m;* **to be in a q. (about sth)** être face à un dilemme (à propos de qch)
quango [ˈkwæŋgəʊ] *(pl* quangoes) *n Br Pol (abbr* **quasi-autonomous non-governmental organization**) = organisme créé par le gouvernement et doté de pouvoirs quasi autonomes

Quango

En Grande-Bretagne, un "quango" est un organisme semi-public principalement financé par l'État mais disposant d'une certaine autonomie. Certains de ces organismes ont un rôle purement consultatif. D'autres sont habilités à prendre des décisions, notamment au niveau local, et c'est pourquoi au cours de ces dernières années les "quangos" ont fait l'objet de critiques, car leurs membres sont nommés par le gouvernement et non pas élus.

quantifier [ˈkwɒntɪfaɪə(r)] *n Math* quantificateur *m*
quantify [ˈkwɒntɪfaɪ] *(pt & pp* quantified) *vt* évaluer
quantitative [ˈkwɒntɪtətɪv] *adj* quantitatif(ive)
quantity [ˈkwɒntɪtɪ] *(pl* quantities) *n* quantité *f;* **q. surveyor** métreur vérificateur *m*
quantum [ˈkwɒntəm] *n Phys* quantum *m; Fig* **q. leap** bond *m* en avant; **q. mechanics** mécanique *f* quantique;

q. physics physique *f* quantique; **q. theory** théorie *f* des quanta

quarantine ['kwɒrəntiːn] **1** *n* quarantaine *f*; **to be in q.** être en quarantaine

2 *vt* mettre en quarantaine

quark [kwɑːk] *n Phys* quark *m*

quarrel ['kwɒrəl] **1** *n* (**a**) *(argument)* dispute *f*, querelle *f*; **to have a q.** se disputer; **to pick a q. with sb** chercher querelle à qn (**b**) *(disagreement)* désaccord *m*; **to have no q. with sb** n'avoir rien à reprocher à qn

2 *vi* (*pt & pp* **quarrelled**, *Am* **quarreled**) (**a**) *(argue)* se disputer (**with** avec) (**b**) *(disagree)* **to q. with sth** ne pas être d'accord avec qch

quarrelling, *Am* **quarreling** ['kwɒrəlɪŋ] *n* disputes *fpl*

quarrelsome ['kwɒrəlsəm] *adj* querelleur(euse)

quarry[1] ['kwɒrɪ] (*pl* **quarries**) *n (prey) & Fig* proie *f*

quarry[2] **1** (*pl* **quarries**) *n (for stone)* carrière *f*

2 *vt* (*pt & pp* **quarried**) *(hill)* exploiter; *(stone)* extraire

quart [kwɔːt] *n (liquid measurement) Br* = 1,136 l; *Am* = 0,946 l

quarter ['kwɔːtə(r)] **1** *n* (**a**) *(fraction)* quart *m*; *(of orange, moon)* quartier *m*; **a q. of a century** un quart de siècle; **a q. of an hour** un quart d'heure; **a q. (of a pound)** = 113,4 g, un quart de livre; **three quarters** trois quarts; **three and a q.** trois un quart; **three and a q. litres** trois litres un quart; **a q. full** au quart plein(e) (**b**) *(in telling time)* **a q. to six,** *Am* **a q. of six** six heures moins le quart; **it's a q. to** il est moins le quart; **a q. past six,** *Am* **a q. after six** six heures un ou et quart; **it's a q. past** il est le quart (**c**) *(three-month period)* trimestre *m* (**d**) *(area)* quartier *m* (**e**) *(group)* milieu *m*; **help came from an unexpected q.** nous avons reçu une aide inespérée (**f**) *Mil* **quarters** *(lodgings)* quartiers *mpl* (**g**) *Am (coin)* pièce *f* de 25 cents

2 *vt* (**a**) *(divide into four)* partager en quatre (**b**) *Mil (troops)* loger

quarterback ['kwɔːtəbæk] *n* quarterback *m*, *Can* quart-arrière *m*

quarterdeck ['kwɔːtədek] *n (of ship)* plage *f* arrière

quarterfinal [kwɔːtə'faɪnəl] *n* quart *m* de finale

quarterly ['kwɔːtəlɪ] **1** (*pl* **quarterlies**) publication *f* trimestrielle

2 *adj* trimestriel(elle)

3 *adv* tous les trimestres

quartermaster ['kwɔːtəmɑːstə(r)] *n Mil* intendant *m*

quarter-pounder [kwɔːtə'paʊndə(r)] *n* gros hamburger *m*

quartet [kwɔː'tet] *n* quatuor *m*

quarto ['kwɔːtəʊ] (*pl* **quartos**) *n* in-quarto *m*

quartz [kwɔːts] *n* quartz *m*; **q. watch** montre *f* à quartz

quasar ['kweɪzɑː(r)] *n Astron* quasar *m*

quash [kwɒʃ] *vt (objection, plan)* rejeter; *(revolt, feeling)* réprimer; *Law (sentence)* annuler

quaver ['kweɪvə(r)] **1** *n* (**a**) *Mus* croche *f* (**b**) *(in voice)* tremblement *m*

2 *vi (of voice)* trembler

quay [kiː] *n* quai *m*

quayside ['kiːsaɪd] *n* quai *m*

queasy ['kwiːzɪ] *adj* **to feel q.** avoir mal au cœur

Quebec [kwɪ'bek] *n (province)* le Québec; *(city)* Québec

queen [kwiːn] *n* (**a**) *(of country, in cards, chess)* reine *f*; *Fam Fig* **she's the q. bee around here** c'est elle la patronne ici; *Br* **Q.'s Counsel** = membre haut placé du barreau; **the Q.'s English** l'anglais *m* correct; **the Q. Mother** la reine mère (**b**) *very Fam (homosexual)* tante *f*, folle *f*, = terme injurieux désignant un homosexuel

queer ['kwɪə(r)] **1** *adj* (**a**) *(strange)* bizarre (**b**) *very Fam (homosexual)* homo, pédé

2 *n very Fam (male homosexual)* homo *m*, pédé *m*, = terme injurieux désignant un homosexuel

3 *vt Fam* **to q. the pitch for sb, to q. sb's pitch** bouleverser les plans de qn

quell [kwel] *vt (revolt)* réprimer; *(doubt, worry)* dissiper

quench [kwentʃ] *vt (thirst)* étancher

querulous ['kwerʊləs] *adj (person)* grincheux(euse); *(tone)* maussade, plaintif(ive)

query ['kwɪərɪ] **1** *n* (*pl* **queries**) question *f*

2 *vt* (*pt & pp* **queried**) mettre en question; **to q. if or whether...** mettre en question le fait que...

quest [kwest] *Lit* **1** *n* quête *f*, poursuite *f* (**for** de); **to go or be in q. of sth** être en quête *ou* à la poursuite de qch

2 *vi* **to q. after** *or* **for sth** être en quête *ou* à la poursuite de qch

question ['kwestʃən] **1** *n* (**a**) *(query)* question *f*; **to ask (sb) a q.** poser une question (à qn); **q. mark** point *m* d'interrogation; *Fig* **a q. mark hangs over the future of the project** l'avenir du projet reste en suspens; *Br Pol* **q. time** ≃ session *f* des questions orales *(à l'Assemblée nationale)* (**b**) *(doubt)* doute *m*; **to call sth into q.** mettre qch en doute; **beyond q.** indiscutable; **it's open to q. whether...** reste à savoir si...; **without q.** indiscutablement (**c**) *(matter)* question *f*, problème *m*; **it is a q. of...** il s'agit de...; **there is no q. of our agreeing to that** il n'est pas question que nous acceptions cela; **to be out of the q.** être hors de question; **it's only a q. of time** ce n'est qu'une question de temps; **the matter/person in q.** l'affaire/la personne en question

2 *vt* (**a**) *(put questions to)* interroger (**on** sur) (**b**) *(cast doubt on)* mettre en doute

questionable ['kwestʃənəbəl] *adj* discutable

questioning ['kwestʃənɪŋ] **1** *n (interrogation)* interrogation *f*; **to be held for q.** *(by police)* être interrogé(e)

2 *adj (look)* interrogateur(trice); *(mind)* curieux(euse)

questionnaire [kwestʃə'neə(r)] *n* questionnaire *m*

queue [kjuː] *Br* **1** *n* queue *f*, file *f* (d'attente); **to jump the q.** resquiller

2 *vi* faire la queue

queue-jump ['kjuːdʒʌmp] *vi Br* resquiller

quibble ['kwɪbəl] **1** *n* petite question *f*

2 *vi* chipoter *(about or over à propos de)*

quiche [kiːʃ] *n* quiche *f*

quick [kwɪk] **1** *adj* (**a**) *(rapid)* rapide; **to have a q. bath/drink** prendre un bain/un verre en vitesse; **to be q.** *(hurry)* faire vite; **that was q.!** tu as fait vite!; **to be q. as a flash** *or* **a wink** rapide comme l'éclair; **to be q. to do sth** faire qch vite *ou* rapidement; **to be q. off the mark** *(to act)* réagir vite; *(to understand)* avoir l'esprit vif; **to have a q. temper** s'emporter facilement (**b**) *(clever)* vif (vive)

2 *adv Fam Fam* vite

3 *n* **to bite one's nails to the q.** se ronger les ongles jusqu'au sang; *Fig* **to cut sb to the q.** piquer qn au vif

quicken ['kwɪkən] **1** *vt* (**a**) *(make faster)* accélérer; **to q. one's pace** presser le pas (**b**) *(imagination)* stimuler; *(interest)* éveiller, exciter

2 *vi (of pace, pulse)* s'accélérer

quickfire ['kwɪkfaɪə(r)] *adj* rapide
quickie ['kwɪkɪ] *Fam* **1** *n* **to have a q.** *(drink)* prendre un verre en vitesse; *(sex)* faire l'amour en vitesse
2 *adj* **q. divorce** divorce *m* rapide
quicklime ['kwɪklaɪm] *n* chaux *f* vive
quickly ['kwɪklɪ] *adv* vite, rapidement
quickness ['kwɪknɪs] *n (speed)* rapidité *f*; *(of mind)* vivacité *f*
quicksand ['kwɪksænd] *n* sables *mpl* mouvants
quicksilver ['kwɪksɪlvə(r)] *n Old-fashioned (mercury)* vif-argent *m*
quick-tempered ['kwɪk'tempəd] *adj* emporté(e)
quick-witted ['kwɪk'wɪtɪd] *adj* vif (vive)
quid [kwɪd] *(pl* **quid**) *n Br Fam (pound)* livre *f*
quiescent [kwaɪ'esənt] *adj Formal* passif(ive)
quiet ['kwaɪət] **1** *n* silence *m*; *Fam* **to do sth on the q.** faire qch en douce
2 *adj (not loud)* silencieux(euse); *(voice)* petit(e); *(music)* doux (douce); **to keep sb q.** faire tenir qn tranquille; **to keep q.** *(make no noise)* ne pas faire de bruit; *(say nothing)* se taire; **to keep q. about sth** ne rien dire au sujet de qch; **to keep sth q.** cacher qch; **be q.!** tais-toi!; **as q. as a mouse** *(person)* silencieux (**b**) *(discreet)* discret(ète); **to have a q. laugh at sb/sth** se moquer discrètement de qn/qch (**c**) *(peaceful)* tranquille; **a q. wedding** un mariage célébré dans l'intimité (**d**) *(business, market)* calme
▸**quiet down** = **quieten down**
quieten ['kwaɪətən] *vt* calmer
▸**quieten down 1** *vt sep* calmer
2 *vi* se calmer
quietly ['kwaɪətlɪ] *adv* (**a**) *(silently)* tranquillement, silencieusement (**b**) *(discreetly)* discrètement; **to be q. confident** être optimiste sans excès
quietness ['kwaɪətnɪs] *n (of person, place)* tranquillité *f*; *(of manner)* douceur *f*
quiff [kwɪf] *n (of hair)* toupet *m*
quill [kwɪl] *n (feather)* penne *f*; *(pen)* plume *f* d'oie; *(of porcupine)* piquant *m*
quilt [kwɪlt] **1** *n* édredon *m*; *(duvet)* couette *f*
2 *vt (garment)* matelasser; **quilted jacket** blouson *m* matelassé
quince [kwɪns] *n* coing *m*; **q. jelly** gelée *f* de coing
quinine [kwɪ'niːn] *n* quinine *f*
quintessential [kwɪntɪ'senʃəl] *adj Formal* quintessentiel(elle)
quintessentially [kwɪntɪ'senʃəlɪ] *adv Formal* fondamentalement
quintet [kwɪn'tet] *n* quintette *m*
quintuplet [kwɪn'tʊplɪt] *n* quintuplé(e) *m,f*
quip [kwɪp] **1** *n* boutade *f*
2 *vi (pt & pp* **quipped**) plaisanter

quirk [kwɜːk] *n* (**a**) *(of character)* particularité *f* (**b**) *(of fate, nature)* caprice *m*; **by a q. of fate** par un caprice du destin
quirky ['kwɜːkɪ] *adj* bizarre, insolite
quisling ['kwɪzlɪŋ] *n* collaborateur(trice) *m,f*
quit [kwɪt] **1** *vt (pt & pp* **quit**) *(person, place)* quitter; *Comput (programme)* sortir de; **to q. one's job** démissionner; **to q. doing sth** arreûter de faire qch
2 *vi (give up)* abandonner; *(resign)* démissionner; *Comput* sortir
3 *adj* **to be q. of** être débarrassé(e) de
quite [kwaɪt] *adv* (**a**) *(entirely)* tout à fait; **q. enough** bien assez; **that's q. enough of that!** ça suffit comme ça!; **q. apart from the fact that...** mis à part le fait que...; **q.!** tout à fait!; **that's q. all right** *(it doesn't matter)* ça n'a pas d'importance du tout; *(you're welcome)* mais pas du tout!; **you know q. well what I mean!** vous savez parfaitement ce que je veux dire!; **I q. understand** je comprends parfaitement (**b**) *(fairly)* assez, plutôt; **I q. like him** il me plaît bien; **q. a lot of people** pas mal de monde (**c**) *(for emphasis)* **it was q. a surprise** ça a été une véritable surprise; **it's been q. a day!** quelle journée!; **that film is q. something** ce film, c'est vraiment quelque chose!
quits [kwɪts] *adj* **to be q. (with sb)** être quitte (envers qn); **let's call it q.** restons-en là
quiver¹ ['kwɪvə(r)] *n (for arrows)* carquois *m*
quiver² **1** *n (tremble)* tremblement *m*
2 *vi (tremble)* trembler (**with** de); *(of flame)* vaciller
quivering ['kwɪvərɪŋ] *adj* tremblant(e)
quixotic [kwɪk'sɒtɪk] *adj* chimérique
quiz [kwɪz] **1** *n (pl* **quizzes**) *(on radio)* jeu *m* radiophonique; *(on TV)* jeu *m* télévisé; *(in magazine)* questionnaire *m*
2 *vt (pt & pp* **quizzed**) interroger
quizzical ['kwɪzɪkəl] *adj (look, air)* interrogateur(trice)
Quorn® [kwɔːn] *n* = aliment aux protéines végétales servant de substitut à la viande
quorum ['kwɔːrəm] *n* quorum *m*
quota ['kwəʊtə] *n (share)* quota *m*
quotation [kwəʊ'teɪʃən] *n* (**a**) *(from author)* citation *f*; **q. marks** guillemets *mpl*; **in q. marks** entre guillemets (**b**) *Com (for work)* devis *m*
quote [kwəʊt] **1** *n Fam* (**a**) *(from author)* citation *f*; **in quotes** *(in quotation marks)* entre guillemets (**b**) *Com (for work)* devis *m*
2 *vt* (**a**) *(author, passage)* citer; **she was quoted as saying that...** elle aurait dit que... (**b**) *Com (price)* indiquer; *Fin* **quoted company** société *f* cotée en Bourse
quotient ['kwəʊʃənt] *n Math* quotient *m*

R¹, r [ɑː(r)] *n (letter)* R, r *m inv*; *Fam* **the three R's** = la lecture, l'écriture et l'arithmétique, fondements de l'enseignement primaire

R² *Am Pol (abbr* **Republican***)* républicain(e)

RA [ɑːˈreɪ] *n Br (abbr* **Royal Academy***)* = académie royale des beaux-arts

rabbi [ˈræbaɪ] *n* rabbin *m*

rabbit [ˈræbɪt] *n* lapin *m*; **r. hole** terrier *m*; **r. hutch** clapier *m*

▸**rabbit on** *vi Fam* ne pas cesser de parler

rabble [ˈræbəl] *n* foule *f* bruyante; **r. rouser** agitateur(-trice) *m,f*

rabid [ˈræbɪd] *adj (animal)* & *Fig (person)* enragé(e); *(prejudice)* profondément enraciné(e)

rabies [ˈreɪbiːz] *n* rage *f*

RAC [ɑːreɪˈsiː] *n Aut (abbr* **Royal Automobile Club***)* = club automobile britannique offrant notamment des services de dépannage

raccoon [rəˈkuːn] *n* raton *m* laveur

race¹ [reɪs] **1** *n (contest)* course *f*; *Fig* **a r. against time** une course contre la montre; **the races** *(horseraces)* les courses *fpl*; *Am* **r. car** voiture *f* de course; **r. meeting** *(for horseraces)* courses *fpl* de chevaux
2 *vt* (**a**) *(person)* faire la course avec; **I'll r. you home!** on fait la course jusqu'à la maison! (**b**) *(horse)* faire courir
3 *vi* (**a**) *(of athlete, horse)* courir (**b**) *(move quickly)* aller à toute vitesse; **to r. in/out** entrer/sortir à toute vitesse; **to r. down the street** dévaler la rue à toute vitesse; **to r. by** *(of time)* passer vite, filer (**c**) *(of engine)* s'emballer; *(of pulse, heart)* battre la chamade

race² *n (of people, animals)* race *f*; **the human r.** le genre humain; **r. relations** relations *fpl* interraciales

racecourse [ˈreɪskɔːs] *n* champ *m* de courses

racehorse [ˈreɪshɔːs] *n* cheval *m* de course

racer [ˈreɪsə(r)] *n (person)* coureur(euse) *m,f*; *(bicycle)* vélo *m* de course

racetrack [ˈreɪstræk] *n (for athletes, cars)* piste *f*; *Am (for horses)* champ *m* de courses

racial [ˈreɪʃəl] *adj* racial(e); **r. discrimination** discrimination *f* raciale

racing [ˈreɪsɪŋ] **1** *n* les courses *fpl*
2 *adj Br* **r. car** voiture *f* de course

racism [ˈreɪsɪzəm] *n* racisme *m*

racist [ˈreɪsɪst] **1** *n* raciste *mf*
2 *adj* raciste

rack [ræk] **1** *n* (**a**) *(for bottles)* casier *m*; *(for plates)* égouttoir *m*; *(for goods in shop)* présentoir *m*; *(for luggage)* porte-bagages *m inv*; *(for goods in shop)* présentoir *m*; *(for luggage)* porte-bagages *m inv*; **r. and pinion** crémaillère *f* (**b**) *(for torture)* chevalet *m*; *Fig* **to be on the r.** avoir des ennuis (**c**) *(idioms)* **to go to r. and ruin** aller de mal en pis

2 *vt (torment)* tourmenter; **to be racked with guilt** être rongé(e) par le remords; **to be racked with pain** être tenaillé(e) par la douleur; **to r. one's brains** se creuser la tête

racket¹ [ˈrækɪt] *n (for tennis)* raquette *f*

racket² *n Fam* (**a**) *(noise)* vacarme *m*, tapage *m*; **to make a r.** faire du vacarme *ou* tapage (**b**) *(criminal activity)* racket *m*

racketeer [rækɪˈtɪə(r)] *n* racketteur *m*

racketeering [rækɪˈtɪərɪŋ] *n* racket *m*

racquet [ˈrækɪt] *n (for tennis)* raquette *f*

racy [ˈreɪsɪ] *adj (risqué)* osé(e); *(lively)* savoureux(-euse), piquant(e)

RADA [ˈrɑːdə] *n Br (abbr* **Royal Academy of Dramatic Art***)* ≃ le Conservatoire national d'art dramatique

radar [ˈreɪdɑː(r)] *n* radar *m*; **r. operator** radariste *mf*; **r. screen** écran *m* radar

radial [ˈreɪdɪəl] **1** *n (tyre)* pneu *m* radial
2 *adj* radial(e)

radiance [ˈreɪdɪəns] *n* éclat *m*, rayonnement *m*

radiant [ˈreɪdɪənt] *adj (light)* éclatant(e); *(person)* resplendissant(e)

radiate [ˈreɪdɪeɪt] **1** *vt (heat, light)* émettre; *Fig (happiness, health)* être rayonnant(e) de; *Fig (optimism, enthusiasm)* être débordant(e) de
2 *vi* rayonner (**from** à partir de)

radiation [reɪdɪˈeɪʃən] *n* radiation *f*

radiator [ˈreɪdɪeɪtə(r)] *n (heater)* radiateur *m*

radical [ˈrædɪkəl] **1** *n* radical(e) *m,f*
2 *adj* radical(e)

radicalism [ˈrædɪkəlɪzəm] *n* radicalisme *m*

radii [ˈreɪdɪaɪ] *pl of* **radius**

radio [ˈreɪdɪəʊ] **1** *n (pl* **radios***)* radio *f*; **r. alarm (clock)** radio-réveil *m*; **r. cassette (recorder** *or* **player)** radiocassette *m*; **r. station** station *f* de radio
2 *vt (pt & pp* **radioed***) (information)* communiquer par radio; *(person)* contacter par radio
3 *vi* **to r. for help** demander de l'aide par radio

Radio

Les principales stations de radio de la BBC sont : Radio 1 (musique pop et rock) ; Radio 2 (variétés) ; Radio 3 (musique classique) ; Radio 4 (actualités, reportages, théâtre, programmes éducatifs) ; Radio 5 Live (sport et actualités). La BBC comprend également de très nombreuses stations locales, ainsi que plusieurs stations de radio numériques spécialisées. Il existe d'autre part plus de cent stations indépendantes.

radioactive [reɪdɪəʊ'æktɪv] *adj* radioactif(ive); **r. waste** déchets *mpl* radioactifs
radioactivity [reɪdɪəʊæk'tɪvɪtɪ] *n* radioactivité *f*
radio-controlled [reɪdɪəʊkən'trəʊld] *adj* télécommandé(e)
radiographer [reɪdɪ'ɒɡrəfə(r)] *n* radiologue *mf*
radiography [reɪdɪ'ɒɡrəfɪ] *n* radiographie *f*
radiologist [reɪdɪ'ɒlədʒɪst] *n* radiologue *mf*
radiology [reɪdɪ'ɒlədʒɪ] *n* radiologie *f*
radiotherapy [reɪdɪəʊ'θerəpɪ] *n* radiothérapie *f*
radish ['rædɪʃ] *n* radis *m*
radium ['reɪdɪəm] *n Chem* radium *m*
radius ['reɪdɪəs] (*pl* **radii** ['reɪdɪaɪ]) *n* rayon *m*; **within a r.** of dans un rayon de
radon ['reɪdɒn] *n Chem* radon *m*
RAF [ɑːreɪ'ef] *n Mil* (*abbr* **Royal Air Force**) = armée de l'air britannique
raffia ['ræfɪə] *n* raphia *m*
raffish ['ræfɪʃ] *adj* canaille
raffle ['ræfəl] **1** *n* tombola *f*; **r. ticket** billet *m* de tombola
  2 *vt* donner comme lot à une tombola
raft [rɑːft] *n* radeau *m*
rafter ['rɑːftə(r)] *n* chevron *m*
rag¹ [ræɡ] *n* (**a**) (*piece of cloth*) chiffon *m*; **rags** (*clothes*) haillons *mpl*, guenilles *fpl*; **to go from rags to riches** passer de la misère à la richesse; **hers is a rags to riches story** elle est partie de rien; *Br Fam* **to lose one's r.** piquer une crise; **r. doll** poupée *f* de chiffon; *Fam* **the r. trade** la confection (**b**) *Fam Pej* (*newspaper*) torchon *m*
rag² **1** *n Old-fashioned* (*prank*) farce *f*, canular *m*; *Univ* **r. week** = semaine de divertissements organisés par les étudiants au profit d'œuvres de charité
  2 *vt* (*pt & pp* **ragged**) *Old-fashioned* (*tease*) taquiner
ragamuffin ['ræɡəmʌfɪn] *n* polisson(onne) *m,f*
rag-and-bone man [ræɡən'bəʊnmæn] *n* chiffonnier *m*
ragbag ['ræɡbæɡ] *n* ramassis *m*
rage [reɪdʒ] *n* (**a**) (*fury*) rage *f*, fureur *f*; **to be in a r.** être furieux(euse); **to fly into a r.** piquer une colère (**b**) *Fam* (*fashion*) **to be all the r.** faire fureur
  2 *vi* (**a**) (*of person*) être furieux(euse) (**against** *or* **at** contre) (**b**) (*of sea*) être démonté(e); (*of epidemic, war*) faire rage
ragga ['ræɡə] *n Mus* ragga *m*
ragged ['ræɡɪd] *adj* (*clothes*) en haillons, en lambeaux; (*edge*) irrégulier(ère); (*person*) en haillons; *Fam* **to run oneself r.** s'épuiser
raging ['reɪdʒɪŋ] *adj* (**a**) (*person*) furieux(euse); **to be in a r. temper** être furieux(euse) (**b**) (*sea*) démonté(e); (*fever, headache*) violent(e); (*thirst*) terrible
ragwort ['ræɡwɜːt] *n Bot* séneçon *m*
raid [reɪd] **1** *n* (*on bank*) hold-up *m inv*; (*by army*) raid *m*; (*by police*) descente *f*
  2 *vt* (*of robbers*) attaquer; (*of army*) faire un raid sur; (*of police*) faire une descente dans; *Fig & Hum* **to r. the fridge** faire la razzia dans le frigo
raider ['reɪdə(r)] *n* (*criminal*) voleur(euse) *m,f*
rail¹ [reɪl] *n* (**a**) (*of stairway*) rampe *f*; (*of balcony*) balustrade *f* (**b**) (*train system*) chemin *m* de fer; (*track*) rail *m*; **by r.** par le *ou* en chemin de fer; *Fig* **to go off the rails** (*of person*) s'écarter du droit chemin; **r. network** réseau *m* ferroviaire; **r. strike** grève *f* des chemins de fer
rail² *vi* **to r. at** *or* **against sth** s'insurger contre qch
railcar ['reɪlkɑː(r)] *n Am* wagon *m*

railcard ['reɪlkɑːd] *n* carte *f* d'abonnement de train; *Br* **young person's r.** ≃ carte *f* Jeunes
railings ['reɪlɪŋz] *npl* grille *f*
railroad ['reɪlrəʊd] **1** *n Am* (*system*) chemin *m* de fer; (*track*) voie *f* ferrée
  2 *vt Fam* **to r. sb into doing sth** forcer qn à faire qch
railway ['reɪlweɪ] *n Br* (*system*) chemin *m* de fer; (*track*) voie *f* ferrée; **r. carriage** voiture *f*; **r. line** ligne *f* de chemin de fer; **r. station** gare *f*
railwayman ['reɪlweɪmən] *n Br & Can* cheminot *m*
rain [reɪn] **1** *n* pluie *f*; **in the r.** sous la pluie; **it looks like r.** on dirait qu'il va pleuvoir; **the rains** la saison des pluies; **come r. or shine** (*whatever the weather*) qu'il pleuve ou qu'il vente; (*whatever the circumstances*) quoi qu'il arrive; *Fam Fig* **I'll take a r. check on that** ça sera pour une autre fois; **r. cloud** nuage *m* de pluie; **r. dance** danse *f* de la pluie
  2 *vt* **r. gifts on sb** couvrir qn de cadeaux; **to r. blows on sb** rouer qn de coups
  3 *vi* pleuvoir; **it's raining** il pleut; *Br Fam* **it's raining cats and dogs** il pleut des cordes; *Prov* **it never rains but it pours** un malheur n'arrive jamais seul
rainbow ['reɪnbəʊ] *n* arc-en-ciel *m*; **r. coalition** coalition *f* des minorités; **r. trout** truite *f* arc-en-ciel
raincoat ['reɪnkəʊt] *n* imperméable *m*
raindrop ['reɪndrɒp] *n* goutte *f* de pluie
rainfall ['reɪnfɔːl] *n* précipitations *fpl*
rainforest ['reɪnfɒrɪst] *n* forêt *f* tropicale humide
rainproof ['reɪnpruːf] *adj* imperméable
rainslicker ['reɪnslɪkə(r)] *n Am* ciré *m*
rainstorm ['reɪnstɔːm] *n* pluie *f* torrentielle
rainwater ['reɪnwɔːtə(r)] *n* eau *f* de pluie
rainy ['reɪnɪ] *adj* pluvieux(euse); (*day*) de pluie; *Fig* **to save sth for a r. day** mettre qch de côté; **the r. season** la saison des pluies
raise [reɪz] **1** *vt* (**a**) (*lift*) lever; **to r. one's voice** élever la voix; **to r. one's glass to one's lips** porter son verre à ses lèvres; *Fig* **to r. one's hat to sb** tirer son chapeau à qn; *Fam Fig* **to r. the roof** faire du raffut (**b**) (*price, salary*) augmenter; (*standard*) élever; *Fig* **to r. the stakes** faire monter la mise (**c**) (*problem, subject*) soulever; (**d**) (*fears, doubts*) faire naître; **to r. a smile/laugh** faire sourire/rire; **to r. sb's hopes** donner trop d'espoir à qn; **to r. the alarm** donner l'alarme; *Fam* **to r. hell** *or* **Cain** faire un foin d'enfer (**e**) (*money*) rassembler; (*for charity*) collecter (**f**) (*children, cattle*) élever; (*crops*) cultiver (**g**) (*statue*) dresser
  2 *n Am* (*pay increase*) augmentation *f* (de salaire)
raisin ['reɪzən] *n* raisin *m* sec
rake [reɪk] **1** *n* (**a**) (*garden tool*) râteau *m*; **to be as thin as a r.** être maigre comme un clou (**b**) (*dissolute man*) libertin *m*
  2 *vt* (*leaves, soil*) ratisser; **to r. one's memory** fouiller dans sa mémoire
▸**rake about, rake around** *vi* (*search*) fouiller (**for** pour trouver)
▸**rake in** *vt sep* (*money*) rapporter; **she's raking it in!** elle s'en met plein les poches!
▸**rake off** *vt sep Fam* (*money*) empocher
▸**rake over** *vt sep* (*subject, the past*) ressasser
rakish ['reɪkɪʃ] *adj* (*dissolute*) libertin(e); (*jaunty*) désinvolte
rally ['rælɪ] **1** *n* (*pl* **rallies**) (**a**) (*protest gathering*) manifestation *f* (**b**) (*in tennis*) échange *m* (**c**) (*car race*) rallye *m*; **r. driver** pilote *m* de rallye
  2 *vt* (*pt & pp* **rallied**) (*troops*) rallier; **to r. support for sb/sth** gagner des appuis à la cause de qn/qch; **to r.**

sb's spirits redonner courage à qn; **rallying cry** cri *m* de ralliement
3 *vi (of prices)* se redresser; *(of patient)* aller mieux; **to r. to sb's defence** se porter au secours de qn
▸**rally round 1** *vt insep* soutenir
2 *vi* apporter son soutien
RAM [ræm] *n Comput (abbr* **random access memory**) mémoire *f* vive
ram [ræm] **1** *n* (**a**) *(animal)* bélier *m* (**b**) *(implement)* (**battering**) **r.** bélier *m*
2 *vt (pt & pp* **rammed**) (**a**) *(crash into)* percuter; *(of ship)* aborder (**b**) *(force into place)* tasser; *Fam* **to r. one's views down sb's throat** bassiner qn avec ses opinions
Ramadan [ræmə'dɑːn] *n Rel* le ramadan
ramble ['ræmbəl] **1** *n (walk)* randonnée *f* (pédestre)
2 *vi* (**a**) *(walk)* faire une randonnée (**b**) *(digress)* divaguer
▸**ramble on** *vi* divaguer; **to r. on about sth** radoter à propos de qch
rambler ['ræmblə(r)] *n (walker)* randonneur(euse) *m,f*
rambling ['ræmblɪŋ] **1** *n* (**a**) *(walking)* **to go r.** aller en randonnée (**b**) **ramblings** *(words)* divagations *fpl*
2 *adj* (**a**) *(letter, speech)* décousu(e) (**b**) *(house)* plein(e) de coins et de recoins; **r. rose** rosier *m* grimpant
ramification [ræmɪfɪ'keɪʃən] *n (consequence)* conséquence *f*
ramp [ræmp] *n* rampe *f*; *(to plane)* passerelle *f*; *(on road)* petit dos *m* d'âne
rampage 1 *n* ['ræmpeɪdʒ] **to go on the r.** *(lose control)* se déchaîner; *(cause damage)* tout saccager
2 *vi* [ræm'peɪdʒ] **to r. about** se déchaîner
rampant ['ræmpənt] *adj* endémique; **corruption is r.** la corruption sévit
rampart ['ræmpɑːt] *n* rempart *m*
ramrod ['ræmrɒd] *n (for rifle)* écouvillon *m*; *Fig* **r. straight** raide comme un piquet
ramshackle ['ræmʃækəl] *adj (building)* délabré(e); *(economy, organization)* qui s'effondre
ran [ræn] *pt of* **run**
ranch [rɑːntʃ] *n* ranch *m*; **r. hand** ouvrier(ère) *m,f* agricole; **r. house** maison *f (sur un ranch)*
rancher ['rɑːntʃə(r)] *n* propriétaire *mf* de ranch
rancid ['rænsɪd] *adj* rance; **to go r.** rancir
rancour ['ræŋkə(r)] *n* rancœur *f*
rand [rænd] *n* rand *m*
R & D [ɑːrən'diː] *n (abbr* **research and development**) recherche *f* et développement *m*, R-D *f*
random ['rændəm] **1** *n* **at r.** au hasard
2 *adj (choice, sample)* (fait(e)) au hasard; *Comput* **r. access memory** mémoire *f* vive; **r. sampling** prélèvement *m* d'échantillons au hasard
R & R [ɑːrən'ɑː(r)] *n Mil (abbr* **rest and recreation**) permission *f*
randy ['rændɪ] *adj Br Fam* excité(e)
rang [ræŋ] *pt of* **ring²**
range [reɪndʒ] **1** *n* (**a**) *(of weapon, telescope)* portée *f*; **within r.** *(of fire)* à portée de tir; *(of hearing)* à portée de la voix; **out of r.** hors de portée (**b**) *(of prices, colours, products)* gamme *f*; *(of instrument, voice)* registre *m*; *(of knowledge, research)* étendue *f* (**c**) *(of hills, mountains)* chaîne *f* (**d**) *(practice area)* (**shooting**) **r.** champ *m* de tir (**e**) *(cooker)* fourneau *m*
2 *vt* (**a**) *(arrange in row)* ranger; **to r. oneself with sb** se ranger du côté de qn; **to r. oneself against sb** s'opposer à qn (**b**) *(travel)* parcourir

3 *vi* (**a**) *(extend)* **to r. from... to** aller de... à (**b**) **to r. over** *(include)* porter sur
rangefinder ['reɪndʒfaɪndə(r)] *n* télémètre *m*
ranger ['reɪndʒə(r)] *n (in forest)* garde *m* forestier; *Am Mil* commando *m*
rangy ['reɪndʒɪ] *adj* élancé(e)
rank¹ [ræŋk] **1** *n* (**a**) *(status)* grade *m*; *Fig* **to pull r.** abuser de son rang (**b**) *(row)* rangée *f*; *Mil* **the ranks** les hommes *mpl* du rang; *Fig* **to rise from the ranks** sortir du rang; *Fig* **the ranks of the unemployed** les rangs des chômeurs; *Fig* **to break ranks (with)** se désolidariser (de); *Fig* **to close ranks** se montrer solidaire; (**taxi**) **r.** station *f* de taxis
2 *vt* placer *(among* parmi); **to r. sb/sth as** considérer qn/qch comme
3 *vi* compter *(among* parmi); **to r. as** être considéré(e) comme; **to r. above/below sb** être supérieur(e)/inférieur(e) à qn; **this ranks as a major disaster** on peut qualifier ceci de catastrophe majeure
rank² *adj* (**a**) *(foul-smelling)* fétide (**b**) *(absolute)* total(e); **she's a r. outsider** elle n'est vraiment pas dans la course
rank-and-file [ræŋkən'faɪl] *n* **the r.** *(in army)* les hommes *mpl* du rang; *(of political party)* la base
ranking ['ræŋkɪŋ] *n (classification)* classement *m*
rankle ['ræŋkəl] *vi* **it still rankles with me** cela m'est resté sur l'estomac
ransack ['rænsæk] *vt (house, desk)* mettre sens dessus dessous; *(shop, town)* piller
ransom ['rænsəm] **1** *n* rançon *f*; **to hold sb to r.** rançonner qn; *Fig* retenir qn en otage
2 *vt* rançonner
rant [rænt] *vi Fam* déblatérer (**about/at** au sujet de/ contre); **to r. and rave** tempêter (**about/at** au sujet de/contre)
rap [ræp] **1** *n* (**a**) *(sharp blow)* coup *m* sec; *Fig* **to take the r. for sth** écoper *ou* trinquer pour qch (**b**) *(music)* rap *m*
2 *vt (pt & pp* **rapped**) *(window, door)* frapper à; *(table)* frapper sur; *Fig* **to r. sb's knuckles, to r. sb over the knuckles** taper sur les doigts de qn
3 *vi* (**a**) *(hit)* frapper (**on** à) (**b**) *(sing)* rapper
rapacious [rə'peɪʃəs] *adj* rapace
rape¹ [reɪp] **1** *n (crime)* viol *m*; *Fig (of countryside, environment)* destruction *f*
2 *vt* violer
rape² *n (crop)* colza *m*
rapid ['ræpɪd] *adj* rapide; **r. reaction force** force *f* d'intervention rapide
rapidity [rə'pɪdɪtɪ] *n* rapidité *f*
rapidly ['ræpɪdlɪ] *adv* rapidement
rapids ['ræpɪdz] *npl (in river)* rapides *mpl*
rapier ['reɪpɪə(r)] *n* rapière *f*
rapist ['reɪpɪst] *n* violeur *m*
rappel [rə'pel] *(pt & pp* **rappelled**) *vi Am* **to r. (down)** descendre en rappel
rappelling [rə'pelɪŋ] *n Am* rappel *m*
rapper ['ræpə(r)] *n (singer)* rappeur(euse) *m,f*
rapport [ræ'pɔː(r)] *n* **to have a good r. (with sb)** avoir de bons rapports (avec qn)
rapt [ræpt] *adj (attention)* profond(e); *(look)* absorbé(e); *(smile)* d'extase
rapture ['ræptʃə(r)] *n* extase *f*; **to be in raptures** être ravi(e); **to go into raptures over sb/sth** s'extasier devant qn/sur qch
rapturous ['ræptʃərəs] *adj (cries)* d'extase; *(applause)* frénétique; *(reception, welcome)* enthousiaste

rare [reə(r)] *adj* (**a**) *(animal, stamp)* rare; **to have a r.**
  gift (for sth) être exceptionnellement doué(e) (pour qch) (**b**) *(steak)* saignant(e)
rarefied ['reərɪfaɪd] *adj (air, gas)* raréfié(e); *Fig (atmosphere, ideas)* fermé(e)
rarely ['reəlɪ] *adv* rarement
raring ['reərɪŋ] *adj* **to be r. to do sth** être impatient(e) de faire qch; **to be r. to go** piaffer d'impatience
rarity ['reərɪtɪ] *(pl* **rarities**) *n* rareté *f*; **to be/become a r.** être/devenir rare; **r. value** rareté *f*
rascal ['rɑːskəl] *n (child)* coquin(e) *m,f; Old-fashioned or Hum (scoundrel)* vaurien(enne) *m,f*
rash¹ [ræʃ] *n* (**a**) *(on skin) (spots)* éruption *f; (red area)* rougeurs *fpl* (**b**) *(series)* série *f*
rash² *adj (imprudent)* irréfléchi(e)
rasher ['ræʃə(r)] *n Br (of bacon)* tranche *f*
rashly ['ræʃlɪ] *adv* sans réfléchir
rasp [rɑːsp] **1** *n* (**a**) *(tool)* râpe *f* (**b**) *(sound)* grincement *m*
  2 *vt (say hoarsely)* grogner
raspberry ['rɑːzbərɪ] *(pl* **raspberries**) *n (fruit)* framboise *f; (plant)* framboisier *m; Fam Fig* **to blow a r.** souffler en signe de dérision; **r. jam** confiture *f* de framboises
rat [ræt] **1** *n* (**a**) *(animal)* rat *m*; **r. poison** mort-aux-rats *f inv*; **r. trap** piège *m* à rats, ratière *f* (**b**) *Fam (scoundrel)* dégueulasse *mf* (**c**) *(idioms)* **to smell a r.** flairer quelque chose de louche; **r. race** foire *f* d'empoigne
  2 *vi (pt & pp* **ratted**) *Fam (inform)* **to r. on sb** dénoncer qn
ratchet ['rætʃɪt] *n* rochet *m*; **r. (wheel)** roue *f* à rochet
rate [reɪt] **1** *n* (**a**) *(of inflation, interest)* taux *m; Fin* **r. of return** taux *m* de rendement (**b**) *(speed)* rythme *m*; **at this r.** à ce rythme (**c**) **at any r.** en tout cas (**d**) *(price, charge)* tarif *m* (**e**) *Br Formerly* **rates** *(local tax)* impôts *mpl* locaux
  2 *vt* (**a**) *(classify)* placer (**among** parmi); **to r. sb/sth as** considérer qn/qch comme; **to r. sb/sth highly** tenir qn/qch en haute estime (**b**) *(deserve)* mériter; **to r. a mention** mériter d'être mentionné(e)
  3 *vi* **to r. as** être considéré(e) comme
rateable value ['reɪtəbəl'væljuː] *n Br Formerly* valeur *f* locative nette
ratepayer ['reɪtpeɪə(r)] *n Br Formerly* contribuable *mf (pour les impôts locaux)*
rather ['rɑːðə(r)] *adv* (**a**) *(preferably)* **I'd r. stay** j'aimerais mieux rester; **I'd r. not go** j'aimerais mieux ne pas y aller; **I'd r. not** je n'y tiens pas; **r. you than me!** je n'aimerais pas être à ta place (**b**) *(more exactly)* plutôt; **he sounded surprised or, r., annoyed** il semblait surpris, ou plutôt, fâché (**c**) *(fairly)* assez; **I r. liked it** j'ai bien aimé (**d**) **r. than him** plutôt que lui; **r. than staying** plutôt que de rester
ratification ['rætɪfɪkeɪʃən] *n* ratification *f*
ratify ['rætɪfaɪ] *(pt & pp* **ratified**) *vt* ratifier
rating ['reɪtɪŋ] *n (of popularity)* classement *m*; **the ratings** *(forTV, radio)* l'indice *m* d'écoute, l'Audimat® *m*
ratio ['reɪʃɪəʊ] *(pl* **ratios**) *n* rapport *m*
ration ['ræʃən, *Am* 'reɪʃən] **1** *n* ration *f; Fig (dose)* dose *f*; **rations** *(supplies)* provisions *fpl*; **r. book** carte *f* de rationnement
  2 *vt* rationner
rational ['ræʃənəl] *adj (sensible)* raisonnable, sensé(e); *(sane)* rationnel(elle)
rationalism ['ræʃənəlɪzəm] *n* rationalisme *m*
rationalist ['ræʃənəlɪst] *n* rationaliste *mf*

rationalization [ræʃənəlaɪ'zeɪʃən] *n (of company)* rationalisation *f*
rationalize ['ræʃənəlaɪz] *vt* (**a**) *(action, dislike)* justifier (**b**) *(company)* rationaliser
rationally ['ræʃənəlɪ] *adv (sensibly)* raisonnablement; *(sanely)* rationnellement
rationing [ræʃənɪŋ] *n* rationnement *m*
rattle ['rætəl] **1** *n* (**a**) *(for baby)* hochet *m* (**b**) *(noise) (of train, chains, keys)* cliquetis *m; (of gunfire)* crépitement *m; (of door, window)* frottement *m*
  2 *vt* (**a**) *(chains, keys)* faire cliqueter; *(door, window)* faire vibrer (**b**) *Fam (make nervous)* démonter
  3 *vi (of chains, keys)* cliqueter; *(of door, window)* vibrer
▸**rattle off** *vt sep Fam (list, facts)* débiter
▸**rattle on** *vi Fam* parler sans cesse
▸**rattle through** *vt insep Fam (work, book)* expédier
rattlesnake ['rætəlsneɪk] *n* serpent *m* à sonnette
ratty ['rætɪ] *adj Br Fam (annoyed)* irrité(e); *(irritable)* irritable
raucous ['rɔːkəs] *adj (hoarse)* rauque; *(rowdy)* bruyant(e)
raunchy ['rɔːntʃɪ] *adj Fam (film, scene, lyrics)* osé(e); *(dress)* provocant(e)
ravage ['rævɪdʒ] **1** *n* **ravages** *mpl*
  2 *vt* ravager
rave [reɪv] **1** *n* rave *f*
  2 *adj (review)* dithyrambique
  3 *vi (deliriously)* délirer; **to r. about sb/sth** *(enthusiastically)* être dithyrambique à propos de qn/qch
raven ['reɪvən] **1** *n (bird)* grand corbeau *m*
  2 *adj (colour)* noir de jais *inv*
ravenous ['rævənəs] *adj (animal)* vorace; *(person)* affamé(e)
raver ['reɪvə(r)] *n Br Fam (socially active person)* noceur(euse) *m,f; (who goes to raves)* raver *mf*
rave-up ['reɪvʌp] *n Br Fam* fiesta *f*, nouba *f*
ravine [rə'viːn] *n* ravin *m*
raving ['reɪvɪŋ] *adj* (**a**) *(delirious)* **r. mad** complètement fou (folle); **a r. lunatic** un fou furieux (une folle furieuse) (**b**) *(success)* éclatant(e)
ravish ['rævɪʃ] *vt* (**a**) *Lit (delight)* enchanter, ravir (**b**) *Old-fashioned (rape)* violenter
ravishing ['rævɪʃɪŋ] *adj* magnifique
raw [rɔː] *adj* (**a**) *(food)* cru(e); *(silk, sugar, statistics)* brut(e); **r. materials** matières *fpl* premières; **r. recruit** bleu *m* (**b**) *(skin)* écorché(e); *Fig* **to get a r. deal** être mal traité(e); *Fig* **to touch a r. nerve** toucher un point sensible (**c**) *(weather, wind)* glacial(e)
ray¹ [reɪ] *n (of light, sun)* rayon *m; Fig (of hope)* lueur *f*
ray² *n (fish)* raie *f*
rayon ['reɪɒn] *n (fabric)* rayonne *f*
raze [reɪz] *vt* **to r. sth to the ground** raser qch
razor ['reɪzə(r)] *n* rasoir *m*; **r. blade** lame *f* de rasoir
razor-sharp ['reɪzəʃɑːp] *adj (knife)* effilé(e); *Fig (intelligence, wit)* vif (vive)
razor-shell ['reɪzəʃel] *n* couteau *m*
razzmatazz ['ræzmətæz] *n Fam* tape-à-l'œil *m inv*
RC [ɑː'siː] *(abbr* **Roman Catholic**) **1** *n* catholique *mf*
  2 *adj* catholique
R & D [ɑːrən'diː] *n Com (abbr* **research and development**) recherche et développement
Rd *(abbr* **Road**) rue
RDA [ɑːdiː'eɪ] *n (abbr* **recommended daily allowance**) recommandation *f* quotidienne officielle *(en vitamines, sels minéraux etc)*

RE [ɑːˈriː] n (abbr **Religious Education**) instruction f religieuse

re¹ [riː] prep concernant; **re your letter** suite à votre lettre; **re: 1997 sales figures** Réf: les ventes de 1997

re² [reɪ] n Mus ré m

reach [riːtʃ] **1** n (**a**) (accessibility) portée f; **within r.** (thing) à portée de main; (location) tout(e) proche; **out of r.** hors de portée (**b**) (of river) **the upper reaches** l'amont m
2 vt (destination, conclusion) atteindre, arriver à; (agreement) aboutir à; (decision) prendre; **the news didn't r. her** les nouvelles ne lui sont pas parvenues (**b**) (contact) joindre; **to r. a wider audience** toucher un public plus important (**c**) (stretch as far as) atteindre, arriver jusqu'à
3 vi (extend) (of forest, property) s'étendre (**to** jusqu'à); (of noise, voice) porter (**to** jusqu'à); **to r. for sth** tendre le bras pour prendre qch; Fig **to r. for the sky** or **the stars** viser très haut
▸**reach out** vi tendre le bras

reachable [ˈriːtʃəbəl] adj accessible

react [rɪˈækt] vi réagir (**against/to** contre/à)

reaction [rɪˈækʃən] n réaction f

reactionary [rɪˈækʃənərɪ] (pl **reactionaries**) **1** n réactionnaire mf
2 adj réactionnaire

reactivate [rɪˈæktɪveɪt] vt réactiver

reactor [rɪˈæktə(r)] n réacteur m

read [riːd] **1** n to have a r. lire; **her books are a good r.** ses livres se lisent bien
2 vt (pt & pp **read** [red]) (**a**) (book, newspaper, letter) lire; **do you r. me?** (on radio) est-ce que vous me recevez?; Fig **to take it as read that...** considérer comme acquis que... (**b**) (interpret) interpréter; **to r. sb's mind** lire dans les pensées de qn; **to r. the future** prédire l'avenir (**c**) Br Univ (study) étudier (**d**) (of dial, thermometer) indiquer; (of inscription) être; **the sign read...** sur l'écriteau, on pouvait lire...
3 vi (**a**) (of person) lire; **to r. aloud** lire à haute voix; **I'd read about it in the newspapers** je l'avais lu dans les journaux; Fig **to r. between the lines** lire entre les lignes (**b**) (of text) **to r. well/badly** se lire facilement/difficilement
▸**read out** vt sep lire (à haute voix)
▸**read up on** vt sep étudier

readable [ˈriːdəbəl] adj (book) facile à lire; (handwriting) lisible

reader [ˈriːdə(r)] n (**a**) (of book, newspaper etc) lecteur(trice) m,f (**b**) (reading book) livre m de lecture (**c**) (device) lecteur m (**d**) Am Univ ≃ assistant(e) m,f; Can Univ ≃ chargé(e) m,f de cours

readily [ˈredɪlɪ] adv (willingly) volontiers; (easily) facilement

reading [ˈriːdɪŋ] n (**a**) (action, interpretation, pastime) lecture f; **r. glasses** lunettes fpl de lecture (**b**) (measurement) relevé m

readjust [riːəˈdʒʌst] **1** vt (figures, salaries) réajuster; (instrument) remettre au point; (clothing) rajuster
2 vi se réadapter (**to** à)

readjustment [riːəˈdʒʌstmənt] n (of figures, salaries) réajustement m; (of person) réadaptation f

readmit [riːədˈmɪt] (pt & pp **readmitted**) vt (to club, party) réintégrer (**to** à); **to r. sb (to hospital)** réhospitaliser qn

read-only [ˈriːdˈəʊnlɪ] adj Comput (file) à lecture seule; **r. memory** mémoire f morte

readvertise [riːˈædvətaɪz] vt repasser une annonce pour

ready [ˈredɪ] **1** adj (**a**) (prepared) prêt(e) (**for** pour); **to be r. to do sth** être prêt à faire qch; **to get r.** se préparer; **to get sth r.** préparer qch; **to be r. for bed** être prêt à se coucher; **r.!, steady!, go!** à vos marques, prêts, partez!; **r. cash** argent m liquide (**b**) (willing) **to be r. to do sth** être prêt(e) ou disposé(e) à faire qch (**c**) (quick) **to have a r. wit** avoir l'esprit vif
2 vt (pt & pp **readied**) (prepare) préparer
3 n (**a**) **at the r.** prêt(e) (**b**) Fam **readies** (cash) ronds mpl

ready-made [redɪˈmeɪd] adj (food) tout(e) préparé(e); (excuse, phrase) tout(e) fait(e)

reaffirm [riːəˈfɜːm] vt réaffirmer

reafforestation [riːəfɒrɪˈsteɪʃən] n reboisement m

real [rɪəl] **1** adj (**a**) (authentic) vrai(e); (gold, leather) véritable; (danger, fear, effort) réel(elle); **r. ale** = bière brune de fabrication traditionnelle (**b**) (actual) réel(elle); **the r. world** la réalité; **what does that mean in r. terms?** qu'est-ce que cela signifie en clair?; Com **r. estate** (property) biens mpl immobiliers; (profession) l'immobilier m (**c**) (for emphasis) **a r. idiot** un(e) véritable idiot(e)
2 adv Am Fam (very) très

realism [ˈrɪəlɪzəm] n réalisme m

realist [ˈrɪəlɪst] n réaliste mf

realistic [rɪəˈlɪstɪk] adj réaliste

reality [rɪˈælɪtɪ] (pl **realities**) n réalité f; **in r.** en réalité; Fam **it was a r. check for him** ça l'a ramené à la réalité; TV **r. show** reality show m; **r. television**, Fam **r. TV** télé-réalité f

realize [ˈrɪəlaɪz] vt (**a**) (become aware of) se rendre compte de; **I r. he's busy, but...** j'ai bien conscience qu'il est occupé mais... (**b**) (ambition, dream) réaliser

really [ˈrɪəlɪ] adv vraiment; (in actual fact) en réalité

realm [relm] n (**a**) (kingdom) royaume m (**b**) (field) domaine m

Realtor [ˈrɪəltə(r)] n Am agent m immobilier

ream [riːm] n (of paper) rame f; Fig **reams of** des quantités de

reanimate [riːˈænɪmeɪt] vt r(é)animer

reap [riːp] vt moissonner; **to r. the benefits (of)** récolter les bénéfices (de); Prov **you r. what you sow** comme tu auras semé tu moissonneras

reaper [ˈriːpə(r)] n (machine) moissonneuse f; Lit **the Grim R.** la Faucheuse

reappear [riːəˈpɪə(r)] vi réapparaître

reappearance [riːəˈpɪərəns] n réapparition f

reapply [riːəˈplaɪ] (pt & pp **reapplied**) vi (for job) poser à nouveau sa candidature (**for** à)

reappraise [riːəˈpreɪz] vt réévaluer; (policy) réexaminer

rear¹ [rɪə(r)] n (**a**) (back part) arrière m; **at the r. of** (inside) à l'arrière de; (behind) derrière; **in the r.** à l'arrière; **to bring up the r.** être en queue; **r. admiral** contre-amiral m; **r. entrance** entrée f de derrière; **r. legs** pattes fpl de derrière; **r. lights** feux mpl arrière; **r. window** vitre f arrière (**b**) Fam (buttocks) derrière m

rear² vt (**a**) (child, livestock) élever (**b**) (one's head) relever; Fig **to r. its ugly head** faire son apparition
▸**rear up** vi (of horse) se cabrer

rearguard [ˈrɪəɡɑːd] n Mil arrière-garde f; also Fig **r. action** combat m d'arrière-garde

rearm [riːˈɑːm] vt & vi réarmer

rearmament [riːˈɑːməmənt] n réarmement m

rearrange [riːəˈreɪndʒ] *vt (books, furniture)* changer la disposition de; *(appointment)* changer
reason [ˈriːzən] **1** *n* (**a**) *(cause, motive)* raison *f* (**for** de); **for no particular r.** sans raison précise; **I don't know the r.** why je ne sais pas pourquoi; *Ironic* **for reasons best known to himself** pour une raison connue de lui seul; **give me one good r.** why **I should!** donne-moi une raison valable de le faire! (**b**) *(sanity, common sense)* raison *f*; **to listen to** or **see r.** entendre raison; **it stands to r.** il va de soi ou sans dire; **within r.** dans des limites raisonnables
   2 *vt* **to r.** **that** estimer que
   3 *vi* raisonner (**about/with** sur/avec)
reasonable [ˈriːzənəbəl] *adj* (**a**) *(fair)* raisonnable; *(excuse)* valable (**b**) *(quite good)* passable
reasonably [ˈriːzənəblɪ] *adv* (**a**) *(behave, act)* raisonnablement (**b**) *(quite)* plutôt
reasoning [ˈriːzənɪŋ] *n (thinking)* raisonnement *m*
reassemble [riːəˈsembəl] **1** *vt (people)* rassembler; *(machine)* remonter
   2 *vi (of people)* se rassembler
reassess [riːəˈses] *vt* (**a**) *(policy, situation)* reconsidérer (**b**) *Fin (tax, property)* réévaluer
reassurance [riːəˈʃʊərəns] *n (comfort)* réconfort *m*; *(guarantee)* assurance *f*
reassure [riːəˈʃʊə(r)] *vt* rassurer
reassuring [riːəˈʃʊərɪŋ] *adj* rassurant(e)
reawaken [riːəˈweɪkən] **1** *vt (interest, feeling)* faire renaître
   2 *vi (of person)* se réveiller à nouveau
rebate [ˈriːbeɪt] *n (refund)* remboursement *m*; *(discount)* rabais *m*
rebel 1 *n* [ˈrebəl] rebelle *mf*
   2 *vi* [rɪˈbel] *(pt & pp* **rebelled***)* se rebeller (**against** contre)
rebellion [rɪˈbeljən] *n* rébellion *f*
rebellious [rɪˈbeljəs] *adj* rebelle
rebirth [riːˈbɜːθ] *n* renaissance *f*
reboot [riːˈbuːt] *Comput* **1** *vt* réamorcer
   2 *vi* se réamorcer
reborn [riːˈbɔːn] *adj* **to be r.** renaître
rebound 1 *n* [ˈriːbaʊnd] *(of ball)* rebond *m*; *Fig* **she married him on the r.** elle l'a épousé à la suite d'une déception sentimentale
   2 *vi* [rɪˈbaʊnd] *(of ball)* rebondir; *Fig (of joke, lie)* se retourner (**on** contre)
rebuff [rɪˈbʌf] **1** *n (of person)* rebuffade *f*; *(of suggestion)* refus *m*; **to meet with a r.** *(of person)* essuyer une rebuffade; *(of suggestion)* être repoussé(e)
   2 *vt* repousser
rebuild [riːˈbɪld] *(pt & pp* **rebuilt** [riːˈbɪlt]*)* *vt* reconstruire
rebuke [rɪˈbjuːk] **1** *n* réprimande *f*
   2 *vt* réprimander
rebut [rɪˈbʌt] *(pt & pp* **rebutted***)* *vt* réfuter
rebuttal [rɪˈbʌtəl] *n* réfutation *f*
recalcitrant [rɪˈkælsɪtrənt] *adj* récalcitrant(e)
recall 1 *n* [ˈriːkɔːl] *(memory)* mémoire *f*; **lost beyond r.** irrévocablement perdu(e)
   2 *vt* [rɪˈkɔːl] (**a**) *(remember)* se souvenir de, se rappeler; **to r.** doing sth se souvenir d'avoir fait qch, se rappeler avoir fait qch (**b**) *(defective goods)* rappeler; *(library book)* demander le retour de; *Br Pol* **to r. Parliament** rappeler le Parlement en session extraordinaire
recant [rɪˈkænt] **1** *vt (opinion)* rétracter
   2 *vi* se rétracter

recap 1 *n* [ˈriːkæp] *(summary)* récapitulation *f*
   2 *vi* [riːˈkæp] *(pt & pp* **recapped***)* récapituler
recapitulate [riːkəˈpɪtjʊleɪt] *vt & vi* récapituler
recapture [riːˈkæptʃə(r)] **1** *n (of criminal)* capture *f*; *(of town, territory)* reprise *f*
   2 *vt* (**a**) *(criminal)* capturer; *(town, territory)* reprendre (**b**) *Fig (memory, atmosphere)* faire revivre; *(one's youth)* retrouver
recede [rɪˈsiːd] *vi (of tide)* se retirer; *(of coastline)* reculer; **to have a receding chin** avoir le menton fuyant; **to have a receding hairline** avoir le front qui se dégarnit
receipt [rɪˈsiːt] *n* (**a**) *(act of receiving)* réception *f*; **to be in r. of sth** avoir reçu qch (**b**) *(proof of payment)* reçu *m*; **receipts** *(at box office)* recette *f*, entrées *fpl*
receive [rɪˈsiːv] *vt* recevoir; *(stolen goods)* receler; **to be well/badly received** *(of film, proposal)* être bien/mal reçu(e); **to r. sb into the Church** admettre qn au sein de l'Église
received [rɪˈsiːvd] *adj (idea)* reçu(e); *(opinion)* admis(e); **r. pronunciation** = prononciation standard de l'anglais *(celle du sud-est de l'Angleterre)*
receiver [rɪˈsiːvə(r)] *n* (**a**) *(of stolen goods)* receleur(euse) *m,f* (**b**) *(of telephone, radio set)* récepteur *m*; **to pick up the r.** décrocher; **to replace the r.** raccrocher (**c**) *Fin* administrateur *m* judiciaire
receivership [rɪˈsiːvəʃɪp] *n Fin* **to go into r.** être placé(e) sous règlement judiciaire
receiving [rɪˈsiːvɪŋ] **1** *n (of stolen goods)* recel *m*
   2 *adj Fam* **to be on the r. end (of sth)** faire les frais (de qch)
recent [ˈriːsənt] *adj* récent(e); *(acquaintance)* nouveau(elle); *(development)* dernier(ère); **in r. months** au cours des derniers mois; **in r. times** récemment
recently [ˈriːsəntlɪ] *adv* récemment; **as r. as yesterday** pas plus tard qu'hier; **until quite r.** jusqu'à ces derniers temps
receptacle [rɪˈseptəkəl] *n* récipient *m*
reception [rɪˈsepʃən] *n* (**a**) *(of guests, announcement, book)* accueil *m*; **to get a warm r.** être accueilli(e) chaleureusement; **to get a frosty r.** être reçu froidement; **r. centre** *(for refugees)* centre *m* d'accueil; **room** *(in house)* salon *m* (**b**) *(party)* réception *f*; **(wedding) r.** réception *f* (**c**) *(in hotel)* r. **(desk)** réception *f* (**d**) *(of radio, TV programme)* réception *f*
receptionist [rɪˈsepʃənɪst] *n* réceptionniste *mf*
receptive [rɪˈseptɪv] *adj* réceptif(ive)
recess [ˈriːses] *n* (**a**) *(of law courts, Parliament)* vacances *fpl* (**b**) *(in wall)* renfoncement *m*; *(smaller)* niche *f*; *(of mind, past)* recoins *mpl* (**c**) *Am Sch (between classes)* récréation *f*
recession [rɪˈseʃən] *n* récession *f*
recharge [riːˈtʃɑːdʒ] *vt (battery)* recharger; *Fig* **to r. one's batteries** recharger ses batteries
rechargeable [riːˈtʃɑːdʒəbəl] *adj* rechargeable
recharger [riːˈtʃɑːdʒə(r)] *n (for battery)* chargeur *m*
recidivism [rɪˈsɪdɪvɪzəm] *n Law* récidivisme *m*
recipe [ˈresɪpɪ] *n also Fig* recette *f*; **a r. for success** le secret de la réussite; **to be a r. for disaster** mener à la catastrophe; **r. book** livre *m* de recettes
recipient [rɪˈsɪpɪənt] *n (of gift, letter)* destinataire *mf*; *(of cheque, money)* bénéficiaire *mf*; *(of award, honour)* lauréat(e) *m,f*
reciprocal [rɪˈsɪprəkəl] *adj* réciproque
reciprocate [rɪˈsɪprəkeɪt] **1** *vt* retourner
   2 *vi* rendre la pareille
recital [rɪˈsaɪtəl] *n (of poetry, music)* récital *m*

recitation [resɪ'teɪʃən] n (of poem) récitation f
recite [rɪ'saɪt] **1** vt (poem) réciter; (complaints, details) énumérer
  2 vi réciter
reckless ['reklɪs] adj imprudent(e); **r. driver** chauffard m
reckon ['rekən] **1** vt (**a**) (consider) considérer; **she is reckoned to be...** on la considère comme... (**b**) (calculate) calculer (**c**) Fam (think) penser
  2 vi compter, calculer
▸**reckon on** vt insep compter sur
▸**reckon up** vt sep calculer
▸**reckon with** vt insep compter avec
reckoning ['rekənɪŋ] n estimation f; **by my r.** d'après mes calculs; **day of r.** moment m de vérité
reclaim [rɪ'kleɪm] vt (lost property, waste materials) récupérer; (expenses) se faire rembourser; **to r. land from the sea/the desert** gagner du terrain sur la mer/le désert
reclamation [reklə'meɪʃən] n (of waste materials) récupération f
recline [rɪ'klaɪn] vi s'allonger
reclining [rɪ'klaɪnɪŋ] adj **in a r. position** (person) en position allongée; **r. seat** siège m à dossier inclinable
recluse [rɪ'kluːs] n reclus(e) m,f
recognition [rekəg'nɪʃən] n reconnaissance f; **to have changed beyond** or **out of all r.** être devenu(e) méconnaissable; **in r. of** en reconnaissance de
recognizable [rekəg'naɪzəbəl] adj reconnaissable
recognize ['rekəgnaɪz] vt reconnaître
recognized ['rekəgnaɪzd] adj reconnu(e); **to be a r. authority (on sth)** faire autorité (en matière de qch)
recoil 1 n ['riːkɔɪl] (of gun) recul m
  2 vi [rɪ'kɔɪl] (of gun) reculer; (of person) avoir un mouvement de recul
recollect [rekə'lekt] vt se souvenir de
recollection [rekə'lekʃən] n souvenir m; **to the best of my r.** autant que je m'en souvienne
recommend [rekə'mend] vt (**a**) (praise) recommander; **to r. sth to sb** recommander qch à qn; **the proposal has a lot to r. it** cette proposition présente de nombreux avantages (**b**) (advise) recommander, conseiller; **to r. sb to do sth** conseiller à qn de faire qch; Com **recommended retail price** prix m conseillé
recommendation [rekəmen'deɪʃən] n recommandation f
recompense ['rekəmpens] **1** n dédommagement m; **in r. for** en dédommagement de
  2 vt dédommager
reconcile ['rekənsaɪl] vt (**a**) (person) réconcilier; **to be reconciled with sb** s'être réconcilié(e) avec qn; **to be reconciled to sth** se résigner à qch (**b**) (facts, differences, opinions) concilier
reconciliation [rekənsɪlɪ'eɪʃən] n réconciliation f
reconditioned [riːkən'dɪʃənd] adj (TV, washing machine) remis(e) à neuf
reconnaissance [rɪ'kɒnɪsəns] n Mil reconnaissance f; **r. flight/mission** vol m/mission f de reconnaissance
reconquer [riː'kɒŋkə(r)] vt reconquérir
reconquest [riː'kɒŋkwest] n reconquête f
reconsider [riːkən'sɪdə(r)] **1** vt réexaminer
  2 vi réconsidérer la question
reconstitute [riː'kɒnstɪtjuːt] vt reconstituer
reconstruct [riːkən'strʌkt] vt reconstruire; (crime, event) reconstituer
reconstruction [riːkən'strʌkʃən] n reconstruction f; (of crime, event) reconstitution f

record 1 n ['rekɔːd] (**a**) (account) rapport m; (file) dossier m; **we have no r. of this** nous n'en avons aucune trace; **to keep a r. of sth** garder une trace écrite de qch; **the coldest winter on r.** l'hiver le plus froid qu'on ait jamais enregistré; **she's on r. as saying that...** elle a déclaré officiellement que...; **(just) for the r.** au passage; **to put** or **set the r. straight** mettre les choses au point; **r. office** archives fpl (**b**) (personal history) passé m; (achievements) résultats mpl; (of criminal) casier m judiciaire; **to have a good/bad safety r.** avoir bonne/mauvaise réputation en matière de sécurité (**c**) (musical) disque m; **r. company** maison f de disques; **r. player** tourne-disques m inv (**d**) (best performance) record m; **to set/break a r.** établir/battre un record (**e**) Comput enregistrement m
  2 adj ['rekɔːd] record inv; **in r. time** en un temps record; **unemployment is at a r. high/low** le chômage a atteint son taux le plus haut/bas
  3 vt [rɪ'kɔːd] (**a**) (on video, cassette) enregistrer (**b**) (write down) noter; **to send sth recorded delivery** envoyer qch en recommandé
record-breaking ['rekɔːdbreɪkɪŋ] adj record inv
recorder [rɪ'kɔːdə(r)] n (musical instrument) flûte f à bec
record-holder ['rekɔːdhəʊldə(r)] n détenteur(trice) m,f du record
recording [rɪ'kɔːdɪŋ] n (on tape) enregistrement m; **r. studio** studio m d'enregistrement
recount [rɪ'kaʊnt] vt (relate) raconter
re-count ['riːkaʊnt] n (in election) deuxième décompte m
recoup [rɪ'kuːp] vt récupérer
recourse [rɪ'kɔːs] n recours m; **to have r. to** avoir recours à
recover [rɪ'kʌvə(r)] **1** vt (territory, customers) & Comput récupérer; (one's appetite, balance) retrouver
  2 vi (from illness, setback) se remettre; (after running, travelling) récupérer; Fig (of economy) se redresser; (of sales) reprendre
recoverable [rɪ'kʌvərəbəl] adj (money) recouvrable
recovery [rɪ'kʌvərɪ] (pl recoveries) n (**a**) (of lost or stolen item) récupération f; **r. vehicle** dépanneuse f (**b**) (from illness) rétablissement m; Fig (of economy) redressement m; (of sales) reprise f; **to make a r.** se rétablir
re-create [riːkrɪ'eɪt] vt recréer
recreation [rekrɪ'eɪʃən] n (leisure) divertissement m; Sch (break) récréation f; **r. area** aire f de jeux; **r. ground** terrain m de jeux; **r. room** salle f de jeux
recreational [rekrɪ'eɪʃənəl] adj de loisirs; **r. drug** drogue prise occasionnellement, dans un but récréatif; Am **r. vehicle** mobile home m
recrimination [rɪkrɪmɪ'neɪʃən] n récrimination f
recruit [rɪ'kruːt] also Mil **1** n recrue f
  2 vt recruter
recruitment [rɪ'kruːtmənt] n also Mil recrutement m; **r. agency** agence f de recrutement; **r. campaign** campagne f de recrutement; **r. consultant** conseil m en recrutement; **r. drive** campagne f de recrutement
rectangle ['rektæŋɡəl] n rectangle m
rectangular [rek'tæŋɡjʊlə(r)] adj rectangulaire
rectify ['rektɪfaɪ] (pt & pp rectified) vt rectifier
rectitude ['rektɪtjuːd] n Formal rectitude f
rector ['rektə(r)] n (**a**) Rel pasteur m anglican (**b**) Scot Univ = personnalité élue par les étudiants pour les représenter; Scot Sch ≃ proviseur m

rectory ['rektərɪ] *(pl* **rectories)** *n Rel* presbytère *m*
rectum ['rektəm] *n* rectum *m*
recumbent [rɪ'kʌmbənt] *adj Formal* allongé(e)
recuperate [rɪ'ku:pəreɪt] *vi (from illness)* se rétablir
recuperation [rɪku:pə'reɪʃən] *n (from illness)* rétablissement *m*
recur [rɪ'kɜ:(r)] *(pt & pp* **recurred)** *vi (of event, problem)* se reproduire; *(of theme, illness)* revenir, réapparaître
recurrence [rɪ'kʌrəns] *n* récurrence *f*
recurring [rɪ'kɜ:rɪŋ] *adj (problem)* récurrent(e); *(dream)* qui revient souvent; **six point six r.** six virgule six à l'infini
recyclable [ri:'saɪkləbəl] *adj* recyclable
recycle [ri:'saɪkəl] *vt* recycler; *Comput* **r. bin** corbeille *f*
recycling [ri:'saɪklɪŋ] *n* recyclage *m*; **r. plant** usine *f* de recyclage
red [red] **1** *n (colour)* rouge *m*; *Fam Fig* **to see r.** *(get angry)* voir rouge; **to be in the r.** *(in debt)* être à découvert *ou* dans le rouge
2 *adj* rouge; *(hair)* roux (rousse); **to turn** *or* **go r.** rougir; **to be as r. as a beetroot** être rouge comme une pivoine; **r. alert** alerte *f* rouge; **the R. Army** l'Armée *f* rouge; **r. blood cell** globule *m* rouge, hématie *f*; **r. card** *(in football)* carton *m* rouge; *Fig* **to roll out the r. carpet** dérouler le tapis rouge; **the R. Cross** la Croix-Rouge; *Fig* **r. herring** diversion *f*; *(in film, book)* fausse piste *f*; *Old-fashioned* **R. Indian** Peau-Rouge *mf*; **r. light** feu *m* rouge; **r. light district** quartier *m* chaud; **r. meat** viande *f* rouge; **r. pepper** poivron *m* rouge; **mentioning her name to him is like a r. rag to a bull** le simple fait d'entendre son nom le met dans une colère noire; **(Little) R. Riding Hood** le Petit Chaperon rouge; **the R. Sea** la mer Rouge; **r. squirrel** écureuil *m* roux; **r. tape** paperasserie *f*; **r. wine** vin *m* rouge
red-blooded [red'blʌdɪd] *adj* **a r. male** un homme viril
redbrick ['redbrɪk] *adj (building)* en brique rouge; *Br* **r. university** = université construite à la fin du XIXe siècle
redcurrant ['redkʌrənt] *n* groseille *f*
redden ['redən] **1** *vt* rougir
2 *vi (of sky)* rougeoyer; *(of person)* rougir
reddish ['redɪʃ] *adj (light, colour)* rougeâtre; *(hair)* légèrement roux (rousse)
redecorate [ri:'dekəreɪt] *vt (repaint)* refaire la peinture de; *(re-wallpaper)* retapisser
redeem [rɪ'di:m] *vt (a) (pawned item)* racheter; *(promise)* tenir; *(gift token, coupon)* échanger; *(mortgage, loan)* rembourser (b) *(rescue)* racheter; **to r. oneself** se racheter
Redeemer [rɪ'di:mə(r)] *n Rel* **the R.** le Rédempteur
redeeming [rɪ'di:mɪŋ] *adj* **he has no r. features** il n'a rien pour le racheter; **his one r. feature is...** la seule chose qui le rachète, c'est...
redemption [rɪ'dem(p)ʃən] *n Rel* rédemption *f*; *also Fig* **to be beyond** *or* **past r.** être irrécupérable
redeploy [ri:dɪ'plɔɪ] *vt (troops)* redéployer; *(staff)* réaffecter
redeployment [ri:dɪ'plɔɪmənt] *n (of troops)* redéploiement *m*; *(of staff)* réaffectation *f*
redevelop [ri:dɪ'veləp] *vt* réaménager
red-faced ['red'feɪst] *adj (naturally)* rougeaud(e); *(with anger, embarrassment)* rouge
red-handed ['red'hændɪd] *adj* **to be caught r.** être pris(e) la main dans le sac
redhead ['redhed] *n* roux (rousse) *m,f*

red-hot [red'hɒt] *adj* **(a)** *(very hot)* brûlant(e) **(b)** *Fam (very good)* super bon (bonne); **r. news** des nouvelles de dernière minute
redial [ri:'daɪəl] **1** *n* **r. button** *(on phone)* touche *f* bis
2 *vt (pt & pp* **redialled,** *Am* **redialed)** *(phone number)* recomposer
redid [ri:'dɪd] *pt of* **redo**
redirect [ri:dɪ'rekt, ri:daɪ'rekt] *vt (letter)* faire suivre; *(plane, traffic)* dévier; *(energy)* canaliser
rediscover [ri:dɪs'kʌvə(r)] *vt* redécouvrir
redistribute [ri:dɪs'trɪbju:t] *vt* redistribuer
red-letter day ['red'letədeɪ] *n* journée *f* mémorable
redo [ri:'du:] *(pt* **redid** [ri:'dɪd], *pp* **redone** [ri:'dʌn]) *vt* refaire
redolent ['redələnt] *adj* **to be r. of** *(smell of)* sentir; *(suggest)* avoir un parfum de
redone [ri:'dʌn] *pp of* **redo**
redraft [ri:'drɑ:ft] *vt* rédiger de nouveau
redress [rɪ'dres] **1** *n (of injustice, grievance)* réparation *f*
2 *vt (injustice, grievance)* réparer; **to r. the balance** rétablir l'équilibre
redskin ['redskɪn] *n Old-fashioned* Peau-Rouge *mf*
reduce [rɪ'dju:s] *vt* **(a)** *(cost, amount, tax)* réduire; *(importance)* minimiser; *(price)* baisser; *(number of people)* faire baisser; *(sauce)* faire réduire; **to r. speed** ralentir **(b)** *(bring to a certain state)* **to r. sth to ashes/dust** réduire qch en cendres/poussière; **to r. sb to silence** réduire qn au silence; **to r. sb to tears** faire fondre qn en larmes; **to be reduced to doing sth** être réduit(e) à faire qch
reduced [rɪ'dju:st] *adj* réduit(e); **to live in r. circumstances** vivre dans la gêne
reduction [rɪ'dʌkʃən] *n (of price, temperature)* baisse *f* (in de); *(of spending, on item)* réduction *f* (in/on de/sur)
redundancy [rɪ'dʌndənsɪ] *(pl* **redundancies)** *n (dismissal)* licenciement *m*; **r. notice** avis *m* de licenciement; **r. pay** prime *f* de licenciement
redundant [rɪ'dʌndənt] *adj* **(a)** *(worker)* **to make sb r.** licencier qn; **to be made r.** être licencié(e) **(b)** *(superfluous)* inutile
reed [ri:d] *n* **(a)** *(plant)* roseau *m* **(b)** *(of musical instrument)* anche *f*
reef [ri:f] *n* récif *m*
reek [ri:k] **1** *n* relent *m*
2 *vi also Fig* **to r. (of sth)** puer (qch)
reel [ri:l] **1** *n* **(a)** *Br (for film, thread)* bobine *f*; *(for fishing line)* moulinet *m* **(b)** *(dance, music)* quadrille *m*
2 *vi (sway)* chanceler; *Fig* **my head is reeling** j'ai la tête qui tourne
►**reel off** *vt sep (names, statistics)* débiter
re-elect [ri:ɪ'lekt] *vt* réélire
re-election [ri:ɪ'lekʃən] *n* réélection *f*
re-enact [ri:ɪ'nækt] *vt* reconstituer
re-enter [ri:'entə(r)] **1** *vt* entrer à nouveau dans
2 *vi* rentrer
re-establish [ri:ɪ'stæblɪʃ] *vt* rétablir
re-examine [ri:ɪg'zæmɪn] *vt* réexaminer
ref [ref] *n* **(a)** *(abbr* **reference)** réf **(b)** *Fam (abbr* **referee)** arbitre *m*
refectory [rɪ'fektərɪ] *(pl* **refectories)** *n* réfectoire *m*
refer [rɪ'fɜ:(r)] *(pt & pp* **referred)** *vt* soumettre (**to** à); **to r. a patient to a specialist** envoyer un patient chez un spécialiste
►**refer to** *vt insep* **(a)** *(mention)* parler de; **she never refers to it** elle n'en parle jamais **(b)** *(allude to)* faire

allusion à; **referred to as...** appelé(e)... (**c**) *(consult)* consulter (**d**) *(apply to)* s'appliquer à

referee [refə'ri:] **1** *n* (**a**) *(in sport)* arbitre *m* (**b**) *(for job)* **please give the names of two referees** veuillez fournir deux références
  2 *vt & vi* arbitrer

reference ['refərəns] *n* (**a**) *(consultation, source)* référence *f*; **for future r.** à titre d'information; **I can't do it without r. to Head Office** je ne peux pas le faire sans en référer au bureau central; **r. book** ouvrage *m* de référence; **r. number** (numéro *m* de) référence *f*; **r. point, point of r.** point *m* de repère (**b**) *(allusion)* allusion *f*; **with r. to** *(in letter)* suite à (**c**) *(from employer)* lettre *f* de référence

referendum [refə'rendəm] *n* référendum *m*

refill 1 *n* ['ri:fɪl] *(for notebook)* feuillets *fpl* de rechange; *(for pen)* cartouche *f*; *(for lighter)* recharge *f*; **would you like a r.?** *(of drink)* je te ressers?
  2 *vt* [ri:'fɪl] *(glass)* remplir à nouveau; *(lighter, pen)* recharger

refine [rɪ'faɪn] *vt* (**a**) *(sugar, petroleum)* raffiner (**b**) *(improve)* perfectionner

refined [rɪ'faɪnd] *adj also Fig* raffiné(e)

refinement [rɪ'faɪnmənt] *n* (**a**) *(of manners, taste, person)* raffinement *m* (**b**) *(improvement)* perfectionnement *m*; **to make refinements to sth** perfectionner qch

refinery [rɪ'faɪnərɪ] *(pl* **refineries**) *n* raffinerie *f*

refit 1 *n* ['ri:fɪt] *(of ship)* remise *f* en état
  2 *vt* [ri:'fɪt] *(pt & pp* **refitted**) *(ship)* remettre en état

reflate [ri:'fleɪt] *vt Econ* relancer

reflation [ri:'fleɪʃən] *n Econ* relance *f*

reflect [rɪ'flekt] **1** *vt* (**a**) *(image, light)* réfléchir, refléter; **to be reflected (in)** se réfléchir *ou* se refléter (dans) (**b**) *Fig (portray)* refléter (**c**) *(think)* **to r. that...** se dire que...
  2 *vi* (**a**) *(think)* réfléchir (**on** à) (**b**) **to r. well/badly on sb/sth** faire honneur/du tort à qn/qch

reflection [rɪ'flekʃən] *n* (**a**) *(image, indication)* reflet *m*; *Fig* **it is no r. on your own capabilities** cela ne remet pas en cause vos compétences (**b**) *(thought)* réflexion *f*; **on r.** après réflexion

reflective [rɪ'flektɪv] *adj* (**a**) *(surface)* réfléchissant(e) (**b**) *(person)* réfléchi(e)

reflector [rɪ'flektə(r)] *n (on bicycle, vehicle)* catadioptre *m*

reflex ['ri:fleks] **1** *n* réflexe *m*
  2 *adj* réflexe; **r. action** réflexe *m*; **r. camera** réflex *m*

reflexive [rɪ'fleksɪv] *adj Gram* **r. pronoun** pronom *m* réfléchi; **r. verb** verbe *m* pronominal réfléchi

reflexologist [ri:flek'splədʒɪst] *n* réflexologiste *mf*

reflexology [ri:flek'splədʒɪ] *n* réflexologie *f*

reforestation [ri:fɒrɪ'steɪʃən] *n* reboisement *m*

reform [rɪ'fɔ:m] **1** *n* réforme *f*
  2 *vt* réformer
  3 *vi* se réformer

re-form ['ri:'fɔ:m] *vi (of organization, pop group)* se reformer

re-format ['ri:'fɔ:mæt] *(pt & pp* **re-formatted**) *vt Comput (disk)* reformater

reformation [refə'meɪʃən] *n* réforme *f*; *Hist* **the R.** la Réforme

reformatory [rɪ'fɔ:mətərɪ] *(pl* **reformatories**) *n Br* ≃ maison *f* de redressement; *Am* ≃ centre *m* d'éducation surveillée

reformed [rɪ'fɔ:md] *adj (alcoholic, drug addict)* ancien(enne); **he's a r. character** il s'est assagi

reformer [rɪ'fɔ:mə(r)] *n* réformateur(trice) *m,f*

reformist [rɪ'fɔ:mɪst] **1** *n* réformiste *mf*
  2 *adj* réformiste

refract [rɪ'frækt] *vt* réfracter

refrain [rɪ'freɪn] **1** *n also Fig* refrain *m*
  2 *vi* **to r. from sth/doing sth** s'abstenir de qch/de faire qch

re-freeze [ri:'fri:z] *(pt* **re-froze** [ri:'frəʊz], *pp* **re-frozen** [ri:'frəʊzən]) *vt* recongeler

refresh [rɪ'freʃ] *vt (of drink)* rafraîchir; *(of nap, holiday)* reposer; *(bath)* revigorer; *Comput* actualiser; **to r. one's memory** se rafraîchir la mémoire; **to r. sb's glass** *(top up)* resservir à boire à qn

refreshing [rɪ'freʃɪŋ] *adj (breeze, drink)* rafraîchissant(e); *(nap, holiday)* reposant(e); *(shower)* revigorant(e); *Fig (honesty)* qui fait l'effet d'une bouffée d'air frais

refreshments [rɪ'freʃmənts] *npl* rafraîchissements *mpl*

refrigerate [rɪ'frɪdʒəreɪt] *vt* réfrigérer; **r. after opening** *(on packet)* à conserver au frais après ouverture

refrigeration [rɪfrɪdʒə'reɪʃən] *n* réfrigération *f*

refrigerator [rɪ'frɪdʒəreɪtə(r)] *n (domestic)* réfrigérateur *m*, frigidaire® *m*; *(industrial)* chambre *f* froide

refroze [ri:'frəʊz] *pt of* **refreeze**

refrozen [ri:'frəʊzən] *pp of* **refreeze**

refuel [ri:'fjʊəl] *(pt & pp* **refuelled**, *Am* **refueled**) **1** *vt (ship, aircraft)* ravitailler en carburant
  2 *vi (of ship, aircraft)* se ravitailler en carburant

refuge ['refju:dʒ] *n (from danger, weather)* refuge *m*; *(for battered women)* foyer *m*; **to seek r.** chercher refuge; **to take r.** se réfugier

refugee [refjʊ'dʒi:] *n* réfugié(e) *m,f*; **r. camp** camp *m* de réfugiés; **r. status** statut *m* de réfugié

refund 1 *n* ['ri:fʌnd] remboursement *m*
  2 *vt* [ri:'fʌnd] rembourser

refurbish [ri:'fɜ:bɪʃ] *vt* rénover

refusal [rɪ'fju:zəl] *n* refus *m*; **to give a flat r.** refuser catégoriquement; **to have first r. (on sth)** avoir la priorité (pour qch)

refuse¹ ['refju:s] *n (rubbish)* ordures *fpl*; **r. collection** ramassage *m* des ordures (ménagères); **r. disposal** traitement *m* des ordures; **r. dump** dépôt *m* d'ordures

refuse² [rɪ'fju:z] **1** *vt (invitation, offer)* refuser; *(request)* rejeter; **to r. to do sth** refuser de faire qch; **to r. sb sth** refuser qch à qn
  2 *vi (of person)* refuser; *(of horse)* refuser l'obstacle

refute [rɪ'fju:t] *vt (argument, theory)* réfuter; *(allegation)* nier

regain [rɪ'geɪn] *vt* (**a**) *(get back)* retrouver; *(power, political seat)* reconquérir; **to r. possession of sth** rentrer en possession de qch; **to r. consciousness** revenir à soi; **to r. the lead** *(in contest)* reprendre l'avantage (**b**) *(reach again)* regagner

regal ['ri:gəl] *adj* royal(e)

regale [rɪ'geɪl] *vt* **to r. sb with sth** gratifier qn de qch

regalia [rɪ'geɪlɪə] *npl* insignes *mpl*

regard [rɪ'gɑ:d] **1** *n* (**a**) *(admiration)* respect *m*, estime *f*; **to hold sb in high r.** tenir qn en haute estime (**b**) *(consideration)* égard *m*; **out of r. for** par égard pour; **without r. to** sans tenir compte de (**c**) *(connection)* **in this r.** à cet égard; **in all regards** à tous égards; **with r. to** en ce qui concerne (**d**) **regards** *(good wishes)* amitiés *fpl*; **give her my regards** transmets-lui mes amitiés
  2 *vt* (**a**) *(admire, respect)* estimer (**b**) *(consider)* **to r. sb/sth as** considérer qn/qch comme; **to r. sb/sth**

with suspicion être soupconneux(euse) à l'égard de qn/qch (**c**) *(concern)* concerner; **as regards...** en ce qui concerne..., concernant...

regarding [rɪ'gɑːdɪŋ] *prep* en ce qui concerne, concernant

regardless [rɪ'gɑːdlɪs] *adv* (**a**) *(despite everything)* quand même (**b**) **r. of** *(without considering)* sans tenir compte de; **r. of the expense** sans regarder à la dépense

regatta [rɪ'gætə] *n* régate *f*

regency ['riːdʒənsɪ] *(pl* **regencies**) *n* régence *f*

regenerate [rɪ'dʒenəreɪt] **1** *vt (sector, city)* régénérer; *(interest, enthusiasm)* raviver
2 *vi* se régénérer

regeneration [rɪdʒenə'reɪʃən] *n* régénération *f*

regent ['riːdʒənt] **1** *n* régent(e) *m,f*
2 *adj* régent(e)

reggae ['regeɪ] *n* reggae *m*

regime [reɪ'ʒiːm] *n* régime *m*

regiment 1 *n* ['redʒɪmənt] régiment *m*
2 *vt* ['redʒɪment] enrégimenter

regimental [redʒɪ'mentəl] *adj* du régiment

regimentation [redʒɪmen'teɪʃən] *n* discipline *f* draconienne

regimented ['redʒɪmentɪd] *adj* très strict(e)

region ['riːdʒən] *n* région *f*; *Fig* **in the r. of** environ

regional ['riːdʒənəl] *adj* régional(e)

regionalism ['riːdʒənəlɪzəm] *n* régionalisme *m*

register ['redʒɪstə(r)] **1** *n* registre *m*; *(at school)* cahier *m* d'appel; *(of voters)* liste *f* électorale; **to take the r.** *(at school)* faire l'appel; **r. of births, marriages and deaths** registre *m* de l'état civil; **(cash) r.** caisse *f* (enregistreuse); *Br* **r. office** bureau *m* de l'état civil
2 *vt* (**a**) *(member, student)* inscrire; *(birth, marriage, death)* déclarer; *(complaint)* déposer; **to r. a protest** protester (**b**) *(temperature, speed)* enregistrer; *(astonishment, displeasure)* manifester (**c**) *(realize)* se rendre compte de (**d**) *(achieve) (victory, progress)* enregistrer
3 *vi* (**a**) *(for course)* s'inscrire; *(at hotel)* signer le registre; *(of voter)* s'inscrire sur les listes électorales (**b**) *Fam (of fact)* **I told him but it didn't r.** je lui ai dit mais il n'a pas enregistré

registered ['redʒɪstəd] *adj (charity)* reconnu(e) par l'État; *(childminder)* agréé(e); *(letter)* recommandé(e); **r. trademark** marque *f* déposée

registrar ['redʒɪstrɑː(r)] *n* (**a**) *(record keeper)* officier *m* de l'état civil (**b**) *(in university)* responsable *mf* des inscriptions (**c**) *(in hospital)* chef *m* de clinique

registration [redʒɪs'treɪʃən] *n (of student)* inscription *f*; *(of voter)* inscription *f* sur les listes électorales; *(of birth, death, marriage)* déclaration *f*; **r. number** *(of car)* numéro *m* d'immatriculation

registry office ['redʒɪstrɪ'ɒfɪs] *n* bureau *m* de l'état civil; **to get married at a r.** se marier civilement, ≃ se marier à la mairie

regress [rɪ'gres] *vi* régresser

regression [rɪ'greʃən] *n* régression *f*

regressive [rɪ'gresɪv] *adj* régressif(ive)

regret [rɪ'gret] **1** *n* regret *m*; **to send one's regrets** *(apologies)* envoyer ses excuses; *(condolences)* envoyer ses condoléances
2 *vt (pt & pp* **regretted**) regretter; **to r. doing** *or* **having done sth** regretter d'avoir fait qch; **I r. to (have to) inform you that...** j'ai le regret de vous annoncer que...

regretful [rɪ'gretfʊl] *adj (voice, smile)* plein(e) de regret; *(person)* qui a des regrets

regrettable [rɪ'gretəbəl] *adj* regrettable

regroup [riː'gruːp] **1** *vt* regrouper
2 *vi* se regrouper

regular ['regjʊlə(r)] **1** *n (in bar, restaurant)* habitué(e) *m,f*
2 *adj* (**a**) *(features, pulse, verb)* régulier(ère); **on a r. basis** régulièrement; **he comes twice a week, as r. as clockwork** il vient deux fois par semaine, c'est réglé comme du papier à musique (**b**) *(normal, habitual)* habituel(elle); *(in size)* moyen(enne); *(listener, viewer)* fidèle; *(customer)* régulier(ère); **she was a r. visitor to the house** elle venait régulièrement à la maison (**c**) *(army, soldier)* régulier(ère) (**d**) *Fam (for emphasis)* vrai(e)

regularity [regjʊ'lærɪtɪ] *n* régularité *f*

regulate ['regjʊleɪt] *vt* (**a**) *(adjust)* régler (**b**) *(control)* réglementer

regulating body ['regjʊleɪtɪŋ'bɒdɪ] *n* autorité *f* de régulation

regulation [regjʊ'leɪʃən] **1** *n* (**a**) *(action)* réglementation *f* (**b**) *(rule)* règlement *m*
2 *adj (statutory)* réglementaire

regulator ['regjʊleɪtə(r)] *n* régulateur *m*

regulatory [regjʊ'leɪtərɪ] *adj* de contrôle

regurgitate [rɪ'gɜːdʒɪteɪt] *vt* régurgiter; *Fig* recracher

rehabilitate [riːhə'bɪlɪteɪt] *vt* réhabiliter

rehabilitation [riːhəbɪlɪ'teɪʃən] *n* réhabilitation *f*

rehash *Fam* **1** *n* ['riːhæʃ] resucée *f*
2 *vt* [riː'hæʃ] *(ideas, proposal)* reprendre; *(film, book)* remanier

rehearsal [rɪ'hɜːsəl] *n* répétition *f*

rehearse [rɪ'hɜːs] *vt & vi* répéter

rehouse [riː'haʊz] *vt* reloger

reign [reɪn] **1** *n* règne *m*
2 *vi also Fig* régner

reigning ['reɪnɪŋ] *adj (monarch)* régnant(e); *(champion)* en titre

reimburse [riːɪm'bɜːs] *vt* rembourser

rein [reɪn] *n also Fig* rêne *f*; *Fig* **to give sb free r. to do sth** donner carte blanche à qn pour qu'il/elle fasse qch; *Fig* **to give free r. to one's imagination** donner libre cours à son imagination; *Fig* **to keep a tight r. on sb** tenir la bride haute à qn

▸**rein in** *vt sep (horse) & Fig (person)* ramener au pas; *Fig (emotions)* maîtriser

reincarnate [riːɪnkɑː'neɪt] *vt* **to be reincarnated** être réincarné(e)

reincarnation [riːɪnkɑː'neɪʃən] *n* réincarnation *f*

reindeer ['reɪndɪə(r)] *n* renne *m*

reinforce [riːɪn'fɔːs] *vt also Fig* renforcer; **reinforced concrete** béton *m* armé

reinforcement [riːɪn'fɔːsmənt] *n* renforcement *m*; *also Fig* **reinforcements** renforts *mpl*

reinsert [riːɪn'sɜːt] *vt* réinsérer

reinstate [riːɪn'steɪt] *vt* réintégrer

reinsurance [riːɪn'ʃʊərəns] *n* réassurance *f*

reinsure [riːɪn'ʃʊə(r)] *vt* réassurer

reinvent [riːɪn'vent] *vt* *Fig* **to r. oneself** changer d'image; **to r. the wheel** refaire ce qui a déjà été fait

reinvest [riːɪn'vest] *vt* réinvestir

reissue [riː'ɪʃuː] **1** *n (of book, record)* réédition *f*
2 *vt (book, record)* rééditer

reiterate [riː'ɪtəreɪt] *vt* réitérer

reiteration [riːɪtə'reɪʃən] *n* réitération *f*

reject 1 *n* ['riːdʒekt] *(object)* rebut *m*; *Fam (person)* inadapté(e) *m,f*
2 *vt* [rɪ'dʒekt] rejeter; *(offer, goods)* refuser
rejection [rɪ'dʒekʃən] *n* rejet *m*; *(of offer, goods)* refus *m*; **to meet with r.** être rejeté(e)
rejoice [rɪ'dʒɔɪs] *vi* se réjouir
rejoicing [rɪ'dʒɔɪsɪŋ] *n* réjouissance *f*
rejoin[1] [riː'dʒɔɪn] *vt* (**a**) *(group, motorway)* rejoindre; *(race)* reprendre (**b**) *(join again)* réintégrer
rejoin[2] [rɪ'dʒɔɪn] *vt & vi (retort)* répliquer, rétorquer
rejoinder [rɪ'dʒɔɪndə(r)] *n* réplique *f*
rejuvenate [rɪ'dʒuːvɪneɪt] *vt* rajeunir
rekindle [riː'kɪndəl] *vt* raviver
relapse 1 *n* ['riːlæps] rechute *f*
2 *vi* [rɪ'læps] rechuter; **to r. into** retomber dans
relate [rɪ'leɪt] **1** *vt* (**a**) *(narrate)* raconter (**b**) *(connect)* mettre en rapport (**to** avec)
2 *vi* (**a**) *(be relevant)* **to r. to** avoir rapport à (**b**) **to r. to** *(understand) (person)* avoir des affinités avec; *(music)* apprécier; *(idea)* comprendre
related [rɪ'leɪtɪd] *adj (people, animals, languages)* apparenté(e); *(ideas, events, activities)* lié(e)
relation [rɪ'leɪʃən] *n* (**a**) *(relative)* parent(e) *m,f* (**b**) *(connection)* rapport *m*; **to bear no r. to** n'avoir aucun rapport avec
relationship [rɪ'leɪʃənʃɪp] *n* (**a**) *(between people)* relation *f*; *(romantic, sexual)* relation *f* amoureuse; *(between countries)* relations *fpl*; *(within family)* lien *m* de parenté; **to have a good/bad r. with sb** s'entendre/ ne pas bien s'entendre avec qn (**b**) *(connection)* rapport *m*
relative ['relətɪv] **1** *n (person)* parent(e) *m,f*
2 *adj (comparative)* relatif(ive); **r. to** en rapport avec; *Gram* **r. clause** proposition *f* relative
relatively ['relətɪvlɪ] *adv* relativement
relativity [relə'tɪvɪtɪ] *n Phys* relativité *f*
relax [rɪ'læks] **1** *vt (person)* détendre; *(muscles, discipline)* relâcher; *(law, control)* assouplir; **to r. one's grip (on)** relâcher son étreinte (sur); *Fig* relâcher son emprise (sur)
2 *vi (of person)* se détendre; *(of muscles)* se relâcher; **r.!** *(calm down)* du calme!
relaxation [riːlæk'seɪʃən] *n* (**a**) *(of person)* détente *f*; *(of discipline)* relâchement *m*; *(of control)* assouplissement *m* (**b**) *(as therapy)* relaxation *f*; **r. exercises/ classes** exercices *mpl*/cours *mpl* de relaxation
relaxed [rɪ'lækst] *adj* détendu(e)
relaxing [rɪ'læksɪŋ] *adj* relaxant(e)
relay 1 *n* ['riːleɪ] *(of workers)* équipe *f* de relais; **to work in relays** se relayer; **r. (race)** *(course f de)* relais *m*; *Rad & TV* **r. station** relais *m*
2 *vt* [rɪ'leɪ] retransmettre; *(information)* transmettre
release [rɪ'liːs] **1** *n* (**a**) *(of prisoner)* libération *f*; *(of gas)* émission *f*; *(emotional)* soulagement *m* (**b**) *(of album, film)* sortie *f*; **to be on general r.** *(of film)* être sorti(e) dans toutes les grandes salles de cinéma
2 *vt* (**a**) *(prisoner)* libérer; *(gas, fumes)* émettre; *(balloon, bomb)* lâcher; *(funds)* dégager; *(brake)* desserrer; **to r. sb from an obligation** dégager qn d'une obligation; **to r. sb's hand** lâcher la main de qn (**b**) *(album, film)* sortir; *(news, information)* communiquer
relegate ['relɪgeɪt] *vt* reléguer (**to** à); **to be relegated** *(of team)* descendre en division inférieure
relegation [relɪ'geɪʃən] *n (of person)* relégation *f* (**to** à); *(of team)* descente *f* en division inférieure

relent [rɪ'lent] *vi (of storm, wind)* se calmer; *(of person)* céder
relentless [rɪ'lentlɪs] *adj (person, attitude)* implacable; *(rain, criticism)* incessant(e)
relevance ['reləvəns] *n* pertinence *f*; **to have r. to sth** avoir un rapport avec qch
relevant ['reləvənt] *adj* (**a**) *(apt)* pertinent(e); **to be r. (to sth)** avoir un rapport (avec qch) (**b**) *(appropriate) (chapter)* correspondant(e); *(authorities)* compétent(e); *(experience, qualifications)* requis(e) (**c**) *(topical)* d'actualité
reliability [rɪlaɪə'bɪlɪtɪ] *n (of person, information)* sérieux *m*; *(of machine)* sûreté *f*, fiabilité *f*
reliable [rɪ'laɪəbəl] *adj (person, machine)* fiable; *(information)* sûr(e); **from a r. source** de source sûre
reliably [rɪ'laɪəblɪ] *adv* **to be r. informed that…** savoir de source sûre que…
reliance [rɪ'laɪəns] *n* (**a**) *(dependence)* dépendance *f* (**on** vis-à-vis de) (**b**) *(trust)* confiance *f*; **to place r. on sb/sth** faire confiance à qn/qch
reliant [rɪ'laɪənt] *adj* **to be r. on** être dépendant(e) de
relic ['relɪk] *n Rel* relique *f*; *Fig* vestige *m*
relief [rɪ'liːf] *n* (**a**) *(comfort)* soulagement *m*; **to bring r. to sb** soulager qn (**b**) *(help)* secours *m*, aide *f*; **r. fund** fonds *m* d'aide; **r. worker** humanitaire *mf* (**c**) *(replacement)* remplaçant(e) *m,f* (**d**) *(of besieged city, troops)* libération *f* (**e**) *(in art)* relief *m*; **in r.** en relief; *Fig* **to throw sth into r.** mettre qch en relief; **r. map** carte *f* en relief
relieve [rɪ'liːv] *vt* (**a**) *(alleviate)* soulager; *(boredom)* tromper; *(pressure)* réduire; *Euph* **to r. oneself** se soulager (**b**) *(replace)* remplacer (**c**) *(liberate)* libérer; **to r. sb of his duties** relever qn de ses fonctions; *Hum* **to r. sb of his wallet** soulager qn de son portefeuille
religion [rɪ'lɪdʒən] *n* religion *f*; **what is your r.?** quelle est votre religion?; *(on form)* à quelle confession appartenez-vous?
religious [rɪ'lɪdʒəs] *adj also Fig* religieux(euse); **r. education, r. instruction** instruction *f* religieuse
religiously [rɪ'lɪdʒəslɪ] *adv also Fig* religieusement
relinquish [rɪ'lɪŋkwɪʃ] *vt (hope, habit, thought)* abandonner; *(claim, share)* renoncer à; *Fig* **to r. one's hold on sb/sth** relâcher son emprise sur qn/qch
relish ['relɪʃ] **1** *n* (**a**) *(pleasure)* goût *m* (**for** pour); **to do sth with r.** faire qch avec délectation (**b**) *(pickle)* condiments *mpl*
2 *vt* savourer; **I didn't r. the idea** l'idée ne m'enthousiasmait guère
relive [riː'lɪv] *vt* revivre
relocate [riːləʊ'keɪt] **1** *vt (company)* transférer; *(person)* muter
2 *vi (of company)* être transféré(e); *(of person)* se déplacer
relocation [riːləʊ'keɪʃən] *n* déménagement *m*
reluctance [rɪ'lʌktəns] *n* réticence *f*; **to do sth with r.** faire qch à contrecœur
reluctant [rɪ'lʌktənt] *adj (smile, promise)* accordé(e) à contrecœur; **to be r. to do sth** être réticent(e) à faire qch
▶ **rely on, rely upon** [rɪ'laɪ] *(pt & pp relied)* *vt insep* (**a**) **to r. on sb (to do sth)** compter sur qn (pour faire qch) (**b**) *(be dependent on)* dépendre de
REM [ɑːr'iːem] *n (abbr rapid eye movement)* mouvements *mpl* oculaires rapides
remain [rɪ'meɪn] *vi* (**a**) *(stay behind, continue to be)* rester (**b**) *(be left)* subsister; **it remains to be seen** cela reste à voir

remainder [rɪˈmeɪndə(r)] *n* reste *m*
remaindered [rɪˈmeɪndɜːd] *adj* (*book*) soldé(e)
remaining [rɪˈmeɪnɪŋ] *adj* restant(e)
remains [rɪˈmeɪnz] *npl* (*of meal, fortune*) restes *mpl*; (*of civilization, building*) vestiges *mpl*; (**human**) **r.** restes *mpl/*humains
remake 1 *n* [ˈriːmeɪk] (*of film*) remake *m*
2 *vt* [riːˈmeɪk] (*pt & pp* **remade** [riːˈmeɪd]) (*film*) faire un remake de
remand [rɪˈmɑːnd] *Law* **1** *n* **on r.** en détention préventive; **r. home** maison *f* de détention préventive
2 *vt* **to r. sb** (**in custody**) placer qn en détention préventive
remark [rɪˈmɑːk] **1** *n* remarque *f*; **to make** *or* **pass a r.** faire une remarque
2 *vt* faire remarquer
remarkable [rɪˈmɑːkəbəl] *adj* remarquable
remarkably [rɪˈmɑːkəblɪ] *adv* remarquablement
remarry [riːˈmærɪ] (*pt & pp* **remarried**) *vi* se remarier
remedial [rɪˈmiːdɪəl] *adj* (**a**) (*class*) de rattrapage; **r. education** rattrapage *m* scolaire (**b**) (*corrective*) **to take r. measures** prendre des mesures de redressement
remedy [ˈremɪdɪ] **1** *n* (*pl* **remedies**) *also Fig* remède *m*
2 *vt* (*pt & pp* **remedied**) remédier à
remember [rɪˈmembə(r)] **1** *vt* (**a**) (*recall*) se souvenir de, se rappeler; **to r. doing sth** se souvenir d'avoir fait qch; **to r. to do sth** penser à faire qch; **a night to r.** une nuit mémorable (**b**) (*commemorate*) commémorer; **to r. the dead** rendre hommage aux disparus (**c**) (*speak of*) **to r. sb to sb** rappeler qn au bon souvenir de qn
2 *vi* se souvenir, se rappeler; **as far as I r.** pour autant que je me souvienne
remembrance [rɪˈmembrəns] *n Formal* (*memory*) souvenir *m*; **in r. of** en souvenir de; **R. Day** *or* **Sunday** = commémoration de la fin des deux guerres mondiales, ≃ le 11 novembre
remind [rɪˈmaɪnd] *vt* **to r. sb of sth** rappeler qch à qn; **to r. sb to do sth** rappeler à qn de faire qch; **that reminds me...** à propos...
reminder [rɪˈmaɪndə(r)] *n* rappel *m*
reminisce [remɪˈnɪs] *vi* évoquer des souvenirs; **to r. about sth** évoquer qch
reminiscence [remɪˈnɪsəns] *n* souvenir *m*
reminiscent [remɪˈnɪsənt] *adj* **to be r. of** rappeler
remiss [rɪˈmɪs] *adj* négligent(e); **it was very r. of him not to phone** c'était très négligent de sa part de ne pas téléphoner
remission [rɪˈmɪʃən] *n* (**a**) *Law* remise *f* de peine (**b**) (*of disease*) **to be in r.** être en phase de rémission
remit 1 *n* [ˈriːmɪt] (*area of authority*) attributions *fpl*
2 *vt* [rɪˈmɪt] (*pt & pp* **remitted**) (*payment*) remettre
remittance [rɪˈmɪtəns] *n* versement *m*
remnant [ˈremnənt] *n* reste *m*; (*of civilization, building*) vestige *m*; (*of cloth*) coupon *m*
remonstrate [ˈremənstreɪt] *vi* protester; **to r. with sb** faire des remontrances à qn
remorse [rɪˈmɔːs] *n* remords *m*; **to feel r.** avoir du *ou* des remords
remorseful [rɪˈmɔːsfʊl] *adj* plein(e) de remords
remorseless [rɪˈmɔːslɪs] *adj* impitoyable
remortgage [riːˈmɔːgɪdʒ] *vt* (*house, property*) hypothéquer de nouveau, prendre une nouvelle hypothèque sur
remote [rɪˈməʊt] *adj* (**a**) (*far-off*) (*in space*) éloigné(e) (**from** de); (*in time*) lointain(e) (**from** de); **r. control**

télécommande *f* (**b**) (*aloof*) distant(e) (**c**) (*chance, possibility*) vague; **the remotest chance/idea** la moindre chance/idée
remote-controlled [rɪˈməʊtkənˈtrəʊld] *adj* télécommandé(e)
remotely [rɪˈməʊtlɪ] *adv* (*distantly*) **r.** situated isolé(e) (**b**) (*slightly*) vaguement; **not r.** pas du tout
remould [ˈriːməʊld] *n* (*tyre*) pneu *m* rechapé
removal [rɪˈmuːvəl] *n* (**a**) (*of politician, official*) renvoi *m*; (*of control, doubt, threat*) suppression *f*; (*of stain*) nettoyage *m* (**b**) *Br* (*moving house*) déménagement *m*; **r. man** déménageur *m*; **r. van** camion *m* de déménagement
remove [rɪˈmuːv] *vt* (**a**) (*take away*) (*thing*) enlever; (*doubt*) dissiper; (*stain*) faire partir; (*politician, official*) renvoyer; **to r. one's child from a school** retirer son enfant d'une école (**b**) (*take off*) (*coat, hat*) enlever, retirer; (*tyre*) démonter
remover [rɪˈmuːvə(r)] *n* (**a**) (*for paint*) décapant *m*; (*for nail varnish*) dissolvant *m* (**b**) (**furniture**) **removers** déménageurs *mpl*
remunerate [rɪˈmjuːnəreɪt] *vt Formal* rémunérer
remuneration [rɪmjuːnəˈreɪʃən] *n Formal* rémunération *f*
remunerative [rɪˈmjuːnərətɪv] *adj Formal* rémunérateur(trice)
renaissance [rɪˈneɪsəns] *n* renouveau *m*; **the R.** la Renaissance
renal [ˈriːnəl] *adj* rénal(e)
rename [riːˈneɪm] *vt* rebaptiser
rend [rend] (*pt & pp* **rent** [rent]) *vt Lit* (*tear*) déchirer
render [ˈrendə(r)] *vt Formal* rendre; **to r. homage to sb** rendre hommage à qn; **to r. sth into French** rendre qch en français; **for services rendered** pour services rendus; **the news rendered her speechless** la nouvelle l'a laissée sans voix
rendezvous [ˈrɒndeɪvuː] **1** *n* (*pl* **rendezvous** [ˈrɒndeɪvuːz]) rendez-vous *m inv*
2 *vi* (*pt & pp* **rendezvoused** [ˈrɒndeɪvuːd]) se retrouver
rendition [renˈdɪʃən] *n* interprétation *f*
renegade [ˈrenɪgeɪd] *n* renégat(e) *m,f*
renege [rɪˈniːg] *vi* **to r. on sth** revenir sur qch
renew [rɪˈnjuː] *vt* (*passport, membership*) renouveler; (*activity, negotiations, library book*) reprendre; (*optimism, strength, interest*) raviver; (*speculation*) relancer
renewable [rɪˈnjuːəbəl] *adj* renouvelable
renewal [rɪˈnjuːəl] *n* (*of passport, membership*) renouvellement *m*; (*of activity, negotiations*) reprise *f*; (*of library book*) renouvellement *m* de prêt; (*of optimism, interest*) regain *m*
rennet [ˈrenɪt] *n* présure *f*
renounce [rɪˈnaʊns] *vt* renoncer à; (*treaty*) dénoncer; (*friends, faith, principles*) renier
renovate [ˈrenəveɪt] *vt* rénover
renovation [renəˈveɪʃən] *n* rénovation *f*
renown [rɪˈnaʊn] *n* renommée *f*
renowned [rɪˈnaʊnd] *adj* renommé(e) (**for** pour)
rent¹ [rent] **1** *n* (*on flat, house*) loyer *m*; **for r.** à louer; *Br Fam* **r. boy** jeune prostitué *m*
2 *vt* louer
rent² *pt & pp of* **rend**
rental [ˈrentəl] *n* (**a**) (*hire*) location *f* (**b**) (*money*) (*for house*) loyer *m*; (*for car, equipment, TV*) location *f*; (*for telephone*) abonnement *m*

rent-free [rent'fri:] **1** *adj* exempt(e) de loyer
2 *adv* sans payer de loyer
reopen [ri:'əupən] **1** *vt* rouvrir; *(talks)* reprendre; *Fig*
to r. old wounds rouvrir une plaie
2 *vi (of talks)* reprendre; *(of shop, theatre)* rouvrir;
school reopens on the 21st of August la rentrée
des classes aura lieu le 21 août
reorder [ri:'ɔ:də(r)] *vt* passer une nouvelle commande de
reorganization [ri:ɔ:gənaɪ'zeɪʃən] *n* réorganisation *f*
reorganize [ri:'ɔ:gənaɪz] *vt* réorganiser
rep [rep] *n Fam (abbr* **representative**) VRP *m*
repaid [ri:'peɪd] *pt & pp of* **repay**
repaint [ri:'peɪnt] *vt* repeindre
repair [rɪ'peə(r)] **1** *n* réparation *f*; **to be beyond r.** être
irréparable; **to be in good/bad r.** être en bon/mau-
vais état; **to be under r.** être en réparation; **r. shop**
atelier *m* de réparations
2 *vt* réparer
repairman [rɪ'peəmæn] *n* réparateur *m*
reparation [repə'reɪʃən] *n* (**a**) *Formal (compensation)*
réparation *f*; **to make r. for sth** réparer qch (**b**) *(after
war)* **reparations** réparations *fpl*
repartee [repɑː'tiː] *n* repartie *f*
repast [rɪ'pɑːst] *n Lit* repas *m*
repatriate [ri:'pætrɪeɪt] *vt* rapatrier (**to** vers)
repatriation [ri:pætrɪ'eɪʃən] *n* rapatriement *m*
repay [ri:'peɪ] *(pt & pp* **repaid** [ri:'peɪd]) *vt* (**a**) *(reimburse) (person, money)* rembourser (**b**) *(reward) (person)* remercier (**for** de); *(kindness)* payer de retour;
(loyalty) récompenser
repayable [ri:'peɪəbəl] *adj* remboursable
repayment [ri:'peɪmənt] *n* remboursement *m*; **r. plan**
calendrier *m* des paiements
repeal [rɪ'pi:l] *vt* abroger
repeat [rɪ'pi:t] **1** *n (of event)* répétition *f*; *(of TV or radio
programme)* rediffusion *f*; **r. prescription** ≃ ordonnance *f* renouvelable
2 *vt* répéter; *(attempt)* renouveler; *(TV programme)*
rediffuser; **to r. oneself** se répéter
repeated [rɪ'pi:tɪd] *adj* répété(e)
repeatedly [rɪ'pi:tɪdlɪ] *adv* à maintes reprises
repel [rɪ'pel] *(pt & pp* **repelled**) *vt also Fig* repousser
repellent [rɪ'pelənt] **1** *n (for insects)* anti-moustiques
m inv
2 *adj (disgusting)* repoussant(e)
repent [rɪ'pent] **1** *vt* se repentir de
2 *vi* se repentir (**of** de)
repentance [rɪ'pentəns] *n* repentir *m*
repentant [rɪ'pentənt] *adj* repentant(e) (**of** de)
repercussion [ri:pə'kʌʃən] *n* répercussion *f*
repertoire ['repətwɑː(r)] *n* répertoire *m*
repertory ['repətərɪ] *(pl* **repertories**) *n Theat* répertoire *m*; **r. company** troupe *f* de répertoire
repetition [repɪ'tɪʃən] *n* répétition *f*; *(of attempt)* renouvellement *m*
repetitive [rɪ'petɪtɪv] *adj* répétitif(ive); **r. strain injury**
= douleurs dans les bras et les mains dues à la répétition de certains mouvements
rephrase [ri:'freɪz] *vt* reformuler
replace [rɪ'pleɪs] *vt* (**a**) *(put back)* **to r. sth** remettre
qch à sa place; **to r. the receiver** *(on telephone)* raccrocher (**b**) *(substitute for)* remplacer
replacement [rɪ'pleɪsmənt] *n* (**a**) *(putting back)* remise *f* en place; *(substituting)* remplacement *m*; *Fin*
r. cost coût *m* de remplacement; **r. parts** pièces *fpl*

de remplacement; **r. value** valeur *f* de remplacement
(**b**) *(person)* remplaçant(e) *m,f*
replay 1 *n* ['ri:pleɪ] *(of match)* nouvelle rencontre *f*;
(action) r. *(on TV)* = répétition d'une séquence précédente; *(at slow speed)* ralenti *m*
2 *vt* [ri:'pleɪ] *(match)* rejouer
replenish [rɪ'plenɪʃ] *vt (cup, tank)* remplir à nouveau
(**with** de); **to r. one's supplies** se réapprovisionner
replete [rɪ'pli:t] *adj Formal* rassasié(e) (**with** de)
replica ['replɪkə] *n* réplique *f*; *Fig (of person)* portrait *m*
replicate ['replɪkeɪt] *vt* reproduire
reply [rɪ'plaɪ] **1** *n (pl* **replies**) réponse *f*; **in r. to your
letter** en réponse à votre lettre; **to say sth in r. (to
sth)** répondre qch (à qch); **there was no r.** *(on telephone)* ça ne répondait pas
2 *vt & vi (pt & pp* **replied**) répondre (**to** à)
report [rɪ'pɔːt] **1** *n* (**a**) *(account)* compte rendu *m*;
(analysis) rapport *m*; *(in newspaper, on radio, television)* reportage *m*; *Br Sch* bulletin *m* (scolaire); **there
are reports that...** il paraîtrait que...; **r. card** *(for primary school)* carnet *m* de notes; *(for secondary
school)* bulletin *m* scolaire (**b**) *(sound)* détonation *f*
2 *vt (information)* rapporter; *(accident, theft)* signaler; **to r. sb missing** signaler la disparition de qn; **to
r. sb to the police/the authorities** dénoncer qn à la
police/aux autorités; **to r. one's findings (to sb)** faire
un rapport (à qn); **nothing to r.** rien à signaler
3 *vi* (**a**) *(present oneself)* se présenter (**to** à); **to r. for
duty** prendre son service (**b**) *(give account)* faire un
rapport (**to** à); *(of journalist)* faire un reportage (**on**
sur) (**c**) *(be accountable)* **to r. to sb** rendre compte à
qn
▶**report back** *vi* (**a**) *(return)* rentrer, être de retour; *(of
soldier)* regagner ses quartiers (**b**) *(present report)*
présenter son rapport (**to** à)
reportedly [rɪ'pɔːtɪdlɪ] *adv* **he r. said that...** il aurait
dit que...; **he is r. resident in Paris** il résiderait à Paris
reporter [rɪ'pɔːtə(r)] *n (for newspaper)* journaliste *mf*;
(on television, radio) reporter *m*
repose [rɪ'pəuz] *Formal* **1** *n* repos *m*
2 *vi* reposer
repository [rɪ'pɒzɪtərɪ] *(pl* **repositories**) *n (for books,
furniture)* dépôt *m*
repossess [ri:pə'zes] *vt* saisir
reprehensible [reprɪ'hensɪbəl] *adj* répréhensible
represent [reprɪ'zent] *vt* représenter; *(describe)*
présenter
representation [reprɪzen'teɪʃən] *n (in Parliament)* représentation *f*; *(of facts)* exposé *m*; *Formal* **to make
representations (to sb)** faire des démarches (auprès
de qn)
representative [reprɪ'zentətɪv] **1** *n* représentant(e)
m,f
2 *adj* représentatif(ive)
repress [rɪ'pres] *vt* réprimer; *(memories, feelings)* refouler; **to be repressed** *(of person)* être un(e)
refoulé(e)
repression [rɪ'preʃən] *n* répression *f*; *(of memories,
feelings)* refoulement *m*
repressive [rɪ'presɪv] *adj* répressif(ive)
reprieve [rɪ'pri:v] **1** *n Law (cancellation)* commutation *f* de la peine capitale; *(postponement)* sursis *m*;
Fig **to win a r.** *(of project, company)* bénéficier d'un
sursis
2 *vt Law* **to r. sb** *(cancel punishment of)* commuer la
peine capitale de qn en réclusion à perpétuité; *(postpone punishment of)* accorder un sursis à qn

reprimand ['reprimɑ:nd] **1** *n (to child)* réprimande *f*; *(to employee)* avertissement *m*
2 *vt (child)* réprimander; *(employee)* avertir
reprint 1 *n* ['ri:print] réimpression *f*
2 *vt* [ri:'print] réimprimer
reprisal [rɪ'praɪzəl] *n* représailles *fpl*; **to take reprisals** exercer des représailles; **in r. for** en représailles à
reproach [rɪ'prəʊtʃ] **1** *n* reproche *m*; **a look of r.** un regard plein de reproche; **beyond** *or* **above r.** irréprochable
2 *vt* faire des reproches à; **to r. sb for** *or* **with sth** reprocher qch à qn; **to r. oneself for sth** se reprocher qch
reproachful [rɪ'prəʊtʃfʊl] *adj (tone)* de reproche; *(look)* plein(e) de reproche
reprobate ['reprəbeɪt] *n* réprouvé(e) *m,f*; *Hum* dépravé(e) *m,f*
reproduce [ri:prə'dju:s] **1** *vt* reproduire
2 *vi* se reproduire
reproduction [ri:prə'dʌkʃən] *n* reproduction *f*; **r. furniture** copies *fpl* (de meubles anciens)
reproductive [ri:prə'dʌktɪv] *adj* reproducteur(trice); **r. organs** organes *mpl* reproducteurs
reproof [rɪ'pru:f] *n Formal* réprobation *f*
reprove [rɪ'pru:v] *vt Formal (person)* réprimander; *(action)* condamner
reproving [rɪ'pru:vɪŋ] *adj Formal* réprobateur(trice)
reptile ['reptaɪl] *n* reptile *m*
reptilian [rep'tɪlɪən] *adj* reptilien(enne); *Fig (manner, looks)* de reptile
republic [rɪ'pʌblɪk] *n* république *f*
Republican [rə'pʌblɪkən] **1** *n* républicain(e) *m,f*
2 *adj* républicain(e)

Republican

Aux États-Unis, un "Republican" est un partisan du parti républicain, le plus conservateur des deux principaux partis politiques des États-Unis. En Irlande, le terme "Republican" désigne une personne qui souhaite le rattachement de l'Irlande du Nord à la république d'Irlande. Au Royaume-Uni et en Australie, le terme désigne les personnes favorables à l'abolition de la monarchie et à l'établissement d'une république.

republican [rə'pʌblɪkən] *n & adj* républicain(e) *m,f*
repudiate [rɪ'pju:dɪeɪt] *vt Formal (offer)* rejeter; *(person, belief)* renier; *(wife)* répudier; *(rumour)* démentir
repudiation [rɪpju:dɪ'eɪʃən] *n Formal (of offer)* rejet *m*; *(of person, belief)* reniement *m*; *(of wife)* répudiation *f*; *(of rumour)* démenti *m*
repugnant [rɪ'pʌgnənt] *adj* répugnant(e)
repulse [rɪ'pʌls] *vt* repousser
repulsive [rɪ'pʌlsɪv] *adj* repoussant(e)
reputable ['repjʊtəbəl] *adj* de bonne réputation
reputation [repju:'teɪʃən] *n* réputation *f*; **to have a good/bad r.** avoir (une) bonne/mauvaise réputation; **to have a r. for doing sth** avoir la réputation de faire qch; **to have a r. for frankness** avoir la réputation d'être franc (franche); **to live up to one's r.** être à la hauteur de sa réputation
repute [rɪ'pju:t] **1** *n Formal* réputation *f*; **to be held in high r.** être estimé(e); **of r.** réputé(e)
2 *vt* **she is reputed to be wealthy/a genius** on la dit riche/géniale
reputedly [rɪ'pju:tɪdlɪ] *adv* à ce qu'on dit

request [rɪ'kwest] **1** *n* demande *f* (**for** de); **available on r.** qui peut être obtenu(e) sur simple demande; **to make a r. (for)** faire une demande (de); **at sb's r.** à la demande de qn; **by popular r.** à la demande générale; **r. stop** *(for bus)* arrêt *m* facultatif
2 *vt* demander; **to r. sb to do sth** prier à qn de faire qch
requiem ['rekwɪəm] *n* requiem *m*; **r. (mass)** messe *f* de requiem
require [rɪ'kwaɪə(r)] *vt (of task, problem, situation)* requérir; *(of person)* avoir besoin de; **to be required to do sth** être tenu(e) de faire qch; **if required** si besoin est/était; **when required** quand il le faut/fallait/faudra
requirement [rɪ'kwaɪəmənt] *n (need)* exigence *f*; *(condition)* condition *f* (requise); **to meet** *or* **satisfy sb's requirements** *(needs)* correspondre aux besoins de qn; *(demands)* satisfaire aux exigences de qn
requisite ['rekwɪzɪt] **1** *n* élément *m* essentiel
2 *adj* requis(e)
requisition [rekwɪ'zɪʃən] *vt* réquisitionner
rerun 1 *n* ['ri:rʌn] *(on TV)* rediffusion *f*; *Fig (of situation, conflict)* répétition *f*
2 *vt* [ri:'rʌn] *(pt* reran [ri:'ræn], *pp* rerun) (**a**) *(TV programme)* rediffuser (**b**) *(race)* courir de nouveau
resale [ri:'seɪl] *n* revente *f*
resat [ri:'sæt] *pt & pp of* resit
reschedule [ri:'ʃedju:l] *vt* (**a**) *(meeting, flight) (change time of)* changer l'heure de; *(change date of)* changer la date de (**b**) *(debt)* rééchelonner
rescind [rɪ'sɪnd] *vt (law)* abroger; *(contract)* résilier
rescue ['reskju:] **1** *n* secours *m*; *(from drowning)* sauvetage *m*; **to come to sb's r.** venir au secours de qn; **r. attempt, r. operation** opération *f* de sauvetage; **r. services** secours *mpl*
2 *vt (from death)* sauver; *(from difficulty)* secourir
rescuer ['reskjuə(r)] *n* sauveteur *m*
research [rɪ'sɜ:tʃ] **1** *n* recherche *f*; **to do r.** faire de la recherche; **to do r. into sth** faire des recherches qch; **r. and development** recherche et développement *m*; **r. assistant/laboratory** assistant(e) *m,f*/laboratoire *m* de recherche
2 *vt* faire des recherches sur
3 *vi* faire des recherches (**into** sur)
researcher [rɪ'sɜ:tʃə(r)] *n* chercheur(euse) *m,f*
resemblance [rɪ'zembləns] *n* ressemblance *f* (**to** avec); **to bear a r. to** ressembler à
resemble [rɪ'zembəl] *vt* ressembler à
resend [ri:'send] *vt Comput & Tel (e-mail, text message)* renvoyer
resent [rɪ'zent] *vt (person)* en vouloir à; *(remark, criticism)* ne pas apprécier du tout
resentful [rɪ'zentfʊl] *adj (of) de* ressentiment; **to be** *or* **feel r.** éprouver du ressentiment
resentment [rɪ'zentmənt] *n* ressentiment *m*; **to feel r. towards sb** éprouver du ressentiment à l'égard de qn
reservation [rezə'veɪʃən] *n* (**a**) *(booking)* réservation *f*; **to make a r.** faire une réservation; **r. desk** bureau *m* des réservations (**b**) *(doubt)* réserve *f*; **to have reservations about** avoir des doutes sur (**c**) *(for Native Americans)* réserve *f* (indienne)
reserve [rɪ'zɜ:v] **1** *n* (**a**) *(supply)* réserve *f*; **to draw on one's reserves** puiser dans ses réserves; **to keep sth in r.** garder qch en réserve (**b**) *(in sport)* remplaçant(e) *m,f*; *Mil* **the reserves** les réservistes *mpl* (**c**) *(for birds, game)* réserve *f* (**d**) *(reticence)* réserve *f*
2 *vt (book, keep)* réserver; **to r. the right to do sth**

se réserver le droit de faire qch; **to r. one's strength** ménager ses forces; **to r. judgement (on sth)** réserver son jugement (sur qch)

reserved [rɪ'zɜːvd] *adj* réservé(e)

reservist [rɪ'zɜːvɪst] *n Mil* réserviste *m*

reservoir ['rezəvwɑː(r)] *n (lake)* réservoir *m*; *Fig (of strength, courage)* réserve *f*

reset [riː'set] *(pt & pp* **reset***)* *vt* (**a**) *(clock, watch)* mettre à l'heure; *(counter)* remettre à zéro; **r. button** bouton *m* de remise à zéro (**b**) *(fracture)* réduire

reshape [riː'ʃeɪp] *vt* réorganiser

reshuffle ['riːʃʌfəl] *n* réorganisation *f*; *Br Pol* (**Cabinet**) **r.** remaniement *m* (ministériel)

reside [rɪ'zaɪd] *vi* résider (**at/in** à/dans/en)

residence ['rezɪdəns] *n* (**a**) *(stay)* séjour *m*; **to take up r.** s'installer; **place of r.** lieu *m* de résidence; **r. permit** permis *m* de séjour (**b**) *Formal (home)* demeure *f* (**c**) *Br Univ* (**hall of**) **r.** résidence *f* universitaire

resident ['rezɪdənt] **1** *n (of country, street)* habitant(e) *m,f*; *(of hotel)* pensionnaire *mf*; **residents only** *(sign) (in street)* interdit sauf aux riverains; *(in hotel)* réservé a la clientèle de l'hôtel; **residents' association** = association de propriétaires ou de locataires d'un immeuble ou d'un quartier

  2 *adj* **to be r. in Manchester** résider à Manchester

residential [rezɪ'denʃəl] *adj* (**a**) *(neighbourhood)* résidentiel(elle) (**b**) *(staff)* à demeure; **r. course** = stage qui nécessite un déplacement de plusieurs jours

residual [rɪ'zɪdjʊəl] *adj* résiduel(elle); *Fig (doubt, worry)* qui persiste; *(income)* net (nette)

residue ['rezɪdjuː] *n* (**a**) *(remainder)* reste *m* (**b**) *Chem* résidu *m*

resign [rɪ'zaɪn] **1** *vt* (**a**) *(job, position)* démissionner de (**b**) **to r. oneself to sth/to doing sth** se résigner à qch/à faire qch

  2 *vi* démissionner

resignation [rezɪg'neɪʃən] *n* (**a**) *(from job)* démission *f*; **to hand in one's r.** donner sa démission (**b**) *(attitude)* résignation *f*

resilience [rɪ'zɪlɪəns] *n (of material, metal)* élasticité *f*; *(of person, economy)* résistance *f*

resilient [rɪ'zɪlɪənt] *adj (material, metal)* élastique; *(person)* résistant(e)

resin ['rezɪn] *n* résine *f*

resist [rɪ'zɪst] **1** *vt* résister à; *Law* **to r. arrest** refuser d'obtempérer *(lors d'une arrestation)*; **to r. doing sth** s'empêcher de faire qch

  2 *vi* résister

resistance [rɪ'zɪstəns] *n* résistance *f* (**to** à); **to put up** *or* **offer r.** offrir une résistance; **to meet with r.** rencontrer une résistance; **to take the line of least r.** adopter la solution de facilité; *Hist* **the (French) R.** la Résistance (française); **r. fighter** résistant(e) *m,f*

resistant [rɪ'zɪstənt] *adj* **to be r. to sth** résister à qch

resistor [rɪ'zɪstə(r)] *n Elec* résistance *f*

resit 1 *n* ['riːsɪt] examen *m* de rattrapage; **the resits** la session de rattrapage

  2 *vt* [riː'sɪt] *(pt & pp* **resat** [riː'sæt]*) (exam, driving test)* repasser

resolute ['rezəluːt] *adj* résolu(e); *(refusal, opposition)* clair(e)

resolution [rezə'luːʃən] *n* (**a**) *(decision, solution)* résolution *f*; **to pass** *or* **carry a r.** adopter une résolution (**b**) *(firmness)* fermeté *f*

resolve [rɪ'zɒlv] **1** *n* résolution *f*

  2 *vt* (**a**) *(decide)* **to r. to do sth** *(of individual)* se

résoudre à faire qch; *(of committee)* décider de faire qch (**b**) *(solve)* résoudre

  3 *vi* **to r. on/against doing sth** se résoudre à faire/ne pas faire qch

resonance ['rezənəns] *n* résonance *f*

resonant ['rezənənt] *adj* qui résonne

resonate ['rezəneɪt] *vi* résonner

resort [rɪ'zɔːt] **1** *n (of recourse)* recours *m*; **without r. to** sans avoir recours à; **as a last r.** en dernier recours (**b**) *(holiday place)* lieu *m* de villégiature

  2 *vi* **to r. to sth** recourir à qch; **to r. to doing sth** finir par faire qch

resound [rɪ'zaʊnd] *vi* résonner (**with** de)

resounding [rɪ'zaʊndɪŋ] *adj (crash, applause, failure)* retentissant(e); *(success)* éclatant(e)

resource [rɪ'zɔːs] **1** *n* ressource *f*; **to be left to one's own resources** être livré(e) à soi-même; **r. management** gestion *f* des ressources

  2 *vt* financer

resourceful [rɪ'zɔːsfʊl] *adj* ingénieux(euse)

respect [rɪ'spekt] **1** *n* (**a**) *(admiration, consideration)* respect *m*; **to have r. for** avoir du respect pour; **treat mountains with r.** soyez prudent en montagne; **with all due r.** sauf le respect que je vous dois; **to pay one's last respects to sb** rendre les derniers hommages à qn (**b**) *(aspect)* égard *m*; **in many respects** à bien des égards; **in some** *or* **certain respects** à certains égards; **in all respects** *or* **every r.** à tous les égards; **with r. to, in r. of** concernant

  2 *vt* respecter

respectability [rɪspektə'bɪlɪtɪ] *n* respectabilité *f*

respectable [rɪ'spektəbəl] *adj (decent, fairly large)* respectable; *(fairly good)* honorable

respectably [rɪ'spektəblɪ] *adv* (**a**) *(honourably, decently)* de manière respectable; *(dressed)* convenablement (**b**) *(fairly well)* honorablement

respecter [rɪ'spektə(r)] *n* **to be no r. of** n'avoir aucun respect pour

respectful [rɪ'spektfʊl] *adj* respectueux(euse)

respective [rɪ'spektɪv] *adj* respectif(ive)

respectively [rɪ'spektɪvlɪ] *adv* respectivement

respiration [respɪ'reɪʃən] *n* respiration *f*

respirator ['respɪreɪtə(r)] *n* respirateur *m*; **to be on a r.** être branché(e) sur un respirateur

respiratory [rɪ'spɪrɪtərɪ] *adj* respiratoire

respite ['respaɪt] *n (rest)* répit *m*; *(delay)* sursis *m*

resplendent [rɪ'splendənt] *adj* resplendissant(e)

respond [rɪ'spɒnd] *vi (answer)* répondre (**to** à); *(react)* réagir (**to** à); **to r. (to treatment)** *(of patient)* bien réagir (au traitement)

respondent [rɪ'spɒndənt] *n* (**a**) *Law* défendeur/eresse) *m,f* (**b**) *(to questionnaire)* sondé(e) *m,f*

response [rɪ'spɒns] *n (answer)* réponse *f*; *(reaction)* réaction *f*; **in r.** en réponse à; **the appeal met with a generous r.** le public a répondu généreusement à l'appel; **r. time** temps *m* de réponse

responsibility [rɪspɒnsɪ'bɪlɪtɪ] *n (pl* **responsibilities***)* *n* responsabilité *f* (**for** de); **to take** *or* **accept r. for sth** accepter la responsabilité de qch

responsible [rɪ'spɒnsɪbəl] *adj* responsable (**for** de); *(job)* à responsabilité; **to hold sb r.** tenir qn pour responsable

responsive [rɪ'spɒnsɪv] *adj (to kindness, praise)* sensible (**to** à); *(to idea, suggestion)* réceptif(ive) (**to** à)

rest[1] [rest] **1** *n* (**a**) *(repose)* repos *m*; **to have** *or* **take a r.** se reposer; *Euph* **to be at r.** reposer en paix; **to put**

or set sb's mind at r. rassurer qn; *Fam* **give it a r.!** tu veux bien arrêter cinq minutes!; **to come to r.** *(of ball, car)* s'arrêter (**b**) *(support)* support *m* (**c**) *Mus (pause)* silence *m*
2 *vt* (**a**) *(cause to repose)* **to r. one's eyes/legs** se reposer les yeux/les jambes; **God r. his soul!** que Dieu ait son âme! (**b**) *(lean)* poser (**on** sur) (**c**) *(argument, hopes, confidence)* fonder (**on** sur); *Fig* **I r. my case!** sans commentaire!
3 *vi* (**a**) *(repose)* se reposer, prendre du repos; **I won't r.** until she has been caught je n'aurai de cesse qu'elle ne soit prise; **r. in peace** *(on gravestone)* qu'il/elle repose en paix (**b**) *(lean)* être posé(e) (**on** sur) (**c**) *(remain)* **to r. with sb** *(of decision, responsibility)* incomber à qn; **there the matter rests** l'affaire en est là; **I won't let it r.** at that je n'en resterai pas là; **r. assured...** soyez assuré que... (**d**) *(of argument, theory)* **to r. on** reposer sur
rest² *n* **the r.** *(remainder)* le reste; *(others)* les autres *mfpl*; **the r. of the time/the men** le reste du temps/des hommes; **the r. of them will stay here** les autres resteront ici
restaurant ['restrɒnt] *n* restaurant *m*; **r. car** *(in train)* wagon-restaurant *m*
restful ['restfʊl] *adj* reposant(e)
restive ['restɪv] *adj* agité(e)
restless ['restlɪs] *adj* agité(e); **to have a r. night** passer une nuit agitée
restoration [restə'reɪʃən] *n* *(of furniture, monarchy)* restauration *f*; *(of communications, law and order)* rétablissement *m*; *(of property)* restitution *f*
restore [rɪ'stɔː(r)] *vt* *(furniture, monarchy, faith, calm)* restaurer; *(communications, law and order, confidence)* rétablir; *(property)* restituer (**to** à); **to r. sb to health/strength** redonner la santé/des forces à qn
restrain [rɪ'streɪn] *vt* *(person, dog)* maîtriser; *(passions)* refréner; *(anger, crowd)* contenir; **to r. sb from doing sth** retenir qn pour qu'il/elle ne fasse pas qch; **to r. oneself (from doing sth)** se retenir (de faire qch)
restrained [rɪ'streɪnd] *adj* *(person, manner)* réservé(e); *(tone, terms)* mesuré(e); *(style)* sobre
restraint [rɪ'streɪnt] *n* (**a**) *(moderation)* mesure *f*, modération *f*; **to show** *or* **exercise great r.** faire preuve d'une grande modération (**b**) *(restriction)* restriction *f*; **without r.** sans retenue
restrict [rɪ'strɪkt] *vt* *(person, freedom)* restreindre; **to r. oneself to sth/to doing sth** se limiter à qch/à faire qch
restricted [rɪ'strɪktɪd] *adj* restreint(e), limité(e); *(document)* secret(ète); **r. area** *Mil* zone *f* interdite; *(for parking)* zone *f* bleue
restriction [rɪ'strɪkʃən] *n* restriction *f*; *(of speed)* limitation *f*; **to place restrictions on sth** apporter des restrictions à qch
restrictive [rɪ'strɪktɪv] *adj* restrictif(ive); *Ind* **r. practices** pratiques *fpl* restrictives
restroom ['restruːm] *n Am* toilettes *fpl*
restructure [riː'strʌktʃə(r)] *vt* restructurer
restructuring [riː'strʌktʃərɪŋ] *n* restructuration *f*
result [rɪ'zʌlt] **1** *n* résultat *m*; **as a r.** en conséquence; **as a r. of** à la suite de; **the r. is that...** il en résulte que...; **to yield** *or* **show results** donner des résultats
2 *vi* **to r. from** résulter de; **to r. in** entraîner
resultant [rɪ'zʌltənt] *adj* résultant(e)
resume [rɪ'zjuːm] **1** *vt* reprendre; *(relations)* renouer; *(attempt)* renouveler; *(interest)* retrouver
2 *vi* reprendre

résumé ['rezjʊmeɪ] *n (summary)* résumé *m*; *Am (curriculum vitae)* curriculum vitae *m inv*
resumption [rɪ'zʌmpʃən] *n* reprise *f*
resurface [riː'sɜːfɪs] **1** *vt (road)* refaire le revêtement de
2 *vi also Fig* refaire surface
resurgent [rɪ'sɜːdʒənt] *adj* renaissant(e); *(economy)* qui connaît une reprise
resurrect [rezə'rekt] *vt Rel* ressusciter; *Fig (fashion)* remettre au goût du jour; *(argument)* ressortir; *(tradition)* faire renaître
resurrection [rezə'rekʃən] *n Fig* réapparition *f*; *Rel* **the R.** la Résurrection (du Christ)
resuscitate [rɪ'sʌsɪteɪt] *vt (person)* ranimer; *Fig (career)* redonner un nouvel élan à; *(scheme)* ressortir
retail ['riːteɪl] **1** *n Com (vente f au)* détail *m*; **r. outlet** magasin *m* de détail; **r. price** prix *m* de détail; *Econ* **r. price index** indice *m* des prix de détail; **r. trade** commerce *m* de détail; *Hum* **I did a bit of r. therapy this weekend** j'ai fait un peu de shopping pour me remonter le moral ce week-end
2 *vt (goods)* vendre au détail
3 *vi* se vendre (**at** à)
retailer ['riːteɪlə(r)] *n* détaillant(e) *m,f*
retain [rɪ'teɪn] *vt* (**a**) *(keep)* conserver, garder (**b**) *(hold in place)* maintenir; **retaining wall** mur *m* de soutènement (**c**) *(remember)* retenir
retainer [rɪ'teɪnə(r)] *n* (**a**) *(fee)* appointements *mpl* (**b**) *Old-fashioned (servant)* serviteur *m*, servante *f*
retaliate [rɪ'tælɪeɪt] *vi* riposter
retaliation [rɪtælɪ'eɪʃən] *n* représailles *fpl*; **in r. (for sth)** en représailles (à qch)
retard [rɪ'tɑːd] *vt* retarder
retarded [rɪ'tɑːdɪd] *adj* **(mentally) r.** arriéré(e)
retch [retʃ] *vi* avoir des haut-le-cœur
retention [rɪ'tenʃən] *n (of custom, practice)* maintien *m*; *(of fact, impression)* mémorisation *f*
retentive [rɪ'tentɪv] *adj (memory)* fidèle; *(person)* qui a (une) bonne mémoire
rethink **1** *n* ['riːθɪŋk] **to have a r. (about sth)** réfléchir à nouveau (à qch)
2 *vt* [riː'θɪŋk] *(pt & pp* rethought [riː'θɔːt]) repenser
reticent ['retɪsənt] *adj* réservé(e), réticent(e); **to be r. about sth** parler peu de qch
retina ['retɪnə] *n* rétine *f*
retinue ['retɪnjuː] *n* suite *f*, cortège *m*
retire [rɪ'taɪə(r)] **1** *vt* mettre à la retraite
2 *vi* (**a**) *(of employee)* prendre sa retraite (**b**) *(withdraw)* se retirer; *(go to bed)* (aller) se coucher
retired [rɪ'taɪəd] *adj* retraité(e), à la retraite
retirement [rɪ'taɪəmənt] *n (from work, army)* retraite *f*; **to take early r.** partir en retraite anticipée; **to come out of r.** reprendre sa carrière; **r. age** l'âge *m* de la retraite; **r. home** maison *f* de retraite; **r. pension** *(pension f* de) retraite *f*
retiring [rɪ'taɪərɪŋ] *adj* (**a**) *(reserved)* réservé(e) (**b**) *(chairman, MP)* sortant(e); *(employee)* qui prend sa retraite; **r. age** l'âge *m* de la retraite
retort [rɪ'tɔːt] **1** *n (answer)* réplique *f*
2 *vt & vi* répliquer
retrace [riː'treɪs] *vt* **to r. one's steps** revenir sur ses pas
retract [rɪ'trækt] **1** *vt* (**a**) *(statement, offer)* revenir sur (**b**) *(claws, aircraft undercarriage)* rentrer
2 *vi* (**a**) *(of person)* se rétracter (**b**) *(of claws, aircraft undercarriage)* rentrer
retractable [rɪ'træktəbəl] *adj* rétractable; *(antenna, aircraft undercarriage)* escamotable

retrain [riːˈtreɪn] **1** *vt* recycler
2 *vi* se recycler
retraining [riːˈtreɪnɪŋ] *n* recyclage *m*
retread [ˈriːtred] *n* pneu *m* rechapé
retreat [rɪˈtriːt] **1** *n* (**a**) *(withdrawal)* retraite *f*; *also Fig* **to beat a (hasty) r.** battre en retraite (**b**) *(place)* retraite *f*
2 *vi* battre en retraite; *Fig* se réfugier
retrial [riːˈtraɪəl] *n Law* nouveau procès *m*
retribution [retrɪˈbjuːʃən] *n* châtiment *m*
retrieve [rɪˈtriːv] *vt* récupérer; *Comput (file)* ouvrir
retriever [rɪˈtriːvə(r)] *n (dog)* retriever *m*
retroactive [retrəʊˈæktɪv] *adj Formal* rétroactif(ive)
retrograde [ˈretrəgreɪd] *adj* rétrograde
retrospect [ˈretrəspekt] *n* **in r.** après coup, rétrospectivement
retrospective [retrəˈspektɪv] **1** *n (exhibition)* rétrospective *f*
2 *adj* rétrospectif(ive); *(measure, decision)* à effet rétroactif
return [rɪˈtɜːn] **1** *n* (**a**) *(of person, peace, season, tennis service)* retour *m*; *(of goods)* renvoi *m*; **on my r.** à mon retour; **by r. of post** par retour du courrier; **in r. (for)** en échange (de); **to do sth in r.** faire qch en retour; **many happy returns (of the day)!** bon anniversaire!; **r. journey** (voyage *m* de) retour *m*; **r. match** match *m* retour; **r. ticket** (billet *m*) aller et retour *m* (**b**) *Fin (profit)* rapport *m*; **to bring a good r.** rapporter un bon bénéfice; **r. on investment** retour *m* sur investissement
2 *vt* (**a**) *(give or send back)* rendre; **to r. a favour** rendre la pareille; **r. to sender** *(on letter)* retour à l'envoyeur; **to r. service** *(in tennis)* renvoyer le service; **to r. sb's call** *(on phone)* rappeler qn; *Law* **to r. a verdict of guilty/not guilty** déclarer l'accusé(e) coupable/non coupable (**b**) *Fin (profit)* rapporter
3 *vi (come back)* revenir; *(go back)* retourner; **to r. to work** reprendre son travail
returnable [rɪˈtɜːnəbəl] *adj (bottle)* consigné(e)
reunification [riːjuːnɪfɪˈkeɪʃən] *n* réunification *f*
reunify [riːˈjuːnɪfaɪ] *(pt & pp* **reunified)** *vt* réunifier
reunion [riːˈjuːnɪən] *n* réunion *f*
reunite [riːjʊˈnaɪt] *vt* réconcilier; **to be reunited with sb** retrouver qn
reusable [riːˈjuːzəbəl] *adj* réutilisable
reuse [riːˈjuːz] *vt* réutiliser
Rev *Rel (abbr* **Reverend) R.** Gray le révérend Gray
rev [rev] *Fam* **1** *n (abbr* **revolution)** tour *m*; **r. counter** compte-tours *m inv*
2 *vt (pt & pp* **revved) to r. the engine** faire monter le régime (du moteur)
revalue [riːˈvæljuː] *vt Fin* réévaluer
revamp [riːˈvæmp] *vt Fam (image)* rajeunir; *(company)* restructurer; *(house)* retaper
reveal [rɪˈviːl] *vt* révéler
revealing [rɪˈviːlɪŋ] *adj (sign, comment)* révélateur(trice); *(clothing)* qui ne cache pas grand-chose
revel [ˈrevəl] *(pt & pp* **revelled,** *Am* **reveled)** *vi* faire la fête; **to r. in sth** savourer qch
revelation [revəˈleɪʃən] *n* révélation *f*; **(the Book of)** Revelations l'Apocalypse *f*
reveller, *Am* **reveler** [ˈrevələ(r)] *n* fêtard(e) *m,f*
revenge [rɪˈvendʒ] **1** *n (punishment)* vengeance *f*; *(getting one's own back)* revanche *f*; **to take r. (on sb)** se venger (de qn); *Prov* **r. is sweet** ça fait du bien de se venger!
2 *vt* venger

revenue [ˈrevənjuː] *n* revenu *m*; *(from sales)* recettes *fpl*
reverberate [rɪˈvɜːbəreɪt] *vi* (**a**) *(of sound)* résonner (**b**) *(of news, rumour)* se propager
reverberation [rɪvɜːbəˈreɪʃən] *n* (**a**) *(sound)* réverbération *f* (**b**) *(of news, rumour)* répercussion *f*
revere [rɪˈvɪə(r)] *vt* révérer
reverence [ˈrevərəns] *n* révérence *f*
Reverend [ˈrevərənd] *adj Rel* révérend; **Right R.** très révérend
reverential [revəˈrenʃəl] *adj* révérencieux(euse)
reverie [ˈrevərɪ] *n* rêverie *f*
reversal [rɪˈvɜːsəl] *n (of opinion, policy)* revirement *m*; *(of roles)* renversement *m*; *(of fortune)* revers *m*; *Law (of decision)* annulation *f*
reverse [rɪˈvɜːs] **1** *n* (**a**) *(opposite)* contraire *m*; **quite the r.!** bien au contraire! (**b**) *(of coin)* revers *m*; *(of fabric)* envers *m* (**c**) *(defeat)* échec *m*; *(misfortune)* revers *m*; **to suffer a r.** *(defeat)* subir un échec; *(misfortune)* subir un revers (**d**) *(gear)* marche *f* arrière; **to put the car into r.** passer la marche arrière
2 *adj* inverse; **in r. order** en ordre inverse; **the r. side** *(of coin)* le revers; *(of fabric)* l'envers *m*; *Br* **r.-charge call** communication *f* en PCV, *Can* appel *m* à frais virés; **r. gear** marche *f* arrière
3 *vt* (**a**) *(order, policy, roles)* inverser; *(decision)* revenir sur; *(situation, trend)* renverser; *Br* **to r. the charges** appeler en PCV (**b**) *(vehicle)* **to r. the car** faire marche arrière
reversible [rɪˈvɜːsəbəl] *adj* (**a**) *(jacket)* réversible (**b**) *(decree)* révocable; *(surgery)* réversible; **not r.** *(decision)* irrévocable; *(surgery)* irréversible
▸**revert to** [rɪˈvɜːt] *vt insep* revenir à; **to r. to type** reprendre ses vieilles habitudes
review [rɪˈvjuː] **1** *n* (**a**) *(of policy, salary)* révision *f*; *(of situation)* examen *m*; **to be under r.** faire l'objet d'une révision (**b**) *(of book, play, film)* critique *f* (**c**) *Mil* revue *f*
2 *vt* (**a**) *(policy, salary)* réviser; *(situation)* faire le point sur (**b**) *(book, play, film)* faire la critique de (**c**) *Mil (troops)* passer en revue
reviewer [rɪˈvjuːə(r)] *n (of book, play, film)* critique *mf*
revile [rɪˈvaɪl] *vt Formal* vilipender
revise [rɪˈvaɪz] **1** *vt* (**a**) *(text, law)* réviser; *(decision)* réexaminer; **to r. one's opinion (of)** changer d'opinion (à l'égard de) (**b**) *Br (for exam) (subject, notes)* réviser
2 *vi Br (for exam)* réviser, faire des révisions
revision [rɪˈvɪʒən] *n* (**a**) *(of text, law)* révision *f* (**b**) *Br (for exam)* révisions *fpl*
revisionism [rɪˈvɪʒənɪzəm] *n Pol* révisionnisme *m*
revisit [rɪˈvɪzɪt] *vt (place)* revisiter; *(person)* retourner voir
revitalize [rɪˈvaɪtəlaɪz] *vt (person)* revigorer; *(arts, industry)* donner un nouvel essor à
revival [rɪˈvaɪvəl] *n (of person)* réanimation *f*; *(of hopes)* renaissance *f*; *(of industry, custom, fashion)* renouveau *m*; *(of play)* reprise *f*
revive [rɪˈvaɪv] **1** *vt (person)* ranimer; *(industry, hopes, custom)* faire renaître; *(fashion)* relancer
2 *vi (of person)* reprendre connaissance; *(of industry)* connaître un renouveau; *(of hopes)* renaître
revoke [rɪˈvəʊk] *vt (law)* abroger; *(decision)* revenir sur; *(privilege)* abolir; **to r. sb's licence** retirer son permis à qn

revolt [rɪ'vəʊlt] **1** *n* révolte *f*; **to be in r.** être en révolte **2** *vt (disgust)* dégoûter **3** *vi (rebel)* se révolter (**against** contre)
revolting [rɪ'vəʊltɪŋ] *adj (disgusting)* dégoûtant(e)
revolution [revə'luːʃən] *n* (**a**) *(radical change)* révolution *f* (**b**) *(turn)* tour *m*, révolution *f*
revolutionary [revə'luːʃənərɪ] **1** *n* (*pl* **revolutionaries**) révolutionnaire *mf* **2** *adj* révolutionnaire
revolutionize [revə'luːʃənaɪz] *vt* révolutionner
revolve [rɪ'vɒlv] *vi* tourner (**around** autour de); *Fig* **to r. around sth** s'articuler autour de qch
revolver [rɪ'vɒlvə(r)] *n* revolver *m*
revolving [rɪ'vɒlvɪŋ] *adj (chair)* pivotant(e); *(platform)* tournant(e); *Fin (credit)* revolving *inv*; **r. door** porte *f* à tambour
revue [rɪ'vjuː] *n Theat* revue *f*
revulsion [rɪ'vʌlʃən] *n* dégoût *m*
reward [rɪ'wɔːd] **1** *n* récompense *f*; **as a r. for** en récompense de **2** *vt* récompenser (**for** de *ou* pour)
rewarding [rɪ'wɔːdɪŋ] *adj (experience)* enrichissant(e), intéressant(e); *(job)* gratifiant(e)
rewind [riː'waɪnd] *(pt & pp* **rewound** [riː'waʊnd]) *vt (tape, film)* rembobiner
rewire [riː'waɪə(r)] *vt* refaire l'installation électrique de
reword [riː'wɜːd] *vt* reformuler
rework [riː'wɜːk] *vt* retravailler
rewound [riː'waʊnd] *pt & pp of* **rewind**
rewrite [riː'raɪt] *(pt* **rewrote** [riː'rəʊt], *pp* **rewritten** [riː'rɪtən]) *vt* réécrire
Reykjavik ['rekjəvɪk] *n* Reykjavik
RFU [ɑːref'juː] *n Br Sport (abbr* **Rugby Football Union**) = fédération britannique de rugby
rhapsodic(al) [ræp'sɒdɪk(əl)] *adj (prose, description)* dithyrambique; *(person)* enthousiaste
rhapsodize ['ræpsədaɪz] *vi* s'extasier (**over** *or* **about** sur)
rhapsody ['ræpsədɪ] *(pl* **rhapsodies**) *n Mus* rhapsodie *f*; **to go into rhapsodies over sth** s'extasier sur qch
rhesus ['riːsəs] *n* **r. factor** facteur *m* rhésus; **r. positive/negative** rhésus *m* positif/négatif; **r. monkey** rhésus *m*
rhetoric ['retərɪk] *n* rhétorique *f*; **the speech was nothing but empty r.** le discours ne consistait qu'en de belles phrases creuses
rhetorical [rɪ'tɒrɪkəl] *adj (style, question)* rhétorique; *(term)* de rhétorique
rheumatic [ruː'mætɪk] *adj (pain)* rhumatismal(e); *(joint)* atteint(e) de rhumatisme; **r. fever** rhumatisme *m* articulaire aigu
rheumatism ['ruːmətɪzəm] *n* rhumatisme *m*
rheumatoid arthritis ['ruːmətɔɪdɑːθ'raɪtɪs] *n* polyarthrite *f* rhumatoïde
Rhine [raɪn] *n* **the R.** le Rhin
rhinestone ['raɪnstəʊn] *n* faux diamant *m*
rhino ['raɪnəʊ] *(pl* **rhinos**) *n Fam* rhinocéros *m*
rhinoceros [raɪ'nɒsərəs] *n* rhinocéros *m*
Rhodes [rəʊdz] *n* Rhodes
rhododendron [rəʊdə'dendrən] *n* rhododendron *m*
rhomboid ['rɒmbɔɪd] *n* rhomboïde *m*
rhombus ['rɒmbəs] *(pl* **rhombuses** *or* **rhombi** ['rɒmbaɪ]) *n* losange *m*
Rhone [rəʊn] *n* **the R.** le Rhône

rhubarb ['ruːbɑːb] *n* rhubarbe *f*; **r. jam/tart** confiture *f*/tarte *f* à la rhubarbe
rhyme [raɪm] **1** *n (sound)* rime *f*; *(poem)* vers *mpl*; **without r. or reason** sans rime ni raison **2** *vi* rimer (**with** avec)
rhyming slang ['raɪmɪŋslæŋ] *n* = argot cockney où les mots sont remplacés par des locutions choisies pour la rime

Rhyming slang

Il s'agit d'un procédé complexe consistant à remplacer un mot par une expression dont le dernier terme rime avec le mot en question ; bien souvent n'est prononcé que le premier terme de l'expression, à savoir celui qui ne rime pas avec le mot remplacé. Exemple : kids = dustbin lids = dustbins; head = loaf of bread = loaf. À l'origine ce type d'argot était pratiqué par les Cockneys (habitants de l'est de Londres) mais certains termes sont maintenant passés dans la langue courante et sont connus de la plupart des Britanniques.

rhythm ['rɪðəm] *n* rythme *m*; **r. method** *(of contraception)* méthode *f* du calendrier
rhythmic(al) ['rɪðmɪk(əl)] *adj* rythmé(e), cadencé(e)
rib [rɪb] **1** *n* (**a**) *(of person, animal)* côte *f* (**b**) *(of umbrella)* baleine *f* **2** *vt (pt & pp* **ribbed**) *Fam (tease)* taquiner (**about** à propos de)
ribald ['rɪbəld, 'raɪbəld] *adj* grivois(e), paillard(e)
ribbed [rɪbd] *adj (fabric, jumper)* à côtes
ribbon ['rɪbən] *n (for hair, typewriter)* ruban *m*; *(of land)* bande *f* étroite; **to tear sth to ribbons** déchiqueter qch; *Fig (criticize)* éreinter qch
ribcage ['rɪbkeɪdʒ] *n* cage *f* thoracique
Ribena® [raɪ'biːnə] *n* sirop *m* de cassis
riboflavin(e) [raɪbəʊ'fleɪvɪn] *n Chem* riboflavine *f*
rice [raɪs] *n* riz *m*; **r. field** *or* **paddy** rizière *f*; **r. pudding** riz *m* au lait
rich [rɪtʃ] **1** *npl* (**a**) **the r.** les riches *mpl* (**b**) **riches** *(wealth)* richesses *fpl* **2** *adj* riche; *(harvest, supply)* abondant(e); *(colour)* intense; *(voice)* chaud(e); **to be r. in sth** être riche en qch; *Fam* **that's r. coming from you!** venant de toi, c'est un peu fort!
richly ['rɪtʃlɪ] *adv* richement; **r. deserved** bien mérité(e)
Richter Scale ['rɪktə'skeɪl] *n* échelle *f* de Richter
rick¹ [rɪk] *n (of hay, straw)* meule *f*
rick² *vt* **to r. one's neck** attraper un torticolis; **to r. one's back** se donner un tour de reins
rickets ['rɪkɪts] *npl* rachitisme *m*; **to have r.** être rachitique
rickety ['rɪkɪtɪ] *adj Fam (furniture, staircase)* branlant(e)
ricochet ['rɪkəʃeɪ] **1** *n* ricochet *m* **2** *vi (pt & pp* **ricochetted** ['rɪkəʃeɪd]) ricocher (**off** sur)
rid [rɪd] *(pt* **rid**, *pp* **rid** *or* **ridden** ['rɪdən]) *vt* **to r. sb of sth** débarrasser qn de qch; **to get r. of sth** se débarrasser de qch
riddance ['rɪdəns] *n Fam* **good r.!** bon débarras!
ridden ['rɪdən] *pp of* **rid, ride**
riddle ['rɪdəl] **1** *n (puzzle)* devinette *f*; *(mystery)* énigme *f* **2** *vt* **to r. sb/sth with bullets** cribler qn/qch de balles; **riddled with mistakes** truffé(e) de fautes

ride [raɪd] **1** *n* (**a**) *(on bicycle, in car)* tour *m*; *(on horse)* promenade *f*; **to go for a r.** aller faire un tour; **to give sb a r.** *(in car)* conduire qn en voiture; **it's only a short r. away** ce n'est pas très loin; *Fig* **she was given a rough r.** on lui en a fait voir de toutes les couleurs; *Fig* **to take sb for a r.** mener qn en bateau (**b**) *(at funfair)* attraction *f*
 2 *vt* (*pt* **rode** [rəʊd], *pp* **ridden** ['rɪdən]) *(horse, bicycle)* monter à; *(bus, train)* prendre
 3 *vi* *(on horse)* faire du cheval; *(on bicycle)* faire de la bicyclette; *Fig* **to be riding high** connaître une période de succès; *Fam Fig* **to let it r.** laisser courir
▸**ride out** *vt sep (problem, crisis)* survivre à; *Fig* **to r. out the storm** surmonter la crise
 rider ['raɪdə(r)] *n* (**a**) *(on horse)* cavalier(ère) *m,f*; *(on bicycle)* cycliste *mf*; *(on motorbike)* motocycliste *mf* (**b**) *Law (to document, treaty)* annexe *f*; *(to bill)* clause *f* additionnelle
 ridge [rɪdʒ] *n (of mountain)* crête *f*; *(of roof)* faîte *m*; *(on surface)* strie *f*; *Met* **r. of high pressure** dorsale *f* barométrique
 ridicule ['rɪdɪkjuːl] **1** *n* ridicule *m*; **to hold sb/sth up to r.** tourner qn/qch en ridicule
 2 *vt* ridiculiser, tourner en ridicule
 ridiculous [rɪ'dɪkjʊləs] *adj* ridicule; **to make sb/sth look r.** rendre qn/qch ridicule; **to make oneself look r.** se rendre ridicule, se ridiculiser
 riding ['raɪdɪŋ] *n* équitation *f*; **to go r.** faire du cheval; **r. boots** bottes *fpl* de cheval; **r. crop** *or* **whip** cravache *f*; **r. school** école *f* d'équitation
 rife [raɪf] *adj* **to be r.** être très répandu(e); *(of rumours)* aller bon train
 riffraff ['rɪfræf] *n* racaille *f*
 rifle ['raɪfəl] *n* fusil *m*; **r. range** champ *m* de tir; *(at funfair)* stand *m* de tir; **r. shot** coup *m* de fusil
▸**rifle through** *vt* fouiller dans
 rifleman ['raɪfəlmən] *n Mil* fusilier *m*
 rift [rɪft] *n (in earth, rock)* fissure *f*; *(in relationship)* rupture *f*; *(difference of opinion)* désaccord *m*
 rig [rɪg] **1** *n* (**a**) *(of ship)* gréement *m* (**b**) **(oil) r.** derrick *m*; *(at sea)* plate-forme *f* pétrolière
 2 *vt* (*pt & pp* **rigged**) (**a**) *(ship)* gréer (**b**) *Fam (election, contest)* truquer
▸**rig out** *vt sep Fam* **to be rigged out in** être attifé(e) de
▸**rig up** *vt sep* monter, installer
 Riga ['riːgə] *n* Riga
 rigging ['rɪgɪŋ] *n (of ship)* gréement *m*
 right [raɪt] **1** *n* (**a**) *(morality)* bien *m*; **to be in the r.** avoir raison; **to set things to rights** arranger les choses
 (**b**) *(entitlement)* droit *m*; **to have the r. to do sth** avoir le droit de faire qch; **to be within one's rights** être dans son droit; **all rights reserved** tous droits réservés; **by rights** en principe; **by r.** de droit; **to be famous in one's own r.** être soi-même une célébrité; *Br* **r. to roam** = droit d'emprunter des sentiers sur des terres appartenant à de grands propriétaires terriens; **the r. to vote** le droit de vote; **r. of way** *(on land)* droit *m* de passage; *(on road)* priorité *f*
 (**c**) *(right-hand side)* droite *f*, côté *m* droit; **on** *or* **to the r.** à droite; **on my r.** à *ou* sur ma droite; **the r.** *(in politics)* la droite
 2 *adj* (**a**) *(correct)* exact(e), bon (bonne); *(word)* juste; **to be r.** *(of person)* avoir raison; **to keep on the r. side of sb** veiller à ne pas se mettre qn à dos; **to be on the r. lines** être sur la bonne voie

 (**b**) *(morally good)* bien *inv*; **to do the r. thing** faire ce qu'il faut
 (**c**) *(appropriate)* bon (bonne); **the r. thing to do** la meilleure chose à faire; **to know the r. people** connaître les gens qu'il faut; **to be in the r. place at the r. time** se trouver à au bon moment
 (**d**) *(mentally, physically well)* **I'm not feeling quite r.** je ne me sens pas très bien; **to be as r. as rain** être en parfaite santé; **no one in his r. mind would do that** aucune personne sensée ne ferait cela; **he's not quite r. in the head** il n'a pas toute sa tête
 (**e**) *Br Fam (for emphasis)* véritable; **I felt a r. fool** je me suis vraiment senti stupide; **my hair was in a r. mess** mes cheveux étaient complètement en bataille
 (**f**) *(right-hand)* droit(e); **on the r. side** à *ou* sur la droite; *Pol* **the r. wing** l'aile *f* droite
 (**g**) *Math* **r. angle** angle *m* droit
 3 *adv* (**a**) *(straight)* tout droit; **to put things r.** arranger les choses; **to put sb r.** détromper qn
 (**b**) **r. away** *(immediately)* sur-le-champ, immédiatement; **I'll be r. back** je reviens tout de suite; **r. now** *(immediately)* tout de suite; *(at the moment)* en ce moment
 (**c**) *(completely)* **to go r. through sth** traverser qch de part en part; **to go r. up to sb** se diriger (tout) droit vers qn; **to turn r. round** se retourner; **r. at the top/back** tout en haut/à l'arrière
 (**d**) *(exactly)* **r. here/there** juste ici/là; **r. in the middle** en plein milieu; **r. behind** juste derrière; *Fig* **to be r. behind sb** soutenir qn à fond
 (**e**) *(answer)* correctement; *(guess)* juste; **to understand/remember r.** bien comprendre/se souvenir
 (**f**) *(well)* **I'm sure it'll all come r. for you** je suis sûr que tout s'arrangera pour vous; *Fam* **to see sb r.** veiller à ce que qn ne soit pas à court d'argent; **it was a mistake, r. enough** c'était une erreur
 (**g**) *(look, turn)* à droite; *Fig* **r., left and centre** de tous les côtés
 4 *vt* (**a**) *(put upright)* redresser
 (**b**) *(redress)* **to r. a wrong** réparer un tort
 right-angled ['raɪtæŋgəld] *adj* à angle droit; *(triangle)* rectangle
 righteous ['raɪtʃəs] *adj (person)* droit(e), vertueux(euse); *(indignation)* vertueux(euse)
 rightful ['raɪtfəl] *adj (heir, owner)* légitime; *(share)* auquel (à laquelle) on a droit
 right-hand ['raɪthænd] *adj* de droite; *(corner, side)* droit(e); **r. bend** virage *m* à droite; **r. drive** conduite *f* à droite; **on the r. side** à droite; **to be sb's r. man** être le bras droit de qn
 right-handed [raɪt'hændɪd] **1** *adj* droitier(ère)
 2 *adv* de la main droite
 right-hander [raɪt'hændə(r)] *n (person)* droitier(ère) *m,f*
 rightly ['raɪtlɪ] *adv (correctly)* bien; *(justifiably)* à juste titre; **I don't r. know why...** je ne sais pas exactement pourquoi...; **r. or wrongly** à tort ou à raison; **... and r. so** ... et non sans raison
 right-minded [raɪt'maɪndɪd], **right-thinking** [raɪt-'θɪŋkɪŋ] *adj* sensé(e)
 right-wing [raɪt'wɪŋ] *adj Pol* de droite
 right-winger [raɪt'wɪŋə(r)] *n Pol (man)* homme *m* de droite; *(woman)* femme *f* de droite
 rigid ['rɪdʒɪd] *adj* rigide; *Fig (person, ideas)* inflexible; *Br Fam* **to be bored r.** s'ennuyer ferme
 rigidity [rɪ'dʒɪdɪtɪ] *n* rigidité *f*

rigmarole ['rɪgmərəʊl] n Fam (process) procédure f compliquée; (speech) long discours m
rigor mortis ['rɪgə'mɔːtɪs] n rigidité f cadavérique
rigorous ['rɪgərəs] adj rigoureux(euse)
rigour ['rɪgə(r)] n rigueur f
rigout ['rɪgaʊt] n Fam (outfit) tenue f
rile [raɪl] vt Fam agacer
rim [rɪm] n (of cup, bowl) bord m; (of wheel) jante f; (of spectacles) monture f
rind [raɪnd] n (of fruit) écorce f; (of cheese) croûte f; (of bacon) couenne f
ring¹ [rɪŋ] **1** n (**a**) (for finger) (with stone) bague f; (without stone) anneau m; (for keys) porte-clés m inv; **the rings** (in gymnastics) les anneaux mpl; **r. binder** classeur m à anneaux; **r. finger** annulaire m (**b**) (of people, chairs) cercle m; (on stove) brûleur m; (stain) marque f; **to have rings under one's eyes** avoir des cernes sous les yeux; Fig **to run rings round sb** éclipser qn; Br **r. road** périphérique m (**c**) (for boxing, wrestling) ring m (**d**) (of criminals) bande f; (of spies) réseau m
2 vt (surround) encercler
ring² **1** n (sound) (of doorbell, telephone) sonnerie f; (of small bell, coins) tintement m; **there was a r. at the door** on sonna à la porte; Fam **to give sb a r.** passer un coup de fil à qn; **to have a r. of truth** avoir l'air vrai(e); **the name has a familiar r.** to it ce nom me dit quelque chose
2 vt (pt **rang** [ræŋ], pp **rung** [rʌŋ]) (bell) sonner; (alarm) déclencher; (on phone) appeler; **to r. the doorbell** sonner à la porte; Fig **that rings a bell** cela me dit quelque chose; Fig **to r. the changes** introduire des changements
3 vi (**a**) (of bell, telephone) sonner; **to r. at the door** sonner à la porte; Fig **to r. true** avoir l'air vrai(e); **to r. false** sonner faux (**b**) (resonate) (of ears) bourdonner; **to r. with** (of street, room) retentir de (**c**) (make a phone call) appeler
▶**ring back** vt sep (on phone) rappeler
▶**ring off** vi (on phone) raccrocher
▶**ring out** vi (of voice, shout) retentir
▶**ring up** vt sep (**a**) (on phone) téléphoner à, appeler (**b**) (on cash register) enregistrer; **to r. up a profit** enregistrer un bénéfice
ringleader ['rɪŋliːdə(r)] n (of strike) meneur(euse) m,f; (of gang) chef m de bande
ringlet ['rɪŋlɪt] n anglaise f
ringmaster ['rɪŋmɑːstə(r)] n ≃ Monsieur m Loyal
ring-pull ['rɪŋpʊl] n bague f (d'ouverture)
ringside ['rɪŋsaɪd] n **at the r.** près du ring; **to have a r. seat** avoir une place au premier rang; Fig être aux premières loges
ringworm ['rɪŋwɜːm] n Med teigne f
rink [rɪŋk] n (for roller skating) piste f; (for ice skating) patinoire f
rinse [rɪns] **1** n **to give sth a r.** rincer qch
2 vt (clothes, dishes) rincer; **to r. one's hands/hair** se rincer les mains/les cheveux
▶**rinse out** vt sep rincer
Rio (de Janeiro) ['riːəʊ(dɪdʒə'neərəʊ)] n Rio (de Janeiro)
riot ['raɪət] **1** n (uprising) émeute f; Fig **a r. of colour** une explosion de couleurs; **to run r.** se déchaîner; **her imagination was running r.** elle s'imaginait toutes sortes de choses; **to read sb the r. act** passer un savon à qn; **r. police** police f anti-émeute, ≃ CRS mpl
2 vi faire une émeute; (of prisoners) se mutiner

rioter ['raɪətə(r)] n émeutier(ère) m,f
rioting ['raɪətɪŋ] n émeutes fpl
riotous ['raɪətəs] adj (party, behaviour, event) tapageur(euse); **r. living** vie f déréglée
RIP [ɑːraɪ'piː] (abbr Rest In Peace) qu'il/elle repose en paix
rip [rɪp] **1** n déchirure f
2 vt (pt & pp **ripped**) déchirer; **to r. sth to pieces** (cloth) mettre en lambeaux; (paper) déchirer qch en mille morceaux; Fig (criticize) mettre en pièces
3 vi (**a**) (of cloth, paper) se déchirer (**b**) Fam **to let r.** (in performance) se déchaîner; **to let r. at sb** s'en prendre violemment à qn
▶**rip off** vt sep (**a**) (tear) arracher (**b**) Fam (swindle) arnaquer; (steal) piquer
▶**rip open** vt sep **to r. open a letter** ouvrir une lettre en déchirant l'enveloppe; **to r. open a parcel** ouvrir un paquet en le déchirant
▶**rip up** vt sep (**a**) (letter) déchirer (**b**) (floorboards) arracher; (pavement) creuser des trous dans
ripe [raɪp] adj (fruit) mûr(e); (cheese) fait(e) à point; **to live to a r. old age** vivre jusqu'à un âge avancé; **the time is r. (to do sth)** le temps est venu (de faire qch)
ripen ['raɪpən] vi mûrir; (of cheese) se faire
rip-off ['rɪpɒf] n Fam arnaque f
riposte [rɪ'pɒst] n riposte f, réplique f
ripple ['rɪpəl] **1** n (on water) ride f; (of applause) vague f; (of excitement) frémissement m
2 vi (of water) se rider; **laughter rippled through the audience** des vagues de rires ont parcouru le public
rise [raɪz] **1** n (**a**) (in price, temperature, pressure) hausse f; Br (pay) **r.** augmentation f (de salaire); **to be on the r.** (of prices) être en hausse; (of crime, inflation) être en augmentation; **the r. and fall of** la grandeur et la décadence de (**b**) (of leader, party) ascension f; **r. to power** accession f au pouvoir (**c**) (in road, ground) éminence f (**d**) (idioms) **to give r. to sth** donner lieu à qch; Fam **to get a r. out of sb** faire enrager qn
2 vi (pt **rose** [rəʊz], pp **risen** ['rɪzən]) (**a**) (get up) se lever; (after falling) se relever; Fam **r. and shine!** debout là-dedans! (**b**) (of smoke, balloon, ground) monter; (of sun, moon) se lever; (in career) monter; **a murmur rose from the crowd** un murmure s'éleva de la foule; **to r. to the occasion** se montrer à la hauteur de la situation; **to r. to the position of managing director** accéder au poste de P-DG; **to r. to power** accéder au pouvoir; **to r. in sb's esteem** monter dans l'estime de qn (**c**) (of temperature) s'élever, monter; (of price) augmenter; (of dough) lever; **my spirits rose** je repris courage; **her voice rose in anger** elle a élevé la voix sous l'effet de la colère (**d**) (revolt) se soulever; **to r. in arms** prendre les armes; **to r. in protest (against sth)** se soulever (contre qch)
▶**rise above** vt insep (problem, criticism) surmonter
▶**rise up** vi (revolt) se soulever; **to r. up in arms** prendre les armes; **to r. up in protest (against sth)** se soulever (contre qch)
risible ['rɪzɪbəl] adj Formal risible
rising ['raɪzɪŋ] **1** n (revolt) soulèvement m
2 adj (sun) levant; (temperature) en hausse; (prices, inflation) en augmentation; (artist, politician) qui monte; Fig **r. star** étoile f montante

risk [rɪsk] **1** *n* risque *m*; **to take a r.** prendre un risque; **at r.** *(life, person)* en danger; *(job)* menacé(e); **to put one's health at r.** risquer de s'abîmer la santé; **at the r. of doing sth** au risque de faire qch; **to run the r. of doing sth** courir le risque de faire qch; **at one's own r.** à ses risques et périls; **r. assessment** évaluation *f* des risques; **r. capital** capital *m* à risque; **r. management** gestion *f* des risques
2 *vt* (**a**) *(life, reputation)* risquer; **to r. one's neck** risquer sa peau (**b**) *(take the chance of)* **to r. failure** risquer d'échouer; **to r. death** risquer sa vie; **I can't r. going** je ne peux pas prendre le risque d'y aller; **they r. losing all their money** ils risquent de perdre tout leur argent; **we can't r. it** nous ne pouvons pas courir ce risque
risky ['rɪskɪ] *adj* risqué(e)
risotto [rɪ'zɒtəʊ] *(pl* **risottos**) *n* risotto *m*
risqué ['rɪskeɪ] *adj* osé(e)
rissole ['rɪsəʊl] *n* croquette *f*
rite [raɪt] *n* rite *m*
ritual ['rɪtjʊəl] **1** *n* rituel *m*
2 *adj* rituel(elle)
ritzy ['rɪtsɪ] *adj Fam* chic *inv*
rival ['raɪvəl] **1** *n* rival(e) *m,f*
2 *adj* rival(e)
3 *vt (pt & pp* **rivalled**, *Am* **rivaled**) *(compete with)* rivaliser avec; *(equal)* égaler
rivalry ['raɪvəlrɪ] *n* rivalité *f*
river ['rɪvə(r)] *n* rivière *f*; *(flowing into sea)* fleuve *m*; *Fig (of blood)* flot *m*
riverbed ['rɪvəbed] *n* lit *m* de la rivière
riverside ['rɪvəsaɪd] *n* bord *m* de l'eau; **a r. villa** une villa au bord de l'eau
rivet ['rɪvɪt] **1** *n* rivet *m*
2 *vt* river; **to be riveted (by)** être fasciné(e) (par); *Fig* **to be riveted to the spot** *(with fear, surprise)* être cloué(e) sur place
riveting ['rɪvɪtɪŋ] *adj Fig* fascinant(e)
Riviera [rɪvɪ'eərə] *n* **the (French) R.** la Côte d'Azur
RN [ɑː'en] *Br (abbr* **Royal Navy**) ≃ Marine *f* Nationale
RNA [ɑːren'eɪ] *n (abbr* **ribonucleic acid**) ARN *m*
RNLI [ɑːrenel'aɪ] *n Br (abbr* **Royal National Lifeboat Institution**) ≃ Société *f* nationale de sauvetage en mer
roach [rəʊtʃ] *n* (**a**) *(fish)* gardon *m* (**b**) *Am Fam (cockroach)* cafard *m*
road [rəʊd] *n* route *f*; *(in town)* rue *f*; **they live across or over the r.** ils habitent en face; **by r.** par la route; **to be off the r.** *(of car)* être en panne; **down/up the r.** un peu plus loin dans la rue; *Fam* **one for the r.** *(final drink)* un petit dernier pour la route; **to be on the r.** *(of salesman)* être sur la route; *(of pop group)* être en tournée; **after three hours on the r.** après trois heures de route; **to be on the r. to recovery** être en voie de guérison; *Fig* **to be on the right r.** être sur la bonne voie; *Fam* **let's get this show on the r.!** allez, c'est parti, on y va!; **a few years down the r.** dans quelques années; *Fig* **to come to the end of the r.** *(of relationship)* toucher à sa fin; **r. accident** accident *m* de la route; **r. conditions** états *mpl* des routes; *Fam* **r. hog** chauffard *m*; **r. rage** rage *f* au volant; **r. safety** sécurité *f* routière; **r. sign** panneau *m* de signalisation; **r. tax** ≃ vignette *f* (automobile)
roadblock ['rəʊdblɒk] *n* barrage *m* routier
roadmap ['rəʊdmæp] *n* carte *f* routière; *Fig* **a r. for peace** un plan de paix

roadside ['rəʊdsaɪd] *n* bord *m* de la route; **r. bar/hotel** bar *m*/hôtel *m* situé en bord de route; **r. bomb** = engin piégé placé au bord de la route
road-test ['rəʊdtest] *vt (car)* essayer sur route
roadway ['rəʊdweɪ] *n* chaussée *f*
roadwork ['rəʊdwɜːk] *n Am* = **roadworks**
roadworks ['rəʊdwɜːks] *npl* travaux *mpl* de voirie
roadworthy ['rəʊdwɜːðɪ] *adj* en état de rouler
roam [rəʊm] **1** *vt (streets, world)* parcourir; *(seas)* sillonner
2 *vi* **to r. (about)** errer; **to r. about the streets** traîner dans les rues
roaming ['rəʊmɪŋ] **1** *n* (**a**) *(wandering)* vagabondage *m* (**b**) *Tel (of mobile phone)* roaming *m*, itinérance *f*; *Comput (on Internet)* roaming *m*
2 *adj* vagabond(e), errant(e)
roar [rɔː(r)] **1** *n (of person, crowd)* hurlement *m*; *(of animal, engine)* rugissement *m*; *(of sea, wind)* mugissement *m*; *(of cars)* vacarme *m*
2 *vi (of person, crowd)* hurler; *(of animal, engine)* rugir; *(of sea, wind)* mugir; *(of cars)* vrombir; **to r. with laughter** hurler de rire
roaring ['rɔːrɪŋ] *adj* **r. drunk** ivre mort(e); **a r. fire** une belle flambée; **a r. success** un succès fou; **to do a r. trade** faire des affaires en or
roast [rəʊst] **1** *n (piece of meat)* rôti *m*
2 *adj* rôti(e)
3 *vt* (**a**) *(meat, potatoes)* faire rôtir; *(nuts, coffee)* faire griller (**b**) *Fam (criticize)* éreinter
roasting ['rəʊstɪŋ] *Fam* **1** *n* **to give sb a r.** *(reprimand)* passer un savon à qn; *(criticize)* descendre qn en flammes
2 *adj (hot)* **it's r. in here** il fait une chaleur à crever ici; **I'm r.!** je crève de chaleur!
rob [rɒb] *(pt & pp* **robbed**) *vt (bank)* dévaliser; *(person)* voler; *(house)* cambrioler; **to r. sb of sth** *(money, jewellery)* voler qch à qn; *Fig (youth, opportunity)* priver qn de qch; **we were robbed!** *(after match)* on nous a volé la victoire!
robber ['rɒbə(r)] *n* voleur(euse) *m,f*
robbery ['rɒbərɪ] *(pl* **robberies**) *n* vol *m*
robe [rəʊb] *n (of priest, judge)* robe *f*; *Am (dressing gown)* robe de chambre
robin ['rɒbɪn] *n* rouge-gorge *m*
robot ['rəʊbɒt] *n* robot *m*
robotics [rəʊ'bɒtɪks] *n* robotique *f*
robust [rəʊ'bʌst] *adj (person)* robuste; *(material, suitcase)* solide; *(defence, speech)* musclé(e)
rock [rɒk] *n* (**a**) *(substance)* roche *f*; *(large stone)* rocher *m*; *Fig* **to be on the rocks** *(of marriage, company)* être en pleine débâcle; **on the rocks** *(drink)* avec des glaçons, *Can* sur glace; **the R. of Gibraltar** le Rocher de Gibraltar; **to hit r. bottom** toucher le fond; **r. climbing** varappe *f*; **r. face** paroi *f* rocheuse; **r. garden** rocaille *f*; **r. pool** = flaque d'eau dans les rochers à marée basse; **r. salt** sel *m* gemme; **r. solid** solide comme le roc (**b**) *Br (sweet)* = sucrerie en forme de bâton (**c**) *(rocking motion)* **to give the cradle a r.** balancer un peu le berceau (**d**) *(music)* rock *m*; **r. and roll** rock-and-roll *m*; **r. concert** concert *m* de rock; **r. group** groupe *m* de rock; **r. singer** chanteur(euse) *m,f* de rock
2 *vt (boat, chair)* balancer; *(building)* secouer; **to r. a baby to sleep** bercer un enfant pour qu'il s'endorme; *Fig* **to r. the boat** faire des histoires; *Fig* **the country has been rocked by these revelations** le pays a été secoué par ces révélations

3 *vi (sway)* se balancer; *(of building)* trembler; **to r. with laughter** être secoué(e) par un fou rire

rock-bottom ['rɒkbɒtəm] *adj* **r. prices** prix *mpl* incroyables

rocker ['rɒkə(r)] *n* (**a**) *(chair)* fauteuil *m* à bascule, *Can* berçante *f; Fam* **to be off one's r.** être givré(e) (**b**) *(musician, fan)* rocker(euse) *m,f*

rockery ['rɒkərɪ] *(pl* **rockeries**) *n* rocaille *f*

rocket ['rɒkɪt] **1** *n* (**a**) *Aviat & Astron* fusée *f;* **r.** launcher lance-fusées *m inv* (**b**) *Br Fam Fig (telling-off)* engueulade *f;* **to give sb a r.** engueuler qn
2 *vi (of prices, inflation, unemployment)* monter en flèche

rockfall ['rɒkfɔːl] *n* éboulement *m*

rock-hard [rɒk'hɑːd] *adj* dur(e) comme (de la) pierre

Rockies ['rɒkɪz] *npl* **the R.** les Rocheuses *fpl*

rocking chair ['rɒkɪŋtʃeə(r)] *n* fauteuil *m* à bascule, *Can* berçante *f*

rocky ['rɒkɪ] *adj* (**a**) *(path, soil)* rocailleux(euse); **the R. Mountains** les Montagnes *fpl* Rocheuses (**b**) *Fig (economy, relationship)* instable

rod [rɒd] *n (wooden)* baguette *f; (metal)* tige *f; (for curtain)* tringle *f; (for fishing)* canne *f* à pêche; *Fig* **to rule with a r. of iron** gouverner d'une main de fer; *Fig* **to make a r. for one's own back** se préparer des ennuis

rode [rəʊd] *pt of* **ride**

rodent ['rəʊdənt] *n* rongeur *m*

rodeo ['rəʊdɪəʊ] *(pl* **rodeos**) *n* rodéo *m*

roe¹ [rəʊ] *n* **r. (deer)** chevreuil *m*

roe² *n (of fish)* œufs *mpl* de poisson

roger¹ ['rɒdʒə(r)] *exclam (in radio message)* bien reçu!

roger² *vt Br very Fam (have sex with)* baiser

rogue [rəʊg] *n (dishonest)* filou *m; (mischievous)* coquin(e) *m,f;* **r. elephant** éléphant *m* solitaire; **r. trader** opérateur(trice) *m,f* peu scrupuleux(euse); **r. trading** opérations *fpl* de marché non autorisées

roguish ['rəʊgɪʃ] *adj* canaille

role [rəʊl] *n* rôle *m; Fig* **to play an important/a leading r. (in sth)** jouer un rôle important/prépondérant (dans qch); **r. model** modèle *m*

role-playing ['rəʊlpleɪɪŋ] *n* jeu *m* de rôle

roll [rəʊl] **1** *n* (**a**) *(of paper)* rouleau *m; (of fat)* bourrelet *m; (of banknotes)* liasse *f;* **a r. of film** une pellicule (photo); **r. neck** col *m* roulé (**b**) *(bread)* petit pain *m;* **cheese r.** ≃ sandwich *m* au fromage (**c**) *(of drum, thunder)* roulement *m* (**d**) *(movement)* roulis *m; Fam* **to be on a r.** avoir la chance de son côté (**e**) *(list)* liste *f;* **r. call** appel *m; Mil* **r. of honour** liste *f* de ceux qui sont morts pour la patrie
2 *vt* (**a**) *(ball)* faire rouler; **to r. sth along the ground** faire rouler qch sur le sol; **to r. one's eyes** lever les yeux au ciel; **to r. one's r's** rouler les r; **the animal rolled itself into a ball** l'animal se mit en boule (**b**) *(lawn)* passer au rouleau; *(road)* cylindrer; *(metal)* laminer (**c**) *(cigarette)* rouler
3 *vi* (**a**) *(of ball, ship)* rouler; *(of camera)* tourner; *Fig* **heads will r.** il y a des têtes qui vont tomber; *Fam* **to be rolling in money, to be rolling in it** rouler sur l'or; *Fig* **to start the ball rolling** mettre les choses en route (**b**) *(of thunder)* gronder

▸**roll down 1** *vt sep (sleeves)* redescendre; *(blind, car window)* descendre
2 *vi (of tears, sweat)* couler

▸**roll on** *vi Fam* **r. on Friday/Christmas!** vivement vendredi/Noël!

▸**roll over** *vi (of person) (once)* se retourner; *(several times)* se rouler; *(of car) (once)* capoter; *(several times)* faire des tonneaux

▸**roll up 1** *vt sep (newspaper)* rouler; *(sleeves)* retrousser; *(blind, car window)* remonter; **to r. sth up in paper** envelopper qch dans du papier
2 *vi Fam (arrive)* rappliquer; **r. up!, r. up!** venez nombreux!

rolled-up [rəʊld'ʌp] *adj (sleeves, trousers)* retroussé(e); *(umbrella)* replié(e); *(newspaper)* roulé(e)

roller ['rəʊlə(r)] *n (for paint, garden)* rouleau *m; (for hair)* bigoudi *m;* **r. blind** store *m (à cylindre);* **r. coaster** montagnes *fpl* russes; **r. skates** patins *mpl* à roulettes

rollerblades ['rəʊləbleɪdz] *npl* rollers *mpl*, patins *mpl* en ligne

rollerblading ['rəʊləbleɪdɪŋ] *n* roller *m;* **to go r.** faire du roller

roller-skate ['rəʊləskeɪt] *vi* faire du patin à roulettes

roller-skating ['rəʊləskeɪtɪŋ] *n* **to go r.** faire du patin à roulettes

rolling ['rəʊlɪŋ] *adj (hills, fields)* ondulant(e); *(sea, waves)* gros (grosse); *(thunder)* qui gronde; **r. mill** *(for steel)* laminoir *m;* **r. pin** rouleau *m* à pâtisserie; *Rail* **r. stock** matériel *m* roulant

rollneck ['rəʊlnek] *adj (sweater)* à col roulé

roll-on ['rəʊlɒn] *adj* (**a**) **r. (deodorant)** déodorant *m* à bille (**b**) *Naut* **r.-roll-off ferry** ferry *m* de type roll-on-roll-off

rollover ['rəʊləʊvə(r)] *n (in lottery)* = à la loterie nationale, situation où, personne n'ayant gagné le gros lot, celui-ci est ajouté à l'enjeu du tirage suivant

Rolls [rəʊlz] *n Br Fam (Rolls-Royce)* Rolls-Royce® *f*

roll-top desk ['rəʊltɒp'desk] *n* bureau *m* à cylindre

roll-up ['rəʊlʌp] *n Fam (cigarette)* cigarette *f* roulée

roly-poly ['rəʊlɪ'pəʊlɪ] *adj Fam (plump)* grassouillet(ette)

ROM [rɒm] *n Comput (abbr* **read only memory**) mémoire *f* morte

Roman ['rəʊmən] **1** *n* Romain(e) *m,f*
2 *adj* romain(e); **R. Catholic** catholique; **R. nose** nez *m* aquilin; **R. numerals** chiffres *mpl* romains

roman ['rəʊmən] *Typ* **1** *n* romain *m*
2 *adj* romain(e)

romance ['rəʊmæns, rə'mæns] *n* (**a**) *(book)* roman *m* d'amour; *(film)* histoire *f* d'amour (**b**) *(love affair)* aventure *f* (**c**) *(charm)* charme *m*

Romania [rə'meɪnɪə] *n* la Roumanie

Romanian [rə'meɪnɪən] **1** *n* (**a**) *(person)* Roumain(e) *m,f* (**b**) *(language)* roumain *m*
2 *adj* roumain(e)

romantic [rəʊ'mæntɪk, rə'mæntɪk] **1** *n* romantique *mf*
2 *adj (scheme, notion)* romanesque

romanticism [rəʊ'mæntɪsɪzəm] *n* romantisme *m*

romanticize [rə'mæntɪsaɪz] *vt (incident)* romancer; *(idea, war)* présenter sous un jour romantique

Romany ['rəʊmənɪ] **1** *n (pl* **Romanies**) (**a**) *(person)* Tzigane *mf* (**b**) *(language)* tzigane *m*
2 *adj* tzigane

Rome [rəʊm] *n* Rome; **R. wasn't built in a day** = Paris ne s'est pas fait en un jour; **when in R.(, do as the Romans do)** il faut suivre les usages de l'endroit où l'on se trouve

romp [rɒmp] **1** *n* **to have a r.** chahuter
2 *vi* **to r. (about** *or* **around)** s'ébattre; **to r. through an exam** réussir un examen les doigts dans le nez

romper ['rɒmpə(r)] *n* **r. suit, rompers** barboteuse *f*
roof [ruːf] **1** *n* (*pl* **rooves** [ruːvz] *or* **roofs**) (*of building, car*) toit *m*; (*of tunnel, cave*) plafond *m*; **to have a r. over one's head** avoir un endroit où vivre; **to live under one** *or* **the same r.** vivre sous le même toit; *Fam* **to hit the r.** sortir de ses gonds; *Fam* **to go through the r.** (*prices*) connaître une flambée; **r. of the mouth** voûte *f* du palais; **r. garden** jardin *m* sur le toit; **r. rack** galerie *f*
  2 *vt* couvrir
roofing ['ruːfɪŋ] *n* toiture *f*; **r. material** matériaux *mpl* de couverture
rooftop ['ruːftɒp] *n* toit *m*; *Fig* **to shout sth from the rooftops** crier qch sur les toits
rook [rʊk] *n* (*bird*) freux *m*; (*in chess*) tour *f*
rookery ['rʊkərɪ] (*pl* **rookeries**) *n* colonie *f* de freux
rookie ['rʊkɪ] *n Am Fam* bleu *m*
room [ruːm] **1** *n* (**a**) (*in house*) pièce *f*; (*bedroom, in hotel*) chambre *f*; (*large, public*) salle *f*; **r. and board** chambre et pension *f*; **r. service** service *m* dans les chambres; **r. temperature** température *f* ambiante (**b**) (*space*) place *f*; **there's no r. to move** il n'y a pas de place; **to make r. (for sb)** faire de la place (pour qn); **there's no r. for doubt** cela ne fait aucun doute; **there is r. for improvement** ça pourrait être mieux
  2 *vi Am* **to r. with sb** partager une chambre avec qn
roommate ['ruːmmeɪt] *n* (*sharing bedroom*) camarade *mf* de chambre; *Am* (*sharing apartment*) colocataire *mf*
roomy ['ruːmɪ] *adj* spacieux(euse); (*clothes*) ample
roost [ruːst] **1** *n* perchoir *m*; **to rule the r.** faire la loi
  2 *vi* se percher; *Fig* **her actions have come home to r.** ses actions se sont retournées contre elle
rooster ['ruːstə(r)] *n* coq *m*
root [ruːt] **1** *n* (**a**) (*of plant, tooth, word, hair*) racine *f*; **to pull up by the roots** (*plant*) déraciner; *also Fig* **to take r.** prendre racine; **they destroyed the party r. and branch** ils ont entièrement détruit le parti; *Fig* **to put down roots** s'intégrer; *Fig* **to get back to one's roots** retrouver ses racines; *Am* **r. beer** = boisson gazeuse aux extraits de plantes; **r. crops** racines *fpl* comestibles; **r. vegetables** légumes *mpl* à racine comestible (**b**) (*origin*) origine *f*; *Prov* **money is the r. of all evil** l'argent est la source de tous les maux
  2 *vt* **to be rooted to the spot** être figé(e) sur place
  3 *vi* (**a**) **to r. about** *or* **around (for sth)** fouiller (pour trouver qch) (**b**) *Am* **to r. for sb** appuyer qn
▸**root for** *vt insep* (*support*) être pour
▸**root out** *vt sep* supprimer
rope [rəʊp] **1** *n* (**a**) (*cord*) corde *f*; (*of pearls*) sautoir *m*; (*of onions*) chapelet *m*; **r. ladder** échelle *f* de corde (**b**) (*idioms*) **to be on the ropes** (*of company*) battre de l'aile; **to learn the ropes** apprendre les ficelles; **to show sb the ropes** former qn; **to give sb plenty of r.** donner du mou à qn
  2 *vt* (*fasten*) lier (avec une corde) (**to** à); **they roped themselves together** (*for climbing*) ils se sont encordés
▸**rope in** *vt sep Fam* (*recruit*) recruter; **to get roped in to do sth** se laisser convaincre de faire qch
▸**rope off** *vt sep* **to r. sth off** interdire l'accès de qch avec une corde
rop(e)y ['rəʊpɪ] *adj Br Fam* (*unreliable*) pas terrible; (*ill*) patraque

rosary ['rəʊzərɪ] (*pl* **rosaries**) *n Rel* chapelet *m*; **to say one's r.** dire son chapelet
rose¹ [rəʊz] **1** *n* (**a**) (*flower*) rose *f*; (*on watering can*) pomme *f*; **r. bed** parterre *m* de rosiers; **r. bush** rosier *m*; **r. garden** roseraie *f*; **r. grower** rosiériste *mf*; **r. window** rosace *f* (**b**) (*idioms*) **life isn't a bed of roses** tout n'est pas rose dans la vie; **to come up roses** se passer à merveille
  2 *adj* (*colour*) rose
rose² *pt of* **rise**
rosé ['rəʊzeɪ] *n* rosé *m*
rosebud ['rəʊzbʌd] *n* bouton *m* de rose
rose-coloured ['rəʊzkʌləd], **rose-tinted** ['rəʊztɪntɪd] *adj* **to see things through r. glasses** *or* **spectacles** voir la vie en rose
rosehip ['rəʊzhɪp] *n* gratte-cul *m*
rosemary ['rəʊzmərɪ] *n* romarin *m*
rosette [rəʊ'zet] *n* rosette *f*
rosewater ['rəʊzwɔːtə(r)] *n* eau *f* de rose
rosewood ['rəʊzwʊd] *n* bois *m* de rose
roster ['rɒstə(r)] *n* liste *f* de service
rostrum ['rɒstrəm] (*pl* **rostrums** *or* **rostra** ['rɒstrə]) *n* (*for speaker*) estrade *f*; (*for prizewinner*) podium *m*
rosy ['rəʊzɪ] *adj* (*pink*) rose; (*complexion*) de rose; *Fig* (*future*) prometteur(euse)
rot [rɒt] **1** *n* (**a**) (*in house, wood*) pourriture *f*; *Fig* **the r. has set in** ça se gâte; *Fig* **to stop the r.** empêcher la situation de se dégrader (**b**) *Fam* (*nonsense*) bêtises *fpl*
  2 *vt* (*pt & pp* **rotted**) (faire) pourrir
  3 *vi* pourrir; **to r. in prison** moisir en prison
rota ['rəʊtə] *n* roulement *m*
rotary ['rəʊtərɪ] **1** *n* (*pl* **rotaries**) *Am* (*roundabout*) rond-point *m*
  2 *adj* rotatif(ive)
rotate [rəʊ'teɪt] **1** *vt* (**a**) (*turn*) faire tourner (**b**) (*alternate*) (*duties*) remplir à tour de rôle; (*crops*) alterner
  2 *vi* (**a**) (*turn*) tourner (**b**) (*in job*) remplir des fonctions à tour de rôle
rotation [rəʊ'teɪʃən] *n* (**a**) (*of planet*) rotation *f* (**b**) (*in job*) roulement *m*; (*of crops*) alternance *f*; **in r.** à tour de rôle
rote [rəʊt] *n* **by r.** par cœur; **r. learning** apprentissage *m* par cœur
rotor ['rəʊtə(r)] *n* rotor *m*
rotten ['rɒtən] *adj* (**a**) (*wood, egg, fruit*) pourri(e) (**b**) *Fam* (*bad*) nul (nulle); (*weather*) pourri(e); **to feel r.** (*ill*) ne pas se sentir dans son assiette; (*guilty*) ne pas être fier(ère) (**about** de); **to have r. luck** avoir la guigne (**c**) (*unpleasant*) dégueulasse; **a r. trick** un tour de cochon
rotter ['rɒtə(r)] *n Br Fam Old-fashioned* peau *f* de vache
rottweiler ['rɒtvaɪlə(r)] *n* rottweiler *m*
rotund [rəʊ'tʌnd] *adj* rond(e)
rouble ['ruːbəl] *n* rouble *m*
rouge [ruːʒ] *n* rouge *m* (à joues)
rough [rʌf] **1** *n* (**a**) (*in golf*) rough *m* (**b**) (*difficulty*) **you have to take the r. with the smooth** on ne peut pas tout avoir dans la vie
  2 *adj* (**a**) (*surface, skin*) rugueux(euse); (*terrain*) accidenté(e) (**b**) (*unrefined*) (*manners*) fruste; *Fig* **a r. diamond** un cœur d'or sous des dehors frustes; **r. draft** brouillon *m*; **r. sketch** ébauche *f* (**c**) *Fam* (*ill*) **to feel/look r.** se sentir/avoir l'air patraque (**d**) (*violent*) brutal(e); (*crossing, sea*) agité(e) (**e**) (*harsh*) (*voice*) rude; (*wine, spirits*) âpre; *Fam* **it was r. on her**

c'était dur pour elle; **r. justice** justice *f* sommaire (**f**) *(approximate)* approximatif(ive); **at a r. guess** à vue de nez; **I've got a r. idea of what he wants** j'ai une petite idée de ce qu'il veut **3** *adv* **to play r.** jouer avec brutalité; *Fig* ne pas faire de cadeaux; *Fam* **to sleep r.** coucher à la dure **4** *vt Fam* **to r. it** vivre à la dure

▸**rough up** *vt sep Fam (beat up)* tabasser

roughage ['rʌfɪdʒ] *n* fibres *fpl* (alimentaires)

rough-and-ready [rʌfən'redɪ] *adj (meal, accommodation)* sommaire; *(person)* rustre

rough-and-tumble [rʌfən'tʌmbəl] *n* bousculade *f*; *Fig* **the r. of politics** le monde sans pitié de la politique

roughly ['rʌflɪ] *adv* (**a**) *(violently)* brutalement; **to treat sb r.** rudoyer qn (**b**) *(crudely)* grossièrement (**c**) *(approximately)* à peu près; **r. (speaking)** en gros

roughness ['rʌfnɪs] *n* (**a**) *(of surface, skin)* rugosité *f* (**b**) *(of behaviour)* rudesse *f*

roughshod ['rʌfʃɒd] *adv* **to ride r. over sth** ne faire aucun cas de qch

rough-spoken [rʌf'spəʊkən] *adj* au langage grossier

roulette [ruː'let] *n* roulette *f*; **r. table** table *f* de roulette; **r. wheel** roulette *f*

round [raʊnd] **1** *n* (**a**) *(slice) (of bread)* tranche *f*; **a r. of sandwiches** = un sandwich au pain de mie coupé en deux ou en quatre (**b**) *(stage of match)* manche *f*; *(stage of tournament)* tour *m*; *(in boxing)* round *m*; *(of golf)* partie *f*; **to get/be through to the next r.** se qualifier/s'être qualifié(e) pour le tour suivant (**c**) *(of talks, visits)* série *f*; *(of drinks)* tournée *f*; **r. of applause** applaudissements *mpl*; **to give sb a r. of applause** applaudir qn (**d**) **to do one's rounds** *(of doctor)* faire ses visites; **to do the rounds** *(of rumour, illness)* circuler; **the daily r.** *(of tasks)* le train-train quotidien (**e**) *Mil (bullet)* balle *f* (**f**) *Mus* canon *m*
2 *adj* rond(e); **to have r. shoulders** avoir le dos rond; **a r. dozen** une douzaine exactement; **in r. figures** en arrondissant; **r. table (conference)** table *f* ronde; **trip** aller (et) retour *m*
3 *adv* autour; **all (the) year r.** toute l'année; **all r.** *(on the whole)* dans l'ensemble; **the wrong way r.** à l'envers; **the right way r.** *(not back to front)* à l'endroit; *(in the correct order)* dans le bon ordre; **the other way r.** *(in the other direction)* dans l'autre sens; **do it the other way r.** fais l'inverse; **to go r. (to sb's house)** passer (chez qn); **to invite sb r.** inviter qn
4 *prep* (**a**) *(position)* autour de; **r. here** dans le coin (**b**) *(motion)* **to look r. a room** parcourir une pièce du regard; **to travel r. the world** parcourir le monde; **to go r. an obstacle** contourner un obstacle; **to go r. the corner** *(of person)* tourner le coin; *(of vehicle)* prendre le virage; **it's just r. the corner** c'est juste au coin (de la rue); *Fig* **to drive** *or* **send sb r. the bend** rendre qn maboul(e) (**c**) *(approximately)* **r. about** environ; **r. about midday** vers midi
5 *vt* (**a**) *(make round)* arrondir (**b**) *(obstacle)* contourner; *(corner)* tourner

▸**round down** *vt sep (figure)* arrondir au chiffre inférieur

▸**round off** *vt sep (conclude)* conclure

▸**round up** *vt sep* (**a**) *(cattle)* rassembler; *(criminals, suspects)* ramasser (**b**) *(figure)* arrondir au chiffre supérieur

roundabout ['raʊndəbaʊt] **1** *n* (**a**) *(at fairground)* manège *m* (**b**) *(for cars)* rond-point *m*
2 *adj (approach, route)* détourné(e); **to lead up to a question in a r. way** aborder une question de biais

rounded ['raʊndɪd] *adj* (**a**) *(shape, number)* arrondi(e); *(breasts)* plein(e) (**b**) *Fig (style)* harmonieux(euse); *(education)* complet(ète)

rounders ['raʊndəz] *n Br* = jeu similaire au base-ball

roundly ['raʊndlɪ] *adv (praise, condemn)* vivement; *(beat)* sévèrement

round-trip ['raʊndtrɪp] *adj Am (ticket)* aller (et) retour

roundup ['raʊndʌp] *n (of criminals)* rafle *f*; *(of events, news)* résumé *m*

rouse [raʊz] *vt* réveiller; **to r. oneself (to do sth)** se secouer (et faire qch); **to r. sb to action** pousser qn à agir; **to r. sb to anger** susciter la colère de qn

rousing ['raʊzɪŋ] *adj (music, speech)* exaltant(e); *(welcome, cheers)* enthousiaste

rout [raʊt] **1** *n* déroute *f*
2 *vt* mettre en déroute

▸**rout out** *vt sep (get rid of)* se débarrasser de

route [ruːt] **1** *n (of traveller)* itinéraire *m*; *(of plane, ship)* route *f*; *(of bus, parade)* parcours *m*; *Fig (to success)* voie *f* (**to** de)
2 *vt (parcel, goods)* acheminer; *(bus, train, flight)* faire passer

router ['ruːtə(r)] *n Comput* routeur *m*

routine [ruː'tiːn] **1** *n* (**a**) *(habit)* routine *f*; **the daily r.** le train-train quotidien (**b**) *(of performer, comedian)* numéro *m*; *Fam Fig* **don't give me that r.** arrête ton numéro (**c**) *Comput* sous-programme *m*
2 *adj* (**a**) *(normal)* de routine (**b**) *(dull)* routinier(ère)

routinely [ruː'tiːnlɪ] *adv* systématiquement

rove [rəʊv] **1** *vt* parcourir
2 *vi* rôder, vagabonder; **her eyes roved around the room** son regard parcourait la pièce

roving ['rəʊvɪŋ] *adj* vagabond(e), nomade; *Fig* **he has a r. eye** il aime bien lorgner les filles; **r. reporter** reporter *m* *(qui va sur le terrain)*

row¹ [rəʊ] *n (line)* rangée *f*; **in a r.** en rang; **two Sundays in a r.** deux dimanches d'affilée; **in the front r.** *(of seats)* au premier rang

row² *n (in boat)* promenade *f* en canot; **to go for a r.** canoter
2 *vt (boat)* faire aller à la rame; *(person)* transporter en canot
3 *vi (in boat)* ramer

row³ [raʊ] **1** *n* (**a**) *(noise)* vacarme *m*; *(protest)* tollé *m* (**b**) *(quarrel)* dispute *f*; **to have a r. (with sb)** se disputer (avec qn)
2 *vi (quarrel)* se disputer *(about* à propos de)

rowan ['raʊən] *n* sorbier *m*

rowboat ['rəʊbəʊt] *n Am* bateau *m* à rames

rowdy ['raʊdɪ] **1** *n (pl* **rowdies)** chahuteur(euse) *m,f*
2 *adj (person)* chahuteur(euse); *(event, party)* bruyant(e); **to be r.** chahuter

rower ['rəʊə(r)] *n* rameur(euse) *m,f*

rowing ['rəʊɪŋ] *n* canotage *m*; *(as sport)* aviron *m*; **r. boat** bateau *m* à rames; **r. machine** rameur *m*

royal ['rɔɪəl] **1** *adj* royal(e); *Fig (splendid)* princier(ère); **His/Her R. Highness** Son Altesse Royale; **r. blue** bleu roi *m inv*; **the R. Family** la famille royale; **r. flush** *(in cards)* quinte *f* royale; **r. jelly** gelée *f* royale; **R. Mail** = la Poste britannique; **the R. Navy** = la marine nationale britannique

2 n Fam membre m de la famille royale; **the Royals** la famille royale

royalist ['rɔɪəlɪst] **1** n royaliste mf
2 adj royaliste

royally ['rɔɪəlɪ] adv (entertain, welcome) royalement

royalty ['rɔɪəltɪ] n (**a**) (rank, position) royauté f; **to be r.** faire partie de la famille royale; **to be treated like r.** être traité(e) royalement (**b**) **royalties** (for author, singer) droits mpl d'auteur

RP [ɑː'piː] n Ling (abbr **received pronunciation**) = prononciation standard de l'anglais (celle du sud-est de l'Angleterre)

RPI [ɑːpiː'aɪ] n Econ (abbr **retail price index**) indice m des prix de détail

rpm [ɑːpiː'em] n Aut (abbr **revolutions per minute**) tr/min

RRP [ˌɑːrɑː'piː] n Com (abbr **recommended retail price**) prix m conseillé

RS [ɑːr'es] n Br (abbr **Royal Society**) ≃ Académie f des Sciences

RSA [ɑːres'eɪ] n (abbr **Republic of South Africa**) Afrique f du Sud

RSI [ɑːres'aɪ] n (abbr **repetitive strain injury**) = douleurs dans les bras et les mains dues à la répétition de certains mouvements

RSPB [ɑːrespiː'biː] n Br (abbr **Royal Society for the Protection of Birds**) = ligue pour la protection des oiseaux

RSPCA [ɑːrespiːsiː'eɪ] n Br (abbr **Royal Society for the Prevention of Cruelty to Animals**) ≃ SPA f

RSVP [ɑːresviː'piː] (abbr **répondez s'il vous plaît**) (on invitation) RSVP

Rt Hon Br Parl (abbr **Right Honourable**) = formule accolée au nom des ministres et anciens ministres

rub [rʌb] **1** n **to give sth a r.** frotter qch; Fig **there's the r.!** voilà le hic!
2 vt (pt & pp **rubbed**) frotter; **to r. one's hands together** se frotter les mains; Fig **to r. shoulders with sb** côtoyer qn; Fam **to r. sb up the wrong way** prendre qn à rebrousse-poil
3 vi (of straps, shoes) frotter (**against** contre)

▶**rub along** vi Fam (**a**) (manage) se débrouiller (**b**) (get on) s'entendre (**with** avec)

▶**rub in** vt sep (lotion, ointment) faire pénétrer; Fam **to r. it in** retourner le couteau dans la plaie

▶**rub off 1** vt sep (dirt, stain) enlever en frottant; (writing) effacer
2 vi partir, s'enlever; Fig **to r. off on sb** (of manners, enthusiasm) déteindre sur qn

▶**rub out** vt sep (**a**) (erase) effacer (**b**) Fam (murder) buter

rubber ['rʌbə(r)] n (**a**) (substance) caoutchouc m; **r. ball/gloves** balle f/gants mpl en caoutchouc; **r. band** élastique m; **r. dinghy** canot m pneumatique; **r. plant** caoutchouc m **r. ring** bouée f; **r. stamp** tampon m (**b**) (eraser) gomme f; (for blackboards) brosse f (**c**) Am Fam (condom) capote f

rubber-stamp [rʌbə'stæmp] vt Fig (approve) approuver sans discussion

rubbery ['rʌbərɪ] adj caoutchouteux(euse)

rubbish ['rʌbɪʃ] Br **1** n (**a**) (refuse) détritus mpl; (from house) ordures fpl; (junk) cochonneries fpl; **r. bag** sac m poubelle; **r. bin** poubelle f; **r. collection** ramassage m des ordures; **r. dump** dépotoir m; Fig **to throw sb/sth on the r. heap** mettre qn/qch au rancart (**b**) Fam (nonsense) idioties fpl; **that book/film is a load**

of r. ce livre/film est nul; **r.!** n'importe quoi!
2 vt Fam (book, plan) descendre en flammes

rubble ['rʌbəl] n décombres mpl

rubella [ruː'belə] n rubéole f

rubric ['ruːbrɪk] n instructions fpl

ruby ['ruːbɪ] **1** n (pl **rubies**) rubis m
2 adj (colour) rubis

RUC [ɑːjuː'siː] n (abbr **Royal Ulster Constabulary**) = forces de l'ordre d'Irlande du Nord

ruck¹ [rʌk] n (**a**) (in rugby) mêlée f ouverte (**b**) (fight) bagarre f

ruck² **1** n (in cloth) faux pli m
2 vi **to r. up** (of sheet) se froisser

rucksack ['rʌksæk] n sac m à dos

ructions ['rʌkʃənz] npl Fam grabuge m

rudder ['rʌdə(r)] n gouvernail m

ruddy ['rʌdɪ] adj (**a**) (complexion) rose (**b**) Br Fam Old-fashioned fichu(e); **r. fool!** espèce d'imbécile!

rude [ruːd] adj (**a**) (impolite) impoli(e) (**b**) (vulgar) grossier(ère); (gesture) obscène (**c**) (primitive) rudimentaire (**d**) (shock, surprise) **to receive a r. awakening** être brutalement rappelé(e) à la réalité (**e**) (vigorous) **to be in r. health** jouir d'une santé robuste

rudeness ['ruːdnɪs] n (**a**) (impoliteness) impolitesse f (**b**) (vulgarity) grossièreté f

rudimentary [ruːdɪ'mentərɪ] adj rudimentaire

rudiments ['ruːdɪmənts] npl rudiments mpl

rue [ruː] vt Lit regretter amèrement; **I r. the day I met her** je maudis le jour où je l'ai rencontrée

rueful ['ruːfʊl] adj (voice, smile) de regret; (person) qui a des regrets

ruff [rʌf] n (on costume) fraise f

ruffian ['rʌfɪən] n Old-fashioned voyou m

ruffle ['rʌfəl] vt (water) troubler; (hair) ébouriffer; **to r. sb's feathers** froisser qn; **to r. sb's composure** faire perdre contenance à qn

rug [rʌg] n (**a**) (carpet) tapis m; Fig **to pull the r. from under sb's feet** couper l'herbe sous le pied à qn (**b**) (blanket) couverture f

rugby ['rʌgbɪ] n rugby m; **r. ball** ballon m de rugby; **r. league** rugby m à treize; **r. player** rugbyman m; **r. tackle** plaquage m; **r. union** rugby à quinze m

rugby-tackle ['rʌgbɪtækəl] vt **to r. sb** plaquer qn au sol

rugged ['rʌgɪd] adj (ground, country) accidenté(e); (features, manner) rude; **r. good looks** beauté f un peu rude

rugger ['rʌgə(r)] n Br Fam (rugby) rugby m

rugrat ['rʌgræt] n Fam môme mf

ruin ['ruːɪn] **1** n ruine f; **to fall into ruin(s)** tomber en ruine(s); **it will be the r. of him** ça le perdra
2 vt (suit, shoes) abîmer; (person) ruiner; (meal, evening, holiday) gâcher; **to r. one's health** se ruiner la santé; **to r. one's eyesight** s'user la vue; **tourism has ruined the town** le tourisme a défiguré la ville; **a ruined castle** un château en ruine(s)

ruinous ['ruːɪnəs] adj (expensive) ruineux(euse)

rule [ruːl] **1** n (**a**) (principle) règle f; (regulation) règlement m; **rules** (of club, school) règlement m; **as a r. en** règle générale; **to make it a r. to do sth** se faire un principe de faire qch; **rules and regulations** règles fpl; Ind **to work to r.** faire la grève du zèle; **it's against the rules** c'est contraire au règlement; **as a r. of thumb** pour avoir une idée approximative; **r. book** règlement m (**b**) (government) autorité f (**c**) (for measuring) règle f

2 *vt* (**a**) *(country, people)* gouverner; **to let sth r. one's life** laisser qch dominer toute sa vie; *Fig* **to r. the roost** commander (**b**) *(decide, decree)* décider; **to be ruled illegal** être décrété(e) illégal(e) (**c**) *(paper)* régler

3 *vi* (**a**) *(of monarch)* régner (**b**) *(of judge)* statuer (on sur); **to r. in favour of/against sb** décider en faveur de/contre qn

▶**rule out** *vt sep* exclure

ruler ['ruːlə(r)] *n* (**a**) *(of country)* dirigeant(e) *m,f* (**b**) *(for measuring)* règle *f*

ruling ['ruːlɪŋ] **1** *n* *(of judge, umpire)* décision *f*
2 *adj* (**a**) *(party)* au pouvoir; *(class)* dirigeant(e) (**b**) *(passion)* dominant(e); *(consideration)* premier(ère)

rum¹ [rʌm] *n* *(drink)* rhum *m*

rum² *adj Fam (strange)* bizarre; *(suspect)* louche

Rumania = Romania

Rumanian = Romanian

rumble ['rʌmbəl] **1** *n* *(of thunder, gunfire, traffic)* grondement *m*; *(of voices)* bourdonnement *m*; *(of stomach)* gargouillement *m*; **rumbles of discontent** murmures *mpl* de protestation
2 *vt Fam (find out) (person)* deviner le jeu de; *(plot)* découvrir
3 *vi* *(of thunder, traffic)* gronder; *(of stomach)* gargouiller

rumbustious [rʌm'bʌstjəs] *adj* exubérant(e)

ruminant ['ruːmɪnənt] *n Zool* ruminant *m*

ruminate ['ruːmɪneɪt] *vi Formal* **to r. (about** *or* **on sth)** ruminer (qch)

rummage ['rʌmɪdʒ] **1** *vi* **to r. about** *or* **around (for sth)** farfouiller (à la recherche de qch); **to r. through sth** fouiller qch
2 *n Am* **r. sale** vente *f* de charité

rumour ['ruːmə(r)] **1** *n* rumeur *f*, bruit *m*; **r. has it...** on raconte que...; **there's a r. going round that...** le bruit court que...
2 *vt* **it is rumoured that...** le bruit court que...; **he is rumoured to be very rich/in hiding** le bruit court qu'il est très riche/qu'il se cache

rump [rʌmp] *n* (**a**) *(of animal)* croupe *f*; *Fam (of person)* postérieur *m*; **r. steak** romsteck *m* (**b**) *(of political party, assembly)* restant *m*; **r. state** état *m* croupion

rumple ['rʌmpəl] *vt* *(clothes, sheets)* friper, froisser; *(hair)* ébouriffer

rumpus ['rʌmpəs] *n Fam (noise)* chahut *m*; **to kick up** *or* **cause a r. (about sth)** faire un scandale (à propos de qch)

run [rʌn] **1** *n* (**a**) *(act of running)* course *f*; **at a r.** en courant; **to go for a r.** aller courir; **to be on the r.** être en fuite; *Fig* **we've got them on the r.** nous les avons mis en déroute; **to give sb the r. of the house** mettre sa maison à la disposition de qn; *Fam* **to make a r. for it** *(escape)* se tirer; *(to catch train)* se grouiller; *Fam* **to give sb a r. for his money** donner du fil à retordre à qn; *Fam* **to have the runs** avoir la courante
(**b**) *(trip)* trajet *m*; *(for pleasure)* balade *f*; **to go for a r.** *(in car)* aller se balader en voiture
(**c**) *Com (of book)* tirage *m*; *(of product)* série *f*
(**d**) *(sequence, series)* série *f*; *(in cards)* suite *f*; **a r. of good luck** une période faste; **a r. of bad luck** une série de malheurs; **in the short/long r.** à court/long terme
(**e**) *Fin (on currency, stock exchange)* ruée *f* (**on** sur); *(on bank)* retrait *m* massif
(**f**) *(in stocking)* échelle *f*

(**g**) *(in cricket, baseball)* point *m*
(**h**) *(for skier)* piste *f*
(**i**) *(for chickens, rabbits)* enclos *m*
2 *vt* *(pt* **ran** [ræn], *pp* **run)** (**a**) *(distance, race)* courir; **to r. an errand** faire une course; **to allow things to r. their course** laisser les choses se faire; **to r. sb close** talonner qn; *Fam* **to be run off one's feet** être débordé(e)
(**b**) *(drive)* **to r. sb to the airport** conduire qn à l'aéroport
(**c**) *(drugs, arms)* faire le trafic de
(**d**) *(machine)* faire fonctionner; *(tests)* effectuer; *Comput (program)* exécuter
(**e**) *(business)* diriger; *(hotel)* tenir; *(car)* avoir; **to r. sb's life for them** dire à qn comment vivre sa vie
(**f**) *(cables, pipes)* faire passer; **to r. one's fingers over/through sth** passer la main sur/dans qch; **to r. one's eye over sth** parcourir qch du regard
(**g**) *(water, bath)* faire couler
(**h**) **to r. a temperature** avoir de la température
(**i**) **to r. a deficit** enregistrer un déficit
(**j**) **to r. an article** publier un article
3 *vi* (**a**) *(of person)* courir; **to r. up/down the street** monter/descendre la rue en courant; **to r. about** courir çà et là; **I'll just r. across/round to the shop** je fais juste un saut à l'épicerie; **to r. after sb** courir après qn; **to r. for help** courir chercher de l'aide; **to r. in/out** entrer/sortir en courant
(**b**) *(flee)* s'enfuir, se sauver; **r. for it!** sauve qui peut!
(**c**) *(compete in race)* courir; **to r. for Parliament** se présenter aux législatives
(**d**) *(flow)* couler; **the river runs into a lake** la rivière se jette dans un lac; **my nose is running** j'ai le nez qui coule; **my blood ran cold** mon sang se glaça
(**e**) **to r. aground** *(of ship)* s'échouer; *Fig (of project, economy)* échouer
(**f**) *(of contract, lease)* courir; *(of play)* être à l'affiche; **it runs in the family** c'est de famille; **the total ran to £2,000** le montant total s'élevait à 2000 livres
(**g**) *(of bus, train)* circuler; **to be running late** *(of bus, train)* avoir du retard; *(of person)* être en retard
(**h**) *(operate) (of machine)* marcher, fonctionner; *(of engine)* tourner; **to r. on gas/electricity** marcher *ou* fonctionner au gaz/à l'électricité; **to r. off the mains** marcher *ou* fonctionner sur secteur; **the car runs on unleaded petrol** la voiture roule à l'essence sans plomb; **things are running smoothly** tout marche comme sur des roulettes
(**i**) *(of road, railway)* passer; **the line runs along the coast** la ligne suit *ou* longe la côte
(**j**) **feelings** *or* **tempers are running high** les esprits sont échauffés; **to be running low** *(of funds, supplies)* s'épuiser; **to r. dry** *(of river)* s'assécher
(**k**) *(of colour, dye)* déteindre

▶**run away** *vi* *(of person)* s'enfuir, se sauver (**from** de); **to r. away from home** faire une fugue; *Fig* **to r. away from the facts** refuser l'évidence; *Fig* **don't r. away with the idea that...** ne va pas t'imaginer que...

▶**run down 1** *vt sep* (**a**) *(in car)* renverser (**b**) *(find)* dénicher (**c**) *(criticize)* dénigrer (**d**) *(reduce) (production, stocks)* diminuer, réduire; *(industry, factory)* fermer progressivement
2 *vi* *(of battery)* se décharger

▶**run into** *vt insep* (**a**) *(collide with)* rentrer dans; *Fig (difficulties)* rencontrer; **to r. into trouble** s'attirer des ennuis (**b**) *(meet by chance)* tomber sur

▸**run off 1** *vt sep (print)* imprimer; *(photocopy)* photo-copier; **to r. off a copy of sth** faire une copie de qch **2** *vi (of person)* s'enfuir, se sauver (**with** avec)
▸**run on** *vi (of meeting, talk)* durer
▸**run out** *vi (of lease, contract)* expirer; *(of money, sup-plies)* s'épuiser; **to have run out of sth** ne plus avoir de qch; **time is running out** il ne reste plus beaucoup de temps; *Fig* **to r. out of steam** *(of person, project)* s'essouffler
▸**run over 1** *vt sep (in car)* renverser, écraser **2** *vt insep (speech, lines)* revoir **3** *vi (of speech, TV programme)* déborder
▸**run to** *vt insep (amount to)* s'élever à; **we can't r. to a new car** *(afford)* nous ne pouvons pas nous permet-tre d'acheter une nouvelle voiture
▸**run up** *vt sep* (**a**) *(debts)* accumuler (**b**) *(flag)* hisser (**c**) *(clothes)* confectionner à la hâte

run-around ['rʌnəraʊnd] *n Fam* **to give sb the r.** faire tourner qn en bourrique
runaway ['rʌnəweɪ] **1** *n* fugitif(ive) *m,f*; *(child)* fu-gueur(euse) *m,f* **2** *adj (prisoner, slave)* en fuite; *(train, lorry)* fou (folle); *(inflation)* galopant(e); *(victory)* remporté(e) haut la main; *(success)* fou (folle)
rundown ['rʌndaʊn] *n (summary)* résumé *m*; **to give sb a r. (on sth)** mettre qn au courant (de qch)
run-down [rʌn'daʊn] *adj (building)* délabré(e); *(per-son)* fatigué(e)
rung¹ [rʌŋ] *n (of ladder)* échelon *m*; *Fig* **on the bot-tom/top r.** tout en bas/en haut de l'échelle
rung² *pp of* **ring²**
run-in ['rʌnɪn] *n Fam* **to have a r. with sb** avoir un ac-crochage avec qn
runner ['rʌnə(r)] *n* (**a**) *(athlete)* coureur(euse) *m,f*; *(messenger)* coursier(ère) *m,f*; *(for drugs, guns)* pas-seur(euse) *m,f* (**b**) **r. bean** haricot *m* d'Espagne (**c**) *(on sleigh)* patin *m*; *(on drawer)* glissière *f* (**d**) *Fam* **to do a r.** se tirer
runner-up [rʌnə'rʌp] *(pl* **runners-up)** *n* suivant(e) *m,f*; *(in second place)* second(e) *m,f*
running ['rʌnɪŋ] **1** *n* (**a**) *(activity)* course *f*; **to go r.** courir; *Fig* **to be out of the r.** *(in competition, race)* n'avoir aucune chance; **to be in the r. for sth** être sur les rangs *ou* dans la course pour qch; *Am Pol* **r. mate** = candidat à la vice-présidence accompagnant dans sa campagne le candidat à la présidence des États-Unis; **r. shoe** chaussure *f* de course; **r. track** piste *f* (**b**) *(of machine, car)* **r. costs** frais *mpl* d'entre-tien (**c**) *(management)* gestion *f* **2** *adj (battle, feud)* incessant(e); *Fam* **go take a r. jump!** va voir ailleurs si j'y suis!; **r. board** *(on car)* marchepied *m*; **r. commentary** commentaire *m* en di-rect; **r. repairs** petites réparations *fpl*; **r. sore** plaie *f* qui suppure; **to keep a r. total (of sth)** comptabiliser (qch) au fur et à mesure; **r. water** eau *f* courante
runny ['rʌnɪ] *adj (liquid)* liquide; **to have a r. nose** avoir le nez qui coule
run-off ['rʌnɒf] *n* (**a**) *(election)* deuxième tour *m*; *(contest)* manche *f* pour départager deux candidats (**b**) *(from fields)* eaux *fpl* de ruissellement
run-of-the-mill [rʌnəvðə'mɪl] *adj* ordinaire
runt [rʌnt] *n* (**a**) *(of litter)* **the r.** le (la) plus faible de la portée (**b**) *(weak person)* avorton *m*
run-up ['rʌnʌp] *n (before jump)* course *f* d'élan; **the r. to the wedding/the election** la période précédant le mariage/les élections
runway ['rʌnweɪ] *n* piste *f*

rupee [ruː'piː] *n* roupie *f*
rupture ['rʌptʃə(r)] **1** *n* rupture *f* **2** *vt (relations)* rompre; *(container)* faire éclater **3** *vi also Med* éclater
rural ['rʊərəl] *adj* rural(e)
ruse [ruːz] *n* ruse *f*
rush¹ [rʌʃ] *n (plant)* jonc *m*; **r. matting** natte *f* (de jonc)
rush² **1** *n* (**a**) *(hurry)* **what's the r.?** pourquoi tant de hâte?; **to be in a r.** être pressé(e); **to do sth in a r.** faire qch à toute vitesse; **there's no r.** il n'y a rien qui presse; **to make a r. for sth** se précipiter vers qch; **r. hour** heures *fpl* de pointe; **a r. job** *(urgent)* un travail urgent; *(hurried)* un travail bâclé (**b**) *(surge) (of air)* bouffée *f*; *(of water)* flot *m* soudain; *(of requests)* flot *m* (**c**) *(demand)* ruée *f*; **there's been a r. on tickets** les gens se sont rués sur les billets (**d**) *Cin* **rushes** rush(e)s *mpl* **2** *vt* (**a**) *(hurry) (task)* faire à la hâte; *(person)* bous-culer; **to r. sb into doing sth** bousculer qn pour qu'elle fasse qch; **to be rushed off one's feet** être dé-bordé(e) (**b**) *(transport quickly)* transporter d'ur-gence (**c**) *(attack)* prendre d'assaut **3** *vi (move quickly)* se ruer (**at/towards** sur/vers); *(act quickly)* se dépêcher; **the blood rushed to my head** le sang m'est monté à la tête; **to r. to do sth** s'empresser de faire qch; **to r. into doing sth** faire qch sans réfléchir; **to r. into marriage** se marier sans réfléchir
▸**rush about, rush around** *vi* courir à droite et à gauche
▸**rush in** *vi (enter)* entrer précipitamment
▸**rush off** *vi* partir précipitamment
▸**rush out 1** *vt sep (book)* publier à la hâte **2** *vi (exit)* sortir précipitamment
▸**rush through 1** *vt sep (bill)* faire passer à la hâte; *(decision)* prendre à la hâte **2** *vt insep (book)* lire à toute vitesse; *(meal, work)* expédier
rusk [rʌsk] *n* gros biscuit *m (pour bébés)*
russet ['rʌsɪt] **1** *n (colour)* brun *m* roux **2** *adj* brun roux *inv*
Russia ['rʌʃə] *n* la Russie
Russian ['rʌʃən] **1** *n* (**a**) *(person)* Russe *mf* (**b**) *(lan-guage)* russe *m* **2** *adj* russe; **the R. Federation** la Fédération de Rus-sie; **R. roulette** roulette *f* russe
rust [rʌst] **1** *n* rouille *f* **2** *adj (colour)* rouille *inv* **3** *vi* rouiller
rustic ['rʌstɪk] *adj* rustique
rustle¹ ['rʌsəl] **1** *n (of leaves, paper)* bruissement *m* **2** *vt (leaves, paper)* faire bruire **3** *vi (of leaves, paper)* bruire
rustle² *vt (cattle)* voler
▸**rustle up** *vt sep Fam (meal, snack)* improviser; **to r. up support** rassembler des partisans
rustler ['rʌslə(r)] *n (cattle thief)* voleur(euse) *m,f* de bétail
rustproof ['rʌstpruːf] *adj (paint)* antirouille *inv*; *(me-tal)* inoxydable
rusty ['rʌstɪ] *adj also Fig* rouillé(e); *(colour)* rouille *inv*
rut¹ [rʌt] *n (groove)* ornière *f*; *Fig* **to be in a r.** être pris-onnier(ère) de la routine
rut² **1** *n (of stag)* rut *m* **2** *vi (pt & pp* **rutted)** *(of stag)* être en rut

rutabaga ['ruːtəbeɪgə] *n Am* rutabaga *m*
ruthless ['ruːθlɪs] *adj* impitoyable
RV [ɑːˈviː] *n Am* (*abbr* **recreational vehicle**) mobile home *m*

Rwanda [rəˈwændə] *n* le Rwanda
Rwandan [rəˈwændən] **1** *n* Rwandais(e) *m,f*
    2 *adj* rwandais(e)
rye [raɪ] *n* seigle *m*; **r. bread** pain *m* de seigle

S, s [es] *n* (**a**) *(letter)* S, s *m inv* (**b**) *(abbr* **south**) S
Sabbath ['sæbəθ] *n (Jewish)* (jour *m* du) sabbat *m*; *(Christian)* jour *m* du seigneur
sabbatical [sə'bætɪkəl] *Univ* **1** *n* congé *m* sabbatique; **to be on s.** être en congé sabbatique
   2 *adj (term, year)* sabbatique
sable ['seɪbəl] **1** *n (animal)* zibeline *f*; **s. coat** manteau *m* de ou en zibeline
   2 *adj Lit (black)* noir(e)
sabotage ['sæbətɑːʒ] **1** *n* sabotage *m*
   2 *vt* saboter
saboteur [sæbə'tɜː(r)] *n* saboteur(euse) *m,f*
sabre ['seɪbə(r)] *n* sabre *m*
sac [sæk] *n Biol* sac *m*
saccharin ['sækərɪn] *n* saccharine *f*
saccharine ['sækərɪn] *adj Pej (smile, words)* mielleux(euse); *(film)* à l'eau de rose
sachet ['sæʃeɪ] *n* sachet *m*
sack¹ [sæk] **1** *n* (**a**) *(bag)* sac *m* (**b**) *Fam (dismissal)* renvoi *m*; **to give sb the s.** virer qn; **to get the s.** se faire virer (**c**) *(bed)* pieu *m*; *Fam* **to hit the s.** se pieuter
   2 *vt Fam (dismiss)* virer
sack² **1** *n (plundering)* sac *m*
   2 *vt (plunder)* mettre à sac
sacking ['sækɪŋ] *n* (**a**) *(textile)* grosse toile *f* (**b**) *Fam (dismissal)* renvoi *m*
sacrament ['sækrəmənt] *n Rel* sacrement *m*; **to take** *or* **receive the sacraments** communier
sacred ['seɪkrɪd] *adj* sacré(e); *Fig* **s. cow** *(belief, institution)* véritable institution *f*
sacrifice ['sækrɪfaɪs] **1** *n* sacrifice *m*; **to make sacrifices** faire des sacrifices
   2 *vt* sacrifier (**to** à); **to s. oneself** se sacrifier
sacrificial [sækrɪ'fɪʃəl] *adj* sacrificiel(elle); *Fig* **s. lamb** *or* **victim** bouc *m* émissaire
sacrilege ['sækrɪlɪdʒ] *n also Fig* sacrilège *m*
sacrilegious [sækrɪ'lɪdʒəs] *adj also Fig* sacrilège
sacristan ['sækrɪstən] *n Rel* sacristain *m*
sacrosanct ['sækrəʊsæŋkt] *adj* sacro-saint(e)
SAD [sæd] *n Med (abbr* **Seasonal Affective Disorder**) = dépression due au manque de soleil en hiver
sad [sæd] *adj* (**a**) *(unhappy, depressing)* triste; **to make sb s.** attrister qn (**b**) *Fam (pathetic)* pitoyable
sadden ['sædən] *vt* attrister
saddle ['sædəl] **1** *n (on horse, bicycle)* selle *f*; **to be in the s.** être en selle; *Fig* être aux commandes
   2 *vt (horse)* seller; *Fam Fig* **to s. sb with sb/sth** refiler qn/qch à qn; **to get saddled with sb/sth** se retrouver avec qn/qch sur les bras
saddlebag ['sædəlbæg] *n* sacoche *f*

saddo ['sædəʊ] *n (pl* **saddos**) *Br Fam* ringard(e) *m,f*, nul (nulle) *m,f*
sadism ['seɪdɪzəm] *n* sadisme *m*
sadist ['seɪdɪst] *n* sadique *mf*
sadistic [sə'dɪstɪk] *adj* sadique
sadly ['sædlɪ] *adv* (**a**) *(unhappily)* tristement (**b**) *(unfortunately)* malheureusement (**c**) *(greatly)* **to be s. mistaken** se tromper lourdement; **he is s. missed** il nous/leur/*etc* manque beaucoup
sadness ['sædnɪs] *n* tristesse *f*
sadomasochism [seɪdəʊ'mæsəkɪzəm] *n* sadomasochisme *m*
sadomasochist [seɪdəʊ'mæsəkɪst] *n* sadomasochiste *mf*
SAE [eseɪ'iː] *n (abbr* **stamped addressed envelope**) enveloppe *f* timbrée
safari [sə'fɑːrɪ] *n* safari *m*; **to go on s.** faire un safari; **s. jacket** saharienne *f*; **s. park** réserve *f* d'animaux sauvages
safe [seɪf] **1** *adj* (**a**) *(not in danger)* en sécurité; *(house, activity)* sûr(e); *(topic of conversation)* sans danger; **s. from sth** à l'abri de qch; **s. and sound** sain et sauf (saine et sauve); **as s. as houses** qui ne présente aucun risque; *Prov* **better s. than sorry** deux précautions valent mieux qu'une; **s. deposit box** coffre-fort *m*; **s. seat** *(in parliament)* = siège parlementaire en principe acquis à un parti donné (**b**) *(not dangerous)* **it is s. to say that...** on peut dire sans risque de se tromper que...; **it's a s. bet that...** il y a fort à parier que...; **at a s. distance** à distance respectueuse; **in s. hands** entre de bonnes mains; **to wish sb a s. journey** souhaiter bon voyage à qn; **...to be on the s. side** ...pour plus de sûreté; **s. house** *(for spies)* cachette *f* sûre; **s.** *ou* **safer sex** rapports *mpl* sexuels protégés
   2 *n (for money)* coffre-fort *m*
   3 *adv* **to play (it) s.** ne pas prendre de risques
safe-conduct [seɪf'kɒndʌkt] *n* sauf-conduit *m*
safeguard ['seɪfgɑːd] **1** *n* garantie *f*
   2 *vt* sauvegarder
   3 *vi* **to s. against sth** se protéger contre qch
safe-keeping [seɪf'kiːpɪŋ] *n* **in s.** en lieu sûr; **to give sth to sb for s.** confier qch à la garde de qn
safely ['seɪflɪ] *adv* (**a**) *(without risk)* en toute sécurité; *(drive)* prudemment; **to arrive s.** *(of person)* bien arriver; *(of goods)* arriver sans dommage (**b**) *(with certainty)* avec certitude
safety ['seɪftɪ] *n* sûreté *f*; **for s.'s sake** pour plus de sûreté; **to be s. conscious** se préoccuper beaucoup de la sécurité; *Prov* **(there's) s. in numbers** plus on est nombreux, moins on court de risques; **s. belt** ceinture *f* de sécurité; **s. catch** cran *m* de sûreté; **s. glass**

verre *m* de sécurité; **s. matches** allumettes *fpl* de sûreté; **s. measures** mesures *fpl* de sûreté; **s. net** filet *m*; *Fig* **mesure** *f* de sécurité; **s. pin** épingle *f* de sûreté; *also Fig* **s. valve** soupape *f* de sûreté
saffron ['sæfrən] **1** *n* safran *m*
2 *adj* safran *inv*
sag [sæg] (*pt & pp* **sagged**) *vi* (*of roof, bridge*) s'affaisser; (*of flesh*) être flasque; (*of rope*) pendre; (*of breasts*) être tombant(e); (*of prices, support*) baisser
saga ['sɑːɡə] *n also Fig* (*story*) saga *f*
sagacious [sə'ɡeɪʃəs] *adj Formal* sagace
sagacity [sə'ɡæsɪtɪ] *n Formal* sagacité *f*
sage¹ [seɪdʒ] **1** *n* (*wise man*) sage *m*
2 *adj* (*person, conduct*) sage
sage² *n* (*herb*) sauge *f*
Sagittarius [sædʒɪ'teərɪəs] *n* (*sign of zodiac*) le Sagittaire; **to be (a) S.** être (du) Sagittaire
Sahara [sə'hɑːrə] *n* **the S. (Desert)** le Sahara
said [sed] *pt & pp of* **say**
sail [seɪl] **1** *n* voile *f*; **to set s.** prendre la mer; *Am* **s. boat** voilier *m*
2 *vi* (*of ship, person*) naviguer; (*start voyage*) prendre la mer; *Fig* **the clouds sailed by** les nuages passaient dans le ciel; *Fig* **his book sailed out of the window** son livre vola par la fenêtre; *Fig* **to s. close to the wind** jouer avec le feu; *Fam* **to s. through an examination** réussir un examen les doigts dans le nez
sailing ['seɪlɪŋ] *n* (*activity*) voile *f*; (*departure*) appareillage *m*; **to go s.** faire de la voile; *Br* **s. boat** voilier *m*
sailor ['seɪlə(r)] *n* marin *m*; **to be a good/bad s.** avoir/ne pas avoir le pied marin; **s. suit** costume *m* marin (*d'enfant*)
saint [seɪnt] *n* saint(e) *m,f*; **All Saints' (Day)** la Toussaint; **S. Bernard** (*dog*) saint-bernard *m inv*; **S. Patrick's Day** la Saint Patrick

Saint Patrick's Day

Patrick, le saint patron de l'Irlande, est célébré le 17 mars, qui est le jour de sa mort, en l'an 461. Saint Patrick convertit les Irlandais au christianisme et établit monastères, églises et écoles dans tout le pays. Selon la légende, il aurait également réussi à chasser tous les serpents d'Irlande. Chômée en Irlande, la St Patrick est également fêtée dans certaines villes américaines comptant une forte proportion de personnes d'origine irlandaise.

saintly ['seɪntlɪ] *adj* (*life, behaviour*) de saint; (*smile*) d'ange
sake [seɪk] *n* **for the s. of sb, for sb's s.** (*for the good of*) pour le bien de qn; (*out of respect for*) par égard pour qn; **for God's** *or* **heaven's s.!** mais bon sang!; **for the s. of peace** pour avoir la paix; **for old times' s.** en souvenir du passé; **this is just talking for talking's s.** c'est parler pour parler; **let's say, for the s. of argument...** admettons que...
salacious [sə'leɪʃəs] *adj* salace
salad ['sæləd] *n* salade *f*; **s. bowl** saladier *m*; *Br* **s. cream** = sorte de mayonnaise liquide; *Fig* **s. days** années *fpl* de jeunesse; **s. dressing** = vinaigrette ou sauce pour salade; **s. spinner** essoreuse *f* à salade
salamander ['sæləmændə(r)] *n* salamandre *f*
salami [sə'lɑːmɪ] *n* salami *m*
salaried ['sælərɪd] *adj* salarié(e)
salary ['sælərɪ] (*pl* **salaries**) *n* salaire *m*; **s. earner** salarié(e) *m,f*; **s. grade** échelon *m* de salaire; **s. scale** échelle *f* des salaires

sale [seɪl] *n* (**a**) (*action, event*) vente *f*; **for s.** à vendre; **to put sth up for s.** mettre qch en vente; **on s.** en vente; *Br* **sales assistant** vendeur(euse) *m,f*; **sales department** service *m* commercial; **sales drive** campagne *f* de vente; **sales force** force *f* de vente; **sales forecast** prévision *f* des ventes; **sales manager** directeur(trice) *m,f* commercial(e); **sales pitch** arguments *mpl* de vente; **s. price** prix *m* de vente; **sales representative**, *Fam* **sales rep** représentant(e) *m,f* (de commerce), VRP *m*; **sales target** objectif *m* de vente; *Am* **s. tax** TVA *f*; **s. of work** vente *f* de charité (**b**) (*at reduced prices*) soldes *mpl*; **the sales** les soldes *mpl*; **in the sales** en solde
saleable ['seɪləbəl] *adj* vendable
saleroom ['seɪlruːm] *n* salle *f* des ventes
salesclerk ['seɪlzklɑːk] *n Am* vendeur(euse) *m,f*
salesgirl ['seɪlzɡɜːl] *n* vendeuse *f*
salesman ['seɪlzmən] *n* (*for company*) représentant *m*; (*in shop*) vendeur *m*
salesmanship ['seɪlzmənʃɪp] *n* technique *f* de vente
salesperson ['seɪlzpɜːsən] (*pl* **salespeople**) *n* (*for company*) représentant(e) *m,f*; (*in shop*) vendeur(euse) *m,f*
saleswoman ['seɪlzwʊmən] *n* (*for company*) représentante *f*; (*in shop*) vendeuse *f*
salient ['seɪlɪənt] *adj Formal* (*feature*) marquant(e); (*point*) essentiel(elle)
saline ['seɪlaɪn] *adj* salin(e); **s. drip** perfusion *f* de solution saline; **s. solution** solution *f* saline
saliva [sə'laɪvə] *n* salive *f*
salivate ['sælɪveɪt] *vi also Fig* saliver
sallow ['sæləʊ] *adj* jaunâtre
▶**sally forth** ['sælɪ] (*pt & pp* **sallied**) *vi Lit* partir
salmon ['sæmən] (*pl* **salmon**) *n* saumon *m*; **s. (pink)** (rose *m*) saumon *m*; **s. trout** truite *f* saumonée
salmonella [sælmə'nelə] *n* salmonelle *f*
salon ['sælɒn] *n* (*beauty*) **s.** institut *m* de beauté; (*hair-dressing*) **s.** salon *m* de coiffure
saloon [sə'luːn] *n* (**a**) (*room*) salle *f*; *Am* (*bar*) bar *m* (**b**) *Br* **s. (car)** berline *f*
SALT [sɔːlt] *n* (*abbr* **Strategic Arms Limitation Talks**) SALT *m*
salt [sɔːlt] **1** *n* (**a**) (*substance*) sel *m*; **s. flat** marais *m* salant; **s. mine** mine *f* de sel (**b**) (*idioms*) **to be worth one's s.** être à la hauteur; **to rub s. in sb's wounds** remuer le couteau dans la plaie; *Fig* **that woman is the s. of the earth!** cette femme est la bonté incarnée! (**c**) *Fam* **an old s.** (*sailor*) un vieux loup de mer
2 *adj* **s. beef** bœuf *m* salé; **s. cod** morue *f* salée; **s. water** eau *f* salée
3 *vt* (*food*) saler; (*roads*) sabler
▶**salt away** *vt sep* (*money*) mettre de côté
saltcellar ['sɔːltselə(r)] *n* salière *f*
salt-free ['sɔːltfriː] *adj* sans sel
saltpetre [sɒlt'piːtə(r)] *n* salpêtre *m*
saltwater ['sɔːltwɔːtə(r)] *adj* (*lake*) salé(e); (*fish*) de mer
salty ['sɔːltɪ] *adj* salé(e)
salubrious [sə'luːbrɪəs] *adj Formal* salubre
salutary ['sæljʊtərɪ] *adj* salutaire
salute [sə'luːt] **1** *n* salut *m*; **to take the s.** passer les troupes en revue
2 *vt also Fig* saluer
3 *vi* faire un salut
salvage ['sælvɪdʒ] **1** *n* (*of ship*) sauvetage *m*; (*of waste material*) récupération *f*; **s. vessel** bateau *m* de sauvetage
2 *vt also Fig* sauver

salvation [sæl'veɪʃən] *n* salut *m*; **S. Army** Armée *f* du Salut

salve [sælv] *vt* **to s. one's conscience** soulager sa conscience

salver ['sælvə(r)] *n (tray)* plateau *m* (de présentation)

salvo ['sælvəʊ] *(pl* **salvos** *or* **salvoes)** *n also Fig* salve *f*; *(of questions)* flot *m*; *(of insults)* torrent *m*

Samaritan [sə'mærɪtən] *n also Fig* **the Good S.** le bon Samaritain; **the Samaritans** ≃ S.O.S. Amitié

same [seɪm] **1** *adj* **the s. man** le même homme; **the s. woman** la même femme; **the s. children** les mêmes enfants; **in the s. way** de la même façon; *Fig* **to go the s. way** prendre le même chemin; **the s. day** le même jour; **the** *or* **that (very) s. day** *(for emphasis)* le jour même; **it all comes to the s. thing** cela revient au même; **at the s. time** *(regularly)* au même moment; *(simultaneously)* en même temps, à la fois

2 *pron* **the s.** le même, la même; *(plural)* les mêmes; **I would have done the s.** j'aurais fait la même chose *ou* pareil; **if it's all the s. to you** si cela vous est égal; *Fam* **(the) s. again?** *(in pub)* la même chose?; *Fam* **s. here!** *(so do I)* moi aussi!; *(neither do I)* moi non plus!; *(I did the same thing)* pareil!; **the house isn't the s. without her** la maison n'est plus la même sans elle

3 *adv* **to think/feel the s.** penser/ressentir la même chose; **to look the s.** *(of two things)* sembler pareils; **to taste the s.** avoir le même goût; **all the s.** *(nevertheless)* tout de même

sameness ['seɪmnɪs] *n* monotonie *f*

Samoa [sə'məʊə] *n* Samoa *m*

Samoan [sə'məʊən] **1** *n* (**a**) *(person)* Samoan(e) *m,f* (**b**) *(language)* samoan *m*

2 *adj* samoan(e)

samosa [səm'əʊsə] *n* samosa *m*

sample ['sɑːmpəl] **1** *n* (**a**) *(of product)* échantillon *m*; *(of blood, urine)* prélèvement *m*; **to take a blood s.** faire une prise de sang (**b**) *Mus* sample *m*

2 *vt* (**a**) *(food, experience)* goûter (**b**) *(public opinion)* sonder (**c**) *(piece of music)* sampler

sanatorium [sænə'tɔːrɪəm] *(pl* **sanatoria** [sænə-'tɔːrɪə])* *n (forTB patients)* sanatorium *m*; *(for convalescents)* maison *f* de santé; *(sick bay)* infirmerie *f*

sanctify ['sæŋ(k)tɪfaɪ] *(pt & pp* **sanctified)** *vt* sanctifier; *Fig* consacrer

sanctimonious [sæŋ(k)tɪ'məʊnɪəs] *adj* moralisateur(trice)

sanction ['sæŋ(k)ʃən] **1** *n* (**a**) *(penalty)* sanction *f*; **to impose sanctions on a country** imposer des sanctions à un pays (**b**) *Formal (consent)* consentement *m*, accord *m*

2 *vt Formal (consent to)* sanctionner

sanctity ['sæŋ(k)tɪtɪ] *n* sainteté *f*; *Fig (of life, marriage)* caractère *m* sacré

sanctuary ['sæŋ(k)tj(ʊ)ərɪ] *(pl* **sanctuaries)** *n Rel* sanctuaire *m*; *(for fugitive, refugee)* refuge *m*, asile *m*; *(for birds, wildlife)* réserve *f*; **to seek/find s.** chercher/trouver refuge

sand [sænd] **1** *n* sable *m*; **s. castle** château *m* de sable; **s. dune** dune *f*

2 *vt* (**a**) *(smooth with sandpaper)* poncer (**b**) *(cover with sand)* sabler

sandal ['sændəl] *n* sandale *f*

sandbag ['sændbæg] *n* sac *m* de sable

sandbank ['sændbæŋk] *n* banc *m* de sable

sandblast ['sændblæst] *vt* décaper à la sableuse

S & M [esən'dem] *n Fam (abbr* **sadomasochism)** sadomasochisme *m*

sandpaper ['sændpeɪpə(r)] **1** *n* papier *m* de verre

2 *vt* poncer, passer au papier de verre

sandpit ['sændpɪt] *n* bac *m* à sable

sandstone ['sændstəʊn] *n* grès *m*

sandstorm ['sændstɔːm] *n* tempête *f* de sable

sandwich ['sændwɪtʃ] **1** *n* sandwich *m*; **ham s.** sandwich *m* au jambon; *Br* **s. course** stage *m* de formation (professionnelle) en alternance; **s. loaf** ≃ pain *m* de mie

2 *vt* **to be sandwiched between** *(of layer)* être intercalé(e) entre; *(of person, building)* être coincé(e) entre

sandy ['sændɪ] *adj* (**a**) *(earth)* sablonneux(euse); *(beach)* de sable (**b**) *(hair)* blond roux *inv*

sane [seɪn] *adj (person)* sain(e) d'esprit; *(action, remark)* sensé(e)

San Franciscan ['sænfrən'sɪskən] **1** *n* habitant(e) *m,f* de San Francisco

2 *adj* de San Francisco

San Francisco ['sænfrən'sɪskəʊ] *n* San Francisco

sang [sæŋ] *pt of* **sing**

sanguine ['sæŋgwɪn] *adj* optimiste

sanitary ['sænɪtərɪ] *adj* (**a**) *(clean)* hygiénique (**b**) *(relating to hygiene)* sanitaire; *Br* **s. towel** serviette *f* hygiénique

sanitation [sænɪ'teɪʃən] *n* installations *fpl* sanitaires

sanitize ['sænɪtaɪz] *vt* expurger

sanity ['sænɪtɪ] *n* santé *f* mentale

sank [sæŋk] *pt of* **sink²**

San Marino [sænmə'riːnəʊ] *n* Saint-Marin

Santa (Claus) ['sæntə('klɔːz)] *n* le père Noël

sap¹ [sæp] *n (of plant)* sève *f*

sap² *n Fam (gullible person)* andouille *f*

sap³ *(pt & pp* **sapped)** *vt (weaken)* saper

sapling ['sæplɪŋ] *n* jeune arbre *m*

sapper ['sæpə(r)] *n Br Mil* soldat *m* du génie

sapphire ['sæfaɪə(r)] *n* saphir *m*

Sarajevo [særə'jeɪvəʊ] *n* Sarajevo

sarcasm ['sɑːkæzəm] *n* sarcasme *m*

sarcastic [sɑː'kæstɪk] *adj* sarcastique

sarcastically [sɑː'kæstɪklɪ] *adv* de manière sarcastique; *(speak)* d'un ton sarcastique

sarcophagus [sɑː'kɒfəgəs] *(pl* **sarcophagi** [sɑː'kɒfə-gaɪ])* *n* sarcophage *m*

sardine [sɑː'diːn] *n* sardine *f*; *Fam Fig* **to be packed like sardines** être serrés(es) comme des sardines

Sardinia [sɑː'dɪnɪə] *n* la Sardaigne

Sardinian [sɑː'dɪnɪən] **1** *n* Sarde *mf*

2 *adj* sarde

sardonic [sɑː'dɒnɪk] *adj* sardonique

sari ['sɑːrɪ] *n* sari *m*

sarong [sə'rɒŋ] *n* paréo *m*

SARS [sɑːz] *n Med (abbr* **severe acute respiratory syndrome)** SRAS *m*

sartorial [sɑː'tɔːrɪəl] *adj Formal* vestimentaire

SAS [eseɪ'es] *n Br (abbr* **Special Air Service)** = service d'intervention spécial de l'Armée britannique

SASE [eseɪe'iː] *n Am (abbr* **self-addressed stamped envelope)** enveloppe *f* timbrée *(portant l'adresse à laquelle elle doit être renvoyée)*

sash [sæʃ] *n (around waist)* large ceinture *f* de tissu; *(around shoulder)* écharpe *f*; **s. cord** corde *f* *(actionnant une fenêtre à guillotine)*; **s. window** fenêtre *f* à guillotine

Sassenach ['sæsənæx] *n Scot Pej* Anglais(e) *m,f*

sassy ['sæsɪ] *adj Fam (cheeky)* culotté(e); *(lively)* plein(e) d'entrain

Sat (*abbr* **Saturday**) samedi
sat [sæt] *pt & pp of* **sit**
Satan ['seɪtən] *n* Satan
satanic [sə'tænɪk] *adj* satanique, diabolique
satanist ['seɪtənɪst] **1** *adj* sataniste
   2 *n* sataniste *mf*
satchel ['sætʃəl] *n* cartable *m*
sate [seɪt] *vt Formal* assouvir
satellite ['sætəlaɪt] *n* satellite *m*; **s.** **(state)** (État *m*) satellite *m*; **s. dish** antenne *f* parabolique; **s. navigation** navigation *f* par satellite; **s. television** télévision *f* par satellite; **s. town** ville *f* satellite
satiate ['seɪʃɪeɪt] *vt Formal* assouvir
satin ['sætɪn] *n* satin *m*
satire ['sætaɪə(r)] *n* satire *f*
satirical [sə'tɪrɪkəl] *adj* satirique
satirist ['sætɪrɪst] *n* écrivain *m* satirique
satirize ['sætɪraɪz] *vt* faire la satire de
satisfaction [sætɪs'fækʃən] *n* satisfaction *f*; **to have the s. of doing sth** avoir la satisfaction de faire qch
satisfactory [sætɪs'fæktərɪ] *adj* satisfaisant(e)
satisfied ['sætɪsfaɪd] *adj* satisfait(e)
satisfy ['sætɪsfaɪ] (*pt & pp* **satisfied**) *vt* (**a**) *(meet needs of)* *(person, curiosity)* satisfaire; *(condition)* remplir (**b**) *(convince)* convaincre, persuader
sat nav ['sætnæv] *n Fam* navigation *f* par satellite
saturate ['sætʃəreɪt] *vt* saturer; **to s. the market** saturer le marché; **saturated fats** graisses *fpl* saturées
saturation [sætʃə'reɪʃən] *n* saturation *f*; **to reach s. point** arriver à saturation; *Mil* **s. bombing** bombardement *m* intensif
Saturday ['sætədɪ] *n* samedi *m*; **this S.** samedi prochain *ou* qui vient; **on S.** samedi; **on S. morning/afternoon/evening** samedi matin/après-midi/soir; **on Saturdays** le samedi; **every S.** tous les samedis; **every other S.** un samedi sur deux; **last S.** samedi dernier; **the S. before last** pas samedi dernier mais celui d'avant; **next S.** samedi prochain; **the S. after next, a week on S., S. week** le samedi d'après, samedi en huit; **the following S.** le samedi suivant; **S.'s paper** le journal de samedi; **S. job** petit boulot *m* (*du samedi*)
Saturn ['sætɜːn] *n* *(planet)* Saturne *f*
sauce [sɔːs] *n* (**a**) *(for food)* sauce *f*; **tomato/cheese s.** sauce *f* tomate/au fromage; **s. boat** saucière *f* (**b**) *Fam (impudence)* culot *m*
sauced [sɔːst] *adj Fam (drunk)* bourré(e), pété(e)
saucepan ['sɔːspən] *n* casserole *f*
saucer ['sɔːsə(r)] *n* soucoupe *f*, *Belg & Suisse* sous-tasse *f*
saucy ['sɔːsɪ] *adj Fam (impertinent)* insolent(e); *(risqué)* coquin(e)
Saudi ['saʊdɪ] **1** *n (person)* Saoudien(enne) *m,f*; *Fam (country)* l'Arabie *f* Saoudite
   2 *adj* saoudien(enne)
Saudi Arabia ['saʊdɪə'reɪbɪə] *n* l'Arabie *f* Saoudite
Saudi Arabian ['saʊdɪə'reɪbɪən] **1** *n* Saoudien(enne) *m,f*
   2 *adj* saoudien(enne)
sauna ['sɔːnə] *n* sauna *m*; **to have a s.** aller au sauna
saunter ['sɔːntə(r)] **1** *n* balade *f*; **to go for a s.** partir en balade
   2 *vi* **to s. (along)** flâner
sausage ['sɒsɪdʒ] *n* saucisse *f*; *Fam* **not a s.** *(nothing)* que dalle; *Hum* **you silly s.!** patate, va!; *Fam* **s. dog** saucisson *m* à pattes; **s. meat** chair *f* à saucisse; *Br* **s. roll** feuilleté *m* à la viande

sauté ['səʊteɪ] **1** *adj* sauté(e)
   2 *vt* (*pt &pp* **sautéed**) faire sauter
savage ['sævɪdʒ] **1** *n Old-fashioned* sauvage *mf*
   2 *adj (animal, person)* féroce, brutal(e); *(attack, criticism)* violent(e)
   3 *vt (attack physically)* attaquer; *Fig (criticize)* descendre en flammes
savagely ['sævɪdʒlɪ] *adv (beat, attack)* sauvagement; *Fig (criticize)* violemment, avec virulence
savanna(h) [sə'vænə] *n* savane *f*
save¹ [seɪv] *prep Formal (except)* hormis
save² [seɪv] *vt* (**a**) *(rescue)* sauver; **to s. sb's life** sauver la vie à qn; *Fam* **she can't sing to s. her life** elle chante comme un pied; *Fam* **to s. one's (own) neck** *or* **skin** sauver sa peau; **to s. sb from falling** empêcher qn de tomber; **to s. a goal** arrêter un but; **God s. the King/the Queen!** vive le Roi/la Reine! (**b**) *(keep for future)* garder, conserver; *(money)* mettre de côté; *Comput* sauvegarder; **to s. oneself for sth** se réserver pour qch (**c**) *(not waste)* *(money, space)* économiser; *(time)* gagner; **s. your breath** ne te fatigue pas (**d**) *(spare)* **to s. sb sth** éviter qch à qn; **to s. sb (from) doing sth** éviter à qn de faire qch
   2 *vi* faire des économies (**for/on** pour/sur)
   3 *n (of goalkeeper)* arrêt *m*; **to make a s.** arrêter un but
▶**save up** *vi* mettre de l'argent de côté (**for** pour)
saver ['seɪvə(r)] *n* épargnant(e) *m,f*
saving ['seɪvɪŋ] **1** *n* (**a**) *(economy)* économie *f* (**b**) **savings** *(money saved)* économies *fpl*; **to live off one's savings** vivre sur ses économies; **savings account** compte *m* d'épargne; **savings bank** caisse *f* d'épargne; *Am* **savings and loan association** caisse *f* d'épargne logement
   2 *adj* **her/its s. grace** ce qui la/le sauve
saviour ['seɪvjə(r)] *n* sauveur *m*; **the S.** le Sauveur
savour ['seɪvə(r)] **1** *n* saveur *f*
   2 *vt also Fig* savourer
   3 *vi Formal* **to s. of** sentir
savoury ['seɪvərɪ] *adj* (**a**) *(food)* salé(e) (**b**) *(conduct)* honorable
saw¹ [sɔː] *pt of* **see²**
saw² **1** *n (tool)* scie *f*
   2 *vt (pp* **sawn** [sɔːn] *or* **sawed**) scier
▶**saw off** *vt sep* scier
▶**saw up** *vt sep* découper à la scie
sawdust ['sɔːdʌst] *n* sciure *f*
sawmill ['sɔːmɪl] *n* scierie *f*
sawn [sɔːn] *pp of* **saw²**
sawn-off shotgun ['sɔːnɒf'ʃɒtgʌn] *n* fusil *m* à canon scié
sax [sæks] *n Fam (saxophone)* sax *m*
Saxon ['sæks(ə)n] **1** *n* (**a**) *(person)* Saxon(onne) *m,f* (**b**) *(language)* saxon *m*
   2 *adj* saxon(onne)
Saxony ['sæksənɪ] *n* Saxe *f*
saxophone ['sæksəfəʊn] *n* saxophone *m*
saxophonist [sæk'sɒfənɪst] *n* saxophoniste *mf*
say [seɪ] *vt (pt & pp* **said** [sed]) dire; *(of clock, watch)* indiquer; **to s. sth to sb** dire qch à qn; **it says that...** *(of text, sign)* il y a écrit que...; **I wouldn't s. no to a cup of tea** je prendrais volontiers une tasse de thé; **I didn't s. a word** je n'ai pas dit un mot; **it's not for me to s.** ce n'est pas à moi de le dire; **there's no saying what might happen if...** inutile de vous dire ce qui se passerait si...; **what have you got to s. for yourself?** as-tu une excuse valable?; **there's a lot to be**

said for living in the country il y a bien des avantages à vivre à la campagne; **you're honest, I'll s. that for you** tu es honnête, je te l'accorde; **it says a lot about her** ça en dit long sur sa personne; **don't s. you've forgotten already!** ne me dis pas que tu as déjà oublié!; **you can s. that again!, you said it!** c'est le cas de le dire!, tu l'as dit!; **need I s. more?** ai-je besoin d'en dire plus?; **they s. that..., it is said that...** on dit que...; **s. we won first prize** supposons que nous gagnions le premier prix; **if I had, s., £100,000** si j'avais, mettons, 100 000 livres

2 *vi* I'm not saying je ne dirai rien; **as they s.** comme on dit; **I s.!** dis-donc!; **I'll s.!** absolument!, tout à fait!; *Fam* **you don't s.!** sans blagues!

3 *n* **to have one's s.** avoir son mot à dire; **to have a s./ no s. in sth** avoir/ne pas avoir voix au chapitre concernant qch

saying ['seɪɪŋ] *n* maxime *f*; **as the s. goes** comme dit la maxime

say-so ['seɪsəʊ] *n Fam (permission)* permission *f*

scab [skæb] *n* (**a**) *(on skin)* croûte *f* (**b**) *Fam (strike-breaker)* jaune *mf*

scabbard ['skæbəd] *n* fourreau *m*, gaine *f*

scabies ['skeɪbiːz] *n* gale *f*

scaffold ['skæfəld] *n (outside building)* échafaudage *m*; *(for execution)* échafaud *m*

scaffolding ['skæfəldɪŋ] *n* échafaudage *m*

scalawag *Am* = **scallywag**

scald [skɔːld] **1** *n* brûlure *f*

2 *vt* ébouillanter; **to s. oneself** s'ébouillanter

scalding ['skɔːldɪŋ] *adj* brûlant(e)

scale¹ [skeɪl] **1** *n (on fish, reptile)* écaille *f*; *(in pipes, kettle)* dépôt *m* calcaire

2 *vt (fish)* écailler

scale² *n* (**a**) *(of instrument)* gamme *f*; *(of salaries)* barème *m*; **on a s. of one to ten** sur une échelle allant de un à dix (**b**) *(of map, drawing)* échelle *f*; *Fig (of problem, changes)* étendue *f*; **to s.** à la bonne échelle; **s. drawing** dessin *m* à l'échelle; **s. model** modèle *m* réduit (**c**) *(of ruler, thermometer)* graduation *f*

scale³ *vt (climb)* escalader

▸**scale down** *vt sep (reduce)* revoir à la baisse

▸**scale up** *vt sep (increase)* augmenter

scales [skeɪlz] *npl* **(set of) s.** *(for kitchen)* balance *f*; *(for bathroom)* pèse-personne *m*

scallion ['skæliən] *n Am & Ir (spring onion)* oignon *m* blanc; *(shallot)* échalote *f*

scallop ['skæləp, 'skɒləp] **1** *n* (**a**) *(shellfish)* coquille *f* Saint-Jacques (**b**) *(in sewing)* feston *m*

2 *vt (in sewing)* festonner

scallywag ['skæliwæg] *n Fam* coquin(e) *m,f*

scalp [skælp] **1** *n* cuir *m* chevelu; *(as war trophy)* scalp *m*

2 *vt (in war)* scalper

scalpel ['skælpəl] *n* scalpel *m*

scaly ['skeɪli] *adj (fish)* écailleux(euse); *(skin)* squameux(euse)

scam [skæm] *n Fam* arnaque *f*, magouille *f*

scamp [skæmp] *n (rascal)* coquin(e) *m,f*

scamper ['skæmpə(r)] *vi* gambader, galoper

▸**scamper away, scamper off** *vi* détaler, partir en courant

scampi ['skæmpi] *n* scampi *mpl*

scan [skæn] **1** *vt (pt & pp scanned)* (**a**) *(examine closely)* scruter; *Comput* scanner, passer au scanner *ou* au scanneur; *Med* faire une scanographie de; *(with* ultrasound)* faire une échographie de (**b**) *(glance at)* parcourir

2 *n Med* scanographie *f*; *(with ultrasound)* échographie *f*

scandal ['skændəl] *n* (**a**) *(outrage)* scandale *m*; **to create** *or* **cause a s.** créer *ou* provoquer un scandale (**b**) *(gossip)* ragots *mpl*

scandalize ['skændəlaɪz] *vt* scandaliser, choquer

scandalous ['skændələs] *adj* scandaleux(euse)

Scandinavia [skændɪ'neɪvɪə] *n* la Scandinavie

Scandinavian [skændɪ'neɪvɪən] **1** *n* Scandinave *mf*

2 *adj* scandinave

scanner ['skænə(r)] *n Med & Comput* scanner *m*

scant [skænt] *adj* insuffisant(e)

scantily ['skæntɪli] *adv* insuffisamment, sommairement; **s. dressed** *or* **clad** légèrement vêtu(e)

scanty ['skænti] *adj (dress)* léger(ère); *(amount, information)* maigre, limité(e)

scapegoat ['skeɪpgəʊt] *n* bouc *m* émissaire

scar [skɑː(r)] **1** *n also Fig* cicatrice *f*; **s. tissue** tissu *m* cicatriciel

2 *vt (pt & pp scarred)* marquer de cicatrices; *Fig* marquer; **to be scarred for life** garder des cicatrices toute sa vie; *Fig* être marqué(e) à vie

3 *vi (of wound)* laisser une cicatrice

scarce ['skeəs] *adj* rare; *Fam* **to make oneself s.** filer

scarcely ['skeəsli] *adv* à peine; **she could s. speak** elle pouvait à peine parler; **s. ever/anyone** presque jamais/personne; **it is s. likely that...** il est peu probable que...

scarcity ['skeəsɪti], **scarceness** ['skeəsnɪs] *n* manque *m*, pénurie *f*

scare ['skeə(r)] **1** *n* frayeur *f*; **bomb s.** alerte *f* à la bombe; **you gave me an awful s.** tu m'as fait une belle frayeur

2 *vt* effrayer; *Fam* **to s. the life out of sb, to s. the living daylights out of sb** faire une de ces trouilles à qn

3 *vi* s'effrayer

▸**scare away, scare off** *vt sep* faire fuir

scarecrow ['skeəkrəʊ] *n* épouvantail *m*

scared [skeəd] *adj* effrayé(e); **to be s. of sb/sth** avoir peur de qn/qch; **to be s. stiff, to be s. to death** être mort(e) de peur

scaremongering ['skeəmʌŋgərɪŋ] *n* alarmisme *m*

scarf [skɑːf] *(pl* **scarves** [skɑːvz])* *n (long)* écharpe *f*; *(square)* foulard *m*

scarlet ['skɑːlɪt] **1** *n* écarlate *f*

2 *adj* écarlate; *Fig* **to go** *or* **turn s.** *(with anger, embarrassment)* devenir rouge; **s. fever** scarlatine *f*

scarper ['skɑːpə(r)] *vi Br Fam* ficher le camp, se tailler

scary ['skeərɪ] *adj Fam* effrayant(e)

scat [skæt] *exclam Fam* fiche le camp!, dégage!

scathing ['skeɪðɪŋ] *adj (remark, sarcasm)* acerbe; **to be s. about sb/sth** faire des remarques acerbes sur qn/qch

scatological [skætə'lɒdʒɪkəl] *adj* scatologique

scatter ['skætə(r)] **1** *vt (clouds, demonstrators)* disperser, éparpiller; *(corn, seed)* jeter *ou* semer à la volée; *(crumbs, papers)* laisser traîner

2 *vi (of crowd)* se disperser

scatterbrain ['skætəbreɪn] *n Fam* tête *f* de linotte

scatty ['skæti] *adj Br Fam* farfelu(e)

scavenge ['skævɪndʒ] **1** *vt* récupérer

2 *vi* **to s. for sth** fouiller pour trouver qch; **to s. in the dustbins** fouiller dans *ou* faire les poubelles

scavenger ['skævɪndʒə(r)] *n (animal)* charognard *m*; *Fig (person)* fouilleur(euse) *m,f* de poubelles

scenario [sɪ'nɑːrɪəʊ] *(pl* **scenarios)** *n* (**a**) *(of film)* scénario *m* (**b**) *(situation)* hypothèse *f*

scene [siːn] *n* (**a**) *(in book, film, play)* scène *f*; *also Fig* **a touching/terrifying s.** une scène touchante/terrifiante; *also Fig* **behind the scenes** dans les coulisses; *Theat* **s. shifter** machiniste *mf* (**b**) *(of event)* lieu *m*, endroit *m*; **a change of s.** un changement de décor; **to arrive** *or* **come on the s.** *(of police, ambulance)* arriver sur les lieux; *Fig* faire son apparition; **the s. of the crime/accident** le lieu du crime/de l'accident; **a s. of devastation** un spectacle de dévastation; **I can picture the s.** j'imagine la scène; *Fam* **it's not my s.** ce n'est pas mon truc (**c**) *(fuss)* scandale *m*; **to make a s.** faire un scandale

scenery ['siːnərɪ] *n* (**a**) *(in play)* décor(s) *m(pl)* (**b**) *(landscape)* paysage *m*; *Fam* **to need a change of s.** avoir besoin de changer de décor *ou* d'air

scenic ['siːnɪk] *adj* pittoresque; **s. railway** petit train *m* (touristique); **s. route** route *f* touristique

scent [sent] **1** *n* (**a**) *(smell)* odeur *f* (**b**) *(perfume)* parfum *m* (**c**) *(in hunting)* fumet *m*; **to pick up the s.** trouver la piste; **to be on the s. of sth** être sur la trace de qch; **to lose the s.** perdre la trace; **she threw her pursuers off the s.** elle sema ses poursuivants
2 *vt* (**a**) *(smell)* flairer; *Fig* **to s. blood** sentir que sa victime est affaiblie; *Fig* **to s. danger** flairer le danger (**b**) *(perfume)* parfumer

sceptic, *Am* **skeptic** ['skeptɪk] *n* sceptique *mf*

sceptical, *Am* **skeptical** ['skeptɪkəl] *adj* sceptique

sceptically, *Am* **skeptically** ['skeptɪklɪ] *adv* avec scepticisme

scepticism, *Am* **skepticism** ['skeptɪsɪzəm] *n* scepticisme *m*

sceptre ['septə(r)] *n* sceptre *m*

schedule ['ʃedjuːl, *Am* 'skedjuːl] **1** *n* (**a**) *(plan) (for work, project)* planning *m*; *(for events)* programme *m*, calendrier *m*; *Am (for trains, buses)* horaire *m*; **on s.** *(train, bus)* à l'heure; *(person)* dans les temps; **to be behind/ahead of s.** être en retard/en avance sur le programme; **to go according to s.** se dérouler comme prévu; **to work to a tight s.** avoir un emploi du temps serré (**b**) *Com (list of prices)* barème *m*
2 *vt* prévoir; **we're scheduled to arrive at 21.45** notre arrivée est prévue à 21h45; **the museum is scheduled to open in August** l'ouverture du musée est prévue pour le mois d'août

scheduled ['ʃedjuːld, *Am* 'skedjuːld] *adj* prévu(e); **s. flight** vol *m* régulier

schematic [skɪ'mætɪk] *adj* schématique

scheme [skiːm] **1** *n (arrangement, system)* arrangement *m*; *(plan)* plan *m*; *(plot)* machination *f*, complot *m*; **in the (grand) s. of things** dans le fond; **(housing) s.** lotissement *m*
2 *vi Pej* comploter, intriguer (**against** contre)

schilling ['ʃɪlɪŋ] *n* schilling *m*

schism ['s(k)ɪzəm] *n* schisme *m*

schizoid ['skɪtsɔɪd] **1** *n* schizoïde *mf*
2 *adj* schizoïde

schizophrenia [skɪtsəʊ'friːnɪə] *n* schizophrénie *f*

schizophrenic [skɪtsəʊ'frenɪk] **1** *n* schizophrène *mf*
2 *adj* schizophrène

schmaltzy ['ʃmɔːltsɪ] *adj Fam* à l'eau de rose, cucul *inv*

scholar ['skɒlə(r)] *n (learned person)* érudit(e) *m,f*

scholarly ['skɒləlɪ] *adj* érudit(e)

scholarship ['skɒləʃɪp] *n* (**a**) *(learning)* érudition *f*, savoir *m* (**b**) *(grant)* bourse *f* (d'études)

scholastic [skə'læstɪk] *adj Formal* scolaire

school¹ [skuːl] **1** *n* (**a**) *(for children)* école *f*; **to go to s.** aller à l'école; **s. of art, art s.** école *f* d'art; **of s. age** d'âge scolaire; *Fig* **I went to the s. of hard knocks** j'ai été à rude école; **s. bag** cartable *m*; *Br* **s. board** conseil *m* d'administration de l'établissement; **s. book** manuel *m ou* livre *m* scolaire; **s. day** journée *f* d'école *ou* scolaire; **s. friend** camarade *mf* d'école; **s. leaver** = jeune qui vient de terminer ses études secondaires; **s. report** *(for primary school)* carnet *m* de notes; *(for secondary school)* bulletin *m* scolaire; **s. uniform** uniforme *m* scolaire; **s. year** année *f* scolaire (**b**) *Am (college, university)* faculté *f*, université *f* (**c**) *(of artists, thinkers)* école *f*; **s. of thought** école *f* de pensée; *Fig* **he's one of the old s.** il est de la vieille école
2 *vt (educate)* scolariser; *(train)* former, entraîner; **to s. sb in sth** former qn à qch

school² *n (of fish)* banc *m*

schoolboy ['skuːlbɔɪ] *n* écolier *m*, élève *m*

schoolchild ['skuːltʃaɪld] *n* écolier(ère) *m,f*, élève *mf*

schoolgirl ['skuːlɡɜːl] *n* écolière *f*, élève *f*

schooling ['skuːlɪŋ] *n* scolarité *f*, éducation *f*

schoolmaster ['skuːlmɑːstə(r)] *n Formal (primary)* instituteur *m*, maître *m*; *(secondary)* professeur *m*

schoolmate ['skuːlmeɪt] *n* camarade *mf* de classe

schoolmistress ['skuːlmɪstrɪs] *n Formal (primary)* institutrice *f*, maîtresse *f*; *(secondary)* professeur *m*

schoolroom ['skuːlruːm] *n* salle *f* de classe

schoolteacher ['skuːltiːtʃə(r)] *n (primary)* instituteur(trice) *m,f*, maître(esse) *m,f (secondary)* professeur *m*

schoolyard ['skuːljɑːd] *n Am* cour *f* de récréation

schooner ['skuːnə(r)] *n* (**a**) *(ship)* schooner *m* (**b**) *(glass)* grand verre *m* (à xérès)

sciatica [saɪ'ætɪkə] *n* sciatique *f*

science ['saɪəns] *n* science *f*; **she's good at s.** elle est bonne en sciences; **s. fiction** science-fiction *f*; **s. park** parc *m* scientifique; **s. teacher** professeur *m* de sciences

scientific [saɪən'tɪfɪk] *adj* scientifique

scientist ['saɪəntɪst] *n* scientifique *mf*

sci-fi ['saɪfaɪ] *Fam* **1** *n* SF *f*
2 *adj* de SF

Scilly ['sɪlɪ] *n* **the S. Isles, the Scillies** les Sorlingues *fpl*

scimitar ['sɪmɪtə(r)] *n* cimeterre *m*

scintillating ['sɪntɪleɪtɪŋ] *adj* brillant(e)

scissors ['sɪzəz] *npl* ciseaux *mpl*; **a pair of s.** une paire de ciseaux

sclerosis [sklə'rəʊsɪs] *n Med* sclérose *f*

scoff [skɒf] **1** *vt Br Fam (eat)* bouffer
2 *vi (mock)* se moquer (**at** de)

scold [skəʊld] *vt* gronder

scone [skɒn] *n* scone *m*

scoop [skuːp] **1** *n* (**a**) *(utensil) (for ice cream)* cuillère *f* à glace; *(for flour, sugar)* pelle *f*; *(for mashed potato)* cuillère *f* (**b**) *(portion) (of ice cream)* boule *f*; *(of mashed potato)* portion *f* (**c**) *Fam (in journalism)* scoop *m*
2 *vt* (**a**) *(with hands, spoon)* ramasser (**b**) *(story)* publier en exclusivité

▶**scoop up** *vt sep* ramasser

scoot [skuːt] *vi Fam* **to s. (off** *or* **away)** filer

scooter ['sku:tə(r)] *n (for child)* trottinette *f*; *(small motorbike)* scooter *m*

scope [skəʊp] *n (of action)* possibilité *f*; *(of enquiry)* étendue *f*, portée *f*; **to give s. for...** *(interpretation, explanation)* laisser le champ libre à...; **the book is too narrow in s.** le livre est d'une portée trop limitée; **there's plenty of s. for improvement** les possibilités d'amélioration ne manquent pas; **the job gave him little s.** to demonstrate his talents son travail lui fournissait peu d'occasions de montrer ses talents

scorch [skɔ:tʃ] **1** *vt* roussir; **scorched earth policy** politique *f* de la terre brûlée
2 *n* **s. mark** brûlure *f*

scorcher ['skɔ:tʃə(r)] *n Fam (hot day)* **what a s.!** c'est la canicule!

scorching ['skɔ:tʃɪŋ] *adj (day, weather)* torride; *(sun)* brûlant(e)

score [skɔ:(r)] **1** *n* **(a)** *(in sport, quiz)* score *m*; **there was still no s.** personne n'avait encore marqué; **to keep the s.** compter les points; *Fam Fig* **to know the s.** connaître le topo **(b)** *(line)* rayure *f*, entaille *f* **(c)** *(quarrel)* **to have a s. to settle with sb** avoir un compte à régler avec qn **(d)** *(reason, grounds)* **on that s.** à ce sujet, sur ce point **(e)** *(in music)* partition *f* **(f)** *Old-fashioned (twenty)* **a s.** vingt; *Fam* **scores of** *(a lot)* des tas de
2 *vt* **(a)** *(in sport)* marquer; **to s. a hit** *(hit target)* atteindre la cible; *Fig (of person, film)* remporter un grand succès; *Fig* **to s. points off sb** avoir le dessus **(b)** *(cut line in)* entailler **(c)** *Fam (buy)* **to s. drugs** acheter de la drogue
3 *vi* **(a)** *(score a goal)* marquer un but **(b)** *Fam (sexually)* faire une touche; *(buy drugs)* acheter de la drogue
▸**score off, score out** *vt sep (delete)* biffer, barrer

scoreboard ['skɔ:bɔ:d] *n* tableau *m* d'affichage (des scores)

scorecard ['skɔ:ka:d] *n* carte *f* de score

scorer ['skɔ:rə(r)] *n* marqueur(euse) *m,f*

scorn [skɔ:n] **1** *n* mépris *m*; **to pour s. on sb/sth** n'avoir que du mépris pour qn/qch
2 *vt* mépriser

scornful ['skɔ:nfʊl] *adj* méprisant(e); **to be s. of sb/sth** considérer qn/qch avec mépris

Scorpio ['skɔ:pɪəʊ] *(pl* **Scorpios)** *n (sign of zodiac)* Scorpion *m*; **to be (a) S.** être (du) Scorpion

scorpion ['skɔ:pɪən] *n* scorpion *m*

Scot [skɒt] *n* Écossais(e) *m,f*

Scotch [skɒtʃ] **1** *n (whisky)* scotch *m*
2 *adj* **S. broth** = potage écossais à base de légumes et d'orge perlé; **S. egg** = œuf dur enrobé de chair à saucisse et pané; *Am* **S. tape®** scotch® *m*; **S. terrier** scotch-terrier *m*; **S. whisky** scotch *m*

scotch [skɒtʃ] *vt (rumour)* étouffer

scot-free ['skɒt'fri:] *adj Fam* **to get off s.** s'en tirer sans la moindre punition

Scotland ['skɒtlənd] *n* l'Écosse *f*

Scots [skɒts] **1** *n (dialect)* écossais *m*
2 *adj* écossais(e)

Scotsman ['skɒtsmən] *n* Écossais *m*

Scotswoman ['skɒtswʊmən] *n* Écossaise *f*

Scottie dog ['skɒtɪ'dɒg] *n Fam* scotch-terrier *m*

Scottish ['skɒtɪʃ] *adj* écossais(e); **the S. Parliament** le parlement écossais; **S. terrier** scotch-terrier *m*

Scottish Parliament

Le parlement écossais fut établi dans le cadre du projet de décentralisation ("devolution") du gouvernement travailliste et fut inauguré à Édimbourg en mai 1999. Les 129 membres du parlement écossais (MSPs) siègent sous la houlette du "First Minister". Le parlement est pourvu d'une grande autonomie en matière de fiscalité mais ses pouvoirs législatifs sont néanmoins limités (il n'est pas habilité à légiférer dans certains domaines qui restent le privilège du parlement de Westminster, tels que la politique extérieure et la défense.) *Voir aussi l'encadré sur* **Devolution**.

scoundrel ['skaʊndr(ə)l] *n* crapule *f*; *Fam (child)* coquin(e) *m,f*

scour ['skaʊə(r)] *vt* **(a)** *(pot, surface)* récurer, frotter **(b)** *(area, house)* ratisser, fouiller

scourer ['skaʊərə(r)] *n* tampon *m* à récurer

scourge [skɜ:dʒ] *n* fléau *m*

scout [skaʊt] **1** *n* **(a)** **(boy) s.** (boy-)scout *m*, éclaireur *m*; **(girl) s.** éclaireuse *f*; **(talent) s.** dénicheur(euse) *m,f* de talents **(b)** *Mil (searcher)* éclaireur *m* **(c)** *(action)* **to have a s. around (for sth)** chercher (qch)
2 *vi* **to s. for talent** dénicher des talents

scoutmaster ['skaʊtma:stə(r)] *n* chef *m* scout

scowl [skaʊl] **1** *n* regard *m* noir
2 *vi* lancer des regards noirs (**at** à)

scrabble ['skræbəl] *vi* **to s. about** *or* **around for sth** chercher qch à tâtons

scraggy ['skrægɪ] *adj* maigre, décharné(e)

scram [skræm] *(pt & pp* **scrammed)** *vi Fam* se tirer

scramble ['skræmbəl] **1** *n* **(a)** *(rush)* ruée *f*; *(struggle)* bousculade *f* (**for** pour)
2 *vt Rad, TV & Tel (signal)* brouiller
3 *vi* **to s. for sth** se précipiter pour qch; **to s. up a hill** gravir une colline avec les mains

scrambled eggs ['skræmbəld'egz] *npl* œufs *mpl* brouillés

scrap¹ [skræp] **1** *n* **(a)** *(of material, paper)* bout *m*; *(of information)* bribe *f*; *(of evidence)* semblant *m*; **scraps** *(of food)* restes *mpl*; **a s. of truth** une once de vérité; **s. paper** (papier *m*) brouillon *m* **(b)** **s. (metal)** ferraille *f*; **s. merchant** *or* **dealer** ferrailleur *m*; **to sell sth for s.** vendre qch à la casse
2 *vt (pt & pp* **scrapped)** *(car)* envoyer à la casse; *(submarine, missile)* mettre au rebut; *(project)* abandonner

scrap² *Fam* **1** *n (fight)* bagarre *f*; **to have a s., to get into a s.** se bagarrer
2 *vi (fight)* se bagarrer

scrapbook ['skræpbʊk] *n* album *m (de coupures de presse etc)*

scrape [skreɪp] **1** *n* **(a)** *(action)* coup *m* de grattoir; *(mark)* éraflure *f*; *(sound)* raclement *m*; **to give sth a s.** donner un coup de grattoir à qch **(b)** *Fam* **to get into a s.** se mettre dans le pétrin
2 *vt* **(a)** *(skin, side of car)* érafler; *(dirt, wallpaper, vegetables)* gratter; **to s. one's plate clean** nettoyer son assiette; *Fig* **to s. the bottom of the barrel** être tombé(e) bien bas **(b)** *(barely obtain)* **to s. a living** arriver tout juste à vivre; **to s. a pass** *(in exam)* passer de justesse
3 *vi* **(a)** *(make sound)* gratter, grincer **(b)** *(barely manage)* **to s. home** *(in contest)* réussir de justesse; **to s. into college** passer de justesse à l'université

▶**scrape through** *vt insep* passer de justesse
▶**scrape together** *vt sep (money, resources)* parvenir à rassembler
scraper ['skreɪpə(r)] *n (tool)* grattoir *m*
scrapheap ['skræphiːp] *n* tas *m* de ferraille; *Fig* **to be on the s.** être au rebut
scrappy ['skræpɪ] *adj (performance)* décousu(e); *(knowledge)* limité(e)
scratch [skrætʃ] **1** *n* (**a**) *(on skin)* égratignure *f*; *(on record, furniture)* rayure *f*; *(by claw)* griffure *f* (**b**) *(action)* **to give one's arm a s.** se gratter le bras (**c**) *Fam (idioms)* **to start from s.** partir de rien *ou* de zéro; *(restart)* recommencer à zéro; **to come up** *or* **be up to s.** être à la hauteur; **to bring sth/sb up to s.** mettre qch/qn à niveau
2 *adj (meal, team)* improvisé(e)
3 *vt* (**a**) *(skin) (by accident)* égratigner; *(to relieve itching)* gratter; *(with claw, nail)* griffer; *(glass, record)* rayer; **to s. oneself** se gratter; **to s. one's arm** se gratter le bras; *Fig* **you s. my back and I'll s. yours** un service en vaut un autre; *Fig* **we've only scratched the surface of the problem** nous n'avons fait que survoler le problème (**b**) *(write, draw)* griffonner (**c**) *(in sport)* retirer
4 *vi* (**a**) *(of person)* se gratter; *(of pen, new clothes)* gratter; *(of thorns)* piquer; **the dog was scratching at the door** le chien grattait à la porte (**b**) *(of DJ)* scratcher
▶**scratch out** *vt sep (number, name)* rayer; *Fig* **to s. sb's eyes out** arracher les yeux à qn
scratchcard ['skrætʃkaːd] *n (for lottery)* carte *f* à gratter
scratchy ['skrætʃɪ] *adj (garment, towel)* qui gratte; *(record)* rayé(e)
scrawl [skrɔːl] **1** *n (writing)* gribouillage *m*
2 *vt & vi* gribouiller
scrawny ['skrɔːnɪ] *adj* maigrelet(ette)
scream [skriːm] **1** *n* (**a**) *(of person)* hurlement *m*; **screams of laughter** éclats *mpl* de rire (**b**) *Fam (good fun)* **it/he was a s.** c'était/il était tordant
2 *vt* hurler; **the headlines screamed "guilty"** le mot "coupable" s'étalait en gros à la une des journaux
3 *vi* hurler; **the car screamed past** la voiture est passée en rugissant; **to s. with pain** hurler de douleur; **to s. with laughter** se tordre de rire
screamingly ['skriːmɪŋlɪ] *adv Fam* **s. funny** tordant(e)
scree [skriː] *n* éboulis *m*
screech [skriːtʃ] **1** *n (of bird, person)* cri *m* strident; *(of brakes)* crissement *m*; *(of laughter)* éclat *m*
2 *vt* hurler
3 *vi (of bird)* pousser des cris stridents; *(of person)* hurler; *(of brakes)* crisser; **the car screeched to a halt** la voiture s'est arrêtée dans un crissement de pneus
screen [skriːn] **1** *n* (**a**) *(barrier)* écran *m*; *(folding)* paravent *m*; *Am* **s. door** porte *f* avec moustiquaire (**b**) *(of TV, computer, in cinema)* écran *m*; **the big/small s.** le grand/petit écran; **s. actor/actress** acteur *m*/actrice *f* de cinéma; *Comput* **s. saver** économiseur *m* d'écran; *Cin* **s. test** bout *m* d'essai; *Aut* **s. wash** liquide *m* lave-glace
2 *vt* (**a**) *(protect)* protéger; **to s. sth from view** cacher qch aux regards (**b**) *(film)* projeter; *(TV programme)* diffuser (**c**) *(test) (for security)* effectuer une enquête sur; *(for disease)* tester
screening ['skriːnɪŋ] *n* (**a**) *Cin* projection *f* (**b**) *(for security)* enquête *f*; *(for disease)* dépistage *m*

screenplay ['skriːnpleɪ] *n Cin* scénario *m*
screenwriter ['skriːnraɪtə(r)] *n Cin* scénariste *mf*
screw [skruː] **1** *n* (**a**) *(for fixing)* vis *f*; *Fam Fig* **she's got a s. loose** elle a une case en moins; *Fam Fig* **to put the screws on sb** faire pression sur qn; **s. top** *(of bottle, jar)* couvercle *m* qui se visse (**b**) *(propeller)* hélice *f* (**c**) *very Fam (prison officer)* maton(onne) *m*,*f* (**d**) *Vulg (sex)* **to have a s.** s'envoyer en l'air
2 *vt* (**a**) *(fix)* visser (**to** à); *Fam* **to s. money out of sb** extorquer de l'argent à qn (**b**) *Vulg (have sex with)* baiser; **s. you!** va te faire foutre!
3 *vi Vulg (have sex)* baiser
▶**screw around** *vi Vulg* baiser à droite et à gauche
▶**screw on 1** *vt sep (attach)* visser; *Fam* **she's got her head screwed on** elle a la tête sur les épaules
2 *vi (of lid)* se visser
▶**screw up 1** *vt sep* (**a**) *(paper)* froisser; **to s. up one's face** faire la grimace; *Fig* **to s. up one's courage** prendre son courage à deux mains (**b**) *very Fam (spoil)* foutre en l'air
2 *vi very Fam (fail)* cafouiller
screwdriver ['skruːdraɪvə(r)] *n* tournevis *m*
scribble ['skrɪbəl] **1** *n* gribouillage *m*
2 *vt & vi* griffonner
scribe [skraɪb] *n* scribe *m*
scrimmage ['skrɪmɪdʒ] *n* (**a**) *(pushing)* bousculade *f* (**b**) *Am (in football)* mêlée *f*
scrimp [skrɪmp] *vi* **to s. (and save)** économiser sur tout
script [skrɪpt] *n* (**a**) *(for play)* texte *m*; *(for film, TV programme)* script *m*; *(in exam)* copie *f* d'examen (**b**) *(handwriting)* script *m*
Scripture ['skrɪptʃə(r)] *n (Holy) S.*, **the Scriptures** les saintes Écritures *fpl*
scriptwriter ['skrɪptraɪtə(r)] *n Cin & TV* scénariste *mf*
scroll [skrəʊl] **1** *n* (**a**) *(of paper, parchment)* rouleau *m* (**b**) *Archit* volute *f*
2 *vi Comput* défiler
▶**scroll down** *vi Comput* défiler vers le bas
▶**scroll up** *vi Comput* défiler vers le haut
scrooge [skruːdʒ] *n* avare *mf*
scrotum ['skrəʊtəm] *n* scrotum *m*
scrounge [skraʊndʒ] *Fam* **1** *n* **to be on the s.** venir quémander
2 *vt* **to s. sth from** *or* **off sb** taper qch à qn
3 *vi* **to s. off sb** vivre aux crochets de qn
scrounger ['skraʊndʒə(r)] *n Fam* parasite *m*
scrub [skrʌb] **1** *n* (**a**) *(bushes)* broussailles *fpl* (**b**) *(wash)* **to give sth a (good) s.** (bien) frotter qch (**c**) *(for skin, face)* gommage *m*
2 *vt (pt & pp* **scrubbed)** (**a**) *(floor)* frotter; *(pots)* récurer; **to s. one's hands** se frotter les mains (**b**) *Fam (cancel)* annuler (**c**) *(for face, body)* gommage *m*
▶**scrub up** *vi Med* se brosser les mains
scrubber ['skrʌbə(r)] *n* (**a**) *(for dishes)* tampon *m* à récurer (**b**) *Br very Fam Pej (woman)* pute *f*
scrubbing brush ['skrʌbɪŋbrʌʃ] *n* brosse *f* en chiendent
scrubland ['skrʌblænd] *n* brousse *f*
scruff [skrʌf] *n* (**a**) **by the s. of the neck** par la peau du cou (**b**) *Fam (unkempt person)* **he's a bit of a s.** il n'est pas très soigné
scruffily ['skrʌfɪlɪ] *adv* **to be s. dressed** être dépenaillé(e)
scruffy ['skrʌfɪ] *adj (person)* peu soigné(e); *(clothes)* miteux(euse)

scrum [skrʌm] *n (in rugby)* mêlée *f; Fig* bousculade *f*; **s. half** demi *m* de mêlée

scrumptious ['skrʌm(p)ʃəs] *adj Fam* délicieux(euse)

scrunch [skrʌntʃ] **1** *vt (paper)* froisser en boule; *(can, cigarette)* écraser
2 *vi* crisser

scrunchie ['skrʌntʃi] *n (for hair)* chouchou *m*

scruple ['skru:pəl] *n* scrupule *m*; **to have no scruples** n'avoir aucun scrupule

scrupulous ['skru:pjʊləs] *adj* scrupuleux(euse)

scrupulously ['skru:pjʊləslɪ] *adv* scrupuleusement

scrutineer [skru:tɪ'nɪə(r)] *n* scrutateur(trice) *m,f*

scrutinize ['skru:tɪnaɪz] *vt (document, contract)* éplucher; *(votes)* vérifier

scrutiny ['skru:tɪnɪ] *n (of document, votes)* examen *m* minutieux; **to come under s.** être examiné(e)

scuba ['sku:bə] *n* **s. diver** plongeur(euse) *m,f* sous-marin(e); **s. diving** plongée *f* sous-marine

scuff [skʌf] **1** *n* **s. mark** éraflure *f*
2 *vt (shoe)* érafler

scuffle ['skʌfəl] **1** *n* échauffourée *f*
2 *vi* se bagarrer

scull [skʌl] **1** *n (oar)* aviron *m*
2 *vi* ramer

scullery ['skʌlərɪ] *(pl* **sculleries)** *n Br* arrière-cuisine *f*

sculpt [skʌlpt] *vt* sculpter

sculptor ['skʌlptə(r)] *n* sculpteur *m*

sculpture ['skʌlptʃə(r)] **1** *n* sculpture *f*
2 *vt* sculpter

scum [skʌm] *n* (**a**) *(layer of dirt)* crasse *f; (froth)* écume *f* (**b**) *very Fam Pej (person)* ordure *f; (people)* racaille *f*; **the s. of the earth** le rebut de la société

scupper ['skʌpə(r)] *vt (ship, project)* couler

scurrilous ['skʌrɪləs] *adj* calomnieux(euse)

scurry ['skʌrɪ] *(pt & pp* **scurried)** *vi (dash)* courir
▸**scurry away, scurry off** *vi* se sauver

scurvy ['skɜ:vɪ] *n Med* scorbut *m*

scuttle¹ ['skʌtəl] **1** *n (coal)* **s.** seau *m* à charbon
2 *vt (ship, plan)* saborder

scuttle² *vi (run)* courir
▸**scuttle away, scuttle off** *vi* déguerpir

scuzzy ['skʌzɪ] *adj Fam* dégueulasse, cradingue

scythe [saɪð] **1** *n* faux *f*
2 *vt* faucher

SDLP [esdi:el'pi:] *n Br (abbr* **Social Democratic Labour Party)** = parti démocrate d'Irlande du Nord en faveur de la réunification de l'Irlande

SDP [esdi:'pi:] *n Br Formerly (abbr* **Social Democratic Party)** parti *m* social-démocrate

SE [es'i:] *n (abbr* **southeast)** SE

SEA [esi:'eɪ] *n (abbr* **Single European Act)** AUE *m*

sea [si:] *n* mer *f*; **by the s.** au bord de la mer; **to go to s.** *(become a sailor)* devenir marin; *Fig* **a s. of people** une marée humaine; **heavy seas** mer *f* démontée; **on the high seas, out at s.** en haute mer; **to find** *or* **get one's s. legs** s'habituer au roulis; *Fig* **to be all at s.** être complètement perdu(e); **s. air** air *m* marin; **s. anemone** anémone *f* de mer; **s. breeze** brise *f* de mer; **s. change** changement *m* radical; *Fam* **(old) s. dog** (vieux) loup *m* de mer; **s. horse** hippocampe *m; Naut* **s. lane** couloir *m* maritime; **s. level** niveau *m* de la mer; **s. lion** otarie *f*; **s. salt** sel *m* de mer; **s. urchin** oursin *m*; **s. voyage** voyage *m* en mer

seaboard ['si:bɔ:d] *n* côte *f*

seaborne ['si:bɔ:n] *adj (trade)* maritime; *(invasion)* naval(e)

seafarer ['si:feərə(r)] *n* marin *m*

seafaring ['si:feərɪŋ] *adj (people)* de navigateurs

seafood ['si:fu:d] *n* fruits *mpl* de mer

seafront ['si:frʌnt] *n* front *m* de mer

seagoing ['si:gəʊɪŋ] *adj (boat)* de mer

seagull ['si:gʌl] *n* mouette *f*

seal¹ [si:l] *n (animal)* phoque *m*

seal² **1** *n* (**a**) *(stamp)* sceau *m*; **to give one's s. of approval to sth** donner son approbation à qch; **to set the s. on sth** *(on alliance, friendship)* sceller qch; *(on victory, defeat)* confirmer qch (**b**) *(device)* joint *m* (d'étanchéité); *(on food container)* = fermeture garantissant la fraîcheur d'un produit
2 *vt (document, envelope)* cacheter; *(with official seal)* sceller; *(jar)* fermer hermétiquement; *(joint)* assurer l'étanchéité de; **to s. sb's fate** décider du sort de qn; **my lips are sealed** je ne dirai rien
▸**seal in** *vt sep* enfermer
▸**seal off** *vt sep (area)* boucler; *(people)* isoler

sealing wax ['si:lɪŋ'wæks] *n* cire *f* à cacheter

sealskin ['si:lskɪn] *n* peau *f* de phoque

seam [si:m] *n* (**a**) *(of garment)* couture *f; (in metalwork)* soudure *f*; **to be coming apart at the seams** *(of clothing)* craquer de partout; *Fig (of plan, organization)* s'effondrer (**b**) *(of coal)* veine *f*

seaman ['si:mən] *n Naut* marin *m*

seamanship ['si:mənʃɪp] *n Naut* qualités *fpl* de navigateur

seamstress ['semstrɪs] *n* couturière *f*

seamy ['si:mɪ] *adj* sordide

seance ['seɪɒns] *n* séance *f* de spiritisme

seaplane ['si:pleɪn] *n* hydravion *m*

seaport ['si:pɔ:t] *n* port *m* maritime

sear [sɪə(r)] *vt (skin)* brûler; *Fig* **the image was seared on her memory** l'image était gravée dans sa mémoire

search [sɜ:tʃ] **1** *n* recherches *fpl*; *(of building, room)* fouille *f*; **to have a s. for sth** chercher qch; **in s. of** à la recherche de; **to make a s.** faire des recherches; *Comput* **to do a s.** faire une recherche; *Comput* **s. engine** moteur *m* de recherche; **s. party** équipe *f* de secours; *Law* **s. warrant** mandat *m* de perquisition
2 *vt (person, place)* fouiller; *Comput (file, directory)* rechercher dans; *Fam* **s. me!** je n'en ai pas la moindre idée!
3 *vi* chercher; **to s. for sth** chercher qch; *Comput* **s. and replace** rechercher et remplacer

searching ['sɜ:tʃɪŋ] *adj (examination)* minutieux(-euse); *(look)* pénétrant(e)

searchlight ['sɜ:tʃlaɪt] *n* projecteur *m*

searing ['sɪərɪŋ] *adj (pain, heat)* fulgurant(e); *(criticism, indictment)* virulent(e)

seascape ['si:skeɪp] *n Art* marine *f*

seashell ['si:ʃel] *n* coquillage *m*

seashore ['si:ʃɔ:(r)] *n* rivage *m*

seasick ['si:sɪk] *adj* **to be s.** avoir le mal de mer

seasickness ['si:sɪknɪs] *n* mal *m* de mer

seaside ['si:saɪd] *n* **the s.** le bord de la mer; **at the s.** au bord de la mer; **s. resort** station *f* balnéaire

season¹ ['si:zən] *n* saison *f; (of films)* cycle *m*; **S.'s Greetings** meilleurs vœux de fin d'année; **the high s.** *(for tourism)* la haute saison; **cherries are out of s.** ce n'est pas la saison des cerises; **s. ticket** abonnement *m*

season² *vt* (**a**) *(with salt, pepper)* assaisonner; *(with spice)* épicer (**b**) *(wood)* faire sécher

seasonable ['si:zənəbəl] *adj* **s. weather** un temps de saison

seasonal ['si:zənəl] *adj (work, fluctuations)* saisonnier(ère)

seasoned ['si:zənd] *adj* (**a**) *(food)* assaisonné(e); **a highly s. dish** un plat très relevé (**b**) *(wood)* sec (sèche) (**c**) *(person)* expérimenté(e); *(soldier)* aguerri(e)

seasoning ['si:zənɪŋ] *n Culin* assaisonnement *m*

seat [si:t] **1** *n* (**a**) *(chair)* chaise *f; (on bus, train, in theatre, cinema)* place *f*, siège *m; (in Parliament)* siège *m;* **to take a s.** s'asseoir; **s. belt** ceinture *f* de sécurité (**b**) *(part of chair, toilet)* siège *m; (of trousers)* fond *m* (**c**) *(centre) (of government)* siège *m;* **a s. of learning** un haut lieu du savoir; **country s.** *(of aristocrat)* demeure *f* familiale
2 *vt* (**a**) *(cause to sit) (child)* asseoir; *(guests)* faire asseoir; **to be/remain seated** être/rester assis(e); *Formal* **please be seated** veuillez vous asseoir (**b**) *(accommodate)* **the bus seats thirty** il y a trente places assises dans le bus; **this table seats twelve** on tient douze à cette table; **the hall seats two hundred** la salle compte deux cents places

seating ['si:tɪŋ] *n (seats)* sièges *mpl; (positioning)* placement *m;* **s. capacity** nombre *m* de places assises; **s. plan** plan *m* de table

SEATO ['si:təʊ] *n (abbr* **Southeast Asia Treaty Organization)** OTASE *f*

seaway ['si:weɪ] *n* route *f* (maritime)

seaweed ['si:wi:d] *n* algues *fpl*

seaworthy ['si:wɜ:ðɪ] *adj* en état de naviguer

sebaceous [sɪ'beɪʃəs] *adj* sébacé(e)

sec¹ *(abbr* **second(s)**) s.

sec² [sek] *n Fam (second)* **I'll be there in a s.** j'arrive tout de suite; **wait a s.!** attends une seconde!

secateurs [sekə'tɜ:z] *npl* sécateur *m*

secede [sɪ'si:d] *vi* faire sécession (**from** de)

secession [sɪ'seʃən] *n* sécession *f*

secluded [sɪ'klu:dɪd] *adj (place)* reculé(e); *(life)* de reclus(e)

seclusion [sɪ'klu:ʒən] *n* isolement *m*

second¹ ['sekənd] *n (of time)* seconde *f;* **I won't be a s.** j'en ai pour deux secondes; **s. hand** *(of clock)* trotteuse *f*

second² ['sekənd] **1** *n* (**a**) *(in series)* deuxième *mf*, second(e) *m,f;* **Edward the S.** Edward II; **I was s. in the race** je suis arrivé deuxième à la course (**b**) *(of month)* deux *m;* **the s. of May** le deux mai (**c**) *Com* **seconds** articles *mpl* défectueux (**d**) *(in duel)* témoin *m; (in boxing)* soigneur *m* (**e**) *Br Univ* **to get a s.** *(in degree)* ≃ avoir sa licence avec mention assez bien (**f**) **s. (gear)** seconde *f* (**g**) *Fam* **anyone for seconds?** *(at meal)* quelqu'un veut du rab?
2 *adj* deuxième, second(e); **twenty-s.** vingt-deuxième; **ninety-s.** quatre-vingt-deuxième; **to be s. to none** être sans égal(e); **s. in command** *Mil* commandant *m* en second; *(in organization)* adjoint(e) *m,f;* **the s. largest city in England** la deuxième ville d'Angleterre; **a s. Picasso/Churchill** un nouveau Picasso/Churchill; **on s. thoughts** tout bien réfléchi; **to have s. thoughts (about sth)** ne plus être très sûr(e) (de qch); *Fig* **to play s. fiddle to sb** être dans l'ombre de qn; **it's s. nature to her** elle le fait automatiquement; **to get one's s. wind** trouver un second souffle; **s. chance** deuxième chance *f;* **to be in one's s. childhood** être retombé(e) en enfance; **s. class** *(on train)* deuxième classe *f; Rel* **the S. Coming** le second

avènement; **s. cousin** petit(e) cousin(e) *m,f;* **s. floor** *Br* deuxième étage *m, Am* premier étage *m;* **s. language** seconde langue *f;* **s. name** nom *m* de famille; *Law* **s. offence** récidive *f;* **s. opinion** deuxième avis *m; Gram* **s. person** deuxième personne *f;* **s. sight** don *m* de double vue; **s. violin** second violon *m;* **the S. World War** la Seconde Guerre mondiale
3 *vt (motion)* appuyer

second³ [sɪ'kɒnd] *vt (officer, employee)* détacher (**from/to** de/à)

secondary ['sekəndərɪ] *adj* secondaire; **s. school** établissement *m* secondaire, *Can & Suisse* école *f* secondaire

second-best ['sekənd'best] **1** *n* pis-aller *m;* **to be content with s.** se contenter d'un pis-aller
2 *adv* **to come off s.** être battu(e)

second-class ['sekənd'klɑ:s] **1** *adj (ticket, carriage)* de deuxième classe; **s. citizen** citoyen(enne) *m,f* de second rang; *Br Univ* **s. degree** licence *f* avec mention assez bien; **s. mail** courrier *m* au tarif lent
2 *adv* **to travel s.** voyager en seconde classe

Second-class mail

Le tarif postal réduit est utilisé en Grande-Bretagne pour les lettres et les paquets non urgents. Aux États-Unis, il est réservé aux magazines et aux journaux.

seconder ['sekəndə(r)] *n* = personne qui appuie une motion

second-guess ['sekənd'ges] *vt* **to s. sb** anticiper ce que qn va faire

second-hand ['sekənd'hænd] **1** *adj (car, clothes)* d'occasion; **s. shop** magasin *m* d'articles d'occasion
2 *adv (buy)* d'occasion; **to hear news s.** avoir des nouvelles de seconde main

secondly ['sekəndlɪ] *adv* deuxièmement

secondment [sɪ'kɒndmənt] *n* **to be on s.** être en détachement

second-rate ['sekəndreɪt] *adj* médiocre

secrecy ['si:krɪsɪ] *n* secret *m;* **in s.** en secret; **to swear sb to s.** faire jurer le silence à qn

secret ['si:krɪt] **1** *n* secret *m;* **to do sth in s.** faire qch secrètement; **I make no s. of it** je ne m'en cache pas; **it's no s.** tout le monde le sait
2 *adj* secret(ète); **to keep sth s. from sb** cacher qch à qn; **s. agent** agent *m* secret; **s. police** police *f* secrète; **s. service** services *mpl* secrets; **the S. Service** = service de sécurité du président américain; *also Fig* **s. weapon** arme *f* secrète

secretarial [sekrə'teərɪəl] *adj (work)* administratif(-ive); *(job, college, course)* de secrétariat

secretariat [sekrə'teərɪət] *n* secrétariat *m*

secretary ['sekrətərɪ] *n* (*pl* **secretaries**) (**a**) *(in office)* secrétaire *mf* (**b**) *Pol Br* ministre *m; Am* secrétaire *mf* d'Etat; *Am* **S. of State** ministre *m* des Affaires étrangères

secretary-general ['sekrətərɪ'dʒenərəl] *n Pol* secrétaire *m* général

secrete [sɪ'kri:t] *vt* (**a**) *(discharge)* sécréter (**b**) *(hide)* cacher

secretion [sɪ'kri:ʃən] *n* sécrétion *f*

secretive ['si:krɪtɪv] *adj* secret(ète); **to be s. about sth** faire des cachotteries à propos de qch

secretly ['si:krɪtlɪ] *adv* secrètement

sect [sekt] *n* secte *f*

sectarian [sek'teərɪən] *adj* sectaire

sectarianism [sek'teərɪənɪzəm] *n* sectarisme *m*

section ['sekʃən] **1** *n* (**a**) *(in general)* partie *f*; *(of road, railway)* tronçon *m*; *(of machine)* élément *m*; *(of organization)* département *m*; *(in orchestra)* section *f*; *(of law, treaty)* article *m*; **all sections of society** toutes les catégories sociales (**b**) *(of soldiers)* section *f* (**c**) *(cross-section)* coupe *f*
2 *vt (cut)* sectionner

sector ['sektə(r)] *n* secteur *m*

secular ['sekjʊlə(r)] *adj (history, art)* laïque; *(music)* profane

secure [sɪ'kjʊə(r)] **1** *adj* (**a**) *(free from anxiety)* en sécurité; **s. in the knowledge that...** ayant l'assurance que... (**b**) *(investment, place)* sûr(e); *(foothold)* ferme; *(nomination, future)* assuré(e); *(load, rope)* bien attaché(e); *(foundations, lock)* solide; *Comput* **s. website** site *m* sécurisé
2 *vt* (**a**) *(make safe) (position, future)* assurer (**b**) *(fasten) (load)* bien amarrer; *(door, window)* bien fermer (**c**) *(obtain) (support, promise, loan)* obtenir

securely [sɪ'kjʊəlɪ] *adv* (**a**) *(stored, hidden)* en toute sécurité; *(protected)* bien (**b**) *(firmly)* solidement; **the door was s. fastened** la porte était bien fermée

security [sɪ'kjʊərɪtɪ] (*pl* **securities**) *n* (**a**) *(stability, safety)* sécurité *f*; **s. of tenure** sécurité *f* de l'emploi; **s. blanket** doudou *m*; **the S. Council** le Conseil de sécurité; **s. forces** forces *fpl* de sécurité; **s. guard** garde *m*; **s. officer** agent *m* de sécurité; **to be a s. risk** être un danger pour la sécurité (**b**) *Fin (for loan)* garantie *f* (**c**) *Fin* **securities** titres *mpl*

sedan [sɪ'dæn] *n* (**a**) *Am (car)* berline *f* (**b**) **s. chair** chaise *f* à porteurs

sedate [sɪ'deɪt] **1** *adj* tranquille
2 *vt* donner des calmants à

sedately [sɪ'deɪtlɪ] *adv* tranquillement

sedation [sɪ'deɪʃən] *n* **under s.** sous calmants

sedative ['sedətɪv] *n* sédatif *m*, calmant *m*

sedentary ['sedəntrɪ] *adj* sédentaire

sediment ['sedɪmənt] *n* sédiment *m*

sedition [sɪ'dɪʃən] *n* sédition *f*

seditious [sɪ'dɪʃəs] *adj* séditieux(euse)

seduce [sɪ'djuːs] *vt (sexually)* séduire; *Fig* **to s. sb into doing sth** persuader qn de faire qch

seducer [sɪ'djuːsə(r)] *n* séducteur(trice) *m,f*

seduction [sɪ'dʌkʃən] *n* séduction *f*

seductive [sɪ'dʌktɪv] *adj (look)* séducteur(trice); *(argument, offer)* séduisant(e)

see¹ [siː] *n Rel* évêché *m*

see² [siː] (*pt* **saw** [sɔː], *pp* **seen** [siːn]) **1** *vt* (**a**) *(with eyes, perceive)* voir; **now s. what you've done!** regarde ce que tu as fait!; **s. page 50** voir page 50; **to be seeing things** *(hallucinate)* avoir des visions; **it has to be seen to be believed** il faut le voir pour le croire; **to s. sb do** *or* **doing sth** voir qn faire qch; **I can't s. a way out of this problem** je ne vois pas comment on peut s'en sortir; **could you s. your way to lending me your car?** cela te serait-il possible de me prêter ta voiture?; **to s. sense** *or* **reason** entendre raison; **the city has seen many changes** la ville a connu de grands changements; **I don't know what you s. in her** je ne vois pas ce que tu lui trouves; **it remains to be seen whether...** reste à savoir si...; **I'll s. what I can do** je vais voir ce que je peux faire (**b**) *(understand)* voir; **I s. what you mean** je vois ce que tu veux dire; **I don't s. the point** je n'en vois pas l'intérêt (**c**) *(envisage, imagine)* imaginer, voir; **what do you s. happening next?** à ton avis, qu'est-ce qui va se passer maintenant?;

I can't s. them arriving before six ça m'étonnerait qu'ils arrivent avant six heures; **I can't s. you as a boxer** je ne t'imagine pas boxeur (**d**) *(make sure)* **I shall s. that he comes** je ferai en sorte qu'il vienne; **s. that this doesn't happen again!** fais en sorte que ça ne se reproduise pas! (**e**) *(meet) (person, doctor, solicitor)* voir; **I'm seeing Bill tomorrow** je vois Bill demain; **s. you (soon)!** à bientôt! (**f**) *(accompany)* **to s. sb home** accompagner qn chez lui; **to s. sb to the door** accompagner qn jusqu'à la porte
2 *vi* (**a**) *(with eyes)* voir; **s. for yourself** à toi de juger; **we shall s.** nous verrons bien (**b**) *(understand)* comprendre; **ah, I s.!** ah, je vois! (**c**) *(consider)* **let me s.!**, **let's s.!** voyons!; **have you got a free room? – let me s.** voyons une chambre libre? – voyons voir (**d**) *(find out)* **I'll go and s.** je vais voir

▸**see about** *vt insep* (**a**) *(deal with)* s'occuper de (**b**) *(consider)* voir; *Fam* **we'll (soon) s. about that!** c'est ce qu'on va voir!

▸**see in** *vt sep* **to s. the New Year in** fêter le Nouvel An

▸**see off** *vt sep* (**a**) *(say goodbye to)* dire au revoir à (**b**) *(attacker)* faire fuir

▸**see out** *vt sep* accompagner jusqu'à la porte; **I'll s. myself out** inutile de me raccompagner

▸**see through** **1** *vt sep (project, policy)* mener à bien
2 *vt insep (person, lie, plan)* percer à jour

▸**see to** *vt insep (deal with)* s'occuper de; **to get sth seen to** *(machine, roof)* faire réparer qch; *(wound, injury)* faire examiner qch; **I'll s. to it that you're not disturbed** je ferai en sorte que tu ne sois pas dérangé

seed [siːd] **1** *n* (**a**) *(for sowing)* graine *f*; *(of fruit)* pépin *m*; **to go** *or* **run to s.** *(of plant)* monter en graine; **s. corn** blé *m* de semence; *Fig* capital *m* initial; **s. merchant** grainetier(ère) *m,f*; **s. potatoes** pommes *fpl* de terre de semence (**b**) *Sport (in tournament)* tête *f* de série (**c**) *Lit (semen)* semence *f*
2 *vt* (**a**) *(remove seeds from)* épépiner (**b**) *(lawn)* ensemencer (**c**) *(in tournament)* **seeded players** joueurs *mpl* classés tête de série
3 *vi (of plant)* monter en graine

seedless ['siːdlɪs] *adj* sans pépins

seedling ['siːdlɪŋ] *n* plant *m*

seedy ['siːdɪ] *adj* (**a**) *(shabby) (person, hotel, area)* miteux(euse) (**b**) *Fam (unwell)* mal fichu(e)

seeing ['siːɪŋ] **1** *conj* **s. (that** *or* **how)...** étant donné que...
2 *n* **s. is believing** voir c'est croire

seek [siːk] (*pt & pp* **sought** [sɔːt]) *vt* (**a**) *(look for) (thing lost, job)* chercher; *(someone's friendship, promotion)* essayer d'obtenir (**b**) *(request)* **to s. sth from sb** demander qch à qn; **to s. sb's advice** demander conseil à qn (**c**) *(try)* **to s. to do sth** essayer de faire qch

▸**seek after** *vt insep* **to be much sought after** être très recherché(e)

▸**seek out** *vt sep (person)* dénicher

seem [siːm] *vi* sembler; **to s. tired** avoir l'air fatigué(e); **do what seems best** fais au mieux; **it seemed like a dream** j'avais l'impression de rêver; **I s. to have heard her name somewhere** il me semble avoir entendu son nom quelque part; **I can't s. to get it right** je n'y arrive pas; **it seems (that)..., it would s. that...** il semble que...+ *subjunctive*; **it seems to me that...** il me semble que...; **it seems** *or* **would s. so** il paraît; **it seems** *or* **would s. not** il paraît que non

seeming ['siːmɪŋ] *adj* apparent(e)

seemingly ['siːmɪŋlɪ] *adv* apparemment

seemly ['siːmlɪ] *adj Formal* bienséant(e)

seen [siːn] *pp of* **see²**
seep [siːp] *vi* suinter; **to s. into sth** s'infiltrer dans qch
seepage ['siːpɪdʒ] *n (oozing)* suintement *m*; *(into surface)* infiltration *f*
seer [sɪə(r)] *n Lit* voyant(e) *m,f*
seesaw ['siːsɔː] **1** *n* bascule *m*, tapecul *m*
  2 *vi Fig (of prices)* être en dents de scie
seethe [siːð] *vi (of liquid)* bouillonner; *(of street)* grouiller (**with** de); **to be seething (with anger)** bouillir (de rage)
see-through ['siːθruː] *adj* transparent(e)
segment 1 *n* ['segmənt] segment *m*; *(of orange)* quartier *m*
  2 *vt* [seg'ment] *(orange)* couper en quartiers; *(line)* segmenter
segmentation [segmen'teɪʃən] *n Econ* segmentation *f*
segregate ['segrɪgeɪt] *vt* séparer (**from** de); *(prisoner)* isoler (**from** de)
segregation [segrɪ'geɪʃən] *n* ségrégation *f*; *(of prisoner)* isolement *m*
Seine [seɪn] *n* **the S.** la Seine
seismic ['saɪzmɪk] *adj* sismique
seismograph ['saɪzməgrɑːf] *n* sismographe *m*
seismology [saɪz'mɒlədʒɪ] *n* sismologie *f*
seize [siːz] *vt* (**a**) *(grab) & Fig (opportunity)* saisir; **to s. hold of** saisir (**b**) *(city, territory)* s'emparer de; *(drugs, stolen goods)* saisir
▸**seize on, seize upon** *vt insep* sauter sur
▸**seize up** *vi (of engine, back)* se bloquer
seizure ['siːʒə(r)] *n* (**a**) *(of land, city)* prise *f*; *Law (of property, drugs)* saisie *f* (**b**) *Med* crise *f*
seldom ['seldəm] *adv* rarement; **s. have I seen such courage** j'ai rarement vu un tel courage
select [sɪ'lekt] **1** *adj (exclusive)* sélect(e); **a s. few** quelques privilégiés(ées); *Br Parl* **s. committee** commission *f* d'enquête
  2 *vt* sélectionner
selected [sɪ'lektɪd] *adj* choisi(e)
selection [sɪ'lekʃən] *n* sélection *f*, choix *m*; **to make a s.** faire un choix; **a wide s.** un grand choix
selective [sɪ'lektɪv] *adj* sélectif(ive)
selector [sɪ'lektə(r)] *n (of team)* sélectionneur(euse) *m,f*
self [self] *(pl* **selves** [selvz]*) n* (**a**) **he's quite his old s. again** il est redevenu comme avant; **she was her usual cheerful s.** comme à son habitude, elle était gaie (**b**) *Psy* **the s.** le moi
self-addressed envelope ['selfə'drest'envələʊp] *n* enveloppe *f* libellée à ses nom et adresse
self-appointed ['selfə'pɔɪntɪd] *adj* **he's the s. spokesman** il s'est proclamé porte-parole
self-assessment ['selfə'sesmənt] *n* (**a**) *(of person)* auto-évaluation *f* (**b**) *Br (for taxes)* = système de déclaration des revenus pour le paiement des impôts, par opposition au prélèvement à la source
self-assured ['selfə'ʃʊəd] *adj* plein(e) d'assurance
self-catering ['self'keɪtərɪŋ] *adj (holiday)* en appartement meublé; *(accommodation)* meublé(e)
self-centred ['self'sentəd] *adj* égocentrique
self-confessed ['selfkən'fest] *adj* **he's a s. liar/cheat** il est menteur/tricheur de son propre aveu
self-confidence ['self'kɒnfɪdəns] *n* confiance *f* en soi
self-confident ['self'kɒnfɪdənt] *adj* plein(e) d'assurance
self-conscious ['self'kɒnʃəs] *adj* timide, gêné(e)

self-contained ['selfkən'teɪnd] *adj (person)* réservé(e); *(apartment)* indépendant(e)
self-contradictory ['selfkɒntrə'dɪktərɪ] *adj* qui contient des contradictions
self-control ['selfkən'trəʊl] *n* maîtrise *f* de soi
self-deception ['selfdɪ'sepʃən] *n* aveuglement *m*
self-defeating ['selfdɪ'fiːtɪŋ] *adj* qui va à l'encontre du but recherché
self-defence, *Am* **self-defense** ['selfdɪ'fens] *n* autodéfense *f*; *Law* légitime défense *f*; **in s.** en état de légitime défense
self-denial ['selfdɪ'naɪəl] *n* abnégation *f*
self-destruct ['selfdɪ'strʌkt] *vi* s'autodétruire
self-determination ['selfdɪtɜːmɪ'neɪʃən] *n* autodétermination *f*
self-discipline ['self'dɪsɪplɪn] *n* autodiscipline *f*
self-doubt ['self'daʊt] *n* manque *m* de confiance en soi
self-effacing ['selfɪ'feɪsɪŋ] *adj* effacé(e)
self-employed ['selfɪm'plɔɪd] *adj* indépendant(e)
self-esteem [selfə'stiːm] *n* confiance *f* en soi
self-evident ['self'evɪdənt] *adj* évident(e)
self-explanatory ['selfɪk'splænətərɪ] *adj* **to be s.** se passer d'explications
self-expression ['selfɪk'spreʃən] *n* expression *f* individuelle
self-government ['self'gʌvənmənt] *n* autonomie *f*
self-help ['self'help] *n* **s. book** = guide pour apprendre à résoudre ses problèmes par soi-même; **s. group** groupe *m* d'entraide
self-important ['selfɪm'pɔːtənt] *adj* suffisant(e)
self-indulgent ['selfɪn'dʌldʒənt] *adj (person)* qui ne se refuse rien; *(book, film)* complaisant(e)
self-inflicted ['selfɪn'flɪktɪd] *adj* que l'on s'inflige à soi-même
self-interest ['self'ɪntərest] *n* intérêt *m* personnel
selfish ['selfɪʃ] *adj* égoïste
selfishness ['selfɪʃnɪs] *n* égoïsme *m*
self-knowledge ['self'nɒlɪdʒ] *n* connaissance *f* de soi
selfless ['selflɪs] *adj* désintéressé(e)
self-made man ['selfmeɪd'mæn] *n* self-made-man *m*
self-pity ['self'pɪtɪ] *n* apitoiement *m* sur son propre sort; **to be full of s.** s'apitoyer sur son sort
self-portrait ['self'pɔːtreɪt] *n* autoportrait *m*
self-possessed ['selfpə'zest] *adj* qui a une grande maîtrise de soi
self-preservation ['selfprezə'veɪʃən] *n* **instinct for s.** instinct *m* de conservation
self-raising flour ['selfreɪzɪŋ'flaʊə(r)] *n* farine *f* avec levure incorporée
self-reliant ['selfrɪ'laɪənt] *adj* indépendant(e)
self-respect ['selfrɪ'spekt] *n* amour-propre *m*
self-respecting ['selfrɪ'spektɪŋ] *adj* qui se respecte
self-restraint ['selfrɪs'treɪnt] *n* retenue *f*, maîtrise *f* de soi
self-righteous ['self'raɪtʃəs] *adj* suffisant(e)
self-rising flour ['selfraɪzɪŋ'flaʊə(r)] *Am* = **self-raising flour**
selfsame ['selfseɪm] *adj* **the s. day** le même jour exactement; **the s. thing** la même chose exactement
self-satisfied ['self'sætɪsfaɪd] *adj* suffisant(e), content(e) de soi
self-service ['self'sɜːvɪs] **1** *n* self-service *m*
  2 *adj* self-service
self-starter ['self'stɑːtə(r)] *n (person)* personne *f* pleine d'initiative

self-styled ['selfstaɪld] adj prétendu(e), soi-disant inv
self-sufficient ['selfsə'fɪʃənt] adj (person) indépendant(e); (country) auto-suffisant(e)
self-tan ['self'tæn] n (cream) autobronzant m
self-taught ['self'tɔːt] adj autodidacte
sell [sel] (pt & pp **sold** [səʊld]) **1** vt vendre; **to s. sb sth, to s.** sth to sb vendre qch à qn; **scandal sells newspapers** le scandale fait vendre les journaux; Fig **to s. oneself** (present oneself) se vendre; Fig **to s. sb an idea** faire accepter une idée à qn; Fig **to s. sb down the river** trahir qn
  2 vi (of product) se vendre; (of person) vendre; **to s. like hot cakes** se vendre comme des petits pains
▸**sell off** vt sep (at reduced prices) solder; (clear) liquider; (privatize) privatiser
▸**sell out 1** vt sep (**a**) **to be sold out** (of book, item) être épuisé(e); (of show, concert) afficher complet; **the tickets are sold out** il n'y a plus de billets (**b**) (betray) trahir, vendre
  2 vi (**a**) **to s. out of sth** ne plus avoir de qch (**b**) (betray beliefs) renier ses principes
▸**sell up** vi (sell home, business) tout vendre
sell-by date ['selbaɪdeɪt] n date f limite de vente; Fig **to be past one's s.** avoir fait son temps
seller ['selə(r)] n vendeur(euse) m,f; Econ **s.'s market** marché m favorable au vendeur
selling ['selɪŋ] n vente f; **s. point** atout m; **s. price** prix m de vente
sell-off ['selɒf] n (of state-owned company) vente f
Sellotape® ['seləteɪp] n Scotch® m
sellotape ['seləteɪp] vt scotcher
sellout ['selaʊt] n (**a**) **the play was a s.** il n'y avait plus de places pour cette pièce, la pièce a joué à guichets fermés (**b**) (betrayal) trahison f
semantic [sɪ'mæntɪk] adj sémantique
semantics [sɪ'mæntɪks] n sémantique f
semaphore ['seməfɔː(r)] n signaux mpl à bras
semblance ['sembləns] n semblant m
semen ['siːmən] n sperme m
semester [sɪ'mestə(r)] n semestre m
semi ['semɪ] n Br Fam (semi-detached house) maison f jumelée
semiautomatic ['semɪɔːtə'mætɪk] adj semi-automatique
semicircle ['semɪsɜːkəl] n demi-cercle m
semicircular ['semɪ'sɜːkjʊlə(r)] adj semi-circulaire, en demi-cercle
semicolon ['semɪ'kəʊlən] n point-virgule m
semiconductor ['semɪkən'dʌktə(r)] n Elec semi-conducteur m
semiconscious ['semɪ'kɒnʃəs] adj à demi conscient(e)
semidetached ['semɪdɪ'tætʃt] **1** n maison f jumelée
  2 adj jumelé(e)
semifinal ['semɪ'faɪnəl] n demi-finale f
semifinalist ['semɪ'faɪnəlɪst] n demi-finaliste mf
seminal ['semɪnəl] adj majeur(e), de première importance
seminar ['semɪnɑː(r)] n séminaire m
semi-precious ['semɪ'preʃəs] adj semi-précieux(euse)
semiquaver ['semɪkweɪvə(r)] n Mus double croche f
semi-skimmed [semɪ'skɪmd] adj (milk) demi-écrémé(e)
Semite ['semaɪt] n Sémite mf
Semitic [sɪ'mɪtɪk] adj (language) sémitique; (people) sémite
semitone ['semɪtəʊn] n Mus demi-ton m
semitrailer ['semɪtreɪlə(r)] n Am semi-remorque m

semitropical ['semɪ'trɒpɪkəl] adj semi-tropical(e)
semolina [semə'liːnə] n semoule f
Senate ['senɪt] n the S. le Sénat

Senate

Le Sénat constitue, avec la Chambre des représentants, l'organe législatif américain ; composé de 100 membres (deux par État), il a pour responsabilité d'approuver les nominations présidentielles, de ratifier les traités ainsi que de tenir les audiences en cas de mise en accusation d'un élu.

senator ['senətə(r)] n sénateur m
send [send] (pt & pp **sent** [sent]) vt (letter, message, person) envoyer; **to s. sb sth, to s.** sth to sb envoyer qch à qn; **to s. sb home** renvoyer qn chez soi; **to s. sb to prison** envoyer qn en prison; **to s.** sb on an errand envoyer qn faire une course; Fig **to s. sb/sth flying** envoyer qn/qch valser; **to s. sb into fits of laughter** faire rire qn aux larmes
▸**send away 1** vt sep (person) renvoyer
  2 vi **to s. away for sth** se faire envoyer qch
▸**send back** vt sep renvoyer
▸**send down** vt sep Br (**a**) (expel from university) renvoyer (**b**) Fam (send to prison) mettre en taule (for pour)
▸**send for** vt insep (help, supplies) envoyer chercher; (doctor) faire venir
▸**send in** vt sep envoyer
▸**send off 1** vt sep (**a**) (letter, order) expédier, envoyer (**b**) (player) expulser
  2 vi **to s. off for sth** se faire envoyer qch
▸**send on** vt sep (ahead) expédier; (later) faire suivre
▸**send out 1** vt sep envoyer
  2 vi **to s. out for sth** envoyer chercher qch
▸**send up** vt sep Br Fam (parody) se moquer de
sender ['sendə(r)] n expéditeur(trice) m,f
send-off ['sendɒf] n Fam **to give sb a good s.** faire des adieux en règle à qn
send-up ['sendʌp] n Br Fam parodie f, pastiche m
Senegal [senɪ'gɔːl] n le Sénégal
Senegalese [senɪgə'liːz] **1** n (person) Sénégalais(e) m,f
  2 adj sénégalais(e)
senile ['siːnaɪl] adj sénile; **s. dementia** démence f sénile
senility [sɪ'nɪlɪtɪ] n sénilité f
senior ['siːnjə(r)] **1** n (**a**) (in age) **to be sb's s.** être l'aîné(e) de qn; **she's three years his s.** elle est son aînée de trois ans (**b**) (in rank) supérieur(e) m,f (**c**) Am Sch élève mf de terminale; Am Univ étudiant(e) m,f de licence; Br Sch **the seniors** ≃ les grands mpl
  2 adj (**a**) (in age) aîné(e); **Thomas Smith, S.** Thomas Smith père; **he's two years s. to me** il a deux ans de plus que moi; **s. citizen** personne f du troisième âge; Am Sch & Univ **s. year** dernière année f (**b**) (in rank, position) supérieur(e); **(the) s. management** la direction; **s. officer** officier m supérieur; **s. partner** (in company) associé(e) m,f principal(e)
seniority [siːnɪ'ɒrɪtɪ] n (in age, length of service) ancienneté f; (in rank) supériorité f
sensation [sen'seɪʃən] n (**a**) (feeling) sensation f; **a tingling/burning s.** une sensation de picotement/brûlure (**b**) (excitement) **to cause a s.** faire sensation
sensational [sen'seɪʃənəl] adj sensationnel(elle)

sensationalism [sen'seɪʃənəlɪzəm] *n* sensationnalisme *m*
sense [sens] **1** *n* (**a**) *(faculty)* sens *m*; **to come to one's senses** *(recover consciousness)* revenir à soi; *(see reason)* revenir à la raison; **s. of direction** sens *m* de l'orientation; **s. of duty** sens *m* du devoir; **s. of hearing** ouïe *f*; **s. of humour** sens *m* de l'humour (**b**) *(rationality)* bon sens *m*, intelligence *f*; **there's no s. in staying/leaving** ça ne sert à rien de rester/partir (**c**) *(feeling)* sentiment *m*; **to lose all s. of time/reality** perdre toute notion du temps/de la réalité; **a s. of achievement** un sentiment de satisfaction (**d**) *(meaning)* sens *m*, signification *f*; **to make s.** être logique; **to make no s.** n'avoir aucun sens; **to make s. of sth** comprendre qch; **in a s.** dans un sens **2** *vt (perceive)* sentir, deviner; **to s. that** sentir que
senseless ['senslɪs] *adj* (**a**) *(unconscious)* sans connaissance (**b**) *(pointless)* absurde
sensibilities [sensɪ'bɪlɪtɪz] *npl* susceptibilité *f*
sensible ['sensɪbəl] *adj* (**a**) *(rational)* sensé(e) (**b**) *(practical)* pratique (**c**) *Formal (aware)* **to be s. of sth** être sensible à qch
sensibly ['sensɪblɪ] *adv (rationally)* raisonnablement
sensitive ['sensɪtɪv] *adj* (**a**) *(person)* sensible (**to** à) (**b**) *(subject, issue)* délicat(e); *(document, information)* confidentiel(elle)
sensor ['sensə(r)] *n* détecteur *m*
sensory ['sensərɪ] *adj* sensoriel(elle); **s. organs** organes *mpl* sensoriels
sensual ['sensjʊəl] *adj* sensuel(elle)
sensuality [sensjʊ'ælɪtɪ] *n* sensualité *f*
sensuous ['sensjʊəs] *adj* sensuel(elle)
sent [sent] *pt & pp of* **send**
sentence ['sentəns] **1** *n* (**a**) *(phrase)* phrase *f* (**b**) *(in prison)* peine *f*; **to pass s.** prononcer la sentence **2** *vt (criminal)* condamner (**to** à)
sententious [sen'tenʃəs] *adj Formal* sentencieux(euse)
sentient ['sentɪənt] *adj* sensible
sentiment ['sentɪmənt] *n* (**a**) *(opinion)* sentiment *m*; **my sentiments exactly** je suis tout à fait du même avis (**b**) *(sentimentality)* sentimentalité *f*
sentimental [sentɪ'mentəl] *adj* sentimental(e); **to have s. value** avoir une valeur sentimentale
sentimentality [sentɪmen'tælɪtɪ] *n* sentimentalité *f*, sensiblerie *f*
sentry ['sentrɪ] *(pl* **sentries***)* *n* sentinelle *f*; **to be on s. duty** être de garde; **s. box** guérite *f*
Seoul [səʊl] *n* Séoul
Sep *(abbr* **September***)* septembre
separable ['sepərəbəl] *adj* séparable
separate 1 *adj* ['sepərət] *(parts)* séparé(e), distinct(e); *(box, room, document)* à part; *(occasion, attempt, entrance)* différent(e); *(organization)* indépendant(e); **fish and meat should be kept s.** le poisson et la viande doivent être gardés séparément; **he was kept s. from the others** on le tenait à l'écart *ou* on l'isolait des autres; **to lead s. lives** avoir chacun sa vie; *also Fig* **they went their s. ways** ils sont partis chacun de leur côté; *Can* **s. school** ≃ école *f* libre **2** *n* ['sepərət] **separates** *(clothes)* coordonnés *mpl* **3** *vt* ['sepəreɪt] séparer (**from** de) **4** *vi* ['sepəreɪt] se séparer (**from** de)
separation [sepə'reɪʃən] *n* séparation *f*
separatist ['sepərətɪst] *n Pol* séparatiste *mf*
sepia ['si:pɪə] *n* sépia *f*
sepsis ['sepsɪs] *n* infection *f*

Sept *(abbr* **September***)* septembre
September [sep'tembə(r)] *n* septembre *m*; *see also* **May**
septet [sep'tet] *n* septuor *m*
septic ['septɪk] *adj* septique; **to go s.** s'infecter; **s. tank** fosse *f* septique
septicaemia, *Am* **septicemia** [septɪ'si:mɪə] *n* septicémie *f*
sepulchre, *Am* **sepulcher** ['sepəlkə(r)] *n Formal* sépulcre *m*
sequel ['si:kwəl] *n* (**a**) *(book, film)* suite *f* (**to** de) (**b**) *(result)* conséquence *f* (**to** de)
sequence ['si:kwəns] *n* (**a**) *(order)* ordre *m*, suite *f*; **in s.** par ordre; **out of s.** dans le désordre (**b**) *(of numbers, events)* suite *f*, série *f*; *(in film)* séquence *f*
sequencing ['si:kwənsɪŋ] *n Biol & Chem* séquençage *m*
sequential [sɪ'kwenʃəl] *adj* séquentiel(elle)
sequestrate [sɪ'kwestreɪt] *vt Law* séquestrer
sequestration [si:kwe'streɪʃən] *n Law* mise *f* sous séquestre
sequin ['si:kwɪn] *n* paillette *f*
sequoia [se'kwɔɪə] *n* séquoia *m*
Serbia ['sɜ:bɪə] *n* la Serbie
Serb ['sɜ:b], **Serbian** ['sɜ:bɪən] **1** *n* Serbe *mf* **2** *adj* serbe
Serbo-Croat ['sɜ:bəʊ'krəʊæt] **1** *n* serbo-croate *m* **2** *adj* serbo-croate
serenade [serə'neɪd] **1** *n* sérénade *f* **2** *vt* chanter une sérénade à
serene [sɪ'ri:n] *adj* serein(e)
serenity [sɪ'renɪtɪ] *n* sérénité *f*
serf [sɜ:f] *n Hist* serf (serve) *m,f*
serfdom ['sɜ:fdəm] *n Hist* servage *m*
serge [sɜ:dʒ] *n* serge *f*
sergeant ['sɑ:dʒənt] *n (in police)* brigadier *m*; *Mil* sergent *m*
sergeant-major ['sɑ:dʒənt'meɪdʒə(r)] *n* sergent-major *m*
serial ['sɪərɪəl] **1** *n (in magazine)* roman-feuilleton *m*; *(on TV)* feuilleton *m* **2** *adj* d'une série, en série; **s. killer** tueur(euse) *m,f* en série; **s. number** numéro *m* de série
serialize ['sɪərɪəlaɪz] *vt (in magazine)* publier en feuilleton; *(on TV)* adapter en feuilleton
series ['sɪəri:z] *(pl* **series***)* *n* série *f*
serious ['sɪərɪəs] *adj (person)* sérieux(euse); *(situation, problem, injury)* grave; **to be s. about doing sth** envisager sérieusement de faire qch; **are you s.?** tu parles sérieusement?; *Fam* **s. money** un bon paquet d'argent
seriously ['sɪərɪəslɪ] *adv* (**a**) *(in earnest)* sérieusement; **to take sb/sth s.** prendre qn/qch au sérieux; **to take oneself too s.** se prendre trop au sérieux; **you can't s. expect...** sérieusement, vous ne pensez pas que... (**b**) *(gravely, critically)* gravement
sermon ['sɜ:mən] *n Also Fig* sermon *m*
serotonin [serə'təʊnɪn] *n* sérotonine *f*
serpent ['sɜ:pənt] *n Lit* serpent *m*
serpentine ['sɜ:pəntaɪn] *adj Lit* qui serpente, sinueux(euse)
SERPS [sɜ:ps] *n Br Formerly Fin (abbr* **State Earnings Related Pension Scheme***)* = retraite versée par l'État, calculée sur le salaire
serrated [se'reɪtɪd] *adj* en dents de scie
serum ['sɪərəm] *n* sérum *m*
servant ['sɜ:vənt] *n* domestique *mf*

serve [sɜːv] **1** *vt* (**a**) *(country, cause)* servir; **to s. one's own interests** servir ses propres intérêts (**b**) *(be useful to)* servir à, être utile à; **to s. a purpose** avoir une utilité; **it doesn't s. my purpose** cela ne me sert à rien; **it has served me well** ça m'a fait de l'usage; **if my memory serves me right** si ma mémoire est bonne (**c**) *(prison sentence)* purger; *(apprenticeship)* faire (**d**) *(meal, customer, drink)* servir; **s. chilled** *(dish, drink)* servir frais; **serves four** *(on packet, in recipe)* pour quatre personnes (**e**) *Law* **to s. sb with a summons** remettre une assignation à qn (**f**) **(it) serves her right!** bien fait pour elle!
2 *vi* servir; **to s. as** *(be used as)* servir de
3 *n (in tennis)* service *m*; **(it's) your s.!** à toi de servir!
▸**serve up** *vt sep* servir
server ['sɜːvə(r)] *n* (**a**) *(in tennis)* serveur(euse) *m,f* (**b**) *Comput* serveur *m*
service ['sɜːvɪs] **1** *n* (**a**) *(with army, firm)* service *m*; *Mil* **the services** les forces *fpl* armées; **to do sb a s.** rendre un service à qn; **to be at sb's s.** être au service de qn; **to be of s. to sb** être utile à qn; **to offer one's services** offrir ses services; *Comput* **s. provider** *(for Internet)* fournisseur *m* d'accès (**b**) *(in shop, restaurant)* service *m*; **s. included/not included** service *m* compris/non compris; **s. charge** service *m*; **s. industry** industrie *f* de services; *Br* **s. lift** ascenseur *m* de service (**c**) *(system)* **postal/air/train s.** service *m* postal/aérien/des trains (**d**) *(maintenance) (of machine)* entretien *m*; *(of car)* révision *f*; **the machine is out of s.** la machine est hors service; **s. area** *(on motorway)* aire *f* de service; **s. station** *(on motorway)* station-service *f* (**e**) *(in church)* service *m*, office *m* (**f**) *(in tennis)* service *m*; **s. line** ligne *f* de service (**g**) *Old-fashioned* **to be in/go into s.** *(of servant)* être/devenir domestique
2 *vt (machine)* entretenir; *(car)* réviser
serviceable ['sɜːvɪsəbəl] *adj* (**a**) *(in working order)* en état de marche (**b**) *(durable)* résistant(e)
serviceman ['sɜːvɪsmən] *n* militaire *m*
servicewoman ['sɜːvɪswʊmən] *n* femme *f* soldat
serviette [sɜːvɪ'et] *n Br* serviette *f* (de table)
servile ['sɜːvaɪl] *adj* servile, obséquieux(euse)
serving ['sɜːvɪŋ] *n (portion)* portion *f*; **s. hatch** passe-plat *m*
servitude ['sɜːvɪtjuːd] *n* servitude *f*, asservissement *m*
sesame ['sesəmɪ] *n* (**a**) **s. oil** huile *f* de sésame; **s. seeds** graines *fpl* de sésame (**b**) **open s.!** sésame, ouvre-toi!
session ['seʃən] *n* (**a**) *(period of activity)* séance *f*, session *f* (**b**) *(meeting)* séance *f*; **to be in s.** siéger (**c**) *(university, school term)* trimestre *m*; *(university year)* année *f* universitaire; *(school year)* année scolaire
SET [esiː'tiː] *n Comput (abbr* **secure electronic transaction)** SET *f*
set [set] **1** *n* (**a**) *(of keys)* jeu *m*; *(of saucepans)* série *f*, assortiment *m*; *(of books)* collection *f*; *(of tyres)* train *m*; *(of problems, rules, symptoms)* ensemble *m*; **s. of teeth** dentition *f* (**b**) *(of people)* cercle *m* (**c**) *(TV, radio)* poste *m* (**d**) *(in theatre)* décor *m*; *(in cinema)* plateau *m* (**e**) *(in tennis)* set *m*; **s. point** balle *f* de set
2 *adj* (**a**) *(fixed) (look)* figé(e); *(ideas)* déterminé(e); *(price)* fixe; **to be s. in one's ways** tenir à ses habitudes; **s. menu** menu *m*; **s. phrase** expression *f* figée; **s. piece** *(in play, film)* morceau *m* de bravoure; *(in sport)* tactique *f* (**b**) *(ready)* **to be (all) s. for sth/to do sth** être (fin) prêt(e) pour qch/à faire qch (**c**) *(determined)* **to be (dead) s. on sth** avoir fixé son choix

sur qch; **to be (dead) s. on doing sth** être fermement décidé(e) à faire qch; **to be dead s. against** être formellement opposé(e) à
3 *vt (pt & pp* **set)** (**a**) *(place)* placer, mettre; *(jewel)* sertir; **to s. the table** mettre la table; **to s. a trap (for sb)** tendre un piège (à qn); **the novel/film is set in Edinburgh** le roman/film se passe à Édimbourg (**b**) *(fix) (date, day, limit, price)* fixer, déterminer; *(watch)* régler; *(alarm clock)* mettre; *(record)* établir; **to s. a value on sth** estimer la valeur de qch; **to s. the scene** planter le décor; **the scene was set for the arms negotiations** tout était prêt pour les négociations sur les armements (**c**) *(cause to start)* **to s. sb thinking** faire réfléchir qn; **to s. sb free** libérer qn; **to s. sth on fire** mettre le feu à qch (**d**) *(task)* fixer; *(essay, homework)* donner (**e**) *(bone, fracture)* réduire
4 *vi* (**a**) *(of sun, moon)* se coucher (**b**) *(become firm) (of jelly, concrete)* prendre; *(of broken bone)* se ressouder
▸**set about** *vt insep* (**a**) *(task, job)* se mettre à; **to s. about doing sth** se mettre à faire qch (**b**) *(attack)* attaquer
▸**set against** *vt sep* (**a**) *(cause to oppose)* **to s. sb against sb** monter qn contre qn (**b**) *(compare)* **to s. sth against sth** comparer qch à qch (**c**) *(deduct)* **to s. expenses against tax** déduire les dépenses des impôts
▸**set apart** *vt sep* distinguer (**from** de)
▸**set aside** *vt sep* (**a**) *(put down, disregard)* laisser de côté (**b**) *(save) (money)* mettre de côté; *(time)* réserver
▸**set back** *vt sep* (**a**) *(delay)* retarder (**b**) *Fam (cost)* coûter
▸**set down** *vt sep (put down)* poser, laisser; **to s. sth down in writing** coucher qch par écrit
▸**set forth** *vi Lit (depart)* partir, se mettre en route
▸**set in** *vi (of winter, mood)* s'installer; *(of fog, night)* tomber; *(of infection)* se déclarer
▸**set off 1** *vt sep* (**a**) *(bomb, explosion, alarm)* déclencher; *(argument, chain of events)* provoquer; **to s. sb off (laughing)** faire éclater qn de rire; **to s. sb off (crying)** faire éclater qn en sanglots (**b**) *(enhance)* mettre en valeur, rehausser
2 *vi (depart)* partir, se mettre en route
▸**set out 1** *vt sep (arrange)* disposer
2 *vi* (**a**) *(depart)* partir, se mettre en route; *(in job, task)* démarrer (**b**) *(intend)* **to s. out to do sth** avoir l'intention de faire qch
▸**set to** *vi* (**a**) *(start working)* s'y mettre (**b**) *Fam (start arguing)* recommencer à se disputer
▸**set up 1** *vt sep* (**a**) *(statue)* ériger; *(tent, barrier)* monter; *(roadblock)* mettre en place (**b**) *(meeting)* arranger; *(company)* créer, fonder; *(system)* mettre en place; **to s. up house** *or* **home** s'installer; **to s. sb up in business (as)** installer qn (comme) (**c**) *(trick, frame)* monter un coup contre; **to be set up** être victime d'un coup monté
2 *vi (establish oneself)* s'installer (**as** comme); **to s. up in business (as)** s'installer (comme)
▸**set upon** *vt insep (attack)* attaquer
setback ['setbæk] *n* revers *m*, échec *m*
set-square ['setskweə(r)] *n* équerre *f* (à dessin)
settee [se'tiː] *n* canapé *m*
setter ['setə(r)] *n (dog)* setter *m*
setting ['setɪŋ] **1** *n* (**a**) *(of story, film)* cadre *m* (**b**) *(of sun)* coucher *m* (**c**) *(on machine)* réglage *m* (**d**) **s. lotion**

lotion *f* pour mise en plis (**e**) *Comput* **settings** paramètres *mpl*
2 *adj (sun)* couchant(e)
settle ['setəl] **1** *vt* (**a**) *(put in place)* installer; **to s. oneself** s'installer (**b**) *(nerves)* calmer; **to s. one's stomach** ses douleurs d'estomac (**c**) *(day, venue)* décider, régler (**d**) *(problem, dispute, bill)* régler; **to s. one's affairs** régler ses affaires; *Fam* **that settles it!** c'est décidé!; *Law* **to s. a matter out of court** régler une affaire à l'amiable (**e**) *(colonize)* coloniser
2 *vi* (**a**) *(of bird, insect)* se poser; *(of dust, liquid, beer)* se déposer (**b**) *(of person, family)* s'installer, s'établir; *(of crowd)* se calmer, s'apaiser; **to s. into an armchair** s'installer confortablement dans un fauteuil (**c**) *Law* **to s. out of court** régler l'affaire à l'amiable
▸**settle down 1** *vt sep* (**a**) *(make comfortable)* installer (**b**) *(make calm)* calmer
2 *vi* (**a**) *(make oneself comfortable)* s'installer confortablement; **to s. down to work** se mettre au travail (**b**) *(in new home)* s'installer; *(adopt steady lifestyle)* se ranger, s'assagir; **to s. down with sb** se mettre en couple (**c**) *(of situation, excitement)* se calmer
▸**settle for** *vt insep* accepter, se contenter de
▸**settle in** *vi (in new home)* s'installer; *(in new school, job)* s'adapter
▸**settle on** *vt insep* se décider pour, choisir
▸**settle up** *vi (pay bill)* régler
settled ['setəld] *adj (person, life)* rangé(e), établi(e); *(weather)* stable
settlement ['setəlmənt] *n* (**a**) *(of problem, dispute, bill)* règlement *m*; **to reach a s.** parvenir à un accord (**b**) *(village)* village *m*
settler ['setlə(r)] *n* colon *m*
set-to ['set'tu:] *n Fam* bagarre *f*
set-top box ['settɒp'bɒks] *n TV* décodeur *m* numérique
setup ['setʌp] *n Fam (arrangement)* système *m*
seven ['sevən] **1** *n* sept *m inv*
2 *adj* sept; **the s. deadly sins** les sept péchés capitaux; *Lit* **to sail the s. seas** parcourir les mers; *see also* **eight**
seventeen [sevən'ti:n] **1** *n* dix-sept *m inv*
2 *adj* dix-sept; *see also* **eight**
seventeenth [sevən'ti:nθ] **1** *n* (**a**) *(fraction)* dix-septième *m* (**b**) *(in series)* dix-septième *mf* (**c**) *(of month)* dix-sept *m inv*
2 *adj* dix-septième; *see also* **eighth**
seventh ['sevənθ] **1** *n* (**a**) *(fraction)* septième *m* (**b**) *(in series)* septième *mf* (**c**) *(of month)* sept *m inv*
2 *adj* septième; **to be in s. heaven** être au septième ciel; *see also* **eighth**
seventieth ['sevəntɪθ] **1** *n* (**a**) *(fraction)* soixante-dixième *m* (**b**) *(in series)* soixante-dixième *mf*
2 *adj* soixante-dixième
seventy ['sevəntɪ] **1** *n* soixante-dix *m inv, Belg & Suisse* septante *m inv*
2 *adj* soixante-dix, *Belg & Suisse* septante; *see also* **eighty**
sever ['sevə(r)] *vt (arm, finger)* couper, trancher; *Fig (link, relationship)* rompre
several ['sevərəl] **1** *adj* plusieurs
2 *pron* plusieurs; **s. of us/them** plusieurs d'entre nous/eux
severance ['sevərəns] *n* rupture *f*; **s. pay** indemnité *f* de licenciement

severe [sɪ'vɪə(r)] *adj (person, punishment, criticism)* sévère; *(pain)* vif (vive); *(illness, injury)* grave; *(winter)* rude; *(weather)* très mauvais(e); *(style)* austère, sévère
severity [sɪ'verɪtɪ] *n (of person, punishment, criticism)* sévérité *f*; *(of pain)* intensité *f*; *(of injury, illness)* gravité *f*; *(of winter)* rigueur *f*; *(of style)* austérité *f*, sévérité *f*
sew [səʊ] *(pp* sewn [səʊn]) *vt & vi* coudre
▸**sew up** *vt sep* (**a**) *(stitch)* coudre (**b**) *Fam* **it's all sewn up** *(decided, settled)* l'affaire est dans le sac
sewage ['su:ɪdʒ] *n* eaux *fpl* usées *ou* d'égout; **s. disposal** évacuation *f* des eaux usées; **s. works** champ *m* d'épandage
sewer ['su:ə(r)] *n* égout *m*; *Fam* **to have a mind like a s.** avoir l'esprit mal tourné
sewing ['səʊɪŋ] *n (activity)* couture *f*; *(work)* ouvrage *m*; **s. kit** nécessaire *m* de couture; **s. machine** machine *f* à coudre
sewn [səʊn] *pp of* **sew**
sex [seks] *n* sexe *m*; **to have s. with sb** faire l'amour avec qn; **s. appeal** sex-appeal *m*; **s. education** éducation *f* sexuelle; **s. life** vie *f* sexuelle; **s. maniac** obsédé(e) *m,f* sexuel(elle); **s. shop** sex-shop *m*; **s. symbol** sex-symbol *m*; **s. therapist** sexologue *mf*; **s. tourism** tourisme *m* sexuel
▸**sex up** *vt sep* (**a**) *(image, style)* rendre plus sexy (**b**) *Fig (text, document, story)* enjoliver; **the government is accused of sexing up the report** on accuse le gouvernement d'avoir monté le rapport en épingle
sexagenarian [seksədʒɪ'neərɪən] *n* séxagénaire *mf*
sexism ['seksɪzəm] *n* sexisme *m*
sexist ['seksɪst] **1** *n* sexiste *mf*
2 *adj* sexiste
sexologist [sek'sɒlədʒɪst] *n* sexologue *mf*
sextant ['sekstənt] *n* sextant *m*
sextet [seks'tet] *n* sextuor *m*
sexton ['sekstən] *n* sacristain *m*, bedeau *m*
sexual ['seksjʊəl] *adj* sexuel(elle); **s. assault** agression *f* sexuelle; **s. discrimination** discrimination *f* sexuelle; **s. harassment** harcèlement *m* sexuel; **s. intercourse** rapports *mpl* sexuels; **s. reproduction** reproduction *f* sexuée
sexuality [seksjʊ'ælɪtɪ] *n* sexualité *f*
sexually ['seksjʊəlɪ] *adv* sexuellement; **s. transmitted infection** infection *f* sexuellement transmissible
sexy ['seksɪ] *adj Fam* sexy *inv*; *Fig (car, hi-fi)* branché(e)
Seychelles [seɪ'ʃelz] *npl* **the S.** les Seychelles *fpl*
Sgt *(abbr* **Sergeant**) Sgt
sh [ʃ] *exclam* chut!
shabbily ['ʃæbɪlɪ] *adv* (**a**) *(furnished, dressed)* pauvrement (**b**) *(treat, behave)* avec mesquinerie
shabbiness ['ʃæbɪnɪs] *n* (**a**) *(of person, clothes, area)* apparence *f* miteuse (**b**) *(of treatment, behaviour)* mesquinerie *f*
shabby ['ʃæbɪ] *adj* (**a**) *(dingy, worn out)* miteux(euse) (**b**) *(behaviour, treatment)* minable, mesqui(e)
shack [ʃæk] *n* cabane *f*, hutte *f*
▸**shack up** *vi Fam* **to s. up with sb** se mettre à la colle avec qn
shackle ['ʃækəl] **1** *n* **shackles** chaînes *fpl*, fers *mpl*
2 *vt (prisoner)* enchaîner
shade [ʃeɪd] **1** *n* (**a**) *(shadow)* ombre *f*; **in the s.** à l'ombre; *Fig* **to put sb in the s.** éclipser qn; **shades of 1968/the Beatles** *(reminders, suggestions)* ça rappelle 1968/les Beatles (**b**) *(of colour, meaning, opinion)* nuance *f*, ton *m*; **a s. better/longer** un tout

petit mieux/plus long (**c**) *Fam* **shades** *(sunglasses)* lunettes *fpl* de soleil

2 *vt (from sun)* **to s. one's eyes** se protéger les yeux

shaded ['ʃeɪdɪd] *adj* (**a**) *(garden, path)* à l'ombre, ombragé(e) (**b**) *(area on diagram, map)* hachuré(e)

shading ['ʃeɪdɪŋ] *n (on drawing)* ombres *fpl*; *(on diagram, map)* hachure *f*

shadow ['ʃædəʊ] **1** *n* (**a**) *(dark area)* ombre *f*; **to cast a s.** projeter une ombre; *Fig* **to cast a s. over sth** jeter une ombre sur qch; **to be a s. of one's former self** n'être plus que l'ombre de soi-même; **without a s. of doubt** sans l'ombre d'un doute; **the s. of death/war** le spectre de la mort/de la guerre; **to have shadows under one's eyes** avoir des cernes, avoir les yeux cernés (**b**) *(in workplace)* stagiaire *mf (qui observe un employé expérimenté de façon à apprendre le métier)*

2 *adj Br Pol* **s. cabinet** cabinet *m* fantôme; **s. minister** = député de l'opposition chargé d'un dossier administratif tel que l'Intérieur, les Affaires étrangères etc

3 *vt (follow)* filer, prendre en filature; *(in workplace)* **she's shadowing a senior journalist for a week** elle observe comment travaille un journaliste expérimenté pendant une semaine

Shadow cabinet

En Grande-Bretagne, le "shadow cabinet" est composé de parlementaires de l'opposition qui deviendraient ministres si l'opposition accédait au pouvoir. Chaque ministre du gouvernement dispose de son homologue "fantôme" dans l'opposition (on parle de "shadow minister"), qui étudie les mêmes dossiers et se spécialise ainsi dans un domaine donné. Les ministres fantômes occupent les "frontbenches" de l'opposition à la Chambre des communes.

shadowing ['ʃædəʊɪŋ] *n* = pour un stagiaire, fait d'observer un employé expérimenté de façon à apprendre le métier

shadowy ['ʃædəʊɪ] *adj (dark)* ombragé(e); *(form, outline)* vague

shady ['ʃeɪdɪ] *adj* (**a**) *(garden, lane)* ombragé(e) (**b**) *Fam (suspicious)* louche

shaft [ʃɑːft] **1** *n* (**a**) *(of golf club, tool)* manche *m*; *(of light)* rayon *m* (**b**) *(of mine)* puits *m*; *(for lift)* cage *f*

2 *vt very Fam (cheat)* entuber

shag¹ [ʃæg] *n (tobacco)* tabac *m*

shag² *Br Vulg* **1** *n (sexual intercourse)* **to have a s.** s'envoyer en l'air

2 *vt & vi (pt & pp shagged)* baiser

shagged [ʃægd] *adj Br very Fam (exhausted)* crevé(e)

shaggy ['ʃægɪ] *adj (hairy)* hirsute; *Fam* **s. dog story** histoire *f* sans queue ni tête

shah [ʃɑː] *n* schah *m*

shake [ʃeɪk] **1** *n* (**a**) *(action)* secousse *f*; **to give sb/sth a s.** secouer qn/qch; *Fig* **to give oneself a s.** se secouer; *Fam* **to have the shakes** avoir la tremblote; *Fam* **in two shakes (of a lamb's tail)** en un rien de temps; *Fam* **to be no great shakes** ne pas casser trois pattes à un canard (**b**) **(milk) s.** (milk-)shake *m*

2 *vt (pt shook* [ʃʊk], *pp shaken* ['ʃeɪkən]*) (person, box, bottle)* secouer; *(building)* faire trembler, ébranler; *Fig* **to s. sb's faith/trust** ébranler la foi/la confiance de qn; **to s. one's head** faire non de la tête; **to s. one's fist at sb** menacer qn du poing; **to s. hands**

with sb serrer la main à qn; **to s. hands on a deal** conclure un accord par une poignée de mains

3 *vi* (**a**) *(of person, building, voice)* trembler; **to s. like a leaf** trembler comme une feuille (**b**) *Fam* **to s. on it** *(shake hands)* toper; **s. on it!** tope là!

▶**shake off** *vt sep (illness, depression)* sortir de; *(pursuer)* semer

▶**shake up** *vt sep* (**a**) *(upset)* secouer (**b**) *(reorganize)* réorganiser de fond en comble

shaken ['ʃeɪkən] *pp of* **shake**

Shakespearean [ʃeɪks'pɪərɪən] *adj* shakespearien(enne)

shake-up ['ʃeɪkʌp] *n Fam (reorganization)* chambardement *m*

shakily ['ʃeɪkɪlɪ] *adv (walk)* d'un pas vacillant; *(write)* d'une main tremblante; *(speak)* d'une voix tremblante

shaky ['ʃeɪkɪ] *adj (table, ladder)* branlant(e); *(handwriting)* tremblé(e); *(voice)* tremblant(e); *(health, position)* précaire

shale [ʃeɪl] *n* schiste *m* argileux

shall [*stressed* ʃæl, *unstressed* ʃəl]

> On trouve généralement **I/you/he**/etc **shall** sous leurs formes contractées **I'll/you'll/he'll**/etc. La forme négative correspondante est **shan't**, que l'on écrira **shall not** dans des contextes formels.

modal aux v (**a**) *(with first person) (expressing future tense)* **I s. be there** j'y serai; **where s. I sit?** où veux-tu que je m'asseye?; **I shan't say this more than once** je ne le dirai pas plus d'une fois; **as we s. see** comme nous le verrons (**b**) *(making suggestions, offers)* **s. I make some coffee?** veux-tu que je fasse du café?; **let's go in, s. we?** entrons, tu veux bien? (**c**) *Formal (with 2nd and 3rd person) (expressing determination)* **you s. pay for this!** tu me le paieras! (**d**) *(indicating general truth)* **all members s. be entitled to vote** tous les membres auront le droit de vote

shallot [ʃə'lɒt] *n* échalote *f*

shallow ['ʃæləʊ] *adj* (**a**) *(water, dish)* peu profond(e); **s. end** *(of swimming pool)* petit bain *m* (**b**) *Fig (person, mind)* superficiel(elle)

sham [ʃæm] **1** *n (trial, election)* comédie *f*, farce *f*; *(person)* imposteur *m*

2 *adj* feint(e); **a s. election** un simulacre d'élections

3 *vt (pt & pp shammed)* feindre, simuler

4 *vi* faire semblant

shamble ['ʃæmbəl] *vi* **to s. along** marcher en traînant les pieds

shambles ['ʃæmbəlz] *n* désordre *m*, pagaille *f*; **this place is a s.!** quel désordre!, quelle pagaille!

shambolic [ʃæm'bɒlɪk] *adj Fam* bordélique

shame [ʃeɪm] **1** *n* (**a**) *(disgrace, guilt)* honte *f*; **to my s.** à ma grande honte; **s. on you!** tu devrais avoir honte!; **to put sb to s.** faire honte à qn (**b**) *(pity)* dommage *m*; **it's a s. (that...)** c'est dommage (que... + *subjunctive*); **what a s.!** quel dommage!

2 *vt* (**a**) *(cause to feel ashamed)* faire honte à; **to s. sb into doing sth** obliger qn à faire qch en lui faisant honte (**b**) *(bring shame on)* couvrir de honte

shamefaced ['ʃeɪmfeɪst] *adj* honteux(euse), penaud(e)

shameful ['ʃeɪmfʊl] *adj* honteux(euse), scandaleux(-euse)

shamefully ['ʃeɪmfəlɪ] *adv* honteusement

shameless ['ʃeɪmlɪs] *adj* impudique; **to be s. about doing sth** n'avoir aucun scrupule à faire qch

shammy ['ʃæmɪ] *n* **s. (leather)** peau *f* de chamois

shampoo [ʃæm'puː] **1** n (pl **shampoos**) shampo(o)ing m **2** vt (pt & pp **shampooed**) to s. one's hair se faire un shampo(o)ing
shamrock ['ʃæmrɒk] n trèfle m
shandy ['ʃændɪ] (pl **shandies**) n panaché m
shank [ʃæŋk] n (of lamb, beef) jarret m
shan't [ʃɑːnt] = shall not
shanty¹ ['ʃæntɪ] (pl **shanties**) n (hut) baraque f, cabane f; **s. town** bidonville m
shanty² n (song) chanson f de marins
shape [ʃeɪp] **1** n (**a**) (form) forme f; **what s. is it?** quelle forme cela a-t-il?; **to be the same s. as...** avoir la même forme que...; **to take s.** (of plan) prendre forme; Fig **in any s. or form** quel (quelle) qu'il (elle) soit; Fig **in the s. of** sous la forme de; (person) en la personne de (**b**) (condition) **to be in good/bad s.** (of person) être en bonne/mauvaise forme; (of company, economy) bien/mal marcher; **to get into/keep in s.** (of person) retrouver/garder la forme
2 vt (**a**) (clay) modeler; (wood) façonner (**b**) Fig (perception, events, future) influencer; (character) former
▸**shape up** vi (of person) progresser; (of team, plans) prendre forme
shapeless ['ʃeɪplɪs] adj informe
shapely ['ʃeɪplɪ] adj bien fait(e)
shard [ʃɑːd] n (of glass) éclat m; (of pottery) tesson m
share [ʃeə(r)] **1** n (**a**) (portion) part f; **in equal shares** en parts égales; **to have a s. in sth** avoir une part dans qch; **to do one's s.** mettre la main à la pâte; also Fig **to get one's fair s. of sth** avoir sa part de qch (**b**) Fin action f; **s. capital** capital m social; **s. certificate** certificat m ou titre m d'actions; **s. option** option f d'achat des actions
2 vt partager
3 vi partager; **to s. in sth** partager qch; **s. and s. alike!** chacun sa part!
▸**share out** vt sep partager, répartir
shareholder ['ʃeəhəʊldə(r)] n Fin actionnaire mf
shareholding ['ʃeəhəʊldɪŋ] n Fin actionnariat m
shareware ['ʃeəweə(r)] n Comput shareware m, partagiciel m
shark [ʃɑːk] n also Fig requin m
sharp [ʃɑːp] **1** adj (**a**) (knife) bien aiguisé(e); (pencil) bien taillé(e); (scissors, razor) qui coupe bien; (point) aigu(ë); (claws) acéré(e) (**b**) (features) anguleux(euse); (turning, rise, fall) brusque; (photo, outline, focus) net (nette); (contrast) marqué(e); (hearing) fin(e); (eyesight) perçant(e); Fig **to be at the s. end** être en première ligne (**c**) (intelligent) vif (vive) (**d**) (harsh) (voice, words) cinglant(e); (person) mordant(e); **to have a s. tongue** être mordant (**e**) (taste, sauce) acide; (sound) perçant(e); (pain, wind) vif (vive) (**f**) (in music) **C s.** do dièse
2 adv (**a**) (punctually) pile; **at four o'clock s.** à quatre heures pile ou précises (**b**) (immediately) **to turn s. left/right** tourner tout de suite à gauche/à droite (**c**) (idioms) Fam **look s.!** grouille-toi!
3 n (in music) dièse m
sharpen ['ʃɑːpən] vt (**a**) (knife, tool) aiguiser; (pencil) tailler; Can affiler (**b**) (pain) accentuer; (passion, desire) exacerber; **to s. one's wits** faire travailler sa matière grise
sharpener ['ʃɑːpənə(r)] n (for knife) aiguisoir m (à couteaux); (for pencil) taille-crayon m
sharp-eyed ['ʃɑːpaɪd] adj observateur(trice)

sharply ['ʃɑːplɪ] adv (**a**) (contrast) nettement (**b**) (rise, fall, brake) brusquement
sharpness ['ʃɑːpnɪs] n (**a**) (of knife) tranchant m (**b**) (of outline, photo) netteté f (**c**) (of mind, hearing, sight) acuité f (**d**) (of voice, words) brusquerie f (**e**) (of pain) acuité f; (of wind) âpreté f
sharpshooter ['ʃɑːpʃuːtə(r)] n tireur m d'élite
sharp-sighted [ʃɑːp'saɪtɪd] adj observateur(trice)
sharp-tongued [ʃɑːp'tʌŋd] adj mordant(e)
shat [ʃæt] pt of **shit**
shatter ['ʃætə(r)] **1** vt (**a**) (glass, bone) briser en mille morceaux; Fig (hopes, nerves) briser; (health) ruiner (**b**) Fam **to be shattered** (stunned) être accablé(e); Br (exhausted) être crevé(e)
2 vi se briser en mille morceaux
shattering ['ʃætərɪŋ] adj (**a**) (defeat) accablant(e); **it was a s. blow** ça a été un coup terrible (**b**) Fam (stunning) accablant(e); Br (exhausting) crevant(e)
shatterproof ['ʃætəpruːf] adj (glass) Sécurit®; (windscreen, door) en verre Sécurit®
shave [ʃeɪv] **1** n **to have a s.** se raser; Fig **that was a close s.** il était moins une
2 vt (**a**) (face, legs) raser; **to s. one's legs** se raser les jambes (**b**) (wood) raboter
3 vi se raser
▸**shave off** vt sep se raser
shaven ['ʃeɪvən] adj rasé(e)
shaver ['ʃeɪvə(r)] n rasoir m électrique
shaving ['ʃeɪvɪŋ] n (**a**) **s. brush** blaireau m; **s. foam** mousse f à raser (**b**) (piece of wood) copeau m; (piece of metal) rognure f
shawl [ʃɔːl] n châle m
she [ʃiː] **1** pron elle; **she's Scottish** elle est écossaise; SHE **hasn't got it!** ce n'est pas elle qui l'a!
2 n **it's a s.** (of animal) c'est une femelle
sheaf [ʃiːf] (pl **sheaves** [ʃiːvz]) n (of corn) gerbe f; (of papers) liasse f
shear [ʃɪə(r)] (pp **shorn** [ʃɔːn] or **sheared**) **1** vt (sheep) tondre; Fig **to be shorn of sth** être dépouillé(e) de qch
2 vi (cut) **to s. through sth** couper qch
shears [ʃɪəz] npl cisailles fpl
sheath [ʃiːθ] n (**a**) (for sword, knife) fourreau m; (for electric cable) gaine f; **s. knife** couteau m à gaine (**b**) (contraceptive) préservatif m
sheaves [ʃiːvz] pl of **sheaf**
shed¹ [ʃed] n (in garden) abri m, remise f; (in factory) atelier m
shed² (pt & pp **shed**) vt (leaves) perdre; (tears) verser; **to s. its skin** (of snake) muer; **to s. light on sth** jeter de la lumière sur qch; **to s. weight** perdre du poids; **to s. its load** (of lorry) perdre son chargement
she'd [ʃiːd] = she had, she would
sheen [ʃiːn] n (on metal, silk) lustre m; (on hair) brillant m
sheep [ʃiːp] (pl **sheep**) n mouton m
sheepdog ['ʃiːpdɒg] n chien m de berger
sheepfold ['ʃiːpfəʊld] n parc m à moutons
sheepish ['ʃiːpɪʃ] adj penaud(e)
sheepskin ['ʃiːpskɪn] n peau f de mouton; **s. jacket** veste f en peau de mouton
sheer [ʃɪə(r)] adj (**a**) (pure) pur(e); **it's s. madness** c'est de la folie pure; **by s. chance** tout à fait par hasard (**b**) (steep) à pic inv (**c**) (stockings, fabric) très fin(e)
sheet [ʃiːt] n (on bed) drap m; (of paper) feuille f; (of glass, ice, metal) plaque f; (of flame) rideau m; **s. lightning** éclair m en nappe(s); **s. metal** tôle f; **s. music** partitions fpl

sheetfeed ['ʃiːtfiːd] *n Comput* avancement *m* du papier

sheik(h) [ʃeɪk] *n* cheikh *m*

shekel ['ʃekəl] *n* shekel *m*

shelf [ʃelf] (*pl* **shelves** [ʃelvz]) *n* (**a**) (*in cupboard, bookcase*) étagère *f*; (**set of**) **shelves** étagère *f*; *Fig* **to be left on the s.** rester vieille fille; *Com* **s. life** (*of goods*) durée *f* de conservation avant vente (**b**) (*of cliff, rock face*) rebord *m*

shell [ʃel] **1** *n* (**a**) (*of snail, oyster, egg, nut*) coquille *f*; (*of lobster, tortoise*) carapace *f*; (*on beach*) coquillage *m*; *Fig* **to come out of one's s.** sortir de sa coquille; **s. suit** = survêtement en synthétique brillant (**b**) (*of building*) carcasse *f* (**c**) (*bomb*) obus *m*; **s. shock** psychose *f* traumatique (*à la suite d'une explosion*)
2 *vt* (**a**) (*nuts*) décortiquer; (*peas*) écosser; (*eggs*) écaler (**b**) (*bombard*) bombarder

▶**shell out** *Fam* **1** *vt sep* (*money*) casquer
2 *vi* **to s. out (for sth)** casquer (pour qch)

she'll [ʃiːl] = **she will, she shall**

shellfire ['ʃelfaɪə(r)] *n* tirs *mpl* d'obus

shellfish ['ʃelfɪʃ] *n* (*crustacean*) crustacé *m*; (*mollusc*) coquillage *m*; (*as food*) fruits *mpl* de mer

shelling ['ʃelɪŋ] *n* bombardement *m*

shellshocked ['ʃelʃɒkt] *adj* (*soldier*) commotionné(e) (*à la suite d'une explosion*); *Fig* sous le choc

shelter ['ʃeltə(r)] **1** *n* (*place, protection*) abri *m*; **to take s.** se mettre à l'abri, s'abriter
2 *vt* abriter (**from** de); (*criminal, refugee*) accueillir
3 *vi* s'abriter, se mettre à l'abri (**from** de)

sheltered ['ʃeltəd] *adj* (*place*) abrité(e); (*life, childhood*) protégé(e); **s. housing** = logements spécialement conçus pour les personnes âgées

shelve [ʃelv] *vt* (*postpone*) mettre au placard

shelving ['ʃelvɪŋ] *n* étagères *fpl*

shelves [ʃelvz] *pl of* **shelf**

shepherd ['ʃepəd] **1** *n* berger *m*; **s.'s pie** ≃ hachis *m* Parmentier
2 *vt* (*sheep*) garder; *Fig* (*people*) guider, conduire

shepherdess [ʃepə'des] *n* bergère *f*

sherbet ['ʃɜːbət] *n Br* (*powder*) poudre *f* acidulée; *Am* (*sorbet*) sorbet *m*

sheriff ['ʃerɪf] *n* (**a**) *Br Law* (*in England*) = plus haut fonctionnaire du comté, dont le rôle est essentiellement protocolaire; (*in Scotland*) ≃ juge *m* au tribunal de grande instance (**b**) *Am* sherif *m*

sherry ['ʃerɪ] *n* sherry *m*, xérès *m*

she's [ʃiːz] = **she has, she is**

Shetland ['ʃetlənd] *n* **the S. Islands, the Shetlands** les (îles *fpl*) Shetland *fpl*; **S. pony** poney *m* des Shetland

shiatsu, shiatzu [ʃi'ætsuː] *n* shiatsu *m*

shield [ʃiːld] **1** *n* (*of knight*) & *Fig* (*protection*) bouclier *m*; (*police badge*) badge *m*; (*trophy*) trophée *m* en forme d'écusson
2 *vt* (*protect*) protéger (**from** de); **to s. one's eyes** se protéger les yeux

shift [ʃɪft] **1** *n* (**a**) (*change of position*) changement *m*; **a s. in meaning** un glissement de sens; **a s. to the right/left** (*in politics*) un revirement à droite/gauche; **s. key** (*on typewriter, computer*) touche *f* des majuscules (**b**) (*period*) poste *m*; (*workers*) équipe *f*; **to work (in) shifts** avoir un travail posté (**c**) **s.** (**dress**) robe *f* chasuble
2 *vt* (**a**) (*move*) déplacer; (*stain*) enlever, faire partir; **to s. the blame onto sb** rejeter la responsabilité sur qn (**b**) *Fam* (*sell*) écouler

3 *vi* (*move*) bouger; (*of stain*) partir; *Fam* (*move quickly*) foncer

shiftless ['ʃɪftlɪs] *adj* fainéant(e)

shiftwork ['ʃɪftwɜːk] *n* travail *m* posté

shifty ['ʃɪftɪ] *adj* (*person*) louche; (*look*) fuyant(e)

shilling ['ʃɪlɪŋ] *n* shilling *m*

shimmer ['ʃɪmə(r)] **1** *n* (*of light*) scintillement *m*; (*of water*) miroitement *m*; (*of silk*) chatoiement *m*
2 *vi* (*of light*) scintiller; (*of water*) miroiter; (*of silk*) chatoyer

shimmering ['ʃɪmərɪŋ] *adj* (*light*) scintillant(e); (*water*) miroitant(e); (*silk*) chatoyant(e)

shin [ʃɪn] *n* tibia *m*; **s. guard** *or* **pad** (*in sport*) jambière *f*

▶**shin up** *vt insep* (*climb*) grimper à

shinbone ['ʃɪnbəʊn] *n* tibia *m*

shindig ['ʃɪndɪɡ] *n Fam* (**a**) (*party*) fête *f*; **to have a s.** faire la fiesta (**b**) (*fuss*) tapage *m*; **he kicked up a real s.** il a fait un sacré tapage

shine [ʃaɪn] **1** *n* (**a**) brillant *m*, éclat *m* (**b**) (*idioms*) **to take the s. off sth** faire perdre son éclat à qch, ternir qch; *Fam* **to take a s. to sb** (*take a liking to*) se prendre d'amitié pour qn; (*get a crush on*) s'enticher de qn
2 *vt* (*pt & pp* **shone** [ʃɒn]) (**a**) (*light, torch*) braquer (**on** sur) (**b**) (*pt & pp* **shined**) (*polish*) faire briller
3 *vi* briller; *Fig* **to s. at sth** (*excel*) briller en qch; **her face shone with joy** son visage rayonna de joie

shiner ['ʃaɪnə(r)] *n Fam* (*black eye*) œil *m* au beurre noir

shingle ['ʃɪŋɡəl] *n* (**a**) (*wooden tile*) bardeau *m* (**b**) (*pebbles*) galets *mpl*

shingles ['ʃɪŋɡəlz] *n* (*disease*) zona *m*; **to have s.** avoir un zona

shining ['ʃaɪnɪŋ] *adj* brillant(e); *Fig* **a s. example (of)** un parfait exemple (de)

shiny ['ʃaɪnɪ] *adj* brillant(e)

ship [ʃɪp] **1** *n* navire *m*; *Fig* **when my s. comes in** quand je serai riche
2 *vt* (*pt & pp* **shipped**) (*transport*) transporter; (*send*) expédier; (*take on board*) embarquer

▶**ship off** *vt sep Fam* expédier

shipboard ['ʃɪpbɔːd] *n Naut* **on s.** à bord

shipbuilder ['ʃɪpbɪldə(r)] *n* constructeur *m* naval

shipbuilding ['ʃɪpbɪldɪŋ] *n* construction *f* navale; **the s. industry** (l'industrie *f* de) la construction navale

shipload ['ʃɪpləʊd] *n* cargaison *f*; *Fig* **by the s.** en masse

shipmate ['ʃɪpmeɪt] *n Naut* camarade *m* de bord

shipment ['ʃɪpmənt] *n* cargaison *f*

shipowner ['ʃɪpəʊnə(r)] *n* armateur *m*

shipping ['ʃɪpɪŋ] *n* (*ships*) navires *mpl*; **s. agent** (*person*) agent *m* maritime; (*company*) agence *f* maritime; **s. lane** voie *f* de navigation

shipshape ['ʃɪpʃeɪp] *adj* rangé(e), en ordre

shipwreck ['ʃɪprek] **1** *n* (*disaster*) naufrage *m*; (*ship*) épave *f*
2 *vt* **to be shipwrecked** faire naufrage

shipwrecked ['ʃɪprekt] *adj* naufragé(e)

shipwright ['ʃɪpraɪt] *n Naut* (*company*) constructeur *m* naval; (*worker*) ouvrier(ère) *m,f* de chantier naval

shipyard ['ʃɪpjɑːd] *n* chantier *m* naval

shire ['ʃaɪə(r)] *n Br* comté *m*; **s. horse** shire *m*

shirk [ʃɜːk] **1** *vt* (*task*) éviter de faire; (*obligation, responsibility*) se dérober à
2 *vi* (*avoid work*) tirer au flanc

shirker ['ʃɜːkə(r)] *n* tire-au-flanc *mf inv*

shirt [ʃɜːt] *n* chemise *f*; *Fam* **keep your s. on!** on se calme!

shirtmaker [ˈʃɜːtmeɪkə(r)] *n* fabricant(e) *m,f* de chemises
shirtsleeves [ˈʃɜːtsliːvz] *npl* **to be in s.** être en bras de chemise
shirt-tail [ˈʃɜːteɪl] *n* pan *m* de chemise
shirty [ˈʃɜːtɪ] *adj Br Fam* en rogne; **to get s. (with sb)** se mettre en rogne (contre qn)
shit [ʃɪt] *Vulg* **1** *n* (**a**) *(excrement)* merde *f*; *(mess)* bordel *m*; *(nonsense)* conneries *fpl*; **to have a s.** chier (**b**) *(man)* salaud *m*; *(woman)* salope *f* (**c**) *(idioms)* **to talk s.** dire des conneries; **to be in the s.** être dans la merde; **he doesn't give a s.** il n'en a rien à foutre; **to beat the s. out of sb** casser la gueule à qn; **to scare the s. out of sb** foutre une de ces trouilles à qn
2 *vt (pt & pp* **shitted** *or* **shat** [ʃæt]) **to s. oneself** chier dans son froc
3 *vi* chier
4 *exclam* merde!
shitty [ˈʃɪtɪ] *adj Vulg* (**a**) *(nappies, trousers)* dégueulasse (**b**) *(weather, job)* merdique; *(behaviour, remark)* dégueulasse; **to feel s.** *(ill)* avoir la tête dans le cul; *(guilty)* se sentir merdeux(euse)
shiver [ˈʃɪvə(r)] **1** *n (of cold, fear)* frisson *m*; **to send shivers down sb's spine** donner le frisson à qn
2 *vi* frissonner, trembler (**with** de)
shoal [ʃəʊl] *n (of fish)* banc *m*; *Fig (of people)* foule *f*
shock¹ [ʃɒk] *n (of hair)* crinière *f*
shock² **1** *n* (**a**) *(impact)* choc *m*; *(of earthquake)* secousse *f*; **s. absorber** amortisseur *m*; **s. tactics** tactique *f* de choc; *Mil* **s. troops** troupes *fpl* de choc; *also Fig* **s. wave** onde *f* de choc (**b**) *(emotional blow)* choc *m*, coup *m*; **I got a real s. when...** cela m'a vraiment fait un choc quand...; **to be in s.** être en état de choc (**c**) *(electric)* décharge *f* (électrique); **s. therapy** (traitement *m* par) électrochocs *mpl*
2 *vt (surprise, startle)* stupéfier; *(scandalize)* choquer; **to s. sb into doing sth** pousser qn à faire qch en lui faisant peur
shocked [ʃɒkt] *adj (startled)* stupéfié(e); *(scandalized)* choqué(e)
shocking [ˈʃɒkɪŋ] *adj* (**a**) *(scandalous)* choquant(e); **s. pink** rose *m* bonbon (**b**) *(very bad)* atroce
shockproof [ˈʃɒkpruːf] *adj (watch)* antichoc *inv*
shoddy [ˈʃɒdɪ] *adj (a) (goods)* de mauvaise qualité; *(workmanship)* mal fait(e); *(conduct)* méprisable
shoe [ʃuː] **1** *n* chaussure *f*; *(horseshoe)* fer *m* (à cheval); *Fig* **I wouldn't like to be in her shoes** je n'aimerais pas être à sa place; *Fig* **put yourself in my shoes** mets-toi à ma place; **s. polish** cirage *m*; **s. shop** magasin *m* de chaussures
2 *vt (pt & pp* **shod** [ʃɒd] *or* **shoed**) *(horse)* ferrer
shoebrush [ˈʃuːbrʌʃ] *n* brosse *f* à chaussures
shoehorn [ˈʃuːhɔːn] *n* chausse-pied *m*
shoelace [ˈʃuːleɪs] *n* lacet *m* (de chaussure)
shoemaker [ˈʃuːmeɪkə(r)] *n (manufacturer)* bottier *m*; *(seller)* chausseur *m*
shoeshine [ˈʃuːʃaɪn] *n Am (person)* cireur *m* de chaussures
shoestring [ˈʃuːstrɪŋ] *n* (**a**) *Fam* **on a s.** avec trois fois rien; **s. budget** petit budget *m* (**b**) *Am* lacet *m* (de chaussure)
shone [ʃɒn] *pt & pp of* **shine**
shoo [ʃuː] *exclam* ouste!
▸ **shoo away, shoo off** *vt sep* chasser
shook [ʃʊk] *pt of* **shake**
shoot [ʃuːt] **1** *vt (pt & pp* **shot** [ʃɒt]) (**a**) *(fire) (bullet)* tirer; *(arrow)* & *Fig (glance)* lancer (**b**) *(kill)* **s. sb**

(wound) blesser qn par balle; *(kill)* tuer qn par balle; *(execute)* fusiller qn; **to be shot in the arm** recevoir une balle dans le bras; **to s. rabbits/grouse** chasser le lapin/la grouse; *Fig* **to s. oneself in the foot** compromettre ses chances; *Am Fam* **to s. the breeze** tailler une bavette (**c**) *(film, TV programme)* tourner (**d**) *(pass rapidly)* **to s. the rapids** franchir les rapides; **to s. the lights** *(in car)* brûler *ou* griller le feu rouge (**e**) **to s. dice/pool** jouer aux dés/au billard
2 *vi* (**a**) *(with gun)* tirer (**at** sur); *(in football)* tirer, shooter; *Fam Fig (to questioner)* **s.!** allez-y! (**b**) *(move rapidly)* filer; **he shot into/out of the house** il se précipita dans/hors de la maison; **the pain shot up her arm** elle ressentit soudain une vive douleur au bras
3 *n* (**a**) *(of plant)* pousse *f* (**b**) *(hunting party)* chasse *f*
▸ **shoot down** *vt sep (person)* descendre; *(plane)* abattre
▸ **shoot off** *vi (leave quickly)* filer
▸ **shoot out** *vi (emerge quickly)* jaillir
▸ **shoot up** *vi* (**a**) *(of plant)* pousser vite; *(of child)* monter en graine; *(of buildings)* pousser comme des champignons (**b**) *(of rocket)* s'élever; *(of prices)* monter *ou* grimper en flèche (**c**) *Fam (with drugs)* se shooter
shooting [ˈʃuːtɪŋ] **1** *n* (**a**) *(gunfire)* coups *mpl* de feu; *(incident)* fusillade *f*; **s. stick** canne-siège *f* (**b**) *(of film, TV programme)* tournage *m*
2 *adj* **s. star** étoile *f* filante
shoot-out [ˈʃuːtaʊt] *n* fusillade *f*
shop [ʃɒp] **1** *n* (**a**) *(for goods)* magasin *m*; **s. assistant** vendeur(euse) *m,f*; **s. window** vitrine *f* (**b**) *Fam* **to do a s.** *(go shopping)* faire ses courses (**c**) *(workshop)* atelier *m*; *Fig* **the s. floor** les ouvriers *mpl* (**d**) *(idioms) Fam* **barber shop** barbier, perruquier; *Fam Fig* **all over the s.** *(everywhere)* un peu partout; *Fig* **his explanation was all over the s.** son explication ne tenait pas debout; **my hair was all over the s.** j'étais coiffé n'importe comment; **at the interview he was all over the s.** à l'entretien, il a raconté n'importe quoi
2 *vt (pt & pp* **shopped**) *Br Fam (betray)* balancer
3 *vi* faire ses courses; **to go shopping** faire des courses; *(for food)* faire ses courses; **to s. around** comparer les prix
shopaholic [ʃɒpəˈhɒlɪk] *n* **he's a real s.** il adore faire les magasins
shopgirl [ˈʃɒpgɜːl] *n* vendeuse *f*
shopkeeper [ˈʃɒpkiːpə(r)] *n* commerçant(e) *m,f*
shoplifter [ˈʃɒplɪftə(r)] *n* voleur(euse) *m,f* à l'étalage
shoplifting [ˈʃɒplɪftɪŋ] *n* vol *m* à l'étalage
shopper [ˈʃɒpə(r)] *n* personne *f* qui fait ses courses; *(customer)* client(e) *m,f*
shopping [ˈʃɒpɪŋ] *n* courses *fpl*; **to do the s.** faire les courses; **to do one's s.** faire ses courses; **s. bag** sac *m* à provisions, cabas *m*; **s. basket** panier *m* (à provisions); *Econ* panier *m* de la ménagère; *Am* **s. cart** chariot *m*; *Br* **s. centre** *or* **precinct** centre *m* commercial; **s. list** liste *f* des courses; *Am* **s. mall** centre *m* commercial; *Br* **s. trolley** chariot *m*
shopsoiled [ˈʃɒpsɔɪld] *adj Br* défraîchi(e)
shore [ʃɔː(r)] *n (of sea)* rivage *m*; *(of lake)* bord *m*; **on s.** à terre; **to go on s.** *(from ship)* débarquer; **s. leave** permission *f* à terre
▸ **shore up** *vt sep (house, wall)* étayer; *Fig (reputation)* consolider
shoreline [ˈʃɔːlaɪn] *n* littoral *m*

shorn [ʃɔːn] *pp of* shear
short [ʃɔːt] **1** *adj* (**a**) *(physically)* court(e); *(person)* petit(e); **Bill is s. for William** Bill est le diminutif de William; **the s. answer is no** en deux mots la réponse est non; **to have a s. temper** *or* **fuse** être soupe au lait; **s. story** nouvelle *f* (**b**) *(in time)* court(e), bref (brève); **in s.** en bref; **to make s. work of sb/sth** expédier qn/qch; **s. and sweet** bref (brève) (**c**) *(abrupt)* brusque, sec (sèche) (**with** avec) (**d**) *(insufficient, lacking)* insuffisant(e); **to be in s. supply** manquer; **to be s. of sth** être à court *ou* manquer de qch; **I'm 50 pence s.** il me manque 50 pence; **little** *or* **not far s. of** *(almost)* pas loin de; **he's not far s. of forty** il n'est pas loin de la quarantaine; **it was nothing s. of miraculous that she survived** c'est vraiment un miracle qu'elle ait survécu
2 *adv* (**a**) *(suddenly)* **to stop s.** s'arrêter net; **to bring sb up s.** arrêter net qn (**b**) *(in length, duration)* **to stop s. of doing sth** se retenir tout juste de faire qch; **to cut sb s.** couper la parole à qn, interrompre qn; **to cut sth s.** abréger qch (**c**) *(without)* **to go s. (of sth)** se priver (de qch) (**d**) *(insufficiency)* **to be running s. of sth** n'avoir presque plus de qch; **to fall s. of sth** *(target)* ne pas atteindre qch; *(expectations)* ne pas répondre à qch; *Fig* **to sell sb s.** rouler qn; **to be caught s.** arrêter pris(e) d'un besoin pressant
3 *n Fam* (**a**) *(short film)* court-métrage *m* (**b**) *(drink)* alcool *m* fort (**c**) *(short circuit)* court-circuit *m*
shortage [ʃɔːtɪdʒ] *n* pénurie *f*; **petrol/food s.** pénurie *f* d'essence/de nourriture; **housing s.** crise *f* du logement; **to have no s. of sth** ne pas manquer de qch
shortbread [ʃɔːtbred], **shortcake** [ʃɔːtkeɪk] *n* sablés *mpl* au beurre
short-change [ʃɔːt'(t)ʃeɪndʒ] *vt (in shop)* ne pas rendre assez de monnaie à; *Fig (cheat)* escroquer
short-circuit [ʃɔːt'sɜːkɪt] **1** *n* court-circuit *m*
2 *vt also Fig* court-circuiter
3 *vi* se mettre en court-circuit
shortcomings [ʃɔːtkʌmɪŋz] *npl* défauts *mpl*
shorten [ʃɔːtən] *vt (skirt, text)* raccourcir; *(visit, task)* abréger
shortfall [ʃɔːtfɔːl] *n* manque *m*, insuffisance *f*
shorthaired [ʃɔːtheəd] *adj (cat, dog)* à poil(s) court(s); *(person)* aux cheveux courts
shorthand [ʃɔːthænd] *n* sténographie *f*, sténo *f*; **s. typist** sténodactylo *mf*
short-haul [ʃɔːthɔːl] *adj* moyen-courrier *m*
shortlist [ʃɔːtlɪst] **1** *n* = liste de candidats après une première sélection
2 *vt* **to be shortlisted (for sth)** être parmi les candidats retenus (à qch)
short-lived [ʃɔːt'lɪvd] *adj* de courte durée
shortly [ʃɔːtlɪ] *adv* (**a**) *(soon)* bientôt; **s. after(wards)** peu (de temps) après (**b**) *(abruptly)* sèchement
short-range [ʃɔːtreɪndʒ] *adj (missile)* de courte portée
shorts [ʃɔːts] *npl (short trousers)* short *m*
short-sighted [ʃɔːt'saɪtɪd] *adj* myope; *Fig* peu clairvoyant(e)
short-sleeved [ʃɔːtsliːvd] *adj* à manches courtes
shortstop [ʃɔːtstɒp] *n Am Sport* bloqueur *m*
short-tempered [ʃɔːttempəd] *adj* coléreux(euse)
short-term [ʃɔːttɜːm] *adj* à court terme
shot [ʃɒt] **1** *n* (**a**) *(act of firing, sound)* coup *m* (de feu); **to fire a s.** tirer; *Fig* **like a s.** sans hésiter; *Fig* **to take a s. in the dark** tenter le coup; *Fig* **to call the shots** faire la loi; **to put** lancer *m* du poids (**b**) *(marksman)* tireur

m (**c**) *(in football, rugby)* coup *m* de pied; *(in basketball)* lancer *m*; **good s.!** bien joué! (**d**) *(photograph)* photo *f*; *(of film, TV programme)* prise *f* de vue, plan *m* (**e**) *Fam (injection)* piqûre *f* (**f**) *(attempt)* tentative *f*, essai *m*; **to have a s. at sth/at doing sth** essayer qch/de faire qch (**g**) *(drink)* petit verre *m*
2 *pt & pp of* shoot
shotgun [ʃɒtɡʌn] *n* fusil *m* de chasse; *Fam* **s. wedding** mariage *m* en catastrophe
should [ʃʊd]

La forme négative **should not** s'écrit **shouldn't** en forme contractée.

modal aux v (**a**) *(expressing obligation, desirability)* **you s. do it at once** vous devriez le faire tout de suite; **you s. have come earlier** vous auriez dû venir plus tôt; **she shouldn't have told them** elle n'aurait pas dû leur dire (**b**) *(expressing probability)* **the weather s. improve from now on** le temps devrait s'améliorer à partir de maintenant; **she s. have arrived by this time** elle devrait être arrivée à l'heure qu'il est (**c**) *(in exclamations, rhetorical questions)* **why s. you suspect me?** pourquoi me soupçonnez-vous?; **who s. I meet but Martin!** et qui a-t-il fallu que je rencontre? Martin!; **he apologized – I s. think so, too!** il s'est excusé – j'espère bien! (**d**) *(in subordinate clauses)* **he ordered that they s. be released** il a ordonné leur libération; **she insisted that he s. meet her parents** elle a insisté pour qu'il rencontre ses parents (**e**) *(in conditional clauses)* **if he s. come** *or Formal* **s. he come, let me know** s'il vient, fais-le-moi savoir (**f**) *(expressing opinions, preferences)* **I s. like a drink** je prendrais bien un verre; **I s. imagine he was rather angry** j'imagine qu'il était plutôt en colère; **I shouldn't be surprised if...** cela ne m'étonnerait pas si...
shoulder [ʃəʊldə(r)] **1** *n (of person, meat)* épaule *f*; **to stand s. to s.** *(of two people)* se tenir l'un(e) contre l'autre; **to rub shoulders with sb** côtoyer qn; *Fig* **to be looking over one's s.** être constamment sur ses gardes; *Fig* **to cry on sb's s.** pleurer sur l'épaule de qn; **s. bag** (sac *m*) besace *f*; **s. blade** omoplate *f*; **s. pad** épaulette *f*; **s. strap** *(of bag)* bandoulière *f*; *(of garment)* bretelle *f*
2 *vt* (**a**) *(push)* **to s. one's way through a crowd** se frayer un passage à travers la foule à coups d'épaule; **to s. sb aside** écarter qn d'un coup d'épaule (**b**) *(put on shoulder)* mettre sur son épaule; *Fig* **to s. the responsibility** endosser la responsabilité
shouldn't [ʃʊdənt] = should not
shout [ʃaʊt] **1** *n* cri *m*; **shouts of laughter** des éclats *mpl* de rire; **give me a s. when you're ready** appelle-moi quand tu seras prêt
2 *vt* crier; **to s. sth at sb** crier qch à qn
3 *vi* crier; **to s. at sb** crier après qn; **to s. for help** crier au secours; *Fig* **to have something to s. about** pouvoir être fier(ère) de qch
▸**shout down** *vt sep* **to s. sb down** huer qn
shouting [ʃaʊtɪŋ] *n* cris *mpl*; **s. match** engueulade *f*
shove [ʃʌv] **1** *n* poussée *f*; **to give sb/sth a s.** pousser qn/qch
2 *vt & vi* pousser
▸**shove off** *vi Fam (leave)* dégager
shovel [ʃʌvəl] **1** *n* pelle *f*
2 *vt (pt & pp shovelled)* pelleter; *Fam* **to s. food into one's mouth** enfourner de la nourriture
shovelful [ʃʌvəlfʊl] *n* pelletée *f*

show [ʃəʊ] **1** n (**a**) (exhibition) exposition f; **to be on s.** être exposé(e); **to put sth on s.** exposer qch; **s. house** maison f témoin; **s.** jumper cavalier(ère) m,f spécialisé(e) dans le jumping; **s. jumping** jumping m; Pej **s. trial** procès m à grand spectacle (**b**) (concert, play) spectacle m; (on TV, radio) émission f; Fig **to run the s.** commander; **s. business** show-business m, monde m du spectacle; **s. girl** girl f; Fam **to be a s. stopper** être le clou du spectacle (**c**) (act of showing) démonstration f, manifestation f; **s. of hands** vote m à main levée; **it's all s.** tout ça, c'est de la comédie; **to do sth for s.** faire qch pour épater la galerie; Fam **good s.!** (well done) bravo! **2** vt (pp **shown** [ʃəʊn]) (**a**) (display) montrer; (picture) exposer; (courage, talent) faire preuve de; **to s. sb sth, to s. sth to sb** montrer qch à qn; Fig **to s. one's cards** or **one's hand** abattre ses cartes; **they had nothing to s. for all that work** ils avaient fait tout ce travail pour rien; **he won't s.** his face round here again on ne le reverra pas de sitôt; **to s. oneself** se montrer; **to s. a profit/a loss** enregistrer un bénéfice/une perte; **you're showing your age** ça ne te rajeunit pas!; **to s. oneself to be...** se révéler... (**b**) (indicate) montrer, indiquer (**c**) (prove, demonstrate) démontrer, prouver; **it goes to s. that...** cela montre bien que... (**d**) (teach) montrer; **to s. sb how to do sth** montrer à qn comment faire qch (**e**) (film) passer; (TV programme) diffuser (**f**) (escort, lead) **to s. sb the way** montrer le chemin à qn; **to s. sb to his/her room** conduire qn à sa chambre; **to s. sb (a)round the town** faire visiter la ville à qn **3** vi (**a**) (be visible) se voir (**b**) (of film) passer
▸**show in** vt sep (escort in) faire entrer
▸**show off 1** vt sep exhiber **2** vi frimer
▸**show out** vt sep (escort out) reconduire, raccompagner
▸**show up 1** vt sep (**a**) (reveal) révéler (**b**) (embarrass) faire honte à **2** vi (**a**) (stand out) ressortir, se voir (**b**) Fam (arrive) se pointer
showbiz [ˈʃəʊbɪz] n Fam show-biz m, monde m du spectacle
showcase [ˈʃəʊkeɪs] n vitrine f
showdown [ˈʃəʊdaʊn] n confrontation f
shower [ˈʃaʊə(r)] **1** n (**a**) (of rain) averse f; (of stones, insults) pluie f (**b**) (for washing) douche f; **to have** or **take a s.** prendre une douche; **s. cap** bonnet m de douche; **s. curtain** rideau m de douche; **s. gel** gel m douche; **s. head** pomme f de douche **2** vt **to s. sb with sth, to s. sth on sb** couvrir qn de qch **3** vi (take a shower) se doucher
showery [ˈʃaʊərɪ] adj pluvieux(euse)
showing [ˈʃəʊɪŋ] n (exhibition) exposition f; (of film) séance f
showman [ˈʃəʊmən] n (at circus) forain m; Fig cabotin m
showmanship [ˈʃəʊmənʃɪp] n sens m du spectacle
shown [ʃəʊn] pp of **show**
show-off [ˈʃəʊɒf] n Fam frimeur(euse) m,f
showpiece [ˈʃəʊpiːs] n joyau m
showroom [ˈʃəʊruːm] n magasin m
showstopping [ˈʃəʊstɒpɪŋ] adj sensationnel(elle)
showy [ˈʃəʊɪ] adj voyant(e)
shrank [ʃræŋk] pt of **shrink**
shrapnel [ˈʃræpnəl] n Mil éclats mpl d'obus; Fam (loose change) mitraille f

shred [ʃred] **1** n lambeau m; **in shreds** en lambeaux; **to tear sth to shreds** mettre qch en lambeaux; Fig (criticize) mettre qch en pièces; Fig **there isn't a s. of evidence** il n'y a pas l'ombre d'une preuve **2** vt (pt & pp **shredded**) (documents) déchiqueter; (food) couper grossièrement
shredder [ˈʃredə(r)] n (for paper) déchiqueteuse f
shrew [ʃruː] n (**a**) (animal) musaraigne f (**b**) (nagging woman) mégère f
shrewd [ʃruːd] adj (person) perspicace; (decision) judicieux(euse)
shrewdly [ˈʃruːdlɪ] adv judicieusement
shriek [ʃriːk] **1** n cri m strident; **shrieks of laughter** hurlements mpl de rire; **to give a s.** pousser un cri strident **2** vt hurler **3** vi pousser un cri strident; **to s. with laughter** hurler de rire
shrift [ʃrɪft] n **to give sb short s.** envoyer qn promener
shrill [ʃrɪl] adj strident(e), aigu(ë)
shrimp [ʃrɪmp] n crevette f
shrimping net [ˈʃrɪmpɪŋˈnet] n crevettier m (filet)
shrine [ʃraɪn] n (tomb) tombeau m; (place) lieu m de pèlerinage; Fig haut lieu m
shrink [ʃrɪŋk] **1** vt (pt **shrank** [ʃræŋk], pp **shrunk** [ʃrʌŋk]) faire rétrécir **2** vi (**a**) (of material) rétrécir; (of income, budget) diminuer, se réduire (**b**) (move back) **to s. from sth** se dérober devant qch; **to s. from doing sth** répugner à faire qch **3** n Fam (psychiatrist) psy mf
shrinkage [ˈʃrɪŋkɪdʒ] n (of material) rétrécissement m; Fig (in sales, profit) diminution f
shrink-wrapped [ˈʃrɪŋkˈræpt] adj emballé(e) sous film plastique
shrivel [ˈʃrɪvəl] (pt & pp **shrivelled**, Am **shriveled**) **1** vt dessécher **2** vi se dessécher
▸**shrivel up** vi se dessécher
shroud [ʃraʊd] **1** n linceul m; Fig (of mystery, darkness) voile m **2** vt Fig **to be shrouded in sth** être enveloppé(e) de qch
Shrove Tuesday [ˈʃrəʊvˈtjuːzdɪ] n Mardi m gras
shrub [ʃrʌb] n arbuste m
shrubbery [ˈʃrʌbərɪ] (pl **shrubberies**) n jardin m d'arbustes
shrug [ʃrʌg] **1** n haussement m d'épaules **2** vt (pt & pp **shrugged**) **to s. one's shoulders** hausser les épaules **3** vi hausser les épaules
▸**shrug off** vt sep ignorer
shrunk [ʃrʌŋk] pp of **shrink**
shrunken [ˈʃrʌŋkən] adj rétréci(e)
shudder [ˈʃʌdə(r)] **1** n (of person) frisson m **2** vi (of person) frissonner; (of vehicle) vibrer; **I s. to think!** j'ai des frissons quand j'y pense!
shuffle [ˈʃʌfəl] **1** n (**a**) **to walk with a s.** marcher en traînant les pieds (**b**) **to give the cards a s.** battre les cartes **2** vt (papers) brasser; (cards) battre **3** vi (when walking) traîner les pieds
shun [ʃʌn] (pt & pp **shunned**) vt fuir, éviter
shunt [ʃʌnt] vt (train, carriages) aiguiller; Fam Fig (people) transbahuter
shush [ʃʊʃ] **1** vt faire taire **2** exclam chut!

shut [ʃʌt] **1** *adj* fermé(e); *Fam* **to keep one's mouth s.** se taire

2 *vt* (*pt & pp* **shut**) fermer; **to s. the door on sb** fermer la porte au nez de qn; **to s. one's finger in the door** se coincer le doigt dans la porte; *Fam* **s. your mouth!** ferme-la!

3 *vi* (*of door*) se fermer; (*of shop*) fermer

▸**shut down 1** *vt sep* fermer; (*production*) arrêter

2 *vi* fermer

▸**shut in** *vt sep* (*confine*) enfermer

▸**shut off** *vt sep* (**a**) (*electricity, water, funds*) couper (**b**) (*road, exit*) fermer (**c**) (*isolate*) isoler (**from** de)

▸**shut out** *vt sep* (**a**) (*exclude*) exclure; (*light, view*) bloquer (**b**) (*keep outside*) empêcher d'entrer; **to s. oneself out** s'enfermer dehors

▸**shut up 1** *vt sep* (**a**) (*confine*) enfermer (**b**) (*close*) fermer (**c**) *Fam* (*silence*) faire taire

2 *vi Fam* (*be quiet*) se taire

shutdown ['ʃʌtdaʊn] *n* (*of factory*) fermeture *f*

shut-eye ['ʃʌtaɪ] *n Fam* roupillon *m*; **to get some s.** roupiller

shutter ['ʃʌtə(r)] *n* (**a**) (*on window*) volet *m*; (*of shop*) store *m*; **to put up the shutters** (*of shop*) fermer le magasin (**b**) (*in camera*) obturateur *m*

shuttle ['ʃʌtəl] **1** *n* (**a**) (*in sewing, train, bus, plane*) navette *f*; **s. service** service *m* de navettes (**b**) (*in badminton*) volant *m*

2 *vt* véhiculer

3 *vi* faire la navette (**between** entre)

shuttlecock ['ʃʌtəlkɒk] *n* volant *m*

shy [ʃaɪ] **1** *adj* timide; **to be s. of sb** être intimidé(e) par qn; **to be s. of doing sth** éviter de faire qch à tout prix

2 *vi* (*pt &pp* **shied**) (*of horse*) s'effaroucher (**at** devant)

▸**shy away** *vi* **to s. away from sth/from doing sth** éviter qch/de faire qch

shyly ['ʃaɪlɪ] *adv* timidement

Siamese [saɪə'miːz] **1** *n* (*pl* **Siamese**) (*cat*) siamois *m*

2 *adj* siamois(e); **S. cat** chat *m* siamois; **S. twins** (*boys*) frères *mpl* siamois; (*girls*) sœurs *fpl* siamoises

Siberia [saɪ'bɪərɪə] *n* la Sibérie

Siberian [saɪ'bɪərɪən] **1** *n* Sibérien(enne) *m,f*

2 *adj* sibérien(enne)

sibling ['sɪblɪŋ] *n* (*brother*) frère *m*; (*sister*) sœur *f*; **s. rivalry** rivalité *f* entre frères et sœurs

sic [sɪk] *adv* sic

Sicilian [sɪ'sɪlɪən] **1** *n* Sicilien(enne) *m,f*

2 *adj* sicilien(enne)

Sicily ['sɪsɪlɪ] *n* la Sicile

sick [sɪk] *adj* (**a**) (*ill*) malade; **to be s.** (*be ill*) être malade; (*vomit*) vomir; **to feel s.** avoir envie de vomir; *Fig* **it makes me s.!** ça me dégoûte!; *Fig* **to be worried s.** se faire un sang d'encre; **s. bay** infirmerie *f*; **s. leave** congé *m* de maladie; **s. note** (*from parents*) mot *m* d'absence; (*from doctor*) certificat *m* médical; **s. pay** indemnité *f* de maladie (**b**) (*fed up*) **to be s. of sb/sth** en avoir assez de qn/qch; **to be s. and tired** *or* **s. to death of sb/sth** en avoir ras le bol de qn/qch (**c**) (*humour, joke*) de mauvais goût; (*person*) malsain(e); **to have a s. mind** avoir l'esprit dérangé

2 *n Fam* (*vomit*) vomi *m*

3 *npl* **the s.** les malades *mpl*

▸**sick up** *vt sep Br Fam* (*vomit*) vomir

sicken ['sɪkən] **1** *vt* (*make ill*) rendre malade; *Fig* (*disgust*) écœurer

2 *vi* **to be sickening for something** couver quelque chose

sickening ['sɪknɪŋ] *adj* écœurant(e)

sickle ['sɪkəl] *n* faucille *f*

sickly ['sɪklɪ] *adj* (**a**) (*person, complexion*) maladif(-ive); (*plant*) rabougri(e); (*colour, light, smile*) faible (**b**) (*taste, sentiment*) écœurant(e); **s. sweet** douceâtre

sickness ['sɪknɪs] *n* (*illness*) maladie *f*; (*nausea*) écœurement *m*; **s. benefit** indemnité *f* journalière

sickroom ['sɪkruːm] *n* chambre *f* de malade

side [saɪd] **1** *n* (**a**) (*of person, animal, object*) côté *m*; (*of mountain*) flanc *m*, versant *m*; **by sb's s.** aux côtés de qn; **s. by s.** côte à côte; *Fam* **to split one's sides (laughing)** se tordre de rire; **s. door/entrance** porte *f*/entrée *f* latérale (**b**) (*of record*) face *f*; (*paper*) côté *m* (**c**) (*adjacent area*) côté *m*; **on this/that s. (of)** de ce côté (de); **on the other s. (of)** de l'autre côté (de); **from all sides, from every s.** de toutes parts; **to move from s. to s.** osciller; **the left-/right-hand s.** le côté gauche/droit; **to lean to one s.** se pencher sur le côté; **to stand to one s.** se tenir à l'écart; **s. dish** plat *m* d'accompagnement; **s. salad** salade *f* (*pour accompagner un plat*); **s. view** vue *f* latérale (**d**) (*aspect*) côté *m*; **to look on the bright/gloomy s. (of things)** voir le bon/mauvais côté (des choses) (**e**) (*in game*) camp *m*; (*in dispute*) côté *m*; **to be on sb's s.** être du côté de qn; **to take sides** prendre parti; **to change sides** changer de camp; **he had let the s. down** il nous/les/*etc* avait fait faux bond (**f**) (*secondary*) **s. effects** effets *mpl* secondaires; **s. issue** question *f* d'intérêt secondaire; **s. road** petite route *f*; **s. street** ruelle *f* (**g**) (*idioms*) **on his mother's s.** (*of family*) du côté de sa mère; **to put sth to one s.** mettre qch de côté; **to take sb to one s.** prendre qn à part; **to be on the wrong s. of forty** avoir plus de quarante ans; **to get on the right s. of sb** se faire bien voir de qn; **to get on the wrong s. of sb** prendre qn à rebrousse-poil; **it's a bit on the expensive/long s.** c'est un peu cher(ère)/long(ue); **to do sth on the s.** (*as extra job*) faire qch pour arrondir ses fins de mois; *Fam* **to have a bit on the s.** (*of man*) avoir une maîtresse; (*of woman*) avoir un amant

2 *vi* **to s. with** prendre le parti de; **to s. against** prendre parti contre

sideboard ['saɪdbɔːd] *n* buffet *m*

sideboards ['saɪdbɔːdz], **sideburns** ['saɪdbɜːnz] *npl* (*facial hair*) pattes *fpl*

sidecar ['saɪdkɑː(r)] *n* side-car *m*

sidekick ['saɪdkɪk] *n Fam* acolyte *m*

sidelight ['saɪdlaɪt] *n* feu *m* de position

sideline ['saɪdlaɪn] **1** *n* (**a**) (*of football, rugby pitch*) ligne *f* de touche; *Fig* **to sit on the sidelines** rester sur la touche (**b**) (*business, job*) à-côté *m*; **we sell DVDs as a s.** nous vendons également des DVDs

2 *vt Sport & Fig* mettre sur la touche

side-saddle ['saɪdsædəl] *adv* **to ride s.** monter en amazone

sideshow ['saɪdʃəʊ] *n* (*at fair*) attraction *f*; *Fig* événement *m* mineur

side-splitting ['saɪdsplɪtɪŋ] *adj Fam* tordant(e)

sidestep ['saɪdstep] (*pt & pp* **sidestepped**) **1** *vt* (*tackle, player*) éviter; *Fig* (*question*) éluder

2 *vi* (*in boxing*) esquiver

sideswipe ['saɪdswaɪp] *n* remarque *f* désobligeante

sidetrack ['saɪdtræk] *vt* distraire

sidewalk ['saɪdwɔːk] *n Am* trottoir *m*

sideways ['saɪdweɪz] **1** adj (look, movement) de côté **2** adv (move, walk) latéralement; (turn, fall, lean) sur le côté

siding ['saɪdɪŋ] n (on railway) voie f de garage

sidle ['saɪdəl] vi **to s. up to sb** se glisser vers qn

siege [siːdʒ] n siège m; **to lay s. to a town** assiéger une ville; **under s.** assiégé(e); **to have a s. mentality** se sentir persécuté(e)

Sierra Leone [sɪ'erəlɪ'əʊn] n la Sierra Leone

sieve [sɪv] **1** n crible m; (in kitchen) passoire f; Fam **to have a memory like a s.** avoir la tête comme une passoire **2** vt tamiser

sift [sɪft] **1** vt (flour, sugar) tamiser **2** vi Fig **to s. through sth** passer qch au crible

sigh [saɪ] **1** n soupir m **2** vi soupirer; (of wind) gémir

sight [saɪt] **1** n (**a**) (faculty) vue f; **to lose one's s.** perdre la vue (**b**) (act of seeing) to catch s. of sb/sth apercevoir qn/qch; **to lose s. of sb/sth** perdre qn/qch de vue; **I hate the s. of him** je ne peux pas le voir; **I can't stand the s. of blood** je ne supporte pas la vue du sang; **to shoot on s.** tirer à vue; **at first s.** à première vue; **it was love at first s.** ça a été le coup de foudre; **to know sb by s.** connaître qn de vue; **to buy sth s. unseen** acheter qch sans l'avoir vu (**c**) (range of vision) **to come into s.** apparaître; **in s.** en vue; **to keep sb in s.** garder un œil sur qn; **out of s.** caché(e); **to put sth out of s.** cacher qch; **to keep out of s.** se cacher; Prov **out of s., out of mind** loin des yeux, loin du cœur (**d**) (of instrument, gun) viseur m; Fig **to have sb/sth in one's sights** avoir qn/qch en vue; Fig **to have or set one's sights on sb/sth** avoir des vues sur qn/qch (**e**) (spectacle) spectacle m; **you're/it's a s. for sore eyes** c'est un plaisir de te voir/de voir ça; Fam **to look a s.** ne pas être beau (belle) à voir; **sights** (of city) attractions fpl touristiques (**f**) Fam (for emphasis) **a damn s. easier/longer** bien plus facile/long (longue) **2** vt (see) apercevoir

sighted ['saɪtɪd] **1** npl **the s.** les voyants mpl **2** adj (person) voyant(e)

sighting ['saɪtɪŋ] n **several sightings of the fugitive have been reported** on a aperçu le fugitif à plusieurs reprises; **there have been several UFO sightings in the area** on a aperçu plusieurs OVNIs dans les parages

sightless ['saɪtləs] adj aveugle

sight-read ['saɪtriːd] (pt & pp **sight-read** ['saɪtred]) vt & vi déchiffrer

sightseeing ['saɪtsiːɪŋ] n tourisme m; **to go s.** faire du tourisme

sightseer ['saɪtsiːə(r)] n touriste mf

sign [saɪn] **1** n (**a**) (gesture, symbol, indication) signe m; **to make a s. to sb** faire un signe à qn; **it's a sure s. that...** on peut être sûr que...; **a s. of the times** un signe des temps; **there's no s. of an improvement** il n'y a rien qui annonce une quelconque amélioration; **there's no s. of it/him** je ne le vois nulle part; **she gave no s. of having heard** elle n'a pas semblé avoir entendu; **all the signs are that...** tout laisse à penser que...; **the equipment showed signs of having been used** on voyait qu'on l'équipement avait déjà été utilisé; **s. language** langue f des signes (**b**) (notice) panneau m; (of pub, shop) enseigne f; (on road) panneau m de signalisation routière; **follow the signs for Manchester** suivre la direction de Manchester **2** vt (**a**) (write signature on) signer (**b**) (in sign language) dire en langue des signes (**c**) (in sport) engager **3** vi (**a**) (write signature) signer (**b**) (use sign language) communiquer en langue des signes (**c**) (in sport) signer (**for** avec)

▸**sign away** vt sep (rights) renoncer à

▸**sign for** vt insep (delivery, parcel) signer un reçu pour

▸**sign in** vi (**a**) (in factory) pointer; (in hotel) signer le registre en arrivant (**b**) Comput (on website) entrer

▸**sign off** vi (**a**) (of radio, TV presenter) terminer l'émission (**b**) (close letter) finir la lettre

▸**sign on** vi Fam (for unemployment benefit) (initially) s'inscrire au chômage; (regularly) pointer

▸**sign out 1** vt sep **to s. sth out** (book, equipment) signer un registre pour emprunter qch **2** vi (**a**) (from factory) pointer (en partant); (from hotel) signer le registre à son départ (**b**) Comput (from website) sortir

▸**sign up** vi (**a**) (register) s'inscrire (**for** à) (**b**) (of soldier) s'engager

signal ['sɪɡnəl] **1** n signal m; **radio s.** signal m radiophonique; Fig **to send the wrong signals** ne pas être clair(e); **s. box** poste m d'aiguillage; **s. flare** fusée f éclairante; **s. rocket** fusée de signalisation **2** vt (pt & pp **signalled**, Am **signaled**) (**a**) (make gesture to) faire signe à; **to s. sb to do sth** faire signe à qn de faire qch (**b**) (be sign of) être le signe de **3** vi (**a**) (make gesture) faire signe (**to** à) (**b**) (in car) clignoter

signalman ['sɪɡnəlmən] (pl **signalmen**) n aiguilleur m

signatory ['sɪɡnətərɪ] (pl **signatories**) n signataire mf

signature ['sɪɡnətʃə(r)] n signature f; **s. tune** (of radio, TV programme) indicatif m

signboard ['saɪnbɔːd] n enseigne f

signet ring ['sɪɡnɪtrɪŋ] n chevalière f

significance [sɪɡ'nɪfɪkəns] n (**a**) (importance) importance f; **of great s.** d'une grande importance; **of no s.** sans importance (**b**) (meaning) signification f

significant [sɪɡ'nɪfɪkənt] adj (important) important(e), considérable; (meaningful) significatif(ive); **s. other** partenaire mf (dans une relation affective); Psy = personne dont on se sent très proche

significantly [sɪɡ'nɪfɪkəntlɪ] adv (**a**) (appreciably) nettement; **to vary/change s.** varier/changer considérablement (**b**) (meaningfully) d'une manière significative; **s., no one mentioned it** fait révélateur, personne n'en a parlé

signify ['sɪɡnɪfaɪ] (pt & pp **signified**) vt signifier

signpost ['saɪnpəʊst] **1** n poteau m indicateur; Fig indice m

Sikh [siːk] **1** n sikh mf **2** adj sikh

silage ['saɪlɪdʒ] n ensilage m

silence ['saɪləns] **1** n silence m; **to listen/watch in s.** écouter/regarder en silence; Prov **s. is golden** le silence est d'or **2** vt faire taire

silencer ['saɪlənsə(r)] n (on car, gun) silencieux m

silent ['saɪlənt] adj (person, place) silencieux(euse); (letter) muet(ette); **to fall s.** se taire; **to remain or keep s.** garder le silence; **s. film** film m muet; **s. majority**

majorité f silencieuse; **s. protest** manifestation f silencieuse

silently ['saɪləntlɪ] adv silencieusement

silhouette [sɪluːˈet] **1** n silhouette f
2 vt **she was silhouetted against the light** sa silhouette se détachait à contre-jour

silica ['sɪlɪkə] n silice f

silicon ['sɪlɪkən] n Chem silicium m; **s. chip** puce f électronique

silicone ['sɪlɪkəʊn] n Chem silicone f; **s. implants** implants mpl mammaires en silicone

silk [sɪlk] n soie f; **s. screen printing** sérigraphie f

silkworm ['sɪlkwɜːm] n ver m à soie

silky ['sɪlkɪ] adj soyeux(euse); (voice) suave

sill [sɪl] n (of window) rebord m

silliness ['sɪlɪnɪs] n stupidité f

silly ['sɪlɪ] **1** adj idiot(e), stupide; **the s. thing is that...** ce qui est idiot, c'est que...; **to look s.** avoir l'air ridicule; **to say/do something s.** dire/faire une bêtise; **to laugh/worry oneself s.** mourir de rire/d'inquiétude; **to knock sb s.** assommer qn
2 n Fam bêta(asse) m,f

silo ['saɪləʊ] (pl **silos**) n silo m

silt [sɪlt] n vase f

▸**silt up** vi s'envaser

silver ['sɪlvə(r)] **1** n (**a**) (metal) argent m; Prov **every cloud has a s. lining** à quelque chose malheur est bon; **s. haired** aux cheveux argentés; **s. (medal)** médaille f d'argent; **s. paper** papier m d'argent; **s. plate** (coating) plaqué m argent; (articles) argenterie f; **the s. screen** le grand écran; **s. wedding** noces fpl d'argent (**b**) Br (coins) pièces fpl en argent (**c**) (silverware) argenterie f
2 adj (**a**) (made of silver) en argent (**b**) **s.(-coloured)** argenté(e)

silver-plated [sɪlvəˈpleɪtɪd] adj plaqué(e) argent

silversmith ['sɪlvəsmɪθ] n orfèvre mf

silverware ['sɪlvəweə(r)] n argenterie f

silverwork ['sɪlvəwɜːk] n orfèvrerie f

silvery ['sɪlvərɪ] adj (colour) argenté(e); (sound) argentin(e)

SIM card ['sɪmkɑːd] n Tel (abbr **subscriber identity module**) carte f SIM

simian ['sɪmɪən] adj simien(enne)

similar ['sɪmɪlə(r)] adj semblable, similaire (**to** à); **s. in appearance/size** d'apparence/de taille semblable; **they are very s.** ils se ressemblent beaucoup

similarity [sɪmɪˈlærɪtɪ] (pl **similarities**) n ressemblance f

similarly ['sɪmɪləlɪ] adv de la même façon

simile ['sɪmɪlɪ] n comparaison f

simmer ['sɪmə(r)] **1** n **at a s.** à feu doux
2 vt mijoter
3 vi mijoter; Fig (of revolt, discontent) couver; **to s. with rage** bouillonner de rage

▸**simmer down** vi Fam se calmer

simper ['sɪmpə(r)] vi minauder

simple ['sɪmpəl] adj (**a**) (easy) simple; **in s. terms** dit simplement; **the s. truth** la vérité pure et simple (**b**) (unintelligent) simplet(ette)

simple-minded [sɪmpəlˈmaɪndɪd] adj (person) simple d'esprit; (ideas, belief) naïf(ïve)

simpleton ['sɪmpəltən] n simple mf d'esprit

simplicity [sɪmˈplɪsɪtɪ] n simplicité f

simplification [sɪmplɪfɪˈkeɪʃən] n simplification f

simplify ['sɪmplɪfaɪ] (pt & pp **simplified**) vt simplifier

simplistic [sɪmˈplɪstɪk] adj simpliste

simply ['sɪmplɪ] adv (**a**) (in simple manner) simplement (**b**) (absolutely) absolument (**c**) (just) simplement; **it's s. a question of time** c'est une simple question de temps; **she s. had to snap her fingers and...** elle n'avait qu'à claquer des doigts et...

simulate ['sɪmjʊleɪt] vt simuler

simulated ['sɪmjʊleɪtɪd] adj (leather, marble) faux (fausse); (surprise, anger) simulé(e)

simulation [sɪmjʊˈleɪʃən] n simulation f

simultaneous [sɪməlˈteɪnɪəs, Am saɪməlˈteɪnɪəs] adj simultané(e); **s. broadcast** retransmission f simultanée; **s. translation** traduction f simultanée

simultaneously [sɪməlˈteɪnɪəslɪ, Am saɪməlˈteɪnɪəslɪ] adv simultanément

sin [sɪn] n péché m; Old-fashioned or Hum **to be living in s.** (of unmarried couple) vivre dans le péché; Fam **it would be a s. to...** ce serait un crime de...
2 vi (pt & pp **sinned**) pécher

since [sɪns] **1** adv depuis; **long s.** depuis longtemps
2 prep depuis; **s. June/1984** depuis le mois de juin/1984; **s. then** depuis
3 conj (**a**) (in time) depuis que; **it's a long time s. I saw her** cela fait longtemps que je ne l'ai pas vue (**b**) (because) puisque

sincere [sɪnˈsɪə(r)] adj sincère

sincerely [sɪnˈsɪəlɪ] adv sincèrement; **Yours s.** (ending letter) Veuillez agréer, Monsieur/Madame, l'expression de mes salutations distinguées

sincerity [sɪnˈserɪtɪ] n sincérité f; **in all s.** en toute sincérité

sinecure ['saɪnɪkjʊə(r)] n sinécure f

sinew ['sɪnjuː] n tendon m

sinewy ['sɪnjuːɪ] adj musclé(e)

sinful ['sɪnfʊl] adj (act, life) coupable; (waste) scandaleux(euse); **s. person** pécheur(eresse) m,f

sing [sɪŋ] (pt **sang** [sæŋ], pp **sung** [sʌŋ]) **1** vt (song) chanter
2 vi (of person, bird, kettle) chanter

▸**sing out** vi (sing loudly) chanter fort

Singapore [sɪŋəˈpɔː(r)] n Singapour

Singaporean [sɪŋəˈpɔːrɪən] **1** n Singapourien(enne) m,f
2 adj singapourien(enne)

singe [sɪndʒ] vt roussir

singer ['sɪŋə(r)] n chanteur(euse) m,f; **s. songwriter** auteur-compositeur-interprète m

singing ['sɪŋɪŋ] n chant m; **his s. is awful** il chante atrocement; **s. lessons** cours mpl de chant; **to have a fine s. voice** chanter admirablement

single ['sɪŋɡəl] **1** adj (**a**) (just one) seul(e); **every s. day** tous les jours; **not a s. one** pas un(e); **don't say a s. word** ne dis pas un mot; Br **s. cream** ≃ crème f fraîche liquide; Fin **s. currency** monnaie f unique; Econ **European market** marché m unique européen (**b**) (not double) **in s. figures** inférieur à dix; **in s. file** en file indienne; **s. bed** lit m à une place; **s. room** chambre f pour une personne (**c**) (not married) célibataire; **s. mother** mère f célibataire; **s. parent** parent m isolé; **s. parent family** famille f monoparentale
2 n (**a**) (record) single m (**b**) (ticket) aller m simple (**c**) (hotel room) chambre f pour une personne (**d**) **singles** (in tennis) simple m

▸**single out** vt sep distinguer; **she was singled out for praise** on n'a choisi de faire des compliments qu'à elle

single-breasted ['sɪŋɡəl'brestɪd] *adj (jacket, suit)* droit(e)
single-decker ['sɪŋɡəl'dekə(r)] *n Br (bus)* autobus *m* sans impériale
single-handedly ['sɪŋɡəl'hændɪdlɪ] *adv* tout(e) seul(e)
single-income ['sɪŋɡəl'ɪŋkʌm] *adj (family)* à salaire unique
single-minded ['sɪŋɡəl'maɪndɪd] *adj (person)* résolu(e); *(determination, conviction)* farouche
single-sex school ['sɪŋɡəl'seks'skuːl] *n* école *f* non mixte
singlet ['sɪŋɡlɪt] *n* maillot *m* de corps
single-track railway ['sɪŋɡəl'træk'reɪlweɪ] *n* chemin *m* de fer à une seule voie
singsong ['sɪŋsɒŋ] **1** *n* (**a**) *(voice, tone)* voix *f* chantante (**b**) *Fam (singing session)* **to have a s.** chanter en chœur
2 *adj (voice, tone)* chantant(e)
singular ['sɪŋɡjʊlə(r)] **1** *n Gram* singulier *m*; **in the s.** au singulier
2 *adj* (**a**) *Gram* singulier(ère) (**b**) *(remarkable)* remarquable
singularly ['sɪŋɡjʊləlɪ] *adv* remarquablement
Sinhalese [sɪnə'liːz] **1** *n (pl Sinhalese)* (**a**) *(person)* Cinghalais(e) *m,f* (**b**) *(language)* cinghalais *m*
2 *adj* cinghalais(e)
sinister ['sɪnɪstə(r)] *adj* sinistre
sink¹ [sɪŋk] *n (in kitchen)* évier *m*; *(in bathroom)* lavabo *m*; *Br* **s. estate** cité *f* dépotoir
sink² *(pt sank [sæŋk], pp sunk [sʌŋk])* **1** *vt* (**a**) *(ship)* couler; **to be sunk in thought** être perdu(e) dans ses pensées; *Fam Fig* **to be sunk** être fichu(e) (**b**) *(well)* creuser; **to s. one's teeth into sth** mordre à pleines dents dans qch; **to s. money into sth** investir des capitaux dans qch; *Br Fam* **to s. a pint** s'envoyer une pinte de bière
2 *vi (in water, mud)* couler; **her heart sank** son cœur s'est serré; **his spirits sank** il a perdu tout son courage; **to s. into sb's memory** *(of information)* se graver dans la mémoire de qn; **to s. into oblivion** tomber dans l'oubli; **to s. into a deep sleep** sombrer dans un profond sommeil; **to s. into an armchair** s'affaler dans un fauteuil; **to s. to the ground** s'effondrer par terre; **to s. in sb's estimation** baisser dans l'estime de qn; **how could you s. so low?** comment peux-tu tomber aussi bas?
▸**sink in** *vi (of liquid)* pénétrer; *(of information)* être assimilé(e); *Fig* **it hasn't sunk in yet** je n'ai/il n'a/*etc* pas encore digéré la nouvelle
sinking ['sɪŋkɪŋ] **1** *n* (**a**) *(of ship)* naufrage *m* (**b**) *Fin* **s. fund** fonds *m* d'amortissement
2 *adj (feeling)* d'angoisse; **with a s. heart** avec un serrement de cœur
sinner ['sɪnə(r)] *n* pécheur(eresse) *m,f*
sinuous ['sɪnjʊəs] *adj (river, curves)* sinueux(euse); *(snake, dancer)* qui ondule; *(movement)* ondulant(e)
sinus ['saɪnəs] *n* sinus *m*
sinusitis [saɪnə'saɪtɪs] *n* sinusite *f*
sip [sɪp] **1** *n* petite gorgée *f*; **to take a s. (of sth)** boire une petite gorgée (de qch)
2 *vt (pt & pp sipped)* siroter
3 *vi* **to s. at sth** siroter qch
siphon ['saɪfən] **1** *n* siphon *m*
2 *vt* siphonner
▸**siphon off** *vt sep (liquid)* siphonner; *Fig (money, supplies)* détourner

sir [sɜː(r)] *n* (**a**) *(form of address)* monsieur *m*; **Dear S./ Sirs** *(in letter)* Monsieur/Messieurs (**b**) *(title)* **S. Clyde** sir Clyde *(titre de noblesse masculin)*
sire ['saɪə(r)] **1** *n* (**a**) *(father of animal)* père *m* (**b**) *Old-fashioned (address to sovereign)* sire *m*
2 *vt* engendrer
siren ['saɪərən] *n* sirène *f*
sirloin ['sɜːlɔɪn] *n* **s. (steak)** steak *m* d'aloyau
sissy ['sɪsɪ] *(pl sissies)* *n Fam (weak male)* poule *f* mouillée; *(effeminate male)* garçon *m* efféminé
sister ['sɪstə(r)] *n* (**a**) *(sibling, nun)* sœur *f*; **s. company** société *f* sœur; **s. ship** sister-ship *m* (**b**) *(nurse)* infirmière-chef *f*
sisterhood ['sɪstəhʊd] *n* (**a**) *(community of nuns)* communauté *f* religieuse (**b**) *(solidarity)* solidarité *f* féminine
sister-in-law ['sɪstərɪn'lɔː] *(pl sisters-in-law)* *n* belle-sœur *f*
sisterly ['sɪstəlɪ] *adj (advice, devotion)* de sœur
sit [sɪt] *(pt & pp sat [sæt])* **1** *vt* (**a**) **to s. a child on one's knee** asseoir un enfant sur ses genoux (**b**) *Br (exam)* passer
2 *vi* (**a**) *(of person)* s'asseoir; **to be sitting** être assis(e); **to be sitting reading** être assis en train de lire; **s.!** *(to dog)* assis!; *Fam* **to s. tight** *(not move)* ne pas bouger de sa place; *(not take action)* ne rien faire (**b**) *(of assembly, court)* siéger; **to s. on a jury** faire partie d'un jury (**c**) *(of object)* **to be sitting on the radiator/ outside** être sur le radiateur/dehors
▸**sit about, sit around** *vi* rester assis(e) à ne rien faire
▸**sit back** *vi* (**a**) *(lean back)* **to s. back in one's chair** s'installer confortablement sur sa chaise (**b**) *Fam (relax)* se détendre; *(not intervene)* ne rien faire
▸**sit down 1** *vt sep* asseoir; *Fam* **s. yourself down!** asseds-toi donc!
2 *vi* s'asseoir; **to be sitting down** être assis(e)
▸**sit in** *vi (at meeting)* assister (**on** à)
▸**sit on** *vt insep Fam* (**a**) *(not deal with)* laisser traîner (**b**) *(repress)* rembarrer
▸**sit out 1** *vt sep* (**a**) *(not participate in)* ne pas participer à (**b**) *(endure)* attendre la fin de
2 *vi (in garden)* s'asseoir dehors
▸**sit through** *vt insep* rester jusqu'au bout de
▸**sit up** *vi* (**a**) *(straighten one's back)* se redresser; *(from lying position)* s'asseoir; *Fig* **to make sb s. up (and take notice)** secouer qn (**b**) *(not go to bed)* veiller
sitar ['sɪtɑː(r)] *n* sitar *m*
sitcom ['sɪtkɒm] *n* sitcom *m*
site [saɪt] **1** *n* (**a**) *(of building)* emplacement *m*; *(archaeological)* site *m* (**b**) **(building) s.** chantier *m* (de construction) (**c**) *Comput (on Internet)* site *m*
2 *vt* situer
sit-in ['sɪtɪn] *n* occupation *f* des locaux
sitting ['sɪtɪŋ] **1** *n (of committee, for portrait)* séance *f*; *(for meal)* service *m*; **at one s.** d'un trait; **s. room** *(in house)* salon *m*
2 *adj* (**a**) *(seated)* assis(e); *Fam Fig* **s. duck** or **target** cible *f* facile (**b**) *(current) Pol* **s. member** député *m* en exercice; **s. tenant** locataire *mf* dans les lieux
situate ['sɪtjʊeɪt] *vt* situer
situated ['sɪtjʊeɪtɪd] *adj* situé(e)
situation [sɪtjʊ'eɪʃən] *n* (**a**) *(circumstances)* situation *f*; **s. comedy** *(on TV)* sitcom *m* (**b**) *(job)* **situations vacant/wanted** *(in advertisements)* offres *fpl*/demandes *fpl* d'emploi; (**c**) *(location)* emplacement *m*
sit-up ['sɪtʌp] *n* **to do sit-ups** faire des abdominaux

six [sɪks] **1** *n* six *m inv*; *Fam* **it's s. of one and a half a dozen of the other** c'est kif-kif; **at sixes and sevens** sens dessus dessous; *Fam* **to knock sb for s.** étendre qn
2 *adj* six; *see also* **eight**
six-figure ['sɪks'fɪgə(r)] *adj* **a s. sum** une somme à six chiffres
six-pack ['sɪkspæk] *n* (**a**) *(of beer)* pack *m* de six (**b**) *Fam Hum (stomach muscles)* **to have a s.** avoir les abdos en tablette de chocolat
sixpence ['sɪkspəns] *n Br Formerly* = ancienne pièce de 6 pence
six-shooter ['sɪksʃuːtə(r)] *n* six-coups *m inv*
sixteen [sɪks'tiːn] **1** *n* seize *m inv*
2 *adj* seize; *see also* **eight**
sixteenth [sɪks'tiːnθ] **1** *n* (**a**) *(fraction)* seizième *m* (**b**) *(in series)* seizième *mf* (**c**) *(of month)* seize *m inv*
2 *adj* seizième; *see also* **eighth**
sixth [sɪksθ] **1** *n* (**a**) *(fraction)* sixième *m* (**b**) *(in series)* sixième *mf* (**c**) *(of month)* six *m inv*
2 *adj* sixième; *Br Sch* **the s. form** ≃ les classes *fpl* de première et de terminale; *Br Sch* **s. former** ≃ élève *mf* de première ou de terminale; **s. sense** sixième sens *m*; *see also* **eighth**
sixtieth ['sɪkstɪθ] **1** *n* (**a**) *(fraction)* soixantième *m* (**b**) *(in series)* soixantième *mf*
2 *adj* soixantième
sixty ['sɪkstɪ] **1** *n* soixante *m inv*
2 *adj* soixante; *see also* **eighty**
size [saɪz] *n (of person, clothes)* taille *f*; *(of shoe)* pointure *f*; *(of place, object)* dimensions *fpl*; *(of country)* superficie *f*; *(of problem, undertaking)* ampleur *f*; *Fam* **that's about the s. of it** c'est à peu près ça; **s. 10 shoes** ≃ des chaussures du 44; **what s. do you take?** *(of clothes)* quelle taille faites-vous?; *(of shoes)* quelle est votre pointure?, vous chaussez du combien?; **to try sth (on) for s.** essayer qch pour voir si la taille convient
▸**size up** *vt sep (person)* jauger; *(situation)* évaluer
sizeable ['saɪzəbəl] *adj* non négligeable; *(improvement)* net (nette)
sizzle ['sɪzəl] **1** *n* grésillement *m*
2 *vi* grésiller
skanky ['skæŋkɪ] *adj Fam (ugly)* hyper moche; *(dirty)* crado *inv*
skate¹ [skeɪt] *n (fish)* raie *f*
skate² **1** *n* patin *m*; *Fam Fig* **to get one's skates on** se dépêcher
2 *vi (on ice skates)* faire du patin à glace; *(on roller skates)* faire du patin à roulettes; *(on roller blades)* faire du roller; *Fig* **to s. round sth** tourner autour de qch
▸**skate over** *vt insep (deal with superficially)* survoler
skateboard ['skeɪtbɔːd] *n* planche *f* à roulettes
skateboarder ['skeɪtbɔːdə(r)] *n* skateur(euse) *m,f*
skatepark ['skeɪtpɑːk] *n* skatepark *m*
skater ['skeɪtə(r)] *n (on ice-skates)* patineur(euse) *m,f*; *Fam (on skateboard)* skateur(euse) *m,f*
skating ['skeɪtɪŋ] *n* patinage *m*; **s. rink** *(for ice skating)* patinoire *f*; *(for roller skating)* piste *f*
skeletal ['skelɪtəl] *adj* squelettique
skeleton ['skelɪtən] *n* (**a**) *(of person)* squelette *m*; *(of building)* charpente *f*; *Fig* **to have a s. in the cupboard** *or* **closet** avoir un secret honteux; **s. staff/crew** personnel *m*/équipage *m* réduit; **s. key** passepartout *m inv* (**b**) *Sport* skeleton *m*
skeptic, skeptical *etc Am* = **sceptic, sceptical** *etc*

sketch [sketʃ] **1** *n* (**a**) *(drawing, description)* croquis *m*; **s. pad** bloc *m* à dessin (**b**) *(on stage, TV)* sketch *m*
2 *vt also Fig* esquisser
▸**sketch in** *vt sep also Fig* esquisser
▸**sketch out** *vt sep* ébaucher
sketchbook ['sketʃbʊk] *n* carnet *m* de croquis
sketchily ['sketʃɪlɪ] *adv* vaguement
sketchy ['sketʃɪ] *adj* vague (**about** à propos de)
skew [skjuː] **1** *n* **on the s.** de travers
2 *vt (distort)* fausser
skewer ['skjuːə(r)] **1** *n* brochette *f*
2 *vt* embrocher
ski [skiː] **1** *n* ski *m*; **s. boots** chaussures *fpl* de ski; **s. instructor** moniteur(trice) *m,f* de ski; **s. jump** saut *m* à skis; **s. jumper** sauteur(euse) *m,f* à ski; **s. lift** remontée *f* mécanique; **s. pants** fuseau *m*; **s. resort** station *f* de ski; **s. run** *or* **slope** piste *f* de ski; **s. stick** bâton *m* de ski
2 *vi (pt & pp skied)* skier, faire du ski
skid [skɪd] **1** *n* (**a**) *(of car)* dérapage *m*; **to go into a s.** faire un dérapage (**b**) *(idioms) Fam* **to put the skids under sb/sth** faire accélérer qn/qch; *Fam* **to be on the skids** battre de l'aile; *Am Fam* **to be on s. row** être à la rue
2 *vi (pt & pp skidded)* déraper
skier ['skiːə(r)] *n* skieur(euse) *m,f*
skiing ['skiːɪŋ] *n* ski *m*; **to go s.** aller faire du ski; **s. instructor** moniteur(trice) *m,f* de ski
skilful, *Am* **skillful** ['skɪlfʊl] *adj* habile
skilfully, *Am* **skillfully** ['skɪlfʊlɪ] *adv* habilement
skill [skɪl] *n (ability)* qualités *fpl*; *(technique)* compétence *f*, connaissances *fpl*
skilled [skɪld] *adj (person, work)* qualifié(e); **to be s. in doing sth** être habile à faire qch; **s. worker** ouvrier(-ère) *m,f* qualifié(e)
skillet ['skɪlɪt] *n Am* poêle *f*
skillful, skillfully *Am* = **skilful, skilfully**
skim [skɪm] *(pt & pp skimmed)* **1** *vt* (**a**) *(milk)* écrémer; *(soup)* écumer (**b**) *(surface)* effleurer; **to s. stones on water** faire des ricochets (**c**) *Fam* **to s. a credit card** = récupérer illégalement les données d'une carte bancaire lors d'une transaction grâce à un lecteur caché
2 *vi* **to s. along** *or* **over the ground** voler au ras du sol; **to s. over the water** raser la surface de l'eau
▸**skim off** *vt sep (fat, cream)* enlever; *Fig (money)* ponctionner
▸**skim through** *vt insep (novel, document)* lire en diagonale
skimmed milk ['skɪmd'mɪlk], *Am* **skim milk** ['skɪm'mɪlk] *n* lait *m* écrémé
skimming ['skɪmɪŋ] *n Fam (credit card fraud)* = fraude consistant à récupérer les données d'une carte bancaire lors d'une transaction grâce à un lecteur caché
skimp [skɪmp] **1** *vt* lésiner sur; *(work)* bâcler
2 *vi* **to s. on sth** lésiner sur qch
skimpy ['skɪmpɪ] *adj (meal)* maigre; *(clothes)* étriqué(e)
skin [skɪn] **1** *n* (**a**) *(of person, animal, fruit, on milk, sauce)* peau *f*; **to be all s. and bone** n'avoir que la peau et les os; *Fam* **to jump out of one's s.** sauter au plafond; **by the s. of one's teeth** de justesse; **to save one's (own) s.** sauver sa peau; *Fam* **to get under sb's s.** taper sur les nerfs de qn; *Fam* **it's no s. off my nose** je m'en balance; **s. cancer** cancer *m* de la peau; **s. complaint** problème *m* de peau; **s. cream** crème *f* pour la peau; **s. disease** maladie *f* de peau; **s. diving** plongée *f* sous-marine; *Am Fam* **s. flick** *(porn film)*

film *m* porno; *Med* **s. graft** greffe *f* de peau; **s. patch** timbre *m* transdermique (**b**) *Fam (skinhead)* skin mf
2 *vt (pt & pp* **skinned**) *(animal)* écorcher; *(tomato)* peler; **to s. one's knees** s'écorcher les genoux
▸**skin up** *vi Br very Fam* rouler un joint
skinflint ['skɪnflɪnt] *n Fam* radin(e) *m,f*
skinhead ['skɪnhed] *n* skinhead *mf*
skinny ['skɪnɪ] *adj* maigre
skint [skɪnt] *adj Br Fam* fauché(e)
skintight ['skɪntaɪt] *adj* moulant(e)
skip¹ [skɪp] **1** *n (jump)* saut *m*
2 *vt (pt & pp* **skipped**) *(meal, page, stage)* sauter
3 *vi (of lambs, children)* gambader; *(with rope)* sauter à la corde
skip² *n (for rubbish)* benne *f*
skipper ['skɪpə(r)] **1** *n (of ship, team)* capitaine *m*
2 *vt Fam* commander
skipping ['skɪpɪŋ] *n* saut *m* à la corde; **s. rope** corde *f* à sauter
skirmish ['skɜːmɪʃ] **1** *n Mil* escarmouche *f*; *Fig* accrochage *m*
2 *vi* s'engager dans une escarmouche
skirt [skɜːt] **1** *n* jupe *f*
2 *vt (village, hill)* contourner; **to s. (a)round a problem** contourner un problème
skirting board ['skɜːtɪŋbɔːd] *n Br* plinthe *f*
skit [skɪt] *n* satire *f*
skittish ['skɪtɪʃ] *adj* (**a**) *(nervous)* nerveux(euse) (**b**) *(playful)* espiègle
skittle ['skɪtəl] *n* quille *f*
skive [skaɪv] *vi Br Fam* tirer au flanc
▸**skive off** *vi Br Fam* s'esquiver
skiver ['skaɪvə(r)] *n Br Fam* tire-au-flanc *m inv*
skivvy ['skɪvɪ] *(pl* **skivvies**) *n Br Pej* bonne *f* à tout faire
skulduggery [skʌl'dʌgərɪ] *n* magouille *f*
skulk [skʌlk] *vi* rôder
skull [skʌl] *n* crâne *m*; **s. and crossbones** tête *f* de mort
skullcap ['skʌlkæp] *n* calotte *f*
skunk [skʌŋk] *n (animal)* moufette *f*, *Can* bête *f* puante; *Fam Pej (person)* mufle *m*
sky [skaɪ] *(pl* **skies**) *n* ciel *m*; *Fam* **the s.'s the limit** tout est possible; *Fam* **to praise sb to the skies** porter qn aux nues; **s. high** *(price, costs)* astronomique; **s. marshal** = policier armé embarqué dans un avion de transport de passagers afin d'assurer la sécurité de ces derniers
sky-blue [skaɪ'bluː] *adj* bleu ciel *inv*
skydiver ['skaɪdaɪvə(r)] *n* parachutiste *mf (qui pratique la chute libre)*
skydiving ['skaɪdaɪvɪŋ] *n* parachutisme *m (en chute libre)*
skylark ['skaɪlɑːk] *n* alouette *f* des champs
skylight ['skaɪlaɪt] *n* lucarne *f* faîtière
skyline ['skaɪlaɪn] *n (horizon)* horizon *m*; *(of city)* silhouette *f*
skyscraper ['skaɪskreɪpə(r)] *n* gratte-ciel *m inv*; *Comput* **s. ad** skyscraper *m*
slab [slæb] *n* (**a**) *(of stone, concrete)* dalle *f*; *(of cake)* tranche *f*; *(of meat)* pavé *m*; *(of chocolate)* plaque *f* (**b**) *(in mortuary)* table *f* d'autopsie
slack [slæk] **1** *adj* (**a**) *(not tight)* mou (molle); **trade is s.** le commerce marche mal; **in s. periods** en période creuse (**b**) *(careless)* négligent(e)
2 *n* **to take up the s.** *(in rope)* tendre la corde; *Fig* prendre le relais
3 *vi Fam* se relâcher

▸**slack off** *vi (of rain)* se calmer; *(of trade, demand)* se ralentir
slacken ['slækən] **1** *vt (pace)* ralentir; *(rope)* détendre
2 *vi (of person, rope)* se relâcher; *(of speed)* se ralentir; *(of storm, wind)* se calmer; *(of energy, enthusiasm)* retomber
▸**slacken off** *vi (of rain)* se calmer; *(of trade, demand)* se ralentir
slacker ['slækə(r)] *n Fam* flemmard(e) *m,f*
slackness ['slæknɪs] *n* (**a**) *(negligence)* négligence *f*; *(laziness)* fainéantise *f* (**b**) *(of rope)* mou *m* (**c**) *(of business)* stagnation *f*
slacks [slæks] *npl Am (trousers)* pantalon *m*
slag [slæg] *n* (**a**) *(from coalmine)* scories *fpl*; **s. heap** terril *m* (**b**) *Br very Fam Pej (woman)* salope *f*
▸**slag off** *(pt & pp* **slagged**) *vt sep Br Fam (criticize)* débiner
slain [sleɪn] **1** *npl* **the s.** les morts *mpl*
2 *pp of* **slay**
slake [sleɪk] *vt Lit* **to s. one's thirst** étancher sa soif
slalom ['slɑːləm] *n* slalom *m*
slam [slæm] **1** *n (of door)* claquement *m*
2 *vt (pt & pp* **slammed**) (**a**) *(door)* claquer; *(lid, drawer)* fermer violemment; **to s. the door in sb's face** claquer la porte au nez de qn; **to s. sth down** flanquer qch (**b**) *Fam (criticize)* éreinter
3 *vi (of door)* claquer; **to s. on the brakes** freiner à fond
slander ['slɑːndə(r)] **1** *n* calomnie *f*
2 *vt* calomnier
slanderous ['slɑːndərəs] *adj* calomnieux(euse)
slang [slæŋ] **1** *n* argot *m*
2 *vt Fam (insult)* injurier
slanging match ['slæŋɪŋ'mætʃ] *n* échange *m* d'insultes
slant [slɑːnt] **1** *n* (**a**) *(slope)* pente *f* (**b**) *(point of view)* perspective *f*; *(bias)* parti *m* pris; **to put a s. on sth** présenter qch d'une manière partiale
2 *vt* (**a**) *(set at angle)* incliner (**b**) *(bias)* présenter avec parti pris
3 *vi (slope)* être incliné(e)
slanting ['slɑːntɪŋ] *adj (roof)* en pente; *(writing)* penché(e)
slap [slæp] **1** *n (with hand)* claque *f*; *also Fig* **a s. in the face** gifle; **to get a s. on the wrist** *(reprimand)* se faire taper sur les doigts
2 *adv Fam* **s. (bang) in the middle** en plein milieu
3 *vt (pt & pp* **slapped**) *(person)* donner une claque à; **to s. sb's face, to s. sb on the face** gifler qn; **to s. sb on the back** donner une tape dans le dos à qn; *Fig* **to s. sb down** remettre qn à sa place; **to s. some paint on sth** passer un coup de peinture sur qch
slapdash ['slæpdæʃ] *adj (work)* fait n'importe comment *ou* à la va-vite; *(person)* négligent(e)
slapper ['slæpə(r)] *n Br Fam* pouffiasse *f*, traînée *f*
slapstick ['slæpstɪk] *n* **s. (comedy)** comédie *f* bouffonne
slap-up ['slæpʌp] *adj Br Fam* **s. meal** gueuleton *m*
slash [slæʃ] **1** *n* (**a**) *(cut)* coupure *f*, balafre *f* (**b**) *Typ* barre *f* oblique (**c**) *Br very Fam* **to have a s.** pisser un coup
2 *vt (cut)* taillader, balafrer; *(reduce)* réduire considérablement; **prices slashed** *(sign)* prix sacrifiés
slat [slæt] *n* latte *f*
slate [sleɪt] **1** *n* (**a**) *(stone)* ardoise *f*; **s. grey** ardoise *m inv*; **s. quarry** ardoisière *f* (**b**) *(idioms)* **put it on**

the s. mettez-le-moi sur mon ardoise; **to wipe the s. clean** faire table rase
2 *vt Fam (criticize)* éreinter
slaughter ['slɔːtə(r)] **1** *n (of animals)* abattage *m*; *(of people)* massacre *m*
2 *vt (animals)* abattre; *(people)* massacrer; *Fam (defeat heavily)* massacrer
slaughterhouse ['slɔːtəhaʊs] *n* abattoir *m*
Slav [slɑːv] *n* Slave *mf*
slave [sleɪv] **1** *n* esclave *mf*; *Fam Fig* **s. driver** négrier *m*; **s. labour** travail *m* de forçat; **s. trade** commerce *m* des esclaves
2 *vi* trimer (**over** sur); **I've been slaving over a hot stove all day** j'ai passé ma journée aux fourneaux
slaver ['slævə(r)] *vi* baver
slavery ['sleɪvərɪ] *n* esclavage *m*
Slavic ['slɑːvɪk] *adj* slave
slavish ['sleɪvɪʃ] *adj* servile
Slavonic [slə'vɒnɪk] *adj* slave
slay [sleɪ] (*pt* **slew** [sluː], *pp* **slain** [sleɪn]) *vt Lit (kill)* tuer
sleaze [sliːz] *n Fam* (**a**) *(immorality)* côté *m* scabreux (**b**) *(in politics)* scandales *mpl*
sleazy ['sliːzɪ] *adj Fam (affair, place)* sordide; *(person)* louche
sledge [sledʒ], *Am* **sled** [sled] **1** *n* luge *f*; *(for transporting)* traîneau *m*
2 *vi (Am pt & pp* **sledded**) faire de la luge
sledgehammer ['sledʒhæmə(r)] *n* masse *f*; *Fig* **to use a s. to crack a nut** avoir recours à des moyens démesurés
sleek [sliːk] *adj (hair)* lisse et brillant(e); *(manner)* mielleux(euse)
▸**sleek down** *vt sep* **to s. down one's hair** se lisser les cheveux
sleep [sliːp] **1** *n* (**a**) *(rest)* sommeil *m*; **to go to s.** s'endormir; **to put sb to s.** *(anaesthetize)* endormir qn; **to put an animal to s.** *(kill)* faire piquer un animal; *Fig* **to send sb to s.** *(bore)* endormir qn; **I won't lose any s. over it** cela ne va pas m'empêcher de dormir; **to walk in one's s.** être somnambule; **to talk in one's s.** parler en dormant; **my foot has gone to s.** je ne sens plus mon pied (**b**) *(in eye)* **to have s. in one's eyes** avoir les yeux chassieux
2 *vi (pt & pp* **slept** [slept]) dormir; *Euph* **to s. with sb** coucher avec qn; **I slept through the alarm** je n'ai pas entendu le réveil; **I'll s. on it** la nuit porte conseil; **to s. rough** dormir dehors *ou* dans la rue
3 *vt* **the flat sleeps four** on peut dormir à quatre dans l'appartement; **I haven't slept a wink all night** je n'ai pas fermé l'œil de la nuit
▸**sleep around** *vi Fam* coucher à droite et à gauche
▸**sleep in** *vi* ne pas se réveiller à l'heure
▸**sleep off** *vt sep* **to s. off a hangover** cuver son vin
▸**sleep together** *vi* coucher ensemble
sleeper ['sliːpə(r)] *n* (**a**) *(person)* dormeur(euse) *m,f*; **to be a light/heavy s.** avoir le sommeil léger/lourd (**b**) *Rail (train)* train-couchettes *m*; *Br (on track)* traverse *f*, *Can* dormant *m*
sleepily ['sliːpɪlɪ] *adv* d'un air endormi
sleeping ['sliːpɪŋ] **1** **s. arrangements** couchage *m*; **s. bag** sac *m* de couchage; **s. car** *(on train)* wagon-lit *m*; **s. pill** somnifère *m*
2 *adj* endormi(e); *Prov* **let s. dogs lie** ne réveillez pas le chat qui dort; **s. partner** *(in company)* commanditaire *m*; *Br* **s. policeman** *(in road)* ralentisseur *m*
sleepless ['sliːpləs] *adj* **to have a s. night** passer une nuit blanche, ne pas fermer l'œil de la nuit

sleepover ['sliːpəʊvə(r)] *n* = soirée entre fillettes, où les invitées restent dormir chez leur hôte
sleepwalk ['sliːpwɔːk] *vi* être somnambule
sleepwalker ['sliːpwɔːkə(r)] *n* somnambule *mf*
sleepy ['sliːpɪ] *adj* somnolent(e); **to be** *or* **feel s.** avoir sommeil
sleet [sliːt] **1** *n* neige *f* fondue
2 *vi* **it's sleeting** il tombe de la neige fondue
sleeve [sliːv] *n* (**a**) *(of shirt, jacket)* manche *f*; *Fig* **he's still got something up his s.** il n'a pas encore dit son dernier mot (**b**) *(of record)* pochette *f*
sleeveless ['sliːvlɪs] *adj* sans manches
sleigh [sleɪ] *n* traîneau *m*
sleight [slaɪt] *n* **s. of hand** tour *m* de passe-passe
slender ['slendə(r)] *adj* (**a**) *(person, figure)* svelte; *(waist)* fin(e) (**b**) *(hope)* mince; *(income)* maigre; *(majority)* faible; **of s. means** qui a peu de moyens
slept [slept] *pt & pp of* **sleep**
sleuth [sluːθ] *n Fam* limier *m*
slew [sluː] *pt of* **slay**
slice [slaɪs] **1** *n (of bread, meat, cake)* tranche *f*; *(of pizza)* part *f*; *(of cheese)* lamelle *f*; *(of salami)* rondelle *f*; *Fig* **a s. of the profits** une part des bénéfices
2 *vt* (**a**) *(bread, meat, cake)* couper en tranches; *(cheese)* couper en lamelles; *(salami)* couper en rondelles; **to s. sth in two** *or* **in half** couper qch en deux (**b**) *(in sport)* slicer
▸**slice off** *vt sep* couper
▸**slice through** *vt insep* trancher
▸**slice up** *vt sep* couper en tranches
sliced bread ['slaɪst'bred] *n* pain *m* en tranches; *Fam* **it's the best thing since s.** on n'a rien fait de mieux depuis l'invention du fil à couper le beurre
slick [slɪk] **1** *adj* (**a**) *(campaign, event)* bien mené(e) (**b**) *Pej (reply, person, manner)* habile (**c**) *(surface, tyre)* lisse
2 *n (oil)* **s. marée** *f* noire
▸**slick back** *vt sep* **to s. one's hair back** se lisser les cheveux
slide [slaɪd] **1** *n* (**a**) *(fall) (in prices, popularity)* chute *f*; *Math* **s. rule** règle *f* à calcul (**b**) *(in playground)* toboggan *m* (**c**) *(for microscope)* lame *f*; *(photographic)* diapositive *f*; **s. projector** projecteur *m* de diapositives; **s. show** diaporama *m* (**d**) *Br (for hair)* barrette *f*
2 *vt (pt & pp* **slid** [slɪd]) glisser; **s. the lid off** faites glisser le couvercle
3 *vi* (**a**) *(slip) (of person)* glisser; *(of door, hatch)* coulisser; **the door slid open** la porte coulissante s'est ouverte; *Fig* **to let things s.** laisser les choses se dégrader; **to s. down a rope** glisser le long d'une corde (**b**) *(move quietly)* se glisser
sliding ['slaɪdɪŋ] *adj* coulissant(e); **s. door** porte *f* coulissante; **s. scale** échelle *f* mobile
slight [slaɪt] **1** *adj* (**a**) *(small, unimportant)* léger(ère); **not the slightest danger/interest** pas le moindre danger/intérêt; **not in the slightest** pas du tout (**b**) *(person)* menu(e)
2 *n (affront)* affront *m*
3 *vt* blesser
slightly ['slaɪtlɪ] *adv* (**a**) *(to a small degree)* légèrement (**b**) **s. built** menu(e)
slim [slɪm] **1** *adj (person)* mince, svelte; *(book, chance, hope)* mince; *(majority)* faible
2 *vi (pt & pp* **slimmed**) faire un régime
▸**slim down 1** *vt sep Fig (budget, company)* réduire
2 *vi (of person)* perdre du poids; *Fig (of company)* réduire ses effectifs

slime [slaɪm] *n (mud)* vase *f; (of snail, slug)* bave *f*
slimmer ['slɪmə(r)] *n* personne *f* qui fait un régime amaigrissant
slimming ['slɪmɪŋ] *n* **s. can be bad for you** les régimes amaigrissants peuvent être dangereux pour la santé; **s. diet** régime *m* amaigrissant; **s. product** produit *m* amaigrissant
slimy ['slaɪmɪ] *adj (frog, snail)* visqueux(euse); *Pej (person)* mielleux(euse)
sling [slɪŋ] **1** *n* (**a**) *(for injured arm)* écharpe *f*; **he had his arm in a s.** il avait le bras en écharpe (**b**) *(weapon)* fronde *f*
  2 *vt (pt & pp* **slung** [slʌŋ]*) (throw)* lancer; **to s. sth over one's shoulder** mettre qch sur son épaule; *Br Fam Fig* **s. your hook! dégage!**
▸**sling out** *vt sep Fam (throw away)* balancer; *(person)* vider
▸**slingshot** ['slɪŋʃɒt] *n Am* lance-pierres *m inv*
slink [slɪŋk] *(pt & pp* **slunk** [slʌŋk]*) vi* **to s. off** *or* **away** s'éclipser
slinky ['slɪŋkɪ] *adj (dress)* long (longue) et sexy
slip [slɪp] **1** *n* (**a**) *(fall)* chute *f; (of land)* glissement *m; (in prices, standards)* chute *f* (**b**) *(error)* erreur *f*; **a s. of the pen/tongue** un lapsus (**c**) **to give sb the s.** semer qn (**d**) *(of paper)* bout *m* de papier; *(printed)* bordereau *m* (**e**) *Br* **a s. of a girl** une gamine; **a s. of a lad** un gamin (**f**) *Br Aut* **s. road** bretelle *f* (**g**) *(garment)* combinaison *f*; **(pillow) s.** taie *f* d'oreiller
  2 *vt (pt & pp* **slipped**) (**a**) *(escape)* **her name has slipped my mind** son nom m'échappe; **the ship slipped its moorings** le bateau a quitté son mouillage (**b**) *(put)* glisser; **to s. sth into the conversation** glisser qch dans la conversation; **to s. a coat on/off** enfiler/quitter un manteau (**c**) **to s. a disc** se faire une hernie discale
  3 *vi* (**a**) *(slide) (of person, foot)* glisser; *(of prices, popularity)* chuter; **to s. from sb's hands** *or* **grasp** glisser des mains de qn; *Fig* **to s. through sb's fingers** glisser entre les doigts de qn; **to let one's guard/concentration s.** relâcher sa vigilance/concentration (**b**) *(move quickly)* **to s. into sth** *(bed, room, shoes)* se glisser dans qch; *(clothes)* enfiler qch; **to s. out of sth** *(clothes)* quitter qch (**c**) *(make mistake)* faire une erreur; **you're slipping!** tu baisses! (**d**) **to let sth s.** *(words, information)* lâcher qch
▸**slip away** *vi (leave)* s'éclipser
▸**slip by** *vi (of time, years)* passer vite
▸**slip out** *vi (escape)* s'échapper; **to s. out to the shop** faire un saut au magasin
▸**slip through** *vi (of mistake)* échapper à l'attention
▸**slip up** *vi (make mistake)* se planter
slip-on ['slɪpɒn] **1** *n Fam* **slip-ons** chaussures *fpl* sans lacets
  2 *adj (shoes)* sans lacets
slipper ['slɪpə(r)] *n* pantoufle *f*
slippery ['slɪpərɪ] *adj (road)* glissant(e); *(person)* fuyant(e); *Fig* **to be on a s. slope** être sur une pente savonneuse
slippy ['slɪpɪ] *adj* glissant(e)
slipshod ['slɪpʃɒd] *adj (work)* bâclé(e)
slipstream ['slɪpstriːm] *n* sillage *m*
slip-up ['slɪpʌp] *n* bourde *f*
slipway ['slɪpweɪ] *n Naut (for repairs)* cale *f* de construction; *(for launching)* cale *f* de lancement
slit [slɪt] **1** *n* fente *f*
  2 *vt (pt & pp* **slit**) fendre; **to s. sth open** ouvrir qch; **to s. sb's throat** couper la gorge à qn
slither ['slɪðə(r)] *vi* glisser

sliver ['slɪvə(r)] *n (of ham, cheese)* mince tranche *f; (of wood, glass)* éclat *m*
slob [slɒb] *n Fam (untidy person)* dégueulasse *mf; (lazy person)* flemmard(e) *m,f*
slobber ['slɒbə(r)] *vi* baver
sloe [sləʊ] *n (fruit)* prunelle *f*; **s. gin** alcool *m* de prunelles
slog [slɒg] *Fam* **1** *n* **it was a bit of a s.** ça a été dur; **it's a long s.** *(walk)* ça fait une trotte
  2 *vi (pt & pp* **slogged**) *(work hard)* trimer, bosser (**at** sur)
slogan ['sləʊgən] *n* slogan *m*
slo-mo ['sləʊməʊ] *adj Fam (abbr* **slow-motion***)* au ralenti
sloop [sluːp] *n (ship)* sloop *m*
slop [slɒp] **1** *n* (**a**) *(pig food)* pâtée *f* (**b**) *Fam Pej (sentimentality)* sensiblerie *f*
  2 *vt (pt & pp* **slopped**) renverser
  3 *vi* se renverser
slope [sləʊp] **1** *n* pente *f*
  2 *vi* être en pente
▸**slope off** *vi Fam* se tailler
sloping ['sləʊpɪŋ] *adj (roof, ground)* en pente; *(handwriting)* penché(e); **s. shoulders** épaules *fpl* tombantes
sloppy ['slɒpɪ] *adj* (**a**) *(careless) (person)* sans soin; *(attitude)* négligé(e); *(work)* bâclé(e) (**b**) *Fam Pej (sentimental)* sentimental(e)
slosh [slɒʃ] *vi (of liquid)* clapoter; *(spill)* se renverser
sloshed [slɒʃt] *adj Fam (drunk)* bourré(e); **to get s.** prendre une cuite
slot [slɒt] **1** *n* (**a**) *(in box, machine)* fente *f; (in schedule, list)* créneau *m*; **s. machine** *(for vending)* distributeur *m* automatique; *(for gambling)* machine *f* à sous
  2 *vt (pt & pp* **slotted**) *(part)* insérer
▸**slot in 1** *vt sep (into schedule)* caser
  2 *vi (of part)* rentrer; *(into team)* s'intégrer
sloth [sləʊθ] *n* (**a**) *(laziness)* paresse *f* (**b**) *(animal)* paresseux *m*
slothful ['sləʊθfʊl] *adj* paresseux(euse)
slouch [slaʊtʃ] **1** *n Fam* **he's no s.** il n'est pas empoté
  2 *vi (on chair)* être avachi(e); **she slouched out of the room** elle est sortie de la pièce en traînant les pieds; **don't s.!** tiens-toi droit!
slough [slʌf] *vt* **to s. its skin** *(of reptile)* muer
Slovak ['sləʊvæk] **1** *n* (**a**) *(person)* Slovaque *mf* (**b**) *(language)* slovaque *m*
  2 *adj* slovaque
Slovakia [sləʊ'vækɪə] *n* la Slovaquie
Slovakian [sləʊ'vækɪən] **1** *n* Slovaque *mf*
  2 *adj* slovaque
Slovene [sləʊ'viːn] **1** *n* (**a**) *(person)* Slovène *mf* (**b**) *(language)* slovène *m*
  2 *adj* slovène
Slovenia [sləʊ'viːnɪə] *n* la Slovénie
Slovenian [sləʊ'viːnɪən] **1** *n* Slovène *mf*
  2 *adj* slovène
slovenly ['slʌvənlɪ] *adj (untidy)* négligé(e); *(careless)* négligent(e); *(unkempt)* débraillé(e)
slow [sləʊ] **1** *adj (not fast, stupid)* lent(e); **business is s.** les affaires tournent au ralenti; **my watch is s.** ma montre a du retard; **to be s. to do sth** être lent à faire qch; **to be s. off the mark** *(in race)* être lent à démarrer; *(to understand)* être lent à la détente; *Culin* **in a s. oven** à four doux; **we're making s. progress** nous avançons lentement; **she's a s. worker** elle travaille lentement; *Aut* **s. lane** voie *f* lente; *Cin & TV*

(in) s. motion (au) ralenti *m*; s. train (train *m*) omnibus *m*
  2 *adv* lentement
  3 *vi* ralentir
▸slow down, slow up *vt sep & vi* ralentir
slowcoach ['sləʊkəʊtʃ] *n Br Fam* lambin(e) *m,f*
slowly ['sləʊli] *adv* lentement; s. but surely lentement mais sûrement
slowness ['sləʊnɪs] *n* lenteur *f*
slowpoke ['sləʊpəʊk] *n Am Fam* lambin(e) *m,f*
slow-witted ['sləʊ'wɪtɪd] *adj* à l'esprit lent
slow-worm ['sləʊwɜːm] *n* orvet *m*
SLR [esel'ɑː(r)] *n Phot (abbr* single-lens reflex) reflex *m* monoculaire
sludge [slʌdʒ] *n* vase *f*, boue *f*
slug [slʌg] 1 *n* (a) *(mollusc)* limace *f* (b) *Fam (bullet)* balle *f* (c) *Fam (of drink)* goutte *f*
  2 *vt (pt & pp* slugged) *Fam (hit)* cogner
sluggish ['slʌgɪʃ] *adj (person) (lazy)* paresseux(euse); *(not energetic)* léthargique; *(business, market)* au ralenti
sluice [sluːs] 1 *n* (a) *(channel)* canal *m* (b) *(sluicegate)* écluse *f*
  2 *vt* to s. sth down/out laver qch à grande eau
sluicegate ['sluːsgeɪt] *n* écluse *f*
slum [slʌm] 1 *n (district)* quartier *m* délabré; *(shantytown)* bidonville *m*; *(house)* taudis *m*
  2 *vt (pt & pp* slummed) to s. it s'encanailler
slumber ['slʌmbə(r)] 1 *n* (a) *Lit* sommeil *m* (b) *Am* s. party = soirée entre fillettes, où les invitées restent dormir chez leur hôte
  2 *vi* dormir
slump [slʌmp] 1 *n (in prices, sales)* effondrement *m*; *(economic depression)* crise *f* (économique)
  2 *vi (of person, economy, prices)* s'effondrer
slung [slʌŋ] *pt & pp of* sling
slunk [slʌŋk] *pt & pp of* slink
slur [slɜː(r)] 1 *n* (a) *(insult)* insulte *f*; to cast a s. on sb's reputation entacher la réputation de qn (b) *(in speech)* there was a s. in her voice elle avait du mal à articuler
  2 *vt (pt & pp* slurred) mal articuler
slurp [slɜːp] *vt & vi (drink)* boire bruyamment; *(eat)* manger bruyamment
slush [slʌʃ] *n* (a) *(snow)* neige *f* fondue (b) *Pol* s. fund caisse *f* noire (c) *Fam Pej (sentimentality)* sensiblerie *f*
slushy [slʌʃɪ] *adj* (a) *(snow)* fondu(e) (b) *Fam Pej (film, book)* à l'eau de rose
slut [slʌt] *n (promiscuous woman)* salope *f*
sluttish ['slʌtɪʃ] *adj (slovenly)* négligé(e)
sly [slaɪ] 1 *adj* (a) *(cunning)* rusé(e) (b) *(dishonest)* sournois(e) (c) *(mischievous)* espiègle
  2 *n* on the s. en douce
smack [smæk] 1 *n* (a) *(blow)* claque *f*; *(on bottom)* fessée *f*; *(sound)* claquement *m*; a s. in the face une gifle (b) *Fam (heroin)* héro *f*
  2 *adv Fam* to bump s. into a tree rentrer en plein dans un arbre
  3 *vt (hit)* donner une claque à; *(on bottom)* donner une fessée à; to s. one's lips faire claquer ses lèvres
▸smack of *vt insep (suggest)* avoir des relents de
smacker ['smækə(r)] *n Fam* (a) *(kiss)* grosse bise *f* (b) 50 smackers *(pounds)* 50 livres; *(dollars)* 50 dollars
small [smɔːl] 1 *adj* (a) *(not big)* petit(e); to make sth smaller rapetisser qch; *Fig* it made me feel s. *(inconsequential)* je me suis senti tout petit; the s. hours le

petit matin; *Journ* s. ads petites annonces *fpl*; s. arms armes *fpl* portatives; s. business petite entreprise *f*; s. businessman petit entrepreneur *m*; s. letters *(not capitals)* minuscules *fpl*; s. talk banalités *fpl*; to make s. talk échanger des banalités (b) *(not important)* peu important(e); it's s. wonder that... ce n'est pas très étonnant que...; in a s. way à sa façon; *Fam* to be s. beer *(of money)* être que dalle; s. change petite monnaie *f*; s. fry menu fretin *m*
  2 *adv (chop)* menu; *(write)* petit; to think s. voir petit
  3 *n* (a) the s. of the back la chute des reins (b) *Fam* smalls *(underwear)* sous-vêtements *mpl*
smallholder ['smɔːlhəʊldə(r)] *n* petit(e) exploitant(e) *m,f*
smallholding ['smɔːlhəʊldɪŋ] *n* petite exploitation *f*
small-minded [smɔːl'maɪndɪd] *adj* étroit(e) d'esprit
smallness ['smɔːlnɪs] *n* petitesse *f*
smallpox ['smɔːlpɒks] *n* variole *f*
small-scale ['smɔːlskeɪl] *adj (model)* réduit(e); *(research, project)* à petite échelle
small-time ['smɔːltaɪm] *adj Fam (criminal, businessman)* petit(e)
smarmy ['smɑːmɪ] *adj Fam Pej* mielleux(euse)
smart [smɑːt] 1 *adj* (a) *(clever) (person)* futé(e); *(decision, move)* habile; don't get s. with me n'essaie pas de faire le malin avec moi; *Fam* s. aleck petit malin *m*; s. bomb bombe *f* intelligente; s. card carte *f* à puce; s. drug psychotrope *m*; s. missile missile *m* (télé)guidé (b) *(elegant) (clothes)* élégant(e); *(hotel, area)* chic *inv*; the s. set le beau monde; to be a s. dresser bien s'habiller (c) *(quick) (pace, work)* rapide; look s. (about it)! et que ça saute!
  2 *vi (sting) (of wound, graze)* brûler; *(of eyes)* piquer; *Fig (of person)* être piqué(e) au vif
▸smarten up ['smɑːtən] 1 *vt sep* égayer; to s. oneself up se faire beau
  2 *vi (improve)* se reprendre
smarty-pants ['smɑːtɪpænts] *(pl* smarty-pants) *n Fam Pej* petit(e) malin(igne) *m,f*
smash [smæʃ] 1 *n (blow)* coup *m*; *(noise)* fracas *m*; *(collision)* collision *f*; *(in tennis)* smash *m*; s. (hit) *(record, film)* gros succès *m*
  2 *vt* (a) s. sth (to pieces) fracasser qch; to s. sth open défoncer qch; to s. down a door défoncer une porte (b) *(ruin)* anéantir; to s. a drugs ring démanteler un réseau de trafiquants de drogue; she smashed the world record elle a pulvérisé le record du monde
  3 *vi (strike)* to s. into sth s'écraser contre qch (b) to s. (into pieces) éclater (en morceaux)
▸smash up *vt sep (room, car, furniture)* saccager
smash-and-grab raid ['smæʃən'græbreɪd] *n* pillage *m* de vitrines
smashed [smæʃt] *adj Fam (drunk)* pété(e)
smasher ['smæʃə(r)] *n Br Fam* what a s.! *(person)* il/elle est génial(e)!
smashing ['smæʃɪŋ] *adj* (a) *(blow)* violent(e) (b) *Br Fam (excellent)* génial(e); we had a s. time! on s'est éclatés!
smattering ['smætərɪŋ] *n* notions *fpl*
smear [smɪə(r)] 1 *n* (a) *(stain)* tache *f*; *Med* s. test frottis *m* (b) *(slander)* propos *m* diffamatoire; s. campaign campagne *f* de diffamation
  2 *vt* (a) *(stain)* tacher; *(spread)* enduire, barbouiller; *(smudge) (paint)* salir (b) *(slander)* calomnier
smell [smel] 1 *n* (a) *(sense)* odorat *m* (b) *(odour)* odeur *f*; there's a bad s. ça sent mauvais; to have a s. of sth sentir qch

2 *vt* (*pt & pp* **smelled** *or* **smelt** [smelt]) *also Fig* sentir; *Fig* **I s. a rat** ça sent l'embrouille
3 *vi* sentir; *(stink)* sentir mauvais; **to s. of sth** sentir qch; **his breath smells** il a mauvaise haleine
smelly ['smelɪ] *adj* qui sent mauvais
smelt [smelt] **1** *vt (ore)* fondre
2 *pt & pp of* **smell**
smile [smaɪl] **1** *n* sourire *m*; **to give sb a s.** sourire à qn; **she was all smiles** elle était tout sourire; **to take** *or* **wipe the s. off sb's face** passer l'envie de sourire à qn
2 *vi* sourire (**at** à); **fortune smiled on them** la fortune leur sourit; **s.!** *(for photograph)* un petit sourire!
smiley ['smaɪlɪ] *n Comput* souriant *m*, émoticon *m*, *Can* binette *f*
smiling ['smaɪlɪŋ] *adj* souriant(e)
smirk [smɜːk] **1** *n* sourire *m* en coin
2 *vi* sourire en coin
smite [smaɪt] (*pt* **smote** [sməʊt], *pp* **smitten** ['smɪtən]) *vt* (**a**) *Lit (strike)* frapper (**b**) **smitten with terror** terrorisé(e); **smitten with remorse** envahi(e) par les remords
smith [smɪθ] *n* forgeron *m*
smithereens [smɪðə'riːnz] *npl* **to smash/blow sth to s.** réduire qch en miettes
smithy ['smɪðɪ] (*pl* **smithies**) *n* forge *f*
smitten ['smɪtən] **1** *adj (in love)* très épris(e) (**with** de)
2 *pp of* **smite**
smock [smɒk] *n* blouse *f*
smog [smɒg] *n* smog *m*
smoke [sməʊk] **1** *n* fumée *f*; **to have a s.** fumer une cigarette; *Fig* **to go up in s.** partir en fumée; *Prov* **there's no s. without fire** il n'y a pas de fumée sans feu; **s. bomb** bombe *f* fumigène; **s. detector** détecteur *m* de fumée; *also Fig* **s. screen** rideau *m* de fumée; **s. signals** signaux *mpl* de fumée
2 *vt* (**a**) *(cigarette)* fumer; **to s. a pipe** fumer la pipe (**b**) *(meat, fish)* fumer
3 *vi* (**a**) *(of person)* fumer (**b**) *(of chimney, oil)* fumer
►**smoke out** *vt sep (insects)* enfumer; *Fig (rebels)* débusquer
smoked [sməʊkt] *adj* fumé(e); **s. glass** verre *m* fumé; **s. salmon** saumon *m* fumé
smokeless ['sməʊklɪs] *adj* **s. fuel** combustible *m* non polluant; **s. zone** = zone où l'usage de combustible polluant n'est pas autorisé
smoker ['sməʊkə(r)] *n* fumeur(euse) *m,f*; **to be a cigarette/pipe s.** fumer des cigarettes/la pipe; **to be a heavy s.** être un(e) grand(e) fumeur(euse); **s.'s cough** toux *f* de fumeur
smoking ['sməʊkɪŋ] *n* **s. can damage your health** fumer *ou* le tabac nuit à la santé; **no s.** *(sign)* défense de fumer; **s. ban** interdiction *f* de fumer; **s. compartment** compartiment *m* fumeurs; *Fig* **s. gun** *(clue)* indice *m* flagrant; **s. jacket** veste *f* d'intérieur; **s. room** salle *f* fumeurs

Smoking ban

En 2004, une loi interdisant de fumer dans les lieux de travail et les lieux publics est entrée en vigueur en République d'Irlande. Cette loi concerne également les bars, les clubs et les restaurants, où elle vise à protéger le personnel travaillant dans ce type d'établissement des effets nocifs de la fumée. La même interdiction est entrée en application en Écosse en mars 2006 et doit être étendue au reste du Royaume-Uni en 2007.

smoky ['sməʊkɪ] *adj (atmosphere, room)* enfumé(e); *(fire)* qui dégage de la fumée; *(surface)* noirci(e) par la fumée; *(taste)* de fumée
smolder *Am* = **smoulder**
smooch [smuːtʃ] *vi Fam* se bécoter
smooth [smuːð] **1** *adj* (**a**) *(not rough)* lisse; *(sea)* calme; *(sauce)* homogène; *(skin, wine, whisky)* doux (douce); *(style)* coulant(e); *(flight, crossing)* calme; **a s.** shave un rasage de près (**b**) *(person, manner)* onctueux(euse); **he's a s. talker** c'est un beau parleur; **to be a s. operator** savoir y faire (**c**) *(without problems)* sans problèmes; **to get off to a s. start** commencer sans problèmes
2 *vt (feathers, hair)* lisser; *(pillow, sheet, clothing)* défroisser; *(surface)* égaliser; **to s. the way for sb** faciliter les choses à qn; **to s. the way for sth** faciliter qch
►**smooth back** *vt sep* **to s. back one's hair** lisser ses cheveux en arrière
►**smooth down** *vt sep* lisser
►**smooth out** *vt sep (map, sheets)* défroisser; *(crease)* faire disparaître; *Fig (difficulty)* aplanir
►**smooth over** *vt sep (difficulties)* aplanir; *(differences)* atténuer; **to s. things over** arranger les choses
smoothly ['smuːðlɪ] *adv* sans problèmes; **to go s.** se passer sans problèmes
smoothness ['smuːðnɪs] *n (of skin, wine, whisky)* douceur *f*; *(of surface)* aspect *m* lisse; *(of flight, crossing)* calme *m*; *(of sauce)* homogénéité *f*
smooth-talking ['smuːð'tɔːkɪŋ] *adj* mielleux(euse)
smote [sməʊt] *pt of* **smite**
smother ['smʌðə(r)] *vt* (**a**) *(person, fire, yawn)* étouffer; **to s. sb with kisses** couvrir qn de baisers (**b**) *(cover)* **to s. sth in sth** recouvrir qch de qch
smoulder, *Am* **smolder** ['sməʊldə(r)] *vi (of fire)* couver; *Fig* **to s. with anger/passion** se consumer de colère/passion
SMS [esem'es] *n Tel (abbr* **short message service**) service *m* SMS
smudge [smʌdʒ] **1** *n* tache *f*
2 *vt (ink, lipstick)* étaler; *(drawing)* maculer
3 *vi (of ink, lipstick)* s'étaler
smug [smʌg] *adj* suffisant(e)
smuggle ['smʌgəl] *vt (arms, drugs)* faire de la contrebande de; **to s. sth in/out** faire entrer/sortir qch en contrebande; **to s. sb in/out** faire entrer/sortir qn clandestinement; **to s. sth through customs** passer qch en fraude à la douane
smuggler ['smʌglə(r)] *n* contrebandier(ère) *m,f*; *(of drugs)* trafiquant(e) *m,f*
smuggling ['smʌglɪŋ] *n* contrebande *f*; *(of drugs)* trafic *m*
smut [smʌt] *n* (**a**) *(soot)* tache *f* de suie (**b**) *(obscenity)* cochonneries *fpl*
smutty ['smʌtɪ] *adj* (**a**) *(dirty)* sale, noirci(e) (**b**) *(obscene)* cochon(onne)
snack [snæk] **1** *n* casse-croûte *m inv*; **to have a s.** grignoter quelque chose; **s. bar** snack-bar *m*
2 *vi* **to s. on sth** grignoter qch
snag [snæg] **1** *n (problem)* problème *m*
2 *vt (pt & pp* **snagged**) *(clothing)* faire un accroc à
snail [sneɪl] *n* escargot *m*; **at a s.'s pace** *(move)* comme un escargot; *(change, learn, progress)* très lentement; *Fam* **s. mail** courrier *m* escargot
snake [sneɪk] **1** *n* serpent *m*; *Fig* **s. in the grass** traître(esse) *m,f*; **snakes and ladders** ≃ jeu *m* de l'oie; **s.**

charmer charmeur(euse) *m,f* de serpent; *Am Fig* **s. pit** fosse *f* aux serpents

2 *vi (of road, river)* serpenter

snakebite ['sneɪkbaɪt] *n* (**a**) *(of snake)* morsure *f* de serpent (**b**) *(drink)* = boisson composée d'une mesure de bière et d'une mesure de cidre

snakeskin ['sneɪkskɪn] *n* peau *f* de serpent

snap [snæp] **1** *n* (**a**) *(bite)* coup *m* de dents (**b**) *(sound)* craquement *m*; **a s. of the fingers** un claquement de doigts (**c**) *(of weather)* **a cold s.** une brusque vague de froid (**d**) *Fam (photograph)* photo *f* (**e**) *(card game)* = jeu de cartes dont le but est de crier "snap" lorsque l'on pose sur la table une carte similaire à celle qui vient d'être posée; *Fam* **I'm going to Paris – s.!** je vais à Paris – tiens, moi aussi!

2 *adj (judgement, decision)* hâtif(ive); **to call a s. election** procéder à une élection surprise

3 *vt (pt & pp snapped)* (**a**) *(break)* casser net; **to s. sth in two** casser qch en deux (**b**) **to s. one's fingers** faire claquer ses doigts (**c**) *(say sharply)* dire sèchement (**d**) *Fam (take photograph of)* prendre en photo

4 *vi* (**a**) *(break cleanly)* casser net; *(break noisily)* casser avec un bruit sec (**b**) *(bite)* **to s. (at)** essayer de mordre; **to s. shut** *(of jaws, lid)* se refermer avec un bruit sec (**c**) *(speak abruptly)* parler sèchement (**at** à) (**d**) *(idioms)* **to s. out of it** *(of depression, apathy)* se secouer; *(of sulk)* arrêter de faire la tête

▸**snap off 1** *vt sep* (**a**) *(break)* casser net (**b**) *Fam* **to s. sb's head off** rembarrer qn

2 *vi* casser net

▸**snap up** *vt sep* (**a**) *(seize in jaws)* attraper (**b**) *(buy, take quickly)* rafler

snapdragon ['snæpdrægən] *n* gueule-de-loup *f*

snappy ['snæpɪ] *adj Fam (style, prose)* vif (vive); *(slogan)* accrocheur(euse); **to be a s. dresser** s'habiller toujours à la mode; **make it s.!** *(be quick)* au trot!

snapshot ['snæpʃɒt] *n Fam (photograph)* photo *f*

snare [sneə(r)] **1** *n* collet *m*; *Fig* piège *m*; **s. drum** caisse *f* claire

2 *vt* prendre au collet; *Fig* prendre au piège

snarl [snɑːl] **1** *n* grognement *m*

2 *vi* grogner (**at** après)

▸**snarl up 1** *vt sep (thread, hair)* emmêler; *Br (traffic)* bloquer; **to get snarled up** *(thread)* s'emmêler; *Br (traffic)* se bloquer, bouchonner

2 *vi (of thread, hair)* s'emmêler, *Br (of traffic)* se bloquer

snarl-up ['snɑːlʌp] *n (of traffic)* bouchon *m*; *(in system)* paralysie *f*

snatch [snætʃ] **1** *n (of conversation)* bribe *f*; **to sleep in snatches** avoir un sommeil fragmenté; **a s. of music** quelques notes de musique

2 *vt* (**a**) *(grab)* saisir; **to s. something to eat** avaler quelque chose à la hâte; **to s. some sleep** dormir un peu (**b**) *(steal, abduct) (wallet, handbag)* arracher; *(person)* enlever

3 *vi* **to s. at sth** essayer de saisir qch

▸**snatch away** *vt sep* arracher

snazzy ['snæzɪ] *adj Fam* chicos, classe

sneak [sniːk] **1** *n* (**a**) *Fam (telltale)* mouchard(e) *m,f* (**b**) **to get a s. preview of sth** voir qch en avant-première

2 *vt (pt & pp sneaked, Am snuck [snʌk])* **to s. sth past sb** passer qch subrepticement devant qn; **to s. sb in/out** faire entrer/sortir qn subrepticement; **to s. a glance at sb** jeter un coup d'œil furtif à qn

3 *vi* (**a**) *(tell tales)* rapporter (**b**) *(move furtively)* se

déplacer furtivement; **to s. past sb** passer furtivement devant qn; **to s. in/out** entrer/sortir furtivement

▸**sneak away, sneak off** *vi* s'esquiver

sneaker ['sniːkə(r)] *n Am (running shoe)* chaussure *f* de sport

sneaky ['sniːkɪ] *adj* sournois(e)

sneer [snɪə(r)] **1** *n (expression)* sourire *m* méprisant

2 *vt* **"you couldn't do that,"** he sneered "vous n'en seriez pas capable", dit-il d'un air méprisant

3 *vi* ricaner; **to s. at sb/sth** se moquer de qn/qch

sneering ['snɪərɪŋ] **1** *n (laughter)* ricanement *m*; *(remarks)* sarcasmes *mpl*

2 *adj* méprisant(e)

sneeze [sniːz] **1** *n* éternuement *m*

2 *vi* éternuer; *Fam Fig* **it's not to be sneezed at** il ne faut pas cracher dessus

snicker ['snɪkə(r)] *Am* **1** *n* ricanement *m*

2 *vi* ricaner

snide [snaɪd] *adj* méprisant(e)

sniff [snɪf] **1** *vt* (**a**) *(smell)* sentir; *(detect)* flairer (**b**) *(inhale) (air)* respirer; *(cocaine, glue)* sniffer

2 *vi* renifler; *(disdainfully)* avoir une moue de dédain; *Fam* **it's not to be sniffed at** il ne faut pas cracher dessus

3 *n* **to take a s. at sth** sentir qch; **with a s. of disgust** avec une moue de dégoût

▸**sniff out** *vt sep (of dog)* découvrir à l'odeur; *Fig (of investigator)* découvrir

sniffer dog ['snɪfədɒg] *n* chien *m* renifleur

sniffle ['snɪfəl] **1** *n (slight cold)* petit rhume *m*; *Fam* **to have the sniffles** avoir un petit rhume

2 *vi* (**a**) *(sniff repeatedly)* renifler (**b**) *(cry quietly)* pleurer (doucement)

sniffy ['snɪfɪ] *adj Fam (disdainful)* dédaigneux(euse); **to be s. about sth** éprouver du dédain pour qch

snifter ['snɪftə(r)] *n Br Fam Old-fashioned (drink)* petit verre *m*

snigger ['snɪgə(r)] **1** *n* ricanement *m* étouffé

2 *vi* ricaner

snip [snɪp] **1** *n* (**a**) *(cut)* petite entaille *f* (**b**) *(piece cut off)* bout *m* (**c**) *Br Fam (bargain)* (bonne) affaire *f*

2 *vt (pt & pp snipped)* couper

▸**snip off** *vt sep* couper

snipe¹ [snaɪp] *(pl snipe) n (bird)* bécassine *f*

snipe² *vi (shoot)* tirer (d'une position cachée); **to s. at sb** tirer sur qn (d'une position cachée); *Fig (criticize)* critiquer qn de façon malveillante

sniper ['snaɪpə(r)] *n* tireur(euse) *m,f* embusqué(e)

snippet ['snɪpɪt] *n (of information, conversation)* bribe *f*; **a s. of news** une nouvelle brève

snitch [snɪtʃ] *Fam* **1** *n* (**a**) *(informer)* mouchard(e) *m,f* (**b**) *(nose)* pif *m*

2 *vi* moucharder; **to s. on sb** moucharder qn

snivel ['snɪvəl] *(pt & pp snivelled, Am sniveled) vi* pleurnicher

snivelling, Am sniveling ['snɪvəlɪŋ] *adj* pleurnicheur(euse)

snob [snɒb] *n* snob *mf*

snobbery ['snɒbərɪ] *n* snobisme *m*

snobbish ['snɒbɪʃ] *adj* snob *inv*

snog [snɒg] *Br Fam* **1** *n* **to have a s.** se bécoter

2 *vt (pt & pp snogged)* bécoter

3 *vi* se bécoter

snooker ['snuːkə(r)] **1** *n (game)* snooker *(sorte de billard qui se joue avec vingt-deux billes)*

2 *vt* **to s. sb** *(in game)* laisser qn dans une position difficile; *Fig* mettre qn dans l'embarras

snoop [snu:p] *Fam* **1** *n* (**a**) *(person)* fouineur(euse) *m,f*
(**b**) *(look)* **to have a s.** (**around**) jeter un coup d'œil
2 *vi* fouiner, fureter
snooper ['snu:pə(r)] *n Fam* fouineur(euse) *m,f*
snooty ['snu:tɪ] *adj Fam* prétentieux(euse)
snooze [snu:z] *Fam* **1** *n* petit somme *m*; **to have a s.**
faire un petit somme
2 *vi* faire un petit somme
snore [snɔ:(r)] **1** *n* ronflement *m*
2 *vi* ronfler
snoring ['snɔ:rɪŋ] *n* ronflements *mpl*
snorkel ['snɔ:kəl] **1** *n* tuba *m*
2 *vi* (*pt & pp* **snorkelled**, *Am* **snorkeled**) nager sous
l'eau avec un tuba
snort [snɔ:t] **1** *n* (*of person*) grognement *m*; (*of horse*)
ébrouement *m*
2 *vt Fam* (*drugs*) sniffer
3 *vi* (*of person*) grogner; (*of horse*) s'ébrouer
snot [snɒt] *n Fam* morve *f*
snotty ['snɒtɪ] *adj Fam* (**a**) (*nose*) qui coule (**b**) (*arrogant*) arrogant(e)
snout [snaʊt] *n* (*of pig*) groin *m*; (*of other animal*) museau *m*; *Fam* (*of person*) pif *m*
snow [snəʊ] **1** *n* neige *f*; **s. blindness** cécité *f* des
neiges; *Aut* **s. chains** chaînes *fpl* (à neige); *Am* **s. pea**
mange-tout *m inv*
2 *vi* neiger; **it's snowing** il neige
▸**snow in** *vt sep* **to be snowed in** être bloqué(e) par la
neige
▸**snow under** *vt sep* **to be snowed under (with)**
(*work*) être débordé(e) (de); (*invitations, offers*) être
submergé(e) (de)
snowball ['snəʊbɔ:l] **1** *n* boule *f* de neige, *Can* balle *f*
de neige; **s. fight** bataille *f* de boules de neige; *Fam*
she hasn't a s.'s chance (in hell) elle n'a pas la
moindre chance
2 *vi Fig* faire boule de neige
snowbike ['snəʊbaɪk] *n* motoski *m*
snowboarding ['snəʊbɔ:dɪŋ] *n* snowboard *m*; **to go
s.** faire du snowboard
snowbound ['snəʊbaʊnd] *adj* bloqué(e) par la
neige
snowcapped ['snəʊkæpt] *adj* couronné(e) de neige
snowdome ['snəʊdəʊm] *n* (**a**) (*ornament*) boule *f* à
neige (**b**) (*for skiing, snowboarding*) centre *m* de ski
couvert
snowdrift ['snəʊdrɪft] *n* congère *f*
snowdrop ['snəʊdrɒp] *n*(*flower*) perce-neige *m ou f
inv*
snowfall ['snəʊfɔ:l] *n* chute *f* de neige
snowflake ['snəʊfleɪk] *n* flocon *m* de neige
snowglobe ['snəʊgləʊb] *n* boule *f* à neige
snowman ['snəʊmæn] *n* bonhomme *m* de neige
snowmobile ['snəʊməʊbi:l] *n* (*enclosed*) autoneige *f*;
(*open*) motoneige *f*
snowplough, *Am* **snowplow** ['snəʊplaʊ] *n* chasse-
neige *m inv*
snowshoe ['snəʊʃu:] *n* raquette *f*
snowstorm ['snəʊstɔ:m] *n* tempête *f* de neige
snowsuit ['snəʊsu:t] *n* combinaison *f* de ski (*pour
enfants*)
Snow White ['snəʊ'waɪt] *n* **S. and the Seven Dwarfs**
Blanche-Neige et les sept nains
snowy ['snəʊɪ] *adj* (*landscape, field*) enneigé(e);
(*weather*) neigeux(euse); (*day*) de neige
SNP [esen'pi:] *n Br Pol* (*abbr* **Scottish National Party**) =
parti politique écossais indépendantiste

Snr (*abbr* **Senior**) Jonathan Pye-Finch S. Jonathan
Pye-Finch père
snub [snʌb] **1** *n* (*refusal*) rebuffade *f*; (*insult*) affront *m*
2 *vt* (*pt & pp* **snubbed**) snober
snub nose ['snʌb'nəʊz] *n* nez *m* retroussé
snuck [snʌk] *Am pt & pp of* **sneak**
snuff [snʌf] **1** *n* tabac *m* à priser
2 *vt* (*candle*) moucher; *Br Fam* **to s. it** (*die*) casser sa
pipe
▸**snuff out** *vt sep* (*candle*) moucher; (*life, opposition*)
mettre fin à
snuffbox ['snʌfbɒks] *n* tabatière *f*
snuffle ['snʌfəl] **1** *n* (*sniff*) reniflement *m*
2 *vi* (*sniff*) renifler
snug [snʌg] *adj* (**a**) (*place*) douillet(ette); (*person*)
bien au chaud (**b**) (*tight-fitting*) bien ajusté(e)
▸**snuggle up** ['snʌgəl] *vi* **to s. up to sb** se blottir contre
qn
snugly ['snʌglɪ] *adv* (*comfortably*) confortablement;
to fit s. être bien ajusté(e)
so [səʊ] **1** *adv* (**a**) (*to such an extent*) tellement, si (**that**
que); **I was so angry (that) I almost hit him** j'étais
tellement en colère que j'ai failli le frapper; **he's not
so clever as she is** il n'est pas aussi intelligent qu'elle;
it isn't so very old il n'est pas si vieux; **I'm not so sure
of that** je n'en suis pas si sûr; **so much money/many
people** tant *ou* autant d'argent/de gens; **it was difficult, so much so that...** c'était difficile, à tel point
que...
(**b**) (*for emphasis*) tellement; **I was so disappointed!** j'étais tellement déçu!; **we enjoyed ourselves
so much!** nous nous sommes tellement amusés!
(**c**) (*expressing agreement*) **you're late – so I am!** tu
es en retard – ah oui, tu as raison!; **that's Johnny
Depp – so it is!** c'est Johnny Depp – ah oui, tu as raison!
(**d**) (*referring to statement already mentioned*) **I hope
so** j'espère bien; **I think so** je crois; **I suppose so** je le
suppose; **so I believe** c'est ce que je crois; **I told you
so!** je vous l'avais bien dit!; **I'm not very organized –
so I see!** je ne suis pas très bien organisé – c'est ce
que je vois!; **so be it!** soit!
(**e**) (*also*) **so am I** moi aussi; **so do we** nous aussi;
so can they eux aussi; **so is my brother** mon frère
aussi
(**f**) (*in this way*) ainsi; **do it (like) so** fais-le comme
ça; **and so on, and so forth** et ainsi de suite
2 *conj* (**a**) (*because of this*) donc; **she has a bad temper, so be careful** elle a mauvais caractère, donc fais
attention
(**b**) (*introducing remark*) alors; **so you're not coming?** alors, tu ne viens pas?; **so that's why!** alors, c'est
pour ça!; **so (what)?** et alors?, et après?
(**c**) **so as to** afin de; **we hurried so as not to be late**
nous nous sommes dépêchés afin de ne pas être en
retard
(**d**) **so that** pour que + *subjunctive*; **she sat down so
that I could see better** elle s'est assise pour que je
puisse mieux voir; **we hurried so that we wouldn't
be late** nous nous sommes dépêchés pour ne pas arriver en retard
soak [səʊk] **1** *vt* (*leave in water*) faire *ou* laisser tremper; (*make very wet*) tremper (**with** de)
2 *vi* (*of food, clothes*) tremper; **to leave sth to s.** faire
ou laisser tremper qch
▸**soak in** *vi* (*of liquid*) pénétrer

▶**soak up** *vt sep (liquid)* absorber; *Fig* **to s. up the sun** prendre un bain de soleil

soaked [səʊkt] *adj* trempé(e); **s. to the skin** trempé(e) jusqu'aux os

so-and-so ['səʊənsəʊ] *(pl* **so-and-sos**) *n Fam* (**a**) *(unspecified person)* untel (unetelle) *m,f*; **Mr S.** M. Untel; **Mrs S.** Mme Unetelle (**b**) *(unpleasant person)* peau *f* de vache

soap [səʊp] **1** *n* savon *m*; **a bar of s.** un morceau de savon; **s. (opera)** feuilleton *m* populaire; **s. powder** lessive *f* (en poudre)
   2 *vt* savonner

Soap opera

Les "soap operas" (ou "soaps") (feuilletons télévisés ou radiophoniques) sont une véritable institution en Grande-Bretagne. Les premiers furent diffusés à la radio – le feuilleton radiophonique "The Archers" est diffusé par la BBC depuis 1951. Les feuilletons télévisés les plus connus sont "Coronation Street" (dont l'action se situe dans le Nord de l'Angleterre, diffusé depuis 1960) et "EastEnders" (diffusé depuis le milieu des années 80 et situé dans l'East End londonien). Les vedettes de soap operas acquièrent souvent le statut de célébrités nationales ; les tabloïds et la presse people sont très friands de toute anecdote les concernant. Le terme "soap opera" (littéralement 'opéra-savon') s'explique par le fait qu'au départ, ces feuilletons diffusés pendant la journée pour un public presque uniquement composé de femmes au foyer étaient financés par des marques de détergents.

---

soapbox ['səʊpbɒks] *n* tribune *f* improvisée à l'extérieur; **s. orator** harangueur(euse) *m,f*

soapdish ['səʊpdɪʃ] *n* porte-savon *m*

soapflakes ['səʊpfleɪks] *npl* savon *m* en paillettes

soapsuds ['səʊpsʌdz] *npl* mousse *f* de savon

soapy ['səʊpɪ] *adj (water)* savonneux(euse); *(body)* couvert(e) de savon; *(taste, smell)* de savon

soar [sɔː(r)] *vi (of bird, plane)* & *Fig (of prices)* monter en flèche; *Fig (of building)* se dresser

soaring ['sɔːrɪŋ] *adj Fig (prices)* en forte hausse; *(building)* élancé(e)

sob [sɒb] **1** *n* sanglot *m*; *Fam* **s. story** histoire *f* larmoyante
   2 *vi (pt & pp* **sobbed**) sangloter

s.o.b. [esəʊ'biː] *n Am very Fam (abbr* **son of a bitch)** salaud *m*

sobbing ['sɒbɪŋ] *n* sanglots *mpl*

sober ['səʊbə(r)] *adj* (**a**) *(not drunk)* qui n'a pas bu (**b**) *(sensible)* sobre

▶**sober up** *vt sep & vi* dessoûler

sobering ['səʊbərɪŋ] *adj (news, thought)* qui donne à réfléchir

sobriety [səʊ'braɪətɪ] *n* sobriété *f*

Soc *n (abbr* **society)** club *m*, société *f*

so-called [səʊ'kɔːld] *adj* (**a**) *(supposed)* soi-disant *inv*; **his s. aunt** sa soi-disant tante (**b**) *(so named)* appelé(e) ainsi; **the s. temperate zone** la zone dite tempérée

soccer ['sɒkə(r)] *n* football *m*; **s. match** match *m* de football

sociable ['səʊʃəbəl] *adj* sociable

social ['səʊʃəl] **1** *adj* social(e); *EU* **the S. Chapter** le volet social *(du traité de Maastricht)*; **s. class** classe *f* sociale; **s. climber** arriviste *mf*; *Pol* **s. democrat**

social(e)-démocrate *m,f*; **s. intercourse** relations *fpl* avec les gens; **s. life** vie *f* sociale; **he doesn't have much of a s. life** il ne sort pas beaucoup; **s. outcast** paria *m*; **s. sciences** sciences *fpl* humaines; **s. security** prestations *fpl* sociales; **the s. services** les services *mpl* sociaux; **s. work** assistance *f* sociale; **s. worker** assistant(e) social(e) *m,f*
   2 *n (party)* fête *f*

socialism ['səʊʃəlɪzəm] *n* socialisme *m*

socialist ['səʊʃəlɪst] **1** *n* socialiste *mf*
   2 *adj* socialiste

socialite ['səʊʃəlaɪt] *n* mondain(e) *m,f*

socialize ['səʊʃəlaɪz] *vi* fréquenter des gens; **to s. with sb** fréquenter qn

socially ['səʊʃəlɪ] *adv* socialement; **to see sb s.** fréquenter qn

society [sə'saɪətɪ] *(pl* **societies**) *n* (**a**) *(community)* société *f*; **(high)** s. haute société *f*, (beau) monde *m* (**b**) *(club)* club *m*, société *f*

socioeconomic [səʊsɪəʊiːkə'nɒmɪk] *adj* socioéconomique

sociological [səʊsɪəʊ'lɒdʒɪkəl] *adj* sociologique

sociologist [səʊsɪ'ɒlədʒɪst] *n* sociologue *mf*

sociology [səʊsɪ'ɒlədʒɪ] *n* sociologie *f*

sock [sɒk] **1** *n* (**a**) *(garment)* chaussette *f*; *Br Fam Fig* **to pull one's socks up** se secouer (**b**) *Fam (blow)* coup *m* de poing
   2 *vt Fam (hit)* donner un coup de poing à; *Fig* **to s. it to sb** montrer à qn de quoi on est capable

socket ['sɒkɪt] *n (of eye)* orbite *f*; *(for plug)* prise *f* de courant

sod¹ [sɒd] *n (of earth)* motte *f*

sod² *Br* **1** *n very Fam (man)* salaud *m*; *(woman)* salope *f*; **poor s.!** pauvre bougre!; **s. all** que dalle; **S.'s law** la loi de l'emmerdement maximum
   2 *vt Vulg* **s. it!** merde!; **s. you!** va te faire voir!; **s. the party, I'm tired** tant pis pour la soirée, je suis fatigué

▶**sod off** *(pt & pp* **sodded**) *vi Br Vulg (go away)* aller se faire voir

soda ['səʊdə] *n* (**a**) **s. (water)** eau *f* de Seltz; **s. fountain** cafétéria *f* (**b**) *Am (fizzy drink)* boisson *f* gazeuse (**c**) *Chem* soude *f*

sodden ['sɒdən] *adj* trempé(e)

sodium ['səʊdɪəm] *n Chem* sodium *m*; **s. bicarbonate** bicarbonate *m* de soude; **s. chloride** chlorure *m* de sodium

sodomize ['sɒdəmaɪz] *vt* sodomiser

sodomy ['sɒdəmɪ] *n* sodomie *f*

sofa ['səʊfə] *n* canapé *m*; **s. bed** canapé-lit *m*

Sofia [səʊ'fiːə] *n* Sofia

soft [sɒft] *adj* (**a**) *(in texture)* mou (molle); *(ground)* meuble; *(pillow, carpet)* moelleux(euse); *(fabric, skin)* doux (douce); **s. cheese** fromage *m* frais; *Comput* **s. copy** visualisation *f* sur écran; **s. furnishings** tissus *mpl* d'ameublement; *Comput* **s. return** retour *m* de chariot conditionnel, changement *m* de ligne facultatif; **s. shoulder** *(on road)* accottement *m* non stabilisé; *Anat* **s. tissue** parties *fpl* charnues; **s. toy** peluche *f* (**b**) *(voice)* doux (douce); *(rain)* léger(ère); *(colour)* doux (douce), tendre; **s. currency** devise *f* faible; **s. drinks** boissons *fpl* non alcoolisées; **s. drugs** drogues *fpl* douces; *Phot* **s. focus** flou *m* artistique; *Fin* **s. loan** prêt *m* offrant des conditions avantageuses; **s. porn** soft *m*; *Com* **s. sell** méthode *f* de vente non agressive; **s. skills** savoirs *m* comportementaux (**c**) *(not strict)* indulgent(e), faible; **to have a s. spot for sb** avoir un faible pour qn; **to have a s. heart** avoir

le cœur tendre (**d**) *Fam (stupid)* idiot(e) (**e**) *(easy)* *(job, life)* facile; *Fam* **to be a s.** **touch** être bonne pâte; **s.** option solution *f* de facilité
softback ['sɒftbæk] *n* livre *m* broché
softball ['sɒftbɔːl] *n Am* = sorte de base-ball joué sur un plus petit terrain avec une balle moins dure
soft-boiled ['sɒftbɔɪld] *adj (egg)* à la coque
soften ['sɒfən] **1** *vt (wax, butter)* ramollir; *(leather, fabric)* assouplir; *(skin, light)* adoucir; *Fig* **to s. the blow** amortir le choc
2 *vi (of wax, butter)* ramollir; *Fig (of person)* se radoucir; *(of opinions, resolve, stance)* devenir plus modéré(e)
▸**soften up** *vt sep Fam (before attack)* affaiblir; *(before request)* amadouer
softener ['sɒfənə(r)] *n* adoucissant *m*
softhearted [sɒft'hɑːtɪd] *adj* qui se laisse facilement attendrir
softie = **softy**
softly ['sɒftlɪ] *adv (quietly, gently)* doucement; **to be s. lit** être légèrement éclairé(e)
softly-softly ['sɒftlɪ'sɒftlɪ] *adj Fam (approach, attitude)* en douceur
softness ['sɒftnɪs] *n (of ground)* consistance *f* meuble; *(of fabric, skin, voice)* douceur *f*
soft-pedal [sɒft'pedəl] *(pt & pp* **soft-pedalled,** *Am* **soft-pedaled)** *vi also Fig* mettre la pédale douce
soft-soap ['sɒftsəup] *vt Fam* amadouer
soft-spoken [sɒft'spəukən] *adj* qui a une voix douce
software ['sɒftweə(r)] *n Comput* logiciel *m*; **s. company** éditeur *m* de logiciels; **s. developer** développeur(euse) *m,f*; **s. engineer** ingénieur *m* développement logiciel; **s. package** progiciel *m*
softy ['sɒftɪ] *(pl* **softies)** *n Fam (gentle person)* bonne pâte *f; (coward)* froussard(e) *m,f*
soggy ['sɒgɪ] *adj* trempé(e)
soh [səʊ] *n Mus* sol *m*
soil [sɔɪl] **1** *n (earth)* terre *f;* **on British s.** sur le sol britannique
2 *vt (clothes, sheet)* salir; *Fig* **to s. one's hands** se salir les mains
solace ['sɒləs] *n Lit* réconfort *m*
solar ['səʊlə(r)] *adj* solaire; **s. eclipse** éclipse *f* solaire; **s. plexus** plexus *m* solaire; **s. system** système *m* solaire
sold [səʊld] *pt & pp of* **sell**
solder ['səʊldə(r)] **1** *n* soudure *f*
2 *vt* souder
soldering iron ['səʊldərɪŋ'aɪən] *n* fer *m* à souder
soldier ['səʊldʒə(r)] **1** *n* soldat *m*
2 *vi* être soldat
▸**soldier on** *vi* persévérer
sole¹ [səʊl] **1** *n (of foot)* plante *f; (of shoe)* semelle *f*
2 *vt (shoe)* ressemeler
sole² *n (fish)* sole *f*
sole³ *adj (only)* unique; *Com* **s. agent** agent *m* exclusif
solely ['səʊllɪ] *adv* uniquement
solemn ['sɒləm] *adj* solennel(elle)
solemnity [sə'lemnɪtɪ] *n* solennité *f*
sol-fa [sɒl'fɑː] *n Mus* solfège *m*
solicit [sə'lɪsɪt] **1** *vt (request)* solliciter, demander
2 *vi (of prostitute)* racoler
solicitor [sə'lɪsɪtə(r)] *n Br (for property, wills)* notaire *m; (in court cases)* avocat(e) *m,f;* **S. General** conseil *m* juridique de la Couronne

solicitous [sə'lɪsɪtəs] *adj Formal* empressé(e); *(caring)* plein(e) de sollicitude; *(concerned)* soucieux(euse) (**for** de)
solid ['sɒlɪd] **1** *n* solide *m;* **solids** *(food)* aliments *mpl* solides
2 *adj (***a**) *(not liquid)* solide; **s. food** aliments *mpl* solides; **s. fuel** combustible *m* solide (**b**) *(not hollow)* plein(e); *(gold, silver)* massif(ive); **made of s. brick** construit(e) entièrement en brique (**c**) *(worker)* sérieux(euse)
3 *adv* **ten hours s.** dix heures d'affilée
solidarity [sɒlɪ'dærɪtɪ] *n* solidarité *f*
solidify [sə'lɪdɪfaɪ] *(pt & pp* **solidified)** *vi* se solidifier
solidity [sə'lɪdɪtɪ] *n* solidité *f*
solidly ['sɒlɪdlɪ] *adv (firmly)* solidement; *(without interruption)* sans arrêt
solid-state [sɒlɪd'steɪt] *adj Elec* transistorisé(e)
soliloquy [sə'lɪləkwɪ] *(pl* **soliloquies)** *n* soliloque *m*
solitaire [sɒlɪ'teə(r)] *n (card game)* réussite *f; (board game, jewellery)* solitaire *m*
solitary ['sɒlɪtərɪ] *adj (***a**) *(single)* seul(e) (**b**) *(alone)* solitaire; **s. confinement** isolement *m* cellulaire
solitude ['sɒlɪtjuːd] *n* solitude *f*
solo ['səʊləʊ] **1** *n (pl* **solos)** *(musical)* solo *m*
2 *adj (flight, crossing)* en solitaire; *(performance)* solo
3 *adv* en solitaire; **to go s.** *(of musician)* faire une carrière solo; *(of business partner)* s'établir à son compte
soloist ['səʊləʊɪst] *n* soliste *mf*
Solomon Islands ['sɒləmən'aɪləndz] *npl* **the S.** les îles *fpl* Salomon
solstice ['sɒlstɪs] *n* solstice *m*
soluble ['sɒljʊbəl] *adj* soluble
solution [sə'luːʃən] *n* solution *f*
solve [sɒlv] *vt* résoudre
solvency ['sɒlvənsɪ] *n* solvabilité *f*
solvent ['sɒlvənt] **1** *n* solvant *m,* dissolvant *m;* **s. abuse** usage *m* de solvants hallucinogènes
2 *adj (financially)* solvable
Somali [sə'mɑːlɪ] **1** *n (***a**) *(person)* Somalien(enne) *m,f* (**b**) *(language)* somali *m*
2 *adj* somalien(enne)
Somalia [sə'mɑːlɪə] *n* la Somalie
sombre, *Am* **somber** ['sɒmbə(r)] *adj* sombre
some [sʌm] **1** *pron (***a**) *(certain quantity or number)* **there is/are s. over there** il y en a là-bas; *(a few)* il y en a quelques-uns là-bas; **give me s.** (**of them**) donne-m'en; *(a few)* donne-m'en quelques-uns; **do you want s.?** en veux-tu?; *(a few)* en veux-tu quelques-uns?; **s. of my wine** un peu de mon vin; **s. of my sweets** quelques-uns de mes bonbons; **s. of the time** une partie du temps (**b**) *(as opposed to others)* certains *mpl,* certaines *fpl;* **s. say...** certains disent que..., il y en a qui disent que...; **s. of the guests** certains invités; **they went off, s. one way, s. another** ils sont partis, certains par là, d'autres par là-bas
2 *adj (***a**) *(certain quantity or number of)* **s. wine** du vin; **s. ice-cream** de la glace; **s. water** de l'eau; **s. books** des livres; *(a few)* quelques livres; **s. ways** par certains côtés; **to s. extent** jusqu'à un certain point (**b**) *(as opposed to other)* certain(e); **s. people say...** certains disent que..., il y a des gens qui disent que... (**c**) *(considerable quantity or number of)* **I've been waiting for s. time/hours** ça fait un moment/ plusieurs heures que j'attends; **s. distance away**

assez loin; **s. miles away** à plusieurs kilomètres (**d**) *(unspecified)* **for s. reason or other** pour une raison ou pour une autre; **she'll come s. day** elle viendra un jour (ou l'autre); **at s. time in the future** plus tard; **in s. book or other** dans un livre quelconque; **s. fool left the door open** un imbécile a laissé la porte ouverte (**e**) *Fam (for emphasis)* **that was s. storm/meal!** quel orage/repas!; *Ironic* **s. hope!** je peux/il peut/*etc* toujours y compter!; *Ironic* **s. friend you are!** quel ami tu fais!

3 *adv (approximately)* environ; **s. fifteen minutes** environ quinze minutes

somebody ['sʌmbədɪ] **1** *pron* quelqu'un; **she's s. you can trust** c'est quelqu'un en qui vous pouvez avoir confiance; **s.'s coming** on vient; **s. important/taller** quelqu'un d'important/de plus grand; **s. else** quelqu'un d'autre

2 *n* **she thinks she's s. I want to be s.** elle se croit importante; **I want to be s.** je veux devenir quelqu'un

somehow ['sʌmhaʊ] *adv* (**a**) *(in some way or other)* d'une façon ou d'une autre (**b**) *(for some reason or other)* pour une raison ou pour une autre

someone ['sʌmwʌn] = **somebody**

somersault ['sʌməsɔːlt] **1** *n (on the ground)* roulade *f*; *(in the air)* saut *m* périlleux

2 *vi (of person) (on the ground)* faire une roulade; *(in the air)* faire un saut périlleux; *(of car)* faire un tonneau

something ['sʌmθɪŋ] **1** *pron* quelque chose; **there's s. about him I don't like** il y a quelque chose chez lui que je n'aime pas; **s. tells me she'll be there** quelque chose me dit qu'elle sera là; **s. to drink/to eat/to read** quelque chose à boire/à manger/à lire; **s. red/different/special** quelque chose de rouge/de différent/de spécial; **he's s. in publishing** il a un poste important dans l'édition; **in nineteen-fifty s.** dans les années cinquante; **she's eighty s.** elle a quatre-vingts ans et quelques; **what's his name? – Simon s.** comment s'appelle-t-il? – Simon quelque chose; **at least he apologized, that's s.!** au moins, il s'est excusé, c'est déjà ça!; **there's s. in what you say** il y a quelque chose d'intéressant dans ce que vous dites; **she has s. to do with what happened** elle a quelque chose à voir avec ce qui s'est passé; **that was quite s.!** ce n'était rien du tout!; **he's a mechanic or s. like that** il est mécanicien ou un truc comme ça; **she's got a cold or s. (like that)** elle a un rhume, je crois

2 *adv* (**a**) *(expressing degree)* **there's been s. of an improvement** il y a eu une certaine amélioration; **she's s. of a miser** elle est plutôt avare; **it's s. like a guinea pig** ça ressemble à un cobaye (**b**) *(for emphasis)* **it hurt s. awful!** ça faisait mal, quelque chose de bien!

3 *n* **a little s.** un petit quelque chose

sometime ['sʌmtaɪm] *adv* **see you s.** à un de ces jours; **s. last week** la semaine dernière; **s. before Christmas** avant Noël; **you'll have to make up your mind s.** il faudra bien que tu te décides un jour; **s. soon** d'ici peu, bientôt; **s. or other** un jour ou l'autre

sometimes ['sʌmtaɪmz] *adv* quelquefois

somewhat ['sʌmwɒt] *adv* quelque peu, un peu

somewhere ['sʌmweə(r)] *adv* (**a**) *(some place)* quelque part; **s. else** ailleurs; **do you have s. to stay?** est-ce que tu as trouvé à te loger?; *Fig* **now we're getting s.!** nous voilà enfin sur la bonne route *ou* voie! (**b**) *(approximately)* environ; **she's s. around fifty** elle

a environ cinquante ans; **it costs s. in the region of £500** cela coûte environ 500 livres

somnolent ['sɒmnələnt] *adj Formal* somnolent(e)

son [sʌn] *n* fils *m*; *Am very Fam* **s. of a bitch** salaud *m*

sonar ['səʊnɑː(r)] *n* sonar *m*

sonata [sə'nɑːtə] *n* sonate *f*

song [sɒŋ] *n* (**a**) *(music with words)* chanson *f*; **to burst** *or* **break into s.** se mettre à chanter; **s. book** livre *m* de chansons; **s. thrush** grive *f* musicienne (**b**) *(idioms)* **to buy sth for a s.** acheter qch pour une bouchée de pain; *Br* **to make a s. and dance (about sth)** faire toute une histoire (de qch)

songbird ['sɒŋbɜːd] *n* oiseau *m* chanteur

songwriter ['sɒŋraɪtə(r)] *n* auteur-compositeur *m*

sonic ['sɒnɪk] *adj* sonique; **s. boom** bang *m*

son-in-law ['sʌnɪnlɔː] *(pl* **sons-in-law***) n* gendre *m*

sonnet ['sɒnɪt] *n* sonnet *m*

sonny ['sʌnɪ] *n Fam* fiston *m*

sonorous ['sɒnərəs] *adj (deep)* sonore; *(impressive)* imposant(e)

soon [suːn] *adv* (**a**) *(within a short time)* bientôt; *(in past)* vite; **it will s. be Friday** c'est bientôt vendredi; **she s. changed her mind** elle a vite changé d'avis; **after(wards)** peu après; **s. after four** peu après quatre heures; **no sooner had she left than...** elle n'était pas plus tôt partie que... (**b**) *(early)* tôt; **none too s.** pas trop tôt; **how s. can you get here?** quand pouvez-vous être ici au plus tôt?; **sooner or later** tôt ou tard; **the sooner the better** le plus tôt sera le mieux; **as s. as** aussitôt que, dès que; **as s. as possible** aussitôt que possible, dès que possible (**c**) *(expressing preference)* **I would just as s. stay** j'aimerais autant rester; **I would sooner do it alone** je préférerais le faire seul

soot [sʊt] *n* suie *f*

soothe [suːð] *vt* apaiser

soothing ['suːðɪŋ] *adj* apaisant(e)

soothsayer ['suːθseɪə(r)] *n* devin (devineresse) *m,f*

sooty ['sʊtɪ] *adj (covered in soot)* couvert(e) de suie; *(black)* noir(e) comme de la suie

sop [sɒp] *n (concession)* concession *f* (**to** à)

sophist ['sɒfɪst] *n* sophiste *mf*

sophisticated [sə'fɪstɪkeɪtɪd] *adj (person, taste)* raffiné(e); *(style, humour)* recherché(e); *(machinery, technique)* sophistiqué(e)

sophistication [səfɪstɪ'keɪʃən] *n (of person, taste)* raffinement *m*; *(of style, humour)* recherche *f*; *(of machinery, technique)* sophistication *f*

sophistry ['sɒfɪstrɪ] *n (reasoning)* sophistique *f*; *(argument)* sophisme *m*

sophomore ['sɒfəmɔː(r)] *n Am* étudiant(e) *m,f* de deuxième année

soporific [sɒpə'rɪfɪk] *adj Formal* soporifique

sopping ['sɒpɪŋ] *adj* **s. (wet)** trempé(e)

soppy ['sɒpɪ] *adj Br Fam* sentimental(e)

soprano [sə'prɑːnəʊ] *(pl* **sopranos** *or* **soprani** [sə'prɑːniː]*) n (singer)* soprano *mf*; **s. voice** voix *f* de soprano

sorbet ['sɔːbeɪ] *n* sorbet *m*

sorcerer ['sɔːsərə(r)] *n* sorcier *m*

sorceress ['sɔːsərɪs] *n* sorcière *f*

sorcery ['sɔːsərɪ] *n* sorcellerie *f*

sordid ['sɔːdɪd] *adj* sordide

sore [sɔː(r)] **1** *adj* (**a**) *(painful)* douloureux(euse); **to have a s. throat/back** avoir mal à la gorge/au dos; **my feet are s.** mes pieds me font mal (**b**) *Fam* (annoyed) en colère (**about** à propos de); **it's a s. point (with him)** c'est un sujet douloureux (pour lui) **2** n (wound) plaie f

sorely ['sɔːlɪ] adv (greatly) sérieusement; **she will be s. missed** elle nous/leur manquera beaucoup; **to be s. in need of sth** avoir vraiment besoin de qch; **s. tempted** sérieusement tenté(e)

sorrow ['sɒrəʊ] n chagrin m; **to my great s.** à mon grand regret

sorrowful ['sɒrəfʊl] adj triste

sorry ['sɒrɪ] adj (**a**) (regretful, disappointed) désolé(e); **to be s. about sth** être désolé(e) de qch; **to be s. one did sth** regretter d'avoir fait qch; **to say s.** (**to sb**) s'excuser (auprès de qn); **I'm s. you didn't like it** je suis désolé(e) que tu n'aies pas aimé; **s. to keep you waiting** désolé(e) de vous faire attendre; **I'm s. to hear (that)...** je suis désolé(e) d'apprendre que...; Fam **you'll be s.!** tu vas le regretter!; **s.?** (pardon?) pardon? (**b**) (sympathetic) **to feel s. for sb** plaindre qn; **to feel s. for oneself** s'apitoyer sur son propre sort; **I'm just feeling a bit s. for myself** je suis juste un peu déprimé(e) (**c**) (pathetic) triste; **to be a s. sight** être dans un triste état; **to be in a s. state** être dans un triste état

sort [sɔːt] **1** n (**a**) (kind) sorte f; **all sorts of** toutes sortes de; **what s. of tree is it?** qu'est-ce que c'est comme arbre?; **that s. of thing** ce genre de chose; **she's that s. of person** elle est comme ça; **something of the s.** quelque chose de ce genre; **I did nothing of the s.** je n'ai jamais fait ça; **he's so arrogant – he's nothing of the s.!** il est vraiment arrogant – pas du tout!; **it takes all sorts** il faut de tout pour faire un monde; Fam **she's a good s.** c'est une brave fille; **she's not the s. to give in easily** elle n'est pas du genre à abandonner facilement; **we don't want your s. here** nous ne voulons pas de personnes de votre genre ici; **to be out of sorts** (unwell) ne pas être dans son assiette; (in a bad mood) être de mauvaise humeur; **they served us coffee of a s.** ils nous ont servi du café, si on peut appeler ça du café; **an artist of sorts** une espèce d'artiste (**b**) Fam **this is s. of embarrassing** c'est plutôt gênant; **I s. of expected it** je m'y attendais un peu; **do you like it? – s. of** ça te plaît? – oui, plus ou moins (**c**) (in order to organize) **to have a s. through sth** faire du tri dans qch
2 vt also Comput trier
▸**sort out** vt sep (**a**) (organize) ranger; **to s. oneself out** résoudre ses problèmes (**b**) (problem) régler; Fam **to s. sb out** régler son compte à qn

sorted ['sɔːtɪd] adj Br Fam bien dans sa peau, équilibré(e)

sortie ['sɔːtiː] n Mil sortie f; Fig escapade f

sorting ['sɔːtɪŋ] n tri m; **s. office** bureau m de tri

SOS [esəʊ'es] n S.O.S. m; **to send out an S.** lancer un S.O.S.

soufflé ['suːfleɪ] n soufflé m; **cheese s.** soufflé m au fromage

sought [sɔːt] pt & pp of seek

sought-after ['sɔːtɑːftə(r)] adj recherché(e)

soul [səʊl] n (**a**) (spirit) âme f; **to sell one's s.** vendre son âme au diable; Fig **she's the s. of discretion** c'est la discrétion même; Fig **it lacks s.** cela n'a pas d'âme; **All Souls' Day** le jour des Morts (**b**) (person) âme f, personne f; **he's a good s.** c'est une bonne personne; **there wasn't a s. in the street** il n'y avait pas âme qui vive dans la rue; **poor s.!** le/la pauvre! (**c**) (music) soul f

soul-destroying ['səʊldɪstrɔɪɪŋ] adj démoralisant(e)

soulful ['səʊlfʊl] adj (look, eyes) mélancolique; (song) émouvant(e)

soulless ['səʊllɪs] adj (person) insensible; (place) sans âme

soulmate ['səʊlmeɪt] n âme f sœur

soul-searching ['səʊlsɜːtʃɪŋ] n examen m de conscience

sound¹ [saʊnd] **1** n son m; (noise) bruit m; **not a s. could be heard** on n'entendait pas un bruit; **she likes the s. of her own voice** elle aime s'écouter parler; **to turn the s. up/down** (on TV, radio) monter/baisser le son; Fig **I don't like the s. of it** cela ne me dit rien qui vaille; **she's angry, by the s. of it** elle est en colère, on dirait; **s. barrier** mur m du son; **s. bite** petite phrase f (prononcée par un homme politique à la radio ou à la télévision pour frapper les esprits); Comput **s. card** carte f son; **s. effects** bruitage m; **s. engineer** ingénieur m du son; **s. wave** onde f sonore
2 vt (**a**) (bell) sonner; also Fig (alarm) donner; **to s. one's horn** klaxonner (**b**) (pronounce) prononcer; **the "h" is not sounded** le "h" ne se prononce pas
3 vi (**a**) (make sound) (of trumpet, bell) sonner (**b**) (seem) avoir l'air, sembler; **she sounds French** on dirait qu'elle est française; **that sounds like a good idea** ça me semble une bonne idée; **he sounds like a nice guy** ça a l'air d'être un type bien; **it sounds like Mozart** on dirait du Mozart; **that sounds like trouble!** c'est signe de problèmes!; **how does it s. to you?** (referring to suggestion) qu'en pensez-vous?
▸**sound off** vi Fam se plaindre (**about** de)
▸**sound out** vt sep sonder (**about** à propos de)

sound² **1** adj (**a**) (healthy) sain(e); (in good condition) en bon état; **to be of s. mind** être sain d'esprit (**b**) (sensible, logical) (argument) valable; (basis) solide; (advice) bon (bonne) (**c**) (reliable) (investment) sûr(e); (business) sain(e); (person) compétent(e)
2 adv **to be s. asleep** être profondément endormi(e)

sounding board ['saʊndɪŋbɔːd] n (on pulpit, stage) abat-voix m; Fig **I use John as a s.** j'utilise John pour tester mes idées

soundings ['saʊndɪŋz] npl **to take s.** faire des sondages

soundly ['saʊndlɪ] adv (**a**) (solidly) solidement (**b**) (logically) judicieusement (**c**) (thoroughly) **to sleep s.** dormir profondément; **to thrash sb s.** donner une bonne correction à qn

soundproof ['saʊndpruːf] **1** adj insonorisé(e)
2 vt insonoriser

soundtrack ['saʊndtræk] n bande f sonore

soup [suːp] n soupe f; Fig **to be in the s.** être dans le pétrin; **s. kitchen** soupe f populaire; **s. ladle** louche f; **s. plate** assiette f creuse; **s. spoon** cuillère f à soupe
▸**soup up** vt sep Fam (engine) gonfler; (car) gonfler le moteur de

sour ['saʊə(r)] **1** adj (fruit, milk, taste) aigre; Fig (person) aigri(e); **to turn s.** (of milk) tourner; Fig (of situation, relationship) tourner à l'aigre, mal tourner; **s. cream** crème f aigre; Fig **it was just s. grapes** c'était par dépit
2 vt (milk) faire tourner; Fig (atmosphere, relationship) empoisonner
3 vi (of milk) tourner; Fig (of atmosphere, relationship) détériorer

source [sɔːs] **1** n source f; (of unrest, discontent) origine f; Comput **s. code** code m source
2 vt (products) s'approvisionner en; **all our ingredients**

are sourced from local farms tous nos ingrédients proviennent d'exploitations agricoles locales
sourly ['saʊəlɪ] *adv* avec aigreur
souse [saʊs] *vt* tremper
south [saʊθ] **1** *n* sud *m*; **to the s. of** au sud de
   2 *adj (coast, side)* sud; *(wind)* du sud; **S. Africa** Afrique *f* du Sud; **S. African** sud-africain(e); *(person)* Sud-Africain(e) *m,f*; **S. America** Amérique *f* du Sud; **S. American** sud-américain(e); *(person)* Sud-Américain(e) *m,f*; **S. Carolina** la Caroline du Sud; **S. China Sea** mer *f* de Chine du Sud; **S. Dakota** le Dakota du Sud; **S. Korea** Corée *f* du Sud; **S. Korean** sud-coréen(-enne); *(person)* Sud-Coréen(enne) *m,f*; **S. Pole** pôle *m* sud
   3 *adv* au sud; *(travel)* vers le sud; **to face s.** *(of house)* être exposé(e) au sud
southbound ['saʊθbaʊnd] *adj (train, traffic)* en direction du sud; **s. carriageway** voie *f* sud
southeast [saʊθ'iːst] **1** *n* sud-est *m*
   2 *adj (side)* sud-est; *(wind)* du sud-est
   3 *adv* au sud-est; *(travel)* vers le sud-est
southeasterly [saʊθ'iːstəlɪ] **1** *n (pl southeasterlies) (wind)* vent *m* du sud-est
   2 *adj (direction)* vers le sud-est; *(wind)* du sud-est
southeastern [saʊθ'iːstən] *adj (region)* (du) sud-est
southerly ['sʌðəlɪ] **1** *n (pl southerlies) (wind)* vent *m* du sud
   2 *adj (direction)* vers le sud; *(wind)* du sud; **the most s. point** le point le plus au sud
southern ['sʌðən] *adj (region, accent)* du sud; **s. France** le sud de la France; **s. hemisphere** hémisphère *m* sud
southerner ['sʌðənə(r)] *n* habitant(e) *m,f* du Sud *(de l'Angleterre)*
south-facing ['saʊθ'feɪsɪŋ] *adj* exposé(e) au sud
south-southeast ['saʊθsaʊθ'iːst] *adv* au sud-sud-est; *(travel)* vers le sud-sud-est
south-southwest ['saʊθsaʊθ'west] *adv* au sud-sud-ouest; *(travel)* vers le sud-sud-ouest
southward ['saʊθwəd] **1** *adj* au sud
   2 *adv* vers le sud
southwards ['saʊθwədz] *adv* vers le sud
southwest [saʊθ'west] **1** *n* sud-ouest *m*
   2 *adj (side)* sud-ouest; *(wind)* du sud-ouest
   3 *adv* au sud-ouest; *(travel)* vers le sud-ouest
southwesterly [saʊθ'westəlɪ] **1** *n (pl southwesterlies) (wind)* vent *m* du sud-ouest
   2 *adj (direction)* vers le sud-ouest; *(wind)* du sud-ouest
southwestern [saʊθ'westən] *adj (region)* (du) sud-ouest
souvenir [suːvə'nɪə(r)] *n* souvenir *m*
sovereign ['sɒvrɪn] **1** *n* souverain(e) *m,f*
   2 *adj* souverain(e)
sovereignty ['sɒvrəntɪ] *n* souveraineté *f*
Soviet ['səʊvɪət] **1** *n (person)* Soviétique *mf*
   2 *adj* soviétique; *Formerly* **the S. Union** l'Union *f* soviétique
sow¹ [səʊ] *(pt sowed* [səʊd], *pp sown* [səʊn] *or sowed) vt (seeds)* & *Fig (discord, doubt)* semer; *(field)* ensemencer *(with en)*
sow² [saʊ] *n (female pig)* truie *f*
sown [səʊn] *pp of* **sow¹**
soya ['sɔɪə] *n* soja *m*
soy sauce [sɔɪ'sɔːs] *n* sauce *f* de soja
sozzled ['sɒzəld] *adj Br Fam (drunk)* bourré(e); **to get s.** se cuiter

spa [spɑː] *n (place)* ville *f* d'eau; *(spring)* source *f* thermale
space [speɪs] **1** *n* (**a**) *(room)* place *f*; **to stare into s.** regarder dans le vide (**b**) *(individual place)* place *f*; *(on printed form)* espace *m*; **wide open spaces** grands espaces *mpl*; **s. bar** *(on keyboard)* barre *f* d'espacement (**c**) *(period of time)* espace *m*; **in the s. of a year** en l'espace d'une année (**d**) *(outer space)* espace *m*; **the s. age** l'ère *f* spatiale; *Fam* **to be a s. cadet** planer; **s. rocket** fusée *f* spatiale; **s. shuttle** navette *f* spatiale; **s. suit** combinaison *f* spatiale; **s. travel** voyages *mpl* dans l'espace; **s. tourism** voyages *mpl* dans l'espace (**e**) *(gap)* espace *m*, vide *m*; *(in timetable)* trou *m*
   2 *vt* espacer
▸**space out** *vt sep* espacer
space-age ['speɪseɪdʒ] *adj* futuriste
spacecraft ['speɪskrɑːft] *n* vaisseau *m* spatial
spaced out ['speɪst'aʊt] *adj Fam* **to be s.** planer complètement
spaceman ['speɪsmæn] *n* astronaute *m*
spaceship ['speɪsʃɪp] *n* vaisseau *m* spatial
spacing ['speɪsɪŋ] *n* espacement *m*; *Typ* **single/double s.** simple/double interligne *m*
spacious ['speɪʃəs] *adj* spacieux(euse)
spade [speɪd] *n* (**a**) *(tool)* bêche *f*; **to call a s. a s.** appeler un chat un chat (**b**) *(in cards)* pique *m*
spaghetti [spə'getɪ] *n* spaghetti *mpl*
Spain [speɪn] *n* l'Espagne *f*
spam [spæm] *Comput* **1** *n* spams *mpl*, messages *mpl* publicitaires
   2 *vi (pt & pp spammed)* spammer, envoyer des messages publicitaires en masse
spammer ['spæmə(r)] *n Comput* spammeur *m*, = personne qui envoie des messages publicitaires en masse
spamming ['spæmɪŋ] *n Comput* spamming *m*, = envoi de messages publicitaires en masse
span [spæn] **1** *n* (**a**) *(of hand)* empan *m*; *(of wing)* envergure *f* (**b**) *(of arch)* portée *f*; *(of bridge)* travée *f* (**c**) *(period of time)* période *f* (**d**) *(of knowledge, interests)* étendue *f*
   2 *vt (pt & pp spanned) (of bridge)* franchir; *Fig (of life, knowledge)* couvrir
Spaniard ['spænjəd] *n* Espagnol(e) *m,f*
spaniel ['spænjəl] *n* épagneul *m*
Spanish ['spænɪʃ] **1** *npl (people)* **the S.** les Espagnols *mpl*
   2 *n (language)* espagnol *m*
   3 *adj* espagnol(e); **the S. Inquisition** l'Inquisition *f* espagnole; *Culin* **S. omelette** omelette *f* à l'espagnole
spank [spæŋk] **1** *n* **to give sb a s.** donner une claque sur les fesses à qn
   2 *vt* donner une fessée à
spanking ['spæŋkɪŋ] **1** *n* fessée *f*; **to give sb a s.** donner une fessée à qn
   2 *adv Fam* **s. new** flambant neuf (neuve); **they had a s. good time** ils se sont rudement bien amusés
spanner ['spænə(r)] *n Br* clef *f*; *Fig* **to throw a s. in the works** compliquer les choses
spar¹ [spɑː(r)] *n (on ship)* espar *m*
spar² *(pt & pp sparred) vi (in boxing)* s'entraîner avec qn; *(argue)* se chamailler avec qn
spare ['speə(r)] **1** *n (spare part)* pièce *f* de rechange; *(tyre)* pneu *m* de rechange
   2 *adj* (**a**) *(available)* disponible; *(surplus)* en trop, qui reste; *(reserve)* de rechange; **do you have a s. pen?** tu as un stylo à me prêter?; **to be going s.** être

en trop; **a** s. **moment** un moment de libre; s. **part** pièce f de rechange; s. **ribs** travers mpl de porc; s. **room** chambre f d'amis; s. **time** temps m (de) libre; s. **tyre** pneu m de secours ou de rechange; Fam Fig (around waist) bourrelet m; s. **wheel** roue f de secours (**b**) (frugal) (meal) frugal(e); (style) dépouillé(e); (room) austère (**c**) Br Fam (angry) to go s. sortir de ses gonds

3 vt (**a**) (give away, go without) (person) se passer de; **to have no time to** s. ne pas avoir le temps; **can you** s. **the time?** avez-vous le temps?; **with five minutes to** s. avec cinq minutes d'avance; **to have a few moments to** s. disposer de quelques minutes; **can you** s. **me a few moments?** pouvez-vous m'accorder quelques minutes?; **could you** s. **me some milk?** est-ce que tu peux me donner un peu de lait?; **to** s. **a thought for sb** penser à qn (**b**) (avoid) **to** s. **no expense** ne pas regarder à la dépense (**c**) (save from) **to** s. **sb sth** épargner qch à qn; s. **me the details!** épargnez-moi les détails! (**d**) (show mercy towards) épargner; **to** s. **sb's life** épargner la vie de qn; **to** s. **sb's feelings** ménager les sentiments de qn

sparing ['speərɪŋ] adj économe (**with** avec); **to be** s. **with one's compliments** être avare de compliments

sparingly ['speərɪŋlɪ] adv en petite quantité

spark [spɑːk] **1** n (electrical, from fire) étincelle f; Fig (of intelligence, interest) lueur f; Fig **sparks will fly** cela va faire des étincelles; Fig s. **plug** bougie f

2 vi jeter ou faire des étincelles

▸**spark off** vt sep déclencher

sparkle ['spɑːkəl] **1** n also Fig éclat m

2 vi (of light, eyes) & Fig (of person, conversation) briller; (of diamond) scintiller

sparkler ['spɑːklə(r)] n (**a**) (firework) cierge m magique (**b**) Fam (diamond) diam m

sparkling ['spɑːklɪŋ] adj (light, eyes) & Fig (person, conversation) brillant(e); (diamond) scintillant(e); (wine) pétillant(e)

sparkly ['spɑːklɪ] adj (diamond, dress) scintillant(e)

sparring partner ['spɑːrɪŋ'pɑːtnə(r)] n (in boxing) partenaire mf d'entraînement; Fig adversaire mf

sparrow ['spærəʊ] n moineau m

sparse [spɑːs] adj clairsemé(e)

sparsely ['spɑːslɪ] adv (populated, furnished) peu; s. **covered with trees** aux arbres clairsemés

spartan ['spɑːtən] adj also Fig spartiate

spasm ['spæzəm] n spasme m; Fig (of coughing) quinte f; (of jealousy) crise f

spasmodic [spæz'mɒdɪk] adj (irregular) irrégulier(ère)

spasmodically [spæz'mɒdɪklɪ] adv (irregularly) irrégulièrement

spastic ['spæstɪk] n (**a**) Med handicapé(e) m,f moteur (**b**) very Fam Pej (clumsy, useless person) empoté(e) m,f

spat[1] [spæt] n Fam (quarrel) querelle f

spat[2] pt & pp of **spit**[2]

spate [speɪt] n (of letters, calls) avalanche f; (of crimes) vague f

spatial ['speɪʃəl] adj spatial(e)

spatter ['spætə(r)] vt éclabousser (**with** avec)

spatula ['spætjʊlə] n spatule f

spawn [spɔːn] **1** n (of frog, fish) œufs mpl

2 vt (give rise to) engendrer

3 vi (of frog, fish) frayer

speak [spiːk] (pt spoke [spəʊk], pp spoken ['spəʊkən]) **1** vt (**a**) (utter) dire (**b**) (language) parler

2 vi (talk, give a speech) parler (**to/about** à/de);

they're not speaking (to each other) ils ne se parlent pas; I know her to s. to on se parle quelquefois; legally/morally speaking légalement/moralement parlant; so to s. pour ainsi dire; who's speaking? (on phone) qui est à l'appareil?; Mr Curry? – yes, speaking Mr Curry? – lui-même

▸**speak for** vt insep **to** s. **for sb** (on behalf of) parler pour qn; s. **for yourself!** parle pour toi!; **the facts** s. **for themselves** les faits parlent d'eux-mêmes

▸**speak out** vi parler franchement; **to** s. **out against sth** s'élever contre qch

▸**speak up** vi (**a**) (speak more loudly) parler plus fort (**b**) (speak in favour of) **to** s. **up for sb/sth** parler en faveur de qn/qch; **to** s. **up for oneself** se défendre

speaker ['spiːkə(r)] n (**a**) (at meeting) intervenant(e) m,f; (at conference) conférencier(ère) m,f; **an Italian** s. une personne qui parle italien; **a Spanish/Portuguese** s. un(e) hispanophone/lusophone; **to be a slow/fast** s. parler lentement/vite; Pol **the S.** Br le Président de la Chambre des communes; Am le Président du Congrès (**b**) (loudspeaker) enceinte f

speakerphone ['spiːkəfəʊn] n téléphone m avec haut-parleur; **to put sb on** s. mettre qn sur haut-parleur

speaking ['spiːkɪŋ] adj (doll, robot) parlant(e); s. **clock** horloge f parlante; s. **part** (in play, film) rôle m parlant

spear ['spɪə(r)] **1** n lance f

2 vt transpercer d'un coup de lance

spearhead ['spɪəhed] **1** n also Fig fer m de lance

2 vt (attack, campaign) être le fer de lance de

spearmint ['spɪəmɪnt] n menthe f verte

spec [spek] n Fam **on** s. à tout hasard

special ['speʃəl] **1** adj spécial(e); (friend) proche; (reason, effort, attention) particulier(ère); **what's so** s. **about the 19th of November?** qu'est-ce que le 19 novembre a de si spécial?; s. **agent** agent m secret; Br **S. Branch** = service de renseignements britannique; s. **delivery** envoi m en exprès; s. **effects** effets mpl spéciaux; s. **interest group** groupe m d'intérêt commun; s. **interest holidays** vacances fpl à thème; s. **needs** difficultés fpl d'apprentissage; s. **offer** offre f spéciale; Pol s. **powers** pouvoirs mpl exceptionnels

2 n (on menu) plat m du jour

specialist ['speʃəlɪst] **1** n spécialiste mf; Med **heart** s. cardiologue mf; **lung** s. pneumologue mf

2 adj (skills, equipment) d'un spécialiste; (shop) spécialisé(e)

speciality [speʃɪ'ælɪtɪ] (pl specialities) n Br spécialité f

specialization [speʃəlaɪ'zeɪʃən] n spécialisation f

specialize ['speʃəlaɪz] vi se spécialiser (**in** en)

specially ['speʃəlɪ] adv (expressly) spécialement

specialty ['speʃəltɪ] (pl specialties) Am = speciality

species ['spiːʃiːz] (pl species) n espèce f

specific [spɪ'sɪfɪk] **1** adj précis(e) (**about** au sujet de); **to be** s.,... pour être précis,...; Phys s. **gravity** densité f

2 npl specifics détails mpl

specifically [spɪ'sɪfɪkəlɪ] adv (**a**) (explicitly) expressément (**b**) (specially) spécialement (**c**) (precisely) précisément

specification [spesɪfɪ'keɪʃən] n spécification f

specify ['spesɪfaɪ] (pt & pp specified) vt (**a**) (state exactly) préciser (**b**) (stipulate) stipuler

specimen ['spesɪmɪn] n (**a**) (sample amount) (of handwriting, blood) échantillon m; s. **copy** spécimen m (**b**) (individual example) spécimen m; Fam **he's an odd** s. c'est un drôle de spécimen

specious ['spiːʃəs] *adj* spécieux(euse)
speck [spek] *n (of dust)* grain *m; (of paint, ink)* petite tache *f;* **a s. of dirt** une poussière
speckled ['spekəld] *adj* tacheté(e) (**with** de)
specs [speks] *npl Fam (spectacles)* lunettes *fpl*
spectacle ['spektəkəl] *n* (**a**) *(show, sight)* spectacle *m;* **to make a s. of oneself** se donner en spectacle (**b**) **spectacles** *(glasses)* lunettes *fpl*
spectacular [spek'tækjʊlə(r)] **1** *n* production *f* à grand spectacle **2** *adj* spectaculaire
spectator [spek'teɪtə(r)] *n* spectateur(trice) *m,f;* **s. sport** sport *m* à grand public
specter *Am* = **spectre**
spectra ['spektrə] *pl of* **spectrum**
spectre, Am specter ['spektə(r)] *n* spectre *m*
spectrum ['spektrəm] *(pl* **spectra** ['spektrə]*) n* spectre *m; Fig* éventail *m*
speculate ['spekjʊleɪt] *vi* (**a**) *(hypothesize)* faire des suppositions (**about** au sujet de) (**b**) *Fin* **to s. (on the Stock Market)** spéculer (à la Bourse)
speculation [spekjʊ'leɪʃən] *n* suppositions *fpl*
speculative ['spekjʊlətɪv] *adj* spéculatif(ive)
speculator ['spekjʊleɪtə(r)] *n Fin* spéculateur(trice) *m,f*
sped [sped] *pt & pp of* **speed**
speech [spiːtʃ] *n* (**a**) *(faculty)* parole *f;* **s. defect** *or* **impediment** défaut *m* d'élocution; **s. therapist** orthophoniste *mf, Belg & Suisse* logopède *mf;* **s. therapy** orthophonie *f* (**b**) *(address)* discours *m;* **to give** *or* **make a s.** faire un discours; *Br Sch* **s. day** remise *f* des prix (**c**) *(way of speaking)* langue *f* (**d**) *Gram* **part of s.** partie *f* du discours

Speech day
À la fin de l'année scolaire en Grande-Bretagne, certaines écoles invitent une personnalité à prononcer un discours et à distribuer des prix.

speechless ['spiːtʃlɪs] *adj* muet(ette) (**with** de); **to be left s.** rester sans voix
speechwriter ['spiːtʃraɪtə(r)] *n* personne *f* qui écrit des discours
speed [spiːd] **1** *n* (**a**) *(rapidity)* vitesse *f;* **the s. of light/sound** la vitesse de la lumière/du son; **at s.** à toute vitesse; **to gather** *or* **pick up/lose s.** prendre/perdre de la vitesse; *Fig* **to be up to s. on sth** être au courant de qch; **s. bump** ralentisseur *m;* **s. camera** radar *m; Am Fam* **s. cop** motard *m* (de la police); **s. dating** speed dating *m,* = soirées de rencontre dont chaque participant dispose d'un temps limité pour s'entretenir avec tous les autres; *Tel* **s. dial** numérotation *f* abrégée; **s. limit** limitation *f* de vitesse; **s. skating** patinage *m* de vitesse; **s. trap** contrôle *m* de vitesse (**b**) *(gear)* vitesse *f;* **five-s. gearbox** boîte *f* à cinq vitesses (**c**) *Fam (amphetamine)* amphés *fpl,* speed *m* **2** *vi* (**a**) *(pt & pp* **sped** [sped] *or* **speeded**) *(move quickly)* **to s. along** foncer; **to s. away/out** partir/sortir à toute vitesse; *(exceed speed limit)* faire un excès de vitesse; **to be caught speeding** être arrêté(e) pour excès de vitesse
▸**speed off** *vi* partir à toute vitesse
▸**speed up 1** *vt sep (person)* faire aller plus vite; *(work, project, process)* accélérer **2** *vi* aller plus vite

speedboat ['spiːdbəʊt] *n* vedette *f; (with outboard motor)* hors-bord *m inv*
speedily ['spiːdɪlɪ] *adv* vite, rapidement
speeding ['spiːdɪŋ] *n* excès *m* de vitesse
speedometer [spiː'dɒmɪtə(r)] *n* compteur *m* de vitesse
speedway ['spiːdweɪ] *n* speedway *m*
speedy ['spiːdɪ] *adj* rapide
spell¹ [spel] *n (magic words)* formule *f* magique; **to cast a s.** on sb jeter un sort à qn; **to break the s.** rompre le charme; **to be under a s.** être envoûté(e); **to be under sb's s.** être sous le charme de qn
spell² *(pt & pp* **spelt** [spelt] *or* **spelled**) **1** *vt* (**a**) *(in writing)* écrire, orthographier; *(aloud)* épeler; **how do you s. it?** comment ça s'écrit? (**b**) *(signify)* signifier; **to s. disaster** être un désastre; **to s. trouble** être mauvais signe **2** *vi* **he can s. well** il a une bonne orthographe; **he can't s.** il a une mauvaise orthographe
▸**spell out** *vt sep (address, name)* épeler; *Fig (explain explicitly)* expliquer clairement; **do I have to s. it out for you?** est-ce qu'il faut que je te fasse un dessin?
spell³ *n (period)* période *f;* **after a s. as a teacher, he...** après avoir été professeur pendant un temps, il...; **a cold s.** une période de froid; **a good/bad s.** une bonne/mauvaise période
spellbound ['spelbaʊnd] *adj* fasciné(e)
spell-checker ['speltʃekə(r)] *n Comput* correcteur *m* d'orthographe
speller ['spelə(r)] *n Am* manuel *m* d'orthographe
spelling ['spelɪŋ] *n* orthographe *f;* **to be good/bad at s.** être bon (bonne)/mauvais(e) en orthographe; *Am* **s. bee** concours *m* d'orthographe; **s. mistake** faute *f* d'orthographe
spelt [spelt] *pt & pp of* **spell²**
spelunker [spɪ'lʌŋkə(r)] *n Am* spéléologue *mf*
spelunking [spɪ'lʌŋkɪŋ] *n Am* spéléologie *f;* **to go s.** faire de la spéléologie
spend [spend] *(pt & pp* **spent** [spent]*) vt* (**a**) *(money)* dépenser; **to s. money on sb** dépenser de l'argent pour qn; **to s. money on sth** *(object)* dépenser de l'argent en qch; *(holidays, education)* dépenser de l'argent pour qch (**b**) *(time)* passer; **to s. time on sth/doing sth** passer du temps sur qch/à faire qch
spender ['spendə(r)] *n* **to be a big s.** être très dépensier(ère)
spending ['spendɪŋ] *n* dépenses *fpl;* **s. money** argent *m* de poche; **s. power** pouvoir *m* d'achat; **to go on a s. spree** faire des folies
spendthrift ['spendθrɪft] *n* dépensier(ère) *m,f*
spent [spent] **1** *adj (bullet, match)* utilisé(e); **to be a s. force** ne plus avoir d'influence **2** *pt & pp of* **spend**
sperm [spɜːm] *n (semen)* sperme *m;* **s. bank** banque *f* de sperme; **s. count** nombre *m* de spermatozoïdes; **s. donor** donneur *m* de sperme; **s. whale** cachalot *m*
spermicide ['spɜːmɪsaɪd] *n* spermicide *m*
spew [spjuː] *vt & vi Br Fam (vomit)* dégobiller
sphere [sfɪə(r)] *n also Fig* sphère *f;* **that's outside my s.** ce n'est pas dans mes compétences; **s. of influence** sphère d'influence
spherical ['sferɪkəl] *adj* sphérique
sphincter ['sfɪŋktə(r)] *n Anat* sphincter *m*
sphinx [sfɪŋks] *n* sphinx *m*
spice [spaɪs] **1** *n (seasoning)* épice *f; Fig (excitement)* sel *m,* piquant *m;* **s. rack** présentoir *m* à épices

2 *vt (food)* épicer; *Fig* **to s. sth (up)** *(make more exciting)* ajouter du piquant à qch

spick-and-span [spɪkən'spæn] *adj Fam* nickel, impeccable

spicy ['spaɪsɪ] *adj (food)* épicé(e); *Fig (story, gossip)* croustillant(e)

spider ['spaɪdə(r)] *n* araignée *f*; **s.'s web** toile *f* d'araignée; **s. plant** chlorophytum *m*

spiel [ʃpiːl] *n Fam* baratin *m*

spike [spaɪk] **1** *n* pointe *f*; **spikes** *(running shoes)* pointes *fpl*
2 *vt* **to s. sb's guns** mettre des bâtons dans les roues de qn; **to s. sb's drink** ajouter de l'alcool dans la boisson de qn

spiky ['spaɪkɪ] *adj (plant)* couvert(e) de piquants; *(hair)* en épis

spill [spɪl] **1** *n* **to take a s.** *(fall)* faire une chute
2 *vt (pt & pp* **spilt** [spɪlt] *or* **spilled)** renverser; *Fig* **to s. the beans** vendre la mèche
3 *vi (of liquid)* se répandre

▸**spill over** *vi (of liquid)* déborder; *Fig (of conflict)* s'étendre

spillage ['spɪlɪdʒ] *n* déversement *m*

spilt [spɪlt] *pt & pp of* **spill**

spin [spɪn] **1** *n* **(a)** *(turning movement)* tournoiement *m*; **to go into a s.** *(of car)* faire un tête-à-queue; *Pej Pol* **s. doctor** = spécialiste en communication chargé de présenter l'information de façon à mettre en valeur un parti politique (**b**) *Fam (in car)* **to go for a s.** aller faire un tour (**c**) *(on ball)* effet *m*; **to put s. on a ball** donner de l'effet à une balle
2 *vt (pt & pp* **spun** [spʌn]) (**a**) *(wool, cotton)* filer (**b**) *(wheel, top)* faire tourner, faire tournoyer; **to s. a coin** jouer à pile ou face (**c**) *(spin-dry)* essorer
3 *vi* tourner, tournoyer; **my head's spinning** j'ai la tête qui tourne; **the room's spinning** la pièce tourne (autour de moi)

▸**spin out** *vt sep (speech, debate)* faire traîner (en longueur); *(money)* faire durer

spinach ['spɪnɪtʃ] *n* épinards *mpl*

spinal ['spaɪnəl] *adj* vertébral(e); **s. column** colonne *f* vertébrale; **s. cord** moelle *f* épinière; **s. injury** lésion *f* de la colonne vertébrale

spindly ['spɪndlɪ] *adj (person)* chétif(ive); *(arms, legs)* maigre

spin-dry ['spɪn'draɪ] *(pt & pp* **spin-dried)** *vt* essorer

spin-dryer ['spɪn'draɪə(r)] *n* essoreuse *f*

spine [spaɪn] *n* (**a**) *(backbone)* colonne *f* vertébrale (**b**) *(of book)* dos *m* (**c**) *(of plant, hedgehog)* piquant *m*

spine-chilling ['spaɪntʃɪlɪŋ] *adj* à vous glacer le sang

spineless ['spaɪnlɪs] *adj (weak)* mou (molle)

spinney ['spɪnɪ] *(pl* **spinneys)** *n* bosquet *m*

spinning ['spɪnɪŋ] *n* **s. top** toupie *f*; **s. wheel** rouet *m*

spin-off ['spɪnɒf] *n* (**a**) *(result)* retombée *f* (**b**) *(TV programme)* = feuilleton tiré d'un film ou d'un autre feuilleton

spinster ['spɪnstə(r)] *n* vieille fille *f*

spiny ['spaɪnɪ] *adj* couvert(e) de piquants; **s. lobster** langouste *f*

spiral ['spaɪərəl] **1** *n* spirale *f*; **s. staircase** escalier *m* en colimaçon
2 *vi (pt & pp* **spiralled)** *(of smoke)* s'élever *ou* monter en spirale; *(of prices)* s'envoler

spire ['spaɪə(r)] *n (of church)* flèche *f*

spirit ['spɪrɪt] *n* (**a**) *(soul, being)* esprit *m*; **the Holy S.** le Saint-Esprit (**b**) *(mood, attitude)* esprit *m*; **to enter into the s. of sth** participer de bon cœur à qch; **to take sth in the right/wrong s.** bien/mal prendre qch; **to be in good/poor spirits** être de bonne humeur/déprimé(e); *Fam* **that's the s.!** à la bonne heure! (**c**) *(determination)* courage *m*; **to break sb's s.** entamer le courage de qn (**d**) **spirits** *(drinks)* spiritueux *mpl*; **s. lamp** lampe *f* à alcool; **s. level** niveau *m* (à bulle)

▸**spirit away, spirit off** *vt sep* faire disparaître (comme par enchantement)

spirited ['spɪrɪtɪd] *adj (person, defence)* courageux(-euse); *(reply)* énergique; *(performance)* plein(e) de brio

spiritual ['spɪrɪtʃʊəl] **1** *adj* spirituel(elle); **France is my s. home** c'est en France que je me sens vraiment chez moi
2 *n* **(Negro) s.** Negro spiritual *m*

spiritualism ['spɪrɪtʃʊəlɪzəm] *n* spiritisme *m*

spirituality [spɪrɪtʃʊ'ælɪtɪ] *n* spiritualité *f*

spit[1] [spɪt] *n* (**a**) *(for cooking)* broche *f* (**b**) *(of land)* pointe *f*

spit[2] **1** *n (saliva)* salive *f*; *(spittle)* crachat *m*; *Fam* **s. and polish** astiquage *m*
2 *vt (pt & pp* **spat** [spæt]) cracher
3 *vi (of person, cat)* cracher; *(of hot fat)* sauter; *Fig* **to be within spitting distance (of)** être à deux pas (de); **it's spitting** *(with rain)* il pleuvote

▸**spit out** *vt sep* cracher; *Fam* **s. it out!** *(say what you want to)* allez, accouche!

spite [spaɪt] **1** *n* (**a**) *(malice)* dépit *m*; **out of s.** par dépit (**b**) **in s. of** malgré; **to do sth in s. of oneself** faire qch malgré soi
2 *vt* vexer

spiteful ['spaɪtfʊl] *adj* vexant(e)

spitting image ['spɪtɪŋ'ɪmɪdʒ] *n Fam* **he's the s. of his father** c'est son père tout craché

spittle ['spɪtəl] *n* crachat *m*

spiv [spɪv] *n Br very Fam* aigrefin *m*

splash [splæʃ] **1** *n* (**a**) *(of liquid)* éclaboussure *f*; *(sound)* plouf *m*; *Fam Fig* **to make a s.** faire sensation; *Comput* **s. screen** splash screen *m* (**b**) *(of colour, light)* tache *f*
2 *vt* éclabousser (**with** de); **to s. one's face with water** se passer le visage à l'eau; **the photo was splashed across the front page** la photo était étalée à la une
3 *vi (of liquid, waves)* faire des éclaboussures

▸**splash about, splash around** *vi* patauger

▸**splash down** *vi (of spacecraft)* amerrir

▸**splash out** *vt sep Fam* claquer des ronds (**on** en achetant)

splatter ['splætə(r)] **1** *n* éclaboussure *f*; *(sound)* crépitement *m*
2 *vt* éclabousser (**with** de)

splay [spleɪ] *vt* écarter

spleen [spliːn] *n* (**a**) *(part of body)* rate *f* (**b**) *Formal (anger)* mauvaise humeur *f*; **to vent one's s. (on sb)** passer sa mauvaise humeur (sur qn)

splendid ['splendɪd] *adj* magnifique

splendour, *Am* **splendor** ['splendə(r)] *n* splendeur *f*

splice [splaɪs] *vt (film)* coller; *(rope)* épisser; *Fam* **to get spliced** *(marry)* se caser

splint [splɪnt] *n* attelle *f*

splinter ['splɪntə(r)] **1** *n (of wood, glass)* éclat *m*; *(in finger)* écharde *f*; *(of bone)* esquille *f*; *Pol* **s. group** groupe *m* dissident
2 *vt* briser
3 *vi* se briser; *Fig (of political party)* se scinder

split [splɪt] **1** *n (in wood)* fente *f; (in group)* division *f; (in garment) (tear)* déchirure *f; (by design)* fente *f;* **to do the splits** faire le grand écart
2 *adj* brisé(e); **s. ends** *(in hair)* fourches *fpl;* **s. peas** pois *mpl* cassés; **s. personality** dédoublement *m* de la personnalité; *Cin & Comput* **s. screen** écran *m* divisé; **in a s. second** en quelques dixièmes de seconde
3 *vt (pt & pp* **split**) (**a**) *(wood)* fendre; *(cloth)* déchirer; *(seam)* faire craquer; *(group)* diviser; *(political party)* scinder; **to s. one's head open** se fendre le crâne; **to s. the vote** éparpiller les voix; *Fam* **to s. one's sides (laughing)** se tordre de rire; *Fig* **to s. hairs** couper les cheveux en quatre (**b**) *(share)* partager; **to s. the difference** partager la différence
4 *vi* (**a**) *(of wood)* se fendre; *(of cloth)* se déchirer; *(of seam)* craquer; *(of group)* se diviser; *(of political party)* se scinder (**b**) *very Fam (leave)* se casser
▸**split up 1** *vt sep (share out)* diviser, partager
2 *vi (of couple, group)* se séparer; **to s. up with sb** rompre avec qn
split-second ['splɪtsekənd] *adj (decision)* pris(e) en un rien de temps; *(timing)* au quart de seconde
splitting ['splɪtɪŋ] *adj* **to have a s. headache** avoir un mal de tête atroce
splodge [splɒdʒ] *n Fam* tache *f*
splutter ['splʌtə(r)] *vi (of person)* bredouiller; *(of engine)* tousser; *(of flame, candle)* crépiter
spoil [spɔɪl] *(pt & pp* **spoilt** [spɔɪlt] *or* **spoiled**) **1** *vt* (**a**) *(ruin)* gâcher; **to s. sb's fun** gâcher le plaisir de qn; **to s. sb's appetite** couper l'appétit à qn; *Pol* **spoilt ballot** vote *m* nul (**b**) *(indulge)* gâter; **spoilt child** enfant *mf* gâté(e); **to be spoilt for choice** avoir l'embarras du choix
2 *vi* (**a**) *(of food)* s'abîmer (**b**) **to be spoiling for a fight** chercher la bagarre
spoils [spɔɪlz] *npl (of war, crime)* butin *m*
spoilsport ['spɔɪlspɔːt] *n Fam* rabat-joie *mf inv*
spoilt [spɔɪlt] *pt & pp of* **spoil**
spoke¹ [spəʊk] *n (of wheel)* rayon *m; Fig* **to put a s. in sb's wheel** mettre des bâtons dans les roues à qn
spoke² *pt of* **speak**
spoken ['spəʊkən] *pp of* **speak**
spokesman ['spəʊksmən] *n* porte-parole *m*
spokesperson ['spəʊkspɜːsən] *n* porte-parole *m*
spokeswoman ['spəʊkswʊmən] *n* porte-parole *m*
sponge [spʌndʒ] **1** *n* éponge *f; Fig* **to throw in the s.** jeter l'éponge; **s. bag** trousse *f* de toilette; **s. cake** génoise *f;* **s. pudding** = sorte de génoise, cuite à la vapeur et servie avec de la crème anglaise, de la confiture *etc*
2 *vt* (**a**) *(wash)* nettoyer avec une éponge (**b**) *Fam (scrounge)* taper (**off** *or* **from** à)
3 *vi Fam (scrounge)* taper les autres
▸**sponge down** *vt sep (wash)* nettoyer avec une éponge
▸**sponge off 1** *vt sep (stain)* faire partir d'un coup d'éponge
2 *vt insep Fam (scrounge from)* taper
sponger ['spʌndʒə(r)] *n Fam* tapeur(euse) *m,f*
spongy ['spʌndʒɪ] *adj* spongieux(euse)
sponsor ['spɒnsə(r)] **1** *n* sponsor *m; (of student, club member)* parrain *m*
2 *vt* sponsoriser; *(student)* financer les études de; *(club member)* parrainer; **sponsored walk** marche *f* parrainée

Sponsored event

La Grande-Bretagne compte de très nombreuses organisations caritatives ("charities"). L'un des moyens employés pour rassembler des fonds est de s'engager auprès d'autres gens (généralement des amis, voisins et collègues de travail) à accomplir une épreuve en échange d'une somme d'argent déterminée. Il peut s'agir d'épreuves physiques ("sponsored walk", "sponsored swim") ou de défis saugrenus, tels que se rendre au bureau en pyjama ou bien encore garder le silence pendant toute une journée ("sponsored silence"). Des "sponsored events" sont également organisés par des écoles et des clubs sportifs afin d'obtenir de l'argent pour acheter du matériel.

sponsorship ['spɒnsəʃɪp] *n* sponsoring *m; (of student, club member)* parrainage *m;* **s. deal** *(for athlete, team)* contrat *m* de sponsoring
spontaneity [spɒntə'neɪtɪ] *n* spontanéité *f*
spontaneous [spɒn'teɪnɪəs] *adj* spontané(e)
spoof [spuːf] *Fam* **1** *n* (**a**) *(parody)* parodie *f* (**on** de) (**b**) *(hoax)* canular *m*
2 *adj* **a s. documentary** *(parody)* une parodie de documentaire; **a s. phone call** *(hoax)* un canular téléphonique
spook [spuːk] *Fam* **1** *n* (**a**) *(ghost)* fantôme *m* (**b**) *(spy)* barbouze *mf*
2 *vt* ficher la trouille à
spooky ['spuːkɪ] *adj Fam* qui fait froid dans le dos
spool [spuːl] *n* bobine *f*
spoon [spuːn] **1** *n* cuillère *f*
2 *vt* **to s. sth onto sth** mettre qch sur qch avec une cuillère
spoon-feed ['spuːnfiːd] *(pt & pp* **spoon-fed** ['spuːnfed]) *vt* faire manger à la cuillère; *Fig* mâcher le travail de
spoonful ['spuːnfʊl] *n* cuillerée *f*
sporadic [spə'rædɪk] *adj* sporadique
spore [spɔː(r)] *n* spore *f*
sporran ['spɒrən] *n Scot* = bourse portée sur le devant du kilt
sport [spɔːt] **1** *n* (**a**) *(activity)* sport *m* (**b**) *Fam (person)* **to be a (good) s.** *(man)* être un chic type; *(woman)* être une chic fille; **to be a bad s.** être mauvais(e) joueur(euse)
2 *vt (wear)* arborer
sporting ['spɔːtɪŋ] *adj* (**a**) *(related to sport)* sportif(ive) (**b**) *(fair)* chic *inv;* **to give sb a s. chance** donner sa chance à qn
sports [spɔːts] *adj* **s. bra** soutien-gorge *m* de sport; **s. car** voiture *f* de sport; **s. centre** complexe *m* sportif; **s. day** = compétition sportive annuelle organisée à l'école; **s. ground** terrain *m* de sport; *Br* **s. jacket** veste *f* sport; **s. page** page *f* des sports; **s. science** sciences *fpl* du sport; **s. shop** magasin *m* de sports
sportsman ['spɔːtsmən] *n* sportif *m*
sportsmanship ['spɔːtsmənʃɪp] *n* esprit *m* sportif
sportsperson ['spɔːtspɜːsən] *n* sportif(ive) *m,f*
sportswoman ['spɔːtswʊmən] *n* sportive *f*
sporty ['spɔːtɪ] *adj (person)* sportif(ive); *(car, clothing)* de sport
spot [spɒt] **1** *n* (**a**) *(place)* endroit *m;* **on the s.** sur place; *Fam* **to put sb on the s.** mettre qn en mauvaise posture; *Fam* **to be in a (tight) s.** être dans le pétrin; **s. check** contrôle *m* surprise (**b**) *(stain)* tache *f* (**c**)

(pimple) bouton *m* (**d**) *(forming pattern on cloth)* pois *m*; *(on leopard)* tache *f* (**e**) *Br Fam (small amount)* goutte *f*; **to have a s.** **of lunch** manger un morceau; **a s. of bother** de petits problèmes *mpl* (**f**) *(spotlight)* projecteur *m*; *(smaller)* spot *m* (**g**) *(on TV, radio, in show)* numéro *m*
2 *vt (pt & pp spotted)* (**a**) *(stain, mark)* tacher (**b**) *(notice)* remarquer; *(opportunity, opening)* repérer; **to s. sb doing sth** apercevoir qn en train de faire qch; **well spotted!** bien vu!

spotless ['spɒtlɪs] *adj* impeccable; *Fig (reputation)* irréprochable

spotlight ['spɒtlaɪt] *n* projecteur *m*; *(smaller)* spot *m*; *Fig* être sous le feu des projecteurs

spot-on ['spɒt'ɒn] *adj Fam* tout à fait exact(e)

spotter plane ['spɒtə'pleɪn] *n* avion-espion *m*

spotty ['spɒtɪ] *adj (pimply)* boutonneux(euse)

spouse [spaʊz] *n* époux (épouse) *m,f*

spout [spaʊt] **1** *n (of teapot, kettle)* bec *m*; *Fam Fig* **to be up the s.** être fichu(e); *(of economy, business)* s'être cassé la figure; *(pregnant)* être enceinte
2 *vt (water)* faire jaillir; *Fam Fig (speech, nonsense)* débiter
3 *vi (of liquid)* jaillir; *Fam Fig (of person)* faire des discours

sprain [spreɪn] **1** *n (injury)* entorse *f*
2 *vt* **to s. one's ankle/wrist** se fouler la cheville/le poignet

sprang [spræŋ] *pt of* **spring**

sprat [spræt] *n* sprat *m*

sprawl [sprɔːl] *vi (of person)* s'affaler; *(of town)* s'étendre

sprawling ['sprɔːlɪŋ] *adj (person)* affalé(e); *(town)* tentaculaire

spray¹ [spreɪ] *n (of flowers)* bouquet *m*

spray² **1** *n* (**a**) *(of liquid)* fines gouttelettes *fpl*; *(from sea)* embruns *mpl* (**b**) *(act of spraying)* **to give sth a s.** *(flowers, crops)* pulvériser; *(room)* vaporiser (**c**) *(device)* bombe *f*; *(for perfume)* atomiseur *m*; **s. can** bombe *f* aérosol; **s. gun** *(for paint)* pistolet *m* (à peinture)
2 *vt (flowers, crops)* pulvériser; *(room)* vaporiser; **to s. oneself with perfume** se mettre du parfum *(avec un vaporisateur)*; **to s. sb with sth** asperger qn de qch

spray-on ['spreɪɒn] *adj (product, lotion etc)* en bombe, en aérosol

spray-paint ['spreɪpeɪnt] **1** *n* peinture *f* en bombe
2 *vt (with spray can)* peindre à la bombe; *(with spray gun)* peindre au pistolet

spread [spred] **1** *n* (**a**) *(of idea, religion, language)* diffusion *f*; *(of disease)* propagation *f* (**b**) *(of products, ages)* éventail *m* (**c**) *(in newspaper)* **full-page s.** pleine page *f*; **double-page s.** double page *f* (**d**) *(paste)* **cheese/chocolate s.** fromage *m*/chocolat *m* à tartiner (**e**) *(of wings, sails)* envergure *f* (**f**) *Fam (big meal)* festin *m*
2 *vt (pt & pp spread)* (**a**) *(arms, legs)* écarter; *Fig* **to s. one's wings** acquérir de l'indépendance (**b**) *(sand, sawdust, terror)* répandre; *(rumour, disease, germs)* propager; *(payments)* étaler (**c**) *(butter, ointment)* étaler; **to s. a surface with sth** étaler qch sur une surface
3 *vi* se répandre; *(of rumour, disease, fire)* se propager

▸**spread out 1** *vt sep* (**a**) *(map, newspaper)* étaler (**b**) **to be spread out** *(of fields, city)* s'étendre

2 *vi (of person)* s'étendre; *(of search party)* se disperser

spreadsheet ['spredʃiːt] *n Comput* tableur *m*

spree [spriː] *n Fam* **to go on a s.** *(go drinking)* prendre une cuite; **to go on a shopping** *or* **spending s.** faire des folies dans les magasins

sprig [sprɪg] *n (of parsley)* brin *m*; *(of holly, mistletoe)* branche *f*

sprightly ['spraɪtlɪ] *adj* alerte

spring [sprɪŋ] **1** (**a**) *(of water)* source *f* (**b**) *(season)* printemps *m*; **in (the) s.** au printemps; **s. onion** ciboule *f*; **s. roll** rouleau *m* de printemps; **s. tide** grande marée *f* (**c**) *(leap)* bond *m* (**d**) *(elasticity)* élasticité *f*; **to walk with a s. in one's step** marcher d'un pas souple (**e**) *(device)* ressort *m*
2 *vt (pt sprang [spræŋ], pp sprung [sprʌŋ])* (**a**) *(reveal unexpectedly)* **to s. sth on sb** annoncer qch à qn (**b**) *(develop)* **to s. a surprise on sb** faire une surprise à qn (**b**) *(develop)* **to s. a leak** commencer à fuir; *(of boat)* commencer à prendre l'eau (**c**) *Fam (prisoner)* faire évader
3 *vi* (**a**) *(jump)* bondir, sauter; **to s. to one's feet** se lever d'un bond; **to s. into action** passer rapidement à l'action; **to s. to life** *(of person, town)* s'animer; *(of machine)* se mettre en marche; **to s. to sb's defence** prendre vivement la défense de qn; **to s. open/shut** s'ouvrir/se fermer brusquement; **to s. to mind** venir à l'esprit (**b**) *(originate)* **to s. from** venir de; **to s. into existence** voir le jour; *Fam* **where did you s. from?** d'où sortez-vous?

▸**spring up** *vi* (**a**) *(jump to one's feet)* se lever d'un bond (**b**) *(appear suddenly)* surgir; *(of wind)* se lever; *(of feeling)* prendre naissance

springboard ['sprɪŋbɔːd] *n also Fig* tremplin *m*

spring-clean [sprɪŋ'kliːn] **1** *n* grand nettoyage *m*
2 *vt* nettoyer à fond

spring-cleaning [sprɪŋ'kliːnɪŋ] *n* grand nettoyage *m*; **to do the s.** faire le grand nettoyage

springtime ['sprɪŋtaɪm] *n* printemps *m*

springy ['sprɪŋɪ] *adj* souple

sprinkle ['sprɪŋkəl] **1** *n (of salt, flour)* pincée *f*
2 *vt (with liquid)* arroser, asperger (**with** de); *(with salt, flour)* saupoudrer (**with** de); **to s. liquid on sth** arroser *ou* asperger qch de liquide; **to s. salt/flour on sth** saupoudrer qch de sel/farine

sprinkler ['sprɪŋklə(r)] *n (for lawns)* arroseur *m*; *(for fire prevention)* sprinkler *m*

sprinkling ['sprɪŋklɪŋ] *n* **a s. of** *(liquid)* quelques gouttes de; *(salt, flour)* un peu de; *Fig (people)* quelques

sprint [sprɪnt] **1** *n (fast run)* sprint *m*; *(race)* course *f* (de vitesse); **to put on a s.** piquer un sprint
2 *vi (run fast)* piquer un sprint; **to s. off** partir en courant

sprinter ['sprɪntə(r)] *n* sprinter(euse) *m,f*

sprocket ['sprɒkɪt] *n* **s. (wheel)** pignon *m*

sprout [spraʊt] **1** *n (of plant)* pousse *f*; **(Brussels) s.** chou *m* de Bruxelles
2 *vt (leaves, shoots)* faire; *Fam (moustache, beard)* se laisser pousser
3 *vi (of leaves, hair)* pousser

▸**sprout up** *vi (of plant, child)* pousser; *(of new buildings, towns)* surgir

spruce¹ [spruːs] *n (tree)* épicéa *m*

spruce² *adj* impeccable

▸**spruce up** *vt sep (room)* bien nettoyer; **to s. oneself up** se faire beau (belle)

sprung [sprʌŋ] **1** *adj (mattress)* à ressorts
 2 *pp of* **spring**
spry [spraɪ] *adj* alerte
spud [spʌd] *n Fam (potato)* patate *f*
spun [spʌn] **1** *adj* **s. silk** schappe *f*
 2 *pt & pp of* **spin**
spunk [spʌŋk] *n* (**a**) *Fam (courage)* cran *m* (**b**) *Vulg (semen)* sperme *m*
spur [spɜː(r)] *n* (**a**) *(for riding)* éperon *m*; *Fig (stimulus)* motivation *f*; *Fig* **to win one's spurs** faire ses preuves; **on the s. of the moment** sur un coup de tête (**b**) *(of land, rock)* éperon *m*
 2 *vt (pt & pp* **spurred**) *(horse)* éperonner; *Fig* **to s. sb on** stimuler qn; **to s. sb on to do sth** inciter qn à faire qch; *Fig* **to s. sb into action** inciter qn à agir
spurious ['spjʊərɪəs] *adj (argument, reasoning)* spécieux(euse); *(claim, story, charge)* sans fondement
spurn [spɜːn] *vt* repousser, rejeter
spurt [spɜːt] **1** *n (of liquid)* giclée *f*; *(of activity, energy)* regain *m*; *(increase in speed)* accélération *f*; **to do sth in spurts** faire qch par à-coups; **to put on a s.** accélérer
 2 *vi* **the wound was spurting blood** le sang giclait de la blessure; **the pen spurted ink** l'encre giclait du stylo
 3 *vi* (**a**) *(of liquid)* gicler (**b**) *(move quickly)* **to s. off** s'élancer brusquement
sputter ['spʌtə(r)] *vi (of engine)* toussoter; *(of flame, candle)* crépiter
spy [spaɪ] **1** *n (pl* **spies**) espion(onne) *m,f*; **s. plane** avion *m* espion; **s. ring** réseau *m* d'espionnage; **s. satellite** satellite *m* espion
 2 *vt (pt & pp* **spied**) *(notice)* repérer
 3 *vi* espionner, faire de l'espionnage; **to s. on sb** espionner qn
▸**spy out** *vt sep Fig* **to s. out the land** tâter le terrain
spyware ['spaɪweə(r)] *n Comput* logiciel *m* espion
Sq *(abbr* **Square**) pl
sq *(abbr* **square**) carré; **sq ft** ≃ mètres *mpl* carrés
squabble ['skwɒbəl] **1** *n* querelle *f*
 2 *vi* se quereller (**about** *or* **over** à propos de)
squabbling ['skwɒblɪŋ] *n* querelles *fpl*
squad [skwɒd] *n (of workmen)* équipe *f*; *(of athletes, footballers)* délégation *f*; *(of soldiers)* section *f*; *(of police)* brigade *f*; **s. car** voiture *f* de patrouille
squadron ['skwɒdrən] *n Mil (of planes)* escadron *m*; *(of ships)* escadrille *f*
squalid ['skwɒlɪd] *adj (dirty)* crasseux(euse); *(sordid)* sordide
squall [skwɔːl] **1** *n (of wind)* bourrasque *f*
 2 *vi (cry)* pousser des hurlements
squalor ['skwɒlə(r)] *n (dirtiness)* crasse *f*; *(poverty)* misère *f* noire
squander ['skwɒndə(r)] *vt (money, resources, talents)* gaspiller; *(time)* perdre; *(fortune, inheritance)* dilapider; *(opportunity)* laisser passer
square [skweə(r)] **1** *n* (**a**) *(shape)* carré *m*; *(on chessboard, map)* case *f*; *Fig* **to be back at s. one** être de retour à la case départ (**b**) *Math* carré *m* (**c**) *(of town, village)* place *f* (**d**) *Fam (unfashionable person)* **to be a s.** être ringard(e)
 2 *adj* (**a**) *(in shape)* carré(e) (**b**) *(right-angled)* **s. corner** angle *m* droit (**c**) *Math* carré(e); **s. root** racine *f* carrée (**d**) *Fam (unfashionable)* vieux jeu *inv*, ringard(e) (**e**) *(idioms)* **to be s. with sb** être honnête avec qn; **we're s.** nous sommes quittes; **to feel like a s. peg in a round hole** ne pas se sentir à sa place; **s.**

deal arrangement *m* équitable; **s. meal** bon repas *m*
 3 *adv* **to hit sb s. on the jaw** frapper qn en pleine mâchoire; **to look sb s. in the eye** regarder qn bien en face
 4 *vt* (**a**) *(make square)* mettre en forme de carré; *Math (number)* élever au carré; **squared paper** papier *m* quadrillé (**b**) *(settle) (account, debt)* régler (**c**) *(arrange)* **to s. sth with sb** arranger qch avec qn
 5 *vi (agree)* coller; **to s. with** correspondre à
▸**square up** *vi* (**a**) *(settle debts)* régler ses comptes (**b**) *(of fighters)* se mettre en garde; *Fig* **to s. up to a problem/an opponent** faire face à un problème/un adversaire
squarely ['skweəlɪ] *adv* (**a**) *(directly)* **to hit sb s. in the chest/face** frapper qn en pleine poitrine/figure (**b**) *(honestly)* honnêtement
squash¹ [skwɒʃ] **1** *n* (**a**) *(crush)* cohue *f*; **it was a s.** on était serrés comme des sardines (**b**) *Br (drink)* **orange/lemon s.** ≃ sirop *m* d'orange/de citron (**c**) *(sport)* squash *m*; **s. court** court *m* de squash
 2 *vt* écraser
 3 *vi* **to s. into a room/car** s'entasser dans une pièce/voiture
squash² *n Am (vegetable)* courge *f*
▸**squash up** *vi* se serrer
squat [skwɒt] **1** *n (illegally occupied dwelling)* squat *m*
 2 *adj (person, object, building)* trapu(e)
 3 *vi (pt & pp* **squatted**) (**a**) *(crouch down) (of person)* s'accroupir; *(of animal)* se tapir (**b**) *(occupy illegally)* squatter
squatter ['skwɒtə(r)] *n* squatter *m*
squaw [skwɔː] *n* squaw *f*
squawk [skwɔːk] **1** *n (of bird)* cri *m* rauque; *Fam (of person)* braillement *m*
 2 *vi (of bird)* pousser un cri rauque; *Fam (of person)* brailler
squeak [skwiːk] **1** *n (of animal, person)* cri *m* aigu; *(of door, hinges)* grincement *m*; *Fam* **I don't want to hear another s. out of you** je ne veux plus vous entendre
 2 *vi (of animal, person)* pousser un cri aigu; *(of door, hinges)* grincer; *(of shoes)* craquer
squeaky ['skwiːkɪ] *adj (voice)* aigu(ë); *(door, hinges)* qui grince; *(shoes)* qui craque; **s. clean** impeccable
squeal [skwiːl] **1** *n (of person, animal)* cri *m* perçant; *(of brakes)* crissement *m*
 2 *vt* crier
 3 *vi* (**a**) *(of person, animal)* pousser un cri perçant; *(of brakes)* crisser; *Fam* **to s. about sth** *(complain)* se lamenter au sujet de qch (**b**) *very Fam (inform)* moucharder; **to s. on sb** balancer qn
squeamish ['skwiːmɪʃ] *adj* de nature délicate; **to be s. about sth** ne pas supporter qch
squeeze [skwiːz] **1** *n* pression *f*; **to give sth a s.** presser qch; **to give sb a s.** *(hug)* serrer qn dans ses bras; **a s. of lemon** quelques gouttes de citron; *Fam* **it was a tight s.** nous étions/ils étaient/*etc* serrés comme des sardines; *Fam* **to put the s. on sb** *(pressurize)* faire pression sur qn
 2 *vt (press)* presser; **to s. sb's hand** serrer la main à qn; *Fig* **to s. sb** *(pressurize)* faire pression sur qn (**b**) *(squash)* **to s. sth into sth** faire rentrer qch dans qch; **I think we can just s. you in** je pense qu'on peut vous trouver une place
 3 *vi* **to s. into sth** s'entasser dans qch; **to s. past sb** se glisser devant qn; **s. up a bit!** serrez-vous un peu!
▸**squeeze out** *vt sep (juice)* exprimer

squelch [skweltʃ] *vi* patauger; **to s. through the mud** avancer en pataugeant dans la boue

squib [skwɪb] *n (firework)* pétard *m*; *Fig* **to be a damp s.** être bidon *inv*

squid [skwɪd] *(pl* **squid**) *n* calmar *m*

squiggle ['skwɪgəl] *n* gribouillis *m*

squint [skwɪnt] **1** *n* (**a**) *(eye defect)* strabisme *m*; **to have a s.** loucher (**b**) *(quick look)* coup d'œil *m*; **to have a s. at** jeter un coup d'œil à
2 *vi* (**a**) *(have eye defect)* loucher (**b**) *(narrow one's eyes)* plisser les yeux; **to s. at** plisser les yeux pour voir

squire ['skwaɪə(r)] *n (landowner)* châtelain *m*; *Hist* écuyer *m*

squirm [skwɜːm] *vi (wriggle)* se tortiller; *Fig* **to s. (with embarrassment)** être mal à l'aise

squirrel ['skwɪrəl] *n* écureuil *m*

squirt [skwɜːt] **1** *n* (**a**) *(of liquid)* giclée *f* (**b**) *Fam Pej (insignificant person)* petit(e) morveux(euse) *m,f*
2 *vt (liquid)* faire gicler; **to s. sth on sb/sth, to s. sb/ sth with sth** asperger qn/qch de qch
3 *vi (of liquid)* **to s. out** gicler

Sr (*abbr* **Senior**) **Thomas Smith, Sr** Thomas Smith père

Sri Lanka [sriː'læŋkə] *n* le Sri Lanka

Sri Lankan [sriː'læŋkən] **1** *n* Sri Lankais(e) *m,f*
2 *adj* sri lankais(e)

SSE (*abbr* **south-southeast**) sud-sud-est

SSN [eses'en] *n Am* (*abbr* **social security number**) numéro *m* de sécurité sociale

SSW (*abbr* **south-southwest**) sud-sud-ouest

St (**a**) (*abbr* **Street**) rue *f* (**b**) (*abbr* **Saint**) st(e); *Bot & Med* **St John's wort** millepertuis *m*; *Geog* **St Kitts and Nevis** Saint-Kitts-et-Nevis; **St Lucia** Sainte-Lucie; **St Petersburg** Saint-Petersbourg; **St Vincent and the Grenadines** Saint-Vincent-et-les-Grenadines; *see also* **saint**

stab [stæb] **1** *n* (**a**) *(with knife)* coup *m* de couteau; *Fig* **a s. of pain** un élancement; **a s. of envy** un pincement de jalousie; **a s. of guilt** un accès de culpabilité (**b**) *Fam (attempt)* **to have a s. at sth/at doing sth** essayer qch/de faire qch
2 *vt (pt & pp* **stabbed**) *(with knife)* poignarder; *(with other weapon)* transpercer; **to s. sb to death** tuer qn d'un coup de couteau; *Fig* **to s. sb in the back** poignarder qn dans le dos

stabbing ['stæbɪŋ] **1** *n (attack)* agression *f* au couteau
2 *adj (pain)* lancinant(e)

stability [stə'bɪlɪtɪ] *n* stabilité *f*; *EU* **S. and Growth Pact** pacte *m* de stabilité et de croissance

stabilize ['steɪbɪlaɪz] **1** *vt* stabiliser
2 *vi* se stabiliser

stabilizer ['steɪbɪlaɪzə(r)] *n (on bicycle)* stabilisateur *m*

stable¹ ['steɪbəl] **1** *n* écurie *f*; *Fig* **to lock the s. door after the horse has bolted** prendre des mesures trop tard
2 *vt* mettre à l'écurie

stable² *adj* stable

stack [stæk] **1** *n* (**a**) *(pile)* pile *f*; *Fam* **stacks of** des tas de (**b**) *(chimney)* cheminée *f*
2 *vt* empiler; **to be stacked with sth** *(full of)* être plein(e) de qch; **the odds were stacked against them** ils n'avaient aucune chance

stadium ['steɪdɪəm] *(pl* **stadiums** *or* **stadia** ['steɪdɪə]) *n* stade *m*

staff [stɑːf] **1** *n* (**a**) *(stick)* bâton *m* (**b**) *(personnel)* personnel *m*; **teaching/nursing s.** personnel *m* enseignant/infirmier; **s. meeting** réunion *f* du personnel;

Br **s. nurse** infirmier(ère) *m,f* diplômé(e); **s. room** *(in school)* salle *f* des professeurs (**c**) *(pl* **staves** [steɪvz]) *Mus* portée *f*
2 *vt* **the office is staffed by volunteers** le personnel du bureau est composé de volontaires; **the desk is staffed at all times** il y a a toujours quelqu'un au bureau

stag [stæg] *n (animal)* cerf *m*; **s. beetle** cerf-volant *m*; **s. night** *or* **party** *(before wedding)* enterrement *m* de la vie de garçon

Stag party

En Grande-Bretagne, le phénomène des "stag parties" ou "stag nights" est une tradition bien établie. Il s'agit d'une sorte de rite de passage destiné à enterrer de vie de garçon d'un futur marié, qui a lieu en règle générale quelques semaines avant le mariage. Le futur marié part soit en virée nocturne, soit en week-end avec un groupe d'amis. Les 'stag parties' sont généralement très abondamment arrosées. Cette coutume a donné lieu à une véritable industrie en Grande-Bretagne : il existe désormais des entreprises spécialisées dans l'organisation de ces événements, comportant parfois des activités sportives et d'autres divertissements. L'équivalent féminin de la "stag party" est la "**hen night**" (voir encadré).

stage [steɪdʒ] **1** *n* (**a**) *(platform)* plate-forme *f*; *(in theatre)* scène *f*; **to go on the s.** faire du théâtre; *Fig* **to set the s. for sth** préparer le terrain à qch; **s. directions** indications *fpl* scéniques; **s. door** entrée *f* des artistes; **s. fright** trac *m*; **s. manager** régisseur *m*; **s. name** nom *m* de scène; **s. whisper** aparté *m* (**b**) *(phase)* stade *m*; **at this s. in...** à ce stade de...; **to do sth in stages** faire qch par étapes (**c**) **s. (coach)** diligence *f*
2 *vt (play)* monter, mettre en scène; *Fig (demonstration, invasion)* organiser

stagehand ['steɪdʒhænd] *n* machiniste *m*

stage-manage ['steɪdʒ'mænɪdʒ] *vt (play)* s'occuper de la régie de; *Fig (event, demonstration)* mettre en scène

stage-struck ['steɪdʒstrʌk] *adj* fou (folle) de théâtre

stagflation [stæg'fleɪʃən] *n Econ* stagflation *f*

stagger ['stægə(r)] **1** *vt* (**a**) *(astound)* stupéfier (**b**) *(tea-breaks, holidays)* échelonner
2 *vi (stumble)* tituber; **to s. along/in/out** marcher/ entrer/sortir en titubant; **to s. to one's feet** se relever péniblement

stagnant ['stægnənt] *adj* stagnant(e)

stagnate [stæg'neɪt] *vi* stagner

stagnation [stæg'neɪʃən] *n* stagnation *f*

staid [steɪd] *adj* collet monté *inv*

stain [steɪn] **1** *n (mark)* tache *f*; *(dye)* teinture *f*; **s. remover** détachant *m*
2 *vt (mark)* tacher; *(dye)* teindre; *Fig (reputation)* salir

stained-glass ['steɪndglɑːs] *n* vitrail *m*; **s. window** vitrail

stainless steel ['steɪnlɪs'stiːl] *n* acier *m* inoxydable, inox® *m*

stair [steə(r)] *n (single step)* marche *f*; **stairs** *(staircase)*

staircase ['steəkeɪs] *n* escalier *m*

stairway ['steəweɪ] *n* escalier *m*

stairwell ['steəwel] *n* cage *f* d'escalier

stake [steɪk] **1** *n* (**a**) *(piece of wood)* pieu *m*; *(piece of metal)* piquet *m*; *(for plant)* tuteur *m*; **to be burnt at the s.** périr sur le bûcher (**b**) *(bet)* enjeu *m*; **to be at s.** être en jeu (**c**) *(share)* **to have a s. in sth** avoir des intérêts dans qch; *Fig* être concerné(e) par qch
2 *vt* (**a**) *(money)* miser (**on** sur); *Fig (one's reputation, job)* risquer (**on** sur); **I'd s. my life on it** j'en mettrais ma tête à couper (**b**) **to s. a claim (to sth)** revendiquer un droit (à qch)
stakeout ['steɪkaʊt] *n* surveillance *f*
stalactite ['stæləktaɪt] *n* stalactite *f*
stalagmite ['stæləgmaɪt] *n* stalagmite *f*
stale [steɪl] *adj* (**a**) *(bread, cake)* rassis(e); *(air)* confiné(e); *(smell)* âcre (**b**) *Fig (social life, politics)* sans intérêt; *(excuse, joke)* éculé(e); *(person)* blasé(e)
stalemate ['steɪlmeɪt] *n (in chess)* pat *m*; *(in negotiations)* impasse *f*; **to reach a s.** être dans l'impasse
stalk¹ [stɔːk] **1** *vt (suspect, wild animal)* traquer; *(obsessively)* harceler
2 *vt (of obsessive fan, infatuated person etc)* suivre en permanence *(de façon obsessionelle)*
3 *vi (walk angrily)* **to s. in/out** entrer/sortir d'un air furieux mais digne
stalk² *n (of plant, flower)* tige *f*; *(of fruit)* queue *f*
stalker ['stɔːkə(r)] *n* = admirateur obsessionnel qui harcèle une de ses connaissances ou une célébrité
stall [stɔːl] **1** *n* (**a**) *(in stable)* stalle *f*; *(for shower, toilet)* cabine *f* (**b**) *(in market)* étal *m*; *(at exhibition)* stand *m* (**c**) **the stalls** *(in theatre)* l'orchestre *m*
2 *vt (hold off)* faire patienter
3 *vi* (**a**) *(of car)* caler; *Fig (of campaign)* être interrompu(e) (**b**) *(delay)* **to s. (for time)** essayer de gagner du temps
stallion ['stæljən] *n* étalon *m*
stalwart ['stɔːlwət] **1** *n* fidèle *mf*
2 *adj* résolu(e)
stamen ['steɪmən] *n* étamine *f*
stamina ['stæmɪnə] *n* résistance *f* physique
stammer ['stæmə(r)] **1** *n* bégaiement *m*; **to have a s.** bégayer
2 *vi* bégayer
3 *vt* balbutier
▸**stammer out** *vt insep* balbutier
stamp [stæmp] **1** *n (for letter)* timbre *m*; *(mark)* cachet *m*; *(device)* tampon *m*; *Fig* **to bear the s. of sth** porter l'empreinte de qch; *Fig* **s. of approval** aval *m*, approbation *f*; **s. album** album *m* de timbres; **s. collector** philatéliste *mf*; *Fin* **s. duty** droit *m* de timbre; **s. machine** distributeur *m* de timbres-poste
2 *vt* (**a**) *(document)* tamponner; **to s. the date on sth** tamponner la date sur qch; **stamped addressed envelope** enveloppe *f* timbrée libellée à ses noms et adresse (**b**) **to s. one's foot** taper du pied
3 *vi* **to s. on sth** *(on purpose)* écraser qch avec le pied; *(accidentally)* écraser qch du pied; **to s. off/out** partir/sortir en tapant des pieds
▸**stamp out** *vt sep* (**a**) *(resistance, dissent)* anéantir; *(poverty)* éradiquer (**b**) *(fire)* éteindre en piétinant
stampede [stæm'piːd] **1** *n* débandade *f*; **there was a s. for the door** il y a eu une ruée vers la porte
2 *vi* se ruer
stance [stɑːns] *n also Fig* position *f*
stand [stænd] **1** *n* (**a**) *(opinion)* position *f*; **to take a s. (on sth)** prendre position (sur qch)
(**b**) *(of lamp, microphone)* pied *m*; *(for books, postcards)* présentoir *m*

(**c**) *(stall) (outside)* étalage *m*; *(at exhibition)* stand *m* (**d**) *(at sports ground)* tribune *f* (**e**) *(taxi rank)* station *f*
2 *vt (pt & pp* **stood** [stʊd]) (**a**) *(place)* poser; **to s. sth against sth** mettre qch contre qch
(**b**) *(endure)* supporter; **to s. comparison with sb/sth** soutenir la comparaison avec qn/qch; **to s. one's ground** tenir bon
(**c**) *(pay for)* **to s. sb a drink/meal** payer à boire/manger à qn
(**d**) *(have)* **to s. a chance (of doing sth)** avoir des chances (de faire qch); **she doesn't s. a chance** elle n'a aucune chance
(**e**) *Law* **to s. trial** passer en jugement
3 *vi* (**a**) *(of person) (get up)* se mettre debout; *(be upright)* être debout; *(remain upright)* rester debout; **to s. on one's head** faire le poirier; **I could hardly s.** je tenais à peine debout; **don't just s. there!** ne reste pas planté là les bras ballants!; **to s. fast** *or* **firm** tenir bon; **to s. still** *(of person)* se tenir immobile; **time seemed to s. still** le temps semblait s'être arrêté
(**b**) *(of building)* se dresser; *(of object)* être, se trouver
(**c**) *(be in situation)* **inflation/unemployment stands at...** le taux d'inflation/de chômage s'élève à...; **to s. in need of sth** avoir besoin de qch; **to s. to do sth** risquer de faire qch; **it stands to reason that...** il est clair que...
(**d**) *(idioms)* **to be standing right behind sb** être avec qn; **to s. on one's own two feet** se débrouiller tout(e) seul(e); **I don't know where I s.** je ne sais pas à quoi m'en tenir; **to know how things s.** savoir où en sont les choses; **I s. corrected** autant pour moi; **to s. for Parliament** se présenter aux élections législatives; **the offer still stands** l'offre tient toujours
▸**stand aside** *vi* s'écarter
▸**stand back** *vi (move away)* reculer (**from** de); *Fig* prendre de la distance (**from** par rapport à)
▸**stand by 1** *vt insep* (**a**) *(person, cause)* défendre, soutenir (**b**) *(promise, decision)* maintenir
2 *vi* (**a**) *(be ready)* se tenir prêt(e) (pour qch/à faire qch); *(of vehicle)* être prêt(e) (pour qch/à faire qch) (**b**) *(not get involved)* rester sans rien faire
▸**stand down** *vi (retire)* se retirer
▸**stand for** *vt insep* (**a**) *(mean, represent)* vouloir dire (**b**) *(tolerate)* supporter
▸**stand out** *vi* (**a**) *(be prominent)* ressortir; **to s. out in a crowd** se détacher dans la foule; *Fam* **it stands out a mile** ça se voit comme le nez au milieu de la figure (**b**) *(oppose)* **to s. out against sth** résister à qch
▸**stand up** *vt sep* (**a**) *(put in upright position)* mettre à la verticale (**b**) *Fam* **to s. sb up** *(on date)* poser un lapin à qn
2 *vi* (**a**) *(get up)* se mettre debout; *(be standing)* être debout; *Fig* **to s. up for sb/sth** défendre qn/qch; *Fig* **to s. up to sb** tenir tête à qn (**b**) *(of argument, theory)* faire le poids; **to s. up to sth** résister à qch; **it'll never s. up in court** ça ne sera pas valable au tribunal
standard ['stændəd] **1** *n* (**a**) *(point of reference)* référence *f*; *(set requirement)* norme *f*; *(for weight, measurement)* étalon *m* (**b**) *(required level)* niveau *m*; **to be up to/below s.** être du/en dessous du niveau requis; **s. of living** niveau *m* de vie; **s. of accommodation** qualité *f* du logement (**c**) **standards** *(morals)* principes *mpl* moraux; **to have high/low standards** être/ne pas être exigeant(e) (**d**) *(flag)* étendard *m*; *also Fig* **s. bearer** porte-drapeau *m*

2 adj (**a**) (design, size) standard inv; Math **s. deviation** écart m type; **s. lamp** lampadaire m; **s. measure** mesure f étalon; **s. time** heure f légale (**b**) (usual) habituel(elle); **S. English** anglais m standard; **s. practice** pratique f courante

standardization [stændədaɪˈzeɪʃən] n normalisation f

standardize [ˈstændədaɪz] vt normaliser

stand-by [ˈstændbaɪ] n (**a**) (fuel, food) réserve f; **to have sth as a s.** avoir qch en réserve; **to be on s.** (of troops, emergency services) être en état d'alerte (**b**) (for air travel) **to be on s.** être en stand-by; **s. passenger** passager(ère) m,f en stand-by; **s. ticket** billet m en stand-by

stand-in [ˈstændɪn] n remplaçant(e) m,f; (for actor) doublure f

standing [ˈstændɪŋ] **1** n (**a**) (status) réputation f (**b**) (duration) **of long s.** de longue date
2 adj (**a**) (upright) debout; **to give sb a s. ovation** se lever pour applaudir qn (**b**) (permanent) permanent(e); **I have a s. invitation** je peux y aller quand je veux; **s. army** armée f de métier; **s. charges** (on bill) frais mpl d'abonnement; **s. joke** plaisanterie f classique; Fin **s. order** virement m automatique

standoffish [stændˈɒfɪʃ] adj distant(e)

standpoint [ˈstændpɔɪnt] n point m de vue

standstill [ˈstændstɪl] n **to be at a s.** (of traffic) être immobilisé(e); (of production, economy) être paralysé(e); **to come to a s.** (of traffic) s'immobiliser; (of production) s'arrêter; (of economy) être paralysé(e)

stand-up [ˈstændʌp] adj (**a**) **s. comedian** comique mf (qui se produit seul en scène); **s. comedy** spectacle m comique (**b**) (fight, argument) en règle

stank [stæŋk] pt of stink

stanza [ˈstænzə] n strophe f

staple¹ [ˈsteɪpəl] **1** n (for fastening paper) agrafe f; **s. gun** agrafeuse f
2 vt agrafer

staple² n (basic food) aliment m de base; (basic product) principale production f; Fig **such stories are a s. of the tabloid press** la presse à sensation se nourrit de telles histoires

stapler [ˈsteɪplə(r)] n agrafeuse f

star [stɑː(r)] **1** n (**a**) (heavenly body) étoile f; the Stars and Stripes (US flag) la bannière étoilée; Fig **to reach for the stars** essayer d'atteindre les sommets; Fig **to see stars** (after blow to head) voir trente-six chandelles; **s. fruit** carambole f; **s. sign** signe m du zodiaque (**b**) (famous person) star f, vedette f; **s. player** vedette f (**c**) Fam **stars** (horoscope) horoscope m
2 vt (pt & pp starred) (of film, play) avoir pour vedette
3 vi **to s. in a film/play** jouer dans un film/une pièce

starboard [ˈstɑːbəd] n Naut tribord m

starch [stɑːtʃ] **1** n (for shirts, in food) amidon m
2 vt (shirt) amidonner

starchy [ˈstɑːtʃɪ] adj (**a**) (food) riche en féculents (**b**) Fam (person, manner) guindé(e)

stardom [ˈstɑːdəm] n célébrité f

stare [steə(r)] **1** n regard m fixe
2 vt **to be staring sb in the face** (be obvious) crever les yeux à qn
3 vi **to s. at sb** dévisager qn; **to s. at sth** regarder qch fixement; **to s. into space** regarder dans le vague; **it's rude to s.** ce n'est pas poli de dévisager les gens

starfish [ˈstɑːfɪʃ] (pl starfish or starfishes) n étoile f de mer

stark [stɑːk] **1** adj (contrast) net (nette); (light, colours) cru(e); (truth, facts) brut(e); (landscape) nu(e)
2 adv **s. naked** tout(e) nu(e); Fam **s. raving mad** complètement dingue

starkers [ˈstɑːkəz] adj Br Fam à poil

starlet [ˈstɑːlɪt] n (young actress) starlette f

starlight [ˈstɑːlaɪt] n lumière f des étoiles

starling [ˈstɑːlɪŋ] n étourneau m

starlit [ˈstɑːlɪt] adj étoilé(e)

starry [ˈstɑːrɪ] adj étoilé(e)

starry-eyed [stɑːrɪˈaɪd] adj naïf(ïve)

start [stɑːt] **1** n (**a**) (beginning) début m; (starting place, of journey, race) départ m; **for a s.** pour commencer; **at the s.** au début; **from the s.** dès le départ; **from s. to finish** du début à la fin; **to make a s. on sth** commencer qch; **he lent her £50 to give her a s.** il lui a prêté 50 livres pour l'aider à démarrer; **to give sb a 60-metre s.** (in race) laisser 60 mètres d'avance à qn (**b**) (sudden movement) sursaut m; **to wake with a s.** se réveiller en sursaut; **to give sb a s.** faire sursauter qn
2 vt (**a**) (begin) commencer; (conversation, talks) entamer; (fire) déclencher; (fashion, rumour) lancer; (business) monter; **to s. doing sth, to s. to do sth** commencer de faire qch; **to s. crying/laughing/sneezing** se mettre à pleurer/rire/éternuer; **to get started** démarrer (**b**) (machine, engine) mettre en marche; (car) démarrer
3 vi (**a**) (begin) commencer; **to s. at the beginning** commencer par le commencement; **to s. by doing sth** commencer par faire qch; **to s. on sth** commencer qch; **she had started as a doctor** elle avait commencé sa carrière comme médecin; **to s. with** au début, d'abord; **now don't you s.!** tu ne vas pas t'y mettre aussi! (**b**) (make sudden movement) sursauter (**c**) (begin journey) se mettre en route (**d**) (of car, engine) démarrer

▸**start off 1** vt sep (argument, debate) commencer; **to s. sb off** (in business) aider qn à démarrer; (on a subject) lancer qn
2 vi (begin) commencer; (on journey) se mettre en route

▸**start out** vi (begin) débuter; (on journey) se mettre en route

▸**start up 1** vt sep (car) démarrer; (machine) mettre en marche; (business) monter
2 vi (of engine) démarrer; **to s. up in business** monter son entreprise

starter [ˈstɑːtə(r)] n (**a**) (competitor) partant(e) m,f; (official) starter m (**b**) **to be a late s.** (of child) ne pas être très précoce; **to be a slow s.** (of person) être lent(e) à démarrer (**c**) (device) starter m (**d**) (in meal) hors-d'œuvre m inv; Fig **for starters** pour commencer

starting [ˈstɑːtɪŋ] n (**a**) (in sport) **s. block** starting-block m; **s. line** ligne f de départ; **s. pistol** pistolet m de starter (**b**) (initial) **s. point** or **place** point m de départ; **s. price** (in betting) cote f au départ; **s. salary** salaire m de départ

startle [ˈstɑːtəl] vt faire sursauter

startling [ˈstɑːtlɪŋ] adj (noise) effrayant(e); (news, event) incroyable

start-up [ˈstɑːtʌp] n (**a**) Com démarrage m; **s. costs** coûts mpl d'installation (**b**) (Internet company) start-up f, jeune pousse f

starvation [stɑːˈveɪʃən] n privation f totale de nourriture; **to die of s.** mourir de faim; **to be on a s. diet** (not

have enough to eat) n'avoir presque rien à manger; **s. wages** salaires *mpl* de misère
starve [stɑːv] **1** *vt* priver de nourriture; **to s. sb to death** faire mourir qn de faim; *Fig* **to be starved of sth** être privé(e) de qch **2** *vi (lack food)* souffrir de la faim; **to s. (to death)** mourir de faim; *Fam* **I'm starving!** je meurs de faim!
starving ['stɑːvɪŋ] *adj* famélique
stash [stæʃ] *Fam* **1** *n* réserve *f* **2** *vt* planquer
state [steɪt] **1** *n* (**a**) *(condition)* état *m*; *(situation)* situation *f*; **I'm not in a fit s. to travel** je ne suis pas en état de voyager; **s. of war/emergency** état *m* de guerre/d'urgence; **s. of affaires** situation *f*; **s. of health** état *m* de santé; **s. of mind** état *m* d'esprit; **in a s. of terror** terrifié(e); **in a s. of shock** en état de choc; **to be in a terrible s.** être dans un état lamentable; **to lie in s.** *(of dead person)* être exposé(e) au public (**b**) *(country, administrative region)* État *m*; *Fam* **the States** *(the USA)* les États-Unis; **s. control** étatisme *m*; *Am* **S. Department** ≃ ministère *m* des Affaires étrangères; **s. occasions** cérémonie *f* officielle; **s. school** école *f* publique; **s. secret** secret *m* d'État; **s. sector** secteur *m* public; **S. Supreme Court** = la plus haute instance judiciaire dans chaque État américain; *Am Pol* **S. of the Union address** le discours sur l'état de l'Union; **s. visit** visite *f* officielle **2** *vt (declare)* déclarer; *(address, age)* indiquer, préciser; **to s. the obvious** enfoncer une porte ouverte; **as stated earlier/above** comme mentionné précédemment/ci-dessus; **at the stated times** aux heures prévues

State of the Union
Ce discours radiotélévisé, dans lequel le Président des États-Unis dresse le bilan de son programme et en définit les orientations, est prononcé devant le Congrès. L'allocution présidentielle a lieu tous les ans en janvier.

stateless ['steɪtlɪs] *adj* apatride
stately ['steɪtlɪ] *adj* imposant(e); **s. home** ≃ château *m*
statement ['steɪtmənt] *n* (**a**) *(of opinion)* déclaration *f*; *(of facts)* exposé *m*; **to make a s.** *(of spokesperson)* faire une déclaration; *(of witness)* faire une déposition; *Fig (of lifestyle, behaviour)* faire passer un message (**b**) *(from bank)* relevé *m* de compte
state-of-the-art [steɪtəvðɪ'ɑːt] *adj (technology, computer etc)* de pointe; **it's s.** c'est du dernier cri
state-owned [steɪt'əʊnd] *adj (company)* d'État; *(property)* de l'État
statesman ['steɪtsmən] *n* homme *m* d'État
statesmanlike ['steɪtsmənlaɪk] *adj* digne d'un homme d'État
static ['stætɪk] **1** *adj* statique; **s. electricity** électricité *f* statique **2** *n* électricité *f* statique
station ['steɪʃən] **1** *n* (**a**) *(for trains)* gare *f*; **s. master** chef *m* de gare; *Am* **s. wagon** *(car)* break *m* (**b**) *(post)* poste *m*; **(police) s.** poste *m* (de police); **(radio/television) s.** station *f* de radio/télévision (**c**) *(social condition)* condition *f*; **to have ideas above one's s.** ne pas avoir les moyens de ses ambitions **2** *vt (person)* placer; *(soldier, troops)* poster
stationary ['steɪʃənərɪ] *adj* immobile
stationer ['steɪʃənə(r)] *n* **s.'s (shop)** papeterie *f*

stationery ['steɪʃənərɪ] *n (writing materials)* papeterie *f*; *(writing paper)* papier *m* à lettres
statistic [stə'tɪstɪk] *n* chiffre *m* statistique; **statistics** statistiques *fpl*
statistical [stə'tɪstɪkəl] *adj* statistique
statistician [stætɪs'tɪʃən] *n* statisticien(enne) *m,f*
statue ['stætjuː] *n* statue *f*
statuesque [stætjʊ'esk] *adj* sculptural(e)
statuette [stætjʊ'et] *n* statuette *f*
stature ['stætjə(r)] *n (physical build)* stature *f*; *(reputation)* envergure *f*, réputation *f*
status ['steɪtəs] *n (position, prestige)* statut *m*; *Comput* **s. bar** barre *f* d'état; **s. report** rapport *m* de situation; **s. symbol** marque *f* de prestige
status quo ['steɪtəs'kwəʊ] *n* statu quo *m inv*
statute ['stætjuːt] *n* texte *m* de loi; **by s.** par la loi; **s. book** recueil *m* de lois
statutory ['stætjʊtərɪ] *adj* légal(e); **s. duty** obligation *f* légale; **s. holiday** jour *m* férié; *Am* **s. rape** détournement *m* de mineur
staunch¹ [stɔːntʃ] *adj (resolute)* convaincu(e); *(supporter)* ardent(e)
staunch² *vt (blood)* étancher
staunchly ['stɔːntʃlɪ] *adv* résolument
stave [steɪv] *n* (**a**) *(of barrel)* douve *f* (**b**) *Mus* portée *f*
▸**stave in** *(pt & pp* staved *or* stove [stəʊv]) *vt sep* défoncer; *(ribs)* enfoncer
▸**stave off** *vt sep (problem, disaster)* éviter; *(hunger)* tromper
staves *pl* of **staff 1(c)**
stay [steɪ] **1** *vt (endure)* **to s. the course** *or* **distance** tenir la distance **2** *vi* (**a**) *(not move, remain)* rester; *Fam* **to s. put** rester tranquille; **to s. still** rester tranquille; **computers are here to s.** l'informatique est entrée dans les mœurs (**b**) *(reside temporarily)* séjourner; **I stayed five years in the States** j'ai passé cinq ans aux États-Unis; **to s. with sb** loger chez qn (**c**) *Scot (live)* habiter **3** *n* (**a**) *(visit)* séjour *m* (**b**) *Law & Fig* **s. of execution** sursis *m*
▸**stay away** *vi* **to s. away from sb/sth** ne pas s'approcher de qn/qch; **to s. away from school** ne pas aller à l'école
▸**stay in** *vi (not go out)* rester chez soi
▸**stay on** *vi* rester
▸**stay out** *vi* (**a**) *(not go home)* ne pas rentrer; **to s. out all night** ne pas rentrer de la nuit; **to s. out late** rentrer tard (**b**) *(of strikers)* continuer la grève (**c**) *(not interfere)* **to s. out of sth** ne pas se mêler de qch
▸**stay up** *vi* ne pas aller se coucher
staying power ['steɪɪŋ'paʊə(r)] *n* endurance *f*
STD [estiː'diː] *n* (**a**) *Med (abbr* **sexually transmitted disease)** MST *f* (**b**) *Br Tel (abbr* **subscriber trunk dialling)** indicatif *m*
stead [sted] *n* **to stand sb in good s.** être fort utile à qn; **in sb's s.** à la place de qn
steadfast ['stedfɑːst] *adj* dévoué(e); *(opponent, resistance)* constant(e)
steadily ['stedɪlɪ] *adv (change, grow)* progressivement; *(work)* assidûment; *(walk)* d'un pas régulier; *(look)* fixement; *(breathe, increase)* régulièrement
steady ['stedɪ] **1** *adj* (**a**) *(stable)* stable; **in a s. voice** d'une voix assurée (**b**) *(regular)* régulier(ère); *(progress)* constant(e); *(relationship)* durable; **to have a s. girlfriend** avoir une copine (attitrée); **to drive at a s. 50 mph** ≃ rouler à une vitesse régulière de 80 km/h

2 *adv* **to be going s.** sortir ensemble sérieusement; *Br Fam* **s. (on)!** du calme!
3 *vt* faire tenir; **to s. oneself** trouver son équilibre; **to s. one's nerves** se calmer; **to s. one's voice** contrôler sa voix

steak [steɪk] *n (beef)* steak *m*; *(of fish)* darne *f*; **s. and kidney pie** = tourte à la viande de bœuf et aux rognons

steal [stiːl] *(pt* **stole** [stəʊl], *pp* **stolen** ['stəʊlən]) **1** *vt* (**a**) *(thieve)* voler; **to s. sth from sb** voler qch à qn (**b**) *(idioms)* **to s. a glance at sb** jeter un coup d'œil à qn; **to s. the show** ravir la vedette
2 *vi* (**a**) *(thieve)* voler (**b**) *(move quietly)* **to s. away/in/out** s'en aller/rentrer/sortir sans faire de bruit; **to s. up on sb** s'approcher de qn sans faire de bruit; *Fig* prendre qn par surprise

stealth [stelθ] *n* ruse *f*; **s. tax** = mesure visant à augmenter les recettes du gouvernement par un moyen détourné, afin d'éviter une hausse directe et visible des impôts qui mécontenterait les citoyens

stealthily ['stelθɪlɪ] *adv* furtivement
stealthy ['stelθɪ] *adj* furtif(ive)

steam [stiːm] **1** *n* (**a**) *(water vapour)* vapeur *f*; *(on glass)* buée *f*; **s. bath** bain *m* de vapeur; **s. engine** locomotive *f* à vapeur; **s. iron** fer *m* à vapeur; **s. shovel** pelleteuse *f* (**b**) *(idioms)* **to get up s.** prendre de l'élan; **to run out of s.** s'essouffler; **to let off s.** se défouler; **to do sth under one's own s.** faire qch tout(e) seul(e)
2 *vt (food)* faire cuire à la vapeur
3 *vi (give off steam)* fumer
▶**steam open** *vt sep (envelope)* décacheter à la vapeur
▶**steam up 1** *vt sep* **to get all steamed up (about sth)** *(of person)* se mettre dans tous ses états (à propos de qch)
2 *vi (of window, glasses)* s'embuer

steamer ['stiːmə(r)] *n* (**a**) *(ship)* (bateau *m* à) vapeur *m* (**b**) *(for food)* panier *m* de cuisson à la vapeur
steamroller ['stiːmrəʊlə(r)] **1** *n* rouleau *m* compresseur
2 *vt* **to s. sb into doing sth** forcer qn à faire qch
steamship ['stiːmʃɪp] *n* bateau *m* à vapeur
steamy ['stiːmɪ] *adj* (**a**) *(room)* plein(e) de vapeur; *(mirror)* embué(e) (**b**) *Fam (novel, film)* torride
steel [stiːl] **1** *n* acier *m*; **nerves of s.** nerfs *mpl* d'acier; **the s. industry** la sidérurgie; **s. band** steel band *m*; **s. mill** aciérie *f*, **s. wool** paille *f* de fer
2 *vt* **to s. oneself to do sth** s'armer de courage pour faire qch; **to s. oneself against sth** se blinder contre qch
steelworker ['stiːlwɜːkə(r)] *n* employé(e) *m,f* de la sidérurgie
steep¹ [stiːp] *adj* (**a**) *(path, hill)* pentu(e), escarpé(e); *(climb)* raide; *Fig (increase)* considérable (**b**) *Fam (expensive)* salé(e); *(unreasonable)* raide
steep² *vt (soak)* faire tremper; *Fig* **steeped in history/tradition** imprégné(e) d'histoire/de tradition
steeple ['stiːpəl] *n* clocher *m*
steeplechase ['stiːpəltʃeɪs] *n* steeple-chase *m*
steeplejack ['stiːpəldʒæk] *n* réparateur *m* de clochers et de cheminées d'usines
steer¹ [stɪə(r)] **1** *vt (car)* conduire; *(ship)* barrer; **to s. sb out of trouble** sortir qn du pétrin
2 *vi (of person)* conduire; *(of ship)* se diriger (**for** vers); **to s. clear of sb/sth** éviter qn/qch
steer² *n (bull)* bouvillon *m*

steering ['stɪərɪŋ] *n (mechanism)* direction *f*; **s. column** colonne *f* de direction; *Pol* **s. committee** comité *m* d'organisation; **s. wheel** volant *m*
stem [stem] **1** *n (of plant)* tige *f*; *(of glass)* pied *m*; *(of pipe)* tuyau *m*; *(of word)* radical *m*, *Biol* **s. cell** cellule *f* souche
2 *vt (pt & pp* **stemmed**) *(halt)* stopper; **to s. the tide of sth** enrayer le flot de qch
3 *vi* **to s. from** provenir de
stench [stentʃ] *n* puanteur *f*
stencil ['stensəl] **1** *n* pochoir *m*
2 *vt (pt & pp* **stencilled**, *Am* **stenciled**) dessiner au pochoir
stenographer [stə'nɒgrəfə(r)] *n* sténographe *mf*
step [step] **1** *n* (**a**) *(movement, sound)* pas *m*; **to take a s.** faire un pas; **s. by s.** pas à pas; *Fig* petit à petit; *also Fig* **to watch one's s.** faire attention où l'on met les pieds; **to keep in s.** *(in dance)* danser en mesure; *Fig* **to be out of s. (with sb)** être en décalage (par rapport à qn) (**b**) *(action, measure)* mesure *f*; **to take steps (to do sth)** prendre des mesures (pour faire qch); **the next s. is to...** la prochaine chose à faire, c'est de...; **a s. in the right direction** un pas dans la bonne direction; **at every s.** à chaque étape; **every s. of the way** sur toute la ligne (**d**) *(of staircase)* marche *f*; *(of stepladder)* échelon *m*; **(flight of) steps** escalier *m*; *(on outside of building)* perron *m* (**e**) *(exercise)* step *m*; **s. class** cours *m* de step
2 *vi (pt & pp* **stepped**) *(take a step)* faire un pas; *(walk)* marcher; **to s. on sth** marcher sur qch; **s. this way** venez par ici; *Fam Fig* **to s. on it** se grouiller
▶**step back** *vi* reculer (**from** de); *Fig* prendre du recul (**from** par rapport à)
▶**step down** *vi (resign)* démissionner
▶**step forward** *vi (volunteer)* se porter volontaire
▶**step in** *vi (intervene)* intervenir
▶**step up** *vt sep (increase)* accélérer; *(pressure)* augmenter
stepbrother ['stepbrʌðə(r)] *n* demi-frère *m (fils du conjoint d'un des parents)*
stepchild ['steptʃaɪld] *n (boy)* beau-fils *m*; *(girl)* belle-fille *f*
stepdaughter ['stepdɔːtə(r)] *n* belle-fille *f*
stepfather ['stepfɑːðə(r)] *n* beau-père *m*
stepladder ['steplædə(r)] *n* escabeau *m*
stepmother ['stepmʌðə(r)] *n* belle-mère *f*
stepparent ['steppeərənt] *n (father)* beau-père *m*; *(mother)* belle-mère *f*; **stepparents** beaux-parents *mpl*
steppe [step] *n* steppe *f*
stepper ['stepə(r)] *n (gym equipment)* stepper *m*
stepsister ['stepsɪstə(r)] *n* demi-sœur *(fille du conjoint d'un des parents)*
stepson ['stepsʌn] *n* beau-fils *m*
stereo ['sterɪəʊ] **1** *n (pl* **stereos**) *(equipment)* chaîne *f* stéréo; *(sound)* stéréo *f*, **in s.** en stéréo
2 *adj* stéréo *inv*
stereophonic [sterɪə'fɒnɪk] *adj* stéréophonique
stereoscopic [sterɪəʊ'skɒpɪk] *adj* stéréoscopique
stereotype ['sterɪətaɪp] *n* stéréotype *m*
stereotyped ['sterɪətaɪpt] *adj* stéréotypé(e)
sterile ['steraɪl] *adj* stérile
sterility [ste'rɪlɪtɪ] *n* stérilité *f*
sterilization [sterɪlaɪ'zeɪʃən] *n* stérilisation *f*
sterilize ['sterɪlaɪz] *vt* stériliser

sterling ['stɜːlɪŋ] **1** *n (British currency)* livre *f* sterling **2** *adj* (**a**) *(silver)* fin(e) (**b**) *(effort, quality)* remarquable

stern¹ [stɜːn] *adj (person, look)* sévère

stern² *n (of boat)* poupe *f*

sternum ['stɜːnəm] (*pl* **sternums** *or* **sterna** ['stɜːnə]) *n* sternum *m*

steroid ['stɪərɔɪd] *n* stéroïde *m*

stethoscope ['steθəskəʊp] *n* stéthoscope *m*

stevedore ['stiːvədɔː(r)] *n* docker *m*

stew [stjuː] **1** *n* ragoût *m*; *Br Fam Fig* **to be in a s.** *(of person)* être dans le pétrin **2** *vt (meat)* faire cuire en ragoût; *(fruit)* faire de la compote de **3** *vi (of meat)* mijoter; *Br Fam* **to let sb s.** (**in his/her own juice**) laisser qn mariner

steward ['stjʊəd] *n (on estate)* régisseur *m*; *(on ship, plane)* steward *m*; *(at sporting event)* organisateur *m*; *(at demonstration)* membre *m* du service d'ordre

stewardess [stjʊə'des] *n (on ship, plane)* hôtesse *f*

stewed [stjuːd] *adj* (**a**) *Culin* **s. beef** bœuf *m* en ragoût; **s. fruit** compote *f* de fruits; **this tea is s.** ce thé a trop infusé (**b**) *Fam (drunk)* bourré(e)

STI [estiː'aɪ] *n Med (abbr* **sexually transmitted infection**) IST *f*

stick¹ [stɪk] *n* (**a**) *(of wood, glue, chewing gum)* bâton *m*; *(for walking)* canne *f*; *(of celery, rhubarb)* tige *f*; *Fam Fig* **to get hold of the wrong end of the s.** comprendre de travers; *Fam* **she lives out in the sticks** elle habite dans un trou perdu; **s. insect** phasme *m* (**b**) *Fam (criticism)* **to give sb s.** (**for sth**) taper sur les doigts de qn (à cause de qch); *Br* **to take a lot of s.** se faire beaucoup critiquer

stick² (*pt & pp* **stuck** [stʌk]) **1** *vt* (**a**) *(insert)* **to s. sth in(to) sth** planter qch dans qch (**b**) *Fam (put)* mettre, poser (**c**) *(attach with glue)* coller (**on/in** sur/dans) (**d**) *Fam (endure)* supporter **2** *vi* (**a**) *(adhere)* coller; *Fig* **the name stuck** ce nom lui/leur/*etc* est resté; *Fig* **to s. to** s'en tenir à; **to s. to the facts** s'en tenir aux faits; **to s. to one's principles** rester fidèle à ses principes (**b**) *(become jammed)* se coincer; *Fig* **it sticks in my throat** c'est dur à avaler

▸**stick around** *vi Fam* attendre

▸**stick at** *vt insep (persevere with)* persévérer dans; **to s. at nothing** ne reculer devant rien

▸**stick by** *vt insep (friend)* soutenir; *(promise, statement)* maintenir

▸**stick out 1** *vt sep* (**a**) *(cause to protrude)* faire sortir; **to s. one's tongue out (at sb)** tirer la langue (à qn); *Fam* **to s. one's neck out (for sb)** prendre des risques (pour qn) (**b**) *Fam (endure)* **to s. it out** tenir bon **2** *vi* (**a**) *(protrude)* ressortir; *(of ears)* être décollé(e)s; *(of teeth)* avancer (**b**) *Fam (be noticeable)* se voir; **it sticks out a mile** *or* **like a sore thumb** ça se voit comme le nez au milieu de la figure

▸**stick together 1** *vt sep* coller **2** *vi* (**a**) *(with glue)* être collé(e) (**b**) *(of friends)* rester ensemble

▸**stick up 1** *vt sep (sign, poster)* mettre; *Fam* **s. 'em up!** haut les mains! **2** *vi (of building, hair)* se dresser

▸**stick up for** *vt insep (person, rights)* prendre la défense de

▸**stick with** *vt insep (not give up)* rester avec

sticker ['stɪkə(r)] *n* autocollant *m*

stick-in-the-mud ['stɪkɪnðəmʌd] *n Fam* rabat-joie *m inv*

stickleback ['stɪkəlbæk] *n* épinoche *f*

stickler ['stɪklə(r)] *n* **to be a s. for sth** être à cheval sur qch

stick-on ['stɪkɒn] *adj* autocollant(e)

stick-up ['stɪkʌp] *n Fam (robbery)* braquage *m*

sticky ['stɪkɪ] *adj* (**a**) *(substance)* collant(e); *(climate)* humide, moite; *(label)* adhésif(ive); *Fig* **to have s. fingers** avoir une tendance pickpocket; **s. tape** ruban *m* adhésif (**b**) *Fig (awkward)* délicat(e); **to come to a s. end** mal finir; *Fam* **to be on a s. wicket** être dans une situation délicate

stiff [stɪf] *adj* (**a**) *(rigid)* rigide; *(paste)* ferme; **as s. as a board** tout(e) raide; **to be bored s.** s'ennuyer à mourir; **to be scared s.** avoir une trouille bleue; **to be frozen s.** être frigorifié(e) (**b**) *(joint)* ankylosé(e); **to be s.** *(of person)* avoir des courbatures; **to have a s. neck** avoir un torticolis; **my leg is s.** j'ai la jambe ankylosée (**c**) *(handle, hinge, drawer)* dur(e) (**d**) *(severe) (punishment, fine)* sévère; *(resistance)* opiniâtre; *(competition)* rude; *(exam)* dur(e); *(breeze)* fort(e); **a s. drink** une boisson forte (**e**) *(formal)* rigide; *(smile)* forcé(e)

stiffen ['stɪfən] **1** *vt* renforcer; *(paste)* épaissir **2** *vi* se raidir

stiffly ['stɪflɪ] *adv (bow)* avec raideur; *(answer, greet)* avec froideur

stifle ['staɪfəl] *vt also Fig* étouffer

stifling ['staɪflɪŋ] *adj* étouffant(e)

stigma ['stɪgmə] (*pl* **stigmas**) *n* honte *f*

stigmata [stɪg'mɑːtə] *npl (of saint)* stigmates *mpl*

stigmatize ['stɪgmətaɪz] *vt* stigmatiser

stile [staɪl] *n* échalier *m*

stiletto [stɪ'letəʊ] (*pl* **stilettos**) *n (dagger)* stylet *m*; *(shoe)* talon *m* aiguille; **s. heels** talons *mpl* aiguille

still¹ [stɪl] **1** *adj (motionless)* immobile; *(calm)* calme; *(silent)* silencieux(euse); *(drink)* non gazeux(euse); **to stand s.** ne pas bouger; *Art* **s. life** nature *f* morte; *Prov* **s. waters run deep** il faut se méfier de l'eau qui dort **2** *vt* calmer, apaiser **3** *n* (**a**) **in the s. of the night** dans le silence de la nuit (**b**) *(photograph)* photo *f* de plateau

still² *adv* (**a**) *(up to given point in time)* toujours, encore; **she's s. alive** elle vit toujours; **I s. think/say that...** je continue de penser/dire que...; **I s. have 50 euros** il me reste encore 50 euros (**b**) *(nonetheless)* tout de même; **s., it could have been worse** enfin, ç'aurait pu être pire (**c**) *(even)* encore; **s. more/better** encore plus/mieux

still³ *n (distilling equipment)* alambic *m*

stillbirth ['stɪlbɜːθ] *n* enfant *mf* mort-né(e)

stillborn ['stɪlbɔːn] *adj* mort-né(e)

stillness ['stɪlnɪs] *n* tranquillité *f*

stilt [stɪlt] *n (for walking)* échasse *f*; *(for building)* pilotis *m*

stilted ['stɪltɪd] *adj* guindé(e)

stimulant ['stɪmjʊlənt] *n* stimulant *m*

stimulate ['stɪmjʊleɪt] *vt* stimuler

stimulating ['stɪmjʊleɪtɪŋ] *adj* stimulant(e)

stimulation [stɪmjʊ'leɪʃən] *n* stimulation *f*

stimulus ['stɪmjʊləs] (*pl* **stimuli** ['stɪmjʊlaɪ]) *n* encouragement *m*; *(physiological)* stimulus *m inv*

sting [stɪŋ] **1** *n* (**a**) *(of bee)* dard *m*; *(of scorpion)* aiguillon *m*; *(wound)* piqûre *f* (**b**) *(sensation)* brûlure *f* (**c**) *(idioms)* **to have a s. in the tail** *(of story, proposal)* avoir une fin inattendue (et désagréable); **to take**

the s. out of sth atténuer les effets de qch **2** *vt* (*pt* & *pp* **stung** [stʌŋ]) *(of bee, nettle)* piquer; *Fig (of remark)* blesser, piquer au vif; *Fig* **to s. sb into action** inciter qn à agir; *Fam Fig* **they stung him for £10** ils l'ont arnaqué de 10 livres **3** *vi (of eyes, skin)* piquer

stinging ['stɪŋɪŋ] *adj (pain)* cuisant(e); *(remark, criticism)* cinglant(e); **s. nettle** ortie *f*

stingray ['stɪŋreɪ] *n* pastenague *f*

stingy ['stɪndʒɪ] *adj (person)* pingre; *(portion)* minuscule; **to be s. with one's praise** être avare de compliments

stink [stɪŋk] **1** *n (smell)* puanteur *f*; *Fam Fig* **to kick up a s.** *(about sth)* faire tout un scandale (à propos de qch) **2** *vi (pt* **stank** [stæŋk] *or* **stunk** [stʌŋk], *pp* **stunk**) **(a)** *(smell)* puer; **to s. of sth** puer qch; *Fam Fig* **to s. of corruption** sentir la corruption à plein nez **(b)** *Fam Fig (be of bad quality)* craindre

stinkbomb ['stɪŋkbɒm] *n* boule *f* puante

stinker ['stɪŋkə(r)] *n Fam (person)* peau *f* de vache; *(difficult task)* casse-tête *m*; **a s. of a cold** un rhume carabiné

stinking ['stɪŋkɪŋ] **1** *adj* puant(e); **a s. cold** un rhume carabiné **2** *adv Fam* **to be s. rich** être bourré(e) de fric

stint [stɪnt] **1** *n (period)* période *f*; *(share of work)* part *f* de travail; **to take a s. at the wheel** prendre le volant; **he had a two-year s. in the army** il a fait deux ans d'armée **2** *vt* épargner; **to s. oneself** se sacrifier **3** *vi* **to s. on sth** lésiner sur qch

stipend ['staɪpend] *n* traitement *m*

stipulate ['stɪpjʊleɪt] *vt* stipuler

stipulation [stɪpjʊ'leɪʃən] *n* stipulation *f*

stir [stɜː(r)] **1** *n* **(a) to give sth a s.** remuer qch **(b)** *Fig* **to cause a s.** faire du bruit **2** *vt (pt* & *pp* **stirred**) **(a)** *(liquid, mixture)* remuer; *(leaves)* agiter **(b)** *Fig (person)* émouvoir, remuer; *(emotion)* réveiller; *(curiosity)* exciter; **to s. sb to do sth** inciter qn à faire qch; *Fam* **to s. oneself** se remuer; *Fam* **to s. it** *(make trouble)* envenimer les choses **3** *vi (move)* bouger, remuer

▸**stir up** *vt sep* **(a)** *(dust, leaves)* remuer **(b)** *Fig (rebellion, anger, resentment)* attiser; *(workers, crowd)* inciter à la révolte; **to s. up trouble** semer la zizanie; **to s. things up** envenimer les choses

stir-fry [stɜː'fraɪ] *Culin* **1** *n (pl* **stir-fries)** sauté *m* **2** *vt (pt* & *pp* **stir-fried)** faire sauter

stirrer ['stɜːrə(r)] *n Fam (trouble-maker)* semeur(euse) *m,f* de zizanie

stirring ['stɜːrɪŋ] **1** *n* **the first stirrings of** les premiers signes de **2** *adj (speech, film)* poignant(e)

stirrup ['stɪrəp] *n* étrier *m*

stitch [stɪtʃ] **1** *n* **(a)** *(in sewing)* point *m*; *(in knitting)* maille *f*; *Med* point *m* (de suture); *Fam* **she didn't have a s. on** elle était nue comme un ver; *Prov* **a s. in time saves nine** un point à temps en vaut cent **(b)** *(sharp pain)* point *m* (de côté); **to get a s.** prendre un point **(c)** *Fam* **we were in stitches** *(laughing)* on était pliés **2** *vt (clothing)* coudre; *Med* recoudre

▸**stitch up** *vt sep Fam (falsely incriminate)* faire porter le chapeau à

stoat [stəʊt] *n* hermine *f*

stock [stɒk] **1** *n* **(a)** *(supply)* provisions *fpl*; *Com* stock *m*; *Com* **while stocks last** jusqu'à épuisement des stocks; **to have sth in s.** avoir qch en stock; **to be out of s.** être épuisé(e); *Fig* **to take s.** faire le point; *Com* **s. control** gestion *f* des stocks; *Com* **s. list** inventaire *m* des stocks **(b)** *(livestock)* bétail *m* **(c)** *Fin* valeurs *fpl*, actions *fpl*; *Fig* **her s. is going up/down** sa cote est en hausse/baisse; **stocks and shares** valeurs *fpl* mobilières; **s. exchange** Bourse *f* (des valeurs); **s. market** marché *m* des valeurs; **s. option** stock-option *f*, option *f* de titres **(d)** *(descent)* **of German s.** de souche allemande **(e)** *(of rifle)* fût *m* **(f)** **stocks** *(for punishment)* pilori *m* **(g)** *(in cooking)* bouillon *m*; **s. cube** bouillon cube *m* **2** *adj (argument, excuse)* classique **3** *vt* **(a)** *(goods)* vendre **(b)** *(supply)* *(shop)* approvisionner **(with** en**)**

▸**stock up** *vi* faire des provisions (**with** de)

stockade [stɒ'keɪd] *n* palissade *f*

stockbroker ['stɒkbrəʊkə(r)] *n Fin* agent *m* de change

stockholder ['stɒkhəʊldə(r)] *n Fin* actionnaire *mf*

Stockholm ['stɒkhəʊm] *n* Stockholm

stocking ['stɒkɪŋ] *n (garment)* bas *m*

stockist ['stɒkɪst] *n Com* stockiste *mf*

stockpile ['stɒkpaɪl] **1** *n* réserves *fpl* **2** *vt* faire des réserves de

stockroom ['stɒkruːm] *n* réserve *f*, magasin *m*

stock-still ['stɒk'stɪl] *adv* **to stand s.** se tenir complètement immobile

stocktaking ['stɒkteɪkɪŋ] *n Com* inventaire *m* des stocks; *Fig* **a s. exercise** un examen de situation

stocky ['stɒkɪ] *adj* trapu(e)

stodge [stɒdʒ] *n Fam (food)* aliments *mpl* bourratifs

stodgy ['stɒdʒɪ] *adj (food)* bourratif(ive); *(book)* indigeste

stoic ['stəʊɪk] *adj* stoïque

stoical ['stəʊɪkəl] *adj* stoïque

stoicism ['stəʊɪsɪzəm] *n* stoïcisme *m*

stoke [stəʊk] *vt (fire, boiler)* alimenter; *Fig* entretenir

stole[1] [stəʊl] *n (garment)* étole *f*

stole[2] *pt of* **steal**

stolen ['stəʊlən] **1** *adj* volé(e) **2** *pp of* **steal**

stolid ['stɒlɪd] *adj* impassible

stomach ['stʌmək] **1** *n* ventre *m*; *(organ)* estomac *m*; **on an empty s.** à jeun; *Fig* **it turns my s.** ça m'écœure; *Fig* **I've no s. for his vulgar jokes this evening** je n'ai aucune envie d'écouter ses plaisanteries vulgaires ce soir; **to have (a) s. ache** avoir mal au ventre; *(in organ)* avoir mal à l'estomac; *Med* **s. pump** pompe *f* stomacale **2** *vt Fig (tolerate)* supporter

stomp [stɒmp] *vi* marcher en tapant des pieds; **to s. in/out** entrer/sortir en tapant des pieds

stomping ground ['stɒmpɪŋ'graʊnd] *n* lieu *m* de prédilection; **this was one of my old stomping grounds** j'y allais tout le temps

stone [stəʊn] **1** *n* **(a)** *(material, piece of rock)* pierre *f*; *(smaller)* caillou *m*; *Fig* **to leave no s. unturned** remuer ciel et terre; *Fig* **a s.'s throw from here** à deux pas d'ici; **the S. Age** l'âge *m* de pierre; *Zool* **s. marten** fouine *f* **(b)** *(of fruit)* noyau *m* **(c)** *(unit of weight)* = 6,35kg **2** *adj* en pierre; *(jug)* en grès **3** *vt* **(a)** *(fruit)* dénoyauter **(b)** *(person)* lapider

stone-cold ['stəʊn'kəʊld] *adj* glacé(e)

stoned [stəʊnd] *adj Fam (on drugs)* défoncé(e)

stone-dead ['stəʊn'ded] *adj* raide mort(e)
stone-deaf ['stəʊn'def] *adj* sourd(e) comme un pot
stonemason ['stəʊnmeɪsən] *n* maçon *m*
stonewall [stəʊn'wɔːl] *vi (in game)* pratiquer un jeu défensif; *(in inquiry)* refuser de répondre
stoneware ['stəʊnweə(r)] *n* poterie *f* en grès
stonework ['stəʊnwɜːk] *n* maçonnerie *f*
stonily ['stəʊnɪlɪ] *adv* froidement
stony ['stəʊnɪ] *adj (ground, beach)* caillouteux(euse); *Fig (look, silence)* glacial(e); *Br Fam* **to be s. broke** n'avoir pas un rond
stood [stʊd] *pt & pp of* **stand**
stooge [stuːdʒ] *n (comedian's fall guy)* faire-valoir *m*; *(minion)* larbin *m*
stool [stuːl] *n* (**a**) *(seat)* tabouret *m*; *Fig* **to fall between two stools** être assis(e) entre deux chaises; *Fam* **s. pigeon** balance *f*, indic *m* (**b**) *Med (faeces)* selles *fpl*
stoop¹ [stuːp] **1** *n* **to have a s.** être voûté(e); **to walk with a s.** marcher le dos courbé
2 *vi (bend down)* se pencher; *Fig* **to s. to sth/doing sth** s'abaisser à qch/à faire qch
stoop² *n Am (of house) (with roof)* véranda *f*; *(without roof)* perron *m*
stop [stɒp] **1** *n* (**a**) *(halt)* arrêt *m*; **to put a s. to sth** mettre fin à qch; **to come to a s.** s'arrêter; *Aut* **s. sign** stop *m* (**b**) *(pause) (in work)* pause *f*; *(in journey)* halte *f*; *(of plane)* escale *f*; *(of train)* arrêt *m* (**c**) *(for bus, train)* arrêt *m* (**d**) *(full stop)* point *m*; *(in telegram)* stop *m* (**e**) *Mus (on organ)* jeu *m*; *Fig* **to pull out all the stops** remuer ciel et terre
2 *vt (pt & pp* **stopped**) (**a**) *(halt) (person, vehicle)* arrêter; *(conversation, speaker)* interrompre; *(corruption, abuse)* mettre fin à; *Fin* **to s. a cheque** faire opposition à un chèque; **s., thief!** au voleur! (**b**) *(cease)* arrêter; **to s. doing sth** arrêter de faire qch (**c**) *(prevent)* empêcher; **to s. sb from doing sth** empêcher qn de faire qch; **I couldn't s. myself** je n'ai pas pu m'en empêcher (**d**) *(fill in) (hole, gap)* boucher
3 *vi* (**a**) *(halt) (of moving person, vehicle)* s'arrêter (**b**) *(cease) (of speaker, worker)* s'arrêter; *(of pain, bleeding)* cesser; *(of rain)* s'arrêter, cesser; **she'll s. at nothing** rien ne l'arrêtera; **to s. short** s'arrêter net (**c**) *(stay)* rester
▶**stop by** *vi (visit)* passer; **I'll s. by your place tomorrow** je passerai chez toi demain
▶**stop off** *vi* faire une halte
▶**stop over** *vi Aviat* faire escale
▶**stop up** *vt sep (hole, sink, pipe)* boucher
stopcock ['stɒpkɒk] *n* robinet *m* d'arrêt
stopgap ['stɒpgæp] *n (thing, person)* bouche-trou *m*; **s. measure** mesure *f* transitoire
stoplight ['stɒplaɪt] *n Am Aut* feux *mpl* (tricolores *ou* de signalisation)
stopover ['stɒpəʊvə(r)] *n Aviat* escale *f*
stoppage ['stɒpɪdʒ] *n* (**a**) *(of flow, traffic)* arrêt *m*; *(strike)* débrayage *m* (**b**) *Fin (deduction)* retenue *f*
stopper ['stɒpə(r)] *n* bouchon *m*
stop-press ['stɒppres] *adj Journ* de dernière minute
stopwatch ['stɒpwɒtʃ] *n* chronomètre *m*
storage ['stɔːrɪdʒ] *n* (**a**) *(action)* emmagasinage *m*; *(space available)* (espace *m* de) rangement *m*; **to put sth into s.** entreposer qch; **s. heater** radiateur *m* à accumulation; **s. space** espace *m* de rangement; **s. tank** citerne *f* (**b**) *Comput* mémoire *f*
store [stɔː(r)] **1** *n* (**a**) *(supply) (of goods, food)* provision *f*; *Fig (of knowledge)* fonds *m*; **stores** réserves

fpl (**b**) *(warehouse)* entrepôt *m* (**c**) *Am (shop)* magasin *m*; *also Br* **s. detective** vigile *m*; **s. card** carte *f* de crédit *(d'un grand magasin)* (**d**) *(idioms)* **to hold** *or* **keep sth in s.** tenir *ou* garder qch en réserve; **I have a surprise in s. for her** je lui réserve une surprise; **to set great s. by sth** faire grand cas de qch
2 *vt (put in storage)* entreposer; *(food)* ranger; *(electricity, heat)* emmagasiner; **s. in a cool place** conserver au frais
▶**store up** *vt sep* accumuler
storehouse ['stɔːhaʊs] *n* entrepôt *m*
storeroom ['stɔːruːm] *n (in office, factory)* réserve *f*; *(at home)* débarras *m*
storey, *Am* **story** ['stɔːrɪ] *n* étage *m*; **a four-s. building** un immeuble de quatre étages
stork [stɔːk] *n* cigogne *f*
storm [stɔːm] **1** *n* (**a**) *(bad weather)* tempête *f*; *(thunderstorm)* orage *m*; *Fig* **a s. in a teacup** une tempête dans un verre d'eau; **s. cloud** nuée *f* d'orage; **s. door** double porte *f* (**b**) *Fig (scandal, of protest)* tempête *f*; *(of abuse)* bordée *f* (**c**) *Mil* **to take sth by s.** prendre qch d'assaut; *Fig* **she/the show took London by s.** elle/le spectacle a eu un succès foudroyant à Londres; **s. troops** troupes *fpl* d'assaut
2 *vt (town, fortress)* prendre d'assaut
3 *vi (of person)* tempêter; **to s. in/out** entrer/sortir comme un ouragan
stormy ['stɔːmɪ] *adj also Fig* orageux(euse)
story¹ ['stɔːrɪ] *(pl* **stories**) *n* (**a**) *(account)* histoire *f*; *Fig* **to tell stories** *(lie)* raconter des histoires (**b**) *(plot) (of novel, play)* intrigue *f*, histoire *f* (**c**) *(in newspaper)* article *m* (**d**) *(idioms)* **that's quite another s.** ça c'est une autre histoire; **it's the same old s.** c'est toujours la même histoire; **or so the s. goes** c'est du moins ce que l'on raconte; *Fam* **it's the s. of my life** je suis le/la spécialiste de ce genre de choses; **it's a long s.** c'est une longue histoire; **to cut a long s. short,...** bref, pour résumer...
story² *Am* = **storey**
storybook ['stɔːrɪbʊk] *n* livre *m* d'histoires
storyteller ['stɔːrɪtelə(r)] *n* conteur(euse) *m,f*
stout [staʊt] **1** *n (beer)* stout *f*, bière *f* brune forte
2 *adj* (**a**) *(fat)* corpulent(e) (**b**) *(solid) (door, shoes)* solide (**c**) *(brave) (person, resistance)* acharné(e)
stouthearted [staʊt'hɑːtɪd] *adj Lit* vaillant(e)
stoutly ['staʊtlɪ] *adv (resist, maintain)* avec fermeté
stove [stəʊv] *n (for cooking)* cuisinière *f*; *(for heating)* poêle *m*
stow [stəʊ] *vt (put away)* ranger; *Naut* arrimer
▶**stow away** *vi (on ship)* s'embarquer clandestinement
stowaway ['stəʊəweɪ] *n* passager(ère) *m,f* clandestin(e)
straddle ['strædəl] *vt (horse)* enfourcher; *(chair)* se mettre à califourchon sur; *Fig (period of time, subject)* couvrir
strafe [streɪf] *vt Mil* mitrailler en rase-mottes
straggle ['strægəl] *vi* (**a**) *(lag behind)* être à la traîne (**b**) *(of hair)* pendouiller
straggler ['stræglə(r)] *n* retardataire *mf*
straggly ['stræglɪ] *adj (hair)* épars(e)
straight [streɪt] **1** *adj* (**a**) *(level, not curved) (line, tie, skirt, picture, back)* droit(e); *(hair)* raide; **to keep a s. face** garder son sérieux; **to put things** *or* **matters s.** arranger les choses; **to put sb s. about sth** éclairer qn sur qch (**b**) *(consecutive)* consécutif(ive); **s. flush** *(in cards)* quinte *f* flush (**c**) *(honest) (person)* honnête; *(answer)* clair(e); **to be s. with sb** jouer franc jeu avec

qn (**d**) *(conventional)* conformiste; *Theat* **s. man** faire-valoir *m* (**e**) *Fam (heterosexual)* hétéro (**f**) *(undiluted)* pur(e)
2 *adv* (**a**) *(in straight line)* droit; **sit up s.!** tiens-toi droit sur ton siège!; **to see s.** voir bien; **I can't think s.** je n'ai pas les idées claires; **to look s. ahead** regarder droit devant soi; **go s. on** allez tout droit; *Fig* **to go s.** *(of criminal)* se ranger (**b**) *(immediately)* immédiatement; **I'll be s.** back je reviens tout de suite; **s. away** *or* **off** tout de suite (**c**) *(directly)* directement; **to come** *or* **get s. to the point** allez droit au fait; **to come s. out with sth** dire qch tout net
3 *n* (**a**) **to keep to the s. and narrow** rester sur le droit chemin (**b**) *(on running track, racecourse)* ligne *f* droite
straightaway ['streɪtəweɪ] *adv* tout de suite
straighten ['streɪtən] *vt (bent nail, rod)* redresser; *(picture)* remettre droit; *(tie, hat)* ajuster; **to s. one's back** se redresser
▸**straighten out** *vt sep (problem)* régler; *(one's affairs)* mettre de l'ordre dans
straight-faced ['streɪt'feɪst] *adj* à l'air sérieux
straightforward [streɪt'fɔːwəd] *adj* (**a**) *(honest)* direct(e), franc (franche) (**b**) *(simple)* simple
strain¹ [streɪn] **1** *n* (**a**) *(on rope, beam, economy, friendship)* tension *f*; *(on muscle, ankle)* foulure *f*; **to put a s. on** *(economy)* grever; *(friendship)* éprouver (**b**) *(mental stress)* stress *m*; **to be under a lot of s.** être très stressé(e)
2 *vt* (**a**) *(muscle, ankle)* se fouler; *(economy)* grever; *(friendship)* éprouver; **to s. one's back** se faire mal au dos; **to s. one's ears** tendre l'oreille (**b**) *Culin (liquid)* filtrer, passer; *(vegetables)* égoutter
3 *vi* **to s. at a rope** tirer sur une corde; *Fig* **to s. at the leash** ne plus tenir en place
strain² *n (variety) (of virus)* souche *f*; *(of plant)* variété *f*
strained [streɪnd] *adj (muscle)* froissé(e); *Fig (atmosphere, relationship)* tendu(e)
strainer ['streɪnə(r)] *n* passoire *f*
strait [streɪt] *n* détroit *m*; **the Straits of Gibraltar** le détroit de Gibraltar
straitlaced ['streɪt'leɪst] *adj* collet monté *inv*
strand¹ [strænd] *vt (ship)* échouer; **to be stranded** *(of person)* être bloqué(e)
strand² *n (of rope, cotton)* brin *m*; *(of hair)* mèche *f*; *Fig (of plot)* fil *m*
strange [streɪndʒ] *adj* (**a**) *(odd) (person, behaviour)* bizarre (**b**) *(unfamiliar)* inconnu(e)
strangely ['streɪndʒlɪ] *adv (behave, dress)* bizarrement; **s. enough,...** chose bizarre,...
strangeness ['streɪndʒnɪs] *n* (**a**) *(oddness)* bizarrerie *f* (**b**) *(unfamiliarity)* étrangeté *f*
stranger ['streɪndʒə(r)] *n (unknown person)* inconnu(e) *m,f*; *(from somewhere else)* étranger(ère) *m,f*; **I'm a s. here myself** je ne suis pas d'ici
strangle ['stræŋgəl] *vt also Fig* étrangler
stranglehold ['stræŋgəlhəʊld] *n Fig* **to have a s. on sth** avoir la mainmise sur qch
strangulation [stræŋgjʊ'leɪʃən] *n* strangulation *f*
strap [stræp] **1** *n (of leather, canvas)* sangle *f*, lanière *f*; *(on dress, bra)* bretelle *f*; *(on watch)* bracelet *m*; *(on shoe)* bride *f*
2 *vt (pt & pp strapped)* **to s. sth to sth** sangler qch à qch; *Fam* **to be strapped (for cash)** être un peu juste
▸**strap in** *vt sep* attacher; **to s. oneself in** attacher sa ceinture de sécurité
strapless ['stræplɪs] *adj (dress, bra)* sans bretelles

strapping ['stræpɪŋ] *adj* costaud(e)
Strasbourg ['stræzbɜːg] *n* Strasbourg
strata ['strɑːtə] *pl of* stratum
strategic [strə'tiːdʒɪk] *adj* stratégique
strategist ['strætədʒɪst] *n* stratège *m*
strategy ['strætɪdʒɪ] *(pl* **strategies***) n* stratégie *f*
stratification [strætɪfɪ'keɪʃən] *n* stratification *f*
stratosphere ['strætəsfɪə(r)] *n* stratosphère *f*
stratum ['strɑːtəm] *(pl* **strata** ['strɑːtə]*) n* strate *f*; *Fig* couche *f*
straw [strɔː] *n* (**a**) *(from wheat, for drinking)* paille *f*; **s. hat** chapeau *m* de paille; *Fig* **s. man** homme *m* de paille; **s. poll** sondage *m* d'opinion (**b**) *(idioms)* **to clutch** *or* **grasp at straws** se raccrocher à de faux espoirs; **that's the last s.!** ça c'est le comble!
strawberry ['strɔːbərɪ] *(pl* **strawberries***) n* fraise *f*; **s. jam** confiture *f* de fraises

Strawberries and cream

En Grande-Bretagne, les fraises à la crème sont traditionnellement consommées lors de certaines manifestations en plein air, notamment au tournoi de tennis de Wimbledon.

straw-coloured, *Am* **straw-colored** ['strɔːkʌləd] *adj* jaune paille *inv*
stray [streɪ] **1** *n (dog)* chien *m* errant; *(cat)* chat *m* égaré
2 *adj (animal)* égaré(e); *(dog)* errant(e); *(bullet)* perdu(e)
3 *vi (of person, animal)* s'égarer; **s. from the point** s'écarter du sujet
streak [striːk] **1** *n (stripe) (of paint, dirt)* traînée *f*; *(of light)* rai *m*; *(in hair)* mèche *f*; **a s. of lightning** un éclair; **a s. of luck** une période de chance; **to be on a winning/losing s.** être dans une période de chance/poisse; **to have a mean/cruel s.** avoir un côté mesquin/cruel
2 *vt* **streaked with dirt** plein(e) de traînées sales; **streaked with tears** strié(e) de larmes; **his hair is streaked with silver** ses cheveux sont parsemés de cheveux gris; **to have one's hair streaked** se faire faire des mèches
3 *vi* (**a**) *(move quickly)* **to s. off** partir à toute vitesse; **to s. past** passer en trombe (**b**) *Fam (run naked)* courir nu(e) (en public)
streaker ['striːkə(r)] *n Fam* = personne qui court nue en public
streaky ['striːkɪ] *adj (surface, pattern)* strié(e); **s. bacon** bacon *m* entrelardé
stream [striːm] **1** *n* (**a**) *(brook)* ruisseau *m* (**b**) *(of light, blood, water)* jet *m*; *(of tears, insults)* torrent *m*; *(of people)* flot *m*; **to come on s.** *(of industrial plant)* entrer en production
2 *vt* (**a**) *(spurt)* **to s. blood** ruisseler de sang (**b**) *Br Sch* **to s. pupils** répartir des élèves par niveau
3 *vi* (**a**) *(of liquid)* ruisseler; *(of people)* affluer; *(of traffic)* s'écouler; **her eyes were streaming** ses yeux étaient ruisselants de larmes; (**b**) *(of hair, banner)* flotter
streamer ['striːmə(r)] *n* banderole *f*
streamline ['striːmlaɪn] *vt (vehicle)* caréner; *Fig (system)* rationaliser; *(department)* dégraisser
streamlined ['striːmlaɪnd] *adj (vehicle)* caréné(e); *Fig (system)* rationalisé(e); *(department)* dégraissé(e)
street [striːt] *n* (**a**) *(road)* rue *f*; **on the s.** dans la rue; **to take to the streets** *(of protesters)* descendre dans

la rue; **s. fighting** combats *mpl* de rue; **s. lamp** lampadaire *m*; **s. map** plan *m* (de la ville); **s. market** marché *m* de plein air; **s. sweeper** balayeur(euse) *m,f*; **s. theatre** théâtre *m* de rue; **s. value** *(of drugs)* valeur *f* à la revente (**b**) *(idioms)* **to walk the streets** *(of prostitute)* faire le tapin *ou* le trottoir; **the man in the s.** Monsieur Tout-le-Monde; *Fam* **to be streets ahead** dépasser tout le monde; **that's right up my s.** c'est tout à fait mon rayon; *Fam* **to have s. cred** être très branché(e)

streetcar ['striːtkɑː(r)] *n Am* tramway *m*

streetwalker ['striːtwɔːkə(r)] *n* racoleuse *f*

streetwise ['striːtwaɪz] *adj* dégourdi(e)

strength [streŋθ] *n* (**a**) *(of person, wind, emotion, currency)* force *f*; *(of rope, fabric)* solidité *f*; *(of light, alcohol, army)* puissance *f*; **to be at full s.** *(of department, regiment)* avoir des effectifs complets; **to be under s.** *(of department, regiment)* ne pas avoir des effectifs complets; **in s.** en force; **to go from s. to s.** aller de mieux en mieux; **on the s. of** sur la base de; **on the s. of her qualifications** grâce à ses diplômes (**b**) *(strong point)* point *m* fort

strengthen ['streŋθən] **1** *vt (wall, building)* renforcer, consolider; *(muscle)* affermir; *(friendship)* consolider; *(determination, position)* renforcer

2 *vi (of friendship)* se consolider; *(of determination)* se renforcer; *(of currency)* se raffermir; *(of wind)* souffler plus fort

strenuous ['strenjʊəs] *adj (activity, lifestyle)* fatigant(e); *(effort, opposition)* vigoureux(euse); *(denial)* énergique

strenuously ['strenjʊəslɪ] *adv (campaign, deny)* énergiquement; *(resist)* vigoureusement

stress [stres] **1** *n* (**a**) *(tension) (physical)* tension *f*; *(mental)* stress *m*; **to be under a lot of s.** être très stressé(e); **s. factor** facteur *m* de stress; *Med* **s. fracture** fracture *f* de surmenage (**b**) *(emphasis)* insistance *f*; *Ling* accentuation *f*; **to put s. on sth** insister sur qch

2 *vt (emphasize)* insister sur; *Ling* accentuer

3 *vi Fam* stresser

stressed (out) [strest('aʊt)] *adj Fam* stressé(e)

stressful ['stresfʊl] *adj* stressant(e)

stretch [stretʃ] **1** *n* (**a**) *(of body)* **to have a s.** s'étirer; *Fig* **by no s. of the imagination** même avec beaucoup d'imagination; **s. marks** vergetures *fpl* (**b**) *(of water, land)* étendue *f*; *(of road)* tronçon *m*; *(of time, silence)* période *f*; **at one s.** d'une traite (**c**) *(at full s.* *(factory)* au maximum de ses capacités

2 *vt* (**a**) *(elastic)* étirer; *(belt, arm, hand)* tendre; **to s. the truth** exagérer; **to s. one's legs** se dégourdir les jambes (**b**) *(put demands on) (person)* pousser à son maximum; *(resources)* utiliser au maximum; *(patience)* abuser de; **we're fully stretched at the moment** nous sommes au maximum de notre rendement en ce moment (**c**) *(make last) (income, supplies)* faire durer

3 *vi* (**a**) *(of elastic)* s'étendre; *(of person, fabric)* s'étirer (**b**) *(of road, land, years)* s'étendre, s'étaler (**c**) *(of resources, budget)* **my budget won't s. to a new car** je n'ai pas les moyens de m'acheter une nouvelle voiture

▸**stretch out 1** *vt sep (arm, hand)* tendre

2 *vi* (**a**) *(of person)* s'étirer (**b**) *(of road, land, time)* s'étaler, s'étendre

stretcher ['stretʃə(r)] *n* brancard *m*; **s. bearer** brancardier *m*

stretchy ['stretʃɪ] *adj* extensible

strew [struː] *(pp strewed or strewn [struːn]) vt (objects)* éparpiller; **to be strewn with sth** *(of surface)* être jonché(e) de qch

stricken ['strɪkən] *adj (with grief, guilt)* accablé(e) (**with** de); *(with illness, by disaster)* frappé(e) (**with** par); **the s. city** la ville sinistrée

strict [strɪkt] *adj* (**a**) *(person, instruction, discipline)* strict(e); **s. morals** morale *f* sévère; **a s. Muslim** un(e) musulman(e) de stricte obéissance (**b**) *(meaning, minimum)* strict(e); **in strictest confidence** en toute confidence

strictly ['strɪktlɪ] *adv* (**a**) *(severely, only)* strictement (**b**) *(exactly)* **s. speaking** à proprement parler; **not s. true** pas tout à fait vrai(e)

strictness ['strɪktnɪs] *n (of discipline, rules)* sévérité *f*

stride [straɪd] **1** *n* (**a**) pas *m*; *(when running)* foulée *f* (**b**) *(idioms)* **to make great strides** faire des pas de géant; **to take sth in one's s.** prendre qch calmement; **to get into one's s.** trouver son rythme

2 *vi (pt strode [strəʊd], pp stridden ['strɪdən])* **to s. in/out** entrer/sortir à grands pas

strident ['straɪdənt] *adj* strident(e)

strife [straɪf] *n* conflits *mpl*

strike [straɪk] **1** *n* (**a**) *(refusal to work)* grève *f*; **to be on s.** être en grève; **s. fund** = caisse de prévoyance permettant d'aider les grévistes; **s. pay** indemnité *f* de grève (**b**) *(discovery) (of ore, oil)* découverte *f* (**c**) *(blow)* coup *m*; *Mil* attaque *f*, raid *m*

2 *vt (pt & pp struck [strʌk])* (**a**) *(hit)* frapper; *(collide with)* heurter, taper contre; **to be struck by lightning** être frappé(e) par la foudre; **to s. sb in the face** frapper qn à la figure; **to s. a blow** donner un coup; *Fig* **to s. a blow for freedom** se battre pour défendre sa liberté; **the clock struck ten** l'horloge a sonné dix heures; *Fig* **to s. the right/wrong note** *(of speech, remark)* sonner juste/faux; **to s. terror into sb** frapper qn de terreur; **to be struck dumb/blind** être frappé(e) de mutisme/cécité; **a stray bullet struck him dead** il a été tué par une balle perdue (**b**) *(match)* craquer (**c**) *(coin, medal)* frapper (**d**) *(impress)* frapper; **she strikes me as a reasonable person** elle me paraît raisonnable; **it struck me that...** il m'a semblé que... (**e**) *(discover) (gold, oil)* découvrir; *Fam* **to s. it rich** faire fortune; *Fam* **to s. it lucky** avoir un coup de chance (**f**) *(reach) (bargain, deal)* conclure; **to s. a balance** trouver un équilibre

3 *vi* (**a**) *(attack)* *(of enemy)* attaquer; *(of criminal)* frapper; *(of disaster, earthquake)* se produire; *(of clock)* sonner; **to s. home** *(of criticism)* faire mouche; *Prov* **while the iron is hot** il faut battre le fer pendant qu'il est chaud (**b**) *(of workers)* faire grève

▸**strike back** *vi (retaliate)* riposter

▸**strike down** *vt sep (of disease)* terrasser; *(of bullet)* abattre

▸**strike off** *vt sep (doctor, lawyer)* radier

▸**strike out 1** *vt sep (delete)* rayer

2 *vi* (**a**) *(hit out)* **to s. out at sb** essayer de frapper qn (**b**) *(leave)* s'élancer (**for** vers); **to s. out on one's own** s'établir à son compte

▸**strike up** *vt sep (song)* entonner; *(conversation)* entamer; **to s. up a friendship (with sb)** se lier d'amitié (avec qn)

strikebreaker ['straɪkbreɪkə(r)] *n* briseur(euse) *m,f* de grève

striker ['straɪkə(r)] *n* (**a**) *(striking worker)* gréviste *mf* (**b**) *(in football)* buteur *m*

striking ['straɪkɪŋ] *adj* (**a**) *(similarity, appearance)* frappant(e), saisissant(e) (**b**) *(worker)* en grève (**c**) **she lives within s. distance of New York** elle habite tout près de New York

string [strɪŋ] **1** *n* (**a**) *(for tying)* ficelle *f*; *(of violin, tennis racket, bow)* corde *f*; *(of puppet)* fil *m*; *Mus* **the strings** *(in orchestra)* les cordes; *Fig* **to have more than one s.** *to one's bow* avoir plus d'une corde à son arc; *Fig* **with no strings attached** sans conditions; *Fig* **to pull strings for sb** *(obtain favours)* faire jouer ses relations pour qn; *(get job, promotion)* pistonner qn; *Mus* **s. quartet** quatuor *m* à cordes; *Br* **s. vest** maillot *m* de corps à grosses mailles (**b**) *(of onions, islands)* chapelet *m*; *(of words, shops, defeats)* série *f*; *Comput* série

2 *vt (pp & pt strung* [strʌŋ])(**a**)*(violin)* monter; *(tennis racket)* corder; *(bow)* bander (**b**) *(pearls, beads)* enfiler

▸**string along** *vt sep Fam* mener en bateau

▸**string up** *vt sep Fam (criminal)* pendre

stringed [strɪŋd] *adj (instrument)* à cordes

stringent ['strɪndʒənt] *adj* rigoureux(euse)

strip¹ [strɪp] *n* (**a**) *(of cloth, paper)* bande *f*; *(of metal)* lame *f*; *Fam* **to tear sb off a s.** passer un savon à qn; **s. cartoon** bande *f* dessinée; **s. lighting** éclairage *m* au néon (**b**) *(of sports team)* tenue *f*

strip² **1** *n* **to do a s.** *(undress)* se déshabiller; *(for show)* faire un strip-tease; **s. club** boîte *f* de strip-tease; **s. poker** strip-poker *m*; **s. show** strip-tease *m*

2 *vt (pt & pp stripped) (person)* déshabiller; *(bed)* défaire; *(paint)* gratter; *(wallpaper)* décoller; **to s. sb of sth** dépouiller qn de qch

3 *vi (undress)* se déshabiller

strip off 1 *vt sep (paint)* gratter; *(wallpaper)* décoller **2** *vi (undress)* se déshabiller

stripe [straɪp] *n* (**a**) *(on cloth, animal's coat)* rayure *f*, raie *f*(**b**) *(indicating rank)* galon *m*

striped [straɪpt] *adj* à rayures, rayé(e)

stripling ['strɪplɪŋ] *n* tout jeune homme *m*

stripper ['strɪpə(r)] *n (woman)* strip-teaseuse *f*; **(male) s.** strip-teaseur *m*

strip-search ['strɪpsɜːtʃ] **1** *n* fouille *f* corporelle **2** *vt* **to s. sb** faire subir une fouille corporelle à qn

striptease ['strɪptiːz] *n* strip-tease *m*

strive [straɪv] *(pt strove* [strəʊv], *pp striven* ['strɪvən]) *vi* **to s. to do sth** s'efforcer de faire qch; **to s. for** *or* **after sth** se battre pour obtenir qch

strobe [strəʊb] *n Phys* stroboscope *m*; **s. lighting** lumières *fpl* stroboscopiques

strode [strəʊd] *pt of* stride

stroke [strəʊk] **1** *n* (**a**) *(blow, tennis shot)* coup *m*; *(in rowing, swimming)* *(style)* nage *f*; *(single movement)* mouvement *m*; **a brush s.** un coup de pinceau (**b**) *(of clock, bell)* **on the s. of nine** à neuf heures sonnantes (**c**) *(caress)* caresse *f*; **to give sb/sth a s.** caresser qn/qch (**d**) *Med* attaque *f* (**e**) *(idioms)* **she hasn't done a s. of work** elle n'a rien fichu; **a s. of luck** un coup de chance; **a s. of genius** un coup de génie; **at a s.** d'un seul coup

2 *vt (caress)* caresser

stroll [strəʊl] **1** *n* promenade *f*, tour *m*; **to go for a s.** aller se promener *ou* faire un tour

2 *vi* se promener, flâner

strong [strɒŋ] **1** *adj* (**a**) *(physically, mentally)* fort(e); *(candidate, team)* bon (bonne); *(friendship, argument)* solide; **the pound is s. against the dollar** la livre est solide face au dollar (**b**) *(in degree) (colour,*

light, protest) vif (vive); *(smell, drink, accent, possibility)* fort(e); *(resemblance)* grand(e); *(measures)* énergique; **s. language** grossièretés *fpl*; **s. point** point *m* fort (**c**) *(sturdy) (rope, chair, shoes)* solide

2 *adv* **to be still going s.** *(band, programme)* marcher toujours très bien; *(person)* être toujours d'attaque

3 *npl* **the s.** les forts *mpl*

strong-arm tactics ['strɒŋɑːm'tæktɪks] *npl* manière *f* forte

strong-box ['strɒŋbɒks] *n* coffre-fort *m*

stronghold ['strɒŋhəʊld] *n (fortress)* forteresse *f*; *Fig (of political party, religion)* bastion *m*

strongly ['strɒŋlɪ] *adv (oppose, endorse)* vigoureusement; *(believe)* fermement; **s. built** solide; **a s. worded letter** une lettre bien sentie; **to feel s. about sth** être convaincu(e) de qch

strongman ['strɒŋmæn] *n (in circus)* hercule *m* (de foire); *Fig (dictator)* homme *m* fort

strong-minded [strɒŋ'maɪndɪd] *adj* résolu(e)

strongroom ['strɒŋruːm] *n* chambre *f* forte

strong-willed [strɒŋ'wɪld] *adj* résolu(e)

strontium ['strɒntɪəm] *n Chem* strontium *m*

strop [strɒp] *n* (**a**) *(for razor)* cuir *m* (à rasoir) (**b**) *Br Fam* **to be in a s.** être de mauvais poil

stroppy ['strɒpɪ] *adj Br Fam* hargneux(euse); **to get s.** monter sur ses grands chevaux

strove [strəʊv] *pt of* strive

struck [strʌk] *pt & pp of* strike

structural ['strʌktʃərəl] *adj* structurel(elle); **s. damage** dégâts *mpl* de structure; **s. survey** = inspection pour vérifier la solidité d'un bâtiment

structurally ['strʌktʃərəlɪ] *adv* structurellement

structure ['strʌktʃə(r)] **1** *n* (**a**) *(of society, language, story)* structure *f* (**b**) *(building, monument)* édifice *m*, construction *f*

2 *vt* structurer

struggle ['strʌgəl] **1** *n* lutte *f* (**for** pour); **without a s.** sans résistance; **to be s.** la vie est un combat

2 *vi* lutter (**for** pour); **to s. to do sth** lutter pour faire qch; **to be struggling** *(of person, company)* avoir des difficultés *ou* du mal

strum [strʌm] *(pt & pp strummed) vt (guitar)* gratter

strung [strʌŋ] *pt & pp of* string

strut¹ [strʌt] *n (for frame)* étai *m*; *Aviat* pilier *m*

strut² *(pt & pp strutted)* **1** *vi* se pavaner

2 *vt Fam* **to s. one's stuff** frimer

strychnine ['strɪkniːn] *n* strychnine *f*

stub [stʌb] **1** *n (of pencil)* bout *m*; *(of cigarette)* mégot *m*; *(of cheque)* talon *m*

2 *vt (pt & pp stubbed)* **to s. one's toe (on** *or* **against)** se cogner l'orteil (contre)

▸**stub out** *vt sep (cigarette)* écraser

stubble ['stʌbəl] *n* (**a**) *(in field)* chaume *m* (**b**) *(on face)* barbe *f* de plusieurs jours

stubborn ['stʌbən] *adj (person)* têtu(e); *(determination, resistance)* farouche; *(stain, infection)* rebelle

stubbornness ['stʌbənnɪs] *n (of person)* entêtement *m*, obstination *f*; *(of determination, resistance)* inflexibilité *f*

stubby ['stʌbɪ] *adj* court(e) et boudiné(e)

stucco ['stʌkəʊ] *n* stuc *m*

stuck [stʌk] **1** *adj* bloqué(e), coincé(e); **to get s.** être coincé; *(in mud, sand, with problem)* s'enliser; **to be s. for sth** être à court de qch; *Fam* **to be s. with sb/sth** ne pas pouvoir se débarrasser de qn/qch

2 *pt & pp of* stick²

stuck-up ['stʌk'ʌp] adj Fam snob inv
stud¹ [stʌd] n (fastener) bouton-pression m; (on football, rugby boots) crampon m; (earring) clou m d'oreille
stud² n (**a**) (farm) haras m; (stallion) étalon m (**b**) Fam (man) étalon m
student ['stjuːdənt] n (at university) étudiant(e) m,f; (at school) élève mf; **s. card** carte f d'étudiant; **s. life** vie f étudiante; **s. loan** = prêt bancaire pour étudiants; **s. nurse** élève mf infirmier(ère); **s. teacher** enseignant(e) m,f stagiaire; **students' union** (association) = association d'aide et de services aux étudiants; (place) foyer m des étudiants

Students' union

Dans les universités britanniques et américaines, on appelle "students' union" à la fois le syndicat et les locaux où il se trouve. Le syndicat est chargé de défendre les intérêts des étudiants, sert de centre d'information et de conseil en matière de logement, de santé et de financement, et organise des événements culturels et des activités.

studied ['stʌdɪd] adj (manner, attitude) calculé(e)
studio ['stjuːdɪəʊ] (pl **studios**) n studio m; (of artist) atelier m; TV **s. audience** public m (présent lors de l'enregistrement); Br **s. flat** studio m
studious ['stjuːdɪəs] adj studieux(euse)
study ['stʌdɪ] **1** n (pl **studies**) (**a**) (investigation, by artist) étude f; **to make a s. of sth** faire une étude sur qch; **s. group** groupe m d'étude; **s. trip** voyage m d'études (**b**) (room) bureau m, cabinet m de travail
2 vt (pt & pp **studied**) (facts, evidence) examiner; (behaviour, school subject) étudier; (university subject) faire des études de
3 vi (revise) travailler; (be at university) faire des études
stuff [stʌf] **1** n (**a**) (objects, possessions) affaires fpl; **some s.** (substance) un truc; Fam **he reads all that intellectual s.** il lit tous ces trucs intellos; Fam **she writes good s.** c'est bien, ce qu'elle écrit; Fam **he knows his s.** il s'y connaît; Fam **that's the s.!** c'est bien! (**b**) (cloth) étoffe f
2 vt (fill) (cushion) rembourrer; (chicken, tomatoes) farcir; (pocket) remplir; **to s. sth into sth** fourrer qch dans qch; Fam **to s. oneself** s'empiffrer; Br very Fam **get stuffed!** va te faire foutre!
stuffed [stʌft] adj (**a**) (chicken, pepper) farci(e); **s. animal** (for display) animal m empaillé; Am (soft toy) peluche f (**b**) Br Fam (in trouble) fichu(e)
stuffing ['stʌfɪŋ] n (for furniture) rembourrage m; (for chicken) farce f; Fam **to knock the s. out of sb** ficher un coup à qn
stuffy ['stʌfɪ] adj (**a**) (room) qui sent le renfermé (**b**) (person) vieux jeu inv
stultifying ['stʌltɪfaɪɪŋ] adj abrutissant(e)
stumble ['stʌmbəl] **1** n faux-pas m
2 vi (when walking, speaking) trébucher
▸**stumble across** vt insep (find) tomber par hasard sur
stump [stʌmp] **1** n (**a**) (of tree) souche f; (of arm, leg) moignon m (**b**) (in cricket) piquet m (**c**) Am Fam (of politician) **to be on the s.** être en campagne électorale
2 vt (baffle) laisser perplexe; **to be stumped for an answer** ne pas savoir quoi répondre
▸**stump up** vt insep Br Fam (pay) cracher
stumpy ['stʌmpɪ] adj court(e) et boudiné(e)

stun [stʌn] (pt & pp **stunned**) vt (make unconscious) assommer; Fig (shock) abasourdir
stung [stʌŋ] pt & pp of **sting**
stunk [stʌŋk] pt & pp of **stink**
stunner ['stʌnə(r)] n Br Fam (man, woman) canon m
stunning ['stʌnɪŋ] adj (shocking) étourdissant(e); (excellent) excellent(e); (beautiful) superbe
stunt¹ [stʌnt] vt (person) ralentir la croissance de; (growth) ralentir
stunt² n (in film) cascade f; (for publicity) coup m de pub; **s. man** cascadeur m
stunted [stʌntɪd] adj (plant, person) chétif(ive); (growth) retardé(e)
stupefy ['stjuːpɪfaɪ] (pt & pp **stupefied**) vt (of alcohol, drugs) abrutir; (of news, behaviour) stupéfier
stupefying ['stjuːpɪfaɪɪŋ] adj stupéfiant(e)
stupendous [stjuː'pendəs] adj fantastique
stupid ['stjuːpɪd] adj bête, stupide; **the s.** TV keeps breaking down cette saleté de télé est sans arrêt en panne; **what a s. thing to do!** c'est vraiment idiot d'avoir fait ça!
stupidity [stjuː'pɪdɪtɪ] n bêtise f, stupidité f
stupidly ['stjuːpɪdlɪ] adv bêtement
stupor ['stjuːpə(r)] n état m d'abrutissement
sturdy ['stɜːdɪ] adj (person, object) robuste; (opposition, resistance) résolu(e); (rope, chair, shoes) solide
sturgeon ['stɜːdʒən] n esturgeon m
stutter ['stʌtə(r)] **1** n bégaiement m
2 vi bégayer
sty¹ [staɪ] n (for pigs) & Fig porcherie f
sty², stye [staɪ] n (in eye) orgelet m
style [staɪl] **1** n (**a**) (manner, design) style m (**b**) (sophistication) classe f; **to live in s.** mener grand train
2 vt (design) créer; (hair) coiffer
styli ['staɪlaɪ] pl of **stylus**
stylish ['staɪlɪf] adj élégant(e), chic inv
stylist ['staɪlɪst] n (hairdresser) coiffeur(euse) m,f
stylistic [staɪ'lɪstɪk] adj stylistique
stylized ['staɪəlaɪzd] adj stylisé(e)
stylus ['staɪləs] (pl **styluses** or **styli** ['staɪlaɪ]) n (for engraving) style m; (on record player) pointe f de lecture
stymie ['staɪmɪ] vt Br Fam coincer
suave [swɑːv] adj affable; Pej mielleux(euse)
sub [sʌb] Fam **1** n (**a**) (abbr **subscription**) cotisation f (**b**) (abbr **substitute**) remplaçant(e) m,f (**c**) (abbr **submarine**) sous-marin m (**d**) Journ (abbr **subeditor**) secrétaire mf de rédaction
2 vt (pt & pp **subbed**) Journ (abbr **subedit**) mettre au point
3 vi (abbr **substitute**) **to s. for sb** remplacer qn
subaltern ['sʌbəltən] n Mil officier m subalterne
subcommittee ['sʌbkəmɪtɪ] n sous-comité m
subconscious [sʌb'kɒnʃəs] **1** n **the s.** l'inconscient m
2 adj inconscient(e)
subcontinent [sʌb'kɒntɪnənt] n sous-continent m
subcontract 1 n [sʌb'kɒntrækt] sous-traitance f
2 vt [sʌbkən'trækt] sous-traiter
subcontractor [sʌbkən'træktə(r)] n sous-traitant m
subculture ['sʌbkʌltʃə(r)] n phénomène m de groupe
subdivision [sʌbdɪ'vɪʒən] n subdivision f
subdue [səb'djuː] vt (enemy, rioter) soumettre; (emotions) maîtriser
subdued [səb'djuːd] adj (person, event) inhabituellement calme; (light) tamisé(e); (sound, voice) bas (basse)
subedit ['sʌb'edɪt] vt Journ mettre au point

subeditor [sʌb'edɪtə(r)] *n Journ* secrétaire *mf* de rédaction

subhuman [sʌb'hjuːmən] **1** *n* sous-homme *m* **2** *adj* inférieur(e) (aux humains)

subject 1 *n* ['sʌbdʒekt] (**a**) *(of conversation, book, painting, photograph)* sujet *m*; *(at school, university)* matière *f*; **while we're on the s.** à ce propos; **to change the s.** parler d'autre chose; **s. matter** *(of letter)* contenu *m*; *(of book)* sujet (**b**) *Gram* sujet *m* (**c**) *(of monarch)* sujet(ette) *m,f* **2** *adj* ['sʌbdʒekt] (**a**) *(prone)* **to be s. to** *(illness)* être sujet(ette) à; *(fine, taxation)* être passible de; **to be s. to jealousy/depression** avoir tendance à être jaloux(ouse)/dépressif(ive) (**b**) **s. to** *(dependent on)* sous réserve de **3** *vt* [səb'dʒekt] *(control)* soumettre, assujettir; **to s. sb to sth** *(force to undergo)* soumettre qn à qch

subjective [səb'dʒektɪv] *adj* subjectif(ive)

subjectivity [sʌbdʒek'tɪvɪtɪ] *n* subjectivité *f*

sub judice ['sʌb'dʒuːdɪsɪ] *adj Law* en instance

subjugate ['sʌbdʒʊɡeɪt] *vt* assujettir

subjunctive [səb'dʒʌŋktɪv] *Gram* **1** *n* subjonctif *m* **2** *adj* subjonctif(ive)

sublet [sʌb'let] *(pt & pp* **sublet**) *vt* sous-louer

sublimate ['sʌblɪmeɪt] *vt* sublimer

sublime [sə'blaɪm] **1** *adj* sublime; *(utter)* suprême **2** *n* **from the s. to the ridiculous** du sublime au ridicule

subliminal [sʌb'lɪmɪnəl] *adj* subliminal(e)

sub-machine gun [sʌbmə'ʃiːnɡʌn] *n* mitraillette *f*

submarine [sʌbmə'riːn] *n* sous-marin *m*

submerge [səb'mɜːdʒ] **1** *vt (immerse)* immerger; *(cover)* submerger; *Fig* **to be submerged in sth** être submergé(e) par qch **2** *n* plonger

submersion [səb'mɜːʃən] *n* submersion *f*

submission [səb'mɪʃən] *n* (**a**) *(to will, authority)* soumission *f*; **to starve sb into s.** réduire qn à la soumission en le/la privant de nourriture; **to beat sb into s.** battre qn jusqu'à ce qu'il/elle se soumette (**b**) *(of document)* présentation *f* (**c**) *(report)* soumission *f*

submissive [səb'mɪsɪv] *adj* soumis(e)

submit [səb'mɪt] *(pt & pp* **submitted**) **1** *vt* soumettre (**for** à) **2** *vi (to person, authority)* se soumettre (**to** à)

subnormal [sʌb'nɔːməl] *adj* arriéré(e)

subordinate 1 *n* [sə'bɔːdɪnət] subordonné(e) *m,f* **2** *adj* [sə'bɔːdɪnət] *(rank)* subalterne; *(role)* secondaire; **to be s. to sb** être subordonné(e) à qn; *Gram* **s. clause** proposition *f* subordonnée **3** *vt* [sə'bɔːdɪneɪt] subordonner

subordination [səbɔːdɪ'neɪʃən] *n* subordination *f*

subplot ['sʌbplɒt] *n* intrigue *f* secondaire

subpoena [sə'piːnə] *Law* **1** *n* citation *f ou* assignation *f* à comparaître **2** *vt* citer *ou* assigner à comparaître

subscribe [səb'skraɪb] *vi* (**a**) *(to newspaper, magazine)* s'abonner (**to** à); *(to charity, organization)* être membre (**to** de) (**b**) **s. to** *(opinion, theory)* souscrire à

subscriber [səb'skraɪbə(r)] *n (to newspaper, magazine, telephone, ISP)* abonné(e) *m,f*; *(to charity, organization)* membre *m*

subscript ['sʌbskrɪpt] *n Typ* indice *m*

subscription [səb'skrɪpʃən] *n (to newspaper, magazine, telephone, ISP)* abonnement *m*; *(to charity, organization, club)* cotisation *f*

subsection ['sʌbsekʃən] *n* subdivision *f*

subsequent ['sʌbsɪkwənt] *adj* ultérieur(e)

subsequently ['sʌbsɪkwəntlɪ] *adv* par la suite, ultérieurement

subservient [sʌb'sɜːvɪənt] *adj* servile

subside [səb'saɪd] *vi (of ground, building)* s'affaisser; *(of water)* baisser; *(of bump)* dégonfler; *(of storm, excitement, fever)* s'apaiser; *(of noise, pain)* s'affaiblir

subsidence [səb'saɪdəns] *n (of ground, building)* affaissement *m*; *(of water)* baisse *f*

subsidiarity [sʌbsɪdɪ'ærɪtɪ] *n* subsidiarité *f*

subsidiary [sʌb'sɪdɪərɪ] **1** *n (pl* **subsidiaries**) *(company)* filiale *f* **2** *adj* subsidiaire

subsidize ['sʌbsɪdaɪz] *vt* subventionner

subsidy ['sʌbsɪdɪ] *(pl* **subsidies**) *n* subvention *f*

subsist [səb'sɪst] *vi* **to s. on** vivre de

subsistence [səb'sɪstəns] *n* subsistance *f*; **s. allowance** faux frais *mpl*; **s. wage** salaire *m* à peine suffisant pour vivre

substance ['sʌbstəns] *n* (**a**) *(matter)* substance *f*; **s. abuse** usage *m* de stupéfiants (**b**) *(essential element)* fond *m* (**c**) *(solidity, worth)* fondement *m*

substandard [sʌb'stændəd] *adj* de qualité inférieure

substantial [səb'stænʃəl] *adj* (**a**) *(significant)* important(e); *(meal)* substantiel(elle); **a s. number of** un nombre important de (**b**) *(solid, robust)* solide

substantially [səb'stænʃəlɪ] *adv* (**a**) *(considerably)* considérablement (**b**) *(for the most part)* pour l'essentiel; **they are s. the same** ils sont pareils dans l'ensemble (**c**) *(solidly)* solidement

substantiate [səb'stænʃɪeɪt] *vt (statement)* corroborer; *(claim)* justifier

substantive ['sʌbstəntɪv] **1** *n Gram* substantif *m* **2** *adj* important(e)

substitute ['sʌbstɪtjuːt] **1** *n (person)* remplaçant(e) *m,f*; *(foodstuff, drug)* succédané *m*; **to be a s./no s. for** remplacer/ne pas remplacer **2** *vt* remplaçant(e); *Am & Ir* **s. teacher** suppléant(e) *m,f* **3** *vt* **to s. A for B** remplacer B par A **4** *vi* **to s. for sb** remplacer qn

substitution [sʌbstɪ'tjuːʃən] *n* substitution *f*; *(of person, player)* remplacement *m*

subsume [sʌb'sjuːm] *vt Formal* subsumer

subterfuge ['sʌbtəfjuːdʒ] *n* subterfuge *m*

subterranean [sʌbtə'reɪnɪən] *adj* souterrain(e)

subtitle ['sʌbtaɪtəl] **1** *n* sous-titre *m* **2** *vt* sous-titrer

subtle ['sʌtəl] *adj* subtil(e)

subtlety ['sʌtəltɪ] *(pl* **subtleties**) *n* subtilité *f*

subtly ['sʌtəlɪ] *adv* subtilement

subtotal ['sʌbtəʊtəl] *n* sous-total *m*

subtract [səb'trækt] *vt* soustraire (**from** de)

subtraction [səb'trækʃən] *n* soustraction *f*

subtropical [sʌb'trɒpɪkəl] *adj* subtropical(e)

suburb ['sʌbɜːb] *n* banlieue *f*; **the suburbs** la banlieue

suburban [sə'bɜːbən] *adj* (**a**) *(of suburb)* de banlieue; *(population, development)* suburbain(e) (**b**) *Pej (narrow-minded)* étriqué(e)

suburbia [sə'bɜːbɪə] *n* la banlieue

subversion [səb'vɜːʃən] *n* subversion *f*

subversive [səb'vɜːsɪv] *adj* subversif(ive)

subvert [səb'vɜːt] *vt* renverser, subvertir

subway ['sʌbweɪ] *n* (**a**) *Br (underpass)* passage *m* souterrain (**b**) *Am (underground railway)* métro *m*; **s. station** station *f* de métro

sub-zero [sʌb'zɪərəʊ] *adj* au-dessous de zéro
succeed [sək'siːd] **1** *vt (follow)* succéder à
 2 *vi* (**a**) *(be successful)* réussir; **to s. in doing sth** réussir à faire qch (**b**) **to s. to the throne** monter sur le trône
succeeding [sək'siːdɪŋ] *adj (following)* suivant(e)
success [sək'ses] *n* réussite *f*, succès *m*; **to be a s.** avoir du succès; **s. story** réussite *f*
successful [sək'sesfʊl] *adj (person)* brillant(e); *(project, application)* couronné(e) de succès; **to be s.** réussir; **to be s. in doing sth** réussir à faire qch
successfully [sək'sesfəlɪ] *adv* avec succès
succession [sək'seʃən] *n* succession *f*, série *f*; **two years in s.** deux années de suite
successive [sək'sesɪv] *adj* successif(ive); **on five s. Sundays** cinq dimanches consécutifs
successor [sək'sesə(r)] *n* successeur *m*
succinct [sʌk'sɪŋ(k)t] *adj* succinct(e)
succulent ['sʌkjʊlənt] **1** *adj (delicious)* succulent(e)
 2 *n (plant)* plante *f* grasse
succumb [sə'kʌm] *vi* succomber (**to** à)
such [sʌtʃ] **1** *pron* tel (telle) *m,f*; **if s. were the case** si tel était le cas; **and s.** et des choses comme ça; **as s.** en tant que tel; **s. is life!** c'est la vie!
 2 *adj* tel (telle), pareil(eille); **s. a question** une telle question, une question pareille; **animals s. as the lion or the tiger** des animaux tels que le lion ou le tigre; **s. books as these, books s. as these** de tels livres, des livres pareils; **here's my bedroom, s. as it is** voici ce qui me sert de chambre; **s. as?** par exemple?; **do you have s. a thing as a screwdriver?** est-ce que tu aurais un tournevis, par hasard?; **there's no s. thing as aliens** les extraterrestres n'existent pas; **I said/did no s. thing** je n'ai rien dit/fait de tel; **in s. a way that** d'une façon telle que; **on s. and s. a day** tel jour
 3 *adv* (**a**) *(in comparisons)* **s. a big house** une si *ou* aussi grande maison; **I had never heard s. good music** je n'avais jamais entendu de si bonne musique (**b**) *(for emphasis)* **we had s. a good time** nous nous sommes tellement amusés; **it was s. a long time ago** ça fait tellement longtemps; **s. a lot of people** tant de gens
suchlike ['sʌtʃlaɪk] *pron* **...and s.** ...et autres
suck [sʌk] **1** *vt (lollipop, thumb)* sucer; *(liquid, air)* aspirer; *(mother's milk)* téter
 2 *vi very Fam* **it sucks** *(it's bad)* c'est nul (nulle)
▸**suck in** *vt sep* aspirer; *Fig* **to get sucked into sth** se laisser entraîner dans qch
▸**suck up 1** *vt sep (liquid, dust)* aspirer
 2 *vi Fam* **to s. up to sb** lécher les bottes a qn
sucker ['sʌkə(r)] *n* (**a**) *(of octopus)* suçoir *m*; *(of plant)* rejeton *m* (**b**) *Fam (gullible person)* niais(e) *m,f*; **to be a s. for sth** craquer pour qch
suckle ['sʌkəl] **1** *vt* allaiter
 2 *vi* téter
sucrose ['suːkrəʊs] *n* saccharose *m*
suction ['sʌkʃən] *n* succion *f*
Sudan [suː'dæn] *n* le Soudan
Sudanese [suːdə'niːz] **1** *npl (people)* **the S.** les Soudanais *mpl*
 2 *n* Soudanais(e) *m,f*
 3 *adj* soudanais(e)
sudden ['sʌdən] *adj* soudain(e), subit(e); **all of a s.** tout à coup; *Fig* **s. death** *(in match, contest)* la mort subite
suddenly ['sʌdənlɪ] *adv* soudain, tout à coup; *(die, happen)* subitement

suddenness ['sʌdənnɪs] *n* soudaineté *f*
sudoku [sʊ'dəʊkuː] *n* sudoku *m*
suds [sʌdz] *npl (of soap)* mousse *f*
sue [suː] **1** *vt* intenter un procès à (**for** en)
 2 *vi* **to s. for divorce** entamer une procédure de divorce; **to s. for damages** demander des dommages-intérêts
suede [sweɪd] *n* daim *m*
suet ['suːɪt] *n* graisse *f* de rognon
Suez ['suːɪz] *n* **the S. Canal** le canal de Suez
suffer ['sʌfə(r)] **1** *vt* (**a**) *(loss, defeat, consequence)* subir; *(pain)* avoir (**b**) *(tolerate)* supporter; **she doesn't s. fools gladly** elle ne supporte pas les imbéciles
 2 *vi (of person)* souffrir (**from** de); *(of health, work)* en pâtir
sufferance ['sʌf(ə)rəns] *n* **I'm just here on s.** on me tolère tout juste ici
sufferer ['sʌfərə(r)] *n* victime *f*
suffering ['sʌfərɪŋ] *n* souffrance *f*
suffice [sə'faɪs] *vi Formal* suffire
sufficient [sə'fɪʃənt] *adj* suffisant(e); **to be s.** suffire, être suffisant
sufficiently [sə'fɪʃəntlɪ] *adv* suffisamment
suffix ['sʌfɪks] *n Gram* suffixe *m*
suffocate ['sʌfəkeɪt] *also Fig* **1** *vt* étouffer
 2 *vi* suffoquer
suffocating ['sʌfəkeɪtɪŋ] *adj* suffocant(e)
suffocation [sʌfə'keɪʃən] *n* suffocation *f*
suffrage ['sʌfrɪdʒ] *n* droit *m* de vote
suffragette [sʌfrə'dʒet] *n* suffragette *f*
suffuse [sə'fjuːz] *vt Lit (of light, liquid, colour)* inonder; *(of heat)* envahir
sugar ['ʃʊgə(r)] **1** *n* (**a**) *(food)* sucre *m*; **two sugars, please** deux sucres, s'il te plaît; **s. almond** dragée *f*; **s. beet** betterave *f* sucrière; **s. bowl** sucrier *m*; **s. cane** canne *f* à sucre; *Fam* **s. daddy** vieux *m* plein de fric *(qui entretient une jeune femme)*; **s. lump** morceau *m* de sucre; **s. plantation** plantation *f* de canne à sucre; **s. refinery** raffinerie *f* de sucre (**b**) *Fam (term of address)* mon trésor
 2 *vt (coffee, tea)* sucrer; *Fig* **to s. the pill** dorer la pilule
sugar-coated [ʃʊgə'kəʊtɪd] *adj* recouvert(e) de sucre
sugar-free [ʃʊgə'friː] *adj* sans sucre
sugary ['ʃʊgərɪ] *adj* (**a**) *(containing sugar)* sucré(e) (**b**) *Fig (smile, tone)* mielleux(euse), doucereux(euse)
suggest [sə'dʒest] *vt* (**a**) *(propose)* suggérer (**b**) *(imply)* indiquer
suggestible [sə'dʒestɪbəl] *adj* influençable
suggestion [sə'dʒestʃən] *n* (**a**) *(proposal)* suggestion *f*; **suggestions box** boîte *f* à idées (**b**) *(insinuation, hint)* indication *f*; **there is no s. that...** rien ne dit que...; **a s. of** une pointe de
suggestive [sə'dʒestɪv] *adj* suggestif(ive); **to be s. of** évoquer
suicidal [sʊɪ'saɪdəl] *adj* suicidaire
suicide ['sʊɪsaɪd] *n* suicide *m*; **to commit s.** se suicider; **s. attack** attentat-suicide *m*; **s. attempt** tentative *f* de suicide; **s. bomber** auteur *m* d'un attentat-suicide à la bombe; **s. mission** mission *f* suicide; **s. pact** = accord de suicide collectif entre deux ou plusieurs personnes; **s. note** lettre *f* *(laissée par un suicidé)*
suit [suːt] **1** *n* (**a**) *(clothing) (man's)* costume *m*, complet *m*; *(woman's)* tailleur *m*; **s. of armour** armure *f* complète (**b**) *(in cards)* couleur *f*; *Fig* **to follow s.**

faire de même; *Fig* **politeness is not her strong s.** la politesse n'est pas son fort (**c**) *Law* procès *m* **2** *vt* (**a**) *(of clothes, colours)* aller à (**b**) *(of arrangement, time, job)* convenir à; **to be suited to** *or* **for sth** *(purpose, job)* être fait(e) pour qch; **to s. sb down to the ground** convenir parfaitement à qn; **they are well suited** ils sont vraiment faits l'un pour l'autre; *Fam* **s. yourself** fais comme tu voudras (**c**) *(adapt)* **to s. sth to sth** adapter qch à qch

suitability [suːtə'bɪlɪtɪ] *n (of behaviour)* caractère *m* convenable; *(of clothing)* caractère *m* approprié; *(of person)* aptitude *f*

suitable ['suːtəbəl] *adj (behaviour, subject)* convenable; *(clothing)* approprié(e); *(candidate, date, title)* adéquat(e); **the film is not s. for children** ce n'est pas un film pour les enfants

suitably ['suːtəblɪ] *adv (behave, dress)* convenablement; **s. impressed/embarrassed** vraiment impressionné(e)/gêné(e)

suitcase ['sjuːtkeɪs] *n* valise *f*

suite [swiːt] *n* (**a**) *(of rooms)* suite *f* (**b**) *(of furniture)* **(three-piece) s.** canapé *m* avec deux fauteuils assortis (**c**) *Mus* suite *f*

suitor ['suːtə(r)] *n Old-fashioned (admirer)* soupirant *m*

sulfate, sulfide *etc Am* = **sulphate, sulphide** *etc*

sulk [sʌlk] **1** *n* **to be in a s.** bouder
2 *vi* bouder

sulky ['sʌlkɪ] *adj* boudeur(euse)

sullen ['sʌlən] *adj* renfrogné(e)

sully ['sʌlɪ] *(pt & pp* **sullied)** *vt Lit (reputation)* ternir; *Fig* **to s. one's hands (with sth)** se salir les mains (en faisant qch)

sulphate, *Am* **sulfate** ['sʌlfeɪt] *n Chem* sulfate *m*

sulphide, *Am* **sulfide** ['sʌlfaɪd] *n Chem* sulfure *m*

sulphur, *Am* **sulfur** ['sʌlfə(r)] *n Chem* soufre *m*; **s. dioxide** anyhydride *m* sulfureux

sulphuric, *Am* **sulfuric** [sʌl'fjʊərɪk] *adj Chem* sulfurique; **s. acid** acide *m* sulfurique

sultan ['sʌltən] *n* sultan *m*

sultana [sʌl'tɑːnə] *n* raisin *m* de Smyrne

sultry ['sʌltrɪ] *adj (heat)* étouffant(e); *(weather)* lourd(e); *(look, smile)* sensuel(elle)

sum [sʌm] *n (amount of money)* somme *f*; *(mathematical problem)* problème *m*; **the s. of** la somme de; **s. total** somme totale

▶**sum up** *(pt & pp* **summed) 1** *vt sep* (**a**) *(summarize)* résumer (**b**) *(assess quickly)* jauger, évaluer
2 *vi (summarize)* résumer

summarily ['sʌmərɪlɪ] *adv* sommairement

summarize ['sʌməraɪz] *vt* résumer

summary ['sʌmərɪ] **1** *n (pl* **summaries)** résumé *m*
2 *adj (brief)* sommaire

summer ['sʌmə(r)] **1** *n* été *m*; **in (the) s.** en été; **s. holidays** vacances *fpl* d'été; **s. school** cours *mpl* d'été
2 *vi* passer l'été

summerhouse ['sʌməhaʊs] *n (in garden)* pavillon *m*

summertime ['sʌmətaɪm] *n* été *m*

summery ['sʌmərɪ] *adj* d'été

summing-up [sʌmɪŋ'ʌp] *n Law* résumé *m* des débats

summit ['sʌmɪt] *n* sommet *m*; **to hold a s.** tenir un sommet

summon ['sʌmən] *vt (person, meeting)* convoquer; *(police, doctor, help)* appeler, faire venir; *Law (witness)* assigner *ou* citer à comparaître

▶**summon up** *vt sep* rassembler

summons ['sʌmənz] *Law* **1** *n (pl* **summonses** ['sʌmənzɪz]) assignation *f ou* citation *f* à comparaître
2 *vt* assigner *ou* citer à comparaître

sump [sʌmp] *n* (**a**) *(in engine)* carter *m* à huile (**b**) *(cesspool)* fosse *f* d'aisance

sumptuous ['sʌm(p)tjʊəs] *adj* somptueux(euse)

Sun *(abbr* **Sunday)** dimanche

sun [sʌn] **1** *n* soleil *m*; **in the s.** au soleil; **to catch the s.** prendre le soleil; **there is a lot of sun** *ou* il est possible d'imaginer; **s. block** écran *m* total; **s. cream** crème *f* solaire; **s. lamp** lampe *f* à bronzer; **s. lotion** lotion *f* solaire; **s. shield** *or* **visor** *(in car)* pare-soleil *m*
2 *vt (pt & pp* **sunned) to s. oneself** prendre le soleil

sunbathe ['sʌnbeɪð] *vi* se faire bronzer

sunbeam ['sʌnbiːm] *n* rayon *m* de soleil

sunbed ['sʌnbed] *n* lit *m* à ultraviolets

sunburn ['sʌnbɜːn] *n* coup *m* de soleil; **to have s.** avoir un coup de soleil

sunburnt ['sʌnbɜːnt], **sunburned** ['sʌnbɜːnd] *adj* **to be s.** avoir un coup de soleil

sundae ['sʌndeɪ] *n* coupe *f* glacée

Sunday ['sʌndeɪ] *n* dimanche *m*; **S. best** habits *mpl* du dimanche; **S. paper** journal *m* du dimanche; **S. school** ≃ catéchisme *m*; **S. trading** = ouverture des magasins le dimanche; *see also* **Saturday**

Sunday papers

La lecture des journaux du dimanche constitue une sorte de rituel pour de nombreux Britanniques. Les journaux du dimanche sont très volumineux ; ils comprennent de nombreux suppléments sur des sujets tels que le sport, la mode, les voyages et les arts, ainsi qu'une magazine en couleurs. Ils coûtent plus cher que les journaux vendus en semaine. Certains journaux du dimanche sont des éditions dominicales de quotidiens paraissant en semaine (c'est le cas de "The Sunday Times" et de "The Independent on Sunday" par exemple) tandis que d'autres, comme "The Observer", paraissent uniquement le dimanche.

sundial ['sʌndaɪəl] *n* cadran *m* solaire

sundown ['sʌndaʊn] *n* coucher *m* du soleil

sun-drenched ['sʌndren(t)ʃt] *adj* inondé(e) de soleil

sun-dried ['sʌndraɪd] *adj* séché(e) au soleil

sundry ['sʌndrɪ] **1** *n (pl* **sundries)** (**a**) **all and s.** tout le monde (**b**) **sundries** *(items)* articles *mpl* divers; *(costs)* frais *mpl* divers
2 *adj* divers(e)

sunflower ['sʌnflaʊə(r)] *n* tournesol *m*; **s. oil** huile *f* de tournesol; **s. seeds** *(as snack)* graines *fpl* de tournesol

sung ['sʌŋ] *pp of* **sing**

sunglasses ['sʌnglɑːsɪz] *npl* lunettes *fpl* de soleil, *Belg* lunettes *fpl* solaires

sunhat ['sʌnhæt] *n* chapeau *m* de soleil

sunk ['sʌŋk] *pp of* **sink²**

sunken ['sʌŋkən] *adj (ship)* englouti(e); *(eyes)* enfoncé(e); *(rock)* immergé(e)

sunlight ['sʌnlaɪt] *n* lumière *f* du soleil; **in the s.** au soleil

sunlit ['sʌnlɪt] *adj* éclairé(e) par le soleil

sunny ['sʌnɪ] *adj* (**a**) *(day, place)* ensoleillé(e); **it's s.** il fait du soleil (**b**) *Fig (face)* radieux(euse); **to have a s. personality** être toujours content(e)

sunray lamp ['sʌnreɪ'læmp] *n* lampe *f* à bronzer

sunrise ['sʌnraɪz] *n* lever *m* de soleil; **at s.** au lever du soleil, au soleil levant; *Econ* **s. industry** industrie *f* d'avenir

sunroof ['sʌnruːf] *n* toit *m* ouvrant

sunscreen ['sʌnskriːn] *n* écran *m ou* filtre *m* solaire

sunset ['sʌnset] *n* coucher *m* de soleil; **at s.** au coucher du soleil, au soleil couchant

sunshade ['sʌnʃeɪd] *n* parasol *m*

sunshine ['sʌnʃaɪn] *n* soleil *m*

sunspot ['sʌnspɒt] *n* (**a**) *(on sun)* tache *f* solaire (**b**) *Fam (holiday resort)* destination *f* ensoleillée

sunstroke ['sʌnstrəʊk] *n* insolation *f*; **to have s.** avoir une insolation

suntan ['sʌntæn] *n* bronzage *m*; **to have a s.** être bronzé(e); **s. cream** crème *f* solaire; **s. lotion** lotion *f* solaire

suntrap ['sʌntræp] *n* coin *m* très ensoleillé

sup [sʌp] *(pt & pp* **supped**) *vt* boire à petites gorgées

super ['suːpə(r)] **1** *adj Fam (excellent)* super *inv*; *Am Sport* **the S. Bowl** = la finale du championnat des États-Unis de football américain
  2 *n (petrol)* super *m*

superannuation [suːpərænjʊ'eɪʃən] *n Fin* retraite *f*

superb [suː'pɜːb] *adj* excellent(e)

superbug ['suːpəbʌg] *n Fam Med* infection *f* nosocomiale à bactéries multi-résistantes

supercharger ['suːpətʃɑːdʒə(r)] *n Aut & Aviat* compresseur *m*

supercilious [suːpə'sɪlɪəs] *adj* hautain(e)

superconductor [suːpəkən'dʌktə(r)] *n Phys* supraconducteur *m*

super-duper ['suːpə'duːpə(r)] *adj Fam* super *inv*; génial(e)

superego ['suːpəriːgəʊ] *n Psy* surmoi *m*

superficial [suːpə'fɪʃəl] *adj* superficiel(elle)

superficiality [suːpəfɪʃɪ'ælɪtɪ] *n* superficialité *f*

superficially [suːpə'fɪʃəlɪ] *adv* superficiellement

superfluous [suː'pɜːflʊəs] *adj* superflu(e)

superhuman [suːpə'hjuːmən] *adj* surhumain(e)

superimpose [suːpərɪm'pəʊz] *vt* superposer

superintend [suːpərɪn'tend] *vt (run)* diriger; *(supervise)* surveiller

superintendent [suːpərɪn'tendənt] *n (supervisor)* directeur(trice) *m,f*; *(police officer)* ≃ commissaire *m* de police

superior [suː'pɪərɪə(r)] **1** *adj* (**a**) *(better, more senior)* supérieur(e) *Pej* (**b**) *(arrogant) (person)* qui se croit supérieur(e); *(tone, air, smile)* de supériorité
  2 *n (senior)* supérieur(e) *m,f*

superiority [suːpɪərɪ'ɒrɪtɪ] *n* supériorité *f*

superlative [suː'pɜːlətɪv] **1** *n Gram* superlatif *m*
  2 *adj* (**a**) *(excellent)* excellent(e) (**b**) *Gram* superlatif(ive)

superman ['suːpəmæn] *n* surhomme *m*

supermarket ['suːpəmɑːkɪt] *n* supermarché *m*

supermodel ['suːpəmɒdəl] *n* top model *m*

supernatural [suːpə'nætʃərəl] **1** *n* **the s.** le surnaturel
  2 *adj* surnaturel(elle)

superpower ['suːpəpaʊə(r)] *n* superpuissance *f*

supersede [suːpə'siːd] *vt* supplanter, détrôner

supersonic [suːpə'sɒnɪk] *adj* supersonique

superstar ['suːpəstɑː(r)] *n* superstar *f*

superstition [suːpə'stɪʃən] *n* superstition *f*

superstitious [suːpə'stɪʃəs] *adj* superstitieux(euse)

superstore ['suːpəstɔː(r)] *n* hypermarché *m*

superstructure ['suːpəstrʌktʃə(r)] *n* superstructure *f*

supertanker ['suːpətæŋkə(r)] *n* supertanker *m*

supervise ['suːpəvaɪz] *vt (children)* surveiller; *(staff)* superviser

supervision [suːpə'vɪʒən] *n (of children)* surveillance *f*; *(of staff)* supervision *f*

supervisor ['suːpəvaɪzə(r)] *n* (**a**) *(in office)* chef *m* de service; *(in factory)* chef *m* d'équipe (**b**) *(for thesis)* directeur(trice) *m,f* de thèse

supervisory [suːpə'vaɪzərɪ] *adj* de supervision

supine ['suːpaɪn] **1** *adj* couché(e) sur le dos; *Fig (inactive)* mou (molle)
  2 *adv* **to lie s.** être couché(e) sur le dos

supper ['sʌpə(r)] *n (evening meal)* dîner *m*; *(snack before going to bed)* = casse-croûte pris avant d'aller se coucher

supplant [sə'plɑːnt] *vt* supplanter

supple ['sʌpəl] *adj* souple

supplement ['sʌplɪmənt] **1** *n* supplément *m*
  2 *vt* compléter

supplementary [sʌplɪ'mentərɪ] *adj* supplémentaire

supplication [sʌplɪ'keɪʃən] *n* supplication *f*

supplier [sə'plaɪə(r)] *n* fournisseur(euse) *m,f*

supply [sə'plaɪ] **1** *n (pl* **supplies**) *(stock)* provision *f*; *(act of supplying)* approvisionnement, *m* fourniture *f*; **a week's/month's s. of sth** une provision de qch pour une semaine/un mois; **petrol is in short s.** on manque d'essence; *Econ* **s. and demand** l'offre *f* et la demande; **s. lines** lignes *fpl* de ravitaillement; **s. ship** ravitailleur *m*; **s. teacher** remplaçant(e) *m,f*, suppléant(e) *m,f*
  2 *vt (pt & pp* **supplied**) *(provide)* fournir; **to s. sb with sth** fournir qch à qn

support [sə'pɔːt] **1** *n* (**a**) *(backing)* soutien *m*; **to give sb/sth s.** appuyer qn/qch; **in s. of** *(theory, claim)* à l'appui de; *(cause)* en faveur de; **s. band** *(at concert)* première partie *f* (**b**) *(person supporting)* soutien *m*; *(thing supporting)* support *m*
  2 *vt* (**a**) *(hold up)* supporter, soutenir; **I supported her with my arm** je lui ai donné le bras pour qu'elle s'appuie dessus (**b**) *(encourage, aid)* soutenir, apporter son soutien à; *(team in sport)* supporter (**c**) *(sustain)* pourvoir aux besoins de; **to s. oneself** subvenir à ses propres besoins

supporter [sə'pɔːtə(r)] *n (of opinion, party, policy)* défenseur *m*, sympathisant(e) *m,f*; *(of team)* supporter *m*

supporting [sə'pɔːtɪŋ] *adj (role)* secondaire; *(actor)* qui a un rôle secondaire; **s. film** film *m* qui passe en première partie; **s. cast** seconds rôles *mpl*

supportive [sə'pɔːtɪv] *adj* d'un grand soutien

suppose [sə'pəʊz] *vt* supposer; **I s. so/not** je suppose que oui/non; **s. or supposing he came back** supposons qu'il revienne; **I don't s. you'd consider sharing it?** je suppose que tu ne veux pas partager?; **s. we change the subject?** et si nous changions de sujet?

supposed [sə'pəʊzd] *adj* (**a**) *(meant)* **to be s. to do sth** être censé(e) faire qch; **there's s. to be a meeting today** il est censé y avoir une réunion aujourd'hui (**b**) *(reputed)* **the film's s. to be very good** il paraît que c'est un très bon film

supposition [sʌpə'zɪʃən] *n* supposition *f*; **on the s. that...** en supposant que...

suppository [sə'pɒzɪtrɪ] *(pl* **suppositories**) *n Med* suppositoire *m*

suppress [sə'pres] *vt (revolt)* réprimer; *(fact, evidence)* faire disparaître; *(emotions)* refouler; *(cough, smile)* réprimer

suppressed [sə'prest] *adj (emotion)* refoulé(e)

suppression [sə'preʃən] *n (of revolt)* répression *f; (of fact, evidence)* dissimulation *f; (of emotions)* refoulement *m*

suppurate ['sʌpjʊreɪt] *vi* suppurer

supranational [suːprə'næʃənəl] *adj* supranational(e)

supremacy [suː'preməsɪ] *n* suprématie *f*

supreme [suː'priːm] *adj* suprême; **to make the s. sacrifice** se sacrifier; *Fig* **to reign s.** régner; *Mil* **S. Commander** commandant *m* en chef; *Am Law* **S. Court** Cour *f* suprême

supremely [suː'priːmlɪ] *adv* suprêmement

supremo [suː'priːməʊ] *(pl* **supremos***) n Fam* grand chef *m*

surcharge ['sɜːtʃɑːdʒ] **1** *n* supplément *m*
2 *vt* faire payer un supplément à

sure [ʃʊə(r)] **1** *adj* sûr(e); **to be s. of** *or* **about sth** être sûr(e) de qch; **to be s. to do sth** ne pas oublier de faire qch; **to be s. of oneself** être sûr(e) de soi; **to make s. of sth** s'assurer de qch; **to make s. that...** s'assurer que...; **I don't know for s.** je ne suis pas absolument certain(e); **that's for s.** ça, c'est sûr; *Fam* **s. thing!** bien sûr!
2 *adv* (**a**) *Am Fam (really)* **it s. is cold** il fait vachement froid; **are you tired? – I s. am** tu es fatigué? – ça oui (**b**) *(yes)* bien sûr (**c**) **s. enough he was there** il était bien là

surefooted [ʃʊə'fʊtɪd] *adj* **to be s.** avoir le pied sûr

surely ['ʃʊəlɪ] *adv* (**a**) *(certainly)* sûrement; **s. you don't believe that!** tu ne crois quand même pas ça!; **s. not!** c'est pas vrai! (**b**) *(in a sure manner)* **slowly but s.** lentement mais sûrement

surety ['ʃʊərətɪ] *n Law* caution *f;* **to stand s. (for sb)** se porter caution (pour qn)

surf [sɜːf] **1** *n* surf *m*
2 *vi (go surfing)* faire du surf
3 *vt Comput* **to s. the Net** naviguer sur l'Internet

surface ['sɜːfɪs] **1** *n* surface *f; Fig* **on the s.** en apparence; *Fig* **beneath the s.** au fond; **s. mail** courrier *m* par voie de terre; **s. tension** tension *f* de surface; **s. water** eaux *fpl* de surface
2 *vt (road)* revêtir
3 *vi (from water)* & *Fam Hum (from bed)* faire surface; *Fig (of person, emotion)* réapparaître

surface-to-air missile ['sɜːfɪstʊ'eə'mɪsaɪl] *n Mil* missile *m* sol-air

surface-to-surface missile ['sɜːfɪstə'sɜːfɪs'mɪsaɪl] *n Mil* missile *m* sol-sol

surfboard ['sɜːfbɔːd] *n* (planche *f* de) surf *m*

surfeit ['sɜːfɪt] *n Formal* surabondance *f*

surfer ['sɜːfə(r)] *n* surfer *m*

surfing ['sɜːfɪŋ] *n* surf *m;* **to go s.** faire du surf

surge [sɜːdʒ] **1** *n (of electricity)* surtension *f; (of enthusiasm, support, demand)* sursaut *m; (of profits)* hausse *f* soudaine; *(of crowd)* ruée *f*
2 *vi (of water, crowd)* déferler; *(of feeling)* monter

surgeon ['sɜːdʒən] *n* chirurgien(enne) *m,f*

surgery ['sɜːdʒərɪ] *n* (**a**) *(technique)* chirurgie *f; (operation)* intervention *f* chirurgicale; **to perform s. on sb** opérer qn (**b**) *Br (doctor's office)* cabinet *m* (de consultation); *(period)* heures *fpl* de consultation (**c**) *Br (of MP)* permanence *f*

surgical ['sɜːdʒɪkəl] *adj* chirurgical(e); *Fig* **with s. precision** avec une précision mathématique; **s. instruments** instruments *mpl* de chirurgie; **s. spirit** alcool *m* à 90°; *Mil* **s. strike** frappe *f* chirurgicale

Surinam ['sʊrɪnæm] *n* le Surinam

surly ['sɜːlɪ] *adj* revêche

surmise [sɜː'maɪz] *vt* conjecturer

surmount [sɜː'maʊnt] *vt* surmonter

surname ['sɜːneɪm] *n* nom *m* de famille

surpass [sɜː'pɑːs] *vt (person)* surpasser; *(record)* battre; *(expectation)* dépasser; **to s. oneself** se surpasser

surplice ['sɜːplɪs] *n Rel* surplis *m*

surplus ['sɜːpləs] **1** *n* surplus *m; Econ (of trade)* excédent *m*
2 *adj (items)* en trop, en surplus; **to be s. to requirements** être en trop

surprise [sə'praɪz] **1** *n* surprise *f;* **to take sb by s.** prendre qn par surprise; **to give sb a s.** faire une surprise à qn; **it was no s.** cela n'a étonné personne
2 *adj (attack, defeat)* surprise *inv;* **s. party** soirée *f* surprise
3 *vt* surprendre, étonner; **I'm not surprised** ça ne m'étonne pas

surprising [sə'praɪzɪŋ] *adj* surprenant(e), étonnant(e)

surprisingly [sə'praɪzɪŋlɪ] *adv* étonnamment; **not s.** comme il fallait s'y attendre; **s. enough,...** chose surprenante...

surreal [sə'rɪəl] *adj (surrealist)* surréaliste; *(strange)* délirant(e)

surrealism [sə'rɪəlɪzəm] *n Art* surréalisme *m*

surrealist [sə'rɪəlɪst] *Art* **1** *n* surréaliste *mf*
2 *adj* surréaliste

surrender [sə'rendə(r)] **1** *n* (**a**) *(of army, weapons)* reddition *f;* **no s.!** nous ne nous rendrons pas! (**b**) *Fin* **s. value** valeur *f* de rachat
2 *vt (town)* livrer; *(right, possessions)* abandonner; *(advantage)* perdre; **to s. control of sth** abandonner la direction de qch
3 *vi* se rendre

surreptitious [sʌrəp'tɪʃəs] *adj* furtif(ive)

surrogate ['sʌrəgət] *n* substitut *m;* **s. mother** mère *f* porteuse

surround [sə'raʊnd] **1** *vt* entourer; *(of police)* cerner
2 *n* encadrement *m; Cin & TV* **s. sound** son *m* 3D

surrounding [sə'raʊndɪŋ] *adj* environnant(e)

surroundings [sə'raʊndɪŋz] *npl* environnement *m*

surtax ['sɜːtæks] **1** *n* surtaxe *f*
2 *vt* surtaxer

surveillance [sə'veɪləns] *n* surveillance *f;* **under s.** sous surveillance

survey 1 *n* ['sɜːveɪ] (**a**) *(look at)* contempler (**b**) *(of subject, situation)* étude *f; (of opinions)* sondage *m* (**b**) *(of land)* expertise *f; (of land)* relevé *m*
2 *vt* [sə'veɪ] (**a**) *(look at)* contempler (**b**) *(subject, situation)* étudier, examiner (**c**) *(house)* faire l'expertise de; *(land)* faire un relevé de

surveying [sɜː'veɪɪŋ] *n (of house)* expertise *f; (of land)* relevé *m*

surveyor [sə'veɪə(r)] *n (of building)* expert *m; (of land)* géomètre *mf*

survival [sə'vaɪvəl] *n* (**a**) *(continued existence)* survie *f; also Fig* **the s. of the fittest** la survie du plus apte; **s. kit** équipement *m* de survie (**b**) *(relic)* vestige *m*

survive [sə'vaɪv] **1** *vt (of person)* survivre à; *(of object)* résister à; **he is survived by a wife and son** il laisse une épouse et un fils
2 *vi* survivre

surviving [sə'vaɪvɪŋ] *adj (person)* survivant(e); *(remains, copy)* restant(e)

survivor [sə'vaɪvə(r)] *n* survivant(e) *m,f*

susceptible [sə'septɪbəl] *adj* sensible (**to** à)

suspect 1 *n* ['sʌspekt] suspect(e) *m,f*
2 *adj* ['sʌspekt] suspect(e)

3 *vt* [sə'spekt] (**a**) *(person)* soupçonner (**b**) *(have intuition of)* se douter de; **to s. the truth** soupçonner la vérité (**c**) *(consider likely)* croire

suspend [sə'spend] *vt* (**a**) *(hang)* suspendre (**from** à) (**b**) *(service, employee, player)* suspendre; *(pupil)* renvoyer temporairement

suspended [sə'spendɪd] *adj* suspendu(e); **in s. animation** en hibernation; *Law* **s. sentence** condamnation *f* avec sursis

suspender [sə'spendə(r)] *n* (**a**) *Br (for stocking)* jarretelle *f*; *(for sock)* fixe-chaussette *m*; **s. belt** porte-jarretelles *m inv* (**b**) *Am* **suspenders** *(for trousers)* bretelles *fpl*

suspense [sə'spens] *n (uncertainty)* incertitude *f*; *(in film)* suspense *m*; **to keep sb in s.** tenir qn en haleine

suspension [sə'spenʃən] *n* (**a**) *(of car)* suspension *f*; **s. bridge** pont *m* suspendu (**b**) *(of service, employee)* suspension *f*; *(of pupil)* renvoi *m*

suspicion [sə'spɪʃən] *n* (**a**) *(belief of guilt)* soupçon *m*; **to be under s.** être soupçonné(e); **to be above s.** être au-dessus de tout soupçon; **to have one's suspicions about sb/sth** avoir des doutes sur qn/qch; **to arouse s.** éveiller les soupçons (**b**) *(small amount)* soupçon *m*

suspicious [sə'spɪʃəs] *adj (arousing suspicions)* suspect(e); *(having suspicions)* méfiant(e) (**of** *or* **about** à l'égard de); **to make sb s.** éveiller les soupçons de qn

suspiciously [sə'spɪʃəslɪ] *adv (behave)* d'une manière suspecte; *(ask)* avec méfiance; *Fam* **it looks s. like...** ça ressemble étrangement à...

suss [sʌs] *adj Br Fam* louche

▸**suss out** *vt sep Br Fam* piger; *(person)* cerner

sustain [sə'steɪn] *vt* (**a**) *(maintain)* soutenir; *(life)* maintenir; **a proper breakfast will s. you until lunchtime** un bon petit déjeuner vous permettra de tenir jusqu'à midi; *Law* **objection sustained** objection accordée (**b**) *(loss, attack, damage)* subir; **to s. an injury** être blessé(e)

sustainable [sə'steɪnəbəl] *adj (growth, development)* durable

sustained [sə'steɪnd] *adj* soutenu(e); **s. applause** applaudissements *mpl* prolongés

sustenance ['sʌstɪnəns] *n* subsistance *f*

suture ['suːtʃə(r)] *n* suture *f*

SUV [esjuː'viː] *n Am Aut (abbr* **sport-utility vehicle)** quatre-quatre *m ou f*

svelte [svelt] *adj* svelte

SW *n* (**a**) *(abbr* **southwest)** SO (**b**) *Rad (abbr* **Short Wave)** OC

swab [swɒb] **1** *n (cotton wool)* tampon *m*
2 *vt (pt & pp* **swabbed)** *(wound)* nettoyer; *(floor)* laver

swag [swæg] *n very Fam (of thief)* butin *m*

swagger ['swægə(r)] **1** *n* démarche *f* balancée et crâneuse
2 *vi (strut)* se pavaner

swallow¹ ['swɒləʊ] **1** *n (of drink)* gorgée *f*; *(of food)* bouchée *f*
2 *vt* (**a**) *(food, drink)* avaler; *Fig (pride, anger)* ravaler; **to s. sth whole** avaler qch tout rond (**b**) *Fam (believe)* gober, avaler
3 *vi* avaler; **to s. hard** *(when nervous, afraid)* avaler sa salive

swallow² *n (bird)* hirondelle *f*; *Prov* **one s. doesn't make a summer** une hirondelle ne fait pas le printemps

▸**swallow up** *vt sep Fig (company, country)* engloutir

swam [swæm] *pt of* **swim**

swamp [swɒmp] **1** *n* marais *m*
2 *vt (flood)* inonder; *Fig* **to be swamped with sth** être submergé(e) de qch

swan [swɒn] **1** *n* cygne *m*; *Fig* **s. song** chant *m* du cygne
2 *vi (pt & pp* **swanned)** *Fam* **to s. in/out/off** arriver/sortir/partir tranquillement

▸**swan about, swan around** *vi Fam* musarder

swank [swæŋk] *Fam* **1** *n (ostentation)* épate *f*; *(ostentatious person)* frimeur(euse) *m,f*
2 *vi* frimer

swanky ['swæŋkɪ] *adj Fam* chic *inv*

swap [swɒp] **1** *n* échange *m*; **to do a s.** faire un échange
2 *vt (pt & pp* **swapped)** **to s. sth for sth** échanger qch contre qch; **to s. places with sb** changer de place avec qn; **to s. insults/ideas** échanger des insultes/idées
3 *vi* échanger

swarm [swɔːm] **1** *n (of bees)* essaim *m*; *(of people)* nuée *f*
2 *vi (of bees)* essaimer; *(of people)* accourir en masse; **to be swarming with** *(of place)* grouiller de

swarthy ['swɔːðɪ] *adj* basané(e)

swashbuckling ['swɒʃbʌklɪŋ] *adj* de cape et d'épée

swastika ['swɒstɪkə] *n* svastika *m*

SWAT [swɒt] *n Am (abbr* **Special Weapons and Tactics)** **S. team** = groupe d'intervention d'élite de la police américaine

swat [swɒt] *(pt & pp* **swatted)** *vt* écraser

swatch [swɒtʃ] *n* échantillon *m*

swathe [sweɪð] **1** *n (of grass)* andain *m*; *(of material, land)* bande *f*; *Fig* **to cut a s. through sth** *(of fire, storm)* détruire qch sur son passage
2 *vt* envelopper (**in** de)

sway [sweɪ] **1** *n* (**a**) *(movement)* balancement *m* (**b**) *(influence)* influence *f*; **to be under sb's s.** être sous l'influence de qn; **to hold s. over sb/sth** tenir qn/qch sous sa domination
2 *vt (influence)* influencer
3 *vi* se balancer; **to s. from side to side** se balancer d'un côté à l'autre

Swazi ['swɑːzɪ] **1** *n* (**a**) *(person)* Swazi(e) *m,f* (**b**) *(language)* swazi *m*
2 *adj* swazi(e)

Swaziland ['swɑːzɪlænd] *n* le Swaziland

swear [sweə(r)] *(pt* **swore** [swɔː(r)], *pp* **sworn** [swɔːn]) **1** *vt (vow)* jurer; **to s. to do sth** jurer de faire qch; *Law* **s. an oath** prêter serment
2 *vi (use swearwords)* jurer; **to s. at sb** injurier qn

▸**swear by** *vt insep (have confidence in)* se fier à

▸**swear in** *vt sep Law (jury, witness)* faire prêter serment à

swearing ['sweərɪŋ] *n* grossièretés *fpl*

swearword ['sweəwɜːd] *n* juron *m*, mot *m* grossier

sweat [swet] **1** *n* transpiration *f*, sueur *f*; *Fig* **to be in a s. about sth** avoir des sueurs froides à propos de qch; *Fam* **no s.!** pas de problèmes!; **s. gland** glande *f* sudoripare
2 *vt Fam* **to s. buckets** être en nage; *Fig* **to s. blood** suer sang et eau
3 *vi* (**a**) *(perspire)* transpirer, suer; *Fam* **to s. like a pig** suer comme un bœuf (**b**) *Fam Fig (worry)* se faire de la bile; **to make sb s.** laisser mariner qn

sweatband ['swetbænd] *n (on head)* bandeau *m*; *(on wrist)* poignet *m*

sweater ['swetə(r)] *n* pullover *m*, pull *m*
sweatshirt ['swetʃɜːt] *n* sweatshirt *m*
sweatshop ['swetʃɒp] *n* = atelier de confection où l'on exploite le personnel
sweaty ['swetɪ] *adj (person)* en sueur; *(hands)* moite; *(clothes)* imprégné(e) de sueur; *(work)* qui fait transpirer
Swede [swiːd] *n (person)* Suédois(e) *m,f*
swede [swiːd] *n Br (vegetable)* rutabaga *m*
Sweden ['swiːdən] *n* la Suède
Swedish ['swiːdɪʃ] **1** *npl (people)* **the S.** les Suédois *mpl*
2 *n (language)* suédois *m*
3 *adj* suédois(e)
sweep [swiːp] **1** *n* (**a**) *(action)* coup *m* de balai; **to give sth a s.** donner un coup de balai à qch; *Fig* **at one s.** d'un seul coup; *Fig* **to make a clean s.** *(win everything)* tout gagner (**b**) *(movement)* **with a s. of the arm** d'un geste large (**c**) *(of land, hills)* étendue *f*; *(of road, river)* courbe *f*
2 *vt (pt & pp swept* [swept]) (**a**) *(floor, street)* balayer; *(chimney)* ramoner; **to be swept overboard** être emporté(e) par une vague; **the boat was swept out to sea** le bateau a été emporté vers le large (**b**) *(idioms)* **to s. sth under the carpet** tirer le rideau sur qch; **to s. the board** *(in competition)* rafler tous les prix; **the latest craze to s. the country** la dernière folie qui a envahi le pays; *Fig* **he swept her off her feet** elle est tombée follement amoureuse de lui
3 *vi* (**a**) *(with broom)* balayer (**b**) *(move rapidly)* **to s. in/out** faire une entrée/une sortie majestueuse; **to s. to power** être propulsé(e) au pouvoir; **a wave of nationalism swept through the country** une vague de nationalisme a déferlé sur le pays
▸**sweep aside** *vt sep (opposition, criticism)* écarter
▸**sweep away** *vt sep (building)* emporter; *Fig (obstacle, difficulty)* balayer; *Fig* **to be swept away by sth** *(enthusiasm, passion)* être emporté(e) par qch
▸**sweep up** *vt sep & vi* balayer
sweeper ['swiːpə(r)] *n* (**a**) (**carpet**) **s.** balai *m* mécanique (**b**) *(footballer)* arrière *mf* volant(e)
sweeping ['swiːpɪŋ] *adj (gesture)* large; *(statement)* généralisateur(trice); *(change, proposal)* radical(e)
sweepstake ['swiːpsteɪk] *n* sweepstake *m*
sweet [swiːt] **1** *adj* (**a**) *(sugary)* sucré(e); *(wine)* doux (douce); **to taste s.** avoir un goût sucré; **as s. as honey** doux comme le miel; **to have a s. tooth** aimer les sucreries; **s. pea** pois *m* de senteur; **s. potato** patate *f* douce; **s. william** œillet *m* de poète (**b**) *(smell)* agréable; *(sound)* doux (douce) (**c**) *(pretty, kind)* adorable; **to whisper s. nothings to sb** dire des mots doux à qn
2 *n Br (piece of confectionery)* bonbon *m*; *(dessert)* dessert *m*; **s. shop** confiserie *f*
sweetbreads ['swiːtbredz] *npl* ris *m (de veau, d'agneau)*
sweet-and-sour [swiːtən'saʊə(r)] *adj* aigre-doux (aigre-douce)
sweetcorn ['swiːtkɔːn] *n* maïs *m*
sweeten ['swiːtən] *vt (food)* sucrer; *Fig* **to s. sb up** amadouer qn
sweetener ['swiːtənə(r)] *n* (**a**) *(in food)* édulcorant *m* (**b**) *Fam (bribe)* pot-de-vin *m*
sweetheart ['swiːthɑːt] *n (term of address) (to woman)* chérie *f*; *(to man)* chéri *m*

sweetie ['swiːtɪ] *n Fam* (**a**) *Br (piece of confectionery)* bonbon *m* (**b**) *(darling)* chou *m*; **he's such a s.** il est adorable
sweetly ['swiːtlɪ] *adv (sing)* d'une voix douce; *(smile, answer)* gentiment
sweetness ['swiːtnɪs] *n* douceur *f*; **to be all s. and light** être tout sucre tout miel
sweet-talk ['swiːt'tɔːk] *vt Fam* **to s. sb into doing sth** baratiner qn pour qu'il fasse qch
sweet-tempered [swiːt'tempəd] *adj* doux (douce)
swell [swel] **1** *vt (pp swollen* ['swəʊlən] *or swelled) (numbers, crowd)* gonfler
2 *vi (of part of body)* enfler; *(of number, crowd)* grossir; *(of sea)* se soulever; **to s. with pride** se gonfler d'orgueil
3 *n (of sea)* houle *f*
4 *adj Am Fam (excellent)* super *inv*
▸**swell up** *vi (part of body)* enfler
swelling ['swelɪŋ] *n* gonflement *m*, enflure *f*; **the s. had gone down** ça avait désenflé
sweltering ['sweltərɪŋ] *adj* étouffant(e)
swept [swept] *pt & pp of* sweep
swerve [swɜːv] **1** *n (of car)* embardée *f*; *(of player)* écart *m*
2 *vi (of car, driver)* faire une embardée; *(of player)* faire un écart; *(of ball)* décrire une courbe
swift [swɪft] **1** *n (bird)* martinet *m*
2 *adj* rapide
swift-footed ['swɪftfʊtɪd] *adj* rapide à la course
swiftly ['swɪftlɪ] *adv* rapidement, vite
swiftness ['swɪftnɪs] *n* rapidité *f*
swig [swɪg] *Fam* **1** *n* lampée *f*; **to take a s. from a bottle** boire un coup à une bouteille
2 *vt (pt & pp swigged)* boire à grands traits
swill [swɪl] **1** *n (food) (for pigs)* pâtée *f*; *Pej (for people)* nourriture *f* infâme
2 *vt Fam (drink)* écluser
▸**swill about, swill around** *vi (of liquid)* se répandre
▸**swill out** *vt sep (rinse)* rincer à grande eau
swim [swɪm] **1** *n* **to go for or have a s.** aller nager
2 *vt (pp swam* [swæm]*, pp swum* [swʌm]*)* nager; **to s. the breast stroke** nager la brasse; **to s. the Channel** traverser la Manche à la nage
3 *vi (in water)* nager; **to go swimming** aller nager; **to s. across sth** traverser qch à la nage; *Fig* **to s. with the tide** suivre le courant (**b**) *(be dizzy)* **my head is swimming** j'ai la tête qui tourne
swimmer ['swɪmə(r)] *n* nageur(euse) *m,f*
swimming ['swɪmɪŋ] *n* natation *f*; **s. cap** bonnet *m* de bain; *Br* **s. costume** maillot *m* de bain; **s. lesson** cours *m* de natation; **s. pool** piscine *f*; **s. trunks** slip *m* de bain
swimmingly ['swɪmɪŋlɪ] *adv Br Fam* au mieux; **things are going s.** ça baigne
swimsuit ['swɪmsuːt] *n* maillot *m* de bain
swindle ['swɪndəl] **1** *n* escroquerie *f*
2 *vt* escroquer; **to s. sb out of sth** soutirer qch à qn
swindler ['swɪndlə(r)] *n* escroc *m*
swine [swaɪn] *(pl swine) n* (**a**) *Lit (pig)* porc *m*; **s. fever** peste *f* porcine (**b**) *Fam (man)* salaud *m*; *(woman)* garce *f*
swing [swɪŋ] **1** *n* (**a**) *(movement) (of rope, chain)* balancement *m*; *(in golf)* swing *m*; *Fam* **to take a s. at sb/sth** balancer un coup de poing à qn/qch; **to be in full s.** battre son plein; *Fam* **to go with a s.** *(of party)* swinguer; *Fam* **to get into the s. of things** se mettre dans le bain; **s. door** porte *f*

battante (**b**) *(change) (in opinion)* revirement *m* (**in** de); *(in economy)* fluctuation *f* (**in** de); *(in mood)* saute *f* (**in** de) (**c**) *(in playground)* balançoire *f*; *Fam* **it's swings and roundabouts** ce qu'on gagne d'un côté on le perd de l'autre
   2 *vt* (*pt & pp* **swung** [swʌŋ]) *(arms, racquet, axe)* balancer; **to s. one's hips** balancer les hanches; **to s. sb/sth onto one's shoulder** hisser qn/qch sur ses épaules; *Fam* **to s. it so that...** arranger les choses de manière à ce que... + *subjunctive*
   3 *vi* (**a**) *(move to and fro)* se balancer; **to s. open** *(of door)* s'ouvrir; **to s. into action** passer à l'action; *Fam* **he should s. for this** *(be hanged)* il mérite d'être pendu; *Fam* **the party was really swinging** la fête battait son plein (**b**) *(change direction)* virer; **to s. round** se retourner
swingeing ['swɪndʒɪŋ] *adj* énorme
swipe [swaɪp] **1** *vt* (**a**) *(through electronic reader)* passer dans un lecteur de cartes (**b**) *Fam (steal)* faucher
   2 *vi (hit)* **to s. at** essayer de frapper
   3 *n* (**a**) **to take a s. at** *(aim blow at)* essayer de frapper; *Fig (criticize)* s'en prendre à (**b**) *(for electronic reader)* **s. card** badge *m*
swirl [swɜːl] **1** *n (of cream)* spirale *f*; *(of smoke, leaves, dust)* tourbillon *m*
   2 *vt* remuer
   3 *vi* tourbillonner, tournoyer
swish [swɪʃ] **1** *n (of cane, whip)* sifflement *m*; *(of dress, silk)* froufrou *m*
   2 *adj Fam (elegant)* chic *inv*
   3 *vt (cane)* faire siffler; **to s. its tail** *(of animal)* remuer la queue
   4 *vi (of cane, whip)* siffler; *(of dress, silk)* froufrouter
Swiss [swɪs] **1** *npl* **the S.** *(people)* les Suisses *mpl*
   2 *adj suisse*; **S. army knife** couteau *m* suisse; **S. chard** bette *f*; **S. cheese** emmental; **S. cheese plant** philodendron *m*; **s. roll** roulé *m*
Switch® [swɪtʃ] *n Br* **to pay by S.** ≃ payer par carte bleue®; **S. card** ≃ carte *f* bleue®
switch [swɪtʃ] **1** *n* (**a**) *(electrical)* interrupteur *m* (**b**) *(change)* revirement *m*; **to make a s.** effectuer un changement (**c**) *(stick)* baguette *f*
   2 *vt* (**a**) *(change)* **to s. channels/jobs** changer de chaîne/d'emploi; **they switched their attention to...** leur attention s'est portée sur...; **he's been switched to another department** il a été muté dans un autre service (**b**) *(exchange)* échanger
   3 *vi (change)* **to s. to** passer à; *Comput* basculer vers
▸**switch off 1** *vt sep (appliance, heating)* éteindre
   2 *vi* (**a**) *(of appliance, heating)* s'éteindre (**b**) *Fam (of person)* décrocher
▸**switch on 1** *vt sep (appliance, heating)* allumer
   2 *vi (of appliance, heating)* s'allumer
▸**switch over** *vi (change TV channel)* passer sur une autre chaîne; **to s. over to sth** passer à qch
switchback ['swɪtʃbæk] *n* route *f* en lacets
switchboard ['swɪtʃbɔːd] *n* standard *m*; **s. operator** standardiste *mf*
Switzerland ['swɪtsələnd] *n* la Suisse
swivel ['swɪvəl] **1** *n* pivot *m*; **s. chair** chaise *f* pivotante
   2 *vi (pt & pp* **swivelled**) pivoter
swizz [swɪz] *n Fam* arnaque *f*
swollen ['swəʊlən] **1** *adj* enflé(e)
   2 *pp of* **swell**
swoon [swuːn] **1** *n* évanouissement *m*
   2 *vi* s'évanouir

swoop [swuːp] **1** *n (of bird, plane)* descente *f* en piqué; *(of police)* descente *f*
   2 *vi (of bird, plane)* descendre en piqué; *(of police)* faire une descente
swop = **swap**
sword [sɔːd] *n* épée *f*
swordfish ['sɔːdfɪʃ] *n* espadon *m*
swore [swɔː(r)] *pt of* **swear**
sworn [swɔːn] **1** *adj* **s. enemy** ennemi(e) *m,f* juré(e)
   2 *pp of* **swear**
swot [swɒt] *Br Fam* **1** *n (studious pupil)* bûcheur(euse) *m,f*
   2 *vi (pt & pp* **swotted**) *(study hard)* bûcher
▸**swot up on** *vt insep Br Fam (subject)* potasser
swum [swʌm] *pp of* **swim**
swung [swʌŋ] *pt & pp of* **swing**
sycamore ['sɪkəmɔː(r)] *n* sycomore *m*
sycophant ['sɪkəfənt] *n* flagorneur(euse) *m,f*
sycophantic [sɪkə'fæntɪk] *adj* flagorneur(euse)
Sydney ['sɪdnɪ] *n* Sydney
syllable ['sɪləbəl] *n* syllabe *f*
syllabus ['sɪləbəs] *n* programme *m*
sylph-like ['sɪlflaɪk] *adj Hum* **a s. woman** une sylphide
symbiotic [sɪmb(a)ɪ'ɒtɪk] *adj* symbiotique
symbol ['sɪmbəl] *n* symbole *m*
symbolic [sɪm'bɒlɪk] *adj* symbolique
symbolism ['sɪmbəlɪzəm] *n Art* symbolisme *m*
symbolist ['sɪmbəlɪst] *Art* **1** *n* symboliste *mf*
   2 *adj* symboliste
symbolize ['sɪmbəlaɪz] *vt* symboliser
symmetrical [sɪ'metrɪkəl] *adj* symétrique
symmetry ['sɪmɪtrɪ] *n* symétrie *f*
sympathetic [sɪmpə'θetɪk] *adj (understanding)* compréhensif(ive); *(compassionate)* compatissant(e); **to be s. to a proposal/cause** être favorable à une proposition/cause
sympathize ['sɪmpəθaɪz] *vi* (**a**) *(show compassion)* compatir (**with** avec) (**b**) *(show understanding)* **to s. (with sb)** comprendre (qn)
sympathizer ['sɪmpəθaɪzə(r)] *n* sympathisant(e) *m,f*
sympathy ['sɪmpəθɪ] *(pl* **sympathies**) *n* (**a**) *(pity, compassion)* compassion *f*; **to have s. for sb** éprouver de la compassion pour qn; **with deepest s.** avec toutes mes/nos condoléances (**b**) *(understanding, support)* sympathie *f*; **to feel s. for sb** éprouver de la sympathie pour qn; **s. strike** grève *f* de solidarité
symphony ['sɪmfənɪ] *(pl* **symphonies**) *n* symphonie *f*; **s. orchestra** orchestre *m* symphonique
symposium [sɪm'pəʊzɪəm] *(pl* **symposia** [sɪm'pəʊzɪə]) *n* symposium *m*
symptom ['sɪm(p)təm] *n also Fig* symptôme *m*
symptomatic [sɪm(p)tə'mætɪk] *adj* symptomatique
synagogue ['sɪnəgɒg] *n* synagogue *f*
sync, synch [sɪŋk] *n Fam* synchronisation *f*; **in/out of s. (with)** synchrone/pas synchrone (avec)
synchronization [sɪŋkrənaɪ'zeɪʃən] *n* synchronisation *f*
synchronize ['sɪŋkrənaɪz] *vt* synchroniser
syncopation [sɪŋkə'peɪʃən] *n Mus* syncope *f*
syndicalism ['sɪndɪkəlɪzəm] *n Pol* syndicalisme *m*
syndicalist ['sɪndɪkəlɪst] *Pol* **1** *n* syndicaliste *mf*
   2 *adj* syndicaliste
syndicate 1 *n* ['sɪndɪkət] syndicat *m*
   2 *vt* ['sɪndɪkeɪt] *Journ* publier simultanément dans plusieurs journaux; **syndicated columnist** journaliste *mf* d'agence

syndrome ['sındrəʊm] *n Fig* syndrôme *m*
synergy ['sınədʒı] *(pl* **synergies**) *n* synergie *f*
synod ['sınəd] *n Rel* synode *m*
synonym ['sınənım] *n* synonyme *m*
synonymous [sı'nɒnıməs] *adj* synonyme (**with** de)
synopsis [sı'nɒpsıs] *(pl* **synopses** [sı'nɒpsiːz]) *n* résumé *m*; *(of film)* synopsis *m*
syntax ['sıntæks] *n Ling* syntaxe *f*; *Comput* **s. error** erreur *f* de syntaxe
synthesis ['sınθısıs] *(pl* **syntheses** ['sınθısiːz]) *n* synthèse *f*
synthesize ['sınθəsaız] *vt* synthétiser
synthesizer ['sınθəsaızə(r)] *n* synthétiseur *m*
synthetic [sın'θetık] **1** *adj* synthétique
2 *n* **synthetics** *(materials)* synthétique *m*
syphilis ['sıfılıs] *n* syphilis *f*
syphon = siphon
Syria ['sırıə] *n* la Syrie

Syrian ['sırıən] **1** *n* Syrien(enne) *m,f*
2 *adj* syrien(enne)
syringe [sı'rındʒ] **1** *n* seringue *f*
2 *vt (ears)* déboucher
syrup ['sırəp] *n* sirop *m*
syrupy ['sırəpı] *adj (smile, music)* sirupeux(euse)
SYSOP ['sısɒp] *n Comput (abbr* **Systems Operator**) sysop *m*, opérateur *m* système
system ['sıstəm] *n* (**a**) *(structure)* système *m*; **the S.** *(established order)* le système; *Fam* **it was a shock to the s.** ça a été un choc; *Fam* **to get sb out of one's s.** oublier qn; *Fam* **to get sth out of one's s.** se débarrasser de qch (**b**) *Comput* système *m*; **systems analyst** analyste-programmeur(euse) *m,f* (**c**) *(method)* méthode *f*
systematic [sıstə'mætık] *adj* systématique
systematize ['sıstəmətaız] *vt* systématiser

T, t¹ [ti:] *n* (**a**) *(letter)* T, t *m inv* (**b**) *(idioms)* **that's you to a T** c'est tout à fait toi; **to suit sb to a T** convenir parfaitement à qn

t² *(abbr* **ton(s)**) t

TA [ti:'eɪ] *n Br Mil (abbr* **Territorial Army**) = armée de réserve, constituée de volontaires

ta [tɑ:] *exclam Br Fam* merci!

tab [tæb] *n* (**a**) *(on garment)* étiquette *f; Fam* **to keep tabs on sb/sth** avoir qn/qch à l'œil (**b**) *(on typewriter, word processor)* tabulation *f;* **t. (key)** tabulateur *m* (**c**) *Am Fam (for meal, drinks)* addition *f; also Fig* **to pick up the t.** payer l'addition (**d**) *(of LSD, ecstasy)* pilule *f*

tabbouleh [tæ'bu:leɪ] *n Culin* taboulé *m*

tabby ['tæbɪ] *(pl* **tabbies**) *n* **t. (cat)** chat *m* tigré

tabernacle ['tæbənækəl] *n (church)* temple *m; (on altar)* tabernacle *m*

table ['teɪbəl] **1** *n* (**a**) *(furniture)* table *f;* **to lay** *or* **set the t.** mettre *ou* dresser la table; **to clear the t.** débarrasser la table; **t. lamp** petite lampe *f;* **t. linen** linge *m* de table; **to have good/bad t. manners** bien/mal se tenir à table; **t. dancing** danse *f* aux tables; **t. mat** set *m* de table; **t. salt** sel *m* de table; **t. tennis** tennis *m* de table; **t. wine** vin *m* de table (**b**) *(of facts, figures)* tableau *m*, table *f;* **t. of contents** table *f* des matières; **twelve times t.** table *f* de douze (**c**) *(idioms)* **the offer is still on the t.** l'offre tient toujours; **to turn the tables on sb** renverser les rôles

2 *vt* **to t. a motion/proposal** *Br (present)* présenter une motion/une proposition; *Am (postpone)* ajourner une motion/une proposition

tablecloth ['teɪbəlklɒθ] *n* nappe *f*

tablespoon ['teɪbəlspu:n] *n* cuillère *f* à soupe

tablet ['tæblɪt] *n* (**a**) *(pill)* cachet *m* (**b**) *(inscribed stone)* tablette *f* (**c**) *(of soap)* pain *m*

tableware ['teɪbəlweə(r)] *n* vaisselle *f*

tabloid ['tæblɔɪd] *n (newspaper)* tabloïd *m;* **the t. press** la presse populaire

---

Tabloids

Dans les pays anglo-saxons, le format tabloïd est caractéristique de la presse populaire, bien que certains journaux de qualité aient récemment adopté le même format. En Grande-Bretagne, les plus connus des "tabloids" sont le "Sun", le "Daily Mirror", le "Daily Mail" et le "Daily Express". Ces journaux sont très influents en Grande-Bretagne – le "Sun" affiche ainsi les plus grands tirages de la presse britannique. Les "tabloids" privilégient les histoires à scandale et à sensation, ce qui a suscité un débat sur le code de conduite de la presse et sur la législation à mettre en place pour protéger la vie privée.

---

taboo [tə'bu:] **1** *n (pl* **taboos**) tabou *m*
2 *adj* tabou(e)

tabular ['tæbjʊlə(r)] *adj* **in t. form** sous forme de tableau

tabulate ['tæbjʊleɪt] *vt* présenter sous forme de tableau

tachometer [tæk'ɒmɪtə(r)] *n* compte-tours *m*

tacit ['tæsɪt] *adj* tacite

tacitly ['tæsɪtlɪ] *adv* tacitement

taciturn ['tæsɪtɜ:n] *adj* taciturne

tack [tæk] **1** *n* (**a**) *(small nail)* clou *m; Am (drawing pin)* punaise *f* (**b**) *Naut (course)* bordée *f; Fig* **to change t.** changer de tactique

2 *vt* (**a**) *(fasten)* clouer; *Am (with drawing pin)* punaiser; *Fig* **to t. sth on** *(add)* rajouter qch (**b**) *(in sewing)* faufiler

3 *vi Naut* louvoyer

tackle ['tækəl] **1** *n* (**a**) *(equipment)* matériel *m*, équipement *m* (**b**) *(in football)* tacle *m; (in rugby)* placage *m*

2 *vt* (**a**) *(deal with) (problem)* s'attaquer à; *(subject)* aborder; **to t. sb about sth** *(confront)* confronter qn à propos de qch (**b**) *(in football)* tacler; *(in rugby)* plaquer

tacky ['tækɪ] *adj* (**a**) *(sticky)* collant(e) (**b**) *Fam Pej (tasteless)* de mauvais goût; *(person)* vulgaire

tact [tækt] *n* tact *m*

tactful ['tæktfʊl] *adj (person)* qui a du tact; *(answer, remark)* diplomatique

tactic ['tæktɪk] *n* tactique *f*

tactical ['tæktɪkəl] *adj* tactique; *Pol* **t. voting** vote *m* utile

tactician [tæk'tɪʃən] *n* tacticien(enne) *m,f*

tactile ['tæktaɪl] *adj* tactile

tactless ['tæktlɪs] *adj* dépourvu(e) de tact

tactlessly ['tæktlɪslɪ] *adv* sans tact

tad [tæd] *n Fam* **a t.** un tantinet, un peu

tadpole ['tædpəʊl] *n* têtard *m*

Tadzhikistan [tædʒɪkɪ'stɑ:n] *n* le Tadjikistan

taffeta ['tæfɪtə] *n* taffetas *m*

tag [tæg] **1** *n* (**a**) *(label)* étiquette *f; Gram* **t. question** tag *m* (**b**) *(game)* **to play t.** jouer à chat
2 *vt (pt & pp* **tagged**) *(label)* étiqueter

▸**tag along** *vi* **she always tags along** elle me/le/*etc* suit partout; **to t. along with sb** venir avec qn

▸**tag on** *vt sep* **to t. sth on** rajouter qch

Tagus ['teɪgəs] *n* **the T.** le Tage

Tahiti [tə'hi:tɪ] *n* Tahiti *f*

Tahitian [tə'hi:ʃən] **1** *n* Tahitien(enne) *m,f*
2 *adj* tahitien(enne)

tail [teɪl] **1** n (**a**) (of animal, plane) queue f; (of shirt) pan m; **heads or tails?** (when tossing coin) pile ou face?; **tails, t.** coat queue-de-pie f; **t.** end (last part) fin f; Am Aut **t.** light feu m arrière (**b**) (idioms) **with one's t.** between one's legs la queue entre les jambes; Fam **to turn t.** tourner les talons **2** vt Fam (follow) filer
▸**tail away, tail off** vi décliner; (of voice) baisser
tailback ['teɪlbæk] n (traffic jam) bouchon m
tailboard ['teɪlbɔːd], Am **tailgate** ['teɪlgeɪt] n hayon m
tailor ['teɪlə(r)] **1** n tailleur m; **t.'s dummy** mannequin m; **t.'s shop** atelier m de tailleur **2** vt (suit) faire; Fig (speech, policy) adapter (**to** à)
tailored ['teɪləd] adj ajusté(e)
tailor-made ['teɪləmeɪd] adj also Fig fait(e) sur mesure
tailplane ['teɪlpleɪn] n Aviat stabilisateur m
tailspin ['teɪlspɪn] n Aviat descente f en vrille; **to go into a t.** descendre en vrille; Fig paniquer
tailwind ['teɪlwɪnd] n vent m arrière
taint [teɪnt] **1** n contamination f; Fig tare f **2** vt (contaminate) contaminer; Fig souiller
Taiwan [taɪ'wɑːn] n Taiwan
Taiwanese [taɪwə'niːz] **1** n Taiwanais(e) m,f **2** adj taiwanais(e)
Tajikistan = Tadzhikistan
take [teɪk] **1** vt (pt took [tʊk], pp taken ['teɪkən]) (**a**) (grasp) prendre; **to t.** hold of prendre ou saisir; **to t. sb by the arm** prendre qn par le bras; **to t. sb in one's arms** prendre qn dans ses bras; **to t. the opportunity to do sth** profiter de l'occasion pour faire qch (**b**) (remove) prendre; **to t. sth away from sb** prendre qch à qn; **to t. sth out of sth** prendre qch dans qch (**c**) (tolerate) supporter; **he can't t. a joke** il prend mal la plaisanterie; **I can't t. (it) any more** je n'en peux plus (**d**) (lead, carry) amener; **to t. sb home/to the station** conduire qn chez lui/à la gare; **to t. sb to court** faire un procès à qn; **to t. the dog for a walk** aller promener le chien; **her job takes her all over the world** son travail l'amène à voyager dans le monde entier; **if you can get the money we'll t. it from there** quand tu auras l'argent on verra comment on procède (**e**) (go by) (bus, road, turning) prendre (**f**) (require) prendre; **it takes courage (to do)** il faut du courage (pour faire); **how long does it t.?** combien de temps cela prend-il?; **it took me an hour to get here** il m'a fallu une heure pour venir; **that will t. a lot of explaining** ça ne va pas être facile de se faire pardonner (**g**) (adopt) (precautions, measures) prendre; **to t. legal advice** consulter un avocat; **to t. sth as an example** prendre qch comme exemple (**h**) (record) (temperature, notes) prendre (**i**) (capture) (power, town, chess piece) prendre; **to t. first prize** remporter le premier prix (**j**) (assume) **I t. it (that)...** je suppose que... (**k**) (accept) (cheque, credit card) accepter; **my car only takes unleaded** ma voiture ne marche qu'à l'essence sans plomb; **t. it or leave it!** c'est à prendre ou à laisser!; **to t. sth well/badly** prendre bien/mal qch; **to t. sth the wrong way** mal comprendre qch; **how much** or **what will you t. for it?** combien est-ce que

tu en veux?; **you can t. it from me that...** je peux te garantir que...
(**l**) (contain) avoir une capacité de
(**m**) (subject) faire; (course) suivre; (exam) passer; **he takes them for English** il leur enseigne l'anglais
(**n**) (in phrases) **to t. a bath** prendre un bain; **to t. drugs** se droguer; **to t. fright** prendre peur; **to be taken ill** tomber malade; **to t. a look at sth** jeter un coup d'œil à qch; **to t. a photograph of sb/sth** prendre qn/qch en photo; **to t. a seat** s'asseoir; **to t. a walk** se promener
2 vi (be successful) (of fire, plant cutting, dye) prendre
3 n (**a**) (of film, music) prise f (**b**) (money) recette f; Fam **to be on the t.** toucher des pots-de-vin
▸**take after** vt insep ressembler à
▸**take apart** vt (machine, engine) démonter; (argument) démolir
▸**take away 1** vt sep (remove) enlever, retirer; (deduct) ôter; **to t. sth away from sb** enlever qch à qn; Br **sandwiches to t. away** sandwichs à emporter **2** vi **to t. away from the pleasure/value of sth** diminuer le plaisir/la valeur de qch
▸**take back** vt sep (**a**) (return) ramener, rapporter; **that takes me back to my childhood** cela me rappelle mon enfance (**b**) (accept) reprendre (**c**) (withdraw) retirer; **t. that back!** retire ce que tu viens de dire!
▸**take down** vt sep (**a**) (remove) (from shelf) prendre; (downstairs) descendre; (poster, decorations) enlever (**b**) (lower) baisser; Fam **to t. sb down a peg or two** remettre qn à sa place (**c**) (dismantle) (tent, scaffolding) démonter; (wall, barricade) démolir (**d**) (record) noter; (notes) prendre
▸**take for** vt sep **to t. sb for somebody else** prendre qn pour quelqu'un d'autre; **what do you t. me for?** pour qui est-ce que tu me prends?
▸**take in** vt sep (**a**) (lead, carry) (person) faire entrer; (harvest) rentrer (**b**) (orphan) recueillir; (lodger) prendre (**c**) (garment) reprendre (**d**) (include) inclure, comprendre (**e**) (understand) saisir (**f**) (deceive) tromper, rouler
▸**take off 1** vt sep (**a**) (remove) enlever; **to t. sth off sb's hands** retirer qch des mains de qn; **to t. years off sb** (of clothes, diet) rajeunir qn; **he took £10 off (the price)** il a baissé (le prix) de 10 livres; **he never took his eyes off us** il ne nous a pas quittés des yeux (**b**) (lead) (person) emmener; **to t. oneself off** s'en aller (**c**) (mimic) imiter **2** vi (of plane) décoller (**b**) Fam (of person) se casser (**c**) Fam (succeed) prendre
▸**take on** vt sep (**a**) (task, responsibility) assumer; (problem) s'occuper de; (opponent) défier; (fuel, supplies) prendre (**b**) (employ) embaucher (**c**) (acquire) prendre
▸**take out** vt sep (**a**) (remove) sortir; Fam **to t. it** or **a lot out of sb** épuiser qn; **to t. it out on sb** passer sa colère sur qn (**b**) (person) inviter (à sortir) (**c**) (obtain) (licence) obtenir; (insurance policy) souscrire; (subscription) prendre
▸**take over 1** vt sep (**a**) (become responsible for) (job, business) reprendre (**b**) (take control of) (place) envahir; (company) racheter **2** vi (**a**) (assume power) prendre le pouvoir (**b**) (relieve) prendre la relève (**from** de)

▸**take to** *vt insep* (**a**) *(go to)* **to t. to one's heels** prendre ses jambes à son cou; **to t. to one's bed** s'aliter; **to t. to the hills** se réfugier dans les collines (**b**) *(adopt habit)* **to t. to doing sth** se mettre à faire qch (**c**) *(like)* **to t. to sb** se prendre de sympathie pour qn; **to t. to sth** prendre goût à qch

▸**take up 1** *vt sep* (**a**) *(carry)* monter (**b**) *(lead)* (person) faire monter (**c**) *(lift)* enlever (**d**) *(shorten)* (skirt, hem) raccourcir (**e**) *(challenge)* relever; *(offer, suggestion)* accepter; **to t. sb up on an offer** accepter l'offre de qn (**f**) *(subject, problem)* parler de (**with sb** avec qn) (**g**) *(assume)* (position, post) prendre (**h**) *(hobby, studies)* se mettre à; **we t. up the story just after...** nous reprenons l'histoire juste après... (**i**) *(space, time)* prendre **2** *vi* **to t. up with sb** se lier avec qn

▸**take upon** *vt sep* **to t. it upon oneself to do sth** prendre sur soi de faire qch

takeaway ['teɪkəweɪ] *Br* **1** *n (food)* plat *m* à emporter; *(restaurant)* restaurant *m* qui fait des plats à emporter **2** *adj (food)* à emporter

take-home pay ['teɪkhəʊmpeɪ] *n* salaire *m* net

taken ['teɪkən] **1** *adj* (**a**) *(occupied)* pris(e) (**b**) *(impressed)* **I was very t. with him** il m'a fait très bonne impression **2** *pp of* **take**

takeoff ['teɪkɒf] *n* (**a**) *(imitation)* imitation *f*; **to do a t. of sb** imiter qn (**b**) *(of plane)* décollage *m*

takeover ['teɪkəʊvə(r)] *n* (**a**) *Com (of company)* rachat *m*; **t. bid** offre *f* publique d'achat (**b**) *(of government, country)* prise *f* de pouvoir

taker ['teɪkə(r)] *n (buyer)* acheteur(euse) *m,f*, preneur(euse) *m,f*; **there were no takers** personne n'en voulait; **any takers?** *(for food)* y a-t-il des amateurs?

taking ['teɪkɪŋ] *n* (**a**) **it's yours for the t.** tu n'as plus qu'à accepter (**b**) *Com* **takings** recette *f*

talc [tælk] *n* talc *m*

talcum powder ['tælkəmpaʊdə(r)] *n* talc *m*

tale [teɪl] *n* (**a**) *(story)* histoire *f*; *(legend)* conte *m*; **to live to tell the t.** survivre (**b**) *(lie)* histoire *f*, salades *fpl* (**c**) **to tell tales (on sb)** moucharder (qn)

talent ['tælənt] *n* (**a**) *(person, ability)* talent *m*; **t. scout** *or* **spotter** dénicheur(euse) *m,f* de talents (**b**) *Br Fam (attractive women)* belles nanas *fpl*; *(attractive men)* beaux mecs *mpl*

talented ['tæləntɪd] *adj* talentueux(euse)

talisman ['tælɪzmən] *n* talisman *m*

talk [tɔːk] **1** *n* (**a**) *(conversation)* conversation *f*; **to have a t. with sb** parler *ou* s'entretenir avec qn; *Fam* **to be all t.** parler beaucoup (et ne pas faire grandchose); **t. show** *(on TV, radio)* talk-show *m* (**b**) **talks** *(negotiations)* pourparlers *mpl* (**c**) *(gossip)* **there is some t. of him resigning** le bruit court qu'il va démissionner; **it's the t. of the town** on ne parle que de cela (**d**) *(lecture)* intervention *f* **2** *vt (speak)* parler; **to t. nonsense** dire des bêtises; **to t. business/politics** parler business/politique; **to t. sense** tenir des propos sensés; **to t. (some) sense into sb** faire entendre raison à qn; **she can t. her way out of anything** avec son bagou elle arrive toujours à se tirer d'affaire; **to t. sb into/out of doing sth** convaincre/dissuader qn de faire qch; **to t. shop** parler boutique **3** *vi* (**a**) *(speak)* parler (**to/about** à/de); **to t. to oneself** parler tout(e) seul(e); **talking of embarrassing situations,...** à propos de situations embarrassantes,...; *Fam* **now you're talking!** voilà qui est

mieux!; *Fam* **you can t.!, look who's talking!** tu peux parler! (**b**) *(gossip)* cancaner, jaser (**c**) *(give lecture)* faire une intervention (**on** sur)

▸**talk back** *vi* répondre avec insolence

▸**talk down to** *vt insep* **to t. down to sb** parler à qn sur un ton de supériorité

▸**talk over** *vt sep* discuter

talkative ['tɔːkətɪv] *adj* bavard(e)

talker ['tɔːkə(r)] *n* **he was never much of a t.** il n'a jamais été très bavard

talking ['tɔːkɪŋ] *adj* **t. book** livre *m* enregistré; **t. point** sujet *m* de conversation; *Fam* **t. shop** = organisation où l'on parle beaucoup mais où l'on agit peu

talking-to ['tɔːkɪŋtuː] *n Fam* savon *m*; **to give sb a t.** passer un savon à qn

tall [tɔːl] **1** *adj (person)* grand(e); *(building)* haut(e); **how t. are you?** combien est-ce que tu mesures?; **to be 2 metres t.** *(of person)* mesurer 2 mètres; *(of object)* faire 2 mètres de haut; *Fig* **that's a t. order** c'est beaucoup demander; *Fig* **a t. story** une histoire invraisemblable **2** *adv* **to walk** *or* **stand t.** marcher la tête haute

tallboy ['tɔːlbɔɪ] *n* commode *f* haute

Tallin(n) ['tælɪn] *n* Tallinn

tallow ['tæləʊ] *n* suif *m*

tally ['tælɪ] **1** *n* compte *m*; **to keep a t. of sth** tenir le compte de qch **2** *vi (of figure, report)* concorder

talon ['tælən] *n* serre *f*

tamarind ['tæmərɪnd] *n (fruit)* tamarin *m*; *(tree)* tamarinier *m*

tambourine [tæmbə'riːn] *n* tambourin *m*

tame [teɪm] **1** *adj* (**a**) *(not timid or vicious)* familier(ère); *(domesticated)* apprivoisé(e) (**b**) *(unadventurous)* timide; *(speech, attempt)* mou (molle); *(party, evening)* morne **2** *vt (animal)* apprivoiser; *Fig (emotion)* dominer

tamely ['teɪmlɪ] *adv (say, ask)* timidement; *(accept)* docilement

Tamil ['tæmɪl] **1** *n* (**a**) *(person)* Tamoul(e) *m,f* (**b**) *(language)* tamoul *m* **2** *adj* tamoul(e)

▸**tamper with** ['tæmpə(r)] *vt insep* toucher à; *(lock)* tripoter; *(documents, records)* trafiquer

tampon ['tæmpɒn] *n* tampon *m* (hygiénique)

tan¹ [tæn] *n Math (abbr* tangent) tan *f*, tg *f*

tan² **1** *n* (**a**) *(colour)* marron *m* clair (**b**) *(from sun)* bronzage *m* **2** *adj (colour)* marron clair *inv* **3** *vt (pt & pp* tanned) (**a**) *(of sun)* (skin) hâler (**b**) *(leather)* tanner; *Fam* **to t. sb, to t. sb's hide** tanner le cuir à qn **4** *vi (of person, skin)* bronzer

tandem ['tændəm] *n* (**a**) *(bicycle)* tandem *m* (**b**) **to do sth in t.** faire qch à deux

tang [tæŋ] *n (taste)* saveur *f* acidulée; *(smell)* odeur *f* acidulée

tangent ['tændʒənt] *n Math* tangente *f*; *Fig* **to go off at a t.** changer de sujet

tangerine [tændʒə'riːn] **1** *n (fruit, colour)* mandarine *f* **2** *adj (colour)* mandarine *inv*

tangible ['tændʒɪbəl] *adj* tangible; *Fig (real)* évident(e); *Fin* **t. assets** biens *mpl* corporels

tangibly ['tændʒɪblɪ] *adv* tangiblement

Tangier [tæn'dʒɪə(r)], **Tangiers** [tæn'dʒɪəz] *n* Tanger

tangle ['tæŋgəl] **1** *n* enchevêtrement *m*; **to be in a t.** être emmêlé(e); *Fig (of person, figures, accounts)* être embrouillé(e); **to get into a t.** s'emmêler; *Fig (of person, figures, accounts)* s'embrouiller
2 *vt* **to get tangled up in sth** se prendre dans qch; *Fig* se retrouver mêlé(e) à qch
▸ **tangle with** *vt insep Fam* s'en prendre à
tangled ['tæŋgəld] *adj* emmêlé(e); *Fig* embrouillé(e)
tango ['tæŋgəʊ] **1** *n (pl* **tangos**) *(dance)* tango *m*
2 *vi (pt & pp* **tangoed**) danser le tango; *Fam* **it takes two to t.** chacun a sa part de responsabilité
tangy ['tæŋɪ] *adj* acidulé(e)
tank [tæŋk] *n* (**a**) *(container)* réservoir *m* (**b**) *Mil* tank *m* (**c**) **t. top** *(garment)* débardeur *m* en laine
▸ **tank along** *vi Fam* foncer
▸ **tank up** *vt sep Br Fam* **to be tanked up** être bourré(e); **to get tanked up** se prendre une biture
tankard ['tæŋkəd] *n* chope *f*
tanker ['tæŋkə(r)] *n (ship)* navire-citerne *m*; *(lorry)* camion-citerne *m*
tankini [tæŋ'ki:nɪ] *n* maillot *m* brassière, tankini *m*
tanned [tænd] *adj* bronzé(e)
tanner ['tænə(r)] *n* tanneur(euse) *m,f*
tannery ['tænərɪ] *(pl* **tanneries**) *n* tannerie *f*
tannin ['tænɪn] *n* tan(n)in *m*
tanning ['tænɪŋ] *n* bronzage; **t. salon** *or* **studio** centre *m* de bronzage
tannoy® ['tænɔɪ] *n* système *m* de haut-parleurs; **over the t.** au haut-parleur
tantalize ['tæntəlaɪz] *vt* allécher (**with** avec)
tantalizing ['tæntəlaɪzɪŋ] *adj (smell)* alléchant(e); *(hint, possibility)* tentant(e)
tantamount ['tæntəmaʊnt] *adj* **t. to** équivalent(e) à
Tantric ['tæntrɪk] *adj* tantrique
tantrum ['tæntrəm] *n* caprice *m*; **to throw a t.** faire un caprice
Tanzania [tænzə'nɪə] *n* laTanzanie
Tanzanian [tænzə'nɪən] **1** *n* Tanzanien(enne) *m,f*
2 *adj* tanzanien(enne)
tap[1] [tæp] **1** *n* (**a**) *Br (for water, gas)* robinet *m*; **to be on t.** *(of beer)* être à la pression; *Fig (of person, information)* être toujours disponible; **t. water** eau *f* du robinet (**b**) **to put a t. on a phone** mettre un téléphone sur écoute
2 *vt (pt & pp* **tapped**) (**a**) *(tree)* inciser; *(resources)* puiser dans; *Fam* **to t. sb for money** taper de l'argent à qn (**b**) *(phone)* mettre sur écoute
tap[2] **1** *n* (**a**) *(light blow)* petit coup *m*; *(with hand)* tape *f* (**b**) **t. dancer** danseur(euse) *m,f* de claquettes; **t. dancing** claquettes *fpl*
2 *vt (pt & pp* **tapped**) donner un petit coup à; *(with hand)* donner une tape à
3 *vi* **to t. (at** *or* **on)** frapper doucement (à)
tape [teɪp] **1** *n* (**a**) *(ribbon)* ruban *m*; *(of paper)* bande *f*; **(adhesive** *or Fam* **sticky) t.** ruban *m* adhésif, Scotch® *m*; *Sport* **(finishing) t.** ligne *f* d'arrivée; **t. (measure)** mètre *m* (**b**) *(for recording)* bande *f*; *(cassette)* cassette *f*; **t. deck** platine *f* cassette; **t. recorder** magnétophone *m*; **t. recording** enregistrement *m*
2 *vt* (**a**) *(stick with tape)* scotcher; *Fig* **to have sb taped** connaître qn comme sa poche; **to have sth taped** avoir compris qch (**b**) *(record)* enregistrer
taper ['teɪpə(r)] **1** *n (candle)* bougie *f* filée
2 *vi* s'effiler; **to t. to a point** se terminer en pointe
▸ **taper off** *vi (of object)* s'effiler; *Fig (decrease)* s'amenuiser
tape-record ['teɪprɪkɔ:d] *vt* enregistrer

tapestry ['tæpɪstrɪ] *(pl* **tapestries**) *n* tapisserie *f*
tapeworm ['teɪpwɜ:m] *n* ver *m* solitaire
tapioca [tæpɪ'əʊkə] *n* tapioca *m*
tapping ['tæpɪŋ] *n (sound)* petits coups *mpl*
tar [tɑ:(r)] **1** *n (substance)* goudron *m* (**b**) *Fam Old-fashioned (sailor)* matelot *m*
2 *vt (pt & pp* **tarred**) goudronner; **to t. and feather sb** rouler qn dans le goudron et les plumes; *Fig* **we've been tarred with the same brush** on nous a mis dans le même sac
tarantula [tə'ræntjʊlə] *n* tarentule *f*
tardily ['tɑ:dɪlɪ] *adv Formal (late)* tardivement; *(slowly)* lentement
tardy ['tɑ:dɪ] *adj Formal (late)* tardif(ive); *(slow)* lent(e)
target ['tɑ:gɪt] **1** *n* (**a**) *(of bullet, missile, joke)* cible *f*; **t. language** *(in translating)* langue *f* d'arrivée; **t. practice** exercices *mpl* de tir (**b**) *Fig (goal)* objectif *m*; **to set oneself a t.** se fixer un objectif; **to be on t. (to do sth)** être dans les temps (pour faire qch); **t. audience** type *m* d'écoute ciblé; **t. market** marché *m* ciblé
2 *vt* (**a**) *(aim)* **to t. sth at sth** *(missile)* diriger qch sur qch; *Fig (campaign, TV programme, benefits)* destiner qch à qch (**b**) *also Fig (aim at)* viser
tariff ['tærɪf] *n (tax)* tarif *m*, droit *m* de douane; *(price list)* tarif; **t. barrier** barrière *f* douanière
tarmac® ['tɑ:mæk] **1** *n* macadam *m*; **the t.** *(runway)* le tarmac
2 *vt (pt & pp* **tarmacked**) goudronner
tarnish ['tɑ:nɪʃ] **1** *vt also Fig* ternir
2 *vi* se ternir
tarot ['tærəʊ] *n* tarot *m*; **t. card** carte *f* de tarot
tarpaulin [tɑ:'pɔ:lɪn] *n* bâche *f*
tarragon ['tærəgən] *n* estragon *m*
tart [tɑ:t] **1** *n* (**a**) *(cake) (large)* tarte *f*; *(small)* tartelette *f* (**b**) *Br Fam Pej (promiscuous woman, prostitute)* pute *f*
2 *adj* (**a**) *(in taste)* âpre (**b**) *(tone, remark)* aigrelet(ette)
▸ **tart up** *vt sep Fam (room, pub)* retaper; **to t. oneself up** se faire une beauté
tartan ['tɑ:tən] *n* tartan *m*, écossais *m*; **t. tie/jacket** cravate *f*/veste *f* écossaise
Tartar ['tɑ:tə(r)] *n* Tatar(e) *m,f*
tartar ['tɑ:tə(r)] *n (on teeth)* tartre *m*
tartar(e) sauce ['tɑ:tə'sɔ:s] *n* sauce *f* tartare
tartly ['tɑ:tlɪ] *adv* avec aigreur
task [tɑ:sk] *n* tâche *f*; **to take sb to t. for sth/for doing sth** reprocher qch à qn/à qn d'avoir fait qch
taskforce ['tɑ:skfɔ:s] *n Mil* corps *m* expéditionnaire; *Fig* commission *f*
taskmaster ['tɑ:skmɑ:stə(r)] *n* **to be a hard t.** être très exigeant(e)
Tasmania [tæz'meɪnɪə] *n* laTasmanie
Tasmanian [tæz'meɪnɪən] **1** *n* Tasmanien(enne) *m,f*
2 *adj* tasmanien(enne)
Tasman Sea ['tæzmən'si:] *n* **the T.** la mer de Tasman
tassel ['tæsəl] *n* gland *m*
taste [teɪst] **1** *n* (**a**) *(flavour, sense)* goût *m*; **t. bud** papille *f* gustative (**b**) *(sample) also Fig* **to have a t. of sth** goûter à qch; **a t. of things to come** un avant-goût des choses à venir; **to give sb a t. of his own medicine** rendre la pareille à qn (**c**) *(liking)* goût *m* (**for** pour); **to acquire** *or* **develop a t. for sth** prendre goût à qch; **add sugar to t.** ajouter du sucre à volonté; **violent films are not to my t.** les films violents ne me plaisent pas (**d**) *(judgement)* goût *m*; **in good/bad** *or* **poor t.** de bon/mauvais goût

2 *vt* (**a**) *(detect flavour of)* sentir (le goût de) (**b**) *(sample)* goûter; *Fig (happiness, success)* goûter à **3** *vi* to **t.** of *or* like sth avoir un goût de qch; **to t. good/bad** être bon (bonne)/mauvais(e)
tasteful ['teɪstfəl] *adj* de bon goût
tastefully ['teɪstfəlɪ] *adv* avec goût
tasteless ['teɪstlɪs] *adj* (**a**) *(food)* insipide (**b**) *(remark, clothes)* de mauvais goût
taster ['teɪstə(r)] *n* (**a**) *(person)* goûteur(euse) *m,f* (**b**) *(foretaste)* avant-goût *m*
tasty ['teɪstɪ] *adj* (**a**) *(food)* savoureux(euse) (**b**) *Fam (attractive)* bien foutu(e)
tat [tæt] *n Fam* camelote *f*
ta-ta [tæ'tɑː] *exclam Br Fam* au revoir!
tatters ['tætəz] *npl also Fig* **in t.** en lambeaux
tattered ['tætəd] *adj* déguenillé(e)
tattle ['tætəl] **1** *n* potins *mpl*, commérages *mpl* **2** *vi* commérer
tattoo¹ [tə'tuː] *(pl* **tattoos**) *n* (**a**) *(on drum)* retraite *f* du soir (**b**) *(military show)* parade *f* militaire
tattoo² **1** *n (design)* tatouage *m* **2** *vt* tatouer
tatty ['tætɪ] *adj Br Fam* minable
taught [tɔːt] *pt & pp of* **teach**
taunt [tɔːnt] **1** *n (words)* raillerie *f* **2** *vt* railler
Taurus ['tɔːrəs] *n* leTaureau; **to be (a) T.** êtreTaureau
taut [tɔːt] *adj* tendu(e)
tauten ['tɔːtən] **1** *vt* tendre **2** *vi* se tendre
tautness ['tɔːtnɪs] *n* tension *f*
tautological [tɔːtə'lɒdʒɪkəl] *adj* tautologique
tautology [tɔː'tɒlədʒɪ] *(pl* **tautologies**) *n* tautologie *f*
tavern ['tævən] *n* taverne *f*
tawdry ['tɔːdrɪ] *adj* (**a**) *(conduct, motive)* lâche (**b**) *(decor, jewellery)* tape-à-l'œil *inv*
tawny ['tɔːnɪ] *adj* fauve; **t. owl** chouette *f* hulotte
tax [tæks] **1** *n* impôt *m*, taxe *f*; **t. allowance** abattement *m* fiscal; **t. avoidance** optimisation *f* ou évasion *f* fiscale; **t. bracket** tranche *f* d'imposition; **t. break** allègement *m* fiscal; **t. collector** percepteur(trice) *m,f*; **t. cut** réduction *f* d'impôt; *Br* **t. disc** ≃ vignette *f* automobile; **t. evasion** évasion *f* fiscale; **t. exemption** exonération *f* ou exemption *f* d'impôt; **t. exile** = personne vivant à l'étranger pour échapper au fisc; **t. haven** paradis *m* fiscal; **t. incentive** incitation *f* fiscale; **t. inspector** inspecteur(trice) *m,f* des impôts; **t. relief** dégrèvement *m* fiscal; **t. return** déclaration *f* d'impôt
2 *vt* (**a**) *(subject to tax)* imposer, frapper d'un impôt (**b**) *(put under strain)* mettre à l'épreuve (**c**) *Formal (accuse)* **to t. sb with sth** taxer qn de qch
taxable ['tæksəbl] *adj* imposable
taxation [tæk'seɪʃən] *n* imposition *f*; **an increase in t.** une augmentation des impôts
tax-deductible [tæksdɪ'dʌktɪbəl] *adj* déductible des impôts
tax-exempt [tæksɪg'zempt] *adj (goods)* exonéré(e) de taxes; *(income)* exonéré(e) d'impôts
tax-free [tæks'friː] *adj* exempt(e) d'impôt
taxi ['tæksɪ] **1** *n* taxi *m*; **t. driver** chauffeur *m* de taxi; **t. rank** station *f* de taxi
2 *vi (of aircraft)* rouler
taxidermist ['tæksɪdɜːmɪst] *n* taxidermiste *mf*
taxing ['tæksɪŋ] *adj* ardu(e)
taxonomy [tæk'sɒnəmɪ] *n* taxonomie *f*

taxpayer ['tækspeɪə(r)] *n* contribuable *mf*
TB [tiː'biː] *n (abbr* **tuberculosis**) tuberculose *f*
T-bone steak [tiːbəʊn'steɪk] *n* côte *f* de bœuf à l'os
te [tiː] *n Mus* si *m*
tea [tiː] *n* (**a**) *(plant, drink)* thé *m*; *(herbal infusion)* tisane *f*; **t. break** ≃ pause-café *f*; **t. caddy** boîte *f* à thé; **t. cosy** couvre-théière *m*; **t. leaves** feuilles *fpl* de thé; **t. party** goûter *m*; **t. set** service *m* à thé; **t. strainer** passoire *f* à thé; **t. towel** torchon *m* (pour la vaisselle); **t. tray** plateau *m* (**b**) *Br (evening meal)* dîner *m*; *(afternoon)* **t.** thé *m*

Tea

Bien que, dans certains milieux, le thé ait été récemment supplanté par le café, le thé reste en Grande-Bretagne comme en Irlande une boisson extrêmement populaire. Si la tradition de l'"afternoon tea" a largement disparu, de même que les "tea ladies" qui servaient sur le lieu de travail le thé sur une table roulante, les britanniques et les irlandais restent de grands consommateurs de thé.

teabag ['tiːbæg] *n* sachet *m* de thé
teach [tiːtʃ] *(pt & pp* **taught** [tɔːt]) **1** *vt* enseigner; **to t. sb sth**, **to t. sth to sb** enseigner qch à qn; **to t. sb (how) to do sth** apprendre à qn à faire qch; **t. yourself Spanish** apprendre qch tout seul; *Am* **to t. school** enseigner; *Fig* **to t. sb a lesson** donner une leçon à qn; *Fam* **that'll t. him!** ça lui apprendra!
2 *vi* enseigner
teacher ['tiːtʃə(r)] *n (at primary school)* instituteur(trice) *m,f*; *(at secondary school)* professeur *m*, enseignant(e) *m,f*; **t.'s pet** chouchou(te) *m,f* du professeur; **t. training** formation *f* pédagogique; **t. training college** ≃ IUFM *m*
teaching ['tiːtʃɪŋ] *n* (**a**) *(profession, action)* enseignement *m*; **t. hospital** CHU *m*; **t. practice** stage *m* pratique d'enseignement; **t. staff** personnel *m* enseignant (**b**) *(doctrine)* doctrine *f*
teacup ['tiːkʌp] *n* tasse *f* à thé
teak [tiːk] *n* teck *m*
team [tiːm] *n* équipe *f*; **a t. effort** un travail d'équipe; **t. games** jeux *mpl* d'équipe; **t. leader** chef *m* d'équipe; **t. player** joueur(euse) *m,f* qui a l'esprit d'équipe; **t. spirit** esprit *m* d'équipe
▸**team up** *vi* s'associer (**with** avec)
team-mate ['tiːmmeɪt] *n* coéquipier(ère) *m,f*
teamwork ['tiːmwɜːk] *n* travail *m* d'équipe
teamster ['tiːmstə(r)] *n Am (lorry driver)* routier *m*
teapot ['tiːpɒt] *n* théière *f*
tear¹ [tɪə(r)] *n* larme *f*; **in tears** en larmes; **t. duct** canal *m* lacrymal; **t. gas** gaz *m* lacrymogène
tear² [teə(r)] **1** *vt (pt* **tore** [tɔː(r)], *pp* **torn** [tɔːn]) *(rip)* déchirer; *(snatch)* arracher (**from** à); **to t. sth in two** *or* **in half** déchirer qch en deux; **to t. sth to pieces** déchirer qch en mille morceaux; *Fig* démolir qch; *Fig* **to t. sb to pieces** mettre qn en pièces; **to be torn between two things** se sentir tiraillé(e) entre deux choses; *Fam* **that's torn it!** il ne manquait plus que ça!
2 *vi* (**a**) *(rip)* se déchirer (**b**) **to t. at sth** déchirer qch (**c**) *(move quickly)* **to t. along/past/away** aller/passer/partir à toute vitesse
3 *n* déchirure *f*
▸**tear apart** *vt sep Fig* déchirer
▸**tear away** *vt sep Fig* **to t. oneself away from sth** s'arracher de qch

▶**tear down** *vt sep (building)* démolir; *(statue)* renverser; *(poster)* arracher

▶**tear into** *vt insep* **to t. into sb** *(physically)* se jeter sur qn; *(verbally)* passer un savon à qn

▶**tear off 1** *vt sep (remove)* arracher
  2 *vi (run away)* se sauver à toute vitesse

▶**tear out** *vt sep* arracher; *Fig* **to t. one's hair out** s'arracher les cheveux

▶**tear up** *vt sep (document, photo)* déchirer; *(plant)* déraciner; *(floorboards)* enlever

tearaway ['teərəweɪ] *n* casse-cou *m inv*

teardrop ['tɪədrɒp] *n* larme *f*

tearful ['tɪəfʊl] *adj* en larmes; **in a t. voice** avec des larmes dans la voix

tearfully ['tɪəfəlɪ] *adv* en pleurant

tearjerker ['tɪədʒɜ:kə(r)] *n Fam (film, book)* **it's a real t.** c'est complètement mélo

tearoom ['ti:ru:m] *n* salon *m* de thé

tearstained ['tɪəsteɪnd] *adj* barbouillé(e) de larmes

tease [ti:z] **1** *vt* taquiner (**about** sur *ou* à propos de)
  2 *vi* plaisanter
  3 *n (person)* taquin(e) *m,f*

▶**tease out** *vt sep* clarifier

teaser ['ti:zə(r)] *n Fam* (**a**) *(problem)* colle *f* (**b**) *(advertisement)* aguiche *f*; **t. advertising** aguichage *m*

teashop ['ti:ʃɒp] *n* salon *m* de thé

teasing ['ti:zɪŋ] *n* taquinerie *f*

teaspoon ['ti:spu:n] *n* cuillère *f* à café

teat [ti:t] *n (of animal)* trayon *m*; *(of feeding bottle)* tétine *f*

teatime ['ti:taɪm] *n (in the afternoon)* l'heure *f* du thé; *(in the evening)* l'heure *f* du dîner

technical ['teknɪkəl] *adj* technique; *Br* **t. college** ≃ institut *m* universitaire; **t. drawing** *(school subject)* dessin *m* industriel; **t. hitch** incident *m* technique

technicality [teknɪ'kælɪtɪ] *n* détail *m* technique

technically ['teknɪklɪ] *adv* techniquement

technician [tek'nɪʃən] *n* technicien(enne) *m,f*

technique [tek'ni:k] *n* technique *f*

techno ['teknəʊ] *n Mus* techno *f*

technological [teknə'lɒdʒɪkəl] *adj* technologique

technology [tek'nɒlədʒɪ] *(pl* **technologies***) n* technologie *f*

teddy ['tedɪ] *(pl* **teddies***) n* **t. (bear)** ours *m* en peluche

tedious ['ti:dɪəs] *adj* ennuyeux(euse); *(task)* fastidieux(euse)

tedium ['ti:dɪəm] *n* ennui *m*

tee [ti:] *n (in golf)* tee *m*

▶**tee off** *vi (in golf)* jouer le départ

teem [ti:m] *vi* (**a**) *(rain)* **to t. (down)** pleuvoir à verse (**b**) **to be teeming with sth** *(insects, ideas)* grouiller de qch

teeming ['ti:mɪŋ] *adj* grouillant(e)

teen ['ti:n] **1** *adj* adolescent(e); **t. idol** idole *f* des jeunes
  2 *n Fam* ado *mf*

teenage ['ti:neɪdʒ] *adj* adolescent(e)

teenager ['ti:neɪdʒə(r)] *n* adolescent(e) *m,f*

teens [ti:nz] *npl* adolescence *f*; **to be in one's t.** être adolescent(e)

teensy(-weensy) ['ti:nzɪ('wi:nzɪ)] *adj Fam* tout(e) petit(e)

teeny-bopper ['ti:nɪbɒpə(r)] *n Fam* petite minette *f*

teeny(-weeny) ['ti:nɪ('wi:nɪ)] *adj Fam* tout(e) petit(e)

teeshirt ['ti:ʃɜ:t] *n* tee-shirt *m*

teeter ['ti:tə(r)] *vi* chanceler; *Fig* **to t. on the brink of sth** être au bord de qch

teeth [ti:θ] *pl of* **tooth**

teethe [ti:ð] *vi* **to be teething** faire ses dents

teething ['ti:ðɪŋ] *n* poussée *f* dentaire; *Fig* **t. troubles** *(of project)* difficultés *fpl* initiales

teetotal [ti:'təʊtəl] *adj* qui ne boit jamais d'alcool

teetotaller, *Am* **teetotaler** [ti:'təʊtələ(r)] *n* = personne qui ne boit jamais d'alcool

TEFL ['tefəl] *n (abbr* **Teaching of English as a Foreign Language***)* enseignement *m* de l'anglais langue étrangère

Teh(e)ran [teə'rɑ:n] *n* Téhéran

tel *(abbr* **telephone***)* tél

telebanking ['telɪbæŋkɪŋ] *n* monétique *f*; *(home banking)* banque *f* à domicile

telecommunications [telɪkəmju:nɪ'keɪʃənz] *npl* télécommunications *fpl*

telecommuting [telɪkə'mju:tɪŋ] *n* télétravail *m*

teleconference [telɪ'kɒnfərəns] *n* téléconférence *f*

telegenic [telɪ'dʒenɪk] *adj* télégénique

telegram ['telɪgræm] *n* télégramme *m*

telegraph ['telɪgrɑ:f] **1** *n* télégraphe *m*; **t. pole/wire** poteau *m*/fil *m* télégraphique
  2 *vt* télégraphier

telegraphic [telɪ'græfɪk] *adj* télégraphique

telemarketing [telɪ'mɑ:kɪtɪŋ] *n* télémarketing *m*

telepathic [telɪ'pæθɪk] *adj* télépathique

telepathy [tɪ'lepəθɪ] *n* télépathie *f*

telephone ['telɪfəʊn] **1** *n* téléphone *m*; **to be on the t.** *(talking)* être au téléphone; *(have a telephone)* avoir le téléphone; *Com* **t. banking** opérations *fpl* bancaires par téléphone, banque *f* à domicile; **t. bill** facture *f* de téléphone; **t. box** cabine *f* téléphonique; **t. call** appel *m* téléphonique, coup *m* de téléphone; **t. directory** *or* **book** annuaire *m* (téléphonique); **t. exchange** central *m* téléphonique; **t. number** numéro *m* de téléphone
  2 *vt* téléphoner à
  3 *vi* téléphoner

telephonist [tɪ'lefənɪst] *n Br* téléphoniste *mf*

telephoto lens ['telɪfəʊtəʊlenz] *n* téléobjectif *m*

teleportation [telɪpɔ:'teɪʃən] *n* téléportation *f*

teleprinter ['telɪprɪntə(r)] *n* téléimprimeur *m*

telesales ['telɪseɪlz] *npl Com* téléventes *fpl*

telescope ['telɪskəʊp] *n* télescope *m*

telescopic [telɪs'kɒpɪk] *adj* télescopique; **t. sight** *(of rifle)* lunette *f*

teleshopping ['telɪʃɒpɪŋ] *n* téléachat *m*

teletext ['telɪtekst] *n* Télétexte® *m*

televangelist [telɪ'vændʒəlɪst] *n* = évangéliste qui prêche à la télévision

televise ['telɪvaɪz] *vt* téléviser

television [telɪ'vɪʒən] *n* télévision *f*; **on t.** à la télévision; **t. camera** caméra *f* de télévision; *Br* **t. licence** redevance *f* télévision; **t. programme** émission *f* de télévision; **t. screen** écran *m* de télévision; **t. set** téléviseur *m*, poste *m* de télévision

teleworker ['telɪwɜ:kə(r)] *n* télétravailleur(euse) *m,f*

teleworking ['telɪwɜ:kɪŋ] *n* télétravail *m*

telex ['teleks] **1** *n* télex *m*
  2 *vt (message)* télexer

tell [tel] *(pt & pp* **told** [təʊld]*)* **1** *vt* (**a**) *(say)* dire; *(story, joke)* raconter; **to t. sb sth, to t. sth to sb** dire qch à qn; **to t. the truth/a lie** dire la vérité/un mensonge; **to t. you the truth, I don't know** je t'avouerai que je ne sais pas; **can you t. me the way to the station? I told you so!** est-ce que vous pouvez m'indiquer la gare?; **I told you so!** je te l'avais bien dit!; **you're telling me!** à

qui le dis-tu!; **let me t. you, I was frightened** laisse-moi te dire que j'ai eu peur!; **to t. the time** *(of clock)* donner l'heure; **to t. sb the time** *(of person)* donner l'heure à qn; **he can't t. the time** il ne sait pas lire l'heure **(b)** *(discern)* **I could t. he was lying** je savais qu'il mentait; **you can t. she's lived abroad** ça se voit qu'elle a vécu à l'étranger; **there's no telling what she'll do next** qui sait ce qu'elle va inventer maintenant **(c)** *(distinguish)* **to t. sth from sth** distinguer qch de qch; **to t. two people/things apart** distinguer deux personnes/choses; **to t. right from wrong** discerner le bien du mal; **I can't t. the difference** je ne vois pas la différence **(d)** *(order)* **to t. sb to do sth** dire à qn de faire qch; **do as you're told!** fais ce qu'on te dit!; **I'm not asking you, I'm telling you!** ce n'est pas une question, c'est un ordre!; **he wouldn't be told** il refusait d'écouter ce qu'on lui disait **(e)** *Pol (votes)* compter; **all told** au total
  2 *vi* **(a)** *(say)* dire; **that would be telling!** je ne veux pas cafarder! **(b)** *(discern)* dire; **it's difficult** *or* **hard to t.** c'est difficile à dire; **it's too early to t.** il est trop tôt pour se prononcer; **you never can t.** on ne sait jamais **(c)** *(have effect)* se faire sentir
▸**tell off** *vt sep (scold)* **to t. sb off** disputer qn
▸**tell on** *vt insep Fam (inform on)* dénoncer, balancer
teller ['telə(r)] *n* **(a)** *(of votes)* scrutateur(trice) *m,f* **(b)** *(in bank)* guichetier(ère) *m,f*
telling ['telɪŋ] **1** *n* **(a)** *(of story)* narration *f* **(b)** **t. off** réprimande *f*; **to give sb a t. off** disputer qn
  2 *adj* **(a)** *(revealing)* révélateur(trice) **(b)** *(decisive)* qui porte
telltale ['telteɪl] **1** *n (person)* rapporteur(euse) *m,f*
  2 *adj (revealing)* révélateur(trice)
telly ['telɪ] *(pl* **tellies**) *n Br Fam* télé *f*; **on t.** à la télé; **t. addict** accro *mf* de la télé
temerity [tɪ'merɪtɪ] *n* témérité *f*, audace *f*; **to have the t. to do sth** avoir l'audace de faire qch
temp [temp] *Fam* **1** *n* intérimaire *mf*; **to be a t.** faire de l'intérim
  2 *vi* faire de l'intérim
temper ['tempə(r)] **1** *n (character)* caractère *m*, tempérament *m*; *(mood)* humeur *f*; *(bad mood)* mauvaise humeur *f*; **to be in a good/bad t.** être de bonne/mauvaise humeur; **to have a short t.** être coléreux(euse); **to lose one's t.** se mettre en colère; **to fly into a t.** piquer une colère; *Fam* **t., t.!** on se calme!; **t. tantrum** caprice *m*
  2 *vt* **(a)** *(steel)* tremper **(b)** *(action)* tempérer
temperament ['tempərəmənt] *n* tempérament *m*, caractère *m*
temperamental [tempərə'mentəl] *adj* capricieux(euse)
temperance ['tempərəns] *n* **(a)** *(moderation)* modération *f* **(b)** *(abstinence from alcohol)* tempérance *f*; *Hist* **t. movement** mouvement *m* antialcoolique
temperate ['tempərət] *adj* **(a)** *Geog (climate, zone)* tempéré(e) **(b)** *Formal (language, criticism)* mesuré(e)
temperature ['tempərətʃə(r)] *n* température *f*; **to take sb's t.** prendre la température de qn; **to have a t.** avoir de la température
tempered ['tempəd] *adj (steel)* trempé(e)
tempest ['tempɪst] *n Lit* tempête *f*
tempestuous [tem'pestjʊəs] *adj* tempétueux(euse)
tempi ['tempi:] *pl of* **tempo**
temping ['tempɪŋ] *n* intérim *m*; **to do t.** faire de l'intérim; **t. agency** société *f* d'intérim
template ['templeɪt] *n* gabarit *m*; *Comput* modèle *m*

temple¹ ['tempəl] *n (place of worship)* temple *m*
temple² *n (side of head)* tempe *f*
tempo ['tempəʊ] *(pl* **tempos** *or* **tempi** ['tempi:]) *n Mus* tempo *m*
temporal ['tempərəl] *adj* temporel(elle)
temporarily [tempə'reərɪlɪ] *adv* temporairement
temporary ['tempərərɪ] *adj (accommodation, solution)* temporaire, provisoire; *(employment)* temporaire, intérimaire; *(improvement)* passager(ère)
tempt [tem(p)t] *vt* tenter; **to t. sb to do sth** inciter qn à faire qch; **to be tempted to do sth** être tenté(e) de faire qch; **to t. fate** tenter le diable
temptation [tem(p)'teɪʃən] *n* tentation *f*
tempting ['tem(p)tɪŋ] *adj* tentant(e)
temptress ['tem(p)trɪs] *n Lit* tentatrice *f*
ten [ten] **1** *n* **(a)** dix *m inv* **(b)** *(idioms)* **they're t. a penny** on en trouve à la pelle; **t. to one he'll find out** je te parie qu'il finira par le savoir
  2 *adj* dix; **theT. Commandments** les dix commandements; *see also* **eight**
tenable ['tenəbəl] *adj* défendable
tenacious [te'neɪʃəs] *adj* tenace
tenacity [te'næsɪtɪ] *n* ténacité *f*
tenancy ['tenənsɪ] *(pl* **tenancies**) *n* location *f*; **t. agreement** bail *m* (de location)
tenant ['tenənt] *n* locataire *mf*
tend¹ *vt (look after)* s'occuper de
tend² *vi* pencher *(towards* vers); **to t. to do sth** avoir tendance à faire qch
▸**tend to** *vt insep (look after)* s'occuper de
tendency ['tendənsɪ] *(pl* **tendencies**) *n* tendance *f* *(towards* à); **to have a t. to do sth** avoir tendance à faire qch
tendentious [ten'denʃəs] *adj Formal* tendancieux(euse)
tender¹ *adj* **(a)** *(affectionate)* tendre **(b)** *(sore)* sensible **(c)** *(meat)* tendre **(d)** *(young)* **at the t. age of...** dès l'âge de...
tender² **1** *n Com (bid)* offre *f*, soumission *f*; **to make** *or* **put in a t.** soumissionner
  2 *vt (services, money)* offrir; *(resignation)* donner; *(apology)* présenter
  3 *vi Com* **to t. for a contract** soumissionner à un appel d'offres
tenderhearted [tendə'hɑːtɪd] *adj* au cœur tendre
tenderly ['tendəlɪ] *adv* tendrement
tenderness ['tendənɪs] *n* **(a)** *(affection)* tendresse *f* **(b)** *(soreness)* sensibilité *f* **(c)** *(of meat)* tendreté *f*
tendon ['tendən] *n* tendon *m*
tendril ['tendrɪl] *n* vrille *f*
tenement ['tenɪmənt] *n* immeuble *m*
tenet ['tenət] *n (principle)* dogme *m*; *(belief)* croyance *f*
tenfold ['tenfəʊld] **1** *adj* décuple
  2 *adv* dix fois plus; **to increase t.** être multiplié(e) par dix
tenner ['tenə(r)] *n Br Fam (sum)* dix livres *fpl*; *(note)* billet *m* de dix livres
tennis ['tenɪs] *n* tennis *m*; **t. ball** balle *f* de tennis; **t. club** club *m* de tennis; **t. court** court *m* de tennis; **t. elbow** tennis-elbow *m*; **t. player** joueur(euse) *m,f* de tennis; **t. racquet** *or* **racket** raquette *f* de tennis; **t. shoe** (chaussure *f* de) tennis *m ou f*
tenor ['tenə(r)] *n* **(a)** *(singer)* ténor *m*; **t. saxophone** saxophone *m* ténor **(b)** *Formal (content, sense)* teneur *f*
tenpin bowling ['tenpɪn'bəʊlɪŋ] *n* bowling *m* *(jeu)*

tense¹ [tens] *n Gram* temps *m*

tense² **1** *adj (cord, person, situation)* tendu(e); *(voice)* étranglé(e); *(muscle)* contracté(e)

  2 *vt (cord)* tendre; *(muscle)* contracter; **to t. oneself** se raidir

  3 *vi* se tendre, se raidir

►**tense up** *vi* se crisper

tensely ['tenslɪ] *adv* nerveusement

tension ['tenʃən] *n* tension *f*

tent [tent] *n* tente *f*; **t. peg** piquet *m* de tente; **t. pole** mât *m* de tente

tentacle ['tentəkəl] *n* tentacule *m*

tentative ['tentətɪv] *adj (hesitant)* hésitant(e), timide; *(provisional)* provisoire

tentatively ['tentətɪvlɪ] *adv (hesitantly)* timidement; *(provisionally)* provisoirement

tenterhooks ['tentəhʊks] *npl* **to be on t.** être sur des charbons ardents; **to keep sb on t.** mettre qn au supplice

tenth [tenθ] **1** *n* (**a**) *(fraction)* dixième *m* (**b**) *(in series)* dixième *mf* (**c**) *(of month)* dix *m inv*

  2 *adj* dixième; *see also* **eighth**

tenuous ['tenjʊəs] *adj (connection)* ténu(e); *(comparison)* subtil(e); *(argument)* faible

tenure ['tenjə(r)] *n (of land)* fermage *m*; *(of office)* occupation *f*; *(of university teaching job)* titularisation *f*

tepid ['tepɪd] *adj also Fig* tiède

tequila [tɪ'ki:lə] *n* tequila *f*

term [tɜːm] **1** *n* (**a**) *(word, expression)* terme *m*; **I told her in no uncertain terms** je le lui ai dit carrément (**b**) **to be on good/bad terms (with sb)** *(relations)* être en bons/mauvais termes (avec qn); **to be on friendly terms with sb** avoir des relations amicales avec qn; **to be on speaking terms** *(of two people)* se parler; **to come to terms with sth** accepter qch; **in financial/international terms** sur le plan *ou* d'un point de vue financier/international; **in terms of** en ce qui concerne, du point de vue de; **I was thinking more in terms of a Jaguar** je pensais plutôt à une Jaguar (**c**) *Com* **terms** *(conditions)* conditions *fpl*; *(of contract)* termes *mpl*; **terms and conditions apply** sujet à conditions; **terms of reference** *(of commission)* attributions *fpl*; **terms of payment** conditions *fpl* de paiement (**d**) *(at school, university)* trimestre *m*; **t. of office** *(of politician)* mandat *m*; **t. of imprisonment** peine *f* de prison; **in the long/short t.** à long/court terme; **to have reached (full) t.** *(of pregnancy)* arriver à terme

  2 *vt* appeler

terminal ['tɜːmɪnəl] **1** *n* (**a**) *(of battery)* pôle *m*, borne *f* (**b**) *(rail, bus)* terminus *m*; *(at airport)* terminal *m* (**c**) *Comput* terminal *m*

  2 *adj* terminal(e); *(illness)* en phase terminale

terminally ['tɜːmɪnəlɪ] *adv* **to be t. ill** être condamné(e)

terminate ['tɜːmɪneɪt] **1** *vt* (**a**) *(employment, project)* mettre fin à; *(contract)* résilier (**b**) *(pregnancy)* interrompre

  2 *vi* (**a**) *(of contract)* prendre fin (**b**) *(of bus, train)* aller jusqu'à

termination [tɜːmɪ'neɪʃən] *n* (**a**) *(of employment, project)* fin *f*; *(of contract)* résiliation *f* (**b**) **t. (of pregnancy)** interruption *f* de grossesse

termini ['tɜːmɪnaɪ] *pl of* **terminus**

terminology [tɜːmɪ'nɒlədʒɪ] *n* terminologie *f*

terminus ['tɜːmɪnəs] *(pl* **terminuses** *or* **termini** ['tɜːmɪnaɪ]) *n* terminus *m*

termite ['tɜːmaɪt] *n* termite *m*

tern [tɜːn] *n* sterne *f*

Terr *abbr* **Terrace**

terrace ['terɪs] *n* (**a**) *(beside house, on hillside)* terrasse *f* (**b**) *Br* **the terraces** *(in football ground)* les gradins *mpl* (**c**) *Br (of houses)* = rangée de maisons attenantes

Terrace

Ce mot désigne une rangée de maisons à un ou deux étages. À l'origine, les "terraced houses" étaient surtout des logements ouvriers (équivalents des corons) construits à proximité d'usines ou de mines de charbon.

terraced ['terɪst] *adj* (**a**) *(hillside)* en terrasses (**b**) *Br* **t. house** = maison située dans une rangée d'habitations attenantes

terracotta ['terə'kɒtə] *n* terre *f* cuite

terrain [tə'reɪn] *n* terrain *m*

terrapin ['terəpɪn] *n* tortue *f* d'eau douce

terrestrial [tɪ'restrɪəl] *adj* terrestre; **t. broadcasting, t. television** diffusion *f* hertzienne *ou* terrestre

terrible ['terɪbəl] *adj (shocking)* terrible; *(of poor quality)* épouvantable

terribly ['terɪblɪ] *adv* (**a**) *(badly)* affreusement mal; *(injured)* très gravement (**b**) *Fam (very)* extrêmement

terrier ['terɪə(r)] *n (dog)* terrier *m*; *Fig* **he's a real t.** il n'abandonne jamais

terrific [tə'rɪfɪk] *adj Fam* (**a**) *(excellent)* super *inv* (**b**) *(enormous)* incroyable

terrifically [tə'rɪfɪklɪ] *adv Fam (very)* extrêmement

terrified ['terɪfaɪd] *adj* terrifié(e); **to be t. of** avoir une peur bleue de

terrify ['terɪfaɪ] *(pt & pp* **terrified)** *vt* terrifier

terrifying ['terɪfaɪɪŋ] *adj* terrifiant(e)

territorial [terɪ'tɔːrɪəl] *adj* territorial(e); *(animal)* qui défend son territoire; *Br Mil* **the T. Army** = armée de réserve, constituée de volontaires; **t. waters** eaux *fpl* territoriales

territory ['terɪtərɪ] *(pl* **territories)** *n* territoire *m*; *Fig (area of activity)* domaine *m*

terror ['terə(r)] *n* terreur *f*; **reign of t.** régime *m* de terreur; *Fam* **that child is a t.** cet enfant est une vraie terreur

terrorism ['terərɪzəm] *n* terrorisme *m*

terrorist ['terərɪst] **1** *n* terroriste *mf*

  2 *adj* terroriste

terrorize ['terəraɪz] *vt* terroriser

terror-stricken ['terəstrɪkən] *adj* terrorisé(e)

terse [tɜːs] *adj (person, reply)* sec (sèche); *(style, prose)* concis(e)

terseness ['tɜːsnɪs] *n (of person, reply)* brusquerie *f*; *(of style, prose)* concision *f*

tertiary ['tɜːʃərɪ] *adj* tertiaire; **t. education** enseignement *m* supérieur

TESL ['tesəl] *n (abbr* **Teaching of English as a Second Language)** enseignement *m* de l'anglais deuxième langue

TESOL ['ti:səl] *n (abbr* **Teaching of English to Speakers of Other Languages)** enseignement *m* de l'anglais langue étrangère

test [test] **1** *n* (**a**) *(trial, check)* test *m*; **to put sb/sth to the t.** mettre qn/qch à l'épreuve; **to pass the t.** se montrer à la hauteur; **to stand the t. of time** résister à l'épreuve du temps; **t. ban** interdiction *f* des essais nucléaires; *Law* **t. case** affaire *f* qui fait jurisprudence;

t. drive essai *m* sur route; **t. flight** vol *m* d'essai; **t. pilot** pilote *m* d'essai; **t. tube** tube *m* à essai, éprouvette *f*; **t. tube baby** bébé-éprouvette *m* (**b**) *(examination)* examen *m*; **(driving) t.** examen *m* du permis de conduire; **French/maths t.** examen *m* de français/maths (**c**) *(in cricket, rugby)* **t. (match)** match *m* international
2 *vt* (**a**) *(examine) (pupil)* interroger (**on** sur); *(sight, hearing)* examiner; **to t. sb's knowledge** tester les connaissances de qn; **to t. sb for Aids** faire subir à qn le test de dépistage du sida (**b**) *(try out)* tester, mettre à l'épreuve
3 *vi* **to t. for Aids** faire un test de dépistage du sida; **to t. positive/negative** *(for drugs)* être positif(ive)/négatif(ive); *(for Aids)* être séropositif(ive)/séronégatif(ive)
▶**test out** *vt sep* tester
testament ['testəmənt] *n* (**a**) *Law (will)* testament *m* (**b**) *(tribute)* preuve *f* (**to** de)
test-bed ['testbed] *n* banc *m* d'essai
test-drive ['testdraɪv] *vt* essayer
testes ['testiːz] *pl of* **testis**
testicle ['testɪkəl] *n* testicule *m*
testify ['testɪfaɪ] *(pt & pp* **testified)** *Law* **1** *vt* **to t. that...** attester que...
2 *vi* témoigner (**for/against** en faveur de/contre); *Fig* **to t. to sth** *(be proof of)* témoigner de qch
testily ['testɪlɪ] *adv* d'un ton irrité
testimonial [testɪ'məʊnɪəl] *n* (**a**) *(character reference)* références *fpl* (**b**) *(in football)* **t. (match)** = match en l'honneur d'un footballeur
testimony ['testɪmənɪ] *(pl* **testimonies)** *n* *Law* témoignage *m*, déposition *f*; *Fig* **to be a t. to sth** *(proof of)* témoigner de qch
testing ['testɪŋ] **1** *n* essai *m*; **t. ground** terrain *m* d'essai
2 *adj* éprouvant(e)
testis ['testɪs] *(pl* **testes** ['testiːz]) *n* testicule *m*
testosterone [tes'tɒstərəʊn] *n* testostérone *f*
testy ['testɪ] *adj (person, mood)* irritable; *(tone, manner)* irrité(e)
tetanus ['tetənəs] *n* tétanos *m*
tetchy ['tetʃɪ] *adj Fam* irritable
tether ['teðə(r)] **1** *n (for tying animal)* longe *f*; *Fig* **to be at the end of one's t.** être à bout
2 *vt (animal)* attacher
Texan ['teksən] **1** *n* Texan(e) *m,f*
2 *adj* texan(e)
Texas ['teksəs] *n* le Texas
Tex-Mex [teks'meks] *adj* tex-mex *inv*
text [tekst] **1** *n* texte *f*; *Comput* **t. editor** éditeur *m* de texte; *Tel* **t. message** SMS *m*, texto *m*
2 *vt (send text message to)* envoyer un SMS *ou* un texto à
textbook ['tekstbʊk] *n* manuel *m*; *Fig* **a t. example (of)** un parfait exemple (de)
textile ['tekstaɪl] **1** *n* textile *m*
2 *adj* textile
textual ['tekstjʊəl] *adj* de texte
texture ['tekstʃə(r)] *n* texture *f*
Thai [taɪ] **1** *n* (**a**) *(person)* Thaïlandais(e) *m,f* (**b**) *(language)* thaï *m*
2 *adj* thaïlandais(e)
Thailand ['taɪlænd] *n* la Thaïlande
Thames [temz] *n* **the T.** la Tamise
than [ðæn, *unstressed* ðən] *conj* que; **he's taller t. me** il est plus grand que moi; **he was taller t. I had expected** il était plus grand que je (ne) l'imaginais;

more/less t. ten plus/moins de dix; **more t. once** plus d'une fois
thank [θæŋk] *vt* remercier; **to t. sb for sth/for doing sth** remercier qn pour qch/d'avoir fait qch; **t. God!** Dieu merci!; **t. you** merci; **t. you very much** merci beaucoup; **no, t. you** non merci; **t. you for coming** merci d'être venu; *Ironic* **I'll t. you to mind your own business!** je te prierai de te mêler de tes affaires!; *also Ironic* **we have Mike to t. for this** c'est à Mike que nous devons cela
thankful ['θæŋkfʊl] *adj* reconnaissant(e) (**for** de); **to be t. that...** être heureux(euse) que...
thankfully ['θæŋkfəlɪ] *adv* (**a**) *(gratefully)* avec gratitude (**b**) *(fortunately)* heureusement
thankless ['θæŋklɪs] *adj* ingrat(e)
thanks [θæŋks] **1** *npl* remerciements *mpl*; **t. to** *(because of)* grâce à; **no t. to you/them!** ce n'est pas grâce à toi/eux!
2 *exclam Fam* **t.!** merci!; *Fam* **no t.** non merci; **t. for coming/your letter** merci d'être venu/pour ta lettre; *Fam Ironic* **t. for nothing!** je te remercie!
thanksgiving [θæŋks'gɪvɪŋ] *n* action *f* de grâces; *Am* **T. (Day)** = 4ème jeudi de novembre, fête commémorant la première action de grâce des colons anglais

Thanksgiving

Aux États-Unis, "Thanksgiving" commémore, le quatrième jeudi de novembre, l'installation des premiers colons en Amérique. Ceux-ci remercièrent Dieu de leur avoir permis de survivre dans des conditions difficiles et primitives. Le dîner en famille qui a généralement lieu à cette occasion est traditionnellement composé d'une dinde servie avec une sauce aux airelles accompagnée de patates douces, et se termine par une tarte au potiron.

thank you ['θæŋkjʊ] *n* merci *m*, remerciement *m*; **to say t. to sb** dire merci à qn, remercier qn; **t. letter** lettre *f* de remerciement
that [ðæt] **1** *demonstrative pron (pl* **those** [ðəʊz]) (**a**) *(subject)* ce, cela, ça *(in more informal contexts)*; *(object)* cela, ça *(in more informal contexts)*; **who's t.?** qui est-ce?; **what's t.?** qu'est-ce que c'est?; **t.'s strange** c'est bizarre; **t.'s what she told me** c'est ce qu'elle m'a dit; **is t. all the luggage you're taking?** c'est tout ce que vous prenez comme bagages?; **t.'s where he lives** c'est là qu'il habite; **can you run as fast as t.?** tu peux courir aussi vite que ça?; **t.'s it!** c'est ça!; **and t.'s t.!** un point, c'est tout! (**b**) *(as opposed to* **this**) celui-là (celle-là) *m,f*; **in a case like t.** dans un cas comme celui-là
2 *demonstrative adj (pl* **those**) (**a**) *(indicating person, thing)* ce (cette); **t. book** ce livre; **t. question** cette question; **t. man** cet homme (**b**) *(as opposed to* **this**) ce...-là (cette...-là); **I prefer t. film** je préfère ce film-là; **take t. cup** prends cette tasse-là; **t. one** celui-là (celle-là)
3 *adv* **t. high/big** haut(e)/grand(e) comme ça; **I tasted it but it wasn't t. good** j'y ai goûté mais ce n'était pas si bon que ça; **I've never seen one t. good** je n'en ai jamais vu d'aussi bon que ça; **he's t. stupid he...** il est tellement stupide qu'il...
4 *[unstressed* ðət] *relative pron*

On peut omettre le pronom relatif **that** sauf s'il est en position sujet.

(**a**) *(subject)* qui; *(object)* que; **the letter t. came yesterday** la lettre qui est arrivée hier; **the woman t. I saw** la femme que j'ai vue (**b**) *(with preposition)* **the person t. I gave it to** la personne à qui je l'ai donné; **the woman t. we're talking about** la femme dont nous parlons; **the room t. he's sleeping in** la chambre où il dort (**c**) *(when)* où; **the day t. you arrived** le jour où tu es arrivé
5 *[unstressed ðət] conj*

Sauf dans la langue soutenue, la conjonction **that** est souvent omise.

que; **she said t. she would come** elle a dit qu'elle viendrait

thatch [θætʃ] **1** *n (on roof)* chaume *m*; *Fam (of hair)* tignasse *f*
2 *vt (roof)* couvrir de chaume; **thatched cottage** chaumière *f*; **thatched roof** toit *m* de chaume

thaw [θɔː] **1** *n also Fig* dégel *m*
2 *vt (snow, ice)* faire fondre; *(food)* décongeler
3 *vi (of snow, ice)* fondre; *(of food)* se décongeler; *Fig (of person)* se dérider
▸**thaw out** *vi (of lake)* dégeler; *(of food)* se décongeler; *Fig (of person)* se dérider

the *[before consonant sounds ðə, before vowel sounds ðɪ, stressed ðiː] definite art* (**a**) *(singular)* le (la); *(plural)* les; **t. pen** le stylo; **t. house** la maison; **t. airport** l'aéroport; **in t. summer** *(this summer)* cet été; *(every summer)* l'été; **to have t. measles/flu** avoir la rougeole/la grippe; **at t. time** à ce moment-là; **t. Europe of today** l'Europe d'aujourd'hui; *Fam* **how's t. knee?** et ce genou? (**b**) *(denoting concept, group)* **t. poor/blind** les pauvres/aveugles; **t. Wilsons** les Wilson; **t. supernatural** le surnaturel (**c**) *(with titles)* **Edward t. Eighth** Édouard VIII; **Alexander t. Great** Alexandre le Grand; **Catherine t. Great** la Grande Catherine (**d**) *(with proportions, rates)* **to be paid by t. hour** être payé(e) à l'heure; **15 kilometres to t.** litre 15 kilomètres au litre (**e**) *(in exclamations)* **t. arrogance/stupidity of it!** quelle arrogance/stupidité! (**f**) *[stressed ðiː]* **not THE Professor Branestorm?** pas le célèbre professeur Branestorm?; **it's THE destination this summer** c'est LA destination de cet été (**g**) *(in comparisons)* **t. more I see him, t. more I like him** plus je le vois, plus il me plaît; **t. more I see him, t. less I like him** plus je le vois, moins je l'apprécie; **t. sooner t. better** le plus tôt sera le mieux (**h**) *(with dates)* **t. sixties** les années soixante; **t. eighteen hundreds** le dix-neuvième siècle

theatre, *Am* **theater** [ˈθɪətə(r)] *n* (**a**) *(drama, building)* théâtre *m*; **t. company** compagnie *f* théâtrale, troupe *f* de théâtre (**b**) *Br* **(operating) t.** salle *f* d'opération (**c**) *(area)* **t. of war** théâtre *m* des hostilités

theatre-goer, *Am* **theater-goer** [ˈθɪətəgəʊə(r)] *n* amateur(trice) *m,f* de théâtre

theatrical [θɪˈætrɪkəl] *adj also Fig* théâtral(e); **t. company** compagnie *f* théâtrale, troupe *f* de théâtre

thee [ðiː] *pron Lit or Rel* te; *(after preposition)* toi

theft [θeft] *n* vol *m*

theftproof [ˈθeftpruːf] *adj (lock)* antivol *inv*; *(vehicle)* muni(e) d'un dispositif antivol

their [ˈðeə(r)] *possessive adj* (**a**) *(singular)* leur; *(plural)* leurs; **t. job** leur travail; **t. wives** leurs femmes; **it wasn't THEIR idea!** ce n'est pas eux qui en ont eu l'idée! (**b**) *(for parts of body)* **they hit t. heads** ils se sont

cogné la tête (**c**) *(indefinite use)* **someone's left t. umbrella** quelqu'un a oublié son parapluie

theirs [ðeəz] *possessive pron* (**a**) *(singular)* le leur (la leur) *m,f*; *(plural)* les leurs; **our house is big, but t. is bigger** notre maison est grande, mais la leur est plus grande encore (**b**) *(used attributively)* **this book is t.** ce livre est à eux/à elles; **a friend of t.** un de leurs amis; **where's that brother of t.?** où leur frère a-t-il bien pu passer? (**c**) *(indefinite use)* **if anyone hasn't got t. they can use mine** si quelqu'un n'a pas le sien, il pourra utiliser le mien

theism [ˈθiːɪzəm] *n Rel* théisme *m*

them [ðem, *unstressed* ðəm] *pron* (**a**) *(direct object)* les; **I hate t.** je les déteste; **I can understand their son but not THEM** je comprends leur fils, mais eux, je ne les comprends pas (**b**) *(indirect object)* leur; **I gave t. the book** je leur ai donné le livre; **I gave it to t.** je le leur ai donné (**c**) *(after preposition)* eux/elles *mpl,fpl*; **I'm thinking of t.** je pense à eux/elles (**d**) *(as complement of verb* **to be)** eux (elles) *mpl,fpl*; **it's t.!** ce sont eux/elles!; **it was t. who did it** c'est eux/elles qui l'ont fait (**e**) *(indefinite use)* **if anyone comes, tell t....** si quelqu'un vient, dis-lui...

thematic [θɪˈmætɪk] *adj* thématique

theme [θiːm] *n* thème *m*; **t. bar** bar *m* à thème; **t. park** parc *m* à thème; **t. restaurant** restaurant *m* à thème; **t. song** *or* **tune** chanson *f* du générique

themselves [ðəmˈselvz, *stressed* ðemˈselvz] *pron* (**a**) *(reflexive)* **they hurt t.** ils se sont blessés (**b**) *(emphatic)* eux-mêmes (elles-mêmes) *mpl,fpl*; **they t. have never...** eux-mêmes/elles-mêmes n'ont jamais...; **they told me t.** ils me l'ont dit eux-mêmes; **they're not t. today** ils ne sont pas dans leur état normal aujourd'hui (**c**) *(after preposition)* **they live by t.** ils vivent seuls; **they bought it for t.** ils se le sont acheté; **they talk to t.** ils parlent tout seuls

then [ðen] **1** *adv* (**a**) *(at that time)* alors, à ce moment-là; **since t.** depuis (ce moment-là), depuis (lors); **until t.** *(in future)* jusque-là; *(in past)* jusqu'à ce moment-là; **by t.** *(in future)* d'ici là; *(in past)* entre-temps; **there and t.,** *and* **there** sur-le-champ (**b**) *(next)* ensuite, puis; **what t.?** et alors, qu'est-ce qui va se passer? (**c**) *(in that case)* alors; **if it rains, t. we get wet** s'il pleut, alors on va se mouiller (**d**) *(therefore)* donc; **you already knew, t.?** donc, tu le savais déjà?
2 *adj* **the t. President** le Président de l'époque

thence [ðens] *adv Formal* de là

theologian [θiːəˈləʊdʒ(ɪ)ən] *n* théologien(enne) *m,f*

theological [θiːəˈlɒdʒɪkəl] *adj* théologique

theology [θiːˈɒlədʒɪ] *n* théologie *f*

theorem [ˈθɪərəm] *n* théorème *m*

theoretical [θiːəˈretɪkəl] *adj* théorique

theoretically [θiːəˈretɪklɪ] *adv* théoriquement

theoretician [θiːərɪˈtɪʃən] *n* théoricien(enne) *m,f*

theorist [ˈθiːərɪst] *n* théoricien(enne) *m,f*

theorize [ˈθiːəraɪz] *vi* théoriser (**about** sur)

theory [ˈθɪərɪ] *n* théorie *f*; **in t.** en théorie

therapeutic [θerəˈpjuːtɪk] *adj also Fig* thérapeutique; *Med* **t. cloning** clonage *m* thérapeutique

therapist [ˈθerəpɪst] *n* thérapeute *mf*

therapy [ˈθerəpɪ] *n (pl* **therapies)** *n* thérapie *f*

there [ðeə(r), *unstressed* ðə(r)] **1** *pron* **t. is/are** il y a; **t. was/were** il y avait; **t.'s somebody at the door** il y a quelqu'un à la porte; **t. isn't/aren't any** il n'y en a pas; **t. are** *or Fam* **t.'s two left** il (en) reste deux; **t.'s a page missing** il manque une page; **t. comes a time...** il arrive un moment où...

2 *adv* (**a**) *(in that place)* là; *(over there)* là-bas; **he isn't t.** il n'est pas là; **the weather's nice t.** il fait beau là-bas; **I'm going t. tomorrow** j'y vais demain; **give me that book t.** donne-moi ce livre-là; **do we have time to get t. and back?** avons-nous le temps d'y aller et de revenir?; **t. it is!** le voilà!; **t. you are!** *(I was looking for you)* te voilà!; *(when handing over something)* voilà!; *(expressing triumph, satisfaction)* tu vois!; **t. and then, then and t.** sur-le-champ; *Fam* **he's not all t.** il n'a pas toute sa tête (**b**) *(at that point)* là; **t.'s the difficulty** voilà la difficulté; **we'll stop t. for today** nous nous arrêterons là pour aujourd'hui; *Fam* **you've got me t.!** alors là, vous me posez une colle!
3 *exclam* voilà!; **t., t.!** allons, allons!; **t., I told you so!** et voilà, je te l'avais bien dit!; **t. now, that wasn't so bad!** voilà, ce n'était pas si terrible!
thereabouts ['ðeərə'baʊts] *adv* (**a**) *(with place)* dans les environs; **he's from Stirling or t.** il est de Stirling, ou quelque part par là (**b**) *(with number, quantity, distance)* environ, à peu près; **it costs £500 or t.** ça coûte environ *ou* à peu près 500 livres
thereafter [ðeər'ɑ:ftə(r)] *adv Formal* après cela, par la suite
thereby ['ðeəbaɪ] *adv Formal* ainsi; **t. hangs a tale!** c'est une longue histoire!
therefore ['ðeəfɔ:(r)] *adv* donc
thereupon [ðeərə'pɒn] *adv Formal* sur ce
thermal ['θɜ:məl] **1** *n Met* ascendance *f* thermique
2 *adj* thermique; **t. energy** énergie *f* thermique; **t. springs** sources *fpl* thermales; **t. underwear** sous-vêtements *mpl* en Thermolactyl®
thermodynamics [θɜ:məʊdaɪ'næmɪks] *n* thermodynamique *f*
thermoelectric [θɜ:məʊɪ'lektrɪk] *adj* thermoélectrique
thermometer [θə'mɒmɪtə(r)] *n* thermomètre *m*
Thermos® ['θɜ:məs] *n* **T. (flask)** (bouteille *f*) Thermos® *m ou f*
thermostat ['θɜ:məstæt] *n* thermostat *m*
thesaurus [θɪ'sɔ:rəs] *(pl* **thesauruses** *or* **thesauri** [θɪ'sɔ:raɪ]*) n* dictionnaire *m* de synonymes
these [ði:z] **1** *demonstrative pron* ceux-ci (celles-ci) *mpl,fpl*; **in cases like t.** dans des cas comme ceux-ci; **t. are the ones I want** voici ceux que je veux; **t. are my parents** *(introducing)* je te présente mes parents
2 *demonstrative adj* (**a**) *(indicating people or things)* ces; **t. children** ces enfants (**b**) *(as opposed to* **those**) ces...-ci; **I like t. shoes** j'aime bien ces chaussures-ci; **t. ones** ceux-ci (celles-ci) *mpl,fpl*
thesis ['θi:sɪs] *(pl* **theses** ['θi:si:z]*) n* thèse *f*
thespian ['θespɪən] *n Lit or Hum* comédien(enne) *m,f*
they [ðeɪ] *pron* (**a**) *(subject)* ils (elles) *mpl,fpl*; **they're Scottish** *(masculine)* ils sont écossais; *(feminine)* elles sont écossaises; **THEY haven't got it!** ce ne sont pas eux/elles qui l'ont! (**b**) *(indefinite use)* **somebody called – what did t. want?** quelqu'un a appelé – qu'est-ce qu'il voulait?; **t. say that...** on dit que...
they'd [ðeɪd] = **they had, they would**
they'll [ðeɪl] = **they will, they shall**
they're [ðeə(r)] = **they are**
they've [ðeɪv] = **they have**
thick [θɪk] **1** *adj* (**a**) *(in general)* épais(aisse); **to be a metre t.** faire un mètre d'épaisseur; **the air was t. with smoke** l'air était empli d'une épaisse fumée; **the snow was t. on the ground** il y avait une épaisse couche de neige sur le sol; *Fig* **to be t. on the ground**

(plentiful) être légion (**b**) *(voice)* pâteux(euse); *(accent)* fort(e) (**c**) *Fam (stupid)* bouché(e); **to be as t. as two short planks** *or* **as a brick** être bête comme ses pieds (**d**) *(idioms)* **to have a t. skin** ne pas être susceptible; **to give sb a t. ear** donner une gifle à qn; *Fam* **to be as t. as thieves** s'entendre comme larrons en foire
2 *adv* (**a**) *(cut)* en tranches épaisses; *(spread)* en couche épaisse (**b**) *(idioms)* **to come t. and fast** *(of questions, orders)* pleuvoir; *Fam* **to lay it on a bit t.** exagérer
3 *n* **in the t. of the forest** au beau milieu de la forêt; **to be in the t. of it** *or* **things** être au cœur de l'action; **through t. and thin** quoi qu'il arrive
thicken ['θɪkən] **1** *vt* épaissir
2 *vi* s'épaissir; *Hum* **the plot thickens...** les choses se compliquent...
thicket ['θɪkɪt] *n* fourré *m*
thickly ['θɪklɪ] *adv* (**a**) *(cut)* en tranches épaisses; *(spread)* en couche épaisse (**b**) *(populated)* fortement (**c**) *(speak)* d'une voix pâteuse
thickness ['θɪknɪs] *n* épaisseur *f*
thickset ['θɪk'set] *adj* trapu(e)
thick-skinned [θɪk'skɪnd] *adj Fig* peu susceptible
thief [θi:f] *(pl* **thieves** [θi:vz]*) n* voleur(euse) *m,f*
thieve [θi:v] *vt & vi* voler
thieving ['θi:vɪŋ] **1** *n* vol *m*
2 *adj* voleur(euse)
thigh [θaɪ] *n* cuisse *f*
thighbone ['θaɪbəʊn] *n* fémur *m*
thimble ['θɪmbəl] *n* dé *m* à coudre
thin [θɪn] **1** *adj* (**a**) *(person, wall)* mince; *(paper, slice, layer)* fin(e), mince; *(blanket, clothing)* léger(ère); *(book)* peu épais(aisse); **to get thinner** *(of person)* maigrir (**b**) *(sparse) (hair, crowd, vegetation)* clairsemé(e); *(fog, mist)* léger(ère) (**c**) *(soup, sauce)* liquide; *(paint)* dilué(e); *(blood)* appauvri(e) (**d**) *(voice)* grêle (**e**) *(idioms)* **to vanish into t. air** se volatiliser; **to have a t. time (of it)** avoir la vie dure; **to be t. on the ground** être rare; **it's just the t. end of the wedge** ce n'est qu'un début
2 *adv* *(cut)* en tranches fines *ou* minces; *Fig* **our forces/resources are spread very t.** nos forces/ressources sont très éparpillées
3 *vt* *(pt & pp* **thinned**) *(paint)* diluer; *(sauce)* éclaircir
4 *vi* *(of crowd)* s'éclaircir; *(of fog, mist)* se lever; **his hair is thinning** il perd ses cheveux, il se dégarnit
thing [θɪŋ] *n* (**a**) *(action, remark, fact)* chose *f*; **the important t. is that...** l'important, c'est que...; **that's the only t. we can do** c'est tout ce que nous pouvons faire; **that's another t. altogether** c'est une autre affaire; **the t. is,...** le problème, c'est que...; **that was a silly t. to do/say** c'était stupide de faire/dire ça; **for one t.** d'abord; **what with one t. and another** avec tout ce qui s'est passé; **I don't know a t. about algebra** je n'y connais rien en algèbre; **to know a t. or two (about sth)** s'y connaître (en qch); **to take things too seriously** prendre les choses trop au sérieux; **it's just one of those things** ce sont des choses qui arrivent; **things are going well/badly** les choses vont bien/mal; *Fam* **how are things?, how's things?** comment ça va?; **t.** (**b**) *(object)* chose *f*; *Fam* **what's that t.?** qu'est-ce que c'est que ce truc?; *Fam* **where's that spanner t. I was using?** où est cette espèce de clé dont je me suis servi tout à l'heure?; **things** *(belongings)* affaires *fpl* (**c**) *Fam (person)* **you poor t.!** pauvre de toi!; **you lucky t.!** sacré veinard!; **you silly**

t.! espèce d'imbécile! (**d**) *(idioms)* **to have a t. about sb/sth** *(like)* avoir un faible pour qn/qch; *(dislike)* avoir quelque chose contre qn/qch; **to have a t. about tidiness/punctuality** être très à cheval sur la propreté/la ponctualité; **it's not the done t.** ça ne se fait pas; **the latest t. in shoes** la dernière mode en matière de chaussures

thingummy ['θɪŋəmɪ], **thingumajig** ['θɪŋəmɪdʒɪg], **thingumabob** ['θɪŋəmɪbɒb] *n Fam (object)* truc *m*; *(person)* machin(e) *m,f*

think [θɪŋk] **1** *vt (pt & pp* thought [θɔːt]) (**a**) *(have in mind)* **to t. that...** penser que...; **what are you thinking?** à quoi penses-tu?; **to t. evil thoughts** avoir de mauvaises pensées; **to t. to do sth** penser à faire qch (**b**) *(believe, have as opinion)* croire, penser; **he thinks he knows everything** il croit tout savoir; **anyone would t. she was asleep** on jurerait qu'elle dort; **who'd have thought it!** qui l'eût cru!; **what do you t.?** qu'en penses-tu?; **I t. so** je pense (que oui); **I don't t. so, I t. not** je ne pense pas, je pense que non; **I thought so, I thought as much** c'est ce que je pensais; **I should t. so, too!** j'espère bien!; **that's what you t.!** c'est ce que tu crois!; **what do you t. about that idea?** qu'est-ce que tu penses de cette idée? (**c**) *(imagine)* imaginer; **I can't t. why/what/where...** je me demande bien pourquoi/ce que/où...; **t. what we could do with all that money!** imagine ce qu'on pourrait faire avec tout cet argent!; **to t. that he's only twenty!** et dire qu'il n'a que vingt ans

2 *vi* réfléchir, penser; **to t. ahead** voir loin; **to t. aloud** penser tout haut; **to t. long and hard before doing sth** bien réfléchir avant de faire qch; **to t. on one's feet** réagir vite; **it makes you t.** ça fait réfléchir; **you can t. again!** tu te fourres le doigt dans l'œil!

3 *n* **to have a t.** réfléchir; *Fam* **you've got another t. coming!** tu te fourres le doigt dans l'œil!; **t. tank** groupe *m* de réflexion

▸**think about** *vt insep (have in mind, take into account)* penser à; *(consider)* réfléchir à; **to t. about doing sth** songer à faire qch; **it's quite cheap when you t. about it** ça n'est pas très cher quand on y pense; **that will give them something to t. about** voilà qui va leur donner matière à réflexion

▸**think back to** *vt insep* repenser à

▸**think of** *vt insep* (**a**) *(have in mind, take into account)* penser à; **to t. of doing sth** songer à faire qch; **come to t. of it, I** DID **see her that night** maintenant que j'y pense, je l'ai effectivement vue ce soir-là; **where were you thinking of, walking home alone?** qu'est-ce qui t'a pris de rentrer à pied tout seul? (**b**) *(have opinion about)* **what do you t. of this?** qu'est-ce que tu penses de cela?; **to t. well/badly of sb** avoir une bonne/mauvaise opinion de qn; **I don't t. much of the idea** cette idée ne me dit pas grand-chose (**c**) *(recall)* se rappeler; **I can't t. of the right word** le mot m'échappe

▸**think out** *vt sep* réfléchir à

▸**think over** *vt sep* réfléchir à

▸**think through** *vt sep* **to t. sth through** bien réfléchir à qch

▸**think up** *vt sep* imaginer, inventer

thinker ['θɪŋkə(r)] *n* penseur *m*

thinking ['θɪŋkɪŋ] **1** *n* (**a**) *(process of thought)* réflexion *f*; **to do some t.** réfléchir (**b**) *(opinion)* avis *m*, opinion *f*; **to my (way of) t.** à mon avis

2 *adj Br Hum* **the t. man's crumpet** une jolie fille avec quelque chose dans la tête

thinly ['θɪnlɪ] *adv* (**a**) *(cut)* en tranches fines *ou* minces; *(spread)* en couche fine *ou* mince (**b**) *(populated)* faiblement

thinner ['θɪnə(r)] *n* diluant *m*

thinness ['θɪnɪs] *n (of person, wall)* minceur *f*; *(of paper, slice, layer)* finesse *f*; *(of liquid)* fluidité *f*; *(of blanket, clothing)* légèreté *f*

third [θɜːd] **1** *n* (**a**) *(fraction)* tiers *m inv* (**b**) *(in series)* troisième *mf* (**c**) *(of month)* trois *m inv* (**d**) *Mus* tierce *f* (**e**) *Br Univ* **to get a t.** *(in degree)* ≃ avoir sa licence avec mention passable

2 *adj* troisième; **t. degree burns** brûlures *fpl* au troisième degré; *Fam* **to give sb the t. degree** cuisiner qn; *Law* **t. party** tiers *m*, tierce personne *f*; **t. party cover** *(in insurance)* assurance *f* au tiers; **t. rate** *(mediocre)* très mauvais(e); **the T. World** le tiers-monde; *see also* **eighth**

thirdly ['θɜːdlɪ] *adv* troisièmement

thirst [θɜːst] **1** *n* soif *f*; *Fig* **the t. for sth** la soif de qch

2 *vi Fig* être assoiffé(e) (**for** de)

thirsty ['θɜːstɪ] *adj also Fig* assoifé(e); **to be** *or* **feel t.** avoir soif; *Fam* **it's t. work** ça donne soif

thirteen [θɜː'tiːn] **1** *n* treize *m inv*

2 *adj* treize; *see also* **eight**

thirteenth [θɜː'tiːnθ] **1** *n* (**a**) *(fraction)* treizième *m* (**b**) *(in series)* treizième *mf* (**c**) *(of month)* treize *m inv*

2 *adj* treizième; *see also* **eighth**

thirtieth ['θɜːtɪəθ] **1** *n* (**a**) *(fraction)* trentième *m* (**b**) *(in series)* trentième *mf* (**c**) *(of month)* trente *m inv*

2 *adj* trentième; *see also* **eighth**

thirty ['θɜːtɪ] **1** *n* trente *m inv*

2 *adj* trente; *see also* **eighty**

this [ðɪs] **1** *demonstrative pron (pl* these [ðiːz]) (**a**) *(subject)* ce, ceci; *(object)* ceci; **who's t.?** qui est-ce?; **what's t.?** qu'est-ce que c'est?; **t. is ridiculous!** c'est ridicule!; **t. leads me to believe that...** ceci me mène à croire que...; **I do it like t.** je le fais comme ceci; **t. is what she told me** voici ce qu'elle m'a dit; **listen to t.** écoute ça; **t. is Sarah Jervis** *(on telephone)* c'est Sarah Jervis à l'appareil; *(introducing another person)* je te présente Sarah Jervis; *Fam* **to talk about t. and that** parler de choses et d'autres (**b**) *(as opposed to* that) celui-ci (celle-ci) *m,f*; **in a case like t.** dans un cas comme celui-ci

2 *demonstrative adj (pl* these) (**a**) *(indicating person, thing)* ce (cette); **t. book** ce livre; **t. question** cette question; **t. man** cet homme (**b**) *(as opposed to "that")* ce...-ci (cette...-ci); **I prefer t. film** je préfère ce film-ci; **take t. cup** prends cette tasse-ci; **t. one** celui-ci (celle-ci)

3 *adv* **t. high/big** haut(e)/grand(e) comme ça; **I didn't think it would be t. good** je ne pensais pas que ce serait aussi bon; **I've never seen one t. good** je n'en ai jamais vu d'aussi bon que ça; **t. much is certain,...** une chose est sûre,...

thistle ['θɪsəl] *n* chardon *m*

thither ['ðɪðə(r)] *adv Lit* **hither and t.** ça et là

thong [θɒŋ] *n* (**a**) *(underwear, swimwear)* tanga *m*, string *m* (**b**) *(strip of leather)* lanière *f* (**c**) *Am & Austr* **thongs** *(flip-flops)* tongs *fpl*

thorax ['θɔːræks] *n Anat* thorax *m*

thorn [θɔːn] *n* épine *f*; *Fig* **to be a t. in sb's flesh** *or* **side** être une source d'irritation constante pour qn

thorny ['θɔːnɪ] *adj also Fig* épineux(euse)

thorough ['θʌrə] *adj* (**a**) *(search, cleaning, preparation)* minutieux(euse); *(knowledge, examination, revision)* approfondi(e); **to do** *or* **make a t. job of sth**

faire qch très consciencieusement (**b**) *(work, worker)* consciencieux(euse) (**c**) *(complete)* intégral(e)
thoroughbred ['θʌrəbred] **1** *n* pur-sang *m inv*
2 *adj (horse)* pur-sang *inv*
thoroughfare ['θʌrəfeə(r)] *n* rue *f*; **no t.** *(sign) (no entry)* passage interdit; *(cul-de-sac)* voie sans issue
thoroughgoing ['θʌrəgəʊɪŋ] *adj (search)* minutieux(euse); *(knowledge, revision)* approfondi(e)
thoroughly ['θʌrəlɪ] *adv* (**a**) *(with thoroughness)* à fond (**b**) *(completely)* tout à fait
thoroughness ['θʌrənɪs] *n* minutie *f*
those [ðəʊz] *(plural of* that) **1** *demonstrative pron* ceux-là (celles-là) *mpl,fpl*; **in cases like t.** dans des cas comme ceux-là; **t. are the ones I want** voilà ceux que je veux; **t. of us who...** ceux d'entre nous qui...
2 *demonstrative adj* ces; **t. ones** ceux-là (celles-là) *mpl,fpl*
though [ðəʊ] **1** *conj* bien que + *subjunctive*; **t. I say so myself** sans fausse modestie; **strange t. it may seem** aussi étrange que cela puisse paraître; **even t.** même si; **as t.** comme si
2 *adv* pourtant
thought [θɔːt] **1** *n* (**a**) *(thinking, idea)* pensée *f*; **it's quite a t.!** *(pleasant)* le rêve!; *(unpleasant)* quelle horreur!; **what a kind t.!** quelle délicate attention!; **the very t. of it...** le simple fait d'y penser...; **I didn't give it another t.** je n'y ai plus pensé; **her thoughts were elsewhere** son esprit était ailleurs; **what are your thoughts on the matter?** quelle est votre opinion sur le sujet? (**b**) *(reflection)* réflexion *f*; **after much t.** après mûre réflexion; **to give some/no t. to sth** réfléchir/ne pas réfléchir à qch; **to be deep** *ou* **lost in t.** être perdu(e) *ou* plongé(e) dans ses pensées (**c**) *(intention)* intention *f*; **to have no t. of doing sth** ne pas avoir l'intention de faire qch; **you must give up all t.** *or* **thoughts of seeing him** tu dois renoncer à le voir
2 *pt & pp of* think
thoughtful ['θɔːtfʊl] *adj* (**a**) *(pensive) (person)* pensif(ive); *(book, writer)* sérieux(euse) (**b**) *(considerate) (person)* attentionné(e); *(gesture, remark)* gentil(ille)
thoughtfully ['θɔːtfəlɪ] *adv* (**a**) *(pensively)* pensivement (**b**) *(considerately)* gentiment
thoughtless ['θɔːtlɪs] *adj* irréfléchi(e)
thought-out ['θɔːt'aʊt] *adj* **well/poorly t.** *(plan, scheme)* bien/mal étudié(e)
thought-provoking ['θɔːtprəvəʊkɪŋ] *adj* qui donne à réfléchir
thousand ['θaʊzənd] **1** *n* mille *m inv*; **one** *or* **a t.** mille; **thousands of people** des milliers de gens; **she's one in a t.** elle est unique
2 *adj* mille *inv*; **a t. years** mille ans; **two t. men** deux mille hommes; *Fam* **to have a t. and one things to do** avoir mille choses à faire
thousandth ['θaʊzənθ] **1** *n* (**a**) *(fraction)* millième *m* (**b**) *(in series)* millième *mf*
2 *adj* millième
thrash [θræʃ] *vt (beat)* battre; *Fam Fig (defeat heavily)* écraser, battre à plate(s) couture(s)
▸**thrash about, thrash around 1** *vt sep* **to t. one's arms and legs about** se débattre
2 *vi (move wildly)* se débattre
▸**thrash out** *vt sep* discuter *ou* débattre de
thread [θred] **1** *n* (**a**) *(for sewing)* fil *m*; *Fig* **his life hung by a t.** sa vie ne tenait qu'à un fil; **to lose the t.** **(of sth)** perdre le fil (de qch) (**b**) *(of screw, bolt)* filetage *m*

2 *vt* (**a**) *(needle, beads)* enfiler (**b**) *(move)* **to t. one's way between the cars** se faufiler entre les voitures; **to t. one's way through the crowd** se frayer un chemin à travers la foule
threadbare ['θredbeə(r)] *adj (clothes)* élimé(e); *Fig (argument, joke)* éculé(e)
threat [θret] *n* menace *f*
threaten ['θretən] **1** *vt* menacer; **to t. to do sth** menacer de faire qch; **to t. sb with sth** menacer qn de qch
2 *vi* menacer
threatening ['θretənɪŋ] *adj (look, gesture)* menaçant(e); *(letter)* de menaces
three [θriː] **1** *n* trois *m inv*; **come with us – no, (two's company,) t.'s a crowd** viens avec nous – non, je me sentirais de trop
2 *adj* trois *inv*; *see also* **eight**
three-cornered [θriː'kɔːnəd] *adj* triangulaire
three-course meal ['θriːkɔːs'miːl] *n* repas *m* à trois plats *(entrée, plat principal, dessert)*
three-dimensional [θriːdaɪ'menʃənəl] *adj (object)* tridimensionnel(elle), en trois dimensions; *(character)* qui semble réel; *(film, picture)* en relief
threefold ['θriːfəʊld] **1** *adj* triple
2 *adv* **to increase t.** être multiplié(e) par trois
three-legged [θriː'legɪd] *adj (stool)* à trois pieds; **t. race** = course dont les participants sont attachés deux à deux par une jambe
three-piece ['θriːpiːs] *adj* **t. suit** *(costume m)* trois-pièce *m inv*; **t. suite** canapé *m* avec deux fauteuils assortis
three-point turn ['θriːpɔɪnt'tɜːn] *n* demi-tour *m* en trois manœuvres
threescore ['θriːskɔː(r)] *adj Lit* soixante *inv*; **t. (years) and ten** soixante-dix *inv*
threesome ['θriːsəm] *n* (**a**) groupe *m* de trois personnes (**b**) *Fam (for sex)* partouze *f* à trois
three-wheeler [θriː'wiːlə(r)] *n (car)* voiture *f* à trois roues; *(tricycle)* tricycle *m*
thresh [θreʃ] *vt* battre
threshold ['θreʃəʊld] *n also Fig* seuil *m*; **to cross the t.** franchir le seuil; *Fig* **to be on the t. of sth** être au seuil de qch
threw [θruː] *pt of* throw
thrice [θraɪs] *adv Lit* trois fois
thrift [θrɪft] *n* économie *f*, épargne *f*
thriftless ['θrɪftlɪs] *adj* dépensier(ère)
thrifty ['θrɪftɪ] *adj* économe
thrill [θrɪl] **1** *n (excitement)* sensation *f*; *(trembling)* frisson *m*; **to get a t. out of doing sth** adorer faire qch
2 *vt* exalter, donner des frissons à; **to be thrilled for sb/with sth** être ravi(e) pour qn/de qch
3 *vi Lit* tressaillir, frissonner
thriller ['θrɪlə(r)] *n* thriller *m*
thrilling ['θrɪlɪŋ] *adj (story, film, match)* palpitant(e); *(idea, proposal, situation)* exaltant(e)
thrive [θraɪv] *(pt & pp* thrived [θraɪvd], *pt also* throve [θrəʊv]) *vi (of child, plant)* se développer; *(of adult)* s'épanouir; *(of business)* prospérer; **to t. on sth** *(stress, danger)* avoir besoin de qch pour s'épanouir
thriving ['θraɪvɪŋ] *adj (plant, person, animal)* vigoureux(euse); *(business)* prospère, florissant(e)
throat [θrəʊt] *n* (**a**) *(part of body)* gorge *f*; **to clear one's t.** se racler la gorge, s'éclaircir la voix (**b**) *(idioms)* **to ram** *or* **shove sth down sb's t.** rebattre

les oreilles à qn de qch; **to jump down sb's t.** sauter sur qn; **to be at each other's throats** se battre

throaty ['θrəʊtɪ] *adj* rauque

throb [θrɒb] **1** *n (of heart)* battement *m; (of pain)* élancement *m; (of engine)* vibration *f*
2 *vi (pt & pp* **throbbed**) *(of heart)* battre; *(of engine)* vibrer; **my head is throbbing** j'ai une douleur lancinante dans la tête

throes [θrəʊz] *npl* **t. of death, death t.** affres *fpl* de la mort, l'agonie *f*; **to be in the t. of sth/of doing sth** être en plein qch/en train de faire qch

thrombosis [θrɒm'bəʊsɪs] *(pl* **thromboses**) *n* thrombose *f*

throne [θrəʊn] *n* trône *m*

throng [θrɒŋ] **1** *n* foule *f*
2 *vt* se presser dans; **the streets were thronged with people** les rues étaient noires de monde
3 *vi* affluer, se presser; **to t. round sb** se presser autour de qn

throttle ['θrɒtəl] **1** *n (valve)* papillon *m* des gaz; *(accelerator)* manette *f* des gaz; **at full t.** à pleins gaz
2 *vt also Fig* étrangler

through [θruː] **1** *prep* (**a**) *(with place)* par, à travers; **to go t. a tunnel** passer par un tunnel; **to look t. a hole** regarder par un trou; **to come in t. the window** entrer par la fenêtre; **we went t. Belgium** nous sommes passés par la Belgique (**b**) *(in the course of)* **all t. his life** toute sa vie durant; **halfway t. a book/ film** à la moitié d'un livre/film; **to get t. sth** *(finish)* venir à bout de qch; *Fam* **he's been t. a lot** il en a bavé (**c**) *(by means of)* par; **to send sth t. the post** envoyer qch par la poste; **I found out t. my brother/the newspaper** je l'ai appris par mon frère/le journal (**d**) *(because of)* à cause de; **t. ignorance/carelessness** par ignorance/négligence (**e**) *Am (up to)* **Tuesday t. Thursday** de mardi à jeudi
2 *adv* (**a**) *(to other side)* **to go t.** *(of bullet, nail)* traverser; **to let sb t.** laisser passer qn; **to get t. to the final** être en finale (**b**) *(from start to finish)* **to sleep all night t.** dormir toute la nuit; **to read a book right t.** lire un livre tout entier; **he's bad t. and t.** il est vraiment méchant (**c**) *(in contact)* **to get t. to sb** *(on phone)* joindre qn; **to put sb t. to sb** *(on phone)* passer qn à qn; *Fam* **I just can't get t. to him** *(make myself understood)* je n'arrive pas à le lui faire comprendre
3 *adj* (**a**) *(finished)* fini(e); **to be t. with sb/sth** en avoir fini avec qn/qch (**b**) *(direct)* **t. train** train *m* direct

throughout [θruː'aʊt] **1** *prep (in every part of)* partout dans; *(during)* tout au long de; **t. the country** dans tout le pays; **t. her life** tout au long de sa vie, pendant toute sa vie
2 *adv (everywhere)* partout; *(the whole time)* tout le temps

throughput ['θruːpʊt] *n Comput* débit *m*

throve [θrəʊv] *pt of* thrive

throw [θrəʊ] **1** *vt (pt* **threw** [θruː], *pp* **thrown** [θrəʊn]) (**a**) *(in general)* jeter, lancer; *(javelin, discus)* lancer; **to t. sth at sb/sth** lancer qch à qn/contre qch; **to t. sth in sb's face** lancer qch à la figure de qn; *Fig* jeter qch à la figure de qn; **to t. sb forwards/backwards** projeter qn en avant/en arrière; *Fig* **to t. oneself into sth** *(after traumatic event)* se jeter dans qch; *(enthusiastically)* se lancer dans qch; **to t. oneself at sb** se jeter sur qn; **to t. sb into confusion** plonger qn dans l'embarras; **to t. a switch** appuyer sur un interrupteur; **to t. open the door** ouvrir la porte en grand;

Fam **to t. one's weight about** *or* **around** la ramener (**b**) *(image, shadow)* projeter (**on** sur); *Fig* **to t. light on sth** éclairer qch (**c**) *(have)* **to t. a fit** piquer une crise; *Fam* **to t. a party** organiser une fête (**d**) *(in wrestling)* renverser (**e**) *(of horse)* désarçonner (**f**) *Fam (disconcert)* désarçonner, déconcerter
2 *n* (**a**) *(in general)* jet *m; (of javelin, discus)* lancer *m; (in wrestling)* mise *f* à terre (**b**) *(for furniture, bed)* jeté *m* (**c**) *Fam* **£50 a t.** *(each)* 50 livres chaque

▸**throw away** *vt sep* (**a**) *(discard)* jeter (**b**) *(chance, life)* gâcher; *(money)* gaspiller

▸**throw in** *vt sep* (**a**) *(in general)* jeter; *Fig* **to t. in the sponge** *or* **the towel** jeter l'éponge; *Fig* **to t. in one's lot with sb** s'associer avec qn (**b**) *(add)* placer; *(give as extra)* ajouter, donner en plus

▸**throw out** *vt sep* (**a**) *(eject) (person)* exclure, mettre à la porte; *(thing)* jeter; *(proposal)* rejeter (**b**) *(emit) (light, heat)* émettre

▸**throw together** *vt sep (assemble or gather hurriedly)* assembler à la hâte; *(make hurriedly)* faire à la hâte; **chance had thrown us together** le hasard nous avait réunis

▸**throw up 1** *vt sep* (**a**) *(raise)* **to t. up one's hands** *(in horror, dismay)* lever les bras au ciel (**b**) *(reveal) (facts, information)* révéler (**c**) *(abandon) (career)* abandonner
2 *vi Fam (vomit)* vomir

throwaway ['θrəʊəweɪ] *adj* (**a**) *(disposable)* jetable (**b**) *(line, remark)* fait(e) sans y penser

throwback ['θrəʊbæk] *n Biol* régression *f* (**to** à); *Fig* retour *m* (**to** à)

throw-in ['θrəʊɪn] *n (in football)* remise *f* en jeu

thrown [θrəʊn] *pp of* throw

thru = through

thrush[1] [θrʌʃ] *n (bird)* grive *f*

thrush[2] *n (disease)* muguet *m*

thrust [θrʌst] **1** *n* (**a**) *(forward movement)* mouvement *m* en avant; *(of army)* attaque *f* (**b**) *(of argument)* idée *f* principale (**c**) *(force of engine)* poussée *f*
2 *vt (pt & pp* **thrust**) **to t. sth into sth** enfoncer qch dans qch; **to t. one's way through the crowd** se frayer un chemin à travers la foule

▸**thrust aside** *vt sep* repousser, écarter

▸**thrust forward** *vt sep* pousser en avant; *Fig* **to t. oneself forward** se mettre en avant

▸**thrust on** *vt sep* **to t. sth on sb** imposer qch à qn; **he thrust himself on them** il s'est imposé

▸**thrust out** *vt sep (arm, leg)* allonger; *(chest)* bomber; *(chin)* avancer

▸**thrust upon** = thrust on

thrusting ['θrʌstɪŋ] *adj* entreprenant(e), dynamique

thruway ['θruːweɪ] *n Am* autoroute *f*

thud [θʌd] **1** *n* bruit *m* sourd
2 *vi (pt & pp* **thudded**) faire un bruit sourd; **to t. against sth** frapper qch avec un bruit sourd

thug [θʌg] *n* voyou *m*

thumb [θʌm] **1** *n* pouce *m; Fig* **she's got him under her t.** il est sous sa coupe; *Fam* **to be all thumbs** être maladroit(e); *Fam* **to give sth the thumbs up/down** accepter/rejeter qch
2 *vt* **to t. one's nose at sb** faire un pied de nez à qn; *Fam* **to t. a lift** *or* **ride** faire de l'auto-stop; **a well thumbed book/magazine** un livre/magazine qui a beaucoup servi
3 *vi* **to t. through a book/magazine** feuilleter un livre/magazine

thumbnail [ˈθʌmneɪl] *n* ongle *m* du pouce; **t. sketch** description *f* rapide

thumbprint [ˈθʌmprɪnt] *n* empreinte *f* du pouce

thumbtack [ˈθʌmtæk] *n Am* punaise *f*

thump [θʌmp] **1** *n (blow)* coup *m*; *(sound)* bruit *m* sourd
2 *vt (hit)* cogner, frapper; *(put down heavily)* poser lourdement
3 *vi* (**a**) **to t. on sth** *(table, door)* cogner, frapper qch (**b**) *(walk heavily)* **to t. around** *or* **about** marcher à pas lourds (**c**) *(of heart)* battre la chamade

thumping [ˈθʌmpɪŋ] *Fam* **1** *adj* (**a**) *(very large)* énorme (**b**) *(headache)* lancinant(e)
2 *adv* **a t. great book/salary** un livre/un salaire énorme

thunder [ˈθʌndə(r)] **1** *n* tonnerre *m*; **with a face like t.** le visage déformé par la colère
2 *vi also Fig* tonner; **to t. along** *(of train, lorry)* passer dans un bruit de tonnerre

thunderbolt [ˈθʌndəbəʊlt] *n* éclair *m* suivi d'un coup de tonnerre

thunderclap [ˈθʌndəklæp] *n* coup *m* de tonnerre

thundercloud [ˈθʌndəklaʊd] *n* nuage *m* orageux

thunderous [ˈθʌndərəs] *adj (voice)* tonitruant(e); **t. applause** un tonnerre d'applaudissements

thunderstorm [ˈθʌndəstɔːm] *n* orage *m*

thunderstruck [ˈθʌndəstrʌk] *adj* abasourdi(e)

Thur *(abbr* **Thursday)** jeudi

Thursday [ˈθɜːzdɪ] *n* jeudi *m*; *see also* **Saturday**

thus [ðʌs] *adv Formal* (**a**) *(in this way, therefore)* ainsi (**b**) **t. far** *(in present)* jusqu'ici; *(in past)* jusque-là

thwart [θwɔːt] *vt* contrecarrer

thyme [taɪm] *n* thym *m*

thyroid [ˈθaɪərɔɪd] **1** *n* thyroïde *f*
2 *adj* thyroïde; **t. gland** thyroïde *f*

tiara [tɪˈɑːrə] *n (jewellery)* diadème *m*

Tibet [tɪˈbet] *n* le Tibet

Tibetan [tɪˈbetən] **1** *n* (**a**) *(person)* Tibétain(e) *m,f* (**b**) *(language)* tibétain *m*
2 *adj* tibétain(e)

tibia [ˈtɪbɪə] *n Anat* tibia *m*

tic [tɪk] *n* tic *m*

tick¹ [tɪk] *n (parasite)* tique *f*

tick² *n Br Fam (credit)* **to buy sth on t.** acheter qch à crédit

tick³ **1** *n* (**a**) *(of clock)* tic-tac *m inv*; *Fam (moment)* instant *m* (**b**) *(mark)* coche *f*; **to put a t. beside sth** cocher qch
2 *vt (mark)* cocher
3 *vi (of clock)* faire tic-tac; **the minutes were ticking by** *or* **away** les minutes passaient; *Fam* **I don't know what makes him t.** je ne sais pas ce qui se passe dans sa tête

▸**tick off** *vt sep* (**a**) *(on list)* cocher (**b**) *Br Fam (reprimand)* passer un savon à (**c**) *Am Fam (irritate)* énerver

▸**tick over** *vi (of engine)* tourner au ralenti; *(of business)* tourner

ticket [ˈtɪkɪt] **1** *n* (**a**) *(for train, plane, cinema, lottery)* billet *m*; *(for underground, bus)* ticket *m*; **(parking) t.** P-V *m*; *Br* **t. inspector** contrôleur(euse) *m,f*, *Belg* accompagnateur(trice) *m,f* de train; **t. office** guichet *m*, billetterie *f*; **t. tout** revendeur(euse) *m,f* de billets (**b**) *(label)* **(price) t.** étiquette *f* (**c**) *Am Pol (list of candidates)* liste *f* électorale; **she ran on an anti-corruption t.** elle a fondé son programme électoral sur la

lutte contre la corruption (**d**) *Fam* **it was just the t.!** c'était juste ce qu'il fallait!
2 *vt (goods)* étiqueter

ticketless [ˈtɪkɪtles] *adj* **t. travel** = vol avec reçu de paiement tenant lieu de billet

ticking [ˈtɪkɪŋ] *n* (**a**) *(of clock)* tic-tac *m inv* (**b**) *(fabric)* toile *f* à matelas

ticking off *n Br Fam (reprimand)* savon *m*; **to give sb a t.** passer un savon à qn

tickle [ˈtɪkəl] **1** *n* chatouillement *m*; **to have a t.** in one's throat avoir des picotements dans la gorge
2 *vt* chatouiller; *Fig (amuse)* amuser; **to t. sb's fancy** plaire à qn; **to be tickled pink** être ravi(e)
3 *vi* chatouiller

ticklish [ˈtɪklɪʃ] *adj* (**a**) *(person)* chatouilleux(euse) (**b**) *Fam (situation, problem)* délicat(e)

tic-tac-toe [tɪktæk'təʊ] *n Am (game)* morpion *m*

tidal [ˈtaɪdəl] *adj* régi(e) par les marées; **t. energy** énergie *f* marémotrice; **t. wave** raz de marée *m inv*

tiddler [ˈtɪdlə(r)] *n Br Fam (small fish)* petit poisson *m*; *(child)* mioche *m*

tiddly [ˈtɪdlɪ] *adj Br Fam* (**a**) *(small)* minuscule (**b**) *(drunk)* paf *inv*

tiddlywinks [ˈtɪdlɪwɪŋks] *n* jeu *m* de puce

tide [taɪd] *n* marée *f*; *Fig (of events)* cours *m*; **high/low t.** marée *f* haute/basse; *Fig* **to go against the t.** aller à contre-courant; *Fig* **the t. has turned** le vent a tourné

▸**tide over** *vt sep* **to t. sb over** dépanner qn

tidemark [ˈtaɪdmɑːk] *n (mark left by tide)* laisse *f* de haute mer; *Br Fam (in bath, around neck)* ligne *f* de crasse

tidings [ˈtaɪdɪŋz] *npl Lit* nouvelles *fpl*

tidy [ˈtaɪdɪ] **1** *adj* (**a**) *(room, house)* rangé(e), en ordre; *(hair)* bien coiffé(e); *(appearance, handwriting)* soigné(e); *(person) (in habits)* ordonné(e); *(in appearance)* soigné (**b**) *Fam (considerable)* joli(e)
2 *vt (pt & pp* **tidied)** ranger; *(garden)* nettoyer; **to t. one's hair** se recoiffer

▸**tidy up** *vt sep & vi* ranger

tie [taɪ] **1** *n* (**a**) *(link)* lien *m* (**b**) *(garment)* cravate *f*; **t. rack** porte-cravates *m* (**c**) *(draw) (in match)* match *m* nul; **there was a t. for second place** *(in race, competition)* il y a eu égalité pour la deuxième place (**d**) *(match)* match *m* (**e**) *Am Rail* traverse *f*, *Can* dormant *m*
2 *vt (shoelace, string)* attacher, nouer; **to t. a knot** faire un nœud; **to t. sth to sth** attacher qch à qch; *Fig* **to have one's hands tied** avoir les mains liées; *Fig* **to be tied to one's desk** être cloué(e) à son bureau
3 *vi (in race, contest)* être à égalité; **to t. for first/second place** être premiers(ères)/deuxièmes ex aequo

▸**tie back** *vt sep (hair, curtains)* relever

▸**tie down** *vt sep (immobilize)* attacher; *Fig* **children t. you down** les enfants sont une contrainte; **she didn't want to feel tied down** elle voulait garder sa liberté

▸**tie in** *vi (of facts, story)* concorder, cadrer

▸**tie on** *vt* attacher

▸**tie up** *vt sep* (**a**) *(person, animal)* attacher; *(parcel)* ficeler; *(boat)* amarrer (**b**) *(deal)* conclure; *(money)* immobiliser (**c**) *Fig* **to be tied up** *(busy)* être occupé(e)

tie-break [ˈtaɪbreɪk], **tie-breaker** [ˈtaɪbreɪkə(r)] *n (in tennis)* tie-break *m*; *(in quiz, competition)* question *f* subsidiaire

tie-in ['taɪɪn] *n (link)* lien *m*, rapport *m* (**with** avec); a **film/TV t.** = livre, jouet etc commercialisé à la suite d'un film ou d'une série télévisée

tier [tɪə(r)] *n (of theatre, stadium)* gradin *m*; *(of wedding cake)* étage *m*; *(administrative)* échelon *m*

tiff [tɪf] *n Br Fam* querelle *f*

tiger ['taɪɡə(r)] *n* tigre *m*

tight [taɪt] **1** *adj* (**a**) *(clothes, knot, screw)* serré(e); **to be a t.** fit *(of clothes)* être un peu juste; **to keep a t.** hold *or* grip on sth s'agripper à qch; **it was a t. squeeze** il a fallu se serrer un peu; *Fig* **to be in a t. spot** *or* **corner** être dans une mauvaise passe; *Fig* **to run a t. ship** mener son monde à la baguette (**b**) *(competition, race, bend, schedule)* serré(e); *(restrictions)* strict(e); **a t. finish** *(in race)* une arrivée disputée; *Fam* **money's a bit t. at the moment** je suis un peu à court d'argent en ce moment (**c**) *Fam (mean)* radin(e) (**d**) *Fam (drunk)* bourré(e) **2** *adv (hold, squeeze)* fortement; *(seal, shut)* bien; **hold t.!** tiens bon!; **sleep t.!** dors bien!

tighten ['taɪtən] **1** *vt (screw, knot)* serrer; *(rope)* tendre; *(restrictions, security)* renforcer; *(conditions, rules)* durcir; **to t. one's grip on sth** *(rope, handle)* resserrer sa prise sur qch; *Fig (power, organization)* renforcer son emprise sur qch; **to t. one's belt** se serrer la ceinture **2** *vi (of knot, grip)* se resserrer; *(of rope)* se tendre
▸**tighten up** *vt sep (screw)* resserrer; *(restrictions, security)* renforcer

tightfisted [taɪt'fɪstɪd] *adj Fam* radin(e)

tightknit ['taɪt'nɪt] *adj (community)* uni(e)

tight-lipped ['taɪtlɪpt] *adj (silent)* peu bavard(e); *(angry)* renfrogné(e)

tightly ['taɪtlɪ] *adv (hold, squeeze)* fortement; *(seal, shut)* bien

tightness ['taɪtnɪs] *n (of link, clothing)* étroitesse *f*; *(of regulations, security)* rigueur *f*

tightrope ['taɪtrəʊp] *n* corde *f* raide; *Fig* **to walk a t.** être sur la corde raide; **t. walker** funambule *mf*

tights [taɪts] *npl Br (garment)* collant *m*

tigress ['taɪɡrɪs] *n* tigresse *f*

'til [tɪl] = **until**

tile [taɪl] **1** *n (on roof)* tuile *f*; *(on floor, wall)* carreau *m* **2** *vt (roof)* couvrir de tuiles; *(floor, wall)* carreler

tiled [taɪld] *adj (roof)* de tuiles; *(floor, wall)* carrelé(e)

till¹ [tɪl] *vt (field)* labourer

till² *n (cash register)* caisse *f*; *Fig* **to be caught with one's hand** *or* **fingers in the t.** être pris(e) la main dans le sac

till³ = **until**

tiller ['tɪlə(r)] *n (on boat)* barre *f*

tilt [tɪlt] **1** *n* (**a**) *(angle)* inclinaison *f* (**b**) **at full t.** à toute vitesse **2** *vt (head, chair)* incliner, pencher; **to t. the balance of opinion in favour of** faire pencher l'opinion en faveur de **3** *vi* (**a**) *(incline)* pencher; **to t. backwards/forwards** pencher vers l'arrière/vers l'avant (**b**) *Fig* **to t. at windmills** se battre contre des moulins à vent
▸**tilt over** *vi* basculer

timber ['tɪmbə(r)] *n (wood)* bois *m*; **t. merchant** marchand *m* de bois

time [taɪm] **1** *n* (**a**) *(in general)* temps *m*; *Fig* **to have no t. for sb/sth** ne pas avoir de temps à perdre avec qn/qch; **to take t.** prendre du temps; **to take one's t. (doing sth)** prendre son temps (pour faire qch); **you took your t.!** tu as pris ton temps!; **in one's own t.** *(out of working hours)* pendant son temps libre; *(at one's own pace)* à son rythme; **in t.** *(eventually)* avec le temps; **in t. for sth/to do sth** à temps pour qch/pour faire qch; **in good t.** *(early)* à temps; *(in due course)* en temps voulu; **all in good t.** chaque chose en son temps; **she'll do it in her own good t.** elle le fera quand elle le pourra; **now my t. is my own** maintenant, je suis libre de mon temps; **in no t. at all, in next to no t.** en un rien de temps; **t.'s getting on** l'heure avance; **t.'s up!** c'est l'heure!; **t. will tell** l'avenir le dira; *Prov* **t. is money** le temps, c'est de l'argent; *Fam* **to do t.** *(go to prison)* faire de la taule; *also Fig* **t. bomb** bombe *f* à retardement; **to be in a t. warp** être hors du temps; **t. travel** voyage *m* dans le temps (**b**) *(period)* in a short/long t. dans peu de temps/longtemps; **for some t.** pendant quelque temps; **in three weeks' t.** dans trois semaines; **to take a long t. over sth/to do sth** passer beaucoup de temps sur qch/à faire qch; **for the t. being** pour le moment; **to have a good t.** bien s'amuser; **to give sb a hard t.** faire passer un mauvais moment à qn (**c**) *(age)* époque *f*; **before my t.** avant ma naissance; **to be ahead of one's t.** être en avance sur son temps; **to move with the times** vivre avec son temps; **she was a good singer in her t.** c'était une bonne chanteuse à son époque; **she's seen a few things in her t.** elle a vu pas mal de choses dans sa vie; **t. capsule** capsule *f* témoin *(qui doit servir de témoignage historique aux générations futures)* (**d**) *(moment)* moment *m*; **at the t.** à ce moment-là; **at the present t.** en ce moment; **at one t.** à une époque; **at no t.** jamais, à aucun moment; **at the same t.** en même temps; **at times** parfois, par moments; **by the t. you get this, I'll already be in Paris** quand tu recevras cette lettre, je serai déjà à Paris; **this t. next year** l'année prochaine à la même époque; **from t. to t.** de temps en temps; **at this t. of (the) year** à cette époque de l'année; **the t. has come to...** le moment est venu de...; *Fam* **not before t.!** il était temps!; *Fam* **it's high t. (that)...** il est grand temps que... + *subjunctive* (**e**) *(on clock)* heure *f*; **what's the t.?** quelle heure est-il?; **to pass the t. of day with sb** parler de la pluie et du beau temps avec qn; *Fam* **he wouldn't give you the t. of day** il n'est vraiment pas aimable; **this t. tomorrow** demain à la même heure; **on t.** à l'heure; **it's t. we left** il est temps de partir; **t. difference** décalage *m* horaire; **t. lag** décalage; **t. limit** délai *m*; *Ind* **t. sheet** fiche *f* horaire; **t. switch** minuterie *f* (**f**) *(occasion)* fois *f*; **five times** cinq fois; **t. and t. again, t. after t.** encore et encore (**g**) *(in multiplication)* **four times two is eight** quatre fois deux égalent huit; **three times as big/expensive as** trois fois plus grand(e)/cher (chère) que (**h**) *(in music)* mesure *f*; **to keep t.** rester en mesure **2** *vt* (**a**) *(meeting, visit)* prévoir; *(remark, action)* **well timed** opportun(e); **badly timed** mal venu(e) (**b**) *(remark, action)* well timed opportun(e); **badly timed** mal venu(e) (**c**) *(athlete, race)* chronométrer

time-consuming ['taɪmkənsju:mɪŋ] *adj* qui prend beaucoup de temps

time-honoured ['taɪmɒnəd] *adj* consacré(e) (par l'usage)

timekeeper ['taɪmki:pə(r)] *n (in competition)* chronométreur *m*

timekeeping ['taɪmki:pɪŋ] *n* (**a**) *(in factory)* contrôle *m* de présence (**b**) *(punctuality)* ponctualité *f*

timeless ['taɪmlɪs] *adj* intemporel(elle)

timely ['taɪmlɪ] *adj* opportun(e)

time-out ['taɪmaʊt] *n (in sport)* temps *m* mort; *Fig* pause *f*; **to take t.** faire une pause

timepiece ['taɪmpiːs] *n (clock)* pendule *f*; *(watch)* montre *f*

timer ['taɪmə(r)] *n* minuteur *m*

time-saving ['taɪmseɪvɪŋ] *adj* qui permet de gagner du temps

timescale ['taɪmskeɪl] *n* période *f*

time-share ['taɪmʃeə(r)] *n (flat)* appartement *m* en multipropriété; *(house)* maison *f* en multipropriété

timespan ['taɪmspæn] *n* laps *m* de temps

timetable ['taɪmteɪbəl] **1** *n (at school, university)* emploi *m* du temps; *(for event, project)* calendrier *m*; *(for trains, buses)* horaire *m*; **to work to a t.** suivre un emploi du temps

2 *vt (talks, meeting)* fixer une date pour; *(classes)* établir un emploi du temps pour

time-wasting ['taɪmweɪstɪŋ] *n* perte *f* de temps

timid ['tɪmɪd] *adj* timide

timidity [tɪ'mɪdɪtɪ] *n* timidité *f*

timidly ['tɪmɪdlɪ] *adv* timidement

timing ['taɪmɪŋ] *n* (**a**) *(of announcement, election)* moment *m* choisi (**of** pour) (**b**) *(of remark, action)* **good t.** à-propos *m*; **bad t.** manque *m* d'à-propos; **perfect t.!** ça tombe bien! (**c**) *(of musician)* sens *m* du rythme

timorous ['tɪmərəs] *adj* timoré(e)

tin [tɪn] *n* (**a**) *(metal)* étain *m*; **t. mine** mine *f* d'étain; **t. plate** fer-blanc *m*; **t. soldier** soldat *m* de plomb (**b**) *(mould)* moule *m* (**c**) *(container) (for biscuits, cakes)* boîte *f* en fer; *Br (for preserved food)* boîte *f*; *Br* **t. opener** ouvre-boîte *m*

tinder ['tɪndə(r)] *n* petit bois *m*

tinderbox ['tɪndəbɒks] *n Fig* poudrière *f*

tinfoil ['tɪnfɔɪl] *n Br* papier *m* aluminium

ting-a-ling ['tɪŋəlɪŋ] *n* dring-dring *m inv*

tinge [tɪn(d)ʒ] **1** *n (of colour, emotion)* pointe *f*
2 *vt* **tinged with** teinté(e) de

tingle ['tɪŋgəl] **1** *n (physical sensation)* picotement *m*; *(of fear)* frisson *m*; *(of excitement)* frémissement *m*
2 *vi* picoter; **to t. with fear** frissonner de peur; **to t. with excitement** frémir d'excitation

tingling ['tɪŋglɪŋ] *n* picotement *m*

tinker ['tɪŋkə(r)] **1** *n (travelling person)* rétameur *m*
2 *vi* **to t. with sth** bricoler qch

tinkle ['tɪŋkəl] **1** *n (of bell)* tintement *m*; *Br Fam (phone call)* **to give sb a t.** passer un coup de fil à qn
2 *vi* tinter

tinned [tɪnd] *adj Br (food)* en boîte

tinnitus ['tɪnɪtəs] *n* acouphène *m*

tinny ['tɪnɪ] *adj (sound)* métallique

tinsel ['tɪnsəl] *n* guirlandes *fpl* de Noël

tint [tɪnt] **1** *n* teinte *f*, nuance *f*; *(in hair)* rinçage *m*
2 *vt* teinter

tiny ['taɪnɪ] *adj* minuscule; **a t. bit** un tout petit peu

tip¹ [tɪp] **1** *n (end)* bout *m*; **on the tips of one's toes** sur la pointe des pieds; **it's on the t. of my tongue** je l'ai sur le bout de la langue; *Fig* **that's just the t. of the iceberg** ce n'est que la partie visible de l'iceberg
2 *vt (pt & pp* **tipped)** **to be tipped with sth** avoir le bout recouvert de qch

tip² **1** *n* (**a**) *(payment)* pourboire *m* (**b**) *(piece of advice)* truc *m*
2 *vt (pt & pp* **tipped)** (**a**) *(give money to)* donner un pourboire à (**b**) *(predict)* **to t. a winner** *(in horse race)* pronostiquer un cheval gagnant; **to t. sb for success/**

promotion prédire à qn le succès/une promotion; **the film is tipped to win an Oscar** de l'avis général il y a de fortes chances que le film remporte un Oscar

tip³ **1** *n (for rubbish) & Fig* dépotoir *m*
2 *vt (pt & pp* **tipped)** (**a**) *(pour) (rubbish)* déverser; *(liquid)* verser; **to t. sth over sb/sth** renverser qch sur qn/qch (**b**) **to t. the scales at 95 kg** peser 95 kg; *Fig* **to t. the scales** *or* **balance (in sb's favour)** faire pencher la balance (en faveur de qn)

▸**tip off** *vt sep (warn)* avertir

▸**tip out** *vt sep (empty)* vider; *(discard)* jeter

▸**tip over 1** *vt sep* renverser
2 *vi* se renverser

▸**tip up 1** *vt sep* renverser
2 *vi* basculer

tip-off ['tɪpɒf] *n Fam* tuyau *m*

Tipp-Ex® ['tɪpeks] **1** *n*Tipp-Ex® *m inv*
2 *vt* **to t. sth out** effacer qch avec du Tipp-Ex®

tipple ['tɪpəl] *n Fam* **what's your t.?** qu'est-ce que vous buvez habituellement?; **sherry's her favourite t.** ce qu'elle préfère, c'est le sherry

tipsy ['tɪpsɪ] *adj Fam* pompette

tiptoe ['tɪptəʊ] **1** *n* **on t.** sur la pointe des pieds
2 *vi* marcher sur la pointe des pieds; **to t. in/out** entrer/sortir sur la pointe des pieds

tiptop ['tɪptɒp] *adj* excellent(e)

tirade [taɪ'reɪd] *n* diatribe *f*

tire¹ ['taɪə(r)] **1** *vt* fatiguer
2 *vi* se fatiguer; **to t. of sth/of doing sth** se lasser de qch/de faire qch

▸**tire out** *vt sep (exhaust)* épuiser

tire² *Am* **= tyre**

tired ['taɪəd] *adj* fatigué(e); **to be t. of sth/of doing sth** en avoir assez de qch/de faire qch

tireless ['taɪəlɪs] *adj* infatigable

tiresome ['taɪəsəm] *adj* ennuyeux(euse)

tiring ['taɪərɪŋ] *adj* fatigant(e)

tissue ['tɪʃuː] *n* (**a**) *Biol* tissu *m* (**b**) *(paper handkerchief)* mouchoir *m* en papier; *Fig* **a t. of lies** un tissu de mensonges; **t. paper** papier *m* de soie

tit¹ [tɪt] *n (bird)* mésange *f*

tit² *n* **tit for tat** prêté pour un rendu; **to give sb t. for tat** rendre à qn la monnaie de sa pièce

tit³ *n very Fam* (**a**) *(breast)* nichon *m*; *Br* **to get on sb's tits** courir sur le haricot à qn (**b**) *Br (idiot)* con (conne) *m,f*

titanic [taɪ'tænɪk] *adj (conflict, struggle)* titanesque

titanium [taɪ'teɪnɪəm] *n Chem* titane *m*

titbit ['tɪtbɪt] *n (snack)* morceau *m* de choix; *Fig* **t. of gossip** potin *m*; **t. of information** nouvelle *f*

titch [tɪtʃ] *n Br Fam (small person)* microbe *m*

titchy ['tɪtʃɪ] *adj Br Fam* minuscule

tit-for-tat [tɪtfə'tæt] *adj Fam (murder)* en représailles; **it's just t.** c'est un prêté pour un rendu

titillate ['tɪtɪleɪt] *vt* titiller

titillation [tɪtɪ'leɪʃən] *n* titillation *f*

title ['taɪtəl] **1** *n* titre *m*; **the titles** le générique; **t. deeds** titres de propriété; **t. fight** combat *m* comptant pour le titre; **t. page** page *f* de titre; **t. role** *(in play, film)* rôle-titre *m*; **t. track** *(of album)* morceau *m* qui donne son titre à l'album
2 *vt* intituler

titled ['taɪtəld] *adj (person)* titré(e)

titleholder ['taɪtəlhəʊldə(r)] *n (in sport)* tenant(e) *m,f* du titre

titter ['tɪtə(r)] **1** *n* petit rire *m*
2 *vi* rire bêtement

tittle-tattle ['tɪtəltætəl] *Fam* **1** *n* potins *mpl*, cancans *mpl*
2 *vi* cancaner

titular ['tɪtjʊlə(r)] *adj* en titre

tizzy ['tɪzɪ] (*pl* **tizzies**) *n Fam* **to be in/get into a t.** être/se mettre dans tous ses états

T-junction ['tiːdʒʌŋkʃən] *n* carrefour *m* en T

TLC [tiːel'siː] *n* (*abbr* **tender loving care**) affection *f*, tendresse *f*

TNT [tiːen'tiː] *n Chem* (*abbr* **trinitrotoluene**) TNT *m*

to [tuː, *unstressed* tə] **1** *prep* (**a**) (*towards*) à; **to go to church/school** aller à l'église/à l'école; **to go to France/Japan/the USA** aller en France/au Japon/aux États-Unis; **to go to sb's house** aller chez qn; **to the left/right** à gauche/droite (**b**) (*until*) jusqu'à; **it's ten to (six)** il est (six heures) moins dix; **to count to ten** compter jusqu'à dix; **a year to the day** un an jour pour jour (**c**) (*expressing indirect object*) **to give sth to sb** donner qch à qn; **to speak to sb** parler à qn (**d**) (*with result*) **to my surprise/joy** à ma grande surprise/joie; **to my horror, I discovered that...** et, horreur!, je découvris que... (**e**) (*expressing proportion*) **six votes to four** six voix contre quatre; **there are 2 dollars to the pound** une livre vaut 2 dollars
2 *particle* (**a**) (*with infinitive*) **to go** aller; **to have things to do** avoir des choses à faire; **it's too hot to go out** il fait trop chaud pour sortir; **he came to help me** il est venu m'aider; **I want him to know** je veux qu'il sache; **she told me to stay** elle m'a dit de rester (**b**) (*representing verb*) **I want/ought to** je veux/devrais le faire; **I was told to** on m'a dit de le faire

toad [təʊd] *n* (*animal*) crapaud *m*; *Fam Pej* (*man*) type *m* répugnant; *Br* **t. in the hole** = saucisses cuites au four dans de la pâte à crêpes

toadstool ['təʊdstuːl] *n* champignon *m* non comestible

toady ['təʊdɪ] *Fam* **1** *n* lèche-bottes *mf inv*
2 *vi* (*pt & pp* **toadied**) **to t. to sb** lécher les bottes de qn

toast [təʊst] **1** *n* (**a**) (*toasted bread*) pain *m* grillé; **a slice** *or* **piece of t.** un toast; **t. rack** porte-toasts *m inv* (**b**) (*tribute*) toast *m*; **to drink a t. to sb/sth** porter un toast à qn/qch
2 *vt* (**a**) (*bread*) (faire) griller; **toasted cheese** fromage *m* fondu; **toasted sandwich** sandwich *m* grillé (**b**) (*tribute*) porter un toast à

toaster ['təʊstə(r)] *n* grille-pain *m inv*

toastie ['təʊstɪ] *n Fam* (*toasted sandwich*) sandwich *m* grillé

tobacco [tə'bækəʊ] *n* tabac *m*; **t. pouch** blague *f* à tabac

tobacconist [tə'bækənɪst] *n* marchand(e) *m,f* de tabac; *Br* **t.'s (shop)** (bureau *m* de) tabac *m*

toboggan [tə'bɒgən] **1** *n* luge *f*
2 *vi* faire de la luge

today [tə'deɪ] *adv* aujourd'hui; **a week ago t.** il y a juste une semaine aujourd'hui; **a week from t.** aujourd'hui en huit; **t.'s date** la date d'aujourd'hui; **t.'s paper** le journal du jour

toddle ['tɒdəl] *vi* (*of infant*) commencer à marcher; *Fam* **to t. off** ficher le camp

toddler ['tɒdlə(r)] *n* tout-petit *m* (*qui fait ses premiers pas*)

to-die-for [tə'daɪfɔː(r)] *adj Fam* craquant(e)

to-do [tə'duː] *n Fam* remue-ménage *m inv*; **what a t.!** quelle histoire!

toe [təʊ] **1** *n* (**a**) (*of foot*) orteil *m*, doigt *m* de pied; (*of sock, shoe*) bout *m*; **big/little t.** gros/petit orteil (**b**) (*idioms*) **to be on one's toes** être en alerte; **to keep sb on his/her toes** ne pas laisser de répit à qn; **to tread on sb's toes** marcher sur les pieds de qn
2 *vt* **to t. the line** bien se tenir

toehold ['təʊhəʊld] *n* (*in climbing*) prise *f* de pied; *Fig* **to gain a t. in the market** mettre un pied sur le marché

toenail ['təʊneɪl] *n* ongle *m* de pied

toff [tɒf] *n Br Fam Old-fashioned* aristo *mf*

toffee ['tɒfɪ] *n* caramel *m* (au beurre); *Fam* **he can't sing for t.** il chante comme un pied; **t. apple** pomme *f* d'amour

tofu ['təʊfuː] *n* tofu *m*

together [tə'geðə(r)] **1** *adv* ensemble; **t. with** ainsi que, en même temps que
2 *adj Fam* (*person*) équilibré(e)

togetherness [tə'geðənɪs] *n* unité *f*, harmonie *f*

toggle ['tɒgəl] **1** *n* (*on coat*) olive *f*; *Comput & Elec* **t. switch** commande *f* à bascule
2 *vi Comput* basculer

Togo ['təʊgəʊ] *n* le Togo

Togolese [təʊgə'liːz] **1** *n* Togolais(e) *m,f*
2 *adj* togolais(e)

togs [tɒgz] *npl Br Fam* (*clothes*) fringues *fpl*

toil [tɔɪl] **1** *n Lit* labeur *m*
2 *vi* (*work hard*) travailler dur; **to t. away at sth** peiner sur qch; **to t. up a hill** gravir péniblement une colline

toilet ['tɔɪlɪt] *n* (**a**) (*lavatory*) toilettes *fpl*; **to go to the t.** aller aux toilettes; **t. paper** papier *m* hygiénique; **t. roll** rouleau *m* de papier hygiénique; **t. seat** siège *m* des toilettes (**b**) *Old-fashioned* (*washing and dressing*) toilette *f*; **t. bag** trousse *f* de toilette; **t. soap** savon *m* de toilette

toiletries ['tɔɪlɪtrɪz] *npl* articles *mpl* de toilette

toilet-trained ['tɔɪlɪttreɪnd] *adj* propre

toilet-training ['tɔɪlɪttreɪnɪŋ] *n* apprentissage *m* de la propreté

token ['təʊkən] **1** *n* (**a**) (*symbol*) signe *m*, marque *f*; **as a t. of respect** en signe de respect; **by the same t.** de même, pareillement (**b**) (*for vending machine*) jeton *m*
2 *adj* (*resistance, effort*) symbolique; (*gesture*) symbolique, pour la forme; **I was the t. woman on the committee** j'étais la seule femme de la commission, parce qu'il en fallait une

Tokyo ['təʊkɪəʊ] *n* Tokyo

told [təʊld] *pt & pp of* **tell**

tolerable ['tɒlərəbəl] *adj* (**a**) (*bearable*) tolérable, supportable (**b**) (*reasonably good*) acceptable

tolerance ['tɒlərəns] *n* tolérance *f*; **to have a high/low t. for sth** bien/mal tolérer qch

tolerant ['tɒlərənt] *adj* tolérant(e); **to be t. of sb/sth** tolérer qn/qch

tolerate ['tɒləreɪt] *vt* tolérer

toleration [tɒlə'reɪʃən] *n* tolérance *f*

toll¹ [təʊl] *n* (**a**) (*charge*) péage *m*; **t. bridge** pont *m* à péage; **t. road** route *f* à péage (**b**) (*of dead, injured*) nombre *m* de victimes; *Fig* **to take its t.** faire des dégâts

toll² **1** *vt* (*bell*) sonner
2 *vi* (*of bell*) sonner

toll-free [təʊl'friː] *Am* **1** *adj* **t. number** ≃ numéro *m* vert
2 *adv* (*call*) gratuitement

Tom [tɒm] *pr n Fam* any **T., Dick or Harry** le premier venu

tomahawk ['tɒməhɔːk] *n* tomahawk *m*

tomato [tə'mɑːtəʊ, *Am* tə'meɪtəʊ] (*pl* **tomatoes**) *n* tomate *f*; **t. juice** jus *m* de tomate; **t. ketchup** ketchup *m*; **t. purée** concentré *m* de tomates; **t. sauce** (*for pasta*) sauce *f* tomate; (*ketchup*) ketchup *m*; **t. soup** soupe *f* à la tomate

tomb [tuːm] *n* tombe *f*

tomboy ['tɒmbɔɪ] *n* garçon *m* manqué

tombstone ['tuːmstəʊn] *n* pierre *f* tombale

tomcat ['tɒmkæt] *n* matou *m*

tome [təʊm] *n Formal* gros volume *m*

tomfoolery [tɒm'fuːlərɪ] *n Fam* bêtises *fpl*

tomorrow [tə'mɒrəʊ] **1** *n* demain *m*; *Fam* **to do sth like there's no t.** faire qch frénétiquement
 2 *adv* demain; **t. morning/night** demain matin/soir

tom-tom ['tɒmtɒm] *n* tam-tam *m*

ton [tʌn] *n* tonne *f*; *Fam* **to weigh a t.** peser une tonne; *Fam* **tons of** des tonnes de; *Fam* **to come down on sb like a t. of bricks** tomber dessus à qn

tone [təʊn] *n* (**a**) (*of voice*) ton *m*; (*quality of sound*) sonorité *f*; **don't speak to me in that t. of voice** ne me parle pas sur ce ton; **leave your name and number after the t.** (*on answering machine*) laissez votre nom et votre numéro de téléphone après le signal sonore; *Fig* **it set the t. for the evening** et le ton a été donné pour le reste de la soirée; *Fig* **to raise/lower the t. of the neighbourhood** améliorer/faire baisser le standing du quartier (**b**) (*colour*) ton *m*

▸**tone down** *vt sep* (*colour*) adoucir; *Fig* (*remarks*) modérer

▸**tone up** *vt sep* (*muscles*) raffermir, tonifier

tone-deaf [təʊn'def] *adj* **to be t.** ne pas avoir d'oreille

Tonga ['tɒŋə] *n* les îles *fpl* Tonga

Tongan ['tɒŋən] **1** *n* (**a**) (*person*) Tonguien(enne) *m,f* (**b**) (*language*) tongan *m*
 2 *adj* tonguien(enne)

tongs [tɒŋz] *npl* (**pair of**) **t.** pince *f*; (**curling**) **t.** (*for hair*) fer *m* à friser

tongue [tʌŋ] *n* (**a**) (*in mouth, of land, flame*) langue *f*; (*of shoe*) languette *f*; (*language*) langue *f*; **to stick one's t. out** tirer la langue; **t. twister** = mot ou phrase difficile à prononcer (**b**) (*idioms*) **hold your t.!** tiens ta langue!, tais-toi!; **have you lost your t.?** tu as perdu ta langue?; **to say sth t. in cheek** dire qch en plaisantant

tongue-tied ['tʌŋtaɪd] *adj* muet(ette)

tonic ['tɒnɪk] *n also Fig* tonique *m*, remontant *m*; **t. (water)** Schweppes® *m*

tonight [tə'naɪt] **1** *n* (*evening*) ce soir *m*; (*night*) cette nuit *f*
 2 *adv* (*evening*) ce soir; (*night*) cette nuit

tonnage ['tʌnɪdʒ] *n Naut* (*of ship*) tonnage *m*

tonne [tʌn] *n* tonne *f*

tonsil ['tɒnsəl] *n* amygdale *f*; **to have one's tonsils out** se faire opérer des amygdales

tonsillitis [tɒnsɪ'laɪtɪs] *n* amygdalite *f*; **to have t.** avoir une amygdalite

too [tuː] *adv* (**a**) (*excessively*) trop; **t. many people** trop de gens; **I know her all** *or* **only t. well** je ne la connais que trop; **you're t. kind** vous êtes trop aimable; **he's not t. well today** il ne va pas trop bien aujourd'hui; **t. bad** tant pis; *Fam* **t. right!** et comment! (**b**) (*also*) aussi (**c**) (*moreover*) en plus

took [tʊk] *pt of* take

tool [tuːl] *n* (**a**) (*implement*) outil *m*; (**set of**) **tools** outillage *m*; **t. bag** trousse *f* à outils; *Comput* **t. bar** barre *f* d'outils; *also Comput* **t. box** boîte *f* à outils; **t. kit** trousse *f* à outils; **t. shed** remise *f* (**b**) (*means, instrument*) instrument *m*

toot [tuːt] **1** *n* coup *m* de Klaxon®
 2 *vt* **to t. the horn** klaxonner; **to t. sb** klaxonner qn
 3 *vi* klaxonner

tooth [tuːθ] (*pl* **teeth** [tiːθ]) *n* (**a**) (*of person, saw, comb*) dent *f*; **to cut a t.** percer une dent; **t. decay** carie *f* (**b**) (*idioms*) **to fight t. and nail** se défendre bec et ongles; **to lie through one's teeth** mentir effrontément; **in the teeth of opposition** malgré l'opposition; **armed to the teeth** armé(e) jusqu'aux dents; *Fam* **to get one's teeth into sth** se mettre à fond dans qch; *Fam* **to be fed up to the back teeth with sb/sth** en avoir ras le bol de qn/qch; *Fam* **to be long in the t.** n'être plus tout jeune

toothache ['tuːθeɪk] *n* mal *m* de dents; **to have t.** avoir mal aux dents

toothbrush ['tuːθbrʌʃ] *n* brosse *f* à dents

toothless ['tuːθlɪs] *adj* édenté(e), sans dents; *Fig* (*powerless*) sans pouvoir

toothpaste ['tuːθpeɪst] *n* dentifrice *m*

toothpick ['tuːθpɪk] *n* cure-dents *m inv*

toothy ['tuːθɪ] *adj* **t. grin** large sourire *m*

top¹ [tɒp] *n* (*toy*) toupie *f*

top² **1** *n* (**a**) (*highest part*) (*of tree, mountain, tower, head*) sommet *m*; (*of page, map*) haut *m*; **at the t. of the stairs/street** en haut des escaliers/de la rue; **to be (at the) t. of the class** être premier(ère) de la classe; **from t. to bottom** de haut en bas; *Fig* de fond en comble; **at the t. of one's voice** à tue-tête; **to go over the t.** *Mil* partir à l'assaut; *Fig* aller trop loin; *Fig* **over the t.** (*excessive*) exagéré(e); **to make it to the t.** parvenir au sommet; *Fig* réussir (**b**) (*lid*) (*of box*) couvercle *m*; (*of bottle*) bouchon *m*; (*of pen*) capuchon *m* (**c**) (*surface*) dessus *m* (**d**) (*garment*) haut *m*, top *m* (**e**) (*on*) **t.** dessus; **on t. of** sur; *Fig* **to be on t. of sth** maîtriser qch; **you mustn't let things get on t. of you** il ne faut pas te laisser dépasser par les événements; *Fig* **to come out on t.** prendre le dessus; **to feel on t. of the world** se sentir en pleine forme
 2 *adj* (**a**) (*highest*) (*shelf, drawer*) du haut; (*floor*) dernier(ère); **the t. people** (*in society*) les gens *mpl* en vue; (*in an organization*) la direction *f*; *Fam* **the t. brass** les gros bonnets *mpl*; **t. coat** (*of paint*) dernière couche *f*; **t. deck** (*of bus*) impériale *f*; *Fam Fig* **t. dog** chef *m*; **to feel on t. form** se sentir en pleine forme; *Aut* **t. gear** (*fourth*) quatrième *f* (*vitesse f*); (*fifth*) cinquième *f* (*vitesse f*); **t. hat** haut-de-forme *m*; **t. security** haute sécurité *f*; *Fig* **t. speed** vitesse *f* de pointe; *Fig* **at t. speed** à toute vitesse (**b**) (*best, major*) premier(ère); **the t. ten** les dix premiers; **to come t. in sth** arriver premier en qch
 3 *vt* (**a**) (*place on top of*) couvrir (**with** de); (*pizza*) garnir; (*cake, ice cream*) napper; **and to t. it all** et pour couronner le tout (**b**) (*exceed*) dépasser (**c**) (*be at the top of*) être en tête de; **to t. the bill** être la tête d'affiche (**d**) *Br Fam* **to t. oneself** (*commit suicide*) se foutre en l'air

▸**top up** *vt sep* (*glass, tank*) remplir; *Br* (*mobile phone*) recharger le compte de; (*sum of money*) compléter

top-heavy [tɒp'hevɪ] *adj (structure)* trop lourd(e) du haut, déséquilibré(e); *Fig (organization)* aux dirigeants trop nombreux; *Fam* **to be t.** *(woman)* avoir de gros seins
topic ['tɒpɪk] *n* sujet *m*, thème *m*
topical ['tɒpɪkəl] *adj* d'actualité
topless ['tɒplɪs] *adj (woman)* aux seins nus; **to go t.** faire du monokini
top-level ['tɒplevəl] *adj* au plus haut niveau
topmost ['tɒpməʊst] *adj* le (la) plus haut(e)
top-notch ['tɒpnɒtʃ] *adj Fam* de première classe
topography [tə'pɒgrəfɪ] *n* topographie *f*
topping ['tɒpɪŋ] *n (for pizza)* garniture *f*; *(for cake, ice-cream)* nappage *m*
topple ['tɒpəl] **1** *vt* faire tomber, renverser
2 *vi* tomber
top-quality ['tɒpkwɒlətɪ] *adj* de qualité supérieure
top-secret ['tɒpsiːkrɪt] *adj* top secret(ète)
topsoil ['tɒpsɔɪl] *n* couche *f* arable
topsy-turvy [tɒpsɪ'tɜːvɪ] *Fam* **1** *adj (untidy)* sens dessus dessous; *(confused)* tordu(e)
2 *adv (untidily)* sens dessus dessous
top-up ['tɒpʌp] *n Br (for drink)* **can I give you a t.?** je vous ressers?; *Tel* **t. card** *(for mobile phone)* recharge *f*
torch [tɔːtʃ] **1** *n* **(a)** *(burning)* torche *f*; *Fig* **to carry a t. for sb** aimer qn secrètement **(b)** *Br (electric)* lampe *f* de poche
2 *vt* incendier, mettre le feu à
torchlight ['tɔːtʃlaɪt] *n* **by t.** à la lumière d'une lampe de poche; **t. procession** retraite *f* aux flambeaux
tore [tɔː] *pt of* tear²
torment 1 *n* ['tɔːment] supplice *m*; **to be in t.** être au supplice
2 *vt* [tɔː'ment] tourmenter
tormentor [tɔː'mentə(r)] *n* bourreau *m*
torn [tɔːn] *pp of* tear²
tornado [tɔː'neɪdəʊ] *(pl* tornados *or* tornadoes) *n* tornade *f*
Toronto [tə'rɒntəʊ] *n* Toronto
torpedo [tɔː'piːdəʊ] **1** *(pl* torpedoes) *n* torpille *f*; **t. boat** torpilleur *m*, vedette *f* lance-torpilles
2 *vt (pt & pp* torpedoed) **(a)** *also Fig* torpiller
torpid ['tɔːpɪd] *adj* engourdi(e), léthargique
torpor ['tɔːpə(r)] *n* torpeur *f*
torrent ['tɒrənt] *n* torrent *m*; *Fig (of abuse, insults)* flot *m*; **it's raining in torrents** il pleut à torrents
torrential [tə'renʃəl] *adj* torrentiel(elle)
torrid ['tɒrɪd] *adj also Fig* torride
torso ['tɔːsəʊ] *(pl* torsos) *n* torse *m*
tortoise ['tɔːtəs] *n* tortue *f*
tortoiseshell ['tɔːtəsʃel] *n* écaille *f* (de tortue); **t. (cat)** chat *m* noir, blanc et roux
tortuous ['tɔːtjʊəs] *adj* tortueux(euse)
torture ['tɔːtʃə(r)] **1** *n* torture *f*; *Fig* **it was sheer t.!** c'était un vrai supplice!; **t. chamber** chambre *f* de torture
2 *vt also Fig* torturer
Tory ['tɔːrɪ] **1** *n (pl* Tories) Tory *m*, conservateur(trice) *m,f*
2 *adj* Tory, conservateur(trice)
tosh [tɒʃ] *n Br Fam* bêtises *fpl*
toss [tɒs] **1** *n* **(a)** *(of ball)* lancer *m*; *(of head)* mouvement *m* brusque; **to decide sth on the t. of a coin** décider qch à pile ou face; **to argue the t.** discuter inutilement **(b)** *Br very Fam* **not to give a t.** s'en ficher
2 *vt (throw)* lancer; *(pancake)* faire sauter; *(salad)* remuer; **to t. sth to sb** lancer qch à qn; **to t. a coin** jouer à pile ou face; **to t. one's head** rejeter la tête en arrière; **the ship was tossed by the sea** le bateau était ballotté par la mer
3 *vi* **to t. (up) for sth** jouer qch à pile ou face; **to t. and turn** *(in bed)* se tourner et se retourner *(pour trouver le sommeil)*
▸**toss about, toss around** *vt sep (ship)* ballotter; *Fig (idea)* lancer
▸**toss off** *vt sep* **(a)** *(write)* expédier **(b)** *Vulg (masturbate)* **to t. oneself off** se branler; **to t. sb off** branler qn
▸**toss out** *vt sep* jeter
tosser ['tɒsə(r)] *n Br very Fam* con (conne) *m,f*
toss-up ['tɒsʌp] *n* **to have a t.** jouer à pile ou face; *Fam* **it was a t. between the pub and the cinema** nous n'arrivions pas à nous décider entre le pub et le cinéma; **it's a t. whether or not she'll say yes** je ne sais vraiment pas si elle va dire oui
tot [tɒt] *n* **(a)** *(child)* tout-petit *m* **(b)** *(of drink)* (petite) goutte *f*
▸**tot up** *(pt & pp* totted) *vt sep* additionner
total ['təʊtəl] **1** *n* total *m*; **in t.** au total
2 *adj* total(e); **t. eclipse** éclipse *f* totale
3 *vt* **(a)** *(sum)* se monter à **(b)** *Am Fam (wreck)* bousiller
totalitarian [təʊtælɪ'teərɪən] *adj* totalitaire
totality [təʊ'tælɪtɪ] *n* totalité *f*
totally ['təʊtəlɪ] *adv* totalement
tote¹ [təʊt] *n (in betting)* totalisateur *m*, totaliseur *m*
tote² **1** *n (bag)* fourre-tout *m inv*
2 *vt Fam (carry)* trimbal(l)er
totem pole ['təʊtəm'pəʊl] *n* totem *m*
totter ['tɒtə(r)] *vi also Fig* chanceler; **to t. in/out** entrer/sortir d'un pas chancelant
totty ['tɒtɪ] *n Br Fam (attractive women)* belles nanas *fpl*; *(attractive men)* beaux mecs *mpl*
toucan ['tuːkæn] *n* toucan *m*
touch [tʌtʃ] **1** *n* **(a)** *(act of touching)* toucher *m*, contact *m*; **I felt a t. on my arm** j'ai senti qu'on me touchait le bras; **it was t. and go whether...** il n'était pas certain que... + *subjunctive* **(b)** *(sense)* toucher *m*; *(feel)* contact *m*; **hard/soft to the t.** dur/doux au toucher; **he's lost his t.** il a perdu la main **(c)** *(detail)* **there were some nice touches in the film** il y avait quelques bons passages dans le film **(d)** *(small amount)* pointe *f*; **a t. (too) strong/short** un peu trop fort(e)/court(e); **to have a t. of flu** être un peu grippé(e) **(e)** *(communication)* **to be/get in t. with sb** être/se mettre en contact avec qn; **to stay in/lose t. with sb** rester en/perdre contact avec qn **(f)** *(in football, rugby)* **in t.** en touche; **t. judge** juge *m* de touche
2 *vt (physically, emotionally)* toucher; *(interfere with)* toucher à; **to t. bottom** *(of ship, economy)* toucher le fond; *Fam* **t. wood!** je touche du bois!; **I never t. alcohol** je ne touche jamais à l'alcool; **you haven't touched your meal** tu n'as pas touché à ton repas; **the law can't t. her** la loi ne peut rien contre elle; *Fig* **there's nothing to t. it** c'est sans égal; **there's nothing to t. her** elle est imbattable
▸**touch down** *vi (of plane)* atterrir
▸**touch on** *vt insep* aborder
▸**touch up** *vt sep* **(a)** *(picture)* retoucher **(b)** *Br Fam (molest)* peloter
touchdown ['tʌtʃdaʊn] *n* **(a)** *(of plane)* atterrissage *m* **(b)** *(in American football)* but *m*

touched [tʌtʃt] *adj* (**a**) *(moved)* touché(e), ému(e) (**b**) *Fam (mad)* toqué(e)

touching ['tʌtʃɪŋ] *adj (moving)* touchant(e), émouvant(e)

touchline ['tʌtʃlaɪn] *n* ligne *f* de touche

touch-sensitive screen ['tʌtʃ'sensɪtɪv'skriːn] *n* Comput écran *m* tactile

touchstone ['tʌtʃstəʊn] *n* pierre *f* de touche

touch-tone ['tʌtʃtəʊn] *adj (telephone)* à touches

touch-type ['tʌtʃtaɪp] *vi* taper au toucher

touch-typing ['tʌtʃtaɪpɪŋ] *n* dactylographie *f* au toucher

touchy ['tʌtʃɪ] *adj (subject)* délicat(e); *(person)* susceptible (**about** à propos de)

touchy-feely ['tʌtʃɪfiːlɪ] *adj Pej* qui affectionne les contacts physiques

tough [tʌf] **1** *adj* (**a**) *(strict, severe)* dur(e); *(resistant)* résistant(e), solide; *Fam* **a t. guy** un dur à cuire; **to get t. (with sb)** se montrer plus sévère (avec qn) (**b**) *(difficult)* dur(e), difficile; *(unfair)* dur(e); *Fam* **t. luck!** pas de chance!; *Ironic* tant pis!
2 *adv* **to act t.** jouer au dur
3 *n* dur(e) *m,f*

toughen ['tʌfən] *vt (person, skin)* endurcir; *(penalties, conditions)* durcir; **toughened glass** verre *m* trempé

toughness ['tʌfnɪs] *n (of meat, skin, conditions)* dureté *f*; *(of task)* difficulté *f*; *(of person) (strength)* force *f*; *(hardness)* dureté *f*

toupee ['tuːpeɪ] *n* postiche *m*

tour [tʊə(r)] **1** *n (by tourist)* voyage *m*; *(of building, town)* visite *f*; *(by pop group, theatre company)* tournée *f*; **to go on a t.** *(of tourist)* faire un voyage organisé; **to go on a t.** *(of pop group, theatre company)* partir en tournée; *Mil* **t. of duty** service *m*; **t. of inspection** tournée *f* d'inspection; **t. guide** *(person)* guide *mf*; **t. operator** voyagiste *m*
2 *vt (country, hospital)* visiter; *(of pop group, theatre company)* être en tournée à/en
3 *vi (of tourist)* faire du tourisme, voyager; *(of pop group, theatre company)* être en tournée

tour de force ['tʊədə'fɔːs] *n* tour *m* de force

tourism ['tʊərɪzəm] *n* tourisme *m*

tourist ['tʊərɪst] *n* touriste *mf*; **t. attraction** site *m* touristique; **t. class** classe *f* touriste; **t. (information) office** syndicat *m* d'initiative, office *m* du tourisme; *Fam* **t. trap** piège *m* à touristes

tournament ['tʊənəmənt] *n* tournoi *m*

tourniquet ['tʊənɪkeɪ] *n Med* garrot *m*

tousle ['taʊzəl] *vt (hair)* ébouriffer

tout [taʊt] **1** *n (ticket)* **t.** revendeur(euse) *m,f* de billets *(au marché noir)*
2 *vt (tickets, goods)* revendre
3 *vi* **to t. for trade** racoler des clients

tow [təʊ] **1** *n* **to give sb a t.** remorquer qn; **on t.** en remorque; *Fam* **to have someone in t.** avoir qn dans son sillage; **t. truck** dépanneuse *f*
2 *vt* remorquer; **to t. a car away** enlever une voiture

toward [tə'wɔːd] = **towards**

towards [tə'wɔːdz] *prep* (**a**) *(in space, time)* vers (**b**) *(directed at) (of feelings, behaviour)* envers (**c**) *(contributing to)* **to contribute t. the cost of sth** participer au coût de qch; **15% of the budget will go t. improving safety** 15% du budget sera destiné à l'amélioration de la sécurité

towbar ['təʊbɑː(r)] *n* barre *f* de remorquage

towel ['taʊəl] **1** *n* serviette *f* (de toilette); **t. rail** porte-serviette *m*
2 *vt* **to t. oneself (dry)** se sécher, s'essuyer

towelling ['taʊəlɪŋ] *n* tissu-éponge *m*

tower ['taʊə(r)] **1** *n* tour *f*; *Fig* **a t. of strength** un roc; *Br* **t. block** tour d'habitation; *Comput* **t. system** tour
2 *vi* **to t. over sb/sth** dominer qn/qch

towering ['taʊərɪŋ] *adj* immense

town [taʊn] *n* ville *f*; **to go into t.** aller en ville; **to go out on the t.** faire la fête en ville; *Fam Fig* **to go to t. (on sth)** mettre le paquet (sur qch); **t. centre** centre-ville *m*; **t. clerk** secrétaire *mf* de mairie; **t. council** conseil *m* municipal; **t. hall** mairie *f*; **t. planner** urbaniste *mf*; **t. planning** urbanisme *m*

townsfolk ['taʊnzfəʊk] *npl* citadins *mpl*

township ['taʊnʃɪp] *n (in North America)* municipalité *f*; *(in South Africa)* township *f*

townspeople ['taʊnzpiːpəl] *npl* citadins *mpl*

towpath ['təʊpɑːθ] *n* chemin *m* de halage

towrope ['təʊrəʊp] *n* câble *m* de remorque

toxic ['tɒksɪk] *adj* toxique; *Med* **t. shock syndrome** syndrome *m* du choc toxique; **t. waste** déchets *mpl* toxiques

toxin ['tɒksɪn] *n* toxine *f*

toy [tɔɪ] **1** *n* jouet *m*; **t. soldier** petit soldat *m*; **t. shop** magasin *m* de jouets; **t. train** train *m* miniature
2 *vi* **to t. with sb** jouer avec qn; **to t. with an idea** caresser une idée; **to t. with sb's affections** jouer avec les sentiments de qn

toyboy ['tɔɪbɔɪ] *n Fam* jeune amant *m* (d'une femme plus âgée)

trace [treɪs] **1** *n* trace *f*; **without t.** sans laisser de traces; *Chem* **t. element** oligo-élément *m*
2 *vt* (**a**) *(diagram, picture)* tracer (**b**) *(person)* retrouver (la trace de); *(development, history)* retracer

trachea [trə'kiːə] *(pl* tracheae [trə'kiːiː]*) n Anat* trachée *f*

track [træk] **1** *n* (**a**) *(mark)* trace *f*; *(trail)* piste *f* (**b**) *(path)* piste *f*, chemin *m*; *(in athletics)* piste; *Sport* **t. and field events** épreuves *fpl* d'athlétisme; *Fig* **t. record** passé *m*; **t. shoes** chaussures *fpl* d'athlétisme (**c**) *(on record, CD)* morceau *m* (**d**) *(of tank, tractor)* chenille *f* (**e**) *(railway line)* voie *f* (**f**) *(idioms)* **to be on the right t.** être sur la bonne voie; **to keep t. of sth** surveiller qch; **to lose t. of sb** perdre qn de vue; **I've lost t. of how much money I've spent** je ne sais plus combien d'argent j'ai dépensé; **to stop sb in his/her tracks** stopper qn net; *Fam* **to make tracks** filer, mettre les voiles
2 *vt (animal)* suivre à la trace; *(missile)* suivre la trajectoire de; *(person)* traquer

▸**track down** *vt sep (locate)* trouver

tracked [trækt] *adj (vehicle)* chenillé(e)

tracker dog ['trækə'dɒg] *n* chien *m* policier

tracksuit ['træksuːt] *n* survêtement *m*; **t. top** veste *f* de survêtement; **t. bottoms** pantalon *m* de survêtement

tract[1] [trækt] *n* (**a**) *(of land)* étendue *f* (**b**) *Anat (respiratory, digestive)* appareil *m*

tract[2] *n (pamphlet)* tract *m*

tractable ['træktəbəl] *adj (person, animal)* docile

traction ['trækʃən] *n (force)* traction *f*; *Med* **to be in t.** être en extension; **t. engine** locomobile *f*

tractor ['træktə(r)] *n (vehicle)* tracteur *m*; *Comput* **t. feed** alimentation *f* par entraînement

trade [treɪd] **1** *n* (**a**) *Com (commerce)* commerce *m*; **t. association** association *f* professionnelle; **t. deficit** déficit *m* commercial; **t. discount** remise *f* professionnelle;

t. embargo embargo *m* commercial; **t. fair** foire *f ou* exposition *f* commerciale; **t. gap** déficit *m* commercial; **t. name** *(of product)* nom *m* de marque; *(of firm)* raison *f* commerciale; *also Fig* **t. secret** secret *m* de fabrication; *Geog* **t. winds** alizés *mpl* (**b**) *(swap)* échange *m*; **to do a t.** faire un échange (**c**) *(profession)* métier *m*; **he's a plumber by t.** il est plombier (de son métier); **t. union** syndicat *m*; **t. unionist** syndicaliste *mf*
2 *vt* **to t. sth (for sth)** échanger qch (contre qch); **to t. places with sb** changer de place avec qn; **to t. insults/blows** échanger des insultes/coups
3 *vi* commercer, faire du commerce
▸**trade in** *vt sep* faire reprendre; **I traded my car in for a new one** ils ont repris ma vieille voiture quand j'ai acheté la nouvelle
▸**trade on** *vt insep (exploit)* profiter de
trade-in ['treɪdɪn] *n* reprise *f*
trademark ['treɪdmɑːk] *n* marque *f* (de fabrique); *Fig* signe *m* distinctif
trade-off ['treɪdɒf] *n* compromis *m*
trader ['treɪdə(r)] *n* commerçant(e) *m,f*, marchand(e) *m,f*; *(on stock exchange)* opérateur(trice) *m,f*
tradesman ['treɪdzmən] *n* commerçant(e) *m,f*
trading ['treɪdɪŋ] *n* **t. partner** partenaire *m* commercial; **t. post** comptoir *m* commercial; **t. stamp** timbre-prime *m*
tradition [trə'dɪʃən] *n* tradition *f*
traditional [trə'dɪʃənəl] *adj* traditionnel(elle)
traditionalist [trə'dɪʃənəlɪst] 1 *n* traditionaliste *mf*
2 *adj* traditionaliste
traffic ['træfɪk] 1 *n* (**a**) *(vehicles)* circulation *f*, trafic *m*; **t. cone** cône *m* de signalisation; *Fam* **t. cop** agent *m* de la circulation; **t. island** refuge *m*; **t. jam** embouteillage *m*; *Br* **t. lights** feux *mpl* (tricolores *ou* de signalisation); **t. police** police *f* de la route; *Br* **t. warden** contractuel(elle) *m,f* (**b**) *(trade)* trafic *m*
2 *vt* faire le trafic de
3 *vi* faire du trafic (**in** de)
trafficker ['træfɪkə(r)] *n* trafiquant(e) *m,f*
tragedy ['trædʒɪdɪ] *(pl* **tragedies**) *n* tragédie *f*
tragic ['trædʒɪk] *adj* tragique
tragically ['trædʒɪklɪ] *adv* tragiquement
trail [treɪl] 1 *n* (**a**) *(of smoke, blood)* traînée *f*; **to be on the t. of sb/sth** être sur les traces *ou* la piste de qn/qch (**b**) *(path)* sentier *m*, piste *f*; **t. bike** moto *f* de cross
2 *vt (drag)* traîner
3 *vi* (**a**) *(drag)* traîner (**b**) *(move slowly)* se traîner (**c**) *(in sport, contest)* **to be trailing (behind)** être mené(e)
▸**trail away, trail off** *vi (of voice)* se taire; *(of sound)* s'arrêter
trailblazer ['treɪlbleɪzə(r)] *n* pionnier(ère) *m,f*
trailer ['treɪlə(r)] *n* (**a**) *(vehicle)* remorque *f*; *Am (caravan)* camping-car *m*; *Am* **t. park** = terrain aménagé pour les camping-cars; *Am Fam Pej* **t. trash** prolos *mpl* (qui vivent dans les caravanes) (**b**) *(for film, TV programme)* bande-annonce *f*
train [treɪn] 1 *n* (**a**) *(means of transport)* train *m* (**b**) *(series)* suite *f*, enchaînement *m*; **t. of thought** enchaînement d'idées (**c**) *(retinue)* suite *f* (**d**) *(of dress)* traîne *f*
2 *vt* (**a**) *(person)* former; *(animal)* dresser; **to t. sb for sth/to do sth** former qn à qch/à faire qch (**b**) *(gun, telescope)* braquer (**on** sur)
3 *vi (of athlete, soldier)* s'entraîner; **to t. as a nurse/**

teacher suivre une formation d'infirmière/de professeur
trained [treɪnd] *adj* (**a**) *(animal)* dressé(e) (**b**) *(teacher, nurse)* diplômé(e) (**c**) *(eye, ear)* exercé(e)
trainee [treɪ'niː] *n* stagiaire *mf*
traineeship [treɪ'niːʃɪp] *n* stage *m*
trainer ['treɪnə(r)] *n* (**a**) *(of athlete, team, racehorse)* entraîneur *m*; *(of animals)* dresseur(euse) *m,f* (**b**) *(shoe)* chaussure *f* de sport
training ['treɪnɪŋ] *n* *(in sport)* entraînement *m*; *(for job)* formation *f*; **to be in t. (for)** *(of athlete, team)* s'entraîner (pour); **to be out of t.** manquer d'entraînement; **t. course** stage *m* (de formation); **t. officer** officier *m* instructeur
trainload ['treɪnləʊd] *n* **a t. of** un train plein de
trainspotter ['treɪnspɒtə(r)] *n Br* = personne dont le passe-temps est de noter les numéros des trains; *Fam Pej* **he's a bit of a t.** il est vraiment ringard
traipse [treɪps] *vi Fam* traîner
trait [treɪt] *n* trait *m* (de caractère)
traitor ['treɪtə(r)] *n* traître(esse) *m,f*
trajectory [trə'dʒektərɪ] *(pl* **trajectories**) *n* trajectoire *f*
tram [træm] *n Br* tramway *m*
tramline ['træmlaɪn] *n* ligne *f* de tramway; **tramlines** *(in tennis)* lignes *fpl* de côté
tramp [træmp] 1 (**a**) *Br (vagabond)* clochard(e) *m,f* (**b**) *very Fam (immoral woman)* traînée *f* (**c**) *(walk)* promenade *f*
2 *vt (country)* arpenter, parcourir; **to t. the streets** battre le pavé
3 *vi* marcher (d'un pas lourd)
trample ['træmpəl] 1 *vt* piétiner; **to t. sth underfoot** fouler qch aux pieds
2 *vi* **to t. on sb/sth** piétiner qn/qch
trampoline [træmpə'liːn] *n* trampoline *m*
trance [trɑːns] *n* transe *f*; **to go into a t.** entrer *ou* se mettre en transe
tranquil ['træŋkwɪl] *adj* tranquille, calme
tranquillity, *Am* **tranquility** [træŋ'kwɪlɪtɪ] *n* tranquillité *f*, calme *m*
tranquillizer, *Am* **tranquilizer** ['træŋkwɪlaɪzə(r)] *n* tranquillisant *m*, calmant *m*
transaction [træn'zækʃən] *n* transaction *f*, opération *f*
transatlantic [trænzət'læntɪk] *adj* transatlantique
transcend [træn'send] *vt (go beyond)* transcender; *(be superior to)* surpasser
transcendental [trænsen'dentəl] *adj* transcendantal(e); **t. meditation** méditation *f* transcendantale
transcontinental [trænzkɒntɪ'nentəl] *adj* transcontinental(e)
transcribe [træns'kraɪb] *vt* transcrire
transcript ['trænskrɪpt] *n* transcription *f*
transcription [træns'krɪpʃən] *n* transcription *f*
transfer 1 *n* ['trænsfɜː(r)] (**a**) *(move)* transfert *m*; *(of employee)* mutation *f*; *(of power)* passation *f*; **t. fee** *(for footballer)* prime *f* de transfert; **t. lounge** *(in airport)* salle *f* de transit; **t. passenger** passager *m* en transit; *Comput* **t. speed** vitesse *f* de transfert (**b**) *(sticker)* transfert *m*
2 *vt* [træns'fɜː(r)] transférer; *(employee)* muter; *(attention, affection)* déplacer
3 *vi* [træns'fɜː(r)] être transféré(e) (**to** dans); *(between planes, trains)* changer
transferable [træns'fɜːrəbəl] *adj* transmissible; **not t.** *(on ticket)* titre de transport nominal
transfigure [træns'fɪgə(r)] *vt* transfigurer

transfix [træns'fıks] *vt* transpercer; *Fig* **to be transfixed with fear** être pétrifié(e) par la peur
transform [træns'fɔːm] *vt* transformer (**into** en)
transformation [trænsfə'meıʃən] *n* transformation *f*
transformer [træns'fɔːmə(r)] *n Elec* transformateur *m*
transfusion [træns'fjuːʒən] *n* (**blood**) **t.** transfusion *f* (sanguine)
transgendered [træns'dʒendəd] *adj* transsexuel(elle)
transgenic [trænz'dʒenık] *adj* transgénique
transgress [trænz'gres] *Formal* **1** *vt* (*law*) transgresser, enfreindre
  2 *vi* (*violate law*) transgresser la loi; (*sin*) pécher
transient ['trænzıənt] *adj* éphémère
transistor [træn'zıstə(r)] *n Elec* transistor *m*; **t.** (**radio**) transistor
transit ['trænzıt] *n* transit *m*; **in t.** en transit; **t. camp** camp *m* de transit; **t. visa** visa *m* de transit
transition [træn'zıʃən] *n* transition *f*; **the t. from sth to sth** le passage de qch à qch
transitional [træn'zıʃənəl] *adj* transitoire, de transition
transitive ['trænzıtıv] *adj Gram* transitif(ive)
transitory ['trænzıtərı] *adj* transitoire
translate [trænz'leıt] **1** *vt* traduire (**from/into** de/en); *Fig* **to t. one's ideas into action** mettre ses idées en pratique
  2 *vi* (*of person*) faire de la traduction; (*of word, expression*) se traduire (**as** par)
translation [trænz'leıʃən] *n* (*of language*) traduction *f*
translator [trænz'leıtə(r)] *n* traducteur(trice) *m,f*
transliterate [trænz'lıtəreıt] *vt* transcrire
translucent [trænz'luːsənt] *adj* translucide
transmission [trænz'mıʃən] *n* (*action*) transmission *f*; (*TV, radio programme*) émission *f*; **t. shaft** (*in vehicle*) arbre *m* de transmission
transmit [trænz'mıt] *vt* transmettre; (*TV, radio programme*) diffuser
transmitter [trænz'mıtə(r)] *n* (*emitter*) émetteur *m*; (*relay station*) réémetteur *m*
transparent [træns'pærənt] *adj* (**a**) (*see-through*) transparent(e) (**b**) (*obvious*) évident(e)
transpire [træns'paıə(r)] **1** *vt* (*become apparent*) **it transpired that...** il s'est avéré que...; **she transpired to be...** elle s'est avérée être...
  2 *vi* (*happen*) arriver, se passer
transplant 1 *n* ['trænsplɑːnt] (*of organ*) transplantation *f*, greffe *f*
  2 *vt* [træns'plɑːnt] (**a**) (*organ*) transplanter, greffer (**b**) (*population*) transplanter
transport 1 *n* ['trænspɔːt] transport *m*; *Br* **t. café** routier *m* (*restaurant*); **t. costs** frais *mpl* de transport
  2 *vt* [trænz'pɔːt] transporter
transportation [trænzpɔː'teıʃən] *n* transport *m*; *Hist* (*as punishment*) transportation *f*
transporter [træns'pɔːtə(r)] *n* (*vehicle*) camion *m* pour transport d'automobiles
transpose [træns'pəuz] *vt* transposer
transsexual [træn(z)'seksjuəl] **1** *n* transsexuel(elle) *m,f*
  2 *adj* transsexuel(elle)
Transvaal ['trɑːnzvɑːl] *n* **theT.** leTransvaal
transverse ['trænzvɜːs] *adj* transversal(e)
transvestite [trænz'vestaıt] *n* travesti *m*
trap [træp] **1** *n* (**a**) (*in hunting*) & *Fig* piège *m*; **to set a t.** tendre un piège; *Fig* **to walk** *or* **fall straight into the t.** tomber en plein dans le piège (**b**) *very Fam* (*mouth*) gueule *f*

  2 *vt* (*pt & pp* **trapped**) piéger, prendre au piège; **to t. sb into saying/doing sth** faire dire/faire faire qch à qn en usant de ruse
trapdoor ['træp'dɔː(r)] *n* trappe *f*
trapeze [trə'piːz] *n* trapèze *m*; **t. artist** trapéziste *mf*
trapper ['træpə(r)] *n* trappeur *m*
trappings ['træpıŋz] *npl* signes *mpl* extérieurs
trash [træʃ] **1** *n* (**a**) *Am* (*refuse*) ordures *fpl*; **t. can** poubelle *f* (**b**) (*worthless objects*) camelote *f*; *Fam* **that book/film is a load of t.** ce livre/film est nul
  2 *vt Fam* (**a**) (*vandalize*) saccager (**b**) (*criticize*) descendre en flammes
trashy ['træʃı] *adj Fam* à la noix
trauma ['trɔːmə] *n* traumatisme *m*
traumatic [trɔː'mætık] *adj* traumatisant(e)
traumatize ['trɔːmətaız] *vt* traumatiser
travail ['træveıl] *n Lit* labeur *m*
travel ['trævəl] **1** *n* voyage *m*; **on my travels** au cours de mes voyages; **I spend half my money on t.** (*to and from work*) la moitié de mon argent part dans les transports; **t. agency** agence *f* de voyages; **t. agent** agent *m* de voyages; **t. documents** titre *m* de transport; **t. insurance** assurance-voyage *f*; **t. writer** auteur *m* de récits de voyage
  2 *vt* (*road, country*) parcourir
  3 *vi* (**a**) (*of person*) voyager; (*vehicle, of light, sound, electricity*) se déplacer; **we travelled across France by train** nous avons traversé la France en train; **wine doesn't t. well** le vin supporte mal d'être transporté; *Fam* (**good**) **news travels fast** les nouvelles vont vite
traveller, *Am* **traveler** ['trævələ(r)] *n* voyageur(euse) *m,f*; *Br* (**new age**) **t.** voyageur(euse) *m,f* new age; **t.'s cheque** chèque *m* de voyage
travelling, *Am* **traveling** ['trævəlıŋ] **1** *n* déplacement *m*; **t. bag** sac *m* de voyage; **t. companion** compagnon (compagne) *m,f* de voyage; **t. expenses** frais *mpl* de déplacement; *Br* **t. rug** plaid *m*
  2 *adj* (*performer, circus*) itinérant(e); **t. salesman** voyageur *m* de commerce
traverse [trə'vɜːs] *vt Lit* traverser
travesty ['trævəstı] *n* travestissement *m*; **t. of justice** simulacre *m* de justice
trawl [trɔːl] **1** *n* (**a**) (*net*) chalut *m* (**b**) *Fig* (*search*) **to carry out** *or* **make a t. through sth** passer qch au crible
  2 *vt* (**a**) (*sea*) aller à la pêche au chalut en (**b**) *Fig* (*search through*) passer au crible
  3 *vi* (**a**) (*fish*) pêcher au chalut (**b**) *Fig* **to t. through sth** passer qch au crible
trawler ['trɔːlə(r)] *n* (*ship*) chalutier *m*
tray [treı] *n* plateau *m*; (*in office*) corbeille *f*
treacherous ['tretʃərəs] *adj* traître
treachery ['tretʃərı] *n* traîtrise *f*
treacle [triːkəl] *n* mélasse *f*
tread [tred] **1** *vt* (*pt* **trod** [trɒd], *pp* **trodden** ['trɒdən]) marcher sur; **to t. sth underfoot** fouler qch aux pieds; **to t. sth into the carpet** mettre qch sur le tapis (avec ses chaussures); **to t. the boards** (*appear on stage*) monter sur les planches; **to t. grapes** fouler le raisin; **to t. water** faire du surplace; *Fig* (*of company*) se maintenir à flot
  2 *vi* marcher (**on** sur); *also Fig* **to t. on sb's toes** marcher sur les pieds de qn; *Fig* **to t. carefully** *or* **warily** y aller doucement
  3 *n* (**a**) (*sound of footstep*) pas *m* (**b**) (*of tyre*) chape *f*

treadmill ['tredmɪl] *n (in gym)* tapis *m* roulant de jogging; *Hist (in prison)* = roue ou manège auxquels étaient attachés les prisonniers; *Fig (routine)* routine *f*

treason ['triːzən] *n* trahison *f*

treasonable ['triːzənəbəl] *adj* qui constitue un acte de trahison

treasure ['treʒə(r)] **1** *n also Fig* trésor *m*; **t. hunt** chasse *f* au trésor; **t. trove** *Law* trésor *m*; *Fig* mine *f* **2** *vt (person, possession)* tenir beaucoup à; *(memory)* chérir

treasurer ['treʒərə(r)] *n* trésorier(ère) *m,f*

treasury ['treʒərɪ] *n* trésorerie *f*; **the T.** *(government department)* ≃ le ministère des Finances; *Fin* **t. bond** ≃ bon *m* du Trésor

treat [triːt] **1** *n (pleasure)* plaisir *m*; *(gift)* cadeau *m*; **to give sb a t.** faire plaisir à qn; **it's my t.** *(I'm paying)* c'est moi qui régale; *also Ironic* **you've got a real t. in store** attends-toi à une belle surprise; *Fam* **to work a t.** marcher à merveille
2 *vt* (**a**) *(person, illness, metal)* traiter; **to t. sb well/badly** bien/mal traiter qn; **to t. sth as a joke** prendre qch à la rigolade (**b**) *(give present to)* **to t. sb to sth** offrir qch à qn; **to t. oneself to sth** s'offrir qch; **I'll t. you** *(pay for you)* je t'invite; *Ironic* **she treated us to one of her tantrums** nous avons eu droit à une de ses colères
3 *vi Formal (negotiate)* **to t. with sb/sth** traiter avec qn/qch

treatise ['triːtɪs] *n* traité *m*

treatment ['triːtmənt] *n* traitement *m*

treaty ['triːtɪ] *(pl* **treaties***) n (international)* traité *m*; *(between individuals)* accord *m*, contrat *m*

treble ['trebəl] **1** *n Mus (person, voice)* soprano *m*
2 *adj (triple)* triple; *Mus* **t. clef** clef *f* de sol
3 *vt & vi* tripler

tree [triː] *n* arbre *m*; *Fig* **at the top of the t.** en haut de l'échelle; *Am Fam* **to be out of one's t.** débloquer; *Pej* **t. hugger** écologiste *mf* fanatique; **t. trunk** tronc *m* d'arbre

treetop ['triːtɒp] *n* cime *f* d'un arbre

trek [trek] **1** *n (long walk)* randonnée *f* (pédestre); *Fig* **it's quite a t. to the shops** ça fait loin à pied jusqu'aux magasins
2 *vi* faire de la randonnée; *Fig* **to t. to the shops/home** se taper le chemin à pied jusqu'aux magasins/jusqu'à chez soi

trellis ['trelɪs] *n* treillis *m*, treillage *m*

tremble ['trembəl] **1** *n* tremblement *m*
2 *vi* trembler (**with** de)

tremendous [trɪ'mendəs] *adj* (**a**) *(enormous)* énorme (**b**) *Fam (excellent)* formidable

tremendously [trɪ'mendəslɪ] *adv (very)* extrêmement

tremor ['tremə(r)] *n* tremblement *m*

tremulous ['tremjʊləs] *adj (voice, hand)* tremblant(e); *(person, smile)* timide

trench [trentʃ] *n (ditch)* fossé *m*; *Mil* tranchée *f*; **t. coat** trench-coat *m*; **t. warfare** guerre *f* de tranchées

trenchant ['tren(t)ʃənt] *adj* tranchant(e)

trend [trend] *n (tendency)* tendance *f*; *(fashion)* mode *f*; **to set** *or* **start a t.** lancer une mode

trendsetter ['trendsetə(r)] *n* lanceur(euse) *m,f* de mode

trendspotter ['trendspɒtə(r)] *n* tendanceur *m*, = personne employée par une société commerciale pour identifier les nouvelles tendances de la mode telles qu'elles apparaissent dans la rue, les bars etc

trendy ['trendɪ] *n Br Fam* branché(e)

trepidation [trepɪ'deɪʃən] *n Formal* inquiétude *f*

trespass ['trespəs] *vi Law* s'introduire illégalement dans une propriété privée

trespasser ['trespəsə(r)] *n Law* intrus(e) *m,f*; **trespassers will be prosecuted** *(sign)* défense d'entrer sous peine de poursuites

tresses ['tresɪz] *npl Lit (hair)* chevelure *f*

trestle ['tresəl] *n* tréteau *m*; **t. table** table *f* à tréteaux

trial ['traɪəl] *n* (**a**) *Law* procès *m*; **to bring sb to t.** traduire qn en justice; **to be on t.** *(test)* essai *m*; **on t.** à l'essai; **by t. and error** par tâtonnements; **t. period** période *f* d'essai; **t. run** essai *m*; **t. separation** *(of couple)* séparation *f* à l'essai (**c**) *(ordeal)* épreuve *f*

triangle ['traɪæŋgəl] *n* triangle *m*

triangular [traɪ'æŋgjʊlə(r)] *adj* triangulaire

triathlon [traɪ'æθlɒn] *n* triathlon *m*

tribal ['traɪbəl] *adj* tribal(e)

tribalism ['traɪbəlɪzəm] *n* tribalisme *m*

tribe [traɪb] *n* tribu *f*

tribesman ['traɪbzmən] *n* membre *m* d'une tribu

tribulation [trɪbjʊ'leɪʃən] *n Formal* malheur *m*

tribunal [traɪ'bjuːnəl] *n Law* tribunal *m*

tributary ['trɪbjʊtərɪ] *(pl* **tributaries***) n (of river)* affluent *m*

tribute ['trɪbjuːt] *n* (**a**) *(homage)* hommage *m*; **to pay t. to** rendre hommage à (**b**) *(testimony)* **our success is a t. to all your hard work** c'est grâce à vos efforts soutenus que nous avons réussi

trice [traɪs] *n* **in a t.** en un clin d'œil

triceps ['traɪseps] *n Anat* triceps *m*

trick [trɪk] **1** *n* (**a**) *(ruse)* tour *m*; *(practical joke)* farce *f*; **to play a t. on sb** jouer un tour à qn; *(practical joke)* faire une farce à qn; **t. photography** truquage *m*; **t. question** question *f* piège (**b**) *(by magician)* tour *m* (**c**) *(in card game)* pli *m* (**d**) *(idioms)* **to do the t.** marcher; **to know all the tricks** connaître toutes les astuces; **the tricks of the trade** les ficelles du métier; **she doesn't miss a t.** rien ne lui échappe; **he's been up to his old tricks again** il a encore fait des siennes; *Fam* **how's tricks?** comment va, quoi de neuf?
2 *vt (person)* duper; **to t. sb into doing sth** amener qn à faire qch par la ruse

trickery ['trɪkərɪ] *n* duperie *f*, ruse *f*

trickle ['trɪkəl] **1** *vt (liquid)* faire couler goutte à goutte
2 *vi (of liquid)* couler goutte à goutte; **to t. in/out** *(of people)* entrer/sortir au compte-gouttes
3 *n (of liquid)* filet *m*; *(of complaints, letters)* petit nombre *m*; *Econ* **t.-down theory** = théorie selon laquelle la richesse de quelques-uns finira par profiter à toute la société

tricky ['trɪkɪ] *adj* délicat(e)

tricycle ['traɪsɪkəl] *n* tricycle *m*

trident ['traɪdənt] *n* trident *m*

tried-and-tested ['traɪdən'testɪd] *adj* qui a fait ses preuves

trier ['traɪə(r)] *n Fam* **to be a t.** être persévérant(e)

trifle ['traɪfəl] *n* (**a**) *(insignificant thing)* broutille *f*, bagatelle *f* (**b**) **a t. wide/short** un tantinet trop large/court(e) (**c**) *Br (dessert)* = dessert où alternent une couche de génoise imbibée d'alcool et de fruits en gelée et une couche de crème anglaise, et recouvert de chantilly

▸**trifle with** *vt insep* plaisanter avec

trifling ['traɪflɪŋ] *adj* insignifiant(e)

trigger ['trɪgə(r)] **1** n (of gun) détente f; Fig (of change, decision) élément m déclencheur
  2 vt déclencher
▸**trigger off** vt sep déclencher
trigger-happy ['trɪgəhæpɪ] adj Fam **to be t. happy** avoir la gâchette facile
trigonometry [trɪgə'nɒmɪtrɪ] n trigonométrie f
trilby ['trɪlbɪ] (pl **trilbies**) n Br (chapeau m en) feutre m
trill [trɪl] **1** n trille m
  2 vi triller
trillion ['trɪljən] n billion m; Fam **trillions of** (lots of) un milliard de
trilogy ['trɪlədʒɪ] (pl **trilogies**) n trilogie f
trim [trɪm] **1** n (**a**) **to give sb's hair a t.** faire une coupe d'entretien à qn; **to give the hedge a t.** tailler la haie (**b**) **to be/keep in t.** (keep fit) être en/garder la forme
  2 adj (**a**) (neat) soigné(e) (**b**) (slim) svelte
  3 vt (pt & pp **trimmed**) (**a**) (cut) (hair) rafraîchir; (hedge) tailler, élaguer; (meat) parer; (budget) réduire (**b**) (decorate) orner, décorer (**with** de)
▸**trim down** vt sep (text) élaguer; (company, expenditure) réduire
trimaran ['traɪməræn] n trimaran m
trimester [trɪ'mestə(r)] n trimestre m
trimming ['trɪmɪŋ] n (**a**) (on clothes) garniture f (**b**) **trimmings** (of meal) accompagnements mpl traditionnels
Trinidad and Tobago ['trɪnɪdædəntə'beɪgəʊ] n Trinité-et-Tobago
Trinity ['trɪnɪtɪ] n Rel **the T.** la Trinité
trinket ['trɪŋkɪt] n babiole f
trio ['triːəʊ] (pl **trios**) n trio m
trip [trɪp] **1** n (**a**) (journey) trajet m, voyage m; (for one day) excursion f (**b**) Fam (on drugs) trip m (**c**) (stumble) faux pas m; **t. wire** fil m de détente
  2 vt (pt & pp **tripped**) (**a**) (make stumble) faire un croche-pied à (**b**) **to t. a switch** déclencher un interrupteur (**c**) (idiom) Hum **to t. the light fantastic** danser
  3 vi (**a**) (stumble) trébucher (**b**) (step lightly) marcher d'un pas léger; **to t. off the tongue** (of word, name) être facile à prononcer (**c**) Fam (on drugs) **to be tripping** être en plein trip
▸**trip over 1** vt insep trébucher sur
  2 vi trébucher
▸**trip up 1** vt sep (cause to stumble) faire un croche-pied à; Fig (cause to make mistake) désarçonner
  2 vi (stumble) trébucher
tripe [traɪp] n (food) tripes fpl; Fam (nonsense) foutaises fpl
triple ['trɪpəl] **1** adj triple; **t. jump** triple saut m; Med **t. (combination) therapy** trithérapie f
  2 adv **t. the number/amount** trois fois le nombre/la quantité
  3 vt & vi tripler
triplet ['trɪplɪt] n (**a**) (person) triplé(e) m,f (**b**) Mus triolet m
triplicate ['trɪplɪkət] n **in t.** en trois exemplaires
tripod ['traɪpɒd] n trépied m
Tripoli ['trɪpəlɪ] n Tripoli
trite [traɪt] adj banal(e)
triumph ['traɪəmf] **1** n triomphe m; **in t.** triomphant(e)
  2 vi triompher (**over** de)
triumphant [traɪ'ʌmfənt] adj triomphant(e)

triumvirate [traɪ'ʌmvɪrɪt] n triumvirat m
trivet ['trɪvɪt] n (on open fire) trépied m; (stand) = support métallique surélevé pour plats chauds
trivia ['trɪvɪə] npl (unimportant details) détails mpl; (useless information) futilités fpl
trivial ['trɪvɪəl] adj (detail, matter) sans importance, insignifiant(e); (person) superficiel(elle)
trivialize ['trɪvɪəlaɪz] vt banaliser
trod [trɒd] pt of **tread**
trodden ['trɒdən] pp of **tread**
Trojan ['trəʊdʒən] Hist **1** n Troyen(enne) m,f
  2 adj de Troie, troyen(enne); **T. Horse** cheval m de Troie; **the T. War** la guerre de Troie
troll [trəʊl] **1** n (goblin) & Fam Comput troll m
  2 vi Fam Comput troller
trolley ['trɒlɪ] (pl **trolleys**) n Br chariot m; Fam **to be off one's t.** débloquer; Am **t. car** tramway m
trolleybus ['trɒlɪbʌs] n trolleybus m
trolleyed ['trɒlɪd] adj Br Fam bourré(e), pété(e)
trollop ['trɒləp] n Old-fashioned or Hum gourgandine f, catin f
trombone [trɒm'bəʊn] n trombone m (instrument)
trombonist [trɒm'bəʊnɪst] n trombone m (musicien)
troop [truːp] **1** n (**a**) **troops** (soldiers) troupes fpl (**b**) (of people) groupe m
  2 vi **to t. in/out** entrer/sortir en groupe
trooper ['truːpə(r)] n (soldier) cavalier m; Am (mounted policeman) membre m de la police montée; Fam **to swear like a t.** jurer comme un charretier
trophy ['trəʊfɪ] n trophée m
tropic ['trɒpɪk] n tropique m; **in the tropics** sous les tropiques
tropical ['trɒpɪkəl] adj tropical(e)
trot [trɒt] **1** n trot m; **at a t.** au trot; Fam **on the t.** (consecutively) de suite; Fam **to have the trots** avoir la courante
  2 vi (pt & pp **trotted**) (of horse) aller au trot; (of person) trotter
▸**trot out** vt sep Fam débiter
Trotskyism ['trɒtskɪɪzəm] n trotskisme m
Trotskyist ['trɒtskɪɪst], **Trotskyite** ['trɒtskɪaɪt] **1** n trotskiste mf
  2 adj trotskiste
trotter ['trɒtə(r)] n (of pig) pied m
trouble ['trʌbəl] **1** n (**a**) (problem) ennui m; **to have t. with sb/sth** avoir des problèmes avec qn/qch; **to have t. doing sth** avoir du mal à faire qch; **to be in/get into t.** avoir/s'attirer des ennuis; **to get sb into t.** attirer des ennuis à qn; **to get sb out of t.** tirer qn d'affaire; **to make t. (for sb)** créer des ennuis (à qn); **it's more t. than it's worth** le jeu n'en vaut pas la chandelle; Fam **man/woman t.** ennuis mpl de cœur (**b**) (inconvenience) problème m; **to go to the t. of doing sth** se donner la peine de faire qch; **it's not worth the t.** ça n'en vaut pas la peine; **(it's) no t.** (ça ne pose) aucun problème (**c**) (disorder, unrest) troubles mpl; **t. spot** point m chaud
  2 vt (worry) inquiéter; (inconvenience) déranger
  3 vi **to t. to do sth** se donner la peine de faire qch
troubled ['trʌbəld] adj (person) inquiet(ète); (region) agité(e) de troubles; (period) troublé(e)
trouble-free ['trʌbəlfriː] adj (life) sans soucis; (visit, journey) sans histoires
troublemaker ['trʌbəlmeɪkə(r)] n semeur(euse) m,f de troubles

troubleshooter ['trʌbəlʃuːtə(r)] n (for organizational problems) expert m; (for industrial disputes) conciliateur(trice) m,f; (for machines) dépanneur(euse) m,f

troublesome ['trʌbəlsəm] adj pénible

trough [trɒf] n (for food) mangeoire f; (for drink) abreuvoir m; (of wave, on graph) creux m; (in weather front) dépression f

trounce [traʊns] vt battre à plates coutures

troupe [truːp] n troupe f

trouser press ['traʊzə'prɛs] n presse-pantalon m

trousers ['traʊzəz] npl Br (a) (garment) pantalon m (b) (idioms) Fam to wear the t. porter la culotte; Fam to be caught with one's t. down être pris(e) en flagrant délit

trouser suit ['traʊzə'suːt] n tailleur-pantalon m

trousseau ['truːsəʊ] n trousseau m (de jeune mariée)

trout [traʊt] (pl trout) n truite f

trowel ['traʊəl] n truelle f

truancy ['truːənsɪ] n absentéisme m scolaire

truant ['truːənt] n (pupil) élève mf qui fait l'école buissonnière; to play t. faire l'école buissonnière

truce [truːs] n also Fig trêve f; to call a t. demander une trêve

truck [trʌk] 1 n (a) (lorry) camion m; t. driver conducteur(trice) m,f de camion, camionneur m; Am t. farm exploitation f maraîchère; t. stop relais m routier (b) (rail wagon) wagon m (c) Fam to have no t. with sb/sth ne rien avoir à faire avec qn/qch
2 vt (goods) acheminer par camion
3 vi Am (drive a truck) être conducteur(trice) m,f de camion

trucker ['trʌkə(r)] n Am (truck driver) camionneur m

truculent ['trʌkjʊlənt] adj agressif(ive)

trudge [trʌdʒ] 1 n trajet m pénible
2 vi marcher péniblement, se traîner

true [truː] 1 adj (a) (not fictional) vrai(e); to come t. se réaliser; to hold t. (for) être vrai (de) (b) (genuine) véritable; t. love grand amour m; t. north le nord géographique (c) (faithful) fidèle; to be t. to sb être loyal(e) envers qn; to be t. to sth être fidèle à qch; t. to life fidèle à la réalité; t. to form or type fidèle à soi-même (d) (accurate) exact(e)
2 n out of t. hors d'aplomb

truffle ['trʌfəl] n truffe f

truism ['truːɪzəm] n truisme m

truly ['truːlɪ] adv vraiment; yours t. (at end of letter) = je vous prie d'agréer, Madame/Monsieur, l'expression de mes sentiments distingués; Fam Hum (myself) mézigue

trump [trʌmp] 1 n atout m; spades are trumps c'est atout pique; Fig to play one's t. card jouer son atout; Fam Fig to turn up trumps sauver la mise
2 vt couper à l'atout

trumped up ['trʌmptʌp] adj fabriqué(e)

trumpet ['trʌmpɪt] 1 n trompette f; Fig to blow one's own t. vanter ses propres mérites
2 vt (proclaim) claironner
3 vi (of elephant) barrir

trumpeter ['trʌmpɪtə(r)] n trompettiste mf

truncate [trʌŋ'keɪt] vt tronquer

truncheon ['trʌn(t)ʃən] n Br matraque f

trundle ['trʌndəl] 1 vt pousser péniblement
2 vi rouler péniblement

trunk [trʌŋk] n (a) (of tree, body) tronc m; Br Old-fashioned t. call appel m interurbain; Br t. road route f nationale (b) (case) malle f (c) Am (of car) coffre m (d)
(of elephant) trompe f (e) **trunks** (swimming costume) slip m de bain

truss [trʌs] 1 n (a) (for hernia) bandage m herniaire (b) (for roof, bridge) ferme f
2 vt (tie up) ligoter

▶**truss up** vt sep (person) ligoter; (chicken, turkey) trousser

trust [trʌst] 1 n (a) (faith) confiance f (in en); to put one's t. in sb/sth se fier à qn/qch; to take sth on t. croire qch sur parole (b) Law in t. par fidéicommis; Fin t. fund fonds m en fidéicommis (c) Com (group of companies) trust m
2 vt (a) (believe in) faire confiance à; to t. sb with sth confier qch à qn; to t. sb to do sth laisser à qn le soin de faire qch; Fam t. him to say that! c'est bien de lui! (b) Formal (hope) to t. (that)... espérer que...
3 vi to t. in sb/sth faire confiance à qn/qch; to t. to luck s'en remettre au hasard

trusted ['trʌstɪd] adj de confiance; t. third party (for Internet transactions) tierce partie f de confiance

trustee [trʌs'tiː] n Law (of fund, property) fidéicommissaire m; (of charity) administrateur(trice) m,f

trusting ['trʌstɪŋ] adj qui fait confiance aux gens

trustworthy ['trʌstwɜːðɪ] adj (person) digne de confiance; (thing) fiable

trusty ['trʌstɪ] adj Hum fidèle

truth [truːθ] n vérité f; to tell the t. dire la vérité; to tell (you) the t., I don't care à vrai dire, je m'en moque complètement

truthful ['truːθfʊl] adj (person) sincère; (story) véridique

try [traɪ] 1 vt (pt & pp tried) (a) (sample, attempt) essayer; (food, drink) goûter (à); to t. to do sth essayer de faire qch; I'll t. anything once il faut tout essayer dans la vie (b) Law (case, person) juger (c) (test) tester; (person) mettre à l'épreuve; to t. sb's patience mettre la patience de qn à l'épreuve
2 vi essayer; to t. harder faire plus d'efforts; just you t.! essaie un peu pour voir!
3 n (pl tries) (a) (attempt) essai m; to give sth a t. essayer qch; to have a t. at sth/at doing sth essayer qch/de faire qch; it's worth a t. ça vaut le coup d'essayer (b) (in rugby) essai m

▶**try on** vt sep (a) (clothes) essayer (b) Fam to t. it on (with sb) tenter le coup (avec qn); (sexually) draguer (qn)

▶**try out 1** vt sep essayer; to t. sth out on sb expérimenter qch sur qn
2 vi Am to t. out for a team faire un essai pour se faire engager dans une équipe

trying ['traɪɪŋ] adj difficile

tryout ['traɪaʊt] n Am Sport épreuve f de sélection

tsar [zɑː(r)] n tsar m

tsarist ['zɑːrɪst] 1 n tsariste mf
2 adj tsariste

tsetse ['t(s)etsɪ] n t. (fly) (mouche f) tsé-tsé f inv

T-shirt ['tiːʃɜːt] n tee-shirt m

TTP [tiːtiːpiː] n (abbr trusted third party) (for Internet transactions) TPC f

tub [tʌb] n (a) (for washing clothes) baquet m; (bath) baignoire f (b) (for food, plants) pot m

tuba ['tjuːbə] n tuba m

tubby ['tʌbɪ] adj Fam boulot(otte)

tube [tjuːb] n (a) (cylindrical container) tube m; (pipe) tuyau m; Fam to go down the tubes (of money) être foutu en l'air; (of work, plan) tomber à l'eau (b) Br Fam the t. *(underground railway)* le métro; **t. station** station *f* de métro (**c**) *Am Fam (TV)* télé *f*

tuber ['tjuːbə(r)] *n* tubercule *m*

tuberculosis [tjʊbɜːkjʊ'ləʊsɪs] *n* tuberculose *f*

tubing ['tjuːbɪŋ] *n* tuyaux *mpl*

tubular ['tjuːbjʊlə(r)] *adj* tubulaire; **t. bells** carillon *m*

TUC [tiːjuː'siː] *n Br (abbr* **Trades Union Congress**) = confédération des syndicats britanniques

tuck [tʌk] **1** *n* (**a**) *(in sewing)* pli *m* (**b**) *Br Fam (food)* sucreries *fpl*; **t. shop** *(in school)* boutique *f* de friandises (**c**) *(in cosmetic surgery) (for face)* lifting *m*
  2 *vt* **to t. one's shirt into one's trousers** rentrer sa chemise dans son pantalon; **to t. sth under one's arm** mettre qch sous son bras; **to t. sb up in bed** border qn; **to t. sth into a drawer** glisser qch dans un tiroir

▸**tuck in 1** *vt sep (sheets, child)* border; *(clothes)* rentrer
  2 *vi Fam (start to eat)* attaquer

▸**tuck into** *vt insep Fam (meal)* attaquer

Tudor ['tjuːdə(r)] **1** *n Hist* **the Tudors** les Tudor
  2 *adj* des Tudor

Tue(s) *(abbr* **Tuesday**) mardi

Tuesday ['tjuːzdɪ] *n* mardi *m*; *see also* **Saturday**

tuft [tʌft] *n* touffe *f*

tug [tʌg] **1** *vt (pt & pp* **tugged**) (**a**) *(pull)* tirer sur (**b**) *(tow)* remorquer
  2 *vi* **to t. at sth** tirer sur qch
  3 *n* (**a**) *(pull)* **to give sth a t.** tirer sur qch (**b**) *(boat)* remorqueur *m*

tug-of-love [tʌgəv'lʌv] *n Br* = conflit de parents séparés à propos de la garde d'un enfant

tug-of-war [tʌgəv'wɔː(r)] *n (game)* lutte *f* (de traction) à la corde; *Fig* lutte *f* acharnée

tuition [tjʊ'ɪʃən] *n* cours *mpl*, leçons *fpl*; *Univ* **t. fees** frais *mpl* de scolarité

tulip ['tjuːlɪp] *n* tulipe *f*

tum [tʌm] *n Br Fam* ventre *m*

tumble ['tʌmbəl] **1** *vi (of person)* faire une chute; *Fig (of prices)* chuter
  2 *n (fall)* chute *f*; **to take a t.** *(of person)* faire une chute; *Fig (of prices)* chuter

▸**tumble down** *vi* s'écrouler

tumbledown ['tʌmbəldaʊn] *adj* qui tombe en ruines

tumble-drier [tʌmbəl'draɪə(r)] *n* sèche-linge *m inv*

tumble-dry ['tʌmbəldraɪ] *(pt & pp* **tumble-dried**) *vt* faire sécher au sèche-linge

tumbler ['tʌmblə(r)] *n* verre *m* droit

tummy ['tʌmɪ] *(pl* **tummies**) *n Fam* ventre *m*; **to have (a) t. ache** avoir mal au ventre

tumour, *Am* **tumor** ['tjuːmə(r)] *n* tumeur *f*

tumult ['tjuːmʌlt] *n* tumulte *m*

tumultuous [tjʊ'mʌltjʊəs] *adj* tumultueux(euse)

tuna ['tjuːnə] *n* thon *m*

tundra ['tʌndrə] *n* toundra *f*

tune [tjuːn] **1** *n* (**a**) *(melody)* air *m*, mélodie *f*; **to be in/out of t.** *(of person)* chanter juste/faux; *(of instrument)* être accordé(e)/désaccordé(e) (**b**) *(idioms)* **to be in t. with sb/sth** être en harmonie avec qn/qch; **to call the t.** commander; **to change one's t.** changer de discours; **to be in debt to the t. of £200** avoir 200 livres de dettes
  2 *vt (musical instrument)* accorder; *(engine, TV, radio)* régler

▸**tune in** *vi* brancher son poste

tuneful ['tjuːnfʊl] *adj* mélodieux(euse)

tuneless ['tjuːnlɪs] *adj* discordant(e)

tuner ['tjuːnə(r)] *n* (**a**) *(person)* accordeur(euse) *m,f* (**b**) *(on TV, radio)* tuner *m*

tungsten ['tʌŋstən] *n* tungstène *m*; **t. steel** acier *m* au tungstène

tunic ['tjuːnɪk] *n* tunique *f*

tuning fork ['tjuːnɪŋ'fɔːk] *n* diapason *m*

Tunis ['tjuːnɪs] *n* Tunis

Tunisia [tjuː'nɪzɪə] *n* la Tunisie

Tunisian [tjuː'nɪzɪən] **1** *n* Tunisien(enne) *m,f*
  2 *adj* tunisien(enne)

tunnel ['tʌnəl] **1** *n* tunnel *m*; **to have t. vision** souffrir d'un rétrécissement du champ visuel; *Fig* avoir des œillères
  2 *vt (pt & pp* **tunnelled**) **to t. one's way out of prison** s'échapper de prison en creusant un tunnel
  3 *vi* creuser un tunnel

turban ['tɜːbən] *n* turban *m*

turbine ['tɜːbaɪn] *n* turbine *f*

turbo-charged ['tɜːbəʊtʃɑːdʒd] *adj* turbocompressé(e)

turbo-charger ['tɜːbəʊtʃɑːdʒə(r)] *n* turbocompresseur *m*

turbojet ['tɜːbəʊdʒet] *n (engine)* turboréacteur *m*; *(plane)* avion *m* à turboréacteur

turboprop ['tɜːbəʊprɒp] *n (engine)* turbopropulseur *m*; *(plane)* avion *m* à turbopropulseur

turbot ['tɜːbət] *n* turbot *m*

turbulence ['tɜːbjʊləns] *n* turbulence *f*

turbulent ['tɜːbjʊlənt] *adj* agité(e)

turd [tɜːd] *n very Fam (excrement)* étron *m*

tureen [tjʊə'riːn] *n* soupière *f*

turf [tɜːf] **1** *n (grass-covered earth)* gazon *m*; *Fam (territory)* territoire *m*; *Br* **t. accountant** bookmaker *m*
  2 *vt* gazonner

▸**turf out** *vt sep Br Fam (person)* vider; *(thing)* balancer

Turk [tɜːk] *n* Turc (Turque) *m,f*

Turkey ['tɜːkɪ] *n* la Turquie

turkey ['tɜːkɪ] *(pl* **turkeys**) *n* (**a**) *(bird)* dinde *f* (**b**) *Fam (bad play, film)* navet *m*

Turkish ['tɜːkɪʃ] **1** *n (language)* turc *m*
  2 *adj* turc (turque); **T. bath** bain *m* turc; **T. delight** loukoum *m*

Turkmenistan [tɜːkmenɪ'stɑːn] *n* le Turkménistan

turmeric ['tɜːmərɪk] *n* curcuma *m*

turmoil ['tɜːmɔɪl] *n (of person)* émoi *m*; *(of country)* agitation *f*; **to be in (a) t.** *(of person)* être dans tous ses états; *(of country)* être en ébullition; **his mind was in t.** il était très troublé

turn [tɜːn] **1** *n* (**a**) *(of wheel, screw)* tour *m*; **the meat is done to a t.** la viande est cuite à point
  (**b**) *(change of direction)* demi-tour *m*; *(in road)* virage *m*; **no right/left t.** *(on sign)* défense de tourner à droite/gauche; *Fig* **at every t.** à tout bout de champ; **to take a t. for the better** s'améliorer; **to take a t. for the worse** se détériorer; **events took an unexpected t.** les événements ont pris une tournure inattendue; **the t. of the century** le tournant du siècle; **the t. of the tide** le changement de marée; *Fig* **le renversement de tendances**; *Am Aut* **t. signal** clignotant *m*, *Belg* clignoteur *m*, *Suisse* signafil(e) *m*
  (**c**) *(in game, queue)* tour *m*; **to take (it in) turns (to do sth)** se relayer (pour faire qch); **in t.** à tour de rôle
  (**d**) *Fam (fit)* crise *f*
  (**e**) *Theat (performance)* numéro *m*
  (**f**) *(service)* **to do sb a good t.** rendre un service à qn; **one good t. deserves another** un service en vaut un autre
  (**g**) **t. of phrase** tournure *f* de phrase

2 *vt* (**a**) *(cause to move)* tourner; *Fam Fig* **without turning a hair** sans broncher; *Fam Fig* **success has turned her head** le succès lui a tourné la tête; **to t. sb's stomach** soulever le cœur à qn
(**b**) *(direct)* **to t. the conversation to sb/sth** orienter la conversation sur qn/qch
(**c**) *(go round)* **to t. the corner** tourner au coin de la rue; *Fig* passer le moment critique; **she's just turned forty** elle vient d'avoir quarante ans
(**d**) *(change)* **to t. sth into sth** transformer qch en qch; **to t. sth green/black** verdir/noircir qch; **to t. sb against sb** monter qn contre qn
(**e**) *(on lathe)* tourner
3 *vi* (**a**) *(rotate) (of wheel)* tourner; *(of person)* se retourner; **she turned to me** elle s'est tournée vers moi; **to t. to sb (for help/advice)** se tourner vers qn (pour obtenir de l'aide/des conseils); **to t. (to the) right/left** tourner à droite/gauche
(**b**) *(change)* **to t. against sb** se retourner contre qn; **to t. nasty** *(of person)* devenir méchant(e); *(of situation)* mal tourner; **to t. red** devenir rouge; **to t. sour** *(of milk)* tourner; *Fig (of relationship)* tourner au vinaigre
▸**turn away 1** *vt sep (refuse entry, help to)* refuser
2 *vi* se détourner
▸**turn back 1** *vt sep (person)* refouler; *(sheets)* rabattre; **to t. the clocks back** retarder les pendules; *Fig* revenir en arrière
2 *vi* faire demi-tour; **t. back to page 20** revenez à la page 20
▸**turn down** *vt sep* (**a**) *(volume, heat)* baisser (**b**) *(request, application)* rejeter, refuser
▸**turn in 1** *vt sep (lost property)* rapporter à la police; *(person)* livrer à la police
2 *vi Fam (go to bed)* aller se pieuter
▸**turn into** *vt insep (become)* devenir
▸**turn off 1** *vt sep* (**a**) *(water, gas)* fermer; *(light, TV, engine)* éteindre (**b**) *Fam* **to t. sb off** dégoûter qn; *(sexually)* couper l'envie à qn
2 *vt insep* **to t. off the road** quitter la route
3 *vi (leave road)* sortir
▸**turn on 1** *vt sep* (**a**) *(water, gas)* ouvrir; *(light, TV, engine)* allumer (**b**) *Fam* **to t. sb on** *(excite)* brancher qn; *(sexually)* exciter qn
2 *vt insep* (**a**) *(attack)* **to t. on sb** attaquer qn (**b**) *(depend on)* dépendre de
▸**turn out 1** *vt sep* (**a**) *(light)* éteindre; *(gas)* fermer (**b**) *(eject)* mettre à la porte (**c**) *(pocket, container)* vider (**d**) *(produce)* produire, fabriquer; **to be well turned out** *(of person)* être élégant(e)
2 *vi* (**a**) *(appear, attend)* se déplacer (**b**) *(result)* se terminer; **to t. out to be** s'avérer (être); **it turns out that...** il se trouve que...
▸**turn over 1** *vt sep* (**a**) *(change position of)* retourner; **to t. sth over in one's mind** retourner qch dans sa tête; *Fig* **to t. over a new leaf** tourner la page (**b**) *(hand in)* **to t. sb/sth over to sb** remettre qn/qch entre les mains de qn
2 *vi* (**a**) *(of person)* se retourner; *(of car)* faire un tonneau, capoter (**b**) *(change TV channels)* changer de chaîne
▸**turn round 1** *vt sep (object)* retourner; *(situation)* renverser; *(company, economy)* remettre sur pied
2 *vi (of person)* se retourner
▸**turn up 1** *vt sep* (**a**) *(collar)* relever; *(trousers)* retrousser (**b**) *(volume, heat)* mettre plus fort
2 *vi (of person)* arriver; *(of lost object)* réapparaître;

something is sure to t. up quelque chose finira bien par se présenter
turnabout ['tɜːnəbaʊt] *n (in situation, opinion)* revirement *m*
turnaround ['tɜːnəraʊnd] *n* (**a**) *(in situation, opinion)* revirement *m* (**b**) *Comput* **t. time** temps *m* de rotation
turncoat ['tɜːnkəʊt] *n* renégat(e) *m,f*
turning ['tɜːnɪŋ] *n* (**a**) *(off road) (in country)* route *f* transversale; *(in town)* rue *f* transversale; **the second t. on the left** la deuxième rue à gauche (**b**) **t. circle** *(of car)* rayon *m* de braquage; *Fig* **t. point** tournant *m*
turnip ['tɜːnɪp] *n* navet *m*
turn-off ['tɜːnɒf] *n* (**a**) *(on road)* sortie *f* (**b**) *Fam* **to be a t.** être rébarbatif(ive); *(sexually)* couper l'envie
turn-on ['tɜːnɒn] *n Fam* **to be a t.** *(sexually)* être excitant(e)
turnout ['tɜːnaʊt] *n (attendance)* assistance *f*; *(at election)* taux *m* de participation
turnover ['tɜːnəʊvə(r)] *n* (**a**) *(of company)* chiffre *m* d'affaires (**b**) *(cake)* chausson *m*; **apple t.** chausson *m* aux pommes
turnpike ['tɜːnpaɪk] *n Am (road)* autoroute *f*
turnstile ['tɜːnstaɪl] *n* tourniquet *m*
turntable ['tɜːnteɪbəl] *n* platine *f*
turn-up ['tɜːnʌp] *n* (**a**) *Br (on trousers)* revers *m* (**b**) *Fam* **what a t. for the books!** quel événement!
turpentine ['tɜːpəntaɪn] *n* essence *f* de térébenthine
turquoise ['tɜːkwɔɪz] **1** *n* (**a**) *(stone)* turquoise *f* (**b**) *(colour)* turquoise *m*
2 *adj* turquoise *inv*
turret ['tʌrɪt] *n* tourelle *f*; **(gun) t.** *(on ship, tank)* tourelle *f*
turtle ['tɜːtəl] *n Br* tortue *f* de mer; *Am* tortue *f*; **t. dove** tourterelle *f*; **t. soup** potage *m* à la tortue
turtleneck ['tɜːtəlnek] *n* col *m* montant; **t. sweater** pull *m* à col montant
Tuscan ['tʌskən] *adj* toscan(e)
Tuscany ['tʌskənɪ] *n* la Toscane
tusk [tʌsk] *n* défense *f*
tussle ['tʌsəl] **1** *n* empoignade *f*; **to have a t. (with sb)** *(physically)* se battre (avec qn); *(verbally)* se disputer (avec qn)
2 *vi (physically)* se battre; *(verbally)* se disputer
tutor ['tjuːtə(r)] **1** *n (at university)* directeur(trice) *m,f* d'études; *(for private lessons)* professeur *m* particulier
2 *vt* **to t. sb (in sth)** donner des leçons particulières (de qch) à qn
tutorial [tjuː'tɔːrɪəl] *n* (**a**) *Br Univ* travaux *mpl* dirigés, TD *mpl* (**b**) *Comput* didacticiel *m*
tux [tʌks] *n Fam* smoking *m*
tuxedo [tʌk'siːdəʊ] *(pl* tuxedos) *n* smoking *m*
TV [tiː'viː] *n (television)* télé *f*, TV *f*; **TV dinner** plateau *m* télé; **TV movie** téléfilm *m*
TVP [tiːviː'piː] *n (abbr* **textured vegetable protein)** protéine *f* végétale texturée
twaddle ['twɒdəl] *n Br Fam* fadaises *fpl*
twang [twæŋ] **1** *n (sound)* vibration *f*; *(nasal voice)* ton *m* nasillard
2 *vi (of string)* vibrer
tweak [twiːk] **1** *n* **to give sth a t.** *(nose)* pincer qch; *(ear)* tirer qch; *Fam Fig (statistics, mechanism)* ajuster légèrement qch
2 *vt (nose)* pincer; *(ear)* tirer; *Fam Fig (statistics, mechanism)* ajuster légèrement
twee [twiː] *adj Br Fam Pej* cucul (la praline) *inv*
tweed [twiːd] *n* tweed *m*; **tweeds** *(suit)* costume *m* de tweed

tweet [twiːt] **1** n pépiement m
2 vi pépier
tweezers ['twiːzəz] npl pince f à épiler
twelfth [twelfθ] **1** n (**a**) (fraction) douzième m (**b**) (in series) douzième mf (**c**) (of month) douze m inv
2 adj douzième; **T. Night** ≃ la fête des Rois; see also **eighth**
twelve [twelv] **1** n douze m inv; **half past t.** (in the afternoon) douze heures trente, midi et demi; (at night) zéro heures trente, minuit et demi
2 adj douze; see also **eight**
twentieth ['twentɪθ] **1** n (**a**) (fraction) vingtième m (**b**) (in series) vingtième mf (**c**) (of month) vingt m inv
2 adj vingtième; see also **eighth**
twenty ['twentɪ] **1** n vingt m inv
2 adj vingt; **to have t.-t. vision** avoir dix sur dix à chaque œil; see also **eighty**
twenty-first ['twentɪ'fɜːst] **1** n (**a**) (in series) vingt et unième mf (**b**) (of month) vingt et un m inv (**c**) Br (birthday) vingt-et-unième anniversaire m (anniversaire considéré comme un rite de passage à l'âge adulte, particulièrement fêté en Grande-Bretagne)
2 adj vingt et unième

Twenty-first

En Grande-Bretagne, l'âge de la majorité est passé de 21 ans à 18 ans en 1970. Néanmoins, le vingt-et-unième anniversaire a conservé sa signification symbolique et reste une étape toute aussi importante – voire plus importante – que les 18 ans. Traditionnellement, l'on dit qu'à 21 ans on reçoit la clé de la porte de la maison ("to get the key to the door") et c'est pourquoi les cartes célébrant le vingt-et-unième anniversaire (ainsi que les gâteaux préparés à cette occasion) représentent souvent une clé.

twenty one ['twentɪ'wʌn] **1** n vingt et un m inv
2 adj vingt et un
twerp [twɜːp] n Fam crétin(e) m,f
twice [twaɪs] adv deux fois; **t. a week** deux fois par semaine; **t. as big (as)** deux fois plus grand (que); **it would cost t. as much elsewhere** ça coûterait le double ailleurs; **t. over** à deux reprises; **to think t. before doing sth** réfléchir à deux fois avant de faire qch; **he didn't have to be asked t.** il ne s'est pas fait prier
twiddle ['twɪdəl] **1** vt tripoter; **to t. one's thumbs** se tourner les pouces
2 vi **to t. with sth** tripoter qch
twig¹ [twɪg] n (small branch) brindille f
twig² (pt & pp twigged) vt & vi Br Fam piger
twilight ['twaɪlaɪt] n crépuscule m; **his t. years** les dernières années de sa vie; **t. zone** zone f crépusculaire; Fig zone floue
twin [twɪn] **1** n jumeau(elle) m,f; **t. brother** frère m jumeau; **t. sister** sœur f jumelle
2 adj (paired) jumeau(elle), jumelé(e); **t. beds** lits mpl jumeaux; **t.-engine(d) aircraft** avion m bimoteur
3 vt (pt & pp twinned) (town) jumeler
twine [twaɪn] **1** n (string) ficelle f
2 vt **t. sth around sb/sth** enrouler qch autour de qn/qch
twinge [twɪn(d)ʒ] n (of pain) élancement m; **a t. of conscience** un léger remords
twinkle ['twɪŋkəl] **1** vi (of star, light) scintiller; (of eyes) pétiller

2 n (of star, light) scintillement m; (of eyes) pétillement m
twirl [twɜːl] **1** n (movement) tournoiement m
2 vt faire tournoyer
3 vi (of person) tournoyer
twist [twɪst] **1** n (**a**) (action) tour m; **to give sth a t.** (to open) dévisser qch; (to close) visser qch (**b**) (bend) tortillement m; **twists and turns** (in road) tours mpl et détours; Fig (of events) rebondissements mpl; Br Fam **to be round the t.** être dingue; Br Fam **to drive sb around the t.** rendre qn dingue (**c**) (in story, plot) tour m inattendu; **by a strange t. of fate** par un hasard extraordinaire (**d**) **a t. of lemon** une rondelle de citron (**e**) (dance) **the t.** le twist
2 vt (hair, rope, thread) tordre, tortiller; Fig (words, meaning) déformer; **to t. one's ankle** se fouler la cheville; **to t. sb's arm** tordre le bras à qn; Fig forcer la main à qn; Fig **to t. the knife in the wound** retourner ou remuer le couteau dans la plaie
3 vi (of smoke) faire des volutes; (of road) faire des lacets; **to t. and turn** (of road) être en lacets
►**twist off 1** vt sep (lid) dévisser
2 vi se dévisser
twisted ['twɪstɪd] adj also Fig tordu(e)
twister ['twɪstə(r)] n (**a**) Br Fam (dishonest person) escroc m (**b**) Am (tornado) tornade f
twit [twɪt] n Br Fam andouille f
twitch [twɪtʃ] **1** n (pull) coup m sec; **to have a nervous t.** avoir un tic (nerveux)
2 vt (pull) tirer d'un coup sec
3 vi (of muscle, limb, face) se contracter nerveusement
twitter ['twɪtə(r)] **1** vi (of bird) gazouiller; Fig (of person) jacasser
2 n (of bird) gazouillis m
two [tuː] **1** n (pl twos) deux m; **to break / fold sth in t.** casser/plier qch en deux; **to walk in twos or t. by t.** marcher deux par deux; Fig **to put t. and t. together** faire le rapprochement; Fam **that makes t. of us** comme ça, on est deux
2 adj deux; see also **eight**
two-bit ['tuː'bɪt] adj Am Fam (cheap) de quatre sous
two-dimensional [tuːdaɪ'menʃənəl] adj à deux dimensions; Fig (character, film) simpliste
two-faced ['tuː'feɪst] adj hypocrite
twofold ['tuːfəʊld] adj double
two-legged ['tuː'legɪd] adj bipède
twopence ['tʌpəns] n Br deux pence mpl; Fam **it isn't worth t.** ça ne vaut pas tripette
two-piece ['tuː'piːs] adj (suit, swimsuit) deux pièces
two-pin ['tuːpɪn] adj (plug, socket) à deux fiches
twosome ['tuːsəm] n couple m
two-time ['tuːtaɪm] vt Fam (boyfriend, girlfriend) tromper
two-way ['tuːweɪ] adj **t. mirror** miroir m sans tain; **t. radio** poste m émetteur-récepteur
tycoon [taɪ'kuːn] n magnat m
type [taɪp] **1** n (**a**) (kind) type m, genre m; Fam **he's not my t.** ce n'est pas mon genre de mec (**b**) Typ caractères mpl; **in bold t.** en caractères gras
2 vt & vi taper (à la machine)
►**type up** vt sep taper (à la machine)
typecast ['taɪpkɑːst] (pt & pp typecast) vt **to be typecast** être cantonné(e) dans un rôle
typed [taɪpt] adj (document) écrit(e) à la machine, dactylographié(e)
typeface ['taɪpfeɪs] n police f de caractères
typescript ['taɪpskrɪpt] n texte m dactylographié m

typesetter ['taɪpsetə(r)] *n* typographe *mf*
typewriter ['taɪpraɪtə(r)] *n* machine *f* à écrire
typhoid ['taɪfɔɪd] *n* **t. (fever)** (fièvre *f*) typhoïde *f*; **to have t.** avoir la typhoïde
typhoon [taɪ'fuːn] *n* typhon *m*
typhus ['taɪfəs] *n* typhus *m*
typical ['tɪpɪkəl] *adj* typique; **it was t. of him to offer to pay** c'était bien son genre de proposer de payer; *Pej* **that's t. (of him/her)!** ça ne m'étonne pas (de lui/d'elle)!
typically ['tɪpɪklɪ] *adv* typiquement
typify ['tɪpɪfaɪ] *(pt & pp* **typified)** *vt* caractériser
typing ['taɪpɪŋ] *n* dactylographie *f*, frappe *f*; **t. error** faute *f* de frappe; **t. paper** papier *m* machine; **t. pool** équipe *f* de dactylos; **t. speed** vitesse *f* de frappe

typist ['taɪpɪst] *n* dactylo *mf*
typo ['taɪpəʊ] *(pl* **typos)** *n Fam (in typescript)* faute *f* de frappe; *(in printed text)* coquille *f*
typographic(al) [taɪpə'græfɪk(əl)] *adj* typographique
typography [taɪ'pɒgrəfɪ] *n* typographie *f*
tyrannical [tɪ'rænɪkəl] *adj* tyrannique
tyrannize ['tɪrənaɪz] *vt* tyranniser
tyranny ['tɪrənɪ] *n* tyrannie *f*
tyrant ['taɪrənt] *n* tyran *m*
tyre, *Am* **tire** ['taɪə(r)] *n* pneu *m*; **t. marks** traces *fpl* de pneu; **t. pressure** pression *f* des pneus
tzar, tzarist = tsar, tsarist
T-zone [tiː'zəʊn] *n* zones *fpl* graisses du visage *(front, nez, menton)*

U, u [juː] *n (letter)* U, u *m inv;* **U bend** tuyau *m* U; **U boat** sous-marin *m* allemand; **U turn** *(in car)* demi-tour *m*; *Fig* virage *m* à 180 degrés

UAE [juːeɪˈiː] *n (abbr* **United Arab Emirates**) EAU *mpl*

UB40 [juːbiːˈfɔːtɪ] *n Br* = carte de pointage de demandeur d'emploi

ubiquitous [juːˈbɪkwɪtəs] *adj* omniprésent(e)

UCAS [ˈjuːkæs] *n Br (abbr* **Universities and Colleges Admissions Service**) = centre national d'inscriptions à l'université

UDA [juːdiːˈeɪ] *n Br Pol (abbr* **Ulster Defence Association**) = groupement paramilitaire protestant d'Irlande du Nord

udder [ˈʌdə(r)] *n* pis *m*, mamelle *f*

UDI [juːdiːˈaɪ] *n Pol (abbr* **Unilateral Declaration of Independence**) déclaration *f* unilatérale d'indépendance

UEFA [juːˈeɪfə] *n (abbr* **Union of European Football Associations**) UEFA *f*

UFO [juːefˈəʊ] *n (abbr* **unidentified flying object**) OVNI *m*

Uganda [juːˈgændə] *n* l'Ouganda *m*

Ugandan [juːˈgændən] **1** *n* Ougandais(e) *m,f*
2 *adj* ougandais(e)

ugh [ʌχ] *exclam* berk!

ugly [ˈʌglɪ] *adj* (**a**) *(in appearance)* laid(e); *Fig* **u. duckling** vilain petit canard *m* (**b**) *(unpleasant)* désagréable, déplaisant(e)

UHF [juːeɪtʃˈef] *n (abbr* **ultra-high frequency**) UHF

UHT [juːeɪtʃˈtiː] *adj (abbr* **ultra-heat-treated**) UHT

UK [juːˈkeɪ] *n (abbr* **United Kingdom**) *(written)* RU; *(spoken)* Royaume-Uni *m*

UKIP [ˈjuːkɪp] *n Br Pol (abbr* **UK Independence Party**) = parti politique britannique qui prône le retrait du Royaume-Uni de l'Union européenne

Ukraine [juːˈkreɪn] *n* the U. l'Ukraine *f*

Ukrainian [juːˈkreɪnɪən] **1** *n* (**a**) *(person)* Ukrainien(enne) *m,f* (**b**) *(language)* ukrainien *m*
2 *adj* ukrainien(enne)

ukulele [juːkəˈleɪlɪ] *n* ukulélé *m*

ulcer [ˈʌlsə(r)] *n* ulcère *m; (in mouth)* aphte *m*

ulcerate [ˈʌlsəreɪt] **1** *vt* ulcérer
2 *vi* s'ulcérer

ulna [ˈʌlnə] *n* cubitus *m*

Ulster [ˈʌlstə(r)] *n* l'Ulster *m*

ulterior [ʌlˈtɪərɪə(r)] *adj* ultérieur(e); **u. motive** arrière-pensée *f*

ultimate [ˈʌltɪmət] **1** *adj* (**a**) *(last)* final(e) (**b**) *(supreme, best)* absolu(e); **the u. holiday** les vacances *fpl* idéales
2 *n Fam* **the u. (in)** le summum (de)

ultimately [ˈʌltɪmɪtlɪ] *adv* (**a**) *(finally)* finalement (**b**) *(basically)* en fin de compte

ultimatum [ʌltɪˈmeɪtəm] *n* ultimatum *m;* **to deliver an u. to sb** adresser un ultimatum à qn

ultra- [ˈʌltrə] *pref* ultra-

ultramarine [ʌltrəməˈriːn] *n* bleu *m* outremer

ultramodern [ʌltrəˈmɒdən] *adj* ultramoderne

ultrasound [ˈʌltrəsaʊnd] *n* ultrasons *mpl*

ultraviolet [ʌltrəˈvaɪələt] *adj* ultraviolet(ette)

Ulysses [ˈjuːlɪsiːz] *n* Ulysse *m*

umbilical cord [ʌmˈbɪlɪkəlkɔːd] *n* cordon *m* ombilical

umbrage [ˈʌmbrɪdʒ] *n* **to take u. (at sth)** prendre ombrage (de qch)

umbrella [ʌmˈbrelə] *n* parapluie *m; Fig* **under the u. of** sous les auspices de; **u. organization** organisme *m* de tutelle; **u. stand** porte-parapluie *m*

umpire [ˈʌmpaɪə(r)] **1** *n* arbitre *mf*
2 *vt* arbitrer

umpteen [ʌmpˈtiːn] *adj Fam* je ne sais combien de

umpteenth [ʌmpˈtiːnθ] *adj Fam* énième

UN [juːˈen] *n (abbr* **United Nations**) ONU *f*

unabashed [ʌnəˈbæʃt] *adj* nullement décontenancé(e)

unable [ʌnˈeɪbəl] *adj* **to be u. to do sth** être incapable de faire qch

unabridged [ʌnəˈbrɪdʒd] *adj* intégral(e)

unacceptable [ʌnəkˈseptəbəl] *adj* inacceptable

unaccompanied [ʌnəˈkʌmpənɪd] **1** *adj (person)* non accompagné(e); *(violin, singer)* sans accompagnement
2 *adv (travel)* seul(e); *(play, sing)* sans accompagnement

unaccomplished [ʌnəˈkʌmplɪʃt] *adj* médiocre

unaccountable [ʌnəˈkaʊntəbəl] *adj* (**a**) *(not answerable)* **to be u. (to sb)** ne pas avoir de comptes à rendre (à qn) (**b**) *(puzzling)* inexplicable

unaccounted for [ʌnəˈkaʊntɪdfɔː(r)] *adj* **to be u.** *(of person)* ne pas être retrouvé(e)

unaccustomed [ʌnəˈkʌstəmd] *adj* (**a**) *(not used)* **to be u. to sth/to doing sth** ne pas être habitué(e) à qch/à faire qch (**b**) *(not usual)* inhabituel(elle)

unacknowledged [ʌnəkˈnɒlɪdʒd] **1** *adj* non reconnu(e)
2 *adv* **to go u.** *(of talent, achievement)* ne pas être reconnu(e)

unacquainted [ʌnəˈkweɪntɪd] *adj* **to be u. with sb/sth** ne pas connaître qn/qch

unadulterated [ʌnəˈdʌltəreɪtɪd] *adj* (**a**) *(food)* naturel(elle) (**b**) *(total, sheer)* pur(e)

unadventurous [ʌnədˈventʃərəs] *adj* peu audacieux(euse)

unaffected [ʌnə'fektɪd] *adj* (**a**) *(sincere)* simple (**b**) *(not touched)* **to be u.** (**by sth**) ne pas être affecté(e) (par qch)
unaffiliated [ʌnə'fɪlɪeɪtɪd] *adj* non affilié(e)
unafraid [ʌnə'freɪd] *adj* **to be u.** ne pas avoir peur
unaided [ʌn'eɪdɪd] *adv* sans aide
unaltered [ʌn'ɔːltəd] *adj* inchangé(e)
unambiguous [ʌnæm'bɪgjʊəs] *adj* sans équivoque
unambitious [ʌnæm'bɪʃəs] *adj* sans ambition
unanimity [juːnə'nɪmɪtɪ] *n* unanimité *f*
unanimous [juː'nænɪməs] *adj* unanime
unanimously [juː'nænɪməslɪ] *adv* à l'unanimité
unannounced [ʌnə'naʊnst] **1** *adj* non annoncé(e) **2** *adv* sans prévenir
unanswerable [ʌn'ɑːnsərəbəl] *adj* irréfutable
unanswered [ʌn'ɑːnsəd] **1** *adj* sans réponse **2** *adv* **to go u.** *(of question, letter)* rester sans réponse
unappealing [ʌnə'piːlɪŋ] *adj* peu attrayant(e)
unappetizing [ʌn'æpɪtaɪzɪŋ] *adj* peu appétissant(e)
unappreciated [ʌnə'priːʃɪeɪtɪd] *adj* non reconnu(e)
unapproachable [ʌnə'prəʊtʃəbəl] *adj* inaccessible
unarmed [ʌn'ɑːmd] *adj* non armé(e); **u. combat** combat *m* à mains nues
unashamed [ʌnə'ʃeɪmd] *adj* (joy, greed) non dissimulé(e); **he's u. about his background** il n'a absolument pas honte de ses origines
unassailable [ʌnə'seɪləbəl] *adj (castle, position)* imprenable; *(argument, theory)* inattaquable
unassuming [ʌnə'sjuːmɪŋ] *adj* sans prétention
unattached [ʌnə'tætʃt] *adj* (**a**) *(not connected)* détaché(e) (**b**) *(without partner)* sans attaches
unattainable [ʌnə'teɪnəbəl] *adj* inaccessible
unattractive [ʌnə'træktɪv] *adj (place, habit, prospect)* peu attrayant(e); *(person, appearance)* sans charme
unauthorized [ʌn'ɔːθəraɪzd] *adj* non autorisé(e)
unavailable [ʌnə'veɪləbəl] *adj* non disponible; **to be u.** ne pas être disponible
unavailing [ʌnə'veɪlɪŋ] *adj* vain(e)
unavoidable [ʌnə'vɔɪdəbəl] *adj* inévitable
unaware [ʌnə'weə(r)] *adj* ignorant(e); **to be u. of sth** ignorer qch
unawares [ʌnə'weəz] *adv* **to catch sb u.** prendre qn au dépourvu
unbalanced [ʌn'bælənst] *adj* (**a**) *(person)* instable (**b**) *(biased)* partial(e)
unbearable [ʌn'beərəbəl] *adj* insupportable
unbeatable [ʌn'biːtəbəl] *adj* imbattable
unbecoming [ʌnbɪ'kʌmɪŋ] *adj (behaviour)* inconvenant(e); *(dress)* peu seyant(e)
unbeknown(st) [ʌnbɪ'nəʊn(st)] *adv* **u. to me/him** à mon/son insu
unbelievable [ʌnbɪ'liːvəbəl] *adj* incroyable
unbending [ʌn'bendɪŋ] *adj* inflexible
unbias(s)ed [ʌn'baɪəst] *adj* impartial(e)
unblock [ʌn'blɒk] *vt (sink, pipe)* déboucher; *(road)* dégager
unborn ['ʌnbɔːn] *adj (child)* à naître
unbounded [ʌn'baʊndɪd] *adj* sans bornes
unbreakable [ʌn'breɪkəbəl] *adj* (**a**) *(glass, toy)* incassable (**b**) *(promise, rule)* sacré(e)
unbridled [ʌn'braɪdəld] *adj* débridé(e)
unbroken [ʌn'brəʊkən] *adj* (**a**) *(intact)* intact(e) (**b**) *(uninterrupted)* ininterrompu(e)
unburden [ʌn'bɜːdən] *vt* **to u. oneself to sb** se confier à qn

unbusinesslike [ʌn'bɪznɪslaɪk] *adj* peu professionnel(elle)
unbutton [ʌn'bʌtən] *vt* déboutonner
uncalled-for [ʌn'kɔːldfɔː(r)] *adj (of behaviour, remark)* déplacé(e); *(insult)* gratuit(e)
uncanny [ʌn'kænɪ] *adj* étrange, troublant(e)
uncaring [ʌn'keərɪŋ] *adj* indifférent(e)
unceasing [ʌn'siːsɪŋ] *adj* incessant(e)
uncertain [ʌn'sɜːtən] *adj* incertain(e); **to be u. about sth** ne pas être certain(e) de qch; **it is u. if...** on ne sait pas si...; **in no u. terms** en termes on ne peut plus clairs
uncertainty [ʌn'sɜːtəntɪ] (*pl* **uncertainties**) *n* incertitude *f*
unchallenged [ʌn'tʃælɪndʒd] *adj* incontesté(e)
unchanged [ʌn'tʃeɪndʒd] *adj* inchangé(e)
unchanging [ʌn'tʃeɪndʒɪŋ] *adj* immuable
uncharacteristic [ʌnkærəktə'rɪstɪk] *adj* inhabituel(elle)
uncharitable [ʌn'tʃærɪtəbəl] *adj* peu charitable
uncharted [ʌn'tʃɑːtɪd] *adj* inexploré(e)
unchecked [ʌn'tʃekt] **1** *adj* (**a**) *(not restrained)* incontrôlé(e) (**b**) *(not verified)* non vérifié(e) **2** *adv* **to go u.** rester incontrôlé(e)
UNCHR [juːensiːeɪtʃ'ɑː(r)] *n (abbr* **United Nations Commission on Human Rights**) CDH *f*
uncivil [ʌn'sɪvɪl] *adj* impoli(e)
uncivilized [ʌn'sɪvɪlaɪzd] *adj* non civilisé(e)
unclaimed [ʌn'kleɪmd] *adj* non réclamé(e); **to go u.** ne pas être réclamé(e)
uncle ['ʌŋkəl] *n* oncle *m*; *Am* **U. Sam** l'oncle Sam
unclean [ʌn'kliːn] *adj* sale, souillé(e)
unclear [ʌn'klɪə(r)] *adj* vague
unclothed [ʌn'kləʊðd] *adj* nu(e)
uncoil [ʌn'kɔɪl] *vt* dérouler
uncombed [ʌn'kəʊmd] *adj* pas peigné(e)
uncomfortable [ʌn'kʌmfətəbəl] *adj* inconfortable; *(silence)* gêné(e); **to feel u.** *(physically)* ne pas être à l'aise; *(ill at ease)* être mal à l'aise
uncommitted [ʌnkə'mɪtɪd] *adj* indécis(e)
uncommon [ʌn'kɒmən] *adj* peu commun(e)
uncommunicative [ʌnkə'mjuːnɪkətɪv] *adj* peu communicatif(ive)
uncomplicated [ʌn'kɒmplɪkeɪtɪd] *adj* simple, non compliqué(e)
uncomplimentary [ʌnkɒmplɪ'mentərɪ] *adj* peu flatteur(euse)
uncomprehending [ʌnkɒmprɪ'hendɪŋ] *adj* **to be u. of sth** ne pas comprendre qch; **with an u. look** l'air perplexe
uncompromising [ʌn'kɒmprəmaɪzɪŋ] *adj (person, opposition)* intransigeant(e)
unconcealed [ʌnkən'siːld] *adj* non dissimulé(e)
unconcerned [ʌnkən'sɜːnd] **1** *adj* indifférent(e); **to be u. about sth** ne pas s'inquiéter de qch **2** *adv* avec indifférence
unconditional [ʌnkən'dɪʃənəl] *adj* sans condition
unconfirmed [ʌnkən'fɜːmd] *adj* non confirmé(e)
unconnected [ʌnkə'nektɪd] *adj* sans lien
unconscious [ʌn'kɒnʃəs] **1** *adj* (**a**) *(having fainted)* sans connaissance; *(asleep)* profondément endormi(e) (**b**) *(unaware)* inconscient(e); **to be u. of sth** ne pas avoir conscience de qch **2** *n* **the u.** l'inconscient *m*
unconsciously [ʌn'kɒnʃəslɪ] *adv* inconsciemment
unconstitutional [ʌnkɒnstɪ'tjuːʃənəl] *adj* inconstitutionnel(elle)

uncontaminated [ʌnkən'tæmɪneɪtɪd] *adj* non contaminé(e)
uncontested [ʌnkən'testɪd] *adj* incontesté(e)
uncontrollable [ʌnkən'trəʊləbəl] *adj* incontrôlable
uncontroversial [ʌnkɒntrə'vɜːʃəl] *adj* anodin(e)
unconventional [ʌnkən'venʃənəl] *adj* non-conformiste
unconvinced [ʌnkən'vɪnst] *adj* sceptique
unconvincing [ʌnkən'vɪnsɪŋ] *adj* peu convaincant(e)
uncooked [ʌn'kʊkt] *adj* cru(e)
uncool [ʌn'kuːl] *adj Fam* ringard(e)
uncooperative [ʌnkəʊ'ɒpərətɪv] *adj* peu coopératif(ive)
uncoordinated [ʌnkəʊ'ɔːdɪneɪtɪd] *adj* qui manque de coordination
uncork [ʌn'kɔːk] *vt* déboucher
uncorroborated [ʌnkə'rɒbəreɪtɪd] *adj* non corroboré(e)
uncountable [ʌn'kaʊntəbəl] *adj* indénombrable
uncouth [ʌn'kuːθ] *adj* fruste
uncover [ʌn'kʌvə(r)] *vt also Fig* découvrir
uncritical [ʌn'krɪtɪkəl] *adj* peu critique; **to be u. of sb/sth** ne pas être critique envers qn/qch
UNCTAD ['ʌŋktæd] *n Econ (abbr* **United Nations Conference on Trade and Development**) CNUCED *f*
unction ['ʌŋkʃən] *n Rel* onction *f*
unctuous ['ʌŋktjʊəs] *adj Pej* onctueux(euse)
uncultivated [ʌn'kʌltɪveɪtɪd] *adj* inculte
uncultured [ʌn'kʌltʃəd] *adj* inculte
uncut [ʌn'kʌt] *adj (gem)* brut(e); *(text, film)* intégral(e)
undamaged [ʌn'dæmɪdʒd] *adj* intact(e)
undated [ʌn'deɪtɪd] *adj* non daté(e)
undaunted [ʌn'dɔːntɪd] *adj* qui n'est pas impressionné(e); **to be u. by sth** ne pas se laisser impressionner par qch
undecided [ʌndɪ'saɪdɪd] *adj* (**a**) *(question, problem)* sans réponse; **that's still u.** aucune décision n'a encore été prise (**b**) *(person)* indécis(e) (**about** à propos de)
undefeated [ʌndɪ'fiːtɪd] *adj* invaincu(e)
undefended [ʌndɪ'fendɪd] *adj* sans défense
undemanding [ʌndɪ'mɑːndɪŋ] *adj (job)* peu prenant(e); *(person)* peu exigeant(e)
undemocratic [ʌndemə'krætɪk] *adj* antidémocratique
undemonstrative [ʌndɪ'mɒnstrətɪv] *adj* peu démonstratif(ive)
undeniable [ʌndɪ'naɪəbəl] *adj* indéniable
undeniably [ʌndɪ'naɪəblɪ] *adv* indéniablement
under ['ʌndə(r)] **1** *prep* (**a**) *(beneath)* sous; **u. the table/the stairs** sous la table/l'escalier; *Fam* **to be u. the weather** se sentir patraque (**b**) *(less than)* moins de; **he's u. thirty** il a moins de trente ans; **children u. five** les enfants de moins de cinq ans (**c**) *(under the control of)* sous; **he had a hundred men u. him** il avait cent hommes sous ses ordres; **Spain u. Franco** l'Espagne de Franco (**d**) *(subject to)* **to be u. orders to do sth** avoir pour ordre de faire qch; **u. the terms of the agreement** d'après les termes de l'accord; **u. these conditions** dans ces conditions; **u. the circumstances** dans ces circonstances (**e**) *(in the process of)* **u. repair/observation** en réparation/observation; **to be u. investigation** faire l'objet d'une enquête; **to get u. way** *(of meeting, campaign)* commencer
2 *adv* (**a**) *(underneath)* dessous; *(underwater)* sous l'eau; **to go u.** *(of company)* faire faillite (**b**) *(less)*

au-dessous; **children of five and u.** les enfants de cinq ans et au-dessous
underachiever [ʌndərə'tʃiːvə(r)] *n* = personne qui ne tire pas profit de ses capacités intellectuelles
under-age [ʌndər'eɪdʒ] *adj* mineur(e); **u. drinking** consommation *f* d'alcool par les mineurs; **u. sex** relations *fpl* sexuelles entre personnes mineures
undercarriage ['ʌndəkærɪdʒ] *n* train *m* d'atterrissage
undercharge [ʌndə'tʃɑːdʒ] *vt* se tromper dans l'addition de *(à l'avantage du client)*; **he undercharged me by £5** il aurait dû me faire payer 5 livres de plus
underclass ['ʌndəklɑːs] *n* sous-prolétariat *m*
underclothes ['ʌndəkləʊðz] *npl* sous-vêtements *mpl*
underclothing ['ʌndəkləʊðɪŋ] *n* sous-vêtements *mpl*
undercoat ['ʌndəkəʊt] *n* sous-couche *f*
undercook [ʌndə'kʊk] *vt* ne pas faire cuire assez longtemps
undercover ['ʌndəkʌvə(r)] **1** *adj* secret(ète) **2** *adv* clandestinement
undercurrent ['ʌndəkʌrənt] *n (in sea)* courant *m* sous-marin; *Fig (of emotion, unrest)* courant sous-jacent
undercut [ʌndə'kʌt] *(pt & pp* **undercut**) *vt* vendre moins cher que
underdeveloped [ʌndədɪ'veləpt] *adj* sous-développé(e)
underdog ['ʌndədɒg] *n* (**a**) *(in contest)* celui *m*/celle *f* qui risque de perdre (**b**) *(in society)* **the u.** les opprimés *mpl*
underestimate 1 *n* [ʌndər'estɪmɪt] sous-estimation *f* **2** *vt* [ʌndər'estɪmeɪt] sous-estimer
underexposed ['ʌndərɪks'pəʊzd] *adj* sous-exposé(e)
underfed [ʌndə'fed] *adj* sous-alimenté(e)
underfoot [ʌndə'fʊt] *adv* sous les pieds; **it's wet u.** le sol est mouillé; **to trample sth u.** piétiner qch
underfunding [ʌndə'fʌndɪŋ] *n* insuffisance *f* de financement
undergarment ['ʌndəgɑːmənt] *n* sous-vêtement *m*
undergo [ʌndə'gəʊ] *(pt* **underwent** [ʌndə'went], *pp* **undergone** [ʌndə'gɒn]) *vt (change)* connaître; *(test)* subir; **to u. surgery** être opéré(e); **to u. treatment** *(of patient)* suivre un traitement
undergraduate [ʌndə'grædjʊɪt] *n* étudiant(e) *m,f* qui prépare une licence
underground 1 *adj* ['ʌndəgraʊnd] (**a**) *(below ground)* souterrain(e) (**b**) *(clandestine)* clandestin(e) **2** *adv* [ʌndə'graʊnd] (**a**) *(below ground)* sous terre (**b**) **to go u.** *(into hiding)* passer dans la clandestinité **3** *n* ['ʌndəgraʊnd] (**a**) *Br (railway system)* métro *m* (**b**) *(resistance movement)* mouvement *m* de résistance
undergrowth ['ʌndəgraʊθ] *n* broussailles *fpl*
underhand ['ʌndəhænd] *adj* sournois(e)
underlain [ʌndə'leɪn] *pp of* **underlie**
underlay [ʌndəleɪ] *n (for carpet)* thibaude *f*
underlie [ʌndə'laɪ] *(pt* **underlay** [ʌndə'leɪ], *pp* **underlain** [ʌndə'leɪn]) *vt* sous-tendre
underline [ʌndə'laɪn] *vt also Fig* souligner
underlying [ʌndə'laɪɪŋ] *adj* sous-jacent(e)
undermanning [ʌndə'mænɪŋ] *n* manque *m* de main-d'œuvre
undermentioned ['ʌndəmenʃənd] *adj Formal* ci-dessous
undermine [ʌndə'maɪn] *vt (weaken) (cliff, person, authority)* saper; *(confidence)* ébranler; *(democracy)* fragiliser

underneath [ʌndə'niːθ] **1** *prep* sous
2 *adv* dessous
3 *n* the u. le dessous
undernourished [ʌndə'nʌrɪʃt] *adj* sous-alimenté(e)
underpaid [ʌndə'peɪd] *adj* sous-payé(e)
underpants ['ʌndəpænts] *npl* slip *m*
underpass ['ʌndəpɑːs] *n* passage *m* souterrain
underperform [ʌndəpə'fɔːm] *vi Fin (of shares, investment)* ne pas être performant(e)
underpin [ʌndə'pɪn] *(pt & pp* **underpinned***) vt* étayer
underpopulated [ʌndə'pɒpjʊleɪtɪd] *adj* sous-peuplé(e)
underprivileged [ʌndə'prɪvɪlɪdʒd] *adj* défavorisé(e)
underqualified [ʌndə'kwɒlɪfaɪd] *adj* sous-qualifié(e)
underrate [ʌndə'reɪt] *vt* sous-estimer
underscore 1 *n* ['ʌndəskɔː(r)] *Typ* trait *m* bas; **g u.**
brown at xmail dot com *(in e-mail addresses)* g underscore brown, arobase, xmail, point com
2 *vt* [ʌndə'skɔː(r)] *also Fig* souligner
underside ['ʌndəsaɪd] *n* dessous *m*
undersized [ʌndə'saɪzd] *adj* trop petit(e)
underskirt ['ʌndəskɜːt] *n* jupon *m*; *(full-length)* combinaison *f*
understaffed [ʌndə'stɑːft] *adj* to be u. manquer de personnel
understand [ʌndə'stænd] *(pt & pp* **understood** [ʌndə'stʊd]*)* **1** *vt* **(a)** *(comprehend)* comprendre; **to make oneself understood** se faire comprendre; **they u. each other** ils se comprennent **(b)** *(believe, assume)* **to u. that** croire que; **I u. that you're coming to work here** j'ai appris que vous venez travailler ici; **to give sb to u. that** laisser entendre à qn que; **are we to u. that...?** devons-nous en conclure que...?
2 *vi* comprendre
understandable [ʌndə'stændəbəl] *adj* compréhensible
understandably [ʌndə'stændəblɪ] *adv* naturellement
understanding [ʌndə'stændɪŋ] **1** *n* **(a)** *(comprehension, sympathy)* compréhension *f* **(b)** *(agreement)* accord *m*; **to come to** *or* **to reach an u.** parvenir à un accord; **on the u. that** à condition que + *subjunctive*
2 *adj* compréhensif(ive)
understatement [ʌndə'steɪtmənt] *n* euphémisme *m*; *(in literature)* litote *f*; **that's an u.!** c'est peu dire!
understood [ʌndə'stʊd] *pt & pp of* **understand**
understudy ['ʌndəstʌdɪ] *(pl* **understudies***) n* doublure *f*
undertake [ʌndə'teɪk] *(pt* **undertook** [ʌndə'tʊk]*, pp* **undertaken** [ʌndə'teɪkən]*) vt* entreprendre; **to u. to do sth** entreprendre de faire qch
undertaker ['ʌndəteɪkə(r)] *n Br* entrepreneur *m* de pompes funèbres; **the undertakers** les pompes *fpl* funèbres
undertaking [ʌndə'teɪkɪŋ] *n* **(a)** *(enterprise)* entreprise *f* **(b)** *(promise)* engagement *m*, promesse *f*
undertone ['ʌndətəʊn] *n (low voice)* voix *f* basse; *Fig (hint, suggestion)* fond *m*
undertook [ʌndə'tʊk] *pt of* **undertake**
undertow ['ʌndətəʊ] *n* ressac *m*
undervalue [ʌndə'væljuː] *vt (property)* sous-évaluer; *Fig (person, ability)* sous-estimer
underwater 1 *adj* ['ʌndəwɔːtə(r)] de plongée
2 *adv* [ʌndə'wɔːtə(r)] sous l'eau
underwear ['ʌndəweə(r)] *n* sous-vêtements *mpl*
underweight [ʌndə'weɪt] *adj* trop maigre

underwent [ʌndə'went] *pt of* **undergo**
underworld ['ʌndəwɜːld] *n* **(a)** *(in mythology)* **the U.** les Enfers *mpl* **(b)** *(of criminals)* pègre *f*
underwrite ['ʌndəraɪt] *(pt* **underwrote** [ʌndə'rəʊt]*, pp* **underwritten** [ʌndə'rɪtən]*) vt* souscrire
underwriter ['ʌndəraɪtə(r)] *n (in insurance)* souscripteur *m*
underwritten [ʌndə'rɪtən] *pp of* **underwrite**
underwrote [ʌndə'rəʊt] *pt of* **underwrite**
undeserved [ʌndɪ'zɜːvd] *adj* immérité(e)
undeserving [ʌndɪ'zɜːvɪŋ] *adj* peu méritant(e); **to be u. of sth** ne pas mériter qch
undesirable [ʌndɪ'zaɪərəbəl] **1** *n* indésirable *mf*
2 *adj* indésirable
undetected [ʌndɪ'tektɪd] **1** *adj* non détecté(e)
2 *adv* **to go u.** passer inaperçu(e)
undetermined [ʌndɪ'tɜːmɪnd] *adj* indéterminé(e)
undeterred [ʌndɪ'tɜːd] **1** *adj* **to be u.** (by sth) ne pas se laisser décourager (par qch)
2 *adv* sans se laisser décourager
undeveloped [ʌndɪ'veləpt] *adj* non développé(e); *(land)* inexploité(e)
undid [ʌn'dɪd] *pt of* **undo**
undies ['ʌndɪz] *npl Fam* sous-vêtements *mpl*
undigested [ʌndaɪ'dʒestɪd] *adj also Fig* non digéré(e)
undignified [ʌn'dɪgnɪfaɪd] *adj* indigne
undiluted [ʌndaɪ'luːtɪd] *adj (liquid)* non dilué(e); *Fig (emotion)* pur(e)
undiminished [ʌndɪ'mɪnɪʃt] *adj* intact(e)
undiplomatic [ʌndɪplə'mætɪk] *adj* peu diplomate
undisciplined [ʌn'dɪsɪplɪnd] *adj* indiscipliné(e)
undisclosed [ʌndɪs'kləʊzd] *adj* non révélé(e)
undiscovered [ʌndɪs'kʌvəd] *adj* inconnu(e); **to go/ continue u.** rester ignoré(e)
undiscriminating [ʌndɪs'krɪmɪneɪtɪŋ] *adj* **to be u.** manquer de discernement
undisputed [ʌndɪs'pjuːtɪd] *adj* incontesté(e)
undistinguished [ʌndɪs'tɪŋwɪʃt] *adj* médiocre
undisturbed [ʌndɪs'tɜːbd] *adj (sleep)* paisible; **to leave sth u.** ne pas toucher à qch
undo [ʌn'duː] *(pt* **undid** [ʌn'dɪd]*, pp* **undone** [ʌn'dʌn]*) vt* **(a)** *(mistake, damage)* réparer; *Comput (command)* annuler **(b)** *(knot, button, shoelaces)* défaire; *(parcel, zip)* ouvrir; *(bra, dress)* dégrafer
undoing [ʌn'duːɪŋ] *n* ruine *f*; **her pride was her u.** c'est sa fierté qui l'a perdue
undone [ʌn'dʌn] *pp of* **undo**
undoubted [ʌn'daʊtɪd] *adj* indubitable
undoubtedly [ʌn'daʊtɪdlɪ] *adv* indubitablement
undreamed-of [ʌn'driːmdɒv], **undreamt-of** [ʌn'dremtɒv] *adj* inimaginable
undress [ʌn'dres] **1** *vt* déshabiller; **to get undressed** se déshabiller
2 *vi* se déshabiller
3 *n* **in a state of u.** *(naked)* nu(e); *(nearly naked)* en petite tenue
undue [ʌn'djuː] *adj* excessif(ive)
undulate ['ʌndjʊleɪt] *vi* onduler
undulation [ʌndjʊ'leɪʃən] *n* ondulation *f*
unduly [ʌn'djuːlɪ] *adv* trop
unearned [ʌn'ɜːnd] *adj (reward, punishment)* immérité(e); *Fin* **u. income** rentes *fpl*
unearth [ʌn'ɜːθ] *vt (buried object)* déterrer; *Fig (information, secret)* mettre à jour
unearthly [ʌn'ɜːθlɪ] *adj* **(a)** *(supernatural)* mystérieux(-euse)* **(b)** *Fam* **at an u. hour** à une heure impossible;

an u. din *or* **racket** un vacarme de tous les diables; **for some u. reason** pour une raison étrange
unease [ʌn'iːz] *n* malaise *m*
uneasily [ʌn'iːzɪlɪ] *adv* d'un air gêné
uneasy [ʌn'iːzɪ] *adj (person)* mal à l'aise; *(sleep)* agité(e); *(silence)* gêné(e)
uneconomical [ʌniːkə'nɒmɪkəl] *adj* peu économique
uneducated [ʌn'edjʊkeɪtɪd] *adj* sans instruction; **to be u.** ne pas avoir d'instruction
unemotional [ʌnɪ'məʊʃənəl] *adj* impassible
unemployable [ʌnɪm'plɔɪəbəl] *adj* inemployable
unemployed [ʌnɪm'plɔɪd] **1** *npl* **the u.** les sans-emploi *mpl*, les chômeurs *mpl*
2 *adj* sans emploi, au chômage
unemployment [ʌnɪm'plɔɪmənt] *n* chômage *m; Br* **u. benefit** allocation *f* chômage; **u. rate** taux *m* de chômage
unending [ʌn'endɪŋ] *adj* interminable
unendurable [ʌnɪn'djʊərəbəl] *adj* insupportable
unenlightened [ʌnɪn'laɪtənd] *adj (person)* peu éclairé(e)
unenlightening [ʌnɪn'laɪtnɪŋ] *adj* obscur(e)
unenterprising [ʌn'entəpraɪzɪŋ] *adj* qui manque d'initiative
unenthusiastic [ʌnɪnθjuːzɪ'æstɪk] *adj* peu enthousiaste
unenviable [ʌn'envɪəbəl] *adj* peu enviable
unequal [ʌn'iːkwəl] *adj* inégal(e)
unequivocal [ʌnɪ'kwɪvəkəl] *adj* sans équivoque
unerring [ʌn'ɜːrɪŋ] *adj* infaillible
UNESCO [juː'neskəʊ] *n (abbr* **United Nations Educational, Scientific and Cultural Organization**) Unesco *f*
unethical [ʌn'eθɪkəl] *adj* contraire à l'éthique
uneven [ʌn'iːvən] *adj* inégal(e)
uneventful [ʌnɪ'ventfʊl] *adj* sans histoires
unexceptionable [ʌnɪk'sepʃənəbəl] *adj* tout à fait convenable
unexceptional [ʌnɪk'sepʃənəl] *adj* qui n'a rien d'exceptionnel
unexciting [ʌnɪk'saɪtɪŋ] *adj* peu intéressant(e)
unexpected [ʌnɪks'pektɪd] *adj* inattendu(e), imprévu(e)
unexplained [ʌnɪks'pleɪnd] *adj* inexpliqué(e)
unexplored [ʌnɪks'plɔːd] *adj* inexploré(e)
unfailing [ʌn'feɪlɪŋ] *adj* à toute épreuve
unfair [ʌn'feə(r)] *adj* injuste; **to be u. to sb** être injuste envers qn; **to have an u. advantage (over sb)** être injustement favorisé(e) (par rapport à qn); *Com* **u. competition** concurrence *f* déloyale; *Law* **u. dismissal** licenciement *m* abusif
unfairly [ʌn'feəlɪ] *adv (act, treat)* injustement; *(share, distribute)* inéquitablement; *(dismiss)* abusivement
unfairness [ʌn'feənɪs] *n* injustice *f*
unfaithful [ʌn'feɪθfʊl] *adj* infidèle
unfamiliar [ʌnfə'mɪlɪə(r)] *adj* (**a**) *(unknown)* inconnu(e) (**b**) *(unacquainted)* **to be u. with** ne pas connaître
unfashionable [ʌn'fæʃənəbəl] *adj* démodé(e)
unfasten [ʌn'fɑːsən] **1** *vt* défaire
2 *vi* se défaire
unfathomable [ʌn'fæðəməbəl] *adj* insondable
unfavourable, *Am* **unfavorable** [ʌn'feɪvərəbəl] *adj* défavorable; *(moment)* peu propice
unfazed [ʌn'feɪzd] *adj Fam* **to be u. by sth** n'être pas du tout impressionné(e) par qch

unfeeling [ʌn'fiːlɪŋ] *adj* insensible
unfinished [ʌn'fɪnɪʃt] *adj* inachevé(e); **to have (some) u. business (with sb)** avoir des affaires à régler (avec qn)
unfit [ʌn'fɪt] *adj* (**a**) *(unsuitable)* inapte; **to be u. to do sth** être incapable de faire qch; **he's u. for the job** il est incapable d'assumer ce travail; **u. for human consumption** impropre à la consommation; **u. mother** mère *f* indigne (**b**) *(physically)* qui n'est pas en forme; **to be u.** ne pas être en forme
unflagging [ʌn'flægɪŋ] *adj (optimism, courage, enthusiasm)* inépuisable; *(attention, interest)* sans faille
unflappable [ʌn'flæpəbəl] *adj* imperturbable
unflattering [ʌn'flætərɪŋ] *adj* peu flatteur(euse)
unflinching [ʌn'flɪnʃɪŋ] *adj (courage)* inépuisable; *(resolve, loyalty, support)* à toute épreuve
unfold [ʌn'fəʊld] **1** *vt* (**a**) *(newspaper, map)* déplier (**b**) *(intentions, proposal)* dévoiler
2 *vi (of story, events)* se développer, se dérouler
unforced [ʌn'fɔːst] *adj* naturel(elle)
unforeseeable [ʌnfɔː'siːəbəl] *adj* imprévisible
unforeseen [ʌnfɔː'siːn] *adj* imprévu(e)
unforgettable [ʌnfə'getəbəl] *adj* inoubliable
unforgivable [ʌnfə'gɪvəbəl] *adj* impardonnable
unforgiving [ʌnfə'gɪvɪŋ] *adj* implacable, impitoyable
unformatted [ʌn'fɔːmætɪd] *adj Comput (disk)* non formaté(e); *(text)* non mis(e) en forme
unforthcoming [ʌnfɔːθ'kʌmɪŋ] *adj* réticent(e)
unfortunate [ʌn'fɔːtjənɪt] *adj (person)* malchanceux(euse); *(accident, event)* fâcheux(euse), regrettable; **it is u. that...** il est fâcheux *ou* regrettable que... + *subjunctive*
unfortunately [ʌn'fɔːtjənɪtlɪ] *adv* malheureusement
unfounded [ʌn'faʊndɪd] *adj* infondé(e), sans fondement
unfriendly [ʌn'frendlɪ] *adj (person)* peu sympathique; *(reception, tone, look)* froid(e)
unfulfilled [ʌnfʊl'fɪld] *adj (promise)* non tenu(e); *(desire, ambition)* insatisfait(e); *(potential)* non réalisé(e); **to feel u.** se sentir insatisfait
unfunny [ʌn'fʌnɪ] *adj* qui n'a rien de drôle
unfurl [ʌn'fɜːl] **1** *vt* déployer
2 *vi* se déployer
unfurnished [ʌn'fɜːnɪʃt] *adj* non meublé(e)
ungainly [ʌn'geɪnlɪ] *adj* disgracieux(euse)
ungenerous [ʌn'dʒenərəs] *adj (person)* qui manque de générosité; *(remark)* pas gentil(ille)
ungodly [ʌn'gɒdlɪ] *adj* impie; *Fam* **at an u. hour** à une heure impossible
ungovernable [ʌn'gʌvənəbəl] *adj (people, country)* ingouvernable; *(feelings)* irrépressible
ungracious [ʌn'greɪʃəs] *adj* peu aimable
ungrateful [ʌn'greɪtfʊl] *adj* ingrat(e)
ungrudging [ʌn'grʌdʒɪŋ] *adj* accordé(e) de bon cœur; **to be u. in one's praise** être généreux(euse) avec ses compliments
unguarded [ʌn'gɑːdɪd] *adj* (**a**) *(place)* sans surveillance (**b**) *(remark)* irréfléchi(e); **in an u. moment** dans un moment d'inattention
unhampered [ʌn'hæmpəd] *adj* non entravé(e) (**by** par)
unhappily [ʌn'hæpɪlɪ] *adv* (**a**) *(unfortunately)* malheureusement (**b**) *(sadly)* sans joie, sans bonheur
unhappiness [ʌn'hæpɪnɪs] *n* tristesse *f*
unhappy [ʌn'hæpɪ] *adj* (**a**) *(sad)* triste, malheureux(euse) (**b**) *(worried)* **to be u. about doing sth** ne pas vouloir faire qch (**c**) *(not pleased)* mécontent(e)

(with de) (**d**) *(unfortunate)* malheureux(euse), regrettable

unharmed [ʌnˈhɑːmd] *adj* indemne

UNHCR [juːeneɪtʃsiːˈɑː(r)] *n (abbr* **United Nations High Commission for Refugees**) HCR *m*

unhealthy [ʌnˈhelθɪ] *adj* (**a**) *(person)* maladif(ive); *(environment, climate)* malsain(e) (**b**) *(unwholesome)* malsain(e)

unheard-of [ʌnˈhɜːdɒv] *adj* (**a**) *(unknown)* inconnu(e) (**b**) *(unprecedented)* inouï(e); **it was u. in my youth!** c'était inconcevable dans ma jeunesse!

unheeded [ʌnˈhiːdɪd] *adj* ignoré(e); **to go u.** rester ignoré

unhelpful [ʌnˈhelpfʊl] *adj (person)* peu serviable; *(criticism, advice)* de peu d'utilité

unhesitating [ʌnˈhezɪteɪtɪŋ] *adj (support)* résolu(e), ferme; *(reply, reaction)* immédiat(e)

unhindered [ʌnˈhɪndəd] **1** *adj (progress)* sans encombres; **to be u. by sth** *(doubts, worry)* ne pas être gêné(e) par qch
2 *adv* sans encombres

unhinged [ʌnˈhɪndʒd] *adj (mad)* déséquilibré(e)

unhip [ʌnˈhɪp] *adj Fam (unfashionable)* ringard(e)

unholy [ʌnˈhəʊlɪ] *adj* impie; *Fam* **an u. mess/noise** une pagaille/un bruit invraisemblable; **u. alliance** alliance *f* contre nature

unhurt [ʌnˈhɜːt] *adj* indemne

unhygienic [ʌnhaɪˈdʒiːnɪk] *adj* contraire à l'hygiène; *(person)* qui manque d'hygiène

UNICEF [ˈjuːnɪsef] *n (abbr* **United Nations International Children's Emergency Fund**) Unicef *m*

unicorn [ˈjuːnɪkɔːn] *n* licorne *f*

unidentified [ʌnaɪˈdentɪfaɪd] *adj* non identifié(e); **u. flying object** objet *m* volant non identifié

unification [juːnɪfɪˈkeɪʃən] *n* unification *f*

uniform [ˈjuːnɪfɔːm] **1** *n* uniforme *m*
2 *adj (colour, size)* uniforme; *(temperature)* constant(e)

uniformity [juːnɪˈfɔːmɪtɪ] *n* uniformité *f*

uniformly [ˈjuːnɪfɔːmlɪ] *adv* uniformément

unify [ˈjuːnɪfaɪ] *(pt & pp* **unified**) **1** *vt* unifier
2 *vi* s'unifier

unilateral [juːnɪˈlætərəl] *adj* unilatéral(e)

unimaginable [ʌnɪˈmædʒɪnəbəl] *adj* inimaginable

unimaginative [ʌnɪˈmædʒɪnətɪv] *adj* qui manque d'imagination, peu imaginatif(ive)

unimpaired [ʌnɪmˈpeəd] *adj* intact(e)

unimportant [ʌnɪmˈpɔːtənt] *adj* sans importance

unimpressed [ʌnɪmˈprest] *adj* qui n'est pas impressionné(e); *(unconvinced)* qui n'est pas convaincu(e)

uninformed [ʌnɪnˈfɔːmd] *adj* mal informé(e) (**about** sur)

uninhabitable [ʌnɪnˈhæbɪtəbəl] *adj* inhabitable

uninhabited [ʌnɪnˈhæbɪtɪd] *adj* inhabité(e)

uninhibited [ʌnɪnˈhɪbɪtɪd] *adj (person)* sans complexes; *(feeling)* non refréné(e)

uninitiated [ʌnɪˈnɪʃɪeɪtɪd] *adj* non initié(e)

uninspiring [ʌnɪnˈspaɪrɪŋ] *adj* peu stimulant(e)

unintelligible [ʌnɪnˈtelɪdʒɪbəl] *adj* inintelligible

unintended [ʌnɪnˈtendɪd] *adj* involontaire

unintentional [ʌnɪnˈtenʃənəl] *adj* involontaire

uninterested [ʌnˈɪntərestɪd] *adj* indifférent(e)

uninteresting [ʌnˈɪntərestɪŋ] *adj* inintéressant(e)

uninterrupted [ʌnɪntəˈrʌptɪd] *adj* ininterrompu(e)

uninvited [ʌnɪnˈvaɪtɪd] **1** *adj (comment, advice)* non désiré(e); **u. guest** invité(e)-surprise *m,f*
2 *adv* sans invitation

uninviting [ʌnɪnˈvaɪtɪŋ] *adj* peu attrayant(e); *(food)* peu appétissant(e)

union [ˈjuːnjən] *n* (**a**) *(between countries, people)* union *f*; **the U. Jack** l'Union Jack *m (drapeau du Royaume-Uni)* (**b**) *(trade union)* syndicat *m*

unionist [ˈjuːnjənɪst] *n* (**a**) *(supporter of trade union)* syndicaliste *mf* (**b**) *(in Northern Ireland)* unioniste *mf*

unionize [ˈjuːnjənaɪz] *vt* syndiquer

unique [juːˈniːk] *adj* unique; **to be u. to** être propre à

unisex [ˈjuːniseks] *adj* unisexe

UNISON [ˈjuːnɪsən] *n Br* = principal syndicat de la fonction publique

unison [ˈjuːnɪsən] *n* **in u.** *(sing, play)* à l'unisson; *(speak, reply)* en même temps

unit [ˈjuːnɪt] *n* (**a**) *(in general)* unité *f*; **u. of measurement** unité *f* de mesure; *Com* **u. price** prix *m* à l'unité; *Fin* **u. trust** fonds *m* commun de placement, SICAV *f* (**b**) *(part of system, machine)* bloc *m*, élément *m* (**c**) *(in hospital)* service *m*, département *m*; *(in army)* unité *f* (**d**) *(of furniture)* élément *m*

unitary [ˈjuːnɪtərɪ] *adj* unitaire

unite [juːˈnaɪt] **1** *vt* unir, rassembler
2 *vi* s'unir; **to u. in doing sth** s'unir pour faire qch

united [juːˈnaɪtɪd] *adj* uni(e); **the U. Arab Emirates** les Émirats *mpl* arabes unis; **the U. Kingdom** le Royaume-Uni; **the U. Nations** les Nations *fpl* unies; **the U. States (of America)** les États-Unis *mpl* (d'Amérique)

unity [ˈjuːnɪtɪ] *n* unité *f*

univ *(abbr* **university**) univ

universal [juːnɪˈvɜːsəl] *adj* universel(elle); **u. suffrage** suffrage *m* universel

universally [juːnɪˈvɜːsəlɪ] *adv* universellement

universe [ˈjuːnɪvɜːs] *n* univers *m*

university [juːnɪˈvɜːsɪtɪ] *(pl* **universities**) *n* université *f*; **u. fees** frais *mpl* d'inscription à l'université; **u. student** étudiant(e) *m,f* à l'université, *Belg & Suisse* universitaire *mf*; **u. town** ville *f* universitaire

UNIX [ˈjuːnɪks] *n Comput (abbr* **Uniplexed Information and Computing System**) UNIX *m*

unjust [ʌnˈdʒʌst] *adj* injuste

unjustifiable [ʌndʒʌstɪˈfaɪəbəl] *adj* injustifiable

unjustified [ʌnˈdʒʌstɪfaɪd] *adj* injustifié(e)

unkempt [ʌnˈkem(p)t] *adj* négligé(e)

unkind [ʌnˈkaɪnd] *adj* pas gentil(ille); **to be u. to sb** ne pas être gentil avec qn

unkindly [ʌnˈkaɪndlɪ] *adv* méchamment; **to take u. to sth** mal accepter qch

unknowingly [ʌnˈnəʊɪŋlɪ] *adv* inconsciemment

unknown [ʌnˈnəʊn] **1** *adj* inconnu(e); *Fig* **to be an u. quantity** rester une inconnue; **the U. Soldier** le Soldat inconnu
2 *adv* **u. to me/us** à mon/notre insu
3 *n (person)* inconnu(e) *m,f*; **the u.** l'inconnu *m*

unlace [ʌnˈleɪs] *vt* délacer, défaire

unladylike [ʌnˈleɪdɪlaɪk] *adj (person)* qui ne se conduit pas comme une jeune fille; *(behaviour)* qui n'est pas digne d'une jeune fille

unlawful [ʌnˈlɔːfʊl] *adj* illégal(e), illicite

unleaded [ʌnˈledɪd] **1** *adj* sans plomb
2 *n* sans plomb *m*

unleash [ʌnˈliːʃ] *vt (dog)* détacher, lâcher; *Fig (emotion, criticism)* susciter

unleavened [ʌnˈlevənd] *adj* sans levain

unless [ʌnˈles] *conj* à moins que + *subjunctive*; **u. I hear to the contrary** sauf avis contraire

unlike [ʌn'laɪk] *prep* to be u. sb/sth ne pas être comme qn/qch; he's not u. his sister il ressemble assez à sa sœur; he, u. his father,... lui, à la différence de son père...; it's u. her to do such a thing cela ne lui ressemble pas de faire une chose pareille

unlikely [ʌn'laɪklɪ] *adj* improbable; *(story, explanation)* invraisemblable; it's u. to happen il est peu probable que cela se produise; she's u. to do it il est peu probable qu'elle le fasse; in the u. event of an accident dans le cas fort peu probable d'un accident

unlimited [ʌn'lɪmɪtɪd] *adj* illimité(e), sans limites; *Com* u. liability responsabilité *f* illimitée; u. mileage *(of hired car)* ≃ kilométrage *m* illimité

unlisted [ʌn'lɪstɪd] *adj* (a) *Fin* non inscrit(e) à la cote (b) *AmTel (phone number)* qui est sur liste rouge

unlit [ʌn'lɪt] *adj (fire, cigarette)* non allumé(e); *(place)* non éclairé(e)

unload [ʌn'ləʊd] 1 *vt (boat, gun, goods)* décharger; *Fig* to u. one's problems onto sb se soulager de ses problèmes en en parlant à qn
    2 *vi (of lorry, ship)* décharger

unlock [ʌn'lɒk] *vt* (a) *(door)* ouvrir; *Fig (mystery)* dévoiler, révéler (b) *Tel (mobile phone)* débloquer

unlovable [ʌn'lʌvəbəl] *adj* peu attachant(e)

unloved [ʌn'lʌvd] *adj* mal aimé(e)

unlovely [ʌn'lʌvlɪ] *adj* déplaisant(e)

unluckily [ʌn'lʌkɪlɪ] *adv* malheureusement

unlucky [ʌn'lʌkɪ] *adj (coincidence, decision)* malheureux(euse); *(day)* de malchance; to be u. *(of person)* être malchanceux(euse); *(of thing)* porter malheur

unmanageable [ʌn'mænɪdʒəbəl] *adj (person, situation)* difficile; *(hair)* impossible à coiffer

unmanly [ʌn'mænlɪ] *adj (effeminate)* efféminé(e), peu viril(e); *(cowardly)* lâche

unmanned [ʌn'mænd] *adj (spaceship)* inhabité(e)

unmarked [ʌn'mɑːkt] *adj* (a) *(grave)* sans inscription; u. (police) car voiture *f* (de police) banalisée (b) *(uncorrected)* non corrigé(e)

unmarried [ʌn'mærɪd] *adj* non marié(e)

unmask [ʌn'mɑːsk] *vt* démasquer

unmentionable [ʌn'menʃənəbəl] *adj* à ne pas mentionner

unmissable [ʌn'mɪsəbəl] *adj* inratable

unmistakable [ʌnmɪs'teɪkəbəl] *adj* caractéristique

unmitigated [ʌn'mɪtɪgeɪtɪd] *adj* total(e), absolu(e)

unmoved [ʌn'muːvd] 1 *adj* to be u. by sth rester insensible à qch; he was u. by her elle le laissait complètement indifférent
    2 *adv* sans broncher

unnamed [ʌn'neɪmd] *adj (person)* anonyme; *(thing)* sans nom

unnatural [ʌn'nætjərəl] *adj* (a) *(abnormal)* anormal(e) (b) *(affected)* affecté(e)

unnecessary [ʌn'nesɪsərɪ] *adj* inutile, superflu(e)

unnerve [ʌn'nɜːv] *vt* troubler

unnerving [ʌn'nɜːvɪŋ] *adj* troublant(e)

unnoticed [ʌn'nəʊtɪst] 1 *adj* inaperçu(e)
    2 *adv* to pass *or* go u. passer inaperçu(e)

UNO [juːen'əʊ] *n (abbr* United Nations Organization) ONU *f*

unobservant [ʌnəb'zɜːvənt] *adj* peu observateur(trice)

unobserved [ʌnəb'zɜːvd] 1 *adj* inaperçu(e)
    2 *adv* to do sth u. faire qch sans être vu(e)

unobstructed [ʌnəb'strʌktɪd] *adj* dégagé(e); *(pipe)* non obstrué(e)

unobtainable [ʌnəb'teɪnəbəl] *adj* impossible à obtenir

unobtrusive [ʌnəb'truːsɪv] *adj* discret(ète)

unoccupied [ʌn'ɒkjʊpaɪd] *adj (person)* qui n'est pas occupé(e); *(seat)* libre; *(house)* inhabité(e), inoccupé(e)

unofficial [ʌnə'fɪʃəl] *adj* officieux(euse), non officiel(elle); *Ind* u. strike grève *f* sauvage

unopened [ʌn'əʊpənd] *adj* non ouvert(e)

unopposed [ʌnə'pəʊzd] 1 *adj* sans opposition; to be u. ne pas rencontrer d'opposition
    2 *adv* to go u. ne pas rencontrer d'opposition

unorthodox [ʌn'ɔːθədɒks] *adj* peu orthodoxe

unpack [ʌn'pæk] 1 *vt* (a) *(suitcase)* défaire; *(contents)* déballer; *(box)* ouvrir (b) *Comput* décompresser, décompacter
    2 *vi* défaire ses bagages

unpaid [ʌn'peɪd] *adj* (a) *(work, volunteer)* non rémunéré(e) (b) *(bill, debt)* impayé(e)

unpalatable [ʌn'pælətəbəl] *adj (food)* qui n'est pas très bon (bonne); *Fig (truth)* désagréable à entendre

unparalleled [ʌn'pærəleld] *adj* incomparable, sans pareil(eille)

unpardonable [ʌn'pɑːdənəbəl] *adj* impardonnable

unpatriotic [ʌnpætrɪ'ɒtɪk, ʌnpeɪtrɪ'ɒtɪk] *adj (person)* peu patriote; *(song, remark)* antipatriotique

unperturbed [ʌnpə'tɜːbd] 1 *adj* to be u. by sth ne pas se laisser perturber par qch
    2 *adv* imperturbablement

unplanned [ʌn'plænd] *adj* imprévu(e); *(pregnancy)* accidentel(elle)

unpleasant [ʌn'plezənt] *adj* désagréable, déplaisant(e)

unpleasantness [ʌn'plezəntnɪs] *n* (a) *(unpleasant nature)* côté *m* désagréable (b) *(ill-feeling)* désagréments *mpl*

unplug [ʌn'plʌg] *(pt & pp* unplugged*) vt* débrancher

unpolished [ʌn'pɒlɪʃt] *adj (shoes, surface)* non ciré(e); *Fig (performance, style)* imparfait(e)

unpolluted [ʌnpə'luːtɪd] *adj* non pollué(e)

unpopular [ʌn'pɒpjʊlə(r)] *adj* impopulaire; she's very u. with the boss at the moment elle n'est pas dans les bonnes grâces du patron en ce moment

unpopularity [ʌnpɒpjʊ'lærɪtɪ] *n* impopularité *f*

unpredictability [ʌnprɪdɪktə'bɪlətɪ] *n* imprévisibilité *f*

unpredictable [ʌnprɪ'dɪktəbəl] *adj* imprévisible

unprejudiced [ʌn'predʒʊdɪst] *adj (view, person)* impartial(e)

unprepared [ʌnprɪ'peəd] *adj (speech)* improvisé(e); to be u. for sth être mal préparé(e) à qch; *(not expect)* ne pas s'attendre à qch

unprepossessing [ʌnpriːpə'zesɪŋ] *adj* peu avenant(e)

unpresentable [ʌnprɪ'zentəbəl] *adj* qui n'est pas présentable

unpretentious [ʌnprɪ'tenʃəs] *adj* sans prétention(s)

unprincipled [ʌn'prɪnsɪpəld] *adj* sans scrupules

unprintable [ʌn'prɪntəbəl] *adj* licencieux(euse)

unproductive [ʌnprə'dʌktɪv] *adj* improductif(ive)

unprofessional [ʌnprə'feʃənəl] *adj* qui n'est pas professionnel(elle)

unprofitable [ʌn'prɒfɪtəbəl] *adj* peu rentable

Unprofor [ʌn'prɒfɔː(r)] *n (abbr* United Nations Protection Force) FORPRONU *f*

unpromising [ʌn'prɒmɪsɪŋ] *adj* peu prometteur(euse)

unpronounceable [ʌnprəˈnaʊnsəbəl] *adj* imprononçable

unprotected [ʌnprəˈtektɪd] *adj* sans protection; *(sex)* non protégé(e)

unprovoked [ʌnprəˈvəʊkt] *adj* gratuit(e)

unpublished [ʌnˈpʌblɪʃt] *adj* inédit(e)

unpunished [ʌnˈpʌnɪʃt] **1** *adj* impuni(e)
  2 *adv* **to go u.** rester impuni(e)

unqualified [ʌnˈkwɒlɪfaɪd] *adj* (**a**) *(doctor, teacher)* non qualifié(e); **to be u.** to do sth ne pas être qualifié(e) pour faire qch (**b**) *(support)* inconditionnel(elle), sans réserve; *(disaster, success)* total(e), complet(ète)

unquestionable [ʌnˈkwestʃənəbəl] *adj* indubitable, incontestable

unquestioning [ʌnˈkwestʃənɪŋ] *adj (trust, obedience)* absolu(e), aveugle

unravel [ʌnˈrævəl] (*pt & pp* **unravelled**) **1** *vt (wool, knitting)* démêler; *(threads)* démêler; *Fig (plot)* dénouer; *(mystery)* éclaircir
  2 *vi (of wool, knitting)* se défaire; *Fig (of plan)* péricliter; *(of mystery)* s'éclaircir

unreadable [ʌnˈriːdəbəl] *adj* illisible

unreal [ʌnˈrɪəl] *adj* irréel(elle)

unrealistic [ʌnrɪəˈlɪstɪk] *adj* irréaliste

unreasonable [ʌnˈriːzənəbəl] *adj* déraisonnable

unrecognizable [ʌnrekəgˈnaɪzəbəl] *adj* méconnaissable

unrecognized [ʌnˈrekəgnaɪzd] **1** *adj* méconnu(e)
  2 *adv* **to go u.** rester méconnu(e)

unrecorded [ʌnrɪˈkɔːdɪd] *adj* non enregistré(e)

unrefined [ʌnrɪˈfaɪnd] *adj* (**a**) *(sugar, petrol)* non raffiné(e) (**b**) *(person, taste)* qui manque de raffinement

unregistered [ʌnˈredʒɪstəd] *adj (birth)* non déclaré(e)

unrelated [ʌnrɪˈleɪtɪd] *adj* **to be u.** *(of events)* ne pas avoir de rapport; *(of people)* n'avoir aucun lien de parenté

unrelenting [ʌnrɪˈlentɪŋ] *adj* incessant(e); *(person)* tenace

unreliable [ʌnrɪˈlaɪəbəl] *adj* peu fiable

unrelieved [ʌnrɪˈliːvd] *adj (pain)* constant(e)

unremarkable [ʌnrɪˈmɑːkəbəl] *adj* quelconque

unremitting [ʌnrɪˈmɪtɪŋ] *adj* inlassable, infatigable

unrepentant [ʌnrɪˈpentənt] *adj* impénitent(e)

unreported [ʌnrɪˈpɔːtɪd] **1** *adj* non signalé(e)
  2 *adv* **to go u.** ne pas être signalé(e)

unrepresentative [ʌnreprɪˈzentətɪv] *adj* non représentatif(ive)

unrepresented [ʌnreprɪˈzentɪd] *adj* non représenté(e)

unrequited love [ˈʌnrɪkwaɪtɪdˈlʌv] *n* amour *m* non partagé

unreserved [ʌnrɪˈzɜːvd] *adj* (**a**) *(praise, support)* sans réserve (**b**) *(seat, table)* non réservé(e)

unresponsive [ʌnrɪˈspɒnsɪv] *adj* sans réaction; **to be u. to sth** être insensible à qch

unrest [ʌnˈrest] *n* agitation *f*, troubles *mpl*

unrestricted [ʌnrɪˈstrɪktɪd] *adj* illimité(e); *(access)* libre

unrewarding [ʌnrɪˈwɔːdɪŋ] *adj (financially)* qui ne rapporte pas; *(intellectually)* ingrat(e)

unripe [ʌnˈraɪp] *adj* qui n'est pas mûr(e)

unrivalled [ʌnˈraɪvəld] *adj* sans pareil(eille), incomparable

unromantic [ʌnrəˈmæntɪk] *adj* peu romantique

unruffled [ʌnˈrʌfəld] *adj* imperturbable

unruly [ʌnˈruːlɪ] *adj (child, hair)* indiscipliné(e); *(crowd)* incontrôlé(e)

unsaddle [ʌnˈsædəl] *vt (horse)* desseller

unsafe [ʌnˈseɪf] *adj* (**a**) *(in danger)* en danger (**b**) *(dangerous)* dangereux(euse)

unsaid [ʌnˈsed] *adj* **to leave sth u.** passer qch sous silence; **it's better left u.** il vaut mieux garder le silence là-dessus

unsalted [ʌnˈsɔːltɪd] *adj* sans sel; **u. butter** beurre *m* doux

unsatisfactory [ʌnsætɪsˈfæktərɪ] *adj* peu satisfaisant(e)

unsatisfying [ʌnˈsætɪsfaɪɪŋ] *adj* peu satisfaisant(e)

unsavoury [ʌnˈseɪvərɪ] *adj (person, place)* peu recommandable; *(reputation)* sale

unscathed [ʌnˈskeɪðd] *adj* indemne

unscheduled [ʌnˈʃedjuːld] *adj* imprévu(e)

unscientific [ʌnsaɪənˈtɪfɪk] *adj* non scientifique

unscramble [ʌnˈskræmbəl] *vt* décoder

unscrew [ʌnˈskruː] **1** *vt* dévisser
  2 *vi* se dévisser

unscrupulous [ʌnˈskruːpjʊləs] *adj (person)* sans scrupules; *(action)* malhonnête

unseat [ʌnˈsiːt] *vt (rider)* désarçonner; *Br Fig (MP)* faire perdre son siège à; *(leader)* faire tomber

unseemly [ʌnˈsiːmlɪ] *adj* inconvenant(e), indécent(e)

unseen [ʌnˈsiːn] **1** *adj* invisible; **u. translation** traduction *f* à vue
  2 *adv* **to do sth u.** faire qch sans qu'on vous voie

unselfconscious [ʌnselfˈkɒnʃəs] *adj* naturel(elle); **he's quite u.** about it il n'en est pas du tout complexé

unselfish [ʌnˈselfɪʃ] *adj* généreux(euse)

unsentimental [ʌnsentɪˈmentəl] *adj (person)* peu sentimental(e); *(book, film)* dénué(e) de tout sentimentalisme

unsettle [ʌnˈsetəl] *vt* troubler, perturber

unshakeable [ʌnˈʃeɪkəbəl] *adj* inébranlable

unshaven [ʌnˈʃeɪvən] *adj* pas rasé(e)

unsightly [ʌnˈsaɪtlɪ] *adj* laid(e)

unsigned [ʌnˈsaɪnd] *adj* non signé(e)

unskilful [ʌnˈskɪlfʊl] *adj* maladroit(e), malhabile

unskilled [ʌnˈskɪld] *adj* non qualifié(e)

unsociable [ʌnˈsəʊʃəbəl] *adj (by nature)* sauvage; **she's feeling rather u. at the moment** elle n'a pas envie de voir du monde en ce moment

unsold [ʌnˈsəʊld] *adj* invendu(e)

unsolicited [ʌnsəˈlɪsɪtɪd] *adj* non sollicité(e)

unsolved [ʌnˈsɒlvd] *adj* non résolu(e)

unsophisticated [ʌnsəˈfɪstɪkeɪtɪd] *adj* simple

unsound [ʌnˈsaʊnd] *adj* (**a**) *(health)* précaire; *Law* **to be of u. mind** ne pas jouir de toutes ses facultés mentales (**b**) *(decision, advice)* peu judicieux(euse); *(investment)* hasardeux(euse); **he's ideologically u.** son idéologie est suspecte

unsparing [ʌnˈspeərɪŋ] *adj* **to be u. of one's time/ with one's advice** ne pas être avare de son temps/ de ses conseils

unspeakable [ʌnˈspiːkəbəl] *adj* indescriptible

unspecified [ʌnˈspesɪfaɪd] *adj* non spécifié(e)

unspoilt [ʌnˈspɔɪlt] *adj (beach, landscape)* préservé(e)

unspoken [ʌnˈspəʊkən] *adj (fear, threat)* inexprimé(e); *(agreement)* tacite

unsporting [ʌnˈspɔːtɪŋ], **unsportsmanlike** [ʌn ˈspɔːtsmənlaɪk] *adj* qui n'est pas fair-play

unstable [ʌnˈsteɪbəl] *adj* instable

unsteady [ʌn'stedɪ] *adj (table, chair)* bancal(e); *(hand, voice)* mal assuré(e); **to be u. on one's feet** ne pas être très solide sur ses jambes

unstinting [ʌn'stɪntɪŋ] *adj (praise, effort)* sans réserve

unstressed [ʌn'strest] *adj Ling* inaccentué(e)

unstuck [ʌn'stʌk] *adj Fam* **to come u.** *(of person)* se casser la figure; *(of plan)* tomber à l'eau

unsubscribe [ʌnsʌb'skraɪb] *vi (from mailing list etc)* se désinscrire

unsubstantiated [ʌnsəb'stænʃɪeɪtɪd] *adj (accusation)* sans fondement

unsuccessful [ʌnsək'sesfʊl] *adj* **to be u.** *(of person, project)* ne pas réussir

unsuccessfully [ʌnsək'sesfəlɪ] *adv* en vain, sans succès

unsuitable [ʌn'suːtəbəl] *adj (candidate)* inadéquat(e); *(friend)* pas convenable; *(time)* inopportun(e); *(choice)* inapproprié(e); **to be u. for sth** ne pas convenir à qch; **this film is u. for children** ce n'est pas un film pour les enfants

unsuited [ʌn'suːtɪd] *adj* **to be u. to sth** ne pas être fait(e) pour qch; **to be u.** *(of couple)* être mal assorti(e)

unsupervised [ʌn'suːpəvaɪzd] *adj (child)* non surveillé(e)

unsupported [ʌnsə'pɔːtɪd] *adj* (**a**) *(statement, charges)* sans fondement (**b**) *(structure)* non soutenu(e)

unsure [ʌn'ʃʊə(r)] *adj* incertain(e), peu sûr(e); **to be u. of** *or* **about sth** ne pas être sûr(e) de qch

unsurpassed [ʌnsə'pɑːst] *adj* inégalé(e)

unsuspected [ʌnsəs'pektɪd] *adj* insoupçonné(e)

unsuspecting [ʌnsəs'pektɪŋ] *adj* qui ne se doute de rien

unsustainable [ʌnsə'steɪnəbəl] *adj* non viable

unsweetened [ʌn'swiːtənd] *adj* non sucré(e), sans sucre ajouté

unswerving [ʌn'swɜːvɪŋ] *adj* à toute épreuve

unsympathetic [ʌnsɪmpə'θetɪk] *adj* peu compatissant(e) (**to** à); *(to cause, request)* insensible (**to** à)

unsystematic [ʌnsɪstə'mætɪk] *adj* non systématique

untainted [ʌn'teɪntɪd] *adj (food)* qui n'a pas été contaminé(e); *(reputation)* qui n'a pas été entaché(e)

untalented [ʌn'tæləntɪd] *adj* peu doué(e)

untamed [ʌn'teɪmd] *adj (animal)* sauvage

untangle [ʌn'tæŋgəl] *vt* démêler; *Fig (plot)* dénouer

untapped [ʌn'tæpt] *adj* inexploité(e)

untenable [ʌn'tenəbəl] *adj (position)* intenable; *(theory)* indéfendable

untested [ʌn'testɪd] *adj (drug, product)* non testé(e); *(method, system)* qui n'a pas été mis(e) à l'épreuve

unthinkable [ʌn'θɪŋkəbəl] *adj* impensable, inconcevable

untidiness [ʌn'taɪdɪnɪs] *n* désordre *m*

untidy [ʌn'taɪdɪ] *adj (person)* désordonné(e); *(place)* en désordre

untie [ʌn'taɪ] *vt (knot, shoelaces)* défaire; *(string)* dénouer; *(person, animal)* détacher

until [ʌn'tɪl] **1** *prep* jusqu'à; **u. April** jusqu'en avril; **u. now** jusqu'à présent; **not u. tomorrow** pas avant demain; **I didn't see her u. Sunday** c'est seulement dimanche que je l'ai vue
 2 *conj* jusqu'à ce que + *subjunctive*; **u. she gets back** jusqu'à ce qu'elle revienne; **don't move u. I tell you** ne bouge pas avant que je (ne) te le dise

untimely [ʌn'taɪmlɪ] *adj (death)* prématuré(e); *(remark)* inopportun(e); *(moment)* mauvais(e)

untiring [ʌn'taɪərɪŋ] *adj* infatigable, inlassable

untold [ʌn'təʊld] *adj (wealth, beauty)* immense

untouchable [ʌn'tʌtʃəbəl] **1** *n* intouchable *mf*; *Fig* paria *m*
 2 *adj* intouchable

untouched [ʌn'tʌtʃt] *adj* qui n'a pas été touché(e); **to leave sth u.** ne pas toucher à qch

untoward [ʌntə'wɔːd] *adj Formal* fâcheux(euse), malencontreux(euse)

untrained [ʌn'treɪnd] *adj (animal)* non dressé(e); *(person)* sans formation

untranslatable [ʌntræns'leɪtəbəl] *adj* intraduisible

untried [ʌn'traɪd] *adj* (**a**) *(person, system)* qui n'a pas encore fait ses preuves (**b**) *Law (person, case)* non jugé(e)

untroubled [ʌn'trʌbəld] *adj* tranquille, calme; **to be u. by sth** ne pas être perturbé(e) par qch

untrue [ʌn'truː] *adj* (**a**) *(false)* faux (fausse) (**b**) *(unfaithful)* infidèle (**to** à)

untrustworthy [ʌn'trʌstwɜːðɪ] *adj (person)* qui n'est pas digne de confiance; *(information)* qui n'est pas fiable

untruth [ʌn'truːθ] *n* mensonge *m*

untruthful [ʌn'truːθʊl] *adj (person)* menteur(euse); *(story, reply)* mensonger(ère)

unusable [ʌn'juːzəbəl] *adj* inutilisable

unused *adj* (**a**) [ʌn'juːzd] *(not in use)* inutilisé(e) (**b**) [ʌn'juːzd] *(never yet used)* neuf (neuve) (**c**) [ʌn'juːst] *(unaccustomed)* **to be u. to sth/to doing sth** ne pas avoir l'habitude de qch/de faire qch

unusual [ʌn'juːʒʊəl] *adj (not common)* inhabituel(-elle); *(strange)* bizarre, étrange; **it's u. of her not to notice** c'est rare qu'elle ne s'en rende pas compte

unusually [ʌn'juːʒʊəlɪ] *adv* exceptionnellement

unvaried [ʌn'veərɪd] *adj* monotone

unvarnished [ʌn'vɑːnɪʃt] *adj* non verni(e); *Fig* **the u. truth** la vérité pure et simple

unveil [ʌn'veɪl] *vt also Fig* dévoiler

unverifiable [ʌn'verɪfaɪəbəl] *adj* invérifiable

unvoiced [ʌn'vɔɪst] *adj* (**a**) *Ling* non voisé(e) (**b**) *(unspoken)* inexprimé(e)

unwaged [ʌn'weɪdʒd] **1** *npl* **the u.** ceux qui n'ont pas d'activité rémunérée
 2 *adj* qui n'a pas d'activité rémunérée

unwanted [ʌn'wɒntɪd] *adj* non désiré(e); **to feel u.** se sentir de trop

unwarranted [ʌn'wɒrəntɪd] *adj* injustifié(e)

unwary [ʌn'weərɪ] *adj* sans méfiance

unwashed [ʌn'wɒʃt] **1** *adj (dishes, floor)* non lavé(e); *(person)* qui ne s'est pas lavé(e)
 2 *npl Hum Pej* **the great u.** la populace

unwavering [ʌn'weɪvərɪŋ] *adj (devotion)* inébranlable; *(loyalty, support)* à toute épreuve; *(gaze)* fixe

unwelcome [ʌn'welkəm] *adj (visit, visitor)* importun(e); *(news)* fâcheux(euse); **to make sb feel u.** faire sentir à qn qu'il n'est pas le bienvenu

unwell [ʌn'wel] *adj* souffrant(e)

unwholesome [ʌn'həʊlsəm] *adj* malsain(e)

unwieldy [ʌn'wiːldɪ] *adj (object)* difficile à manier; *Fig (system, method)* lourd(e)

unwilling [ʌn'wɪlɪŋ] *adj* réticent(e); **to be u. to do sth** être réticent à faire qch

unwillingness [ʌn'wɪlɪŋnɪs] *n* réticence *f*

unwind [ʌn'waɪnd] *(pt & pp* **unwound** [ʌn'waʊnd]*)* **1** *vt (string, wool)* dérouler

2 *vi* (**a**) *(of string, wool)* se dérouler (**b**) *Fam (relax)* se détendre, se relaxer

unwise [ʌnˈwaɪz] *adj (person)* imprudent(e); *(decision, action)* peu judicieux(euse)

unwitting [ʌnˈwɪtɪŋ] *adj* involontaire

unworkable [ʌnˈwɜːkəbəl] *adj* impraticable

unworthy [ʌnˈwɜːðɪ] *adj* indigne (**of** de)

unwound [ʌnˈwaʊnd] *pt & pp of* unwind

unwrap [ʌnˈræp] *(pt & pp* unwrapped) *vt* déballer

unwritten [ʌnˈrɪtən] *adj (language)* non écrit(e); *(agreement)* verbal(e); **it's an u. rule that...** il est entendu que...

unyielding [ʌnˈjiːldɪŋ] *adj* inflexible

unzip [ʌnˈzɪp] *(pt & pp* unzipped) *vt* (**a**) *(garment, bag etc)* ouvrir (la fermeture Éclair® de) (**b**) *Comput (file)* décompresser, dézipper

up [ʌp] **1** *adv* (**a**) *(with motion)* **to come/go up** monter; **to go up to sb** s'approcher de qn; **to go up north** aller au nord; **to put one's hand up** lever la main; **to put a poster up** accrocher un poster; **petrol has gone up in price** l'essence a augmenté
(**b**) *(with position)* en haut; **up here** ici; **up there** là-haut; **up above** au-dessus; **further up** plus haut; **petrol is up in price** l'essence a augmenté
(**c**) *(ahead)* **to be one goal/five points up** avoir un but/cinq points d'avance
(**d**) *(in phrases with* to) **up to now/the age of seven** jusqu'à maintenant/l'âge de sept ans; **what are the children up to?** que fabriquent les enfants?; **she's up to something** elle manigance quelque chose; **what have you been up to?** qu'est-ce que tu deviens?; **it's up to you to do it** c'est à vous de le faire; **it's up to you** *(you decide)* c'est à vous de décider; **he's not up to the job** il n'est pas à la hauteur de la tâche; **I don't feel up to it** je ne m'en sens pas capable; **it's not up to much** *(not very good)* ce n'est pas extraordinaire
2 *prep* (**a**) *(with motion)* **to go up the stairs/the street** monter les escaliers/la rue; **to run up the stairs/the street** monter les escaliers/la rue en courant; **to climb up a hill** monter à une colline; *Vulg* **up yours!** va te faire foutre!
(**b**) *(with position)* **to be up a tree/ladder** être dans un arbre/sur une échelle; **to live up the street (from sb)** habiter plus haut dans la rue (que qn); *Fig* **to be up against sth** avoir affaire à qch
3 *adj* (**a**) *(out of bed)* levé(e); **I was up at seven** j'étais levé à sept heures; **she was up late last night** elle a veillé tard hier soir; **we were up all night** nous sommes restés debout toute la nuit; **to be up and about** être debout; *(after illness)* être sur pied
(**b**) *(finished)* **the two weeks were up** les deux semaines étaient terminées; **(your) time's up** c'est terminé
(**c**) *Fam (wrong)* **something's up** quelque chose ne va pas; **what's up?** qu'est-ce qu'il y a?; **what's up with her?** qu'est-ce qu'elle a?
(**d**) *(idiom)* **to be up and running** *(of machine, system)* être opérationnel(elle)
4 *n* **ups and downs** des hauts et des bas
5 *vt (pt & pp* upped) *Fam (price, offer)* augmenter
6 *vi Fam* **to up and go** *or* **leave** filer

up-and-coming [ˈʌpəndˈkʌmɪŋ] *adj (star, politician)* qui monte

upbeat [ʌpˈbiːt] *adj* optimiste

upbraid [ʌpˈbreɪd] *vt Formal* réprimander; **to u. sb for sth** reprocher qch à qn; **to u. sb for doing sth** reprocher à qn d'avoir fait qch

upbringing [ˈʌpbrɪŋɪŋ] *n* éducation *f*

upcoming [ˈʌpkʌmɪŋ] *adj (event)* à venir, prochain(e)

update 1 *n* [ˈʌpdeɪt] mise *f* à jour, actualisation *f*
2 *vt* [ʌpˈdeɪt] mettre à jour, actualiser; **to u. sb on sth** mettre qn au courant de qch

upend [ʌpˈend] *vt* renverser

upfront [ʌpˈfrʌnt] **1** *adj Fam (frank)* franc (franche), direct(e)
2 *adv (in advance)* d'avance

upgradable [ʌpˈɡreɪdəbəl] *adj Comput (hardware, system)* évolutif(ive); *(memory)* extensible

upgrade 1 *n* [ˈʌpɡreɪd] *Comput (of hardware)* augmentation *f* de puissance; *(of software)* nouvelle version *f*
2 *vt* [ʌpˈɡreɪd] (**a**) *(improve)* améliorer; *(promote)* promouvoir; augmenter; **I was upgraded to business class** *(on plane)* on m'a mis en classe affaires (**b**) *Comput (hardware)* augmenter la puissance de; *(software)* acquérir la dernière version de

upheaval [ʌpˈhiːvəl] *n* bouleversement *m*

upheld [ʌpˈheld] *pt & pp of* uphold

uphill [ˈʌphɪl] **1** *adj* qui monte; *Fig (struggle)* ardu(e), pénible
2 *adv* **to go u.** monter

uphold [ʌpˈhəʊld] *(pt & pp* upheld [ʌpˈheld]) *vt (opinion, principle)* soutenir; *(decision)* maintenir; **to u. the law** faire respecter la loi

upholstered [ʌpˈhəʊlstəd] *adj* tapissé(e)

upholstery [ʌpˈhəʊlstərɪ] *n* tapisserie *f*; *(in car)* sièges *mpl*

upkeep [ˈʌpkiːp] *n* entretien *m*

uplift *n* [ˈʌplɪft] élévation *f* morale *ou* spirituelle
2 *vt* [ʌpˈlɪft] élever

uplifting [ʌpˈlɪftɪŋ] *adj* édifiant(e)

upload *Comput* **1** *n* [ˈʌpləʊd] téléchargement *m* (vers le serveur)
2 *vt* [ʌpˈləʊd] télécharger *(vers le serveur)*

upmarket [ˈʌpmɑːkɪt] *adj (product)* haut de gamme *inv*; *(area, place)* chic *inv*

upon [əˈpɒn] *prep* sur; **u. my word!** ma parole!

upper [ˈʌpə(r)] **1** *adj* supérieur(e); **the u. class** l'aristocratie *f*; **to get/have the u. hand** prendre/avoir le dessus; *Br Pol* **the U. House** la Chambre des Lords
2 *n (of shoe)* empeigne *f*; *Fam* **to be on one's uppers** manger de la vache enragée

upper-class [ˈʌpəklɑːs] *adj* aristocratique

upper-crust [ˈʌpəkrʌst] *adj Fam* aristo

uppermost [ˈʌpəməʊst] *adj* le (la) plus haut(e); *Fig* **it was u. in my mind** c'était la première de mes préoccupations

uppity [ˈʌpɪtɪ] *adj Fam* crâneur(euse); **to get u.** crâner

upright [ˈʌpraɪt] **1** *adj* (**a**) *(vertical)* droit(e); **u. piano** piano *m* droit; **u. vacuum cleaner** aspirateur *m* balai (**b**) *(honest)* droit(e)
2 *adv* droit; **to set** *or* **stand sth u.** mettre qch debout *ou* d'aplomb
3 *n (beam)* montant *m*

uprising [ˈʌpraɪzɪŋ] *n* soulèvement *m*, révolte *f*

uproar [ˈʌprɔː(r)] *n (noise, protest)* tumulte *m*; **the house was in an u.** ce fut le tumulte dans la maison

uproarious [ʌpˈrɔːrɪəs] *adj (noisy)* tonitruant(e); *(funny)* hilarant(e)

uproot [ʌpˈruːt] *vt* déraciner

upset 1 *vt* [ʌp'set] (*pt & pp* **upset**) (**a**) *(liquid, container)* renverser (**b**) *(person, plans, schedule)* bouleverser

2 *n* ['ʌpset] *(disturbance)* bouleversement *m*; *(surprise)* défaite *f*; **to have a stomach u.** avoir l'estomac dérangé

3 *adj* [ʌp'set] *(unhappy)* bouleversé(e) (**about** par); **to have an u. stomach** avoir l'estomac dérangé

upsetting [ʌp'setɪŋ] *adj* bouleversant(e)

upshot ['ʌpʃɒt] *n* conséquence *f*, résultat *m*

upside down ['ʌpsaɪd'daʊn] **1** *adj* à l'envers **2** *adv* à l'envers; **to turn sth u.** retourner qch; *Fig* mettre qch sens dessus dessous

upstage [ʌp'steɪdʒ] **1** *adv Theat (move)* vers le fond de la scène; **u. of sb/sth** à l'arrière-plan par rapport à qn/qch **2** *vt Theat & Fig* éclipser, voler la vedette à

upstairs 1 *adj* ['ʌpsteəz] de l'étage du dessus; **u. neighbours** les voisins du dessus; **the u. bathroom** la salle de bains du haut **2** *adv* [ʌp'steəz] en haut; **to come/go u.** monter; **he lives u.** il habite à l'étage au-dessus **3** *n* [ʌp'steəz] **the u.** l'étage *m*

upstanding [ʌp'stændɪŋ] *adj* droit(e)

upstart ['ʌpstɑːt] *n* parvenu(e) *m,f*

upstream [ʌp'striːm] *adv* en amont; *(with movement)* vers l'amont

upsurge ['ʌpsɜːdʒ] *n (of anger, enthusiasm)* vague *f*; *(of interest)* recrudescence *f*

upswing ['ʌpswɪŋ] *n* amélioration *f* (**in** de); *(in economy)* redressement *m* (**in** de)

uptake ['ʌpteɪk] *n Fam* **to be quick on the u.** piger vite; **to be slow on the u.** être lent(e) à la détente

uptight [ʌp'taɪt] *adj Fam (nervous)* tendu(e), crispé(e); *(inhibited)* coincé(e)

up-to-date [ʌptə'deɪt] *adj* (**a**) *(most recent)* à jour; *(news)* récent(e); **to bring sb u. (on sth)** mettre qn au courant (de qch) (**b**) *(modern)* à la mode

up-to-the-minute [ʌptəðə'mɪnɪt] *adj (news, information)* de dernière minute; *(style, fashion)* dernier cri *inv*

upturn ['ʌptɜːn] *n* amélioration *f* (**in** de); *(in economy)* redressement *m* (**in** de)

upturned ['ʌptɜːnd] *adj (bucket, box)* retourné(e); *(nose)* retroussé(e)

upward ['ʌpwəd] **1** *adj* vers le haut; **u. mobility** ascension *f* sociale; **an u. trend** une tendance à la hausse **2** *adv* = **upwards**

upwardly mobile ['ʌpwədlɪ'məʊbaɪl] *adj* qui connaît une ascension sociale rapide

upwards ['ʌpwədz] *adv* vers le haut; **from £100 u.** à partir de 100 livres; **u. of** plus de

Urals ['jʊərəlz] *npl* **the U.** l'Oural *m*

uranium [jʊ'reɪnɪəm] *n* uranium *m*

Uranus [jʊ'reɪnəs] *n (planet)* Uranus *f*

urban ['ɜːbən] *adj* urbain(e); **u. legend** *or* **myth** = anecdote souvent inventée mais qui passe pour vraie; **u. renewal** rénovations *fpl* urbaines; **u. sprawl** étalement *m* urbain

urbane [ɜː'beɪn] *adj* urbain(e), courtois(e)

urbanization [ɜːbənaɪ'zeɪʃən] *n (process)* urbanisation *f*

urchin ['ɜːtʃɪn] *n* galopin(e) *m,f*

Urdu ['ʊədu:] *n* ourdou *m*

urethra [jʊ'riːθrə] *n* urètre *m*

urge [ɜːdʒ] **1** *n* terrible envie *f*; **to have an u. to do sth** avoir très envie de faire qch **2** *vt* (**a**) *(encourage)* **to u. sb to do sth** presser qn de faire qch (**b**) *(recommend)* conseiller; **to u. that sth be done** insister pour que qch soit fait

▸**urge on** *vt sep* encourager; **to u. sb on to do sth** encourager qn à faire qch

urgency ['ɜːdʒənsɪ] *n* urgence *f*; **it's a matter of u.** il y a urgence

urgent ['ɜːdʒənt] *adj* urgent(e); **to be in u. need of sth** avoir un besoin urgent de qch

urgently ['ɜːdʒəntlɪ] *adv* d'urgence

urinal [jə'raɪnəl] *n* urinoir *m*

urinary ['jʊərɪnərɪ] *adj* urinaire

urinate ['jʊərɪneɪt] *vi* uriner

urine ['jʊərɪn] *n* urine *f*

URL [juːɑː'rel] *n Comput (abbr* **uniform resource locator***)* (adresse *f*) URL *m*

urn [ɜːn] *n* urne *f*; **(tea) u.** fontaine *f* (à thé)

urology [jʊ'rɒlədʒɪ] *n Med* urologie *f*

Uruguay ['jʊərəgwaɪ] *n* l'Uruguay *m*

Uruguayan [jʊərə'gwaɪən] **1** *n* Uruguayen(enne) *m,f* **2** *adj* uruguayen(enne)

us [*stressed* ʌs, *unstressed* əs] *pron* (**a**) *(direct object)* nous; **she hates us** elle nous déteste; **she can understand our son but not us** elle comprend notre fils, mais nous, elle ne nous comprend pas (**b**) *(indirect object)* nous; **she gave us the book** elle nous a donné le livre; **she gave it to us** elle nous l'a donné (**c**) *(after preposition)* nous; **she's thinking of us** elle pense à nous (**d**) *(as complement of verb* **to be***)* nous; **it's us!** c'est nous!; **it was us who did it** c'est nous qui l'avons fait

US [juː'es] **1** *n (abbr* **United States***)* **the US** les USA *mpl* **2** *adj (forces, officials)* américain(e), des États-Unis

USA [juːes'eɪ] *n* (**a**) *(abbr* **United States of America***)* **the U.** les USA *mpl* (**b**) *Am (abbr* **United States Army***)* armée *f* de terre des États-Unis

usable ['juːzəbəl] *adj* utilisable

USAF [juːeseɪ'ef] *n Am (abbr* **United States Air Force***)* armée *f* de l'air des États-Unis

usage ['juːsɪdʒ] *n* usage *m*

use 1 *n* [juːs] *(utilization)* utilisation *f*, emploi *m*; **to make (good) u. of sth** faire (bon) usage de qch; **to be in u.** être utilisé(e); **not in u., out of u.** hors d'usage (**b**) *(ability, permission to use)* usage *m*; **to have the u. of sth** pouvoir utiliser qch; **she has full u. of her faculties** elle jouit de toutes ses facultés (**c**) *(usefulness)* **to be of u.** être utile; **can I be of any u. to you?** puis-je vous être d'une quelconque utilité?; **it's not much u.** cela ne sert pas à grand-chose; **to have no u. for sth** ne pas avoir l'usage de qch; *Fam* **he's no u.** il n'est bon à rien; **it's no u.** cela ne sert à rien; **it's no u. crying** cela ne sert à rien de pleurer; **what's the u. of worrying?** à quoi bon s'inquiéter?

2 *vt* [juːz] (**a**) *(utilize)* utiliser, se servir de; *(force, diplomacy)* avoir recours à; *Fam* **u. your head!** réfléchis un peu!; *Fam* **I could u. some sleep** un peu de sommeil ne me ferait pas de mal (**b**) *(exploit)* utiliser, se servir de (**c**) *(consume)* *(petrol, electricity)* consommer; **who's used all the milk?** qui a pris tout le lait?

3 *v aux* **used to** ['juːstə] *(translated by imperfect of main verb)* **we used to live abroad** (autrefois,) nous vivions à l'étranger; **I didn't u. to like him** avant, je ne l'aimais pas; **do you travel much? – I used to** tu voyages beaucoup? – autrefois, oui

▶**use up** *vt sep (food, fuel)* finir; *(ideas)* épuiser; *(money)* dépenser

use-by date ['juːzbaɪdeɪt] *n* date *f* limite de consommation

used *adj* (**a**) [juːzd] *(second-hand)* d'occasion (**b**) [juːst] *(accustomed)* **to be u. to sth/to doing sth** être habitué(e) à qch/à faire qch; **to get u. to sb/sth** s'habituer à qn/qch

useful ['juːsfʊl] *adj* utile; **to make oneself u.** se rendre utile

usefully ['juːsfəlɪ] *adv* utilement

usefulness ['juːsfʊlnɪs] *n* utilité *f*

useless ['juːslɪs] *adj* (**a**) *(not useful)* inutile; **to be worse than u.** ne servir strictement à rien (**b**) *(incompetent)* nul (nulle) (**at** en)

user ['juːzə(r)] *n (of road, dictionary)* utilisateur(trice) *m,f*; *(of telephone)* usager *m*; *(of drugs)* consommateur(trice) *m,f*; *Comput* **u. name** nom *m* de l'utilisateur

user-friendly [juːzə'frendlɪ] *adj* convivial(e)

usher ['ʌʃə(r)] **1** *n (in court)* huissier *m*; *(in theatre, cinema)* ouvreur *m*; *(at wedding)* placeur *m*
2 *vt* **to u. sb in/out** faire entrer/sortir qn

usherette [ʌʃə'ret] *n* ouvreuse *f*

USIA [juːesaɪ'eɪ] *n Am (abbr* **United States Information Agency***)* renseignements *mpl* généraux américains

USN [juːes'en] *n Am (abbr* **United States Navy***)* marine *f* de guerre des États-Unis

USP [juːes'piː] *n Com (abbr* **unique selling point** *or* **proposition***)* avantage *m* unique

USS [juːes'es] *n Am (abbr* **United States Ship***)* **U. Lexington** le Lexington *(bâtiment de la marine américaine)*

USSR [juːeses'aː(r)] *n Formerly (abbr* **Union of Soviet Socialist Republics***)* URSS *f*

usual ['juːʒʊəl] **1** *adj* habituel(elle); **you're not your u. cheery self today** tu n'es pas aussi gai que d'habitude aujourd'hui; **earlier/later than u.** plus tôt/tard que d'habitude; **as u.** comme d'habitude
2 *n Fam (drink)* **the u., sir?** comme d'habitude, monsieur?

usually ['juːʒʊəlɪ] *adv* habituellement, d'habitude; **he was more than u. polite** il était plus poli que d'habitude

usurer ['juːʒərə(r)] *n* usurier(ère) *m,f*

usurp [juː'zɜːp] *vt* usurper

usurper [juː'zɜːpə(r)] *n* usurpateur(trice) *m,f*

usury ['juːʒʊrɪ] *n* usure *f*

utensil [juː'tensəl] *n* ustensile *m*

uterus ['juːtərəs] *(pl* uteri ['juːtəraɪ]*) n* utérus *m*

utilitarian [juːtɪlɪ'teərɪən] **1** *adj (approach, design)* utilitaire; *(in philosophy)* utilitariste
2 *n (in philosophy)* utilitariste *mf*

utility [juː'tɪlɪtɪ] *(pl* **utilities***) n* (**a**) *(usefulness)* utilité *f*; *Comput* **u. program** (programme *m*) utilitaire *m*; **u. room** pièce *f* de rangement (**b**) **(public) utilities** services *mpl* (publics) (**c**) *Am* **utilities** *(service charges)* charges *fpl*

utilize ['juːtɪlaɪz] *vt* utiliser, se servir de

utmost ['ʌtməʊst] **1** *n* **to the u.** au plus haut point; **to do one's u. (to do sth)** faire de son mieux (pour faire qch)
2 *adj* (**a**) *(greatest)* **the u.** le (la) plus grand(e); **it is of the u. importance that...** il est de la plus haute importance que... + *subjunctive* (**b**) *(furthest)* **to the u. ends of the earth** au bout du monde

utopia [juː'təʊpɪə] *n* utopie *f*

utopian [juː'təʊpɪən] **1** *n* utopiste *mf*
2 *adj* utopique

utter¹ ['ʌtə(r)] *adj* total(e); **it's u. madness** c'est de la folie pure; **it's u. rubbish** c'est complètement absurde

utter² *vt (cry)* pousser; *(word)* prononcer

utterance ['ʌtərəns] *n (act)* énonciation *f*; *(words spoken)* paroles *fpl*, déclaration *f*

utterly ['ʌtəlɪ] *adv* complètement, tout à fait

uttermost ['ʌtəməʊst] *adj* = **utmost**

UV [juː'viː] *adj Phys (abbr* **ultra-violet***)* UV *inv*; **UV rays** UV *mpl*

uvula ['juːvjələ] *n* luette *f*

Uzbekistan [ʊzbekɪ'staːn] *n* l'Ouzbékistan *m*

V¹, v [viː] *n* (**a**) *(letter)* V, v *m inv*; **V sign** *(for victory)* signe *m* de la victoire; *(as insult)* cornes *fpl* (**b**) *(abbr very)* t (**c**) *(abbr versus)* contre (**d**) *(abbr verse)* *(pl* vv) V

V² *(abbr* **volt**) V

VA [viːˈeɪ] *n Am (abbr* **Veterans Administration**) ≃ ministère *m* des Anciens Combattants

vacancy [ˈveɪkənsɪ] *n* (**a**) *(position, job)* poste *m* vacant (**b**) *(at hotel)* chambre *f* libre *ou* à louer; **no vacancies** *(sign)* complet

vacant [ˈveɪkənt] *adj* (**a**) *(seat, space)* libre, inoccupé(e); *Am* **v. lot** terrain *m* vague (**b**) *(expression, look)* absent(e)

vacantly [ˈveɪkəntlɪ] *adv* d'un air absent

vacate [vəˈkeɪt] *vt (seat, flat)* libérer, quitter; *(one's post)* démissionner de

vacation [vəˈkeɪʃən] *n Br Univ & Am* vacances *fpl*; *Am* **to take a v.** prendre des vacances; *Am* **on v.** en vacances

vaccinate [ˈvæksɪneɪt] *vt* vacciner

vaccination [væksɪˈneɪʃən] *n* vaccination *f*

vaccine [ˈvæksiːn] *n* vaccin *m*

vacillate [ˈvæsɪleɪt] *vi* hésiter (**between** entre)

vacuous [ˈvækjʊəs] *adj (person, look)* vide, sans expression; *(book, remark)* dénué(e) de sens

vacuum [ˈvækjʊm] **1** *n Phys* vacuum *m*; *Fig* vide *m*; **v. cleaner** aspirateur *m*; **v. flask** Thermos® *m ou f*
  2 *vt (room)* passer l'aspirateur dans
  3 *vi* passer l'aspirateur

vacuum-packed [vækjʊmˈpækt] *adj* (emballé(e)) sous vide

vagabond [ˈvægəbɒnd] *n* vagabond(e) *m,f*

vagary [ˈveɪɡərɪ] *(pl* **vagaries**) *n* caprice *m*

vagina [vəˈdʒaɪnə] *n* vagin *m*

vagrancy [ˈveɪɡrənsɪ] *n* vagabondage *m*

vagrant [ˈveɪɡrənt] *n* vagabond(e) *m,f*

vague [veɪg] *adj (idea, feeling)* vague; *(shape, outline)* flou(e), indistinct(e); **I haven't the vaguest idea** je n'en ai pas la moindre idée

vaguely [ˈveɪglɪ] *adv* vaguement

vagueness [ˈveɪɡnɪs] *n* imprécision *f*, flou *m*

vain [veɪn] **1** *adj* (**a**) *(conceited)* vaniteux(euse) (**b**) *(hopeless)* vain(e)
  2 *n* **in v.** en vain

vale [veɪl] *n Lit* val *m*, vallée *f*; *Fig* **v. of tears** vallée *f* de larmes

valency [ˈveɪlənsɪ] *n Chem* valence *f*

valentine [ˈvæləntaɪn] *n* **v.**, **v.'s card** carte *f* de la Saint-Valentin; **V.'s Day** la Saint-Valentin

valet [ˈvæleɪ] *n* valet *m* de chambre

valiant [ˈvælɪənt] *adj Lit* vaillant(e)

valiantly [ˈvælɪəntlɪ] *adv* vaillamment

valid [ˈvælɪd] *adj* valable; **v. for six months** valable six mois; **no longer v.** périmé(e)

validate [ˈvælɪdeɪt] *vt (document)* valider; *(theory)* confirmer

validation [vælɪˈdeɪʃən] *n (of document)* validation *f*; *(of theory)* confirmation *f*

validity [vəˈlɪdɪtɪ] *n* validité *f*

valise [væˈliːz] *n Am* mallette *f*

valley [ˈvælɪ] *(pl* **valleys**) *n* vallée *f*

valour, *Am* **valor** [ˈvælə(r)] *n* bravoure *f*

valuable [ˈvæljʊəbəl] **1** *adj (object)* de valeur; *(advice, time, contribution)* précieux(euse) (**to** à)
  2 *n* **valuables** objets *mpl* de valeur

valuation [væljʊˈeɪʃən] *n* (**a**) *(act)* estimation *f* (**b**) *(price)* évaluation *f*

value [ˈvæljuː] **1** *n* (**a**) *(worth)* valeur *f*; **to be of v.** avoir de la valeur; **to be good/poor v. (for money)** être d'un bon/mauvais rapport qualité-prix; **to set a v. upon sth** estimer la valeur de qch; **to make a v. of** pour une valeur de; **to make a v. judgment** faire un jugement de valeur (**b**) **values** *(principles)* valeurs *fpl*
  2 *vt* (**a**) *(evaluate)* estimer (**b**) *(appreciate)* apprécier

value-added tax [ˈvæljuːædɪdˈtæks] *n* taxe *f* sur la valeur ajoutée, *Can* taxe *f* sur les ventes

valued [ˈvæljuːd] *adj* précieux(euse)

valueless [ˈvæljʊlɪs] *adj* sans valeur

valve [vælv] *n* (**a**) *Anat* valve *f* (**b**) *Tech (in pipe, tube, air chamber)* valve *f*; *(in machine)* soupape *f*

vampire [ˈvæmpaɪə(r)] *n* vampire *m*; **v. bat** vampire *m*

van¹ [væn] *n* (**a**) *(vehicle)* camionnette *f*, fourgonnette *f*; **v. driver** chauffeur *m* de camionnette (**b**) *Br Rail* fourgon *m*

van² = **vanguard**

Vancouver [vænˈkuːvə(r)] *n* Vancouver

vandal [ˈvændəl] *n* vandale *mf*

vandalism [ˈvændəlɪzəm] *n* vandalisme *m*

vandalize [ˈvændəlaɪz] *vt* saccager

vane [veɪn] *n* girouette *f*

vanguard [ˈvænɡɑːd] *n* avant-garde *f*; **to be in the v. of** être à l'avant-garde de

vanilla [vəˈnɪlə] *n* vanille *f*; **v. essence** extrait *m* de vanille; **v. ice cream** glace *f* à la vanille

vanish [ˈvænɪʃ] *vi* disparaître

vanishing [ˈvænɪʃɪŋ] *adj* **to do a v. act** disparaître dans la nature; **v. point** point *m* de fuite

vanity [ˈvænɪtɪ] *n* vanité *f*; **v. case** vanity-case *m*, mallette *f* de toilette; **v. plate** plaque *f* d'immatriculation personnalisée

vanquish [ˈvæŋkwɪʃ] *vt Lit* vaincre

vantage point ['vɑːntɪdʒpɔɪnt] n point m de vue; Fig position f objective
Vanuatu [vænuːˈætuː] n Vanuatu m
vapid ['væpɪd] adj insipide
vapor Am = vapour
vaporize ['veɪpəraɪz] **1** vt vaporiser **2** vi se vaporiser
vapour, Am **vapor** ['veɪpə(r)] n vapeur f; **v. trail** traînée f de condensation
variable ['veərɪəbəl] **1** n variable f **2** adj variable
variance ['veərɪəns] n désaccord m; **to be at v. with sb** être en désaccord avec qn; **to be at v. with sth** ne pas concorder avec qch
variant ['veərɪənt] **1** n variante f **2** adj différent(e)
variation [veərɪˈeɪʃən] n variation f
varicose vein ['værɪkəʊsˈveɪn] n varice f
varied ['veərɪːd] adj varié(e)
variegated ['veərɪɡeɪtɪd] adj panaché(e)
variety [vəˈraɪətɪ] (pl **varieties**) n (**a**) (diversity) variété f; **a v. of** toutes sortes de; Prov **v. is the spice of life** la diversité est le sel de la vie (**b**) (of plant) variété f (**c**) (in theatre, on TV) variétés fpl; **v. show** spectacle m de variétés
various ['veərɪəs] adj (different) divers(e); (several) plusieurs
variously ['veərɪəslɪ] adv **v. described as a hero or a rogue** parfois décrit comme un héros, d'autres fois comme un escroc
varnish ['vɑːnɪʃ] **1** n vernis m **2** vt vernir
▸ **varnish over** vt sep Fig maquiller, dissimuler
vary ['veərɪ] (pt & pp **varied**) **1** vt varier **2** vi varier (in/with en/selon)
varying ['veərɪŋ] adj qui varie, variable
vase [vɑːz, Am veɪz] n vase m
vasectomy [vəˈsektəmɪ] (pl **vasectomies**) n vasectomie f; **to have a v.** subir une vasectomie
Vaseline® ['væsəliːn] n vaseline f
vast [vɑːst] adj immense
vastly ['vɑːstlɪ] adv à l'extrême; (superior) infiniment
VAT [viːeɪˈtiː, væt] n (abbr **value added tax**) TVA f
vat [væt] n (container) cuve f, bac m
Vatican ['vætɪkən] n **the V.** le Vatican; **V. City** la cité du Vatican, le Vatican
vaudeville ['vɔːdəvɪl] n music-hall m
vault¹ [vɔːlt] n (**a**) (roof) voûte f (**b**) (cellar) cave f; (for burial) caveau m; (of bank) chambre f forte, salle f des coffres
vault² vt & vi sauter
vaulted ['vɔːltɪd] adj (ceiling) voûté(e)
vaulting horse ['vɔːltɪŋˈhɔːs] n cheval m d'arçons
vaunt [vɔːnt] vt vanter; **his much vaunted reputation as...** sa réputation tant vantée de...
VC [viːˈsiː] n (**a**) (abbr **Vice-Chairman**) vice-président m (**b**) (abbr **Victoria Cross**) = la plus haute distinction militaire britannique
vCJD [viːsiːdʒeɪˈdiː] n Med (abbr **new-variant Creutzfeldt-Jakob disease**) vMCJ m
VCR [viːsiːˈɑː(r)] n (abbr **video cassette recorder**) magnétoscope m
VD [viːˈdiː] n (abbr **venereal disease**) maladie f vénérienne
VDU [viːdiːˈjuː] n Comput (abbr **visual display unit**) console f de visualisation
veal [viːl] n veau m

vector ['vektə(r)] n vecteur m
veer ['vɪə(r)] vi virer; **to v. to the left/right** virer à gauche/droite
▸ **veer round** vi tourner, changer de direction; Fig **she has veered round to our point of view** elle s'est ralliée à notre point de vue
veg [vedʒ] Fam **1** npl Br (abbr **vegetables**) légumes mpl, verdure f **2** vi (do nothing) **to v. (out) in front of the TV** comater devant la télé
vegan ['viːɡən] n végétalien(enne) m,f
vegetable ['vedʒtəbəl] n (**a**) (food) légume m; **v. garden** potager m (**b**) (brain-damaged person) légume m
vegetarian [vedʒɪˈteərɪən] **1** n végétarien(enne) m,f **2** adj végétarien(enne)
vegetarianism [vedʒɪˈteərɪənɪzəm] n végétarisme m

Vegetarianism

Que ce soit pour des raisons éthiques, religieuses ou diététiques, le végétarisme s'est considérablement répandu au cours des dernières années en Grande-Bretagne – sensiblement plus que dans les autres pays européens ou aux États-Unis. Aujourd'hui, la majorité des restaurants proposent un menu avec un ou plusieurs plats sans viande, et lorsque l'on invite des gens à dîner, il est d'usage de s'enquérir s'ils sont végétariens ou non.

vegetate ['vedʒɪteɪt] vi végéter
vegetation [vedʒɪˈteɪʃən] n végétation f
veggie ['vedʒɪ] Fam **1** n (**a**) Br (abbr **vegetarian**) végétarien(enne) m,f (**b**) (abbr **vegetable**) **veggies** légumes mpl, verdure f **2** adj Br (abbr **vegetarian**) végétarien(enne)
vehemence ['viːm…] n véhémence f
vehement ['viːmənt] adj véhément(e)
vehicle ['viːɪkəl] n also Fig véhicule m
vehicular [vɪˈhɪkjʊlə(r)] adj de véhicules; **v. traffic** circulation f automobile
veil [veɪl] **1** n also Fig voile m; Fig **to draw a v. over sth** jeter un voile sur qch; Fig **under a v. of secrecy** sous le voile du secret **2** vt voiler; Fig **veiled in secrecy** secret(ète)
veiled [veɪld] adj also Fig voilé(e)
vein [veɪn] n (**a**) (in body, wood, marble) veine f; (in leaf) nervure f; (in rock) filon m (**b**) (idioms) **and now, in a lighter v....** et maintenant, dans un registre plus léger...; **in (a) similar v.** de la même veine
Velcro® ['velkrəʊ] n (bande f) Velcro® m
vellum ['veləm] n vélin m; **v. (paper)** papier m vélin
velocity [vɪˈlɒsɪtɪ] n vélocité f
velvet ['velvɪt] n velours m; **v. jacket** veste f en velours Fig **an iron fist** or **hand in a v. glove** une main de fer dans un gant de velours
velveteen [velvɪˈtiːn] n velvantine f
velvety ['velvɪtɪ] adj velouté(e)
venal ['viːnəl] adj vénal(e)
vendetta [venˈdetə] n vendetta f; **to carry on a v. against sb** mener une vendetta contre qn
vending machine ['vendɪŋməˈʃiːn] n distributeur m automatique
vendor ['vendɔː(r)] n vendeur(euse) m,f
veneer [vəˈnɪə(r)] n placage m; Fig vernis m, apparence f
venerable ['venərəbəl] adj vénérable
venerate ['venəreɪt] vt vénérer
veneration [venəˈreɪʃən] n vénération f

venereal [vɪ'nɪərɪəl] *adj* vénérien(enne); **v. disease** maladie *f* vénérienne
Venetian [vɪ'niːʃən] **1** *n* Vénitien(enne) *m,f* **2** *adj* vénitien(enne); **V. blind** store *m* vénitien
Venezuela [vene'zweɪlə] *n* le Vénézuela
Venezuelan [vene'zweɪlən] **1** *n* Vénézuélien(enne) *m,f* **2** *adj* vénézuélien(enne)
vengeance ['vendʒəns] *n* vengeance *f*; **to take v. on sb** se venger de qn; *Fig* **it started to rain with a v.** il s'est mis à pleuvoir de plus belle; **she's back with a v.** elle fait un retour en force
vengeful ['vendʒful] *adj* vengeur(eresse)
venial ['viːnɪəl] *adj* véniel(elle)
Venice ['venɪs] *n* Venise
venison ['venɪsən] *n* viande *f* de chevreuil
venom ['venəm] *n also Fig* venin *m*
venomous ['venəməs] *adj also Fig* venimeux(euse)
vent [vent] **1** *n* conduit *m*; *Fig* **to give v. to sth** donner *ou* laisser libre cours à qch **2** *vt* **to v. one's anger (on)** décharger sa colère (sur)
ventilate ['ventɪleɪt] *vt* ventiler, aérer
ventilation [ventɪ'leɪʃən] *n* ventilation *f*, aération *f*
ventilator ['ventɪleɪtə(r)] *n* (**a**) *Tech* ventilateur *m* (**b**) *Med* respirateur *m*; **to be on a v.** être branché(e) sur respirateur
ventriloquism [ven'trɪləkwɪzəm] *n* ventriloquie *f*
ventriloquist [ven'trɪləkwɪst] *n* ventriloque *mf*; **v.'s dummy** marionnette *f* de ventriloque
venture ['ventʃə(r)] **1** *n* entreprise *f* hasardeuse; *(in business)* entreprise; *Fin* **v. capital** capital-risque *m* **2** *vt (fortune, life)* risquer; *(opinion, suggestion)* hasarder; **to v. to do sth** se risquer à faire qch; *Prov* **nothing ventured, nothing gained** qui ne risque rien n'a rien **3** *vi* s'aventurer
▸**venture on, venture upon** *vt insep* s'aventurer dans
venue ['venjuː] *n (for meeting, concert)* salle *f*; *(for football match)* stade *m*
Venus ['viːnəs] *n (planet)* Vénus *f*
veracity [və'ræsɪtɪ] *n Formal* véracité *f*
veranda(h) [və'rændə] *n* véranda *f*
verb [vɜːb] *n* verbe *m*
verbal ['vɜːbəl] *adj* verbal(e); **v. abuse** insultes *fpl* verbales
verbalize ['vɜːbəlaɪz] *vt* verbaliser
verbally ['vɜːbəlɪ] *adv* verbalement
verbatim [vɜː'beɪtɪm] **1** *adj* textuel(elle) **2** *adv* mot pour mot
verbiage ['vɜːbɪdʒ] *n* verbiage *m*
verbose [vɜː'bəʊs] *adj* verbeux(euse)
verbosity [vɜː'bɒsɪtɪ] *n* verbosité *f*
verdict ['vɜːdɪkt] *n also Fig* verdict *m*; **to return a v. of guilty/not guilty** rendre un verdict de culpabilité/ non-culpabilité; **to give one's v. on sth** se prononcer sur qch
verge [vɜːdʒ] *n (of road)* bord *m*; *Fig* **on the v. of sth** au bord de qch; *(victory, defeat)* à deux doigts de qch; *Fig* **to be on the v. of doing sth** être sur le point de faire qch
▸**verge on** *vt insep* friser
verger ['vɜːdʒə(r)] *n (in Church of England)* bedeau *m*
verifiable [verɪ'faɪəbəl] *adj* vérifiable
verification [verɪfɪ'keɪʃən] *n* vérification *f*
verify ['verɪfaɪ] *(pt & pp verified)* *vt* vérifier

verisimilitude [verɪsɪ'mɪlɪtjuːd] *n Formal* vraisemblance *f*
veritable ['verɪtəbəl] *adj Formal* véritable
vermilion [və'mɪljən] **1** *n* vermillon *m* **2** *adj* vermillon *inv*
vermin ['vɜːmɪn] *npl also Fig* vermine *f*
vermouth ['vɜːməθ] *n* vermouth *m*
vernacular [və'nækjʊlə(r)] **1** *n* langue *f* vernaculaire **2** *adj* vernaculaire
verruca [ve'ruːkə] *n* verrue *f* plantaire
versatile ['vɜːsətaɪl] *adj (person)* aux talents variés; *(tool)* polyvalent(e)
versatility [vɜːsə'tɪlɪtɪ] *n (of person)* variété *f* de talents; *(of tool)* polyvalence *f*
verse [vɜːs] *n* (**a**) *(poetry)* vers *mpl* (**b**) *(stanza)* strophe *f* (**c**) *(of Bible)* verset *m*
versed [vɜːst] *adj* **to be (well) v. in sth** être versé(e) dans qch
version ['vɜːʃən] *n* version *f*
versus ['vɜːsəs] *prep* (**a**) *(in law, sport)* contre (**b**) *(compared to)* comparé(e) à
vertebra ['vɜːtɪbrə] *(pl* **vertebrae** ['vɜːtɪbriː]*)* *n* vertèbre *f*
vertebral column ['vɜːtɪbrəl'kɒləm] *n* colonne *f* vertébrale
vertebrate ['vɜːtɪbrɪt] **1** *n* vertébré *m* **2** *adj* vertébré(e)
vertex ['vɜːteks] *(pl* **vertices** ['vɜːtɪsiːz]*)* *n* sommet *m*
vertical ['vɜːtɪkəl] **1** *n* verticale *f* **2** *adj* vertical(e)
vertically ['vɜːtɪklɪ] *adv* à la verticale
vertices ['vɜːtɪsiːz] *pl of* **vertex**
vertigo ['vɜːtɪgəʊ] *n* vertige *m*
verve [vɜːv] *n* verve *f*
very ['verɪ] **1** *adv* (**a**) *(extremely)* très; **v. little** très peu; **v. much** beaucoup; **are you hungry? – yes, v.** as-tu faim? – oui, très; *Rad* **v. high frequency** hyperfréquences *fpl* (**b**) *(emphatic use)* **the v. first/last** le (la) tout(e) premier(ère)/dernier(ère); **the v. best** tout ce qu'il y a de mieux; **at the v. most/least** tout au plus/moins; **at the v. earliest/latest** au plus tôt/ tard; **the v. same** exactement le même; **I v. nearly died** j'ai bien failli mourir; **the v. next day** le lendemain même **2** *adj (emphatic use)* **this v. house** cette maison même; **this v. day** aujourd'hui même; **those were her v. words** c'est ce qu'elle a dit mot pour mot; **at the v. beginning** au tout début; **the v. thought of it!** rien que d'y penser!
vessel ['vesəl] *n* (**a**) *(ship)* vaisseau *m* (**b**) *(container)* récipient *m*
vest [vest] *n Br (undershirt)* maillot *m* de corps; *Am (waistcoat)* gilet *m*
vested ['vestɪd] *adj* **to have a v. interest in sth/in doing sth** avoir un intérêt personnel dans qch/à faire qch
vestibule ['vestɪbjuːl] *n* hall *m*
vestige ['vestɪdʒ] *n* vestige *m*
vestments ['vestmənts] *npl Rel* habits *mpl* sacerdotaux
vestry ['vestrɪ] *(pl* **vestries***)* *n Rel* sacristie *f*
vet¹ [vet] *n (veterinary surgeon)* vétérinaire *mf*
vet² [vet] *(pt & pp vetted)* *vt (person)* effectuer une enquête sur; *(application)* examiner minutieusement; *(figures)* vérifier soigneusement
vet³ *n Am Fam Mil (veteran)* ancien combattant *m*

veteran ['vetərən] **1** *n Mil* ancien combattant *m*; *Fig* vétéran *m*
 2 *adj* de longue date
veterinarian [vetərɪ'neərɪən] *n Am* vétérinaire *mf*
veterinary ['vetərɪnərɪ] *adj* vétérinaire; **v. medicine** médecine *f* vétérinaire; *Formal* **v. surgeon** vétérinaire *mf*
veto ['viːtəʊ] **1** *n* (*pl* **vetoes**) veto *m*; **right** *or* **power of v.** droit *m* de veto; **to impose a v. on sth** mettre son veto à qch
 2 *vt* (*pt & pp* **vetoed**) mettre son veto à
vetting ['vetɪŋ] *n* (*of person*) enquête *f* (**of** sur); (*of things*) contrôle *m* (**of** de)
vex [veks] *vt* contrarier
vexation [vek'seɪʃən] *n* (*annoyance*) contrariété *f*
vexed [vekst] *adj* (**a**) (*annoyed*) très contrarié(e) (**b**) **v. question** question *f* controversée
VHF [viːeɪtʃ'ef] *n* (*abbr* **very high frequency**) VHF *f*
VHS [viːeɪtʃ'es] *n* (*abbr* **video home system**) VHS *m*
via ['vaɪə] *prep* par, via
viability [vaɪə'bɪlɪtɪ] *n* viabilité *f*
viable ['vaɪəbəl] *adj* viable
viaduct ['vaɪədʌkt] *n* viaduc *m*
Viagra® [vaɪ'ægrə] *n* Viagra® *m*
vibe [vaɪb] *n Fam* (*abbr* **vibration**) atmosphère *f*, ambiance *f*; **this bar's got a nice relaxed v.** l'ambiance est très cool dans ce bar; **their new album's got a bit of an R&B v.** leur nouvel album a un petit côté R&B; **I got good/bad vibes from her** je la sentais/je ne la sentais pas bien
vibrant ['vaɪbrənt] *adj* très actif(ive)
vibrate [vaɪ'breɪt] *vi* vibrer
vibration [vaɪ'breɪʃən] *n* vibration *f*
vibrator [vaɪ'breɪtə(r)] *n* vibromasseur *m*
vicar ['vɪkə(r)] *n* (*in Church of England*) pasteur *m*
vicarage ['vɪkərɪdʒ] *n* presbytère *m*
vicarious [vɪ'keərɪəs] *adj* indirect(e), **to lead a v. existence** vivre par procuration
vice[1] [vaɪs] *n* (*immorality, immoral activity*) vice *m*; **the V. Squad** ≃ la brigade des mœurs
vice[2] *n* (*tool*) étau *m*
vice-chairman [vaɪs'tʃeəmən] *n* vice-président(e) *m,f*
vice-president [vaɪs'prezɪdənt] *n* vice-président(e) *m,f*
viceroy ['vaɪsrɔɪ] *n* vice-roi *m*
vice versa [vaɪs'vɜːsə] *adv* vice versa
vicinity [vɪ'sɪnɪtɪ] *n* (*surrounding area*) environs *mpl*; (*proximity*) proximité *f*; **in the v. (of)** dans les alentours (de); **a sum in the v. of £25,000** un chiffre aux alentours de 25 000 livres
vicious ['vɪʃəs] *adj* (*violent*) violent(e); (*malicious, cruel*) malveillant(e); **v. circle** cercle *m* vicieux
vicissitudes [vɪ'sɪsɪtjuːdz] *npl Formal* vicissitudes *fpl*
victim ['vɪktɪm] *n* victime *f*; **to be the v. of sth** être victime de qch
victimization [vɪktɪmaɪ'zeɪʃən] *n* brimades *fpl*
victimize ['vɪktɪmaɪz] *vt* (*bully*) prendre comme tête de Turc; (*penalize*) pénaliser
victor ['vɪktə(r)] *n* vainqueur *m*
Victorian [vɪk'tɔːrɪən] **1** *n* Victorien(enne) *m,f*
 2 *adj* victorien(enne)
victorious [vɪk'tɔːrɪəs] *adj* victorieux(euse); **to be v. over sb** vaincre qn
victory ['vɪktərɪ] (*pl* **victories**) *n* victoire *f*; **v. celebrations** ≃ fêtes pour célébrer une victoire

victuals ['vɪtəlz] *npl Old-fashioned* (*food*) victuailles *fpl*
vid [vɪd] *n Fam* (*abbr* **video**) vidéo *f*, vidéocassette *f*
video ['vɪdɪəʊ] **1** *n* (*pl* **videos**) (*medium*) vidéo *f*; (*cassette*) (cassette *f*) vidéo; (*recorder*) magnétoscope *m*; **v. camera** caméra *f* vidéo; **v. cassette** *or* **tape** cassette *f* vidéo; **v. (cassette) recorder** magnétoscope *m*; **v. game** jeu *m* vidéo; **v. library** vidéothèque *f*; **v. nasty** = film vidéo à contenu très violent ou pornographique; **v. projector** vidéoprojecteur *m*; **v. shop** magasin *m* vidéo
 2 *vt* (*pt & pp* **videoed**) (**a**) (*on video recorder*) enregistrer (**b**) (*on camcorder*) filmer en vidéo
videotape ['vɪdɪəʊteɪp] **1** *n* bande *f* vidéo
 2 *vt* enregistrer sur magnétoscope
vie [vaɪ] (*pt & pp* **vied** [vaɪd]) *vi* **to v. with sb (for sth/ to do sth)** rivaliser avec qn (pour qch/pour faire qch)
Vienna [vɪ'enə] *n* Vienne
Viennese [vɪə'niːz] **1** *n* Viennois(e) *m,f*
 2 *adj* viennois(e)
Vietnam [vɪet'næm] *n* le Viêt Nam; **the V. War** la guerre du Viêt Nam
Vietnamese [vɪetnə'miːz] **1** *npl* (*people*) **the V.** les Vietnamiens *mpl*
 2 *n* (**a**) (*person*) Vietnamien(enne) *m,f* (**b**) (*language*) vietnamien *m*
 3 *adj* vietnamien(enne)
view [vjuː] **1** *n* (**a**) (*sight, scene, prospect*) vue *f*; **a room with a v.** une chambre avec vue; **to have a good v. of sth** avoir une belle vue de qch; **in full v. of** sous les yeux de; *Fig* **in v. of** (*considering*) compte tenu de, étant donné (**b**) (*opinion*) opinion *f*; **in my v.** à mon avis (**c**) (*intention*) intention *f*; **with this in v.** dans cette intention; **with a v. to doing sth** dans l'intention de faire qch
 2 *vt* (**a**) (*look at*) voir; (*prospective property, exhibition*) visiter (**b**) (*consider*) voir, considérer; **to v. sth with horror/delight** envisager qch avec horreur/ ravissement
viewer ['vjuːə(r)] *n* (**a**) (*of TV*) téléspectateur(trice) *m,f* (**b**) (*for slides*) visionneuse *f*
viewfinder ['vjuːfaɪndə(r)] *n* viseur *m*
viewpoint ['vjuːpɔɪnt] *n* point *m* de vue
vigil ['vɪdʒɪl] *n* veillée *f*; **to keep v.** veiller
vigilance ['vɪdʒɪləns] *n* vigilance *f*
vigilant ['vɪdʒɪlənt] *adj* vigilant(e)
vigilante [vɪdʒɪ'læntɪ] *n* = membre d'une milice privée
vignette [vɪn'jet] *n* (*photo, picture*) buste *m* sur un fond dégradé; (*short essay*) court portrait *m*
vigor *Am* = **vigour**
vigorous ['vɪgərəs] *adj* vigoureux(euse)
vigour, *Am* **vigor** ['vɪgə(r)] *n* vigueur *f*
Viking ['vaɪkɪŋ] **1** *n* Viking *mf*
 2 *adj* viking *inv*
vile [vaɪl] *adj* (*weather, person, thought*) abominable; (*food, drink*) infecte; (*temper*) exécrable
vilification [vɪlɪfɪ'keɪʃən] *n* calomnie *f*
vilify ['vɪlɪfaɪ] (*pt & pp* **vilified**) *vt* calomnier
villa ['vɪlə] *n* villa *f*
village ['vɪlɪdʒ] *n* village *m*; **v. hall** salle *f* des fêtes; **v. idiot** idiot *m* du village
villager ['vɪlɪdʒə(r)] *n* villageois(e) *m,f*
villain ['vɪlən] *n* (*scoundrel*) scélérat *m*; *Hum* **the v. of the piece** le/la coupable
villainous ['vɪlənəs] *adj* diabolique
villainy ['vɪlənɪ] *n* infamie *f*
Vilnius ['vɪlnɪəs] *n* Vilnius

vindicate ['vɪndɪkeɪt] *vt (decision, action)* donner raison à; *(right, claim)* justifier

vindication [vɪndɪ'keɪʃən] *n (of decision, action)* bienfondé *m*; *(of right, claim)* justification *f*

vindictive [vɪn'dɪktɪv] *adj* vindicatif(ive)

vine [vaɪn] *n* vigne *f*; **v. leaf** feuille *f* de vigne

vinegar ['vɪnɪɡə(r)] *n* vinaigre *m*

vineyard ['vɪnjəd] *n* vigne *f*

vintage ['vɪntɪdʒ] *n (year)* année *f*; *(wine)* cru *m*; *Fig* **a v. year (for)** une grande année (pour); *Fig* **it was v.** Agatha Christie c'était de l'Agatha Christie du meilleur style; **v. car** = voiture construite entre 1919 et 1930; **v. wine** vin *m* de cru

vinyl ['vaɪnɪl] *n* vinyle *m*

viola [vɪ'əʊlə] *n* alto *m*

violate ['vaɪəleɪt] *vt (agreement)* violer; *(rule, law)* enfreindre

violation [vaɪə'leɪʃən] *n* violation *f*

violence ['vaɪələns] *n* violence *f*

violent ['vaɪələnt] *adj* violent(e); **to die a v. death** mourir de mort violente; **to take a v. dislike to sb/sth** se prendre d'une aversion violente pour qn/qch

violently ['vaɪələntlɪ] *adv* violemment; *(die)* de mort violente; **to be v. sick** être pris(e) de violents vomissements

violet ['vaɪələt] **1** *n* (**a**) *(flower)* violette *f* (**b**) *(colour)* violet *m*
2 *adj* **v.(-coloured)** violet(ette)

violin [vaɪə'lɪn] *n* violon *m*

violinist [vaɪə'lɪnɪst] *n* violoniste *mf*

VIP [viːaɪ'piː] *n (abbr* **very important person**) VIP *mf*; **V. lounge** salon *m* de luxe; **to get V. treatment** recevoir un accueil princier

viper ['vaɪpə(r)] *n* vipère *f*

viral ['vaɪrəl] *adj* viral(e)

virgin ['vɜːdʒɪn] **1** *n* vierge *mf*; **the (Blessed) V.** la Sainte Vierge; **the V. Islands** les îles *fpl* Vierges
2 *adj* vierge

Virginia [vɜː'dʒɪnjə] *n* la Virginie

virginity [və'dʒɪnɪtɪ] *n* virginité *f*

Virgo ['vɜːɡəʊ] *(pl* **Virgos** *or* **Virgoes**) *n (sign of zodiac)* la Vierge; **to be (a) V.** être Vierge

virile ['vɪraɪl] *adj* viril(e)

virility [vɪ'rɪlɪtɪ] *n* virilité *f*

virology [vaɪ'rɒlədʒɪ] *n* virologie *f*

virtual ['vɜːtjʊəl] *adj* (**a**) *(near)* quasi; **it's a v. impossibility** c'est quasiment impossible (**b**) *Comput* virtuel(elle); **v. reality** réalité *f* virtuelle

virtually ['vɜːtjʊəlɪ] *adv* quasiment, pratiquement

virtue ['vɜːtjuː] *n* (**a**) *(goodness)* vertu *f*; **by v. of** en vertu de; **to make a v. of necessity** faire de nécessité vertu (**b**) *(advantage)* avantage *m*

virtuoso [vɜːtjʊ'əʊzəʊ] *(pl* **virtuosos** *or* **virtuosi** [vɜːtjʊ'əʊziː]) *n* virtuose *mf*

virtuous ['vɜːtjʊəs] *adj* vertueux(euse)

virulent ['vɪr(j)ʊlənt] *adj* virulent(e)

virus ['vaɪrəs] *n Med & Comput* virus *m*

visa ['viːzə] *n* visa *m*

vis-à-vis ['viːzɑːviː] *prep* par rapport à, vis-à-vis de

visceral ['vɪsərəl] *adj* viscéral(e)

viscount ['vaɪkaʊnt] *n* vicomte *m*

viscous ['vɪskəs] *adj* visqueux(euse)

visibility [vɪzɪ'bɪlɪtɪ] *n* visibilité *f*

visible ['vɪzɪbəl] *adj* visible

visibly ['vɪzɪblɪ] *adv* visiblement

vision ['vɪʒən] *n* (**a**) *(eyesight)* vue *f*; **to have good/poor v.** avoir une bonne/mauvaise vue (**b**) *(foresight,*

imagination) clairvoyance *f*; **a man of v.** un visionnaire (**c**) *(apparition)* vision *f*; **I had visions of being left homeless** je me suis vu devenir sans-abri

visionary ['vɪʒənərɪ] **1** *n (pl* **visionaries**) visionnaire *mf*
2 *adj* visionnaire

visit ['vɪzɪt] **1** *n* visite *f*; **to pay sb a v.** rendre visite à qn; **to be on a v.** être en visite
2 *vt (person)* rendre visite à; *(museum, monument)* visiter
3 *vi* **to be visiting** être de passage

visiting ['vɪzɪtɪŋ] *adj (circus)* de passage; *(lecturer)* invité(e); **v. card** carte *f* de visite; **v. hours** heures *fpl* de visite; **v. professor** professeur *m* invité; **v. rights** *(of divorced parent)* droits *mpl* de visite

visitor ['vɪzɪtə(r)] *n* visiteur(euse) *m,f*; **visitors' book** livre *m* d'or

visor ['vaɪzə(r)] *n* visière *f*

vista ['vɪstə] *n* vue *f*; *Fig* perspective *f*

visual ['vɪʒʊəl] *adj* visuel(elle); **v. aid** support *m* visuel; **v. arts** arts *mpl* plastiques; *Comput* **v. display unit** console *f* de visualisation

visualize ['vɪʒʊəlaɪz] *vt (imagine)* visualiser, se représenter; *(foresee)* envisager

visually ['vɪʒʊəlɪ] *adv* visuellement; **v. handicapped** malvoyant(e)

vital ['vaɪtəl] *adj* (**a**) *(essential)* vital(e); **v. organ** organe *m* vital; *Hum* **v. statistics** *(of woman)* mensurations *fpl* (**b**) *(vigorous)* vigoureux(euse)

vitality [vaɪ'tælɪtɪ] *n* vitalité *f*

vitally ['vaɪtəlɪ] *adv* **supplies are v. needed** on a un besoin vital de vivres; **v. important** d'une importance vitale *ou* capitale

vitamin ['vɪtəmɪn, *Am* 'vaɪtəmɪn] *n* vitamine *f*; **v. C/E** vitamine C/E; **with added vitamins** vitaminé(e)

vitreous ['vɪtrɪəs] *adj* **v. enamel** émail *m* vitrifié; **v. humour** humeur *f* vitrée

vitriol ['vɪtrɪəl] *n also Fig* vitriol *m*

vitriolic [vɪtrɪ'ɒlɪk] *adj Chem* de vitriol; *Fig* au vitriol

vituperative [vɪ'tjuːpərətɪv] *adj Formal* injurieux(euse)

viva ['vaɪvə] *n Br Univ* **v. (voce)** *(oral exam)* oral *m*; *(for thesis)* soutenance *f* de thèse

vivacious [vɪ'veɪʃəs] *adj* enjoué(e)

vivacity [vɪ'væsɪtɪ] *n* vivacité *f*

vivid ['vɪvɪd] *adj* vif (vive); *(memory)* clair(e)

vividly ['vɪvɪdlɪ] *adv* vivement; *(remember)* clairement; *(describe)* de manière vivante

vivisection [vɪvɪ'sekʃən] *n* vivisection *f*

vixen ['vɪksən] *n* renarde *f*

viz [vɪz] *adv (abbr* **videlicet**) à savoir

VOA [viːəʊ'eɪ] *n Am (abbr* **Voice of America**) = station de radio américaine de diffusion mondiale

vocabulary [və'kæbjʊlərɪ] *n* vocabulaire *m*

vocal ['vəʊkəl] **1** *adj* (**a**) *(relating to the voice)* vocal(e); **v. cords** cordes *fpl* vocales (**b**) *(outspoken)* franc (franche); **to be v. about sth** se faire entendre à propos de qch
2 *n* **vocals** chant *m*; **on vocals** au chant

vocalist ['vəʊkəlɪst] *n* chanteur(euse) *m,f*

vocation [vəʊ'keɪʃən] *n* vocation *f*; **to have a v. (for sth)** avoir une vocation (pour qch)

vocational [vəʊ'keɪʃənəl] *adj* professionnel(elle)

vocative ['vɒkətɪv] *n* vocatif

vociferous [və'sɪfərəs] *adj* bruyant(e)

vociferously [və'sɪfərəslɪ] *adv* bruyamment

vodka ['vɒdkə] *n* vodka *f*

vogue [vəʊɡ] *n* vogue *f*; **to be in v.** être en vogue

voice [vɔɪs] **1** *n* (**a**) *(of person)* voix *f*; **to raise/lower one's v.** élever/baisser la voix; **at the top of one's v.** à tue-tête; **I've lost my v.** je n'ai plus de voix; **v. box** larynx *m*; *Comput* **v. recognition** reconnaissance *f* de la parole; *Mus* **v. training** cours *mpl* de chant (**b**) *Gram* **active/passive v.** voix *f* active/passive (**c**) *(idioms)* **the v. of reason** la voix de la raison; **with one v.** d'une seule voix; **to make one's v. heard** se faire entendre; **these reforms would give small parties a v.** ces réformes donneraient voix au chapitre aux petits partis **2** *vt* (**a**) *(opinion, feelings)* exprimer (**b**) *(consonant)* sonoriser

voiced [vɔɪst] *adj (consonant)* sonore

voiceless ['vɔɪslɪs] *adj (consonant)* sans voix

voicemail ['vɔɪsmeɪl] *n Tel (message service)* messagerie *f* vocale; *(message)* message *m* vocal

voice-over ['vɔɪsəʊvə(r)] *n* voix *f* off

void [vɔɪd] **1** *n* vide *m*; **to fill the v.** combler le vide **2** *adj* (**a**) *(devoid)* **v. of** dépourvu(e) de (**b**) *Law (deed, contract)* **(null and) v.** nul (nulle) et non avenu(e)

volatile ['vɒlətaɪl] *adj* (**a**) *(person) (fickle)* inconstant(e); *(temperamental)* lunatique; *(situation)* explosif(ive); *(economy, market)* instable (**b**) *Chem* volatil(e)

volcanic [vɒl'kænɪk] *adj* volcanique

volcano [vɒl'keɪnəʊ] *(pl* **volcanoes**) *n* volcan *m*

vole [vəʊl] *n* campagnol *m*

volition [və'lɪʃən] *n Formal* **of one's own v.** de son propre gré

volley ['vɒlɪ] *(pl* **volleys**) *n* (**a**) *(of gunfire, blows, stones)* volée *f*; *Fig (of insults)* bordée *f* (**b**) *(in tennis)* volée *f*

volleyball ['vɒlɪbɔːl] *n* volley(-ball *m*) *m*

volt [vəʊlt] *n* volt *m*

voltage ['vəʊltɪdʒ] *n* voltage *m*; **high/low v.** haute/basse tension *f*

volte-face ['vɒltfɑːs] *n* volte-face *f inv*

voluble ['vɒljʊbəl] *adj* volubile

volubly ['vɒljʊblɪ] *adv* avec volubilité

volume ['vɒljuːm] *n* (**a**) *(book)* volume *m*, tome *m*; *Fig* **to speak volumes (about)** *(of action, expression)* en dire long (sur) (**b**) *(amount, space occupied)* volume *m*; *(of work)* quantité *f* (**c**) *(loudness)* volume *m*; **to turn the v. up/down** *(on TV, radio)* monter/baisser le volume; **v. control** bouton *m* de réglage du volume (**d**) *(of hair)* volume *m*

voluminous [və'ljuːmɪnəs] *adj (garment)* ample; *(container)* volumineux(euse)

voluntarily [vɒlʌn'teərɪlɪ] *adv* de plein gré

voluntary ['vɒləntərɪ] *adj* volontaire; **v. redundancy** départ *m* volontaire; **v. work** travail *m* bénévole

volunteer [vɒlən'tɪə(r)] **1** *n* volontaire *mf*; *(for charity)* bénévole *mf* **2** *vt (information)* donner spontanément; *(advice)* offrir; **to v. to do sth** se porter volontaire pour faire qch

3 *vi* (**a**) *(for military service)* s'engager (**b**) *(to help, for charity)* se porter volontaire (**for** pour)

voluptuous [və'lʌptjʊəs] *adj* voluptueux(euse)

vomit ['vɒmɪt] **1** *n* vomi *m* **2** *vt & vi* vomir

voodoo ['vuːduː] *n* vaudou *m*

voracious [və'reɪʃəs] *adj* vorace

vortex ['vɔːteks] *(pl* **vortices** ['vɔːtɪsiːz]) *n* vortex *m*; *Fig* tourbillon *m*

vote [vəʊt] **1** *n (choice)* vote *m*; *(election)* scrutin *m*; *(paper)* voix *f*; **to put sth to the v.** soumettre qch au vote; **to take a v. on sth** voter sur qch; **to have the v.** avoir le droit de vote; **they got 52% of the v.** ils ont remporté 52% des voix; **the party has increased its share of the v.** le parti a amélioré ses résultats aux élections; **v. of confidence** vote de confiance; **v. of no confidence** motion *f* de censure

2 *vt* **to v. Communist** voter communiste; **to v. to do sth** voter pour faire qch; **to v. sth down** voter contre qch; **to v. sb in** élire qn; **to v. sb out** ne pas réélire qn; **I v. (that) we go** je propose qu'on y aille

3 *vi* voter (**for/against** pour/contre); **to v. on sth** voter sur qch; *Fig* **to v. with one's feet** manifester son mécontentement en partant

voter ['vəʊtə(r)] *n* électeur(trice) *m,f*

voting ['vəʊtɪŋ] **1** *n* scrutin *m*; **v. booth** isoloir *m* **2** *adj (member)* votant(e)

votive ['vəʊtɪv] *adj Rel* votif(ive)

▸**vouch for** [vaʊtʃ] *vt insep (person)* se porter garant(e) de; *(quality, truth)* attester de

voucher ['vaʊtʃə(r)] *n* coupon *m*, bon *m*; **(gift) v.** chèque-cadeau *m*

vow [vaʊ] **1** *n* vœu *m*; **to make a v.** faire un vœu; **to take a v. of poverty/silence** faire vœu de pauvreté/silence

2 *vt* jurer; **to v. to do sth** jurer de faire qch; **to v. that** jurer que

vowel ['vaʊəl] *n* voyelle *f*; **v. sound** son *m* vocalique

voyage ['vɔɪdʒ] *n* voyage *m*

voyager ['vɔɪdʒə(r)] *n* voyageur(euse) *m,f*

voyeur [vwaː'jɜː(r)] *n* voyeur(euse) *m,f*

voyeuristic [vwaːjʊə'rɪstɪk] *adj* voyeuriste

vs *(abbr* **versus**) contre

VSO [viːes'əʊ] *n Br (abbr* **Voluntary Service Overseas**) ≃ service *m* de la coopération

VTR [viːtiː'ɑː(r)] *n (abbr* **video tape recorder**) magnétoscope *m*

vulgar ['vʌlgə(r)] *adj* vulgaire; *Math* **v. fraction** fraction *f* ordinaire

vulgarity [vʌl'gærɪtɪ] *n* vulgarité *f*

vulnerability [vʌlnərə'bɪlɪtɪ] *n* vulnérabilité *f*

vulnerable ['vʌlnərəbəl] *adj* vulnérable

vulture ['vʌltʃə(r)] *n also Fig* vautour *m*

vulva ['vʌlvə] *(pl* **vulvas** *or* **vulvae** ['vʌlviː]) *n* vulve *f*

W¹, w [ˈdʌbəljuː] n (**a**) (letter) W, w m inv (**b**) (abbr west) O

W² n (abbr **watt(s)**) W

WAAF [wæf] n Hist (abbr **Women's Auxiliary Air Force**) = groupe de femmes, auxiliaires de l'armée de l'air britannique durant la Seconde Guerre mondiale

wacky [ˈwækɪ] adj Fam farfelu(e)

wad [wɒd] n (of cotton wool) morceau m; (of paper, bank notes) liasse f

wadding [ˈwɒdɪŋ] n ouate f

waddle [ˈwɒdəl] vi se dandiner

wade [weɪd] vi (in water) marcher dans l'eau; **to w. across a stream** traverser une rivière à gué; Fam Fig **to w. in** intervenir; Fig **it took me a month to w. through that book** il m'a fallu un mois pour venir à bout de ce livre

▸**wade into** vt insep Fam Fig (task) s'attaquer à; (person) tomber sur

wader [ˈweɪdə(r)] n (**a**) (bird) échassier m (**b**) **waders** (boots) bottes fpl de pêcheur

wafer [ˈweɪfə(r)] n (**a**) (biscuit) gaufrette f, Belg galette f (**b**) Rel (for communion) hostie f

wafer-thin [weɪfəˈθɪn] adj ultramince

waffle¹ [ˈwɒfəl] n (food) gaufre f, **w. iron** gaufrier m

waffle² Br Fam **1** n (spoken) baratin m; (written) remplissage m

2 vi (in speaking) baratiner; (in writing) faire du remplissage

waft [wɒft] **1** vt (smell, sound) porter

2 vi (of smell, sound) parvenir

wag¹ [wæg] **1** vt (pt & pp **wagged**) agiter, remuer; **to w. one's finger at sb** menacer qn du doigt; **to w. its tail** (of dog) remuer la queue

2 vi frétiller, remuer; **its tail was wagging** (of dog) il remuait la queue; Fam **tongues will w.** les langues vont aller bon train

3 n (action) frétillement m; **with a w. of its tail** la queue frétillante

wag² n Fam (joker) farceur(euse) m,f

wage [weɪdʒ] **1** n (pay) **wage(s)** salaire m, paie f; **w. claim** revendication f salariale; **w. cut** diminution f de salaire; Br **w. differential** écart m salarial; **w. earner** salarié(e) m,f; **w. freeze** gel m des salaires; **w. packet** (envelope) enveloppe f de paie; (money) paie f

2 vt **to w. war (on)** faire la guerre (à); **to w. a campaign against smoking** mener une campagne anti-tabac

wager [ˈweɪdʒə(r)] **1** n pari m

2 vt parier

waggle [ˈwægəl] vt & vi remuer

wag(g)on [ˈwægən] n (horse-drawn) charrette f; Br (for railway freight) wagon m (découvert); Fam Fig **to be on the w.** être au régime sec

waif [weɪf] n (abandoned child) enfant mf abandonné(e); (very thin girl) fille f excessivement maigre; **waifs and strays** (children) enfants mpl abandonnés; (animals) animaux mpl abandonnés

wail [weɪl] **1** n (of person) gémissement m; (of siren) hurlement m

2 vi (of person) gémir, pousser des gémissements; (of siren) hurler

waist [weɪst] n taille f; **w. measurement** tour m de taille

waistband [ˈweɪstbænd] n ceinture f

waistcoat [ˈweɪskəʊt] n Br gilet m

waistline [ˈweɪstlaɪn] n taille f; **to watch one's w.** surveiller sa ligne

wait [weɪt] **1** n attente f; **to have a long w.** attendre longtemps; **to lie in w. for sb** guetter qn

2 vt attendre; **to w. one's turn** attendre son tour

3 vi (**a**) (remain in expectation) attendre; **to w. for sb/sth** attendre qn/qch; **to keep sb waiting** faire attendre qn; **I can't w. to see her** j'ai vraiment hâte de la voir; **repairs while you w.** (sign) réparations minute; **we must w. and see** on verra bien (**b**) **to w. at table** (serve) faire le service

▸**wait about, wait around** vi attendre

▸**wait on** vt insep (serve) servir; **to w. on sb hand and foot** être aux petits soins pour qn

▸**wait up** vi (**a**) (stay up) **to w. up for sb** attendre qn pour aller se coucher (**b**) Fam (wait) **w. up!** attendez-moi!

waiter [ˈweɪtə(r)] n serveur m

waiting [ˈweɪtɪŋ] n attente f; **to play the w. game** faire de l'attentisme; **w. list** liste f d'attente; **w. room** salle f d'attente

waitress [ˈweɪtrɪs] n serveuse f

waive [weɪv] vt (rights, claim) renoncer à; (rule) ignorer

wake¹ [weɪk] n (of ship) sillage m; Fig **in the w. of sth** à la suite de qch; Fig **to follow in sb's w.** suivre l'exemple de qn

wake² n (on night before funeral) veillée f de corps

wake³ (pt **woke** [wəʊk] or **waked**, pp **woken** [ˈwəʊkən] or **waked**) **1** vt réveiller

2 vi se réveiller

▸**wake up 1** vt sep réveiller

2 vi se réveiller; Fig **to w. up to sth** prendre conscience de qch

wakeful [ˈweɪkfʊl] adj (**a**) (sleepless) éveillé(e); **to have a w. night** ne pas fermer l'œil de la nuit (**b**) (vigilant) vigilant(e)

waken ['weɪkən] *vt* réveiller
wake-up call ['weɪkʌpkɔːl] *n (in hotel)* réveil *m* téléphonique; *Fig* **the bomb scare was a w. to the government to tighten security** avec cette alerte à la bombe, le gouvernement a compris qu'il devait renforcer les mesures de sécurité
wakey wakey ['weɪkɪ'weɪkɪ] *exclam Br Fam* réveille-toi!
Wales [weɪlz] *n* le pays de Galles
walk [wɔːk] **1** *n* (**a**) *(short)* promenade *f*; *(long)* marche *f*; **it's a long w.** c'est loin à pied; **it's a ten-minute w.** c'est à dix minutes à pied; **to go for a w.** aller se promener (**b**) *(gait)* démarche *f*; **I know her by her w.** je la reconnais à sa démarche (**c**) *(speed)* **at a w.** au pas (**d**) *(path)* avenue *f* (**e**) *(profession, situation)* **people from all walks of life** des gens de tous les milieux
2 *vt* **to w. the dog** promener le chien; **to w. sb home** raccompagner qn; **to w. the streets** battre le pavé; *Euph (of prostitute)* faire le trottoir
3 *vi (move on foot)* marcher; *(as opposed to riding, driving)* aller à pied; *(for exercise, pleasure)* se promener (à pied); **to w. home** rentrer à pied
▸ **walk away** *vi* s'en aller; *Fig* **to w. away from trouble** éviter les ennuis; *Fig* **to w. away with a prize** remporter un prix
▸ **walk in** *vi* entrer
▸ **walk into** *vt insep* (**a**) *(enter)* entrer dans (**b**) *(collide with)* rentrer dans
▸ **walk off** *vi* s'en aller; **to w. off with sth** *(steal)* partir avec qch; *(win easily)* remporter qch
▸ **walk out** *vi* (**a**) *(leave)* sortir; **to w. out on sb** quitter qn (**b**) *(go on strike)* se mettre en grève
▸ **walk over** *vt insep Fam* **to w. all over sb** marcher sur les pieds de qn
walkabout ['wɔːkəbaʊt] *n (of politician)* bain *m* de foule
walker ['wɔːkə(r)] *n* (**a**) *(person)* marcheur(euse) *m,f* (**b**) *Am (device)* déambulateur *m*
walkie-talkie [wɔːkɪ'tɔːkɪ] *n* talkie-walkie *m*
walk-in cupboard ['wɔːkɪn'kʌbəd] *n (for clothes)* débarras *m*; *(for food)* cellier *m*
walking ['wɔːkɪŋ] **1** *n* marche *f*; **w. frame** déambulateur *m*; **w. shoes** chaussures *fpl* de marche; **w. stick** canne *f*
2 *adj* **at a w. pace** au pas; *Fam* **she's a w. encyclopedia** c'est une encyclopédie ambulante; **the w. wounded** les blessés *mpl* en état de marcher
Walkman® ['wɔːkmən] *n* baladeur *m*
walk-on part ['wɔːkɒn'pɑːt] *n (in film, play)* rôle *m* de figurant(e)
walkout ['wɔːkaʊt] *n (strike)* débrayage *m*; *(from meeting)* départ *m* en signe de protestation
walkover ['wɔːkəʊvə(r)] *n Fam* **it was a w.!** c'était du gâteau!
walkway ['wɔːkweɪ] *n* passage *m* (couvert)
wall [wɔːl] *n* (**a**) *(of building, room)* mur *m*; **the Great W. of China** la grande muraille de Chine; **w. cupboard** placard *m* mural; **w. hanging** tenture *f* murale (**b**) *(idioms)* **a w. of silence** un mur de silence; **to go to the w.** faire faillite; *Fam* **to drive sb up the w.** rendre qn dingue; *Fam* **I might as well talk to the w.!** c'est comme parler à un mur
▸ **wall in** *vt sep* entourer
▸ **wall off** *vt sep* séparer
▸ **wall up** *vt sep* murer
wallaby ['wɒləbɪ] *(pl* **wallabies)** *n* wallaby *m*

wallet ['wɒlɪt] *n* portefeuille *m*
wallflower ['wɔːlflaʊə(r)] *n (plant)* giroflée *f*; *Fig* **to be a w.** *(of person)* faire tapisserie
Walloon [wɒ'luːn] **1** *n* (**a**) *(person)* Wallon(onne) *m, f* (**b**) *(language)* wallon *m*
2 *adj* wallon(onne)
wallop ['wɒləp] *Fam* **1** *n* beigne *f*, grand coup *m*
2 *vt* filer un grand coup à
walloping ['wɒləpɪŋ] *Fam* **1** *n* raclée *f*
2 *adv (for emphasis)* super; **a w. great lie** un mensonge gros comme ça
wallow ['wɒləʊ] *vi* se vautrer; **to w. in self-pity** s'apitoyer sur son propre sort
wallpaper ['wɔːlpeɪpə(r)] **1** *n* papier *m* peint
2 *vt* tapisser
wall-to-wall ['wɔːltəwɔːl] *adj* **w. carpeting** moquette *f*; *Fig* **w. coverage** couverture *f* complète
wally ['wɒlɪ] *(pl* **wallies)** *n Br Fam (idiot)* andouille *f*
walnut ['wɔːlnʌt] *n (fruit)* noix *f*; *(tree, wood)* noyer *m*
walrus ['wɔːlrəs] *n* morse *m*
waltz [wɔːls] **1** *n* valse *f*
2 *vi* (**a**) *(dance)* valser (**b**) *Fam (move confidently)* **to w. in/out** entrer/sortir avec désinvolture; *Fam* **to w. off with sth** partir avec qch
WAN [dʌbəljuːeɪ'en] *n Comput (abbr* **wide area network)** grand réseau *m*
wan [wɒn] *adj* blême
wand [wɒnd] *n* baguette *f*
wander ['wɒndə(r)] **1** *n* balade *f*; **to go for a w.** aller faire un tour
2 *vt (streets)* traîner dans; *(world)* courir
3 *vi* (**a**) *(roam)* errer; **to w. around the town** se promener dans la ville; **she had wandered from the path** elle s'était éloignée du chemin (**b**) *(verbally)* radoter; *(mentally)* dérailler; **to w. from the subject** s'écarter du sujet
wanderer ['wɒndərə(r)] *n* vagabond(e) *m, f*
wandering ['wɒndərɪŋ] *adj (person, life)* errant(e); *(tribe)* nomade
wanderlust ['wɒndəlʌst] *n* soif *f* de voyages
wane [weɪn] **1** *vi (of moon)* décroître; *(of popularity, enthusiasm, power)* décliner
2 *n* **to be on the w.** *(of moon)* décroître; *(of popularity, enthusiasm, power)* être en déclin
wangle ['wæŋgəl] *vt Fam* se débrouiller pour avoir; **to w. sb sth, to w. sth for sb** se débrouiller pour avoir qch à qn; **to w. it so that** se débrouiller pour que + *subjunctive*
wank [wæŋk] *Br Vulg* **1** *n* branlette *f*; **to have a w.** se branler
2 *vi* se branler
wanker ['wæŋkə(r)] *n Br Vulg* connard *m*
wanna ['wɒnə] (**a**) = want to (**b**) = want a
want [wɒnt] **1** *vt* (**a**) *(wish, desire)* vouloir; **to w. to do sth** vouloir faire qch; **to w. sb to do sth** vouloir que qn fasse qch; **that's the last thing we w.** nous ne voulons surtout pas cela; **I know when I'm not wanted** je sais quand je suis de trop; **what does she w. with me?** qu'est-ce qu'elle me veut? (**b**) *Fam (need)* avoir besoin de; **the lawn wants cutting** la pelouse a besoin d'être tondue; **you w. to be careful with him** il faut que tu fasses attention avec lui (**c**) *(seek)* **to be wanted by the police** être recherché(e) par la police; **you're wanted on the phone** on te demande au téléphone; **accommodation wanted** *(in advertisement)* cherche appartement
2 *vi* **to w. for nothing** ne manquer de rien

3 *n* (**a**) *(need)* besoin *m*; *Am* **w. ad** petite annonce *f* (**b**) *(lack)* manque *m* (**of** de); **for w. of sth/of doing sth** faute de qch/de faire qch; **for w. of anything better** faute de mieux

wanting ['wɒntɪŋ] *adj* **to be w. in sth** manquer de qch; **to be found w.** *(of person)* se révéler incapable; *(of thing)* laisser à désirer

wanton ['wɒntən] *adj* (**a**) *(unjustified)* gratuit(e) (**b**) *(unrestrained)* dévergondé(e); *(sexually)* licencieux(euse)

war [wɔː(r)] *n* guerre *f*; **to be at w.** (**with**) être en guerre (avec); **to go to w.** (**with/over**) entrer en guerre (contre/à propos de); *Fig* **w. of words** altercation *f*; *Fam Fig* **you look as if you've been through the wars** tu es dans un bel état!; **w. cabinet** cabinet *m* de guerre; **w. correspondent** correspondant(e) *mf* de guerre; **w. crime** crime *m* de guerre; **w. criminal** criminel *m* de guerre; **w. cry** cri *m* de guerre; **w. games** *Mil* manœuvres *fpl*; *(with model soldiers)* wargame *m*; **w. memorial** monument *m* aux morts

warble ['wɔːbəl] **1** *n* gazouillement *m*
2 *vi* gazouiller

warbler ['wɔːblə(r)] *n* fauvette *f*

ward [wɔːd] *n* (**a**) *(in hospital)* salle *f* (**b**) *(electoral division)* circonscription *f* (**c**) *Law* **w. of court** pupille *mf* sous tutelle judiciaire

▸ **ward off** *vt sep (blow)* éviter; *(danger)* chasser

warden ['wɔːdən] *n (of institution, hostel)* directeur(-trice) *m,f*; *(of park)* gardien(enne) *mf*

warder ['wɔːdə(r)] *n Br (of prison)* gardien(enne) *m,f*

wardrobe ['wɔːdrəʊb] *n* (**a**) *(cupboard)* armoire *f* (**b**) *(clothes)* garde-robe *f*; **to have a large w.** avoir une garde-robe importante (**c**) *(theatrical costumes)* costumes *mpl*; **w. mistress** habilleuse *f*

warehouse ['weəhaʊs] *n* entrepôt *m*

wares [weə(r)z] *npl* articles *mpl*

warfare ['wɔːfeə(r)] *n* guerre *f*; **class w.** lutte *f* des classes

warhead ['wɔːhed] *n* ogive *f*

warhorse ['wɔːhɔːs] *n Fig* **an old w.** un vétéran

warily ['weərɪlɪ] *adv* avec une prudence circonspecte

wariness ['weərɪnɪs] *n* prudence *f* circonspecte

warlike ['wɔːlaɪk] *adj* guerrier(ère)

warm [wɔːm] **1** *adj* (**a**) *(in temperature)* chaud(e); **to be w.** *(of person)* avoir chaud; *(of object, water, clothing)* être chaud(e); **it's w.** *(of weather)* il fait chaud; **you're getting warmer** *(in guessing game)* tu chauffes (**b**) *(kind, friendly)* chaleureux(euse)
2 *vt* chauffer; **to w. oneself by the fire** se chauffer près du feu
3 *vi* **to w. to sb** se prendre de sympathie pour qn; **to w. to sth** se laisser séduire par qch

▸ **warm up 1** *vt sep (food)* réchauffer
2 *vi* (**a**) *(of person, room)* se réchauffer (**b**) *(of dancer, athlete)* s'échauffer (**c**) *(of engine)* chauffer

warm-blooded [wɔːm'blʌdɪd] *adj* à sang chaud

warm-hearted [wɔːm'hɑːtɪd] *adj* chaleureux(euse)

warmly ['wɔːmlɪ] *adv* (**a**) *(dress)* chaudement (**b**) *(applaud, thank)* chaleureusement

warmonger ['wɔːmʌŋgə(r)] *n* belliciste *mf*

warmth [wɔːmθ] *n* chaleur *f*

warm-up ['wɔːmʌp] *n (of dancer, athlete)* échauffement *m*

warn [wɔːn] *vt* avertir, prévenir; **to w. sb about sb/sth** mettre qn en garde contre qn/qch; **to w. sb about doing sth** dire à qn de ne pas faire qch; **to w. sb not**

to do sth déconseiller à qn de faire qch; **you have been warned!** te voilà prévenu(e)!

warning ['wɔːnɪŋ] *n* (**a**) *(caution)* avertissement *m*; *(against danger)* mise *f* en garde; **to give sb a w.** donner un avertissement à qn; *(against danger)* mettre qn en garde; *Fig* **w. sign** signe *m* (**b**) *(advance notice)* avis *m*; **without w.** sans prévenir

warp [wɔːp] **1** *vt* (**a**) *(wood, metal)* gauchir (**b**) *(person, mind)* pervertir
2 *vi (of wood, metal)* gauchir

warpath ['wɔːpɑːθ] *n Fam* **to be on the w.** en vouloir à tout le monde

warped [wɔːpt] *adj* (**a**) *(wood, metal)* gauchi(e) (**b**) *(person)* perverti(e); *(mind, humour)* tordu(e)

warrant ['wɒrənt] **1** *n Law* mandat *m*; *Mil* **w. officer** adjudant *m*
2 *vt* (**a**) *(justify)* justifier (**b**) *(guarantee)* garantir

warranty ['wɒrəntɪ] *(pl* **warranties**) *n* garantie *f*; **under w.** sous garantie

warren ['wɒrən] *n (of rabbit)* garenne *f*; *Fig (of streets)* labyrinthe *m*

warring ['wɔːrɪŋ] *adj* en guerre

warrior ['wɒrɪə(r)] *n* guerrier(ère) *m,f*

Warsaw ['wɔːsɔː] *n* Varsovie; *Formerly* **the W. Pact** le pacte de Varsovie

warship ['wɔːʃɪp] *n* navire *m* de guerre

wart [wɔːt] *n* verrue *f*; **warts and all** *(biography, portrait)* sans complaisance

warthog ['wɔːthɒg] *n* phacochère *m*

wartime ['wɔːtaɪm] *n* temps *m* de guerre; **in w.** en temps de guerre

wary ['weərɪ] *adj* méfiant(e); **to be w. of sb/sth** se méfier de qn/qch

was [wɒz] *pt of* **be**

wash [wɒʃ] **1** *n* (**a**) *(action)* lavage *m*; **to have a w.** se laver; **to give sth a w.** laver qch; **your jeans are in the w.** ton jean est au lavage; *Fig* **it will all come out in the w.** tout va s'arranger (**b**) *(of ship)* remous *m*
2 *vt* (**a**) *(clean)* laver; **to w. oneself** se laver; **to w. one's face/one's hands** se laver la figure/les mains; *Fig* **to w. one's hands of sth** se laver les mains de qch; **to w. one's hands of sb** ne plus se préoccuper de qn (**b**) *(carry)* **to w. sb/sth ashore** rejeter qn/qch sur le rivage; **he was washed overboard** une vague l'a emporté par-dessus bord
3 *vi (wash oneself)* se laver; *Br Fam* **that won't w.!** ça ne marche pas!; *Br Fam* **his story just doesn't w. with me!** il ne me fera pas avaler cette histoire!

▸ **wash away** *vt sep* emporter

▸ **wash down** *vt sep* (**a**) *(walls, car)* laver à grande eau (**b**) *(pill)* faire descendre (**with** avec); **to w. down one's dinner with a bottle of wine** arroser son dîner d'une bouteille de vin

▸ **wash off 1** *vt sep* enlever
2 *vi* partir

▸ **wash out 1** *vt sep* (**a**) *(cup, bottle)* rincer (**b**) *(stain, dirt)* faire partir; **to be completely washed out** *(exhausted)* être complètement lessivé(e)
2 *vi (of stain, dirt)* partir

▸ **wash over** *vt insep (of waves)* balayer; *Fig (have no effect on)* ne faire aucun effet à

▸ **wash up 1** *vt sep* (**a**) *Br (clean)* laver (**b**) *(carry ashore)* rejeter sur le rivage
2 *vi* (**a**) *Br (do dishes)* faire la vaisselle (**b**) *Am (have a wash)* se débarbouiller

washbasin ['wɒʃbeɪsən] *n* (cuvette *f* de) lavabo *m*

washboard ['wɒʃbɔːd] *n* planche *f* à laver

washbowl ['wɒʃbəʊl] *n (small)* cuvette *f; (large)* bassine *f*

washcloth ['wɒʃklɒθ] *n Am (face cloth)* lingette *f*

washer ['wɒʃə(r)] *n* (**a**) *Fam (for clothes)* machine *f* à laver (**b**) *(for screw)* rondelle *f; (made of rubber)* joint *m*

washer-dryer [wɒʃə'draɪə(r)] *n* machine *f* à laver qui fait sèche-linge

wash(-)hand basin ['wɒʃhænd'beɪsən] *n* lavabo *m*

washing ['wɒʃɪŋ] *n* (**a**) *(action)* lavage *m*; **to do the w.** faire la lessive; **w. machine** machine *f* à laver; **w. powder** poudre *f* à laver, lessive *f* (en poudre) (**b**) *(dirty clothes)* linge *m* sale; *(clean clothes)* linge *m* (propre)

Washington ['wɒʃɪŋtən] *n* Washington; **W. (State)** l'État *m* de Washington; **W. DC** Washington

washing-up [wɒʃɪŋ'ʌp] *n Br* vaisselle *f*; **to do the w.** faire la vaisselle; **w. bowl** cuvette *f*; **w. liquid** liquide *f* vaisselle

washout ['wɒʃaʊt] *n Fam* bide *m*

washroom ['wɒʃruːm] *n Am* toilettes *fpl*

wasn't [wɒzənt] = was not

Wasp, WASP [wɒsp] *n Am (abbr* **White Anglo-Saxon Protestant)** = Blanc d'origine anglo-saxonne et protestante, appartenant aux classes aisées et influentes

wasp [wɒsp] *n* guêpe *f*; **w.'s nest** guêpier *m*

waspish ['wɒspɪʃ] *adj* hargneux(euse)

wastage ['weɪstɪdʒ] *n* gaspillage *m*

waste [weɪst] **1** *n* (**a**) *(of food, effort)* gaspillage *m*; *(of time, money)* perte *f*; **to go to w.** être gaspillé(e) (**b**) *(rubbish)* déchets *mpl*; **w. bin** *(in kitchen)* poubelle *f*; *(for paper)* corbeille *f*; **w. disposal unit** broyeur *m* d'ordures (**c**) **wastes** *(desert)* étendues *fpl* désertiques

2 *adj (heat, fuel)* gaspillé(e); *(water)* usé(e)

3 *vt (money)* gaspiller; *(time)* perdre; *(opportunity)* gâcher; **to w. no time doing sth** ne pas perdre de temps pour faire qch; *Prov* **w. not, want not** = il ne faut pas gaspiller

▸**waste away** *vi* dépérir

wastebasket ['weɪstbɑːskɪt] *n (for paper)* & *Comput* corbeille *f*

wasted ['weɪstɪd] *adj* (**a**) *(effort)* gaspillé(e); *(opportunity)* gaché(e) (**b**) *Fam (drunk)* bourré(e), pété(e); *(on drugs)* défoncé(e)

wasteful ['weɪstfʊl] *adj* **to be w.** *(of process, practice)* ne pas être rentable; *(of person)* être gaspilleur(euse)

wasteland ['weɪstlænd] *n (disused)* terrain *m* vague; *(of desert, snow)* désert *m*

wastepaper [weɪst'peɪpə(r)] *n* vieux papiers *mpl*; **w. basket** *or* **bin** corbeille *f* à papier

waster ['weɪstə(r)] *n Br Fam (idle person)* bon (bonne) *m,f*, à rien

wasting disease ['weɪstɪŋdɪ'ziːz] *n* maladie *f* dégénérative

watch [wɒtʃ] **1** *n* (**a**) *(timepiece)* montre *f* (**b**) *(period of guard duty)* garde *f*; *(guard)* sentinelle *f*; **to be on w.** monter la garde; **to keep a close w. on sb/sth** surveiller qn/qch de près

2 *vt* (**a**) *(observe)* regarder; **to w. television** regarder la télévision; **to w. sb doing sth** regarder qn faire qch (**b**) *(keep an eye on)* surveiller (**c**) *(be careful of)* faire attention à; **w. your language!** surveille ton langage!; *Fam* **w. it!** attention!

3 *vi* regarder

▸**watch out** *vi* faire attention; **w. out!** attention!

▸**watch out for** *vt insep* (**a**) *(look for) (person)* guetter; *(thing)* chercher (**b**) *(be on guard for)* faire attention à

▸**watch over** *vt insep* veiller sur

watchdog ['wɒtʃdɒg] *n* chien *m* de garde; *Fig (organization)* organisme *m* de contrôle

watchful ['wɒtʃfʊl] *adj* vigilant(e)

watchmaker ['wɒtʃmeɪkə(r)] *n* horloger(ère) *m,f*

watchman ['wɒtʃmən] *n* gardien *m*

watchstrap ['wɒtʃstræp] *n* bracelet *m* de montre

watchtower ['wɒtʃtaʊə(r)] *n* tour *f* de guet

watchword ['wɒtʃwɜːd] *n* mot *m* d'ordre

water ['wɔːtə(r)] **1** *n* (**a**) *(substance)* eau *f*; **to pass w.** *(urinate)* uriner; **w. bed** matelas *m* d'eau; **w. biscuit** = biscuit sec non salé; **w. bottle** gourde *f*; **w. chestnut** macre *f*; *Old-fashioned* **w. closet** waters *mpl*; **w. cooler** distributeur *m* d'eau fraîche; **w. heater** chauffeeau *m*; **w. level** niveau *m* d'eau; **w. lily** nénuphar *m*; **w. meter** compteur *m* d'eau; **w. pistol** pistolet *m* à eau; **w. polo** water-polo *m*; **w. rat** rat *m* d'eau; **w. skiing** ski *m* nautique; **w. tank** réservoir *m* d'eau; **w. tower** château *m* d'eau; **w. wings** brassards *mpl* de natation (**b**) *(idioms)* **to spend money like w.** jeter l'argent par les fenêtres; **the argument doesn't hold w.** cet argument ne tient pas debout; **to keep one's head above w.** garder la tête hors de l'eau; **that's all w. under the bridge now** c'est de l'histoire ancienne; **a lot of w. has passed under the bridge since then** il a coulé beaucoup d'eau sous les ponts depuis

2 *vt* (**a**) *(fields, plants)* arroser (**b**) *(horse)* donner à boire à

3 *vi (of eyes)* pleurer; **it makes my mouth w.** ça me met l'eau à la bouche; **my mouth is watering** j'en ai l'eau à la bouche

▸**water down** *vt sep (liquid, chemical)* diluer; *Fig (criticism, legislation)* atténuer

waterborne ['wɔːtəbɔːn] *adj (goods)* transporté(e) par voie d'eau; *(disease)* d'origine hydrique

watercourse ['wɔːtəkɔːs] *n* cours *m* d'eau

watercolour ['wɔːtəkʌlə(r)] *n* aquarelle *f*

watercress ['wɔːtəkres] *n* cresson *m* (de fontaine)

waterfall ['wɔːtəfɔːl] *n* cascade *f*

waterfowl ['wɔːtəfaʊl] *(pl* **waterfowl***) n* gibier *m* d'eau

waterfront ['wɔːtəfrʌnt] *n (by river)* bord *m* de l'eau; *(by sea)* front *m* de mer

watering ['wɔːtərɪŋ] *n (of garden, plant)* arrosage *m*; **w. can** arrosoir *m*; **w. hole** *(for animals)* point *m* d'eau; *Fam (bar)* bar *m*

waterlogged ['wɔːtəlɒgd] *adj (shoes, clothes)* trempé(e); *(land)* détrempé(e)

watermark ['wɔːtəmɑːk] *n* filigrane *m*

watermelon ['wɔːtəmelən] *n* pastèque *f*

waterproof ['wɔːtəpruːf] **1** *adj* imperméable; *(watch, joint, seal)* étanche; *(make-up)* waterproof *inv*; *(sun lotion)* résistant(e) à l'eau

2 *n (raincoat)* imperméable *m*

3 *vt* imperméabiliser

water-resistant ['wɔːtərɪzɪstənt] *adj (watch)* étanche; *(fabric)* qui résiste à l'eau

watershed ['wɔːtəʃed] *n Geog* ligne *f* de partage des eaux; *Fig (turning point)* tournant *m*; *Br* **the (nine o'clock) w.** *(on television)* = heure après laquelle sont diffusés des programmes ne convenant pas aux enfants

waterside ['wɔːtəsaɪd] *n* bord *m* de l'eau

water-ski ['wɔːtəskiː] *vi* faire du ski nautique

watertight ['wɔːtətaɪt] *adj (seal)* hermétique; *(compartment)* étanche; *Fig (argument, alibi)* inattaquable
waterway ['wɔːtəweɪ] *n* voie *f* navigable
waterworks ['wɔːtəwɜːks] *n* station *f* hydraulique; *Br Euph (urinary system)* voies *fpl* urinaires; *Fam* **to turn on the w.** *(cry)* se mettre à pleurer comme une madeleine
watery ['wɔːtərɪ] *adj (soup)* trop liquide; *(beer, tea, coffee)* insipide, fade; *(eyes)* qui pleure; *(colour)* délavé(e)
watt [wɒt] *n* watt *m*
wattage ['wɒtɪdʒ] *n* puissance *f* en watts
wave [weɪv] **1** *n* (**a**) *(of water, dislike, crime)* vague *f*; *Fig* **to make waves** faire des vagues (**b**) *(gesture)* signe *m* (de la main); **to give sb a w.** faire signe à qn (**c**) *(in hair)* ondulation *f* (**d**) *(in physics)* onde *f*
2 *vt (arm, flag)* agiter; *(stick)* brandir; **to w. one's arms about** agiter les bras; **to w. goodbye to sb** faire au revoir de la main à qn
3 *vi* (**a**) *(of person)* faire signe; **to w. to sb** faire signe à qn (**b**) *(of flag)* flotter au vent
▸**wave aside** *vt insep Fig (objection, criticism)* écarter
waveband ['weɪvbænd] *n* bande *f* de fréquences
wavelength ['weɪvleŋθ] *n* longueur *f* d'ondes; *Fig* **to be on the same w.** être sur la même longueur d'ondes
waver ['weɪvə(r)] *vi (of person)* vaciller; *(of voice)* trembler; *(of courage)* faiblir
waverer ['weɪvərə(r)] *n* indécis(e) *m,f*
wavy ['weɪvɪ] *adj* ondulé(e)
wax¹ [wæks] **1** *n (for candles, polishing)* cire *f*; *(in ear)* cérumen *m*
2 *vt* (**a**) *(polish)* cirer (**b**) *(legs)* épiler (à la cire); **to w. one's legs** s'épiler les jambes (à la cire)
wax² *vi* (**a**) *(of moon)* croître (**b**) *(become)* **to w. lyrical (about sth)** devenir lyrique (à propos de qch)
waxed [wækst] *adj* ciré(e)
waxen ['wæksən] *adj (complexion)* de cire
waxwork ['wækswɜːk] *n* **w. (dummy)** mannequin *m* de cire; **waxworks** musée *m* de cire
way [weɪ] **1** *n* (**a**) *(route)* & *Fig* chemin *m*; **the w. in** l'entrée *f*; **the w. out** la sortie; **the w. to the station** le chemin pour aller à la gare; **to ask sb the w.** demander son chemin à qn; **to show sb the w.** montrer le chemin à qn; **to lose one's w.** se perdre; **to know one's w. about** savoir se débrouiller; **on the w.** en chemin, en route; *Fam* **they've got a baby on the w.** ils ont un bébé en route; **I must be on my w.** je dois partir; **out of the w.** isolé(e); *Fig* **to go out of one's w. to help sb** se mettre en quatre pour aider qn; *Fig* **to find a w. out of a problem** trouver une issue à un problème; *Fig* **she is well on the w. to success** elle est bien partie pour réussir; **to make one's w. to a place** se diriger vers un endroit; **to make one's w. through the crowd** se frayer un chemin à travers la foule; *Fig* **to make w. for sb** laisser la place à qn; *Fig* **to make one's w. in the world** réussir dans la vie; *also Fig* **to stand in sb's w.** barrer le passage à qn; *also Fig* **to be/get in the w.** gêner; *also Fig* **to get out of the w.** s'écarter; *also Fig* **to keep out of the w.** se tenir à l'écart
(**b**) *(manner)* manière *f*, façon *f*; **in this w.** de cette manière; **to do things in one's own w.** faire les choses à sa manière; **I don't like the w. things are going** je n'aime pas la façon dont les choses tournent; **one w. or another** d'une manière ou d'une autre; **to find a w. of doing sth** trouver un moyen de

faire qch; **to get into the w. of doing sth** s'habituer à faire qch; **to have a w. with children/animals** savoir s'y prendre avec les enfants/les animaux; **to get one's (own) w.** arriver à ses fins; **he's used to getting his own w.** il n'a pas l'habitude qu'on le contrarie; **to get used to sb's ways** se faire aux habitudes de qn
(**c**) *(distance)* **to go a part of the w.** faire un bout de chemin; **to go all the w.** aller jusqu'au bout; *Fig* **I'm with you all the w.** je suis tout à fait d'accord avec toi; **San Francisco is a long w. from New York** San Francisco est loin de New York; **we've still got a long w. to go** nous avons encore du chemin à faire; **to be a little/long w. off** être proche/loin
(**d**) *(direction)* direction *f*, sens *m*; **which w. ...?** dans quel sens...?; **this/that w.** par ici/là; *Fig* **to look the other w.** se boucher les yeux; *Fam* **round our w.** chez nous; *Fig* **it works both ways** cela marche dans les deux sens; **to split sth three ways** partager qch en trois
(**e**) *(street)* rue *f*
(**f**) *(respect)* égard *m*; **in a w.** d'une certaine manière; **in every w.** en tous points; **in no w.** en aucune façon
(**g**) *(state, condition)* **to be in a good w.** bien aller; **to be in a bad w.** être mal en point
2 *adv Fam* **w. back in the 1920s** dans les années vingt; **Lucy and I go w. back** Lucy et moi sommes des amis de longue date; **w. ahead** devant tout le monde; **w. down south** tout au sud; **your guess was w. out** tu étais loin de la vérité
wayfarer ['weɪfeərə(r)] *n* voyageur(euse) *m,f*
waylay [weɪ'leɪ] *(pt & pp* **waylaid** [weɪ'leɪd]*) vt (attack)* agresser; *Fig (stop)* arrêter au passage
way-out [weɪ'aʊt] *adj Fam (person)* excentrique; *(ideas, beliefs)* bizarre, curieux(euse)
wayside ['weɪsaɪd] *n* bord *m* de la route; *Fig* **to fall by the w.** se retrouver à la traîne
wayward ['weɪwəd] *adj* difficile
WBA [dʌbəljuːbiː'eɪ] *n (abbr* **World Boxing Association**) WBA, = association mondiale de boxe
WC [dʌbəljuː'siː] *n (abbr* **water closet**) WC *mpl*
we [wiː] *pron* nous; **we're Scottish** nous sommes écossais; **we haven't got it!** ce n'est pas nous qui l'avons!; **as we say in England** comme on dit en Angleterre; **we French are...** nous autres Français, nous sommes...
weak [wiːk] *adj (person, currency, character)* faible; *(heart)* fragile; *(argument, excuse)* peu convaincant(e); *(tea, coffee)* peu fort(e); **to grow w.** s'affaiblir; **to be w. at sth** *(school subject)* être faible en qch; *Fig* **to go w. at the knees** avoir les jambes en coton; *Fig* **w. spot** point *m* faible
weaken ['wiːkən] **1** *vt* affaiblir
2 *vi* s'affaiblir
weak-kneed [wiːk'niːd] *adj Fig* mou (molle)
weakling ['wiːklɪŋ] *n* mauviette *f*, faible *mf*
weakly ['wiːklɪ] *adv* faiblement
weakness ['wiːknɪs] *n* faiblesse *f*; **to have a w. for sb/ sth** avoir un faible pour qn/qch
weak-willed [wiːk'wɪld] *adj* sans volonté
weal [wiːl] *n (mark)* trace *f* de coup
wealth [welθ] *n* richesse *f*; *Fig* **a w. of sth** une abondance de qch
wealthy ['welθɪ] **1** *npl* **the w.** les riches
2 *adj* riche
wean [wiːn] *vt (baby)* sevrer; *Fig* **to w. sb off sth** *(bad habit)* faire passer qch à qn; *(alcohol, drugs)* sevrer qn de qch

weapon ['wepən] *n* arme *f*; **weapons of mass destruction** armes de destruction massive

wear [weə(r)] **1** *vt* (*pt* **wore** [wɔː(r)], *pp* **worn** [wɔːn]) (**a**) (*garment, glasses*) porter; **to w. black** porter du noir; **to w. one's hair up** avoir les cheveux relevés (**b**) (*erode*) user; **to w. a hole in sth** faire un trou dans qch (**c**) *Fam* (*believe, accept*) avaler **2** *vi* (*of clothing*) s'user; **to w. thin** s'user; *Fig* **that excuse is wearing thin** cette excuse ne prend plus; **my patience is wearing thin** je suis à bout de patience; **to w. smooth** devenir lisse; **to w. well** (*of clothing, person, film*) bien vieillir **3** *n* (**a**) (*clothing*) vêtements *mpl*; **evening w.** habits *mpl* de soirée; **children's w.** vêtements *mpl* pour enfants (**b**) (*use*) usure *f*; **to get a lot of w. out of sth** porter qch longtemps; *Fam* **to be the worse for w.** être bien éméché(e); **w. and tear** usure *f* naturelle
▸**wear away 1** *vt sep* user
  2 *vi* s'user
▸**wear down 1** *vt sep* user; *Fig* **to w. sb down** avoir qn à l'usure
  2 *vi* s'user
▸**wear off** *vi* (*of pain*) disparaître; (*of effect*) cesser; (*of anaesthetic*) cesser de faire effet; **the novelty soon wore off** l'attrait de la nouveauté n'a pas duré
▸**wear on** *vi* (*of time*) s'écouler
▸**wear out** *vt sep* user; **to w. sb out** épuiser qn; **to w. oneself out** s'épuiser

wearily ['wɪərɪlɪ] *adv* avec lassitude
weariness ['wɪərɪnɪs] *n* lassitude *f*
wearing ['weərɪŋ] *adj* lassant(e)
wearisome ['wɪərɪsəm] *adj* fatigant(e)
weary ['wɪərɪ] **1** *adj* las (lasse); **to be w. of sth/of doing sth** être las de qch/de faire qch; **to grow w. of sth** se lasser de qch **2** *vt* (*pt & pp* **wearied**) fatiguer, lasser **3** *vi* se lasser (**of** de)
weasel ['wiːzəl] *n* belette *f*
weather ['weðə(r)] **1** *n* (**a**) (*atmospheric conditions*) temps *m*; **what's the w. like?** quel temps fait-il?; **the w. is good/bad** il fait beau/mauvais; **in this w.** par un temps pareil; **w. permitting** si le temps le permet; **w. forecast** prévisions *fpl* météorologiques; **w. map** ou **chart** carte *f* météorologique (**b**) (*idioms*) **to make heavy w. of sth** faire tout un plat de qch; **to be under the w.** se sentir patraque **2** *vt* (**a**) (*rock*) éroder (**b**) (*problem, situation*) surmonter; *Fig* **to w. the storm** tenir le coup **3** *vi* (*of rock*) s'éroder
weatherbeaten ['weðəbiːtən] *adj* (*person, face*) hâlé(e); (*cliff, rock*) battu(e) par les vents
weathercock ['weðəkɒk] *n* girouette *f*
weathergirl ['weðəɡɜːl] *n* présentatrice *f* de la météo
weatherman ['weðəmæn] *n* présentateur *m* de la météo
weatherproof ['weðəpruːf] *adj* résistant(e) aux intempéries
weave [wiːv] **1** *vt* (*pt* **wove** [wəʊv] *or* **weaved**, *pp* **woven** ['wəʊvən]) tisser; *Fig* **a skilfully woven plot** une intrigue bien ficelée **2** *vi* tisser; *Fig* **to w. through the traffic** se faufiler parmi les voitures **3** *n* (*pattern*) tissage *m*
weaver ['wiːvə(r)] *n* tisserand(e) *m,f*
weaving ['wiːvɪŋ] *n* tissage *m*
web [web] *n* (**a**) (*of spider*) toile *f*; *Fig* (*of lies*) tissu *m*; (*of intrigue*) nid *m* (**b**) (*of duck, frog*) palmure *f* (**c**)

Comput **the W.** le Web; **W. designer** concepteur(trice) *m,f* de sites Web; **W. page** page *f* Web; **W. site** site *m* Web
webbed [webd] *adj* (*foot*) palmé(e)
webbing ['webɪŋ] *n* (*on chair, bed*) sangles *fpl*
webcam ['webkæm] *n* *Comput* webcam *f*, caméra *f* Internet
webcast ['webkɑːst] *n* *Comput* webcast *m*
web-footed [web'fʊtɪd] *adj* palmipède
weblog ['weblɒɡ] *n* *Comput* weblog *m*
webmaster ['webmɑːstə(r)] *n* Webmestre *m*, Webmaster *m*
website ['websaɪt] *n* site *m* Web
webzine ['webziːn] *n* *Comput* webzine *m*
Wed (*abbr* **Wednesday**) mercredi
wed [wed] (*pt & pp* **wedded**) **1** *vt* épouser; *Fig* **to be wedded to sth** être totalement dévoué(e) à qch **2** *vi* se marier
we'd [wiːd] = **we had, we would**
wedding ['wedɪŋ] *n* mariage *m*; **w. anniversary** anniversaire *m* de mariage; **w. breakfast** repas *m* de noces; **w. cake** gâteau *m* de mariage; **w. day** jour *m* du mariage; **w. dress** robe *f* de mariée; **w. night** nuit *f* de noces; **w. planner** organisateur(trice) *m,f* de mariages; **w. ring** alliance *f*
wedge [wedʒ] **1** *n* (*for door, wheel*) cale *f*; (*of cake*) part *f*; (*of cheese*) morceau *m*; *Fig* **it has driven a w. between them** ça les a éloignés l'un de l'autre **2** *vt* coincer; **to w. a door open** maintenir une porte ouverte avec une cale
wedlock ['wedlɒk] *n* *Law* mariage *m*; **to be born out of w.** naître de parents non mariés
Wednesday ['wenzdɪ] *n* mercredi *m*; *see also* **Saturday**
wee¹ [wiː] *adj* *Scot* (*small*) petit(e); **a w. bit** un petit peu
wee² *Br Fam* **1** *n* pipi *m*; **to do a w.** faire pipi **2** *vi* faire pipi
weed [wiːd] **1** *n* (**a**) (*plant*) mauvaise herbe *f* (**b**) *Pej* (*weak person*) (*physically*) gringalet *m*; (*in character*) mauviette *f* **2** *vt* désherber
▸**weed out** *vt sep* *Fig* éliminer
weedkiller ['wiːdkɪlə(r)] *n* désherbant *m*
weeds [wiːdz] *npl* (*mourning clothes*) vêtements *mpl* de deuil; **in widow's w.** en deuil
weedy ['wiːdɪ] *adj* *Pej* (*person*) malingre
week [wiːk] *n* semaine *f*; **next/last w.** la semaine prochaine/dernière; **once/twice a w.** une fois/deux fois par semaine; **in a w., in a w.'s time** dans huit jours; **within a w.** sous huitaine; **w. in w. out** chaque semaine; **tomorrow/Tuesday w.** demain/mardi en huit
weekday ['wiːkdeɪ] *n* jour *m* de semaine
weekend [wiːk'end] *n* week-end *m*; *Br* at *or Am* **on the w.** ce week-end; (*every weekend*) le week-end; **a long w.** un weekend prolongé; **w. break** week-end
weekly ['wiːklɪ] **1** *n* (*pl* **weeklies**) (*magazine*) hebdomadaire *m* **2** *adj* hebdomadaire **3** *adv* chaque semaine; **twice w.** deux fois par semaine
weeknight ['wiːknaɪt] *n* soir *m* de semaine
weep [wiːp] **1** *vt & vi* (*pt & pp* **wept** [wept]) pleurer; **to have a w.** pleurer un coup **2** *vt & vi* (*pt & pp* **wept** [wept]) pleurer
weeping ['wiːpɪŋ] **1** *n* pleurs *mpl* **2** *adj* qui pleure; **w. willow** saule *m* pleureur

weepy ['wiːpɪ] *Fam* **1** *n (pl* **weepies**) *(book, film)* mélo *m*
2 *adj (book, film)* mélo *m*; **to be w.** *(of person)* avoir envie de pleurer
wee(-)wee ['wiːwiː] *n Br Fam* pipi *m*; **to do a w.** faire pipi
weft [weft] *n* trame *f*
weigh [weɪ] **1** *vt* (**a**) *(measure)* peser; **to w.** oneself se peser (**b**) *(consider)* mesurer; **to w. sth against sth** mettre qch en balance avec qch (**c**) *Naut* **to w. anchor** lever l'ancre
2 *vi (of person, parcel)* peser; **how much do you w.?** combien tu pèses?; **it's weighing on my conscience** ça me pèse sur la conscience; **her experience weighed in her favour** son expérience a fait pencher la balance en sa faveur
▸**weigh down** *vt sep* lester; *Fig* **to be weighed down with sth** *(grief, responsibilities)* être accablé(e) de qch
▸**weigh in** *vi (of boxer, jockey)* être pesé(e); **to w. in at 75 kilos** peser 75 kilos
▸**weigh out** *vt sep* peser
▸**weigh up** *vt sep (consider)* mesurer; **to w. up the pros and cons** peser la pour et le contre
weighbridge ['weɪbrɪdʒ] *n* pont-bascule *m*
weight [weɪt] **1** *n* (**a**) *(of person, thing)* poids *m*; **they're the same w.** ils font le même poids; **to lose/put on w.** perdre/prendre du poids; **to have a w. problem** avoir un problème de poids; **weights and measures** poids et mesures; **w. training** entraînement *m* aux haltères (**b**) *(idioms)* **to throw one's w. about** affirmer son autorité; **to pull one's w.** faire sa part de travail; **that's a w. off my mind** ça m'ôte un poids; **to carry w.** avoir du poids
2 *vt Fig* **to be weighted in favour of sb/sth** favoriser/ne pas favoriser qn/qch
▸**weight down** *vt sep (to keep in place)* maintenir avec un poids; *(to make sink)* lester
weighting ['weɪtɪŋ] *n Fin* pondération *f*; **London w.** *(in salary)* indemnité *f* de résidence à Londres
weightless ['weɪtlɪs] *adj (astronaut)* en apesanteur; *(conditions)* d'apesanteur
weightlifter ['weɪtlɪftə(r)] *n* haltérophile *mf*
weightlifting ['weɪtlɪftɪŋ] *n* haltérophilie *f*
weighty ['weɪtɪ] *adj (heavy)* lourd(e); *Fig (serious, important)* grave
weir [wɪə(r)] *n* barrage *m*
weird [wɪəd] *adj* bizarre
weirdo ['wɪədəʊ] *(pl* **weirdos**) *n Fam* type *m* bizarre
welcome ['welkəm] **1** *adj (person, news, change)* bienvenu(e); **to make sb w.** faire un bon accueil à qn; **to feel w.** se sentir le (la) bienvenu(e); **you're always w.** elle est toujours la bienvenue; **w. home!** ça fait plaisir de te revoir!; **w. to Scotland!** bienvenue en Écosse!; **you're w!** *(acknowledgement of thanks)* je vous en prie!, *Suisse* service!; **you're w. to borrow it** n'hésite pas à l'emprunter si tu veux
2 *vt (person)* souhaiter la bienvenue à; *(news, change)* accueillir favorablement; *(opportunity)* profiter de
3 *n* accueil *m*; **to give sb a warm w.** faire un accueil chaleureux à qn
welcoming ['welkəmɪŋ] *adj* accueillant(e)
weld [weld] *vt* souder
welder ['weldə(r)] *n* soudeur(euse) *m,f*
welding ['weldɪŋ] *n* soudure *f*
welfare ['welfeə(r)] *n* (**a**) *(wellbeing)* bien-être *m*; *Br* **the W. State** l'État *m* providence; **w. work** assistance

f sociale (**b**) *Am (social security)* **to be on w.** recevoir l'aide sociale
well¹ [wel] *n (for water, oil)* puits *m*; *(for lift, stairwell)* cage *f*
▸**well up** *vi (of tears)* monter
well² *(comparative* **better** ['betə(r)], *superlative* **best** [best]) **1** *adj* bien; **to be w.** aller bien; **to get w.** se remettre; **it's just as w....** heureusement que...; **that's all very w., but...** tout ça, c'est très bien, mais...; **it's all very w. for you to say that** c'est facile pour toi de dire ça
2 *adv* (**a**) *(satisfactorily)* bien; **to speak w. of sb** dire du bien de qn; **I did as w. as I could** j'ai fait de mon mieux; **w. done!** bravo!; **you would do w. to keep quiet about it** vous feriez bien de vous taire à ce sujet; **he apologized, as w. he might** il s'est excusé, et c'était bien la moindre des choses; **very w.!** *(OK)* très bien! (**b**) *(for emphasis)* **to be w. able to do sth** être parfaitement capable de faire qch; **to be w. aware of sth** avoir parfaitement conscience de qch; **to leave w. alone** ne pas s'en mêler; *Fam* **to be w. in with sb** être dans les petits papiers de qn; **it is w. known that...** il est bien connu que...; **it's w. worth the effort** ça vaut vraiment la peine; **I can w. believe it** je n'ai aucun mal à le croire; **w. before/after** bien avant/après (**c**) **as w.** *(also)* aussi, également; **she has a flat in town as w. as a house in the country** elle a un appartement en ville ainsi qu'une maison à la campagne
3 *exclam (expressing surprise, enquiry)* eh bien!; *(expressing resignation, qualifying previous remark)* enfin; **w., who would have believed it!** eh bien, qui l'eût cru!; **w., who was it?** eh bien, qui était-ce?; **w., if you must!** enfin, si tu es vraiment obligé!; **he's nice, w. sometimes** il est gentil, enfin quelquefois
we'll [wiːl] = **we will, we shall**
well-adjusted [welə'dʒʌstɪd] *adj* équilibré(e)
well-advised [weləd'vaɪzd] *adj* sage; **you'd be w. to stay indoors today** tu ferais bien de ne pas sortir aujourd'hui
well-appointed [welə'pɔɪntɪd] *adj* bien équipé(e)
well-argued [wel'ɑːgjuːd] *adj* bien argumenté(e)
well-balanced [wel'bælənst] *adj* équilibré(e)
well-behaved [welbɪ'heɪvd] *adj* sage
wellbeing ['welbiːŋ] *n* bien-être *m*
well-built [wel'bɪlt] *adj (building)* solide; *(person)* bien bâti(e)
well-chosen [wel'tʃəʊzən] *adj* bien choisi(e)
well-disposed [weldɪs'pəʊzd] *adj* **to be w. towards sb** être bien disposé(e) envers qn; **to be w. towards sth** être favorable à qch
well-dressed [wel'drest] *adj* bien habillé(e)
well-earned [wel'ɜːnd] *adj* bien mérité(e)
well-fed [wel'fed] *adj* bien nourri(e)
well-founded [wel'faʊndɪd] *adj* fondé(e)
well-heeled [wel'hiːld] *adj Fam* cossu(e)
well-informed [welɪn'fɔːmd] *adj* bien informé(e)
wellington ['welɪŋtən] *n Br* **wellingtons, w. boots** bottes *fpl* en caoutchouc
well-intentioned [welɪn'tenʃənd] *adj* bien intentionné(e)
well-kept [wel'kept] *adj (garden)* bien entretenu(e); *(secret)* bien gardé(e)
well-known [wel'nəʊn] *adj* connu(e)
well-loved [wel'lʌvd] *adj* très aimé(e)
well-made [wel'meɪd] *adj* bien fait(e)
well-meaning [wel'miːnɪŋ] *adj* bien intentionné(e)

well-nigh ['welnaɪ] *adv* pratiquement
well-off [wel'ɒf] *adj Br (wealthy)* riche; *Fig* **you don't know when you're w.** tu ne connais pas ton bonheur
well-paid [wel'peɪd] *adj* bien payé(e)
well-read [wel'red] *adj* cultivé(e)
well-spoken [wel'spəʊkən] *adj* qui s'exprime bien
well-timed [wel'taɪmd] *adj* opportun(e)
well-to-do [weltə'duː] *adj* aisé(e)
wellwisher ['welwɪʃə(r)] *n* sympathisant(e) *m,f*
well-worn [wel'wɔːn] *adj (garment)* très usé(e); *(argument)* éculé(e)
well-written [wel'rɪtən] *adj* bien écrit(e)
Welsh [welʃ] **1** *npl (people)* **the W.** les Gallois *mpl*
  2 *n (language)* gallois *m*
  3 *adj* gallois(e); **the W. Assembly** l'Assemblée *f* galloise *ou* du pays de Galles; **W. dresser** vaisselier *m*

Welsh Assembly

L'assemblée nationale du pays de Galles fut établie dans le cadre de la décentralisation engagée par le gouvernement travailliste et fut inaugurée à Cardiff en mai 1999 *(voir encadré à* **Devolution***)*. Les soixante membres de l'assemblée forment le "Welsh Cabinet" et siègent sous la houlette du "First Secretary" qui représente les intérêts gallois au parlement de Westminster. L'assemblée nationale du pays de Galles, la première depuis six siècles, a toutefois moins de pouvoirs que le parlement écossais *(voir encadré à* **Scottish Parliament***)* mis en place en même temps.

Welshman ['welʃmən] *n* Gallois *m*
Welshwoman ['welʃwʊmən] *n* Galloise *f*
welt [welt] *n* trace *f* de coup
welter ['weltə(r)] *n (of forms, details)* masse *f*; *(of ideas, activities)* multitude *f*
welterweight ['weltəweɪt] *n Sport* poids *m* welter
wench [wentʃ] *n Old-fashioned or Hum* jeune fille *f*, jeune femme *f*
wend [wend] *vt Lit* **to w. one's way homewards** prendre le chemin du retour
went [went] *pt of* **go**
wept [wept] *pt & pp of* **weep**
we're [wɪə(r)] = **we are**
were [wɜː(r)] *pt of* **be**
weren't [wɜːnt] = **were not**
werewolf ['wɪəwʊlf] *(pl* **werewolves** ['wɪəwʊlvz]*) n* loup-garou *m*
west [west] **1** *n* ouest *m*; **to the w. (of)** à l'ouest (de); **the W.** l'Occident *m*, l'Ouest *m*
  2 *adj (coast, side)* ouest *inv*; *(wind)* d'ouest; **W. Africa** l'Afrique *f* de l'Ouest; **the W. Bank** la Cisjordanie; **the W. Country** le sud-ouest de l'Angleterre; **the W. End** = quartier chic de Londres et Glasgow où l'on trouve théâtres et restaurants; *Formerly* **W. Germany** l'Allemagne *f* de l'Ouest; **W. Indian** antillais(e); *(person)* Antillais(e) *m,f*; **the W. Indies** les Antilles *fpl*; **the W. Side** = les quartiers ouest de New York; **W. Virginia** la Virginie occidentale
  3 *adv* à l'ouest; *(travel)* vers l'ouest; *Fam Fig* **to go w.** *(of TV, car)* rendre l'âme
westbound ['westbaʊnd] *adj (train, traffic)* en direction de l'ouest
westerly ['westəlɪ] **1** *n (pl* **westerlies***) (wind)* vent *m* d'ouest
  2 *adj (point)* à l'ouest; *(wind)* d'ouest, qui vient de l'ouest; **in a w. direction** vers l'ouest

western ['westən] **1** *n (film)* western *m*; *(novel)* roman-western *m*
  2 *adj (region)* de l'ouest; *(in politics, sociology)* occidental(e); **w. France** l'ouest *m* de la France; **W. Europe** l'Europe *f* de l'Ouest; **the W. Isles** *(of Scotland)* les Hébrides *fpl*; **W. Samoa** les Samoa *fpl* occidentales; **W. Samoan** samoan(e); *(person)* Samoan(e) *m,f*
westernized ['westənaɪzd] *adj* occidentalisé(e)
Westminster ['westmɪnstə(r)] *n* Westminster *m*

Westminster

C'est dans ce quartier que se trouvent le Parlement et le palais de Buckingham. Le nom de "Westminster" est également employé pour désigner le Parlement lui-même.

westward ['westwəd] **1** *adj (in the west)* à l'ouest, dans l'ouest
  2 *adv* = **westwards**
westwards ['westwədz] *adv (face, point)* à l'ouest; *(go, travel)* vers l'ouest
wet [wet] **1** *adj (a) (not dry)* mouillé(e); *(weather)* pluvieux(euse); **to get w.** se mouiller; **the ink/paint was still w.** l'encre/la peinture n'était pas sèche; *Fam Fig* **to be still w. behind the ears** manquer d'expérience; *Fig* **w. blanket** rabat-joie *mf*; **w. dream** pollution *f* nocturne; **w. paint** *(sign)* peinture fraîche; **w. suit** combinaison *f* de plongée **(b)** *Br Fam (feeble)* minable
  2 *vt (pt & pp* **wet** *or* wetted*)* mouiller; **to w. the bed** faire pipi au lit; **to w. oneself** mouiller sa culotte
  3 *n* **(a)** *(dampness)* humidité *f*; *(rain)* pluie *f* **(b)** *Br Pol* modéré(e) *m,f*
WEU [dʌbəljuːiːˈuː] *n (abbr* **Western European Union***)* UEO *f*
we've [wiːv] = **we have**
whack [wæk] *Fam* **1** *n* **(a)** *(blow)* grand coup *m*; **to give sb/sth a w.** donner un grand coup à qn/qch **(b)** *(share)* part *f*
  2 *vt* **(a)** *(hit)* donner un grand coup à; **to w. sb on** *or* **over the head** donner un grand coup sur la tête de qn **(b)** *Am very Fam (murder)* liquider
whacked [wækt] *adj Fam (exhausted)* nase, vanné(e)
whacking ['wækɪŋ] *adv Fam* **a w. great increase/fine** une vache d'augmentation/d'amende
whale [weɪl] *n* baleine *f*; *Fam* **to have a w. of a time** s'éclater
whaler ['weɪlə(r)] *n* baleinier *m*
whaling ['weɪlɪŋ] *n* pêche *f ou* chasse *f* à la baleine
wharf [wɔːf] *(pl* **wharves** [wɔːvz]*) n* quai *m*
what [wɒt] **1** *pron* **(a)** *(in questions) (subject)* qu'est-ce qui; *(object)* qu'est-ce que, que; *(after preposition)* quoi; **w.'s happening?** qu'est-ce qui se passe?; **w. do you want?** qu'est-ce que tu veux?, que veux-tu?; **w. are you thinking about?** à quoi penses-tu?; **w.'s that?** qu'est-ce que c'est?; **w.'s it to you?** qu'est-ce que ça peut vous faire?; **w. for?** *(for what purpose?)* pour quoi faire?; *(why)* pourquoi?; **w.'s a modem for?** à quoi ça sert, un modem?; **w. did he do that for?** pourquoi est-ce qu'il a fait ça?; **w.'s French for "dog?"** comment dit-on "dog" en français?; **w.'s he like?** comment est-il?; **w. about the money I lent you?** et l'argent que je vous ai prêté?; **w. about a game of tennis?** et si on faisait une partie de tennis?; **w. about me?** et moi?; **if that doesn't work, w. then?** si ça ne marche pas, qu'est-ce qui reste?; *Fam* **w. of it?** et alors?; *Fam* **are you coming or w.?** tu viens ou

quoi? (**b**) *(in relative constructions) (subject)* ce qui; *(object)* ce que; **I don't know w. has happened** je ne sais pas ce qui s'est passé; **I can't remember w. you told me** je ne me souviens plus de ce que tu m'as dit; **w. is surprising is that...** ce qu'il y a de surprenant, c'est que...; **w. I like is...** ce que j'aime, c'est...; *Fam* **he knows w.'s w.** il sait ce qu'il en est; *Fam* **to give sb w.** for passer un savon à qn

2 *adj* (**a**) *(in questions)* quel (quelle); *(plural)* quels (quelles); **w. time is it?** quelle heure est-il?; **tell me w. time it is** dis-moi l'heure qu'il est; **show me w. books you want** montre-moi quels livres tu veux (**b**) *(in relative constructions)* **I'll give you w. money I have** je vais vous donner l'argent que j'ai; **he took w. little food was left** il a pris le peu de nourriture qui restait (**c**) *(in exclamations)* **w. an idea!** quelle idée!; **w. a fool he is!** qu'il est bête!; **w. a lot of people!** quel monde!

3 *exclam* quoi?; **w. next!** et quoi encore!

what-d'ye-call-her ['wɒtjəkɔːlə(r)] *n Fam (person)* Machine *f*

what-d'ye-call-him ['wɒtjəkɔːlɪm] *n Fam (person)* Machin *m*

what-d'ye-call-it ['wɒtjəkɔːlɪt] *n Fam (thing)* machin *m*, truc *m*

whatever [wɒt'evə(r)] **1** *pron* (**a**) *(no matter what)* quoi que + *subjunctive*; **w. it is, w. it may be** quoi que ce soit; **w. happens** quoi qu'il arrive (**b**) *(anything)* ce que; **do w. you like** fais ce que tu veux; **give him w. he wants** donne-lui tout ce qu'il veut; **w. you say** comme tu voudras (**c**) *(in questions)* **w. does that mean?** qu'est-ce que ça peut bien vouloir dire?

2 *adj* (**a**) *(no matter what)* **take w. food you want** prends toute la nourriture que tu veux; **pay w. price they ask** donne-leur le prix qu'ils en demandent, quel qu'il soit (**b**) *(emphatic)* **for no reason w.** sans aucune raison; **nothing w.** absolument rien

what's-her-name ['wɒtsəneɪm], **what's-his-name** ['wɒtsɪzneɪm], **what's-its-name** ['wɒtsɪtsneɪm] = **what-d'ye-call-her/him/it**

whatsit ['wɒtsɪt] *n Fam* machin *m*, truc *m*

whatsoever [wɒtsəʊ'evə(r)] *adj* **for no reason w.** sans aucune raison; **none w.** aucun(e); **nothing w.** absolument rien

wheat [wiːt] *n* blé *m*; **w. germ** germe *m* de blé

wheaten ['wiːtən] *adj (loaf, roll)* de blé *ou* froment

wheatfield ['wiːtfiːld] *n* champ *m* de blé

wheedle ['wiːdəl] *vt* **to w. sth out of sb** soutirer qch à qn par des cajoleries; **to w. sb into doing sth** amadouer qn pour qu'il/elle fasse qch

wheel [wiːl] **1** *n* (**a**) *(on car, bike, pram)* roue *f*; *(on trolley, suitcase)* roulette *f* (**b**) *(steering wheel)* volant *m*; **to be at the w.** être au volant

2 *vt (push)* pousser

3 *vi (turn)* **to w. (about** *or* **around)** *(of person)* se retourner brusquement; *(of plane)* tourner; *(of bird)* tournoyer

wheelbarrow ['wiːlbærəʊ] *n* brouette *f*

wheelbase ['wiːlbeɪs] *n* empattement *m*

wheelchair ['wiːltʃeə(r)] *n* fauteuil *m* roulant

-wheeled [wiːld] *suff* **two/three/four-w.** à deux/trois/quatre roues

wheelie ['wiːlɪ] *n Fam* **to do a w.** faire une roue arrière

wheelie bin ['wiːlɪ'bɪn] *n Br* poubelle *f (avec des roues)*

wheeling and dealing ['wiːlɪŋəndiːlɪŋ] *n* tractations *fpl*

wheeze [wiːz] **1** *n* (**a**) *(noise)* respiration *f* sifflante (**b**) *Fam (trick)* astuce *f*, combine *f*

2 *vi (breathe heavily)* respirer péniblement

whelk [welk] *n* bulot *m*

whelp [welp] *n* petit *m*

when [wen] **1** *adv (in questions)* quand; **w. will you come?** quand viendras-tu?; **tell me w. it happened** dis-moi quand cela s'est produit; *Fam* **say w.!** *(when serving food, drink)* tu me dis stop!

2 *conj* (**a**) *(with time)* quand, lorsque; **w. I came into the room** quand *ou* lorsque je suis entré dans la pièce; **tell me w. you've finished** dis-moi quand tu auras terminé; **what's the good of talking w. you never listen?** à quoi sert de parler puisque tu n'écoutes jamais? (**b**) *(whereas)* alors que

whence [wens] *adv Lit* d'où

whenever [wen'evə(r)] **1** *conj* (**a**) *(every time that)* chaque fois que; **I go w. I can** j'y vais aussi souvent que je peux (**b**) *(no matter when)* n'importe quand; **come w. you like** viens quand tu veux

2 *adv* (**a**) *(referring to unspecified time)* n'importe quand; **Sunday, Monday or w.** dimanche, lundi ou n'importe quel autre jour (**b**) *(in questions)* **w. did you do that?** quand est-ce que tu as fait ça?

where [weə(r)] **1** *adv (in questions)* où; **w. are you going?** où vas-tu?; **w. does he come from?** d'où vient-il?; **tell me w. she is** dis-moi où elle est; **w. would we be if...?** que serions-nous devenus si...?

2 *conj* où; **I'll stay w. I am** je reste (là) où je suis; **that's w. he lives** c'est là qu'il habite; **that is w. you are mistaken** c'est là que vous vous trompez; **they went to Paris, w. they stayed a week** ils sont allés à Paris, où ils ont séjourné une semaine

whereabouts 1 *npl* ['weərəbaʊts] **nobody knows her w., her w. are unknown** personne ne sait où elle est

2 *adv* [weərə'baʊts] *(where)* où

whereas [weə'ræz] *conj* alors que, tandis que

whereby [weə'baɪ] *adv Formal* par lequel (laquelle)

whereupon [weərə'pɒn] *conj Lit* sur quoi

wherever [weə'revə(r)] **1** *conj* (**a**) *(everywhere that)* où que; **I see him w. I go** où que j'aille, je le vois; **w. possible** partout où cela est possible (**b**) *(no matter where)* n'importe où; **we'll go w. you want** nous irons où tu voudras

2 *adv* (**a**) *(referring to unknown or unspecified place)* **at home, in the office or w.** chez soi, au bureau ou n'importe où; **it's in Nairn, w. that is** c'est à Nairn, mais je ne sais pas où se trouve Nairn (**b**) *(in questions)* **w. can he be?** où peut-il bien être?

wherewithal ['weəwɪðɔːl] *n* **to have the w. (to do sth)** avoir les moyens (de faire qch)

whet [wet] *(pt & pp* **whetted**) *vt (tool, blade, appetite)* aiguiser

whether ['weðə(r)] *conj* (**a**) *(with indirect questions)* si; **I don't know w. it's true** je ne sais pas si c'est vrai (**b**) *(conditional)* **w. she comes or not we shall leave** qu'elle vienne ou non, nous partirons

whew [hjuː] *exclam (of relief)* ouf!; *(of fatigue)* pff!; *(of astonishment)* dis donc!

whey [weɪ] *n* petit-lait *m*

which [wɪtʃ] **1** *pron* (**a**) *(in questions)* lequel (laquelle) *m,f*; *(plural)* lesquels (lesquelles) *mpl,fpl*; **w. (one) is better?** lequel est le meilleur?; **w. of you is going?** qui d'entre vous y va?; **I can never remember w. is w.** je ne me rappelle jamais la différence (**b**) *(relative) (subject)* qui; *(object)* que; **the house w. is for**

sale la maison qui est à vendre; **the film w. I saw last week** le film que j'ai vu la semaine dernière (**c**) *(referring back to whole clause) (subject)* ce qui; *(object)* ce que; **he's getting married, w. surprises me** il va se marier, ce qui m'étonne; **she was back in London, w. I didn't know** elle était de retour à Londres, ce que je ne savais pas (**d**) *(with prepositions)* **behind/in front of w.** derrière/devant lequel (laquelle); **beside/above w.** à côté/au-dessus duquel (de laquelle); **the countries w. we are going to** les pays où nous allons; **the town w. we live in** la ville où nous habitons; **after w. he went out** après quoi, il est sorti
2 *adj* (**a**) *(in questions)* quel (quelle); *(plural)* quels (quelles); **w. colour do you like best?** quelle couleur préférez-vous?; **w. way do we go?** de quel côté allons-nous?; **w. one?** lequel (laquelle)?; **w. ones?** lesquels (lesquelles)? (**b**) *(in relative constructions)* **I was there for a week, during w. time...** j'y suis resté une semaine, période pendant laquelle...; **she came at noon, by w. time I had left** elle est arrivée à midi, heure à laquelle j'étais déjà parti

whichever [wɪtʃ'evə(r)] **1** *pron* (**a**) *(no matter which)* quel (quelle) que soit celui (celle) qui; **w. you choose, I'm sure she'll like it** quel que soit celui que tu choisisses, je suis sûr que ça lui plaira (**b**) *(any)* **take w. you want** prends celui (celle) que tu voudras (**c**) *(according to which)* **come on Saturday or Sunday, w. suits you** viens samedi ou dimanche, suivant ce qui t'arrange
2 *adj (no matter which)* **take w. book you like best** choisis le livre que tu préfères

whiff [wɪf] *n* odeur *f*; **to catch a w. of sth** sentir qch; *Fig* **a w. of scandal** un parfum de scandale

while [waɪl] **1** *n* (**a**) *(time)* **a w.** un moment; **after/in a w.** après/dans un moment; **a short** *or* **little w. ago** il y a un petit moment; **a good w., quite a w.** un bon moment; **a long w.** longtemps; **once in a w.** de temps en temps (**b**) **it's not worth my w.** ça n'en vaut pas la peine; **it's not worth my w. going** ça ne vaut pas la peine que j'y aille; **I'll make it worth your w.** vous serez récompensé de votre peine
2 *conj* (**a**) *(during the time that)* pendant que; **w. reading I fell asleep** je me suis endormi(e) en lisant (**b**) *(as long as)* tant que; **it won't happen w. I'm in charge!** ça ne se produira pas tant que ce sera moi le responsable! (**c**) *(although)* bien que + *subjunctive*; **w. I admit it's difficult,...** bien que j'admette que ce soit difficile... (**d**) *(whereas)* alors que; **one wore white, w. the other was in black** l'un portait du blanc, alors que l'autre était en noir

▸ **while away** *vt sep* **to w. away the time** passer le temps

whilst [waɪlst] *conj Br* = **while**

whim [wɪm] *n* lubie *f*, fantaisie *f*; **to do sth on a w.** faire qch sur un coup de tête

whimper ['wɪmpə(r)] **1** *n* gémissement *m*, geignement *m*; *Fig* **without a w.** sans broncher
2 *vi* gémir, geindre

whimsical ['wɪmzɪkəl] *adj (person, behaviour)* fantasque; *(remark, story)* saugrenu(e)

whine [waɪn] **1** *n (of person, animal)* gémissement *m*; *(of machine)* grincement *m*
2 *vi also Fig* gémir (**about** à propos de)

whinge [wɪndʒ] *vi Br & Austr Fam* pleurnicher

whinger ['wɪndʒə(r)] *n Br & Austr Fam* râleur(euse) *m,f*

whinny ['wɪnɪ] **1** *n (pl* **whinnies**) hennissement *m*
2 *vi (pt & pp* **whinnied**) hennir

whip [wɪp] **1** *n* (**a**) *(for punishment)* fouet *m* (**b**) *Pol* chef *m* de file *(chargé de la discipline de son parti)*
2 *vt (pt & pp* **whipped**) (**a**) *(beat with whip)* fouetter; **whipped cream** crème *f* fouettée; *Fig* **she whipped the crowd into a frenzy** son discours rendit la foule frénétique (**b**) *Fam (defeat)* battre à plates coutures (**c**) *Fam (steal)* faucher

▸ **whip off** *vt sep Fam (clothes)* ôter rapidement

▸ **whip out** *vt sep Fam* sortir soudainement

▸ **whip round** *vi Fam (turn quickly)* se retourner brusquement

▸ **whip up** *vt sep* (**a**) *(support, enthusiasm)* susciter; *(audience)* galvaniser (**b**) *(prepare quickly) (dish, meal)* préparer vite fait

whiplash ['wɪplæʃ] *n* lésion *f* des cervicales

whippersnapper ['wɪpəsnæpə(r)] *n Fam* garnement *m*

whippet ['wɪpɪt] *n* whippet *m*

whipround ['wɪpraʊnd] *n Br Fam* **to have a w. (for sb)** organiser une collecte (pour qn)

whirl [wɜːl] **1** *n also Fig* tourbillon *m*; **the social w.** le tourbillon de la vie mondaine; **my head's in a w.** j'ai la tête qui tourne; *Fam* **let's give it a w.** on va tenter le coup
2 *vt* **to w. sb/sth around** faire tournoyer qn/qch
3 *vi* tourbillonner; **my head's whirling** j'ai la tête qui tourne

▸ **whirl along** *vi (of car, train)* filer à toute vitesse

▸ **whirl round** *vi* se retourner brusquement

whirlpool ['wɜːlpuːl] *n* tourbillon *m*; **w. bath** bain *m* à remous

whirlwind ['wɜːlwɪnd] *n* tourbillon *m*; **w. romance** passion *f* enivrante; **w. tour** visite *f* éclair

whirr [wɜː(r)] **1** *n* ronflement *m*
2 *vi* ronfler

whisk [wɪsk] **1** *n* batteur *m*, fouet *m*
2 *vt* (**a**) *(eggs)* battre (**b**) *(move quickly)* **to w. sb into hospital** transporter qn d'urgence à l'hôpital
3 *vi (move quickly)* **she whisked past me** elle est passée devant moi comme un éclair

▸ **whisk away, whisk off** *vt sep (person)* emmener rapidement; *(object)* enlever rapidement

whisker ['wɪskə(r)] *n* **whiskers** *(of cat, mouse)* moustaches *fpl*; *(of man)* favoris *mpl*; *Fam* **to win by a w.** gagner de justesse

whisky, *Am & Ir* **whiskey** ['wɪskɪ] *n* whisky *m*

whisper ['wɪspə(r)] **1** *n* chuchotement *m*; **to speak in a w.** chuchoter
2 *vt* chuchoter; **to w. sth to sb** chuchoter qch à qn; **it's being whispered that...** le bruit court que...
3 *vi* chuchoter; **to w. to sb** chuchoter à l'oreille de qn

whist [wɪst] *n* whist *m*

whistle ['wɪsəl] **1** *n* (**a**) *(noise)* sifflement *m* (**b**) *(musical instrument)* flageolet *m*; *(of referee, policeman)* sifflet *m*
2 *vt (tune)* siffler
3 *vi* siffler; *Fam* **he can w. for his money** s'il compte récupérer son argent, il peut toujours courir

whistleblower ['wɪsəlbləʊə(r)] *n* dénonciateur(trice) *m,f*, = personne qui tire la sonnette d'alarme

whistle-stop tour ['wɪsəlstɒp'tʊə(r)] *n* tournée *f* rapide

Whit [wɪt] *n* Pentecôte *f*; **W. Sunday** la Pentecôte

whit [wɪt] *n* it doesn't matter a w. ça n'a aucune importance; it won't make a w. of difference ça ne changera absolument rien

white [waɪt] **1** *n* (**a**) *(colour, of egg, eye)* blanc *m*; w. doesn't suit her le blanc ne lui va pas (**b**) *(person)* Blanc (Blanche) *m,f*
2 *adj* blanc (blanche); a w. man un Blanc; a w. woman une Blanche; to turn *or* go w. *(person)* devenir blême; *(object, hair)* blanchir; w. with fear vert(e) de peur; w. as a ghost/sheet pâle comme la mort/un linge; *Biol* w. blood cell globule *m* blanc; w. chocolate chocolat *m* blanc; w. coffee café *m* au lait; *Fig* w. elephant = chose coûteuse et peu rentable; w. fish poisson *m* à chair blanche; w. flag drapeau *m* blanc; w. flour farine *f* blanche; w. goods produits *mpl* blancs; the W. House la Maison-Blanche; w. lie pieux mensonge *m*; w. meat viande *f* blanche; *Am* W. Out® correcteur *m* liquide; *Pol* w. paper livre *m* blanc; w. sauce sauce *f* blanche; w. spirit white-spirit *m*; w. stick canne *f* blanche; w. supremacist partisan(e) *m,f* de la suprématie blanche; w. tie *(formal dress)* tenue *f* de soirée; *Am Pej* w. trash pauvres blancs *mpl*; w. wedding mariage *m* en blanc

whitebait ['waɪtbeɪt] *n* friture *f*

white-collar worker ['waɪt'kɒlə'wɜːkə(r)] *n* col *m* blanc

white-haired ['waɪt'heəd] *adj* aux cheveux blancs

Whitehall ['waɪthɔːl] *n* = rue de Londres où se trouvent les ministères

Whitehall

De nombreux services gouvernementaux ont leurs bureaux dans cette rue londonienne dont le nom est souvent employé pour désigner le gouvernement lui-même.

white-hot ['waɪt'hɒt] *adj* chauffé(e) à blanc
whiteness ['waɪtnɪs] *n* blancheur *f*
whitewash ['waɪtwɒʃ] **1** *n (paint)* badigeon *m* à la chaux; *Fig (cover-up)* blanchiment *m*
2 *vt (paint)* badigeonner à la chaux; *Fig (cover up)* blanchir
whitewater rafting ['waɪtwɔːtə'rɑːftɪŋ] *n* descente *f* en eau vive, rafting *m*
whither ['wɪðə(r)] *adv Lit* w. Britain/education? où va la Grande-Bretagne/l'enseignement?
whiting ['waɪtɪŋ] *n (fish)* merlan *m*
whitish ['waɪtɪʃ] *adj* blanchâtre
Whitsun ['wɪtsən] *n* Pentecôte *f*
whittle ['wɪtəl] *vt* tailler (au couteau); *Fig* to w. sth down réduire qch
► **whittle away** *vt sep Fig* to w. sth away réduire qch à presque rien
whizz [wɪz] **1** *n Fam (expert)* crack *m*; w. kid jeune prodige *m*
2 *vi (of bullet)* siffler; *(of person, car)* passer à toute vitesse; to w. through a book/meal lire un livre/manger à toute vitesse
WHO [dʌbəljuːeɪtʃ'əʊ] *n (abbr* World Health Organization) OMS *f*
who [huː] *pron* (**a**) *(in questions)* qui; w. is it? qui est-ce?; w. with? avec qui?; do you know w. she is? sais-tu qui elle est?; w.'s speaking? *(on phone)* qui est à l'appareil?; w. did you say was there? qui était là, déjà?; w. does he think he is? pour qui se prend-il? (**b**) *(relative)* qui; the people w. came yesterday les gens qui sont venus hier; those w. have already paid

can leave ceux qui ont déjà payé peuvent s'en aller; Louise's father, w. is a doctor, was there le père de Louise, qui est médecin, était là

whodun(n)it [huː'dʌnɪt] *n Fam* polar *m*
whoever [huː'evə(r)] *pron* (**a**) *(no matter who)* qui que + *subjunctive*; w. you are qui que vous soyez; w. wrote that letter la personne qui a écrit cette lettre; *Fam* ask Simon *or* Chris *or* w. demande à Simon ou à Chris ou à n'importe qui d'autre (**b**) *(anyone that)* celui (celle) qui; w. finds it may keep it celui qui le trouvera pourra le garder (**c**) *(in questions)* w. can that be? qui cela peut-il être?
whole [həʊl] **1** *adj* (**a**) *(entire, intact)* entier(ère); the w. truth toute la vérité; the w. world le monde entier; a w. week toute une semaine, une semaine entière; to swallow sth w. avaler qch; w. milk lait *m* entier (**b**) *Fam (for emphasis)* a w. lot of tout un tas de; the w. lot of you vous tous
2 *n* totalité *f*, ensemble *m*; the w. of the village/the money tout le village/l'argent; as a w. dans sa totalité; on the w. dans l'ensemble
wholefood ['həʊlfuːd] *n Br* aliments *mpl* complets; w. restaurant restaurant *m* bio
wholehearted [həʊl'hɑːtɪd] *adj* sans réserve, total(e)
wholemeal ['həʊlmiːl] *adj Br* w. bread pain *m* complet; w. flour farine *f* complète
wholesale ['həʊlseɪl] **1** *adj* de gros; *Fig (large-scale)* à grande échelle
2 *adv* en gros; *Fig (on a large scale)* à grande échelle
3 *n (vente f* en) gros *m*
wholesaler ['həʊlseɪlə(r)] *n* grossiste *mf*
wholesome ['həʊlsəm] *adj (food, entertainment)* sain(e); *(air, climate)* salubre; *(person)* comme il faut
wholewheat ['həʊlwiːt] *esp Am* = wholemeal
wholly ['həʊllɪ] *adv* entièrement
whom [huːm] *pron Formal* (**a**) *(in questions)* qui; w. did you see? qui avez-vous vu?; for/to/of w.? pour/à/de qui? (**b**) *(relative)* que; the woman w. you saw la femme que vous avez vue; the man w. you gave the money to l'homme à qui vous avez donné l'argent; the person of w. we were speaking la personne dont nous parlions; the men, both of w. were quite young,... les hommes, tous deux assez jeunes...
whoop [wuːp] **1** *n* cri *m* de joie
2 *vi* crier de joie
whoopee 1 *n* ['wʊpiː] *Fam* to make w. *(have fun)* faire la bombe; *(have sex)* faire crac-crac
2 *exclam* [wʊ'piː] youpi!
whooping cough ['huːpɪŋkɒf] *n* coqueluche *f*
whoops [wuːps] *exclam* houp-là!
whopper ['wɒpə(r)] *n Fam* (**a**) *(huge thing)* truc *m* énorme (**b**) *(lie)* gros bobard *m*
whopping ['wɒpɪŋ] *adj Fam* w. (great) énorme
whore [hɔː(r)] *n very Fam* putain *f*
whorehouse ['hɔːhaʊs] *n* bordel *m*
whose [huːz] **1** *possessive pron (in questions)* à qui; w. are these gloves? à qui sont ces gants?; w. is this? à qui est-ce?; tell me w. they are dis-moi à qui ils sont
2 *possessive adj* (**a**) *(in questions)* à qui; w. gloves are these? à qui sont ces gants?; w. daughter are you? de qui es-tu la fille? (**b**) *(relative)* dont; the pupil w. work I showed you l'élève dont je t'ai montré le travail; the man to w. wife I gave the money l'homme à la femme de qui j'ai donné l'argent

why [waɪ] **1** adv (**a**) (in questions) pourquoi; **w. didn't you say so?** pourquoi ne l'as-tu pas dit?; **w. get angry?** pourquoi se mettre en colère?; **w. not?** pourquoi pas? (**b**) (in suggestions) **w. don't you phone him?** pourquoi ne lui téléphones-tu pas?; **w. don't I come with you?** pourquoi est-ce que je ne viendrais pas avec toi?; **w. not sell the car?** pourquoi ne pas vendre la voiture?
2 conj pourquoi; **I'll tell you w. I don't like her** je vais vous dire pourquoi je ne l'aime pas; **that's w....** voilà pourquoi...; **the reason w....** la raison pour laquelle...
3 n **the whys and wherefores (of sth)** le pourquoi et le comment (de qch)
4 exclam **w., it's David!** mais voilà David!

WI [dʌblju:ˈaɪ] n Br (abbr **Women's Institute**) = association de femmes en milieu rural qui organise diverses activités

wick [wɪk] n (**a**) (of lamp, candle) mèche f (**b**) Br Fam **to get on sb's w.** taper sur les nerfs à qn
wicked [ˈwɪkɪd] adj (**a**) (evil) méchant(e); Fig (dreadful) affreux(euse) (**b**) Fam (excellent) génial(e)
wickedness [ˈwɪkɪdnɪs] n méchanceté f
wicker [ˈwɪkə(r)] n osier m
wickerwork [ˈwɪkəwɜːk] n vannerie f
wicket [ˈwɪkɪt] n (in cricket) guichet m
wicketkeeper [ˈwɪkɪtkiːpə(r)] n (in cricket) gardien m de guichet
wide [waɪd] **1** adj (**a**) (broad) large; **to be 100 metres w.** faire 100 mètres de large; **in the whole w. world** dans le monde entier; Br Fam Pej **w. boy** escroc m (**b**) (extensive) vaste
2 adv **w. open** (eyes, mouth, door) grand ouvert(e); **to be w. open to criticism** prêter le flanc à la critique; **w. apart** très espacé(e); (legs) très écarté(e); **w. awake** complètement réveillé(e); **the shot went w.** la balle est passée à côté; Fig **w. of the mark** loin de la vérité
wide-angle [ˈwaɪdæŋɡəl] adj **grand angle** inv
wide-eyed [ˈwaɪdaɪd] adj aux yeux écarquillés
widely [ˈwaɪdlɪ] adv (**a**) (extensively) largement; **it is w. believed that...** beaucoup de gens pensent que...; **w. known** connu(e) de tout le monde (**b**) (at a distance) **w. spaced** très espacé(e)
widen [ˈwaɪdən] **1** vt agrandir; (garment) élargir; Fig (influence, scope) étendre; **to w. one's horizons** élargir son horizon
2 vi s'élargir; (of gap, eyes) s'agrandir
widescreen [ˈwaɪdskriːn] n Cin & TV grand écran m; **in w.** en grand écran
widespread [ˈwaɪdspred] adj répandu(e)
widow [ˈwɪdəʊ] **1** n veuve f; **w.'s pension** allocation f veuvage
2 vt **to be widowed** devenir veuf (veuve)
widowed [ˈwɪdəʊd] adj veuf (veuve)
widower [ˈwɪdəʊə(r)] n veuf m
width [wɪdθ] n largeur f
wield [wiːld] vt (**a**) (sword, pen) manier (**b**) (power, influence) exercer
wife [waɪf] (pl **wives** [waɪvz]) n femme f, épouse f
wifely [ˈwaɪflɪ] adj de bonne épouse
WiFi [ˈwaɪfaɪ] Comput **1** n WiFi m
2 adj WiFi
wig [wɪɡ] n perruque f
wiggle [ˈwɪɡəl] **1** n trémoussement m
2 vt remuer
3 vi se trémousser
wiggly [ˈwɪɡlɪ] adj Fam (line) ondulé(e)

wigwam [ˈwɪɡwæm] n wigwam m
wild [waɪld] **1** adj (**a**) (not domesticated) (animal, flower, countryside) sauvage; Fig **it was a w. goose chase** ça n'a rien donné; Fam **w. horses wouldn't drag it out of me** rien au monde ne me le ferait dire; Fig **to sow one's w. oats** jeter sa gourme; **the W. West** le Far West (**b**) (unrestrained) (wind) violent(e); (weather) très mauvais(e); (hair) en bataille; (child) turbulent(e); (enthusiasm) délirant(e); (promise) insensé(e); **w. eyes** regard m fou; **to be w.** (person) mener une vie agitée; **to drive sb w.** rendre qn fou (folle) (**c**) (random) **it was just a w. guess** j'ai dit ça au hasard; Comput & Fig **w. card** joker m (**d**) Fam (enthusiastic) **to be w. about sb/sth** être dingue de qn/qch (**e**) Fam (excellent) génial(e)
2 adv **to grow w.** (of plant) pousser à l'état sauvage; **to run w.** être livré(e) à soi-même; **the audience went w.** le public s'est déchaîné
3 n **in the w.** à l'état sauvage; **in the wilds** en pleine brousse
wildcat [ˈwaɪldkæt] n chat m sauvage; Ind **w. strike** grève f sauvage
wilderness [ˈwɪldənɪs] n région f sauvage; Fig (overgrown garden) jungle f; Fig **to be in the w.** être en pleine traversée du désert
wildfire [ˈwaɪldfaɪə(r)] n **to spread like w.** se répandre comme une traînée de poudre
wildfowl [ˈwaɪldfaʊl] (pl **wildfowl**) n gibier m d'eau
wildlife [ˈwaɪldlaɪf] n nature f; **w. programme** (on TV) émission f sur les animaux
wildly [ˈwaɪldlɪ] adv (**a**) (cheer, applaud) frénétiquement; **to rush about w.** courir dans tous les sens (**b**) (guess) au hasard (**c**) (for emphasis) extrêmement; (inaccurate, exaggerated) complètement
wildness [ˈwaɪldnɪs] n (of countryside, animal) état m sauvage; (of wind, waves) fureur f; (of applause) frénésie f; (of ideas, words) extravagance f
wilful [ˈwɪlfʊl] adj (**a**) (stubborn) têtu(e); Law **w. murder** homicide m volontaire
2 adv **to w. sb to do sth** souhaiter ardemment que qn fasse qch; **to w. oneself to do sth** faire un effort de volonté pour faire qch (**b**) (leave in one's will) **to w. sth to sb** léguer qch à qn par testament
wilfully [ˈwɪlfəlɪ] adv (**a**) (stubbornly) avec entêtement (**b**) (deliberately) délibérément
will¹ [wɪl] **1** n (**a**) (resolve, determination) volonté f (**to do** de faire); **at w.** à volonté!; (cry) à la demande; (fire) au hasard; Mil **fire at w.!** feu à volonté; **to show good w.** faire preuve de bonne volonté; **with the best w. in the world** avec la meilleure volonté du monde; Prov **where there's a w. there's a way** vouloir, c'est pouvoir (**b**) (document) testament m; **the last w. and testament of...** les dernières volontés de...; **to make one's w.** faire son testament
will²

modal aux v (**a**) (expressing future tense) **I'll do it tomorrow** je le ferai demain; **it won't take long** ça ne prendra pas longtemps; **when w. he be coming?** quand viendra-t-il?; **I'll have finished by five** j'aurai fini avant cinq heures; **w. you be there?** – **yes I w./no I won't** tu seras là? – oui/non; **you'll write to me, won't you?** tu m'écriras, n'est-ce pas? (**b**) (expressing *wish, determination)* **I won't allow it!** je ne le permettrai pas!; **w. you help me?** tu veux bien m'aider?; **she won't let me see him** elle refuse que je le voie; **won't you sit down?** vous ne voulez pas vous asseoir?; **be quiet, w. you!** tais-toi, s'il te plaît!; **if she WILL insist on doing everything herself...** si elle continue à tout vouloir faire elle-même...; **WILL you go away!** va-t'en, je te dis!; **it won't open** ça ne s'ouvre pas (**c**) *(expressing general truth)* **these things w.** happen ça arrive parfois; **the restaurant w.** seat a hundred people le restaurant peut accueillir cent personnes (**d**) *(expressing conjecture)* **you'll be tired** vous devez être fatigué; **they'll be home by now** ils ont dû arriver chez eux maintenant

William ['wɪliəm] *pr n* Guillaume; **W. the Conqueror** Guillaume le Conquérant

willies ['wɪlɪz] *npl Fam* **to have the w.** avoir la trouille; **to give sb the w.** flanquer la trouille à qn

willing ['wɪlɪŋ] *adj (assistant, participant)* plein(e) de bonne volonté; **he was a w.** accomplice c'est de son plein gré qu'il est devenu complice; **to be w. to do** sth bien vouloir faire qch; **to show w.** faire preuve de bonne volonté

willingly ['wɪlɪŋlɪ] *adv (voluntarily)* de son plein gré; *(with pleasure)* volontiers

willingness ['wɪlɪŋnɪs] *n* bonne volonté *f*

will-o'-the-wisp [wɪləðə'wɪsp] *n also Fig* feu *m* follet

willow ['wɪləʊ] *n* **w. (tree)** saule *m*

willowy ['wɪləʊɪ] *adj (person, figure)* élancé(e)

willpower ['wɪlpaʊə(r)] *n* volonté *f*

willy ['wɪlɪ] *(pl* willies*) n Br Fam (penis)* zizi *m*

willy-nilly ['wɪlɪ'nɪlɪ] *adv* bon gré, mal gré

wilt [wɪlt] *vi (of plant)* se flétrir; *Fig (of person)* fatiguer

wily ['waɪlɪ] *adj* rusé(e)

wimp [wɪmp] *n Fam* mauviette *f*

wimpy ['wɪmpɪ] *adj Fam* mauviette *f*

win [wɪn] **1** *n* victoire *f*

2 *vt (pt & pp* won [wʌn]*)* (**a**) *(battle, race, prize)* gagner; **to w. an argument** avoir le dernier mot; *Fam* **you can't w. them all, you w. some you lose** some on ne peut pas toujours être gagnant (**b**) *(popularity, recognition)* acquérir; *(confidence, love)* gagner (**c**) *(parliamentary seat, election)* remporter

3 *vi* gagner; *Fam* **you can't w.** j'aurai/tu auras/*etc* toujours tort; **OK, you w.!** bon, d'accord!

▸ **win back** *vt sep* reconquérir

▸ **win out** *vi* triompher

▸ **win over, win round** *vt sep* persuader

▸ **win through** *vi* réussir

wince [wɪns] **1** *n* grimace *f*

2 *vi* **to w. (with pain/embarrassment)** grimacer de douleur/d'embarras

winch [wɪntʃ] **1** *n* treuil *m*

2 *vt* hisser

wind¹ [wɪnd] **1** *n* (**a**) *(air current)* vent *m*; **to sail into** or **against the w.** naviguer vent debout; *Fig* **to sail close to the w.** *(take risks)* jouer avec le feu; *(be risqué)* friser l'indécence; **w. energy** or **power** énergie *f* éolienne; **w. instrument** instrument *m* à vent; **w. pump, w. turbine** aéolienne *f*; **w. tunnel** soufflerie *f* (**b**) *(breath)* souffle *m*; *also Fig* **to get one's second w.** trouver son second souffle (**c**) *(abdominal)* gaz *m*, vent *m*; **to have the w.** avoir des gaz; **to break w.** lâcher un vent (**d**) *(idioms) Fam* **to put the w. up sb** faire une peur bleue à qn; **to take the w. out of sb's sails** couper l'herbe sous le pied à qn; **to get w. of sth**

avoir vent de qch; **to be scattered to the four winds** être éparpillé(e)s aux quatre vents

2 *vt* **to w. sb** *(with punch)* couper la respiration à qn

wind² [waɪnd] *(pt & pp* wound [waʊnd]*)* **1** *vt* (**a**) *(thread, string)* enrouler (**round** autour de) (**b**) *(handle)* tourner; *(clock, watch)* remonter; **to w. a cassette on/back** faire avancer/rembobiner une cassette

2 *vi (of path, river)* serpenter

▸ **wind down** **1** *vt sep* (**a**) *(car window)* baisser (**b**) *(reduce) (production)* réduire progressivement; *(company)* fermer progressivement

2 *vi (of party)* se calmer; *(of meeting)* tirer à sa fin; *Fam (of person)* se détendre, décompresser

▸ **wind up** **1** *vt sep* (**a**) *(car window)* remonter (**b**) *(finish) (speech, meeting)* terminer (**c**) *Fam (tease)* faire marcher; *(annoy)* mettre en boîte

2 *vi* (**a**) *(end speech, meeting)* terminer (**b**) *Fam (end up)* finir; **to w. up doing sth** finir par faire qch; **she'll w. up in prison** elle va finir en prison

windbag ['wɪndbæg] *n Fam Pej* moulin *m* à paroles

windbreak ['wɪndbreɪk] *n* brise-vent *m inv*

windcheater ['wɪndtʃiːtə(r)] *n (jacket)* coupe-vent *m inv*

windchill factor ['wɪndtʃɪlfæktə(r)] *n* facteur *m* de refroidissement au vent

winder ['waɪndə(r)] *n (on watch)* remontoir *m*; *(on car door)* lève-glace *m inv*

windfall ['wɪndfɔːl] *n (fruit)* fruit *m* abattu par le vent; *Fig (money)* aubaine *f*; *Fin* **w. profits** *(of company)* bénéfices *mpl* exceptionnels; **w. tax** impôt *m* sur les bénéfices exceptionnels

winding ['waɪndɪŋ] *adj (path, stream)* sinueux(euse); *(staircase)* en colimaçon

windmill ['wɪndmɪl] *n* moulin *m* à vent

window ['wɪndəʊ] *n* (**a**) *(of house)* & *Comput* fenêtre *f*; *(of vehicle)* vitre *f*, glace *f*; *(of shop)* vitrine *f*; **w. box** jardinière *f*; **w. cleaner** laveur(euse) *m,f* de carreaux; **w. display** étalage *m*; **w. frame** châssis *m*; **w. ledge** rebord *m* de fenêtre; **w. seat** *(in vehicle, plane)* place *f* côté fenêtre (**b**) *(idioms)* **to provide a w. on sth** procurer une ouverture sur qch; **w. of opportunity** ouverture *f*; *Fam* **that's my holiday out of the w.** voilà mes vacances fichues en l'air

window-dressing ['wɪndəʊdresɪŋ] *n (in shop)* présentation de l'étalage; *Fig* façade *f*

windowpane ['wɪndəʊpeɪn] *n* vitre *f*, carreau *m*

window-shopping ['wɪndəʊʃɒpɪŋ] *n* **to go w.** faire du lèche-vitrines

windowsill ['wɪndəʊsɪl] *n* rebord *m* de fenêtre

windpipe ['wɪndpaɪp] *n* trachée *f*

windscreen ['wɪndskriːn], *Am* **windshield** ['wɪndʃiːld] *n* pare-brise *m inv*; **w. wiper** essuie-glace *m inv*

windsock ['wɪndsɒk] *n Aviat* manche *f* à air

windsurf ['wɪndsɜːf] *vi* faire de la planche à voile

windsurfing ['wɪndsɜːfɪŋ] *n* planche *f* à voile; **to go w.** faire de la planche à voile

windswept ['wɪndswept] *adj (hillside, scene)* balayé(e) par le vent; *(hair)* décoiffé(e) par le vent; *(person)* échevelé(e)

wind-up ['waɪndʌp] *n Fam* plaisanterie *f*

windward ['wɪndwəd] *adj* au vent; **the W. Islands** les îles *fpl* du Vent

windy ['wɪndɪ] *adj (day)* venteux(euse); *(place)* venté(e); **I hate w. weather** je déteste le vent

windy² ['waɪndɪ] *adj (road)* sinueux(euse)

wine [waɪn] **1** *n* vin *m*; **w. bar** bar *m* à vin; **w. bottle** bouteille *f* de vin; **w. box** cubitainer *m* de vin; **w. cellar** cave *f* à vin; **w. gum** bonbon *m* à la gomme; **w. list** carte *f* des vins; **w. tasting** dégustation *f* (de vins); **w. vinegar** vinaigre *m* de vin
2 *vt* **to w. and dine sb** inviter qn dans de bons restaurants
wineglass ['waɪnglɑːs] *n* verre *m* à vin
wing [wɪŋ] **1** *n* (**a**) (of bird, plane) aile *f*; Fig **to take sb under one's w.** prendre qn sous son aile; Fig **to spread** or **stretch one's wings** élargir son horizon; Tech **w. nut** papillon *m* (**b**) (of car) aile *f*; **w. mirror** rétroviseur *m* extérieur (**c**) (of building, hospital) aile *f* (**d**) (in football, rugby) (player) ailier *m*; (area) aile *f* (**e**) **the wings** (in theatre) les coulisses *fpl*; Fig **to be waiting in the wings** attendre son heure (**f**) Pol **the left/right w.** l'aile *f* gauche/droite
2 *vt* (**a**) (injure) (bird) blesser à l'aile; (person) blesser au bras (**b**) Fam (improvise) **to w. it** improviser (**c**) (fly) **to w. its way towards sth** (of bird) voler vers qch; Fig **my report should be winging its way towards you** j'ai posté mon rapport, tu devrais l'avoir bientôt
winger ['wɪŋə(r)] *n* (in football, rugby) ailier *m*
wingspan ['wɪŋspæn] *n* envergure *f*
wink [wɪŋk] **1** *n* clin *m* d'œil; **to give sb a w.** faire un clin d'œil à qn; Fam **to tip sb the w.** refiler un tuyau à qn; Fam **I didn't sleep a w.** je n'ai pas fermé l'œil
2 *vi* cligner de l'œil; (of star, light) clignoter
▸ **wink at** *vt insep* (person) faire un clin d'œil à; Fig (offence, illegal practice) fermer les yeux sur
winkle ['wɪŋkəl] *n* (mollusc) bigorneau *m*
▸ **winkle out** *vt sep* Fam **to w. sth out of sb** soutirer qch à qn
winner ['wɪnə(r)] *n* gagnant(e) *m,f*; **this book will be a w.** ce livre est assuré d'avoir du succès
winning ['wɪnɪŋ] **1** *n* **winnings** gains *mpl*
2 *adj* (**a**) (victorious) gagnant(e); **w. post** poteau *m* d'arrivée (**b**) (attractive) charmant(e)
winnow ['wɪnəʊ] *vt* vanner
wino ['waɪnəʊ] (pl winos) *n* Fam (alcoholic) poivrot(e)
winsome ['wɪnsəm] *adj* charmant(e)
winter ['wɪntə(r)] **1** *n* hiver *m*; **in (the) w.** en hiver; **w. break** vacances *fpl* d'hiver; **w. clothing** vêtements *mpl* d'hiver; **w. sports** sports *mpl* d'hiver
2 *vi* passer l'hiver
wintertime ['wɪntətaɪm] *n* hiver *m*
wint(e)ry ['wɪnt(ə)rɪ] *adj* (weather) d'hiver; Fig (hostile) glacial(e)
wipe [waɪp] **1** *n* (**a**) (action) **to give sth a w.** essuyer qch (**b**) (moist tissue) lingette *f*
2 *vt* (**a**) (table, plate) essuyer; **to w. one's nose** s'essuyer le nez; **to w. one's hands (on)** s'essuyer les mains (avec); **to w. one's shoes (on)** s'essuyer les pieds (sur); Fam Fig **to w. the floor with sb** ne faire qu'une bouchée de qn (**b**) (recording, tape) effacer
▸ **wipe away** *vt sep* (tears) essuyer; (mark) enlever
▸ **wipe off 1** *vt sep* effacer; Fam **that'll w. the smile off his face!** ça lui fera passer l'envie de rire!
2 *vi* (of stain) partir
▸ **wipe out** *vt sep* (**a**) (erase) effacer; (debt) liquider (**b**) (destroy) décimer
▸ **wipe up** *vt sep* essuyer
wiper ['waɪpə(r)] *n* essuie-glace *m inv*
wire ['waɪə(r)] **1** *n* (**a**) (of metal) fil *m* de fer; (electrical) fil *m* (électrique); **w. brush** brosse *f* métallique; **w. fence** clôture *f* en fil de fer; **w. mesh** toile *f* métallique;

w. wool paille *f* de fer (**b**) Am (telegram) télégramme *m* (**c**) (idioms) Fam **to get one's wires crossed** s'emmêler les pinceaux; **the tournament went right down to the w.** l'issue du tournoi a été incertaine jusqu'au bout
2 *vt* (**a**) (house) faire l'installation électrique de; **to w. sth to sth** (connect electrically) relier qch à qch; (attach with wire) attacher qch à qch avec du fil de fer (**b**) (send telegram to) télégraphier à
▸ **wire up** *vt sep* (**a**) (attach with wire) attacher avec du fil de fer (**b**) Am Fam (make nervous) énerver
wirecutters ['waɪəkʌtəz] *npl* (pair of) **w.** pince *f* coupante
wireless ['waɪəlɪs] **1** *n* Br Old-fashioned **w. (set)** (poste *m* de) TSF *f*
2 *adj* Comput sans fil
wiretapping ['waɪətæpɪŋ] *n* mise *f* sur écoute d'une ligne téléphonique
wiring ['waɪərɪŋ] *n* installation *f* électrique
wiry ['waɪərɪ] *adj* (hair) crépu(e); (person) petit(e) et musclé(e)
wisdom ['wɪzdəm] *n* sagesse *f*; **w. tooth** dent *f* de sagesse
wise [waɪz] *adj* (knowledgeable) sage; (advisable) prudent(e); Fam Pej **a w. guy** un gros malin; **the Three W. Men** les Rois *mpl* mages; **it's easy to be w. after the event** c'est facile de savoir ce qui est bien ou pas bien après coup; Fam **to be none the wiser** ne pas être plus avancé(e); Fam **to get w. to sth** se rendre compte de qch; Fam **to get w. to sb** percer qn à jour
▸ **wise up** *vi* Fam **to w. up to sb** voir qn sous son vrai jour; **to w. up to sth** se rendre compte de qch; **w. up!** ouvre les yeux!
-wise [waɪz] *suff* Fam (as regards) **health-/salary-w.** du point de vue de la santé/du salaire
wisecrack ['waɪzkræk] Fam **1** *n* vanne *f*, blague *f*
2 *vi* sortir des vannes
wisely ['waɪzlɪ] *adv* sagement
wish [wɪʃ] **1** *n* (**a**) (desire) désir *m*; (thing desired) vœu *m*; **to make a w.** faire un vœu; **to do sth against sb's wishes** faire qch contre le souhait de qn; **w. list** liste *f* de vœux (**b**) (greeting) **best wishes** meilleurs vœux; (in letter) amicalement
2 *vt* (**a**) (want) désirer; **to w. to do sth** désirer faire qch; **to w. sb well** souhaiter à qn que tout se passe bien; **to w. sb luck/a pleasant journey** souhaiter bonne chance/bon voyage à qn; **to w. sth on sb** souhaiter qch à qn (**b**) (want something impossible, unlikely) **I w. she could come** j'aurais bien aimé qu'elle vienne; **I w. I had seen it!** j'aurais bien voulu voir ça!; **I w. I hadn't left so early** je regrette d'être parti aussi tôt; **I w. she wouldn't say things like that** je préférerais qu'elle s'abstienne de dire des choses pareilles; **w. you were here!** (on postcard) je pense/nous pensons bien à toi
3 *vi* **to w. for sth** souhaiter qch; **what more could you w. for?** que souhaiter de plus?; **as you w.** comme tu voudras
wishbone ['wɪʃbəʊn] *n* bréchet *m*
wishful ['wɪʃfʊl] *adj* **that's w. thinking** tu te fais/il se fait/etc des illusions
wishy-washy ['wɪʃɪwɒʃɪ] *adj* Fam mou (molle); (colour) délavé(e)
wisp [wɪsp] *n* (of straw, wool) brin *m*; (of hair) mèche *f*; (of smoke, cloud) traînée *f*
wistful ['wɪstfʊl] *adj* nostalgique

wit [wɪt] *n* (**a**) *(intelligence, presence of mind)* esprit *m*; **to have the w.** **to do sth** être assez intelligent(e) pour faire qch; **to have quick wits** avoir l'esprit vif; **to have lost one's wits** avoir perdu l'esprit; **to have/keep one's wits about one** être/rester très vigilant(e); **to be at one's wits' end** ne plus savoir que faire; **to live by one's wits** vivre d'expédients; **to scare sb out of his/her wits** faire une peur bleue à qn (**b**) *(humour)* esprit *m* (**c**) *(witty person) (man)* homme *m* d'esprit; *(woman)* femme *f* d'esprit

witch [wɪtʃ] *n* sorcière *f*; **w. doctor** sorcier *m*

witchcraft ['wɪtʃkrɑːft] *n* sorcellerie *f*

witch-hunt ['wɪtʃhʌnt] *n Pol* chasse *f* aux sorcières

with [wɪð] *prep* (**a**) *(expressing accompaniment)* avec; **w. me/him** avec moi/lui; **to live w. one's parents** vivre chez ses parents; **I was left w. nobody to talk to** je me suis retrouvé sans personne à qui parler (**b**) *(having)* **the girl w. glasses/blue eyes** la fille aux lunettes/aux yeux bleus; **w. one's hands in one's pockets** les mains dans les poches (**c**) *(expressing association)* **to be pleased w. sb** être content(e) de qn; **to be angry w. sb** être en colère contre qn; **to fight/compete w. sb** se battre/être en concurrence avec qn; **to be in love w. sb** être amoureux(euse) de qn; **covered w. mud** couvert(e) de boue (**d**) *(expressing manner)* **w. pleasure/difficulty** avec plaisir/difficulté; **to say sth w. a smile** dire qch avec un sourire (**e**) *(expressing instrument, agent)* **to hit sb w. sth** frapper qn avec qch; **to cut sth w. a knife** couper qch avec un couteau; **it's pouring w. rain** il pleut à verse (**f**) *(because of)* **to tremble w. rage** trembler de rage; **to cry w. laughter** pleurer de rire; **w. her money, she can surely afford it** avec l'argent qu'elle a, elle peut bien se permettre ça (**g**) *(expressing simultaneity)* **to improve w. age** s'améliorer avec l'âge; **w. those words, he left** sur ces mots, il partit; **w. Christmas coming,...** puisque c'est bientôt Noël,... (**h**) *(idioms)* **to be w. it** être dans le vent; **get w. it!** *(wake up)* réveille-toi!; *(face reality)* ouvre les yeux!; **I'm w. you** *(I support you)* je suis avec vous; **I'm not w. you** *(I don't understand)* je ne vous suis pas

withdraw [wɪð'drɔː] *(pt* **withdrew** [wɪð'druː], *pp* **withdrawn** [wɪð'drɔːn]) **1** *vt* retirer (**from** de) **2** *vi* se retirer (**from** de); **to w. in favour of sb** se désister en faveur de qn; **to w. into oneself** se replier sur soi-même

withdrawal [wɪð'drɔːəl] *n* retrait *m*; **to make a w.** *(from bank)* faire un retrait; **w. symptoms** symptômes *mpl* de manque; **to have w. symptoms** être (en état de) manque

withdrawn [wɪð'drɔːn] *adj* replié(e) sur soi-même

wither ['wɪðə(r)] *vi* *(of plant)* se flétrir; *(of limb)* s'atrophier

withered ['wɪðəd] *adj (plant)* flétri(e); *(limb)* atrophié(e)

withering ['wɪðərɪŋ] *adj (look)* foudroyant(e); *(tone)* cinglant(e)

withhold [wɪð'həʊld] *(pt & pp* **withheld** [wɪð'held]) *vt (consent, help)* refuser; *(money)* retenir; *(truth)* cacher; *(information)* faire de la rétention de

within [wɪð'ɪn] **1** *prep* (**a**) *(inside)* à l'intérieur de; **problems w. the company** des problèmes au sein de l'entreprise (**b**) *(not beyond)* **w. 10 miles of the town** ≃ à moins de 16 km de la ville; **w. a radius of** dans un rayon de; **w. limits** jusqu'à un certain point; **w. reason** dans des limites raisonnables; **to stay w. budget** rester dans les limites du budget; **to come w. an inch of doing sth** bien faillir faire qch (**c**) *(with expressions of time)* **w. an hour/a week** en moins d'une heure/d'une semaine; **w. minutes** en quelques minutes; **w. the next five years** *(in the space of) (in future)* au cours des cinq années à venir; *(in past)* au cours des cinq années suivantes; *(before the end of) (in future)* avant cinq ans; *(in past)* en moins de cinq ans; **they died w. a few days of each other** ils sont morts à quelques jours d'intervalle **2** *adv* à l'intérieur; **from w.** de l'intérieur

without [wɪð'aʊt] **1** *prep* sans; **w. any money/difficulty** sans argent/difficulté; **w. doing sth** sans faire qch; **do it w. him knowing** fais-le sans qu'il le sache; **it goes w. saying that...** il va sans dire que...; **to do or go w. sth** se passer de qch **2** *adv* **to do or go w.** se priver

withstand [wɪð'stænd] *(pt & pp* **withstood** [wɪð'stʊd]) *vt* supporter

witless ['wɪtlɪs] *adj (person, remark)* stupide; **to scare sb w.** faire une peur bleue à qn

witness ['wɪtnɪs] **1** *n* (**a**) *(person)* témoin *m*; **to call sb as w.** citer qn comme témoin; **w. for the defence/prosecution** témoin *m* à décharge/charge; **w. box** barre *f* des témoins (**b**) *(testimony)* **to bear w. (to sth)** témoigner (de qch) **2** *vt* être témoin de; **I witnessed the whole thing** j'ai assisté à tout ce qui s'est passé; *Fig* **this town has witnessed many battles** cette ville a été le théâtre de nombreuses batailles **3** *vi Law* **to w. to sth** témoigner de qch

witter ['wɪtə(r)] *vi Br Fam* **to w. (on)** bavasser

witticism ['wɪtɪsɪzəm] *n* mot *m* d'esprit

wittily ['wɪtɪlɪ] *adv* avec esprit

wittingly ['wɪtɪŋlɪ] *adv* sciemment

witty ['wɪtɪ] *adj* spirituel(elle), plein(e) d'esprit

wives [waɪvz] *pl of* **wife**

wizard ['wɪzəd] *n* (**a**) magicien *m*; *Fig* as *m* (**b**) *Comput* assistant *m*

wizened ['wɪzənd] *adj* ratatiné(e)

wk *(abbr* **week)** semaine

wknd *(abbr* **weekend)** week-end

WMD [dʌbəljuːem'diː] *npl Mil (abbr* **weapons of mass destruction)** ADM *fpl*

wobble ['wɒbəl] *vi (of chair, table)* branler; *(of building, jelly)* trembler; *(of person)* être chancelant(e)

wobbly ['wɒblɪ] **1** *n (pl* **wobblies)** *Br Fam* **to throw a w.** piquer une crise **2** *adj (chair, table)* bancal(e); *(shelf, ladder)* branlant(e); *(person)* chancelant(e)

woe [wəʊ] *n Lit* malheur *m*; *Hum* **w. betide you if you're late** malheur à toi si tu es en retard

woebegone ['wəʊbɪɡɒn] *adj* abattu(e)

woeful ['wəʊfʊl] *adj* (**a**) *(sad)* affligé(e) (**b**) *(very bad)* déplorable

wog [wɒɡ] *n Br very Fam* = terme injurieux désignant une personne qui n'est pas blanche

wok [wɒk] *n* poêle *f* chinoise

woke [wəʊk] *pt of* **wake**³

woken ['wəʊkən] *pp of* **wake**³

wolf [wʊlf] *(pl* **wolves** [wʊlvz]) *n* (**a**) loup *m*; **w. cub** louveteau *m*; **w. whistle** = sifflement admiratif au passage de quelqu'un (**b**) *(idioms)* **I don't earn much but it keeps the w. from the door** je ne gagne pas beaucoup mais ça me met à l'abri du besoin; **to throw sb to the wolves** abandonner qn à son sort; **a w. in sheep's clothing** un loup déguisé en brebis; **to cry w.** crier au loup

▸**wolf down** *vt sep* engloutir

woman ['wʊmən] (*pl* **women** ['wɪmɪn]) *n* femme *f*; **women's magazine** magazine *m* féminin; **women's movement** mouvement *m* de libération de la femme; **women's page** page *f* des lectrices; **women's refuge, women's shelter** centre *m* d'accueil pour les femmes; **w. doctor** femme médecin *f*; **w. driver** conductrice *f*

womanizer ['wʊmənaɪzə(r)] *n* coureur *m* (de jupons)

womanly ['wʊmənlɪ] *adj* féminin(e)

womb [wu:m] *n* utérus *m*

women ['wɪmɪn] *pl of* **woman**

womenfolk ['wɪmɪnfəʊk] *n* femmes *fpl*

won [wʌn] *pt & pp of* **win**

wonder ['wʌndə(r)] **1** *n* (**a**) *(miracle)* miracle *m*, merveille *f*; **to work** *or* **do wonders** faire des miracles; **it's a w. (that)...** c'est un miracle que... + *subjunctive*; **(it's) no w....** ce n'est pas étonnant que... + *subjunctive*; **w. drug** remède *m* miracle (**b**) *(astonishment)* émerveillement *m*; **in w.** avec émerveillement
2 *vt* se demander; **one wonders whether...** c'est à se demander si...; **I was wondering if you were free tonight** je voulais savoir si tu étais libre ce soir
3 *vi* (**a**) *(be curious)* se demander; *Fam* **I w. about her sometimes!** je me pose parfois des questions à son sujet! (**b**) *Lit (be amazed)* s'étonner (**at** de)

wonderful ['wʌndəfʊl] *adj* merveilleux(euse), formidable

wonky ['wɒŋkɪ] *adj Br Fam* déglingué(e)

wont [wəʊnt] *Formal* **1** *n* habitude *f*; **as is her w.** comme à son habitude
2 *adj* **to be w. to do sth** avoir l'habitude de faire qch

won't [wəʊnt] = **will not**

woo [wu:] *(pt & pp* **wooed***) vt* (**a**) *Lit (woman)* courtiser (**b**) *Fig (supporters, investors)* attirer

wood [wʊd] *n* (**a**) *(forest, material)* bois *m*; **w. carving** sculpture *f* sur bois (**b**) *(idioms)* **she can't see the w. for the trees** elle se perd dans les détails; **we're not out of the woods yet** nous ne sommes pas encore tirés d'affaire; *Br* **touch w.!,** *Am* **knock on w.!** je touche du bois!

woodbine ['wʊdbaɪn] *n (plant)* vigne *f* vierge

woodcock ['wʊdkɒk] *n* bécasse *f*

woodcut ['wʊdkʌt] *n* gravure *f* sur bois

woodcutter ['wʊdkʌtə(r)] *n* bûcheron *m*

wooded ['wʊdɪd] *adj* boisé(e)

wooden ['wʊdən] *adj (made of wood)* en bois; *Fig (unexpressive)* impassible; **w. spoon** cuillère *f* de bois; *Fig* **to get the w. spoon** *(in contest)* arriver dernier(ère) au classement

woodland ['wʊdlənd] *n (woods)* bois *mpl*; *(wooded area)* région *f* boisée

woodlouse ['wʊdlaʊs] *(pl* **woodlice** ['wʊdlaɪs]*) n* cloporte *m*

woodpecker ['wʊdpekə(r)] *n* pic *m*

woodpile ['wʊdpaɪl] *n* tas *m* de bois

woodshed ['wʊdʃed] *n* remise *f* à bois

woodwind ['wʊdwɪnd] *n Mus* **the w.** *(instruments)* les bois *mpl*; **w. instrument** bois *m*

woodwork ['wʊdwɜːk] *n (craft)* travail *m* du bois; *(in house)* boiserie *f*; *Fig* **to come** *or* **crawl out of the w.** faire soudain surface

woodworm ['wʊdwɜːm] *n* ver *m* à bois

woof [wʊf] **1** *n* aboiement *m*
2 *exclam* ouah!

wool [wʊl] *n* laine *f*; *Fam* **to pull the w. over sb's eyes** embobiner qn

woollen, *Am* **woolen** ['wʊlən] **1** *n* **woollens** lainages *mpl*
2 *adj (garment)* en laine

woolly, *Am* **wooly** ['wʊlɪ] **1** *n Br Fam (garment)* woollies lainages *mpl*
2 *adj (garment)* en laine; *Fig (idea, theory)* nébuleux(euse)

woozy ['wu:zɪ] *adj Fam* dans les vapes

wop [wɒp] *n very Fam* rital(e) *m,f,* = terme raciste désignant un Italien

word [wɜːd] **1** *n* (**a**) *(in general)* mot *m*; **w. for w.** mot pour mot; **in a w.** en un mot; **in other words** autrement dit; **not in so many words** pas en ces termes-là; **not a w.** pas un mot; **in one's own words** à sa façon; **I can't put it into words** je n'arrive pas à trouver les mots; **he's a man of few words** c'est un homme qui parle peu; **I couldn't get a w. in (edgeways)** je n'ai pas pu placer un mot; **the w. of God** la parole de Dieu; **I'll take your w. for it** je te crois sur parole; **to take sb at his/her w.** prendre qn au mot; **it was too ridiculous for words** c'était d'un ridicule sans nom; **my w.!** ma parole!; *Comput* **w. count** nombre *m* de mots; **w. processor** machine *f* à traitement de texte (**b**) *(remarks, conversation)* **to have a w. with sb** parler à qn; **to have words with sb** avoir des mots avec qn; **just say the w.** tu n'as qu'à me faire signe; **you're putting words into my mouth** tu me fais dire des choses que je n'ai pas voulu dire; **you took the words right out of my mouth** c'est justement ce que j'allais dire; **to put in a good w. for sb** glisser un mot en faveur de qn; **he never has a good w. for anyone** il ne peut pas s'empêcher de dire du mal des gens; **a w. of warning** une mise en garde; **a w. of advice** un petit conseil (**c**) *(news)* **to receive w. from sb** avoir des nouvelles de qn; **to send sb w. of sth** faire part à qn de qch; **the w. is that...** on raconte que...; **by w. of mouth** de bouche à oreille (**d**) *(promise)* parole *f*; **w. of honour** parole *f* d'honneur; **to give sb one's w.** donner sa parole à qn; **to keep one's w.** tenir sa promesse; **to go back on one's w.** manquer à sa parole (**e**) **words** *(lyrics)* paroles *fpl*
2 *vt (express in words)* formuler

wording ['wɜːdɪŋ] *n* formulation *f*

word-processing [wɜːd'prəʊsesɪŋ] *n Comput* traitement *m* de texte

wordy ['wɜːdɪ] *adj* prolixe

wore [wɔː(r)] *pt of* **wear**

work [wɜːk] **1** *n* (**a**) *(labour)* travail *m*; **to be at w. on sth** travailler à *ou* sur qch; **to get to w.** se mettre au travail; **w. ethic** = exaltation des valeurs liées au travail; **w. in progress** *(sign)* travaux; *Comput* **w. station** poste *m* de travail (**b**) *(task)* travail *m*; **to have a lot of w. into sth** beaucoup travailler à qch; **to have one's w. cut out (to do sth)** avoir du mal (à faire qch); **to make quick** *or* **short w. of sth** venir rapidement à bout de qch; **get to w.!** c'est du bon travail! (**c**) *(literary, artistic)* œuvre *f*; **a w. of art** une œuvre d'art (**d**) *(employment)* travail *m*; **to be out of w.** être sans travail; **w. experience** stage *m* (en entreprise); **w. permit** permis *m* de travail (**e**) *Ind* **works council** comité *m* d'entreprise; **works outing** sortie *f* organisée par le comité d'entreprise (**f**) **works** *(construction)* travaux *mpl*; **road works ahead** *(sign)* attention travaux (**g**) **works** *(mechanism)* mécanisme *m* (**h**) *Fam* **the works** *(everything)* le grand jeu; **to give sb the works** *(beating)* passer qn à tabac; *(luxury treatment)* jouer le grand jeu à qn

2 *vt* (**a**) *(person)* **to w. sb hard** exiger beaucoup de qn; **to w. oneself to death** se tuer à la tâche (**b**) *(operate) (machine)* faire fonctionner (**c**) *(bring about) (miracle, cure, change)* opérer; **to w. it** *or* **things so that** faire en sorte que (**d**) *(move)* **to w. one's hands free** se libérer les mains; **to w. one's way through a book/list** avancer progressivement dans la lecture d'un livre/dans une liste (**e**) *(exploit) (mine, quarry)* exploiter; *(land)* travailler
3 *vi* (**a**) *(of person)* travailler; **to w. against sb/in sb's favour** jouer en la défaveur/la faveur de qn (**b**) *(function) (of machine, system)* marcher, fonctionner (**c**) *(have effect) (of medicine)* faire effet; *(of plan, method)* marcher
▸**work in** *vt sep (include)* introduire, glisser
▸**work off** *vt sep (anger)* évacuer; **he worked off 5 kilos** il a perdu 5 kilos en faisant de l'exercice
▸**work on 1** *vt insep* **to w. on sth** travailler à *ou* sur qch
2 *vi (continue to work)* continuer à travailler
▸**work out 1** *vt sep (cost, total)* calculer; *(answer)* trouver; **to w. out how to do sth** trouver comment faire qch; **I'm sure we can w. this thing out** je suis sûr(e) qu'on peut arranger ça
2 *vi* (**a**) *(turn out)* **to w. out well/badly (for sb)** bien/mal se passer (pour qn); **it all worked out in the end** finalement, tout s'est arrangé (**b**) *(total)* **to w. out at** revenir à (**c**) *(exercise)* s'entraîner
▸**work up** *vt sep* (**a**) *(develop)* **to w. up enthusiasm/interest for sth** s'enthousiasmer pour/s'intéresser à qch; **I worked up an appetite** ça m'a ouvert l'appétit (**b**) *(excite)* **to get worked up (about sth)** se mettre dans tous ses états (à propos de qch)
▸**work up to** *vt insep* se préparer à
workable ['wɜːkəbəl] *adj* possible
workaday ['wɜːkədeɪ] *adj* de tous les jours
workaholic [wɜːkə'hɒlɪk] *n Fam* bourreau *m* de travail
workbench ['wɜːkbentʃ] *n* établi *m*
workday ['wɜːkdeɪ] *n Am* jour *m* ouvrable
worker ['wɜːkə(r)] *n* travailleur(euse) *m,f*; *(in industry)* ouvrier(ère) *m,f*; **to be a fast/slow w.** travailler vite/lentement; **w. bee** ouvrière *f*; **w. participation** participation *f* des travailleurs à la gestion
workfare ['wɜːkfeə(r)] *n Pol* = principe selon lequel les bénéficiaires de l'allocation de chômage doivent fournir un travail en échange
workforce ['wɜːkfɔːs] *n* (**a**) *(labour force as a whole)* population *f* active (**b**) *(in industry)* main-d'œuvre *f*; *(in company)* personnel *m*
workhouse ['wɜːkhaʊs] *n Hist* asile *m* des pauvres
working ['wɜːkɪŋ] **1** *n* (**a**) *(operation) (of machine)* fonctionnement *m* (**b**) **workings** *(mechanism)* mécanisme *m*
2 *adj (person)* qui travaille; **to have a w. knowledge of sth** avoir de bonnes bases en qch; **in w. order** en état de marche; **the w. class(es)** la classe ouvrière; **w. clothes** vêtements *mpl* de travail; **w. hours** heures *fpl* de travail; **w. lunch** déjeuner *m* d'affaires; **w. majority** majorité *f* suffisante; **w. model** maquette *f* animée; **w. party** groupe *m* de travail
working-class ['wɜːkɪŋ'klɑːs] *adj* ouvrier(ère); *(accent)* prolétaire
workload ['wɜːkləʊd] *n* charge *f* de travail
workman ['wɜːkmən] *n* ouvrier *m*
workmanlike ['wɜːkmənlaɪk] *adj* de professionnel
workmanship ['wɜːkmənʃɪp] *n* travail *m*; **a fine piece of w.** du beau travail

workout ['wɜːkaʊt] *n* séance *f* d'entraînement
workplace ['wɜːkpleɪs] *n* lieu *m* de travail
workshop ['wɜːkʃɒp] *n* atelier *m*
workshy ['wɜːkʃaɪ] *adj* fainéant(e)
worktop ['wɜːktɒp] *n (in kitchen)* plan *m* de travail, *Can* comptoir *m* de cuisine
work-to-rule [wɜːktə'ruːl] *n Ind* grève *f* du zèle
world [wɜːld] *n* (**a**) *(the earth)* monde *m*; **the best/biggest in the w.** le (la) meilleur(e)/plus grand(e) du monde; **the w. over, all over the w.** dans le monde entier; **the W. Bank** la Banque mondiale; **w. champion** champion(onne) *m,f* du monde; **the W. Cup** la Coupe du monde; **w. map** mappemonde *f*; **w. music** world music *f*; **w. record** record *m* du monde; **W. Series** = championnat national américain de base-ball; **w. tour** *(by traveller)* tour *m* du monde; *(by band, entertainer)* tournée *f* mondiale; **W. War One/Two** la Première/Seconde *ou* Deuxième Guerre mondiale (**b**) *(sphere of activity)* **the literary/political/business w.** le monde littéraire/politique/des affaires (**c**) *(society)* **man of the w.** homme *m* d'expérience; **to go up in the w.** faire du chemin; **to come down in the w.** déchoir; **to have the w. at one's feet** avoir le monde à ses pieds (**d**) *(for emphasis)* **to do sb the w. of good** faire le plus grand bien à qn; **a w. of difference** une différence énorme; **to think the w. of sb** admirer énormément qn; **they carried on for all the w. as if nothing had happened** ils ont continué comme si de rien n'était (**e**) *(idioms)* **she's not long for this w.** elle n'en a plus pour longtemps; **to bring a child into the w.** mettre un enfant au monde; **to have the best of both worlds** avoir tous les avantages et aucun des inconvénients; **she lives in a w. of her own** elle vit dans un monde à elle; *Fam* **it's out of this w.** c'est extraordinaire; **not for (anything in) the w.** pour rien au monde; **it's a small w.!** le monde est petit!; **what is the w. coming to?** où va-t-on?
world-beater ['wɜːldbiːtə(r)] *n* leader *m* mondial
world-famous ['wɜːld'feɪməs] *adj* célèbre dans le monde entier
worldly ['wɜːldlɪ] *adj (pleasure, goods)* matériel(elle)
worldly-wise ['wɜːldlɪ'waɪz] *adj* qui a de l'expérience
world-weary ['wɜːldwɪərɪ] *adj* désabusé(e)
worldwide ['wɜːldwaɪd] **1** *adj* mondial(e); *Comput* **the W. Web** le Worldwide Web
2 *adv* dans le monde entier
WORM [wɜːm] *Comput (abbr* **write once read many times)** WORM
worm [wɜːm] **1** *n* ver *m*; *(maggot)* asticot *m*; **to have worms** *(of person, animal)* avoir des vers; *Fig* **the w. has turned** il/elle/etc a fini par se rebiffer
2 *vt* (**a**) *(animal)* traiter contre les vers (**b**) **to w. one's way out of a situation** réussir à se tirer d'une situation; **to w. oneself into sb's favour/confidence** s'insinuer dans les bonnes grâces/la confiance de qn; **to w. a secret out of sb** arracher un secret à qn
wormeaten ['wɜːmiːtən] *adj (wood)* vermoulu(e); *(fruit)* véreux(euse)
worn [wɔːn] *pp of* **wear**
worried ['wʌrɪd] *adj* inquiet(ète); **to be w. about sb** être inquiet(ète) pour qn; **I'm w. about his safety** je m'inquiète pour sa sécurité; **he's w. about losing his job** il a peur de perdre son emploi
worrier ['wʌrɪə(r)] *n* anxieux(euse) *m,f*
worry ['wʌrɪ] **1** *n (pl* **worries)** souci *m*; **that's the least of my worries** c'est le cadet de mes soucis

2 *vt (pt & pp* **worried)** *(cause anxiety to)* inquiéter; **to w. oneself sick (about sth)** se faire un sang d'encre (à propos de qch)

3 *vi* s'inquiéter, se faire du souci; **to w. about sb** s'inquiéter pour qn; **to w. about the future** s'inquiéter pour l'avenir; **to w. about doing sth** avoir peur de faire qch; **not to w.!** ce n'est pas grave!; **there's/it's nothing to w. about** il n'y a pas de quoi s'inquiéter

worrying ['wʌrɪŋ] *adj* inquiétant(e)

worse [wɜːs] **1** *adj (comparative of* **bad)** pire (**than** que); **there's nothing w. than...** il n'y a rien de pire que...; **to get w.** aller en empirant; **things could be w.** les choses pourraient aller plus mal; **and to make matters w.** et, pour tout arranger...; **to go from bad to w.,...** aller de mal en pis; **I'm none the w. for it** je ne m'en porte pas plus mal; **to be the w. for drink** être éméché(e); *Fam* **to be the w. for wear** *(of car, book)* être en mauvais état; *(of drunk person)* être dans un sale état; **w. luck!** quelle poisse!

2 *adv (comparative of* **badly)** plus mal; **you could do w.** tu aurais pu tomber plus mal; **I don't think any w. of her for it** elle n'a pas pour autant baissé dans mon estime; **he is w. off than before** sa situation a empiré

3 *n* **there was w. to come** le pire restait à venir; **I've seen w.** j'ai vu pire; **a change for the w.** une détérioration

worsen ['wɜːsən] **1** *vt* aggraver
2 *vi* empirer

Worship ['wɜːʃɪp] *n (title)* **His/Her W.** *(referring to mayor)* monsieur/madame le maire; *(referring to magistrate)* monsieur/madame le juge

worship ['wɜːʃɪp] **1** *n (of deity)* vénération *f*, culte *m*; *(of person)* adoration *f*; **place of w.** lieu *m* de culte
2 *vt (pt & pp* **worshipped)** *(deity)* vénérer; *(person)* adorer

worst [wɜːst] **1** *adj (superlative of bad)* **the w.** le (la) pire; **the w. book I've ever read** le plus mauvais livre que j'aie jamais lu; **her w. mistake** sa plus grave erreur; **the w. thing was...** le pire, c'était que...

2 *adv (superlative of badly)* le plus mal; **the elderly are the w. off** ce sont les personnes âgées qui sont le plus mal loties

3 *n* **the w.** le pire; **the w. that could happen** le pire qui puisse arriver; **the w. of it is that...** le pire dans tout ça, c'est que...; **if the w. comes to the w.** au pire; *Fam* **do your w.!** essaie un peu pour voir!; **the w. is over** on a passé le plus dur

worst-case scenario ['wɜːstkeɪsɪ'nɑːrɪəʊ] *(pl* **worst-case scenarios)** *n* le pire qui puisse se produire

worsted ['wʊstɪd] *n* peigné *m*

worth [wɜːθ] **1** *prep* (**a**) *(having a value of)* **to be w. sth** valoir qch; **how much is it w.?** combien est-ce que cela vaut?; **that's my opinion, for what it's w.** c'est mon opinion, elle vaut ce qu'elle vaut; **he's w. millions** il est millionnaire; **he was pulling for all he was w.** il tirait de toutes ses forces (**b**) *(meriting)* **the museum is w. a visit** le musée vaut le détour; **this book is not w. buying** ce livre ne vaut pas la peine d'être acheté; **it's w.it/it isn't w.** it ça en vaut/ça n'en vaut pas la peine; **it's w. thinking about** ça vaut le coup d'y réfléchir

2 *n* valeur *f*; **give me £20 w. of petrol** donnez-moi pour 20 livres d'essence; **to get one's money's w.** en avoir pour son argent

worthless ['wɜːθlɪs] *adj* **to be w.** *(of object)* ne rien valoir; *(of person)* être un(e) bon (bonne) à rien

worthwhile [wɜːθ'waɪl] *adj* **to be w.** valoir la peine *ou* le coup

worthy ['wɜːðɪ] **1** *adj (person, life)* digne; **to be w. of sth** être digne de qch
2 *n* notable *m*

would [wʊd]

On trouve généralement **I/you/he**/etc **would** sous leurs formes contractées **I'd/you'd/he'd**/etc. La forme négative correspondante est **wouldn't**, que l'on écrira **would not** dans des contextes formels.

modal aux v (**a**) *(expressing conditional tense)* **she w. come if you invited her** elle viendrait si vous l'invitiez; **if he had let go, he w. have fallen** s'il avait lâché prise, il serait tombé; **if she had asked me, I w. have refused** si elle m'avait demandé, j'aurais refusé; **w. you do it? – yes I w./no I wouldn't** tu le ferais? – oui/non; **you wouldn't do it, w. you?** tu ne le ferais pas, dis? (**b**) *(expressing wish, determination)* **w. you pass the salt, please?** pourrais-tu passer le sel, s'il te plaît?; **w. you like a drink?** tu veux boire quelque chose?; **she wouldn't let me speak to him** elle m'empêchait de lui parler; **be quiet, w. you!** tais-toi, s'il te plaît!; **the car wouldn't start** la voiture ne démarrait pas (**c**) *(for emphasis)* **you WOULD insist on going!** il fallait que tu insistes pour y aller!; **I forgot – you WOULD!** j'ai oublié – c'est bien (de) toi! (**d**) *(expressing past habit)* **she w. often return home exhausted** il lui arrivait souvent de rentrer épuisée; **there w. always be some left over** il en restait toujours (**e**) *(in reported speech)* **she told me she w. be there** elle m'a dit qu'elle serait là; **I said I w. do it** j'ai dit que je le ferais (**f**) *(expressing conjecture)* **w. that be my pen you're using?** est-ce que, par hasard, ce serait mon stylo que vous utilisez?; **they w. have been tired after their journey** ils devaient être fatigués après leur voyage; **I wouldn't know** je n'en ai aucune idée

would-be ['wʊdbiː] *adj* (**a**) *(aspiring)* **a w. writer** une personne qui veut être écrivain (**b**) *Pej (so-called)* prétendu(e), soi-disant *inv*

wouldn't ['wʊdənt] = **would not**

wound[1] [wuːnd] **1** *n* blessure *f*
2 *vt also Fig* blesser; **to w. sb's feelings** blesser qn, heurter la sensibilité de qn

wound[2] [waʊnd] *pt & pp of* **wind**[2]

wounded ['wuːndɪd] **1** *adj* blessé(e)
2 *npl* **the w.** les blessés *mpl*

wounding ['wuːndɪŋ] *adj* blessant(e)

wove [wəʊv] *pt of* **weave**

woven ['wəʊvən] *pp of* **weave**

wow [waʊ] *Fam* **1** *vt* séduire, emballer
2 *exclam* la vache!

WP [dʌbəljuː'piː] *n Comput* (**a**) *(abbr* **word processor)** *(machine)* machine *f* à traitement de texte; *(software)* logiciel *m* de traitement de texte (**b**) *(abbr* **word-processing)** *(skill)* traitement *m* de texte

WPC [dʌbəljuːpiː'siː] *n (abbr* **woman police constable)** = femme agent de police

wpm [dʌbəljuːpiː'em] *(abbr* **words per minute)** mots par minute

WRAC [ræk] *n Br Mil (abbr* **Women's Royal Army Corps)** = section féminine de l'armée britannique

wrangle ['ræŋgəl] **1** *n* dispute *f*
2 *vi* se disputer (**about** or **over** à propos de)

wrap [ræp] **1** *n* (**a**) *(shawl)* châle *m*; *Fig* **to keep sth under wraps** garder qch secret (**b**) *Culin (sandwich)* = tortilla fourrée
2 *vt (pt & pp* **wrapped)** envelopper, emballer (**in**

dans); **to w. sth around sth** enrouler qch autour de qch; *Fig* **wrapped in mystery** enveloppé(e) de mystère

▸**wrap up 1** *vt sep* (**a**) *(parcel, present)* envelopper; *Fig* **to be wrapped up in sth** être absorbé(e) par qch (**b**) *Fam (bring to an end)* conclure

2 *vi (dress warmly)* s'emmitoufler

wraparound ['ræpəraʊnd] *adj* **w. skirt** jupe *f* portefeuille; **w. sunglasses** lunettes *fpl* de soleil panoramiques

wrapper ['ræpə(r)] *n (of sweet)* papier *m*

wrapping ['ræpɪŋ] *n* emballage *m*; **w. paper** papier *m* d'emballage

wrath [rɒθ] *n Lit* courroux *m*

wreak [ri:k] *vt* **to w. havoc** faire des ravages; **to w. vengeance on sb** assouvir sa vengeance sur qn

wreath [ri:θ] *n* couronne *f*

wreathe [ri:ð] *vt Lit* couronner

wreck [rek] **1** *n (ship, car, train, plane)* épave *f*; *Fig* **to be a physical/nervous w.** être physiquement/nerveusement au bout du rouleau

2 *vt (ship)* faire faire naufrage à; *(car)* démolir; *(room, house)* saccager; *Fig (plans, hopes, happiness)* ruiner, anéantir; *(marriage, career)* ruiner; **to w. one's health** se ruiner la santé

wreckage ['rekɪdʒ] *n (debris) (of plane, car, ship)* débris *mpl*; *(of building)* décombres *mpl*

wrecked [rekt] *adj* (**a**) *(ship)* naufragé(e); *(car, plane)* complètement détruit(e) (**b**) *Fam (drunk)* bourré(e), pété(e) (**c**) *Fam (exhausted)* crevé(e)

wrecker ['rekə(r)] *n Am (salvage vehicle)* dépanneuse *f*

wren [ren] *n* roitelet *m*

wrench [rentʃ] **1** *n* (**a**) *(pull) (to ankle, shoulder)* faux mouvement *m*; *Fig (emotional)* déchirement *m* (**b**) *(tool)* clef *f*

2 *vt* **to w. one's ankle/shoulder** se fouler la cheville/l'épaule; **to w. sth out of sb's hands** arracher qch des mains de qn

wrest [rest] *vt* **to w. sth from sb** arracher qch à qn

wrestle ['resəl] *vi (with person)* lutter (**with** contre); *Fig* **to w. with sth** se débattre avec qch

wrestler ['reslə(r)] *n* lutteur(euse) *m,f*

wrestling ['reslɪŋ] *n* lutte *f*, catch *m*; **w. match** match *m* de catch

wretch [retʃ] *n* malheureux(euse) *m,f*

wretched ['retʃɪd] *adj* (**a**) *(very bad)* atroce (**b**) *(unhappy)* démoralisé(e) (**c**) *Fam (for emphasis)* **I can't find the w. umbrella!** je ne trouve pas ce maudit parapluie!

wriggle ['rɪɡəl] **1** *vt* **to w. one's way out of a situation** se sortir d'une situation

2 *vi* **to w. (about)** gigoter, se tortiller; **to w. out of sth** couper à qch; **he managed to w. out of paying me back** il s'est débrouillé pour ne pas me rembourser

wring [rɪŋ] *vt (pt & pp wrung* [rʌŋ]*) (clothes)* essorer; **to w. one's hands** se tordre les mains; **to w. sb's neck** tordre le cou à qn; *Fam* **I'd like to w. his neck** j'ai envie de lui tordre le cou; *Fig* **to w. sth from sb** réussir à arracher qch à qn

▸**wring out** *vt sep (clothes)* essorer

wringer ['rɪŋə(r)] *n* essoreuse *f*, *Fam Fig* **to put sb through the w.** faire passer un mauvais quart d'heure à qn

wringing ['rɪŋɪŋ] *adj* **w. (wet)** trempé(e)

wrinkle ['rɪŋkəl] **1** *n (on skin, paper)* ride *f*; *(in cloth)* faux pli *m*

2 *vi* se froisser

wrinkled ['rɪŋkəld] *adj (skin)* ridé(e); *(clothes, fabric)* froissé(e)

wrinkly ['rɪŋklɪ] *adj* fripé(e)

wrist [rɪst] *n* poignet *m*; **w. rest** repose-poignets *m*

wristwatch ['rɪstwɒtʃ] *n* montre-bracelet *f*

writ [rɪt] *n Law* ordre *m*, assignation *f*; **to serve a w. on sb** assigner qn en justice

write [raɪt] *(pt wrote* [rəʊt]*, pp written* ['rɪtən]*)* **1** *vt (answer, name)* écrire; *(cheque)* faire; *Am* **to w. sb** écrire à qn; **she had guilt written all over her face** la culpabilité se lisait sur son visage

2 *vi* écrire; *Br* **to w. to sb** écrire à qn; *Fam* **it's nothing to w. home about** ça n'a rien d'extraordinaire

▸**write away for** *vt insep* **to w. away for sth** écrire pour recevoir qch

▸**write back** *vi* répondre

▸**write down** *vt sep* noter

▸**write in 1** *vt sep (insert)* inscrire

2 *vi (send letter)* écrire

▸**write off 1** *vt sep* (**a**) *(debt)* annuler (**b**) *Br Fam (car)* bousiller (**c**) *Fam (person)* enterrer; **to w. sb off as a has-been** considérer qn comme un(e) ringard(e)

2 *vi* **to w. off for sth** écrire pour recevoir qch

▸**write out** *vt sep (instructions, recipe)* noter; *(cheque)* faire

▸**write up** *vt sep (notes, thesis)* rédiger; *(diary, journal)* tenir

write-off ['raɪtɒf] *n* (**a**) *Br Fam (car)* **to be a w.** être bon (bonne) pour la casse (**b**) *(of debt)* annulation *f*

write-protected ['raɪtprə'tektɪd] *adj Comput* protégé(e) en écriture

writer ['raɪtə(r)] *n (by profession)* écrivain *m*, auteur *m*; *(of article, book)* auteur *m*; **w.'s block** angoisse *f* de la page blanche

write-up ['raɪtʌp] *n (of play)* critique *f*

writhe [raɪð] *vi* se tordre (**in** de)

writing ['raɪtɪŋ] *n* (**a**) *(action, profession)* écriture *f*; **w. desk** bureau *m*, secrétaire *m*; **w. pad** bloc-notes *m*; **w. paper** papier *m* à lettres (**b**) *(handwriting)* écriture *f*; **in w.** par écrit (**c**) *(thing written)* écrit *m*; *Fig* **the w. is on the wall** la fin est proche

written ['rɪtən] **1** *adj* écrit(e); **w. consent** consentement *m* par écrit; **w. examination** écrit *m*, épreuve *f* écrite

2 *pp of* **write**

WRNS [renz] *n Br Mil (abbr* **Women's Royal Naval Service***)* = section féminine de la marine britannique

wrong [rɒŋ] **1** *n (immoral action)* mal *m*; **to know right from w.** distinguer le bien du mal; *Ironic* **he can do no w.** il est parfait; **to do sb w.** faire du tort à qn; *Prov* **two wrongs don't make a right** on ne répare pas le mal par le mal; **to be in the w.** être dans son tort

2 *adj* (**a**) *(morally bad)* mauvais(e); **stealing is w.** c'est mal de voler; **it was w. of you not to tell me** ce n'est pas bien de ta part de ne pas me l'avoir dit (**b**) *(incorrect, mistaken)* mauvais(e); **to be w.** *(of person)* avoir tort; **my watch is w.** ma montre n'est pas à l'heure; **don't get the w. idea** ne te fais pas de fausses idées; **I did/said the w. thing** j'ai fait/dit ce qu'il ne fallait pas; *Fig* **to go the w. way about doing sth** mal s'y prendre pour faire qch; *Fig* **to get on the w. side of sb** se faire mal voir de qn; **you've got the w. number** *(on phone)* vous vous êtes trompé(e) de numéro (**c**) *(amiss)* **what's w.?** qu'est-ce qui ne va pas?; **what's w. with you?** qu'est-ce que tu as?; **is anything w.?** quelque chose ne va pas?; **there's**

something w. **with the car** il y a quelque chose qui ne va pas dans cette voiture; *Fam* **he's w. in the head** il ne tourne pas rond
3 *adv* (**a**) *(morally)* mal; **to do w.** mal agir (**b**) *(incorrectly)* mal; **to go w.** se gâter; **where did I go w.?** qu'est-ce que j'ai fait qui n'allait pas?; **don't get me w., I like her** je n'ai pas dit que je ne l'aimais pas
4 *vt* faire du tort à, léser
wrongdoer ['rɒŋduːə(r)] *n* auteur *m* d'un tort
wrongdoing ['rɒŋduːɪŋ] *n (immoral action)* méfait *m*; *(crime)* infraction *f*
wrongful ['rɒŋfʊl] *adj* arbitraire; **w. dismissal** licenciement *m* abusif
wrong-headed [rɒŋ'hedɪd] *adj* buté(e), borné(e)
wrongly ['rɒŋlɪ] *adv* (**a**) *(unjustly)* à tort (**b**) *(incorrectly)* incorrectement
wrote [rəʊt] *pt of* **write**

wrought-iron ['rɔːt'aɪən] *adj* en fer forgé
wrought-up ['rɔːt'ʌp] *adj* **to be w.** être dans tous ses états
wrung [rʌŋ] *pt & pp of* **wring**
wry [raɪ] *adj* ironique
wt *(abbr* **weight)** p.
WTO [dʌbəljuːtiː'əʊ] *n (abbr* **World Trade Organization)** OMC *f*
WW *(abbr* **World War) WWI/II** la Première/Deuxième *ou* Seconde Guerre mondiale
WWF [dʌbəljuːdʌbəljuː'ef] *n (abbr* **WorldWildlife Fund, Worldwide Fund for Nature)** WWF *m*
WWW ['dʌbəljuːdʌbəljuː'dʌbəljuː] *n Comput (abbr* **worldwide web)** WWW, W3
WYSIWYG ['wɪzɪwɪg] *n Comput (abbr* **what you see is what you get)** WYSIWYG *m*

X, x [eks] *n (letter)* X, x *m inv*; **for x number of years** pendant x années; *Formerly* **X (certificate) film** film *m* classé X

xenon ['zenɒn] *n Chem* xénon *m*

xenophobia [zenə'fəʊbɪə] *n* xénophobie *f*

xenophobic [zenə'fəʊbɪk] *adj* xénophobe

Xerox® ['zɪərɒks] **1** *n (machine)* photocopieuse *f*; *(copy)* photocopie *f*
2 *vt* photocopier

XL ['eks'el] *(abbr extra large)* XL

Xmas ['eksməs] *n (abbr Christmas)* Noël *m*

X-rated [eks'reɪtɪd] *adj Formerly Cin (film)* interdit aux mineurs *ou* aux moins de dix-huit ans; *Fam* **some of the stuff she told me was pretty X.** elle m'a dit des choses assez corsées

X-ray ['eksreɪ] **1** *n (radiation)* rayon *m* X; *(picture)* radio *f*; **to have an X.** passer une radio
2 *vt* radiographier

xylophone ['zaɪləfəʊn] *n* xylophone *m*

Y, y [waɪ] *n (letter)* Y, y *m inv*; **Y-fronts** slip *m* ouvert
yacht [jɒt] *n (sailing boat)* voilier *m*; *(large private boat)* yacht *m*; **y. club** club *m* de voile; **y. race** régate *f*
yachting ['jɒtɪŋ] *n* voile *f*; **to go y.** faire de la voile
yachtsman ['jɒtsmən] *n* navigateur *m*
yachtswoman ['jɒtswʊmən] *n* navigatrice *f*
yack [jæk] *Fam* **1** *n* papotage *m*
  2 *vi* papoter
yak [jæk] *n* (**a**) *Zool* yack *m* (**b**) = yack
yam [jæm] *n Br* igname *f*; *Am* patate *f* douce
Yank [jæŋk], **Yankee** ['jæŋkɪ] *n Br Fam (person from the USA)* Ricain(e) *m,f*; *Am Fam (person from northeastern states of the USA)* habitant(e) *m,f* des États du Nord
yank [jæŋk] *Fam* **1** *n* **to give sth a y.** tirer qch d'un coup sec
  2 *vt* tirer d'un coup sec; **to y. sth open/out** ouvrir/arracher qch d'un coup sec
yap [jæp] *(pt & pp yapped) vi (of dog)* japper; *Fam (of person)* jacasser
yard¹ [jɑːd] *n (unit of measurement)* = 0,914 m, yard *m*
yard² *n* (**a**) *(of house, school, farm)* cour *f*; *Am (garden)* jardin *m*; *Am* **y. sale** vide-grenier *m* (**b**) *(for working)* chantier *m*; **(builder's) y.** chantier de construction (**c**) *(for storage)* dépôt *m* de marchandises
Yardie ['jɑːdɪ] *n* = membre d'un gang d'origine jamaïcaine
yardstick ['jɑːdstɪk] *n (standard)* point *m* de référence
yarn [jɑːn] *n* (**a**) *(thread, wool)* fil *m* (à tricoter) (**b**) *Fam (story)* histoire *f* à dormir debout; **to spin a y.** raconter une histoire
yawn [jɔːn] **1** *n* bâillement *m*; *Fam (boring thing)* plaie *f*
  2 *vi* (**a**) *(of person)* bâiller (**b**) *(of chasm)* béer
yd *(abbr* **yard(s))** yard *m*
ye [jiː] **1** *pron Lit* = you
  2 *definite art Lit or Hum* = the
yea [jeɪ] **1** *n* **yeas and nays** voix *fpl* pour et voix contre
  2 *adv Lit* = yes
yeah [jeə] *adv Fam* ouais
year [jɪə(r)] *n (twelve-month period)* an *m*; *(referring to duration)* année *f*; **in the y. 1931** en 1931; **this y.** cette année; **last/next y.** l'année dernière/prochaine; **every y.** chaque année, tous les ans; **twice a y.** deux fois par an; **to earn £20,000 a y.** gagner 20 000 livres par an; **to be ten years old** avoir dix ans; **he got five years** *(prison sentence)* il en a pris pour cinq ans; **for many years** pendant des années; **y. in y. out** chaque année; **over the years** au fil des ans, avec les années; **years ago** il y a des années; **it's years since I saw him, I haven't seen him for** *or* **in years** ça fait des années que je ne l'ai pas vu; **from her earliest years** dès son plus jeune âge; **to be getting on in years** prendre de l'âge
yearbook ['jɪəbʊk] *n* almanach *m*
yearlong ['jɪəlɒŋ] *adj* d'un an
yearly ['jɪəlɪ] **1** *adj* annuel(elle)
  2 *adv* annuellement; **twice y.** deux fois par an
yearn [jɜːn] *vi* **to y. for sth** désirer qch ardemment; **to y. to do sth** brûler de faire qch
yearning ['jɜːnɪŋ] *n* désir *m* ardent
yeast [jiːst] *n* levure *f*
yell [jel] **1** *n* hurlement *m*; **to give a y.** pousser un hurlement
  2 *vt & vi* hurler
yellow ['jeləʊ] **1** *n* jaune *m*
  2 *adj* (**a**) *(in colour)* jaune; **to turn** *or* **go y.** jaunir; **y. card** *(in football)* carton *m* jaune, *Belg* carte *f* jaune; **y. fever** fièvre *f* jaune; **y. line** bande *f* jaune; **to park on a y. line** ≃ se mettre en stationnement irrégulier; **double y. line(s)** double ligne *f* jaune; **the Y. Pages®** les Pages *fpl* Jaunes; **the Y. River** le fleuve Jaune (**b**) *Fam (cowardly)* trouillard(e)
  3 *vi* jaunir

Yellow lines

En Grande-Bretagne, une ligne jaune parallèle au trottoir signifie "arrêt autorisé réglementé" ; une double ligne jaune signifie "stationnement interdit".

yelp [jelp] **1** *n* jappement *m*
  2 *vi* japper
Yemen ['jemən] *n* le Yémen
Yemeni ['jemənɪ] **1** *n* Yéménite *mf*
  2 *adj* yéménite
yen¹ [jen] *n (Japanese currency)* yen *m*
yen² *n Fam* **to have a y. for sth/to do sth** avoir envie de qch/de faire qch
Yerevan [jerə'væn] *n* Erevan
yes [jes] **1** *adv* oui; *(after negative question)* si; **haven't you seen the film? – y.(, I have)** tu n'as pas vu ce film? – mais si(, je l'ai vue)
  2 *n* oui *m inv*
yes-man ['jesmæn] *n Fam* béni-oui-oui *m inv*
yesterday ['jestədeɪ] **1** *n* hier *m*
  2 *adv* hier; **y. morning/evening** hier matin/soir
yet [jet] **1** *adv* (**a**) *(still)* encore; **I haven't finished y.** je n'ai pas encore fini; **don't go y.** ne pars pas tout de suite; **I'll catch her y.!** je finirai bien par l'attraper!; **as y.** jusqu'à présent; **not y.** pas encore; **y. again**

encore une fois; **y. more** encore plus; **y. another mistake** encore une erreur (**b**) *(in questions)* **have they decided y.?** est-ce qu'ils ont décidé? **2** *conj* cependant; **small y. strong** petit(e) mais fort(e); **and y. I like her** et pourtant, je l'aime bien

yeti ['jetɪ] *n* yéti *m*

yew [juː] *n* if *m*

YHA *n (abbr* **Youth Hostels Association)** = association des auberges de jeunesse

Yiddish ['jɪdɪʃ] **1** *n* yiddish *m* **2** *adj* yiddish *inv*

yield [jiːld] **1** *n (of field, shares)* rendement *m*; *(of mine)* production *f* **2** *vt* (*interest)* rapporter; *(results)* donner; **to y. a profit** rapporter (**b**) *(territory, right)* céder **3** *vi (surrender)* se rendre; **to y. to force** céder devant la force; **to y. to reason** se rendre à la raison; **to y. to temptation** céder à la tentation

yippee [jɪˈpiː] *exclam* youpi!

YMCA [waɪemsiːˈeɪ] *n (abbr* **Young Men's Christian Association)** = association chrétienne proposant hébergement et activités sportives

yob [jɒb], **yobbo** ['jɒbəʊ] *(pl* yobbos *or* yobboes) *n Fam* loubard *m*

yodel ['jəʊdəl] *(pt & pp* yodelled) *vi* iodler

yoga ['jəʊɡə] *n* yoga *m*; **y. mat** tapis *m* de yoga

yoghurt, yogurt ['jɒɡət] *n* yaourt *m*

yoke [jəʊk] **1** *n* (**a**) *(for oxen) & Fig* joug *m* (**b**) *(for carrying)* palanche *f* **2** *vt (oxen)* atteler; *Fig* **to be yoked to sth** être lié(e) à qch

yokel ['jəʊkəl] *n Pej or Hum* péquenaud(e) *m,f*

yolk [jəʊk] *n* jaune *m* (d'œuf)

yonder ['jɒndə(r)] *adv* (over) **y.** là-bas

yonks [jɒŋks] *npl Br Fam* une éternité; **it was y. ago** ça fait une paye

Yorkshire pudding ['jɔːkʃɪəˈpʊdɪŋ] *n* = crêpe épaisse salée traditionnellement servie avec du rôti de bœuf

you [juː] *pron* (**a**) *(subject) (familiar)* tu; *(formal, familiar plural)* vous; **you're late** tu es/vous êtes en retard; **have you got it?** c'est toi qui l'as/vous qui l'avez? (**b**) *(direct object) (familiar)* te; *(formal, familiar plural)* vous; **I hate you** je te/vous déteste; **I love y.** je t'aime/ je vous aime; **I can understand your son but not you** je comprends ton fils, mais toi, je ne te comprends pas (**c**) *(indirect object) (familiar)* te; *(formal, familiar plural)* vous; **I gave y. the book** je t'ai/vous ai donné le livre; **I gave it to y.** je te/vous l'ai donné (**d**) *(after preposition) (familiar)* toi; *(formal, familiar plural)* vous; **I'm thinking of y.** je pense à toi/vous (**e**) *(as complement of verb to be) (familiar)* toi; *(formal, familiar plural)* vous; **it's y.** c'est toi/vous; **it was y. who did it** c'est toi qui l'as fait/vous qui l'avez fait (**f**) *(impersonal)* on; **y. never know** on ne sait jamais; **y. have to be careful with her** il faut faire attention avec elle; **smoking is bad for y.** fumer est mauvais pour la santé (**g**) *(in apposition)* **y. men/French** vous les hommes/les Français; **y. idiot!** espèce d'idiot! (**h**) *(with imperative)* **y. sit down here** toi, tu t'assois ici; **don't y. dare!** je t'interdis de le faire! (**i**) *(with interjections)* **silly y.!** que tu es bête!; **poor y.!** pauvre de toi!

you'd [juːd] = you had, you would

you-know-who [juːnəʊˈhuː] *n* qui-tu-sais

you'll [juːl] = you will, you shall

young [jʌŋ] **1** *adj* jeune; **she's younger than me** elle est plus jeune que moi; **she's two years younger than me** elle a deux ans de moins que moi; **you're only y. once** on n'a qu'une jeunesse; **when I was a y. man/woman** quand j'étais jeune; **in his younger days** dans sa jeunesse; **the night is y.!** la soirée ne fait que commencer!; **y. people** les jeunes *mpl*; **she's y. for her age** elle fait plus jeune que son âge; **y. in spirit** *or* **at heart** jeune d'esprit **2** *npl* (**a**) *(people)* **the y.** les jeunes *mpl* (**b**) *(animals)* petits *mpl*

youngster ['jʌŋstə(r)] *n* jeune *mf*

your [jɔː(r)] *possessive adj* (**a**) *(with singular possession) (familiar)* ton (ta); *(formal, familiar plural)* votre; *(with plural possession) (familiar)* tes; *(formal, familiar plural)* vos; **y. job** ton/votre travail; **y. wife** ta/votre femme; **y. parents** tes/vos parents; **it wasn't YOUR idea!** ce n'est pas toi qui en as eu l'idée! (**b**) *(for parts of body)* **did you hit y. head?** vous vous êtes cogné la tête? (**c**) *(impersonal)* **you should buy y. ticket first** on doit acheter son billet d'abord; **smoking is bad for y. health** fumer est mauvais pour la santé; *Fam* **y. average Frenchman** le Français moyen

you're [jɔː(r)] = you are

yours [jɔːz] *possessive pron* (**a**) *(replacing singular possession) (familiar)* le tien (la tienne) *m,f*; *(formal, familiar plural)* le vôtre (la vôtre) *m,f*; *(replacing plural possession) (familiar)* les tiens (les tiennes) *mpl,fpl*; *(formal, familiar plural)* les vôtres *mfpl*; **my house is big, but y. is bigger** ma maison est grande, mais la tienne est plus grande encore (**b**) *(used attributively)* **this book is y.** ce livre est à toi/à vous; **a friend of y.** un de tes/vos amis; **where's that brother of y.?** où ton frère a-t-il bien pu passer?

yourself [jɔːˈself] *pron* (**a**) *(reflexive)* **did you hurt y.?** *(familiar)* tu t'es blessé(e)?; *(formal)* vous vous êtes blessé(e)? (**b**) *(emphatic) (familiar)* toi-même; *(formal)* vous-même; **you y. have never...** vous-même n'avez jamais...; **you told me y.** vous me l'avez dit vous-même; **you're not y. today** tu n'es pas dans ton état normal aujourd'hui (**c**) *(after preposition)* **do you live by y.?** vous vivez seul(e)?; **did you buy it for y.?** vous l'avez acheté pour vous-même?; **are you talking to y.?** tu parles tout(e) seul(e)?

yourselves [jɔːˈselvz] *pron* (**a**) *(reflexive)* **have you hurt y.?** vous vous êtes blessé(e)s? (**b**) *(emphatic)* vous-mêmes; **you y. have never...** vous-mêmes n'avez jamais...; **you told me y.** vous me l'avez dit vous-mêmes; **you're not y. today** vous n'êtes pas dans votre état normal aujourd'hui (**c**) *(after preposition)* **do you live by y.?** vous vivez seul(e)s?; **did you buy it for y.?** vous l'avez acheté pour vous-mêmes?; **do you talk to y.?** vous parlez tout(es) seul(e)s?

youth [juːθ] *n* (**a**) *(period)* jeunesse *f* (**b**) *(young man)* adolescent *m*, jeune *m* (**c**) *(young people)* jeunes *mpl*; **y. club** centre *m* de loisir pour les jeunes; **y. hostel** auberge *f* de jeunesse; **y. worker** éducateur(trice) *m,f*

youthful ['juːθfʊl] *adj (person, looks)* jeune; *(enthusiasm)* juvénile

you've [juːv] = you have

yowl [jaʊl] **1** *n* hurlement *m* **2** *vi* hurler

yo-yo® ['jəʊjəʊ] *(pl* yo-yos) *n* yo-yo® *m*

yr *(abbr* year) année *f*

yuan [juːˈæn] *n* yuan *m*

yucca ['jʌkə] *n* yucca *m*

yuck [jʌk] *exclam Fam* berk!
yucky [ˈjʌkɪ] *adj Fam* dégoûtant(e)
Yugoslav [ˈjuːɡəʊslɑːv] **1** *n* Yougoslave *mf*
2 *adj* yougoslave
Yugoslavia [juːɡəʊˈslɑːvɪə] *n* la Yougoslavie
Yugoslavian [juːɡəʊˈslɑːvɪən] *adj* yougoslave
yuletide [ˈjuːltaɪd] *n* Noël *m*
yummy [ˈjʌmɪ] *adj Fam* délicieux(euse)

yuppie [ˈjʌpɪ] *n* yuppie *mf*; **y. area** quartier *m* riche et branché; *Fam* **y. flu** syndrome *m* de la fatigue chronique
yuppify [ˈjʌpɪfaɪ] (*pt & pp* **yuppified**) *vt* to become **yuppified** s'embourgeoiser
YWCA [waɪdʌbəljuːsiːˈeɪ] *n* (*abbr* **Young Women's Christian Association**) = association chrétienne proposant hébergement et activités sportives

Z, z [zed, *Am* ziː] *n (letter)* Z, z *m inv*
Zaire [zɑːˈɪə(r)] *n Formerly* le Zaïre
Zairean [zɑːˈɪərɪən] **1** *n* Zaïrois(oise) *m,f*
 2 *adj* zaïrois(oise)
Zambia [ˈzæmbɪə] *n* la Zambie
Zambian [ˈzæmbɪən] **1** *n* Zambien(enne) *m,f*
 2 *adj* zambien(enne)
zany [ˈzeɪnɪ] *adj* loufoque
zap [zæp] *(pt & pp* **zapped)** *Fam* **1** *vt (destroy, disable)*
 éliminer
 2 *vi (change TV channel)* zapper
zapper [ˈzæpə(r)] *n Fam (TV remote control)* télécommande *f*
zeal [ziːl] *n* zèle *m*
zealot [ˈzelət] *n* fanatique *mf*
zealous [ˈzeləs] *adj* zélé(e); *(campaigner, supporter)*
 fervent(e)
zebra [*Br* ˈzebrə, *Am* ˈziːbrə] *n* zèbre *m; Br* **z. crossing**
 passage *m* pour piétons
zeds [zedz] *npl Fam (sleep)* **to catch some z.** piquer un
 roupillon
zenith [ˈzenɪθ] *n also Fig* zénith *m;* **at the z. of her**
 powers/influence au sommet de son pouvoir/
 influence
zephyr [ˈzefə(r)] *n* zéphyr *m*
zero [ˈzɪərəʊ] **1** *n (pl* **zeros)** zéro *m;* **22 degrees below**
 z. 22 degrés en dessous de zéro
 2 *adj Fam* aucun(e); **to have z. charm** n'avoir aucun
 charme; **z. tolerance** tolérance *f* zéro *(politique d'in-*
 transigeance à l'égard de toute infraction à la loi ou au
 règlement)
 3 *vi (pt & pp* **zeroed) to z. in on sb** foncer sur qn; **to**
 z. in on sth se concentrer sur qch
zero-rated [ˈzɪərəʊreɪtɪd] *adj Fin (for VAT)* exonéré(e)
 de TVA
zest [zest] *n* (**a**) *(enjoyment)* enthousiasme *m* (**b**) *(of*
 orange, lemon) zeste *m*
zigzag [ˈzɪgzæg] **1** *n* zigzag *m*
 2 *vi (pt & pp* **zigzagged)** zigzaguer
zilch [zɪltʃ] *n Fam* que dalle
Zimbabwe [zɪmˈbɑːbweɪ] *n* le Zimbabwe
Zimbabwean [zɪmˈbɑːbweɪən] **1** *n* Zimbabwéen (enne)
 m,f
 2 *adj* zimbabwéen(enne)

zinc [zɪŋk] *n* zinc *m*
Zionism [ˈzaɪənɪzəm] *n* sionisme *m*
Zionist [ˈzaɪənɪst] **1** *n* sioniste *mf*
 2 *adj* sioniste
zip [zɪp] **1** *n* (**a**) *Br* **z. (fastener)** fermeture *f* Éclair®
 (**b**) *Fam (vigour)* punch *m* (**c**) *Am* **z. code** code *m*
 postal
 2 *vt Comput* zipper, compresser
 3 *vi (pt & pp* **zipped) to z. past** *(of car)* passer en
 trombe; *(of bullet)* passer en sifflant
▶**zip through** *vt insep Fam* **I zipped through the book**
 j'ai lu le livre à toute vitesse; **we zipped through the**
 work nous avons fait le travail à toute vitesse
▶**zip up 1** *vt sep (clothes)* remonter la fermeture Éclair®
 de
 2 *vi* se fermer par une fermeture Éclair®
Zip® *n Comput* Zip®; **Z. disk** cartouche *f* Zip®; **Z.**
 drive lecteur *m* Zip®
zipper [ˈzɪpə(r)] *n Am* fermeture *f* Éclair®
zippy [ˈzɪpɪ] *adj Fam* plein(e) de punch
zit [zɪt] *n Am Fam* bouton *m*
zither [ˈzɪðə(r)] *n* cithare *f*
zodiac [ˈzəʊdɪæk] *n* zodiaque *m*
zombie [ˈzɒmbɪ] *n* zombi *m*
zone [zəʊn] **1** *n* zone *f*
 2 *vt* diviser en zones
zonked (out) [zɒŋkt(ˈaʊt)] *adj Fam (exhausted)* cassé(e); *(drugged)* défoncé(e); *(drunk)* pété(e)
zoo [zuː] *(pl* **zoos)** *n* zoo *m*
zoological [zəʊəˈlɒdʒɪkəl] *adj* zoologique; **z. gar-**
 den(s) jardin *m* zoologique
zoologist [zəʊˈɒlədʒɪst] *n* zoologiste *mf*
zoology [zəʊˈɒlədʒɪ] *n* zoologie *f*
zoom [zuːm] **1** *n* (**a**) *(noise)* vrombissement *m* (**b**) **z.**
 lens zoom *m*
 2 *vi Fam* (**a**) *(move quickly)* **to z. in/out/past** entrer/
 sortir/passer comme une flèche (**b**) *(increase*
 quickly) monter en flèche
▶**zoom in** *vi (of camera)* faire un zoom avant (**on** sur)
zucchini [zuːˈkiːnɪ] *(pl* **zucchini** *or* **zucchinis)** *n Am*
 courgette *f*
Zulu [ˈzuːluː] **1** *n* Zoulou *mf*
 2 *adj* zoulou(e)

Supplement
Supplément

Verbes anglais irréguliers
English Irregular Verbs

Infinitif	Prétérit	Participe passé
arise	arose	arisen
awake	awoke	awoken
awaken	awoke, awakened	awakened, awoken
be	were/was	been
bear	bore	borne
beat	beat	beaten
become	became	become
begin	began	begun
bend	bent	bent
beseech	besought, beseeched	besought, beseeched
bet	bet, betted	bet, betted
bid	bade, bid	bidden, bid
bind	bound	bound
bite	bit	bitten
bleed	bled	bled
blow	blew	blown
break	broke	broken
breed	bred	bred
bring	brought	brought
build	built	built
burn	burnt, burned	burnt, burned
burst	burst	burst
bust	bust, busted	bust, busted
buy	bought	bought
cast	cast	cast
catch	caught	caught
chide	chided, chid	chided, chidden
choose	chose	chosen
cleave	cleaved, cleft, clove	cleaved, cleft, cloven
cling	clung	clung
clothe	clad, clothed	clad, clothed
come	came	come
cost	cost	cost
creep	crept	crept
crow	crowed, crew	crowed
cut	cut	cut
deal	dealt	dealt
dig	dug	dug
dive	dived, *Am* dove	dived
do	did	done
draw	drew	drawn
dream	dreamt, dreamed	dreamt, dreamed
drink	drank	drunk
drive	drove	driven
dwell	dwelt	dwelt
eat	ate	eaten
fall	fell	fallen
feed	fed	fed
feel	felt	felt

Verbes anglais irréguliers

Infinitif	Prétérit	Participe passé
fight	fought	fought
find	found	found
flee	fled	fled
fling	flung	flung
fly	flew	flown
forget	forgot	forgotten
forgive	forgave	forgiven
forsake	forsook	forsaken
freeze	froze	frozen
get	got	got, *Am* gotten
gild	gilded, gilt	gilded, gilt
gird	girded, girt	girded, girt
give	gave	given
go	went	gone
grind	ground	ground
grow	grew	grown
hang	hung/hanged	hung/hanged
have	had	had
hear	heard	heard
hew	hewed	hewn, hewed
hide	hid	hidden
hit	hit	hit
hold	held	held
hurt	hurt	hurt
keep	kept	kept
kneel	knelt	knelt
knit	knitted, knit	knitted, knit
know	knew	known
lay	laid	laid
lead	led	led
lean	leant, leaned	leant, leaned
leap	leapt, leaped	leapt, leaped
learn	learnt, learned	learnt, learned
leave	left	left
lend	lent	lent
let	let	let
lie	lay	lain
light	lit	lit
lose	lost	lost
make	made	made
mean	meant	meant
meet	met	met
mow	mowed	mown
pay	paid	paid
plead	pleaded, *Am* pled	pleaded, *Am* pled
prove	proved	proved, proven
put	put	put
quit	quit	quit
read	read	read
rend	rent	rent
rid	rid	rid
ride	rode	ridden
ring	rang	rung
rise	rose	risen
run	ran	run
saw	sawed	sawn, sawed
say	said	said

Infinitif	Prétérit	Participe passé
see	saw	seen
seek	sought	sought
sell	sold	sold
send	sent	sent
set	set	set
sew	sewed	sewn
shake	shook	shaken
shear	sheared	shorn, sheared
shed	shed	shed
shine	shone	shone
shit	shitted, shat	shitted, shat
shoe	shod	shod
shoot	shot	shot
show	showed	shown
shrink	shrank	shrunk
shut	shut	shut
sing	sang	sung
sink	sank	sunk
sit	sat	sat
slay	slew	slain
sleep	slept	slept
slide	slid	slid
sling	slung	slung
slink	slunk	slunk
slit	slit	slit
smell	smelled, smelt	smelled, smelt
smite	smote	smitten
sow	sowed	sown, sowed
speak	spoke	spoken
speed	sped	sped
spell	spelt, spelled	spelt, spelled
spend	spent	spent
spill	spilt, spilled	spilt, spilled
spin	span	spun
spit	spat, *Am* spit	spat, *Am* spit
split	split	split
spoil	spoilt, spoiled	spoilt, spoiled
spread	spread	spread
spring	sprang	sprung
stand	stood	stood
stave in	staved in, stove in	staved in, stove in
steal	stole	stolen
stick	stuck	stuck
sting	stung	stung
stink	stank, stunk	stunk
strew	strewed	strewed, strewn
stride	strode	stridden
strike	struck	struck
string	strung	strung
strive	strove	striven
swear	swore	sworn
sweep	swept	swept
swell	swelled	swollen, swelled
swim	swam	swum
swing	swung	swung
take	took	taken
teach	taught	taught

Verbes anglais irréguliers

Infinitif	Prétérit	Participe passé
tear	tore	torn
tell	told	told
think	thought	thought
thrive	thrived, throve	thrived
throw	threw	thrown
thrust	thrust	thrust
tread	trod	trodden
wake	woke	woken
wear	wore	worn
weave	wove, weaved	woven, weaved
weep	wept	wept
wet	wet, wetted	wet, wetted
win	won	won
wind	wound	wound
wring	wrung	wrung
write	wrote	written

French Conjugation Tables
Conjugaisons françaises

Full listings of the conjugations of French regular -er, -ir and -re verbs are given on pages (8) and (9). On the following pages you will find a list of model irregular verbs. Numbers after verbs in the French-English side of the dictionary, eg [20], refer you to these tables where you will find their irregular forms.

The more common verbs such as **aller, avoir, être** and **faire** are shown in full for all persons and all tenses. In other cases, where complete forms have not been shown they follow the pattern indicated by the first person singular and/or plural.

As the perfect tense is always formed simply by **avoir** or **être** plus the past participle, this has not been shown apart from the verbs mentioned above. Similarly, the conditional tense can always be formed in the same way as the future tense but with the endings **-ais, -ais, -ait, -ions, -iez** and **-aient**. When not shown, the imperative has the same form as the present tense ("tu", "nous" and "vous" forms).

Toutes les formes des verbes réguliers en **-er, -ir** et **-re** sont données pages (8) et (9), suivies d'une liste de conjugaisons irrégulières types. Les nombres apparaissant après les verbes dans la partie français-anglais du dictionnaire, par exemple [20], renvoient à cette liste.

Toutes les personnes et tous les temps sont donnés systématiquement pour les verbes d'usage fréquent tels qu'**aller, avoir, être** et **faire**. Dans tous les autres cas, seules les formes particulières, c'est-à-dire celles qui ne suivent pas le modèle déterminé par la première personne du singulier et/ou du pluriel, sont indiquées.

Le passé composé étant toujours formé sur le modèle **avoir/être** + participe passé, il n'a pas été inclus dans nos listes, sauf pour les verbes mentionnés ci-dessus. De même, le conditionnel se construira à partir du futur.

INDICATIVE

Present	Imperfect	Perfect	Past Historic	Future
REGULAR -er verb aimer				
j'aime	j'aimais	j'ai aimé	j'aimai	j'aimerai
tu aimes	tu aimais	tu as aimé	tu aimas	tu aimeras
il aime	il aimait	il a aimé	il aima	il aimera
nous aimons	nous aimions	nous avons aimé	nous aimâmes	nous aimerons
vous aimez	vous aimiez	vous avez aimé	vous aimâtes	vous aimerez
ils aiment	ils aimaient	ils ont aimé	ils aimèrent	ils aimeront
REGULAR -ir verb choisir				
je choisis	je choisissais	j'ai choisi	je choisis	je choisirai
tu choisis	tu choisissais	tu as choisi	tu choisis	tu choisiras
il choisit	il choisissait	il a choisi	il choisit	il choisira
nous choisissons	nous choisissions	nous avons choisi	nous choisîmes	nous choisirons
vous choisissez	vous choisissiez	vous avez choisi	vous choisîtes	vous choisirez
ils choisissent	ils choisissaient	ils ont choisi	ils choisirent	ils choisiront
REGULAR -re verb attendre				
j'attends	j'attendais	j'ai attendu	j'attendis	j'attendrai
tu attends	tu attendais	tu as attendu	tu attendis	tu attendras
il attend	il attendait	il a attendu	il attendit	il attendra
nous attendons	nous attendions	nous avons attendu	nous attendîmes	nous attendrons
vous attendez	vous attendiez	vous avez attendu	vous attendîtes	vous attendrez
ils attendent	ils attendaient	ils ont attendu	ils attendirent	ils attendront

CONDITIONAL	SUBJUNCTIVE			IMPERATIVE	PARTICIPLE	
Present	Present	Imperfect			Present	Past
j'aimerais	j'aime	j'aimasse			aimant	aimé
tu aimerais	tu aimes	tu aimasses	aime			
il aimerait	il aime	il aimât				
nous aimerions	nous aimions	nous aimassions	aimons			
vous aimeriez	vous aimiez	vous aimassiez	aimez			
ils aimeraient	ils aiment	ils aimassent				
je choisirais	je choisisse	je choisisse			choisissant	choisi
tu choisirais	tu choisisses	tu choisisses	choisis			
il choisirait	il choisisse	il choisît				
nous choisirions	nous choisissions	nous choisissions	choisissons			
vous choisiriez	vous choisissiez	vous choisissiez	choisissez			
ils choisiraient	ils choisissent	ils choisissent				
j'attendrais	j'attende	j'attendisse			attendant	attendu
tu attendrais	tu attendes	tu attendisses	attends			
il attendrait	il attende	il attendît				
nous attendrions	nous attendions	nous attendissions	attendons			
vous attendriez	vous attendiez	vous attendissiez	attendez			
ils attendraient	ils attendent	ils attendissent				

INDICATIVE

Present	Imperfect	Perfect	Past Historic	Future

1. avoir

Present	Imperfect	Perfect	Past Historic	Future
j'ai	j'avais	j'ai eu	j'eus	j'aurai
tu as	tu avais	tu as eu	tu eus	tu auras
il a	il avait	il a eu	il eut	il aura
nous avons	nous avions	nous avons eu	nous eûmes	nous aurons
vous avez	vous aviez	vous avez eu	vous eûtes	vous aurez
ils ont	ils avaient	ils ont eu	ils eurent	ils auront

2. être

Present	Imperfect	Perfect	Past Historic	Future
je suis	j'étais	j'ai été	je fus	je serai
tu es	tu étais	tu as été	tu fus	tu seras
il est	il était	il a été	il fut	il sera
nous sommes	nous étions	nous avons été	nous fûmes	nous serons
vous êtes	vous étiez	vous avez été	vous fûtes	vous serez
ils sont	ils étaient	ils ont été	ils furent	ils seront

3a. absoudre

Present	Imperfect	Perfect	Past Historic	Future
j'absous	j'absolvais		j'absolus	j'absoudrai
il absout				
nous absolvons				

3b. résoudre PAST PARTICIPLE résolu

4a. accroître

Present	Imperfect	Perfect	Past Historic	Future
j'accrois	j'accroissais		j'accrus	j'accroîtrai
il accroît				
nous accroissons				

4b. croître *follows the above pattern except for the following*

Present	Imperfect	Perfect	Past Historic	Future
je croîs			je crûs	

5. accueillir

Present	Imperfect	Perfect	Past Historic	Future
j'accueille	j'accueillais		j'accueillis	j'accueillerai
nous accueillons				

6. acheter

Present	Imperfect	Perfect	Past Historic	Future
j'achète	j'achetais		j'achetai	j'achèterai
nous achetons				
ils achètent				

7. acquérir

Present	Imperfect	Perfect	Past Historic	Future
j'acquiers	j'acquérais		j'acquis	j'acquerrai
il acquiert				
nous acquérons				
ils acquièrent				

8. aller

Present	Imperfect	Perfect	Past Historic	Future
je vais	j'allais	je suis allé	j'allai	j'irai
tu vas	tu allais	tu es allé	tu allas	tu iras
il va	il allait	il est allé	il alla	il ira
nous allons	nous allions	nous sommes allés	nous allâmes	nous irons
vous allez	vous alliez	vous êtes allés	vous allâtes	vous irez
ils vont	ils allaient	ils sont allés	ils allèrent	ils iront

CONDITIONAL Present	SUBJUNCTIVE Present	Imperfect	IMPERATIVE	PARTICIPLE Present	Past
j'aurais	j'aie	j'eusse		ayant	eu
tu aurais	tu aies	tu eusses	aie		
il aurait	il ait	il eût			
nous aurions	nous ayons	nous eussions	ayons		
vous auriez	vous ayez	vous eussiez	ayez		
ils auraient	ils aient	ils eussent			
je serais	je sois	je fusse		étant	été
tu serais	tu sois	tu fusses	sois		
il serait	il soit	il fût			
nous serions	nous soyons	nous fussions	soyons		
vous seriez	vous soyez	vous fussiez	soyez		
ils seraient	ils soient	ils fussent			
	j'absolve	*not used*		absolvant	absous (oute)
	nous absolvions				
	j'accroisse	j'accrusse		accroissant	accru
	nous accroissions	nous accrussions			
		je crûsse			crû
	j'accueille	j'accueillisse		accueillant	accueilli
			accueille		
	nous accueillions	nous accueillissions	accueillons		
			accueillez		
	j'achète	j'achetasse		achetant	acheté
	nous achetions	nous achetassions			
	j'acquière	j'acquisse		acquérant	acquis
	nous acquérions	nous acquissions			
j'irais	j'aille	j'allasse		allant	allé
tu irais	tu ailles	tu allasses	va		
il irait	il aille	il allât			
nous irions	nous allions	nous allassions	allons		
vous iriez	vous alliez	vous allassiez	allez		
ils iraient	ils aillent	ils allassent			

INDICATIVE

Present	Imperfect	Perfect	Past Historic	Future
9. appeler				
j'appelle	j'appelais		j'appelai	j'appellerai
nous appelons				
ils appellent				
10a. s'asseoir				
je m'assieds/	je m'asseyais/		je m'assis	je m'assiérai/assoirai
assois	assoyais			
il s'assied/assoit				
nous nous				
asseyons/				
assoyons				
10b. surseoir *follows pattern of* oi *forms of* s'asseoir				
				je surseoirai
11. battre				
je bats	je battais		je battis	je battrai
il bat				
nous battons				
12. boire				
je bois	je buvais		je bus	je boirai
il boit				
nous buvons				
ils boivent				
13. bouillir				
je bous	je bouillais		je bouillis	je bouillirai
il bout				
nous bouillons				
14. choir				
je chois				
il chut			il chût	
ils choient				
15. clore				
je clos				je clorai
il clôt				
ils closent				
16. commencer				
je commence	je commençais		je commençai	je commencerai
nous commençons				
vous commencez				
ils commencent				
17a. conclure				
je conclus	je concluais		je conclus	je conclurai
il conclut				
nous concluons				
17b. inclure PAST PARTICIPLE inclus				

CONDITIONAL	SUBJUNCTIVE		IMPERATIVE	PARTICIPLE	
Present	Present	Imperfect		Present	Past
	j'appelle	j'appelasse		appelant	appelé
	nous appelions	nous appelassions			
	je m'asseye/ assoie	je m'assisse		asseyant/ assoyant	assis
	nous nous asseyions/ assoyions	nous nous assissions			
je surseoirais					
	je batte	je battisse		battant	battu
	nous battions	nous battissions			
	je boive	je busse		buvant	bu
	nous buvions	nous bussions			
	je bouille	je bouillisse		bouillant	bouilli
	nous bouillions	nous bouillissions			
					chu
	je close				clos
	nous closions				
	je commence	je commençasse		commençant	commencé
	nous commencions	nous commençassions			
	je conclue	je conclusse		concluant	conclu
	nous concluions	nous conclussions			

INDICATIVE

Present	Imperfect	Perfect	Past Historic	Future
18. conduire				
je conduis	je conduisais		je conduisis	je conduirai
il conduit				
nous conduisons				
19a. confire				
je confis	je confisais		je confis	je confira
il confit				
nous confisons				
19b. suffire PAST PARTICIPLE suffi (invariable)				
20. connaître				
je connais	je connaissais		je connus	je connaîtrai
il connaît				
nous connaissons				
21. coudre				
je couds	je cousais		je cousis	je coudrai
il coud				
nous cousons				
22. courir				
je cours	je courais		je courus	je courrai
il court				
nous courons				
23. craindre				
je crains	je craignais		je craignis	je craindrai
il craint				
nous craignons				
24. créer				
je crée	je créais		je créai	je créerai
nous créons				
25. croire				
je crois	je croyais		je crus	je croirai
il croit				
nous croyons				
ils croient				
26. devoir				
je dois	je devais		je dus	je devrai
il doit				
nous devons				
ils doivent				
27a. dire				
je dis	je disais		je dis	je dirai
il dit				
nous disons				
vous dites				

CONDITIONAL Present	SUBJUNCTIVE Present	Imperfect	IMPERATIVE	PARTICIPLE Present	Past
	je conduise	je conduisisse		conduisant	conduit
	nous conduisions	nous conduisissions			
	je confise	je confisse		confisant	confit
	nous confisions	nous confissions			
	je connaisse	je connusse		connaissant	connu
	nous connaissions	nous connussions			
	je couse	je cousisse		cousant	cousu
	nous cousions	nous cousissions			
	je coure	je courusse		courant	couru
	nous courions	nous courussions			
	je craigne	je craignisse		craignant	craint
	nous craignions	nous craignissions			
	je crée	je créasse		créant	créé
	nous créions	nous créassions			
	je croie	je crusse		croyant	cru
	nous croyions	nous crussions			
	je doive	je dusse		devant	dû (due), dus (dues)
	nous devions	nous dussions			
	je dise	je disse		disant	dit
	nous disions	nous dissions			

INDICATIVE

Present	Imperfect	Perfect	Past Historic	Future

27b. contredire, interdire etc PRESENT vous contredisez, interdisez

28. distraire

Present	Imperfect	Perfect	Past Historic	Future
je distrais	je distrayais			je distrairai
il distrait				
nous distrayons				
ils distraient				

29. dormir

Present	Imperfect	Perfect	Past Historic	Future
je dors	je dormais		je dormis	je dormirai
il dort				
nous dormons				

30. écrire

Present	Imperfect	Perfect	Past Historic	Future
j'écris	j'écrivais		j'écrivis	j'écrirai
il écrit				
nous écrivons				

31a. émouvoir

Present	Imperfect	Perfect	Past Historic	Future
j'émeus	j'émouvais		j'émus	j'émouvrai
il émeut				
nous émouvons				
ils émeuvent				

31b. mouvoir PAST PARTICIPLE mû (mue), mus (mues)

32. employer

Present	Imperfect	Perfect	Past Historic	Future
j'emploie	j'employais		j'employai	j'emploierai
nous employons				
ils emploient				

33. envoyer

Present	Imperfect	Perfect	Past Historic	Future
j'envoie	j'envoyais		j'envoyai	j'enverrai
nous envoyons				
ils envoient				

34. espérer

Present	Imperfect	Perfect	Past Historic	Future
j'espère	j'espérais		j'espérai	j'espérerai
nous espérons				
ils espèrent				

35. faillir

Present	Imperfect	Perfect	Past Historic	Future
je faillis				je faillirai

36. faire

Present	Imperfect	Perfect	Past Historic	Future
je fais	je faisais	j'ai fait	je fis	je ferai
tu fais	tu faisais	tu as fait	tu fis	tu feras
il fait	il faisait	il a fait	il fit	il fera
nous faisons	nous faisions	nous avons fait	nous fîmes	nous ferons
vous faites	vous faisiez	vous avez fait	vous fîtes	vous ferez
ils font	ils faisaient	ils ont fait	ils firent	ils feront

37. falloir

Present	Imperfect	Perfect	Past Historic	Future
il faut	il fallait		il fallut	il faudra

CONDITIONAL Present	SUBJUNCTIVE Present	Imperfect	IMPERATIVE	PARTICIPLE Present	Past
	je distraie			distrayant	distrait
	nous distrayions				
	je dorme	je dormisse		dormant	dormi
	nous dormions	nous dormissions			
	j'écrive	j'écrivisse		écrivant	écrit
	nous écrivions	nous écrivissions			
	j'émeuve	j'émusse		émouvant	ému
	nous émouvions	nous émussions			
	j'emploie	j'employasse		employant	employé
	nous employions	nous employassions			
	j'envoie	j'envoyasse		envoyant	envoyé
	nous envoyions	nous envoyassions			
	j'espère	j'espérasse		espérant	espéré
	nous espérions	nous espérassions			
				faillant	failli
je ferais	je fasse	je fisse		faisant	fait
tu ferais	tu fasses	tu fisses	fais		
il ferait	il fasse	il fît			
nous ferions	nous fassions	nous fissions	faisons		
vous feriez	vous fassiez	vous fissiez	faites		
ils feraient	ils fassent	ils fissent			
					fallu
	il faille	il fallût			

INDICATIVE

Present	Imperfect	Perfect	Past Historic	Future
38. fuir				
je fuis	je fuyais		je fuis	je fuirai
il fuit				
nous fuyons				
ils fuient				
39. geler				
je gèle	je gelais		je gelai	je gèlerai
nous gelons	nous gelions			
ils gèlent				
40. gésir				
je gis	je gisais			
il gît				
nous gisons				
41. haïr				
je hais	je haïssais		je haïs	je haïrai
il hait				
nous haïssons				
42. jeter				
je jette	je jetais		je jetai	je jetterai
nous jetons				
ils jettent				
43. joindre				
je joins	je joignais		je joignis	je joindrai
nous joignons				
44. lire				
je lis	je lisais		je lus	je lirai
nous lisons				
45. manger				
je mange	je mangeais		je mangeai	je mangerai
nous mangeons				
46. mener				
je mène	je menais		je menai	je mènerai
nous menons				
ils mènent				
47. mettre				
je mets	je mettais		je mis	je mettrai
il met				
nous mettons				
48. moudre				
je mouds	je moulais		je moulus	je moudrai
il moud				
nous moulons				

CONDITIONAL Present	SUBJUNCTIVE Present	Imperfect	IMPERATIVE	PARTICIPLE Present	Past
	je fuie	je fuisse		fuyant	fui
	nous fuyions	nous fuissions			
	je gèle	je gelasse		gelant	gelé
		nous gelassions			
				gisant	
	je haïsse	je haïsse		haïssant	haï
	nous haïssions	nous haïssions			
	je jette	je jetasse		jetant	jeté
	nous jetions	nous jetassions			
	je joigne	je joignisse		joignant	joint
	nous joignions	nous joignissions			
	je lise	je lusse		lisant	lu
	nous lisions	nous lussions			
	je mange	je mangeasse		mangeant	mangé
	nous mangions	nous mangeassions			
	je mène	je menasse		menant	mené
	nous menions	nous menassions			
	je mette	je misse		mettant	mis
	nous mettions	nous missions			
	je moule	je moulusse		moulant	moulu
	nous moulions	nous moulussions			

INDICATIVE

Present	Imperfect	Perfect	Past Historic	Future
49. mourir				
je meurs	je mourais		je mourus	je mourrai
il meurt				
nous mourons				
ils meurent				
50a. naître				
je nais	je naissais		je naquis	je naîtrai
il naît				
nous naissons				

50b. paître no PAST HISTORIC; PAST PARTICIPLE pu (invariable; rare)

50c. repaître as paître but PAST HISTORIC je repus

Present	Imperfect	Perfect	Past Historic	Future
51. ouïr				
j'ois	j'oyais		j'ouïs	j'ouïrai
il oit				
nous oyons				
ils oient				
52. ouvrir				
j'ouvre	j'ouvrais		j'ouvris	j'ouvrirai
nous ouvrons				
53. payer				
je paie/paye	je payais		je payai	je paierai/payerai
nous payons				
ils paient/payent				
54. peindre				
je peins	je peignais		je peignis	je peindrai
il peint				
nous peignons				
55a. plaire				
je plais	je plaisais		je plus	je plairai
il plaît	nous plaisions			

55b. taire PRESENT il tait

Present	Imperfect	Perfect	Past Historic	Future
56. pleuvoir				
il pleut	il pleuvait		il plut	il pleuvra
57. pouvoir				
je peux/puis	je pouvais		je pus	je pourrai
il peut				
nous pouvons				

| CONDITIONAL | SUBJUNCTIVE | | IMPERATIVE | PARTICIPLE | |
Present	Present	Imperfect		Present	Past
	je meure	je mourusse		mourant	mort
	nous mourions	nous mourussions			
	je naisse	je naquisse		naissant	né
	nous naissions	nous naquissions			
	j'oie	j'ouïsse		oyant	ouï
	nous oyions				
	j'ouvre			ouvrant	ouvert
	nous ouvrions		ouvre ouvrons ouvrez		
	je paie/paye	je payasse		payant	payé
	nous payions	nous payassions			
	je peigne	je peignisse		peignant	peint
	nous peignions	nous peignissions			
	je plaise	je plusse		plaisant	plu
	nous plaisions	nous plussions			
				pleuvant	plu
	il pleuve	il plût			
	je puisse	je pusse		pouvant	pu
	nous puissions	nous pussions			

INDICATIVE

Present	Imperfect	Perfect	Past Historic	Future
58. prendre				
je prends	je prenais		je pris	je prendrai
il prend				
nous prenons				
ils prennent				
59. protéger				
je protège	je protégeais		je protégeai	je protégerai
nous protégeons				
ils protègent				
60. recevoir				
je reçois	je recevais		je reçus	je recevrai
il reçoit				
nous recevons				
ils reçoivent				
61. rire				
je ris	je riais		je ris	je rirai
il rit				
nous rions				
62. savoir				
je sais	je savais		je sus	je saurai
il sait				
nous savons				
63. servir				
je sers	je servais		je servis	je servirai
il sert				
nous servons				
64a. sortir				
je sors	je sortais		je sortis	je sortirai
il sort				
nous sortons				
64b. mentir PAST PARTICIPLE is invariable				
65. suivre				
je suis	je suivais		je suivis	je suivrai
il suit				
nous suivons				
66. supplier				
je supplie	je suppliais		je suppliai	je supplierai
nous supplions				
67. tressaillir				
je tressaille	je tressaillais		je tressaillis	je tressaillirai
nous tressaillons				

CONDITIONAL Present	SUBJUNCTIVE Present	Imperfect	IMPERATIVE	PARTICIPLE Present	Past
	je prenne	je prisse		prenant	pris
	nous prenions	nous prissions			
	je protège	je protégeasse		protégeant	protégé
	nous protégions	nous protégeassions			
	je reçoive	je reçusse		recevant	reçu
	nous recevions	nous reçussions			
	je rie	je risse		riant	ri
	nous riions	nous rissions			
	je sache	je susse		sachant	su
			sache		
	nous sachions	nous sussions	sachons sachez		
	je serve	je servisse		servant	servi
	nous servions	nous servissions			
	je sorte	je sortisse		sortant	sorti
	nous sortions	nous sortissions			
	je suive	je suivisse		suivant	suivi
	nous suivions	nous suivissions			
	je supplie	je suppliasse		suppliant	supplié
	nous suppliions	nous suppliassions			
	je tressaille	je tressaillisse		tressaillant	tressailli
	nous tressaillions	nous tressaillissions			

INDICATIVE

Present	Imperfect	Perfect	Past Historic	Future
68. vaincre				
je vaincs il vainc nous vainquons	je vainquais		je vainquis	je vaincrai
69a. valoir				
je vaux il vaut nous valons	je valais		je valus	je vaudrai
69b. prévaloir *follows the above pattern except for the following*				
70. venir				
je viens il vient nous venons ils viennent	je venais		je vins	je viendrai
71. vêtir				
je vêts il vêt nous vêtons	je vêtais		je vêtis	je vêtirai
72. vivre				
je vis il vit nous vivons	je vivais		je vécus	je vivrai
73a. voir				
je vois il voit nous voyons ils voient	je voyais		je vis	je verrai
73b. pourvoir *follows the above pattern except for the following*				
			je pourvus	je pourvoirai
73c. prévoir *follows the above pattern except for the following*				
			je prévus	je prévoirai
74. vouloir				
je veux il veut nous voulons ils veulent	je voulais		je voulus	je voudrai

| CONDITIONAL | SUBJUNCTIVE | | IMPERATIVE | PARTICIPLE | |
Present	Present	Imperfect		Present	Past
	je vainque	je vainquisse		vainquant	vaincu
	nous vainquions	nous vainquissions			
	je vaille	je valusse		valant	valu
	nous valions	nous valussions			
	je prévale				
	je vienne	je vinsse		venant	venu
	nous venions	nous vinssions			
	je vête	je vêtisse		vêtant	vêtu
	nous vêtions	nous vêtissions			
	je vive	je vécusse		vivant	vécu
	nous vivions	nous vécussions			
	je voie	je visse		voyant	vu
	nous voyions	nous vissions			
je pourvoirais					
je prévoirais					
	je veuille	je voulusse		voulant	voulu
			veuille		
	nous voulions	nous voulussions	veuillons		
			veuillez		

Guide de communication en anglais

La correspondance

Ce guide a pour objectif de vous aider à rédiger un courrier en anglais : vous y trouverez des conseils sur la mise en page, les formules d'appel et de politesse, la rédaction de l'adresse ainsi que de nombreux modèles de lettres et suggestions de tournures à employer dans la correspondance privée ou commerciale, le courrier électronique et les documents transmis par télécopie.

Formules d'appel et formules de politesse

La formule de politesse varie en fonction de la formule d'appel utilisée.

▪ **formule d'appel**	▪ **formule de politesse**

Lorsque l'on ne connaît pas le nom de la personne à qui l'on s'adresse :

Dear Sir
Dear Madam

Lorsque l'on ne sait pas s'il s'agit d'un homme ou d'une femme :
Dear Sir or Madam
Dear Sir/Madam

Lorsque l'on s'adresse à une société ou à un organisme sans préciser le nom du destinataire:
Dear Sirs (Br)
Dear Gentlemen (Am)

Yours faithfully (Br)

En anglais américain, la formule de politesse est toujours inversée :
Faithfully yours (Am)

Lorsque l'on connaît le nom de la personne à qui l'on s'adresse :

Dear Mr Jameson
Dear Mrs Lucas
Dear Miss Crookshaw
Dear Ms Greening

(L'abréviation Ms est de plus en plus employée lorsque l'on s'adresse à une femme car elle permet de ne pas préciser s'il s'agit d'une femme mariée (Mrs) ou non (Miss).)
Dear Dr Illingworth

Aux États-Unis, l'abréviation est généralement suivie d'un point : Mr., Mrs., Ms., Dr.

Lorsqu'on s'adresse au rédacteur en chef d'un journal :
Sir

à un professeur titulaire de chaire :
Dear Professor Smith

à un député :
Dear Mr/Mrs Brown

à un représentant ou membre du Congrès :
Sir/Madam
Dear Congressman/Congresswoman Fox

Yours sincerely (Br)
Sincerely yours (Am)
Sincerely (Am)

Ton plus amical :
Yours very sincerely (Br)

Style moins soutenu :
With best wishes
With kind regards
Kindest regards

Plus rare et très soutenu :
Yours respectfully (Br)
Respectfully yours (Am)
Respectfully (Am)

Lorsque l'on s'adresse à de la famille ou à des amis :

- **En début de lettre**

  Dear Bill
  Dear Helen
  Dear Tom and Barbara
  Dear all
  Dear Mum and Dad
  Dear Uncle Ralph/Auntie Ann
  My dear Alex
  Dearest/My dearest Kate

  Très familier :
  Hi John!
  Hello there

- **En fin de lettre**

  With love
  Love
  Love from

  Plus affectueux :
  With all my/our love
  Much love

  Plus familier :
  Lots of love

  Plus soutenu :
  Yours
  All the best (Br)
  Best wishes
  Regards

  Familier :
  See you soon
  Bye for now

Présentation d'une lettre dactylographiée

Les paragraphes sont alignés à gauche, sans retrait, et séparés par une ligne de blanc.

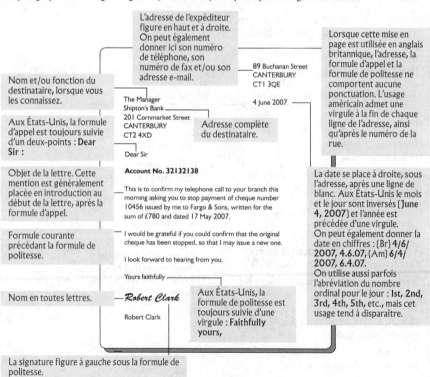

L'adresse de l'expéditeur figure en haut et à droite. On peut également donner ici son numéro de téléphone, son numéro de fax et/ou son adresse e-mail.

Nom et/ou fonction du destinataire, lorsque vous les connaissez.

Aux États-Unis, la formule d'appel est toujours suivie d'un deux-points : **Dear Sir :**

Objet de la lettre. Cette mention est généralement placée en introduction au début de la lettre, après la formule d'appel.

Formule courante précédant la formule de politesse.

Nom en toutes lettres.

La signature figure à gauche sous la formule de politesse.

Lorsque cette mise en page est utilisée en anglais britannique, l'adresse, la formule d'appel et la formule de politesse ne comportent aucune ponctuation. L'usage américain admet une virgule à la fin de chaque ligne de l'adresse, ainsi qu'après le numéro de la rue.

La date se place à droite, sous l'adresse, après une ligne de blanc. Aux États-Unis le mois et le jour sont inversés (**June 4, 2007**) et l'année est précédée d'une virgule. On peut également donner la date en chiffres : (Br) **4/6/2007, 4.6.07,** (Am) **6/4/2007, 6.4.07.** On utilise aussi parfois l'abréviation du nombre ordinal pour le jour : **1st, 2nd, 3rd, 4th, 5th,** etc., mais cet usage tend à disparaître.

Adresse complète du destinataire.

Aux États-Unis, la formule de politesse est toujours suivie d'une virgule : **Faithfully yours,**

89 Buchanan Street
CANTERBURY
CT1 3QE

The Manager
Shipton's Bank
201 Cornmarket Street
CANTERBURY
CT2 4XD

4 June 2007

Dear Sir

Account No. 32132138

This is to confirm my telephone call to your branch this morning asking you to stop payment of cheque number 10456 issued by me to Fargo & Sons, written for the sum of £780 and dated 17 May 2007.

I would be grateful if you could confirm that the original cheque has been stopped, so that I may issue a new one.

I look forward to hearing from you.

Yours faithfully

Robert Clark

Robert Clark

Présentation d'une lettre manuscrite à un ami

Dans une lettre manuscrite, on peut commencer chaque paragraphe par un alinéa.

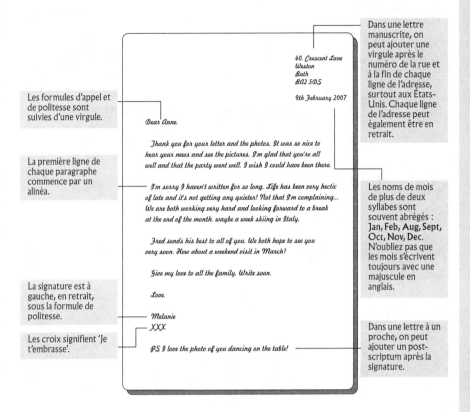

Les formules d'appel et de politesse sont suivies d'une virgule.

La première ligne de chaque paragraphe commence par un alinéa.

La signature est à gauche, en retrait, sous la formule de politesse.

Les croix signifient 'Je t'embrasse'.

Dans une lettre manuscrite, on peut ajouter une virgule après le numéro de la rue et à la fin de chaque ligne de l'adresse, surtout aux États-Unis. Chaque ligne de l'adresse peut également être en retrait.

Les noms de mois de plus de deux syllabes sont souvent abrégés : Jan, Feb, Aug, Sept, Oct, Nov, Dec. N'oubliez pas que les mois s'écrivent toujours avec une majuscule en anglais.

Dans une lettre à un proche, on peut ajouter un post-scriptum après la signature.

40, Crescent Lane
Weston
Bath
BA2 5DS

9th February 2007

Dear Anne,

Thank you for your letter and the photos. It was so nice to hear your news and see the pictures. I'm glad that you're all well and that the party went well. I wish I could have been there.

I'm sorry I haven't written for so long. Life has been very hectic of late and it's not getting any quieter! Not that I'm complaining... We are both working very hard and looking forward to a break at the end of the month, maybe a week skiing in Italy.

Fred sends his best to all of you. We both hope to see you very soon. How about a weekend visit in March?

Give my love to all the family. Write soon.

Love,

Melanie
XXX

PS I love the photo of you dancing on the table!

Enveloppes et adresses

L'adresse doit être aussi précise que possible. Les sites Web des services postaux des différents pays peuvent être utiles pour trouver l'adresse complète d'un particulier, d'un organisme ou d'une entreprise, y compris le code postal précis.

Royaume-Uni : www.royalmail.com
Canada : www.canadapost.ca
Irlande : www.anpost.ie
États-Unis : www.usps.gov
Australie : www.auspost.com.au
Nouvelle-Zélande : www.nzpost.co.nz

Il est recommandé de n'inclure aucun signe de ponctuation et, surtout aux États-Unis et au Canada, de rédiger l'adresse en majuscules (voir les modèles suivants).

▪ Au Royaume-Uni :

L'adresse doit figurer au centre de l'enveloppe, légèrement décalée vers la gauche.

L'adresse de l'expéditeur peut être précisée au verso. Cet usage est moins répandu qu'en France.

On peut aussi utiliser l'abréviation **Rd** pour **Road**. Voir ci-dessous la liste des abréviations utilisées dans les adresses.

Pour les grandes villes, telles que **LONDON** ou **LIVERPOOL**, il suffit de donner le nom de la ville en majuscules, suivi du code postal.

Le code postal (postcode) s'écrit en majuscules.

Ou : **United Kingdom**. On peut également préciser **England, Scotland, Wales** ou **N. Ireland**, selon le cas.

Le comté s'écrit de préférence en majuscules et peut être abrégé. Voir ci-contre la liste des abréviations des comtés du Royaume-Uni.

▪ Aux États-Unis :

L'adresse de l'expéditeur se place en haut et à gauche.

Le code postal (**ZIP code**) à cinq chiffres identifie un secteur de livraison. Depuis 1983, les services postaux le font suivre d'un code à quatre chiffres appelé **ZIP+4**. Ce code facultatif correspond à une adresse ou à une boîte postale, par exemple : **Washington DC 20260-0123**.

Les abréviations et les initiales sont suivies d'un point : **Mr., Mrs., Ms., Dr.**

La municipalité, l'État et le code postal figurent sur la même ligne.

MO = **Missouri**. Voir ci-contre la liste des abréviations des États américains.

▪ Abréviations utilisées dans les adresses

Les abréviations suivantes s'emploient couramment dans les adresses. Elles peuvent figurer aussi bien dans l'en-tête de la lettre que sur l'enveloppe.

Apt	Apartment	Mtn	Mountain
Av, Ave	Avenue	Pde	Parade
Blvd	Boulevard	Pk	Park
Cir	Circle	Pkwy	Parkway
Cl	Close	Pl	Place
Cres	Crescent	Plz	Plaza
Ct	Court	Rdg	Ridge
Dr	Drive	Rd	Road
Est	Estate	Rm	Room
Gdns	Gardens	Rt	Route
Gr, Grv	Grove	Sq	Square
Hts	Heights	St	Street
Jct	Junction	Ter	Terrace
La, Ln	Lane		

■ Abréviations des comtés en Angleterre

En règle générale, pour les noms des comtés se terminant en **-shire**, on ne garde que la première syllabe à laquelle on ajoute un **'s'** : Beds = Bedfordshire, Berks = Berkshire, Bucks = Buckinghamshire, Cambs = Cambridgeshire, Ches = Cheshire, Herts = Hertfordshire, Lancs = Lancashire, Leics = Leicestershire, Lincs = Lincolnshire, Notts = Nottinghamshire, Staffs = Staffordshire, Wilts = Wiltshire, Yorks = Yorkshire (divisé en **N Yorks, S Yorks** et **W Yorks**).

Exceptions :
Glos = Gloucestershire, Hants = Hampshire, Northants = Northamptonshire, Oxon = Oxfordshire, War (ou **Warks**) = Warwickshire.

D'autres abréviations à noter sont : Corn = Cornwall, Dur (ou **Co Durham**) = County Durham, IOW = Isle of Wight, Northumb = Northumberland, Som = Somerset.

Les autre comtés ne s'abrègent pas.

■ Abréviations des États américains

AK	Alaska	MT	Montana
AL	Alabama	NC	North Carolina
AR	Arkansas	ND	North Dakota
AZ	Arizona	NE	Nebraska
CA	California	NH	New Hampshire
CO	Colorado	NJ	New Jersey
CT	Connecticut	NM	New Mexico
DC	District of Columbia	NV	Nevada
DE	Delaware	NY	New York
FL	Florida	OH	Ohio
GA	Georgia	OK	Oklahoma
HI	Hawaii	OR	Oregon
IA	Iowa	PA	Pennsylvania
ID	Idaho	RI	Rhode Island
IL	Illinois	SC	South Carolina
IN	Indiana	SD	South Dakota
KS	Kansas	TN	Tennessee
KY	Kentucky	TX	Texas
LA	Louisiana	UT	Utah
MA	Massachusetts	VA	Virginia
MD	Maryland	VT	Vermont
ME	Maine	WA	Washington
MI	Michigan	WI	Wisconsin
MN	Minnesota	WV	West Virginia
MO	Missouri	WY	Wyoming
MS	Mississippi		

Modèles de lettres

Lettre à un ami

23, Juniper Close,
Lower Benefield,
Wykeham,
WE8 5AF

7th April 2007

The et of ne sont jamais écrits dans les dates, bien qu'ils doivent être prononcés : 7th April se lit: the seventh of April.

Ou: How are you?
Autres formules courantes: Thank you for your letter.
It was lovely/great/nice to hear from you.
I'm sorry/Sorry I haven't written for so long.

Dear Alain,

How are things with you? I hope you're well and not too unhappy that your holidays are now over! I guess it's time to go back to work and start saving for the next trip.

It was great to see you in Paris, even if it was for such a short time. Let's hope that we can spend more time together next time. I'm planning a trip to France next month and will be spending a few days in both Paris and Nancy. Any chance of staying with you for a couple of nights? I haven't finalized dates yet, but will let you know as soon as I have. Probably around 16th May.

The weather here is absolutely beautiful! Yes, it can be good in England! I'm making the most of it and walking every day, getting in training for the trek to Nepal in August.

Cheryl and Pierre send their love. They are both well and are sorry to have missed you

Anyway, that's about all for now. Will no doubt be in touch again very soon. Say hello to your parents from me. Take care of yourself and don't work too hard!

With love,
Joanna
xxx

Utilisation des formes contractées : you're, don't, I've etc.

Style télégraphique : Any chance of ... au lieu de Is there any chance of ...

Style télégraphique : le pronom personnel est omis.

Ou : X and Y send you (their) best wishes.
X asks me to give you his/her love/best wishes.
X sends his/her love/regards.

Ou : I look forward to seeing you/hearing from you soon.
Write soon.
Do keep in touch.
Hope to hear from you soon.
Let me/us have your news.

Ou : Please remember me to ...
Give my love/my regards/my best wishes to ...

Cartes de vœux

Dans les pays anglo-saxons, les cartes de vœux s'envoient au mois de décembre, avant Noël, et non en janvier comme en France. Elles peuvent être envoyées au destinataire ou lui être remises en mains propres.

To Haydn and Ann,

Merry Christmas and a Happy New Year!

Best wishes,

Harry and Dinah

Ou : Wishing you a Happy Christmas.
Merry Christmas to you both and health and happiness in the New Year/in 2008.
With all our best wishes for 2008.
All the best for 2008.

▪ Pour souhaiter un anniversaire

Dear Paul,

Happy Birthday!

Have a great day and enjoy the party. Hope you like your present!

With all our love,

Mum and Dad
XXX

Ou : Many Happy Returns (en anglais britannique). Vous pouvez aussi préciser l'âge de la personne : Happy 21st Birthday! ; Happy 60th!

Autres tournures utiles : Happy Anniversary ; Happy Easter ; Happy Mother's/Father's Day ; Happy Valentines (Day) ; Wishing you happiness in your new home ; Sorry you're leaving ; Enjoy your retirement.

▪ Pour souhaiter bonne chance

Ou : I'll be thinking of you.

Good luck with your driving test.
I shall keep my fingers crossed for you.
Love from Mary

Ou : Good luck for the interview/in your exams/in your new job.
Best of luck with …

▪ Pour féliciter

Dear Sandra and George,

Congratulations on your wedding day!
We wish you both every happiness in your new life together.

With love and best wishes,
Susie and Dan

Ou : … on your engagement/your silver wedding anniversary/the birth of your baby/passing your driving test.

Invitations et réponses

▪ Carton d'invitation à un mariage

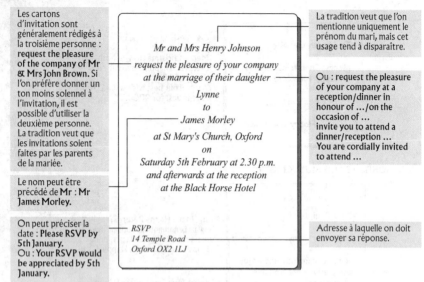

Les cartons d'invitation sont généralement rédigés à la troisième personne : **request the pleasure of the company of Mr & Mrs John Brown.** Si l'on préfère donner un ton moins solennel à l'invitation, il est possible d'utiliser la deuxième personne. La tradition veut que les invitations soient faites par les parents de la mariée.

Le nom peut être précédé de **Mr** : **Mr James Morley.**

On peut préciser la date : **Please RSVP by 5th January.** Ou : **Your RSVP would be appreciated by 5th January.**

Mr and Mrs Henry Johnson
request the pleasure of your company
at the marriage of their daughter
Lynne
to
James Morley
at St Mary's Church, Oxford
on
Saturday 5th February at 2.30 p.m.
and afterwards at the reception
at the Black Horse Hotel

RSVP
14 Temple Road
Oxford OX2 1LJ

La tradition veut que l'on mentionne uniquement le prénom du mari, mais cet usage tend à disparaître.

Ou : **request the pleasure of your company at a reception/dinner in honour of …/on the occasion of …**
invite you to attend a dinner/reception …
You are cordially invited to attend …

Adresse à laquelle on doit envoyer sa réponse.

▪ Réponse à une invitation officielle

La réponse doit toujours être manuscrite.

Ou : **It is with great/much pleasure that we/they accept.**
… thank you for your kind invitation to …, but regret that we/they are unable to attend.

We thank you for your kind invitation to the marriage of your daughter Lynne on 5th February, and to the reception afterwards. We have great pleasure in accepting.
George & Alison Adams

Lorsque l'on répond à ce type d'invitation, il n'est pas nécessaire d'indiquer la date ni d'employer les formules d'appel et de politesse. Si l'invitation est rédigée à la troisième personne, il faut utiliser la troisième personne dans la réponse : **Mr & Mrs George Adams thank Mr & Mrs Henry Johnson for their kind invitation to the marriage of their daughter Lynne on 5th February, and to the reception afterwards. They have great pleasure in accepting.**

▪ Carton d'invitation : soirée entre amis

James and Fiona
INVITE YOU TO
a house-warming party

ON: Friday 13th September
AT: 45 Rowan Crescent
FROM: 8pm onwards

Please bring a bottle   RSVP

Autres tournures utiles : **We're giving a dinner party/cocktail party/birthday party next Friday and hope you will be able to come.**
We are celebrating our engagement by holding a dinner dance at the … on …, and would be delighted if you could join us.
I'm having a party – come along, and bring a friend.

Réponse à une invitation : soirée entre amis

> 46 Hatton Street
> Bath
> BA5 2GA
>
> 23 August 2007
>
> Dear James and Fiona,
>
> Thank you so much for the invitation to your house-warming party. I'd love to come. It will be great to see you and, of course, your new home.
>
> If you need any help with food, I'd be only too glad to bring something along, as well as a bottle, of course!
>
> Thanks once again for the kind invitation. I look forward to seeing you.
>
> Love,
>
> Emily

Autres tournures utiles :
I'd love to come to your party. It was very kind of you to invite me.
Thank you for your invitation to dinner/for the weekend – I look forward to it very much.
Thank you so much for your invitation, but I'm afraid I/we won't be able to come.
I was/We were delighted to get your invitation but unfortunately I/we can't come.

Remerciements

> 167 Ecclesall Road
> South Sheffield
> S11 9PN
>
> 31st May 2007
>
> Dear Ann and Ralph
>
> Thank you so much for the beautiful crystal decanter and wine glasses you sent us as a wedding present. They will look wonderful on our dinner table and I intend to make good use of them.
>
> I was so glad that you could come to the wedding. I hope you enjoyed it as much as we did. It was quite a hectic day really, but of course a wonderful one! Give my thanks to Tracey for the catering, everyone said how delicious the food was.
>
> We had a lovely honeymoon and are now busy settling into our new home. You must come very soon for a meal to try out the glasses.
>
> Many thanks once again!
>
> With much love,
>
> Katie
>
> xxx

Ou : bought us

Ou : We were both delighted you could come...;
It was really nice to see you at the wedding.

Ou : I can't thank you enough for...
Thank you very much for ...

Ou : Say thank you to ...

Condoléances

> Dear Grace,
>
> We were very sad to hear of your husband's death last Tuesday, and we wish to extend our deepest sympathy on your sad loss.
> Alan was greatly liked and respected in the village and he will be greatly missed by all who knew him. If there is anything we can do to help at this difficult time, please don't hesitate to get in touch.
>
> With deepest sympathy,
>
> Susan and Mike

Ou : It was with great sadness that I/we heard the news of your husband's death.

Ou : All our love and deepest sympathy (lorsque l'on écrit à un proche).

Ou : We offer our sincere condolences to you and your family.

Ou : We will miss him greatly/very much.
He will not be forgotten.

Réservations

Les réservations de billets ou de chambres d'hôtel se font de plus en plus par Internet et par courrier électronique. Pour toute réservation faite par téléphone, il est recommandé de confirmer par écrit.

▪ Lettre de réservation

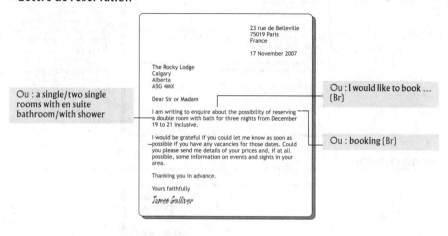

▪ Pour confirmer une réservation

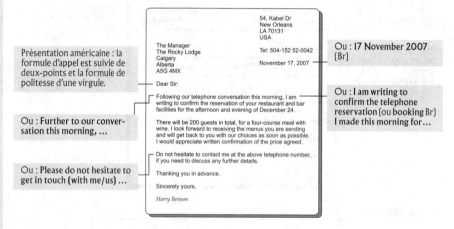

▪ Pour annuler une réservation

Demande de renseignements

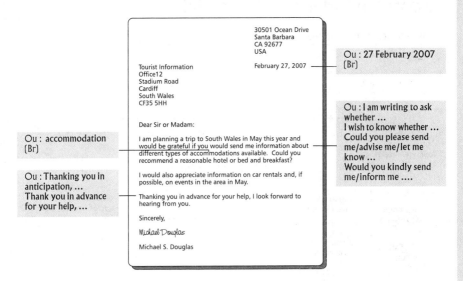

Ou : accommodation (Br)

Ou : Thanking you in anticipation, ...
Thank you in advance for your help, ...

Ou : 27 February 2007 (Br)

Ou : I am writing to ask whether ...
I wish to know whether ...
Could you please send me/advise me/let me know ...
Would you kindly send me/inform me ....

30501 Ocean Drive
Santa Barbara
CA 92677
USA

Tourist Information
Office12
Stadium Road
Cardiff
South Wales
CF35 5HH

February 27, 2007

Dear Sir or Madam:

I am planning a trip to South Wales in May this year and would be grateful if you would send me information about different types of accommodations available. Could you recommend a reasonable hotel or bed and breakfast?

I would also appreciate information on car rentals and, if possible, on events in the area in May.

Thanking you in advance for your help, I look forward to hearing from you.

Sincerely,

Michael Douglas

Michael S. Douglas

Réclamations

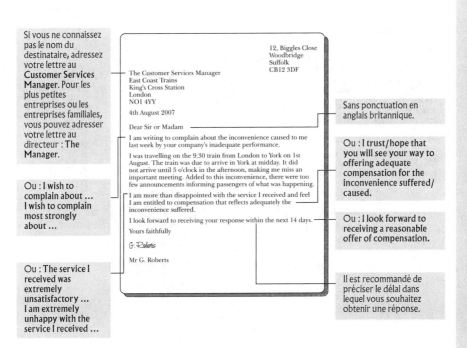

Si vous ne connaissez pas le nom du destinataire, adressez votre lettre au **Customer Services Manager**. Pour les plus petites entreprises ou les entreprises familiales, vous pouvez adresser votre lettre au directeur : **The Manager.**

Ou : I wish to complain about ...
I wish to complain most strongly about ...

Ou : The service I received was extremely unsatisfactory ...
I am extremely unhappy with the service I received ...

Sans ponctuation en anglais britannique.

Ou : I trust/hope that you will see your way to offering adequate compensation for the inconvenience suffered/caused.

Ou : I look forward to receiving a reasonable offer of compensation.

Il est recommandé de préciser le délai dans lequel vous souhaitez obtenir une réponse.

12, Biggles Close
Woodbridge
Suffolk
CB12 3DF

The Customer Services Manager
East Coast Trains
King's Cross Station
London
NO1 4YY

4th August 2007

Dear Sir or Madam

I am writing to complain about the inconvenience caused to me last week by your company's inadequate performance.

I was travelling on the 9.30 train from London to York on 1st August. The train was due to arrive in York at midday. It did not arrive until 5 o'clock in the afternoon, making me miss an important meeting. Added to this inconvenience, there were too few announcements informing passengers of what was happening.

I am more than disappointed with the service I received and feel I am entitled to compensation that reflects adequately the inconvenience suffered.

I look forward to receiving your response within the next 14 days.

Yours faithfully

G. Roberts

Mr G. Roberts

La correspondance commerciale

Pour prendre rendez-vous

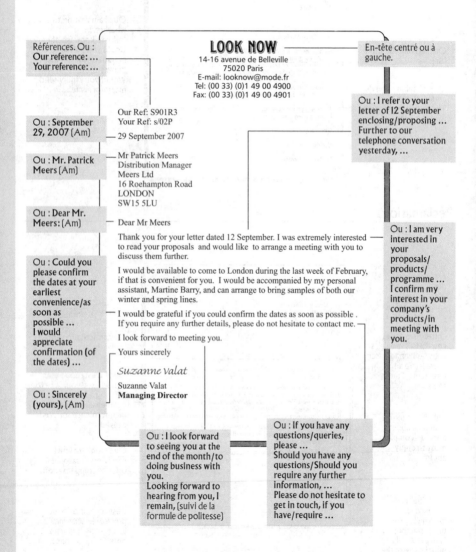

Références. Ou :
Our reference: ...
Your reference: ...

Ou : September
29, 2007 [Am]

Ou : Mr. Patrick
Meers [Am]

Ou : Dear Mr.
Meers: [Am]

Ou : Could you
please confirm
the dates at your
earliest
convenience/as
soon as
possible ...
I would
appreciate
confirmation (of
the dates) ...

Ou : Sincerely
(yours), [Am]

LOOK NOW
14-16 avenue de Belleville
75020 Paris
E-mail: looknow@mode.fr
Tel: (00 33) (0)1 49 00 4900
Fax: (00 33) (0)1 49 00 4901

En-tête centré ou à
gauche.

Our Ref: S901R3
Your Ref: s/02P

29 September 2007

Mr Patrick Meers
Distribution Manager
Meers Ltd
16 Roehampton Road
LONDON
SW15 5LU

Dear Mr Meers

Thank you for your letter dated 12 September. I was extremely interested
to read your proposals and would like to arrange a meeting with you to
discuss them further.

I would be available to come to London during the last week of February,
if that is convenient for you. I would be accompanied by my personal
assistant, Martine Barry, and can arrange to bring samples of both our
winter and spring lines.

I would be grateful if you could confirm the dates as soon as possible .
If you require any further details, please do not hesitate to contact me.

I look forward to meeting you.

Yours sincerely

Suzanne Valat

Suzanne Valat
Managing Director

Ou : I refer to your
letter of 12 September
enclosing/proposing ...
Further to our
telephone conversation
yesterday, ...

Ou : I am very
interested in
your
proposals/
products/
programme ...
I confirm my
interest in your
company's
products/in
meeting with
you.

Ou : I look forward
to seeing you at the
end of the month/to
doing business with
you.
Looking forward to
hearing from you, I
remain, (suivi de la
formule de politesse)

Ou : If you have any
questions/queries,
please ...
Should you have any
questions/Should you
require any further
information, ...
Please do not hesitate to
get in touch, if you
have/require ...

Réponse à une demande de renseignements

Ou : I am enclosing our catalogue for your review.

Ou : If you require/Should you require any further information, please contact me. I look forward to hearing from you soon. After you have reviewed our material, we would appreciate your comments, and we will look forward to answering any questions you have about our products.

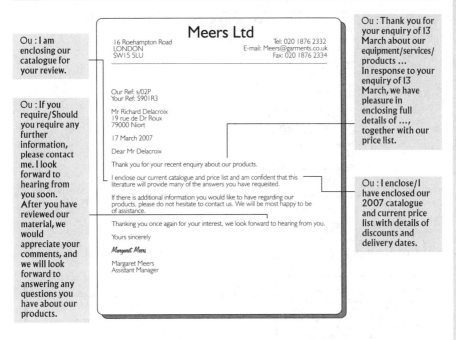

Meers Ltd

16 Roehampton Road
LONDON
SW15 5LU

Tel: 020 1876 2332
E-mail: Meers@garments.co.uk
Fax: 020 1876 2334

Our Ref: s/02P
Your Ref: S901R3

Mr Richard Delacroix
19 rue de Dr Roux
79000 Niort

17 March 2007

Dear Mr Delacroix

Thank you for your recent enquiry about our products.

I enclose our current catalogue and price list and am confident that this literature will provide many of the answers you have requested.

If there is additional information you would like to have regarding our products, please do not hesitate to contact us. We will be most happy to be of assistance.

Thanking you once again for your interest, we look forward to hearing from you.

Yours sincerely

Margaret Meers

Margaret Meers
Assistant Manager

Ou : Thank you for your enquiry of 13 March about our equipment/services/products ...
In response to your enquiry of 13 March, we have pleasure in enclosing full details of ..., together with our price list.

Ou : I enclose/I have enclosed our 2007 catalogue and current price list with details of discounts and delivery dates.

Commande

Ou : Dear Sir/Madam (Br)/Dear Gentlemen (Am)

Ou : The enclosed order is based on your current price list, assuming our usual discount of ... on bulk orders.

Ou : postage and handling (Am)

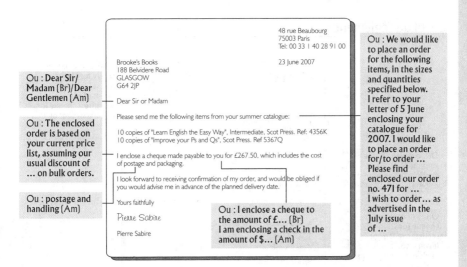

48 rue Beaubourg
75003 Paris
Tel: 00 33 1 40 28 91 00

Brooke's Books
188 Belvidere Road
GLASGOW
G64 2JP

23 June 2007

Dear Sir or Madam

Please send me the following items from your summer catalogue:

10 copies of "Learn English the Easy Way", Intermediate, Scot Press. Ref: 4356K
10 copies of "Improve your Ps and Qs", Scot Press. Ref 5367Q

I enclose a cheque made payable to you for £267.50, which includes the cost of postage and packaging.

I look forward to receiving confirmation of my order, and would be obliged if you would advise me in advance of the planned delivery date.

Yours faithfully

Pierre Sabire

Pierre Sabire

Ou : I enclose a cheque to the amount of £... (Br)
I am enclosing a check in the amount of $... (Am)

Ou : We would like to place an order for the following items, in the sizes and quantities specified below.
I refer to your letter of 5 June enclosing your catalogue for 2007. I would like to place an order for/to order ...
Please find enclosed our order no. 471 for ...
I wish to order... as advertised in the July issue of ...

Guide de communication en anglais

Facture

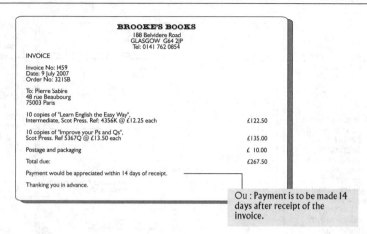

BROOKE'S BOOKS
188 Belvidere Road
GLASGOW G64 2JP
Tel: 0141 762 0854

INVOICE

Invoice No: 1459
Date: 9 July 2007
Order No: 321SB

To: Pierre Sabire
48 rue Beaubourg
75003 Paris

10 copies of "Learn English the Easy Way", Intermediate, Scot Press. Ref: 4356K @ £12.25 each	£122.50
10 copies of "Improve your Ps and Qs", Scot Press. Ref 5367Q @ £13.50 each	£135.00
Postage and packaging	£ 10.00
Total due:	£267.50

Payment would be appreciated within 14 days of receipt.

Thanking you in advance.

> Ou : Payment is to be made 14 days after receipt of the invoice.

▪ Lettre de rappel

Our records indicate that payment on your account is overdue to the amount of £ ... If the amount has already been paid, please disregard this notice. If you have not yet posted your payment, please use the enclosed envelope to send payment in full.

Thank you in advance for your anticipated co-operation in this matter.

> Ou : in the amount of $... (Am)

> Ou : mailed (Am)

▪ Deuxième rappel

On 12 July 2007 we notified you of your overdue account for order no. ...

To date we still have not received payment for the above order.

Please give this matter your most urgent attention. Payment must be made within the next ten days.

Envoi du règlement

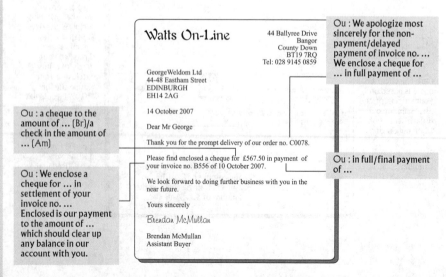

> Ou : We apologize most sincerely for the non-payment/delayed payment of invoice no. ... We enclose a cheque for ... in full payment of ...

Watts On-Line

44 Ballyree Drive
Bangor
County Down
BT19 7RQ
Tel: 028 9145 0859

GeorgeWeldom Ltd
44-48 Eastham Street
EDINBURGH
EH14 2AG

14 October 2007

Dear Mr George

Thank you for the prompt delivery of our order no. C0078.

Please find enclosed a cheque for £567.50 in payment of your invoice no. B556 of 10 October 2007.

We look forward to doing further business with you in the near future.

Yours sincerely

Brendan McMullan

Brendan McMullan
Assistant Buyer

> Ou : a cheque to the amount of ... (Br)/a check in the amount of ... (Am)

> Ou : We enclose a cheque for ... in settlement of your invoice no. ... Enclosed is our payment to the amount of ... which should clear up any balance in our account with you.

> Ou : in full/final payment of ...

(42)

Recherche d'emploi

Lettre de motivation

Dans les pays anglo-saxons, la lettre de candidature (**covering letter** en anglais britannique ou **cover letter** en anglais américain) doit toujours être dactylographiée, sauf si l'annonce spécifie qu'il faut envoyer une lettre manuscrite.

- ## Réponse à une annonce

Financial Analyst

Dunworkin Investments is a forward-looking London-based company specializing in long-term investment strategies. We currently require a Financial Analyst to help progress the commercial potential of the company. You should have at least three years' experience in a similar post and a thorough understanding of corporate finance and capital markets. A knowledge of Excel and Lotus is essential, as is the ability to communicate effectively with all levels of management. A working knowledge of at least one foreign language is desirable.

To apply, please send a CV with current salary details to: David Smithwick, Chief Analyst, Dunworkin Investments, Threadneedle Street, London E3 6PG. Closing date: 31 May 2007.

Coordonnées de l'expéditeur à droite.

8 rue de Renac
44200 Nantes
France

Tel: 0033 2 47 89 22 22
E-mail: jaka@hotmail.com

David Smithwick
Chief Analyst
Dunworkin Investments
Threadneedle Street
LONDON
E3 6PG
UK

19 May 2007

Dear Mr Smithwick

Financial Analyst

I would like to apply for the above post as advertised in "Le Monde" of 14 May, and I enclose my CV for your attention.

I am an experienced financial analyst and consultant, having worked extensively in this sector in Nantes and Paris, and as a lecturer at Nantes University. I am currently looking for a position that will allow me to develop my skills and experience in a small, dynamic commercial team such as Dunworkin Investments.

I believe that my financial and academic background would be of benefit to your company. Should you consider me suitable for the post, I can provide the names of three referees.

I thank you for your consideration and remain at your disposal for any further information.

Your sincerely

Jacques Kahn

Jacques Kahn
Financial Investment Analyst

Enc.

Nom et fonction du destinataire.

On peut mettre la date à gauche, ou à droite, sous les coordonnées de l'expéditeur.

Objet de la lettre : fonction ou poste.

Ou : I am confident that I can perform effectively in this position and am excited about the idea of working for a dynamic firm. My degree in ... and my work placement (Br)/internship (Am) experiences have taught me how to ...

Ou : I should like to apply for the above post as advertised in the July issue of .../which was advertised in today's Daily Post.
I am writing to apply for the above post/for the post of ... as advertised in ...
I am writing in response to your advertisement in ... for ...

Ou : The position seems to fit very well with my education, experience and career interests. According to the advertisement, your position requires excellent communication skills and an MA degree in ..., both of which I possess.

Ou : Thank you for considering my application/for your consideration. If you would like to arrange an interview, please call me at ... I will be available at your convenience. I would be pleased to meet you at any time that is convenient. You may reach me at the above telephone number or e-mail address.

Candidature spontanée

Si vous connaissez quelqu'un travaillant déjà dans l'entreprise, signalez-le.

Ou : **As you will note from the enclosed CV (Br)/résumé (Am), I have specialized in/ majored in (Am) physics and have participated in significant research.**

Ou : **at your convenience.**

Ou : **I would like to/I wish to inquire about the possibility of becoming a ... at your factory/in your company.**

Ou : **I have been/I was given your address by a colleague of mine/of yours,** (nom de la personne) **who advised me that you may be recruiting staff (for your sales team). I am seeking a position in sales/publishing at a (high technology) company such as yours.**

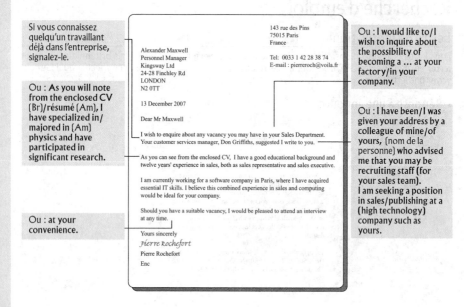

143 rue des Pins
75015 Paris
France

Alexander Maxwell
Personnel Manager
Kingsway Ltd
24-28 Finchley Rd
LONDON
N2 0TT

Tel: 0033 1 42 28 38 74
E-mail : pierreroch@voila.fr

13 December 2007

Dear Mr Maxwell

I wish to enquire about any vacancy you may have in your Sales Department. Your customer services manager, Don Griffiths, suggested I write to you.

As you can see from the enclosed CV, I have a good educational background and twelve years' experience in sales, both as sales representative and sales executive.

I am currently working for a software company in Paris, where I have acquired essential IT skills. I believe this combined experience in sales and computing would be ideal for your company.

Should you have a suitable vacancy, I would be pleased to attend an interview at any time.

Yours sincerely
Pierre Rochefort
Pierre Rochefort
Enc

Demande de stage

Nom et fonction du destinataire.

Date à gauche, ou à droite, sous le numéro de téléphone et l'adresse électronique.

Coordonnées de l'expéditeur à droite.

Si on s'adresse à une entreprise américaine on utilisera le terme **internship** à la place de **work placement.**

Situation actuelle, expérience, diplômes.

Compétences, points forts et motivation.

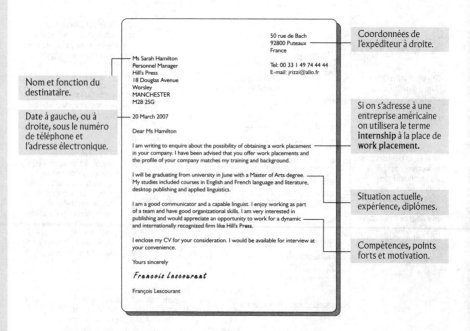

50 rue de Bach
92800 Puteaux
France

Ms Sarah Hamilton
Personnel Manager
Hill's Press
18 Douglas Avenue
Worsley
MANCHESTER
M28 2SG

Tel: 00 33 1 49 74 44 44
E-mail: jrizzi@allo.fr

20 March 2007

Dear Ms Hamilton

I am writing to enquire about the possibility of obtaining a work placement in your company. I have been advised that you offer work placements and the profile of your company matches my training and background.

I will be graduating from university in June with a Master of Arts degree. My studies included courses in English and French language and literature, desktop publishing and applied linguistics.

I am a good communicator and a capable linguist. I enjoy working as part of a team and have good organizational skills. I am very interested in publishing and would appreciate an opportunity to work for a dynamic and internationally recognized firm like Hill's Press.

I enclose my CV for your consideration. I would be available for interview at your convenience.

Yours sincerely

François Lescourant

François Lescourant

Tournures utiles :

I know how to/I can operate a cash register/a switchboard/power equipment.
I am computer literate/a good communicator/well-organised.
I am a capable linguist/can speak fluent English and German.
I have good computer/IT/language/communication/organizational/leadership skills.
I can learn new tasks and enjoy/can accept a challenge.
I enjoy working/can work with a variety of people.
I work well in a team/can handle multiple tasks simultaneously.
I perform well under pressure/am good with difficult customers/am self-motivated.
I have (wide) experience in sales/in dealing with the public.
I have two years' experience of office work/of working with children.

Dossier de candidature

Certains entreprises demandent aux candidats de compléter un formulaire ou un dossier de candidature spécialement conçu pour les besoins de l'entreprise, au lieu d'un CV. Si cette information est précisée dans l'annonce qui vous intéresse, il vous faudra demander les formulaires le plus tôt possible.

33 rue de la Marne
75 013 Paris
France
Tel: 0033 1 41 26 78 95
E-mail: carigib@yahoo.fr

Mr J Jones
Jones Enterprises
Woodside Industrial Estate
Woodside Lane
LEEDS
LS15 5HH

7 February 2007

Dear Mr Jones

Bilingual Secretary

Ou : I am writing in response to … I would be grateful if you could send me …

I am responding to your advertisement in yesterday's Guardian for a bilingual secretary. Could you please send me an application form.

I look forward to hearing from you.

Yours sincerely

Carine Gibert

Carine Gibert

Curriculum vitae

Notez que le mot **CV** s'emploi des deux côtés de l'Atlantique mais que les Américains utilisent plus souvent le terme **résumé**.

▪ Diplômés français ayant une première expérience

Vous n'êtes pas obligé de préciser votre nationalité ou votre âge. Ces informations, tout comme la situation de famille, sont souvent omises ou données à la fin du CV pour leur donner moins d'importance.

On commence par les études et les diplômes les plus récents.

Isabelle Murat
40, impasse de la Colline
75003 Paris
Tel: 00 33 (0)1 40 30 40 40
E-mail: imurat@ubet.fr

Date of Birth 13/2/1987
Nationality French

Professional Experience

April/May 2007	Three-month placement at Cabinet Desmoulin, Paris Customer Services
Summer 2006	Organiser in school summer camp, Port-de-Bouc

Education

2006-2007	Ecole Technique Supérieure, Bordeaux Three-year diploma course in Civil Engineering
2004-2005	Baccalauréat S (equivalent A Levels) in: Maths, Physics, Chemistry, Biology, French, English, Geography, History

Languages French, English (fluent)
German, Greek (basic)

Interests Horse-riding, mountaineering
Opera singing

References available on request

Cette formule n'est pas obligatoire. Vous pouvez inclure sur une deuxième page les coordonnées des personnes pouvant fournir des références.

La date de naissance est facultative mais souvent précisée. Le lieu de naissance est moins courant.

MARC DUFOUR
42 rue Alsace-Lorraine
69 000 Lyon
France
0033 (0)4 78 55 32 14
madufo@voila.fr
Born: 26/2/84 in Nice, France

OBJECTIVE
A post using my IT knowledge and communication skills to train others

Ou : Target. Cette partie n'est pas obligatoire, mais elle est très courante aux États-Unis.

WORK EXPERIENCE
2005 – present Helpdesk Operator (French/English)
QCX Systems, Lyon
Provide telephone assistance with computer problems to international clients
Troubleshoot computer problems within the company
Train company staff in using new software

2002 – 2003 Student Computer Assistant
Université de Lyon 1
Assisted students with computer problems
Carried out minor installations/repairs

Summer 2004 Work placement at Softworld, Leeds
Tested new software and provided feedback

EDUCATION
2001 – 2005 Bachelor's Degree in Computer Science with English,
Université de Lyon 1
(2003 – 2004 Exchange year at University of Leeds)
2001: French "Baccalauréat"

LANGUAGES
French, English
JAVA, HTML, SQL, BASIC

ACTIVITIES
Running (Paris Marathon 2005), tae kwondo, online gaming

Cadre français

> **Name: Laurent Marie**
> **Address:** 25, rue des Arquebusiers   Tel: 0033 (0)2 24 24 45 73
> 76000 Rouen   E-mail: mariel@battisto.com
>
> **Human Resources Consultant**
>
> *Work Experience*
> 1997 – present   Human Resources Consultant, Cabinet Battisto-Langlade, Rouen
>   Advising companies on accounting, recruitment strategies
> 1993 – 1996   Personnel Manager, Conseil général, Le Havre
>   Recruiting, planning of training programmes, staff follow-up
> 1991 – 1992   Assistant to Personnel Manager, Société Pierre et Fils, Le Havre
>
> *Education*
> 1989   Master of Business Administration, Boston University
> 1987 – 1988   DEA 'Langage et Médias' - Paris X
> 1986   Master's Degree in History - Paris IV
> 1982   Baccalauréat (equivalent A Levels), specialising in Maths,
>   Académie de Paris.
>
> *Other Experience*
> Year spent in Africa (1990–91) as part of a mission with the voluntary medical aid
> organisation "Médecins sans frontières"
> Member of a voluntary association promoting adult literacy
>
> *Languages*   Fluent English and Spanish
>
> *Computer Skills*   Mac OS, Word, Excel

On commence par le poste actuel et on termine par le plus ancien. Certain cadres décident parfois de mentionner leur salaire.

Précisez pour chaque emploi les tâches principales que vous deviez effectuer.

Personne française souhaitant changer de profession

> **Hélène Moreau**
> 48 rue Mazarine
> 75 006 Paris, France
> Tel.: 0033 1 43 26 27 64   D.o.b.: 15 July 1975
> E-mail: helemo@hotmail.com   Nationality: French
>
> **Profile**
> Dynamic human resources professional looking to apply my creative and
> interpersonal skills to a career in marketing. Highly organized, goal-oriented
> team player fluent in French and English.
>
> **Professional experience**
> 2003 – present **Assistant Human Resources Manager**, BelleVie insurance
> company, Paris
> - Play a key role in planning recruitment campaigns
> - Write and place job advertisements (press and online)
> - Assist with candidate selection
> - Organize staff training
>
> 2000 – 2003 **Human Resources Executive**, Software Solutions, Paris
> - Worked with the HR team on all aspects of recruitment
> - Responsible for payroll
>
> 1998 – 2000 **Administrator**, Software Solutions, Paris
> - Processed client orders and enquiries
> - Handled varied administrative tasks
>
> **Education**
> 1994 – 1997 Bachelor's degree in Business Studies and English, Université de Nantes
> 1993 Baccalauréat (equivalent A levels), main subjects: economics, history, English
>
> **Language skills**
> French, English: fluent
> German: good knowledge
>
> **IT skills**
> Word, Excel, PowerPoint, Access, Internet
>
> **Other experience**
> 1997 – 1998 Voluntary conservation work in Brazil
>
> **Interests**
> Tango, environmental issues, poker

Date of birth.

Mettez en avant les compétences et les qualités dont l'entreprise pourra bénéficier.

Utilisez le présent simple pour décrire votre emploi actuel.

Utilisez le prétérit pour décrire vos emplois antérieurs.

La télécopie

Dans une entreprise

Ou : **Attn:** (À l'attention de)
FAO: (= for the attention of)

Objet du fax.

Abréviations de **Tuesday** et **September**.

= Wednesday morning

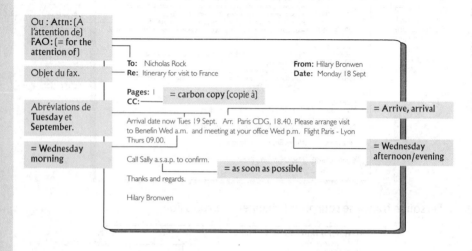

To: Nicholas Rock   **From:** Hilary Bronwen
Re: Itinerary for visit to France   **Date:** Monday 18 Sept

Pages: 1   = carbon copy (copie à)
CC:

= Arrive, arrival

Arrival date now Tues 19 Sept. Arr. Paris CDG, 18.40. Please arrange visit to Benefin Wed a.m. and meeting at your office Wed p.m. Flight Paris - Lyon Thurs 09.00.

= Wednesday afternoon/evening

Call Sally a.s.a.p. to confirm.

= as soon as possible

Thanks and regards.

Hilary Bronwen

Pour confirmer une réservation

Les formules d'appel et de politesse ne changent pas.

Ou : **Further to our conversation this morning, I would like to confirm ...**

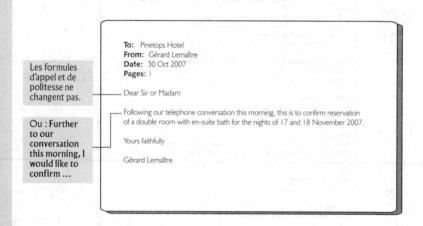

To: Pinetops Hotel
From: Gérard Lemaître
Date: 30 Oct 2007
Pages: 1

Dear Sir or Madam

Following our telephone conversation this morning, this is to confirm reservation of a double room with en-suite bath for the nights of 17 and 18 November 2007.

Yours faithfully

Gérard Lemaître

Le courrier électronique

Le courrier électronique étant un moyen de communication rapide, le style des messages est souvent familier et télégraphique et l'emploi des abréviations et des acronymes est très courant. Selon la netiquette, ou code de conduite sur le réseau, il est déconseillé d'écrire un message tout en majuscules car cela pourrait être interprété comme un signe de mauvaise humeur.

Les formules d'appel traditionnelles (**Dear ...**) sont généralement omises. Si vous connaissez bien votre correspondant, vous pouvez commencer par une formule familière telle que **Hello** ou **Hi**, suivie du prénom de la personne.

Abréviations et acronymes utilisés dans le courrier électronique et les forums

Les abréviations et acronymes qui suivent sont couramment employés dans le courrier électronique et les forums de discussion. Il est cependant conseillé de ne les utiliser que lorsque l'on est sûr que le destinataire connaît leur signification. Les abréviations suivies de la mention *Fam* appartiennent à un registre plus familier et doivent être réservées à une correspondance plus relâchée.

Adv	advice (conseil)	**IOW** *Fam*	in other words (autrement dit)
AFAICT *Fam*	as far as I can tell (pour autant que je sache)	**ISTM** *Fam*	it seems to me (il me semble que)
AFAIK *Fam*	as far as I know (pour autant que je sache)	**ITRO** *Fam*	in the region of (environ)
AFK	away from keyboard (indique que l'on va quitter son poste)	**LOL** *Fam*	laughing out loud (mort de rire)
AIUI *Fam*	as far as I understand (si j'ai bien compris)	**NRN** *Fam*	no reply necessasry (réponse facultative)
B4 *Fam*	before (avant)	**NW!** *Fam*	no way! (sûrement pas!)
BAK	back at keyboard (de retour devant l'écran)	**OMG!** *Fam*	oh my God! (mon Dieu!, j'y crois pas!)
BBL *Fam*	be back later (je reviens)	**OTOH** *Fam*	on the other hand (d'un autre côté)
BTW *Fam*	by the way (à propos)	**OTT** *Fam*	over the top (excessif)
cd, cld	could	**PD**	public domain (domaine public)
Doc	document	**POV**	point of view (point de vue)
EOF	end of file (fin de fichier)	**prhps**	perhaps (peut-être)
F2F *Fam*	face to face (en face, face à face)	**RTFM** *très Fam*	read the f***ing manual (regarde dans le manuel, nom de Dieu!)
FAQ	frequently asked questions (foire aux questions)	**RUOK** *Fam*	are you OK? (ça va?)
FOC	free of charge (gratuit, gratuitement)	**TIA** *Fam*	thanks in advance (merci d'avance)
Foll	following, to follow (suivant, à suivre)	**TNX** *Fam*	thanks (merci)
FYI	for your information (pour ton information)	**TVM** *Fam*	thanks very much (merci beaucoup)
HTH *Fam*	hope this helps (j'espère que cela te sera utile)	**urgt**	urgent
IIRC *Fam*	if I recall correctly (si mes souvenirs sont bons)	**VR**	virtual reality (réalité virtuelle)
IMO, IMHO *Fam*	in my (humble) opinion (à mon (humble) avis)	**WRT** *Fam*	with regard to (en ce qui concerne)

Message interne

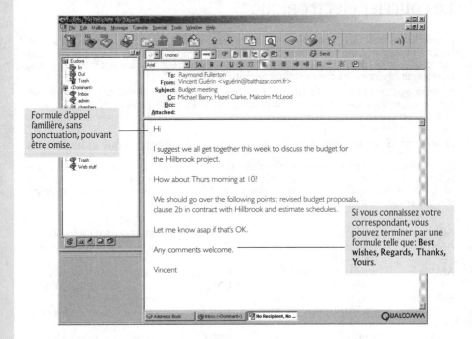

Formule d'appel familière, sans ponctuation, pouvant être omise.

Si vous connaissez votre correspondant, vous pouvez terminer par une formule telle que: **Best wishes, Regards, Thanks, Yours.**

Message d'une entreprise à une autre

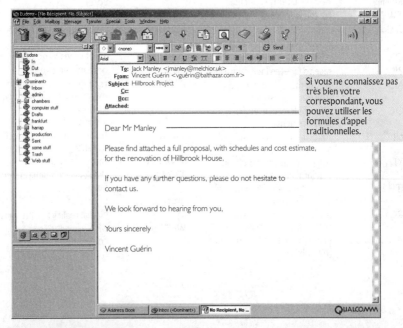

Si vous ne connaissez pas très bien votre correspondant, vous pouvez utiliser les formules d'appel traditionnelles.

Les petites annonces

Emploi

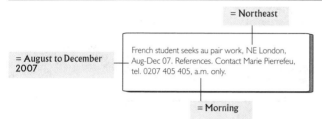

= Northeast

= August to December 2007

French student seeks au pair work, NE London, Aug-Dec 07. References. Contact Marie Pierrefeu, tel. 0207 405 405, a.m. only.

= Morning

= Part time = Including, inclusive of

= Male or Female

= Please

Sales Assistant M/F, good presentation, French-speaking, at least 1 yr experience preferred. P/T, incl. Sats. Sal. negotiable. Pls send CV to Personnel Manager, Stanhopes, 14 Benson Rd, London N3 5RP

= Year
= Salary
= Saturdays

Vente

= Excellent condition

DRYER: Kenmore electric. Exc. cond. $95. Call 364-9999, between 6-8pm.

= inch

DVD PLAYER, VCR, and TV14" screen. As new. £380 ono. 530 7949 leave msg.

= or nearest offer Ou : OBO (= or best offer) (Am)

= Message

Olympus, super VHS camera, high resolution, digital effects, auto/manual focusing, etc., orig. $2500, asking $995. 4383 Powell St. 0121 445 443.

= Original price, originally

Immobilier

= Large
= Room
= Week

Lg. rm to rent in shared house, SE London, £80 per wk. + CT + bills. Deposit reqd. Suit young NS prof.
Tel: 0206 555655

= Southeast
= professional
= Non smoking

Ou : C/T = council tax (Br)
= Required

= Apartment
= Kitchen
= With

2-rm. apt. to rent in city centre. All mod cons. TV, fitted kit., bathroom w/ shower. £555 per month.
Tel: 0786 554321

= All modern conveniences (Br) (tout confort)

Rencontres

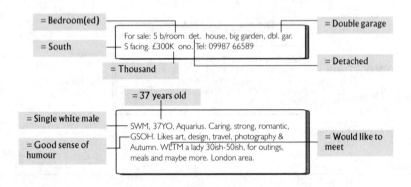

= Bedroom(ed)
= South
= Thousand

For sale: 5 b/room det. house, big garden, dbl. gar. S facing. £300K ono. Tel: 09987 66589

= Double garage
= Detached

= 37 years old

= Single white male
= Good sense of humour

SWM, 37YO, Aquarius. Caring, strong, romantic, GSOH. Likes art, design, travel, photography & Autumn. WLTM a lady 30ish-50ish, for outings, meals and maybe more. London area.

= Would like to meet

Abréviations utilisées dans les petites annonces

AC	air conditioning	gar.	garage
adj.	adjoining	GCH	gas central heating
appt.	appointment	H/CW	hot/cold water
apt.	apartment	hr.	hour
avail.	available	kit.	kitchen
bedrm., BR	bedroom	m.	month
bldg.	building	nr.	near
bsmt.	basement	obo	or best offer
bus.	business	ono	or nearest offer
c/h	central heating	opt.	optional
cond.	condition	pkg.	parking
dbl.	double	ref.	reference
del.	deliver; delivery	rm.	room
det.	detached	sal.	salary
din.	dining	sgl.	single
ea.	each	unfurn.	unfurnished
elec.	electric	vac.	vacancy
exch.	exchange	wk.	week
ft.	foot, feet	wpm	words per minute
furn.	furniture, furnished	yr	year

Le téléphone

Prononciation des numéros de téléphone

En anglais, on donne généralement son numéro chiffre par chiffre :
461 2816 = four six one two eight one six

Le chiffre O se prononce oh en anglais britannique et zéro en anglais américain :
0131 = oh one three one (Br)/zero one three one (Am)

Lorsque l'on répète deux fois le même chiffre, on peut utiliser l'adjectif double :
2992 = two double nine two

Pour obtenir un renseignement

Can I have directory enquiries (Br)/directory assistance (Am), please?
I'm trying to get through to a London number.
What is the (country) code for Canada?
How do I get an outside line?

Pour demander un interlocuteur

Hello,
...could I speak to ...?
...can I speak to ...?
...I'd like to speak to ...
...(could I have) extension 593, please?
...could you put me through to the manager, please?

Pour répondre à un appel

Robert McQueen speaking, can I help you?
Hello, this is ...
Yes, speaking (pour confirmer que l'on est bien la personne demandée).
Hold on/hold please, I'll (just) get him/her.
I'm sorry, he's/she's not here. Can I take a message?
I'm afraid he's away on business/out of the office/off sick/on holiday (Br)/on vacation (Am).

Pour laisser un message

Sur un répondeur :
I'm returning your call.
I'll be in London next week, perhaps we can ...
I'd like to talk to you about ...
Could you call me back, so we can discuss ...?

À une autre personne :
Could you ask him/her to call me on ...?
Could you tell him/her I won't be able to ...?
I'll call back later.
I need to speak to him/her urgently.
Please ask him/her to confirm. Thank you.

Pour demander une confirmation

Could you spell that, please?
Could you speak a bit more slowly, please?
I'm sorry, I didn't catch that. Could you repeat that, please?
Let me check, 11 a.m. on Wednesday 10th. Yes, that's fine.

Pour conclure un appel

Thank you, I look forward to seeing you on Wednesday. (Good)bye.
Thank you for your help.

Message de répondeur téléphonique

We are unable to take your call at the moment/I am not here at the moment. Please leave a message after the tone (and we/I will get back to you as soon as possible).

French Communication Guide

Letters

Model letters

Business correspondence

Employment

Faxes

E-mail

Advertisements

Telephone calls

Letters

When sending a letter or other written communication, particular attention should be paid to the grammar and spelling as these are sensitive topics. Spelling mistakes and grammatical errors in a letter are considered very bad form, even in private correspondence.

The style should be simple and clear. It is a good idea to keep sentences short and to use active rather than passive verbs. Each paragraph should deal with one idea only. The idea is presented in the first sentence of the paragraph and is then developed. A new idea is expressed in a new paragraph.

Layout

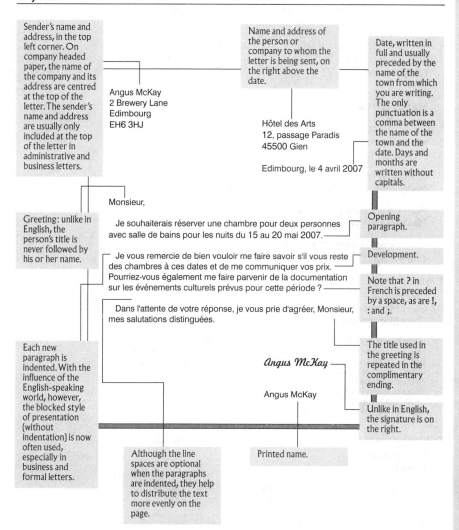

Sender's name and address, in the top left corner. On company headed paper, the name of the company and its address are centred at the top of the letter. The sender's name and address are usually only included at the top of the letter in administrative and business letters.

Name and address of the person or company to whom the letter is being sent, on the right above the date.

Date, written in full and usually preceded by the name of the town from which you are writing. The only punctuation is a comma between the name of the town and the date. Days and months are written without capitals.

Angus McKay
2 Brewery Lane
Edimbourg
EH6 3HJ

Hôtel des Arts
12, passage Paradis
45500 Gien

Edimbourg, le 4 avril 2007

Monsieur,

Greeting: unlike in English, the person's title is never followed by his or her name.

Je souhaiterais réserver une chambre pour deux personnes avec salle de bains pour les nuits du 15 au 20 mai 2007.

Opening paragraph.

Je vous remercie de bien vouloir me faire savoir s'il vous reste des chambres à ces dates et de me communiquer vos prix. Pourriez-vous également me faire parvenir de la documentation sur les événements culturels prévus pour cette période ?

Development.

Note that ? in French is preceded by a space, as are !, : and ;.

Dans l'attente de votre réponse, je vous prie d'agréer, Monsieur, mes salutations distinguées.

Each new paragraph is indented. With the influence of the English-speaking world, however, the blocked style of presentation (without indentation) is now often used, especially in business and formal letters.

Angus McKay

Angus McKay

The title used in the greeting is repeated in the complimentary ending.

Unlike in English, the signature is on the right.

Although the line spaces are optional when the paragraphs are indented, they help to distribute the text more evenly on the page.

Printed name.

Beginnings

The opening greetings and endings used in letters written in French follow certain well-established rules:

■ If you do not know the person you are writing to, whether you know their name or not, or if you know them only slightly:

Monsieur
Madame

> The greetings **Monsieur** and **Madame** are equivalent to "Dear Sir" and "Dear Madam" in English.

Mademoiselle

> **Mademoiselle** is used for an unmarried young woman. If in doubt, use **Madame**.

■ When you are unsure whether the recipient of the letter is male or female:

Madame, Monsieur

■ When the letter is addressed to a company rather than to an individual:

Messieurs

■ When writing to the head of a company or institution:

Monsieur le Directeur
Madame la Directrice

Monsieur le Président
Madame la Présidente

■ When writing to a minister, to the Prime Minister or the President:

Monsieur le Ministre
Madame le Ministre

> The form **Madame la Ministre** is equally acceptable now.

Monsieur le Premier Ministre
Madame le Premier Ministre

Monsieur le Président de la République
Madame la Présidente de la République

■ When writing to a lawyer or solicitor:

Cher Maître

> This form is used irrespective of whether one is addressing a man or woman in this context.

■ When you know the person you are writing to and want to sound less formal:

Cher Monsieur
Chère Madame
Chère Mademoiselle (for an unmarried young woman)

> These greetings are never followed by the name of the person. The equivalent of "Dear Mr Allen" is **Monsieur** if you don't know him very well, or **Cher Monsieur** if you know him better and want to sound less formal. Always write the title in full and avoid abbreviations like **M.**, **Mme** and **Mlle**.

> If you are writing to more than one person, you need to repeat **Cher** before each title: **Cher Monsieur, Chère Madame,**.

■ When writing to a colleague you do not know or know only slightly:

Cher collègue
Chère collègue

Cher confrère
Chère consœur

> The titles **Cher confrère** and **Chère consœur** are used between professionals such as doctors and lawyers.

Cher ami
Chère amie

> The titles **Cher ami** and **Chère amie** are not used between friends but between colleagues or acquaintances. They are slightly formal and old-fashioned.

- When writing to a relative or a friend, or to a colleague with whom you are on first name terms:
  Cher Olivier
  Chère Sandrine

- When writing to a relative or close friend, especially if they are younger than you, you can also use:
  Mon cher Olivier
  Ma chère Sandrine

Endings

The complimentary ending should correspond in form and tone to the opening greeting. The title used at the beginning (**Monsieur, Cher Monsieur**, etc.) is always repeated in the ending of the letter:

- The most neutral endings are:
  Veuillez agréer, Monsieur (Madame), mes salutations distinguées.
  Veuillez recevoir, Monsieur (Madame), mes salutations distinguées.
  Veuillez agréer, Monsieur (Madame), l'expression de mes sentiments distingués.
  Je vous prie d'agréer, Monsieur le Directeur (Madame la Directrice), mes salutations distinguées.
  Je vous prie d'agréer, cher Maître, mes salutations distinguées.
  Je vous remercie d'avance et vous prie d'agréer, Monsieur (Madame), mes salutations distinguées.
  Dans l'attente d'une réponse de votre part, veuillez agréer, Messieurs, nos salutations distinguées.

  > This form is used when addressing a lawyer or solicitor specifically.

- If you want to end on a more respectful note, such as when writing to a superior:
  Veuillez agréer, Monsieur (Madame), l'expression de ma considération distinguée.
  Je vous prie d'agréer, Monsieur (Madame), l'expression de mon profond respect.
  Veuillez agréer, je vous prie, Monsieur le Président (Madame la Présidente), l'expression de ma respectueuse considération.

- If you want to show your gratitude:
  Veuillez agréer, Monsieur (Madame), l'expression de ma profonde gratitude.
  Veuillez agréer, Monsieur (Madame), l'expression de ma respectueuse reconnaissance.
  Croyez, Monsieur (Madame), à toute ma reconnaissance.
  Croyez, Monsieur (Madame), à ma sincère gratitude.

  > As noted above, the expression cher ami, although more friendly, is still formal and should not be used for a friend.

- Although still formal, the following endings are more friendly:
  Veuillez agréer, cher Monsieur (chère Madame), l'expression de mes sentiments les plus cordiaux.
  Veuillez croire, cher Monsieur (chère Madame), à mon meilleur souvenir.
  Veuillez recevoir, cher ami (chère amie), mes plus cordiales salutations.
  Croyez, cher Olivier (chère Sandrine), à mon amical souvenir.

- Simplified and more informal endings are becoming more common. The following endings can be found more and more in everyday business letters, e-mails and faxes:
  Salutations distinguées.
  Cordialement. (more friendly)
  Bien à vous. (even more friendly)

- The following endings are used when writing to friends or relatives:

Polite:	Friendly:	Informal:
Amitiés.	Je t'embrasse.	Grosses bises.
Amicalement.	À bientôt.	Bisous.
Bien amicalement.	Embrasse Pierre de ma	
Bien affectueusement.	part.	
Bien à toi.		

Addresses and postcodes

▪ You might see the words **bis** and **ter** after the street number in a French address. For example:

> 3 bis, rue des Lilas
> 11 ter, avenue de Bernay

They indicate that there is more than one residence, whether in the form of a self-contained apartment or an annexe to the main house or premises, at the address in question. **Bis** is used to indicate that there is a second residential (or business) unit, **ter** a third. The examples above are equivalent to 3A and 11B in English.

▪ The first two numbers of a French postcode correspond to the administrative code number of the relevant "département". All postcodes for Paris begin with 75. This system also applies to vehicle licence plates. For example:

> 20, boulevard Arago
> 75013 Paris

In the example above, the first two numbers indicate the city of Paris while the last two figures indicate that the address is located in the thirteenth "arrondissement" (district) of the city. Note that in French addresses the postcode is usually written before the town, on the same line.

▪ The abbreviation "Cedex" is often found in French business addresses. For example:

> Société Delacour
> 77170 Fontainebleau Cedex

This is a special postcode ensuring rapid delivery of mail to businesses and certain institutions. The first two figures, as in other postcodes, denote geographical location but the following three figures denote an individual code assigned to the company in question.

▪ In Belgium addresses are often written with the building number coming after the street name. For an apartment or a house where there are more than three letterboxes it is usual to add the letterbox number (not the apartment number) after the street number. For example:

> Monsieur Luc Dujardin
> rue du Clocher 143, bte 12   The abbreviation for **boîte**.
> 1040 Bruxelles

▪ Swiss addresses are also usually written with the street number appearing after the street name, and the postcode before the town. When writing from outside Switzerland the abbreviation **CH** (for **Confederatio Helvetica** or the Swiss Confederation) is often added. For example:

> Monsieur André Roux
> Avenue du Peyrou 4
> CH - 2000 Neuchâtel

▪ In Canada, it is usual to write the name of the town or municipality, followed by the province in which it is located, followed by the postcode, all on the same line. For example:

> Madame Chantal Lemoine   The name of the province is usually given in brackets
> 3567 rue Drummond   after the name of the town or municipality.
> Montréal (Québec) H3G 1M8   Alternatively an abbreviation can be used to designate
>   the province: for example **QC** for **Québec**. If the
>   abbreviated form is used then there is no need for
>   brackets.

▪ The websites of the various postal services in French-speaking countries are a useful source of information regarding addresses and postcodes in particular.

> France: www.laposte.fr
> Belgium: www.post.be
> Luxembourg: www.pt.lu
> Switzerland: www.poste.ch
> Canada: www.canadapost.ca

Envelopes

The top left corner can be used by the sender to add any special comment, such as **personnel** or **faire suivre** (please forward).

In administrative letters, the surname usually precedes the forename: **Madame Guimard Annie.**

The recipient's name and address are written towards the right-hand side of the lower half of the envelope.

Madame Annie Guimard
325 rue Consolat
13100 AIX EN PROVENCE

The French postal services recommend that no punctuation be used on the envelope (no commas at the ends of lines, no comma after the street number etc) and that the name of the town should be written in capital letters, without any accents or hyphens.

Note that **rue** is never written with a capital **R**, unlike Street or the abbreviated form St in English.

It is standard practice to write a return address on the back of the envelope at the top, in case the letter gets lost.

Model letters

Chatty letter to a friend or relative

When writing to friends and relatives, as in English, a more informal style is perfectly acceptable.

In letters to friends and relatives, the sender does not usually put his or her name and address at the top of the letter.

Note that unlike in English, months do not start with a capital letter.

Rennes, le 15 juin 2007

Chère Élodie,

The greeting is always followed by a comma.

Je suis désolée d'avoir mis si longtemps à te répondre, mais c'est que je suis très occupée en ce moment. Comme tu le sais déjà, je viens de déménager et je n'ai pas encore fini de défaire mes cartons.

Mon nouvel appart me plaît beaucoup, il est très spacieux, ça me change du studio. Le quartier est également très sympa. J'ai bien l'intention de pendre la crémaillère dès que j'aurai fini de m'installer. J'espère que tu pourras venir !

The style is colloquial: note the use of abbreviated forms.

Pour l'instant, je pense surtout aux vacances et j'attends avec impatience mon départ pour l'Écosse au mois de juillet. Tu te souviens de Fiona, mon amie écossaise ? Nous allons camper dans les Highlands avec quelques amis. J'espère qu'il fera aussi beau que l'année dernière, j'étais rentrée bronzée ! Donne-moi vite de tes nouvelles. Au fait, que fais-tu cet été ?

The ending is always followed by a full stop, unlike in English.

Je t'embrasse.

Marie-Claire

Greetings cards

■ Season's greetings

The use of greetings cards is not as widespread in France as in English-speaking countries. Greetings cards are usually sent for New Year rather than Christmas. You can send a New Year's card at any time from before Christmas until the end of January, although usually before the middle of January. They are mostly sent to friends and relatives who live far away, and to business acquaintances. They are always posted and are never handed to the recipient.

> *Bonne et heureuse année 2008 à tous les trois.*
>
> *À très bientôt, j'espère.*
>
> *Laurence*

> *Cher Simon, chère Odile,*
>
> *Tous nos vœux de bonheur pour l'année 2008 !*
>
> *Bien à vous.*
>
> *Vincent et Sylvie*

> Chère Mathilde,
>
> Que cette nouvelle année t'apporte joie et bonheur et soit l'occasion de nous voir souvent !
>
> Irène

> Cher Jérôme, chère Nicole,
>
> Nous vous remercions de vos vœux et nous vous souhaitons à notre tour une nouvelle année pleine de joie et de bonheur.
>
> Affectueusement
>
> Pascale et Jean-Pierre

■ Birthdays

Birthday cards are not as popular in France as in English-speaking countries. As with other types of greetings cards, they are mostly sent to friends and relatives who live far away rather than to people one sees regularly. Birthday cards are not usually handed directly to the recipient and presents are not systematically accompanied by a card.

> *Cher Thomas,*
>
> *Bon anniversaire ! Dommage que nous ne puissions pas célébrer ensemble tes 30 ans. Je penserai à toi dimanche en buvant un verre à ta santé !*
>
> *Je t'embrasse.*
>
> *Julie*

Useful phrases:

Joyeux anniversaire !
Pierre se joint à moi pour te souhaiter un très bon anniversaire.

■ Congratulations

Written congratulations are usually sent after the announcement of a birth, engagement, wedding or promotion.

> *Grenoble, le 2 juillet 2007*
>
> *Bravo ! Tes parents m'ont appris que tu as été reçu à tes examens. Quel soulagement, tu vas enfin pouvoir profiter de vacances bien méritées. Toutes mes félicitations et bon courage pour la suite de tes études !*
>
> *Je t'embrasse.*
>
> *Marie*

Useful phrases:

For an engagement/a wedding:
C'est avec grand plaisir que j'ai appris tes fiançailles avec Pierre.
Tous nos vœux de bonheur à tous les deux. [less formal]

For a birth:
C'est avec joie que nous avons appris la naissance de Matthieu.
Félicitations à tous les deux et tous nos vœux de bonheur pour votre bébé. [less formal]

For a promotion/success:
C'est avec grand plaisir que j'ai appris votre promotion/nomination au poste de …
Je vous adresse mes sincères félicitations, ainsi que celles de mes collègues. [formal]

Letter of complaint

As in English, it is essential to remain clear and polite. For serious complaints, or if a first letter has been ignored, it is standard practice to send this type of letter by recorded delivery ("lettre recommandée avec accusé de réception").

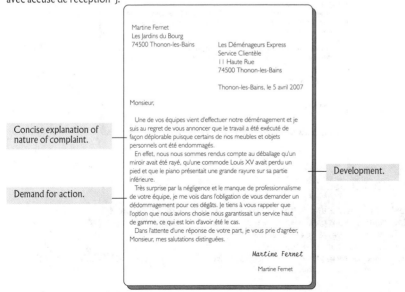

Martine Fernet
Les Jardins du Bourg
74500 Thonon-les-Bains

Les Déménageurs Express
Service Clientèle
11 Haute Rue
74500 Thonon-les-Bains

Thonon-les-Bains, le 5 avril 2007

Monsieur,

Concise explanation of nature of complaint.

Une de vos équipes vient d'effectuer notre déménagement et je suis au regret de vous annoncer que le travail a été exécuté de façon déplorable puisque certains de nos meubles et objets personnels ont été endommagés.

Development.

En effet, nous nous sommes rendus compte au déballage qu'un miroir avait été rayé, qu'une commode Louis XV avait perdu un pied et que le piano présentait une grande rayure sur sa partie inférieure.

Demand for action.

Très surprise par la négligence et le manque de professionnalisme de votre équipe, je me vois dans l'obligation de vous demander un dédommagement pour ces dégâts. Je tiens à vous rappeler que l'option que nous avions choisie nous garantissait un service haut de gamme, ce qui est loin d'avoir été le cas.

Dans l'attente d'une réponse de votre part, je vous prie d'agréer, Monsieur, mes salutations distinguées.

Martine Fernet

Martine Fernet

Useful phrases:

Je vous ai commandé le 20 décembre dernier une armoire que vous deviez me livrer dans les quinze jours. Or je n'ai toujours rien reçu trois semaines plus tard.
Je suis surpris de constater que ... / Je m'étonne de ...
Je suis vivement surpris de ... (stronger)
J'ai le regret de vous signaler que ...
Nous regrettons de devoir vous signaler une erreur dans ...
Nous vous demandons donc de bien vouloir ...
Je vous prie de bien vouloir faire le nécessaire/d'annuler ma commande et de me rembourser la somme de ...

Apologizing

Even if you have already apologized by telephone, in some situations, for example if you have missed a formal appointment, a letter of apology is expected.

Apologize and recall briefly what happened.

Give the specific reason for the mishap.

End on a hopeful note: you hope the person you are apologizing to will excuse you.

Ann Thorne
10, rue des Acacias
75017 Paris

TECHNO-MEDIA
À l'attention de Madame Dubreuil
14, rue du Vieux Marché
78100 Saint-Germain-en-Laye

Paris, le 3 septembre 2007

Madame,

Je suis vraiment navrée de n'avoir pas pu me présenter à l'entretien que vous m'aviez fixé le lundi 3 septembre 2007, à 14 heures. En effet, ainsi que je vous l'ai expliqué lors de mon appel hier matin, aucun train ne circulait en direction de Saint-Germain-en-Laye, en raison d'une grève surprise du personnel de la SNCF.

Je ne peux que vous renouveler mes excuses pour ce fâcheux incident indépendant de ma volonté. Vous serait-il possible de me proposer un nouveau rendez-vous, au jour et à l'heure qui vous conviendraient ?

Je vous remercie à l'avance de votre compréhension et je vous prie d'agréer, Madame, l'expression de ma considération distinguée.

Ann Thorne

Ann Thorne

Useful phrases:

Veuillez accepter toutes nos excuses pour ce malencontreux incident. (formal)
Nous tenons à vous présenter nos excuses pour ... (formal)
Je suis vraiment navré de ce malentendu.
J'espère que vous ne me tiendrez pas rigueur de cet oubli.
Excuse-moi de ne pas t'avoir prévenu plus tôt/de t'avoir fait faux bond hier soir. (informal)

Making a reservation

Specify all your requirements.

Mention that you expect a written response.

Useful phrases:

Je vous confirme ma réservation de votre appartement … pour la période du …
Je vous remercie de bien vouloir me faire savoir s'il vous reste des chambres à ces dates et de me communiquer vos prix.
Veuillez trouver ci-joint comme convenu un chèque de … euros à titre d'arrhes.
Dans l'attente de votre réponse …

Letter of thanks to a friend or relative

Be specific: recall the circumstances.

Thank the person explicitly.

Useful phrases:

Merci pour ton cadeau si généreux/pour ton aide si précieuse.
Merci pour cette magnifique écharpe qui m'a fait très plaisir.
Nous tenons à vous remercier pour la belle lampe que vous nous avez offerte.
Nous vous remercions de tout cœur pour ce magnifique cadeau/de nous avoir si gentiment aidés.

Invitations and replies

- Letter of invitation

> *Paris, le 25 mai 2007*
>
> *Cher Andrew,*
> *Que dirais-tu de venir passer quelques*
> *jours à la campagne ? Nous louons une maison*
> *en Normandie avec des amis du 7 au 15*
> *juillet. Thomas nous a promis d'être des*
> *nôtres. Cela nous ferait très plaisir que tu*
> *te joignes à nous.*
> *Tu trouveras ci-joint un plan détaillé de la*
> *région.*
> *Donne-nous vite ta réponse !*
> *À bientôt.*
>
> *Pierre*

Useful phrases:

À l'occasion du week-end du 1er mai, nous invitons quelques amis dans notre maison de campagne.
Pour fêter l'anniversaire de Simon, nous organisons une soirée le ..., à partir de ...
Nous comptons sur votre présence.

- Invitation card

These are usually made by a printer, who can suggest standard formulas.

> *M. et Mme Tessier*
> *seront heureux de vous recevoir à*
> *l'occasion du baptême*
> *de leur fils*
>
> **Nicolas**
>
> *le samedi 16 juin*
> *à partir de 15 heures*
>
> *4, villa du Puits - 26500 Crest*   *R.S.V.P.*

Useful phrases:

Sophie Tessier recevra ses amis le ... à partir de ...
Jacques Tessier vous invite à venir assister à sa soutenance de thèse le ... à partir de ...
Nous organisons une soirée le ... à l'occasion de ... Nous serions très heureux si vous pouviez vous joindre à nous.

- **Wedding invitation**

Monsieur et Madame Tessier Monsieur et Madame Legrand

ont le plaisir de vous faire part
du mariage de leurs enfants

Nathalie et Sylvain

et vous prient d'assister à la bénédiction nuptiale qui
leur sera donnée
le samedi 16 juin 2007 à 16 heures en l'église
Saint-Christophe à Crest
ainsi qu'au dîner organisé à partir de 20 heures
au restaurant Les Tilleuls de Crest.

Réponse souhaitée avant le 10 mai

4, villa du Puits   6, rue des Bains
26500 Crest   25000 Besançon

> For traditional weddings, the invitation is made by the parents of the couple.

Useful phrases:

Monsieur et Madame X vous prient d'assister à la messe de mariage qui sera célébrée le … en l'église …
Monsieur et Madame X recevront à l'hôtel Les Tilleuls à l'issue de la cérémonie religieuse.
Nathalie Tessier et Sylvain Legrand sont heureux de vous annoncer leur mariage qui sera célébré le … à … à la mairie de Crest.
Un vin d'honneur sera servi à l'issue de la cérémonie à la salle des fêtes de Crest.

- **Declining an invitation**

Valence, le 15 juillet 2007

Chère Aude,

Je viens de recevoir ta lettre, et je suis très touché que tu aies pensé à m'inviter pour ton anniversaire, mais, malheureusement, je dois partir à Londres dès la semaine prochaine pour raisons professionnelles et je ne pourrai pas me joindre à vous.

J'espère bien sûr que tes 30 ans seront dignement célébrés, et dans la bonne humeur ; je penserai à toi ce jour-là, en buvant un verre à ta santé !

Comme cadeau d'anniversaire, je serai ravi de t'accueillir à Londres. On met à ma disposition un grand appartement et un week-end serait suffisant pour te dépayser.

J'attends donc ta réponse et je te souhaite un très bon anniversaire.

Je t'embrasse.

Simon

> Express your pleasure at being invited.

> Explain briefly why you are unable to attend.

Useful phrases:

Je suis vraiment déçu de ne pouvoir accepter mais je ne pourrai pas me libérer car …
Nous regrettons de ne pouvoir nous libérer et nous espérons avoir très prochainement l'occasion de nous réunir.
Nous vous remercions de votre aimable invitation que nous avons le regret de ne pouvoir accepter, étant déjà retenus ce jour-là. [formal]

- **Accepting an invitation**

Express your pleasure at being invited.

Thank the sender for the invitation.

Nantes, le 14 janvier 2007

Cher Vincent,

Je viens de recevoir ta lettre et je suis ravi ! C'est vraiment gentil d'avoir pensé à moi. Ça faisait très longtemps que je rêvais de vacances et l'idée de faire du ski à Serre-Chevalier dans moins d'un mois me rend fou de joie – espérons qu'il continuera à neiger d'ici là !
Tout va bien ici. Mon nouveau travail me plaît énormément et l'équipe est jeune et sympa. Et toi ? Dois-tu repartir aux États-Unis avant les vacances ?
Je te téléphonerai bientôt pour préciser mon jour d'arrivée.
Je te remercie encore et je t'embrasse.

Michel

Useful phrases:

C'est avec grand plaisir que j'accepte votre invitation pour le … / je me joindrais à vous le …
Nous vous remercions de votre invitation au mariage de Sylvain, que nous acceptons avec joie / auquel nous viendrons avec grand plaisir.

Letter of condolence

Name the person who died and, if you knew them, recall their qualities.

You can offer your support.

Toulon, le 3 décembre 2007

Cher Nicolas,

C'est avec beaucoup de peine que nous venons d'apprendre la triste nouvelle du décès de ton frère.
Nous savons à quel point vous étiez proches et nous imaginons ta douleur. Tout le monde appréciait Julien pour sa gentillesse et son enthousiasme. Il nous manquera beaucoup et nous ne l'oublierons pas.
Nous pensons beaucoup à toi. Si nous pouvons t'aider en quoi que ce soit dans ces moments difficiles, n'hésite pas à faire appel à nous.
Transmets à toute ta famille nos sincères condoléances.
Nous t'embrassons avec toute notre affection.

Olivier et Sandrine

Useful phrases:

C'est avec émotion que nous apprenons le malheur qui vient de vous frapper.
Nous prenons part à / Nous partageons votre peine.
Croyez, cher Nicolas / cher Monsieur, à l'expression de ma très sincère sympathie. [formal]

Asking for information

Angus McKay
2 Brewery Lane
Edimbourg EH6 3HJ

Office du tourisme
11 place du Général de Gaulle
06600 Antibes

Edimbourg, le 4 avril 2007

Madame, Monsieur,

Souhaitant passer mes vacances (du 1er au 16 juillet) dans la région d'Antibes, je vous serais reconnaissant de bien vouloir me faire parvenir une liste des hôtels et des chambresd'hôte, à Antibes même ou dans les environs.
Pourriez-vous également me faire parvenir de la documentation sur les événements culturels prévus pour cette période ?
Je vous remercie d'avance et je vous prie d'agréer, Madame, Monsieur, mes salutations distinguées.

Angus McKay

Angus McKay

Business correspondence

Business to business (general)

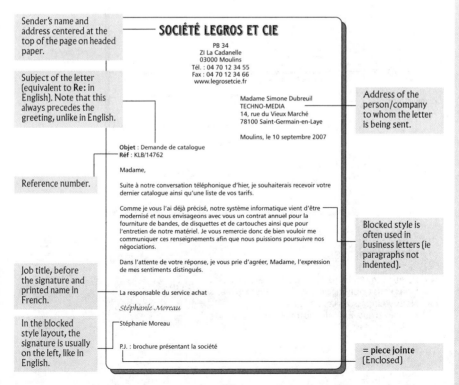

Sender's name and address centered at the top of the page on headed paper.

Subject of the letter (equivalent to **Re:** in English). Note that this always precedes the greeting, unlike in English.

Reference number.

Job title, before the signature and printed name in French.

In the blocked style layout, the signature is usually on the left, like in English.

SOCIÉTÉ LEGROS ET CIE

PB 34
ZI La Cadanelle
03000 Moulins
Tél. : 04 70 12 34 55
Fax : 04 70 12 34 66
www.legrosetcie.fr

Madame Simone Dubreuil
TECHNO-MEDIA
14, rue du Vieux Marché
78100 Saint-Germain-en-Laye

Moulins, le 10 septembre 2007

Objet : Demande de catalogue
Réf : KLB/14762

Madame,

Suite à notre conversation téléphonique d'hier, je souhaiterais recevoir votre dernier catalogue ainsi qu'une liste de vos tarifs.

Comme je vous l'ai déjà précisé, notre système informatique vient d'être modernisé et nous envisageons avec vous un contrat annuel pour la fourniture de bandes, de disquettes et de cartouches ainsi que pour l'entretien de notre matériel. Je vous remercie donc de bien vouloir me communiquer ces renseignements afin que nous puissions poursuivre nos négociations.

Dans l'attente de votre réponse, je vous prie d'agréer, Madame, l'expression de mes sentiments distingués.

La responsable du service achat

Stéphanie Moreau

Stéphanie Moreau

P.J. : brochure présentant la société

Address of the person/company to whom the letter is being sent.

Blocked style is often used in business letters (ie paragraphs not indented).

= **pièce jointe** (Enclosed)

Useful phrases:

En réponse à votre lettre du ...,
Nous avons bien reçu votre lettre du ... et nous vous en remercions.
Nous sommes tout particulièrement intéressés par ...
Nous vous remercions de l'intérêt que vous portez à notre société et nous restons à votre disposition pour toutes informations complémentaires.

Placing an order

A letter placing an order needs to specify the items required, as well as the conditions of delivery and payment.

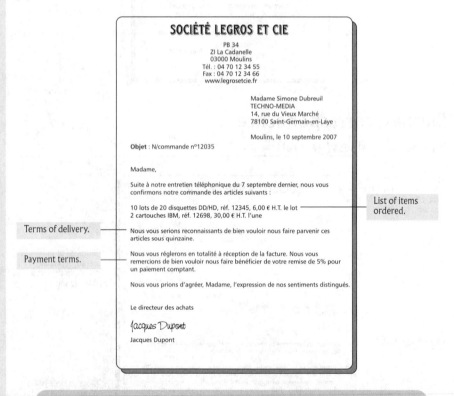

SOCIÉTÉ LEGROS ET CIE

PB 34
ZI La Cadanelle
03000 Moulins
Tél. : 04 70 12 34 55
Fax : 04 70 12 34 66
www.legrosetcie.fr

Madame Simone Dubreuil
TECHNO-MEDIA
14, rue du Vieux Marché
78100 Saint-Germain-en-Laye

Moulins, le 10 septembre 2007

Objet : N/commande n°12035

Madame,

Suite à notre entretien téléphonique du 7 septembre dernier, nous vous confirmons notre commande des articles suivants :

10 lots de 20 disquettes DD/HD, réf. 12345, 6,00 € H.T. le lot
2 cartouches IBM, réf. 12698, 30,00 € H.T. l'une

List of items ordered.

Nous vous serions reconnaissants de bien vouloir nous faire parvenir ces articles sous quinzaine.

Terms of delivery.

Nous vous réglerons en totalité à réception de la facture. Nous vous remercions de bien vouloir nous faire bénéficier de votre remise de 5% pour un paiement comptant.

Payment terms.

Nous vous prions d'agréer, Madame, l'expression de nos sentiments distingués.

Le directeur des achats

Jacques Dupont

Jacques Dupont

Useful phrases:

Veuillez nous faire parvenir les articles suivants ...
Nous vous prions de bien vouloir nous expédier ...
Nous vous passons commande de ...
Veuillez trouver ci-joint notre bon de commande n° ...

Informing a customer

TECHNO-MEDIA
14, rue du Vieux Marché
78100 Saint-Germain-en-Laye
Tél. : 01 34 22 44 66/Fax : 01 34 22 44 67
www.technomedia.fr

Saint-Germain-en-Laye, le 10 septembre 2007

Monsieur,

Nous avons le plaisir de vous informer que vous pouvez désormais consulter notre catalogue et passer vos commandes sur notre site Web.

Notre site est entièrement sécurisé. Si vous souhaitez bénéficier de nos services en ligne, il suffit de vous enregistrer en vous connectant à :
http:\\www.technomedia.fr

Dans l'espoir que ce nouveau service vous donnera entière satisfaction, nous vous prions d'agréer, Monsieur, nos meilleures salutations.

La responsable du site Web

Sylvie Legrand

Sylvie Legrand

Useful phrases:

Nous vous informons que …
Nous tenons à vous signaler que …
Nous restons à votre entière disposition pour tous renseignements complémentaires.
Veuillez noter notre nouvelle adresse à partir du …

Dealing with a customer complaint

Strasbourg, le 31 octobre 2007

Monsieur,

Dans votre lettre du 25 octobre dernier, vous nous signalez un défaut de quantité dans notre livraison n° 2983. Or, notre agent à Cherbourg qui a personnellement supervisé le chargement à bord du navire nous certifie que la quantité a bien été embarquée.

Reference to letter of complaint.

Nous considérons donc que nous ne pouvons être tenus pour responsables et qu'il s'agit probablement d'un vol qui a pu se produire en cours de transport ou lors du stockage au débarquement et nous vous conseillons de prendre contact avec votre assureur.

Explanation of cause of problem.

Nous vous prions d'agréer, Monsieur, nos salutations distinguées.

La directrice des ventes

Isabelle Durand

Isabelle Durand

Useful phrases:

Nous vous prions de bien vouloir nous excuser pour cette regrettable erreur.
Veuillez accepter nos excuses pour le dérangement que nous avons pu vous causer.
Nous avons pris des mesures pour que cela ne se reproduise plus.

Invoice

Company name, registered office, telephone and fax numbers, e-mail address and often company registration number.

Date of invoice.

Reference number of listed items.

Precise description of products or services.

Total including VAT (TTC = toutes taxes comprises).

Name and address of client.

Client reference number and order number.

Unit price not including VAT (HT = hors taxe).

Quantity.

VAT rate.

Total price not including VAT.

Reply to invoice

If you are sent an incorrect invoice, you can contest it and ask for a new one.

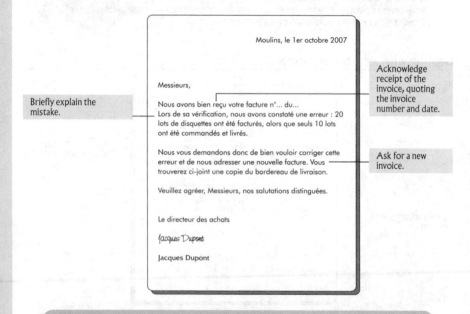

Briefly explain the mistake.

Acknowledge receipt of the invoice, quoting the invoice number and date.

Ask for a new invoice.

Useful phrases:

Nous accusons réception de votre facture n° ...
Les prix ne sont pas ceux qui ont été convenus lors de la commande, à savoir : ....
En vérifiant la facture que vous venez de nous faire parvenir, nous constatons que le montant ne correspond pas à notre commande.
Nous avons décelé l'erreur suivante : ...

Employment

Covering letter

When applying for a job in France, it is customary to write the covering letter (**lettre de motivation**) by hand. Apart from adding a more personal touch, it is not unusual for French companies to use the services of a graphologist who analyses the applicants' handwriting. A letter of application is quite formal in its presentation. It should be concise, properly structured in paragraphs and have the standard opening and closing formulas. You should cover the following points:

- Emphasize what you consider important in your CV
- Add information about your objectives
- Explain why you are interested in the company
- Convince the reader that you are the right person for the job

Replying to an advertisement

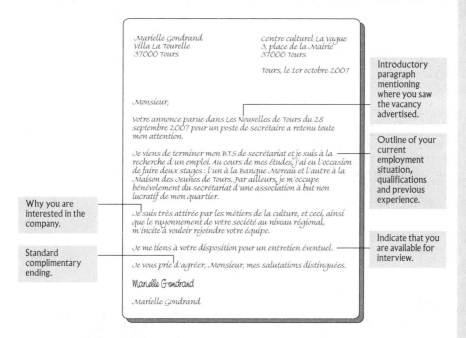

Marielle Gondrand
Villa La Tourelle
37000 Tours

Centre culturel La Vague
3, place de la Mairie
37000 Tours

Tours, le 1er octobre 2007

Monsieur,

votre annonce parue dans Les Nouvelles de Tours du 28 septembre 2007 pour un poste de secrétaire a retenu toute mon attention.

Je viens de terminer mon BTS de secrétariat et je suis à la recherche d'un emploi. Au cours de mes études, j'ai eu l'occasion de faire deux stages : l'un à la Banque Moreau et l'autre à la Maison des Jeunes de Tours. Par ailleurs, je m'occupe bénévolement du secrétariat d'une association à but non lucratif de mon quartier.

Je suis très attirée par les métiers de la culture, et ceci, ainsi que le rayonnement de votre société au niveau régional, m'incite à vouloir rejoindre votre équipe.

Je me tiens à votre disposition pour un entretien éventuel.

Je vous prie d'agréer, Monsieur, mes salutations distinguées.

Marielle Gondrand

Marielle Gondrand

Introductory paragraph mentioning where you saw the vacancy advertised.

Outline of your current employment situation, qualifications and previous experience.

Why you are interested in the company.

Indicate that you are available for interview.

Standard complimentary ending.

Useful phrases:

En réponse à votre annonce parue dans Les Nouvelles de Tours du ..., je me permets de vous adresser mon curriculum vitae pour le poste de secrétaire.
Je dispose de plusieurs années d'expérience dans différentes entreprises.
Au cours de mes cinq années d'expérience auprès de la société X, j'ai acquis une bonne maîtrise de ...
En espérant que ma candidature retiendra votre attention, je vous prie d'agréer, Madame, Monsieur, l'expression de mes sentiments distingués.

Unsolicited application

Wilfrid Garnier
10, impasse des Petites Écuries
37000 Tours
Tél : 02 47 30 60 30
E-mail : wilf.garnier@free.fr

Tours, le 17 févier 2007

M. le Directeur des Ressources
Humaines
Supermarchés Guévara
Z. I. de la Gravière
37042 TOURS CEDEX

Monsieur,

Explain what you can offer the company.

Titulaire d'un BTS de gestion et après une expérience réussie en tant qu'assistant du responsable de la gestion des stocks de la société des Engrais Santic (voir CV ci-joint), je vous écris pour vous proposer mes services. Je souhaiterais désormais élargir mon expérience en utilisant mes compétences dans le domaine de la grande distribution. Ce secteur m'a toujours intéressé et je crois disposer des aptitudes nécessaires pour donner entière satisfaction dans toute mission que vous voudriez bien me confier.

Votre société m'intéresse particulièrement car elle jouit d'une réputation d'excellence sans pareil, et j'admire les efforts qu'elle a fournis pour le développement du commerce éthique.

Show your interest in this particular company.

Je me tiens à votre entière disposition pour vous fournir tout renseignement complémentaire.

Dans l'attente de vous lire, je vous prie d'agréer, Monsieur, l'expression de mes sentiments les meilleurs.

W Garnier

W Garnier

PJ : un CV avec photo

Asking for a work placement

Work placements are very popular in France and are a compulsory part of many courses. It is therefore advisable to send your request well in advance.

This type of letter is always handwritten in French (see Covering letter on previous page).

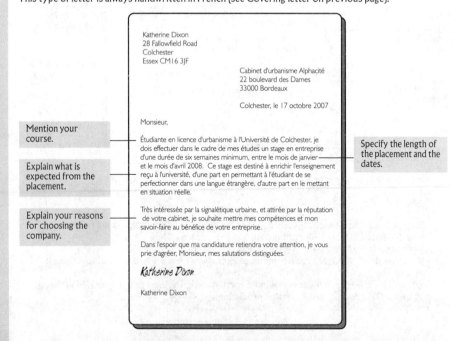

Katherine Dixon
28 Fallowfield Road
Colchester
Essex CM16 3JF

Cabinet d'urbanisme Alphacité
22 boulevard des Dames
33000 Bordeaux

Colchester, le 17 octobre 2007

Monsieur,

Mention your course.

Étudiante en licence d'urbanisme à l'Université de Colchester, je dois effectuer dans le cadre de mes études un stage en entreprise d'une durée de six semaines minimum, entre le mois de janvier et le mois d'avril 2008. Ce stage est destiné à enrichir l'enseignement reçu à l'université, d'une part en permettant à l'étudiant de se perfectionner dans une langue étrangère, d'autre part en le mettant en situation réelle.

Specify the length of the placement and the dates.

Explain what is expected from the placement.

Très intéressée par la signalétique urbaine, et attirée par la réputation de votre cabinet, je souhaite mettre mes compétences et mon savoir-faire au bénéfice de votre entreprise.

Explain your reasons for choosing the company.

Dans l'espoir que ma candidature retiendra votre attention, je vous prie d'agréer, Monsieur, mes salutations distinguées.

Katherine Dixon

Katherine Dixon

Useful phrases:

Vous trouverez ci-joint mon curriculum vitae.

Je vous remercie de l'attention que vous porterez à ma demande et reste à votre disposition pour un entretien.

Je reste à votre disposition pour vous rencontrer et vous fournir tout autre renseignement.

En vous remerciant à l'avance de bien vouloir examiner ma demande, je vous prie d'agréer ...

Curriculum vitae

The presentation of a CV in French is in many ways similar to an English or American CV. The following differences should be respected.

- The title "Curriculum Vitae" should never be included in a French CV.
- Only mention hobbies if they add something personal to your profile or if they are particularly relevant to the job.
- Do not include referees on your CV: references are not commonly used in France apart from certain jobs where personal recommendation would be expected such as catering, cleaning, child care, etc.
- Even if you do not complete your degree, you can mention the fact that you studied for it by using the word **niveau**, ie **niveau licence**.

■ Recent graduate (British)

Stephen Forbes
81 Lincoln Walk
STEVENAGE
Herts SE19 2DN
Tél: 00 44 1283 456789
E-mail: sforbes@teaser.org.uk

23 ans, célibataire
Nationalité britannique

Formation

2004 - 2007	BSc (équivalent de la licence) en Biologie, Université de York
2003	A Levels (équivalent du baccalauréat) : Mathématiques, Chimie, Biologie et Français, Lycée Whitton Comprehensive, Bristol.
2001	GCSE (premier examen de fin de scolarité) : Anglais, Mathématiques, Chimie, Biologie, Français, Histoire et Informatique, Lycée Whitton Comprehensive, Bristol.

Expérience professionnelle

juillet - septembre 2006	Stage de 3 mois auprès du service d'hématologie de l'hôpital Frenchay de Bristol : analyse de prélèvements sanguins.
septembre 2003 - juin 2004	Enseignement de l'anglais langue étrangère, École de langues Babel, Osaka, Japon.

Langues
Anglais : langue maternelle
Français : courant
Japonais : notions

Divers
Bonnes connaissances informatiques : animateur du club d'informatique d'une maison des jeunes et de la culture (Bristol)

Titulaire du brevet de secourisme

Recent graduate (American)

Martha Jacobs
493 Huntington Avenue
Boston
MA 02575
États-Unis
Tél : (617) 267-1680
E-mail: mjacobs@totem.com

25 ans, célibataire
Nationalité américaine

Traductrice anglais/français/espagnol
Début de spécialisation en informatique

FORMATION

2005 - 2007 — Diplôme de traducteur technique
Université McGill, Montréal

2002 - 2005 — BA (équivalent de la licence) en français et espagnol,
mention très bien Université de Boston

2001 — High school diploma (équivalent du baccalauréat)

EXPÉRIENCE PROFESSIONNELLE

2005 - 2006 — Éditions Dulis, Montréal
Travaux de traduction en free-lance

juillet 2004 - septembre 2005 — Société AX Networks, Boston
Stage de 3 mois dans le service de traduction :
adaptation de logiciels pour le marché européen

2003 - 2004 — Lycée Dupuis, Grenoble
Assistante de français

LANGUES
Anglais : langue maternelle
Français : bilingue (2 ans à Montréal, 1 an à Grenoble)
Espagnol : courant

CONNAISSANCES INFORMATIQUES
Word, Excel et Access (sur PC et Mac)

LOISIRS
Escrime, violoncelle

Experienced (British)

Mary Grant
198 Francis Avenue
LEICESTER LE4 9PQ
Grande-Bretagne
Tél : 00 44 1493 767 33 36
E-mail: mgrant@uk.net

36 ans, célibataire
Nationalité britannique

EXPÉRIENCE PROFESSIONNELLE
Depuis septembre 1994 — Directrice des exportations, Gannett UK Ltd, Leicester
(Fabrication et distribution de produits cosmétiques)
» mise en place d'un réseau commercial (40 représentants et 10 agents)
» négociations avec les points de vente
» études de marchés

1990 - 1994 — Responsable des exportations Europe, Simon & Co plc, Leicester
(prêt-à-porter enfants)
» prospection
» contrôle des ventes
» ouverture de deux nouveaux marchés (Espagne et Italie)

FORMATION
1989 - 1993 — MA (équivalent de la Maîtrise) en Gestion, Université d'Édimbourg

1989 — A Levels (équivalent du baccalauréat) : économie, mathématiques,
histoire et français (Lycée Harfield Comprehensive, Leicester)

1988 — GCSE (premier examen de fin de scolarité) : anglais, mathématiques,
français, économie, informatique et histoire (Lycée Harfield
Comprehensive, Leicester)

AUTRES ACTIVITÉS
1993 - 1994 — Séjour d'une année à Paris : enseignement de l'anglais commercial à la
Chambre de commerce et d'industrie franco-britannique

LANGUES
Anglais : langue maternelle
Bilingue français (mère française)
Espagnol : lu, écrit, parlé

DIVERS
Bonne maîtrise de l'outil informatique sur PC et sur Mac
Chant choral

▪ Experienced (American)

John Farmer
18 rue de Turenne
75004 Paris
Tél: 01 42 22 37 89
E-mail: jfarmer@nxl.fr

Né le 17 juin 1962
Marié, 2 enfants (11 et 14 ans)
Nationalité américaine

Directeur des ventes : 11 ans d'expérience
20 ans d'expérience dans la fonction commerciale
Connaissance approfondie du marché informatique

Depuis 1996   Softlux France, Paris
Directeur des ventes Europe
· Encadrement d'une équipe de 20 commerciaux
· Diversification et développement des marchés existants
· Augmentation du chiffre d'affaires (+ 53 %)

1988 - 1996   ICN Europe, Amsterdam
Directeur commercial
· Responsable de la politique commerciale et du marketing
· Recrutement et encadrement d'une équipe de 7 commerciaux
· Dépassement des objectifs fixés: 1994:118 %, 1993: 110%

1984 - 1987   Société ADB, Paris
Ingénieur commercial grands comptes
· Responsable du développement des ventes pour le secteur de
la grande distribution sur la région parisienne
· Ouverture de nouveaux comptes

Formation
1988   MBA, Harvard Business School
1984   MS (équivalent de la maîtrise) en Économie et Gestion,
Université de Boston
1980   High school diploma (équivalent du baccalauréat)

Langues
Anglais : langue maternelle
Français : bilingue

Faxes

Faxes, which are by definition a form of rapid communication, can generally be drafted in a more casual and concise way than letters. The endings are usually short and simplified.

Business

It is not necessary to use an opening greeting when you know the person well.

Short ending.

À l'attention de : Nicolas Roche
Téléphone :   05 40 92 90 32
Télécopie :   05 40 92 97 35

De la part de : Pierre Lenoir
Téléphone :   01 40 36 08 60
Télécopie :   01 40 36 10 30

Date : 10/10/2007
Nombre de pages (y compris celle-ci) : 1

Objet : La réunion a été reportée au mardi 16 octobre. Nous nous chargeons de la réservation de votre billet d'avion ainsi que de votre chambre d'hôtel.

Cordialement.
P. Lenoir

Booking a hotel room

The greeting should be used if you don't know the person or if you know them only slightly.

Short ending.

À l'attention de : Hôtel Le Richelieu
Téléphone :   01 42 36 16 22
Télécopie :   01 42 36 16 24

De la part de : Pierre Lenoir
Téléphone :   01 40 36 08 60
Télécopie :   01 40 36 10 30

Date : 01/10/2007
Nombre de pages (y compris celle-ci) : 1

Monsieur,

Suite à notre conversation téléphonique de ce jour, je vous confirme ma réservation d'une chambre pour une personne avec salle de bains pour les nuits du 15 et 16 octobre 2007.

M. Roche arrivera en fin d'après-midi le lundi 15 octobre.

Nous vous réglerons comme convenu à réception de la facture.

Cordialement.

P. Lenoir

■ Alternative endings:

Salutations.
Salutations distinguées.
Bien à vous. (more friendly)

E-mail

- Because of the nature of the medium, e-mails are not subject to the formal code of letter-writing that is prevalent in French.

- E-mails in French are often written in slightly less telegraphic style than tends to be the case in English, this being mainly due to the fact that French contains fewer of the abbreviated forms that characterize so much of this type of communication in English. Endings are usually rather informal.

- The same rules of "netiquette" apply as in English, so avoid typing entire words in capitals as this is equalivant to shouting.

- The symbol @ is pronounced [arobas] or [arobaz] in French.

Within a company

Business to business

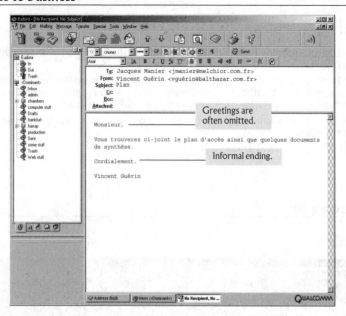

Abbreviations and acronyms: e-mail and Internet

Below is a list of French abbreviations that are used in e-mail correspondence, in newsgroups and chat-rooms. These abbreviations should only be used when you are sure that the person to whom you are sending the message understands what they mean. Some are familiar in register (labelled *Fam*) and therefore should only be used in casual correspondence with friends or very close colleagues.

Note that because English is the main language of the Internet, English abbreviations are much more well established than French ones.

A+ *Fam*	à plus tard (see you/talk to you later)	**info** *Fam*	information
actu *Fam*	actualités (news/current affairs)	**ltr**	lettre (letter)
alp *Fam*	à la prochaine (see you!, till the next time!)	**m**	même (same; even)
ama *Fam*	à mon avis (in my opinion)	**mdr** *Fam*	mort de rire (laughing out loud)
amha *Fam*	à mon humble avis (in my humble opinion)	**MMS** *Fam*	mes meilleurs souvenirs (best regards)
BAL	boîte à lettres (mailbox)	**nvx**	nouveaux (new)
bcp *Fam*	beaucoup (a lot; many)	**p**	pour (for)
B.D.	base de données (database)	**pb, pbm**	problème (problem)
cad	c'est-à-dire (that is to say, ie)	**pr**	pour (for)
dc	donc (then, therefore)	**quoi 2/9** *Fam*	quoi de neuf ? (what's new?)
doc.	document	**RAS** *Fam*	rien à signaler (nothing to report)
doss	dossier (file)	**stp**	s'il te plaît (please)
ds	dans (in)	**suiv.**	suivant (following)
envoy.	envoyer (send)	**svp**	s'il vous plaît (please)
err	erreur (error)	**svt**	souvent (often)
ex.	exemple (example)	**urgt**	urgent
impr.	impression/imprimer/imprimante (printout; print; printer)	**we**	week-end

Advertisements

Job advertisement

Offering goods for sale

Accommodation to rent

Apartments in France are described in terms of the number of rooms (excluding kitchen and bathroom) and their size in square metres (m²). Rent may or may not include **charges** (monthly building maintenance charges).

Personal advertisement

Abbreviations used in advertisments

à déb.	à débattre	park.	parking
appt.	appartement	pces.	pièces
balc.	balcon	px	prix
c.c.	charges comprises/chauffage central	rdc.	rez-de-chaussée
		sdb.	salle de bains
ch.	chambre/cherche	séj.	séjour
compr.	comprenant	sér.	sérieux
cuis.	cuisine	tbe	très bon état
env.	envoyer	tt. conf.	tout confort
équip.	équipé	se prés.	se présenter
gar.	garage	Sté.	société
gren.	grenier		

Telephone calls

Pronunciation of telephone numbers

When giving their phone numbers, French people say them two by two: 01 45 67 44 32 = zéro un, quarante-cinq, soixante-sept, quarante-quatre, trente-deux.

This can be a little disconcerting for the English speaker and you may have to ask them to say it again one number at a time.

Asking for information from the operator or switchboard

Est-ce que vous pouvez me passer les renseignements, s'il vous plaît ?
J'essaie d'obtenir un numéro à Marseille.
Quel est l'indicatif pour le Maroc, s'il vous plaît ?
Comment fait-on pour appeler à l'extérieur ?

Answering the telephone

Informally:
Allô ?

To which the caller replies:
Allô, (c'est) Georges ?/Salut, Georges, c'est Christophe etc.

More formally:
Allô, Hélène Chapsal à l'appareil(, je vous écoute).

In a company or institution:
Éditions Paoli, bonjour.

Asking to speak to someone

Je voudrais parler à Monsieur Dupont.
Pouvez-vous me passer le service du/des …, s'il vous plaît ?
Pouvez-vous me passer le poste 321, s'il vous plaît ? (pronounced **trois cent vingt-et-un**)

Phrases used by a receptionist or secretary taking a call

When asking for the caller's name:
Qui dois-je annoncer ?
C'est de la part de qui ?

When putting a caller through:
(Ne quittez pas,) je vous le passe.

When the caller cannot be connected immediately:
C'est occupé.
Il/Elle est en communication, voulez-vous patienter ?

Asking the caller if he or she wishes to leave a message:
Voulez-vous lui laisser un message ?

To which the caller may reply:
Pouvez-vous lui demander de me rappeler ?
Non merci, je rappellerai plus tard.

Recorded messages

If you are put on hold, the standard recorded message while waiting is :

Nous vous demandons de bien vouloir patienter quelques instants. Nous allons donner suite à votre appel.

If you have to leave a message, you will hear the following standard set of sentences:

Vous êtes bien en communication avec ... Nous ne pouvons répondre à votre appel. Veuillez nous laisser votre nom et numéro de téléphone après le signal sonore et nous vous rappellerons dès que possible. Merci.

Nations of the World
États du monde

Please note that the French name for the countries has been given in the second column. In order to find the French terms for the currencies and languages, please refer to the corresponding table in the French supplement.

English name	French name	Local name	Official language(s)
Afghanistan	Afghanistan	Afghānestān	Dari, Pushtu
Albania	Albanie	Shqīpëri	Albanian
Algeria	Algérie	Al-Jazā'ir (Arabic), Algérie (French)	Arabic
Andorra	Andorre	Andorra	Catalan, French, Spanish
Angola	Angola	Angola	Portuguese
Argentina	Argentine	Argentina	Spanish
Armenia	Arménie	Hayastani	Armenian
Australia	Australie	Australia	English
Austria	Autriche	Österreich	German
Azerbaijan	Azerbaïdjan	Azarbaijan	Azeri (Azerbaijan)
Bahamas, The	Bahamas	Bahamas	English
Bahrain	Bahreïn	Dawlat al-Bahrayn	Arabic
Bangladesh	Bangladesh	Gana Prajatantri Bangladesh	Bengali
Barbados	Barbade	Barbados	English
Belarus	Biélorussie	Belarus	Belarussian
Belgium	Belgique	Belgique (French), Belgïe (Flemish)	Flemish, French, German
Belize	Belize	Belize	English
Benin	Bénin	Bénin	French
Bhutan	Bhoutan	Druk-Yul	Dzongkha
Bolivia	Bolivie	Bolivia	Spanish
Bosnia-Herzegovina	Bosnie-Herzégovine	Bosnia-Herzegovina	Serbo-Croat
Botswana	Botswana	Botswana	English
Brazil	Brésil	Brasil	Portuguese
Brunei	Brunei	Brunei	Malay
Bulgaria	Bulgarie	Bălgarija	Bulgarian
Burkina Faso	Burkina	Burkina Faso	French
Burma ▶ Myanmar	Birmanie		
Burundi	Burundi	Burundi	French, Kirundi
Cambodia	Cambodge	Preah Reach Ana Pak Kampuchea	Khmer
Cameroon	Cameroun	Cameroon	English, French
Canada	Canada	Canada	English, French
Cape Verde	Cap-Vert	Cabo Verde	Portuguese
Central African Republic	République centrafricaine	République centrafricaine	French, Sango
Chad	Tchad	Tchad	French, Arabic
Chile	Chili	Chile	Spanish
China	Chine	Zhongguo	Chinese
Colombia	Colombie	Colombia	Spanish

English name	French name	Local name	Official language(s)
Comoros	Comores	Comores	French, Comorian
Congo, Democratic Republic of the	Congo, République démocratique du	Congo, République démocratique du	French, Lingala, Monokutuba
Costa Rica	Costa Rica	Costa Rica	Spanish
Côte d'Ivoire	Côte d'Ivoire	Côte d'Ivoire	French
Croatia	Croatie	Hrvatska	Serbo-Croat
Cuba	Cuba	Cuba	Spanish
Cyprus	Chypre	Kipros (Greek), Kibris (Turkish)	Greek, Turkish
Czech Republic	République tchèque	Česká Republika	Czech
Denmark	Danemark	Danmark	Danish
Djibouti	Djibouti	Djibouti	Arabic, French
Dominica	Dominique	Dominica	English, French, Creole
Dominican Republic	République Dominicaine	República dominicana	Spanish
Ecuador	Équateur	Ecuador	Spanish
Egypt	Égypte	Jumhuriyat Misr Al-Arabiya	Arabic
El Salvador	Salvador	El Salvador	Spanish
Equatorial Guinea	Guinée équatoriale	Guinea Ecuatorial	Spanish
Eritrea	Érythrée	Eritrea	Tigrinya, Arabic
Estonia	Estonie	Eesti Vabariik	Estonian
Ethiopia	Éthiopie	Ityopiya	Amharic
Faroe Islands	Îles Féroé	Faroyar/Faeroerne	Faroese, Danish
Fiji	Îles Fidji	Matanitu Ko Viti	English
Finland	Finlande	Suomen Tasavalta	Finnish, Swedish
France	France	République française	French
French Guiana	Guyane	Guyane française	French, French Creole
French Polynesia	Polynésie française	Territoire de la Polynésie française	Polynesian, French
Gabon	Gabon	République gabonaise	French
Gambia, The	Gambie	Gambia	English
Georgia	Géorgie	Sakartvelos Respublika	Georgian, Russian
Germany	Allemagne	Bundesrepublik Deutschland	German
Ghana	Ghana	Ghana	English
Greece	Grèce	Elliniki Dimokratia	Greek
Greenland	Groenland	Grønland (Danish), Kalaallit Nunaat	Danish, Greenlandic
Guatemala	Guatemala	Guatemala	Spanish
Guinea	Guinée	République de Guinée	French
Guinea-Bissau	Guinée-Bissau	Republica da Guiné-Bissau	Portuguese
Guyana	Guyana	Guyana	English
Haiti	Haïti	République d'Haïti	French
Holland ▶ Netherlands, The	Hollande		
Honduras	Honduras	Honduras	Spanish
Hungary	Hongrie	Magyar Koztarsasag	Hungarian
Iceland	Islande	Ísland	Icelandic
India	Inde	Bhārat (Hindi)	Hindi, English
Indonesia	Indonésie	Republik Indonesia	Bahasa Indonesia
Iran	Iran	Jomhoori-e-Islami-e-Iran	Farsi
Iraq	Irak	Jumhouriya al Iraquia	Arabic
Ireland	Irlande	Poblacht na hEireann	Irish, English

English name	French name	Local name	Official language(s)
Israel	Israël	Medinat Israel	Hebrew, Arabic
Italy	Italie	Repubblica Italiana	Italian
Ivory Coast ▶ Côte d Ivoire	Côte d Ivoire		
Jamaica	Jamaïque	Jamaica	English
Japan	Japon	Nihon	Japanese
Jordan	Jordanie	Al'Urdun	Arabic
Kazakhstan	Kazakhstan	Kazak Respublikasy	Kazakh, Russian
Kenya	Kenya	Jamhuri ya Kenya	(Ki)Swahili, English
Korea, North	Corée du Nord	Chosōn Minjujuüi In'min Konghwaguk	Korean
Korea, South	Corée du Sud	Taehan-Min'guk	Korean
Kuwait	Koweït	Dowlat al-Kuwayt	Arabic
Kyrgyzstan	Kirghizistan	Kyrgyz Respublikasy	Kyrgyz
Laos	Laos	Lao	Lao
Latvia	Lettonie	Latvijas Republika	Latvian
Lebanon	Liban	Al-Lubnān	Arabic
Lesotho	Lesotho	Lesotho	English, Sesotho
Liberia	Liberia	Liberia	English
Libya	Libye	Lībyā	Arabic
Liechtenstein	Liechtenstein	Furstentum Liechtenstein	German
Lithuania	Lituanie	Lietuva	Lithuanian
Luxembourg	Luxembourg	Lëtzebuerg (Lëtz.), Luxembourg (French), Luxemburg (German)	French, German, Lëtzebuergesch
Macedonia	Macédoine	Republika Makedonija	Macedonian
Madagascar	Madagascar	Republikan'i Madagasikara	Malagasy, French
Malawi	Malawi	Dziko la Malaŵi	Chichewa, English
Malaysia	Malaisie	Federation of Malaysia	Bahasa Melayu
Maldives	Maldives	Maldives Divehi Jumhuriya	Divehi
Mali	Mali	Mali	French
Malta	Malte	Malta	English, Maltese
Martinique	Martinique	Martinique	French, French Creole
Mauritania	Mauritanie	Mauritanie (French), Mūrītāniyā (Arabic)	Arabic
Mauritius	Île Maurice	Mauritius	English
Mexico	Mexique	México	Spanish
Micronesia	Micronésie	Micronesia	English
Moldova	Moldavie	Republica Moldovenească	Moldavian
Monaco	Monaco	Principauté de Monaco	French
Mongolia	Mongolie	Mongol Ard Uls	Halh Mongol
Morocco	Maroc	Mamlaka al-Maghrebia	Arabic
Mozambique	Mozambique	República de Moçambique	Portuguese
Myanmar	Myanmar	Myanmar	Burmese
Namibia	Namibie	Namibia	English
Nauru	Nauru	Naeoro (Nauruan), Nauru (English)	Nauruan, English
Nepal	Népal	Nepal Adhirajya	Napali
Netherlands, The	Pays-Bas	Koninkrijk der Nederlanden	Dutch
New Zealand	Nouvelle-Zélande	New Zealand	English

English name	French name	Local name	Official language(s)
Nicaragua	Nicaragua	Nicaragua	Spanish
Niger	Niger	Niger	French
Nigeria	Nigéria	Nigeria	English, French
Norway	Norvège	Kongeriket Norge	Norwegian
Oman	Oman	Saltanat 'Uman	Arabic
Pakistan	Pakistan	Pākistān	Urdu, English
Panama	Panamá	Panamá	Spanish
Papua New Guinea	Papouasie-Nouvelle-Guinée	Papua New Guinea	English, Tok Písin, Hiri Motu
Paraguay	Paraguay	Paraguay	Spanish
Peru	Pérou	Perú	Spanish
Philippines	Philippines	Pilipinas	Filipino, English
Poland	Pologne	Rzeczpospolita Polska	Polish
Portugal	Portugal	Portugal	Portuguese
Puerto Rico	Porto Rico	Puerto Rico	Spanish, English
Qatar	Qatar	Dowlat Qatar	Arabic
Romania	Roumanie	Romănia	Romanian
Russia	Russie	Rossiya	Russian
Rwanda	Rwanda	Rwanda	(Kinya) Rwanda, French, English
Samoa	Samoa	Samoa	Samoan, English
San Marino	Saint-Marin	San Marino	Italian
Saudi Arabia	Arabie Saoudite	Al-'Arabīyah as Sa'ūdīyah	Arabic
Senegal	Sénégal	Sénégal	French, Wolof
Seychelles, The	Seychelles	Seychelles	Creole French, English, French
Sierra Leone	Sierra Leone	Sierra Leone	English
Singapore	Singapour	Singapore	Chinese, English, Malay, Tamil
Slovakia	Slovaquie	Slovenska Republika	Slovak
Slovenia	Slovénie	Republika Slovenija	Slovene
Solomon Islands	Îles Salomon	Solomon Islands	English
Somalia	Somalie	Somaliya	Arabic, Somali
South Africa	Afrique du Sud	South Africa	English, Afrikaans
Spain	Espagne	España	Spanish
Sri Lanka	Sri Lanka	Sri Lanka	Sinhala, Tamil
Sudan	Soudan	As-Sūdān	Arabic
Surinam	Surinam(e)	Suriname	Dutch
Swaziland	Swaziland	Umbouso we Swatini	Swazi, English
Sweden	Suède	Konungariket Sverige	Swedish
Switzerland	Suisse	Schweiz (German), Suisse (French), Svizzera (Italian)	French, German, Italian, Romansch
Syria	Syrie	As-Sūrīyah	Arabic
Taiwan	Taïwan	T'aiwan	Chinese
Tajikistan	Tadjikistan	Jumkhurii Tojikistan	Tajik
Tanzania	Tanzanie	Tanzania	(Ki)Swahili, English
Thailand	Thaïlande	Prathet Thai	Thai
Togo	Togo	Togo	French
Tonga	Tonga	Tonga	English, Tongan
Trinidad and Tobago	Trinité-et-Tobago	Trinidad and Tobago	English
Tunisia	Tunisie	Tunisiya	Arabic, French
Turkey	Turquie	Türkiye	Turkish
Turkmenistan	Turkménistan	Turkmenostan	Turkmenian
Uganda	Ouganda	Uganda	English, Kiswahili

English name	French name	Local name	Official language(s)
Ukraine	Ukraine	Ukraina	Ukrainian, Russian
United Arab Emirates	Émirats Arabes Unis	Ittihād al-Imārāt al-'Arabīyah	Arabic, English
United Kingdom	Royaume-Uni	United Kingdom	English
United States of America	États-Unis	United States of America	English
Uruguay	Uruguay	Uruguay	Spanish
Uzbekistan	Ouzbékistan	Uzbekistan	Uzbek
Vanuatu	Vanuatu	Vanuatu	Bislama, English, French
Vatican City	cité du Vatican	Citta' del Vaticano	Italian
Venezuela	Venezuela	Venezuela	Spanish
Vietnam	Vietnam	Viêt-nam	Vietnamese
Yemen	Yémen	Al-Yamaniya	Arabic
Yugoslavia	Yougoslavie	Jugoslavija	Serbo-Croat
Zaire ▶ Congo, Democratic Republic of the	Zaïre		
Zambia	Zambie	Zambia	English
Zimbabwe	Zimbabwe	Zimbabwe	English

États du monde
Nations of the World

On trouvera le nom anglais des pays dans la deuxième colonne. Pour la traduction anglaise des monnaies et des langues officielles, se reporter au tableau correspondant dans le supplément anglais.

Nom français	Nom anglais	Nom local	Langue(s) officielle(s)
Afghanistan	Afghanistan	Afghānestān	dari, pachto
Afrique du Sud	South Africa	South Africa	anglais, afrikaans
Albanie	Albania	Shqïpëri	albanais
Algérie	Algeria	Al-Jazā'ir (arabe), Algérie (français)	arabe
Allemagne	Germany	Bundesrepublik Deutschland	allemand
Andorre	Andorra	Andorra	catalan, français, espagnol
Angola	Angola	Angola	portugais
Arabie Saoudite	Saudi Arabia	Al-'Arabīyah as Sa'ūdīyah	arabe
Argentine	Argentina	Argentina	espagnol
Arménie	Armenia	Hayastani Hanrapetut'yun	arménien
Australie	Australia	Australia	anglais
Autriche	Austria	Österreich	allemand
Azerbaïdjan	Azerbaijan	Azarbaijan	azeri
Bahamas	Bahamas, The	Bahamas	anglais
Bahreïn	Bahrain	Dawlat al-Bahrayn	arabe
Bangladesh	Bangladesh	Gana Prajatantri Bangladesh	bengali
Barbade	Barbados	Barbados	anglais
Belgique	Belgium	Belgique (français), Belgïe (flamand)	flamand, français, allemand
Belize	Belize	Belize	anglais
Bénin	Benin	Bénin	français
Bhoutan	Bhutan	Druk-Yul	tibétain
Biélorussie	Belarus	Belarus	biélorusse
Birmanie ▶ Myanmar	Burma		
Bolivie	Bolivia	Bolivia	espagnol
Bosnie-Herzégovine	Bosnia-Herzegovina	Bosnia-Herzegovina	serbo-croate
Botswana	Botswana	Botswana	anglais
Brésil	Brazil	Brasil	portugais
Brunei	Brunei	Brunei	malais
Bulgarie	Bulgaria	Bǎlgarija	bulgare
Burkina	Burkina Faso	Burkina Faso	français
Burundi	Burundi	Burundi	français, kirundi
Cambodge	Cambodia	Preah Reach Ana Pak Kampuchea	khmer
Cameroun	Cameroon	Cameroon	français, anglais
Canada	Canada	Canada	français, anglais
Cap-Vert	Cape Verde	Cabo Verde	portugais

États du monde

Nom français	Nom anglais	Nom local	Langue(s) officielle(s)
Centrafricaine, République	Central African Republic	République Centrafricaine	français, sango
Chili	Chile	Chile	espagnol
Chine	China	Zhongguo	chinois
Chypre	Cyprus	Kipros (grec), Kibris (turc)	grec, turc
Colombie	Colombia	Colombia	espagnol
	Comores	ComorosComores	français, comorien
Congo, République démocratique du	Congo, Demcratic Republic of	Congo, République démocratique du	français, lingala monokutuba
Corée du Nord	Korea, North	Chosŏn Minjujuüi In'min Konghwaguk	coréen
Corée du Sud	Korea, South	Taehan-Min'guk	coréen
Costa Rica	Costa Rica	Costa Rica	espagnol
Côte d'Ivoire	Côte d'Ivoire (Ivory Coast)	Côte d'Ivoire	français
Croatie	Croatia	Hrvatska	serbo-croate
Cuba	Cuba	Cuba	espagnol
Danemark	Denmark	Danmark	danois
Djibouti	Djibouti	Djibouti	arabe, français
Dominique	Dominica	Dominica	anglais, français, créole
Égypte	Egypt	Jumhuriyat Misr Al-Arabiya	arabe
Émirats Arabes Unis	United Arab Emirates	Ittihād al-Imārāt al-'Arabīyah	arabe, anglais
Équateur	Ecuador	Ecuador	espagnol
Érythrée	Eritrea	Eritrea	tigrinya, arabe
Espagne	Spain	España	espagnol
Estonie	Estonia	Eesti Vabariik	estonien
États-Unis	United States of America	United States of America	anglais
Éthiopie	Ethiopia	Ityopiya	amharique
Îles Féroé	Faroe Islands	Faroyar/Faeroerne	féroïen, danois
Îles Fidji	Fiji	Matanitu Ko Viti	anglais
Finlande	Finland	Suomen Tasavalta	finnois, suédois
France	France	République française	français
Gabon	Gabon	République gabonaise	français
Gambie	Gambia, The	Gambia	anglais
Géorgie	Georgia	Sakartvelos Respublika	géorgien, russe
Ghana	Ghana	Ghana	anglais
Grèce	Greece	Elliniki Dimokratia	grec
Groenland	Greenland	Grønland (danois), Kalaallit Nunaat	danois, groenlandais
Guatemala	Guatemala	Guatemala	espagnol
Guinée	Guinea	République de Guinée	français
Guinée-Bissau	Guinea-Bissau	Republica da Guiné-Bissau	portugais
Guinée équatoriale	Equatorial Guinea	Guinea Ecuatorial	espagnol
Guyana	Guyana	Guyana	anglais
Guyane	French Guiana	Guyane française	français, creole
Haïti	Haiti	République d'Haïti	français
Hollande ▶ Pays-Bas	Holland		
Honduras	Honduras	Honduras	espagnol
Hongrie	Hungary	Magyar Koztarsasag	hongrois
Inde	India	Bhārat (hindi)	hindi, anglais
Indonésie	Indonesia	Republik Indonesia	indonésien

[92]

Nom français	Nom anglais	Nom local	Langue(s) officielle(s)
Irak	Iraq	Jumhouriya al Iraquia	arabe
Iran	Iran	Jomhoori-e-Islami-e-Iran	persan
Irlande	Ireland	Poblacht na hEireann	irlandais, anglais
Islande	Iceland	Ísland	islandais
Israël	Israel	Medinat Israel	hébreu, arabe
Italie	Italy	Repubblica italiana	italien
Jamaïque	Jamaica	Jamaica	anglais
Japon	Japan	Nihon	japonais
Jordanie	Jordan	Al'Urdun	arabe
Kazakhstan	Kazakhstan	Kazak Respublikasy	kazakh, russe
Kenya	Kenya	Jamhuri ya Kenya	swahili, anglais
Kirghizistan	Kyrgyzstan	Kyrgyz Respublikasy	kirghiz
Koweït	Kuwait	Dowlat al-Kuwayt	arabe
Laos	Laos	Lao	laotien
Lesotho	Lesotho	Lesotho	anglais, sotho
Lettonie	Latvia	Latvijas Republika	letton
Liban	Lebanon	Al-Lubnān	arabe
Liberia	Liberia	Liberia	anglais
Libye	Libya	Lībyā	arabe
Liechtenstein	Liechtenstein	Furstentum Liechtenstein	allemand
Lituanie	Lithuania	Lietuva	lithuanien
Luxembourg	Luxembourg	Lëtzebuerg (Lëtz.), Luxembourg (français), Luxemburg (allemand)	français, allemand, lëtzebuergesch
Macédoine	Macedonia	Republika Makedonija	macédonien
Madagascar	Madagascar	Republikan'i Madagasikara	malgache, français
Malaisie	Malaysia	Federation of Malaysia	malais
Malawi	Malawi	Dziko la Malawi	chichewa, anglais
Maldives	Maldives	Maldives Divehi Jumhuriya	divehi
Mali	Mali	Mali	français
Malte	Malta	Malta	anglais, maltais
Maroc	Morocco	Mamlaka al-Maghrebia	arabe
Martinique	Martinique	Martinique	français, creole
Île Maurice	Mauritius	Mauritius	anglais
Mauritanie	Mauritania	Mauritanie (français), Mūrītāniyā (arabe)	arabe
Mexique	Mexico	México	espagnol
Micronésie	Micronesia	Micronesia	anglais
Moldavie	Moldova	Republica Moldovenească	roumain
Monaco	Monaco	Principauté de Monaco	français
Mongolie	Mongolia	Mongol Ard Uls	khalkha
Mozambique	Mozambique	República de Moçambique	portugais
Myanmar	Myanmar	Myanmar	birman
Namibie	Namibia	Namibia	anglais
Nauru	Nauru	Naeoro (nauruan), Nauru (anglais)	nauruan, anglais
Népal	Nepal	Nepal Adhirajya	népalais
Nicaragua	Nicaragua	Nicaragua	espagnol
Niger	Niger	Niger	français
Nigéria	Nigeria	Nigeria	anglais, français

États du monde

Nom français	Nom anglais	Nom local	Langue(s) officielle(s)
Norvège	Norway	Kongeriket Norge	norvégien
Nouvelle-Zélande	New Zealand	New Zealand	anglais
Oman	Oman	Saltanat 'Uman	arabe
Ouganda	Uganda	Uganda	anglais, swahili
Ouzbékistan	Uzbekistan	Uzbekistan	ouzbek
Pakistan	Pakistan	Pākistān	urdu, anglais
Panamá	Panama	Panamá	espagnol
Papouasie-Nouvelle-Guinée	Papua New Guinea	Papua New Guinea	anglais, neo-melanaisien
Paraguay	Paraguay	Paraguay	espagnol
Pays-Bas	Netherlands, The	Koninkrijk der Nederlanden	néerlandais
Pérou	Peru	Perú	espagnol
Philippines	Philippines	Pilipinas	tagalog, anglais
Pologne	Poland	Rzeczpospolita Polska	polonais
Polynésie française	French Polynesia	Territoire de la Polynésie française	polynésien, français
Porto Rico	Puerto Rico	Puerto Rico	espagnol, anglais
Portugal	Portugal	Portugal	portugais
Qatar	Qatar	Dowlat Qatar	arabe
République Dominicaine	Dominican Republic	República dominicana	espagnol
République tchèque	Czech Republic	Česká Republika	tchèque
Roumanie	Romania	Romănia	roumain
Royaume-Uni	United Kingdom	United Kingdom	anglais
Russie	Russia	Rossiya	russe
Rwanda	Rwanda	Rwanda	kinyarwanda, français, anglais
Saint-Marin	San Marino	San Marino	italien
Îles Salomon	Solomon Islands	Solomon Islands	anglais
Salvador	El Salvador	El Salvador	espagnol
Samoa	Samoa	Samoa	samoan, anglais
Sénégal	Senegal	Sénégal	français, ouolof
Seychelles	Seychelles, The	Seychelles	français, anglais créole
Sierra Leone	Sierra Leone	Sierra Leone	anglais
Singapour	Singapore	Singapore	chinois, anglais, malais, tamoul
Slovaquie	Slovakia	Slovenska Republika	slovaque
Slovénie	Slovenia	Republika Slovenija	slovène
Somalie	Somalia	Somaliya	arabe, somali
Soudan	Sudan	As-Sūdān	arabe
Sri Lanka	Sri Lanka	Sri Lanka	cinghalais, tamoul
Suède	Sweden	Konungariket Sverige	suédois
Suisse	Switzerland	Schweiz (allemand), Suisse (français), Svizzera (italien)	français, allemand, italien, romanche
Surinam(e)	Surinam	Suriname	néerlandais
Swaziland	Swaziland	Umbouso we Swatini	swazi, anglais
Syrie	Syria	As-Sūrīyah	arabe
Tadjikistan	Tajikistan	Jumkhurii Tojikistan	tadjik
Taïwan	Taiwan	T'aiwan	chinois
Tanzanie	Tanzania	Tanzania	swahili, anglais
Tchad	Chad	Tchad	français, arabe
Thaïlande	Thailand	Prathet Thai	thaï
Togo	Togo	Togo	français
Tonga	Tonga	Tonga	anglais, tongan
Trinité-et-Tobago	Trinidad and Tobago	Trinidad and Tobago	anglais

Nom français	Nom anglais	Nom local	Langue(s) officielle(s)
Tunisie	Tunisia	Tunisiya	arabe, français
Turkménistan	Turkmenistan	Turkmenostan	turkmène
Turquie	Turkey	Türkiye	turc
Ukraine	Ukraine	Ukraina	ukrainien, russe
Uruguay	Uruguay	Uruguay	espagnol
Vanuatu	Vanuatu	Vanuatu	bichlamar, anglais, français
Vatican, cité du	Vatican City	Citta' del Vaticano	italien
Venezuela	Venezuela	Venezuela	espagnol
Vietnam	Vietnam	Viêt-nam	vietnamien
Yémen	Yemen	Al-Yamaniya	arabe
Yougoslavie	Yugoslavia	Jugoslavija	serbo-croat (serbe)
Zaïre	Zaire		
▶ Congo, République démocratique du			
Zambie	Zambia	Zambia	anglais
Zimbabwe	Zimbabwe	Zimbabwe	anglais

Français-Anglais
French-English

A¹, a¹ [ɑ] *nm inv* A, a; **connaître un sujet de A à Z** to know a subject inside out; **prouver qch par A plus B** to prove sth conclusively

A² [ɑ] *nf (abrév* **autoroute**) A1 *Br* ≃ M1, *Am* ≃ I1

a² *voir* **avoir¹**

à [a] *prép*

> **à + le** contracts to form **au** [o], **à + les** contracts to form **aux** [o].

(**a**) *(indique la direction)* to; **aller/venir à Paris** to go/come to Paris; **aller à la pêche** to go fishing; **partir au Venezuela** to leave for Venezuela; **rentrer à la maison** to go/come home; **au lit!** off to bed!

(**b**) *(indique la position)* at; **être à la maison/à la campagne/à Marseille** to be at home/in the country-side/in Marseilles; **j'habite au 3, place des Cardeurs** I live at number 3, place des Cardeurs; **à la page 2** on page 2; **à 2 kilomètres/dix minutes d'ici** 2 kilometres/ten minutes from here; **à la télévision** on (the) television; **un livre à la main** with a book in his/her hand

(**c**) *(dans l'expression du temps)* **à huit heures** at eight (o'clock); **au vingtième siècle** in the twentieth century; **à la tombée de la nuit** at nightfall; **au printemps** in the spring; **à mon arrivée** when I arrive/arrived; **le 2 au soir** on the evening of the 2nd; **à lundi!/ce soir!** see you Monday!/tonight!

(**d**) *(avec de)* to; **de Paris à Lyon** from Paris to Lyons; **du lundi au vendredi** from Monday to Friday, *Am* Monday to *or* thru Friday; **de 2 à 4** *(heure)* from 2 till *or* to 4; **de 10 à 15%** *(environ)* between 10 and 15%

(**e**) *(introduit le complément d'objet indirect)* to; **donner/prêter qch à qn** to give/lend sth to sb, to give/lend sb sth; **penser à qn/qch** to think of *or* about sb/sth

(**f**) *(indique l'appartenance)* **c'est à lui/à Paul** it's his/Paul's; *Fam* **un ami à moi** a friend of mine; **c'est à vous de...** *(il vous incombe de)* it's up to you to...; *(c'est votre tour de)* it's your turn to...; **à toi!** your turn!

(**g**) *(indique le moyen, la manière)* **à bicyclette** by bicycle; **à pied/cheval** on foot/horseback; **au crayon** in pencil; **à la française** in the French style; **fonctionner à l'électricité** to run on electricity; **jouer un air au violon** to play a tune on the violin

(**h**) *(distributif)* **faire qch à deux/trois** to do sth in twos/threes; **se mettre à plusieurs pour faire qch** to team up to do sth; **100 km à l'heure** 100 km an *or* per hour; **être payé à l'heure** to be paid by the hour

(**i**) *(indique la caractéristique)* **l'homme à la barbe/aux lunettes noires** the man with a beard/with the dark glasses; **un timbre à 50 cents** a 50-cent stamp

(**j**) *(indique le but)* **maison à vendre** house for sale; **à louer** *(sur panneau) Br* to let, *Am* to rent; **j'ai une lettre à écrire/des courses à faire** I've got a letter to write/some errands to run

(**k**) *(indique la conséquence)* **c'était à mourir de rire** it was hilarious; **laid à faire peur** hideously ugly; **c'est à se demander si...** you begin to wonder if...

abaisser [abese] *vt* (**a**) *(levier, manette, pont-levis)* to lower; *(store)* to pull down (**b**) *(prix, coût, pression)* to reduce (**c**) *Litt (humilier)* to humble, to abase (**d**) *Culin (pâte)* to roll out
2 s'abaisser *vpr* (**a**) *(descendre)* to slope down (**b**) **s'a. à faire qch** to lower oneself to do sth

abandon [abɑ̃dɔ̃] *nm* (**a**) *(d'un enfant, d'un projet)* abandonment; **exiger l'a. des hostilités** to call for an end to hostilities; *Jur* **a. du domicile conjugal** desertion; *Mil* **a. de poste** desertion of one's post (**b**) *(en sport)* **gagner par a.** to win by default; **être contraint à l'a.** to be forced to withdraw (**c**) *(d'un lieu)* neglect; **être à l'a.** to be neglected; **laisser qch à l'a.** to neglect sth (**d**) *(nonchalance)* abandon (**e**) *Ordinat* abort

abandonner [abɑ̃dɔne] **1** *vt* (**a**) *(personne, village)* to desert, to abandon; *(voiture)* to abandon; **a. le navire** to abandon ship; **a. le domicile conjugal** to desert the marital home; **mes forces m'abandonnent** my strength is failing me (**b**) *(privilège, pouvoir, combat)* to give up; *(projet)* to abandon; *(course)* to withdraw from; **a. ses études** to drop out (of school/university); **a. ses études de médecine** to give up medicine; *aussi Fig* **a. la partie** to throw in one's hand; **j'abandonne** I give up (**c**) *(céder)* to give (**à** to) (**d**) *Ordinat* to abort
2 s'abandonner *vpr (se laisser aller)* to let oneself go; **s'a. au sommeil** to drift off to sleep

abasourdi, -e [abazurdi] *adj* stunned

abat-jour [abaʒur] *nm inv* lampshade

abats [aba] *nmpl Br* offal, *Am* variety meat; *(de volaille)* giblets

abattage [abataʒ] *nm* (**a**) *(d'animal)* slaughter, slaughtering (**b**) **avoir de l'a.** *(acteur, politicien)* to be full of go

abattant [abatɑ̃] *nm (d'une table)* flap; *(des toilettes)* lid

abattement [abatmɑ̃] *nm* (**a**) *(physique)* exhaustion (**b**) *(moral)* dejection, depression (**c**) *Fin* **a. (fiscal)** tax allowance

abattis [abati] *nmpl* (**a**) *(de volaille)* giblets (**b**) *Fam* **numéroter ses a.** to start saying one's prayers

abattoir [abatwar] *nm* slaughterhouse, abattoir; *Fig* **envoyer qn à l'a.** to send sb to the slaughter

abattre [11] [abatr] **1** vt (**a**) (faire tomber) (mur, cloison) to knock down, to pull down; (arbre) to fell, to cut down; (avion) to bring down; (sujet: vent) (arbre) to blow down; Fam Fig **a. de la besogne** to get through a lot of work (**b**) (tuer) (personne) to kill; (animal de boucherie) to slaughter; (animal malade ou dangereux) to destroy; Fig **c'est l'homme à a.** he needs to be removed (**c**) Fig (fatiguer) (sujet: maladie) to lay low; **la chaleur nous a complètement abattus** the heat completely knocked us out (**d**) Fig (démoraliser) to dishearten, to depress; **ne vous laissez pas a.!** keep your chin up! (**e**) aussi Fig **a. ses cartes** ou **son jeu** to lay one's cards on the table
2 s'abattre vpr (arbre, mur) to crash down (**sur** on); (pluie) to pour down (**sur** on); (oiseau) to swoop down (**sur** on)
abattu, -e [abaty] adj dejected, depressed
abbaye [abei] nf abbey
abbé [abe] nm (**a**) (d'une abbaye) abbot (**b**) (prêtre) priest; **j'en parlerai à Monsieur l'a.** I'll mention it to the priest; **l'a. Martin** Father Martin
abc [abese] nm inv (rudiments) basics
abcès [apsɛ] nm abscess; Fig **crever** ou **vider l'a.** to resolve the situation
abdiquer [abdike] vt (trône) to abdicate; (droits) to renounce, to surrender; **être contraint d'a.** to be forced to abdicate
abdomen [abdɔmɛn] nm abdomen
abdominal, -e, -aux, -ales [abdɔminal, -o] **1** adj abdominal
   2 nmpl **abdominaux** (muscles) stomach muscles; **faire des abdominaux** to do stomach or abdominal exercises
abdos [abdo] nmpl Fam (muscles) stomach muscles, abs; **faire des a.** to do abs or sit-ups
abécédaire [abesedɛr] nm ABC, alphabet book
abeille [abɛj] nf bee
aberrant, -e [abɛrã, -ãt] adj (**a**) (insensé) absurd (**b**) Biol aberrant
aberration [abɛrasjɔ̃] nf aberration; **c'est une a.!** it's absurd!
abêtir [abɛtir] **1** vt **a. qn** to dull sb's mind
   2 s'abêtir vpr to become stupid
abêtissant, -e [abetisã, -ãt] adj mind-numbing
abhorrer [abɔre] vt Litt to abhor
Abidjan [abidʒã] n Abidjan
abîme [abim] nm (de l'océan) abyss, depths; Fig (entre deux personnes) gulf; Fig **être au bord de l'a.** to be on the brink of disaster
abîmer [abime] **1** vt (objet) to spoil, to damage; (vêtement, chaussures) to ruin
   2 s'abîmer vpr (**a**) (fruit) to go bad; (objet) to get damaged; (vêtement, chaussures) to get ruined (**b**) **s'a. les yeux** to ruin one's eyesight (**c**) Litt **s'a. en mer** to be engulfed by the sea
abject, -e [abʒɛkt] adj Péj contemptible, despicable
abjurer [abʒyre] vt (religion) to abjure
ablation [ablasjɔ̃] nf removal
ablette [ablɛt] nf bleak (fish)
ablutions [ablysjɔ̃] nfpl Litt ou Hum **faire ses a.** to perform one's ablutions
abnégation [abnegasjɔ̃] nf abnegation, self-sacrifice
aboiement [abwamã] nm bark; **des aboiements** barking
abois [abwa] nmpl **être aux a.** (cerf) to be at bay; Fig **il est aux a.** (personne) the net's closing in on him
abolir [abɔlir] vt to abolish

abolition [abɔlisjɔ̃] nf abolition
abominable [abɔminabl] adj (temps) appalling, abominable; (crime) heinous; (odeur) foul; **l'a. homme des neiges** the abominable snowman
abominablement [abɔminabləmã] adv abominably; (laid) hideously
abomination [abɔminasjɔ̃] nf abomination; Litt **avoir qn/qch en a.** to loathe sb/sth
abondamment [abɔ̃damã] adv (parler, critiquer) at length; (pleuvoir) heavily; (manger, illustrer) copiously; **se servir a.** to help oneself to a large portion of food
abondance [abɔ̃dɑ̃s] nf abundance; (d'informations, de détails) wealth; **il y avait des fruits en a.** there was plenty of fruit; **vivre dans l'a.** to live a life of ease
abondant, -e [abɔ̃dɑ̃, -ãt] adj abundant, plentiful; (repas) hearty; (pluie) heavy; (saignement) profuse; **une chevelure abondante** a thick head of hair; **peu a.** (récolte, chevelure) poor; (pluie) light; (repas) frugal
abonder [abɔ̃de] vi (**a**) (foisonner) to be plentiful; **a. en qch** to abound in sth (**b**) **a. dans le sens de qn** to agree entirely with sb
abonné, -e [abɔne] **1** nm,f (d'une revue) subscriber; (du gaz, de l'électricité) consumer; (de la SNCF, d'un théâtre) season-ticket holder; Tél **il n'y a pas d'a. au numéro que vous avez demandé** ≃ the number you have dialled has not been recognized
   2 adj **être a. à qch** (revue) to have a subscription to sth; (SNCF, théâtre) to have a season ticket for sth; Fam (être sujet à) to be prone to sth
abonnement [abɔnmã] nm (à une revue) subscription (à to); (de train, de théâtre) season ticket; (au téléphone) line rental; **prendre un a.** (à une revue) to take out a subscription; (pour le train, pour le théâtre) to buy a season ticket
abonner [abɔne] **1** vt **a. qn à une revue** to take out a subscription to a magazine for sb
   2 s'abonner vpr (à une revue) to take out a subscription (à to); (au théâtre) to buy a season ticket (à for)
abord [abɔr] nm (**a**) (d'un lieu) **l'île est d'un a. difficile** the island is not easily accessible (**b**) **abords** (d'un bâtiment) surroundings; (d'une ville) outskirts (**c**) (d'une personne) **être d'un a. facile/difficile** to be approachable/unapproachable; **au premier a., de prime a.** at first sight (**d**) **d'a., tout d'a.** (pour commencer) at first, to begin with; (premièrement) first (and foremost), in the first place; Fam **toi, d'a., je ne te parle plus!** I'm not talking to you, so there!
abordable [abɔrdabl] adj (**a**) (lieu) accessible (**b**) (prix) affordable (**c**) (personne) approachable
abordage [abɔrdaʒ] nm (pour attaquer) boarding; (pour s'amarrer) coming alongside; **monter à l'a.** to board a ship
aborder [abɔrde] **1** vt (**a**) (personne) to approach; **se faire a.** to be approached (**b**) (question) to deal with; (virage) to approach (**c**) (navire) (attaquer) to board; (se mettre le long de) to come alongside
   2 vi to land
aborigène [abɔriʒɛn] **1** nmf (d'un pays) native; **les aborigènes d'Australie** the (Australian) Aborigines
   2 adj (indigène) native, indigenous (de to); (des peuplades australiennes) Aboriginal
abortif, -ive [abɔrtif, -iv] adj voir **pilule**

abouler [abule] *Fam* **1** *vt* to hand over **2** s'**abouler** *upr* to turn up, to show up; **alors, tu t'aboules?** well, are you coming or not?

aboutir [abutir] *vi* (**a**) *(réussir)* to be successful; **ne pas a.** to fall through (**b**) *(dans l'espace)* **a. à/dans** *(sujet: personne)* to end up at/in; **a. à** *(sujet: chemin, escalier)* to lead to; *Fig (sujet: efforts, recherches)* to result in; **n'a. à rien** *(personne)* to get nowhere; *(efforts, recherches)* to come to nothing

aboutissants [abutisɑ̃] *nmpl voir* **tenant**

aboutissement [abutismɑ̃] *nm* result, outcome

aboyer [32] [abwaje] *vi* to bark

abracadabrant, -e [abrakadabrɑ̃, -ɑ̃t] *adj Fam* bewildering

abrasif, -ive [abrazif, -iv] *adj & nm* abrasive

abrégé [abreʒe] *nm* (**a**) *(livre)* **un a. d'histoire de France** a short history of France; **un a. de philosophie** a short guide to philosophy (**b**) **écrire en a.** to write in abbreviated form

abréger [59] [abreʒe] *vt (article, exposé)* to shorten, to cut down; *(visite)* to cut short; *(mot)* to abbreviate; *Fam* **allez, abrège!** come on, cut to the chase!

abreuver [abrœve] **1** *vt (chevaux, bétail)* to water; *Fig* **a. qn d'injures** to shower sb with insults **2** s'**abreuver** *upr (cheval, bétail)* to drink

abreuvoir [abrœvwar] *nm (dans une rivière)* watering place; *(baquet)* drinking trough

abréviation [abrevjasjɔ̃] *nf* abbreviation

abri [abri] *nm* shelter; **mettre qn/qch à l'a.** to shelter sb/sth; **se mettre à l'a.** to (take) shelter; **être à l'a. (de qch)** to be sheltered (from sth); **être à l'a. du besoin** to have no financial worries; **personne n'est à l'a. d'une erreur** anybody can make a mistake; **a. antiatomique** fallout shelter; **a. à vélos** bike shed

abribus® [abribys] *nm* bus shelter

abricot [abriko] *nm* apricot **2** *adj inv* apricot-coloured

abricotier [abrikɔtje] *nm* apricot tree

abrier [66] [abrije] *Can* **1** *vt* to wrap up (well) **2** s'**abrier** *upr* to wrap oneself up (well)

abriter [abrite] **1** *vt* (**a**) *(protéger)* to shelter (**de** from) (**b**) *(loger) (personnes)* to house, to accommodate; *(société, machine)* to house **2** s'**abriter** *upr* s'**a. (de la pluie)** to (take) shelter (from the rain); s'**a. (du soleil)** to shade oneself (from the sun)

abrogation [abrɔgasjɔ̃] *nf (d'une loi)* repeal

abroger [45] [abrɔʒe] *vt (loi)* to repeal

abrupt, -e [abrypt] *adj (rocher, pente)* steep; *Fig (manière)* abrupt, blunt; **d'un ton a.** abruptly

abruti, -e [abryti] **1** *nm,f Fam* idiot, fool **2** *adj* (**a**) *(hébété)* stupefied, dazed; **a. par l'alcool** stupefied with drink (**b**) *Fam (bête)* stupid, idiotic

abrutir [abrytir] **1** *vt* (**a**) *(hébéter)* to daze; **a. qn de travail** to work sb to the point of exhaustion (**b**) *(abêtir)* to stultify **2** s'**abrutir** *upr* s'**a. de travail** to work oneself to the point of exhaustion; **on s'abrutit à trop regarder la télévision** too much television numbs the brain

abrutissant, -e [abrytisɑ̃, -ɑ̃t] *adj (travail)* stultifying, mind-numbing; *(bruit)* wearing

ABS [abeɛs] *nm Aut* **(système) A. ABS**

abscisse [apsis] *nf Math* x-axis

abscons, -e [apskɔ̃, -ɔ̃s] *adj Litt* abstruse

absence [apsɑ̃s] *nf* (**a**) *(d'une personne)* absence; **en ou pendant mon a.** in or during my absence, while I am/was away (**b**) *(manque)* lack (**c**) **avoir des ab-** sences to be prone to absent-mindedness; **dans un moment d'a.** in a moment of absent-mindedness

absent, -e [apsɑ̃, -ɑ̃t] **1** *adj* (**a**) *(qui n'est pas présent)* absent (**de** from) (**b**) *(inexistant)* missing (**c**) *(distrait)* **avoir un air a.** to be miles away **2** *nm,f* absentee; **les absents ont toujours tort** it's always those who aren't there who get the blame

absentéisme [apsɑ̃teism] *nm* absenteeism

absenter [apsɑ̃te] s'**absenter** *upr (sortir)* to go away (**de** from); **elle a dû s'a. quelques minutes** she had to go out for a few minutes

absinthe [apsɛ̃t] *nf* absinthe

absolu, -e [apsɔly] **1** *nm* **l'a.** the absolute; **dans l'a.,...** in principle,... **2** *adj* absolute; *(règle)* hard-and-fast; **être dans l'impossibilité absolue de faire qch** to be quite unable to do sth

absolument [apsɔlymɑ̃] *adv* (**a**) *(complètement)* absolutely; **a. pas!** absolutely not! (**b**) *(sans faute)* **vous devez a. y aller!** you really MUST go!

absolution [apsɔlysjɔ̃] *nf Rel* absolution

absolvais *etc voir* **absoudre**

absorbant, -e [apsɔrbɑ̃, -ɑ̃t] *adj (matériau)* absorbent (**b**) *(livre, tâche)* absorbing

absorber [apsɔrbe] *vt* (**a**) *(liquide)* to absorb, to soak up (**b**) *(nourriture)* to eat; *(boisson)* to drink; *(médicament)* to take (**c**) *(entreprise)* to take over (**d**) *(sujet: lecture)* to absorb, to engross; **son travail l'absorbe** he/she is absorbed *or* engrossed in his/her work; **être absorbé dans ses pensées** to be lost in thought

absorption [apsɔrpsjɔ̃] *nf* (**a**) *(de liquide)* absorption (**b**) *(de nourriture)* eating; *(d'une boisson)* drinking; *(d'un médicament)* taking (**c**) *(d'une entreprise)* takeover

absoudre [3a] [apsudr] *vt Litt ou Rel* **a. qn de qch** to forgive sb sth

abstenir [70] [apstənir] s'**abstenir** *upr (ne pas voter)* to abstain (from voting); s'**a. de faire qch** to refrain from doing sth; **dans le doute, abstiens-toi** when in doubt, don't; **pas sérieux s'a.** *(dans une petite annonce)* no timewasters

abstention [apstɑ̃sjɔ̃] *nf* abstention

abstentionniste [apstɑ̃sjɔnist] *nmf* abstainer

abstinence [apstinɑ̃s] *nf* abstinence

abstraction [apstraksjɔ̃] *nf* (**a**) **faire a. de qch** to disregard sth; **a. faite de cette dépense** leaving aside this expense (**b**) *(idée abstraite)* abstract idea, abstraction

abstrait, -e [apstrɛ, -ɛt] **1** *adj* abstract **2** *nm* **dans l'a.** in the abstract

absurde [apsyrd] **1** *adj* absurd **2** *nm* **l'a.** *(d'une situation, d'une remarque)* absurdity; **démonstration par l'a.** reductio ad absurdum

absurdité [apsyrdite] *nf* (**a**) *(caractère absurde)* absurdity (**b**) *(chose absurde)* absurdity, piece of nonsense; **dire des absurdités** to talk nonsense

abus [aby] *nm* (**a**) *(excès)* overindulgence (**de** in); **l'a. d'alcool** alcohol abuse; **l'a. de médicaments est dangereux** taking too much medication is dangerous (**b**) *(pratique)* abuse; *Fam* **il y a de l'a.!** that's going too far! (**c**) *Jur* **a. de biens sociaux** misappropriation of funds; **a. de confiance** breach of trust; **a. de pouvoir** abuse of power

abuser [abyze] **1** *vt Litt* to deceive **2** **abuser de** *vt ind (exploiter, violer)* to take advantage of; **a. du tabac** to smoke too much; **a. de ses forces** to overexert oneself; **il ne faut pas a. des**

bonnes choses good things should be enjoyed in moderation; **je ne voudrais pas a.** I don't want to cause you any inconvenience; **alors là, vous abusez!** this is a bit much!

3 s'abuser *vpr* **si je ne m'abuse** if I'm not mistaken
abusif, -ive [abyzif, -iv] *adj* (**a**) *(emploi d'un mot)* incorrect (**b**) *(excessif)* excessive; *(mère)* possessive
abysse [abis] *nm* abyssal zone
acabit [akabi] *nm Péj* **du même a.** of that type
acacia [akasja] *nm* acacia
académicien, -enne [akademisjɛ̃, -ɛn] *nm,f* = member of the "Académie française"
académie [akademi] *nf* (**a**) *(des lettres, des sciences, d'art)* academy; **l'A. française** = learned society responsible for promoting the French language and imposing standards (**b**) *(école)* school, academy; **a. de musique/dessin** music/art school (**c**) *(dans l'Éducation nationale) Br* ≃ local education authority, *Am* ≃ school district

Académie française

This was originally a group of men of letters who were encouraged by Cardinal Richelieu in 1635 to become an official body. Consisting of forty distinguished writers ("les Quarante" or "les Immortels"), the Académie's chief task was, and is, to produce a definitive dictionary and to be the ultimate authority in matters concerning the French language.

académique [akademik] *adj* (**a**) *Scol* = relating to a local education authority (**b**) *Péj (style)* conventional (**c**) *Belg, Suisse & Can* **l'année a.** the academic year
acajou [akaʒu] **1** *nm* mahogany
2 *adj inv* reddish-brown
a cap(p)ella [akapela] *adv* a cappella
acariâtre [akarjɑtr] *adj* cantankerous
acarien [akarjɛ̃] *nm* dust mite
accablant, -e [akablɑ̃, -ɑ̃t] *adj* (**a**) *(responsabilités)* overwhelming; *(chaleur)* oppressive (**b**) *(témoignage)* damning
accablement [akabləmɑ̃] *nm* dejection, depression
accabler [akable] *vt* (**a**) *(sujet: chaleur, malheur)* to overwhelm; **a. qn de travail** to overload sb with work; **a. qn de reproches** to heap criticism on sb (**b**) *(sujet: témoignage)* to damn
accalmie [akalmi] *nf* lull
accaparer [akapare] *vt (personne, conversation)* to monopolize; *(places, morceaux de choix)* to grab
accédant, -e [aksedɑ̃, -ɑ̃t] *nm,f* **a. à la propriété** new home-owner, first-time buyer
accéder [34] [aksede] **accéder à** *vt ind* (**a**) *(atteindre)* to reach, to get to (**b**) *Fig (responsabilités, rang)* to gain; **a. à la propriété** to become a home-owner; **a. au trône** to accede to the throne (**c**) *(requête)* to comply with (**d**) *Ordinat (programme)* to access
accélérateur [akseleratœr] *nm (de voiture, d'ordinateur)* accelerator; **appuyer sur l'a.** *Br* to step on the accelerator, *Am* to step on the gas; *Ordinat* **a. graphique** graphic(s) accelerator; *Phys* **a. de particules** particle accelerator
accélération [akselerasjɔ̃] *nf* acceleration
accéléré, -e [akselere] **1** *nm Cin* **en a.** speeded-up
2 *adj* quick, fast; *(mouvement)* accelerated; **cours a.** crash course

accélérer [34] [akselere] **1** *vt* to speed up; *Fig* **a. le mouvement** to get a move on
2 *vi (en voiture)* to accelerate
3 s'accélérer *vpr* to accelerate, to speed up
accent [aksɑ̃] *nm* (**a**) *(sur une lettre)* accent; **a. aigu/grave/circonflexe** acute/grave/circumflex (accent); **e a. circonflexe** e circumflex (**b**) *(en phonétique)* stress; **a. tonique** *(primary)* stress (**c**) *(prononciation)* accent; **elle parle anglais sans a.** she speaks English without an accent (**d**) *Fig (inflexion)* **avoir des accents de vérité** to have a ring of truth; **mettre l'a. sur qch** to stress or emphasize sth
accentuation [aksɑ̃tɥasjɔ̃] *nf* (**a**) *(en phonétique)* stress (**b**) *(à l'écrit)* accentuation (**c**) *(d'un phénomène)* intensification
accentué, -e [aksɑ̃tɥe] *adj* (**a**) *(syllabe)* stressed (**b**) *(lettre)* accented (**c**) *Fig (net)* pronounced, marked
accentuer [aksɑ̃tɥe] **1** *vt* (**a**) *(syllabe)* to stress (**b**) *(lettre)* to put an accent on (**c**) *Fig (renforcer)* to emphasize; *(avance)* to increase
2 s'accentuer *vpr* to become more pronounced or marked
acceptable [akseptabl] *adj* (**a**) *(recevable)* acceptable (**b**) *(passable)* satisfactory
acceptation [akseptasjɔ̃] *nf* acceptance
accepter [aksepte] *vt* to accept; **a. de faire qch** to agree to do sth; **il est hors de question que j'accepte** I can't possibly accept; **allez, accepte!** go on, say yes!
acception [aksepsjɔ̃] *nf Sout* (**a**) *(d'un mot)* meaning, sense (**b**) **sans a. de race/de sexe** irrespective of race/sex
accès [aksɛ] *nm* (**a**) *(approche)* access, approach (à to); **être facile/difficile d'a.** to be easy/hard to reach; **avoir a. à qch** to have access to sth; **donner a. à qch** *(sujet: porte, chemin)* to lead to sth; *(sujet: ticket)* to allow entry to sth; **a. aux quais** *(sur panneau)* to the trains (**b**) *(d'une personne)* **être d'un a. facile/difficile** to be approachable/unapproachable (**c**) *(poussée)* fit, attack; **a. de colère** fit of anger; **a. de fièvre** bout of fever; **a. de toux** coughing fit (**d**) *Ordinat* access; *(sur Internet)* hit; **avoir a. à** to have access to , to be able to access
accessible [aksesibl] *adj* (**a**) *(lieu, livre)* accessible; *(prix)* affordable (**b**) *(personne)* approachable
accession [aksesjɔ̃] *nf* **a. au pouvoir/au trône** accession (to power)/to the throne; **l'a. à la propriété** home ownership
accessoire [akseswar] **1** *nm (d'appareil ménager, de mode)* accessory; *Can* **a. électrique** domestic appliance; *Théât* **accessoires** props
2 *adj* minor; **c'est a.** it's a minor detail
accessoirement [akseswarmɑ̃] *adv* if necessary, if need be; *(en plus)* also
accessoiriste [akseswarist] *nmf Théât* prop man, f prop woman
accident [aksidɑ̃] *nm* (**a**) *(collision, malheur)* accident; **a. d'avion** plane or air crash; **a. de chemin de fer** train crash; **a. de la circulation** traffic accident; **a. de la route** road accident; **a. du travail** industrial accident; **a. de voiture** car accident or crash (**b**) *(événement inattendu)* mishap; **par a.** by accident, by chance; **a. de parcours** hitch (**c**) **a. de terrain** *(bosse)* bump; *(trou)* hole
accidenté, -e [aksidɑ̃te] **1** *nm,f* accident victim; **accidentés de la route** road accident victims
2 *adj* (**a**) *(terrain)* uneven (**b**) *(voiture)* damaged

accidentel, -elle [aksidɑ̃tɛl] *adj* accidental
accidentellement [aksidɑ̃tɛlmɑ̃] *adv (par hasard)* accidentally, by chance; *(mourir)* in an accident
acclamation [aklamasjɔ̃] *nf* cheer; **sous les acclamations de la foule** to the cheers of the crowd
acclamer [aklame] *vt* to cheer
acclimatation [aklimatasjɔ̃] *nf* acclimatization, *Am* acclimation (**à** to)
acclimater [aklimate] **1** *vt* to acclimatize, *Am* to acclimate (**à** to)
 2 s'acclimater *vpr* to become *or* get acclimatized *or Am* acclimated (**à** to)
accointances [akwɛ̃tɑ̃s] *nfpl* contacts
accolade [akɔlad] *nf* (**a**) *(embrassade)* (formal) embrace; **donner l'a. à qn** to embrace sb (**b**) *(signe typographique)* curly bracket, brace
accoler [akɔle] *vt (mettre côte à côte)* to put side by side
accommodant, -e [akɔmɔdɑ̃, -ɑ̃t] *adj* accommodating
accommoder [akɔmɔde] **1** *vt (nourriture)* to prepare; *(restes)* to use up
 2 *vi (œil)* to focus
 3 s'accommoder *vpr* **s'a. de qch** to put up with sth
accompagnateur, -trice [akɔ̃paɲatœr, -tris] *nm,f* (**a**) *(pianiste)* accompanist (**b**) *(d'un voyage organisé)* courier, tour guide; *(d'une sortie scolaire)* accompanying adult (**c**) *Belg* **a. de train** ticket inspector
accompagnement [akɔ̃paɲmɑ̃] *nm* (**a**) *(de morceau de musique)* accompaniment; **chanter sans a.** to sing unaccompanied (**b**) *(légumes)* accompaniment
accompagner [akɔ̃paɲe] **1** *vt* (**a**) *(venir avec)* to come with, to accompany; *(aller avec)* to go with, to accompany; **il est venu accompagné d'une amie** he came with a friend (**b**) *(conduire)* **a. qn à la gare** to take sb to the station (**c**) *(chanteur)* to accompany (**à** on) (**d**) *(ajouter à)* **il a accompagné ses mots d'un sourire** he said it with a smile; **elle a accompagné son exposé de diapositives** she complemented her talk with a slide show; **un rôti accompagné de légumes** a roast served with vegetables
 2 s'accompagner *vpr* (**a**) **s'a. au piano** to accompany oneself on the piano (**b**) *(se produire simultanément)* **s'a. de qch** to be accompanied by sth
accompli, -e [akɔ̃pli] *adj (excellent)* accomplished
accomplir [akɔ̃plir] **1** *vt* (**a**) *(tâche)* to carry out; *(bonne action)* to do; *(exploit)* to accomplish; *(souhait, promesse)* to fulfil (**b**) *(terminer)* to complete, to finish
 2 s'accomplir *vpr (souhait)* to come true
accord [akɔr] *nm* (**a**) *(traité)* agreement; *(non formel)* understanding; *(pour résoudre un conflit)* settlement; **arriver** *ou* **parvenir à un a.** to come to *or* reach an agreement; *Com* **a. de confidentialité** confidentiality agreement (**b**) *(entente)* agreement (**sur** on); **être d'a. avec qn** to agree with sb; **se mettre d'a.** *ou* **tomber d'a. avec qn** to come to an agreement with sb; **(c'est) d'a.!** all right!, OK!; **d'un commun a.** by common consent, by mutual agreement; **faire qch en a. avec qn** to do sth in agreement with sb (**c**) *(autorisation)* consent (**d**) *Gram* agreement (**avec** with) (**e**) *(en musique)* chord; **a. parfait** common chord
accord-cadre (*pl* **accords-cadres**) [akɔrkadr] *nm* outline agreement
accordéon [akɔrdeɔ̃] *nm* accordion; *Fig* **en a.** *(chaussettes)* at half-mast

accordéoniste [akɔrdeɔnist] *nmf* accordionist, accordion player
accorder [akɔrde] **1** *vt* (**a**) **a. qch à qn** *(faveur)* to grant sb sth; *(augmentation, dommages-intérêts)* to award sb sth; *(prêt, découvert bancaire)* to authorize sth to sb; **a. son pardon à qn** to pardon sb; **a. la plus grande importance à qch** to attach the utmost importance to sth; **pouvez-vous m'a. quelques minutes?** can you spare me a few minutes?; *Sout* **je ne l'aime pas, je vous l'accorde** I don't like him/her, I must admit (**b**) *Gram* **a. qch avec qch** to make sth agree with sth (**c**) *(instrument de musique)* to tune; *Fig* **il faudrait a. nos violons** we'd better get our stories straight (**d**) *(couleurs)* to coordinate
 2 s'accorder *vpr* (**a**) *(se mettre d'accord)* to agree, to come to an agreement (**avec/sur** with/on); **on s'accorde à penser que...** there is a general belief *or* it is generally believed that... (**b**) *Gram* to agree (**avec** with) (**c**) *(couleurs)* to go together (**d**) *(à soi-même)* **s'a. qch** to allow *or* give oneself sth
accordeur [akɔrdœr] *nm* (piano) tuner
accoster [akɔste] **1** *vt (personne)* to approach
 2 *vi Naut* to dock
accotement [akɔtmɑ̃] *nm* (**a**) *(d'une route)* verge; **accotements non stabilisés** *(sur panneau)* soft verges (**b**) *(de voie ferrée)* shoulder
accouchement [akuʃmɑ̃] *nm* childbirth, delivery; **avoir un a. difficile** to have a difficult birth; **a. sans douleur** = childbirth made less painful by the use of relaxation techniques
accoucher [akuʃe] **1** *vt* **a. qn** to deliver sb's baby
 2 *vi* (**a**) *(avoir un bébé)* to have a baby, to give birth; **elle doit a. dans un mois** her baby's due in a month (**b**) *Fam* **accouche!** come on, spit it out!
 3 accoucher de *vt ind* (**a**) *(enfant)* to give birth to (**b**) *Fam (produire)* to come up with, to produce; **il a accouché de deux minables paragraphes** he produced two measly paragraphs
accoucheur [akuʃœr] *nm* **(médecin) a.** obstetrician
accoucheuse [akuʃøz] *nf* midwife
accouder [akude] **s'accouder** *vpr* **s'a. à** *ou* **sur qch** to lean one's elbow(s) on sth
accoudoir [akudwar] *nm* armrest
accouplement [akuplɔmɑ̃] *nm (d'animaux)* pairing, mating
accoupler [akuple] **s'accoupler** *vpr (animaux)* to mate
accourir [22] [akurir] *vi* to run up, to rush up
accoutrement [akutrɔmɑ̃] *nm* rig-out, get-up
accoutrer [akutre] **1** *vt* to rig out (**de** in)
 2 s'accoutrer *vpr* to rig oneself out (**de** in)
accoutumance [akutymɑ̃s] *nf (adaptation)* familiarization (**à** with); *(à l'alcool, à la drogue)* addiction; **créer une a.** to be addictive
accoutumé, -e [akutyme] *adj* usual; **comme à l'accoutumée** as usual
accoutumer [akutyme] **1** *vt* **a. qn à qch** to accustom sb to sth, to get sb used to sth
 2 s'accoutumer *vpr* **s'a. à** to get used *or* accustomed to
accréditer [akredite] *vt* (**a**) *(ambassadeur, journaliste)* to accredit (**b**) *(rendre plausible)* to substantiate
accro [akro] *Fam* **1** *adj (drogué)* & *Fig* addicted (**à** to), hooked (**à** on)
 2 *nmf (toxicomane)* addict, junkie; *Fig (passionné)* fanatic
accroc [akro] *nm* (**a**) *(à un tissu)* tear, catch (**b**) *Fig* hitch, snag; **sans a.** without a hitch

accrochage [akrɔʃaʒ] *nm* (**a**) *(accident)* minor accident (**b**) *(dispute)* row; *Mil* skirmish

accroche [akrɔʃ] *nf* slogan

accroche-cœur (*pl* **accroche-cœurs**) [akrɔʃkœr] *nm* kiss curl

accrocher [akrɔʃe] **1** *vt* (**a**) *(suspendre)* to hang up (**à** on); *(wagon)* to hitch on, to couple; *Fig* **une robe qui accroche le regard** an eye-catching dress; **avoir le cœur bien accroché** to have strong nerves *or* a strong stomach (**b**) *(abîmer)* *(vêtement)* to catch (**à** on); *(pare-chocs)* to clip
2 *vi* *(achopper)* to hit a stumbling block; **un titre qui accroche** an eye-catching title; *Fam* **ça n'a pas du tout accroché entre eux** they didn't hit it off at all; *Fam* **je n'accroche pas du tout en maths** I just can't get into maths at all, *Br* I can't get my head around maths
3 **s'accrocher** *vpr* (**a**) *aussi Fig (s'agripper)* **s'a. à qn/qch** to cling to sb/sth; *Fam* **accroche-toi, tu n'as pas tout entendu!** brace yourself, you haven't heard everything yet! (**b**) *Fam (persévérer)* to stick at it (**c**) *(voitures)* to crash into each other (**d**) *Fam (se disputer)* to have a row (**avec** with) (**e**) *(se fixer)* to fasten

accrocheur, -euse [akrɔʃœr, -øz] *adj* (**a**) *(tenace)* tenacious, stubborn (**b**) *(titre, slogan)* catchy

accroissement [akrwasmɑ̃] *nm* increase (**de** in)

accroître [akrwatr] [4a] **1** *vt* to increase, to enlarge
2 **s'accroître** *vpr* to increase, to grow

accroupir [akrupir] **s'accroupir** *vpr* to squat (down), to crouch (down); **être accroupi** to be squatting *or* crouching

accu [aky] *nm* battery

accueil [akœj] *nm* *(façon d'accueillir)* reception, welcome; *(lieu)* reception; **faire bon a. à qn** to welcome sb; **faire mauvais a. à qn** to give sb a cool reception

accueillant, -e [akœjɑ̃, -ɑ̃t] *adj* welcoming

accueillir [5] [akœjir] *vt* (**a**) *(personne, proposition)* to greet; **bien a. qn** to give sb a warm welcome; **nous avons été mal accueillis** we weren't given a very warm welcome; **le film a été mal accueilli par le public** the film was badly received by the public (**b**) *(loger)* *(sujet: ami)* to put up; *(sujet: hôtel)* to accommodate

acculer [akyle] *vt* to drive back (**contre** against); *Fig* **a. qn à faire qch** to give sb no choice but to do sth; *Fig* **être acculé à la faillite** to be forced into bankruptcy

accumulateur [akymylatœr] *nm Élec* battery

accumulation [akymylasjɔ̃] *nf* accumulation; *(d'énergie)* storage; **chauffage par a.** storage heating

accumuler [akymyle] **1** *vt* to accumulate, to amass; *(énergie)* to store; **a. les erreurs** to make a series of mistakes
2 **s'accumuler** *vpr* to accumulate; *(nuages)* to gather, to build up; *Fin (intérêts)* to accrue; **les preuves s'accumulent contre elle** the evidence against her is growing

accusateur, -trice [akyzatœr, -tris] **1** *adj (regard, doigt)* accusing
2 *nm,f* accuser

accusation [akyzasjɔ̃] *nf* accusation; **lancer** *ou* **porter une a. contre qn** to make an accusation against sb; *Jur* **mettre qn en a.** to commit sb for trial

accusé, -e [akyze] **1** *adj (trait)* prominent, pronounced
2 *nm,f (d'un crime)* accused; *(au tribunal)* defendant

3 *nm* **a. de réception** *(pour une lettre)* acknowledgement (of receipt); *Ordinat* acknowledgement

accuser [akyze] **1** *vt* (**a**) *(incriminer)* to accuse; **a. qn de qch/de faire qch** to accuse sb of sth/of doing sth (**b**) *(tendance, baisse)* to show; **a. le coup** to be obviously shaken (**c**) **a. réception de qch** to acknowledge (receipt of) sth
2 **s'accuser** *vpr* (**a**) *(se déclarer coupable)* to confess (**de** to) (**b**) *(se renforcer)* to become more pronounced *or* marked

acerbe [asɛrb] *adj* acerbic; **d'un ton a.** sharply

acéré, -e [asere] *adj (lame)* sharp; *Fig (remarque)* cutting

acériculteur [aserikyltœr] *nm Can* maple syrup and sugar producer

acériculture [aserikyltyr] *nf Can* production of maple syrup and sugar

acétone [asetɔn] *nf* acetone

ACF [aseɛf] *nm (abrév* **Automobile Club de France***)* = French motoring organization

achalandé, -e [aʃalɑ̃de] *adj* **magasin bien/mal a.** well/poorly stocked shop

achaler [aʃale] *vt Can* to annoy, to bother

acharné, -e [aʃarne] *adj (lutte, concurrence)* fierce; *(travail)* relentless; *(joueur)* inveterate

acharnement [aʃarnəmɑ̃] *nm* relentlessness; **avec a.** relentlessly; **se battre avec a.** to fight tooth and nail

acharner [aʃarne] **s'acharner** *vpr* **s'a. après** *ou* **contre** *ou* **sur qn** *(persécuter)* to be always after sb; **s'a. sur qn** *(sujet: meurtrier)* to savage sb; *(sujet: examinateur)* to give sb a hard time; **s'a. sur qch** to work away at sth; **s'a. à faire qch** to try very hard to do sth

achat [aʃa] *nm* (**a**) *(action)* purchase, buying; **faire un a.** to make a purchase, to buy something; **faire l'a. de qch** to buy sth; **achats par Internet** online shopping (**b**) *(ce qu'on a acheté)* purchase; **achats** *(provisions, paquets)* shopping; **aller faire ses achats** to go shopping

acheminement [aʃminmɑ̃] *nm (de troupes)* transportation *(sur ou vers to)*; *(de marchandises)* shipping *(sur ou vers to)*; **a. du courrier** mail handling

acheminer [aʃmine] **1** *vt (troupes)* to transport (**sur** *ou* **vers** to); *(marchandises)* to ship (**sur** *ou* **vers** to); *(courrier)* to handle
2 **s'acheminer** *vpr* **s'a. vers** *(endroit)* to make one's way towards; *Fig (accord, solution)* to move towards; *(victoire)* to head towards

acheter [6] [aʃte] **1** *vt* (**a**) *(acquérir)* to buy, to purchase; **a. qch à qn** *(faire une transaction)* to buy sth from sb; *(en cadeau)* to buy sb sth; **je vais lui a. un livre** I'm going to buy him/her a book; **j'ai acheté ce livre 8 euros** I bought this book for 8 euros (**b**) *Fam (corrompre)* to buy off
2 **s'acheter** *vpr* (**a**) *(pour soi-même)* **je vais m'a. une glace** I'm going to buy (myself) an ice cream (**b**) *(être acheté)* **ça s'achète en pharmacie** you can buy it/them in any pharmacy; **l'amour, ça ne s'achète pas** money can't buy love

acheteur, -euse [aʃtœr, -øz] *nm,f* buyer, purchaser; **je suis a.!** I'm interested!

achevé, -e [aʃve] *adj (artiste, style)* accomplished; *(travail)* perfect; **c'est d'un ridicule a.!** it's utterly ridiculous!

achèvement [aʃɛvmɑ̃] *nm* completion

achever [46] [aʃve] **1** *vt* (**a**) *(finir)* *(discours)* to end, to conclude; *(travail)* to complete (**b**) *(tuer)* *(personne,* *proie)* to finish off; *(animal malade ou blessé)* to put out of its misery; *Fam* **ça m'a achevé!** that really finished me (off)!

2 s'achever *vpr (finir)* to end
achigan [aʃigã] *nm Can* (black) bass
achoppement [aʃɔpmã] *nm voir* **pierre**
acide [asid] **1** *adj* acid(ic); *(au goût)* sour; *Fig (propos)* acid, caustic
2 *nm* acid
acidité [asidite] *nf* acidity; *(au goût)* sourness; *Fig (de propos)* acidity
acidulé, -e [asidyle] *adj* slightly acid; **bonbons acidulés** acid drops
acier [asje] *nm* steel; **a. inoxydable** stainless steel
aciérie [asjeri] *nf* steelworks *(singulier)*
acné [akne] *nf* acne; **a. juvénile** (teenage) acne
acolyte [akɔlit] *nm Péj* accomplice
acompte [akɔ̃t] *nm* deposit, down payment; **recevoir un a.** to receive something on account; **verser un a.** to make a down payment
acoquiner [akɔkine] **s'acoquiner** *vpr* **s'a. avec qn** to team up with sb
Açores [asɔr] *nfpl* **les A.** the Azores
à-côté *(pl* à-côtés) [akote] *nm* **(a)** *(élément secondaire)* side issue **(b)** *(financier)* extra
à-coup *(pl* à-coups) [aku] *nm* jolt; **travailler par à-coups** to work in fits and starts; **le moteur a des à-coups** the engine judders
acoustique [akustik] **1** *adj* acoustic
2 *nf (discipline)* acoustics *(singulier); (qualité)* acoustics *(pluriel)*
acquéreur [akerœr] *nm* purchaser, buyer; **notre voiture n'a pas trouvé a.** we couldn't find a buyer for our car
acquérir [7] [akerir] *vt* **(a)** *(obtenir, prendre)* to acquire; **nous avons acquis la certitude de son innocence** we have established beyond doubt that he/she is innocent; **a. de la valeur** to increase in value **(b)** *(acheter)* to purchase, to buy
acquière, acquiers *etc voir* **acquérir**
acquiescer [16] [akjese] *vi* to acquiesce (**à** to); **a. d'un signe de tête** to nod in agreement
acquis, -e [aki, -iz] **1** *pp de* **acquérir**
2 *adj (savoir, caractères)* acquired; **tenir qch pour a.** to take sth for granted; **son aide nous est acquise** we can take it for granted that he/she will help us; **cela est a.** that's been established
3 *nm (connaissances)* knowledge; **il ne fonctionne que sur ses a.** he gets by on what he knows already; *UE* **a. communautaire** acquis communautaire; **les a. sociaux** social benefits
acquisition [akizisjɔ̃] *nf* **(a)** *(action)* acquisition; **faire l'a. de qch** *(acheter)* to purchase sth **(b)** *(bien acheté)* purchase
acquit [aki] *nm Com* receipt; **pour a.** received (with thanks), paid; **par a. de conscience** to ease one's conscience
acquittement [akitmã] *nm* **(a)** *Jur* acquittal **(b)** *(d'une dette)* payment
acquitter [akite] **1** *vt* **(a)** *(accusé)* to acquit **(b)** *(dette, facture)* to pay
2 s'acquitter *vpr* **s'a. d'une obligation/d'un devoir** to fulfil an obligation/a duty; **s'a. envers qn** to repay sb
acre [akr] *nm ou nf Can* acre
âcre [akr] *adj (goût)* bitter; *(odeur)* acrid
acrobate [akrɔbat] *nmf* acrobat

acrobatie [akrɔbasi] *nf (art)* acrobatics *(singulier)*; **faire des acrobaties** to perform acrobatics; **a. aérienne** aerobatics *(singulier)*
acrobatique [akrɔbatik] *adj* acrobatic
acronyme [akrɔnim] *nm* acronym
Acropole [akrɔpɔl] *nf* **l'A.** the Acropolis
acrylique [akrilik] *adj & nm* acrylic
acte [akt] *nm* **(a)** *(action)* act; **faire a. d'autorité** to exercise one's authority; **faire a. de candidature à un emploi** to apply for a job; **faire a. de présence** to put in an appearance; **passer aux actes** to take action; **c'était peut-être un a. manqué** maybe subconsciously I/he/*etc* did it deliberately; **a. de terrorisme** terrorist act **(b)** *Jur* deed, title; **dont a.** duly noted *or* acknowledged; **prendre a. de qch** to take note of sth; *Sout* **nous prenons a. de votre candidature** we acknowledge your application; **a. d'accusation** bill of indictment, charges; **a. de propriété** title deed; *UE* **a. unique européen** Single European Act; **a. de vente** bill of sale **(c)** *(certificat)* record; **a. de décès** death certificate; **a. d'état civil** = certificate of birth, marriage or death; **a. de mariage** marriage certificate; **a. de naissance** birth certificate **(d)** *actes (d'un procès, d'un colloque)* proceedings; *(d'un organisme scientifique)* transactions **(e)** *Théât* act
acter [akte] *vt Belg (noter)* to take a note of, to note; *Jur* to record
acteur [aktœr] *nm* **(a)** *(artiste)* actor; **a. de cinéma/de théâtre** film/stage actor **(b)** *(d'un événement)* **les différents acteurs de la négociation** the different participants in *or* parties involved in the negotiations; **a. économique** economic player; **les acteurs sociaux** = employers, workers and trade unions
actif, -ive [aktif, -iv] **1** *adj* **(a)** *(défenseur, participation, substance)* active; **la population active** the working population; **entrer dans la vie active** to start working **(b)** *(énergique) (personne)* active **(c)** *Gram* active
2 *nm* **(a)** *Com* assets; *Fig* **avoir qch à son a.** to have sth to one's name; **il faut mettre sa patience à son a.** you have to give him/her credit for patience **(b)** **les actifs** *(personnes)* the active *or* working population **(c)** *Gram* **verbe à l'a.** verb in the active voice
action [aksjɔ̃] *nf* **(a)** *(acte)* action, act; **bonne/mauvaise a.** good/bad deed **(b)** *(influence, effet) (d'une substance)* action, effect *(sur* on) **(c)** *(activité)* **entrer en a.** *(loi)* to come into force; **mettre qch en a.** to put sth into operation; **passer à l'a.** to take action, to act; **homme d'a.** man of action **(d)** *(histoire)* action; *TV & Cin* **a.!** action! **(e)** *Fin* share **(f)** *Jur* action; **intenter une a. judiciaire** *ou* **en justice contre** to take legal action against **(g)** *Mil* action **(h)** *Suisse (vente promotionnelle)* sale, special offer
actionnaire [aksjɔnɛr] *nmf Fin* shareholder
actionner [aksjɔne] *vt (mettre en marche)* to start up, to turn on; *(faire fonctionner)* to operate, to drive
activement [aktivmã] *adv* actively
activer [aktive] **1** *vt* **(a)** *(accélérer)* to speed up; *(feu)* to stoke **(b)** *Ordinat* to activate; **a. une option** to select an option
2 *vi Fam* to get a move on
3 s'activer *vpr* to be busy
activiste [aktivist] *adj & nmf* activist
activité [aktivite] *nf* activity; **en a.** *(volcan)* active; *(usine)* in production; *(personne)* working
actrice [aktris] *nf* actress

actualisation [aktµalizasjɔ̃] *nf (d'un texte, d'une méthode de travail)* updating

actualiser [aktµalize] *vt (texte, méthode de travail)* to update

actualité [aktµalite] *nf* **l'a.** the news, current affairs; **l'a. politique française** the current French political scene; **cette question est toujours d'a.** this is still a topical question; **les actualités** *(à la télé, à la radio)* the news; **les actualités télévisées** the television news

actuel, -elle [aktµɛl] *adj* (**a**) *(présent)* present, current; **dans la situation actuelle** as things are *or* stand at the moment (**b**) *(d'actualité)* topical

actuellement [aktµɛlmɑ̃] *adv* at present, at the present time

acuité [akµite] *nf (de la douleur)* acuteness; *(d'un argument)* pointedness; *(d'un son)* shrillness; **a. visuelle/auditive** keenness of vision/hearing

acuponcteur, -trice [akypɔ̃ktœr, -tris] *nm,f* acupuncturist

acuponcture [akypɔ̃ktyr] *nf* acupuncture

acupuncteur, -trice = acuponcteur, -trice

acupuncture = acuponcture

adage [adaʒ] *nm* adage, (common) saying; **selon l'a.** as the saying goes

adaptateur, -trice [adaptatœr, -tris] **1** *nm* (**a**) *(dispositif)* adapter (**b**) *TV (pour TNT)* digital receiver, *Br* set-top box
  2 *nm,f (d'une œuvre)* adapter

adaptation [adaptasjɔ̃] *nf* (**a**) *(à une situation)* adaptation (à to); **faire un effort d'a.** to try to adapt; **faculté d'a.** adaptability (**b**) *(d'une œuvre)* adaptation; **a. théâtrale** stage adaptation

adapter [adapte] **1** *vt* (**a**) *(ajuster)* to adapt (à to); **est-ce vraiment adapté à la situation?** is it really suitable for the situation? (**b**) *(œuvre)* to adapt
  2 **s'adapter** *vpr* (**a**) *(s'acclimater)* to adapt (à to); **savoir s'a.** to be very adaptable *or* flexible (**b**) *(être compatible)* **la prise s'adapte à toutes les télévisions** the plug fits all types of television

Addis-Abeba [adisabeba] *n* Addis Ababa

additif [aditif] *nm* (**a**) *(ajout)* addition (**b**) *(substance)* additive; **sans additifs** additive-free

addition [adisjɔ̃] *nf* (**a**) *(fait d'ajouter)* addition, adding (à to); *(pour faire un total)* adding up; **faire une a.** to do a sum (**b**) *(extension)* addition, extension (**c**) *(au restaurant) Br* bill, *Am* check

additionnel, -elle [adisjɔnɛl] *adj* additional, extra; *Ordinat* add-on

additionner [adisjɔne] **1** *vt* to add (up); **lait additionné d'eau** watered-down milk; **café additionné d'eau-de-vie** coffee laced with brandy
  2 **s'additionner** *vpr* to add up; **aux longues heures de travail s'additionnent celles passées dans le métro** along with the long working hours, there are those spent on the metro

adduction [adyksjɔ̃] *nf Tech* admission, intake; *Constr* **a. d'eau** canalization

adepte [adɛpt] *nmf (d'une doctrine, d'une personnalité)* follower; *(d'une activité)* enthusiast; **faire des adeptes** to attract a following

adéquat, -e [adekwa, -at] *adj (personne, lieu, expression, méthode)* appropriate, suitable; *(montant, quantité)* adequate

adéquation [adekwasjɔ̃] *nf* appropriateness, suitability

adhérence [aderɑ̃s] *nf* adhesion, adherence; *(de pneus)* grip

adhérent, -e [aderɑ̃, -ɑ̃t] **1** *adj (substance, propriétés)* adhesive
  2 *nm,f* member

adhérer [34] [adere] *vi* (**a**) *(coller)* to adhere, to stick (à to); **a. à la route** *(pneus)* to grip the road (**b**) **a. à** *(opinion, doctrine)* to subscribe to (**c**) *(s'inscrire)* **a. à un parti** to join a party

adhésif, -ive [adezif, -iv] **1** *adj* adhesive, sticky
  2 *nm* (**a**) *(substance)* adhesive (**b**) *(ruban)* sticky tape, *Br* Sellotape®, *Am* Scotch® tape

adhésion [adezjɔ̃] *nf* (**a**) *(accord)* support (à for) (**b**) *(inscription)* joining (à of)

ad hoc [adɔk] *adj & adv* ad hoc

adieu, -x [adjø] **1** *exclam* goodbye!, farewell!; **dire a. à qn** to say goodbye to sb; *Fam Fig* **dire a. à qch** to kiss *or* say goodbye to sth
  2 *nm* farewell; **faire ses adieux** to say one's goodbyes; **faire ses adieux à qn** to say goodbye to sb

adipeux, -euse [adipø, -øz] *adj (tissu)* adipose; *(visage)* fat

adjacent, -e [adʒasɑ̃, ɑ̃t] *adj* adjacent (à to)

adjectif [adʒɛktif] *nm* adjective

adjoint, -e [adʒwɛ̃, -ɛ̃t] **1** *adj* assistant, deputy
  2 *nm,f* assistant; **a. au maire** deputy mayor

adjonction [adʒɔ̃ksjɔ̃] *nf* addition; **produit sans a. de sucre** product with no added sugar

adjudant [adʒydɑ̃] *nm Br* warrant officer class II, *Am* warrant officer (junior grade); **a.-chef** *Br* warrant officer class I, *Am* chief warrant officer

adjudication [adʒydikasjɔ̃] *nf* sale by auction

adjuger [45] [adʒyʒe] **1** *vt* **a. qch à qn** *(prix, contrat)* to award sth to sb; *(aux enchères)* to knock sth down to sb; **une fois, deux fois, trois fois, adjugé, vendu!** going, going, gone!
  2 **s'adjuger** *vpr* **s'a. qch** to appropriate sth

ADM [adeɛm] *nfpl Mil (abrév armes de destruction massive)* WMD

admettre [47] [admɛtr] *vt* (**a**) *(accueillir)* **a. qn** to admit sb, to let sb in; **les chiens ne sont pas admis** *(sur la porte d'un magasin)* no dogs allowed; **être admis à l'université** to win a place at university; **être admis à un concours** to pass an examination (**b**) *(accepter)* to allow; **je n'admets pas qu'on me mente** I won't tolerate being lied to; **cette règle n'admet aucune exception** there can be no exceptions to this rule (**c**) *(reconnaître)* to admit, to accept; **admettons que ce soit possible** assuming it's possible; **admettons que j'ai tort** *(pour clore une discussion)* I stand corrected

administrateur, -trice [administratœr, -tris] *nm,f* (**a**) *(d'une société, d'une banque)* director (**b**) *(de fondation)* trustee

administratif, -ive [administratif, -iv] *adj* administrative

administration [administrasjɔ̃] *nf* (**a**) *(d'affaires)* administration, management; *(d'un pays)* governing (**b**) *(ensemble des directeurs)* board of directors; *(d'une institution)* governing body (**c**) **l'A.** *(service public)* ≃ the Civil Service; *(fonctionnaires)* civil servants

administré, -e [administre] *nm,f* citizen

administrer [administre] *vt* (**a**) *(propriété)* to administer, to manage; *(pays)* to govern (**b**) *(justice)* to dispense; *Rel (sacrements)* to administer; *(remède)* to

administer; **je vais lui a. une bonne correction** I'm going to give him/her a good hiding

admirable [admirabl] *adj* admirable; *(très compétent)* wonderful; **elle a été a. de courage** she showed admirable courage

admirablement [admirabləmɑ̃] *adv* admirably; *(très bien)* **a. bien** wonderfully

admirateur, -trice [admiratœr, -tris] *nm,f* admirer

admiratif, -ive [admiratif, -iv] *adj* admiring

admiration [admirasjɔ̃] *nf* admiration; **avoir de l'a. pour qn** to admire sb; **être en a.** devant qch to be filled with admiration for sth; **tomber en a. devant qch** to be stopped in one's tracks by the beauty of sth; **faire l'a. de tous** to be universally admired

admirer [admire] *vt* to admire

admis, -e [admi, -iz] **1** *adj* **(a)** *(autorisé à entrer)* admitted, allowed (in) **(b)** *(accepté)* allowed, accepted

2 *nm,f (à un examen)* successful candidate

admissible [admisibl] *adj (excuse, preuve, conduite)* admissible, allowable; **(candidats) admissibles** candidates who have qualified for the oral examination

admission [admisjɔ̃] *nf* **(a)** *(entrée)* admission (**à/dans** to) **(b)** *Tech* intake; *Aut* induction

ADN [adeɛn] *nm (abrév* **acide désoxyribonucléique)** DNA

ado [ado] *nmf Fam* teenager, teen

adolescence [adɔlesɑ̃s] *nf* adolescence; **pendant mon a.** when I was a teenager

adolescent, -e [adɔlesɑ̃, -ɑ̃t] **1** *nm,f* adolescent, teenager

2 *adj* adolescent, teenage

adon [adɔ̃] *nm Can Fam* coincidence

adonner [adɔne] **s'adonner** *vpr* **s'a. à qch** to devote oneself to sth; **s'a. à la boisson** to be an alcoholic

adopter [adɔpte] *vt* **(a)** *(enfant)* to adopt **(b)** *(accepter)* to accept **(c)** *(choisir)* to adopt **(d)** *(projet de loi, résolution)* to adopt, to pass

adoptif, -ive [adɔptif, -iv] *adj (enfant)* adopted; *(parent)* adoptive

adoption [adɔpsjɔ̃] *nf* **(a)** *(d'un enfant)* adoption **(b)** *(d'une idée, d'une mode)* adoption; **mon pays d'a.** my adopted country **(c)** *(d'un projet de loi)* adoption, passing

adorable [adɔrabl] *adj* adorable, charming

adoration [adɔrasjɔ̃] *nf aussi Fig* adoration; **être en a. devant qn** to worship sb

adorer [adɔre] **1** *vt aussi Fig* to adore; **j'adore monter à cheval** I love *or* adore riding

2 **s'adorer** *vpr* to adore each other

adosser [adose] **1** *vt* **a. qch à** *ou* **contre qch** to lean sth (with its back) against sth

2 **s'adosser** *vpr* **s'a. à** *ou* **contre qch** to lean (back) against sth; **le village est adossé à la colline** the village stands at the foot of the hill

adoucir [adusir] **1** *vt* **(a)** *(voix, eau, linge, peau)* to soften; *(contraste, couleur)* to tone down; **sa nouvelle coiffure adoucit son visage** his/her new haircut softens his/her face **(b)** *(douleur, chagrin)* to ease; *Prov* **la musique adoucit les mœurs** music hath charms to soothe the savage breast

2 **s'adoucir** *vpr* **(a)** *(voix, ton)* to soften **(b)** *(personne, caractère)* to mellow

adoucissant, -e [adusisɑ̃, ɑ̃t] **1** *adj* softening

2 *nm (pour le linge)* fabric softener

adoucisseur [adusisœr] *nm* (water) softener

adr. *(abrév* **adresse)** address

adrénaline [adrenalin] *nf* adrenalin(e)

adresse [adrɛs] *nf* **(a)** *(coordonnées)* address; **changer d'a.** to change one's address; *Fig* **tu te trompes d'a.** you've come to the wrong person; **il connaît de bonnes adresses** *(de restaurants, de magasins)* he knows all the good places to go to; **je l'ai dit à l'a. de ceux qui...** I said it for the benefit of those who... **(b)** *(habileté)* skill; *(savoir-faire)* diplomacy; **avec a.** skilfully **(c)** *Ordinat* address; **a. électronique, a. e-mail,** *Can* **a. de courriel** e-mail address; **a. Internet** Internet address; **a. URL** URL; **a. virtuelle** virtual address

adresser [adrese] **1** *vt* **(a)** *(lettre)* to address; **a. qch à qn** to send sth to sb **(b)** *(personne)* **on m'a adressé à vous** I have been referred to you **(c)** **a. qch à qn** *(compliments, remerciements)* to present sth to sb; **cette remarque était adressée à Martin** that remark was aimed at *or* meant for Martin; **a. un sourire à qn** to smile at sb; **a. la parole à qn** to speak to sb

2 **s'adresser** *vpr* **s'a. à qn** *(sujet: personne)* to speak to sb; *(pour un renseignement)* to ask sb; *(sujet: remarque, recommandation)* to apply to sb; **s'a. ici** *(sur écriteau)* enquire within

Adriatique [adrijatik] *nf* **l'A.** the Adriatic

adroit, -e [adrwa, -at] *adj* **(a)** *(habile)* skilful; **être a. de ses mains** to be clever with one's hands **(b)** *(réponse, diplomate)* shrewd, clever

adroitement [adrwatmɑ̃] *adv* **(a)** *(avec des gestes habiles)* skilfully **(b)** *(astucieusement)* cleverly

ADSL [adeɛsɛl] *nm Ordinat & Tél (abrév* **Asymmetric Digital Subscriber Line)** ADSL; **est-ce que tu as l'A. chez toi?** have you got broadband at home?

aduler [adyle] *vt* to worship

adulte [adylt] **1** *adj (personne)* adult, grown-up; *(plante, animal)* fully grown

2 *nm* adult, grown-up

adultère [adyltɛr] *nm* adultery

advenir [70] [advənir] *v impersonnel (aux* **être)** to happen; **or, il advint que...** it so happened that...; **quoi qu'il advienne** no matter what happens; **advienne que pourra** come what may; **qu'est-il advenu de lui?** whatever became of him?

adverbe [advɛrb] *nm* adverb

adverbial, -e, -aux, -ales [advɛrbjal, -o] *adj* adverbial

adversaire [advɛrsɛr] *nmf* opponent; *(dans un conflit, dans une guerre)* enemy

adverse [advɛrs] *adj (équipe)* opposing; *Jur* **la partie a.** the other side

AELE [aɛlə] *nf (abrév* **Association européenne de libre-échange) l'A.** EFTA

aérateur [aeratœr] *nm* ventilator

aération [aerasjɔ̃] *nf (d'une pièce)* ventilation

aéré, -e [aere] *adj* **(a)** *(chambre)* airy, well-ventilated **(b)** *(présentation, texte)* well-spaced

aérer [34] [aere] **1** *vt* **(a)** *(pièce, linge)* to air **(b)** *(texte, exposé)* to lighten

2 **s'aérer** *vpr* to get some fresh air

aérien, -enne [aerjɛ̃, -ɛn] *adj* **(a)** *(défense, attaque, transport)* air **(b)** *(texture)* (light and) airy; *(grâce, allure)* ethereal **(c)** *(câble)* overhead; *(voie ferrée)* elevated

aérobic [aerɔbik] *nm* aerobics *(singulier)*

aérodrome [aerɔdrom] *nm* aerodrome, airfield

aérodynamique [aerɔdinamik] *adj (forme, voiture)* streamlined

aérogare [aerɔgar] *nf* (air) terminal

aéroglisseur [aerɔglisœr] *nm* hovercraft

aérogramme [aerɔgram] *nm* aerogramme, airmail letter

aéromodélisme [aerɔmɔdelism] *nm* making model aircraft

aéronautique [aerɔnotik] **1** *adj* aeronautic(al)   **2** *nf* aeronautics *(singulier)*

aéronaval, -e, -als, -ales [aerɔnaval] **1** *adj (forces)* air and sea   **2** *nf* l'**Aéronavale** *Br* ≃ the Fleet Air Arm, *Am* ≃ the Naval Air Service

aéronef [aerɔnɛf] *nm* aircraft

aérophagie [aerɔfaʒi] *nf* flatulence; **avoir** *ou* **faire de l'a.** to suffer from flatulence

aéroport [aerɔpɔr] *nm* airport

aéroporté, -e [aerɔpɔrte] *adj* airborne

aérosol [aerɔsɔl] *nm* aerosol; **vendu en a.** sold in spray form

aérospatial, -e, -aux, -ales [aerɔspasjal, -o] **1** *adj* aerospace   **2** *nf* l'**aérospatiale** aerospace science

aérostat [aerɔsta] *nm (montgolfière)* hot-air balloon; *(dirigeable)* airship

affabilité [afabilite] *nf* affability

affable [afabl] *adj* affable

affabulation [afabylasjɔ̃] *nf* fabrication

affabuler [afabyle] *vi* to make things up

affaiblir [afeblir] **1** *vt* (**a**) *(sujet: maladie)* to weaken (**b**) *(réduire)* to lessen, to reduce   **2** *s'***affaiblir** *vpr (personne)* to get weaker; *(vue, ouïe)* to get worse, to deteriorate; *(sentiment)* to wane; *(son)* to grow fainter; **le sens du mot s'est affaibli** the word has lost much of its meaning

affaiblissement [afeblismɑ̃] *nm (d'une personne, d'un gouvernement, de l'économie)* weakening; *(d'un sentiment)* waning; *(d'une lumière, d'un son)* fading

affaire [afɛr] *nf* (**a**) *(occupation)* business, concern; **ce n'est pas votre a.** it's none of your business; **j'en fais mon a.** I'll handle it; **c'est une a. de goût** it's a matter *or* question of taste; **c'est l'a. d'une minute** it won't take a minute; **ça, c'est une autre a.** that's another matter; **avoir a. à qn** *(s'adresser à quelqu'un)* to be dealt with by sb; **s'il continue à mentir, il aura a. à moi!** if he carries on lying, he'll have me to deal with! (**b**) *(usage)* **cela fera parfaitement l'a.** that will do nicely; *Fam* **faire son a. à qn** to do sb in (**c**) *(histoire, problème)* affair, business; **une a. de pots-de-vin** a bribery scandal; **a. de cœur** love affair; **ça n'a pas été une mince a.** it wasn't easy; **c'est toute une a.** it's quite a business; **la belle a.!** big deal!; **ça ne change rien à l'a.** that doesn't change anything; **tirer qn d'a.** to get sb out of trouble; **ce n'est pas une a. d'État!** it's no big deal! (**d**) *(transaction)* deal; *(achat à bon marché)* bargain; **il a fait une a. en achetant cette voiture** he got a bargain when he bought that car; **faire a. avec qn** to make a deal with sb; **une a. en or** the bargain of the century (**e**) *(entreprise)* firm, business (**f**) **affaires** *(effets personnels)* things, belongings (**g**) **les affaires** *(activités commerciales)* business *(singulier)*; **comment vont les affaires?** how's business?; **il est dur en affaires** he's a hard-headed businessman; **les affaires sont les affaires** business is business (**h**)

les Affaires étrangères *Br* ≃ the Foreign (and Commonwealth) Office, *Am* ≃ the State Department

affairé, -e [afere] *adj* busy

affairer [afere] **s'affairer** *vpr* to busy oneself; **s'a. autour de qn** to fuss (a)round sb

affairiste [aferist] *nmf* wheeler-dealer

affaissement [afɛsmɑ̃] *nm (de terrain)* subsidence; *(du plancher, d'une poutre)* sagging

affaisser [afɛse] **s'affaisser** *vpr* (**a**) *(s'enfoncer) (terrain)* to subside; *(poutre, fauteuil)* to sag (**b**) *(tomber, s'écrouler)* to collapse

affalé, -e [afale] *adj* **être a. dans un fauteuil** to be slumped in an armchair

affaler [afale] **s'affaler** *vpr* to collapse

affamé, -e [afame] *adj* starving

affectation [afɛktasjɔ̃] *nf* (**a**) *Péj (pose)* affectation, affectedness; *(simulacre)* pretence, affectation; **avec a.** affectedly; **sans a.** unaffectedly (**b**) *(de fonds, de crédits, de locaux)* assignment, allocation (**à** to) (**c**) *(à un poste)* appointment (**à** to); *(d'un soldat)* posting (**à** to) (**d**) *Ordinat (de touche)* assignment; **a. de mémoire** memory allocation

affecté, -e [afɛkte] *adj Péj (personne, manière)* affected

affecter [afɛkte] *vt* (**a**) *(fonds, crédits, locaux)* to assign (**à** to), to allocate (**à** to) (**b**) *(employé)* to appoint (**à** to); *(soldat)* to post (**à** to) (**c**) *(feindre)* to affect; **a. de faire qch** to pretend to do sth (**d**) *(émouvoir)* to affect, to move (**e**) *(frapper) (carrière, santé)* to affect, to have an effect on; **la grève a affecté plusieurs usines** the strike has affected *or* hit several factories

affectif, -ive [afɛktif, -iv] *adj* emotional, *Spéc* affective

affection [afɛksjɔ̃] *nf* (**a**) *(attachement)* affection (**pour** for); **prendre qn en a.** to become fond of sb; **avoir de l'a. pour qn** to be fond of sb (**b**) *Litt (maladie)* ailment

affectionner [afɛksjɔne] *vt* to be fond of; **votre cousin affectionné** *(dans une lettre)* your affectionate cousin

affectivité [afɛktivite] *nf* feelings

affectueusement [afɛktɥøzmɑ̃] *adv* affectionately; *(dans une lettre)* love (from)

affectueux, -euse [afɛktɥø, -øz] *adj* affectionate

afférent, -e [aferɑ̃, -ɑ̃t] *adj* **a. à** *(concernant)* relating to

affermir [afɛrmir] **1** *vt* (**a**) *(muscles, chairs)* to tone (up) (**b**) *(pouvoir, position, autorité)* to strengthen, to consolidate   **2** **s'affermir** *vpr (chairs, muscles)* to tone up; *(pouvoir, position, autorité)* to be strengthened

affichage [afiʃaʒ] *nm* (**a**) *(pose d'affiches)* billsticking, billposting; **a. interdit** *(sur panneau)* stick no bills (**b**) *Ordinat* display; **montre à a. digital** *ou* **numérique** digital watch; **a. à cristaux liquides** liquid crystal display

affiche [afiʃ] *nf* notice; *(de publicité)* poster; **être à l'a.** *(spectacle)* to be on; **être en tête d'a.** to be top of the bill; **a. électorale** election poster

afficher [afiʃe] **1** *vt* (**a**) *(annonce, poster)* to put up; *(prix, horaires, résultats)* to display; **défense d'a.** *(sur panneau)* stick no bills; **a. complet** *(spectacle)* to be sold out (**b**) *(mépris, indifférence)* to show, to display; *(savoir)* to flaunt; *(déficit, excédent)* to show (**c**) *Ordinat (message)* to display

2 s'afficher *vpr* (**a**) *(personne)* to flaunt oneself (**b**) *(sur un écran)* to be displayed

affichette [afiʃɛt] *nf* small notice; *(publicitaire)* poster

afficheur [afiʃœr] *nm (personne)* billsticker, billposter; *(société)* publicity company

affilée [afile] **d'affilée** *adv* in a row; **cinq heures d'a.** five hours solid *or* at a stretch

affiler [afile] *vt* to sharpen

affiliation [afiljasjɔ̃] *nf* joining (**à** of)

affilier [66] [afilje] **s'affilier** *vpr* to join; **s'a. à un parti** to join a party

affiner [afine] **1** *vt* (**a**) *(métal)* to refine; *(fromage)* to mature (**b**) *(esprit)* to sharpen; *(goût)* to refine

2 s'affiner *vpr (goût)* to become more refined; *(visage)* to get thinner; *(traits)* to become better defined; *(esprit)* to become sharper

affinité [afinite] *nf* affinity (**entre** between)

affirmatif, -ive [afirmatif, -iv] **1** *adj* (**a**) *(réponse)* affirmative, positive; **faire un signe a. de la tête** to nod in agreement (**b**) *(personne)* positive

2 *nf* **dans l'affirmative** if so, if the answer is yes; **répondre par l'affirmative** to answer yes

3 *exclam* affirmative!

affirmation [afirmasjɔ̃] *nf* assertion

affirmer [afirme] **1** *vt* (**a**) *(soutenir)* to maintain; **il affirme vous connaître** he maintains that he knows you (**b**) *(manifester)* to assert; **a. sa volonté de faire qch** to declare one's willingness to do sth

2 s'affirmer *vpr (personnalité)* to assert itself; *(tendance, talent)* to be confirmed

affleurer [aflœre] *vi (récif)* to be near the surface; *Géol (filon)* to outcrop; *Fig (mépris, racisme)* to come to the surface

affliction [afliksjɔ̃] *nf* affliction

affligé, -e [afliʒe] *adj* (**a**) **être a. de** *(atteint)* to be afflicted with (**b**) *(peiné)* distressed

affligeant, -e [afliʒã, -ãt] *adj (nouvelle, vision)* distressing; *(bêtise, ignorance, résultats)* appalling

affliger [45] [afliʒe] **1** *vt* (**a**) *(atteindre)* to afflict; **région affligée par le choléra** area afflicted with cholera; **la nature l'a affligé d'un grand nez** nature has cursed him with a big nose (**b**) *(peiner)* (sujet: nouvelle, événement) to distress

2 s'affliger *vpr* to be distressed (**de** about)

affluence [aflyãs] *nf (de personnes)* crowd; *(de marchandises)* abundance

affluent [aflyã] *nm* tributary

affluer [aflye] *vi (liquide)* to flow (**vers/dans** to/into); *(sang)* to rush (**à** to); *(foule)* to flock (**vers** to)

afflux [afly] *nm (de sang)* rush; *(de visiteurs)* flood; *(de capitaux)* influx

affolant, -e [afolã, -ãt] *adj (spectacle, nouvelle)* distressing; *Fam* **c'est a.!** it's incredible!

affolé, -e [afole] *adj (personne)* panic-stricken

affolement [afolmã] *nm* panic; **pas d'a.!** don't panic!

affoler [afole] **1** *vt* to throw into a panic

2 s'affoler *vpr* (**a**) *(paniquer)* to panic (**b**) *(aiguille de boussole)* to spin (**c**) *(machine)* to race

affranchir [afrãʃir] **1** *vt* (**a**) *(lettre, colis)* to put a stamp/stamps on; *(avec une machine)* to frank (**b**) *(esclave)* to free

2 s'affranchir *vpr* (**a**) *(peuple, personne)* to free oneself (**de** from) (**b**) *Belg (prendre de l'assurance)* to become (more) self-confident

affranchissement [afrãʃismã] *nm* (**a**) *(montant payé) (de lettre, paquet)* postage (**b**) *(d'un esclave)* freeing

affres [afr] *nfpl Litt (du doute, de la jalousie, de la faim)* pangs; **les a. de la mort** death throes

affréter [34] [afrete] *vt* to charter

affreusement [afrøzmã] *adv* horribly; **a. laid** hideously ugly; **il parle a. mal l'anglais** his English is awful

affreux, -euse [afrø, -øz] *adj* (**a**) *(laid)* hideous (**b**) *(atroce) (nouvelle, pauvreté, crime)* dreadful (**c**) *Fam (épouvantable) (temps, migraine)* awful, dreadful; **qu'est-ce que ça a augmenté, c'est a.!** it's dreadful *or* shocking how the price has gone up!; **un a. jojo** a little horror

affriolant, -e [afriolã, -ãt] *adj* alluring

affront [afrɔ̃] *nm* affront, insult; **faire un a. à qn** to affront *or* insult sb

affrontement [afrɔ̃tmã] *nm* clash, confrontation

affronter [afrɔ̃te] **1** *vt (adversaire, danger, mort)* to face, to confront; **a. la colère de qn** to brave the wrath of sb

2 s'affronter *vpr (ennemis)* to clash; *(équipes, joueurs)* to clash; **deux thèses s'affrontent** there are two conflicting theories

affubler [afyble] **1** *vt* **a. qn de qch** to attire sb in sth

2 s'affubler *vpr* **s'a. de qch** to get oneself up in sth

affût [afy] **à l'affût** *adv* **être à l'a.** *(à la chasse)* to lie in wait; *Fig* **être à l'a. de qch** to be on the lookout for sth

affûter [afyte] *vt* to sharpen

afghan, -e [afgã, -an] **1** *adj* Afghan

2 *nm,f* **A.** Afghan

3 *nm (langue)* Afghan

Afghanistan [afganistã] *nm* **l'A.** Afghanistan

afin [afɛ̃] *adv* **a. de faire qch** (in order) to do sth, so as to do sth; **a. que** + *subjunctive* so that; **a. que les autres puissent le voir** so that the others may see it

AFNOR [afnɔr] *nf (abrév* **Association française de normalisation)** = French industrial standards authority, *Br* ≃ BSI, *Am* ≃ ANSI

a fortiori [afɔrsjɔri] *adv* all the more so

AF-P [aɛfpe] *nf (abrév* **Agence France-Presse)** = French international news agency

africain, -e [afrikɛ̃, -ɛn] **1** *adj* African

2 *nm,f* **A.** African

Afrique [afrik] *nf* **l'A.** Africa; **l'A. noire** Black Africa; **l'A. du Nord** North Africa; **l'A. du Sud** South Africa

afro-américain, -e *(mpl* afro-américains, *fpl* afro-américaines) [afroamerikɛ̃, -ɛn] **1** *adj* African American

2 *nm,f* **A.-A.** African American

after [aftœr] *nm ou nf Fam (soirée)* after party; **on a décidé d'aller faire l'a. chez Alex** we finished the night off at Alex's place

after-shave [aftœrʃɛv] *nm inv* aftershave

2 *adj* **lotion a.** aftershave (lotion)

A.G. [aʒe] *nf (abrév* **assemblée générale)** AGM

agaçant, -e [agasã, -ãt] *adj* annoying, irritating

agacer [16] [agase] *vt* (**a**) *(énerver)* to annoy, to irritate; **il m'agace avec ses questions** he's getting on my nerves, asking all those questions (**b**) *(dents, nerfs)* to set on edge

agapes [agap] *nfpl Litt* feast; *Hum* **nous allons faire des a. chez Jeannot** we're going to have a real slap-up meal at Jeannot's

agate [agat] *nf (pierre)* agate; *(bille)* marble

âge [ɑʒ] *nm* (**a**) *(d'une personne)* age; **quel â. avez-vous?** how old are you?; **à ton â.**, **je travaillais** when I was your age, I was working; **à l'â. de six ans** at the age of six; **on ne lui donne pas son â.** he/she doesn't look his/her age; **faire son â.** to look one's age; **un homme d'un grand â.** a very old man; **entre deux âges** middle-aged; **être en â. de faire qch, être d'â. à faire qch** to be old enough to do sth; **ce n'est plus de mon â.** I'm too old for that type of thing; **un whisky de quinze ans d'â.** a fifteen-year-old whisky; **l'â. adulte** adulthood; **l'â. bête** *ou* **ingrat** the awkward *or* difficult age; **â. mental** mental age; **une femme d'â. mur** a mature woman; **avoir l'â. de raison** to have reached the age of reason (**b**) *(époque)* age; **l'â. de (la) pierre** the Stone Age; **l'â. d'or du cinéma muet** the golden age of silent movies

âgé, -e [ɑʒe] *adj* (**a**) *(qui a tel âge)* **être â. de dix ans** to be ten years old; **un enfant â. de deux ans** a two-year-old child (**b**) *(vieux)* old; **être plus/moins â. que qn** to be older/younger than sb

agence [aʒɑ̃s] *nf* agency; *(de banque)* branch; **a. immobilière** *Br* estate agent's *or* agency, *Am* real estate agency; **a. d'intérim** temping agency; **a. matrimoniale** dating agency; **A. nationale pour l'emploi** = French national employment bureau, *Br* ≃ job centre; **a. de presse** press *or* news agency; **a. de recrutement** recruitment agency; **a. de voyages** travel agent's *or* agency

agencé, -e [aʒɑ̃se] *adj Suisse (cuisine)* fitted

agencement [aʒɑ̃smɑ̃] *nm (d'éléments)* arrangement; *(d'une maison, d'une pièce)* layout

agencer [16] [aʒɑ̃se] **1** *vt (éléments)* to arrange; *(maison, pièce)* to lay out, to design
  2 s'agencer *vpr* **les parties du discours s'agencent bien/mal** the different parts of the speech hang/don't hang together well

agenda [aʒɛ̃da] *nm* diary; **a. électronique** personal organizer

agenouiller [aʒnuje] **s'agenouiller** *vpr* to kneel (down) (**devant** in front of)

agent [aʒɑ̃] *nm* (**a**) *(employé, espion)* agent; **a. (de police)** police officer; **pardon, Monsieur l'a.** excuse me, officer; **a. d'assurance(s)** insurance broker; **a. de change** stockbroker; **a. de la circulation** traffic policeman; **a. double** double agent; *Belg* **a. du quartier** community policeman; **a. immobilier** *Br* estate agent, *Am* realtor; **a. secret** secret agent (**b**) *(facteur)* factor (**c**) *Gram* agent

agglomération [aglɔmerasjɔ̃] *nf (ville)* town, built-up area; **l'a. lyonnaise/parisienne** Lyons/Paris and its suburbs

aggloméré [aglɔmere] *nm* chipboard

agglomérer [34] [aglɔmere] **1** *vt* to bind together
  2 s'agglomérer *vpr* to bind together

agglutiner [aglytine] **s'agglutiner** *vpr (personnes)* to congregate, to gather

aggravant, -e [agravɑ̃, -ɑ̃t] *adj* aggravating

aggravation [agravasjɔ̃] *nf (d'une maladie)* aggravation; *(du temps, d'un conflit)* worsening

aggraver [agrave] **1** *vt (situation, état de santé)* to make worse; *(difficultés)* to increase; **pour a. les choses** to make matters worse
  2 s'aggraver *vpr (situation)* to get worse; *(état de santé)* to deteriorate; *(difficultés)* to increase

agile [aʒil] *adj* agile, nimble

agilement [aʒilmɑ̃] *adv* agilely, nimbly

agilité [aʒilite] *nf* agility

agios [aʒjo] *nmpl* bank charges

agir [aʒir] **1** *vi* (**a**) *(faire quelque chose)* to act; **bien/mal a. envers qn** to behave well/badly towards sb; **je n'aime pas sa façon** *ou* **manière d'a.** I don't like his/her behaviour (**b**) *(produire un effet) (médicament, substance)* to act (**sur** on); **a. sur le moral** to have a demoralizing effect (**c**) *Jur* **a. au nom de qn** to act on behalf of sb
  2 s'agir de *v impersonnel* (**a**) *(être question de)* **de quoi s'agit-il?** what's it about?; **l'affaire dont il s'agit** the matter in hand; **il ne s'agit pas d'argent** it's not a question of money; **quand il s'agit d'aider, il est toujours occupé!** when it comes to helping, he always seems to be busy! (**b**) *(falloir)* **s'agit de prendre une décision** we have to take a decision; **il s'agirait de savoir si...** the question is whether...; **il s'agirait de se dépêcher** we've got to hurry

agissements [aʒismɑ̃] *nmpl* dealings

agitateur, -trice [aʒitatœr, -tris] *nm,f Pol* agitator

agitation [aʒitasjɔ̃] *nf (inquiétude)* agitation; *(bougeotte)* restlessness; *(troubles)* unrest

agité, -e [aʒite] *adj (mer)* rough; *(patient, nuit)* restless; *(sommeil)* troubled; *(enfant)* fidgety; *(époque)* unsettled; *(vie)* hectic

agiter [aʒite] **1** *vt (mouchoir, drapeau, bras)* to wave; *(bouteille)* to shake; *(sujet: vent) (arbre, branches)* to sway; **a. la queue** *(chien)* to wag its tail; *(cheval)* to flick its tail (**b**) *(inquiéter)* to trouble; *(malade)* to excite
  2 s'agiter *vpr* (**a**) *(bouger)* to fidget; *(s'affairer)* to bustle around; **s'a. dans son sommeil** to toss and turn in one's sleep (**b**) *(s'énerver)* to get excited

agneau, -x [aɲo] *nm* lamb; **(peau d')a.** lambskin

agnelle [aɲɛl] *nf* ewe lamb

agnostique [agnɔstik] *adj & nmf* agnostic

agonie [agɔni] *nf aussi Fig* death throes; **être à l'a.** to be at death's door; *Fig (régime)* to be in its death throes

agonisant, -e [agɔnizɑ̃, -ɑ̃t] **1** *adj* dying
  2 *nm,f* dying person

agoniser [agɔnize] *vi* to be dying; *Fig (régime)* to be in its death throes

agoraphobie [agɔrafɔbi] *nf Méd* agoraphobia; **souffrir d'a.** to be agoraphobic

agrafe [agraf] *nf* (**a**) *(de bureau)* staple; *(de robe)* hook; *Méd* clip (**b**) *Constr* cramp (iron)

agrafer [agrafe] *vt* (**a**) *(avec une agrafeuse)* to staple; *(robe)* to fasten (**b**) *Fam (arrêter) Br* to nick, *Am* to bust; **se faire a.** to get *Br* nicked *or Am* busted

agrafeuse [agraføz] *nf* stapler

agraire [agrɛr] *adj (économie, société)* agrarian

agrandir [agrɑ̃dir] **1** *vt* (**a**) *(rendre plus grand)* to enlarge; *(maison, influence)* to extend; *(cercle de relations)* to widen (**b**) *(sujet: loupe, microscope)* to magnify; **ce papier peint agrandit la pièce** this wallpaper makes the room look bigger
  2 s'agrandir *vpr (ville)* to grow, to get bigger; *(nombre, influence)* to increase; *(entreprise)* to expand

agrandissement [agrɑ̃dismɑ̃] *nm (a) (d'une maison)* extension; *(d'une ville)* growth; *(d'une entreprise)* expansion (**b**) *(cliché)* enlargement

agréable [agreabl] *adj (personne, endroit, journée)* nice, pleasant; *(apparence)* pleasing; **a. au goût** tasty; **a. à regarder** nice to look at

agréablement [agreabləmɑ̃] *adv* pleasantly
agréer [24] [agree] *vt (fournisseur, équipement)* to approve; **veuillez a.** **l'expression de mes sentiments distingués** *(à une personne dont on connaît le nom)* yours sincerely; *(à une personne dont on ne connaît pas le nom)* yours faithfully
agrégation [agregasjɔ̃] *nf* **(le concours de) l'a.** = competitive examination for posts on the teaching staff of lycées and universities

Agrégation
This is a prestigious professional qualification for teachers in France. Those who pass the challenging competitive exam for the "agrég" become teachers in secondary education or universities and are entitled to higher pay and a less onerous timetable than those who have passed the "**CAPES**" *(see box at this entry)*.

agrégé, -e [agreʒe] **1** *adj* = who has passed the "agrégation" examination
 2 *nm,f* = graduate who has passed the "agrégation" examination
agrément [agremɑ̃] *nm* **(a)** *(plaisir)* **voyage d'a.** pleasure trip **(b)** *(charme)* **une ville sans a.** an unattractive town **(c)** *(accord)* approval, consent
agrémenter [agremɑ̃te] *vt* **a. qch de** *(décorer)* to adorn sth with; **texte agrémenté de citations** text laced with quotations
agrès [agrɛ] *nmpl* **(a)** *Sport* (gymnastics) apparatus; **faire des a.** to do apparatus work **(b)** *Naut* tackle
agresser [agrese] *vt* to attack, to assault; *(en paroles)* to attack; *(tympans)* to assault; *(yeux)* to hurt; *(peau)* to damage; **se faire a.** to be attacked *or (pour son argent)* to be mugged
agresseur [agresœr] *nm* attacker
agressif, -ive [agresif, -iv] *adj* aggressive
agression [agresjɔ̃] *nf (d'une personne)* attack, assault; *(pour son argent)* mugging; *(d'un pays)* act of aggression; **être victime d'une a.** to be attacked *or* assaulted; *(pour son argent)* to be mugged; **les agressions de la vie moderne** the stresses of modern life; **a. sexuelle** sexual assault
agressivement [agresivmɑ̃] *adv* aggressively
agressivité [agresivite] *nf* aggressiveness
agricole [agrikɔl] *adj* agricultural; *(population)* farming; *(produits)* farm
agriculteur, -trice [agrikyltœr, -tris] *nm,f* farmer
agriculture [agrikyltyr] *nf* farming, agriculture
agripper [agripe] **1** *vt* to clutch
 2 s'agripper *vpr* to cling on (**à** to)
agroalimentaire [agroalimɑ̃tɛr] **1** *adj (industrie, secteur)* food
 2 *nm* **l'a.** the food-processing industry
agronome [agrɔnɔm] *nmf* agronomist
agronomie [agrɔnɔmi] *nf* agronomy
agrotourisme [agroturism] *nm* agrotourism
agrume [agrym] *nm* citrus fruit
aguets [agɛ] *nmpl* **aux aguets** *adv* on the lookout; **être** *ou* **se tenir aux a.** to be on the lookout
aguichage [agiʃaʒ] *nm Com* teaser advertising
aguichant, -e [agiʃɑ̃, -ɑ̃t] *adj* seductive
aguiche [agiʃ] *nf Com* teaser (ad)
aguicher [agiʃe] *vt* to seduce
ahuri, -e [ayri] **1** *adj* astounded
 2 *nm,f* numbskull
ahurissant, -e [ayrisɑ̃, -ɑ̃t] *adj* astounding

aide [ɛd] **1** *nf* help, assistance; *Ordinat* help; **demander de l'a. à qn** to ask sb for help; **venir en a. à qn** to help sb; **appeler à l'a.** to call for help; **à l'a.!** help!; **à l'a. de qch** with the aid of sth; **a. de l'État** government aid; **a. humanitaire** (humanitarian) aid; **a. judiciaire** legal aid; *Ordinat* **a. en ligne** online help; **a. sociale** *Br* social security, *Am* welfare
 2 *nmf* assistant; **un a. de camp** an aide-de-camp; **une a. familiale** a home help; **une a. ménagère** a home help
aide-mémoire [ɛdmemwar] *nm inv* aide-mémoire
aider [ede] **1** *vt* to help; *(sujet: gouvernement)* to aid; **que puis-je faire pour vous a.?** how may I help you?; **je me suis fait a. par un ami** I got a friend to help me; **a. qn à faire qch** to help sb to do sth; **a. qn à monter/sortir** to help sb up/out; *Ironique* **tu veux que je t'aide?** stop that!; **elle n'aide jamais** she never helps (out)
 2 aider à *vt ind* to contribute towards; **a. à faire qch** to help to do sth
 3 s'aider *vpr* **(a)** *(soi-même)* **s'a. de qch** to use sth; **marcher en s'aidant d'une canne/de béquilles** to walk with the aid of a stick/crutches; *Prov* **aide-toi et le ciel t'aidera** God helps those who help themselves **(b)** *(l'un l'autre)* to help each other
aide-soignant, -e *(mpl* **aides-soignants,** *fpl* **aides-soignantes)** [ɛdswaɲɑ̃, -ɑ̃t] *nm,f* nursing auxiliary
aïe [aj] *exclam (cri de douleur)* ow!, ouch!; *Fig* **a., j'ai fait une gaffe!** oh no, I've put my foot in it!
AIEA [aiəa] *nf (abrév* **Agence internationale de l'énergie atomique)** IAEA
aïeul, -e [ajœl] *nm,f Vieilli* grandfather, *f* grandmother; **aïeuls** grandparents
aïeux [ajø] *nmpl Litt* ancestors
aigle [ɛgl] *nm* eagle; *Fig* **ce n'est pas un a.** he's no genius; **avoir un œil d'a.** to be eagle-eyed
aiglefin [ɛgləfɛ̃] *nm* haddock
aigre [ɛgr] *adj (goût, lait)* sour; *Fig (propos)* cutting; **d'un ton a.** sharply
aigre-doux, -douce *(mpl* **aigres-doux,** *fpl* **aigres-douces)** [ɛgrədu, -dus] *adj (sauce)* sweet-and-sour; *Fig (remarque)* snide
aigrelet, -ette [ɛgrəlɛ, -ɛt] *adj (vin, goût)* (rather) sour; *(son, voix)* shrill
aigrette [ɛgrɛt] *nf* **(a)** *(d'un oiseau)* crest **(b)** *(panache)* plume
aigreur [ɛgrœr] *nf* **(a)** *(d'un goût)* sourness; *(d'une remarque)* sharpness, bitterness **(b)** *Méd* **aigreurs (d'estomac)** heartburn
aigri, -e [ɛgri] *adj* embittered
aigu, -ë [ɛgy] *adj* **(a)** *(douleur)* acute, sharp; *(regard)* penetrating; *(esprit)* keen; **avoir un sens a. de qch** to have a keen sense of sth **(b)** *(instrument)* sharp; *(angle)* acute **(c)** *(son)* high-pitched **(d)** *Méd* acute
aigue-marine *(pl* **aigues-marines)** [ɛgmarin] *nf* aquamarine
aiguillage [egɥijaʒ] *nm* **(a)** *(manœuvre)* Br shunting, *Am* switching; *(appareil) Br* points, *Am* switches **(b)** *Fig* **faire une erreur d'a.** to take the wrong course
aiguille [egɥij] *nf* **(a)** *(instrument, objet pointu)* needle; *Fig* **chercher une a. dans une botte de foin** to look for a needle in a haystack; **a. à coudre/repriser/tricoter** sewing/darning/knitting needle; *Méd* **a. hypodermique** hypodermic needle; **a. de pin** pine needle **(b)** *(de boussole, de compteur de vitesse)* needle; *(de montre, d'horloge)* hand; **petite a.** hour hand;

grande a. minute hand (**c**) *(d'une église)* spire (**d**) *(sommet)* sharp peak

aiguiller [eguije] *vt (train) Br* to shunt, *Am* to switch; *Fig* **a. qn vers** *(profession)* to steer sb towards; **a. ses recherches vers** to direct one's investigations towards; **a. la police sur une fausse piste** to put the police off the scent; **il a été mal aiguillé dans ses études** he was badly advised about his studies

aiguilleur [eguijœr] *nm (de trains)* signalman; **a. du ciel** air-traffic controller

aiguillon [eguijɔ̃] *nm* (**a**) *(pique-bœuf)* goad; *Fig* spur (**b**) *(d'une guêpe)* sting

aiguiser [egize] *vt* (**a**) *(outil, couteau)* to sharpen (**b**) *Fig (curiosité, jalousie)* to arouse; *(appétit)* to whet

aïkido [ajkido] *nm* aikido; **faire de l'a.** to do aikido

ail [aj] *(pl* **ails** [aj], *Vieilli* **aulx** [o]) *nm* garlic; *Can* **a. des bois** wild garlic

aile [ɛl] *nf* (**a**) *(d'oiseau, de papillon)* wing; *Fig* **battre de l'a.** to be struggling; **la peur nous donnait des ailes** fear lent us wings; *Fam* **avoir un coup dans l'a.** to have had one too many, *Br* to be a bit the worse for wear (**b**) *(d'une voiture) Br* wing, *Am* fender; *(d'un bâtiment)* wing; *(d'une armée)* flank (**c**) *(d'un avion)* wing; *(d'un moulin)* sail; *(d'une hélice, d'une turbine)* blade (**d**) *(au football, au rugby)* wing

ailé, -e [ele] *adj* winged

aileron [ɛlrɔ̃] *nm* (**a**) *(d'oiseau)* pinion; *(de requin)* fin (**b**) *Aviat* aileron

ailette [ɛlɛt] *nf (d'une turbine, d'un ventilateur)* blade; *(d'une bombe, d'un missile)* wing, fin

ailier [elje] *nm (au football)* winger; *(au rugby, au basket)* wing

aille *etc voir* **aller**

ailler [aje] *vt* to put garlic in

ailleurs [ajœr] *adv* (**a**) *(à un autre endroit)* elsewhere, somewhere else; *Fig* **être a., avoir l'esprit a.** to be miles away; **partout a.** everywhere else; *(n'importe où)* anywhere else; **nulle part a.** nowhere else; **vous mangerez ici comme nulle part a.** you'll eat better here than anywhere else; *Fam* **va voir a. si j'y suis!** take a hike! (**b**) **d'a.** *(de plus)* besides, anyway; *(au fait)* by the way (**c**) **par a.** *(par d'autres côtés)* in other respects; *(d'autre part)* moreover

ailloli [ajɔli] = **aïoli**

aimable [ɛmabl] *adj (gentil)* kind, nice; **vous êtes bien a., c'est très a. de votre part** it's very kind of you; **peu a.** *(personne)* not very nice; *(propos)* unkind

aimablement [ɛmabləmɑ̃] *adv* kindly

aimant¹ [ɛmɑ̃] *nm* magnet

aimant², -e [ɛmɑ̃, -ɑ̃t] *adj (personne)* loving

aimanter [ɛmɑ̃te] *vt* to magnetize

aimer [eme] **1** *vt* (**a**) *(d'amour)* to love (**b**) *(apprécier, avoir de l'affection pour)* to like; **a. beaucoup qn/qch** to like sb/sth a lot, to be very fond of sb/sth; **a. bien qn/qch** to like sb/sth; **a. faire qch** to like doing sth; **j'aurais aimé le voir** I would like to have seen him; **je n'aime pas que tu fréquentes ces gens** I don't like you mixing with those people; **j'aime(rais) autant rester ici** I would rather stay here; **j'aime autant qu'il ne m'attende pas** I would rather he didn't wait for me; **a. mieux** to prefer; **ah, j'aime mieux ça!** now that's more like it!; **j'aime mieux lui en parler moi-même** I'd rather talk to him/her about it myself; *Fam* **j'aime mieux pas** I'd rather not; **je vais prendre un pot – qui m'aime me suive!** I'm going for a drink – anyone want to join me?

2 aimer à *vt ind Litt* **a. à faire qch** to take pleasure in doing sth; **j'aime à croire que...** I like to think (that)...

3 s'aimer *vpr* (**a**) *(l'un l'autre)* to love each other (**b**) *(être fier de soi)* to be in love with oneself; **je m'aime pas dans cette veste** I don't like myself in this jacket

aine [ɛn] *nf* groin

aîné, -e [ene] **1** *adj (de deux enfants)* elder; *(de plus de deux enfants)* eldest

2 *nm,f (de deux enfants)* elder (child); *(de plus de deux enfants)* eldest (child); **nos aînés** our elders; **il est mon a.** he is older than me; **il est mon a. de deux ans** he is two years older than me

aînesse [ɛnɛs] *nf voir* **droit³**

ainsi [ɛ̃si] *adv* (**a**) *(de cette façon)* like this, in this way; **c'est a. qu'il est devenu soldat** that's how he became a soldier; **et a. de suite** and so on, and so forth; **pour a. dire** so to speak, as it were; *Rel* **a. soit-il** amen (**b**) **a. (donc)** *(alors)* so; **a. vous ne venez pas?** so you're not coming? (**c**) *(par exemple)* for example, for instance (**d**) **a. que** *(et)* as well as, and

aïoli [ajɔli] *nm Culin* aïoli, garlic mayonnaise

air [ɛr] *nm* (**a**) *(gaz)* air; **cela manque d'a. ici** it's stuffy in here; **faire de l'a.** to let some air in; **sortir prendre l'a.** to go out for some fresh air; **laisser qch à l'a.** to leave sth uncovered; **au grand a.** in the fresh air; **en plein a., à l'a. libre** outside; **concert en plein a.** open-air concert; **activités de plein a.** outdoor pursuits; *Fam* **allez, de l'a.!** go on, clear off!; **a. comprimé** compressed air; **avoir l'a. conditionné** to have air-conditioning (**b**) *(ciel)* **l'a.** the air; **s'élever dans les airs** to rise into the air; **regarder en l'a.** to look up (**c**) *Fig (atmosphère)* **changer d'a.** to have a change of scene; **il y a de la dispute/de l'orage dans l'a.** there's an argument/a storm brewing (**d**) *(vent)* **il y a ou il fait de l'a.** there's a breeze (**e**) *(allure)* look; *(mine)* expression; **avoir un drôle d'a.** to look odd or funny; **avoir l'a. fatigué/de s'ennuyer** to look tired/bored; *Fam* **avoir l'a. fin** to look stupid; **tu as l'a. de ne pas comprendre** you look as if you don't understand; **n'avoir l'a. de rien** *(travail)* to look (deceptively) easy; **il n'a l'a. de rien, mais...** he doesn't look much, but...; **sans avoir l'a. de rien** inconspicuously; **prendre ou se donner des airs** to give oneself airs; **ne prends pas tes grands airs!** don't get on your high horse!; **a. de famille** family likeness; *Can* **avoir l'a. de qn** to look like sb (**f**) *(musique)* tune; **un a. d'opéra** an (operatic) aria (**g**) *(locutions) Fam* **ficher qch en l'a.** to mess sth up; **mettre qch en l'a.** *(en désordre)* to make an awful mess of sth; **c'est dans l'a. du temps** it's the in thing

air-air [ɛrɛr] *adj inv Mil* air-to-air

Airbag® [ɛrbag] *nm* (**a**) *Aut* Airbag® (**b**) *Fam* **airbags** *(seins)* tits, jugs

aire [ɛr] *nf* (**a**) *(surface plane)* area; **a. (de battage)** threshing floor; **a. d'atterrissage** *(pour avions)* landing strip; *(pour hélicoptères)* helipad; **a. de jeux** play area; **a. de lancement** *(de fusée)* launch pad; **a. de repos** *(sur l'autoroute)* rest area; **a. de stationnement** lay-by (**b**) *(d'un champ, d'un triangle, d'un bâtiment)* area; *Fig* **a. d'influence** sphere of influence (**c**) *(d'un aigle)* eyrie

airelle [ɛrɛl] *nf (rouge)* cranberry

air-sol [ɛrsɔl] *adj inv Mil* air-to-ground

aisance [ɛzɑ̃s] *nf* (**a**) *(facilité, grâce)* ease (**b**) *(financière)* **vivre dans l'a.** to live comfortably

aise [ɛz] **1** nf être à l'a. *(bien installé)* to be comfortable; *(avoir beaucoup de place)* to have plenty of room; *(financièrement)* to be comfortably off; *(dans une situation)* to feel comfortable or at ease; **on tient à l'a. à six dans cette voiture** this car holds six comfortably; *Fam* **à l'a.!** *(c'est facile)* no sweat!; **ne pas être à son a., se sentir mal à l'a.** to feel uncomfortable; **il me met mal à l'a.** he makes me feel uneasy or uncomfortable; **mettre qn à l'a.** to put sb at his/her ease; **se mettre à l'a.** to make oneself comfortable; *Ironique* **elle peut en parler à son a.!** it's easy (enough) for her to say that!; **à ton a.!** suit yourself!; **prendre ses aises** to make oneself at home **2** adj *Litt* **être bien** ou **tout a. de faire qch** to be delighted to do sth

aisé, -e [eze] adj (**a**) *(financièrement)* comfortably off (**b**) *(tâche, mouvements)* easy

aisément [ezemã] adv easily

aisselle [ɛsɛl] nf armpit

Aix-la-Chapelle [ɛkslaʃapɛl] n Aachen, Aix-la-Chapelle

AJ [aʒi] nf *(abrév* **auberge de jeunesse)** youth hostel

ajonc [aʒɔ̃] nm gorse

ajouré, -e [aʒure] adj *(pull)* loose-knit; *(broderie, en architecture)* openwork

ajourner [aʒurne] vt *(réunion, décision, voyage)* to postpone, to put off; *(après le début de la séance)* to adjourn; *Scol (candidat)* to refer

ajout [aʒu] nm addition (**à** to)

ajouter [aʒute] **1** vt to add (**à** to) **2 ajouter à** vt ind to add to **3 s'ajouter** vpr **s'a. à** to be added to; **à ceci viennent s'a. les frais de déplacement** on top of this there are travel expenses (to be added)

ajustable [aʒystabl] adj adjustable

ajustage [aʒystaʒ] nm fitting

ajuster [aʒyste] **1** vt (**a**) *(régler) (appareil, outil)* to adjust; *(chapeau, coiffure)* to adjust; **a. le tir** to aim (**b**) *(adapter)* to fit (**à** to); *(vêtement)* to alter; **veste ajustée** fitted jacket **2 s'ajuster** vpr (**a**) *(personne)* to straighten one's clothes (**b**) *(s'adapter)* **s'a. à** to fit; **s'a. sur** to fit onto

ajusteur [aʒystœr] nm fitter

alaise [alɛz] nf undersheet

alambic [alɑ̃bik] nm still

alambiqué, -e [alɑ̃bike] adj convoluted

alangui, -e [alɑ̃gi] adj languid

alarmant, -e [alarmã, -ãt] adj alarming; **son état est a.** his condition is giving serious cause for concern

alarme [alarm] nf alarm; **donner/sonner l'a.** to give/sound the alarm; **une fausse a.** a false alarm; **a. antivol** car alarm; **a. incendie** fire alarm

alarmer [alarme] **1** vt to alarm **2 s'alarmer** vpr to get alarmed; **il n'y a pas lieu de s'a.** there is no cause for alarm

albanais, -e [albanɛ, -ɛz] **1** adj Albanian **2** nm,f **A.** Albanian **3** nm *(langue)* Albanian

Albanie [albani] nf **l'A.** Albania

albâtre [albɑtr] nm alabaster

albatros [albatros] nm albatross

albinos [albinos] adj & nmf albino

album [albɔm] nm album; **a. de timbres/de photos** stamp/photo album

albumen [albymɛn] nm *Biol* albumen

albumine [albymin] nf *Chim* albumin

alcalin, -e [alkalɛ̃, -in] adj *Chim* alkaline

alchimie [alʃimi] nf alchemy

alchimiste [alʃimist] nm alchemist

alcolo [alkɔlo] *Fam* **1** nmf drunk, alky **2** adj **être a.** to be a drunk

alcool [alkɔl] nm (**a**) *Chim* alcohol; **a. à 90°** *Br* surgical spirit, *Am* rubbing alcohol; **a. à brûler** methylated spirits (**b**) *(digestif)* liqueur; **l'a.** *(boissons alcoolisées)* alcohol; **il ne tient pas l'a.** he can't hold his drink; **l'a. au volant** drink-driving; **a. de poire** pear brandy

alcoolémie [alkɔlemi] nf **taux d'a.** blood alcohol level

alcoolique [alkɔlik] **1** nmf alcoholic **2** adj alcoholic; **être a.** to be an alcoholic

alcoolisé, -e [alkɔlize] adj alcoholic

alcoolisme [alkɔlism] nm alcoholism

alcopop [alkopɔp] nm alcopop

Alcotest® [alkɔtɛst] nm breath test; **faire passer un A. à qn** to breathalyze sb

alcôve [alkov] nf recess *(for bed)*

aléa [alea] nm hazard

aléatoire [aleatwar] adj random; *(résultat)* uncertain

alémanique [alemanik] adj **la Suisse a.** German-speaking Switzerland

ALENA [alena] nm *(abrév* **Accord de libre-échange nord-américain)** **l'A.** NAFTA

alentour [alɑ̃tur] **1** adv around, round about; **les villages a.** the surrounding villages **2 alentours** nmpl *(voisinage)* surroundings; **aux alentours** in the vicinity; **aux alentours de la ville/300 euros** in the vicinity of the town/300 euros; **aux alentours de midi** (some time) around midday

Aléoutiennes [aleusjɛn] adj & nfpl **les (îles) A.** the Aleutian Islands

alerte [alɛrt] **1** nf (**a**) *(avertissement)* alarm; **donner/sonner l'a.** to give/sound the alarm; **a. à la bombe** bomb scare (**b**) *(menace)* threat; *(problème de santé)* scare; **à la première a.** at the first sign of danger; **fausse a.** false alarm **2** adj *(personne) (physiquement)* sprightly; *(mentalement)* alert; *(esprit, style)* lively; **d'un pas a.** at a brisk pace **3** exclam look out!

alerter [alɛrte] vt to alert *(sur* to)

alèse [alɛz] = **alaise**

alevin [alvɛ̃] nm young fish

Alexandre [alɛksɑ̃dr] npr **A. le Grand** Alexander the Great

Alexandrie [alɛksɑ̃dri] n Alexandria

alexandrin [alɛksɑ̃drɛ̃] nm alexandrine

alezan, -e [alzã, -an] **1** adj *(cheval)* chestnut **2** nm chestnut (horse)

algèbre [alʒɛbr] nf algebra

algébrique [alʒebrik] adj algebraic

Alger [alʒe] n Algiers

Algérie [alʒeri] nf **l'A.** Algeria

algérien, -enne [alʒerjɛ̃, -ɛn] **1** adj Algerian **2** nm,f **A.** Algerian

algérois, -e [alʒerwa, -az] **1** adj of Algiers **2** nm,f **A.** person from Algiers

algorithme [algɔritm] nm *Math & Ordinat* algorithm

algothérapie [algoterapi] nf = alternative medicine based on marine plant extracts

algue [alg] nf piece of seaweed; **algues** seaweed

alias [aljas] adv alias

alibi [alibi] nm alibi

aliénation [aljenasjɔ̃] *nf* (**a**) *(de l'esprit)* alienation; *Psy* **a. mentale** insanity (**b**) *(de liberté)* loss; *Jur (des droits, de biens)* alienation

aliéné, -e [aljene] **1** *adj* insane
2 *nm,f* insane person

aliéner [34] [aljene] **1** *vt* (**a**) *(personne)* to alienate; **ce commentaire vous a aliéné la sympathie de l'auditoire** you lost the audience's sympathy when you made that comment (**b**) *Jur (biens, droits)* to alienate
2 s'aliéner *vpr* **s'a. la sympathie de l'électorat** to lose the goodwill of the electorate; **s'a. un ami** to alienate a friend

alignement [aliɲəmɑ̃] *nm* (**a**) *(opération)* alignment, aligning; *Pol (sur un pays, une politique)* alignment (**sur** with) (**b**) *(ligne)* line; **être dans l'a. de qch** to be in line with sth (**c**) *(de monolithes)* = line of standing stones

aligner [aliɲe] **1** *vt* (**a**) *(mettre en ligne)* to align, to line up; *(politique, monnaie)* to align (**sur** with) (**b**) *(mettre à la suite) (arguments)* to reel off; **je passe ma journée à a. des chiffres** I spend my day producing lists of figures
2 s'aligner *vpr (se mettre en rang)* to line up; *Pol (sur un pays, une politique)* to align oneself (**sur** with); *Fam* **tu peux toujours t'a.!** not a chance!

aliment [alimɑ̃] *nm* (**a**) *(nourriture)* food (**b**) *Jur* **aliments** alimony

alimentaire [alimɑ̃tɛr] *adj* (**a**) *(plante)* edible; **habitudes alimentaires** eating habits; **l'industrie a.** the food industry (**b**) *Fig* **ce n'est qu'un travail a.** I just do this job to keep body and soul together

alimentation [alimɑ̃tasjɔ̃] *nf* (**a**) *(régime alimentaire)* diet; **avoir une a. équilibrée** to have a balanced diet; **(magasin d')a.** grocer's; **(rayon) a.** grocery department (**b**) *(action) (de personne, de plante, d'animal)* feeding; *(d'une ville, d'un marché)* supply; **l'a. d'une ville en eau** the water supply to a town (**c**) *Tech (d'une chaudière)* feeding; *(en électricité)* power supply; **a. papier** *(d'une imprimante)* sheetfeed, paper feed

alimenter [alimɑ̃te] **1** *vt (personne, plante, animal, chaudière)* to feed; *(cours d'eau)* to flow into; *Fin (compte)* to pay money into; *Fig (conversation)* to keep going; *(sentiment)* to fuel; **a. une usine en courant** to supply a factory with power
2 s'alimenter *vpr* to eat

alinéa [alinea] *nm* (**a**) *(renfoncement)* indent (**b**) *(texte)* paragraph

aliter [alite] **s'aliter** *vpr* to take to one's bed; **être alité** *(temporairement)* to be confined to one's bed; *(en permanence)* to be bedridden

alizé [alize] *adj & nm* **les (vents) alizés** the trade winds

Allah [ala] *npr* Allah

allaitement [alɛtmɑ̃] *nm* feeding; *(d'un animal)* suckling; **a. au biberon** bottle-feeding; **a. maternel** breast-feeding

allaiter [alete] *vt (enfant)* to breast-feed; *(sujet: animal)* to suckle; **est-ce que vous allaitez?** are you breast-feeding?

allant [alɑ̃] *nm* **avoir de l'a., être plein d'a.** to be full of energy

alléchant, -e [aleʃɑ̃, -ɑ̃t] *adj (offre)* tempting; *(odeur, plat)* appetizing

allécher [34] [aleʃe] *vt* to tempt

allée [ale] *nf* (**a**) *(dans un jardin)* path; *(devant une résidence)* driveway; *(dans une ville)* avenue; *(dans un* supermarché, un cinéma) aisle (**b**) **allées et venues** coming(s) and going(s); **faire des allées et venues** to go back and forth

allégation [alegasjɔ̃] *nf* allegation

allégé, -e [aleʒe] *adj (en matières grasses)* low-fat; *(en sucre)* low-sugar

allègement [alɛʒmɑ̃] *nm* (**a**) *(d'impôts, de charges)* reduction; *(des emplois du temps scolaires)* streamlining; **a. fiscal** tax relief (**b**) *(d'un véhicule, d'un fardeau)* lightening

alléger [59] [aleʒe] *vt* (**a**) *(impôts, charges)* to reduce; *(douleur, chagrin)* to soothe (**b**) *(véhicule, fardeau)* to lighten; *(emploi du temps scolaire)* to streamline

allégorie [alegɔri] *nf* allegory

allégorique [alegɔrik] *adj* allegorical

allègre [alɛgr] *adj* lively, cheerful; **d'un ton a.** cheerfully, light-heartedly; **d'un pas a.** with a spring in one's step

allègrement [alɛgrəmɑ̃] *adv* cheerfully; *(marcher)* with a spring in one's step; **il m'a a. refilé ses enfants pour le week-end** he blithely palmed his children off on me for the weekend

allégresse [alegrɛs] *nf* joy; **a. générale** general rejoicing

alléluia [aleluja] *nm & exclam Rel* hallelujah

Allemagne [alman] *nf* **l'A.** Germany; *Anciennement* **l'A. de l'Ouest/de l'Est** West/East Germany

allemand, -e [almɑ̃, -ɑ̃d] **1** *adj* German
2 *nm,f* **A.** German
3 *nm (langue)* German

aller¹ [8] [ale] *(aux être)* **1** *vi* (**a**) *(se déplacer)* to go; **a. à Toulon** to go to Toulon; **ce train va à Lille** this train goes to Lille; **a. à la pêche** to go fishing; **a. et venir** to come and go
(**b**) *(sujet: chemin, route)* **a. à** to go to
(**c**) *(arriver)* **a. jusqu'à** *(dans l'espace)* to go as far as; *(dans le temps)* to last until; **jusqu'où ira-t-il?** *(pour atteindre son but)* to what lengths will he go?; **a. jusqu'à faire qch** to go so far as to do sth
(**d**) *(fonctionner)* to go; *(bien fonctionner)* to go well; **si tu touches à mes affaires, ça va. mal!** touch my things and there'll be trouble!; **ça va (comme ça), merci** *(à table)* that's enough, thanks; **je vous en offre 100 euros, ça va?** I'll give you 100 euros for it, OK?; *Fam* **non mais ça va pas(, la tête)!** are you crazy?
(**e**) *(se porter)* **a. bien/mal** to be well/ill; **comment allez-vous?** how are you?; **ça va? – ça va!** how's things? – OK!
(**f**) *(indique le but)* **a. faire qch** to go and do sth; **a. se coucher** to go to bed; **a. se promener** to go for a walk; **va voir!** go and see!; **n'allez pas vous imaginer que...** don't you go thinking that...; **cet imbécile est allé tout lui raconter** that fool went and told him/her everything
(**g**) *(convenir)* **a. à qn** to suit sb; **a. bien à qn** *(vêtement, couleur)* to look good on sb; **a. (bien) avec qch** *(vêtement, couleur)* to go (well) with sth, to match sth; *Fam* **ça lui va mal de donner des conseils** he's a fine one to be giving advice
(**h**) *(se ranger, s'adapter)* **où vont les couteaux?** where do the knives go or belong?; **un plat qui va au four** an ovenproof dish
(**i**) *(agir)* **il est allé un peu vite dans cette affaire** he was a bit hasty; *Fam* **vas-y doucement** take it easy; *Fam* **comme tu y vas!** that's a bit much!
(**j**) *(locutions)* **y a.** *(partir)* to go; *(commencer)* to

get on with it; **allez!** *(pour encourager)* come on!; *(pour consoler)* come now!; **allons!** *(pour encourager, réprimander)* come on!; **ça passera, va** don't worry, you'll get over it; **va pour 1000 euros/mardi prochain** 1,000 euros/nextTuesday, that's fine; **a. de soi** to be obvious; **a. sur ses quarante ans** to be nearing forty

2 *v aux* (**a**) *(indique le futur proche)* **a. faire qch** to be going to do sth; **il va s'en occuper** he's going to deal with it; **j'allais m'endormir quand...** I was about to fall asleep when...

(**b**) *(indique la progression)* **a. en empirant** to be getting worse and worse

3 *v impersonnel* **il en va de même pour moi/lui** it's the same for me/him

4 s'en aller *vpr* (**a**) *(personne)* to go (away)

(**b**) *(tache)* to come out; *(couleur)* to fade; *(peinture)* to flake off

aller² *nm* (**a**) *(trajet)* outward journey; **à l'a.** on the way there (**b**) *(billet)* **a. (simple)** *Br* single (ticket), *Am* one-way ticket; **a. (et) retour** *Br* return *or Am* round-trip (ticket); *Fam Fig* **un a. et retour** *(gifle)* a slap in the face

allergie [alɛrʒi] *nf* allergy; **avoir** *ou* **faire une a. à qch** to be allergic to sth

allergique [alɛrʒik] *adj aussi Fig* allergic (**à** to)

allergologiste [alɛrgɔlɔʒist], **allergologue** [alɛrgɔlɔg] *nmf Méd* allergist

alliage [aljaʒ] *nm (métallique)* alloy

alliance [aljɑ̃s] *nf* (**a**) *(entente)* alliance; *(d'un couple)* marriage; **parent par a.** relative by marriage (**b**) *(bague)* wedding ring (**c**) *(combinaison)* *(de parfums, de couleurs)* combination (**d**) **l'A. française** = organization promoting French language and culture abroad

Alliance française

In many respects, the activities of the "Alliance française" are similar to those of the British Council, although it is a private body. It organizes classes in French language and civilization and has branches all over the world.

allié, -e [alje] **1** *adj* (**a**) *(nation)* allied (**b**) *Hist* Allied **2** *nm,f (partisan)* ally; **parents et alliés** extended family; *Hist* **les Alliés** the Allies

allier [66] [alje] **1** *vt* (**a**) *(pays)* to ally; *(familles)* to unite by marriage (**b**) *(métaux)* to alloy; *(couleurs)* to combine; **a. l'intelligence à la beauté** to combine intelligence and beauty

2 s'allier *vpr* (**a**) *(s'unir)* to become allies (**avec** with); **s'a. contre qn/qch** to unite against sb/sth (**b**) *(goûts, parfums, couleurs)* to combine

alligator [aligatɔr] *nm* alligator

allitération [aliterasjɔ̃] *nf* alliteration; **a. en s** alliteration of the letter s

allô, allo [alo] *exclam* hello!

allocation [alɔkasjɔ̃] *nf* (**a**) *(d'argent, de terres)* allocation; *(de titres financiers)* allotment (**b**) *(prestation financière)* allowance; **les allocations (familiales)** child benefit; **a. (de) chômage** unemployment benefit; **a. (de) logement** housing benefit

allocs [alɔk] *nfpl Fam Br* child benefit, *Am* welfare

allocution [alɔkysjɔ̃] *nf* address

allongé, -e [alɔ̃ʒe] *adj* (**a**) *(forme, silhouette)* elongated; **avoir le visage a.** to have a long face (**b**) *(couché)* **être a.** to be lying down

allongement [alɔ̃ʒmɑ̃] *nm* (**a**) *(agrandissement)* lengthening (**b**) *(dans le temps)* extension; **a. de l'espérance de vie** increase in life expectancy

allonger [45] [alɔ̃ʒe] **1** *vt* (**a**) *(rendre plus long)* to lengthen; *(vêtement)* to let down; *(sauce)* to thin (down); **cette robe t'allonge la silhouette** this dress makes you look taller (**b**) *(bras)* to stretch out; *(cou)* to crane; **a. le pas** to quicken one's pace; *Sport* **a. l'allure** to increase the pace (**c**) *(personne)* to lie down (**d**) *(vacances, délai)* to extend (**e**) *Fam* **a. une gifle à qn** to give sb a slap; **a. le fric/1000 euros** to hand over the money/1,000 euros

2 *vi (jours)* to get longer

3 s'allonger *vpr* (**a**) *(ombres, jours)* to get longer; *Fig (enfant)* to grow (**b**) *(se coucher)* to lie down; *Fam* **s'a. (par terre)** *(tomber)* to fall flat on the ground

allopathie [alɔpati] *nf Méd* allopathy

allouer [alwe] *vt* **a. qch à qn** *(salaire, indemnité, délai)* to grant sb sth; *(actions, ration)* to allocate sb sth

allumage [alymaʒ] *nm (d'un feu)* lighting; *(d'une lampe)* switching on; *(d'un moteur)* ignition

allume-cigare *(pl* **allume-cigares)** [alymsigar] *nm* cigar lighter

allume-gaz [alymgaz] *nm inv* gas lighter

allumer [alyme] **1** *vt* (**a**) *(cigarette, briquet, feu)* to light; *(lampe, télévision, électricité)* to switch on, to turn on; *(incendie)* to start; **a. (la lumière)** to switch *or* turn the light on; **a. le salon** to switch *or* turn the light on in the lounge; **laisser la cuisinière allumée** to leave the cooker on (**b**) *Fig (passions)* to arouse; *Fam (séduire)* to tease

2 s'allumer *vpr (lumière, lampe, téléviseur)* to come on; **où est-ce que ça s'allume?** where does it switch *or* turn on?

allumette [alymɛt] *nf* match

allumeuse [alymøz] *nf Fam* tease

allure [alyr] *nf* (**a**) *(vitesse)* speed; **à toute a.** at top speed (**b**) *(démarche)* walk, gait; *(manière de se tenir)* bearing; **avoir de l'a.** to be stylish; **avoir fière a.** to cut a fine figure; **avoir une drôle d'a.** to look funny; **avoir des allures de malfrat** to look like a crook; *Belg* **n'avoir pas d'a.** to be unsophisticated (**c**) *Can* **avoir d'a.** *(être vraisemblable)* to be likely

allusion [alyzjɔ̃] *nf* allusion (**à** to); **faire a. à** to refer to, to allude to

alluvial, -e, -aux, -ales [alyvjal, -o] *adj* alluvial

alluvions [alyvjɔ̃] *nfpl* alluvium

almanach [almana] *nm* almanac

aloès [alɔɛs] *nm* aloe

aloi [alwa] *nm* **de bon a.** *(succès)* deserved; *(plaisanterie)* in good taste; **de mauvais a.** *(succès)* undeserved; *(plaisanterie)* in bad taste

alors [alɔr] *adv* (**a**) *(à ce moment-là)* then; *(dans ce cas)* then, in that case; **jusqu'a.** (up) until then; **le ministre d'a.** the minister at the time; **et a.?** so what?; **et a., qu'est-ce qu'il a répondu?** so what did he say?; *Fam* **a., tu viens?** are you coming?; *Fam* **non mais a., pour qui il se prend, celui-là?** really, just who does he think he is?; *Fam* **ça a.!** *Br* blimey!, *Am* jeez!; **a. là, il exagère!** he's going a bit far there! (**b**) *(donc)* so; **il n'était pas là, a. je suis revenu** he wasn't there, so I came back (**c**) **a. que** *(au moment où)* when; *(bien que)* even though; **il a une maison, a. que moi j'habite dans un appartement** he's got a house, whereas I live in a flat

alouette [alwɛt] *nf* lark

alourdir [alurdir] **1** *vt (chose)* to make heavier; *Fig (phrase)* to make cumbersome; *(charges sociales)* to increase
  2 s'alourdir *vpr* to get heavy; *(taille)* to get bigger
aloyau, -x [alwajo] *nm* sirloin
alpaga [alpaga] *nm* alpaca
alpage [alpaʒ] *nm* mountain pasture
alpaguer [alpage] *vt très Fam* to collar; **se faire a. par qn** to get collared by sb
Alpes [alp] *nfpl* **les A.** the Alps; **les A. suisses** the Swiss Alps
alphabet [alfabɛ] *nm* alphabet
alphabétique [alfabetik] *adj* alphabetical
alphabétiquement [alfabetikmã] *adv* alphabetically
alphabétisation [alfabetizasjɔ̃] *nf* teaching of literacy
alphanumérique [alfanymerik] *adj* alphanumeric
alphapage [alfapaʒ] *nm* bleeper
alpin, -e [alpɛ̃, -in] *adj* alpine
alpinisme [alpinism] *nm* mountaineering, climbing; **faire de l'a.** to go mountaineering *or* climbing
alpiniste [alpinist] *nmf* mountaineer, climber
Alsace [alzas] *nf* **l'A.** Alsace
alsacien, -enne [alzasjɛ̃, -ɛn] **1** *adj* of Alsace, Alsatian
  2 *nm,f* **A.** Alsatian
altercation [altɛrkasjɔ̃] *nf* altercation
alter ego [altɛrego] *nm inv* alter ego
altérer [34] [altere] **1** *vt* (**a**) *(détériorer) (viande, vin)* to spoil; *(santé)* to damage (**b**) *(changer)* to affect
  2 s'altérer *vpr (denrée)* to spoil, to go off; *(sentiment, amitié)* to deteriorate
altermondialisme [altɛrmɔ̃djalism] *nm* alterglobalism, ethical globalization movement
altermondialiste [altɛrmɔ̃djalist] *adj & nmf* alterglobalist
alternance [altɛrnɑ̃s] *nf* alternation; *Pol* change of government; **en a.** alternately
alternateur [altɛrnatœr] *nm Élec* alternator
alternatif, -ive [altɛrnatif, -iv] **1** *adj* (**a**) *(successif) & Élec* alternating (**b**) *(de remplacement)* alternative
  2 *nf* **alternative** alternative
alternativement [altɛrnativmã] *adv* alternately, in turn
alterner [altɛrne] **1** *vt (cultures)* to rotate
  2 *vi (se succéder)* to alternate (**avec** with); *(personnes)* to take turns (**avec** with)
altesse [altɛs] *nf* **son A. royale** His/Her Royal Highness
altier, -ère [altje, -ɛr] *adj* haughty
altimètre [altimɛtr] *nm* altimeter
altitude [altityd] *nf* altitude; **à basse/haute a.** at low/high altitude; **à 100 mètres d'a.** at an altitude of 100 metres; **en a.** at altitude; **prendre de l'a.** to climb
alto [alto] *Mus* **1** *nm (instrument)* viola
  2 *nf (chanteuse)* alto
altruisme [altrɥism] *nm* altruism
altruiste [altrɥist] *adj* altruistic
aluminium [alyminjɔm] *nm* aluminium
alunir [alynir] *vi* to land on the moon
alunissage [alynisaʒ] *nm* moon landing
alvéole [alveɔl] *nf (de ruche)* cell; *(pulmonaire)* alveolus; *(de dent)* socket
amabilité [amabilite] *nf* kindness; **auriez-vous l'a. de me le faire savoir?** would you be so kind as to let me know?

amadouer [amadwe] *vt* to coax
amaigrir [amɛgrir] **1** *vt* to make thin; **la maladie l'a beaucoup amaigri** he's much thinner following his illness
  2 s'amaigrir *vpr* to get thinner
amaigrissant, -e [amɛgrisã, -ãt] *adj (régime)* slimming
amaigrissement [amɛgrismã] *nm (involontaire)* weight loss; *(volontaire)* slimming
amalgame [amalgam] *nm* combination
amalgamer [amalgame] *vt (confondre)* to lump together
amanché, -e [amãʃe] *adj Can* **mal a.** badly dressed
amande [amãd] *nf (fruit)* almond; *(dans un noyau)* kernel; **des yeux en a.** almond(-shaped) eyes
amandier [amãdje] *nm* almond tree
amanite [amanit] *nf* **a. phalloïde** death cap; **a. tue-mouches** fly agaric
amant [amã] *nm* lover
amarrage [amaraʒ] *nm Naut* mooring
amarre [amar] *nf Naut* (mooring) rope; **rompre ses amarres** to break its moorings
amarrer [amare] *vt Naut* to moor
amaryllis [amarilis] *nf* amaryllis
amas [ama] *nm* heap, pile
amasser [amase] **1** *vt* to amass
  2 s'amasser *vpr (preuves, foule)* to build up; *(neige)* to pile up; *(troupes)* to mass
amateur [amatœr] **1** *nm* (**a**) *(passionné)* **a. de tennis/de jardinage** tennis/gardening enthusiast; **a. d'art** art lover; **a. de bons vins** connoisseur of fine wines; *Fig* **est-ce qu'il y a des amateurs?** any takers?; **avis aux amateurs!** anyone interested? (**b**) *(non professionnel)* amateur; **faire de la photo en a.** to be an amateur photographer; *Péj* **c'est du travail d'a.** it's amateurish work
  2 *adj* amateur; **photographe a.** amateur photographer
amateurisme [amatœrism] *nm* amateurism
Amazone [amazon] *nf* **l'A.** the Amazon
amazone [amazon] *nf* (**a**) *(dans la mythologie)* **les Amazones** the Amazons (**b**) *(cavalière)* horsewoman; **monter en a.** to ride side-saddle
Amazonie [amazɔni] *nf* **l'A.** the Amazon (Basin)
amazonien, -enne [amazɔnjɛ̃, -ɛn] *adj* Amazonian; *(forêt)* Amazon
ambages [ãbaʒ] **sans ambages** *adv* without beating about the bush
ambassade [ãbasad] *nf* embassy; **l'a. de France au Japon** the French embassy in Japan
ambassadeur, -drice [ãbasadœr, -dris] **1** *nm,f* ambassador; **l'a. de France au Japon** the French ambassador to Japan; *Fig* **être l'a. de son pays** to be an ambassador for one's country
  2 *nf* **ambassadrice** *(épouse)* ambassador's wife
ambiance [ãbjãs] *nf* atmosphere, ambience; *Fam* **mettre de l'a.** to liven things up; *Fam* **il y a de l'a. ici** there's a good atmosphere here
ambiant, -e [ãbjã, -ãt] *adj (gaieté, enthousiasme)* pervading; **température ambiante** room temperature
ambidextre [ãbidɛkstr] *adj* ambidextrous
ambigu, -ë [ãbigy] *adj* ambiguous
ambiguïté [ãbigɥite] *nf* ambiguity; **répondre sans a.** to give an unambiguous answer
ambitieux, -euse [ãbisjø, -øz] **1** *adj* ambitious
  2 *nm,f* ambitious person

ambition [ãbisjɔ̃] *nf* ambition; **avoir de l'a.** to be ambitious; **j'ai l'a. de devenir médecin** my ambition is to be a doctor

ambitionner [ãbisjɔne] **1** *vt (poste)* to aspire to; **il ambitionne de gagner le Tour de France** his ambition is to win the Tour de France
2 *vi Can (exagérer)* to overdo it

ambivalent, -e [ãbivalã, -ãt] *adj* ambivalent

ambre [ãbr] *nm (résine)* amber

ambulance [ãbylãs] *nf* ambulance

ambulancier, -ère [ãbylãsje, -ɛr] *nm,f* ambulanceman, *f* ambulancewoman

ambulant, -e [ãbylã, -ãt] *adj* itinerant, travelling; *Fam* **c'est un dictionnaire a.** he's a walking dictionary

AME [aɛmə] *nm (abrév accord monétaire européen)* EMA

âme [ɑm] *nf* (**a**) *Rel & Phil* soul; *Fig (animateur)* moving spirit; **être artiste dans l'â.** to have an artistic temperament; **rendre l'â.** to give up the ghost; **aller comme une â.** en peine to wander around like a lost soul; **trouver l'â. sœur** to find one's soulmate; **de toute mon â.** with all my heart; **en mon â. et conscience** to the best of my knowledge and belief (**b**) *(personne)* **une bonne â.** a kind soul; **ils ne rencontrèrent â. qui vive** they didn't meet a (living) soul; **un hameau de cinquante âmes** a hamlet of fifty inhabitants; **â. damnée** devoted servant; *Hum* partner in crime (**c**) *(d'un câble)* core

amélioration [ameljɔrasjɔ̃] *nf* improvement; **apporter des améliorations à qch** to make improvements to sth

améliorer [ameljɔre] **1** *vt* to improve
2 s'améliorer *vpr* to improve; **ça ne s'améliore pas** it's not getting any better

amen [amɛn] *nm inv* amen; *Fig* **dire a. à qch** to go along with sth

aménagement [amenaʒmã] *nm (changement)* adjustment; *(d'une pièce)* conversion (**en** into); *(d'une ville, d'une région)* development; **a. du temps de travail** flexibility of working hours; **a. du territoire** regional development, physical planning

aménager [45] [amenaʒe] *vt (changer)* to adjust; *(pièce, maison)* to convert (**en** into)

amende [amãd] *nf* (**a**) *(contravention)* fine; **avoir 200 euros d'a.** to get a 200-euro fine (**b**) **faire a. honorable** to apologize

amendement [amãdmã] *nm Pol* amendment

amender [amãde] **1** *vt* (**a**) *(loi, texte)* to amend (**b**) *Suisse (mettre une amende à)* to fine
2 s'amender *vpr* to turn over a new leaf

amener [46] [amne] **1** *vt* (**a**) *(apporter)* to bring; **a. l'eau à ébullition** to bring the water to the boil; **a. qn à faire qch** to get sb to do sth; *(sujet: circonstances)* to lead sb to do sth; **...ce qui nous amène à parler du chômage** ...which brings us to the issue of unemployment (**b**) *(occasionner)* to bring about (**c**) *(tirer à soi)* to pull in; *(voile)* to lower
2 s'amener *vpr Fam (arriver)* to turn up; **amène-toi!** come here!

amenuiser [amənɥize] **1** *vt* to wear down
2 s'amenuiser *vpr* to dwindle; *(écart)* to get smaller

amer, -ère [amɛr] *adj* bitter

amèrement [amɛrmã] *adv* bitterly

américain, -e [amerikɛ̃, -ɛn] **1** *adj* American
2 *nm,f* **A.** American
3 *nm (langue)* American (English)
4 *nf* **américaine** *Culin* **homard à l'américaine** = lobster cooked in a tomato, white wine and brandy sauce

américaniser [amerikanize] **1** *vt* to Americanize
2 s'américaniser *vpr* to become Americanized

américanisme [amerikanism] *nm Ling* Americanism

amérindien, -enne [amerɛ̃djɛ̃, -ɛn] **1** *adj* Amerindian, American Indian
2 *nm,f* **A.** Amerindian, American Indian

Amérique [amerik] *nf* **l'A.** America; **l'A. centrale** Central America; **l'A. latine** Latin America; **l'A. du Nord/ du Sud** North/South America

Amerloque [amɛrlɔk] *nmf Fam (Américain)* Yank

amerrir [amerir] *vi* to make a landing at sea; *(vaisseau spatial)* to splash down

amerrissage [amerisaʒ] *nm* landing at sea; *(d'un vaisseau spatial)* splashdown

amertume [amɛrtym] *nf* bitterness

améthyste [ametist] *nf* amethyst

ameublement [amœbləmã] *nm* (**a**) *(action de meubler)* furnishing (**b**) *(meubles)* furniture; **magasin d'a.** furniture shop

ameuter [amøte] *vt (gens)* to bring out; **elle va a. tout le voisinage si elle continue à hurler comme ça!** she'll have the whole neighbourhood out if she carries on shouting like that!

ami, -e [ami] **1** *nm,f* friend; **(petit) a.** *(amant)* boyfriend; **(petite) amie** *(maîtresse)* girlfriend; **a. d'enfance** childhood friend; **a. intime** close friend; **les amis des bêtes** animal lovers
2 *adj* friendly; **être a. avec qn** to be friends with sb

amiable [amjabl] *Jur* **1** *adj* amicable
2 à l'amiable *adv* out of court

amiante [amjãt] *nm* asbestos

amical, -e, -aux, -ales [amikal, -o] **1** *adj* friendly; **peu a.** unfriendly
2 *nf* **amicale** association

amicalement [amikalmã] *adv* in a friendly way

amidon [amidɔ̃] *nm* starch

amidonner [amidɔne] *vt* to starch

amieuter [amjøte] **s'amieuter** *vpr Can* to improve, to get better

amincir [amɛ̃sir] **1** *vt* to make thinner; **cette robe t'amincit** that dress makes you look thinner
2 s'amincir *vpr* to get thinner

amincissant, -e [amɛ̃sisã, -ãt] *adj (produit, crème)* slimming

amincissement [amɛ̃sismã] *nm (d'une personne)* slimming

aminé, -e [amine] *adj Chim* **acide a.** amino acid

amiral, -aux [amiral, -o] *nm* admiral

amitié [amitje] *nf* (**a**) *(sentiment)* friendship; **avoir de l'a. pour qn** to be fond of sb; **se lier d'a. avec qn** to make friends with sb; **prendre qn en a.** to befriend sb (**b**) *(dans les formules de politesse)* **faites-moi l'a. de lui dire** would you be so kind as to tell him/her?; **mes amitiés à votre sœur** my best wishes to your sister; **amitiés, Luc** *(en fin de lettre)* regards *or* yours, Luc

amitieux, -euse [amitjø, -øz] *adj Belg* friendly

ammoniaque [amɔnjak] *nf* ammonia

amnésie [amnezi] *nf* amnesia; **souffrir d'a.** to have amnesia

amnésique [amnezik] **1** *adj* amnesic; **être a.** to have amnesia
2 *nmf* amnesiac

amniocentèse [amnjosɛ̃tɛz] *nf Méd* amniocentesis

amniotique [amnjɔtik] *adj* amniotic

amnistie [amnisti] *nf* amnesty; **l'a. des contraventions** = traditional waiving of parking fines by the president following his/her election

Amnistie

Parking fines as well as some prison sentences are traditionally waived by the French president immediately after a presidential election. The latter is known as "la grâce présidentielle".

amnistier [66] [amnistje] *vt* to grant an amnesty to
amocher [amɔʃe] *Fam* **1** *vt (personne)* to beat up; *(objet)* to ruin; **se faire (sérieusement) a.** to get (badly) beaten up
  2 s'amocher *vpr* to smash oneself up
amoindrir [amwɛ̃drir] **1** *vt* to diminish
  2 s'amoindrir *vpr* to diminish
amollir [amɔlir] **1** *vt* to soften
  2 s'amollir *vpr* to soften
amonceler [11] [amɔ̃sle] **1** *vt* to pile up; *(preuves)* to accumulate
  2 s'amonceler *vpr* to pile up; *(preuves)* to accumulate
amoncellement [amɔ̃sɛlmɑ̃] *nm (pile)* heap, pile
amont [amɔ̃] *nm* upstream section; *aussi Ind* **en a. (de)** upstream (from); **la Seine en a. de Paris** the Seine above Paris
amoral, -e, -aux, -ales [amɔral, -o] *adj* amoral
amorçage [amɔrsaʒ] *nm* (**a**) *Ordinat* booting; **système d'a.** *(d'une bombe)* detonating system (**b**) *(pour pêcher)* baiting
amorce [amɔrs] *nf* (**a**) *(commencement)* beginning (**b**) *(détonateur)* detonator; *(d'une petite arme)* cap; **pistolet à amorces** cap gun (**c**) *(appât)* bait
amorcer [16] [amɔrse] **1** *vt* (**a**) *(commencer)* to begin (**b**) *Ordinat* to boot (up); **a. de nouveau** to reboot (**c**) *(bombe)* to arm (**d**) *(hameçon)* to bait
  2 s'amorcer *vpr* (**a**) *(commencer)* to begin; *(tendance)* to develop (**b**) *Ordinat* to boot (up)
amorphe [amɔrf] *adj* lifeless, apathetic
amortir [amɔrtir] *vt* (**a**) *(bruit)* to deaden; *(chute)* to break; *(choc)* to absorb; *(au football)* to trap; *(au tennis)* to kill (**b**) *Fin (dette)* to pay off (**c**) *(rentabiliser)* **il a amorti sa nouvelle voiture en six mois** he recouped the cost of his new car in six months; **le matériel a été amorti dès la première année** the equipment started to pay for itself after the first year
amortissement [amɔrtismɑ̃] *nm* (**a**) *(de matériel)* depreciation (**b**) *(d'un bruit)* deadening; *(d'une chute)* breaking; *(d'un choc)* absorption (**c**) *Fin (d'une dette)* paying off
amortisseur [amɔrtisœr] *nm (d'une voiture)* shock absorber
amour [amur] **1** *nm* (**a**) *(sentiment)* love; **avec a.** lovingly; **être fou d'a. pour qn** to be madly in love with sb; **faire qch par a. pour qn** to do sth out of love for sb; **faire l'a. (avec)** to make love (with); **pour l'a. du Ciel!** for heaven's sake!; **l'a. maternel/filial** a mother's/child's love; **l'a. du prochain** love of one's neighbour; **le grand a.** true love (**b**) *(personne)* **mon a.** my love, my darling; **tu es un a.!** you're an angel!; **quel a. d'enfant!** what an adorable child!
  2 *nfpl* **amours** *(vie amoureuse)* love life; **à tes amours!** *(en buvant)* your health!, cheers!; *(quand on éternue)* bless you!
amouracher [amuraʃe] **s'amouracher** *vpr* **s'a. de qn** to become infatuated with sb

amourette [amurɛt] *nf* fling
amoureusement [amurøzmɑ̃] *adv* lovingly
amoureux, -euse [amurø, -øz] **1** *nm,f (amateur)* **un a. de** a lover of; **un a. de la nature** a nature lover
  2 *nm,f (petit ami, petite amie)* boyfriend, *f* girlfriend; **un couple d'a.** a pair of lovers
  3 *adj (soin, regard)* loving; **vie amoureuse** love life; **tomber a. (de)** to fall in love (with); **être a. de qn** to be in love with sb
amour-propre [amurprɔpr] *nm* self-respect, pride; **elle est blessée dans son a.** her pride is hurt
amovible [amɔvibl] *adj* removable
ampère [ɑ̃pɛr] *nm Élec* ampere
amphés [ɑ̃fe] *nfpl Fam* speed
amphétamine [ɑ̃fetamin] *nf* amphetamine
amphi [ɑ̃fi] *nm Fam* lecture hall *or* theatre
amphibie [ɑ̃fibi] *adj* amphibious
amphibien [ɑ̃fibjɛ̃] *nm Zool* amphibian
amphithéâtre [ɑ̃fiteatr] *nm* (**a**) *(d'université)* lecture hall (**b**) *Archit* amphitheatre; **en a.** in a semicircle
amphore [ɑ̃fɔr] *nf* urn
ample [ɑ̃pl] *adj (robe, jupe)* full; *(geste)* sweeping; *Fig* **de plus amples renseignements** more detailed information; **jusqu'à plus a. informé** until further information is available
amplement [ɑ̃pləmɑ̃] *adv* amply, fully; **nous avons a. le temps** we have plenty of time; **c'est a. suffisant** it's more than enough
ampleur [ɑ̃plœr] *nf* (**a**) *(d'un vêtement)* fullness; *(d'un geste)* expansiveness (**b**) *(importance)* scale, extent; **prendre de l'a.** to grow in size
ampli [ɑ̃pli] *nm Fam* amp
amplificateur [ɑ̃plifikatœr] *nm* amplifier
amplification [ɑ̃plifikasjɔ̃] *nf (d'un son)* amplification; *(d'une tendance, d'un phénomène)* intensification
amplifier [66] [ɑ̃plifje] **1** *vt (son)* to amplify; *(tendance, phénomène)* to intensify
  2 s'amplifier *vpr (son)* to increase; *(tendance, phénomène)* to intensify
amplitude [ɑ̃plityd] *nf* (**a**) *(d'un désastre)* magnitude, scale (**b**) *(d'un geste)* expansiveness (**c**) *(variation)* range; **a. thermique** temperature range (**d**) *(d'une oscillation)* amplitude
ampoule [ɑ̃pul] *nf* (**a**) *(d'une lampe)* (light) bulb; **a. à baïonnette/vis** bayonet/screw-in light bulb (**b**) *(sur la peau)* blister (**c**) *(fiole)* phial
ampoulé, -e [ɑ̃pule] *adj* bombastic
amputation [ɑ̃pytasjɔ̃] *nf* amputation
amputer [ɑ̃pyte] *vt* to amputate; *Fig* to slash; **il fut amputé du bras gauche** his left arm was amputated
Amsterdam [amstɛrdam] *n* Amsterdam
amulette [amylɛt] *nf* amulet
amusant, -e [amyzɑ̃, -ɑ̃t] **1** *adj* amusing, funny; *(divertissant)* entertaining; *(bizarre)* weird
  2 *nm* **le plus a., c'est que...** the funniest thing is that...
amuse-gueule [amyzgœl] *nm inv* appetizer
amusement [amyzmɑ̃] *nm* amusement
amuser [amyze] **1** *vt* to amuse; **cette histoire m'a beaucoup amusé** I found the story very amusing; **si tu crois que ça m'amuse!** do you think I enjoy it?
  2 s'amuser *vpr (se distraire)* to amuse oneself; **bien s'a.** to have a good time; **s'a. avec qn** to play with sb; **s'a. à faire qch** to amuse oneself doing sth; **faire qch pour s'a.** to do sth for the fun of it
amuseur, -euse [amyzœr, -øz] *nm,f* entertainer

amygdales [amidal] *nfpl* tonsils; **se faire opérer des a.** to have one's tonsils out

an [ã] *nm* year; **l'an passé** *ou* **dernier** last year; **l'an prochain** next year; **tous les ans** every year; **tous les trois ans** every three years; **en l'an 2000** in the year 2000; **en l'an de grâce 1172** in the year of Our Lord 1172; **dans trois ans** in three years' time, three years from now; **par an** per year; **Fin** per annum; **avoir dix ans** to be ten (years old); **bon an, mal an** on average over the years

anabolisant [anabɔlizã] *nm* anabolic steroid
anachronique [anakrɔnik] *adj* anachronistic
anachronisme [anakrɔnism] *nm* anachronism
anagramme [anagram] *nf* anagram
anal, -e, -aux, -ales [anal, -o] *adj* anal; *Psy* **stade a.** anal stage
analgésique [analʒezik] *nm* analgesic
anallergique [analɛrʒik] *adj* hypoallergenic
analogie [analɔʒi] *nf* analogy; **par a. avec** by analogy with
analogique [analɔʒik] *adj* (**a**) *(dictionnaire)* analogical (**b**) *Élec* analogue
analogue [analɔg] *adj* similar (**à** to)
analphabète [analfabɛt] **1** *adj* illiterate **2** *nmf* illiterate person
analyse [analiz] *nf* (**a**) *(étude)* analysis; **en dernière a.** in the final analysis; **faire l'a. de qch** to analyse sth (**b**) *Méd* test; **a. de sang/d'urine** blood/urine test; **faire une a. de sang** to have a blood test (**c**) *Psy* (psycho)analysis; **faire une a.** to undergo analysis
analyser [analize] *vt* to analyse; *Méd (sang, urine)* to test
analyseur [analizœr] *nm Ordinat* **a. logique** logic analyser; *Ordinat* **a. syntaxique** parser
analyste [analist] *nmf* (**a**) *Ordinat* analyst (**b**) *Psy* (psycho)analyst
analyste-programmeur *(pl* **analystes-programmeurs)** [analistprɔgramœr] *nm Ordinat* systems analyst
analytique [analitik] *adj* analytical
ananas [anana(s)] *nm* pineapple
anarchie [anarʃi] *nf aussi Fig* anarchy
anarchique [anarʃik] *adj aussi Fig* anarchic
anarchisant, -e [anarʃizã, -ãt] *adj (discours)* advocating anarchy
anarchisme [anarʃism] *nm* anarchism
anarchiste [anarʃist] *adj & nmf* anarchist
anatomie [anatɔmi] *nf* anatomy
anatomique [anatɔmik] *adj* anatomical
ancestral, -e, -aux, -ales [ãsɛstral, -o] *adj* ancestral
ancêtre [ãsɛtr] *nmf* ancestor; *Fam (vieillard)* granddad, *f* grandma
anche [ãʃ] *nf Mus* reed
anchois [ãʃwa] *nm* anchovy
ancien, -enne [ãsjɛ̃, -ɛn] **1** *adj* (**a**) *(vieux)* old; **livre a.** antiquarian book; **meubles anciens** antique furniture; **dans l'a. temps** in the old days; **je suis plus a. que vous dans la profession** I've been in the profession longer than you (**b**) *(d'autrefois) (professeur, voisin)* former, old; *(voiture, maison)* old; **c'est un a. boxeur** he used to be a boxer; **a. combattant** *Br* ex-serviceman, *Am* veteran; **a. élève** former student; *Hist* **l'A. Régime** the Ancien Régime **2** *nm* (**a**) *Rel & Pol* elder (**b**) **l'a.** *(meubles)* antiques; *(immobilier)* old(er) buildings **3** *nm,f (par l'expérience)* **c'est un a. de la maison** he's been with the firm a long time

L'Ancien Régime

This refers to the government and social structure of France before the Revolution of 1789, an absolutist monarchy consisting of three "estates": the nobility, the clergy (both enjoying institutional privileges) and the "Third Estate", or commoners. The privileges which characterized the Ancien Régime were abolished on 4 August 1789.

anciennement [ãsjɛnmã] *adv* formerly
ancienneté [ãsjɛnte] *nf* (**a**) *(âge)* age (**b**) *(expérience)* seniority; **avoir quinze ans d'a.** to have fifteen years' service; **être promu à l'a.** to be promoted by seniority
ancrage [ãkraʒ] *nm Naut* anchoring
ancre [ãkr] *nf* anchor; **lever l'a.** to weigh anchor; **jeter l'a.** to anchor
ancrer [ãkre] **1** *vt (navire)* to anchor; **cette idée est profondément ancrée en lui** this idea is firmly rooted in his mind **2 s'ancrer** *vpr Fig (idée, concept)* to become rooted
andalou, -se [ãdalu, -uz] **1** *adj* Andalusian **2** *nm,f* **A.** Andalusian
Andalousie [ãdaluzi] *nf* **l'A.** Andalusia
Andes [ãd] *nfpl* **les A.** the Andes
andorran, -e [ãdɔrã, -an] **1** *adj* Andorran **2** *nm,f* **A.** Andorran
Andorre [ãdɔr] *nf* Andorra; **la principauté d'A.** the Principality of Andorra
Andorre-la-Vieille [ãdɔrlavjɛj] *n* Andorra la Vella
andouille [ãduj] *nf* (**a**) *Culin* chitterlings sausage *(eaten cold)* (**b**) *Fam (imbécile)* idiot, *Am* jerk; **faire l'a.** to play the fool
andouillette [ãdujɛt] *nf Culin* chitterlings sausage *(for grilling)*
androgyne [ãdrɔʒin] *adj* androgynous
âne [an] *nm* (**a**) *(animal)* donkey; **à dos d'â.** by donkey (**b**) *Fam (idiot)* idiot, fool; *(ignare)* dunce
anéantir [aneãtir] *vt (ville)* to destroy; *(armée)* to crush; *(espoirs)* to shatter; **la nouvelle l'a anéantie** she was staggered by the news
anéantissement [aneãtismã] *nm* (**a**) *(d'une ville, d'un empire)* destruction; *(d'un espoir)* shattering (**b**) *(abattement)* **dans un état d'a. total** completely crushed
anecdote [anɛkdɔt] *nf* anecdote
anecdotique [anɛkdɔtik] *adj* anecdotal
anémie [anemi] *nf* anaemia; **faire de l'a.** to have anaemia
anémique [anemik] *adj* anaemic; *Fig* feeble, weak
anémone [anemɔn] *nf* anemone; **a. de mer** sea anemone
ânerie [ɑnri] *nf (paroles)* stupid remark; *(acte)* stupid act; **dire des âneries** to talk rubbish; **faire des âneries** to behave stupidly
ânesse [ɑnɛs] *nf* she-ass
anesthésie [anɛstezi] *nf* anaesthesia; **être sous a.** to be under anaesthetic; **a. générale/locale** general/local anaesthetic
anesthésier [66] [anɛstezje] *vt* to anaesthetize
anesthésiste [anɛstezist] *nmf Br* anaesthetist, *Am* anesthesiologist
aneth [anɛt] *nm* dill
ange [ãʒ] *nm aussi Fig* angel; **un visage d'a.** an angelic face; **mon a.** my darling *or* angel; **être aux anges** to be in seventh heaven; **un a. passe** someone must

have walked over my grave; **a. gardien** guardian angel

angélique [ãʒelik] **1** *adj* angelic
 2 *nf Culin* angelica

angine [ãʒin] *nf* sore throat; **a. de poitrine** angina (pectoris)

angiome [ãʒjom] *nm Méd* angioma

anglais, -e [ãglε, -εz] **1** *adj* English; *(britannique)* British
 2 *nm,f* **A.** Englishman; *f* Englishwoman; *(Britannique)* British man, *f* British woman; **les A.** the English; *(Britanniques)* the British
 3 *nm (langue)* English
 4 *nf* **anglaise** (**a**) *Fam* **filer à l'anglaise** to slip away (**b**) **anglaises** *(boucles)* ringlets

angle [ãgl] *nm* (**a**) *(d'une pièce, d'une rue, d'une table)* corner; **elle fait l'a. avec la rue du Bac** it intersects the rue du Bac; **la maison qui fait l'a.** the house on the corner (**b**) *(point de vue)* angle (**c**) *(en géométrie)* angle; **a. droit** right angle; **se couper à angles droits** to cross at right angles; *Aut* **a. mort** blind spot

Angleterre [ãglǝtεr] *nf* **l'A.** England; *(Grande-Bretagne)* Britain

anglican, -e [ãglikã, -ãn] *adj & nm,f* Anglican

anglicisme [ãglisism] *nm Ling* Anglicism

anglo-américain, -e *(mpl* **anglo-américains**, *fpl* **anglo-américaines)** [ãgloamerikε̃, -εn] *adj* Anglo-American

anglo-irlandais, -e *(mpl* **anglo-irlandais**, *fpl* **anglo-irlandaises)** [ãgloirlãdε, -εz] *adj* Anglo-Irish

anglo-normand, -e *(mpl* **anglo-normands**, *fpl* **anglo-normandes)** [ãglonɔrmã, -ãd] *adj voir* **île**

anglophone [ãglofɔn] **1** *adj* English-speaking
 2 *nmf* English speaker

anglo-saxon, -onne *(mpl* **anglo-saxons**, *fpl* **anglo-saxonnes)** [ãglosaksɔ̃, -ɔn] **1** *adj* (**a**) *Hist* Anglo-Saxon (**b**) *(culture, civilisation etc)* Anglo-American, British and American
 2 *nm,f* **A.-S.** Anglo-Saxon; **les Anglo-Saxons** *(peuples)* British and American people; *Hist* the Anglo-Saxons

Anglo-saxon
Note that the adjective "anglo-saxon" and the noun "Anglo-Saxon" are often used in French to refer to British and American people, culture, customs etc: "la musique anglo-saxonne", "la littérature anglo-saxonne".

angoissant, -e [ãgwasã, -ãt] *adj (nouvelle)* distressing; *(attente)* agonizing; *(film, livre)* frightening; *(situation)* alarming

angoisse [ãgwas] *nf* anguish, distress; *Méd* **une crise d'a.** an anxiety attack; *Fam* **c'est l'a.!** what a drag!

angoissé, -e [ãgwase] **1** *adj* anxious
 2 *nm,f* anxious person

angoisser [ãgwase] **1** *vt* **a. qn** to make sb anxious
 2 *vi Fam* to worry, to get worked up
 3 **s'angoisser** *vpr* to get anxious; **s'a. pour un rien** to get worked up over nothing

Angola [ãgɔla] *nm* **l'A.** Angola

angolais, -e [ãgɔlε, -εz] **1** *adj* Angolan
 2 *nm,f* **A.** Angolan

angora [ãgɔra] **1** *nm* (**a**) *(lapin)* angora rabbit; *(chat)* Persian cat (**b**) *(laine)* angora (wool)
 2 *adj* angora

anguille [ãgij] *nf* eel; *Fig* **il y a a. sous roche** there's something going on

angulaire [ãgylεr] *adj* angular

anguleux, -euse [ãgylø, -øz] *adj (visage)* angular; *(contours)* rugged

anicroche [anikrɔʃ] *nf* hitch, snag; **sans a.** without a hitch

animal, -e, -aux, -ales [animal, -o] **1** *nm aussi Fig* animal; **animaux de boucherie** animals raised for slaughter; **a. domestique** pet; **a. sauvage** wild animal
 2 *adj* animal

animalerie [animalri] *nf Can* pet shop

animalier, -ère [animalje, -εr] *adj* **parc a.** safari park; **peintre a.** wildlife painter

animateur, -trice [animatœr, -tris] *nm,f* (**a**) *(de télé, de radio)* presenter (**b**) *(dans un club)* leader

animation [animasjɔ̃] *nf* (**a**) *(vie)* life; **une ville pleine d'a.** a lively town; **parler avec a.** to speak animatedly; **mettre de l'a. dans une soirée** to liven up a party (**b**) *(divertissement)* event; **faire de l'a.** *(de centre aéré)* to be an activity leader; *(de télévision, de radio)* to be a presenter (**c**) *Cin* animation (**d**) *Météo* **a. satellite** satellite picture

animé, -e [anime] *adj (personne, discussion)* lively, animated; *(rue, quartier)* busy, bustling

animer [anime] **1** *vt* (**a**) *(sujet: désir, ambition)* to drive; **être animé des meilleures intentions** to have the best of intentions (**b**) *(conversation, quartier, soirée)* to liven up (**c**) *(débat)* to conduct; *(jeu télévisé)* to present
 2 **s'animer** *vpr (personne)* to come to life; *(conversation, soirée)* to get more lively; *(visage)* to light up

animisme [animism] *nm* animism

animosité [animozite] *nf* animosity (**contre** towards), hostility (**contre** towards); **dire qch sans a.** to say sth calmly

anis [ani(s)] *nm (plante)* anise; **(sirop d')a.** aniseed cordial; **(graine d')a.** *(en cuisine)* aniseed; **à l'a.** aniseed-flavoured

anisette [anizεt] *nf* anisette

Ankara [ãkara] *n* Ankara

ankylose [ãkiloz] *nf* stiffness, *Spéc* ankylosis

ankyloser [ãkiloze] **1** *vt* **être ankylosé** to be stiff
 2 **s'ankyloser** *vpr* to get stiff; *Fig (dans un métier, des habitudes)* to get into a rut

annales [anal] *nfpl* annals; **les a. du bac** = past baccalauréat examination papers (with sample answers); **a. de géographie/littéraires** geographical/literary review; *Fig* **ça restera dans les a.** it will go down in history

anneau, -x [ano] *nm* (**a**) *(cercle, bague)* ring; *(de chaîne)* link; **a. nuptial** *ou* **de mariage** wedding ring; **a. de rideau** curtain ring; **les anneaux** *(en gymnastique)* the rings (**b**) *(d'un serpent)* coil (**c**) *Astron* ring

année [ane] *nf* year; **bonne a.!** happy New Year!; **a. de vacances** a year's holiday; **d'a. en a.** year by year; **les années 80** the 80s; **en quelle a....?** in what year...?; **l'a. prochaine/dernière** next/last year; **elle entre dans sa trentième a.** she's just turned twenty-nine; **entrer en troisième a. de médecine** to start the third year of one's medical course; **a. civile** calendar year; **a. comptable** *Br* accounting *or* financial year, *Am* fiscal year; **a. scolaire** school year; **a. universitaire** academic year

année-lumière *(pl* **années-lumière)** [anelymjεr] *nf* light year; **à des années-lumière** *(étoile, planète)* light years away; *Fig* **nous sommes à des années-lumière l'un de l'autre** we're light years apart

annexe [anɛks] **1** *nf* (**a**) *(bâtiment)* annexe (**b**) *(de lettre)* enclosure; *(de livre, de rapport)* appendix; *(de projet de loi)* rider; *(de loi)* schedule; **en a. veuillez trouver...** please find enclosed...
2 *adj* (**a**) *(complémentaire) (pièces)* enclosed; *(revenus)* supplementary; *(industries)* subsidiary (**b**) *(mineur)* secondary

annexer [anɛkse] **1** *vt* (**a**) *(territoire)* to annex (**b**) *(document)* to append (**à** to); **pièces annexées** *(à une lettre)* enclosures
2 s'annexer *vpr* **s'a. qch** to get hold of sth for oneself

annexion [anɛksjɔ̃] *nf* annexation

annihilation [aniilasjɔ̃] *nf* *(d'une ville, d'une armée)* annihilation; *(d'efforts, d'espoirs)* destruction

annihiler [aniile] *vt* *(ville, armée)* to annihilate; *(efforts, espoirs)* to destroy

anniversaire [anivɛrsɛr] **1** *nm* *(d'une naissance)* birthday; *(d'une victoire, d'une mort)* anniversary; **bon** *ou* **joyeux a.!** happy birthday!; **gâteau/carte d'a.** birthday cake/card; **a. de mariage** wedding anniversary
2 *adj* anniversary; **date a.** anniversary

annonce [anɔ̃s] *nf* (**a**) *(déclaration)* announcement; *(par écrit)* notice; *(aux cartes)* declaration, bid; *Fig* sign, indication (**de** of) (**b**) *(publicitaire, de vente)* advert, advertisement; **passer une (petite) a. dans un journal** to put an advert in a newspaper; **petites annonces** *Br* small ads, *Am* want ads; **annonces classées** classified ads

annoncer [16] [anɔ̃se] **1** *vt* (**a**) *(déclarer)* to announce; **a. la nouvelle à qn** to tell sb the news (**b**) *(dans la presse) (soldes, exposition)* to advertise (**c**) *(indiquer)* to herald; **cela n'annonce rien de bon** things aren't looking too good (**d**) **a. qn** *(visiteur)* to show sb in; *(lors d'une occasion officielle)* to announce sb; **se faire a.** to give one's name
2 s'annoncer *vpr* (**a**) *(prévenir de sa visite)* to announce one's arrival (**b**) *(situation)* **cela s'annonce bien/mal** things aren't looking too bad/good; **les négociations s'annoncent difficiles** the negotiations look like they're going to be difficult; **l'avènement de la démocratie s'annonce dans plusieurs pays** there are signs in several countries that democracy is on the way

annonceur [anɔ̃sœr] *nm* *(de publicité)* advertiser

annonciateur, -trice [anɔ̃sjatœr, -tris] *adj* **signes annonciateurs de crise** signs that a crisis is on the way

Annonciation [anɔ̃sjasjɔ̃] *nf* **l'A.** the Annunciation

annoncier [anɔ̃sje] *nm Can (feuille d'annonces)* advertisements page

annotation [anɔtasjɔ̃] *nf* annotation; **faire des annotations dans un texte** to annotate a text

annoter [anɔte] *vt* to annotate

annuaire [anɥɛr] *nm* *(d'un organisme)* yearbook; *(liste d'adresses)* directory; **l'a. du téléphone** *ou* **téléphonique** the telephone directory; **je suis dans l'a.** I'm in the (phone) book; **a. électronique** electronic telephone directory; **a. des marées** tide table

annuel, -elle [anɥɛl] *adj* annual, yearly

annuellement [anɥɛlmɑ̃] *adv* annually, yearly

annuité [anɥite] *nf* (**a**) *(sur un emprunt)* annual repayment (**b**) *Can & Suisse (rente)* annuity

annulaire [anɥlɛr] **1** *nm* ring finger
2 *adj* annular, ring-shaped

annulation [anylasjɔ̃] *nf* (**a**) *(d'une commande, d'un rendez-vous, de vacances)* cancellation; *(d'une dette)* writing off; *(d'un mariage, d'un contrat)* annulment; *(d'un jugement)* quashing (**b**) *Ordinat* deletion; **a. d'entrée** *(commande)* cancel entry

annuler [anyle] *vt* (**a**) *(commande, rendez-vous, vacances)* to cancel; *(dette)* to write off; *(mariage, contrat)* to annul; *(jugement)* to quash (**b**) *(remplacer)* to supersede (**c**) *Sport (but, essai)* to disallow
2 s'annuler *vpr* to cancel each other out

anoblir [anɔblir] *vt* to ennoble

anode [anɔd] *nf Élec* anode

anodin, -e [anɔdɛ̃, -in] *adj (remarque)* harmless; *(personne)* insignificant; *(blessure, changement)* slight, minor; *(infection)* mild

anomalie [anɔmali] *nf* anomaly; *Méd* abnormality

ânon [anɔ̃] *nm* little donkey

ânonner [anɔne] *vt* to stumble through; **il a lu le poème en ânonnant** he read the poem haltingly

anonymat [anɔnima] *nm* anonymity; **garder l'a.** to remain anonymous

anonyme [anɔnim] *adj* anonymous; *Fig (décor, intérieur)* impersonal

anorak [anɔrak] *nm* anorak

anorexie [anɔrɛksi] *nf* anorexia; **faire de l'a.** to suffer from anorexia; **a. mentale** anorexia nervosa

anorexique [anɔrɛksik] *adj & nmf* anorexic

anormal, -e, -aux, -ales, -o] **1** *adj* (**a**) *(non conforme)* abnormal; *(mentalement)* educationally subnormal; **il fait une chaleur anormale** it's abnormally hot (**b**) *(injuste)* unfair; **il est a. que tu sois si peu payé** it's unfair that you're paid so little
2 *nm,f (mentalement)* educationally subnormal person

anormalement [anɔrmalmɑ̃] *adv* abnormally

ANP [ɑenpe] *nm (abrév* **assistant numérique personnel)** PDA

ANPE [ɑenpeə] *nf (abrév* **Agence nationale pour l'emploi)** = French state employment agency; **pointer à l'A.** *Br* to sign on, *Am* to register as unemployed

anse [ɑ̃s] *nf* (**a**) *(d'une cruche, d'un panier)* handle (**b**) *(crique)* cove

antagonisme [ɑ̃tagɔnism] *nm* antagonism

antagoniste [ɑ̃tagɔnist] **1** *nmf* antagonist
2 *adj (opinions, parties)* antagonistic

antalgique [ɑ̃talʒik] *adj & nm Méd* analgesic

antan [ɑ̃tɑ̃] **d'antan** *adj Litt* of yesteryear

antarctique [ɑ̃tarktik] **1** *adj* Antarctic
2 *nm* **l'A.** the Antarctic, Antarctica

antécédent [ɑ̃tesedɑ̃] *nm* (**a**) **antécédents** *(d'une personne)* previous history, past record; **il y a des antécédents cancéreux dans ma famille** my family has a history of cancer; **avoir de bons/mauvais antécédents** to have a good/bad record; **antécédents médicaux** medical history (**b**) *Ling* antecedent

Antéchrist [ɑ̃tekrist] *nm* Antichrist

antédiluvien, -enne [ɑ̃tedilyvjɛ̃, -ɛn] *adj Hum* **ma télévision est antédiluvienne** my television is an antique

anténatal, -e, -als, -ales [ɑ̃tenatal] *adj Méd* antenatal

antenne [ɑ̃tɛn] *nf* (**a**) *(de radio)* aerial, antenna; *(d'un satellite, d'un robot)* antenna; **être à l'a.** to be on the air; **passer à l'a.** *(émission)* to be broadcast; *(personne)* to be on the television/radio; **rendre l'a.** to hand over; **à vous l'a.** over to you; **hors a.** off the air; **a. parabolique** *(satellite)* dish (**b**) *(d'un insecte)* antenna, feeler; *Fig* **avoir des antennes** *(de l'intuition)* to have a sixth sense (**c**) *Mil* **a. chirurgicale** field hospital (**d**) *(de société)* branch

antépénultième [ãtepenyltjɛm] *adj* antepenultimate

antérieur, -e [ãterjœr] *adj* (**a**) *(période)* former; *(date)* earlier; *(année)* previous; *(engagement)* prior; **tous ces événements sont antérieurs à la révolution** all these events took place before the revolution; **dans une vie antérieure** in a previous life (**b**) *(muscle)* anterior; *(membre)* fore

anthologie [ãtɔlɔʒi] *nf* anthology

anthracite [ãtrasit] **1** *nm* (**a**) *(minerai)* anthracite (**b**) *(couleur)* charcoal grey
  2 *adj inv* charcoal grey

anthropologie [ãtrɔpɔlɔʒi] *nf* anthropology

anthropologiste [ãtrɔpɔlɔʒist], **anthropologue** [ãtrɔpɔlɔg] *nmf* anthropologist

anthropophage [ãtrɔpɔfaʒ] **1** *nmf* cannibal
  2 *adj* cannibalistic

anti- [ãti] *préf (contre)* anti-

antiadhésif, -ive [ãtiadezif, -iv] **1** *adj (revêtement, poêle)* nonstick
  2 *nm* antiadhesive

antiaérien, -enne [ãtiaerjɛ̃, -ɛn] *adj* anti-aircraft

anti-âge [ãtiaʒ] *adj inv* anti-aging

antialcoolique [ãtialkɔlik] *adj (ligue)* temperance

antiatomique [ãtiatɔmik] *adj* antinuclear

antiavortement [ãtiavɔrtəmã] *adj inv* pro-life, anti-abortion

antibactérien, -enne [ãtibakterjɛ̃, -ɛn] *adj* antibacterial

antibiotique [ãtibjɔtik] **1** *nm* antibiotic; **être sous antibiotiques** to be on antibiotics
  2 *adj* antibiotic

antiblocage [ãtiblɔkaʒ] *adj inv Aut* **système a. (des roues)** anti-lock brakes

antibrouillard [ãtibrujar] *adj inv & nm Aut* **(phare) a.** fog lamp

antibruit [ãtibrɥi] *adj inv (mur)* soundproof; **lutte a.** noise abatement campaign

antibuée [ãtibɥe] *adj inv & nm Aut* **(dispositif) a.** demister

anticalcaire [ãtikalkɛr] *adj inv* **produit a.** *(pour machine à laver)* water softener

anticancéreux, -euse [ãtikãserø, -øz] *adj* **centre/ sérum a.** cancer hospital/serum

anticasseurs [ãtikasœr] *adj inv* **loi a.** = law banning violent behaviour during demonstrations

antichambre [ãtiʃãbr] *nf* waiting room, antechamber; *Fig* **dans les antichambres du pouvoir** on the fringes of power

antichar [ãtiʃar] *adj inv Mil* anti-tank

antichoc [ãtiʃɔk] *adj inv* shock-proof

anticipation [ãtisipasjɔ̃] *nf* anticipation; **payer par a.** to pay in advance; **littérature d'a.** science fiction; **film d'a.** science-fiction movie *or Br* film

anticipé, -e [ãtisipe] *adj (paiement)* advance; *(départ, retour)* early; **avec mes remerciements anticipés** thanking you in advance

anticiper [ãtisipe] **1** *vt (réaction, réponse)* to anticipate; *(action)* to forestall; *(tendance, résultat d'élections)* to forecast; **j'anticipais déjà le pire** I was expecting the worst
  2 *vi* to anticipate, to look *or* think ahead; *(en sport, aux échecs)* to anticipate what one's opponent will

do next; **n'anticipons pas** let's not look too far ahead; **a. sur qch** to anticipate sth

anticlérical, -e, -aux, -ales [ãtiklerikal, -o] *adj & nm,f* anticlerical

anticoagulant, -e [ãtikɔagylã, -ãt] *adj & nm* anticoagulant

anticolonialiste [ãtikɔlɔnjalist] *adj* anti-colonialist

anticommunisme [ãtikɔmynism] *nm* anti-communism

anticommuniste [ãtikɔmynist] *adj & nmf* anti-communist

anticonceptionnel, -elle [ãtikɔ̃sɛpsjɔnɛl] *adj (pilule)* contraceptive

anticonformiste [ãtikɔ̃fɔrmist] *adj & nmf* non-conformist

anticonstitutionnel, -elle [ãtikɔ̃stitysjɔnɛl] *adj* unconstitutional

anticorps [ãtikɔr] *nm* antibody

anticyclone [ãtisiklɔn] *nm Météo* anticyclone

antidater [ãtidate] *vt* to backdate, to antedate

antidémocratique [ãtidemɔkratik] *adj* undemocratic

antidépresseur [ãtideprɛsœr] *adj m & nm* antidepressant; **être sous antidépresseurs** to be on antidepressants

antidérapant, -e [ãtiderapã, -ãt] *adj (pneu, route)* non-skid; *(semelle, tapis)* non-slip

anti-discriminatoire [ãtidiskriminatwar] *adj (mesures, politique)* anti-discriminatory

antidopage [ãtidɔpaʒ], **antidoping** [ãtidɔpiŋ] *adj inv Sport* **contrôle a.** drug(s) test

antidote [ãtidɔt] *nm aussi Fig* antidote (**contre** for)

anti-dumping [ãtidœmpiŋ] *adj inv (loi, législation)* anti-dumping

antiémeute [ãtiemøt] *adj inv* antiriot; **brigade a.** riot squad

antiesclavagiste [ãtiɛsklavaʒist] *adj* anti-slavery

antifasciste [ãtifaʃist] *adj* anti-fascist

antifongique [ãtifɔ̃ʒik] **1** *adj* fungicidal
  2 *nm* fungicide

antigel [ãtiʒɛl] *nm* antifreeze

antigrippal, -e, -aux, -ales [ãtigripal, -o] *adj* anti-flu

antihéros [ãtiero] *nm* antihero

antihistaminique [ãtiistaminik] *adj & nm Pharm* antihistamine

anti-inflammatoire [ãtiɛ̃flamatwar] *adj & nm Méd* anti-inflammatory

anti-inflationniste [ãtiɛ̃flasjɔnist] *adj* anti-inflationary

antillais, -e [ãtijɛ, -ɛz] **1** *adj* West Indian
  2 *nm,f* **A.** West Indian

Antilles [ãtij] *nfpl* **les A.** the West Indies

Antilles

The French West Indies include the overseas "départements" of Martinique and Guadeloupe, the latter including the islands of La Désirade, Marie-Galante, Saint-Barthélemy (Saint Bart), Les Saintes and part of Saint-Martin.

antilope [ãtilɔp] *nf* antelope

antimatière [ãtimatjɛr] *nf Phys* antimatter

antimilitariste [ãtimilitarist] *adj & nmf* antimilitarist

antimite [ãtimit] **1** *adj inv (produit)* moth-repellent; **bombe a.** moth spray
  2 *nm* mothkiller

antimondialisation [ãtimɔ̃djalizasjɔ̃] *nf* antiglobalization

antimondialiste [ãtimɔ̃djalist] *adj & nmf* antiglobalist

antinazi, -e [ãtinazi] *adj & nm,f* anti-Nazi

antinomie [ãtinɔmi] *nf* antinomy

antinucléaire [ãtinyklɛɛr] *adj* anti-nuclear

Antiope® [ãtjɔp] *n* = French teletext system, providing subtitles for the deaf

antioxydant, -e [ãtiɔksidã, -ãt] *adj & nm* antioxidant

antipathie [ãtipati] *nf* antipathy; **avoir** *ou* **éprouver de l'a. pour qn** to dislike sb

antipathique [ãtipatik] *adj* unpleasant; **il m'est très a.** I don't like him at all

antipelliculaire [ãtipelikylɛr] *adj* **shampooing a.** (anti-)dandruff shampoo

antiphrase [ãtifraz] *nf Ling* antiphrasis

antipodes [ãtipɔd] *nmpl Géog* antipodes; **être aux a. de** to be on the other side of the world from; *Fig* to be the exact opposite of

antipoison [ãtipwazɔ̃] *adj inv Méd* **centre a.** poisons unit

antiprotéase [ãtiprɔteaz] *nf Méd* protease inhibitor

antiquaire [ãtikɛr] *nmf* antique dealer

antique [ãtik] *adj (de l'Antiquité)* ancient; *(mobilier)* antique; *Hum (voiture, télévision)* antiquated; **la Grèce/la Rome a.** ancient Greece/Rome

antiquité [ãtikite] *nf* (**a**) *Hist* **l'a. grecque/romaine** ancient Greece/Rome (**b**) **antiquités** *(meubles et objets anciens)* antiques; **magasin d'antiquités** antique shop (**c**) **antiquités** *(dans un musée)* antiquities

antirabique [ãtirabik] *adj Méd* anti-rabies

antiracisme [ãtirasism] *nm* anti-racism

antiraciste [ãtirasist] *adj & nmf* anti-racist

antiradar [ãtiradar] *nm* anti-radar device

antireflet [ãtirəflɛ] *adj inv* non-reflecting; *Ordinat* antiglare

antirides [ãtirid] *adj inv* anti-wrinkle

antirouille [ãtiruj] **1** *adj inv* rustproofing
  2 *nm* rustproofing agent

antiroulis [ãtiruli] *adj Aut* **barre a.** anti-roll bar

anti-scintillements [ãtisɛ̃tijmã] *adj inv Ordinat* flicker-free

antisèche [ãtisɛʃ] *nf Fam* crib sheet

antisémite [ãtisemit] **1** *adj* anti-Semitic
  2 *nmf* anti-Semite

antisémitisme [ãtisemitism] *nm* anti-Semitism

antiseptique [ãtisɛptik] *adj & nm* antiseptic

antisocial, -e, -aux, -ales [ãtisɔsjal, -o] *adj* antisocial

antispasmodique [ãtispasmɔdik] *adj & nm Méd* antispasmodic

antitabac [ãtitaba] *adj inv* **lutte** *ou* **campagne a.** anti-smoking campaign

antiterroriste [ãtitɛrɔrist] *adj* anti-terrorist

antithèse [ãtitɛz] *nf* antithesis; *Fig* **être l'a. de** to be the opposite of

antitrust [ãtitrœst] *adj inv Br* anti-monopoly, *Am* antitrust

antivariolique [ãtivarjɔlik] *adj Méd* **vaccin a.** smallpox vaccine

antivenimeux, -euse [ãtivənimø, -øz] *adj Méd* anti-venin

antivieillissement [ãtivjɛjismã] *nm (produit qui ralentit le vieillissement)* anti-ageing product

antivol [ãtivɔl] **1** *adj inv (dispositif)* anti-theft
  2 *nm* anti-theft device

antre [ãtr] *nm (caverne)* cave, cavern; *(d'animaux, de brigands)* den, lair; *Fig (d'une personne)* den

anus [anys] *nm* anus

Anvers [ãvɛr(s)] *n* Antwerp

anxiété [ãksjete] *nf* anxiety; **éprouver de l'a.** to feel anxious; **avec a.** anxiously

anxieux, -euse [ãksjø, -øz] **1** *adj* anxious, worried; **a. de faire qch** anxious to do sth
  2 *nm,f* worrier

anxiolytique [ãksjɔlitik] *Méd* **1** *adj* anxiety-reducing
  2 *nm* tranquillizer

AOC [aɔse] *nf (abrév* **appellation d'origine contrôlée)** = (guarantee of) high-quality wine from an identified vineyard

aorte [aɔrt] *nf* aorta

août [u(t)] *nm* August; **le quinze a.** *(fête)* Assumption Day; *voir aussi* janvier

aoûtat [auta] *nm Br* harvest mite, *Am* chigger

aoûtien, -enne [ausjɛ̃, -ɛn] *nm,f* August *Br* holidaymaker *or Am* vacationer

apache [apaʃ] **1** *nm* **A.** Apache
  2 *adj* Apache

apaisant, -e [apɛzã, -ãt] *adj* soothing, calming

apaisement [apɛzmã] *nm (de la douleur)* alleviation; *(calme)* calm

apaiser [apeze] **1** *vt (personne)* to calm (down); *(douleur)* to soothe; *(faim)* to satisfy; *(soif)* to quench; *(craintes)* to allay
  2 **s'apaiser** *vpr (personne)* to calm down; *(vent, douleur, craintes)* to subside

apanage [apanaʒ] *nm* prerogative; **elle croit avoir l'a. de la sagesse** she thinks she has a monopoly on wisdom

aparté [aparte] *nm* (**a**) *Théât* aside; **en a.** in an aside (**b**) *(entre deux personnes)* private conversation; **en a.** in private

apartheid [apartɛd] *nm* apartheid

apathie [apati] *nf* apathy, listlessness

apathique [apatik] *adj* apathetic, listless

apatride [apatrid] **1** *adj* stateless
  2 *nmf* stateless person

APEC [apɛk] *nf (abrév* **Association pour l'emploi des cadres)** = employment agency for executives and graduates

apercevoir [60] [apɛrsəvwar] **1** *vt* to see; *(soudain, rapidement)* to catch sight of; **laisser a. qch** to let sth show
  2 **s'apercevoir** *vpr* **s'a. de qch** *(comprendre, réaliser)* to realize *or* notice sth; **s'a. que...** to realize *or* notice that...; **sans s'en a.** inadvertently, without realizing it

aperçu [apɛrsy] *nm (idée générale)* general idea; *Ordinat* **a. avant impression** print preview

apéritif [aperitif] *nm* aperitif; **prendre l'a.** to have a drink before the meal

Apéritif
In France, the "apéritif", or "apéro", is an informal social ritual. It is quite usual to invite people for before-dinner drinks without actually providing dinner, or to arrange to meet someone in a café "pour l'apéritif" before going out for a meal.

apéro [apero] *Fam* = **apéritif**

apesanteur [apəzãtœr] *nf* weightlessness; **en (état d')a.** in weightless conditions

à-peu-près [apøprɛ] *nm inv* vague approximation; **il y a trop d'à. dans votre exposé** there is too much vagueness in your report

apeuré, -e [apœre] *adj* frightened, scared

apeurer [apœre] *vt* to frighten, to scare

aphasie [afazi] *nf Méd* aphasia

aphasique [afazik] *adj & nmf Méd* aphasic

aphone [afɔn] *adj Méd* voiceless; **elle était a. d'avoir trop crié** she'd lost her voice because she'd been shouting too much

aphorisme [afɔrism] *nm* aphorism; *Péj* platitude

aphrodisiaque [afrɔdizjak] *adj & nm* aphrodisiac

aphte [aft] *nm* mouth ulcer

aphteux, -euse [aftø, -øz] *adj* **fièvre aphteuse** foot-and-mouth disease

à-pic [apik] *nm inv* sheer face

apiculteur, -trice [apikyltœr, -tris] *nm,f* beekeeper

apiculture [apikyltyr] *nf* beekeeping

apitoiement [apitwamɑ̃] *nm* pity; **pas d'a.!** *(ne sois pas indulgent)* don't feel sorry for him/her/*etc*!; *(sois sans pitié)* show no mercy!

apitoyer [32] [apitwaje] **1** *vt* **a. qn** to move sb to pity **2** **s'apitoyer** *vpr* **s'a. sur (le sort de) qn** to feel sorry for sb; **s'a. sur soi-même** *ou* **sur son sort** to feel sorry for oneself

APL [apeɛl] *nf (abrév* **Aide personnalisée au logement)** housing benefit

aplanir [aplanir] **1** *vt (bois)* to plane; *(route)* to level; *Fig (difficultés)* to iron out **2** **s'aplanir** *vpr (sol)* to level out

aplati, -e [aplati] *adj (ballon, nez)* flat; *(figure géométrique)* oblate

aplatir [aplatir] **1** *vt (objet)* to flatten; **a. qch à coups de marteau** to hammer sth flat **2** **s'aplatir** *vpr (coiffure)* to go flat; *(chapeau)* to get flattened; **s'a. contre un mur** to flatten oneself against a wall; *Fig* **s'a. devant qn** to grovel to sb

aplomb [aplɔ̃] *nm* **(a)** *(ligne droite)* perpendicularity; **mettre qch d'a.** to stand sth up straight; **les étagères ne sont pas d'a.** the shelves aren't level; **je ne me sens pas d'a. aujourd'hui** I'm feeling out of sorts today; **remettre qn d'a.** to perk sb up **(b)** *(assurance)* (self-)confidence; *Péj* nerve, cheek; *Péj* **il ne manque pas d'a.** he's got a nerve *or* a cheek

apnée [apne] *nf* **plonger en a.** to dive without breathing apparatus

apocalypse [apɔkalips] *nf* apocalypse; **l'A.** *(dans la Bible)* the Book of Revelation; *Fig* **une vision d'a.** an apocalyptic vision

apocalyptique [apɔkaliptik] *adj* apocalyptic

apogée [apɔʒe] *nm Astron* apogee; *Fig* **être à l'a. de sa carrière** to be at the height of one's career

apolitique [apɔlitik] *adj* apolitical

apollon [apɔlɔ̃] *nm (bel homme)* Adonis

apologie [apɔlɔʒi] *nf (défense)* apologia (**de** for); *(éloge)* eulogy; **faire l'a. de** *(défendre)* to (seek to) justify; *(louer)* to eulogize

apoplectique [apɔplɛktik] *adj & nmf Méd* apoplectic

apoplexie [apɔplɛksi] *nf Méd* apoplexy; **attaque d'a.** apoplectic seizure, stroke

a posteriori [apɔsterjɔri] *adv* with hindsight

apostolat [apɔstɔla] *nm (mission)* vocation

apostrophe [apɔstrɔf] *nf* **(a)** *(signe, figure de style)* apostrophe **(b)** *(interpellation)* rude remark

apostropher [apɔstrɔfe] **1** *vt (pour attirer l'attention)* to shout to; *(être impoli envers)* to shout at **2** **s'apostropher** *vpr* to shout at one another

apothéose [apɔteoz] *nf (consécration)* crowning glory; **finir en a.** to end spectacularly

apothicaire [apɔtikɛr] *nm Vieilli* apothecary; *Fig* **tenir des comptes d'a.** to know where every penny goes

apôtre [apotr] *nm* apostle; *Fig* **se faire l'a. de qch** to become an advocate of sth

Appalaches [apalaʃ] *nmpl* **les (monts) A.** the Appalachians

apparaître [20] [aparɛtr] *(aux être)* **1** *vi* **(a)** *(devenir visible)* to appear; **il lui est apparu en rêve** he came *or* appeared to him/her in a dream **(b)** *(phénomène, espèce)* to appear **(c)** *(vérité, solution)* to become apparent **(d)** *(sembler)* to seem; **il m'apparaît comme le seul capable d'y parvenir** he seems to me to be the only person capable of doing it **2** *v impersonnel* **il apparaît que...** it appears (that)...

apparat [apara] *nm* pomp, show; **tenue d'a.** ceremonial dress; **en grand a.** with great pomp and ceremony

appareil [aparɛj] *nm* **(a)** *(instrument)* apparatus; **a. (dentaire)** *(correctif)* brace; *(dentier)* dentures; **appareils ménagers** household appliances; **a. (photographique), a. photo** camera; **a. photo numérique** digital camera **(b)** *(téléphone)* telephone; **Paul à l'a.** Paul speaking *or* here; **qui est à l'a.?** who's speaking? **(c)** *(avion)* aircraft, plane **(d)** *(structure, système)* apparatus; **l'a. de la justice** the legal system; *Pol* **l'a. du parti** the party machine; **a. de production** *(industriel)* production facilities **(e)** *Anat* system; **a. digestif** digestive system; **a. génital** genital system; **a. respiratoire** respiratory system **(f)** *Litt ou Hum* **dans le plus simple a.** in one's birthday suit

appareillage [aparɛjaʒ] *nm* **(a)** *Naut* getting under way **(b)** *(matériel)* equipment; *Ind* plant

appareiller [aparɛje] *vi Naut* to get under way

apparemment [aparamɑ̃] *adv* apparently

apparence [aparɑ̃s] *nf* **(a)** *(aspect extérieur)* appearance, look; **un homme à l'a. négligée/soignée** an untidy-looking/a tidy-looking man; **en dépit des apparences** in spite of appearances **(b)** *(aspect trompeur)* **il ne faut pas se fier aux apparences** appearances can be deceptive; **il a l'air gentil, mais ce n'est qu'une a.** he seems nice, but it's only a façade; **en a.** outwardly; **pour sauver les apparences** to keep up appearances

apparent, -e [aparɑ̃, -ɑ̃t] *adj* **(a)** *(visible)* visible, apparent; **peu a.** hardly noticeable; **sans raison apparente** for no apparent reason **(b)** *(prétendu)* apparent; **sous cette apparente bonté se cache un grand égoïsme** beneath that kind exterior there lies great selfishness

apparenté, -e [aparɑ̃te] *adj* **(a)** *(par le mariage)* related; *(en rapport)* related, connected **(b)** *Pol* **candidat a. à un parti** = candidate who, though not a member of a party, can count on its support in an election

apparenter [aparɑ̃te] **s'apparenter** *vpr (ressembler)* to have something in common (**à** with)

appariteur [aparitœr] *nm (d'université)* porter

apparition [aparisjɔ̃] *nf* **(a)** *(manifestation)* appearance; **faire son a.** *(personne)* to make one's appearance **(b)** *(fantôme)* apparition; **avoir des apparitions** to see things

appartement [apartəmɑ̃] *nm Br* flat, *Am* apartment; *(dans un hôtel)* suite; **vivre en a.** to live in *Br* a flat *or*

Am an apartment; **les grands appartements** *(d'un château)* the state apartments

appartenance [apartənɑ̃s] *nf* belonging (**à** to); *(à un parti)* membership (**à** of)

appartenir [70] [apartənir] **appartenir à 1** *vt ind* (**a**) *(être possédé par)* to belong to (**b**) *(faire partie de) (club, parti, espèce)* to belong to, to be a member of; **elle appartient à une famille très riche** she comes from a very wealthy family

2 *v impersonnel* **il appartient au comité de prendre la décision** it is up to the committee to decide

appât [apɑ] *nm (de pêche)* bait; *Fig (du succès)* lure; **l'a. du gain** the lure of money

appâter [apɑte] *vt* (**a**) *(animaux)* to lure; *Fig (personne)* to entice (**b**) *(hameçon)* to bait

appauvrir [apovrir] **1** *vt* to impoverish

2 s'appauvrir *vpr* to get poorer; *(sol, langue)* to become impoverished

appeau, -x [apo] *nm* birdcall *(instrument)*

appel [apɛl] *nm* (**a**) *(invitation, sollicitation)* appeal; **faire a. à qn** to appeal to sb; *(plombier, médecin)* to send for sb; **faire a. à la générosité de qn** to appeal to sb's generosity; **cette formation fait a. à des connaissances commerciales** this training course calls for some knowledge of business; **faire a. à ses souvenirs** to search one's memory; **un a. à la révolte** a call to revolt; *Com* **lancer un a. d'offres** to invite bids (**b**) *(cri)* call; **a. au secours** call for help; **faire un a. de phares à qn** to flash one's headlights at sb; *Fig* **a. du pied** veiled hint (**c**) *(attirance)* call; **l'a. du large/de la nature** the call of the sea/of the wild; **a. d'air** *(courant d'air)* draught (**d**) **a. (téléphonique)** (tele)phone call; **a. gratuit** *Br* Freefone® call, *Am* toll-free call; **a. en PCV,** *Can* **a. à frais virés** *Br* reverse-charge call, *Am* collect call (**e**) *(pour vérifier)* **faire l'a.** to have a roll call; *Scol* to take the register; **manquer/répondre à l'a.** to be absent/present (**f**) *Jur* appeal; **faire a. d'une décision** to appeal against a decision; *Fig* **être sans a.** *(décision)* to be final (**g**) *Typ* **a. de note** reference figure (**h**) *(pour sauter)* take-off (**i**) *Ordinat* call; *(de commande)* selection

appelé [aple] *nm* (**a**) *Mil* conscript (**b**) *Fig* **il y a beaucoup d'appelés, mais peu d'élus** many are called, but few are chosen

appeler [9] [aple] **1** *vt* (**a**) *(personne, chien)* to call (to); *(taxi)* to hail; **a. (qn) au secours** to call (to sb) for help; **il arrive qu'il appelle la nuit** he sometimes calls out in the night (**b**) **a. qn (au téléphone)** to call sb, to ring sb (up); **a. un taxi/un médecin** to call *or* ring for a taxi/a doctor; **laisse-la a. la première** wait for her to call you (**c**) *(faire venir)* to send for; *(ascenseur)* to call; **faire a. un médecin** to send for a doctor; **a. qn à faire qch** *(inviter)* to call on sb to do sth; *aussi Hum* **le devoir t'appelle** duty calls (**d**) *(désigner)* to call (**e**) **être appelé à faire qch** *(être destiné à)* to be destined to do sth; *(avoir l'obligation de)* to be called upon to do sth (**f**) *(demander, réclamer) (solution, mesures)* to call for; *(critique)* to invite

2 en appeler à *vt ind* to appeal to

3 s'appeler *vpr* (**a**) *(avoir pour nom)* to be called; **comment vous appelez-vous?** what's your name?; **je m'appelle David** my name's David (**b**) *(se téléphoner)* to call each other; **alors, on s'appelle, hein?** talk to you on the phone, okay?

appellation [apɛlasjɔ̃] *nf* name; *(de produit)* designation; **a. contrôlée** *(de vin)* guaranteed vintage; **a. d'origine** = guarantee of wine quality

appendice [apɛ̃dis] *nm* (**a**) *Anat* appendix; *Zool & Bot* appendage (**b**) *(d'un livre)* appendix

appendicite [apɛ̃disit] *nf* appendicitis; **avoir l'a.** *ou* **une crise d'a.** to have appendicitis; **se faire opérer de l'a.** to have one's appendix out

appesantir [apəzɑ̃tir] **1** *vt (démarche)* to slow down; **les paupières appesanties par le sommeil** eyes heavy with sleep

2 s'appesantir *vpr (démarche)* to slow down; *Fig* **s'a. sur qch** *(sujet)* to dwell at length on sth

appétissant, -e [apetisɑ̃, -ɑ̃t] *adj (nourriture)* appetizing, tempting; *Hum (personne)* attractive

appétit [apeti] *nm* (**a**) *(de nourriture)* appetite; **couper l'a. à qn** to spoil sb's appetite; **donner de l'a. à qn, mettre qn en a.** to give sb an appetite; **perdre l'a.** to lose one's appetite; **manger de bon a.** to tuck in; **avoir un a. d'oiseau** to have a poor appetite; **avoir bon** *ou* **un gros a.** to have a good appetite; **bon a.!** enjoy your meal!; *Prov* **l'a. vient en mangeant** it's only when you start eating that you realize you're hungry (**b**) *(désir) (de culture, de connaissances)* appetite (**de** for)

applaudimètre [aplodimɛtr] *nm* clapometer

applaudir [aplodir] **1** *vt* to applaud

2 *vi* to applaud, to clap

3 applaudir à *vt ind (décision, changement)* to applaud

applaudissements [aplodismɑ̃] *nmpl* applause, clapping; **un tonnerre** *ou* **une tempête d'a.** thunderous applause

applicable [aplikabl] *adj* applicable (**à** to)

applicateur [aplikatœr] *nm (dispositif)* applicator

application [aplikasjɔ̃] *nf* (**a**) *(de peinture, de pommade)* application (**b**) *(d'un règlement)* application; *(de la loi, d'une peine)* enforcement; **mettre une théorie en a.** to put a theory into practice; **mettre une loi en a.** to enforce a law; **entrer en a.** to come into force (**c**) *(emploi)* application (**d**) *(assiduité)* application; **travailler avec a.** to apply oneself to one's work (**e**) *Ordinat* application

applique [aplik] *nf (lampe)* wall light

appliqué, -e [aplike] *adj* (**a**) *(personne)* hard-working, diligent; *(écriture)* careful (**b**) *(sciences)* applied

appliquer [aplike] **1** *vt* (**a**) *(mettre)* to apply (**sur** to) (**b**) *(utiliser)* to apply (**à** to); *(loi, peine)* to enforce

2 s'appliquer *vpr* (**a**) *(se concentrer)* to apply oneself (**à** to); **s'a. à faire qch** to take pains to do sth (**b**) **s'a. à** *(concerner)* to apply to (**c**) *(se placer)* to be applied; **cette crème doit s'a. avant le coucher** this cream should be applied at bedtime

appoint [apwɛ̃] *nm* (**a**) *(monnaie)* exact money *or* change; **faire l'a.** to give the exact money (**b**) *(revenu supplémentaire)* extra income; **d'a.** *(chauffage, éclairage)* additional

appointements [apwɛ̃tmɑ̃] *nmpl* salary

apport [apɔr] *nm (contribution)* contribution (**à** to); *Fin* **a. en capital/numéraire** capital/cash contribution; **a. calorique** *(d'un aliment)* calorie content

apporter [apɔrte] *vt* (**a**) *(porter)* to bring (**à** to); *(capitaux)* to bring in; **je t'ai apporté le DVD** I've brought you the DVD (**b**) *(mettre)* **a. du soin à faire qch** to exercise care in doing sth (**c**) *(bonheur, soulagement)* to bring (**à** to); *(preuve)* to provide; *(changements)* to bring about; **ce travail ne m'apporte pas grand-chose** I don't get very much out of this work

apposer [apoze] *vt (affiche)* to put up; *(signature, scellés, sceau)* to affix (**à** to)
apposition [apozisjɔ̃] *nf* (**a**) *(d'un sceau, de scellés, de signature)* affixing (**à** to) (**b**) *Gram* apposition; **en a.** in apposition
appréciable [apresjabl] *adj* (**a**) *(visible)* appreciable, noticeable (**b**) *(non négligeable)* considerable, appreciable (**c**) *(agréable) (qualités)* praiseworthy; *(changement)* welcome
appréciation [apresjasjɔ̃] *nf* (**a**) *(évaluation)* valuation (**b**) *(opinion)* judgement, opinion; *(sur devoir scolaire)* comment; **laisser qch à l'a. de qn** to leave sth to sb's discretion (**c**) *(augmentation de valeur)* appreciation
apprécier [66] [apresje] **1** *vt* (**a**) *(température, distance, son)* to estimate; *(différences, nuances)* to appreciate; **tu ne l'apprécies pas à sa juste valeur** you don't appreciate his/her true worth (**b**) *(aimer)* to like; *Fam* **elle n'a pas apprécié** she wasn't too pleased
2 s'apprécier *vpr* (**a**) *(personnes)* to like each other (**b**) *(monnaie)* to appreciate
appréhender [apreɑ̃de] *vt* (**a**) *Jur (arrêter)* to arrest, to apprehend (**b**) *(craindre)* to dread; **a. de faire qch** to dread doing sth (**c**) *(comprendre)* to grasp
appréhensif, -ive [apreɑ̃sif, -iv] *adj* apprehensive
appréhension [apreɑ̃sjɔ̃] *nf (crainte)* apprehension (**de** about); **avoir une a.** to be apprehensive
apprendre [58] [aprɑ̃dr] *vt* (**a**) *(leçon, langue, instrument de musique)* to learn; **a. à faire qch** to learn how to do sth; **a. vite/lentement** to be a fast/slow learner (**b**) *(nouvelle)* to hear; *(mort, mariage)* to hear of; **a. que...** to hear that... (**c**) *(enseigner)* to teach sb sth; **a. à qn à faire qch** to teach sb how to do sth; *Fam* **je t'apprendrai à me parler sur ce ton!** I'll teach you to speak to me like that!; *Fam* **ça vous apprendra!** that'll teach you! (**d**) *(informer de)* **a. qch à qn** to tell sb sth; **vous ne m'apprenez rien!** you're telling me! (**e**) *Belg (former)* to train
2 s'apprendre *vpr* **ça s'apprend vite** it can be learned quickly; **ça s'apprend facilement** it's easy to learn
apprenti, -e [aprɑ̃ti] *nm,f* apprentice; **a. menuisier** carpenter's apprentice; *Fig* **jouer les apprentis sorciers** to bite off more than one can chew
apprentissage [aprɑ̃tisaʒ] *nm* (**a**) *(professionnel)* training; *(chez un artisan)* apprenticeship; **être en a. chez qn** to be apprenticed to sb (**b**) *(d'une matière, d'une langue)* **l'a. de qch** learning sth; *Fig* **faire l'a. de qch** to learn about sth
apprêté, -e [aprete] *adj (style, attitude)* affected
apprêter [aprete] **1** *vt* (**a**) *(repas)* to prepare (**b**) *(tissu, cuir)* to finish
2 s'apprêter *vpr (se préparer)* to get ready; **s'a. à faire qch** to get ready to do sth
apprivoisé, -e [aprivwaze] *adj* tame
apprivoiser [aprivwaze] **1** *vt (animal)* to tame; *Fig (personne)* to win over
2 s'apprivoiser *vpr (animal)* to become tame; *Fig (personne)* to become more sociable
approbateur, -trice [aprɔbatœr, -tris] *adj* approving
approbation [aprɔbasjɔ̃] *nf* approval (**de** of); **soumettre qch à l'a. de qn** to submit sth to sb for approval; **le film a reçu l'a. du public** the film was well received by the public; **pour a.** *(sur document)* for approval
approchant [aprɔʃɑ̃] *adj m* **je n'ai jamais rien vu d'a.** I've never seen anything like it; **voilà ce qu'il a dit ou**

quelque chose d'a. that's what he said, or something similar
approche [aprɔʃ] *nf* (**a**) *(dans le temps)* approach; **à l'a. de la vieillesse** as old age draws/drew near; **aux approches de la trentaine elle a voulu avoir des enfants** as she approached thirty she wanted children (**b**) *(dans l'espace)* **à son a.** as he/she approached; *Fig* **d'une a. difficile** *(personne)* unapproachable; *(livre)* hard to understand (**c**) *(d'une question, d'un problème)* approach (**de** to) (**d**) **approches** *(d'une ville, d'un village)* outskirts (**e**) *Aviat* approach
approcher [aprɔʃe] **1** *vt* (**a**) *(mettre plus près)* to bring up; **a. qch de qn/qch** to bring sth near (to) sb/sth (**b**) *(venir près de)* to approach, to get closer to; *(aborder)* to go up to
2 *vi* (**a**) *(dans l'espace, dans le temps)* to approach, to get closer; **l'heure** *ou* **le moment approche** it will soon be time; **la nuit approchait** it was beginning to get dark; **approche, je vais te montrer quelque chose** come (over) here, I've got something to show you; **a. de qn/qch** to approach sb/sth; **a. du but** to be nearing one's goal; **il approche de la trentaine** he's getting on for thirty (**b**) *Fig* **a. de qch** *(être semblable à)* to be close to sth
3 s'approcher *vpr* to approach, to get closer; **s'a. de qn/qch** to approach sb/sth; *Fig* **s'a. de qch** *(être semblable à)* to be close to sth
approfondi, -e [aprɔfɔ̃di] *adj (recherche)* detailed, extensive; *(connaissances, enquête)* thorough, in-depth
approfondir [aprɔfɔ̃dir] *vt (examiner)* to go thoroughly into
approprié, -e [aprɔprije] *adj* appropriate (**à** for)
approprier [66] [aprɔprije] **1** *vt Belg (nettoyer)* to clean; *(ranger)* to tidy
2 s'approprier *vpr* **s'a. qch** to appropriate sth
approuver [apruve] *vt* (**a**) *(décision, choix)* to approve of; **a. qn (d'avoir fait qch)** to think sb is right (to have done sth) (**b**) *(facture, contrat, projet de loi)* to approve
approvisionnement [aprɔvizjɔnmɑ̃] *nm* (**a**) *(ravitaillement) (d'une ville, d'une armée)* supplying (**en** with); *(d'un magasin)* stocking (**en** with) (**b**) **approvisionnements** *(stocks)* supplies
approvisionner [aprɔvizjɔne] **1** *vt* (**a**) *(ville, armée, personne)* to supply (**en** with); *(magasin)* to stock (**en** with) (**b**) *(compte bancaire)* to pay money into; **son compte en banque n'est plus approvisionné** his/her bank account is no longer in credit
2 s'approvisionner *vpr* to get in supplies (**en** of); **s'a. chez qn** to get one's supplies from sb; *(faire ses courses)* to shop at sb's
approximatif, -ive [aprɔksimatif, -iv] *adj (calcul, estimation)* approximate; **dans un anglais a.** in broken English
approximation [aprɔksimasjɔ̃] *nf* approximation
approximativement [aprɔksimativmɑ̃] *adv* approximately
appt *(abrév* **appartement**) *Br* flat, *Am* apartment
appui [apɥi] *nm* (**a**) *(support)* support; **prendre a. sur qch** *(personne)* to lean on sth; **prendre a. sur le pied gauche** *(pour sauter)* to take off from the left foot; **a. de fenêtre** window ledge *or* sill (**b**) *(moral)* support, backing; **à l'a. de qch** in support of sth; **preuves à l'a.** with supporting evidence
appui-tête *(pl* **appuis-tête**) [apɥitɛt] *nm* headrest

appuyé, -e [apЧije] *adj (plaisanterie, ironie)* laboured; **il lui lançait des regards appuyés** he stared at him/her intently

appuyer [32] [apЧije] **1** *vt* (**a**) *(poser)* to lean, to rest (**contre** against) (**b**) *(appliquer)* **a. qch sur qch** to press sth on sth; **a. le pied sur la pédale de frein** to put one's foot on the brake (**c**) *Fig (demande, pétition, candidat)* to support, to back; *(proposition)* to second

  2 *vi* (**a**) *(presser)* to press; **a. sur un bouton** to press a button (**b**) **a. sur** *(accentuer) (mot, syllabe)* to stress; *Fig (insister)* to emphasize, to stress

  3 s'appuyer *vpr* (**a**) *(reposer)* **s'a. sur/contre** to lean on/against; *Fig* **s'a. sur qch** *(être basé sur)* to be based on sth; *(se servir de)* to draw on sth (**b**) *Fam* **s'a. qch** *(corvée)* to get lumbered with sth

âpre [apr] *adj* (**a**) *(aigre)* bitter; *(vin)* rough (**b**) *(vent)* raw (**c**) *(concurrence)* fierce; **être â. au gain** to be money-grabbing

âprement [aprəmã] *adv* fiercely

après [aprɛ] **1** *prép* (**a**) *(dans le temps, dans l'espace)* after; **jour a. jour** day after day; **a. s'être rasé** after shaving; **a. vous, Monsieur/Madame!** after you!; *Fam* **courir a. qn** to run after sb; *Fig (faire la cour à)* to chase sb; **il est toujours a. moi** he's always nagging me; *Fam* **en avoir a. qn** to have it in for sb; **a. coup** after the event; **a. tout** after all (**b**) **d'a.** *(selon)* according to; **d'a. moi** in my opinion; **d'a. l'article 12** under article 12

  2 *adv* afterwards; **six semaines a.** six weeks later; **a. que** after, when; **avec lui, la famille, ça passe a.** his family takes second place; **le jour d'a.** the next *or* following day; **et a.?** *(que s'est-il passé?)* what happened next?; *Fam* **et (puis) a.?** so what?

après- [aprɛ] *préf* post-; **l'a.-68** the post-1968 period; **l'a.-Gorbatchev** the post-Gorbachev era

après-demain [aprɛdəmɛ̃] *adv* the day after tomorrow

après-guerre *(pl* **après-guerres)** [aprɛgɛr] *nm* post-war period

après-midi [aprɛmidi] *nm inv ou nf inv* afternoon; **trois heures de l'a.** three (o'clock) in the afternoon

après-rasage *(pl* **après-rasages)** [aprɛrazaʒ] *nm & adj inv* aftershave

après-ski *(pl* **après-skis)** [aprɛski] *nm* snowboot

après-soleil [aprɛsɔlɛj] *adj inv voir* **lait**

après-vente [aprɛvɑ̃t] *adj inv Com* **service a.** after-sales service

âpreté [aprəte] *nf* (**a**) *(aigreur)* bitterness; *(du vin)* roughness (**b**) *(du vent)* rawness (**c**) *(de la concurrence)* fierceness

a priori [aprijɔri] **1** *adv* in principle

  2 *nm inv* preconception; **avoir des a. (contre/en faveur de qch)** to be prejudiced (against/in favour of sth); **être sans a.** to be impartial

apr. J.-C. *(abrév* **après Jésus-Christ)** AD; **en 55 a.** in 55 AD

à-propos [aprɔpo] *nm (d'une remarque, d'une réaction)* appropriateness; **avoir l'esprit d'à.** to have presence of mind; **répondre avec à.** to give an appropriate reply

apte [apt] *adj* **a. à qch/à faire qch** fit for sth/for doing sth; *Mil* **a. au service** fit for military service

aptitude [aptityd] *nf (capacité)* aptitude, ability (**à** *ou* **pour** for)

Aquagym® [akwaʒim] *nf* aquarobics *(singulier)*

aquaplanage [akwaplanaʒ], **aquaplaning** [akwaplaniŋ] *nm Aut* aquaplaning

aquarelle [akwarɛl] *nf* watercolour; **peindre à l'a.** to paint in watercolors

aquarelliste [akwarelist] *nmf* watercolourist

aquarium [akwarjɔm] *nm* aquarium

aquatique [akwatik] *adj* aquatic

aqueduc [akədyk] *nm* aqueduct

aqueux, -euse [akø, -øz] *adj Anat & Chim* aqueous; *(soupe)* watery

aquilin, -e [akilɛ̃, -in] *adj* aquiline

Aquitaine [akitɛn] *nf* **l'A.** Aquitaine

arabe [arab] **1** *adj (monde, littérature, pays)* Arab, Arabic; *(chiffres, langue)* Arabic; *(cheval)* Arab; *(coutumes, civilisation)* Arabian, Arabic

  2 *nmf* **A.** Arab

  3 *nm (langue)* Arabic

Arabe

Note that in a French context this word usually refers to people from the former colonies of North Africa, who make up the largest ethnic minority in France.

arabesque [arabɛsk] *nf* arabesque

arabica [arabika] *nm* arabica

Arabie [arabi] *nf* **l'A.** Arabia; **l'A. saoudite** Saudi Arabia

arable [arabl] *adj* arable

arachide [araʃid] *nf (plante)* peanut, groundnut; **huile d'a.** peanut *or* groundnut oil

araignée [arɛɲe] *nf* spider; *Fam* **avoir une a. au plafond** to have a screw loose; **a. de mer** spider crab

Aral [aral] *n voir* **mer**

arbalète [arbalɛt] *nf* crossbow

arbitrage [arbitraʒ] *nm* (**a**) *(au tennis)* umpiring; *(au football)* refereeing (**b**) *(dans un conflit)* arbitration

arbitraire [arbitrɛr] *adj* arbitrary

arbitrairement [arbitrɛrmɑ̃] *adv* arbitrarily

arbitre [arbitr] *nm* (**a**) *(au tennis)* umpire; *(au football)* referee (**b**) *(dans un conflit)* arbitrator (**c**) *Phil* **libre a.** free will

arbitrer [arbitre] *vt* (**a**) *(match de tennis)* to umpire; *(match de football)* to referee (**b**) *(dans un conflit)* to arbitrate

arborer [arbɔre] *vt (porter, exhiber)* to wear, to sport

arborescence [arbɔresɑ̃s] *nf Math & Ordinat* tree diagram

arborescent, -e [arbɔresɑ̃, -ɑ̃t] *adj* (**a**) *Bot* arborescent (**b**) *Math & Ordinat* **structure arborescente** tree diagram

arboriculteur, -trice [arbɔrikyltœr, -tris] *nm,f* tree grower

arboriculture [arbɔrikyltyr] *nf* tree growing

arbre [arbr] *nm* (**a**) *(végétal)* tree; *Fig* **les arbres cachent la forêt** you can't see the wood for the trees; **a. fruitier** fruit tree; **a. de Noël** Christmas tree (**b**) **a. généalogique** family tree; **faire son a. généalogique** to trace one's family tree (**c**) *Tech* shaft; **a. à cames** camshaft; **a. de transmission** transmission shaft

arbrisseau, -x [arbriso] *nm* shrub

arbuste [arbyst] *nm* shrub

arc [ark] *nm* (**a**) *(arme)* bow (**b**) *Archit & Anat* arch; **a. de triomphe** triumphal arch (**c**) *(de cercle)* arc; **assis en a. de cercle** sitting in a semicircle

arcade [arkad] *nf* (**a**) *Archit* archway; **arcades** *(d'une place)* arcade (**b**) *Anat* **a. sourcilière** arch of the eyebrows

arc-bouter [arkbute] **s'arc-bouter** *vpr* to brace oneself

arceau, -x [arso] *nm* (**a**) *(d'une voûte)* arch (**b**) *(au croquet)* hoop (**c**) *Aut* **a. de sécurité** roll bar

arc-en-ciel (*pl* **arcs-en-ciel**) [arkɑ̃sjɛl] *nm* rainbow

archaïque [arkaik] *adj* archaic

archaïsme [arkaism] *nm* archaism

archange [arkɑ̃ʒ] *nm* archangel

arche¹ [arʃ] *nf* **l'a. de Noé** Noah's ark

arche² *nf (d'un pont)* arch

archéologie [arkeɔlɔʒi] *nf* archaeology

archéologique [arkeɔlɔʒik] *adj* archaeological

archéologue [arkeɔlɔg] *nmf* archaeologist

archer [arʃe] *nm* archer

archet [arʃɛ] *nm* bow *(for violin)*

archétype [arketip] *nm* archetype; **c'est l'a. du père de famille** he is the archetypal father figure

archevêque [arʃəvɛk] *nm* archbishop

archiconnu, -e [arʃikɔny] *adj Fam* really well-known; **c'est a.!** that's common knowledge!

archiduc [arʃidyk] *nm* archduke

archiduchesse [arʃidyʃɛs] *nf* archduchess

archifaux, -fausse [arʃifo, -fos] *adj Fam* totally wrong

Archimède [arʃimɛd] *npr* Archimedes

archipel [arʃipɛl] *nm* archipelago

architecte [arʃitɛkt] *nm* architect; *Ordinat* **a. de réseaux** network architect

architectural, -e, -aux, -ales [arʃitɛktyral, -o] *adj* architectural

architecture [arʃitɛktyr] *nf aussi Ordinat* architecture; *Fig* structure

archiver [arʃive] *vt (documents officiels)* to archive; *(factures)* to file

archives [arʃiv] *nfpl* archives, records; **les a. nationales** ≃ the (Public) Record Office

archiviste [arʃivist] *nmf* archivist; *(employé de bureau)* filing clerk

arçon [arsɔ̃] *nm* saddle bow

arctique [arktik] **1** *adj* arctic
2 *nm* **l'A.** the Arctic

ardemment [ardamɑ̃] *adv (aimer)* passionately; **désirer a. qch** to long for sth

ardent, -e [ardɑ̃, -ɑ̃t] *adj* (**a**) *(braises, soleil)* scorching, blazing; *(soif, fièvre)* raging (**b**) *(tempérament, jeunesse)* fiery; *(désir)* burning; *(lutte, défenseur)* fierce; *(admirateur)* ardent, fervent

ardeur [ardœr] *nf* (**a**) *(enthousiasme)* ardour, fervour; **travailler avec a.** to work enthusiastically (**b**) *(du soleil, du feu)* intense heat

ardoise [ardwaz] *nf* (**a**) *(matière, plaque, pour écrire)* slate; **toit d'ardoises** slate roof (**b**) *Fam (compte)* tab; **il a des ardoises dans tous les bars de la ville** he owes money in every bar in town

ardu, -e [ardy] *adj* arduous

are [ar] *nm* are, = 100 m²

aréna [arena] *nm ou nf Can* = sports centre including an ice rink

arène [arɛn] *nf (d'amphithéâtre)* arena; *(de tauromachie)* bullring; **arènes** *(antiques)* amphitheatre; *Fig* **descendre dans l'a.** to enter the fray; *Fig* **l'a. politique** the political arena

arête [arɛt] *nf* (**a**) *(de poisson)* bone; **sans arêtes** boneless; **enlever les arêtes d'un poisson** to fillet a

fish (**b**) *(du nez)* bridge (**c**) *(d'un solide)* edge (**d**) *Géog* ridge

argent [arʒɑ̃] **1** *nm* (**a**) *(métal)* silver; **bracelet d'a.** *ou* **en a.** silver bracelet (**b**) *(monnaie)* money; **en avoir pour son a.** to get one's money's worth; *Fig* **prendre qch pour a. comptant** to take sth at face value; *Prov* **l'a. ne fait pas le bonheur** money can't buy you happiness; *Prov* **l'a. n'a pas d'odeur** it's all money; **a. liquide** cash; **a. de poche** pocket money; **a. électronique** e-cash, electronic money (**c**) *(couleur)* silver
2 *adj inv* silver

argenté, -e [arʒɑ̃te] *adj* (**a**) *(couleur)* silver (**b**) *(plaqué)* silver-plated

argenterie [arʒɑ̃tri] *nf* (silver) plate, silverware

argentin, -e [arʒɑ̃tɛ̃, -in] **1** *adj* Argentinian, Argentine
2 *nm,f* **A.** Argentinian, Argentine

Argentine [arʒɑ̃tin] *nf* **l'A.** Argentina

argile [arʒil] *nf* clay

argileux, -euse [arʒilø, -øz] *adj* clayey

argot [argo] *nm* slang

Argot

This term can refer both to "la langue verte" (the slang of the underworld) or the jargon of particular social or professional groups (such as butchers, soldiers, students etc). Some "argot" has evolved from being part of the secret language of a select group to becoming part of everyday speech, while other terms have become obsolete, supplanted by "verlan" *(see box at this entry)*, the slang used by young people in the suburbs of big cities.

argotique [argɔtik] *adj* slang, slangy

arguer [arge, argɥe] **arguer de** *vt ind Litt* **a. de qch** to give sth as a reason

argument [argymɑ̃] *nm* argument; **a. de vente** selling point

argumentaire [argymɑ̃tɛr] *nm* sales blurb

argumentation [argymɑ̃tasjɔ̃] *nf (arguments)* argument

argumenter [argymɑ̃te] *vi* to argue (**contre/en faveur de** against/for)

argus [argys] *nm* = guide to used car prices

aria [arja] *nf Mus* aria

aride [arid] *adj (pays)* arid, barren; *(œuvre, sujet)* dry

aridité [aridite] *nf* aridity, barrenness

aristocrate [aristɔkrat] *nmf* aristocrat

aristocratie [aristɔkrasi] *nf* aristocracy

aristocratique [aristɔkratik] *adj* aristocratic

Aristote [aristɔt] *npr* Aristotle

arithmétique [aritmetik] **1** *adj* arithmetical
2 *nf (matière, calculs)* arithmetic

arlequin [arləkɛ̃] *nm Théât* Harlequin

armagnac [armaɲak] *nm* Armagnac

armateur [armatœr] *nm* shipowner

armature [armatyr] *nf* framework; *(dans le béton)* reinforcement; *(de tente, d'abat-jour)* frame; *(de soutien-gorge)* underwiring

arme [arm] *nf* (**a**) *(de combat)* arm, weapon; *Fig* weapon; **peuple/ville en armes** nation/town in arms; **prendre les armes** to take up arms (**contre** against); **aux armes!** to arms!; **le métier** *ou* **la carrière des armes** the military profession; **passer qn par les armes** to send sb to the firing squad; *Fam* **passer l'a. à gauche** to snuff it, to kick the bucket; **faire**

ses premières armes to earn one's spurs; à armes égales on equal terms; avec armes et bagages with bag and baggage; armes biologiques biological weapons; a. blanche knife; armes de destruction massive weapons of mass destruction; a. à feu firearm; armes nucléaires nuclear weapons (**b**) (section de l'armée) service (**c**) armes (blason) (coat of) arms

armé, -e¹ [arme] adj (**a**) (muni d'une arme) armed; a. jusqu'aux dents armed to the teeth; aussi Fig être a. de qch to be armed with sth; Fig être a. pour qch (préparé) to be equipped for sth (**b**) (renforcé) fortified, strengthened

armée² nf aussi Fig army; être dans l'a. to be in the army; être à l'a. to be doing one's military service; l'a. de l'air the air force; a. de métier professional army; a. régulière ou active regular army; a. de réserve reserves; l'A. du salut the Salvation Army; l'a. de terre the army

armement [arməmɑ̃] nm (**a**) (action) (d'un pays, d'une région) armament; (d'une armée) arming (**b**) armements (armes) armaments, weaponry (**c**) (d'une arme à feu) cocking; (d'un appareil photo) setting (**d**) (de navire) commissioning, fitting out

Arménie [armeni] nf l'A. Armenia

arménien, -enne [armenjɛ̃, -ɛn] **1** adj Armenian
2 nm,f A. Armenian
3 nm (langue) Armenian

armer [arme] **1** vt (**a**) (munir d'armes) to arm (**de** with); je sors toujours armé I always carry a weapon when I go out (**b**) (navire) to commission, to fit out (**c**) (arme à feu) to cock; (appareil photo) to set
2 s'armer vpr to arm oneself; s'a. de courage/de patience to summon up (one's) courage/patience

armistice [armistis] nm armistice

armoire [armwar] nf (placard) Br cupboard, Am closet; (pour les vêtements) Br wardrobe, Am closet; a. à glace mirrored wardrobe; Hum c'est une a. à glace he's built like a tank; a. de toilette ou de salle de bain bathroom cabinet

armoiries [armwari] nfpl (coat of) arms

armure [armyr] nf armour

armurier [armyrje] nm (**a**) (vendeur) gun dealer (**b**) (dans une caserne) armourer

ARN [aɛrɛn] nm (abrév acide ribonucléique) RNA

arnaque [arnak] nf Fam rip-off; c'est de l'a.! what a rip-off!

arnaquer [arnake] vt Fam to rip off; se faire a. to get ripped off

arnaqueur, -euse [arnakœr, -øz] nm,f Fam rip-off merchant

arnica [arnika] nm ou nf arnica

arobas [arobas], **arobase** [arobaz] = arrobas

aromate [arɔmat] nm (herbe) herb; (épice) spice

aromathérapie [arɔmaterapi] nf aromatherapy

aromatique [arɔmatik] adj aromatic

aromatisé, -e [arɔmatize] adj flavoured; a. à la vanille vanilla-flavoured

arôme [arom] nm (parfum) aroma; (goût) flavour; crème glacée, a. vanille vanilla ice cream

arpège [arpɛʒ] nm Mus arpeggio

arpent [arpɑ̃] nm = former land measurement approximately equivalent to one acre

arpenter [arpɑ̃te] vt (**a**) (mesurer) to survey, to measure (**b**) (parcourir) to pace up and down

arqué, -e [arke] adj (sourcils) arched; (nez) hooked; jambes arquées bow legs

arquer [arke] s'arquer vpr to bend, to curve

arrachage [araʃaʒ] nm (de plantes) uprooting; (de pommes de terre) lifting; (d'une dent, d'un clou, de piquets) pulling out

arraché [araʃe] nm (en haltérophilie) snatch; Fig gagner à l'a. to snatch victory; Fig ils ont obtenu le contrat à l'a. it was a struggle for them to get the contract

arrachement [araʃmɑ̃] nm (peine) wrench

arrache-pied [araʃpje] d'arrache-pied adv relentlessly

arracher [araʃe] **1** vt (**a**) (arbre) to uproot; (légumes) to lift; (dent, mauvaises herbes, piquets) to pull out; (page) to tear out; (affiche) to tear down; (vêtement, membre, toit) to tear off; se faire a. une dent to have a tooth out; a. qch à qn/des mains de qn to snatch sth from sb/from sb's hands; Fig je vais lui a. les yeux! I'll scratch his/her eyes out! (**b**) (obtenir) a. qch à qn (argent) to get sth off sb; (secret) to drag sth out of sb; (promesse, sourire) to force sth out of sb; Fig nous sommes finalement parvenus à lui a. quelques mots we did eventually manage to get a few words out of him/her (**c**) (séparer) a. un enfant à sa mère to take a child away from its mother; a. qn à la mort to snatch sb from the jaws of death; a. qn à son travail to tear or drag sb away from his/her work (**d**) Fam (sujet: alcool, piment) ça arrache! it blows your head off!
2 vi Can en a. to have a hard time (of it)
3 s'arracher vpr (**a**) (se disputer) s'a. qn/qch to fight over sb/sth (**b**) (se retirer) c'est à s'a. les cheveux! it's enough to make you tear your hair out!; s'a. à son travail to tear oneself away from one's work (**c**) très Fam (partir) to hit the road

arracheur [araʃœr] nm mentir comme un a. de dents to lie through one's teeth

arraisonner [arɛzɔne] vt to stop and examine

arrangeant, -e [arɑ̃ʒɑ̃, -ɑ̃t] adj helpful

arrangement [arɑ̃ʒmɑ̃] nm (**a**) (fait de disposer) arranging; (manière d'être disposé) arrangement (**b**) (accord) agreement, settlement (**c**) Mus arrangement

arranger [45] [arɑ̃ʒe] **1** vt (**a**) (meubles, fleurs) to arrange; (pièce, maison) to put in order; (cravate, col) to straighten (**b**) (réparer) to repair (**c**) (organiser) to arrange, to organize; j'ai tout arrangé I've made all the arrangements (**d**) (régler) (problème) to settle; cela n'arrangera pas les choses that won't help things; Ironique pour tout a., il s'est mis à pleuvoir just to help matters, it started to rain (**e**) Fam a. qn (maltraiter) to give sb a going over; (critiquer) to tear sb to pieces (**f**) (convenir à) to suit; faire qch pour a. qn to do sth to help sb out (**g**) Mus to arrange
2 s'arranger vpr (**a**) (s'organiser) to manage; arrangez-vous pour être là/finir à temps make sure you're there/you finish on time; Fam je ne sais pas comment tu t'arranges, tu es toujours en retard I don't know how you manage it, but you're always late (**b**) (s'améliorer) to work out; ça ne s'arrange pas! things aren't getting any better! (**c**) (rectifier son apparence) to tidy oneself up (**d**) (se mettre d'accord) to come to an agreement (avec with); ça ne me regarde pas, arrange-toi avec elle it's got nothing to do with me, sort it out with her (**e**) (se contenter) s'a. de qch to make do with sth

arrestation [arɛstasjɔ̃] *nf* arrest; **en état d'a.** under arrest

arrêt [arɛ] *nm* (**a**) *(interruption) (des combats, des hostilités, de la production)* stop; **Clermont-Ferrand, dix minutes d'a.** *(en train)* this is Clermont-Ferrand, there will be a ten-minute stop; **sans a.** continuously; **tomber en a.** devant qn/qch to stop and stare at sb/sth; **marquer un temps d'a.** to pause; **a. du cœur** heart failure; *Ordinat* **a. de fin de session** shutdown; *TV & Cin* **a. sur image** freeze frame; **a. de jeu** stoppage; **a. de travail** sick leave; **être en a. de travail** to be on sick leave (**b**) *(de véhicule)* stop; **ne pas descendre avant l'a. complet du train** *(sur la portière)* do not alight until the train has come to a complete stop; **le train est sans a. jusqu'à Hendaye** the train is nonstop to Hendaye; **je descends au prochain a.** I'm getting off at the next stop; **a. de bus** bus stop; **a. facultatif** request stop (**c**) *Jur* judgement; *aussi Fig* **a. de mort** death sentence

arrêté, -e [arete] **1** *adj (idées)* fixed
2 *nm (décret)* order, decree; **a. ministériel** ministerial order; **a. municipal** bylaw; **a. préfectoral** bylaw

arrêter [arete] **1** *vt* (**a**) *(personne, animal, véhicule)* to stop; *(machine, moteur, musique)* to turn off; *(fuite)* to stem; *(études)* to give up; **là je vous arrête, je ne suis pas d'accord!** hold it right there, I don't agree!; **arrête-moi au carrefour** drop me off at the crossroads; **rien ne l'arrête** nothing will stop him/her; **a. de faire qch** to stop doing sth; **elle n'arrête pas de me déranger** she keeps disturbing me; **ce détail arrêta mon attention** this detail caught my attention (**b**) *(criminel)* to arrest (**c**) *(déterminer)* to decide; *(date, prix)* to fix
2 *vi* to stop; **arrête!** stop it!
3 **s'arrêter** *vpr* (**a**) *(cesser, s'immobiliser)* to stop; **s'a. de faire qch** to stop doing sth; **s'a. chez qn** to call in at sb's house (**b**) **s'a. à qch** *(faire attention à)* to pay attention to sth

arrhes [ar] *nfpl* deposit

arrière [arjɛr] **1** *adj inv* back; **feu a.** rear light; **roue a.** rear *or* back wheel
2 *nm* (**a**) *(d'une maison, d'un avion)* back; *(d'un bateau)* stern; **à l'a. de la voiture** in the back of the car (**b**) *Mil* **l'a.** the rear; *Fig* **protéger ses arrières** to leave oneself a way out (**c**) *(au football, au rugby)* full back
3 *exclam* stand back!
4 **en arrière** *adv* (**a**) *(derrière)* behind; **rester en a.** to lag behind; **en a. de qn/qch** behind sb/sth (**b**) *(dans la direction inverse)* backwards; **pencher la tête en a.** to lean one's head back; **retourner en a.** to go *or* turn back (**c**) *Suisse* **il y a un siècle en a.** a century ago

arriéré, -e [arjere] **1** *adj* (**a**) *(paiement)* overdue (**b**) *(dans ses idées, son développement)* backward
2 *nm* arrears

arrière-boutique *(pl* **arrière-boutiques)** [arjɛrbutik] *nf Br* back shop, *Am* back store

arrière-cour *(pl* **arrière-cours)** [arjɛrkur] *nf* backyard

arrière-garde *(pl* **arrière-gardes)** [arjɛrgard] *nf* rearguard

arrière-goût *(pl* **arrière-goûts)** [arjɛrgu] *nm aussi Fig* aftertaste

arrière-grand-mère *(pl* **arrière-grands-mères)** [arjɛrgrɑ̃mɛr] *nf* great-grandmother

arrière-grand-père *(pl* **arrière-grands-pères)** [arjɛrgrɑ̃pɛr] *nm* great-grandfather

arrière-grands-parents [arjɛrgrɑ̃parɑ̃] *nmpl* great-grandparents

arrière-pays [arjɛrpei] *nm inv* hinterland

arrière-pensée *(pl* **arrière-pensées)** [arjɛrpɑ̃se] *nf* ulterior motive

arrière-petite-fille *(pl* **arrière-petites-filles)** [arjɛrpətitfij] *nf* great-granddaughter

arrière-petit-fils *(pl* **arrière-petits-fils)** [arjɛrpətifis] *nm* great-grandson

arrière-petits-enfants [arjɛrpətizɑ̃fɑ̃] *nmpl* great-grandchildren

arrière-plan *(pl* **arrière-plans)** [arjɛrplɑ̃] *nm aussi Fig* background; **à l'a.** in the background

arrière-saison *(pl* **arrière-saisons)** [arjɛrsɛzɔ̃] *nf* late autumn, *Am* late fall

arrière-train *(pl* **arrière-trains)** [arjɛrtrɛ̃] *nm (d'un animal)* (hind)quarters; *Fam (d'une personne)* rump, rear

arrimer [arime] *vt* (**a**) *Naut (cargaison)* to stow (**b**) *(fixer)* to secure *or* fasten (**à** to)

arrivage [arivaʒ] *nm* consignment

arrivant, -e [arivɑ̃, -ɑ̃t] *nm,f* arrival; **les nouveaux arrivants** the new arrivals, the newcomers

arrivé, -e [arive] **1** *adj* **être a.** *(socialement)* to have arrived, to have made it
2 *nm,f (personne)* **le premier/dernier a.** the first/last (person) to arrive

arrivée [arive] *nf* (**a**) *(venue)* arrival; **depuis son a. au pouvoir** since he/she came to power; **à mon a.** when I arrive/arrived; **arrivées** *(sur panneau)* arrivals (**b**) *Tech* inlet (**c**) *(d'une course)* winning post, finish

arriver [arive] *(aux être)* **1** *vi* (**a**) *(venir)* to arrive; **a. à Lyon/en France** to arrive in Lyons/in France; **a. le premier/dernier** *(à une soirée)* to arrive first/last; **a. premier/second** *(dans un concours, une course)* to come first/second; **j'arrive!** (I'm) coming!; **c'est à cette heure-là que tu arrives?** and what time do you call this?; **nous sommes presque arrivés** we're almost there (**b**) *(atteindre)* **l'eau m'arrive aux chevilles** the water comes up to my ankles; **ses cheveux lui arrivent aux épaules** his/her hair comes down to his/her shoulders *or* is shoulder-length (**c**) **en a. à faire qch** to get to the stage of doing sth; **c'est malheureux d'en a. là** it's a shame it's got to that stage; **elle en arrive même à ne plus le souhaiter** she's even starting not to want it anymore; **j'en arrive à penser que.../me demander si...** I'm beginning to think.../wonder if... (**d**) *(socialement)* to arrive, to make it (**e**) *(parvenir)* **a. à un résultat** to achieve a result; **a. à faire qch** to manage to do sth; **je n'arrive pas à l'ouvrir** I can't get it open; **il n'arrivera jamais à rien** he'll never make anything of himself (**f**) *(se produire)* to happen (**à** to)
2 *v impersonnel* **quoi qu'il arrive** whatever happens; **il lui est arrivé quelque chose** something's happened to him/her; **il m'arrive d'y penser** I sometimes think about it; **il arrive à tout le monde de se tromper** anyone can make a mistake; **qu'est-ce qu'il t'arrive?** what's wrong (with you)?

arrivisme [arivism] *nm* unscrupulous ambition

arriviste [arivist] *nmf* social climber, arriviste

arrobas [arɔbas], **arrobase** [arɔbaz] *nf Ordinat (dans une adresse électronique)* at-sign

arrogance [arɔgɑ̃s] *nf* arrogance; **avec a.** arrogantly

arrogant, -e [arɔgɑ̃, -ɑ̃t] *adj* arrogant

arroger [45] [aʁɔʒe] s'**arroger** *vpr* s'**a. un droit/un privilège** to claim a right/a privilege; s'**a. le droit de faire qch** to assume the right to do sth
arrondi, -e [aʁɔ̃di] **1** *adj (objet, visage)* round
2 *nm* (**a**) *(forme)* roundness, rounded form (**b**) *(d'une jupe)* hemline
arrondir [aʁɔ̃diʁ] **1** *vt* (**a**) *(forme)* **a. qch** to make sth round; **cette coiffure lui arrondit le visage** that haircut makes his/her face look round; *Fig* **a. les angles** to smooth things over (**b**) *(chiffre, somme) (vers le haut)* to round up; *(vers le bas)* to round down; *Fam* **a. ses fins de mois** to make a bit of money on the side; **a. à l'euro supérieur/inférieur** to round up/down to the nearest euro
2 s'**arrondir** *vpr (corps, visage)* to fill out
arrondissement [aʁɔ̃dismɑ̃] *nm* = administrative subdivision of Paris, Lyons and Marseilles

Arrondissement
In Paris, Lyons and Marseilles, the number of the "arrondissement" corresponds to the last two digits in a postcode: thus, you can tell from the postcode 75012 that it refers to the 12th arrondissement of Paris.

arrosage [aʁozaʒ] *nm (des plantes, du sol)* watering; *(des rues)* spraying; *(d'une pelouse)* sprinkling
arroser [aʁoze] **1** *vt* (**a**) *(plantes, sol)* to water; *(pelouse)* to sprinkle; *(rues)* to spray; *(rôti)* to baste; **région très peu arrosée** area with little rainfall; **a. qch d'essence** to douse sth in petrol (**b**) *(fêter)* to drink to; **un repas bien arrosé** a meal washed down with plenty of alcohol (**c**) *(sujet: rivière)* to flow through
2 s'**arroser** *vpr (se fêter)* **ça s'arrose!** that calls for a celebration!
arroseur [aʁozœʁ] *nm (appareil)* sprinkler
arrosoir [aʁozwaʁ] *nm* watering can
arsenal, -aux [aʁsənal, -o] *nm* (**a**) *Mil* arsenal; **a. maritime** *ou* **de la marine** naval dockyard (**b**) *Fam (attirail)* gear
arsenic [aʁsənik] *nm* arsenic
art [aʁ] *nm* (**a**) *(esthétique)* art; **c'est du grand a.!** it's a work of art!; **le septième a.** cinema; **a. dramatique** drama, dramatic art; **les arts graphiques** graphic arts; **l'a. lyrique** opera; **arts martiaux** martial arts; **arts plastiques** fine art; **les arts du spectacle** the performing arts (**b**) *(savoir-faire)* **l'a. de faire qch** the art of doing sth; **cultiver l'a. de vivre** to enjoy the finer things in life; **préparer le café, c'est tout un a.** there's quite an art to making coffee; *Fig* **avoir l'a. de faire qch** to have a knack for doing sth
Arte [aʁte] *n* = French-German TV channel showing cultural programmes
artère [aʁtɛʁ] *nf* (**a**) *(vaisseau)* artery (**b**) **(grande) a.** *(route)* arterial road; *(en ville)* main thoroughfare
artériel, -elle [aʁteʁjɛl] *adj (système, maladie)* arterial
artériosclérose [aʁteʁjosklɛʁoz] *nf* hardening of the arteries, *Spéc* arteriosclerosis
arthrite [aʁtʁit] *nf* arthritis
arthrose [aʁtʁoz] *nf* osteoarthritis
Arthur [aʁtyʁ] *npr Fam* **je vais me faire appeler A.!** I'm going to get a real telling-off!
artichaut [aʁtiʃo] *nm* artichoke
article [aʁtikl] *nm* (**a**) *Com* item; **articles de toilette** toiletries; **faire l'a.** to make a sales pitch (**b**) *Journ* article; *(de dictionnaire)* entry (**c**) *(d'un traité, d'un règle-*

ment) article (**d**) *Gram* article; **a. défini/indéfini** definite/indefinite article (**e**) **être à l'a. de la mort** to be on the point of death (**f**) *Ordinat (dans base de données)* record; *(commande)* command
articulaire [aʁtikylɛʁ] *adj Anat* articular, articulatory
articulation [aʁtikylasjɔ̃] *nf* (**a**) *Anat & Tech* joint (**b**) *(prononciation)* articulation (**c**) *(organisation)* structure
articuler [aʁtikyle] **1** *vt* (**a**) *(idées, arguments)* to link (**b**) *(mots)* to articulate; **articule!** speak clearly!
2 s'**articuler** *vpr (pièces, idées)* to be linked; **les différentes parties du texte s'articulent bien** the different parts of the text hang well together; s'**a. autour de qch** *(théorie)* to centre on sth
artifice [aʁtifis] *nm* trick
artificiel, -elle [aʁtifisjɛl] *adj* (**a**) *(non naturel)* artificial; *Fig (personne)* false; *(rire)* forced (**b**) *(arbitraire)* arbitrary
artificiellement [aʁtifisjɛlmɑ̃] *adv* (**a**) *(de façon non naturelle)* artificially (**b**) *(arbitrairement)* arbitrarily
artificier [aʁtifisje] *nm (fabricant)* firework manufacturer; *(dans un feu d'artifice)* master of ceremonies
artillerie [aʁtijʁi] *nf* artillery; **a. légère/lourde** light/ heavy artillery; **pièce d'a.** artillery cannon
artilleur [aʁtijœʁ] *nm* artilleryman
artisan [aʁtizɑ̃] *nm* craftsman, *f* craftswoman; *Fig* architect
artisanal, -e, -aux, -ales [aʁtizanal, -o] *adj* traditionally made; *(à la main)* hand-made; **métier a.** craft
artisanat [aʁtizana] *nm* craft industry
artiste [aʁtist] **1** *adj (tempérament, style)* artistic; **se donner un genre a.** to cultivate an arty image
2 *nmf* (**a**) *(personne créative)* artist (**b**) *(interprète) (musicien)* performer; *(acteur)* actor, *f* actress; *(chanteur)* singer; *(danseur)* dancer; **a. (peintre)** artist
artistique [aʁtistik] *adj* artistic
as¹ *voir* **avoir¹**
as² [as] *nm* (**a**) *(aux cartes)* ace; *(aux dominos, aux dés)* one; *Fam* **être ficelé** *ou* **fichu comme l'as de pique** to look like *Br* a tramp *or Am* a bum; **être plein aux as** to be rolling in it; *Fam* **passer à l'as** to go out of the window (**b**) *Fam (champion)* whizz; **as du volant** crack racing driver; **un as du bricolage** a DIY expert
ascendance [asɑ̃dɑ̃s] *nf (ancêtres)* ancestry
ascendant, -e [asɑ̃dɑ̃, -ɑ̃t] **1** *adj (échelle)* rising; *(mouvement, courant)* upward
2 *nm* (**a**) *(influence)* influence; **avoir de l'a. sur qn** to have influence over sb (**b**) **ascendants** *(ancêtres)* ancestry
ascenseur [asɑ̃sœʁ] *nm* (**a**) *(dans un bâtiment) Br* lift, *Am* elevator; *Fig* **je lui renverrai l'a.** I'll return the favour (**b**) *Ordinat* scroll box
ascension [asɑ̃sjɔ̃] *nf* (**a**) *(escalade)* ascent; **faire l'a. d'une montagne** to climb a mountain (**b**) *(progression)* **a. sociale** social climbing (**c**) *Rel* **(la fête** *ou* **le jeudi de) l'A.** Ascension Day

Ascension
Ascension Day is on the fortieth day after Easter and is a public holiday in France. Many people take an extended weekend break during this period.

ascensionnel, -elle [asɑ̃sjɔnɛl] *adj (mouvement)* upward
ascète [asɛt] *nmf* ascetic
ASCII [aski] *nm (abrév* **American standard code for information interchange) (code) a.** ASCII (code)

ascorbique [askɔrbik] *adj (acide)* ascorbic
aseptique [asɛptik] *adj* aseptic
aseptiser [asɛptize] *vt (blessure)* to sterilize; *(pièce)* to disinfect; *Fig & Péj* **un univers aseptisé** a sterile environment
asexué, -e [asɛksɥe], **asexuel, -elle** [asɛksɥɛl] *adj aussi Fig* asexual
ashkénaze [aʃkenaz] *adj & nmf* Ashkenazi
asiatique [azjatik] **1** *adj* oriental
2 *nmf* **A.** Oriental

Asiatique
This word tends to refer to Oriental people (ie from countries such as China, Japan, Laos etc), rather than Asia as a whole. Note that it is not used like the word "Asian" in British English, meaning someone from the Indian subcontinent.

Asie [azi] *nf* **l'A.** Asia; **l'A. centrale** Central Asia; **l'A. du Sud-Est** Southeast Asia
asile [azil] *nm* (**a**) *(abri)* refuge; *Vieilli* **a. (d'aliénés)** mental hospital; **a. de nuit** night shelter; **a. de vieillards** old people's home (**b**) *(statut)* **a. politique/diplomatique** political/diplomatic asylum; **demander l'a. politique** to ask for political asylum
asocial, -e, -aux, -ales [asɔsjal, -o] **1** *adj* asocial
2 *nm,f* asocial person
aspartam(e) [aspartam] *nm* aspartame
aspect [aspɛ] *nm* (**a**) *(air)* appearance, look; **un bar d'a. louche** a shady-looking bar (**b**) *(angle)* angle, point of view; **sous tous ses aspects** from every angle, from all points of view (**c**) *Gram* aspect
asperge [aspɛrʒ] *nf* (**a**) *(plante)* asparagus (**b**) *Fam (personne)* beanpole
asperger [45] [aspɛrʒe] **1** *vt (linge, plante)* to spray with water; **a. qn de qch** to splash sb with sth; **se faire a.** to get splashed
2 **s'asperger** *vpr* (**a**) *(soi-même)* **s'a. de qch** to splash oneself with sth (**b**) *(mutuellement)* to splash *or* spray one another
aspérité [asperite] *nf* (**a**) *(d'une surface)* rough part (**b**) *(d'un caractère)* harshness
aspersion [aspɛrsjɔ̃] *nf* spraying
asphalte [asfalt] *nm* asphalt
asphyxiant, -e [asfiksjɑ̃, -ɑ̃t] *adj* asphyxiating, suffocating; *Fig* stifling, suffocating; **gaz a.** poison gas
asphyxie [asfiksi] *nf* asphyxiation
asphyxier [66] [asfiksje] **1** *vt* (**a**) *(personne, animal)* to asphyxiate (**b**) *Fig (économie, industrie)* to paralyse
2 **s'asphyxier** *vpr (suffoquer)* to choke; *(se suicider)* to gas oneself
aspirateur [aspiratœr] *nm* vacuum cleaner, *Br* Hoover®; **passer l'a. dans la maison** to vacuum *or Br* hoover the house
aspiration [aspirasjɔ̃] *nf* (**a**) *(inhalation)* inhalation; *Tech (d'eau dans une pompe)* suction (**b**) *(désir)* yearning (**à** for); *(ambition)* aspiration (**à** for) (**c**) *Ling* aspiration
aspiré, -e [aspire] *adj Ling* aspirate(d)
aspirer [aspire] **1** *vt* (**a**) *(air, parfum)* to inhale, to breathe (in) (**b**) *(liquide)* to suck up (**c**) *Ling* to aspirate
2 **aspirer à** *vt ind* to aspire to; **a. à faire qch** to aspire to do sth
aspirine [aspirin] *nf* aspirin; **un cachet d'a.** an aspirin; **blanc comme un cachet d'a.** white as a ghost

assagir [asaʒir] **1** *vt* to quieten down
2 **s'assagir** *vpr* to settle down
assaillant, -e [asajɑ̃, -ɑ̃t] *nm,f* assailant, attacker
assaillir [67] [asajir] *vt* to assault, to attack; *Fig (sujet: difficultés, remords, doute)* to beset; **a. qn de questions** to bombard sb with questions; **il a été assailli par les journalistes** he was set upon by the journalists
assainir [asenir] *vt (maison, rivière)* to clean up; *(atmosphère)* to purify; *(marais)* to drain; *(économie)* to stabilize
assainissement [asenismɑ̃] *nm (d'une maison, d'une rivière)* cleaning up; *(de l'atmosphère)* purifying; *(d'un marais)* drainage; *(de l'économie)* stabilization
assaisonnement [asɛzɔnmɑ̃] *nm (de plat)* seasoning; *(de salade)* dressing
assaisonner [asɛzɔne] *vt (plat)* to season (**de** with); *(salade)* to dress; *Fam Fig* **se faire a.** to get a good telling-off
assassin, -e [asasɛ̃, -in] **1** *nm* murderer; *(d'une personnalité politique)* assassin; **à l'a.!** murder!
2 *adj* (**a**) *(méchant) (regard)* murderous; *(remarque)* crushing (**b**) *(provocant) (sourire, œillade)* provocative
assassinat [asasina] *nm* murder; *(d'une personnalité politique)* assassination
assassiner [asasine] *vt* to murder; *(personnalité politique)* to assassinate; *Fig (chanson, texte)* to murder; *(sujet: critique)* to crucify
assaut [aso] *nm (attaque)* assault, attack; *Mil* charge; **donner l'a. à** to storm, to launch an attack on; **monter à l'a.** to attack; **prendre qch d'a.** *Mil* to storm sth; *Fig (buffet, guichets)* to make a run for sth
assèchement [asɛʃmɑ̃] *nm (d'un terrain, d'un marécage)* drainage; *(d'un cours d'eau)* drying out
assécher [34] [aseʃe] **1** *vt (terrain, marécage)* to drain; *(cours d'eau)* to dry out
2 **s'assécher** *vpr* to dry up
ASSEDIC [asedik] *nfpl (abrév* **Association pour l'emploi dans l'industrie et le commerce)** = French unemployment benefits department, *Br* ≃ Unemployment Benefit Office; **toucher les A.** to get *Br* unemployment benefit *or Am* welfare
assemblage [asɑ̃blaʒ] *nm* (**a**) *(de pièces détachées)* assembly; *(en menuiserie)* joint; *(en couture)* making up; *(de feuillets)* collating (**b**) *(structure)* assembly
assemblée [asɑ̃ble] *nf* (**a**) *(réunion)* assembly; *(plus petite)* meeting; **a. générale** annual general meeting (**b**) *Pol* **l'A. nationale** the National Assembly, *Br* ≃ the House of Commons, *Am* ≃ the House of Representatives (**c**) *(foule)* crowd

Assemblée nationale
The French parliament has two chambers: the National Assembly and the Senate. The members of the National Assembly (the "députés") are elected in the "élections législatives" held every five years.

assembler [asɑ̃ble] **1** *vt* (**a**) *(machine, meuble en kit)* to assemble, to put together; *(feuillets)* to collate (**b**) *(pièces)* to join (**c**) *Ordinat* to assemble
2 **s'assembler** *vpr (foule)* to gather
assembleur, -euse [asɑ̃blœr, -øz] **1** *nm,f (ouvrier)* fitter
2 *nm Ordinat* assembler (language)
asséner [34] [asene] *vt* **a. qch à qn** *(coup)* to deliver sth to sb; *(remarque)* to hurl sth at sb

assentiment [asɑ̃timɑ̃] *nm* assent

asseoir [10a] [aswar] **1** *vt* (**a**) *(installer) (personne)* to seat, to sit; **être assis** to be sitting (down) (**b**) *Fig (autorité, réputation)* to establish

2 *vi* **faire a. qn** to ask sb to sit down *or* to take a seat **3** **s'asseoir** *vpr* to sit (down); *(depuis la position allongée)* to sit up; **s'a. sur une chaise/dans un fauteuil** to sit on a chair/in an armchair; *Fam Fig* **ses problèmes, je m'assois dessus!** I don't give a damn about his/her problems!

assermenté, -e [asɛrmɑ̃te] *adj* sworn (in); *(témoin)* under *or* on oath; **fonctionnaire a.** sworn official; *Hist* **(prêtre) non a.** non-juring (priest)

assertion [asɛrsjɔ̃] *nf* assertion

asservir [asɛrvir] *vt* to enslave; *Tech* **moteur asservi** servomotor

asservissement [asɛrvismɑ̃] *nm* enslavement; **a. à qn/qch** subjection to sb/sth

assesseur [asɛsœr] *nm* assessor

asseyais *etc voir* **asseoir**

assez [ase] *adv* (**a**) *(suffisamment)* enough; **a. grand/intelligent (pour faire qch)** big/clever enough (to do sth); **a. bien** well enough; *(appréciation scolaire)* fair; **tu as a. mangé** you've eaten enough; **a.!** that's enough!; **a. parlé!** that's enough talk!; **nous sommes a. de trois** three of us is enough (**b**) **a. de** enough; **il y a a. de pain/de pâtes** there's enough bread/pasta; **j'en ai a.** *(suffisamment)* I've got enough; *(je suis agacé)* I've had enough (**c**) *(plutôt)* quite, rather

assidu, -e [asidy] *adj* (**a**) *(toujours présent)* regular; **être a. aux cours** to attend classes regularly (**b**) *(appliqué)* diligent; **un soin a.** painstaking care (**c**) *(attentionné)* **être a. auprès de qn** to be attentive to sb; **faire une cour assidue à qn** to pay constant court to sb

assiduité [asidɥite] *nf* (**a**) *(présence régulière)* regularity; **a. aux cours** regular attendance at classes (**b**) *(zèle)* diligence (**c**) **poursuivre qn de ses assiduités** to force one's attentions on sb

assidûment [asidymɑ̃] *adv* (**a**) *(régulièrement)* regularly (**b**) *(avec application)* diligently

assied *etc voir* **asseoir**

assiéger [59] [asjeʒe] *vt aussi Fig* to besiege

assiéra *etc voir* **asseoir**

assiette [asjɛt] *nf* (**a**) *(vaisselle)* plate; *(contenu)* plateful; *Culin* **a. anglaise** assorted cold meats; **a. creuse** soup plate; **a. à dessert** dessert plate; **a. plate** dinner plate (**b**) *(d'un impôt, d'un taux)* base (**c**) *(d'un cavalier)* seat (**d**) **ne pas être dans son a.** to be out of sorts

assiettée [asjete] *nf* plateful

assignation [asiɲasjɔ̃] *nf* (**a**) *(d'une tâche)* assignment (à to); *(de fonds, d'une part)* allotment (à to) (**b**) *Jur* summons; **a. à résidence** house arrest

assigner [asiɲe] *vt* (**a**) *(tâche)* to assign (à to); *(fonds, part)* to allot (à to) (**b**) *Jur (témoin)* to summon; **a. qn à résidence** to place sb under house arrest

assimilable [asimilabl] *adj (comparable)* comparable (à to)

assimilation [asimilasjɔ̃] *nf* (**a**) *(absorption)* & *Fig* assimilation (**b**) *(comparaison)* comparison (à with)

assimilé, -e [asimile] *adj (de même nature)* similar; **cadres et assimilés** executives and those in similar categories

assimiler [asimile] **1** *vt* (**a**) *(aliment, connaissances, immigrés)* to assimilate; **un élève qui a du mal à a.** a pupil who finds it hard to take things in (**b**) *(comparer)* to compare (à with)

2 **s'assimiler** *vpr* (**a**) *(immigré)* to assimilate (**b**) *(être comparable)* to be comparable (à with)

assis, -e [asi, -iz] **1** *pp de* **asseoir**

2 *adj* sitting, seated; **je travaille a. toute la journée** I spend the whole day at work sitting down; *Fig* **une situation/réputation bien assise** a secure job/an established reputation

assise [asiz] *nf (d'une théorie)* basis, foundation

assises [asiz] *nfpl* (**a**) *(congrès)* conference (**b**) *Jur* **les a.** the assizes

assistanat [asistana] *nm* (**a**) *(gen)* assistantship (**b**) *Scol* (foreign) assistant exchange scheme

assistance [asistɑ̃s] *nf* (**a**) *(public)* audience (**b**) *(aide)* assistance; **prêter a. à qn** to give sb assistance; *Méd* **a. médicale à la procréation** assisted conception (**c**) **être à l'A. (publique)** to be in care

assistant, -e [asistɑ̃, -ɑ̃t] **1** *nm,f (personne)* assistant; *(de langue)* language assistant; **a. de direction** personal assistant, PA; **a. metteur en scène** assistant director; **a. maternelle** child minder; **a. social** social worker

2 *nm Ordinat* wizard; **a. numérique personnel** personal digital assistant, PDA

assisté, -e [asiste] **1** *nm,f Péj* person living on handouts

2 *adj* **a. par ordinateur** computer-aided, computer-assisted

assister [asiste] **1** *vt (personne)* to assist

2 **assister à** *vt ind* to be (present) at, to attend; *(accident)* to witness; **je ne peux pas vous répondre, je n'ai pas assisté à la scène** I can't give you an answer, I wasn't there

associatif, -ive [asɔsjatif, -iv] *adj* **mouvement a.** associations; **la vie associative est tres développée dans ce pays** a lot of people in this country belong to clubs and associations

association [asɔsjasjɔ̃] *nf* (**a**) *(groupe, société)* association; *Com* partnership; **a. à but non lucratif** *Br* non-profit-making *or Am* not-for-profit organization; **A. européenne de libre-échange** European Free Trade Association; **a. de parents d'élèves** parent-teacher association; **a. sportive** sports club (**b**) *(de mots, d'idées)* association; *(d'aliments, de substances, de couleurs)* combination (**c**) *Jur* **a. de malfaiteurs** criminal conspiracy

associé, -e [asɔsje] **1** *nm,f* associate; *Com* partner

2 *adj* **membre a.** associate member

associer [66] [asɔsje] **1** *vt* (**a**) *(lier)* to combine (à with) (**b**) *(mentalement)* to associate (à with)

2 **s'associer** *vpr* (**a**) **s'a. à un projet** to join in a project; **s'a. à** *ou* **avec qn** *(dans une lutte)* to join forces with sb; *Com* to enter into partnership with sb; **je m'associe à votre douleur** I share your grief (**b**) *(se mêler)* to combine (à with)

assoiffé, -e [aswafe] *adj* thirsty; *Fig* **a. de sang** bloodthirsty; **a. de savoir** thirsty for knowledge

assolement [asɔlmɑ̃] *nm* crop rotation

assombrir [asɔ̃brir] **1** *vt* to darken; *(avenir)* to cast a shadow over

2 **s'assombrir** *vpr* (ciel, visage) to darken, to cloud over; *(personne)* to become gloomy

assommant, -e [asɔmɑ̃, -ɑ̃t] *adj* very boring

assommer [asɔme] *vt* **a. qn** *(étourdir)* to knock sb senseless; *(engourdir)* to make sb lethargic; *(ennuyer)* to bore sb to death

Assomption [asɔ̃psjɔ̃] *nf* **(la fête de) l'A.** (the feast of) the Assumption

Assomption
The Feast of the Assumption, on the 15th of August, is a Catholic feast day and an important holiday in France.

assonance [asɔnɑ̃s] *nf* assonance
assorti, -e [asɔrti] *adj* (**a**) *(en harmonie)* matching; **bien a.** well-matched; **mal a.** ill-matched; **pull avec jupe assortie** sweater with matching skirt; **le pull n'était pas a. à la jupe** the sweater didn't match the skirt (**b**) *(bonbons)* assorted, mixed (**c**) **bien a.** *(magasin)* well-stocked (**d**) *(accompagné)* **a. de** accompanied by
assortiment [asɔrtimɑ̃] *nm (de produits)* assortment
assortir [asɔrtir] *vt* (**a**) *(couleurs)* to match (**à** to) (**b**) *Com* to restock
assoupir [asupir] **s'assoupir** *vpr* to doze off
assouplir [asuplir] **1** *vt (chaussures, cuir, corps)* to make supple; *Fig (réglementation)* to relax
  2 s'assouplir *vpr (chaussures, cuir, corps)* to get supple; *(personne)* to loosen up
assouplissant [asuplisɑ̃] *nm* fabric softener
assouplissement [asuplismɑ̃] *nm (du corps)* making supple; *Fig (de la réglementation)* relaxing; **exercices d'a.**, **assouplissements** limbering-up exercises
assourdir [asurdir] *vt* (**a**) *(personne)* to deafen (**b**) *(son)* to deaden
assourdissant, -e [asurdisɑ̃, -ɑ̃t] *adj* deafening
assouvir [asuvir] *vt (faim, désir)* to satisfy
assouvissement [asuvismɑ̃] *nm (de la faim, du désir)* satisfaction
assoyant *voir* **asseoir**
assujettir [asyʒetir] *vt* (**a**) *(province)* to subjugate (**b**) *(soumettre)* **a. qn à qch** to subject sb to sth; **être assujetti à l'impôt** to be liable for tax (**c**) *(objet)* to fix, to fasten (**à** to)
assujettissement [asyʒetismɑ̃] *nm* (**a**) *(dépendance)* subjection (**à** to) (**b**) *(à l'impôt)* liability (**à** for)
assumer [asyme] **1** *vt* (**a**) *(responsabilité)* to assume, to take on; *(risque)* to take (**b**) *(accepter) (conséquences)* to take; *Fam* **tu vas devoir a.** you'll have to live with it
  2 s'assumer *vpr* to come to terms with oneself
assurance [asyrɑ̃s] *nf* (**a**) *(confiance)* (self-)assurance (**b**) *(garantie)* assurance; **je vous donne l'a. que tout sera fini demain** I assure you that everything will be finished tomorrow; **demander/recevoir des assurances** to ask for/to receive assurance (**c**) *(contre le vol, les accidents)* insurance; **prendre une a.** to take out insurance; *Fam* **je vais écrire à mon a.** I'm going to write to my insurance company; **a. auto** car insurance; **a. maladie** health insurance; **a. au tiers** third-party insurance; **a. tous risques** comprehensive insurance; **a. sur la vie, a.-vie** life insurance; **a. vieillesse** retirement pension
assuré, -e [asyre] **1** *adj* (**a**) *(pas, voix)* firm; *(air, personne)* assured, confident; **d'une voix mal assurée** in an unsteady voice (**b**) *(succès, victoire)* guaranteed, certain
  2 *nm,f* **l'a.** the insured; **les assurés sociaux** ≃ people who pay *Br* national insurance *or Am* social security
assurément [asyremɑ̃] *adv Vieilli* certainly
assurer [asyre] **1** *vt* (**a**) *(garantir)* to ensure, to guarantee; **a. une rente à qn** to settle an annuity on sb; **ma retraite m'assure de quoi vivre** my pension gives me enough to live on; **a. ses arrières** to leave oneself

a way out (**b**) *(certifier)* **a. qch à qn, a. qn de qch** to assure sb of sth; **a. qn que** to assure sb that; **c'est bien vrai, je t'assure** it's absolutely true, I assure you; **mais si, je t'assure!** yes, I swear! (**c**) *(se charger de)* to be in charge of; **a. les fonctions de directeur de la production** to be production manager; **un service régulier est assuré entre Paris et Londres** there is a regular service between Paris and London; **j'assure la permanence ce matin** I'm on duty this morning; **a. la défense de qn** *(sujet: avocat)* to defend sb (**d**) *(immobiliser)* to steady; *(attacher)* to secure (**e**) *(par contrat d'assurance)* to insure (**contre** against)
  2 *vi Fam* **a. en maths** to be brilliant at maths; **à l'entretien, j'ai assuré un max** I did brilliantly at the interview; **il n'assure pas** he's useless, he hasn't got a clue
  3 s'assurer *vpr* (**a**) **s'a. de qch** *(vérifier)* to make sure of sth; **s'a. que** to check *or* make sure (that); **je vais m'en a.** I'll check (**b**) *(par contrat d'assurance)* to insure oneself (**contre** against); **s'a. au tiers/sur la vie** to take out third-party/life insurance (**c**) *(se procurer)* **s'a. la collaboration de qn** to secure sb's collaboration; **les Allemands se sont assuré la victoire** the Germans are assured of victory
assureur [asyrœr] *nm* insurer
astérisque [asterisk] *nm* asterisk
astéroïde [asterɔid] *nm* asteroid
asteure, astheure [astœr] *Can Fam* **1** *adv* now
  2 asteure que *conj* now that
asthmatique [asmatik] *adj & nmf* asthmatic
asthme [asm] *nm* asthma; **avoir de l'a.** to have asthma; **crise d'a.** asthma attack
asticot [astiko] *nm* maggot
asticoter [astikɔte] *vt Fam* to bug
astigmate [astigmat] *adj & nmf* astigmatic
astiquer [astike] *vt (faire briller)* to polish; *(récurer)* to scour; **a. sa maison** to get one's house spotlessly clean
astrakan [astrakɑ̃] *nm* astrakhan
astre [astr] *nm* star; **beau comme un a.** radiantly handsome *or* beautiful
astreignant, -e [astrɛɲɑ̃, -ɑ̃t] *adj* exacting, demanding
astreindre [54] [astrɛ̃dr] **1** *vt* **a. qn à faire qch** to compel *or* oblige sb to do sth
  2 s'astreindre *vpr* **s'a. à un régime sévère** to strictly follow a diet; **s'a. à faire qch** to force oneself to do sth
astreinte [astrɛ̃t] *nf* constraint
astrologie [astrɔlɔʒi] *nf* astrology
astrologique [astrɔlɔʒik] *adj* astrological
astrologue [astrɔlɔɡ] *nmf* astrologer
astronaute [astronot] *nmf* astronaut
astronautique [astronotik] *nf* astronautics *(singulier)*
astronome [astronɔm] *nmf* astronomer
astronomie [astronɔmi] *nf* astronomy
astronomique [astronɔmik] *adj aussi Fig* astronomical
astrophysique [astrofizik] *nf* astrophysics *(singulier)*
astuce [astys] *nf* (**a**) *(finesse)* shrewdness (**b**) *(truc)* trick; *(conseil)* tip; **il doit y avoir une a.** there must be a trick to it (**c**) *(plaisanterie)* witticism; *(jeu de mots)* pun; **je ne saisis pas l'a.** I don't get it
astucieusement [astysjøzmɑ̃] *adv* shrewdly
astucieux, -euse [astysjø, -øz] *adj (personne)* shrewd; *(solution)* clever
asymétrie [asimetri] *nf* asymmetry
asymétrique [asimetrik] *adj* asymmetrical

asynchrone [asɛ̃krɔn] *adj Ordinat* asynchronous
ataca [ataka] *nm Can* cranberry
atavisme [atavism] *nm* atavism; **faire qch par a.** to do sth because it's in one's genes
atchoum [atʃum] *exclam* atishoo!
atelier [atəlje] *nm* (**a**) *(lieu)* workshop; *(dans une maison)* workroom; *(d'artiste)* studio; **a. de carrosserie** bodyshop; **a. de montage** assembly shop; *TV & Cin* **a. de production** production studio; **a. de réparations** repair shop (**b**) *(personnel)* workshop staff (**c**) *(groupe de travail)* work-group
atermoiements [atɛrmwamɑ̃] *nmpl* procrastination
athée [ate] **1** *adj* atheistic
  2 *nmf* atheist
athéisme [ateism] *nm* atheism
athénée [atene] *nm Belg* secondary *or* high school
Athènes [atɛn] *n* Athens
athénien, -enne [atenjɛ̃, -ɛn] **1** *adj* Athenian
  2 *nm,f* **A.** Athenian
athlète [atlɛt] *nmf* athlete
athlétique [atletik] *adj* athletic
athlétisme [atletism] *nm* athletics *(singulier)*; **épreuves d'a.** athletic events
atlantique [atlɑ̃tik] **1** *adj* Atlantic
  2 *nm* **l'A.** the Atlantic (Ocean)
atlas [atlas] *nm (livre)* atlas
atmosphère [atmɔsfɛr] *nf aussi Fig* atmosphere
atmosphérique [atmɔsferik] *adj* atmospheric
atoca [atɔka] *nm Can* cranberry
atoll [atɔl] *nm* atoll
atome [atom] *nm* atom; *Fig* **avoir des atomes crochus avec qn** to hit it off with sb; **elle n'a pas un a. de bon sens** she doesn't have an ounce of common sense
atomique [atɔmik] *adj* atomic
atomiser [atɔmize] *vt* (**a**) *(pulvériser)* to atomize (**b**) *(ville, région)* to destroy with nuclear weapons
atomiseur [atɔmizœr] *nm* atomizer, spray; **parfum en a.** perfume spray
atone [atɔn] *adj* (**a**) *(inerte)* lacklustre (**b**) *(voyelle)* unstressed
atours [atur] *nmpl Litt ou Hum* finery; **parée de ses plus beaux a.** in all her finery
atout [atu] *nm (aux cartes)* trump; *Fig* asset; **a. carreau** diamonds are trumps; **a. maître** master trump; *Fig* trump card; *aussi Fig* **avoir tous les atouts dans son jeu** to hold all the winning cards
âtre [atr] *nm Litt* hearth; **au coin de l'â.** by the fireplace
atrique, -e [atrike] *adj Can* **mal a.** badly dressed
atroce [atrɔs] *adj (crime)* atrocious; *(douleur)* excruciating; *(odeur, cauchemar, repas)* dreadful, horrible; **j'avais une peur a. de le rencontrer** I dreaded meeting him
atrocement [atrɔsmɑ̃] *adv (cruellement)* atrociously; *(très mal)* dreadfully, horribly; **avoir a. mal** to be in dreadful pain; **sentir a. mauvais** to smell really horrible
atrocité [atrɔsite] *nf* atrocity
atrophie [atrɔfi] *nf* atrophy
atrophier [66] [atrɔfje] **1** *vt* to atrophy
  2 *s'atrophier vpr* to atrophy
attabler [atable] *s'attabler vpr* to sit down at the/a table
attachant, -e [ataʃɑ̃, -ɑ̃t] *adj* engaging
attache [ataʃ] *nf* (**a**) *(lien)* fastener; *Fig* **attaches** *(amis)* links; *Fig* **sans attaches** unattached; **je n'avais plus aucune a. dans cette ville** there was nothing to

keep me in the town (**b**) **avoir les attaches fines** *(chevilles et poignets)* to have delicate wrists and ankles
attaché, -e [ataʃe] **1** *adj* (**a**) *(fixé)* fastened; *(chien)* chained up (**b**) *(affectivement)* **a. à** attached to (**c**) *(dépendant)* **les avantages attachés à une fonction** the benefits attached to a post
  2 *nm,f* attaché; **a. d'ambassade** attaché; **a. culturel** cultural attaché; **a. militaire** military attaché; **a. de presse** press officer
attaché-case *(pl* **attachés-cases)** [ataʃekɛz] *nm* attaché case
attachement [ataʃmɑ̃] *nm* attachment (**à** to)
attacher [ataʃe] **1** *vt* (**a**) **a. qch à qch** *(fixer)* to fasten sth to sth; *(avec de la ficelle, avec une corde)* to tie sth to sth; *(avec une chaîne)* to chain sth to sth; **a. ses cheveux** to tie one's hair back; **a. ses lacets** *ou* **chaussures** to tie one's shoelaces (**b**) *(accorder)* **a. de l'importance/de la valeur à qch** to attach importance/great value to sth
  2 *vi (dans une poêle, une casserole)* to stick to the pan; **une casserole qui n'attache pas** a non-stick saucepan
  3 *s'attacher vpr* (**a**) *(se fixer)* to be fastened (**à** to); **cette jupe s'attache par derrière** this skirt does up at the back (**b**) *(affectivement)* **s'a. à qn/qch** to get attached to sb/sth; **je ne veux pas m'a.** I don't want to commit myself (**c**) *(se concentrer)* **s'a. aux faits** to stick to the facts; **s'a. à faire qch** to strive to do sth (**d**) *(s'assurer)* **s'a. les services de qn** to procure sb's services
attaquant, -e [atakɑ̃, -ɑ̃t] **1** *adj* attacking
  2 *nm,f Sport* attacker
attaque [atak] *nf* (**a**) *(agression, en sport)* attack; *aussi Fig* **passer à l'a.** to go on the offensive; **à l'a.!** attack!; **a. aérienne** air raid; **a. à main armée** armed robbery (**b**) *Fam* **être d'a.** to be on top form; **se sentir d'a. pour faire qch** to feel up to doing sth (**c**) *Méd (crise)* attack; **une a.** *(apoplexie)* a stroke; *(crise cardiaque)* a heart attack
attaquer [atake] **1** *vt* (**a**) *(physiquement, verbalement)* to attack; *(sujet: acide)* to attack; *Jur* **a. qn en justice** to bring an action against sb (**b**) *(repas, sujet, travail)* to tackle; *Fam* **on attaque?** *(à table)* shall we get stuck in? (**c**) *Mus (morceau)* to strike up; *(note)* to attack
  2 *s'attaquer vpr* **s'a. à** *(adversaire)* to attack; *(problème)* to tackle; **s'a. à plus fort que soi** to bite off more than one can chew
attardé, -e [atarde] **1** *adj* (**a**) *(qui flâne)* **il ne restait plus que quelques passants attardés** there were only a few people still about (**b**) *(vieux)* old-fashioned (**c**) *(mentalement)* (mentally) retarded
  2 *nm,f* **a. (mental)** (mentally) retarded person
attarder [atarde] *s'attarder vpr* to linger; **s'a. à des détails** to dwell over details; **ne nous attardons pas sur ce point** let's not dwell on this point
atteignais *etc voir* **atteindre**
atteindre [54] [atɛ̃dr] **1** *vt* to reach; *(cible)* to hit; **être atteint d'une maladie** to be suffering from a disease; **il a été atteint dans son amour-propre** his pride has been wounded; **le poumon est atteint** the lung is affected; *Fig* **rien ne l'atteint** nothing affects him; *Fam* **il est très atteint** *(fou)* he's not right in the head
  2 *atteindre à vt ind* **a. à la perfection** to be close to perfection
atteinte [atɛ̃t] *nf (attaque)* **a. à** attack on; **porter a. à** to undermine

attelage [atəlaʒ] *nm (animaux)* team

atteler [9] [atəle] **1** *vt (chevaux)* to harness; *(bœufs)* to yoke; **a. une voiture** to hitch horses up to a carriage

2 s'atteler *vpr* **s'a. à une tâche** to buckle down to a task

attelle [atɛl] *nf* splint

attenant, -e [atənɑ̃, -ɑ̃t] *adj* adjoining; **a. à** adjoining

attendre [atɑ̃dr] **1** *vt* to wait for; **a. son tour** to wait one's turn; **a. un bébé** to be expecting (a baby); **se faire a.** *(personne)* to keep people waiting; **la réponse ne s'est pas fait a.** the reply wasn't long in coming; **je l'attends d'une minute à l'autre** I'm expecting him/her any minute now; **a. qch de qn/qch** to expect sth from sb/sth; **qu'est-ce que tu attends pour le lui dire?** what are you waiting for? go and tell him/her; **a. que qn fasse qch** to wait for sb to do sth; **attends de lui avoir parlé avant de prendre une décision** wait until you've spoken to him/her before you take a decision; *Fig* **a. qn au tournant** to be waiting to catch sb out

2 *vi* to wait; **a. une heure** to wait (for) an hour; **sans plus a.** without further ado; **faire a. qn** to keep sb waiting; *Fam* **on ne va pas a. cent sept ans** we're not going to wait forever; **en attendant** meanwhile; *(néanmoins)* all the same; **en attendant son arrivée** until he/she arrives/arrived

3 s'attendre *vpr* **s'a. à qch** to expect sth; **je m'attends à tout** I'm ready for anything; **je m'y attendais** I expected as much; **il fallait s'y a.** it was only to be expected; **je m'attendais à ce que tu le lui dises** I was expecting you to tell him/her

attendrir [atɑ̃drir] **1** *vt* (**a**) *(émouvoir)* to move; *(rendre indulgent)* to soften (**b**) *(viande)* to tenderize

2 s'attendrir *vpr* to be moved (**sur** by)

attendrissant, -e [atɑ̃drisɑ̃, -ɑ̃t] *adj* moving

attendu, -e [atɑ̃dy] **1** *adj* expected; **le jour tant a. est arrivé** the long-awaited day has arrived

2 *prép Sout* **a. les circonstances** considering the circumstances

3 attendu que *conj Sout* considering that; *Jur* whereas

attentat [atɑ̃ta] *nm* attack; **a. à la bombe** bombing; **a. à la pudeur** indecent assault; **a. à la sûreté de l'État** high treason; **a. à la voiture piégée** car-bomb attack

attentat-suicide *(pl* **attentats-suicides)** [atɑ̃tasɥisid] *nm* suicide (bomb) attack

attente [atɑ̃t] *nf* (**a**) *(fait d'attendre)* waiting; *(période)* wait; **être dans l'a. de qch** to be waiting for sth; **en a.** *(au téléphone)* on hold; *Ordinat* **liste de fichiers à imprimer en a.** print queue (**b**) *(espoir)* expectations; **contre toute a.** against all expectations; **répondre à l'a.** *ou* **aux attentes de qn** to live up to sb's expectations; **dans l'a. de votre réponse/de vous rencontrer** *(dans une lettre)* I look forward to receiving your reply/to meeting you

attenter [atɑ̃te] **attenter à** *vt ind* to make an attempt on; **a. à ses jours** to attempt suicide

attentif, -ive [atɑ̃tif, -iv] *adj* attentive; **être a. aux autres** to be attentive to others; **être a. à qch** to pay attention to sth; *(ses intérêts, sa santé)* to look after sth; **écouter d'une oreille attentive** to listen attentively

attention [atɑ̃sjɔ̃] *nf* (**a**) *(soin)* attention; **écouter avec a.** to listen attentively; **faire a. à qch** to pay attention to sth; *(sa santé, ses intérêts)* to look after sth; **il a fait a. de ne pas la blesser** he took care not to hurt her; **ne pas prêter la moindre a. à** to take no notice of; **(faites) a.!** look out!; **a. si je t'attrape!** if I catch

you there'll be trouble!; **a., peinture fraîche** *(sur écriteau)* wet paint; **a. à la fermeture des portières, a. au départ!** stand clear of the doors, the train is about to depart!; **à l'a. de qn** *(sur une lettre)* for the attention of sb (**b**) *(amabilité)* attention; **être plein d'attentions envers qn** to be very attentive towards sb

attentionné, -e [atɑ̃sjɔne] *adj* attentive (**auprès de** towards)

attentisme [atɑ̃tism] *nm* wait-and-see policy

attentiste [atɑ̃tist] **1** *adj* **attitude a.** wait-and-see attitude

2 *nmf* **les attentistes** those who play a waiting game

attentivement [atɑ̃tivmɑ̃] *adv* attentively

atténuation [atenɥasjɔ̃] *nf (d'un effet, de la douleur)* reduction; *(d'une lumière)* dimming; *(d'une couleur)* toning down; *(d'une chute)* breaking

atténuer [atenɥe] **1** *vt (effet, douleur)* to reduce; *(lumière)* to dim; *(couleur)* to tone down; *(chute)* to break

2 s'atténuer *vpr (douleur)* to ease; *(lumière, couleurs, bruit)* to fade

atterrant, -e [atɛrɑ̃, -ɑ̃t] *adj* appalling

atterrer [atere] *vt* to appal

atterrir [aterir] *vi* to land; **a. en catastrophe** to make an emergency landing; *Fam* **a. dans un bar/en prison** to wind up in a bar/in prison

atterrissage [aterisaʒ] *nm* landing; **a. en douceur** soft landing; **a. forcé** forced landing

attestation [atɛstasjɔ̃] *nf* certificate

attester [atɛste] *vt (témoigner)* to testify to; **a. que** to testify that; **aucun dictionnaire n'atteste l'existence de ce mot** this word is not attested in any dictionary

attifer [atife] *Fam* **1** *vt* to dress (**de** in)

2 s'attifer *vpr* to dress; **s'a. de qch** to put sth on

attirail [atiraj] *nm* paraphernalia

attirance [atirɑ̃s] *nf* attraction; **éprouver de l'a. pour** *ou* **envers qn** to be attracted to sb

attirant, -e [atirɑ̃, -ɑ̃t] *adj* attractive

attirer [atire] **1** *vt* (**a**) *(sujet: aimant, planète)* to attract; *Fig* **a. qn dans un piège** to lure sb into a trap; **a. qn dans un coin** to take sb into a corner; **a. l'attention de qn** *(sujet: chose)* to catch sb's attention; **a. l'attention de qn sur qch** to draw sb's attention to sth; **a. les regards** to catch the eye (**b**) *(séduire)* to attract; *(sujet: matière, pays)* to appeal to

2 s'attirer *vpr* (**a**) *(mutuellement)* to be attracted to each other (**b**) *(sur soi)* **s'a. des critiques** to come in for criticism; **s'a. des ennuis** to get oneself into trouble; **s'a. la colère de qn** to incur sb's anger

attiser [atize] *vt* (**a**) *(feu)* to poke (**b**) *Fig (désir, colère, racisme)* to stir up

attitré, -e [atitre] *adj* (**a**) *(habituel)* usual (**b**) *(chargé d'une fonction)* appointed

attitude [atityd] *nf* (**a**) *(conduite, position)* attitude (**envers** *ou* **à l'égard de** towards); **tu as eu une a. déplorable** your behaviour was appalling (**b**) *(maintien)* bearing, demeanour (**c**) *(affectation)* pose

attouchement [atuʃmɑ̃] *nm* fondling; **se livrer à des attouchements sur qn** to fondle sb

attraction [atraksjɔ̃] *nf* (**a**) *(d'un aimant)* attraction; **l'a. terrestre** the earth's gravitational pull (**b**) *aussi Fig (spectacle)* attraction

attrait [atrɛ] *nm* attraction

attrape [atrap] *nf (farce)* trick

attrape-nigaud *(pl* **attrape-nigauds)** [atrapnigo] *nm* trick

attraper [atrape] **1** *vt* (**a**) *(capturer, saisir)* to catch; **se faire a.** to be caught; *Fam* **a. qn à faire qch** to catch sb doing sth (**b**) *(maladie)* to catch; **a. froid** to catch cold; **a. mal** to catch a chill (**c**) *(tromper)* **a. qn** to take sb in; **là, tu es bien attrapé** you fell for it good and proper (**d**) *Fam (gronder)* **se faire a.** to get a good telling-off

2 s'attraper *vpr (maladie)* to be caught; *(habitude)* to be picked up

attrayant, -e [atrɛjɑ̃, -ɑ̃t] *adj* attractive; **peu a.** unattractive

attribuable [atribɥabl] *adj* attributable (**à** to)

attribuer [atribɥe] **1** *vt* (**a**) *(allouer)* to assign, to allot (**à** to); *(prix, récompense, bourse)* to award (**à** to) (**b**) *(œuvre, crime, erreur)* to attribute (**à** to); **a. de l'importance à qch** to attach importance to sth

2 s'attribuer *vpr* **s'a. qch** to claim sth; **il s'en est attribué tout le mérite** he claimed all the credit for it

attribut [atriby] **1** *nm* attribute

2 *adj m Gram* attributive

attribution [atribysjɔ̃] *nf* (**a**) *(allocation)* assigning, allocation (**à** to); *(d'un prix, d'une récompense, d'une bourse)* awarding (**à** to); **attributions** *(fonctions)* duties; **entrer dans les attributions de qn** to be part of sb's duties (**b**) *(d'une œuvre, d'un crime, d'une erreur)* attribution (**à** to)

attristant, -e [atristɑ̃, -ɑ̃t] *adj* depressing

attrister [atriste] **1** *vt* to sadden; **cela m'attriste** it makes me sad

2 s'attrister *vpr* to be saddened (**de** by)

attroupement [atrupmɑ̃] *nm* crowd; **provoquer un a.** to draw a crowd

attrouper [atrupe] **s'attrouper** *vpr* to gather

atypique [atipik] *adj* atypical

au [o] *voir* à

aubaine [obɛn] *nf* godsend; **profiter de l'a.** to take advantage of one's good luck; *Can* **à prix d'a.** at a reduced price

aube [ob] *nf* (**a**) *(matin)* dawn; **à l'a.** at dawn; *Fig* **l'a. de la civilisation** the dawn of civilization (**b**) *Rel* alb

aubépine [obepin] *nf* hawthorn; **fleurs d'a.** may blossom

auberge [obɛrʒ] *nf* inn; *Fig* **ici, c'est l'a. espagnole** you have to bring everything yourself here; *Fam* **on n'est pas sorti de l'a.** we're not out of the woods yet; **a. de jeunesse** youth hostel

aubergine [obɛrʒin] *nf* (**a**) *(plante) Br* aubergine, *Am* eggplant (**b**) *Fam (contractuelle)* (female) traffic warden

aubergiste [obɛrʒist] *nmf* innkeeper

auburn [obœrn] *adj inv* auburn

aucun, -e [okœ̃, -yn] **1** *pron indéfini* (**a**) *(personne, rien)* none; **a. des deux** neither (of them); **a. d'entre eux** none of them; **je ne me fie à a. d'entre eux** I don't trust any of them (**b**) *Litt* **d'aucuns** some people

2 *adj indéfini* (**a**) *(négatif)* no, not any; **je n'en ai aucune idée** I've (got) no idea; **sans aucune exception** without any exception; **sans a. doute** without a doubt (**b**) *(positif)* any; **plus rapide qu'a. autre coureur** faster than any other runner

aucunement [okynmɑ̃] *adv* not at all, not in the slightest

audace [odas] *nf* (**a**) *(courage)* boldness, daring (**b**) *(culot)* audacity, impudence (**c**) *(originalité)* boldness (**d**) *(action audacieuse)* **avoir toutes les audaces** to do the most daring things

audacieusement [odasjøzmɑ̃] *adv* (**a**) *(avec courage)* boldly, daringly (**b**) *(avec culot)* impudently

audacieux, -euse [odasjø, -øz] *adj* (**a**) *(courageux)* bold, daring (**b**) *(culotté)* impudent (**c**) *(original)* bold

au-dedans [odədɑ̃] *adv* inside; **a. de** inside

au-dehors [odəor] *adv* outside; **a. de** outside

au-delà [odəla] **1** *nm* **l'a.** the next world

2 *prép* **a. de** beyond

3 *adv* beyond; **jusqu'à une certaine somme mais pas a.** up to a certain sum but no more

au-dessous [odəsu] *adv* below, underneath; *(à l'étage inférieur)* downstairs; **on en trouve à 8 euros et même a.** you can get them for 8 euros or even less; **a. de** *(dans l'espace)* below, under; *(nombre, somme)* under; *(dans une hiérarchie)* below; **15 degrés a. de zéro** 15 degrees below zero; *Fig* **être a. de tout** to be beneath contempt

au-dessus [odəsy] *adv* above; *(à l'étage supérieur)* upstairs; **une terrasse avec une marquise a.** a terrace with an awning over it; **1000 euros et a.** 1,000 euros and upwards; **a. de** *(dans l'espace, dans une hiérarchie)* above; *(nombre, somme)* over; **a. de nos têtes** *(dans le ciel)* overhead; **c'est a. de mes forces** it's beyond me; **vivre a. de ses moyens** to live beyond one's means; *Fig* **je suis a. de ça** I'm above all that

au-devant [odəvɑ̃] **au-devant de** *prép* **aller/courir a. de qn** to go/run to meet sb; **aller a. des désirs de qn** to anticipate sb's wishes; **aller a. du danger** to court danger

audible [odibl] *adj* audible

audience [odjɑ̃s] *nf* (**a**) *(entrevue)* audience; *Jur* hearing; **l'a. est suspendue** the case is adjourned (**b**) *(intérêt)* **trouver a. auprès des jeunes** to find a following among young people (**c**) *(public)* audience

Audimat® [odimat] *nm (appareil)* = device for calculating television audience ratings; *(résultats)* audience ratings; **faire de l'A.** to increase audience ratings

audioconférence [odjokɔ̃ferɑ̃s] *nf* audioconference

audioguide [odjogid] *nf* audioguide, headset

audionumérique [odjonymerik] *adj* digital audio; **disque a.** compact disc

audiovisuel, -elle [odjovizɥɛl] **1** *adj* (**a**) *(méthodes)* audiovisual (**b**) *TV & Rad* television and radio

2 *nm TV & Rad* **l'a.** television and radio

auditeur, -trice [oditœr, -tris] *nm,f* (**a**) *(d'un programme de radio)* listener (**b**) *Univ* **suivre un cours en a. libre** = to follow a course without being officially registered as a student, *Am* to audit a course

auditif, -ive [oditif, -iv] *adj (nerf)* auditory; *(troubles)* hearing

audition [odisjɔ̃] *nf* (**a**) *(faculté)* hearing (**b**) *(de chanteur, d'acteur)* audition; **passer une a.** to have an audition (**c**) *Jur* **a. des témoins** examination of the witnesses

auditionner [odisjɔne] *vt & vi* to audition

auditoire [oditwar] *nm* (**a**) *(public)* audience (**b**) *Belg & Suisse (amphithéâtre)* auditorium; *(salle de cours)* lecture hall or theatre

auditorium [oditɔrjɔm] *nm* auditorium; *Rad & TV* recording studio

AUE [ayə] *nm (abrév* **acte unique européen**) SEA

auge [oʒ] *nf (mangeoire)* trough

augmentation [ɔgmɑ̃tasjɔ̃] *nf* (**a**) *(accroissement)* increase (**de** in); **a. (de salaire)** *Br* (pay) rise, *Am* raise; **demander une a.** to ask for a *Br* (pay) rise or *Am* raise; **être en a.** to be on the increase (**b**) *Ordinat* **a. de puissance** upgrade

augmenter [ɔgmãte] **1** *vt* to increase; **édition augmentée** enlarged edition; **a. qn** to raise sb's salary **2** *vi* to increase (**de** by)

augure [ogyr] *nm* (**a**) *(devin)* augur (**b**) *(présage)* omen; **de bon a.** auspicious; **de mauvais a.** ominous

augurer [ogyre] *vt* **a. bien/mal de qch** to augur well/ill for sth

auguste [ogyst] *adj* august

aujourd'hui [oʒurdɥi] *adv* (**a**) *(ce jour)* today; **le journal d'a.** today's paper; *Fam* **c'est pour a. ou pour demain?** I/we haven't got all day! (**b**) *(à l'heure actuelle)* nowadays, today; **les jeunes gens d'a.** young people today; **l'Europe d'a.** present-day Europe

aulne [on] *nm* alder

aumône [omon] *nf* alms; **demander l'a.** to ask for charity; **faire l'a. à qn** to give alms to sb

aumônier [omonje] *nm* chaplain

aune [on] *nm* alder

auparavant [oparavã] *adv (avant)* before(hand); *(d'abord)* first

auprès [oprɛ] **auprès de** *prép* (**a**) *(près de)* by, next to; **ambassadeur a. des Nations unies** ambassador to the United Nations (**b**) *(en comparaison de)* compared with (**c**) *(en s'adressant à)* **se renseigner a. de qn** to ask sb

auquel [okɛl] *voir* **lequel**

aura¹ *etc voir* **avoir¹**

aura² [ɔra] *nf* aura

auréole [ɔreɔl] *nf* (**a**) *(d'un saint, d'un astre)* halo; *Fig* **parer qn d'une a.** to idolize sb (**b**) *(trace)* ring

auréoler [ɔreɔle] *vt* **tout auréolé de gloire** crowned with glory

auriculaire [ɔrikylɛr] *nm* little finger

aurifère [ɔrifɛr] *adj* gold-bearing; **gisement a.** goldfield

Aurigny [ɔriɲi] *n* Alderney

aurore [ɔrɔr] *nf* dawn, daybreak; **à l'a.** at dawn; *Fam* **aux aurores** at the crack of dawn; **a. boréale** aurora borealis, northern lights

auscultation [ɔskyltasjɔ̃] *nf* auscultation

ausculter [ɔskylte] *vt (malade, cœur)* to listen to

auspices [ɔspis] *nmpl* **sous les a. de** *(sous l'égide de)* under the auspices of; **sous d'heureux a.** auspiciously; **sous de fâcheux a.** inauspiciously

aussi [osi] **1** *adv* (**a**) *(également)* too, as well; **lui a. il sait le faire** he, too, knows how to do it, he knows how to do it as well (**b**) *(tellement)* so; **une a. belle journée** such a nice day (**c**) *(dans les phrases comparatives)* as; **a. grand que moi** as tall as me; **pas a. gros que** not as big as, not so big as; **a. bien que moi** as well as me (**d**) *(quelque)* however; **a. bizarre que cela soit** however odd it may be **2** *conj* therefore, so

aussitôt [osito] **1** *adv* immediately, straight away; **a. avant/après** immediately before/after; **a. après son retour je suis parti** as soon as he/she returned I left; **a. l'argent reçu je vous paierai** as soon as I get the money I'll pay you; **a. dit, a. fait** no sooner said than done **2** *conj* **a. que** as soon as

austère [ostɛr] *adj (vie, style)* austere; *(vêtement)* severe; *(expression)* stern

austérité [osterite] *nf (de la vie, d'un style)* austerity; *(d'un vêtement)* severity; *(d'une expression)* sternness; **mesures d'a.** austerity measures

austral, -e, -als *ou* **-aux** [ostral, -o] *adj* southern

Australasie [ostralazi] *nf* **l'A.** Australasia

Australie [ostrali] *nf* **l'A.** Australia

australien, -enne [ostraljɛ̃, -ɛn] **1** *adj* Australian **2** *nm,f* **A.** Australian

autant [otã] *adv* (**a**) *(tellement)* so much; **a. de** *(quantité)* so much; *(nombre)* so many; **je n'avais jamais vu a. de neige/de bateaux** I had never seen so much snow/so many boats (**b**) *(la même quantité, le même nombre)* **remettez-m'en encore a.** give me the same again; **il m'en veut, mais je lui en veux tout a.** he's angry with me, but I'm just as angry with him; **le coût de la vie a augmenté de 5% mais les salaires n'ont pas augmenté d'a.** the cost of living has increased by 5% but salaries have not risen by the same amount; **a. que** *(quantité)* as much as; *(nombre)* as many as; **a. que possible** as far as possible; **a. de... que** *(quantité)* as much... as; *(nombre)* as many... as; **ils ont a. de terrain/d'amis que vous** they have as much land/as many friends as you (**c**) *(de même)* **on ne peut pas en dire a. de tout le monde** you can't say the same for everybody; **essaie un peu d'en faire a.** try to do the same (**d**) *(locutions)* **a. elle est expansive, a. il est réservé** she's as extroverted as he is shy; **a. pour moi!** I stand corrected!; **(pour) a. que je sache** as far as I know, to the best of my knowledge; **ce sera a. de moins à payer** it will be that much less to pay; **a. rester ici** we may as well stay here; **a. dire que...** which amounts to saying that...; **j'aimerais a. aller au cinéma** I'd rather go to the cinema; **j'aime a. te dire que je n'étais pas contente!** I wasn't too happy, I can tell you!; **..., d'a. (plus) que... ...,** especially since...; **d'a. plus/moins que** all the more/less because; **cela vous sera d'a. plus facile que vous êtes jeune** it will be that much easier for you since you are young; **pour a.** *(malgré cela)* for all that

autarcie [otarsi] *nf Pol* autarky; **vivre en a.** to be self-sufficient

autel [otɛl] *nm aussi Fig* altar; **conduire sa fille à l'a.** to give one's daughter away

auteur [otœr] *nm* (**a**) *(de livre)* author, writer; *(de chanson)* composer; *(de tableau)* painter (**b**) *(responsable)* author; *(d'un crime)* perpetrator; *(d'un projet)* instigator

authenticité [otãtisite] *nf* authenticity

authentification [otãtifikasjɔ̃] *nf* authentication

authentifier [66] [otãtifje] *vt* to authenticate

authentique [otãtik] *adj* authentic, genuine; *(fait, histoire)* true

authentiquement [otãtikmã] *adv* authentically, genuinely

autisme [otism] *nm* autism

autiste [otist] **1** *adj* autistic **2** *nmf* person with autism

auto [oto] *nf* car; **autos tamponneuses** bumper cars, *Br* Dodgems®; **petite a.** *(jouet)* toy car

auto- [oto] *préf* auto-, self-

autoaccusation [otoakyzasjɔ̃] *nf* self-accusation

autobiographie [otobjɔgrafi] *nf* autobiography

autobiographique [otobjɔgrafik] *adj* autobiographical

autobronzant, -e [otobrɔ̃zã, -ãt] **1** *adj* self-tanning **2** *nm* self-tan, self-tanning cream

autobus [otobys] *nm* bus; **a. à impériale** double-decker (bus); **a. à soufflet** articulated bus, *Br* bendy bus

autocar [otokar] *nm* bus, *Br* coach; **a. de luxe** luxury coach

autocassable [otokasabl] *adj* **ampoule a.** break-open phial

autocensurer [otosãsyre] **s'autocensurer** *vpr* to practise self-censorship
autochtone [otɔkton] **1** *nmf aussi Hum* native **2** *adj* native
autocollant, -e [otokɔlã, -ãt] **1** *adj* self-adhesive; *(enveloppe)* self-seal **2** *nm* sticker
autocorrecteur, -trice [otokɔrɛktœr, -tris] *adj Ordinat* self-correcting
autocouchette(s) [otokuʃɛt] *adj inv voir* train
autocrate [otokrat] *nmf* autocrat
autocratie [otokrasi] *nf* autocracy
autocratique [otokratik] *adj* autocratic
autocritique [otokritik] *nf* self-criticism; **faire son a.** to criticize oneself
autocuiseur [otokɥizœr] *nm* pressure cooker
autodafé [otodafe] *nm Hist* auto-da-fé
autodéfense [otodefãs] *nf* self-defence
autodestructeur, -trice [otodɛstryktœr, -tris] *adj* self-destructive
autodestruction [otodɛstryksjɔ̃] *nf* self-destruction
autodétermination [otodetɛrminasjɔ̃] *nf Pol* self-determination
autodidacte [otodidakt] **1** *adj* self-taught **2** *nmf* self-taught person
autodrome [otodrom] *nm* motor-racing track; *(pour les essais)* car-testing track
auto-école (*pl* **auto-écoles**) [otoekɔl] *nf* driving school
autofinancement [otofinãsmã] *nm* self-financing
autofinancer [45] [otofinãse] **s'autofinancer** *vpr* to be self-financing
autofocus [otofɔkys] *adj & nm Phot* autofocus
autogéré, -e [otoʒere] *adj* self-managed
autogestion [otoʒɛstjɔ̃] *nf* self-management
autographe [otograf] *nm & adj* autograph
automate [otomat] *nm* (**a**) *aussi Fig (robot)* automaton (**b**) *Suisse (machine)* vending machine; *(à billets)* cash dispenser
automation [otomajɔ̃] *nf* automation
automatique [otomatik] **1** *adj* automatic; **il est absent tous les lundis, c'est a.** he's off every Monday without fail **2** *nm* (**a**) *Tél* direct dialling (**b**) *(pistolet)* automatic
automatiquement [otomatikmã] *adv* automatically
automatisation [otomatizasjɔ̃] *nf* automation
automatiser [otomatize] *vt* to automate
automatisme [otomatism] *nm* (**a**) *(réflexe)* automatism; **agir par a.** to act automatically; **fermer la porte à double tour est devenu un a.** double-locking the door has become automatic (**b**) *(dispositif)* automatic device
automédication [otomedikasjɔ̃] *nf* self-medication
automitrailleuse [otomitrajøz] *nf* armoured car
automnal, -e, -aux, -ales [otɔnal, -o] *adj* autumnal
automne [otɔn] *nm* autumn, *Am* fall; **en a., à l'a.** in autumn; **une soirée d'a.** an autumn evening; *Fig* **à l'a. de sa vie** in the autumn of his/her life
automobile [otomɔbil] **1** *nf* (**a**) *(voiture)* car, *Am* automobile (**b**) *(industrie)* **l'a.** the car industry **2** *adj* (**a**) *(véhicule)* self-propelling (**b**) *(industrie, accessoires)* car, *Am* automobile
automobiliste [otomɔbilist] *nmf* motorist
autoneige [otonɛʒ] *nf Can* snowmobile
autonettoyant, -e [otonetwajã, -ãt] *adj* self-cleaning

autonome [otonɔm] *adj (état, région)* autonomous, self-governing; *(personne)* self-sufficient; *(appareil)* self-contained; *Ordinat* stand-alone
autonomie [otonɔmi] *nf* (**a**) *Pol* autonomy, self-government (**b**) *(de personne)* self-sufficiency (**c**) *(de voiture)* range; *(de batterie)* life; *Aviat* **a. (de vol)** *(flight)* range
autonomiste [otonɔmist] *nmf Pol* separatist
autoportrait [otopɔrtrɛ] *nm* self-portrait
autopsie [otɔpsi] *nf* autopsy, post-mortem; *Fig* **faire l'a. d'une œuvre** to dissect a work
autopsier [66] [otɔpsje] *vt* to perform an autopsy *or* a post-mortem on
autopunition [otopynisjɔ̃] *nf* self-punishment
autoradio [otoradjo] *nm* car radio
autorail [otorɑj] *nm* railcar
autorégulation [otoregylasjɔ̃] *nf* self-regulation
autoreverse [otorivœrs] *adj* **appareil a.** auto-reverse
autorisation [otorizasjɔ̃] *nf* (**a**) *(permission)* authorization, permission; **donner à qn l'a. de faire qch** to give sb permission to do sth; **demander (à qn) l'a. de faire qch** to ask (sb) permission to do sth; *Ordinat* **a. d'accès** access authorization; **a. de sortie du territoire** = parental authorization for a minor to travel abroad; *Aviat* **a. de vol** flight clearance (**b**) *(document)* authorization
autorisé, -e [otorize] *adj* (**a**) *(qualifié)* **tenir qch de source autorisée** to have sth from an authoritative source; **les milieux autorisés** official circles (**b**) *(permis)* permitted, allowed
autoriser [otorize] *vt* (**a**) *(permettre à)* **a. qn à faire qch** to authorize *or* permit sb to do sth; **je ne vous autorise pas à me parler sur ce ton** I won't have you talk to me like that (**b**) *(permettre)* **ces découvertes (nous) autorisent à penser que...** these discoveries entitle us to believe that...
autoritaire [otoritɛr] *adj* authoritarian
autoritairement [otoritɛrmã] *adv* in an authoritarian manner
autoritarisme [otoritarism] *nm* authoritarianism
autorité [otorite] *nf* (**a**) *(domination, fermeté)* authority; **avoir de l'a. sur qn** to have authority over sb; **faire qch d'a.** to do sth on one's own authority (**b**) *(poids)* **faire a. en qch** *(personne)* to be an authority on sth; **ce livre fait a.** this book is the authoritative work (**c**) *(gouvernement)* **les représentants de l'a.** the representatives of authority; **les autorités** the authorities (**d**) *(personne respectée)* authority
autoroute [otorut] *nf* (**a**) *Aut Br* motorway, *Am* freeway; **a. à péage** *Br* toll motorway, *Am* turnpike (road) (**b**) *Ordinat* **a. de l'information** information superhighway
autoroutier, -ère [otorutje, -ɛr] *adj* **réseau a.** *Br* motorway *or Am* freeway system
autosatisfaction [otosatisfaksjɔ̃] *nf* self-satisfaction
auto-stop [otostɔp] *nm* hitch-hiking, hitching; **faire de l'a.** to hitch-hike, to hitch; **prendre qn en a.** to give sb a lift; **faire le tour de l'Europe en a.** to hitch-hike around Europe
auto-stoppeur, -euse (*mpl* **auto-stoppeurs**, *fpl* **auto-stoppeuses**) [otostɔpœr, -øz] *nm,f* hitch-hiker, hitcher
autosuggestion [otosygʒɛstjɔ̃] *nf* auto-suggestion
autour [otur] *adv* around; **une ville avec des murs tout a.** a town with walls all around it; **a. de** *(dans l'espace)* around, round; *(environ)* about; *Fig* **discuter qch a. d'un verre** to discuss sth over a drink

autre [otr] **1** *adj indéfini* (**a**) *(différent)* other; **l'a. côté** the other side; **un a. jour** another day; **as-tu d'autres questions?** do you have any other questions?; **les choux et autres légumes** cabbages and other vegetables; **je l'ai vu l'a. jour/soir** I saw him the other day/evening
(**b**) *(avec un pronom personnel)* **nous autres Français** we French (people); *Fam* **eh, vous autres, venez par ici!** hey, you lot *or* you guys, come over here!
(**c**) *(locutions)* **a. chose** something else; **avez-vous a. chose à faire?** have you got anything else to do?; *Fig* **il est assez bon musicien, mais sa femme c'est autre c.!** he's not a bad musician, but his wife's in another league!; **a. part** somewhere else
2 *pron indéfini* (**a**) **l'a.** *(personne, chose)* the other (one); *Fam* **et l'a. qui se plaint tout le temps!** and then there's him/her and his/her constant complaining!; *Fam* **comme dit l'a.** as the saying goes, as they say; **un a.** *(personne, chose)* another (one); **il n'est pas plus bête qu'un a.** he is no more stupid than anyone else; **c'était un touriste comme un a.** he was just an ordinary tourist; **c'est une raison comme une a.** it's as good a reason as any; **les autres** *(personnes, choses)* the others, the other ones; **tu devrais penser un peu aux autres** you should think of others; *Fam* **à d'autres!** who do you think you're kidding?; *Fam* **j'en ai vu d'autres** I've seen worse than that
(**b**) *(avec l'un, les uns)* **l'un et l'a.** both; **l'un dit ceci, l'a. dit cela** one says this and the other says that; **les uns disent ceci, les autres disent cela** some say this and others say that; **les uns et les autres** *(deux groupes)* both parties; **l'un ou l'a.** either; **c'est l'un ou l'autre** *(il faut choisir)* it's one or the other; **ni l'un ni l'a.** neither; **je ne les connais ni l'un ni l'a.** I don't know either of them; **ni les uns ni les autres** none of them; **je n'ai vu ni les uns ni les autres** I didn't see any of them; **l'un l'a.** each other, one another; **les uns les autres** one another; **ils dépendent l'un de l'a.** they depend on each other; *Fig* **l'un dans l'a.** on the whole
(**c**) *(avec de)* **quelque chose d'a.** something else; *(dans les questions)* anything else; **rien d'autre** nothing else; **il n'y en a pas d'a.** there aren't any others; **personne d'a.** nobody else; **quelqu'un d'a.** somebody else; *(dans les questions)* anybody else; **que pouvait-il faire d'a.?** what else could he do?; **qui d'a. sera là?** who else will be there?
autrefois [otrəfwa] *adv* in the past, once; **d'a.** of long ago
autrement [otrəmã] *adv* (**a**) *(différemment)* differently; **il ne put faire a. que d'obéir** he had no alternative but to obey; **a. dit** in other words (**b**) *(sinon)* otherwise (**c**) *(bien plus)* far more; **a. plus dangereux (que)** far more dangerous (than) (**d**) **pas a.** not particularly; **cela ne me surprend pas a.** that doesn't particularly surprise me
Autriche [otriʃ] *nf* **l'A.** Austria
autrichien, -enne [otriʃjɛ̃, -ɛn] **1** *adj* Austrian
2 *nm,f* **A.** Austrian
autruche [otryʃ] *nf* ostrich; **sac en a.** ostrich-skin handbag; *Fig* **avoir un estomac d'a.** to have a cast-iron stomach; **pratiquer la politique de l'a., faire l'a.** to bury one's head in the sand
autrui [otrɥi] *pron indéfini* others, other people; **ne fais pas à a. ce que tu ne voudrais pas qu'on te fît** do as you would be done by

auvent [ovã] *nm (toit)* porch roof; *(de tente)* canopy, awning
auvergnat, -e [ovɛrɲa, -at] **1** *adj* of the Auvergne
2 *nm,f* **A.** person from the Auvergne
aux [o] *voir* à
auxiliaire [ɔksiljɛr] **1** *adj* auxiliary
2 *nmf (aide)* assistant; *(dans les hôpitaux)* auxiliary, *(dans l'administration)* temporary worker; **a. familiale** mother's help
3 *nm Gram* auxiliary verb
auxquels, auxquelles [okɛl] *voir* **lequel**
av. *(abrév* **avenue)** Ave
avachi, -e [avaʃi] *adj* (**a**) *(vêtement, bottes, canapé)* misshapen (**b**) *(personne, muscles)* flabby; **être a. dans un fauteuil** to be slumped in an armchair
avachir [avaʃir] **s'avachir** *vpr* (**a**) *(vêtement, bottes, canapé)* to lose its shape (**b**) *(personne) (physiquement)* to get flabby; *(moralement)* to let oneself go; **s'a. dans un fauteuil** to flop into an armchair
avais *etc voir* **avoir¹**
aval¹, -als [aval] *nm Fin (d'un effet de commerce)* endorsement; **a. bancaire** bank guarantee; *Fig* **donner son a. à un projet** to give a project one's backing *or* support
aval², -als *nm (d'un cours d'eau)* downstream section; *aussi Ind* **en a. (de)** downstream (from); **la Seine en a. de Paris** the Seine below Paris
avalanche [avalɑ̃ʃ] *nf* avalanche; *Fig (d'injures)* shower; *(de lettres, de compliments)* flood
avaler [avale] *vt* to swallow; *(goulûment) (nourriture)* to bolt; *(boisson)* to gulp down; *Fig (livre)* to devour; *(croire)* to swallow; **j'ai avalé de travers** it went down the wrong way; **je meurs de faim, je n'ai rien avalé depuis hier** I'm starving, I haven't had a thing to eat since yesterday; **on lui fait avaler n'importe quoi** he's/she's very gullible, he/she believes anything you tell him/her; **a. la fumée** to inhale; *Fig* **a. ses mots** to mumble; **une carte de crédit** *(distributeur automatique)* to swallow a credit card; **a. les kilomètres** to eat up the miles; **tu as avalé ta langue?** have you lost your tongue?
avaleur [avalœr] *nm* **a. de sabres** sword swallower
avance [avɑ̃s] *nf* (**a**) *(progression)* advance; **a. rapide** *(sur magnétophone)* fast-forwarding (**b**) *(avantage)* lead; **avoir de l'a. sur qn** to be ahead of sb; **prendre de l'a. sur qn** to take the lead over sb; **avoir deux minutes/deux km d'a. sur qn** to have a two-minute/two-km lead over sb; **avoir un but/point d'a. (sur qn)** to be one goal/point ahead (of sb); *Scol* **avoir un an d'a.** to be a year ahead; **arriver avec cinq minutes d'a.** to arrive five minutes early; **d'a., à l'a., par a.** in advance; **d'a. merci** *(dans une lettre)* thanking you in advance; *(dans une conversation)* thanks; **en a.** early; **être en a. d'une demi-heure** to be half an hour early; **être en a. pour son âge** to be advanced for one's age; **être en a. sur son temps** to be ahead of one's time (**c**) *(d'argent)* advance; **faire une a. à qn** to give sb an advance (**d**) **faire des avances à qn** *(chercher à séduire)* to make advances to sb
avancé, -e [avɑ̃se] *adj* (**a**) *(dans l'espace)* advanced (**b**) *(précoce)* **être a. pour son âge** to be advanced for one's age (**c**) *(idées, technologie)* advanced (**d**) *(tardif)* **à une heure avancée de la nuit** late in the night; **à un âge a.** at an advanced age (**e**) *(presque à terme)* **à un stade a.** at an advanced stage; **mon travail est bien a.** I'm making good progress with my

work; *Fig* **vous voilà bien a.**! a lot of good that's done you!

avancée [avɑ̃se] *nf* (**a**) *(saillie)* projection; *Constr* **a. du toit** eaves (**b**) *(de troupes, de la recherche)* advance

avancement [avɑ̃smɑ̃] *nm* (**a**) *(d'un projet)* progress; **état d'a.** des travaux progress report (**b**) *(promotion)* promotion; **avoir** *ou* **obtenir de l'a.** to be promoted (**c**) *Ordinat* **a. automatique** automatic feed; **a. ligne par ligne** line feed; **a. du papier** paper feed; **a. par friction** friction feed

avancer [16] [avɑ̃se] **1** *vt* (**a**) *(mettre en avant)* to move forward; *(pion)* to advance; *(présenter) (main, verre, assiette)* to hold out; *Sout ou Hum* **l'automobile de Monsieur est avancée** Sir's carriage awaits (**b**) *Fig (thèse)* to advance, to put forward (**c**) *(dans le temps)* to bring forward; **a. sa montre d'une heure** to put one's watch forward one hour (**d**) *(argent)* **a. qch à qn** to advance sb sth; *(prêter)* to lend sb sth (**e**) *(faire progresser)* **à quoi cela vous avancera-t-il?** what good will that do you?; **ça ne t'avancera à rien de te mettre en colère** losing your temper won't get you anywhere; **ses réponses ne m'ont pas beaucoup avancé** his/her answers didn't leave me much the wiser
2 *vi* (**a**) *(aller de l'avant)* to move forward; *(armée)* to advance; **a. d'un pas** to take a step forward; **faire a. qn** to advance sb along; **allez, avance!** on va être en retard come on, move! we're going to be late (**b**) *(faire des progrès)* to progress; **alors, ça avance?** so, how's it coming along?; **faire a. les choses** to get things moving (**c**) *(montre)* to be fast; **ma montre avance d'une minute par jour** my watch gains a minute a day; **vous avancez de dix minutes** your watch is ten minutes fast (**d**) *(promontoire, toit)* to jut out
3 *s'avancer* *vpr* (**a**) *(aller devant)* to move forward; **s'a. vers qch** to head towards sth; **s'a. d'un pas** to take a step forward (**b**) *(faire son travail à l'avance)* to get ahead (**c**) *Fig (s'engager hâtivement)* to commit oneself

avant [avɑ̃] **1** *prép* (**a**) *(dans le temps, dans l'espace)* before; **a. une heure** by one o'clock; *(dans moins d'une heure)* within an hour; **800 a. Jésus-Christ** 800 BC; **a. impôt** before tax; **je vous reverrai a. de partir** I'll see you before I leave; **ne fais rien a. d'être tout à fait sûr** don't do anything until you're absolutely sure; **je vous reverrai a. que vous (ne) partiez** I'll see you before you leave; **je serai parti a. que vous ayez fini** I'll have left by the time you've finished; **ne partez pas a. qu'on vous le dise** don't go until you are told; *Fam* **celle-là, a. qu'elle se décide!** she takes forever to make her mind up! (**b**) *(par ordre de priorité)* before; **faire passer qch a. le reste** to put sth before everything else; **pour lui, la famille passe a. tout** for him, (the) family comes first; **a. tout** *(surtout)* above all; **a. toute chose** before anything else
2 *adv* (**a**) *(auparavant)* before; *(d'abord)* beforehand; **a. j'avais les cheveux longs** I used to have long hair; **tu ferais mieux de téléphoner a.** you'd better phone first; **le jour d'a.** the day before (**b**) *(dans l'espace)* **vous voyez l'église? sa maison est juste a.** you see the church? his/her house is just before you get to it (**c**) *Litt (loin)* far; *(tard)* late; *Fig* **poussons plus a.** notre enquête let's take our investigation further (**d**) **en a.** *(devant les autres)* in front, ahead; *(se pencher, tomber)* forwards; *Mil* **en a., marche!** forward march!; **partir en a.** to go on ahead; **faire deux pas en a.** to take two steps forward; *Fig* **se mettre en**

a. to push oneself forward; **en a. de** in front of
3 *adj inv* front
4 *nm* (**a**) *(d'un véhicule, d'une salle)* front; **à l'a.** *(d'un véhicule)* in the front; **aller de l'a.** to get on with it (**b**) *(en sport)* forward; **jouer a.** to be a forward

avantage [avɑ̃taʒ] *nm* (**a**) *(intérêt)* advantage; **cette solution** *ou* **présente l'a. d'être rapide** this solution has the advantage of being quick (**b**) *(supériorité)* advantage; **(sur** over); **être à son a.** *(physiquement)* to look one's best (**c**) *(profit)* advantage; **tu aurais a. à être poli** you'd do well to be polite; **être/tourner à l'a. de qn** to be/to turn to sb's advantage; **tirer a. de qch** to turn sth to one's advantage; **a. fiscal** tax benefit; **a. en nature** benefit in kind; **avantages sociaux** social security benefits (**d**) *Sport* advantage; **prendre/conserver l'a.** to gain/retain the advantage

avantager [45] [avɑ̃taʒe] *vt* (**a**) *(favoriser)* **a. qn (par rapport à)** to give sb an advantage (over); **être avantagé par rapport à qn** to have an advantage over sb (**b**) *(physiquement)* **a. qn** to show sb off to advantage; **il n'a pas été avantagé par la nature** he hasn't been favoured by nature

avantageux, -euse [avɑ̃taʒø, -øz] *adj* (**a**) *(offre)* attractive; *(conditions)* favourable; *(prix)* reasonable; *(produit)* good value (**b**) *(vaniteux) (ton)* superior

avant-bras [avɑ̃bra] *nm inv* forearm

avant-centre *(pl* avants-centres) [avɑ̃sɑ̃tr] *nm (au football)* centre forward

avant-coureur *(pl* avant-coureurs) [avɑ̃kurœr] *adj m voir* **signe**

avant-dernier, -ère *(mpl* avant-derniers, *fpl* avant-dernières) [avɑ̃dɛrnje, -ɛr] **1** *adj* last but one, second to last; **l'avant-dernière fois** the time before last
2 *nm,f* last but one, second to last

avant-garde *(pl* avant-gardes) [avɑ̃gard] *nf* (**a**) *Mil* advance guard (**b**) **l'a.** *(modernité)* the avant-garde; **d'a.** *(œuvre, théâtre)* avant-garde; **être à l'a. de la mode** to be at the cutting edge of fashion

avant-goût *(pl* avant-goûts) [avɑ̃gu] *nm* foretaste (**de** of)

avant-guerre *(pl* avant-guerres) [avɑ̃gɛr] *nm ou nf* pre-war period

avant-hier [avɑ̃tjɛr] *adv* the day before yesterday; **a. au soir** the evening before last

avant-midi [avɑ̃midi] *nm inv ou nf inv Belg & Can* morning

avant-plan *(pl* avant-plans) [avɑ̃plɑ̃] *nm Belg* foreground

avant-poste *(pl* avant-postes) [avɑ̃pɔst] *nm Mil* outpost

avant-première *(pl* avant-premières) [avɑ̃prəmjɛr] *nf* preview; **(présenté) en a.** *(film, pièce)* previewed

avant-propos [avɑ̃prɔpo] *nm inv* foreword, preface

avant-scène *(pl* avant-scènes) [avɑ̃sɛn] *nf Théât* apron

avant-toit *(pl* avant-toits) [avɑ̃twa] *nm* eaves

avant-veille *(pl* avant-veilles) [avɑ̃vɛj] *nf* **l'a. (de qch)** two days before (sth)

avare [avar] **1** *adj* mean, miserly; *Fig* **il n'est pas a. de compliments** he's generous with his compliments
2 *nmf* miser

avarice [avaris] *nf* miserliness, avarice

avarie [avari] *nf* damage; **subir une a.** to be damaged

avarié, -e [avarje] *adj (nourriture)* rotten

avarier [66] [avarje] **s'avarier** *vpr (nourriture)* to go off, to go bad

avatar [avatar] *nm* (**a**) *(incarnation)* incarnation (**b**) *(mésaventure)* mishap, misadventure

avec [avɛk] **1** *prép* (**a**) *(en compagnie de)* with; **être gentil/méchant a. qn** to be nice/nasty to sb; **être bien/mal a. qn** *(s'entendre bien/mal)* to get on well/ badly with sb; **je suis a. vous** *(je vous soutiens)* I'm right behind you; *Fam* **et a. ça?** *(au magasin)* anything else? (**b**) *(indique la manière)* **a. enthousiasme** enthusiastically, with enthusiasm; **a. beaucoup de gentillesse** very kindly, with great kindness; **c'est a. émotion que j'accepte** I'm thrilled to accept (**c**) *(indique la simultanéité)* **diminuer a. l'âge** to decrease with age; **cela viendra a. le temps** it will come in time (**d**) *(indique le moyen)* with; **ouvrir qch a. une clef** to open sth with a key; **j'ai eu un accident a. cette voiture** I had an accident in this car (**e**) *(à cause de)* **a. tous les ennuis que j'ai en ce moment...** with all the problems I have at the moment...; **impossible de sortir a. cette pluie** it's impossible to go out in this rain (**f**) *(en ce qui concerne)* **a. elle, on ne sait jamais** you never can tell with her (**g**) **divorcer d'a. qn** to divorce sb

2 *adv* **je suis venu a.** *(mon parapluie, mes gants)* I came with it/them; **il faut bien faire a.** I'll/we'll just have to put up with it

avenant, -e [avnɑ̃, -ɑ̃t] **1** *adj (personne, manières)* pleasant

2 *nm* (**a**) *(de police d'assurance)* endorsement (**b**) **le bâtiment est beau et le jardin est à l'a.** the building is beautiful and the garden is in keeping with it

avènement [avɛnmɑ̃] *nm (du Christ, d'une ère)* advent; *(d'un roi)* accession

avenir [avnir] *nm* future; **assurer l'a. de qn** to make provision for sb; **dans un très proche a.** in the very near future; **avoir de l'a.** *(personne, technique)* to have a future; **un métier d'a.** a career with good prospects; **un avocat d'a.** a lawyer with a great future; **à l'a.** in future

Avent [avɑ̃] *nm* **l'A.** Advent

aventure [avɑ̃tyr] *nf* (**a**) *(histoire)* adventure; **pour trouver des fruits en hiver, c'est tout une a.** it's quite a job finding fruit in winter (**b**) *(liaison)* (love) affair (**c**) **l'a.** *(le risque)* adventure; **tenter l'a.** to seek adventure; **partir à l'a.** to set off in search of adventure; *(sans préparation)* to set out without making plans (**d**) **dire la bonne a. à qn** to tell sb's fortune

aventurer [avɑ̃tyre] **s'aventurer** *vpr* to venture (**dans** into); **je ne m'aventurerai pas à dire que...** I wouldn't go so far as to say (that)...

aventureux, -euse [avɑ̃tyrø, -øz] *adj (vie, personne)* adventurous; *(projet)* risky

aventurier, -ère [avɑ̃tyrje, -ɛr] *nm,f* adventurer, *f* adventuress

avenue [avny] *nf* avenue

avérer [34] [avere] **s'avérer** *vpr (se révéler)* to prove to be; **il s'est avéré que...** it turned out that...

averse [avɛrs] *nf* shower; *Can* **a. de neige** snow flurry

aversion [avɛrsjɔ̃] *nf* aversion (**pour** to), dislike (**pour** of); **prendre qn en a.** to take a dislike to sb

averti, -e [avɛrti] *adj (bien informé)* (well-)informed; **vous voilà a.!** don't say I didn't warn you!; *Prov* **un homme a. en vaut deux** forewarned is forearmed

avertir [avɛrtir] *vt* **a. qn de qch** *(informer)* to inform sb of sth; *(d'un danger)* to warn sb of sth; **je vais me mettre en colère, je t'avertis!** I'm going to get angry, I'm warning you!

avertissement [avɛrtismɑ̃] *nm* (**a**) *(avis préalable)* warning; **a. (au lecteur)** foreword (**b**) *(réprimande)* warning; *Sport (de l'arbitre)* warning, caution (**c**) *(signal)* warning sign

avertisseur [avɛrtisœr] *nm (dispositif)* alarm; *(Klaxon®)* horn; **a. d'incendie** fire alarm

aveu, -x [avø] *nm* confession; **passer aux aveux** to make a confession; **je dois vous faire un a...** I must confess...; **de l'a. de tout le monde...** it is commonly acknowledged that...

aveuglant, -e [avœglɑ̃, -ɑ̃t] *adj* blinding, dazzling; *Fig (preuve)* blindingly obvious

aveugle [avœgl] **1** *adj aussi Fig* blind; **a. d'un œil** blind in one eye; **avoir une confiance a. en qn** to trust sb implicitly

2 *nmf* blind man, *f* blind woman; **les aveugles** the blind

aveuglement [avœgləmɑ̃] *nm (moral, mental)* blindness

aveuglément [avœglemɑ̃] *adv* blindly

aveugle-né, -e [avœglɔne] *(mpl* **aveugles-nés,** *fpl* **aveugles-nées)** [avœglɔne] **1** *adj* blind from birth

2 *nm,f* person blind from birth

aveugler [avœgle] *vt aussi Fig* to blind; **aveuglé par la colère** blind with rage

aveuglette [avœglɛt] **à l'aveuglette** *adv* blindly; **aller à l'a.** to grope one's way

aviateur, -trice [avjatœr, -tris] *nm,f* aviator

aviation [avjasjɔ̃] *nf* (**a**) *(activité)* flying; **faire de l'a.** to go flying (**b**) *(secteur)* aviation; **a. civile/commerciale** civil/commercial aviation; **a. de tourisme** civil aviation (**c**) *Mil* air force

aviculteur, -trice [avikyltœr, -tris] *nm,f (de volailles)* poultry farmer

aviculture [avikyltyr] *nf (de volailles)* poultry farming

avide [avid] *adj* (**a**) *(passionné)* eager (**de** for); **a. de sang** bloodthirsty (**b**) *Péj (cupide)* greedy

avidement [avidmɑ̃] *adv (voracement)* greedily; *(avec passion)* eagerly

avidité [avidite] *nf (voracité, cupidité)* greed; *(passion)* eagerness; **avec a.** *(manger)* greedily; *(écouter, regarder)* eagerly

aviez *etc voir* **avoir**[1]

Avignon [aviɲɔ̃] *nf* Avignon; *Théât* **le festival d'A.** the Avignon festival

Le festival d'Avignon

Founded by Jean Vilar in 1947 and held every summer in Avignon in the South of France, this arts festival is a showcase for new theatre and dance performances: "La pièce sera donnée d'abord en Avignon". Along with the programme of official shows ("le in") performed in prestigious venues such as the Court of Honour of the "Palais des Papes", a programme comprising numerous fringe shows, referred to as "le off", has also been performed since the 1970s.

avilir [avilir] **1** *vt (dégrader)* to degrade, to demean

2 s'avilir *vpr (personne)* to demean oneself

avilissant, -e [avilisɑ̃, -ɑ̃t] *adj* degrading

avilissement [avilismɑ̃] *nm (dégradation)* degradation

aviné, -e [avine] *adj (personne)* inebriated; *(haleine)* reeking of wine

avion [avjɔ̃] *nm* plane, *Br* aeroplane, *Am* airplane; **par a.** *(sur lettre)* airmail; **voyager en a.** to travel by plane *or* by air; **a. charter** charter plane; **a. de chasse** fighter (plane); **a. gros-porteur** jumbo jet; **a. de ligne** airliner; **a. à réaction** jet (plane); **a. supersonique** supersonic plane; **a. de tourisme** private plane

avion-cargo (*pl* **avions-cargos**) [avjɔ̃kargo] *nm* freight plane, cargo plane

avion-espion (*pl* **avions-espions**) [avjɔ̃ɛspjɔ̃] *nm* spy plane

avions *etc voir* **avoir¹**

aviron [avirɔ̃] *nm* (**a**) *(rame)* oar; *Can* paddle (**b**) *(sport)* **l'a.** rowing; **faire de l'a.** to row

avironner [avirɔne] *vi Can* to paddle

avis [avi] *nm* (**a**) *(opinion)* opinion; **changer d'a.** to change one's mind; **les a. sont partagés** opinion is divided; **à mon a.** in my opinion; **tu vas accepter? – à ton a.?** are you going to accept? – what do you think?; **être de l'a. de qn** to be of the same opinion as sb; **de l'a. de tous...** the general opinion is that...; **être d'a. de faire qch** to be of a mind to do sth; *Prov* **deux a. valent mieux qu'un** two heads are better than one (**b**) *(conseils)* advice; **suivre l'a. de qn** to follow sb's advice (**c**) *(avertissement)* notice; **jusqu'à nouvel a.** until further notice; **sauf a. contraire** unless I/you/*etc* hear to the contrary; **a. de livraison** delivery note; **a. de prélèvement** direct debit advice; **a. de réception** acknowledgement of receipt

avisé, -e [avize] *adj (sage)* sensible, wise; *(acheteur, consommateur)* shrewd; **tu serais bien/mal a. de...** you'd be well-/ill-advised to...

aviser [avize] **1** *vt* (**a**) *(informer)* **a. qn de qch** to inform sb of sth; **a. qn que...** to inform sb that... (**b**) *Fam (entrevoir)* to spot
2 *vi (prendre une décision)* to make up one's mind
3 s'aviser *vpr* (**a**) *(se rendre compte)* **s'a. que** to notice that (**b**) *(oser)* **s'a. de faire qch** to get it into one's head to do sth; **et ne t'avise pas de recommencer!** don't you dare start again!

aviver [avive] *vt (couleurs)* to brighten up; *(passion, querelle, feu)* to stir up; *(appétit)* to sharpen

av. J.-C. *(abrév* avant Jésus-Christ) BC; **en 106 a.** in 106 BC

avocat¹, -e [avɔka, -at] *nm,f* (**a**) *Jur* lawyer; **a. d'affaires** business lawyer; **a. général** assistant public prosecutor *(in a Court of Appeal)* (**b**) *Fig* advocate; **se faire l'a. du diable** to play devil's advocate

avocat² *nm (fruit)* avocado (pear)

avocette [avɔsɛt] *nf* avocet

avoine [avwan] *nf* (**a**) *(céréale)* oats (**b**) *Fam (argent)* dough

avoir¹ [1] [avwar] **1** *v aux* to have; **je ne l'ai pas encore fini** I haven't finished it yet; **je te l'ai dit hier** I told you yesterday; **j'avais déjà vu ce film** I had already seen the film; **il faut que je l'aie fini pour demain** I have to finish it by tomorrow; **est-ce que tu auras terminé ce soir?** will you get it finished tonight?; **il aurait réussi s'il avait travaillé plus** he would have passed if he had worked harder
2 *vt* (**a**) *(posséder)* to have; **il a une fille** he has *or* he's got a daughter; **a. les yeux bleus** to have blue eyes; **a. une drôle de forme** to have a funny shape; **a. un rhume** to have a cold; **a. du diabète** to be diabetic; **a. mal au cœur** to feel sick; **j'ai le nez qui pique** I've got an itchy nose; **a. de l'ambition** to be ambitious; **a. de l'humour** to have a sense of humour; **a. 20 ans** to be 20 (years old); **a. de quoi manger** to have something to eat; **elle a Guy pour voisin** Guy is her neigh-

bour; **qui as-tu comme prof de math?** who's your maths teacher?
(**b**) *(obtenir)* to get; **a. qn au téléphone** to speak to sb on the telephone; **a. son train** to catch one's train; **je l'ai eu pour 50 euros** I bought it for 50 euros; **j'ai eu mon bac en 1995** I passed my "bac" in 1995
(**c**) *(porter) (vêtement)* to wear; *(objet)* to carry
(**d**) *(faire)* **il a eu un sourire étrange** he smiled strangely
(**e**) *(atteindre) (cible)* to hit
(**f**) *Fam (duper) (personne)* to take for a ride, to con; **tu nous a bien eus!** you really had us going!; **se faire a.** to be conned; **se faire a. de 100 euros** to be conned *or* done out of 100 euros
(**g**) *(locutions)* **a. faim/froid** to be hungry/cold; **a. quelque chose à faire** to have something to do; **j'ai à faire** I've got things to do; **j'ai à lui parler** I've got to talk to him/her; **tu n'as qu'à le lui dire** just tell him/her; **tu en as pour combien de temps?** how long will you be?; **j'en ai pour 10 minutes** I'll be 10 minutes; **je n'en ai pas pour longtemps** I won't be long; **qu'est-ce que tu as?** what's wrong?; **j'ai que je suis fatigué** I'm tired, that's all; **qu'est-ce qu'il a à se plaindre sans arrêt?** why is he complaining all the time?; **on les aura!** we'll have them!
3 *il y a* **v** *impersonnel* there is/are; **il y a un problème** there's a problem; **il y a des problèmes** there are some problems; **il y a six ans** six years ago; **il y a un mois que je suis ici** I've been here for a month; **il n'y a qu'à le faire** we'll just have to do it; **il n'y a pas que ça dans la vie** there's more to life than that; **il n'y a pas de quoi!** don't mention it!; **qu'y a-t-il?, qu'est-ce qu'il y a?** what is it?, what's wrong?; **il y a que j'en ai assez** I've had enough, that's all

avoir² *nm (d'une compagnie)* assets; *(d'un compte)* credit; *(dans un magasin)* voucher

avoisinant, -e [avwazinã, -ãt] *adj* neighbouring, nearby

avoisiner [avwazine] *vt* **une somme avoisinant les 500 euros** a sum in the region of 500 euros

avons *voir* **avoir¹**

avortement [avɔrtəmã] *nm* (**a**) *(chez une femme)* **a. (provoqué)** abortion; **a. spontané** miscarriage; **a. thérapeutique** termination for medical reasons (**b**) *(chez un animal)* casting (**c**) *Fig (d'un projet)* failure

avorter [avɔrte] **1** *vi* (**a**) *(subir une IVG)* to have an abortion; *(faire une fausse couche)* to miscarry (**b**) *(animal)* to cast (**c**) *Fig (projet)* to fall through
2 *vt (sujet: médecin)* to abort; **se faire a.** to have an abortion

avorteur, -euse [avɔrtœr, -øz] *nm,f* abortionist

avorton [avɔrtɔ̃] *nm Péj* runt

avoué¹ [avwe] *nm Jur Br* ≃ solicitor, *Am* ≃ attorney

avoué², -e *adj* (**a**) *(auteur, partisan)* confessed (**b**) *(but)* declared

avouer [avwe] **1** *vt (faute, crime)* to confess to, to own up to; **il a fini par a.** he finally confessed; **a. que** to admit that; **ceci me surprend, je l'avoue** this surprises me, I must confess; **il faut bien a. que...** it must be admitted that...
2 **s'avouer** *vpr* **s'a. coupable** to admit one's guilt; **s'a. vaincu** to acknowledge defeat

avril [avril] *nm* April; **le premier a.** *(jour des farces)* April Fools' Day; *Prov* **en a., ne te découvre pas d'un fil** ne'er cast a clout till May be out; *voir aussi* **janvier**

axe [aks] *nm* (**a**) *(géométrique)* axis; **a. des abscisses/des ordonnées** x-/y-axis; **être dans l'a. de qch** to be in line with sth; **(grand) a.** *(routier)* main road; *Fig* **les grands axes de sa politique** the main thrust of his/her policy (**b**) *(de machine, de roue de vélo)* axle (**c**) *Hist* **l'A. (Rome-Berlin)** the (Rome-Berlin) Axis

axer [akse] *vt* to centre; **être axé sur** *ou* **autour de** to centre on

axiome [aksjom] *nm* axiom

ayant *etc voir* **avoir¹**

ayant droit *(pl* **ayants droit**) [ɛjãdrwa] *nm Jur* beneficiary

ayatollah [ajatɔla] *nm* ayatollah

azalée [azale] *nf* azalea

Azerbaïdjan [azɛrbajdʒɑ̃] *nm* **l'A.** Azerbaijan

azerbaïdjanais, -e [azɛrbajdʒanɛ, -ɛz] **1** *adj* Azerbaijani
  2 *nm,f* **A.** Azerbaijani

azéri, -e [azeri] **1** *adj* Azeri
  2 *nm,f* **A.** Azeri

azimuts [azimyt] *nmpl Fam* **une campagne électorale tous a.** an all-out electoral campaign

azote [azɔt] *nm* nitrogen

AZT® [azɛdte] *nm Méd (abrév* **azidothymidine)** AZT

aztèque [aztɛk] **1** *adj* Aztec
  2 *nmf* **A.** Aztec

azur [azyr] *nm Litt* (**a**) *(couleur)* azure (**b**) **l'a.** *(ciel)* the sky

azyme [azim] *adj m voir* **pain**

B, b [be] *nm inv* B, b
baba¹ [baba] *nm* **b. au rhum** rum baba; *Fam* **elle l'a dans le b.** she's had it
baba² *adj inv Fam* flabbergasted; **j'en suis resté b.** I was flabbergasted
baba cool (*pl* **babas cool**) [babakul] *nmf* hippie
Babel [babɛl] *n* **la tour de B.** the Tower of Babel
babil [babil] *nm* (*d'un enfant*) prattling; (*des oiseaux*) twittering; (*d'un ruisseau*) babbling
babillard [babijar] *nm Ordinat* bulletin board, BBS
babiller [babije] *vi* (*enfant*) to prattle; (*oiseau*) to twitter; (*ruisseau*) to babble
babines [babin] *nfpl aussi Hum* chops; **d'avance, je m'en lèche les b.** my mouth's watering in anticipation
babiole [babjɔl] *nf* (**a**) (*bibelot*) knick-knack, trinket (**b**) (*broutille*) trifle
bâbord [babɔr] *nm* port (side); **à b.** to port
babouche [babuʃ] *nf* Turkish slipper
babouin [babwɛ̃] *nm* baboon
baboune [babun] *nf Can Fam* **faire la b.** to sulk
baby-boom (*pl* **baby-booms**) [bebibum] *nm* baby boom
baby-foot [babifut] *nm inv* table football
baby-sitter (*pl* **baby-sitters**) [bebisitœr] *nmf* baby-sitter
baby-sitting [bebisitiŋ] *nm* baby-sitting; **faire du b.** to baby-sit
bac¹ [bak] *nm* (**a**) (*bateau*) ferry(-boat) (**b**) (*récipient*) tank; (*d'imprimeur, de photographe*) tray; (*d'alimentation*) sheet feed; **b. à glace** ice tray; **b. à légumes** salad drawer; *Belg* **b. à ordures** *Br* dustbin, *Am* garbage can; **b. de** *ou* **à papier** (*d'imprimante*) paper tray; **b. à sable** sandpit
bac² *Fam* = baccalauréat
baccalauréat [bakalɔrea] *nm* = secondary school examination qualifying for entry to university, *Br* ≃ A levels, *Am* ≃ high school diploma; **b. L** *ou* **littéraire** = arts-based "baccalauréat"; **b. S** *ou* **scientifique** = science-based "baccalauréat"

Baccalauréat

The "baccalauréat", or "bac", is taken by pupils who have completed their final year at the "lycée"; successful candidates may go to university. Pupils may choose to study for a "baccalauréat général", "technologique" (vocational) or "professionnel" (vocational and including professional training). There are three main types of "baccalauréat général", each corresponding to a specific field: "bac L" (arts subjects), "bac ES" (economics and social studies) and "bac S" (sciences).

---

bacchantes [bakɑ̃t] *nfpl Hum* moustache
bâche [baʃ] *nf* (*toile*) tarpaulin
bachelier, -ère [baʃəlje, -ɛr] *nm,f* = student who has passed the "baccalauréat"
bâcher [baʃe] *vt* **b. qch** to cover sth with a tarpaulin
bachot [baʃo] *Fam Vieilli* = baccalauréat
bachotage [baʃɔtaʒ] *nm Fam Vieilli* cramming, *Br* swotting
bachoter [baʃɔte] *vi Fam Vieilli* to cram, *Br* to swot
bacille [basil] *nm Biol* bacillus
bâcler [bɑkle] *vt Fam* to botch
bacon [bekɔn] *nm* (**a**) (*viande*) bacon (**b**) *Can Fam* **avoir du b.** to be loaded
bactérie [bakteri] *nf* bacterium
bactériologique [bakterjɔlɔʒik] *adj* bacteriological; **guerre b.** germ warfare
badaboum [badabum] *exclam Fam* **et b., il est tombé!** he fell down, crash, bang, wallop!
badaud [bado] *nm* (*promeneur*) stroller; (*curieux*) *Br* gawper, *Am* rubberneck
badge [badʒ] *nm* (**a**) (*insigne, d'identité*) *Br* badge, *Am* button (**b**) (*carte magnétique*) swipe card
badigeonner [badiʒɔne] *vt* (**a**) (*surface*) to daub (**de** with); (*mur*) to whitewash; *Culin* to brush (**de** with) (**b**) (*gorge, plaie*) to paint (**de** with)
badin, -e [badɛ̃, -in] *adj* playful
badinage [badinaʒ] *nm* banter
badine [badin] *nf* switch
badiner [badine] *vi* to jest, to joke; **il ne badine pas avec la ponctualité** he's very strict about punctuality
badinerie [badinri] *nf* jest
badminton [badminton] *nm* badminton
bâdrant, -e [badrɑ̃, -ɑ̃t] *adj Can* bothersome
bâdrer [badre] *vt Can* to bother
baffe [baf] *nf Fam* clout, smack; **flanquer une b. à qn** to give sb a smack in the face
baffle [bafl] *nm* baffle
bafouer [bafwe] *vt* (*personne*) to jeer at; (*règlement, autorité*) to flout
bafouiller [bafuje] *vt & vi* to stammer
bâfrer [bafre] *vi très Fam* to stuff oneself, to pig out
bagage [bagaʒ] *nm* (**a**) (*sac, valise*) **bagages** luggage, baggage; **faire ses bagages** to pack one's bags; **b. à main** piece of hand luggage (**b**) *Fig* (*connaissances*) knowledge (**en** of)
bagagiste [bagaʒist] *nm* baggage handler
bagarre [bagar] *nf* fight, brawl; **chercher la b.** to look for a fight
bagarrer [bagare] **se bagarrer** *vpr Fam* to fight

bagarreur, -euse [bagarœr, -øz] *Fam* **1** *adj (personne, caractère)* aggressive
2 *nm,f* brawler

bagatelle [bagatɛl] *nf (chose sans importance)* trifle; **pour la b. de 400 euros** for a mere 400 euros

Bagdad [bagdad] *n* Baghdad

bagnard [baɲar] *nm* convict

bagne [baɲ] *nm Hist (prison)* convict prison; *(peine)* penal servitude; *Fig* **c'est le b., ici!** they work you to death in this place!

bagnole [baɲɔl] *nf Fam* car

bagou(t) [bagu] *nm* glibness; **avoir du b.** to have the gift of the gab

bague [bag] *nf* (**a**) *(bijou)* ring; *Fig* **passer la b. au doigt à qn** to marry sb; **b. de fiançailles** engagement ring (**b**) *(d'une boîte de conserve)* ring-pull; *(de cigare)* band (**c**) *(d'oiseau)* ring (**d**) *Tech* bush, ring; **b. de serrage** jubilee clip

baguenauder [bagnode] **1** *vi* to saunter around
2 se baguenauder *vpr* to saunter around

baguer [bage] *vt (oiseau, arbre)* to ring

baguette [bagɛt] *nf (tige)* stick; *(de chef d'orchestre)* baton; *(pain)* baguette, French loaf; **baguettes** *(pour manger)* chopsticks; **mener** *ou* **faire marcher qn à la b.** to rule sb with a rod of iron; **b. magique** magic wand; **d'un coup de b. magique** with a wave of my/his/*etc* magic wand; **baguettes de tambour** drumsticks; **avoir des cheveux raides comme des baguettes de tambour** to have poker-straight hair

bah [ba] *exclam* bah!

Bahamas [baamas] *nfpl* **les B., l'archipel des B.** the Bahamas

Bahreïn [barajn], **Bahrayn** [barɛ̃] *n* Bahrain

bahut [bay] *nm* (**a**) *(coffre)* chest; *(buffet)* sideboard (**b**) *Fam (collège, lycée)* school (**c**) *Fam (camion)* truck, *Br* lorry

bai, -e¹ [bɛ] *adj (cheval)* bay

baie² *nf Géog* bay; **la b. d'Hudson** Hudson Bay

baie³ *nf* **b. vitrée** picture window

baie⁴ *nf (fruit)* berry

baignade [bɛɲad] *nf* (**a**) *(activité)* swimming, *Br* bathing; **b. interdite** *(sur panneau)* no swimming (**b**) *(endroit)* swimming *or Br* bathing place

baigner [beɲe] **1** *vt (pieds, œil, blessure)* to bathe; *(bébé, chien) Br* to bath, *Am* to bathe; *(sujet: mer)* to wash; *(sujet: rivière)* to water; **être baigné de sueur** to be bathed in sweat; **visage baigné de larmes** face streaming with tears; **baigné de lumière** bathed in light
2 *vi (tremper)* to soak, to steep (**dans** in); **les légumes baignent dans la sauce** the vegetables are swimming in sauce; **il baignait dans son sang** he was lying in a pool of his own blood; *Fam* **ça baigne (dans l'huile)!** everything's hunky dory!
3 se baigner *vpr* (**a**) *(se laver)* to have *or* take a bath (**b**) *(nager)* to have a swim

baigneur, -euse [bɛɲœr, -øz] **1** *nm,f* swimmer, *Br* bather
2 *nm (poupée)* doll

baignoire [bɛɲwar] *nf* (**a**) *(dans la salle de bains)* bath (**b**) *Théât* ground-floor box

Baïkal [bajkal] *n voir* lac

bail [baj] *(pl* **baux** [bo]*) nm* lease; *Fam* **ça fait un b. que je ne l'ai pas vu** I haven't seen him for ages

bâillement [bajmɑ̃] *nm* yawn

bâiller [baje] *vi* (**a**) *(personne)* to yawn; *Fam* **b. à s'en ou se décrocher la mâchoire** to yawn one's head off (**b**) *(coutures, col)* to gape; *(porte)* to be ajar

bâillon [bajɔ̃] *nm* gag; **mettre un b. à qn** to gag sb

bâillonner [bajɔne] *vt aussi Fig* to gag

bain [bɛ̃] *nm* (**a**) *(pour se laver)* bath; **prendre un b.** to have *or* take a bath; *Fam Fig* **être/se mettre dans le b.** to be in/get into the swing of things; **b. de bouche** mouthwash; **faire un b. de bouche** to use mouthwash; **b. de boue** mud bath; **prendre un b. de foule** *(personnalité)* to go on a walkabout; **b. moussant** bubble bath; **prendre un b. de pieds** to soak one's feet; **prendre un b. de soleil** to sunbathe; **b. turc** Turkish bath; **b. de vapeur** steam bath (**b**) *Can (baignoire)* bathtub, *Br* bath (**c**) *(à la piscine)* **petit/grand b.** small/large pool (**d**) *(à la mer, en rivière)* swim, *Br* bathe; *Vieilli* **bains de mer** swimming in the sea (**e**) *Phot* bath (**f**) *Tex* dye

bain-marie [bɛ̃mari] *(pl* **bains-marie**[bɛ̃mari]*) nm* bain-marie *(cooking pan set over second pan of boiling water)*; **faire cuire qch au b.** to cook sth in a bain-marie

baïonnette [bajɔnɛt] *nf* bayonet

baisemain [bɛzmɛ̃] *nm* **faire le b. à qn** to kiss sb's hand

baiser¹ [beze] **1** *vt* (**a**) *Litt (embrasser)* to kiss (**b**) *Vulg (coucher avec)* to fuck (**c**) *Vulg (tromper)* to screw; **se faire b.** to get screwed
2 *vi Vulg* to fuck

baiser² *nm* kiss; **gros baisers** *(dans une lettre)* love and kisses

baisse [bɛs] *nf* fall, drop (**de** in); **être en b.** *(température, actions)* to be falling; *(popularité)* to be on the decline

baisser [bese] **1** *vt* (**a**) *(rideau, store, vitre de voiture)* to lower; **b. la tête** to lower one's head; *(de honte, de découragement)* to hang one's head; **b. les yeux** to look down; *Fig* **b. les bras** to give in (**b**) *(lumière, son, chauffage)* to turn down; *(prix)* to lower; **b. la voix** to lower one's voice; **je vous prie de b. le ton!** please keep your voice down!
2 *vi* (**a**) *(diminuer) (température, niveau de l'eau, prix)* to fall; *(marée)* to ebb; **elle a baissé dans mon estime** she's gone down in my estimation (**b**) *(s'affaiblir) (malade)* to get weaker; *(enthousiasme)* to fall off; *(feu)* to burn low; *(vue, mémoire)* to fail; **le jour baisse** night is falling
3 se baisser *vpr* to bend down; *(pour éviter un coup)* to duck; *Fig* **il n'y a qu'à se b. pour les ramasser** there are loads of them around

baissier [besje] *adj m voir* **marché**

bajoues [baʒu] *nfpl (d'animal)* chops; *Péj (d'une personne)* flabby cheeks

Bakou [baku] *n* Baku

bal *(pl* **bals**) [bal] *nm (populaire)* dance; *(élégant)* ball; **b. costumé** *ou* **masqué** fancy dress ball; **b. musette** = dance to accordion music; **b. populaire** = public dance held outdoors

balade [balad] *nf Fam (à pied)* walk; *(en voiture)* drive; *(à bicyclette, à moto)* ride; **faire une b.** *(à pied)* to go for a walk; *(en voiture)* to go for a drive; *(à bicyclette, à moto)* to go for a ride

balader [balade] *Fam* **1** *vt (personne, chien)* to take for a walk; *(avoir avec soi) (objet)* to drag around
2 *vi* **envoyer b. qn** to send sb packing
3 se balader *vpr (à pied)* to go for a walk; *(en voiture)* to go for a drive; *(à bicyclette, à moto)* to go for a ride

baladeur, -euse [baladœr, -øz] **1** *adj Fam* **avoir les mains baladeuses** to have wandering hands **2** *nm* personal stereo, Walkman® **3** *nf* **baladeuse** *(lampe)* inspection lamp

baladin [baladɛ̃] *nm* strolling player

balafre [balafr] *nf* (**a**) *(coupure)* gash (**b**) *(cicatrice)* scar

balafré [balafre] *nm* scarface

balafrer [balafre] *vt* to gash; **visage balafré** scarred face

balai [balɛ] *nm* (**a**) *(de ménage)* broom; **passer le b.** to give the floor a sweep; **donner un coup de b.** *(balayer)* to give the floor a sweep; *Fig (dans une entreprise)* to have a shake-out; **du b.!** clear off!; **b. mécanique** carpet sweeper (**b**) *Aut (d'essuie-glace)* blade (**c**) *(percussion)* brush (**d**) *Fam (an)* **avoir quarante/cinquante balais** to be forty/fifty

balai-brosse *(pl* **balais-brosses** *)* [balɛbrɔs] *nm* long-handled scrubbing brush

balaise [balɛz] = **balèze**

balalaïka [balalaika] *nf* balalaika

balance [balɑ̃s] *nf* (**a**) *(appareil)* (pair of) scales; *(publique)* weighing machine; *Fig* **ce facteur pèse dans la b.** this factor carries some weight; **faire pencher la b.** to tip the scales (**b**) *Astron & Astrol* **la B.** Libra; **être B.** to be a Libran (**c**) *Écon* balance; **b. commerciale** balance of trade; **b. des paiements** balance of payments (**d**) *Fam (mouchard)* squealer, *Br* grass

balancé, -e [balɑ̃se] *adj Fam* **être bien b.** *(personne)* to have a good body

balancelle [balɑ̃sɛl] *nf (de jardin) Br* swing hammock, *Am* glider

balancement [balɑ̃smɑ̃] *nm* swaying

balancer [16] [balɑ̃se] **1** *vt* (**a**) *(bras, jambes, trompe, pendule)* to swing; *(hanches)* to sway (**b**) *Fam (projectile, objet)* to chuck, to throw; **b. des vannes/remarques** to make snide/unpleasant remarks (**c**) *Com (compte)* to balance (**d**) *Fam (se débarrasser de) (objet)* to chuck *or* throw out; **b. qn** to give sb the push; **elle a tout balancé** *(tout abandonné)* she's given it all up (**e**) *Fam (dénoncer)* to squeal on, *Br* to grass up **2** *vi Litt (hésiter)* to waver **3 se balancer** *vpr* (**a**) *(arbres, blés)* to sway; **se b. sur sa chaise** to rock backwards and forwards on one's chair; **se b. d'un pied sur l'autre** to rock from one foot to the other (**b**) *(sur une balançoire)* to swing (**c**) *très Fam* **je m'en balance!** I don't *or Am* a toss *or Am* a rat's ass! (**d**) *Fam* **il s'est balancé du haut de la tour Eiffel** he chucked himself off the top of the Eiffel Tower

balancier [balɑ̃sje] *nm* (**a**) *(d'un funambule)* balancing pole (**b**) *(d'horloge)* pendulum

balançoire [balɑ̃swar] *nf (suspendue)* swing; *(bascule)* seesaw

balayage [balɛjaʒ] *nm* (**a**) *(pour nettoyer)* sweeping (**b**) *Rad, Élec & TV* scanning

balayer [53] [balɛje] *vt* (**a**) *(nettoyer)* to sweep; *(saletés)* to sweep up; *Fig (objections, obstacles)* to brush aside; **le vent a balayé les nuages** the wind has swept the clouds away; *Fig* **b. devant sa porte** to put one's own house in order (**b**) *Rad, Élec & TV* to scan; *(sujet: projecteurs)* to sweep

balayette [balɛjɛt] *nf* small brush; *(des WC)* toilet brush

balayeur, -euse [balɛjœr, -øz] **1** *nm,f* road-sweeper **2** *nf* **balayeuse** *Can (aspirateur)* vacuum cleaner

balbutiement [balbysimɑ̃] *nm* (**a**) *(en parlant)* stammering (**b**) **balbutiements** *(d'une science, d'une discipline)* early stages

balbutier [66] [balbysje] **1** *vi* to stammer **2** *vt* to stammer (out)

balcon [balkɔ̃] *nm* (**a**) *(d'édifice)* balcony (**b**) *(dans un théâtre)* circle; **premier/deuxième b.** dress/upper circle

baldaquin [baldakɛ̃] *nm* canopy

Bâle [bɑl] *n* Basel

Baléares [balear] *nfpl* **les (îles)** B. the Balearic Islands

baleine [balɛn] *nf* (**a**) *(animal)* whale; **b. blanche/ bleue** white/blue whale (**b**) *(d'un parapluie)* rib; *(d'un corset)* (whale)bone

baleineau, -x [balɛno] *nm* whale calf

baleinière [balɛnjɛr] *nf* whaleboat

balèze [balɛz] *adj Fam (grand et fort)* hefty; *(intelligent)* brainy; **b. en maths** brilliant at maths

balisage [balizaʒ] *nm* (**a**) *(signaux)* Naut & Rad beacons; *Aviat* lights (**b**) *(action)* Naut & Rad beaconing; *Aviat* lighting

balise [baliz] *nf Naut & Rad* beacon; *Aviat* light; *(de piste de ski, d'épave)* marker; *Ordinat* tag; *Naut* **b. flottante** buoy; *Rad* **b. radar** radar beacon

baliser [balize] *vt (chenal)* to beacon; *(aéroport)* to equip with lights; *(route)* to mark out with beacons; *(piste de ski)* to mark out

balistique [balistik] **1** *adj (missile)* ballistic **2** *nf* ballistics *(singulier)*

balivernes [balivɛrn] *nfpl* twaddle

balkanisation [balkanizasjɔ̃] *nf aussi Fig* Balkanization

Balkans [balkɑ̃] *nmpl* **les B.** the Balkans

ballade [balad] *nf* ballad

ballant, -e [balɑ̃, -ɑ̃t] *adj (bras, jambes)* dangling; **ne reste pas là, les bras ballants** don't just stand there like an idiot

ballast [balast] *nm* (**a**) *Constr (d'une route, d'une voie ferrée)* ballast (**b**) *Naut* ballast tank

balle[1] [bal] *nf* (**a**) *(pour jouer)* ball; **jouer à la b.** to play ball; *Fig* **prendre** *ou* **saisir la b. au bond** to seize the opportunity; *Fig* **se renvoyer la b.** to pass the buck; *Fig* **la b. est dans votre camp** the ball's in your court; **b. de golf/de tennis** golf/tennis ball; **b. de break/de match** break/match point (**b**) *(d'arme)* bullet; **b. à blanc** blank; **b. perdue** stray bullet (**c**) *Anciennement Fam* **balles** *(francs)* francs

balle[2] *nf (de coton, de laine)* bale

balle[3] *nf (de blé)* husk

ballerine [balrin] *nf* (**a**) *(danseuse)* ballerina (**b**) *(chaussure)* pump

ballet [balɛ] *nm* ballet

ballon [balɔ̃] *nm* (**a**) *(aéronef)* balloon; **b. d'essai** pilot balloon (**b**) *(balle)* ball; **jouer au b.** to play with a ball; **b. de football** football; **le b. ovale** rugby; **le b. rond** football (**c**) *(pour boire)* **(verre) b.** round wine glass (**d**) **b. (de baudruche)** balloon; **souffler dans le b.** *(d'Alcootest)* to blow into the bag; **b. d'oxygène** oxygen bottle (**e**) *Suisse (petit pain)* (bread) roll

ballonné, -e [balɔne] *adj (ventre, personne)* bloated

ballon-panier [balɔ̃panje] *nm inv Can Sport* basketball

ballon-sonde *(pl* **ballons-sondes** *)* [balɔ̃sɔ̃d] *nm Météo* sounding balloon

ballot [balo] *nm* (**a**) *(paquet)* bundle (**b**) *Fam (imbécile)* idiot, fool

ballottage [balɔtaʒ] *nm Pol* **il y a b.** there will be a second ballot

ballottement [balɔtmã] *nm (de train)* rocking; *(des passagers)* shaking; *(de navire)* tossing

ballotter [balɔte] **1** *vt (bateau)* to toss about; *(passagers)* to shake about; *Fig* **un enfant ballotté entre son père et sa mère** a child passed backwards and forwards between its father and mother
2 *vi (bagages, bateau)* to be tossed about; *(poitrine)* to bounce up and down

ball-trap [baltrap] *nm (sport)* clay-pigeon shooting

balluchon [balyʃɔ̃] *nm Fam (de vêtements)* bundle; **faire son b.** to pack one's bags

balnéaire [balneɛr] *adj voir* **station**

balourd, -e [balur, -urd] **1** *adj (personne)* oafish
2 *nm,f* clumsy oaf

balsa [balza] *nm* balsawood

balte [balt] **1** *adj* Baltic; **les pays Baltes** the Baltic states
2 *nmf* **B.** Balt

Baltique [baltik] *nf* **la (mer) B.** the Baltic (Sea)

baluchon [balyʃɔ̃] = **balluchon**

balustrade [balystrad] *nf* (**a**) *Archit* balustrade (**b**) *(clôture)* railing

bambin [bãbɛ̃] *nm Fam* toddler, tot

bambou [bãbu] *nm (plante)* bamboo; *Fam* **c'est le coup de b.!** it's a rip-off!

bamboula [bãbula] *nf Fam* spree; **faire la b.** to live it up

ban [bã] *nm* (**a**) *(applaudissements)* round of applause (**b**) **bans** *(de mariage)* banns; **publier les bans** to publish the (wedding) banns (**c**) **être au b. de la société** to be an outcast from society; **le b. et l'arrière-b.** *(tout le monde)* the world and his wife (**d**) *Suisse* **mettre qch au b.** to forbid access to sth

banal, -e, -als, -ales [banal] *adj (objet, gens, occupation)* ordinary; *(idée, remarque, style)* trite, banal; *(accident, exemple)* common; **pas b.** unusual

banalisation [banalizasjɔ̃] *nf (généralisation)* spread; *Péj (perte d'originalité)* trivialization; **la b. des transports aériens** the fact that air travel has become commonplace *or* an everyday phenomenon

banaliser [banalize] **1** *vt (rendre commun)* to trivialize; **véhicule banalisé** unmarked police car
2 se banaliser *vpr* to become more common

banalité [banalite] *nf* (**a**) *(d'un objet, de gens, d'une occupation)* ordinariness; *(d'une idée, d'une remarque, d'un style)* triteness, banality; *(d'un accident, d'un exemple)* commonness (**b**) **banalités** *(propos banals)* platitudes

banane [banan] *nf* (**a**) *(fruit)* banana; **b. plantain** plantain (**b**) *(coiffure)* quiff (**c**) *(petit sac) Br* bum bag, *Am* fanny pack

bananier, -ère [bananje, -ɛr] **1** *adj (plantation, production)* banana
2 *nm (arbre)* banana tree

banc [bã] *nm* (**a**) *(siège)* bench; **ils se sont connus sur les bancs de l'école** they got to know each other at school; **b. des accusés** dock; **b. d'église** pew; **b. des témoins** *Br* witness box, *Am* witness stand (**b**) *(de roche)* layer; *Can* **b. de neige** snowdrift; *(entassé mécaniquement)* bank of snow; **b. de sable** sandbank (**c**) *(de poissons)* shoal; **b. d'huîtres** oyster bed (**d**) *(établi)* (work)bench (**e**) **b. d'essai** *Ind* test bed; *Ordinat* benchmark; *Fig* testing ground; *Ordinat* **b. de mémoire** memory bank

bancaire [bãkɛr] *adj (opération)* banking; *(chèque, compte)* bank

bancal, -e, -als, -ales [bãkal] *adj (meuble)* wobbly; *Fig (raisonnement, projet)* unsound

bandage [bãdaʒ] *nm (pansement)* bandage; *(action)* bandaging

bandana [bãdana] *nm* bandana

bande¹ [bãd] *nf* (**a**) *(de tissu, de papier, de terre)* strip; *(motif)* stripe; **b. dessinée** comic strip (**b**) *(pansement)* bandage; **b. Velpeau®** crêpe bandage (**c**) *(magnétique)* tape; *(pellicule)* film; *Ordinat* **b. de défilement** scroll bar; **b. originale** *(d'un film)* original soundtrack; **b. sonore** soundtrack (**d**) *Aut* **b. d'arrêt d'urgence** *Br* hard shoulder, *Am* shoulder; **b. médiane** *(sur la route)* central line; **b. de roulement** *(de pneu)* tread (**e**) *Rad* **b. (de fréquence)** (frequency) band; *Phys & Tél* **b. passante** pass-band (**f**) *(d'une mitrailleuse)* cartridge belt (**g**) *Naut* **donner de la b.** to list

bande² *nf (de personnes)* band, group; *(de voleurs)* gang, band; **faire b. à part** *(agir seul)* to do one's own thing; **viens avec nous, ne fais pas b. à part** come with us, don't stay on all your own; **faire qch en b.** to do sth in a group; **une b. d'incapables/d'imbéciles** a bunch of incompetents/idiots

bande-annonce *(pl* **bandes-annonces)** [bãdanɔ̃s] *nf* trailer (**de** for)

bandeau, -x [bãdo] *nm* (**a**) *(pour les cheveux)* headband (**b**) *(sur les yeux)* blindfold; **mettre un b. à qn** to blindfold sb (**c**) *Ordinat (dans un site Web)* banner

bandelette [bãdlɛt] *nf (de tissu)* strip; **bandelettes** *(de momie)* bandages

bander [bãde] **1** *vt* (**a**) *(blessure, main)* to bandage; **b. les yeux à qn** to blindfold sb (**b**) *(ressort)* to tighten; *(arc)* to bend; *(muscles)* to flex
2 *vi Vulg* to have a hard-on

banderille [bãdrij] *nf* banderilla

banderole [bãdrɔl] *nf* banner

bande-son *(pl* **bandes-son)** [bãdsɔ̃] *nf* soundtrack

bandit [bãdi] *nm (escroc)* crook; *Vieilli (brigand)* bandit; **b. de grand chemin** highwayman

banditisme [bãditism] *nm* crime; **le grand b.** organized crime

bandoulière [bãduljɛr] *nf (d'un sac)* shoulder strap; **en b.** over one's shoulder

bang [bãg] *nm inv Aviat* sonic boom; *Astron* **le big b.** the big bang

Bangkok [bãkɔk] *n* Bangkok

Bangladesh [bãgladɛʃ, bɛ̃gladɛʃ] *nm* **le B.** Bangladesh

banjo [bãdʒo] *nm* banjo

banlieue [bãljø] *nf* suburbs; **la b. parisienne/marseillaise** the suburbs of Paris/Marseilles; **la grande/proche b.** the outer/inner suburbs; **vivre en b.** to live in the suburbs; **de b.** suburban

Banlieue

In France the word "banlieue" often refers not to the upmarket areas of a city – as the word "suburbia" suggests in English-speaking countries – but to the impoverished suburban areas on the outskirts of some cities. These neighbourhoods are culturally and ethnically diverse and are frequently associated with social problems such as delinquency, unemployment and unrest.

banlieusard, -e [bãljøzar, -ard] *nm,f* suburbanite

bannière [banjɛr] *nf* (**a**) *(drapeau)* banner; **la b. étoilée** the Star-spangled Banner (**b**) *Ordinat (dans un siteWeb)* banner

bannir [banir] *vt (personne, idée)* to banish (**de** from); *(sujet de conversation)* to ban (**de** from); **vous devez b. le sucre de votre alimentation** you must exclude sugar from your diet

bannissement [banismɑ̃] *nm* banishment

banque [bɑ̃k] *nf* (**a**) *(établissement)* bank; **employé/ directeur de b.** bank clerk/manager; **b. d'affaires** *Br* merchant bank, *Am* investment bank; **b. centrale** central bank; **B. centrale européenne** European central bank; **B. européenne pour la reconstruction et le développement** European Bank for Reconstruction and Development; **la B. de France** the Bank of France; **B. internationale pour la reconstruction et le développement** International Bank for Reconstruction and Development; **la B. mondiale** theWorld Bank (**b**) *(activité)* banking; **travailler dans la b.** to be *or* work in banking; **b. à domicile** telebanking, home banking; **b. en ligne** online banking (**c**) *(au jeu)* bank; **faire sauter la b.** to break the bank (**d**) *Ordinat* **b. de données** data bank; **b. d'organes/du sperme** organ/sperm bank

banquer [bɑ̃ke] *vi Fam* to cough up

banqueroute [bɑ̃krut] *nf Jur* bankruptcy; **faire b.** to go bankrupt

banquet [bɑ̃kɛ] *nm* banquet

banquette [bɑ̃kɛt] *nf* (**a**) *(siège)* seat; **la b. arrière** *(d'une voiture)* the back seat (**b**) *(d'un couloir d'autobus)* = kerb separating a bus lane from the rest of the roadway

banquier, -ère [bɑ̃kje, -ɛr] *nm,f* banker

banquise [bɑ̃kiz] *nf* ice floe

bantou, -e [bɑ̃tu] **1** *adj* Bantu
  2 *nm,f* **B.** Bantu

baobab [baɔbab] *nm* baobab (tree)

baptême [batɛm] *nm* (**a**) *Rel* baptism, christening; **donner le b. à qn** to baptize *or* christen sb (**b**) *(d'un navire)* naming; *(d'une cloche)* blessing (**c**) **b. de l'air** first flight; **b. du feu** baptism of fire (**d**) *Belg* = **bizutage**

baptiser [batize] *vt* (**a**) *Rel* to baptize, to christen (**b**) *(nommer)* to name; *(surnommer)* to christen (**c**) *(navire)* to name; *(cloche)* to bless

baptismal, -e, -aux, -ales [batismal, -o] *adj* baptismal

baptistère [batistɛr] *nm Rel* baptistry

baquet [bakɛ] *nm (cuve)* tub

bar¹ [bar] *nm (café, comptoir)* bar; **b. à thème** theme bar

bar² *nm (poisson)* bass

bar³ *nm Phys* bar

barachois [baraʃwa] *nm Can (dans une rivière)* sandbar

baragouiner [baragwine] *Fam* **1** *vt (langue étrangère)* to speak badly; **qu'est-ce qu'il baragouine?** what's he jabbering about?
  2 *vi* to jabber

baraque [barak] *nf* (**a**) *(cabane)* hut, shack; *(de forain)* stall, stand (**b**) *Fam (maison)* place

baraqué, -e [barake] *adj Fam* hefty

baraquement [barakmɑ̃] *nm* shacks; *Mil* camp

baratin [baratɛ̃] *nm Fam* (**a**) *(d'un vendeur)* sales talk, patter; *(d'un séducteur)* smooth talk (**b**) *(verbiage)* waffle

baratiner [baratine] *Fam* **1** *vt (sujet: vendeur)* to give the sales talk to; *(sujet: séducteur) Br* to chat up, *Am* to hit on
  2 *vi* to waffle

baratineur, -euse [baratinœr, -øz] *nm,f Fam* smooth talker

baratte [barat] *nf* churn

Barbade [barbad] *nf* **la B.** Barbados

barbant, -e [barbɑ̃, -ɑ̃t] *adj Fam* deadly boring

barbare [barbar] **1** *adj (cruel, sauvage)* barbaric
  2 *nmf* barbarian

barbarie [barbari] *nf* (**a**) *(cruauté)* barbarity (**b**) *(manque de civilisation)* barbarism

barbarisme [barbarism] *nm* barbarism

barbe [barb] *nf* (**a**) *(d'homme)* beard; **b. de trois jours** stubble; *Fig* **à la b. de qn** right under sb's nose; **parler dans sa b.** to mutter, to mumble; **rire dans sa b.** to laugh up one's sleeve; *Fam* **la b.!** what a pain *or* drag!; *Fam* **quelle b.!** what a drag!; **b. à papa** *Br* candy floss, *Am* cotton candy (**b**) *(de chèvre, d'épi)* beard; *(de plume, d'hameçon)* barb (**c**) *Tech (de métal)* burr; *(de papier)* ragged edge

barbecue [barbəkju] *nm* barbecue; **faire un b.** to have a barbecue

barbelé [barbəle] **1** *adj m voir* **fil**
  2 *nmpl* **barbelés** barbed wire

barber [barbe] *Fam* **1** *vt* **b. qn** to bore sb stiff
  2 **se barber** *vpr* to be bored stiff

barbeuc, barbeuk [barbœk] *nm Fam (barbecue)* BBQ, *Br* barbie

barbeux, -euse [barbœ, -øz] *adj Can Fam* **être b.** to be a pain in the neck

barbiche [barbiʃ] *nf* goatee (beard)

barbichette [barbiʃɛt] *nf Fam* small goatee (beard)

barbier [barbje] *nm* (**a**) *Vieilli* barber (**b**) *Can (coiffeur pour hommes)* (men's) hairdresser

barbiturique [barbityrik] *nm* barbiturate

barboter [barbɔte] **1** *vi* to splash about
  2 *vt Fam (voler)* to pinch

barboteuse [barbɔtøz] *nf* (**a**) *(vêtement)* romper suit (**b**) *Can (piscine gonflable) Br* paddling pool, *Am* wading pool

barbouiller [barbuje] *vt* (**a**) *(salir)* to smear (**de** with); *(peindre)* to daub (**b**) *Fam* **b. l'estomac** *ou* **le cœur à qn** to make sb feel queasy; **se sentir barbouillé** to feel queasy

barbouze [barbuz] *nf Fam (agent secret)* secret agent

barbu, -e [barby] **1** *adj* bearded
  2 *nm* bearded man

Barcelone [barsəlɔn] *n* Barcelona

barda [barda] *nm Fam* (**a**) *(affaires)* gear; *Mil* kit (**b**) *Can (pagaille)* shambles (**c**) *Can (bruit)* **faire du b.** to make a racket

barde¹ [bard] *nf Culin (sur un rôti)* bard

barde² *nm (poète)* bard

barder¹ [barde] *v impersonnel Fam* **ça va b.!** there's going to be trouble!

barder² *vt* (**a**) *Culin* to bard (**b**) **bardé de fer/cuir** steel-/leather-clad; **être bardé de décorations** to be covered with decorations; **être bardé de diplômes** to have a whole string of qualifications

barème [barɛm] *nm* (**a**) *(de notes, de salaires, de prix)* scale (**b**) *(pour calcul rapide)* ready reckoner

barge [barʒ] *nf (péniche)* barge

baril [baril] *nm (de vin, de pétrole)* barrel; *(de poudre)* keg; *(de lessive)* drum

barillet [barijɛ] *nm (de revolver)* cylinder

bariolé, -e [barjɔle] *adj* multicoloured

barjo(t) [barʒo] *adj Fam* nutty

barman [barman] (*pl* **barmans** *ou* **barmen** [barmɛn]) *nm Br* barman, *Am* bartender

baromètre [barɔmɛtr] *nm aussi Fig* barometer

baron [barɔ̃] *nm (seigneur)* baron; *Fig* **les barons de la finance/de l'industrie** financial/industrial tycoons

baronne [barɔn] *nf* baroness

baroque [barɔk] **1** *adj (architecture, art, musique)* baroque; *(idées)* bizarre, odd
2 *nm* **le b.** the Baroque

baroud [barud] *nm* **b. d'honneur** last stand

barouder [barude] *vi Fam (voyager)* to knock about, to bum around

baroudeur [barudœr] *nm Fam* (**a**) *(combattant)* fighter (**b**) *(voyageur)* keen traveller

barouf(le) [baruf(l)] *nm Fam* din, racket

barque [bark] *nf* boat; *Fig* **bien mener** *ou* **bien conduire sa b.** to manage one's affairs well; *Fig* **c'est elle qui mène la b.** she's the boss

barquette [barkɛt] *nf* (**a**) *(pour plat à emporter)* container; *(de fruits)* punnet (**b**) *(gâteau)* pastry boat

barrage [baraʒ] *nm (sur l'eau)* dam; **b. de police** roadblock; **b. routier** roadblock

barre [bar] *nf* (**a**) *(de métal)* bar, rod; *(de bois)* rod; **b. d'appui** *(d'une fenêtre)* rail; **b. de céréales** cereal *or* muesli bar; **b. de chocolat, b. chocolatée** bar of chocolate; **b. à mine** = metal bar used for breaking stone surfaces (**b**) *(pour la danse)* barre; *Sport* **barres asymétriques** asymmetric bars; **b. fixe** horizontal bar; **barres parallèles** parallel bars; **b. transversale** *(de but)* crossbar; *Fig* **placer la b. trop haut** to set too high a standard (**c**) *(trait)* line, stroke; *(d'un t)* cross; **b. oblique** oblique, slash; *Mus* **b. de mesure** bar (line) (**d**) *Naut (à l'arrière)* tiller; *(volant)* helm; *aussi Fig* **être à** *ou* **tenir la b.** to be at the helm (**e**) *Jur (de tribunal)* bar; **b. des témoins** *Br* witness box, *Am* witness stand; **être appelé à la b.** to be called to the witness box (**f**) *(de clavier)* **b. d'espacement** space bar (**g**) *Ordinat* **b. d'outils** tool bar; **b. de sélection** menu bar; **b. de titre** title bar (**h**) **b. HLM** *Br* large block of council flats, *Am* large apartment building on a housing project (**i**) *Can* **la b. du jour** dawn, daybreak

barreau, -x [baro] *nm* (**a**) *(d'une fenêtre, d'une cage)* bar; *(d'une échelle, d'une chaise)* rung; *Fig* **b. de chaise** fat cigar; **être derrière les barreaux** to be behind bars (**b**) *Jur* **le b.** the bar

barrer [bare] **1** *vt* (**a**) *(route, passage, chemin)* to block off; *(porte, fenêtre)* to bar; *Can (fermer à clef)* to lock; **route barrée** *(sur panneau)* road closed; **b. le passage** *ou* **la route à qn** to bar sb's way (**b**) *(chèque)* to cross (**c**) *(mot, paragraphe)* to cross out (**d**) *Naut (bateau)* to steer; *(à l'aviron)* to cox (**e**) *Fam* **on est mal barrés** things don't look good
2 se barrer *vpr Fam* to clear off, to beat it

barrette [barɛt] *nf* (**a**) *(pour les cheveux) Br* (hair) slide, *Am* barrette (**b**) *(broche)* brooch (**c**) *Fam (de haschisch)* thin strip (**d**) *Ordinat* **b. de mémoire vive** RAM module

barreur [barœr] *nm Naut* helmsman; *(à l'aviron)* cox

barricade [barikad] *nf* barricade

barricader [barikade] **1** *vt (rue, porte)* to barricade
2 se barricader *vpr* to barricade oneself in

barrière [barjɛr] *nf (obstacle)* barrier; *(clôture)* fence; *(d'un passage à niveau)* gate; *Aut* **b. de dégel** = ban on the use of a road by heavy traffic during a thaw; *Com* **barrières douanières** trade barriers; **b. Nadar** crowd barrier; **la Grande B. de Corail** the Great Barrier Reef; *Belg* **b. Vauban** security barrier

barrique [barik] *nf* barrel; *Fam Fig* **plein** *ou* **rond comme une b.** drunk as a skunk

barrir [barir] *vi (éléphant)* to trumpet

barrissements [barismɑ̃] *nmpl (d'un éléphant)* trumpeting

bar-tabac (*pl* **bars-tabacs**) [bartaba] *nm* = bar that also sells cigarettes and tobacco

baryton [baritɔ̃] *nm Mus* baritone

baryum [barjɔm] *nm Chim* barium

bas¹ [bɑ], **basse** [bɑs] **1** *adj* (**a**) *(dans l'espace, en quantité, en intensité)* low; *(marée)* out, low; **à b. prix** cheaply; **avoir la vue basse** to be short-sighted (**b**) *(dans une hiérarchie)* low; *Péj ou Hum* **le b. peuple** the hoi polloi; **les b. quartiers** the poor districts (**c**) *(note)* low; *(instrument de musique)* bass (**d**) *(dans le temps)* late; **le b. Moyen Âge** the late Middle Ages (**e**) *Péj (acte)* mean, low; *(besognes)* menial
2 *adv* (**a**) *(dans l'espace)* low (down); **voir plus b.** *(dans un article)* see below; *Fig* **mettre qn plus b. que terre** to treat sb like dirt; **tomber b.** *(température, prix d'une action)* to plummet; *Fam* **b. les mains** *ou* **les pattes!** hands off!, keep your paws off! (**b**) *(dans une hiérarchie)* low (**c**) *(parler)* quietly; *(chanter) (dans le registre)* low; *(doucement)* softly; **rire tout b.** to chuckle to oneself (**d**) **en b.** at the bottom; *(à l'étage inférieur)* downstairs; **les gens d'en b.** the people below *or* downstairs; **la tête en b.** upside down; **en b. de** at the bottom of (**e**) **à b. la dictature/la police!** down with dictatorship/the police!
3 *nm (partie inférieure)* bottom; **l'étagère du b.** the bottom shelf; **le b. du dos** the small of the back; **au b. de** at the bottom; **en b. en haut** upwards
4 *nf* **basse** *Mus* (**a**) *(partie)* bass part; *(voix, chanteur)* bass (**b**) *(contrebasse)* (double) bass; *(guitare)* bass (guitar)

bas² *nm (vêtement)* stocking; *Can* sock; **b. de contention** elastic stocking; *Fig* **b. de laine** nest egg; **b. nylon** nylons; **b. résille** fishnet stockings; **b. à varices** support stocking

basalte [bazalt] *nm* basalt

basané, -e [bazane] *adj (bronzé)* tanned; *(tanné)* weatherbeaten; *(naturellement)* swarthy

bas-côté (*pl* **bas-côtés**) [bakote] *nm* (**a**) *(d'une route)* verge (**b**) *(d'une église)* (side) aisle

basculant, -e [baskylɑ̃, -ɑ̃t] *adj* **benne basculante** *(de camion)* tipping body; **pont b.** drawbridge

bascule [baskyl] *nf* (**a**) *(balançoire)* seesaw (**b**) *(balance)* weighing machine (**c**) *Ordinat* toggle (**d**) *Can* **donner la b. à qn** to give sb the bumps

basculer [baskyle] **1** *vt* (**a**) *(brouette, charrette)* to tip up; *(chargement)* to tip over (**b**) *Ordinat* to toggle
2 *vi* (**a**) *(tomber)* to topple over; **faire b.** *(personne)* to knock over; *(chargement)* to tip over; **le pays a basculé dans l'anarchie** the country tipped over into anarchy (**b**) *Ordinat* to toggle

base [bɑz] *nf* (**a**) *(partie inférieure)* base; *Fig (d'un syndicat, d'un parti politique)* rank and file; **b. de maquillage** foundation (**b**) *Mil (d'opérations)* base; **b. aérienne/navale** air/naval base; **b. de lancement** launch site (**c**) *(principe)* basis; **jeter** *ou* **poser les bases de qch** to lay the foundations for sth; **de b.** basic; **denrées de b.** staple commodities; **à b. d'amidon/de gin** starch-/gin-based (**d**) *Math & Chim* (**e**) *Ordinat* **b. de données** database

base-ball [bɛzbol] *nm* baseball

baser [baze] **1** *vt* to base; **être basé sur qch** to be based on sth
2 se baser *vpr* **se b. sur qch** *(sujet: personne)* to base one's argument on sth; **sur quoi te bases-tu pour dire que...?** what basis do you have for saying that...?
bas-fond *(pl* **bas-fonds)** [bafɔ̃] *nm (dans la mer, la rivière)* shallow; **les bas-fonds** *(d'une ville)* the rough areas
basic [bazik] *nm Ordinat* BASIC
basilic [bazilik] *nm (plante)* basil
basilique [bazilik] *nf* basilica
basket [baskɛt] **1** *nm ou nf (chaussure)* **baskets** *Br* trainers, *Am* sneakers; *Fam* **être bien dans ses baskets** to be very together
2 *nm (sport)* basketball
basket-ball [baskɛtbol] *nm* basketball
basketteur, -euse [baskɛtœr, -øz] *nm,f* basketball player
basque¹ [bask] **1** *adj* Basque
2 *nmf* **B.** Basque
3 *nm (langue)* Basque

Basque

The area covered by the Basque Country includes the far south-western corner of France. The French portion shares with its Spanish counterpart a common language and a strong sense of separate identity. Nevertheless, nationalist sentiment is much less radical there and Basque is not as widely spoken as it is on the other side of the Pyrenees. Basque, or "Euskera", stands out as one of the very few non-Indo-European languages surviving in Europe.

basque² *nf (d'une veste)* tail; *Fig* **être toujours pendu aux basques de qn** to be always at sb's heels
bas-relief *(pl* **bas-reliefs)** [baʁəljɛf] *nm* bas-relief
basse [bɑs] *voir* **bas¹**
basse-cour *(pl* **basses-cours)** [baskur] *nf* **(a)** *(cour)* farmyard **(b)** *(volaille)* poultry
bassement [bɑsmɑ̃] *adv* **être b. intéressé** to have one's own interests at heart
bassesse [bɑsɛs] *nf* **(a)** *(d'une action, d'un caractère)* lowness **(b)** *(action)* low act
basset [bɑsɛ] *nm (chien)* basset (hound)
bassin [bɑsɛ̃] *nm* **(a)** *(récipient)* basin, bowl; **b. (hygiénique)** bedpan **(b)** *(dans un jardin)* ornamental lake; *(de fontaine)* basin; *(réservoir)* tank; **petit b.** *(de la piscine)* children's pool; **grand b.** *(de la piscine)* large pool **(c)** *(d'un port)* dock, basin **(d)** *Géol* basin; **b. houiller** coal basin; **b. minier** mining area; **le B. parisien** the Paris Basin **(e)** *(partie du corps)* pelvis
bassine [bɑsin] *nf* **(a)** *(en plastique)* basin, bowl; *(contenu)* basinful, bowlful **(b)** *(en cuivre)* pan; *(contenu)* panful
bassiner [bɑsine] *vt Fam (ennuyer)* to bore stiff
bassiste [bɑsist] *nmf (contrebassiste)* double bass player; *(guitariste)* bass guitarist
basson [bɑsɔ̃] *nm* **(a)** *(instrument)* bassoon **(b)** *(joueur)* bassoonist
basta [basta] *exclam Fam* that'll do!
bastide [bastid] *nf* **(a)** *(maison)* country house; *(ferme)* farm **(b)** *Hist (ville fortifiée)* fortified town
bastille [bastij] *nf* fortress; *Hist* **la B.** the Bastille; **la prise de la B.** the storming of the Bastille
bastingage [bastɛ̃gaʒ] *nm Naut (garde-corps)* rail
bastion [bastjɔ̃] *nm aussi Fig* bastion

baston [bastɔ̃] *nm ou nf Fam* fistfight, *Br* punch-up
bastonner [bastone] **se bastonner** *vpr Fam* to fight
bastringue [bastʁɛ̃g] *nm Fam* **(a)** *(dancing)* (seedy) dance hall **(b)** *(affaires)* gear, stuff; **et tout le b.** and the whole caboodle
bas-ventre *(pl* **bas-ventres)** [bavɑ̃tr] *nm* lower abdomen
bât [bɑ] *nm* packsaddle; *Fig* **c'est là que le b. blesse** there's the rub
bataclan [bataklɑ̃] *nm Fam (affaires)* stuff, gear; **et tout le b.** and the whole caboodle
bataille [bataj] *nf* **(a)** *(lutte)* battle, fight; *(électorale)* contest; **b. terrestre/aérienne/navale** land/air/naval battle; **cheveux en b.** dishevelled hair **(b)** *(jeu de cartes)* beggar-my-neighbour
batailler [bataje] *vi Fam* **b. pour faire qch** to battle to do sth
batailleur, -euse [batajœr, -øz] *adj* aggressive
bataillon [batajɔ̃] *nm Mil* battalion; *Fam* **un b. de** a troop of
bâtard, -e [bɑtar, -ard] **1** *adj (enfant)* illegitimate; *Péj* bastard; *(style, solution)* hybrid
2 *nm,f (enfant)* illegitimate child; *Péj* bastard
3 *nm (chien)* mongrel; *(pain)* = small French loaf
batavia [batavja] *nf* batavia lettuce
bateau, -x [bato] **1** *nm* **(a)** *(embarcation)* boat; **faire du b.** to go boating; **prendre le b.** to go/come by boat; **en** *ou* **par b.** by boat; *Fam Fig* **mener qn en b.,** **monter un b. à qn** to wind sb up; **b. à moteur** motorboat; **b. de pêche** fishing boat; **b. de plaisance** pleasure boat; **b. à vapeur** steamboat, steamer; **b. à voiles** *Br* sailing boat, *Am* sailboat **(b)** *(sur le trottoir)* driveway entrance **(c)** **encolure b.** boat neck
2 *adj inv Fam (banal)* hackneyed
bateau-mouche *(pl* **bateaux-mouches)** [batomuʃ] *nm* river boat *(on the Seine)*
bateleur, -euse [batlœr, -øz] *nm,f Vieilli (jongleur)* juggler; *(acrobate)* acrobat
batelier, -ère [batəlje, -ɛr] *nm,f* boatman, *f* boatwoman; *(sur un bac)* ferryman, *f* ferrywoman
bat-flanc [baflɑ̃] *nm inv (dans un dortoir, une prison)* wooden partition
bâti, -e [bɑti] **1** *adj (personne)* **être bien b.** to be well-built; **être mal b.** to have an odd shape
2 *nm* **(a)** *Constr* frame, framework **(b)** *(en couture)* tacking, basting
batifoler [batifole] *vi Fam* to fool around
batik [batik] *nm* batik
bâtiment [batimɑ̃] *nm* **(a)** *(immeuble)* building; **b. d'habitation** residential building **(b)** *(secteur)* **le b.** building; **être dans le b.** to be in the building trade; **bâtiments et travaux publics** building and civil engineering **(c)** *Naut* ship; **b. de guerre** warship, battleship
bâtir [bɑtir] **1** *vt* **(a)** *(maison, ville)* to build; *Fig (fortune, hypothèse)* to build (up); **(se) faire b. une maison** to have a house built; **terrain bâti** developed *or* built-up site **(b)** *(en couture)* to tack, to baste
2 se bâtir *vpr* **se b. une réputation (de)** to build up a reputation (as)
bâtisse [bɑtis] *nf* ugly building
batiste [batist] *nf* batiste
bâton [bɑtɔ̃] *nm* **(a)** *(en bois, de colle, de craie)* stick; *(d'agent de police)* *Br* truncheon, *Am* nightstick; *(de majorette)* baton; **mener une vie de b. de chaise** to lead a wild life; **mettre des bâtons dans les roues à qn** to put a spoke in sb's wheel; **parler à bâtons**

rompus to talk about this and that; **conversation à bâtons rompus** rambling conversation; **b. de rouge à lèvres** lipstick; **bâtons de ski** ski sticks *or* poles (**b**) *(trait vertical)* vertical line (**c**) *Can & Suisse* **b. (de hockey)** *Br* ice-hockey stick, *Am* hockey stick

bâtonnet [batɔnɛ] *nm* stick

batracien [batrasjɛ̃] *nm Zool* amphibian

battage [bataʒ] *nm* (**a**) *Fam (publicité)* hype; **faire du b.** autour de qch to hype sth up (**b**) *(du blé)* threshing

battant, -e [batɑ̃, -ɑ̃t] **1** *adj (pluie)* lashing; **le cœur b.** with a pounding heart
2 *nm,f (personne combative)* fighter
3 *nm* (**a**) *(d'une cloche)* clapper, tongue (**b**) *(d'une porte, d'un volet)* leaf; **porte à double b.** double door

batte [bat] *nf* bat; **b. de base-ball/de cricket** baseball/cricket bat

battement [batmɑ̃] *nm* (**a**) *(de tambour)* beat, beating; *(de mains)* clapping; *(d'ailes, de voiles)* flapping; *(de porte)* banging; **j'entendais les battements de son cœur** I could hear his/her heart beating (**b**) *(entre deux événements)* gap; **deux heures de b.** a two-hour gap

batterie [batri] *nf* (**a**) *(dans un orchestre)* drums; **être à la b.** to be on drums (**b**) *Mil* battery; *Fig* **dévoiler ses batteries** to show one's hand; **b. antiaérienne/anti-chars** anti-aircraft/antitank battery (**c**) *(ensemble, groupe)* battery; *(de tests, de questions)* series; **élevage en b.** battery farming; **poulet de b.** battery hen; **b. de cuisine** kitchen utensils (**d**) *Élec* battery; **fonctionner sur b.** to be battery-operated *or* battery-powered; **b. de secours** emergency battery

batteur [batœr] *nm* (**a**) *(dans un groupe)* drummer (**b**) *(au cricket)* batsman; *(au base-ball)* batter, striker (**c**) *(de cuisine)* mixer

batteuse [batøz] *nf (machine agricole)* threshing machine, thresher

battoir [batwar] *nm* (**a**) *(pour les tapis)* (carpet) beater; *(pour le linge)* beetle (**b**) *Fam (grande main)* great paw *or* mitt

battre [11] [batr] **1** *vt* (**a**) *(frapper)* *(personne, chien, tapis)* to beat; *(blé)* to thresh; *(métal)* to hammer; **b. qn à coups de poings** to punch sb; **b. le tambour** to beat the drum; **b. le rappel** *Mil* to call to arms; *Fig* to call everyone together; **b. la campagne** to scour *or* comb the countryside; *(esprit)* to wander; *Prov* **il faut b. le fer quand il** *ou* **pendant qu'il est chaud** strike while the iron is hot (**b**) *(cartes)* to shuffle; *(beurre)* to churn; *(œufs, préparation culinaire)* to beat, to whisk; **b. les blancs en neige** to beat the whites stiffly (**c**) *(adversaire)* to beat; *(record)* to break; **b. qn à plate(s) couture(s)** to beat sb hollow; *Fig* **b. tous les records** to take some beating (**d**) *Mus* **b. la mesure** to beat time (**e**) *Naut* **b. pavillon français/britannique** to fly the French/British flag
2 *vi* (**a**) *(cœur)* to beat; *(porte, volet)* to bang; *(voile)* to flap; **il a le cœur qui bat** *(d'émotion)* his heart is pounding (**b**) **b. en retraite** to beat a retreat
3 battre de *vt ind* **b. des mains** to clap one's hands; **b. des cils** to flutter one's eyelashes
4 se battre *vpr aussi Fig* to fight *(avec/contre* with/against); **se b. comme des chiffonniers** to fight like cat and dog; **se b. au couteau** to fight with knives; *très Fam* **je m'en bats l'œil** I don't give *Br* a toss *or Am* a rat's ass

battu, -e [baty] *adj (femme, enfant)* battered; **un air** *ou* **regard de chien b.** a hangdog look; **avoir les yeux battus** to have dark circles under one's eyes

battue [baty] *nf (à la chasse)* beat; *(pour retrouver quelqu'un)* search

batture [batyr] *nf Can* sandbank

baud [bo] *nm Tél & Ordinat* baud

baudet [bodɛ] *nm* ass, donkey; **chargé comme un b.** loaded down like a packhorse

baudrier [bodrije] *nm* shoulder strap; *(pour épée)* baldric; *(d'escalade)* harness

baudroie [bodrwa] *nf* monkfish

baudruche [bodryʃ] *nf* **(ballon de) b.** balloon

baume [bom] *nm aussi Fig* balm; **mettre du b. au cœur de qn** *(événement)* to be a consolation for sb; **b. pour les lèvres** lip balm

baux [bo] *voir* **bail**

bauxite [boksit] *nf* bauxite

bavard, -e [bavar, -ard] **1** *adj* (**a**) *(qui parle beaucoup)* chatty; *(style, essai)* wordy; **il est b. comme une pie** he'd talk the hind legs off a donkey (**b**) *(indiscret)* indiscreet
2 *nm,f* (**a**) *(qui parle beaucoup)* chatterbox (**b**) *(indiscret)* gossip

bavardage [bavardaʒ] *nm* (**a**) *(action)* chatting; *(commérage)* gossiping (**b**) *Ordinat (sur Internet)* chat (**c**) **bavardages** *(paroles)* chat; *(commérage)* gossip

bavarder [bavarde] *vi* (**a**) *(parler)* to chat; *(commérer)* to gossip (**b**) *Ordinat (sur Internet)* to chat

bavardoir [bavardwar] *nm Can Ordinat* chat room

bavarois, -e [bavarwa, -az] **1** *adj* Bavarian
2 *nm,f* **B.** Bavarian
3 *nm Culin* bavarois, = dessert consisting of set custard and whipped cream mixed with fruit purée

bave [bav] *nf (de personne)* dribble; *(de chien)* slaver; *(de cheval, de chien enragé)* froth, foam; *(d'escargot)* slime; *(de crapaud)* spittle

baver [bave] *vi (personne)* to dribble; *(chien)* to slaver; *(chien enragé)* to foam at the mouth; *(stylo)* to leak, to run; *(encre)* to smudge; *Fam* **en b. (des ronds de chapeaux)** to have a hard time of it; *Fam* **en faire b. (des ronds de chapeaux) à qn** to give sb a hard time

bavette [bavɛt] *nf* (**a**) *(d'un bébé, d'un tablier)* bib (**b**) *Culin* skirt (of beef) (**c**) *Fam* **tailler une b.** to have a chat

baveux, -euse [bavø, -øz] **1** *adj (bouche, enfant)* dribbling; *(omelette)* runny
2 *nm,f Can (morveux)* pain, pest

Bavière [bavjɛr] *nf* la B. Bavaria

bavoir [bavwar] *nm* bib

bavure [bavyr] *nf* (**a**) *(tache)* smudge, smear (**b**) *(erreur)* slip-up; **sans bavure(s)** faultless; **b. policière** case of police misconduct

bayer [53] [baje] *vi* **b. aux corneilles** to stare into space

bazar [bazar] *nm* (**a**) *(marché)* bazaar (**b**) *(magasin)* general store (**c**) *Fam (désordre)* shambles *(singulier)*; *(bruit)* racket; *(affaires)* stuff, gear; **et tout le b.** and the whole caboodle; **mettre du** *ou* **le b. dans qch** to make a shambles of sth (**d**) *Belg Fam (chose)* thing, thingy

bazarder [bazarde] *vt Fam (se débarrasser de)* to get shot of; *(jeter)* to chuck out; *(vendre)* to flog

bazooka [bazuka] *nm* bazooka

BCBG [besebeʒe] *adj inv (abrév* **bon chic bon genre**) *Br* ≃ Sloany, *Am* ≃ preppy

BCE [besea] *nf (abrév* **Banque centrale européenne**) European central bank

BCG® [beseʒe] *nm Méd* BCG®

BD [bede] *nf* (**a**) *(abrév* **bande dessinée**) comic strip, cartoon (**b**) *Ordinat (abrév* **base de données**) dbase

BD

This is a common abbreviation for "bande dessi-née", or "comic book". Considered a serious and important art form in France, the comic book has become popular among teenagers and intellectuals alike. An annual festival of comic book art is held in Angoulême.

bd *abrév* **boulevard**

beach-volley [bitʃvɔlɛ] *nm Sport* beach volleyball

béant, -e [beã, -ãt] *adj (bouche, porte)* wide open; *(blessure, gouffre)* gaping

béat, -e [bea, -at] *adj Rel* blessed; *(heureux)* blissful; *Péj (niais)* inane; **être b. d'admiration** to be open-mouthed in admiration; **elle nous observait d'un air b.** she watched us open-mouthed

béatement [beatmã] *adv (sourire)* inanely

béatifier [66] [beatifje] *vt Rel* to beatify

béatitude [beatityd] *nf* (**a**) *Rel* beatitude (**b**) *(bonheur parfait)* bliss

beau, belle [bo, bɛl]

bel is used before masculine singular nouns beginning with a vowel or h mute.

1 *adj* (**a**) *(d'apparence) (femme, enfant)* beautiful, good-looking; *(homme)* handsome, good-looking; *(objet, maison)* lovely, beautiful; **b. comme un dieu** like a Greek god; **ce n'est pas b. à voir** it's not a pretty sight; **se faire b.** to smarten oneself up

(**b**) *(de qualité) (œuvre, spectacle, discours)* fine; **avoir une belle situation** to have a good job

(**c**) *(moralement)* fine, noble; **un b. geste** a noble gesture; **ce n'est pas b. de mentir** it isn't nice to tell lies

(**d**) *(bien)* **c'est trop b. pour être vrai** it's too good to be true; **ce serait trop b.!** that would be too much (to hope for)!; **le plus b. jour de ma vie** the best day of my life

(**e**) *Ironique* **une belle grippe** a nasty dose of the flu; **une belle correction** a good thrashing; **te voilà b.!** you're in a fine mess!; **te voilà dans un bel état!** look at the state of you!; **j'ai eu une belle peur** I had an awful fright; **vous avez fait du b. travail!** well done!; *très Fam* **un b. salaud** a total bastard; **j'en ai entendu de belles sur votre compte!** I've heard some fine things about you!; **il en a fait de belles** he got up to some real tricks

(**f**) *(intensif)* **au b. milieu de la rue** right or bang in the middle of the road; **une belle somme** a tidy sum; **un b. poulet** a nice big chicken

(**g**) *(locutions)* **bel et bien** *(complètement)* well and truly; **il est bel et bien venu** he really did come; **il s'est bel et bien trompé** he has indeed made a mistake; **de plus belle** with a vengeance; **il reprit l'entraînement de plus belle** he resumed training with a vengeance or more enthusiastically than ever

2 *adv* **il fait b.** it's fine; **il ferait b. voir ça!** that'll be the day!; **j'ai b. le lui expliquer...** no matter how many times I explain it to him...; **j'ai b. pousser, la porte ne bouge pas** no matter how hard I push or try as I might, I can't get the door to open

3 *nm* **le b.** *(beauté)* beauty; **mais le plus b., c'est que...** but the best bit or part is that ...; *Fam Ironique* **c'est du b.!** that's great!; **le temps est au b. (fixe)** the weather is set fair; *Fig* **avoir le moral au b. fixe** to be permanently in a good mood; **un vieux b.** an old roué; **faire le b.** *(chien)* to sit up and beg; *Can*

(homme) to strut about

4 *nf* **belle** (**a**) *(partie)* decider (**b**) *Hum (amie)* lady friend (**c**) *Fam (locutions)* **se faire la belle** to run away, *Br* to do a runner; *(de prison)* to escape; *Belg* **avoir belle à faire qch** to have no trouble doing sth

beaucoup [boku] *adv* (**a**) *(intensément, en grande quantité)* a lot; **ça te plaît? – pas b.** do you like it? – not much or not a lot (**b**) *(une grande quantité, un grand nombre)* **il reste encore b. à faire** there's still a lot to do; **c'est déjà b. qu'il veuille bien vous parler** it's quite something that he condescended to speak to you; **il y est pour b.** he has had a lot or a great deal to do with it; **b. pensent que...** a lot of or many people think that...; **b. d'entre nous** a lot of or many of us; **de b. (de loin)** by far; **il s'en faut de b. que je sois riche** I'm far from rich (**c**) **b. de** *(quantité)* a lot of; *(nombre)* a lot of, many; **b. de vin/chance** a lot of wine/luck; **b. de fautes** a lot of or many mistakes; **pas b. de** *(argent, courage)* not much; *(gens, problèmes)* not many; **avec b. de soin** with great care, very carefully; **j'en veux b.!** I want a lot! (**d**) *(avec des comparatifs)* a lot, much; **b. moins/plus vite** a lot or much slower/faster; **il parle b. trop** he talks far too much; **b. moins d'enfants** a lot or many fewer children; **b. moins de temps** a lot or much less time

beauf [bof] *Fam* **1** *adj Péj* **il est un peu b.** he's a bit of a narrow-minded average Frenchman

2 *nm* (**a**) *(beau-frère)* brother-in-law (**b**) *Péj* = stereotypical narrow-minded average Frenchman

beau-fils *(pl* **beaux-fils**) [bofis] *nm* (**a**) *(gendre)* son-in-law (**b**) *(après remariage)* stepson

beau-frère *(pl* **beaux-frères**) [bofrɛr] *nm* brother-in-law

beaujolais [boʒɔlɛ] *nm* Beaujolais

beau-père *(pl* **beaux-pères**) [bopɛr] *nm* (**a**) *(père du conjoint)* father-in-law (**b**) *(après remariage)* stepfather

beaupré [bopre] *nm Naut* bowsprit

beauté [bote] *nf* beauty; **être en b.** to be looking magnificent; **de toute b.** magnificent; **finir en b.** to end on a high note; **faire qch pour la b. du geste** to do sth for the sake of it; **se refaire une b.** to put one's face on

beaux-arts [bozar] *nmpl* fine art; **école des b., B.** art school

beaux-parents [boparã] *nmpl* parents-in-law

bébé [bebe] *nm* (**a**) *(nourrisson)* baby; **faire le b.** to behave like a baby; **être très b.** to be very babyish (**b**) *(animal)* **b. gazelle/lapin** baby gazelle/rabbit

bébé-éprouvette *(pl* **bébés-éprouvette**) [bebeepruvɛt] *nm* test-tube baby

bébelle [bebɛl] *nf Can (gadget)* gadget; *(bibelot)* ornament; *(jouet)* toy

bébête [bebɛt] *Fam* **1** *adj* silly

2 *nf* creepy-crawly

bec [bɛk] *nm* (**a**) *(d'oiseau, de tortue, de pieuvre)* beak (**b**) *Fam (bouche)* mouth; **il n'a pas ouvert le b. de la journée** he hasn't opened his mouth all day; **la clope au b.** with a *Br* fag or *Am* smoke in his/her mouth; **rester le b. dans l'eau** to be left high and dry; **b. fin** gourmet; *Can* **faire le b. fin** to be picky (**c**) *(de pot)* lip; *(de cafetière)* spout; *(d'instrument à vent)* mouthpiece; **b. Bunsen** Bunsen burner; **b. de gaz** *(réverbère)* gas lamp; **b. verseur** spout (**d**) *Belg, Suisse & Can (baiser)* **donner un b. à qn** to give sb a kiss

bécane [bekan] *nf Fam (vélo)* bike; *(machine, ordinateur)* machine

bécarre [bekar] *adj & nm Mus* natural

bécasse [bekas] *nf* (**a**) *(oiseau)* woodcock (**b**) *Fam (idiote)* silly thing

bec-de-lièvre *(pl* becs-de-lièvre) [bɛkdəljɛvr] *nm* harelip

béchamel [beʃamɛl] *nf* (**sauce**) **b. béchamel** sauce

bêche [bɛʃ] *nf* spade

bêcher [beʃe] *vt* to dig, to turn over

bêcheur, -euse [beʃœr, -øz] *nm,f Fam (snob)* snob

bécosses [bekɔs] *nfpl Can Fam Br* bog, *Am* john

bécoter [bekɔte] *Fam* **1** *vt Br* to snog, *Am* to make out with
  2 se bécoter *vpr Br* to snog, *Am* to make out

becqueter [42] [bɛkte] **1** *vt (sujet: oiseau)* to peck at
  2 *vi très Fam (personne)* to eat

becter [bɛkte] *vi* = **becqueter**

bedaine [bədɛn] *nf Fam* pot-belly, paunch; **prendre de la b.** to get a pot-belly *or* a paunch

bédé [bede] *nf Fam* comic strip, cartoon

bedeau, -x [bədo] *nm* verger

bedon [bədɔ̃] *nm Fam* pot-belly, paunch

bedonnant, -e [bədɔnɑ̃, -ɑ̃t] *adj Fam* pot-bellied, paunchy

bédouin, -e [bedwɛ̃, -in] **1** *adj* Bedouin
  2 *nm,f* **B.** Bedouin

bée [be] *adj f* **bouche b.** open-mouthed; **j'en suis restée bouche b.** I was speechless; **regarder qch bouche b.** to gape at sth

beffroi [befrwa] *nm* belfry

bégaiement [begɛmɑ̃] *nm* stuttering, stammering

bégayer [53] [begeje] **1** *vi* to stutter, to stammer
  2 *vt* to stammer (out)

bégonia [begɔnja] *nm* begonia

bègue [bɛg] **1** *adj* **être b.** to stutter, to stammer
  2 *nmf* stutterer, stammerer

bégueule [begœl] *adj* prudish

béguin [begɛ̃] *nm Fam (personne)* crush; **avoir le b. pour qn** to have a crush on sb; **avoir le b. pour qch** to have taken a fancy to sth

BEI [beəi] *nf (abrév* **Banque européenne d'investissement)** EIB

beige [bɛʒ] *adj & nm* beige

beigne[1] [bɛɲ] *nf Fam* clout; **filer une b. à qn** to give sb a clout

beigne[2] *nm Can* doughnut

beignet [bɛɲɛ] *nm (salé)* fritter; *(au sucre, à la confiture)* doughnut; **b. de** *ou* **aux pommes** apple fritter

bel [bɛl] *voir* **beau**

bêlement [bɛlmɑ̃] *nm aussi Fig* bleat; **des bêlements** bleating

bêler [bɛle] *vi aussi Fig* to bleat

bel-étage, bel étage [bɛletaʒ] *(pl* beaux-étages) [bozetaʒ] *nm Belg* (**a**) *(rez-de-chaussée surélevé)* mezzanine *Br* ground *or Am* first floor (**b**) *(maison)* house with mezzanine *Br* ground *or Am* first floor

belette [bəlɛt] *nf* weasel

Belfast [bɛlfast] *n* Belfast

belge [bɛlʒ] **1** *adj* Belgian
  2 *nm* **B.** Belgian

belgicisme [bɛlʒisism] *nm (mot)* Belgian-French word; *(tournure)* Belgian-French expression

Belgique [bɛlʒik] *nf* **la B.** Belgium

Belgrade [bɛlgrad] *n* Belgrade

bélier [belje] *nm* (**a**) *(animal)* ram (**b**) *Mil* battering ram (**c**) *Astron & Astrol* **le B.** Aries; **être B.** to be (an) Aries

Belize [beliz] *nm* **le B.** Belize

belladone [beladɔn] *nf* belladonna, deadly nightshade

bellâtre [bɛlɑtr] *nm Péj* smoothie

belle [bɛl] *voir* **beau**

belle-famille *(pl* belles-familles) [bɛlfamij] *nf* in-laws

belle-fille *(pl* belles-filles) [bɛlfij] *nf* (**a**) *(épouse du fils)* daughter-in-law (**b**) *(après remariage)* stepdaughter

belle-mère *(pl* belles-mères) [bɛlmɛr] *nf* (**a**) *(mère du conjoint)* mother-in-law (**b**) *(après remariage)* stepmother

belle-sœur *(pl* belles-sœurs) [bɛlsœr] *nf* sister-in-law

belligérant, -e [beliʒerɑ̃, -ɑ̃t] **1** *adj* belligerent
  2 *nm* **les belligérants** the warring nations

belliqueux, -euse [beliko, -øz] *adj (pays, peuple)* warlike; *(personne, humeur)* aggressive

belote [bəlɔt] *nf* = type of card game

bélouga [beluga], **béluga** [belyga] *nm* beluga whale

belvédère [bɛlvedɛr] *nm* (**a**) *(construction)* belvedere, gazebo (**b**) *(sur un site naturel)* viewpoint

bémol [bemɔl] *Mus* **1** *nm* flat; *Fam Fig* **mettre un b.** to tone it down
  2 *adj* flat; **mi b.** E flat

ben [bɛ̃] *adv Fam* **b. oui!** well, yes!; **b. voilà, euh...** yeah, well, er...

bénédictin, -e [benediktɛ̃, -in] **1** *adj* Benedictine
  2 *nm,f* **B.** Benedictine
  3 *nf* **Bénédictine** *(alcool)* Benedictine

bénédiction [benediksjɔ̃] *nf Rel* blessing, benediction; *(d'une église)* consecration; *Fig* blessing

bénéfice [benefis] *nm* (**a**) *(gain)* profit; **b. d'exploitation** operating profit (**b**) *(avantage)* benefit, advantage; **tirer un certain b. de qch** to derive some benefit *or* advantage from sth; **avoir le b. de l'âge** to have the benefit of age; **accorder** *ou* **laisser le b. du doute à qn** to give sb the benefit of the doubt; **au b. de** *(œuvre charitable)* in aid of

bénéficiaire [benefisjɛr] **1** *adj Com (entreprise)* profit-making; *(compte)* in credit
  2 *nmf (d'un chèque)* payee; *Jur* beneficiary

bénéficier [66] [benefisje] **bénéficier de** *vt ind* (**a**) *(profiter de)* to benefit from; **faire b. qn de son expérience** to give sb the benefit of one's experience (**b**) *(avoir)* to have; **cette carte d'abonnement vous fait b. d'une remise** this season ticket entitles you to a reduction

bénéfique [benefik] *adj* beneficial (**à** to)

Benelux [benelyks] *nm* **le B.** Benelux

benêt [bənɛ] *adj m* simple
  2 *nm* simpleton

bénévolat [benevɔla] *nm* voluntary work

bénévole [benevɔl] **1** *adj (travail, infirmière)* voluntary
  2 *nmf* volunteer, voluntary worker

Bengale [bɛ̃gal] *nm* **le B.** Bengal

Bénin [benɛ̃] *nm* **le B.** Benin

bénin, -igne [benɛ̃, -iɲ] *adj (accident, opération)* minor; *(tumeur)* benign

béninois, -e [beninwa, -az] **1** *adj* Beninese
  2 *nm,f* **B.** Beninese

bénir [benir] *vt aussi Fig* to bless; *(église)* to consecrate; **(que) Dieu vous bénisse!** (may) God bless you!; **être béni des dieux** to have been touched by God

bénit, -e [beni, -it] *adj voir* **eau, pain**

bénitier [benitje] *nm Rel* holy-water stoup

benjamin, -e [bɛ̃ʒamɛ̃, -in] *nm,f* (**a**) *(le plus jeune)* youngest (**b**) *Sport* junior *(10 to 12 years old)*

benjoin [bɛ̃ʒwɛ̃] *nm* (gum) benzoin, benjamin

benne [bɛn] *nf (de camion)* tipping *or* dump body; *(dans une mine)* tub, truck; *(de téléphérique)* (cable) car; **b. à ordures** bin lorry

benzine [bɛ̃zin] *nf* benzine

BEP [beape] *nm Scol (abrév* **brevet d'études professionnelles**) = vocational diploma taken at age eighteen

BEPC [beapese] *nm Anciennement Scol (abrév* **brevet d'études du premier cycle**) = school-leaving certificate taken at age fifteen

béquille [bekij] *nf* (**a**) *(pour marcher)* crutch; **marcher avec des béquilles** to be on crutches (**b**) *(d'un vélo, d'une moto)* stand

berbère [bɛrbɛr] **1** *adj* Berber
2 *nmf* **B.** Berber
3 *nm (langue)* Berber

bercail [bɛrkaj] *nm (de l'Église)* fold; *Hum* **rentrer au b.** to return to the fold

berçante [bɛrsɑ̃t] *adj f & nf Can* (**chaise**) **b.** rocking chair

berce [bɛrs] *nf Belg & Suisse (berceau)* cradle

berceau, -x [bɛrso] *nm (de bébé)* cradle; *Fig (d'une civilisation, d'un mouvement)* birthplace; **dès la b.** from the cradle, from birth; *Fam* **il les prend au b.** he's a cradle-snatcher

bercer [16] [bɛrse] **1** *vt* (**a**) *(bébé, passager)* to rock; *Fig* **mon enfance a été bercée par la musique de Debussy** I was brought up listening to Debussy (**b**) *Fig* **b. qn de promesses** to delude sb with promises
2 se bercer *vpr* **se b. d'illusions** to delude oneself

berceuse [bɛrsøz] *nf* (**a**) *(chanson)* lullaby (**b**) *Can (fauteuil à bascule)* rocking-chair

BERD [bɛrd] *nf (abrév* **Banque européenne pour la reconstruction et le développement**) EBRD

béret [berɛ] *nm* beret

bergamote [bɛrgamɔt] *nf* bergamot; **thé à la b.** bergamot-flavoured tea

berge¹ [bɛrʒ] *nf (bord)* bank

berge² *nf Fam (an)* **il a quarante berges** he's forty

berger, -ère [bɛrʒe, -ɛr] **1** *nm,f* shepherd, *f* shepherdess
2 *nm (chien)* **b. allemand** German shepherd, *Br* Alsatian; **b. des Pyrénées** Pyrenean mountain dog
3 *nf* **bergère** *(fauteuil)* wing chair

bergerie [bɛrʒəri] *nf* sheepfold

bergeronnette [bɛrʒərɔnɛt] *nf* wagtail

Béring [beriŋ] *n voir* **détroit**

berk [bɛrk] *exclam* yuk!

Berlin [bɛrlɛ̃] *n* Berlin; *Hist* **B.-Ouest/-Est** West/East Berlin

berline [bɛrlin] *nf Aut Br* (four-door) saloon, *Am* (four-door) sedan

berlingot [bɛrlɛ̃go] *nm* (**a**) *(bonbon) Br* boiled sweet, *Am* hard candy (**b**) *(de lait)* carton; *(de produit d'entretien)* pack

berlinois, -e [bɛrlinwa, -az] **1** *adj* from Berlin
2 *nm,f* **B.** Berliner

berloque [bɛrlɔk] *nf Belg* **battre la b.** to beat *or* pound wildly

berlue [bɛrly] *nf Fam* **avoir la b.** to be seeing things

berme [bɛrm] *nf Belg & Suisse (terre-plein)* **b. centrale** *Br* central reservation, *Am* median (strip)

bermuda [bɛrmyda] *nm* Bermuda shorts, Bermudas

Bermudes [bɛrmyd] *nfpl* **les (îles) B.** Bermuda

bernard-l'(h)ermite [bɛrnarlɛrmit] *nm inv* hermit crab

Berne [bɛrn] *n* Bern

berne [bɛrn] *nf* **en berne** *adj Naut* at *Br* half mast *or Am* half staff; *Mil* furled

berner [bɛrne] *vt* to fool

bernois, -e [bɛrnwa, -az] **1** *adj* Bernese
2 *nm,f* **B.** Bernese

berzingue [bɛrzɛ̃g] **à tout(e) b.** *adv Fam* at full speed, double quick

besace [bəzas] *nf (de mendiant)* bag; *(de pèlerin)* scrip; **sac b.** = large, soft handbag

bésef [bezɛf] = **bézef**

besogne [bəzɔɲ] *nf* job, task; **aller vite en b.** to get things done quickly; *Fig & Péj* to jump the gun

besoin [bəzwɛ̃] *nm* (**a**) *(nécessité)* need (**de qch** for sth); **avoir b. de qn/qch** to need sb/sth; **avoir b. de faire qch** to need to do sth; **j'ai b. que tu m'aides** I need you to help me; **éprouver le b. de faire qch** to feel the need to do sth; **pour les besoins de la cause** for the sake of the cause; **au b.** if necessary, if need be; **en cas de b.** if need be; **si b. est** if necessary, if need be (**b**) **faire ses besoins** *(personne)* to relieve oneself; *(animal)* to do its business (**c**) *(misère)* **être dans le b.** to be in need

bestial, -e, -aux¹, -ales [bɛstjal, -o] *adj* bestial

bestiaux² [bɛstjo] *nmpl* livestock

bestiole [bɛstjɔl] *nf* small animal; *(insecte)* creepy-crawly

best-seller *(pl* best-sellers) [bɛstsɛlœr] *nm* best-seller

bêta, -asse [bɛta, -as] *Fam* **1** *adj* silly
2 *nm,f Br* silly-billy, *Am* silly-willy

bêtabloquant [betablɔkɑ̃] *nm Méd* beta-blocker

bétail [betaj] *nm* livestock; **gros b.** cattle and horses

bétaillère [betajɛr] *nf* cattle truck

bêta-test *(pl* bêta-tests) [betatɛst] *nm Ordinat* beta test; **bêta-tests** *(procédure)* beta testing

bête [bɛt] **1** *adj* stupid, silly; **c'est b., on a loupé le film!** what a pity *or* a shame, we've missed the film!; **ce n'est pas b.** *(suggestion)* that's not a bad idea; **rester tout b.** *(décontenancé)* to be open-mouthed; *Fam* **être b. comme ses pieds** *Br* to be as thick as two short planks, *Am* to be as dumb as they come; **être b. à pleurer** to be pathetically stupid; **c'est b. comme chou, c'est tout b.** it's as easy as pie
2 *nf* (**a**) *(animal)* animal; **travailler comme une b.** to work flat out; **elle m'a regardé comme une b. curieuse** she looked at me as if I was from another planet; *Péj* **b. à concours** *Br* swot, *Am* grind; **b. à cornes** horned animal; **b. fauve** big cat; **b. féroce** wild animal; **b. noire** *(personne)* bête noire; *(chose)* pet hate; *Can* **b. puante** skunk; **b. de somme** beast of burden (**b**) *(insecte)* insect; *Fig* **chercher la petite b.** to nitpick; **b. à bon Dieu** *Br* ladybird, *Am* ladybug

bêtement [bɛtmɑ̃] *adv (rire, regarder)* stupidly; **mourir b.** to die senselessly; **tout b.** quite simply, purely and simply

bêtifier [66] [betifje] *vi (avec un enfant)* to use baby-talk

bêtise [betiz] *nf* (**a**) *(manque d'intelligence)* stupidity, silliness (**b**) *(action idiote)* stupid thing (to do); *(parole idiote)* stupid thing to say; **dire/faire une b.** to say/do something stupid; **dire des bêtises** to talk nonsense (**c**) *(chose sans importance)* trivial thing; **se disputer pour des bêtises** to argue over nothing (**d**) *Can* **bêtises** *(injures)* insults (**e**) **bêtises de Cambrai** *Br* ≃ mint humbugs, *Am* ≃ hard mint candies

bêtisier [betizje] *nm (écrit)* collection of howlers; *(à la télévision)* collection of humorous out-takes

béton [betɔ̃] *nm* (**a**) *(matériau)* concrete; *Fig* **des muscles en b.** rock-hard muscles; **un alibi en b.** a cast-iron alibi; **b. armé** reinforced concrete (**b**) *Fam* **laisse b.!** drop it!

bétonner [betɔne] *vt* to concrete

bétonneuse [betɔnøz], **bétonnière** [betɔnjɛr] *nf* cement mixer, concrete mixer

bette [bɛt] *nf* (Swiss) chard

betterave [bɛtrav] *nf* **b. (rouge)** *Br* beetroot, *Am* beet; **b. fourragère** mangel-wurzel; **b. sucrière** sugar beet

beuglement [bøɡləmɑ̃] *nm (d'une vache)* moo; *(d'un taureau)* bellow; *(de la radio, de la télé)* blaring; **des beuglements** mooing/bellowing; **pousser des beuglements** *(personne)* to bellow

beugler [bøɡle] **1** *vi (vache)* to moo; *(taureau, personne)* to bellow; *(radio, télé)* to blare
2 *vt (chanson)* to bawl out, to bellow out

beur [bœr] **1** *nmf* = North African born in France of immigrant parents
2 *adj inv* = of North Africans born in France of immigrant parents

beurre [bœr] *nm* butter; **au b.** *(pâtisserie)* made with butter; *Fam* **ça compte pour du b.** that doesn't count; *Fam* **faire son b.** to make a packet; **ça mettra du b. dans les épinards** that will make life a bit easier; **elle veut le b. et l'argent du b.** she wants to have her cake and eat it; **b. d'anchois** anchovy paste; **b. de cacahouètes** peanut butter; **b. de cacao** cocoa butter; **b. salé/demi-sel** salted/slightly salted butter

beurré, -e [bœre] *adj très Fam (ivre) Br* pissed, *Am* wasted

beurrer [bœre] *vt* to butter

beurrier [bœrje] *nm* butter dish

beuverie [bøvri] *nf* binge, drinking session

bévue [bevy] *nf* slip-up

Beyrouth [berut] *n* Beirut

bézef [bezɛf] *adv Fam* **il n'y en a pas b.** *(pain, confiture)* there's not much *or* a lot (of it); *(légumes, livres)* there aren't many *or* a lot (of them)

Bhoutan [butɑ̃] *nm* **le B.** Bhutan

bi- [bi] *préf* bi-

biais [bjɛ] *nm* (**a**) *(d'un mur)* slant; **regarder qn de b.** to look sideways at sb; **en b.** at an angle; **tailler un tissu dans le b.** to cut material on the bias (**b**) *(moyen)* way; **par le b. de** through (**c**) *(aspect)* angle; **par quel b. envisager la chose?** from what angle should we look at the issue?

biaiser [bjeze] *vi (ruser)* to dodge the issue

biathlon [bjatlɔ̃] *nm* biathlon

bibande [bibɑ̃d] *Tél* **1** *adj* dual-band
2 *nm (téléphone portable)* dual-band *Br* mobile phone *or Am* cellphone

bibelot [biblo] *nm* curio, knick-knack

biberon [bibrɔ̃] *nm* (baby's *or* feeding) bottle; **nourrir** *ou* **élever un enfant au b.** to bottle-feed a child; **c'est l'heure du b.** it's the baby's feeding time

bibi¹ [bibi] *nm (chapeau)* (woman's) hat

bibi² *pron Fam (moi)* yours truly; **la vaisselle, c'est encore pour b.!** yours truly gets stuck doing the dishes again!

bibine [bibin] *nf Fam (boisson)* dishwater

bibite [bibit] *nf Can Fam* bug, insect

bible [bibl] *nf aussi Fig* bible; **la B.** the Bible

bibliographie [bibliɔɡrafi] *nf* bibliography

bibliographique [bibliɔɡrafik] *adj* bibliographical

bibliophile [bibliɔfil] *nmf* book-lover

bibliothécaire [bibliɔtekɛr] *nmf* librarian

bibliothèque [bibliɔtɛk] *nf* (**a**) *(bâtiment, salle)* library; **b. municipale** public library; **b. de prêt** lending library; **b. universitaire** university library (**b**) *(meuble)* bookcase

biblique [biblik] *adj* biblical

Bic® [bik] **1** *adj* **stylo B.**, **pointe B.** ballpoint (pen), *Br* Biro®
2 *nm* ballpoint (pen), *Br* Biro®

bicarbonate [bikarbɔnat] *nm Chim* bicarbonate; **b. de soude** bicarbonate of soda

bicentenaire [bisɑ̃tnɛr] *nm Br* bicentenary, *Am* bicentennial

biceps [bisɛps] *nm* biceps; *Fam* **avoir des b.** to have big biceps

biche [biʃ] *nf* (**a**) *(animal)* hind, doe (**b**) *Fam* **ma b.** darling

bicher [biʃe] *vi Fam Vieilli (se réjouir)* to be tickled pink

bichonner [biʃɔne] **1** *vt* (**a**) *(préparer)* to doll up (**b**) *(soigner)* to pamper
2 **se bichonner** *vpr* to doll oneself up

bicolore [bikɔlɔr] *adj* two-colour(ed)

bicoque [bikɔk] *nf Fam (maison)* house, place

bicorne [bikɔrn] *nm* cocked hat

bicyclette [bisiklɛt] *nf* bicycle; **aller en ville à** *ou* **en b.** to cycle into town, to go into town by bicycle; **faire de la b.** to go cycling; **il ne sait pas faire de la b.** he can't ride a bicycle

bidasse [bidas] *nm très Fam Br* squaddie, *Am* GI

bide [bid] *nm Fam* (**a**) *(ventre)* belly; **avoir/prendre du b.** to have/develop a belly (**b**) *(échec)* flop, washout; **faire un b.** *Br* to flop, *Am* to bomb

bidet [bidɛ] *nm* (**a**) *(de toilette)* bidet (**b**) *Hum (cheval)* nag

bidimensionnel, -elle [bidimɑ̃sjɔnɛl] *adj* bidimensional

bidoche [bidɔʃ] *nf très Fam* meat

bidon [bidɔ̃] **1** *adj inv Fam (excuse, argument)* phoney, fake; *(élections)* rigged
2 *nm* (**a**) *(d'huile, d'essence)* can; *(de lait)* churn; *(gourde)* water bottle; **b. d'essence** petrol can, jerry can (**b**) *Fam (ventre)* belly (**c**) *Fam (bluff)* **c'est du b.** *Br* it's a load of tosh, *Am* it's baloney (**d**) *Belg Fam* **bidons** *(vêtements)* gear, threads; *(affaires)* gear, stuff

bidonnant, -e [bidɔnɑ̃, -ɑ̃t] *adj Fam* hilarious

bidonner [bidɔne] **se bidonner** *vpr Fam* to laugh one's head off

bidonville [bidɔ̃vil] *nm* shantytown

bidouillage [bidujaʒ], **bidouille** [biduj] *nm Fam* tinkering; *Ordinat (d'un logiciel)* patching

bidouiller [biduje] *vt Fam* to tinker with; *Ordinat (logiciel)* to patch

bidule [bidyl] *nm Fam* thingy, whatsit; **B.** *(personne)* what's-his-name, *f* what's-her-name

bielle [bjɛl] *nf Aut* connecting rod, con-rod

biélorusse [bjelɔrys] **1** *adj* Byelorussian
2 *nmf* **B.** Byelorussian

Biélorussie [bjelɔrysi] *nf* **la B.** Belarus

bien [bjɛ̃] **1** *adv* (**a**) *(convenablement)* well; **un livre b. écrit** a well-written book; **écoutez-moi b.** listen carefully; *Ironique* **ça commence b.!** that's a good start!

(**b**) *(moralement)* right; **se conduire** *ou* **se tenir b.** to behave (well); **vous avez b. fait** you did the right thing; **tu fais b. de me le dire** it's a good thing you've told me; **tu ferais b. de te méfier** you'd be wise to watch out

(**c**) *(emphatique)* **regarder qn b. en face** to look sb right in the face; **c'est b. cela** that's right; **c'est b. une erreur** that's definitely a mistake; **est-ce b. le train pour Paris?** is this the right train for Paris?; **j'ai b. dû lire dix de ses livres** I must have read at least ten of his/her books; **j'irais b. avec vous mais...** I'd love to go with you but...; **j'y suis b. obligé** I just have to; **je sais b.** I'm well aware of it; **je vous l'avais b. dit!** I told you so!; **c'est b. ce que je pensais** that's what I thought; **nous verrons b.!** we'll see!; **qu'est-ce que ça peut b. être/vouloir dire?** what on earth can it be/mean?; **est-ce b. raisonnable?** is that really reasonable?; **B. à vous** *(dans une lettre)* Regards, Yours

(**d**) *(très)* very; **vous arrivez b. tard** you're very late; **que ce soit b. clair, je...** let's get this clear, I...

(**e**) *(beaucoup)* *(réfléchir, changer)* a lot, a great deal; **b. plus** much *or* a lot more; **b. moins** much *or* a lot less; **b. des gens** a lot of people; **b. d'autres** many others; **b. des fois** often; **avoir b. de la peine** *ou* **du mal à faire qch** to have a lot of difficulty doing sth; **tu as b. de la chance!** you're really lucky!

(**f**) *(locutions)* **b. que** although, though; **b. que je le sache** although I know it; **b. entendu, b. sûr, b. évidemment** of course; **b. sûr que je viendrai** of course I'll come; **b. sûr que non!** of course not!

2 *exclam* **eh b.!** well!; **b.! je vous appelle demain!** OK, I'll call you tomorrow!

3 *adj inv* (**a**) *(satisfaisant)* good; **c'est b.!** *(bravo)* good!

(**b**) *(à l'aise)* comfortable; **être b. avec qn** *(en bons termes)* to be on good terms with sb; **se mettre b. avec qn** to get into sb's good books; *Fam* **nous voilà b.!** we're in a right mess!

(**c**) *(en forme)* well

(**d**) *(moral)* decent; **ce n'est pas b. de vous moquer de lui** it's not nice *or* kind of you to make fun of him

(**e**) *(beau)* *(personne)* good-looking, attractive; **elle est b. sur cette photo** she looks good in this photo

4 *nm* (**a**) *Phil & Rel* good; **le b. et le mal** good and evil, right and wrong; **faire le b.** to do good; **faire du b. à qn** to do sb good; **grand b. vous fasse!** much good may it do you!; **dire du b. de qn** to speak well of sb; **c'est pour ton b.** it's for your own good; **c'était en tout b.** tout honneur it was quite innocent

(**b**) *(chose matérielle)* possession; *Jur* assets; **biens** possessions, property; **avoir du b.** to have property; *Prov* **b. mal acquis ne profite jamais** ill-gotten gains never enrich; **biens de consommation** consumer goods; **biens immobiliers** *ou* **immeubles** real estate *or* property

bien-aimé, -e *(mpl* **bien-aimés**, *fpl* **bien-aimées)** [bjɛ̃neme] *adj* beloved

bien-être [bjɛ̃nɛtr] *nm* well-being

bienfaisance [bjɛ̃fəzɑ̃s] *nf* **œuvre de b.** charity, charitable organization

bienfaisant, -e [bjɛ̃fəzɑ̃, -ɑ̃t] *adj* (**a**) *(personne)* charitable (**b**) *(remède)* beneficial; *(vent, pluie)* refreshing

bienfait [bjɛ̃fɛ] *nm* (**a**) *(acte)* kindness (**b**) *(avantage)* benefit

bienfaiteur, -trice [bjɛ̃fɛtœr, -tris] *nm,f* benefactor, *f* benefactress

bien-fondé [bjɛ̃fɔ̃de] *nm* validity; *Jur* cogency

bienheureux, -euse [bjɛ̃nørø, -øz] *adj* blissful; *Rel* blessed

biennal, -e, -aux, -ales [bjenal, -o] *adj* biennial

bien-pensant, -e *(mpl* **bien-pensants,** *fpl* **bien-pensantes)** [bjɛ̃pɑ̃sɑ̃, -ɑ̃t] *adj* & *nm,f* conformist

bienséance [bjɛ̃seɑ̃s] *nf* propriety, decorum

bientôt [bjɛ̃to] *adv* soon; **il est b. deux heures** it's nearly two o'clock; **on est b. arrivés?** will we soon be there?; *Fam* **tu n'as pas b. fini?** have you quite finished?; **à b.!** see you soon!

bienveillance [bjɛ̃vɛjɑ̃s] *nf* kindness; **avec b.** kindly

bienveillant, -e [bjɛ̃vɛjɑ̃, -ɑ̃t] *adj* kind

bienvenu, -e¹ [bjɛ̃vny] **1** *adj* *(remarque)* apposite; *(repas, explication)* welcome

2 *nm,f* **soyez le b.!** welcome!; **vous serez toujours la bienvenue** you're always welcome

bienvenue² [bjɛ̃vny] *nf* welcome; **souhaiter la b. à qn** to welcome sb

2 *exclam* welcome! (**à** to); *Can (de rien)* you're welcome!

bière¹ [bjɛr] *nf* *(boisson)* beer; *Fam* **ce n'est pas de la petite b.** it's no small thing; **b. blonde** lager; **b. brune** *Br* brown ale, *Am* dark beer; **b. pression** *Br* draught beer, *Am* draft beer

bière² *nf* *(cercueil)* coffin; **assister à la mise en b.** to be present when the body is placed in the coffin

biffer [bife] *vt* to cross out; **b. un nom d'une liste** to cross a name off a list

biffure [bifyr] *nf* crossing out

bifidus [bifidys] *nm* live culture

bifocal, -e, -aux, -ales [bifɔkal, -o] *adj* *(lentille)* bifocal; **lunettes bifocales** bifocals

bifteck [biftɛk] *nm* (beef)steak; **b. haché** *Br* mince, *Am* mincemeat; *Fam* **gagner son b.** to earn one's bread and butter

bifurcation [bifyrkasjɔ̃] *nf* fork

bifurquer [bifyrke] *vi* *(route, chemin)* to fork; *(automobiliste)* to fork off; **bifurquez à droite** take the right fork

bigame [bigam] *adj* bigamous

bigamie [bigami] *nf* bigamy

bigarré, -e [bigare] *adj* *(tissu)* multicoloured; **une foule bigarrée** a motley crew

bigarreau, -x [bigaro] *nm* = type of cherry

bigler [bigle] *Fam* **1** *vi* (**a**) *(loucher)* to have a squint

(**b**) **b. sur qch** to have a good look at sth

2 *vt* *(personne)* to eye up

bigleux, -euse [biglø, -øz] *adj Fam (qui louche)* cross-eyed; *(myope)* short-sighted

bigophone [bigɔfɔn] *nm Fam Br* blower, *Am* horn

bigorneau, -x [bigɔrno] *nm* winkle

bigot, -e [bigo, -ɔt] **1** *nm,f* *(religious)* bigot

2 *adj* sanctimonious

bigoterie [bigɔtri] *nf* *(religious)* bigotry

bigoudi [bigudi] *nm* (hair) curler *or* roller; **se mettre des bigoudis** to put one's hair in curlers

bigre [bigr] *exclam Fam Vieilli* gosh!

bigrement [bigrəmɑ̃] *adv Fam (très)* awfully; *(beaucoup)* a hell of a lot

bihebdomadaire [biɛbdɔmadɛr] *adj* twice-weekly

bijou, -x [biʒu] *nm* jewel; *Fig* gem; **des bijoux** jewellery, jewels; **b. de famille** family jewel; **un b. fantaisie** a piece of costume jewellery

bijouterie [biʒutri] *nf (boutique)* jeweller's (shop); *(commerce, fabrication)* jeweller's trade

bijoutier, -ère [biʒutje, -ɛr] *nm,f* jeweller

bikini® [bikini] *nm* bikini

bilan [bilã] *nm* (**a**) *Fin* balance sheet; **faire** *ou* **dresser un b.** to draw up a balance sheet; *Com* **déposer son b.** to file one's petition (in bankruptcy); *Com* **un dépôt de b.** a petition in bankruptcy; **b. comptable** balance sheet (**b**) *(appréciation) (d'une situation, de faits)* assessment, evaluation; *(résultats)* results; *(d'une catastrophe)* toll; **faire le b. de la situation** to take stock of the situation; **accident sur l'autoroute, b. quatre morts** *(titre)* motorway accident, four dead; **b. de santé** complete check-up

bilatéral, -e, -aux, -ales [bilateral, -o] *adj* bilateral

bilboquet [bilbɔkɛ] *nm* cup-and-ball

bile [bil] *nf* bile; **décharger sa b. sur qn** to vent one's spleen on sb; *Fam* **se faire de la b. (pour)** to fret (about)

biler [bile] **se biler** *vpr Fam* to fret

biliaire [biljɛr] *adj* biliary

bilingue [bilɛ̃g] *adj* bilingual

billard [bijar] *nm* (**a**) *(jeu)* billiards; **faire un b.** *ou* **une partie de b.** to have a game of billiards; **b. américain** pool; **b. électrique** pinball (**b**) *(table)* billiard table (**c**) *Fam* **passer sur le b.** to go under the knife

bille¹ [bij] *nf* (**a**) *(de verre)* marble; *Fig* **reprendre ses billes** to pull out; *Fam* **toucher sa b. en qch** to know a thing or two about sth (**b**) *(de billard)* (billiard) ball; *Fig* **y aller b. en tête** not to beat about the bush (**c**) *Tech* ball (**d**) *très Fam (visage)* mug; **avoir une bonne b.** to look pleasant enough

bille² *nf (pièce de bois)* billet

billet [bijɛ] *nm* (**a**) *(argent)* **b. (de banque)** *Br* (bank)note, *Am* bill; **un b. de 100 euros** a 100-euro *Br* note *or Am* bill; **un faux b.** a forged banknote; **le b. vert** the dollar; *Fam* **je te fiche mon b. qu'il ne viendra pas!** you can bet your bottom dollar he won't come! (**b**) *(pour voyager, pour le cinéma)* ticket; **b. d'avion/de train** plane/train ticket; **b. de première/de seconde** first-/second-class ticket; **b. simple** *Br* single *or Am* one-way ticket; **b. aller (et) retour** *Br* return *or Am* round-trip ticket; **b. électronique** e-ticket (**c**) *Com & Fin (effet)* bill; **b. au porteur** bill payable to bearer (**d**) *Litt (lettre)* note; *Scol* **b. d'absence** absence slip; **b. doux** love letter; *Scol* **b. de retard** = note given to pupil who is late, specifying the time of arrival

billetterie [bijɛtri] *nf* (**a**) *(lieu)* ticket office (**b**) *(de billets de transport)* **b. automatique** ticket machine

billion [biljɔ̃] *nm* trillion

billot [bijo] *nm* block

bimensuel, -elle [bimãsɥɛl] **1** *adj Br* fortnightly, *Am* semimonthly
2 *nm Br* fortnightly *or Am* semimonthly magazine

bimestriel, -elle [bimɛstriɛl] *adj & nm* bimonthly

bimoteur [bimɔtœr] *adj & nm* **(avion) b.** twin-engine aircraft

binaire [binɛr] *adj Math* binary; **langage b.** binary notation

biner [bine] *vt* to hoe

binette¹ [binɛt] *nf (outil)* hoe

binette² *nf Fam (visage)* mug; *Can Ordinat* smiley, emoticon

biniou [binju] *nm* Breton bagpipes

binoclard, -e [binɔklar, -ard] *nm,f Fam* four-eyes, *Br* speccy

binocle [binɔkl] *nm* pince-nez *inv*; *Fam* **binocles** *(lunettes)* specs

binôme [binom] *nm* (**a**) *Math* binomial (**b**) *Scol (étudiant)* partner; **travailler en b.** to work in pairs *or* twos

binouze [binuz] *nf Fam (bière)* beer

bio [bjo] *adj inv Fam (aliment)* organic; *(yaourt)* bio

biocarburant [bjokarbyrã] *nm* biofuel

biochimie [bjoʃimi] *nf* biochemistry

biodégradable [bjodegradabl] *adj* biodegradable

biodiversité [bjodivɛrsite] *nf* biodiversity

biographe [bjograf] *nmf* biographer

biographie [bjografi] *nf* biography

biographique [bjografik] *adj* biographical

bio-industrie *(pl* **bio-industries)** [bjoɛ̃dystri] *nf* biotechnology industry

biologie [bjɔlɔʒi] *nf* biology

biologique [bjɔlɔʒik] *adj* biological; *(sans engrais chimiques)* organic

biologiste [bjɔlɔʒist] *nmf* biologist

biomasse [bjomas] *nf* biomass

biophysique [bjofizik] *nf* biophysics *(singulier)*

biopsie [bjɔpsi] *nf* biopsy

biorythme [bjoritm] *nm* biorhythm

biosphère [bjosfɛr] *nf* biosphere

biotechnique [bjotɛknik], **biotechnologie** [bjotɛknɔlɔʒi] *nf* biotechnology

bioterrorisme [bjɔtɛrɔrism] *nm* bioterrorism

bioterroriste [bjɔtɛrɔrist] *adj & nmf* bioterrorist

bip [bip] **1** *exclam* beep!
2 *nm* (**a**) *(son)* beep; **faire b.** to beep (**b**) *(appareil)* beeper, pager

biparti, -e [biparti], **bipartite** [bipartit] *adj* bipartite

bipède [bipɛd] *adj & nm* biped

biper [bipe] *vt* to page

biplace [biplas] *adj & nm Aut & Aviat* two-seater

biplan [biplã] *nm* biplane

bipolaire [bipɔlɛr] *adj Élec & Phys* bipolar

bique [bik] *nf Fam* (**a**) *(chèvre)* nanny goat (**b**) *Péj (femme)* **vieille b.** old bag

biquet, -ette [bikɛ, -ɛt] *nm,f* (**a**) *(chevreau)* kid (**b**) *Fam* **mon b.** my pet

bircher [birʃɛr] *nm Suisse* muesli

BIRD [bird] *nf (abrév* **banque internationale pour la reconstruction et le développement)** IBRD

biréacteur [bireaktœr] *nm* twin-engine jet

birman, -e [birmã, -an] **1** *adj* Burmese
2 *nm,f* **B.** Burmese
3 *nm (langue)* Burmese

Birmanie [birmani] *nf* **la B.** Burma

bis¹, -e¹ [bi, biz] *adj* greyish-brown

bis² [bis] *adv* (**a**) *Théât* encore; *Mus* repeat (**b**) *(d'une adresse)* **10 b.** ≃ 10A

bisaïeul, -e [bizajœl] *nm,f Litt* great-grandfather, *f* great-grandmother

bisannuel, -elle [bizanɥɛl] *adj* biennial

bisbille [bisbij] *nf Fam* squabble; **être en b. avec qn** to be at loggerheads with sb

bisbrouille [bisbruj] *nf Belg* tiff

biscornu, -e [biskɔrny] *adj* (**a**) *(chapeau)* misshapen; *(bâtiment, objet)* oddly shaped (**b**) *Fam (idées)* cranky; *(raisonnement, esprit)* tortuous

biscoteaux [biskɔto] *nmpl Fam* biceps; **avoir des b.** to have bulging biceps

biscotte [biskɔt] *nf* rusk

biscuit [biskɥi] *nm* (**a**) *(gâteau) Br* biscuit, *Am* cookie; **b. à la cuiller** *Br* sponge finger, *Am* lady finger; **biscuits salés** crackers (**b**) *(porcelaine)* biscuit

bise² [biz] *nf (vent)* north wind
bise³ *nf Fam (baiser)* kiss; **donner** *ou* **faire une b.** **à qn**
to give sb a kiss; **se faire la b.** to give each other a kiss; **grosses bises** *(sur une lettre)* love and kisses
biseau, -x [bizo] *nm* (**a**) *(bord)* bevel; **taillé en b.** bevel-edged (**b**) *(outil)* bevel
biseauter [bizote] *vt* (**a**) *(tailler)* to bevel (**b**) *(cartes à jouer)* to mark
bisexualité [bisɛksɥalite] *nf* bisexuality
bisexuel, -elle [bisɛksɥɛl] *adj & nm,f* bisexual
bismuth [bismyt] *nm* bismuth
bison [bizɔ̃] *nm* bison
Bison Futé [bizɔ̃fyte] *n* = organization which advises drivers of driving conditions on French motorways
bisou [bizu] *nm Fam* kiss; **bisous** *(sur une lettre)* love
bisque [bisk] *nf Culin* **b. de homard** lobster bisque
bisquer [biske] *vi Fam* **faire b. qn** to wind sb up
bissectrice [bisɛktris] *nf* bisector
bisser [bise] *vt* (**a**) *(sujet: artiste) (chanson)* to give an encore of (**b**) *(sujet: spectateur) (chanson)* to call for an encore of; **b. un chanteur** to call on a singer to give an encore (**c**) *Belg Scol (redoubler)* to repeat
bissextile [bisɛkstil] *adj* **année b.** leap year
bistouri [bisturi] *nm* lancet
bistro(t) [bistro] *nm Fam* bar

Bistrot

This word can refer either to a small café or to a cosy restaurant, especially one frequented by regulars. These establishments are usually not as up-market as bistros in English-speaking countries. The "style bistrot" refers to a style of furnishing inspired by the chairs, tables and zinc countertops typical of the traditional "bistrot".

BIT [beite] *nm (abrév* **Bureau international du travail)** ILO
bit [bit] *nm Ordinat* bit; **b. d'arrêt** stop bit; **b. de contrôle** control bit; **b. de départ** start bit
bite [bit] *nf Vulg* dick, cock
bitoniau [bitɔnjo] *nm Fam* thingy
bitte¹ [bit] = **bite**
bitte² *nf Naut* **b. d'amarrage** bollard
bitture [bityr] *nf très Fam* **prendre une b.** to get *Br* pissed *orAm* wasted
bitturer [bityre] **se bitturer** *vpr très Fam* to get *Br* pissed *orAm* wasted
bitume [bitym] *nm (revêtement)* asphalt
bitumer [bityme] *vt (route)* to asphalt
bitumeux, -euse [bitymø, -øz], **bitumineux, -euse** [bityminø, -øz] *adj* bituminous
biture [bityr] = **bitture**
biturer [bityre] = **bitturer**
bivouac [bivwak] *nm* bivouac
bivouaquer [bivwake] *vi* to bivouac
bizarre [bizar] *adj* strange, odd
bizarrement [bizarmɑ̃] *adv* strangely, oddly
bizarrerie [bizarri] *nf (d'une situation, d'une idée, d'une attitude)* strangeness, oddness; **bizarreries** *(d'une personne)* eccentricities
bizarroïde [bizarɔid] *adj Fam* weird
bizut [bizy] *nm Fam Scol & Univ* = first-year student on whom practical jokes are played
bizutage [bizytaʒ] *nm Fam Scol & Univ* = practical jokes played on first-year students, *Br* ≃ ragging, *Am* ≃ hazing

Bizutage

In some French schools and colleges, students in fancy dress take to the streets and play practical jokes, sometimes of a very cruel nature, on each other and on passers-by at the beginning of the school year. This is part of the traditional initiation ceremony known as "bizutage". As a consequence of the excessive behaviour to which it has often led, a law was passed in 1998 to make it an offence.

---

bizuter [bizyte] *vt Fam Scol & Univ (étudiant)* to play practical jokes on, *Br* ≃ to rag, *Am* ≃ to haze
bizuth [bizy] = **bizut**
bla-bla [blabla] *nm Fam* claptrap
black [blak] *Fam* **1** *adj* black **2** *nmf* B. Black
blackbouler [blakbule] *vt Fam (à un examen)* to fail; **se faire b.** to fail, *Am* to flunk
blafard, -e [blafar, -ard] *adj* pallid
blague [blag] *nf* (**a**) *(plaisanterie)* joke; **faire une b. à qn** to play a joke on sb; **b. à part** joking apart; **sans b.?** no kidding? (**b**) *(mensonge)* **raconter des blagues** to lie
blaguer [blage] *vi Fam* to joke; **aimer b.** to like a joke
blagueur, -euse [blagœr, -øz] *Fam* **1** *adj* **il est très b.** he really likes a joke **2** *nm,f (qui dit des blagues)* joker; *(qui fait des blagues)* practical joker
blair [blɛr] *nm très Fam Br* conk, *Am* schnozzle
blaireau, -x [blɛro] *nm* (**a**) *(animal)* badger (**b**) *(pinceau)* shaving brush (**c**) *Fam Pej (personne)* jerk, *Br* prat
blairer [blere] *vt Fam* **je ne peux pas le b.** I can't stand him
blâme [blɑm] *nm* (**a**) *(reproche)* blame (**b**) *(sanction)* reprimand
blâmer [blɑme] *vt* (**a**) *(désapprouver)* to blame (**b**) *(sanctionner)* to reprimand
blanc, blanche [blɑ̃, blɑ̃ʃ] **1** *adj* (**a**) *(couleur)* white; **b. comme neige** snow-white, as white as snow; *Fig* (as) pure as the driven snow (**b**) *(peau)* pale; *(pas bronzé)* white; **b. comme un linge** as white as a sheet (**c**) *(page)* blank (**d**) *(sourd)* **d'une voix blanche** in a toneless voice
2 *nm* (**a**) *(couleur)* white; **le b. est à la mode** white is in; **b. cassé** off-white (**b**) *(partie blanche) (d'une cible)* bull's-eye; **le b. des yeux** the whites of the eyes; **regarder qn dans le b. des yeux** to look sb straight in the eye; **b. d'œuf** egg white; **b. de poulet** chicken breast (**c**) *(espace)* blank (**d**) *(aux dominos)* blank (**e**) **chauffé à b.** white-hot; **tirer à b.** to fire a blank/blanks (**f**) *(linge)* **(articles de) b.** linen; **je lave le b. séparément** I wash my whites separately (**g**) *(vin)* white wine
3 *nm,f* **B.** White (man), *f* White (woman); **les Blancs** the Whites
4 *nf* **blanche** *Mus Br* minim, *Am* half note
blanc-bec *(pl* **blancs-becs)** [blɑ̃bɛk] *nm* total novice
blanchâtre [blɑ̃ʃɑtr] *adj* whitish
blanche [blɑ̃ʃ] *voir* **blanc**
Blanche-Neige [blɑ̃ʃnɛʒ] *npr* Snow White
blancheur [blɑ̃ʃœr] *nf* whiteness
blanchiment [blɑ̃ʃimɑ̃] *nm (d'argent)* laundering
blanchir [blɑ̃ʃir] **1** *vt* (**a**) *(rendre blanc)* to whiten; *(linge)* to launder; **b. à la chaux** to whitewash (**b**) *(disculper)* to clear (**c**) *(argent)* to launder (**d**) *Culin* to blanch

2 *vi* (**a**) *(devenir blanc)* to turn *or* go white (**b**) *(pâlir)* to blanch

blanchissage [blɑ̃ʃisaʒ] *nm* (**a**) *(du linge)* laundering (**b**) *Can Sport* shutout

blanchissement [blɑ̃ʃismɑ̃] *nm* whitening

blanchisserie [blɑ̃ʃisri] *nf* laundry

blanchisseur, -euse [blɑ̃ʃisœr, -øz] *nm,f* laundryman, *f* laundrywoman

blanchon [blɑ̃ʃɔ̃] *nm Can* whitecoat *(seal pup)*

blanquette¹ [blɑ̃kɛt] *nf Culin* **b. (de veau)** = veal stew in a white sauce

blanquette² *nf* **b. de Limoux** = sparkling white wine from Limoux

blasé, -e [blaze] *adj* blasé

blason [blazɔ̃] *nm* coat of arms

blasphème [blasfɛm] *nm* blasphemy

blasphémer [34] [blasfeme] *vi* to blaspheme

blatte [blat] *nf* cockroach

blazer [blazɛr, blazœr] *nm* blazer

bld *abrév* boulevard

blé [ble] *nm* (**a**) *(céréale)* wheat, *Br* corn; **b. dur** durum wheat; **b. en herbe** wheat in the blade; *Fig* **manger son b. en herbe** to eat one's seed corn; *Can* **b. d'Inde** *Br* maize, *Am* (Indian) corn (**b**) *Fam (argent)* dough

bled [blɛd] *nm* (**a**) *(en Afrique du Nord)* **le b.** the interior of the country (**b**) *Fam (lieu isolé)* dump, hole; **dans un b. perdu** in the middle of nowhere

blême [blɛm] *adj (personne, matin)* pale; **b. de colère** livid with anger; **devenir b.** to turn *or* go pale

blêmir [blemir] *vi* to turn *or* go pale; **b. de colère** to turn livid with anger

blennorragie [blɛnoraʒi] *nf* gonorrhoea

blessant, -e [blesɑ̃, -ɑ̃t] *adj* hurtful

blessé, -e [blese] **1** *adj (dans un accident)* injured; *(par arme)* wounded; *(moralement)* hurt; **être b. dans son amour-propre** to have had one's pride hurt; **êtes-vous b.?** are you hurt?

2 *nm,f (victime d'un accident)* injured person; *(victime d'une agression)* wounded person; **les blessés** the injured/wounded

blesser [blese] **1** *vt* (**a**) *(dans un accident)* to injure, to hurt; *(par arme)* to wound; *(sujet: chaussures)* to hurt; **il a été blessé au bras** *(dans un accident)* his arm was injured; *(par arme)* he was wounded in the arm (**b**) *(moralement)* to hurt

2 se blesser *vpr (accidentellement)* to hurt *or* injure oneself (**avec** with); *(avec une arme)* to wound oneself; **se b. à la tête** *(accidentellement)* to hurt one's head; *(avec une arme)* to wound oneself in the head

blessure [blesyr] *nf (dans un accident)* injury; *(par arme)* wound; *Fig (morale)* wound, hurt

blette [blɛt] *nf* = bette

bleu, -e [blø] **1** *adj* blue; *(bifteck)* very rare; **b. de froid** blue with cold

2 *nm* (**a**) *(couleur)* blue; **le b. est à la mode** blue is in; **b. canard** peacock blue; **b. ciel** sky blue; **b. électrique** electric blue; **b. marine** navy (blue); **b. nuit** midnight blue; **b. de Prusse** Prussian blue; **b. roi** royal blue (**b**) *(ecchymose)* bruise; **se faire un b.** to bruise oneself (**c**) *Fam (novice)* novice; *Mil* rookie (**d**) *(fromage)* blue cheese; **b. d'Auvergne/de Bresse** = blue cheese from Auvergne/Bresse (**e**) **b. (de chauffe** *ou* **de travail)** *Br* overalls *Am* coveralls; *(salopette) Br* dungarees, *Am* overall (**f**) *Suisse Fam (permis de conduire) Br* driving licence, *Am* driver's license

bleuâtre [bløɑtr] *adj* blu(e)ish

bleuet [bløɛ] *nm* (**a**) *(plante)* cornflower (**b**) *Can (baie)* blueberry

bleuetière [bløtjɛr] *nf Can* blueberry field

bleuté, -e [bløte] *adj* bluish; *(verres)* blue-tinted

blindage [blɛ̃daʒ] *nm Mil* armour-plating

blinde [blɛ̃d] **à toute blinde** *adv Fam* at full speed, like lightning

blindé, -e [blɛ̃de] **1** *adj* (**a**) *(véhicule militaire)* armoured, armour-plated; *(voiture)* bulletproof; **porte blindée** steel security door (**b**) *Fam* **je suis b.** I'm hardened to it

2 *nm Mil* armoured vehicle

blinder [blɛ̃de] *vt* (**a**) *(véhicule)* to armour-plate; *(porte)* to reinforce with steel (**b**) *Fam (personne)* to harden (**contre** to)

blini [blini] *nm* blini

blizzard [blizar] *nm* blizzard

bloc [blɔk] *nm* (**a**) *(de bois, de pierre)* block (**b**) *(de maisons)* block (**c**) *Pol* bloc; **faire b. (avec/contre qn)** to join forces (with/against sb); *Écon* **b. monétaire** monetary bloc (**d**) *(de papier)* pad; **b. de papier à lettres** writing pad (**e**) *(ensemble d'éléments)* unit; **b. opératoire** operating theatre (**f**) *très Fam (prison)* clink, slammer; **être au b.** to be in the clink *or* the slammer (**g**) *Ordinat* block; **b. d'alimentation secteur** mains power unit; **b. de données** data block; **b. de touches** keypad (**h**) *(locutions)* **tout refuser en b.** to reject everything in its entirety; **serrer qch à b.** to screw sth as tightly as possible

blocage [blɔkaʒ] *nm* (**a**) *(d'un mécanisme)* jamming; *(des freins)* locking; *(des prix, des salaires)* freezing; *Psy* (mental) block; *Psy* **faire un b.** to get a (mental) block (**b**) *Ordinat (dans réseau)* lockout; **b. majuscule** caps lock

bloc-appartement *(pl* blocs-appartements) [blɔkapartəmɑ̃] *nm Can Br* block of flats, *Am* apartment building

blockhaus [blɔkos] *nm* blockhouse

bloc-moteur *(pl* blocs-moteurs) [blɔkmɔtœr] *nm* engine block

bloc-notes *(pl* blocs-notes) [blɔknɔt] *nm* notepad

blocus [blɔkys] *nm* blockade; **lever/forcer le b.** to raise/run the blockade

blog [blɔg] *nm Ordinat (abrév* weblog**)** blog

blogeur, -euse [blɔgœr, -øz] *nm,f Ordinat* blogger

bloggeur, -euse = blogeur, -euse

blogging [blɔgiŋ] *nm Ordinat* blogging

blond, -e [blɔ̃, -ɔ̃d] **1** *adj (cheveux)* fair, blond; *(personne)* fair-haired, blond; *(sable, blés)* golden; **être b. comme les blés** *(sujet: personne)* to have golden-blond hair

2 *nm,f (personne)* **un b.** a fair-haired man; **une blonde** a blonde, a fair-haired woman; **une blonde décolorée** a peroxide blonde

3 *nm (couleur)* **b. cendré** ash blond; **b. platine** platinum blond; **b. vénitien** strawberry blond

4 *nf* **blonde** (**a**) *(bière)* lager (**b**) *(cigarette)* Virginia cigarette (**c**) *Can Fam (amie)* girlfriend

blondinet, -ette [blɔ̃dinɛ, -ɛt] *nm,f* fair-haired child

blondir [blɔ̃dir] **1** *vt (cheveux)* to bleach

2 *vi (cheveux, personne)* to go *or* turn blond; **faire b. des oignons** to cook onions until transparent

bloquer [blɔke] **1** *vt* (**a**) *(mécanisme, porte)* to jam; **il m'a bloqué contre un mur** he jammed me up against a wall; *Fam* **je suis bloqué à l'hôpital** I'm stuck in hospital (**b**) *(réunir)* to group together; *(jours de congé)* to lump together (**c**) *(compte bancaire, prix, salaires)* to freeze (**d**) *(route, ballon)* to block; **b. le chemin** *ou* **le passage à qn** to block sb's way (**e**) *Belg Fam (sujet)* to bone up on (**f**) *Can Fam (examen) Br* to fail, *Am* to flunk (**g**) *Psy* **ça me bloque de me sentir observé** I get a (mental) block if I feel I'm being watched; **être bloqué** to have a (mental) block **2 se bloquer** *vpr* (**a**) *(machine, ascenseur)* to get stuck (**b**) *Psy* to get a (mental) block

blottir [blɔtir] **se blottir** *vpr* to snuggle up; **se b. contre qn/dans les bras de qn** to snuggle up to sb/in sb's arms; **blottis les uns contre les autres** huddled up together

blousant, -e [bluzã, -ãt] *adj* loose-fitting

blouse [bluz] *nf* (**a**) *(tablier)* overall; **b. de laboratoire/blanche** lab/white coat; *Fig* **les blouses blanches** doctors and nurses (**b**) *(de femme)* blouse

blouser [bluze] **1** *vi (corsage)* to be loose-fitting **2** *vt Fam (personne)* to con

blouson [bluzɔ̃] *nm* (lumber-)jacket; *(plus léger)* blouson; **b. en** *ou* **de cuir** leather jacket; **b. d'aviateur** bomber jacket; *Fam Vieilli* **b. noir** young hoodlum *(wearing a black leather jacket)*; **b. de rappeur** Puffa jacket®

blue-jean [bludʒin] *(pl* **blue-jeans)** *nm Vieilli* jeans

blues [bluz] *nm* blues

bluff [blœf] *nm* bluff; **y aller au b.** to try and bluff

bluffer [blœfe] **1** *vt (aux cartes)* to bluff; *Fam (personne)* to take in **2** *vi (aux cartes) & Fam* to bluff

blush [blœʃ] *nm* blusher

BN [beɛn] *nf (abrév* **Bibliothèque nationale)** = the former French national library

BNF [beɛnɛf] *nf (abrév* **bibliothèque nationale de France)** = French national library, comprising the "Bibliothèque de France" and the "Bibliothèque nationale"

BO [beo] **1** *nf (abrév* **bande originale)** (original) soundtrack **2** *nm (abrév* **bulletin officiel)** = official listing of all new laws and decrees

boa [bɔa] *nm* (**a**) *(serpent)* boa; **b. constricteur** boa constrictor (**b**) *(en plumes)* boa

boat people [botpipœl] *nmpl* boat people

bob [bɔb] *nm Fam (chapeau)* sun hat

bobard [bɔbar] *nm Fam* tall story

bobine [bɔbin] *nf* (**a**) *(de ruban, de fil)* reel; *(de machine à coudre)* bobbin; *(de machine à écrire, d'appareil photo)* spool; *(de film, de papier)* roll (**b**) *Élec* coil (**c**) *Fam (visage)* mug

bobo [bobo] *nm (langage enfantin) (coupure)* cut; *(piqûre)* sting; **ça fait b.?** does it hurt?; **se faire b.** to hurt oneself

bobsleigh [bɔbslɛ(g)] *nm* bobsleigh

bocage [bɔkaʒ] *nm* bocage *(countryside with many hedges, trees and small fields)*

bocal, -aux [bɔkal, -o] *nm* jar; *(aquarium)* (fish)bowl

Boche [bɔʃ] *nmf Fam Péj* Kraut, = offensive term referring to a German

bock [bɔk] *nm* beer glass

body [bɔdi] *nm (vêtement)* body

body-building [bɔdibildiŋ] *nm* body building; **faire du b.** to do body building

bœuf [bœf, *pl* bø] **1** *nm* (**a**) *(animal)* bullock; *(de trait)* ox; *Fam* **on n'est pas des bœufs** we're not superhuman (**b**) *(viande)* beef; **b. bourguignon** bœuf bourguignon; **b. mode** stewed beef (**c**) *Fam (improvisation)* jam session; **faire un b.** to jam

2 *adj inv Fam* **avoir un succès b.** to be incredibly successful; **faire un effet b.** to make a really big impression

bof [bɔf] *exclam Fam* **ça te plaît? – b., pas tellement** do you like it? – not really, no; **il est chouette, hein, mon nouveau pull? – b.** my new sweater's great, isn't it? – I suppose so

Bogota [bogota] *n* Bogota

bogue [bɔg] *nf* (**a**) *(de châtaigne) Br* burr, *Am* shuck (**b**) *Ordinat* bug; **dépourvu/plein de bogues** bug-free/-ridden; **b. de l'an 2000** millennium bug; **b. de logiciel** software bug

bohème [bɔɛm] **1** *adj* bohemian **2** *nmf* **mener une vie de b.** to lead a bohemian life

Bohême [bɔɛm] *nf* **la B.** Bohemia

bohémien, -enne [bɔemjɛ̃, -ɛn] *nm,f* gypsy

boire¹ [12] [bwar] **1** *vt* (**a**) *(sujet: personne)* to drink; *Fig* **b. les paroles de qn** to drink in sb's every word (**b**) *(sujet: plante, matière poreuse)* to soak up, to absorb **2** *vi (personne)* to drink; *(plante)* to soak up *or* absorb water; *Can (bébé)* to feed; **b. comme un trou** to drink like a fish; **b. à la bouteille** to drink from the bottle; **b. au succès de qn/qch** to drink to the success of sb/sth; **donner à b. à qn** to give sb a drink; **faire b. qn** to give sb something to drink; **faire b. les chevaux** to water the horses; *Fig* **il y a à b. et à manger là-dedans** it's a bit of a mixed bag; *Prov* **qui a bu boira** old habits die hard **3 se boire** *vpr* to be drunk

boire² *nm* **le b. et le manger** food and drink

bois [bwa] *nm* (**a**) *(forêt)* wood (**b**) *(matériau)* wood; **des meubles en b.** wooden furniture; *Fig* **elle n'est pas de b.** she's only human; *Fig* **je vais leur faire voir de quel b. je me chauffe!** I'll show them (what I'm made of)!; **petit b.** kindling; **b. de charpente** *ou* **de construction** *Br* timber, *Am* lumber; **b. de chauffage** firewood; **b. mort** deadwood; *Can* **b. de poêle** firewood; *Can* **b. rond** log; **b. de rose** rosewood (**c**) *(de chaise, de raquette)* frame; **faire un b.** *(au tennis)* to hit the ball off the frame; **b. de lit** bed frame (**d**) *Mus* **les b.** the woodwind (**e**) **les b.** *(d'un cerf)* the antlers

boisé, -e [bwaze] *adj (région)* wooded

boisement [bwazmã] *nm* afforestation

boiseries [bwazri] *nfpl* panelling

boisson [bwasɔ̃] *nf* drink; *Can (spiritueux)* hard liquor, spirits; **b. alcoolisée/non alcoolisée** alcoholic/soft drink; **b. chaude** hot drink; **b. gazeuse** fizzy drink

boîte [bwat] *nf* (**a**) *(récipient)* box; **des haricots en b.** canned *or Br* tinned beans; **mettre qch en b.** *(marchandises)* to box sth; *(aliments)* to can sth, *Br* to tin sth; *Fam* **mettre qn en b.** to pull sb's leg; **b. d'allumettes** *(pleine)* box of matches; *(vide)* matchbox; **b. à bijoux** jewel box; **b. de conserve** can, *Br* tin; **b. à couture** *ou* **ouvrage** sewing box; **b. de dialogue** dialogue box; *Ordinat & Tél* **b. d'envoi** *(pour e-mails, SMS)* outbox; **b. à gants** glove compartment; **b. à** *ou* **aux lettres** *Br* postbox, *Am* mailbox; *(chez soi) Br* letterbox, *Am* mailbox; *Ordinat* **b. à lettres électronique** mailbox; **b. à musique** music box; *Aviat* **b. noire** black box; **b. à outils** toolbox; **b. postale** Post Office Box; *Ordinat & Tél* **b. de réception** *(pour e-mails, SMS)* inbox; *Aut* **b. de vitesses** gearbox; **b. vocale** voicemail (**b**) *Fam (entreprise)* firm; *(école)* school (**c**) **b. (de nuit)** nightclub; **aller** *ou* **sortir en b.** to go to a nightclub

boiter [bwate] *vi* to limp

boiteux, -euse [bwatø, -øz] *adj (personne, cheval, explication)* lame; *(raisonnement)* shaky; *(phrase)* badly constructed
boîtier [bwatje] *nm* case; *Phot* (camera) body; *Ordinat* **b. de commande** command box; *Ordinat* **b. commutateur** data switch
boitiller [bwatije] *vi* to limp slightly
boive *voir* **boire**[1]
bol [bɔl] *nm* (**a**) *(récipient)* bowl (**b**) *(contenu)* bowl(-ful); **prendre un b. d'air frais** *ou* **pur** to get a good breath of fresh air (**c**) *Fam (chance)* luck; **avoir du b.** to be lucky; **ne pas avoir de b.** to be unlucky; **manque de b., il avait déjà demandé!** just my luck, he'd already asked! (**d**) **le B. d'or** = 24-hour motorcycle race
bolchevique [bɔlʃəvik, bɔlʃevik] *adj & nmf* Bolshevik
bolduc [bɔldyk] *nm* gift-wrap ribbon
bolée [bɔle] *nf* bowl(ful)
boléro [bɔlero] *nm (vêtement, pièce musicale)* bolero
bolet [bɔlɛ] *nm* boletus
bolide [bɔlid] *nm (voiture)* racing car; **comme un b.** like a rocket
Bolivie [bɔlivi] *nf* **la B.** Bolivia
bolivien, -enne [bɔlivjɛ̃, -ɛn] **1** *adj* Bolivian **2** *nm,f* **B.** Bolivian
bolognais, -e [bɔlɔɲɛ, -ɛz] *adj* Bolognese; *Culin* **spaghetti bolognaise** spaghetti bolognese
Bologne [bɔlɔɲ] *n* Bologna
bombage [bɔ̃baʒ] *nm Fam* (aerosol) graffiti; **faire des bombages sur un mur** to spray-paint a wall with graffiti
bombance [bɔ̃bɑ̃s] *nf Fam* **faire b.** to feast
bombardement [bɔ̃bardəmɑ̃] *nm (avec des obus)* shelling; *(avec des bombes)* bombing; **b. aérien** air raid
bombarder [bɔ̃barde] *vt* (**a**) *(avec des obus)* to shell; *(avec des bombes)* to bomb; **b. qn de questions/de lettres** to bombard sb with questions/letters (**b**) *Fam* **on l'a bombardé ministre** he's been pitchforked into the post of minister
bombardier [bɔ̃bardje] *nm (avion)* bomber; *(aviateur)* bombardier
bombe [bɔ̃b] *nf* (**a**) *(explosif)* bomb; *Fig* **faire l'effet d'une b.** to be a bombshell; **b. atomique** atom(ic) bomb; **b. à eau** water bomb; *Culin* **b. glacée** bombe glacée; **b. H** H bomb; **b. incendiaire** incendiary device, fire bomb; **b. lacrymogène** tear-gas grenade; **b. à retardement** time bomb (**b**) *(atomiseur)* spray, aerosol (**c**) *(chapeau)* riding hat (**d**) *Can (bouilloire)* kettle (**e**) *Fam* **faire la b.** to live it up
bombé, -e [bɔ̃be] *adj* bulging
bomber [bɔ̃be] **1** *vt (gonfler)* **b. qch** to cause sth to bulge; **b. le torse** to throw out one's chest; *Fig* to swagger (around) **2** *vi (mur)* to bulge; *(planche)* to warp
bombeur, -euse [bɔ̃bœr, -øz] *nm,f* graffiti artist *(who uses spray paint)*
bombonne [bɔ̃bɔn] = **bonbonne**
bôme [bom] *nf Naut* boom
bon[1]**, bonne** [bɔ̃, bɔn] **1** *adj* (**a**) *(agréable)* good; **passer une bonne soirée** to spend a pleasant evening; **l'eau est bonne** *(en se baignant)* the water's lovely; **de bons petits plats** nice little meals; **souhaiter une** *ou* **la bonne année à qn** to wish sb a happy New Year; **bonnes vacances!** have a good holiday! (**b**) *(satisfaisant) (travail, qualité)* good; **c'est b.**

(*d'accord*) that's fine; **c'est b., j'ai compris** all right *or* OK, I understand (**c**) *(correct)* right; **c'est la bonne réponse/le b. bus** that's the right answer/bus; **un intellectuel, au b. sens du terme** an intellectual in the true sense of the word (**d**) *(compétent)* good (**en** at); **un b. médecin/père** a good doctor/father (**e**) *(profitable) (investissement, conseil, idée)* good; **cet exercice est b. pour le dos** this exercise is good for the back; **c'est b. à savoir** it's worth knowing; **il serait b. que vous lui en parliez** it would be a good idea if you spoke to him/her about it; **à quoi b.?** what's the point *or* the use?; **à quoi b. se plaindre?** what's the point *or* the use of complaining?; **quand b. vous semble** whenever you like (**f**) *(apte)* **b.** *à* manger *or* safe to eat; **b. pour le service** *Mil* fit for duty; *Fig* serviceable; **elle n'est bonne à rien** she's useless; **tu es b. pour une contravention** you're in for a fine (**g**) *(valable) (billet, abonnement)* valid; **la balle est bonne** *(au tennis)* the ball is in *or* good; **les yaourts sont-ils encore bons?** are the yoghurts still all right to eat? (**h**) *(moralement)* good; *(généreux)* good, kind (**envers** *ou* **avec** to) (**i**) *(en intensif)* good; **j'ai attendu deux bonnes heures** I waited for a good two hours; **il m'a fallu un b. moment pour comprendre** it took me a while to understand; **un b. rhume** a bad cold (**j**) *(locutions)* **elle est bien bonne!** that's a good one!; **il en a de bonnes!** he must be joking *or* kidding!; *Fam* **avoir qn à la bonne** to have a soft spot for sb; **pour de b.** *(partir, revenir)* for good **2** *exclam (d'accord)* right!, fine!; **b., on y va?** right, shall we go?; **allons b.!** what!; **ah b., je ne le savais pas** really? I didn't know; **sors d'ici!** – **b., b., c'est pas la peine de crier!** get out of here! – OK, OK, no need to shout!
3 *adv (sentir)* good, nice; **il fait b.** it's lovely; **un pays où il fait b. vivre** a country that's good to live in
4 *nm,f* **les bons et les méchants** *(dans un film)* the goodies and the baddies; **b. à rien** a good-for-nothing
5 *nm* **cela a du b.** it has some good points
bon[2] *nm* (**a**) *(papier)* voucher, coupon; **b. d'achat** gift voucher; **b. de commande** order form; **b. de garantie** guarantee; **b. de livraison** delivery note; **b. de réduction** money-off coupon (**b**) *Fin* bond; **b. du Trésor** treasury bond
bonard, -e [bɔnar, -ard] *adj Fam* **c'est b.!** that's pretty good!
bonasse [bɔnas] *adj* soft; **d'un ton b.** meekly
bonbon [bɔ̃bɔ̃] **1** *nm* (**a**) *(sucrerie)* Br sweet, Am candy; **b. à la menthe** mint (**b**) *Belg (biscuit)* Br biscuit, Am cookie **2** *adv Fam* **coûter b.** to cost an arm and a leg *or* a bundle
bonbonne [bɔ̃bɔn] *nf* demijohn; *(de gaz)* cylinder
bonbonnière [bɔ̃bɔnjɛr] *nf Br* sweet *or Am* candy box
bond [bɔ̃] *nm* (**a**) *(saut)* leap, jump; **faire un b.** to leap up; *Fig* to shoot up; **faire un b. en avant/en arrière** to leap forwards/back; **franchir qch d'un b.** to clear sth at one leap; **se lever d'un b.** to jump to one's feet (**b**) *(d'une balle)* bounce; **faire faux b. à qn** to leave sb in the lurch

bonde [bɔ̃d] *nf* (**a**) *(bouchon)* *(d'un évier, d'une baignoire)* plug; *(d'un tonneau)* bung; *(d'un bassin)* sluice gate (**b**) *(trou)* *(d'un évier, d'une baignoire)* plughole; *(d'un tonneau)* bunghole; *(d'un bassin)* drainage hole

bondé, -e [bɔ̃de] *adj* packed, crammed

bondir [bɔ̃dir] *vi* to leap, to jump; **b. sur** to pounce on; *Fig* **cela me fait b.** it makes me hopping mad

bon enfant [bɔ̃nɑ̃fɑ̃] *adj inv* easy-going

bonheur [bɔnœr] *nm* (**a**) *(bien-être)* happiness; **faire le b. de qn** to make sb happy (**b**) *(chance)* good fortune, (good) luck; **j'ai le b. de la connaître** I have the good fortune to know her; **porter b. à qn** to bring sb (good) luck; **il ne connaît pas son b.** he doesn't know how lucky he is; **par b.** luckily; **au petit b. (la chance)** at random (**c**) *Litt (réussite)* **avec b.** felicitously

bonhomie [bɔnɔmi] *nf* good-naturedness; **avec b.** good-naturedly

bonhomme [bɔnɔm] *(pl* **bonshommes** [bɔ̃zɔm]*) nm Fam* (**a**) *(homme)* fellow, guy; **c'est un sacré b.** he's a hell of a guy; **on se retrouvera, mon b.!** I'll get even with you, my friend!; **aller son petit b. de chemin** to be jogging along nicely; **b. de neige** snowman (**b**) *(figure)* man; **dessiner des bonshommes** to draw little men *or* people

boniche [bɔniʃ] *nf Fam* maid, *Br* skivvy

bonification [bɔnifikasjɔ̃] *nf* (**a**) *(d'une terre, d'un vin)* improvement (**b**) *Com* bonus (**c**) *Sport* advantage

bonifier [66] [bɔnifje] **1** *vt (terre, caractère)* to improve **2 se bonifier** *vpr* to improve

boniment [bɔnimɑ̃] *nm* (**a**) *(discours)* sales talk, patter; *Fam* **faire du b. à qn** *Br* to chat sb up, *Am* to hit on sb (**b**) *Fam (mensonges)* tall story; **tout ça, c'est du b.** that's all claptrap

bonite [bɔnit] *nf bonito*

bonjour [bɔ̃ʒur] *nm* hello; *(le matin)* good morning; *(l'après-midi)* good afternoon; **dire b. à qn** to say hello/good morning/good afternoon to sb; **dis b. à ta mère de ma part** say hello to your mother for me; **facile ou simple comme b.** easy as pie; *Fam* **b. l'ambiance!** there was one hell of an atmosphere!; *Fam* **b. la soirée!** what an evening!; *Fam* **le périphérique à six heures du soir, b.!** the ring road at six o'clock at night, forget it!

bon marché [bɔ̃marʃe] *adj inv* cheap; **acheter/vendre qch (à) b.** to buy/sell sth cheap(ly)

bonnard, -e [bɔnar, -ard] = **bonard, bonarde**

bonne [bɔn] **1** *voir* **bon¹**
2 *nf (domestique)* maid, *Vieilli* maidservant; *Fam* **dis-donc, je ne suis pas ta b.!** I'm not your maid, you know!; **b. à tout faire** maid, *Vieilli* maidservant; **b. d'enfants** nanny

Bonne-Espérance [bɔnɛsperɑ̃s] *voir* **cap**

bonne-main *(pl* **bonnes-mains**) [bɔnmɛ̃] *nf Suisse* tip

bonnement [bɔnmɑ̃] *adv* **tout b.** simply

bonnet [bɔnɛ] *nm* (**a**) *(coiffure)* hat; **c'est b. blanc et blanc b.** it's six of one and half a dozen of the other; **b. d'âne** dunce's cap; **b. de bain** bathing cap; **b. de nuit** nightcap; *Fig Péj* wet blanket; **b. de ski** ski cap (**b**) *(d'un soutien-gorge)* cup; **quelle profondeur de b.?** what cup size?

bonneterie [bɔnɛtri] *nf* (**a**) *(bas)* hosiery (**b**) *(commerce)* hosiery trade; *(magasin)* hosier's (shop)

bonniche [bɔniʃ] = **boniche**

bonsaï [bɔnzaj, bɔ̃zaj] *nm* bonsai

bonsoir [bɔ̃swar] *nm* good evening; *(quand on se quitte tard, quand on se couche)* goodnight; **dire b. à qn** to say good evening/goodnight to sb

bonté [bɔ̃te] *nf* (**a**) *(gentillesse)* kindness, goodness; **une femme d'une grande b.** a very kind woman; **un sourire plein de b.** a kind smile; **avoir la b. de faire qch** to be so good as to do sth; **faire qch par b. d'âme** to do sth out of the goodness of one's heart; *Vieilli* **b. divine!** good heavens! (**b**) *(acte)* **remercier qn pour ses bontés** to thank sb for his/her kindness

bonus [bɔnys] *nm* (**a**) *(prime de salaire)* bonus; *(d'assurance)* no-claims bonus (**b**) *(sur un DVD)* special feature

bon vivant [bɔ̃vivɑ̃] *adj m* **être b.** to enjoy life

bonze [bɔ̃z] *nm* Buddhist priest

bookmaker [bukmɛkœr] *nm* bookmaker

booléen, -enne [buleɛ̃, -ɛn] *adj Math & Ordinat* Boolean

boom [bum] *nm* boom

boomerang [bumrãg] *nm* boomerang

booter [bute] *vi Ordinat* **b. (sur le lecteur B)** to boot up (off the B drive)

boots [buts] *nmpl* ankle boots

borborygmes [bɔrbɔrigm] *nmpl* rumbling

bord [bɔr] *nm* (**a**) *(limite)* edge; *(d'un chapeau)* brim; *(d'une tasse, d'un verre)* rim; **un chapeau à larges bords** a wide-brimmed hat; **le b. du trottoir** *Br* the kerb, *Am* the curb; **sur le** *ou* **au b. de** *(route)* at the side of; *(lac, rivière)* beside; **aller au b. de la mer** to go to the seaside; **une maison en b. de mer** a house beside the sea; *Can* **l'autre b.** *(outre-Atlantique)* Europe; **au b. des larmes/de la catastrophe** on the verge of tears/of disaster; *Fam* **un peu voleur sur les bords** a bit light-fingered; **b. à b.** edge to edge; *Ordinat* **b. de reliure** inside margin (**b**) **à b. de** *(bateau, avion)* on board; **prendre qn à son b.** to take sb on board; **par-dessus b.** overboard; *Fig* **être du même b.** to be on the same side

bordages [bɔrdaʒ] *nmpl Can (glace)* inshore ice

bordeaux [bɔrdo] **1** *nm* Bordeaux (wine); **b. rouge** claret
2 *adj inv* maroon

bordée [bɔrde] *nf* (**a**) *Naut (de coups de feu)* broadside; *Fig* **b. de jurons** torrent of swearwords (**b**) *Fam* **être en b.** to be on a binge (**c**) *Can* **b. (de neige)** heavy snowfall

bordel [bɔrdɛl] *nm très Fam (hôtel de passe)* brothel; *(désordre)* mess; *(vacarme)* racket; **mettre** *ou* **foutre le b. dans qch** to make a mess of sth; **mettre** *ou* **foutre le b. en classe** to create mayhem in the classroom; **et tout le b.** and the whole damn lot; *Vulg* **b.! shit!**

bordelais, -e [bɔrdəlɛ, -ɛz] **1** *adj* of Bordeaux
2 *nm/f* **B.** person from Bordeaux
3 *nm* **le B.** *(région)* the Bordeaux region

bordélique [bɔrdelik] *adj Fam (pièce, organisation)* shambolic; **être b.** *(personne)* to be a slob

border [bɔrde] *vt* (**a**) *(garnir)* **b. qch de** to edge sth with (**b**) *(sujet: arbres) (route)* to line; *(sujet: bateau) (côte)* to skirt (**c**) *(lit, draps)* to tuck in; **b. qn (dans son lit)** to tuck sb in

bordereau, -x [bɔrdəro] *nm (liste)* schedule; **b. de livraison** delivery note

bordure [bɔrdyr] *nf* (**a**) *(bord)* edge; *(d'un vêtement)* border; **en b. de route/de mer** by the roadside/the sea (**b**) *(d'un miroir, d'un tableau)* frame

boréal, -e, -als *ou* **-aux, -ales** [bɔreal, -o] *adj* northern

borgne [bɔrɲ] **1** *adj* (**a**) *(personne)* one-eyed; *(mur)* blind; *(fenêtre)* obstructed (**b**) *(louche)* shady
2 *nmf* one-eyed man, *f* one-eyed woman

borne [bɔrn] *nf* (**a**) *(limite)* boundary marker; *(pierre)* boundary stone; *Fig* **sans bornes** boundless; **b. d'incendie** *Br* (fire) hydrant, *Am* fireplug; **b. kilométrique** kilometre marker, ≃ milestone (**b**) *Fam (kilomètre)* kilometre (**c**) *Élec* terminal (**d**) *Ordinat* **b. (interactive)** terminal; **b. d'accès** *(à Internet)* access point

borné, -e [bɔrne] *adj (esprit)* narrow; *(personne)* narrow-minded

borne-fontaine *(pl* **bornes-fontaines)** [bɔrnfɔ̃tɛn] *nf Can (bouche d'incendie) Br* (fire) hydrant, *Am* fireplug

borner [bɔrne] **1** *vt (terrain)* to mark out
2 se borner *vpr* (**a**) **se b. à qch/à faire qch** *(personne)* to restrict oneself to sth/to doing sth (**b**) **se b. à qch** *(choses)* to be limited to sth

borsalino [bɔrsalino] *nm* fedora

bosniaque [bɔsnjak] **1** *adj* Bosnian
2 *nmf* **B.** Bosnian

Bosnie [bɔsni] *nf* **la B.** Bosnia; **la B.-Herzégovine** Bosnia-Herzegovina

bosquet [bɔskɛ] *nm* copse, grove

bosse [bɔs] *nf* (**a**) *(d'un bossu, d'un chameau)* hump; *Fig* **avoir la b. du commerce/des maths** to have a good head for business/maths; *Fam* **il a roulé sa b.** he's knocked about a bit (**b**) *(sur la tête)* bump, lump; *(sur le sol)* bump; *(sur une piste de ski)* mogul; **se faire une b.** to get a bump

bosselé, -e [bɔsle] *adj (casserole, pare-chocs)* dented

bosser [bɔse] *Fam* **1** *vi* to work
2 *vt Scol* to bone up on, *Br* to swot up

bosseur, -euse [bɔsœr, -øz] *Fam* **1** *adj* hardworking
2 *nm,f* hard worker

bossu, -e [bɔsy] **1** *adj (personne)* hunchbacked; *(animal)* humped
2 *nm,f* hunchback

bot [bo] *adj m voir* **pied**

botanique [bɔtanik] **1** *adj* botanical
2 *nf* botany

botaniste [bɔtanist] *nmf* botanist

Botox® [bɔtɔks] *nm Pharm* Botox®; **se faire faire des injections de B.** to have Botox® (injections)

Botswana [bɔtswana] *nm* **le B.** Botswana

botte¹ [bɔt] *nf (de fleurs, de carottes, de radis)* bunch; *(de foin, de paille)* bale

botte² *nf (chaussure)* boot; *Fig* **sous la b. de** under the heel of; *Fam* **en avoir plein les bottes (de)** to be fed up to the back teeth (with); **bottes de** *ou* **en caoutchouc** rubber boots, *Br* wellingtons; **bottes de cavalier** *ou* **de cheval** riding boots

botte³ *nf (en escrime)* thrust; **porter une b. à qn** to make a thrust at sb; *Fig* **b. secrète** secret weapon; *Fam* **il lui a proposé la b.** he asked her straight out to sleep with him

botter [bɔte] *vt* (**a**) *(chausser)* **botté de cuir** wearing leather boots (**b**) *Fam* **b. les fesses** *ou* **le derrière à qn** to boot sb up the backside (**c**) *Fam (plaire à)* **ça me botte** I like it; **ça te botterait d'y aller?** d'you want to go?, *Br* d'you fancy going? (**d**) *Sport* **b. la balle en touche** to kick the ball into touch; *Fig* to dodge the issue

bottier [bɔtje] *nm* bootmaker

bottillon [bɔtijɔ̃] *nm* ankle boot

Bottin® [bɔtɛ̃] *nm (annuaire téléphonique)* phone book, telephone directory; **B. mondain** ≃ Who's Who

bottine [bɔtin] *nf* ankle boot

botulisme [bɔtylism] *nm Méd* botulism

boubou [bubu] *nm* = long traditional African robe

bouc [buk] *nm (animal)* (billy) goat; *(barbe)* goatee (beard); *Fam* **puer comme un b., puer le b.** to stink to high heaven; **b. émissaire** scapegoat

boucan [bukɑ̃] *nm Fam* racket, din; **faire du b.** to make a racket

boucane [bukan] *nf Can* smoke

boucané, -e [bukane] *adj (teint)* weatherbeaten

boucanier [bukanje] *nm* buccaneer

bouche [buʃ] *nf* (**a**) *(de personne, d'animal)* mouth; **avoir/parler la b. pleine** to have/to talk with one's mouth full; **une pipe à la b.** with a pipe in his/her mouth; *Fig* **faire la fine b.** to be fussy; **c'est une fine b.** he's/she's a gourmet; **elle n'a pas ouvert la b. de la soirée** she didn't say a word all evening; **b. cousue!** mum's the word!; **de b. à oreille** by word of mouth (**b**) *(d'une rivière, d'un cratère, d'un four)* mouth; *(d'un fusil, d'un canon)* muzzle; **b. d'égout** manhole; **b. d'incendie** *Br* (fire) hydrant, *Am* fireplug; **b. de métro** *Br* underground *or Am* subway entrance

bouché, e [buʃe] *adj (conduite, rue)* blocked; *(temps)* cloudy, overcast; **j'ai le nez b.** my nose is stuffed up; **j'ai les oreilles bouchées** my ears are blocked up; *Fam* **être b.** *(personne)* to be dense; *Fam* **être b. à l'émeri** to be a complete moron

bouche-à-bouche [buʃabuʃ] *nm inv* mouth-to-mouth resuscitation, *Br* kiss of life; **faire du b. à qn** to give sb mouth-to-mouth resuscitation *or Br* the kiss of life

bouchée [buʃe] *nf* (**a**) *(quantité)* mouthful; *Fig* **ne faire qu'une b. de qn/qch** to make short work of sb/sth; **acheter qch pour une b. de pain** to buy sth for a song; **mettre les bouchées doubles** to really get a move on (**b**) *Culin* **b. (au chocolat)** chocolate; **b. à la reine** chicken vol-au-vent

boucher¹ [buʃe] **1** *vt (fente, trou)* to fill in; *(conduite, fenêtre)* to block up; *(vue)* to block; *(bouteille)* to cork; **b. le passage à qn** to block sb's way; *Fam* **elle/ça m'en a bouché un coin** she/that took the wind out of my sails
2 se boucher *vpr (conduite)* to get blocked up; **se b. le nez** to hold one's nose; **se b. les oreilles** to put one's fingers in one's ears

boucher², -ère¹ [buʃe, -ɛr] *nm,f aussi Fig* butcher

bouchère² [buʃɛr] *nf Suisse (sur la lèvre)* cold sore

boucherie [buʃri] *nf (boutique)* butcher's (shop); *(activité)* butchery; *Fig (massacre)* slaughter; **b. chevaline** horse butcher's (shop)

bouche-trou *(pl* **bouche-trous)** [buʃtru] *nm Fam* stopgap; **être un b.** to act as a stopgap

bouchon [buʃɔ̃] *nm* (**a**) *(à vis)* cap, top; *(d'un tonneau)* stopper; **b. (de liège)** cork; **vin qui sent le b.** corked wine; *Aut* **b. de réservoir** *Br* petrol cap, *Am* fuel cap; *Fig* **tu pousses le b. un peu loin!** you're going a bit too far! (**b**) *(embouteillage)* traffic jam; **3 kilomètres de b.** a 3-kilometre tailback (**c**) *(d'une ligne de pêche)* float (**d**) *(de paille)* wisp

bouchonné, -e [buʃɔne] *adj (vin)* corked

bouchonner [buʃɔne] **1** *vt (cheval)* to rub down
2 *vi Fam* **ça bouchonne** *(sur la route)* there's congestion

bouchot [buʃo] *nm* mussel bank

boucle [bukl] *nf* (**a**) *(de ceinture, de chaussure, de harnais)* buckle; **b. d'oreille** earring (**b**) *(nœud, méandre, looping)* loop; **faire une b.** *(en marchant, en voiture)* to loop back (**c**) *(de cheveux)* curl (**d**) *Sport* lap (**e**) *Ordinat* loop

bouclé, -e [bukle] *adj (cheveux)* curly; *(personne)* curly-haired; *Ordinat* **système b.** looped system

boucler [bukle] **1** *vt* (**a**) *(ceinture, valise)* to buckle; *Fam (dossier, travail)* to finish off; **b. sa valise** *(se préparer à partir)* to pack one's bags; **avoir du mal à b. ses fins de mois** to find it hard to make ends meet at the end of the month; *Fam* **boucle-la!** shut it! (**b**) *(quartier)* to seal off; *Fam (chambre, maison)* to lock up; *Fam (prisonnier)* to bang up (**c**) **b. la boucle** *Aviat* to loop the loop; *Fig* to come full circle
2 *vi (cheveux)* to be curly; *(personne)* to have curly hair

bouclette [buklɛt] *nf (de cheveux)* small curl; *(de laine, de moquette)* curl

bouclier [buklije] *nm aussi Fig* shield; **b. atomique** *ou* **nucléaire** nuclear shield; **b. humain** human shield; **b. thermique** *(d'engin spatial)* heat shield

Bouddha [buda] *npr* Buddha

bouddhisme [budism] *nm* Buddhism

bouddhiste [budist] *adj & nmf* Buddhist

bouder [bude] **1** *vi* to sulk
2 *vt* **b. qn/qch** to refuse to have anything to do with sb/sth; **en été, les Parisiens boudent les salles de cinéma** Parisians stay away from the cinema in summer

boudeur, -euse [budœr, -øz] **1** *adj* sulky
2 *nm,f* sulky person

boudin [budɛ̃] *nm* (**a**) *(charcuterie)* **b. (noir)** *Br* black pudding, *Am* blood sausage; **b. blanc** white pudding (**b**) *(de pâte à modeler, de terre)* roll (**c**) *(traversin)* bolster (**d**) *Fam Péj (femme)* fat lump

boudiné, -e [budine] *adj* (**a**) **je suis b. dans ce pantalon** I'm bursting out of these *Br* trousers *or Am* pants (**b**) *(doigts)* podgy

boudoir [budwar] *nm* (**a**) *(salon)* boudoir (**b**) *(biscuit) Br* sponge finger, *Am* lady finger

boue [bu] *nf* (**a**) *(terre détrempée)* mud; *Fig* **traîner qn dans la b.** to drag sb through the mud (**b**) *(dans une rivière)* silt; *(dans l'océan)* ooze; *Méd* **boues activées** activated sludge

bouée [bwe] *nf Naut* buoy; *(pour nager)* rubber ring; **b. de sauvetage** lifebelt; *Fig* lifeline

boueux, -euse [buø, -øz] **1** *adj* muddy
2 *nm Fam Br* dustman, *Am* garbage man

bouffant, -e [bufɑ̃, -ɑ̃t] **1** *adj (manche)* puff(ed); *(jupe)* full; *(pantalon)* baggy; **cheveux bouffants** bouffant hair-do
2 *nm (des cheveux)* body

bouffe [buf] *nf Fam (nourriture)* grub; *(repas)* meal; **on se fait une b. samedi?** do you fancy getting together for a meal on Saturday?

bouffée [bufe] *nf* (**a**) *(de fumée)* puff; *(de parfum)* whiff; *(d'air)* breath; *aussi Fig* **une b. d'air pur** a breath of fresh air; *Méd* **b. de chaleur** *Br* hot flush, *Am* hot flash (**b**) *(d'éloquence, de colère)* outburst; *(d'orgueil)* fit

bouffer [bufe] **1** *vt Fam* (**a**) *(manger)* to eat; *Fig* **je l'aurais bouffé** I could have killed him; **elle se laisse b. par ses enfants/son travail** she has no time for anything but her children/her work; **b. du curé** to rant against the clergy; **elle a bouffé du lion!** she's full of beans! (**b**) *(argent, économies)* to blow; **b. de**

l'essence *(voiture)* to be heavy on petrol
2 *vi* (**a**) *Fam (manger)* to eat (**b**) *(manche, jupe)* to puff out; *(cheveux)* to have body; **faire b. ses cheveux** to give body to one's hair
3 **se bouffer** *vpr Fam* **se b. le nez** *(une fois)* to have a go at one another; *(constamment)* to be at daggers drawn

bouffi, -e [bufi] *adj (yeux, visage)* puffy, swollen; **b. d'orgueil** puffed up with pride

bouffon, -onne [bufɔ̃, -ɔn] **1** *nm* buffoon; *Hist* jester
2 *adj* farcical

bouge [buʒ] *nm Péj (maison)* hovel; *(bar)* dive

bougeoir [buʒwar] *nm (plat)* candleholder; *(haut)* candlestick

bougeotte [buʒɔt] *nf Fam* **avoir la b.** to be fidgety; *(envie de voyager)* to have itchy feet

bouger [45] [buʒe] **1** *vt* to move, to shift
2 *vi (remuer, se déplacer)* to move; **rester sans b.** to keep still; **ne bougeons plus!** *(pour une photo)* hold it there!; **je n'ai pas bougé (de chez moi) pendant deux jours** I haven't been out for two days; *Fig* **cette chemise ne bouge pas au lavage** *(ne déteint pas)* this shirt doesn't run in the wash; *(ne rétrécit pas)* this shirt doesn't shrink in the wash; *Fam* **ça bouge pas mal dans cette ville** this town's pretty lively
3 **se bouger** *vpr Fam (se déplacer)* to move; *(s'activer)* to get a move on; **bouge-toi de là!** shift yourself!

bougie [buʒi] *nf* (**a**) *(en cire)* candle; **s'éclairer à la b.** to use candles for lighting (**b**) *Aut* **b. (d'allumage)** spark plug

bougnat [buɲa] *nm Fam Vieilli* coal-merchant

bougnoul(e) [buɲul] *nmf* = racist term referring to a North African person

bougon, -onne [bugɔ̃, -ɔn] *Fam* **1** *adj* grumpy
2 *nm,f* grumbler

bougonner [bugɔne] *vi Fam* to grumble

bougre [bugr] *nm Fam* (**a**) *Vieilli (individu)* **le pauvre b.** the poor devil; **ce n'est pas un mauvais b.** he's not a bad sort (**b**) **b. d'imbécile** damn(ed) fool

bougrement [bugrəmɑ̃] *adv* damn(ed)

boui-boui *(pl* bouis-bouis*)* [bwibwi] *nm Fam* dingy café, *Br* greasy spoon

bouillabaisse [bujabɛs] *nf* bouillabaisse *(Provençal fish soup)*

bouillant, -e [bujɑ̃, -ɑ̃t] *adj* (**a**) *(qui bout)* boiling; *(très chaud, fiévreux)* boiling hot (**b**) *Fig (ardent)* fiery

bouille [buj] *nf Fam (visage)* mug; **il a une bonne b.** he looks a good sort

bouilleur [bujœr] *nm* **b. de cru** home distiller

bouilli, -e [buji] **1** *adj* boiled
2 *nm* boiled meat; *Can* = stew made with beans, cabbage, potatoes, salt pork and ham; **b. de bœuf** boiled beef

bouillie [buji] *nf (pour bébés)* baby food; *(à base de céréales)* baby cereal; **b. de légumes** mashed vegetables; **réduire qch en b.** *(légumes, fruits)* to mash sth; *(au mixer)* to liquidize sth; *Fam (voiture, visage)* to smash sth up; *Fam* **mettre** *ou* **réduire qn en b.** to beat sb to a pulp

bouillir [13] [bujir] *vi* to boil; **faire b. qch** to boil sth; **b. de colère** to seethe with anger; **b. d'impatience** to burst with impatience; **cela me fait b.** that makes my blood boil

bouilloire [bujwar] *nf* kettle

bouillon [bujɔ̃] *nm* (**a**) *(d'un liquide en ébullition)* bubble; **bouillir à gros bouillons** to boil hard; **le sang sortait à gros bouillons** the blood was gushing out

(**b**) *Culin (liquide)* stock; *Fam* **boire un b.** *(en nageant)* to get a mouthful; *(professionnellement)* to come to grief; **b. cube** stock cube; **b. de culture** culture medium; **b. de légumes** vegetable stock
bouillonnant, -e [bujɔnɑ̃, -ɑ̃t] *adj* bubbling; *(torrent)* foaming; *Fig* **b. de colère** seething; *Fig* **b. de vie/ d'idées** bubbling over with life/ideas
bouillonner [bujɔne] *vi (eau, soupe, bain)* to bubble; *(torrent)* to foam; **b. de colère** to seethe with anger; **b. d'idées** to bubble over with ideas
bouillotte [bujɔt] *nf* hot-water bottle
boul. *abrév* boulevard
boulanger, -ère [bulɑ̃ʒe, -ɛr] *nm,f* baker
boulangerie [bulɑ̃ʒri] *nf (magasin)* baker's (shop); *(industrie)* bakery trade; **b.-pâtisserie** baker's and confectioner's (shop)
boule [bul] *nf* (**a**) *(sphère)* ball; *Fam (tête)* nut; **se rouler** *ou* **se mettre en b.** *(animal)* to roll up into a ball; *Fig* **se mettre en b.** *(en colère)* to fly off the handle; *Fam* **avoir la b. à zéro** to be a skinhead; *Fam* **avoir les boules** *(être énervé)* to be pissed off; *(être déprimé)* to be down in the dumps; *Fam* **foutre les boules à qn** *(faire peur à)* to put the wind up sb; *(énerver)* to upset sb; *Fam* **perdre la b.** to lose the plot; *Suisse* **b. de Berlin** doughnut; **b. à neige** *(objet décoratif)* snowdome, snowglobe; **b. de neige** snowball; *Fig* **faire b. de neige** to snowball; **c'est une b. de nerfs** he's/she's a bundle of nerves; **b. puante** stink bomb; **b. Quiès®** earplug (**b**) *(de pétanque, de bowling)* bowl; *(de billard)* ball; **jouer aux boules** to play bowls (**c**) *(de machine à écrire)* golf ball
bouleau, -x [bulo] *nm* (silver) birch; *(bois)* birch(-wood)
bouledogue [buldɔg] *nm* bulldog
bouler [bule] *vi Fam* **envoyer b. qn** to send sb packing
boulet [bulɛ] *nm* (**a**) *(projectile)* **b. (de canon)** cannonball; **passer comme un b. (de canon)** to hurtle past; **tirer à boulets rouges sur qn** to go for sb hammer and tongs (**b**) *(de bagnard)* ball and chain; *Fig* **c'est un b. qu'il traînera toute sa vie** it'll be a millstone round his neck all his life
boulette [bulɛt] *nf* (**a**) *(de papier, de pâte)* small ball (**b**) *Culin* meatball (**c**) *Fam (gaffe) Br* boob, *Am* booboo; **faire une b.** to blunder, to put one's foot in it
boulevard [bulvar] *nm* boulevard; **les Grands Boulevards** *(à Paris)* the main boulevards; **b. périphérique** *Br* ring road, *Am* beltway
bouleversant, -e [bulvɛrsɑ̃, -ɑ̃t] *adj (émouvant)* deeply moving; *(perturbant)* distressing
bouleversement [bulvɛrsəmɑ̃] *nm* (**a**) *(de projets, d'habitudes)* disruption; **bouleversements politiques/économiques** political/economic upheavals (**b**) *(d'une personne)* emotion
bouleverser [bulvɛrse] *vt* (**a**) *(projets, habitudes)* to disrupt; *(vie)* to turn upside down (**b**) *(émouvoir)* to move deeply; *(perturber)* to distress
boulier [bulje] *nm* abacus
boulimie [bulimi] *nf Méd* bulimia
boulimique [bulimik] *adj & nmf Méd* bulimic; **être b.** to be bulimic, to have bulimia
bouliste [bulist] *nmf* bowls player
boulocher [bulɔʃe] *vi (vêtement)* to pill
boulodrome [bulɔdrom] *nm* bowling alley
boulon [bulɔ̃] *nm* bolt
boulonner [bulɔne] **1** *vt* to bolt **2** *vi Fam (travailler)* to slog away
boulot¹, -otte [bulo, -ɔt] *adj Fam* tubby

boulot² [bulo] *Fam* **1** *nm (travail, lieu de travail)* work; *(emploi)* job; **allez, au b.!** come on, get to work!; **refaire les peintures dans une maison, c'est du b.** repaint a whole house is quite a job; *Fig* **faire le sale b.** to do the dirty work **2** *adj inv* **être b. b.** to be a workaholic
boum [bum] **1** *exclam* bang! **2** *nm Fam* (**a**) *(bruit)* bang (**b**) *(succès)* **le b. du multimédia/de l'informatique** the multimedia/computer boom; **en plein b.** in full swing **3** *nf Fam (fête)* party *(for teenagers)*
boumer [bume] *vi Fam Vieilli* **ça boume?** how's things?
bouquet¹ [bukɛ] *nm* (**a**) *(fleurs)* bunch of flowers; *(imposant)* bouquet; *(petit)* posy; *(d'arbres)* clump; **un b. de roses** a bunch/bouquet of roses; **le b. de la mariée** the bride's bouquet; *Culin* **b. garni** bouquet garni *(bunch of mixed herbs)* (**b**) *(d'un vin)* bouquet, nose (**c**) *(d'un feu d'artifice)* grand finale; *Fam Fig* **ça, c'est le b.!** that takes the *Br* biscuit *or Am* cake! (**d**) *TV* (multichannel) package; **b. numérique** digital package
bouquet² *nm (crevette)* prawn
bouquetin [buktɛ̃] *nm* ibex
bouquin [bukɛ̃] *nm Fam* book
bouquiner [bukine] *vi Fam* to read
bouquiniste [bukinist] *nmf* second-hand bookseller
bourbeux, -euse [burbø, -øz] *adj* muddy
bourbier [burbje] *nm aussi Fig* quagmire
bourbon [burbɔ̃] *nm (whisky)* bourbon
bourde [burd] *nf Fam* (**a**) *(balivernes)* fib (**b**) *(gaffe)* blunder; **faire une b.** to put one's foot in it
bourdon [burdɔ̃] *nm* (**a**) *(insecte)* bumblebee; *Fam* **avoir le b.** to be down (in the dumps) (**b**) *(cloche)* great bell (**c**) *Mus (de cornemuse)* drone; *(d'orgue)* bourdon stop
bourdonnement [burdɔnmɑ̃] *nm (d'insectes)* buzz(ing); *(de machine, de moteur)* hum(ming); **avoir des bourdonnements d'oreilles** to have a buzzing in one's ears
bourdonner [burdɔne] *vi (insectes, oreilles)* to buzz; *(machine, moteur)* to hum
bourg [bur] *nm* market town
bourgade [burgad] *nf* village
bourge [burʒ] *Fam* **1** *adj* (**a**) *(de la bourgeoisie)* upper-class, *Br* posh (**b**) *Péj* snobby **2** *nmf* (**a**) *(de la bourgeoisie)* upper-class person, *Br* toff (**b**) *Péj* snob
bourgeois, -e [burʒwa, -az] **1** *adj* (**a**) *(personne)* middle-class; **cuisine bourgeoise** home cooking (**b**) *Péj (conventionnel)* middle-class, bourgeois **2** *nm,f* (**a**) *(de la classe moyenne)* middle-class person; **les grands/petits b.** the upper/lower middle class (**b**) *Hist (roturier)* commoner (**c**) *Suisse (citoyen)* citizen
bourgeoisie [burʒwazi] *nf* middle class, bourgeoisie; **la haute/petite b.** the upper/lower middle class
bourgeon [burʒɔ̃] *nm* bud; **en bourgeons** in bud
bourgeonner [burʒɔne] *vi* (**a**) *(plante, arbre)* to bud (**b**) *Fam (avoir des boutons)* to come out in spots
bourgmestre [burgmɛstr] *nm* burgomaster
Bourgogne [burgɔɲ] **1** *nf* **la B.** Burgundy **2** *nm (vin)* Burgundy
bourguignon, -onne [burgiɲɔ̃, -ɔn] **1** *adj* Burgundian **2** *nm,f* **B.** Burgundian

bourlinguer [burlɛ̃ge] *vi (personne) (naviguer)* to sail the seven seas; *Fam (voyager)* to knock about, to bum around

bourrade [burad] *nf* push, shove

bourrasque [burask] *nf* squall, gust (of wind); **b. de neige** snow flurry; **souffler en bourrasques** to gust

bourratif, -ive [buratif, -iv] *adj Fam* stodgy

bourre [bur] *nf* (**a**) *(pour rembourrer)* stuffing, padding; *(de coton, de soie)* waste (**b**) *(des bourgeons)* down (**c**) *(d'arme à feu)* wad (**d**) *Fam* **de première b.** first-rate; **à la b.** in a rush

bourré, -e¹ [bure] *adj* (**a**) *(plein)* packed, crammed (**de** with); **b. à craquer** full to bursting; *Fam* **être b. de complexes** to be a mass of complexes; *Fam* **être b. de fric** to have pots of money (**b**) *très Fam (ivre) Br* pissed, *Am* wasted

bourreau, -x [buro] *nm* (**a**) *(exécuteur)* executioner; *(qui pend)* hangman; *(tortionnaire)* torturer (**b**) *Fig* tormentor; **b. des cœurs** ladykiller; **b. d'enfants** child-beater; *Hum* child tormentor; **b. de travail** workaholic

bourrée² [bure] *nf (danse)* bourrée

bourrée³ *nf Suisse* (**a**) *(grande affluence)* crowd (**b**) *(grande quantité)* **une b. de** masses of, loads of

bourrelé, -e [burle] *adj* **b. de remords** stricken with remorse

bourrelet [burlɛ] *nm* (**a**) *Fam* **b. (de graisse)** *(au ventre)* spare tyre (**b**) *(contre les courants d'air)* weather strip, *Br* draught excluder

bourrer [bure] **1** *vt* (**a**) *(chaise, coussin)* to stuff, to pad (**b**) *(placard, sac)* to cram (**de** with); *(pipe)* to fill; **ça bourre** *(aliment)* it's filling; **b. qn de qch** *(gaver)* to fill sb up with sth; **b. qn de coups** to beat sb up; *Fam* **b. le crâne à qn** *(élève)* to stuff sb's head with facts; *(politiquement)* to brainwash sb; *Fam* **b. le mou à qn** to pull the wool over sb's eyes

2 se bourrer *vpr* (**a**) **se b. de qch** *(se gaver)* to stuff oneself with sth (**b**) *très Fam* **se b. la gueule** to get *Br* pissed or *Am* wasted

bourriche [buriʃ] *nf (d'huîtres)* basket

bourrichon [buriʃɔ̃] *nm Fam* **se monter le b.** to get worked up

bourricot [buriko] *nm* (small) donkey

bourrin [burɛ̃] *nm Fam (cheval)* nag

bourrique [burik] *nf (ânesse)* she-ass; *Fam (personne têtue)* pigheaded person; **faire tourner qn en b.** to drive sb crazy

bourru, -e [bury] *adj* surly

bourse [burs] *nf* (**a**) *(porte-monnaie)* purse; **la b. ou la vie!** your money or your life!; **sans b. délier** without spending a penny; **faire b. commune** to pool one's money (**b**) *Scol & Univ* **b. (d'études)** grant (**c**) *Fin* **la B. (des valeurs)** the Stock Exchange, the Stock Market; **jouer à la B.** to play the market; **b. de commerce** commodities exchange (**d**) *Anat* **bourses** scrotum

boursicoter [bursikɔte] *vi* to dabble on the Stock Market

boursier, -ère [bursje, -ɛr] **1** *adj* (**a**) *Fin* Stock Exchange, Stock Market (**b**) *Scol & Univ* **étudiant b.** grant holder

2 *nm,f* (**a**) *Scol & Univ* grant holder (**b**) *Fin* (Stock Exchange) operator (**c**) *Suisse (trésorier)* treasurer

boursouflé, -e [bursufle] *adj (visage, yeux)* swollen, puffy; *(peinture)* blistered; *Fig (style, discours)* turgid

bous *voir* **bouillir**

bousculade [buskylad] *nf (agitation)* pushing and shoving; **être pris dans la b.** to be caught up in the rush

bousculer [buskyle] **1** *vt* (**a**) *(pousser)* to jostle; *Fig (habitudes)* to disrupt; *(préjugés)* to overturn (**b**) *(presser)* to rush

2 se bousculer *vpr (foule)* to push and shove; **les idées se bousculaient dans sa tête** his/her head was buzzing with ideas; *Fig* **les candidats ne se bousculent pas au portillon** applicants aren't exactly queuing up for the job

bouse [buz] *nf* **de la b. (de vache)** cow dung; **une b. a** cowpat

bouseux [buzø] *nm Fam Péj Br* yokel, *Am* hick

bousiller [buzije] *Fam* **1** *vt (voiture, appareil photo)* to wreck; *(travail)* to botch (up), to bungle

2 se bousiller *vpr* **se b. la santé** to ruin one's health

boussole [busɔl] *nf* compass; **s'orienter à la b.** to use a compass to get one's bearings; *Fam Fig* **perdre la b.** to lose the plot

boustifaille [bustifaj] *nf très Fam* grub

bout¹ [bu] *voir* **bouillir**

bout² [bu] *nm* (**a**) *(extrémité)* end; **b. à b.** end to end; **de b. en b., d'un b. à l'autre** *(dans l'espace)* from one end to the other; *(reprendre un travail, lire)* from start to finish; **à l'autre b., au b. du fil** *(au téléphone)* on the other end; *Fig* **je n'en vois pas le b.** I'm nowhere near the end of it; *Fig* **voir le b. du tunnel** to see the light at the end of the tunnel; **au b. de la rue** at the end of the street; **aller au b. du monde** to go to the ends of the earth; *Fig* **ce n'est pas le b. du monde** it's not exactly difficult; **au b. d'une heure/de quelques jours** after an hour/a few days (**b**) *(du doigt, du nez)* tip, end; *(d'une pipe)* mouthpiece; *(d'une chaussure)* toe; **b. filtre** *(d'une cigarette)* filter tip; **b. du sein** nipple (**c**) *(morceau)* bit; **elle en connaît un b. sur la question** she knows a thing or two about it; **faire un b. de chemin** to go part of the way; **un b. de temps** a little while; **ça fait un bon b. de temps que je ne l'ai pas vu** I haven't seen him for quite a while; *Fig* **b. de chou** little child; *Cin & TV* **b. d'essai** screen test (**d**) *(locutions)* **être à b.** *(épuisé)* to be exhausted; *(exaspéré)* to be at the end of one's patience; **pousser qn à b.** to push sb too far; **être à b. d'arguments** to have run out of arguments; **venir à b. de qch** *(travail)* to get through sth; *(obstacle)* to overcome sth; **à b. de bras** at arm's length; **Fig porter une entreprise à b. de bras** to carry a firm; **à b. portant** point-blank; **on ne sait jamais par quel b. le prendre** it's hard to know how to handle him; **avoir un mot sur le b. de la langue** to have a word on the tip of one's tongue; **tenir le bon b.** to be well on the way to success

boutade [butad] *nf (trait d'esprit)* quip

boute-en-train [butɑ̃trɛ̃] *nm inv* live wire

bouteille [butɛj] *nf* bottle; *(de gaz, d'oxygène)* cylinder; *(contenu)* bottle(ful); **c'est une bonne b.** it's a good bottle of wine; **mettre du vin en bouteilles** to bottle wine; *Fam* **prendre de la b.** to be getting long in the tooth

boutique [butik] *nf Br* shop, *Am* store; **fermer b.** to shut up shop; **parler b.** to talk shop; **b. hors taxes** duty-free shop; **b. (de mode)** fashion shop, boutique

boutiquier, -ère [butikje, -ɛr] *nm,f Br* shopkeeper, *Am* storekeeper

bouton [butɔ̃] *nm* (**a**) *(de fleur)* bud; **b. de rose** rosebud; **en b.** in bud (**b**) *(sur un vêtement)* button; *(de col)* stud; **boutons de manchette** cufflinks (**c**) *(de*

porte, de radio) knob; *(qu'on pousse)* & *Ordinat* button; *(interrupteur)* switch; *Ordinat* **b. de réinitialisation** reset button (**d**) *(sur le visage)* spot
bouton-d'or *(pl* **boutons-d'or)** [butɔ̃dɔr] *nm* buttercup
boutonnage [butɔnaʒ] *nm* buttoning (up); **veste à double b.** double-breasted jacket
boutonner [butɔne] **1** *vt (vêtement)* to button (up), to fasten (up)
  2 se boutonner *vpr (vêtement)* to button (up)
boutonneux, -euse [butɔnø, -øz] *adj* spotty
boutonnière [butɔnjɛr] *nf (de vêtement)* buttonhole; **porter une fleur à la b.** to wear a *Br* buttonhole *orAm* boutonnière
bouton-pression *(pl* **boutons-pression)** [butɔ̃presjɔ̃] *nm Br* press stud, *Am* snap fastener
bouture [butyr] *nf* cutting; **faire des boutures** to take cuttings
bouturer [butyre] *vt* to propagate by cuttings
bouvier, -ère [buvje, -ɛr] **1** *nm,f* cowherd
  2 *nm (chien)* sheepdog
bouvreuil [buvrœj] *nm* bullfinch
bovin, -e [bɔvɛ̃, -in] **1** *adj aussi Fig* bovine
  2 *nm Zool* bovine
bowling [buliŋ] *nm* (**a**) *(jeu)* (tenpin) bowling (**b**) *(lieu)* (tenpin) bowling alley
box *(pl* **boxes)** [bɔks] *nm (dans un dortoir, un bureau)* cubicle; *(dans une écurie)* stall; *(garage)* lock-up (garage); *Jur* **b. des accusés** dock
boxe [bɔks] *nf* boxing; **faire de la b.** to box; **b. anglaise** boxing; **b. française** kick boxing
boxer¹ [bɔkse] **1** *vi* to box
  2 *vt Fam (frapper)* to punch up
boxer² [bɔksɛr] *nm (chien)* boxer
boxeur [bɔksœr] *nm* boxer
box-office *(pl* **box-offices)** [bɔksɔfis] *nm* box office; **être en tête du b.** to be a box-office hit
boyau, -x [bwajo] *nm* (**a**) *(d'animal)* gut; *(corde)* (cat)gut (**b**) *(de vélo)* tubular tyre (**c**) *(allée)* narrow alleyway; *(de mine)* narrow gallery; *Mil* communication trench
boycott(age) [bɔjkɔt(aʒ)] *nm* boycott(ing)
boycotter [bɔjkɔte] *vt* to boycott
boys band [bɔjzbãd] *nm* boy band
boy-scout *(pl* **boy-scouts)** [bɔjskut] *nm Vieilli* boy scout; *Fig* **mentalité de b.** boy-scout mentality
BP [bepe] *nf (abrév* **boîte postale)** PO Box
bracelet [braslɛ] *nm* (**a**) *(bijou)* bracelet; *(rigide)* bangle; *(de montre)* strap (**b**) *(élastique)* rubber *or* elastic band
bracelet-montre *(pl* **bracelets-montres)** [braslɛmɔ̃tr] *nm* wristwatch
braconnage [brakɔnaʒ] *nm* poaching
braconner [brakɔne] *vi* to poach
braconnier [brakɔnje] *nm* poacher
bradé, -e [brade] *adj (soldé)* cut-price
brader [brade] *vt (solder)* to sell off
braderie [bradri] *nf (liquidation)* clearance sale; *(vente par des particuliers) Br* ≃ car boot sale, *Am* ≃ garage sale; *(magasin)* discount store
braguette [bragɛt] *nf Br* flies, *Am* fly
braille [braj] *nm* Braille; **lire en b.** to read Braille
braillements [brajmã] *nmpl* yelling; *(d'enfant)* howling
brailler [braje] **1** *vi* to yell; *(enfant)* to howl
  2 *vt (chanson)* to bawl out; *(slogan)* to chant
braire [28] [brɛr] *vi (âne)* to bray; *Fam Fig* to yell

braise [brɛz] *nf (charbons)* (glowing) embers; **des yeux de b.** glowing eyes
braiser [brɛze] *vt Culin* to braise
bramer [brame] *vi (cerf)* to bell; *Fig (hurler)* to howl
brancard [brɑ̃kar] *nm* (**a**) *(d'une civière, d'une charrette)* shaft; *Fig* **ruer dans les brancards** to kick over the traces (**b**) *(civière)* stretcher
brancardier, -ère [brɑ̃kardje, -ɛr] *nm,f* stretcher bearer
branchage [brɑ̃ʃaʒ] *nm (des arbres)* branches; **branchages** *(coupés)* cut branches
branche [brɑ̃ʃ] *nf* (**a**) *(d'un arbre)* branch; *(de céleri)* stick; *Fig (de l'industrie, de la science, d'une famille)* branch; *(professionnelle)* line of business; **la b. maternelle** the mother's side; *Fam* **vieille b.** old stick (**b**) *(d'un compas)* leg; *(de lunettes)* side piece; *(d'un chandelier)* branch (**c**) *Suisse Univ (matière)* subject
branché, -e [brɑ̃ʃe] *adj Fam (à la mode)* trendy, hip; **il est b. tennis/techno** he's really into tennis/techno music
branchement [brɑ̃ʃmã] *nm (sur un réseau)* connecting (up) (**sur** to); *(à une prise)* plugging in; *(assemblage de fils)* connection
brancher [brɑ̃ʃe] **1** *vt* (**a**) *(à un réseau)* to connect (up) (**sur** to); *(à une prise)* to plug in; *Fig* **b. qn sur un sujet** to get sb onto a subject (**b**) *Fam (plaire à)* **l'art moderne, ça ne me branche pas tellement** I'm not really into modern art; **on se fait un resto ce soir, ça te branche?** fancy going out for a meal tonight?
  2 se brancher *vpr* (**a**) *(appareil électrique)* to plug in (**b**) *Can Fam (se décider)* to decide, to make up one's mind (**c**) **se b. sur** *(une station de radio)* to tune in to
branchie [brɑ̃ʃi] *nf* gill
brandade [brɑ̃dad] *nf Culin* **b. (de morue)** = salt cod puréed with garlic, oil and cream
brandebourg [brɑ̃dbur] *nm* frog *(on uniform)*
brandir [brɑ̃dir] *vt* to brandish
brandy [brɑ̃di] *nm* brandy
branlant, -e [brɑ̃lã, -ãt] *adj (dent)* loose; *(chaise, escalier)* rickety
branle [brɑ̃l] *nm* **mettre qch en b.** *(processus)* to set sth in motion; **se mettre en b.** *(partir)* to get moving; *(entrer en fonctionnement)* to get going
branle-bas [brɑ̃lba] *nm inv* **b.** *(de combat) (agitation)* commotion
branlée [brɑ̃le] *nf Fam* thrashing; **prendre** *ou* **recevoir une b.** to get a thrashing
branler [brɑ̃le] **1** *vt Vulg (masturber)* to jerk off, *Br* to wank; *Fig* **mais qu'est-ce qu'il branle** what the hell's he up to?
  2 *vi (dent)* to be loose; *(chaise, escalier)* to be rickety
  3 se branler *vpr Vulg (se masturber)* to jerk off, *Br* to wank; *Fig* **je m'en branle!** I don't give a shit!
branleur, -euse¹ [brɑ̃lœr, -øz] *nm,f Vulg (bon à rien)* jerk, *Br* wanker
branleux, -euse² [brɑ̃lø, øz] *adj Can Fam (qui hésite)* dithering; *(lâche)* cowardly
branque [brɑ̃k] *Fam* **1** *adj* nuts, *Br* bonkers
  2 *nmf (imbécile)* dope, jerk; *(fou)* headcase, *Br* nutter
braquage [brakaʒ] *nm* (**a**) *Aut (des roues)* turning; **(angle de) b.** *Fam (vol)* steering lock (**b**) *Fam (vol)* hold-up; **faire un b.** to do a hold-up
braque [brak] *nm (chien)* pointer
braquer [brake] **1** *vt* (**a**) *(diriger)* to point (**sur** at); *(regard)* to fix (**sur** on) (**b**) *(rendre hostile)* **b. qn contre qn/qch** to turn sb against sb/sth (**c**) *Fam (banque)* to hold up

2 *vi Aut* to turn the (steering) wheel; **b. à fond** to apply full lock; **voiture qui braque mal** car that has a poor lock
3 se braquer *vpr* to dig one's heels in; **se b. contre qn** to set one's face against sb
braquet [brakɛ] *nm* gear ratio; **changer de b.** to change gear
bras [bra] *nm* (**a**) *(membre)* arm; **donner le b. à qn** to give sb one's arm; **un panier au b.** with a basket on one's arm; **les b. croisés** with one's arms folded; *Fig* **rester les b. croisés** *(être passif)* to stand by with one's arms folded; **b. dessus, b. dessous** arm in arm; **être le b. droit de qn** to be sb's right-hand man/woman; **accueillir qn à b. ouverts** to welcome sb with open arms; *Fam* **tomber sur qn à b. raccourcis** to lay into sb; *Fig* **avoir le b. long** to have a lot of influence; *Fig* **avoir qn/qch sur les b.** to have sb/sth on one's hands; **les b. m'en tombent!** I'm flabbergasted!; **en b. de chemise** in (one's) shirtsleeves; **une partie de b. de fer** an arm-wrestling match; *Fig* **un b. de fer entre la direction et les syndicats** a trial of strength between the management and the unions; **faire un b. d'honneur à qn** ≃ to stick two fingers up at sb (**b**) *(d'un fauteuil, d'un levier, d'une ancre)* arm; *(d'une grue)* jib; *(d'une croix)* limb; *Can* **b. d'escalier** banister; **b. de lecture** pickup arm; *Can* **b. de vitesse** *Br* gear lever, *Am* stick shift (**c**) *(de fleuve)* arm; **b. de mer** arm of the sea
brasero [brazero] *nm* brazier
brasier [brazje] *nm (incendie)* blaze, inferno
Brasilia [brazilja] *n* Brasilia
bras-le-corps [brɑlkɔr] **à bras-le-corps** *adv* **saisir qn à b.** to seize sb round the waist; **prendre un problème à b.** to get to grips with a problem
brassage [brasaʒ] *nm* (**a**) *(de la bière)* brewing (**b**) *(mélange)* mixing
brassard [brasar] *nm* armband; **b. de deuil** black armband
brasse [bras] *nf Sport (style)* breaststroke; *(mouvement)* stroke; **nager la b.** to swim breaststroke; **b. coulée** = breaststroke in which face is submerged; **b. papillon** butterfly (stroke)
brassée [brase] *nf* armful
brasser [brase] *vt* (**a**) *(bière)* to brew (**b**) *(mélanger)* to mix; *Fig* **b. de l'argent** to handle large amounts of money; **b. de l'air** *ou* **du vent** to work without getting anything done
brasserie [brasri] *nf* (**a**) *(fabrique)* brewery; *(industrie)* brewing (**b**) *(restaurant)* brasserie
brasseur, -euse [brasœr, -øz] *nm,f* (**a**) *(fabricant de bière)* brewer (**b**) *Fig* **b. d'affaires** big businessman
brassière [brasjɛr] *nf* (**a**) *(de bébé) Br* vest, *Am* undershirt (**b**) *Can (soutien-gorge)* bra
Bratislava [bratislava] *n* Bratislava
bravade [bravad] *nf* bravado; **par b.** out of bravado
brave [brav] **1** *adj* (**a**) *(courageux)* brave, courageous (**b**) *(bon)* good; **de braves gens** good people (**c**) *Péj* **il est bien b.** *(pas futé)* he means well
2 *nm* (**a**) *(héros)* brave man (**b**) *Vieilli* **mon b.** my good man
bravement [bravmɑ̃] *adv* (**a**) *(courageusement)* bravely, courageously (**b**) *(avec résolution)* boldly
braver [brave] *vt (mort, danger)* to brave; *(personne, lois, règlements)* to defy
bravo [bravo] **1** *exclam* bravo!; *(dans un débat)* hear, hear!; *Ironique* well done!

2 *nm* **un grand b. à toute l'équipe technique** a big hand for all the technical crew; **des bravos** cheers
bravoure [bravur] *nf* bravery, courage
Brazzaville [brazavil] *n* Brazzaville
break¹ [brɛk] *nm (voiture) Br* estate car, *Am* station wagon
break² *nm (pause) & Sport* break
brebis [brəbi] *nf* (**a**) *(animal)* ewe; *Fig* **b. galeuse** black sheep (**b**) *Rel* sheep
brèche [brɛʃ] *nf (dans un mur, une haie)* gap; *(dans la coque d'un bateau)* hole; *Mil* breach; *Fig* **être toujours sur la b.** to be always on the go; **battre qch en b.** to demolish sth
bréchet [breʃɛ] *nm* breastbone
bredouille [brəduj] *adj* empty-handed
bredouiller [brəduje] *vt & vi* to mumble, to mutter
bref, -ève [brɛf, brɛv] **1** *adj* brief, short; *Ling (voyelle)* short; **soyez b.!** be brief!
2 *adv* in short; **une cousine ou une tante, enfin b., quelqu'un de sa famille** a cousin or an aunt, well anyway, one of his/her relatives; **l'actualité en b.** the news in brief
3 *nf* **brève** *(nouvelle)* short news item
brelan [brəlɑ̃] *nm* three of a kind; **b. d'as** three aces
breloque [brələk] *nf (sur un bracelet)* charm
brème [brɛm] *nf* bream
Brême [brɛm] *n* Bremen
Brésil [brezil] *nm* **le B.** Brazil
brésilien, -enne [brezìljɛ̃, -ɛn] **1** *adj* Brazilian
2 *nm,f* **B.** Brazilian
Bretagne [brətaɲ] *nf* **la B.** Brittany
bretelle [brətɛl] *nf* (**a**) *(de soutien-gorge, de robe)* (shoulder) strap; **(paire de) bretelles** *(pour pantalon)* (pair of) *Br* braces *or Am* suspenders (**b**) *(lanière)* strap; *(de fusil)* sling (**c**) *(route)* **b. (d'accès)** access road; **b. (d'autoroute)** *Br* (motorway) slip road, *Am* (highway) access road
breton, -onne [brətɔ̃, -ɔn] **1** *adj* Breton
2 *nm,f* **B.** Breton
3 *nm (langue)* Breton

Breton

Breton belongs to the Celtic family of languages along with Welsh and Gaelic. For generations it was banned in favour of French, but has come back into favour in recent decades with the revival of the Celtic identity and culture. However, despite efforts to promote its use, Breton is still spoken principally by the older generations of Western Brittany.

bretzel [brɛdzɛl] *nm* pretzel
breuvage [brœvaʒ] *nm (potion)* potion; *Hum (boisson)* concoction
brève [brɛv] *voir* bref
brevet [brəvɛ] *nm (certificat)* certificate; *(diplôme)* diploma; *Scol* **b. (des collèges)** = general exam taken at fifteen; **b. d'études professionnelles** = vocational diploma; **b. (d'invention)** patent; **b. de pilote** *Aviat* pilot's licence; *Mil* wings; **b. de technicien supérieur** = advanced vocational training certificate
breveter [brəvte] *vt (invention)* to patent; **faire b. qch** to take out a patent on sth
bréviaire [brevjɛr] *nm Rel* breviary
briard [brijar] *nm (chien)* Briard
bribes [brib] *nfpl* **b. de conversation** snatches of conversation; **des b. de finlandais** a few scraps of Finnish

bric-à-brac [brikabrak] *nm inv (vieux objets)* odds and ends, bric-à-brac; *(mélange)* jumble (**de** of); (**boutique de**) **b.** second-hand shop

bric et de broc [brikedəbrɔk] **de bric et de broc** *adv* haphazardly

brick [brik] *nm (carton)* carton

bricolage [brikɔlaʒ] *nm* (**a**) *(travail)* do-it-yourself, *Br* DIY; **faire du b.** to do some DIY (**b**) *Péj (réparation)* botch-up

bricole [brikɔl] *nf (objet)* trinket; *(chose sans importance)* trifle; *Fam* **il va lui arriver des bricoles** he's/she's going to get into a pickle

bricoler [brikɔle] **1** *vt (construire)* to put together; *(réparer)* to tinker with
  2 *vi* to do do-it-yourself *or Br* DIY; **j'ai passé la matinée à b. dans la maison** I spent the morning doing odd jobs about the house

bricoleur, -euse [brikɔlœr, -øz] **1** *adj* **être b.** to be good with one's hands
  2 *nm,f* handyman, *f* handywoman

bride [brid] *nf* (**a**) *(de harnais)* bridle; *Fig* **lâcher la b. à qn** to give sb his/her head; *Fig* **avoir la b. sur le cou** to have a free rein; **aller à b. abattue** to ride full tilt (**b**) *(de boutonnière)* bar

bridé, -e [bride] *adj (yeux)* slanting

brider [bride] *vt (cheval)* to bridle; *(personne, passions, impulsion)* to curb, to restrain

bridge [bridʒ] *nm (jeu, prothèse)* bridge

brie [bri] *nm* Brie

brièvement [brievmɑ̃] *adv* briefly

brièveté [brievte] *nf* brevity, briefness

brigade [brigad] *nf* (**a**) *Mil* brigade; *(de police, de gendarmerie)* squad; **b. antigang** organized crime squad; *Hist* **les Brigades internationales** the International Brigades; **b. des stupéfiants** *ou Fam* **des stups** drug squad (**b**) *(d'ouvriers)* team

brigadier [brigadje] *nm* (**a**) *Mil* corporal; *(d'artillerie)* bombardier (**b**) **b.** (**de police**) (police) sergeant

brigand [brigɑ̃] *nm (bandit)* brigand; *(personne malhonnête)* crook; **petit b.!** *(enfant)* little rascal! or rogue!

briguer [brige] *vt (honneur, poste)* to solicit

brillamment [brijamɑ̃] *adv* brilliantly

brillant, -e [brijɑ̃, -ɑ̃t] **1** *adj* (**a**) *(lumière, couleur)* bright, brilliant; *(pierre précieuse)* sparkling; *(cheveux, chaussures, cuir)* shiny; **les yeux brillants de fièvre** eyes bright with fever (**b**) *(carrière, élève, avenir)* brilliant; *(conversation)* sparkling
  2 *nm* (**a**) *(d'un métal)* brilliance, brightness; *(d'une pierre précieuse)* sparkle; *(d'un papier, d'un tissu, de cheveux)* shininess (**b**) *(diamant)* brilliant (**c**) **b. à lèvres** lip gloss

brillantine [brijɑ̃tin] *nf* brilliantine

briller [brije] *vi* (**a**) *(soleil, étoiles, yeux)* to shine; *(bougie)* to glimmer; *(pierre précieuse)* to sparkle; *(eau, satin)* to shimmer; *(braises)* to glow; **faire b. ses chaussures** to shine or polish one's shoes; **des yeux qui brillent de colère/de joie** eyes shining with anger/happiness; **b. de mille feux** to sparkle brilliantly; *Prov* **tout ce qui brille n'est pas or** all that glitters is not gold (**b**) *(exceller)* to shine; **b. par son absence** to be conspicuous by one's absence; **elle ne brille pas par sa ponctualité** she's not noted for her punctuality

brimade [brimad] *nf* instance of bullying; **faire subir des brimades à qn** to bully sb

brimbaler [brɛ̃bale] = **bringuebaler**

brimer [brime] *vt* to bully; **se sentir brimé** to feel victimized

brin [brɛ̃] **1** *nm* (**a**) *(de persil, de romarin)* sprig; *(de mimosa, de muguet)* spray; *(de paille)* wisp; **un b. d'herbe** a blade of grass (**b**) *Fam (petite quantité)* **un b. de qch** a bit of sth; **un b. d'ironie/de jalousie** a touch of irony/jealousy; **faire un b. de toilette** to have a quick wash (and brush-up); **un beau b. de fille** a fine-looking girl (**c**) *(de laine, corde, fil)* strand
  2 *adv Fam* **un b.** *(un peu)* a bit

brindille [brɛ̃dij] *nf* twig

bringue¹ [brɛ̃g] *nf Fam* **grande b.** *(fille)* beanpole

bringue² *nf Fam (fête)* binge; **faire la b.** to go on a binge

bringue³ *nf Suisse* (**a**) *(querelle)* row (**b**) *(rengaine)* refrain

bringuebaler [brɛ̃gbale], **brinquebaler** [brɛ̃kbale] *vt & vi Fam* to shake about

brio [brijo] *nm* brilliance; **avec b.** brilliantly

brioche [brijɔʃ] *nf* brioche; *Fam Fig* **avoir/prendre de la b.** to have/develop a paunch

brioché, -e [brijɔʃe] *adj* **pain b.** milk bread

brique [brik] **1** *nf* (**a**) *(de construction)* brick; **mur de ou en briques** brick wall (**b**) *Anciennement très Fam (10 000 francs)* 10,000 francs
  2 *adj inv* (**rouge**) **b.** brick-red

briquer [brike] *vt* (**a**) *(nettoyer)* to scrub down; *(pont de navire)* to holystone (**b**) *Suisse (briser)* to break, to smash

briquet [brikɛ] *nm* (cigarette) lighter

briqueterie [brikɛtri] *nf* brickyard

briquette [brikɛt] *nf* (**a**) *(petite brique)* small brick (**b**) *(de jus de fruit)* small carton (**c**) *(de charbon)* briquette

bris [bri] *nm (de verre, de scellés)* breaking; **b. de glaces** broken windows

brisant [brizɑ̃] *nm (écueil)* reef; **brisants** *(vagues)* breakers

brise [briz] *nf* breeze; *Naut* **forte b.** stiff breeze

brise-glace [brizglas] *nm inv* (**a**) *(navire)* ice breaker (**b**) *(d'une pile de pont)* ice breaker; *(d'un navire)* ice beam

brise-lames [brizlam] *nm inv* breakwater

briser [brize] **1** *vt (casser)* to break; *(opposition, résistance, espérances)* to crush; *(carrière)* to wreck; *(grève)* to break; **b. qn** *(sujet: effort, marche)* to shatter sb; **brisé par la douleur** crushed by grief; **la voix brisée par l'émotion** his/her voice choked with emotion; **cela me brise le cœur** it breaks my heart
  2 **se briser** *vpr (vagues, porcelaine, verre)* to break; *(voix)* to break; *Fig (espoirs)* to be shattered

brise-tout [briztu] *nmf inv* clumsy person *(who is always breaking things)*

briseur, -euse [brizœr, -øz] *nm,f* **b. de grève** strike breaker

brise-vent [brizvɑ̃] *nm inv* windbreak

bristol [bristɔl] *nm* Bristol board; *(carte de visite)* visiting card

britannique [britanik] **1** *adj* British; **les îles Britanniques** the British Isles
  2 *nmf* **B.** Briton; **les Britanniques** the British

broc [bro] *nm* pitcher, jug

brocante [brɔkɑ̃t] *nf (commerce)* secondhand trade; *(magasin)* secondhand shop; *(marché aux puces)* secondhand market

brocanteur, -euse [brɔkɑ̃tœr, -øz] *nm,f* secondhand dealer

brocarder [brɔkarde] *vt Litt* to gibe at
brocart [brɔkar] *nm* brocade
broche [brɔʃ] *nf* (**a**) *(pour rôtir)* spit; **faire cuire qch à la b.** to spit-roast sth (**b**) *(bijou)* brooch (**c**) *Tech, Élec & Méd* pin
brocher [brɔʃe] *vt* (**a**) *(livre)* to stitch (**b**) *(tissu)* to brocade
brochet [brɔʃɛ] *nm* pike
brochette [brɔʃɛt] *nf (broche)* skewer; *(plat)* kebab
brochure [brɔʃyr] *nf* brochure, pamphlet
brocoli [brɔkɔli] *nm* broccoli; **des brocolis** broccoli
brodequin [brɔdkɛ̃] *nm* laced boot
broder [brɔde] *vt & vi aussi Fig* to embroider
broderie [brɔdri] *nf* (**a**) *(ouvrage)* piece of embroidery; **broderies** embroidery; **b. anglaise** broderie anglaise (**b**) *(activité)* embroidery
broie *voir* **broyer**
bromure [brɔmyr] *nm* bromide
bronche [brɔ̃ʃ] *nf* bronchial tube; **être fragile des bronches** to have a weak chest
broncher [brɔ̃ʃe] *vi* (**a**) *(réagir)* **sans b.** without batting an eyelid; **il n'a pas bronché** he didn't bat an eyelid (**b**) *(cheval)* to stumble
bronchite [brɔ̃ʃit] *nf* bronchitis; **avoir une b.** to have bronchitis
broncho-pneumonie *(pl* **broncho-pneumonies)** [brɔ̃kopnømɔni] *nf Méd* bronchopneumonia
bronzage [brɔ̃zaʒ] *nm (activité)* tanning; *(hâle)* (sun)tan; **b. intégral** all-over tan
bronze [brɔ̃z] *nm (métal, objet d'art)* bronze
bronzé, -e [brɔ̃ze] *adj (peau)* (sun)tanned; *Euph ou Péj (personne)* coloured
bronzer [brɔ̃ze] *vi (personne)* to go brown, to tan
bronzette [brɔ̃zɛt] *nf Fam* sunbathing; **faire b.** to do a bit of sunbathing, to catch some rays
brosse [brɔs] *nf* (**a**) *(ustensile)* brush; **donner un coup de b. à qch** to give sth a brush; **donner un coup de b. à qn** *(coiffer)* to give sb's hair a brush; **avoir les cheveux en b.** to have a crew cut; *Can Fam* **être en b.** to be *Br* pissed *or Am* wasted; *Fig* **manier la b. à reluire** to bow and scrape; **b. à cheveux** hairbrush; **b. à dents** toothbrush; **b. à habits** clothes brush; **b. à ongles** nailbrush (**b**) *(pinceau large)* (paint)brush
brosser [brɔse] **1** *vt* (**a**) *(tapis, manteau, cheveux)* to brush; *(sol)* to scrub; *(cheval)* to brush down; *Belg* **b. un cours** *Br* to skive off, *Am* to cut a class (**b**) *(décrire)* **b. un tableau optimiste de la situation** to paint an optimistic picture of the situation
  2 se brosser *vpr (se nettoyer)* to brush oneself down; **se b. les dents/les cheveux** to brush one's teeth/one's hair; *Fam* **tu peux toujours te b.!** not a chance!
brou [bru] *nm* (**a**) *(enveloppe)* husk, *Am* shuck (**b**) *(teinture)* **b. de noix** walnut stain
broue [bru] *nf Can* froth; *très Fam Fig* **faire** *ou* **péter de la b.** to talk big
brouette [bruɛt] *nf* wheelbarrow
brouhaha [bruaa] *nm* hubbub
brouillard [brujar] *nm* fog; **il y a du b.** it's foggy; *Fig* **être dans le b.** to be in a fog; **b. givrant** freezing fog
brouille [bruj] *nf* quarrel, disagreement
brouillé, -e [bruje] *adj* (**a**) *(teint)* blotchy (**b**) **être b. avec qn** to have fallen out with sb; **être b. avec les dates/la grammaire** to be hopeless at dates/grammar
brouiller [bruje] **1** *vt* (**a**) *(rendre trouble) (idées)* to muddle up; *(vue)* to blur; **yeux brouillés de larmes** eyes blurred with tears; *Fig* **b. les cartes** to confuse

the issue; *Fig* **b. les pistes** to cover one's tracks (**b**) *(fâcher)* **b. qn avec qn** to set sb against sb (**c**) *Rad & Élec (accidentellement)* to cause interference to; *(intentionnellement)* to jam
  2 se brouiller *vpr* (**a**) *(idées, dates)* to get muddled up (**b**) *(vue)* to get blurred (**c**) *(se détériorer)* **le temps se brouille** it's clouding over (**d**) *(se disputer)* to fall out *(avec qn* with sb)
brouillon, -onne [brujɔ̃, -ɔn] **1** *adj (mal organisé)* disorganized, unmethodical; *(mal présenté)* untidy
  2 *nm (ébauche)* (rough) draft; **(papier) b.** *Br* scrap *or Am* scratch paper; **faire un exercice au b.** to do an exercise in rough; **(cahier de) b.** rough book; *Ordinat* **version b.** draft version
broussaille [brusɑj] *nf* **broussailles** scrub; **en b.** *(cheveux)* tousled; *(sourcils)* bushy
broussailleux, -euse [brusɑjø, -øz] *adj (terrain)* scrubby; *(cheveux)* tousled; *(sourcils)* bushy
brousse [brus] *nf* **la b.** the bush
brouter [brute] **1** *vt (herbe)* to graze
  2 *vi* (**a**) *(animal)* to graze (**b**) *(embrayage)* to judder
broutille [brutij] *nf* trifle
broyer [32] [brwaje] *vt (pierre, aliments, couleurs)* to grind; *(membre, main, personne)* to crush; *Fig* **b. du noir** to be down in the dumps
broyeur, -euse [brwajœr, -øz] **1** *adj (appareil)* grinding
  2 *nm (machine)* grinder; **b. à ordures** *Br* waste *or Am* garbage disposal unit
bru [bry] *nf* daughter-in-law
brugnon [brynɔ̃] *nm* nectarine
bruine [brɥin] *nf* drizzle
bruiner [brɥine] *v impersonnel* to drizzle
bruire [brɥir] *vi Litt (feuilles, étoffe)* to rustle; *(ruisseau, vent)* to murmur
bruissement [brɥismɑ̃] *nm (des feuilles, d'une étoffe)* rustle, rustling; *(d'un ruisseau, du vent)* murmur(ing)
bruit [brɥi] *nm* (**a**) *(son)* sound, noise; **b. de pas** (sound of) footsteps; **des bruits de voix** the sound of voices; **sans b.** without a sound (**b**) *(vacarme)* noise; **faire du b.** *(être bruyant)* to make a noise; *Fig (affaire, histoire)* to cause a sensation; **b. de fond** background noise; **beaucoup de b. pour rien** a lot of fuss over nothing (**c**) *(rumeur)* rumour; **faire courir un b.** to spread a rumour; **le b. court que...** the rumour has it that...
bruitage [brɥitaʒ] *nm* sound effects
bruiteur, -euse [brɥitœr, -øz] *nm,f* sound-effects man, *f* sound-effects woman
brûlant, -e [brylɑ̃, -ɑ̃t] *adj (plat, casserole)* red-hot; *(café)* boiling (hot); *(soleil)* scorching; *Fig* **b. de désir** burning with desire; **question brûlante** burning question; **le sujet est d'une actualité brûlante** it's one of the burning issues of the day
brûlé, -e [bryle] **1** *nm,f (accidenté)* burns victim; *Méd* **les grands brûlés** people with third-degree burns
  2 *nm* **sentir le b.** to smell burnt; **une odeur de b.** a burnt smell; **avoir un goût de b.** to taste burnt
brûle-parfum *(pl* **brûle-parfums)** [brylparfœ̃] *nm* perfume burner
brûle-pourpoint [brylpurpwɛ̃] **à brûle-pourpoint** *adv* point-blank
brûler [bryle] **1** *vt* (**a**) *(sujet: flamme, acide)* to burn; *(sujet: eau bouillante)* to scald; *(sujet: fer à repasser)* to scorch; *(café)* to roast; **gazon brûlé par le soleil** lawn scorched by the sun; **être brûlé vif** *(dans un accident)* to be burnt alive; *(être supplicié)* to be burnt at

the stake; **l'argent lui brûle les doigts** money burns a hole in his/her pocket (**b**) *(consommer) (électricité, combustible)* to use; *(calories)* to burn (**c**) **b. un feu rouge** to go through a red light; **b. un stop** to go straight past a stop sign
2 *vi* (**a**) *(flamber, être carbonisé)* to burn; *(être très chaud)* to be red-hot; *(liquide)* to be boiling (hot); *(blessure)* to smart; **attention, ça brûle!** careful, it's hot!; **tu brûles** *(dans un jeu)* you're getting hot (**b**) *Fig* **b. de faire qch** to be burning to do sth; **b. d'impatience** to be bursting with impatience; **b. de désir** to be burning with desire
3 se brûler *vpr (par accident)* to burn oneself (**avec** on); **se b. la langue/la main** to burn one's tongue/hand
brûleur [brylœr] *nm* burner
brûlot [brylo] *nm* (**a**) *(article polémique)* scathing article (**b**) *Can (moustique)* gnat, midge
brûlure [brylyr] *nf (blessure)* burn; *(sensation)* burning; **b. de cigarette** cigarette burn; **brûlures d'estomac** heartburn
brume [brym] *nf* mist, haze; **b. de chaleur** heat haze
brumeux, -euse [brymø, -øz] *adj* misty, hazy; *Fig (idées, explication)* hazy
Brumisateur® [brymizatœr] *nm* spray containing Evian® mineral water
brun, -e [brœ̃, bryn] **1** *adj (cheveux)* dark, brown; *(peau, personne) (naturellement)* dark; *(bronzé)* brown; **être b. de peau** to be dark-skinned; *Can* **il fait b.** it's getting dark
2 *nm,f (personne)* dark-haired man, *f* dark-haired woman
3 *nm (couleur)* brown
4 *nf* **brune** (**a**) *(bière)* brown ale (**b**) *(cigarette)* brown tobacco cigarette (**c**) *Litt* **à la brune** at dusk
brunante [brynɑ̃t] *nf Can* dusk
brunâtre [brynɑtr] *adj* brownish
brunch [brœntʃ] *nm* brunch
bruncher [brœntʃe] *vi* to have brunch
Brunei [brynei] *nm* **le B.** Brunei
brunir [brynir] *vi (peau, personne)* to tan; *(cheveux)* to darken
brushing® [brœʃiŋ] *nm* blow-dry; **se faire faire un b.** to have a blow-dry
brusque [brysk] *adj* abrupt
brusquement [bryskəmɑ̃] *adv* abruptly
brusquer [bryske] *vt* (**a**) **b. qn** *(être impoli envers)* to be abrupt with sb; *(maltraiter)* to treat sb harshly (**b**) *(hâter) (décision)* to rush; **il ne faut rien b.** we mustn't rush things
brusquerie [bryskəri] *nf* abruptness; **avec b.** abruptly
brut, -e¹ [bryt] **1** *adj* (**a**) *(pétrole, minerai)* crude; *(sucre)* unrefined; *(pierre précieuse)* uncut; *(champagne)* extra-dry; *(cidre)* dry; **à l'état b.** in its raw state (**b**) *(bénéfice, poids, salaire)* gross
2 *nm* (**a**) *(pétrole)* crude (oil); **b. léger** light crude (**b**) *(champagne)* extra-dry champagne
3 *adv* gross
brutal, -e, -aux, -ales [brytal, -o] *adj* (**a**) *(personne, paroles, manières)* brutal; *(choc)* violent; **être b. avec qn** to be rough with sb (**b**) *(changement)* abrupt
brutalement [brytalmɑ̃] *adv (violemment)* brutally; *(avec brusquerie)* roughly; *(soudainement)* abruptly
brutaliser [brytalize] *vt* to ill-treat
brutalité [brytalite] *nf (violence, brusquerie)* brutality; *(soudaineté)* abruptness; **brutalités** brutality

brute² [bryt] *nf (personne violente)* brute; *(personne grossière)* boor; **taper sur qch comme une b.** to bang at sth like a madman; **une b. épaisse** a great brute; **grosse b.!** you big brute!
Bruxelles [brysɛl, bryksɛl] *n* Brussels
bruxellois, -e [brysɛlwa, -az, bryksɛlwa, -az] **1** *adj* of Brussels
2 *nm,f* **B.** person from Brussels
bruyamment [brɥijamɑ̃] *adv (parler, rire)* loudly; *(manger)* noisily
bruyant, -e [brɥijɑ̃, -ɑ̃t] *adj (rue, voisin)* noisy; *(rire, applaudissements)* loud
bruyère [bryjɛr] *nf (plante)* heather; *(terre)* heath; **pipe de b.** briar pipe; **terre de b.** peat
BTP [betepe] *nm (abrév* **bâtiment et travaux publics***)* = building and public works sector
BTS [beteɛs] *nm (abrév* **brevet de technicien supérieur***)* = advanced vocational training certificate
bu, -e *pp de* **boire¹**
buanderette [bɥɑ̃drɛt] *nf Can Br* launderette, *Am* Laundromat®
buanderie [bɥɑ̃dri] *nf* (**a**) *(pièce)* laundry (room) (**b**) *Can (laverie)* (dry) cleaner's, laundry
Buba [byba] *nf (abrév* **Bundesbank***)* **la Buba** the Bundesbank
bubonique [bybɔnik] *adj voir* **peste**
Bucarest [bykarɛst] *n* Bucharest
buccal, -e, -aux, -ales [bykal, -o] *adj* buccal; **par voie buccale** orally
bûche [byʃ] *nf* (**a**) *(morceau de bois)* log; **b. de Noël** Yule log (**b**) *Fam (chute)* fall; **prendre une b.** *Br* to come a cropper, *Am* to take a spill
bûcher¹ [byʃe] **1** *nm* (**a**) *(pour le bois)* woodshed (**b**) *(de supplice)* stake (**c**) *(funéraire)* (funeral) pyre
2 *vt Can (arbre)* to fell, to cut down
bûcher² *Fam Scol* **1** *vt* to bone up on, *Br* to swot up
2 *vi Br* to swot, *Am* to grind
bûcheron [byʃrɔ̃] *nm* woodcutter
bûcheur, -euse [byʃœr, -øz] *Fam Scol* **1** *adj* hardworking
2 *nm,f Br* swot, *Am* grind
bucolique [bykɔlik] *adj* pastoral
Budapest [bydapɛst] *n* Budapest
budget [bydʒɛ] *nm* budget
budgétaire [bydʒetɛr] *adj (dépenses, contrôle)* budgetary; *(année)* financial; **déficit/excédent b.** budget deficit/surplus
buée [bɥe] *nf (sur les vitres)* condensation; *(sur un miroir)* mist
Buenos Aires [bɥenɔzɛr] *n* Buenos Aires
buffet [byfɛ] *nm* (**a**) *(meuble) (bas)* sideboard; *(haut)* dresser (**b**) *(repas)* buffet; **b. campagnard** = cold buffet made with country produce; **b. froid** cold buffet (**c**) *Fam (ventre)* belly
buffle [byfl] *nm* buffalo
building [bildiŋ] *nm* tower block
buis [bɥi] *nm (arbre)* box (tree); *(bois)* box(wood)
buisson [bɥisɔ̃] *nm* bush
buissonnière [bɥisɔnjɛr] *adj f voir* **école**
bulbe [bylb] *nm* (**a**) *Bot* bulb (**b**) *Anat* **b. pileux** hair bulb; **b. rachidien** medulla oblongata (**c**) *Archit* onion dome
bulgare [bylgar] **1** *adj* Bulgarian
2 *nmf* **B.** Bulgarian
3 *nm (langue)* Bulgarian
Bulgarie [bylgari] *nf* **la B.** Bulgaria
bulldozer [byldozœr] *nm* bulldozer

bulle [byl] *nf* (**a**) *(d'air, de savon, stérile)* bubble; *(de bandes dessinées)* balloon; **faire des bulles** to blow bubbles; *Fam* **coincer la b.** to sleep, *Br* to kip; *Ordinat* **b. d'aide** help pop-up (**b**) *(lettre du pape)* (papal) bull
buller [byle] *vi Fam* to laze around
bulletin [byltɛ̃] *nm (communiqué)* bulletin; *(d'entreprise)* newsletter; *(formulaire)* form; *Scol* **b. (scolaire)** (school) report; **b. blanc** blank ballot paper; **b. d'informations** news bulletin; **b. météorologique** weather report; **b. officiel** official listing of all new laws and decrees; **b. de paie** *ou* **de salaire** pay slip; *Méd* **b. de santé** medical bulletin; **b. trimestriel** end-of-term report; *Suisse* **b. de versement** money order; **b. de vote** ballot paper; **b. (de vote) nul** spoiled ballot paper
bulletin-réponse *(pl* bulletins-réponse) [byltɛ̃repɔ̃s] *nm* reply form
bungalow [bœ̃galo] *nm* bungalow
bunker [bunkœr] *nm Mil* bunker; *(en golf) Br* bunker, *Am* sand trap
buraliste [byralist] *nmf* (**a**) *(de bureau de tabac)* tobacconist (**b**) *(dans un bureau)* clerk
bure [byr] *nf (étoffe)* frieze; *(habit religieux)* frock
bureau, -x [byro] *nm* (**a**) *(meuble)* desk (**b**) *(lieu)* office; *(à la maison)* study (**c**) *(comité)* committee (**d**) *(agence)* office; **b. de change** bureau de change; **b. d'études** design office; *(de recherche)* R & D department; **B. international du travail** International Labour Office; **b. de poste** post office; **b. de tabac** tobacconist's (shop) (**e**) *(organisme)* **b. d'aide sociale** welfare office (**f**) *Ordinat (écran)* desktop
bureaucrate [byrokrat] *nmf* bureaucrat
bureaucratie [byrokrasi] *nf (système)* bureaucracy; *(ensemble des fonctionnaires)* bureaucrats
bureaucratique [byrokratik] *adj* bureaucratic
Bureautique® [byrotik] *nf* office automation
burette [byrɛt] *nf* (**a**) *(pour l'huile)* oilcan; *(de chimiste)* burette (**b**) *très Fam* **burettes** *(testicules)* balls, *Br* bollocks
burin [byrɛ̃] *nm* (**a**) *(de graveur)* burin (**b**) *(pour découper)* (cold) chisel
buriné, -e [byrine] *adj (visage)* deeply lined
burka [burka] = **burqa**
Burkina [byrkina] *nm* **le B.** Burkina Faso
burkinabé [byrkinabe] **1** *adj* of Burkina Faso
2 *nmf* **B.** person from Burkina Faso
burlesque [byrlɛsk] **1** *adj* (**a**) *(ridicule)* ludicrous, ridiculous (**b**) *(film, genre)* burlesque
2 *nm (genre)* **le b.** the burlesque
burqa [burka] *nf* burka, burkha, burqa
Burundi [burundi] *nm* **le B.** Burundi

bus [bys] *nm (autobus)* & *Ordinat* bus
buse [byz] *nf* (**a**) *(oiseau)* buzzard (**b**) *(conduit)* duct (**c**) *Belg (échec)* failure
busqué, -e [byske] *adj (nez)* hook(ed)
buste [byst] *nm (torse)* chest; *(seins, sculpture)* bust
bustier [bystje] *nm (corsage)* bustier; *(soutien-gorge)* long-line (strapless) bra
but [by, byt] *nm* (**a**) *(objectif)* aim, goal; *(intention)* purpose; *(d'un trajet)* destination, goal; **dans ce b.** with this aim in view; **dans le b. de faire qch** with the aim of doing sth; **c'est le b. de l'opération** that's the point of the operation; **errer sans b.** to wander about aimlessly (**b**) *Sport* goal; **marquer un b.** to score a goal; **gagner/perdre (par) 3 buts à 1** to win/lose by 3 goals to 1; **les buts** *(zone)* the goal (**c**) **demander/dire qch de b. en blanc** to ask/say sth straight out
butane [bytan] *nm* butane
buté, -e¹ [byte] *adj* stubborn, obstinate
butée² [byte] *nf* (**a**) *(pièce)* **b. (d'arrêt)** stop (**b**) *Archit* abutment
buter [byte] **1** *vt* (**a**) *(braquer)* **b. qn** to put sb's back up (**b**) *très Fam (tuer)* to bump off
2 *vi* **b. contre qch** *(cogner)* to bump into sth; *(trébucher)* to stumble over sth; **b. sur un problème/une difficulté** to come up against a problem/a difficulty
3 se buter *vpr (s'entêter)* to dig one's heels in
buteur [bytœr] *nm (au football)* goalscorer; *(au rugby)* kicker
butin [bytɛ̃] *nm* (**a**) *(d'une armée)* booty; *(de pillards)* spoils; *(de voleur)* loot (**b**) *Can Fam (affaires personnelles)* gear, stuff
butiner [bytine] **1** *vi (abeille)* to gather pollen
2 *vt (sujet: abeille)* to gather pollen from; *(renseignements)* to gather
butineur [bytinœr] *nm Ordinat* browser
butoir [bytwar] *nm Rail* buffer; *(de porte)* door stop; **date b.** deadline
butte [byt] *nf (colline)* hillock; *Fig* **être en b. à qch** to be exposed to sth
buvable [byvabl] *adj* (**a**) *(potable)* drinkable (**b**) *(médicament)* to be taken orally
buvard [byvar] *nm (feuille)* sheet of blotting paper; *(sous-main)* blotter; **(papier) b.** blotting paper
buvette [byvɛt] *nf (dans une gare, à une fête)* refreshment bar
buveur, -euse [byvœr, -øz] *nm,f* drinker; **un gros b.** a heavy drinker
buviez *etc voir* **boire¹**
Byzance [bizɑ̃s] *n* Byzantium; *Fam* **c'est B.** it's the last word in luxury; *Fam* **ce n'est pas B.** it's not exactly luxurious

C¹, c [se] *nm inv* C, c; **c cédille** c cedilla
C² (*abrév* **Celsius**) C
c' *voir* **ce¹**
C4 [sekatr] *nm inv Belg* = official document given to an employee who is being laid off by his or her employer, *Br* ≃ P45
CA [sea] *nm* (**a**) *Élec* (*abrév* **courant alternatif**) AC (**b**) *Com* (*abrév* **chiffre d'affaires**) turnover
ça [sa] *pron démonstratif* (**a**) (*en désignant*) (*cela*) that; (*ceci*) this; **donne-moi ça** give that to me; **c'est bien vrai ça!** that's very true!; **écoute-moi ça!** just listen to this!; **ce n'est pas si facile que ça** it isn't as easy as that; **ça oui!** oh yes!; **à part ça** apart from that; **qui/quand/où ça?** who/when/where?; **c'est ça!** that's right!; *Ironique* if you say so!; **comment ça, elle est partie?** what do you mean she's gone?; **ça alors!, ça par exemple!** my goodness!; **ça y est, j'ai fini** that's it, I'm finished; **et insolent avec ça!** AND you're/he's/*etc* rude! (**b**) (*sujet indéterminé*) it; **ça m'ennuie/me choque** it annoys/shocks me; **ça m'amuse** I find it funny; **ça me ferait plaisir** I'd enjoy it (**c**) *Fam* **ça criait dans tous les coins** there was shouting going on everywhere; *Hum* **ça travaille là-dedans!** you're not just a pretty face!
çà [sa] **çà et là** *adv* here and there
cabale [kabal] *nf* (**a**) (*complot, comploteurs*) cabal; **monter une c. contre qn** to plot against sb (**b**) *Rel* cabbala
cabalistique [kabalistik] *adj* cabbalistic
caban [kabã] *nm* reefer
cabane [kaban] *nf* (**a**) (*baraque*) hut; (*en rondins*) cabin; (*à outils*) shed; **c. à lapins** rabbit hutch; *Can* **c. à sucre** sugar shack (**b**) *très Fam* (*prison*) **en c.** in the clink *or* the slammer; **faire de la c.** to do time
cabanon [kabanõ] *nm* (**a**) (*petite cabane*) hut, shed (**b**) (*en Provence*) (*maison de campagne*) (country) cottage
cabaret [kabarɛ] *nm* cabaret
cabas [kaba] *nm* shopping bag
cabestan [kabɛstã] *nm* capstan
cabillaud [kabijo] *nm* (fresh) cod
cabine [kabin] *nf* (**a**) (*de bateau, de vaisseau spatial*) cabin; **c. de pilotage** (*de petit avion*) cockpit; (*de gros avion*) flight deck (**b**) **c. de douche** (*pièce*) shower room; (*installation*) shower cubicle; **c. de bain(s)** (*de plage*) beach hut; (*de piscine*) changing cubicle; **c. d'essayage** fitting room; **c. Internet** Internet booth (**c**) (*de grue, de locomotive, de camion*) cab; (*d'ascenseur*) *Br* cage, *Am* car; **c. téléphonique** phone box
cabinet [kabinɛ] *nm* (**a**) (*petite pièce*) small room; *Fam* **les cabinets** *Br* the loo, *Am* the john; **c. noir** cubby-

hole; **c. de toilette** (small) bathroom; **c. de travail** study (**b**) (*de pub*) agency; (*d'architectes, de notaire*) office; (*de médecin*) *Br* surgery, practice, *Am* office; **c. dentaire** dental surgery *or* practice (**c**) (*entreprise*) **c. conseil** consultancy; **c. juridique** law firm (**d**) *Pol* (*d'un ministre*) departmental staff
câble [kabl] *nm* (**a**) (*fil*) cable; **c. métallique** wire cable (**b**) *TV* **le c.** cableTV; **avoir le c.** to have cable (TV) (**c**) *Vieilli* (*message*) cable
câblé, -e [kable] *adj* (**a**) *TV* (*ville, région*) with cable television; *Ordinat & Tél* hard-wired; **réseau c.** cable (TV) network; **l'immeuble est c.** the building is wired for cableTV (**b**) (*à fonctionnement fixe*) cabled
câbler [kable] *vt* (**a**) *TV* (*ville, quartier*) to install cable television in (**b**) *Vieilli* (*message*) to cable
câblo-opérateur (*pl* **câblo-opérateurs**) [kablooperatœr] *nm* cable company
cabochard, -e [kabɔʃar, -ard] *Fam* **1** *adj* pigheaded **2** *nm,f* pigheaded person
caboche [kabɔʃ] *nf Fam* (*tête*) nut; **mets-le-toi dans la c.!** get that into your thick skull!
cabosser [kabɔse] *vt* (*métal, voiture*) to bash up; (*chapeau*) to bash in; **un vieux chapeau cabossé** a battered old hat
cabot [kabo] *nm Fam* (**a**) (*chien*) pooch (**b**) (*acteur*) ham (actor)
cabotage [kabotaʒ] *nm Naut* coasting
caboteur [kabotœr] *nm Naut* coaster
cabotin, -e [kabɔtɛ̃, -in] **1** *adj* (*acteur*) ham **2** *nm,f* (**a**) (*acteur*) ham (actor, *f* actress) (**b**) (*vantard*) show-off
cabrer [kabre] **se cabrer** *vpr* (*cheval*) to rear (up); *Fig* (*personne*) to recoil
cabriole [kabrijɔl] *nf* (*saut, bond*) caper; (*en danse*) cabriole; (*en équitation*) capriole; (*de gymnaste*) somersault; **faire des cabrioles** to caper about
cabriolet [kabrijɔlɛ] *nm* (**a**) (*auto*) convertible (**b**) (*voiture à cheval*) cabriolet
CAC [kak] *n* (*abrév* **Compagnie des agents de change**) **le C.-40** = the Paris Stock Exchange index
caca [kaka] *nm* (*langage enfantin*) (*excrément*) poo; **faire c.** to do a poo; **c. d'oie** yellowish green
cacah(o)uète [kakawɛt] *nf* peanut
cacao [kakao] *nm* (*boisson, poudre*) cocoa; (*fève*) cocoa bean
cacaoui [kakawi] *nm Can* long-tailed duck
cacatoès [kakatɔɛs] *nm* cockatoo
cacatois [kakatwa] *nm Naut* (*voile*) royal sail; (**mât de**) **c.** royal mast
cachalot [kaʃalo] *nm* sperm whale

cache [kaʃ] **1** *nf* hiding place; **c. d'armes** arms cache **2** *nm (sur un texte)* masking card
caché, -e [kaʃe] *adj* hidden; *(sentiment)* secret
cache-cache [kaʃkaʃ] *nm* **jouer à c.** to play hide-and-seek
cache-col [kaʃkɔl] *nm inv Vieilli* scarf
Cachemire [kaʃmir] *nm* **le C.** Kashmir
cachemire [kaʃmir] *nm (laine)* cashmere; **à impression c.** paisley
cache-nez [kaʃne] *nm inv* scarf
cache-pot [kaʃpo] *nm inv* flowerpot holder
cacher [kaʃe] **1** *vt* to hide; **il ne cache pas que...** he makes no secret of the fact that...; **c. qch à qn** *(omettre de lui dire)* to hide sth from sb; **pour ne rien te c.** to be completely open with you; **je ne vous cache pas que j'ai été surpris** I won't pretend (that) I wasn't surprised; **le mur nous cache la vue** the wall hides our view
2 se cacher *vpr (personne, soleil)* to hide; **se c. de qn** to hide from sb; **sa timidité se cache derrière une certaine rudesse** his/her shyness is hidden behind a bluff exterior; **je ne m'en cache pas** I make no secret of it; **en se cachant** secretly; **sans se c.** openly
cache-sexe [kaʃsɛks] *nm inv* G-string, thong; *(d'indigène)* apron
cachet [kaʃɛ] *nm* (**a**) *(médicament)* tablet, pill (**b**) *(tampon)* stamp; *(sceau)* seal; *(de fabricant)* (trade)mark; **c. de la poste** postmark (**c**) *(style) (d'un endroit)* character; *(d'un vêtement)* style (**d**) *(salaire)* fee
cacheter [42] [kaʃte] *vt* to seal
cachette [kaʃɛt] *nf* (**a**) hiding place; **en c.** secretly; **boire en c.** *(habituellement)* to be a secret drinker; **faire qch en c. de qn** to do sth without sb's knowing (**b**) *Can* **jouer à la c.** to play hide-and-seek
cachot [kaʃo] *nm* (**a**) *(cellule)* dungeon (**b**) *(isolement)* solitary confinement
cachotterie [kaʃɔtri] *nf* **faire des cachotteries** to be secretive
cachottier, -ère [kaʃɔtje, -ɛr] **1** *adj* secretive **2** *nm,f* secretive person; **petit c.!** you secretive little thing!
cachou [kaʃu] *nm (bonbon)* cachou *(liquorice sweet)*
cacophonie [kakɔfɔni] *nf* cacophony
cactus [kaktys] *nm* cactus
c.-à-d. *(abrév* **c'est-à-dire**) ie
cadastre [kadastr] *nm (registre)* cadastre; *(administration)* cadastral survey office
cadavérique [kadaverik] *adj (teint)* deathly pale; *Méd* cadaveric
cadavre [kadavr] *nm* (**a**) *(de personne)* corpse, (dead) body; *(d'animal)* carcass, body; *Fam* **c'est un c. ambulant** he's a walking skeleton (**b**) *Fam (bouteille)* empty
caddie [kadi] *nm* (**a**) *Sport* caddie (**b**) *(chariot) Br* trolley, *Am* cart
cadeau, -x [kado] *nm* present, gift; *(avec un achat)* free gift; **en c.** as a present; **en c. avec** *(achat)* free with; **faire c. à qn de qch** *(donner)* to make sb a present of sth; *Fam Fig* **il ne lui a pas fait de cadeaux** he didn't spare him/her; *Fam* **ton frère, ce n'est pas un c.** your brother's a real pain; **c'est un c. empoisonné** it's more trouble than it's worth
cadenas [kadna] *nm* padlock

cadenasser [kadnase] **1** *vt (porte, pièce)* to padlock **2 se cadenasser** *vpr (personne)* to lock oneself away
cadence [kadɑ̃s] *nf (rythme régulier)* rhythm; *(vitesse)* rate; **en c.** in time; **c. de production** rate of production; **c. de tir** rate of fire
cadencé, -e [kadɑ̃se] *adj* (**a**) *(rythmé)* rhythmic(al); **marcher au pas c.** to walk in time (**b**) *Ordinat* **c. à** running at
cadet, -ette [kadɛ, -ɛt] **1** *adj (de deux)* younger; *(de plus de deux)* youngest **2** *nm,f* (**a**) *(de deux)* younger (one); *(de plus de deux)* youngest (one); **il est mon c. de deux ans** he's two years younger than I am; **c'est le c. de mes soucis** that's the least of my worries (**b**) *Sport* junior *(16 to 18 years old)* (**c**) *Hist & Mil* cadet
cadrage [kadraʒ] *nm Cin & Phot (de l'image)* centring; *(plan)* frame; *Ordinat* positioning
cadran [kadrɑ̃] *nm (d'horloge, de baromètre)* face; *(d'instrument, de téléphone)* dial; *Fig* **faire le tour du c.** *(dormir)* to sleep round the clock; *Aut* **cadrans (de bord)** display panels; **c. solaire** sundial
cadre [kadr] *nm* (**a**) *(de tableau, de porte, de vélo)* frame (**b**) *(domaine)* limits; *(structure)* framework; **dans le c. de** within the framework of (**c**) *(décor)* setting; **c. (de vie)** environment (**d**) *(dans un formulaire)* box; *Ordinat (pour graphique)* box; **c. réservé à l'administration** *(sur formulaire)* for official use only (**e**) *(dans une entreprise)* executive, manager; **les cadres** the management; *Mil* the officers; **c. moyen** middle manager; **c. supérieur** senior executive; **jeune c. dynamique** dynamic young executive (**f**) **être rayé des cadres** to be dismissed (**g**) *Can (tableau)* painting, picture

Cadre

In French companies, employees are divided into two categories, "employés" and "cadres". "Cadres", who are better qualified, tend to occupy more senior posts and consequently enjoy higher salaries, more benefits and more prestige. They are also expected to work longer hours.

cadre-adresse *(pl* **cadres-adresses**) [kadradrɛs] *nm* address space
cadrer [kadre] **1** *vt (photo)* to centre; *(plan)* to frame; *Ordinat* to position **2** *vi (correspondre)* to tally (**avec** with)
cadreur [kadrœr] *nm TV & Cin* cameraman
caduc, caduque [kadyk] *adj* (**a**) *(feuille)* deciduous (**b**) *Jur (accord)* lapsed; *(loi)* null and void
caducée [kadyse] *nm* caduceus
CAF [seaɛf] *(abrév* **Caisse d'allocations familiales**) = child benefit office
cafard [kafar] *nm* (**a**) *(insecte)* cockroach (**b**) *Fam* **avoir le c.** *ou* **un coup de c.** to feel down *or* low (**c**) *Fam (rapporteur)* sneak
cafarder [kafarde] *vi Fam* (**a**) *(rapporter)* to sneak (**b**) *(avoir le cafard)* to feel down *or* low
cafardeur, -euse [kafardœr, -øz] *nm,f Fam* sneak
cafardeux, -euse [kafardø, -øz] *adj Fam* **se sentir** *ou* **être c.** to feel down *or* low
café [kafe] **1** *nm* (**a**) *(produit, boisson)* coffee; **glace au c.** coffee ice cream; **c. crème** white coffee; **c. décaféiné** decaffeinated coffee; **c. en grains** coffee beans; **c. au lait** white coffee; **c. liégeois** = coffee ice cream topped with whipped cream; **c. moulu** ground coffee; *Suisse* **c. nature** black coffee; **c. noir**

black coffee; **c. en poudre** *ou* **instantané** instant coffee (**b**) *(bar)* café *(also serving alcoholic drinks)*; **c. tabac** = café-cum-tobacconist's
2 *adj inv (couleur)* **c. (au lait)** coffee-coloured

Café

In French cafés, a small cup of strong black coffee is called "un (petit) café", "un express" or, colloquially, "un petit noir". This may be served "serré" (extrastrong), "léger" (weak) or "allongé" (diluted with hot water). An "express" with a dash of milk is called "une noisette". A large cup of black coffee is "un grand café", "un double express" or, colloquially, "un grand noir". Coffee with frothy, steam-heated milk is called "un (grand/petit) crème". The term "café au lait" is almost never used in cafés. Parisian cafés have traditionally played an important part in the intellectual and artistic life of the city. The Café de Flore, for example, was a favourite meeting place for the existentialists.

---

caféine [kafein] *nf* caffeine
cafétéria [kafeterja] *nf* cafeteria
café-théâtre *(pl* **cafés-théâtres)** [kafeteatr] *nm* café where theatre performances take place
cafetier [kaftje] *nm* café owner
cafetière [kaftjɛr] *nf (récipient)* coffee pot; *(électrique)* coffee machine; **c. à piston** cafetière; **c. à pression** percolator
cafouillage [kafujaʒ] *nm Fam* (**a**) *(confusion)* muddle, shambles (**b**) *(de moteur de voiture)* misfiring
cafouiller [kafuje] *vi Fam* (**a**) *(personne)* to get into a muddle; *(projet)* to fall apart (**b**) *(moteur de voiture)* to misfire; *(poste de télévision)* to be on the blink
cafter [kafte] *vi Fam* to sneak, to tell tales, *Am* to snitch
cage [kaʒ] *nf* (**a**) *(pour oiseaux, dans un zoo)* cage; *(pour poules)* coop; *(pour lapins)* hutch; **mettre un oiseau en c.** to put a bird in a cage; *Fam Fig* **c. à lapins** rabbit hutch (**b**) *(de foot)* goal (**c**) **c. d'ascenseur** lift *or Am* elevator shaft; **c. d'escalier** stairwell (**d**) *Anat* **c. thoracique** rib cage
cageot [kaʒo] *nm* (**a**) *(caisse)* crate (**b**) *Fam Péj (femme)* dog
cagette [kaʒɛt] *nf* crate
cagibi [kaʒibi] *nm Fam* storage room
cagnard [kaɲar] *nm Fam* blazing sunshine
cagneux, -euse [kaɲø, -øz] *adj* **avoir les genoux c.** to have knock-knees
cagnotte [kaɲɔt] *nf (caisse commune)* kitty; *(de jeux)* pool; *(économies)* nest egg
cagoule [kagul] *nf (de moine)* cowl; *(de pénitent, de terroriste)* hood
cahier [kaje] *nm* (**a**) *(livre)* notebook; *(d'écolier)* exercise book; **c. de brouillon** rough book; **c. de textes** homework book (**b**) *Typ* signature (**c**) *(d'un journal)* section (**d**) **Cahiers de...** *(revue)* Journal of... (**e**) *Com* **c. des charges** *(d'un contrat)* terms and conditions; *(de fabrication)* specifications
cahin-caha [kaɛ̃kaa] *adv Fam* **aller c.** *(se déplacer)* to struggle along; **ça va, la santé? – ça va, c.** how are you keeping? – oh, so-so
cahot [kao] *nm (secousse)* jolt
cahoter [kaote] **1** *vt* **être cahoté** *(dans un véhicule)* to be jolted about
2 *vi* to jolt along
cahoteux, -euse [kaotø, -øz] *adj* bumpy
cahute [kayt] *nf* shack

caïd [kaid] *nm Fam (chef de bande)* gang leader; **un c. de la drogue** a drugs baron; **faire le c., jouer les caïds** to act high and mighty
caillasse [kajas] *nf Fam* loose stones
caille [kaj] *nf* quail; *Fam* **ma petite c.** my little dove
caillé [kaje] *nm* curds
caillebotis [kajbɔti] *nm* (**a**) *Naut* grating (**b**) *(plancher)* duckboard
caillebotte [kajbɔt] *nf* curds
cailler [kaje] **1** *vt (lait)* to curdle; *(sang)* to clot
2 *vi* (**a**) *(lait)* to curdle; *(sang)* to clot; **faire c. du lait** to curdle milk (**b**) *Fam* **ça caille** it's freezing
3 se cailler *vpr Fam* **on se (les) caille** it's freezing
caillot [kajo] *nm (de sang)* clot
caillou, -x [kaju] *nm* (**a**) *(petite pierre)* stone; *(sur la plage)* pebble (**b**) *Fam (pierre précieuse)* stone, rock (**c**) *Fam (tête)* nut; **il n'a plus un poil sur le c.** he's as bald as a coot
caillouteux, -euse [kajutø, -øz] *adj (route)* stony; *(plage)* pebbly
caïman [kaimã] *nm* cayman
Caire [kɛr] *n* **Le C.** Cairo
cairote [kerɔt] **1** *adj* of Cairo
2 *nmf* **C.** person from Cairo, Cairene
caisse [kɛs] *nf* (**a**) *(pour marchandises)* case; *(à outils)* box; *(de champagne, de vin)* case; *(pour plantes)* tub; *(de fruits)* crate (**b**) *Com & Fin (coffre)* cash box; *(d'une caisse enregistreuse)* till; *(où l'on paie) (dans un magasin)* cash desk; *(dans un supermarché)* checkout; **les caisses de l'État** the coffers of the State; **tenir la c.** *(dans un restaurant, dans un magasin)* to be the cashier; **passer à la c.** *(se faire licencier)* to be paid off; *Fam (payer)* to pay; *Fam (se faire payer)* to be paid; **c. (enregistreuse)** cash register; *Pol* **c. noire** slush fund (**c**) *(argent)* cash (in hand); **faire la** *ou* **sa c.** to do the till (**d**) *(organisme)* **c. d'allocations familiales** = child benefit office; **c. d'épargne** savings bank; *Can* **c. populaire** credit union; **c. primaire d'assurance maladie** = French government department dealing with health insurance; **c. de retraite** pension fund (**e**) *Mus* **c. claire** snare drum; **c. de résonance** sound box (**f**) *(de piano, d'horloge)* case; *(de véhicule)* body (**g**) *très Fam (voiture)* car
caissette [kɛsɛt] *nf* small box
caissier, -ère [kɛsje, -ɛr] *nm,f* cashier; *(dans un supermarché)* checkout operator
caisson [kɛsɔ̃] *nm* (**a**) *très Fam* **se faire sauter le c.** to blow one's brains out (**b**) *Archit* **plafond à caissons** coffered ceiling (**c**) *(de plongée)* caisson
cajoler [kaʒɔle] *vt* to cuddle
cajolerie [kaʒɔlri] *nf* cuddle
cajou [kaʒu] *nm voir* **noix**
cake [kɛk] *nm* fruit cake
cal *(pl* **cals)** [kal] *nm (durillon)* callus
calamar [kalamar] = **calmar**
calamine [kalamin] *nf (dépôt)* carbon deposits
calamité [kalamite] *nf (fléau)* calamity; *(malheur)* great misfortune; *Fam* **ce mec, c'est une vraie c.!** that guy's a walking disaster!
calamiteux, -euse [kalamitø -øz] *adj* calamitous
calancher [kalɑ̃ʃe] *vi très Fam* to croak, *Br* to snuff it, *Am* to check out
calandre [kalɑ̃dr] *nf* (**a**) *(machine)* calender (**b**) *Aut* radiator grille
calanque [kalɑ̃k] *nf* deep narrow creek *(in the Mediterranean)*
calao [kalao] *nm* hornbill

calcaire [kalkɛr] **1** *adj (sol, terrain)* chalky; *(roche)* calcareous; *(eau)* hard **2** *nm* (**a**) *Géol* limestone (**b**) *(dépôt)* fur
calcification [kalsifikasjɔ̃] *nf Méd* calcification
calciner [kalsine] **1** *vt (brûler)* to char; **calciné** *(trop cuit)* burnt to a cinder **2 se calciner** *vpr* to burn
calcium [kalsjɔm] *nm* calcium
calcul¹ [kalkyl] *nm* (**a**) *(compte)* calculation; **faire un c.** to make a calculation (**b**) *Scol* **le c.** arithmetic; **c. mental** mental arithmetic (**c**) *Math* **c. différentiel/intégral** differential/integral calculus (**d**) *(prévision)* calculation; **agir par c.** to act from selfish motives; **faire un mauvais c.** to miscalculate
calcul² *nm Méd* stone, *Spéc* calculus; **c. biliaire/rénal** gall/kidney stone
calculateur, -trice [kalkylatœr, -tris] **1** *adj (personne, politique)* calculating **2** *nm Vieilli Ordinat* computer **3** *nf* **calculatrice (de poche)** (pocket) calculator
calculé, -e [kalkyle] *adj (insulte, risque)* calculated; *(méchanceté)* premeditated; *(insolence)* deliberate
calculer [kalkyle] **1** *vt (compter) (prix, superficie)* to work out, to calculate; *(comportement, propos)* to plan; *(conséquences, chances)* to weigh (up); **tout bien calculé** taking everything into account **2** *vi* to calculate; *Péj (économiser)* to count every penny
calculette [kalkylɛt] *nf* (pocket) calculator
Calcutta [kalkyta] *n* Calcutta
caldoche [kaldɔʃ] **1** *adj* White New Caledonian **2** *nmf* **C.** New Caledonian
cale¹ [kal] *nf Naut* (**a**) *(de navire)* hold; **à fond de c.** down in the hold (**b**) *(rampe)* **c. sèche** dry dock
cale² *nf (pour meuble, pour porte)* wedge; *(pour bloquer une roue)* chock
calé, -e [kale] *adj Fam* (**a**) *(personne)* **être c. en qch** to be well up in sth (**b**) *(problème, question, devoir)* tough (**c**) *Belg (prêt)* ready
calebasse [kalbas] *nf* calabash
calèche [kalɛʃ] *nf* barouche
calecif [kalsif] *nm Fam Br* boxers, *Am* shorts
caleçon [kalsɔ̃] *nm* boxer shorts; *(de femme)* leggings; *Vieilli* **c. de bain** bathing trunks; *Vieilli* **c. long** long johns
calédonien, -enne [kaledɔnjɛ̃, -ɛn] **1** *adj* Caledonian **2** *nm,f* **C.** Caledonian
calembour [kalɑ̃bur] *nm* pun, play on words; **faire des calembours** to make puns
calendes [kalɑ̃d] *nfpl* **renvoyer qch aux c. grecques** to put sth off indefinitely
calendrier [kalɑ̃drije] *nm* (**a**) *(système, tableau)* calendar (**b**) *(de voyage, de travail)* timetable
cale-pied (*pl* **cale-pieds**) [kalpje] *nm* toe clip
calepin [kalpɛ̃] *nm* (**a**) *(carnet)* notebook (**b**) *Belg (serviette)* briefcase
caler¹ [kale] **1** *vt* (**a**) *(meuble, porte)* to wedge; *(roue)* to chock; *(chargement)* to secure; **c. un malade avec des coussins** to prop up a patient with cushions (**b**) *Fam (remplir)* **ça cale (l'estomac)** it fills you up; **je suis calé** I'm full up **2** *vi (moteur)* to stall **3 se caler** *vpr (dans un fauteuil)* to settle oneself comfortably
caler² *vi* (**a**) *Fam (abandonner)* to give up (**b**) *Can (se dégarnir)* to have a receding hairline
calfater [kalfate] *vt Naut* to caulk

calfeutrer [kalføtre] **1** *vt* (**a**) *(brèches)* to block up (**b**) *(pièce, fenêtre)* to draught-proof **2 se calfeutrer** *vpr (pour avoir chaud)* to make oneself snug; *(pour être seul)* to shut oneself away
calibre [kalibr] *nm* (**a**) *(d'arme à feu, de tuyau, de balle)* calibre; *(d'œufs, de fruits)* grade; *Fig* **sa sœur est d'un autre c.** his sister is of quite a different calibre (**b**) *(outil)* gauge (**c**) *très Fam (revolver)* shooter
calibrer [kalibre] *vt (pièce)* to gauge; *(instrument de mesure)* to calibrate; *Com (œufs, fruits)* to grade
calice¹ [kalis] *nm Rel* chalice; *Fig* **boire le c. jusqu'à la lie** to drain the cup to the dregs
calice² *nm Bot* calyx
calife [kalif] *nm* caliph
Californie [kalifɔrni] *nf* **la C.** California
californien, -enne [kalifɔrnjɛ̃, -ɛn] **1** *adj* Californian **2** *nm,f* **C.** Californian
califourchon [kalifurʃɔ̃] **à califourchon** *adv* astride; **se mettre à c. sur qch** to sit astride sth
câlin, -e [kalɛ̃, -in] **1** *adj* affectionate **2** *nm* cuddle; **faire un c. à qn** to give sb a cuddle
câliner [kaline] *vt* to cuddle
calisson [kalisɔ̃] *nm* = lozenge-shaped sweet made of marzipan
calleux, -euse [kalø, -øz] *adj* callous
call-girl (*pl* **call-girls**) [kolgœrl] *nf* call girl
calligramme [kaligram] *nm* calligram
calligraphe [kaligraf] *nmf* calligrapher
calligraphie [kaligrafi] *nf* calligraphy
calmant, -e [kalmɑ̃, -ɑ̃t] *Méd* **1** *adj (pour les nerfs)* tranquilizing, sedative; *(pour la douleur)* painkilling **2** *nm (pour les nerfs)* tranquilizer; *(pour la douleur)* painkiller; **sous calmants** on tranquilizers
calmar [kalmar] *nm* squid
calme [kalm] **1** *adj* (**a**) *(personne) (qui garde son sang-froid)* calm; *(tranquille)* quiet (**b**) *(mer) (ciel)* clear; **les affaires sont calmes en août** business is quiet in August **2** *nm (absence d'agitation)* calm, calmness; *(sang-froid)* composure; *(du paysage)* peace and quiet; **être au c.** to have peace and quiet; **du c.!** *(taisez-vous)* keep quiet!; *(ne vous affolez pas)* keep calm!; **garder/perdre son c.** to keep/lose one's composure; *Naut* **c. plat** dead calm; **c'est le c. plat dans ma vie sentimentale** my love life is in the doldrums
calmement [kalməmɑ̃] *adv* calmly
calmer [kalme] **1** *vt (personne)* to calm (down); *(craintes)* to calm; *(douleur)* to soothe; *(fièvre)* to reduce; *(soif)* to quench; *(faim)* to appease; *(ardeur, passion)* to cool; *Fig* **c. le jeu** to calm things down **2 se calmer** *vpr (personne)* to calm down; *(tempête, vent)* to die down; *(mer)* to become calm; *(pluie)* to ease off; *(douleur, fièvre)* to subside
calmos [kalmos] *exclam Fam* chill (out)!, take it easy!
calomnie [kalɔmni] *nf (en paroles)* slander; *(par écrit)* libel
calomnier [66] [kalɔmnje] *vt (en paroles)* to slander; *(par écrit)* to libel
calomnieux, -euse [kalɔmnjø, -øz] *adj (paroles)* slanderous; *(écrits)* libellous
calorie [kalɔri] *nf* calorie; **régime basses calories** low-calorie diet
calorifère [kalɔrifɛr] **1** *adj* heat-conveying **2** *nm Vieilli* (slow-combustion) stove; *Can* radiator
calorifique [kalɔrifik] *adj* calorific

calorifuge [kalɔrifyʒ] **1** *adj* (heat-)insulating **2** *nm* heat insulation; *(pour chaudière, tuyau)* lagging

calorique [kalɔrik] *adj* calorific

calot [kalo] *nm (coiffure militaire) Br* forage cap, *Am* garrison cap

calotte [kalɔt] *nf* (**a**) *(chapeau rond)* skullcap; *Rel* calotte; *(de chapeau)* crown; *très Fam* **Pёj la c.** *(le clergé)* the clergy (**b**) *Fam (gifle)* clout (**c**) *Anat* **c. crânienne** skullcap (**d**) *Géol* **c. glaciaire** ice cap

calque [kalk] *nm (copie)* tracing; *Fig (de poème, de portrait)* exact copy; *(traduction)* calque; **prendre un c. de qch** to make a tracing of sth; **(papier) c.** tracing paper

calquer [kalke] *vt (reproduire)* to trace; *Fig* to copy exactly; **expression calquée sur l'anglais** expression copied from the English; **il calque sa conduite sur celle de son frère** he models his behaviour on his brother's

calumet [kalymɛ] *nm* peace pipe; *Fig* **fumer le c. de la paix** to bury the hatchet

calvados [kalvados] *nm* Calvados

calvaire [kalvɛr] *nm* (**a**) *(du Christ)* calvary; *Fig (épreuve pénible)* ordeal (**b**) *(croix)* calvary

calviniste [kalvinist] *adj & nmf* Calvinist

calvitie [kalvisi] *nf* baldness; **avoir un début de c.** to be starting to go bald; **c. précoce** premature baldness

camaïeu, -x [kamajø] *nm (peinture)* monochrome; *(gravure)* tint drawing; **un c. de bleu** *(papiers peints, vêtements)* different shades of blue

camarade [kamarad] *nmf* friend; *Pol (terme d'adresse)* comrade; **c. de chambre** roommate; **c. de classe** classmate; **c. d'école** school friend

camaraderie [kamaradri] *nf* camaraderie

camber [kɑ̃be] *vt Suisse* to stride over

cambiste [kɑ̃bist] *nmf Fin* foreign exchange dealer

Cambodge [kɑ̃bɔdʒ] *nm* **le C.** Cambodia

cambodgien, -enne [kɑ̃bɔdʒjɛ̃, -ɛn] **1** *adj* Cambodian **2** *nm,f* **C.** Cambodian

cambouis [kɑ̃bwi] *nm* dirty oil

cambré, -e [kɑ̃bre] *adj (pied)* with a high instep; *(personne)* with an arched back

cambrer [kɑ̃bre] **1** *vt (dos, pied)* to arch; **c. la taille** *ou* **les reins** to arch one's back **2** **se cambrer** *vpr* to arch one's back

cambrien, -enne [kɑ̃mbrijɛ̃, -ɛn] *Géol* **1** *adj* Cambrian **2** *nm* **le c.** the Cambrian period

cambriolage [kɑ̃brijɔlaʒ] *nm* burglary, break-in

cambrioler [kɑ̃brijɔle] *vt (maison, personne) Br* to burgle, *Am* to burglarize

cambrioleur, -euse [kɑ̃brijɔlœr, -øz] *nm,f* burglar

cambrousse [kɑ̃brus], **cambrouse** [kɑ̃bruz] *nf Fam* country; **en pleine c.** in the middle of nowhere

cambrure [kɑ̃bryr] *nf (du pied, du dos)* arch; **c. des reins** small of the back

cambuse [kɑ̃byz] *nf* (**a**) *Naut* storeroom (**b**) *Fam Vieilli (chambre, maison)* dump, hole

came¹ [kam] *nf Tech* cam

came² *nf très Fam (drogue)* dope

camé, -e¹ [kame] *très Fam* **1** *adj* high, wasted **2** *nm,f* junkie, druggie

camée² *nm* cameo

caméléon [kameleɔ̃] *nm aussi Fig* chameleon

camélia [kamelja] *nm* camellia

camelote [kamlɔt] *nf Fam* (**a**) *(pacotille)* junk (**b**) *(marchandise)* stuff

camembert [kamɑ̃bɛr] *nm* (**a**) *(fromage)* Camembert (**b**) *(diagramme)* pie-chart

camer [kame] **se camer** *vpr très Fam* to do drugs; **se c. à l'héroïne** to do heroin

caméra [kamera] *nf Cin & TV* camera; **c. cachée** *(appareil)* hidden camera; *(émission)* candid camera; **c. infrarouge** infrared camera; **c. Internet** webcam; **c. de télévision** television camera; **c. vidéo** video camera

cameraman [kameraman] *(pl* **cameramans** *ou* **cameramen** [kameramɛn]) *nm Cin & TV* cameraman

Cameroun [kamrun] *nm* **le C.** Cameroon

camerounais, -e [kamrunɛ, -ɛz] **1** *adj* Cameroonian **2** *nm,f* **C.** Cameroonian

Caméscope® [kameskɔp] *nm* camcorder

camion [kamjɔ̃] *nm Br* lorry, *Am* truck; **c. à benne** dump truck; **c. de déménagement** removal van; **c. de dépannage** breakdown truck; **c. frigorifique** *ou* **réfrigéré** refrigerated lorry

camion-benne *(pl* **camions-bennes**) [kamjɔ̃bɛn] *nm* dumper truck

camion-citerne *(pl* **camions-citernes**) [kamjɔ̃sitɛrn] *nm* tanker

camionnette [kamjɔnɛt] *nf* van; **c. de livraison** delivery van

camionneur [kamjɔnœr] *nm* (**a**) *(conducteur) Br* lorry driver, *Am* truck driver (**b**) *(transporteur) Br* haulier, *Am* trucker

camisole [kamizɔl] *nf* (**a**) *Can (tricot de corps) Br* vest, *Am* undershirt (**b**) *(chemise de nuit)* nightshirt (**c**) **c. de force** straitjacket

camomille [kamɔmij] *nf* camomile; *(tisane)* camomile tea

camouflage [kamuflaʒ] *nm Mil* camouflage; *(de la vérité, d'intentions)* disguising; *(de bénéfices)* concealment

camoufler [kamufle] **1** *vt Mil* to camouflage; *(vérité, intentions)* to disguise; *(bénéfices)* to conceal; **c. un meurtre en suicide** to make a murder look like suicide **2** **se camoufler** *vpr* to camouflage oneself

camp [kɑ̃] *nm* (**a**) *(campement)* camp; **établir un c.** to pitch camp; **lever le c.** to strike camp; *Fam Fig (partir)* to hit the road; **c. (de vacances)** *Br* (children's) holiday camp, *Am* summer camp; **c. de concentration** concentration camp; **c. de loisirs** holiday camp; **c. de prisonniers** prison camp; **c. de réfugiés** refugee camp (**b**) *(parti)* camp, side (**c**) *(de jeux)* side; **faire deux camps** to form two teams

campagnard, -e [kɑ̃paɲar, -ard] *adj* country

campagne [kɑ̃paɲ] *nf* (**a**) *(par opposition à la ville)* country; *(paysage)* countryside; **à la c.** in the country; **en pleine c.** deep in the countryside; **en rase c.** in the open country (**b**) *Mil, Pol & Com* campaign; *Pol* **entrer en c.** to go on the campaign trail; **faire c. pour/contre** to campaign for/against; **partir en c. contre le tabac** to launch an anti-smoking campaign; **c. électorale** election campaign; **c. de presse** press campaign; **c. publicitaire** *ou* **de publicité** advertising campaign

campanile [kɑ̃panil] *nm Archit* bell tower

campanule [kɑ̃panyl] *nf* campanula

campement [kɑ̃pmɑ̃] *nm (installation)* camp; *(lieu)* camping place; **établir un c.** to pitch camp

camper [kɑ̃pe] **1** *vi* (**a**) *(faire du camping)* to camp (**b**) *Fig (chez quelqu'un)* to camp out

2 *vt* (**a**) *Vieilli* **c. son chapeau sur sa tête** to plant one's hat on one's head (**b**) (*décrire*) to put in context; **c. un personnage** (*sujet: acteur*) to play a part effectively

3 se camper *vpr* **se c. devant qn** to plant oneself in front of sb

campeur, -euse [kãpœr, -øz] *nm,f* camper

camphre [kãfr] *nm* camphor

camphré, -e [kãfre] *adj* camphorated

camping [kãpiŋ] *nm* (**a**) (*activité*) camping; **faire du c.** to go camping; **c. à la ferme** farm camping; **c. sauvage** unauthorized camping (**b**) (*lieu*) campsite; **c. aménagé** campsite with facilities

camping-car (*pl* **camping-cars**) [kãpiŋkar] *nm* camper

camping-caravaning [kãpiŋkaravaniŋ] *nm* camping-caravanning

Camping-Gaz® [kãpiŋgaz] *nm inv* camping stove

campus [kãpys] *nm* campus; **habiter sur le c.** to live on campus

camus [kamy] *adj m* (*nez*) flat

Canada [kanada] *nm* **le C.** Canada

Canadair® [kanadɛr] *nm* fire-fighting plane

canadianisme [kanadjanism] *nm Ling* Canadianism

canadien, -enne [kanadjɛ̃, -ɛn] **1** *adj* Canadian
2 *nm,f* **C.** Canadian
3 *nf* **canadienne** (*veste*) sheepskin jacket; (*tente*) ridge tent

canaille [kanɑj] **1** *adj* (*chanson, paroles*) vulgar; (*air*) roguish
2 *nf* (*crapule*) scoundrel; **petite c.!** (*à un enfant*) you little devil!

canal, -aux [kanal, -o] *nm* (**a**) (*cours d'eau*) canal; **c. d'irrigation** irrigation canal; **le c. de Panama/de Suez** the Panama/Suez Canal (**b**) (*conduite*) conduit (**c**) *Anat & Bot* duct (**d**) *Rad & TV* French pay television channel (**e**) *Fig* (*moyen*) channel; **par le c. de la poste** through the post (**f**) *Com* channel; **c. de distribution** distribution channel

---

Canal+
Canal+, France's first private television channel, was established in 1982 and started broadcasting in 1984. It broadcasts programmes that have to be unscrambled using a special decoding unit, although for part of the day its programmes can be seen without this device. Canal+ also plays a prominent role in funding international films.

---

canalisation [kanalizasjɔ̃] *nf* (**a**) (*conduite*) pipe; (*pour pétrole*) pipeline (**b**) (*de rivière*) canalization

canaliser [kanalize] *vt* (**a**) (*région, rivière*) to canalize (**b**) (*énergie*) to channel; (*trafic, foule*) to direct

canapé [kanape] *nm* (**a**) (*meuble*) sofa, couch; **c. convertible** sofa bed; **c. deux places** two-seater sofa (**b**) (*pour l'apéritif*) canapé

canapé-lit (*pl* **canapés-lits**) [kanapeli] *nm* sofa bed

canaque [kanak] **1** *adj* Kanak (*of New Caledonia*)
2 *nmf* **C.** Kanak (*from New Caledonia*)

canard [kanar] *nm* (**a**) (*oiseau*) duck; (*mâle*) drake; *Fam* **mon petit c.** my pet; **marcher en c.** to walk with one's feet turned out; **c. laqué** Peking duck; **c. à l'orange** duck à l'orange; **c. sauvage** wild duck (**b**) *Fam* (*journal*) rag (**c**) (*morceau de sucre*) = sugar lump dipped in coffee or alcoholic drink (**d**) *Mus* false note (**e**) *Can* (*bouilloire*) kettle

canarder [kanarde] *vt Fam* to snipe on

canari [kanari] *nm* canary

Canaries [kanari] *nfpl* **les (îles) C.** the Canary Islands, the Canaries

canasson [kanasɔ̃] *nm Fam* (*cheval*) nag

cancan [kãkã] *nm* (**a**) **cancans** (*ragots*) gossip (*sur* about) (**b**) (*danse*) cancan

cancaner [kãkane] *vi* (**a**) (*médire*) to gossip (*sur* about) (**b**) (*canard*) to quack

cancanier, -ère [kãkanje, -ɛr] *Fam* **1** *adj* gossipy
2 *nm,f* gossip

cancer [kãsɛr] *nm* (**a**) *Méd & Fig* cancer; **c. du poumon/du sein** lung/breast cancer; **avoir un c.** to have cancer (**b**) *Astron & Astrol* **le C.** Cancer; **être C.** to be (a) Cancer

cancéreux, -euse [kãserø, -øz] **1** *adj* (*tumeur*) cancerous
2 *nm,f* cancer sufferer

cancérigène [kãseriʒɛn] *adj* carcinogenic; **produit c.** carcinogen

cancérologie [kãserɔlɔʒi] *nf* cancerology

cancérologue [kãserɔlɔg] *nmf* cancer specialist

cancre [kãkr] *nm Fam* dunce

cancrelat [kãkrəla] *nm* cockroach

candélabre [kãdelabr] *nm* (*chandelier*) candelabra

candeur [kãdœr] *nf* guilelessness; **un regard plein de c.** a guileless look

candi [kãdi] *adj m voir* **sucre**

candidat, -e [kãdida, -at] *nm,f* (*à un poste*) applicant (*à* for); (*à un examen*) candidate (*à* for); **être c. aux élections** to stand *or* run for election

candidature [kãdidatyr] *nf* (*aux élections*) candidature; (*à un poste*) application (*à* for); **poser sa c. à un poste** to apply for a post; **c. spontanée** unsolicited application

candide [kãdid] *adj* guileless

candidement [kãdidmã] *adv* guilelessly

candidose [kãdidoz] *nf Méd* candidiasis

cane [kan] *nf* (*female*) duck

caneton [kantɔ̃] *nm* (*male*) duckling

canette¹ [kanɛt] *nf* (*petite cane*) (*female*) duckling

canette² = **cannette**

canevas [kanva] *nm* (**a**) (*trame*) canvas (**b**) (*de film, de roman*) outline

caniche [kaniʃ] *nm* poodle

caniculaire [kanikylɛr] *adj* (*chaleur, été*) scorching

canicule [kanikyl] *nf* heatwave; **quelle c.!** what a scorcher!

canif [kanif] *nm* penknife

canin, -e [kanɛ̃, -in] **1** *adj* canine; **exposition canine** dog show
2 *nf* **canine** canine (tooth)

caniveau, -x [kanivo] *nm* gutter

cannabis [kanabis] *nm* cannabis

cannage [kanaʒ] *nm* (*partie en rotin*) canework

canne [kan] *nf* (**a**) (*tige*) cane; **c. à pêche** fishing rod; **c. à sucre** sugar cane (**b**) (*pour s'appuyer*) (walking) stick; **c. blanche** white stick (**c**) *très Fam* (*jambe*) leg, pin (**d**) *Suisse* (*au hockey sur glace*) *Br* ice hockey stick, *Am* hockey stick

canné, -e [kane] *adj* (*chaise*) cane

canneberge [kanbɛrʒ] *nf* cranberry

cannelé, -e [kanle] *adj* (*colonne*) fluted; (*pneu*) grooved

cannelle [kanɛl] *nf* cinnamon; **bâton de c.** cinnamon stick; **à la c.** cinnamon(-flavoured)

cannellonis [kanɛlɔni] *nmpl* cannelloni

cannelure [kanlyr] *nf (rainure)* groove; *(de colonne)* fluting

cannette [kanɛt] *nf* (**a**) *(petite bouteille)* bottle; *(boîte)* can (**b**) *Tex* spool

cannibale [kanibal] **1** *nmf* cannibal
2 *adj (pratiques)* cannibalistic; **tribu c.** tribe of cannibals

cannibalisme [kanibalism] *nm* cannibalism

canoë [kanɔe] *nm* canoe; **faire du c.** to go canoeing

canoë-kayak [kanɔekajak] *nm* canoeing

canon¹ [kanɔ̃] *nm* (**a**) *(pièce d'artillerie)* gun; *Hist* cannon (**b**) *(de carabine)* barrel (**c**) *Anciennement (mesure)* = wine measure equivalent to 0.058 l; *Fam* **boire un c.** to have a glass of wine

canon² **1** *nm* (**a**) *Rel & Fig (règle)* canon (**b**) *Mus* canon; **c. à deux/trois voix** canon for two/three voices; **chanter qch en c.** to sing sth in canon (**c**) *Fam (personne)* babe, hottie
2 *adj inv Fam (beau)* gorgeous, hot, *Br* fit

canonique [kanɔnik] *adj* canonical; *Fig* **être d'un âge c.** to be advanced in years

canoniser [kanɔnize] *vt Rel* to canonize

canonnade [kanɔnad] *nf* gunfire; **une c.** a burst of gunfire

canot [kano] *nm Naut* (**a**) *(petit bateau)* boat; **c. pneumatique** rubber dinghy; **c. de sauvetage** lifeboat (**b**) *Can (canoë)* canoe

canotage [kanɔtaʒ] *nm* boating; *Can (en canoë)* canoeing; **faire du c.** to go boating/canoeing

canoter [kanɔte] *vi Naut* to go boating; *Can (en canoë)* to go canoeing

canotier [kanɔtje] *nm* (**a**) *(rameur)* rower (**b**) *(chapeau)* boater

cantal, -als [kãtal] *nm* Cantal

cantate [kãtat] *nf* cantata

cantatrice [kãtatris] *nf (chanteuse d'opéra)* opera singer; *(de concert)* (concert) singer

cantine [kãtin] *nf* (**a**) *(réfectoire)* canteen; *(à l'école)* dining hall; **déjeuner à la c.** *(de l'école)* to have school meals (**b**) *(malle)* trunk (**c**) *Suisse (boîte)* lunchbox (**d**) *Suisse (tente)* marquee

cantique [kãtik] *nm Rel* hymn; **le C. des cantiques** the Song of Solomon

canton [kãtɔ̃] *nm (en France)* canton *(administrative division of a department)*; *(en Suisse)* canton *(semi-autonomous administrative region of Switzerland)*; *Can* **les cantons de l'Est** the Eastern Townships

cantonade [kãtɔnad] **à la cantonade** *adv* to everybody present; *(au théâtre)* off

cantonais, -e [kãtɔnɛ, -ɛz] **1** *adj* Cantonese
2 *nm,f* **C.** Cantonese
3 *nm (langue)* Cantonese

cantonal, -e, -aux, -ales [kãtɔnal, -o] *adj* cantonal; **les (élections) cantonales** the cantonal elections

cantonnement [kãtɔnmã] *nm Mil (des troupes)* quartering; *(lieu)* quarters

cantonner [kãtɔne] *vt* (**a**) *Mil (troupes)* to quarter (**b**) **c. qn dans/à** to confine sb to
2 se cantonner *vpr (se limiter)* **se c. dans/à** to confine oneself to

cantonnier [kãtɔnje] *nm* roadmender; *Rail* lineman

canular [kanylar] *nm Fam* hoax; **monter un c.** to play a hoax

canule [kanyl] *nf Méd* cannula

canyon [kanjɔ̃] *nm* canyon; **le Grand C.** the Grand Canyon

canyoning [kanjɔniŋ] *nm* canyoning

CAO [seao] *nf Ordinat (abrév* **conception assistée par ordinateur***)* CAD

caoutchouc [kautʃu] *nm* (**a**) *(substance)* rubber; **c. Mousse®** foam rubber; **c. synthétique** synthetic rubber (**b**) *(plante)* rubber plant

caoutchouteux, -euse [kautʃutø, -øz] *adj Péj* rubbery

CAP [seape] *nm (abrév* **certificat d'aptitude professionnelle***)* = vocational training certificate

Cap [kap] *n* **le C.** Cape Town

cap [kap] *nm* (**a**) *Géog* cape, headland; **passer** *ou* **franchir** *ou* **doubler un c.** to round a cape; **quand on a franchi le c. de la quarantaine** when you've turned forty; **notre usine va passer le c. des mille employés** our factory will soon pass the thousand-employee mark; **le c. de Bonne-Espérance** the Cape of Good Hope; **le c. Horn** Cape Horn (**b**) *Naut & Aviat (direction)* course; **mettre le c. sur...** to set course for...

capable [kapabl] *adj* (**a**) *(susceptible)* **être c. de qch** to be capable of sth; **être c. de faire qch** to be capable of doing sth, to be able to do sth; **il est c. de tout** he's capable of anything; **c. du meilleur comme du pire** capable of the best as well as the worst; **elle est bien c. d'oublier les clefs!** she's quite capable of forgetting the keys! (**b**) *(compétent)* capable, able (**c**) *Jur* competent (**de faire** to do)

capacité [kapasite] *nf* (**a**) *(contenance)* capacity; **c. d'accueil** *(d'un hôtel)* accommodation capacity (**b**) *(aptitude)* ability, capability; **de grandes capacités (intellectuelles)** great intellectual abilities; **c. de concentration** attention span; *Ordinat* **c. de mémoire** memory capacity (**c**) *Jur* capacity; **avoir c. pour faire qch** to be (legally) entitled to do sth (**d**) *Univ* **c. en droit** = certificate entitling holder to practise in some branches of the legal profession

cape [kap] *nf (vêtement)* cape; *(plus longue)* cloak; **roman/film de c. et d'épée** swashbuckling novel/film; *Fig* **rire sous c.** to laugh up one's sleeve

capeline [kaplin] *nf (chapeau)* floppy hat

CAPES [kapɛs] *nm (abrév* **certificat d'aptitude au professorat de l'enseignement du second degré***)* = postgraduate teaching certificate

CAPES

This is a required qualification for state teachers in France. Candidates who pass this competitive exam become "professeurs certifiés" and are entitled to teach in secondary education.

CAPET [kapɛt] *nm (abrév* **certificat d'aptitude au professorat de l'enseignement technique***)* = postgraduate technical teaching certificate

capétien, -enne [kapesjɛ̃, -ɛn] **1** *adj* Capetian
2 *nmpl* **les Capétiens** the Capetians

capharnaüm [kafarnaɔm] *nm Fam (pièce en désordre)* pigsty; *(désordre)* mess

capillaire [kapilɛr] **1** *adj* capillary
2 *nm* (**a**) *(plante)* maidenhair (fern) (**b**) *Anat* capillary

capillarité [kapilarite] *nf Phys* capillarity

capilotade [kapilɔtad] **en capilotade** *adv* **j'ai le dos en c.** my back's killing me

capitaine [kapitɛn] *nm* (**a**) *Mil & Naut* captain; *Aviat Br* flight lieutenant, *Am* captain; **c. de gendarmerie** police superintendent; **c. des pompiers** fire chief; **c. de port** harbour master (**b**) *Sport* captain

capitainerie [kapitɛnri] *nf* harbour master's office

capital, -e, -aux, -ales [kapital, -o] **1** *adj* (**a**) *(essentiel)* major; **il est c. qu'il soit présent à la réunion** it is essential for him to be at the meeting (**b**) *Typ* **lettre capitale** capital letter
2 *nm Fin* capital; *Fig (culturel, artistique)* wealth; **posséder un c.** to have some capital; **capitaux propres** equity; **c. social** (issued) share capital
3 *nf* **capitale** (**a**) *(ville)* capital (city) (**b**) *Typ* capital; **écrire en capitales d'imprimerie** to write in block letters
capitalisable [kapitalizabl] *adj (intérêts)* capitalizable
capitalisation [kapitalizasjɔ̃] *nf (d'intérêts)* capitalization
capitaliser [kapitalize] **1** *vt (intérêts)* to capitalize
2 *vi* (**a**) *Fin* to save (**b**) **c. sur qch** *(jouer sur)* to capitalize on sth
capitalisme [kapitalism] *nm* capitalism; **c. sauvage** ruthless capitalism
capitaliste [kapitalist] *adj & nmf* capitalist
capite [kapit] *nf Suisse (dans un vignoble, un jardin)* shed
capiteux, -euse [kapitø, -øz] *adj (vin, parfum)* heady; *(charme)* sensuous; *(femme)* alluring
capitonnage [kapitɔnaʒ] *nm (action, matière)* padding, stuffing
capitonné, -e [kapitɔne] *adj (siège, cellule)* padded
capitulation [kapitylasjɔ̃] *nf* surrender; **c. sans conditions** unconditional surrender
capituler [kapityle] *vi* to surrender
caporal, -aux [kapɔral, -o] *nm Mil Br* lance corporal, *Am* private first class
capot¹ [kapo] *nm Aut Br* bonnet, *Am* hood; *Aviat (de moteur d'avion)* cowl; *Naut (bâche)* tarpaulin; *Ordinat* **c. d'imprimante** printer hood
capot² *adj inv* **être c.** *(aux cartes)* to have made no tricks at all
capote [kapɔt] *nf* (**a**) *Aut (de décapotable) Br* hood, *Am* top; **baisser la c.** to put the hood down (**b**) *Mil (manteau)* greatcoat (**c**) *Fam* **c. (anglaise)** condom, rubber
capoté, -e [kapɔte] *adj Can Fam* annoyed
capoter [kapɔte] *vi Naut* to capsize; *Aut & Aviat* to overturn; *Fig (échouer) (projet)* to fall through
cappuccino [kaputʃino] *nm* cappuccino
câpre [kɑpr] *nf* caper
caprice [kapris] *nm* (**a**) *(fantaisie)* whim, caprice; **on lui passe tous ses caprices** they indulge his/her every whim; **par un c. du destin** by a whim of fate (**b**) *(crise de colère)* tantrum; **faire un c.** to throw a tantrum
capricieux, -euse [kaprisjø, -øz] *adj (personne, courant, vent)* capricious; *(moteur)* temperamental; *(temps)* changeable
capricorne [kaprikɔrn] *nm* (**a**) *(insecte)* capricorn beetle (**b**) *Astron & Astrol* **le C.** Capricorn; **être C.** to be (a) Capricorn
caprin, -e [kaprɛ̃, -in] *adj Zool* goat, *Spéc* caprine
capsule [kapsyl] *nf* (**a**) *Anat, Bot & Méd* capsule (**b**) *(de bouteille)* cap, top (**c**) **c. (spatiale)** (space) capsule
capter [kapte] *vt* (**a**) *(l'attention de quelqu'un)* to gain, to capture (**b**) *(courant électrique)* to pick up; *(eaux)* to harness (**c**) *Rad & Tél (messages, station)* to pick up
capteur [kaptœr] *nm Phys* sensor; *Ordinat* **c. photosensible** photosensitive sensor; **c. solaire** solar panel
captif, -ive [kaptif, -iv] *adj & nm,f* captive
captivant, -e [kaptivɑ̃, -ɑ̃t] *adj* captivating

captiver [kaptive] *vt* to captivate
captivité [kaptivite] *nf* captivity; **en c.** in captivity
capture [kaptyr] *nf* (**a**) *(d'un ennemi, d'un animal)* capture (**b**) *(proie)* catch (**c**) *Ordinat* **c. vidéo** video capture
capturer [kaptyre] *vt* to capture
capuche [kapyʃ] *nf* hood; *(de poche)* rainhood
capuchon [kapyʃɔ̃] *nm* (**a**) *(de manteau)* hood; *(de moine)* cowl (**b**) *(de stylo, de tube de dentifrice)* cap, top; *(de cheminée)* cowl
capucine [kapysin] *nf* nasturtium
capverdien, -enne [kapvɛrdjɛ̃, -ɛn] **1** *adj* of Cape Verde
2 *nm,f* **C.** person from Cape Verde
Cap-Vert [kapvɛr] *nm* **le C., les îles du C.** Cape Verde
caquelon [kaklɔ̃] *nm* fondue dish
caquet [kakɛ] *nm* (**a**) *(de poules)* cackle (**b**) *Fam (bavardage)* prattle; **quel c. elle a!** she doesn't half prattle on!; **rabattre** *ou* **rabaisser le c. à qn** to shut sb up
caqueter [42] [kakte] *vi* (**a**) *(poule)* to cackle (**b**) *Fam (bavarder)* to prattle
car¹ [kar] *conj* for, because
car² *nm (véhicule)* bus, *Br* coach; **c. de police** police van; **c. de ramassage scolaire** school bus
carabine [karabin] *nf* rifle; **c. à air comprimé** air gun
carabiné, -e [karabine] *adj Fam (vent)* stiff; *(orage, fièvre)* violent; *(rhume)* stinking
carabinier [karabinje] *nm* (**a**) *(en Espagne)* frontier guard (**b**) *(en Italie)* carabiniere (**c**) *Hist* carabineer
Caracas [karakas] *n* Caracas
caraco [karako] *nm* camisole
caracoler [karakɔle] *vi (cheval)* to caracole; *Fam (sautiller)* to prance about; **c. en tête des sondages** to be riding high in the opinion polls
caractère [karaktɛr] *nm* (**a**) *(nature)* character, nature; *(détermination, style)* character; **avoir du c.** to have character; **avoir bon c.** to be good-natured; **avoir mauvais** *ou* **sale c.** to be bad-tempered; *Fam* **avoir un c. de cochon** to have a foul temper; **ce n'est pas dans son c. de...** it's not in his/her nature to... (**b**) *(attribut)* characteristic, feature; *(aspect)* nature, character; **publication à c. officiel** publication of an official nature; *Biol* **c. héréditaire/acquis** hereditary/acquired characteristic (**c**) *(signe)* character, letter; *Typ* **caractères** *(en métal)* type; **en petits caractères** in small print; **écrivez en caractères d'imprimerie** *(sur formulaire)* write in block letters (**d**) *Ordinat* character; **c. de contrôle** control character; **c. imprimable** printable character; **c. en mode point** bitmap character; **c. à sept bits** seven-bit character
caractériel, -elle [karakterjɛl] *Psy* **1** *adj (troubles)* emotional; **enfant c.** problem child
2 *nm,f* emotionally disturbed person; *(enfant)* problem child
caractérisé, -e [karakterize] *adj* **une rougeole caractérisée** a clear case of measles; **c'est de la méchanceté caractérisée** it's sheer spite
caractériser [karakterize] **1** *vt* to characterize; **avec la bonté qui la caractérise, elle...** with characteristic kindness, she...
2 se caractériser *vpr* **se c. par** to be characterized by
caractéristique [karakteristik] **1** *adj* characteristic (**de** of)
2 *nf (particularité)* characteristic, feature; **caractéristiques** *(d'une voiture, d'un avion)* specifications

carafe [karaf] *nf* (**a**) *(pour le vin, l'eau)* carafe; *(pour le whisky)* decanter (**b**) *Fam* **rester en c.** to be (left) stranded

carafon [karafɔ̃] *nm (pour le vin)* small carafe; *(pour le whisky)* small decanter

Caraïbes [karaib] *nfpl* **les C.** the Caribbean

carambolage [karãbɔlaʒ] *nm* (multiple) pile-up

caramboler [karãbɔle] **se caramboler** *vpr Fam* to collide

caramel [karamɛl] *nm (sucre brûlé)* caramel; **des caramels** *(mous)* fudge; *(durs)* toffees

caraméliser [karamelize] **1** *vt* (**a**) *(sucre)* to caramelize (**b**) *(mets, moule)* to coat with caramel **2** *vi* to caramelize **3** **se caraméliser** *vpr (sucre, oignons)* to caramelize

carapace [karapas] *nf aussi Fig* shell

carapater [karapate] **se carapater** *vpr Fam* to beat it

carat [kara] *nm* carat; **or (à) 18 carats** 18-carat gold; *Fam* **tu as jusqu'à trois heures, dernier c.** you've got until three o'clock at the latest

caravanage [karavanaʒ] = **caravaning**

caravane [karavan] *nf* (**a**) *(de tourisme)* caravan, *Am* trailer (**b**) *(du désert)* caravan

caravaning [karavaniŋ] *nm* caravanning; **faire du c.** to go caravanning

carbonate [karbɔnat] *nm Chim* carbonate; **c. de soude** sodium carbonate; *(dans le commerce)* washing soda

carbone [karbɔn] *nm Chim* carbon; **c. 14** carbon-14; **datation au c. 14** carbon dating; **(papier) c.** carbon (paper)

carbonique [karbɔnik] *adj* carbonic; **gaz c.** carbon dioxide; **neige c.** dry ice

carbonisé, -e [karbɔnize] *adj (nourriture)* burnt to a cinder; *(corps)* charred; **mourir c.** to burn to death

carburant [karbyrã] *nm* fuel

carburateur [karbyratœr] *nm Aut* carburettor

carbure [karbyr] *nm Chim* carbide; **c. d'hydrogène** hydrogen carbide

carburer [karbyre] *vi* (**a**) *(moteur)* **mal c.** to be badly tuned (**b**) *Fam* **ça carbure ici** everyone here's working like mad; **il carbure au café** coffee keeps him going

carcajou [karkaʒu] *nm* wolverine

carcan [karkã] *nm Fig* yoke; **le c. des horaires** scheduling constraints; **le c. des conventions** the straitjacket of convention

carcasse [karkas] *nf* (**a**) *(d'animal mort)* carcass; *Fam (de personne)* body (**b**) *(de maison, de bateau)* shell; **à c. radiale** *(pneu)* radial-ply

carcéral, -e, -aux, -ales [karseral, -o] *adj* prison

carcinogène [karsinɔʒɛn] *adj Méd* carcinogenic

cardan [kardã] *nm* universal joint

carder [karde] *vt* to card

cardiaque [kardjak] **1** *adj (arrêt, massage)* cardiac; **être c.** to have a heart condition **2** *nmf* person with a heart condition

cardigan [kardigã] *nm* cardigan

cardinal, -e, -aux, -ales [kardinal, -o] **1** *adj (point, nombre, vertu)* cardinal **2** *nm (religieux)* cardinal

cardiologie [kardjɔlɔʒi] *nf* cardiology

cardiologue [kardjɔlɔg] *nmf* cardiologist

cardio-training [kardjotrɛniŋ] *nm* cardio-training, CV training

cardio-vasculaire (*pl* **cardio-vasculaires**) [kardjovaskylɛr] *adj* cardiovascular

carême [karɛm] *nm* (**a**) *(période)* **le c.** Lent (**b**) *(jeûne)* fast; **faire c.** to fast

carence [karãs] *nf (manque)* deficiency; **c. en vitamine E** vitamin E deficiency; **c. alimentaire** nutritional deficiency; **c. affective** emotional deprivation

carène [karɛn] *nf* hull

caréner [34] [karene] *vt* (**a**) *Naut* to careen (**b**) *Aviat & Aut* to streamline

caressant, -e [karɛsã, -ãt] *adj* affectionate; **d'une voix caressante** affectionately

caresse [karɛs] *nf* caress; **faire des caresses à** *(personne)* to caress; *(animal)* to stroke

caresser [karese] *vt (personne)* to caress; *(animal)* to stroke; *Fig (espoir, rêve)* to cherish

car-ferry (*pl* **car-ferrys**) [karferi] *nm* car ferry

cargaison [kargɛzɔ̃] *nf* cargo; *Fam* **il est arrivé avec une c. de cadeaux** he arrived weighed down with presents

cargo [kargo] *nm Naut* freighter

cariatide [karjatid] *nf* caryatid

caribou [karibu] *nm* caribou

caricatural, -e, -aux, -ales [karikatyral, -o] *adj (récit, description)* caricatured

caricature [karikatyr] *nf* caricature

caricaturer [karikatyre] *vt* to caricature

caricaturiste [karikatyrist] *nmf* caricaturist

caricole [karikɔl] *nf Belg* periwinkle

carie [kari] *nf* **c. (dentaire)** tooth decay, *Spéc* dental caries; **avoir une c.** to have a cavity

carié, -e [karje] *adj* decayed

carier [66] [karje] **se carier** *vpr* to rot, to decay

carillon [karijɔ̃] *nm* (**a**) *(sonnerie)* chimes; **c. électrique** doorbell (**b**) *(ensemble de cloches)* bells (**c**) *(horloge)* chiming clock

carillonner [karijɔne] **1** *vi (cloches)* to chime; **c. à la porte** to ring the (door)bell loudly **2** *vt (air)* to chime; *(fête religieuse)* to announce with a peal of bells

carioca [karjɔka] **1** *adj* of Rio de Janeiro **2** *nmf* **C.** person from Rio de Janeiro

caritatif, -ive [karitatif, -iv] *adj* charitable; **association caritative** charity

carlingue [karlɛ̃g] *nf* (**a**) *Aviat* cabin (**b**) *Naut* keelson

carmélite [karmelit] *nf* Carmelite (nun)

carmin [karmɛ̃] **1** *nm* carmine **2** *adj inv* **(rouge) c.** carmine, crimson

carnage [karnaʒ] *nm* carnage

carnassier, -ère [karnasje, -ɛr] **1** *adj (animal)* flesh-eating; *Fig (sourire)* cruel **2** *nm* carnivore

carnaval, -als [karnaval] *nm* carnival; **un masque de c.** a carnival mask

carnet [karnɛ] *nm* (**a**) *(cahier)* notebook; *(de tickets de métro)* = book of ten tickets; *Scol* **c. (de notes)** report card; **c. d'adresses** address book; **c. de chèques** cheque book; *Scol* **c. de correspondance** = book of forms to be completed by parents of schoolchildren in the event of absence; *Journ* **c. mondain** society column; *Journ* **c. rose** births column; **c. de santé** health record; **c. de timbres** book of stamps (**b**) *Fin* **c. de banque** bankbook; *Br* savings book; *Belg & Suisse* **c. d'épargne** *(compte)* savings account

carnivore [karnivɔr] **1** *adj (animal)* carnivorous **2** *nm* carnivore

Caroline [karɔlin] *nf* **la C. du Nord/du Sud** North/South Carolina

carolingien, -enne [karɔlɛ̃ʒjɛ̃, -ɛn] **1** *adj* Carolingian
2 *nmpl* **les Carolingiens** the Carolingians
carotène [karɔtɛn] *nm* carotene
carotide [karɔtid] *nf* carotid
carotte [karɔt] **1** *nf* (**a**) *(légume)* carrot; *Suisse* **c. rouge** *Br* beetroot, *Am* beet; **la c. et** *ou* **ou le bâton** the carrot and the stick; *Fam* **les carottes sont cuites** you've/he's/*etc* had it (**b**) *(enseigne)* tobacconist's sign
2 *adj inv* **cheveux (roux) c.** carroty hair
carotter [karɔte] *vt Fam (objet, argent)* to pinch, *Br* to nick; **il m'a carotté 50 euros** he did me out of 50 euros
caroube [karub] *nf* carob (bean)
Carpates [karpat] *nfpl* **les C.** the Carpathians
carpe¹ [karp] *nm Anat* carpus
carpe² *nf (poisson)* carp
carpette [karpɛt] *nf* rug; *Fam Péj* **c'est une vraie c.** he's a doormat
carquois [karkwa] *nm* quiver
carre [kar] *nf (de patin, de ski)* edge
carré, -e [kare] **1** *adj* (**a**) *(figure, jardin, visage)* square; *(épaules)* square, broad (**b**) *Math* **10 mètres carrés** 10 square metres (**c**) *(tranché) (personne)* straightforward; **être c. en affaires** to be straightforward in one's business dealings
2 *nm* (**a**) *(forme)* square; *Can (place)* (public) square; **c. de soie** silk scarf; *Naut* **c. des officiers** wardroom; **c. de valets** *(aux cartes)* four jacks; **avoir une coupe au c.** *ou* **un c.** to have one's hair in a bob; *Fam* **faire la tête au c. à qn** to punch sb in the face (**b**) *Math (d'un nombre)* square; **élever au c.** to square; **le c. de six, six au c.** six squared (**c**) *Culin* **c. d'agneau** rack of lamb
carreau, -x [karo] *nm* (**a**) *(motif)* square; *(sur du tissu)* check; **tissu à carreaux** check(ed) material (**b**) *(de céramique)* tile (**c**) *(vitre)* (window) pane; *Fam* **carreaux** *(lunettes)* specs, glasses (**d**) *(carte)* diamond; *(couleur)* diamonds; *Fam* **se tenir à c.** to keep a low profile (**e**) *(locutions) Fam* **rester sur le c.** *(être tué)* to get killed; *(être blessé)* to be badly injured; *(être éliminé)* to be given the boot
carreauté, -e [karote] *adj Can (chemise)* check(ed)
carrefour [karfur] *nm* (**a**) *(croisement)* crossroads *(singulier)*; *Fig* **être à un c.** to be at a crossroads (**b**) *(réunion)* forum
carrelage [karlaʒ] *nm (carreaux)* tiles; *(sol)* (tiled) floor
carreler [9] [karle] *vt* to tile
carrelet [karlɛ] *nm* plaice
carreleur [karlœr] *nm* tiler
carrément [karemɑ̃] *adv Fam* (**a**) *(franchement)* straight out; **vas-y c.** get on with it (**b**) *(très)* really; **c'était c. immangeable** it was absolutely inedible
carrière¹ [karjɛr] *nf (profession)* career; **faire c. (dans)** to make a career (in)
carrière² *nf (lieu)* quarry
carriériste [karjerist] *nmf Péj* careerist
carriole [karjɔl] *nf* (**a**) *(petite charrette)* light cart (**b**) *(traîneau) Can* sleigh, sled
carrossable [karɔsabl] *adj (chemin, route)* suitable for motor vehicles
carrosse [karɔs] *nm* (**a**) *(véhicule)* (horse-drawn) coach (**b**) *Can (voiture d'enfant) Br* pram, *Am* baby carriage
carrosser [karɔse] *vt* to fit the body to; **une voiture bien carrossée** a sturdily built car

carrosserie [karɔsri] *nf (de voiture)* bodywork
carrossier [karɔsje] *nm* coachbuilder
carrousel [karuzɛl] *nm* (**a**) *(d'une aérogare)* carousel (**b**) *Can, Belg & Suisse (manège)* merry-go-round
carrure [karyr] *nf (de personne)* build; *(de vêtement)* width across the shoulders; **un homme à la forte c.** a broad-shouldered man; *Fig* **un homme d'une c. exceptionnelle** a man of exceptional qualities; **elle est d'une autre c. que son prédécesseur** she is of quite a different calibre from her predecessor
cartable [kartabl] *nm* school bag
carte [kart] *nf* (**a**) *(pour la correspondance)* card; *Fig* **donner c. blanche à qn** to give sb carte blanche; *Can* **c. d'affaires** business card; **c. d'anniversaire** birthday card; **c. postale** postcard; **c. de visite** *Br* visiting *or Am* calling card; *(d'une entreprise)* business card; **c. de vœux** *Br* greetings card, *Am* greeting card (**b**) *(document officiel)* card; **c. d'abonnement** *(de bibliothèque)* library card; *(de transports, de théâtre)* season ticket; **c. d'adhérent** membership card; **c. d'électeur** voting card; **c. d'embarquement** boarding pass; **c. d'étudiant** student card; **c. de fidélité** loyalty card; *Aut* **c. grise** ≃ (vehicle) registration document; **c. d'identité** identity card; *Rail* **c. Jeunes** = reduced-rate railcard for young people, valid in certain European countries; **C. Orange** *(à Paris)* = combined monthly season ticket for the underground, bus and suburban train; **c. de presse** press card; **c. de Sécurité sociale** ≃ National Insurance Card; **c. de séjour** residence permit; *Rail* **C. Vermeil** = reduced-rate railcard for people over sixty within France; *Aut* **c. verte** green card
(**c**) *(document informatisé)* card; **c. bancaire** bank card; **c. Bleue®** debit card, *Br* ≃ Switch® card; **c. de crédit** credit card; **c. de paiement** payment card; **c. à puce** smart card; *Tél* **c. SIM** SIM card; **c. de téléphone** phonecard
(**d**) *(pour jouer)* **c. (à jouer)** (playing) card; **jouer aux cartes** to play cards; **donner les cartes** to deal (the cards); *Fig* **jouer cartes sur table** to lay one's cards on the table; **c. à gratter** scratchcard; **c. maîtresse** trump card
(**e**) *(géographique)* map; *Naut* chart; **faire la c. d'une région** to map (out) an area; *Astrol* **c. du ciel** astronomical chart; **c. d'état-major** *Br* ≃ Ordnance Survey map, *Am* ≃ Geological Survey map; **c. routière** road map
(**f**) *(de restaurant)* menu; **manger à la c.** to eat à la carte; **c. des vins** wine list
(**g**) *Ordinat* card; *(de clavier)* map; **c. accélératrice** accelerator card; **c. à circuit imprimé** *ou* **de circuits imprimés** printed circuit board, PCB; **c. à circuit(s) intégré(s)** integrated circuit card, IC card; **c. d'extension** expansion card *or* board; **c. mémoire** memory card; **c. mère** motherboard; **c. modem** modem card; **c. de polices de caractères** font card; **c. processeur** processor card; **c. réseau** network card; **c. SCSI** SCSI card; **c. son** *ou* **sonore** sound card; **c. unité centrale** CPU board; **c. vidéo** video card; **c. vocale** voice card
carte-adaptateur *(pl* **cartes-adaptateurs)** [kartadaptatœr] *nf Ordinat* **c. réseau** network adaptor card
cartel [kartɛl] *nm Écon* cartel; **c. de l'acier/de la drogue** steel/drug cartel
carte-lettre *(pl* **cartes-lettres)** [kartəlɛtr] *nf* letter-card
carter [kartɛr] *nm (d'engrenages)* casing; *(de bicyclette)* chain guard; *Aut (de vilebrequin)* crankcase

carte-réponse (*pl* **cartes-réponses**) [kartrepɔ̃s] *nf* reply card
carterie [kartəri] *nf* card shop
cartésien, -enne [kartezjɛ̃, -ɛn] *adj* (**a**) *Math* Cartesian (**b**) *(logique)* logical
carte-vue (*pl* **cartes-vues**) [kartəvy] *nf Belg* (picture) postcard
cartilage [kartilaʒ] *nm* cartilage
cartilagineux, -euse [kartilaʒinø, -øz] *adj* cartilaginous; *(viande)* gristly
cartographe [kartɔgraf] *nmf* cartographer
cartographie [kartɔgrafi] *nf* cartography
cartomancien, -enne [kartɔmɑ̃sjɛ̃, -ɛn] *nm,f* fortune-teller *(who uses cards)*
carton [kartɔ̃] *nm* (**a**) *(matière)* cardboard; *(feuille)* piece of cardboard; **c. d'invitation** invitation (card); **c. jaune/rouge** *(au football)* yellow/red card (**b**) *(boîte)* (cardboard) box; **faire des cartons** to pack one's things up in cardboard boxes; **c. à chapeau(x)** hatbox (**c**) *Art (dessin)* cartoon, sketch; **c. à dessin** portfolio (**d**) *(locutions)* **faire un c.** *(au tir)* to have a shot; *Fam (sur quelqu'un)* to shoot somebody; *Fam (à un examen)* to pass with flying colours; *Fam Scol* (**se**) **prendre un c.** *(une mauvaise note)* to get a bad mark
cartonner [kartɔne] **1** *vt (livre)* to case; **livre cartonné** hardback (book)
2 *vi Fam* (**a**) *(à l'école)* to get excellent marks (**en** in) (**b**) *(musique)* to be mind-blowing
cartonneux, -euse [kartɔnø, -øz] *adj* like cardboard
carton-pâte [kartɔ̃pɑt] *nm* pasteboard
cartouche [kartuʃ] *nf (de fusil, de stylo, d'imprimante)* cartridge; *(de cigarettes)* carton; *Ordinat* **c. Zip®** Zip® disk
cartouchière [kartuʃjɛr] *nf* cartridge belt
caryatide [karjatid] = **cariatide**
cas [kɑ] *nm* (**a**) *(situation)* case, situation; *Jur & Méd* case; **c. particulier** exception; **envisager tous les c. possibles** to consider all the possibilities; **examiner qch au c. par c.** to examine sth on a case by case basis; **c'est le c. de le dire** you can say that again; **en pareil c.** in a similar situation; **si tel est votre c.** if that applies to you; **il parle trois langues mais ce n'est pas mon c.** he speaks three languages but I don't; *Fam* **c'est un c.!** he is a case!; **un c. social** a person with social problems (**b**) *Gram* case (**c**) *(locutions)* **en aucun c.** under no circumstances, on no account; **en tout c., dans tous les c.** in any case, anyway; **dans ce c.** *(puisqu'il en est ainsi)* in that case; **dans tous les c. de figure** in all cases; **le c. échéant** if necessary, if need be; **selon le c.** as the case may be; **en c. d'urgence** in an emergency; **en c. de besoin** if need be; **j'ai pris un pull supplémentaire en c. de besoin** I took an extra sweater just in case; **au c. où il viendrait** in case he comes; *Fam* **je te le laisse au c. où** I'll leave it for you just in case; **faire grand c. de qn/qch** to have a high opinion of sb/sth; **faire peu de c. de qch** to have a low opinion of sb/sth; **ne faire aucun c. de qch** to take no notice of sth
Casablanca [kazablɑ̃ka] *n* Casablanca
casanier, -ère [kazanje, -ɛr] *adj* home-loving; *Péj* stay-at-home
casaque [kazak] *nf (de jockey)* blouse; *Fig* **tourner c.** *(partir)* to turn tail; *(changer d'opinion)* to change sides
cascade [kaskad] *nf* (**a**) *(chute d'eau)* waterfall; *Fig* **des rires en c.** peals of laughter; *Ordinat* **ouvrir des fenêtres en c.** to cascade windows (**b**) *(au cinéma)* stunt

cascadeur, -euse [kaskadœr, -øz] *nm,f* stuntman, f stuntwoman
case [kɑz] *nf* (**a**) *(de tiroir)* compartment; *(de formulaire)* box; *(de mots croisés, de damier)* square; *Fam* **il lui manque une c., il a une c. de vide** he's got a screw loose; **c. départ** *(dans les jeux)* start; *Fig* **retour à la c. départ** back to square one (**b**) *(hutte)* hut (**c**) *Ordinat* button; *(en forme de boîte)* box (**d**) *Suisse* **c. (postale)** postbox
casemate [kazmat] *nf* blockhouse
caser [kɑze] **1** *vt* (**a**) *(placer)* to fit in (**b**) *Fam* **c. qn** *(établir)* to fix sb up with a job; *(marier)* to marry sb off
2 se caser *vpr Fam (trouver un emploi)* to get oneself a job; *(se marier)* to get married and settle down
caserne [kazɛrn] *nf* barracks; **c. de pompiers** fire station
cash [kaʃ] *adv Fam* **payer c.** to pay cash (down)
cash-flow (*pl* **cash-flows**) [kaʃflo] *nm Com* cash flow
casier [kazje] *nm* (**a**) *(compartiment)* compartment; *(pour le courrier)* pigeonhole; *(à vêtements)* locker; **c. à bouteilles** bottle rack (**b**) *Jur* **c. judiciaire** police *or* criminal record; **avoir un c. (judiciaire)** to have a record (**c**) *(pour pêcher)* pot; **casiers à homards** lobster pots
casino [kazino] *nm* casino
Caspienne [kaspjɛn] *adj f voir* **mer**
casque [kask] *nm* (**a**) *(de soldat, de pompier)* helmet; *(de motocycliste)* (crash) helmet; **le port du c. est obligatoire** *(sur panneau)* safety helmets must be worn; **c. intégral** full-face crash helmet; **les Casques bleus** the Blue Berets (**b**) *(écouteurs)* headphones, headset (**c**) *(de salon de coiffure)* hood hairdryer
casqué, -e [kaske] *adj* helmeted
casquer [kaske] *vi Fam (payer)* to fork out
casquette [kaskɛt] *nf* cap
cassable [kasabl] *adj* breakable
cassant, -e [kasɑ̃, -ɑ̃t] *adj* brittle; *Fig (personne, ton)* brusque
cassation [kasasjɔ̃] *nf Jur* annulment
casse¹ [kas] *nf Typ* case; **bas/haut de c.** lower/upper case
casse² *nf* (**a**) *(action de casser)* **il va y avoir de la c.** something will get broken; *Fam (des ennuis)* there'll be trouble; **aller** *ou* **partir à la c.** *(voiture)* to go for scrap (**b**) *(objets cassés)* breakages
casse³ *nm très Fam (cambriolage)* break-in
cassé, -e [kase] *adj (objet, jambe)* broken; *(voix)* cracked; *très Fam (ivre) Br* pissed, *Am* wasted; *(drogué)* high, wasted
casse-cou [kasku] **1** *adj inv (personne)* reckless
2 *nmf inv (personne)* daredevil
casse-croûte [kaskrut] *nm inv* (**a**) *Fam (repas)* snack, bite; *(sandwich)* sandwich, *Br* sarnie (**b**) *Can (snack)* snack bar
casse-cul [kasky] *très Fam* **1** *adj inv* (**a**) *(ennuyeux)* boring as hell (**b**) *(agaçant)* **être c.** to be a pain in the *Br* arse *or Am* ass
2 *nmf inv* pain in the *Br* arse *or Am* ass
casse-gueule [kasgœl] *très Fam* **1** *adj inv (endroit)* dangerous; *(entreprise)* risky
2 *nm inv (endroit)* danger spot; *(entreprise)* risky business
casse-noisettes [kasnwazɛt] *nm inv* nutcrackers
casse-noix [kasnwa] *nm inv* nutcrackers
casse-pieds [kaspje] *Fam* **1** *adj inv* **ce qu'il peut être c.!** he can be a real pain (in the neck)!
2 *nmf inv* pain (in the neck)

casse-pipe [kaspip] *nm inv Fam* **aller au c.** to go to the front

casser [kase] **1** *vt* (**a**) *(briser)* to break; *(noix)* to crack; *(voix)* to strain; *(chaussures)* to break in; *Fam (personne)* to humiliate; **c. les prix** to slash prices; *aussi Fig* **c. le moral des troupes** to discourage the ranks; *Fig* **c. du sucre sur le dos de qn** to talk about sb behind his/her back; *Fam* **c. la croûte** *ou* **la graine** to have a bite to eat; *Fam* **ça ne casse pas trois pattes à un canard, ça ne casse pas des briques** it's nothing to write home about; *Fam* **c. la baraque** *(pièce, acteur)* to bring the house down; *Fam* **à tout c.** *(au maximum)* at the very most (**b**) *Fam (locutions avec parties du corps)* **c. les pieds à qn** *(ennuyer)* to bore the pants off sb; *(agacer)* to get on sb's nerves; **ça fait deux mois qu'elle me casse les pieds pour que j'y aille** she's been bugging me to go for two months now; **c. les oreilles à qn** to deafen sb; **c. la figure** *ou très Fam* **la gueule à qn** to smash sb's face in; *Fam* **c. sa pipe** to kick the bucket, to snuff it; *Vulg* **il nous casse les couilles, il nous les casse** he's pissing us off, *Br* he's getting on our tits (**c**) *Jur (verdict)* to quash; *(mariage)* to annul; *(fiançailles)* to break off **2** *vi* (**a**) *(se briser)* to break; **attention, ça casse!** be careful, it's fragile! (**b**) *Fam (se séparer)* to split up, to break up **3** *se casser vpr* (**a**) *(se briser)* to break (**b**) **se c. une** *ou* **la jambe** to break one's leg; *Fig* **se c. le nez** to fail; *Fig* **se c. la tête** to rack one's brains; *Fam* **se c. la figure** *ou très Fam* **la gueule** *(tomber)* to fall flat on one's face; *(échouer)* to fail (**c**) *Fam (se fatiguer)* **il ne s'est pas cassé pour m'aider** he didn't exactly strain himself helping me; *Vulg* **se c. le cul à faire qch** to bust a gut *or Am* to bust one's ass trying to do sth (**d**) *Fam (partir)* to split, to clear off; **tu viens? on se casse** we're off, are you coming?; **casse-toi!** piss off!

casserole [kasrɔl] *nf* (**a**) *(de cuisine)* (sauce)pan; *très Fam* **passer à la c.** *(sexuellement)* to get screwed; *(être tué)* to get bumped off (**b**) *Fam* **chanter comme une c.** to be a lousy singer

casse-tête [kastɛt] *nm inv* (**a**) *(jeu)* puzzle (**b**) *(problème)* headache

cassette [kasɛt] *nf* cassette, tape; **enregistrer qch sur c.** to tape sth; **c. vidéo** video (cassette)

casseur, -euse [kasœr, -øz] *nm,f* (**a**) *(manifestant)* rioter (**b**) *très Fam (cambrioleur)* burglar

cassis [kasis] *nm* (**a**) *(baie)* blackcurrant (**b**) *(arbuste)* blackcurrant bush (**c**) *(liqueur)* blackcurrant liqueur (**d**) *Fam (tête)* nut

cassonade [kasɔnad] *nf* brown sugar

cassoulet [kasulɛ] *nm* cassoulet *(stew of beans, pork, goose etc, a speciality of Languedoc)*

cassure [kasyr] *nf* break; *Géol* fault

castagne [kastaɲ] *nf Fam* fighting; **aimer la c.** *(la bagarre)* to like fighting, *Br* to like a good scrap

castagnettes [kastaɲɛt] *nfpl* castanets; *Fam Fig* **ses dents/genoux jouaient des castagnettes** his/her teeth were chattering/knees were knocking

caste [kast] *nf* caste

castillan, -e [kastijɑ̃, -an] **1** *adj* Castilian **2** *nm,f* **C.** Castilian **3** *nm (langue)* Castilian

Castille [kastij] *nf* **la C.** Castile

casting [kastiŋ] *nm Cin & Théât* casting

castor [kastɔr] *nm* beaver

castrat [kastra] *nm Mus* castrato

castrer [kastre] *vt* to castrate; *(chat, chien)* to neuter

cata [kata] *nf Fam* **c'est la c.** it's a disaster

cataclysme [kataklism] *nm* cataclysm

cataclysmique [kataklismik] *adj* cataclysmic

catacombes [katakɔ̃b] *nfpl* catacombs

catadioptre [katadjɔptr] *nm (de véhicule)* reflector; *(sur la route)* cat's-eye®

catafalque [katafalk] *nm* catafalque

catalan, -e [katalɑ̃, -an] **1** *adj* Catalan **2** *nm,f* **C.** Catalan **3** *nm (langue)* Catalan

Catalogne [katalɔɲ] *nf* **la C.** Catalonia

catalogue [katalɔg] *nm* catalogue; **faire le c. de** to catalogue; **acheter sur c.** to buy things from a catalogue

cataloguer [katalɔge] *vt* to catalogue; *Fig & Péj* to label

catalyser [katalize] *vt aussi Fig* to catalyse

catalyseur [katalizœr] *nm aussi Fig* catalyst

catalytique [katalitik] *adj Chim* catalytic

catamaran [katamarɑ̃] *nm Naut* catamaran

Cataphote® [katafɔt] = **catadioptre**

cataplasme [kataplasm] *nm* poultice

catapulte [katapylt] *nf* catapult

catapulter [katapylte] *vt* to catapult; *Fig* **c. qn à un poste** to catapult sb into a post

cataracte [katarakt] *nf (maladie, chute d'eau)* cataract

catastrophe [katastrɔf] *nf* disaster, catastrophe; **c. ferroviaire/aérienne** rail/air disaster; **c'est la c.!** a disaster!; **c.! il est déjà là!** panic stations! he's here already!; **en c.** *(à toute vitesse)* in a mad rush *or* panic

catastrophé, -e [katastrɔfe] *adj Fam* stunned

catastrophique [katastrɔfik] *adj* disastrous, catastrophic

catch [katʃ] *nm* wrestling; **faire du c.** to wrestle

catcheur, -euse [katʃœr, -øz] *nm,f* wrestler

catéchisme [kateʃism] *nm* catechism

catégorie [kategɔri] *nf* category, type; *(d'hôtel, de personne)* grade; *(de boxeur)* class; **c. sociale** social class; **c. socioprofessionnelle** socio-professional group

catégorique [kategɔrik] *adj (réponse, refus)* categoric(al); **je suis absolument c., c'est lui** I'm absolutely positive it's him

catégoriquement [kategɔrikmɑ̃] *adv* categorically

catégoriser [kategɔrize] *vt* to categorize

Cathares [katar] *nmpl Hist* **les C.** the Cathars

catharsis [katarsis] *nf* catharsis

cathédrale [katedral] *nf* cathedral

cathéter [katetɛr] *nm Méd* catheter

catho [kato] *adj Fam* Catholic

cathode [katɔd] *nf Élec* cathode

cathodique [katɔdik] *adj Élec* cathodic; **tube c.** cathode ray tube

catholicisme [katɔlisism] *nm* (Roman) Catholicism

catholique [katɔlik] **1** *adj* (Roman) Catholic; *Fam* **ce n'est pas très c.** it's a bit shady **2** *nm,f* (Roman) Catholic

catimini [katimini] **en catimini** *adv* on the sly

catin [katɛ̃] *nf* (**a**) *Vieilli (prostituée)* trollop (**b**) *Can (poupée)* doll

catogan [katɔgɑ̃] *nm (nœud)* hair ribbon *(for ponytail)*; *(queue de cheval)* ponytail

Caucase [kokaz] *nm* **le C.** the Caucasus

caucasien, -enne [kokazjɛ̃, -ɛn] *adj* Caucasian

cauchemar [koʃmar] *nm aussi Fig* nightmare; **une vision de c.** a nightmarish vision; **faire un c.** to have a nightmare

cauchemarder [koʃmarde] *vi* to have nightmares
cauchemardesque [koʃmardɛsk] *adj* nightmarish
causal, -e, -als *ou* **-aux, -ales** [kozal, -o] *adj* causal
causant, -e [kozɑ̃, -ɑ̃t] *adj Fam* chatty
cause [koz] *nf* (**a**) *(origine)* cause; **quelle est la c. de son départ?** why is he/she leaving?; **il s'est mis en colère, et pour c.** he got angry, and with good reason; **fermé pour c. d'inventaire/de décès** *(sur panneau)* closed for stocktaking/due to bereavement; **à c. de** because of (**b**) *Jur* case; *Fig* **la c. est entendue** there's nothing more to be said; **être en c.** *(sujet à caution)* to be in question; **mettre qch en c.** to doubt sth, to question sth; **mettre qn en c.** *(impliquer)* to implicate sb; **mettre qn hors de c.** to clear sb; **en tout état de c.** in any case (**c**) *(parti)* cause; **faire c. commune avec qn** to join forces with sb; **c'est pour une bonne c.** it's all in a good cause
causer¹ [koze] *vt (provoquer)* to cause; **c. des ennuis à qn** to cause sb problems
causer² *vi* (**a**) *(parler)* to chat, to talk (**de** about); **c. affaires** to talk business; **c. avec** *ou* **à qn** to chat with sb; *Fam* **je ne lui cause plus!** I'm not talking to him/her!; *Ironique* **cause toujours(, tu m'intéresses)!** yeah, yeah(, whatever)! (**b**) *(cancaner)* to talk, to gossip; **on en cause au village** it's the talk of the village
causerie [kozri] *nf* (**a**) *(discussion)* chat, talk (**b**) *(conférence)* (informal) talk
causette [kozɛt] *nf Fam* little chat; **faire la c.** *ou* **un brin de c. avec qn** to have a little chat with sb
causse [kos] *nm* = limestone plateau in central and southern France
caustique [kostik] *adj aussi Fig* caustic
cautériser [koterize] *vt* to cauterize
caution [kosjɔ̃] *nf* (**a**) *(pour appartement)* deposit; *Jur* bail; *Fig (appui)* support, backing; *Jur* **sous c.** on bail; **sujet à c.** *(information)* unconfirmed (**b**) *(personne)* guarantor
cautionner [kosjone] *vt (personne)* to stand surety for; *Jur* to stand bail for; *Fig (approuver)* to support, to back
cavalcade [kavalkad] *nf Fam (bousculade)* stampede
cavale [kaval] *nf Fam (évasion)* escape; **être en c.** to be on the run
cavaler [kavale] *vi Fam (se démener)* to rush around; *(fuir)* to run off; **c. après qn** to chase after sb
cavalerie [kavalri] *nf Mil* cavalry
cavaleur, -euse [kavalœr, -øz] *Fam* **1** *adj (homme)* womanizing; *(femme)* man-chasing
2 *nm,f* (**a**) skirt-chaser; *(femme)* man-chaser
cavalier, -ère [kavalje, -ɛr] **1** *adj (manière, personne)* cavalier
2 *nm,f* (**a**) *(à cheval)* rider, horseman, *f* horsewoman (**b**) *(de bal)* partner; *Fig* **faire c. seul** to go it alone **3** *nm* (**a**) *(aux échecs)* knight (**b**) *(accompagnateur)* escort (**c**) *Can (amoureux)* boyfriend
cavalièrement [kavaljɛrmɑ̃] *adv* in a cavalier manner
cave¹ [kav] *adj (joues, yeux)* hollow, sunken
cave² *nf* (**a**) *(cellier)* cellar; **c. à charbon/vin** coal/wine cellar; *Fig* **de la c. au grenier** from top to bottom (**b**) *Can (sous-sol)* basement
caveau, -x [kavo] *nm* (**a**) *(petite cave)* small cellar (**b**) *(funéraire)* burial vault
caverne [kavɛrn] *nf* cave, cavern; **homme des cavernes** caveman
caverneux, -euse [kavɛrnø, -øz] *adj (voix)* deep
caviar [kavjar] *nm* caviar

caviarder [kavjarde] *vt* to censor
caviste [kavist] *nm* cellarman
cavité [kavite] *nf* cavity, hollow; **c. buccale** oral cavity
Cayenne [kajɛn] *n* (**a**) *(ville)* Cayenne (**b**) **poivre de C.** cayenne pepper
CB [sibi] *nf (abrév* **citizen band***)* CB
CC [sese] *nm (abrév* **compte courant***)* CA
CCI [sesei] *nf (abrév* **Chambre de commerce et d'industrie***)* Chamber of Commerce and Industry
CCP [sesepe] *nm (abrév* **compte courant postal, compte chèque postal***)* *Br* ≃ Giro account, *Am* ≃ Post Office checking account
CD [sede] *nm* (**a**) *(abrév* **Compact Disc***)* CD (**b**) *(abrév* **corps diplomatique***)* CD
CDD [sedede] *nm (abrév* **contrat à durée déterminée***)* fixed-term contract
CDI [sedei] *nm inv* (**a**) *(abrév* **centre des impôts***)* tax office (**b**) *(abrév* **contrat à durée indéterminée***)* permanent contract (**c**) *(abrév* **centre de documentation et d'information***)* school library *(with special resources on how to find information)*
CD-I [sedei] *(abrév* **Compact Disc interactif***)* CDI
CD-R [sedeɛr] *nm (abrév* **Compact Disc recordable***)* CD-R
CD-ROM [sederɔm] *nm inv* CD-ROM; **C. d'installation** installation CD-ROM
CD-RW [sedeɛrdublǝve] *nm (abrév* **Compact Disc Rewritable***)* CD-RW
CE [seǝ] **1** *nf* (**a**) *(abrév* **Conseil de l'Europe***)* Council of Europe (**b**) *(abrév* **cours élémentaire***)* CE1 = second year of primary school; CE2 = third year of primary school
2 *nf (abrév* **Communauté européenne***)* EC
ce¹ [sǝ] *pron démonstratif*

---

ce becomes **c'** before a vowel.

(**a**) *(pour désigner)* **c'est mon père** that's my father; *(au téléphone)* it's my father; **ce sont** *ou Fam* **c'est mes amis** those are my friends; *(qui arrivent)* there are my friends; **c'était mon idée** it was my idea; **c'est le plus beau jour de ma vie** this is the best day of my life; **c'est moi** it's me; **qui est-ce?,** *Fam* **qui c'est?** who is it?; **c'est lui qui l'a écrit** HE wrote it; **qui a fait ça? – c'est moi!** who did that? – I did!; **c'est un bon traducteur** he's a good translator; **c'est la première voiture que j'aie eue** that was my first car; **c'est ici que je suis né** this is where I was born, I was born here; **c'est jeudi aujourd'hui** today's Thursday, it's Thursday today; **c'était il y a longtemps** it was a long time ago (**b**) *(pour qualifier ou pour expliquer)* **c'est facile/joli** it's easy/nice; **c'est exact!** that's right!; **c'est que maman est déjà partie** the thing is, Mum's already left; **s'il chante, (alors) c'est qu'il est de bonne humeur** if he's singing, it means he's in a good mood; *Fam* **c'est bizarre qu'il n'ait pas appelé!** it's strange that he hasn't called!; *Fam* **ce qu'il est pénible!** he's such a pain! (**c**) *(avec des pronoms relatifs)* **ce qui..., ce que...** what...; **je sais ce qui s'est passé** I know what happened; **ce que je crois, c'est que...** what I think is...; **voici ce dont il s'agit** this is what it's all about; **voilà ce à quoi j'avais pensé** that's what I thought of; **ce qui compte, c'est que...** what counts is that...; **j'ai appris tout ce qui se trouve dans le chapitre 4** I've learned everything in chapter 4; **j'ai oublié tout ce qu'elle m'a dit** I've forgotten everything she told me; **pour ce qui est de la qualité** with regard to or as regards quality (**d**) *(locutions)* **ce faisant** in so doing, whilst doing so; **il y est allé, et ce malgré mon interdiction** he went despite the fact that I had forbidden him; **sur ce, je m'en vais** on that note, I'm leaving; **... et, sur ce, il sortit son album de photos** ... whereupon he brought out his photo album

ce², **cet**, **cette**, **ces** [sə, sɛt, se] *adj démonstratif*

cet is used before a masculine singular noun or adjective beginning with a vowel or mute h.

(**a**) *(par référence)* **ce garçon** this boy; **cet enfant** this child; **cette fille** this girl; **ces gens/animaux/couleurs** these people/animals/colours (**b**) *(en désignant)* **ce vin-ci** this wine; **ce vin-là** that wine; **ces voitures-ci** these cars; **ces voitures-là** those cars (**c**) *Fam (intensif)* **alors, cette lettre, tu me la montres?** so do I get to see this *or* that letter of yours?; **et ce café, il arrive?** is that coffee on its way or what?; **je lui ai envoyé une de ces lettres!** I wrote him/her such a letter!; **j'ai une de ces faims!** I'm so hungry!

CEA [seəa] *nm (abrév* **commissariat à l'énergie atomique)** = French atomic energy commission, *Br* ≃ AEA, *Am* ≃ AEC

CEAM [seəaɛm] *nf (abrév* **carte européenne d'assurance maladie)** EHIC, European Health Insurance Card

ceci [səsi] *pron démonstratif* this; **c. (étant) dit** having said that; **c. n'explique pas cela** that's no explanation

cécité [sesite] *nf* blindness; **être atteint de c.** to be blind

CED [seəde] *nf (abrév* **Communauté européenne de défense)** EDC

céder [34] [sede] **1** *vt* (**a**) *(donner) (objet, droit)* to give up (**à** to); *(dans un testament)* to leave (**à** to); **c. sa place à qn** to give up one's seat to sb; **c. du terrain** to give ground; **cédez le passage** *(sur panneau) Br* give way, *Am* yield (**b**) *(vendre)* to sell; **à c.** *(sur panneau)* for sale

2 *vi* (**a**) *(plancher, branche)* to give way (**b**) *(se soumettre)* to give in (**devant** to)

3 *céder à vt ind (personne, tentation, revendication)* to give in to

cédérom [sederɔm] *nm Ordinat* CD-Rom

Cedex [sedɛks] *nm (abrév* **Courrier d'entreprise à distribution exceptionnelle)** = postal code ensuring rapid delivery of business mail

cédille [sedij] *nf* cedilla

cédrat [sedra] *nm (fruit)* citron

cèdre [sɛdr] *nm (arbre, bois)* cedar; **c. du Liban** cedar of Lebanon

CEE [seəə] *nf (abrév* **Communauté économique européenne)** EEC

CEEA [seəəa] *nf (abrév* **Communauté européenne de l'énergie atomique)** Euratom

CÉGEP, cégep [seʒɛp] *nm Can (abrév* **collège d'enseignement général et professionnel)** = college of further education

CEI [seəi] *nf (abrév* **Communauté d'États indépendants)** CIS

ceindre [54] [sɛdr] *vt Litt* (**a**) *(épée)* to strap on (**b**) *(sujet: couronne)* to encircle

ceinture [sɛtyr] *nf* (**a**) *(accessoire)* belt; **être c. noire de judo** to be a black belt in judo; *Fam* **se serrer la c., faire c.** to tighten one's belt; **c. de chasteté** chastity belt; **c. de sécurité** seat belt; **attacher sa c. (de sécurité)** to fasten one's seat belt (**b**) *(taille) (de vêtement)* waistband; *(d'une personne)* waist; **frapper au-des-**

sous de la c. to hit below the belt (**c**) **la petite C.** = circular bus route around centre of Paris

ceinturer [sɛtyre] *vt* to grab around the waist

ceinturon [sɛtyrɔ̃] *nm* belt

cela [səla, sla] *pron démonstratif* that; **c'est c.!** *(c'est exact)* that's right!; **c'est pour c. que je viens** that's what I've come for *or* why I've come; **il y a deux ans de c.** that was two years ago; **et pourquoi c.?** why is that?; **s'il n'y avait que c.** if that were the only problem; **et avec c.?** *(dans un magasin)* (will there be) anything else?; **c. (étant) dit** having said that

célébration [selebrasjɔ̃] *nf* celebration

célèbre [selɛbr] *adj* famous (**pour** for); **se rendre c.** to become famous for sth; **tristement c.** notorious

célébrer [34] [selebre] *vt* (**a**) *(fêter) (anniversaire, victoire, messe)* to celebrate (**b**) *(vanter)* **c. les mérites/le talent de qn** to extol sb's merits/talent

célébrité [selebrite] *nf (notoriété)* fame; *(personne)* celebrity

céleri [selri] *nm* celery; *Culin* **c. rémoulade** = grated celeriac in mayonnaise

céleri-rave *(pl* **céleris-raves)** [selrirav] *nm* celeriac

céleste [selɛst] *adj* (**a**) *(du firmament) (phénomènes, corps)* celestial, heavenly (**b**) *Rel* heavenly

célibat [seliba] *nm* single life; *(des prêtres)* celibacy

célibataire [selibatɛr] **1** *adj (non marié)* unmarried, single

2 *nm* bachelor; **un c. endurci** a confirmed bachelor

3 *nf* single woman

celle [sɛl] *voir* **celui**

cellier [selje] *nm* storeroom; *(cave)* cellar

Cellophane® [selɔfan] *nf* cellophane®; **sous C.** cellophane-wrapped

cellulaire [selylɛr] **1** *adj* (**a**) *Biol* cell (**b**) *Jur* **régime c.** solitary confinement (**c**) *Tél* cellular

2 *nm Can Tél Br* mobile (phone), *Am* cell(phone)

cellule [selyl] *nf* (**a**) *(d'une prison, d'un couvent)* cell; *Hum* **il a passé la nuit en c. de dégrisement** he spent the night in the cells to sober up (**b**) *Biol* cell; **c. nerveuse** nerve cell; **c. souche** stem cell (**c**) *Fig (élément)* unit; *(de parti politique)* cell; **c. dormante** *ou* **en sommeil** sleeper cell (**d**) *Élec* **c. photoélectrique** photo-electric cell

cellulite [selylit] *nf* cellulite

Celluloïd® [selylɔid] *nm* celluloid®

cellulose [selyloz] *nf* cellulose

celte [sɛlt] **1** *adj* Celtic

2 *nmf* **C.** Celt

celtique [sɛltik] *adj & nm* Celtic

celui, celle [səlɥi, sɛl] *(mpl* **ceux** [sø]*, fpl* **celles**) *pron démonstratif* the one; **mon livre et c. de Paul** my book and Paul's; **mes livres et ceux de Paul** my books and Paul's; **c. que je t'ai donné** the one I gave you; **celles dont je t'ai parlé** the ones I talked to you about; **c.-ci** this one; *(ce dernier)* the latter; **c.-là** that one; *(le premier)* the former; **ceux-ci** these ones; *(ces derniers)* the latter; **ceux-là** those ones; *(les premiers)* the former; **ah, c.-là, quel idiot!** he's such an idiot, that one!; **autre exemple, plus technique c.-là** another example, a more technical one this time; **elle est bien bonne, celle-là!** that's a good one!

cendre [sɑ̃dr] *nf* ash(es); **faire cuire des pommes de terre sous la c.** to roast potatoes in the ashes; **réduire qch en cendres** to reduce sth to ashes; **cendres** *(après incinération)* ashes; *Rel* **le mercredi des Cendres** Ash Wednesday

cendré, -e¹ [sɑ̃dre] *adj voir* **blond**
cendrée² [sɑ̃dre] *nf Sport (piste)* cinder track; *(mâche-fer)* cinders
cendrier [sɑ̃drije] *nm* ashtray
Cendrillon [sɑ̃drijɔ̃] *npr* Cinderella
Cène [sɛn] *nf* **la C.** the Last Supper
censé, -e [sɑ̃se] *adj* **être c. faire qch** to be supposed to do sth
censeur [sɑ̃sœr] *nm* (**a**) *Scol (d'un lycée) Br* deputy head, *Am* assistant principal (**b**) *(dans les médias)* censor (**c**) *Litt (juge)* critic
censure [sɑ̃syr] *nf (activité)* censorship; *(personnes)* (board of) censors
censurer [sɑ̃syre] *vt* (**a**) *(film, livre, scène)* to censor (**b**) *Litt (critiquer)* to censure
cent¹ [sɑ̃] **1** *adj* a *or* one hundred; **deux cents hommes** two hundred men; **deux c. cinquante** two hundred and fifty; **je te l'ai dit c. fois** I've told you a hundred times; **vous avez c. fois raison** you're absolutely right; *Fam* **je ne vais pas t'attendre (pendant) c. sept ans** I'm not going to wait for you forever; **faire les c. pas** to pace up and down; *Fam* **être aux c. coups** to be frantic; *Fam* **faire les quatre cents coups** to get up to all sorts of tricks
    2 *nm* (**a**) *(nombre)* hundred; a hundred; **pour c.** per cent; **c. pour c.** a hundred per cent; *voir aussi* **trois** (**b**) *(division de l'euro)* cent
cent² [sɛnt] *nm (monnaie)* cent
centaine [sɑ̃tɛn] *nf* **une c. (de)** about a hundred, a hundred or so; **des centaines de livres** hundreds of books; **plusieurs centaines de personnes** several hundred people
centaure [sɑ̃tor] *nm* centaur
centenaire [sɑ̃tnɛr] **1** *adj (personne, arbre)* hundred-year-old; **être c.** *(avoir cent ans)* to be a hundred (years old); *(avoir plus de cent ans)* to be over a hundred (years old); **plusieurs fois c.** hundreds of years old
    2 *nmf (vieillard)* centenarian
    3 *nm (anniversaire)* centenary, *Am & Can* centennial
centième [sɑ̃tjɛm] **1** *nmf, nm & adj* hundredth; *voir aussi* **cinquième**
    2 *nf Théât* hundredth performance
centigrade [sɑ̃tigrad] *adj* **degré c.** degree centigrade
centigramme [sɑ̃tigram] *nm* centigram
centilitre [sɑ̃tilitr] *nm* centilitre
centime [sɑ̃tim] *nm* (**a**) *(d'euro)* cent; **je ne lui donnerai pas un c.!** I won't give him/her *Br* a penny *or Am* a cent! (**b**) *Anciennement (de franc)* centime
centimètre [sɑ̃timɛtr] *nm* (**a**) *(unité de mesure)* centimetre (**b**) *(ruban)* tape measure
centrafricain, -e [sɑ̃trafrikɛ̃, -ɛn] **1** *adj* of the Central African Republic
    2 *nm,f* **C.** person from the Central African Republic
central, -e, -aux, -ales [sɑ̃tral, -o] **1** *adj* (**a**) *(au centre)* central (**b**) *(principal)* central, main (**c**) **(l'École) Centrale** = "Grande École" specializing in engineering
    2 *nm* **c. téléphonique** telephone exchange
    3 *nf* **centrale** (**a**) *(usine)* **centrale (électrique)** power station; **centrale thermique/nucléaire** thermal/nuclear power station (**b**) *(prison)* county jail (**c**) *(groupement)* **centrale (syndicale)** group of affiliated trade unions; *Com* **centrale d'achat** (central) purchasing group
centralisation [sɑ̃tralizasjɔ̃] *nf* centralization
centraliser [sɑ̃tralize] *vt* to centralize

centralisme [sɑ̃tralism] *nm Pol* centralism
centre [sɑ̃tr] *nm* (**a**) *(milieu)* centre; **il se prend pour le c. du monde** he thinks the world revolves round him; **cette question est au c. du débat** this question is at the heart of the debate; *Phys* **c. de gravité** centre of gravity; **c. d'intérêt** centre of interest (**b**) *Pol* centre; **le c. droit/gauche** the centre right/left (**c**) *(au football) (passe)* cross; **faire un c.** to make a cross (**d**) *(organisme, lieu)* centre; **les grands centres urbains** large conurbations; **c. aéré** outdoor activity centre; **c. d'appels** call centre; **c. commercial** shopping centre; **c. culturel** arts centre; **c. hospitalier** hospital complex; **c. des impôts** tax office; **c. de loisirs** leisure centre; **c. de tri** sorting office
centré, -e [sɑ̃tre] *adj Suisse (magasin, appartement)* central
centrer [sɑ̃tre] *vt (ballon, mécanisme)* to centre; **c. une discussion sur un sujet** to focus a discussion on a subject
centre-ville *(pl* **centres-villes)** [sɑ̃trəvil] *nm* town centre; *(d'une grande ville) Br* city centre, *Am* downtown area; **aller au c.** to go into town; **habiter au c.** to live in the town/city centre, *Am* to live downtown
centrifuge [sɑ̃trifyʒ] *adj* centrifugal
centrifuger [45] [sɑ̃trifyʒe] *vt* to centrifuge
centrifugeur [sɑ̃trifyʒœr] *nm*, **centrifugeuse** [sɑ̃trifyʒøz] *nf (en chimie, en biologie)* centrifuge; *(pour jus de fruits)* juice extractor
centripète [sɑ̃tripɛt] *adj* centripetal
centrisme [sɑ̃trism] *nm Pol* centrism
centriste [sɑ̃trist] *adj & nmf Pol* centrist
centuple [sɑ̃typl] *nm* **le c. de dix** a hundred times ten; **je te le rendrai au c.** I'll repay you a hundred times over
cep [sɛp] *nm* **c. (de vigne)** vine-stock
cépage [sepaʒ] *nm* variety of vine
cèpe [sɛp] *nm* cep
cependant [səpɑ̃dɑ̃] **1** *conj* however, nevertheless; **le directeur, c., n'est pas d'accord** the manager, however, does not agree; **c., vous ne m'avez pas averti** nevertheless, you didn't tell me
    2 *adv Litt* meanwhile; **c. que** while
céphalée [sefale] *nf Méd* headache, *Spéc* cephalalgia
céramique [seramik] *nf (art)* ceramics *(singulier)*; *(matière, objet)* ceramic
cerceau, -x [sɛrso] *nm* hoop
cercle [sɛrkl] *nm* (**a**) *(figure)* circle; **en c.** in a circle; **c. vicieux** vicious circle; **décrire des cercles** *(avion, oiseau)* to circle (**b**) *(groupe de personnes)* circle (**c**) *(association)* club; **c. de lecture** book group *or* club; **c. littéraire** literary society (**d**) *(objet circulaire)* hoop, ring (**e**) *Géog* **c. (polaire) arctique** Arctic Circle
cerclé, -e [sɛrkle] *adj* **lunettes cerclées d'écaille** horn-rimmed spectacles; **un tonneau c. de fer** a barrel with iron hoops
cercueil [sɛrkœj] *nm* coffin
céréale [sereal] *nf* cereal, grain; **céréales** *(au petit déjeuner)* cereal
céréalier, -ère [serealje, -ɛr] *adj (production, culture)* cereal; *(région)* cereal-growing
cérébral, -e, -aux, -ales [serebral, -o] *adj* cerebral; **hémorragie cérébrale** brain haemorrhage
cérémonial, -als [seremɔnjal] *nm* ceremonial
cérémonie [seremɔni] *nf* ceremony; **habit de c.** dress suit; **uniforme de c.** dress uniform; *Fig* **sans cérémonies** *(réception, repas)* informal; *(recevoir quelqu'un)* informally; *(renvoyer quelqu'un)* unceremoniously;

faire des cérémonies to stand on ceremony; **sans plus de c.** without further ado
cérémonieux, -euse [seremɔnjø, -øz] adj ceremonious
cerf [sɛr] nm stag
cerfeuil [sɛrfœj] nm chervil
cerf-volant (pl cerfs-volants) [sɛrvɔlã] nm (a) (jeu) kite (b) (insecte) stag beetle
cerise [səriz] **1** nf cherry
2 adj inv (rouge) c. cherry(-red)
cerisier [sərizje] nm (arbre) cherry tree; (bois) cherrywood
CERN [sɛrn] nm (abrév Conseil européen pour la recherche nucléaire) CERN
cerne [sɛrn] nm ring
cerné, -e [sɛrne] adj avoir les yeux cernés to have rings under one's eyes
cerner [sɛrne] vt (a) (encercler) to surround (b) (définir) (problème) to identify; une personne difficile à c. a difficult person to figure out
certain, -e [sɛrtɛ̃, -ɛn] **1** adj (sûr) certain; il viendra, c'est c. he'll definitely come; être c. de qch to be certain of sth; aller à une mort certaine to be heading for certain death
2 adj indéfini (avant le nom) certain; il a un c. charme he has a certain charm; un c. temps a while; jusqu'à un c. point up to a (certain) point; d'une certaine façon in a way; dans une certaine mesure to a certain extent; dans certaines circonstances in some or certain circumstances; d'un c. âge elderly; avoir un c. âge to be getting on; cela demande un c. culot/courage it takes some nerve/courage; une certaine Martine someone called Martine
3 pron indéfini certains pensent que... some (people) think (that)...; certaines d'entre nous/vous some of us/you
certainement [sɛrtɛnmã] adv (probablement) most probably; c.! (bien sûr) of course!; c. pas! certainly not!
certes [sɛrt] adv certainly; il n'est pas sans défauts, c., mais... he has his faults, certainly, but...; c. oui! yes indeed!; c. non! certainly not!
certificat [sɛrtifika] nm certificate; c. d'assurance insurance certificate; c. de garantie certificate of guarantee; c. médical medical certificate; c. de scolarité school attendance record; c. de travail certificate of employment
certifié, -e [sɛrtifje] adj professeur c. = qualified (graduate) teacher
certifier [66] [sɛrtifje] vt (a) (authentifier) to certify; (signature) to witness (b) (assurer) c. à qn que... to assure sb that...
certitude [sɛrtityd] nf certainty; j'en ai la c. I'm certain of it
cérumen [serymɛn] nm earwax, Spéc cerumen
cerveau [sɛrvo] nm Anat & Fig brain; (esprit) mind, brains; (personne intelligente) brainy person; (d'un projet) mastermind
cervelas [sɛrvəla] nm saveloy
cervelet [sɛrvəlɛ] nm Anat cerebellum
cervelle [sɛrvɛl] nf Anat (substance) brain; se brûler ou se faire sauter la c. to blow one's brains out; il n'a rien dans la c. he's got nothing between his ears; avoir une c. de moineau to be bird-brained; Culin c. d'agneau lamb's brains
cervical, -e, -aux, -ales [sɛrvikal, -o] adj Anat cervical

CES [seaɛs] nm (a) (abrév collège d'enseignement secondaire) = former secondary school for pupils aged 12 to 15 (b) Anciennement (abrév contrat emploi-solidarité) = short-term contract subsidized by the government
ces [se] voir ce²
César [sezar] **1** npr Jules C. Julius Caesar
2 nm Cin = French cinema award
césarienne [sezarjɛn] nf Caesarean (section)
cessant, -e [sesã, -ãt] adj toutes affaires cessantes forthwith
cessation [sesasjɔ̃] nf cessation; c. des hostilités cease-fire; c. de paiements suspension of payments
cesse [sɛs] nf (a) sans c. constantly, continually (b) Litt il n'aura (pas) de c. qu'il ne réussisse he won't rest until he has succeeded
cesser [sese] **1** vi to stop, to cease; (vent) to die down; faire c. qch to put a stop to sth; il faudra que ça cesse this has to stop
2 vt (interrompre) to stop; Mil cessez le feu! cease fire!; c. de faire qch to stop doing sth; il ne cesse de me contredire he's forever contradicting me
cessez-le-feu [seselfø] nm inv cease-fire
cession [sesjɔ̃] nf Jur transfer
c'est-à-dire [sɛtadir] conj that is (to say); vous l'avez prévenu? – eh bien, c. que non did you let him know? – well, actually, no; c. que je n'étais pas au courant the thing is that no one told me; il faut aller de l'avant! – c.? we must forge ahead! – what do you mean by that?
césure [sezyr] nf (en poésie) caesura; Ordinat break, hyphenation
cet [sɛt] voir ce²
cétacé [setase] nm cetacean
cette [sɛt] voir ce²
ceux [sø] voir celui
Ceylan [selã] n Ceylon
cf (abrév confer) cf
CFA [seɛfa] (abrév Communauté financière africaine) African Financial Community; franc C. = currency used in former French African colonies
CFAO [seɛfao] nf (abrév conception et fabrication assistées par ordinateur) CADCAM
CFC [seɛfse] nm (abrév chlorofluorocarbone) CFC
CFDT [seɛfdete] nf (abrév Confédération française démocratique du travail) = French trade union
CFTC [seɛftese] nf (abrév Confédération française des travailleurs chrétiens) = French trade union
CGC [seʒese] nf (abrév Confédération générale des cadres) = French trade union for managerial staff
CGT [seʒete] nf (abrév Confédération générale du travail) = French trade union
chacal, -als [ʃakal] nm jackal; Fig vulture
chacun, -e [ʃakœ̃, -yn] pron indéfini (a) (chaque personne) each (one), every one; 3 euros c. 3 euros each; nous avons pris c. notre chapeau each of us took our hat (b) (tout le monde) everyone, everybody; c. pour soi every man for himself; c. ses goûts everyone to their own taste; c. son tour (dans une file d'attente) each in turn; c. son tour! wait your turn!; tout un c. everyone
chagrin, -e [ʃagrɛ̃, -in] **1** nm (peine) grief, sorrow; avoir du c. to be upset; avoir un gros c. (langage enfantin) to be very unhappy; faire du c. à qn to distress sb; un c. d'amour an unhappy love affair
2 adj Litt woeful; esprits chagrins malcontents

chagriner [ʃagrine] **1** *vt (peiner)* to grieve; *(contrarier)* to bother
2 se chagriner *vpr Can* **le temps se chagrine** it's getting cloudy
chahut [ʃay] *nm Fam* racket, din; **faire du c.** to make a racket
chahuter [ʃayte] *Fam* **1** *vi (faire du tapage)* to make a racket; *(jouer brutalement)* to be rowdy
2 *vt (professeur)* to bait; *(orateur)* to heckle; **se faire c.** *(professeur)* to get baited; *(orateur)* to get heckled
chai [ʃɛ] *nm* wine and spirits storehouse
chaîne [ʃɛn] *nf* (**a**) *(pour attacher, pour décorer)* chain; **faire la c.** to form a chain; **chaînes** *Aut* (snow) chains; *Fig (contraintes)* chains, shackles (**b**) *(de transmission)* chain; **c. de vélo** bicycle chain (**c**) *(série) (d'hôtels, de magasins)* chain; **c. alimentaire** food chain; **c. de montagnes** range *or* chain of mountains (**d**) *TV* channel; **c. de télévision** television channel (**e**) *(dans l'industrie)* **c. (de montage)** assembly line, production line; **travail à la c.** assembly line work; **travailler à la c.** to work on the assembly line (**f**) *Tex* warp (**g**) *Ordinat* string; **c. de caractères** character string; **c. de recherche** search string (**h**) **c. (haute-fidélité)** hi-fi (**i**) *Can* **c. du trottoir** *Br* kerb, *Am* curb
chaînette [ʃɛnɛt] *nf* small chain
chaînon [ʃɛnɔ̃] *nm* link; *Fig* **le c. manquant** the missing link
chair [ʃɛr] **1** *nf (d'humain, d'animal, de fruit)* flesh; **en c. et en os** in the flesh; **être bien en c.** to be plump; **la c. est faible** the flesh is weak; **c. à canon** cannon fodder; **avoir la c. de poule** to have *Br* goose pimples *or Am* goose bumps; **donner la c. de poule à qn** to give sb goose pimples; **c. à saucisse** sausagemeat; *Fam Fig* **je vais en faire de la c. à saucisse** I'll make mincemeat of him/her
2 *adj inv* **(couleur) c.** flesh-coloured
chaire [ʃɛr] *nf* (**a**) *(dans une église)* pulpit (**b**) *Univ (fonction, tribune)* chair; **être titulaire d'une c.** to hold a chair
chaise [ʃɛz] *nf* chair; *Fig* **être assis** *ou* **très Fam avoir le cul entre deux chaises** to be in an awkward position; *Can* **c. berçante** rocking chair; **chaises musicales** musical chairs; **c. électrique** electric chair; **c. haute** high chair; **c. longue** deckchair; **c. à porteurs** sedan chair; **c. roulante** wheelchair
chaland [ʃalɑ̃] *nm* barge
châle [ʃal] *nm* shawl
chalet [ʃalɛ] *nm* (**a**) *(de montagne)* chalet (**b**) *Can* cottage
chaleur [ʃalœr] *nf* (**a**) *(température)* heat; **les grandes chaleurs** the hot season; **il fait une c. terrible** it's terribly hot; **coup de c.** heatstroke (**b**) *(d'une personne, d'une couleur, d'une voix, d'un accueil)* warmth; **c. humaine** human warmth; **avec c.** warmly (**c**) *Zool* **être en c.** to be *Br* on heat *or Am* in heat
chaleureusement [ʃalørøzmɑ̃] *adv* warmly
chaleureux, -euse [ʃalørø, -øz] *adj (accueil, atmosphère)* warm; *(paroles)* glowing
challenge [ʃalɑ̃ʒ] *nm* (**a**) *Sport* tournament (**b**) *(défi)* challenge
challenger [tʃalɑ̃ʒœr] *nm* challenger
chaloupe [ʃalup] *nf* (**a**) *Naut* launch; *(à rames) Br* rowing boat, *Am* rowboat; **c. à moteur** motor launch; **c. de sauvetage** lifeboat (**b**) *Can (couvre-chaussure)* rubber overshoe
chaloupé, -e [ʃalupe] *adj* swaying

chalumeau, -x [ʃalymo] *nm* (**a**) *Tech Br* blowlamp, *Am* blowtorch (**b**) *Can* spout *(for collecting sap of maple tree)*
chalut [ʃaly] *nm* trawl; **pêcher au c.** to trawl
chalutier [ʃalytje] *nm* trawler
chamade [ʃamad] *nf* **battre la c.** to beat wildly
chamailler [ʃamaje] **se chamailler** *vpr* to squabble
chamailleur, -euse [ʃamajœr, -øz] **1** *adj* quarrelsome
2 *nm,f* squabbler
chamarré, -e [ʃamare] *adj* richly coloured
chambardement [ʃɑ̃bardəmɑ̃] *nm Fam* upheaval
chambarder [ʃɑ̃barde] *vt Fam (projets, maison)* to turn upside down
chambouler [ʃɑ̃bule] *vt Fam (projets, maison)* to turn upside down
chambranle [ʃɑ̃brɑ̃l] *nm (d'une porte, d'une fenêtre)* frame
chambre [ʃɑ̃br] *nf* (**a**) *(pièce)* bedroom; *(d'un hôtel)* room; **c. à un lit/deux lits** single/twin room; **vous auriez une c. (de) libre?** do you have any vacancies?; **faire c. à part** to sleep in separate rooms; **faire sa c.** to tidy (up) one's room; **garder la c.** to keep to one's room; **sportif/politicien en c.** armchair sportsman/politician; **c. d'amis** spare room; **c. de bonne** maid's room; **c. à coucher** *(pièce)* bedroom; *(mobilier)* bedroom furniture; **c. forte** strongroom; **c. frigorifique** *ou* **froide** cold store; **c. à gaz** gas chamber; **c. d'hôte** ≃ guest house; **c. meublée** furnished room, *Br* bedsit(ter) (**b**) *Jur (d'un tribunal)* division; **c. d'accusation** Court of Criminal Appeal; **C. de commerce** Chamber of Commerce (**c**) *Pol* **la C.** the House; **siéger à la C.** to sit in the House; **C. des députés** = lower chamber of Parliament (**d**) *Tech (d'un fusil, d'un appareil photo)* chamber; **c. à air** inner tube
chambrée [ʃɑ̃bre] *nf* (**a**) *(occupants d'une chambre)* room(ful) (**b**) *Mil* barrackroom
chambrer [ʃɑ̃bre] *vt* (**a**) **c. qch** *(bouteille, vin)* to bring sth to room temperature (**b**) *Fam* **c. qn** to pull sb's leg
chambreur, -euse [ʃɑ̃brœr, -øz] *nm,f Can & Suisse* lodger
chameau, -x [ʃamo] *nm* (**a**) *(animal)* camel (**b**) *Fam (homme)* bastard; *(femme)* bitch
chamelier [ʃaməlje] *nm* camel-driver
chamelle [ʃamɛl] *nf* she-camel
chamois [ʃamwa] *nm* (**a**) *(animal)* chamois (**b**) *Sport* **c. d'or/d'argent/de bronze** = gold/silver/bronze skiing proficiency medal
chamoisette [ʃamwazɛt] *nf Belg* duster
champ [ʃɑ̃] *nm* (**a**) *(étendue)* field; **c. de blé** field of wheat, wheatfield; **prendre** *ou* **couper à travers champs** to cut across country; **à tout bout de c.** at every possible opportunity; *Fig* **laisser le c. libre à qn** to leave the field free for sb; **c. de bataille** battlefield; **c. de courses** *Br* racecourse, *Am* racetrack; **c. de foire** fairground; **mort** *ou* **tombé au c. d'honneur** killed in action; **c. de mines** minefield; **c. de tir** rifle range; *Mil* practice ground; *(d'un fusil)* field of fire (**b**) *Fig (portée)* scope; **c. d'action** field of activity; **élargir le c. de ses activités** to extend the scope of one's activities (**c**) *Phot* shot, picture; *(d'un instrument optique)* field; **être dans le c.** to be in shot; **c. visuel** field of vision (**d**) *Élec & Rad* field; **c. magnétique** magnetic field (**e**) *Ordinat* field; **c. numérique** numeric field; **c. de texte** text field
champagne [ʃɑ̃paɲ] *nm* champagne

champenois, -e [ʃãpənwa, -az] **1** *adj* (**a**) *(de la région)* of Champagne (**b**) **méthode champenoise** champagne method **2** *nm,f* **C.** person from Champagne
champêtre [ʃãpɛtr] *adj* rustic, rural
champignon [ʃãpiɲɔ̃] *nm* (**a**) *(plante)* mushroom; *Fig* **pousser comme un c.** *(enfant)* to shoot up; *(ville)* to mushroom; **c. atomique** mushroom cloud; **c. hallucinogène** magic mushroom; **c. de Paris** button mushroom; **c. vénéneux** poisonous mushroom, toadstool (**b**) *Méd* fungus (**c**) *Fam (accélérateur)* appuyer sur le c. *Br* to put one's foot down, *Am* to step on the gas
champion, -onne [ʃãpjɔ̃, -ɔn] **1** *nm,f* (**a**) *(dans une discipline)* champion; **le c. du monde d'escrime** the world fencing champion; *Fam* **c'est un c. du bricolage** he's a whizz at DIY (**b**) *(d'une cause)* champion **2** *adj* (**a**) *Sport* **l'équipe championne du monde** the world champions (**b**) *Fam* great; **pour les gaffes, il est c.!** he's a great one for putting his foot in it!
championnat [ʃãpjɔna] *nm* championship; **le championnat du monde d'athlétisme** the world athletics championships
champlure [ʃãplyr] *nf Can (robinet) Br* tap, *Am* faucet
chance [ʃãs] *nf* (**a**) *(sort favorable)* (good) luck, (good) fortune; **la c. lui sourit** fortune favours him/her; **souhaiter bonne c. à qn** to wish sb luck; **bonne c.!** good luck!; **quelle c.!** what a stroke of luck!; **avec un peu de c....** with a bit of luck...; **avoir de la c.** to be lucky *or* fortunate; **ne pas avoir de c.** to be unlucky; **porter c. à qn** to bring sb luck; **c'est mon jour de c.** it's my lucky day; **c'est bien ma c.!** just my luck!; **pas de c.!** hard luck!; **par c.** luckily, fortunately (**b**) *(possibilité)* chance; **avoir des chances de faire qch** to stand a (good) chance of doing sth; **avoir peu de chances de faire qch** to have little chance of doing sth; **donner une** *ou* **sa c. à qn** to give sb a chance; **elle a une c. sur deux de gagner** she has a fifty-fifty chance of winning; *Fam* **il y a des chances** probably; **il y a de grandes** *ou* **fortes chances (pour) qu'on le lui propose** there's every chance that he/she will be offered it
chancelant, -e [ʃãslã, -ãt] *adj (pas)* unsteady; *(mémoire)* shaky; *(santé)* delicate; *(pouvoir, gouvernement)* tottering; *(détermination)* wavering
chanceler [42] [ʃãsle] *vi (personne)* to stagger, to totter; *(objet)* to wobble; *(régime, gouvernement)* to totter; **l'uppercut le fit c.** the uppercut sent him reeling
chancelier [ʃãsəlje] *nm Pol* chancellor; *(d'ambassade)* chief secretary
chancellerie [ʃãsɛlri] *nf* (**a**) *(d'une ambassade)* chancery (**b**) *(ministère de la Justice)* ≃ *Br* Lord Chancellor's Department, ≃ *Am* Department of Justice
chanceux, -euse [ʃãsø, -øz] *adj* lucky
chancre [ʃãkr] *nm Méd & Fig* canker
chandail [ʃãdaj] *nm* sweater, jumper
Chandeleur [ʃãdlœr] *nf* **la C.** Candlemas

La Chandeleur
This Catholic feast, celebrated on 2 February, is traditionally marked by eating sweet crêpes.

chandelier [ʃãdəlje] *nm (à une branche)* candlestick; *(à plusieurs branches)* candelabra
chandelle [ʃãdɛl] *nf* (**a**) *(bougie)* candle; **s'éclairer à la c.** to use candlelight; **un dîner aux chandelles** a candlelit dinner; **faire des économies de bouts de**

c. to make cheeseparing economies; **brûler la c. par les deux bouts** to burn the candle at both ends; **le jeu n'en vaut pas la c.** the game is not worth the candle; **tenir la c.** *Br* to play gooseberry, *Am* to feel like a fifth wheel; **voir trente-six chandelles** to see stars; **devoir une fière c. à qn** to owe sb a great debt (**b**) *(en gymnastique)* **faire la c.** to do a shoulder stand (**c**) *Aviat* **(montée en) c.** vertical climb
chanfrein [ʃãfrɛ̃] *nm (de cheval)* nose
change [ʃãʒ] *nm* (**a**) *Fin* exchange; **le c. est avantageux** the exchange rate is good; *Fig* **gagner/ne pas perdre au c.** to gain on/not to lose on the exchange (**b**) *Fig* **donner le c. à qn** to put sb off the scent (**c**) *(couche-culotte)* **c. (complet)** disposable *Br* nappy *or Am* diaper
changeant, -e [ʃãʒã, -ãt] *adj (temps)* unsettled; **d'humeur changeante** moody
changement [ʃãʒmã] *nm* (**a**) *(modification)* change; **ça va te faire un drôle de c.** it'll be quite a change for you; **c. de décor** *Théât* scene change; *Fig* change of scenery; **c. de direction** *(sur un écriteau)* under new management (**b**) *(dans les transports)* change; **il y a un c. à Valence** you have to change at Valence (**c**) **c. de vitesse** *(action)* change of gear; *(levier) Br* gear lever, *Am* gear shift; *Ordinat* **c. de ligne** line feed
changer [45] [ʃãʒe] **1** *vt* (**a**) *(remplacer) (draps, couche de bébé, roue)* to change; **c. qch contre qch** to change *or* exchange sth for sth (**b**) *(enfant, bébé)* to change (**c**) *(convertir) (argent)* to change (**en** into) (**d**) *(transformer)* **c. qn/qch en** to change sb/sth into (**e**) *(modifier)* to change, to alter; **ça va les c.!** that'll be a change for them!; **ça lui changera les idées** that'll take his/her mind off things; **ça nous change du café du coin!** that makes a change from the local!; **cela ne change rien à l'affaire** that makes no difference; **sa nouvelle coiffure la change** she looks different with her new hairstyle; **mais cela change tout!** that changes everything!; **c. qch de place** to move sth **2** *vi* (**a**) *(se modifier)* to change; **c. en bien** *ou* **en mieux** to change for the better; **c. en mal** *ou* **en pire** to change for the worse; *Ironique* **pour c.** for a change (**b**) *(dans les transports)* to change **3** **changer de** *vt ind* to change; **c. de train/de travail** to change trains/jobs; **c. de place avec qn** to change places with sb; **c. de coiffure** to change one's hairstyle; **c. de vêtements** to change (one's clothes), to get changed; **c. de couleur** to change colour; *Aut* **c. de vitesse** to change gear; **je te prie de c. de ton!** don't talk to me in that tone of voice!; *Fam Fig* **change de disque!** change the record! **4** **se changer** *vpr* (**a**) *(mettre d'autres vêtements)* to change (**b**) **se c. les idées** to change one's ideas (**c**) *(se transformer)* **se c. en** to change *or* turn into
chanoine [ʃanwan] *nm Rel* canon
chanson [ʃãsɔ̃] *nf* (**a**) *(air)* song; *Fam* **c'est toujours la même c.!** it's always the same old story!; *Fam* **on connaît la c.!** I've heard that one before!; **c. d'amour** love song; **c. à boire** drinking song (**b**) *(genre littéraire)* song; **la c. française** French song
chansonnette [ʃãsɔnɛt] *nf* ditty
chansonnier [ʃãsɔnje] *nm* satirical cabaret singer
chant [ʃã] *nm* (**a**) *(chanson)* song; *(d'un instrument de musique, de la mer, du vent)* sound; *(d'un oiseau)* singing; *(du grillon, de la cigale)* chirping; *(du coq)* crowing; **au c. du coq** at cockcrow; *Fig* **c. du cygne** swan song; **c. funèbre** dirge; **c. de Noël** Christmas carol; **c. sacré** hymn (**b**) *(art)* singing; **leçon/professeur de c.**

singing lesson/teacher; **apprendre le c.** to take singing lessons; **c. choral** choral singing; **c. grégorien** Gregorian chant (**c**) *(d'un poème)* canto
chantage [ʃɑ̃taʒ] *nm* blackmail; **faire du c.** à qn to blackmail sb; **il lui fait du c. au suicide** he's blackmailing him/her with suicide threats
chantant, -e [ʃɑ̃tɑ̃, -ɑ̃t] *adj (musique, air)* tuneful; *(accent, voix)* lilting
chanter [ʃɑ̃te] **1** *vt (chanson)* to sing; *Fam* **qu'est-ce que vous me chantez là?** what are you on about?; *Fam* **elle le chante sur tous les tons** she's always going on about it
  2 *vi* (**a**) *(personne, oiseau)* to sing; *(coq)* to crow; *(grillon, cigale)* to chirp; **c. juste/faux** to sing in tune/out of tune (**b**) **faire c. qn** *(exercer un chantage sur)* to blackmail sb (**c**) *(plaire)* **viens, si ça te chante** come along, if you fancy the idea; **il vient quand ça lui chante** he comes when he feels like it
chanterelle[1] [ʃɑ̃trɛl] *nf Mus (corde)* top string
chanterelle[2] *nf (champignon)* chanterelle
chanteur, -euse [ʃɑ̃tœr, -øz] *nm,f* singer; **c. de charme** crooner; **c. des rues** street singer
chantier [ʃɑ̃tje] *nm* (**a**) *(lieu de construction)* (building) site; *(sur la route)* roadworks; **c. interdit au public** *(sur panneau)* no admittance to the public; **mettre qch en c.** to get sth under way; **c. naval** shipyard (**b**) *Fig (projet d'envergure)* major project *or* piece of work (**c**) *Fam (désordre)* **quel c.!** what a shambles!; **ils ont tout laissé en c.** they left the place in a complete shambles
chantilly [ʃɑ̃tiji] *nf* (**crème**) **c.** whipped cream
chantonner [ʃɑ̃tɔne] *vt & vi* to sing softly; *(sans paroles)* to hum
chantre [ʃɑ̃tr] *nm (défenseur)* champion
chanvre [ʃɑ̃vr] *nm* hemp; **c. indien** Indian hemp
chaos [kao] *nm* chaos
chaotique [kaɔtik] *adj* chaotic
chaparder [ʃaparde] *vt Fam* to pinch
chapardeur, -euse [ʃapardœr, -øz] *nm,f Fam* thief
chape [ʃap] *nf (de béton)* screed; *(d'un pneu)* tread; **la chaleur pèse sur la ville comme une c. de plomb** the heat lies on the town like a dead weight
chapeau, -x [ʃapo] *nm* (**a**) *(coiffure)* hat; *Fig* **porter le c.** to carry the can; *Fig* **tirer son c. à qn** to take off one's hat to sb; **c.!** well done!; **c. de cow-boy** cowboy hat; **c. melon** bowler hat; **c. mou** *Br* trilby, *Am* fedora; **c. de paille** straw hat (**b**) *(d'un champignon)* cap (**c**) *(partie supérieure) (de vol-au-vent, de bouchée à la reine)* lid; **prendre un virage sur les chapeaux de roues** to take a corner at top speed; **démarrer sur les chapeaux de roues** *(projet, soirée)* to get off to a cracking start (**d**) *Typ & Journ* lead-in
chapeauter [ʃapote] *vt (contrôler)* to head
chapelain [ʃaplɛ̃] *nm Rel* chaplain
chapelet [ʃaplɛ] *nm (de prière)* rosary; *Fig (d'invectives, d'insultes)* stream; *(d'objets)* string; **dire son c.** *Br* to say the rosary, *Am* to tell one's beads
chapelier, -ère [ʃapəlje, -ɛr] *nm,f* hatter
chapelle [ʃapɛl] *nf* (**a**) *Rel* chapel; **c. ardente** chapel of rest (**b**) *Belg (café)* café
chapelure [ʃaplyr] *nf* breadcrumbs
chaperon [ʃaprɔ̃] *nm* (**a**) *(personne)* chaperon (**b**) **le Petit C. rouge** Little Red Riding Hood
chaperonner [ʃaprɔne] *vt aussi Fig* to chaperon
chapiteau, -x [ʃapito] *nm* (**a**) *Archit (d'une colonne)* capital (**b**) *(d'un cirque)* big top; **sous c.** in a marquee

chapitre [ʃapitr] *nm* (**a**) *(d'un livre)* chapter; *(d'un budget)* item; **inscrire une somme au c. des recettes/dépenses** to enter a sum under revenue/expenditure; **elle est sévère sur le c. de la discipline** she is strict in the matter of discipline; **en voilà assez sur ce c.** that's enough of that; **et maintenant, au c. des faits divers...** and now for the news in brief... (**b**) *Rel (assemblée)* chapter; *Fig* **avoir voix au c.** to have a say in the matter
chapitrer [ʃapitre] *vt* **c. qn** *(réprimander)* to tell sb off; *(faire la morale à)* to lecture sb
chapon [ʃapɔ̃] *nm (coq)* capon
chaptaliser [ʃaptalize] *vt* to chaptalize
chaque [ʃak] *adj indéfini* each, every; **c. femme doit pouvoir travailler et élever ses enfants** every woman should be able to work as well as bring up her children; **ces livres coûtent 15 euros c.** these books cost 15 euros each; **c. chose à sa place** everything in its place; **c. chose en son temps** all in good time; **c. fois qu'il vient** every time *or* whenever he comes; **j'y pense à c. instant** I think about it all the time
char [ʃar] *nm* (**a**) *Mil* **c. (d'assaut** *ou* **de combat)** tank (**b**) *(romain)* chariot (**c**) **c. de carnaval** float (**d**) *Can Fam (voiture)* car (**e**) *Sport* **c. à voile** sand yacht; **faire du c. à voile** to go sand yachting (**f**) *Fam* **arrête ton c.!** come off it!
charabia [ʃarabja] *nm Fam* gibberish
charade [ʃarad] *nf* (**a**) *(devinette)* riddle (**b**) *(mime)* (game of) charades
charançon [ʃarɑ̃sɔ̃] *nm* weevil
charbon [ʃarbɔ̃] *nm* (**a**) *(combustible)* coal; **c. (de bois)** charcoal; **chauffage au c.** coal-fired heating; *Fig* **être sur des charbons ardents** to be on tenterhooks (**b**) *Art* charcoal; **dessin au c.** charcoal drawing (**c**) *Méd (médicament)* charcoal
charbonnage [ʃarbɔnaʒ] *nm* (**a**) *(exploitation)* coal mining (**b**) **charbonnages** *(houillères)* collieries
charbonneux, -euse [ʃarbɔnø, -øz] *adj (noir)* coalblack; *(yeux)* heavy with black make-up
charbonnier, -ère [ʃarbɔnje, -ɛr] **1** *adj (industrie)* coal
  2 *nm,f* (**a**) *(marchand de charbon)* coal merchant; *Prov* **c. est maître dans sa maison** *ou* **chez soi** a man is master in his own home (**b**) *Naut* coaler
  3 *nf* **charbonnière** *(mésange)* great tit
charcuter [ʃarkyte] *Fam* **1** *vt* **c. qn** to butcher sb
  2 **se charcuter** *vpr* to cut oneself to ribbons; **se c. le menton/le doigt** to cut one's chin/finger to ribbons
charcuterie [ʃarkytri] *nf* (**a**) *(magasin)* pork butcher's (shop) (**b**) *(activité)* cooked meats trade (**c**) *(produits)* cooked meats

Charcuterie

A "charcuterie" sells mainly food prepared with pork: sausages, pâtés, ham etc, collectively also known as "charcuterie". Ready-prepared dishes to take away are usually also sold.

charcutier, -ère [ʃarkytje, -ɛr] *nm,f* (**a**) *(commerçant, fabricant)* pork butcher (**b**) *Fam Péj (chirurgien)* butcher
chardon [ʃardɔ̃] *nm (plante)* thistle
chardonneret [ʃardɔnrɛ] *nm* goldfinch
charentais, -e [ʃarɑ̃tɛ, -ɛz] **1** *adj* of Charente
  2 *nm,f* **C.** person from Charente
  3 *nf* **charentaise** *(chausson)* slipper

charge [ʃarʒ] *nf* (**a**) *(poids)* load; *(sur bateau)* cargo; *Fig* **être une c. pour qn** to be a burden to sb; **c. utile** *(d'un véhicule)* capacity (**b**) *(responsabilité)* responsibility; **être en c.** **de qch** to be in charge of sth; **prendre qn/qch en c.** to take charge of sb/sth; **se prendre en c.** to be responsible for oneself (**c**) *(fonction)* office; *(d'avoué)* practice (**d**) *(obligation financière)* **être à la c. de qn** *(personne)* to be dependent on sb; *(appel, transport, réparations)* to be chargeable to sb; **avoir deux enfants à c.** to have two dependent children; **prendre un client en c.** *(taxi)* to pick up a fare; **être pris en c. à cent pour cent par la Sécurité sociale** to have one's medical expenses fully paid for by Social Security; **charges (locatives)** *(d'un appartement)* maintenance charges; **charges d'exploitation** operating costs; **charges sociales** *Br* national insurance contributions, *Am* social security charges *(paid by the employer)* (**e**) *(d'une arme, d'explosifs)* charge (**f**) *Constr (pression)* load (**g**) *Élec (d'une batterie, d'une particule)* charge (**h**) *Mil* charge; *Fig* **revenir à la c.** to return to the attack (**i**) *Jur (preuve)* charge

Charges
Householders and tenants in blocks of flats are required to pay "charges", a monthly contribution to pay for the general upkeep of the building. In estate agencies, rent is expressed either including this sum ("charges comprises" or "cc") or excluding it ("hors charges" or "charges en sus"). Sometimes, the "charges" include heating costs.

chargé, -e [ʃarʒe] **1** *adj* (**a**) *(camion, navire)* loaded, laden (**de** with); *(revolver, appareil photo)* loaded; *Fig (style)* ornate; **la voiture est trop chargée** the car is overloaded; **être c. comme un bourricot** *ou* **un mulet** to be loaded down; **avoir la langue chargée** to have a furred tongue; **un regard c. de reconnaissance** a look full of gratitude (**b**) *(occupé) (journée, programme)* full (**c**) *(responsable)* **être c. de qch** *(mission)* to be entrusted with sth; *(tâche)* to be responsible for sth; **c. de famille** to have family responsibilities; **être c. de faire qch** to be responsible for doing sth (**d**) *Phys* charged **2** *nm* **c. d'affaires** chargé d'affaires; **c. de mission** official representative **3** *nm,f Univ* **c. de cours** = part-time lecturer; *Can* lecturer

chargement [ʃarʒəmɑ̃] *nm* (**a**) *(action)* loading; *Élec (d'une batterie)* charging; **machine à laver à c. frontal** front-loading washing machine (**b**) *(marchandises)* load; *(sur bateau)* cargo

charger [45] [ʃarʒe] **1** *vt* (**a**) *(camion, navire, marchandises)* to load (**b**) *(remplir)* to fill (**de** with) (**c**) *(fusil, appareil photo)* to load; *Élec (batterie)* to charge; *Ordinat* to load (up) (**d**) *(donner une responsabilité à)* **c. qn de qch** to entrust sb with sth; **c. qn de faire qch** to give sb the responsibility for doing sth; **il m'a chargé de vous transmettre un message** he asked me to give you a message (**e**) *(attaquer)* to charge (at) **2** *vi* (**a**) *Ordinat* to load up (**b**) *Mil* to charge **3 se charger** *vpr* (**a**) *(s'alourdir)* to weigh oneself down (**b**) **se c. de qch/qn** *(prendre la responsabilité de)* to take care of sb/sth; **se c. de faire qch** to undertake to do sth; **laisse tomber, je m'en charge** don't worry about it, I'll take care of it

chargeur [ʃarʒœr] *nm (d'arme)* magazine; *Phot* cartridge; *Élec* (battery) charger; *Ordinat* loader; **c. automatique** self loader

chariot [ʃarjo] *nm (petite charrette)* wagon; *(de supermarché) Br* trolley, *Am* cart; *(pour diapositives)* cartridge; *(pour la manutention)* truck; *(d'hôpital) Br* trolley, *Am* gurney; *Cin* dolly; *(d'une machine à écrire)* carriage; **c. à bagages** luggage trolley

charismatique [karismatik] *adj* charismatic

charisme [karism] *nm* charisma

charitable [ʃaritabl] *adj* charitable (**envers** towards); *(conseil)* friendly

charité [ʃarite] *nf* (**a**) *(altruisme)* charity; **faites-moi ou ayez la c. de...** please be kind enough to...; *Prov* **c. bien ordonnée commence par soi-même** charity begins at home (**b**) *(don)* charity; **faire la c. à qn** to give money to sb; **demander la c.** to ask for charity; **la c., Messieurs Dames** *(dans la rue)* can you spare some change, please?

charlatan [ʃarlatɑ̃] *nm Péj (mauvais médecin)* quack; *(escroc)* charlatan

Charles [ʃarl] *npr* **C. Quint** Charles the Fifth

charlot [ʃarlo] *nm Fam (personne peu sérieuse)* clown

charlotte [ʃarlɔt] *nf Culin* charlotte; **c. aux poires/au chocolat** pear/chocolate charlotte

charmant, -e [ʃarmɑ̃, -ɑ̃t] *adj (personne, chose, soirée)* charming, delightful; *Ironique* **et voilà qu'il pleut, ah, c'est c.!** now it's raining, marvellous!

charme¹ [ʃarm] *nm* (**a**) *(attrait)* charm; **avoir du c.** to have charm; **c'est ce qui en fait le c.** that's what makes it so attractive; **faire du c. à qn** to turn on the charm with sb; **charmes** *(d'une femme)* charms; **vivre de ses charmes** to sell one's charms (**b**) *(magie)* spell; **être/tomber sous le c.** to be/fall under the spell; *Fig* **se porter comme un c.** to be as fit as a fiddle

charme² *nm (arbre)* hornbeam

charmer [ʃarme] *vt* (**a**) *(plaire à)* to charm; **j'ai été charmé de vous rencontrer** it's been a pleasure to meet you (**b**) *(envoûter)* to charm

charmeur, -euse [ʃarmœr, -øz] **1** *nm,f* charmer; **c. de serpents** snake charmer **2** *adj (regard, sourire)* charming

charnel, -elle [ʃarnɛl] *adj* carnal

charnier [ʃarnje] *nm* mass grave

charnière [ʃarnjɛr] *nf (de porte, de fenêtre)* hinge; *Fig* **à la c. de deux grandes périodes** at the junction of two great eras; **époque/œuvre c.** transitional period/work

charnu, -e [ʃarny] *adj (partie du corps, lèvres)* fleshy; *(fruit)* pulpy; *Hum* **la partie charnue de son anatomie** his posterior

charognard [ʃarɔɲar] *nm* (**a**) *Zool* carrion-eater (**b**) *(exploiteur)* vulture

charogne [ʃarɔɲ] *nf* (**a**) *(d'animal)* carrion (**b**) *Fam (homme)* bastard; *(femme)* bitch

charpente [ʃarpɑ̃t] *nf (d'un bâtiment, d'un roman)* framework; *(du corps)* frame; **avoir une solide c.** *(personne)* to be solidly built

charpenterie [ʃarpɑ̃tri] *nf (métier)* carpentry

charpentier [ʃarpɑ̃tje] *nm* carpenter

charpie [ʃarpi] *nf* **mettre qch en c.** to tear sth to shreds; *Fam* **mettre qn en c.** to make mincemeat out of sb

charretier [ʃartje] *nm* **jurer comme un c.** to swear like a trooper

charrette [ʃarɛt] *nf* (**a**) *(véhicule)* cart (**b**) *(de licenciements)* round of redundancies (**c**) *Suisse Fam* **c. de Paul!** *Br* bloody Paul!, *Am* goddamn Paul!

charrier [66] [ʃarje] **1** *vt* (**a**) *(transporter)* to cart (**b**) *(entraîner)* to carry along (**c**) *Fam (se moquer de)* **c. qn** to wind sb up, to pull sb's leg **2** *vi Fam (exagérer)* to go too far; **faut pas c.!** *(n'exagère pas)* come off it!

charrue [ʃary] *nf* (**a**) *(pour labourer)* plough; *Fig* **mettre la c. avant les bœufs** to put the cart before the horse (**b**) *Can (chasse-neige)* snowplough

charte [ʃart] *nf* charter

charter [ʃartɛr] *nm* (**avion**) **c.** charter plane

chartreux, -euse [ʃartrø, -øz] **1** *nm,f Rel* Carthusian **2** *nf* **chartreuse** (**a**) *(couvent)* Carthusian monastery (**b**) *(alcool)* Chartreuse

chas [ʃa] *nm* eye *(of needle)*

chasse [ʃas] *nf* (**a**) *(activité)* hunting; *(au fusil)* shooting; **aller à la c.** to go hunting/shooting; **la c. est ouverte/fermée** the shooting season has begun/ended; *Prov* **qui va à la c. perd sa place** if you leave your place someone will take it; **c. à courre** hunting; **c. au lapin** rabbit shooting (**b**) *(événement)* hunt; *(au fusil)* shoot (**c**) *(réserve)* **c. gardée** private game preserve; *Fig (domaine)* preserve (**d**) *(poursuite)* chase; **donner la c. à qn/qch, prendre qn/qch en c.** to give chase to sb/sth; **c. à l'homme** manhunt; *Pol* **c. aux sorcières** witch hunt; **c. au trésor** treasure hunt (**e**) **c. (d'eau)** flush; **tirer la c. (d'eau)** to flush the toilet (**f**) **être en c.** *(chienne, chatte)* to be *Br* on heat *or Am* in heat

châsse [ʃas] *nf Rel* shrine

chassé-croisé *(pl* chassés-croisés) [ʃasekrwaze] *nm (de personnes)* comings and goings; *(de conversations)* babble

chasse-neige [ʃasnɛʒ] *nm inv* (**a**) *(engin)* snowplough (**b**) *(en ski)* snowplough; **descendre une piste en c.** to snowplough down a ski slope

chasser [ʃase] **1** *vt* (**a**) *(animaux)* to hunt; **c. le renard/la perdrix** to go foxhunting/partridge shooting (**b**) *(expulser)* to drive *or* chase away (**de** from); *(employé)* to dismiss; *(mouches)* to brush away; *(sujet: vent) (nuages)* to blow away; *(idées noires)* to forget; **je ne veux pas vous c. mais il est tard** I'm not trying to get rid of you but it's getting late; *Fig* **c. qn/qch de son esprit** to dismiss sb/sth from one's thoughts **2** *vi* (**a**) *(aller à la chasse)* to hunt, to go hunting; *(au fusil)* to shoot (**b**) *Aut* to skid

chasseur, -euse [ʃasœr, -øz] **1** *nm,f* hunter; **c. de primes** bounty hunter; *aussi Fig* **c. de têtes** headhunter **2** *nm* (**a**) *(dans un hôtel) Br* pageboy, *Am* bellboy (**b**) *(avion de chasse)* fighter (**c**) *Mil* **les chasseurs alpins** the mountain light infantry

châssis [ʃasi] *nm* (**a**) *(charpente)* frame (**b**) *Art* stretcher (**c**) *(de jardin)* (cold) frame (**d**) *Aut* chassis (**e**) *Can (fenêtre)* window

chaste [ʃast] *adj* chaste

chastement [ʃastəmã] *adv* chastely

chasteté [ʃastəte] *nf* chastity

chasuble [ʃazybl] *nf* (**a**) *(robe)* **c.** *Br* pinafore dress, *Am* jumper (**b**) *Rel* chasuble

chat¹, chatte [ʃa, ʃat] **1** *nm,f* cat; **petit c.** kitten; *Fam* **mon petit c., ma petite chatte** my pet; *Fig* **il n'y avait pas un c.** there wasn't a soul there; **appeler un c. un c.** to call a spade a spade; **avoir un c. dans la gorge** to have a frog in one's throat; **jouer au c. et à la souris avec qn** to play cat and mouse with sb; *Prov* **c. échaudé craint l'eau froide** once bitten, twice shy; **quand le c. n'est pas là, les souris dansent** when

the cat's away the mice will play; **c. de gouttière** alley cat; **c. persan** Persian (cat); **c. sauvage** wildcat; *Can (raton laveur)* raccoon; **c. siamois** Siamese (cat) **2** *nf* **chatte** *Vulg (sexe féminin)* pussy

chat² [tʃat] *nm Ordinat (sur Internet)* chat

châtaigne [ʃatɛɲ] *nf* (**a**) *(fruit)* (sweet) chestnut (**b**) *très Fam (coup de poing)* clout; **flanquer une c. à qn** to clout sb; **se prendre une c.** *(décharge)* to get a shock

châtaignier [ʃatɛɲe] *nm (arbre, bois)* chestnut

châtain [ʃatɛ̃] **1** *adj (cheveux)* (chestnut-)brown; *(personne)* brown-haired **2** *nm* chestnut brown

château, -x [ʃato] *nm* (**a**) *(forteresse)* castle; *(manoir)* mansion; *(de famille aristocratique)* stately home; *(palais)* palace; **les châteaux de la Loire** the châteaux of the Loire; *Fig* **bâtir des châteaux en Espagne** to build castles in the air; **c. de cartes** house of cards; **c. d'eau** water tower; **c. fort** castle; **c. gonflable** bouncy castle (**b**) *(exploitation vinicole)* château; **mis en bouteille au c.** *(sur bouteille)* = indicates that wine was bottled at source

châtelain [ʃatlɛ̃] *nm (au Moyen Âge)* lord of the manor; *(propriétaire d'un château)* château owner

châtelaine [ʃatlɛn] *nf (au Moyen Âge)* lady of the manor; *(propriétaire d'un château)* (woman) château owner; *(épouse du propriétaire)* wife of a/the château owner

chat-huant *(pl* chats-huants) [ʃayã] *nm* tawny owl

châtié, -e [ʃatje] *adj (style)* polished; *(langage)* refined

châtier [66] [ʃatje] *vt Litt (personne)* to chastise; *Prov* **qui aime bien châtie bien** spare the rod and spoil the child

chatière [ʃatjɛr] *nf* (**a**) *(pour chat)* cat flap (**b**) *(pour aération)* ventilation hole

châtiment [ʃatimã] *nm* (**a**) *Litt* chastisement (**b**) **c. corporel** corporal punishment

chaton¹ [ʃatɔ̃] *nm* (**a**) *(petit chat)* kitten (**b**) *Bot* catkin

chaton² *nm* (**a**) *(d'une bague)* bezel (**b**) *(pierre)* stone

chatouille [ʃatuj] *nf* **faire des chatouilles à qn** to tickle sb; **craindre les chatouilles** to be ticklish

chatouiller [ʃatuje] *vt* to tickle; *Fig (curiosité)* to arouse; *(amour-propre)* to flatter; **ah, ça chatouille!** oh, that tickles!

chatouilleux, -euse [ʃatujø, -øz] *adj* ticklish; *Fig* sensitive (**sur** about)

chatoyant, -e [ʃatwajã, -ãt] *adj* shimmering; *(pierre, imagination)* sparkling

chatoyer [32] [ʃatwaje] *vi* to shimmer; *(pierre)* to sparkle

châtrer [ʃatre] *vt (homme, taureau)* to castrate; *(étalon)* to geld; *(chat)* to neuter

chatte [ʃat] *nf voir* **chat¹**

chatter [tʃate] *vi Ordinat (sur l'Internet)* to chat (online)

chatterton [ʃatɛrtɔ̃] *nm Br* insulating tape, *Am* friction tape

chaud, -e [ʃo, ʃod] **1** *adj* (**a**) *(modérément)* warm; *(intensément)* hot; *Fig (voix)* sultry; *(couleur)* warm; **la soupe est toute chaude** the soup is piping hot; **l'été va être c.** it'll be a hot summer; *Fig* there'll be a lot of unrest this summer; **l'alerte fut chaude** it was a close thing; **une nouvelle toute chaude** some hot news (**b**) *(passionné) (discussion)* heated; *(partisan)* keen; **elle n'est pas chaude pour le projet** she's not too keen on the plan; **je ne suis pas très c. pour aller au cinéma** I don't really feel like going to the cinema

2 *adv* **j'aime manger c.** I like my food hot
3 *nm (modéré)* warmth; *(intense)* heat; **garder** *ou* **tenir qch au c.** to keep sth warm; **chez soi, au c.** at home, in the warmth; **avoir c.** to be *or* feel hot; *Fam (échapper de justesse)* to have a narrow escape; **il fait c.** it's hot; *Fig* **cela ne me fait ni c. ni froid** it's all the same to me; **interroger les spectateurs à c.** to question the audience on the spot; **attraper un c. et froid** to catch a chill

chaudement [ʃodmɑ̃] *adv (s'habiller, féliciter, recommander)* warmly

chaudière [ʃodjɛr] *nf* (**a**) *(de chauffage)* boiler; **c. à mazout/à gaz** oil-fired/gas boiler (**b**) *Can (seau)* bucket

chaudron [ʃodrɔ̃] *nm* cauldron

chaudronnier, -ère [ʃodrɔnje, -ɛr] *nm,f* boiler maker

chauffage [ʃofaʒ] *nm (d'une pièce, d'un bâtiment)* heating; *(appareils)* heating (system); *(dans une voiture)* heater; **c. à l'électricité/au gaz/au mazout** electric/gas/oil-fired heating; **c. central** central heating

chauffagiste [ʃofaʒist] *nm* heating engineer

chauffant, -e [ʃofɑ̃, -ɑ̃t] *adj voir* **couverture, plaque**

chauffard [ʃofar] *nm* reckless driver

chauffe-biberon *(pl* **chauffe-biberons**) [ʃofbibrɔ̃] *nm* bottle-warmer

chauffe-eau [ʃofo] *nm inv* water heater; **c. électrique** immersion heater

chauffe-plat *(pl* **chauffe-plats**) [ʃofpla] *nm* hot plate

chauffer [ʃofe] **1** *vt (pièce, bâtiment)* to heat (up); *(moteur)* to warm up; **c. une maison au gaz** to heat a house with gas; **la chambre n'est pas chauffée** there's no heating in the bedroom; *Fig* **c. la salle** to warm up one's audience
2 *vi* (**a**) *(devenir chaud)* to heat up; **ce radiateur chauffe bien/mal** this radiator gives out/doesn't give out a lot of heat; **faire c. qch, mettre qch à c.** to heat sth up (**b**) *(s'échauffer) (moteur)* to overheat (**c**) *Fam* **ça va c. s'il est en retard!** there'll be trouble if he's late!; **tu chauffes!** *(dans un jeu)* you're getting warmer!
3 **se chauffer** *vpr* to warm oneself; **se c. (les muscles)** to warm up; **se c. au mazout/à l'électricité** to have oil-fired/electric heating

chaufferette [ʃofrɛt] *nf (pour les pieds)* footwarmer

chaufferie [ʃofri] *nf* boiler room

chauffeur [ʃofœr] *nm (de voiture, de bus)* driver; *(employé)* chauffeur; **les chauffeurs du dimanche** Sunday drivers; **c. de camion** *Br* lorry driver, *Am* truck driver; **c. de taxi** taxi driver

chauffeuse [ʃoføz] *nf (fauteuil)* low armless chair

chauler [ʃole] *vt (murs)* to whitewash; *(terres)* to treat with lime

chaume [ʃom] *nm* (**a**) *(pour toits)* thatch (**b**) *(des céréales)* stubble

chaumière [ʃomjɛr] *nf (maison pauvre)* cottage; *(maison à toit de chaume)* thatched cottage

chaussée [ʃose] *nf (route)* roadway

chausse-pied *(pl* **chausse-pieds**) [ʃospje] *nm* shoehorn

chausser [ʃose] *vt* **1** (**a**) *(chaussures, lunettes, skis)* to put on; **chaussé de pantoufles** wearing slippers; **elle chausse du 37** she takes a size 37 (**b**) *(mettre des chaussures à)* to put shoes on (**c**) *(aller à)* to fit; **souliers qui chaussent bien** shoes that fit well
2 **se chausser** *vpr (mettre ses chaussures)* to put one's shoes on

chausses [ʃos] *nfpl (vêtement)* breeches

chaussette [ʃosɛt] *nf* sock; **en chaussettes** in one's socks; **laisser tomber qn comme une vieille c.** to cast sb aside like an old rag

chausseur [ʃosœr] *nm (magasin)* shoe shop; *(fabricant)* shoe manufacturer

chausson [ʃosɔ̃] *nm* (**a**) *(pantoufle)* slipper; *(de danse)* ballet shoe; *(de bébé)* bootee (**b**) *Culin* **c. aux pommes** apple turnover

chaussure [ʃosyr] *nf* shoe; **(l'industrie de) la c.** the shoe industry; **chaussures de ville/de sport/habillées** town/sports/dress shoes; **chaussures à lacets** lace-up shoes; **chaussures de marche** *ou* de montagne walking boots; **chaussures montantes** ankle boots; **chaussures de ski** ski boots; **chaussures à talons** high-heeled shoes; *Fig* **trouver c. à son pied** to find the right woman/man

chauve [ʃov] **1** *adj* bald
2 *nm* bald(-headed) man

chauve-souris *(pl* **chauves-souris**) [ʃovsuri] *nf* bat

chauvin, -e [ʃovɛ̃, -in] **1** *adj* chauvinistic
2 *nm,f* chauvinist

chauvinisme [ʃovinism] *nm* chauvinism

chaux [ʃo] *nf* lime; **blanchir un mur à la c.** to whitewash a wall; **c. vive** quicklime

chavirer [ʃavire] **1** *vi* (**a**) *(bateau)* to capsize; **faire c. un bateau** to capsize a boat (**b**) *(tourner)* **tout chavire autour de moi** everything's spinning
2 *vt (bouleverser)* to overwhelm

check-up [tʃɛkœp] *nm inv Méd* check-up; **se faire faire un c.** to have a check-up

chef [ʃɛf] *nm* (**a**) *(d'un parti politique, d'une bande)* leader; *(d'une tribu)* chief; *Fam (patron)* boss; **ingénieur/rédacteur en c.** chief engineer/editor; **se débrouiller comme un c.** to be getting on very well; **c. d'atelier** (shop) foreman; **c. comptable** *Br* chief accountant, *Am* chief financial officer; **c. d'entreprise** company manager; **c. d'équipe** team leader; **c. d'État** head of state; **c. de famille** head of the family; **c. de file** leader; **c. de gare** station manager; **le c. du gouvernement** the head of government; **c. d'orchestre** conductor; **c. de service** departmental head; *Belg Univ* **c. de travaux** *Br* ≃ (senior) lecturer, *Am* ≃ assistant professor (**b**) *(cuisinier)* chef (**c**) *Jur* **c. d'accusation** charge (**d**) *(tête)* head; **faire qch de son propre c.** to do sth on one's own authority

chefaillon [ʃɛfajɔ̃] *nm Fam Péj* little Hitler

chef-garde *(pl* **chefs-gardes**) [ʃɛfgard] *nm Belg Rail* ticket inspector

chef-d'œuvre *(pl* **chefs-d'œuvre**) [ʃɛdœvr] *nm* masterpiece

chef-lieu *(pl* **chefs-lieux**) [ʃɛfljø] *nm* = administrative centre of a "département"

cheik(h) [ʃɛk] *nm* sheik(h)

chelem [ʃlɛm] *nm Sport* **grand c.** grand slam

chelou [ʃəlu] *adj inv Fam (verlan de* **louche***)* shady, *Br* dodgy, *Am* sketchy

chemin [ʃəmɛ̃] *nm* (**a**) *(route étroite)* path, track; **c. de grande randonnée** hiking trail; **c. de ronde** parapet walk; **c. de terre** track; **c. de traverse** path across the fields (**b**) *(itinéraire)* way (**de** to); *Fig (de la gloire, du bonheur)* road (**de** to); **sur le c. du retour** on the way back; **en c.** on the way; **se mettre en c.** to set out *or* off; **nous ne pouvons pas nous arrêter en si bon c.** we can't give up now when we're doing so well; **ne pas y aller par quatre chemins** to get straight to the point; **prendre le c. des écoliers** to take the long way round; **suivre le droit c.** to stay on the straight and narrow (**c**) *(distance)* way; *aussi Fig* **avoir beaucoup de c. à faire** to have a long way to go; **nous avons fait la moitié du c. ensemble/à pied** we went half the way together/on foot; *Fig* **faire son c.** *(idée)* to gain ground (**d**) *Ordinat* path; **c. d'accès** path

chemin de fer (*pl* **chemins de fer**) [ʃəmɛ̃dfɛr] *nm Br* railway, *Am* railroad; **les chemins de fer** *(société d'exploitation)* the railway

cheminée [ʃəmine] *nf* (**a**) *(dans une maison)* fireplace; *(dessus)* mantelpiece (**b**) *(conduit) (de maison, d'usine)* chimney; *(de bateau à vapeur)* funnel (**c**) *Géol* chimney

cheminement [ʃəminmɑ̃] *nm (de personnes)* movement; *Fig* **le c. de la pensée** the development of thought

cheminer [ʃəmine] *vi (personne)* to make one's way; *Fig (idée)* to gain ground

cheminot [ʃəmino] *nm Br* railwayman, *Am* railroader

chemise [ʃəmiz] *nf* (**a**) *(vêtement)* shirt; **c. à manches longues/courtes** long-/short-sleeved shirt; *Fig* **changer de qch comme de c.** to change sth at the drop of a hat; **c. de nuit** *(de femme)* nightdress; *(d'homme)* nightshirt (**b**) *(classeur)* folder

chemisette [ʃəmizɛt] *nf (d'homme)* short-sleeved shirt

chemisier [ʃəmizje] *nm* (**a**) *(corsage)* blouse (**b**) *(fabricant)* shirt-maker; *(marchand)* men's outfitter

chenal, -aux [ʃənal, -o] *nm (d'une rivière, d'un port)* channel

chenapan [ʃənapɑ̃] *nm Vieilli* scoundrel

chêne [ʃɛn] *nm* oak; **table en c. massif** solid oak table; **c. vert** holm oak

chêne-liège (*pl* **chênes-lièges**) [ʃɛnljɛʒ] *nm* cork oak

chenet [ʃənɛ] *nm* firedog

chenil [ʃənil] *nm* (**a**) *(abri, élevage)* kennels (**b**) *Suisse (désordre)* shambles

chenille [ʃənij] *nf* (**a**) *(insecte)* caterpillar (**b**) *(de char, d'autoneige)* caterpillar track; **véhicule à chenilles** tracked vehicle (**c**) *(tissu)* chenille

chenu, -e [ʃəny] *adj Litt (personne, tête)* hoary; *(arbre)* leafless

cheptel [ʃɛptɛl] *nm (d'un agriculteur)* livestock

chèque [ʃɛk] *nm* **c. (bancaire)** *Br* cheque, *Am* check; **c. de 60 euros** cheque for 60 euros; **faire un c. à qn** to write sb a cheque; **payer qch par c.** to pay for sth by cheque; **c. de banque** banker's draft, *Am* cashier's check; **c. barré** crossed cheque; **c. en blanc** blank cheque; *Fam* **c. en bois** rubber cheque; **c. sans provision** bad cheque; **j'ai fait un c. sans provision** my cheque bounced; **c. de voyage** traveller's cheque

chèque-cadeau (*pl* **chèques-cadeaux**) [ʃɛkkado] *nm* gift token

chèque-repas (*pl* **chèques-repas**) [ʃɛkrəpa], **chèque-restaurant** (*pl* **chèques-restaurant**) [ʃɛkrɛstɔrɑ̃] *nm* luncheon voucher

chéquier [ʃekje] *nm Br* cheque book, *Am* check book

cher, -ère¹ [ʃɛr] **1** *adj* (**a**) *(coûteux)* dear, expensive; *Fam* **pas c.** cheap; **la vie est chère en ville** it's expensive to live in town (**b**) *(aimé)* dear; *Litt* **être c. à qn** to be dear to sb; **c'est mon vœu le plus c.** it's my dearest wish; **il a retrouvé sa chère maison/son c. bureau** he's back in his beloved house/office; **C. Monsieur** *(dans une lettre)* Dear Mr X; *(officiel)* Dear Sir

2 *adv* **payer qch c./trop c.** to pay a high price/too much for sth; *Fam* **je l'ai eu pour pas c.** I got it cheap; **coûter c.** to cost a lot; **je donnerais c. pour savoir ce qu'il leur a dit** I'd give anything to know what he said to them

3 *nm,f* **mon c., ma chère** my dear

chercher [ʃɛrʃe] *vt* (**a**) *(objet, personne, emploi, solution)* to look for; *(dans un dictionnaire)* to look up; *(dans ses souvenirs)* to try to think of; **c. qn du regard** *ou* **des yeux** to look around for sb; **c. ses mots** to search for words; **cherche!** *(à un chien)* fetch!; *Fig* **où va-t-il donc c. tout cela?** where on earth does he get that from?; **il l'a bien cherché** he was asking for it; **c. midi à quatorze heures** to look for problems where there are none (**b**) *(prendre)* **aller/venir c. qn/qch** to (go/come and) fetch sb/sth (**c**) *(essayer)* **c. à faire qch** to try to do sth (**d**) *Fam (atteindre)* **cela va c. dans les 10 000 euros** you're talking about something like 10,000 euros (**e**) *Fam (provoquer)* to get at; **tu me cherches?** are you looking for a fight?

2 se chercher *vpr (chercher son identité)* to try to find oneself

chercheur, -euse [ʃɛrʃœr, -øz] *nm,f* (**a**) *(scientifique)* researcher (**b**) **c. d'or** gold digger

chère² [ʃɛr] *nf Litt* **aimer la bonne c.** to be a lover of good food

chèrement [ʃɛrmɑ̃] *adv* **vendre c. sa peau** to sell one's life dearly

chéri, -e [ʃeri] **1** *adj* dear; **à notre grand-mère chérie** *(sur une couronne mortuaire)* to our beloved grandmother

2 *nm,f* darling; **mon c., ma chérie** darling

chérir [ʃerir] *vt Litt* to cherish

cherra *etc voir* **choir**

cherry (*pl* **cherrys** *ou* **cherries**) [ʃeri] *nm* cherry brandy

cherté [ʃerte] *nf* high cost; **la c. de la vie** the high cost of living

chérubin [ʃerybɛ̃] *nm aussi Fig* cherub

chétif, -ive [ʃetif, -iv] *adj (personne)* puny, sickly; *(arbuste)* stunted

cheval, -aux [ʃəval, -o] *nm* (**a**) *(animal)* horse; *Péj (femme)* carthorse; **à c.** on horseback; **monter à c.** to ride; *aussi Fig* **être à c. sur qch** to straddle sth; **être à c. sur l'étiquette** to be a stickler for etiquette; *Fam* **ce n'est pas un mauvais c.** he's not such a bad sort; **monter sur ses grands chevaux** to get on one's high horse; **petits chevaux** = type of board game; **c. d'arçons** (vaulting) horse; **c. à bascule** rocking horse; **c'est son c. de bataille** that's his/her hobbyhorse; **chevaux de bois** *Br* roundabout, *Am* carousel; **c. de course** racehorse; **c. de labour** workhorse; **c. de trait** carthorse (**b**) *Aut* horsepower; **une automobile de 20 chevaux** a 20-horsepower car

chevalerie [ʃəvalri] *nf* (**a**) *(dignité)* knighthood (**b**) *(institution)* chivalry

chevalet [ʃəvalɛ] *nm* (**a**) *(de peintre)* easel; *(de menuisier, de charpentier)* trestle (**b**) *Mus (de violon)* bridge

chevalier [ʃəvalje] *nm* (**a**) *(seigneur)* knight; **c. servant** faithful admirer (**b**) *(de la Légion d'honneur)* chevalier

chevalière [ʃəvaljɛr] *nf* signet ring

chevalin, -e [ʃəvalɛ̃, -in] *adj* equine; *Fig (traits)* horsey

cheval-vapeur (*pl* **chevaux-vapeur**) [ʃəvalvapœr] [ʃovovapœr] *nm* horsepower

chevauchée [ʃəvoʃe] *nf (course)* ride

chevaucher [ʃəvoʃe] **1** *vt (mur, chaise)* to straddle; *Litt (cheval, âne)* to ride

2 *vi Litt* to ride

3 se chevaucher *vpr* to overlap

chevelu, -e [ʃəvly] *adj Péj* long-haired

chevelure [ʃəvlyr] *nf* (head of) hair; **femme à la c.**
rousse/blonde red-haired/blonde woman
chevet [ʃəvɛ] *nm* (**a**) *(tête de lit)* bedhead; **rester au c.**
de qn to stay at sb's bedside (**b**) *Archit (d'une église)*
chevet
cheveu, -x [ʃəvø] *nm* (**a**) *(poil)* hair; **avoir le c.**
terne to have dull hair; **un c.** **blanc** a grey hair; **arriver**
comme un c. **sur la soupe** to come at an awkward
moment; **il s'en est fallu d'un c.** **qu'il n'éclate de rire**
he very nearly burst out laughing; **rater qch d'un c.** to
miss sth by a whisker; **à un c.** **près, je ratais mon train**
I caught my train by a hair's breadth (**b**) **cheveux**
hair; **avoir les cheveux longs/courts** to have long/
short hair; **un vieillard à cheveux blancs** a white-
haired old man; **argument tiré par les cheveux** far-
fetched argument; **cheveux d'ange** *(pâtes)* angel-
hair pasta
cheville [ʃəvij] *nf* (**a**) *(partie du corps)* ankle; *Fig* **il ne**
vous arrive pas à la c. he can't hold a candle to you;
Fam Péj **tu as les chevilles qui enflent** you're getting
too big for your *Br* boots *or Am* britches (**b**) *(pour ac-*
crocher) peg; *(pour boucher un trou)* plug; *(de violon,*
de guitare) peg; *Fam* **être en c.** **avec qn** to be in cahoots with sb; *Fig* **c.** **ouvrière** mainspring
chèvre [ʃɛvr] **1** *nf* goat; *Fam* **devenir c.** to go round the
bend; *Fam* **rendre qn c.** to drive sb round the bend
2 *nm* goat's cheese
chevreau, -x [ʃəvro] *nm* kid; **gants en c.** kid gloves
chèvrefeuille [ʃɛvrəfœj] *nm* honeysuckle
chevreuil [ʃəvrœj] *nm* roe deer; *Can* deer; *(gibier)* venison
chevron [ʃəvrɔ̃] *nm* (**a**) *Constr (d'un toit)* rafter (**b**) *Mil*
stripe, chevron (**c**) *(motif)* **tissu à chevrons** herring-
bone-pattern material
chevronné, -e [ʃəvrɔne] *adj (qui a de l'expérience)* experienced
chevrotant, -e [ʃəvrɔtɑ̃, -ɑ̃t] *adj (voix)* quavering
chevroter [ʃəvrɔte] *vi (voix)* to quaver
chevrotine [ʃəvrɔtin] *nf* buckshot
chewing-gum *(pl* **chewing-gums)** [ʃwiŋɡɔm] *nm*
chewing-gum
chez [ʃe] *prép* (**a**) *(dans la maison de)* **il n'est pas c.** **lui**
he's not at home, he's not in; **elle est rentrée c.** **elle**
she's gone home; **faites comme c.** **vous** make yourself at home; **je vais c.** **ma sœur** I'm going to my sister's; **venez c.** **nous** come to our place; **il vit c.** **nous** he
lives with us; **aller c.** **le dentiste** to go to the dentist;
chez... *(sur une lettre)* c/o... (**b**) *(en, dans)* **c'est deve-**
nu une habitude c. **moi** it's become a habit with me;
ce que j'admire c. **cet homme, c'est...** what I admire
about the man is...; **c. les Espagnols, on dîne tard** the
Spaniards have dinner late (**c**) *(au temps de)* during
the time of (**d**) *(parmi)* among; **cette expression est**
courante c. **les jeunes** this expression is common
among young people
chez-soi [ʃeswa] *nm inv* **son petit c.** one's own little
home
chialer [ʃjale] *vi très Fam* to blubber
chiant, -e [ʃjɑ̃, -ɑ̃t] *adj très Fam* (**a**) *(ennuyeux)* boring
as hell (**b**) *(agaçant)* damned annoying; **c'est c.!** it's a
real pain in the neck *or Br* arse!
chianti [kjɑ̃ti] *nm* Chianti
chiasse [ʃjas] *nf Vulg* **avoir la c.** *(la diarrhée)* to have
the shits; *(avoir peur)* to be shit-scared
chic [ʃik] **1** *adj inv* (**a**) *(élégant)* stylish, smart; **les gens**
c. the smart set (**b**) *Fam Vieilli (aimable)* decent
2 *nm* (**a**) *(savoir-faire)* **avoir le c.** **pour faire qch** to

have the knack of doing sth (**b**) *(élégance)* style; **bon**
c. bon genre *Br* ≃ Sloany, *Am* ≃ preppy
3 *exclam Fam Vieilli* **c. (alors)!** great!
Chicago [ʃikago] *n* Chicago
chicaner [ʃikane] **1** *vt (chercher querelle à)* to quibble
with (**sur** about)
2 chicaner sur *vt ind* to quibble over
3 se chicaner *vpr* to squabble
chicaneur, -euse [ʃikanœr, -øz], **chicanier, -ère**
[ʃikanje, -ɛr] *nm,f* quibbler
chiche [ʃiʃ] *adj (repas)* scanty; *(personne)* mean; **être**
c. de louanges to be sparing in one's praise; *Fam* **tu**
n'es pas c. d'y aller! I bet you don't go!; *Fam* **c.!** *(pour*
défier) I dare you!; *(pour relever le défi)* you're on!
chichement [ʃiʃmɑ̃] *adv* meanly
chichi [ʃiʃi] *nm Fam* **faire du c.** *ou* **des chichis** *(se don-*
ner des airs) to put on airs; *(compliquer les choses)* to
make a fuss; **repas sans c.** informal meal
chicorée [ʃikɔre] *nf* (**a**) *(plante)* **c. (frisée)** endive; **c.**
sauvage chicory (**b**) *(en poudre)* chicory
chicos [ʃikos] *adj Fam* smart
chicot [ʃiko] *nm (dent)* stump
chié, -e¹ [ʃje] *adj Fam (culotté)* **il est c., lui!** he's got a
nerve!
chiée² *nf très Fam* **(toute) une c. de** a hell of a lot of
chien, chienne [ʃjɛ̃, ʃjɛn] **1** *nm,f* dog, *f* bitch; **jeune c.**
puppy, pup; **(attention) c. méchant** *(sur écriteau)* beware of the dog; **traiter qn comme un c.** to treat sb
like a dog; *Fam* **quel temps de c.!** what foul weather!;
Fam **vie de c.** dog's life; *Fam* **chienne de vie!** life's a
bitch!; **être comme c. et chat** to fight like cat and
dog; **entre c. et loup** at dusk; **se regarder en chiens**
de faïence to stare at one another; **c. d'arrêt** pointer;
c. d'aveugle guide dog; **c. de berger** sheepdog; **c. de**
chasse retriever; **c. de garde** guard dog; **c. policier**
police dog; **c. de race** pedigree dog; **c. savant** *(dans*
un cirque) performing dog; *Fig* performing monkey;
c. de traîneau husky
2 *nm* (**a**) *Fam (style)* **avoir du c.** to have a certain
something (**b**) *(d'un fusil)* hammer; **dormir en c. de**
fusil to sleep curled up
chiendent [ʃjɛ̃dɑ̃] *nm* couch grass; **brosse en** *ou* **de c.**
scrubbing brush; **pousser comme du c.** to sprout up
chien-loup *(pl* **chiens-loups)** [ʃjɛ̃lu] *nm* wolfhound
chienne [ʃjɛn] *nf voir* **chien**
chier [66] [ʃje] *vi Vulg* to shit, to crap; **faire c. qn** *(éner-*
ver) to piss sb off; *(ennuyer)* to bore sb shitless; **se**
faire c. *(s'ennuyer)* to be bored shitless; **se faire c. (à**
faire qch) *(avoir du mal)* to bust a gut (doing sth); **je**
vais pas me faire c. à tout recopier! I can't be bothered *or Br* arsed writing it all out again!
chiffe [ʃif] *nf Fam* **c'est une c. molle** he's a drip
chiffon [ʃifɔ̃] *nm* rag; **c. à poussière** duster; **passer un**
coup de c. to have a dust; **passer un coup de c. sur**
qch to give sth a dust; *Fam* **parler chiffons** to talk
clothes
chiffonner [ʃifɔne] **1** *vt* (**a**) *(robe, morceau de papier)*
to crumple (**b**) *Fam (ennuyer)* to bug
2 se chiffonner *vpr* to crumple
chiffonnier, -ère [ʃifɔnje, -ɛr] *nm,f* (**a**) **1** *nm,f* rag picker;
disputer comme des chiffonniers to go at it hammer
and tongs
2 *nm (meuble)* chiffonier
chiffrable [ʃifrabl] *adj* **facilement/difficilement c.**
easy/difficult to calculate; **ne pas être c.** to be impossible to calculate

chiffre [ʃifr] *nm* (**a**) *(nombre)* figure, number; **chiffres arabes/romains** Arabic/Roman numerals; **nombre à trois chiffres** three-figure number; *Ordinat* **c. binaire** binary digit; *Ordinat* **c. ASCII** ASCII number (**b**) *(total)* total; **c. d'affaires (annuel)** (annual) turnover; **faire un c. d'affaires de 4 millions d'euros** to have a turnover of 4 million euros

chiffrement [ʃifrəmɑ̃] *nm Ordinat* **c. de données** data encryption

chiffrer [ʃifre] **1** *vt* (**a**) *(montant, coût)* to work out, to calculate; *(réparations)* to assess (**b**) **message chiffré** coded message
  2 se chiffrer *vpr* **se c. à** to add up to, to amount to

chignole [ʃiɲɔl] *nf* hand drill; *(électrique)* electric drill

chignon [ʃiɲɔ̃] *nm* bun, chignon; **se faire un c.** to put one's hair in a bun

chihuahua [ʃiwawa] *nm* chihuahua

chiite [ʃiit] *adj & nmf Rel* Shiite

Chili [ʃili] *nm* **le C.** Chile

chili (con carne) [ʃili(kɔnkarne)] *nm Culin* chilli (con carne)

chilien, -enne [ʃiljɛ̃, -ɛn] **1** *adj* Chilean
  2 *nm,f* **C.** Chilean

chimère [ʃimɛr] *nf (monstre)* chimera; *Fig (rêve)* pipe dream

chimie [ʃimi] *nf* chemistry

chimio [ʃimjo] *nf Fam Méd* chemo; **faire une c.** to have chemo

chimiothérapie [ʃimjoterapi] *nf Méd* chemotherapy; **faire une c.** to have chemotherapy

chimique [ʃimik] *adj* chemical

chimiste [ʃimist] *nmf* chemist; **ingénieur c.** chemical engineer

chimpanzé [ʃɛ̃pɑ̃ze] *nm* chimpanzee

chinchilla [ʃɛ̃ʃila] *nm (animal, fourrure)* chinchilla; **veste en c.** chinchilla jacket

Chine [ʃin] *nf* **la C.** China

chiné, -e [ʃine] *adj (tissu)* flecked

chiner [ʃine] **1** *vt Fam (personne)* to kid
  2 *vi* to hunt for second-hand goods

chinetoque [ʃintɔk] *nmf très Fam* Chink, = racist term used to refer to a Chinese person

chinois, -e [ʃinwa, -az] **1** *adj* Chinese
  2 *nm,f* **C.** Chinese; **les C.** the Chinese
  3 *nm* (**a**) *(langue)* Chinese; *Fam Fig* **c'est du c. pour moi** it's all Greek to me (**b**) *(ustensile)* conical strainer

chinoiserie [ʃinwazri] *nf* (**a**) *(objet)* Chinese curio (**b**) *Fam* **chinoiseries** *(complications)* pointless complications

chintz [ʃints] *nm* chintz; **des rideaux en c.** chintz curtains

chiot [ʃjo] *nm* puppy, pup

chiottes [ʃjɔt] *nfpl très Fam Br* bog, *Am* john; *Vulg* **aux c., l'arbitre!** the referee's a dickhead *or Br* a wanker!

chiper [ʃipe] *vt Fam* to pinch, to swipe

chipie [ʃipi] *nf Fam* minx

chipolata [ʃipɔlata] *nf* chipolata (sausage)

chipoter [ʃipɔte] *vi* (**a**) *(picorer)* to pick at one's food (**b**) *(contester)* to quibble (**sur** about)

chips [ʃips] *nf Br* crisp, *Am* chip; **des (pommes) c.** *Br* crisps, *Am* chips

chique [ʃik] *nf* (**a**) *(de tabac)* quid (**b**) *Fam* **avoir la c.** *(la joue enflée)* to have a swollen cheek *(due to toothache)* (**c**) *Belg (bonbon)* sweet

chiqué [ʃike] *nm Fam* **faire du c.** to put on an act; **c'est du c.** it's all put on

chiquenaude [ʃiknod] *nf* flick; **d'une c., il l'envoya sur le bureau** he flicked it onto the desk

chiquer [ʃike] **1** *vt* to chew
  2 *vi* to chew tobacco

chiromancien, -enne [kirɔmɑ̃sjɛ̃, -ɛn] *nm,f* palmist

chirurgical, -e, -aux, -ales [ʃiryrʒikal, -o] *adj* surgical

chirurgie [ʃiryrʒi] *nf* surgery; **c. esthétique** plastic *or* cosmetic surgery; **c. au laser** laser surgery

chirurgien [ʃiryrʒjɛ̃] *nm* surgeon

chirurgien-dentiste (*pl* **chirurgiens-dentistes**) [ʃiryrʒjɛ̃dɑ̃tist] *nm* dental surgeon

chiure [ʃjyr] *nf* **c. de mouche** fly-speck

ch-l. *(abrév* **chef-lieu)** = administrative centre of a "département"

chleuh, -e [ʃlø] *adj & nm,f très Fam* Kraut, = offensive term used to refer to a German

chlinguer [ʃlɛ̃ge] *vi très Fam* to stink

chlorate [klɔrat] *nm Chim* chlorate

chlore [klɔr] *nm* chlorine

chlorer [klɔre] *vt* to chlorinate

chlorhydrique [klɔridrik] *adj (acide)* hydrochloric

chlorofluorocarbure [klɔrɔflyɔrɔkarbyr] *nm Chim* chlorofluorocarbon

chloroforme [klɔrɔfɔrm] *nm* chloroform

chloroformer [klɔrɔfɔrme] *vt* to chloroform

chlorophylle [klɔrɔfil] *nf* chlorophyll

chlorure [klɔryr] *nm Chim* chloride; **c. de sodium** sodium chloride

chnoque [ʃnɔk] = schnock

choc [ʃɔk] *nm* (**a**) *(coup)* impact; *Fig (conflit)* clash; *(forte impression)* impact; *Écon* **c. pétrolier** oil crisis (**b**) *Méd* shock; **c. opératoire** post-operative shock (**c**) *(émotion brutale)* shock; **faire un c. à qn** to give sb a shock; **être en état de c.** to be in a state of shock; **être sous le c.** to be in shock (**d**) **équipe de c.** team of troubleshooters; **troupes de c.** shock troops
-choc [ʃɔk] *suff* **image-c.** shocking image; **prix-chocs** *(sur une vitrine)* drastic reductions

chochotte [ʃɔʃɔt] *Fam Péj* **1** *adj (homme)* camp
  2 *nf* la-di-da type; *(homme)* namby-pamby; **faire sa c.** to put on airs

chocolat [ʃɔkɔla] **1** *nm* (**a**) *(produit)* chocolate; **gâteau au c.** chocolate cake; **c. blanc** white chocolate; **un c. (chaud)** a hot chocolate; **c. à cuire** cooking chocolate; **c. au lait** milk chocolate; **c. noir** *ou* **à croquer** plain *or* dark chocolate; **c. aux noisettes** hazelnut chocolate; **c. en poudre** drinking chocolate (**b**) *(bonbon)* chocolate
  2 *adj inv* chocolate-coloured; *Fam Fig* **être c.** to have lost out

chocolaté, -e [ʃɔkɔlate] *adj* chocolate

chocolatier, -ère [ʃɔkɔlatje, -ɛr] **1** *nm,f (fabricant)* chocolate-maker; *(vendeur)* chocolate-seller
  2 *adj (industrie)* chocolate

chocottes [ʃɔkɔt] *nfpl Fam* **avoir les c.** to have the jitters

chœur [kœr] *nm* choir; *(d'opéra)* chorus; **les chœurs** *(d'un opéra, d'un spectacle)* the chorus; **chanter en c.** to sing in chorus; **répétez tous en c.** (repeat all) together now

choir [14] [ʃwar] *vi (aux* être*) Litt (tomber)* to fall; **se laisser c.** to sink down; *Fam* **laisser c. qn** to drop sb

choisi, -e [ʃwazi] *adj* (**a**) *(sélectionné)* **morceaux choisis de...** selected extracts from... (**b**) *(langage, termes)* careful

choisir [ʃwazir] *vt* to choose, to pick; **c. de faire qch** to choose to do sth; **il a bien choisi son moment!** he really picked his moment!; **à toi de c.**, **cette fois** it's your turn to choose now

choix [ʃwa] *nm* choice; **un grand c. de cravates** a wide choice *or* selection of ties; **avoir le c.** to have a choice; **faire son c.** to take one's pick; **faire le bon c.** to make the right choice; **mon c. est fait** I've made my choice; **laisser le c. à qn** to let sb choose; **viande ou poisson au c.** *(sur un menu)* choice of meat or fish; **de premier c.** top-grade; **de second c.** second-grade

choléra [kɔlera] *nm* cholera; **avoir le c.** to have cholera

cholestérol [kɔlɛsterɔl] *nm* cholesterol; **taux de c.** cholesterol level; *Fam* **avoir du c.** to have a high cholesterol level

cholestérolémie [kɔlɛsterɔlemi] *nf Méd* cholesterol level

chômage [ʃomaʒ] *nm* unemployment; **être au c.** to be unemployed, to be out of work; **toucher le c.** to claim unemployment benefit; **s'inscrire au c.** to sign on; **le c. des jeunes** youth unemployment; **être en c. technique** to have been laid off; **c. de longue durée** long-term unemployment

chômé, -e [ʃome] *adj* **jour c.** public holiday, *Br* bank holiday

chômedu [ʃomdy] *nm Fam* unemployment; **être au c.** to be unemployed

chômer [ʃome] *vi* **vous n'avez pas chômé!** you've not been idle!

chômeur, -euse [ʃomœr, -øz] *nm,f* unemployed person; **les chômeurs** the unemployed; **les chômeurs de longue durée** the long-term unemployed

chope [ʃɔp] *nf (récipient)* beer mug, tankard; *(contenu)* ≃ pint

choper [ʃɔpe] *vt Fam* (**a**) *(arrêter, prendre)* to nab; **se faire c.** to get nabbed (**b**) *(maladie)* to catch

chopine [ʃɔpin] *nf Fam (bouteille)* half-litre bottle; **tu viens boire une c.?** are you coming for a drink?

choquant, -e [ʃɔkɑ̃, -ɑ̃t] *adj* shocking

choquer [ʃɔke] *vt* (**a**) *(indigner)* to shock (**b**) *(traumatiser)* **c. qn** to shake sb badly

choral, -e, -aux *ou* **-als, -ales** [kɔral] **1** *adj* choral **2** *nf* **chorale** *(club)* choral society; *(chanteurs)* choir

chorégraphe [kɔregraf] *nmf* choreographer

chorégraphie [kɔregrafi] *nf* choreography; **faire la c. d'un spectacle** to choreograph a show

chorégraphier [66] [kɔregrafje] *vt* to choreograph

chorégraphique [kɔregrafik] *adj* choreographic

choriste [kɔrist] *nmf* choir member; *(d'église)* chorister; *(d'opéra)* chorus member; *(d'un chanteur)* backing singer

chorizo [tʃorizo] *nm* chorizo

chorus [kɔrys] *nm (de jazz)* chorus

chose [ʃoz] **1** *nf* (**a**) *(objet, parole, événement)* thing; **il s'est passé une c. incroyable** something unbelievable has happened; **je vais te dire une c.** I'm going to tell you something; **il a très bien pris la c.** he took it very well (**b**) *(locutions)* **avant toute c.** first of all; **les choses étant ce qu'elles sont** with things as they are; **aller au fond des choses** to get to the heart of the matter; **bien faire les choses** to do things in style; **il ne fait pas les choses à moitié** he doesn't do things by halves; **parler de choses et d'autres** to talk about this and that; **c'est ça, c'est done; de deux choses l'une, soit il parle, soit…** either he talks or…; **c. curieuse, personne n'en savait rien** curiously enough,

nobody knew anything about it; **et, c. rare, il a demandé pardon** he apologized for once; **dites bien des choses de ma part à… remember me to…**

2 *nm Fam (truc)* whatsit, thingummy; **Monsieur/Madame C.** Mr/Mrs thingummy

3 *adj inv Fam* **se sentir tout c.** to feel a bit funny

chou¹, -x [ʃu] *nm* (**a**) *(légume)* cabbage; **faire ses choux gras de qch** to have a field day with sth; **faire c. blanc** to draw a blank; **mon petit c.** darling; **c. de Bruxelles** Brussels sprout; **c. rouge** red cabbage (**b**) *(gâteau)* **c. à la crème** cream puff

chou² *adj inv Fam (mignon)* cute; *(gentil)* nice, kind

chouchou, -oute [ʃuʃu, -ut] **1** *nm,f Fam* **c'est le c. (de la maîtresse)** he's (the) teacher's pet; **c'est le c. de sa maman** he's a mummy's boy

2 *nm (pour les cheveux)* scrunchie

chouchouter [ʃuʃute] *vt Fam* to pamper; **elle aime se faire c.** she enjoys being pampered

choucroute [ʃukrut] *nf (chou)* sauerkraut; **c. (garnie)** = sauerkraut served with different types of sausages and bacon

chouette¹ [ʃwɛt] *nf* owl; **c. hulotte** tawny owl; *Fam Péj* **une vieille c.** an old shrew

chouette² *Fam* **1** *adj* great, terrific; **il a été très c. avec elle** he's been really nice to her

2 *exclam* great!, terrific!

chou-fleur *(pl* **choux-fleurs)** [ʃuflœr] *nm* cauliflower; **oreille en c.** cauliflower ear

chouia [ʃuja] *nm Fam* **un c. (de qch)** a tiny bit (of sth)

chouraver [ʃurave], **chourer** [ʃure] *vt très Fam* to swipe; **se faire c. qch** to have sth swiped

choyer [32] [ʃwaje] *vt* to pamper

CHR [seaɛr] *nm (abrév* **centre hospitalier régional)** regional hospital

chrétien, -enne [kretjɛ̃, -ɛn] *adj & nm,f* Christian

chrétienté [kretjɛ̃te] *nf* Christendom

Christ [krist] *nm* (**a**) **le C.** Christ (**b**) *(crucifix)* **c.** crucifix

christianisme [kristjanism] *nm* Christianity

chromatique [krɔmatik] *adj* (**a**) *(des couleurs) & Mus* chromatic (**b**) *Biol* chromosomal

chrome [krom] *nm Chim* chromium; **chromes** *(d'une voiture)* chrome

chromé, -e [krome] *adj* chromium-plated; **acier c.** chrome steel

chromosome [krɔmozom] *nm* chromosome

chromosomique [krɔmozomik] *adj* chromosomal

chronique¹ [krɔnik] *adj* chronic

chronique² *nf* (**a**) *Journ* column; **tenir la c. sportive** to write the sports column (**b**) *(annale)* chronicle

chroniqueur, -euse [krɔnikœr, -øz] *nm,f Journ* columnist; **c. sportif** sports reporter

chrono [krɔno] *nm Fam* stopwatch; **faire du 220 km/h c.** to be timed at 220 kph

chronologie [krɔnɔlɔʒi] *nf* chronology

chronologique [krɔnɔlɔʒik] *adj* chronological

chronomètre [krɔnɔmɛtr] *nm (montre de précision)* chronometer; *(pour le sport)* stopwatch

chronométrer [34] [krɔnɔmetre] *vt Sport* to time

chrysalide [krizalid] *nf* chrysalis

chrysanthème [krizɑ̃tɛm] *nm* chrysanthemum

Chrysanthèmes

Chrysanthemums are often associated with funerals in France, and so are never given as gifts. They are traditionally used to decorate graves, especially on All Saints' Day.

ch'timi [ʃtimi] **1** *nmf Fam* Northerner *(from Northern France)*
  2 *nm (patois)* = dialect spoken in Northern France
CHU [seaʃy] *nm inv (abrév* **centre hospitalo-universitaire**) teaching hospital
chu *voir* **choir**
chuchotement [ʃyʃɔtmɑ̃] *nm* whisper; **des chuchotements** whispering
chuchoter [ʃyʃɔte] *vt & vi* to whisper
chuintement [ʃɥɛ̃tmɑ̃] *nm* hissing
chuinter [ʃɥɛ̃te] *vi (siffler)* to hiss
chut [ʃyt] *exclam* sh!, hush!
chute [ʃyt] *nf* (**a**) *(fait de tomber) & Fig* fall; *(diminution)* drop, fall; **faire une c.** (**de cheval/moto**) to have a fall (from one's horse/motorbike); **prévenir la c. des cheveux** to prevent hair loss; **il m'a entraîné dans sa c.** he has dragged me down with him; **c. libre** free fall; **descendre en c. libre** to be in free fall; **c. de neige** snowfall (**b**) **c. d'eau** waterfall; **les chutes Victoria** the Victoria Falls (**c**) *(d'histoire drôle)* punchline (**d**) *(de tissu, de métal)* scrap; *(de bois)* off-cut
chuter [ʃyte] *vi (diminuer)* to fall, to drop; *Fam (tomber)* to fall (down)
Chypre [ʃipr] *n* Cyprus
chypriote [ʃiprijɔt] **1** *adj* Cypriot
  2 *nmf* **C.** Cypriot
ci¹ [si] *adv* **ce livre-ci** this book; **ces jours-ci** these days; **de-ci de-là** here and there; **par-ci par-là** here and there
ci² *pron démonstratif Fam* **faire ci et ça** to do this and that
CIA [seia] *nf* **la C.** the CIA
ciao [tʃao] *exclam Fam* ciao!
ci-après [siaprɛ] *adv* below; *Jur* hereinafter
cibiste [sibist] *nmf* CB user
cible [sibl] *nf aussi Fig* target
ciblé, -e [sible] *adj* well-targeted
ciboire [sibwar] *nm Rel* ciborium
ciboulette [sibulɛt] *nf* chives
ciboulot [sibulo] *nm très Fam (tête)* nut; **il n'a rien dans le c.** he doesn't have much upstairs; **se creuser le c.** to rack one's brains
cicatrice [sikatris] *nf aussi Fig* scar
cicatrisant, -e [sikatrizɑ̃, -ɑ̃t] *adj* healing
cicatrisation [sikatrizasjɔ̃] *nf* healing
cicatriser [sikatrize] **1** *vt & vi* to heal
  2 se cicatriser *vpr* to heal
ci-contre [sikɔ̃tr] *adv* opposite
ci-dessous [sidəsu] *adv* below
ci-dessus [sidəsy] *adv* above
ci-devant [sidəvɑ̃] *adv Vieilli* formerly
CIDEX [sidɛks] *nm (abrév* **courrier individuel à distribution exceptionelle**) = system grouping letter boxes in country areas
CIDJ [seideʒi] *nm (abrév* **centre d'information et de documentation de la jeunesse**) = library offering careers information and literature to young people
cidre [sidr] *nm Br* cider, *Am* hard cider; **c. bouché** = traditionally made cider, fermented twice; **c. doux/brut** sweet/dry cider
Cie *(abrév* **compagnie**) Co
ciel [sjɛl] *nm* (**a**) *(air)* sky; **les ciels de Turner** Turner's skies; **à c. ouvert** open-air; **sous d'autres cieux** in other climes; **lever les bras/les yeux au c.** to raise one's arms/one's eyes heavenwards; *Fam* **être au septième c.** to be in seventh heaven; *Fam* **tomber du c. (à qn)** *(héritage)* to be a godsend (to sb); *(solu-*

tion) to come (to sb) out of the blue (**b**) *(pl* **cieux** [sjø]) *(paradis)* heaven; **il est au c.** he's in heaven; **notre Père qui êtes aux cieux** our Father which art in Heaven (**c**) **c. de lit** canopy
cierge [sjɛrʒ] *nm Rel* candle; **brûler un c.** to light a candle
cigale [sigal] *nf* cicada
cigare [sigar] *nm* (**a**) *(à fumer)* cigar (**b**) *très Fam (tête)* **ne rien avoir dans le c.** to be completely brainless
cigarette [sigarɛt] *nf* cigarette; *Culin* **c. russe** = shortcake biscuit shaped like a brandy snap
ci-gît [siʒi] *voir* **gésir**
cigogne [sigɔɲ] *nf* stork
ciguë [sigy] *nf* hemlock
ci-inclus, -e *(mpl* **ci-inclus**, *fpl* **ci-incluses**) [siɛ̃kly, -yz] **1** *adj* **la copie ci-incluse** the enclosed copy
  2 *adv* (**vous trouverez**) **c. copie de votre lettre** please find enclosed a copy of your letter
ci-joint, -e *(mpl* **ci-joints**, *fpl* **ci-jointes**) [siʒwɛ̃, -ɛ̃t] *adj* **les pièces ci-jointes** the enclosed documents
  2 *adv* (**vous trouverez**) **c. copie de votre lettre** please find enclosed a copy of your letter
cil [sil] *nm* eyelash; **faux cils** false eyelashes
ciller [sije] *vi* to blink; *Fig* **il n'a pas cillé** he didn't bat an eyelid
cime [sim] *nf (d'une montagne)* summit; *(pic)* peak; *(d'un arbre, d'un mât)* top
ciment [simɑ̃] *nm* cement
cimenter [simɑ̃te] *vt aussi Fig* to cement
cimetière [simtjɛr] *nm* cemetery; *(d'église)* graveyard; **c. de voitures** scrapyard
ciné [sine] *nm Fam Br* flicks, *Am* movies
cinéaste [sineast] *nmf* film maker
ciné-club *(pl* **ciné-clubs**) [sineklœb] *nm* film club
cinéma [sinema] *nm* (**a**) *(art, industrie) Br* cinema, *Am* movies; **faire du c.** to be a movie *or Br* film actor; *Fam (faire semblant)* to put on an act; *Fam* **c'est du c.** it's all an act; *Fam* **arrête ton c.!** stop making such a fuss!; **c. d'art et d'essai** *Br* art films, *Am* arthouse movies; **c. muet/parlant** silent/talking movies *or Br* films (**b**) *(salle) Br* cinema, *Am* movie theater; **aller au c.** to go to the *Br* cinema *or Am* movies
CinémaScope® [sinemaskɔp] *nm* CinemaScope®
cinémathèque [sinematɛk] *nf* film library
cinématographie [sinematɔgrafi] *nf* cinematography
cinématographique [sinematɔgrafik] *adj* cinema, film
ciné-parc *(pl* **cinés-parcs**) [sinepark] *nm Can* drive-in movie theater
cinéphile [sinefil] **1** *adj* **être c.** to be a movie *or Br* film buff
  2 *nmf* movie *or Br* film enthusiast
cinéraire [sinerɛr] *adj (urne)* cinerary
cinétique [sinetik] *adj (énergie)* kinetic
cinglant, -e [sɛ̃glɑ̃, -ɑ̃t] *adj (pluie)* lashing; *(vent, marque)* cutting
cinglé, -e [sɛ̃gle] *Fam* **1** *adj* crazy
  2 *nmf* loony
cingler¹ [sɛ̃gle] *vi Naut* **c. vers** to make for
cingler² *vt (frapper)* to lash; **la grêle lui cinglait le visage** the hail was stinging his/her face
cinoche [sinɔʃ] *nm Fam Br* cinema; **aller au c.** to go to the *Br* flicks *or Am* movies
cinq [sɛ̃k] **1** *adj inv* five
  2 *nm inv* five; **recevoir qn c. sur c.** to receive sb loud

and clear; *Fam* **c'était moins c.** it was a close shave; *voir aussi* **trois**
cinquantaine [sɛ̃kɑ̃tɛn] *nf* **une c. de personnes** about fifty people, fifty or so people; **avoir la c.** to be about fifty
cinquante [sɛ̃kɑ̃t] *adj & nm inv* fifty; *voir aussi* **trois**
cinquantenaire [sɛ̃kɑ̃tnɛr] **1** *nm (anniversaire)* fiftieth anniversary, golden jubilee
2 *adj* **être c.** to be fifty years old
cinquantième [sɛ̃kɑ̃tjɛm] *nmf, nm & adj* fiftieth; *voir aussi* **cinquième**
cinquième [sɛ̃kjɛm] **1** *adj* fifth; **le c. jour** the fifth day; **arriver c.** to finish fifth
2 *nmf* fifth; **le c. en partant de la droite** the fifth from the right; **arriver le c.** to finish fifth
3 *nm* (**a**) *(fraction)* fifth (**b**) *(étage) Br* fifth floor, *Am* sixth floor; **habiter au c.** to live on the *Br* fifth *or Am* sixth floor (**c**) *(arrondissement)* fifth arrondissement
4 *nf* (**a**) *(classe) Br* ≃ second year of secondary school, *Am* ≃ sixth grade (**b**) *(vitesse)* fifth (gear); **passer la c.** to go into fifth (gear)
cinquièmement [sɛ̃kjɛmmɑ̃] *adv* fifthly
cintre [sɛ̃tr] *nm* (coat)hanger
cintré, -e [sɛ̃tre] *adj (veste)* fitted; *(taille)* nipped-in
CIO [seio] *nm (abrév* **Comité international olympique)** IOC
cirage [siraʒ] *nm* (shoe) polish; *Fam* **être dans le c.** to be feeling woozy
circoncire [sirkɔ̃sir] *vt* to circumcise
circoncision [sirkɔ̃sizjɔ̃] *nf* circumcision
circonférence [sirkɔ̃ferɑ̃s] *nf* circumference; **avoir 10 centimètres de c.** to have a circumference of 10 centimetres
circonflexe [sirkɔ̃flɛks] *adj voir* **accent**
circonlocution [sirkɔ̃lɔkysjɔ̃] *nf* circumlocution; **parler par circonlocutions** to speak in a roundabout way
circonscription [sirkɔ̃skripsjɔ̃] *nf* division, district; **c. électorale** *(au niveau municipal)* ward; *(au niveau national)* constituency
circonscrire [30] [sirkɔ̃skrir] *vt Math* to circumscribe; *(encercler)* to encircle; *(incendie)* to contain
circonspect, -e [sirkɔ̃spɛ, -ɛkt] *adj* circumspect, cautious
circonstance [sirkɔ̃stɑ̃s] *nf* circumstance; **dans les circonstances actuelles** in the present circumstances; **en pareille c.** under such circumstances; **être à la hauteur des circonstances** to be equal to the occasion; **des paroles de c.** appropriate words; **habillé pour la c.** appropriately dressed; **circonstances aggravantes** aggravating circumstances; *Jur* **circonstances atténuantes** extenuating circumstances
circonstancié, -e [sirkɔ̃stɑ̃sje] *adj* detailed
circonstanciel, -elle [sirkɔ̃stɑ̃sjɛl] *adj voir* **complément**
circonvolution [sirkɔ̃vɔlysjɔ̃] *nf* convolution
circuit [sirkɥi] *nm* (**a**) *(chemin)* way; *(boucle)* tour; *Fig* **ça fait longtemps que je ne suis plus dans le c.** I've been out of circulation for ages; **c. touristique** (organized) tour (**b**) *(de course automobile, de cyclisme)* circuit; **c. automobile** racing circuit (**c**) *Élec* circuit (**d**) *Tech* **c. de refroidissement** cooling system (**e**) *Ordinat* **c. de commande** command circuit; **c. imprimé** printed circuit; **c. intégré** integrated circuit; **c. de liaison** link circuit; **c. logique** logic circuit (**f**) *Écon* **c. de distribution** distribution network; **circuits de vente** commercial channels

circulaire [sirkylɛr] **1** *nf* circular
2 *adj* circular; **billet c.** round-trip ticket
circulation [sirkylasjɔ̃] *nf* (**a**) *(d'autos, d'avions)* traffic; **c. interdite** *(sur panneau)* no thoroughfare; **c. aérienne** air traffic; **c. routière** road traffic (**b**) *(du sang, de l'information, des marchandises)* circulation; *Méd* **avoir une mauvaise c.** to have bad circulation; **mettre qch en c.** to put sth into circulation; **retirer un produit de la c.** to take a product off the market (**c**) *Fin (des billets, des capitaux)* circulation (**d**) *Pol & Écon* **libre c. des personnes et des biens** free movement of persons and goods
circulatoire [sirkylatwar] *adj* circulatory
circuler [sirkyle] *vi* (**a**) *(sang, air, rumeur)* to circulate; **faire c. un plat** to pass or hand a dish round; **faire c. une pétition** to circulate a petition (**b**) *(voyageur)* to travel; *(train, autobus)* to run; **on circule très mal dans Paris** it's very difficult to drive about in Paris; **circulez, il n'y a rien à voir!** move along now, there's nothing to see!
cire [sir] *nf* wax; *(pour le bois)* polish; *(dans l'oreille)* (ear)wax; **c. d'abeille** beeswax; **c. à cacheter** sealing wax; **personnage en c.** waxwork (model)
ciré [sire] *nm* oilskin
cirer [sire] *vt (chaussures, meubles)* to polish; *Fam* **c. les pompes à qn** to lick sb's boots; *très Fam* **il en a rien à c. (de ces histoires)** he doesn't give a damn (about your stories)
cireur, -euse[1] [sirœr, -øz] **1** *nm,f (de chaussures)* shoeblack
2 *nf* **cireuse** *(machine)* (floor) polisher
cireux, -euse[2] [sirø, -øz] *adj* waxy
cirque [sirk] *nm* (**a**) *(spectacle)* circus; *Fam* **quel c. dans ce bureau!** it's like a zoo in this office!; *Fam* **faire tout un c.** to make a scene; *Fig* **c. médiatique** media circus (**b**) *Géol* corrie
cirrhose [siroz] *nf* **c. (du foie)** cirrhosis (of the liver); **avoir une c.** to have cirrhosis
cisaille [sizaj] *nf* **c., cisailles** *(de jardinier)* shears
cisailler [sizaje] *vt (branches, haie)* to prune
ciseau, -x [sizo] *nm* (**a**) *(de jardin)* shears; **(une paire de) ciseaux** *(pour papier, pour tissu)* (a pair of) scissors; **des ciseaux à ongles** nail scissors (**b**) *Sport* **sauter en ciseaux** to do a scissors jump (**c**) *Tech* chisel
ciseler [39] [sizle] *vt (or, argent)* to chase; *(marbre)* to chisel; *(bijou)* to engrave a design on
Cisjordanie [sisʒɔrdani] *nf* **la C.** the West Bank
cisjordanien, -enne [sisʒɔrdanjɛ̃, -ɛn] **1** *adj* from the West Bank
2 *nm,f* **C.** person from the West Bank
cistercien, -enne [sistɛrsjɛ̃, -ɛn] *adj & nm Rel* Cistercian
citadelle [sitadɛl] *nf* citadel
citadin, -e [sitadɛ̃, -in] **1** *nm,f* city-dweller
2 *adj* city
citation [sitasjɔ̃] *nf* (**a**) *(extrait)* quotation; **fin de c.** unquote (**b**) *Jur* **c. à comparaître** *(d'un accusé)* summons; *(d'un témoin)* subpoena
cité [site] *nf* (**a**) *(ville)* city (**b**) *(groupe d'immeubles)* (housing) *Br* estate *or Am* development; **c. universitaire** *Br* halls of residence, *Am* dormitory complex
cité-dortoir (*pl* **cités-dortoirs**) [sitedɔrtwar] *nf* dormitory town
citer [site] *vt* (**a**) *(rapporter)* to quote; *(auteur)* to quote (from); **c. qn en exemple** to quote sb as an example; **il a dit, je cite...** he said, and I quote,... (**b**) *(énumérer)* to name (**c**) *Jur (personne en justice)* to summons; *(té-*

moin) to subpoena (**d**) *Mil* **c. qn (à l'ordre du jour)** to mention sb in dispatches

citerne [sitɛrn] *nf* tank; **c. à mazout** oil tank

cithare [sitar] *nf (instrument moderne)* zither

citizen band [sitizənbɑ̃d] *nf* Citizens' Band, CB

citoyen, -enne [sitwajɛ̃, -ɛn] *nm,f* citizen; **c. d'honneur** freeman *(of a city)*

citoyenneté [sitwajɛnte] *nf* citizenship; **la c. française** French citizenship

citrique [sitrik] *adj (acide)* citric

citron [sitrɔ̃] *nm* (**a**) *(fruit)* lemon; **un c. givré** = lemon sorbet served inside the skin of a whole lemon; **un c. pressé** = freshly squeezed lemon juice served with water and sugar; **c. vert** lime (**b**) *Fam (tête)* nut

citronnade [sitrɔnad] *nf Br* lemon squash, *Am* lemonade

citronnelle [sitrɔnɛl] *nf (plante, huile)* citronella

citronnier [sitrɔnje] *nm* lemon tree

citrouille [sitruj] *nf* (**a**) *(plante)* pumpkin (**b**) *Fam (tête)* nut

civelle [sivɛl] *nf* elver

civet [sivɛ] *nm Culin* **c. de lapin** rabbit stew; **c. de lièvre** ≃ jugged hare

civière [sivjɛr] *nf* stretcher

civil, -e [sivil] **1** *adj* (**a**) *(du citoyen, non ecclésiastique)* civil (**b**) *(non militaire)* civilian; **dans la vie civile** in civilian life (**c**) *Litt (courtois)* civil
2 *nm* (**a**) *(personne) (non ecclésiastique)* layman, civilian (**b**) **dans le c.** in civilian life; **en c.** *(policier)* in plain clothes; *(militaire)* in civilian clothes (**c**) *Jur* **poursuivre qn au c.** to bring a civil action against sb

civilement [sivilmɑ̃] *adv* (**a**) *Jur* **se marier c.** to have a civil wedding (**b**) *Litt (avec courtoisie)* civilly

civilisation [sivilizasjɔ̃] *nf* civilization

civilisé, -e [sivilize] *adj* civilized

civilité [sivilite] *nf Litt* (**a**) *(courtoisie)* civility (**b**) **civilités** *(politesses)* courtesies

civique [sivik] *adj* civic; **avoir le sens c.** to have a sense of civic responsibility

civisme [sivism] *nm* sense of civic responsibility

cl *(abrév* **centilitre(s))** cl

clac [klak] *exclam (d'un fouet)* crack!; *(d'un objet qui se casse)* snap!; *(d'une porte)* slam!

clafoutis [klafuti] *nm* clafoutis *(fruit, usually cherries, baked in a dish of batter)*

claie [klɛ] *nf* (**a**) *(treillis)* rack (**b**) *(clôture)* fence

clair, -e [klɛr] **1** *adj* (**a**) *(transparent) (eau, teint, voix)* clear; **par temps c.** on a clear day (**b**) *(pièce, couleur)* light (**c**) *(sens, explication)* clear; **il a été très c. là-dessus** he was very clear about it; **il est c. qu'il a tort** he's clearly wrong; **être c. comme de l'eau de roche** to be crystal clear; **avoir les idées claires** to have a clear head; **c'est c. et net** there are no two ways about it; *Fam* **un individu pas très c.** a bit of a shady character (**d**) *(soupe)* thin
2 *adv* clearly; **il fait c.** it's light; *Fig* **je commence à y voir c.** I'm beginning to understand
3 *nm* (**a**) *(lumière)* **c. de lune** moonlight; **au c. de lune** in the moonlight (**b**) **en c.** *(autrement dit)* in plain language; **émission en c.** non-crypted broadcast (**c**) *Fig* **tirer une affaire au c.** to clear a matter up; **passer le plus c. de son temps à faire qch** to spend the better part of one's time doing sth

clairement [klɛrmɑ̃] *adv* clearly

claire-voie *(pl* **claires-voies)** [klɛrvwa] *nf* (**a**) *(treillage)* **à c.** open-work (**b**) *Archit* clerestory

clairière [klɛrjɛr] *nf* clearing, glade

clair-obscur *(pl* **clairs-obscurs)** [klɛrɔpskyr] *nm (en peinture)* chiaroscuro

clairon [klɛrɔ̃] *nm* (**a**) *(instrument)* bugle; **sonner le c.** to sound the bugle (**b**) *(joueur)* bugler

claironner [klɛrɔne] *vt (nouvelle)* to trumpet forth

clairsemé, -e [klɛrsəme] *adj (population, cheveux, gazon)* sparse; *(arbres)* scattered

clairvoyant, -e [klɛrvwajɑ̃, -ɑ̃t] *adj* perceptive

clamer [klame] *vt* to proclaim

clameur [klamœr] *nf* clamour; **une c. de joie** a shout of joy; **les clameurs de la foule** the clamour of the crowd

clamser [klamse] *vi très Fam (mourir)* to kick the bucket, to snuff it

clan [klɑ̃] *nm (tribu)* clan; *Péj (groupe)* clique

clandestin, -e [klɑ̃dɛstɛ̃, -in] **1** *adj (réunion, atelier)* clandestine; *(travailleur, immigré)* illegal; *(mouvement)* underground
2 *nm* (**a**) *(voyageur)* stowaway; *(immigré)* illegal immigrant; *(travailleur)* illegal worker

clandestinement [klɑ̃dɛstinmɑ̃] *adv (secrètement)* clandestinely; *(illégalement)* illegally

clandestinité [klɑ̃dɛstinite] *nf* **dans la c.** *(secrètement)* clandestinely; *(illégalement)* illegally; **entrer dans/sortir de la c.** to go into/to come out of hiding

clap [klap] *nm Cin* clapperboard; **c. de fin** end board

clapet [klapɛ] *nm* (**a**) *Tech* valve (**b**) *Fam* **ferme ton c.!** shut your trap!

clapier [klapje] *nm (rabbit)* hutch

clapoter [klapɔte] *vi* to lap

clapotis [klapɔti] *nm* lapping

claquage [klakaʒ] *nm (blessure)* pulled muscle; **se faire un c.** to pull a muscle

claque¹ [klak] *nf* (**a**) *(gifle)* slap; **donner une c. à qn** to give sb a slap; *Fam Fig* **il va se prendre une c.** it'll be a slap in the face for him; **une paire de claques** a slap (**b**) *Fam* **j'en ai ma c.** I've had it up to here (**c**) *Can (chaussure)* **claques** galoshes

claque² *nm très Fam (maison de passe)* Br knocking shop, *Am* cathouse

claqué, -e [klake] *adj Fam (fatigué)* Br shattered, *Am* bushed

claquement [klakmɑ̃] *nm (de porte)* slam(ming); *(de dents)* chattering; *(d'un fouet)* crack(ing); *(d'un drapeau)* flap(ping); *(de doigts)* snap(ping); *(de talons, de la langue)* click(ing); *(de sabots)* clatter(ing)

claquer [klake] **1** *vt* (**a**) *(porte)* to slam; **c. la langue** to click one's tongue (**b**) *Fam (dépenser)* to blow; **il claque un fric monstre chez le coiffeur** he spends a fortune at the hairdresser's
2 *vi* (**a**) *(porte)* to slam; *(drapeau)* to flap; *(talons)* to click; *(sabots)* to clatter; **c. des mains** to clap; **c. des doigts** to snap one's fingers; **elle claque des dents** her teeth are chattering; **faire c. sa langue** to click one's tongue (**b**) *(ampoule électrique)* to go; *(élastique)* to snap; *Fam (personne)* to kick the bucket, to snuff it
3 **se claquer** *vpr* **se c. un muscle** to pull a muscle

claquettes [klakɛt] *nfpl* tap dancing; **faire des c.** to do tap dancing; **danseur de c.** tap dancer

clarification [klarifikasjɔ̃] *nf aussi Fig* clarification

clarifier [66] [klarifje] **1** *vt (liquide, situation)* to clarify
2 **se clarifier** *vpr (situation)* to become clear

clarinette [klarinɛt] *nf* clarinet

clarinettiste [klarinɛtist] *nmf* clarinettist

clarté [klarte] nf (**a**) (lumière) light (**b**) (transparence) clearness (**c**) Fig (du style) clarity; **avec c.** clearly; **manquer de c.** (personne) not to make oneself clear; (texte, argument) to be unclear

classe [klas] **1** nf (**a**) (catégorie) class; (dans une hiérarchie) grade; **c. affaires/économique** business/economy class; **c. d'âge** age group; **la c. dirigeante** the ruling class; **les classes moyennes** the middle class(es); **la c. ouvrière** the working class(es); **c. sociale** social class (**b**) (qualité) class; **un sportif de c. internationale** a world-class sportsman; **avoir de la c.** (personne) to have class; (objet, vêtement) to be classy; Fam **ce type, c'est la c.**! he's got real class! (**c**) (à l'école) (niveau) year; (groupe d'élèves) class; **les grandes classes, les classes supérieures** the senior school; **les petites classes** the junior school; **c. de mer/de neige** school study trip to the seaside/to the mountains; **partir en c. de mer** to go on a school study trip to the seaside; **c. préparatoire (aux grandes écoles)** = preparatory class for the entrance examinations for the Grandes Écoles; **c. unique** = class where pupils belonging to different years are taught together by one teacher; **c. verte** school study trip to the countryside (**d**) (leçon) class; **la c. de français** the French class; **aller en c.** to go to school; **être en c.** (à l'école) to be at school; (en cours) to be in class; **faire la c.** to teach (**e**) (pièce) **(salle de) c.** classroom (**f**) Mil (de conscrits) levy; **faire ses classes** to undergo basic training

2 adj inv Fam classy

Classes préparatoires

This term refers to the two years of intensive preparation required for students who have passed their baccalauréat and wish to enter the "grandes écoles". These two years of study are extremely competitive and highly demanding. Students are completely immersed in their subject, which can be in humanities, economics or the sciences, and do little other than study for the "grandes écoles" exams. For students who are not successful in these exams, two years of "prépa" are considered equivalent to a "**DEUG**" (see box at this entry), and these students often go on to study at a university.

classé, -e [klase] adj (monument) listed

classement [klasmã] nm (**a**) (dans une classe ou une course) position, place; (liste d'équipes, de concurrents) classification; (au foot, au rugby) table; (des plantes) classification; **être troisième au c.** to be in third place; **c. général** overall classification (**b**) (rangement) (de documents) filing; (d'articles) sorting out; **faire du c.** to do some filing; **c. (par ordre) alphabétique** alphabetical classification

classer [klase] **1** vt (**a**) (classifier) to classify; (étudiants) to grade; **être classés par pays** to be classified according to country (**b**) (ranger) (documents) to file; (articles) to sort out; **c. une affaire** to consider a matter closed; **c'est une affaire classée** the matter's closed
2 se classer vpr **se c. parmi les meilleurs** to rank among the best; Sport **se c. troisième** to be placed third

classeur [klasœr] nm (**a**) (dossier) ring binder (**b**) (meuble) filing cabinet (**c**) Ordinat filer

classicisme [klasisism] nm classicism

classification [klasifikasjɔ̃] nf classification; Chim **c. périodique des éléments** periodic table

classifier [66] [klasifje] vt to classify

classique [klasik] **1** adj (**a**) (période) classical; (beauté) classic (**b**) (conventionnel) (vêtement, style, exemple, plaisanterie) classic; (arme, guerre) conventional; Fam **c'est le coup c.** it's the same old story
2 nm (**a**) (auteur) classical author; **connaître ses classiques** to be well-read (**b**) (œuvre, film, chanson) classic; **c'est un c.** du genre it's a classic of its kind (**c**) (style musical) **le c.** classical music

claudication [klodikasjɔ̃] nf limp

clause [kloz] nf Jur clause; **c. d'exclusivité** exclusivity clause; **c. de la nation la plus favorisée** most-favoured-nation status

claustrophobe [klostrofob] adj claustrophobic

claustrophobie [klostrofobi] nf claustrophobia

clavecin [klavsɛ̃] nm harpsichord

claveciniste [klavsinist] nmf harpsichordist

clavicule [klavikyl] nf collarbone, Spéc clavicle

clavier [klavje] nm keyboard; Ordinat **c. multifonction** multifunctional keyboard; **c. numérique** numerical or numeric keypad

claviste [klavist] nmf Ordinat keyboarder; Typ typesetter

clé [kle] = **clef**

clean [klin] adj inv Fam (**a**) (BCBG) clean-cut (**b**) (qui ne se drogue pas) clean

clébard [klebar], **clebs** [klɛps] nm Fam pooch, mutt

clef [kle] **1** nf (**a**) (d'une porte, d'un cadenas) key; **fermer qch à c.** to lock sth; **tenir/mettre qch sous c.** to keep/put sth under lock and key; **usine clefs en main** turnkey factory; **prix clefs en main** (d'une voiture) on-the-road price; (d'une maison) all-inclusive price; Fig **mettre la c. sous la porte** to move away; (commerçant) to shut up shop; **prendre la c. des champs** (prisonnier) to make a bid for freedom; **c. de contact** ignition key; **c. passe-partout** passkey, master key (**b**) (outil) spanner; **c. anglaise** monkey wrench; **c. à molette** adjustable spanner; **c. plate** open-end Br spanner or Am wrench (**c**) Mus (d'un instrument à cordes) peg; (d'un instrument à vent) key; **c. de sol/de fa** treble/bass clef; Fig **il y a une forte somme d'argent à la c.** there is a large sum of money at the end of it (**d**) (moyen d'accès, solution) key; **la c. du mystère** the key to the mystery (**e**) **c. de voûte** (d'une arche) keystone; Fig cornerstone (**f**) Ordinat key; (du DOS) switch; **c. de contrôle** control key; **c. gigogne** dongle; **c. à puce** computerized key; **c. USB** memory stick, flash drive
2 adj (vital) key; **un secteur(-)c. de la recherche** a key area of research

clématite [klematit] nf clematis

clémence [klemɑ̃s] nf (**a**) (de la température) mildness (**b**) (d'un juge, d'un maître) clemency (**envers** towards)

clément, -e [klemɑ̃, -ɑ̃t] adj (**a**) (température) mild (**b**) (juge, maître) clement (**envers** towards)

clémentine [klemɑ̃tin] nf clementine

Cléopâtre [kleopatr] npr Cleopatra

cleptomane [klɛptɔman] adj & nmf kleptomaniac

cleptomanie [klɛptɔmani] nf kleptomania

clerc [klɛr] nm (**a**) (dans un bureau) **c. de notaire** ≃ solicitor's clerk (**b**) Rel cleric (**c**) Litt **il n'est pas besoin d'être grand c. pour...** you don't have to be a genius in order to...

clergé [klɛrʒe] nm clergy

clérical, -e, -aux, -ales [klerikal, -o] *adj* clerical
clic [klik] *nm* (**a**) *(bruit)* click; **faire c.** to click (**b**) *Ordinat* click; **double c.** double click
clic-clac [klikklak] *nm inv* (**a**) *(d'un appareil photo)* click; *(des talons)* click-clack (**b**) *(canapé)* spring-action sofa bed
cliché [kliʃe] *nm* (**a**) *(photo)* photo; *(négatif)* negative (**b**) *(lieu commun)* cliché
client, -e [klijɑ̃, -ɑ̃t] *nm,f* *(d'un magasin, d'une entreprise)* customer; *(d'un médecin)* patient; *(d'un avocat)* client; *(d'un hôtel)* guest; *(d'un taxi)* fare; **ici, le c. est roi** the customer is always right
clientèle [klijɑ̃tɛl] *nf* (**a**) *(d'un magasin, d'une entreprise)* customers; *(d'un médecin, d'un avocat)* practice; *(d'un hôtel)* clientèle; *(d'un taxi)* fares; **c. de passage** passing trade (**b**) *(fait d'acheter)* custom; **accorder sa c. à** to give one's custom to
cligner [kliɲe] *vi* **c. des yeux** to blink; **c. de l'œil** to wink
clignotant, -e [kliɲɔtɑ̃, -ɑ̃t] **1** *adj (étoile)* twinkling; *(lumière)* flashing
　2 *nm (de voiture)* Br indicator, Am turn signal; **mettre son c.** (à gauche/droite) to indicate (left/right)
clignoter [kliɲɔte] *vi (étoile)* to twinkle; *(lumière, voyant)* to flash; *Ordinat (marqueur)* to flash, to blink
clignoteur [kliɲɔtœr] *nm Belg Aut Br* indicator, Am turn signal
clim [klim] *nf Fam (climatisation)* air-conditioning
climat [klima] *nm aussi Fig* climate; **sous des climats plus ensoleillés** in sunnier climes; **c. de détente** relaxed climate
climatique [klimatik] *adj (conditions)* climatic
climatisation [klimatizasjɔ̃] *nf* air conditioning
climatisé, -e [klimatize] *adj* air-conditioned
climatiser [klimatize] *vt* to air-condition
climatiseur [klimatizœr] *nm* air-conditioner
clin d'œil (*pl* clins d'œil) [klɛ̃dœj] *nm* wink; **faire un c. à qn** to wink at sb; **en un c.** in a flash
clinique [klinik] **1** *nf* (**a**) *(hôpital privé)* clinic (**b**) *(médecine)* clinical medicine
　2 *adj* clinical
clinquant, -e [klɛ̃kɑ̃, -ɑ̃t] **1** *adj* flashy
　2 *nm (éclat trompeur)* flashiness
clip [klip] *nm* (**a**) *(vidéo)* (music) video (**b**) *(broche)* brooch; *(boucle d'oreille)* clip-on earring
clipart [klipart] *nm Ordinat* clip art
cliquable [klikabl] *adj Ordinat* clickable
clique [klik] *nf* (**a**) *Fam (gang)* clique, gang; **et toute la c.** and the rest of the gang (**b**) *(d'une fanfare militaire)* drum-and-bugle band
cliquer [klike] *vi Ordinat* to click (**sur** on); **c. deux fois** to double-click
cliques [klik] *nfpl Fam* **prendre ses c. et ses claques** to pack one's bags and go
cliqueter [42] [klikte] *vi (chaînes)* to rattle; *(épées, aiguilles à tricoter)* to click; *(monnaie, clefs)* to jingle
cliquetis [klikti] *nm (de chaînes)* rattling; *(de pièces de monnaie, de clefs)* jingling; *(d'épées, d'aiguilles à tricoter)* clicking
clitoris [klitɔris] *nm* clitoris
clivage [klivaʒ] *nm (dans la société)* divide; *(dans un parti politique)* split
cloaque [klɔak] *nm aussi Fig* cesspool
clochard, -e [klɔʃar, -ard] *nm,f* tramp, Am hobo
clochardiser [klɔʃardize] **1** *vt* to turn into a tramp
　2 **se clochardiser** *vpr* to turn into a tramp

cloche [klɔʃ] **1** *nf* (**a**) *(d'église, de bétail)* bell; **déménager à la c. de bois** to do a moonlight flit; *Fig* **entendre plusieurs sons de c.** to hear several different versions of events (**b**) *(pour couvrir)* Chim bell jar; *(pour cultures)* cloche; *(pour garder au chaud)* dish cover; **c. à fromage(s)** covered cheese dish; **c. à plongeur** diving bell (**c**) *Fam (imbécile)* idiot, fool (**d**) **(chapeau) c.** cloche (hat) (**e**) *Fam* **être de la c.** *(être clochard)* to be a tramp *or Am* hobo (**f**) *Belg Méd* blister
　2 *adj Fam* stupid
cloche-pied [klɔʃpje] **à cloche-pied** *adv* **sauter à c.** to hop
clocher¹ [klɔʃe] *nm (d'une église)* bell tower, steeple
clocher² *vi Fam* **il y a quelque chose qui cloche** there's something wrong somewhere; **il y a quelque chose qui cloche dans son histoire** there's something not quite right about his/her story
clochette [klɔʃɛt] *nf* (**a**) *(petite cloche)* small bell (**b**) *(fleur)* bell-flower; *(corolle)* bell-shaped flower
clodo [klodo] *nm Fam* tramp, Am bum
cloison [klwazɔ̃] *nf* (**a**) *(entre des pièces)* partition (**b**) *Anat* **c. nasale** nasal septum
cloisonner [klwazɔne] *vt (pièce)* to partition (off); *Fig* to compartmentalize
cloître [klwatr] *nm* (**a**) *(partie d'un monastère)* cloister (**b**) *(bâtiment)* *(pour moines)* monastery; *(pour religieuses)* convent
cloîtrer [klwatre] **1** *vt Rel* to cloister; *Fig* to shut up *or* away; **nonne cloîtrée** nun in an enclosed order
　2 **se cloîtrer** *vpr (moine)* to enter a monastery; *(religieuse)* to enter a convent; *Fig* to shut oneself away
clonage [klonaʒ] *nm Biol* cloning; **c. humain** human cloning; *Méd* **c. reproductif/thérapeutique** reproductive/therapeutic cloning
clone [klon] *nm Biol* clone
cloner [klone] *vt Biol* to clone
clope [klɔp] *nf Fam Br* fag, Am smoke
clopin-clopant [klɔpɛ̃klɔpɑ̃] *adv* **aller c.** to hobble along; *Fig (commerce)* to struggle along
clopiner [klɔpine] *vi* to hobble
clopinettes [klɔpinɛt] *nfpl Fam* **des c.** Br sweet FA, Am zilch; **travailler pour des c.** to work for peanuts
cloporte [klɔpɔrt] *nm (insecte)* woodlouse
cloque [klɔk] *nf* (**a**) *(sur la peau, sur la peinture)* blister; **faire des cloques** to blister (**b**) *très Fam* **être en c.** *(enceinte)* to be knocked up
clore [15] [klɔr] **1** *vt (réunion, discussion)* to conclude, to end; *(débat, compte)* to close; *Ordinat* **c. une session** to log off, to log out
　2 **se clore** *vpr (réunion, film, livre)* to end (**sur** with)
clos, -e [klo, kloz] **1** *pp de* **clore**
　2 *adj* (**a**) *(fermé)* *(porte, volets)* closed (**b**) *(achevé)* finished, concluded; **l'incident est c.** the matter is closed; **les inscriptions seront closes le 5 mars** the closing date for applications is 5 March (**c**) *(clôturé)* *(jardin)* enclosed
　3 *nm* enclosure; **c. (de vigne)** vineyard
clôture [klotyr] *nf* (**a**) *(barrière)* fence (**b**) *(d'une réunion, d'une discussion)* conclusion, end; *(d'un débat, d'un compte)* closing; **c. des inscriptions le 3 mars** closing date for applications is 3 March; **c. de la chasse** close of the hunting season; *Fin* **c. de l'exercice** end of the financial year (**c**) *(à la Bourse)* close; **à la c.** at the close (**d**) *Ordinat* close; **c. de session** logging off

clôturer [klotyre] **1** vt (**a**) (champ, terrain) to enclose, to fence in (**b**) (session, débats) to close (**c**) Fin (comptes) to close **2** vi (valeur, indice) **c.** à to close at

clou [klu] nm (**a**) (pointe) nail; **être maigre comme un c.** to be as thin as a rake; Fam **ça ne vaut pas un c.** it's not worth a penny; Fam **des clous!** not a sausage!; Fam **travailler pour des clous** to work for peanuts (**b**) Culin **c. de girofle** clove (**c**) (d'un spectacle) main attraction; **ç'a été le c. de la soirée** it was the highlight of the evening (**d**) **les clous** (passage piéton) Br the pedestrian crossing, Am the crosswalk (**e**) Fam (vieux) **c.** (voiture) old banger; (vélo) old boneshaker (**f**) Fam **mettre qn au c.** (en prison) to lock sb up; Vieilli **mettre qch au c.** (en gage) to pawn sth

clouer [klue] vt (**a**) (au mur) to nail up; (ensemble) to nail together; (caisse) to nail down; Fam **c. le bec à qn** to shut sb up (**b**) Fig (immobiliser) **c. qn au sol** to pin sb down; **rester cloué sur place** to be rooted to the spot; **être cloué au lit** to be stuck in bed

clouté, -e [klute] adj (chaussures) studded

clown [klun] nm aussi Fig clown; **faire le c.** to clown around

club [klœb] nm (**a**) (culturel, sportif, politique) club; **c. automobile** car club; **c. de foot** football club; **c. d'investissement** investment club; **c. de vacances** Br holiday club, Am vacation center (**b**) (canne de golf) club

CM [seɛm] nm (abrév **cours moyen**) **CM1** = fourth year of primary school; **CM2** = fifth year of primary school

cm (abrév **centimètre(s)**) cm

CNPF [seɛnpeɛf] nm Anciennement (abrév **Conseil national du patronat français**) = national employers' association

CNRS [seɛnɛrɛs] nm (abrév **Centre national de la recherche scientifique**) = national organization for scientific research

coach [kotʃ] nm (entraîneur) coach; **c. personnel** life coach

coagulant, -e [kɔagylɑ̃, -ɑ̃t] **1** adj coagulating **2** nm coagulant

coagulation [kɔagylasjɔ̃] nf coagulation

coaguler [kɔagyle] **1** vt & vi (sang) to clot; (lait) to curdle **2 se coaguler** vpr (sang) to clot; (lait) to curdle

coaliser [kɔalize] **se coaliser** vpr to unite; (partis, pays) to form a coalition

coalition [kɔalisjɔ̃] nf (**a**) (alliance) coalition (**b**) Fig & Péj conspiracy; **former une c. contre** to join forces against

coaltar [kɔltar] nm coaltar; Fam **être dans le c.** to be in a daze

coasser [kɔase] vi (grenouille) to croak

coassurance [kɔasyrɑ̃s] nf mutual assurance

coauteur [kootœr] nm (**a**) (d'un livre) co-author (**b**) Jur accomplice

COB [kɔb] nf Fin (abrév **Commission des opérations de Bourse**) = French Stock Exchange watchdog

cobalt [kɔbalt] nm cobalt

cobaye [kɔbaj] nm aussi Fig guinea pig

cobol [kɔbɔl] nm Ordinat COBOL

cobra [kɔbra] nm cobra

Coca® [kɔka] nm inv Fam (boisson) Coke®

coca [kɔka] **1** nm (plante) coca **2** nf (feuilles) coca

Coca-Cola® [kɔkakɔla] nm inv Coca-Cola®

cocagne [kɔkaɲ] nf voir **mât, pays**

cocaïne [kɔkain] nf cocaine

cocaïnomane [kɔkainɔman] nmf cocaine addict

cocarde [kɔkard] nf (insigne) rosette; Hist (sur un chapeau) cockade

cocasse [kɔkas] adj Fam comical

coccinelle [kɔksinɛl] nf (**a**) (insecte) Br ladybird, Am ladybug (**b**) (voiture) beetle

coccyx [kɔksis] nm coccyx

coche [kɔʃ] nm Vieilli stagecoach; Fam **rater** ou **louper le c.** to miss the boat

cochenille [kɔʃnij] nf cochineal

cocher¹ [kɔʃe] nm coachman

cocher² vt Br to tick (off), Am to check

cochère [kɔʃɛr] adj f voir **porte**

cochon, -onne [kɔʃɔ̃, -ɔn] **1** nm (**a**) (animal, personne sale) pig; (viande) pork; **sale comme un c.** filthy; **gros** ou **gras comme un c.** as round as a barrel; **manger comme un c.** to eat like a pig; **tu écris comme un c.** your writing's an absolute mess; Fig **nous n'avons pas gardé les cochons ensemble!** but we hardly know each other!; Fam Fig **eh ben, mon c.!** you old devil!; **c. de lait** suck(l)ing pig (**b**) **c. d'Inde** guinea pig (**c**) (personne malfaisante) swine (**d**) (personne grivoise) dirty devil; **un vieux c.** a dirty old man (**e**) Can (tirelire) piggy bank **2** adj (histoire, film) dirty

cochonner [kɔʃɔne] vt Fam (travail) to bungle, to botch

cochonnerie [kɔʃɔnri] nf (**a**) (chose sans valeur) trash, rubbish (**b**) (nourriture de mauvaise qualité) muck (**c**) (saleté) mess; **faire des cochonneries** to make a mess (**d**) (obscénité) smutty remark; **dire des cochonneries** to say smutty things

cochonnet [kɔʃɔnɛ] nm (**a**) (aux boules) jack (**b**) (petit cochon) piglet

cocker [kɔkɛr] nm cocker spaniel

cockpit [kɔkpit] nm Naut & Aviat cockpit

cocktail [kɔktɛl] nm (boisson) & Fig cocktail; (soirée) cocktail party; **c. de fruits** fruit cocktail; **c. Molotov** Molotov cocktail

coco¹ [koko] nm (**a**) (plante) coconut (**b**) Fam **mets-toi ça dans le c.!** (dans la tête) get that into your thick skull!; (dans l'estomac) get that inside you!

coco² nm (**a**) Fam (type) **un drôle de c.** a strange character; **toi, mon c., je t'ai à l'œil** just watch it, Br mate or Am buddy (**b**) (terme d'affection) **mon petit c.** my pet

coco³ adj & nmf Fam (communiste) commie

cocon [kɔkɔ̃] nm aussi Fig cocoon; Fig **le c. familial** family nest

cocorico [kɔkɔriko] **1** exclam cock-a-doodle-doo! **2** nm (cri du coq) cock-a-doodle-doo; aussi Fig **faire c.** to crow

cocoter [kɔkɔte] vi Fam to stink

cocotier [kɔkɔtje] nm (arbre) coconut palm

cocotte [kɔkɔt] nf (**a**) (marmite) large casserole dish (**b**) (poule) hen (**c**) (pliage) paper bird (**d**) (terme d'affection) **ma c.** darling (**e**) Fam **hue, c.!** gee up! (**f**) Fam Vieilli (femme) tart, slut (**g**) Can (de pin) pine cone

Cocotte-Minute® (pl **Cocottes-Minute**) [kɔkɔtminyt] nf pressure cooker

cocu, -e [kɔky] **1** adj **un mari c.** a cuckold; **je suis c./cocue** my wife's/husband's cheating on me **2** nm cuckold; **faire son mari c.** to cheat on one's husband

cocufier [66] [kɔkyfje] vt to be unfaithful to

coda [kɔda] *nf Mus* coda
codage [kɔdaʒ] *nm* coding
code [kɔd] *nm* (**a**) *(symboles)* code; **mettre qch en c.** to put sth into code; **c. confidentiel** security code; *(d'une carte bancaire)* PIN; **c. postal** *Br* postcode, *Am* zip code (**b**) *Ordinat* code; **c. d'accès** access code; **c. d'autorisation d'accès** access authorization code; **c. de caractère** character code; **c. de commande** command code; **c. de contrôle** control code; **c. d'erreur** error code; **c. d'imprimante** printer code; **c. natif** source code; **c. source** source code (**c**) *(ensemble de lois, livre)* code; **passer le c.** *(du permis de conduire)* to sit the written part of one's driving test; **c. civil** civil code, ≃ common law; **c. de la nationalité** = laws governing French nationality; **c. pénal** penal code; **c. de la route** Highway Code; **c. du travail** employment legislation (**d**) *(phare)* **codes** *Br* dipped headlights, *Am* low beams; **se mettre en codes** *Br* to dip one's headlights, *Am* to switch on one's low beams; **rouler en codes** to drive with *Br* dipped headlights *or Am* low beams (**e**) *Biol* **c. génétique** genetic code

Code postal
In France, the first two numbers of a given postcode correspond to the administrative code number of the relevant "département". Thus all postal codes for Paris begin with 75.

code-barres (*pl* **codes-barres**) [kɔdbar] *nm* bar code
codéine [kɔdein] *nf* codeine
coder [kɔde] *vt* to code
codétenu, -e [kɔdetny] *nm,f* fellow prisoner
CODEVI [kɔdevi] *nm* = type of government savings account
codicille [kɔdisil] *nm Jur* codicil
codification [kɔdifikasjɔ̃] *nf Ordinat* **c. binaire** binary code; **c. décimale** decimal coding
codifier [66] [kɔdifje] *vt* to codify
codirecteur, -trice [kɔdirɛktœr, -tris] *nm,f* joint manager
coéditer [koedite] *vt* to copublish
coédition [koedisjɔ̃] *nf (procédé)* copublishing; *(livre)* joint publication
coefficient [kɔefisjɑ̃] *nm* coefficient; *Aut* **c. aérodynamique** *ou* de pénétration dans l'air drag coefficient
coentreprise [koɑ̃trəpriz] *nf* joint venture
coéquipier, -ère [koekipje, -ɛr] *nm,f* team-mate
coercitif, -ive [kɔɛrsitif, -iv] *adj* coercive
coercition [kɔɛrsisjɔ̃] *nf* coercion
cœur [kœr] *nm* (**a**) *(organe)* heart; **être malade du c.** to have a weak heart; **être opéré à c. ouvert** to have open-heart surgery; **recevoir une balle en plein c.** to get a bullet right in the heart; **en (forme de) c.** heart-shaped
(**b**) *(poitrine)* **serrer** *ou* **presser qn contre son c.** to hold sb close
(**c**) *(estomac)* **avoir mal au c.** to feel sick; **soulever le c. à qn** to turn sb's stomach; *Fig* **avoir le c. solide** *ou* **bien accroché** to have a strong stomach
(**d**) *(symbole de la bonté)* **avoir bon c.** to be kind-hearted; **ne pas avoir de c.** to be heartless; **avoir un c. d'or/de pierre** to have a heart of gold/stone; **avoir le c. sur la main** to be very generous; **à votre bon c., M'sieurs Dames** can you spare a few coins?
(**e**) *(siège des sentiments)* **donner son c. à qn** to lose one's heart to sb; **de tout (son) c.** with all one's heart; **aller droit au c. de qn** to go straight to sb's heart;

avoir le **c. brisé** to be heartbroken *or* broken-hearted; *Fig* **ça (me) fait mal au c.** it's sickening; **faire qch le c. léger** to do sth with a light heart; **avoir le c. gros** *ou* **serré** to have a heavy heart; **si tu aimes les pâtes, tu vas t'en donner à c. joie** if you like pasta, you'll be able to eat it to your heart's content; **ne pas porter qn dans son c.** to be not very fond of sb; **du fond du c.** from the bottom of one's heart; **au fond de mon c.** in my heart of hearts; *Prov* **le c. a ses raisons que la raison ne connaît point** the heart has its reasons
(**f**) *(pensées intimes)* **dire ce qu'on a sur le c.** to say what's on one's mind; **en avoir le c. net** to get to the bottom of it; **ouvrir son c. à qn** to open one's heart to sb
(**g**) **par c.** by heart; *Fam* **connaître qn par c.** to know sb inside out
(**h**) *(courage)* courage; **ne pas avoir le c. de faire qch** not to have the heart to do sth; *Fam* **avoir du c. au ventre** to have plenty of guts
(**i**) *(envie, désir)* **ils n'ont pas le c. à l'ouvrage** their hearts aren't in it; **le c. n'y est pas** his/my/*etc* heart isn't in it; **elle n'a plus le c. à rien** she hasn't the heart for anything any more; **avoir le c. à rire** to be in the mood for laughing; **si le c. vous en dit** if you feel like it; **avoir à c. de faire qch** to have one's heart set on doing sth; **ce projet lui tient à c.** this project is close to his/her heart; **de bon c.** *(volontiers)* willingly; *(rire)* heartily; **y aller de bon c.** to get down to it
(**j**) *(personne)* **c'est un c. d'or** she's got a heart of gold; **merci, mon c.** thank you, darling
(**k**) *(centre)* heart; **fromage fait à c.** ripe cheese; **au c. de l'hiver/l'été** in the depths of winter/height of summer; **au c. de la ville** in the heart of the town; **au c. du débat** in the heart of the debate; **c. d'artichaut** artichoke heart; *Fig* **avoir un c. d'artichaut** to be always falling in love; **c. de palmier** palm heart
(**l**) *(objet en forme de cœur)* heart; *(carte)* heart; *(couleur)* hearts

coexistence [kɔɛgzistɑ̃s] *nf* coexistence (**avec** with); *Pol* **c. pacifique** peaceful coexistence
coexister [kɔɛgziste] *vi* to coexist (**avec** with)
coffrage [kɔfraʒ] *nm (pour ouvrages en béton)* formwork
coffre [kɔfr] *nm* (**a**) *(meuble)* chest; **c. à jouets** toy box; **c. à linge** linen chest (**b**) *(pour objets de valeur)* safe; *(à la banque)* safe deposit box; **les coffres de l'État** the coffers of the State (**c**) *Fam* **avoir du c.** to have a good set of lungs (**d**) *(d'une voiture) Br* boot, *Am* trunk; **c. à bagages** *(d'un avion)* baggage compartment
coffre-fort (*pl* **coffres-forts**) [kɔfrəfɔr] *nm* safe
coffrer [kɔfre] *vt Fam (mettre en prison)* to put inside; **se faire c.** to get put inside
coffret [kɔfrɛ] *nm* (**a**) *(petit coffre)* box; **c. à bijoux** jewellery box (**b**) *(de livres, de disques)* box; **c. cadeau** gift box (**c**) *Ordinat* case
cogérant, -e [kɔʒerɑ̃, -ɑ̃t] *nm,f* joint manager, *f* joint manageress
cogestion [kɔʒɛstjɔ̃] *nf* joint management
cogitation [kɔʒitasjɔ̃] *nf Hum* cogitation
cogiter [kɔʒite] *vi Hum* to cogitate
cognac [kɔɲak] *nm* cognac
cognement [kɔɲəmɑ̃] *nm (bruit)* banging; *(d'un moteur)* knocking
cogner [kɔɲe] **1** *vt* (**a**) *(heurter)* to knock (**b**) *Fam (battre)* to knock about
2 *vi* (**a**) *(buter)* to bang (**sur/contre** on); **sa tête a**

cogné contre le mur he/she banged his/her head on the wall; **c. du poing sur la table** to bang (one's fist) on the table; **c. à une porte** to bang on a door (**b**) *Fam (frapper)* **il cogne dur** he's handy with his fists; **se faire c. dessus** to get knocked about (**c**) *Fam* **ça cogne** *(il fait chaud)* it's scorching (**d**) *(moteur)* to knock
3 se cogner *vpr* to bang oneself; **se c. à** *ou* **contre qch** to bang into sth; **se c. la tête contre qch** to bang one's head on sth; *Fig* **se c. la tête contre les murs** to bang one's head against a brick wall
cohabitation [kɔabitasjɔ̃] *nf* living together, cohabitation; *Pol* cohabitation

Cohabitation
Originally, this term referred to the period (1986–1988) during which the socialist President (François Mitterrand) had a right-wing Prime Minister (Jacques Chirac), following the victory of the RPR in the legislative elections and Mitterrand's decision not to resign as President. It has since been used to refer to the similar situation which arose following the 1993 elections (with Édouard Balladur as Prime Minister) and more recently the 1997 elections (with the left-wing government of Lionel Jospin co-ruling with the President Jacques Chirac).

cohabiter [kɔabite] *vi* to live together; **c. avec qn** to live with sb
cohérence [kɔerɑ̃s] *nf (d'une argumentation, d'un discours)* coherence; *(d'une attitude)* consistency
cohérent, -e [kɔerɑ̃, -ɑ̃t] *adj (argumentation, discours)* coherent; *(attitude)* consistent
cohéritier, -ère [kɔeritje, -ɛr] *nm,f* joint heir, *f* joint heiress
cohésion [kɔezjɔ̃] *nf* cohesion
cohorte [kɔɔrt] *nf (de gens)* horde
cohue [kɔy] *nf* crowd
coi, coite [kwa, kwat] *adj* **se tenir c.** to keep quiet; **en rester c.** to be speechless
coiffe [kwaf] *nf (coiffure régionale, religieuse)* headdress
coiffé, -e [kwafe] *adj* (**a**) **je ne suis pas encore coiffée** I haven't done my hair yet; **elle est bien coiffée** her hair is lovely; **il est mal c.** his hair's a mess (**b**) **être c. de qch** to be wearing sth *(on one's head)*
coiffer [kwafe] **1** *vt* (**a**) *(peigner)* **c. qn** to do sb's hair; **il coiffe bien** he's a good hairdresser; **se faire c.** (chez/par qn) to have one's hair done (at sb's/by sb) (**b**) *(mettre un chapeau à)* **c. qn de qch** to put sth on sb's head; *Fig* **c. sainte Catherine** to be twenty-five and still unmarried (**c**) *(service)* to head (**d**) *Sport & Fig* **se faire c. (au poteau)** to be pipped at the post
2 se coiffer *vpr* (**a**) *(se peigner)* to do one's hair (**b**) *(mettre)* **se c. de qch** to put sth on
coiffeur, -euse [kwafœr, -øz] **1** *nm,f* hairdresser
2 *nf* **coiffeuse** *(meuble)* dressing-table
coiffure [kwafyr] *nf* (**a**) *(coupe de cheveux)* hairstyle (**b**) *(activité)* hairdressing (**c**) *(chapeau)* headgear; *(de costume régional)* headdress
coin [kwɛ̃] *nm* (**a**) *(angle)* corner; **faire le c.** to be on the corner; **à tous les coins de rue** on every street corner; **aux quatre coins du monde** in all corners of the earth; **mettre un enfant au c.** *(pour le punir)* to make a child stand in the corner; *Fig* **rester dans son c.** to keep to oneself; **les coins et les recoins de qch** the nooks and crannies of sth; **je ne voudrais pas**

le rencontrer au c. d'un bois I wouldn't like to meet him on a dark night; *Aviat & Rail* **c. fenêtre/couloir** window/aisle seat; **au c. du feu** by the fire(side); **lancer un regard en c. à qn** to give sb a sidelong glance; **sourire en c.** half smile; **regarder qn du c. de l'œil** to look at sb out of the corner of one's eye (**b**) *(endroit quelconque)* spot, place; **un petit c. tranquille** a quiet little spot; *Euph* **le petit c.** the smallest room (in the house); **dans un c. de ma mémoire** in a corner of my mind; **j'ai dû le mettre dans un c.** I must have put it somewhere; **chercher qch dans tous les coins** to look high and low for sth (**c**) *(voisinage)* **du c.** local; **il habite dans le c.** he lives around here (**d**) *(parcelle)* patch; **c. de ciel bleu** patch of blue sky (**e**) *(cale)* wedge
coincé, -e [kwɛ̃se] *adj* (**a**) *(fermeture, porte, mécanisme)* jammed, stuck (**b**) *Fam (inhibé)* hung up (**c**) *(acculé)* **il faut que je paie, je suis c.** I'll have to pay, I've no choice
coincer [16] [kwɛ̃se] **1** *vt* (**a**) *(accidentellement) (tiroir, clef)* to jam; **j'ai coincé mes cheveux dans ma fermeture Éclair®** I got my hair caught in my zip; **la voiture est coincée entre deux camions** *(en stationnement)* the car is boxed in by two lorries; **être coincé** *(personne) (dans un embouteillage, un endroit)* to be stuck; *(être occupé)* to be tied up (**b**) *(volontairement) (porte)* to wedge; **elle l'a coincé dans le couloir** she cornered him in the corridor; **il m'a coincé** *(je n'ai pas su répondre)* he had me cornered (**c**) *Fam (arrêter)* *Br* to nick, *Am* to bust; **se faire c.** to get *Br* nicked *or Am* busted
2 *vi (tiroir, mécanisme)* to jam, to stick; *Fam* **ça coince** there's a hitch
3 se coincer *vpr (tiroir, mécanisme)* to jam, to stick; **se c. le doigt dans la porte** to catch one's finger in the door; **je me suis coincé le dos** my back's seized up
coïncidence [kɔɛ̃sidɑ̃s] *nf* coincidence
coïncider [kɔɛ̃side] *vi (événements, versions)* to coincide (**avec** with); **leurs intérêts coïncident** they have similar interests; **tous les témoignages coïncident** the witnesses all bear each other out
coin-coin [kwɛ̃kwɛ̃] **1** *nm inv (des canards)* quacking
2 *exclam* quack! quack!
coin-cuisine *(pl* coins-cuisines*)* [kwɛ̃kɥizin] *nm* kitchen area
coïnculpé, -e [kɔɛ̃kylpe] *nm,f* co-defendant
coing [kwɛ̃] *nm* quince
coin-repas *(pl* coins-repas*)* [kwɛ̃rəpa] *nm* dining area
coït [kɔit] *nm* coitus
coite [kwat] *voir* coi
coke [kɔk] **1** *nm (combustible)* coke
2 *nf Fam (cocaïne)* coke
col [kɔl] *nm* (**a**) *(d'une robe, d'une chemise)* collar; **c. de fourrure/de dentelle** fur/lace collar; **c. blanc** *(employé de bureau)* white-collar worker; **c. bleu** *(ouvrier)* blue-collar worker; **c. cheminée** *ou* **montant** *Br* turtleneck, *Am* mock turtleneck; **c. rond** round neck; **c. roulé** *Br* polo neck, *Am* turtleneck; **c. en V** V-neck; **faux c.** false collar (**b**) *(d'une bouteille)* neck (**c**) *Géog* col (**d**) *Anat (d'un os)* neck; **c. de l'utérus** cervix
colchique [kɔlʃik] *nm* autumn crocus
coléoptère [kɔleɔptɛr] *nm* beetle, *Spéc* coleopteran
colère [kɔlɛr] *nf* anger; **être en c. (contre qn)** to be angry (with sb); **mettre qn en c.** to make sb angry; **se mettre en c.** to get angry; **se mettre dans une c. bleue** *ou* **noire** to fly into a towering rage; **piquer une c.** to fly into a rage; **passer sa c. sur qn** to take one's

anger out on sb; **avec c.** angrily; *Litt* **la c. de Dieu** the wrath of God; **c. froide** cold fury

coléreux, -euse [kɔlerø, -øz], **colérique** [kɔlerik] *adj (personne)* quick-tempered; *(disposition)* irritable

colibri [kɔlibri] *nm* humming-bird

colifichet [kɔlifiʃɛ] *nm* trinket, knick-knack

colimaçon [kɔlimasɔ̃] *nm voir* **escalier**

colin [kɔlɛ̃] *nm (merlu)* hake; *(lieu noir)* coley

colin-maillard [kɔlɛ̃majar] *nm* blind man's buff; **jouer à c.** to play blind man's buff

colique [kɔlik] *nf* (**a**) *(diarrhée)* diarrhoea; **avoir la c.** to have diarrhoea (**b**) *(douleur)* **coliques** stomach pains, colic; **c. néphrétique** renal colic

colis [kɔli] *nm* parcel; **par c. postal** by parcel post

Colisée [kɔlize] *nm* **le C.** the Coliseum

colistier, -ère [kɔlistje, -ɛr] *nm,f Pol* fellow candidate

colite [kɔlit] *nf Méd* colitis

collabo [kɔlabo] *nmf Fam Hist* collaborator

collaborateur, -trice [kɔlabɔratœr, -tris] *nm,f* (**a**) *(aide)* assistant (**b**) *Journ* contributor (**de** to) (**c**) *Hist* collaborator

collaboration [kɔlabɔrasjɔ̃] *nf* (**a**) *(aide)* collaboration (**a** on); **travailler en étroite c. (avec qn)** to work closely (with sb) (**b**) *Journ* contribution (**c**) *Hist* collaboration

collaborer [kɔlabɔre] *vi* (**a**) *(travailler ensemble)* to collaborate (**avec** with); **c. à qch** *(projet)* to take part in sth; *(journal)* to contribute to sth (**b**) *Hist* to collaborate

collage [kɔlaʒ] *nm* (**a**) *(d'affiches)* sticking up; *(de bois)* gluing; *(de papier)* pasting (**b**) *(composition)* collage

collagène [kɔlaʒɛn] *nm* collagen

collant, -e [kɔlɑ̃, -ɑ̃t] **1** *adj* (**a**) *(adhésif)* sticky (**b**) *(poisseux)* sticky (**c**) *(moulant)* skin-tight (**d**) *Fam (personne)* **qu'est-ce qu'il est c.!** you just can't shake him off!

2 *nm* (**a**) *(bas) Br* (pair of) tights, *Am* pantihose (**b**) *Can* **c. à mouches** flypaper

collation [kɔlasjɔ̃] *nf (repas)* light meal

colle [kɔl] *nf* (**a**) *(transparente)* glue; *(blanche)* paste; **c. à bois** woodworking glue; **c. forte** strong glue; **de la c. en pot/stick/tube** a pot/stick/tube of glue (**b**) *Fam (question difficile)* poser; **là, tu me poses une c.** you've got me there (**c**) *Fam (punition)* detention (**d**) *Fam (examen oral)* oral test (**e**) *très Fam* **vivre** *ou* **être à la c.** to be shacked up together

collecte [kɔlɛkt] *nf* collection; **faire une c. (au profit de)** to make a collection (in aid of); **c. de fonds** fundraising; **faire une c. de fonds** to raise funds, to fundraise

collecter [kɔlɛkte] *vt* to collect

collecteur, -trice [kɔlɛktœr, -tris] **1** *nm,f* collector; **c. d'impôts** tax collector

2 *nm* (**a**) *(d'eaux pluviales)* main sewer (**b**) *Aut* **c. d'échappement** exhaust manifold

collectif, -ive [kɔlɛktif, -iv] **1** *adj (action, travail, responsabilité)* collective; *(billet)* group; *(licenciements)* mass

2 *nm* (**a**) *Fin* **c. budgétaire** bill of supply (**b**) *(association)* collective

collection [kɔlɛksjɔ̃] *nf* (**a**) *(action)* collecting; **faire la c. de qch** to collect sth (**b**) *(série) (de timbres, de papillons, d'œuvres d'art)* collection; *(de périodiques)* series; *(d'échantillons)* line; **j'en ai toute une c.** I've got a whole collection of them (**c**) *(de haute couture, de prêt-à-porter)* collection

collectionner [kɔlɛksjɔne] *vt* to collect

collectionneur, -euse [kɔlɛksjɔnœr, -øz] *nm,f* collector

collectivisme [kɔlɛktivism] *nm Écon* collectivism

collectivité [kɔlɛktivite] *nf* (**a**) *(groupe)* community (**b**) **collectivités locales** local communities; **c. d'outre-mer** = French overseas collectivity

collège [kɔlɛʒ] *nm* (**a**) *(école)* school; **c. d'enseignement secondaire** = former secondary school for pupils aged 12 to 15; **c. d'enseignement technique** technical school; **le C. de France** the Collège de France *(prestigious higher education institution)* (**b**) *Pol* **c. électoral** electoral college

collégial, -e, -aux, -ales [kɔleʒjal, -o] **1** *adj* collegiate

2 *nf* **collégiale** collegiate church

collégien, -enne [kɔleʒjɛ̃, -ɛn] *nm,f* schoolboy, *f* schoolgirl; **je me suis fait avoir comme un c.** I fell for it like a fool

collègue [kɔlɛg] *nmf* **c. (de travail)** colleague; *Fam* **salut, c.!** how's things?

coller [kɔle] **1** *vt* (**a**) *(faire adhérer)* to stick (**à/sur** to/on); **il avait les cheveux collés par la sueur/la peinture** his hair was matted with sweat/paint; **il est resté collé à la télé toute la soirée** he was glued to the TV all evening (**b**) *(appuyer)* **c. qch à** *ou* **contre qch** to press sth against sth (**c**) *Fam (mettre)* to stick; **colle ton sac là** stick *or* dump your bag over there; **ils ont collé le bébé à la grand-mère** they've dumped the baby on the grandmother; **on m'a collé à la comptabilité sans que j'aie dit oui** I got shoved in accounts without any say in the matter; **c. une gifle à qn** to slap sb in the face; **si tu continues, je t'en colle une!** if you don't stop, I'll thump you one!; **c. une contravention à qn** to slap a fine on sb (**d**) *Fam (retenir en punition)* to keep in; **se faire c.** to be kept in (**e**) *(refuser) (candidat)* to fail; **se faire c.** to fail (**f**) *Fam (suivre)* to follow closely; **il me colle!** he sticks to me like glue! (**g**) *Ordinat* to paste

2 *vi Fam* (**a**) *(coïncider)* to tally (**avec** with) (**b**) *(aller bien)* **ça colle!** that's OK!; **ça ne va pas c. pour mercredi** it's no go for Wednesday; **ça ne colle pas entre eux** they don't hit it off

3 coller à *vt ind aussi Fig* to stick to; *Fam* **c. aux fesses à qn** to stick to sb's tail; **sa réputation lui colle à la peau** he/she can't shake off his/her reputation

4 se coller *upr* (**a**) *(adhérer les uns aux autres)* to stick (**b**) *(s'aplatir)* **se c. contre un mur** to flatten oneself against a wall; **se c. contre qn** to cling to sb; *Fam* **se c. devant la télé** to plonk oneself down in front of the TV; *Fam* **c'est encore toi qui t'y colles** you're landed with it again

collerette [kɔlrɛt] *nf* (**a**) *(de vêtement)* collar; *Hist (fraise)* ruff (**b**) *Bot (de champignon)* annulus (**c**) *(de tuyau)* flange

collet [kɔlɛ] *nm* (**a**) *(de vêtement)* collar; **saisir** *ou* **prendre qn au c.** to grab sb by the scruff of the neck; **mettre la main au c. à qn** *(l'arrêter)* to get hold of sb; **être c. monté** to be strait-laced (**b**) *(piège)* snare

colleter [42] [kɔlte] **se colleter** *upr Fam* to tussle (**avec** qn with sb); **se c. avec qch** to grapple with sth

collier [kɔlje] *nm* (**a**) *(bijou)* necklace; **c. de perles** pearl necklace; **c. de fleurs** garland of flowers (**b**) *(de chien)* collar; *Fig* **donner un coup de c.** to put one's back into it (**c**) *(barbe)* **c. (de barbe)** fringe of beard (**d**) *Culin (de bœuf, de mouton)* neck (**e**) *Zool (d'oiseau)* collar

collimateur [kɔlimatœr] *nm Fig* **avoir qn dans le c.** to keep one's eye on sb
colline [kɔlin] *nf* hill
collision [kɔlizjɔ̃] *nf (entre véhicules, entre objets)* collision; **entrer en c. avec qch** to collide with sth; *Aut* **c. frontale/latérale** head-on/side-on collision
colloque [kɔlɔk] *nm (conférence)* seminar
collusion [kɔlyzjɔ̃] *nf* collusion
collutoire [kɔlytwar] *nm* throat spray
collyre [kɔlir] *nm* eyewash
colmater [kɔlmate] *vt* to fill in
colo [kɔlo] *nf Fam Br* (children's) holiday camp, *Am* summer camp
colocataire [kɔlɔkatɛr] *nmf (dans une maison) Br* housemate, *Am* roommate; *(dans un appartement) Br* flatmate, *Am* roommate
Colomb [kɔlɔ̃] *npr* **Christophe C.** Christopher Columbus
colombage [kɔlɔ̃baʒ] *nm Constr* half-timbering; **maison à colombages** half-timbered house
colombe [kɔlɔ̃b] *nf* dove
Colombie [kɔlɔ̃bi] *nf* **la C.** Colombia
Colombie-Britannique [kɔlɔ̃bibritanik] *nf* **la C.** British Columbia
colombien, -enne [kɔlɔ̃bjɛ̃, -ɛn] **1** *adj* Colombian **2** *nm,f* **C.** Colombian
colombier [kɔlɔ̃bje] *nm (pigeonnier)* dovecote
colon [kɔlɔ̃] *nm* (**a**) *(pionnier)* settler, colonist (**b**) *(dans une colonie de vacances)* child (at camp)
côlon [kɔlɔ̃] *nm* colon
colonel [kɔlɔnɛl] *nm (dans l'armée de terre)* colonel; *(dans l'armée de l'air) Br* group captain, *Am* colonel
colonial, -e, -aux, -ales [kɔlɔnjal, -o] **1** *adj* colonial **2** *nf Hist* **la coloniale** the Colonial Army
colonialisme [kɔlɔnjalism] *nm* colonialism
colonialiste [kɔlɔnjalist] *adj & nmf* colonialist
colonie [kɔlɔni] *nf* (**a**) *(territoire, immigrés)* colony (**b**) **c. (de vacances)** *Br* (children's) holiday camp, *Am* summer camp; **envoyer ses enfants en c.** to send one's children to camp

<hr>

Colonie de vacances
The "colonie de vacances" or "colo" is an integral part of childhood for many French people. The children's parents do not stay with them at the "colonie", the group being supervised by "moniteurs" or "animateurs" (group leaders), who organize games and activities.

<hr>

colonisation [kɔlɔnizasjɔ̃] *nf* colonization
coloniser [kɔlɔnize] *vt* to colonize
colonnade [kɔlɔnad] *nf* colonnade
colonne [kɔlɔn] *nf* (**a**) *(pilier)* column, pillar; **c. Morris** = pillar used to advertise forthcoming events (**b**) *(file)* column; **en c. par deux/trois** in columns of two/three (**c**) *(d'un dictionnaire, d'un journal)* column (**d**) *(de fumée, de mercure)* column (**e**) *Anat* **c. vertébrale** spine, spinal column (**f**) *Aut* **c. de direction** steering column
coloquinte [kɔlɔkɛ̃t] *nf (plante)* bitter apple
colorant, -e [kɔlɔrɑ̃, -ɑ̃t] **1** *adj* colouring **2** *nm* (**a**) *(pour teindre)* colorant (**b**) *(alimentaire)* colouring; **sans colorants** *(sur étiquette)* no artificial colouring
coloration [kɔlɔrasjɔ̃] *nf* (**a**) *(fait de colorer)* colouring; **se faire faire une c.** to have one's hair tinted (**b**) *(de la peau)* colouring (**c**) *Fig* **c. politique** political colour
coloré, -e [kɔlɔre] *adj* coloured; *(teint)* ruddy; *Fig (style)* colourful
colorer [kɔlɔre] **1** *vt* to colour; *Fig (récit)* to lend colour to; **c. qch en vert** to colour sth green **2 se colorer** *vpr (visage)* to become flushed
coloriage [kɔlɔrjaʒ] *nm (action)* colouring (in); *(dessin)* drawing; **album** *ou* **livre de c.** colouring (in) book
colorier [66] [kɔlɔrje] *vt* to colour (in)
coloris [kɔlɔri] *nm* shade
coloriser [kɔlɔrize] *vt Cin* to colourize
colossal, -e, -aux, -ales [kɔlɔsal, -o] *adj* colossal, huge
colosse [kɔlɔs] *nm (homme)* giant; *Fig* **un c. aux pieds d'argile** a giant with feet of clay
colostomie [kɔlɔstɔmi] *nf Méd* colostomy
colporter [kɔlpɔrte] *vt (marchandises)* to hawk; *(nouvelle, rumeurs)* to spread
colporteur, -euse [kɔlpɔrtœr, -øz] *nm,f* hawker
colt [kɔlt] *nm* Colt®
coltiner [kɔltine] **se coltiner** *vpr Fam* **se c. qn/qch** to get landed with sb/sth
colvert [kɔlvɛr] *nm* mallard
colza [kɔlza] *nm* rape
COM [kɔm] *nf (abrév* **collectivité d'outre-mer)** = French overseas collectivity

<hr>

COM
There are four "COM"s or "collectivités d'outre-mer": French Polynesia, Mayotte (in the Indian Ocean), St Pierre and Miquelon (off Newfoundland) and Wallis and Futuna Islands (in the Pacific Ocean).

<hr>

coma [kɔma] *nm* coma; **être/tomber dans le c.** to be in/go into a coma
comateux, -euse [kɔmatø, -øz] **1** *adj* comatose **2** *nm,f* patient in a coma
combat [kɔba] *nm* (**a**) *Mil (bataille)* fight; *(activité)* combat; **c. aérien** dog fight; *aussi Fig* **c. d'arrière-garde** rearguard action (**b**) *(dispute)* fight; **c. de boxe** boxing match; **c. de coqs** cockfight (**c**) *Fig (lutte)* fight (**contre** against)
combatif, -ive [kɔbatif, -iv] *adj* combative
combativité [kɔbativite] *nf* combativeness
combattant, -e [kɔbatɑ̃, -ɑ̃t] **1** *nm,f* combatant; **anciens combattants** veterans **2** *adj (troupes, unité)* fighting
combattre [11] [kɔbatr] **1** *vt (ennemi)* to fight (against); *(maladie, inflation, racisme)* to fight **2** *vi* to fight (**pour/contre** for/against)
combi [kɔbi] *nm Belg* police van
combien [kɔbjɛ̃] **1** *adv* (**a**) *(comme)* how (much); **j'ai pu constater c. tu avais changé** I could see how much you'd changed (**b**) *(en nombre)* how many; **c. sont-ils?** how many (of them) are there?; **c. de** how many; **c. de gens furent tués dans cette guerre!** what a lot of people were killed in that war! (**c**) *(en quantité, en poids)* how much; **ça fait c.?** *(d'argent)* how much is that?; **c. y a-t-il d'ici à Londres?** how far is it to London?; **à c. sommes-nous de Paris?** how far are we from Paris?; **c. mesure-t-il?** how tall is he?; **elle est enceinte – de c.?** she's pregnant – how far gone is she?; **c. de temps** how long; **c. de temps how long 2** *nm inv Fam* **le c. sommes-nous?** what's the date (today)?; **il y a un car tous les c.?** how often do the

buses run?; **tu chausses du c.?** what size shoe do you take?
combientième [kɔ̃bjɛ̃tjɛm] *Fam* **1** *nmf* **c'est le c. sur la liste?** where is it on the list?
2 *adj* **tu as été reçu c. à l'examen?** where did you come in the exam?; **c'est la c. fois que tu viens?** how often have you been now?
combinaison [kɔ̃binɛzɔ̃] *nf* (**a**) *(assemblage)* combination; **la c. gagnante** *(au tiercé)* the winning combination; *Ordinat* **c. de touches** key combination (**b**) *(vêtement) (de travail) Br* boiler suit, *Am* coveralls; *Aviat* flying suit; *(de femme)* catsuit; *(sous-vêtement)* slip; **c. de plongée** wet suit; **c. de ski** ski suit; **c. spatiale** space suit
combine [kɔ̃bin] *nf Fam* trick; **il a une c. pour entrer sans payer** he knows a way of getting in without paying; **mettre qn dans la c.** to let sb in on it
combiné, -e [kɔ̃bine] **1** *adj (action, efforts)* combined
2 *nm* (**a**) **c. (téléphonique)** receiver (**b**) *(en ski)* **c. alpin** alpine competition
combiner [kɔ̃bine] **1** *vt* (**a**) *(unir)* to combine (**b**) *Fam (plan)* to concoct; **qu'est-ce que tu combines encore?** what are you cooking up now?
2 se combiner *vpr* to combine
comble [kɔ̃bl] **1** *adj* (jam-)packed; **faire salle c.** *(au théâtre)* to have a full house
2 *nm* (**a**) *(maximum)* **le c. de** the height of; *(du désespoir)* the depth of; **ça, c'est le** *ou* **un c.!** that's the last straw!; **être au c. de la joie** to be overjoyed (**b**) *Archit (en bois)* roof timbers; *(en métal)* roof structure; **les combles** *(grenier)* the attic; **loger sous les combles** to live in an attic
combler [kɔ̃ble] *vt* (**a**) *(puits, fossé, trou)* to fill in; *(perte)* to make good; *(découvert)* to pay off; *(lacune)* to fill; **c. son retard** to make up for lost time (**b**) *(satisfaire)* to satisfy; **c. qn de cadeaux** to shower sb with gifts; **un mari comblé** a happily married man
combustible [kɔ̃bystibl] **1** *nm* fuel; **c. fossile/nucléaire** fossil/nuclear fuel
2 *adj* combustible
combustion [kɔ̃bystjɔ̃] *nf* combustion
comédie [kɔmedi] *nf (pièce, film, genre)* comedy; **jouer** *ou* **faire la c.** to act; *Fig* to put on an act; **allons, pas de c.!** *(caprice)* come on, stop your nonsense!; **c'est une vraie c. quand il faut aller à l'école** it's a real fuss when it's time to go to school; **c. de mœurs** comedy of manners; **c. musicale** musical
Comédie-Française [kɔmedifrɑ̃sɛz] *nf* **la C. =** state-run theatre company presenting plays from the established repertoire

Comédie-Française

This state-subsidized company dates back to the seventeenth century; the theatre itself, officially called "leThéâtre-Français" or "le Français", is situated in the rue Richelieu in Paris. Its repertoire consists mainly of classical works, although modern plays are often staged. Actors who perform in the Comédie-Française fall into two categories: the "sociétaires" who are fully-fledged members of the company, and the "pensionnaires" who work with the company on a fixed salary but are not shareholders in it.

comédien, -enne [kɔmedjɛ̃, -ɛn] **1** *nm,f (acteur)* actor, *f* actress; *Fig* **c'est une comédienne** she's always

putting on an act; **comédiens ambulants** strolling players
2 *adj* **elle est très comédienne** she's always putting on an act
comédon [kɔmedɔ̃] *nm* blackhead
comestible [kɔmɛstibl] *adj* edible; **denrées comestibles** foodstuffs
comète [kɔmɛt] *nf* comet; *Fig* **tirer** *ou* **faire des plans sur la c.** to build castles in the air
comice [kɔmis] *nm* **c. agricole** agricultural association; **comices agricoles** *(foire)* agricultural show
comique [kɔmik] **1** *adj* (**a**) *(acteur, film, rôle)* comedy; **le genre c.** comedy (**b**) *(amusant)* comical, funny
2 *nm* (**a**) *(genre)* comedy; **c. de situation** situation comedy (**b**) *(acteur)* comic actor; *Péj (bouffon)* comedian (**c**) **le c. de l'histoire, c'est que...** the funny part is that...
comité [kɔmite] *nm* committee; **faire partie d'un c.** to sit on a committee; *Fig* **nous serons en petit c.** we'll just have a small get-together; **c. d'entreprise** works council; **C. international olympique** International Olympic Committee

Comité d'entreprise

The "Comité d'entreprise" or "CE" looks after the general welfare of company employees and organizes subsidised leisure activities, outings, holidays etc. It also deals with industrial problems.

commandant [kɔmɑ̃dɑ̃] *nm* (**a**) *(officier) (d'unité)* commander; *(de camp, de base)* commandant; *(de bateau)* captain *(whatever his rank)*; *Aviat* **c. de bord** captain; **c. en chef** commander-in-chief; *Naut* executive officer (**b**) *(rang) (dans l'armée de terre)* major; *(dans l'armée de l'air) Br* squadron leader, *Am* major
commande [kɔmɑ̃d] *nf* (**a**) *Com* order; **faire** *ou* **passer une c.** to put in *or* place an order; **sur c.** *aussi Fig* to order; **on ne peut pas rire sur c.** you can't laugh to order; **ouvrage de c.** commissioned work (**b**) *(action, manette)* control; *(mécanisme)* drive; **c. à distance** remote control; **commandes** *(d'un avion)* controls; **prendre les commandes** *(d'un avion)* to take over the controls; *(d'une société)* to take control (**c**) *Ordinat* command; **c. d'annulation/d'effacement** undo/delete command; **à c. vocale** voice-activated
commandement [kɔmɑ̃dmɑ̃] *nm* (**a**) *(ordre) Mil* command; **à mon c.** when I give/gave the command; *Rel* **les dix commandements** theTen Commandments (**b**) *(pouvoir)* command; **avoir/prendre la c.** to be in/ to take command; **c. suprême, haut c.** high command
commander [kɔmɑ̃de] **1** *vt* (**a**) *(diriger, ordonner)* to command; *Fam* **sans rire, c., est-ce que vous pourriez fermer la fenêtre?** I wonder if you'd mind closing the window? (**b**) *(marchandises, dîner)* to order; *(peinture, ouvrage)* to commission; **c. qch à qn** to order/commission sth from sb (**c**) *(mouvement, valve)* to control; *(machine)* to drive (**d**) *Ordinat* to drive; **commandé par menu** menu-driven
2 *vi* **c. à qn de faire qch** to order sb to do sth; **qui est-ce qui commande ici?** who's in charge here?
3 se commander *vpr* **ces choses-là ne se commandent pas** *(sont incontrôlables)* these things are beyond our control
commanditaire [kɔmɑ̃ditɛr] *adj & nm Com (associé)* **c.** *Br* sleeping *or Am* silent partner; **les commanditaires de l'attentat** the people behind the attack

commandite [kɔmãdit] *nf Com* **(société en) c.** mixed liability company

commandité [kɔmãdite] *adj & nm Com* **(associé) c.** active partner

commanditer [kɔmãdite] *vt Com* to finance; *(meurtre, attentat)* to be behind

commando [kɔmãdo] *nm (groupe)* commando (unit)

comme [kɔm] **1** *adv* (**a**) *(devant un nom, un pronom)* like; **il n'est pas c.** **les autres** he isn't like the others; **c. ça** like that; *(du coup)* that way; **c'est c. ça, un point c'est tout!** too bad, that's the way it is!; **alors c. ça, vous venez de Paris?** you come from Paris, don't you?; *Fam* **c. ça!** *(formidable)* great!, fab!; **quelque chose c. deux cents personnes** something like two hundred people

(**b**) *(devant une proposition)* as; **il écrit c. il parle** he writes as he speaks; **insolent c. il est...** insolent as he is...; **il leva la main c. pour me frapper** he lifted his hand as if *or* as though to strike me; **c. il faut** *(se conduire)* properly; **des gens très c. il faut** very respectable people; **c. si** as if, as though; **c. si je ne le savais pas!** as if I didn't know!

(**c**) *(dans des images)* as; **doux c. un agneau** (as) gentle as a lamb

(**d**) *(et)* **les femmes c. les hommes** men and women alike; **tout le monde fera la vaisselle, toi c. les autres** everyone's going to do the dishes, and you're no exception

(**e**) *(tel que)* such as, like; **les bois durs c. le chêne** hard woods like *or* such as oak; **P c. pomme** P as in peach

(**f**) *(en tant que)* as; **je l'ai eue c. professeur** she was my teacher; **qu'est-ce que vous avez c. desserts?** what have you got in the way of desserts?; **ce n'est pas mal c. roman** it's not a bad novel

(**g**) *(en quelque sorte)* **elle a eu c. une hésitation** she seemed to hesitate; **j'étais c. hypnotisé** it was as if *or* as though I was hypnotized

(**h**) *(comment)* how; **tu sais bien c. il est** you know what he's like; *Fam* **elle a fait les carreaux, faut voir c.!** you should see the way she's done the windows!

(**i**) *(exclamatif)* how; **c. tu as grandi!** how you've grown!; **c. elle est bête!** she's so stupid!; **c. elle a de beaux cheveux!** what lovely hair she has!

(**j**) *Fam (locutions)* **c'est tout c.** it amounts to the same thing; **c. ci c. ça** so-so; **c. qui dirait** as it were; **c. quoi** *(disant que)* to the effect that; *(ce qui prouve que)* which goes to show that; **drôle c. tout** as funny as anything

2 *conj* (**a**) *(puisque)* as, since; **c. vous êtes mon ami, je vais tout vous dire** as you're my friend I'll tell you everything

(**b**) *(alors que)* **c. il allait frapper, la porte s'ouvrit** he was just about to knock when the door opened

commémoratif, -ive [kɔmemɔratif, -iv] *adj (plaque, cérémonie)* commemorative; *(service)* memorial; **monument c.** memorial

commémoration [kɔmemɔrasjɔ̃] *nf* commemoration; **en c. de** in commemoration of

commémorer [kɔmemɔre] *vt* to commemorate

commencement [kɔmãsmã] *nm* beginning, start; **au c.** at the beginning *or* start; **il faut un c. à tout** you've got to start somewhere; *Fam* **c'est le c. de la fin** it's the beginning of the end

commencer [16] [kɔmãse] **1** *vt* (**a**) *(entreprendre)* to begin, to start; *(traitement, régime)* to go on, to start; **nous avons mal commencé l'année** we've made a

bad start to the year (**b**) *(être au début de)* to begin, to start

2 *vi* to begin, to start; **pour c., je dois vous dire...** to begin with, I must tell you...; *Ironique* **ça commence bien!** that's a good start!; **c. par qch/par faire qch** to begin *or* start with sth/by doing sth; **par où c.?** where shall I begin?; **à c. par...** beginning with...

3 commencer à *vt ind* **c. à faire qch** to begin *or* start to do sth, to begin *or* start doing sth; *Fam* **je commence à en avoir assez!** I've had just about enough!; *Fam* **ça commence à bien faire** it's getting a bit too much

comment [kɔmã] **1** *adv* how; **c. allez-vous?** how are you?; **c.?** *(pour faire répéter)* sorry?, pardon?; **c. ça, tu ne veux pas?** what do you mean, you don't want to?; **c. faire?** what can I/we/*etc* do?; **c. est-il, ce garçon?** what's this young man like?; **elle me dira c. faire** she'll tell me how to do it

2 *exclam* what!; **mais c. donc!** why, of course!; *Fam* **ça vous a plu? – et c.!** did you like it? – you bet I did!

commentaire [kɔmãtɛr] *nm* (**a**) *(remarque)* comment, remark; **faire des commentaires** to make comments; **cela se passe de c.** it speaks for itself; *Fam* **sans c.!** no comment!; *Scol* **c. de texte** textual commentary (**b**) *(à la radio, à la télévision)* commentary; **c. sportif** sports commentary

commentateur, -trice [kɔmãtatœr, -tris] *nm,f (à la radio, à la télévision)* commentator; **c. sportif** sports commentator

commenter [kɔmãte] *vt (expliquer, donner son avis sur)* to comment on; *(à la radio, à la télévision) (compétition)* to commentate on; **c. l'actualité** to comment on current affairs

commérage [kɔmeraʒ] *nm* (piece of) gossip; **commérages** gossip

commerçant, -e [kɔmɛrsã, -ãt] **1** *nm,f* trader; *(qui tient un magasin)* shopkeeper; **petits commerçants** small traders

2 *adj* **quartier c.** shopping area; **rue très commerçante** busy shopping street; **il n'est pas très c.** he doesn't look after his customers very well

commerce [kɔmɛrs] *nm* (**a**) **le c.** *(activité, secteur)* trade; *(affaires)* business; **ça se trouve dans le c.** you can buy it in the shops; **faire du c. avec** to do business with; **hors c.** not for (general) sale; **c. de détail** retail trade; **c. électronique** e-commerce; **c. équitable** fair trade; **c. en ou de gros** wholesale trade; **c. intérieur/extérieur** home/foreign trade; **c. international** world trade; **c. maritime** seaborne trade; **le petit c.** small traders (**b**) *(magasin)* business

commercer [16] [kɔmɛrse] *vi* to trade (**avec** with)

commercial, -e, -aux, -ales [kɔmɛrsjal, -o] **1** *adj (rapports, pratiques)* business, commercial; *(embargo, tribunal)* trade; *(droit)* commercial; *Péj (film, chanson)* commercial; **suivre une formation commerciale** to do a business studies course

2 *nm,f* salesman, *f* saleswoman

3 *nf* **commerciale** *(voiture) Br* estate car, *Am* station wagon

commercialisation [kɔmɛrsjalizasjɔ̃] *nf* marketing

commercialiser [kɔmɛrsjalize] *vt (produit)* to market

commère [kɔmɛr] *nf* gossip

commettre [47] [kɔmɛtr] **1** *vt* (**a**) *(crime, péché, injustice)* to commit; *(erreur)* to make; *Hum* **il a déjà commis deux pièces de théâtre** he's already to blame for two plays (**b**) *Jur* **avocat commis d'office** counsel appointed by the court

2 se commettre *vpr Litt* **se c.** avec qn to compromise oneself by associating with sb

commis¹, -e *voir* **commettre**

commis² [kɔmi] *nm* (**a**) *(employé)* clerk; *(dans un magasin)* (shop) assistant (**b**) *Vieilli* **c. voyageur** commercial traveller

commisération [kɔmizerasjɔ̃] *nf* commiseration; **témoigner de la c. à qn** to commiserate with sb

commissaire [kɔmisɛr] *nm* (**a**) **c. (de police)** *Br* ≃ (police) superintendent, *Am* ≃ (police) captain (**b**) *Fin* **c. aux comptes** government auditor (**c**) *(membre d'une commission)* commissioner (**d**) *Sport* steward (**e**) *(d'une exposition)* organizer

commissaire-priseur (*pl* **commissaires-priseurs**) [kɔmisɛrprizœr] *nm* auctioneer

commissariat [kɔmisarja] *nm* (**a**) **c. (de police)** police station (**b**) *(fonction)* commissionership (**c**) *(service)* commission; **le C. à l'énergie atomique** the Atomic Energy Commission

commission [kɔmisjɔ̃] *nf* (**a**) *(course)* **faire les commissions** to go shopping (**b**) *(service)* errand; *(message)* message; **faire une c.** to run an errand; **faire une c. à qn** to give sb a message (**c**) *(comité)* commission, committee; **c. d'enquête** board of inquiry; **C. européenne** European Commission; **C. des opérations de Bourse** = French Stock Exchange watchdog (**d**) *(pourcentage)* *Com* commission; *Fin* brokerage; **être payé à la c.** to be paid on a commission basis; **c. bancaire** bank commission (**e**) *Fam* **la petite/grosse c.** number one/two

commissionnaire [kɔmisjɔnɛr] *nm* (**a**) *(messager)* messenger; *(à l'hôtel, au théâtre)* commissionaire (**b**) *Com* (commission) agent

commissionner [kɔmisjɔne] *vt* to commission

commissures [kɔmisyr] *nfpl* **c. des lèvres** *ou* **de la bouche** corners of the mouth

commode [kɔmɔd] **1** *adj* (**a**) *(heure, lieu)* convenient; *(outil, système)* handy (**b**) **pas c.** *(difficile)* tricky (**c**) **pas c.** *(peu aimable)* awkward
2 *nf* chest of drawers

commodément [kɔmɔdemɑ̃] *adv (assis, installé)* comfortably

commodité [kɔmɔdite] *nf* (**a**) *(facilité)* convenience; **pour plus de c.** for greater convenience; **les commodités de la vie moderne** the comforts of modern life (**b**) *Vieilli* **commodités** *(toilettes)* *Br* toilet, *Am* restroom

commotion [kɔmosjɔ̃] *nf* (**a**) *Méd* **c. cérébrale** concussion (**b**) *(émotion)* shock

commotionner [kɔmosjɔne] *vt* (**a**) *Méd* to concuss (**b**) *(choquer)* to shake (up)

commuer [kɔmɥe] *vt Jur (peine)* to commute (**en** to)

commun, -e [kɔmœ̃, -yn] **1** *adj* (**a**) *(non exclusif)* common (**à** to); *(travail)* joint; *(ami)* mutual; **jardin c. à deux maisons** garden shared by two houses; **en c.** *(travailler)* communally; *(vivre)* communally; **avoir des choses en c.** *(se ressembler)* to have things in common; **nous n'avons aucun point c.** we have nothing in common; **se mettre** *ou* **mettre de l'argent en c.** **pour acheter un cadeau** to club together to buy a present (**b**) *(répandu)* common; **il est d'une force peu commune** he's unusually strong (**c**) *(vulgaire)* common
2 *nm* (**a**) *(majorité)* **le c. des mortels** the ordinary man; **hors du c.** out of the ordinary (**b**) **communs** *(dépendances)* outbuildings

communal, -e, -aux, -ales [kɔmynal, -o] *adj (de la commune) (terrain, salle)* *Br* ≃ council, *Am* ≃ district; **école communale** ≃ local *Br* primary *or Am* grade school; *Belg* **maison communale** town hall

communautaire [kɔmynotɛr] *adj (en commun)* communal; *(de la Communauté européenne)* Community

communauté [kɔmynote] *nf* (**a**) *(collectivité)* & *Rel* community; *(de hippies)* commune; **vivre en c.** to live in a commune; **la C. économique européenne** the European Economic Community; **la C. d'États indépendants** the Commonwealth of Independent States (**b**) *(d'intérêts, d'idées)* similarity; *Jur* **être mariés sous le régime de la c.** to be married on the basis of a joint settlement of property

commune [kɔmyn] *nf* (**a**) *(municipalité)* commune *(smallest territorial division)* (**b**) *(administration)* local authority, *Br* (town) council (**c**) *Hist* **la C. (de Paris)** the Commune *(in 1789 and 1871)*

Commune

There are over 36,000 "communes" or administrative districts in France, some with fewer than 25 inhabitants. Each "commune" has an elected mayor and a town council.

communément [kɔmynemɑ̃] *adv* commonly

communiant, -e [kɔmynjɑ̃, -ɑ̃t] *nm,f Rel* communicant; **premier c.** person taking his first communion

communicatif, -ive [kɔmynikatif, -iv] *adj* (**a**) *(qui parle)* communicative; **peu c.** uncommunicative (**b**) *(rire, bonne humeur)* infectious

communication [kɔmynikasjɔ̃] *nf* (**a**) *(échange)* communication; **entrer** *ou* **se mettre en c. avec qn** to get in touch *or* in contact with sb; **toutes les communications sont coupées** all lines of communication are cut; **c. de masse** mass communication (**b**) **c. (téléphonique)** (telephone) call; **je vous passe la c.** I'll put you through; **la c. est mauvaise** the line is bad (**c**) *(message)* communication, message; **faire une c.** *(dans un colloque)* to read a paper

communier [kɔmynje] *vi Rel* to receive Communion

communion [kɔmynjɔ̃] *nf* (**a**) *(communauté)* communion; **être en c. avec la nature** to commune with nature (**b**) *Rel* Communion; **première c.** first Communion; **c. solennelle** solemn Communion; **faire sa c.** to make one's first/solemn Communion

communiqué [kɔmynike] *nm* communiqué; **c. de presse** press release

communiquer [kɔmynike] **1** *vt* to communicate (**à** to); *(maladie)* to pass on (**à** to)
2 *vi* (**a**) *(être en relation)* to communicate (**avec** with) (**b**) *(pièce)* to communicate (**avec** with); **porte qui communique avec le jardin** door that leads into the garden
3 se communiquer *vpr (se transmettre)* to spread (**à** to)

communisme [kɔmynism] *nm* communism

communiste [kɔmynist] *adj & nmf* communist

commutateur [kɔmytatœr] *nm Élec (bouton)* switch; *Ordinat* **c. de données** data switch

commutation [kɔmytasjɔ̃] *nf* (**a**) *Jur (de peine)* commutation (**b**) *(changement)* & *Gram* substitution; *(entre documents)* switching (**c**) *Ordinat* **c. de message/ de paquets** message/packet switching

Comores [kɔmɔr] *nfpl* **les C., l'archipel des C.** the Comoros

comorien, -enne [kɔmɔrjɛ̃, -ɛn] **1** *adj* Comoran **2** *nm,f* C. Comoran

compact, -e [kɔ̃pakt] **1** *adj* (**a**) *(de petit format)* compact (**b**) *(masse, terre)* compact; *(foule)* dense **2** *nm (CD)* compact disc **Compact Disc®** *(pl* **Compact Discs**) [kɔ̃paktdisk] *nm* compact disc

compacter [kɔ̃pakte] *vt Ordinat (fichier, données)* to compress; *(base de données)* to pack

compacteur [kɔ̃paktœr] *nm Ordinat* compressor; **c. de données** data compressor

compagne [kɔ̃paɲ] *nf* (**a**) *(camarade)* companion; **mes compagnes de captivité** my fellow captives (**b**) *(concubine)* partner

compagnie [kɔ̃paɲi] *nf* (**a**) *(présence)* company; **tenir c. à qn** to keep sb company; **en c. de qn** with sb (**b**) *(groupe)* **et toute la c.** and everybody; *Fam* **salut, la c.!** hi, guys *or* everybody! (**c**) *Com & Théât* company; *Com* **Thomas et C.** Thomas and Company; **c. aérienne** airline; **c. d'assurances** insurance company; **c. maritime** shipping line; **c. pétrolière** oil company; **Compagnies républicaines de sécurité** *Br* ≃ riot police, *Am* ≃ state troopers; **c. de transports** carrier (**d**) *Mil* company (**e**) *(de perdrix)* covey

compagnon [kɔ̃paɲɔ̃] *nm* (**a**) *(camarade)* companion; **c. de voyage** travelling companion (**b**) *(ouvrier)* journeyman (**c**) *(concubin)* partner

comparable [kɔ̃parabl] *adj* comparable (**à** *ou* **avec** to *or* with); **ce n'est pas c.** there's no comparison

comparaison [kɔ̃parɛzɔ̃] *nf* (**a**) *(action de comparer)* comparison; **faire la c. entre** to make a comparison between; **c'est sans c. avec...** it can't be compared with...; **il est sans c. le plus grand** he is by far the tallest; **en c. de...** in comparison with...; **par c.** by comparison; **par c. avec** *ou* **à** compared with *or* to (**b**) *(figure de style)* simile

comparaître [50a] [kɔ̃parɛtr] *vi Jur* **c. (en justice)** to appear (in court); **être appelé à c.** to be summoned to appear

comparatif, -ive [kɔ̃paratif, -iv] **1** *adj* comparative **2** *Gram* comparative; **c. de supériorité/d'infériorité** comparative of greater/lesser degree

comparativement [kɔ̃parativmɑ̃] *adv* comparatively

comparé, -e [kɔ̃pare] *adj (anatomie, histoire, littérature)* comparative; **c. à** compared with *or* to

comparer [kɔ̃pare] **1** *vt* to compare (**à** *ou* **avec** to *or* with) **2 se comparer** *vpr* (**a**) *(soi-même)* **se c. à** *ou* **avec** to compare oneself to *or* with (**b**) *(être comparé)* **Händel ne peut pas se c. à Mozart** Handel can't be compared with Mozart

comparse [kɔ̃pars] *nmf Péj* associate

compartiment [kɔ̃partimɑ̃] *nm (de wagon, de boîte, de tiroir)* compartment; **c. fumeurs** smoking compartment, smoker; **c. non-fumeurs** no-smoking compartment, non-smoker; **c. à bagages** *(d'autocar)* luggage compartment

compartimenter [kɔ̃partimɑ̃te] *vt (diviser en espaces)* to partition; *Fig* **une société compartimentée** a compartmentalized society

comparution [kɔ̃parysjɔ̃] *nf Jur* appearance

compas [kɔ̃pa] *nm* (**a**) *Math* (pair of) compasses; *Fig* **avoir le c. dans l'œil** to have an accurate eye; **c. à pointes sèches** dividers (**b**) *Naut* compass

compassé, -e [kɔ̃pase] *adj* stiff, starchy

compassion [kɔ̃pasjɔ̃] *nf* compassion; **avec c.** compassionately

compatibilité [kɔ̃patibilite] *nf* compatibility

compatible [kɔ̃patibl] *adj aussi Ordinat* compatible (**avec** with)

compatir [kɔ̃patir] *vi* to sympathize; **c. au chagrin de qn** to sympathize with sb in his/her grief

compatissant, -e [kɔ̃patisɑ̃, -ɑ̃t] *adj* compassionate, sympathetic

compatriote [kɔ̃patriɔt] *nmf* compatriot

compensable [kɔ̃pɑ̃sabl] *adj (chèque)* clearable

compensation [kɔ̃pɑ̃sasjɔ̃] *nf* (**a**) *(d'une perte, d'un inconvénient)* compensation; **en c. de qch** as compensation for (**b**) *(de chèque)* clearing

compensé, -e [kɔ̃pɑ̃se] *adj* **chaussures à semelles compensées** platform shoes

compenser [kɔ̃pɑ̃se] **1** *vt* (**a**) *(perte, défaut)* to compensate for, to make up for (**b**) *(chèque)* to clear **2 se compenser** *vpr* to make up for each other

compère [kɔ̃pɛr] *nm Vieilli (camarade)* friend

compétence [kɔ̃petɑ̃s] *nf* (**a**) *(capacité)* competence; **compétences** *(connaissances)* ability, skills; **cela n'entre pas dans mes compétences** it's beyond my capabilities; **compétences transférables** transferable skills (**b**) *Jur (d'un tribunal, d'un maire)* competence; **cela n'est pas de sa c.** that doesn't come within his/her province

compétent, -e [kɔ̃petɑ̃, -ɑ̃t] *adj* (**a**) *(capable)* competent; **c. en qch** conversant with sth (**b**) *Jur (tribunal, autorité)* competent; **adressez-vous au service c.** apply to the relevant department

compétitif, -ive [kɔ̃petitif, -iv] *adj* competitive

compétition [kɔ̃petisjɔ̃] *nf* (**a**) *(rivalité)* competition; **être en c. avec qn** to compete with sb (**b**) *Sport (épreuve)* **c. (sportive)** *(sporting)* event; **faire de la c.** to go in for competitive sport

compétitivité [kɔ̃petitivite] *nf* competitiveness

compilateur [kɔ̃pilatœr] *nm Ordinat* compiler

compilation [kɔ̃pilasjɔ̃] *nf* compilation

compiler [kɔ̃pile] *vt aussi Ordinat* to compile

complaire [55a] [kɔ̃plɛr] **se complaire** *vpr* **se c. dans qch/à faire qch** to delight *or* revel in sth/in doing sth

complaisance [kɔ̃plɛzɑ̃s] *nf* (**a**) *(bienveillance)* kindness; **faire qch par c.** to do sth out of kindness (**b**) *Péj (indulgence)* indulgence; **certificat médical de c.** = medical certificate to which one is not entitled (**c**) *(autosatisfaction)* complacency, smugness

complaisant, -e [kɔ̃plɛzɑ̃, -ɑ̃t] *adj* (**a**) *(bienveillant)* obliging, kind (**envers** towards) (**b**) *Péj (indulgent)* indulgent (**c**) *(satisfait)* complacent, smug

complément [kɔ̃plemɑ̃] *nm* (**a**) *(reste)* rest, remainder; **demander un c. d'information** to ask for further information (**b**) *Gram* complement; **c. d'attribution** indirect object; **c. circonstanciel de temps/de manière** adverbial phrase of time/of manner; **c. de nom** possessive phrase; **c. d'objet direct/indirect** direct/indirect object

complémentaire [kɔ̃plemɑ̃tɛr] *adj (couleur)* complementary; **pour tout renseignement c., s'adresser à...** for further information, apply to...

complet, -ète [kɔ̃plɛ, -ɛt] **1** *adj* (**a**) *(entier, intégral) (tenue, service)* complete, whole; **deux jours complets** two full *or* whole days; **formation très complète** thorough training; *Fam* **c'est c.!** that's the last straw! (**b**) *(détaillé)* full (**c**) *(absolu)* complete; **un c. abruti** a complete moron; **ce fut un échec c.** it was a complete failure (**d**) *(bus, salle de théâtre)* full; **c.** *(sur pan-*

neau) (parking) full; *(pension, hôtel)* no vacancies (**e**) *(pain, pâtes)* wholemeal; *(riz)* brown **2** *nm* (**a**) **c.(-veston)** suit (**b**) **est-ce que nous sommes au c.?** are we all here?; **j'ai invité la famille au (grand) c. pour Noël** I've invited the whole family for Christmas

complètement [kɔ̃plɛtmɑ̃] *adv* (**a**) *(terminé, guéri)* completely, totally; **je n'ai pas c. fini** I haven't quite finished (**b**) *(vraiment) (perdu, idiot)* completely, totally

compléter [34] [kɔ̃plete] **1** *vt (collection, formation)* to complete; *(somme)* to make up; *(formulaire)* to complete, to fill in **2 se compléter** *vpr* to complement one another

complexe [kɔ̃plɛks] **1** *adj (compliqué)* complex **2** *nm* (**a**) *(ensemble de bâtiments, d'industries)* complex; **c. hôtelier** hotel complex; **c. sportif** sports complex (**b**) *(gêne)* hang-up; *Psy* complex; **avoir des complexes (à cause de qch)** to have a hang-up (about sth); **être sans c.** to have no hang-ups; **c. d'infériorité** inferiority complex; **c. d'Œdipe** Oedipus complex

complexé, -e [kɔ̃plɛkse] *adj* hung up (**par** about)
complexer [kɔ̃plɛkse] *vt* **c. qn** to give sb a hang-up
complexité [kɔ̃plɛksite] *nf* complexity
complication [kɔ̃plikasjɔ̃] *nf* (**a**) *(ennui)* complication; **faire des complications** to create complications (**b**) *(complexité)* complexity (**c**) *Méd* **complications** complications

complice [kɔ̃plis] **1** *nmf* accomplice **2** *adj (regard, sourire)* knowing; **être c. de qch** to be party to sth

complicité [kɔ̃plisite] *nf* complicity; **agir en c. avec qn** to act in collusion with sb; **accusé de c. de meurtre** accused of being an accessory to murder

compliment [kɔ̃plimɑ̃] *nm* compliment; **faire des compliments à qn (sur qch)** to pay sb compliments (on sth); **(je vous fais) mes compliments!** I congratulate you!; *Ironique* **mes compliments!** congratulations!

complimenter [kɔ̃plimɑ̃te] *vt* **c. qn pour** *(courage, présence d'esprit)* to congratulate sb on; **c. qn sur** *(toilette, coiffure)* to compliment sb on

compliqué, -e [kɔ̃plike] *adj* complicated; **ce n'est pourtant pas c.!** it's quite simple!

compliquer [kɔ̃plike] **1** *vt* to complicate; **c. les choses** to complicate matters **2 se compliquer** *vpr (situation, problème)* to get complicated; **se c. l'existence** to make life complicated for oneself

complot [kɔ̃plo] *nm* plot, conspiracy
comploter [kɔ̃plɔte] **1** *vt* to plot; **c. de faire qch** to plot to do sth **2** *vi* to plot (**contre** against)

comportement [kɔ̃pɔrtəmɑ̃] *nm* behaviour; *Écon* **c. d'achat** buying behaviour

comporter [kɔ̃pɔrte] **1** *vt* (**a**) *(être constitué de)* to consist of, to be made up of (**b**) *(contenir)* to contain (**c**) *(difficultés, inconvénients)* to involve **2 se comporter** *vpr* (**a**) *(agir)* to behave (**vis-à-vis de** *ou* **envers** towards) (**b**) *(fonctionner) (voiture)* to handle

composant [kɔ̃pozɑ̃] *nm* component
composante [kɔ̃pozɑ̃t] *nf* component
composé, -e [kɔ̃poze] *adj & nm* compound
composer [kɔ̃poze] **1** *vt* (**a**) *(symphonie, poème)* to compose, to write; *(bouquet)* to make up (**b**) *(faire*

partie de) to make up; **être composé de qch** to be made up *or* composed of sth (**c**) *(numéro de téléphone)* to dial (**d**) *Typ* to set (**e**) **c. son visage** to compose one's features **2** *vi* (**a**) *(s'entendre)* to compromise (**avec** with) (**b**) *Scol* to take a test **3 se composer** *vpr* (**a**) **se c. de qch** to be made up *or* composed of sth (**b**) **se c. un visage de circonstance** to put on a suitable expression

composite [kɔ̃pozit] *adj* composite
compositeur, -trice [kɔ̃pozitœr, -tris] *nm,f* (**a**) *Mus* composer (**b**) *Typ* typesetter

composition [kɔ̃pozisjɔ̃] *nf* (**a**) *(d'une symphonie, d'un poème)* composition, writing; **un poème de ma c.** a poem I wrote (myself); *Cin & Théât* **rôle de c.** character part (**b**) *(éléments)* composition; *(d'un aliment)* ingredients; **la c. des équipes n'est pas encore connue** the teams haven't been announced yet (**c**) *(œuvre musicale, littéraire)* composition (**d**) *(rédaction)* essay; *(examen)* test (**e**) *(caractère)* **être de bonne c.** to be good-natured (**f**) *Typ* typesetting

compost [kɔ̃pɔst] *nm* compost
composter [kɔ̃pɔste] *vt* (**a**) *(pour dater)* to date-stamp (**b**) *(pour valider)* to punch

Composter

Rail passengers in France are required to insert their ticket into a special punching machine ("composteur") on the platform before beginning their journey. The words "à composter" printed across the ticket mean that the passenger must do this before getting on the train.

compote [kɔ̃pɔt] *nf* compote, stewed fruit; **c. de pommes** apple compote, stewed apples; *Fam* **j'ai les jambes en c.** my legs feel like jelly

compotier [kɔ̃pɔtje] *nm* fruit dish
compréhensible [kɔ̃preɑ̃sibl] *adj* (**a**) *(clair)* comprehensible (**par** to) (**b**) *(justifié)* understandable

compréhensif, -ive [kɔ̃preɑ̃sif, -iv] *adj* understanding

compréhension [kɔ̃preɑ̃sjɔ̃] *nf* (**a**) *(fait de comprendre)* comprehension, understanding (**b**) *(bienveillance)* understanding

comprendre [58] [kɔ̃prɑ̃dr] **1** *vt* (**a**) *(par l'esprit)* to understand; **dois-je c. que...?** am I to understand that...?; **mal c. qn/qch** to misunderstand sb/sth; **je ne le comprends pas** *(il est étrange, il n'articule pas)* I can't understand him; **il faut la c.** you have to see things from her point of view; **je n'y comprends rien** I can't make head nor tail of it; **c'est à n'y rien c.** it's incomprehensible; **ne cherche pas, il n'y a rien à c.** don't even try to understand; **va y c. quelque chose!** YOU try to make head or tail of it!; **faire c. à qn que...** to give sb to understand that...; *(avec autorité)* to make it clear to sb that...; **se faire c.** to make oneself understood; **me suis-je bien fait c.?** have I made myself clear?; **elle comprend vite** she's quick on the uptake; **ça va, j'ai compris!** OK, I understand!; **tu comprends...** you see... (**b**) *(être composé de)* to consist of, to be made up of (**c**) *(inclure)* to include **2 se comprendre** *vpr (l'un l'autre)* to understand each other; **ça se comprend** it's understandable; **je me comprends!** I know what I mean!

comprenure [kɔ̃prənyr] *nf Belg & Can Fam* **être dur de c.** to be slow on the uptake

compresse [kɔ̃prɛs] *nf* compress

compresser [kɔ̃prɛse] *vt* to compress; *Ordinat* to zip
compresseur [kɔ̃prɛsœr] *nm* (**a**) *Tech (de gaz, de vapeur)* compressor; *(de moteur)* supercharger (**b**) *Ordinat* **c. de données** data compressor
compression [kɔ̃prɛsjɔ̃] *nf* (**a**) *(de gaz, de vapeur)* compression (**b**) *(réduction)* reduction; **c. des dépenses** spending cuts
comprimé, -e [kɔ̃prime] **1** *adj (gaz)* compressed
     2 *nm (médicament)* tablet; **un c. d'aspirine** an aspirin
comprimer [kɔ̃prime] *vt* (**a**) *(gaz, artère, fichier informatique)* to compress; **cette jupe me comprime la taille** this skirt is too tight round my waist (**b**) *Fig (dépenses)* to reduce
compris, -e [kɔ̃pri, -iz] **1** *pp de* **comprendre**
     2 *adj* (**a**) *(enregistré)* **bien c.** (fully) understood; **mal c.** misunderstood; **alors, c'est c.?** so, do you understand?; *Fam* **tu fais tes devoirs immédiatement, c.?** you'll do your homework right now, (is that) understood? (**b**) *(inclus)* included; **service non c.** service not included; **tout c.** all in; **y c.** including (**c**) *(situé)* **être c. entre** to be between
compromettant, -e [kɔ̃prɔmɛtɑ̃, -ɑ̃t] *adj* compromising
compromettre [47] [kɔ̃prɔmɛtr] **1** *vt* (**a**) *(personne, réputation)* to compromise; **être compromis dans qch** to be implicated in sth (**b**) *(sécurité, vacances, chances)* to jeopardize
     2 se compromettre *vpr* to compromise oneself; **se c. dans qch** to be implicated in sth
compromis [kɔ̃prɔmi] *nm (arrangement)* compromise
compromission [kɔ̃prɔmisjɔ̃] *nf Péj* compromise
comptabiliser [kɔ̃tabilize] *vt (recettes, dépenses)* to enter in the accounts; *(points)* to count
comptabilité [kɔ̃tabilite] *nf* (**a**) *(livres)* accounts; *(technique)* book-keeping, accounting; **tenir la c.** to keep the accounts (**b**) *(service)* accounts department
comptable [kɔ̃tabl] **1** *adj (travail, technique)* book-keeping, accounting
     2 *nmf* accountant; **c. agréé** *Br* chartered accountant, *Am* certified public accountant
comptage [kɔ̃taʒ] *nm* counting
comptant [kɔ̃tɑ̃] **1** *adv* **payer c.** to pay (in) cash
     2 *nm* cash; **payer/acheter au c.** to pay (in)/buy for cash
compte [kɔ̃t] *nm* (**a**) *(dans une banque, chez un commerçant)* account; **comptes** *(comptabilité)* accounts; **tenir les comptes** to keep the accounts; **faire ses comptes** to do one's accounts; **verser une somme sur son c.** to pay a sum into one's account; **se mettre ou s'installer à son c.** to start one's own business; **faire qch pour le c. de qn** to do sth on sb's behalf; **c. en banque** *ou* **bancaire** bank account; **c. chèques** *Br* current account, *Am* checking account; **c. chèques postal** ≃ giro account; **c. courant** *Br* current account, *Am* checking account; **c. de dépôt** deposit account; **c. épargne** savings account; **c. épargne logement** savings account *(for purchasing a property)*; **c. étranger** non-resident *or* foreign account; **c. joint** joint account (**b**) *(calcul)* calculation; **faire le c. de** *(dépenses)* to add up; *(temps restant)* to calculate; *(objets, personnes)* to count; **le c. y est** *(somme)* it's the right amount; *(objets, personnes)* they're all here; **c. à rebours** countdown (**c**) *(explication)* **demander des comptes à qn** to

ask sb for an explanation; **rendre des comptes** to explain oneself; **je n'ai de comptes à rendre à personne** I'm not answerable to anyone; **rendre c. de qch** to account for sth (**d**) *(locutions) Fam* **avoir son c.** to have had enough; **être loin du c.** *(se tromper)* to be wide of the mark; *Fam* **régler son c. à qn** to sort sb out; **on réglera nos comptes plus tard** we'll settle scores later; **apprendre qch sur le c. de qn** to learn sth about sb; **j'en ai appris de belles sur son c.!** I heard some fine things about him/her!; *Fam* **son c. est bon** he's/she's for it; **tenir c. de qch** to take sth into account; **il n'a tenu aucun c. de mes conseils** he took no heed of my advice; **c. tenu de** considering; **s'en tirer à bon c.** to get off lightly; **y trouver son c.** to get something out of it; **à ce c.-là** in that case; **au bout du c., en fin de c.** in the end; **tout c. fait** all things considered; *Prov* **les bons comptes font les bons amis** pay your debts and keep your friends
compte-gouttes [kɔ̃tgut] *nm inv* dropper; *Fig* **au c.** in dribs and drabs
compter [kɔ̃te] **1** *vt* (**a**) *(dénombrer)* to count; **on ne compte plus les mécontents** we've lost count of the malcontents; *Fig* **c. les points** to watch from the sidelines (**b**) *(donner avec parcimonie)* **il compte chaque sou** he begrudges every penny he spends; **ses jours sont comptés** his/her days are numbered (**c**) *(inclure)* to include; **sans c....** not counting...; **sans c. que...** besides the fact that...; **je le compte parmi mes meilleurs amis** I number him among my best friends (**d**) *(prévoir)* to allow; **j'ai compté 200 grammes par personne** I've allowed 200 grams per person; **c. faire qch** *(espérer)* to expect to do sth; *(avoir l'intention de)* to intend to do sth (**e**) *(facturer)* **c. qch à qn** to charge sb for sth (**f**) *Can (marquer)* to score
     2 *vi* (**a**) *(calculer)* to count; **dépenser sans c.** *(dépenser trop)* to spend money like water; **à c. du 1er janvier** (with effect) from 1 January (**b**) *(être parcimonieux)* to count the pennies (**c**) *(être important)* to count, to matter; **il compte beaucoup pour elle** he means a lot to her; **c. double** to count double; **à table, il compte pour deux** he eats enough for two (**d**) *(figurer)* **c. parmi les meilleurs** to rank among the best (**e**) **c. avec qn/qch** to reckon with sb/sth (**f**) **c. sur qn/qch** to count *or* rely on sb/sth; **j'y compte bien!** I should hope so!; *Fam* **compte là-dessus et bois de l'eau!** you'll be lucky!
     3 se compter *vpr* **les membres de cette secte se comptent par milliers** this sect has thousands of members
compte rendu *(pl* **comptes rendus)** [kɔ̃trɑ̃dy] *nm* report; *(d'un roman, d'un film)* review; *(d'une réunion)* minutes
compte-tours [kɔ̃ttur] *nm inv* rev counter
compteur [kɔ̃tœr] *nm* meter; **c. d'eau/d'électricité/à gaz** water/electricity/gas meter; **c. (de) Geiger** Geiger counter; *Aut* **c. kilométrique** *Br* mileometer, *Am* odometer; *Can* **c. de stationnement** parking meter; *Aut* **c. de vitesse** speedometer
comptine [kɔ̃tin] *nf* nursery rhyme
comptoir [kɔ̃twar] *nm* (**a**) *(dans un magasin)* counter; *(dans un bar)* bar; **prendre une consommation au c.** to have a drink at the bar; **c. d'enregistrement** check-in desk; **c. d'information** information desk; **c. de réception** reception desk; **c. de vente** sales counter (**b**) *(dans un pays éloigné)* trading post

compulser [kɔ̃pylse] *vt (documents, livres)* to consult
comte [kɔ̃t] *nm* count; *(en Grande-Bretagne)* earl
comté [kɔ̃te] *nm* (**a**) *Hist* earldom (**b**) *(subdivision administrative)* county (**c**) *(fromage)* = type of hard cheese (**d**) *Can Pol* riding
comtesse [kɔ̃tɛs] *nf* countess
con, conne [kɔ̃, kɔn] **1** *adj très Fam* (**a**) *(stupide) Br* bloody *or Am* goddamn stupid; *Fam* **être c. comme la lune** *ou* **un balai** to be *Br* as thick as two short planks *or Am* as dumb as they come; **c'est pas c.!** that's pretty smart! (**b**) *(facile)* **c'est tout c.!** it's dead easy!
2 *nm,f très Fam* stupid bastard, *f* stupid bitch; **faire le c.** to arse around; **pauvre c.!** stupid bastard!; **à la c.** *(ordinateur, voiture)* crap, lousy; *(idée, histoire) Br* bloody *or Am* goddamn stupid
3 *nm Vulg (sexe)* cunt
conard [kɔnar] *nm très Fam* jerk
conasse [kɔnas] *nf très Fam* silly bitch
concasser [kɔ̃kase] *vt (roche)* to crush; *(poivre)* to grind
concave [kɔ̃kav] *adj* concave
concéder [34] [kɔ̃sede] *vt* (**a**) *(privilège, droit, terrain, concession)* **c. qch à qn** to grant sb sth, to grant sth to sb (**b**) *(reconnaître)* **c. qu'on a tort** to admit that one is wrong; **il fait chaud, je vous le concède** it's warm, I grant you (**c**) *Sport (point, but, victoire)* to concede
concentration [kɔ̃sɑ̃trasjɔ̃] *nf* concentration
concentrationnaire [kɔ̃sɑ̃trasjɔnɛr] *adj* of concentration camps; **la vie c.** life in a concentration camp
concentré, -e [kɔ̃sɑ̃tre] **1** *adj* (**a**) *(solution)* concentrated; *(lait)* condensed (**b**) *(intellectuellement)* **il était très c.** he was concentrating hard
2 *nm Chim & Culin* concentrate; **c. de tomate** tomato purée
concentrer [kɔ̃sɑ̃tre] **1** *vt (troupes, forces, efforts)* to concentrate; *(rayons du soleil)* to focus
2 se concentrer *vpr* (**a**) *(être attentif)* to concentrate (**sur** on) (**b**) *(s'assembler) (foule)* to gather; **la population se concentre dans les grandes villes** the population is concentrated in the big cities
concentrique [kɔ̃sɑ̃trik] *adj* concentric
concept [kɔ̃sɛpt] *nm* concept
concepteur, -trice [kɔ̃sɛptœr, -tris] *nm,f* designer; **c. graphiste** graphic designer; **c. rédacteur** copywriter; **c. de sites Web** web designer
conception [kɔ̃sɛpsjɔ̃] *nf* (**a**) *(d'un enfant, d'une idée)* conception (**b**) *(idée)* concept (**c**) *(création)* design; **c. assistée par ordinateur** computer-aided *or* computer-assisted design; **c. graphique** graphic design; **c. de sites Web** web design
concernant [kɔ̃sɛrnɑ̃] *prép* concerning
concerner [kɔ̃sɛrne] *vt* to concern; **en ce qui me concerne** as far as I am concerned; **cela ne vous concerne pas** *(cela ne vous regarde pas)* it's none of your business; *(vous n'êtes pas visé)* it doesn't concern you
concert [kɔ̃sɛr] *nm* (**a**) *(de musique)* concert (**b**) *(accord)* **agir de c. avec qn** to act jointly with sb
concertation [kɔ̃sɛrtasjɔ̃] *nf* consultation
concerté, -e [kɔ̃sɛrte] *adj (action)* concerted
concerter [kɔ̃sɛrte] **1** *vt (projet)* to devise together
2 se concerter *vpr* to consult together
concertiste [kɔ̃sɛrtist] *nmf* concert performer
concerto [kɔ̃sɛrto] *nm* concerto; **c. pour violon** violin concerto

concession [kɔ̃sɛsjɔ̃] *nf* (**a**) *(compromis)* concession; **faire des concessions** to make concessions; **sans concessions** uncompromising (**b**) *(attribution) (de terrain)* granting (**c**) *(terrain)* concession; *(au cimetière)* plot (**d**) *(droit exclusif de vente)* dealership
concessionnaire [kɔ̃sɛsjɔnɛr] *nmf* dealer
concevable [kɔ̃səvabl] *adj* conceivable
concevoir [60] [kɔ̃səvwar] **1** *vt* (**a**) *(enfant, plan, idée)* to conceive; *(produit)* to design (**b**) *(comprendre)* to understand; **je conçois que tu sois fâché, mais...** I can understand *or* see why you are angry, but...; **c'est ainsi que je conçois l'amour** this is my idea of love (**c**) *(éprouver)* **c. de l'amitié pour qn** to take a liking to sb
2 se concevoir *vpr* **ça se conçoit** that's understandable
concierge [kɔ̃sjɛrʒ] *nmf (d'immeuble, d'appartements) & Scol Br* caretaker, *Am* janitor; *(dans un hôtel)* porter; *Fam* **c'est une vraie c.** she's a terrible gossip
concile [kɔ̃sil] *nm Rel* council
conciliabule [kɔ̃siljabyl] *nm (conversation)* confab
conciliant, -e [kɔ̃siljɑ̃, -ɑ̃t] *adj* conciliatory
conciliation [kɔ̃siljasjɔ̃] *nf* reconciliation
concilier [66] [kɔ̃silje] **1** *vt (deux choses)* to reconcile; **c. sa vie professionnelle et sa vie de famille** to balance one's professional life with one's family life
2 se concilier *vpr* (**a**) *(être compatible)* **se c. avec** to go with (**b**) **se c. qn** *ou* **la faveur de qn** to win sb's goodwill
concis, -e [kɔ̃si, -iz] *adj* concise
concision [kɔ̃sizjɔ̃] *nf* conciseness; **avec c.** concisely
concitoyen, -enne [kɔ̃sitwajɛ̃, -ɛn] *nm,f* fellow citizen
concluant, -e [kɔ̃klyɑ̃, -ɑ̃t] *adj* conclusive; **peu c.** inconclusive
conclure [17a] [kɔ̃klyr] **1** *vt* (**a**) *(terminer)* to conclude, to end (**par** with) (**b**) *(accord, pacte)* to finalize; *(marché)* to clinch; **marché conclu!, affaire conclue!** it's a deal! (**c**) *(déduire)* to conclude (**de** from); **dois-je en c. que...?** am I to conclude that...?
2 conclure à *vt ind* **ils ont conclu au suicide/meurtre** they concluded it was suicide/murder
conclusion [kɔ̃klyzjɔ̃] *nf* (**a**) *(fin) (d'un discours, d'une réunion)* conclusion, end (**b**) *(déduction)* conclusion; **tirer une c. de qch** to draw a conclusion from sth; *Fam* **c., l'échafaudage s'est écroulé** the result was that the scaffolding collapsed
concocter [kɔ̃kɔkte] *vt Fam* to concoct
concombre [kɔ̃kɔ̃br] *nm* cucumber
concordance [kɔ̃kɔrdɑ̃s] *nf* (**a**) *(de preuves, de témoignages, de dates)* tallying (**b**) *Gram* **c. des temps** sequence of tenses
concorder [kɔ̃kɔrde] *vi (preuves, dates, témoignages)* to tally (**avec** with)
concourir [22] [kɔ̃kurir] *vi* (**a**) *Sport* to compete (**b**) *(lignes)* to converge
2 concourir à *vt ind* **c. à qch/à faire qch** to contribute to sth/to doing sth
concours [kɔ̃kur] *nm* (**a**) *(compétition)* competition, contest; *(examen)* competitive examination; **c. agricole/hippique** agricultural/horse show; **c. de beauté** beauty contest; **c. d'entrée (à)** entrance examination (to) (**b**) *(aide)* aid, assistance; **avec le c. de** with the participation of, in association with (**c**) **c. de circonstances** combination of circumstances; **par un heureux c. de circonstances** by a lucky coincidence

Concours

Unlike an ordinary examination, passing a "concours" does not lead to a degree, but rather to a teaching post in the state education system (for example the "**CAPES**" and "**agrégation**", *see boxes at these entries*), an appointment or promotion in the civil service, or a place in a "**Grande École**" (*see box at* **école**). "Concours" are extremely competitive examinations, and the quota of successful candidates is determined in advance. They are usually held over a period of several days, and comprise a series of written and oral examinations requiring a high level of preparation.

concret, -ète [kɔ̃krɛ, -ɛt] **1** *adj* concrete **2** *nm* **ce que je veux, c'est du c.** what I want is something concrete *or* something I can get my teeth into

concrètement [kɔ̃krɛtmɑ̃] *adv* in concrete terms

concrétiser [kɔ̃kretize] **1** *vt (rêve)* to realize; *(projet, promesse)* to carry out **2 se concrétiser** *vpr* to materialize

conçu, -e *voir* concevoir

concubin, -e [kɔ̃kybɛ̃, -in] *nm,f Jur* cohabitant

concubinage [kɔ̃kybinaʒ] *nm* cohabitation; **vivre en c.** to cohabit

concupiscent, -e [kɔ̃kypisɑ̃, -ɑ̃t] *adj* concupiscent

concurrence [kɔ̃kyrɑ̃s] *nf* (**a**) *(rivalité, concurrents)* competition; **faire c. à** to compete with; **faire jouer la c.** to shop around (**b**) **jusqu'à c. de...** up to...

concurrencer [16] [kɔ̃kyrɑ̃se] *vt* to compete with

concurrent, -e [kɔ̃kyrɑ̃, -ɑ̃t] **1** *adj (industries, produits)* competing, rival **2** *nm,f* (**a**) *Com* competitor (**b**) *(dans une épreuve, un concours)* competitor

concurrentiel, -elle [kɔ̃kyrɑ̃sjɛl] *adj* competitive

condamnation [kɔ̃danasjɔ̃] *nf* (**a**) *Jur (jugement)* conviction (**pour** for); *(peine)* sentence (**à** to); **c. à mort** death sentence (**b**) *(critique)* condemnation

condamné, -e [kɔ̃dane] **1** *adj (malade)* terminally ill **2** *nm,f* convicted person; **un c. à mort** a condemned man

condamner [kɔ̃dane] *vt* (**a**) *Jur* to sentence (**à** to); **c. qn à 1000 euros d'amende** to fine sb 1,000 euros (**b**) *(obliger à)* **c. qn à qch** to force sb into sth; **être condamné à la solitude** to be condemned to loneliness; **je suis condamnée à les attendre** I have to wait for them (**c**) *(blâmer)* to condemn (**d**) *(porte)* to block up; *(pièce)* to seal up (**e**) *(interdire)* to forbid

condensateur [kɔ̃dɑ̃satœr] *nm Élec* condenser

condensation [kɔ̃dɑ̃sasjɔ̃] *nf* condensation

condensé, -e [kɔ̃dɑ̃se] **1** *adj* condensed **2** *nm* digest

condenser [kɔ̃dɑ̃se] **1** *vt (article, récit)* to condense **2 se condenser** *vpr* to condense

condescendant, -e [kɔ̃desɑ̃dɑ̃, -ɑ̃t] *adj* condescending

condescendre [kɔ̃desɑ̃dr] *vi* **c. à faire qch** to condescend to do sth

condiment [kɔ̃dimɑ̃] *nm* condiment

condisciple [kɔ̃disipl] *nmf Univ* fellow student; *Scol* schoolmate

condition [kɔ̃disjɔ̃] *nf* (**a**) *(stipulation)* condition; **sans c.** unconditionally; **à une c....** on one condition...; **à c. que tu viennes avec moi** providing *or* on condition that you come with me; **tu peux y aller à c. de rentrer pour minuit** you can go providing that *or* on condition that you're home by midnight (**b**) **conditions** *(circonstances)* conditions; *(d'une vente, d'un accord)* terms; **dans ces conditions, je n'y vais pas** if that's the way it is, I'm not going; **conditions atmosphériques** atmospheric conditions; **conditions de paiement** terms of payment; **conditions de vie/travail** living/working conditions (**c**) *(état)* condition; **être en bonne/ mauvaise c. physique** to be in good/bad shape (**d**) *(sort)* condition; **la c. humaine** the human condition; **la c. des ouvriers/des paysans** the workers'/ farmers' lot (**e**) *(classe sociale)* station, status; **une personne de c. modeste** a person from a humble background

conditionnel, -elle [kɔ̃disjɔnɛl] **1** *adj* conditional **2** *nm Gram* conditional

conditionnement [kɔ̃disjɔnmɑ̃] *nm* (**a**) *(fait d'emballer, emballage)* packaging (**b**) *Psy* conditioning

conditionner [kɔ̃disjɔne] *vt* (**a**) *(être la condition de)* to govern (**b**) *(emballer)* to package (**c**) *Psy (personne)* to condition

condoléances [kɔ̃dɔleɑ̃s] *nfpl* condolences; **présenter ses c. à qn** to offer one's condolences to sb; **toutes mes c.** (please accept) my condolences

condominium [kɔ̃dɔminjɔm] *nm Pol* condominium

condor [kɔ̃dɔr] *nm* condor

conducteur, -trice [kɔ̃dyktœr, -tris] **1** *nm,f (d'une voiture, d'un train)* driver; *(de machine)* operator; **c. de travaux** clerk of works **2** *nm Élec & Phys* conductor **3** *adj Élec & Phys* conductive

conduction [kɔ̃dyksjɔ̃] *nf Élec* conduction

conductivité [kɔ̃dyktivite] *nf Élec* conductivity

conduire [18] [kɔ̃dɥir] **1** *vt* (**a**) *(emmener)* to take; *(en voiture)* to drive, to take (**b**) *(mener) (troupeau, aveugle)* to lead (**c**) *(entraîner)* **c. qn à faire qch** to lead sb to do sth; **c. qn au désespoir/suicide** to drive sb to despair/suicide (**d**) *(voiture, camion)* to drive; *(moto)* to ride; *(bateau)* to steer (**e**) *(acheminer) (eau, gaz)* to carry (**f**) *(diriger) (opérations)* to manage, to run **2** *vi* (**a**) *(en voiture)* to drive; *(en moto)* to ride; **elle conduit bien** she's a good driver (**b**) *(sujet: porte, couloir, études)* **c. à** to lead to **3 se conduire** *vpr (se comporter)* to behave; **se c. mal** *(d'un enfant)* to misbehave; **se c. bien/mal avec qn** to behave well/badly towards sb

conduit [kɔ̃dɥi] *nm* (**a**) *(tuyau)* conduit, pipe; **c. d'aération** air duct; **c. de ventilation** ventilation shaft (**b**) *Anat* **c. auditif** auditory canal

conduite [kɔ̃dɥit] *nf* (**a**) *(de voiture, de camion)* driving; *(de moto)* riding; **leçons de c.** driving lessons; **c. à gauche/droite** *(position du volant)* left-/right-hand drive; *(sur la route)* driving on the left/right; **c. accompagnée** = learning to drive accompanied by someone holding a full driving licence; **conduite en état d'ivresse** *Br* drink-driving, *Am* drunk-driving; **c. intérieure** *Br* saloon (car), *Am* sedan; **c. sur route** driving on the open road (**b**) *(des affaires, des opérations)* management, running; *(d'une armée)* command; *(de travaux)* supervision (**c**) *(comportement)* behaviour, conduct; *Hum* **s'acheter une c.** to turn over a new leaf (**d**) *(tuyau)* pipe; **c. d'eau/de gaz** water/gas main

cône [kon] *nm* cone

confection [kɔ̃fɛksjɔ̃] *nf* (**a**) (*d'un vêtement, d'un repas*) making (**b**) (*industrie*) (ready-made) clothing industry; **vêtements de c.** ready-made clothes
confectionner [kɔ̃fɛksjɔne] *vt* to make
confédération [kɔ̃federasjɔ̃] *nf* confederation; **la C. helvétique** the Swiss Confederation
conférence [kɔ̃ferɑ̃s] *nf* (**a**) (*congrès, colloque*) conference; **c. de presse** press conference; **c. au sommet** summit (conference) (**b**) (*exposé*) lecture; **faire une c. sur...** to give a lecture on...
conférencier, -ère [kɔ̃ferɑ̃sje, -ɛr] *nm,f* lecturer
conférer [34] [kɔ̃fere] **1** *vt* (*titre*) to confer (**à** on); **l'âge confère certains privilèges** age brings with it certain privileges **2** *vi* to confer (**avec** with)
confesser [kɔ̃fɛse] **1** *vt* (**a**) *Rel* to confess (**b**) (*reconnaître*) to confess, to admit **2 se confesser** *vpr* to confess; (**aller**) **se c.** to go to confession
confession [kɔ̃fɛsjɔ̃] *nf* (**a**) *Rel & Fig* confession; *Fam* **on lui donnerait le bon Dieu sans c.** he/she looks as though butter wouldn't melt in his/her mouth (**b**) (*croyance*) denomination
confessionnal, -aux [kɔ̃fɛsjɔnal, -o] *nm* confessional
confetti [kɔ̃feti] *nm* (piece of) confetti; **confettis** confetti
confiance [kɔ̃fjɑ̃s] *nf* (**a**) (*foi*) trust, confidence; **avoir c. en qn/qch, faire c. à qn/qch** to trust sb/sth, to have confidence in sb/sth; **faites-moi c.** trust me; *Fam* (*croyez-moi*) believe me; **se sentir en c.** (**avec qn**) to feel safe (with sb); **digne de c.** trustworthy; **de c.** (*mission*) of trust; (*personne*) trustworthy (**b**) (*assurance*) confidence; **c. en soi** self-confidence; **avoir c. en soi** to be self-confident
confiant, -e [kɔ̃fjɑ̃, -ɑ̃t] *adj* (**a**) (*qui fait confiance*) trusting (**b**) (*optimiste*) confident (**dans** in) (**c**) (*qui a confiance en soi*) self-confident
confidence [kɔ̃fidɑ̃s] *nf* confidence; **faire une c./des confidences à qn** to confide in sb; **mettre qn dans la c.** to let sb into the secret
confident, -e [kɔ̃fidɑ̃, -ɑ̃t] *nm,f* confidant, *f* confidante
confidentiel, -elle [kɔ̃fidɑ̃sjɛl] *adj* confidential
confidentiellement [kɔ̃fidɑ̃sjɛlmɑ̃] *adv* confidentially
confier [66] [kɔ̃fje] **1** *vt* (**a**) (*laisser*) **c. qch à qn** to entrust sb with sth; **je leur ai confié les enfants** I left the children with them (**b**) (*dire*) **c. qch à qn** to confide sth to sb; **c. un secret à qn** to share a secret with sb **2 se confier** *vpr* **se c. à qn** to confide in sb
configuration [kɔ̃figyrasjɔ̃] *nf* (**a**) (*disposition*) configuration; (*de bâtiment*) layout; **la c. du terrain** the lie of the land (**b**) *Ordinat* configuration; **c. matérielle** hardware configuration
configurer [kɔ̃figyre] *vt Ordinat* to configure
confiné, -e [kɔ̃fine] *adj* (**a**) (*atmosphère*) enclosed; (*air*) stale (**b**) (*enfermé*) shut up
confiner [kɔ̃fine] **1** *vt* (*enfermer*) to confine, to shut up **2 confiner à** *vt ind* to border on **3 se confiner** *vpr* **se c. chez soi** to shut oneself up indoors
confins [kɔ̃fɛ̃] *nmpl* (*de région, d'État*) confines, borders; **aux c. de** on the edge of
confire [19a] [kɔ̃fir] *vt* (*dans du sucre*) to preserve, to candy; (*dans du vinaigre*) to pickle

confirmation [kɔ̃firmasjɔ̃] *nf* confirmation
confirmer [kɔ̃firme] **1** *vt* (*nouvelle, jugement*) to confirm; **c. qn dans son opinion** to confirm sb in his/her opinion **2 se confirmer** *vpr* (*nouvelle, bruit*) to be confirmed; (*tendance*) to continue
confiserie [kɔ̃fizri] *nf* (**a**) (*magasin*) *Br* sweetshop, *Am* candy store (**b**) (*bonbon*) **confiseries** *Br* sweets, *Am* candy (**c**) (*secteur*) confectionery
confiseur, -euse [kɔ̃fizœr, -øz] *nm,f* confectioner
confisquer [kɔ̃fiske] *vt* to confiscate; **c. qch à qn** to confiscate sth from sb
confit, -e [kɔ̃fi, -it] **1** *adj* (*fruits*) crystallized, candied **2** *nm* **c. d'oie/de canard** potted goose/duck
confiture [kɔ̃fityr] *nf* jam; **c. de fraises** strawberry jam; **c. d'oranges** (orange) marmalade; *Fig* **ce serait donner de la c. aux cochons** that would be throwing pearls before swine
conflictuel, -elle [kɔ̃fliktɥɛl] *adj* (*témoignages, intérêts*) conflicting; **situation conflictuelle** situation of potential conflict; **ils ont des rapports conflictuels** they have a tempestuous relationship
conflit [kɔ̃fli] *nm* conflict; **c. armé** armed conflict; **conflits sociaux** industrial disputes
confluent [kɔ̃flyɑ̃] *nm* confluence; **au c. du Cher et de la Loire** where the Cher and the Loire meet
confondre [kɔ̃fɔ̃dr] **1** *vt* (**a**) (*personnes, noms, dates*) to confuse, to mix up; **je l'ai confondu avec son frère** I mistook him for his brother; **toutes catégories confondues** all categories taken together (**b**) (*sidérer*) to astound (**c**) (*démasquer*) to confound **2 se confondre** *vpr* (**a**) (*couleurs, formes*) to merge, to blend (**en** into) (**b**) (*être similaire*) (*intérêts*) to merge (**c**) (*se répandre*) **se c. en excuses** to apologize profusely; **se c. en remerciements** to be profuse in one's thanks
conforme [kɔ̃fɔrm] *adj* (**a**) (*identique*) **copie c. à l'original** exact copy; **pour copie c.** (*sur document*) certified true copy; *Fig* **c'est la copie c. de sa mère** she's the image of her mother (**b**) (*qui correspond*) **être c. à** to be in accordance with
conformément [kɔ̃fɔrmemɑ̃] **conformément à** *prép* in accordance with
conformer [kɔ̃fɔrme] **1** *vt* to model (**à** on) **2 se conformer** *vpr* **se c. à qch** to conform to sth
conformisme [kɔ̃fɔrmism] *nm* conformism
conformiste [kɔ̃fɔrmist] *adj & nmf* conformist
conformité [kɔ̃fɔrmite] *nf* (*d'un produit aux normes*) compliance (**à** with); **en c. avec** in accordance with
confort [kɔ̃fɔr] *nm* comfort; **maison/hôtel tout c.** house/hotel with every modern convenience; **améliorer le c. d'écoute** to improve the sound quality; **c. d'emploi** (*d'un ordinateur*) user-friendliness
confortable [kɔ̃fɔrtabl] *adj* comfortable
confortablement [kɔ̃fɔrtabləmɑ̃] *adv* comfortably; **installe-toi c.** make yourself comfortable
conforter [kɔ̃fɔrte] *vt* (*position, avance*) to consolidate; **c. qn dans son opinion** to confirm sb's opinion
confrère [kɔ̃frɛr] *nm* (*de profession*) colleague; (*de société*) fellow member
confrérie [kɔ̃freri] *nf Rel* brotherhood
confrontation [kɔ̃frɔ̃tasjɔ̃] *nf* (**a**) (*face-à-face*) confrontation; *Fig* (*d'opinions, d'idéaux*) clash, conflict (**b**) (*comparaison*) comparison
confronter [kɔ̃frɔ̃te] *vt* (**a**) (*personnes*) to confront; **être confronté à** to be confronted with (**b**) (*comparer*) to compare

confucianisme [kɔ̃fysjanism] *nm* Confucianism

confus, -e [kɔ̃fy, -yz] *adj* (**a**) *(indistinct) (masse, explication, idées)* confused; *(bruit)* indistinct; *(style, texte)* obscure (**b**) *(gêné)* embarrassed

confusément [kɔ̃fyzemã] *adv* vaguely

confusion [kɔ̃fyzjɔ̃] *nf* (**a**) *(désordre)* confusion; **jeter la c. dans les esprits** to confuse people (**b**) *(méprise)* mix-up, confusion (**c**) *(gêne)* embarrassment

congé [kɔ̃ʒe] *nm* (**a**) *(vacances) Br* holiday, *Am* vacation; **en c. on holiday; un jour/une semaine de c.** a day/a week off; **congés payés** paid holiday (**b**) *(arrêt de travail)* leave; **c. de maladie** sick leave; **c. de maternité** maternity leave; **c. de paternité** paternity leave; **être en c. de maladie/maternité** to be on sick/maternity leave; **c. sans solde** unpaid leave (**c**) *(avis de renvoi)* notice; **donner son c. à qn** to give sb his/her notice; **demander son c.** to hand in one's notice (**d**) **prendre c. de qn** to take one's leave of sb

congédier [66] [kɔ̃ʒedje] *vt* to dismiss

congélateur [kɔ̃ʒelatœr] *nm* freezer

congélation [kɔ̃ʒelasjɔ̃] *nf* freezing

congeler [39] [kɔ̃ʒle] **1** *vt (aliments)* to freeze
2 se congeler *vpr* to freeze

congénital, -e, -aux, -ales [kɔ̃ʒenital, -o] *adj* congenital

congère [kɔ̃ʒɛr] *nf* snowdrift

congestion [kɔ̃ʒɛstjɔ̃] *nf* congestion; **c. cérébrale** stroke; **c. pulmonaire** congestion of the lungs

congestionné, -e [kɔ̃ʒɛstjɔne] *adj (visage)* flushed; *(routes)* congested

conglomérat [kɔ̃glɔmera] *nm* conglomerate

Congo [kɔ̃go] *nm* **le C.** the Congo

congolais, -e [kɔ̃gɔlɛ, -ɛz] **1** *adj* Congolese
2 *nm,f* **C.** Congolese
3 *nm (pâtisserie)* coconut cake

congratuler [kɔ̃gratyle] **1** *vt* to congratulate
2 se congratuler *vpr* to congratulate each other

congre [kɔ̃gr] *nm* conger (eel)

congrégation [kɔ̃gregasjɔ̃] *nf Rel* congregation

congrès [kɔ̃grɛ] *nm* conference; **le C.** *(aux États-Unis)* Congress

congru, -e [kɔ̃gry] *adj voir* **portion**

conifère [kɔnifɛr] *nm* conifer

conique [kɔnik] *adj* conical

conjecture [kɔ̃ʒɛktyr] *nf* conjecture

conjecturer [kɔ̃ʒɛktyre] *vi* to conjecture

conjoint, -e [kɔ̃ʒwɛ̃, -ɛ̃t] **1** *adj* joint
2 *nm* spouse; **les conjoints** the husband and wife

conjointement [kɔ̃ʒwɛ̃tmã] *adv* jointly

conjonctif, -ive [kɔ̃ʒɔ̃ktif, -iv] *adj* (**a**) *Gram* conjunctive (**b**) *Anat* connective

conjonction [kɔ̃ʒɔ̃ksjɔ̃] *nf* (**a**) *(union)* union; **la c. de nos efforts** our combined efforts (**b**) *Gram* conjunction; **c. de coordination/subordination** coordinating/subordinating conjunction

conjonctivite [kɔ̃ʒɔ̃ktivit] *nf* conjunctivitis

conjoncture [kɔ̃ʒɔ̃ktyr] *nf (situation)* circumstances, situation; **dans la c. actuelle** in the present circumstances

conjugaison [kɔ̃ʒygɛzɔ̃] *nf* (**a**) *(d'un verbe)* conjugation (**b**) *(union)* combination

conjugal, -e, -aux, -ales [kɔ̃ʒygal, -o] *adj (devoir)* conjugal; **bonheur c.** wedded bliss; **le domicile c.** the matrimonial home; **le lit c.** the marital bed; **la vie conjugale** married life

conjuguer [kɔ̃ʒyge] *vt* (**a**) *(verbe)* to conjugate (**b**) *(unir)* to combine

conjurer [kɔ̃ʒyre] **1** *vt* (**a**) *(implorer)* **c. qn de faire qch** to beg or implore sb to do sth; **je t'en conjure** I beg you (**b**) *(écarter) (danger, mauvais sort)* to avert, to ward off
2 se conjurer *vpr* to conspire (together) (**contre** against)

connaissance [kɔnɛsãs] *nf* (**a**) *(fait de connaître)* knowledge; **avoir c. de qch** to be aware of sth; **prendre c. de qch** to acquaint oneself with sth; **à ma c.** to my knowledge; **en (toute) c. de cause** with full knowledge of the facts (**b**) *(contact)* **faire la c. de qn** to make sb's acquaintance; **faire c. avec qn** to get to know sb; **quelqu'un de ma c.** someone I know, an acquaintance of mine (**c**) *(personne)* acquaintance (**d**) *(savoir)* knowledge; **elle a de bonnes connaissances en astronomie** she has a good knowledge of astronomy (**e**) *(conscience)* consciousness; **sans c.** unconscious

connaisseur, -euse [kɔnɛsœr, -øz] **1** *nm,f* connoisseur, expert
2 *adj* expert

connaître [20] [kɔnɛtr] **1** *vt* (**a**) *(personne, détails, endroit)* to know; **c. qn de nom/de vue** to know sb by name/by sight; **il n'y connaît rien** he doesn't know anything about it; **c'est ce livre qui l'a fait c.** this is the book that made his/her name; **tu connais la nouvelle?** have you heard the news?; **c'est mal le c.** you/they/*etc* don't know him; *Fam* **je connais la musique** *ou* **la chanson** I've heard it all before; *Fam* **si tu fais ça, je ne te connais plus** if you do that, I'll have nothing more to do with you (**b**) *(rencontrer)* to meet (**c**) *(éprouver) (famine, guerre civile)* to experience; *(amour, peur, faim)* to know; **c. des moments difficiles** to go through some difficult times; **c. un destin tragique** to have a tragic fate; **c. un succès considérable** to enjoy considerable success (**d**) *(avoir)* **ne pas c. de limites** to know no bounds
2 se connaître *vpr* (**a**) **se c. (soi-même)** to know oneself (**b**) **s'y c. en qch** to know a lot about sth (**c**) *(mutuellement)* to know each other (**d**) *(se rencontrer)* to meet

connard [kɔnar] = **conard**

conne [kɔn] *voir* **con**

connecter [kɔnɛkte] *vt Élec* to connect; *Ordinat* **connecté** *(sur Internet)* on line; **connecté en anneau/bus/étoile** in a ring/bus/star configuration

connerie [kɔnri] *nf très Fam* (**a**) *(acte stupide)* **faire une c./des conneries** to do a bloody stupid thing/ some bloody stupid things (**b**) *(remarque stupide)* bloody stupid thing; **dire** *ou* **raconter des conneries** to talk bullshit (**c**) *(caractère stupide)* stupidity

connexion [kɔnɛksjɔ̃] *nf* connection

connivence [kɔnivãs] *nf* connivance; **agir/être de c. avec qn** to act/be in connivance with sb; **des regards de c.** conniving looks

connotation [kɔnɔtasjɔ̃] *nf* connotation

connu, -e [kɔny] **1** *pp de* **connaître**
2 *adj (écrivain, chanteur)* well-known; **c'est bien c.!** everyone knows that!

conquérant, -e [kɔ̃kerã, -ãt] **1** *adj (air)* triumphant
2 *nm,f* conqueror

conquérir [7] [kɔ̃kerir] *vt (pays, territoire, sommet)* to conquer; *(marché)* to capture; **ils ont été conquis par son charme** they were won over by his/her charm

conquête [kɔ̃kɛt] *nf* conquest; **faire la c. de** *(pays)* to conquer; *(personne)* to make a conquest of; **se lancer à la c.** *(pouvoir)* to make a bid for; *(sommet)* to set out to conquer

conquis, -e *voir* **conquérir**

conquistador [kɔ̃kistadɔr] *nm* conquistador

consacré, -e [kɔ̃sakre] *adj (coutume)* established; **selon l'expression consacrée** as the saying goes; **c. par l'usage** sanctioned by usage

consacrer [kɔ̃sakre] **1** *vt* (**a**) *Rel* to consecrate (**b**) *(temps, énergie)* **c. qch à** to devote sth to; **combien de temps pouvez-vous me c.?** how much time can you spare me? (**c**) *(entériner) (coutume)* to establish; *(usage)* to sanction
2 se consacrer *vpr* **se c. à son travail/sa famille** to devote oneself to one's work/family

consanguin, -e [kɔ̃sãgɛ̃, -in] *adj* **frère c.** half-brother *(on the father's side)*; **sœur consanguine** half-sister *(on the father's side)*; **mariage c.** intermarriage

consciemment [kɔ̃sjamã] *adv* consciously

conscience [kɔ̃sjãs] *nf* (**a**) *(esprit)* consciousness; **perdre/reprendre c.** to lose/regain consciousness; **avoir/prendre c. de qch** to be/become aware or conscious of sth (**b**) *(morale)* conscience; **avoir bonne/mauvaise c.** to have a clear/bad conscience; **se donner bonne c.** to ease one's conscience; **avoir la c. tranquille, avoir sa c. pour soi** to have a clear conscience; **avoir qch sur la c.** to have sth on one's conscience (**c**) **c. professionnelle** professional integrity

consciencieusement [kɔ̃sjãsjøzmã] *adv* conscientiously

consciencieux, -euse [kɔ̃sjãsjø, -øz] *adj* conscientious

conscient, -e [kɔ̃sjã, -ãt] *adj* (**a**) *(décision, choix)* conscious; **être c. de qch** to be aware or conscious of sth (**b**) *(lucide)* conscious

consécration [kɔ̃sekrasjɔ̃] *nf* (**a**) *(d'une église, d'un évêque)* consecration; *(d'un prêtre)* ordination (**b**) *(aboutissement) (des efforts, d'une œuvre)* recognition; *(d'une carrière)* crowning moment

consécutif, -ive [kɔ̃sekytif, -iv] *adj* consecutive; **c. à** resulting from

consécutivement [kɔ̃sekytivmã] *adv* consecutively; **c. à** following

conseil [kɔ̃sɛj] *nm* (**a**) *(recommandation)* piece of advice; **des conseils** advice; **donner un c. à qn** to give sb a piece of advice; **être de bon c.** to give good advice (**b**) *(assemblée)* council, committee; *(d'une entreprise)* board; *(réunion)* meeting; **c. d'administration** board of directors; **c. de classe** = staff meeting with participation of class representatives to discuss school matters; **C. constitutionnel** = independent body which pronounces on the constitutionality of government decisions; **c. de discipline** disciplinary committee; **C. d'État** Council of State; **C. de l'Europe** Council of Europe; *Can* **C. Exécutif** ≃ Cabinet; **C. général** regional council; **c. de guerre** *(réunion)* council of war; *(tribunal)* court martial; **le c. des ministres** ≃ the Cabinet; *UE* the (European) Council of Ministers; **c. municipal** local council; *Can* **C. national des autochtones du Canada** Native Council of Canada; **C. de sécurité** *(de l'ONU)* Security Council (**c**) *(personne)* consultant **c. en communication** PR consultant; **c. en gestion** management consultant; **c. en recrutement** recruitment consultant

Conseil de classe

The French school year is divided into three terms. In secondary schools, a "conseil de classe", or staff meeting, is held at the end of each term to discuss the progress made by pupils in a given class. A report containing the marks obtained during the term with teachers' comments is filled in for each pupil. The "conseil de classe" is initially held behind closed doors, attended by the teachers of a given class and the head teacher, and then with two elected class representatives present. During the last "conseil de classe" of the year, decisions are taken such as which pupils repeat a year and which should change courses.

conseiller¹ [kɔ̃seje] *vt* (**a**) *(guider) (personne)* to advise; **il m'a bien conseillé** he gave me good or sound advice (**b**) *(recommander)* **c. qch à qn** to recommend sth to sb; **c. à qn de faire qch** to advise sb to do sth; **il est conseillé de ne pas fumer** it is advisable not to smoke

conseiller², -ère [kɔ̃seje, -ɛr] *nm,f* (**a**) *(spécialiste)* adviser, consultant; **c. en gestion** management consultant; **c. d'insertion et de probation** probation officer; **c. d'orientation** *Br* careers adviser, *Am* career counselor; **c. technique** technical adviser (**b**) *Pol* *(d'un chef d'État)* advisor; **c. général** regional councillor; **c. municipal** local councillor

consensuel, -elle [kɔ̃sãsɥɛl] *adj* consensual

consensus [kɔ̃sɛsys] *nm* consensus (of opinion)

consentant, -e [kɔ̃sãtã, -ãt] *adj* consenting; **être c.** to consent

consentement [kɔ̃sãtmã] *nm* consent; **donner son c. à qch** to give one's consent to sth; **divorce par c. mutuel** divorce by mutual consent

consentir [64a] [kɔ̃sãtir] **1** *vi* to consent, to agree (**à qch/à faire qch** to sth/to do sth); **je consens (à ce) qu'il vienne** I consent to his coming
2 *vt* **c. un prêt à qn** to grant sb a loan; **c. une remise à qn** to allow sb a discount

conséquence [kɔ̃sekãs] *nf* consequence; **une erreur sans c.** an inconsequential mistake; **tirer les conséquences de qch** to draw conclusions from sth; **la baisse des taxes a eu pour c. de créer des emplois** the tax reduction resulted in the creation of jobs; **agir en c.** to take appropriate action; **en c. (de quoi)** consequently

conséquent, -e [kɔ̃sekã, -ãt] *adj* (**a**) *(cohérent)* consistent (**b**) *Fam (somme)* tidy (**c**) **par c.** consequently

conservateur, -trice [kɔ̃sɛrvatœr, -tris] **1** *adj Pol* Conservative
2 *nm,f* (**a**) *(de musée)* curator; *(de bibliothèque)* librarian (**b**) *Pol* Conservative
3 *nm (alimentaire)* preservative; **sans c.** *(sur emballage)* free of preservatives

conservation [kɔ̃sɛrvasjɔ̃] *nf (de fruits, de viande)* preserving; *(de bâtiments)* preservation; *(d'archives)* keeping

conservatoire [kɔ̃sɛrvatwar] *nm (de musique, d'art dramatique)* school, academy; **le C. (de Paris)** the (Paris) Conservatoire; **le C. des arts et métiers** = museum and college of applied sciences

conserve [kɔ̃sɛrv] *nf (aliment)* canned or *Br* tinned food; *(en bocal)* preserve; *(boîte)* can, *Br* tin; **en c.** canned, *Br* tinned; *(en bocal)* preserved; **mettre qch en c.** to can sth, *Br* to tin sth; *(en bocal)* to preserve sth

conserver [kɔ̃sɛrve] **1** *vt* (**a**) *(aliment)* to keep; *(dans le sel, le vinaigre)* to preserve; **c. à l'abri de la lumière** *(sur emballage)* keep away from direct sunlight; **c. au froid** *(sur emballage)* keep in a cold place; **être bien conservé** *(personne)* to be well preserved (**b**) *(garder) (objet, emploi, sang-froid)* to keep; *(droits)* to retain; **c. un bon souvenir de qch** to have good memories of sth
2 se conserver *vpr (aliment)* to keep
considérable [kɔ̃siderabl] *adj* considerable
considérablement [kɔ̃siderabləmɑ̃] *adv* considerably
considération [kɔ̃siderasjɔ̃] *nf* (**a**) *(examen)* **prendre qch en c.** to take sth into consideration; *(offre, demande d'emploi)* to consider sth (**b**) *(estime)* regard, esteem; **agir avec/sans c.** to act considerately/inconsiderately; **jouir d'une grande c.** to be highly regarded (**c**) **considérations (sur)** *(observations)* observations (on); **je ne peux pas entrer dans ces considérations** I can't go into that
considérer [34] [kɔ̃sidere] **1** *vt* (**a**) *(étudier, regarder)* to consider; **tout bien considéré** all things considered (**b**) *(estimer)* **c. que** to consider that; **c. qn/qch comme...** to regard sb/sth as...
2 se considérer *vpr* **se c. désavantagé** to consider oneself disadvantaged; **se c. comme un artiste/un révolutionnaire** to consider oneself an artist/a revolutionary
consigne [kɔ̃siɲ] *nf* (**a**) *(ordres)* orders; **avoir pour c. de...** to have orders to...; **passer la c.** to pass on the orders; **consignes en cas d'incendie** fire notice (**b**) *(punition) Mil* confinement to barracks; *Scol* detention (**c**) *(pour les bagages)* **c. (à bagages)** *Br* left-luggage office, *Am* checkroom; **c. automatique** lockers (**d**) *(de bouteille)* deposit
consigner [kɔ̃siɲe] *vt* (**a**) *(bouteille, emballage)* to charge a deposit on; **bouteille consignée** returnable bottle (**b**) *(noter)* to record (**c**) *(punir) (soldat)* to confine to barracks; *(élève)* to keep in (**d**) *(laisser à la consigne) Br* to deposit in the left-luggage office, *Am* to check
consistance [kɔ̃sistɑ̃s] *nf (d'un corps)* consistency; **sans c.** *(pâte, fromage)* too soft; *Fig (personne)* bland; *(personnage de fiction)* insubstantial
consistant, -e [kɔ̃sistɑ̃, -ɑ̃t] *adj (substance)* firm; *(sauce, soupe)* thick; *(repas)* substantial; *(argument)* sound
consister [kɔ̃siste] *vi* **c. en qch** to consist of sth; **c. à faire qch** to consist in doing sth
consœur [kɔ̃sœr] *nf (female)* colleague
consolation [kɔ̃sɔlasjɔ̃] *nf* consolation, comfort
console [kɔ̃sɔl] *nf* console; **c. de jeux** games console; **c. de visualisation** *(visual)* display unit
consoler [kɔ̃sɔle] **1** *vt* to console, to comfort; **si ça peut te c.** if that's any consolation to you
2 se consoler *vpr* to console oneself; *(l'un l'autre)* to console each other; **se c. d'une perte/d'un échec** to get over a loss/a failure; **elles se sont consolées mutuellement** they consoled each other
consolidation [kɔ̃sɔlidasjɔ̃] *nf* (**a**) *aussi Fig (renforcement)* strengthening (**b**) *Méd (d'une fracture)* knitting
consolider [kɔ̃sɔlide] **1** *vt* (**a**) *aussi Fig (renforcer)* to strengthen (**b**) *(fracture)* to knit (**c**) *Fin (dette)* to fund; *(bilan)* to consolidate
2 se consolider *vpr* (**a**) *(régime)* to strengthen its position; *(amitié, liens)* to become stronger (**b**) *(fracture)* to knit

consommateur, -trice [kɔ̃sɔmatœr, -tris] *nm,f Écon* consumer; *(dans un restaurant, un café)* customer; **je suis un grand c. de café** I'm a great coffee drinker; *Écon* **c. final** end-user
consommation [kɔ̃sɔmasjɔ̃] *nf* (**a**) *(d'électricité, de pétrole, de nourriture)* consumption; *(d'une voiture)* (fuel) consumption; **faire une grande c. de qch** to consume great quantities of sth (**b**) *(dans un café)* drink (**c**) *(du mariage)* consummation
consommé, -e [kɔ̃sɔme] **1** *nm Culin* consommé
2 *adj (accompli)* consummate
consommer [kɔ̃sɔme] **1** *vt* (**a**) *(électricité, pétrole, nourriture)* to consume; **à c. avant fin novembre** *(sur emballage)* best before end November; **cette voiture consomme trop (d'essence)** this car is heavy on fuel; **c. au bar** to drink at the bar (**b**) *(mariage)* to consummate
2 se consommer *vpr* **ce plat se consomme froid** this dish is eaten cold
consonance [kɔ̃sɔnɑ̃s] *nf Mus & Ling* consonance; **langue à c. germanique** German-sounding language
consonne [kɔ̃sɔn] *nf* consonant
consortium [kɔ̃sɔrsjɔm] *nm Com & Fin* consortium
conspirateur, -trice [kɔ̃spiratœr, -tris] **1** *nm,f* conspirator
2 *adj* conspiratorial
conspiration [kɔ̃spirasjɔ̃] *nf* conspiracy, plot
conspirer [kɔ̃spire] *vi* (**a**) *(comploter)* to conspire, to plot (**contre** against) (**b**) *(contribuer)* to conspire (**à faire qch** to do sth)
constamment [kɔ̃stamɑ̃] *adv* constantly
constance [kɔ̃stɑ̃s] *nf* (**a**) *(dans une tâche)* perseverance; *(en amour)* constancy; **travailler avec c.** to work steadily (**b**) *(de la température, d'un phénomène)* constancy
constant, -e [kɔ̃stɑ̃, -ɑ̃t] *adj* (**a**) *(souci, température, va-et-vient)* constant; *(effort)* persistent; *(amitié, intérêt)* steady (**b**) *(personne)* **être c. dans ses opinions** to stick to one's opinions; **être c. dans ses amitiés** to be faithful to one's friends
2 *nf* **constante** (**a**) *(en sciences)* constant (**b**) *(caractéristique)* stable *or* permanent trait
constat [kɔ̃sta] *nm* (**a**) *Jur* official report; **dresser un c. d'accident** to write out an accident report; **c. amiable** = report of road accident agreed by parties involved (**b**) *(bilan)* assessment; **faire un c. d'échec** to acknowledge failure
constatation [kɔ̃statasjɔ̃] *nf* (**a**) *(observation)* observation; **c'est une simple c.** it's a simple statement of fact (**b**) **constatations** *(d'une enquête)* findings
constater [kɔ̃state] *vt* (**a**) *(observer)* to note (**que** that); **vous pouvez c. vous-même qu'elle est partie** you can see for yourself that she's gone (**b**) *Jur (enregistrer)* to record; *(décès)* to certify; *(dégâts)* to assess
constellation [kɔ̃stelasjɔ̃] *nf* constellation
constellé, -e [kɔ̃stele] *adj* **un ciel c. d'étoiles** a star-studded sky; **c. de taches** spattered with stains
consternant, -e [kɔ̃stɛrnɑ̃, -ɑ̃t] *adj (nouvelle)* dismaying; **d'une bêtise consternante** appallingly stupid
consternation [kɔ̃stɛrnasjɔ̃] *nf* dismay, consternation; **jeter la c. dans/parmi** to fill with dismay; **à la c. générale** to everyone's dismay
consterner [kɔ̃stɛrne] *vt* to dismay
constipation [kɔ̃stipasjɔ̃] *nf* constipation
constipé, -e [kɔ̃stipe] *adj* constipated; *Fam (mal à l'aise)* ill at ease

constituer [kɔ̃stitɥe] **1** *vt* (**a**) *(composer)* to make up; **être constitué de** to be made up of (**b**) *(équivaloir à)* to constitute (**c**) *(comité, gouvernement, équipe)* to form; *(bibliothèque, fortune, stocks)* to build up; **c. une rente/une dot à qn** to settle an annuity/a dowry on sb
2 se constituer *vpr* (**a**) *(devenir)* **se c. prisonnier** to give oneself up; *Jur* **se c. partie civile** to bring a civil suit for damages (**b**) *(se réunir)* **se c. en commission/en association** to form a committee/an association

constitution [kɔ̃stitysjɔ̃] *nf* (**a**) *(physique, d'un pays)* constitution; **avoir une bonne c.** to have a sound constitution (**b**) *(de comité, de société, de gouvernement)* formation; *(de stocks, de bibliothèque)* building up

constitutionnel, -elle [kɔ̃stitysjɔnɛl] *adj* constitutional

constructeur [kɔ̃stryktœr] *nm (bâtisseur)* builder; **c. automobile** car manufacturer; **c. naval** shipbuilder

constructif, -ive [kɔ̃stryktif, -iv] *adj* constructive

construction [kɔ̃stryksjɔ̃] *nf* (**a**) *(d'une maison, d'une route, d'un voilier)* building, construction; *(d'une phrase)* structure; **en c.** under construction; **c. navale** shipbuilding (**b**) *(bâtiment)* building

construire [18] [kɔ̃strɥir] **1** *vt* to build, to construct; *(roman, phrase, théorie)* to construct
2 se construire *vpr Gram* **"après que" se construit avec l'indicatif** "après que" takes the indicative

consul [kɔ̃syl] *nm* consul; **le c. de France** the French consul; **c. général** consul general

consulaire [kɔ̃sylɛr] *adj* consular

consulat [kɔ̃syla] *nm (lieu)* consulate; *(charge)* consulship

consultant, -e [kɔ̃syltɑ̃, -ɑ̃t] **1** *nm,f* consultant
2 *adj* consulting; **médecin c.** consultant

consultation [kɔ̃syltasjɔ̃] *nf* (**a**) *(d'un expert, d'un médecin)* consultation; **le médecin est en c.** the doctor is with a patient; **heures de c.** consulting *or Br* surgery hours (**b**) *(de livre)* consultation (**c**) *Pol* **c. populaire** consultation of the people

consulter [kɔ̃sylte] **1** *vt* to consult
2 *vi (docteur)* to see patients, *Br* to take surgery
3 se consulter *vpr* to consult each other

consumer [kɔ̃syme] **1** *vt (brûler)* to consume; *Fig* **consumé par le remords** consumed with remorse
2 se consumer *vpr (brûler)* to burn; *Fig* **se c. d'inquiétude/de chagrin** to be consumed with worry/with grief

contact [kɔ̃takt] *nm* (**a**) *(relation, personne)* contact; **garder/perdre le c. avec qn** to keep in touch/lose touch with sb; **prendre c.** *ou* **se mettre en c. avec qn** to get in touch *or* in contact with sb; **être/entrer en c. avec qn** to be in/come into contact with sb; **être d'un c. facile/difficile** to be approachable/unapproachable; **il a changé a mon c.** he's changed since he met me (**b**) *(toucher)* contact; **au c. agréable** pleasant to the touch; **être/entrer en c. avec qch** to be in/come into contact with sth; **au c. de qch** on contact with sth (**c**) *Élec* contact (**d**) *Aut* contact; **mettre/couper le c.** to switch the ignition on/off

contacter [kɔ̃takte] *vt* to contact

contagieux, -euse [kɔ̃taʒjø, -øz] *adj (maladie, virus, personne)* contagious; *(rire, enthousiasme)* infectious

contagion [kɔ̃taʒjɔ̃] *nf Méd* contagion

container [kɔ̃tɛnɛr] *nm* container

contamination [kɔ̃taminasjɔ̃] *nf (pollution)* contamination; *Méd* infection

contaminer [kɔ̃tamine] *vt (polluer)* to contaminate; *Méd* to infect

conte [kɔ̃t] *nm* story, tale; **c. de fées** fairy tale; *Fig* **elle vit un c. de fées** her life is a fairy tale

contemplatif, -ive [kɔ̃tɑ̃platif, -iv] *adj & nm,f* contemplative

contemplation [kɔ̃tɑ̃plasjɔ̃] *nf* contemplation; **être en c. devant qch** to gaze at sth

contempler [kɔ̃tɑ̃ple] **1** *vt* to contemplate, to gaze at
2 se contempler *vpr (soi-même)* to gaze at oneself

contemporain, -e [kɔ̃tɑ̃pɔrɛ̃, -ɛn] **1** *adj* (**a**) *(moderne)* contemporary (**b**) *(du même âge)* contemporary (**de** with); **être c. de qn** to be a contemporary of sb; **ils sont contemporains** they are contemporaries
2 *nm,f* contemporary

contenance [kɔ̃tnɑ̃s] *nf* (**a**) *(d'un récipient)* capacity (**b**) *(allure)* attitude, bearing; **faire qch pour se donner une c.** to do sth to give an impression of composure; **faire bonne c.** to put on a bold front; **perdre c.** to lose one's composure

contenant [kɔ̃tnɑ̃] *nm* container

conteneur [kɔ̃tnœr] *nm* container

contenir [70] [kɔ̃tnir] **1** *vt* (**a**) *(renfermer)* to contain; **le théâtre contient mille places** the theatre holds *or* seats a thousand (**b**) *(foule, ennemi)* to contain, to keep in check; *(colère)* to curb; *(larmes)* to hold back
2 se contenir *vpr* to contain oneself

content, -e [kɔ̃tɑ̃, -ɑ̃t] **1** *adj (satisfait)* happy, content (**de** with); *(joyeux)* glad (**de faire** to do); **je suis très c. de vous voir** I'm very pleased *or* glad to see you; **être c. de soi** to be pleased with oneself; **tu peux être c. de toi, tu as vu ce que tu as fait!** I hope you're happy, just look what you've done!; **non c. de mentir, il vole!** not content with lying, he steals as well!; **je suis vraiment c. que vous soyez venu** I'm so glad you've come; *Fam* **et si tu n'es pas c., c'est pareil** you can like it or lump it
2 *nm* **manger tout son c.** to eat one's fill; **avoir son c. de qch** to have had one's fill of sth

contentement [kɔ̃tɑ̃tmɑ̃] *nm (état)* satisfaction, contentment; **un sourire de c.** a contented smile

contenter [kɔ̃tɑ̃te] **1** *vt (personne)* to satisfy, to please
2 se contenter *vpr* **se c. de qch/de faire qch** to content oneself with sth/with doing sth; **se c. de peu** to be easily satisfied; **je me contenterai de faire remarquer que...** I will merely point out that...

contentieux [kɔ̃tɑ̃sjø] *nm (querelle)* dispute; *Jur* litigation; *(service)* legal department; **avoir un c. avec qn** to be in dispute with sb

contenu, -e [kɔ̃tny] **1** *nm (d'un paquet, d'une bouteille, d'une boîte)* contents; *(d'une lettre, d'un livre)* content
2 *adj (émotion)* restrained

conter [kɔ̃te] *vt* to tell; **elle ne s'en laisse pas c.** you can't fool her

contestataire [kɔ̃tɛstatɛr] **1** *adj Pol* anti-establishment; *(mécontent)* rebellious
2 *nmf Pol* protester; *(mécontent)* rebel

contestation [kɔ̃tɛstasjɔ̃] *nf* (**a**) *(protestation)* protest; **il y a matière** *ou* **sujet à c.** there are grounds for dispute; **sans c. possible** beyond dispute (**b**) *Pol* protest

conteste [kɔ̃tɛst] **sans conteste** *adv* indisputably

contester [kɔ̃tɛste] *vt* to dispute; **je lui conteste le droit de...** I dispute his/her right to...; **elle est très contestée** she is very controversial; **faire qch sans c.** to do sth without protest

conteur, -euse [kɔ̃tœr, -øz] *nm,f* storyteller
contexte [kɔ̃tɛkst] *nm* context; **dans le c. de** in the context of; **hors c.** out of context
contextualiser [kɔ̃tɛkstɥalize] *vt* to contextualize
contigu, -ë [kɔ̃tigy] *adj (maisons, pièces)* adjoining; **c. à qch** adjoining sth
continent [kɔ̃tinɑ̃] *nm* (**a**) *(étendue)* continent; **l'Ancien/le Nouveau C.** the Old/the New World (**b**) *(par rapport à une île)* mainland
continental, -e, -aux, -ales [kɔ̃tinɑ̃tal, -o] **1** *adj (climat, plateau)* continental; *(par rapport à une île)* mainland
2 *nm,f* mainlander
contingent [kɔ̃tɛ̃ʒɑ̃] *nm* (**a**) *Mil* contingent; **les soldats du c.** the conscripted soldiers (**b**) *(quota)* quota
continu, -e [kɔ̃tiny] *adj (ligne, effort)* continuous; *(soin, attention)* constant; **en c.** continuously; *Ordinat* **papier en c.** continuous paper
continuation [kɔ̃tinɥasjɔ̃] *nf* continuation; **bonne c.!** all the best!
continuel, -elle [kɔ̃tinɥɛl] *adj (ininterrompu)* continuous; *(qui se répète)* continual
continuellement [kɔ̃tinɥɛlmɑ̃] *adv (de façon ininterrompue)* continuously; *(de façon répétitive)* continually
continuer [kɔ̃tinɥe] **1** *vt (études, efforts, politique)* to continue (with), to carry on with; *(trait, route)* to continue; **c. sa route** *ou* **son chemin** to continue on one's way; **continuez!** carry on!; **si tu continues comme ça,...** if you carry on like that,...
2 *vi* to continue
3 continuer à *ou* **de** *vt ind* **c. à** *ou* **de faire qch** to continue doing sth, to carry on doing sth; **si tu continues à m'embêter, je vais me fâcher** if you carry *or* keep on annoying me I'm going to get cross; **je continue à** *ou* **de me demander si...** I keep wondering if...
4 se continuer *vpr* to continue
continuité [kɔ̃tinɥite] *nf (d'une action)* continuity; *(d'une tradition, d'une politique)* continuation
contondant, -e [kɔ̃tɔ̃dɑ̃, -ɑ̃t] *adj* blunt
contorsion [kɔ̃tɔrsjɔ̃] *nf* contortion
contorsionner [kɔ̃tɔrsjɔne] **se contorsionner** *vpr* to contort oneself
contorsionniste [kɔ̃tɔrsjɔnist] *nmf* contortionist
contour [kɔ̃tur] *nm* (**a**) *(silhouette)* outline (**b**) *Suisse (virage)* bend
contourner [kɔ̃turne] *vt* to go round; *Fig (loi, difficulté)* to get round
contraceptif, -ive [kɔ̃trasɛptif, -iv] *Méd* **1** *adj* contraceptive
2 *nm* contraceptive; **c. oral** oral contraceptive
contraception [kɔ̃trasɛpsjɔ̃] *nf* contraception; **c. d'urgence** emergency contraception
contractant, -e [kɔ̃traktɑ̃, -ɑ̃t] *adj Jur (partie)* contracting
contracté, -e [kɔ̃trakte] *adj* (**a**) *(muscles, visage, personne)* tense (**b**) *Ling* contracted
contracter[1] [kɔ̃trakte] *vt* (**a**) *(alliance, dette)* to contract; *(assurance)* to take out (**b**) *(habitude, goût, manie)* to acquire; *(maladie)* to contract
contracter[2] **1** *vt (muscles, visage)* to tense; **visage contracté par la douleur** face drawn with pain
2 se contracter *vpr* (**a**) *(cœur, muscle)* to contract; *(personne)* to tense (up) (**b**) *Ling* to contract
contraction [kɔ̃traksjɔ̃] *nf* (**a**) *(d'un muscle, d'un gaz, d'un mot)* contraction; **contractions** *(à l'accouche-*

ment) contractions (**b**) *Scol* **c. de texte** précis; **faire une c. de texte** to summarize a text
contractuel, -elle [kɔ̃traktɥɛl] **1** *adj (obligations)* contractual; **agent c.** = contractor working for the local council
2 *nm,f (auxiliaire de police) Br* ≃ traffic warden, *Am* ≃ traffic policeman, *f* traffic policewoman
contracture [kɔ̃traktyr] *nf Méd* spasm
contradiction [kɔ̃tradiksjɔ̃] *nf* (**a**) *(opposition)* contradiction; **avoir l'esprit de c.** to be contrary; **il ne supporte pas la c.** he can't stand being contradicted (**b**) *(illogisme)* contradiction; **être en c. avec qch** to contradict sth; **être en c. avec soi-même** to contradict oneself
contradictoire [kɔ̃tradiktwar] *adj* contradictory (**avec** to); **débat c.** debate
contraignant, -e [kɔ̃trɛɲ ɑ̃, -ɑ̃t] *adj* restricting
contraindre [23] [kɔ̃trɛ̃dr] **1** *vt (obliger)* **c. qn à faire qch** to force *or* compel sb to do sth; **être contraint de faire qch** to be forced *or* compelled to do sth; **contraint et forcé** under duress
2 se contraindre *vpr* **se c. à faire qch** to force oneself to do sth
contrainte [kɔ̃trɛ̃t] *nf* (**a**) *(obligation, limitation, retenue)* constraint; **parler sans c.** to speak freely (**b**) *(force)* force; **obtenir qch par la c.** to get sth by force; **faire qch sous la c.** to do sth under duress (**c**) *Tech* stress
contraire [kɔ̃trɛr] **1** *adj* (**a**) *(opposé) (intérêts, avis)* conflicting; **vent c.** headwind; **c. à** contrary to; **en sens c.** in the opposite direction (**b**) *(défavorable)* **le sort nous/m'est c.** fate is against us/me
2 *nm* opposite; **le c. de** the opposite of; **sa sœur est tout le c. de lui** his sister is the exact opposite of him; **(bien) au c.** on the contrary
contrairement [kɔ̃trɛrmɑ̃] **contrairement à** *prép* contrary to; **c. à moi,...** unlike me,...
contralto [kɔ̃tralto] *nm Mus* contralto
contrariant, -e [kɔ̃trarjɑ̃, -ɑ̃t] *adj* (**a**) *(personne)* contrary; **elle n'est pas contrariante** she's easy-going; *Péj* she says yes to everything (**b**) *(situation)* annoying, irritating
contrarier [66] [kɔ̃trarje] *vt* (**a**) *(ennuyer)* to annoy, to irritate (**b**) *(contrecarrer) (projets, desseins)* to thwart, to frustrate
contrariété [kɔ̃trarjete] *nf* annoyance; **éprouver une vive c.** to feel extremely annoyed
contraste [kɔ̃trast] *nm* contrast; **faire c. (avec)** to contrast (with); **par c. avec** in contrast to; **effet de c.** contrasting effect
contrasté, -e [kɔ̃traste] *adj* (**a**) *(différencié)* contrasting; **photo bien/mal contrastée** photo with the right amount of/with not enough contrast (**b**) *Ordinat* highlighted
contraster [kɔ̃traste] *vi* to contrast (**avec** with)
contrat [kɔ̃tra] *nm* (**a**) *(accord)* contract, agreement; **passer un c. (avec qn)** to enter into an agreement (with sb); **c. d'assurance** contract of insurance; **c. collectif** collective agreement; **c. à durée déterminée/indéterminée** fixed-term/permanent contract; **c. emploi-solidarité** = short-term contract subsidized by the government; **c. de mariage** marriage contract; **c. première embauche** = employment contract for people under 26 which could be terminated without justification in the first two years, proposed by the French government but abandoned under public

pressure; **c. de travail** *Br* contract of employment, *Am* labor contract (**b**) *(au bridge)* contract

contravention [kɔ̃travɑ̃sjɔ̃] *nf (envers un règlement)* contravention; *(amende)* fine; *(pour stationnement non autorisé) (amende)* parking fine; *(avis)* (parking) ticket; **être en c.** to be in breach of the law

contre [kɔ̃tr] **1** *prép* (**a**) *(se battre, jouer)* against; **se fâcher c. qn** to get angry with sb; **la campagne c. l'avortement** the anti-abortion campaign; **je suis c.!** I'm against it!; **je n'ai rien c., je ne suis pas c.** I've got nothing against it; **par c.** on the other hand (**b**) *(pour se protéger de)* **sirop c. la toux** cough mixture; **être assuré c. le vol** to be insured against theft (**c**) *(en échange de)* (in exchange) for; **échanger une chose c. une autre** to exchange one thing for another (**d**) *(en proportion de)* to; **parier à cinq c. un** to bet five to one; **10 voix c. 2** 10 votes to 2 (**e**) *(en contact avec)* against; **s'appuyer c. qch** to lean against sth; **leur maison est tout c. la mienne** their house is right next to mine; **joue c. joue** cheek to cheek; **le radiateur est allumé, assieds-toi tout c.** the heater is on, sit right next to it (**f**) *(en dépit de)* **c. toute logique** against all logic; **c. toute attente** against all expectations (**g**) *(en comparaison de)* compared to; **la livre était à 1,5 euros c. 1,3 euros le mois précédent** the pound stood at 1.5 euros compared to 1.3 euros the previous month **2** *nm* (**a**) **peser le pour et le c.** to weigh up the pros and cons (**b**) *(au volley, au basket)* block

contre-allée *(pl* **contre-allées**) [kɔ̃trale] *nf* sideroad

contre-attaque *(pl* **contre-attaques**) [kɔ̃tratak] *nf* counter-attack

contre-attaquer [kɔ̃tratake] *vi* to counter-attack

contrebalancer [16] [kɔ̃trəbalɑ̃se] **1** *vt (poids)* to counterbalance; *(inconvénient)* to offset **2 se contrebalancer** *vpr Fam* **se c. de qch** not to give a damn about sth

contrebande [kɔ̃trəbɑ̃d] *nf* (**a**) *(activité)* smuggling; **faire de la c.** to smuggle goods; **faire entrer des marchandises en c.** to smuggle in goods; **de c.** smuggled (**b**) *(marchandises)* contraband

contrebandier, -ère [kɔ̃trəbɑ̃dje, -ɛr] *nm,f* smuggler

contrebas [kɔ̃trəba] **en contrebas** *adv* (down) below; **en c. de** below

contrebasse [kɔ̃trəbas] *nf (instrument)* (double) bass; *(musicien)* (double) bass player

contrebassiste [kɔ̃trəbasist] *nmf* (double) bass player

contre-braquer [kɔ̃trəbrake] *vi Aut* to steer into the skid

contrecarrer [kɔ̃trəkare] *vt* to thwart

contrechamp [kɔ̃trəʃɑ̃] *nm Cin* reverse shot

contre-chant *(pl* **contre-chants**) [kɔ̃trəʃɑ̃] *nm Mus* counterpoint

contrecœur [kɔ̃trəkœr] **à contrecœur** *adv* reluctantly, unwillingly

contrecoup [kɔ̃trəku] *nm (conséquence)* repercussions

contre-courant [kɔ̃trəkurɑ̃] **à contre-courant** *adv (nager)* against the current; *(sur la route)* in the wrong direction; *Fig* **aller à c. de qch** to go against the current of sth

contredanse [kɔ̃trədɑ̃s] *nf Fam (amende)* parking fine; *(avis)* (parking) ticket; **flanquer une c. à qn** to give sb a (parking) ticket

contredire [27b] [kɔ̃trədir] **1** *vt* to contradict **2 se contredire** *vpr (soi-même)* to contradict oneself; *(l'un l'autre)* to contradict each other

contrée [kɔ̃tre] *nf Litt (région)* region; *(pays)* land

contre-emploi *(pl* **contre-emplois**) [kɔ̃trɑ̃plwa] *nm Théât & Cin* miscasting; **utiliser qn à c.** to miscast sb

contre-enquête *(pl* **contre-enquêtes**) [kɔ̃trɑ̃kɛt] *nf Jur* counter-inquiry

contre-espionnage [kɔ̃trɛspjɔnaʒ] *nm* counterespionage

contre-exemple *(pl* **contre-exemples**) [kɔ̃trɛgzɑ̃pl] *nm* counter-example

contre-expertise *(pl* **contre-expertises**) [kɔ̃trɛkspɛrtiz] *nf* second valuation

contrefaçon [kɔ̃trəfasɔ̃] *nf* (**a**) *(pratique)* counterfeiting; *(de signature)* forging (**b**) *(produit)* fake, imitation

contrefaire [36] [kɔ̃trəfɛr] *vt* (**a**) *(voix, écriture)* to disguise (**b**) *(pièce, produit de marque)* to counterfeit; *(signature)* to forge

contrefait, -e [kɔ̃trəfɛ, -ɛt] *adj* (**a**) *(difforme)* deformed, misshapen (**b**) *(falsifié) (signature, argent)* counterfeit, forged

contreficher [kɔ̃trəfiʃe] **se contreficher** *vpr très Fam* **se c. de qch** not to give a damn about sth

contre-filet *(pl* **contre-filets**) [kɔ̃trəfilɛ] *nm Culin* sirloin

contrefort [kɔ̃trəfɔr] *nm* (**a**) *Archit* buttress (**b**) *Géog* **contreforts** foothills (**c**) *(de chaussure)* stiffener

contre-indication *(pl* **contre-indications**) [kɔ̃trɛ̃dikasjɔ̃] *nf* contraindication

contre-interrogatoire *(pl* **contre-interrogatoires**) [kɔ̃trɛ̃terɔgatwar] *nm Jur* cross-examination

contre-jour *(pl* **contre-jours**) [kɔ̃trəʒur] *nm* (**a**) *(éclairage défavorable)* light from behind; **à c.** against the light (**b**) *Art, Cin & Phot* backlighting

contre-la-montre [kɔ̃trəlamɔ̃tr] *nm inv Sport* timetrial

contremaître, -maîtresse [kɔ̃trəmɛtr, -mɛtrɛs] *nm,f* foreman, *f* forewoman

contre-manifestation *(pl* **contre-manifestations**) [kɔ̃trəmanifɛstasjɔ̃] *nf* counter-demonstration

contremarche [kɔ̃trəmarʃ] *nf (d'un escalier)* riser

contremarque [kɔ̃trəmark] *nf (au spectacle)* passout ticket

contre-mesure *(pl* **contre-mesures**) [kɔ̃trəməzyr] *nf* countermeasure

contre-offensive *(pl* **contre-offensives**) [kɔ̃trɔfɑ̃siv] *nf* counter-offensive

contrepartie [kɔ̃trəparti] *nf (compensation)* compensation; **en c. (de)** in return (for)

contre-performance *(pl* **contre-performances**) [kɔ̃trəpɛrfɔrmɑ̃s] *nf* substandard performance

contrepèterie [kɔ̃trəpɛtri] *nf* spoonerism

contre-pied [kɔ̃trəpje] *nm* (**a**) **prendre le c. de qch** *(faire le contraire)* to do the opposite of sth; *(dire le contraire)* to take the opposite view to sth (**b**) *Sport* **prendre son adversaire à c.** to wrong-foot one's opponent; **prendre la balle à c.** to take the ball on the wrong foot

contreplaqué [kɔ̃trəplake] *nm* plywood

contre-plongée *(pl* **contre-plongées**) [kɔ̃trəplɔ̃ʒe] *nf Cin & TV* low-angle shot; **filmer qch en c.** to film sth from below

contrepoids [kɔ̃trəpwa] *nm aussi Fig* counterbalance; *Fig* **faire c. à qch** to counterbalance sth

contre-poil [kɔ̃trəpwal] **à contre-poil** *adv* the wrong way; *Fam* **prendre qn à c.** to rub sb up the wrong way

contrepoison [kɔ̃trəpwazɔ̃] *nm* antidote

contre-pouvoir (*pl* contre-pouvoirs) [kɔ̃trəpuvwar] *nm* anti-establishment force

contre-proposition (*pl* contre-propositions) [kɔ̃trəprɔpozisjɔ̃] *nf* counter-proposal

contrer [kɔ̃tre] *vt* (**a**) *(attaque, argument, personne)* to counter (**b**) *(au volley, au basket)* to block (**c**) *(aux cartes)* to double

contre-révolution (*pl* contre-révolutions) [kɔ̃trərevɔlysjɔ̃] *nf* counter-revolution

contre-révolutionnaire (*pl* contre-révolutionnaires) [kɔ̃trərevɔlysjɔnɛr] *adj & nmf* counter-revolutionary

contresens [kɔ̃trəsɑ̃s] *nm* (**a**) *(mauvaise compréhension)* misinterpretation; *(mauvaise traduction)* mistranslation; **faire un c.** *(mal comprendre)* to make a mistake in interpretation; *(mal traduire)* to make a mistake in translation (**b**) **Aut à c.** the wrong way; **prendre une rue à c.** to go the wrong way down a street

contresigner [kɔ̃trəsiɲe] *vt* to countersign

contretemps [kɔ̃trətɑ̃] *nm* (**a**) *(ennui)* hitch, mishap (**b**) *Mus* offbeat; **à c.** off the beat; *Fig* at the wrong moment

contre-ténor (*pl* contre-ténors) [kɔ̃trətenɔr] *nm* counter-tenor

contre-torpilleur (*pl* contre-torpilleurs) [kɔ̃trətɔrpijœr] *nm* destroyer

contrevenant, -e [kɔ̃trəvənɑ̃, -ɑ̃t] *nm,f* offender

contrevenir [70] [kɔ̃trəvənir] **contrevenir à** *vt ind* to contravene

contrevent [kɔ̃trəvɑ̃] *nm (volet)* (outside) shutter

contrevérité [kɔ̃trəverite] *nf* untruth, falsehood

contribuable [kɔ̃tribɥabl] *nmf* taxpayer

contribuer [kɔ̃tribɥe] **contribuer à** *vt ind* to contribute to; **c. financièrement à qch** to contribute (money) to sth; **c. à faire qch** to help (to) do sth

contribution [kɔ̃tribysjɔ̃] *nf* (**a**) *(impôt)* tax; **contributions** *(à l'État)* taxes; *(à la collectivité locale) Br* rates, *Am* local taxes; **(bureau des) contributions** tax office, *Br* ≃ Inland Revenue, *Am* ≃ Internal Revenue; **contributions directes/indirectes** direct/indirect taxation; **c. sociale généralisée** = income-based tax deducted at source (**b**) *(collaboration, aide financière)* contribution (**à** to); **mettre qn à c.** to call on sb's services

contrit, -e [kɔ̃tri, -it] *adj* contrite

contrôle [kɔ̃trol] *nm* (**a**) *(vérification)* checking; *Scol* test; *Scol & Univ* **c. des connaissances** assessment; *Univ* **c. continu** continuous assessment; **c. douanier** customs control; **c. fiscal** tax inspection; **c. d'identité** identity check; **c. des passeports** passport control; **c. de police** police check; **c. radar** *(sur la route)* radar speed check; *Aut* **c. technique** test of roadworthiness, *Br* ≃ MOT (test) (**b**) *(surveillance) (d'opérations)* monitoring; *Fin* **c. des changes** exchange control; **sous c. judiciaire** on probation; **sous c. médical** under medical supervision; **c. des prix** price control (**c**) *(maîtrise)* control; **avoir le c. de qch** to have control of sth, to be in control of sth; **perdre le c. de son véhicule** to lose control of one's vehicle; **prendre le c. d'une entreprise** to take over a company; **c. de soi** self-control; **sous c. israélien** under Israeli control; **c. des naissances** birth control (**d**) *Ordinat* **touche c.** control key; **c. d'accès** access control; **faire un c. croisé de** to cross-check

contrôler [kɔ̃trole] **1** *vt* (**a**) *(vérifier)* to check (**b**) *(surveiller) (opérations)* to monitor (**c**) *(maîtriser)* to

control (**d**) *Ordinat* **contrôlé par le logiciel** software-controlled; **contrôlé par menu** menu-driven, menu-controlled
2 se contrôler *vpr* to control oneself

contrôleur, -euse [kɔ̃trolœr, -øz] **1** *nm,f (dans les trains, les bus)* ticket inspector; **c. aérien** air-traffic controller; **c. des impôts** tax inspector **2** *nm Ordinat* **c. d'affichage** display *or* screen controller

contrordre [kɔ̃trɔrdr] *nm* countermand; **il y a c.** the orders have been changed; **sauf c.** unless otherwise directed

controverse [kɔ̃trɔvɛrs] *nf* controversy; **prêter à c.** to be controversial

controversé, -e [kɔ̃trɔvɛrse] *adj* controversial

contumace [kɔ̃tymas] **par contumace** *adv Jur* in absentia

contusion [kɔ̃tyzjɔ̃] *nf* bruise, *Spéc* contusion

contusionné, -e [kɔ̃tyzjɔne] *adj* bruised

convaincant, -e [kɔ̃vɛ̃kɑ̃, -ɑ̃t] *adj* convincing

convaincre [68] [kɔ̃vɛ̃kr] *vt* (**a**) *(persuader)* to convince (**de/que** of/that); **c. qn de faire qch** to persuade sb to do sth; **se laisser c.** to let oneself be persuaded (**b**) *(prouver la culpabilité de)* **être convaincu de meurtre** to be convicted *or* found guilty of murder

convaincu, -e [kɔ̃vɛ̃ky] **1** *pp de* convaincre **2** *adj* convinced; *(pacifiste, partisan)* committed; **être c. de/que** to be convinced of/that; **d'un ton c.** with conviction

convalescence [kɔ̃valɛsɑ̃s] *nf* convalescence; **être en c.** to be convalescing

convalescent, -e [kɔ̃valɛsɑ̃, -ɑ̃t] *adj & nm,f* convalescent

convecteur [kɔ̃vɛktœr] *nm* convector (heater)

convenable [kɔ̃vnabl] *adj* (**a**) *(décent)* decent, respectable; **il n'est pas c. de faire du bruit en mangeant** it is not polite to make a noise when eating (**b**) *(acceptable) (salaire, délai)* decent (**c**) *(approprié)* appropriate, suitable

convenablement [kɔ̃vnabləmɑ̃] *adv* decently

convenance [kɔ̃vnɑ̃s] *nf* (**a**) *(fait de convenir)* **pour (des raisons de) c. personnelle** for personal reasons; **trouver qch à sa c.** to find sth to one's liking; **il le fera à sa c.** he'll do it at his own convenience (**b**) **les convenances** the proprieties; **contraire aux convenances** improper

convenir [70] [kɔ̃vnir] **1 convenir à** *vt ind (aller à, plaire à)* to suit; **il est difficile de trouver le mot qui convient** it's hard to find the right word **2 convenir de** *vt ind* (**a**) *(reconnaître)* to admit; **j'ai eu tort, j'en conviens** I was wrong, I admit it; **il convient qu'il a eu tort** he admits that he was wrong (**b**) *(décider de)* to agree on; **c. de faire qch** to agree to do sth **3** *v impersonnel* (**a**) **il convient de...** *(il est souhaitable de)* it is advisable to...; *(il est de bon ton de)* it is proper to... (**b**) *(être décidé)* **il fut convenu qu'ils le feraient venir** it was agreed that they would send for him

convention [kɔ̃vɑ̃sjɔ̃] *nf* (**a**) *(accord)* agreement; **c. collective** collective agreement (**b**) *(règle arbitraire)* convention; **les conventions (sociales)** the (social) conventions; *Péj* **amabilité/sourire de c.** superficial courtesy/smile (**c**) *Pol (assemblée)* assembly; *Hist* **la C.** the French National Convention *(1792–95)*

conventionné, -e [kɔ̃vɑ̃sjɔne] *adj (médecin, clinique)* attached to the health system, *Br* ≃ NHS; **médecin non c.** private doctor

conventionnel, -elle [kɔ̃vɑ̃sjɔnɛl] *adj* (**a**) *(style, personne, armes)* conventional (**b**) *Jur (clause)* contractual

convenu, -e [kɔ̃vny] **1** *pp de* **convenir**
2 *adj* (**a**) *(décidé)* agreed; **comme c.** as agreed (**b**) *Péj (peu original)* conventional

convergence [kɔ̃vɛrʒɑ̃s] *nf* convergence

convergent, -e [kɔ̃vɛrʒɑ̃, -ɑ̃t] *adj* convergent

converger [45] [kɔ̃vɛrʒe] *vi (routes, lignes)* to converge (**vers** on); **c. vers** *(efforts)* to be focused on; **leurs opinions convergent** they were of like mind

conversation [kɔ̃vɛrsasjɔ̃] *nf* (**a**) *(discussion)* conversation; **être en grande c.** (**avec qn**) to be deep in conversation (with sb); **engager la c.** to start a conversation; **faire la c. (à qn)** to make conversation (with sb); **n'avoir aucune c.** to be a poor conversationalist; **c. téléphonique** telephone conversation (**b**) *(pourparlers)* **conversations diplomatiques** diplomatic talks *or* negotiations

conversationnel, -elle [kɔ̃vɛrsasjɔnɛl] *adj Ordinat* **mode c.** conversational *or* interactive mode

converser [kɔ̃vɛrse] *vi Sout* to converse (**avec** with)

conversion [kɔ̃vɛrsjɔ̃] *nf* (**a**) *(changement)* conversion (**en** into); *Ordinat* **c. de fichier** file conversion (**b**) *(à une doctrine)* conversion (**à** to)

converti, -e [kɔ̃vɛrti] **1** *pp de* **convertir**
2 *adj* converted
3 *nm,f Rel* convert; *Fig* **prêcher un c.** to preach to the converted

convertibilité [kɔ̃vɛrtibilite] *nf Fin* convertibility

convertible [kɔ̃vɛrtibl] **1** *adj* convertible (**en** into)
2 *nm (canapé)* sofa bed

convertir [kɔ̃vɛrtir] **1** *vt* (**a**) *(changer)* to convert (**en** into) (**b**) *(à une doctrine)* to convert (**à** to)
2 se convertir *vpr* (**a**) *(à une doctrine)* to be converted (**à** to) (**b**) **se c. en** *(se changer en)* to be converted into

convertisseur [kɔ̃vɛrtisœr] *nm Tech* converter; **c. catalytique** catalytic converter; *Ordinat* **c. analogique numérique** digitizer; **c. de monnaie** currency converter

convexe [kɔ̃vɛks] *adj* convex

conviction [kɔ̃viksjɔ̃] *nf* (**a**) *(certitude)* conviction; **avoir la c. que...** to be convinced that... (**b**) **convictions** *(opinions)* convictions

convier [66] [kɔ̃vje] *vt Sout (inviter)* to invite (**à** to); **c. qn à faire qch** to invite sb to do sth

convive [kɔ̃viv] *nmf* guest

convivial, -e, -aux, -ales [kɔ̃vivjal, -o] *adj* convivial; *Ordinat* user-friendly

convivialité [kɔ̃vivjalite] *nf* conviviality; ≃ *Ordinat* user-friendliness

convocation [kɔ̃vɔkasjɔ̃] *nf* (**a**) *(lettre)* notice to attend; *Jur* summons; **c. à un examen** notification of an examination (**b**) *(d'une assemblée)* convening

convoi [kɔ̃vwa] *nm* (**a**) *(de véhicules, de troupes, de prisonniers)* convoy; **c. exceptionnel** *(sur un camion) (dangereux)* dangerous load; *(large)* wide load (**b**) *(train)* train; **c. de marchandises** goods *or* freight train; **c. postal** mail train (**c**) *(cortège)* **c. funèbre** funeral procession

convoiter [kɔ̃vwate] *vt (poste, richesse)* to covet; *(femme)* to lust after

convoitise [kɔ̃vwatiz] *nf* covetousness; **regarder qch avec c.** to look covetously at sth; **exciter les convoitises** to excite envy

convoler [kɔ̃vɔle] *vi Hum* **c. (en justes noces)** to marry

convoquer [kɔ̃vɔke] *vt* (**a**) *(assemblée)* to convene; **c. les actionnaires** to call the shareholders to a meeting (**b**) *(témoin)* to summon; *(employé)* to call in; **c. qn à un examen** to notify sb of an examination

convoyer [32] [kɔ̃vwaje] *vt (troupes)* to convoy; *(fonds)* to transport under armed guard

convoyeur [kɔ̃vwajœr] *nm* (**a**) *(personne)* **c. de fonds** security guard (**b**) *Ind* conveyer

convulser [kɔ̃vylse] **1** *vt* to convulse
2 se convulser *vpr* to be convulsed

convulsif, -ive [kɔ̃vylsif, -iv] *adj* convulsive

convulsion [kɔ̃vylsjɔ̃] *nf* convulsion; **être pris de convulsions** to go into convulsions

convulsivement [kɔ̃vylsivmɑ̃] *adv* convulsively

cookie [kuki] *nm* (**a**) *(biscuit) Br* biscuit, *Am* cookie (**b**) *Ordinat* cookie

cool [kul] *adj inv Fam* cool

coopérant, -e [kɔɔperɑ̃, -ɑ̃t] **1** *nm,f (à l'étranger)* aid worker
2 *nm Anciennement (pendant le service militaire)* = man doing voluntary work overseas instead of military service

coopératif, -ive [kɔɔperatif, -iv] **1** *adj (société, personne)* co-operative
2 *nf* **coopérative** *(association, magasin)* co-operative, co-op; **coopérative d'achat** wholesale co-operative

coopération [kɔɔperasjɔ̃] *nf* (**a**) *(appui)* co-operation; **en c. avec qn** in co-operation with sb (**b**) *Pol* overseas development; *Anciennement (comme alternative au service militaire)* = voluntary work overseas instead of military service

coopérer [34] [kɔɔpere] *vi* to co-operate (**à** in)

cooptation [kɔɔptasjɔ̃] *nf* co-option; **par c.** by co-option

coordinateur, -trice [kɔɔrdinatœr, -tris] = **coordonnateur**

coordination [kɔɔrdinasjɔ̃] *nf (d'un projet, des mouvements)* coordination

coordonnateur, -trice [kɔɔrdɔnatœr, -tris] *nm,f* coordinator

coordonné, -e [kɔɔrdɔne] **1** *adj (mouvement, efforts)* coordinated; *(draps, vêtements)* matching
2 *nmpl* **coordonnés** *(vêtements)* coordinates, separates
3 *nfpl* **coordonnées** (**a**) *Math, Géog & Astron* coordinates (**b**) *(d'une personne)* contact details, address and phone number

coordonner [kɔɔrdɔne] *vt* to coordinate (**à** *ou* **avec** with)

copain, copine [kɔpɛ̃, kɔpin] *Fam* **1** *nm,f* (**a**) *(camarade)* pal, mate; **salut les copains!** *(en arrivant)* hi guys!; *(en partant)* see you guys!; **c. de classe** classmate (**b**) *(fiancé)* **(petit) c.** boyfriend; **(petite) copine** girlfriend
2 *adj* **ils sont très copains** they're great pals; **être copains comme cochons** to be thick as thieves; **ils sont très c.-c.** they're very pally

copeau, -x [kɔpo] *nm (de bois, de chocolat)* shaving; *(de métal)* cutting

Copenhague [kɔpɛnag] *n* Copenhagen

copie [kɔpi] *nf* (**a**) *(double, manuscrit)* copy (**b**) *Scol (d'examen)* paper; **rendre c. blanche** to hand in a blank paper; *Fig* **revoir sa c.** to go back to the drawing board; **c. simple/double** single/double sheet of paper (**c**) *(d'une œuvre d'art)* copy, reproduction; *(d'un roman, d'un style)* imitation (**d**) *TV & Cin* copy (**e**) *Ordinat* **c. sur papier** hard copy, printout; **c. de sauvegarde** *ou* **de secours** backup (copy) **copier** [66] [kɔpje] *vt* (**a**) *(texte, musique, document informatique)* to copy; **c. qch au propre** *ou* **au net** to make a fair copy of sth, to copy sth out neatly (**b**) *(œuvre d'art)* to copy, to reproduce; *(personne, style)* to imitate (**c**) *(à un devoir sur table)* to copy (**sur** from) **copier-coller** [kɔpjekɔle] *nm inv Ordinat* copy-and-paste

copieur, -euse¹ [kɔpjœr, -øz] **1** *nm,f (élève)* copier **2** *nm (photocopieuse)* (photo)copier

copieusement [kɔpjøzmɑ̃] *adv (manger, boire)* copiously; **il s'est servi c.** he took a generous helping; **un repas c. arrosé** a meal washed down with a lot of wine; **je me suis fait c. insulter** I got well and truly insulted

copieux, -euse² [kɔpjø, -øz] *adj (repas)* copious; *(portion, part, pourboire)* generous

copilote [kɔpilɔt] *nmf (d'avion)* co-pilot; *(de rallye automobile)* navigator

copinage [kɔpinaʒ] *nm Fam* **obtenir un poste par c.** to get a job through one's connections

copiste [kɔpist] *nmf (scribe)* copyist

coprésentateur, -trice [kɔprezɑ̃tatœr, -tris] *nm,f* co-presenter

coprésidence [kɔprezidɑ̃s] *nf* co-chairmanship

coprésident, -e [kɔprezidɑ̃, -ɑ̃t] *nm,f* co-chairman, *f* co-chairwoman

coprocesseur [kɔprɔsesœr] *nm Ordinat* co-processor **coproduction** [kɔprɔdyksjɔ̃] *nf* coproduction **coproduire** [18] [kɔprɔdɥir] *vt* to coproduce **copropriétaire** [kɔprɔprijetɛr] *nmf* co-owner, joint owner

copropriété [kɔprɔprijete] *nf* co-ownership, joint ownership; **acheter/posséder une maison en c.** to buy/own a house jointly

copte [kɔpt] **1** *adj* Coptic **2** *nmf* **C.** Copt

copulation [kɔpylasjɔ̃] *nf* copulation **copuler** [kɔpyle] *vi* to copulate **copyright** [kɔpirajt] *nm* copyright **coq¹** [kɔk] *nm* (**a**) *(oiseau)* cock, *Am* rooster; **jeune c.** cockerel; *Fig* young upstart; **le c.** gaulois the French cockerel; *Fig* **le c. du village** the local Casanova; *Fig* **passer** *ou* **sauter du c. à l'âne** to jump from one subject to another; **être comme un c. en pâte** to be in clover; **c. de bruyère** capercaillie; **c. de combat** fighting cock; *Culin* **c. au vin** coq au vin *(chicken cooked in red wine)* (**b**) *(girouette)* weathercock

coq² *nm Naut* (ship's) cook

coq-à-l'âne [kɔkalan] *nm inv* **faire un c.** to jump from one subject to another

coquard, coquart [kɔkar] *nm Fam* shiner, black eye

coque [kɔk] *nf* (**a**) *(d'une noix, d'un fruit)* shell; *Fig* **c. de noix** flimsy craft (**b**) *(d'un navire)* hull; *(d'un avion)* fuselage; *(d'une voiture)* body (**c**) *(mollusque)* cockle

coquelet [kɔklɛ] *nm* cockerel

coquelicot [kɔkliko] *nm* (red) poppy

coqueluche [kɔklyʃ] *nf (maladie)* whooping cough; **avoir la c.** to have whooping cough; **il est devenu la c. de ces dames** he's become a heart-throb

coquet, -ette [kɔkɛ, -ɛt] **1** *adj (ville, intérieur)* charming; **elle est coquette** she's very clothes-conscious;

Fam **une coquette somme** a tidy sum **2** *nf* **coquette** *Vieilli* coquette

coquetier [kɔktje] *nm* egg-cup; *Fam* **gagner** *ou* **décrocher le c.** to hit the jackpot

coquetterie [kɔkɛtri] *nf* (**a**) *(vestimentaire)* consciousness of one's appearance; *Vieilli (désir de plaire)* coquetry; **avec c.** *(s'habiller)* stylishly (**b**) *Fam* **avoir une c. dans l'œil** to have a cast in one's eye

coquillage [kɔkijaʒ] *nm* (**a**) *(mollusque)* shellfish; **manger des coquillages** to eat shellfish (**b**) *(coque vide)* shell

coquille [kɔkij] *nf* (**a**) *(de mollusque, d'œuf, de noix)* shell; *Fig* **rentrer dans/sortir de sa c.** to withdraw into/to come out of one's shell; *Fig* **c. de noix** flimsy craft; **c. d'œuf** *(couleur)* eggshell; **c. Saint-Jacques** *Culin* scallop; *(coquillage)* scallop shell (**b**) *Typ* misprint, typo

coquillettes [kɔkijɛt] *nfpl* pasta shells **coquin, -e** [kɔkɛ̃, -in] **1** *adj (sourire, air)* mischievous; *(sous-vêtement)* sexy, naughty; *(histoire)* risqué **2** *nm,f (garnement)* rascal; **petit c.!** little rascal *or* scamp!

cor [kɔr] *nm* (**a**) *(instrument)* horn; **c. de chasse** hunting horn; **sonner du c.** to sound *or* blow the horn; *Fig* **réclamer qch à c. et à cri** to clamour for sth (**b**) *(durillon)* corn

corail, -aux [kɔraj, -o] **1** *nm* coral **2** *adj inv* **(rouge) c.** coral(-red)

Coran [kɔrɑ̃] *nm* **le C.** the Koran **coranique** [kɔranik] *adj* Koranic

corbeau, -x [kɔrbo] *nm* (**a**) *(oiseau)* crow (**b**) *(auteur de lettres anonymes)* poison-pen letter writer

corbeille [kɔrbɛj] *nf* (**a**) *(panier)* basket; **c. à linge** laundry basket; **c. de mariage** wedding presents; **c. à ouvrage** workbasket; **c. à pain** breadbasket; **c. à papier** wastepaper basket (**b**) *(à la Bourse de Paris)* trading floor (**c**) *Théât* dress circle (**d**) *Ordinat* wastebasket, *Am* trash; **c. d'arrivée** *(pour courrier électronique)* inbox; **c. de départ** *(pour courrier électronique)* outbox

corbillard [kɔrbijar] *nm* hearse **cordage** [kɔrdaʒ] *nm (corde)* rope; *(d'une raquette)* stringing; *Naut* **cordages** rigging

corde [kɔrd] *nf* (**a**) *(lien)* rope; **échelle de c.** rope ladder; **c. à linge** clothes *or* washing line; **c. lisse** climbing rope; **c. à nœuds** knotted climbing rope; **c. raide** tightrope; **Fig être sur la c. raide** to be walking a tightrope; **c. à sauter** *Br* skipping rope, *Am* jump-rope; **il ne vaut pas la c. pour le pendre** hanging's too good for him (**b**) *(d'instrument, de raquette)* string; **les cordes** *(d'un orchestre)* the strings; *Fig* **avoir plus d'une c. à son arc** to have more than one string to one's bow; *Fig* **j'ai dû toucher la c. sensible** I must have touched a raw nerve (**c**) *Sport* **tenir la c.** *(coureur)* to be on the inside; *(cheval)* to hug the rails; **les cordes** *(d'un ring)* the ropes (**d**) *Anat* **cordes vocales** vocal cords; *Fig* **ce n'est pas dans mes cordes** it's not in my line

cordeau, -x [kɔrdo] *nm (corde)* string; *Fig* **tiré au c.** as straight as a die

cordée [kɔrde] *nf (d'alpinistes)* roped party; **premier de c.** leader

cordelette [kɔrdəlɛt] *nf* cord **cordelière** [kɔrdəljɛr] *nf (ceinture)* cord **cordial, -e, -aux, -ales** [kɔrdjal, -o] **1** *adj (accueil, personne)* cordial **2** *nm (médicament)* tonic

cordialement [kɔrdjalmã] *adv* cordially; **détester c. qn** to heartily dislike sb; **bien c.** *(dans une lettre)* best wishes

cordier [kɔrdje] *nm (de violon)* tailpiece

cordillère [kɔrdijɛr] *nf* mountain range; **la c. des Andes** the Andes

cordon [kɔrdɔ̃] *nm* (**a**) *(lien)* cord, string; *Fig* **tenir les cordons de la bourse** to hold the purse-strings; *Anat* **c. ombilical** umbilical cord; *aussi Fig* **couper le c. (ombilical)** to cut the umbilical cord (**b**) *(de policiers, de soldats)* cordon

cordon-bleu *(pl* **cordons-bleus)** [kɔrdɔ̃blø] *nm Fam* cordon bleu (cook)

cordonnerie [kɔrdɔnri] *nf* (**a**) *(métier)* shoe-repairing (**b**) *(boutique)* shoe repairer's (shop)

cordonnier, -ère [kɔrdɔnje, -ɛr] *nm,f* shoe repairer; *Prov* **les cordonniers sont toujours les plus mal chaussés** the shoemaker's wife is always the worst shod

Corée [kɔre] *nf* **la C. du Nord/du Sud** North/South Korea

coréen, -enne [kɔreɛ̃, -ɛn] **1** *adj* Korean **2** *nm,f* **C.** Korean

Corfou [kɔrfu] *n* Corfu

coriace [kɔrjas] *adj* (**a**) *(viande)* tough (**b**) *(personne, adversaire)* tough

coriandre [kɔrjãdr] *nf* coriander

Corinthe [kɔrɛ̃t] *n voir* raisin

cormoran [kɔrmɔrã] *nm* cormorant

corne [kɔrn] *nf* (**a**) *(d'animal)* horn; **c. d'abondance** horn of plenty, cornucopia; **c. de brume** foghorn; **la C. de l'Afrique** the Horn of Africa; *Fam Fig* **avoir** *ou* **porter des cornes** to be a cuckold; *Fam Fig* **faire porter des cornes à qn** to cuckold sb (**b**) *(matériau)* horn; **peigne de c.** horn comb (**c**) *(d'un croissant)* end; **faire une c. à une page** to turn down the corner of a page (**d**) *(aux pieds, aux mains)* hard skin

corned-beef [kɔrnbif] *nm* corned beef

cornée [kɔrne] *nf* cornea

cornéen, -enne [kɔrneɛ̃, -ɛn] *adj* corneal

corneille [kɔrnɛj] *nf* crow

cornemuse [kɔrnəmyz] *nf* bagpipes

corner¹ [kɔrne] *vt* (**a**) *(page)* to turn down the corner of; *(abîmer)* to make dog-eared (**b**) *Fam* **c. qch aux oreilles de qn** to shout sth into sb's ear

corner² [kɔrnɛr] *nm (au football)* corner; **tirer un c.** to take a corner

cornet [kɔrnɛ] *nm* (**a**) *(de papier)* cone; *(de marrons, de frites)* cornet; **mettre les mains en c.** to cup one's hands together; **c. (à pistons)** cornet; **c. de glace** ice cream cone *or Br* cornet (**b**) *Suisse (sac en papier)* paper bag; *(sac en plastique)* plastic bag

cornette [kɔrnɛt] *nf (coiffe)* cornet

cornettiste [kɔrnɛtist] *nmf* cornetist

corn flakes [kɔrnflɛks] *nmpl* cornflakes

corniaud [kɔrnjo] *nm* (**a**) *(chien)* mongrel (**b**) *Fam (personne)* idiot, fool

corniche [kɔrniʃ] *nf* (**a**) *(de bâtiment)* cornice (**b**) *(de rochers)* ledge; *(de glace, de neige)* cornice; **(route de) c.** coast road

cornichon [kɔrniʃɔ̃] *nm* gherkin

Cornouailles [kɔrnwaj] *nf* **la C.** Cornwall

cornu, -e [kɔrny] *adj (animal, diable)* horned

corollaire [kɔrɔlɛr] *nm (suite)* consequence

corolle [kɔrɔl] *nf* corolla

coron [kɔrɔ̃] *nm* mining village

coronaire [kɔrɔnɛr] *adj* coronary

coronarien, -enne [kɔrɔnarjɛ̃, -ɛn] *adj* coronary

corporation [kɔrpɔrasjɔ̃] *nf* corporate body

corporatiste [kɔrpɔratist] *adj* corporatist

corporel, -elle [kɔrpɔrɛl] *adj (punition)* corporal; *(besoins)* bodily; *(hygiène)* personal

corps [kɔr] *nm* (**a**) *(organisme)* body; **trembler de tout son c.** to tremble all over; **lutter c. à c.** to fight hand to hand; *Fig* **faire qch à son c. défendant** to do sth reluctantly; *Fig* **se jeter à c. perdu dans qch** to throw oneself into sth; *Fig* **se donner c. et âme à qn/qch** to give oneself body and soul to sb/sth (**b**) *(cadavre)* body, corpse (**c**) *Chim & Phys* body; *Astron* **c. céleste** heavenly body; **c. composé** compound; **c. gras** fat; **c. simple** element (**d**) *(consistance)* **avoir du c.** *(vin)* to have body; *Fig* **prendre c.** *(projet, idée)* to take shape (**e**) *(partie principale)* main part; *(d'un texte)* body; *Naut* **perdu c. et biens** lost with all hands; *Jur* **le c. du délit** the corpus delicti (**f**) *(groupe)* **c. d'armée** army corps; **c. de ballet** corps de ballet; **c. diplomatique** diplomatic corps; **c. électoral** electorate; **plaisanterie de c. de garde** barrackroom joke; **le c. médical/enseignant** the medical/teaching profession; **c. de métier** trade; *Hist* corporation; **les grands c. de l'État** = the highest sections of the French administration *(Conseil d'État, Cour des comptes etc)*

corpulence [kɔrpylãs] *nf* stoutness, corpulence

corpulent, -e [kɔrpylã, -ãt] *adj* stout, corpulent

corpus [kɔrpys] *nm Jur & Ling* corpus

corpuscule [kɔrpyskyl] *nm* corpuscle

correct, -e [kɔrɛkt] *adj* (**a**) *(sans fautes)* correct (**b**) *(courtois) (personne)* correct; **cela n'est pas c. de sa part** that's not right of him/her; **elle a été correcte avec moi** she behaved properly towards me (**c**) *Fam (acceptable) (repas, travail, salaire)* reasonable

correctement [kɔrɛktəmã] *adv* (**a**) *(sans faire d'erreur, décemment)* correctly (**b**) *Fam (de façon acceptable)* reasonably; **gagner c. sa vie** to make a reasonable living

correcteur, -trice [kɔrɛktœr, -tris] **1** *nm,f (de copies d'examen)* examiner; *(en typographie)* proofreader; *(dans la presse)* copyreader **2** *nm Ordinat* checker; **c. liquide** correcting fluid; *Ordinat* **c. d'orthographe** *ou* **orthographique** spell-checker **3** *adj (verres)* correcting

correction [kɔrɛksjɔ̃] *nf* (**a**) *(d'une faute)* correction; *Scol (d'un exercice)* correcting, marking; *Typ (d'épreuves)* proofreading (**b**) *(punition)* beating (**c**) *(décence, courtoisie)* correctness

correctionnel, -elle [kɔrɛksjɔnɛl] *Jur* **1** *adj* **peine correctionnelle** = penalty of more than five days' (but less than five years') imprisonment; **tribunal c.** criminal court **2** *nf* **correctionnelle** criminal court; **passer en correctionnelle** to go before the criminal court

corrélation [kɔrelasjɔ̃] *nf* correlation; **être en c. étroite** to be closely connected *or* related

correspondance [kɔrɛspɔ̃dãs] *nf* (**a**) *(lettres)* correspondence (**b**) *(entre trains, avions)* connection; **assurer la c. avec...** *(train, bateau)* to connect with... (**c**) *(entre deux choses)* correspondence; *(d'idées, de principes)* conformity

correspondant, -e [kɔrɛspɔ̃dã, -ãt] **1** *adj* corresponding (**a**) *(journaliste)* correspondent; **c. de guerre** war correspondent; **c. permanent à Londres** London correspondent (**b**) *(au téléphone)* caller; *(par lettre)* penfriend; **le numéro de votre c. a changé** *(au téléphone)* the number you have dialled has been changed

correspondre [kɔrɛspɔ̃dr] *vi* (**a**) *(être conforme, équivaloir)* **c. à qch** to correspond to sth; **les vis et les écrous qui correspondent** the screws and the nuts that go with them (**b**) *(par lettres)* **c. avec qn** to correspond with sb

corrida [kɔrida] *nf* bullfight; *Fam (problèmes)* hassle

corridor [kɔridɔr] *nm* corridor

corrigé, -e [kɔriʒe] **1** *adj* corrected; **en données corrigées des variations saisonnières** seasonally adjusted
2 *nm Scol (d'un exercice)* correct answers (**de** to); *(à la fin d'un ouvrage)* key (**de** to)

corriger [45] [kɔriʒe] **1** *vt* (**a**) *(erreur, faute d'orthographe, myopie, défauts)* to correct; *(exercice, examen)* to correct, to mark; *(épreuves typographiques)* to read; *(article de journal)* to subedit; **c. qn de qch** to cure sb of sth (**b**) *(pour punir)* **c. qn** to give sb a beating
2 se corriger *vpr (personne)* to mend one's ways; **se c. de qch** to cure oneself of sth

corroborer [kɔrɔbɔre] *vt* to corroborate

corroder [kɔrɔde] *vt* to corrode

corrompre [kɔrɔ̃pr] *vt* (**a**) *(personne, goût)* to corrupt (**b**) *(soudoyer)* to bribe

corrompu, -e [kɔrɔ̃py] *adj* corrupt

corrosif, -ive [kɔrozif, -iv] *adj* corrosive; *Fig (propos, humour)* caustic

corrosion [kɔrozjɔ̃] *nf (d'un métal)* corrosion

corruption [kɔrypsjɔ̃] *nf (perversion)* corruption; *(fait de soudoyer)* bribery

corsage [kɔrsaʒ] *nm* blouse

corsaire [kɔrsɛr] **1** *nm* (**a**) *Hist (navire, homme)* corsair (**b**) *(pantalon)* breeches
2 *adj* **pantalon c.** breeches

Corse [kɔrs] *nf* **la C.** Corsica

La Corse

Since the 1970s, the Corsican independence movement has become more radical, with the FLNC (the Corsican Liberation Movement) engaged in a sometimes violent struggle against the French government. In 1982, as part of the law on decentralization, Corsica was attributed a "statut spécial" (special statute) allowing for the election of its own assembly, and became a "collectivité locale" in 1991. However, in 1998 tension between the French authorities and the pro-independence movement reached new heights following the assassination of the prefect of Corsica. In 2003, Corsicans rejected offers of greater autonomy in a referendum, so the problem of the island's status is no nearer to a resolution.

corse [kɔrs] **1** *adj* Corsican
2 *nmf* **C.** Corsican
3 *nm (langue)* Corsican

corsé, -e [kɔrse] *adj (vin)* full-bodied; *(sauce, plat)* spicy; *(café)* full-flavoured; *Fig (histoire)* spicy

corser [kɔrse] **1** *vt (plat)* to spice up; *Fig (récit)* to liven up
2 se corser *vpr (intrigue)* to thicken; **ça se corse** things are getting complicated

corset [kɔrsɛ] *nm* corset; **c. orthopédique** surgical corset

cortège [kɔrtɛʒ] *nm* procession; *Fig* **la vie de famille et son c. de problèmes** family life and its attendant problems; **c. funèbre** funeral cortège

cortex [kɔrtɛks] *nm Anat & Bot* cortex

corticoïde [kɔrtikɔid] *nm* corticoid

cortisone [kɔrtizɔn] *nf* cortisone

corvée [kɔrve] *nf* (**a**) *(obligation pénible)* chore; **je suis de c. de vaisselle ce soir** I'm on washing-up duty tonight; **quelle c.!** what a drag! (**b**) *Mil* fatigue duty; **être de c.** to be on fatigue duty (**c**) *Hist* corvée

corvette [kɔrvɛt] *nf* corvette

coryza [kɔriza] *nm* head cold, *Spéc* coryza

cosaque [kɔzak] *nm* cossack

cosignataire [kosiɲatɛr] *adj & nmf* cosignatory

cosinus [kɔsinys] *nm* cosine

cosmétique [kɔsmetik] *adj & nm* cosmetic

cosmique [kɔsmik] *adj* cosmic

cosmologie [kɔsmɔlɔʒi] *nf* cosmology

cosmonaute [kɔsmɔnot] *nmf* cosmonaut

cosmopolite [kɔsmɔpɔlit] *adj* cosmopolitan

cosmos [kɔsmos] *nm (univers)* cosmos; *(espace)* outer space

cosse [kɔs] *nf (de petits pois)* pod

cossu, -e [kɔsy] *adj (maison, intérieur)* opulent; *(personne)* well-to-do

costard [kɔstar] *nm Fam* suit; **tailler un c. à qn** *Br* to slag sb off, *Am* to badmouth sb

Costa Rica [kɔstarika] *nm* **le C.** Costa Rica

costaud, -e [kɔsto, -od] *Fam* **1** *adj* (**a**) *(fort, solide) (personne)* sturdy (**b**) *(problème)* tough (**c**) *(alcool, café)* strong
2 *nm,f* sturdy man, *f* sturdy woman

costume [kɔstym] *nm (habit)* costume; *(complet)* suit

costumé, -e [kɔstyme] *adj voir* **bal**

costumier, -ère [kɔstymje, -ɛr] *nm,f (de théâtre)* wardrobe master, *f* wardrobe mistress; *(de cinéma)* costume supervisor

cotation [kɔtasjɔ̃] *nf* **c. (en Bourse)** quotation (on the Stock Exchange)

cote [kɔt] *nf* (**a**) *(d'une action) (valeur)* quotation; *(liste)* share index; *(d'un cheval)* odds; **hors c.** *(actions)* unlisted; *(marché) Br* unofficial, *Am* over-the-counter; **c. de popularité** popularity rating; *Fam* **avoir la c. (avec** *ou* **auprès de qn)** to be popular (with) (**b**) *(servant à classer)* classification mark (**c**) *(altitude)* altitude; **atteindre la c. d'alerte** *(fleuve)* to reach danger level; *Fig* to reach crisis point

coté, -e [kɔte] *adj* (**a**) *(estimé)* **bien/très/mal c.** highly/very highly/not highly thought of (**b**) **action cotée en Bourse** share quoted on the Stock Exchange; **être c. à 100 euros** to be trading at 100 euros; **être c. à l'argus** to be listed in the car buyer's guide

côte [kɔt] *nf* (**a**) *(os)* rib; **c. à c.** side by side; *Fam* **on lui voit les côtes** he's/she's nothing but skin and bone; **c. d'agneau/de porc** lamb/pork chop; **c. de bœuf** rib of beef (**b**) *(de melon, de feuille)* rib; **tissu à côtes** ribbed material (**c**) *(d'une montagne)* slope; **monter/descendre une c.** to go up/down a hill (**d**) *(rivage)* coast; **la C. (d'Azur)** the (French) Riviera

côté [kote] *nm* (**a**) *(du corps humain)* side; **couché sur le c.** lying on one's side; *Fig* **être aux côtés de qn** to be at sb's side (**b**) *(d'une route, d'un triangle, d'une feuille)* side; **de l'autre c. (de qch)** on the other side (of sth); **siège c. couloir/fenêtre** aisle/window seat; *Théât* **jardin/cour** stage right/left (**c**) *(aspect)* side; **il a de bons côtés** he's got a good side to him; **prendre la vie du bon c.** to look on the bright side of life (**d**) *(end-*

roit) **de tous côtés** *(cerné)* on all sides; *(affluer)* from all directions; **du c. de** *(près de)* near; **ils s'en allèrent chacun de son c.** they went their separate ways; **de quel c.?** *(direction)* which way?; *(position)* which side?; *Fig* **être du c. de qn** to be on sb's side; **ma tante du c. maternel** my aunt on my mother's side; **d'un c...., d'un autre c....** on the one hand..., on the other hand... **(e)** *(en ce qui concerne)* **Fam c.** **argent, ça va** things are OK moneywise; **de ce c., il n'y a rien à craindre** there's nothing to worry about on that score **(f)** **à c.** *(près)* nearby; **à c. de** *(près de)* next to; *(comparé à)* compared with; **les voisins d'à c.** the next-door neighbours; **à c. l'un de l'autre** side by side; *Fig* **passer à c. de qch** to miss out on sth **(g)** **faire un saut de c.** to leap to one side *or* aside; *Fig* **mettre qch de c.** to put sth aside; *Fig* **laisser qn/qch de c.** to leave sb/sth out

coteau, -x [kɔto] *nm (versant)* hillside; *(colline)* hill

Côte d'Ivoire [kotdivwar] *nf* **la C.** the Ivory Coast

côtelé, -e [kotle] *adj voir* **velours**

côtelette [kotlɛt, kɔtlɛt] *nf* chop; **c. d'agneau/de porc** lamb/pork chop

coter [kɔte] *vt* **(a)** *(prix, actions)* to quote **(b)** *(documents)* to classify

côtier, -ère [kotje, -ɛr] *adj (fleuve, navigation)* coastal; *(pêche)* inshore

cotillon [kɔtijɔ̃] *nm* **accessoires de c., cotillons** party novelties

cotisation [kɔtizasjɔ̃] *nf* **(a)** *(à une caisse)* contribution; **cotisations de Sécurité Sociale** ≃ National Insurance contributions **(b)** *(à un club)* subscription

cotiser [kɔtize] **1** *vi (à une caisse de retraite, à une mutuelle)* to contribute (**à** to) **2 se cotiser** *vpr* to club together

coton [kɔtɔ̃] **1** *nm* **(a)** *(plante, tissu)* cotton; **chemise 100% c.** 100% cotton shirt; *Fam* **filer un mauvais c.** *(financièrement, physiquement)* to be in a bad way **(b)** **c. (hydrophile)** *Br* cotton wool, *Am* absorbent cotton; **un c.** a piece of *Br* cotton wool *or Am* absorbent cotton; *Fig* **élever un enfant dans du c.** to wrap a child in cotton wool; *Fam* **j'ai les jambes en c.** my legs feel like jelly **2** *adj Fam* tough, tricky

cotonnade [kɔtɔnad] *nf* cotton fabric

cotonneux, -euse [kɔtɔnø, -øz] *adj (feuille)* downy; *(nuage)* fluffy; *(fruit)* mushy

Coton-Tige® *(pl* **Cotons-Tiges)** [kɔtɔ̃tiʒ] *nm* cotton bud

côtoyer [32] [kotwaje] *vt* **(a)** *(personnes)* to mix with **(b)** *(rivière, forêt)* to border on

cotte [kɔt] *nf* **c. de mailles** coat of mail

cou [ku] *nm* neck; **tendre le c.** to crane one's neck; **avoir un c. de taureau** to have a neck like a bull; **se jeter au c. de qn** to throw one's arms round sb's neck; *Fam* **endetté jusqu'au c.** up to one's eyes in debt

couac [kwak] *nm (fausse note)* false note; *Fig* discordant note; **faire un c.** to play a false note; *(chanteur)* to sing a false note

couchage [kuʃaʒ] *nm voir* **sac¹**

couchant, -e [kuʃɑ̃, -ɑ̃t] **1** *adj* **le soleil c.** the setting sun **2** *nm (ouest)* west; **dans la direction du c.** in a westerly direction

couche [kuʃ] *nf* **(a)** *(de peinture)* coat; *(de beurre, de crème, de poussière)* layer; *(classe sociale)* level; *Géol* layer, stratum; **la c. d'ozone** the ozone layer; *Fam* **il en tient une c.!** he's really stupid! **(b)** *(de bébé) Br* nappy,

Am diaper **(c)** *Vieilli* **femme en couches** woman in labour; **mourir en couches** to die in childbirth **(d)** *Litt (lit)* bed

couché, -e [kuʃe] *adj* **(a)** *(allongé)* lying (down); *(au lit)* in bed **(b)** *(écriture)* slanting, sloping

couche-culotte *(pl* **couches-culottes)** [kuʃkylɔt] *nf* disposable *Br* nappy *or Am* diaper

coucher¹ [kuʃe] *nm* **(a)** *(fait d'aller au lit)* **l'heure du c.** bedtime; **prendre deux comprimés au c.** take two tablets at bedtime **(b)** *(gîte)* accommodation **(c)** *(du soleil)* setting; **un superbe c. de soleil** a magnificent sunset; **au c. du soleil** at sunset

coucher² **1** *vt* **(a)** *(mettre au lit)* **c. qn** to put sb to bed **(b)** *(allonger, poser)* to lay down **(c)** *(écrire)* **c. qn sur son testament** to mention sb in one's will **2** *vi* **(a)** *(passer la nuit)* to sleep; *Fig* **c. sous les ponts** to sleep rough **(b)** *Fam* **c. avec qn** to sleep with sb; **c. ensemble** to sleep together **(c)** *(à un chien)* **couché!** (lie) down! **3 se coucher** *vpr* **(a)** *(au lit)* to go to bed; **aller se c.** to go to bed; *Fam* **se c. avec les poules** to go to bed early; *Prov* **comme on fait son lit, on se couche** as we make our bed, so we must lie in it **(b)** *(s'allonger)* to lie down; **se c. à plat ventre** to lie flat on one's stomach **(c)** **se c. sur le flanc** *(navire)* to keel over **(d)** *(soleil, lune)* to set, to go down

coucheries [kuʃri] *nfpl Fam* sleeping around

couchette [kuʃɛt] *nf (de navire)* bunk; *(de train)* couchette

coucheur, -euse [kuʃœr, -øz] *nmf Fam* **c'est un c.** he sleeps around; **c'est un mauvais c.** he's an awkward customer

couci-couça [kusikusa] *adv Fam* so-so

coucou [kuku] **1** *nm* **(a)** *(oiseau)* cuckoo **(b)** *(horloge)* cuckoo clock **(c)** *(plante)* cowslip **(d)** *Fam (avion)* old crate **2** *exclam (langage enfantin)* peekaboo!; *(bonjour)* cooee!

coude [kud] *nm* **(a)** *(articulation)* elbow; **être au c. à c.** to be neck and neck; **jouer des coudes** to push and shove; *Fig* to manœuvre; *Fig* **se serrer les coudes** to stick together; *Fig* **garder qch sous le c.** to hold on to sth; *Fam* **lever le c.** to booze **(b)** *(tournant)* sharp bend; *(de barre, de tuyau)* bend; *(d'arbre)* crank

coudé, -e¹ [kude] *adj* bent

coudée² [kude] *nf* **avoir les coudées franches** to have plenty of elbow room

cou-de-pied *(pl* **cous-de-pied)** [kudəpje] *nm* instep

coudre [21] [kudr] *vt (ourlet)* to sew; *(bouton)* to sew on; *(deux morceaux d'étoffe)* to sew together; *(jupe, plaie)* to sew up; **c. un bouton à une robe** to sew a button on a dress; **je ne sais pas c.** I can't sew

coudrier [kudrije] *nm* hazel (tree); **baguette de c.** hazel stick *or* switch

couenne [kwan] *nf* rind

couette¹ [kwɛt] *nf (édredon)* duvet, continental quilt

couette² *nf (coiffure)* bunch; **se faire des couettes** to put one's hair in bunches

couille [kuj] *nf Vulg (testicule)* ball; *(problème)* balls-up

couillon, -onne [kujɔ̃, -ɔn] *très Fam* **1** *adj* damned stupid **2** *nm,f Br* twat, *Am* jerk

couillonner [kujɔne] *vt très Fam (personne)* to con; **se faire c.** to be conned

couiner [kwine] *vi (animal)* to squeak; *(enfant)* to whine

coulant, -e [kulɑ̃, -ɑ̃t] *adj (fromage)* runny; *Fig (style)* flowing; *Fam (personne)* easy-going

coulée [kule] *nf* **c. de boue** mudslide; **c. de lave** lava flow

coulemelle [kulmɛl] *nf* parasol mushroom

couler [kule] **1** *vt* (**a**) *(liquide, cire, ciment)* to pour; *(métal, statue)* to cast (**b**) *(navire)* to sink; *Fig* **c. qn** to bring sb down (**c**) *(passer)* **c. des jours heureux** to lead a happy life; *Fam* **se la c. douce** to take things easy

2 *vi* (**a**) *(liquide, rivière)* to flow, to run; *(fromage, maquillage)* to run; *(style)* to flow; **la sueur coulait sur son front** sweat was trickling down his/her forehead; **cette affaire a fait c. beaucoup d'encre** a lot has been written about this affair; **faire c. un bain à qn** to run a bath for sb; *Fig* **c. de source** to be obvious (**b**) *(navire)* to sink, to go down; *(entreprise)* to go under (**c**) *(tonneau, stylo)* to leak; *(nez)* to run; **avoir le nez qui coule** to have a runny nose

3 se couler *vpr (se glisser)* to slip

couleur [kulœr] **1** *nf* (**a**) *(teinte, orientation politique)* colour; **de quelle c. est...?** what colour is...?; **de c.** coloured; **de c.** jaune/verte yellow-/green-coloured; **télévision/photographie en c.** *ou* **couleurs** colour television/photography; **les couleurs** *(linge)* coloureds; *Fig* **pour faire c. locale** to add a bit of local colour; *Fam* **elle nous en a fait voir de toutes les couleurs** she gave us a hard time; *Fam* **je n'en ai pas encore vu la c.** I've seen no sign of it yet (**b**) *(teint)* **prendre des couleurs** to get some colour in one's cheeks (**c**) *Mil* **couleurs** *(drapeau)* colours (**d**) **couleurs** *(d'un club, d'une écurie)* colours; **défendre les couleurs de** to represent (**e**) *(peinture)* paint; **une boîte de couleurs** a paintbox (**f**) *(aux cartes)* suit; **annoncer la c.** to call (trumps); *Fam* to lay one's cards on the table (**g**) *(en coiffure)* dye; **se faire une c.** to dye one's hair; **se faire faire une c.** to have one's hair dyed

2 *adj inv (télévision, pellicule)* colour; **une chevelure c. de feu** flame-coloured hair

couleuvre [kulœvr] *nf* **c. (à collier)** grass snake; *Fig* **avaler des couleuvres** *(se faire humilier)* to eat humble pie; *(être naïf)* to swallow anything

coulis [kuli] *nm* **c. de tomates/framboises** tomato/raspberry coulis

coulissant, -e [kulisɑ̃, -ɑ̃t] *adj* sliding

coulisse [kulis] *nf* (**a**) *(glissière)* runner; **porte à c.** sliding door (**b**) *Théât* **les coulisses** the wings; **en coulisses, dans les coulisses** in the wings; *Fig* behind the scenes

coulisser [kulise] *vi* to slide

couloir [kulwar] *nm* (**a**) *(de maison)* corridor, passage; *(de train)* corridor; *(en athlétisme, en natation)* lane; *(au tennis)* Br tramlines, Am alley; **c. aérien** air corridor; **c. d'autobus** bus lane; **c. à vélos** cycle lane (**b**) *Géog* gully

coulommiers [kulɔmje] *nm* = type of soft cheese

coulon [kulɔ̃] *nm Belg* pigeon

coulpe [kulp] *nf* **battre sa c.** to beat one's breast

coup [ku] *nm* (**a**) *(choc)* blow; **donner un c. à qn** to hit sb; **se donner un c. contre qch** to knock against sth; **j'ai pris un coup sur la tête** I got a knock *or* a bang on the head; **donner un c. de bâton à qn** to hit sb with a stick; **donner un c. de coude à qn** to nudge sb; **donner un c. de couteau à qn** to knife sb; **donner un c. de griffe à qn/qch** to claw at sb/sth; **c. de pied** kick; **donner un c. de pied à qn/qch** to kick sb/sth; **c. de poing** punch; **donner un c. de poing à qn** to punch sb; **c. de poing américain** knuckle-duster; *Fig* **donner un c. de pouce à qn** to push sb; **c. de tête** header;

Fam **faire qch sur un c. de tête** to do sth on the spur of the moment; **rendre c. pour c.** to give as good as one gets; *Fig* **tous les coups sont permis** there are no holds barred; *Fig* **c'était un c. bas** that was below the belt; *Jur* **coups et blessures** grievous bodily harm (**b**) *(choc émotionnel)* blow; **ça m'a fait un c.** *(émotion)* it gave me a shock; *(déception)* it was a blow; **accuser le c.** to show that one has been affected; *Fam* **tenir le c.** to hold out; *Fam* **en prendre un c.** to be devastated; **un c. dur** a setback

(**c**) *(action soudaine, événement soudain)* **c. de vent** gust of wind; *Fam* **passer en c. de vent** to pay a flying visit; **donner un c. de frein** to brake; **donner un c. de volant** to turn the wheel sharply; **donner un c. d'arrêt à qch** to call a halt to sth; *Fam* **prendre un c. de vieux** to age; *Fam* **avoir un c. de barre** *ou* **de pompe** to feel tired all of a sudden; **c. de chance** *ou Fam* **de bol** *ou* **de pot** stroke of luck; *Fam* **avoir un c. de cœur pour qch** to absolutely love sth; **c. d'État** coup (d'État); *Fig* **ça été le c. de foudre** it was love at first sight; **avoir le c. de foudre pour qn** to fall head over heels in love with sb; **attraper un c. de froid** to catch a cold; *Fam* **pousser un c. de gueule** to yell; *Fam* **un c. de pub** a publicity stunt; **prendre un c. de soleil** to get sunburned; **c. de théâtre** coup de théâtre; *(dans la vie)* sudden turn of events

(**d**) *(bruit)* **c. de feu** shot; **c. de fusil** shot; **c. de sifflet** whistle; **c. de sonnette** ring; **c. de tonnerre** clap of thunder; **tirer deux coups** to fire twice; **l'horloge sonna trois coups** the clock struck three; *Fig* **sur le c. de midi** on the stroke of twelve; **les trois coups** *(au théâtre)* = the three knocks given just before the curtain rises

(**e**) *(influence)* **sous le c. de la colère** in a fit of anger; **tomber sous le c. de la loi** to be an offence

(**f**) *(essai)* attempt, go; *Fig* **réussir son c.** to be a great success; **d'un seul c.** in one go; **du premier c.** at the first attempt; *Fam* **à tous les coups, à tous les coups on va se faire repérer** the boss is bound to see us; **il n'en est pas à son c. d'essai** it's not the first time he's done it; **c. de maître** masterstroke

(**g**) *(au golf)* stroke; *(aux échecs)* move; **c. droit** *(au tennis)* forehand; *Fig* **faire c. double** to kill two birds with one stone; **c. d'envoi** *(au football, au rugby)* kick-off; *Fig* **donner le c. d'envoi de qch** to launch sth; **c. franc** *(au football)* free kick; **c. de pied de réparation** penalty kick

(**h**) *Fam (tour, combine)* **réussir un bon c.** to do well for oneself; **faire un sale c. à qn** to play a dirty trick on sb; **être sur un c.** to be on to a good thing; **être dans le c.** *(impliqué)* to be involved; *(à la mode)* to be trendy; **c. fourré, c. de Jarnac** dirty trick; **c. monté** put-up job

(**i**) *Vulg* **tirer un c.** to get laid

(**j**) *(locutions)* **tout à c., tout d'un c.** suddenly, all of a sudden; **c. sûr** for certain, definitely; **au c. par c.** step by step; **c. sur c.** one after the other; **après c.** after the event; *Fam* **du c.** and so; **pleurer un bon c.** to have a good cry; **mourir sur le c.** to die on the spot; **sur le c., je n'ai pas compris** at the time I didn't understand; **faire les quatre cents coups** to sow one's wild oats; **donner le c. de grâce à qn** to finish sb off; **avoir le c. de main (pour faire qch)** to have the knack (of doing sth); **donner un c. de main à qn** to give sb a hand; *Fam* **boire un c.** to have a drink; *Fam* **avoir un c. dans le nez** to be *Br* pissed *or Am* wasted; *Fam* **valoir le c.** to be worth it; *Fam* **il va falloir en mettre un c.** we're going to have to pull out all the stops

coupable [kupabl] **1** *adj (personne)* guilty (**de** of); *(action, négligence)* culpable; *(faiblesse)* reprehensible; **se sentir c. (de faire qch)** to feel guilty (about doing sth) **2** *nmf* culprit

coupant, -e [kupã, -ãt] *adj* sharp

coupe¹ [kup] *nf* (**a**) *(récipient)* bowl; **c. à champagne** champagne glass; *Fig* **la c. est pleine** that's the limit; *Prov* **il y a loin de la c. aux lèvres** there's many a slip 'twixt cup and lip (**b**) *(trophée)* cup; **la C. du monde de football** the Football World Cup; **la c. Davis** the Davis Cup

coupe² *nf* (**a**) *(action) (du blé)* cutting; *(de tissu)* cutting out; *(d'arbres)* cutting down; **c. (de cheveux)** haircut; **acheter du fromage à la c.** to buy cheese from the fresh cheese counter; **c. sombre** *(dans une forêt)* slight thinning; *(du personnel, des dépenses)* drastic cut (**b**) *(d'un vêtement)* cut (**c**) *(plan)* section (**d**) *(aux cartes)* cut; *Fig* **être sous la c. de qn** to be under sb's thumb; **tomber sous la c. de qn** to fall into sb's clutches

coupé, -e [kupe] **1** *adj* (**a**) *(taillé)* cut; **un costume mal c.** a badly cut suit (**b**) *(au tennis)* **une balle coupée** a slice (**c**) *(castré) (chat)* neutered (**d**) *(dilué)* **c. d'eau** watered down, diluted **2** *nm (voiture)* coupé; **c. sport** sports coupé

coupe-coupe [kupkup] *nm inv* machete

coupe-faim [kupfɛ̃] *nm inv* appetite suppressant

coupe-feu [kupfø] *nm inv* firebreak; *Ordinat* **mur c.** firewall; **porte c.** fire door

coupe-gorge [kupgɔrʒ] *nm inv* dangerous back alley

coupe-légumes [kuplegym] *nm inv* vegetable slicer

coupelle [kupɛl] *nf* (**a**) *(petite coupe)* small dish (**b**) *(de laboratoire)* cupel

coupe-ongles [kupɔ̃gl] *nm inv* nail clippers

coupe-papier [kuppapje] *nm inv* paper knife, letter opener

couper [kupe] **1** *vt* (**a**) *(trancher)* to cut; *(arbre)* to cut down; *(vêtement)* to cut out; **c. qch en morceaux** to cut sth up (into pieces); **c. qch en trois** to cut sth into three; **c. les cheveux à qn** to cut sb's hair; **c. la tête à qn** to cut off sb's head; *Fig* **c. les cheveux en quatre** to split hairs; **un brouillard à c. au couteau** fog you could cut with a knife; **j'en donnerais ma main** *ou* **ma tête à c.** I'd stake my life on it (**b**) *(supprimer, raccourcir)* to cut; **c. dans le vif** to take drastic measures (**c**) *(traverser)* to cut across; **c. la route à qn** to cut in in front of sb; **c. à travers champs** to cut across country; **c. par le jardin** to cut through the garden (**d**) *(séparer)* to divide (**en deux** in two); **être coupé du monde** to be cut off from the outside world (**e**) *(interrompre) (personne)* to cut in on; *(son)* to turn right down; **c. l'eau** *(pour réparation)* to turn off the water; *(pour non-paiement)* to cut off the water; **c. le courant** *ou* **l'électricité** *(pour réparation)* to switch off the current; *(pour non-paiement)* to cut off the power; **c. le téléphone à qn** to cut off sb's telephone; **nous avons été coupés, la communication a été coupée** we were cut off; **c. le contact** *(d'une voiture)* to switch off the ignition; **c. l'appétit à qn** to spoil sb's appetite; **ces bas me coupent la circulation** these stockings are cutting off my circulation; *Fam* **ça te la coupe!** that's taken the wind out of your sails! (**f**) *(châtrer) (chat)* to neuter (**g**) **c. du vin** *(en mélangeant)* to blend wine; *(avec de l'eau)* to water down wine (**h**) *(paquet de cartes)* to cut; *(prendre avec l'atout)* to trump; **à toi de c.** it's your turn to cut; **c. à carreau** to trump with a

diamond (**i**) *(au tennis) (balle)* to slice **2** *vi (être tranchant)* to be sharp; **le couteau coupe bien** the knife cuts well **3 couper à** *vt ind* (**a**) *Fam* **c. à qch** *(se dérober)* to get out of sth (**b**) **c. court à qch** to cut sth short **4 se couper** *vpr* (**a**) *(se blesser)* to cut oneself; **se c. le** *ou* **au doigt** to cut one's finger; **se c. les veines** to slash one's wrists (**b**) *(tailler)* **se c. les ongles/les cheveux** to cut one's nails/hair (**c**) *(routes)* to intersect, to cross (**d**) **se c. de qn** to cut oneself off from sb

couper-coller [kupekɔle] *nm inv* *Ordinat* cut-and-paste

couperet [kuprɛ] *nm* (**a**) *(pour la viande)* cleaver (**b**) *(de la guillotine)* blade

couperose [kuproz] *nf* blotches

couperosé, -e [kuproze] *adj* blotchy

coupe-vent [kupvã] *nm inv* (**a**) *(dispositif)* windbreak (**b**) *(blouson)* *Br* windcheater, *Am* Windbreaker®

couple [kupl] *nm (de personnes)* couple; *(d'animaux)* pair; **vivre en c.** to live together; **un c. sans enfants** a childless couple

couplet [kuplɛ] *nm (de chanson)* verse; *Fam* tirade (**sur** about)

coupole [kupɔl] *nf* dome, cupola

coupon [kupɔ̃] *nm* (**a**) *(ticket)* **c. de réduction** money-off coupon (**b**) *(de tissu)* remnant (**c**) *Fin* **c. d'action** coupon

coupon-réponse *(pl* **coupons-réponse)** [kupɔ̃repɔ̃s] *nm* reply coupon

coupure [kupyr] *nf* (**a**) *(blessure)* cut (**b**) *(suppression)* cut (**c**) **c. (de courant)** power cut (**d**) *Fig (séparation)* break (**e**) *(pause)* break (**f**) **c. de journal** *ou* **de presse** newspaper *or* press cutting (**g**) *Fin* denomination; **50 000 euros en petites coupures** 50,000 euros in small notes or denominations

cour [kur] *nf* (**a**) *(de maison, de ferme)* yard; *Can* **c. à bois** lumber yard; **c. d'honneur** main courtyard; **c. de récréation** *Br* playground, *Am* schoolyard; *Fig* **jouer dans la c. des grands** to be up there with the leaders (**b**) *(de souverain)* court; **vivre à la c.** to live at court (**c**) *(tribunal)* court; **Messieurs, la C.!** all rise!; **Haute C.** High Court *(for impeachment of president or ministers)*; **c. d'appel** court of appeal; **c. d'assises** court of assizes; **c. de cassation** ≃ Supreme Court of Appeal; **la C. des comptes** the Audit Office; **la C. internationale de justice** the International Court of Justice; **c. martiale** court martial; **passer en c. martiale** *(pour qch)* to be court-martialled (for sth); *Can* **la C. suprême** the Supreme Court (**d**) **faire la c. à qn** to court sb

courage [kuraʒ] *nm* courage, bravery; **avec c.** bravely, courageously; **perdre c.** to lose heart; **prendre son c. à deux mains** to pluck up courage; **avoir le c. de ses opinions** to have the courage of one's convictions; **avoir/se sentir le c. de faire qch** to be/to feel up to doing sth; **bon c.!** good luck!

courageusement [kuraʒøzmã] *adv (bravement)* courageously, bravely; *(résolument)* with a will

courageux, -euse [kuraʒø, -øz] *adj* (**a**) *(brave)* courageous, brave (**b**) *(énergique)* energetic

courailler [kuraje] *vi* *Can Fam* to chase women

courailleur [kurajœr] *nm* *Can Fam* womanizer

couramment [kuramã] *adv* (**a**) *(parler)* fluently (**b**) *(généralement)* commonly; **ce mot s'emploie c.** this word is in common use

courant, -e [kurɑ̃, -ɑ̃t] **1** *adj* (**a**) *(commun)* common; **dans la vie courante** in everyday life (**b**) *(en cours)* current; **le 5 c.** the 5th inst.
2 *nm* (**a**) *(dans une rivière)* current; *Fig (tendance)* trend; **suivre/remonter le c.** to go with/against the current; **c. d'air** draught; **c. de pensée** way of thinking (**b**) *Élec* **c.** *(électrique)* (electric) current; **c. continu/ alternatif** direct/alternating current; *Fig* **le c. ne passe pas** we're/they're/you're not on the same wavelength (**c**) *(durée)* **dans le c. de** in the course of; **c. janvier** during the month of January (**d**) **être au c. (de qch)** to know (about sth); **mettre qn au c. (de qch)** to tell sb (about sth); **tenir qn au c. (de qch)** to keep sb up-to-date (on sth)
3 *nf* **courante** *Fam* **avoir la courante** to have the runs
courbatu, -e [kurbaty] *adj* aching (all over)
courbature [kurbatyr] *nf* ache; **avoir des courbatures** to be aching (all over)
courbaturé, -e [kurbatyre] *adj* aching (all over)
courbe [kurb] **1** *adj* curved
2 *nf* curve; *(graphe)* graph; **c. de niveau** contour (line); **c. des prix/des salaires** price/salary curve; **c. de température** temperature curve
courber [kurbe] **1** *vt* to bend; **c. la tête** to bow *or* bend one's head; *Fig* **c. l'échine** to submit
2 *vi* to bend
3 se courber *vpr (personne)* to bend down, to stoop; **se c. en deux** to bend double
courbette [kurbɛt] *nf (salut)* bow; *Fig* **faire des courbettes (à qn)** to bow and scrape (to sb)
courbure [kurbyr] *nf (d'une surface, d'une ligne)* curvature; *(d'un morceau de bois, du dos)* curve
coureur, -euse [kurœr, -øz] **1** *nm,f (à pied)* runner; **c. (automobile)** (racing) driver; **c. (cycliste)** (racing) cyclist
2 *adj (homme)* womanizing; *(femme)* manhunting
3 *nm* **c. (de jupons)** womanizer
4 *nf* **coureuse** *(dévergondée)* manhunter
courge [kurʒ] *nf* (**a**) *(plante) Br* marrow, *Am* squash (**b**) *Fam (imbécile)* idiot, fool
courgette [kurʒɛt] *nf Br* courgette, *Am* zucchini
courir [22] [kurir] **1** *vi* (**a**) *(personne)* to run; **monter/ descendre la colline en courant** to run up/down the hill; **arriver en courant** to come running (up); **je cours le prévenir** I'll run and warn him; **c. après qn/ qch** to run after sb/sth; **c. après la gloire** to chase after glory; **c. à sa perte** to be heading for disaster; **l'assassin court toujours** the murderer is still at large; *Fam* **tu peux toujours c.!** not a chance!; *Fam* **laisse c.!** forget it!; *Prov* **rien ne sert de c., il faut partir à point** slow and steady wins the race (**b**) *(se propager)* **le bruit court que...** rumour has it that...; **faire c. un bruit** to spread a rumour (**c**) *(eau, ruisseau)* to rush (**d**) *(participer à une course) (à pied)* to run; *(automobile)* to drive; *(cycliste)* to ride
2 *vt* (**a**) *(tenter)* **c. un risque** to run a risk (**b**) *Sport* **c. le 100 mètres** to run the 100 metres (**c**) *(parcourir, fréquenter)* **c. le monde** to roam the world; **c. les théâtres** to go to the theatre all the time; **ça ne court pas les rues** *(personnes)* they're thin on the ground; *(objets)* you don't see that every day (**d**) *(chasser)* **c. les filles** to chase women; *Fig* **c. deux lièvres à la fois** to have two irons in the fire
3 *v impersonnel* **il court des bruits sur lui** there are rumours going round about him
courlis [kurli] *nm* curlew

couronne [kurɔn] *nf* (**a**) *(de fleurs, de lauriers)* wreath; **c. funéraire** *ou* **mortuaire** (funeral) wreath (**b**) *(de souverain)* crown; *(de noble)* coronet; **la C. de France** the French Crown (**c**) *(monnaie)* crown (**d**) *(pain)* ring-shaped loaf(e); *(de dent)* crown; **se faire poser une c.** to have a tooth crowned
couronnement [kurɔnmɑ̃] *nm (de souverain)* coronation; *Fig (réussite)* crowning achievement
couronner [kurɔne] *vt* (**a**) *(sacrer)* to crown; *Fig* **mes efforts furent couronnés de succès** my efforts were crowned with success; **et pour c. le tout...** and to crown it all... (**b**) *(dent)* to crown
courra *etc voir* **courir**
courre [kur] *voir* **chasse**
courriel [kurjɛl] *nm Can Ordinat* e-mail
courrier [kurje] *nm* (**a**) *(lettres)* mail, *Br* post; **c. électronique** e-mail; *Fam Hum* **c. escargot** snail mail; **c. interne** internal mail (**b**) *Journ* **c. du cœur** problem page; **c. des lecteurs** letters to the Editor (**c**) *Vieilli (messager)* courier
courroie [kurwa] *nf* (**a**) *(de cuir, de toile)* strap (**b**) *Méc* belt; **c. de transmission** driving belt; **c. de ventilateur** fanbelt
courroucé, -e [kuruse] *adj Litt* incensed
courroux [kuru] *nm Litt* ire, wrath
cours¹ [kur] *nm* (**a**) *(leçon) Univ* lecture; *Scol* lesson; *(ensemble des leçons)* course; **aller en c.** *Univ* to go to lectures; *Scol* to go to school; **prendre** *ou* **suivre un c.** to take *or* do a course; **donner des c.** *Univ* to give lectures; *Scol* to give classes; **c. par correspondance** correspondence course; **c. intensif** crash course; **c. magistral** lecture; **c. particulier** private lesson; **c. du soir** evening class (**b**) *(classe)* **c. élémentaire** = second and third years of primary school; **c. moyen** = fourth and fifth years of primary school; **c. préparatoire** = first year of primary school (**c**) *(de rivière, d'un astre)* course; **suivre le c. de ses pensées** to follow one's train of thought; **donner libre c. à qch** to give free rein to sth; **c. d'eau** waterway (**d**) *(évolution)* course; **suivre son c.** to run its course; **en c.** *(affaires)* in hand; *(travaux)* in progress, *(année)* current; **en c. de route** on the way; **au c. de qch** in the course of sth (**e**) *(d'une monnaie)* currency; **avoir c.** *(monnaie)* to be legal tender; *(pratique)* to be current (**f**) *Fin (d'une action)* price; *(de devises)* rate; **c. des changes** exchange rate; **c. pivot** central rate
cours² *voir* **courir**
course [kurs] *nf* (**a**) *Sport (épreuve)* race; *(discipline)* racing; **faire la c. avec qn** to race with sb; **les courses (de chevaux)** the races; *Fam* **ça va encore être la c.** it's going to be another mad rush; **la c. aux armements** the arms race; **c. automobile** motor race; *(discipline)* motor racing; **c. de chevaux** horse race; *Sport & Fig* **c. contre la montre** race against the clock; **c. cycliste** cycle race; **c. de haies** *(en athlétisme)* hurdles; *(course de chevaux)* steeplechase; **c. d'obstacles** steeplechase; **c. d'orientation** orienteering; **c. à pied** race; *(discipline)* running; **c. de taureaux** *(corrida)* bullfight (**b**) *(action de courir)* running (**c**) *(achat)* **faire une c.** to get something from the shops; **courses** shopping; **faire des courses** to go shopping (**d**) *(trajet en taxi)* journey; *(prix)* fare (**e**) *(de planète, de projectile)* course (**f**) *Suisse (trajet)* trip *(by train or boat)*; *(excursion)* excursion
courser [kurse] *vt Fam* to chase after
coursier, -ère [kursje, -ɛr] *nm,f* messenger; *(en moto)* motorcycle courier

coursive [kursiv] *nf Naut* gangway

court¹, -e [kur, kurt] **1** *adj* short; *Fam* **15 euros, c'est un peu c.** 15 euros, that's not very much **2** *adv* short; **pour faire c.** to cut a long story short; **on l'appelle Charles tout c.** people just call him Charles; **prendre qn de c.** *(en lui laissant peu de temps)* to give sb short notice; *(sans le prévenir)* to catch sb unawares; **à c. de** short of

court² *nm* **c. (de tennis)** (tennis) court

court³ *voir* **courir**

court-bouillon *(pl* **courts-bouillons**) [kurbujɔ̃] *nm* court-bouillon

court-circuit *(pl* **courts-circuits**) [kursirkɥi] *nm* short circuit

court-circuiter [kursirkɥite] *vt Élec & Fam Fig* to short-circuit

courtier, -ère [kurtje, -ɛr] *nm,f* broker; **c. d'assurances** insurance broker

courtisan [kurtizɑ̃] *nm* **(a)** *Hist* courtier **(b)** *Péj (flatteur)* sycophant

courtisane [kurtizan] *nf Litt* courtesan

courtiser [kurtize] *vt* **(a)** *(femme)* to court **(b)** *(flatter)* to fawn on

courtois, -e [kurtwa, -az] *adj (poli)* courteous (**envers** *ou* **avec** towards)

courtoisement [kurtwazmɑ̃] *adv* courteously

courtoisie [kurtwazi] *nf* courtesy (**envers** towards)

court-vêtu, -e *(mpl* **court-vêtus,** *fpl* **court-vêtues**) [kurvety] *adj* in a short skirt; **être c.** to be wearing a short skirt

couru, -e [kury] *adj* **(a)** *(lieu, spectacle)* popular **(b)** *Fam* **c'est c. (d'avance)** it's a sure thing

cousais *etc voir* **coudre**

couscous [kuskus] *nm* couscous

cousin¹, -e [kuzɛ̃, -in] *nm,f* cousin; **c. germain** first cousin

cousin² *nm (insecte)* mosquito

coussin [kusɛ̃] *nm* **(a)** *(de siège)* cushion; *Belg & Suisse (oreiller)* pillow **(b) c. d'air** air cushion

coussinet [kusinɛ] *nm* **(a)** *(coussin)* small cushion **(b)** *(d'animal)* pad

cousu, -e [kuzy] **1** *pp de* **coudre 2** *adj* sewn; **c. (à la) main** hand-sewn; *Fam Fig* **c'est du c. main** it's first-rate; **une histoire cousue de fil blanc** a blatant lie

coût [ku] *nm aussi Fig* cost; **le c. de la vie** the cost of living

coûtant [kutɑ̃] *adj m voir* **prix**

couteau, -x [kuto] *nm* **(a)** *(ustensile)* knife; **être à couteaux tirés (avec qn)** to be at daggers drawn (with sb); *Fig* **avoir le c. sous la gorge** to have a gun at one's head; **c. de cuisine** kitchen knife; **c. à fromage** cheese-knife; **c. à pain** breadknife; **c. suisse** Swiss army knife **(b)** *(mollusque)* razor shell **(c)** *Fig* **deuxième** *ou* **second c.** *(en politique, dans la Mafia)* minion

couteau-scie *(pl* **couteaux-scies**) [kutosi] *nm* serrated knife

coutelas [kutla] *nm* large knife

coûter [kute] *vi* to cost; **combien ça coûte?** how much is it?, how much does it cost?; **ça coûte 100 euros** it costs 100 euros, it's 100 euros; **c. les yeux de la tête** to cost a fortune; **ça ne coûte rien d'essayer** there's no harm in trying; **c. cher** to cost a lot, to be expensive; **cela vous coûtera cher** it'll cost you a lot; *Fig* you'll pay for that; **c. la vie à qn** to cost sb his/her life; **ça m'a beaucoup coûté** it was very painful for me; **coûte que coûte** at all costs

coûteux, -euse [kutø, -øz] *adj* costly, expensive; **peu c.** inexpensive

coutume [kutym] *nf* **(a)** *(habitude)* custom; **avoir c. de faire qch** to be accustomed to doing sth; **plus aimable que de c.** nicer than usual; **comme de c.** as usual; **une fois n'est pas c.** it won't hurt for once **(b)** *(tradition)* custom

coutumier, -ère [kutymje, -ɛr] *adj* **(a)** *(habituel)* customary, usual **(b)** *(personne)* **il est c. du fait** it's not the first time he's done that **(c)** *Jur* **droit c.** common law

couture [kutyr] **1** *nf* **(a)** *(de vêtement)* seam; *Fig* **examiner qn/qch sous toutes les coutures** to examine sb/sth from every angle **(b)** *(activité)* sewing, needlework; **faire de la c.** to sew **2** *adj inv (collection)* designer

couturier [kutyrje] *nm* fashion designer, couturier; **grand c.** big fashion designer

couturière [kutyrjɛr] *nf* dressmaker

couvaison [kuvɛzɔ̃] *nf* incubation

couvée [kuve] *nf* **(a)** *(œufs)* clutch **(b)** *(d'oisillons, d'enfants)* brood

couvent [kuvɑ̃] *nm* **(a)** *(communauté religieuse)* *(de femmes)* convent; *(d'hommes)* monastery **(b)** *(pensionnat)* convent school

couver [kuve] **1** *vt* **(a)** *(œufs)* to sit on; *Fig (personne)* to mollycoddle; **c. qn des yeux** to look fondly at sb **(b)** *(maladie)* to be coming down with **2** *vi (poule)* to brood; *(feu, passion)* to smoulder; *(émeute)* to be brewing

couvercle [kuvɛrkl] *nm* lid; *(qui se visse)* cap, top

couvert¹, -e [kuvɛr, -ɛrt] **1** *pp voir* **couvrir 2** *adj* **(a)** *(allée, marché)* covered; *(piscine)* indoor; **(b)** *(jonché, plein)* **c. de** covered with or in **(c)** *(habillé)* covered up; **chaudement** *ou* **bien c.** warmly dressed **(d)** *(ciel)* overcast

couvert² *nm* **(a)** *(ustensiles)* **un c. en argent** a silver knife, fork and spoon; **couverts** cutlery **(b)** *(pour chaque convive)* place setting; **mettre le c.** to set or *Br* lay the table; **mettre trois couverts** to set or *Br* lay the table for three; **mets deux couverts de plus** set or *Br* lay two extra places **(c) sous le c. de** *(sous l'apparence de)* under the cover of

couverture [kuvɛrtyr] *nf* **(a)** *(de lit)* blanket; *Fig* **tirer la c. à soi** to take all the credit; **c. chauffante** electric blanket **(b)** *(d'un livre, d'un magazine, d'un cahier)* cover; **en c.** on the cover **(c)** *(protection)* **c. sociale** social security cover **(d)** *(d'un bâtiment)* roofing **(e)** *(d'un événement médiatique)* coverage

couveuse [kuvøz] *nf* **(a)** *(pour nouveau-nés)* incubator **(b)** *(poule)* brooder

couvre-chef *(pl* **couvre-chefs**) [kuvrəʃɛf] *nm Hum* hat

couvre-feu *(pl* **couvre-feux**) [kuvrəfø] *nm Mil* curfew

couvre-lit *(pl* **couvre-lits**) [kuvrəli] *nm* bedspread

couvre-pied(s) *(pl* **couvre-pieds**) [kuvrəpje] *nm* quilt

couvreur [kuvrœr] *nm* roofer

couvrir [52] [kuvrir] **1** *vt* **(a)** *(casserole, meuble, livre)* to cover (**de** with) **(b) c. qn de** *(cadeaux, honneurs, compliments)* to shower sb with **(c)** *(protéger, justifier)* to cover; **être couvert par ses supérieurs** to be acting with the authority of one's superiors **(d)** *(parcourir, englober) & Journ* to cover **(e)** *(bruit, voix)* to drown (out) **(f)** *(sujet: assurance)* to cover **(g)** *Zool (femelle)* to cover **2 se couvrir** *vpr* **(a)** *(pour sortir)* to wrap up; *(pour cacher sa nudité)* to cover oneself up; *(mettre son chapeau)* to put on one's hat **(b)** *(ciel)* to cloud over; **le**

temps *ou* **ça se couvre** it's clouding over (**c**) **se c. de** *(honte, ridicule)* to cover oneself with; **se c. de feuilles** *(arbre)* to come into leaf; **se c. de boutons** *(visage)* to come out *or* to become covered in spots

covoiturage [kɔvwatyraʒ] *nm* car pooling *(for commuting to the workplace)*

cow-boy *(pl* **cow-boys**) [kobɔj] *nm* cowboy

coyote [kɔjɔt] *nm* coyote

CP [sepe] *nm (abrév* **cours préparatoire**) = first year of primary school

CPAM [sepeaɛm] *nf (abrév* **caisse primaire d'assurance maladie**) = French government department dealing with health insurance

CPE [sepeə] *nm (abrév* **contrat première embauche**) = employment contract for people under 26 which could be terminated without justification in the first two years, proposed by the French government but abandoned under public pressure

cpp *Ordinat (abrév* **caractères par pouce**) cpi

cps *Ordinat (abrév* **caractères par seconde**) cps

crabe [krab] *nm* crab; **marcher en c.** to walk sideways

crac [krak] **1** *exclam (bruit de cassure)* crack!; *Fam* **et c., elle est tombée malade!** and what do you know, she fell ill!
  2 *nm* crack

crachat [kraʃa] *nm* gob of spit; **crachats** spit

craché [kraʃe] *adj inv Fam* **c'est sa mère tout c., c'est le portrait (tout) c. de sa mère** she's the spitting image of her mother; **c'est lui tout c.!** that's just like him!

cracher [kraʃe] **1** *vi* (**a**) *(personne)* to spit; **c. sur qn** to spit at sb; *Fam Fig* **ne pas c. sur qch** not to say no to sth; *Fam Fig* **c. dans la soupe** to bite the hand that feeds one (**b**) *(stylo)* to splutter (**c**) *(haut-parleur, téléphone, radio)* to crackle
  2 *vt* (**a**) *(chewing-gum, nourriture)* to spit out; **c. du sang** to spit blood (**b**) *(fumée)* to belch out (**c**) *très Fam (somme d'argent)* to cough up

cracheur, -euse [kraʃœr, -øz] *nm,f* **c. de feu** fire-eater

crachin [kraʃɛ̃] *nm* (fine) drizzle

crachoir [kraʃwar] *nm* spittoon; *Fam Fig* **tenir le c.** to monopolize the conversation; *Fam Fig* **tenir le c. à qn** to listen to sb rambling on and on

crachoter [kraʃɔte] *vi (feu)* to splutter; *(radio, téléphone)* to crackle

crack [krak] *nm* (**a**) *Fam (personne)* ace (**en** at) (**b**) *(drogue)* crack

cracker [krakœr] *nm* cracker

Cracovie [krakɔvi] *n* Cracow

cracra [krakra] *adj inv Fam* filthy

crade [krad], **cradingue** [kradɛ̃g], **crado** [krado] *adj Fam* filthy

craie [krɛ] *nf (matière)* chalk; *(bâtonnet)* stick of chalk

craignais *etc voir* **craindre**

craignos [krɛɲos] *adj Fam (laid)* hideous; *(louche)* dodgy

craindre [23] [krɛ̃dr] **1** *vt* (**a**) *(redouter)* to fear, to be afraid of; **ne craignez rien!** *(n'ayez pas peur)* don't be frightened!; *(ne vous inquiétez pas)* don't worry!; **je crains qu'il (ne) soit parti** I'm afraid he's left; **c. de faire qch** to be afraid of doing sth (**b**) *(ne pas supporter)* **ces plantes craignent le gel** these plants don't like frost; **craint l'humidité/la chaleur** *(sur emballage)* keep dry/cool
  2 *vi Fam* **ça craint!** *(c'est ennuyeux)* what a pain!; *(c'est très laid)* it's hideous!; *(c'est louche)* it's shady *or Br* dodgy

craint, -e¹ *voir* **craindre**

crainte² [krɛ̃t] *nf* fear; **de c. de tomber** for fear of falling; **de c. qu'on ne l'entende** for fear of being overheard; **soyez sans c., n'ayez c.** have no fear

craintif, -ive [krɛ̃tif, -iv] *adj* timid

cramer [krame] *Fam* **1** *vi & vt* to burn
  2 se cramer *vpr* to burn oneself; **se c. les doigts** to burn one's fingers

cramoisi, -e [kramwazi] *adj* crimson

crampe [krɑ̃p] *nf* cramp; **j'ai une c. au pied** I've got cramp in my foot; **crampes d'estomac** stomach cramps

crampon [krɑ̃pɔ̃] *nm* (**a**) *(de chaussure de sport)* stud; *(pour alpinisme)* crampon; **crampons** *(chaussures)* boots with studs (**b**) *Constr* cramp (iron) (**c**) *Fam (personne)* leech

cramponner [krɑ̃pɔne] **se cramponner** *vpr* to hold on; **se c. à** to hold on to; *Fig (vie, espoir)* to cling to; *(fonction)* to hang on to

cran [krɑ̃] *nm* (**a**) *(entaille)* notch; *(de ceinture)* hole; **serrer sa ceinture d'un c.** to take one's belt in a notch; **c. de sûreté** *ou* **d'arrêt** safety catch; **(couteau à) c. d'arrêt** *Br* flick knife, *Am* switchblade (**b**) *Fig (degré)* **avancer/reculer d'un c.** to go up/come down a notch (**c**) *Fam* **être à c.** to be wound up (**d**) *Fam (courage)* guts; **avoir du c.** to have guts (**e**) *(dans les cheveux)* crimp

crâne [krɑn] *nm* skull, *Spéc* cranium; *Fam* **avoir mal au c.** to have a headache; *Fam* **mets-toi ça dans le c.!** get that into your thick skull!

crâner [krɑne] *vi Fam* to swagger, to show off

crâneur, -euse [krɑnœr, -øz] *Fam* **1** *adj* swaggering; **être c.** to be a show-off
  2 *nm,f* show-off

crânien, -enne [krɑnjɛ̃, -ɛn] *adj Anat* cranial

crapahuter [krapayte] *vi Fam* (**a**) *(marcher)* to traipse about (**b**) *Mil (soldat)* to trudge along

crapaud [krapo] *nm* (**a**) *(animal)* toad (**b**) *(défaut)* flaw

crapule [krapyl] *nf* scoundrel, villain

crapuleux, -euse [krapylø, -øz] *adj voir* **crime**

craquant, -e [krakɑ̃, -ɑ̃t] *adj Fam (personne)* gorgeous

craque [krak] *nf Fam (mensonge)* fib, lie

craqueler [42] [krakle] **1** *vt* to crack
  2 se craqueler *vpr* to crack

craquement [krakmɑ̃] *nm (de branche)* crack; *(d'escalier, de plancher)* creak; **des craquements** cracking/creaking

craquer [krake] **1** *vi* (**a**) *(branche)* to crack; *(escalier, plancher)* to creak; **faire c. ses doigts** to crack one's fingers (**b**) *(se déchirer)* to rip; *(se casser)* to snap (**c**) *(perdre le contrôle de soi)* to crack up (**d**) *Fam (succomber)* **c. pour qn** to fall for sb; **ce mec me fait c.** *Br* I really fancy that guy, *Am* I have a major crush on that guy
  2 *vt* (**a**) *(allumette)* to strike (**b**) *(déchirer)* to rip

crasse [kras] **1** *adj (ignorance)* crass
  2 *nf* (**a**) *(saleté)* filth (**b**) *Fam (mauvais tour)* dirty trick; **faire une c. à qn** to play a dirty trick on sb

crasseux, -euse [krasø, -øz] *adj* filthy

cratère [kratɛr] *nm* crater

cravache [kravaʃ] *nf (riding)* crop; *Fig* **mener qn à la c.** to rule sb with a rod of iron

cravacher [kravaʃe] **1** *vt (cheval)* to use the crop on
  2 *vi Fam (travailler vite)* to work like mad

cravate [kravat] *nf* tie; *Fam* **s'en jeter un derrière la c.** to knock back a drink

crawl [krol] *nm* crawl; **nager le c.** to do the crawl
crayeux, -euse [krɛjø, -øz] *adj (matière, teint)* chalky
crayon [krɛjɔ̃] *nm* (**a**) *(pour écrire)* pencil; **écrire au c.**
to write in pencil; **c. de couleur** coloured pencil, crayon; **c. gras** soft lead pencil; *Ordinat* **c. lumineux** *ou* **optique** light pen (**b**) *(bâton)* stick; **c. à lèvres** lip pencil (**c**) *(œuvre)* pencil drawing
créance [kreɑ̃s] *nf* debt; **c. douteuse** bad debt
créancier, -ère [kreɑ̃sje, -ɛr] *nm,f* creditor
créateur, -trice [kreatœr, -tris] **1** *adj (génie)* creative; **industrie créatrice d'emplois** job-creating industry **2** *nm,f* creator; **c. (de mode)** (fashion) designer; *Rel* **le C.** the Creator
créatif, -ive [kreatif, -iv] *adj* creative
création [kreasjɔ̃] *nf* (**a**) *(fait de créer)* creation; **c. d'emplois** job creation (**b**) *(produit)* new product; *(d'un couturier)* creation (**c**) *(univers)* **la c.** creation (**d**) *(première représentation) (d'une pièce)* first production; *(d'un rôle)* creation; *(d'une œuvre musicale)* first performance
créativité [kreativite] *nf* creativity
créature [kreatyr] *nf* (**a**) *(être vivant)* creature; *Hum* **une c. de rêve** *(femme)* a magnificent woman (**b**) *Péj (protégé)* creature
crécelle [kresɛl] *nf* rattle; **une voix de c.** a rasping voice
crèche [krɛʃ] *nf* (**a**) *(garderie)* crèche, day nursery (**b**) *(de Noël)* crib

Crèche
State-subsidized care for children under three years of age of working families is well established in France, although this is subject to the availability of places.

crécher [34] [kreʃe] *vi Fam (habiter)* to live; *(temporairement)* to crash
crédibilité [kredibilite] *nf* credibility
crédible [kredibl] *adj* credible
crédit [kredi] *nm* (**a**) *(prêt)* credit; **à c.** on credit; **faire c. à qn** to give sb credit; **la maison ne fait pas c.** *(sur panneau)* we do not give credit; **c. à la consommation** consumer credit; **c. gratuit** interest-free credit; **c. immobilier** home loan, mortgage (**b**) *(en comptabilité)* credit side; **porter une somme au c. de qn** to credit sb with a sum; *Écol* **crédits de carbone** carbon credits (**c**) **crédits** *(somme d'argent)* funds (**d**) *Litt (influence)* credit
crédit-bail *(pl* **crédits-bails)** [kredibaj] *nm* leasing
créditer [kredite] *vt* (**a**) *Fin (compte)* to credit (**de** with) (**b**) *Fig* **c. qn de qch** to give sb credit for sth
créditeur, -trice [kreditœr, -tris] *adj (solde, compte)* credit; **être c.** to be in credit
crédit-relais *(pl* **crédits-relais)** [kredirəlɛ] *nm* bridging loan
credo [kredo] *nm inv* credo, creed
crédule [kredyl] *adj* credulous
crédulité [kredylite] *nf* credulity
créer [24] [kree] **1** *vt* (**a**) *(emplois, poste)* to create; *(entreprise)* to set up (**b**) *(œuvre, nouveau produit, vêtement)* to create (**c**) *(difficultés, problème)* to create (**à** for) (**d**) *(interpréter pour la première fois) (rôle)* to create; *(pièce de théâtre)* to produce for the first time; *(œuvre musicale)* to perform for the first time **2 se créer** *vpr* (**a**) *(être créé)* to be created (**b**) *(pour soi-même)* **se c. une clientèle** to build up a clientèle; **se c. des problèmes** to create problems for oneself

crémaillère [kremajɛr] *nf (dans la cheminée)* trammel (hook); *Fig* **pendre la c.** to have a housewarming (party)
crémant [kremɑ̃] *nm* slightly sparkling champagne
crémation [kremasjɔ̃] *nf* cremation
crématoire [krematwar] *adj voir* **four**
crématorium [krematɔrjɔm] *nm* crematorium
crème [krɛm] *nf* (**a**) *(du lait, dessert)* cream; *Fig* **c'est la c. des hommes** he's the best of men; **c. anglaise** custard; **c. au beurre** ≃ butter cream; **c. brûlée** crème brûlée; **c. (au) caramel** caramel custard, crème caramel; **c. Chantilly** whipped cream *(with sugar added)*; **c. fouettée** whipped cream; **c. fraîche** crème fraîche; **c. glacée** ice cream; **c. pâtissière** confectioner's custard; **c. renversée** crème caramel *(turned out of its mould)* (**b**) *(produit cosmétique)* cream; **c. antirides** anti-wrinkle cream; **c. hydratante** moisturizing cream; **c. à raser** shaving cream; **c. solaire** suncream (**c**) *(liqueur)* **c. de menthe** crème de menthe; **c. de cassis** blackcurrant liqueur **2** *nm Fam* **un grand c.** a large white coffee **3** *adj inv* cream(-coloured)
crémerie [krɛmri] *nf (magasin)* dairy; *Fam Fig* **changer de c.** to go somewhere else, to move on
crémeux, -euse [kremø, -øz] *adj* creamy
crémier, -ère [kremje, -ɛr] *nm,f* dairyman, *f* dairywoman
crémone [kremɔn] *nf* espagnolette
créneau, -x [kreno] *nm* (**a**) *(de rempart)* crenel; *Fig* **monter au c.** to step into the breach (**b**) *(manœuvre)* **faire un c.** to reverse into a (parking) space (**c**) *Com* niche (**d**) *(dans un programme, un emploi du temps)* slot; **c. horaire** time slot
crénelé, -e [krɛnle] *adj* crenellated
créole [kreɔl] **1** *adj* Creole **2** *nmf* **C.** Creole **3** *nm (langue)* Creole **4** *nfpl* **créoles** *(boucles d'oreille)* hoop earrings
crêpe [krɛp] **1** *nf* pancake **2** *nm* (**a**) *(tissu)* crêpe (**b**) *(caoutchouc)* crêpe (rubber); **semelles (de) c.** crêpe soles
crêper [krepe] **1** *vt* (**a**) *(cheveux)* to backcomb (**b**) *(tissu)* to crimp **2 se crêper** *vpr Fam Fig* **se c. le chignon** to have a cat-fight
crêperie [krɛpri] *nf* pancake restaurant
crépi, -e [krepi] *adj & nm Constr* roughcast
crépir [krepir] *vt Constr* to roughcast
crépitement [krepitmɑ̃] *nm (du feu)* crackling
crépiter [krepite] *vi (feu)* to crackle
crépon [krepɔ̃] *nm (papier)* crêpe paper
crépu, -e [krepy] *adj* frizzy
crépuscule [krepyskyl] *nm aussi Fig* twilight; **au c.** at twilight
crescendo [kreʃɛndo] **1** *adv* crescendo; **aller c.** to get louder and louder; *Fig (difficultés)* to get worse and worse **2** *nm* crescendo
cresson [kresɔ̃, krəsɔ̃] *nm* watercress
crétacé, -e [kretase] *Géol* **1** *adj* Cretaceous **2** *nm* **le C.** the Cretaceous period
Crète [krɛt] *nf* **la C.** Crete
crête [krɛt] *nf* (**a**) *(d'oiseau)* crest; *(de coq)* comb (**b**) *(de montagne, de vague, de toit)* crest
crétin, -e [kretɛ̃, -in] *nm,f Fam* cretin
crétois, -e [kretwa, -az] **1** *adj* Cretan **2** *nm,f* **C.** Cretan

cretonne [krətɔn] *nf* cretonne

cretons [krɔtɔ̃] *nmpl Can* potted pork

creuser [krøze] **1** *vt* (**a**) *(trou, tranchée, puits)* to dig; *Fig* **c. l'écart entre** to widen the gap between; *Fig* **c. un abîme entre deux personnes** to create a gulf between two people (**b**) *(évider)* to hollow (out); **c. la terre** to dig (**c**) *(problème, question)* to look into (**d**) *(donner faim à)* **c. qn** to give sb an appetite; **le grand air, ça creuse** the fresh air gives you an appetite (**e**) *(cambrer)* **c. les reins** to arch one's back (**f**) *(amaigrir)* **il avait le visage creusé par la fatigue/la maladie** his face was gaunt with exhaustion/illness
2 *vi* to dig
3 **se creuser** *vpr* (**a**) *(s'agrandir) (écart)* to widen (**b**) **se c. (la tête** *ou* **la cervelle) (pour faire qch)** to *Br* rack *or Am* cudgel one's brains (to do sth) (**c**) *(visage)* to grow hollow

creuset [krøzɛ] *nm* (**a**) *Chim* crucible (**b**) *Fig* melting pot

creux, -euse [krø, krøz] **1** *adj* (**a**) *(vide) (arbre, mur, dent)* hollow; *(chemin)* sunken; *Fig* **avoir le ventre c.** to be hungry (**b**) *(période, heures)* off-peak (**c**) *(joues)* hollow; *(visage)* gaunt (**d**) *Péj (débat, discours, personne)* hollow
2 *adv* **sonner c.** to sound hollow; *Fig* to sound empty
3 *nm* (**a**) *(de la main, dans le sol, sur une route)* hollow; **le c. des reins** the small of the back (**b**) *(d'une vague, d'une courbe)* trough; *Fig* **être au c. de la vague** to have hit rock bottom (**c**) *Fam* **avoir un (petit) c.** to be feeling (a bit) *Br* peckish *or Am* snackish

crevaison [krəvɛzɔ̃] *nf (d'un pneu)* puncture, flat

crevant, -e [krəvɑ̃, -ɑ̃t] *adj Fam* (**a**) *(fatigant)* exhausting (**b**) *(drôle)* priceless

crevasse [krəvas] *nf* (**a**) *(sur la peau)* crack; **avoir des crevasses aux mains** to have chapped hands (**b**) *(dans un mur, le sol)* crack; *(dans un glacier)* crevasse

crevé, -e [krəve] *adj* (**a**) *(éclaté) (ballon, pneu)* burst (**b**) *Fam (fatigué)* dead beat (**c**) *très Fam (mort)* dead

crève [krɛv] *nf très Fam* **avoir la c.** *(gros rhume)* to have a stinking cold; **attraper la c.** to catch one's death of cold

crève-cœur [krɛvkœr] *nm inv* heartbreak; **c'est un c. de partir** it's heartbreaking to leave

crève-la-faim [krɛvlafɛ̃] *nm inv Fam* down-and-out

crever [46] [krəve] **1** *vt* (**a**) *(ballon, sac, pneu)* to burst; **c. un œil à qn** to put sb's eye out; **ça me crève le cœur** I'm heartbroken about it; *Fig* **ça crève les yeux** it sticks out a mile; *Fig* **c. l'écran** to have great screen presence (**b**) *Fam (épuiser)* to wear out (**c**) *très Fam* **c. la dalle** to be starving
2 *vi* (**a**) *(éclater)* to burst; **mon pneu a** *ou Fam* **j'ai crevé** I've got a puncture; **c. de** *(jalousie, orgueil)* to be bursting with (**b**) *(mourir) (bête, plante)* to die; *très Fam (personne)* to kick the bucket, to snuff it; *Fam* **il fait une chaleur à c.** it's boiling hot; *Fam* **c. d'envie de faire qch** to be dying to do sth; *Fam* **c. de faim** *(mourir)* to starve to death; *(avoir faim)* to be starving; *Fam* **c. de soif** to be parched; *Fam* **c. de froid/de chaud** to be freezing/boiling; *Fam* **c. de rire** to split one's sides laughing; *Fam* **qu'il crève!** he can go to hell!; *Fam* **plutôt c.!** I'd rather die!
3 **se crever** *vpr Fam* to wear oneself out

crevette [krəvɛt] *nf* **c. (rose)** prawn; **c. grise** shrimp

cri [kri] *nm* (**a**) *(d'une personne)* cry, shout; *(perçant)* scream; **j'ai entendu des cris** I heard shouting; *Fig* **pousser les hauts cris** to kick up a fuss; **c'est le c. du**

cœur it's a cry from the heart; *Mil* **c. de guerre** war cry (**b**) *(d'un animal, d'un oiseau)* cry

criailler [kriaje] *vi* (**a**) *(crier sans arrêt)* to bawl (**b**) *(faisan, pintade)* to cry; *(oie)* to honk

criant, -e [krijɑ̃, -ɑ̃t] *adj (erreur)* glaring; *(preuve, contraste)* striking; *(vérité)* obvious; *(abus, injustice)* blatant; **c. de vérité** *(témoignage, reportage)* obviously true

criard, -e [krijar, -ard] *adj* (**a**) *(aigu) (voix)* shrill (**b**) *(couleur)* loud (**c**) *(enfant)* noisy

crible [kribl] *nm* sieve; *Fig* **passer qch au c.** to go through sth with a fine-tooth comb

criblé, -e [krible] *adj* **c. de** *(trous, balles)* riddled with; *Fig* **être c. de dettes** to be up to one's eyes in debt

cric [krik] *nm* jack

cricket [krikɛt] *nm* cricket

criée [krije] *nf (vente)* (sale by) auction; *(salle)* auction room; *(dehors)* auction area; **à la c.** by auction

crier [66] [krije] **1** *vi* (**a**) *(personne)* to shout, to cry (out); *(fort)* to scream; *(parler très fort)* to shout; **c. de douleur** to cry out *or* scream with pain; **c. contre** *ou* **après qn** to shout at sb; **c. au secours** to shout for help; **c. au scandale** to protest, to be up in arms; **c. qch sur les toits** to shout sth from the rooftops (**b**) *(souris)* to squeak; *(oiseau)* to call
2 *vt (ordre, injures)* to shout (**à** at); **c. à qn de faire qch** to shout to sb to do sth; **c. son innocence** to protest one's innocence

crime [krim] *nm* (**a**) *Jur & Fig* crime; **ce n'est pas un c.!** it's not a crime!; **c. crapuleux** crime committed for financial gain; **c. d'État** treason; **crimes de guerre** war crimes; **c. contre l'humanité** crime against humanity (**b**) *(meurtre)* murder; **c. passionnel** crime of passion

criminalité [kriminalite] *nf* crime

criminel, -elle [kriminɛl] **1** *adj (acte)* criminal; *Fam* **ce serait c. de la jeter** it would be criminal to throw it away
2 *nm,f* (**a**) *(malfaiteur)* criminal; **c. de guerre** war criminal (**b**) *(assassin)* murderer

criminologie [kriminɔlɔʒi] *nf* criminology

crin [krɛ̃] *nm* horsehair; *Fig* **à tout c., à tous crins** out-and-out

crinière [krinjɛr] *nf aussi Fig* mane

crinoline [krinɔlin] *nf* crinoline

crique [krik] *nf* creek

criquet [krikɛ] *nm* locust

crise [kriz] *nf* (**a**) *(marasme, période d'instabilité)* crisis; **c. de l'énergie** energy crisis; **c. du logement** housing crisis *or* shortage (**b**) *(d'une maladie)* attack; **c. cardiaque** heart attack; **c. de foie** bilious attack (**c**) *(accès)* **c. de colère** fit of anger; **c. de conscience** attack of conscience; **c. de larmes** crying fit; **c. de nerfs** attack of nerves, fit of hysterics; *Fam* **la c. (de rire)!** what a hoot! (**d**) *Fam (colère)* fit of rage; **piquer** *ou* **faire une c.** to throw a fit

crispant, -e [krispɑ̃, -ɑ̃t] *adj Fam* irritating, annoying

crispé, -e [krispe] *adj (visage, personne)* tense; *(sourire, rire)* forced

crisper [krispe] **1** *vt* (**a**) *(poings, mains)* to clench; *(corps)* to tense (**b**) *(énerver)* to irritate, to annoy
2 **se crisper** *vpr (muscle, visage)* to tense; *(sourire)* to become strained; *(personne)* to get tense

crissement [krismɑ̃] *nm (de la craie sur le tableau)* squeak; *(des pneus, des freins)* squeal; *(du gravier, de la neige)* crunch

crisser [krise] *vi (pneus, freins)* to squeal; *(gravier, neige)* to crunch; *(craie)* to squeak

cristal, -aux [kristal, -o] *nm* crystal; **c. de roche** rock crystal; **cristaux** *(verre)* crystal(ware); *(de sel, de glace)* crystals; *Tech* **cristaux liquides** liquid crystal

cristallin, -e [kristalɛ̃, -in] **1** *adj* (**a**) *(roche)* crystalline (**b**) *Fig (eau, voix)* crystal-clear; *(son, note)* ringing
  2 *nm (de l'œil)* crystalline lens

cristalliser [kristalize] **1** *vi* to crystallize
  2 se cristalliser *vpr* to crystallize

critère [kritɛr] *nm* criterion; *Ordinat* **c. de tri** sort criterion; *UE* **critères de convergence** convergence criteria

critérium [kriterjɔm] *nm Sport* heat

critique¹ [kritik] *adj (décisif, crucial)* critical

critique² **1** *adj (esprit, personne, édition)* critical
  2 *nmf* critic; **c. d'art/de cinéma** art/film critic; **c. gastronomique** restaurant critic
  3 *nf* (**a**) *(condamnation)* criticism; **si je peux me permettre de vous faire une c.,...** if I could just make one criticism,...; **il n'accepte pas la c.** he can't take criticism (**b**) *(article)* critical article; *Théât & Cin* review; **faire la c. de qch** to review sth (**c**) **la c.** *(l'ensemble des critiques)* the critics

critiquer [kritike] *vt (personne, attitude)* to criticize (**pour** for); **ce n'est pas pour te c., mais...** I don't mean to criticize, but...; **c'est facile de c.** it's easy to criticize

croassement [krɔasmɑ̃] *nm* caw; **des croassements** cawing

croasser [krɔase] *vi* to caw

croate [krɔat] **1** *adj* Croatian
  2 *nmf* **C.** Croat, Croatian

Croatie [krɔasi] *nf* **la C.** Croatia

croc [kro] *nm* (**a**) *(de loup, de chien)* fang; *Fam Fig* **avoir les crocs** to be famished (**b**) *(crochet)* hook

croc-en-jambe (*pl* **crocs-en-jambes**) [krɔkɑ̃ʒɑ̃b] *nm* trip; **faire un c. à qn** to trip sb up

croche [krɔʃ] *nf Mus Br* quaver, *Am* eighth note

croche-pied (*pl* **croche-pieds**) [krɔʃpje] = **croc-en-jambe**

crochet [krɔʃɛ] *nm* (**a**) *(pour accrocher)* hook; *Fig* **vivre aux crochets de qn** to live off sb (**b**) *(pour tricoter)* crochet hook; *(technique)* crochet; **faire du c.** to (do) crochet (**c**) *(détour)* **faire un c. (par)** *(personne)* to make a detour (through) (**d**) *Typ* square bracket; **entre crochets** in square brackets (**e**) *(coup de poing)* **c. du gauche/du droit** left/right hook (**f**) *(d'un serpent)* fang

crocheter [39] [krɔʃte] *vt (serrure)* to pick; *(porte)* to pick the lock on

crochu, -e [krɔʃy] *adj (nez, bec)* hooked; *(doigts)* claw-like

crocodile [krɔkɔdil] *nm* crocodile; **en c.** *(sac, chaussures)* crocodile(-skin)

crocus [krɔkys] *nm* crocus

croire [25] [krwar] **1** *vt* (**a**) *(accepter, faire confiance à)* to believe; *Fam Ironique* **c'est ça, je te crois!** is that so?; *Fam* **faut pas c.!** don't you believe it!; **croyez-moi, ce n'était pas facile** believe (you) me, it wasn't easy; **à l'en c.,...** to hear him/her, you'd think...; **si on en croit la rumeur,...** if the rumour is to be believed,...; **je n'en croyais pas mes yeux/mes oreilles** I couldn't believe my eyes/my ears (**b**) *(penser)* to think; **je crois que oui** I think so; **je crois que non** I don't think so; **je ne crois pas** I don't think so; **vous**

croyez? do you really think so?; **je vous croyais anglais/riche** I thought you were English/rich; **j'ai cru nécessaire de...** I thought it necessary to...; **j'ai cru bien faire** I thought or believed I was doing the right thing; **elle ne croyait pas si bien dire** she didn't know how right she was; **je n'aurais pas cru cela de lui** I would never have thought it of him; **on croirait qu'il dort** you'd think he was asleep
  2 *vi (avoir la foi)* to be a believer
  3 croire à *vt ind* (**a**) *(envisager)* **le médecin crut à une rougeole** the doctor thought it was measles (**b**) *(accepter)* to believe; **veuillez c. ou je vous prie de c. à l'expression de mes sentiments distingués** yours sincerely (**c**) *(avoir confiance en, adhérer à)* to believe in
  4 croire en *vt ind (personne, talent, Dieu)* to believe in
  5 se croire *vpr* **il se croit intelligent** he thinks he's clever; **il se croit tout permis** he thinks he can get away with anything; **on se serait cru en octobre** it felt like October; *Fam* **se c. sorti de la cuisse de Jupiter** to think a lot of oneself, to think one is God's gift; *Fam* **il s'y croit** he thinks a lot of himself

croisade [krwazad] *nf Hist & Fig* crusade; **partir en c.** to go on a crusade

croisé, -e [krwaze] **1** *adj (manteau, veste)* double-breasted
  2 *nm Hist* crusader

croisement [krwazmɑ̃] *nm* (**a**) *(carrefour)* crossroads *(singulier)*, intersection (**b**) *(d'animaux)* crossing; *(animal)* cross (**entre** between)

croiser [krwaze] **1** *vt* (**a**) *(couper) (ligne, route)* to cross; **c. le regard de qn** to meet sb's gaze (**b**) *(passer à côté de)* *(véhicule, personne)* to pass (**c**) *(mettre l'un sur l'autre)* **c. les jambes** to cross one's legs; **c. les bras** to fold one's arms; *Fig* **c. les doigts** to keep one's fingers crossed; **je croise les doigts** fingers crossed (**d**) *(animaux, espèces)* to cross(breed)
  2 *vi (navire)* to cruise
  3 se croiser *vpr* (**a**) *(lignes, routes)* to cross, to intersect; *(regards)* to meet (**b**) *(personnes) (dans la rue)* to walk past each other; *(se voir rapidement)* to meet briefly; *(lettres)* to cross

croiseur [krwazœr] *nm Naut* cruiser

croisière [krwazjɛr] *nf* cruise; **faire une c.** to go on a cruise

croisillon [krwazijɔ̃] *nm* (**a**) *(de croix)* crosspiece (**b**) **croisillons** *(de fenêtre, de barrière)* latticework; *(sur une tarte)* lattice

croissais *etc voir* **croître**

croissance [krwasɑ̃s] *nf (d'un enfant)* & *Écon* growth; **en pleine c.** growing rapidly; **finir sa c.** *(enfant)* to stop growing

croissant¹, -e [krwasɑ̃, -ɑ̃t] *adj (plante, tendance, angoisse)* growing; *(ordre)* ascending; *(chaleur, température)* increasing

croissant² *nm* (**a**) *(arc de cercle)* crescent; **un c. de lune** a crescent moon; **en c.** crescent-shaped (**b**) *(pâtisserie)* croissant; **c. au beurre/ordinaire** croissant made with/without butter

croissant³ *voir* **croître**

croître [4b] [krwatr] *vi* (**a**) *(enfant, plantes)* to grow (**b**) *(vente, chiffre)* to grow, to increase (**de** by); *(jours)* to get longer; *(lune)* to wax; **aller croissant** *(succès)* to grow and grow; *(suspense)* to get worse and worse

croix [krwa] *nf* cross; **signer d'une c.** to make one's mark; *Fam Fig* **faire une c. sur qch** to say goodbye to sth; **en (forme de) c.** cross-shaped; **les bras en c.** with one's arms stretched out at the sides; **c. de bois c.** de fer, **si je mens je vais en enfer** cross my heart and hope to die; **c'est la c. et la bannière** it's the devil of a job; **c. gammée** swastika; **la c. de Lorraine** the cross of Lorraine *(symbol of the Gaullist movement)*; **la C.-Rouge** the Red Cross

croquant, -e [krɔkã, -ãt] *adj* crisp, crunchy

croque-au-sel [krɔkosɛl] **à la croque-au-sel** *adv* = raw and seasoned only with salt

croque-madame [krɔkmadam] *nm inv* = toasted cheese and ham sandwich topped with a fried egg

croque-monsieur [krɔkməsjø] *nm inv* = toasted cheese and ham sandwich

croque-mort *(pl* **croque-morts)** [krɔkmɔr] *nm Fam* undertaker

croquer [krɔke] **1** *vt* **(a)** *(pomme, bonbon)* to crunch; *Fig (fortune, héritage)* to squander; **à sucer ou à c.** *(sur boîte de médicaments)* may be sucked or chewed; *Fig* **c. la vie à belles dents** to make the most of life; **il est à c.** *(enfant)* he looks good enough to eat; **joli** *ou* **mignon à c.** as pretty as a picture **(b)** *(faire un croquis de)* to sketch **2** *vi* **(a)** *(pomme, salade)* to be crunchy **(b)** *(mordre)* **c. dans** to bite into

croquet [krɔkɛ] *nm (jeu)* croquet

croquette [krɔkɛt] *nf (de pomme de terre, de viande, de poisson)* croquette; **croquettes** *(pour chien, chat)* biscuits

croquis [krɔki] *nm* sketch; **faire un c. de qch** to make a sketch of sth

cross [krɔs] *nm (sport)* cross-country running; *(événement)* cross-country run

crosse [krɔs] *nf* **(a)** *(de fusil)* butt; *(de pistolet)* grip; *(d'évêque)* crook **(b)** *(de hockey)* stick; *Fam Fig* **chercher des crosses à qn** to try to pick a fight with sb **(c)** *Can (jeu)* lacrosse

crotte [krɔt] *nf* **(a)** *(de cheval, de mouton, de lapin)* dung, droppings; **une c. de chien** dog dirt; **c. de nez** *Br* bogey, *Am* booger; *Fam* **c.!** *Br* blast!, *Am* darn it! **(b)** **une c. de chocolat** a chocolate **(c)** *Vieilli (boue)* mud

crotter [krɔte] **1** *vt (chaussures, manteau)* to cover in mud **2 se crotter** *vpr* to get covered in mud

crottin [krɔtɛ̃] *nm* **(a)** *(excrément) (de cheval)* dung **(b)** *(fromage)* small goat's-milk cheese

croulant, -e [krulã, -ãt] **1** *adj (bâtiment)* crumbling **2** *nm,f très Fam* **vieux c.** old fossil

crouler [krule] *vi (bâtiment)* to crumble; **c. sous le poids de qch** to give way under the weight of sth; **c. sous le travail** to be snowed under with work; **la salle croulait sous les applaudissements** the audience brought the house down

croupe [krup] *nf* rump; **monter en c.** to ride behind

croupi, -e [krupi] *adj (eau)* stagnant

croupier [krupje] *nm* croupier

croupion [krupjɔ̃] *nm (d'oiseau)* rump; *(d'une volaille) Br* parson's *ou Am* pope's nose

croupir [krupir] *vi* **(a)** *(eau)* to stagnate **(b)** *(végéter)* **c. en prison** to rot in prison

croupissant, -e [krupisã, -ãt] *adj (eau, vie)* stagnant

CROUS [krus] *nm (abrév* **Centre régional des œuvres universitaires et scolaires)** = organization responsible for student accommodation and catering etc

croustillant, -e [krustijã, -ãt] *adj* **(a)** *(biscuit, pâte)* crisp; *(pain)* crusty **(b)** *Fig (histoire, détails)* spicy

croustiller [krustije] *vi (biscuit, pâte)* to be crisp; *(pain)* to be crusty

croustilles [krustij] *nfpl Can Br* crisps, *Am* chips

croûte [krut] *nf* **(a)** *(de pain, de tarte)* crust; *(de fromage)* rind; *(d'une plaie)* scab; **la c. terrestre** the earth's crust; *Fam* **gagner sa c.** to earn one's bread and butter **(b)** *Fam (mauvaise peinture)* daub

croûton [krutɔ̃] *nm* **(a)** *(de pain)* end **(b)** *(dans la soupe, les salades)* crouton **(c)** *Fam* **(vieux) c.** old fossil

croyable [krwajabl] *adj* believable, credible; **ce n'est pas c.!** it's unbelievable!, it's incredible!

croyais *etc voir* **croire**

croyance [krwajãs] *nf* belief **(en** in)

croyant, -e [krwajã, -ãt] **1** *adj* **être c.** to be a believer **2** *nm,f* believer

CRS [sɛɛrɛs] *nm (abrév* **compagnie républicaine de sécurité)** *Br* ≃ riot policeman, *Am* ≃ state trooper; **les C.** *Br* ≃ the riot police, *Am* ≃ the state troopers

CRS

The CRS is the Minister of the Interior's police force, whose primary responsibility is to ensure public order at demonstrations and deal with riots. They have been criticized for certain strong-arm tactics.

cru¹, -e¹ [kry] *adj* **(a)** *(viande, poisson, légumes)* raw; *(lait)* unpasteurized **(b)** *(couleur, lumière)* garish **(c)** *(licencieux) (langage)* crude **(d)** *(direct) (réponse, personne)* blunt **(e)** **monter à c.** to ride bareback **(f)** *Belg, Can & Suisse (temps, bâtiment)* damp and cold

cru² *nm (terroir)* vineyard; *(vin)* wine; **un grand c.** a vintage wine; **du c.** local; *Fig* **une histoire de son (propre) c.** a story of his/her own invention

cru³, -e² *voir* **croire**

cruauté [kryote] *nf* **(a)** *(dureté)* cruelty **(envers** to) **(b)** *(acte)* (act of) cruelty

cruche [kryʃ] **1** *nf* **(a)** *(récipient, contenu) Br* jug, *Am* pitcher; *Prov* **tant va la c. à l'eau qu'à la fin elle se casse** the pitcher has gone to the well once too often **(b)** *Fam (imbécile)* idiot, fool **2** *adj Fam (bête)* dumb, stupid

cruchon [kryʃɔ̃] *nm (récipient, contenu)* small *Br* jug *or Am* pitcher

crucial, -e, -aux, -ales [krysjal, -o] *adj* crucial

crucifier [66] [krysifje] *vt* to crucify

crucifix [krysifi] *nm* crucifix

crucifixion [krysifiksjɔ̃] *nf* crucifixion

cruciforme [krysifɔrm] *adj* cruciform; **vis/tournevis c.** Phillips® screw/screwdriver

cruciverbiste [krysivɛrbist] *nmf* crossword enthusiast

crudité [krydite] *nf* **(a)** **crudités** *(légumes)* assorted raw vegetables **(b)** *(d'une couleur, d'une lumière)* garishness **(c)** *(d'une expression)* crudeness

crue³ [kry] *nf (montée)* swelling; *(inondation)* flood; **rivière en c.** river in spate

cruel, -elle [kryɛl] *adj* cruel **(envers** *ou* **avec** to)

cruellement [kryɛlmã] *adv* cruelly; **être c. éprouvé** to be deeply affected; **faire c. défaut** to be sadly lacking

crûment [krymã] *adv* **(a)** *(parler) (sans détours)* bluntly; *(grossièrement)* crudely **(b)** *(éclairé)* **c.** garishly lit

crustacé, -e [krystase] *nm Zool* crustacean; **crustacés** crustaceans; *Culin* seafood

cruzado [kruzado] *nm* cruzado

cryogénie [krijoʒeni] *nf* cryogenics *(singulier)*
cryogénique [krijoʒenik] *adj* cryogenic
cryothérapie [krijoterapi] *nf* cryotherapy
cryptage [kriptaʒ] *nm* encoding
crypte [kript] *nf* crypt
crypté, -e [kripte] *adj (message)* & *TV* coded
crypter [kripte] *vt* to encode
CSA [sɛɛsa] *nm (abrév* **Conseil supérieur de l'audiovi-suel)** = organization regulating French broadcasting, *Br* ≃ ITC
CSG [sɛɛsʒe] *nf (abrév* **Contribution sociale générali-sée)** = income-based tax deducted at source
Cuba [kyba] *n* Cuba
cubain, -e [kybɛ̃, -ɛn] **1** *adj* Cuban
   2 *nm,f* **C.** Cuban
cube [kyb] **1** *nm* cube; *(de jeu)* building block; **élever un nombre au c.** to cube a number
   2 *adj (mètre, centimètre)* cubic
cubique [kybik] *adj* cubic
cubisme [kybism] *nm* cubism
cubiste [kybist] *adj* & *nmf* Cubist
cubitus [kybitys] *nm* ulna
cucul [kyky] *adj inv Fam* **c. (la praline)** *(personne, dé-coration)* twee; *(film, livre)* corny
cueillette [kœjɛt] *nf (action)* gathering, picking; *(fruits, noisettes, baies)* harvest
cueillir [5] [kœjir] *vt (fleurs, fruits)* to gather, to pick; *Fig* **la mort l'a cueilli en pleine jeunesse** he was cut down in his prime; *Fam* **c. qn** to pick sb up
cui-cui [kɥikɥi] **1** *nm* cheeping
   2 *exclam* cheep!
cuiller, cuillère [kɥijɛr] *nf* (**a**) *(couvert)* spoon; *(con-tenu)* spoon(ful); *Fam Fig* **il n'y va pas avec le dos de la c.** he doesn't do things by halves; *Fam Fig* **en deux** *ou* **trois coups de c. à pot** in two shakes (of a lamb's tail); *Fam* **être à ramasser à la petite c.** *(épuisé)* to be all in; *(déprimé)* to be down in the dumps; **c. à café, petite c.** teaspoon; **c. à soupe,** *Can* **c. à table** soup spoon; *(pour mesurer)* tablespoon (**b**) *(pour la pêche)* spoon (bait); **pêcher la truite à la c.** to troll for trout
cuillerée [kɥijere] *nf* spoonful; **une c. à café** a tea-spoonful; **une c. à soupe** a tablespoonful
cuir [kɥir] *nm* (**a**) *(matière)* leather; *(veste)* leather jacket; **chaussures/veste en c.** leather shoes/jacket (**b**) *(d'un éléphant, d'un rhinocéros)* hide (**c**) **c. cheve-lu** scalp
cuirasse [kɥiras] *nf* (**a**) *(protection)* breastplate; *Fig* **trouver le défaut dans la c. de qn** to find the chink in sb's armour (**b**) *(d'un navire de guerre, d'un blindé)* armour (plating)
cuirassé [kɥirase] *nm* battleship
cuirassier [kɥirasje] *nm* cuirassier
cuire [18] [kɥir] **1** *vt* (**a**) *(aliment)* to cook; **c. qch à l'eau** to boil sth; **c. qch à la vapeur** to steam sth; **c. qch au four** to bake sth (**b**) *(briques, poterie)* to fire (**c**) *(chauffer) (sujet: soleil)* to bake
   2 *vi* (**a**) *(aliments, plat)* to cook; **faire trop c. qch** to overcook sth; **faire c. qch à feu doux** to cook sth over a low heat (**b**) *(brûler)* **les joues me cuisent** my cheeks are burning (**c**) *Fam (avoir très chaud)* to be boiling
   3 *v impersonnel* **il vous en cuira** you'll regret it
cuisais *etc voir* **cuire**
cuisant, -e [kɥizɑ̃, -ɑ̃t] *adj (douleur)* burning; *(froid)* biting; *(déception, échec)* bitter
cuisine [kɥizin] *nf* (**a**) *(pièce)* kitchen; *(sur un navire)* galley (**b**) *(art)* cooking, cookery; **faire la c.** to do the

cooking; **bien faire la c.** to be a good cook; **c. au beurre/à l'huile** cooking with butter/oil; **la c. fran-çaise/chinoise** French/Chinese cooking *or* cuisine (**c**) *(meubles)* kitchen (furniture); **c. intégrée,** *Suisse* **c. agencée** fitted kitchen (**d**) *Fam (magouilles)* scheming
cuisiner [kɥizine] **1** *vi* to cook; **bien c.** to be a good cook
   2 *vt* (**a**) *(préparer)* to cook; **plats cuisinés** ready-cooked meals (**b**) *Fam (interroger)* to grill
cuisinette [kɥizinɛt] *nf Offic* & *Can* & *Suisse* kitchen-ette
cuisinier, -ère [kɥizinje, -ɛr] **1** *nm,f* cook
   2 *nf* **cuisinière** stove, *Br* cooker; **cuisinière électri-que/à gaz** electric/gas stove *or Br* cooker; **c. mixte** combined gas and electric stove *or Br* cooker
cuissardes [kɥisard] *nfpl (bottes de femme)* thigh boots; *(de pêche)* waders
cuisse [kɥis] *nf* thigh; **cuisses de grenouilles** frogs' legs; **c. de poulet** chicken leg
cuisson [kɥisɔ̃] *nf* (**a**) *(d'aliments)* cooking; *(de pain, de gâteau)* baking; **temps de c.** cooking time; **c. à la vapeur** steaming (**b**) *(des briques, de la porcelaine)* firing
cuissot [kɥiso] *nm (de venaison)* haunch
cuistot [kɥisto] *nm Fam* cook
cuit, -e¹ [kɥi, kɥit] *adj* (**a**) *(aliment)* cooked; **bien c.** well done; **c. à point** done to a turn; **trop c.** over-cooked; **pas assez c.** undercooked; **c. au four** baked; **c. à la vapeur** steamed (**b**) *Fam Fig* **être c.** *(perdu)* to have had it; **c'est c.!** we've had it!; **c'est du tout c.** it's a cinch
cuite² [kɥit] *nf Fam* **avoir/prendre une c.** to be/get *Br* pissed *or Am* wasted
cuivre [kɥivr] *nm* (**a**) *(métal)* **c. (rouge)** copper; **c. jaune** brass; **les cuivres** *(objets)* copper(ware); *(en cuivre jaune)* brasses (**b**) *Mus* **les cuivres** the brass (section)
cuivré, -e [kɥivre] *adj (peau, teint) (naturellement)* copper-coloured; *(par le soleil)* bronzed
cul [ky] **1** *nm* (**a**) *tres Fam (d'une personne) Br* arse, *Am* ass; **en rester** *ou* **tomber sur le c.** to be flabbergasted; **c'est à se taper le c. par terre** it's an absolute scream; **de c.** *(magazine, film)* porn; **être comme c. et che-mise** to be as thick as thieves; *Vulg* **l'avoir dans le c.** to be screwed up; *Vulg* **en avoir plein le c.** to be pissed off; **avoir qn au c.** to have sb on one's tail (**b**) *Fam (chance)* **avoir du c.** to be a lucky devil, *Br* to be jammy (**c**) *(d'un sac, d'un tonneau, d'une bouteille)* bottom; **boire le sec** to down one's drink in one go; **c. sec!** bottoms up!
   2 *adj Fam (personne, décoration)* twee; *(livre)* corny
culasse [kylas] *nf* (**a**) *(de fusil, de pistolet)* breech (**b**) *(de moteur)* cylinder head
culbute [kylbyt] *nf* (**a**) *(cabriole)* somersault; **faire la c.** to do a somersault (**b**) *(chute)* tumble; **faire la c.** to take a tumble
culbuter [kylbyte] **1** *vi (vase, statue)* to topple over; *(personne)* to take a tumble; *(voiture)* to overturn
   2 *vt (objet)* to knock over
cul-de-jatte (*pl* **culs-de-jatte**) [kydʒat] *nmf* legless cripple
cul-de-poule [kydpul] *nm* **avoir la bouche en c.** to have pursed lips
cul-de-sac (*pl* **culs-de-sac**) [kydsak] *nm* dead end, cul-de-sac; *Fig* dead end
culinaire [kylinɛr] *adj* culinary

culminant, -e [kylminɑ̃, -ɑ̃t] *adj* point **c.** *(d'une chaîne de montagnes)* highest point; *(de la gloire, d'une carrière)* height, peak

culminer [kylmine] *vi* (**a**) **le mont Blanc culmine à 4807 mètres** Mont Blanc is 4,807 metres at its highest point (**b**) *(crise, tension)* to peak

culot [kylo] *nm* (**a**) *Fam (audace)* cheek, nerve; **il a un de ces culots!** he's got a nerve!; **y aller au c.** to brazen it out (**b**) *(de douille, de cartouche)* base

culotte [kylɔt] *nf* (**a**) *(sous-vêtement)* Br knickers, pants, Am panties (**b**) *(pantalon)* **c. courte** short Br trousers or Am pants; **c. de cheval** jodhpurs; *Fam Fig* jodhpur thighs; **c. de golf** plus-fours; *Fam Fig* **c'est elle qui porte la c.** she's the one who wears the Br trousers or Am pants; *Fam* **faire dans sa c.** to mess one's pants; *Fig* to be scared stiff, to wet oneself (**c**) *(de bœuf)* rump

culotté, -e [kylɔte] *adj Fam* cheeky

culpabiliser [kylpabilize] **1** *vt* **c. qn** to make sb feel guilty
   2 *vi* to feel guilty

culpabilité [kylpabilite] *nf* guilt

culte [kylt] *nm* (**a**) *(vénération)* worship; *Fig* cult; *Fig* **vouer un c. à qn** to (hero-)worship sb; **c. de la personnalité** personality cult (**b**) *(religion)* religion; **liberté du c.** freedom of worship (**c**) *(service protestant)* (church) service

cul-terreux *(pl* **culs-terreux**) [kytɛrø] *nm Fam Péj Br* yokel, Am hick

cultivable [kyltivabl] *adj* suitable for cultivation

cultivateur, -trice [kyltivatœr, -tris] **1** *nm,f* farmer; **petits cultivateurs** small farmers; Br smallholders
   2 *nm (machine)* cultivator

cultivé, -e [kyltive] *adj* (**a**) *(terre, champs)* cultivated (**b**) *(personne)* cultured, cultivated

cultiver [kyltive] **1** *vt* (**a**) *(sol, champ)* to cultivate, to farm; *(plantes)* to grow (**b**) *(art, relations, amitié, image)* to cultivate
   2 **se cultiver** *vpr* to improve one's mind

culture [kyltyr] *nf* (**a**) *(du sol)* cultivation; *(de plantes)* growing; **cultures** land under cultivation (**b**) *(espèce cultivée)* crop (**c**) *(connaissances)* culture; **un homme d'une grande c.** a highly cultured man; **c. générale** general knowledge (**d**) *(civilisation)* culture (**e**) *Biol* **c. microbienne/de tissus** bacteria/tissue culture (**f**) **c. physique** physical training

culturel, -elle [kyltyrɛl] *adj* cultural

culturisme [kyltyrism] *nm* body building

culturiste [kyltyrist] *nmf* body builder

cumin [kymɛ̃] *nm* cumin

cumul [kymyl] *nm* **c. des fonctions** plurality of offices; **c. des traitements** drawing of more than one salary

cumulable [kymylabl] *adj (fonctions)* which can be held concurrently; *(traitements)* which can be drawn concurrently

cumulatif, -ive [kymylatif, -iv] *adj* cumulative

cumuler [kymyle] *vt* **c. des fonctions** to hold more than one office; **c. plusieurs traitements** to draw several salaries; **c. plusieurs emplois** to have several jobs

cumulo-nimbus [kymylonɛ̃bys] *nm inv* cumulo-nimbus

cumulus [kymylys] *nm inv* cumulus

cupide [kypid] *adj* avaricious

cupidité [kypidite] *nf* cupidity

Cupidon [kypidɔ̃] *npr* Cupid

curable [kyrabl] *adj (maladie)* curable

curaçao [kyraso] *nm* curaçao (liqueur)

curage [kyraʒ] *nm* cleaning out

curare [kyrar] *nm* curare

cure [kyr] *nf* (**a**) *(traitement)* (course of) treatment; **c. d'amaigrissement** (course of) slimming treatment; **faire une c. de désintoxication** *(alcoolique)* to receive treatment for alcohol dependency; *(toxicomane)* to receive treatment for drug dependency; **faire une c. de vitamines** to go/be on a course of vitamins; **faire une c. de fruits** to eat a lot of fruit; **faire une c. de repos/de sommeil** to go/be on a rest cure/sleep cure (**b**) *(dans une ville d'eau)* **c. (thermale)** spa cure; **faire une c.** to take the waters (**c**) *(fonction de curé)* office of a parish priest

curé [kyre] *nm* parish priest; **aller à l'école chez les curés** to be educated by priests

cure-dents [kyrdɑ̃] *nm inv* toothpick

curée [kyre] *nf (lutte)* scramble; **ce fut la c. entre les héritiers** the heirs started to fight over the spoils

cure-pipe *(pl* **cure-pipes**) [kyrpip] *nm* pipe cleaner

curer [kyre] **1** *vt* to clean out
   2 **se curer** *vpr* **se c. les ongles/les oreilles** to clean one's nails/one's ears

curetage [kyrtaʒ] *nm (en chirurgie)* D&C

curieusement [kyrjøzmɑ̃] *adv (bizarrement)* curiously (enough)

curieux, -euse [kyrjø, -øz] **1** *adj* (**a**) *(intéressé)* curious; **je serais c. de voir cela** I'd be curious to see that (**b**) *(indiscret)* curious, inquisitive (**c**) *(étrange)* curious, strange; **chose curieuse,...** curiously enough,...
   2 *nm,f* inquisitive person; *(badaud)* onlooker

curiosité [kyrjozite] *nf* (**a**) *(intellectuelle)* curiosity; **avec c.** curiously (**b**) *(indiscrétion)* curiosity, inquisitiveness; **par c.** out of curiosity; *Prov* **la c. est un vilain défaut** curiosity killed the cat (**c**) *(objet)* curio; **les curiosités d'une ville** the interesting sights of a town

curiste [kyrist] *nmf* = patient taking a spa cure

curriculum vitae [kyrikylɔmvite] *nm inv* Br curriculum vitae, Am résumé

curry [kyri] *nm* curry; **poulet au c., c. de poulet** chicken curry

curseur [kyrsœr] *nm aussi Ordinat* cursor

cursif, -ive [kyrsif, -iv] *adj (écriture)* cursive

cursus [kyrsys] *nm Univ* degree course

cutané, -e [kytane] *adj* skin, *Spéc* cutaneous

cuti [kyti] *nf* skin test; **virer sa c.** to have a positive skin test; *Fam Fig* to change radically

cuti-réaction *(pl* **cuti-réactions**) [kytireaksjɔ̃] *nf* skin test

cutter [kœtœr, kytɛr] *nm* Stanley knife®

cuve [kyv] *nf (réservoir)* (storage) tank; *(de machine à laver)* tub; *(pour la fermentation des alcools, du vin)* vat; *(en photographie)* tank

cuvée [kyve] *nf* (**a**) *(quantité)* vatful (**b**) *(produit)* vintage; *Fig* batch

cuver [kyve] *vt Fam* **c. (son vin)** to sleep it off

cuvette [kyvɛt] *nf* (**a**) *(récipient)* basin, bowl (**b**) *(de W.-C.)* bowl (**c**) *Géog* basin

CV¹ [seve] *Aut (abrév* **cheval-vapeur)** hp

CV² *nm (abrév* **curriculum vitae)** CV, Am résumé

cyanure [sjanyr] *nm* cyanide

cybercafé [sibɛrkafe] *nm* cybercafé

cyberespace [sibɛrɛspas] *nm* cyberspace

cyberharcèlement [sibɛrarsɛlmɑ̃] *nm* cyberstalking

cybernétique [sibɛrnetik] **1** *adj* cybernetic
   2 *nf* cybernetics *(singulier)*

cybersexe [sibɛrsɛks] *nm* cybersex

cyberterrorisme [sibɛrtɛrɔrism] *nm* cyberterrorism
cyberterroriste [sibɛrtɛrɔrist] *adj & nmf* cyberterrorist
cyclable [siklabl] *adj voir* **piste**
cyclamen [siklamɛn] *nm* cyclamen
cycle [sikl] *nm* (**a**) *(suite, mouvement)* cycle; **c. menstruel** menstrual cycle (**b**) *(dans l'éducation)* **premier/second c.** *Scol* lower/upper classes *(in secondary school)*; *Univ* first/last two years *(of degree course)*; *Univ* **troisième c.** postgraduate studies; **c. I/ II/III** = subdivisions of primary school (between the ages of 2 and 4, 5 and 7, and 8 and 10 respectively) (**c**) *(bicyclette)* cycle
cyclique [siklik] *adj* cyclical
cyclisme [siklism] *nm* cycling
cycliste [siklist] **1** *nmf* cyclist
 2 *adj voir* **coureur, course**
cyclo-cross [siklokrɔs] *nm inv* cyclo-cross
cyclomoteur [siklomɔtœr] *nm* moped
cyclone [siklon] *nm* cyclone
cyclope [siklɔp] *nm* cyclops
cyclothymique [siklotimik] *adj Psy* manic-depressive

cyclotourisme [sikloturism] *nm* bicycle touring
cygne [siɲ] *nm* swan
cylindre [silɛ̃dr] *nm* (**a**) *aussi Aut* cylinder; **une quatre cylindres** a four-cylinder car (**b**) *(rouleau)* roller
cylindrée [silɛ̃dre] *nf* (cubic) capacity; **petite/grosse c.** *(moto)* motorbike with a small/large engine; *(voiture)* car with a small/large engine
cylindrique [silɛ̃drik] *adj* cylindrical
cymbale [sɛ̃bal] *nf* cymbal
cynique [sinik] **1** *adj* cynical
 2 *nmf* cynic
cyniquement [sinikmɑ̃] *adv* cynically
cynisme [sinism] *nm* cynicism
cyprès [siprɛ] *nm* cypress (tree)
cypriote [siprijɔt] **1** *adj* Cypriot
 2 *nmf* **C.** Cypriot
cyrillique [sirilik] *adj (alphabet, caractères)* Cyrillic
cystite [sistit] *nf* cystitis
cytomégalovirus [sitomegalovirys] *nm Méd* cytomegalovirus, CMV
cytoplasme [sitɔplasm] *nm Biol* cytoplasm

D¹, d [de] *nm inv* D, d
D² [de] *nf (abrév* **route départementale**) = designation of secondary road
DAB [deabe] *nm (abrév* **distributeur automatique de billets**) ATM
dactylo [daktilo] **1** *nmf (abrév* **dactylographe**) typist
2 *nf (abrév* **dactylographie**) typing
dactylographe [daktilograf] *nmf* typist
dactylographie [daktilografi] *nf* typing
dactylographier [66] [daktilografje] *vt* to type
dada [dada] *nm* (**a**) *(langage enfantin) (cheval)* geegee; **à d.** on horseback (**b**) *Fam (sujet favori)* hobbyhorse
dadais [dadɛ] *nm Fam* **un grand d.** a big clumsy oaf
dague [dag] *nf (épée)* dagger
dahlia [dalja] *nm* dahlia
daigner [deɲe] *vt* **d. faire qch** to deign to do sth
daim [dɛ̃] *nm* (**a**) *(animal)* (fallow) deer; *(mâle)* buck (**b**) *(peau)* suede; **gants/veste en d.** suede gloves/jacket
dais [dɛ] *nm* canopy
Dakar [dakar] *n* Dakar
dalaï-lama *(pl* **dalaï-lamas**) [dalailama] *nm* dalai lama
dallage [dalaʒ] *nm (action, revêtement)* paving
dalle [dal] *nf* (**a**) *(de pierre)* paving stone; *(de marbre)* slab; *(de moquette, de lino)* tile (**b**) *Fam* **que d.** *(rien)* zilch, *Br* sod all; **j'y vois que d.** I can't see a damn thing (**c**) *Fam* **avoir** *ou* **crever la d.** to be starving
daller [dale] *vt* to pave
dalmatien, -enne [dalmasjɛ̃, -ɛn] *nm,f (chien)* Dalmatian
daltonien, -enne [daltɔnjɛ̃, -ɛn] **1** *adj* colour-blind
2 *nm,f* colour-blind person
daltonisme [daltɔnism] *nm* colour blindness
dam [dã] *nm* **au grand d. de qn** to sb's great displeasure
damage [damaʒ] *nm (de la terre, de la neige)* packing down
Damas [damas] *n* Damascus; *Fig* **trouver son chemin de D.** to see the light
damas [damas] *nm* damask
damassine [damasin] *nf Suisse (fruit)* plum; *(eau de vie)* plum brandy
dame [dam] *nf* (**a**) *(femme)* lady; **d. de compagnie** lady's companion; **d. d'honneur** lady-in-waiting (**b**) *(aux cartes, aux échecs)* queen; *(au jeu de dames)* king (**c**) **dames** *(jeu)* Br draughts, *Am* checkers
damer [dame] *vt* (**a**) *Jeu Fig* **d. le pion à qn** to get one over on sb (**b**) *(terre, neige)* to pack down
dameuse [damøz] *nf* piste basher

damier [damje] *nm Br* draughtboard, *Am* checkerboard; **tissu à damiers** *Br* checked *or Am* checkered material
damnation [danasjɔ̃] *nf* damnation
damné, -e [dane] **1** *adj* damned
2 *nm,f* damned soul; *Fig* **souffrir comme un d.** to suffer sheer torture
damner [dane] **1** *vt* to damn
2 **se damner** *vpr* to damn oneself; **il se damnerait pour...** he'd sell his soul to the devil for...
Damoclès [damɔklɛs] *voir* **épée**
dancing [dãsiŋ] *nm Vieilli* dance hall
dandinement [dãdinmã] *nm* waddle
dandiner [dãdine] **se dandiner** *vpr* to waddle; **se d. d'un pied sur l'autre** to shift from foot to foot
dandy [dãdi] *nm* dandy
Danemark [danmark] *nm* **le D.** Denmark
danger [dãʒe] *nm* danger; **être en d.** to be in danger; **mettre en d. la vie de qn** to endanger sb's life; **d. de mort** *(sur panneau)* danger of death; **hors de d.** out of danger; **d. public** public menace
dangereusement [dãʒrøzmã] *adv* dangerously
dangereux, -euse [dãʒrø, -øz] *adj* dangerous
danois, -e [danwa, -az] **1** *adj* Danish
2 *nm,f* **D.** Dane
3 *nm* (**a**) *(langue)* Danish (**b**) *(chien)* Great Dane
dans [dã] *prép* (**a**) *(à l'intérieur de)* in; **d. une boîte** in(side) a box; **il est d. sa chambre** he's in his room; **lire qch d. un journal** to read sth in a newspaper; **tomber d. l'escalier** to fall down the stairs; **il pleut d. tout le pays** it's raining all over the country; **être d. le commerce/l'informatique** to be in business/computers; **travailler d. le bruit/la saleté** to work in noisy/dirty surroundings (**b**) *(avec mouvement)* into; **il est entré d. leur chambre** he went into their room (**c**) *(exprime la temporalité)* in; **d. vingt ans** in twenty years, in twenty years' time; **d. peu de temps** soon, shortly (**d**) *(indique une provenance)* out of; **boire d. un verre** to drink out of a glass; **découper un article d. le journal** to cut an article out of the paper (**e**) *(indique une approximation)* **d. les quarante ans/les 3000 euros** about forty (years old)/3,000 euros (**f**) *(pour indiquer un état)* in; **d. mon excitation/ma hâte** in my excitement/hurry
dansant, -e [dãsã, -ãt] *adj voir* **soirée, thé**
danse [dãs] *nf (ensemble de mouvements, musique)* dance; **la d.** *(art)* dancing; **d. classique** ballet; **d. contemporaine** contemporary dance; **d. folklorique** folk dance/dancing; *Méd* **d. de Saint-Guy** St Vitus's dance; **d. aux tables** table dancing; **la d. du ventre** belly dancing

danser [dãse] **1** *vi* to dance; **le bouchon/le bateau danse sur l'eau** the cork/the boat is bobbing up and down on the water; *Fig* **avec lui je ne sais jamais sur quel pied d.** I never know where I am with him **2** *vt (valse, tango)* to dance
danseur, -euse [dãsœr, -øz] *nm,f* dancer; **d. (classique** *ou* **de ballet)** ballet dancer; **d. étoile** lead dancer; **danseuse étoile** prima ballerina; **être en danseuse** *(en cyclisme)* to stand on the pedals
Danube [danyb] *nm* **le D.** the Danube
dard [dar] *nm (d'insecte, de scorpion)* sting
darder [darde] *vt* **il a dardé sur moi un regard furieux** he shot me a furious look; **le soleil darde ses rayons** the sun is beating down
dare-dare [dardar] *adv Fam* at the double
darne [darn] *nf (de poisson)* steak
dartre [dartr] *nf* dry patch of skin
darwinisme [darwinism] *nm* Darwinism
datation [datasjɔ̃] *nf* dating
date [dat] *nf* date; **prendre d. pour qch** to fix a date for sth; **faire d.** to be a landmark; **amitié de fraîche/ longue d.** recent/long-standing friendship; **je la connais de longue d.** I've known her (for) a long time; **d. limite** deadline; **d. limite de consommation/de vente/de fraîcheur** use-by/sell-by/best-before date; **d. de naissance** date of birth
dater [date] *vt (lettre)* to date **2** *vi* **à d. du 15** as from the 15th; **ça date un peu** it's a bit dated; **ça ne date pas d'hier** that's nothing new
dateur [datœr] *adj m* **tampon** *ou* **timbre d.** date stamp
datte [dat] *nf* date
dattier [datje] *nm* date palm
dauphin [dofɛ̃] *nm* (**a**) *(animal)* dolphin (**b**) *Hist* D. Dauphin (**c**) *Fig (successeur)* heir apparent
daurade [dɔrad] *nf* sea bream
davantage [davãtaʒ] *adv* more; **elle est jolie, mais tu l'es bien d.** she's pretty but you're even prettier; **nous ne resterons pas d.** we won't stay any longer
DCA [desea] *nf Mil (abrév* **Défense contre avions)** anti-aircraft defence
DD *Ordinat (abrév* **disque dur)** HD
DDASS [das] *nf (abrév* **Direction départementale de l'action sanitaire et sociale)** = local social work department, one of whose tasks is to deal with children who have been abandoned or ill-treated
DDT [dedete] *nm (abrév* **dichloro-diphényl-trichloréthane)** DDT
de [də]

> **de** becomes **d'** before a vowel and h mute; **de + le** contracts to form **du**, and **de + les** to form **des**.

1 *prép* (**a**) *(indique l'origine)* from; **venir/être de** to come/be from; **sortir de chez soi** to leave the house; **l'idée est de vous** it's your idea; **de vous à moi...** between ourselves...
(**b**) *(indique une progression)* **de... à...** from... to...; **du matin au soir** from morning till night; **de vingt à trente personnes** between twenty and thirty people; **de... en...** from... to...; **errer de ville en ville** to go from town to town
(**c**) *(introduit l'agent, l'auteur)* by; *(introduit l'instrument)* with; **accompagné de ses amis** accompanied by his friends; **la statue est de Rodin** the statue is by Rodin; **un concerto de Beethoven** a Beethoven concerto; **armé de pierres** armed with stones; **couvert de puces** covered in fleas
(**d**) *(indique la manière)* **d'un air amusé** with an

amused expression; **d'une voix douce** gently, in a gentle voice
(**e**) *(indique la cause)* **sauter de joie** to jump for joy; **resplendissant de santé** blooming with health
(**f**) *(introduit une mesure)* **un enfant de dix ans** a child of ten, a ten-year-old child; **il est plus grand que moi de 5 cm** he's 5 cm taller than I am; **une pièce de 20 centimes** a 20-centime coin; **la terrasse fait 20 mètres de long** the terrace is 20 metres long; **20 euros de l'heure** 20 euros an hour
(**g**) *(indique l'appartenance)* of; **le livre de Pierre** Pierre's book; **le toit de la maison** the roof of the house; **le règlement de l'école** the school rules
(**h**) *(pour préciser la nature, la matière)* **un problème d'algèbre** an algebra problem; **un hôtel de la rive gauche** a hotel on the left bank; **le journal d'hier** yesterday's paper; **à quatre heures de l'après-midi** at four (o'clock) in the afternoon; **une robe de soie** a silk dress; **un verre de vin** a glass of wine
(**i**) *(dans, parmi)* of; **l'un d'eux** one of them; **le meilleur élève de la classe** the best pupil in the class; **la moitié de ses économies** half (of) his/her savings
(**j**) *(pendant)* **je ne l'ai pas vu de la soirée** I haven't seen him all evening; **de nuit** by night
(**k**) *(introduit un infinitif)* **il est honteux de mentir** it is shameful to lie; **j'aime mieux attendre que de me faire mouiller** I would rather wait than get wet
(**l**) *(pour insister)* **c'est d'un ridicule!** it's utterly ridiculous!
(**m**) *(dans un titre)* **de l'amour** (on) love
2 *art partitif* some; **je bois du café tous les matins** I drink coffee every morning; **donnez-moi du vin** give me some wine; **c'est du Bach** it's Bach; **avez-vous du pain?** do you have any bread?
3 *art indéfini* **je n'ai plus d'amis/de problèmes** I haven't got any friends/problems any more
dé¹ [de] *nm (pour joueur)* dice; **joueur aux dés** to play dice; **couper un dés** *(légumes)* to dice sth
dé² *nm* **dé (à coudre)** thimble
DEA [deəa] *nm (abrév* **diplôme d'études approfondies)** = postgraduate qualification which is a prerequisite for PhD candidates
dealer [dilœr] *nm Fam (de drogue)* dealer
déambulateur [deãbylatœr] *nm Br* Zimmer® frame, *Am* walker
déambuler [deãbyle] *vi* to stroll (about)
débâcle [debakl] *nf* (**a**) *(d'un cours d'eau gelé)* breaking up (**b**) *Mil* rout; *Fig (d'une affaire, d'une monnaie)* collapse
déballage [debalaʒ] *nm* (**a**) *(action)* unpacking (**b**) *Fam (aveu)* outpouring
déballer [debale] *vt* (**a**) *(affaires, produits, caisses)* to unpack (**b**) *Fam (sa vie privée, ses sentiments)* to pour out
débandade [debãdad] *nf (d'une armée, d'une équipe)* rout; **c'est la d. dans l'entreprise** the company's in disarray
débaptiser [debatize] *vt (personne, rue)* to rename
débarbouillage [debarbujaʒ] *nm* face wash
débarbouiller [debarbuje] **1** *vt* **d. qn** to wash sb's face
2 se débarbouiller *vpr* to wash one's face
débarbouillette [debarbujɛt] *nf Can* (face) flannel, face cloth, *Am* washcloth
débarcadère [debarkadɛr] *nm* landing stage; *(pour les marchandises)* wharf

débardeur [debardœr] *nm* (**a**) *(vêtement)* vest top (**b**) *(personne)* docker, stevedore
débarquement [debarkəmã] *nm* (**a**) *(de cargaison)* unloading; *(de passagers)* landing (**b**) *(de troupes)* landing; *Hist* **le D.** the Normandy landings
débarquer [debarke] **1** *vt (cargaison)* to unload; *(passagers)* to land
  2 *vi* (**a**) *(d'un bateau, d'un avion)* to disembark (**b**) *Fam Fig (arriver)* to turn up; **il a toujours l'air de d.** he never seems to know what's going on
débarras [debara] *nm* (**a**) *(endroit)* junk room (**b**) *Fam* **bon d.!** good riddance!
débarrasser [debarase] **1** *vt (table, bureau, pièce)* to clear; **d. qn de qch** to relieve sb of sth; **d. qn de qn** to rid sb of sb; *Fam Fig* **d.** to clear out
  2 se débarrasser *vpr* **se d. de** to get rid of
débat [deba] *nm* debate; *Pol* **débats (parlementaires)** (parliamentary) proceedings
débattre [11] [debatr] **1** *vt (discuter)* to debate, to discuss; **prix à d.** price negotiable
  2 débattre de *vt ind* to discuss
  3 se débattre *vpr* to struggle; **se d. contre les difficultés** to be up against difficulties
débauche [deboʃ] *nf* debauchery; **lieu de d.** den of vice; *Fig* **une d. de couleurs** a riot of colour
débauché, -e [deboʃe] **1** *adj* debauched
  2 *nm,f* debauchee
débaucher [deboʃe] *vt* (**a**) *(inciter à la débauche)* to corrupt (**b**) *(licencier)* to lay off
débecter [debɛkte] *vt très Fam* **ça me débecte** it makes me want to throw up
débile [debil] **1** *adj* (**a**) *(qui manque de vigueur) (enfant)* sickly; *(corps)* weak; *(santé)* poor (**b**) *Fam (stupide)* stupid
  2 *nmf* **d. mental** mental defective; *Fam Fig* complete idiot
débilitant, -e [debilitã, -ãt] *adj* debilitating; *Fig* demoralizing
débilité [debilite] *nf* (**a**) *(faiblesse)* debility; **d. mentale** mental deficiency (**b**) *Fam (stupidité)* stupidity
débiliter [debilite] *vt* to debilitate
débiner [debine] *Fam* **1** *vt Br* to slag off, *Am* to badmouth
  2 se débiner *vpr* to clear off
débit [debi] *nm* (**a**) *Fin* debit (**b**) *(ventes)* turnover (**c**) *(commerce)* **d. de boissons** bar; **d. de tabac** tobacconist's (shop) (**d**) *(de bois)* cutting up (**e**) *(d'une rivière, de liquide)* flow; *(d'une machine)* output; *Ordinat* **d. de données** data throughput; *Ordinat* **haut d.** broadband (**f**) *(d'un orateur)* delivery; *Fam* **il a un de ces débits!** he's really got the gift of the gab!
débitant, -e [debitã, -ãt] *nm,f* **d. de boissons** bar owner; **d. de tabac** tobacconist
débiter [debite] *vt* (**a**) *(sujet: usine)* to produce; *(sujet: cours d'eau)* to have a flow rate of (**b**) *Fin (somme, compte)* to debit; **d. une somme d'un compte** to debit an account with an amount, to debit an amount to an account (**c**) *(bois, viande)* to cut up (**d**) *(vendre)* to sell (**e**) *Péj (dire)* to spout
débiteur, -trice [debitœr, -tris] **1** *adj (compte)* debit
  2 *nm,f* debtor
déblaiement [deblɛmã] *nm* clearing
déblatérer [34] [deblatere] *vi Fam* **d. contre** *ou* **sur qn/qch** to rail against sb/sth
déblayage [deblɛjaʒ] *nm* clearing

déblayer [53] [debleje] *vt* (**a**) *(terre, gravats, neige)* to clear (**b**) *(terrain)* to clear; *Fig* **d. le terrain** *(faire des préparatifs)* to prepare the ground
déblocage [deblɔkaʒ] *nm* *(d'une porte, d'un tiroir, d'un mécanisme)* unjamming; *(des prix, des salaires)* unfreezing; *Tél (de téléphone portable)* unlocking
débloquer [deblɔke] **1** *vt* (**a**) *(porte, tiroir, mécanisme)* to unjam; *(prix, salaires)* to unfreeze; *Tél (téléphone portable)* to unlock; **d. des fonds** to release funds (**b**) *Psy* **d. qn** *(lui ôter ses complexes)* to rid sb of his/her complexes; *(le rendre moins timide)* to make sb less inhibited
  2 *vi (être fou)* to be off one's rocker; *(raconter n'importe quoi)* to talk drivel; *(être gâteux)* to be gaga
déboguer [debɔge] *vt Ordinat* to debug
débogueur [debɔgœr] *nm Ordinat* debugger
déboires [debwar] *nmpl (déceptions)* disappointments; *(ennuis)* problems; **essuyer des d.** to suffer disappointments *or* setbacks
déboisement [debwazmã] *nm* deforestation
déboiser [debwaze] *vt* to deforest
déboîtement [debwatmã] *nm* (**a**) *(d'un membre, d'une articulation)* dislocation (**b**) *(en voiture)* pulling out
déboîter [debwate] **1** *vt* (**a**) *(objets encastrés)* to disconnect (**b**) *(articulation, membre)* to dislocate
  2 *vi (en voiture)* to pull out
  3 se déboîter *vpr (articulation, membre)* to become dislocated; **se d. l'épaule/le genou** to dislocate one's shoulder/knee
débonnaire [debɔnɛr] *adj (personne)* good-natured, easy-going; **répondre d'un ton d.** to answer good-naturedly
débordant, -e [debɔrdã, -ãt] *adj (activité)* tireless; *(imagination)* boundless; **d. de santé/d'enthousiasme** bursting with health/with enthusiasm
débordé, -e [debɔrde] *adj* **d. (de travail)** snowed under (with work)
débordement [debɔrdəmã] *nm (d'une rivière)* overflowing; *Fig (d'enthousiasme, de joie)* outburst (**b**) **débordements** *(excès)* excesses (**c**) *Mil (de l'ennemi)* outflanking
déborder [debɔrde] **1** *vi* (**a**) *(liquide, rivière, baignoire)* to overflow; **l'eau déborde du vase** the vase is overflowing; **les papiers débordent de la corbeille** the wastepaper basket is overflowing with paper; **d. sur le temps prévu** to overrun (**b**) *Fig* **d. de vie** to be bursting with vitality; **d. d'imagination** to have boundless imagination
  2 *vt (dépasser) (alignement)* to stick out from; *(limite)* to go beyond; *Mil (l'ennemi)* to outflank; *Sport (coureur)* to overtake; **cela déborde le cadre de...** that is beyond the scope of...
débouchage [debuʃaʒ] *nm* (**a**) *(d'un tuyau, d'un évier)* unblocking (**b**) *(d'une bouteille)* uncorking
débouché [debuʃe] *nm (professionnel)* opening, job opportunity; *Com* outlet
déboucher [debuʃe] *vt* (**a**) *(tuyau, évier)* to unblock (**b**) *(bouteille)* to uncork
  2 *vi* (**a**) *(dans l'espace) (personne, voiture)* to emerge (**de** from), to come out (**de** of); **d. dans/sur** to lead to (**b**) *Fig* **d. sur qch** *(avoir pour résultat)* to lead to sth
  3 se déboucher *vpr (tuyau, évier, oreilles)* to clear; **la bouteille se débouche facilement** the bottle opens easily
débouler [debule] *Fam* **1** *vt* **d. l'escalier** to race down the stairs

2 *vi* (**a**) *(descendre)* to race down (**b**) *(arriver)* to turn up

déboulonner [debulɔne] *vt* (**a**) *Tech* to unbolt; *(statue)* to take down (**b**) *Fam Fig (critiquer)* to debunk; *(de son poste)* to kick out

débourser [deburse] *vt (argent)* to lay out; **sans rien d.** without spending a penny

déboussoler [debusɔle] *vt Fam* to throw, to confuse

debout [dəbu] *adv* (**a**) *(verticalement) (chose)* upright; *(personne)* standing; **cent ans plus tard, la maison est encore d.** the house is still standing a hundred years later; **elle est d.** **toute la journée** she's on her feet all day; **mettre qch d.** to stand sth up; **se mettre d.** to stand up; **rester d.** to stand; **tenir d.** *(objet)* to stay upright; *(personne)* to stay on one's feet; **il ne tient plus d.** *(fatigué)* he's dead on his feet; *(ivre)* he's legless; *Fig* **un argument qui ne tient pas d.** an argument that won't stand up; **se tenir d.** to stand; **conte** *ou* **histoire à dormir d.** cock-and-bull story (**b**) *(hors du lit)* **être d.** to be up; **allons, d.!** come on, get up!

débouter [debute] *vt Jur* to dismiss, *Br* to nonsuit

déboutonner [debutɔne] **1** *vt* to unbutton

2 se déboutonner *vpr (personne)* to undo one's coat/jacket/*etc*; *(vêtement)* to unbutton; *Fig (se confier)* to open up

débraillé, -e [debraje] *adj* slovenly

débrancher [debrɑ̃ʃe] *vt (appareil électrique)* to unplug; *(tuyau)* to diconnect

débrayage [debrɛjaʒ] *nm* (**a**) *Aut* declutching (**b**) *(grève)* stoppage, walkout

débrayer [53] [debrɛje] *vi* (**a**) *Aut* to release the clutch (**b**) *(se mettre en grève)* to stop work

débridé, -e [debride] *adj (passion)* unbridled; *(imagination)* vivid

débris [debri] **1** *nmpl (d'un avion, d'une voiture)* debris, wreckage; *(de verre, de bois)* fragments; **d. de métal** scrap (metal)

2 *nm Fam* **un vieux d.** *(personne)* an old wreck

débrouillard, -e [debrujar, -ard] *Fam* **1** *adj* resourceful

2 *nm,f* resourceful person

débrouillardise [debrujardiz] *nf* resourcefulness

débrouiller [debruje] **1** *vt (fil, mystère)* to unravel

2 se débrouiller *vpr* to manage, to cope; *(dans une langue, un domaine)* to get by; **débrouillez-vous!** you'll just have to manage!; **elle s'est débrouillée pour rencontrer le directeur** she worked it so that she got to meet the director; **débrouille-toi pour arriver à l'heure** make sure you get there on time

débroussailler [debrusaje] *vt* to clear of undergrowth; *Fig (question)* to clarify

débusquer [debyske] *vt* to flush out

début [deby] *nm* (**a**) *(commencement)* beginning, start; **au d. (de)** at the start or beginning (of); **au tout d., tout au d.** at the very start or beginning; **dès le d.** from the start; **je le savais depuis le d.** I knew all along; **du d. à la fin** from start to finish; **en d. de** at the start of; *Hum* **il faut** *ou* **il y a un d. à tout** there's a first time for everything (**b**) **débuts** *(d'un acteur, d'un chanteur)* debut, first appearance; **faire ses débuts** to make one's debut; **faire des débuts prometteurs** to get off to a promising start; **en être à ses débuts** *(société, projet)* to be in its early stages (**c**) *Ordinat* home; **aller au d.** *(commande)* go top

débutant, -e [debytɑ̃, -ɑ̃t] **1** *adj* novice

2 *nm,f (dans une discipline)* beginner; **grand d.** complete beginner

débuter [debyte] **1** *vi* (**a**) *(commencer)* to begin, to start (**par** with) (**b**) *(dans le spectacle)* to make one's debut; *(dans la vie professionnelle)* to start out; **mal/ bien d. dans la vie** to get off to a bad/good start in life

2 *vt Fam* to start, to begin (**par** with)

deçà [dəsa] **en deçà de** *prép (dans l'espace)* (on) this side of; **rester (très) en d. de la vérité** to be (very) short of the truth

déca [deka] *nm Fam (café)* decaf

décacheter [42] [dekaʃte] *vt* to unseal, to open

décadenasser [dekadnase] *vt* to take the padlock off

décadence [dekadɑ̃s] *nf (état)* decadence; *(processus)* decline; **tomber en d.** to go into decline

décadent, -e [dekadɑ̃, -ɑ̃t] *adj* decadent

décaféiné [dekafeine] **1** *adj m (café)* decaffeinated

2 *nm* decaffeinated coffee

décagonal, -e, -aux, -ales [dekagɔnal, -o] *adj* decagonal

décagone [dekagon] *nm Math* decagon

décalage [dekalaʒ] *nm* (**a**) *(désaccord)* gap (**b**) *(dans le temps)* time lag; **d. horaire** time difference; **souffrir du d. horaire** to have jet lag

décalaminer [dekalamine] *vt* to decoke

décalcification [dekalsifikasjɔ̃] *nf Méd* decalcification

décalcifier [66] [dekalsifje] *Méd* **1** *vt* to decalcify

2 se décalcifier *vpr* to become decalcified

décalcomanie [dekalkɔmani] *nf (procédé) Br* transfer process, *Am* decal; *(image) Br* transfer, *Am* decal; **faire de la d.** to do *Br* transfers or *Am* decals

décalé, -e [dekale] *adj (humour, style)* offbeat, quirky

décaler [dekale] **1** *vt* (**a**) *(dans l'espace)* to move, to shift (**de** from) (**b**) *(dans le temps) (avancer)* to bring forward (**de** by); *(reculer)* to put back (**de** by)

2 se décaler *vpr* to move, to shift; **vous pourriez vous d. d'un rang/vers la gauche?** could you move up a row/move to the left?

décalitre [dekalitr] *nm* decalitre

décalquer [dekalke] *vt* to trace

décamètre [dekamɛtr] *nm* decametre

décamper [dekɑ̃pe] *vi Fam* to clear off

décan [dekɑ̃] *nm* = one of three divisions of each sign of the zodiac

décaniller [dekanije] *vi Fam* to clear off

décanter [dekɑ̃te] **1** *vt (vin)* to decant

2 se décanter *vpr (vin)* to settle; *Fig (situation)* to become clearer

décapage [dekapaʒ] *nm (avec un produit)* stripping; *(au papier de verre)* sanding (down); *(d'un four)* cleaning

décapant, -e [dekapɑ̃, -ɑ̃t] **1** *adj* (**a**) **produit d.** *(pour vernis, peinture)* paint stripper; *(pour four)* oven cleaner (**b**) *Fig (humour)* caustic

2 *nm (pour vernis, peinture)* paint stripper; *(pour four)* oven cleaner

décaper [dekape] *vt* (**a**) *(avec un produit)* to strip; *(au papier de verre)* to sand (down); *(four)* to clean (**b**) *Fam Fig* **ça décape!** *(alcool)* it blows your head off!

décapeuse [dekapøz] *nf* scraper

décapitation [dekapitasjɔ̃] *nf* decapitation

décapiter [dekapite] *vt (personne)* to decapitate; *(arbre)* to pollard

décapotable [dekapɔtabl] **1** adj convertible; (coupé) drop-head
2 nf convertible
décapoter [dekapɔte] vt to lower the top of
décapsuler [dekapsyle] vt to take the top off
décapsuleur [dekapsylœr] nm bottle opener
décarcasser [dekarkase] **se décarcasser** vpr Fam to sweat blood, to bust a gut (**pour faire** to do)
décasyllabe [dekasilab] **1** adj decasyllabic
2 nm decasyllable
décathlon [dekatlɔ̃] nm decathlon
décati, -e [dekati] adj (visage) age-worn; (personne) decrepit
décatir [dekatir] **se décatir** vpr to become decrepit
décédé, -e [desede] adj deceased
décéder [34] [desede] vi to die
décelable [deslabl] adj detectable
déceler [39] [desle] vt (**a**) (découvrir) to detect (**b**) (indiquer) to indicate
décélération [deselerasjɔ̃] nf deceleration
décélérer [34] [deselere] vi to decelerate
décembre [desãbr] nm December; voir aussi janvier
décemment [desamã] adv (**a**) (convenablement) (se comporter) properly; (s'habiller) decently (**b**) (passablement) reasonably well (**c**) (raisonnablement) reasonably; **je ne pouvais pas d. refuser** I couldn't reasonably refuse
décence [desãs] nf (**a**) (bienséance) (de comportement) propriety; (d'habillement) decency (**b**) (tact) decency; **avoir la d. de faire qch** to have the decency to do sth
décennal, -e, -aux, -ales [desenal, -o] adj ten-year
décennie [deseni] nf decade
décent, -e [desã, -ãt] adj (**a**) (comportement) proper; (vêtements) decent; **peu d.** improper/indecent (**b**) (passable) reasonable
décentralisation [desãtralizasjɔ̃] nf decentralization
décentraliser [desãtralize] vt to decentralize
décentré, -e [desãtre] adj (**a**) **être d.** to be off-centre (**b**) Suisse (quartier, endroit) outlying
décentrer [desãtre] **1** vt to move off centre
2 se décentrer vpr to move off centre
déception [desepsjɔ̃] nf disappointment; **d. sentimentale** disappointment in love
décerner [deserne] vt (prix, médaille) to award (**à** to)
décès [desɛ] nm death; **fermé pour cause de d.** (sur la porte d'un magasin) closed due to bereavement
décevant, -e [desvã, -ãt] adj disappointing
décevoir [60] [desvwar] vt to disappoint; **il/ce voyage m'a beaucoup déçu** I was very disappointed in him/with the trip
déchaîné, -e [deʃene] adj (passion) unbridled; (mer, vent) raging; (personne) wild
déchaînement [deʃɛnmã] nm (des éléments) fury; (des passions) outburst
déchaîner [deʃene] **1** vt (passions, colère) to unleash; **d. l'hilarité** to provoke laughter
2 se déchaîner vpr (tempête, vent) to rage; (personne) to fly into a rage (**contre** with)
déchanter [deʃãte] vi Fam to become disillusioned
décharge [deʃarʒ] nf (**a**) (tirs) discharge (**b**) **d. (électrique)** (electric) shock; **prendre une d.** to get an electric shock; **d. d'adrénaline** rush of adrenaline (**c**) (d'ordures) **d. (publique)** Br rubbish or Am garbage dump; **d. interdite** (sur panneau) no dumping (**d**) Jur (d'un accusé) acquittal; (d'une obligation) dis-

charge; Fig **dire qch à la d. de qn** to say sth in sb's defence
déchargement [deʃarʒəmã] nm unloading
décharger [45] [deʃarʒe] **1** vt (**a**) (vider) (camion, bateau, cargaison) to unload; (sujet: camion) (sable, gravier) to dump; (arme à feu) to fire, to discharge; Fig **d. sa conscience** to unburden one's conscience (**de** of) (**b**) (soulager) **d. qn de qch** (tâche, responsabilité) to relieve sb of sth; Jur (d'une accusation) to acquit sb of sth
2 se décharger vpr (**a**) (personne) **se d. d'une tâche/d'une responsabilité sur qn** to offload a task/a responsibility onto sb (**b**) (pile, batterie) to go flat
décharné, -e [deʃarne] adj (corps, membres, visage) emaciated; Fig (arbre) bare
déchaussé, -e [deʃose] adj (**a**) (sans chaussures) barefoot (**b**) (dent) loose
déchausser [deʃose] **1** vt (enlever ses chaussures à) **d. qn** to take off sb's shoes; **d. ses skis** to take off one's skis
2 se déchausser vpr (**a**) (enlever ses chaussures) to take off one's shoes (**b**) (dent) to work loose
dèche [dɛʃ] nf Fam **être dans la d.** to be Br stony broke or Am flat broke; **c'est la d.** I'm/we're/etc Br stony broke orAm flat broke
déchéance [deʃeãs] nf (**a**) (physique, morale) decline (**b**) Jur (de droits) forfeiture; **d. de l'autorité parentale** loss of parental rights
déchet [deʃɛ] nm (**a**) **déchets** waste; **déchets radioactifs/industriels** radioactive/industrial waste (**b**) (perte) **il y a du d.** there's some wastage (**c**) Péj (personne) down-and-out; **un d. de la société** a social outcast
déchiffrable [deʃifrabl] adj decipherable
déchiffrage [deʃifraʒ] nm Mus sight-reading
déchiffrement [deʃifrəmã] nm deciphering; Ordinat decryption
déchiffrer [deʃifre] vt (**a**) (inscription, écriture, message) to decipher; (signaux) to interpret; Fig (pensées, sentiments, mystère) to fathom (**b**) (musique) to sight-read
déchiqueté, -e [deʃikte] adj (**a**) (irrégulier) jagged (**b**) (vêtements, papiers) torn to shreds; (corps) (dans une explosion) blown to pieces
déchiqueter [42] [deʃikte] vt (vêtements, papiers) to tear to shreds; (sujet: explosion) (corps) to blow to pieces
déchirant, -e [deʃirã, -ãt] adj (spectacle, adieux) heartrending
déchiré, -e [deʃire] adj aussi Méd & Fig torn; **être d. entre deux personnes** to be torn between two people
déchirement [deʃirmã] nm (peine) heartbreak
déchirer [deʃire] **1** vt (**a**) (accidentellement) to tear; (volontairement) to tear up; (enveloppe) to tear open (**b**) Fig (famille, pays) to tear apart; (silence) to pierce; **des sons qui déchirent le tympan** ear-splitting sounds
2 se déchirer vpr (**a**) (tissu, papier) to tear (**b**) Méd **se d. un muscle** to tear a muscle (**c**) Fig (couple) to tear each other apart
déchirure [deʃiryr] nf (dans un tissu) & Méd tear; Fig (peine) heartbreak; **se faire une d. musculaire** to tear a muscle
déchoir [14] [deʃwar] vi **ce serait d. (que de...)** it would be demeaning (to...); **par ce mariage il déchoit de son rang** he is marrying beneath him

déchu, -e [deʃy] *adj (dépossédé) (roi)* deposed; **être d. de qch** *(droit, nationalité)* to be stripped of sth
décibel [desibɛl] *nm* decibel
décidé, -e [deside] *adj* (**a**) *(fixé)* settled (**b**) *(caractère, personne, manière)* determined; **d'un ton d.** in a decisive tone; **être d. à faire qch** to be determined to do sth
décidément [desidemã] *adv* really; **d. je n'ai pas de chance!, je n'ai d. pas de chance!** I really don't have any luck!
décider [deside] **1** *vt* (**a**) *(déterminer)* **d. que/quand/si** to decide that/when/if; **il fut décidé qu'on attendrait** it was decided that we/they/*etc* should wait; **c'est moi qui décide ici** I'm the one who makes the decisions here; **je déciderai pour toi** I'll decide for you (**b**) *(convaincre)* **d. qn à faire qch** to persuade sb to do sth
2 décider de *vt ind* **d. de qch** to decide on sth; **un événement qui a décidé de sa carrière** an event that determined his/her career; **d. de faire qch** to decide to do sth
3 se décider *vpr* (**a**) *(prendre une décision)* to make up one's mind, to come to a decision; **bon, décide-toi!** right, make up your mind!; **se d. à faire qch** to make up one's mind to do sth; **je ne peux pas me d. à le faire** I can't bring myself to do it; *Fig* **il ne se décide pas à faire beau** the weather can't make up its mind whether to be nice or not; **se d. pour qn/qch** to decide on sb/sth (**b**) *(problème, question)* to be settled
décideur, -euse [desidœr, -øz] *nm,f* decision-maker
décigramme [desigram] *nm* decigram
décilitre [desilitr] *nm* decilitre
décimal, -e, -aux, -ales [desimal, -o] **1** *adj* decimal **2** *nf* **décimale** decimal
décimer [desime] *vt* to decimate
décimètre [desimɛtr] *nm* decimetre; **double d.** *(règle)* ruler *(20 cm long)*
décisif, -ive [desizif, -iv] *adj (bataille, argument)* decisive; *(preuve)* conclusive; *(moment)* critical
décision [desizjɔ̃] *nf* (**a**) *(choix)* decision; *Jur* ruling; **arriver à/prendre une d.** to come to/to make a decision; **prendre la d. de faire qch** to decide to do sth; **la d. ne m'appartient pas** it's not my decision (**b**) *(détermination)* determination; **avec d.** decisively; **esprit de d.** decisiveness
déclamation [deklamasjɔ̃] *nf (éloquence)* declamation
déclamatoire [deklamatwar] *adj Péj (style)* declamatory; *(discours)* bombastic
déclamer [deklame] *vt (discours, vers)* to declaim; *Péj* to spout
déclaration [deklarasjɔ̃] *nf* (**a**) *(annonce orale, écrite)* statement; **d. (d'amour)** declaration of love; **faire une ou sa d. à qn** to declare one's love to sb; **le chef de l'État a une importante d. à faire** the President has an important announcement to make; **faire une d. à la police** to make a statement to the police; **D. des droits de l'homme** Declaration of Human Rights; **d. de guerre** declaration of war; *Hist* **D. d'indépendance** Declaration of Independence; **d. de principe** statement of principle (**b**) *(acte officiel) (de naissance, de décès)* registration; *(à une compagnie d'assurances)* claim *(de for)*; *(à la police)* report; **d. en douane** customs declaration; **d. d'impôts** tax return; **faire sa d. d'impôts** to *Br* fill in *or Am* file one's tax re-

turn; **d. de revenus** income tax return (**c**) *Ordinat* **d. de champ** field definition

Déclaration d'impôts

People in France are required to declare their taxable earnings at the beginning of the year. Thrice-yearly tax payments ("tiers provisionnels") are based on one third of the previous year's total, the final payment being adjusted according to the actual tax owed. It is also possible to pay tax on a monthly basis. This is known as "mensualisation".

déclaré, -e [deklare] *adj (ennemi, intention)* declared; *(partisan)* avowed
déclarer [deklare] **1** *vt (annoncer)* to declare; *(revenus, décès, naissance)* to register; *(à une compagnie d'assurances)* to make a claim for; *(à la police)* to report; **d. que** to declare (that); *Sport* **d. forfait** to scratch; **d. la guerre à qn** to declare war on sb; **rien à d.** *(en douane)* nothing to declare; **être déclaré coupable** to be found guilty
2 se déclarer *vpr* (**a**) *(feu, maladie, guerre)* to break out (**b**) *(se prononcer)* **se d. pour/contre qch** to declare oneself in favour of/against sth (**c**) *(se dire)* **se d. satisfait/surpris** to declare oneself satisfied/surprised; **se d. coupable** to admit one's guilt (**d**) *(faire une déclaration d'amour)* to declare one's love *(à à to)*
déclasser [deklase] *vt* (**a**) *(faire changer de classe) Sport* to relegate; *(hôtel)* to downgrade; *(passagers)* to transfer from one class to another (**b**) *(déranger)* to get out of order
déclenchement [deklãʃmã] *nm (d'un appareil)* starting; *(d'un mécanisme)* activation; *(d'une sonnerie)* setting off; *(d'un événement)* triggering
déclencher [deklãʃe] **1** *vt (appareil)* to start; *(mécanisme)* to activate; *(sonnerie)* to set off; *(événement, critiques, questions)* to trigger; *Mil (attaque)* to launch
2 se déclencher *vpr* (**a**) *(sonnerie, sirène, bombe)* to go off (**b**) *(commencer) (douleur, incendie)* to start
déclencheur [deklãʃœr] *nm Phot* shutter release
déclic [deklik] *nm (bruit)* click; **la vue de cette photo a été pour elle un véritable d.** when she looked at the photo things fell into place
déclin [deklɛ̃] *nm (du talent, de la santé, d'une civilisation)* decline; *(de la beauté)* fading; *(du jour)* close; **être en d.** to be in decline; **le soleil est à son d.** the sun is setting; **au d. de sa vie** in his/her declining years
déclinaison [deklinɛzɔ̃] *nf Gram* declension
déclinant, -e [deklinã, -ãt] *adj (beauté, lumière)* fading; *(pouvoirs)* declining
décliner [dekline] **1** *vi (jour)* to draw to a close; *(talent, santé)* to decline; *(beauté)* to fade
2 *vt* (**a**) *Sout (refuser) (offre, invitation)* to decline; **d. toute responsabilité** to accept no liability (**b**) *Gram* to decline (**c**) *(réciter) (identité)* to state
3 se décliner *vpr Gram* to be declined
déclivité [deklivite] *nf* slope, incline
décloisonnement [deklwazɔnmã] *nm* decompartmentalization
décloisonner [deklwazɔne] *vt* to decompartmentalize
déco [deko] *nf Fam (d'une pièce)* décor; *(métier)* (interior) decorating; **j'aime beaucoup faire de la d.** I love decorating
décocher [dekɔʃe] *vt* (**a**) *(flèche)* to shoot; **d. un coup/une ruade à qn** to hit out at/to kick sb (**b**)

Fig (remarque) to fire off (**à** at); *(sourire, œillade)* to flash (**à** at)
décoction [dekɔksjɔ̃] *nf* decoction
décodage [dekɔdaʒ] *nm* decoding
décoder [dekɔde] *vt* to decode
décodeur [dekɔdœr] *nm TV* decoder; **d. numérique** set-top box
décoiffer [dekwafe] **1** *vt (ébouriffer)* **d. qn** to mess up sb's hair; **tu es tout décoiffé** your hair's in a mess; *Fam Fig* **un film qui décoiffe** a mind-blowing film
2 se décoiffer *vpr* (**a**) *(se dépeigner)* to mess up one's hair (**b**) *(ôter son chapeau)* to remove one's hat
décoincer [16] [dekwɛ̃se] **1** *vt (tiroir, mécanisme)* to loosen; *Fam (personne)* to loosen up
2 se décoincer *vpr (tiroir, mécanisme)* to loosen; *Fam Fig (personne)* to loosen up
déçois *etc voir* **décevoir**
décolérer [34] [dekɔlere] *vi* to calm down; **il ne décolérait pas** he was still angry; **il n'a pas décoléré depuis huit jours** he's been angry for a week
décollage [dekɔlaʒ] *nm* (**a**) *aussi Fig (démarrage)* takeoff (**b**) *(d'un timbre, de papier peint, d'une affiche)* peeling off
décollement [dekɔlmɑ̃] *nm* (**a**) *Méd* **d. de la rétine** detachment of the retina (**b**) *(d'un timbre, de papier peint, d'une affiche)* peeling off
décoller [dekɔle] **1** *vt (timbre, papier peint, affiche)* to peel off; **d. une enveloppe à la vapeur** to steam open an envelope; *Fam Fig* **d. qn de la télé/du bar** to tear sb away from the TV/the bar
2 *vi* (**a**) *(avion, fusée, économie)* to take off (**b**) *Fam (partir)* to leave; **bon, on décolle?** shall we get moving?; **je ne décollerai pas d'ici tant que...** I'm not budging until...; *Sport* **d. du peloton** to pull away from the pack
3 se décoller *vpr (se détacher)* to peel off; *Méd (rétine)* to become detached
décolleté, -e [dekɔlte] **1** *adj (vêtement)* low-cut; **une femme très décolletée** a woman in a very low-cut dress; **robe décolletée dans le dos** dress cut low at the back
2 *nm (de vêtement)* low neckline; *(haut des seins)* cleavage
décolonisation [dekɔlɔnizasjɔ̃] *nf* decolonization
décoloniser [dekɔlɔnize] *vt* to decolonize
décolorant, -e [dekɔlɔrɑ̃, -ɑ̃t] **1** *adj* bleaching
2 *nm* bleaching agent
décoloration [dekɔlɔrasjɔ̃] *nf (d'un tissu)* fading; *(des cheveux)* bleaching; **se faire faire une d.** to have one's hair bleached
décolorer [dekɔlɔre] **1** *vt (tissu)* to fade; *(cheveux)* to bleach
2 se décolorer *vpr (tissu)* to fade; **se d. les cheveux** to bleach one's hair
décombres [dekɔ̃br] *nmpl* ruins, debris
décommander [dekɔmɑ̃de] **1** *vt (réunion, dîner)* to cancel, to call off; *(invité)* to put off
2 se décommander *vpr* to cancel
décompacter [dekɔ̃pakte] *vt Ordinat (données)* to unpack
décomplexer [dekɔ̃plɛkse] *vt Fam* **d. qn** to cure sb of his/her hang-ups
décomposer [dekɔ̃poze] **1** *vt* (**a**) *(élément chimique)* to decompose; *(problème, phrase, mouvement)* to break down (**en** into) (**b**) *(matière organique)* to decompose (**c**) *(traits, visage)* to distort; **il est arrivé complètement décomposé** *(par l'émotion)* he arrived

quite distraught
2 se décomposer *vpr* (**a**) *(corps, viande, feuilles)* to decompose; *Fig (tomber en décadence)* to decay (**b**) *(visage, traits)* to become distorted
décomposition [dekɔ̃pozisjɔ̃] *nf* (**a**) *(d'un élément chimique)* decomposition; *(d'un problème, d'une phrase, d'un mouvement)* breaking down (**en** into) (**b**) *(de viande, de feuilles, de corps)* decomposition; *Fig (décadence)* decay; **en d.** *(cadavre)* decomposing; *Fig (société)* decaying
décompresser [dekɔ̃prese] **1** *vt Tech* to decompress; *Ordinat* to decompress, to unzip
2 *vi Fam* to unwind
décompression [dekɔ̃presjɔ̃] *nf* decompression; *Ordinat* decompression, unbundling; **avoir un accident de d.** *(plongeur)* to get the bends
décompte [dekɔ̃t] *nm (sur une somme à payer)* deduction; *(calcul)* calculation; **faire le d. des voix** to count the votes; **faire le d. des points** to add up *or* to reckon up the score
décompter [dekɔ̃te] *vt* to deduct (**de** from)
déconcentrer [dekɔ̃sɑ̃tre] **1** *vt* (**a**) *(pouvoirs, administration)* to devolve, to decentralize (**b**) *(distraire)* to distract
2 se déconcentrer *vpr* to lose concentration
déconcertant, -e [dekɔ̃sɛrtɑ̃, -ɑ̃t] *adj* disconcerting
déconcerté, -e [dekɔ̃sɛrte] *adj* disconcerted
déconcerter [dekɔ̃sɛrte] *vt* to disconcert
déconfit, -e [dekɔ̃fi, -it] *adj (personne, mine)* crestfallen
déconfiture [dekɔ̃fityr] *nf (échec)* defeat
décongeler [39] [dekɔ̃ʒle] *vt* to defrost, to thaw
décongestionner [dekɔ̃ʒɛstjɔne] *vt aussi Fig* to relieve congestion in
déconnecter [dekɔnɛkte] *vt (fil)* to disconnect; *Fig* **déconnecté de la réalité** out of touch with the real world
déconner [dekɔne] *vi très Fam* (**a**) *(dire des bêtises)* to talk garbage; *(faire des bêtises)* to piss around; **faire qch pour d.** *(pour rire)* to do sth for a laugh; **sans d., c'était super** no kidding, it was great; **sans d.!** *(en réponse)* no kidding! (**b**) *(mal fonctionner)* to play up
déconneur, -euse [dekɔnœr, -øz] *nm,f très Fam* clown
déconseiller [dekɔ̃seje] *vt* **d. qch à qn** to advise sb against sth; **d. à qn de faire qch** to advise sb against doing sth; **un livre à d. aux jeunes** an unsuitable book for young people; **il est déconseillé de...** it is inadvisable to...
déconsidérer [34] [dekɔ̃sidere] **1** *vt* to discredit
2 se déconsidérer *vpr* to bring discredit on oneself
décontamination [dekɔ̃taminasjɔ̃] *nf* decontamination
décontaminer [dekɔ̃tamine] *vt* to decontaminate
décontenancer [16] [dekɔ̃tnɑ̃se] **1** *vt* to disconcert
2 se décontenancer *vpr* to become disconcerted
décontracté, -e [dekɔ̃trakte] *adj (ambiance, attitude, personne)* relaxed; *(vêtement)* casual; *Péj (désinvolte)* casual
décontracter [dekɔ̃trakte] **1** *vt (muscle)* to relax; *(personne)* to put at ease
2 se décontracter *vpr* to relax
décontraction [dekɔ̃traksjɔ̃] *nf* relaxation; **faire qch avec d.** to do sth casually
déconvenue [dekɔ̃vny] *nf Sout* disappointment; **quelle ne fut pas ma d. quand...** I was so disappointed when...

décor [dekɔr] *nm* (**a**) *(d'une maison, d'un restaurant)* décor (**b**) *Théât, Cin & TV* **décors** set, scenery; **en d. naturel** on location; *Fam* **aller/envoyer qn dans le d.** *(en voiture)* to go/knock sb off the road (**c**) *(environnement)* surroundings; *Fig* **il aurait besoin d'un changement** *ou* **de changer de d.** he needs a change of scene

décorateur, -trice [dekɔratœr, -tris] *nm,f* (**a**) *(d'intérieur)* (interior) decorator (**b**) *Théât* set designer

décoratif, -ive [dekɔratif, -iv] *adj* decorative; *(arbre)* ornamental; *Péj* **n'avoir qu'un rôle d.** to have a purely decorative role

décoration [dekɔrasjɔ̃] *nf* (**a**) *(d'une maison, d'un restaurant)* decoration; **faire de la d.** to decorate; **d. d'intérieur** interior decorating; **décorations de Noël** Christmas decorations (**b**) *(médaille)* decoration

décorer [dekɔre] *vt* (**a**) *(pièce, maison)* to decorate (**de** with) (**b**) *(médailler)* to decorate (**de** with)

décorticage [dekɔrtikaʒ] *nm (de crevettes, de noisettes)* shelling; *(de riz, d'orge)* hulling; *Fig (d'un texte, d'un auteur)* detailed analysis

décortiquer [dekɔrtike] *vt (crevettes, noisettes)* to shell; *(riz, orge)* to hull; *Fig (texte)* to analyse in detail

décorum [dekɔrɔm] *nm* decorum

découcher [dekuʃe] *vi* to stay out all night

découdre [21] [dekudr] **1** *vt (vêtement, poche, ourlet)* to unpick, to unstitch; *(bouton)* to take off
2 *vi* **en d.** to fight
3 se découdre *vpr (vêtement, poche, ourlet)* to come unstitched; *(bouton)* to come off

découler [dekule] *vi* to follow (**de** from); **il en découle que...** it follows that...

découpage [dekupaʒ] *nm* (**a**) *(de gâteau)* cutting up; *(de viande)* carving; *(de métaux, du cuir)* punching; *Ordinat (de fichier, d'image)* splitting; *Pol* **d. électoral** division into constituencies (**b**) *(image découpée)* cutout; **faire du d.** *ou* **des découpages** to do some cutting out (**c**) *Fig (d'un texte)* division (**en** into); *Cin (scénario)* shooting script

découpé, -e [dekupe] *adj (irrégulier)* jagged

découper [dekupe] **1** *vt* (**a**) *(gâteau, papier)* to cut up; *(viande)* to carve; *(métaux, cuir)* to punch; *Ordinat (fichier, image)* to split; **d. un article dans un journal** to cut an article out of a newspaper (**b**) *Fig (texte)* to divide (**en** into)
2 se découper *vpr* **se d. sur** to stand out against

décourageant, -e [dekuraʒɑ̃, -ɑ̃t] *adj (nouvelle, situation, travail)* disheartening; *(personne)* hopeless

découragement [dekuraʒmɑ̃] *nm* discouragement

décourager [45] [dekuraʒe] **1** *vt* (**a**) *(démoraliser)* to discourage, to dishearten; **se laisser d.** to be discouraged *or* disheartened (**b**) *(dissuader)* to discourage; **d. qn de faire qch** to discourage sb from doing sth
2 se décourager *vpr* to get discouraged *or* disheartened

décousu, -e [dekuzy] *adj (ourlet, poche, vêtement)* unstitched; *Fig (phrases, idées)* disjointed; *(conversation)* rambling; *(travail)* unmethodical

découvert, -e [dekuvɛr, -ɛrt] **1** *adj (épaules)* bare; *(terrain)* open; **dormir à d.** to sleep without any covers; **la tête découverte** bareheaded
2 *nm* (**a**) *Fin* **d. (bancaire)** overdraft; **être à d. (de 200 euros)** *(personne, compte)* to be overdrawn (by 200 euros) (**b**) **agir à d.** to act openly; **s'avancer à d.** to move forward without restraint

découverte [dekuvɛrt] *nf* discovery; **aller** *ou* **partir à la d. de qch** to go off to explore sth; **faire une d. to** make a discovery; *Hum* **ce n'est pas une d.!** that's nothing new!

découvrir [52] [dekuvrir] **1** *vt* (**a**) *(trouver)* to discover (**b**) *(mettre à jour) (secret, complot)* to uncover; **d. qch à qn** *(projets, secrets)* to disclose *or* reveal sth to sb (**c**) *(apprendre à connaître) (domaine, art, sentiment)* to discover; *(personne)* to get to know (**d**) *(casserole, statue)* to uncover; *(dents, bras)* to bare; **une robe avec un décolleté qui découvre les épaules** an off-the-shoulder dress; *aussi Fig* **d. son jeu** to show one's hand (**e**) *(apercevoir)* to have a view of
2 se découvrir *vpr* (**a**) *(enlever son chapeau)* to take off one's hat (**b**) *(en dormant)* **le malade s'est découvert** the patient threw off his bedclothes (**c**) *(ciel)* to clear (**d**) *(se trouver)* to discover; **se d. des parents éloignés** to discover some distant relatives; **il s'est découvert une passion pour le jardinage** he discovered he had a passion for gardening

décrasser [dekrase] **1** *vt* to clean; *Fam Fig* **d. qn** to knock the rough edges off sb
2 se décrasser *vpr* to clean oneself up; *Fig (en faisant de l'exercice)* to clean out one's system

décrêper [dekrepe] *vt (cheveux)* to straighten; **se faire d. les cheveux** to have one's hair straightened

décrépit, -ite [dekrepi, -it] *adj (maison, mur, personne)* decrepit

décrépitude [dekrepityd] *nf* decrepitude; *(décadence)* decay; **tomber en d.** *(civilisation)* to decay; *(institution)* to become obsolete

décret [dekrɛ] *nm* decree

décréter [34] [dekrete] *vt* (**a**) *Jur (état d'urgence, nomination)* to decree (**b**) *(décider)* **d. que** to vow (that)

décrié, -e [dekrije] *adj* disparaged

décrire [30] [dekrir] *vt* (**a**) *(représenter)* to describe (**b**) **d. un cercle** to circle; **d. une courbe** to curve

décrispation [dekrispasjɔ̃] *nf Pol* détente

décrisper [dekrispe] **1** *vt (personne)* to relax; *(atmosphère)* to lighten
2 se décrisper *vpr* to relax

décrocher [dekrɔʃe] **1** *vt* (**a**) *(détacher) (vêtement d'une patère, rideau, tableau)* to take down (**de** from); *(wagons)* to uncouple; **d. (le téléphone)** *(pour répondre)* to pick up the phone; *(pour ne pas être dérangé)* to take the phone off the hook; **décrochez** *(dans cabine téléphonique)* lift the receiver (**b**) *(recevoir) (poste, prix, contrat)* to land; *Fam* **d. la timbale** to hit the jackpot
2 *vi Fam* (**a**) *(ne plus se concentrer)* to switch off; *(être à la traîne)* to fail to keep up (**b**) *(arrêter de se droguer)* to kick the habit
3 se décrocher *vpr (rideau, tableau)* to come unhooked (**de** from); *(vêtement)* to fall down (**de** from); *(collier)* to come undone; *(wagon)* to come uncoupled (**de** from); **se d. la mâchoire** to dislocate one's jaw

décrocheur, -euse [dekrɔʃœr, -øz] *nm,f Can* dropout

décroiser [dekrwaze] *vt (jambes, bras)* to uncross

décroissant, -e [dekrwasɑ̃, -ɑ̃t] *adj* decreasing; **par ordre d.** in descending order

décroître [4a] [dekrwatr] *vi (forces, population, nombre, intensité)* to decrease; *(journées)* to draw in; to get shorter; *(lune)* to wane; *(eaux)* to subside; **aller (en) décroissant** to be decreasing

décrotter [dekrɔte] *vt (chaussures, semelles)* to clean the mud off; *Fam Fig (personne)* to knock the rough edges off

décrue [dekry] *nf (de rivière)* drop in level

décrypter [dekripte] *vt* to decipher

déçu, -e [desy] **1** *pp de* **décevoir**
2 *adj* disappointed; *Fig & Ironique* **elle ne va pas être déçue (du voyage)** she's in for a disappointment

déculottée [dekylɔte] *nf Fam* hammering

déculotter [dekylɔte] **1** *vt* **d. qn** *(enlever son slip)* to take sb's underpants off; *(enlever son pantalon)* to take sb's *Br* trousers *or Am* pants off
2 se déculotter *vpr (enlever son slip)* to take one's underpants off; *(enlever son pantalon)* to take one's *Br* trousers *or Am* pants off; *Fig (s'abaisser)* to grovel (**devant** to)

déculpabiliser [dekylpabilize] **1** *vt* **d. qn** to stop sb feeling guilty
2 se déculpabiliser *vpr* to stop feeling guilty

décuple [dekypl] *nm* **le d. de qch** ten times sth

décupler [dekyple] **1** *vt* to increase tenfold; *Fig* **la terreur décupla ses forces** terror gave him/her the strength of ten people
2 *vi* to increase tenfold

dédaigner [dedɛɲe] *vt (offre)* to scorn; *(injure, conseil, gloire)* to disregard; *(personne)* to despise; **il ne dédaigne pas un cigare de temps en temps** he is not averse to the occasional cigar

dédaigneusement [dedɛɲøzmɑ̃] *adv* scornfully, disdainfully

dédaigneux, -euse [dedɛɲø, -øz] *adj* scornful, disdainful (**de** of)

dédain [dedɛ̃] *nm* scorn, disdain (**pour qn/de qch** for sb/sth); **avec d.** scornfully, with disdain

dédale [dedal] *nm aussi Fig* maze

dedans [dədɑ̃] **1** *adv* inside; **la lettre est d.** the letter is inside; **c'est un bon film mais il y a trop de violence d.** it's a good film but there's too much violence in it; **de d.** *(depuis l'intérieur)* from inside; **en d.** *(d'un objet)* (on the) inside; *(en son for intérieur)* inwardly; **marcher les pieds en d.** to be pigeon-toed; **en d. de** inside
2 *nm (d'une maison, d'une boîte)* inside; **du d.** *(depuis l'intérieur)* from inside

dédicace [dedikas] *nf* (**a**) *(de livre, de photo)* dedication (**b**) *(à la radio)* dedication

dédicacer [16] [dedikase] *vt* (**a**) *(signer)* to sign (**à** for); *(écrire dans) (livre)* to write a dedication in (**à** to); *(photo)* to write a dedication on (**à** to) (**b**) *(chanson)* to dedicate (**à** to)

dédier [66] [dedje] *vt* to dedicate (**à** to)

dédire [27b] [dedir] **se dédire** *vpr* **se d. d'une déclaration** to retract *or* withdraw a statement; **se d. d'une promesse** to go back on one's word

dédommagement [dedɔmaʒmɑ̃] *nm* compensation; **500 000 euros de d.** 500,000 euros (in) compensation; **en d. de qch** in compensation for sth

dédommager [45] [dedɔmaʒe] *vt (financièrement)* to compensate (**de** for); **pour me d., il m'a invité au restaurant** he took me out for a meal to make up for it

dédouanement [dedwanmɑ̃] *nm* clearance through customs

dédouaner [dedwane] **1** *vt (marchandise)* to clear (through customs); *Fig (personne)* to clear
2 se dédouaner *vpr* to clear one's name

dédoublement [dedublǝmɑ̃] *nm* **d. de la personnalité** split personality

dédoubler [deduble] **1** *vt (partager)* to divide *or* split into two
2 se dédoubler *vpr Psy* to have a split personality; *Hum* **je ne peux pas me d.** I can't be in two places at once

dédramatiser [dedramatize] *vt* **d. qch** to make sth less dramatic

déductible [dedyktibl] *adj* deductible; **d. des impôts** tax-deductible

déduction [dedyksjɔ̃] *nf* (**a**) *(soustraction, abattement)* deduction; **d. faite des frais d'essence** after deduction of petrol costs (**b**) *(conclusion)* deduction

déduire [18] [dedɥir] *vt* (**a**) *(enlever)* to deduct (**de** from) (**b**) *(conclure)* to deduce, to infer (**de** from)

déesse [deɛs] *nf* goddess

défaillance [defajɑ̃s] *nf* (**a**) *(insuffisance) (morale)* failing; *(physique)* deficiency; *(d'une machine)* failure; **avoir des défaillances en** *(intellectuelles)* to have problems with; **courage sans d.** unfailing courage; **d. cardiaque** heart failure (**b**) *(évanouissement)* fainting fit; *(faiblesse)* feeling of weakness; **avoir une d.** *(s'évanouir)* to faint; *(se sentir faible)* to feel weak

défaillant, -e [defajɑ̃, -ɑ̃t] *adj* (**a**) *(forces, mémoire, santé)* failing; *(cœur)* weak; *(voix)* faltering (**b**) *(qui s'évanouit)* faint

défaillir [35] [defajir] *vi* (**a**) *(faiblir) (mémoire, forces)* to fail; **à cette nouvelle, son cœur défaillit** his/her heart sank at the news (**b**) *(s'évanouir)* to faint; **d. de faim/de bonheur** to feel faint with hunger/happiness

défaire [36] [defɛr] **1** *vt* (**a**) *(ouvrir, détacher)* to undo; *(valise)* to unpack; **d. le lit** *(enlever les draps)* to strip the bed; *(le mettre en désordre)* to rumple the bedclothes; **d. ses cheveux** to let one's hair down (**b**) *(désassembler) (puzzle)* to take apart; *(ourlet)* to undo
2 se défaire *vpr* (**a**) *(se dénouer) (vêtement, nœud)* to come undone; *(cheveux)* to come down (**b**) *(se désagréger) (puzzle)* to come apart; *(ourlet)* to come undone; *Fig (alliance, mariage)* to break up (**c**) **se d. de qn/qch** to get rid of sb/sth; **je ne veux pas m'en d.** I don't want to part with it (**d**) *(s'altérer) (visage)* to drop

défait, -e¹ [defɛ, -ɛt] *adj (traits, visage)* haggard; **il est arrivé à l'hôpital, complètement d.** he arrived in a state of total distress

défaite² [defɛt] *nf* defeat

défaitisme [defɛtism] *nm* defeatism

défaitiste [defɛtist] *adj & nmf* defeatist

défalquer [defalke] *vt* to deduct (**de** from)

défausser [defose] **se défausser** *vpr (aux cartes)* to discard; **se d. à cœur** to discard a heart/some hearts; **se d. d'un dix** to discard a ten

défaut [defo] *nm* (**a**) *(imperfection) (d'une personne)* fault, shortcoming; *(d'une pierre précieuse, d'un verre, d'un tissu)* flaw; *(d'une machine)* defect; *(d'un raisonnement)* flaw; *(inconvénient)* drawback; **c'est là son moindre d.** that's the least of his/her faults; **sans d.** faultless, flawless; **prendre qn en d.** to catch sb napping; **d. de fabrication** manufacturing fault; **d. de prononciation** *ou* **d'élocution** speech impediment (**b**) *(manque)* lack; **le courage lui a fait d.** his/her courage failed him/her; **l'argent lui fait cruellement d.** he/she is very short of money; **le bon sens lui fait cruellement d.** he/she is sorely lacking in common sense; **ou à d.,...** or, failing that,...; **à d. de qch** for lack of sth; **à d. d'un salaire conséquent, elle a au moins un travail intéressant** she might not have a very good salary, but at least her work is interesting (**c**) *Jur* default; **faire d.** to default; **d. de paiement** default on payment (**d**) *Math* **total approché par d.** total rounded down; *Ordinat* **lecteur par d.** default drive

défaveur [defavœr] *nf* être en d. (auprès de qn) to be in disfavour (with sb); s'attirer la d. de qn to incur sb's disfavour

défavorable [defavɔrabl] *adj* unfavourable (à to)

défavorisé, -e [defavɔrize] *adj (milieu, pays)* under-privileged

défavoriser [defavɔrize] *vt* to put at a disadvantage (par rapport à compared to)

défectif, -ive [defɛktif, -iv] *adj* defective

défection [defɛksjɔ̃] *nf* (a) *(d'un espion, d'un soldat)* defection (b) *(annulation)* cancellation

défectueux, -euse [defɛktɥø, -øz] *adj* defective, faulty

défendable [defɑ̃dabl] *adj* defensible

défendre [defɑ̃dr] **1** *vt* (a) *(soutenir)* to defend (contre against) (b) *(protéger) (personne, pays, propriété)* to defend (contre against *ou* from); *(intérêts)* to protect; d. qn contre le froid *ou* du froid to protect sb from the cold; *Fig* d. son bifteck to look after number one; *Sport* Durant défendra les buts de l'équipe d'Aix Durant will be in goal for Aix (c) *(interdire)* to forbid, to prohibit; ce médicament est défendu aux enfants this medicine must not be given to children; d. à qn de faire qch to forbid sb to do sth; il m'est défendu de fumer I'm not allowed to smoke; il est défendu de fumer smoking is prohibited

2 se défendre *vpr* (a) *(se protéger)* to defend oneself (de *ou* contre against); se d. comme un beau diable to fight like a mad thing (b) *Fam (se débrouiller)* je me défends (en anglais/en tennis) I can get by (in English/at tennis) (c) *(se justifier)* ça se défend there's something to be said for it (d) *(s'empêcher)* se d. de faire qch to refrain from doing sth; on ne peut se d. de les aimer you can't help liking them

défenestrer [defɔnɛstre] **1** *vt* d. qn to throw sb out of a/the window

2 se défenestrer *vpr* to jump out of a/the window

défense¹ [defɑ̃s] *nf* (a) *(soutien) (d'une théorie, d'une politique, d'un accusé)* defence; prendre la d. de qn to come to sb's defence; sans d. defenceless; *Jur* assurer la d. de qn to defend sb; qu'avez-vous à dire pour votre d.? what do you have to say in your defence?; d. des consommateurs consumer protection (b) *(protection) (d'une personne, d'un pays, en sport)* defence; d. aérienne/nationale/passive air/national/civil defence; *Méd* défenses immunitaires immune defences (c) *(interdiction)* d. d'entrer/de fumer *(sur panneau)* no entry/smoking; et d. d'en parler à ton père! don't go telling your father about it!

défense² *nf (d'éléphant, de sanglier)* tusk

défenseur [defɑ̃sœr] *nm* (a) *(d'une personne, d'une ville, d'une cause, en sport)* defender; jouer les défenseurs de la veuve et de l'orphelin to protect the weak and oppressed (b) *Jur* counsel for the defence

défensif, -ive [defɑ̃sif, -iv] **1** *adj* defensive

2 être *ou* se tenir sur la défensive to be on the defensive

déféquer [34] [defeke] *vi* to defecate

déférence [deferɑ̃s] *nf* deference (pour for)

déférer [34] [defere] *vt Jur* d. une affaire à un tribunal to refer a case to a court; d. qn à la justice to hand sb over to the police

déferlante [defɛrlɑ̃t] *adj f & nf* (vague) d. breaker; *Fig* tidal wave

déferlement [defɛrləmɑ̃] *nm (des vagues)* breaking; *Fig (de personnes)* invasion; *(d'enthousiasme, de violence, de racisme)* wave

déferler [defɛrle] *vi (vagues)* to break; la foule déferle dans les rues the crowd is surging along the streets; les vacanciers déferlent sur les routes holiday-makers are taking to the roads in droves

défi [defi] *nm* (a) *(acte de provocation)* challenge (à to); lancer *ou* jeter un d. à qn to throw out a challenge to sb; mettre qn au d. de faire qch to defy sb to do sth; relever un d. to take up a challenge (b) *(bravade)* defiance

défiance [defjɑ̃s] *nf* mistrust

déficience [defisjɑ̃s] *nf* deficiency; d. immunologique immune deficiency

déficient, -e [defisjɑ̃, -ɑ̃t] **1** *adj* deficient; *(raisonnement, théorie)* weak

2 *nm,f* d. moteur person with motor deficiency; d. mental mentally deficient person

déficit [defisit] *nm* (a) *Fin* deficit; être en d. to be in deficit; d. budgétaire/commercial budget/trade deficit (b) *Méd (mental)* deficiency; d. immunitaire immunodeficiency

déficitaire [defisitɛr] *adj (entreprise)* loss-making; *(compte)* in debit; *(budget)* in deficit

défier [66] [defje] **1** *vt* (a) *(provoquer)* to challenge; d. qn aux échecs to challenge sb to a game of chess (b) *(inciter)* d. qn de faire qch to defy sb to do sth (c) *(braver) (personne, danger, mort)* to defy (d) *(résister à)* d. l'imagination to defy the imagination; des prix qui défient toute concurrence unbeatable prices

2 se défier *vpr Litt* se d. de to mistrust

défigurer [defigyre] *vt (personne, paysage)* to disfigure; *Fig (vérité, sens)* to distort; *(pensée, intentions)* to misrepresent

défilé [defile] *nm* (a) *Géog (mountain)* pass (b) *(de manifestants)* march; *(de chars de carnaval)* procession; *Mil* parade; un d. ininterrompu de touristes/voitures an endless stream of tourists/cars; d. aérien flypast; d. de mode fashion show

défilement [defilmɑ̃] *nm Ordinat* scrolling

défiler¹ [defile] se défiler *vpr Fam (se dérober)* to slope off

défiler² *vi* (a) *(manifestants)* to march; *(chars de carnaval)* to drive in procession; *(touristes, voitures)* to stream; *Mil* to parade (b) *(avancer) (bande)* to wind on; *Ordinat* faire d. un document to scroll through a document; *Ordinat* d. vers le bas/le haut to scroll down/up (c) *(se succéder) (images, souvenirs)* to pass; le paysage défile à toute vitesse the countryside is speeding past

défini, -e [defini] *adj* (a) *(précis)* definite; bien d. clearly defined; *Ordinat* d. par l'utilisateur user-defined (b) *Gram* definite

définir [definir] **1** *vt* to define

2 se définir *vpr* (a) *(concept)* se d. comme to be defined as (b) *(soi-même)* to describe oneself (comme as)

définissable [definisabl] *adj* definable

définitif, -ive [definitif, -iv] *adj* (a) *(irrévocable) (jugement, décision, version)* final (b) *(pour toujours) (séparation, fermeture)* permanent (c) *(qui fait autorité)* definitive *(à la fin)* in the end

définition [definisjɔ̃] *nf* (a) *(d'un mot, de conditions)* definition; *(de mots croisés)* clue; par d. by definition (b) *(d'une image sur écran)* definition

définitivement [definitivmɑ̃] *adv (décider)* definitely; *(partir, s'installer)* for good; *(nommé)* permanently

défiscaliser [defiskalize] *vt* to exempt from tax

déflagration [deflagrasjɔ̃] *nf (explosion)* explosion
déflation [deflasjɔ̃] *nf Écon* deflation
déflecteur [deflɛktœr] *nm (d'une voiture) Br* quarter-light, *Am* vent
déflocage [deflɔkaʒ] *nm* removal of asbestos
déflorer [deflɔre] *vt* (**a**) *(vierge)* to deflower (**b**) *Fig (sujet)* to spoil
défoliant [defɔljɑ̃] *nm* defoliant
défonce [defɔ̃s] *nf Fam* **la d.** getting high
défoncé, -e [defɔ̃se] *adj* (**a**) *(chemin)* bumpy (**b**) *Fam (drogué)* high (**à** on)
défoncer [16] [defɔ̃se] **1** *vt (boîte, porte)* to smash in; *(matelas)* to ruin; *(mur)* to knock down; *(tonneau, bateau)* to stave in; *(chaussée)* to break up
  2 se défoncer *vpr Fam* (**a**) *(se droguer)* to get high (**à** on) (**b**) *(faire un grand effort)* to sweat blood, to bust a gut (**pour faire qch** to do sth)
déforestation [defɔrɛstasjɔ̃] *nf* deforestation
déformant, -e [defɔrmɑ̃, -ɑ̃t] *adj (glace)* distorting
déformation [defɔrmasjɔ̃] *nf (d'un membre)* deformation; *(d'un vêtement, de chaussures)* putting out of shape; *(de métal)* buckling; *(de bois)* warping; *(des traits, d'une image, des faits)* distortion; *(de propos)* twisting; **d. professionnelle** = habits acquired through the type of work one does; *Hum* **ne fais pas attention, c'est la d. professionnelle!** don't worry, it's just my job!
déformer [defɔrme] **1** *vt (membre)* to deform; *(vêtement, chaussures)* to put out of shape; *(métal)* to buckle; *(bois)* to warp; *(traits, image, faits)* to distort; *(propos)* to twist; *(pensée)* to misrepresent
  2 se déformer *vpr (corps, vêtement, chaussures)* to get out of shape; *(bois)* to warp; *(métal)* to buckle
défoulement [defulmɑ̃] *nm Fam* letting off steam; **avoir besoin de d.** to need to let off steam
défouler [defule] *Fam* **1** *vt (agressivité)* to vent (**sur** on); **d. qn** to help sb let off steam; **ça défoule** it helps you let off steam
  2 se défouler *vpr* to let off steam; **se d. sur qn** to take it out on sb
défraîchi, -e [defrɛʃi] *adj (fleur, beauté)* faded; *(vêtement)* shabby
défrayer [53] [defreje] *vt* (**a**) *(rembourser)* **d. qn** to pay sb's expenses (**b**) **d. la chronique** to be widely talked about
défrichage [defriʃaʒ], **défrichement** [defriʃmɑ̃] *nm (de terrain)* clearing
défricher [defriʃe] *vt* to clear; *Fig (domaine)* to open up; *Fig* **d. le terrain** to prepare the ground
défriser [defrize] *vt (cheveux)* to straighten; *Fam Fig (agacer)* to bug
défriseur [defrizœr] *nm (pour les cheveux)* hair straighteners
défroisser [defrwase] *vt* to smooth out
défroqué, -e [defrɔke] *adj* defrocked
défunt, -e [defœ̃, -œ̃t] **1** *adj* **mon d. mari** my late husband; *Litt* **des amours défuntes** lost loves
  2 *nm,f* deceased; **prier pour les défunts** to pray for the dead
dégagé, -e [degaʒe] *adj (ton, air)* casual; *(ciel, route)* clear; *(vue)* open; **une coupe avec la nuque très dégagée** a haircut that is very short at the back
dégagement [degaʒmɑ̃] *nm* (**a**) *(d'une route, des poumons)* clearing (**b**) *(au football)* clearance (**c**) *(de vapeur, de gaz, de chaleur)* emission
dégager [45] [degaʒe] **1** *vt* (**a**) *(libérer)* to free (**de** from); *(d'une voiture accidentée, de décombres)* to pull

clear (**de** of); **une robe qui dégage les épaules** an off-the-shoulder dress (**b**) *(désencombrer) (route, passage)* to clear; *Fam* **dégage!** clear off! (**c**) *Fam (enlever)* to clear away; **tu vas me d. toutes ces bricoles de tes étagères** I want you to clear all these odds and ends off your shelves (**d**) *(laisser échapper) (vapeur, odeur, chaleur)* to emit; *Fig (impression)* to give off (**e**) *(au football)* **d. (le ballon) en touche** to kick the ball into touch (**f**) *Fin (crédits)* to release; *(profit)* to show
  2 se dégager *vpr* (**a**) *(se libérer)* to free oneself (**de** from); *(d'une situation difficile)* to extricate oneself (**de** from) (**b**) *(se débloquer) (ciel, nez)* to clear (**c**) *(gaz, odeur, chaleur)* to be given off (**de** by); *Fig* **le magnétisme qui se dégage d'elle** the magnetism she radiates
dégaine [degɛn] *nf Fam (démarche)* awkward way of walking; *(apparence)* strange appearance
dégainer [degene] *vt (arme)* to draw
dégarni, -e [degarni] *adj (personne)* balding; **avoir le front d.** to have a receding hairline
dégarnir [degarnir] **1** *vt (frigidaire, rayons)* to empty
  2 se dégarnir *vpr (personne)* to go bald; *(arbre)* to lose its leaves; *(salle)* to empty; *(rayons)* to be emptied
dégât [dega] *nm* damage; **faire du d.** *ou* **des dégâts** to cause damage; *Fig* **limiter les dégâts** to limit the damage; *Mil* **dégâts collatéraux** collateral damage; **dégâts des eaux** water damage; **dégâts matériels** material damage
dégel [deʒɛl] *nm Météo & Pol* thaw; *Écon (des prix, des salaires, des crédits)* unfreezing
dégeler [39] [deʒle] **1** *vt* (**a**) *(réchauffer)* to thaw; *(surgelé)* to defrost; *Fig (public)* to warm up; **d. l'atmosphère** to thaw out the atmosphere (**b**) *Écon (prix, salaires, crédits)* to unfreeze
  2 *vi (neige, surgelé)* to thaw; **faire d. qch** *(surgelé)* to defrost sth
  3 *v impersonnel* to thaw
  4 se dégeler *vpr* (**a**) *(étang)* to thaw (**b**) *Fig (atmosphère)* to thaw; *(personne)* to thaw out, to relax
dégénératif, -ive [deʒeneratif, -iv] *adj* degenerative
dégénéré, -e [deʒenere] **1** *adj* (**a**) *(arriéré)* mentally defective (**b**) *(dépravé)* degenerate
  2 *nm,f* (**a**) *(arriéré)* mental defective (**b**) *(dépravé)* degenerate
dégénérer [34] [deʒenere] *vi (mal tourner) (situation, conversation)* to degenerate (**en** into); **son rhume a dégénéré en bronchite** his/her cold developed into bronchitis
dégénérescence [deʒenerɛsɑ̃s] *nf Méd & Fig* degeneration
dégingandé, -e [deʒɛ̃gɑ̃de] *adj* gangling, lanky
dégivrage [deʒivraʒ] *nm* (**a**) *(action) (d'un pare-brise)* de-icing; *(d'un réfrigérateur)* defrosting (**b**) *(dispositif) (d'un pare-brise)* de-icer; *(d'un réfrigérateur)* defroster
dégivrer [deʒivre] *vt (pare-brise)* to de-ice; *(réfrigérateur)* to defrost
déglacer [16] [deglase] *vt Culin (poêle à frire)* to deglaze
déglinguer [deglɛ̃ge] *Fam* **1** *vt (appareil)* to bust; **ma moto est toute déglinguée** my motorbike is falling to pieces
  2 se déglinguer *vpr (appareil)* to go; *(véhicule)* to fall to pieces
déglutir [deglytir] *vi* to swallow
déglutition [deglytisjɔ̃] *nf* swallowing
dégobiller [degɔbije] *très Fam* **1** *vi* to puke
  2 *vt* to puke up

dégonflé, -e [degɔ̃fle] **1** adj (**a**) (pneu, ballon) flat (**b**) Fam (lâche) chicken
2 nm,f Fam chicken
dégonfler [degɔ̃fle] **1** vt (pneu, ballon) to let the air out of, to deflate
2 vi (partie du corps) to go down
3 se dégonfler vpr (**a**) (pneu, ballon) to go flat (**b**) Fam (personne) to chicken out
dégorger [45] [degɔrʒe] **1** vt (**a**) (évacuer) to discharge; **la rue a dégorgé un flot de gens** a crowd of people surged from the street (**b**) (passage, tuyau, évier) to unblock
2 vi **faire d. des concombres** = to remove water from cucumbers by sprinkling them with salt
dégot(t)er [degɔte] vt Fam to dig up
dégouliner [deguline] vi (liquide) to trickle; **je dégouline** I'm dripping wet
dégoupiller [degupije] vt (grenade) to pull the pin out of
dégourdi, -e [degurdi] **1** adj smart, bright
2 nm,f **c'est un d.** he's a smart one
dégourdir [degurdir] **1** vt (membres) to remove the stiffness from; Fig **d. qn** to teach sb a thing or two
2 se dégourdir vpr (**a**) (membres) **se d. les jambes** to stretch one's legs (**b**) Fig to learn a thing or two
dégoût [degu] nm (**a**) (aversion) disgust, distaste; **éprouver du d. pour qch** to be disgusted by sth; **prendre qch en d.** to take a strong dislike to sth (**b**) (lassitude) weariness; **le d. de la vie** world-weariness
dégoûtant, -e [degutɑ̃, -ɑ̃t] **1** adj disgusting
2 nm,f disgusting person; **un vieux d.** a dirty old man
dégoûté, -e [degute] adj (**a**) (écœuré) (air) disgusted; Ironique **vous n'êtes pas d.!** you're not fussy! (**b**) (choqué) disgusted (**c**) (las) weary; **être d. de qch** to be weary or sick of sth
2 nm,f **faire le d.** to turn up one's nose
dégoûter [degute] vt **d. qn** (physiquement) to turn sb's stomach; (moralement) to disgust sb, to make sb sick; **d. qn de qch** to put sb off sth; **c'est à vous d. de l'Espagne/des hommes!** it's enough to put you off Spain/men for life!
dégoutter [degute] **dégoutter de** vt ind (laisser couler) to drip with
dégradant, -e [degradɑ̃] adj degrading
dégradation [degradasjɔ̃] nf (d'un monument) defacement; (de matériel scolaire, de l'environnement) damage (de to); Fig (de la santé, de relations, d'une situation) deterioration
dégradé [degrade] nm (de couleurs) gradation; **un d. de bleus** blues shading off into each other; **se faire faire un d.** (chez le coiffeur) to have one's hair layered; Ordinat **d. de couleur** colour scale
dégrader [degrade] **1** vt (**a**) (abîmer) (monument) to deface; (matériel, maison) to damage; Ordinat (données) to corrupt (**b**) Fig (humilier) to degrade (**c**) Mil to demote
2 se dégrader vpr (**a**) (se détériorer) (santé, relations, situation) to deteriorate; (bâtiment) to fall into disrepair (**b**) (s'abaisser) to degrade oneself
dégrafer [degrafe] **1** vt (vêtement, bracelet) to undo
2 se dégrafer vpr (**a**) (vêtement, bracelet) to come undone (**b**) (femme) to undo one's dress
dégraffitage [degrafitaʒ] nm graffiti removal
dégraissage [degrɛsaʒ] nm (d'une entreprise) downsizing
dégraisser [degrese] **1** vt (bouillon) to skim the fat off; Fig (entreprise) to downsize; **d. les effectifs** to cut

back on staff
2 vi (entreprise) to downsize
degré [dəgre] nm (**a**) (d'un angle, de chaleur) degree; (de boisson alcoolisée) proof; **combien de degrés fait ce whisky?** what proof is this whisky?; **d. Celsius/Fahrenheit** degree Celsius/Fahrenheit (**b**) (stade, niveau) stage; **d. de parenté** family relationship; **cousins au second d.** second cousins; **brûlure au deuxième/troisième d.** second/third degree burn; **au plus haut d.** (extrêmement) in the extreme; **jusqu'à un certain d.** up to a point; **par degrés** by degrees; **prendre une plaisanterie au premier d.** to take a joke seriously (**c**) (d'escalier) step; (d'échelle) rung
dégressif, -ive [degresif, -iv] adj **tarif d.** tapering rate; **impôt d.** degressive taxation
dégrèvement [degrɛvmɑ̃] nm **d. (fiscal)** tax relief
dégriffé, -e [degrife] **1** adj = with its designer label removed and reduced in price
2 nm = reduced-price designer item with its label removed
dégringolade [degrɛ̃gɔlad] nf Fam (chute) tumble; Fig (d'une entreprise) collapse; (des prix, des cours) slump (**de** in)
dégringoler [degrɛ̃gɔle] Fam **1** vt to rush down
2 vi (personne) to tumble; Fig (entreprise) to collapse; (prix, cours) to slump
dégripper [degripe] vt (mécanisme) to unjam
dégriser [degrize] **1** vt to sober up; Fig to bring down to earth
2 se dégriser vpr to sober up
dégrossir [degrosir] vt (bois) to trim; (pierre) to roughhew; Fig (travail) to rough out; **d. qn** to knock the rough edges off sb; **être mal dégrossi** to be uncouth
dégrouper [degrupe] vt to divide into groups
déguenillé, -e [degənije] adj ragged
déguerpir [degɛrpir] vi to clear off; **faire d. qn** to chase sb away
dégueulasse [degœlas] très Fam **1** adj (sale) filthy; (mauvais, désagréable) disgusting, gross; **c'est pas d.** (bon) it's not bad at all; **être d. avec qn** to be mean to sb; **se balader en d.** to go around in sloppy old clothes
2 nmf **un gros d.** (sale) a filthy pig; (débauché) a filthy swine
dégueulasser [degœlase] vt très Fam to mess up
dégueuler [degœle] vi très Fam to puke
dégueulis [degœli] nm très Fam puke
déguisé, -e [degize] adj (pour tromper) disguised; (pour s'amuser) dressed up; **avec une joie non déguisée** with unconcealed delight
déguisement [degizmɑ̃] nm (pour tromper) disguise; (pour s'amuser) fancy dress
déguiser [degize] **1** vt (**a**) (costumer) to dress up; **d. qn en clown** to dress sb up as a clown (**b**) (voix, écriture, vérité, pensée) to disguise
2 se déguiser vpr (pour tromper) to disguise oneself; (pour s'amuser) to dress up; **se d. en pompier** to dress up as a fireman
dégurgiter [degyrʒite] vt aussi Fig to regurgitate
dégustation [degystasjɔ̃] nf tasting; **d. de vin** wine tasting; **d. d'huîtres** (panneau devant un restaurant) oysters served here
déguster [degyste] vt (**a**) (tester) (vin, alcool) to taste (**b**) (savourer) (aliment, livre) to savour (**c**) très Fam **toute sa vie, elle a dégusté** (souffert) she's had a rough time of it all her life; **tu vas d.!** you're in for it!
déhanché, -e [deɑ̃ʃe] adj lopsided

déhanchement [deɑ̃ʃmɑ̃] *nm (en marchant)* swaying of the hips; *(à l'arrêt)* standing with one's weight on one foot

déhancher [deɑ̃ʃe] **se déhancher** *vpr (en marchant)* to sway one's hips; *(à l'arrêt)* to stand with one's weight on one foot

dehors [dəɔr] **1** *adv (à l'extérieur)* outside; *(en plein air)* out of doors; *(pas chez soi)* out; *Fam* **ficher** *ou* **foutre qn d.** to kick sb out; **ne pas mettre le nez** *ou* **les pieds d.** to set foot outside; **en d.** *(s'ouvrir, tourner)* outwards; **marcher les pieds en d.** to walk with one's feet turned out; **en d. de** *(à l'extérieur de)* outside; *(à part)* apart from; **rester en d. d'une dispute** to keep out of an argument; **en d. du sujet** *(remarque)* irrelevant
2 *nm* (**a**) *(extérieur)* outside; **au d.** on the outside; *(se pencher, se répandre)* out (**b**) *(apparence)* **une maison aux d. imposants** a house with an imposing exterior; **sous des d. aimables** under a pleasant exterior

déhoussable [deusabl] *adj (canapé, siège)* with loose covers

déj [deʒ] *nm Fam* **petit d.** breakfast, *Br* brekkie

déjà [deʒa] *adv* (**a**) *(dès maintenant)* already; *(si tôt)* yet; **il est d. trois heures** it's already three o'clock; **faut-il que vous partiez d.?** do you have to go so soon? (**b**) *(auparavant)* before; **j'avais d. lu ce livre** I'd read that book before; **d. en 1900** as early as 1900 (**c**) *(intensif)* **j'aurais dû le faire il y a d. trois jours** I should have done it three days ago as it is; **c'est d. ça!, c'est d. pas mal!** that's not bad at all!; **vous avez d. trop de travail** you have too much work as it is; **d. que je n'en ai pas beaucoup, si tu m'en prends la moitié...** I haven't got much as it is, so if you take half... (**d**) *(interrogatif)* **qu'est-ce que vous faites, d.?** what did you say your job was?; **c'est quoi, d., ton nom?** what was your name again?

déjanté, -e [deʒɑ̃te] *adj très Fam* **être (complètement) d.** to be off one's rocker

déjanter [deʒɑ̃te] **1** *vi très Fam* **(être fou)** to be off one's rocker; *(devenir fou)* to flip one's lid
2 se déjanter *vpr (pneu)* to come off the rim

déjà-vu [deʒavy] *nm inv* **une impression de d.** a feeling of déjà vu; **c'est du d.** *(ce n'est pas original)* it's the same old thing

déjeuner [deʒœne] **1** *nm* (**a**) *(repas de midi)* lunch; **prendre son d.** to have lunch; **d. d'affaires/de travail** business/working lunch (**b**) *(repas du matin)* **(petit) d.** breakfast (**c**) *(tasse et soucoupe)* breakfast cup and saucer
2 *vi* (**a**) *(le matin)* to have breakfast (**b**) *(à midi)* to have lunch; **nous avons les Dupont à d. dimanche** the Duponts are coming for lunch on Sunday; **d. d'un sandwich** to have a sandwich for lunch

déjouer [deʒwe] *vt (complot, plans)* to foil

délabré, -e [delabre] *adj (bâtiment, meuble)* dilapidated; *(santé)* ruined

délabrement [delabrəmɑ̃] *nm (d'un bâtiment, d'un meuble)* dilapidated state; *(d'une entreprise)* ruin; **dans un état de grand d.** *(bâtiment)* in a state of total disrepair

délabrer [delabre] **se délabrer** *vpr (bâtiment)* to fall into disrepair; *(meuble)* to fall to pieces; *(entreprise)* to go to rack and ruin; *(santé)* to deteriorate

délacer [16] [delase] **1** *vt (chaussures)* to untie; *(corset)* to unlace
2 se délacer *vpr (chaussures)* to come untied; *(corset)* to come unlaced; *(femme)* to unlace one's corset

délai [dele] *nm* (**a**) *(laps de temps)* time allowed; **dans un d. de dix jours** within ten days; **il faut compter un d. de dix jours** you should allow ten days; **respecter** *ou* **tenir les délais** to meet the deadline; **dans les délais** on time; **dans les plus brefs délais** as soon as possible; **lundi dernier d.** by Monday at the very latest; **d. de livraison: un mois** allow one month for delivery; **d. de paiement** *(fixé par contrat)* term of payment (**b**) *(prolongation)* extension; **laisser à qn un d. de réflexion** to give sb time to think; **sans d.** without delay, immediately

délaisser [delese] *vt (abandonner)* to desert, to abandon; *(négliger)* to neglect

délassant, -e [delasɑ̃, -ɑ̃t] *adj (bain, massage)* relaxing; *(lecture)* entertaining

délassement [delasmɑ̃] *nm* relaxation

délasser [delase] **1** *vt* to relax
2 se délasser *vpr* to relax

délateur, -trice [delatœr, -tris] *nm,f* informer

délation [delasjɔ̃] *nf* denouncement

délavé, -e [delave] *adj (tissu, jean)* faded; *(couleur)* watery

délayage [delɛjaʒ] *nm Péj* padding

délayer [53] [deleje] *vt* (**a**) *(poudre)* to add water to; *(peinture)* to thin; *(liquide)* to water down; **d. de la farine dans du lait** to mix flour with milk (**b**) *Fig (discours, texte)* to pad out

Delco® [dɛlko] *nm Aut* distributor

délectable [delɛktabl] *adj* delectable

délecter [delɛkte] **se délecter** *vpr* **se d. de qch/à faire qch** to take delight in sth/in doing sth

délégation [delegasjɔ̃] *nf* (**a**) *(action de déléguer) (de représentants)* delegation; **agir par d.** to act on the authority invested in one; **d. de pouvoir** delegation of authority (**b**) *(groupe)* delegation

délégué, -e [delege] *nm,f* delegate; *Scol* **d. (de classe)** class representative *(at class meetings)*; **d. du personnel** staff representative; **d. syndical** union representative; *(d'usine)* shop steward

déléguer [34] [delege] *vt* (**a**) *(personne)* to delegate (**b**) *(transmettre) (pouvoirs)* to delegate (à to); **c'est un patron qui sait d.** he's a boss who knows how to delegate

délestage [delɛstaʒ] *nm (d'un navire, d'un ballon)* unballasting; **pour assurer le d. des grandes artères** to relieve congestion on the main roads; **itinéraire de d.** relief route

délester [delɛste] *vt (navire, ballon)* to unballast; *(voie de communication)* to relieve congestion on; *aussi Hum* **d. qn de qch** to relieve sb of sth

délibération [deliberasjɔ̃] *nf* (**a**) *(débat)* deliberation; **être en d.** to be under discussion (**b**) *(réflexion)* deliberation; **après mûre d.** after careful consideration

délibéré, -e [delibere] **1** *adj (intentionnel)* deliberate
2 *nm Jur (de juges)* deliberation

délibérément [deliberemɑ̃] *adv* deliberately

délibérer [34] [delibere] *vi* (**a**) *(discuter)* to deliberate (**de** *ou* **sur** on); *Jur (jury)* to consider its verdict (**b**) *(réfléchir)* to deliberate

délicat, -e [delika, -at] *adj* (**a**) *(fragile, fin)* delicate; *(peau)* sensitive; *(travail)* fine (**b**) *(raffiné) (goûts)* refined; *(gestes)* graceful; *(plat)* sophisticated; **avoir le palais d.** to have a discerning palate (**c**) *(plein de tact)* tactful; **quelle attention délicate!** how thoughtful!; **peu d.** *(peu scrupuleux)* unscrupulous (**d**) *(exigeant)* fussy; **faire le d.** to turn up one's nose

délicatement [delikatmã] *adv (légèrement)* gently; *(finement)* finely

délicatesse [delikatɛs] *nf* (**a**) *(d'un objet)* fragility; *(d'une fleur, d'un tissu, d'un coloris)* delicacy; *(de la peau)* sensitivity; *(de la santé)* frailty (**b**) *(des goûts)* refinement; *(des gestes)* grace; *(d'un plat)* sophistication; **avec d.** *(légèrement)* gently; *(finement)* finely (**c**) *(difficulté)* delicacy (**d**) *(tact)* tact; **avec d.** tactfully

délice [delis] *nm (plaisir)* delight; **cette tarte est un vrai d.** this tart is absolutely delicious

délices [delis] *nfpl Litt ou Hum* delights; **faire ses d. de qch** to delight in sth

délicieusement [delisjøzmã] *adv (agréablement)* delightfully; **d. bon** *(plat)* absolutely delicious

délicieux, -euse [delisjø, -øz] *adj (nourriture, sensation, chaleur)* delicious; *(personne, robe)* delightful

délictueux, -euse [deliktɥø, -øz] *adj Jur* **acte d.** offence

délié, -e [delje] **1** *adj (taille)* slim; *(doigts)* nimble **2** *nm (de l'écriture)* thin stroke

délier [66] [delje] **1** *vt* to untie; **d. qn d'une promesse** to release sb from a promise; *Fig* **le vin lui a délié la langue** the wine loosened his/her tongue **2 se délier** *vpr (se défaire)* to come untied; *Fig* **sa langue s'est déliée** he/she found his/her tongue

délimiter [delimite] *vt (territoire)* to demarcate; *(responsabilité, sujet)* to define

délinquance [delɛ̃kɑ̃s] *nf* delinquency; **d. juvénile** juvenile delinquency; **la petite d. des banlieues** petty crime in the suburbs

délinquant, -e [delɛ̃kɑ̃, -ɑ̃t] **1** *adj* delinquent **2** *nm,f* offender; **d. juvénile** juvenile delinquent; **d. sexuel** sex offender

déliquescence [delikɛsɑ̃s] *nf Péj (d'une civilisation, des mœurs)* decay; **tomber en d.** to fall into decay

déliquescent, -e [delikɛsɑ̃, -ɑ̃t] *adj Péj (civilisation, mœurs)* decadent

délirant, -e [delirã, -ɑ̃t] *adj Méd* delirious; *Fig (joie, imagination)* frenzied; **c'est d. de leur demander de tout payer!** it's crazy asking them to pay for everything!

délire [delir] *nm* (**a**) *Méd* delirium; **avoir le d.** to be delirious; *Fig* **c'est du d.!** it's crazy!; **d. de grandeur** delusions of grandeur; *Psy* **d. de persécution** persecution complex (**b**) *(frénésie)* frenzy; **foule en d.** frenzied crowd; *Fam* **cette soirée, c'est le d.!** this is a wild party!

délirer [delire] *vi* (**a**) *(être malade)* to be delirious; *(dire n'importe quoi)* to rave; *Fig* **tu délires!** you're out of your mind! (**b**) *(s'amuser)* to have a blast

delirium tremens [delirjɔmtremɛ̃s] *nm* delirium tremens; **avoir le d.** to have delirium tremens

délit [deli] *nm* offence; **d. de fuite** failure to report an accident; **d. d'initié** insider dealing *or* trading

délivrance [delivrãs] *nf* (**a**) *(soulagement)* relief; **leur départ fut une vraie d.** it was a real relief when they left (**b**) *(accouchement)* delivery (**c**) *(d'un certificat, d'un passeport, d'un permis)* issue

délivrer [delivre] **1** *vt* (**a**) *(libérer) (captif, otage)* to rescue; *(ville)* to liberate; *(peuple)* to set free; **d. qn de ses liens** to free sb from his/her bonds (**b**) *(soulager)* **d. qn d'un secret trop lourd** to share the burden of a secret with sb; **d. qn d'un grand poids** to take a weight off sb's shoulders (**c**) *(remettre) (marchandises)* to deliver; *(certificat, passeport, permis)* to issue **2 se délivrer** *vpr* to free oneself (**de** from)

délocalisation [delɔkalizasjɔ̃] *nf* relocation

délocaliser [delɔkalize] *vt* to relocate

déloger [45] [delɔʒe] *vt (envahisseur)* to drive out (**de** from); *(locataire)* to evict; *(objet coincé)* to dislodge (**de** from)

déloyal, -e, -aux, -ales [delwajal, -o] *adj (ami)* disloyal, unfaithful; *(adversaire, pratique, concurrence)* unfair; *(coup)* illegal

delta [dɛlta] *nm* (**a**) *(d'un fleuve)* delta (**b**) *Aviat* **(aile) d.** delta wing

deltaplane [dɛltaplan] *nm* hang-glider; **faire du d.** to go hang-gliding

deltiste [dɛltist] *nmf* hang-glider *(person)*

déluge [delyʒ] *nm (de pluie)* downpour; *(d'injures)* torrent; *(de larmes)* flood; *Rel* **le D.** the Flood; **noyer qn sous un d. de compliments** to shower sb with compliments; **après moi le d.!** when I'm gone I don't care what happens!

déluré, -e [delyre] *adj (vif)* sharp, smart; *Péj (provocant)* forward

démagogie [demagɔʒi] *nf* demagogy

démagogique [demagɔʒik] *adj* demagogic

démagogue [demagɔg] *nmf* demagogue

demain [dəmɛ̃] **1** *adv* tomorrow; **d. soir** tomorrow evening; **d. en huit** a week tomorrow, tomorrow week; **à d.!** see you tomorrow!; **le journal de d.** tomorrow's paper; *Fam* **ce n'est pas pour d., ce n'est pas d. la veille** that won't happen for a long time yet; *Fig* **d. il fera jour** tomorrow is another day; *Fig* **de d.** *(de l'avenir)* of tomorrow **2** *nm* tomorrow; **tu as tout d. pour y réfléchir** you've got all tomorrow to think about it

demande [dəmɑ̃d] *nf* (**a**) *(requête)* request (**de** for); *(formulaire)* application form; **faire une d. de qch** *(de permis, de prêt)* to apply for sth; **faire qch à** *ou* **sur la d. de qn** to do sth at sb's request; **à la d. générale** by popular demand; **sur d.** on request; **demandes d'emploi** *(titre de rubrique)* situations wanted; **d. (en mariage)** proposal (of marriage); **faire sa d. (en mariage)** to propose; **d. de rançon** ransom demand (**b**) *Écon* demand; **d. des consommateurs** consumer demand (**c**) *Jur* **d. en divorce** divorce petition; **d. de dommages-intérêts** claim for damages (**d**) *(besoin) (de soins, d'affection)* need

demander [dəmɑ̃de] **1** *vt* (**a**) *(réclamer) (augmentation, addition, preuves)* to ask for; *(dommages et intérêts)* to claim; **d. qch à qn** to ask sb for sth; *(service)* to ask sb sth; **d. à qn de faire qch** to ask sb to do sth; **d. à manger/boire** to ask for something to eat/drink; **d. son avis à qn** to ask sb's opinion; **d. le divorce** to file for divorce; **d. la main de qn** to ask for sb's hand (in marriage); **d. qn en mariage** to propose to sb; **d. la parole** to ask to speak; **d. la permission de faire qch** to ask (for) permission to do sth; **combien demandez-vous de l'heure?** how much do you charge an hour?; **combien en demande-t-elle?** how much is she asking for it?; **je ne demande pas mieux que de vous aider** I'll be only too pleased to help you; **il ne demande que ça** he'd be only too pleased!; *Hum* **que demande le peuple?** what more could I/he/*etc* ask?; **je ne demande qu'une seule chose: qu'on me laisse tranquille** all I ask is to be left alone; **on demande un maçon** *(dans une petite annonce)* builder wanted; **être très demandé** to be in great demand; **il n'y a qu'à** *ou* **il suffit de d.** you/he/*etc* only have/has to ask (**b**) *(nécessiter) (tact, réflexion, attention)* to require; **ça demande de gros sacrifices** great sacrifices are called for (**c**) *(exiger)* to demand; **en d. trop à qn**

to ask too much of sb; **d. l'impossible** to ask the impossible (**d**) *(s'enquérir de) (prix, cause, raison)* to ask; **d. qch à qn** to ask sb sth; **il m'a demandé de tes nouvelles** he asked after you; *Fam* **je ne t'ai rien demandé!** I didn't ask for your advice!; **je vous (le) demande, je vous demande un peu!** I ask you! (**e**) *(appeler) (médecin, prêtre)* to ask for; **on vous demande** you're wanted; **on vous demande au téléphone** there's a call for you

2 demander à *vt ind* **d. à faire qch** to ask to do sth; **les suspects ne demandaient qu'à parler** the suspects were only too willing to speak; **demande à ce qu'on vienne te chercher** ask someone to come and collect you

3 se demander *vpr* to wonder, to ask oneself; **je me demande pourquoi elle a dit ça** I wonder why she said that; **c'est à se d. si...** it makes you wonder whether...; **des choses comme ça, ça ne se demande pas!** you don't ask that sort of question!

demandeur, -euse [dəmɑ̃dœr, -øz] *nm,f* **d. d'asile** asylum-seeker; **d. d'emploi** job seeker

démangeaison [demɑ̃ʒɛzɔ̃] *nf* itch; **avoir une d.** to have an itch, to be itching; **j'ai des démangeaisons dans les jambes** my legs are itchy

démanger [45] [demɑ̃ʒe] *vi* to itch; **l'épaule me démange** my shoulder's itching; *Fig* **méfie-toi, la main me démange!** *(à un enfant)* watch out or you'll feel the back of my hand!; **ça me démange de lui dire ce que je pense** I'm itching to tell him/her what I think

démantèlement [demɑ̃tɛlmɑ̃] *nm* breaking up

démanteler [39] [demɑ̃tle] *vt* to break up

démantibuler [demɑ̃tibyle] *Fam* **1** *vt* to break up

2 se démantibuler *vpr* to come to pieces

démaquillage [demakijaʒ] *nm* removal of make-up

démaquillant, -e [demakijɑ̃, -ɑ̃t] **1** *adj* cleansing

2 *nm* cleanser; **d. pour les yeux** eye make-up remover

démaquiller [demakije] **1** *vt* **d. qn** to remove sb's make-up

2 se démaquiller *vpr* to remove one's make-up; **se d. les yeux** to remove one's eye make-up

démarcation [demarkasjɔ̃] *nf* demarcation

démarchage [demarʃaʒ] *nm (porte-à-porte)* door-to-door selling; **d. électoral** canvassing; **d. par téléphone** telesales

démarche [demarʃ] *nf* (**a**) *(allure)* gait, walk (**b**) *(requête)* step; **faire une d. auprès de qn** to approach sb; **faire les démarches nécessaires pour faire qch** to take the necessary steps to do sth (**c**) *Fig (cheminement)* process; **d. intellectuelle** thought process

démarcher [demarʃe] *vt* to canvass for

démarcheur, -euse [demarʃœr, -øz] *nm,f* door-to-door salesman, *f* door-to-door saleswoman

démarque [demark] *nf Com* markdown; **la d. inconnue** shrinkage

démarquer [demarke] **1** *vt (marchandises)* to mark down

2 se démarquer *vpr Sport* to lose one's marker; *Fig* **se d. de qn** *(se distinguer)* to distinguish oneself from sb

démarrage [demaraʒ] *nm (d'un moteur)* starting; *(d'une entreprise)* start-up; *(d'un projet, d'une campagne publicitaire)* start; **au d.** *(d'un véhicule)* when moving off; **faire un d.** *(coureur)* to put on a spurt; *Ordinat* **d. à chaud/froid** warm/cold start; **d. en côte** hill start

démarrer [demare] **1** *vi* (**a**) *(véhicule)* to move off; *(moteur)* to start; *(conducteur)* to drive off (**b**) *(commencer)* to start; **bien/mal d.** to get off to a good/bad start (**c**) *(commencer à réussir)* to take off

2 *vt* to start; *Ordinat* to boot (up), to start up

démarreur [demarœr] *nm Aut* starter (motor)

démasquer [demaske] *vt aussi Fig* to unmask

démâter [demɑte] **1** *vt* to dismast

2 *vi* to lose its mast

démêlant [demɛlɑ̃] *adj m & nm* **(produit) d.** conditioner, detangler

démêlé [demele] *nm* disagreement (**avec** with); **avoir des démêlés avec la justice** to be in trouble with the law

démêler [demele] **1** *vt (fil, laine, cheveux)* to untangle; *(mystère)* to unravel; **d. le vrai du faux** to disentangle the truth from the lies

2 se démêler *vpr* **se d. de** to extricate oneself from

démembrement [demɑ̃brəmɑ̃] *nm (d'un empire)* breaking up; *(d'une propriété agricole)* division

démembrer [demɑ̃bre] *vt (empire)* to break up; *(propriété agricole)* to divide (up)

déménagement [demenaʒmɑ̃] *nm* move; **c'est pour quand le d.?** when are you/we/etc moving?

déménager [45] [demenaʒe] **1** *vi* (**a**) *(personne, entreprise)* to move; **où déménage-t-il?** where's he moving to?; **d. à la cloche de bois** to do a moonlight flit; *Fam* **allez, déménagez!** beat it! (**b**) *Fam Fig (musique)* to be mind-blowing; *(alcool)* to pack a punch

2 *vt (meubles)* to move

déménageur [demenaʒœr] *nm Br* removal man, *Am* furniture mover; **avoir des épaules de d.** to have strong broad shoulders

démence [demɑ̃s] *nf* insanity; *Méd* dementia; *Fam* **c'est de la d.!** it's madness!

démener [46] [demne] **se démener** *vpr* (**a**) *(s'agiter)* to thrash about; **se d. comme un beau diable** *(pour se libérer)* to struggle like a madman (**b**) *(se dépenser)* to exert oneself (**c**) *(faire des efforts)* **se d. pour faire qch** to go to great lengths to do sth

dément, -e [demɑ̃, -ɑ̃t] **1** *adj (fou)* insane; *Fam (formidable)* fantastic; *Fam* **c'est d.!** it's unbelievable!

2 *nm,f* lunatic; *Méd* demented person

démenti [demɑ̃ti] *nm* denial; *Journ* disclaimer; **opposer un d. formel à qch** to issue a firm denial of sth

démentiel, -elle [demɑ̃sjɛl] *adj (idée, projet)* insane; *Fam (incroyable)* crazy

démentir [64a] [demɑ̃tir] **1** *vt* to deny; *(être en contradiction avec)* to belie

2 se démentir *vpr (cesser)* **leur honnêteté ne s'est jamais démentie** they've always been unfailing in their honesty

démerder [demɛrde] **se démerder** *vpr très Fam* to get by, to manage; **démerde-toi tout seul!** sort it out yourself!; **elle est assez grande pour se d. seule** she's old enough to take care of herself; **elle se démerde pas mal en cuisine/tennis** she's not a bad cook/tennis player; **se d. pour faire qch** to manage to do sth

démériter [demerite] *vi* to be at fault; **je ne vois pas en quoi il a démérité** I don't see how he is at fault

démesure [deməzyr] *nf* excess

démesuré, -e [deməzyre] *adj (en taille)* enormous; *(orgueil, ambition)* excessive

démesurément [deməzyremɑ̃] *adv* enormously

démettre¹ [47] [demɛtr] **1** *vt* **il m'a démis l'épaule** he dislocated my shoulder

2 se démettre *vpr* **se d. l'épaule/le genou** to dislocate one's shoulder/knee

démettre² **1** *vt* **d. qn de ses fonctions** to remove sb from his/her post

2 se démettre *vpr* **se d. de ses fonctions** to resign from one's post

demeurant [dəmœrɑ̃] **au demeurant** *adv (malgré tout)* for all that; *(d'ailleurs)* after all

demeure [dəmœr] *nf* (**a**) *(château)* mansion; *Litt (résidence)* (place of) residence; *Euph* **dernière d.** last resting place (**b**) **mettre qn en d. de faire qch** to instruct sb to do sth; *Jur* to give sb notice to do sth (**c**) **à d.** permanently

demeuré, -e [dəmœre] **1** *adj Vieilli* mentally retarded; *Fam Péj* halfwitted

2 *nm,f Vieilli* mentally retarded person; *Fam Péj* halfwit

demeurer [dəmœre] *vi* (**a**) *(aux être) (rester)* to remain; **d. convaincu que...** to remain convinced that...; **d. fidèle à qn** to remain faithful to sb; **demeurons-en là** let's leave it at that; **il n'en demeure pas moins que...** the fact remains that... (**b**) *Sout (aux avoir) (habiter)* to reside

demi, -e [dəmi] **1** *adj* (**a**) *(après un nom)* **deux heures et demie** *(durée)* two and a half hours; *(moment)* half past two; **un litre/kilo et d.** a litre/kilo and a half; **il gagne trois fois et demie ce que je gagne** he earns three and a half times as much as I do (**b**) *(avant un nom ou un adjectif)* half; **une d.-cuillère de sucre** half a teaspoon of sugar

2 *nm* (**a**) *(moitié)* half (**b**) *(bière)* **un d.** a beer, *Br* ≃ a half (**c**) *Sport (au football)* midfielder; **d. de mêlée** *(au rugby)* scrum half; **d. d'ouverture** *(au rugby)* fly half

3 *nf* **demie** *(heure)* **il est la demie** it's half past; **à la demie** at half past

4 *adv* half; **d. plein** half full; **à d.** half; **à d. mort** half dead; **faire les choses à d.** to do things by halves; **croire qn à d.** to half believe sb; **ouvrir qch à d.** to half open sth

demiard [dəmjar] *nm Can* half pint

demi-cercle *(pl* demi-cercles) [dəmisɛrkl] *nm* semicircle, half circle; **en d.** in a semicircle

demi-dieu *(pl* demi-dieux) [dəmidjø] *nm* demigod

demi-douzaine *(pl* demi-douzaines) [dəmiduzɛn] *nf* half-dozen; **une d. d'œufs** half a dozen eggs

demi-droite *(pl* demi-droites) [dəmidrwat] *nf Math* half-line

demi-écrémé, -e *(mpl* demi-écrémés, *fpl* demi-écrémées) [dəmiekreme] *adj* semi-skimmed

demi-finale *(pl* demi-finales) [dəmifinal] *nf* semifinal

demi-fond [dəmifɔ̃] *nm inv Sport* **(course de) d.** middle-distance race

demi-frère *(pl* demi-frères) [dəmifrɛr] *nm* half-brother

demi-gros [dəmigro] *nm inv* **(commerce de) d.** cash and carry

demi-heure *(pl* demi-heures) [dəmijœr] *nf* **une d.** half an hour; **toutes les demi-heures** every half-hour

demi-jour *(pl* demi-jours) [dəmiʒur] *nm* half-light

demi-journée *(pl* demi-journées) [dəmiʒurne] *nf* half-day

démilitariser [demilitarize] *vt* to demilitarize

demi-litre *(pl* demi-litres) [dəmilitr] *nm* half-litre; **un d. de vin** half a litre of wine

demi-lune *(pl* demi-lunes) [dəmilyn] *nf* half-moon

demi-mesure *(pl* demi-mesures) [dəmiməzyr] *nf (compromis)* half-measure

demi-mort, -e *(mpl* demi-morts, *fpl* demi-mortes) [dəmimɔr, -mɔrt] *adj* half-dead

demi-mot [dəmimo] **à demi-mot** *adv* **comprendre à d.** to take the hint; **nous nous comprenons à d.** we don't have to spell everything out to each other

déminage [deminaʒ] *nm* mine clearance; *(en mer)* minesweeping

déminer [demine] *vt* to clear of mines

démineur [deminœr] *nm (personne)* bomb disposal expert; *(navire)* minesweeper

demi-pause *(pl* demi-pauses) [dəmipoz] *nf Mus Br* minim rest, *Am* half-note rest

demi-pension [dəmipɑ̃sjɔ̃] *nf (à l'hôtel) Br* half-board, *Am* modified American plan; **sept jours en d.** seven days *Br* half-board *or Am* modified American plan; *Scol* **être en d.** to be a *Br* day boarder *or Am* day student

demi-pensionnaire *(pl* demi-pensionnaires) [dəmipɑ̃sjɔnɛr] *nmf (écolier) Br* day boarder, *Am* day student

demi-portion *(pl* demi-portions) [dəmipɔrsjɔ̃] *nf Fam Péj* weed, runt

demi-queue *(pl* demi-queues) [dəmikø] *adj & nm* **(piano) d.** baby grand (piano)

démis, -e [demi, -iz] *adj (membre)* dislocated

demi-saison *(pl* demi-saisons) [dəmisɛzɔ̃] *nf* spring or autumn; **vêtements de d.** spring or autumn clothes

demi-sel [dəmisɛl] *adj inv (beurre)* slightly salted; **fromage d.** slightly salted cream cheese

demi-sœur *(pl* demi-sœurs) [dəmisœr] *nf* half-sister

demi-sommeil *(pl* demi-sommeils) [dəmisɔmɛj] *nm* half-sleep; **être dans un d.** to be half-asleep

demi-soupir *(pl* demi-soupirs) [dəmisupir] *nm Mus Br* quaver rest, *Am* eighth-note rest

démission [demisjɔ̃] *nf* resignation; *Fig* renunciation; **donner sa d.** to hand in one's resignation

démissionnaire [demisjɔnɛr] *adj* resigning

démissionner [demisjɔne] *vi* to resign (**de** from); *Fig* to give up

demi-tarif [dəmitarif] **1** *nm* *(pl* demi-tarifs) half-price

2 *adj inv* **billet d.** *(de transports)* half-fare (ticket); *(de spectacle)* half-price ticket

demi-teinte *(pl* demi-teintes) [dəmitɛ̃t] *nf* halftone; *Fig* **être tout en demi-teintes** to be subtle in character

demi-ton *(pl* demi-tons) [dəmitɔ̃] *nm Mus Br* semitone, *Am* half step

demi-tour *(pl* demi-tours) [dəmitur] *nm* half-turn; *(en voiture)* U-turn; *Mil* about-turn; **faire d.** to turn back; **faire un d.** *(en voiture)* to do a U-turn; *Mil* **d. droite!** right about-turn!

démiurge [demjyrʒ] *nm* demiurge

demi-volée *(pl* demi-volées) [dəmivɔle] *nf (au tennis, au football)* half-volley

démobilisation [demɔbilizasjɔ̃] *nf* (**a**) *(de troupes)* demobilization (**b**) *Fig (désintérêt)* apathy

démobiliser [demɔbilize] *vt* (**a**) *(troupes)* to demobilize (**b**) *Fig (désintéresser)* to demobilize

démocrate [demɔkrat] **1** *adj* democratic

2 *nmf* democrat

démocrate-chrétien, -enne *(mpl* démocrates-chrétiens, *fpl* démocrates-chrétiennes) [demɔkratkretjɛ̃, -ɛn] *adj & nm,f Pol* Christian Democrat

démocratie [demɔkrasi] *nf* democracy

démocratique [demɔkratik] *adj* democratic
démocratiquement [demɔkratikmã] *adv* democratically
démocratisation [demɔkratizasjɔ̃] *nf* democratization
démocratiser [demɔkratize] **1** *vt* to democratize
2 se démocratiser *vpr* to become (more) democratic
démodé, -e [demɔde] *adj* old-fashioned
démoder [demɔde] **se démoder** *vpr* to go out of fashion
démographie [demɔgrafi] *nf* demography
démographique [demɔgrafik] *adj* demographic
demoiselle [dəmwazɛl] *nf* (**a**) *(jeune fille)* young lady; **d. de compagnie** lady's companion; **d. d'honneur** *(d'une souveraine)* lady-in-waiting; *(d'une mariée)* bridesmaid (**b**) *Vieilli (célibataire)* maiden lady; **c'est une vieille d.** she's never married (**c**) *(insecte)* dragonfly
démolir [demɔlir] *vt* (**a**) *(abattre)* to demolish, to pull down; *(mettre en pièces)* to demolish, to wreck; **d. une porte à coups de hache** to smash in a door with an axe; **l'alcool lui a démoli le foie** alcohol has ruined his/her liver (**b**) *Fig (théorie, adversaire)* to demolish; *(autorité)* to undermine; *(auteur, cinéaste, roman, film)* to slate (**c**) *Fam (battre)* to beat up; **d. le portrait à qn** to smash sb's face in; **se faire d. (le portrait)** to get beaten up
démolition [demɔlisjɔ̃] *nf* demolition; **chantier de d.** demolition site; **entreprise de d.** demolition contractors; **en d.** being demolished
démon [demɔ̃] *nm aussi Fig* demon, devil; **le d. the** Devil; **le d. de midi** the mid-life crisis; *Can* **être en d.** to be furious *or* mad
démoniaque [demɔnjak] *adj* demonic; *Fig (pervers)* fiendish
démonstratif, -ive [demɔ̃stratif, -iv] **1** *adj (affectueux)* & *Gram* demonstrative
2 *nm Gram* demonstrative
démonstration [demɔ̃strasjɔ̃] *nf* (**a**) *Math* demonstration; **d. par l'absurde** reductio ad absurdum; **faire la d. de qch** to demonstrate sth (**b**) *(d'appareil)* demonstration; **être en d.** to be a display model (**c**) *(manifestation)* show; **d. de force** show of force; **faire de grandes démonstrations d'amitié** to make a great show of friendship
démontable [demɔ̃tabl] *adj* that can be dismantled
démontage [demɔ̃taʒ] *nm* dismantling
démonté, -e [demɔ̃te] *adj (mer)* raging
démonter [demɔ̃te] **1** *vt* (**a**) *(machine, meuble, tente)* to dismantle; *(pneu)* to remove (**b**) *Fam (déconcerter)* to throw; **se laisser d.** to get thrown (**c**) *Can (décourager)* to discourage
2 se démonter *vpr* (**a**) *(machine, meuble)* to come apart (**b**) *Fam* **elle ne s'est pas démontée pour si peu** she wasn't so easily thrown
démontrable [demɔ̃trabl] *adj* demonstrable
démontrer [demɔ̃tre] *vt* to demonstrate
démoralisant, -e [demɔralizɑ̃, -ɑ̃t] *adj* demoralizing
démoralisation [demɔralizasjɔ̃] *nf* demoralization
démoraliser [demɔralize] **1** *vt* to demoralize
2 se démoraliser *vpr* to become demoralized
démordre [demɔrdr] **démordre de** *vt ind* **ne pas d. de qch** to stick to sth; **elle n'en démord pas** she's sticking to her guns
démotiver [demɔtive] *vt* to demotivate; **se laisser d. par qch** to be put off by sth

démoulage [demulaʒ] *nm (d'un moulage)* removal from the mould; *(d'un gâteau)* turning out
démouler [demule] *vt (moulage)* to remove from the mould; *(gâteau)* to turn out
démuni, -e [demyni] *adj (pauvre)* destitute, penniless
démunir [demynir] **1** *vt* **d. qn de qch** to deprive sb of sth
2 se démunir *vpr* **se d. de qch** to part with sth
démystification [demistifikasjɔ̃] *nf* demystification
démystifier [66] [demistifje] *vt* to demystify
dénatalité [denatalite] *nf* fall in the birth rate
dénationaliser [denasjɔnalize] *vt* to denationalize
dénaturé, -e [denatyre] *adj* (**a**) *(parents, goût, mœurs)* unnatural (**b**) *Chim* denatured
dénaturer [denatyre] *vt (faits, propos)* to distort; *Chim* to denature
dénégation [denegasjɔ̃] *nf* denial
déneiger [45] [deneʒe] *vt* to clear the snow from
déneigeuse [deneʒøz] *nf Can* snowblower
déni [deni] *nm Jur* **d. de justice** denial of justice
déniaiser [denjeze] *vt Fam* **d. qn** *(dépuceler)* to take away sb's innocence; *(dégourdir)* to teach sb a thing or two
dénicher [deniʃe] *vt Fam (objet)* to unearth; *(personne)* to track down
denier [dənje] *nm* (**a**) *(monnaie française)* denier; *Fig* **deniers** funds; **le d. du culte** contribution to parish costs (**b**) *(de bas)* **bas de 30 deniers** 30-denier stockings
dénier [66] [denje] *vt* (**a**) *(nier) (faute, responsabilité)* to deny (**b**) *(refuser)* **d. à qn le droit de faire qch** to deny sb the right to do sth
dénigrement [denigrəmã] *nm* denigration; **une campagne de d.** a smear campaign
dénigrer [denigre] *vt* to denigrate
dénivelé [denivle] *nm* difference in level
dénivellation [denivɛlasjɔ̃] *nf* difference in level
dénombrable [denɔ̃brabl] *adj* countable
dénombrer [denɔ̃bre] *vt* to count
dénominateur [denɔminatœr] *nm Math* denominator; **le plus petit d. commun** the lowest common denominator
dénomination [denɔminasjɔ̃] *nf* designation
dénommé, -e [denɔme] *adj* **un d. Charles** someone by the name of Charles
dénoncer [16] [denɔ̃se] **1** *vt* (**a**) *(trahir) (malfaiteur)* to denounce (à to); *(élève)* to tell on (à to) (**b**) *(protester contre)* to denounce (**c**) *(annuler)* to terminate
2 se dénoncer *vpr (malfaiteur)* to give oneself up (à to); *(élève)* to own up (à to)
dénonciation [denɔ̃sjasjɔ̃] *nf* denunciation
dénoter [denɔte] *vt* to denote, to indicate
dénouement [denumã] *nm (d'un livre)* ending; *(d'une pièce)* dénouement; *(d'une affaire)* outcome
dénouer [denwe] **1** *vt (nœud)* to untie, to undo; *(cheveux)* to undo, to let down; *Fig (intrigue)* to unravel
2 se dénouer *vpr (nœud)* to come undone; *(cheveux)* to come down
dénoyauter [denwajote] *vt (fruit)* to stone, *Am* to pit
denrée [dãre] *nf* foodstuff; **denrées alimentaires** foodstuffs; **denrées de consommation courante** staple foods; **denrées périssables** perishable goods
dense [dãs] *adj* dense
densité [dãsite] *nf (de population)* & *Phys* density

dent [dɑ̃] *nf* (**a**) *(d'homme, d'animal)* tooth; **faire ses dents** *(enfant)* to be teething; **se faire les dents sur qch** *(chat, enfant)* to cut one's teeth on sth; **manger du bout des dents** to pick at one's food; **mordre à belles dents dans qch** to take a good bite out of sth; **parler entre ses dents** to mumble, to mutter; *Fig* **se casser les dents sur qch** to come a cropper over sth; *aussi Fig* **serrer les dents** to grit one's teeth; *Fig* **avoir les dents longues** to have great ambitions; *Fig* **avoir la d. dure** to have a sharp tongue; *Fig* **il n'a pas desserré les dents de la soirée** he hasn't opened his mouth all evening; *Fam* **être sur les dents** *(sur le qui-vive)* to be on the alert; *(surmené)* to be overworked; *Fam* **avoir une d. contre qn** to have a grudge against sb; *Fam* **avoir la d.** to be starving; **d. de lait/de sagesse** milk/wisdom tooth (**b**) *(de peigne, de scie)* tooth; *(de roue)* cog; *(de fourchette)* prong; *(de timbre)* perforation; **en dents de scie** serrated; *Fig (évolution, progrès)* uneven

dentaire [dɑ̃tɛr] *adj* dental

denté, -e [dɑ̃te] *adj Tech* toothed; *(feuille)* jagged

dentelé, -e [dɑ̃tle] *adj (rivage, feuille)* jagged

dentelle [dɑ̃tɛl] *nf* lace; **robe de** *ou* **en d.** lace dress; **des crêpes d.** wafer-thin pancakes; *Fam* **ne pas faire dans la d.** *(en paroles)* not to beat about the bush; *(en actions)* not to mess about

dentellière [dɑ̃təljɛr] *nf (personne)* lacemaker

dentelure [dɑ̃tlyr] *nf (d'un rivage, d'une feuille)* jagged outline; **dentelures** *(d'un timbre)* perforations

dentier [dɑ̃tje] *nm* (set of) false teeth, dentures

dentifrice [dɑ̃tifris] **1** *nm* toothpaste **2** *adj* **pâte d.** toothpaste

dentiste [dɑ̃tist] *nmf* dentist

dentition [dɑ̃tisjɔ̃] *nf* (**a**) *(croissance)* dentition (**b**) *(denture)* set of teeth

denture [dɑ̃tyr] *nf* set of teeth

dénudé, -e [denyde] *adj (campagne, arbre, fil)* bare

dénuder [denyde] **1** *vt (colline, arbre, fil)* to strip; **cette robe dénude le dos** this dress leaves the back bare **2 se dénuder** *vpr* (**a**) *(colline)* to grow bare; *(arbre)* to lose its leaves (**b**) *(se déshabiller)* to strip (naked)

dénué, -e [denye] *adj* **d. de** *(intelligence, intérêt)* devoid of; **d. de tout fondement** totally without foundation

dénuement [denymɑ̃] *nm* destitution; **être dans le d.** to be destitute

déodorant [deɔdɔrɑ̃] *nm* deodorant

déodoriser [deɔdɔrize] *vt* to deodorize

déontologie [deɔ̃tɔlɔʒi] *nf* professional ethics

dépannage [depanaʒ] *nm (d'une machine)* (emergency) repairs; *(remorquage)* recovery; *Ordinat* troubleshooting; **service de d.** breakdown service

dépanner [depane] *vt (machine)* to repair; *Fam (personne)* to help out (**de** with)

dépanneur [depanœr] *nm* (**a**) *(de voitures)* breakdown mechanic; *(de téléviseurs)* (television) repairman; *Ordinat* troubleshooter (**b**) *Can (magasin)* Br corner shop, *Am* convenience store

dépanneuse [depanøz] *nf (véhicule) Br* breakdown lorry, *Am* wrecker

dépareillé, -e [depareje] *adj (gant)* odd; *(service de table)* incomplete

déparer [depare] *vt* to spoil, to mar; **ce tableau ne dépare pas dans le salon** this painting looks pretty good in the living room

départ [depar] *nm* (**a**) *(d'une personne, d'un véhicule, d'un bateau)* departure; **les grands départs** the great *Br* holiday *orAm* vacation exodus; **être sur le d.** to be on the point of leaving; **excursions au d. de Nice** trips departing from Nice; **je regrette votre d.** I'm sorry you're leaving; **d. volontaire** *(d'employé)* voluntary redundancy (**b**) *(d'une course)* start; **ligne de d.** starting line; **faux d.** false start; **donner le d. (d'une course)** to give the starting signal (for a race); *aussi Fig* **prendre un bon/mauvais d.** to get off to a good/bad start (**c**) *(début)* start, beginning; **salaire de d.** starting salary; **au d.** at first, to start with

départager [45] [departaʒe] *vt* to decide between

département [departəmɑ̃] *nm* (**a**) *(de la France)* department *(division of local government)* (**b**) *(dans un ministère)* department; **le d. d'anglais** *(d'une faculté)* the English department

Département

A "département" is the chief administrative division of France. There are 95 "départements" in metropolitan France and 4 overseas (Guadeloupe, Martinique, Guiana and Réunion) and each is administered by a "conseil général" and a "préfet". The number of the "département" corresponds to the first two figures in a postcode and the last two figures on a car registration number.

départemental, -e, -aux, -ales [departəmɑ̃tal, -o] **1** *adj* departmental **2** *nf* **départementale** secondary road, *Br* ≃ B road

départir [64a] [departir] **se départir** *vpr Litt* **il ne s'est jamais départi de son calme/sa bonne humeur** his calm/his good humour never deserted him

dépassé, -e [depase] *adj* (**a**) *(démodé) (vêtement, technique)* old-fashioned (**b**) *(perdu)* overwhelmed; **être d. par les événements** to be overtaken by events

dépassement [depasmɑ̃] *nm* (**a**) *(en voiture) Br* overtaking, *Am* passing (**b**) *Fin* **il y a un d. de crédit de plusieurs millions** the budget has been exceeded by several million

dépasser [depase] **1** *vt* (**a**) *(aller plus loin que)* to go past (**b**) *(doubler) Br* to overtake, *Am* to pass (**c**) *(excéder) (limite de vitesse, temps imparti, poids)* to exceed; **d. la date limite de vente** *(produit)* to be past its sell-by date; **d. dix minutes** to last longer than ten minutes; **ne pas d. la dose prescrite** *(sur notice)* do not exceed the stated dose; **cela dépasse l'entendement** it's beyond belief (**d**) *(surpasser)* to outstrip; **qn d'une tête** to stand a head taller than sb; **d. qn en beauté** to be more beautiful than sb; **d. les espérances de qn** to exceed sb's expectations (**e**) *(exagérer)* **d. les bornes** to overstep the mark; **cela me dépasse** it's beyond me **2** *vi* (**a**) *(en voiture) Br* to overtake, *Am* to pass (**b**) *(se voir)* to stick out *(de* of); *(jupon)* to show **3 se dépasser** *vpr* to surpass oneself

dépassionner [depasjɔne] *vt (débat)* to take the heat out of

dépatouiller [depatuje] **se dépatouiller** *vpr Fam* to cope, to manage; **se d. d'une situation** to get out of or to wriggle one's way out of a situation

dépaysé, -e [depeize] *adj* out of one's element

dépaysement [depeizmɑ̃] *nm (positif)* change of scene; *(négatif)* disorientation

dépayser [depeize] *vt (positivement)* to be a change of scene for; *(négativement)* to disorientate

dépecer [16/46] [depəse] *vt (sujet: boucher)* to cut up; *(sujet: animal)* to tear up

dépêche [depɛʃ] *nf* dispatch; **d. d'agence** agency news item

dépêcher [depeʃe] **1** *vt (messager)* to dispatch **2 se dépêcher** *vpr* to hurry; **dépêchez-vous!** hurry up!; **se d. de faire qch** to hurry to do sth; **dépêche-toi de finir ton travail** hurry up and finish your work

dépeindre [54] [depɛ̃dr] *vt* to depict

dépenaillé, -e [depənaje] *adj* ragged

dépénalisation [depenalizasjɔ̃] *nf* decriminalization

dépénaliser [depenalize] *vt* to decriminalize

dépendance [depɑ̃dɑ̃s] *nf* (**a**) *(asservissement)* dependence (**à** on); **être sous la d. de qn** to be under sb's domination (**b**) *(bâtiment)* outbuilding

dépendant, -e [depɑ̃dɑ̃, -ɑ̃t] *adj* dependent (**de** on)

dépendre [depɑ̃dr] *vi* to depend (**de** on); **cela ne dépend pas de nous** it's not up to us; *Fam* **ça dépend (des fois)** it depends

dépens [depɑ̃] *nmpl* (**a**) **aux d. de** at the expense of; **apprendre qch à ses d.** to learn sth to one's cost (**b**) *Jur* **être condamné aux d.** to be ordered to pay costs

dépense [depɑ̃s] *nf* (**a**) *(frais)* expenditure, expense; **dépenses** spending; **les dépenses du ménage** household expenses; **faire des dépenses** to spend money; **pousser (les gens) à la d.** to encourage people to spend; **il ne regarde pas à la d.** he spares no expense (**b**) **d. physique** physical exertion

dépenser [depɑ̃se] **1** *vt (argent)* to spend; *Fig* **d. toute son énergie (à faire qch)** to use up all one's energy (in doing sth) **2** *vi* to spend (money); **d. sans compter** to spend lavishly **3 se dépenser** *vpr* to burn up energy

dépensier, -ère [depɑ̃sje, -ɛr] *adj* extravagant

déperdition [depɛrdisjɔ̃] *nf (de chaleur, d'énergie)* loss

dépérir [deperir] *vi (personne)* to waste away; *(plante)* to wither; *(arbre)* to decay

dépêtrer [depetre] *Fam* **1** *vt* **d. qn de qch** to free sb from sth **2 se dépêtrer** *vpr (se dégager)* to free oneself (**de** from); *Fig* **se d. de qch** to get oneself out of sth; *Fig* **se d. de qn** to get rid of sb

dépeuplement [depœpləmɑ̃] *nm (d'un pays)* depopulation

dépeupler [depœple] **1** *vt (pays)* to depopulate **2 se dépeupler** *vpr (pays)* to become depopulated

déphasé, -e [defaze] *adj* (**a**) *Élec* out of phase (**b**) *Fam (désorienté)* disorientated

dépiauter [depjote] *vt Fam (animal)* to skin; *Fig* **d. un texte** to pull a text to pieces

dépilatoire [depilatwar] *adj* **crème d.** hair-removing cream

dépistage [depistaʒ] *nm (d'une maladie)* screening; **d. du sida** Aids screening

dépister [depiste] *vt (gibier, criminel)* to track down; *(maladie)* to detect

dépit [depi] *nm* (**a**) *(ressentiment)* spite; **par d.** out of spite (**b**) **en d. de** in spite of, despite; **en d. du bon sens** contrary to common sense

dépité, -e [depite] *adj* annoyed

déplacé, -e [deplase] *adj* (**a**) *(dérangé)* out of place; **avoir une vertèbre déplacée** to have a slipped disc (**b**) *(inconvenant) (observation)* uncalled-for

déplacement [deplasmɑ̃] *nm* (**a**) *(réarrangement)* moving; *(mutation)* transfer; **d. de vertèbre** slipped

disc; *Ordinat* **d. du curseur** cursor movement; *Ordinat* **d. entre fichiers** movement between files (**b**) *(voyage)* trip; **déplacements** travel; **être en d.** to be on a (business) trip; *Fig* **valoir le d.** to be worth the trip

déplacer [16] [deplase] **1** *vt (objet)* to move; *(fonctionnaire, service)* to transfer; *Fig* **d. le problème** *(volontairement)* to avoid the issue; *(involontairement)* to miss the point **2 se déplacer** *vpr* (**a**) *(changer de place)* to move around (**b**) *(voyager)* to travel (**c**) **se d. une vertèbre** to slip a disc

déplafonner [deplafɔne] *vt (prix, crédit)* to remove the ceiling on

déplaire [55a] [deplɛr] **1** *vi* **d. à qn** *(irriter)* to displease sb; **cet homme/cette maison me déplaît** I don't like that man/that house; **cela ne me déplairait pas** I wouldn't mind it; *Ironique* **ne vous/leur en déplaise** whether you/they like it or not **2 se déplaire** *vpr* **il se déplaît à Paris** he doesn't like it in Paris; **elle ne se déplaît pas à Paris** she quite likes it in Paris

déplaisant, -e [deplɛzɑ̃, -ɑ̃t] *adj* unpleasant

déplaisir [deplezir] *nm* displeasure, annoyance; **à son grand d.** to his/her great annoyance

dépliant [deplijɑ̃] *nm* leaflet; *(d'un livre)* fold-out page

déplier [66] [deplije] **1** *vt (journal, lettre, mouchoir)* to unfold; *(canapé)* to open out; **d. les jambes** to stretch one's legs **2 se déplier** *vpr* to unfold, to open out

déplisser [deplise] **1** *vt* to take the creases out of **2 se déplisser** *vpr* to lose its creases

déploiement [deplwamɑ̃] *nm (d'ailes)* spreading; *(de troupes)* deployment; *Fig (de force)* display

déplorable [deplɔrabl] *adj* deplorable

déplorer [deplɔre] *vt* to deplore; **nous devrons travailler plus, (et) je le déplore, mais...** we'll have to do more work, I'm sorry to say, but...; **d. la mort de qn** to mourn sb's death; **d. la perte de qch** to lament the loss of sth

déployer [32] [deplwaje] **1** *vt (journal, carte)* to unfold, to open out; *(voiles, ailes)* to spread; *(troupes, police)* to deploy; *Fig (étaler)* to display **2 se déployer** *vpr (voile)* to unfurl; *(troupes, police)* to deploy

déplumé, -e [deplyme] *adj* featherless; *Fam (chauve)* bald

déplumer [deplyme] **se déplumer** *vpr (oiseau)* to moult; *Fam (personne)* to go bald

dépoitraillé, -e [depwatraje] *adj Fam* with one's shirt open

dépoli, -e [depɔli] *adj (verre)* frosted

dépolitiser [depɔlitize] *vt* to depoliticize

dépolluer [depɔlɥe] *vt* to clean up

déportation [depɔrtasjɔ̃] *nf (en camp de concentration)* internment

déporté, -e [depɔrte] *nm,f (de camp de concentration)* internee

déporter [depɔrte] **1** *vt* **d. qn** *(en camp de concentration)* to send sb to a concentration camp **2 se déporter** *vpr* **se d. vers la droite/gauche** to veer off to the right/left

déposer [depoze] **1** *vt* (**a**) *(mettre à terre)* to put down; *aussi Fig* **d. les armes** to lay down one's arms (**b**) *(laisser) (personne)* to drop (off); **d. qch chez qn** to drop sth off at sb's house; **d. une gerbe sur une tombe** to lay a wreath on a grave; **d. un baiser sur le front de**

qn to plant a kiss on sb's forehead; **d. la clé à la réception** to leave the key at reception; **d. une caution** to leave a deposit; **d. de l'argent (à la banque)** to deposit money (at the bank); *Jur* **d. une plainte (contre qn)** to lodge a complaint (against sb); *Pol* **d. un projet de loi** to introduce a bill (**c**) *(marque, brevet)* to register; **marque déposée** registered trademark (**d**) *(monarque)* to depose
  2 *vt Jur* **d. (en justice)** to give evidence (**contre** against)
  3 se déposer *vpr (substance)* to settle
dépositaire [depozitɛr] *nmf* (**a**) *(de papiers)* depositary; *Fig (d'un secret)* guardian (**b**) *Com (de produits)* agent
déposition [depozisjɔ̃] *nf* (**a**) *Jur* statement *(made by witness)*; **faire/recueillir une d.** to make/take a statement (**b**) *(d'un monarque)* deposing
déposséder [34] [depɔsede] *vt* to dispossess, to deprive (**de** of)
dépôt [depo] *nm* (**a**) *(action)* depositing; *(somme)* deposit; **faire un d.** *(à la banque)* to make a deposit; **mettre qch en d.** to put sth into storage; *Fin* **d. d'espèces** cash deposit; *Jur* **d. légal** registration of copyright; *Fin* **d. à vue** cash deposit (**b**) *(entrepôt)* depot; *(de trains)* engine shed; **d. de munitions** munitions depot; **d. d'ordures** *Br* rubbish dump, *Am* garbage dump (**c**) *(prison)* prison (**d**) *(substance)* deposit; *(limon)* silt; *(de bouilloire)* fur
dépoter [depɔte] *vt (plantes)* to repot
dépotoir [depɔtwar] *nm (dépôt d'ordures)* dump; *Fam (chambre)* dump; *(classe)* dumping ground
dépôt-vente *(pl* **dépôts-ventes**) [depovɑ̃t] *nm* second-hand shop *(where items are sold on commission)*
dépouille [depuj] *nf* (**a**) *(d'animal)* skin, hide; **d. (mortelle)** (mortal) remains (**b**) **dépouilles** *(trésor de guerre)* spoils, loot
dépouillé, -e [depuje] *adj (style)* bald; *(arbre)* bare
dépouillement [depujmɑ̃] *nm* (**a**) *(examen)* **d. du scrutin** counting of the votes; **d. du courrier** sorting through the mail (**b**) *(pauvreté)* poverty; *(sobriété)* austerity
dépouiller [depuje] **1** *vt* (**a**) *(priver)* to deprive (**de** of); **d. qn de ses vêtements** to strip sb; **se faire d.** *(dans une affaire)* to lose all one's money (**b**) *(examiner) (courrier)* to sort through; **d. le scrutin** to count the votes (**c**) *(animal)* to skin
  2 se dépouiller *vpr* **se d. de qch** to rid oneself of sth; **les arbres se dépouillent de leurs feuilles** the trees are shedding their leaves
dépourvu, -e [depurvy] *adj* (**a**) **d. de qch** devoid of sth (**b**) **être pris au d.** to be caught off (one's) guard
dépoussiérer [34] [depusjere] *vt* to dust; *Fig (institution)* to dust down
dépravation [depravasjɔ̃] *nf* depravity
dépravé, -e [deprave] **1** *adj* depraved
  2 *nm,f* degenerate
dépraver [deprave] *vt* to deprave
dépréciation [depresjasjɔ̃] *nf* depreciation
déprécier [66] [depresje] **1** *vt* to undervalue
  2 se déprécier *vpr (valeurs, marchandises)* to depreciate
déprédation [depredasjɔ̃] *nf* depredation
dépressif, -ive [depresif, -iv] *adj* depressive
dépression [depresjɔ̃] *nf* (**a**) *(creux)* depression; **d. (atmosphérique)** low, trough (**b**) *Psy* depression; **faire de la d.** to be suffering from depression; **faire**

une d. to be depressed; **d. nerveuse** nervous breakdown
dépressurisation [depresyrizasjɔ̃] *nf* depressurization
dépressuriser [depresyrize] *vt (avion)* to depressurize
déprimant, -e [deprimɑ̃, -ɑ̃t] *adj* depressing
déprime [deprim] *nf Fam* depression; **avoir un (petit) coup de d.** to be feeling (a bit) low
déprimé, -e [deprime] *adj Psy* depressed
déprimer [deprime] **1** *vt (démoraliser)* to depress
  2 *vi Fam* to be feeling low
déprogrammer [deprɔgrame] *vt (émission)* to cancel; *Ordinat* to remove from a program
dépuceler [9] [depysle] *vt Fam* to deflower
depuis [dəpɥi] **1** *prép* (**a**) *(indiquant le point de départ)* **d. hier/ce matin/2001** since yesterday/this morning/2001; **d. l'âge de cinq ans** from the age of five; **d. ce temps-là** since then; **d. quand êtes-vous ici?** how long have you been here? (**b**) *(durée)* for; **je suis ici d. trois jours** I've been here for three days; **d. combien de temps êtes-vous mariés?** how long have you been married (for)?; **il l'aime d. toujours** he has always loved her; **d. longtemps** for a long time; **d. la nuit des temps** since the dawn of time (**c**) *(lieu)* from; **il ne m'a pas parlé de Rouen** he hasn't spoken to me since (we left) Rouen
  2 *adv* since (then)
  3 *conj* **d. que** since; **d. que le monde est monde** since time *or* the world began
député, -e [depyte] *nm,f Pol* deputy; *Br* ≃ MP, *Am* ≃ representative (**de** for); **d. (du Parlement) européen** Member of the European Parliament, MEP
déraciné, -e [derasine] **1** *adj* uprooted
  2 *nm,f* person who has been uprooted
déraciner [derasine] *vt (arbre, personne)* to uproot
déraillement [derajmɑ̃] *nm* derailment
dérailler [deraje] *vi* (**a**) *(train, tram)* to leave the rails; **faire d. un train** to derail a train (**b**) *Fam (personne)* to talk drivel
dérailleur [derajœr] *nm (de bicyclette)* derailleur (gears)
déraison [derɛzɔ̃] *nf Litt* folly
déraisonnable [derɛzɔnabl] *adj* foolish
déraisonner [derɛzɔne] *vi Litt* to talk nonsense
dérangé, -e [derɑ̃ʒe] *adj (fou)* deranged
dérangeant, -e [derɑ̃ʒɑ̃, -ɑ̃t] *adj (film, personnage)* disturbing
dérangement [derɑ̃ʒmɑ̃] *nm* (**a**) *(gêne)* trouble; **je ne veux pas vous causer de d.** I don't want to put you to any trouble; **excusez-moi pour le d.** I'm sorry to trouble you (**b**) *(panne)* **la ligne est en d.** the line is out of order
déranger [45] [derɑ̃ʒe] **1** *vt* (**a**) *(papiers, livres)* to disturb; *(pièce)* to mess up (**b**) *(gêner) (personne)* to disturb; **ne pas d.** *(sur panneau)* do not disturb; **cela vous dérange si j'ouvre la fenêtre?** would you mind if I opened the window?; **si cela ne vous dérange pas** if that's all right by you; *Ironique* **je ne te dérange pas trop?** am I in your way?; *Fam* **et alors, ça te dérange?** what's it to you? (**c**) *(perturber)* to upset; **avoir le cerveau dérangé** to be deranged
  2 *vi (choquer)* to be disturbing
  3 se déranger *vpr* **merci de vous être dérangé** thank you for your trouble; **ne vous dérangez pas pour moi** please don't go to any trouble on my account

dérapage [derapaʒ] *nm (en voiture)* skid; *(à skis)* sideslip; *Fig* mistake; *Fig* **le d. des prix** spiralling prices; **le d. de l'économie** the downward spiral of the economy
déraper [derape] *vi (voiture)* to skid; *(à skis)* to sideslip; *Fig (prix)* to be rising uncontrollably; *(situation)* to go wrong
dératé, -e [derate] *nm,f Fam* **courir comme un d.** to run flat out
dératiser [deratize] *vt* **d. qch** to clear sth of rats
derechef [dərəʃɛf] *adv Litt* once more
déréglé, -e [deregle] *adj* (**a**) *(mécanisme)* not working properly (**b**) *(estomac)* upset
dérèglement [derɛgləmã] *nm (d'un mécanisme)* malfunctioning; **d. hormonal** hormonal disorder
dérégler [34] [deregle] **1** *vt (mécanisme)* to cause to malfunction
2 se dérégler *vpr (mécanisme)* to go wrong; **elle s'est déréglé le système digestif** she's ruined her digestive system
déridage [deridaʒ] *nm Méd* facelift
dérider [deride] **1** *vt* to cheer up
2 se dérider *vpr* to cheer up
dérision [derizjõ] *nf* derision; **tourner qch en d.** to deride sth
dérisoire [derizwar] *adj (salaire, somme)* derisory; *(prix)* rock-bottom
dérivatif [derivatif] *nm* distraction (à from)
dérivation [derivasjõ] *nf* (**a**) *(route, cours d'eau)* diversion; *Élec* **monté en d.** shunt connected (**b**) *Math* derivation
dérive [deriv] *nf Naut & Aviat* drift; **à la d., en d.** adrift; **aller à la d.** to drift, to go adrift; *Fig* to go downhill; **la d. des continents** continental drift
dérivé, -e [derive] **1** *adj* (**a**) *(sens, fonction)* derived; **produit d.** *Chim* by-product; *Fin* derivative (**b**) *Élec* **courant d.** shunt current
2 *nm* (**a**) *Chim* derivative (**b**) *(produit)* by-product
3 *nf Math* **dérivée** derivative
dériver¹ [derive] **1** *vt* (**a**) *(cours d'eau)* to divert; *Élec (courant)* to shunt (**b**) *Math (fonction)* to derive
2 dériver de *vt ind (mot)* to be derived from
dériver² *vi Naut & Aviat* to drift
dériveur [derivœr] *nm Naut* sailing dinghy *(with centreboard)*
dermatite [dɛrmatit] *nf Méd* dermatitis
dermato [dɛrmato] *nmf Fam* dermatologist
dermatologie [dɛrmatɔlɔʒi] *nf* dermatology
dermatologique [dɛrmatɔlɔʒik] *adj* dermatological
dermatologiste [dɛrmatɔlɔʒist], **dermatologue** [dɛrmatɔlɔg] *nmf* dermatologist
derme [dɛrm] *nm* dermis
dernier, -ère [dɛrnje, -ɛr] **1** *adj* (**a**) *(ultime)* last; *(marquant la fin)* final; **au d. moment** at the last moment (**b**) *(passé)* last; *(le plus récent) (livre, nouvelles, mode)* latest; **au cours des dernières années** over the past *or* last few years (**c**) *(dans l'espace)* last; **le d. rang** the back *or* last row; **la dernière marche de l'escalier** *(en haut)* the top step; *(en bas)* the bottom step; **au d. étage** on the top floor (**d**) *Litt (extrême)* utmost; **de la dernière importance** of the utmost importance; **c'est du d. chic** it's the height of elegance (**e**) *(le pire)* worst; **de d. ordre** very inferior; **être reçu d. au concours** to come last in the competition; **c'était la dernière chose à faire** that's the last thing you/he/etc should have done
2 *nm,f* (**a**) *(dans un classement)* last; **les six derniers**

the last six; **arriver dans les derniers** to be one of the last to finish; **il est arrivé le d.** *ou* **bon d.** he came in last; **c'est le d. de sa classe** he's bottom of his class; *Fam* **c'est le d. de mes soucis** that's the least of my worries (**b**) *(dans une chronologie) (l'ultime)* last; *(le plus récent)* latest; **le d. en date** the most recent; **ce d. répondit...** the latter answered...; **c'est toujours le d. à sortir** he's always last out; **comment va la petite dernière?** how's the little one? (**c**) *Péj* **on la traite comme la dernière des dernières** they treat her like the lowest of the low; **c'est vraiment le d. des menteurs** he's the world's biggest liar
3 *nf* **dernière** (**a**) *(spectacle)* last night (**b**) *(nouveauté)* **tu as entendu la dernière de ton frère?** have you heard your brother's latest?
4 *adv* **en d.** last (of all); **il sort toujours en d.** he's always last out
dernièrement [dɛrnjɛrmã] *adv* lately, recently
dernier-né, dernière-née *(mpl* **derniers-nés,** *fpl* **dernières-nées)** [dɛrnjene, dɛrnjɛrne] *nm,f* youngest *(child)*
dérobade [derɔbad] *nf (esquive)* evasion (**b**) *(d'un cheval)* swerve
dérobé, -e¹ [derɔbe] *adj* (**a**) *(escalier, porte)* hidden, secret (**b**) *(volé)* stolen
dérobée² [derɔbe] **à la dérobée** *adv* secretly, on the sly; **regarder qn à la d.** to steal a glance at sb
dérober [derɔbe] **1** *vt* (**a**) *(voler)* to steal (à from) (**b**) *(cacher)* to hide (à from)
2 se dérober *vpr* (**a**) *(s'échapper)* to slip away (à from); **se d. à la curiosité de qn** to avoid sb's prying eyes (**b**) *(éviter de répondre)* to be evasive (**c**) *(manquer) (sol, jambes)* to give way (**sous** beneath) (**d**) *(cheval)* to swerve
dérogation [derɔgasjõ] *nf* exemption (à from); *Jur* waiver; *(à une loi)* derogation (à of)
déroger [45] [derɔʒe] *vi* **d. à l'usage/à la loi** to depart from custom/the law
dérouillée [deruje] *nf très Fam* thrashing, hammering; **prendre une d.** to get thrashed *or* hammered
dérouiller [deruje] **1** *vi très Fam* (**a**) *(être battu)* to get a belting (**b**) *(souffrir)* to have a hard time of it
2 se dérouiller *vpr Fam* **se d. les jambes** to stretch one's legs
déroulement [derulmã] *nm (d'événement)* unfolding; **pendant tout le d. de la cérémonie** throughout the ceremony
dérouler [derule] **1** *vt (rouleau)* to unroll; *(store)* to let down; *(câble)* to unwind; *Ordinat* **d. un menu** to pull down a menu
2 se dérouler *vpr* (**a**) *(rouleau)* to unroll; *(store)* to come down; *(câble)* to unwind (**b**) *Fig (événement)* to unfold; **la manifestation s'est déroulée dans le calme** the demonstration passed off peacefully
déroutant, -e [derutã, -ãt] *adj* disconcerting
déroute [derut] *nf Aussi Fig* rout; **l'ennemi fut mis en d.** the enemy was routed
dérouter [derute] *vt* (**a**) *(navire, avion)* to divert, to reroute (**b**) *(égarer) (poursuivants)* to throw off the scent (**c**) *Fig (étonner)* to throw
derrière [dɛrjɛr] **1** *prép* behind; **les uns d. les autres** one behind the other; **sortir de d. un buisson** to come out from behind a bush; *aussi Fig* **les autres sont loin d. elle** the others are way behind her; *Fig* **il faut toujours être d. elle** you always have to be on her back; *Fig* **c'est lui qui est d. tout ça** he's the one behind it all

2 adv behind; **aller** ou **monter d.** (en voiture) to sit Br in the back or Am in back
3 nm (**a**) (de bâtiment) back, rear; **le mur de d.** the back wall (**b**) (de personne) behind, backside; (d'animal) hindquarters; **recevoir des coups de pied dans le** ou **au d.** to get kicked in the behind

des [de] voir **de, un**

dès [dɛ] prép (à partir de) from; **d. 1840** as far back as 1840; **d. le matin** first thing in the morning; **d. leur arrivée** as soon as they arrive/arrived; **d. maintenant, d. à présent** from now on; **d. que tu seras là** as soon as you're here; **d. lors** (dans le temps) from then on; (par conséquent) consequently; **d. lors que...** since...

désabusé, -e [dezabyze] adj disillusioned

désaccord [dezakɔr] nm disagreement; **être en d. avec qn** (sur qch) to disagree with sb (about sth)

désaccordé, -e [dezakɔrde] adj out of tune

désaccoutumer [dezakutyme] **se désaccoutumer** vpr to get out of the habit (**de** of)

désaffecté, -e [dezafɛkte] adj disused

désaffection [dezafɛksjɔ̃] nf disaffection (**à l'égard de** with)

désagréable [dezagreabl] adj unpleasant

désagrégation [dezagregasjɔ̃] nf (désintégration) disintegration

désagréger [59] [dezagreʒe] **1** vt (désintégrer) to cause to disintegrate
2 se désagréger vpr to disintegrate

désagrément [dezagremã] nm (**a**) (gêne) trouble; **causer du d. à qn** to inconvenience sb (**b**) (souci, aspect négatif) problem

désaltérant, -e [dezalterɑ̃, -ɑ̃t] adj thirst-quenching

désaltérer [34] [dezaltere] **1** vt **d. qn** to quench sb's thirst; **c'est une boisson qui désaltère** it's a thirst-quenching drink
2 se désaltérer vpr to quench one's thirst

désambiguïser [dezɑ̃bigɥize] vt (situation) to clarify; (mot) to disambiguate

désamorçage [dezamɔrsaʒ] nm (**a**) (d'une bombe, d'un conflit) defusing (**b**) (d'une pompe) draining

désamorcer [16] [dezamɔrse] vt (**a**) (bombe, conflit, querelle) to defuse (**b**) (pompe) to drain

désappointer [dezapwɛ̃te] vt Litt to disappoint

désapprobateur, -trice [dezaprɔbatœr, -tris] adj disapproving

désapprobation [dezaprɔbasjɔ̃] nf disapproval

désapprouver [dezapruve] vt to disapprove of

désarçonner [dezarsɔne] vt (**a**) (jeter bas) to unseat, to throw (**b**) Fig (déconcerter) to throw

désargenté, -e [dezarʒɑ̃te] adj Fam (personne) broke

désarmant, -e [dezarmɑ̃, -ɑ̃t] adj disarming

désarmé, -e [dezarme] adj (touché) disarmed; (sans défense) defenceless, helpless

désarmement [dezarməmɑ̃] nm (**a**) (d'un pays, d'une région) disarmament; **d. multilatéral** multilateral disarmament (**b**) (de soldats) disarming

désarmer [dezarme] **1** vt (**a**) (malfaiteur) to disarm (**b**) Fig (toucher) to disarm (**c**) (navire) to lay up
2 vi (**a**) (pays, région) to disarm (**b**) (cesser) **sa colère ne désarme pas** he/she is still angry

désarroi [dezarwa] nm confusion; **jeter qn dans le d.** to throw sb into confusion; **il est en plein d.** ou **dans un grand d.** he's in a state of utter confusion

désarticuler [dezartikyle] **1** vt to dislocate
2 se désarticuler vpr to contort oneself; **se d. l'épaule** to dislocate one's shoulder

désastre [dezastr] nm disaster

désastreux, -euse [dezastrø, -øz] adj disastrous

désavantage [dezavɑ̃taʒ] nm disadvantage; **avoir un d. par rapport à qn** to be at a disadvantage compared with sb; **voir qn à son d.** to see sb in an unfavourable light

désavantager [45] [dezavɑ̃taʒe] vt to put at a disadvantage, to disadvantage; **être désavantagé par rapport à qn** to be at a disadvantage compared with sb

désavantageux, -euse [dezavɑ̃taʒø, -øz] adj disadvantageous

désaveu [dezavø] nm (**a**) (reniement) disowning (**b**) (condamnation) disapproval

désavouer [dezavwe] vt (**a**) (renier) to disown (**b**) (condamner) to disapprove of (**c**) Jur (enfant) to disown

désaxé, -e [dezakse] **1** adj (psychiquement) unbalanced, unhinged
2 nm,f lunatic

desceller [desele] vt (**a**) (pierre) to loosen (**b**) (acte, document) to unseal

descendance [desɑ̃dɑ̃s] nf (**a**) (filiation) descent (**b**) (postérité) descendants

descendant, -e [desɑ̃dɑ̃, -ɑ̃t] **1** adj (mouvement) downward
2 nm,f descendant

descendre [desɑ̃dr] **1** vi (aux **être**) (**a**) (en s'approchant) to come down; (en s'éloignant) to go down; **d. de qch** to come down from sth; **faire d. qn de qch** to get sb down from sth; **aider qn à d.** to help sb down; **d. à 150 m de profondeur** to go down to a depth of 150 m; **d. en dessous des dix secondes** to get below ten seconds; **d. à Marseille/dans le Midi** to go down to Marseilles/to the South; Fig **d. dans la rue** to take to the streets (**b**) (d'un escalier) (en s'approchant) to come downstairs; (en s'éloignant) to go downstairs; **d. à la cave** to go down to the cellar (**c**) (d'un véhicule) **d. d'un train/d'une voiture** to get off a train/out of a car; **d. de cheval/de vélo/de moto** to dismount; **tout le monde descend!** (au terminus) all change! (**d**) (baisser) (marée) to go out; **faire d. la fièvre** to reduce fever (**e**) (tomber) (brouillard) to come down (**f**) (s'étendre) to go down; (route, rue) to go downhill; **d. jusqu'à la taille/jusqu'aux chevilles** to come down to the waist/to the ankles; **ce chemin descend au village** this path goes down to the village (**g**) (loger) **d. chez qn** to stay with sb; **d. à l'hôtel** to put up or stay at a hotel (**h**) (être issu) **d. de** to be descended from
2 vt (aux **avoir**) (**a**) (dévaler) **d. un escalier/la rue/la rivière** (en s'éloignant) to go down a staircase/the street/the river; (en s'approchant) to come down a staircase/the street/the river (**b**) (porter vers le bas) (en s'éloignant) to take down; (en s'approchant) to bring down; **d. la poubelle** to take the Br rubbish or Am garbage down; **peux-tu me d. mon pull?** can you bring me down my sweater? (**c**) (abaisser) (store, étagère) to lower (**d**) Fam (abattre) (avion, personne) to shoot down (**e**) Fam (consommer) (repas, boisson) to put away; **qu'est-ce qu'il descend!** he's really putting it away!

descente [desɑ̃t] nf (**a**) (action de descendre) descent; **d. en rappel** abseiling (**b**) (sortie) **accueillir qn à sa d. du train** to meet sb off the train (**c**) (incursion) raid; **d. de police** police raid (**d**) (route en pente) slope; **ralentir dans la d.** to slow down when going downhill (**e**) (en ski) (course) downhill (race); **faire de la d.** to do downhill (skiing) (**f**) **d. de lit** bedside rug (**g**) (tuyau)

downpipe (**h**) *Fam* **il a une bonne d.** he can really put it away
descriptible [dɛskriptibl] *adj* describable
descriptif, -ive [dɛskriptif, -iv] **1** *adj* descriptive **2** *nm* description
description [dɛskripsjɔ̃] *nf* description; **faire la d. de** to give a description of; **d. de poste** job description
désembourber [dezɑ̃burbe] *vt* to pull out of the mud
désembuage [dezɑ̃bɥaʒ] *nm* demisting
désemparé, -e [dezɑ̃pare] *adj (personne)* at a loss
désemparer [dezɑ̃pare] *vi* **sans d.** without stopping
désemplir [dezɑ̃plir] *vi* **ne pas d.** to be always full
désenchanté, -e [dezɑ̃ʃɑ̃te] *adj (personne)* disillusioned; *(sourire)* wistful
désenchantement [dezɑ̃ʃɑ̃tmɑ̃] *nm* disillusion
désenchanter [dezɑ̃ʃɑ̃te] *vt* to disillusion
désenclaver [dezɑ̃klave] *vt (région)* to open up
désencombrer [dezɑ̃kɔ̃bre] *vt (passage)* to clear (**de** of)
désendettement [dezɑ̃dɛtmɑ̃] *nm* debt clearing
désenfler [dezɑ̃fle] *vi* to go down, to become less swollen
désengagement [dezɑ̃gaʒmɑ̃] *nm* disengagement
désengager [45] [dezɑ̃gaʒe] **1** *vt (d'une obligation)* to free (**de** from); *Mil (d'un conflit)* to withdraw **2 se désengager** *vpr (d'une obligation)* to free oneself (**de** from); *Mil (d'un conflit)* to withdraw
désensabler [dezɑ̃sable] *vt* (**a**) *(chenal, port)* to clear of sand (**b**) *(bateau)* to get off the sand; *(voiture)* to dig out of the sand
désensibiliser [dezɑ̃sibilize] *vt aussi Fig* to desensitize
désépaissir [dezepɛsir] *vt* (**a**) *(sauce)* to thin down (**b**) *(cheveux)* to thin out
déséquilibre [dezekilibr] *nm* imbalance; **être en d.** to be unsteady
déséquilibré, -e [dezekilibre] **1** *adj* unbalanced **2** *nm,f* unbalanced person
déséquilibrer [dezekilibre] *vt* (**a**) *(objet, personne)* to throw off balance (**b**) *Psy* to unbalance
désert, -e [dezɛr, -ɛrt] **1** *adj (lieu)* deserted; *(pays, région)* uninhabited **2** *nm* desert; *Fig* **d. culturel** cultural desert *or* wasteland; **le d. de Gobi** the Gobi Desert; **d. de sable** sandy desert
déserter [dezɛrte] **1** *vt* (**a**) *(lieu, fonction)* to desert; *Mil* **d. son poste** to desert one's post (**b**) *Fig (cause)* to desert, to abandon **2** *vi (soldat)* to desert
déserteur [dezɛrtœr] *nm* deserter
désertification [dezɛrtifikasjɔ̃] *nf* (**a**) *(transformation en désert)* desertification (**b**) *(dépeuplement)* depopulation
désertion [dezɛrsjɔ̃] *nf* desertion
désertique [dezɛrtik] *adj* desert
désespérant, -e [dezɛspera, -ɑ̃t] *adj (situation, personne)* hopeless; **être d'une lenteur/bêtise désespérante** to be incredibly slow/stupid
désespéré, -e [dezɛspere] **1** *adj* (**a**) *(qui ne laisse aucun espoir)* desperate; *(inconsolable)* in despair (**b**) *(exprimant le désespoir)* desperate (**c**) *(extrême) (mesure, solution)* desperate **2** *nm,f* desperate person
désespérément [dezɛsperemɑ̃] *adv* desperately
désespérer [34] [dezɛspere] **1** *vt (personne)* to drive to despair **2** *vi* to despair

3 désespérer de *vt ind* to despair of; **d. de faire qch** to despair of doing sth; **il ne désespère pas d'y arriver** he hasn't given up hope of getting there **4 se désespérer** *vpr* to despair
désespoir [dezɛspwar] *nm* despair; **être au d.** to be in despair; **être au d. de faire qch** to be extremely sorry to do sth; **faire** *ou* **être le d. de qn** *(personne)* to be the despair of sb; **réduire qn au d.** to drive sb to despair
déshabillé [dezabije] *nm* negligee
déshabiller [dezabije] **1** *vt (personne)* to undress; **qn du regard** to undress sb with one's eyes **2 se déshabiller** *vpr* (**a**) *(pour être nu)* to undress, to take off one's clothes (**b**) *(ôter son manteau)* to take off one's coat
déshabituer [dezabitɥe] **1** *vt* **d. qn de qch/de faire qch** to get sb out of the habit of sth/of doing sth **2 se déshabituer** *vpr* **se d. de qch/de faire qch** to get out of the habit of sth/of doing sth
désherbage [dezɛrbaʒ] *nm* weeding
désherbant [dezɛrbɑ̃] *nm* weedkiller
désherber [dezɛrbe] *vt* to weed
déshérité, -e [dezerite] **1** *adj (démuni)* deprived **2** *nm,f* **les déshérités** the underprivileged
déshériter [dezerite] *vt* to disinherit
déshonneur [dezɔnœr] *nm* dishonour
déshonorant, -e [dezɔnɔrɑ̃, -ɑ̃t] *adj* dishonourable
déshonorer [dezɔnɔre] **1** *vt* to disgrace; **se croire/sentir déshonoré de faire qch** to think/feel it beneath oneself to do sth **2 se déshonorer** *vpr* to disgrace oneself
déshumaniser [dezymanize] *vt* to dehumanize
déshydratation [dezidratasjɔ̃] *nf* dehydration
déshydraté, -e [dezidrate] *adj* dehydrated
déshydrater [dezidrate] **1** *vt* to dehydrate **2 se déshydrater** *vpr* to become dehydrated
desiderata [deziderata] *nmpl* desiderata
design [dizajn] **1** *nm* design; **d. industriel** industrial design **2** *adj inv* designer; **un intérieur d.** a designer interior
désignation [dezinasjɔ̃] *nf* (**a**) *(appellation)* designation (**b**) *(choix)* appointment
désigner [dezine] *vt* (**a**) *(montrer)* to point out; **d. qn/qch du doigt** to point to sb/sth (**b**) *(dénommer)* to refer to (**c**) *(choisir)* to designate, to appoint (**d**) **il est tout désigné pour le faire** he's just the man for the job
désillusion [dezilyzjɔ̃] *nf* disillusion
désillusionner [dezilyzjɔne] *vt* to disillusion
désincrustant, -e [dezɛ̃krystɑ̃, -ɑ̃t] **1** *adj* (**a**) *Tech (substance)* scaling (**b**) *(masque, savon)* cleansing **2** *nm* (**a**) *Tech* scale preventive (**b**) *(savon)* cleanser
désindustrialisation [dezɛ̃dystrijalizasjɔ̃] *nf* deindustrialization
désinence [dezinɑ̃s] *nf Gram* ending
désinfectant, -e [dezɛ̃fɛktɑ̃, -ɑ̃t] *adj & nm* disinfectant
désinfecter [dezɛ̃fɛkte] *vt* to disinfect
désinfection [dezɛ̃fɛksjɔ̃] *nf* disinfection
désinflation [dezɛ̃flasjɔ̃] *nf Écon* disinflation
désinformation [dezɛ̃fɔrmasjɔ̃] *nf* disinformation
désinformer [dezɛ̃fɔrme] *vt* to disinform
désinscrire [dezɛ̃skrir] **se désinscrire** *vpr Ordinat* to unsubscribe
désintégration [dezɛ̃tegrasjɔ̃] *nf* (**a**) *(des roches)* weathering (**b**) *(d'un groupe, de la famille)* break-up (**c**) *Phys (de matière)* disintegration

désintégrer [34] [dezɛ̃tegre] **1** *vt* (**a**) *(roches)* to weather (**b**) *(groupe, famille)* to break up (**c**) *Phys (matière)* to disintegrate; *(atome)* to split **2 se désintégrer** *vpr* (**a**) *(roches)* to weather (**b**) *(groupe, famille)* to break up (**c**) *Phys (matière)* to disintegrate

désintéressé, -e [dezɛ̃terese] *adj* disinterested

désintéresser [dezɛ̃terese] **se désintéresser** *vpr* **se d. de qn/qch** *(ne pas s'y intéresser)* to have no interest in sb/sth; *(s'en détacher)* to lose interest in sb/sth

désintérêt [dezɛ̃terɛ] *nm* disinterest

désintoxication [dezɛ̃tɔksikasjɔ̃] *nf Méd* detoxication

désintoxiquer [dezɛ̃tɔksike] **1** *vt (alcoolique)* to treat for alcoholism; *(drogué)* to treat for drug addiction **2 se désintoxiquer** *vpr* (**a**) *(alcoolique)* to come off alcohol; *(drogué)* to come off drugs (**b**) *Fig (se remettre en forme)* to clean out one's system; *(perdre une habitude)* to get out of the habit

désinvolte [dezɛ̃vɔlt] *adj* (**a**) *(négligeant)* casual, off-hand (**b**) *(à l'aise) (manière)* unselfconscious; *(mouvements)* easy

désinvolture [dezɛ̃vɔltyr] *nf* (**a**) *(excès de liberté)* casualness; **avec d.** casually (**b**) *(naturel) (de manières)* unselfconsciousness; *(de mouvement)* ease

désir [dezir] *nm* (**a**) *(souhait)* desire; **selon le d. de qn** in accordance with sb's wishes; **prendre ses désirs pour des réalités** to indulge in wishful thinking; **tes désirs sont des ordres** your wish is my command (**b**) **d. (sexuel)** (sexual) desire

désirable [dezirabl] *adj* desirable

désirer [dezire] *vt* (**a**) *(souhaiter)* to wish; **d. faire qch** to wish to do sth; **je désire qu'il vienne** I want him to come; **cela laisse à d.** it leaves a lot to be desired; **elle se fait d.** *(elle n'arrive pas)* she's keeping us waiting; **que désirez-vous?**, *Fam* **vous désirez?** *(dans un magasin)* can I help you?; *(qu'est-ce que je vous sers?)* what would you like? (**b**) *(sexuellement)* to desire

désireux, -euse [dezirø, -øz] *adj* **être d. de faire qch** to be anxious to do sth

désistement [dezistəmɑ̃] *nm* withdrawal

désister [deziste] **se désister** *vpr* to withdraw

désobéir [dezɔbeir] *vi* to disobey; **d. à qn/qch** to disobey sb/sth

désobéissance [dezɔbeisɑ̃s] *nf* disobedience (**à** to); **d. civile** civil disobedience

désobéissant, -e [dezɔbeisɑ̃, -ɑ̃t] *adj* disobedient (**à** to)

désobligeant, -e [dezɔbliʒɑ̃, -ɑ̃t] *adj* disagreeable

désodorisant, -e [dezɔdɔrizɑ̃, -ɑ̃t] *adj & nm* deodorant

désodoriser [dezɔdɔrize] *vt* to deodorize

désœuvré, -e [dezœvre] *adj* idle

désœuvrement [dezœvrəmɑ̃] *nm* idleness; **par d.** for something to do

désolant, -e [dezɔlɑ̃, -ɑ̃t] *adj* (**a**) *(affligeant)* distressing (**b**) *(contrariant)* annoying

désolé, -e [dezɔle] *adj* (**a**) *(navré)* sorry; **je suis d. de vous déranger** I'm sorry to disturb you; **d., je n'ai pas le temps** sorry, I haven't got the time (**b**) *(affligé)* upset (**c**) *(région)* desolate

désoler [dezɔle] **1** *vt* (**a**) *(navrer)* to upset (**b**) *(affliger)* to distress **2 se désoler** *vpr* to be upset

désolidariser [desɔlidarize] **se désolidariser** *vpr* **se d. de** to dissociate oneself from

désopilant, -e [dezɔpilɑ̃, -ɑ̃t] *adj* hilarious

désordonné, -e [dezɔrdɔne] *adj* (**a**) *(chambre, bureau, personne)* untidy (**b**) *(désorganisé) (personne, article, pensées)* disorganized; *(mouvements)* uncoordinated (**c**) *(vie)* disorderly

désordre [dezɔrdr] *nm* (**a**) *(manque d'ordre)* untidiness, mess; **en d.** untidy; **mettre qch en d.** to make a mess of sth (**b**) *(manque d'organisation)* disorder (**c**) *(trouble)* commotion; **mettre le d. dans une réunion** to disrupt a meeting (**d**) *(agitation)* **désordres** disturbances (**e**) *Méd* disorder

désorganisation [dezɔrganizasjɔ̃] *nf* disorganization

désorganisé, -e [dezɔrganize] *adj (personne)* disorganized

désorganiser [dezɔrganize] *vt* to disrupt

désorienté, -e [dezɔrjɑ̃te] *adj* (**a**) *(égaré)* disorientated (**b**) *(déconcerté)* bewildered

désorienter [dezɔrjɑ̃te] *vt (déconcerter)* to bewilder

désormais [dezɔrmɛ] *adv* from now on, in future

désosser [dezɔse] **1** *vt (viande, poisson)* to bone **2 se désosser** *vpr* to contort oneself

despote [dɛspɔt] *nm aussi Fig* despot

despotique [dɛspɔtik] *adj* despotic

desquamation [dɛskwamasjɔ̃] *nf* peeling, *Spéc* desquamation

desquels, desquelles [dekɛl] *voir* lequel

DESS [deǝɛsɛs] *nm (abrév* **diplôme d'études supérieures spécialisées)** = postgraduate diploma

dessaisir [desezir] **1** *vt* (**a**) *(déposséder)* **d. qn de qch** to confiscate sth from sb (**b**) **d. un juge d'une affaire** to withdraw a judge from a case **2 se dessaisir** *vpr* **se d. de qch** to relinquish sth, to part with sth

dessaler [desale] **1** *vt* (**a**) *(viande, poisson)* to remove the salt from *(by soaking)*; *(eau de mer)* to desalinate (**b**) *Fam* **d. qn** to teach sb a thing or two **2** *vi* (**a**) *(voilier)* to capsize (**b**) **mettre qch à d.** *(viande, poisson)* to soak sth to remove the salt **3 se dessaler** *vpr Fam* to learn a thing or two

dessaouler [desule] *Fam* = dessoûler

dessèchement [desɛ∫mɑ̃] *nm (de la peau)* drying up; *(de la végétation)* withering

dessécher [34] [dese∫e] **1** *vt (déshydrater) (peau)* to dry up; *(végétation)* to wither **2 se dessécher** *vpr (peau)* to dry up; *(végétation)* to wither

dessein [desɛ̃] *nm* intention, purpose; **à d.** intentionally; **dans ce d.** with this intention; **dans le d. de faire qch** with the intention of doing sth

desseller [desele] *vt (cheval)* to unsaddle

desserrer [desere] **1** *vt* (**a**) *(relâcher) (vis, ceinture, nœud)* to loosen; *(frein à main)* to release (**b**) *(décrisper) (poing)* to unclench; *(étreinte)* to relax; *Fig* **il n'a pas desserré les dents** he didn't open his mouth **2 se desserrer** *vpr* (**a**) *(vis, ceinture, nœud)* to come loose (**b**) *(étreinte)* to relax

dessert [desɛr] *nm* dessert; **qu'est-ce qu'il y a comme ou au d.?** what's for dessert?

desserte [desɛrt] *nf (meuble)* sideboard

desservir¹ [63] [desɛrvir] *vt* (**a**) *(passer par) (ville, localité)* to serve; **ce train dessert les gares de... ***(annonce)* this train stops at...; **ville bien desservie** town with efficient public transport (**b**) *(conduire à) (pièce)* to lead to

desservir² *vt* (**a**) *(débarrasser) (table)* to clear; **vous pouvez d.** you may clear the table (**b**) *(nuire à)* **d. qn** to do sb a disservice

dessiller [desije] *vt Fig & Litt* **d. les yeux de qn** to open sb's eyes

dessin [desɛ̃] *nm* (**a**) *(technique, art)* drawing; **faire du d.** to draw; **d. industriel** industrial drawing (**b**) *(représentation)* drawing; **faire un d.** to do a drawing; *Fam Fig* **tu veux que je te fasse un d.?** do you want me to spell it out for you?; *Cin* **d. animé** cartoon; **d. humoristique** cartoon *(in a newspaper etc)* (**c**) *(motif) (sur tissu)* design, pattern; **un tissu à dessins géométriques** a fabric with geometric patterns *or* a geometric design (**d**) *(contour) (de la bouche, du visage)* outline

dessinateur, -trice [desinatœr, -tris] *nm,f* (**a**) *(artiste)* drawer; **d. de bandes dessinées** cartoonist; **d. humoristique** cartoonist *(for a newspaper etc)* (**b**) *(concepteur)* designer (**c**) *Tech* **d. industriel** draughtsman

dessiner [desine] **1** *vt* (**a**) *(faire un dessin de)* to draw; **d. à l'encre/à la craie** to draw in ink/chalk (**b**) *(concevoir)* to design (**c**) *Fig (tracer) (lignes)* to outline; **vêtement qui dessine la taille** garment that shows off the waist; **visage bien dessiné** finely chiselled face

2 se dessiner *vpr* (**a**) *(apparaître)* to stand out; **se d. à l'horizon** to stand out on the horizon; **un sourire se dessine sur ses lèvres** a smile flickers over his/her lips (**b**) *Fig (prendre forme) (changement, résultat)* to become apparent; *(projet)* to take shape

dessoûler [desule] *vt & vi Fam* to sober up

dessous [dəsu] **1** *adv* (**a**) *(sous)* underneath (**b**) **en d.** underneath; **l'appartement d'en d.** the downstairs *Br* flat *or Am* apartment, the *Br* flat *or Am* apartment downstairs; **en d. de** below; **tu es très en d. de la vérité** you're not even close; *Fam* **être en d. de tout** to be worse than useless (**c**) **prendre/porter qch par (en) d.** to take hold of/carry sth from underneath; *Fig* **regarder qn par en d.** to look at sb furtively

2 *nm* (*partie inférieure*) *(d'une assiette, d'une table)* underside; *(du pied)* bottom; **les gens du d.** the people below; *Fig* **avoir le d.** to get the worst of it

3 *nmpl* (**a**) *(partie cachée) (d'une affaire)* hidden side (**b**) *(sous-vêtements)* underwear

dessous-de-plat [dəsudpla] *nm inv* table mat

dessous-de-table [dəsudtabl] *nm inv* backhander, bribe; **verser un d. à qn** to give sb a backhander, to bribe sb

dessous-de-verre [dəsudvɛr] *nm inv* coaster; *(en carton)* beer mat

dessus [dəsy] **1** *adv* on (it/them); **il a marché d.** he trod on it; **mais il n'y a pas l'adresse d.** but the address isn't on it

2 *nm* (**a**) *(d'une table, du pied)* top; *(d'une assiette)* upper side; **l'étage du d.** the top floor (**b**) *Fig* **avoir le d.** to have the upper hand; **reprendre le d.** *(se remettre)* to get over it

dessus-de-lit [dəsydli] *nm inv* bedspread

déstabiliser [destabilize] *vt* to destabilize

destin [dɛstɛ̃] *nm* fate, destiny

destinataire [dɛstinatɛr] *nmf (d'une lettre)* addressee; *(de marchandises)* consignee; *(d'un mandat postal)* payee

destination [dɛstinasjɔ̃] *nf* destination; **trains/vols à d. de Paris** trains/flights to Paris; **arriver à d.** to reach one's destination

destinée [dɛstine] *nf* (**a**) *(vie)* destiny (**b**) *Litt* **être promis à de grandes** *ou* **hautes destinées** to be destined for great things (**c**) *(fatalité)* fate, destiny

destiner [dɛstine] **1** *vt* (**a**) *(réserver)* **d. qch à qn** *(bien, somme d'argent, emploi)* to intend sth for sb (**b**) *(adresser)* **être destiné à qn** *(remarque, paquet)* to

be meant for sb (**c**) *(assigner)* **d. une somme d'argent à qch** to allot *or* assign a sum of money to sth; **cet argent est destiné à la recherche contre le sida** this money is going towards Aids research (**d**) *(concevoir pour)* **destiné à qch** (intended) for sth; **cette salle est destinée aux répétitions** this room is for rehearsing in (**e**) *(vouer)* **d. qn à qch** to destine sb for sth; *Litt* **le sort les destinait à se rencontrer** they were destined to meet

2 se destiner *vpr* **se d. à qch** to intend to take up sth

destituer [dɛstitɥe] *vt (renvoyer) (officier)* to discharge; *(fonctionnaire)* to remove from office; *(souverain)* to depose

destitution [dɛstitysjɔ̃] *nf (d'un officier)* discharge; *(d'un fonctionnaire)* removal from office; *(d'un souverain)* deposition

destructeur, -trice [dɛstryktœr, -tris] *adj* destructive

destruction [dɛstryksjɔ̃] *nf* destruction

désuet, -ète [dezɥɛ, -ɛt, desɥɛ, -ɛt] *adj* (**a**) *(dépassé)* obsolete (**b**) *(démodé)* old-fashioned

désuétude [dezɥetyd, desɥetyd] *nf* disuse; **tomber en d.** *(mot, expression, pratique)* to become obsolete

désuni, -e [dezyni] *adj (famille, amis, amants)* divided

désunir [dezynir] *vt (personnes, famille)* to divide

désynchronisé, -e [desɛ̃krɔnize] *adj* out of synch

détachable [detaʃabl] *adj* detachable

détachant, -e [detaʃɑ̃, -ɑ̃t] **1** *adj* stain-removing

2 *nm* stain remover

détaché, -e [detaʃe] *adj* (**a**) *(ton, air, manière)* detached (**b**) *(fonctionnaire)* seconded

détachement [detaʃmɑ̃] *nm* (**a**) *(indifférence)* detachment (**de** from) (**b**) *(d'un fonctionnaire)* secondment; **être en d.** to be on secondment (**c**) *(troupes)* detachment

détacher¹ [detaʃe] **1** *vt* (**a**) *(défaire) (étiquette, page perforée)* to detach; *(ceinture, liens)* to undo; *(rideau)* to take down; *(wagon)* to uncouple; **d. ses yeux de qch** to take one's eyes off sth (**b**) *(libérer) (prisonnier, animal)* to untie (**c**) *(déléguer) (fonctionnaire)* to second; *(militaire)* to detach (**d**) *Fig* **d. qn de qch** to turn sb away from sth (**e**) *(faire sonner)* **d. les syllabes d'un mot** to pronounce each syllable of a word separately

2 se détacher *vpr* (**a**) *(étiquette, bouton, page)* to come off; *(ceinture)* to come undone; *(écorce)* to peel off (**b**) *(se libérer) (animal)* to get loose (**c**) *Fig* **se d. de qn** *(en devenant adulte)* to break away from sb; *(par manque d'intérêt)* to grow apart from sb; **se d. de qch** to turn one's back on sth (**d**) *(se séparer) (groupe de coureurs)* to break away (**de** from) (**e**) *(ressortir)* to stand out (**sur** against)

détacher² *vt (nettoyer)* to remove stains from

détail [detaj] *nm* (**a**) *(élément)* detail (**b**) *(énumération) (d'un compte, d'un inventaire)* items; *(d'une facture)* breakdown; **elle m'a fait le d. de sa soirée** she gave me a detailed account of her party; *Fam Fig* **il n'a pas fait de d.!** he didn't make any exceptions!; *Fam Fig* **il n'a pas fait dans le d.** he didn't go into detail; **en d.** in detail; **se perdre dans les détails** to get bogged down in detail (**c**) *Com* retail; **vendre/acheter au d.** to sell/buy retail

détaillant, -e [detajɑ̃, -ɑ̃t] *nm,f Com* retailer

détaillé, -e [detaje] *adj (récit, description)* detailed; *(facture)* itemized

détaler [detale] *vi Fam (personne)* to take off; **faire d. qn** to send sb packing

détartrage [detartraʒ] *nm* (**a**) *(de dents)* scaling; **se faire faire un d.** to have one's teeth scaled (**b**) *(de bouilloire, de cafetière, de chaudière)* descaling

détartrer [detartre] *vt* (**a**) *(dents)* to scale (**b**) *(bouilloire, cafetière, chaudière)* to descale

détaxe [detaks] *nf* tax refund

détaxer [detakse] *vt* to exempt from tax; **marchandises détaxées** duty-free goods

détectable [detɛktabl] *adj* detectable

détecter [detɛkte] *vt* to detect

détecteur, -trice [detɛktœr, -tris] **1** *adj* detecting **2** *nm* detector; **d. de faux billets** forged banknote detector; **d. de fumée** smoke detector; **d. de mensonges** lie detector; **d. de mines** mine detector; *Ordinat* **d. de virus** virus detector

détection [detɛksjɔ̃] *nf* detection; *Ordinat* **d. d'erreurs** error detection; *Ordinat* **d. virale** virus detection

détective [detɛktiv] *nm* detective; **d. privé** private detective

déteindre [54] [detɛ̃dr] *vi* *(tissu)* to run (**sur** over); **d. au lavage** to run in the wash; *Fig* **cela a déteint sur eux** it's rubbed off on them

dételer [9] [detle] **1** *vt* *(chevaux)* to unharness; *(bœufs)* to unyoke **2** *vi Fam* to stop working; **sans d.** non-stop

détendre [detɑ̃dr] **1** *vt* (**a**) *(relâcher) (corde)* to slacken; *(arc)* to unbend; *(ressort)* to release (**b**) *(décontracter) (personne)* to relax; **le yoga, ça détend** yoga is relaxing (**c**) **d. l'atmosphère** to make the atmosphere less tense **2 se détendre** *vpr* (**a**) *(corde)* to slacken; *(arc)* to unbend; *(ressort)* to lose its tension (**b**) *(se relaxer) (personne, visage)* to relax (**c**) *(atmosphère, situation)* to become less tense

détendu, -e [detɑ̃dy] *adj (personne, conversation)* relaxed

détenir [70] [detnir] *vt* (**a**) *(avoir en sa possession) (passeport, titres, pouvoir, record)* to hold; *(secret, preuve)* to have (**b**) *(garder prisonnier)* to hold

détente [detɑ̃t] *nf* (**a**) *(relaxation)* relaxation (**b**) *Pol* détente (**c**) *(d'une arme)* trigger (**d**) *(d'un athlète)* spring; **avoir de la d.** to jump well (**e**) *(d'un gaz)* expansion (**f**) **être dur** *ou* **long à la d.** to be slow on the uptake

détenteur, -trice [detɑ̃tœr, -tris] *nm,f (d'argent, de titres, de record)* holder; *(d'arme)* possessor

détention [detɑ̃sjɔ̃] *nf* (**a**) *(de titres)* holding; *(d'armes)* possession (**b**) *(incarcération)* detention; **d. provisoire** detention pending trial

détenu, -e [detny] *nm,f* prisoner

détergent, -e [detɛrʒɑ̃, -ɑ̃t] *adj & nm* detergent

détérioration [deterjɔrasjɔ̃] *nf* deterioration

détériorer [deterjɔre] **1** *vt* to damage **2 se détériorer** *vpr* to deteriorate

déterminant, -e [detɛrminɑ̃, -ɑ̃t] **1** *adj* decisive **2** *nm* (**a**) *Ling* determiner (**b**) *Math* determinant

détermination [detɛrminasjɔ̃] *nf* (**a**) *(fermeté)* determination (**b**) *(d'une date, d'un lieu, d'un prix)* determination, fixing; *(du sang, d'une bactérie)* typing

déterminé, -e [detɛrmine] *adj* (**a**) *(résolu)* determined; **être d. à faire qch** to be determined to do sth (**b**) *(défini)* specific

déterminer [detɛrmine] **1** *vt* (**a**) *(définir)* to determine, to fix; *(sang, bactérie)* to type (**b**) *(décider)* **d. qn à faire qch** to induce sb to do sth (**c**) *(causer) (changement)* to cause; *(action, décision)* to determine (**d**) *Gram* to determine

2 se déterminer *vpr* **se d. à faire qch** to make up one's mind to do sth

déterré, -e [detere] *nm,f Fam* **avoir une mine de d.** to look like death warmed up

déterrer [detere] *vt aussi Fig* to dig up

détestable [detɛstabl] *adj* foul

détester [detɛste] **1** *vt* to detest, to hate; **je déteste être dérangé** I hate being disturbed; **ne pas d. faire qch** to quite like doing sth **2 se détester** *vpr (soi-même)* to hate oneself; *(l'un l'autre)* to hate each other

détonant, -e [detɔnɑ̃, -ɑ̃t] **1** *adj aussi Fig* explosive **2** *nm* explosive

détonateur [detɔnatœr] *nm* detonator; *Fig* **servir de d. à qch** to spark sth off

détonation [detɔnasjɔ̃] *nf* *(bruit)* explosion; *(bruit d'arme à feu)* bang

détoner [detɔne] *vi (explosif)* to detonate; **faire d. qch** to detonate sth

détonner [detɔne] *vi* (**a**) *(chanteur)* to sing out of tune; *(instrumentiste)* to play out of tune (**b**) *(trancher) (couleurs)* to clash; *Fig* **il détonne dans ce milieu** he's out of place in that environment

détordre [detɔrdr] *vt (fil)* to untwist

détour [detur] *nm* (**a**) *(parcours)* detour; **faire un d. (par)** to make a detour (via); **valoir le d.** *(site)* to be worth the trip (**b**) *Fig (biais)* roundabout means; **user de détours pour faire qch** to do sth in a roundabout way; **sans d.** without beating about the bush (**c**) *(tracé) (d'une route, d'une rivière)* bend; **faire un d.** to bend; *Fig* **au d. de la conversation** in the course of the conversation

détourné, -e [deturne] *adj aussi Fig (indirect)* roundabout, indirect

détournement [deturnəmɑ̃] *nm* (**a**) **d. d'avion** hijacking (**b**) *(d'un cours d'eau)* diversion (**c**) *Jur* **d. de fonds** embezzlement; **d. de mineur** corruption of a minor

détourner [deturne] **1** *vt* (**a**) *(circulation, rivière)* to divert; *(avion)* to hijack (**b**) *(éloigner)* **d. qn de** *(ami, famille)* to take sb away from; *(préoccupation, engagement)* to divert sb from; **d. qn du droit chemin** to lead sb astray; **d. l'attention de qn** to divert or distract sb's attention; **d. la conversation** to change the subject; **d. les soupçons** to avert suspicion (**c**) *(voler) (fonds)* to embezzle (**à** from) (**d**) *(tourner)* **d. la tête** to turn one's head away; **d. les yeux** *ou* **le regard** to look away **2 se détourner** *vpr aussi Fig* to turn away (**de** from)

détracteur, -trice [detraktœr, -tris] *nm,f* detractor

détraqué, -e [detrake] **1** *adj (appareil)* out of order; *(estomac)* upset; *(temps)* unsettled; *Fam (personne) (psychologiquement)* unhinged **2** *nm,f Fam* maniac

détraquer [detrake] **1** *vt (appareil)* to put out of order; *(santé)* to ruin; *(estomac)* to upset **2 se détraquer** *vpr (appareil, santé)* to break down; *(temps)* to become unsettled; **se d. l'estomac** to upset one's stomach

détrempé, -e [detrɑ̃pe] *adj (terre, sol)* sodden, waterlogged

détresse [detrɛs] *nf* (**a**) *(angoisse)* distress (**b**) *(dénuement)* financial difficulties; **les familles dans la d.** families in dire need *or* dire straits (**c**) *(perdition)* **en d.** *(navire)* in distress; *(voiture, avion)* in difficulties (**d**) *Méd* **d. respiratoire** respiratory distress

détriment [detrimɑ̃] *nm* **au d.** de to the detriment of; **je l'ai appris à mon d.** I found it out to my cost

détritus [detritys] *nm Br* rubbish, *Am* garbage

détroit [detrwa] *nm* strait; **le d. de Béring** the Bering Strait; **le d. de Gibraltar** the Strait of Gibraltar

détromper [detrɔ̃pe] **1** *vt.* **qn** to put sb right (**sur** about)
2 se détromper *vpr* to realize that one was wrong; **détrompez-vous!** think again!

détrôner [detrone] *vt* (**a**) *(monarque)* to dethrone (**b**) *(théorie, méthode, produit)* to supersede

détrousser [detruse] *vt Hum* **d. qn** to relieve sb of his/ her valuables

détruire [18] [detrμir] **1** *vt* (**a**) *(démolir) (édifice, empire, avion)* to destroy (**b**) *(anéantir) (espoir, mariage, santé)* to ruin, to wreck (**c**) *(tuer)* to kill
2 se détruire *vpr (se faire du mal)* to ruin one's health

dette [dɛt] *nf aussi Fig* **avoir des dettes** to be in debt; **être couvert** *ou* **criblé de dettes** to be crippled with debt; **d. extérieure** foreign debt; **la d. publique** *ou* **de l'État** the National Debt; **payer sa d. à la société** to pay one's debt to society

DEUG [dœg] *nm* *(abrév* **diplôme d'études universitaires générales**) = degree gained after a two-year course

DEUG, DEUST

In French universities, students take the "DEUG" or the "DEUST" ("diplôme d'études universitaires scientifiques et techniques") after two years of courses. They may then take further courses leading to the "licence" (the equivalent of a bachelor's degree). Most students who obtain the "DEUG" choose to do this, while the majority of students who obtain the "DEUST" leave university and go straight into employment.

deuil [dœj] *nm* (**a**) *(décès)* bereavement; **il y a eu un d. dans leur famille** there has been a death in their family (**b**) *(tristesse)* mourning; **être en d.** to be in mourning; **journée de d. national** day of national mourning (**c**) *(tenue)* **porter le d. (de qn)** to be in mourning (for sb); **prendre/quitter le d.** to go into/ come out of mourning; *Fam Fig* **avoir les ongles en d.** to have dirty fingernails (**d**) **faire son d. de qch** to give sth up as lost

DEUST [døst] *nm* *(abrév* **diplôme d'études universitaires scientifiques et techniques**) = university diploma taken after two years of science courses; *voir aussi encadré sous* **DEUG**

Deutsche Mark [dɔjtʃmark, døtʃmark] *nm Anciennement* Deutschmark

deux [dø] **1** *adj inv* (**a**) *(chiffre)* two; **d. fois** twice; **des d. côtés du fleuve** on either side *or* on both sides of the river; **tous (les) d.** both; **tous les d. jours** every other day, every two days; **nous/vous/eux d.** the two of us/you/them; **vivre à d.** to live together; **les ordinateurs et moi, ça fait d.** I know absolutely nothing about computers (**b**) *(peu de)* **c'est à d. pas d'ici** it's only a short distance away, it's two minutes away; **je reviens dans d. minutes** I'll be back in a minute; **tu peux venir? – d. secondes!** can you come here? – just a minute!
2 *nm inv* two; **casser qch en d.** to break sth in two; **marcher par d.** to walk in pairs *or* twos; *(dans une procession)* to march two abreast; *Fam* **en moins de d.** in next to no time; *voir aussi* **trois**

deuxième [døzjɛm] *adj & nmf* second; *voir aussi* **cinquième**

deuxièmement [døzjɛmmɑ̃] *adv* secondly

deux-mâts [døma] *nm inv* two-master

deux-pièces [døpjɛs] *nm inv* (**a**) *(maillot de bain)* two-piece (swimsuit) (**b**) *(tailleur)* two-piece (**c**) *(appartement)* two-room *Br* flat *or Am* apartment

deux-points [døpwɛ̃] *nm inv* colon

deux-roues [døru] *nm inv* two-wheeled vehicle

deux-temps [døtɑ̃] *nm inv (moteur)* two-stroke (engine)

deuzio [døzjo] *adv Fam* second

dévaler [devale] **1** *vt (escalier, pente)* to hurtle down
2 *vi (personne, pierres)* to hurtle down; *(eau, lave, boue)* to rush down

dévaliser [devalize] *vt* (**a**) *(cambrioler) (banque)* to rob; *(maison)* to burgle; *Fig (commerçant)* to clean out (**b**) *(vider) (réfrigérateur, placard)* to raid

dévalorisation [devalɔrizasjɔ̃] *nf* (**a**) *(action) (de la monnaie)* devaluation; *(de marchandises)* marking down; *(résultat) (de la monnaie)* depreciation; *(de marchandises)* mark-down (**b**) *Fig (d'une personne, d'une politique)* discrediting; *(d'un diplôme, d'une profession)* devaluation

dévaloriser [devalɔrize] **1** *vt* (**a**) *(monnaie)* to devalue (**b**) *(personne, politique)* to discredit; *(qualification, diplôme)* to devalue
2 se dévaloriser *vpr* (**a**) *(monnaie)* to depreciate (**b**) *(personne)* to put oneself down

dévaluation [devalμasjɔ̃] *nf Fin* devaluation

dévaluer [devalμe] **1** *vt (monnaie)* to devalue
2 se dévaluer *vpr* to fall in value

devancer [16] [dəvɑ̃se] *vt* (**a**) *(être devant) (concurrent)* to be/get ahead of; **d. son époque** to be ahead of one's time (**b**) *(arriver avant)* to arrive before (**c**) *(prévoir) (personne, critiques)* to forestall; *(demande)* to anticipate (**d**) *(faire avant)* Mil **d. l'appel** to enlist before call-up; *Fin* **d. une échéance** to settle an account early

devant [dəvɑ̃] **1** *prép* (**a**) *(en face de, en avant de)* in front of; **assis d. moi** sitting in front of me; **marcher droit d. soi** to walk straight on; **regardez d. vous!** look where you're going!; **passer d. qn/qch** *(dans la rue)* to go past sb/sth; **passer d. qn** *(dans une file d'attente)* to go in front of sb; **avoir du temps/de l'argent d. soi** to have time/money to spare; **tu as la vie d. toi** you've got your whole life ahead of you; **d. derrière** back to front (**b**) *(face à)* **d. le danger** in the face of danger; **égaux d. la loi** equal in the eyes of the law; **que faire d. tant d'injustice?** what can one do faced with so much injustice?
2 *adv* (**a**) *(en face)* in front; **je cherchais la gare et j'étais juste d.** I was looking for the station when I was standing right in front of it; **où est Martin? – je crois qu'il est d.** where's Martin? – I think he's up ahead (**b**) *(en avant) (dans les premiers rangs)* at the front; *(en voiture)* in the front; **aller d.** to go in front; **marcher/courir d.** to walk on/run on ahead; **passez d.!** you go ahead of me!
3 *nm* front; *Fig* **prendre les devants** to make the first move

devanture [dəvɑ̃tyr] *nf (vitrine)* window; *(façade)* front

dévastateur, -trice [devastatœr, -tris] *adj* devastating

dévastation [devastasjɔ̃] *nf* devastation

dévaster [devaste] *vt* to devastate

déveine [devɛn] *nf Fam* bad luck; **être dans la d.** to be down on one's luck

développement [devlɔpmɑ̃] *nm* development; *(de pellicule)* developing; **en plein d.** *(entreprise)* growing fast; *(pays)* developing rapidly; **développements** *(d'une affaire)* developments; *Fig* **se lancer dans de grands développements** to go into detailed explanation

développer [devlɔpe] **1** *vt* to develop **2 se développer** *vpr* to develop; *(s'étendre)* to spread

devenir[1] [dəvnir] *nm Litt* (**a**) *(évolution)* evolution; **être en perpétuel d.** to be constantly evolving (**b**) *(futur)* future

devenir[2] [70] *(aux être) vi* to become; **il devint général** he became a general; **il était devenu (un) homme** he had grown into a man; **ça devient difficile** it's getting difficult; **d. vieux** to get *or* grow old; **d. fou** to go mad; **c'est à d. fou!** it's enough to drive you mad!; **d. tout rouge** to go all red; **que devient-il?** how is he getting on?; **qu'est-il devenu?** what's become of him?

dévergondé, -e [devɛrgɔ̃de] **1** *adj* shameless **2** *nm,f* shameless person

dévergonder [devɛrgɔ̃de] **se dévergonder** *vpr* to get into bad ways

déversement [devɛrsəmɑ̃] *nm (écoulement)* discharge; *(action)* pouring

déverser [devɛrse] **1** *vt* (**a**) *(eau)* to pour; *(sable, gravier, déchets)* to dump; *Fig (touristes, voyageurs)* to disgorge (**b**) **d. sa colère sur qn** to vent one's anger on sb; **d. des insultes sur qn** to hurl abuse at sb **2 se déverser** *vpr (rivière)* to empty (**dans** into)

dévestiture [devɛstityr] *nf Suisse* access; (**chemin de**) **d.** access road

dévêtir [71] **1** *vt* to undress **2 se dévêtir** *vpr* to undress

devez *voir* **devoir**[2]

déviation [devjasjɔ̃] *nf* (**a**) *(itinéraire modifié) Br* diversion, *Am* detour (**b**) *(modification)* deviation (**par rapport à** from)

dévier [66] [devje] **1** *vt* (**a**) *(circulation)* to divert (**b**) *(balle, coup)* to deflect **2** *vi (véhicule, missile)* to veer (**vers** towards); *(balle)* to deflect (**vers** towards); **d. de sa route** *(véhicule, missile)* to veer off course; *Fig* **d. de son sujet** to digress

devin [dəvɛ̃] *nm* soothsayer; *Fam* **je ne suis pas d.!** I'm not a mind-reader!

deviner [dəvine] *vt (énigme, secret)* to guess; *(futur)* to predict; *(pensée)* to read; **devine qui j'ai vu** guess who I saw; **je ne pouvais pas d.!** how was I supposed to know?

devinette [dəvinɛt] *nf* riddle; **jouer aux devinettes** to play at riddles; *Fig* to speak in riddles; **poser une d. à qn** to ask sb a riddle

devis [dəvi] *nm* estimate, quote; **faire faire un d. pour qch** to get an estimate *or* a quote for sth

dévisager [45] [devizaʒe] *vt* to stare at

devise [dəviz] *nf* (**a**) *(d'une personne)* motto (**b**) *(monnaie)* currency; **devises étrangères** foreign currency; **d. forte** hard currency

deviser [dəvize] *vi Litt* to converse

dévisser [devise] **1** *vt* to unscrew **2** *vi (alpiniste)* to fall **3 se dévisser** *vpr* to unscrew; *(par accident)* to come unscrewed; *Fig* **se d. la tête** *ou* **le cou** to screw one's head round

de visu [devizy] *adv* with one's own eyes

dévitaliser [devitalize] *vt (dent)* to remove the nerve from

dévoiler [devwale] **1** *vt (visage, statue, plaque)* to unveil; *Fig (nom, secret, complot)* to disclose **2 se dévoiler** *vpr (secret, complot)* to come to light

devoir[1] [dəvwar] *nm* (**a**) *(obligation)* duty; **faire qch par d.** to do sth out of a sense of duty; **un homme/ une femme de d.** a man/a woman with a sense of duty; **faire** *ou* **remplir son d.** (**by**); **il est de mon d. de vous le dire** it is my duty to tell you (**b**) *(exercices) (en classe)* test; **devoirs** *(à la maison)* homework; **faire ses devoirs** to do one's homework; **devoirs de vacances** *Br* holiday *or Am* vacation homework (**c**) *Sout* **rendre les derniers devoirs à qn** to pay one's last respects to sb

devoir[2] [26] **1** *vt (être redevable de)* **d. qch à qn** to owe sb sth, to owe sth to sb; **il me doit mille euros** he owes me a thousand euros; **je lui dois bien cela** it's the least I can do for him/her, I owe him/her that at least **2** *v aux* (**a**) *(indique l'obligation)* **d. faire qch** to have to do sth; **vous devez être là à trois heures** you must be *or* you have to be there by three o'clock; **elle a cru d. refuser** she thought it advisable to refuse; **les commandes doivent être adressées à...** orders should be sent to...; **vous devriez rester** you should stay, you ought to stay; **il aurait dû m'avertir** he should have warned me, he ought to have warned me (**b**) *(indique la nécessité)* **tu dois absolument lui en parler** you really must talk to him/her about it; **finalement, j'ai dû céder** I had to give way in the end; **il ne devait plus les revoir** *(il ne les reverrait plus)* he was (destined) never to see them again; **cela devait arriver!** it was bound to *or* it had to happen! (**c**) *(indique l'intention)* **je devais partir lundi, mais...** I was meant to leave on Monday, but...; **le train doit arriver à midi** the train is due (to arrive) at twelve o'clock (**d**) *(indique la supposition)* **vous devez avoir faim** you must be hungry; **il ne doit pas avoir plus de 40 ans** he can't be more than 40; **il a dû me prendre pour un autre** he must have mistaken me for someone else; **la pollution devrait s'accroître d'ici la fin du siècle** pollution is expected to increase by the end of the century **3 se devoir** *vpr* **je me dois à ma famille/mon travail** I must devote myself to my family/my work; **je me dois de le faire** it's my duty to do it; **comme il se doit** as is (only) right and proper

dévolu, -e [devɔly] **1** *adj (somme, responsabilités)* assigned (**à** to) **2** *nm* **jeter son d. sur** to set one's heart on

devons *voir* **devoir**[2]

dévorant, -e [devɔrɑ̃, -ɑ̃t] *adj (jalousie, passion)* consuming; *(envie)* overwhelming; *(curiosité)* burning; **avoir une faim dévorante** to be ravenous

dévorer [devɔre] *vt* (**a**) *(proie, nourriture, livre)* to devour; **être dévoré par les moustiques** to be eaten alive by mosquitoes; **d. qn des yeux** *ou* **du regard** to devour sb with one's eyes (**b**) *Fig (détruire)* **l'ambition/la jalousie la dévore** she is consumed by ambition/jealousy; **dévoré de remords** consumed with remorse (**c**) *Fig (fortune, kilomètres)* to eat up

dévot, -e [devo, -ɔt] **1** *adj* devout **2** *nm,f* devout person

dévotion [devosjɔ̃] *nf* (**a**) *(ferveur)* devoutness (**b**) *(adoration)* devotion; **avoir une d. pour** to be devoted to (**c**) **dévotions** *(prières)* devotions

dévoué, -e [devwe] *adj* devoted (**à** to)

dévouement [devumɑ̃] *nm* (**a**) *(abnégation)* devotion to duty (**b**) *(amour)* devotion (**à** to); **avec d.** devotedly

dévouer [devwe] **se dévouer** *vpr (se sacrifier)* to volunteer (**pour faire qch** to do sth); *(se consacrer)* to devote oneself (**à** to); **il faut que quelqu'un se dévoue** somebody has to do it; *Hum* **vous voulez que je finisse la tarte? bon, je me dévoue!** you want me to finish the tart? oh well, if I must!

dévoyé, -e [devwaje] *adj & nm,f* delinquent

dévoyer [32] [devwaje] **se dévoyer** *vpr Litt* to go astray

devra *etc voir* **devoir²**

dextérité [dɛksterite] *nf* dexterity, skill; **avec d.** skilfully

dézipper [dezipe] *vt Ordinat* to unzip

DGSE [deʒeɛsə] *nf (abrév* **direction générale de la sécurité extérieure**) = French military intelligence service, *Br* ≃ MI6

diabète [djabɛt] *nm* diabetes; **avoir du d.** to have diabetes

diabétique [djabetik] *adj & nmf* diabetic

diable [djɑbl] *nm* (**a**) *(démon)* devil; **le d.** the Devil; **un petit d.** *(enfant)* a little devil; **une faim de tous les diables** to be absolutely ravenous; **un bruit de tous les diables** a hell of a din; *Fig* **avoir le d. au corps** to be possessed; *Can Fam* **être au d.** to be fed up; *Fig* **tirer le d. par la queue** to live from hand to mouth; **au d. l'avarice!** to hell with the expense!; **allez au d.!** go to hell!, **au d. (vauvert)** miles away; **que le d. l'emporte!** he can go to hell!; **ce serait bien le d. si...** it would be surprising if... (**b**) *(marque la surprise, l'agacement)* **d.!** goodness me!; **où d. est-elle allée?** where the devil has she gone?; **que d.!** for goodness sake! (**c**) *(chariot)* (two-wheeled) trolley (**d**) *(jouet)* jack-in-the-box

diablement [djɑbləmɑ̃] *adv Fam* damned

diablesse [djɑblɛs] *nf (démon, méchante femme)* she-devil; *Vieilli (jeune fille)* devil

diablotin [djɑblɔtɛ̃] *nm* imp

diabolique [djabɔlik] *adj* diabolical

diaboliser [djabɔlize] *vt* to demonize

diabolo [djabɔlo] *nm (boisson)* **d. menthe/fraise** mint/strawberry syrup and lemonade

diadème [djadɛm] *nm* tiara

diagnostic [djagnɔstik] *nm* diagnosis; **faire un d.** to make a diagnosis; **ce médecin a un d. très sûr** this doctor makes very reliable diagnoses; *Ordinat* **d. d'autotest** self-test diagnosis

diagnostiquer [djagnɔstike] *vt* to diagnose

diagonal, -e, -aux, -ales [djagɔnal, -o] **1** *adj* diagonal
2 *nf* **diagonale** diagonal; **en diagonale** diagonally; *Fig* **lire qch en diagonale** to skim through sth

diagonalement [djagɔnalmɑ̃] *adv* diagonally

diagramme [djagram] *nm* diagram

dialecte [djalɛkt] *nm* (**a**) *(variante régionale)* dialect (**b**) *Suisse (allemand)* Swiss German

dialectique [djalɛktik] *adj* dialectical

dialogue [djalɔg] *nm* dialogue; *(conversation)* conversation; **c'est un d. de sourds** it's a dialogue of the deaf; *Ordinat* **mode de d.** interactive mode

dialoguer [djalɔge] *vi* to communicate; *(avec un ordinateur)* to interact

dialyse [djaliz] *nf Méd* dialysis

diamant [djamɑ̃] *nm* diamond; **diamants de la guerre** conflict diamonds

diamantaire [djamɑ̃tɛr] *nm (tailleur)* diamond cutter; *(vendeur)* diamond merchant

diamétralement [djametralmɑ̃] *adv* **d. opposés** diametrically opposed

diamètre [djamɛtr] *nm* diameter

diapason [djapazɔ̃] *nm Mus* (**a**) *(note)* pitch; *Fig* **se mettre au d.** to fall in with the others (**b**) *(appareil)* tuning fork

diaphane [djafan] *adj* diaphanous

diaphragme [djafragm] *nm Anat & (contraceptif)* diaphragm

diapo [djapo] *nf Fam* slide

diaporama [djaporama] *nm* slide show

diapositive [djapozitiv] *nf* slide

diarrhée [djare] *nf* diarrhoea; **avoir la d.** to have diarrhoea

diaspora [djaspɔra] *nf* diaspora

diatonique [djatɔnik] *adj* diatonic

diatribe [djatrib] *nf* diatribe (**contre** against)

dichotomie [dikɔtɔmi] *nf* dichotomy

dico [diko] *nm Fam* dictionary

Dictaphone® [diktafɔn] *nm* Dictaphone®

dictateur [diktatœr] *nm* dictator

dictatorial, -e, -aux, -ales [diktatɔrjal, -o] *adj* dictatorial

dictature [diktatyr] *nf* dictatorship

dictée [dikte] *nf* dictation; **écrire qch sous la d. de qn** to write sth at sb's dictation; **d. musicale** musical dictation

dicter [dikte] *vt* to dictate

diction [diksjɔ̃] *nf* diction

dictionnaire [diksjɔnɛr] *nm* dictionary; **d. électronique** electronic dictionary; **d. de langue** language dictionary

dicton [diktɔ̃] *nm* saying

didacticiel [didaktisjɛl] *nm Ordinat* tutorial

didactique [didaktik] *adj* (**a**) *(ouvrage, voyage)* educational (**b**) *(terme, langage)* technical

dièse [djɛz] **1** *nm Mus* sharp; *Typ & Ordinat* hash (sign)
2 *adj Mus* sharp; **fa d.** F sharp

diesel [djezɛl] **1** *adj* **moteur d.** diesel engine
2 *nm (carburant)* diesel
3 *nf (voiture)* diesel

diète [djɛt] *nf (régime) (partiel)* diet; *(total)* fast; **être à la d.** *(partielle)* to be on a diet; *(totale)* to be fasting

diététicien, -enne [djetetisjɛ̃, -ɛn] *nm,f* dietitian

diététique [djetetik] **1** *adj (menu, repas)* diet; **magasin/restaurant d.** health-food shop/restaurant
2 *nf* dietetics *(singulier)*

dieu, -x [djø] **1** *nm* (**a**) *(divinité)* god; *Fam* **comme un d.** *(chanter, jouer)* like a god (**b**) *(dans la religion chrétienne)* **D.** God; **le bon D.** God; **D. merci!, D. soit loué!** thank God!; **D. sait si j'ai travaillé** God knows I've worked hard enough!; **D. seul le sait** God only knows (**b**) *(dans la religion chrétienne)* **D.** God; **D. merci!, D. soit loué!**; **2** *exclam* **mon D.!** Good God!; **D. qu'elle est petite!** God, she's small!; *Fam* **c'est pas D. possible!** it's just not possible!; *Fam* **bon D.!** for God's sake!; *très Fam* **nom de D.!** Christ almighty!

diffamation [difamasjɔ̃] *nf (paroles)* slander; *(écrits)* libel; **procès en d.** slander/libel trial

diffamatoire [difamatwar] *adj (paroles)* slanderous; *(écrits)* libellous

différé, -e [difere] **1** *adj Ordinat* **traitement d.** off-line processing
2 *nm* **en d.** *(émission)* pre-recorded

différemment [diferamɑ̃] *adv* differently

différence [diferɑ̃s] nf difference (**entre** between); **d. d'âge/de prix** age/price difference; **faire la d.** (entre) to make a distinction (between); **cela ne fait aucune** ou **pas de d.** it makes no difference; **à la d. de** unlike

différenciation [diferɑ̃sjasjɔ̃] nf differentiation

différencier [66] [diferɑ̃sje] **1** vt to differentiate (**de** ou **d'avec** from)
2 se différencier vpr (**a**) (être différent) to differ (**de/ par** from/in) (**b**) (chercher à être différent) to differentiate oneself (**de** from)

différend [diferɑ̃] nm difference of opinion, disagreement (**entre** between); Jur dispute; **avoir un d. avec qn** to have a disagreement with sb

différent, -e [diferɑ̃, -ɑ̃t] adj different (**de** from); **différents cas** (plusieurs) various cases

différentiel, -elle [diferɑ̃sjɛl] **1** adj & nm differential
2 nf **différentielle** Math differential

différer [34] [difere] **1** vt (jugement, paiement) to defer; (décision, départ) to postpone
2 vi (être différent) to differ (**par** in)

difficile [difisil] **1** adj difficult; (exigeant) fussy; **le plus d. est fait** the most difficult part is over; **il est d. de le joindre** it's difficult to contact him; **il m'est d. d'accepter** it's difficult for me to accept; **être d. à vivre** to be difficult to get on with; **être d. sur qch** to be particular about sth
2 nmf **faire le d.** to be fussy

difficilement [difisilmɑ̃] adv with difficulty, not easily; **on peut d. le lui dire** you can hardly tell him/her that

difficulté [difikylte] nf difficulty; **être en d.** to be in difficulty or trouble; **faire des difficultés** to create difficulties; **avoir de la d. à faire qch** to have difficulty (in) doing sth; **avoir des difficultés en anglais** to have difficulties with English

difforme [difɔrm] adj deformed, misshapen

difformité [difɔrmite] nf deformity

diffus, -e [dify, -yz] adj (lumière) diffuse; (impression, souvenir) vague; (douleur) dull

diffuser [difyze] vt (**a**) (lumière, chaleur) to diffuse; (livres) to distribute; (idée, nouvelle) to spread (**b**) (émission) to broadcast

diffuseur [difyzœr] nm (de lumière, de chaleur) diffuser; **d. de parfum** air freshener, room freshener

diffusion [difyzjɔ̃] nf (**a**) (de lumière, de chaleur) diffusion; (de livres) distribution; (d'une idée, d'une nouvelle) spreading (**b**) (d'une émission) broadcasting; **d. audionumérique** digital audio broadcasting; **d. numérique/satellite/terrestre** digital/satellite/terrestrial broadcasting

digérer [34] [diʒere] vt (**a**) (aliment) to digest; **je ne digère pas le lait** I can't digest milk (**b**) (assimiler intellectuellement) to digest; Fam (accepter) to stomach, to take; **des vérités dures à d.** unpalatable truths

digeste [diʒɛst] adj aussi Fig easily digestible

digestif, -ive [diʒɛstif, -iv] **1** adj digestive
2 nm liqueur

digestion [diʒɛstjɔ̃] nf digestion; **avoir une d. difficile** to have problems with one's digestion

Digicode® [diʒikɔd] nm door code (for entry to a building)

digital¹, -e, -aux, -ales [diʒital, -o] adj (numérique) digital

digital², -e, -aux, -ales 1 adj voir **empreinte**
2 nf **digitale** Bot digitalis

digne [diɲ] adj (**a**) (méritant) **d. de** worthy of; **d. d'éloges** praiseworthy; **d. de foi** reliable; **être d. de**

faire qch to be fit to do sth (**b**) (approprié) **d. de** worthy of; **peu d. de qn** unworthy of sb; **d. de ce nom** worthy of the name; Hum **tu es bien le d. fils de ton père** you're your father's son all right (**c**) (grave) dignified

dignement [diɲəmɑ̃] adv (**a**) (avec dignité) with dignity (**b**) (de façon appropriée) fittingly; **être d. récompensé** to be justly rewarded

dignitaire [diɲitɛr] nm dignitary

dignité [diɲite] nf dignity

digression [digrɛsjɔ̃] nf digression; **faire une d.** to digress

digue [dig] nf (**a**) (dans un port) dike; (contre l'érosion) sea wall (**b**) (de billes de bois) logjam

dilapider [dilapide] vt (fortune) to squander; (fonds publics) to embezzle

dilatation [dilatasjɔ̃] nf (**a**) (des pupilles) dilation; (de l'estomac) distension (**b**) (d'un gaz) expansion

dilater [dilate] **1** vt (**a**) (pupilles) to dilate; (estomac) to distend (**b**) (gaz) to expand
2 se dilater vpr (**a**) (pupilles) to dilate; (estomac) to distend (**b**) (gaz) to expand

dilemme [dilɛm] nm dilemma

dilettante [diletɑ̃t] nmf dilettante; **faire qch en d.** to dabble in sth

diligence [diliʒɑ̃s] nf (**a**) (véhicule) (stage)coach (**b**) Litt (soin) diligence

diligent, -e [diliʒɑ̃, -ɑ̃t] adj Litt (zélé) diligent

diluant [dilɥɑ̃] nm thinner

diluer [dilɥe] vt (boisson) to dilute; (peinture) to thin down; Fig (discours, dissertation) to pad out

dilution [dilysjɔ̃] nf (de peinture) thinning down; (d'une boisson) dilution

diluvien, -enne [dilyvjɛ̃, -ɛn] adj (pluies) torrential

dimanche [dimɑ̃ʃ] nm Sunday; **le d. des Rameaux/ de Pâques** Palm/Easter Sunday; Fig **conducteur du d.** Sunday driver; voir aussi **samedi**

dîme [dim] nf Hist tithe

dimension [dimɑ̃sjɔ̃] nf (**a**) (grandeur) dimension, size; **à deux/trois dimensions** two-/three-dimensional; **prendre les dimensions de qch** (objet) to take the measurements of sth (**b**) (importance) magnitude (**c**) (aspect) dimension

diminué, -e [diminɥe] adj **être d.** to have gone downhill

diminuer [diminɥe] **1** vt (**a**) (réduire) to reduce, to decrease (**b**) (affaiblir) to weaken (**c**) (dénigrer) (personne) to belittle; (action) to undermine
2 vi to decrease; (fièvre) to drop
3 se diminuer vpr to belittle oneself

diminutif, -ive [diminytif, -iv] adj & nm diminutive

diminution [diminysjɔ̃] nf reduction, decrease; **être en d.** (effectifs) to be dwindling; (naissances, ventes) to be falling

dinar [dinar] nm dinar

dinde [dɛ̃d] nf (**a**) (volaille, viande) turkey (**b**) Fam (femme sotte) silly goose

dindon [dɛ̃dɔ̃] nm turkey (cock); Fig **être le d. de la farce** to be made a fool of

dindonneau, -x [dɛ̃dɔno] nm young turkey

dîner¹ [dine] nm (**a**) (repas du soir) dinner; (soirée) dinner party; **il y a des pâtes pour le** ou **au** ou **à d.** it's pasta for dinner (**b**) (repas de midi) lunch

dîner² vi (**a**) (le soir) to have dinner, to dine; **il dîna d'une tranche de jambon** he had a slice of ham for dinner (**b**) (à midi) to have lunch

dînette [dinɛt] *nf (service)* doll's tea set; **jouer à la d.** to have a dolls' tea party

dingo [dɛ̃go] **1** *adj Fam* crazy
2 *nm (chien sauvage d'Australie)* dingo
3 *nmf Fam* nutcase

dingue [dɛ̃g] *Fam* **1** *adj* **(a)** *(fou)* crazy; **être d. de qn/qch** to be crazy about sb/sth **(b)** *(incroyable)* incredible **2** *nmf (fou)* nutcase; **être un(e) d.** de moto/golf to be a motorbike/golf nut

dinguer [dɛ̃ge] *vi Fam* **aller d. contre qch** to go crashing into sth; **envoyer d. qn** *(éconduire)* to send sb packing; **envoyer d. qch** to send sth flying

dinosaure [dinɔzɔr] *nm aussi Fig* dinosaur

diocèse [djɔsɛz] *nm Rel* diocese

diode [djɔd] *nf Élec* diode; **d. électroluminescente** light-emitting diode

dioxyde [diɔksid] *nm Chim* dioxide; **d. de carbone** carbon dioxide

diphtérie [difteri] *nf Méd* diphtheria; **avoir la d.** to have diphtheria

diphtongue [diftɔ̃g] *nf Ling* diphthong

diplomate [diplɔmat] **1** *adj* diplomatic **2** *nm Culin* = dessert made with sponge cake, custard and fruit, *Br* ≃ trifle **3** *nmf* diplomat

diplomatie [diplɔmasi] *nf* **(a)** *(habileté)* diplomacy; **user de d.** to be diplomatic **(b)** *(service)* diplomatic service

diplomatique [diplɔmatik] *adj* diplomatic

diplomatiquement [diplɔmatikmɑ̃] *adv* diplomatically

diplôme [diplom] *nm* diploma; *Univ* degree; **avoir des diplômes** to have qualifications

diplômé, -e [diplome] **1** *adj* qualified; *Univ* graduate; **un ingénieur d. de l'École polytechnique** an engineering graduate of the École Polytechnique **2** *nm,f* holder of a diploma; *Univ* graduate

dire¹ [dir] *nm* **au d. de qn** according to sb; **selon ses dires** according to him/her

dire² [27a] **1** *vt* **(a)** *(exprimer)* to say; **comment dit-on "soleil" en anglais?** how do you say "soleil" in English?; **il ne savait plus quoi d.** he didn't know what to say; **je sais ce que je dis!** I know what I'm talking about!; **laisse-les d., ils sont stupides!** let them talk, they're stupid!; **elle a dit qu'elle arriverait en retard** she said she would be late; **comment dirais-je?** how shall I put it?; **comme on dit** as the saying goes; **cela dit...** having said that...; **il est un peu lent, pour ne pas d. complètement idiot** he's a bit slow, or to put it bluntly he's a complete idiot; **qui dit mieux?** *(à une vente aux enchères)* any advance?; **c'est vite dit** it's easier said than done
(b) *(communiquer)* **d. qch à qn** to tell sb sth; **d. à qn que...** to tell sb (that)...; **je t'ai déjà dit que oui!** I've already said yes!; **je vous l'avais bien dit!** I told you so!; *Fam* **c'est elle, je te dis** it's her, I tell you; **je lui ai fait d. de venir** I sent for him/her; **elle ne se le fit pas d. deux fois** she didn't wait to be told twice
(c) *(ordonner)* **d. à qn de faire qch** to tell sb to do sth; **faites ce qu'on vous dit** do as you're told; **taisez-vous, j'ai dit!** be quiet, I said!
(d) *(prétendre)* to say; **à ce qu'elle dit** according to her; **on le dit mort** he is said to have died
(e) *(langage enfantin) (rapporter)* to tell; **je vais le d. à ma mère** I'm going to tell my mum on you
(f) *(décider)* **disons à quatre heures** let's say four o'clock; **il est dit que je resterai célibataire** I'm destined to stay single

(g) *(penser)* **alors, qu'est-ce que tu en dis?** well, what do you think?; **qu'est-ce que tu dirais d'aller au cinéma?** how about going to the cinema?; **on dirait qu'il pleut** it looks as if it's raining; **on dirait du Mozart** it sounds like Mozart; **on dirait du gin** *(au goût)* it tastes like gin; **on aurait dit qu'elle était hypnotisée** it looked as if she was hypnotized; **et d. que...!** and to think (that)...!
(h) *(objecter)* to say; **j'ai eu une augmentation conséquente, je n'ai rien à d.** I got a decent rise, I can't complain; **vous avez beau d.,...** you can say what you like, but...; **ce n'est pas pour d., mais...** I don't want to be rude, but...
(i) *(indiquer) (sujet: statistiques)* to show; **que dit le baromètre?** what does the barometer say?; **qu'est-ce qui vous dit qu'il viendra?** what makes you think he'll come?; **ce nom ne me dit rien** the name doesn't ring a bell; **quelque chose me dit que...** something tells me (that)...
(j) *(plaire)* **ça te dit de partir en vacances avec nous?** *Br* do you fancy coming on holiday with us?, *Am* would you like to come on vacation with us?; **ça ne me dit trop rien de manger chinois** I don't really fancy Chinese food; **ça ne me dit rien qui vaille** I don't like the look of it
(k) *(prière, messe)* to say; *(poésie)* to recite
(l) *(signifier)* **qui dit bordeaux dit bon vin** Bordeaux is synonymous with good wine
(m) *(locutions)* **c'est (tout) d.** need I say more?; **c'est d. s'il t'aime** that shows how much he loves you; **c'est beaucoup d.** that's saying (quite) a lot; **c'est peu d.** that's putting it mildly; **il n'y a pas à d.,...** there are no two ways about it,...; **pour ainsi d.** so to speak, as it were; **pour tout (vous) d.,...** to be honest (with you),...; **quelques jours, je ne dis pas, mais un mois!** a few days, that's fair enough, but a whole month!; *Fam* **je te dis pas la tête qu'il a faite!** you should have seen his face!; *Fam* **je ne te dis que ça** say no more, enough said; **c'est moi qui vous le dis** let me tell you, believe me; *Fam* **à qui le dites-vous!** you're telling ME!; **vous m'en direz tant!** you don't say!; *Fam* **je ne te le fais pas d.!** tell me something I don't know!; *Fam* **tu l'as dit(, bouffi)!** you said it!; **cela va sans d.** that goes without saying; **dis donc!** *(au fait)* hey!; *(marque la surprise)* gosh!; *(marque l'indignation)* do you mind!; **tu me le donnes, dis?** give it to me, will you?
2 *se dire vpr* **(a)** *(l'un à l'autre)* **on se dit bonjour** we say hello
(b) *(penser)* **se d. que...** to think that...; **dis-toi bien que ça aurait pu être plus grave** it could have been worse, you know; **je me disais bien que je l'avais déjà vu quelque part** I knew I'd seen him somewhere before
(c) *(être exprimé)* **comment ça se dit en anglais?** how do you say it in English?; **ça se dit en français?** can you say that in French?
(d) *(se prétendre)* **elle se dit écossaise** she says she's Scottish

direct, -e [dirɛkt] **1** *adj* direct **2** *nm* **(a)** *(à la radio, à la télévision)* live broadcasting; **en d. de l'Opéra de Paris** live from the Paris Opera House **(b)** *(en boxe)* jab; **d. du droit/du gauche** straight right/left **(c)** *(train)* direct train **(pour** to) **3** *adv Fam* straight

directement [dirɛktəmɑ̃] *adv* **(a)** *(sans détour)* straight **(b)** *(sans intermédiaire)* directly

directeur, -trice [dirɛktœr, -tris] **1** *nm,f* **(a)** *(d'un magasin, d'un service)* manager; **d. artistique** *(d'un*

film) artistic director; *(à la télévision)* production designer; *(d'un journal)* art editor; **d. commercial** sales director; **d. général** *(d'une entreprise)* managing director; **d. de la rédaction** editorial director; **d. des ressources humaines** *ou* **du personnel** personnel manager (**b**) *(d'une école) Br* headmaster, *f* headmistress, *Am* principal (**c**) *(d'une prison) Br* governor, *Am* warden (**d**) *Univ* **d. de thèse** thesis supervisor
  2 *adj (équipe, instances)* management; *(idée)* main; *(principe, force)* guiding
direction [dirɛksjɔ̃] *nf* (**a**) *(d'une entreprise, d'un théâtre)* management; *(d'une école)* running; *(d'un parti, d'un pays)* leadership; **sous la d. de qn** under the supervision of sb; *(orchestre)* conducted by sb (**b**) *(ensemble des cadres)* management; **d. commerciale** sales management; **d. générale** general management; **d. des ressources humaines** *ou* **du personnel** *(service)* personnel department (**c**) *(orientation)* direction; **toutes/autres directions** *(sur panneau)* all/other directions; **quelle d. ont-ils prise?** which way did they go?; **le train en d. de Strasbourg** the train to Strasbourg, the Strasbourg train (**d**) *(d'un véhicule)* steering; **d. assistée** power steering
directive [dirɛktiv] *nf* directive
directoire [dirɛktwar] *nm* (**a**) *Com (d'une société anonyme)* board of directors (**b**) *Hist* **le D.** the (French) Directory
dirham [diram] *nm* dirham
dirigeable [diriʒabl] *adj & nm* (**ballon**) **d.** dirigible, airship
dirigeant, -e [diriʒɑ̃, ɑ̃t] **1** *adj voir* **classe**
  2 *nm,f (d'un parti, d'un pays)* leader; *(d'une entreprise)* manager; **d. syndical** union leader
diriger [45] [diriʒe] **1** *vt* (**a**) *(entreprise, équipe, projet)* to manage, to run; *(pays, parti)* to lead; *(séance)* to conduct; *(travaux)* to supervise; *(acteurs)* to direct; *(orchestre)* to conduct (**b**) *(arme, télescope, lumière)* to point (**sur** at) (**c**) *(pas)* to direct (**vers** towards); *(regard)* to turn (**vers** to); *(attention)* to turn (**sur** to); *(conversation)* to steer (**sur** onto) (**d**) *(orienter professionnellement)* to steer (**sur** *ou* **vers** towards)
  2 se diriger *vpr* (**a**) *(aller)* **se d. vers** *(endroit)* to head for; *(personne)* to go up to; *(carrière, secteur)* to go into (**b**) *(s'orienter)* to find one's way around
dirigisme [diriʒism] *nm* state control
dirlo [dirlo] *nm Fam Br* head, *Am* principal
disais *etc voir* **dire²**
discernement [disɛrnəmɑ̃] *nm (jugement)* discernment; **sans d.** rashly
discerner [disɛrne] *vt* (**a**) *(percevoir)* to make out (**b**) *(différencier)* **d. qch de** to distinguish sth from (**c**) *(deviner)* to discern
disciple [disipl] *nmf* disciple
disciplinaire [disiplinɛr] *adj* disciplinary
discipline [disiplin] *nf (ordre, matière)* discipline
discipliné, -e [disipline] *adj* disciplined
discipliner [disipline] **1** *vt (enfant)* to control
  2 se discipliner *vpr* to discipline oneself
disc-jockey *(pl* **disc-jockeys***)* [diskʒɔkɛ] *nm* disc jockey
discographie [diskɔgrafi] *nf* discography
discontinu, -e [diskɔ̃tiny] *adj* intermittent; *(ligne)* broken
discontinuer [diskɔ̃tinɥe] **sans discontinuer** *adv* without stopping

disconvenir [70] [diskɔ̃vnir] *vi Litt* **ne pas d. de qch** not to deny sth
discordant, -e [diskɔrdɑ̃, -ɑ̃t] *adj* (**a**) *(son, bruit)* discordant (**b**) *(couleurs)* clashing; *(opinions)* conflicting
discorde [diskɔrd] *nf* discord; **semer la d.** to make trouble
discothèque [diskɔtɛk] *nf* (**a**) *(boîte de nuit)* disco (**b**) *(organisme)* record library; *(collection)* record collection
discount [diskunt] **1** *nm (rabais)* discount
  2 *adj* discount; **prix d.** discount price
discourir [22] [diskurir] *vi* **d. sur qch** to discourse on sth; *Péj* to air one's opinions on sth
discours [diskur] *nm* (**a**) *(allocution)* speech; **prononcer** *ou* **faire un d.** to make a speech; **d. de clôture/d'ouverture** closing/opening speech (**b**) *Gram* speech; **d. indirect/direct** reported *or* indirect/direct speech (**c**) *(paroles)* talk; **il m'a tenu un grand d. sur la tolérance** he gave me a great long speech about tolerance; **tous ces beaux d. ne nous avancent à rien** all this talking isn't getting us anywhere
discrédit [diskredi] *nm* discredit; **jeter le d. sur qn** to bring discredit on sb
discréditer [diskredite] **1** *vt* to discredit
  2 se discréditer *vpr (personne)* to discredit oneself; **se d. auprès de** *ou* **aux yeux de qn** to discredit oneself with sb
discret, -ète [diskrɛ, -ɛt] *adj* (**a**) *(plein de retenue)* discreet; **tu sauras rester d.?** you'll keep it to yourself, won't you? (**b**) *(sobre) (personne)* unassuming; *(vêtements)* simple; *(maquillage)* natural (**c**) *(endroit)* quiet
discrètement [diskrɛtmɑ̃] *adv* (**a**) *(avec retenue)* discreetly; **il lui a parlé d.** he had a quiet word with him/her (**b**) *(sobrement) (habillé)* simply; **être d. maquillée** to be wearing natural make-up
discrétion [diskresjɔ̃] *nf* (**a**) *(retenue)* discretion; **manquer de d.** to be tactless (**b**) *(sobriété)* simplicity; **avec d.** *(s'habiller)* simply; *(se maquiller)* discreetly (**c**) **champagne à d.** unlimited champagne
discrimination [diskriminasjɔ̃] *nf* discrimination; **d. raciale/sexuelle** racial/sexual discrimination; **sans d. d'âge ni de sexe** regardless of age or sex
discriminatoire [diskriminatwar] *adj* discriminatory
disculper [diskylpe] **1** *vt* to exonerate (**de** from)
  2 se disculper *vpr* to exonerate oneself (**de** from)
discussion [diskysjɔ̃] *nf* discussion; **avoir une d.** (**sur** *ou* **à propos de**) to have a discussion (about); **pas de d., au travail!** don't argue, get to work!
discutable [diskytabl] *adj* questionable
discutailler [diskytaje] *vi Fam Péj* to quibble
discuté, -e [diskyte] *adj (question)* disputed; *(livre, sujet)* much discussed
discuter [diskyte] **1** *vt (examiner)* to discuss; *(contester)* to question; *Fam* **d. le coup, d. le bout de gras** to have a chat
  2 *vi* (**a**) *(parler)* to discuss; **d. avec qn sur** *ou* **de qch** to discuss sth with sb (**b**) *(protester)* to argue; **suis-moi sans d.** follow me and don't argue
  3 se discuter *vpr* **ça se discute** that's debatable
dise *etc voir* **dire²**
disette [dizɛt] *nf* food shortage
diseuse [dizøz] *nf* **d. de bonne aventure** fortune-teller

disgrâce [disgrɑs] *nf* **tomber en d.** to fall into disfavour

disgracieux, -euse [disgrasjø, -øz] *adj (personne)* ungainly; *(visage, moue)* ugly

disjoindre [43] [disʒwɛ̃dr] **1** *vt* to separate **2 se disjoindre** *vpr* to come apart

disjoint, -e [disʒwɛ̃, -ɛ̃t] *adj (pièces)* separated

disjoncter [disʒɔ̃kte] **1** *vt (circuit électrique)* to break **2** *vi (circuit électrique)* to fuse; *Fam Fig* to crack up

disjoncteur [disʒɔ̃ktœr] *nm Élec* circuit breaker

dislocation [dislɔkasjɔ̃] *nf (d'une articulation)* dislocation

disloquer [dislɔke] **1** *vt* (**a**) **il m'a disloqué l'épaule** he dislocated my shoulder (**b**) *(empire, État)* to break up **2 se disloquer** *vpr (empire, État)* to break up; **se d. l'épaule/le genou** to dislocate one's shoulder/knee

disparaître [20] [disparɛtr] *vi* (**a**) *(devenir invisible)* to disappear, to vanish; **d. dans la foule** to disappear into the crowd; *Fam* **d. de la circulation** to drop out of circulation; *Fam* **disparais!** clear off! (**b**) *(mourir)* to die (**c**) *(douleur, sentiment)* to disappear; *(maladie, tradition)* to die out; **faire d. qch** to get rid of sth

disparate [disparat] *adj (éléments)* disparate; *(couleurs, objets, mobilier)* ill-matched

disparité [disparite] *nf (d'éléments)* disparity; *(de couleurs, d'objets, de mobilier)* mismatch; *(des salaires, des revenus)* inequality

disparition [disparisjɔ̃] *nf* (**a**) *(absence)* disappearance (**b**) *(décès)* death

disparu, -e [dispary] **1** *adj (personne)* missing; **être porté d.** to be reported missing **2** *nm,f (mort)* dead person; *(absent)* missing person

dispensaire [dispɑ̃sɛr] *nm* community health centre

dispense [dispɑ̃s] *nf* (**a**) *(d'une obligation)* exemption (**b**) *(certificat)* certificate of exemption

dispenser [dispɑ̃se] **1** *vt* (**a**) **d. qn de qch/de faire qch** to exempt sb from sth/from doing sth; **se faire d. de qch** to be excused *or* let off sth; *Euph* **je vous dispense de vos commentaires** you can keep your remarks to yourself (**b**) *(soins, charité, faveurs)* to dispense **2 se dispenser** *vpr* **se d. de qch/de faire qch** to get out of sth/of doing sth; **tu pourrais te d. de ce genre de commentaire!** you can keep that sort of remark to yourself!

dispersé, -e [dispɛrse] *adj (épars)* scattered

disperser [dispɛrse] **1** *vt (foule, famille, feuilles)* to scatter **2 se disperser** *vpr (nuages, foule, famille)* to scatter, to disperse; *Fig (intellectuellement)* to spread oneself too thinly

dispersion [dispɛrsjɔ̃] *nf* (**a**) *(de manifestants, de nuages, d'une armée)* scattering, dispersal; *Fig (inattention)* lack of focus (**b**) *Suisse (peinture)* emulsion (paint)

disponibilité [disponibilite] *nf* (**a**) *(d'une personne, de places, d'un capital)* availability; **d. d'esprit** receptiveness (**b**) *(d'un fonctionnaire)* leave of absence; **être en d.** to be on leave of absence (**c**) *Fin* **disponibilités** available funds

disponible [disponibl] *adj* (**a**) *(personne, place, capital)* available; **êtes-vous d. ce soir?** are you free tonight? (**b**) *(fonctionnaire)* on leave of absence

dispos, -e [dispo, -oz] *adj (personne)* fit and well

disposé, -e [dispoze] *adj (personne)* **être bien/mal d.** to be in a good/bad mood; **être bien d. envers qn** to be well disposed towards sb; **être d. à faire qch** to feel disposed *or* willing to do sth

disposer [dispoze] **1** *vt* (**a**) *(objets, fleurs)* to arrange; *(table)* to lay, to set (**b**) **d. qn à (faire) qch** to dispose *or* incline sb to (do) sth **2** *vi* (**a**) *Sout* **vous pouvez d.** you may go (**b**) *(décider) Prov* **l'homme propose, Dieu dispose** man proposes, God disposes **3 disposer de** *vt ind* to have at one's disposal; **les renseignements dont je dispose** the information at my disposal; **le droit des peuples à d. d'eux-mêmes** the right of people to self-determination **4 se disposer** *vpr* **se d. à faire qch** to get ready to do sth

dispositif [dispozitif] *nm* (**a**) *(appareil)* device (**b**) *(ensemble de moyens)* system; **d. policier** police presence (**c**) *Ordinat* **d. d'alimentation** power unit; *(pour papier)* sheet feed; **d. d'alimentation papier** *(d'une imprimante)* sheet feed, paper feed

disposition [dispozisjɔ̃] *nf* (**a**) *(arrangement)* arrangement (**b**) *(disponibilité)* **à la d. de qn** at sb's disposal; **mettre qch à la d. de qn** to put sth at sb's disposal; **je suis** *ou* **je me tiens à votre d.** I am at your service (**c**) *(tendance)* tendency (**à** to) (**d**) *(intentions)* **être dans de bonnes/mauvaises dispositions** to be in a good/bad mood; **être dans de bonnes dispositions à l'égard de qn** to be favourably disposed towards sb (**e**) *(dons)* **avoir des dispositions pour qch** to have an aptitude for sth (**f**) **dispositions** *(préparatifs)* arrangements; **prendre des dispositions pour faire qch** to make arrangements to do sth; **prendre ses dispositions** to make arrangements (**g**) *Jur* **dispositions** *(d'une loi)* clauses

disproportion [disprɔpɔrsjɔ̃] *nf* disproportion (**entre** between)

disproportionné, -e [disprɔpɔrsjɔne] *adj* disproportionate (**par rapport à** to)

dispute [dispyt] *nf* quarrel, argument

disputé, -e [dispyte] *adj (question)* controversial; *(match)* hard-fought; **ce poste sera très d.** there will be a lot of competition for this post

disputer [dispyte] **1** *vt* (**a**) *(match)* to play; *(combat)* to fight (**b**) *(se battre pour)* **d. qch à qn** to fight with sb over sth (**c**) *Fam (réprimander)* to tell off; **se faire d.** to get told off **2 se disputer** *vpr* (**a**) *(se quereller)* to quarrel, to argue (**pour/avec** over/with) (**b**) *(avoir lieu)* **le match se disputera à Wimbledon** the match will be played at Wimbledon (**c**) *(se battre pour)* **se d. qch** to fight over sth

disquaire [diskɛr] *nmf* record dealer

disqualification [diskalifikasjɔ̃] *nf* disqualification

disqualifier [66] [diskalifje] *vt (sportif)* to disqualify

disque [disk] *nm* (**a**) *(enregistrement)* record; **mettre un d.** to play a record; **d. audionumérique** compact disc; **d. compact** compact disc, CD; **d. compact vidéo** video compact disc; **d. laser** laser disc; **d. vidéo numérique** digital video disc (**b**) *Ordinat* disc; **d. amovible** removable disk; **d. dur** hard disk; **d. fixe** fixed disk (**c**) *(cartilage)* disc (**d**) *(objet rond)* disc; **d. de stationnement** parking disc (**e**) *(en sport)* discus (**f**) *Tech* disc; **d. d'embrayage** clutch plate

disquette [diskɛt] *nf Ordinat* diskette, floppy (disk); **sur d.** on diskette, on floppy; **d. de démonstration,** *Fam* **d. démo** demo disk; **d. haute densité** high-density disk; **d. optique** optical disk, floptical disk

dissection [disɛksjɔ̃] *nf aussi Fig* dissection

dissemblable [disãblabl] *adj* dissimilar

dissémination [diseminasjɔ̃] *nf (de graines, de peuple)* scattering; *(de germes)* spreading

disséminer [disemine] **1** *vt (graines, peuple)* to scatter; *(germes)* to spread; **les écoles sont très disséminées** the schools are very thin on the ground
 2 se disséminer *vpr* to be scattered

dissension [disãsjɔ̃] *nf* dissension

disséquer [34] [diseke] *vt aussi Fig* to dissect

dissertation [disɛrtasjɔ̃] *nf* essay; **faire une d.** to write an essay

disserter [disɛrte] *vi (parler)* **d. sur qch** to discourse on sth, *Péj* to hold forth on sth; *(écrire)* to write about sth

dissidence [disidãs] *nf* dissidence; **la d.** *(les opposants)* the dissidents

dissident, -e [disidã, -ãt] **1** *adj (en politique)* dissident; *(en religion)* dissenting
 2 *nm,f (en politique)* dissident; *(en religion)* dissenter

dissimulateur, -trice [disimylatœr, -tris] **1** *adj* dissembling
 2 *nm,f* dissembler

dissimulation [disimylasjɔ̃] *nf* (**a**) *(hypocrisie)* dissembling, deceit; **agir avec d.** to act in an underhand way (**b**) *(des sentiments, de la vérité)* concealment

dissimuler [disimyle] **1** *vt* to cover up, to conceal; *(sujet: rideau)* to screen off; **d. qch à qn** to conceal sth from sb; **avec un plaisir non dissimulé** with unconcealed delight
 2 se dissimuler *vpr* to be hidden

dissipation [disipasjɔ̃] *nf* (**a**) *(de craintes, de soupçons)* dispelling; *(d'un malentendu)* clearing up; **après d. des brouillards matinaux** after the early fog has cleared (**b**) *(à l'école)* unruly behaviour (**c**) *Litt (débauche)* dissipation

dissipé, -e [disipe] *adj* (**a**) *(élève)* unruly (**b**) *Litt (débauche)* dissipated

dissiper [disipe] **1** *vt* (**a**) *(nuages)* to disperse; *(brouillard)* to clear; *(malentendu)* to clear up; *(craintes, soupçons)* to dispel (**b**) *(distraire)* to lead astray
 2 se dissiper *vpr* (**a**) *(nuages)* to disperse; *(brouillard)* to clear; *(craintes, soupçons)* to vanish (**b**) *(se laisser distraire)* to be unruly

dissociable [disɔsjabl] *adj* separable

dissocier [66] [disɔsje] **1** *vt* to separate
 2 se dissocier *vpr* **se d. de qch** to dissociate oneself from sth

dissolu, -e [disɔly] *adj Litt* dissolute

dissolution [disɔlysjɔ̃] *nf* (**a**) *(d'un parlement, d'un mariage)* dissolution; *(d'une association)* breaking up (**b**) *(dans un liquide)* dissolving

dissolvais *etc voir* **dissoudre**

dissolvant, -e [disɔlvã, -ãt] *adj & nm* (**produit**) **d.** solvent; *(pour ongles)* nail polish remover

dissonant, -e [disɔnã, -ãt] *adj (sons)* dissonant; *Fig* clashing

dissoudre [3a] [disudr] **1** *vt* (**a**) *(substance)* to dissolve (**b**) *(parlement, mariage)* to dissolve; *(association)* to break up
 2 se dissoudre *vpr (substance)* to dissolve; *(association)* to break up

dissuader [disɥade] *vt* **d. qn de faire qch** to dissuade sb from doing sth

dissuasif, -ive [disɥazif, -iv] *adj* deterrent; *(prix)* prohibitive; **avoir un effet d.** to be a deterrent

dissuasion [disɥazjɔ̃] *nf* dissuasion; *Mil* **force de d.** deterrent

dissymétrie [disimetri] *nf* asymmetry

distance [distãs] *nf* distance; **suivre qn à d.** to follow sb at a distance; **à quelle d. sommes-nous de la ville?** how far are we from the town?; **à une courte d. (de)** short distance away (from); **à d.** *(déclencher)* by remote control; *(rester, observer)* at a distance; *aussi Fig* **tenir qn à d.** to keep sb at a distance; **conserver** *ou* **garder ses distances, se tenir à d.** to hold oneself aloof; **prendre ses distances, prendre de la d.** to stand back; *Sport & Fig* **tenir la d.** to go the distance

distancer [16] [distãse] *vt aussi Fig* to outstrip, to outdistance; **se laisser d.** to fall *or* lag behind; **d. qn de deux points/de 10 mètres** to go two points/10 metres ahead of sb

distant, -e [distã, -ãt] *adj* (**a**) *(éloigné)* distant; **nos deux maisons sont distantes d'un kilomètre** our two houses are a kilometre apart (**b**) *Fig (froid)* distant, standoffish (**avec** with)

distendre [distãdr] **1** *vt (corde, élastique, vêtement)* to stretch; *(muscle)* to strain
 2 se distendre *vpr (corde, élastique, vêtement)* to stretch; *(muscle)* to slacken

distillation [distilasjɔ̃] *nf* distillation

distiller [distile] *vt* (**a**) *(alcool, pétrole)* to distil; **eau distillée** distilled water (**b**) *(poison)* to distil; *Fig (colère, ennui)* to exude

distillerie [distilri] *nf (lieu)* distillery; *(procédé)* distilling

distinct, -e [distɛ̃, -ɛ̃kt] *adj* (**a**) *(séparé)* distinct, separate (**de** from) (**b**) *(clair) (silhouette, voix)* distinct, clear

distinctement [distɛ̃ktəmã] *adv* distinctly, clearly

distinctif, -ive [distɛ̃ktif, -iv] *adj* distinctive

distinction [distɛ̃ksjɔ̃] *nf* (**a**) *(différence)* distinction; **faire une d. entre deux choses** to make a distinction between two things; **sans d.** without distinction, indiscriminately; **sans d. de race ou de couleur** regardless of race or colour (**b**) *(élégance)* distinction; **avoir de la d.** to be distinguished

distingué, -e [distɛ̃ge] *adj* distinguished

distinguer [distɛ̃ge] **1** *vt* (**a**) *(différencier)* to distinguish (**de** from); **il a appris à d. les champignons** he has learnt how to tell the various kinds of mushroom apart; **on peut à peine les d. l'un de l'autre** you can hardly tell them apart (**b**) *(discerner) (objet, silhouette)* to make out; *(personne)* to pick out; **d. une nuance d'amertume dans la voix de qn** to detect a trace of bitterness in sb's voice
 2 se distinguer *vpr* (**a**) *(s'illustrer)* to distinguish oneself (**par** by); **on ne peut vraiment pas dire qu'il se distingue par son intelligence** he hardly stands out as being very intelligent (**b**) *(se différencier)* **se d. de qn/qch (par)** to be distinguishable from sb/sth (by) (**c**) *(être perçu)* **au loin se distinguait la côte** the coastline could be made out in the distance

distinguo [distɛ̃go] *nm* distinction; **faire un d. entre** to make a distinction between

distordre [distɔrdr] *vt* to distort

distorsion [distɔrsjɔ̃] *nf* distortion; *(entre deux facteurs, deux salaires)* imbalance

distraction [distraksjɔ̃] *nf* (**a**) *(inattention)* absent-mindedness; **par d.** inadvertently, absent-mindedly (**b**) *(loisir)* activity; **ça manque de distractions, ici** there's nothing to do here

distraire [28] [distrɛr] **1** *vt* (**a**) *(détourner)* to distract (**de** from) (**b**) *(divertir)* to entertain, to amuse

2 se distraire *vpr (s'occuper)* to amuse oneself; *(se détendre)* to enjoy oneself

distrait, -e [distrɛ, -ɛt] *adj* (**a**) *(étourdi)* absent-minded; **d'un air d.** absent-mindedly (**b**) *(inattentif)* inattentive; **d'une oreille distraite** with only half an ear

distraitement [distrɛtmɑ̃] *adv* absent-mindedly

distrayais *etc voir* **distraire**

distrayant, -e [distrɛjɑ̃, -ɑ̃t] *adj* entertaining

distribuer [distribɥe] *vt* (**a**) *(donner) (prix, bonbons, provisions, vivres)* to distribute (**à** to); *(dividendes)* to pay (**à** to); *(cartes)* to deal (**à** to); *(courrier)* to deliver (**à** to); *(eau, gaz, électricité)* to supply (**à** to); *(sourires, compliments)* to bestow (**à** on); **d. des coups** to lash out with one's fists (**b**) *(répartir) (tâches)* to allocate; **d. les rôles** to cast a play (**c**) *(commercialiser)* to distribute

distributeur, -trice [distribytœr, -tris] **1** *nm,f Com* distributor; **d. agréé** authorized distributor **2** *nm (appareil)* (vending) machine; **d. (automatique) de billets** *Br* cash dispenser *or* machine, *Am* ATM; **d. (automatique) de boissons/de cigarettes** drinks/cigarette machine; **d. d'eau fraîche** water cooler

distribution [distribysjɔ̃] *nf* (**a**) *(remise)* distribution; *(de lettres, de marchandises)* delivery; **d. des prix** *(à l'école)* prizegiving (**b**) *(répartition) (de tâches)* allocation; *(d'une maison, d'un appartement)* layout; *(d'un film, d'une pièce) (action)* casting; *(acteurs)* cast (**c**) *Com* distribution; **grande d.** large-scale distribution (**d**) *(approvisionnement)* supply; **d. des eaux** water supply

district [distrikt] *nm* district

dit, -e [di, dit] **1** *pp de* **dire²** **2** *adj* (**a**) *(décidé)* **à l'heure dite** at the agreed time (**b**) *(appelé)* known as

dithyrambique [ditirɑ̃bik] *adj* eulogistic

diurétique [djyretik] *adj & nm* diuretic

diurne [djyrn] *adj* diurnal

diva [diva] *nf* diva

divagations [divagasjɔ̃] *nfpl* raving

divaguer [divage] *vi* to rave

divan [divɑ̃] *nm* divan, couch

divergence [divɛrʒɑ̃s] *nf (de lignes, de rayons)* divergence; *(d'opinions)* difference

divergent, -e [divɛrʒɑ̃, -ɑ̃t] *adj (lignes)* divergent; *(opinions)* differing

diverger [45] [divɛrʒe] *vi (opinions, lignes, rayons)* to diverge (**de** from)

divers, -e [divɛr, -ɛrs] *adj* (**a**) *(différents)* varied; **d.** *(rubrique)* miscellaneous (**b**) *(plusieurs)* various; **diverses solutions sont possibles** there are various possible solutions

diversement [divɛrsəmɑ̃] *adv* in various ways

diversification [divɛrsifikasjɔ̃] *nf* diversification

diversifier [66] [divɛrsifje] **1** *vt (économie, cultures, activités)* to diversify; *(intérêts, couleurs)* to vary **2 se diversifier** *vpr (entreprise, activités)* to diversify

diversion [divɛrsjɔ̃] *nf* diversion; **faire d.** to create a diversion

diversité [divɛrsite] *nf (variété)* variety, diversity

divertir [divɛrtir] **1** *vt (amuser)* to entertain, to amuse **2 se divertir** *vpr* to enjoy oneself; **se d. de qch** to laugh at sth

divertissant, -e [divɛrtisɑ̃, -ɑ̃t] *adj* amusing, entertaining

divertissement [divɛrtismɑ̃] *nm* entertainment, amusement

dividende [dividɑ̃d] *nm Math & Fin* dividend

divin, -e [divɛ̃, -in] *adj aussi Fig* divine; **le d. Enfant** the Holy Child

divinement [divinmɑ̃] *adv* divinely

divinité [divinite] *nf* (**a**) *(nature de Dieu)* divinity (**b**) *(dieu)* deity

diviser [divize] **1** *vt* (**a**) *(partager)* to divide (**en/entre** into/among); **d. 15 par 3** to divide 15 by 3 (**b**) *(opposer)* to divide; **l'opinion est divisée au sujet de cette affaire** opinion on the matter is divided; **d. pour mieux régner** divide and rule **2 se diviser** *vpr* to divide (**en** into); **l'examen se divise en trois parties** the examination is divided into three parts; **le chemin se divise en deux** the road divides *or* forks

diviseur [divizœr] *nm Math* divisor; **plus grand commun d.** highest common factor

divisible [divizibl] *adj* divisible

division [divizjɔ̃] *nf* (**a**) *(séparation) & Math* division (**en** into); **faire une d.** to do a division; *Biol* **d. cellulaire** cell division; **d. du travail** division of labour (**b**) *(partie)* part, section; *Mil* division; **d. blindée** armoured division (**c**) *(désaccord)* division

divisionnaire [divizjɔnɛr] **1** *adj* divisional **2** *nm* (**a**) *(commissaire) Br* ≃ chief superintendent, *Am* ≃ police chief (**b**) *Mil* major general

divorce [divɔrs] *nm* divorce; *Fig (désaccord)* gulf; **demander le d.** to ask for a divorce; **obtenir le d.** to get a divorce

divorcé, -e [divɔrse] **1** *adj* divorced **2** *nm,f* divorcee

divorcer [16] [divɔrse] *vi* to get divorced, to get a divorce; **d. d'avec** *ou* **de qn** to divorce sb

divulgation [divylgasjɔ̃] *nf* disclosure (**de** of)

divulguer [divylge] *vt* to divulge, to disclose

dix [dis] *adj & nm inv* ten; *voir aussi* **trois**

dix-huit [dizɥit] *adj & nm inv* eighteen; *voir aussi* **trois**

dix-huitième [dizɥitjɛm] *nmf, nm & adj* eighteenth; *voir aussi* **cinquième**

dixième [dizjɛm] *nmf, nm & adj* tenth; *voir aussi* **cinquième**

dixit [diksit] **d. Paul** so Paul says

dix-neuf [diznœf] *adj & nm inv* nineteen; *voir aussi* **trois**

dix-neuvième [diznœvjɛm] *nmf, nm & adj* nineteenth; *voir aussi* **cinquième**

dix-sept [dis(s)ɛt] *adj & nm inv* seventeen; *voir aussi* **trois**

dix-septième [dis(s)ɛtjɛm] *nmf, nm & adj* seventeenth; *voir aussi* **cinquième**

dizaine [dizɛn] *nf* **une d. (de)** about ten, ten or so; *Math* **la colonne des dizaines** the tens column

djeune [dʒœn] *Fam Ironique* **1** *adj* young and hip **2** *nmf* hip young person

Djibouti [dʒibuti] *n* Djibouti

do [do] *nm inv (note)* C; *(chantée)* doh

doberman [dɔbɛrman] *nm* doberman

docile [dɔsil] *adj (enfant, animal)* docile

docilement [dɔsilmɑ̃] *adv* docilely

docilité [dɔsilite] *nf* docility

dock [dɔk] *nm* (**a**) *(bassin)* dock (**b**) *(entrepôt)* warehouse

docker [dɔkɛr] *nm* docker

docte [dɔkt] *adj Litt* learned

docteur [dɔktœr] *nm* (**a**) *(médecin)* doctor (**b**) *Univ* **être d. ès lettres/ès sciences** ≃ to have a PhD in arts/science; **être d. en droit** ≃ to have an LLD **doctoral, -e, -aux, -ales** [dɔktɔral, -o] *adj Péj (air, ton)* pompous **doctorat** [dɔktɔra] *nm Univ* doctorate; **d. d'État** = highest postgraduate research degree; **d. de 3ᵉ cycle** ≃ PhD

doctoresse [dɔktɔrɛs] *nf Vieilli* lady doctor
doctrine [dɔktrin] *nf* doctrine
document [dɔkymɑ̃] *nm* document
documentaire [dɔkymɑ̃tɛr] *adj & nm* documentary
documentaliste [dɔkymɑ̃talist] *nmf (d'archives)* archivist; *(dans les écoles)* librarian
documentation [dɔkymɑ̃tasjɔ̃] *nf (action)* research; *(documents)* documentation (**sur** on)
documenté, -e [dɔkymɑ̃te] *adj (personne)* well-informed; *(étude, thèse)* documented
documenter [dɔkymɑ̃te] **se documenter** *vpr* to gather information *or* material (**sur** on)
dodeliner [dɔdɔline] *vi* **il dodelinait de la tête** his head kept nodding
dodo [dodo] *nm (langage enfantin)* **faire d.** to sleep; **aller au d.** to go to bye-byes
dodu, -e [dɔdy] *adj* plump, chubby
doge [dɔʒ] *nm Hist* doge
dogmatique [dɔgmatik] *adj* dogmatic
dogmatisme [dɔgmatism] *nm* dogmatism
dogme [dɔgm] *nm* dogma
dogue [dɔg] *nm* mastiff
doigt [dwa] *nm* (**a**) *(de la main)* finger; **d. de pied** toe; **le petit d.** the little finger; **lever le d.** *(en classe)* to put one's hand up; **porter une bague au d.** to wear a ring on one's finger; **faire signe à qn du d.** to beckon to sb; **être comme les (deux) doigts de la main** to be as thick as thieves; **on peut les compter sur les doigts de la main** you can count them on the fingers of one hand; *Fig* **se faire taper sur les doigts** to get a rap over the knuckles; **filer** *ou* **glisser entre les doigts de qn** to slip through sb's fingers; **vous avez mis le d. dessus** you've put your finger on it; **obéir à qn au d. et à l'œil** to obey sb blindly; **savoir qch sur le bout des doigts** to have sth at one's fingertips; **mon petit d. me l'a dit** a little bird told me; **avoir des doigts de fée** to have nimble fingers; *Fig* **ne pas lever ou bouger le petit d.** not to lift a finger; *Fam* **tu te mets le d. dans l'œil (jusqu'au coude)** you couldn't be more wrong; *Fam* **faire qch les doigts dans le nez** to do sth standing on one's head; *Fam* **gagner les doigts dans le nez** to win hands down (**b**) *(petite quantité) (d'alcool)* drop; **être à deux doigts de qch/de faire qch** to be within a hair's breadth of sth/of doing sth
doigté [dwate] *nm* (**a**) *Mus (d'un morceau de musique)* fingering (**b**) *Fig (adresse)* dexterity; *(tact)* tact
dois, doive *etc voir* **devoir²**
doléances [dɔleɑ̃s] *nfpl* complaints; **présenter ses doléances** to air one's grievances
dollar [dɔlar] *nm* dollar
dolmen [dɔlmɛn] *nm* dolmen
domaine [dɔmɛn] *nm* (**a**) *(propriété)* estate, property; **être du d. public** to be in the public domain; **d. skiable** skiing area (**b**) *(matière)* field, domain; **c'est du d. du possible** it's within the realms of possibility (**c**) *Ordinat* domain; **nom de d.** domain name
domanial, -e, -aux, -ales [dɔmanjal, -o] *adj* state-owned
dôme [dom] *nm Archit & Géog* dome

domestication [dɔmɛstikasjɔ̃] *nf* domestication
domestique [dɔmɛstik] **1** *adj (vie, soucis, querelle)* domestic; *(tâches, déchets)* household; **accidents domestiques** accidents in the home **2** *nmf* servant
domestiquer [dɔmɛstike] *vt (animal)* to domesticate; *(éléments)* to harness
domicile [dɔmisil] *nm* (place of) residence, home; **sans d. fixe** of no fixed abode; **travailler à d.** to work from home; **livrer à d.** to do home deliveries; *Jur* **d. conjugal** marital home
domicilié, -e [dɔmisilje] *adj* **d. à** resident at
dominant, -e [dɔminɑ̃, -ɑ̃t] **1** *adj (opinion)* prevailing; *(couleur, trait, idée)* dominant; *Biol* **caractère d.** dominant characteristic **2** *nf* **dominante** *(ce qui domine)* chief characteristic; **une tenue pâle, avec une dominante de rose** a pale, mainly pink outfit
dominateur, -trice [dɔminatœr, -tris] *adj (personne, ton, attitude)* domineering
domination [dɔminasjɔ̃] *nf* domination (**sur** over); **être sous la d. de qn** to be dominated by sb
dominer [dɔmine] **1** *vt* (**a**) *(assujettir) (personne)* to dominate; *(empire)* to rule over (**b**) *(surpasser) (adversaire, concurrent)* to surpass (**c**) *(prédominer dans)* to be the dominant feature of (**d**) *(maîtriser) (timidité, passions, larmes, sujet)* to master; *(paresse, envie)* to overcome; *(match)* to dominate; **d. la situation** to keep the situation under control (**e**) *(surplomber)* to dominate; **de leur terrasse, on domine la mer** their balcony overlooks the sea **2** *vi* (**a**) *(l'emporter)* to be dominant (**b**) *(prédominer)* to predominate **3** **se dominer** *vpr* to control oneself
dominicain, -e [dɔminikɛ̃, -ɛn] **1** *adj* Dominican **2** *nm,f* (**a**) *Rel* Dominican (**b**) *(de la République Dominicaine)* **D.** Dominican
dominical, -e, -aux, -ales [dɔminikal, -o] *adj* Sunday; **repos d.** day of rest; **ouverture dominicale des magasins** Sunday opening
Dominique [dɔminik] *nf* **la D.** Dominica
domino [dɔmino] *nm (plaquette)* domino; **jouer aux dominos** to play dominoes
dommage [dɔmaʒ] *nm* (**a**) *(préjudice)* harm; **causer un d. à qn** to do sb harm; **d. corporel** physical injury; **dommages et intérêts, dommages-intérêts** damages; **d. matériel** material damage (**b**) **dommages** *(dégâts matériels)* damage; *Mil* **dommages collatéraux** collateral damage (**c**) **(quel) d.!** what a pity!, what a shame!; **c'est (bien) d. qu'elle ne soit pas venue** it's a (great) pity that she didn't come (**d**) *Can* **beau d!** of course!, you bet!
dommageable [dɔmaʒabl] *adj* detrimental (**à** to)
dompter [dɔ̃(p)te] *vt (fauve, fleuve, nature)* to tame; *(sentiments, passions, personne)* to subdue
dompteur, -euse [dɔ̃(p)tœr, -øz] *nm,f* tamer
DOM-TOM [dɔmtɔm] *nmpl Anciennement (abrév* **départements et territoires d'outre-mer**) = French overseas "départements" and territories
don [dɔ̃] *nm* (**a**) *(cadeau)* gift; *(à un musée, une œuvre)* donation; **faire d. à qn de qch** to make a gift of sth to sb; **d. du sang/de sperme** blood/sperm donation; *Fig* **d. du ciel** godsend; **le d. de soi** self-sacrifice (**b**) *(aptitude)* gift, talent; *aussi Ironique* **avoir le d. de faire qch** to have a knack for doing sth
donateur, -trice [dɔnatœr, -tris] *nm,f* donor

donation [dɔnasjɔ̃] *nf* donation; *Jur* **d. entre vifs** donation inter vivos

donc [dɔ̃k] *conj* (**a**) *(marque la conséquence)* so (**b**) *(emphatique)* **tu le savais d. depuis le début?** so you knew from the start?; **que voulez-vous d.?** whatever do you want?; **mais taisez-vous d.!** do be quiet!; **allons d.!** come on! (**c**) *(après interruption ou digression)* **je disais d. que...** I was saying, then, that...

dondon [dɔ̃dɔ̃] *nf Fam Péj* **grosse d.** great fat lump

donf [dɔ̃f] **à donf** *adv Fam (vite) Br* like the clappers, *Am* like sixty; *(très fort)* at full blast; *(beaucoup)* really, like crazy

donjon [dɔ̃ʒɔ̃] *nm* keep

don Juan *(pl* **dons Juans**) [dɔ̃ʒɥɑ̃] *nm* Don Juan

donne [dɔn] *nf (aux cartes)* deal

donné, -e¹ [dɔne] *adj* (**a**) *(offert)* given; *Fam* **c'est d.** it's dirt cheap; *Fam* **ce n'est pas d.** it doesn't come cheap (**b**) *(défini)* given; **à un moment d.** *(dans le passé)* at one point; *(dans le futur)* at some point; **étant d. la situation** given the situation; **étant d. que...** seeing that...

donnée² [dɔne] *nf* (**a**) *(élément)* piece of information; **avoir toutes les données du problème** to have all the data *or* information on the problem (**b**) *Ordinat* **données** data; **données numériques** digital data

donner [dɔne] **1** *vt* (**a**) *(offrir, distribuer)* to give; **d. qch à qn** to give sth to sb, to give sb sth; **d. à boire à qn** to give sb something to drink; **d. à manger à** *(animal)* to feed; **c'est à qui de d.?** *(aux cartes)* whose deal is it? (**b**) *(faire don de) (temps, vie)* to give; *(corps, organe)* to donate; **d. son sang** to give blood (**c**) *(céder)* to give; *Fam (dénoncer)* to grass on (**à** to); **en d. à qn pour son argent** to give sb his/her money's worth (**d**) *(payer)* **je lui donne 15 euros de l'heure** I pay him/her 15 euros an hour; **je vous en donne 10 euros** I'll give you 10 euros for it (**e**) *(confier)* **d. qch à garder à qn** to give sb sth to look after; **d. un vêtement à nettoyer** to hand in a garment to be dry-cleaned (**f**) *(avis, ordre, conseil)* to give; **d. l'heure à qn** to tell sb the time; **tu lui donneras le bonjour de ma part** say hello to him/her for me; **d. des** *ou* **de ses nouvelles à qn** to keep in touch with sb (**g**) *(chance, délai, occasion)* to give; **je vous donne une semaine, pas plus** I'll give you a week and no more (**h**) *(causer)* **d. de l'appétit à qn** to give sb an appetite; **d. des boutons à qn** to bring sb out in a rash; **d. mal à la tête à qn** to give sb a headache; **d. faim/sommeil/chaud à qn** to make sb hungry/sleepy/hot; **d. du souci à qn** to cause sb worry; **toute cette histoire m'a donné à réfléchir** the whole business made me think again (**i**) *(produire) (récoltes)* to yield; *(fruits)* to bear; **les blés vont d. cette année** there will be a good crop of wheat this year; **ça n'a rien donné** nothing came of it; **qu'est-ce que ça donne?** *(comment ça se présente?)* how does it look? (**j**) *(administrer)* to give; **d. un baiser/une gifle à qn** to give sb a kiss/a slap in the face; **tu peux d. un coup de balai dans la cuisine?** can you give the kitchen a sweep? (**k**) *(bal, dîner, conférence)* to give; *(pièce de théâtre)* to put on, to perform; **qu'est-ce qu'on donne au cinéma?** *Br* what's on at the cinema?, *Am* what's playing at the movies?

(**l**) *(attribuer)* **je lui donne vingt ans** I'd say he's/she's twenty; **les médecins lui donnent deux jours (à vivre)** the doctors give him/her two days (to live) (**m**) *(maladie)* to give

2 *vi (cogner)* **d. de la tête contre qch** to hit one's head against sth; *Fig* **je ne savais pas où d. de la tête** I didn't know where to start

3 *v impersonnel* **le spectacle le plus épouvantable qu'il m'ait été donné de voir** the most horrifying sight I've ever been unfortunate enough to witness; **il n'est pas donné à tout le monde d'être écrivain** not everyone can be a writer

4 **donner dans** *vt ind* (**a**) *(tomber)* **d. dans le piège** *ou* **le panneau** to fall into the trap (**b**) *(avoir un penchant pour)* to have a tendency for **5** **donner sur** *vt ind (sujet: fenêtre)* to look onto; *(sujet: porte)* to lead into **6** **se donner** *vpr* (**a**) *(faire don de soi)* to give of oneself; **se d. à qch** to devote oneself to sth; **se d. en spectacle** to make an exhibition of oneself (**b**) *(à soi-même)* **se d. un coup de peigne/brosse** to give one's hair a quick comb/brush; **se d. un coup de marteau sur le pouce** to hit one's thumb with a hammer; **se d. le temps de réfléchir** to give oneself time to think; **se d. pour tâche de faire qch** to set oneself the task of doing sth (**c**) *Litt (sexuellement)* to give oneself (**à** to) (**d**) *(l'un l'autre)* **se d. des coups** to exchange blows; **se d. des baisers** to kiss (each other)

donneur, -euse [dɔnœr, -øz] *nm,f* (**a**) *(d'organe)* donor; **d. de sang/de sperme** blood/sperm donor (**b**) *(aux cartes)* dealer

dont [dɔ̃] *pron relatif* (**a**) *(introduit le complément du verbe)* **la famille d. je descends** the family I'm descended from; **la façon d. il me regardait** the way (in which) he looked at me; **le livre d. j'ai besoin** the book (that) I need; **un groupe d. on parle beaucoup** a band that is being talked about a lot; **l'homme d. elle se moque** the man she's making fun of (**b**) *(introduit le complément du nom)* **la dame d. je connais le fils** the woman whose son I know; **la maison d. on voit le toit** the house whose roof can be seen; **un livre d. voici le résumé** a book of which this is a summary; **quelques-uns d. votre frère** there were a few people here, including your brother (**c**) *(introduit le complément de l'adjectif)* **la femme d. il est amoureux** the woman he is in love with; **le groupe d'enfants d. vous êtes responsable** the group of children you are responsible for; **le souvenir d. elle est si honteuse** the memory she is so ashamed of

dopage [dɔpaʒ] *nm* doping; *(de sportif)* drug-taking

doper [dɔpe] **1** *vt (droguer)* to dope **2 se doper** *vpr* to take drugs

dorade [dɔrad] *nf* sea bream

doré, -e [dɔre] **1** *adj* (**a**) *(recouvert d'or)* gilded, gilt; **d. sur tranche** gilt-edged (**b**) *(couleur d'or) (blé, lumière, peau, cheveux)* golden; *(gâteau passé au jaune d'œuf)* glazed; *(viande, pommes de terre, gâteau cuit)* browned **2** *nm Can (poisson)* wall-eyed pike, yellow pike

dorénavant [dɔrenavɑ̃] *adv* from now on

dorer [dɔre] **1** *vt* (**a**) *(recouvrir d'or)* to gild; *Fig* **d. la pilule à qn** to sweeten the pill for sb (**b**) *(donner une couleur dorée à) (peau)* to turn golden; *(gâteau)* to glaze; *(viande, pommes de terre)* to brown **2** *vi (plat, gâteau)* to brown

3 se dorer *vpr* **se d. au soleil** to sunbathe; *Fig* **se d. la pilule** to catch some rays

dorloter [dɔrlɔte] *vt* to pamper, to coddle

dormant, -e [dɔrmɑ̃, -ɑ̃t] **1** *adj* **eaux dormantes** stagnant water
2 *nm Can Rail Br* sleeper, *Am* tie

dormeur, -euse [dɔrmœr, -øz] *nm,f (personne endormie)* sleeper; **être un gros d.** to need a lot of sleep

dormir [29] [dɔrmir] *vi* (**a**) *(sommeiller)* to sleep; **elle dort** she's sleeping, she's asleep; **d. profondément** to be fast asleep; **je n'ai pas dormi de la nuit** I didn't sleep a wink (all night); **le café m'empêche de d.** coffee keeps me awake; *Fam* **ce n'est pas ça qui va m'empêcher de d.** I won't lose any sleep over it; **d. à poings fermés, d. comme un loir** to sleep like a log; **ne d. que d'un œil** to sleep with one eye open; **vous pouvez d. tranquille** *ou* **sur vos deux oreil-les** you can rest easy; **avoir envie de d.** to be *or* feel sleepy; **d. debout** to be asleep on one's feet; *Prov* **qui dort, dîne** he who sleeps forgets his hunger (**b**) *Fig (ville, forêt)* to be sleeping; *(capitaux)* to lie idle

dorsal, -e, -aux, -ales [dɔrsal, -o] *adj* dorsal

dortoir [dɔrtwar] *nm* dormitory

dorure [dɔryr] *nf* (**a**) *(couche d'or)* gilding (**b**) *(ornement)* gilt

doryphore [dɔrifɔr] *nm* Colorado beetle

DOS [dɔs] *nm Ordinat* DOS

dos [do] *nm* (**a**) *(d'une personne, d'un animal)* back; **sur le d.** on one's back; **je n'ai rien à me mettre sur le d.** I haven't a thing to wear; **à d. d'âne** on a donkey; **je ne l'ai vu que de d.** I only saw him from the back; **d. à d.** back to back; **faire le gros d.** *(chat)* to arch its back; **faire qch derrière** *ou* **dans le d. de qn** to do sth behind sb's back; *Fam* **je l'ai tout le temps sur le d.** he's/she's always on my back; **s'enrichir sur le d. de qn** to get rich off sb; **avoir bon d.** *(personne)* to have a broad back; **elle a bon d., la grève des postes, dis plutôt que tu n'as pas écrit** why don't you admit you haven't written instead of blaming it on the postal strike?; *Fam* **en avoir plein le d.** to be sick of it, to be fed up with it; **se mettre qn à d.** to get sb's back up; **tourner le d. à qn** *(debout)* to stand with one's back to sb; *(assis)* to sit with one's back to sb; *(volontairement)* to turn one's back on sb; **dès qu'il a le d. tourné** as soon as his back is turned (**b**) *(d'une chaise, d'une page, d'un chèque, de la main)* back; *(d'un livre)* spine; **voir au d.** (please) turn over, PTO (**c**) **d. (crawlé)** backstroke

dosage [dozaʒ] *nm (d'ingrédients)* proportioning; *(de médicaments)* dosage

dos-d'âne [dodan] *nm inv* bump; **pont en d.** humpbacked bridge

dose [doz] *nf (d'un élément dans un mélange)* proportion; *(de médicament)* dose; *Fig* **à petites doses** in small doses; *Fam* **il faut une sacrée d. de culot pour faire cela** it takes a hell of a nerve to do that; **forcer la d.** to overdo it; *Fam* **avoir sa d. (de qch)** to have had more than enough (of sth)

doser [doze] *vt (médicament, ingrédient)* to measure out

doseur [dozœr] *nm* measure

dossard [dosar] *nm* number *(worn by competitor)*

dossier [dosje] *nm* (**a**) *(d'un siège)* back (**b**) *(documents)* file, dossier; *(d'un prisonnier, d'un malade, d'un élève)* record; *(chemise)* folder, file; *Ordinat (répertoire)* folder; *(fichier)* file; **constituer un d. sur**

qn/qch to build up a file on sb/sth; *Ordinat* **d. système** system folder (**c**) *Fig (sujet)* question

dot [dɔt] *nf* dowry

dotation [dɔtasjɔ̃] *nf (fonds) (d'hôpital, de collège)* endowment; *(versés à un chef d'État)* allowance

doter [dɔte] *vt (équiper)* to equip (**de** with); **elle est dotée d'une intelligence remarquable** she is endowed with great intelligence

douairière [dwɛrjɛr] *adj & nf* dowager

douane [dwan] *nf* customs; **passer à la d.** to go through customs; **droits de d.** customs duty

douanier, -ère [dwanje, -ɛr] **1** *adj* customs; **union douanière** customs union; **barrières douanières** tariff barriers
2 *nm* customs officer

doublage [dublaʒ] *nm* (**a**) *(d'un vêtement)* lining (**b**) *(d'un film, d'une voix)* dubbing; *(par une doublure)* doubling

double [dubl] **1** *adj* (**a**) *(quantité, lit, chambre)* double; **en d. exemplaire** in duplicate; **fermer une porte à d. tour** to double-lock a door; **avoir la d. nationalité** to have dual nationality; *Mus* **d. croche** *Br* semiquaver, *Am* sixteenth note; *Ordinat* **d. densité** double density; **d. mètre** 2-metre rule; **d. vitrage** double glazing (**b**) *(ambigu)* **mener une d. vie** to lead a double life; **mot à d. sens** ambiguous word
2 *adv* double
3 *nm* (**a**) **le d. (de)** *(quantité, prix)* twice as much (as); *(nombre)* twice as many (as); **dix est le d. de cinq** ten is two times five; **mettre qch en d.** to fold sth in two *or* half (**b**) *(exemplaire)* duplicate, copy; *(d'une clef)* duplicate; *Ordinat* backup; **avoir qch en d.** to have two of sth; *(lettre, devoir)* to make two copies of sth (**c**) *(personne)* double (**d**) *(au tennis)* **d. messieurs/dames/mixte** men's/ladies'/mixed doubles

doublé, -e [duble] **1** *adj* (**a**) *(veste, gants)* lined (**de** with) (**b**) *(film)* dubbed
2 *nm (victoires)* double

double-clic *(pl* **doubles-clics)** [dubləklik] *nm Ordinat* double-click; **faire un d. (sur)** to double-click (on)

double-cliquer [dubləklike] *vi Ordinat* to double-click

doublement¹ [dubləmɑ̃] *adv* doubly

doublement² *nm (d'un nombre, d'une somme, d'une lettre)* doubling

doubler [duble] **1** *vt* (**a**) *(multiplier par deux)* to double (**b**) *(plier)* to fold in two *or* in half (**c**) *(vêtement)* to line (**d**) *(film, voix)* to dub; *(sujet: acteur)* to dub the voice of; *(sujet: cascadeur)* to stand in for (**e**) *(passer) (véhicule) Br* to overtake, *Am* to pass (**f**) *Fam (trahir)* to double-cross
2 *vi* (**a**) *(population, salaire)* to double; **d. de valeur** to double in value (**b**) *(véhicule) Br* to overtake, *Am* to pass
3 se doubler *vpr* **se doubler de** to be coupled with

doublure [dublyr] *nf* (**a**) *(d'un vêtement, d'un sac)* lining (**b**) *(au théâtre)* understudy; *(au cinéma)* stand-in

douce [dus] *voir* **doux**

douceâtre [dusɑtr] *adj (saveur)* sickly sweet; *(ton)* smarmy

doucement [dusmɑ̃] *adv (délicatement)* gently; *(bas)* softly; **allez-y d.!** gently does it!; *Fam* **(allez-y) d. avec le vin!** go easy on the wine!

doucereux, -euse [dusrø, -øz] *adj (personne, voix, ton)* smarmy

douceur [dusœr] *nf* (**a**) *(d'un son, d'une matière)* softness; *(d'un climat)* mildness; *(du miel, d'un parfum)* sweetness (**b**) *(de caractère)* gentleness; *(d'un sourire)* sweetness; **traiter qn avec d.** to treat sb gently; **en d.** gently; **la voiture a démarré en d.** the car started smoothly (**c**) **douceurs** *(sucreries) Br* sweets, *Am* candy

douche [duʃ] *nf* shower; **prendre une d.** to have *or* take a shower; *Fig* **avec lui, c'est la d. écossaise** you never know where you are with him; *Fig* **d. froide** terrible disappointment

doucher [duʃe] **1** *vt (pour laver)* **d. qn** to give sb a shower
  2 se doucher *vpr* to have *or* take a shower

doudoune [dudun] *nf (anorak)* padded jacket

doué, -e [dwe] *adj* gifted, talented; **être d. pour** to have a gift for

douille [duj] *nf (d'une ampoule)* lamp socket; *(d'une cartouche)* case

douillet, -ette [dujɛ, -ɛt] *adj* (**a**) *(lit)* cosy (**b**) *(délicat)* **ne sois pas si d.!** don't be such a baby!

douillettement [dujɛtmɑ̃] *adv (confortablement)* cosily

douleur [dulœr] *nf (physique)* pain; *(diffuse)* ache; *(morale)* sorrow, grief; **nous avons la d. de vous faire part de...** we regret to inform you of...; *Fam* **j'ai compris ma d.** my worst fears came true

douloureux, -euse [dulurø, -øz] *adj* (**a**) *(coup, maladie, opération)* painful; *(au contact)* sore, tender; **mon dos est d.** my back is sore *or* aching (**b**) *(perte, événement)* sad; *(séparation, circonstances)* painful

doute [dut] *nm* (**a**) *(incertitude)* doubt; **être dans le d. (au sujet de qch)** to be doubtful (about sth); **mettre qch en d.** to question sth, to cast doubt on sth; **mettre en d. la parole de qn** to doubt sb's word; **il n'y a pas de** *ou* **aucun d.** there's no doubt about it; **sans d.** no doubt, probably; **sans aucun d.** without (any) doubt (**b**) *(soupçon)* doubt; **avoir des doutes sur** *ou* **au sujet de qn/qch** to have doubts about sb/sth

douter [dute] **1** *vi* to doubt; **d. de qn/qch** to doubt sb/sth; **elle ne doute de rien** she isn't backward in coming forward; **j'en doute** I doubt it
  2 *vt* **je doute qu'il soit assez fort** I doubt whether he's strong enough; **je n'ai jamais douté que tu viendrais** I never doubted that you'd come
  3 se douter *vpr* **se d. de qch** to suspect sth; **je m'en doutais (bien)** I thought as much; *Fam* **on s'en serait douté!** I might have known!

douteux, -euse [dutø, -øz] *adj* (**a**) *(incertain)* doubtful (**b**) *(suspect)* dubious; **d'un goût d.** *(plaisanteries, vêtements)* in dubious taste; **vêtements d.** *ou* **d'une propreté douteuse** clothes that are not too clean

douve [duv] *nf (d'un château)* moat

Douvres [duvr] *n* Dover

doux, douce [du, dus] **1** *adj* (**a**) *(au toucher)* soft; *(au goût)* mild (**b**) *(couleur, son, lumière)* soft; *(climat, hiver, tabac)* mild; *(vin, cidre)* sweet; *(pente)* gentle; **les médecines douces** alternative medicine (**c**) *(nature, regard, voix)* gentle; **faire les yeux d. à qn** to make eyes at sb; **d. comme un agneau** as gentle as a lamb
  2 *adv Fam* **filer d.** to toe the line
  3 *nf* **douce** *Fam* **en douce** on the quiet

douzaine [duzɛn] *nf* **une d. (de)** *(environ)* around a dozen, a dozen or so; **trois douzaines d'œufs** three dozen eggs

douze [duz] *adj & nm inv* twelve; *voir aussi* **trois**

douzième [duzjɛm] *nmf, nm & adj* twelfth; *voir aussi* **cinquième**

doyen, -enne [dwajɛ̃, -ɛn] *nm,f* (**a**) *(personne la plus âgée)* most senior member (**b**) *(d'une faculté)* dean

drachme [drakm] *nf Anciennement* drachma

draconien, -enne [drakɔnjɛ̃, -ɛn] *adj* draconian

dragage [dragaʒ] *nm (nettoyage)* dredging

dragée [draʒe] *nf (confiserie)* sugared almond; *(médicament)* sugar-coated pill

dragon [dragɔ̃] *nm* (**a**) *(animal mythologique, femme acariâtre)* dragon (**b**) *(soldat)* dragoon

drague [drag] *nf* (**a**) *(pour nettoyer)* dredge (**b**) *Fam (flirt)* **ce mec-là, c'est un pro de la d.** that guy's a real pro at *Br* chatting up *or Am* hitting on women; **c'est un lieu de d. idéal** it's an ideal place for *Br* chatting people up *or Am* hitting on people

draguer [drage] **1** *vt* (**a**) *(nettoyer)* to dredge (**b**) *Fam (hommes, femmes) Br* to chat up, *Am* to hit on
  2 *vi Fam* to be *Br* on the pull *or Am* on the make

dragueur, -euse [dragœr, -øz] **1** *nm (bateau)* dredger; **d. de mines** minesweeper
  2 *nm,f Fam* **c'est un d.** he's always *Br* on the pull or *Am* on the make; **sa sœur est une sacrée dragueuse** his/her sister's always chasing after men
  3 *adj* **il n'a jamais été très d.** he's never been for *Br* chatting up *or Am* hitting on women

drain [drɛ̃] *nm* (**a**) *(conduit)* drain (**b**) *Méd* drainage tube

drainage [drɛnaʒ] *nm (d'un champ, d'une plaie)* draining

drainer [drene] *vt (sol, abcès)* to drain

dramatique [dramatik] **1** *adj* (**a**) *(de théâtre)* dramatic; **auteur d.** playwright (**b**) *(grave)* tragic
  2 *nf* TV drama

dramatiser [dramatize] *vt* to dramatize

dramaturge [dramatyrʒ] *nm* dramatist, playwright

drame [dram] *nm* (**a**) *(genre littéraire, pièce)* drama (**b**) *Fig* tragedy; **faire un d. de qch** to make a drama out of sth

drap [dra] *nm* (**a**) *(linge)* **d. (de lit)** sheet; **d. de dessous/dessus** bottom/top sheet; *Fig* **être dans de beaux draps** to be in a real mess; **d. de bain** bath sheet (**b**) *(tissu)* cloth (**c**) *Belg (serviette)* towel

drapeau, -x [drapo] *nm* flag; *Fig* **être sous les drapeaux** to serve in the armed forces; **d. blanc** white flag; **d. tricolore** tricolour

draper [drape] **1** *vt (étoffe)* to drape
  2 se draper *vpr* **se d. dans** to drape oneself in; *Fig* **se d. dans sa dignité** to stand on one's dignity

draperie [drapri] *nf (tenture)* drapery

drap-housse (*pl* **draps-housses**) [draus] *nm* fitted sheet

drapier, -ère [drapje, -ɛr] **1** *nm,f (marchand)* draper; *(fabricant)* cloth manufacturer
  2 *adj* cloth

drastique [drastik] *adj* drastic

drave [drav] *nf Can (de rondins)* drive

draver [drave] *vt Can (rondins)* to float, to drive

draveur [dravœr] *nm Can* driver, raftsman

Dresde [drɛzd] *n* Dresden

dressage [drɛsaʒ] *nm (d'un animal de cirque)* training; *(d'un animal sauvage)* breaking in; *(d'un cheval de parade)* dressage

dresser [drese] **1** *vt* (**a**) *(élever)* to put up, to erect; **d. la tête** to raise *or* lift one's head; *(pour regarder)* to look up; **d. les oreilles** *(animal)* to prick up its ears; *Fig* **d. l'oreille** to prick up one's ears (**b**) *(plan, rapport, liste)*

to prepare, to draw up (**c**) *(animal de cirque)* to train (**à faire qch** to do sth); *(cheval sauvage)* to break in; *Fam* **ça va le d.!** that'll put him in his place! (**d**) *(exciter)* **d. qn contre qn** to set sb against sb
2 se dresser *vpr* (**a**) *(se lever)* to stand up, to rise (**b**) *(monument)* to stand; *(montagne)* to rise up; *Fig* **les obstacles qui se dressent sur notre chemin** the obstacles that stand in our way
dresseur, -euse [drɛsœr, -øz] *nmf (d'animaux de cirque)* trainer; *(de chevaux sauvages)* horsebreaker
DRH [deɛraʃ] **1** *nf (abrév* **direction des ressources humaines**) human resources department
2 *nmf (abrév* **directeur, -trice des ressources humaines**) human resources manager
dribble [dribl] *nm Sport* dribble
dribbler [drible] *Sport* **1** *vi* to dribble
2 *vt (joueur)* to dribble round
drille [drij] *nm Fam* **c'est un joyeux d.** he's always good for a laugh
drogue [drɔg] *nf* (**a**) *(stupéfiant)* drug; **d. dure/douce** hard/soft drug; **la d.** *(usage)* drug-taking, drugs (**b**) *Vieilli (médicament)* medicine
drogué, -e [drɔge] *nm,f* drug addict
droguer [drɔge] **1** *vt* (**a**) *(victime)* to drug; *(cheval)* to dope (**b**) *(malade)* to dose with drugs
2 se droguer *vpr* to take drugs; **se d. à qch** to be on sth
droguerie [drɔgri] *nf* hardware store
droguiste [drɔgist] *nmf* hardware dealer
droit¹, -e [drwa, drwat] **1** *adj* (**a**) *(rectiligne, vertical)* straight; **se tenir d.** *(debout)* to stand (up) straight; *(assis)* to sit (up) straight; **d. comme un i** *ou* **un piquet** poker-straight (**b**) *(honnête)* upright
2 *nf* **droite** straight line
3 *adv* **écrire/marcher d.** to write/walk straight; **aller d. devant soi** to go straight ahead; **aller d. au but** to get to the point; **aller d. à la catastrophe** to be heading straight for disaster; **c'est tout d.** it's straight ahead
droit², -e 1 *adj (main, jambe, gant)* right; **du côté d.** on the right-hand side
2 *nf* **droite** (**a**) *(côté)* right; **tourner à droite** to turn (to the) right; **rouler à droite** to drive on the right; **le placard de droite** the right-hand cupboard, the cupboard on the right; **à ma droite, le château** to *or* on my right is the castle; *Fig* **courir à droite et à gauche** to run about all over the place (**b**) *Pol* **la droite** the right (wing); **de droite** *(candidat, journal)* right-wing; **voter à droite** to vote for the right
droit³ *nm* (**a**) *(prérogative)* right; **avoir d. à qch** to have a right to sth; **avoir le d. de faire qch** to have the right to do sth; **donner d. à qch à qn** *(carte, abonnement)* to entitle sb to sth; **être dans son (bon) d.** to be within one's rights; **avoir des droits sur qn/qch** to have rights over sb/sth; **tous droits (de reproduction) réservés** *(sur livre)* all rights reserved; **de quel d. me critiques-tu?** what gives you the right to criticize me?; **d. d'aînesse** birthright; **d. d'asile** right of asylum; **avoir un d. de regard sur qch** to have the right to know about sth; **d. de réponse** right of reply; **d. de visite** *(d'un parent)* visiting rights; **d. de vote** right to vote; **les droits de l'homme** human rights (**b**) *(en argent)* fee; *(imposition)* duty; *(taxe)* tax; **droits d'auteur** royalties; **droits de douane** (customs) duty; **d. d'entrée** admission fee; **droits d'inscription** registration fee; **droits de succession** death duties; **d. de timbre** stamp duty (**c**) *Jur* law;

faire son d. to study *or* read law; **d. administratif** administrative law; **d. des affaires** business law; **d. canon** canon law; **d. civil** civil law; **d. commercial** commercial law; **d. commun** common law; **d. communautaire** Community law; **d. constitutionnel** constitutional law; **d. international** international law; **d. pénal** criminal law; **d. privé** private law; **d. public** public law; **d. du travail** labour laws
droitier, -ère [drwatje, -ɛr] **1** *adj* right-handed
2 *nm,f* right-handed person
droiture [drwatyr] *nf* rectitude
drôle [drol] *adj* (**a**) *(amusant)* funny (**b**) *(étrange)* funny; **un d. de type** a funny sort; **faire une d. de tête** to pull a face; *Fam* **ça me fait tout d. de te voir ici** it feels really funny seeing you here (**c**) *Fam (en intensif)* **il faut un d. de courage pour faire ça** you need a hell of a lot of courage to do that; **j'ai eu une d. de grippe!** I had a bad case of flu
drôlement [drolmɑ̃] *adv* funnily; *Fam (très)* really; *Fam* **les prix ont d. augmenté** prices have gone up an awful lot; *Fam* **elle est d. bien** *(remarquable)* she's a terrific person; *(belle)* she's great-looking
drôlerie [drolri] *nf* funniness
DROM [drom] *nm (abrév* **Département et Région d'outre-mer**) = French overseas "département" and region

---
DROM

The acronym "DROM" replaced the acronym "DOM" in 2003 *(see also entries* **DOM-TOM** *and* **COM**). The "départements et régions d'outre-mer" are Guadeloupe, Martinique, Guiana and La Réunion.

---

dromadaire [drɔmadɛr] *nm* dromedary
dru, -e [dry] **1** *adj (herbe, blé, cheveux, barbe)* thick; *(pluie)* heavy
2 *adv* **pousser d.** to grow thickly; **tomber d.** *(pluie)* to fall heavily
druide [drɥid] *nm* druid
DST [deɛste] *nf (abrév* **Direction de la surveillance du territoire**) = French Secret Service
DTP [detepe] *nm Méd (abrév* **diphtérie, tétanos, polio**) diphtheria, tetanus and polio vaccination
du [dy] *voir* **de**
dû, due *(mpl* dus, *fpl* dues) [dy] **1** *pp de* devoir²
2 *adj* (**a**) *(que l'on doit)* due, owed; **en port dû** carriage forward (**b**) *(causé)* **être dû à qch** to be due to sth (**c**) **en bonne et due forme** in due form
3 *nm* due
dualisme [dɥalism] *nm* dualism
dualité [dɥalite] *nf* duality
dubitatif, -ive [dybitatif, -iv] *adj* doubtful
Dublin [dyblɛ̃] *n* Dublin
dublinois, -e [dyblinwa, -az] **1** *adj* of Dublin
2 *nm,f* **D.** Dubliner
duc [dyk] *nm* duke
ducal, -e, -aux, -ales [dykal, -o] *adj* ducal
duché [dyʃe] *nm* duchy
duchesse [dyʃɛs] *nf (femme)* duchess
due *voir* dû
duel [dɥɛl] *nm* duel; **se battre en d.** to fight a duel
dulcinée [dylsine] *nf Litt ou Hum* ladylove
dûment [dymɑ̃] *adv* duly
dumping [dœmpiŋ] *nm* dumping; **faire du d.** to dump
dune [dyn] *nf* dune
Dunkerque [dœ̃kɛrk] *n* Dunkirk

duo [dɥo] *nm* (*chanson*) duet; (*de comiques, de musiciens*) duo
duodénum [dɥɔdenɔm] *nm* duodenum
dupe [dyp] **1** *nf* dupe
 2 *adj* **être d. (de)** to be taken in (by)
duper [dype] *vt* to dupe, to fool
duperie [dypri] *nf* deception
duplex [dyplɛks] *nm* (**a**) (**émission en**) **d.** link-up (**b**) (*appartement*) *Br* maisonette, *Am* duplex
duplicata [dyplikata] *nm* duplicate
duplication [dyplikasjɔ̃] *nf* (**a**) *Biol* doubling (**b**) *Ordinat* **d. de logiciel** software copying
duplicité [dyplisite] *nf* duplicity
duquel [dykɛl] *voir* **lequel**
dur, -e [dyr] **1** *adj* (**a**) (*rigide*) hard; (*viande*) tough; (*pain*) stale (**b**) (*difficile, pénible*) (*travail, hiver*) hard; (*scène, film*) distressing (**c**) (*sévère, cruel*) harsh (**avec** with) (**d**) *Fam* **être d. de la feuille** to be hard of hearing
 2 *nm,f Fam* (*personne*) tough type; *Pol* hard liner; **un d. à cuire** a tough nut; **jouer les durs** to act tough
 3 *nm* permanent building
 4 *nf Fam* **élever qn à la dure** to bring sb up the hard way
 5 *adv* (*travailler*) hard
durable [dyrabl] *adj* lasting
durablement [dyrabləmɑ̃] *adv* for a long time
duraille [dyraj] *adj Fam* hard
durant [dyrɑ̃] *prép* **d. le mois de mai** during May; **d. plusieurs années** for several years; **d. toute sa vie, sa vie d.** throughout his/her life; **parler des heures d.** to talk for hours on end
durcir [dyrsir] **1** *vt aussi Fig* to harden
 2 *vi* to harden
 3 se durcir *vpr aussi Fig* to harden
durcissement [dyrsismɑ̃] *nm aussi Fig* hardening
durée [dyre] *nf* (*d'un règne, d'une guerre, d'un séjour*) duration, length; (*d'une note*) length, value; **de courte d.** (*bonheur, soulagement*) short-lived; **d. de connexion** (*sur Internet*) on-line time; **d. de projec-**tion** (*d'un film*) running time; **d. de validité** (*d'un billet*) period of validity; **d. de vie** (*de personne*) life span; (*d'une pile*) life; (*d'une machine*) useful life; **d. de vol** flight time
durement [dyrmɑ̃] *adv* (*répondre, parler*) harshly; **d. éprouvé** sorely tried
durer [dyre] *vi* to last; **voilà trois ans que cela dure** it's been going on for three years; **ça ne peut pas d.** this can't go on; *Hum* **faire d. le plaisir** to prolong the agony
dureté [dyrte] *nf* (**a**) (*rigidité*) hardness; (*d'une viande*) toughness (**b**) (*d'un hiver*) severity (**c**) (*cruauté*) harshness; **parler avec d.** to speak harshly
durillon [dyrijɔ̃] *nm* (*de la main*) callus; (*du pied*) corn
Durit® [dyrit] *nf* flexible pipe; *Fam* **péter une D.** to hit the *Br* roof *or Am* ceiling
DUT [deyte] *nm* (*abrév* **diplôme universitaire de technologie**) = post-baccalauréat technical qualification awarded after two years
duvet [dyvɛ] *nm* (**a**) (*poil*) down (**b**) (*sac de couchage*) sleeping bag (**c**) *Belg & Suisse* (*couette*) duvet
duveteux, -euse [dyvtø, -øz] *adj* downy
DVD [devede] *nm* (*abrév* **Digital Versatile Disk, Digital Video Disk**) DVD
DVD-ROM, DVD-Rom [devederɔm] *nm inv* (*abrév* **Digital Versatile Disk read-only memory**) DVD-ROM
dynamique [dinamik] **1** *adj* dynamic
 2 *nf* (**a**) (*science*) dynamics (*singulier*) (**b**) (*progrès*) dynamic
dynamiser [dinamize] *vt* to energize
dynamisme [dinamism] *nm* dynamism
dynamite [dinamit] *nf aussi Fig* dynamite
dynamiter [dinamite] *vt* to dynamite
dynamo [dinamo] *nf* dynamo
dynastie [dinasti] *nf* dynasty
dysenterie [disɑ̃tri] *nf* dysentery
dysfonctionnement [disfɔ̃ksjɔnmɑ̃] *nm* dysfunction
dyslexie [dislɛksi] *nf* dyslexia
dyslexique [dislɛksik] *adj* dyslexic

E¹, e [ə] *nm inv* E, e
E² *(abrév* **Est**) E
EAO [aao] *nm inv (abrév* **enseignement assisté par ordinateur)** CAL
eau, -x [o] *nf* (**a**) *(liquide)* water; **laver qch à grande e.** to wash sth down; **prendre l'e.** to let in water; **avoir l'e. courante** to have running water; *Fig* **mettre de l'e. dans son vin** to tone it down a bit; *Fig* **apporter de l'e. au moulin de qn** to strengthen sb's case; *Fig* **dans ces eaux-là** or thereabouts; *Fam* **partir en e. de boudin** to go down the pan; *Can* **s'en aller à l'e.** to be going bankrupt; *Fam* **il y a de l'e. dans le gaz** there's trouble brewing; **e. bénite** holy water; **e. de Cologne** eau de Cologne; **e. douce** fresh water; **e. de Javel** bleach; **e. lourde** heavy water; **e. de mer** *ou* **salée** salt water; **e. minérale** mineral water; **e. oxygénée** hydrogen peroxide; **e. de pluie** rainwater; **e. du robinet** tap water; *Fig* **roman à l'e. de rose** sentimental novel; **e. de Seltz** soda water, *Am* club soda; **e. de source** spring water; **eaux thermales** hot springs; *Vieilli* **prendre les eaux** to take the waters; **e. de toilette** eau de toilette; *aussi Fig* **e. de vaisselle** dishwater (**b**) *(étendue)* water; **au bord de l'e.** by the water's edge; **tomber à l'e.** to fall into the water; *Fig* to fall through; *Fig* **se jeter à l'e.** to take the plunge; **les eaux territoriales françaises** French waters (**c**) *(sécrétion)* **être tout en e.** to be dripping with perspiration; **ça me met l'e. à la bouche!** it makes my mouth water!; **elle a perdu les eaux** her waters have broken (**d**) *(d'une pierre précieuse)* **un diamant de la plus belle e.** a diamond of the first water
eau-de-vie *(pl* **eaux-de-vie)** [odvi] *nf* brandy
eau-forte *(pl* **eaux-fortes)** [ofɔrt] *nf (estampe)* etching
ébahi, -e [ebai] *adj* astounded
ébats [eba] *nmpl* frolicking; **é. amoureux** lovemaking
ébattre [11] [ebatr] **s'ébattre** *vpr* to frolic
ébauche [eboʃ] *nf (dessin)* rough sketch; *(d'un roman)* outline; *(d'une lettre)* draft; *Fig* **l'é. d'un sourire** the ghost of a smile
ébaucher [eboʃe] *vt (tableau, roman)* to rough out; *(lettre)* to draft; *Fig* **é. un sourire** to give a faint smile; *Fig* **é. un geste** to make a movement
ébène [ebɛn] *nf* ebony; **(d'un noir) d'é., (noir) é.** jet black
ébéniste [ebenist] *nmf* cabinet maker
éberlué, -e [ebɛrlɥe] *adj* flabbergasted
éblouir [ebluir] *vt aussi Fig* to dazzle
éblouissant, -e [ebluisã, -ãt] *adj aussi Fig* dazzling; **d'une beauté éblouissante** dazzlingly beautiful

éblouissement [ebluismã] *nm* dazzle, glare; *(malaise)* fit of dizziness; *Fig* **ce fut un é.** it was dazzling
éborgner [ebɔrɲe] **1** *vt* **é. qn** to put sb's eye out
  2 s'éborgner *vpr* to put one's eye out
éboueur [ebwœr] *nm Br* dustman, *Am* garbage man
ébouillanter [ebujãte] **1** *vt* to scald
  2 s'ébouillanter *vpr* to scald oneself
éboulement [ebulmã] *nm* (**a**) *(écroulement)* collapse; *(de mine)* cave-in; **deux personnes sont mortes dans l'é. de la falaise** two people were killed when the cliff collapsed (**b**) *(gravats)* mass of fallen rocks
ébouler [ebule] **s'ébouler** *vpr (falaise, remblai)* to collapse; *(tunnel)* to cave in
éboulis [ebuli] *nm* mass of fallen rocks
ébouriffé, -e [eburife] *adj (cheveux, personne)* dishevelled
ébouriffer [eburife] *vt (cheveux)* to ruffle; **é. qn** to ruffle sb's hair
ébranler [ebrãle] **1** *vt aussi Fig* to shake
  2 s'ébranler *vpr* to move off
Èbre [ɛbr] *nm* **l'È.** the Ebro
ébrécher [34] [ebreʃe] *vt (verre, porcelaine)* to chip; *(lame)* to nick
ébriété [ebriete] *nf* **en état d'é.** in a state of inebriation
ébrouer [ebrue] **s'ébrouer** *vpr* (**a**) *(cheval)* to snort (**b**) *(chien)* to shake itself
ébruiter [ebrɥite] **1** *vt (secret)* to give away; *(nouvelle)* to spread
  2 s'ébruiter *vpr (nouvelle)* to spread
EBS [abɛɛs] *nf (abrév* **encéphalite bovine spongiforme)** BSE
ébullition [ebylisjɔ̃] *nf* boiling; **arriver à é.** to come to the boil; **amener qch à é.** to bring sth to the boil; *Fig* **en é.** in turmoil
écaille [ekaj] *nf (de poisson)* scale; *(de tortue, d'huître)* shell; *(de peinture)* flake; **peigne en é.** tortoiseshell comb; **des lunettes d'é.** *ou* **en é.** tortoiseshell-rimmed glasses
écailler [ekaje] **1** *vt* (**a**) *(poisson)* to scale (**b**) *(huître)* to open
  2 s'écailler *vpr (émail, vernis à ongles)* to chip (off); *(peinture)* to peel (off)
écarlate [ekarlat] *adj* scarlet; *Fig* **devenir é.** to go bright red
écarquiller [ekarkije] *vt* **é. les yeux** to open one's eyes wide
écart [ekar] *nm* (**a**) *(entre deux chiffres)* difference (**entre** between); *(entre deux points)* gap, distance; *(en distance, en temps, dans un classement)* gap (**entre** between); **ils ont trois ans d'é.** there's a three-year gap between them; **é. de niveau**

(dans une classe) difference in ability; **é. de salaires** wage differential (**b**) **faire le grand é.** to do the splits (**c**) *(déviation)* **faire un é.** *(personne)* to jump aside; *(cheval)* to shy; *(voiture)* to swerve; *Fig* **écarts de conduite** misbehaviour; *Fig* **écarts de langage** bad language (**d**) **mettre qn à l'é.** to keep sb out of things; **tenir qn à l'é.** to keep qn out of things; **se tenir à l'é.** to keep out of things; **un terrain à l'é.** de la ville a piece of land away from the town

écarté, -e [ekarte] *adj* (**a**) *(loin l'un de l'autre) (bras, pieds)* apart; *(yeux)* widely spaced; **avoir les dents écartées** to be gap-toothed (**b**) *Can (personne)* lost

écarteler [39] [ekartəle] *vt* to quarter; *Fig* **être écartelé** to be torn (between)

écartement [ekartəmã] *nm (distance)* space, gap

écarter [ekarte] **1** *vt* (**a**) *(séparer) (doigts, bras, jambes)* to spread; *(rideaux)* to draw (back); *(personnes, objets)* to move apart (**b**) *(repousser) (objet, branches)* to move aside; *(danger, soupçons)* to avert; **é. qn/qch de** to move sb/sth away from; **é. qn de son chemin** to push sb out of one's way (**c**) *(exclure) (candidat, proposition)* to turn down

2 s'écarter *vpr* (**a**) *(se séparer) (personnes)* to move apart; *(foule)* to part; *(routes)* to diverge (**b**) *(s'éloigner) (piéton)* to move away (**de** from); *(voiture)* to swerve (**de** from); *Fig* **s'é. du sujet** to wander from the subject (**c**) *Can (s'égarer)* to get lost

ecchymose [ekimoz] *nf* bruise

ecclésiastique [eklezjastik] **1** *adj* ecclesiastical **2** *nm* clergyman

écervelé, -e [esɛrvəle] **1** *adj* scatterbrained **2** *nm,f* scatterbrain

ECG [əseʒe] *nm Méd (abrév* **électrocardiogramme)** ECG

échafaud [eʃafo] *nm* scaffold; *Fig* **monter à l'é.** to go to the scaffold

échafaudage [eʃafodaʒ] *nm* scaffolding; **des échafaudages** scaffolding

échafauder [eʃafode] *vt (empiler)* to pile up; *Fig (système, argumentation)* to put together, to construct

échalas [eʃala] *nm Fam* **grand é.** beanpole

échalote [eʃalɔt] *nf* shallot

échancré, -e [eʃãkre] *adj* (**a**) *(vêtement)* low-cut (**b**) *(littoral)* jagged, indented

échancrer [eʃãkre] *vt* to cut out the neckline of

échancrure [eʃãkryr] *nf (décolleté)* low neckline

échange [eʃãʒ] *nm* (**a**) *(d'objets, de prisonniers, d'idées)* exchange; **voulez-vous (me) faire l'é.?** could you exchange it/them (for me)?; **recevoir/donner qch en é. (de qch)** to receive/give sth in exchange (for sth); **de violents échanges** *(physiques)* violent clashes; *(verbaux)* violent exchanges; **échanges culturels** cultural exchanges (**b**) **échanges commerciaux** trade; **échanges internationaux** international trade (**c**) *(au tennis)* rally; **faire des échanges** to knock up (**d**) *Ordinat* **é. de données** data exchange; **é. de données informatisé** electronic data interchange

échanger [45] [eʃãʒe] *vt (objets, articles)* to exchange, to swap (**contre** for); *Fig (coups, idées)* to exchange; *(injures)* to trade

échangeur [eʃãʒœr] *nm* interchange

échantillon [eʃãtijɔ̃] *nm* sample; **prélever un é. de qch** to take a sample of sth; **é. gratuit** free sample

échantillonnage [eʃãtijɔnaʒ] *nm* (**a**) *(action)* sampling (**b**) *(échantillons)* selection of samples

échantillonner [eʃãtijɔne] *vt (pour sondage)* to sample

échappatoire [eʃapatwar] *nf* way out

échappée [eʃape] *nf* (**a**) *(de coureurs)* breakaway; **être dans l'é.** to be part of the breakaway group (**b**) *(espace libre)* **une é. sur la mer** a sea view

échappement [eʃapmã] *nm* (**a**) *(de voiture)* exhaust; **des gaz d'é.** exhaust fumes (**b**) *Ordinat* escape

échapper [eʃape] **1 échapper à** *vt ind* **é. à qn** *(sujet: personne)* to get away from sb; **é. à qch** *(punition, mort)* to escape sth; *(corvée)* to get out of sth; **son nom m'échappe** his/her name escapes me; **je n'aurais pas dû le dire mais ça m'a échappé** I shouldn't have said it but it just slipped out; **rien ne lui échappe** he/she doesn't miss a thing; **la victoire nous a échappé** victory eluded us; **le vase m'a échappé des mains** the vase slipped out of my hands

2 *vi* **laisser é.** *(personne, animal)* to let escape; *(objet)* to drop; *(de l'air)* to let out; *(de la vapeur)* to let off; *(larme)* to let fall; *(secret, soupir, cri)* to let out; *(détail)* to overlook

3 *vt* **il l'a échappé belle** he had a narrow escape

4 s'échapper *vpr* (**a**) *(s'évader)* to escape (**de** from) (**b**) *(sortir) (eau, gaz)* to escape (**de** from); **un cri s'échappa de ses lèvres** he/she let out a cry

écharde [eʃard] *nf* splinter

écharpe [eʃarp] *nf* scarf; **l'é. tricolore** the tricolour sash; **avoir le bras en é.** to have one's arm in a sling

écharper [eʃarpe] *vt Fam* **se faire é.** to get torn to pieces

échasse [eʃas] *nf* (**a**) *(bâton)* stilt; **être monté sur des échasses** to be on stilts (**b**) *(oiseau)* stilt

échassier [eʃasje] *nm* wader

échaudé, -e [eʃode] *adj Fig* **être é.** to get one's fingers burnt

échauffement [eʃofmã] *nm* (**a**) *(d'un moteur)* overheating (**b**) *(excitation)* overexcitement (**c**) *(d'athlète)* warm-up

échauffer [eʃofe] **1** *vt* (**a**) *(moteur)* to overheat (**b**) *(exciter)* **é. les esprits** to get people worked up; **les esprits sont échauffés** feelings are running high; *Fam* **é. les oreilles à qn** to get up sb's nose (**c**) *(athlète)* to warm up

2 s'échauffer *vpr* (**a**) *(moteur)* to get overheated (**b**) *(athlète)* to warm up (**c**) *(s'énerver) (personne)* to get worked up

échauffourée [eʃofure] *nf* brawl; *Mil* skirmish

échéance [eʃeãs] *nf (de dette, de facture)* date of payment; **à courte/longue é.** *(prêt)* short-/long-term; **venir à é.** to fall due; **faire face à ses échéances** to meet one's financial obligations; *Fig* **une é. électorale** an election

échéancier [eʃeãsje] *nm (livre)* billbook (**b**) *(calendrier)* timetable

échéant [eʃeã] *adj m voir* **cas**

échec [eʃɛk] *nm* (**a**) *(défaite)* failure; *(revers)* setback; **subir un é.** *(défaite)* to fail; *(revers)* to suffer a setback; *Can* **mettre en é.** *(au hockey)* to check; **faire é. à qch** to foil sth; **faire é. à qn** to frustrate sb; **l'é. scolaire** doing badly at school (**b**) *(jeu)* **échecs** chess; **é.!** check!; **é. et mat!** checkmate!

échelle [eʃɛl] *nf* (**a**) *(pour grimper)* ladder; **l'é. des pompiers** the fireman's ladder; *Fig* **l'é. sociale** the social ladder; *Fig* **é. des salaires** salary scale; **é. des valeurs** scale of values; **faire la courte é. à qn** to give sb *Br* a leg up *or Am* a boost; **5 sur l'é. de Richter** 5 on the Richter scale (**b**) *(d'une carte)* scale; **l'é. est de**

1/10 000 the scale is 1:10,000; *Fig* **sur une grande é.** on a large scale; **à l'é. nationale** on a national scale; *Ordinat* **intégration à grande/petite é.** large-/small-scale integration (**c**) *(dans un collant) Br* ladder, *Am* run; **faire une é. à son collant** *Br* to ladder one's tights, *Am* to get a run in one's pantyhose

échelon [eʃlɔ̃] *nm* (**a**) *(d'une échelle)* rung (**b**) *(d'une hiérarchie)* grade; **gravir tous les échelons** to climb to the top of the ladder (**c**) *(niveau)* level; **à l'é. national** on a national level; **à tous les échelons** at every level

échelonnement [eʃlɔnmɑ̃] *nm* (**a**) *(de paiements)* spreading; *(de vacances)* staggering (**b**) *(d'objets)* spacing

échelonner [eʃlɔne] **1** *vt* (**a**) *(paiements)* to spread; *(vacances)* to stagger (**b**) *(objets)* to space out
2 s'échelonner *vpr* (**a**) **les paiements s'échelonnent sur deux ans** the payments are spread over two years (**b**) *(objets)* to be spaced out

écheveau, -x [eʃvo] *nm (de fil)* skein; *Fig* **démêler l'é. d'une affaire compliquée** to untangle a complicated business

échevelé, -e [eʃəvle] *adj (personne)* dishevelled; *Fig (course)* mad

échevin [eʃəvɛ̃] *nm Belg* deputy mayor

échinacée [eʃinase] *nf Bot & Méd* echinacea

échine [eʃin] *nf* (**a**) *(colonne vertébrale)* spine, backbone (**b**) *(de porc)* loin

échiné, -e [eʃine] *adj Can* exhausted

échiner [eʃine] **s'échiner** *vpr* **s'é. à faire qch** to wear oneself out doing sth

échiquier [eʃikje] *nm (d'échecs)* chessboard; *Fig* **l'é. politique** the political scene

écho [eko] *nm* (**a**) *(bruit)* echo; **il y a de l'é.** there's an echo; *Fig* **trouver un é.** to get a response; *Fig* **se faire l'é. de qch** to echo sth; *Fig* **j'en ai eu de très bons échos** I've had some very good feedback (**b**) **les échos** *(de journal)* gossip column

échographe [ekograf] *nf Méd* (ultrasound) scanner
échographie [ekografi] *nf* (ultrasound) scan; **passer une é.** to have a scan

échoir [14] [eʃwar] **1** *vi (dette)* to fall due; *(investissement)* to mature
2 échoir à *vt ind* to fall to

échoppe [eʃɔp] *nf shop*

échotier, -ère [ekɔtje, -ɛr] *nm,f* gossip columnist

échouer [eʃwe] **1** *vi* (**a**) *(navire)* to run aground; *(baleine)* to get stranded; **navire échoué** stranded ship; *Fam* **é. dans un bar** to wind up in a bar (**b**) *(rater) (projet, personne)* to fail; **é. à un examen** to fail an exam; **faire é.** *(projet)* to wreck; *(complot)* to foil
2 *vt (navire)* to beach
3 s'échouer *vpr (navire)* to run aground; *(baleine)* to get stranded

éclabousser [eklabuse] **1** *vt* to splash, to spatter (**avec** with); *Fig* **le scandale a éclaboussé certains de ses collègues** the scandal tarnished the reputation of some of his/her colleagues
2 s'éclabousser *vpr* to splash oneself

éclaboussure [eklabusyr] *nf* splash

éclair [eklɛr] **1** *nm* (**a**) *(lumière)* flash; *(pendant un orage)* flash of lightning; **éclairs** lightning; **être rapide comme l'é.** to be as quick as a flash; *Fig* **en un é.** in a flash (**b**) *Fig (de lucidité, de génie)* flash; **lancer des éclairs** *(yeux)* to flash (**c**) *(gâteau)* éclair
2 *adj inv (visite, attaque)* lightning

éclairage [eklɛraʒ] *nm* lighting; *(par projecteurs)* floodlighting

éclairagiste [eklɛraʒist] *nmf (de cinéma, de théâtre)* lighting technician

éclaircie [eklɛrsi] *nf* sunny spell

éclaircir [eklɛrsir] **1** *vt* (**a**) *(rendre plus clair) (couleur, cheveux)* to lighten; *(teint)* to clear (**b**) *(rendre moins épais) (sauce)* to thin (**c**) *Fig (élucider) (mystère)* to clear up
2 s'éclaircir *vpr* (**a**) *(temps, ciel)* to clear; *(visage)* to brighten up (**b**) *(se dissiper) (brouillard)* to clear; *Fig (mystère)* to be cleared up (**c**) *(cheveux)* to thin (**d**) **s'é. la voix** to clear one's throat

éclaircissement [eklɛrsismɑ̃] *nm* (**a**) *(explication)* explanation; **demander des éclaircissements (à qn) sur qch** to ask (sb) for an explanation of sth (**b**) *(de cheveux)* lightening

éclairé, -e [eklere] *adj* lit; *Fig* enlightened

éclairer [eklere] **1** *vt* (**a**) *(pièce, vitrine)* to light; **e. qn** to give sb some light; **éclairé au néon** neon-lit; *Fig* **é. qch d'un jour nouveau** to shed or throw new light on sth; *Fig* **un sourire éclairait son visage** a smile lit up his/her face (**b**) *Fig (informer)* to enlighten; *Fam* **é. la lanterne de qn (sur qch)** to put sb in the picture (about sth)
2 *vi* **cette lampe éclaire mal** this lamp doesn't give much light
3 s'éclairer *vpr* (**a**) *(personne)* **s'é. au pétrole/gaz** to use oil lamps/gaslight; **s'é. à la bougie** to use candles for lighting (**b**) *(devenir lumineux) (bâtiment, visage)* to light up (**c**) *Fig* **tout s'éclaire!** everything's becoming clear!

éclaireur, -euse [eklɛrœr, -øz] **1** *nm Mil* scout; *Mil & Fig* **partir en é.** to go off for a scout around
2 *nm,f (boy)* scout, *f (girl)* guide

éclat [ekla] *nm* (**a**) *(fragment) (de bois, de verre)* splinter; *(de pierre)* chip; **é. d'obus** piece of shrapnel; **des éclats d'obus** shrapnel; **des éclats de verre** *(bris)* broken glass; *(projeté)* flying glass; **voler en éclats** to shatter (**b**) *(son)* **é. de rire** burst of laughter; **partir d'un grand é. de rire** to burst out laughing; **rire aux éclats** to roar with laughter; **des éclats de voix** loud voices (**c**) *Fig (scandale)* scandal; **faire un é.** to create a scandal (**d**) *(du soleil)* glare; *(d'un diamant)* flash; *(de couleurs)* brilliance; **l'é. de ses yeux** the sparkle in his/her eyes; *Fig* **l'é. de la jeunesse** the bloom of youth (**e**) *(d'une cérémonie, d'une époque)* splendour; **action** *ou* **coup d'é.** brilliant feat

éclatant, -e [eklatɑ̃, -ɑ̃t] *adj* (**a**) *(lumière, couleur, succès)* brilliant; *(teint)* glowing; *(preuve)* striking; **être é. de santé** to be glowing with health; **être dans une forme éclatante** to be on brilliant form (**b**) *(son, rire)* loud

éclate [eklat] *nf Fam* **c'est l'é.** it's a laugh *or* hoot

éclaté, -e [eklate] *adj (vision)* fragmented

éclatement [eklatmɑ̃] *nm (d'un obus, d'un pneu)* bursting; *(d'un verre)* shattering; *Fig (d'un groupe)* break-up

éclater [eklate] **1** *vi* (**a**) *(exploser) (obus, pneu, ballon)* to burst; *(verre)* to shatter; *Fig (groupe)* to break up; **faire é. qch** to burst/shatter sth; **faire é. un pétard** to let off a firework (**b**) *Fig* **é. de rire** to burst out laughing; **é. en sanglots** to burst into tears; **é. en applaudissements** to burst into applause (**c**) *(se déclencher) (guerre, incendie)* to break out; *(orage, scandale)* to break
2 *vt Fam* **é. la tête à qn** to smash sb's head in
3 s'éclater *vpr Fam* to have a really good time

éclectique [eklɛktik] *adj* eclectic

éclipse [eklips] *nf (de soleil, de lune)* eclipse
éclipser [eklipse] **1** *vt aussi Fig* to eclipse
  2 s'éclipser *vpr Fam (s'esquiver)* to slip away
éclopé, -e [eklɔpe] **1** *adj* lame
  2 *nm,f* lame person
éclore [eklɔr] *vi* (**a**) *(œuf, poussin)* to hatch (**b**) *(fleur)* to open (**c**) *Fig (talent)* to be born, to appear
éclosion [eklozjɔ̃] *nf* (**a**) *(d'œuf, de poussin)* hatching (**b**) *(de fleurs)* opening (**c**) *Fig (d'un talent)* birth
écluse [eklyz] *nf* lock; **(porte d')é.** lock gate
éclusier, -ère [eklyzje, -ɛr] *nm,f* lock keeper
écœurant, -e [ekœrɑ̃, -ɑ̃t] *adj* (**a**) *(nourriture)* nauseating; *Fig (révoltant)* disgusting (**b**) *Fam (décourageant)* sickening
écœurement [ekœrmɑ̃] *nm* (**a**) *(nausée)* nausea; *Fig (indignation)* disgust; **manger qch jusqu'à l'é.** to eat sth until one feels sick (**b**) *Fam (découragement)* discouragement
écœurer [ekœre] *vt* (**a**) **é. qn** *(donner la nausée à)* to make sb feel sick; *Fig (indigner)* to disgust sb (**b**) *Fam (décourager)* to sicken
écoguerrier, -ère [ekɔgɛrje, -ɛr] *nm,f Écol* ecowarrior
écolabel [ekolabɛl] *nm* ecolabel
école [ekɔl] *nf* (**a**) *(établissement, enseignement)* school; **être à l'é.** to be at school; **aller à l'é.** to go to school; **reprendre l'é.** to go back to school; **faire l'é. buissonnière** to play *Br* truant *or Am* hookey; *Fig* **être à bonne é.** to be in good hands; *Fam* **je n'ai pas é. aujourd'hui** I don't have any classes today; **les grandes écoles** = university-level colleges specializing in professional training; **É. des beaux-arts** = art school in Paris; **é. de commerce** business school; **é. de conduite** driving school; **é. de danse** dancing school; **é. de dessin** art school; **é. hôtelière** hotel school; **é. libre** independent *or* private school; **é. maternelle,** *Suisse* **é. enfantine** nursery school; **é. militaire** military academy; **é. de musique** music school; **É. nationale d'administration** = university-level college preparing students for senior posts in law and economics; *Anciennement* **é. normale** teacher training college; **É. normale supérieure** = university-level college preparing students for senior posts in teaching; **é. primaire** *(bâtiment)* primary school; *(enseignement)* primary education; **é. privée** private school; **é. publique** *Br* state *or Am* public school; *Can & Suisse* **é. secondaire** *Br* secondary school, *Am* high school (**b**) *(de pensée, d'art)* school; **faire é.** to win a following

▨▨▨▨▨▨▨▨▨▨▨▨▨▨▨▨▨▨▨▨▨▨▨▨▨▨▨▨▨▨

Grandes écoles

These are highly selective establishments which exist in parallel to the universities. Admission is usually only possible after two years of intensive preparatory studies ("écoles préparatoires") and a "**concours**" *(see box at this entry)*. Graduates from these institutions typically go on to work in senior and executive posts in the civil service or the private sector. The "grandes écoles" include HEC (management), Polytechnique, Centrale, the École des Mines and the École des Ponts et Chaussées (engineering), the ENA (senior civil service) and the École normale supérieure (humanities or science). Having been to a "grande école" is comparable in prestige to having an Oxbridge degree in Britain or a degree from Harvard or Yale in the US.

▨▨▨▨▨▨▨▨▨▨▨▨▨▨▨▨▨▨▨▨▨▨▨▨▨▨▨▨▨▨

écolier, -ère [ekɔlje, -ɛr] *nm,f* schoolchild, schoolboy, *f* schoolgirl *(at primary school)*

écolo [ekɔlo] *adj & nmf Fam* green
écologie [ekɔlɔʒi] *nf* ecology
écologique [ekɔlɔʒik] *adj* ecological; *(produit)* eco-friendly, environmentally friendly; *(politique, parti)* green
écologiste [ekɔlɔʒist] *adj & nmf* environmentalist
écomusée [ekomyze] *nm* living museum *(showing man in his natural and social environment)*
éconduire [18] [ekɔ̃dɥir] *vt Litt* (**a**) *(congédier)* to dismiss (**b**) *(refuser) (prétendant)* to reject
économat [ekɔnɔma] *nm* (**a**) *(fonction)* bursarship (**b**) *(bureau)* bursar's office
économe [ekɔnɔm] **1** *adj* economical, thrifty
  2 *nmf (de collège)* bursar
  3 *nm* **(couteau) é.** potato peeler
économie [ekɔnɔmi] *nf* (**a**) *(système)* economy; **é. dirigée** planned economy; **é. libérale** open market economy; **é. de marché** market economy; **é. mondiale** global economy (**b**) *(gain)* saving; *(vertu)* economy, thrift; **avoir le sens de l'é.** to be thrifty; **faire une é. de temps/de 20%** to save time/20%; **faire l'é. d'un coup de fil** to save oneself a phone call (**c**) *(discipline)* economics *(singulier)*; **il enseigne l'é.** he teaches economics (**d**) **économies** savings; **faire des économies** to save money; **faire des économies de chauffage** to save money on heating; **faire des économies d'énergie** to save energy; **prendre sur ses économies** to dip into one's savings; **il n'y a pas de petites économies** every little helps
économique [ekɔnɔmik] *adj* (**a**) *(relatif à l'économie)* economic (**b**) *(avantageux)* economical
économiser [ekɔnɔmize] *vt (argent, temps, énergie)* to save; *(électricité, nourriture)* to economize on, to save on; **é. ses forces** to conserve one's strength; **é. sa salive** to save one's breath; **é. pour ses vacances** to save up for one's *Br* holiday *or Am* vacation
économiseur [ekɔnɔmizœr] *nm Ordinat* **é. d'écran** screen saver
économiste [ekɔnɔmist] *nmf* economist
écoper [ekɔpe] **1** *vt (barque)* to bale (out); **nous avons dû é.** we had to bale out
  2 écoper de *vt ind Fam (être puni)* **é. d'une amende/de cinq ans de prison** to get a fine/five years in prison; **c'est encore moi qui vais é.** I'm going to get the blame again
écoproduit [ekɔprɔdɥi] *nm* eco-friendly *or* environmentally friendly product
écorce [ekɔrs] *nf* (**a**) *(d'arbre)* bark; *(d'orange)* peel (**b**) **l'é. terrestre** the earth's crust
écorché, -e [ekɔrʃe] **1** *nm* anatomical model
  2 *nm,f Fig* **é. (vif)** tortured soul
écorcher [ekɔrʃe] **1** *vt* (**a**) *(animal)* to skin; *(criminel)* to flay (**b**) *(érafler)* to graze; *Fig (nom)* to mispronounce; *Fig* **é. les oreilles à qn** to grate on sb's ears
  2 s'écorcher *vpr* to graze oneself; **s'é. le genou** to graze one's knee
écorchure [ekɔrʃyr] *nf* graze
écorecharge [ekɔrəʃarʒ] *nf* eco-refill
écorner [ekɔrne] *vt (meuble)* to damage the corner(s) of; **livre écorné** dog-eared book
écossais, -e [ekɔsɛ, -ɛz] **1** *adj (coutume, lande, personne)* Scottish; *(whisky)* Scotch; **une jupe écossaise** a tartan skirt
  2 *nm,f* **É.** Scot
  3 *nm (tissu)* tartan
Écosse [ekɔs] *nf* **l'É.** Scotland
écosser [ekɔse] *vt* to shell

écosystème [ekosistɛm] *nm* ecosystem

écot [eko] *nm* **payer son é.** to pay one's share

écotaxe [ekɔtaks] *nf* ecotax

écotourisme [ekɔturism] *nm Écol* ecotourism

écoulement [ekulmɑ̃] *nm* (**a**) *(de liquide)* flow (**b**) *(de blessure)* discharge (**c**) *(de marchandises)* sale; *(de faux billets)* circulation (**d**) *(du temps)* passage

écouler [ekule] **1** *vt (marchandises)* to dispose of; *(faux billets)* to circulate
2 s'écouler *vpr* (**a**) *(liquide)* to flow out, to run out (**de** of) (**b**) *(marchandises)* to sell (**c**) *(temps)* to pass

écourter [ekurte] *vt (robe, texte)* to shorten; *(visite, discours)* to cut short

écoute [ekut] *nf* (**a**) *(d'une radio)* **être à l'é. (de)** to be listening in (to); **rester à l'é.** to stay tuned; **heure de grande é.** *Rad & TV* prime time; **indice d'é.** ratings; **écoutes téléphoniques** telephone tapping; **elle est sur é.** her phone's been tapped (**b**) **être à l'é. des autres** to be willing to lend a sympathetic ear

écouter [ekute] **1** *vt* (**a**) *(entendre)* to listen to; **é. qn jusqu'au bout** to hear sb out; **savoir é.** to be a good listener; **é. aux portes** to listen at doors; **faire é. qch à qn** to play sb sth; **écoute, ça suffit maintenant!** listen *or* look here, that's quite enough now! (**b**) *(suivre) (personne)* to listen to; **é. sa conscience** to listen to one's conscience
2 s'écouter *vpr* **il s'écoute trop** he coddles himself; **si je m'écoutais** if I did what I wanted; **s'é. parler** to like the sound of one's own voice

écouteur [ekutœr] *nm (du téléphone)* earpiece; **écouteurs** *(casque)* headphones

écoutille [ekutij] *nf Naut* hatchway

écouvillon [ekuvijɔ̃] *nm (pour bouteille, biberon)* bottle brush

écrabouiller [ekrabuje] *vt Fam* to squash, to crush; **se faire é. par une voiture** to get flattened by a car

écran [ekrɑ̃] *nm* (**a**) *(de télévision, de cinéma)* screen; **porter une pièce à l'é.** to adapt a play for the screen; **prochainement sur vos écrans** coming soon to a *Br* cinema *or Am* movie theater near you; **le grand/petit é.** the big/small screen; **é. panoramique** wide screen; **é. plat** flat screen (**b**) *Ordinat* screen, display; **à l'é.** on screen; **é. d'accueil** start-up screen; **é. d'aide** help screen; **é. couleur** colour screen *or* display; **é. à cristaux liquides** liquid crystal screen; **é. à fenêtres** split screen; **é. monochrome** monochrome screen; **é. rétro-éclairé** back-lit screen; **é. tactile** touch(-sensitive) screen; **é. de visualisation** VDU (**c**) *(pour protéger)* screen; **on ne peut pas voir le lac car les arbres font é.** you can't see the lake because it's screened by the trees; **é. de fumée** smoke screen; **é. solaire** sunscreen, sunblock; **é. total** total sun block

écrasant, -e [ekrazɑ̃, -ɑ̃t] *adj (poids, défaite, responsabilité)* crushing; *(majorité, victoire)* overwhelming

écrasé, -e [ekraze] *adj (nez)* flat; *Fig* **é. de travail** snowed under with work

écraser [ekraze] **1** *vt* (**a**) *(fruit, ail, membre)* to crush; *(insecte)* to squash; *(cigarette)* to stub out; *(piéton, chien)* to run over; **se faire é.** *(par une voiture)* to get run over; *Fam* **é. l'accélérateur** *ou* **le champignon** *Br* to put one's foot down, *Am* to step on the gas (**b**) *(vaincre) (adversaire, troupes)* to crush; **se faire é.** to be crushed (**c**) *Fam* **en é.** to sleep like a log (**d**) *très Fam* **écrase!** shut it!
2 s'écraser *vpr* (**a**) *(avion)* to crash (**b**) *Fam (ne rien dire)* to keep quiet

écrémage [ekremaʒ] *nm (sélection)* creaming off

écrémer [34] [ekreme] *vt (lait)* to skim; *Fig (sélectionner)* to cream off the best of

écrevisse [ekrəvis] *nf* crayfish

écrier [66] [ekrije] **s'écrier** *vpr* to cry out, to exclaim

écrin [ekrɛ̃] *nm* (jewel) case

écrire [30] [ekrir] **1** *vt (lettre, livre, chanson)* to write; *(noter)* to write down; **é. à qn** to write to sb; **é. un mot à qn** to drop sb a line; **je leur ai écrit de venir** I've written asking them to come; **il écrit bien** his handwriting is good; *(écrivain)* he writes well; **ce stylo écrit très bien** this pen writes very well
2 s'écrire *vpr* (**a**) *(s'orthographier)* to be spelt; **comment ça s'écrit?** how do you spell it? (**b**) *(correspondre)* to write to each other

écrit [ekri] *nm* (**a**) **mettre qch par é.** to put sth down in writing (**b**) *(texte)* (written) document; **écrits** *(œuvre)* writings (**c**) *(examen)* written examination

écriteau, -x [ekrito] *nm* notice

écritoire [ekritwar] *nf* writing case

écriture [ekrityr] *nf* (**a**) *(système, caractères)* writing; *Ordinat* write; *Tél* **é. prédictive** predictive text (input) (**b**) *(façon d'écrire)* (hand)writing; **elle a une belle é.** she has nice handwriting (**c**) *(littérature)* writing; *TV & Cin* **é. de scénarios** scriptwriting (**d**) *écritures (comptabilité)* accounts; **tenir les écritures** to keep the accounts (**e**) *Rel* **l'É. sainte, les saintes Écritures** the Scriptures

écrivain [ekrivɛ̃] *nm* writer; **é. public** (public) letter writer

écrivais *etc voir* **écrire**

écrou [ekru] *nm (de boulon)* nut

écrouer [ekrue] *vt Jur* to imprison

écroulé, -e [ekrule] *adj Fam* **é. (de rire)** doubled up with laughter

écroulement [ekrulmɑ̃] *nm* collapse

écrouler [ekrule] **s'écrouler** *vpr (bâtiment, prix, empire)* to collapse; *(espoirs)* to crumble away; **s'é. sur une chaise** to flop onto a chair; **s'é. de fatigue** to collapse with exhaustion

écru, -e [ekry] *adj (beige)* ecru; *(naturel)* unbleached

ecsta [ɛksta] *nf Fam* E

ecstasy [ɛkstazi] *nf* ecstasy

ECU, ÉCU [eky] *nm Anciennement (abrév* **European Currency Unit)** ECU

écu [eky] *nm* (**a**) *Hist* crown (**b**) *(bouclier)* shield

écueil [ekœj] *nm (rocher)* reef; *Fig (danger)* pitfall

écuelle [ekɥɛl] *nf* bowl

éculé, -e [ekyle] *adj (chaussure)* down-at-heel; *Fig (plaisanterie, argument)* hackneyed

écume [ekym] *nf (bave, sur la mer)* foam; *(sur la soupe, la confiture)* scum; **avoir l'é. à la bouche** to be foaming at the mouth; **é. (de mer)** *(magnésite)* meerschaum

écumer [ekyme] **1** *vt* (**a**) *(soupe, confiture)* to skim (**b**) *(piller)* to plunder; *Fig (parcourir)* to scour; **é. les mers** *(pirates)* to scour the seas
2 *vi* **é. (de rage)** to foam (with rage)

écumoire [ekymwar] *nf* skimmer; *Fig* **troué comme une é.** riddled with holes

écureuil [ekyrœj] *nm* squirrel; **é. roux/gris** red/grey squirrel

écurie [ekyri] *nf* stable; **é. (de courses)** *(de chevaux, de voitures)* (racing) stable

écusson [ekysɔ̃] *nm* (**a**) *(armoiries)* escutcheon (**b**) *(de tissu)* badge

écuyer, -ère [ekyije, -ɛr] **1** *nm Hist (gentilhomme)* squire **2** *nm,f* rider; **é. de cirque** circus rider
eczéma [egzema] *nm* eczema; **avoir** *ou* **faire de l'é.** to have eczema
édam [edam] *nm* Edam
edelweiss [edɛlvɛs] *nm* edelweiss
Éden [edɛn] *nm* **l'É.** Eden; *Fig* **un é.** a paradise
édenté, -e [edɑ̃te] *adj* toothless
EDF [ødɛɛf] *nf (abrév* **Électricité de France)** French electricity company
EDI [ødei] *nm Ordinat (abrév* **échange de données informatisé)** EDI
édifiant, -e [edifjɑ̃, -ɑ̃t] *adj* edifying
édification [edifikasjɔ̃] *nf* **(a)** *(d'un monument)* erection; *Fig (d'un empire, d'une fortune)* building up **(b)** *(instruction morale)* edification
édifice [edifis] *nm* building; *Fig* **apporter sa pierre à l'é.** to make a contribution; *Fig* **l'é. social** the social fabric
édifier [66] [edifje] *vt* **(a)** *(monument)* to erect; *Fig (empire, fortune)* to build up **(b)** *(instruire)* to edify
Édimbourg [edɛ̃bur] *n* Edinburgh
édimbourgeois, -e [edɛ̃burʒwa, -az] **1** *adj* of Edinburgh **2** *nm,f* **É.** person from Edinburgh
édit [edi] *nm Hist* edict
éditer [edite] *vt* **(a)** *(publier)* to publish **(b)** *(commenter) (texte)* to edit **(c)** *Ordinat* to edit
éditeur, -trice [editœr, -tris] **1** *nm,f* **(a)** *(d'une maison d'édition)* publisher; **é. de disques** record producer; **é. de logiciels** software producer **(b)** *(commentateur)* editor **2** *nm Ordinat (de programme)* editor; **é. d'icônes** icon editor; **é. HTML** HTML editor; **é. de texte** text editor
édition [edisjɔ̃] *nf* **(a)** *(activité)* publishing; **é. électronique** electronic publishing **(b)** *(texte, exemplaire)* edition; *Hum* **où est le sucre? – dans le placard, troisième é.!** where's the sugar? – for the third time, it's in the cupboard!; **é. originale** first edition **(c)** *(d'un journal)* edition; **dernière é.** final edition; **é. spéciale** special edition **(d)** *Ordinat* editing; **é. de liens** linking; **é. pleine page** full page editing
édito [edito] *nm Fam* editorial, *Br* leader
éditorial, -e, -aux, -ales [editɔrjal, -o] **1** *adj* editorial **2** *nm* editorial, *Br* leader
éditorialiste [editɔrjalist] *nmf* editorial writer, *Br* leader writer
édredon [edrədɔ̃] *nm* eiderdown
éducateur, -trice [edykatœr, -tris] *nm,f* teacher; **é. spécialisé** special needs teacher
éducatif, -ive [edykatif, -iv] *adj* educational
éducation [edykasjɔ̃] *nf* **(a)** *(enseignement)* education; *(par les parents)* upbringing; **faire l'é. de qn** to educate sb; **é. manuelle et technique** handicraft classes; **l'É. nationale** the Department of Education; **é. physique** physical training *or* education; **é. religieuse** religious instruction; **é. sexuelle** sex education **(b)** *(savoir-vivre)* good manners; **avoir de l'é.** to have good manners; **manquer d'é.** to have no manners **(c)** *Fig (des réflexes, du goût)* training
édulcorant, -e [edylkɔrɑ̃, -ɑ̃t] **1** *adj* sweetening **2** *nm* sweetener; **é. de synthèse** artificial sweetener
édulcorer [edylkɔre] *vt (discours, compte rendu)* to water down; *(roman pornographique)* to tone down

éduquer [edyke] *vt* **(a)** *(donner un enseignement à) (enfant, peuple)* to educate; *(élever)* to bring up; **mal éduqué** ill-mannered **(b)** *Fig (réflexes, goût)* to train
EEE [øøø] *nm Pol (abrév* **Espace économique européen)** EEA
EEG *nm (abrév* **électroencéphalogramme)** EEG
effaçable [efasabl] *adj* erasable
effacé, -e [efase] *adj* **(a)** *(personne, manières)* self-effacing **(b)** *(menton)* receding
effacement [efasmɑ̃] *nm* **(a)** *(d'un mot, d'un message, d'une bande)* erasing; *Ordinat* deletion; *(d'une tache)* removal; *(par le temps) (d'une inscription)* wearing away; *(des souvenirs)* fading **(b)** *(d'une personne)* self-effacement
effacer [16] [efase] **1** *vt* **(a)** *(mot, enregistrement, bande)* to erase; *(tableau)* to clean; *(tache, traces)* to remove; *Ordinat (données)* to delete; *(écran)* to clear; *(sujet: temps) (inscription)* to wear away **(b)** *Fig* **e. qch de sa mémoire** to erase sth from one's memory; **on efface tout et on recommence** we'll wipe the slate clean and make a fresh start **2 s'effacer** *vpr* **(a)** *(disparaître) (inscription)* to wear away; *Fig (sentiment, souvenir)* to fade (away) **(b)** *(s'écarter)* to move aside; *Fig (se faire discret)* to keep in the background
effaceur [efasœr] *nm* **e. (d'encre)** ink eraser
effarant, -e [efarɑ̃, -ɑ̃t] *adj* astounding
effaré, -e [efare] *adj* astounded
effarement [efarmɑ̃] *nm* astonishment
effarer [efare] *vt* to astound
effaroucher [efaruʃe] **1** *vt* **(a)** *(effrayer)* to scare; *(faire reculer)* to scare away **(b)** *(choquer)* to shock **2 s'effaroucher** *vpr* **(a)** *(s'effrayer)* to take fright (**de** at) **(b)** *(s'offusquer)* to be shocked (**de** by)
effectif, -ive [efɛktif, -iv] **1** *adj (réel)* effective **2** *nm (employés)* staff; *(d'un club, d'un bataillon)* strength; *(d'une classe)* size
effectivement [efɛktivmɑ̃] *adv* **(a)** *(en effet)* actually; **c'est pratique, hein? – e.!** it's practical, isn't it? – it certainly is! **(b)** *(réellement, de manière effective)* actually
effectuer [efɛktɥe] **1** *vt (mouvement, opération)* to perform; *(paiement, parcours, calcul, réservation)* to make; *(démarches)* to take; *(commande)* to place **2 s'effectuer** *vpr (mouvement, opération)* to be performed; *(paiement, parcours)* to be made
efféminé, -e [efemine] *adj* effeminate
effervescence [efɛrvɛsɑ̃s] *nf* excitement; **être en e.** *(ville, bureau)* to be buzzing with excitement
effervescent, -e [efɛrvɛsɑ̃, -ɑ̃t] *adj (médicament)* effervescent
effet [efɛ] *nm* **(a)** *(résultat, conséquence)* effect (**sur** on); **avoir pour e. de faire qch** to have the effect of doing sth; **faire e.** to take effect; **à cet e.** with that in mind; **rester** *ou* **demeurer sans e.** to have no effect; **sous l'e. de l'alcool/la drogue** under the influence of alcohol/drugs; **les feuilles sont tombées sous l'e. de la chaleur** the heat caused the leaves to drop off; **e. pervers** undesired effect; *Méd* **side effect; e. de serre** greenhouse effect; **e. secondaire** side effect; *Ordinat* **e. de transition** melt **(b)** *(impression)* impression; **quel e. ça te fait qu'elle revienne?** how do you feel about her coming back?; **ne faire aucun e. à qn** to make no impression on sb; **elle me fait l'e. d'une fille plutôt équilibrée** she strikes me as being a fairly well-balanced girl; **il me fait de l'e.** he does something for me; **faire un drôle d'e. à qn** to give sb a

funny feeling; **faire bon/mauvais e.** (à qn) to make a good/bad impression (on sb) (**c**) *(but recherché)* **manquer son e.** *(plaisanterie)* to fall flat; **faire des effets de voix** to make striking use of one's voice; *Cin* **effets spéciaux** special effects; **e. de style** stylistic effect (**d**) *(application)* **prendre e.** to take effect (**e**) *(au tennis)* spin; **donner de l'e. à une balle** to put spin on a ball (**f**) *Fin* bill; **e. de commerce** bill of exchange (**g**) **effets (personnels)** *(affaires)* belongings (**h**) **en e., je m'en souviens** yes, I do remember; **en e.,** c'est ce que je me suis dit that's just what I thought; **mais c'est monstrueux! – en e.!** it's appalling! – isn't it just!; **j'ai dû partir, en e.** j'étais pressé I had to leave because I was in a hurry

effeuiller [efœje] *vt (fleur)* to pull the petals off; *(sujet: vent) (arbre)* to blow the leaves off; *Fig* **e. la marguerite** to play "he/she loves me, he/she loves me not"

efficace [efikas] *adj (méthode, remède)* effective; *(personne)* efficient

efficacement [efikasmɑ̃] *adv (avec succès)* effectively; *(de façon productive)* efficiently

efficacité [efikasite] *nf (d'une méthode, d'un remède)* effectiveness; *(d'une personne)* efficiency

effigie [efiʒi] *nf* effigy; **à l'e. de qn** bearing the image of sb

effilé, -e [efile] *adj (frange)* ragged; *(doigts)* tapering; *(outil, lame)* tapered; *(amandes)* slivered

effilocher [efilɔʃe] **s'effilocher** *vpr* to fray

efflanqué, -e [eflɑ̃ke] *adj* skinny

effleurement [eflœrmɑ̃] *nm* light touch

effleurer [eflœre] *vt (frôler)* to touch lightly; *(accidentellement)* to brush (against); *(surface de l'eau)* to skim; *Fig (sujet)* to touch on; **cette idée ne m'a jamais effleuré** the idea never crossed my mind

effluent [eflyɑ̃] *nm* **e. urbain** (sewage) effluent; **effluents radioactifs** radioactive waste

effluve [eflyv] *nm* emanation

effondré, -e [efɔ̃dre] *adj (peiné)* grief-stricken; *(déçu)* shattered

effondrement [efɔ̃drəmɑ̃] *nm (d'un bâtiment, d'un mur, d'un toit)* collapse; *Fig (d'un plan)* falling through; *(d'un empire, des prix)* collapse; *(d'une personne)* dejection

effondrer [efɔ̃dre] **s'effondrer** *vpr (bâtiment, mur, toit)* to collapse; *Fig (plan)* to fall through; *(empire, prix)* to collapse; *(personne)* to go to pieces; **s'e. dans un fauteuil** to sink or slump into an armchair

efforcer [16] [eforse] **s'efforcer** *vpr* **s'e. de faire qch** to do one's best to do sth

effort [efɔr] *nm* (**a**) *(physique, intellectuel)* effort; **allons, encore un (petit) e.** come on, try again; **son médecin lui a interdit tout e.** his/her doctor has forbidden any exertion; **sans e.** effortlessly; **faire un e. (pour faire qch)** to make an effort (to do sth); **faire des efforts** to make an effort; **faire l'e. de faire qch** to make the effort to do sth; **après l'e., le réconfort** I/you/etc deserve this; **il est partisan du moindre e.** he doesn't believe in exerting himself (**b**) *Tech* strain, stress

effraction [efraksjɔ̃] *nf Jur* breaking and entering; **entrer par e.** to break in

effraie [efrɛ] *nf (oiseau)* barn owl

effranger [45] [efrɑ̃ʒe] **1** *vt* to fray
2 s'effranger *vpr* to fray

effrayant, -e [efrɛjɑ̃, -ɑ̃t] *adj* frightening; *(chaleur, appétit)* tremendous

effrayer [53] [efreje] **1** *vt (faire peur à)* to frighten, to scare; *(inquiéter)* to alarm
2 s'effrayer *vpr* to be frightened (**de** at); **elle s'effraie pour un rien** the least little thing frightens her

effréné, -e [efrene] *adj (passion, luxe)* unbridled; *(galop, course)* frantic

effritement [efritmɑ̃] *nm (d'un mur, d'un revêtement)* crumbling; *(de la roche)* weathering; *Fig (de l'autorité, d'une majorité, de fonds)* erosion

effriter [efrite] **1** *vt (pain, fromage)* to crumble; *(roche)* to weather
2 s'effriter *vpr (mur, revêtement)* to crumble; *(roche)* to weather; *Fig (autorité, majorité, fonds)* to be eroded

effroi [efrwa] *nm Litt* terror, dread

effronté, -e [efrɔ̃te] *adj (personne, manières)* impudent; *(mensonge, menteur)* brazen

effrontément [efrɔ̃temɑ̃] *adv* impudently; *(mentir)* brazenly

effronterie [efrɔ̃tri] *nf (d'une personne, de manières)* impudence; *(d'un mensonge)* brazenness

effroyable [efrwajabl] *adj* dreadful

effroyablement [efrwajabləmɑ̃] *adv* dreadfully

effusion [efyzjɔ̃] *nf* (**a**) **e. de sang** bloodshed (**b**) *(exubérance)* effusiveness; **avec e.** effusively

égailler [egaje] **s'égailler** *vpr* to disperse

égal, -e, -aux, -ales [egal, -o] **1** *adj* (**a**) *(équivalent)* equal (**à** to); **la partie n'est pas égale** they/we/you are not evenly matched; **ils sont de force/d'intelligence égale** they are equally strong/intelligent; **à prix é., tu peux trouver mieux** for the same price, you can find something better (**b**) *(constant) (respiration, son)* even; *(allure, pouls)* steady; *(sol)* level; *(climat)* equable; **être d'humeur égale** to be even-tempered; **rester é. à soi-même** to be still one's old self (**c**) **cela m'est é.** it's all the same to me; *(cela ne m'intéresse pas)* I don't care
2 *nm,f* equal; **être l'é. de qn** to be sb's equal; **traiter qn d'é. à é.** to treat sb as an equal; **sans é.** unequalled

également [egalmɑ̃] *adv (aussi)* as well, too

égaler [egale] *vt (personne, score, record)* to equal; **deux et deux égalent quatre** two and two equal four

égalisation [egalizasjɔ̃] *nf* (**a**) *(équilibrage)* equalization; *Sport* (**but/point d'**)**é.** equalizer (**b**) *(d'une surface)* levelling

égaliser [egalize] **1** *vt* (**a**) *(salaires, pression)* to equalize; *(cheveux)* to trim (**b**) *(sol)* to level
2 *vi Sport* to equalize

égalitaire [egalitɛr] *adj* egalitarian

égalité [egalite] *nf* (**a**) *(entre des quantités, des personnes)* equality; *(au tennis)* deuce; **être à é.** *(équipes)* to be level; **é. des chances** equal opportunities; **é. des salaires** equal pay (**b**) *(constance) (de la respiration, d'un son)* evenness; *(de l'allure, du pouls)* steadiness; *(du sol)* levelness; *(du climat)* equability; **é. d'humeur** even-temperedness

égard [egar] *nm* (**a**) *(respect)* consideration; **par é. pour qn** out of consideration for sb; **égards** *(attentions)* consideration (**b**) *(aspect)* **à cet é.,...** in this respect,...; **je n'ai pas d'opinion à cet é.** I've no opinion on that score; **à certains/tous les égards** in some/all respects (**c**) *(locutions)* **à l'é. de qn** towards sb; **eu é. à** considering

égaré, -e [egare] *adj* (**a**) *(personne, animal)* lost (**b**) *(hagard) (air, regard)* distraught

égarement [egarmɑ̃] *nm* (**a**) *(folie)* distraction (**b**) **égarements** *(dérèglements de conduite)* wild behaviour

égarer [egare] **1** *vt (objet)* to mislay; *(personne) (volontairement)* to mislead; *(soupçons)* to avert **2 s'égarer** *vpr* (**a**) *(se perdre) (personne, lettre)* to get lost (**b**) *(sortir du sujet)* to wander from the point

égayer [53] [egeje] **1** *vt (personne)* to cheer up; *(conversation)* to liven up; *(pièce, vêtement)* to brighten up **2 s'égayer** *vpr (s'animer)* to cheer up

Égée [eʒe] *n voir* **mer**

égérie [eʒeri] *nf* muse

égide [eʒid] *nf* **sous l'é. de** under the aegis of

églantier [eglɑ̃tje] *nm* wild rose (bush)

églantine [eglɑ̃tin] *nf* wild rose

églefin [egləfɛ̃] *nm* haddock

église [egliz] *nf* (**a**) *(bâtiment)* church; **aller à l'é.** *(à la messe)* to go to church; **se marier à l'é.** to get married in church, to have a church wedding (**b**) **l'É.** the Church; **l'É. catholique** the Catholic Church; **l'É. anglicane** the Church of England, the Anglican Church

ego [ego] *nm inv* ego

égocentrique [egosɑ̃trik] **1** *adj* self-centred, egocentric **2** *nmf* self-centred person

égoïsme [egɔism] *nm* selfishness, egoism

égoïste [egɔist] **1** *adj* selfish, egoistic **2** *nmf* selfish person, egoist

égorger [45] [egɔrʒe] *vt* to cut the throat of

égosiller [egozije] **s'égosiller** *vpr (en parlant)* to shout oneself hoarse; *(en chantant)* to sing at the top of one's voice

égout [egu] *nm* sewer

égoutier [egutje] *nm* sewerman

égoutter [egute] **1** *vt* to drain **2** *vi* **laisser é. qch** to leave sth to drain **3 s'égoutter** *vpr* to drain

égouttoir [egutwar] *nm* (**a**) *(dans l'évier)* draining board; *(mobile)* drainer (**b**) *(passoire)* colander

égratigner [egratiɲe] **1** *vt* to scratch; *Fig* to have a dig at **2 s'égratigner** *vpr* to scratch oneself; **s'é. la joue** to scratch one's cheek

égratignure [egratiɲyr] *nf* scratch; *Fig* dig

égrener [46] [egrəne] *vt* (**a**) *(maïs, pois)* to shell; *(grappe)* to pick the grapes off (**b**) *Fig* **é. son chapelet** to tell one's beads

égrillard, -e [egrijar, -ard] *adj* bawdy

Égypte [eʒipt] *nf* **l'É.** Egypt

égyptien, -enne [eʒipsjɛ̃, -ɛn] **1** *adj* Egyptian **2** *nm,f* **É.** Egyptian

eh [e] *exclam* hey!; **eh bien** well; **eh oui!** that's right!

éhonté, -e [eɔ̃te] *adj* shameless

éjaculation [eʒakylasjɔ̃] *nf* ejaculation; **é. précoce** premature ejaculation

éjaculer [eʒakyle] *vi* to ejaculate

éjectable [eʒɛktabl] *adj* **siège é.** ejector seat

éjecter [eʒɛkte] *vt (cartouche, pilote)* to eject; *Fam (expulser)* to throw out (**de** of)

éjection [eʒɛksjɔ̃] *nf (d'une cartouche, du pilote)* ejection; *Fam (expulsion)* throwing out

élaboration [elabɔrasjɔ̃] *nf (d'un plan, d'une idée)* development; *(d'une constitution, d'une loi)* drawing up

élaboré, -e [elabɔre] *adj (technique, machine)* sophisticated; *(plan)* elaborate

élaborer [elabɔre] *vt (plan, idée)* to develop; *(constitution, loi)* to draw up

élagage [elagaʒ] *nm aussi Fig* pruning

élaguer [elage] *vt aussi Fig* to prune

élan¹ [elɑ̃] *nm* (**a**) *(course)* run-up; *(vitesse)* momentum; *Fig (impulsion)* boost; **prendre de l'é.** *ou* **son é.** to take a run-up; **saut sans/avec é.** standing/running jump; *Fig* **d'un seul é.** all in one go; *Fig* **emporté par son é.** carried away (**b**) *(transport) (d'enthousiasme)* burst; *(de tendresse, de passion)* surge (**c**) *(ferveur)* fervour

élan² *nm (cerf)* elk

élancé, -e [elɑ̃se] *adj* slim, slender

élancement [elɑ̃smɑ̃] *nm (douleur)* shooting pain

élancer [16] [elɑ̃se] **1** *vi* **la jambe m'élance** I've got shooting pains in my leg **2 s'élancer** *vpr (se précipiter)* to rush forward; *Sport* to take a run-up

élargir [elarʒir] **1** *vt* (**a**) *(route, rue)* to widen; *(vêtement)* to let out; *(trou)* to enlarge (**b**) *Fig (groupe, gamme de produits)* to expand; *(connaissances, débat)* to broaden; **é. l'Union européenne** to enlarge the European Union (**c**) *Jur (prisonnier)* to release **2** *vi Fam (personne)* to get bigger **3 s'élargir** *vpr* (**a**) *(route, rue)* to widen; *(chaussures, vêtement)* to stretch; *(trou)* to enlarge (**b**) *Fig (groupe, gamme de produits)* to expand; *(connaissances, débat)* to broaden

élargissement [elarʒismɑ̃] *nm* (**a**) *(d'une route, d'une rue)* widening; *(d'un trou)* enlargement (**b**) *Fig (d'un groupe, d'une gamme de produits)* expansion; *(des connaissances, d'un débat)* broadening; **l'é. de l'Union européenne** the enlargement of the European Union (**c**) *Jur (d'un prisonnier)* release

élastique [elastik] **1** *adj (corps, matière)* elastic; *Fig (démarche)* springy; *(règlement, principes)* flexible; *(conscience)* accommodating **2** *nm* (**a**) *(pour la couture)* elastic (**b**) *(de bureau)* elastic *or* rubber band (**c**) *(jeu)* **jouer à l'é.** to play elastics

électeur, -trice [elɛktœr, -tris] *nm,f* voter, elector; **mes électeurs** the people who voted for me

élection [elɛksjɔ̃] *nf* (**a**) *(d'un candidat)* election; **élections législatives** general election; **élections municipales** local elections; **é. présidentielle, élections présidentielles** presidential election (**b**) *(choix)* **mon pays d'é.** my adopted country

Élections

All French citizens of eighteen or over are entitled to vote in elections, which take place on a Sunday. Polling stations are often set up in local schools. Voters collect leaflets (each corresponding to the different political parties or candidates), go to a booth and put their chosen leaflet into the envelope provided, which is then placed in the ballot box ("l'urne") supervised by an "assesseur", who then utters the words "a voté!". Unlike Britain with its first-past-the-post system, the French electoral system is based on a type of proportional representation. As from 2002 presidential elections take place every five years. General elections are also held every five years.

électoral, -e, -aux, -ales [elɛktɔral, -o] *adj (campagne, comité, promesses)* election

électorat [elɛktɔra] *nm* voters, electorate; **l'é. communiste/féminin** communist/female voters

électricien, -enne [elɛktrisjɛ̃, -ɛn] *nm,f* electrician

électricité [elɛktrisite] *nf* electricity; *(installation)* wiring; *Fig* **il y a de l'é. dans l'air** the atmosphere is electric; **é. statique** static (electricity)
électrifier [66] [elɛktrifje] *vt (chemin de fer)* to electrify; *(village)* to bring electricity to
électrique [elɛktrik] *adj aussi Fig* electric
électrisant, -e [elɛktrizɑ̃, -ɑ̃t] *adj (exaltant)* electrifying
électriser [elɛktrize] *vt aussi Fig* to electrify
électroaimant [elɛktrɔɛmɑ̃] *nm* electromagnet
électrocardiogramme [elɛktrokardjɔgram] *nm* electrocardiogram
électrochoc [elɛktroʃɔk] *nm* electric shock; **traitement par électrochocs** electric shock treatment; **faire des électrochocs à qn** to give sb electric shock treatment
électrocuter [elɛktrɔkyte] **1** *vt* to electrocute; **se faire é.** to be electrocuted
2 s'électrocuter *vpr* to electrocute oneself
électrocution [elɛktrokysjɔ̃] *nf* electrocution
électrode [elɛktrɔd] *nf* electrode
électroencéphalogramme [elɛktrɔɑ̃sefalɔgram] *nm* electroencephalogram
électrogène [elɛktrɔʒɛn] *adj* **groupe é.** generating unit
électrolyse [elɛktrɔliz] *nf* electrolysis
électroménager [elɛktromenaʒe] **1** *adj m* **appareils électroménagers** household appliances
2 *nm* household appliances
électron [elɛktrɔ̃] *nm* electron; **é. libre** free electron; *Fig* maverick
électronicien, -enne [elɛktrɔnisjɛ̃, -ɛn] *nm,f* electronics engineer
électronique [elɛktrɔnik] **1** *adj (composant, jeu)* electronic; *(microscope, télescope)* electron; *(industrie)* electronics
2 *nf* electronics *(singulier)*
électrophone [elɛktrɔfɔn] *nm* record player
élégamment [elegamɑ̃] *adv (vêtu, maquillée)* elegantly, smartly
élégance [elegɑ̃s] *nf (d'une personne, d'un restaurant, d'un style)* elegance, smartness; *(d'un geste, d'un comportement)* courtesy; *(d'une méthode, d'une solution)* neatness; **habillé avec é.** elegantly *or* smartly dressed; **savoir perdre avec é.** to be a good loser
élégant, -e [elegɑ̃, -ɑ̃t] *adj (vêtements, restaurant, style)* elegant, smart; *(geste, comportement)* courteous; *(méthode, solution)* neat; **un procédé peu é.** callous behaviour
élégie [eleʒi] *nf* elegy
élément [elemɑ̃] *nm* (**a**) *(partie) (d'une structure, d'un problème)* element; *(meuble)* unit; *Ordinat* **é. de menu** menu item (**b**) *(personne)* element; **j'ai de bons éléments dans ma classe** I've got some good pupils in my class (**c**) *(naturel)* element; **les quatre éléments** the four elements; *Fig* **être dans son é.** to be in one's element (**d**) *Chim* element (**e**) *(d'une batterie, d'un accumulateur)* cell
élémentaire [elemɑ̃tɛr] *adj* (**a**) *(de base) (connaissance, cours, problème)* elementary; *(minimal) (habitation)* basic; **c'est é.!** *(évident)* it's elementary! (**b**) *Chim & Phys* elementary
éléphant [elefɑ̃] *nm* elephant; **é. mâle/femelle** bull/cow elephant; **é. de mer** sea elephant; **é. d'Afrique/d'Asie** African/Indian elephant
éléphanteau, -x [elefɑ̃to] *nm* baby elephant

élevage [elvaʒ] *nm* (**a**) *(production)* breeding; *(d'abeilles, de volaille)* keeping; **faire de l'é.** *(de bétail)* to breed cattle; **é. intensif/en batterie** intensive/battery farming (**b**) *(ferme)* farm; **é. de poulets/de visons** poultry/mink farm
élévateur, -trice [elevatœr, -tris] **1** *adj* **chariot é.** forklift truck
2 *nm (appareil)* elevator
élévation [elevasjɔ̃] *nf* (**a**) *(action d'élever) (de la voix, des prix, de la température)* raising; *(d'une statue)* erection; *Rel (de l'hostie)* elevation (**b**) *(dans l'air)* rising (up) (**c**) *(augmentation)* rise (**de** in) (**d**) *Litt (des sentiments)* nobility (**e**) *Archit (projection)* elevation (**f**) *(relief)* rise
élevé, -e [elve] *adj* (**a**) *(haut, important)* high; *(rythme, pouls)* rapid; *Fig (style, esprit)* elevated (**b**) *(éduqué)* **bien/mal é.** well-/ill-mannered; **c'est très mal é. de parler la bouche pleine** it's very bad manners to speak with your mouth full
élève [elɛv] *nmf* student, pupil; **é. infirmière** student nurse; *Mil* **é. officier** cadet
élever¹ [46] [elve] *vt* (**a**) *(éduquer)* to bring up, to raise; **bébé élevé au sein/au biberon** breast-/bottle-fed baby (**b**) *(faire l'élevage de)* to breed; *(abeilles, volaille)* to keep
élever² *vt* (**a**) *(faire monter) (niveau d'eau, voix, prix, température)* to raise; **é. un nombre au carré/au cube** to square/cube a number; **é. un nombre à la puissance 4** to raise a number to the power of 4 (**b**) *(dresser) (monument, statue)* to erect; *(bras, poing, yeux)* to raise; *Fig (objection)* to raise (**c**) *(rehausser) (plafond, plancher)* to raise; **é. qch de 20 cm** to raise sth by 20 cm (**d**) *(promouvoir)* to promote (**au rang de** to) (**e**) *(édifier) (esprit)* to improve; **é. le débat** to raise the tone of the debate
2 s'élever *vpr* (**a**) *(avec mouvement)* to rise (up); *(cri)* to go up (**b**) *(se dresser) (bâtiment, montagnes)* to stand (**c**) *(monter) (température, prix)* to rise (**d**) *(protester)* **s'é. contre** to rise up against (**e**) **s'é. à** *(atteindre)* to amount to
éleveur, -euse [elvœr, -øz] *nm,f (de bovins)* cattle farmer; **é. de chevaux/chiens** horse/dog breeder; **é. de moutons/poulets** sheep/poultry farmer
elfe [ɛlf] *nm* elf
éligibilité [eliʒibilite] *nf* eligibility
éligible [eliʒibl] *adj* eligible
élimé, -e [elime] *adj* worn, threadbare
élimination [eliminasjɔ̃] *nf* elimination; **procéder par é.** to use a process of elimination
éliminatoire [eliminatwar] **1** *adj* **5 est une note é.** counts as a fail; **il a eu une note é.** he didn't get a pass mark
2 *adj & nf (épreuve)* **é.** qualifying heat
éliminer [elimine] *vt (candidat, suspect, toxines)* to eliminate (**de** from); *Sport (pour faute, dopage)* to disqualify; *(possibilité, théorie)* to rule out; **faites de l'exercice pour é.** do some exercise to clear your system
élire [44] [elir] *vt* (**a**) *(candidat, représentant)* to elect (**b**) **é. domicile** to take up residence
élision [elizjɔ̃] *nf Ling* elision
élite [elit] *nf* elite; **d'é.** *(personnel)* top; *(régiment)* crack
élitisme [elitism] *nm* elitism
élitiste [elitist] *adj & nmf* elitist
élixir [eliksir] *nm* elixir; **é. d'amour** elixir of love
elle [ɛl] *pron personnel* (**a**) *(sujet) (personne)* she; *(chose, animal)* it; **ton amie viendra-t-e.?** is your

friend coming?; **e., e. n'aurait pas levé le petit doigt** SHE wouldn't have lifted a finger; **la France, e.,** a exprimé clairement sa position France, for its part, has clearly expressed its position; **si j'étais e., je me méfierais** if I were her, I'd be careful (**b**) *(objet direct) (personne)* her; *(chose)* it; **et e., tu l'oublies?** and what about her, have you forgotten her? (**c**) *(avec préposition) (personne)* her; *(réfléchi)* herself; *(chose, animal)* it; **dis-le-lui, à e.** tell HER; **ce n'est pas à moi, c'est à e.** it's not mine, it's hers; **elle possède une entreprise à e.** she has her own company; *Fam* **une relation à e.** a relation of hers; **e. ne pense qu'à e.** she only thinks about herself (**d**) *(dans les comparaisons)* her; **il boit plus qu'e.** he drinks more than she does *or* than her **elle-même** [ɛlmɛm] *pron personnel (personne)* herself; *(chose, animal)* itself

elles [ɛl] *pron personnel* (**a**) *(sujet)* they; **nos chambres sont-e. prêtes?** are our rooms ready?; **e., e. seraient déjà parties** THEY would have left by now; **mes filles, e.,** ont fait des études my daughters, for their part, have been to university; **si j'étais e., je me méfierais** if I were them, I'd be careful (**b**) *(objet direct)* them; **et e., tu les oublies?** and what about them, have you forgotten them? (**c**) *(avec préposition)* them; *(réfléchi)* themselves; **dis-le-leur, à e.** tell THEM; **ce CD est à e.** this CD is theirs; **e. ont un appartement à e.** they have their own flat; *Fam* **un parent à e.** a relative of theirs; **e. ne pensent qu'à e.** they only think about themselves (**d**) *(dans les comparaisons)* them; **je mange plus qu'e.** I eat more than they do *or* than them **elles-mêmes** [ɛlmɛm] *pron personnel* themselves

ellipse [elips] *nf* (**a**) *Gram* ellipsis (**b**) *(courbe)* ellipse

elliptique [eliptik] *adj* elliptical

élocution [elɔkysjɔ̃] *nf* (**a**) *(diction)* diction (**b**) *Belg Scol (exposé)* talk, presentation

éloge [elɔʒ] *nm* (**a**) *(louange)* praise; **faire l'é. de qn/ qch** to praise sb/sth; **digne d'éloges** praiseworthy (**b**) *(discours)* eulogy; **é. funèbre** funeral oration

élogieux, -euse [elɔʒjø, -øz] *adj (discours, article)* complimentary; **parler de qn/qch en termes é.** to speak very highly of sb/sth

éloigné, -e [elwaɲe] *adj (dans l'espace, dans le temps)* distant, remote; *(parent)* distant; **ils sont éloignés d'un kilomètre** they're one kilometre apart; **être é. de qch** to be a long way (away) from sth; **se tenir é. de** to keep away from

éloignement [elwaɲəmã] *nm* (**a**) *(séparation)* separation; **l'é. est difficile à vivre** being apart is difficult (**b**) *(distance) (dans l'espace, dans le temps)* distance, remoteness

éloigner [elwaɲe] **1** *vt* (**a**) *(dans l'espace) (personne, objet)* to move away (**de** from); *(moustiques)* to keep away; **ce trajet nous éloigne du centre-ville** this route takes us away from the centre of town (**b**) *(distraire, détourner) (crainte, pensée)* to dismiss; *(soupçons)* to avert; *(personne) (de son travail, d'une autre personne)* to keep away (**de** from) **2 s'éloigner** *upr* (**a**) *(s'écarter)* to move away (**de** from); *(partir)* to go away (**de** from); *(orage)* to pass (**b**) *(se distraire, se détourner)* **s'é. de** *(vérité, sujet)* to wander from; *(famille, amis)* to distance oneself from; *(dans un couple)* to grow away from

élongation [elɔ̃gasjɔ̃] *nf* pulled muscle; **se faire une é.** to pull a muscle

éloquence [elɔkãs] *nf (expressivité)* eloquence

éloquent, -e [elɔkã, -ãt] *adj aussi Fig* eloquent; **ces chiffres sont éloquents** these figures speak for themselves

élu, -e [ely] **1** *adj (à un poste)* elected; *Rel* chosen **2** *nm,f* (**a**) *Rel* **les élus** the chosen ones (**b**) *(responsable)* elected representative (**c**) *Hum* **qui est l'heureuse élue?** who's the lucky lady?; **l'é. de son cœur** her beloved

élucider [elyside] *vt* to elucidate

élucubrations [elykybrasjɔ̃] *nfpl Péj* flights of fancy

éluder [elyde] *vt* to evade

Élysée [elize] *nm* **(le palais de) l'É.** the Élysée Palace *(residence of the President of the French Republic)*

Élysée

This eighteenth-century palace near the Champs-Élysées in Paris is the official residence of the French President. The name is often used to refer to the presidency itself.

émacié, -e [emasje] *adj* emaciated

émail, -aux [emaj, -o] *nm* enamel; *(sur porcelaine)* glaze; **en é.** *(ustensile de cuisine)* enamel

e-mail *(pl* e-mails) [imɛl] *nm Ordinat* e-mail; **envoyer un e. à qn** to e-mail sb, to send sb an e-mail; **par e.** by e-mail

émaillé, -e [emaje] *adj* (**a**) *(métal, ustensile de cuisine)* enamelled (**b**) *(porcelaine)* glazed (**c**) *Fig* **é. de** *(plein de)* studded with

émanation [emanasjɔ̃] *nf* **émanations** emanations; **émanations toxiques** toxic fumes; *Fig* **être l'é. de qch** to emanate from sth

émancipation [emãsipasjɔ̃] *nf* emancipation; *Fig (de l'esprit, de la pensée)* liberation

émancipé, -e [emãsipe] *adj* emancipated

émanciper [emãsipe] **1** *vt* to emancipate **2 s'émanciper** *upr* to become emancipated

émaner [emane] **émaner de** *vt ind aussi Fig* to emanate from

émarger [45] [emarʒe] **1** *vi* to draw one's salary **2** *vt (apposer ses initiales sur)* to initial; *(signer)* to sign

émasculation [emaskylasjɔ̃] *nf* emasculation

émasculer [emaskyle] *vt* to emasculate

emballage [ãbalaʒ] *nm* (**a**) *(action)* packing; *(dans du papier)* wrapping; **e. sous vide** vacuum-packing (**b**) *(contenant)* packaging; *(papier)* wrapping

emballé, -e [ãbale] *adj Fam (enthousiaste)* mad keen (**par** on)

emballer [ãbale] **1** *vt* (**a**) *(empaqueter)* to pack; *(dans du papier)* to wrap; *(pour la vente)* to package (**b**) *(moteur)* to race (**c**) *Fam (enthousiasmer)* to grab (**d**) *Fam (séduire)* to pick up **2 s'emballer** *upr* (**a**) *(moteur)* to race; *(cheval)* to bolt (**b**) *Fam (s'enthousiasmer)* to get carried away (**c**) *(cours, monnaie)* to spiral out of control

embarcadère [ãbarkadɛr] *nm* landing stage

embarcation [ãbarkasjɔ̃] *nf* (small) boat

embardée [ãbarde] *nf (d'une voiture)* swerve; *(d'un bateau)* yaw; **faire une e.** *(voiture)* to swerve; *(bateau)* to yaw

embargo [ãbargo] *nm* embargo; **mettre l'e. sur** to put an embargo on; **lever l'e. sur** to lift the embargo on

embarquement [ãbarkəmã] *nm (de passagers)* boarding; *(de marchandises)* loading; **e. immédiat porte 5** *(annonce)* now boarding at gate 5

embarquer [ãbarke] **1** vt (**a**) (passagers) to take on board; (marchandises) to load (**b**) Fam (emporter) to take (with one) (**c**) Fam (entraîner) (en week-end, au cinéma) to take off; (arrêter) to nick; **se laisser e. dans** (affaire, discussion) to get caught up in **2** vi (sur un bateau) (monter) to go on board, to board; (pour une destination) to embark **3** s'embarquer vpr (**a**) (sur un bateau) (monter) to go on board, to board; (pour une destination) to embark (**b**) Fam Fig **s'e. dans** (entreprise, discussion) to embark on

embarras [ãbara] nm (**a**) (situation difficile) **mettre qn dans l'e.** to put sb in an awkward situation; **tirer qn d'e.** to get sb out of an awkward situation; **n'avoir que l'e. du choix** to be spoilt for choice (**b**) (difficulté financière) **être dans l'e.** to be in financial difficulties (**c**) (gêne) embarrassment (**d**) (obstacle) **être un e. pour qn** to be a bother to sb (**e**) Méd **e. gastrique** upset stomach

embarrassant, -e [ãbarasã, -ãt] adj (**a**) (qui gêne) (question, situation) embarrassing (**b**) (qui encombre) cumbersome

embarrassé, -e [ãbarase] adj (**a**) (gêné) embarrassed; **je suis très e. de devoir le leur dire** I'm very embarrassed about having to tell them (**b**) (encombré) (table, pièce) cluttered (**de** with); **avoir les mains embarrassées** to have one's hands full

embarrasser [ãbarase] **1** vt (**a**) (gêner) to embarrass (**b**) (encombrer) (table, pièce) to clutter up (**de** with); **e. qn** (vêtement, achats) to hamper sb; (empêcher le passage de) to be in sb's way **2** s'embarrasser vpr (s'encombrer) **s'e. de** to burden oneself with; Fig **elle ne s'embarrasse pas de douceur** she doesn't worry about being gentle

embauche [ãboʃ] nf (**a**) (action) taking on, hiring (**b**) (emploi) employment

embaucher [ãboʃe] vt (**a**) (engager) to take on, to hire; **l'entreprise embauche en ce moment** the company is currently recruiting (**b**) Fam (pour corvée) to recruit (**pour faire** to do)

embaumer [ãbome] vt (**a**) (corps) to embalm (**b**) (répandre une odeur de) to be fragrant with; **son parfum embaumait la pièce** the scent of her perfume filled the room; **le chèvrefeuille embaumait** there was a fragrant smell of honeysuckle

embaumeur [ãbomœr] nm (de corps) embalmer

embellie [ãbɛli] nf (éclaircie) bright spell; Naut calm spell, lull; Fig (de l'économie, d'une situation etc) improvement; **courte e.** bright interval

embellir [ãbɛlir] **1** vt (pièce, parc, personne) to make more attractive; Fig (histoire, vérité) to embellish **2** vi to grow more attractive

embellissement [ãbɛlismã] nm (d'un lieu) improvement; (d'un récit) embellishment

emberlificoter [ãbɛrlifikɔte] Fam **1** vt (**a**) (fil) to tangle up (**b**) (duper) to take in **2** s'emberlificoter vpr **s'e. dans** (vêtements, mensonges) to get tangled up in

embêtant, -e [ãbɛtã, -ãt] adj Fam annoying

embêtement [ãbɛtmã] nm Fam problem; **faire des embêtements à qn** to make trouble for sb

embêter [ãbete] Fam **1** vt (contrarier, agacer) to annoy; (ennuyer) to bore **2** s'embêter vpr (s'ennuyer) to be bored; Ironique **tu ne t'embêtes pas!** you don't do badly for yourself!; **s'e. à faire qch** (prendre la peine de le faire) to bother doing sth

emblée [ãble] **d'emblée** adv right away, straight away

emblématique [ãblematik] adj emblematic; Fig symbolic

emblème [ãblɛm] nm aussi Fig emblem

embobiner [ãbɔbine] vt Fam (duper) to take in

emboîter [ãbwate] **1** vt (assembler) to fit together; **e. qch dans qch** to fit sth into sth; **e. le pas à qn** to follow close on sb's heels; Fig to follow sb's lead **2** s'emboîter vpr to fit together

embolie [ãbɔli] nf embolism; **e. gazeuse/pulmonaire** air/pulmonary embolism; **e. cérébrale** clot on the brain, Spéc cerebral embolism

embonpoint [ãbɔ̃pwɛ̃] nm stoutness; **avoir/prendre de l'e.** to be/get stout

embouché, -e [ãbuʃe] adj Fam **mal e.** foul-tempered

embouchure [ãbuʃyr] nf (**a**) (d'un instrument à vent) mouthpiece (**b**) (d'un cours d'eau) mouth

embourber [ãburbe] **s'embourber** vpr (**a**) (véhicule) to get stuck in the mud (**b**) Fig & Péj to get bogged down

embourgeoisement [ãburʒwazmã] nm (d'une personne) attainment of middle-class respectability; (d'un quartier) gentrification, yuppification

embourgeoiser [ãburʒwaze] **s'embourgeoiser** vpr (personne) to become middle-class; (quartier) to become gentrified or yuppified

embout [ãbu] nm (d'un parapluie, d'une canne) tip; (d'un tuyau) nozzle

embouteillage [ãbutɛjaʒ] nm traffic jam, hold-up

embouteiller [ãbuteje] vt (route) to clog up

emboutir [ãbutir] vt (**a**) (véhicule) to crash into (**b**) (métal) to stamp

embranchement [ãbrãʃmã] nm (**a**) (croisement) junction; (bifurcation) (d'une route) fork (**b**) (voie secondaire) (de route) side road; (de chemin de fer) branch line (**c**) Bot & Zool subkingdom

embraser [ãbraze] Litt **1** vt (**a**) (incendier) to set ablaze (**b**) (éclairer) to set aglow (**c**) Fig (exalter) (foule) to set alight **2** s'embraser vpr (**a**) (prendre feu) to blaze up (**b**) (rougeoyer) to glow

embrassade [ãbrasad] nf embrace, hug

embrasser [ãbrase] **1** vt (**a**) (donner un baiser à) to kiss (**b**) (étreindre) to embrace, to hug; **qui trop embrasse mal étreint** one shouldn't spread oneself too thinly (**c**) (adopter) (religion, doctrine, cause) to embrace; (carrière) to take up (**d**) (englober) (sujets, questions) to embrace, to take in; **e. qch du regard** to take sth in at a glance **2** s'embrasser vpr to kiss (each other)

embrasure [ãbrazyr] nf Constr aperture; **se tenir dans l'e. de la porte** to stand in the doorway

embrayage [ãbrɛjaʒ] nm (**a**) (mécanisme) clutch (**b**) (action) engaging the clutch

embrayer [53] [ãbreje] vi (**a**) Aut to engage the clutch (**b**) Fam (commencer) to get going (**sur** on)

embrigadement [ãbrigadmã] nm dragooning (**dans** into)

embrigader [ãbrigade] vt to dragoon (**dans** into)

embringuer [ãbrɛ̃ge] Fam **1** vt **e. qn dans qch** to get sb mixed up in sth **2** s'embringuer vpr **s'e. dans qch** to get mixed up in sth

embrocher [ãbrɔʃe] vt (**a**) Culin (viande) to put on a spit (**b**) Fam (transpercer) **e. qn** to skewer sb

embrouillamini [ãbrujamini] nm Fam muddle

embrouillé, -e [ãbruje] *adj* (**a**) *(fils)* tangled (**b**) *Fig (idées, raisonnement, esprit)* muddled; *(affaire)* complicated
embrouiller [ãbruje] **1** *vt* (**a**) *(fils)* to tangle (up) (**b**) *Fig (personne, situation, idées)* to muddle (up)
   2 s'embrouiller *vpr (personne, idées)* to get muddled (up)
embroussaillé, -e [ãbrusaje] *adj (allée, jardin)* overgrown; *(cheveux)* messed up
embrumé, -e [ãbryme] *adj (horizon)* hazy; *(esprit)* fuddled
embruns [ãbrõ] *nmpl* spray
embryologie [ãbrijɔlɔʒi] *nf* embryology
embryon [ãbrijõ] *nm* embryo
embryonnaire [ãbrijɔnɛr] *adj* embryonic
embûches [ãbyʃ] *nfpl* traps; **semé d'e.** full of pitfalls
embuer [ãbɥe] *vt (miroir, vitre)* to mist up; **yeux embués de larmes** eyes misted over with tears
embuscade [ãbyskad] *nf* ambush; **tendre une e. à qn** to set an ambush for sb; **tomber dans une e.** to be ambushed
embusquer [ãbyske] **s'embusquer** *vpr* (**a**) *(se mettre en embuscade)* to lie in ambush (**b**) *(se faire affecter loin du front)* to get a cushy posting
éméché, -e [emeʃe] *adj Fam* tipsy
émeraude [emrod] **1** *nf (pierre)* emerald
   2 *nm & adj inv* emerald green
émergence [emɛrʒãs] *nf (apparition)* emergence
émerger [45] [emɛrʒe] *vi* (**a**) *(apparaître)* to emerge (**de** from) (**b**) *Fam (se lever)* to surface
émeri [emri] *nm* emery; **papier** *ou* **toile é.** emery paper
émérite [emerit] *adj* (**a**) *(expert)* highly skilled (**b**) *(professeur)* emeritus
émerveillement [emɛrvɛjmã] *nm* wonder
émerveiller [emɛrveje] **1** *vt (enchanter)* to fill with wonder; **être émerveillé par** to marvel at
   2 s'émerveiller *vpr* **s'é. de** *ou* **devant** *(s'enchanter de)* to marvel at
émetteur, -trice [emɛtœr, -tris] **1** *adj* (**a**) *Fin (banque, organisme)* issuing (**b**) *Rad* **poste é.** transmitter; **station émettrice** transmitting station
   2 *nm* transmitter
émettre [47] [emɛtr] **1** *vt* (**a**) *(cri, rot, soupir)* to give; *(son, lumière)* to give out, to emit; *(fumée, chaleur)* to give off, to emit (**b**) *Fig (opinion, objection, idée)* to voice (**c**) *Rad & TV* to transmit, to broadcast (**d**) *(billets de banque, actions, timbres-poste)* to issue
   2 *vi Rad & TV* to transmit, to broadcast
émeu [emø] *nm* emu
émeus, émeut *voir* **émouvoir**
émeute [emøt] *nf* riot
émeutier, -ère [emøtje, -ɛr] *nm,f* rioter
émeuve *etc voir* **émouvoir**
émietter [emjete] **1** *vt* (**a**) *(pain)* to crumble (**b**) *Fig (domaine, empire)* to break up
   2 s'émietter *vpr (pain, roche)* to crumble
émigrant, -e [emigrã, -ãt] *nm,f* emigrant
émigration [emigrasjõ] *nf* emigration
émigré, -e [emigre] **1** *nm,f* emigrant; *Hist* émigré
   2 *adj (travailleur, population)* migrant
émigrer [emigre] *vi* to emigrate
émincer [16] [emɛ̃se] *vt (viande, légumes)* to slice thinly
éminemment [eminamã] *adv* eminently
éminence [eminãs] *nf* (**a**) *(de relief)* hill (**b**) *Rel* **É.** Eminence; *Fig* **l'é. grise** the éminence grise

éminent, -e [eminã, -ãt] *adj (personne)* eminent; **il nous a rendu d'éminents services** he rendered us outstanding service
émir [emir] *nm* emir
émirat [emira] *nm* emirate; **les Émirats arabes unis** the United Arab Emirates
émissaire [emisɛr] *nm (envoyé)* emissary
émission [emisjõ] *nf* (**a**) *(de son, de substance)* emission; *(électricité, chaleur, connaissances)* to store up
emmagasiner [ãmagazine] *vt (marchandises)* to store; *(électricité, chaleur, connaissances)* to store up
emmailloter [ãmajɔte] *vt (nourrisson)* to swaddle
emmancher [ãmãʃe] **1** *vt* (**a**) *(outil)* to fit a handle on (**b**) *(tuyaux)* to fit together; *(pièce)* to fit (**dans** into)
   2 s'emmancher *vpr (pièces)* to fit together; *Fam Fig* **bien/mal s'e.** to get off to a good/bad start
emmanchure [ãmãʃyr] *nf* armhole
emmêler [ãmɛle] **1** *vt (fils, cheveux)* to tangle
   2 s'emmêler *vpr (fils, cheveux)* to get tangled; *Fam* **s'e. les pédales** *ou* **les pinceaux** to get all muddled up
emménager [45] [ãmenaʒe] *vi* to move in
emmener [46] [ãmne] *vt* (**a**) *(prendre avec soi) (personne)* to take; *(prisonnier)* to take away; *Fam (objet)* to take; **e. qn en voiture** to give sb a *Br* lift *orAm* ride (**b**) *(entraîner) (équipier, peloton, sprint)* to lead
emmenthal [emɛtal] *nm* Emmenthal
emmerdant, -e [ãmɛrdã, -ãt] *adj très Fam* (**a**) *(contrariant, agaçant)* damn *or Br* bloody annoying (**b**) *(ennuyeux) Br* bloody *or Am* goddamn boring
emmerdement [ãmɛrdəmã] *nm très Fam* damn *or Br* bloody nuisance; **avoir des emmerdements** to have a hell of a lot of trouble
emmerder [ãmɛrde] **1** *vt très Fam* **e. qn** *(contrarier, agacer)* to piss sb off; *(ennuyer)* to bore sb stiff; **je l'emmerde!** screw him!, *Br* sod him!
   2 s'emmerder *vpr très Fam (s'ennuyer)* to be bored stiff; **s'e. à faire qch** *(prendre la peine de le faire)* to bother doing sth; *Ironique* **tu ne t'emmerdes pas!** you're not doing badly for yourself!; *(tu as du culot)* you've got a *Br* bloody *orAm* goddamn nerve!
emmerdeur, -euse [ãmɛrdœr, -øz] *nm,f très Fam* pain in the *Br* arse *orAm* ass
emmitoufler [ãmitufle] **1** *vt* to wrap up (**dans** in)
   2 s'emmitoufler *vpr* to wrap oneself up (**dans** in)
emmurer [ãmyre] *vt* to wall up
émoi [emwa] *nm (trouble)* emotion; *(plaisir)* excitement; **être (tout) en é.** *(troublé)* to be in a flutter
émollient, -e [emɔljã, -ãt] *adj & nm* emollient
émoluments [emɔlymã] *nmpl* remuneration
émonder [emõde] *vt (arbre, texte)* to prune
émoticon [emɔtikõ] *nm Ordinat* smiley, emoticon
émotif, -ive [emɔtif, -iv] **1** *adj* emotional
   2 *nm,f* emotional person
émotion [emosjõ] *nf* emotion; *(frayeur)* fright; **donner des émotions à qn** to give sb a real fright
émotivité [emotivite] *nf* **être d'une grande é.** to be highly emotional
émoulu, -e [emuly] *adj* **frais é. de l'université** fresh out of university
émoussé, -e [emuse] *adj (pointe, lame)* blunt; *Fig (sentiment, intérêt)* blunted
émoustiller [emustije] *vt* to arouse
émouvant, -e [emuvã, -ãt] *adj* moving

émouvoir [31a] [emuvwar] **1** *vt (toucher)* to move, to touch; *(troubler)* to upset **2 s'émouvoir** *vpr (être touché)* to be moved *or* touched; **s'é. de qch** *(s'en inquiéter)* to be concerned about sth

empailler [ɑ̃paje] *vt* (**a**) *(animal)* to stuff (**b**) **e. une chaise** to bottom a chair with straw

empaler [ɑ̃pale] **1** *vt* to impale **2 s'empaler** *vpr* to impale oneself

empaqueter [42] [ɑ̃pakte] *vt* to pack

emparer [ɑ̃pare] **s'emparer** *vpr* **s'e. de** *(lieu, personne, objet)* to seize; *(sujet: sentiment, doute)* to take hold of

empâter [ɑ̃pɑte] **1** *vt* to bloat **2 s'empâter** *vpr* to become bloated

empattement [ɑ̃patmɑ̃] *nm* (**a**) *(d'une voiture)* wheelbase (**b**) *Typ* serif

empêché, -e [ɑ̃peʃe] *adj (retenu)* held up, detained

empêchement [ɑ̃pɛʃmɑ̃] *nm* hitch; **il a eu un e.** something came up

empêcher [ɑ̃peʃe] **1** *vt (action, événement)* to prevent, to stop; *(mouvement, passage)* to obstruct; **e. qn de faire qch** to prevent *or* stop sb (from) doing sth; *Fam* **ça ne m'empêchera pas de dormir** I won't lose any sleep over it; **il n'y a rien qui t'en empêche** there's nothing stopping you; **cela n'empêche que...**, **il n'empêche que...**, all the same,...; *Fam* **(il) n'empêche** all the same **2 s'empêcher** *vpr* **je ne peux pas m'en e.** I can't help it; **je ne pouvais pas m'e. de rire** I couldn't help laughing

empêcheur, -euse [ɑ̃peʃœr, -øz] *nm,f Fam* **e. de tourner en rond** spoilsport

empennage [ɑ̃pɛnaʒ] *nm (de flèche)* feathering, feathers; *(d'avion)* tail section

empereur [ɑ̃prœr] *nm* emperor

empesé, -e [ɑ̃paze] *adj* (**a**) *(col, chemise)* starched (**b**) *Fig (personne, air, style)* stiff

empester [ɑ̃pɛste] **1** *vt (frigo, pièce)* to stink out; **e. l'alcool/le fromage** to stink of alcohol/cheese **2** *vi* to stink

empêtrer [ɑ̃petre] **s'empêtrer** *vpr* to get entangled; **s'e. les pieds dans qch** to get one's feet caught in sth; *Fig* **s'e. dans** *(explications, mensonges)* to get tangled up in; *Fig* **s'e. dans une affaire** to get mixed up in a business; **s'e. de qn** to land oneself with sb

emphase [ɑ̃fɑz] *nf* pomposity; **avec e.** pompously

emphatique [ɑ̃fatik] *adj* pompous

emphysème [ɑ̃fizɛm] *nm* emphysema

empiècement [ɑ̃pjɛsmɑ̃] *nm (d'un vêtement)* yoke

empiétement [ɑ̃pjɛtmɑ̃] *nm* encroachment (**sur** on)

empiéter [34] [ɑ̃pjete] *vi* **e. sur** *(terrain, horaire, vie privée)* to encroach on

empiffrer [ɑ̃pifre] **s'empiffrer** *vpr Fam* to stuff oneself (**de** with)

empiler [ɑ̃pile] **1** *vt (livres, bois, boîtes)* to stack, to pile (up) **2 s'empiler** *vpr* (**a**) *(livres, dossiers)* to pile up (**b**) *(passagers)* **s'e. dans** to cram into

empire [ɑ̃pir] *nm* (**a**) *Hist & Fig* empire; **un e. commercial** a business empire; **pas pour un e.!** not for all the tea in China!; **le premier E.**, **l'E.** the First Empire; **le second E.** the Second Empire; **style/meubles E.** Empire style/furniture; **l'E. du milieu** the Middle Kingdom, the Celestial Empire (**b**) *Litt (influence)* influence; **avoir de l'e. sur qn** to have influence over sb;

faire qch sous l'e. de la boisson/de la colère to do sth under the influence of drink/in a fit of anger

empirer [ɑ̃pire] *vi* to worsen, to get worse

empirique [ɑ̃pirik] *adj* empirical

emplacement [ɑ̃plasmɑ̃] *nm* (**a**) *(endroit)* site, location; *(sur un marché, dans un parking)* space (**b**) *Ordinat* slot; **e. pour carte d'extension** expansion slot; **e. (pour) périphériques** extension slot

emplafonner [ɑ̃plafɔne] *vt Fam* to crash into

emplâtre [ɑ̃plɑtr] *nm* (**a**) *(pansement)* plaster (**b**) *Fam (personne)* drip

emplette [ɑ̃plɛt] *nf* purchase; **faire ses emplettes** to go shopping; **faire l'e. de qch** to purchase sth

emplir [ɑ̃plir] **1** *vt* to fill (**de** with) **2 s'emplir** *vpr* to fill (up) (**de** with)

emploi [ɑ̃plwa] *nm* (**a**) *(utilisation)* use; **prêt à l'e.** ready to use; **e. du temps** timetable, schedule; **faire double e.** to be redundant (**b**) *(situation)* job; *(embauche)* employment; **être sans e.** to be out of work, to be unemployed; **la crise/situation de l'e.** the employment crisis/situation; *Fig* **il a le physique** *ou* **la tête** *ou Fam* **la gueule de l'e.** he looks the part; **e. de bureau** desk job, office job; **e. à plein temps** full-time job; **e. saisonnier** seasonal job; **e. à temps partiel** part-time job

emploi-jeunes [ɑ̃plwaʒœn] *nm inv* = job, usually in the public sector or in education, created for a young person as part of a programme to combat unemployment

employable [ɑ̃plwajabl] *adj* employable

employé, -e [ɑ̃plwaje] *nm,f* employee; **e. de banque** bank clerk; **e. de bureau** office worker; **e. de maison** domestic employee

employer [32] [ɑ̃plwaje] **1** *vt* (**a**) *(utiliser) (outil, mot, technique, force)* to use; **e. les grands moyens** to take drastic measures; **e. son temps à faire qch** to spend one's time doing sth (**b**) *(faire travailler) (personne)* to employ; **elle l'emploie comme secrétaire** she employs him/her as a secretary **2 s'employer** *vpr* (**a**) *(personne)* **s'e. à faire qch** to work on doing sth; **je m'y emploie** I'm working on it (**b**) *(être utilisé)* to be used

employeur, -euse [ɑ̃plwajœr, -øz] *nm,f* employer

empocher [ɑ̃pɔʃe] *vt* to pocket

empoignade [ɑ̃pwaɲad] *nf Fam* dust-up

empoigne [ɑ̃pwaɲ] *nf voir* **foire**

empoigner [ɑ̃pwaɲe] **1** *vt* to grab (hold of) **2 s'empoigner** *vpr* to have a dust-up

empoisonnant, -e [ɑ̃pwazɔnɑ̃, -ɑ̃t] *adj Fam* irritating

empoisonnement [ɑ̃pwazɔnmɑ̃] *nm* (**a**) *(par une substance nocive)* poisoning (**b**) *Fam (ennui)* problem

empoisonner [ɑ̃pwazɔne] **1** *vt* (**a**) *(avec une substance nocive) (personne, nourriture, lieu)* to poison; *Fig* **empoisonné** *(paroles)* poisonous (**b**) *(empester) (lieu)* to stink out (**c**) *Fam (irriter)* **e. qn** to get on sb's nerves (**d**) *(altérer) (existence, relations)* to poison; **e. la vie de qn** to make sb's life a misery **2 s'empoisonner** *vpr* to poison oneself; **s'e. l'existence** to make one's life a misery

emporté, -e [ɑ̃pɔrte] *adj* quick-tempered

emportement [ɑ̃pɔrtəmɑ̃] *nm* anger

emporte-pièce [ɑ̃pɔrtəpjɛs] **1** *nm inv Tech* punch; *Culin* pastry cutter **2 à l'emporte-pièce** *adj (jugement, style)* incisive

emporter [ɑ̃pɔrte] **1** *vt* (**a**) *(prendre avec soi)* to take; **plats à e.** *ou Suisse* **à l'e.** takeaway meals (**b**) *(trans-*

porter) to take away (**c**) (*entraîner*) (*sujet: courant*) to sweep away; (*sujet: vent*) to blow off; **il a eu une jambe emportée par un obus** a shell took one of his legs off; **e. qn** (*maladie*) to carry sb off; **ça emporte la bouche** *ou Fam* **la gueule** (*moutarde, plat épicé*) it blows your head off; *Fig* **se laisser e. par la colère/ son imagination** to let one's anger/one's imagination get the better of one (**d**) (*conquérir*) (*position*) to take (**e**) **l'e.** (*gagner*) to win; (*prédominer*) to prevail; **l'e. sur qn** to beat sb; **l'e. sur qch** to prevail over sth
  2 s'emporter *vpr* to lose one's temper (**contre qn** with sb)
empoté, -e [ɑ̃pɔte] *Fam* **1** *adj* cack-handed
  2 *nm,f* cack-handed idiot
empourprer [ɑ̃purpre] **1** *vt* to tinge with crimson
  2 s'empourprer *vpr* to turn crimson
empoussiéré, -e [ɑ̃pusjere] *adj* dusty
empreinte [ɑ̃prɛ̃t] *nf* (**a**) (*trace*) (*de pas*) footprint; (*d'animal*) track; **e. digitale** fingerprint; **e. génétique** genetic fingerprint (**b**) *Fig* (*de l'éducation, du milieu*) stamp, mark
empressé, -e [ɑ̃prese] **1** *adj* (*prévenant*) attentive
  2 *nm,f Péj* **faire l'e. auprès de qn** to dance attendance on sb
empressement [ɑ̃prɛsmɑ̃] *nm* (**a**) (*prévenance*) attentiveness (**b**) (*hâte*) eagerness (**à faire qch** to do sth); **il montre peu d'e. à faire les travaux** he doesn't seem very eager to do the work; **avec e.** eagerly; **mettre beaucoup d'e. à faire qch** to hasten to do sth
empresser [ɑ̃prese] **s'empresser** *vpr* (**a**) (*se dépêcher*) **s'e. de faire qch** to hasten to do sth (**b**) (*être prévenant*) **s'e. auprès de qn** to be attentive to sb
emprise [ɑ̃priz] *nf* hold (**sur** over); **avoir de l'e. sur qn** to have a hold over sb; **sous l'e. de la colère** in a fit of anger
emprisonnement [ɑ̃prizɔnmɑ̃] *nm* imprisonment; **peine d'e.** prison sentence
emprisonner [ɑ̃prizɔne] *vt* to imprison
emprunt [ɑ̃prœ̃] *nm* (**a**) (*action*) borrowing (**b**) (*somme*) loan; **faire un e.** (*auprès d'une banque*) to take out a loan; **e. d'État** government loan; **lancer un e.** to issue a bond (**c**) *Ling* borrowing
emprunté, -e [ɑ̃prœ̃te] *adj* self-conscious, awkward
emprunter [ɑ̃prœ̃te] *vt* (**a**) (*objet, argent*) to borrow (**à** from) (**b**) (*route, chemin*) to take
emprunteur, -euse [ɑ̃prœ̃tœr, -øz] *nm,f* borrower
empuantir [ɑ̃pyɑ̃tir] *vt* (*lieu*) to stink out
ému, -e [emy] **1** *pp de* **émouvoir**
  2 *adj* (*touché*) moved, touched; (*intimidé*) nervous; **voix émue** voice filled with emotion; **garder un souvenir é. de qch** to have fond memories of sth
émulation [emylasjɔ̃] *nf aussi Ordinat* emulation
émule [emyl] *nmf* emulator; **j'ai fait des émules** people followed my example
émuler [emyle] *vt aussi Ordinat* to emulate
émulsifiant [emylsifjɑ̃] *nm* emulsifier
émulsion [emylsjɔ̃] *nf* emulsion
en¹ [ɑ̃] *prép* (**a**) (*indique la date ou la durée*) in; **en 1800** in 1800; **en hiver/été** in winter/summer; **en une minute/trois jours** in a minute/three days (**b**) (*indique la destination*) to; **aller en Allemagne** to go to Germany; **partir en vacances** to go on *Br* holiday *or Am* vacation (**c**) (*indique le lieu*) in; **vivre en France** to live in France; **en altitude** at altitude; **se promener en forêt** to walk in the forest; **en pleine mer** out at sea; **il y a**

quelque chose en lui qui me déplaît there's something about him I don't like (**d**) (*indique le moyen*) by; **en voiture/avion/train** by car/plane/train (**e**) (*décrit un état*) in; **écrit en français** written in French; **en ruines** ruined; **être en colère/en larmes** to be angry/crying; **être en transe/en danger** to be in a trance/in danger; **être en arrêt maladie** to be on sick leave; **en trois parties** in three parts; **montre en or/en argent** gold/silver watch; **disponible en rouge/38** available in red/in size 38; **être bon en physique** to be good at physics; **payer en euros** to pay in euros; **la même chose en mieux/en moins bien** the same thing but better/but not as good (**f**) (*indique une transformation, une progression*) into; **traduire qch en français** to translate sth into French; **transformer une chambre en bureau** to convert a bedroom into an office; **casser qch en deux** to break sth in two *or* in half; **peindre qch en rouge** to paint sth red; **réduire qch en poudre** to reduce sth to a powder; **se mettre en colère** to get angry; **aller de ville en ville** to go from town to town; **de jour en jour** by the day; **changer en bien/mal** to change for the better/for the worse (**g**) (*en tant que*) as; **parler à qn en ami** to speak to sb as a friend; **parler en connaisseur** to speak as an expert; **agir en traître** to be disloyal (**h**) (*avec un participe présent*) **entrer en criant** to come in shouting; **il s'est coupé en se rasant** he cut himself shaving; **c'est impoli de lire en mangeant** it's rude to read while you're eating; **traverser en courant** to run across; **répondre en maugréant** to grumble in reply; **dire qch en plaisantant** to say sth as a joke; **elle s'est cassé la jambe en tombant** she fell and broke her leg; **c'est en s'entraînant qu'il s'améliorera** he'll only get better if he practises
en² *pron* (**a**) (*avec les adjectifs construits avec de*) **il en est bien capable** he's quite capable of it; **et ta voiture? – j'en suis très content** how's your car? – I'm very pleased with it (**b**) (*avec les verbes construits avec de*) **qu'en penses-tu?** what do you think of it?; **je ne m'en souviens plus** I can't remember; **on en reparlera** we'll talk about it later; **j'espère en tirer 200 euros** I hope to get 200 euros for it (**c**) (*remplace le complément du nom*) **nous en avons la possibilité** we can do it; **elle en a mangé un morceau** she ate a piece of it; **j'en ai acheté 3 kilos** I bought 3 kilos (**d**) (*remplace le nom*) **il y en a plusieurs** there are several of them; **elle en a cassé deux** she broke two of them; **est-ce que tu en veux?** do you want some?; **je n'en ai jamais vu** I've never seen one/any; **est-ce de l'or? – non, ce n'en est pas** is it gold? – no, it's not (**e**) (*indique la cause*) **il en a perdu la raison** it made him lose his mind; **j'en suis tout retourné** I'm really upset about it (**f**) *Fam* (*pour insister*) **il en a fait une histoire!** he made a real song and dance about it!; **des balayeurs, il en faut** someone has to sweep the streets (**g**) (*indique la provenance*) from there; **justement, j'en viens** I've just come from there
ENA [ena] *nf* (*abrév* **École nationale d'administration**) = university-level college preparing students for senior posts in law and economics
énamouré, -e [ɑ̃namure], **énamouré, -e** [enamure] *adj Vieilli ou Hum* amorous
énamourer [ɑ̃namure], **énamourer** [enamure] **s'énamourer** *vpr* **s'é. de** to become enamoured of
énarque [enark] *nmf* = graduate of the ENA

encabaner [ãkabane] s'**encabaner** vpr Can to shut oneself away

encadré [ãkadre] nm (dans un texte) box; Ordinat **e. graphique** graphics box; Ordinat **e. texte** text box

encadrement [ãkadrəmã] nm (**a**) (cadre) frame; **dans l'e. de la porte** in the doorway (**b**) (fonction) (de personnel) management; (d'élèves, d'enfants) supervision; (personnes qui encadrent) (du personnel) management; Mil officers (**c**) Écon **e. du crédit** credit squeeze

encadrer [ãkadre] vt (**a**) (tableau, photo) to frame (**b**) (entourer) (mots, paragraphe) to circle; **encadré par deux gendarmes** flanked by two policemen (**c**) (guider) (personnel, équipe) to manage; (enfants, handicapés) to supervise; Mil (soldats) to officer (**d**) Fam (supporter) **je ne peux pas l'e.** I can't stand him/her

encadreur, -euse [ãkadrœr, -øz] nm,f picture framer

encaissé, -e [ãkese] adj (vallée) deep; (rivière) with steep sides; (route) cut into the hillside

encaissement [ãkesmã] nm (**a**) (d'un chèque) cashing; (d'argent) collection (**b**) (d'une vallée) depth

encaisser [ãkese] vt (**a**) (chèque) to cash; (argent) to collect (**b**) Fam (supporter) (coups, critiques) to take; **je ne peux pas l'e.** I can't stand him/her; **il sait e.** he can take it; **qu'est-ce qu'il a encaissé!** he took a lot of punishment!

encanailler [ãkanaje] s'**encanailler** vpr to slum it

encart [ãkar] nm (feuille) insert; **e. publicitaire** advertising insert

en-cas [ãka] nm inv snack

encastrable [ãkastrabl] adj (machine à laver, cuisinière) that can be built in

encastré, -e [ãkastre] adj built-in

encastrer [ãkastre] **1** vt to build in

2 s'**encastrer** vpr (éléments) to fit together; (machine à laver, cuisinière) to fit (**dans** into); **la voiture s'est encastrée sous un camion** the car embedded itself under a lorry

encaustique [ãkostik] nf wax, polish

enceinte¹ [ãsɛ̃t] nf (**a**) (mur) (surrounding) wall; (palissade) fence (**b**) (espace) enclosure; (d'église, de couvent) precinct(s); **dans l'e. du parc** within the park (**c**) (baffle) **e. (acoustique)** speaker

enceinte² adj f pregnant; **e. de cinq mois** five months pregnant; **être e. de jumeaux** to be expecting twins; **elle est e. de Marc** she's pregnant by Marc

encens [ãsã] nm incense

encenser [ãsãse] vt **e. qn** to praise sb to the skies

encensoir [ãsãswar] nm censer

encéphalite [ãsefalit] nf encephalitis; **e. bovine spongiforme** bovine spongiform encephalopathy

encéphalogramme [ãsefalɔgram] nm encephalogram

encercler [ãsɛrkle] vt (**a**) (ennemi, lieu) to encircle, to surround (**b**) (mot) to circle, to ring

enchaînement [ãʃɛnmã] nm (**a**) (série) (d'événements, de circonstances) series, chain (**b**) (liaison) (d'idées, de séquences) linking (**c**) (en danse) sequence (of steps); (en ballet) enchaînement (**d**) Ordinat concatenation

enchaîner [ãʃene] **1** vt (**a**) (animal, prisonnier) to chain up; Fig (peuple) to enslave; (presse) to curb; **e. qn à** to chain sb (up) to (**b**) (lier) (épisodes, séquences) to link (up)

2 vi to move on; **e. sur un sujet** to move on to a subject

3 s'**enchaîner** vpr (**a**) (personne) s'e. à to chain one-self (up) to (**b**) (séquences, épisodes) to be linked together; **les événements se sont enchaînés rapidement** events happened very quickly

enchanté, -e [ãʃãte] adj (**a**) (ravi) delighted (**de** with); **e. (de faire votre connaissance)!** pleased to meet you! (**b**) (magique) enchanted

enchantement [ãʃãtmã] nm (**a**) (sortilège) (magic) spell; **comme par e.** as if by magic (**b**) (ravissement, merveille) delight

enchanter [ãʃãte] vt (**a**) (ravir) to delight; **cette idée ne l'enchante pas** he's/she's not keen on the idea (**b**) (ensorceler) to bewitch

enchanteur, -eresse [ãʃãtœr, -trɛs] **1** adj (sourire) bewitching; (spectacle, endroit) enchanting, delightful

2 nm (**a**) (sorcier) sorcerer (**b**) Fig (charmeur) charmer

3 nf enchanteresse sorceress

enchâsser [ãʃase] vt (**a**) (bijou) to set (**b**) (relique) to enshrine

enchère [ãʃɛr] nf bid; **les enchères** the bidding; **vente aux enchères** auction; **faire monter les enchères** to up the bidding; Fig to raise the stakes; **vendre qch aux enchères** to sell sth at auction

enchérir [ãʃerir] vi to make a higher bid; **e. sur qn** to outbid sb; Fig to go one better than sb

enchevêtré, -e [ãʃəvetre] adj (branchages, fils, explications) tangled

enchevêtrement [ãʃəvɛtrəmã] nm (de fils, branchages) tangle

enchevêtrer [ãʃəvetre] **1** vt (fils, branchages) to tangle (up)

2 s'**enchevêtrer** vpr (fils) to get tangled (up)

enclave [ãklav] nf enclave

enclenchement [ãklãʃmã] nm (d'une vitesse, d'un mécanisme) engaging

enclencher [ãklãʃe] **1** vt (vitesse, mécanisme) to engage; Fig (processus) to get under way

2 s'**enclencher** vpr (vitesse, mécanisme) to engage; Fig (processus) to get under way

enclin, -e [ãklɛ̃, -in] adj être e. à faire qch to be inclined to do sth; être e. à la paresse/la méfiance to be inclined to be lazy/wary; **il est peu e. à partager ses secrets** he is reluctant to share his secrets; **peu e. au bavardage** not very talkative

enclos [ãklo] nm (espace) enclosure; (pour chevaux) paddock

enclume [ãklym] nf anvil; Fig **être entre l'e. et le marteau** to be between the devil and the deep blue sea

encoche [ãkɔʃ] nf notch; Ordinat **e. de protection contre l'écriture** write-protect notch

encodage [ãkɔdaʒ] nm Ling & Ordinat encoding

encoder [ãkɔde] vt Ling & Ordinat to encode

encoignure [ãkwanyr] nf (**a**) (d'une pièce) corner (**b**) (meuble) corner cupboard

encoller [ãkɔle] vt (papier peint) to paste

encolure [ãkɔlyr] nf (**a**) (d'animal) neck; **gagner d'une e.** to win by a neck (**b**) (tour de cou) collar size (**c**) (d'un vêtement) neck

encombrant, -e [ãkɔ̃brã, -ãt] adj (meuble, valise, paquet) cumbersome, bulky; Fig (personne, témoin) undesirable

encombre [ãkɔ̃br] nm sans e. without mishap

encombrement [ãkɔ̃brəmã] nm (**a**) (état) (d'une pièce) clutter; (de lignes téléphoniques) jamming; (embouteillage) traffic jam (**b**) (volume) (d'un objet) (overall) dimensions (**c**) *Ordinat* **faible e. sur le disque dur** low use of hard disk space

encombrer [ãkɔ̃bre] **1** *vt (pièce)* to clutter (up); *(passage, route)* to block; *(lignes téléphoniques)* to jam; **tu m'encombres, sors d'ici!** you're getting under my feet, get out!
2 s'encombrer *vpr* **s'e. de** *(colis, équipement)* to load oneself down with; *Fig (obligations, personne)* to saddle oneself with; **elle ne s'encombre pas de scrupules** she is quite unscrupulous

encontre [ãkɔ̃tr] **à l'encontre de** *prép* **aller à l'e. de** to go against

encorbellement [ãkɔrbɛlmã] *nm* corbelled structure

encorder [ãkɔrde] **s'encorder** *vpr* to rope up

encore [ãkɔr] *adv* (**a**) *(toujours)* still; **pas e.** not yet; **elle n'est pas e.** arrivée she hasn't arrived yet; **je n'avais e.** jamais vu ça I'd never seen that before; **qu'il m'appelle par mon prénom, passe e., mais...** his calling me by my Christian name is one thing, but...; **e. heureux que les enfants n'aient pas été là!** it's just as well the children weren't there! (**b**) *(davantage)* more; **en voulez-vous e.?** would you like some more?; **e. une tasse de café** another cup of coffee; **e. trois mois** three more months, another three months; **e. plus/moins** even more/less; **e. plus froid** even colder; **c'est e.** pire/mieux it's even worse/better; **mais e.?** and apart from that? (**c**) *(de nouveau)* again; **il a e.** cassé un verre he's broken another glass; **qu'est-ce qu'il a e. fait?** what's he done this time?; **quoi e.?** now what?; **et puis quoi e.?** is that all?; **e. une fois** once more, once again; **e. vous!** you again! (**d**) *(restrictif)* **si e....** if only...; **il vous en donnera 10 euros, et e.!** he'll give you 10 euros for it, if that!; **et e., ce n'est même pas sûr** even then, it's not certain; **e. faudrait-il qu'elle accepte/qu'il le sache!** she has to agree/he has to know about it first! (**e**) *(seulement)* only; **hier e.** elle me disait que... only yesterday she was telling me that... (**f**) **e. que** although, even though

encorner [ãkɔrne] *vt* to gore

encoubler [ãkuble] **s'encoubler** *vpr Suisse* to trip over

encourageant, -e [ãkuraʒã, -ãt] *adj* encouraging

encouragement [ãkuraʒmã] *nm* encouragement; **des encouragements** encouragement

encourager [45] [ãkuraʒe] *vt* (**a**) *(personne)* to encourage; *(athlète, équipe)* to cheer on; **e. qn à faire qch** to encourage sb to do sth (**b**) *(promouvoir) (arts)* to encourage

encourir [22] [ãkurir] *vt* to incur

encrasser [ãkrase] **1** *vt (vêtements, mains)* to dirty; *Aut (bougie)* to soot up; *(moteur)* to clog
2 s'encrasser *vpr* to get dirty; *Aut (bougie)* to soot up; *(moteur)* to get clogged

encre [ãkr] *nf* ink; *Fig* **nuit d'e.** inky black night; **e. de Chine** Indian ink; **e. sympathique** invisible ink

encrier [ãkrije] *nm* inkpot; *(de pupitre)* inkwell

encroûter [ãkrute] **s'encroûter** *vpr Fam (personne)* to get into a rut

encrypter [ãkripte] *vt Ordinat (données)* to encrypt

enculé, -e [ãkyle] *nm,f Vulg Br* arsehole, *Am* asshole

enculer [ãkyle] *vt Vulg* to bugger; **va te faire e.!** fuck off!; *Fig* **e. les mouches** to nit-pick

encyclique [ãsiklik] *nf Rel* encyclical

encyclopédie [ãsiklɔpedi] *nf* encyclopedia

encyclopédique [ãsiklɔpedik] *adj* encyclopedic

endémie [ãdemi] *nf* endemic disease

endémique [ãdemik] *adj* endemic

endetté, -e [ãdɛte] *adj* in debt; **très e.** heavily in debt

endettement [ãdɛtmã] *nm* debt

endetter [ãdɛte] **1** *vt* **e. qn** to get sb into debt
2 s'endetter *vpr* to get into debt

endeuiller [ãdœje] *vt (famille, nation)* to plunge into mourning; *(événement)* to cast a gloom over

endiablé, -e [ãdjable] *adj (personne, musique, rythme)* wild

endiguer [ãdige] *vt* (**a**) *(cours d'eau)* to dyke (up) (**b**) *Fig (révolte, inflation, chômage)* to contain

endimanché, -e [ãdimãʃe] *adj* in one's Sunday best

endive [ãdiv] *nf* chicory

endocrine [ãdɔkrin] *adj (glande)* endocrine

endoctrinement [ãdɔktrinmã] *nm* indoctrination

endoctriner [ãdɔktrine] *vt* to indoctrinate

endogène [ãdɔʒɛn] *adj Biol & Géol* endogenous

endolori, -e [ãdɔlɔri] *adj* painful

endommager [45] [ãdɔmaʒe] *vt* (**a**) *(abîmer)* to damage (**b**) *Ordinat* to corrupt

endormi, -e [ãdɔrmi] **1** *adj* (**a**) *(qui dort) (personne)* sleeping; *(voix, village)* sleepy; **être e.** *(personne)* to be asleep *or* sleeping; **avoir l'air e.** to look sleepy (**b**) *(inerte, lent) (personne)* sluggish (**c**) *Fig (passion, intérêt)* dormant
2 *nm,f (personne inerte, lente)* slowcoach

endormir [29] [ãdɔrmir] **1** *vt* (**a**) **e. qn** *(bébé)* to send sb to sleep; *(anesthésier)* to put sb to sleep; *(ennuyer)* to send sb to sleep (**b**) *(apaiser) (douleur)* to deaden; **e. les soupçons** to allay suspicion (**c**) *(mettre en confiance) (électeurs, public)* to lull into a false sense of security
2 s'endormir *vpr* to fall asleep, to go to sleep

endossable [ãdosabl] *adj (chèque)* endorsable

endossement [ãdosmã] *nm (d'un chèque)* endorsement

endosser [ãdose] *vt* (**a**) *(vêtement)* to put on (**b**) *(responsabilité)* to assume (**c**) *(chèque)* to endorse

endroit [ãdrwa] *nm* (**a**) *(lieu)* place, spot; **à quel e.?** where?; **c'est à cet e. que...** this is where...; **par endroits** here and there, in places (**b**) *(d'un vêtement)* right side; **à l'e.** the right way round (**c**) *Litt* **à l'e. de** *(personne)* towards; *(événement, objet)* with regard to

enduire [18] [ãdɥir] **1** *vt* to coat, to cover (**de** with)
2 s'enduire *vpr* **s'e. de** to cover oneself with

enduit [ãdɥi] *nm* coating; *(pour boucher)* filler

endurance [ãdyrãs] *nf* (**a**) *(physique)* stamina (**b**) *Sport* **épreuve/course d'e.** endurance race

endurant, -e [ãdyrã, -ãt] *adj* tough

endurci, -e [ãdyrsi] *adj* (**a**) *(dur) (personne)* hard (**b**) *(invétéré) (criminel)* hardened; *(célibataire)* confirmed

endurcir [ãdyrsir] **1** *vt* (**a**) *(moralement)* to harden (**b**) *(physiquement)* to toughen (up)
2 s'endurcir *vpr* (**a**) *(moralement)* to become hard (**b**) *(physiquement)* to toughen up

endurer [ãdyre] *vt* to endure, to bear

enduro [ãdyro] *nm Sport* enduro

énergétique [enɛrʒetik] *adj* (**a**) *(nourriture)* energy-giving (**b**) *(ressources, besoins)* energy

énergie [enɛrʒi] *nf* (**a**) *(dynamisme)* energy; **mettre toute son é. à qch/à faire qch** to devote all one's energy to sth/to doing sth; **avec é.** *(nier)* strongly; *(refuser, répondre)* forcefully; **sans é.** *(enfant)* listless; *(jouer)* listlessly (**b**) *(force)* energy, power; **é. hydroélectrique** hydroelectric power; **é. nucléaire** *ou* **ato-**

mique nuclear power; **é. solaire** solar power *or* energy

énergique [enɛrʒik] *adj* (**a**) *(personne)* energetic, dynamic; *(geste)* brisk; *(visage)* strong (**b**) *(mesures)* strong; *(remède)* powerful

énergiquement [enɛrʒikmɑ̃] *adv (nier)* strongly; *(refuser)* forcefully; **serrer é. la main à qn** to shake sb's hand warmly

énergivore [enɛrʒivɔr] *adj (industrie)* energy-guzzling; *(véhicule)* gaz-guzzling

énergumène [enɛrgymɛn] *nmf* eccentric

énervant, -e [enɛrvɑ̃, -ɑ̃t] *adj* irritating

énervé, -e [enɛrve] *adj (agacé)* irritated; *(excité)* edgy, agitated

énervement [enɛrvəmɑ̃] *nm (agacement)* irritation; *(excitation)* agitation

énerver [enɛrve] **1** *vt* **é. qn** *(agacer)* to get on sb's nerves, to irritate sb; *(exciter)* to make sb nervous **2 s'énerver** *vpr* to get worked up

enfance [ɑ̃fɑ̃s] *nf (jeunesse)* childhood; *(de garçon)* boyhood; *(de fille)* girlhood; **la petite e.** early childhood; *Fam* **c'est l'e. de l'art** it's child's play

enfant [ɑ̃fɑ̃] *nmf* child; **faire l'e.** to act like a child; **je l'ai connu e.** I knew him when he was a child; **il lui a fait un e.** she had a child by him; **viens ici, mon e.** come here, my child; *Fam* **salut, les enfants!** hi guys!; *Fam* **il n'y a plus d'enfants!** honestly, kids nowadays!; **e. en bas âge** infant; **e. bleu** blue baby; *Rel* **e. de chœur** altar boy; *Fig* **ce n'est pas un e. de chœur** he's no angel; **e. terrible** enfant terrible; **e. trouvé** foundling; **e.unique** only child

enfantement [ɑ̃fɑ̃tmɑ̃] *nm Litt* childbirth

enfanter [ɑ̃fɑ̃te] *vt Litt* to give birth to

enfantillages [ɑ̃fɑ̃tijaʒ] *nmpl* childish behaviour; **faire des e.** to be childish

enfantin, -e [ɑ̃fɑ̃tɛ̃, -in] *adj (voix)* child's; *(littérature)* children's; *(très facile)* childishly simple; *Péj (remarque, conduite)* childish

enfarger [45][ɑ̃farʒe] *vi Can* to trip

enfariné, -e [ɑ̃farine] *adj (visage, cheveux)* covered with flour; *Fam* **arriver la gueule enfarinée** to arrive blithely ignorant of the facts

enfer [ɑ̃fɛr] *nm aussi Fig* **l'e.** hell; **aller à un train d'e.** to go like a bat out of hell; *Fig* **elle a vécu un véritable e.** she's been through sheer hell; *Fam* **c'est l'e. pour se garer ici** it's hell trying to park here; *Fam* **une soirée d'e.** one hell of a party; **l'e. est pavé de bonnes intentions** the road to hell is paved with good intentions

enfermement [ɑ̃fɛrməmɑ̃] *nm* imprisonment

enfermer [ɑ̃fɛrme] **1** *vt (personne, chose)* to shut up; **e. qn/qch à clef** to lock sb/sth up; **je suis enfermé toute la journée** I'm cooped up all day; *Fam* **elle est bonne à e.** she should be locked up **2 s'enfermer** *vpr* to shut oneself up; **s'e. à clef** to lock oneself in; *Fig* **s'e. dans le silence** to retreat into silence

enferrer [ɑ̃fere] **s'enferrer** *vpr Fig* to get tangled up (**dans** in)

enfiévré, -e [ɑ̃fjevre] *adj (front, imagination)* fevered

enfiévrer [34] [ɑ̃fjevre] **1** *vt (personne, imagination)* to excite **2 s'enfiévrer** *vpr* to get excited

enfilade [ɑ̃filad] *nf (de portes, de pièces)* series; **être en e.** to be adjoining

enfiler [ɑ̃file] **1** *vt* (**a**) *(aiguille, perles)* to thread (**b**) *(vêtements)* to slip on

2 s'enfiler *vpr* (**a**) *(gants, bottes)* to go on (**b**) *Fam (boisson, nourriture)* to put away

enfin [ɑ̃fɛ̃] *adv* (**a**) *(en dernier lieu)* finally, lastly (**b**) *(à la fin)* at last, finally (**c**) *(de résignation)* **e., n'en parlons plus!** look, let's forget about it!; **e., ce qui est fait est fait!** what's done is done! (**d**) *(d'exaspération)* **e. quoi, tu n'as plus dix ans!** for God's sake, you're not ten any more!; **mais e., je te l'avais dit!** but I told you, for God's sake! (**e**) *(d'hésitation, pour résumer)* well; **e., je ne dis pas non, mais...** well, I'm not saying no, but...; **elle n'est pas mal, e. pour son âge** she's not bad, for her age that is; **e. (bref), c'était la panique!** in short, it was panic!

enflammé, -e [ɑ̃flame] *adj* (**a**) *(brindille, torche, allumette)* burning (**b**) *(joues)* *(de froid)* glowing; *(de fièvre, de gêne)* burning (**c**) *Fig (discours)* fiery, passionate

enflammer [ɑ̃flame] **1** *vt* (**a**) *(mettre le feu à)* to set light to; *(allumette)* to strike (**b**) *Fig (imagination)* to stir; **la colère enflammait son regard** his/her eyes were blazing with anger **2 s'enflammer** *vpr* (**a**) *(prendre feu)* to catch fire (**b**) *Fig (imagination)* to be stirred

enflé, -e [ɑ̃fle] *adj (rivière, membre)* swollen

enfler [ɑ̃fle] **1** *vt* (**a**) *(rivière, membre)* to swell; **e. les joues** to puff out one's cheeks (**b**) *Fig (exagérer) (histoire, succès)* to exaggerate **2** *vi (membre)* to swell (up)

enflure [ɑ̃flyr] *nf* (**a**) *(d'un membre)* swelling (**b**) *très Fam (imbécile)* jerk, *Br* prat

enfoiré, -e [ɑ̃fware] *nm,f Vulg* bugger, bastard

enfoncé, -e [ɑ̃fɔ̃se] *adj (yeux)* deep-set

enfoncement [ɑ̃fɔ̃smɑ̃] *nm (dans le sol)* dip; *(dans un mur)* recess

enfoncer [16] [ɑ̃fɔ̃se] **1** *vt* (**a**) *(clou)* to bang in; *(pieu)* to drive in; *(aiguille)* to stick in, to push in; **e. un couteau dans qch** to stick a knife into sth; **e. la main dans sa poche** to thrust one's hand into one's pocket; **e. son chapeau sur sa tête** to jam one's hat on one's head (**b**) *(porte)* to break down (**c**) *Fam (personne)* to humiliate **2 s'enfoncer** *vpr (clou, couteau)* to go in; *(bateau)* to sink; **s'e. dans son fauteuil** to sink into one's armchair; **s'e. dans un bois** to go into the depths of a wood; *Fam* **enfonce-toi ça dans le crâne!** get that into your thick skull!

enfouir [ɑ̃fwir] **1** *vt* to bury (**dans/sous** in/under) **2 s'enfouir** *vpr* to bury oneself

enfourcher [ɑ̃furʃe] *vt (cheval, vélo)* to get on, to mount

enfourner [ɑ̃furne] *vt (pain)* to put in the oven; *(poteries, briques)* to put in the kiln; *Fam (manger)* to shovel down

enfreindre [54] [ɑ̃frɛ̃dr] *vt* to infringe, to break

enfuir [38] [ɑ̃fɥir] **s'enfuir** *vpr* to run away (**de** from); *(d'une prison)* to escape (**de** from)

enfumé, -e [ɑ̃fyme] *adj (pièce, atmosphère)* smoky

enfumer [ɑ̃fyme] *vt* (**a**) *(pièce)* to fill with smoke (**b**) *(personne, abeilles)* to smoke out

enfuyais *etc voir* enfuir

engagé, -e [ɑ̃gaʒe] **1** *adj (littérature, écrivain)* committed **2** *nm (soldat)* **e. (volontaire)** enlisted man

engageant, -e [ɑ̃gaʒɑ̃, -ɑ̃t] *adj (manière, sourire)* engaging

engagement [ɑ̃gaʒmɑ̃] *nm* (**a**) *(promesse)* undertaking, commitment; **prendre un e.** to enter into an undertaking; **prendre l'e. de faire qch** to undertake to do sth; **tenir ses engagements** to honour one's commitments; **sans e.** (de votre part) without obligation (on your part) (**b**) *(à une cause)* commitment (**c**) *(coup d'envoi) (au football, au rugby)* kick-off; *(au hockey)* bully-off; *(au basket)* tip-off (**d**) *(commencement)* start; *(de poursuites)* institution (**e**) *(d'un employé)* appointment; *(d'un soldat)* enlistment

engager [45] [ãgaʒe] **1** *vt* (**a**) *(lier)* to commit; **e. sa parole** to give one's word; **cela ne vous engage à rien** it doesn't commit you to anything; **cela n'engage que moi** that's just my opinion (**b**) *(mettre en gage)* to pawn (**c**) *(embaucher) (employé)* to appoint; *(soldat)* to enlist (**d**) *(commencer) (conversation, négociations)* to begin, to start; *(poursuites)* to institute; **e. la partie** to start the match; **la partie est maintenant bien engagée** the match is now well under way (**e**) *(introduire) (clef)* to insert (**dans** in) (**f**) *(inciter)* **e. qn à faire qch** to urge sb to do sth

2 s'engager *vpr* (**a**) *(promettre)* **s'e. à faire qch** to promise to do sth, to undertake to do sth (**b**) *(prendre position)* to commit oneself (**c**) *(se lancer)* **s'e. dans une aventure** to get involved in an adventure (**d**) *(soldat)* to enlist, to join up (**e**) *(pénétrer)* **s'e. dans une rue** to turn into a street; **s'e. dans une forêt** to enter a forest (**f**) *(commencer) (négociations, conversation)* to begin

engeance [ãʒãs] *nf Fam* crew, bunch

engelure [ãʒlyr] *nf* chilblain

engendrer [ãʒãdre] *vt* to father; *Fig (maladie, pauvreté)* to cause

engin [ãʒɛ̃] *nm (machine)* machine; *(outil)* device; *Fam (objet)* thing, thingy; **e. blindé** armoured vehicle; **e. de mort** deadly weapon; **e. spatial** spacecraft

englober [ãglɔbe] *vt* to include (**dans** in)

engloutir [ãglutir] *vt* (**a**) *(avaler) (boisson)* to gulp down; *(nourriture)* to wolf down (**b**) *(submerger) (bateau, village)* to submerge; *Fig (fortune)* to swallow up

engoncé, -e [ãgɔ̃se] *adj* **il avait l'air e. dans son manteau** his coat looked too tight for him

engorgement [ãgɔrʒəmã] *nm (blocage)* blocking; *(d'un marché)* glutting; *Méd (d'un organe)* congestion

engorger [45] [ãgɔrʒe] **1** *vt (bloquer)* to block, to clog; *(marché)* to glut

2 s'engorger *vpr (tuyau)* to be blocked *or* clogged; *Méd (organe)* to become engorged *or* congested

engouement [ãgumã] *nm* craze (**pour** for)

engouffrer [ãgufre] **1** *vt Fam (nourriture)* to devour

2 s'engouffrer *vpr* **s'e. dans** to rush into; **le vent s'engouffra par la porte** the wind rushed in through the door

engourdi, -e [ãgurdi] *adj* numb (**par** with)

engourdir [ãgurdir] **1** *vt* (**a**) *(membre)* to numb (**b**) *(douleur)* to dull

2 s'engourdir *vpr* to go numb, to go to sleep

engourdissement [ãgurdismã] *nm* numbness

engrais [ãgrɛ] *nm* fertilizer

engraisser [ãgrese] **1** *vt (animaux, personne)* to fatten up

2 *vi Fam* to get fatter

engranger [45] [ãgrãʒe] *vt (céréales)* to bring in; *Fig* to build up

engrenage [ãgrənaʒ] *nm* (**a**) *(roues dentées)* gears (**b**) *Fig (d'événements)* chain; **l'e. de la violence** the cycle of violence; **être pris dans un e.** to get caught up in a system; **mettre le doigt dans l'e.** to get caught up in it

engrosser [ãgrose] *vt très Fam (femme)* to knock up; **se faire e.** (par) to get knocked up (by)

engueulade [ãgœlad] *nf Fam (réprimande)* earbashing; *(querelle)* row, *Br* slanging match

engueuler [ãgœle] *Fam* **1** *vt* **e. qn** to give sb an earbashing; **se faire e.** to get an earbashing; **e. qn comme du poisson pourri** to call sb every name under the sun

2 s'engueuler *vpr* to have a row *or Br* slanging match

enguirlander [ãgirlãde] *vt* (**a**) *Fam* **e. qn** to give sb an earbashing; **se faire e.** to get an earbashing (**b**) *(décorer)* to garland (**de** with)

enhardir [ãardir] **1** *vt* to embolden

2 s'enhardir *vpr* to become bolder; **s'e. à faire qch** to pluck up the courage to do sth

énième [enjɛm] *adj* **après une é. tentative** after countless attempts; **pour la é. fois** for the umpteenth time

énigmatique [enigmatik] *adj* enigmatic

énigme [enigm] *nf (mystère)* enigma, mystery; *(devinette)* riddle

enivrant, -e [ãnivrã, -ãt] *adj (parfum)* heady; *(vitesse)* exhilarating

enivrement [ãnivrəmã] *nm* (**a**) *(par l'alcool)* intoxication (**b**) *Fig* exhilaration

enivrer [ãnivre] **1** *vt* (**a**) *(soûler)* to intoxicate, to make drunk (**b**) *Fig (exalter)* to exhilarate; **enivré par le succès** intoxicated with success

2 s'enivrer *vpr (se soûler)* to become intoxicated (**de** with), to get drunk (**de** on)

enjambée [ãʒãbe] *nf* stride; **marcher à grandes enjambées** to stride along

enjambement [ãʒãbmã] *nm* enjambment

enjamber [ãʒãbe] *vt (obstacle)* to step over; *(sujet: pont) (rivière)* to span

enjeu, -x [ãʒø] *nm (au jeu)* stake; *Fig (d'une guerre)* stakes; **quel est l'e. de cette élection?** what's at stake in this election?

enjoignais *etc voir* **enjoindre**

enjoindre [43] [ãʒwɛ̃dr] *vt Litt* **e. à qn de faire qch** to enjoin sb to do sth

enjôler [ãʒole] *vt* to cajole

enjôleur, -euse [ãʒolœr, -øz] **1** *adj* cajoling

2 *nm,f* charmer

enjoliver [ãʒɔlive] *vt* to embellish

enjoliveur [ãʒɔlivœr] *nm* hubcap

enjoué, -e [ãʒwe] *adj* playful

enjouement [ãʒumã] *nm* playfulness

enlacement [ãlasmã] *nm* (**a**) *(de rubans, de branches)* intertwining (**b**) *(étreinte)* embrace

enlacer [16] [ãlase] **1** *vt* (**a**) *(rubans, branches)* to intertwine (**b**) *(étreindre)* to embrace

2 s'enlacer *vpr (s'étreindre)* to embrace

enlaidir [ãledir] **1** *vt (personne)* to make ugly, to disfigure; *(paysage, ville)* to disfigure

2 s'enlaidir *vpr* to make oneself look ugly

enlevé, -e [ãlve] *adj (style, rythme)* lively

enlèvement [ãlɛvmã] *nm* (**a**) *(de meubles, d'une tache)* removal, removing; *(de bagages)* collection; **e. des ordures** *Br* rubbish *or Am* garbage collection (**b**) *(kidnapping)* kidnapping, abduction

enlever [46] [ãlve] **1** *vt* (**a**) *(vêtements, couvercle)* to remove, to take off; *(meubles)* to remove, to take away; *(tapis)* to take up; *(rideaux)* to take down; *(papier peint, étiquette, tache)* to remove; **e. qch à qn** to take sth away from sb; **elle me l'a enlevé des mains** she took it from me; **e. à qn la garde d'un enfant** to

remove a child from sb's care; **e. à qn le goût de qch** to take away sb's taste for sth (**b**) *(kidnapper)* to kidnap, to abduct (**c**) *(remporter) (prix)* to carry off; *(victoire, contrat)* to win
2 s'enlever *vpr (couvercle, peinture)* to come off; *(tache)* to come out
enlisement [ãlizmã] *nm* sinking
enliser [ãlize] **1** *vt* e. **une voiture** to get a car stuck
2 s'enliser *vpr (personne, voiture)* to get stuck; *Fig* **s'e. dans ses explications** to get bogged down in explanations
enluminure [ãlyminyr] *nf* illumination
enneigé, -e [ãneʒe] *adj (montagne, champ, route)* snow-covered; *(village)* snowbound
enneigement [ãnɛʒmã] *nm* snow cover
ennemi, -e [ɛnmi] **1** *nm,f* enemy; **se faire un e. de qn** to make an enemy of sb; **passer à l'e.** to defect; *Prov* **le mieux est l'e. du bien** it's better to leave well alone; **e. public numéro un** public enemy number one
2 *adj* **en pays e.** in enemy country
ennui [ãnɥi] *nm* (**a**) *(souci)* worry; *(problème)* problem; **avoir des ennuis** *(soucis)* to be worried; *(problèmes)* to have problems; **avoir des ennuis de santé** to have health problems; **avoir des ennuis avec la police** to be in trouble with the police; **attirer des ennuis à qn** to get sb into trouble; **faire des ennuis à qn** to bother sb (**b**) *(lassitude)* boredom; **il est d'un e.!** his conversation is so boring!
ennuyé, -e [ãnɥije] *adj* (**a**) *(contrarié)* annoyed (**de** about) (**b**) *(las)* bored
ennuyer [32] [ãnɥije] **1** *vt* (**a**) *(contrarier)* to bother; **cela vous ennuierait-il d'attendre?** would you mind waiting? (**b**) *(agacer)* to annoy, to irritate (**c**) *(lasser)* to bore (**avec** with)
2 s'ennuyer *vpr* to be bored; **qu'est-ce qu'on s'ennuie ici!** it's so boring here!; **s'e. à cent sous de l'heure** to be bored to death
ennuyeux, -euse [ãnɥijø, -øz] *adj* (**a**) *(contrariant)* annoying, irritating; **comme c'est e.!** it's so annoying! (**b**) *(lassant)* boring
énoncé [enɔ̃se] *nm* (**a**) *(des faits)* statement; *(d'une sentence)* pronouncement (**b**) *(d'une question)* wording
énoncer [16] [enɔ̃se] *vt (opinion, conditions)* to state
énonciation [enɔ̃sjasjɔ̃] *nf (de faits)* statement
enorgueillir [ãnɔrgœjir] **1** *vt* to make proud
2 s'enorgueillir *vpr* **s'e. de qch/de faire qch** to pride oneself on sth/on doing sth
énorme [enɔrm] *adj* enormous, huge
énormément [enɔrmemã] *adv (lire, travailler, pleurer)* an awful lot; **je le regrette é.** I'm terribly sorry; **s'amuser é.** to have a great time; **il n'a pas é. d'argent** he hasn't got a huge amount of money
énormité [enɔrmite] *nf* (**a**) *(d'une demande, d'un crime)* enormity, outrageousness (**b**) *(d'une personne, d'une somme)* huge size (**c**) *(erreur)* glaring mistake; *(propos choquants)* outrageous statement
enquérir [7] [ãkerir] **s'enquérir** *vpr* to inquire (**de** about)
enquête [ãkɛt] *nf* (**a**) *(recherches)* inquiry; *(de journalistes, de policiers)* investigation (**sur** into); *Fam* **faire sa petite e.** to do a bit of investigating (**b**) *(sondage)* survey
enquêter [ãkete] *vi* (**a**) *(faire des recherches)* to hold an inquiry; *(police, journaliste)* to investigate; **e. sur qch** to investigate sth (**b**) *(faire un sondage)* to conduct a survey (**sur/auprès de** into/among)

enquêteur, -trice [ãkɛtœr, -tris] *nm,f* (**a**) *(policier)* investigator (**b**) *(sondeur)* researcher
enquiers, enquiert *voir* enquérir
enquiquinant, -e [ãkikinã, -ãt] *adj Fam (agaçant)* irritating, annoying
enquiquiner [ãkikine] *vt Fam (agacer)* to irritate, to annoy
enquiquineur, -euse [ãkikinœr, -øz] *nm,f Fam* nuisance, pain
enquis, -e *voir* enquérir
enraciné, -e [ãrasine] *adj (habitude, haine)* deep-rooted, deep-seated
enraciner [ãrasine] **s'enraciner** *vpr aussi Fig* to take root
enragé, -e [ãraʒe] **1** *adj (animal)* rabid
2 *nm,f Fam* fanatic
enrager [45] [ãraʒe] *vi* to be furious; **e. de devoir faire qch** to be really angry at having to do sth; **faire e. qn** *(taquiner)* to tease sb
enrayer [ãreje] [53] **1** *vt (machine)* to jam; *Fig (épidémie)* to check; *(inflation)* to curb
2 s'enrayer *vpr (machine)* to jam
enrégimenter [ãreʒimãte] *vt Péj (dans une organisation)* to enrol
enregistrement [ãrəʒistrəmã] *nm* (**a**) *(d'une naissance, d'un acte)* registration; *(de bagages)* check-in (**b**) *(disque)* recording; **e. vidéo** video recording; **e. sur bande/cassette** tape/cassette recording (**c**) *Ordinat (de données)* logging, recording; **e. de transactions** transaction logging
enregistrer [ãreʒistre] **1** *vt* (**a**) *(naissance, acte)* to register; *(bagages)* to check in; **les meilleures ventes jamais enregistrées** the best sales ever recorded (**b**) *(disque, émission)* to record, to tape; *(données)* to store (**c**) *Fam (mémoriser)* to note, to register
2 s'enregistrer *vpr (personne)* to record oneself
enregistreur, -euse [ãreʒistrœr, -øz] **1** *adj (appareil)* recording
2 *nm* recorder, recording device; *Belg (magnétophone)* tape recorder
enrhumé, -e [ãryme] *adj* **être e.** to have a cold
enrhumer [ãryme] **s'enrhumer** *vpr* to catch a cold
enrichi, -e [ãriʃi] *adj* (**a**) *(personne)* wealthy (**b**) *(céréales)* enriched (**en** with)
enrichir [ãriʃir] **1** *vt (personne, pays)* to make richer; *Fig (collection)* to enhance (**de** with); *(esprit)* to enrich, to improve
2 s'enrichir *vpr* (**a**) *(personne, pays)* to get richer; *Fig (collection)* to be enhanced (**de** by) (**b**) **s'e. l'esprit** to improve one's mind
enrichissant, -e [ãriʃisã, -ãt] *adj (expérience)* rewarding
enrichissement [ãriʃismã] *nm* (**a**) *(en argent)* acquisition of wealth (**b**) *(de l'esprit, d'une collection)* enrichment
enrober [ãrɔbe] *vt* (**a**) *(bonbon)* to coat (**de** with) (**b**) *Hum* **il est un peu enrobé** he's a bit chubby
enrôlement [ãrolmã] *nm* enrolment; *(d'un soldat)* enlistment
enrôler [ãrole] **1** *vt* to enrol, to recruit; *(soldat)* to enlist
2 s'enrôler *vpr* to enrol; *(soldat)* to enlist
enroué, -e [ãrwe] *adj* hoarse, husky; **avoir la voix enrouée** to have a husky voice
enrouer [ãrwe] **1** *vt (voix, personne)* to make hoarse
2 s'enrouer *vpr* to get hoarse

enrouler [ɑ̃rule] **1** *vt* (**a**) *(rouler) (carte, tapis)* to roll up; *(câble, ruban)* to wind (**b**) *(envelopper)* to wrap up (**dans** in)
2 s'enrouler *vpr* (**a**) *(serpent)* to coil up; *(fil)* to wind (**b**) **s'e. dans une couverture** to wrap oneself up in a blanket

ENS [əɛnɛs] *nf (abrév* **École normale supérieure**) = university-level college preparing students for senior posts in teaching

ENSA [ɛnsa] *nf (abrév* **École nationale supérieure d'agronomie**) = one of five competitive-entry agricultural engineering schools

ensablement [ɑ̃sabləmɑ̃] *nm* (**a**) *(d'un port)* silting up (**b**) *(dépôt) (dû à l'eau)* sandbank; *(dû au vent)* sand dune

ensabler [ɑ̃sable] **1** *vt (port)* to silt up
2 s'ensabler *vpr* (**a**) *(véhicule)* to get stuck in the sand (**b**) *(port)* to silt up

ensanglanter [ɑ̃sɑ̃glɑ̃te] *vt* to cover with blood; **des mains ensanglantées** bloodstained *or* bloody hands; **un festival ensanglanté par un attentat** a festival marred by an attempted murder

enseignant, -e [ɑ̃sɛɲɑ̃, -ɑ̃t] **1** *nm,f* teacher
2 *adj* **le corps e.** the teaching profession

enseigne [ɑ̃sɛɲ] **1** *nf* (**a**) *(panonceau)* sign; **e. lumineuse** illuminated sign; *Fig* **nous sommes tous logés à la même e.** we're all in the same boat (**b**) *Litt* **à telle e. que...** so much so that...
2 *nm* **e. (de vaisseau)** *Br* sub-lieutenant, *Am* ensign

enseignement [ɑ̃sɛɲmɑ̃] *nm* (**a**) *(profession)* teaching; **être dans l'e.** to be a teacher (**b**) *(formation)* education; *Fig* **tirer un e. de qch** to learn a lesson from sth; **e. assisté par ordinateur** computer-aided *or* computer-assisted learning; **e. par correspondance** distance learning; **e. primaire/secondaire** primary/secondary education; **e. professionnel/technique** vocational/technical education; **e. supérieur** higher education

enseigner [ɑ̃seɲe] **1** *vt* to teach; **e. qch à qn** to teach sb sth
2 *vi* to be a teacher, to teach

ensemble [ɑ̃sɑ̃bl] **1** *adv* together; **aller bien e.** *(personnes)* to be well matched; *(couleurs)* to go together; **ils sont partis tous e.** they left en masse; *Hum* **ne répondez pas tous e.** don't all answer at once
2 *nm* (**a**) *(totalité)* **l'e. des personnes présentes** all the people present; **l'e. de sa fortune** his/her whole fortune; **dans l'e.** on the whole (**b**) *(unité)* unity; **avec un parfait e.** *(répondre)* as one; *(danser)* in unison (**c**) *(groupe) (de gens)* group; *(d'objets, de faits)* set; *(de services)* package (**d**) *(tenue)* outfit; **e. pantalon** *Br* trouser suit, *Am* pant suit (**e**) *(immeubles)* block; **grand e.** residential estate (**f**) *Math* set

ensemblier [ɑ̃sɑ̃blije] *nm* interior designer; *(pour la télévision)* set designer

ensemencer [16] [ɑ̃səmɑ̃se] *vt* (**a**) *(champ)* to sow (**b**) *Biol* to culture

ensevelir [ɑ̃səvlir] *vt Litt* to bury

ensoleillé, -e [ɑ̃sɔleje] *adj* sunny

ensoleillement [ɑ̃sɔlɛjmɑ̃] *nm* **en raison de l'e. d'une pièce** because the room gets a lot of sun; **cinq heures d'e. par jour** five hours of sunshine a day; **jouir d'un e. exceptionnel** to get a lot of sun

ensommeillé, -e [ɑ̃sɔmeje] *adj* sleepy

ensorceler [9] [ɑ̃sɔrsəle] *vt* to cast *or* put a spell on; *Fig* to bewitch, to captivate

ensorcellement [ɑ̃sɔrsɛlmɑ̃] *nm (action)* bewitching; *(état)* bewitchment; *Fig (charme)* charm

ensuite [ɑ̃sɥit] *adv (plus tard)* later; *(puis)* then, next; **et e., qu'est-ce qu'on fait?** what do you do next?; *Fam* **d'abord, c'est très cher, et e. ça ne te va pas du tout** for one thing it's very expensive, and for another it doesn't suit you at all

ensuivre [65] [ɑ̃sɥivr] **s'ensuivre** *vpr* **jusqu'à ce que mort s'ensuive** until dead; **il s'ensuit que...** it follows that...; **et tout ce qui s'ensuit** and all that goes with it

entacher [ɑ̃taʃe] *vt (réputation)* to sully

entaille [ɑ̃taj] *nf* (**a**) *(dans du bois)* notch; *(longue)* groove (**b**) *(blessure)* gash; **se faire une e. au doigt** to cut one's finger open

entailler [ɑ̃taje] *vt (blesser)* to gash

entame [ɑ̃tam] *nf* (**a**) *(de pain, de jambon)* first slice (**b**) *(aux cartes)* lead

entamer [ɑ̃tame] *vt* (**a**) *(blesser)* to cut into; *Fig (conviction, détermination)* to undermine (**b**) *(commencer) (pain, jambon)* to start on; *(bouteille, pot de confiture)* to open; *(travail, recherches, conversation, négociations)* to start; *(démarches)* to initiate; *(poursuites)* to institute (**c**) *(aux cartes)* **e. à trèfle** to open clubs

entartrer [ɑ̃tartre] **1** *vt (chaudière)* to fur (up)
2 s'entartrer *vpr (chaudière)* to fur (up); *(dents)* to scale up

entassement [ɑ̃tasmɑ̃] *nm* (**a**) *(de pierres) (action)* piling up; *(tas)* pile (**b**) *(de passagers, du bétail)* crowding together

entasser [ɑ̃tase] **1** *vt* (**a**) *(pierres, livres, vêtements)* to pile up (**b**) *(passagers, bétail)* to crowd together
2 s'entasser *vpr* (**a**) *(objets)* to pile up (**b**) *(personnes)* to crowd together

entendement [ɑ̃tɑ̃dmɑ̃] *nm* **dépasser l'e.** to be beyond comprehension

entendeur [ɑ̃tɑ̃dœr] *nm* **à bon e., salut!** mark my words!

entendre [ɑ̃tɑ̃dr] **1** *vt* (**a**) *(ouïr)* to hear; **je n'entends rien (de ce que tu dis)** I can't hear a thing (you're saying); **je l'entends rire** I can hear him/her laughing; **e. dire que...** to hear that...; **e. qn dire qch** to hear sb say sth; **e. parler de** *(connaître l'existence de)* to hear of; *(être au courant de)* to hear about; **elle ne veut pas en e. parler!** she doesn't want to hear another word about it!; **il va m'e.!** I'll give him a talking-to!; **elle répétait à qui voulait l'e. que...** she'd tell anyone who'd listen that...; *Fam* **ce qu'il ne faut pas e.!** I've heard it all now! (**b**) *(écouter) (témoin, suppliant)* to hear; **e. qn en confession** to hear sb's confession; **à vous e., il a eu tort** from what you say, he was in the wrong; **il n'a rien voulu e.** he wouldn't listen; **que Dieu vous entende** may God answer your prayers (**c**) *(comprendre)* to understand; **laisser e. qch** to imply sth; **elle m'a laissé e. que...** she gave me to understand that...; **ce n'est pas ainsi qu'il l'entend** he doesn't see it like that (**d**) *(vouloir dire)* to mean; **qu'entendez-vous par là?** what do you mean by that? (**e**) *(vouloir)* **e. faire qch** to intend *or* mean to do sth; **faites comme vous l'entendez** do as you think best; **il ne l'entendait pas ainsi** he wouldn't hear of it
2 *vi* to hear; **e. mal** to be hard of hearing; **j'ai mal entendu!** *(je n'ai pas entendu)* I didn't hear you properly!; *(je suis choqué)* I don't think I heard you right!; **tu entends?** *(menace)* got it?
3 s'entendre *vpr* (**a**) *(sympathiser)* to get on (**avec** with) (**b**) *(se mettre d'accord)* to agree; **entendons-**

nous bien! let's be clear about this! (**c**) *(être entendu)* to be heard; **on ne s'entend plus ici** you can't hear yourself think in here (**d**) *(être compris)* to be understood (**e**) **s'e. aux affaires** to have a good head for business; **il s'y entend** he knows what he's talking about

entendu, -e [ãtãdy] *adj* (**a**) *(complice) (sourire)* knowing; **d'un air e.** knowingly (**b**) *(décidé)* (**c'est**) **e.!** fine!, all right! (**c**) **bien e.** of course

entente [ãtãt] *nf* (**a**) *(accord)* agreement, understanding (**entre** between) (**b**) *(harmonie)* **bonne e.** harmony

entériner [ãterine] *vt* to ratify

entérite [ãterit] *nf Méd* enteritis

enterrement [ãtɛrmã] *nm* (**a**) *(mise en terre)* burial (**b**) *(cérémonie)* funeral; *Fam* **faire une tête d'e.** to look miserable (**c**) *(cortège)* funeral procession

enterrer [ãtere] **1** *vt* (**a**) *(trésor, corps)* to bury; *Hum* **il nous enterrera tous** he'll outlive us all (**b**) *Fig (projet)* to scrap; *(affaire)* to bury; **e. sa vie de garçon** to have a stag party

  2 s'enterrer *vpr Fig* to hide oneself away

entêtant, -e [ãtɛtã, -ãt] *adj (parfum, musique)* heady

en-tête (*pl* **en-têtes**) [ãtɛt] *nm (sur papier à écrire)* heading, letterhead; *Ordinat* header; **papier à e.** headed paper

entêté, -e [ãtete] **1** *adj* obstinate, stubborn

  2 *nm,f* obstinate *or* stubborn person

entêtement [ãtɛtmã] *nm* obstinacy, stubbornness; **e. à faire qch** persistence in doing sth

entêter [ãtete] **s'entêter** *vpr* to persist; **s'e. à faire qch** to persist in doing sth

enthousiasmant, -e [ãtuzjasmã, -ãt] *adj* exciting

enthousiasme [ãtuzjasm] *nm* enthusiasm (**pour** for); **avec e.** enthusiastically; **sans e.** unenthusiastically

enthousiasmer [ãtuzjasme] **1** *vt (personne)* to fill with enthusiasm

  2 s'enthousiasmer *vpr* to get enthusiastic (**pour** about)

enthousiaste [ãtuzjast] **1** *adj* enthusiastic

  2 *nmf* enthusiast

enticher [ãtiʃe] **s'enticher** *vpr* **s'e. de qn/qch** to become infatuated with sb/sth

entier, -ère [ãtje, -ɛr] **1** *adj* (**a**) *(complet)* whole, entire; **la France entière** the whole of France; **il a mangé le gâteau tout e.** he ate the whole cake; **des heures entières** for hours on end; **le mystère reste e.** the mystery remains unsolved (**b**) *(responsabilité)* full; *(confiance)* complete; **jouir d'une entière liberté** to have absolute freedom; **donner entière satisfaction à qn** *(produit)* to give sb complete satisfaction (**c**) *(sans compromis) (personne)* uncompromising (**d**) *Math (nombre)* whole

  2 *nm* (**a**) **j'ai écouté le disque en e.** I listened to the whole record; **le pays dans son e.** the whole country (**b**) *Math (nombre)* integer, whole number

entièrement [ãtjɛrmã] *adv* entirely; **je ne l'ai pas lu e.** I didn't read all of it

entité [ãtite] *nf* entity

entonner [ãtɔne] *vt* to start singing

entonnoir [ãtɔnwar] *nm* funnel

entorse [ãtɔrs] *nf* (**a**) sprain, wrench; **se faire une e. au poignet** to sprain one's wrist; *Fig* **faire une e. au règlement** to stretch the rules; **faire une e. a son régime** to break one's diet

entortiller [ãtɔrtije] **1** *vt (envelopper)* to wrap (**dans** in); *(enrouler)* to wind (**autour de** round)

  2 s'entortiller *vpr* (**a**) *(serpent, lierre)* to coil (**autour de** round) (**b**) *(s'empêtrer)* to get tangled up (**dans** in) (**c**) *(s'enrouler)* to wrap oneself up (**dans** in)

entour [ãtur] *nm* **à l'e. de** round

entourage [ãturaʒ] *nm (amis)* circle (of friends); *(de ministre, de souverain)* entourage; **dans son e.** **proche** amongst those close to him/her

entourer [ãture] **1** *vt* (**a**) *(border, enceindre)* to surround (**de** with) (**b**) *(être autour de)* to surround; **les gens qui vous entourent** the people around *or* about you; **le monde qui nous entoure** the world about us; **entouré de mystère** shrouded in mystery; **un rang de perles entourait son cou** she had a string of pearls round her neck (**c**) *(soutenir) (personne)* to rally round; **elle est très entourée** she has a lot of people she can turn to for support

  2 s'entourer *vpr* **s'e. d'amis/de belles choses** to surround oneself with friends/with beautiful things

entourloupe [ãturlup], **entourloupette** [ãturlupɛt] *nf Fam* dirty trick; **faire une e. à qn** to play a dirty trick on sb

entournure [ãturnyr] *nf Fam* **être gêné aux entournures** *(mal à l'aise)* to feel awkward; *(financièrement)* to feel the pinch

entracte [ãtrakt] *nm* intermission, *Br* interval

entraide [ãtrɛd] *nf* mutual aid

entraider [ãtrede] **s'entraider** *vpr* to help one another

entrailles [ãtraj] *nfpl* entrails

entrain [ãtrɛ̃] *nm* get-up-and-go; **être plein d'e.** to be full of life; **travailler avec e.** to beaver away; **faire qch sans e.** to do sth half-heartedly

entraînant, -e [ãtrɛnã, -ãt] *adj (air, rythme)* lively

entraînement [ãtrɛnmã] *nm* (**a**) *(en sport)* training; **un e.** a training session; **à l'e.** in training; **avoir de l'e.** to be well trained; **manquer d'e.** to be out of practice (**b**) *Tech* drive

entraîner [ãtrɛne] **1** *vt* (**a**) *(sujet: rivière)* to carry away; *(sujet: locomotive)* to pull; **e. qn quelque part** to take sb off somewhere; **il l'a entraînée dans sa chute** he dragged her down with him (**b**) *(exercer une influence sur)* to influence; **e. qn à faire qch** to lead sb to do sth; **e. qn dans un piège** to lure sb into a trap; **se laisser e.** to allow oneself to be led astray (**c**) *(causer) (dépense, modification)* to entail, to lead to; **e. un retard** to result in a delay (**d**) *(athlète, équipe)* to coach, to train; *(cheval)* to train; **e. qn à faire qch** to train sb to do sth (**e**) *Tech* to drive

  2 s'entraîner *vpr (athlète)* to train; **s'e. à faire qch** to practise doing sth

entraîneur [ãtrɛnœr] *nm (d'un athlète, d'une équipe)* coach; *(d'un cheval)* trainer

entraîneuse [ãtrɛnøz] *nf* (**a**) *(de boîte de nuit)* hostess (**b**) *(d'un athlète, d'une équipe)* coach; *(d'un cheval)* trainer

entrapercevoir [60] [ãtrapɛrsəvwar] *vt* to catch a fleeting glimpse of

entrave [ãtrav] *nf (obstacle)* hindrance, impediment (**à** to)

entraver [ãtrave] *vt* (**a**) *(mouvement, processus)* to hinder, to impede (**b**) *Fam* **j'y entrave que dalle** it beats me

entre [ãtr] *prép* (**a**) *(au milieu de)* between; *Fig* **les deux** *(ni l'un ni l'autre)* in between; **être e. la vie et la mort** to hover between life and death; **être e. deux âges** to be middle-aged; *Fig* **faire qch e. deux portes**

to do sth in passing (**b**) *(parmi)* among(st); **hésiter e. plusieurs solutions** to hesitate between several solutions; **plusieurs d'e. nous** several of us; **être dangereux e. tous** to be extremely dangerous; **e. autres** among others (**c**) *(rapport réciproque) (deux personnes)* between; *(plusieurs personnes)* among(st); **se marier e. cousins** to intermarry with cousins; **ils se battent e. eux** they fight with each other; **qu'y a-t-il e. eux exactement?** what exactly is going on between them?; **soit dit e. nous** between you and me; *Fam* **il faut que je te parle e.** quat'z'yeux I've got to talk to you in private (**d**) *(dans)* **tenir qch e. ses mains** to hold sth in one's hands; **e. ces murs** within these walls (**e**) *(à travers)* through; **se faufiler e. les arbres** to thread one's way through the trees
entrebâillement [ãtrəbajmã] *nm* **par l'e. de la porte** through the half-open door
entrebâiller [ãtrəbaje] *vt (porte, fenêtre)* to half-open; **la porte était entrebâillée** the door was ajar
entrechat [ãtrəʃa] *nm (pas de danse)* entrechat
entrechoquer [ãtrəʃɔke] **1** *vt* to knock together; **e. des verres** to chink glasses
  2 s'entrechoquer *vpr* to knock against one another; *(verres)* to chink
entrecôte [ãtrəkot] *nf* rib steak; **e. à la bordelaise** rib steak in a shallots and red wine sauce
entrecoupé, -e [ãtrəkupe] *adj (voix)* broken
entrecouper [ãtrəkupe] *vt* to interrupt (**de** with)
entrecroiser [ãtrəkrwaze] **1** *vt (ligne)* to intersect; *(fils)* to interlace
  2 s'entrecroiser *vpr (lignes, routes)* to intersect; *(fils)* to interlace
entre-déchirer [ãtrədeʃire] **s'entre-déchirer** *vpr* to tear each other to pieces
entre-deux [ãtrədø] *nm inv* (**a**) *(intervalle)* intervening period (**b**) *Sport* jump ball
entre-deux-guerres [ãtrədøgɛr] *nm inv* **l'e.** the inter-war period
entre-dévorer [ãtrədevɔre] **s'entre-dévorer** *vpr* to devour one another *or* each other
entrée [ãtre] *nf* (**a**) *(action)* entry, entrance; *(de marchandises)* import; **faire son e.** to make one's entrance; **l'e. de la Pologne dans la UE** Poland's entry into the EU; **avant mon e. à l'université** before I go/ went to university; **un ordinateur d'e. de gamme** an entry-level computer; **e. en scène** entrance (on to the stage); **e. en fonction** assumption of one's duties; **e. en matière** introduction; **e. en vigueur** coming into force; *Fig* **à l'e. de l'hiver** at the beginning of winter; *Fig* **d'e. (de jeu)** from the outset (**b**) *(accès)* admission, admittance (**dans** *ou* **de** to); **avoir ses entrées dans un lieu** to have contacts in a place; **e. à l'hôpital** admission to hospital; **e. interdite** *(sur panneau)* no admittance, no entry; **e. libre** *(dans un musée)* admission free; *(dans une boutique)* browsers welcome (**c**) *(voie d'accès)* way in, entrance (**de** to); *(vestibule)* entrance hall; **e. des artistes** stage door; **e. principale** main entrance; **e. de service** service entrance (**d**) *(hors-d'œuvre)* starter (**e**) **faire 1000 entrées** *(film)* to sell 1,000 tickets (**f**) *Ordinat (processus)* input, entry; *(information)* entry; *(touche)* enter (key); **données d'e.** input (data); **e. (par le) clavier** keyboard input; **e. de papier** paper input; **e./sortie** input/output; **e./sortie parallèles** parallel input/output
entrefaites [ãtrəfɛt] *nfpl* **sur ces e.** at that moment
entrefilet [ãtrəfilɛ] *nm* short (news) item
entrejambe [ãtrəʒãb] *nm* crotch

entrelacer [16] [ãtrəlase] **1** *vt (rubans, branches)* to intertwine; *Ordinat* **écran entrelacé** interlaced screen
  2 s'entrelacer *vpr* to intertwine
entrelacs [ãtrəla] *nm* interlaced design, tracery
entrelarder [ãtrəlarde] *vt Culin (viande)* to lard; *Fig* **e. un discours de citations** to lace a speech with quotations
entremêler [ãtrəmele] **1** *vt* to interweave (**de** with)
  2 s'entremêler *vpr* to be interwoven
entremets [ãtrəmɛ] *nm* dessert, *Br* sweet
entremetteur, -euse [ãtrəmɛtœr, -øz] *nm,f* go-between
entremise [ãtrəmiz] *nf* intervention; **par l'e. de qn** through sb
entrepont [ãtrəpɔ̃] *nm* 'tweendecks; *(pour voyageurs)* steerage
entreposer [ãtrəpoze] *vt* to store; *(marchandises)* to warehouse
entrepôt [ãtrəpo] *nm* warehouse
entreprenant, -e [ãtrəprənã, -ãt] *adj* enterprising; *(auprès des femmes)* forward
entreprendre [58] [ãtrəprãdr] *vt* (**a**) *(commencer)* to undertake; **e. des démarches** to take steps; **e. de faire qch** to undertake to do sth (**b**) *(entretenir)* **e. qn sur qch** to engage sb in conversation about sth
entrepreneur, -euse [ãtrəprənœr, -øz] *nm,f* (**a**) *(dans le bâtiment)* contractor (**b**) *(patron)* entrepreneur (**c**) **e. de pompes funèbres** *Br* undertaker, *Am* mortician
entrepreneuriat [ãtrəprənœrja] *nm* entrepreneurship
entrepris, -e¹ *voir* entreprendre
entreprise² [ãtrəpriz] *nf* (**a**) *(action, initiative)* enterprise, undertaking; **la libre e.** free enterprise (**b**) *(firme)* company, firm; **e. privée** private company; (**c**) **e. publique** public corporation
entrer [ãtre] **1** *vi (aux* **être**) (**a**) *(aller)* to go in, to enter; *(venir)* to come in, to enter; **e. dans qch** to go/come into sth, to enter sth; **e. dans une voiture/un ascenseur** to get into a car/lift; **e. par la fenêtre** to get in *or* enter through the window; **e. en courant** to run in; **e. sans payer** to get in without paying; **e. en gare** to come into the station; **e. au port** to come into harbour; **laisser e. qn/qch** to let sb/sth in; **empêcher qn d'e.** to keep sb out; **faire e. qn** to let sb in; *(sujet: secrétaire, majordome)* to show sb in; **faire e. qch dans une pièce** to get sth into a room; *Théât* **Hamlet entre en scène** enter Hamlet; **entrez!** come/go in!
  (**b**) *(pénétrer) (eau, air)* to go/come in; **le clou entra dans le mur** the nail went into the wall; **la clef n'entre pas dans la serrure** the key won't go in the lock
  (**c**) *(heurter)* **e. dans qch** to go into sth, to run into sth; *Fam* **e. dans le décor** to go off the road
  (**d**) *(faire tenir)* **faire e. qch dans qch** to insert sth in sth; **on n'y entrera jamais à vingt** we'll never get twenty people in; **il n'entre pas le carton** it won't go in the box
  (**e**) *(devenir membre)* **e. dans l'armée** to join the army; **e. en religion** to take (holy) orders; **e. aux PTT/chez Renault** to start working for the Post Office/for Renault; **e. au service de qn** to enter sb's service; **e. dans la Communauté européenne** to join the European Community
  (**f**) *(être admis)* **e. à l'université** to go to university; **e. à l'hôpital** to go into hospital; **e. en maternelle** to start nursery school
  (**g**) *(faire partie de)* **e. dans une catégorie** to fall into

a category; **e. dans la légende** to become a legend; **e. dans l'histoire** to go down in history; **e. en ligne de compte** to be taken into account; **e. dans les projets de qn** to be part of sb's plans; **e. dans la vie de qn** to come into sb's life; **e. dans la composition de qch** to go into the making of sth; **cela n'entre pas dans mes idées** I don't go along with that
(**h**) *(commencer)* **e. dans une colère terrible** to get extremely angry; **e. en campagne** *Mil* to take the field; *Pol* to go on the campaign trail; **e. en guerre** to enter the war; **e. en fonction** to take up one's duties; **e. en vigueur** to come into force *or* effect; **e. dans la vie active** to start one's working life; **e. dans une ère nouvelle** to enter a new era; **e. dans les détails** to go into detail; **on entre dans l'hiver** winter is just beginning
(**i**) *Ordinat* to log in *or* on
2 *vt (aux* **avoir**) (**a**) *(introduire)* **e. des marchandises en fraude** to smuggle in goods
(**b**) *(enfoncer)* **e. ses ongles dans le cou de qn** to sink one's nails into sb's neck
(**c**) *Ordinat (données)* to enter, to input; *(au clavier)* to key in
3 *v impersonnel* **il n'entre pas dans mes projets de le faire** it's not part of my plans to do it
entresol [ãtrəsɔl] *nm* mezzanine (floor)
entre-temps [ãtrətã] *adv* meanwhile, in the meantime
entretenir [70] [ãtrətənir] **1** *vt* (**a**) *(soigner) (maison, jardin, routes, machine)* to maintain; **une moquette facile à e.** a carpet which is easy to look after; **e. sa forme** to keep fit (**b**) *(payer pour) (famille, maîtresse)* to maintain, to support (**c**) *(maintenir)* **e. une correspondance avec qn** to keep up a correspondence with sb; **e. de bonnes relations avec qn** to remain on good terms with sb; **cela entretient leur amitié** that keeps their friendship going *or* alive (**d**) *(parler à)* **e. qn de qch** to converse with sb about sth
2 *s'entretenir* *vpr* **s'e. avec qn (de qch)** to converse with sb (about sth)
entretenu, -e [ãtrətəny] *adj* (**a**) **bien/mal e.** *(maison, jardin)* well-kept/badly kept (**b**) **une femme entretenue** a kept woman
entretien [ãtrətjẽ] *nm* (**a**) *(soins) (d'une maison, d'un jardin, des routes, d'une machine)* maintenance; **facile/difficile d'e., d'e.** facile/difficile easy/difficult to maintain; **produits d'e.** (household) cleaning materials (**b**) *(subsistance) (d'une famille, d'une armée)* support, maintenance (**c**) *(conversation)* conversation; *(audience)* interview; **entretiens** *(négociations)* discussions, talks
entre-tuer [ãtrətчe] **s'entre-tuer** *vpr* to kill each other
entreverrai *etc voir* entrevoir
entrevoir [73a] [ãtrəvwar] *vt (rapidement)* to catch sight of; to catch a glimpse of; *(indistinctement)* to make out; **e. des difficultés** to foresee difficulties
entrevoyons *etc voir* entrevoir
entrevu, -e¹ *voir* entrevoir
entrevue² [ãtrəvy] *nf (rendez-vous)* interview; *(réunion)* meeting
entrouvert, -e [ãtruvɛr, -ɛrt] *adj* half-open
entrouvrir [52] [ãtruvrir] **1** *vt* to half-open
2 *s'entrouvrir* *vpr* to half-open
entuber [ãtybe] *vt Fam (duper)* to con; **se faire e.** to be conned
énumération [enymerasjɔ̃] *nf* listing

énumérer [34] [enymere] *vt* to list
envahir [ãvair] *vt (pays)* to invade; *(marché)* to flood; **un jardin envahi par les mauvaises herbes** a garden overgrown with weeds; *Fig* **un doute m'a envahi** I was overcome with doubt; *Fam* **e. qn** *(sujet: personne)* to intrude on sb
envahissant, -e [ãvaisã, -ãt] *adj (plantes)* invasive; *(odeur)* overwhelming; *Fam (personne)* intrusive
envahisseur [ãvaisœr] *nm* invader
enveloppant, -e [ãvlɔpã, -ãt] *adj* (**a**) *(couvrant)* **regard e.** look that takes/took everything in (**b**) *Fig (séduisant) (manières)* captivating
enveloppe [ãvlɔp] *nf* (**a**) *(de lettre)* envelope; **e. à fenêtre** window envelope; **envoyer qch sous e.** to send sth under cover; *Fig* **e. budgétaire** budget; *Fig* **e. de la recherche** the research budget (**b**) *(de paquet)* wrapping (**c**) *(de graines)* husk (**d**) *Fig (apparence)* **sous une e. de rudesse** beneath a rough exterior
enveloppé, -e [ãvlɔpe] *adj Fam* **(bien) e.** *(personne)* well-padded
envelopper [ãvlɔpe] **1** *vt* (**a**) *(marchandises, bébé)* to wrap (up); **enveloppé dans des bandages** swathed in bandages (**b**) *(entourer)* **e. qch du regard** to take sth in with one's gaze; **la nuit nous enveloppa** darkness closed in on us; **enveloppé de mystère/brume** shrouded in mystery/mist
2 *s'envelopper* *vpr* **s'e. dans une couverture** to wrap oneself up in a blanket
envenimer [ãvnime] **1** *vt (plaie)* to make septic; *Fig (querelle, discussion)* to embitter
2 *s'envenimer* *vpr (plaie)* to turn septic; *Fig (querelle, discussion)* to get acrimonious
envergure [ãvɛrgyr] *nf* (**a**) *(d'un oiseau, d'un avion)* wingspan (**b**) *Fig (ampleur)* scope; **de grande e., d'e.** *(réforme)* far-reaching; *(opération)* large-scale (**c**) *(de personne)* calibre; **manquer d'e.** to be of a low calibre
enverrai *etc voir* envoyer
envers¹ [ãvɛr] *nm (d'un document, d'une assiette)* back; *(d'une médaille, d'une pièce)* reverse; **à l'e.** *(l'extérieur à l'intérieur)* inside out; *(de haut en bas)* the wrong way up, upside down; *(devant derrière)* the wrong way round, back to front; *Fig* **l'e. du décor** the other side of the picture; *Fam* **c'est le monde à l'e.!** what's the world coming to!
envers² *prép* towards; **e. et contre tous** in the face of all opposition
envi [ãvi] **à l'envi** *adv* **faire qch à l'e.** to vie with one another in doing sth
enviable [ãvjabl] *adj* enviable
envie [ãvi] *nf* (**a**) *(désir)* desire; *(caprice)* craving (**de** for); **avoir (très) e. de qch/de faire qch** to (really) want sth/to do sth; **avoir e. de dormir** to feel sleepy; **avoir e. de rire/pleurer** to feel like laughing/crying; **être pris d'une terrible e. de rire** to have a terrible urge to laugh; **donner à qn l'e. de faire qch** to make sb want to do sth; **il a e. que je le fasse** he wants me to do it; **je vais lui ôter l'e. de s'amuser** I'll stop him/her messing around; **ce gâteau me fait e.** that cake is tempting; **avoir e. de qn** *(sexuellement)* to want *or* desire sb; **faire e. à qn** *(sujet: personne)* to tempt sb; *Fam* **ça lui a pris comme une e. de pisser** he/she just got a sudden urge (**b**) *(jalousie)* envy; **regarder qch avec e.** to look enviously at sth (**c**) *(au doigt)* hangnail; *(sur la peau)* birthmark

envier [66] [ãvje] *vt* to envy; **e. qch à qn** to envy sb sth; **n'avoir rien à e. à personne** to have no cause to be envious of anyone

envieux, -euse [ãvjø, -øz] **1** *adj* envious (**de** of) **2** *nm,f* envious person; **faire des e.** to make people envious

environ [ãvirɔ̃] **1** *adv* (*à peu près*) about, around **2 environs** *nmpl* (*alentours*) surrounding area; **aux** *ou* **dans les environs de Paris** in the vicinity of Paris; **aux environs de cinq heures** round about five o'clock

environnant, -e [ãvirɔnã, -ãt] *adj* surrounding

environnement [ãvirɔnmã] *nm* (**a**) (*milieu*) environment (**b**) *Ordinat* environment; **e. partagé** shared environment

environner [ãvirɔne] **1** *vt* to surround; **environné de qch** surrounded by sth **2 s'environner** *vpr* **s'e. de** to surround oneself with

envisageable [ãvizaʒabl] *adj* conceivable

envisager [45] [ãvizaʒe] *vt* (*considérer*) (*question, situation, solution*) to consider; (*projeter*) (*conséquence, événement*) to envisage; **e. l'avenir** to foresee the future; **e. de faire qch** to consider doing sth

envoi [ãvwa] *nm* (**a**) (*action*) sending; **e. recommandé** recorded delivery (**b**) (*colis*) parcel; (*lettre*) letter; (*marchandises*) consignment (**de** of)

envol [ãvɔl] *nm* (*d'avion*) take-off; (*d'oiseau*) taking off

envolée [ãvɔle] *nf* flight; *Fig* **e. lyrique** flight of fancy; *Fig* **l'e. du dollar** the soaring price of the dollar

envoler [ãvɔle] **s'envoler** *vpr* (**a**) (*oiseau*) to fly away; (*avion*) to take off; **je m'envole dans une heure** my plane leaves in an hour; *Fig* **s'e. dans les sondages** to shoot up the opinion polls (**b**) (*emporté par le vent*) (*chapeau*) to blow off; (*papiers*) to blow away (**c**) *Fam* (*disparaître*) (*personne, sac*) to vanish

envoûtant, -e [ãvutã, -ãt] *adj* (*fascinant*) bewitching

envoûtement [ãvutmã] *nm aussi Fig* bewitchment

envoûter [ãvute] *vt aussi Fig* to bewitch

envoyé, -e [ãvwaje] *nm,f* (*messager*) messenger; (*d'un gouvernement*) envoy; **e. spécial** (*journaliste*) special correspondent

envoyer [33] [ãvwaje] **1** *vt* to send; (*lancer*) to throw; **e. qch par courrier** to mail sth, *Br* to post sth; **e. qch à qn** to send sb sth; (*lancer*) to throw sth to sb; **e. un baiser à qn** to blow sb a kiss; **e. chercher qn** to send for sb; **e. qn faire qch** to send sb to do sth; *Fam* **e. promener** *ou* **balader** *ou* **paître qn, e. qn sur les roses** to send sb packing; *Fam* **je vais tout e. promener** I'm going to chuck it all in; *Fig* **e. des fleurs à qn** to pat sb on the back **2 s'envoyer** *vpr* (**a**) (*l'un l'autre*) **ils s'envoient des cartes postales** they send postcards to each other; *Fig* **s'e. des fleurs** (*mutuellement*) to sing one another's praises, to pat one another on the back; (*à soi-même*) to pat oneself on the back (**b**) *Fam* **s'e. un verre de vin** to knock back a glass of wine; *très Fam* **s'e. qn** to do it with sb, *Br* to have it off with sb; *très Fam* **s'e. en l'air** to do it, *Br* to have it off

envoyeur, -euse [ãvwajœr, -øz] *nm,f* sender; **retour à l'e.** return to sender

enzyme [ãzim] *nf* enzyme; **lessive aux enzymes** biological washing powder

éolien, -enne [eɔljɛ̃, -ɛn] **1** *adj* **énergie éolienne** wind energy; **moteur é.** wind-powered engine **2** *nf* **éolienne** wind turbine

épagneul, -e [epaɲœl] *nm,f* spaniel; **é. breton** Brittany spaniel

épais, -aisse [epɛ, -ɛs] **1** *adj* thick; **é. de 2 mètres** 2 metres thick; *Fam* **elle n'est pas bien épaisse** she hasn't got much on her **2** *adv* (**a**) (*pousser*) thick(ly) (**b**) *Fam* (*beaucoup*) **il n'y en a pas é.** there's not much of it **3** *nm* **au plus é. de la forêt** in the depths of the forest

épaisseur [epɛsœr] *nf* thickness; *Fig* (*d'une personne*) depth; **avoir 2 mètres d'é.** to be 2 metres thick

épaissir [epesir] **1** *vt* (*sauce, peinture*) to thicken; (*ombre, mystère*) to deepen **2** *vi* (*sauce*) to thicken; (*personne*) to fill out **3 s'épaissir** *vpr* (*cheveux, brouillard, sauce*) to thicken; (*personne*) to fill out; (*ombre, mystère*) to deepen

épaississant [epesisã] *nm* (*substance*) thickener

épaississement [epesismã] *nm* (*du brouillard, d'une sauce*) thickening

épanchement [epãʃmã] *nm* (**a**) **é. de synovie** water on the knee (**b**) *Fig* (*de sentiments*) outpouring

épancher [epãʃe] **1** *vt* **é. sa bile** to vent one's spleen; **é. son cœur** to pour out one's heart **2 s'épancher** *vpr* (*personne*) to pour out one's heart

épandage [epãdaʒ] *nm Agr* manure spreading, manuring

épandre [epãdr] **1** *vt Agr* to spread **2 s'épandre** *vpr Litt* to spread (**sur** over)

épanoui, -e [epanwi] *adj* (*fleur*) in full bloom; (*visage, sourire*) beaming; (*personne*) well-adjusted

épanouir [epanwir] **1** *vt* (*fleur, pétales*) to open out **2 s'épanouir** *vpr* (**a**) (*fleur*) to bloom (**b**) (*visage*) to light up (**c**) (*personne*) to blossom

épanouissant, -e [epanwisã, -ãt] *adj* (*travail, vie*) fulfilling

épanouissement [epanwismã] *nm* (**a**) (*action*) (*d'une fleur*) blooming; (*d'un visage*) lighting up; (*d'une personne*) blossoming (**b**) (*plénitude*) bloom

épargnant, -e [eparɲã, -ãt] *nm,f* saver; **les petits épargnants** small investors

épargne [eparɲ] *nf* (**a**) (*action, vertu*) saving (**b**) (*sommes*) savings (**c**) (*épargnants*) **l'é. privée** private investors

épargner [eparɲe] **1** *vt* (**a**) (*argent, provisions*) to save (**b**) (*énergie, temps*) to save; **é. à qn la peine de faire qch** to save sb the trouble of doing sth; **épargne-moi les détails!** spare me the details! (**c**) (*prisonnier*) to spare **2** *vi* to save (**sur** on) **3 s'épargner** *vpr* **s'é. la peine de faire qch** to save oneself the trouble of doing sth

éparpiller [eparpije] **1** *vt* (*objets, foule*) to scatter **2 s'éparpiller** *vpr* (*objets, foule*) to scatter; *Fig* (*personne*) to take on too much

épars, -e [epar, -ars] *adj* (*maisons*) scattered; (*végétation, population, informations*) sparse; (*cheveux*) loose

épatant, -e [epatã, -ãt] *adj Fam* splendid

épaté, -e [epate] *adj Fam* dumbfounded, *Br* gobsmacked

épater [epate] *vt Fam* to astound

épaule [epol] *nf* shoulder; **être large d'épaules** to be broad-shouldered; *Culin* **é. d'agneau** shoulder of lamb

épauler [epole] **1** *vt* (**a**) (*fusil*) to raise to one's shoulder (**b**) (*aider*) **é. qn** to back sb up **2** *vi* to take aim

épaulette [epolɛt] *nf* (**a**) (*rembourrage*) shoulder pad (**b**) (*bretelle*) shoulder strap

épave [epav] *nf aussi Fig* wreck

épée [epe] *nf* sword; *Sport* épée; **coup d'é.** sword-thrust; *Fig* **un coup d'é. dans l'eau** a wasted effort; *Fig* **une é. de Damoclès** a sword of Damocles

épeler [42] [eple] *vt & vi* to spell

éperdu, -e [epɛrdy] *adj (regard)* distraught; *(amour)* passionate

éperdument [epɛrdymã] *adv (aimer)* madly; **é. amoureux** head over heels in love, madly in love; *Fam* **je m'en fiche é.** I couldn't care less

éperlan [epɛrlã] *nm* smelt

éperon [eprɔ̃] *nm* spur

éperonner [eprɔne] *vt* to spur on

épervier [epɛrvje] *nm* sparrowhawk

épeurant, -e [epœrã, -ãt] *adj Can* scary, frightening

éphèbe [efɛb] *nm* Adonis

éphémère [efemɛr] **1** *adj* short-lived, ephemeral **2** *nm* mayfly

épi [epi] *nm* (**a**) *(de grain)* ear; *(de fleur)* spike; **é. de maïs** corncob (**b**) *(de cheveux)* tuft of hair

épice [epis] *nf* spice; **quatre épices** allspice

épicé, -e [epise] *adj* spicy

épicéa [episea] *nm* spruce

épicentre [episãtr] *nm* epicentre

épicer [16] [epise] *vt* to spice

épicerie [episri] *nf* (**a**) *(magasin)* grocer's (shop); **é. fine** delicatessen (**b**) *(produits)* groceries (**c**) *Can Fig* **liste d'é.** *(de griefs)* shopping list

épicier, -ère [episje, -ɛr] *nm,f* grocer; *Péj* **d'é.** *(mentalité)* small-town, parochial

épicurien, -enne [epikyrjɛ̃, -ɛn] **1** *adj* epicurean; *Phil* Epicurean **2** *nm,f* epicure; *Phil* Epicurean

épidémie [epidemi] *nf* epidemic

épidémique [epidemik] *adj* epidemic

épiderme [epidɛrm] *nm* skin, *Spéc* epidermis

épidermique [epidɛrmik] *adj* epidermal; *Fig* **une réaction é.** a kneejerk reaction

épier [66] [epje] *vt (espionner) (personne, activités)* to spy on; *(observer) (signe, occasion)* to watch out for

épilation [epilasjɔ̃] *nf (des jambes)* hair removal; *(des sourcils)* plucking; **é. à la cire** waxing; **é. maillot** bikini wax; **é. maillot brésilienne** Brazilian (wax)

épilatoire [epilatwar] *adj (crème)* hair-removing

épilepsie [epilɛpsi] *nf* epilepsy; **crise d'é.** epileptic fit

épileptique [epilɛptik] *adj & nmf* epileptic

épiler [epile] **1** *vt (jambes)* to remove the unwanted hair from; *(sourcils)* to pluck; **se faire é. les jambes à la cire** to have one's legs waxed **2** **s'épiler** *vpr* **s'é. les jambes/le maillot** to remove hair from one's legs/bikini line; **s'é. les sourcils** to pluck one's eyebrows; **s'é. les jambes à la cire** to wax one's legs

épilogue [epilɔg] *nm* epilogue

épiloguer [epilɔge] *vi* to hold forth (**sur** about)

épinard [epinar] *nm (plante)* spinach; **épinards** spinach; **épinards en branches** leaf spinach

épine [epin] *nf (piquant)* thorn; *(d'un animal)* spine, prickle; *Fig* **tirer une é. du pied à qn** *(tirer d'embarras)* to get sb out of a mess; *(soulager)* to relieve sb's mind; **é. dorsale** backbone

épinette [epinɛt] *nf* (**a**) *Can Bot* spruce (**b**) *(instrument)* spinet

épineux, -euse [epinø, -øz] *adj (arbuste, problème)* thorny; *(poisson)* spiny

épingle [epɛ̃gl] *nf* pin; **attacher qch avec des épingles** *(cheveux)* to pin sth up; *(tissu, feuilles)* to pin sth together; *Fig* **tirer son é. du jeu** to extricate oneself; *Fig* **être tiré à quatre épingles** to be dressed up to the nines; *Fig* **chercher une é. dans une botte de foin** to look for a needle in a haystack; *Fig* **monter qch en é.** to make too much of sth; **é. à chapeau** hatpin; **é. à cheveux** hairpin; **virage en é. à cheveux** hairpin *Br* bend *or Am* turn; **é. à linge** clothes *Br* peg *or Am* pin; **é. de ou à nourrice, é. de sûreté** safety pin

épingler [epɛ̃gle] *vt* (**a**) *(attacher)* to pin (**à/sur** to/on) (**b**) *Fam (arrêter)* to nab; **se faire é.** to get nabbed

épinoche [epinɔʃ] *nf* stickleback

Épiphanie [epifani] *nf Rel* **l'É.** Epiphany

épique [epik] *adj* epic

épiscopal, -e, -aux, -ales [episkɔpal, -o] *adj* episcopal

épiscopat [episkɔpa] *nm (fonction, évêques)* episcopate

épisode [epizɔd] *nm aussi Fig* episode

épisodique [epizɔdik] *adj (intermittent)* occasional; *(accessoire)* minor

épisodiquement [epizɔdikmã] *adv* occasionally

épistémologie [epistemɔlɔʒi] *nf* epistemology

épistolaire [epistɔlɛr] *adj* epistolary; **être en relation é. avec qn** to correspond with sb

épitaphe [epitaf] *nf* epitaph

épithélium [epiteljɔm] *nm* epithelium

épithète [epitɛt] *nf* epithet; *Gram* attribute

épître [epitr] *nf* epistle

éploré, -e [eplɔre] *adj* tearful

épluchage [eplyʃaʒ] *nm* peeling; *Fig* detailed examination

épluche-légumes [eplyʃlegym] *nm inv* potato *or* vegetable peeler

éplucher [eplyʃe] *vt (peler)* to peel; *Fig (texte, journal)* to go through in detail

épluchette [eplyʃɛt] *nf Can* **é. de blé d'Inde** cornhusking party

éplucheur [eplyʃœr] *nm* potato *or* vegetable peeler

épluchure [eplyʃyr] *nf (pelure)* peeling

éponge [epɔ̃ʒ] **1** *nf* sponge; **donner un coup d'é. à qch** to wipe sth with a sponge; **d'un coup d'é.** with a sponge; **jeter l'é.** *(à la boxe)* & *Fig* to throw in the towel *or* sponge; *Fig* **passer l'é.** to forget all about it **2** *adj inv* **tissu é.** (terry) towelling; **serviette é.** terry towel

éponger [45] [epɔ̃ʒe] **1** *vt* (**a**) *(liquide)* to mop up (**b**) *(surface)* to sponge (down); *(le front de quelqu'un)* to mop (**c**) *Fig (déficit)* to mop up **2** **s'éponger** *vpr* **s'é. le front** to mop one's brow

épopée [epɔpe] *nf aussi Fig* epic

époque [epɔk] *nf* (**a**) *(historique)* era, age; *Géol* period; **la Belle É.** ≃ the Edwardian era; **quelle é. (nous vivons)!** what times we live in!; **être de son é.** to be in tune with the times; **meubles d'é.** period furniture (**b**) *(moment précis)* time; **à l'é.** at the time

La Belle Époque

This refers to the period of apparent stability and prosperity from the closing years of the 19th century to the beginning of the First World War, which found its expression in café and theatre society, fashion, art and architecture. Its chief surviving monument is the area on the south side of the Champs-Élysées containing the "Petit Palais" and the "Grand Palais", erected at the time of the Universal Exhibition of 1900.

épouiller [epuje] *vt* to delouse
époumoner [epumɔne] **s'époumoner** *vpr (en criant)* to shout oneself hoarse; *(en chantant)* to sing oneself hoarse
épouse [epuz] *nf* wife
épouser [epuze] *vt* to marry; *Fig (cause)* to espouse; *Fig* **é. la forme de qch** to take on the exact shape of sth
épousseter [42] [epuste] *vt* to dust
époustouflant, -e [epustuflɑ̃, -ɑ̃t] *adj Fam* astounding
époustoufler [epustufle] *vt Fam* to astound
épouvantable [epuvɑ̃tabl] *adj* dreadful, appalling
épouvantail [epuvɑ̃taj] *nm (de jardin)* scarecrow; *Péj (personne laide)* fright; *(personne terrifiante)* bogey
épouvante [epuvɑ̃t] *nf* terror
épouvanté, -e [epuvɑ̃te] *adj* terror-stricken
épouvanter [epuvɑ̃te] *vt* to terrify
époux [epu] *nm* husband; **les é.** the married couple; **les é. Thomas** Mr and MrsThomas
éprendre [58] [eprɑ̃dr] **s'éprendre** *vpr* **s'é. de qn** to fall in love with sb
épreuve [eprœv] *nf* (**a**) *(essai)* test; **mettre qn/qch à l'é.** to put sb/sth to the test; **à l'é. du feu** fireproof; **à l'é. des balles** bulletproof; **un courage à toute é.** unfailing courage; **être mis à rude é.** *(personne, patience)* to be severely tested; **les bateaux furent mis à rude é. par la tempête** the boats took a battering from the storm; *Fig* **é. de force** trial of strength (**b**) *(examen) (écrit)* (examination) paper; *(oral)* test (**c**) *(d'athlétisme)* event; **é. contre la montre** time trial; **é. éliminatoire** heat (**d**) *(adversité)* trial, ordeal; **dans l'é.** in adversity (**e**) *Typ* proof (**f**) *Phot* print
épris, -e [epri, -iz] *adj* **é. de qn** in love with sb; **é. de qch** passionate about sth
éprouvant, -e [epruvɑ̃, -ɑ̃t] *adj* trying
éprouvé, -e [epruve] *adj* (**a**) *(testé) (remède)* proven, well-tried; *(matériaux)* tested (**b**) *(famille)* sorely tried; *(région)* hard-hit
éprouver [epruve] *vt* (**a**) *(essayer) (méthode, personne, courage)* to test (**b**) *(ressentir) (sensation, sentiment, douleur)* to feel (**c**) *(subir) (perte)* to suffer; *(difficultés)* to meet with
éprouvette [epruvɛt] **1** *nf* test tube **2** *adj* **bébé é.** test-tube baby
EPS [əpeɛs] *nf (abrév* **éducation physique et sportive**) *Br* PE, *Am* Phys. Ed.
épuisant, -e [epɥizɑ̃, -ɑ̃t] *adj* exhausting
épuisé, -e [epɥize] *adj* (**a**) *(très fatigué)* exhausted (**b**) *(sol)* exhausted (**c**) *(livre, édition)* out of print; *(marchandises)* sold out
épuisement [epɥizmɑ̃] *nm* (**a**) *(fatigue)* exhaustion; **danser jusqu'à l'é.** to dance till one drops (**b**) *(d'un sol, d'un stock, de ressources)* exhaustion; **jusqu'à. é. des stocks** while stocks last
épuiser [epɥize] **1** *vt* (**a**) *(fatiguer)* to exhaust (**b**) *(sol, stock, ressources, sujet)* to exhaust **2** **s'épuiser** *vpr* (**a**) *(se fatiguer)* to exhaust oneself, to wear oneself out; **s'é. à faire qch** to wear oneself out doing sth (**b**) *(source)* to dry up; *(stock, ressources)* to run out
épuisette [epɥizɛt] *nf* landing net
épuration [epyrasjɔ̃] *nf (de l'eau, du gaz)* purification; *(du pétrole, d'un minerai)* refining; *Fig (d'une langue)* refining; *Pol* purge
épurer [epyre] *vt (eau, gaz)* to purify; *(pétrole, minerai)* to refine; *Fig (langue)* to refine; *Pol (parti)* to purge

équarrir [ekarir] *vt* (**a**) *(bois, pierre)* to square (**b**) *(animal)* to quarter
équarrissage [ekarisaʒ] *nm* (**a**) *(du bois, de la pierre)* squaring (**b**) *(d'animaux)* quartering
Équateur [ekwatœr] *nm* **l'É.** Ecuador
équateur [ekwatœr] *nm* equator; **sous l'é.** at the equator
équation [ekwasjɔ̃] *nf* equation; **é. du premier/ deuxième degré** simple/quadratic equation
équatorial, -e, -aux, -ales [ekwatɔrjal, -o] *adj* equatorial
équatorien, -enne [ekwatɔrjɛ̃, -ɛn] **1** *adj* Ecuadorian **2** *nm,f* **É.** Ecuadorian
équerre [ekɛr] *nf* **é. (à dessin)** set square; **en é., à l'é.** at right angles; **d'é.** square, straight
équestre [ekɛstr] *adj (statue, sports)* equestrian; *(exercices)* horseriding
équidés [ekɥide, ekide] *nmpl* horse family, *Spéc* Equidae
équidistant, -e [ekɥidistɑ̃, -ɑ̃t] *adj* equidistant (**de** from)
équilatéral, -e, -aux, -ales [ekɥilateral, -o] *adj* equilateral
équilibrage [ekilibraʒ] *nm* balancing
équilibre [ekilibr] *nm* (**a**) *(d'un corps, d'un objet)* balance; **mettre qch en é.** to balance sth; **perdre l'é.** to lose one's balance; **faire perdre l'é. à qn** to throw sb off balance; **faire de l'é. sur qch** to balance on sth; **être en é. instable** to be precariously balanced (**b**) *(mental)* (mental) balance, equilibrium (**c**) *budget* **en é.** balanced budget; **é. budgétaire** balanced budget (**d**) *(d'un ensemble)* balance
équilibré, -e [ekilibre] *adj (chargement, alimentation)* balanced; *(personne)* well-balanced; *(vie)* stable
équilibrer [ekilibre] **1** *vt (charge, composition)* to balance; *(bateau, avion)* to trim; **é. un budget** to balance a budget **2** **s'équilibrer** *vpr (l'un l'autre)* to balance each other out
équilibriste [ekilibrist] *nmf (funambule)* tightrope walker
équinoxe [ekinɔks] *nm* equinox
équipage [ekipaʒ] *nm* (**a**) *(d'un navire, d'un avion)* crew; **les hommes d'é.** the crew; **les membres de l'é.** the crew (**b**) *(voiture et chevaux)* equipage
équipe [ekip] *nf* (**a**) *Sport* team; **une é. de football** a football team (**b**) *(de chercheurs, de médecins)* team; *(d'ouvriers)* gang; *(à l'usine)* shift; *Mil* working party; **travailler en é.** to work as a team; **faire é. avec qn** to team up with sb; **é. dirigeante** management team; **é. de jour/nuit** day/night shift; **é. de secours** rescue team
équipée [ekipe] *nf (frasque)* escapade; *(promenade, voyage)* jaunt
équipement [ekipmɑ̃] *nm* (**a**) *(action) (d'un atelier, d'une cuisine)* equipping, fitting out (**b**) *(matériel)* equipment; *(de soldat)* kit (**c**) *(installations)* facilities; **équipements collectifs** public facilities; *Ordinat* **é. informatique** computer equipment
équiper [ekipe] **1** *vt (atelier, cuisine)* to equip, to fit out (**de** with); *(sportif, armée)* to equip, *Br* to kit out (**de** with); **appartement avec cuisine équipée** *Br* flat *or Am* apartment with cooking facilities **2** **s'équiper** *vpr* to equip oneself (**de** with)
équipier, -ère [ekipje, -ɛr] *nm,f* team member
équitable [ekitabl] *adj* fair

équitablement [ekitabləmã] *adv* fairly

équitation [ekitasjɔ̃] *nf Br* (horse)riding, *Am* (horseback) riding; **faire de l'é.** to go *Br* (horse)riding *or* (horseback) riding

équivalence [ekivalɑ̃s] *nf* equivalence; *Univ* **avoir/obtenir une é.** to have/get an equivalent diploma

équivalent, -e [ekivalɑ̃, -ɑ̃t] **1** *adj* equivalent (**à** to) **2** *nm* equivalent; **sans é.** without equal

équivaloir [69a] [ekivalwar] *vi* **é. à qch** (*valoir*) to be equivalent to sth; (*revenir à*) to amount to sth

équivaut *voir* **équivaloir**

équivoque [ekivɔk] **1** *adj* (**a**) (*ambigu*) (*terme, attitude*) equivocal, ambiguous (**b**) (*douteux*) (*conduite, passé*) dubious **2** *nf* ambiguity; **sans é.** (*réponse, situation*) unequivocal; (*répondre*) unequivocally

érable [erabl] *nm* (*arbre, bois*) maple; **sirop d'é.** maple syrup

érablière [erablijɛr] *nf Can* maple grove

éradication [eradikasjɔ̃] *nf* eradication

éradiquer [eradike] *vt* to eradicate

érafler [erafle] **1** *vt* (*genou*) to graze; (*cuir*) to scuff; (*bois, meuble*) to scratch **2 s'érafler** *vpr* **s'é. le coude** to graze one's elbow

éraflure [eraflyr] *nf* (*au genou*) graze; (*sur cuir*) scuff mark; (*sur bois, sur meuble*) scratch

éraillé, -e [eraje] *adj* (**a**) (*voix*) hoarse (**b**) (*surface*) scratched

ère [ɛr] *nf* era; **en l'an 1150 de notre è.** in the year 1150 AD; **avant notre è.** BC

érection [erɛksjɔ̃] *nf* (**a**) (*construction*) erection (**b**) (*gonflement*) erection; **être en é.** (*personne*) to have an erection; (*verge*) to be erect

éreintant, -e [erɛ̃tɑ̃, -ɑ̃t] *adj Fam* exhausting

éreinté, -e [erɛ̃te] *adj Fam* exhausted

éreinter [erɛ̃te] **1** *vt* (**a**) (*fatiguer*) (*personne, animal*) to exhaust, to wear out (**b**) (*critiquer*) (*livre, auteur*) to tear to pieces **2 s'éreinter** *vpr* **s'é. à faire qch** to wear oneself out doing sth

érémiste [eremist] = **RMiste**

Erevan [erevan] *n* Yerevan

ergot [ɛrgo] *nm* (**a**) (*d'un coq*) spur (**b**) (*d'un chien*) dewclaw (**c**) *Tech* pin

ergoter [ɛrgɔte] *vi* to quibble (**sur** about)

Érié [erje] *n voir* **lac**

ériger [45] [eriʒe] **1** *vt* (**a**) (*dresser*) (*statue, temple, mât*) to erect (**b**) (*créer*) (*tribunal*) to establish, to set up (**c**) *Fig* **é. qn en qch** to set sb up as sth; **é. qch en qch** to elevate sth to the status of sth **2 s'ériger** *vpr* **s'é. en qch** to set oneself up as sth

ermitage [ɛrmitaʒ] *nm* hermitage

ermite [ɛrmit] *nm* hermit; **vivre en e.** to live the life of a recluse

érogène [erɔʒɛn] *adj* erogenous

érosion [erozjɔ̃] *nf* erosion

érotique [erɔtik] *adj* erotic

érotisme [erɔtism] *nm* eroticism

errance [erɑ̃s] *nf Litt* roving, wandering

errant, -e [erɑ̃, -ɑ̃t] *adj* (*vie*) roving, wandering; **chevalier e.** knight errant; **chien e.** stray dog

errata [erata] *nmpl voir* **erratum**

erratique [eratik] *adj* erratic

erratum [eratɔm] (*pl* **errata** [erata]) *nm* erratum

errements [ermã] *nmpl* bad ways; **retomber dans ses e. passés** to fall back into one's bad old ways

errer [ɛre] *vi* (*marcher*) to wander; **e. par les rues** to roam the streets; **e. comme une âme en peine** to wander about like a lost soul

erreur [ɛrœr] *nf* (**a**) (*faute*) mistake, error; **faire** *or* **commettre une e.** to make a mistake; **faire e.** to be mistaken; **être dans l'e.** to be mistaken; **induire qn en e.** to mislead sb; **par e.** by mistake; **sauf e. de ma part** if I'm not mistaken; **il y a e. sur la personne** you've/they've/*etc* got the wrong person; **il n'y a pas d'e. (possible)** there's no doubt about it; **l'e. est humaine** to err is human; **e. de calcul** miscalculation; **e. de jeunesse** youthful indiscretion; **e. judiciaire** miscarriage of justice; **e. de jugement** error of judgement (**b**) *Ordinat* error; **message d'e.** error message; **correction des erreurs** error correction; **e. d'analyse (syntaxique)** parse error; **e. disque** disk error; **e. d'écriture** write error; **e. de lecture** read error; **e. de logiciel** software *or* system error; **e. de programmation** programming error; **e. de saisie** keying error

erroné, -e [ɛrɔne] *adj* erroneous

ersatz [ɛrzats] *nm inv* ersatz, substitute

éructer [erykte] **1** *vi* to belch **2** *vt Fig* **é. des injures** to hurl abuse

érudit, -e [erydi, -it] **1** *adj* erudite, scholarly **2** *nm,f* scholar

érudition [erydisjɔ̃] *nf* erudition, scholarship

éruption [erypsjɔ̃] *nf* (**a**) (*d'un volcan*) eruption; **entrer en é.** to erupt (**b**) (*de boutons*) rash

érythème [eritɛm] *nm Méd* rash; **é. fessier** *Br* nappy *or Am* diaper rash; **é. solaire** sunburn

Érythrée [eritre] *nf* l'É. Eritrea

érythréen, -enne [eritreɛ̃, -ɛn] **1** *adj* Eritrean **2** *nm,f* É. Eritrean

E/S *Ordinat* (*abrév* **entrée/sortie**) I/O

es *voir* **être²**

ès [ɛs] *prép* **docteur ès lettres/sciences** ≃ PhD; **licencié ès lettres** ≃ BA; **licencié ès sciences** ≃ BSc

ESB [əɛsbe] *nf* (*abrév* **encéphalite spongiforme bovine**) BSE

esbroufe [ɛzbruf] *nf Fam* bluffing; **faire de l'e.** to bluff

escabeau, -x [ɛskabo] *nm* (**a**) (*tabouret*) stool (**b**) (*marchepied*) stepladder

escadre [ɛskadr] *nf Naut* squadron; *Aviat* **e. aérienne** wing; **chef d'e.** *Naut* squadron commander; *Aviat* wing commander

escadrille [ɛskadrij] *nf* (**a**) *Naut* flotilla (**b**) *Aviat* (*unité*) flight

escadron [ɛskadrɔ̃] *nm* (**a**) *Mil* squadron; **chef d'e.** major (**b**) *Aviat* squadron (**c**) *Fig* (*groupe*) (*de personnes*) troop, band

escalade [ɛskalad] *nf* (**a**) (*d'un mur, d'une falaise*) climbing, scaling; *Sport* climbing; **faire de l'e.** to go climbing (**b**) *Fig* (*d'une guerre, des prix, de la violence*) escalation

escalader [ɛskalade] *vt* to climb, to scale

escalator® [ɛskalatɔr] *nm* escalator

escale [ɛskal] *nf* (**a**) (*arrêt*) stopover; **faire e.** (*en bateau*) to put into port; (*en avion*) to touch down; **faire e. à Athènes** (*en bateau*) to put in at Athens; (*en avion*) to stop over at Athens; **vol sans e.** nonstop flight; **e. technique** refuelling stop (**b**) (*lieu*) (*pour bateau*) port of call; (*pour avion*) stopover

escalier [ɛskalje] *nm* (*marches*) stairs; (*cage*) staircase; **dans l'e., dans les escaliers** on the stairs; **monter e.** (*en ski*) to sidestep; **e. en colimaçon** spiral staircase; **e. mécanique, e. roulant,** *Can* **e. mobile** esca-

lator; **e. de secours** fire escape; **e. de service** backstairs
escalope [ɛskalɔp] *nf* escalope
escamotable [ɛskamɔtabl] *adj (antenne, train d'atterrissage, phares)* retractable; *(meuble)* foldaway
escamotage [ɛskamɔtaʒ] *nm* (**a**) *(par un illusionniste)* vanishing (**b**) *(d'un train d'atterrissage)* retraction (**c**) *Fig (d'un problème)* dodging
escamoter [ɛskamɔte] *vt* (**a**) **e. qch** *(sujet: illusionniste)* to make sth vanish (**b**) *(voler)* to sneak off with (**c**) *(train d'atterrissage)* to retract (**d**) *Fig (problème)* to dodge
escampette [ɛskɑ̃pɛt] *nf Fam* **prendre la poudre d'e.** to make off
escapade [ɛskapad] *nf* jaunt; **faire une e.** to go on a jaunt
escarbille [ɛskarbij] *nf* cinder
escargot [ɛskargo] *nm* snail; **aller à une allure d'e.** *ou* **à la vitesse d'un e.** to go at a snail's pace; **marcher comme un e.** to walk at a snail's pace; *Fig* **opération e.** = slowing down of traffic by protesting truck drivers
escarmouche [ɛskarmuʃ] *nf* skirmish
escarpé, -e [ɛskarpe] *adj (route, montagne)* steep
escarpement [ɛskarpəmɑ̃] *nm (versant)* steep slope; *Géog* escarpment
escarpin [ɛskarpɛ̃] *nm* pump, *Br* court shoe
escarpolette [ɛskarpɔlɛt] *nf Vieilli (balançoire)* swing
escarre [ɛskar] *nf Méd* scab; *(due aux draps)* bedsore
escient [ɛsjɑ̃] *nm* **à bon e.** wisely; **à mauvais e.** unwisely
esclaffer [ɛsklafe] **s'esclaffer** *vpr* to burst out laughing, to roar with laughter
esclandre [ɛsklɑ̃dr] *nm (scandale, tapage)* scene; **faire** *ou* **causer un e.** to make a scene
esclavage [ɛsklavaʒ] *nm* slavery; **réduire qn en e.** to enslave sb
esclavagisme [ɛsklavaʒism] *nm* slavery; *(doctrine)* pro-slavery
esclave [ɛsklav] **1** *nmf* slave; **être vendu comme e.** to be sold into slavery; *Fig* **être l'e. de qn/qch** to be a slave to sb/sth
2 *adj* **Fig être e. de ses habitudes** to be a slave to one's habits
escogriffe [ɛskɔgrif] *nm* **(grand) e.** beanpole
escompte [ɛskɔ̃t] *nm* discount; *Fin* **taux d'e.** (bank) discount rate
escompter [ɛskɔ̃te] *vt (espérer)* to expect, to anticipate (**que** that); **e. faire qch** to expect to do sth
escorte [ɛskɔrt] *nf* escort; **sous (bonne) e.** under escort
escorter [ɛskɔrte] *vt* to escort
escouade [ɛskwad] *nf Mil* squad
escrime [ɛskrim] *nf Sport* fencing; **faire de l'e.** to fence
escrimer [ɛskrime] **s'escrimer** *vpr* to fight; **s'e. à faire qch** to struggle to do sth
escrimeur, -euse [ɛskrimœr, -øz] *nm,f* fencer
escroc [ɛskro] *nm* crook, swindler
escroquer [ɛskrɔke] *vt (personne)* to swindle, to cheat; **e. qch à qn, e. qn de qch** to swindle *or* to cheat sb out of sth
escroquerie [ɛskrɔkri] *nf (action)* swindling; *(résultat)* swindle; *(délit)* fraud; *Fam* **mais c'est de l'e.!** it's a rip-off!
escudo [ɛskydo] *nm* escudo
eskimo [ɛskimo] = **esquimau**

ésotérique [ezɔterik] *adj* esoteric
espace [ɛspas] *nm* (**a**) *(étendue, distance)* space; **laisser de l'e.** to leave space; **e. blanc** space; **E. économique européen** European Economic Area; **e. publicitaire** advertising space; **e. de rangement** storage space; **e. vital** living space; **espaces verts** parks, green spaces (**b**) *(durée)* **en l'e. d'une semaine** within a week (**c**) *(atmosphère)* space; **e. aérien** airspace (**d**) *Math* space; **e. à trois/quatre dimensions** three-/four-dimensional space (**e**) *Ordinat* **e. disque** disk space; **e. mémoire** memory space; **e. de stockage** storage space
espacement [ɛspasmɑ̃] *nm (action)* spacing out; *(résultat)* spacing; *(distance)* space; *Ordinat* **e. arrière** backspace
espacer [16] [ɛspase] **1** *vt (objets, paiements, visites)* to space out
2 **s'espacer** *vpr* (**a**) *(visites, lettres)* to become less frequent (**b**) *(personnes)* **espacez-vous** space yourselves out
espace-temps *(pl* **espaces-temps)** [ɛspastɑ̃] *nm Math & Phys* space-time (continuum)
espadon [ɛspadɔ̃] *nm* swordfish
espadrille [ɛspadrij] *nf* espadrille
Espagne [ɛspaɲ] *nf* **l'E.** Spain
espagnol, -e [ɛspaɲɔl] **1** *adj* Spanish
2 *nm,f* **E.** Spaniard; **les Espagnols** the Spanish
3 *nm (langue)* Spanish
espagnolette [ɛspaɲɔlɛt] *nf* window fastener *(long vertical bar with pivoting central catch)*
espalier [ɛspalje] *nm* (**a**) *(mur)* espalier wall (**b**) *(de gymnase)* wall bars
espèce [ɛspɛs] *nf* (**a**) *(sorte)* kind, sort; **les gens de son e.** people like him/her, people of his/her kind; **de la pire e.** of the worst sort; **cela n'a aucune e. d'importance** that's of no importance whatsoever; *Fam* **cette e. d'idiot** that stupid idiot; *Fam* **e. d'idiot!** you idiot! (**b**) *Jur* **cas d'e.** specific case; **la loi applicable en l'e.** the law applicable to the case in point (**c**) **espèces** *(argent)* cash; **payer en espèces** to pay in cash; **espèces sonnantes et trébuchantes** hard cash (**d**) *Bot & Zool* species; **l'e. humaine** the human race, mankind
espérance [ɛsperɑ̃s] *nf* hope; **dans l'e. de faire qch** in the hope of doing sth; **dans l'e. que...** in the hope that...; **au-delà de nos espérances** beyond our expectations; **répondre aux espérances de qn** to live up to sb's expectations; **e. de vie** life expectancy
espérer [34] [ɛspere] **1** *vt* to hope for; **e. faire qch** to hope to do sth; **e. que** to hope that; **je ne vous espérais plus** I'd given you up
2 *vi* **j'espère bien** I hope so; **espérons!** let's hope so!
espiègle [ɛspjɛgl] *adj* mischievous
espion, -onne [ɛspjɔ̃, -ɔn] *nm,f* spy
espionnage [ɛspjɔnaʒ] *nm* espionage, spying; **faire de l'e.** to spy; **l'e. industriel** industrial espionage
espionner [ɛspjɔne] **1** *vt* to spy on
2 *vi* to spy
esplanade [ɛsplanad] *nf* esplanade
espoir [ɛspwar] *nm* (**a**) *(espérance)* hope; **avoir l'e. de faire qch** to have hopes of doing sth; **avoir bon e.** to be full of hope; **reprendre e.** to become hopeful again; **nourrir l'e. de faire qch** to live in hope of doing sth; **dans l'e. de faire qch** in the hope of doing sth; **dans l'e. de faire qch** in the hope of doing sth; **dans l'e. de vous voir bientôt** hoping to see you soon; **tous les espoirs sont permis** things look hopeful; **c'est sans e.** it's hopeless; *Ironique* **l'e. fait vivre**

hope springs eternal (**b**) *(personne)* hope; **un e. du tennis français** one of the most promising French tennis players

esprit [ɛspri] *nm* (**a**) *(intellectuel)* mind; **avoir l'e. large/étroit** to be broad-/narrow-minded; **avoir l'e. tranquille** to be easy in one's mind; **avoir l'e. mal tourné** to have a dirty mind; **avoir l'e. d'analyse/ scientifique** to have an analytical/a scientific (turn of) mind; **perdre l'e.** to go out of one's mind; **reprendre ses esprits** to regain consciousness; **elle avait l'e. ailleurs** her thoughts were elsewhere; **elle n'a pas l'e. à ce qu'elle fait** her mind isn't on what she's doing; **je n'ai pas l'e. à plaisanter** I'm not in the mood for joking; **une pareille idée ne me serait jamais venue à l'e.** such an idea would never have crossed my mind; **qu'avez-vous à l'e.?** what are you thinking about? (**b**) *(attitude mentale)* spirit; **avoir mauvais e.** to be a malicious sort; **faire du mauvais e.** to be malicious; **e. de caste** class-consciousness; **e. de clocher** parochialism; **e. de compétition** competitive spirit; **e. de corps** esprit de corps; **e. d'entreprise** enterprise spirit; **e. d'équipe** team spirit; **e. de famille** family feeling (**c**) *(humour)* wit; **avoir de l'e.** to be witty; **mots** *ou* **traits d'e.** witticisms; **faire de l'e.** to display one's wit (**d**) *(personne)* person; **un e. fort** a freethinker; *Prov* **les grands esprits se rencontrent** great minds think alike (**e**) *(sens)* spirit; **l'e. de la loi** the spirit of the law (**f**) *(fantôme)* spirit; **e., es-tu là?** *(dans une séance de spiritisme)* is there anybody there?; **e. frappeur** poltergeist (**g**) *Chim* (volatile) spirit

esquif [ɛskif] *nm* skiff; **un frêle e.** a frail barque

esquimau, -aude, -x, -audes [ɛskimo, -od] **1** *adj* Eskimo, *Am* Inuit
 2 *nm,f* **E.** Eskimo, *Am* Inuit
 3 *nm (glace)* **E.**® *Br* ≃ choc-ice *(on a stick), Am* ≃ ice-cream bar

esquinté, -e [ɛskɛ̃te] *adj Fam (abîmé)* wrecked, *Br* knackered

esquinter [ɛskɛ̃te] *Fam* **1** *vt (abîmer)* to wreck; *(blesser)* to hurt
 2 s'esquinter *vpr (s'abîmer)* **s'e. la jambe** to hurt one's leg, *Br* to do one's leg in; **s'e. la santé/les yeux (à faire qch)** to ruin one's health/eyes (doing sth)

esquisse [ɛskis] *nf (dessin)* sketch; *Fig (d'un projet, d'un roman)* outline; *(d'un sourire)* suggestion

esquisser [ɛskise] **1** *vt (dessiner)* to sketch; *Fig (plan, roman)* to outline; *Fig* **e. un sourire** to give a slight smile
 2 s'esquisser *vpr (idée, projet)* to take shape

esquiver [ɛskive] **1** *vt aussi Fig* to dodge, to evade
 2 s'esquiver *vpr* to slip away

essai [ɛsɛ] *nm* (**a**) *(tentative)* try; **faire un e.** to have a try (**b**) *(test) (d'un produit, d'une voiture)* test, trial; **à l'e.** on a trial basis; *Ordinat* **e. approfondi** beta test; **e. nucléaire** nuclear test; *Ordinat* **e. de performance** benchmark (**c**) *(ouvrage)* essay (**d**) *(au rugby)* try

essaim [ɛsɛ̃] *nm aussi Fig* swarm

essaimer [ɛseme] *vi (abeilles)* to swarm; *Fig (population, famille)* to spread; *(entreprise)* to expand

essayage [ɛsɛjaʒ] *nm* fitting

essayer [53] [ɛseje] **1** *vt* (**a**) *(pour la première fois) (gadget, restaurant)* to try (out); *(voiture)* to test-drive; *(vin, plat)* to try, to taste; *(vêtement, chaussures)* to try on (**b**) *(tester) (machine, produit)* to test (**c**) *(tenter)* **e. de faire qch** to try to do sth

2 s'essayer *vpr* **s'e. à qch/à faire qch** to try one's hand at sth/at doing sth

ESSEC [ɛsɛk] *nf (abrév* **École supérieure des sciences économiques et commerciales**) = university-level business school

essence [ɛsɑ̃s] *nf* (**a**) *(combustible) Br* petrol, *Am* gas(oline); **e. ordinaire** *Br* two-star petrol, *Am* regular gas; **e. sans plomb** unleaded *(Br* petrol *or Am* gas) (**b**) *(extrait) (de plantes, de café)* essence; **e. de térébenthine** spirits of turpentine (**c**) *(caractère fondamental)* essence; **par e.** essentially (**d**) *(espèce)* species

essentiel, -elle [ɛsɑ̃sjɛl] **1** *adj* (**a**) *(nécessaire)* essential, necessary (**à/pour** for) (**b**) *(principal) (condition, caractère)* essential; *(raison)* basic, main
 2 l'e. *(le plus important)* the main thing; *(le minimum)* the essentials; **l'e. de** *(la majeure partie de)* the majority of

essentiellement [ɛsɑ̃sjɛlmɑ̃] *adv* (**a**) *(principalement)* essentially mainly (**b**) *(par nature)* essentially

esseulé, -e [ɛsœle] *adj* isolated

essieu, -x [ɛsjø] *nm* axle

essor [ɛsɔr] *nm* (**a**) *(d'un oiseau)* flight; **prendre son e.** to fly off (**b**) *Fig (d'une industrie, d'une économie)* (rapid) growth; **en plein e.** booming; **prendre son e.** to take off

essorage [ɛsɔraʒ] *nm (à la machine)* spin-drying; *(à la main)* wringing

essorer [ɛsɔre] *vt (vêtements) (à la machine)* to spin(-dry); *(à la main)* to wring out; *(salade)* to spin

essoreuse [ɛsɔrøz] *nf (à tambour)* spin-drier

essoufflé, -e [ɛsufle] *adj* out of breath

essoufflement [ɛsufləmɑ̃] *nm* breathlessness; *Fig (de l'économie, d'une activité)* running down

essouffler [ɛsufle] **1** *vt* to make out of breath
 2 s'essouffler *vpr* to get out of breath; *Fig (économie, activité)* to run down

essuie [ɛsɥi] *nm Belg (essuie-mains)* hand towel; *(torchon)* cloth, tea towel; *(serviette de bain)* bath towel

essuie-glace *(pl* **essuie-glaces)** [ɛsɥiglas] *nm Br* windscreen *or Am* windshield wiper

essuie-mains [ɛsɥimɛ̃] *nm inv* hand towel

essuie-tout [ɛsɥitu] *nm inv* kitchen paper

essuyer [32] [ɛsɥije] **1** *vt* (**a**) *(surface)* to wipe; *(liquide)* to wipe up; *(larmes)* to wipe away; **e. la vaisselle** to dry the dishes, to dry up (**b**) *(subir) (défaite, perte, insultes)* to suffer; *(refus)* to meet with; *(tempête)* to run into
 2 s'essuyer *vpr* to wipe oneself; *(après un bain)* to dry oneself; **s'e. la bouche/les yeux** to wipe one's mouth/ eyes

est¹ [ɛ] *voir* **être²**

est² [ɛst] **1** *nm* east; **un vent d'e.** an easterly wind; **le vent d'e.** the east wind; **à l'e.** in the east; **à l'e. de** (to the) east of; *Géog & Pol* **l'E.** the East
 2 *adj inv (côte, face, régions)* eastern

estafilade [ɛstafilad] *nf* gash

estaminet [ɛstaminɛ] *nm Belg* (small) café

estampe [ɛstɑ̃p] *nf* print

estampille [ɛstɑ̃pij] *nf (sur un document)* stamp; *(sur un produit)* mark

est-ce que [ɛskə] *adv interrogatif* **e. je peux entrer?** can I come in?; **est-ce qu'il est là?** is he here?; **e. tu la connais?** do you know her?; **est-ce qu'il connaissait la réponse?** did he know the answer?

esthète [ɛstɛt] *nmf* aesthete

esthéticien, -enne [ɛstetisjɛ̃, -ɛn] *nm,f* beautician
esthétique [ɛstetik] **1** *adj* aesthetic; *(beau)* aesthetically pleasing
  2 *nf (beauté)* aesthetic quality
estimable [ɛstimabl] *adj* (**a**) *(digne de respect)* estimable (**b**) *(assez bon)* fairly good
estimation [ɛstimasjɔ̃] *nf* (**a**) *(détermination) (d'un prix, d'une distance, d'un poids)* estimation; *(de marchandises, d'une œuvre d'art)* valuation; *(de dommages, de besoins)* assessment (**b**) *(valeur, quantité estimée)* estimate
estime [ɛstim] *nf* (**a**) *(respect)* esteem, regard; **avoir de l'e.** **pour qn/qch** to esteem sb/sth; **baisser/remonter dans l'e.** **de qn** to go down/up in sb's estimation; **avoir un succès d'e.** to be a critical (though not a popular) success (**b**) *Naut* **à l'e.** by dead reckoning
estimer [ɛstime] **1** *vt* (**a**) *(déterminer) (prix, distance, poids)* to estimate; *(marchandises, œuvre d'art)* to value; *(dommages, besoins)* to assess (**b**) *(considérer)* to consider, to think (**que** that); **il n'a pas estimé nécessaire de me prévenir** he didn't consider it necessary to warn me (**c**) *(respecter) (personne)* to have a high opinion of; **e. qn à sa juste valeur** to value sb
  2 **s'estimer** *vpr* **s'e.** **satisfait/heureux** to consider oneself satisfied/lucky
estival, -e, -aux, -ales [ɛstival, -o] *adj* summer
estivant, -e [ɛstivã, -ãt] *nm,f Br* holidaymaker, *Am* vacationer
estocade [ɛstɔkad] *nf aussi Fig* death-blow; **donner l'e. à** to deal the death-blow to
estomac [ɛstɔma] *nm* (**a**) *(ventre)* stomach; **avoir l'e. vide** to have an empty stomach; **avoir l'e. dans les talons** to be starving (**b**) *Fam Fig (courage)* guts
estomaquer [ɛstɔmake] *vt Fam* to flabbergast
estomper [ɛstɔ̃pe] **1** *vt Art (dessin)* to shade off; *Fig (paysage, contour, souvenir)* to blur
  2 **s'estomper** *vpr (paysage, contour, souvenir)* to become blurred; *(peine)* to ease; *(rides)* to be smoothed out
Estonie [ɛstɔni] *nf* l'E. Estonia
estonien, -enne [ɛstɔnjɛ̃, -ɛn] **1** *adj* Estonian
  2 *nm,f* E. Estonian
  3 *nm (langue)* Estonian
estourbir [ɛsturbir] *vt Fam* (**a**) *(tuer)* to bump off (**b**) *(étonner)* to astound
estrade [ɛstrad] *nf* platform
estragon [ɛstragɔ̃] *nm* tarragon
estropié, -e [ɛstrɔpje] **1** *adj* crippled
  2 *nm,f* cripple
estropier [66] [ɛstrɔpje] *vt* (**a**) *(personne)* to cripple, to maim (**b**) *Fig (morceau de musique, langue étrangère)* to murder; *(mot, nom)* to mispronounce; *(texte)* to mutilate
estuaire [ɛstɥɛr] *nm* estuary
estudiantin, -e [ɛstydjãtɛ̃, -in] *adj* student
esturgeon [ɛstyrʒɔ̃] *nm* sturgeon
et [e] **1** *conj* (**a**) *(exprime l'addition, la simultanéité)* and; **et son frère et sa sœur** both his/her brother and his/her sister; **et d'un, il pleut, et de deux, je n'ai pas envie d'y aller** in the first place it's raining, and in the second place I don't want to go; **j'aime le café, et vous?** I like coffee, do you?; **et moi, alors?** what about me? (**b**) *(dans les nombres, les heures)* **vingt/trente et un** twenty-/thirty-one; **une livre et demie** a pound and a half; **il est quatre heures et demie/et quart** it's half past/a quarter past four
  2 *nm (symbole)* **et commercial** ampersand

ETA [ətea] *nf (abrév* **Euskadi ta Askatasuna)** ETA
étable [etabl] *nf* cowshed
établi¹ [etabli] *nm* workbench
établi², -e *adj* established; **considérer qch comme une chose établie** to take sth for granted
établir [etablir] **1** *vt* (**a**) *(paix, relations, principe)* to establish; *(agence)* to set up; *(camp)* to pitch; *(prix)* to fix; *(devis, liste)* to draw up; *(record)* to set (**b**) *(démontrer)* to establish, to prove (**c**) *(autorité, réputation)* to establish (**sur** on)
  2 **s'établir** *vpr* (**a**) *(dans une ville, un pays)* to settle (**b**) *(pour exercer un métier)* to set up in business (**c**) *(s'instaurer)* to become established
établissement [etablismã] *nm* (**a**) *(de la paix, de relations, d'un principe)* establishment; *(d'une agence)* setting up; *(d'un camp)* pitching; *(d'un prix)* fixing; *(d'un devis, d'une liste)* drawing up (**b**) *(démonstration)* establishment (**c**) *(installation) (d'une personne)* settlement (**d**) *(institution)* establishment, institution; *(école)* school; **é. bancaire** bank; **é. de crédit** credit institution; **é. financier** financial institution; **é. hospitalier** hospital; **é. scolaire** school (**e**) *(entreprise)* business, firm; **les établissements Martin** Martin & Co
étage [etaʒ] *nm* (**a**) *(d'un bâtiment)* floor, storey; **à deux étages** two-storeyed; **au troisième é.** on the *Br* third *or Am* fourth floor; **à l'é.** upstairs (**b**) *(d'un terrain)* level; *(d'un gâteau)* tier (**c**) *(d'une fusée)* stage
étager [45] [etaʒe] **s'étager** *vpr* to rise in tiers
étagère [etaʒɛr] *nf (meuble)* (set of) shelves; *(planche)* shelf
étai [etɛ] *nm Constr* prop
étain [etɛ̃] *nm* (**a**) *(métal)* tin (**b**) *(matériau pour vaisselle)* pewter; **un é.** a piece of pewter
étais, était *voir* **être²**
étal *(pl* **étals)** [etal] *nm* (**a**) *(au marché)* stall (**b**) *(de boucher)* butcher's block
étalage [etalaʒ] *nm* (**a**) *(vitrine)* window display (**b**) *Fig (ostentation)* display; **faire é. de son savoir/sa richesse** to show off one's knowledge/wealth
étalagiste [etalaʒist] *nmf* window dresser
étalement [etalmã] *nm (dans le temps)* staggering (**sur** over)
étaler [etale] **1** *vt* (**a**) *(étendre) (journal, papiers)* to spread out; *(nappe, beurre)* to spread; *(peinture, pommade)* to apply (**sur** to); *(cartes)* to lay down (**b**) *Fig (montrer) (richesse, connaissances)* to show off; *(vie privée)* to make a display of; **é. une affaire au grand jour** to make a matter public (**c**) *(dans le temps)* to stagger (**sur** over)
  2 **s'étaler** *vpr* (**a**) *(village, parc)* to spread out (**b**) *(dans le temps)* to be spread (**sur** over) (**c**) *(se vautrer)* to sprawl (**d**) *Fam (tomber)* to fall flat on the ground; **s'é. de tout son long** to fall flat on one's face
étalon¹ [etalɔ̃] *nm (cheval)* stallion
étalon² [etalɔ̃] *nm* (**a**) *(de mesure, monétaire)* standard; *Fig (modèle)* yardstick; *Écon* **l'é.-or** the gold standard
étamine [etamin] *nf Bot* stamen
étanche [etɑ̃ʃ] *adj (bateau, récipient)* watertight; *(montre, bottes)* waterproof
étanchéité [etɑ̃ʃeite] *nf (d'un bateau, d'un récipient)* watertightness; *(d'une montre, de bottes)* waterproofness
étancher [etɑ̃ʃe] *vt* (**a**) *(liquide)* to stop the flow of; *(sang)* to staunch; *(larmes)* to dry (**b**) *(soif)* to quench
étang [etɑ̃] *nm* pond, pool
étant *voir* **être²**

étape [etap] *nf* (**a**) *(lieu)* stopover; **faire é.** to stop; *Fig* **brûler les étapes** *(dans la hiérarchie)* to shoot to the top; *(dans une tâche)* to cut corners (**b**) *(distance)* stage (**c**) *Fig (phase)* stage, step; **par étapes** in stages

état [eta] *nm* (**a**) *(façon d'être)* state, condition; *Phys* state; **l'é. des routes** road conditions; **à l'é. solide/ naturel** in its solid/natural state; **à l'é. neuf** as good as new; **à l'é. pur** *(substance)* unalloyed; *Fig (bêtise, incompétence)* sheer, downright; **dans l'é. actuel des choses** as things stand; **être dans un triste é.** to be in a sorry state; **être dans tous ses états** to be in a state; **en bon/mauvais é.** in good/bad condition; **remettre qch en é.** to repair sth; *(moteur)* to overhaul sth; **laisser les choses en l'é.** to leave things as they are; **être en é. de marche** to be in working order; *(voiture)* to be roadworthy; **être/se sentir en é. de faire qch** to be/ feel up to doing sth; **é. d'alerte** state of alert; **faire qch sans états d'âme** *(sans scrupules)* to have no qualms about doing sth; **é. de choses** state of affairs; **é. d'esprit** state of mind; **c'est un é. de fait** it's an undeniable fact; **l'é. de guerre a été déclaré** a state of war has been declared; **é. de santé** state of health; **être dans un é. second** to be spaced out; **é. de siège** martial law; **é. d'urgence** state of emergency (**b**) *Vieilli ou Hum (profession)* **épicier de son é.** grocer by trade (**c**) *(autorité centrale)* **l'É.** the State; **É. membre** member state (**d**) *(inventaire) (des dépenses, des ventes)* statement; **faire é. de qch** to mention sth; **é. civil** *(à la mairie)* register office; **é. des lieux** inventory of fixtures *(in rented premises)*; **dresser** *ou* **faire un é. des lieux** to draw up an inventory of fixtures; *Fig* to take stock of the situation; **états de service** service record (**e**) *Hist* **les États généraux** the States General (**f**) *Ordinat* **é. d'attente** wait state; **en é. de veille** in standby mode

étatique [etatik] *adj* state

étatiser [etatize] *vt* to bring under state control

état-major *(pl* **états-majors)** [etamaʒɔr] *nm* (**a**) *Mil (officiers)* (general) staff; *(lieu)* headquarters (**b**) *(d'une firme)* management; *(d'un parti politique)* leadership

États-Unis [etazyni] *nmpl* **les É.** (**d'Amérique**) the United States (of America)

étau, -x [eto] *nm* (**a**) *Tech* vice (**b**) *Fig (restrictions)* stranglehold; **l'é. se resserre** the net is closing in

étayer [53] [eteje] *vt* (**a**) *(mur, plafond)* to shore up (**b**) *Fig (argumentation, théorie)* to support

etc [ɛtsetera] *adv* etc

et cætera, et cetera [ɛtsetera] *adv* et cetera

été¹ [ete] *nm* summer; **en é.** in (the) summer; **un jour d'é.** a summer's day; **é. indien** *ou* *Can* **des Indiens** Indian summer

été² *voir* **être²**

éteindre [54] [etɛ̃dr] **1** *vt (incendie, bougie, cigarette)* to put out, to extinguish; *(gaz)* to turn off; *(lumière, radio, radiateur)* to switch off, to turn off; **éteins dans le salon, s'il te plaît** can you switch the light off in the lounge, please?
2 s'éteindre *vpr* (**a**) *(incendie, cigarette, lampe)* to go out (**b**) *(passion)* to fade; *(son, rires, voix)* to die away (**c**) *(disparaître) (personne)* to pass away; *(race)* to die out

éteint, -e [etɛ̃, -ɛ̃t] *adj* (**a**) **être é.** *(incendie, cigarette)* to be out; *(lampe, électricité, radio)* to be off (**b**) *(race, famille, volcan)* extinct (**c**) *(terne) (couleur)* dull; *(regard)* blank; *(voix)* faint; *(personne)* subdued

étendard [etɑ̃dar] *nm* (**a**) *(drapeau)* standard (**b**) *Fig (symbole)* **lever l'é. de la révolte** to raise the standard of revolt; **se ranger sous l'é. de qn** to join sb's camp

étendoir [etɑ̃dwar] *nm* *(à linge)* clothes-line

étendre [etɑ̃dr] **1** *vt* (**a**) *(déployer) (carte, nappe)* to spread out; *(linge)* to hang up; *(beurre, pommade, ailes)* to spread; *(pâte)* to roll out; **é. les bras** to open one's arms wide; *(à un examen)* to fail (**b**) *(coucher)* to lay down (**c**) *(influence, pouvoir, connaissances)* to extend (**à** to) (**d**) *(diluer)* to dilute (**e**) *Ordinat (mémoire)* to upgrade
2 s'étendre *vpr* (**a**) *(s'allonger)* to lie down (**b**) *(aller)* to stretch (**c**) *(incendie, épidémie, grève)* to spread; *(pouvoir, influence, connaissances)* to grow (**d**) *(s'attarder)* **s'é. sur un sujet** to dwell on a subject

étendu, -e [etɑ̃dy] **1** *adj* (**a**) *(large, important) (plaine, connaissances)* extensive; *(pouvoirs)* far-reaching (**b**) *(bras, jambes)* outstretched (**c**) *(personne)* lying (**d**) *(dilué)* diluted (**de** with)
2 *nf* **étendue** *(d'un champ, d'une région)* area; *(d'une grève, d'une épidémie, d'un problème)* scale, extent; *(d'eau, de sable, de terre)* expanse; *(des connaissances, du vocabulaire, des pouvoirs)* range

éternel, -elle [etɛrnɛl] **1** *adj* eternal; *(discussion, bavardages)* never-ending; **tu es un é. mécontent** you're never satisfied
2 *nm* (**a**) **l'É.** *(Dieu)* the Lord; *Hum* **c'est un grand fumeur/paresseux devant l'É.** he's an incurable smoker/incurably lazy (**b**) **l'é. féminin** the archetypal female

éternellement [etɛrnɛlmɑ̃] *adv* for ever; *(reconnaissant)* eternally; **elle est é. mécontente** she's never satisfied

éterniser [etɛrnize] **s'éterniser** *vpr (durer)* to drag on (for ever); *(chez quelqu'un)* to outstay one's welcome

éternité [etɛrnite] *nf* eternity; **il y a une é.** *ou* **des éternités que je ne vous ai vu** I haven't seen you for ages

éternuement [etɛrnymɑ̃] *nm* sneeze

éternuer [etɛrnɥe] *vi* to sneeze

êtes *voir* **être²**

éther [etɛr] *nm* ether

éthéré, -e [etere] *adj* ethereal

Éthiopie [etjɔpi] *nf* **l'É.** Ethiopia

éthiopien, -enne [etjɔpjɛ̃, -ɛn] **1** *adj* Ethiopian
2 *nm,f* **É.** Ethiopian

éthique [etik] **1** *adj* ethical
2 *nf* ethics *(singulier)*

ethnie [ɛtni] *nf* ethnic group

ethnique [ɛtnik] *adj* ethnic

ethnologie [ɛtnɔlɔʒi] *nf* ethnology

ethnologique [ɛtnɔlɔʒik] *adj* ethnological

ethnologue [ɛtnɔlɔg] *nmf* ethnologist

éthylique [etilik] *adj* **alcool é.** ethyl alcohol; **coma é.** alcohol-induced coma

éthylisme [etilism] *nm* *Méd* alcoholism

étiez *etc voir* **être²**

étincelant, -e [etɛ̃slɑ̃, -ɑ̃t] *adj* sparkling; *(étoile)* twinkling

étinceler [9] [etɛ̃sle] *vi (diamant, métal, lac)* to sparkle; *(étoile)* to twinkle; *(yeux) (de joie)* to sparkle (**de** with); *(de colère)* to glint (**de** with)

étincelle [etɛ̃sɛl] *nf aussi Fig* spark; **lancer des étincelles** to throw out sparks; *(diamant, yeux)* to sparkle; *Fig* **ça va faire des étincelles** sparks will fly; **avoir une é. de génie** to have a stroke of genius

étioler [etjɔle] **s'étioler** *vpr (plante)* to wilt; *(personne)* to grow sickly; *(esprit, mémoire)* to deteriorate

étions *etc voir* **être²**

étiqueter [42] [etikte] *vt aussi Fig* to label (**comme** as)

étiquette [etikɛt] *nf* (**a**) *(sur une valise, un produit)* label (**b**) *Fig (d'une personne)* label; **coller une é. à qn** to label sb; **é. politique** political affiliation (**c**) *(protocole)* **l'é.** etiquette

étirement [etirmã] *nm (des membres, du corps)* stretching; **faire des étirements** to do stretching exercises

étirer [etire] **1** *vt* to stretch
2 s'étirer *vpr (personne, tissu, vêtement)* to stretch; *(journée, réunion)* to drag on (for ever)

étoffe [etɔf] *nf* material, fabric; *Fig* **avoir l'é. d'un chef d'État** to have the makings of a statesman; **avoir l'é. d'un héros** to be the stuff heroes are made of

étoffer [etɔfe] **1** *vt (discours, livre, personnage)* to flesh out
2 s'étoffer *vpr (personne)* to fill out

étoile [etwal] *nf* (**a**) *(astre)* star; **un ciel sans étoiles** a starless sky; **coucher** *ou* **dormir à la belle é.** to sleep out (in the open); **né sous une bonne/mauvaise é.** born under a lucky/an unlucky star; **l'é. du berger** *(vue le matin)* the morning star; *(vue le soir)* the evening star; **é. filante** shooting star; **l'é. Polaire** the Pole star (**b**) *(ornement, objet)* star; *(astérisque)* asterisk; **hôtel trois étoiles** three-star hotel; **é. de David** Star of David (**c**) *(vedette)* star (**d**) **é. de mer** starfish (**e**) *Ordinat* **connecté en é.** in a star configuration

étoilé, -e [etwale] *adj* (**a**) *(ciel, nuit)* starry (**b**) *(parebrise)* starred

étonnamment [etɔnamã] *adv* surprisingly

étonnant, -e [etɔnã, -ãt] *adj* surprising; **ce n'est pas é. qu'il soit malade** it's not surprising that he's ill; **chose étonnante, elle est arrivée à l'heure** amazingly enough, she arrived on time

étonné, -e [etɔne] *adj* surprised (**de** at)

étonnement [etɔnmã] *nm* surprise; **à mon grand é.** to my amazement

étonner [etɔne] **1** *vt* to surprise; **elle n'est pas venue? ça m'étonne** she didn't come? I'm surprised; *Fam* **alors ça, ça m'étonnerait!** that'll be the day!; **ça m'étonne de toi** I'm surprised at you; *Fam* **tu m'étonnes!** you don't say!; **tu m'étonneras toujours!** you never cease to amaze me!
2 s'étonner *vpr* to be surprised (**de** at); **je ne m'étonne plus de rien** nothing surprises me any more

étouffant, -e [etufã, -ãt] *adj (air, chaleur, atmosphère)* stifling; *(temps)* oppressive

étouffe-chrétien [etufkretjẽ] *Fam* **1** *adj inv* stodgy
2 *nm inv* **c'est de l'é., cette tarte** this tart is pure stodge

étouffée [etufe] **à l'étouffée 1** *adj* braised
2 *adv* **cuire qch à l'é.** to braise sth

étouffement [etufmã] *nm (asphyxie)* suffocation

étouffer [etufe] **1** *vt* (**a**) *(personne)* to suffocate; *Euph* **ce ne sont pas les scrupules qui l'étouffent** she's not exactly overscrupulous (**b**) *Fig (cri, bâillement, rire)* to stifle; *(son)* to muffle; *(feu)* to smother; *(révolte)* to suppress; *(scandale, affaire)* to hush up
2 *vi* to suffocate; **é. de rire/colère** to choke with laughter/anger; **on étouffe ici** it's stuffy in here
3 s'étouffer *vpr* to suffocate; *(en mangeant)* to choke (**avec** on)

étourderie [eturdəri] *nf* (**a**) *(caractère)* absent-mindedness (**b**) *(faute)* careless mistake

étourdi, -e [eturdi] **1** *adj (distrait)* scatterbrained
2 *nm,f* scatterbrain

étourdir [eturdir] *vt (assommer)* to stun, to daze; *Fig (sujet: vin, éloges)* to make dizzy

étourdissant, -e [eturdisã, -ãt] *adj (bruit)* deafening; *(nouvelles, succès)* staggering; *(beauté)* stunning

étourdissement [eturdismã] *nm* **avoir un é.** to feel dizzy

étourneau, -x [eturno] *nm* starling

étrange [etrãʒ] *adj* strange, odd; **chose é., il est revenu** strangely enough, he came back

étrangement [etrãʒmã] *adv* strangely, oddly; **ressembler é. à qch** to look suspiciously like sth

étranger, -ère [etrãʒe, -ɛr] **1** *adj* (**a**) *(d'un autre pays)* foreign (**b**) *(inconnu)* strange, unfamiliar (**à** to) (**c**) *(extérieur)* **des éléments étrangers** outsiders; **elle est étrangère à cette société/au projet** she isn't involved with this company/the plan
2 *nm,f* (**a**) *(d'un autre pays)* foreigner (**b**) *(d'un autre groupe)* stranger, outsider
3 *nm* **l'é.** *(pays étrangers)* foreign countries; **aller/vivre à l'é.** to go/live abroad

étrangeté [etrãʒte] *nf* strangeness, oddness

étranglé, -e [etrãgle] *adj (passage, vallée)* narrow; *(voix)* choked; *Méd (hernie)* strangulated

étranglement [etrãgləmã] *nm* (**a**) *(d'une personne)* strangling, strangulation; **mourir par é.** to be strangled (**b**) *(partie resserrée) (d'une rivière)* narrow part; *(d'une route)* bottleneck

étrangler [etrãgle] **1** *vt* (**a**) *(personne)* to strangle; *Fig (ruiner)* to cripple (**b**) *(resserrer) (taille, tube)* to constrict
2 s'étrangler *vpr* (**a**) *(en mangeant)* to choke (**avec** on); **s'é. de colère/rire** to choke with anger/laughter (**b**) *(voix)* to choke; **les mots s'étranglèrent dans sa gorge** the words stuck in his/her throat

étrave [etrav] *nf Naut* stem

être¹ [ɛtr] *nm (personne, âme)* being; **un ê. cher** a loved one; **c'est un ê. méprisable** he's a despicable creature; **ê. humain** human being; **ê. vivant** living creature

être² [2] **1** *vi* (**a**) *(indique la nature)* to be; **ê. professeur/informaticien** to be a teacher/computer expert; **ceci est un reptile** this is a reptile
(**b**) *(indique l'état)* to be; **é. bien/mal** *(en bonne/ mauvaise santé)* to be well/ill; **le temps est à l'orage** there's a storm brewing; **il serait mieux avec les cheveux courts** he would look better with short hair
(**c**) *(indique le lieu)* to be; **il est chez elle** she's at home; **Rabat est au Maroc** Rabat is in Morocco; **j'en suis au chapitre IV** I'm on chapter IV; **où en es-tu dans ton travail?** how far have you got with your work?; **je ne sais plus où j'en suis** I don't know what I'm doing any more; **j'en suis à me demander si...** I'm beginning to wonder whether...
(**d**) *(indique le moment)* **nous sommes mercredi/le 16** it's Wednesday/the 16th today
(**e**) *(indique l'appartenance)* **ê. à qn** to belong to sb; *Fig* **je suis à vous** I'm all yours; **elle est de la famille** she's one of the family
(**f**) *(indique la provenance)* **ê. de** to be; **je suis de Lyon/du sud** I'm from Lyons/from the South; **l'enfant n'est pas de lui** it's not his child; **ce tableau est de Cézanne** this picture is by Cézanne
(**g**) *(indique l'obligation)* **ceci est à lire pour demain**

this has to be read for tomorrow; **ce film est à voir absolument** this film is unmissable
 (**h**) *(aller)* to go; **as-tu déjà été à Brighton?** have you ever been to Brighton?; *Fam* **ç'a été** it went OK
 (**i**) *(exister)* to be; **la plus belle voiture qui soit** the most beautiful car in the world; *Litt* **elle n'est plus** she is no longer with us
 (**j**) *(locutions)* **ê. tout le temps à se plaindre/à médire** to be always complaining/criticizing; **ne serait-ce que** if only
 2 *v aux* (**a**) *(avec des verbes à l'actif)* to have/to be; **je suis sorti hier soir** I went out last night; **es-tu déjà allé en Chine?** have you ever been to China?; **elle est née en 1967** she was born in 1967; **j'étais parti très tôt** I had left very early; **il serait parti plus tôt s'il avait pu** he would have left earlier if he could; **ils se sont aimés** they loved each other; **nous nous étions trompés** we had made a mistake
 (**b**) *(avec des verbes au passif)* to be; **nous y sommes/étions toujours bien reçus** we are/were always warmly welcomed
 3 *v impersonnel* to be; **il est cinq heures** it's five (o'clock); **il est difficile de juger** it's hard to tell; **il m'est impossible de vous répondre** it's impossible for me to give you an answer

étreindre [54] [etʀɛ̃dʀ] *vt* to embrace; *(sujet: peur, douleur)* to grip

étreinte [etʀɛ̃t] *nf (embrassade)* embrace; *(sexuelle)* coupling

étrenner [etʀene] *vt (objet)* to use for the first time, to christen; *(vêtement)* to wear for the first time

étrennes [etʀɛn] *nfpl* New Year's gift; *(pour facteur, éboueur) Br* ≃ Christmas box, *Am* ≃ Christmas bonus

étrier [etʀije] *nm* (**a**) *(en équitation)* stirrup; **vider les étriers** to be thrown; *Fig* **mettre le pied à l'é. à qn** to give sb a leg up (**b**) *(sur table d'examen)* stirrup

étriller [etʀije] *vt* (**a**) *(cheval)* to curry (**b**) *Fig (critiquer)* to pan

étriper [etʀipe] **1** *vt (poisson, volaille)* to gut; *Fam Fig* **je vais l'é.!** I'll murder him!
 2 s'étriper *vpr Fam (se battre)* to tear each other apart

étriqué, -e [etʀike] *adj* (**a**) *(vêtement)* tight (**b**) *Fig (esprit, vie)* narrow

étroit, -e [etʀwa, -at] *adj* (**a**) *(peu large)* narrow; *Fig* **avoir l'esprit é.** to be narrow-minded (**b**) *(serré)* tight; *Fig (liens, collaboration, surveillance)* close (**c**) *(logement, pièce)* poky; **être à l'é.** to be cramped for room

étroitement [etʀwatmã] *adv (nouer, tenir)* tightly; *Fig (unir, collaborer, surveiller)* closely

étroitesse [etʀwatɛs] *nf* narrowness; *(d'un logement, d'une pièce)* pokiness; *Fig* **é. d'esprit** narrow-mindedness

étron [etʀɔ̃] *nm* piece of excrement

étrusque [etʀysk] **1** *adj* Etruscan
 2 *nmf* **É.** Etruscan

étude [etyd] *nf* (**a**) *(examen)* study, survey; **mettre qch à l'é.** to study *or* investigate sth; **é. de cas** case study; **é. de faisabilité** feasibility study; **faire une é. de marché** to do market research (**b**) **études** *(éducation)* studies; **j'ai arrêté mes études à seize ans** I left school at sixteen; **faire des études (de français/de droit)** to study French/law; **elle a fait ses études à Oxford** she studied at Oxford (**c**) *Scol (heure)* study period; *(salle)* study room (**d**) *(morceau de musique, peinture)* study (**e**) *(bureau)* office

étudiant, -e [etydjã, -ãt] **1** *nm,f* student; **é. en médecine/en droit** medical/law student; **é. de première/seconde année** first-/second-year student, *Am* freshman/sophomore
 2 *adj (vie, mouvement)* student

étudié, -e [etydje] *adj* (**a**) *(recherché) (tenue, style)* carefully chosen (**b**) *Péj (affecté)* studied (**c**) *Com* **prix très étudiés** very reasonable prices

étudier [66] [etydje] **1** *vt* to study; *(leçon)* to prepare
 2 *vi* to study
 3 s'étudier *vpr (l'un l'autre)* to study each other

étui [etɥi] *nm* case; *(de revolver)* holster; **é. à lunettes** glasses case

étuve [etyv] *nf* (**a**) *(aux thermes)* steam room; *Fig* oven (**b**) *(pour sécher)* drying oven; *(pour stériliser)* sterilizer

étuvée [etyve] **à l'étuvée 1** *adj* braised
 2 *adv* **cuire qch à l'é.** to braise sth

étymologie [etimɔlɔʒi] *nf* etymology

EU [əy] *nmpl (abrév* **États-Unis**) USA

eu, -e *pp de* **avoir¹**

eucalyptus [økaliptys] *nm* eucalyptus

eucharistie [økaʀisti] *nf Rel* **l'e.** the Eucharist

euh [ø] *exclam* er!

eunuque [ønyk] *nm* eunuch

euphémisme [øfemism] *nm* euphemism

euphorie [øfɔʀi] *nf* euphoria

euphorique [øfɔʀik] *adj* euphoric

euphorisant, -e [øfɔʀizã, -ãt] **1** *adj (effet, atmosphère)* exhilarating; *(médicament)* antidepressant; *(drogue)* that produces a feeling of euphoria
 2 *nm* antidepressant; *(drogue)* drug that produces a feeling of euphoria

Euphrate [øfʀat] *nm* **l'E.** the Euphrates

eurasien, -enne [øʀazjɛ̃, -ɛn] **1** *adj* Eurasian
 2 *nm,f* **E.** Eurasian

eurêka [øʀeka] *exclam* eureka!

euro [øʀo] *nm (monnaie)* euro

euro- [øʀo] *préf* Euro-

Eurocorps [øʀokɔʀ] *nm Mil* Eurocorps

eurocrate [øʀokʀat] *nmf* Eurocrat

eurodéputé, -e [øʀodepyte] *nm,f* Euro MP

eurodevise [øʀodəviz] *nf* Eurocurrency

eurodollar [øʀodɔlaʀ] *nm* Eurodollar

Europe [øʀɔp] *nf* **l'E.** Europe; **l'E. centrale** central Europe; **l'E. de l'Est/de l'Ouest** Eastern/Western Europe; **l'E. du Nord** Northern Europe; **l'E. occidentale** Western Europe; **l'E. sociale** social Europe *(a united Europe committed to a progressive social and welfare policy)*; **l'E. verte** European agriculture

européen, -enne [øʀopeɛ̃, -ɛn] **1** *adj* European
 2 *nm,f* **E.** European

eurosceptique [øʀosɛptik] *nmf Pol* Eurosceptic

Eurovision [øʀovizjɔ̃] *nf* Eurovision

eurozone [øʀozon] *nf* Eurozone

eut *voir* **avoir¹**

euthanasie [øtanazi] *nf* euthanasia

eux [ø] *pron personnel* (**a**) *(sujet)* they; **ils apprécient mon travail, e.!** THEY like my work!; **les enfants, e., se sont amusés** the children, for their part, enjoyed themselves; **si j'étais e., je me méfierais** if I were them, I'd be careful (**b**) *(objet direct)* them; **et e., tu les oublies?** and what about them, have you forgotten them? (**c**) *(avec préposition)* them; *(réfléchi)* themselves; **dis-le-leur, à e.** to tell THEM; **ils ne pensent qu'à e.** they only think of themselves; **les deux maisons sont à e.** both houses are theirs; **ils ont leurs**

méthodes à e. they have their own methods; *Fam* **un copain à e.** a friend of theirs (**d**) *(dans les comparaisons)* them; **je dépense plus qu'e.** I spend more than they do *or* than them

eux-mêmes [ømɛm] *pron personnel* themselves

évacuation [evakɥasjɔ̃] *nf* (**a**) *(de matières du corps)* discharge; *(des eaux de pluie, des eaux usées)* drainage (**b**) *(de personnes, d'un lieu)* evacuation

évacuer [evakɥe] *vt* (**a**) *(matières du corps)* to discharge; *(eaux de pluie, eaux usées)* to drain off (**b**) *(personnes, lieu)* to evacuate; **faire é. une salle** to evacuate a hall (**c**) *Fig (problème)* to solve

évadé, -e [evade] *nm,f* escaped prisoner

évader [evade] **s'évader** *vpr aussi Fig* to escape (**de** from)

évaluation [evalɥasjɔ̃] *nf (d'une propriété, d'un bien)* valuation; *(de dommages)* assessment; *(d'un poids, d'un nombre, des risques)* estimation

évaluer [evalɥe] *vt (propriété, bien)* to value; *(dommages)* to assess; *(poids, nombre, risques)* to estimate

évangéliser [evɑ̃ʒelize] *vt* to evangelize

évangéliste [evɑ̃ʒelist] *nm (prédicateur)* evangelist; *(de la Bible)* Evangelist

évangile [evɑ̃ʒil] *nm Rel* **l'É.** the Gospel; **l'É. selon saint Marc** the Gospel according to St Mark; *Fig* **prendre qch pour parole d'é.** to take sth as gospel (truth)

évanoui, -e [evanwi] *adj* unconscious; **tomber é.** to fall down in a faint

évanouir [evanwir] **s'évanouir** *vpr* (**a**) *(perdre conscience)* to faint (**b**) *(disparaître)* to fade (away)

évanouissement [evanwismɑ̃] *nm (syncope)* fainting fit

évaporation [evapɔrasjɔ̃] *nf* evaporation

évaporé, -e [evapɔre] *Péj* **1** *adj* scatterbrained **2** *nm,f* airhead

évaporer [evapɔre] **s'évaporer** *vpr* (**a**) *(liquide)* to evaporate (**b**) *Fig (disparaître)* to vanish (into thin air)

évasé, -e [evaze] *adj (récipient)* wide-mouthed; *(jupe)* flared

évaser [evaze] **s'évaser** *vpr* to widen; *(jupe)* to be flared

évasif, -ive [evazif, -iv] *adj* evasive

évasion [evazjɔ̃] *nf* (**a**) *(fuite)* escape (**de** from); **é. de capitaux** flight of capital; **é. fiscale** tax evasion (**b**) *Fig (distraction)* escapism; **avoir besoin d'é.** to need to escape

Ève [ɛv] *npr* Eve; *Fam* **je ne le connais ni d'È. ni d'Adam** I don't know him from Adam

évêché [eveʃe] *nm (diocèse)* bishopric; *(palais)* bishop's palace

éveil [evɛj] *nm* awakening; **être en é.** to be alert

éveillé, -e [eveje] *adj* (**a**) *(non endormi)* awake (**b**) *(vif)* alert

éveiller [eveje] **1** *vt* (**a**) *(curiosité, soupçons, jalousie)* to arouse; *(intelligence, imagination)* to stimulate (**b**) *Litt (personne)* to wake **2** **s'éveiller** *vpr* (**a**) *Litt (personne)* to awake (**b**) *Fig (curiosité, soupçons, jalousie)* to be aroused; *(intelligence, imagination)* to develop

événement [evɛnmɑ̃] *nm* event; **attendre la suite des événements** to wait and see what happens; **créer l'é.** to make big news; *Hum* **quand il fait la vaisselle, c'est (tout) un é.** it's a major event when he does the dishes

éventail [evɑ̃taj] *nm* (**a**) *(pour se rafraîchir)* fan; **en é.** fan-shaped (**b**) *(choix)* range

éventaire [evɑ̃tɛr] *nm* (**a**) *(étal)* stall (**b**) *(d'un marchand ambulant)* tray

éventé, -e [evɑ̃te] *adj (vin, parfum)* stale; *(bière)* flat

éventer [evɑ̃te] **1** *vt* (**a**) *(avec un éventail)* to fan (**b**) *(secret, complot)* to discover **2** **s'éventer** *vpr* (**a**) *(avec un éventail)* to fan oneself (**b**) *(vin, parfum)* to go stale; *(bière)* to go flat

éventrer [evɑ̃tre] *vt (personne, animal)* to disembowel; *(colis, matelas)* to rip open; *(fût, boîte)* to break open

éventualité [evɑ̃tɥalite] *nf* (**a**) *(circonstance)* eventuality; **parer à toute é.** to be prepared for all eventualities; **dans l'é. de** (**b**) *(possibilité)* possibility

éventuel, -elle [evɑ̃tɥɛl] *adj* possible

éventuellement [evɑ̃tɥɛlmɑ̃] *adv* possibly; **j'aurais é. besoin de votre concours** I may need your help

évêque [evɛk] *nm* bishop

Everest [evərɛst] *nm* **l'E., le mont E.** (Mount) Everest

évertuer [evɛrtɥe] **s'évertuer** *vpr* **s'é. à faire qch** to endeavour to do sth

éviction [eviksjɔ̃] *nf (d'un rival, d'une tête de parti)* ousting; *(d'un locataire)* eviction

évidemment [evidamɑ̃] *adv* of course, obviously

évidence [evidɑ̃s] *nf* (**a**) *(d'un fait, de la vérité)* obviousness; **c'est une é.!** obviously!; **nier l'é.** to deny the obvious; **se rendre à l'é.** to face facts; **de toute é., à l'é.** obviously (**b**) **en é.** *(visible)* in a prominent position; **mettre qch en é.** *(phénomène)* to highlight sth; **se mettre en é.** to try to get oneself noticed

évident, -e [evidɑ̃, -ɑ̃t] *adj* obvious; **tu crois qu'on va réussir? – c'est é.!** do you think we'll succeed? – of course (we will)!; **elle va se rendre compte, c'est é.** she's bound to notice; *Fam* **c'est pas é.!** *(pas facile)* it's not so easy!

évider [evide] *vt* to hollow out

évier [evje] *nm* sink

évincer [evɛ̃se] *vt (rival)* to oust (**de** from)

éviter [evite] **1** *vt* (**a**) *(s'écarter de)* to avoid; **é. de faire qch** to avoid doing sth; **il faut é. qu'il le voie** he mustn't be allowed to see it; **évite que ça se sache** don't let it get out (**b**) *(épargner)* **é. qch à qn** to save *or* spare sb sth; **ça m'évitera d'avoir à le faire** it will save me having to do it **2** **s'éviter** *vpr* **s'é. qch** to avoid sth (**b**) *(se fuir mutuellement)* to avoid each other

évocateur, -trice [evɔkatœr, -tris] *adj* evocative (**de** of)

évocation [evɔkasjɔ̃] *nf* evocation; **le pouvoir d'é. d'un lieu/mot** the evocative power of a place/word

évolué, -e [evɔlɥe] *adj (société)* advanced; *(personne)* broadminded

évoluer [evɔlɥe] *vi* (**a**) *(se déplacer)* to move around; *Fig* **é. dans le milieu des artistes** to move in artistic circles (**b**) *(se développer)* to develop (**c**) *Ordinat* **faire é.** to upgrade

évolutif, -ive [evɔlytif, -iv] *adj* progressive; *Ordinat* upgradeable

évolution [evɔlysjɔ̃] *nf* (**a**) *(développement)* development (**b**) *Biol* evolution (**c**) **évolutions** *(déplacements)* movements

évoquer [evɔke] *vt* (**a**) *(se remémorer)* *(passé)* to recall, to evoke (**b**) *(faire penser à)* to be reminiscent of; **son nom ne m'évoque rien** his/her name means nothing to me (**c**) *(aborder)* to touch on, to mention (**d**) *(par la magie)* to call up, to invoke

ex [ɛks] *nmf Fam* ex

ex- [ɛks] *préf* ex-; **ex-femme/ministre** ex-wife/minister

exacerbation [ɛgzasɛrbasjɔ̃] *nf* exacerbation

exacerber [ɛgzasɛrbe] **1** *vt* to exacerbate
2 s'exacerber *vpr* to become acute

exact, -e [ɛgzakt] *adj* (**a**) *(quantité, poids, nombre)* exact, precise; *(rapport, description)* exact, accurate; *(mot, réponse, heure, date)* right, correct; **c'est e.** *(vrai)* it's quite true; **il s'appelle bien Martin? –** **e.!** his name's Martin, isn't it? – that's right! (**b**) *(ponctuel)* punctual, on time

exactement [ɛgzaktəmɑ̃] *adv* exactly

exactions [ɛgzaksjɔ̃] *nfpl* atrocities

exactitude [ɛgzaktityd] *nf* (**a**) *(précision, fidélité)* exactness; *(justesse)* correctness; **avec. e.** accurately (**b**) *(ponctualité)* punctuality; *Prov* **l'e. est la politesse des rois** punctuality is the politeness of kings

ex æquo [ɛgzeko] **1** *adj inv* **être e.** to tie, to be equally placed (**avec** with)
2 *nmf inv* **il y a deux e.** there's a two-way tie; **départager les e.** to break the tie
3 *adv* **être troisième e.** to tie for third place

exagération [ɛgzaʒerasjɔ̃] *nf* exaggeration

exagéré, -e [ɛgzaʒere] *adj (récit, geste)* exaggerated; *(prix, salaire, pessimisme)* excessive; **il n'est pas e. de dire que...** it's no exaggeration to say that...

exagérément [ɛgzaʒeremɑ̃] *adv* excessively

exagérer [34] [ɛgzaʒere] **1** *vt* to exaggerate; **il ne faut rien e., n'exagérons rien** let's not exaggerate
2 *vi (amplifier)* to exaggerate; *(abuser)* to go too far

exaltant, -e [ɛgzaltɑ̃, -ɑ̃t] *adj* stirring

exaltation [ɛgzaltasjɔ̃] *nf (excitation)* intense excitement

exalté, -e [ɛgzalte] **1** *adj (discours, sentiment)* impassioned; *(personne)* fanatical
2 *nm,f* fanatic

exalter [ɛgzalte] *vt* (**a**) *(exciter) (imagination)* to stir; *(ressentiment, orgueil)* to intensify (**b**) *(louer) (personne)* to exalt

exam [ɛgzam] *nm Fam* exam

examen [ɛgzamɛ̃] *nm* (**a**) *(d'un document, de faits)* examination; *(d'une machine)* checking; *(d'un local)* inspection; *(d'une demande)* consideration; **e. de conscience** soul-searching (**b**) **e. (médical)** (medical) examination; **e. de la vue** sight *or* eye test (**c**) *Scol & Univ* exam, examination; **e. blanc** mock exam; **e. d'entrée** entrance exam; **e. de passage** *Br* end-of-year exam, *Am* final exam

examinateur, -trice [ɛgzaminatœr, -tris] *nm,f* examiner

examiner [ɛgzamine] **1** *vt* (**a**) *(étudier) (document, faits)* to examine; *(machine)* to check; *(local)* to inspect; *(demande)* to consider (**b**) *(observer)* to examine; *(horizon)* to scan; **e. qn de la tête aux pieds** to look sb up and down (**c**) *(patient)* to examine; **se faire e. par un médecin** to be examined by a doctor
2 s'examiner *vpr* (**a**) *(dans une glace)* to examine oneself (**b**) *(l'un l'autre)* to examine each other

exaspérant, -e [ɛgzasperɑ̃, -ɑ̃t] *adj* exasperating

exaspération [ɛgzasperasjɔ̃] *nf* exasperation

exaspérer [34] [ɛgzaspere] *vt* (**a**) *(personne)* to exasperate (**b**) *Litt (douleur, sentiment)* to aggravate

exaucement [ɛgzosmɑ̃] *nm* granting

exaucer [16] [ɛgzose] *vt* (**a**) *(souhait)* to grant (**b**) **e. qn** to grant sb's wish

excavateur [ɛkskavatœr] *nm* excavator, (mechanical) digger

excavation [ɛkskavasjɔ̃] *nf* (**a**) *(trou)* excavation; *(creusée par une bombe)* crater (**b**) *(action)* excavation

excavatrice [ɛkskavatris] *nf* = **excavateur**

excédant, -e [ɛksedɑ̃, -ɑ̃t] *adj* exasperating

excédent [ɛksedɑ̃] *nm* surplus; **budget en e.** surplus budget; **e. de poids** excess weight; **e. de bagages** excess baggage; **être en e.** to show a surplus

excédentaire [ɛksedɑ̃tɛr] *adj (production, poids)* excess; *(budget)* surplus; **balance commerciale e.** trade surplus

excéder [34] [ɛksede] *vt* (**a**) *(quantité, somme, limite)* to exceed; *(forces, compétences)* to be beyond; **e. ses pouvoirs** to exceed one's powers (**b**) *(irriter)* to exasperate

excellence [ɛksɛlɑ̃s] *nf* excellence; *Scol* **prix d'e.** class prize *(for all-round standard)*; **par e.** par excellence; **Son/Votre E.** *(titre)* His/Her/Your Excellency

excellent, -e [ɛksɛlɑ̃, -ɑ̃t] *adj* excellent (**en** at)

exceller [ɛksele] *vi* to excel (**en** at)

excentré [ɛksɑ̃tre] *adj* (**a**) *(quartier)* outlying (**b**) *Tech* off centre

excentricité [ɛksɑ̃trisite] *nf (de caractère, acte bizarre)* eccentricity

excentrique [ɛksɑ̃trik] **1** *adj (bizarre)* eccentric
2 *nmf (personne)* eccentric

excepté, -e [ɛksɛpte] **1** *prép* except, apart from
2 *adj* **les femmes exceptées** except for *or* apart from the women

excepter [ɛksɛpte] *vt* to except (**de** from); **sans e. les enfants** not forgetting the children

exception [ɛksɛpsjɔ̃] *nf* exception (**à** to); **c'est l'e. qui confirme la règle** it's the exception that proves the rule; **à quelques exceptions près** with a few exceptions; **un être d'e.** an exceptional person

L'exception française

This phrase is used to describe France's individual status in terms of economic development. It is characterized by a large public sector, a larger degree of state intervention in the economy than in Britain or the US and a relatively generous welfare State coupled with greater investment in public services. France is also keen to safeguard its film industry and has been campaigning in favour of "l'exception culturelle" – the notion that cultural products should not be treated in the same way as other commercial products and that consequently governments should be authorized to subsidize their film industries.

exceptionnel, -elle [ɛksɛpsjɔnɛl] *adj* exceptional; **ne rien avoir d'e.** to be nothing special

exceptionnellement [ɛksɛpsjɔnɛlmɑ̃] *adv* exceptionally

excès [ɛksɛ] *nm* (**a**) *(excédent)* excess; **pécher par e. de zèle** to be overzealous; **avec e.** excessively, to excess; **sans e.** in moderation; **(jusqu')à l'e.** to excess, excessively; **tomber dans l'e. inverse** to go to the other extreme; **e. de vitesse** speeding; **faire un e. de vitesse** to speed (**b**) *(abus)* excess; **faire des e.** to overindulge

excessif, -ive [ɛksɛsif, -iv] *adj* excessive; **il est e.** he does things to excess

excessivement [ɛksɛsivmɑ̃] *adv (extrêmement)* extremely; *(avec excès)* excessively

excision [ɛksizjɔ̃] *nf* excision

excitant, -e [ɛksitɑ̃, -ɑ̃t] **1** *adj (fascinant, provocant)* exciting; *(tonique)* stimulating **2** *nm* stimulant
excitation [ɛksitasjɔ̃] *nf* (**a**) *(incitation)* incitement (**à** to) (**b**) *(état)* excitement (**c**) *Méd* excitation
excité, -e [ɛksite] **1** *adj* excited **2** *nm,f (personne)* hothead
exciter [ɛksite] **1** *vt* (**a**) *(attiser) (curiosité, jalousie, pitié)* to arouse (**b**) *(encourager)* to urge on; **e. qn à la révolte** to incite sb to revolt (**c**) *(énerver)* to excite (**d**) *(nerf, muscle)* to excite **2 s'exciter** *vpr* to get excited
exclamation [ɛksklamasjɔ̃] *nf* exclamation
exclamer [ɛksklame] **s'exclamer** *vpr* **s'e. de joie/douleur** to cry out with joy/pain; **"jamais!" s'exclama-t-il** "never!" he exclaimed
exclu, -e [ɛkskly] **1** *adj* (**a**) *(non compris)* **TVA exclue** excluding VAT (**b**) *(impensable)* out of the question; **il est e. qu'elle vienne avec nous** there's no question of her coming with us **2** *nm,f* outcast
exclure [17b] [ɛksklyr] *vt* (**a**) *(expulser)* **e. qn de qch** *(parti, école)* to expel sb from sth; *(fonction publique)* to remove sb from sth; *(salle, réunion)* to eject sb from sth (**b**) *(mettre à l'écart)* **e. qn de qch** to exclude sb from sth (**c**) *(ne pas considérer) (hypothèse, solution)* to rule out; **cela n'exclut pas que vous puissiez enseigner** that doesn't rule out the possibility of your teaching
exclusif, -ive [ɛksklyzif, -iv] *adj* exclusive; *(but, mission)* sole; **être e. dans ses amitiés** to be selective in one's choice of friends
exclusion [ɛksklyzjɔ̃] *nf* (**a**) *(d'un parti, d'une école)* expulsion; *(d'une fonction publique)* removal; *(d'une salle, d'une réunion)* ejection (**de** from) (**b**) **à l'e. de** with the exception of
exclusivement [ɛksklyzivmɑ̃] *adv* exclusively
exclusivité [ɛksklyzivite] *nf* (**a**) *(droit)* exclusive rights (**de** to); **en e.** exclusively; **film en première e.** recent release; *Fig* **ne pas avoir l'e. de l'intelligence** not to have a monopoly on intelligence (**b**) *(information)* exclusive, scoop
excommunier [66] [ɛkskɔmynje] *vt* to excommunicate
excréments [ɛkskremɑ̃] *nmpl* excrement
excrétion [ɛkskresjɔ̃] *nf* (**a**) *(action)* excretion (**b**) **excrétions** *(déchets)* excreta
excroissance [ɛkskrwasɑ̃s] *nf* excrescence
excursion [ɛkskyrsjɔ̃] *nf* *(en car, en voiture)* excursion, trip; *(d'une journée)* day trip; *(de plusieurs jours)* tour; **faire une e., partir en e.** to go on a trip/a tour
excursionniste [ɛkskyrsjɔnist] *nmf* *Br* day-tripper, *Am* excursionist
excusable [ɛkskyzabl] *adj* excusable, forgivable
excuse [ɛkskyz] *nf* (**a**) *(raison)* excuse; **trouver des excuses à qn** to find excuses for sb; **ce n'est pas une e.!** that's no excuse! (**b**) **excuses** *(regrets)* apology; **faire** *ou* **présenter ses excuses à qn** to make one's apologies to sb
excuser [ɛkskyze] **1** *vt* (**a**) *(justifier) (personne, action)* to excuse; **e. qn auprès de qn** to apologize for sb to sb (**b**) *(pardonner) (personne, erreur, colère)* to excuse; **excusez-moi** *(j'ai fait une faute)* I'm sorry; *(pour attirer l'attention)* excuse me; **excuse-moi de te déranger** I'm sorry to disturb you; **excuse-moi de ne pas t'avoir téléphoné** I'm sorry I didn't phone you; *Sout* **je vous prie de m'e.** I do beg your pardon; **tu es tout excusé**

there's no need to apologize; *Hum* **excusez du peu!** if you please! (**c**) *(dispenser)* to excuse; **se faire e.** to ask to be excused **2 s'excuser** *vpr* to apologize; **s'e. auprès de qn** to apologize to sb; **s'e. de qch/de faire qch** to apologize for sth/for doing sth; **je m'excuse!** I'm sorry!
exécrable [ɛgzekrabl] *adj* atrocious
exécrer [34] [ɛgzekre] *vt Litt* to loathe
exécutable [ɛgzekytabl] *adj* (**a**) *(réalisable)* possible, feasible (**b**) *Ordinat* executable
exécutant, -e [ɛgzekytɑ̃, -ɑ̃t] *nm,f* (**a**) *(employé)* subordinate; **ce n'est qu'un simple e.** he just carries out orders (**b**) *(musicien)* performer
exécuter [ɛgzekyte] **1** *vt* (**a**) *(effectuer) (travail, ordres)* to carry out; *(danse, morceau de musique)* to perform; *(peinture)* to execute (**b**) *Ordinat (programme)* to run; *(commande)* to execute (**c**) *(mettre à mort)* to execute; *Fam (battre)* to slaughter; *Fam (critiquer)* to savage **2 s'exécuter** *vpr* to comply
exécuteur, -trice [ɛgzekytœr, -tris] *nm,f Jur* **e. testamentaire** executor; **exécutrice testamentaire** executrix
exécutif, -ive [ɛgzekytif, -iv] **1** *adj (pouvoir)* executive **2** *nm* **l'e.** the executive
exécution [ɛgzekysjɔ̃] *nf* (**a**) *(d'un travail, d'ordres)* carrying out; *(d'une danse, d'un morceau de musique)* performance; *(d'une peinture)* execution; **mettre qch à e.** to carry sth out (**b**) *Ordinat* execution (**c**) *(mise à mort)* execution
exécutoire [ɛgzekytwar] *adj* (**a**) **jugement e.** enforceable decision (**b**) **formule e.** executory formula
exégèse [ɛgzeʒɛz] *nf* exegesis; **faire l'e. de** to write a critical interpretation of
exemplaire¹ [ɛgzɑ̃plɛr] *adj* (**a**) *(comportement, courage)* exemplary (**b**) *(punition)* exemplary
exemplaire² *nm* *(livre, gravure)* copy; **en deux/trois exemplaires** in duplicate/triplicate; **photocopier qch en vingt exemplaires** to make twenty photocopies of sth; **le livre a été tiré à dix mille exemplaires** ten thousand copies of the book were printed
exemple [ɛgzɑ̃pl] *nm* (**a**) *(modèle)* example (**pour** for); **donner l'e. (à qn)** to set (sb) an example; **suivre l'e. de qn** to follow sb's example; **prendre qn en e.** to model oneself on sb; **citer qn/qch en e.** to quote sb/sth as an example; **faire un e.** *(en punissant)* to set an example (**b**) *(cas, mot, phrase)* example; **être l'e. même de la bêtise** to be stupidity itself (**c**) **par e.** for example, for instance; *Fam* **ah ça par e.!** well I never!
exempt, -e [ɛgzɑ̃, -ɑ̃t] *adj* **e. de** *(service militaire)* exempt from; *(danger, problème)* free from; **e. de droits de douane** duty-free; **sa remarque n'était pas exempte d'une certaine amertume** his/her remark wasn't without a trace of bitterness
exempter [ɛgzɑ̃te] *vt (dispenser)* to exempt (**de** from)
exemption [ɛgzɑ̃psjɔ̃] *nf* exemption (**de** from)
exercé, -e [ɛgzɛrse] *adj (œil, oreille)* trained; *(main)* practised
exercer [16] [ɛgzɛrse] **1** *vt* (**a**) *(entraîner) (corps, esprit, mémoire)* to train; **e. qn à qch/à faire qch** to train sb in sth/to do sth (**b**) *(user de) (autorité, talent, droit)* to exercise; **e. une influence sur qn** to exert an influence on sb; **e. une pression sur qn/qch** to exert pressure on sb/sth; **e. un contrôle sur qch** to exercise control over sth (**c**) *(profession)* to practise; **e. ses fonctions** to carry out one's duties; **e. le métier de**

journaliste to work as a journalist **2** *vi (médecin, juriste)* to practise **3 s'exercer** *vpr* (**a**) *(s'entraîner)* to practise; **s'e. à qch/à faire qch** to practise sth/doing sth (**b**) *(se manifester) (autorité, pouvoir)* to make itself felt

exercice [ɛgzɛrsis] *nm* (**a**) *(entraînement sportif ou scolaire)* exercise; **faire des exercices** to do (some) exercises; **prendre de l'e.** to (take) exercise (**b**) *Mil* drill; **être à l'e.** to be on parade (**c**) *(du pouvoir, d'un droit)* exercise (**d**) *(d'une profession)* practice; **dans l'e. de ses fonctions** in the exercise of one's duties; **être en e.** *(avocat, médecin)* to be in practice; *(président)* to be in office; **le président en e.** the incumbent president (**e**) **l'e. du culte** public worship (**f**) *(en comptabilité) Br* financial year, *Am* fiscal year

exergue [ɛgzɛrg] *nm (de médaille)* inscription; *(d'un texte)* epigraph; **en e.** *(citation)* as an epigraph

exfoliant, -e [ɛksfɔljɑ̃, -ɑ̃t] **1** *adj* exfoliating **2** *nm* exfoliant

exfolier [66] [ɛksfɔlje] *vt* to exfoliate

exhaler [ɛgzale] **1** *vt (odeur)* to give off; *Fig (joie, colère)* to give vent to; *Fig* **cette maison exhale la tristesse** sadness pervades this house **2 s'exhaler** *vpr (odeur)* to be given off

exhausser [ɛgzose] *vt (mur, édifice)* to heighten; **e. une maison d'un étage** to add a storey to a house

exhaustif, -ive [ɛgzostif, -iv] *adj* exhaustive

exhiber [ɛgzibe] **1** *vt* (**a**) *(documents, passeport)* to produce (**b**) *Péj (savoir, richesses)* to show off, to flaunt **2 s'exhiber** *vpr* to flaunt oneself

exhibition [ɛgzibisjɔ̃] *nf Péj (de savoir, de richesses)* flaunting

exhibitionniste [ɛgzibisjɔnist] *nmf* exhibitionist

exhortation [ɛgzɔrtasjɔ̃] *nf* exhortation (**à** to)

exhorter [ɛgzɔrte] *vt* **e. qn à qch/à faire qch** to exhort sb to sth/to do sth

exhumation [ɛgzymasjɔ̃] *nf (d'un corps)* exhumation; *(d'un trésor, de vestiges)* excavation

exhumer [ɛgzyme] *vt (corps)* to exhume; *(trésor, vestiges)* to excavate

exigeant, -e [ɛgziʒɑ̃, -ɑ̃t] *adj (personne, travail)* exacting

exigence [ɛgziʒɑ̃s] *nf* (**a**) *(caractère)* exacting nature (**b**) *(condition)* requirement, demand; **satisfaire aux exigences de qch** to meet the requirements of sth (**c**) **exigences** *(salaire)* expected salary; **quelles sont vos exigences?** what salary do you expect?

exiger [45] [ɛgziʒe] *vt* (**a**) *(demander en insistant)* to demand (**de** from); **e. que qch soit fait** to demand that sth be done (**b**) *(nécessiter) (soin, action)* to require

exigible [ɛgziʒibl] *adj (dette, impôt)* payable

exigu, -ë [ɛgzigy] *adj* cramped, tiny

exiguïté [ɛgziguite] *nf* crampedness

exil [ɛgzil] *nm* exile; **envoyer qn en e.** to send sb into exile; **être en e.** to be in exile

exilé, -e [ɛgzile] *nm,f* exile

exiler [ɛgzile] **1** *vt* to exile (**de** from) **2 s'exiler** *vpr* to go into exile; *Fig* **s'e. de la ville** to cut oneself off from the town

existant, -e [ɛgzistɑ̃, -ɑ̃t] *adj* existing

existence [ɛgzistɑ̃s] *nf* (**a**) *Phil (être)* existence (**b**) *(vie)* life; **mener une e. tranquille** to lead a quiet life; **dans l'e.** in life (**c**) *(présence)* existence (**de** of) (**d**) *(durée) (d'une institution)* life

existentialisme [ɛgzistɑ̃sjalism] *nm Phil* existentialism

existentiel, -elle [ɛgzistɑ̃sjɛl] *adj* existential

exister [ɛgziste] **1** *vi* to exist; **rien n'existe pour lui que l'art** art is all that matters to him; **et l'amitié, cela existe, non?** there's such a thing as friendship, isn't there? **2** *v impersonnel* **il existe** there is/are

exode [ɛgzɔd] *nm* exodus; **e. rural** rural depopulation

exogène [ɛgzɔʒɛn] *adj Biol & Géol* exogenous

exonération [ɛgzɔnerasjɔ̃] *nf* exemption; **e. fiscale** tax exemption

exonérer [34] [ɛgzɔnere] *vt (personne)* to exempt; *(marchandises)* to exempt from tax; **être exonéré d'impôts** to be exempt from tax

exorbitant, -e [ɛgzɔrbitɑ̃, -ɑ̃t] *adj (prix, demande)* exorbitant

exorbité, -e [ɛgzɔrbite] *adj (yeux)* protruding; *Fig* **ils regardaient, les yeux exorbités** they watched with bulging eyes

exorciser [ɛgzɔrsize] *vt aussi Fig* to exorcize

exorcisme [ɛgzɔrsism] *nm* exorcism

exorciste [ɛgzɔrsist] *nmf* exorcist

exotique [ɛgzɔtik] *adj* exotic; **poisson e.** tropical fish

expansé, -e [ɛkspɑ̃se] *adj (polystyrène)* expanded

expansif, -ive [ɛkspɑ̃sif, -iv] *adj (exubérant)* expansive

expansion [ɛkspɑ̃sjɔ̃] *nf* (**a**) *(de gaz, de l'univers)* expansion; **l'univers en e.** the expanding universe (**b**) *(développement) (d'une ville, d'une industrie)* expansion; **taux d'e.** growth rate; **être en pleine e.** *(économie, entreprise)* to be booming

expansionnisme [ɛkspɑ̃sjɔnism] *nm* expansionism

expatriation [ɛkspatrijasjɔ̃] *nf* expatriation

expatrié, -e [ɛkspatrije] *adj & nm,f* expatriate

expatrier [66] [ɛkspatrije] **1** *vt (personne)* to expatriate **2 s'expatrier** *vpr* to leave one's country

expectative [ɛkspɛktativ] *nf* **être dans l'e.** to be waiting to see what happens

expectorant, -e [ɛkspɛktɔrɑ̃, -ɑ̃t] *adj & nm* expectorant

expectorer [ɛkspɛktɔre] *vt* to expectorate

expédient [ɛkspedjɑ̃] *nm* expedient; **vivre d'expédients** to live by one's wits

expédier [66] [ɛkspedje] *vt* (**a**) *(envoyer)* to send, to dispatch; **e. qch par bateau/par avion/par le train** to send sth by sea/air/rail (**b**) *(se débarrasser de)* to dispose of; **elle les a expédiés en colonie de vacances** she packed them off to camp (**c**) *(faire rapidement) (tâche)* to deal promptly with; *(devoirs, dissertation)* to dash off; **e. les affaires courantes** to deal with the day-to-day matters

expéditeur, -trice [ɛkspeditœr, -tris] **1** *nm,f* sender **2** *adj (bureau, gare)* dispatching

expéditif, -ive [ɛkspeditif, -iv] *adj* hasty

expédition [ɛkspedisjɔ̃] *nf* (**a**) *(envoi)* dispatch, sending (**b**) *(marchandises)* consignment (**c**) *(voyage, opération militaire) & Fig* expedition; **partir en e.** to go on an expedition

expéditionnaire [ɛkspedisjɔnɛr] *adj Mil* expeditionary

expérience [ɛksperjɑ̃s] *nf* (**a**) *(pratique)* experience; **avoir de l'e.** to have experience; **avoir l'e. de qch** to have experience of sth; **savoir qch par e.** to know sth from experience; **faire l'e. de qch** to experience sth; **tenter l'e.** to give it a try (**b**) *(test scientifique)* ex-

periment; **e. en laboratoire** laboratory experiment; **faire une e.** (**sur**) to carry out an experiment (on)
expérimental, -e, -aux, -ales [ɛksperimɑ̃tal, -o] *adj* experimental
expérimentalement [ɛksperimɑ̃talmɑ̃] *adv* experimentally
expérimentation [ɛksperimɑ̃tasjɔ̃] *nf* experimentation; **e. sur l'homme** human experiments
expérimenté, -e [ɛksperimɑ̃te] *adj* experienced
expérimenter [ɛksperimɑ̃te] *vt* (*remède, vaccin*) to test, to try out (**sur** on)
expert, -e [ɛkspɛr, -ɛrt] **1** *adj* expert, skilled (**en/dans** in); **être e. en la matière** to be an expert on the subject
2 *nm* expert; (*d'assurance*) valuer
expert-comptable (*pl* **experts-comptables**) [ɛkspɛrkɔ̃tabl] *nm Br* ≃ chartered accountant, *Am* ≃ certified public accountant, CPA
expertise [ɛkspɛrtiz] *nf* (**a**) (*évaluation*) (*d'une œuvre d'art*) valuation; (*de dommages*) assessment (**b**) (*rapport*) expert's report (**de** on) (**c**) (*compétence*) expertise
expertiser [ɛkspɛrtize] *vt* (*œuvre d'art*) to value; (*dommages*) to assess
expiation [ɛkspjasjɔ̃] *nf* expiation (**de** of)
expiatoire [ɛkspjatwar] *adj* expiatory
expier [66] [ɛkspje] *vt* to atone for, to expiate
expiration [ɛkspirasjɔ̃] *nf* (**a**) (*respiration*) breathing out (**b**) (*d'un contrat, d'un bail*) *Br* expiry, *Am* expiration; **venir** *ou* **arriver à e.** to expire
expirer [ɛkspire] **1** *vi* (**a**) *Litt* (*mourir*) to expire (**b**) (*contrat, bail*) to expire (**c**) (*respirer*) to breathe out
2 *vt* to breathe out
explicatif, -ive [ɛksplikatif, -iv] *adj* explanatory; **notice explicative** directions for use
explication [ɛksplikasjɔ̃] *nf* explanation; **donner une e. à qch** to give an explanation for sth; **exiger des explications** to demand an explanation; **avoir une e. avec qn** (*discuter*) to talk things over with sb; (*se disputer*) to have it out with sb; **e. de textes** critical *or* textual analysis
explicite [ɛksplisit] *adj* explicit
explicitement [ɛksplisitmɑ̃] *adv* explicitly
expliquer [ɛksplike] **1** *vt* to explain; (*texte*) to analyse
2 s'expliquer *vpr* (**a**) (*communiquer ses idées, se justifier*) to explain oneself; **je m'explique** let me explain (**b**) (*comprendre*) **je ne m'explique pas pourquoi il...** I can't understand why he... (**c**) (*être explicable*) **cela s'explique facilement** that's easily explained; **tout s'explique!** there's a reason for everything! (**d**) (*se parler*) to talk things over; **s'e. avec qn** (*discuter*) to talk things over with sb; (*se disputer*) to have it out with sb
exploit [ɛksplwa] *nm* feat
exploitant, -e [ɛksplwatɑ̃, -ɑ̃t] *nm,f* (**a**) **e.** (**agricole**) farmer; **petits exploitants** small farmers (**b**) *Cin* exhibitor
exploitation [ɛksplwatasjɔ̃] *nf* (**a**) (*d'une mine, d'une forêt*) working; (*d'une ligne de chemin de fer, d'une ferme*) running; (*d'une terre*) farming; (*des ressources naturelles, d'un brevet*) & *Fig Péj* exploitation; *Ordinat* **système d'e.** operating system; *Fig* **c'est de l'e.!** it's exploitation!; **l'e. de l'homme par l'homme** man's exploitation of man (**b**) (*entreprise*) concern; **e. agricole** farm; **e. minière** mine
exploiter [ɛksplwate] *vt* (**a**) (*mine, forêt*) to work; (*ressources naturelles, brevet*) to exploit; (*ligne de chemin

de fer, ferme*) to run; (*terre*) to farm; *Fig* (*situation, talent, idée*) to exploit (**b**) *Péj* (*abuser de*) (*personne*) to exploit
exploiteur, -euse [ɛksplwatœr, -øz] *nm,f Péj* exploiter
explorateur, -trice [ɛksplɔratœr, -tris] *nm,f* (*personne*) explorer
exploration [ɛksplɔrasjɔ̃] *nf* exploration; **partir en e.** to go off exploring
exploratoire [ɛksplɔratwar] *adj* exploratory
explorer [ɛksplɔre] *vt* to explore
exploser [ɛksploze] *vi* (**a**) (*bombe, avion, chaudière*) to explode; **faire e. une bombe** to explode a bomb (**b**) *Fig* (*se mettre en colère*) to explode
explosif, -ive [ɛksplozif, -iv] **1** *adj aussi Fig* explosive
2 *nm* explosive
explosion [ɛksplozjɔ̃] *nf aussi Fig* explosion; **une e. de joie** an outburst of joy; **e. démographique** population explosion
exponentiel, -elle [ɛkspɔnɑ̃sjɛl] **1** *adj* exponential
2 *nf* **exponentielle** exponential
export [ɛkspɔr] *nm* export; *Ordinat* **e. de données** data export
exportateur, -trice [ɛkspɔrtatœr, -tris] **1** *adj* exporting; **pays e. de vin** wine-exporting country
2 *nm,f* exporter
exportation [ɛkspɔrtasjɔ̃] *nf* (*action*) export(ation); (*produit*) export; *Ordinat* (*d'un fichier*) exporting; *Ordinat* (*données exportées*) exported data
exporter [ɛkspɔrte] *vt aussi Ordinat* to export (**vers** to)
exposant, -e [ɛkspozɑ̃, -ɑ̃t] **1** *nm,f* (*artiste, firme*) exhibitor
2 *nm* (**a**) *Math* exponent (**b**) *Typ* (*chiffre, lettre*) superscript; **3 en e.** superscript 3
exposé [ɛkspoze] *nm* (*de faits, d'une situation*) account; *Scol & Univ* talk; **après un bref e. de la situation** after outlining the situation; **faire un e.** to give a talk
exposer [ɛkspoze] **1** *vt* (**a**) (*montrer*) (*marchandises*) to display; (*œuvres d'art*) to exhibit (**b**) (*expliquer*) (*raisons, projet*) to set out; (*griefs, point de vue*) to air; **je leur ai exposé ma situation** I explained my situation to them (**c**) (*présenter*) **e. qch à la lumière/au soleil** to expose sth to the light/to the sun; **e. un film to** expose a film (**d**) **e. qn à la critique/au danger** to expose sb to criticism/to danger; **exposé au nord** north-facing
2 s'exposer *vpr* **s'e. au danger** to put oneself in danger; **s'e. à la critique/à des poursuites** to lay oneself open to criticism/to prosecution; **ne t'expose pas trop longtemps** don't stay in the sun too long
exposition [ɛkspozisjɔ̃] *nf* (**a**) (*action*) (*de marchandises, de fleurs*) display; (*d'œuvres d'art*) exhibition (**b**) (*de musée*) exhibition (**c**) (*salon, foire*) exhibition, show; **l'E. universelle** the World Fair (**d**) (*de faits, de raisons*) exposition (**e**) (*au froid, au danger, au soleil*) exposure (**à** to); (*d'une maison*) aspect; *Phot* exposure; **durée de e.** exposure time
exprès[1], -esse [ɛksprɛs] *adj* (*explicite*) express
exprès[2] *adj inv* **lettre/paquet e.** special delivery letter/parcel; **en e.** by special delivery
exprès[3] [ɛksprɛ] *adv* (**à** *dessein*) on purpose, deliberately; (*spécialement*) specially; **je l'ai allumé sans le faire e.** I switched it on without meaning to; **c'est fait e.** it's deliberate; **on dirait un fait e.** you'd think it was

done on purpose; **comme (par) un fait e.**, **il pleuvait** and wouldn't you know it, it was raining
express [ɛksprɛs] **1** adj (train) express
2 nm (**a**) (train) express (**b**) (café) espresso
expressément [ɛksprɛsemɑ̃] adv (**a**) (catégoriquement) expressly (**b**) (spécialement) specially
expressif, -ive [ɛksprɛsif, -iv] adj expressive
expression [ɛksprɛsjɔ̃] nf (**a**) (d'un sentiment, d'une opinion) expression; (du visage) expression, look; **l'e. de son visage** the expression or look on his/her face; **sans e.** expressionless; **e. corporelle** self-expression through movement (**b**) (locution) expression (**c**) Math expression; Fig **réduit à sa plus simple e.** reduced to its simplest form; Ordinat **e. logique** logical expression
expressionnisme [ɛksprɛsjɔnism] nm expressionism
expressionniste [ɛksprɛsjɔnist] adj & nmf expressionist
exprimable [ɛksprimabl] adj expressible
exprimer [ɛksprime] **1** vt (**a**) (sentiment, opinion) & Math to express (**b**) (jus) to squeeze (**de** from)
2 s'exprimer vpr (en parlant, en agissant) to express oneself; **s'e. par gestes** to use sign language; **si je peux m'e. ainsi** if I can put it like that; **le président ne s'est pas encore exprimé sur ce sujet** the president has yet to voice an opinion on the matter
expropriation [ɛksprɔprijasjɔ̃] nf expropriation
exproprier [66] [ɛksprɔprije] vt to expropriate
expulser [ɛkspylse] vt (étranger) to deport, to expel (**de** from); (locataire) to evict (**de** from); (élève, membre de parti) to expel (**de** from); (joueur) to send off
expulsion [ɛkspylsjɔ̃] nf (d'un étranger) deportation (**de** from); (d'un locataire) eviction (**de** from); (d'un élève, d'un membre de parti) expulsion (**de** from); (d'un joueur) sending off
expurger [45] [ɛkspyrʒe] vt to expurgate
exquis, -e [ɛkski, -iz] adj exquisite; (personne, sourire, temps) delightful
exsangue [ɛksɑ̃g, ɛgzɑ̃g] adj (patient, visage) anaemic; Fig (pays, région) bled white
extase [ɛkstaz] nf (**a**) Rel & Psy ecstasy (**b**) (admiration) rapture, ecstasy; **être en e. devant qn/qch** to be in raptures over sb/sth
extasier [66] [ɛkstazje] **s'extasier** vpr (s'exclamer) to go into raptures (**sur/devant** about/over); (être en extase) to be in raptures (**sur/devant** about/over)
extatique [ɛkstatik] adj ecstatic
extenseur [ɛkstɑ̃sœr] **1** adj m (muscle) extensor
2 nm (appareil) chest expander
extensible [ɛkstɑ̃sibl] adj (**a**) (métal) tensile; (vêtement, tissu) stretchy (**b**) Ordinat upgradeable
extensif, -ive [ɛkstɑ̃sif, -iv] adj **culture extensive** extensive farming
extension [ɛkstɑ̃sjɔ̃] nf (**a**) (d'un muscle, d'un ressort) stretching; **être en e.** (ressort) to be released; (gymnaste) to be fully stretched (**b**) Fig (d'un territoire, d'une firme) expansion; (d'un contrat) extension; (d'une maladie, d'une langue) spread; **prendre de l'e.** (entreprise) to expand; (maladie, incendie) to spread (**c**) **par e.** by extension (**d**) Ordinat expansion; **e. mémoire** memory upgrade
exténuer [ɛkstenɥe] **1** vt to exhaust
2 s'exténuer vpr **s'e. à faire qch** to exhaust oneself doing sth
extérieur, -e [ɛksterjœr] **1** adj (**a**) (surface, partie) outer, external; (escalier, éclairage, intérêts) outside;

(signe, fragilité) outward; (facteur, cause) external; **le monde e.** the outside world; **sans aide extérieure** without outside help (**b**) (étranger) (commerce, politique) foreign, external
2 nm (**a**) (d'un bâtiment, d'une boîte) outside, exterior; **vu de l'e.** seen from the outside; **à l'e.** (d'un bâtiment) outside; (d'une boîte) on the outside; **à l'e. de la gare/ville** outside the station/town; Fig **juger de l'e.** to judge by appearances; **match à l'e.** away match; **jouer à l'e.** to play away (**b**) **l'e.** (pays étrangers) foreign countries; **à l'e.** abroad; **de l'e.** from abroad (**c**) Cin location shot; **tourner en e.** to film on location (**d**) Belg Sport (joueur) winger
extérieurement [ɛksterjœrmɑ̃] adv (**a**) (dehors) on the outside, externally (**b**) (en apparence) outwardly
extérioriser [ɛksterjɔrize] **1** vt (sentiment) to express; Psy to externalize
2 s'extérioriser vpr (sentiment) to express itself; (personne) to express oneself
exterminateur, -trice [ɛkstɛrminatœr, -tris] **1** adj (rage) destructive
2 nm,f exterminator
extermination [ɛkstɛrminasjɔ̃] nf extermination
exterminer [ɛkstɛrmine] vt to exterminate
externaliser [ɛkstɛrnalize] vt Écon to outsource
externat [ɛkstɛrna] nm (**a**) (école) day school (**b**) (élèves) day pupils (**c**) (à l'hôpital) non-resident (medical) studentship
externe [ɛkstɛrn] **1** adj (**a**) (surface, partie) external, outer; (cause) external; Ordinat **dispositif e.** external device; **à usage e.** (médicament) for external use only (**b**) **élève e.** day pupil
2 nmf (**a**) (élève) day pupil (**b**) (étudiant en médecine) **e. (des hôpitaux)** non-resident medical student, Am extern
extincteur [ɛkstɛ̃ktœr] nm fire extinguisher
extinction [ɛkstɛ̃ksjɔ̃] nf (**a**) **e. des feux** lights out (**b**) (d'une espèce) extinction; **espèce en voie d'e.** endangered species (**c**) **e. de voix** loss of voice; **avoir une e. de voix** to have lost one's voice
extirper [ɛkstirpe] **1** vt (plante) to uproot; Fig (vices) to eradicate, to root out; **e. qn de son lit** to drag sb out of bed; **je n'ai pas pu lui e. le moindre renseignement** I couldn't get a single piece of information out of him/her
2 s'extirper vpr **s'e. de qch** to extricate oneself from sth; **s'e. de son lit** to drag oneself out of bed
extorquer [ɛkstɔrke] vt (argent, promesse) to extort (**à** from)
extorsion [ɛkstɔrsjɔ̃] nf extortion; **e. de fonds** extortion of funds
extra [ɛkstra] **1** adj inv (**a**) (de qualité supérieure) top-quality (**b**) Fam (remarquable) great, fantastic
2 nm inv (**a**) (gâterie) (special) treat; **s'offrir un e.** to treat oneself (**b**) (serviteur) extra hand; **faire des e. chez qn** to do occasional work for sb
extra- [ɛkstra] préf extra-
extraconjugal, -e, -aux, -ales [ɛkstrakɔ̃ʒygal, -o] adj extramarital
extracteur [ɛkstraktœr] nm extractor
extraction [ɛkstraksjɔ̃] nf aussi Math extraction; (d'une balle) removal; Fig **de haute/basse e.** of noble/humble extraction
extrader [ɛkstrade] vt to extradite
extradition [ɛkstradisjɔ̃] nf extradition
extrafin, -e [ɛkstrafɛ̃, -in] adj (**a**) (petit pois) extrafine (**b**) (de qualité supérieure) top-quality

extrafort, -e [ɛkstrafɔr, -ɔrt] **1** *adj* extra-strong **2** *nm* bias binding

extraire [28] [ɛkstrɛr] **1** *vt aussi Math* to extract (**de** from); *(balle)* to remove (**de** from); *(épingle, clou)* to pull out (**de** of); *(personne)* to free (**de** from); **cette citation est extraite de...** this quotation is taken from... **2 s'extraire** *vpr* **s'e. de qch** to extricate oneself from sth

extrait [ɛkstrɛ] *nm* (**a**) *(essence)* extract (**b**) *(de texte, de film)* extract; *(d'un acte)* abstract; **e. de casier judiciaire** = documentary evidence showing whether one has a criminal record; **e. de naissance** birth certificate

extralucide [ɛkstralysid] *adj & nmf* **(voyant(e))** **e.** clairvoyant

Extranet [ɛkstranɛt] *nm Ordinat* Extranet

extraordinaire [ɛkstraɔrdinɛr] *adj* (**a**) *(spécial) (mesures, messager, mission)* special (**b**) *(étonnant, remarquable)* extraordinary; *Fam (excellent)* fantastic; **cela n'a rien d'e.** that's nothing out of the ordinary; **si par e.** if by some remote chance

extraordinairement [ɛkstraɔrdinɛrmɑ̃] *adv* extraordinarily

extraplat, -e [ɛkstrapla, -at] *adj (montre, calculette)* slimline

extrapoler [ɛkstrapɔle] *vi* to extrapolate

extrascolaire [ɛkstraskɔlɛr] *adj (activités)* extra-curricular

extraterrestre [ɛkstratɛrɛstr] *adj & nmf* extraterrestrial

extra-utérin, -e [ɛkstrayterɛ̃, -in] *adj voir* **grossesse**

extravagance [ɛkstravagɑ̃s] *nf* (**a**) *(d'un comportement, de vêtements)* extravagance; *(d'une personne)* eccentricity; **des idées d'une telle e.** such extravagant ideas (**b**) *(action, remarque)* piece of nonsense

extravagant, -e [ɛkstravagɑ̃, -ɑ̃t] *adj (idée, comportement, vêtements)* extravagant; *(personne)* eccentric

extraverti, -e [ɛkstravɛrti] *adj & nm,f* extrovert

extrême [ɛkstrɛm] **1** *adj* (**a**) *(point, limite)* furthest; *(jeunesse, vieillesse, froid, plaisir)* extreme; **en cas d'e. urgence** if it's extremely urgent; **d'une maigreur e.** extremely thin; *Pol* **e. droite/gauche** far *or* extreme right/left (**b**) *(excessif)* extreme **2** *nm* extreme; **passer d'un e. à l'autre** to go from one extreme to the other; **prudent à l'e.** cautious in the extreme

extrêmement [ɛkstrɛmmɑ̃] *adv* extremely

extrême-onction (*pl* **extrêmes-onctions**) [ɛkstrɛm-ɔ̃ksjɔ̃] *nf Rel* extreme unction

Extrême-Orient [ɛkstrɛmɔrjɑ̃] *nm* **l'E.** the Far East

extrémisme [ɛkstremism] *nm* extremism

extrémité [ɛkstremite] *nf* (**a**) *(bout)* *(d'une jambe, d'une corde)* end; *(d'un doigt)* tip; *(d'une aiguille, d'une épée)* point; **les extrémités** *(pieds et mains)* the extremities (**b**) *(acte désespéré)* **se livrer à une e.** to do something desperate (**c**) *(situation désespérée)* extremity; **être à la dernière e.** to be on the point of death

exubérance [ɛgzyberɑ̃s] *nf (d'une personne)* exuberance; *(d'une végétation)* lushness; **avec e.** exuberantly

exubérant, -e [ɛgzyberɑ̃, -ɑ̃t] *adj (personne, joie)* exuberant; *(végétation)* lush

exultation [ɛgzyltasjɔ̃] *nf* exultation

exulter [ɛgzylte] *vi* to exult, to rejoice

exutoire [ɛgzytwar] *nm* outlet (**à** for)

ex-voto [ɛksvɔto] *nm inv Rel* votive offering

e-zine, ezine [izin] *nm Ordinat* e-zine, ezine

F¹, f [ɛf] *nm inv* F, f; **un F2/F3** *(appartement)* a two-/three-roomed *Br* flat *or Am* apartment

F² (**a**) *(abrév* **franc(s)**) F, fr (**b**) *(abrév* **Fahrenheit**) F

fa [fa] *nm inv (note de musique)* F; *(chantée)* fa

fable [fabl] *nf* (**a**) *(récit)* fable (**b**) *(invention)* story

fabricant, -e [fabrikɑ̃, -ɑ̃t] *nm,f* manufacturer

fabrication [fabrikasjɔ̃] *nf (industrielle)* manufacture; *(manuelle)* making; **f. artisanale** production by craftsmen; **bombe de f. artisanale** home-made bomb; **f. assistée par ordinateur** computer-aided *or* computer-assisted manufacture; **de f. française** French-made

fabrique [fabrik] *nf* factory

fabriquer [fabrike] *vt* (**a**) *(industriellement)* to manufacture; *(manuellement)* to make; *Fam* **qu'est-ce qu'elle fabrique?** what's she up to? (**b**) *(inventer)* to make up, to fabricate

fabulation [fabylasjɔ̃] *nf* fantasizing

fabuleusement [fabyløzmɑ̃] *adv* fabulously

fabuleux, -euse [fabylø, -øz] *adj* fabulous

fac [fak] *nf Fam Br* uni, *Am* college, school; **à la f.** at *Br* uni *or Am* college; **être en f. d'allemand** to be studying German at *Br* uni *or Am* college

façade [fasad] *nf aussi Fig* façade

face [fas] *nf* (**a**) *(visage)* face; *Fig* **perdre/sauver la f.** to lose/save face (**b**) *(côté) (d'un disque)* side; *(d'une pièce de monnaie)* head (side); **changer un disque de f.** to turn a record over (**c**) *Fig (aspect)* side; **changer la f. des choses** to change the face of things (**d**) *(locutions)* **f. à** *(dans l'espace)* facing; *(difficultés, situation)* faced with; *(adversaire)* confronted with; **f. à f. (avec)** face to face (with); **faire f. à** *(lieu, personne)* to face, to be opposite; *(responsabilités, dépenses)* to meet; *(situation, difficultés)* to face up to; **de f.** face on; *(attaquer)* from the front; **en f.** opposite; *(de l'autre côté de la rue)* across the road; **regarder qn en f.** to look sb in the face; **dire qch en f. à qn** to tell sb sth to his/her face; **la maison (d')en f.** the house across the road; **en f. de** opposite, facing; **l'un en f. de l'autre** opposite *or* facing each other

face-à-face [fasafas] *nm inv (public)* face-to-face debate; *(privé)* one-to-one meeting

facétie [fasesi] *nf Litt* joke

facétieux, -euse [fasesjø, -øz] *adj Litt (personne)* mischievous

facette [fasɛt] *nf aussi Fig* facet; **à facettes** facetted; *(personnalité)* multi-faceted

fâché, -e [fɑʃe] *adj* (**a**) *(en colère)* angry (**contre** with) (**b**) *(brouillé)* on bad terms (**avec** with); *Fam* **elle est fâchée avec les maths** she's hopeless at maths (**c**)

(contrarié) sorry; **je ne suis pas f. que ça soit terminé** I'm not sorry that it's finished

fâcher [fɑʃe] **1** *vt (mettre en colère)* to make angry, to anger; **un sujet qui fâche** a controversial topic
2 se fâcher *vpr* (**a**) *(se mettre en colère)* to get angry (**contre** with) (**b**) *(se brouiller)* to fall out (**avec** with)

fâcheux, -euse [fɑʃø, -øz] *adj* unfortunate

facho [faʃo] *adj & nmf Fam* fascist

faciès [fasjɛs] *nm* features

facile [fasil] **1** *adj* (**a**) *(simple)* easy; **être f. à faire** to be easy to do; **c'est f. à dire** that's easily said; **f. d'emploi** easy to use (**b**) *(agréable)* easy-going; **être f. à vivre** to be easy to get on with (**c**) *Péj (superficiel)* facile (**d**) *Péj (femme, fille)* easy
2 *adv Fam (au moins)* easily

facilement [fasilmɑ̃] *adv* easily

facilité [fasilite] *nf* (**a**) *(simplicité)* easiness; **choisir la f.** to take the easy way out (**b**) *(aisance)* ease; **avoir des facilités pour qch** to have a talent for sth (**c**) *facilités de paiement* payment facilities

faciliter [fasilite] *vt* to make easier; **f. qch à qn** to make sth easier for sb; **tu ne me facilites pas la tâche** you're not making things easy for me!

façon [fasɔ̃] *nf* (**a**) *(manière)* way, manner; **faire qch à sa f.** to do sth (in) one's own way; **de cette f.** (in) this way; **de f. à faire qch** so as to do sth; **de f. à ce qu'il t'entende** so that he hears you; **de telle f. que** in such a way that; **d'une ou de f. générale** generally speaking; **d'une f. ou d'une autre** one way or another; **de toute f.** anyway, in any case; *Sout* **vous ne me dérangez en aucune f.** you're not disturbing me in the least; **c'est une f. de parler** in a manner of speaking; **je ne tolère pas ces façons de parler!** I won't tolerate that sort of language!; *Can* **avoir de f.** *(avoir des manières agréables)* to have pleasant manners; *(être beau parleur)* to speak well (**b**) *(imitation)* **f. cuir** imitation leather (**c**) *(fabrication)* making; *(facture)* craftsmanship, workmanship; *(main-d'œuvre)* labour (**d**) *façons (comportement)* manners, behaviour; **en voilà des façons!** what a way to behave!; **faire des façons** *(minauder)* to put on airs; **faire des façons pour accepter qch** to make a fuss about accepting sth; **sans façons** *(personne, repas)* unpretentious; **non merci, sans façons!** no thanks, really!

façonner [fasɔne] *vt* (**a**) *(travailler)* to shape (**b**) *(fabriquer)* to make (**c**) *Fig (personne, caractère)* to mould

fac-similé (*pl* **fac-similés**) [faksimile] *nm* facsimile

facteur¹, -trice [faktœr, -tris] **1** *nm,f (employé des Postes) Br* postman, *f* postwoman, *Am* mailman, *f* mailwoman

2 *nm (de pianos, de clavecins)* maker; *(d'orgues)* builder

facteur² *nm* (**a**) *(élément)* factor; **le f. temps** the time factor (**b**) *Math* factor

factice [faktis] *adj* (**a**) *(faux)* imitation (**b**) *Fig (sourire)* forced; *(gaieté)* false

faction [faksjɔ̃] *nf* (**a**) *(groupe)* faction (**b**) *Mil* guard duty; **être de** *ou* **en f.** to be on guard duty

factotum [faktɔtɔm] *nm* factotum

factuel, -elle [faktɥɛl] *adj* factual

facturation [faktyrasjɔ̃] *nf* invoicing, billing

facture¹ [faktyr] *nf* (**a**) *(style) (d'une œuvre)* construction; *(d'un artiste)* style (**b**) *(de pianos, de clavecins)* making; *(d'orgues)* building

facture² *nf (document)* invoice, bill; **faire** *ou* **dresser une f.** to make out an invoice; **f. d'électricité/de gaz** electricity/gas bill; **f. détaillée** itemized bill

facturer [faktyre] *vt* to invoice

facturette [faktyrɛt] *nf* credit card sales slip

facultatif, -ive [fakyltatif, -iv] *adj* optional

faculté [fakylte] *nf* (**a**) *(de médecine, de droit)* faculty (**b**) *(pouvoir)* capacity (**de** for) (**c**) **facultés mentales** faculties; **ne plus avoir toutes ses facultés** to no longer have all one's faculties

fada [fada] *Fam* **1** *adj* crazy
2 *nmf* nutcase

fadaise [fadɛz] *nf* silly remark; **dire des fadaises** to talk nonsense

fadasse [fadas] *adj Fam* bland

fade [fad] *adj* insipid

fadeur [fadœr] *nf* insipidness

fagot [fago] *nm* bundle of firewood; *Fig* **de derrière les fagots** *(bouteille de vin)* for special occasions; *(compliment, idée)* remarkable

fagoté, -e [fagɔte] *adj Péj* **mal/bizarrement f.** badly/oddly dressed

faiblard, -e [fɛblar, -ard] *adj Fam* a bit weak

faible [fɛbl] **1** *adj* (**a**) *(physiquement, moralement)* weak; (**b**) *(raisonnement, plaisanterie)* weak; **être f. en qch** *(élève)* to be weak at sth (**c**) *(voix, odeur, lumière)* faint; *(vent)* light; **et le terme est f.!** and that's putting it mildly! (**d**) *(quantité)* small; *(prix, revenu)* low; *(avantage, chance, espoir)* slight; *(vitesse)* low; **à une f. hauteur/profondeur** not very high up/deep down
2 *nmf* weakling; **les faibles d'esprit** the feeble-minded
3 *nm* **avoir un f. pour qn/qch** to have a soft spot for sb/a weakness for sth

faiblement [fɛbləmã] *adv (résister, protester)* weakly, feebly; *(éclairer)* faintly

faiblesse [fɛblɛs] *nf* (**a**) *(physique, morale)* weakness; **avoir la f. de faire qch** to be weak enough to do sth; **donner des signes de f.** *(appareil)* to be showing signs of wear and tear; *(personne)* to be looking weak (**b**) *(médiocrité)* weakness (**en** at) (**c**) *(malaise)* **avoir une f.** to feel faint

faiblir [fɛblir] *vi* (**a**) *(devenir faible) (personne, monnaie)* to weaken; *(lumière)* to grow weaker; *(vent)* to drop (**b**) *(niveau scolaire)* to decrease; *(élève)* to get weaker

faïence [fajãs] *nf* (**a**) *(matière)* earthenware (**b**) *(objet)* piece of earthenware; **faïences** earthenware

faïencerie [fajãsri] *nf* (**a**) *(articles)* earthenware (**b**) *(fabrique)* pottery (works) (**c**) *(commerce)* pottery (trade)

faille [faj] *nf* (**a**) *(dans un raisonnement)* flaw; *(dans une amitié)* rift; **sans f.** *(raisonnement)* flawless; *(fidélité)* unwavering (**b**) *Géol* fault

faillir [35] [fajir] **1** *vi* **j'ai failli tomber** I nearly *or* almost fell; **j'ai bien failli me noyer** I very nearly drowned
2 faillir à *vt ind Litt (réputation)* not to live up to; *(devoir)* to fail in

faillite [fajit] *nf* (**a**) *(d'entreprise)* bankruptcy; **être en f.** to be bankrupt; **faire f.** to go bankrupt (**b**) *(échec)* failure

faim [fɛ̃] *nf* hunger; **avoir f.** to be hungry; *Fig* **avoir f. de qch** to hunger for sth; *Fam* **avoir une grosse/petite f.** to be very hungry/a bit hungry; **avoir une f. de loup** to be ravenous; **rester sur sa f.** to remain hungry; *Fig* to be left unsatisfied

fainéant, -e [fɛneã, -ãt] **1** *adj* lazy, idle
2 *nm,f* idler

fainéanter [fɛneãte] *vi* to idle about

fainéantise [fɛneãtiz] *nf* laziness, idleness

faire [36] [fɛr] **1** *vt* (**a**) *(fabriquer, produire)* to make; *(tache, trace)* to leave; **f. du bruit** to make some noise; **f. de la fumée** to give off smoke; **f. une erreur** to make a mistake; **f. de la betterave/du colza** to grow beetroot/rape; *Fam* **des femmes comme ça, on n'en fait plus** they don't make women like that any more; **f. un enfant à qn** to get sb pregnant; **f. des compliments à qn** to compliment sb; **je ferai de lui un homme/un avocat** I'll make a man/a lawyer of him; **qu'est-ce que je vais f. de lui?** what am I going to do with him?; **qu'est-ce que tu vas f. de ce vieux bidon?** what are you going to do with that old can?; **qu'est-ce que j'ai fait de mes lunettes?** what have I done with my glasses?

(**b**) *(effectuer) (changements, effort, grimace, mouvement)* to make; **f. le ménage/la vaisselle** to do the housework/the washing-up; **f. un pas en avant** to step forward; **faire demi-tour** to turn round; **f. une école de commerce** to study at a business school; **f. une licence** to study for a degree; **c'est moi qui fais tout ici** I have to do everything round here; **voilà une bonne chose de faite** that's one thing out of the way; **ce qui est fait est fait** what's done is done; **c'est bien fait pour elle** it serves her right

(**c**) *(occasionner)* **f. de la peine à qn** to hurt sb; **qu'est-ce que tu lui as fait?** what have you done to him/her? *Fam* **f. des ennuis à qn** to make trouble for sb; **ça m'a fait quelque chose/un choc** it upset/shocked me; **ça a fait du scandale** it caused a scandal; **ça ne fait rien** it doesn't matter; **qu'est-ce que ça peut faire?** what difference does it make?; **ça fait mauvais effet** it gives a bad impression; **le médicament n'a pas fait effet** the medicine didn't take effect (**d**) *(changer)* **on ne peut rien y f.** nothing can be done about it; *Fam* **rien à f.!** no way!, *Br* nothing doing!

(**e**) *(subir)* to have; **f. une dépression** to have depression; *Fam* **f. une pneumonie/une grippe** to have pneumonia/flu; *Fam* **il m'a encore fait une grippe!** he's gone and got the flu again!

(**f**) *(pratiquer)* **f. du tennis/football** to play tennis/football; **f. de la voile** to sail; **f. du violon/piano** to play the violin/the piano; **f. du russe/de l'espagnol** to do Russian/Spanish

(**g**) *(constituer)* to make; **il ferait un excellent mari/pompier** he would make an excellent husband/fireman; **f. l'affaire** to do the trick; **c'est cela qui fait ton**

charme that's what gives you your charm; **cette chambre fait aussi bureau** this bedroom also serves as an office

(**h**) *(s'occuper à)* to do; **qu'est-ce qu'il fait dans la vie?** what does he do for a job?; **qu'est-ce que tu fais demain?** what are you doing tomorrow?; **f. des études** to study; **qu'est-ce que tu fais ici?** what are you doing here?

(**i**) *(parcourir)* to do; **f. 100 kilomètres par jour** to do 100 kilometres a day; **il a fait toute la ville pour la retrouver** he searched the whole town for her; **f. du cent à l'heure** to do 100 km/h

(**j**) *(indique une mesure, une quantité)* to be; **la table fait 1 mètre de long** the table is 1 metre long; **deux et deux font quatre** two and two are *or* make four; **combien ça fait en dollars?** how much is that in dollars?; **le bébé fait 5 kilos** the baby weighs 5 kilos

(**k**) *(agir comme)* **f. l'imbécile** to play the fool; **f. l'innocent** to play the innocent; **f. l'important** to act important; **il fait celui qui n'a pas entendu** he pretends he hasn't heard

(**l**) *(sembler)* to look; **il fait jeune/anglais** he looks young/English

(**m**) *(dire)* to say; **"à bientôt!", fit-elle** "see you soon!" she said; **ça a fait plouf** it went splash

(**n**) *(suivi d'un infinitif)* **f. voir qch à qn** to show sb sth; **f. traverser qn** to help sb across; **f. faire qch à qn** to make sb do sth; **elle m'a fait ranger ma chambre** she made me tidy up my bedroom; **f. réparer qch** to get *or* have sth repaired; **f. construire une maison** to have a house built; **elle ne fait que se plaindre** she's always complaining; **je ne fais que répéter ses paroles** I'm just repeating what he/she said

(**o**) *(pour remplacer un verbe)* **il devait arroser les plantes mais il ne l'a pas fait** he was meant to water the plants but he didn't; **mais faites donc!** please do!

2 *vi* (**a**) *(agir)* to do; **f. vite** to be quick; **fais comme tu voudras** do as you like; **f. pour le mieux** to do one's best; **f. comme chez soi** to make oneself at home; **comment f.?** how can I/we do it?; *Fam* **il faut f. avec** it'll have to do

(**b**) *Fam (faire ses besoins)* to go to the *Br* toilet *or Am* bathroom

3 *v impersonnel* (**a**) *(indique un état)* to be; **il fait froid/chaud** it's cold/hot; **il fait beau** it's fine; **il fait 20 degrés** it's 20 degrees; **il fait jour/nuit** it's light/night

(**b**) *(indique la distance, la durée)* **ça fait un mois qu'il est parti** he's been gone for a month; **ça fait une heure que je t'attends** I've been waiting for you for an hour; **ça fait 200 kilomètres que nous roulons** we've been driving for 200 kilometres

4 se faire *vpr* (**a**) *(avoir lieu)* **finalement ça ne s'est jamais fait** nothing happened in the end; **comment se fait-il que...?** how is it that...?

(**b**) *(être pratiqué)* to be done; **ça se fait beaucoup cette année** it's the in thing this year

(**c**) *(être acceptable)* **ça se fait** it's the done thing; **ça ne se fait pas** it's not the done thing

(**d**) *(être fabriqué)* to be made

(**e**) *(se confectionner)* **se f. un lit** to make a bed for oneself; **se f. une bibliothèque** to build up a library; **se f. un œuf sur le plat** to make oneself a fried egg; **se f. les ongles** to do one's nails

(**f**) *(fromage, vin)* to mature; *(chaussures)* to wear in

(**g**) *(provoquer)* **se f. mal** to hurt oneself; **se f. une entorse au poignet** to sprain one's wrist; **se f. du sou-**

ci to worry; **se f. une opinion** to form an opinion; **se f. des amis/des ennemis** to make friends/enemies; *Fam* **s'en f.** to worry; **elle ne s'en fait pas celle-là!** *(elle a du culot)* she's got a nerve!; *(elle a beaucoup d'argent)* she hasn't got a care in the world!

(**h**) *(s'ériger en)* **se f. le défenseur des opprimés** to become established as a defender of the oppressed

(**i**) *(devenir)* **se f. vieux** to get old; **se f. beau** to do oneself up; **se f. moine** to become a monk; **il se fait tard** it's getting late

(**j**) *(avec un infinitif)* **se f. insulter** to get abused; **se f. couper les cheveux** to have one's hair cut; **se f. prêter qch** to borrow sth; **se f. refaire le nez** to have a nose job

(**k**) *(s'habituer)* **se f. à qch** to get used to sth

(**l**) *(l'un l'autre)* **se f. des cadeaux** to give each other presents; **se f. des reproches** to blame each other

(**m**) *Fam* **il faut se f. celui-là!** what a pain in the neck!

faire-part [fɛrpar] *nm inv* announcement

faire-valoir [fɛrvalwar] *nm inv (personne)* foil

fair-play [fɛrplɛ] **1** *adj inv* **être f.** to play fair

2 *nm* fair play

fais *voir* **faire**

faisabilité [fəzabilite] *nf* feasibility

faisable [fəzabl] *adj* feasible

faisan [fəzã] *nm* pheasant

faisandé, -e [fəzãde] *adj (gibier)* high

faisane [fəzan] *adj f & nf* (**poule**) **f.** hen pheasant

faisceau, -x [fɛso] *nm* (**a**) *(rayons)* beam; **f. hertzien** electromagnetic wave; **f. lumineux** beam of light (**b**) *Fig (de preuves)* body

faiseur, -euse [fəzœr, -øz] **1** *nm,f* maker; **f. d'embarras** fusspot; **f. de miracles** miracle worker

2 *nf* **faiseuse d'anges** backstreet abortionist

faisons *voir* **faire**

faisselle [fɛsɛl] *nf (fromage)* = type of soft white cheese; *(récipient)* cheese drainer

fait¹, -e [fɛ, fɛt] *adj* (**a**) *(fabriqué)* **tout f.** *(idée, expression)* fixed (**b**) *(adapté)* **être f. pour qn/qch** to be made for sb/sth; **ils sont faits l'un pour l'autre** they're made for each other; **être f. pour faire qch** *(personne)* to be cut out to do sth (**c**) *(bâti)* *Litt ou Hum* **être bien f. de sa personne** to be good-looking (**d**) *(maquillé)* **avoir les ongles/les yeux faits** to be wearing nail polish/eye make-up (**e**) *(fromage)* ripe

fait³ *nm* (**a**) *(acte)* act; **les faits et gestes de qn** sb's every move; **prendre qn sur le f.** to catch sb in the act *or* red-handed; **prendre f. et cause pour qn** to stand up for sb (**b**) *(réalité)* fact; **le f. d'habiter en ville** living in town; **mettre qn devant le f. accompli** to present sb with a fait accompli; **c'est un f. acquis** it's an established fact (**c**) *(point précis)* **aller droit au f.** to get straight to the point; **en venir au f.** to come to the point (**d**) *(événement)* event; **un f. nouveau s'est produit** there was a new development; **un f. divers** a news item; **faits divers** *(rubrique)* ≃ news in brief (**e**) *(locutions)* **au f.** *(à propos)* by the way; **être au f. de qch** to know *or* be informed about sth; **en f., de f.** in fact, as a matter of fact; **de ce f.** for that reason; **expert en f. de vins** expert as regards wine *or* when it comes to wine

faîte [fɛt] *nm* (**a**) *(d'un toit)* ridge; *(d'un arbre, d'une maison)* top; *(d'une montagne)* summit (**b**) *Fig* **le f. de la gloire** the height of glory

faites *voir* **faire**

faîtier, -ère [fɛtje, -ɛr] *adj Suisse (organisation, association)* umbrella

faitout *nm*, **fait-tout** *nm inv* [fɛtu] stewpot

fakir [fakir] *nm* fakir

falaise [falɛz] *nf* cliff

fallacieux, -euse [falasjø, -øz] *adj (prétexte)* false; *(argument, raisonnement)* specious; *(apparence)* misleading

falloir [37] [falwar] **1** *v impersonnel* (**a**) *(être nécessaire)* **faut-il tout cela?** is all that necessary?; **je l'ai fait parce qu'il le fallait** I did it because I had to; **il lui faut un nouveau pardessus** he needs a new coat; **il me faudrait un kilo de pommes** I need a kilo of apples; **je lui ai tout donné, qu'est-ce qu'il lui faut de plus!** I've given him/her everything, what more does he/she want!; **il m'a fallu trois jours pour le faire** it took me three days to do it; **il faut partir** I/we/you/*etc* must go *or* have to go; **il lui faut se dépêcher** she has to hurry; **il fallait le dire!** why didn't you say so?; **je vous en prie, il ne fallait pas!** you shouldn't have!; **il faudrait qu'elle reste** she ought to stay; **il ne faudrait pas que je vous mette en retard** I'd better not make you late; **il faut toujours que tu fasses des histoires!** why do you always have to cause such a fuss!; **il a fallu qu'elle le raconte à tout le quartier!** she had to go and tell the whole neighbourhood! (**b**) *(locutions) Fam* **il faut ce qu'il faut!** you might as well do things in style!; **il faut voir** *(il faut attendre)* we'll have to wait and see; *(il faut réfléchir)* I/we will have to think about it; *Fam* **elle lui a répondu, faut voir comment!** you wouldn't believe the way she answered him/her!

2 s'en falloir *vpr* **il s'en est fallu de peu** *ou* **peu s'en est fallu qu'elle ne meure** she very nearly died; **10 livres ou peu s'en faut** the best part of £10; **loin** *ou* **tant s'en faut** far from it

fallu *voir* falloir

falot¹ [falo] *nm (lanterne)* lantern

falot², -e [falo, -ɔt] *adj* dreary, drab

falsification [falsifikasjɔ̃] *nf (de documents, de comptes)* falsification; *(d'une signature)* forging

falsifier [66] [falsifje] *vt (document, comptes)* to falsify; *(signature)* to forge

falzar [falzar] *nm Fam Br* trousers, *Am* pants

famé, -e [fame] *adj* **mal f.** disreputable

famélique [famelik] *adj* half-starved

fameusement [faməzmɑ̃] *adv Fam (très)* incredibly

fameux, -euse [famø, -øz] *adj* (**a**) *(célèbre)* famous (**pour** for); **c'est donc ça, ton f. régime!** so this is your famous diet! (**b**) *Fam (excellent)* brilliant; **pas f.** not much good

familial, -e, -aux, -ales [familjal, -o] **1** *adj (vie, atmosphère)* family; *(entreprise, hôtel)* family-run; *(paquet, format)* family-size

2 *nf* **familiale** *(auto) Br* estate car, *Am* station wagon

familiariser [familjarize] **1** *vt* **f. qn avec qch** to familiarize sb with sth, to get sb used to sth

2 se familiariser *vpr* **se f. avec qch** *(en le pratiquant)* to familiarize oneself with sth; *(en s'y habituant)* to get used to sth; *(lieu)* to get to know sth

familiarité [familjarite] *nf* (**a**) *(désinvolture)* informality (**b**) **familiarités** *(libertés)* familiarities

familier, -ère [familje, -ɛr] **1** *adj* (**a**) *(désinvolte)* informal *(avec* with) (**b**) *(langage, expression)* colloquial (**c**) *(connu)* familiar (**à** to)

2 *nm,f (client)* regular visitor (**de** to)

familièrement [familjɛrmɑ̃] *adv* familiarly; **parler f. à qn** to be familiar with sb

famille [famij] *nf* (**a**) *(proches)* family; **de bonne f.** from a good family; **en f.** with one's family; *Fam* **un repas des familles** a cosy little meal; **f. monoparentale** one-parent family; **f. nombreuse,** *Suisse* **grande f.** large family (**b**) *(d'animaux, de langues, de plantes)* family; **f. littéraire/politique** literary/political circle

famine [famin] *nf* famine; **crier f.** to be starving

fan [fan], **fana** [fana] *nmf Fam* fan

fanal, -aux [fanal, -o] *nm (lanterne)* lantern

fanatique [fanatik] **1** *adj* fanatical (**de** about)

2 *nmf* fanatic; **f. de football** football fanatic

fanatiser [fanatize] *vt* to make fanatical

fanatisme [fanatism] *nm* fanaticism

faner [fane] **1** *vi (fleur)* to wither; *Fig (beauté, teint)* to fade

2 se faner *vpr (fleur)* to wither; *Fig (beauté, teint)* to fade

fanes [fan] *nfpl (de carottes, de radis)* tops

fanfare [fɑ̃far] *nf (orchestre)* brass band; **réveil en f.** brutal awakening

fanfaron, -onne [fɑ̃farɔ̃, -ɔn] **1** *adj* boastful

2 *nm,f* braggart; **faire le f.** to brag, to boast

fanfaronnades [fɑ̃farɔnad] *nfpl* bragging, boasting

fanfaronner [fɑ̃farɔne] *vi* to brag, to boast

fanfreluches [fɑ̃frəlyʃ] *nfpl Péj* frills

fange [fɑ̃ʒ] *nf Litt* mire; **élevé dans la f.** brought up in the gutter

fanion [fanjɔ̃] *nm (d'un club)* pennant; *(balise)* flag; **fanions** *(guirlandes)* bunting

fanon [fanɔ̃] *nm (de baleine)* whalebone

fantaisie [fɑ̃tezi] **1** *adj inv* **collants f.** patterned tights; **kirsch f.** kirsch-flavoured liqueur

2 *nf (envie)* whim; **faire qch à sa f.** to do sth as the fancy takes one (**b**) *(créativité)* imagination (**c**) *(œuvre musicale)* fantasia (**d**) *(bibelot)* novelty; **bijoux de f.** costume jewellery

fantaisiste [fɑ̃tezist] **1** *adj (personne)* eccentric; *(interprétation)* fanciful; *(horaires, mode de vie)* unorthodox

2 *nmf (comédien)* variety artist

fantasmagorique [fɑ̃tasmagɔrik] *adj* phantasmagorical

fantasme [fɑ̃tasm] *nm* fantasy

fantasmer [fɑ̃tasme] *vi* to fantasize (**sur** about)

fantasque [fɑ̃task] *adj* whimsical

fantassin [fɑ̃tasɛ̃] *nm* foot soldier, infantryman

fantastique [fɑ̃tastik] **1** *adj* (**a**) *(littérature, conte, film)* fantasy (**b**) *Fam (excellent)* fantastic (**c**) *(créature)* fantastic

2 *nm* **le f.** the fantastic; *(littérature)* fantasy literature

fantoche [fɑ̃tɔʃ] **1** *nm* puppet

2 *adj* **gouvernement f.** puppet government

fantomatique [fɑ̃tɔmatik] *adj* ghostly

fantôme [fɑ̃tom] **1** *nm* ghost, phantom

2 *adj (ville, train)* ghost

fanzine [fɑ̃zin] *nm* fanzine

FAO [ɛfao] *nf* (**a**) *(abrév* **fabrication assistée par ordinateur**) CAM (**b**) *(abrév* **Food and Agricultural Organization**) FAO

faon [fɑ̃] *nm* fawn

FAQ [fak] *Ordinat (abrév* **frequently asked questions, foire aux questions**) FAQ

far [far] *nm* **f. breton** custard flan with prunes

faramineux, -euse [faraminø, -øz] *adj Fam* phenomenal

farandole [farãdɔl] *nf* farandole

farce [fars] *nf* (**a**) *(tour)* (practical) joke, prank; **faire une f. à qn** to play a (practical) joke on sb; **magasin de farces et attrapes** joke shop; *Can Fam* **c'est pas des farces!** I'm not kidding! (**b**) *(préparation culinaire)* stuffing (**c**) *(pièce de théâtre)* farce

farceur, -euse [farsœr, -øz] **1** *adj* mischievous **2** *nm,f* (practical) joker, prankster

farcir [farsir] **1** *vt* (**a**) *(volaille, légume)* to stuff (**b**) *Fam (remplir)* to cram (**de** with) **2 se farcir** *vpr Fam* **se f. qch** *(corvée)* to get landed with sth; **se f. qn/qch** *(supporter)* to put up with sb/sth

fard [far] *nm* make-up; *Fam* **piquer un f.** to go red; **f. à joues** blusher; **f. à paupières** eye shadow

fardeau, -x [fardo] *nm* load; *Fig* burden

farder [farde] **1** *vt (maquiller)* to make up **2 se farder** *vpr* to put on one's make-up; **se f. les yeux** to put eye shadow on

farfadet [farfadɛ] *nm* goblin

farfelu, -e [farfəly] *Fam* **1** *adj (personne, idée)* weird **2** *nm,f* weirdo

farfouiller [farfuje] *vi Fam* to rummage (**dans** through)

farine [farin] *nf* flour; **f. de blé** wheat flour; **f. de maïs** *Br* cornflour, *Am* cornstarch

farineux, -euse [farinø, -øz] **1** *adj* (**a**) *Péj (pommes de terre, banane)* floury (**b**) *(contenant de la fécule)* starchy **2** *nmpl* starchy food

farniente [farnjɛnte] *nm* idleness

farouche [faruʃ] *adj* (**a**) *(animal)* timid; *(personne)* shy (**b**) *(haine, air, regard)* fierce

farouchement [faruʃmã] *adv* fiercely

fart [fart] *nm* (ski) wax

fascicule [fasikyl] *nm (d'une publication)* instalment; *(brochure)* brochure

fascinant, -e [fasinã, -ãt] *adj* fascinating

fascination [fasinasjɔ̃] *nf* fascination; **exercer une f. sur qn** to fascinate sb

fasciner [fasine] *vt* (**a**) *(impressionner)* to fascinate (**b**) *(charmer)* to captivate

fascisme [faʃism] *nm* fascism

fasciste [faʃist] *adj & nmf* fascist

fashion [faʃœn] *adj inv Fam* trendy

fasse *etc voir* **faire**

faste¹ [fast] *nm* splendour

faste² *adj (jour)* lucky; *(période)* good

fast-food *(pl* **fast-foods**) [fastfud] *nm* fast-food restaurant

fastidieux, -euse [fastidjø, -øz] *adj* tedious

fastoche [fastɔʃ] *adj Fam* dead easy

fastueux, -euse [fastɥø, -øz] *adj* sumptuous

fat [fa(t)] *nm* conceited person

fatal, -e, -als, -ales [fatal] *adj* (**a**) *(mortel)* fatal; *Fig* fatal (**à** for); **le choc lui a été f.** the shock killed him/her; *Ordinat* **erreur fatale** fatal error (**b**) *(inévitable)* inevitable

fatalement [fatalmã] *adv* inevitably

fatalisme [fatalism] *nm* fatalism

fataliste [fatalist] **1** *adj* fatalistic **2** *nmf* fatalist

fatalité [fatalite] *nf* (**a**) *(malédiction)* bad luck (**b**) *(inévitabilité)* inevitability

fatidique [fatidik] *adj* fateful

fatigant, -e [fatigã, -ãt] *adj* (**a**) *(épuisant)* tiring; **c'est f. pour le cœur/les yeux** it's a strain on the heart/the eyes (**b**) *(ennuyeux)* tiresome

fatigue [fatig] *nf* tiredness; **tomber** *ou* **être mort de f.** to be dead tired; **f. nerveuse** nervous exhaustion; **f. oculaire** eyestrain

fatigué, -e [fatige] *adj* (**a**) *(las)* tired; **f. par sa promenade** tired from one's walk; **f. par le voyage** travelworn; **f. de qn/qch** tired of sb/sth; **f. de faire qch** tired or weary of doing sth (**b**) *(estomac, foie)* upset; *(cœur)* strained

fatiguer [fatige] **1** *vt* (**a**) *(personne)* to tire (out); *(yeux, cœur)* to strain; *(estomac, foie)* to upset; *Ironique* **si ça ne te fatigue pas trop** if it's not too much of an effort (**b**) *(ennuyer)* to wear out (**c**) *Fam* **f. la salade** to toss the salad **2** *vi (personne)* to get tired; *(moteur, voiture)* to labour **3 se fatiguer** *vpr* (**a**) *(s'épuiser)* to get tired; **se f. à faire qch** to tire oneself out doing sth; **se f. les yeux/le cœur** to strain one's eyes/heart; *Ironique* **tu ne t'es pas fatigué** you didn't exactly strain yourself; **ne te fatigue pas, je m'en charge** don't bother, I'll see to it (**b**) *(se lasser)* **se f. de qn/qch** to get tired of sb/sth

fatras [fatra] *nm* jumble, muddle

fatwa [fatwa] *nf Rel* fatwa; **prononcer une f. contre qn** to declare or issue a fatwa against sb

faubourg [fobur] *nm* suburb

fauche [foʃ] *nf Fam* thieving; **il y a de la f.** there are thieves about

fauché, -e [foʃe] *adj Fam* **f. (comme les blés)** *Br* (stony) broke, *Am* (flat) broke

faucher [foʃe] *vt* (**a**) *(herbe, champ)* to mow; *(blé)* to reap (**b**) *(piéton)* to mow down; **se faire f. par une voiture** to get mown down by a car (**c**) *Fam (voler)* to pinch; **se faire f. qch** to get sth pinched

faucheur, -euse [foʃœr, -øz] **1** *nm,f (de blé)* reaper; *(d'herbe)* mower **2** *nm (insecte) Br* harvestman, *Am* daddy-long-legs **3** *nf* **faucheuse** *(machine) (pour le blé)* reaper; *(pour l'herbe)* mower; **la Faucheuse** *(la Mort)* the Grim Reaper

faucheux [foʃø] *nm Br* harvestman, *Am* daddy-long-legs

faucille [fosij] *nf* sickle; **la f. et le marteau** the hammer and sickle

faucon [fokɔ̃] *nm* falcon, hawk; **f. pèlerin** peregrine falcon

faudra *etc voir* **falloir**

faufiler [fofile] **1** *vt* to tack, to baste **2 se faufiler** *vpr (à travers la foule)* to work one's way (**à travers** through); **il s'était faufilé parmi les invités** he had slipped in with the guests

faune [fon] *nf (animaux)* fauna, animal life; *Fig & Péj* **f. des boîtes de nuit** the nightclub set; **elle fréquente une f. bizarre** she mixes with a funny crowd

faussaire [fosɛr] *nmf* forger

fausse [fos] *adj voir* **faux¹**

faussement [fosmã] *adv* (**a**) *(injustement)* wrongly, falsely (**b**) *(de façon hypocrite)* deceptively

fausser [fose] **1** *vt* (**a**) *(clef, axe)* to buckle, to bend (**b**) *(réalité, résultat)* to distort (**c**) **f. compagnie à qn** to give sb the slip **2 se fausser** *vpr* (**a**) *(voix)* to become strained (**b**) *(clef, axe)* to buckle, to bend

fausset [fosɛ] *nm Mus* falsetto; **voix de f.** falsetto voice

fausseté [foste] *nf* (**a**) *(d'une information, d'un raisonnement)* falseness (**b**) *(hypocrisie)* duplicity
faut *voir* falloir
faute [fot] *nf* (**a**) *(erreur)* mistake, error; *(au football)* foul; *(au tennis)* fault; **faire une f.** to make a mistake *or* an error; **être en f.** to be at fault; **prendre qn en f.** to catch sb out; **c'est de ma f.!** it's my fault!; **f. d'étourderie** *ou* **d'inattention** careless mistake; **f. de français** grammatical mistake; **f. de frappe** typing mistake; **f. d'orthographe** spelling mistake; **f. professionnelle** professional misconduct (**b**) *(manque)* **sans f.** without fail; **f. de temps** for lack of time; **f. de mieux** for lack *or* want of anything better; **f. de quoi** failing which, otherwise; **ce n'est pas f. d'avoir essayé** it's not for want of trying
fauteuil [fotœj] *nm* (**a**) *(siège)* armchair, easy chair; **f. à bascule** rocking chair; **f. d'orchestre** seat in the *Br* stalls *or Am* orchestra; **f. pivotant** swivel chair; **f. roulant** wheelchair (**b**) *Fig (à l'Académie française)* seat
fauteur [fotœr] *nm* **f. de troubles** troublemaker
fautif, -ive [fotif, -iv] **1** *adj* (**a**) *(coupable)* at fault, in the wrong (**b**) *(incorrect)* faulty
2 *nm,f (coupable)* person at fault *or* in the wrong
fauve [fov] **1** *adj* (**a**) *(roux)* fawn (**b**) *(odeur)* musky (**c**) *(en peinture)* Fauvist
2 *nm* (**a**) *(grand félin)* big cat; **sentir le f.** to smell of sweat (**b**) *(couleur)* fawn (**c**) *(en peinture)* Fauvist
fauvette [fovɛt] *nf* warbler
fauvisme [fovism] *nm* Fauvism
faux¹, fausse [fo, fos] **1** *adj* (**a**) *(incorrect)* wrong; **c'est un f. problème** that's not the real problem; *Fam* **t'as tout f.** you're completely wrong; **f. ami** false friend; **faire une fausse couche** to have a miscarriage; **faire une fausse note** to hit a wrong note; **faire fausse route** to take the wrong road; *Fig* to be on the wrong track; **faire un f. sens** *(en traduisant)* to give an inaccurate translation; *(en français)* to give an inaccurate definition (**b**) *(mensonger)* false, untrue; *Fam* **c'est un f. jeton** *ou* **cul** he's two-faced; **f. témoignage** perjury (**c**) *(injustifié)* (alerte, espoirs)* false (**d**) *(postiche)* false (**e**) *(billet, pièce, document)* forged; *(tableau, bijoux)* fake; *(plafond)* false (**f**) *Péj (hypocrite)* false
2 *adv (chanter, sonner)* out of tune, off key; *Fig* **sonner f.** not to ring true
3 *nm* (**a**) *(tableau, sculpture)* fake (**b**) *(document)* forgery; **f. en écriture** forgery
faux² *nf* scythe
faux-cul *(pl* **faux-culs)** [foky] *très Fam* **1** *adj* **il est f.** he's a two-faced bastard
2 *nmf* two-faced bastard, *f* two-faced bitch
faux-filet *(pl* **faux-filets)** [fofilɛ] *nm* sirloin
faux-fuyant *(pl* **faux-fuyants)** [fofчijã] *nm (prétexte)* subterfuge
faux-monnayeur *(pl* **faux-monnayeurs)** [fomɔnɛjœr] *nm* forger, counterfeiter
faux-semblant *(pl* **faux-semblants)** [fosãblã] *nm* pretence, sham
faveur [favœr] *nf* (**a**) *(considération)* favour; **avoir la f. de qn** to be in favour with sb; **de f.** *(régime, traitement)* special (**b**) *(privilège)* favour; **faire une f. à qn** to do sb a favour (**c**) **être en f. de qch** *(être favorable à)* to be in favour of sth; **en ma/sa f.** *(à mon/son avantage)* in my/his/her favour, to my/his/her advantage (**d**) *(ruban)* favour
favorable [favɔrabl] *adj* favourable (**à** to)
favorablement [favɔrabləmã] *adv* favourably

favori, -ite [favɔri, -it] *adj & nm,f* favourite
favoris [favɔri] *nmpl* sideburns
favorisé, -e [favɔrize] *adj (milieu, famille)* fortunate
favoriser [favɔrize] *vt* (**a**) *(avantager)(personne)* to favour (**b**) *(encourager)(croissance, emploi)* to encourage, to promote
favoritisme [favɔritism] *nm* favouritism
fax [faks] *nm (appareil)* fax (machine); *(message)* fax; **envoyer qch par f.** to send sth by fax; **f. modem** fax modem
faxer [fakse] *vt* to fax
fayot [fajo] *Fam nm* (**a**) *(haricot sec)* bean (**b**) *(élève)* crawler
fayotage [fajotaʒ] *nm Fam* crawling
fayoter [fajote] *vi Fam* to crawl
fébrile [febril] *adj aussi Fig* feverish
fébrilement [febrilmã] *adv* feverishly
fébrilité [febrilite] *nf* feverishness
fécond, -e [fekɔ̃, -ɔ̃d] *adj (femme, femelle, terre, imagination)* fertile; *(écrivain)* prolific; *Fig* **f. en qch** *(période, moment)* full of sth
fécondation [fekɔ̃dasjɔ̃] *nf (d'une femme, d'une femelle)* impregnation; *(d'un œuf, d'un ovule)* fertilization; **f. artificielle** artificial insemination; **f. in vitro** in vitro fertilization
féconder [fekɔ̃de] *vt (femme, femelle)* to impregnate; *(œuf, ovule)* to fertilize
fécondité [fekɔ̃dite] *nf* (**a**) *(d'une femme, d'une femelle)* fertility (**b**) *(d'un écrivain)* productiveness
fécule [fekyl] *nf* starch
féculent, -e [fekylã, -ãt] **1** *adj* starchy
2 *nm* starchy food
FED [ɛfəde] *nm (abrév* **Fonds européen de développement)** EDF
FEDER [fedɛr] *nm (abrév* **Fonds européen de développement régional)** ERDF
fédéral, -e, -aux, -ales [federal, -o] *adj* federal
fédéralisme [federalism] *nm* federalism
fédéraliste [federalist] *adj & nmf* federalist
fédérateur, -trice [federatœr, -tris] *adj* federal
fédération [federasjɔ̃] *nf* federation
fédéré, -e [federe] *adj* federate
fée [fe] *nf* fairy; *Hum* **f. du logis** domestic goddess; *Suisse* **f. verte** absinthe
feed-back [fidbak] *nm* feedback
féerie [feri, feeri] *nf (spectacle magnifique)* enchanting display
féerique [ferik, feerik] *adj (personnage, monde)* fairy; *(vision)* enchanting
feignais *etc voir* feindre
feignant, -e [fɛɲã, -ãt] *Fam* **1** *adj* bone idle
2 *nm,f* idler
feindre [54] [fɛ̃dr] *vt (maladie, sentiment)* to feign; **inutile de f.** it's no use pretending; **f. de faire qch** to pretend to do sth
feint, -e [fɛ̃, fɛ̃t] *adj (maladie, joie)* feigned
feinte² [fɛ̃t] *nf* (**a**) *(ruse)* ruse (**b**) *(au football, au rugby)* dummy
feinter [fɛ̃te] **1** *vt Fam (duper)* to take in
2 *vi (au football, au rugby)* to dummy
fêlé, -e [fele] *adj* (**a**) *(verre, voix)* cracked (**b**) *Fam (fou)* cracked, nuts
fêler [fele] *vt* to crack
félicitations [felisitasjɔ̃] *nfpl* congratulations (**pour** on)
féliciter [felisite] **1** *vt* to congratulate (**de/pour** on); **f. qn d'avoir fait qch** to congratulate sb on having done sth

2 se féliciter *vpr* **se f.** **de qch/d'avoir fait qch** to congratulate oneself on sth/on having done sth
félin, -e [felɛ̃, -in] *adj & nm* feline
fêlure [felyr] *nf aussi Fig* crack
femelle [fəmɛl] *adj & nf* female
féminin, -e [feminɛ̃, -in] **1** *adj (personne, charme, visage)* feminine; *(hormone, population, sexe)* female; *(équipe, magazine, mode)* women's
2 *nm Gram* feminine; **au f.** in the feminine
féminiser [feminize] **1** *vt* (**a**) *(ouvrir aux femmes)* to increase the number of women in (**b**) *(rendre efféminé)* to make effeminate
2 se féminiser *vpr* (**a**) *(profession, institution, carrière)* to attract more women (**b**) *(homme)* to become effeminate
féminisme [feminism] *nm* feminism
féministe [feminist] *adj & nmf* feminist
féminité [feminite] *nf* femininity
femme [fam] *nf* (**a**) *(adulte de sexe féminin)* woman; **des femmes, de la f.** *(libération, émancipation, droits)* women's; **la f. de ma vie** the love of my life; **elle est très f.** she's very feminine; *Fam* **une bonne f.** a woman; **f. d'affaires** businesswoman; **f. de chambre** *(dans un hôtel)* (chamber)maid; **f. fatale** femme fatale; **f. au foyer** housewife; **f. de ménage,** *Belg* **f. d'ouvrage** cleaning lady; **f. du monde** society woman; **f. de tête** forceful woman (**b**) *(épouse)* wife
femmelette [famlɛt] *nf Péj (homme)* weakling
fémur [femyr] *nm* thighbone, *Spéc* femur
FEN [fɛn] *nf (abrév* **Fédération de l'Éducation Nationale***)* = largest French teachers' union
fenaison [fənɛzɔ̃] *nf* haymaking
fendant, -e [fɑ̃dɑ̃, -ɑ̃t] *adj Fam* hilarious
fendiller [fɑ̃dije] **1** *vt (bois, vernis)* to crack; *(peau, lèvres)* to chap
2 se fendiller *vpr (bois, vernis)* to crack; *(peau, lèvres)* to chap
fendre [fɑ̃dr] **1** *vt* (**a**) *(bois)* to split; *(pierre, sol)* to crack; **f. le cœur à qn** to break sb's heart (**b**) *(traverser) (flots, mer)* to plough through; *(air)* to cut through
2 se fendre *vpr* (**a**) *(bois)* to split; *(pierre, sol)* to crack (**b**) *Fam* **se f. de qch** *(d'une somme)* to fork out sth; *(d'un cadeau)* to fork out on sth; **tu ne t'es pas fendu** *(ce n'était pas cher)* it didn't break the bank; *(tu ne t'es pas fatigué)* you didn't strain yourself (**c**) *Fam* **se f. la pipe** *ou* **la pêche** *ou* **la poire** to split one's sides (laughing)
fendu, -e [fɑ̃dy] *adj (jupe)* slit
fenêtre [fənɛtr] *nf* (**a**) *(ouverture)* window; **f. à guillotine** sash window (**b**) *Ordinat* window; **f. d'aide** help window; **f. déroulante** pull-down window
fennec [fenɛk] *nm* fennec
fenouil [fənuj] *nm* fennel
fente [fɑ̃t] *nf* (**a**) *(dans le bois)* split; *(dans le sol, dans un mur)* crack (**b**) *(d'une tirelire, d'une boîte aux lettres)* slot
féodal, -e, -aux, -ales [feɔdal, -o] *adj* feudal
féodalité [feɔdalite] *nf* feudalism
fer [fɛr] *nm* (**a**) *(métal)* iron; *Fig* **de f.** *(discipline, volonté)* iron; *(santé)* cast-iron; **croire qch dur comme f.** to believe very firmly in sth; **f. forgé** wrought iron (**b**) *(objet en fer)* **f. à cheval** horseshoe; *Fam* **les quatre fers en l'air** flat on one's back; *Fig* **f. de lance** spearhead (**c**) *(outil)* **f. à repasser** iron; **donner un coup de f. à qch** to iron sth; **marquer qch au f. rouge** to brand sth; **f. à souder** soldering iron (**d**) **fers** *(chaînes)* irons

ferai *etc voir* **faire**
fer-blanc (*pl* **fers-blancs**) [fɛrblɑ̃] *nm* tin(plate); **en f. tin**
ferblanterie [fɛrblɑ̃tri] *nf* (**a**) *(commerce)* tinplate trade (**b**) *(articles)* tinware
férié, -e [ferje] *adj* **lundi prochain est f.** next Monday is a (public) holiday
férir [ferir] *vt* **sans coup f.** without any difficulty
ferme¹ [fɛrm] **1** *adj* (**a**) *(dur)* firm (**b**) *Jur* **trois ans de prison f., trois ans fermes** three years' imprisonment
2 *adv (travailler)* hard; *(discuter)* keenly; **s'ennuyer f.** to be bored stiff
ferme² *nf* farm; **produits de la f.** farm produce
fermé, -e [fɛrme] *adj* (**a**) *(porte, récipient, boutique)* closed, shut; *(route)* closed (**b**) *(expression, visage)* impassive; **être f. à qch** *(ne pas être sensible à)* to have no appreciation of sth (**c**) *(société, club, milieu)* exclusive, select
fermement [fɛrməmɑ̃] *adv* firmly
ferment [fɛrmɑ̃] *nm aussi Fig* ferment
fermentation [fɛrmɑ̃tasjɔ̃] *nf* fermentation
fermenter [fɛrmɑ̃te] *vi* to ferment
fermer [fɛrme] **1** *vt* (**a**) *(porte, boîte, livre)* to close, to shut; *(maison)* to shut up; *(rideaux)* to close, to draw; *(vêtement)* to fasten, to do up; *(parenthèse)* to close; *(enveloppe)* to seal; **f. sa porte à qn** to close one's door to sb; **f. les yeux/la bouche** to close one's eyes/mouth; *Fig* **f. les yeux sur qch** to turn a blind eye to sth; *Fam* **je n'ai pas fermé l'œil** I didn't sleep a wink; *Fam* **f. sa gueule, la f.** to shut up, to shut one's mouth (**b**) *(frontière, pays)* to close off (**c**) *(robinet, eau, électricité)* to turn off (**d**) *(compte bancaire)* to close (**e**) *(entreprise) (temporairement)* to close, to shut; *(définitivement)* to close down; **f. boutique** to shut up shop
2 *vi* (**a**) *(porte, boîte)* to close, to shut; **f. bien/mal** to close/not to close properly (**b**) *(entreprise, magasin) (temporairement)* to close, to shut; *(définitivement)* to close down
3 se fermer *vpr (porte, boîte, yeux)* to close, to shut; *(vêtement)* to fasten, to do up (**b**) *(visage)* to freeze; *(personne)* to clam up
fermeté [fɛrməte] *nf* firmness; **avec f.** firmly
fermeture [fɛrmətyr] *nf* (**a**) *(d'une porte)* closing, shutting; *(d'une route, d'une frontière, d'un débat)* closing (**b**) *(cessation d'activité)* closing; **heure de f.** closing time (**c**) *(d'un compte bancaire)* closing (**d**) **f. Éclair®** *ou* **à glissière** *Br* zip, *Am* zipper (**e**) *Ordinat (d'un fichier, d'une fenêtre)* closing; *(d'une commande)* ending
fermier, -ère [fɛrmje, -ɛr] **1** *adj (poulet)* free-range; *(beurre)* dairy
2 *nm,f* farmer
fermoir [fɛrmwar] *nm (de collier, de sac)* clasp; *Can (fermeture à glissière) Br* zip, *Am* zipper
féroce [ferɔs] *adj (animal, personne, critique)* ferocious; *(joie, moquerie)* savage; *(appétit)* ravenous
férocement [ferɔsmɑ̃] *adv* ferociously
férocité [ferɔsite] *nf* ferocity
Féroé [ferɔe] *nfpl* **les (îles) F.** the Faroe Islands, the Faroes
ferraille [fɛraj] *nf* (**a**) *(débris de fer)* scrap (iron); **mettre qch à la f.** to put sth on the scrap heap (**b**) *Fam (petite monnaie)* small change, *Br* shrapnel

ferré, -e [fɛre] *adj* (**a**) *(chaussure)* hobnailed; *(canne)* metal-tipped (**b**) *(calé)* **être f. en qch** to be well up in sth

ferrer [fɛre] *vt* (**a**) *(cheval)* to shoe (**b**) *(poisson)* to strike

ferreux, -euse [fɛrø, -øz] *adj* ferrous

ferronnerie [fɛrɔnri] *nf* (**a**) *(objets)* **f. (d'art)** (decorative) ironwork (**b**) *(travail)* ironwork (**c**) *(atelier)* ironworks *(singulier)*

ferronnier, -ère [fɛrɔnje, -ɛr] *nm,f* **f. (d'art)** worker in wrought iron

ferroviaire [fɛrɔvjɛr] *adj (réseau, trafic, ligne)* Br railway, *Am* railroad; *(transports)* rail

ferrugineux, -euse [fɛryʒinø, -øz] *adj* ferruginous

ferrure [fɛryr] *nf* (**a**) *(garniture)* fitting (**b**) *(d'un cheval)* shoeing

ferry [fɛri] *nm* ferry

ferry-boat *(pl* **ferry-boats**) [fɛribot] *nm* ferry

fertile [fɛrtil] *adj aussi Fig* fertile; *Fig* **f. en qch** *(période)* full of sth

fertilisation [fɛrtilizasjɔ̃] *nf* fertilization

fertiliser [fɛrtilize] *vt* to fertilize

fertilité [fɛrtilite] *nf* fertility

féru, -e [fery] *adj* **f. de qch** passionately interested in sth

férule [feryl] *nf Litt* **être sous la f. de qn** to be under sb's sway

fervent, -e [fɛrvɑ̃, -ɑ̃t] **1** *adj* fervent; *(catholique)* devout
2 *nm,f* devotee (**de** of)

ferveur [fɛrvœr] *nf* fervour; **avec f.** fervently

fesse [fɛs] *nf* buttock; **fesses** *Br* bottom, *Am* butt

fessée [fese] *nf* spanking; **donner une f. à qn** to give sb a spanking

fessier, -ère [fesje, -ɛr] **1** *adj (muscle)* buttock, *Spéc* gluteal
2 *nm (muscle)* gluteal muscle

festif, -ive [fɛstif, -iv] *adj* festive

festin [fɛstɛ̃] *nm* feast, banquet

festival, -als [fɛstival] *nm* festival; **le f. d'Avignon** = theatre festival held in Avignon; **le f. de Cannes** the Cannes film festival

festivités [fɛstivite] *nfpl* festivities

feston [fɛstɔ̃] *nm* (**a**) *(en broderie)* scallop; **à festons** scalloped (**b**) *(guirlande)* & *Archit* festoon

festoyer [32] [fɛstwaje] *vi* to feast

feta [feta] *nf* feta (cheese)

fêtard, -e [fetar, -ard] *nm,f Fam* party animal

fête [fɛt] *nf* (**a**) *(célébration publique)* fête, fair; *(événement culturel)* festival; **f. foraine** funfair; **la f. des Mères/Pères** Mother's/Father's Day; **la f. de la Musique** = annual music festival held on 21 June; **la f. des Rois** Twelfth Night (**b**) *(soirée)* party; **organiser** *ou* **faire une f.** to have a party (**c**) *(manifestation de joie)* **en f.** in a festive mood; **avoir le cœur en f.** to be over the moon; *Fam* **faire la f.** to party; **être de la f.** to be one of the party; **faire f. à qn** to make a fuss of sb (**d**) *(du saint dont on porte le nom)* saint's day; *Ironique* **ça va être ta f.!** you're in for it!; *Fam* **faire sa f. à qn** to give sb a good hiding (**e**) *(jour chômé)* holiday; **les fêtes (de fin d'année)** Christmas and New Year, *Am* the holidays; **f. légale** *Br* bank holiday, *Am* legal holiday; **f. nationale** national holiday; **la f. du Travail** Labour Day

Fête

The French traditionally wish "bonne fête" to a person who has the same name as the saint commemorated on that particular day.

Fête de la Musique

This annual event takes place throughout France on 21 June, the summer solstice. Both amateur and professional musicians take to the streets and there are many impromptu live performances, with bars and restaurants as well as museums and hospitals serving as free venues for jazz, classical, rock and many other styles of music. The festival was originally launched in 1982 by the minister of culture, Jack Lang, following the election of François Mitterand's socialist government. Such is its success and popularity in France that the event has now spread to many other European countries.

Fête-Dieu *(pl* **Fêtes-Dieu**) [fɛtdjø] *nf* **la F.** Corpus Christi

fêter [fete] **1** *(a) (anniversaire, événement)* to celebrate (**b**) *(personne)* to fête
2 se fêter *vpr* **ça se fête!** this calls for a celebration!

fétiche [fetiʃ] **1** *adj* lucky
2 *nm (objet de culte)* fetish; *(mascotte)* mascot

fétichisme [fetiʃism] *nm* fetishism

fétichiste [fetiʃist] **1** *adj* fetishistic
2 *nmf* fetishist

fétide [fetid] *adj* fetid

fétu [fety] *nm* **f. (de paille)** wisp of straw

feu¹, -x [fø] **1** *nm* (**a**) *(élément, flammes, incendie)* fire; **mettre (le) f. à qch** to set fire to sth; **prendre f.** to catch fire; **allumer** *ou* **faire un f.** to make a fire; **au f.!** fire!; **en f.** *(lieu)* on fire; *Fig (joues, visage)* burning; **mettre une ville à f. et à sang** to ransack a town; **être tout f. tout flamme** to be burning with enthusiasm; **ne pas faire long f.** not to last long; **dans le f. de l'action** in the heat of the action; *Fig* **sous le f. des projecteurs** in the limelight; *Vulg* **avoir le f. au cul** *(être pressé)* to be in a mad rush; *(sexuellement)* to be always gagging for it; **f. d'artifice** *(spectacle)* fireworks display; **f. de Bengale** Bengal light; **f. de camp** campfire; **f. de cheminée** fire in the hearth; **f. de forêt** forest fire; **f. de joie** bonfire; *Fig* **f. de paille** flash in the pan; *Can* **f. sauvage** cold sore (**b**) *(pour allumer une cigarette)* **avez-vous du f.?** have you got a light? (**c**) *(brûleur)* burner; **à f. doux** *ou* **à petit f.** over a low heat; **à f. vif** over a high heat (**d**) *(sur la chaussée)* **f. rouge/vert** red/green light; **feux de signalisation** *ou* **tricolores** traffic lights; *Fig* **donner le f. vert à qn** to give sb the green light (**e**) *(phare)* **feux de brouillard** *ou* **antibrouillard** fog lamps; **feux de croisement** *Am* dipped headlights, *Am* low beams; **feux de détresse** hazard (warning) lights; **feux de position** sidelights; **feux de stationnement** parking lights (**f**) *(tirs)* **faire f.** to fire, to shoot; **ouvrir le f.** to open fire; *Fig* **être pris entre deux feux** to be caught in the crossfire
2 *adj inv* **noir et f.** black-and-tan

feu², -e *adj* **f. M. Perrin** the late Mr Perrin; **f. mon mari** my late husband

feuillage [fœjaʒ] *nm* leaves, foliage

feuille [fœj] *nf* (**a**) *(de plante, d'arbre)* leaf; **f. morte** dead leaf; **f. de vigne** fig leaf (**b**) *(de papier)* sheet; **f. volante** loose sheet (**c**) *(journal)* paper; *Péj* **f. de chou** rag (**d**) *(document)* **f. d'heures** time sheet; **f. d'impôt** tax return; **f. de maladie** = form given by doctor to patient for claiming reimbursement from Social Security; **f. de paie** *ou* **paye** payslip; **f. de soins**

medical expenses claim form (**e**) *Ordinat* **f. de calcul** spreadsheet

feuillet [fœjɛ] *nm* leaf

feuilleté, -e [fœjte] **1** *adj* (**a**) *(pâte)* flaky (**b**) *(verre)* laminated
2 *nm* **f. au jambon/au fromage** ham/cheese pasty

feuilleter [42] [fœjte] *vt* (**a**) *(livre)* to leaf through (**b**) *Ordinat* **f. en arrière** to page up; **f. en avant** to page down

feuilleton [fœjtɔ̃] *nm* serial; **f. télévisé** *(sur plusieurs semaines)* television serial; *(sur plusieurs années)* soap opera

feuillu, -e [fœjy] **1** *adj* (**a**) *(ayant beaucoup de feuilles)* leafy (**b**) *Bot* broad-leaved
2 *nm Bot* broad-leaved tree

feutre [føtr] *nm* (**a**) *(matière)* felt (**b**) *(chapeau)* felt hat (**c**) *(stylo)* felt-tip (pen)

feutré, -e [føtre] *adj* (**a**) *(garni de feutre)* felt(-covered) (**b**) *(assourdi)* muffled; **à pas feutrés** stealthily (**c**) *(vêtement)* matted

feutrer [føtre] **1** *vt* (**a**) *(garnir de feutre)* to cover with felt (**b**) *(assourdir)* to muffle (**c**) *(vêtement)* to mat
2 *vi (vêtement)* to felt
3 se feutrer *vpr (vêtement)* to felt

feutrine [føtrin] *nf* felt

fève [fɛv] *nf* (**a**) *(plante, graine)* broad bean (**b**) *(dans la galette des Rois)* charm (**c**) *Can (haricot)* bean

février [fevrije] *nm* February; *voir aussi* **janvier**

FF *Anciennement (abrév* **franc(s) français**) FF

FFI [ɛfɛfi] *nfpl Hist (abrév* **Forces françaises de l'intérieur**) = French Resistance forces in France during World War Two

FFL [ɛfɛfɛl] *nfpl Hist (abrév* **Forces françaises libres**) Free French Army

fiabilité [fjabilite] *nf* reliability

fiable [fjabl] *adj* reliable

fiacre [fjakr] *nm* hackney carriage

fiançailles [fjɑ̃saj] *nfpl* engagement

fiancé, -e [fjɑ̃se] *nm,f* fiancé, f fiancée

fiancer [16] [fjɑ̃se] **se fiancer** *vpr* to get engaged (**avec** to); **être fiancés** to be engaged

fiasco [fjasko] *nm* fiasco

fibre [fibr] *nf* fibre; *Fig* **avoir la f. maternelle** to be the maternal sort; **f. optique** fibre optics *(singulier)*; **f. de verre** fibreglass

fibreux, -euse [fibrø, -øz] *adj (tissu)* fibrous; *(viande)* stringy

fibrome [fibrom] *nm* fibroma

fibroscopie [fibrɔskɔpi] *nf Méd* fibre-optic endoscopy

ficelé, -e [fisəle] *adj Fam* (**a**) *(construit)* **bien/mal f.** *(scénario)* well/poorly put together (**b**) *(habillé)* dolled up

ficeler [9] [fisəle] *vt* (**a**) *(attacher)* to tie up; **ficelé comme un saucisson** trussed up like a chicken (**b**) *Fam (construire)* to put together

ficelle [fisɛl] *nf* (**a**) *(cordelette)* string; *Fig* **les ficelles du métier** the tricks of the trade (**b**) *(pain)* small French loaf

fiche¹ [fiʃ] *nf* (**a**) *(formulaire)* form; **f. d'état civil** = administrative record of birth details and marital status; **f. de paie** payslip; **f. signalétique** personal details card (**b**) *(carte)* (index) card; **mettre qch sur fiches** to card-index sth; **f. cartonnée** index card; **f. cuisine** *(dans un magazine)* recipe card (**c**) *(prise)* plug; *(broche)* pin

fiche² = **ficher³**

ficher¹ [fiʃe] *vt (mettre sur fiches) (informations)* to file; *(personne)* to put on file

ficher² **1** *vt (enfoncer)* **f. qch dans qch** to stick sth into sth
2 se ficher *vpr (balle, clou)* **se f. dans qch** to go into sth

ficher³ *Fam* **1** *vt* (**a**) *(mettre)* to stick; **f. qn par terre** to send sb sprawling; **f. qch par terre** *(exprès)* to chuck sth on the floor; *(accidentellement)* to knock sth over; *Fig* to mess sth up; **f. qn à la porte** to kick sb out; **f. une gifle à qn** to give sb a slap in the face (**b**) *Fam (faire)* to do; **qu'est-ce que tu fiches?** what are you up to? (**c**) *Fam* **f. le camp** to clear off
2 se ficher *vpr* (**a**) *(se mettre)* **se f. un coup** to wallop oneself; **se f. par terre** to go sprawling; **se f. dedans** to screw up (**b**) *(se moquer)* **se f. de qn** to poke fun at sb; **se f. du monde** to take the piss; **se f. de qch** not to give a damn about sth; **je m'en fiche** I don't give a damn

fichier [fiʃje] *nm* (**a**) *(ensemble de fiches)* (card-index) file (**b**) *(boîte)* card-index box; *(meuble)* card-index cabinet (**c**) *Ordinat* file; **f. joint** *(de courrier électronique)* attachment

fichu¹, -e [fiʃy] *adj Fam* (**a**) *(insupportable)* damn; *(caractère)* rotten (**b**) *(abîmé)* **être f.** to have had it; **c'est f. maintenant!** *(c'est raté)* we can forget it!; **c'est f. pour dimanche** we can forget Sunday (**c**) **être bien/mal f.** *(bien/mal bâti)* to have/not to have a nice body; *(bien/mal conçu)* to be well/badly designed; **être mal f.** *(malade)* to be under the weather (**d**) *(capable)* **être f. de faire qch** to be capable of doing sth

fichu² *nm* headscarf

fictif, -ive [fiktif, -iv] *adj* fictitious

fiction [fiksjɔ̃] *nf* fiction; **œuvre de f.** work of fiction; **la réalité dépasse la f.** truth is stranger than fiction

ficus [fikys] *nm* ficus

fidèle [fidɛl] **1** *adj* (**a**) *(ami, époux)* faithful; *(lecteur, auditeur, client)* regular; **être f. à qn** to be faithful to sb; **être f. à qch** to be loyal *or* true to sth; *Fig* **être f. au poste** to be always there (**b**) *(copie, traduction, récit)* faithful (**à** to); *(mémoire, souvenir)* reliable
2 *nmf* (**a**) *(croyant)* believer; **les fidèles** the faithful; *(à l'église)* the congregation (**b**) *(partisan)* loyal supporter (**de** of) (**c**) *(d'un programme télévisé)* regular viewer (**de** of); *(d'un programme radio)* regular listener (**de** to)

fidèlement [fidɛlmɑ̃] *adv* faithfully

fidélisation [fidelizasjɔ̃] *nf* **f. de la clientèle** building of customer loyalty

fidéliser [fidelize] *vt* to win the loyalty of; **f. la clientèle** to create customer loyalty

fidélité [fidelite] *nf* (**a**) *(d'un époux, d'un ami)* faithfulness (**à** to); *(d'un client, à un principe)* loyalty (**à** to) (**b**) *(d'une traduction, d'une reproduction)* faithfulness; *(de la mémoire)* reliability

Fidji [fidʒi] *nfpl* **les îles F.** Fiji

fiduciaire [fidysjɛr] *adj Fin* **monnaie f.** paper money

fief [fjɛf] *nm* fief; *Fig* **un f. du parti socialiste** a safe Socialist seat

fieffé, -e [fjɛfe] *adj* inveterate

fiel [fjɛl] *nm aussi Fig* gall

fier¹, fière [fjɛr] **1** *adj* (**a**) *(satisfait)* proud (**de** of); **être f. de faire qch** to be proud to do sth; **f. comme un paon** proud as a peacock (**b**) *(hautain, noble)* proud
2 *nm,f Péj* **faire le f.** to put on airs

fier² [66] [fje] **se fier** *vpr* **se f.** **à qn/qch** *(avoir confiance en)* to trust sb/sth; *(compter sur)* to rely on sb/sth
fièrement [fjɛrmɑ̃] *adv* proudly
fierté [fjɛrte] *nf* (**a**) *(satisfaction)* pride; **avec f.** proudly; **tirer f.** **de qch** to take pride in sth (**b**) *(amour-propre)* pride
fiesta [fjɛsta] *nf Fam* wild party
fièvre [fjɛvr] *nf* (**a**) *(élévation de la température)* fever; **avoir de la f.** to have a fever *or* a temperature; **elle a 40 de f.** she's got a temperature of 40 degrees; **avoir une f. de cheval** to have a raging fever (**b**) *(excitation)* frenzy; **dans la f. de la campagne électorale** in the heat *or* excitement of the election campaign
fiévreusement [fjevrøzmɑ̃] *adv* feverishly
fiévreux, -euse [fjevrø, -øz] *adj aussi Fig* feverish
fifre [fifr] *nm (instrument)* fife; *(joueur)* fife player
figé, -e [fiʒe] *adj* (**a**) *(locution)* set (**b**) *(sourire)* fixed (**c**) *(sauce)* congealed
figer [45] [fiʒe] **1** *vt* (**a**) *(immobiliser)* to paralyse; **figé sur place** rooted to the spot (**b**) *(solidifier)* to congeal **2 se figer** *vpr (huile, sauce)* to congeal; *(regard, traits, sourire)* to freeze
fignoler [fiɲɔle] *vt Fam* to put the finishing touches to; **il ne reste plus qu'à f.** it's just a matter now of adding the finishing touches
figue [fig] *nf* fig; **f. de Barbarie** prickly pear
figuier [fiɡje] *nm* fig tree; **f. de Barbarie** prickly pear
figurant, -e [fiɡyrɑ̃, -ɑ̃t] *nm,f (dans une pièce de théâtre)* walk-on; *(dans un film)* extra
figuratif, -ive [fiɡyratif, -iv] *adj* figurative
figuration [fiɡyrasjɔ̃] *nf* **faire de la f.** to play bit parts
figure [fiɡyr] *nf* (**a**) *(visage)* face; **faire bonne f.** to make a good impression; **faire f. d'intellectuel/de patriarche** to be seen as an intellectual/a patriarchal figure (**b**) *(représentation)* figure; *aussi Fig* **f. de proue** figurehead (**c**) *(personnage)* figure (**d**) *(en danse, en patinage artistique)* figure; **figures imposées** compulsory figures; **figures libres** freestyle (**e**) *Ling* **f. de rhétorique** figure of speech; **f. de style** stylistic device
figuré, -e [fiɡyre] **1** *adj (sens)* figurative **2** *nm* **au f.** in the figurative sense
figurer [fiɡyre] **1** *vt* to represent **2** *vi* (**a**) *(apparaître)* to appear (**sur/dans** on/in) (**b**) *(faire partie)* to figure (**parmi** among) **3 se figurer** *vpr* **se f. que** to imagine that; **il se figure qu'il va gagner de l'argent** he thinks *or* believes that he's going to make money; **je suis à sec, figure-toi** believe it or not, I'm broke
figurine [fiɡyrin] *nf* figurine
fil [fil] *nm* (**a**) *(brin, de toile d'araignée)* thread; **de f. en aiguille** little by little, bit by bit; *Fig* **ne tenir qu'à un f.** to hang by a thread; **f. conducteur** unifying thread; **f. à coudre** (sewing) thread; **f. dentaire** dental floss; **f. d'Écosse** lisle thread; **f. à plomb** plumb line; *Fig* **f. rouge** recurring theme (**b**) *(métallique, électrique)* wire; *Fig* **donner du f. à retordre à qn** to give sb trouble; **sans f.** *(rasoir, téléphone)* cordless; *(télégraphie, téléphonie)* wireless; **f. de fer** wire; **f. de fer barbelé** barbed wire (**c**) *Fam (téléphone)* **au bout du f.** on the line; **coup de f.** call; **donner** *ou* **passer un coup de f. à qn** to give sb a call, to call sb (up) (**d**) *(cours)* **au f. de l'eau** with the current; **au f. des jours/semaines** with the passing days/weeks; **perdre/reprendre le f. de qch** to lose/pick up the thread of sth (**e**) *(tissu)* linen (**f**) *(tranchant)* edge
filaire [filɛr] *adj (téléphone)* corded, plug-in

filament [filamɑ̃] *nm* (**a**) *(d'une ampoule électrique)* filament (**b**) *(de viande)* fibre (**c**) *Biol* filament
filandreux, -euse [filɑ̃drø, -øz] *adj (viande, légumes)* stringy
filant, -e [filɑ̃, -ɑ̃t] *adj voir* **étoile**
filasse [filas] **1** *nf* tow **2** *adj inv* tow-coloured
filature [filatyr] *nf* (**a**) *(fabrique)* (spinning) mill (**b**) *(surveillance)* shadowing; **prendre qn en f.** to shadow sb
file [fil] *nf* (**a**) *(queue)* Br queue, Am line; **en f. indienne** in single file; **trois jours à la f.** three days in a row; **f. d'attente** Br queue, Am line; Ordinat print queue (**b**) *(sur la route)* lane; **se garer en double f.** to double-park
filé, -e [file] *adj* (**a**) *(bas, collant)* with a run, Br laddered (**b**) *(verre)* spun (**c**) *(métaphore)* extended
filer [file] **1** *vt* (**a**) *(coton, verre)* to spin (**b**) *(développer)* *(image, métaphore)* to draw *or* spin out (**c**) *Fam (donner)* **f. qch à qn** to give sb sth (**d**) *(surveiller)* *(suspect)* to shadow, to tail (**e**) *(bas, collant)* to put a run in, Br to ladder (**f**) **f. le parfait amour** to live love's dream **2** *vi* (**a**) *(passer vite)* *(temps)* to fly; *(véhicule)* to speed along; **f. entre les mains** *ou* **les doigts à qn** *(argent)* to run through sb's fingers like water; *(personne)* to slip through sb's fingers (**b**) *Fam (partir)* **il faut que je file** I must dash; **allez, file!** off you go! (**c**) *(bas, collant)* to run, Br to ladder
filet¹ [filɛ] *nm* (**a**) *(de lumière)* thin streak; *(d'air)* thin stream; *(d'eau)* trickle (**b**) *(petite quantité)* dash (**c**) *(d'une vis)* thread (**d**) *(de viande, de poisson)* fillet; **f. mignon** filet mignon *(small fillet steak)*
filet² *nm* (**a**) *(en mailles)* net; **f. à bagages** luggage rack; **f. à papillons** butterfly net; **f. de pêche** fishing net; **f. à provisions** string bag (**b**) *(au cirque)* (safety) net; **travailler sans f.** *(trapéziste)* to work without a net; *Fig* to take risks (**c**) *(au tennis)* net
filial, -e, -aux, -ales [filjal, -o] **1** *adj* filial **2** *nf* **filiale** subsidiary (company)
filiation [filjasjɔ̃] *nf* (**a**) *(lien de parenté)* filiation (**b**) *Fig (relation)* relationship (**avec** to)
filière [filjɛr] *nf* (**a**) *(voie obligée)* channels (**b**) *(domaine d'études)* field of study; **suivre une f. scientifique/commerciale** to study scientific/business subjects (**c**) *(organisation clandestine)* network
filiforme [filifɔrm] *adj* spindly
filigrane [filigran] *nm (dessin)* watermark; *Fig* **en f.** implicit
filin [filɛ̃] *nm* rope
fille [fij] *nf* (**a**) *(descendante)* daughter (**b**) *(enfant)* girl; **petite f.** little girl (**c**) *(femme)* **salut les filles!** hi, girls!; **f. de joie** prostitute; **jeune f.** girl; **vieille f.** old maid
fillette [fijɛt] *nf* little girl
filleul, -e [fijœl] *nm,f* godson, *f* goddaughter
film [film] *nm* (**a**) *(œuvre)* movie, Br film; **f. d'action** action movie *or* Br film; **f. d'animation** animated movie *or* Br film; **f. d'aventures** adventure movie *or* Br film; **f. d'épouvante** *ou* **d'horreur** horror movie *or* Br film; **f. policier** detective movie *or* Br film (**b**) *(déroulement)* **revoir le f. de sa vie** to see one's life flashing before one's eyes (**c**) *(emballage)* film, wrap; **f. alimentaire** Br clingfilm, Am Saran® wrap (**d**) *(fine pellicule)* film
filmer [filme] *vt* to film
filmographie [filmɔɡrafi] *nf* filmography

filon [filɔ̃] *nm* (**a**) *(de minéraux)* vein, seam (**b**) *Fam* **trouver le f.** to strike it rich

filou [filu] *nm (escroc)* rogue; *(enfant)* rascal

fils [fis] *nm* son; **f. de famille** young man of good social standing; *Péj* **f. à papa** daddy's boy

filtrage [filtraʒ] *nm* (**a**) *(contrôle)* screening (**b**) *(d'un liquide)* filtering

filtrant, -e [filtrɑ̃, -ɑ̃t] *adj (pouvoir)* filtering; *(verres, papier)* filter

filtre [filtr] **1** *adj (cigarette, café, papier)* filter
2 *nm* filter; **f. à air** air filter; **f. à café** coffee filter; *Phot* **f. coloré** colour filter; *Ordinat* **f. écran** screen filter; **f. solaire** sunscreen

filtrer [filtre] **1** *vt* (**a**) *(liquide, son, lumière)* to filter (**b**) *(informations, visiteurs)* to screen
2 *vi (liquide)* to filter (**à travers** through); *(nouvelle)* to leak out; **laisser f. qch** to let sth filter through; *Fig* to leak sth

fin¹ [fɛ̃] *nf* (**a**) *(conclusion)* end; **"f."** *(au cinéma)* "the end"; **f. juillet** at the end of July; **à la f.** in the end; *Fam* **tu m'ennuies à la f.!** you're really annoying me!; **en f. de qch, à la f. de qch** at the end of sth; **chômeur en f. de droits** = unemployed person about to lose their entitlement to benefit; **mettre f. à qch** to put an end to sth; **prendre f.** to come to an end; **toucher** *ou* **tirer à sa f.** to draw to a close; **avoir des fins de mois difficiles** to be always short of money at the end of the month; **f. de série** discontinued line; **f. de semaine** end of the week, *Can* weekend (**b**) *(mort)* end, death (**c**) *(but)* end, aim; **arriver** *ou* **parvenir à ses fins** to achieve one's ends; **à cette f.** to this end; **à toutes fins utiles** just in case (**d**) *Ordinat* **f. de ligne** line end; **f. de page** pagebreak; **f. de session** logoff, logout

fin², fine¹ [fɛ̃, fin] **1** *adj* (**a**) *(papier, tranche, taille)* thin; *(cheveux, sable, pointe)* fine; **une petite pluie fine** drizzle (**b**) *(traits)* fine (**c**) *(de première qualité)* fine (**d**) **fines herbes** mixed herbs (**e**) **un f. connaisseur** a connoisseur (**f**) *(vue, odorat)* keen; **avoir l'ouïe fine** to have keen hearing (**g**) *(subtil)* subtle (**h**) *Can (gentil)* kind, sweet(-natured) (**i**) **le f. mot de l'histoire** the truth of the matter
2 *nm* **le f. du f.** the ultimate
3 *adv* (**a**) **f. prêt** all ready (**b**) *(finement)* finely

final, -e¹, -als *ou* **-aux, -ales** [final, -o] *adj* final

finale² [final] **1** *nf* (**a**) *(compétition sportive)* final; **aller/être en f.** to go through to/to be in the finals (**b**) *(de mot)* final syllable
2 *nm (d'un morceau de musique)* finale

finalement [finalmɑ̃] *adv* in the end, finally

finaliser [finalize] *vt* to finalize

finaliste [finalist] *adj & nmf* finalist

finalité [finalite] *nf* (**a**) *(objectif)* aim (**b**) *(en biologie)* finality

finance [finɑ̃s] *nf* (**a**) *(profession)* finance; **la haute f.** high finance (**b**) *(argent)* **moyennant f.** for a fee; **finances** finances

financement [finɑ̃smɑ̃] *nm* financing

financer [16] [finɑ̃se] *vt* to finance

financier, -ère [finɑ̃sje, -ɛr] **1** *adj* financial
2 *nm* (**a**) *Fin* financier (**b**) *(gâteau)* = rectangular sponge finger made with almonds

financièrement [finɑ̃sjɛrmɑ̃] *adv* financially

finasser [finase] *vi Fam* to resort to trickery

finaud, -e [fino, -od] **1** *adj* crafty
2 *nm,f* crafty devil

fine² [fin] *nf* liqueur brandy

finement [finmɑ̃] *adv* (**a**) *(adroitement)* cleverly (**b**) *(délicatement)* finely

finesse [fines] *nf* (**a**) *(minceur)* fineness; *(de la taille)* slenderness, slimness (**b**) *(d'un visage)* fineness; *(d'un travail fait à la main)* delicacy (**c**) *(subtilité)* subtlety

fini, -e [fini] **1** *adj* (**a**) *(usé, à bout)* finished (**b**) *Péj (imbécile, escroc)* absolute (**c**) *(espace, temps, nombre)* finite
2 *nm (d'un objet manufacturé)* finish

finir [finir] **1** *vt* to finish; *(vie)* to end; **f. son assiette** to clear one's plate
2 *vi* to end, to finish; **f. bien/mal** to end well/badly; *(film, roman)* to have a happy/sad ending; **mal f.** *(personne)* to come to a bad end; **f. de faire qch** to finish doing sth; **f. par faire qch** to end up doing sth; **en f. avec qn/qch** to have done with sb/sth; **à n'en plus f.** endless; **pour f.** *(en résumé)* to cut a long story short; *(finalement)* in the end

finish [finiʃ] *nm inv* finish

finition [finisjɔ̃] *nf* finishing touch; **travail de f.** finishing touches; **les finitions de cette robe sont mal faites** this dress is badly finished

finlandais, -e [fɛ̃lɑ̃dɛ, -ɛz] **1** *adj* Finnish
2 *nm,f* **F.** Finn

Finlande [fɛ̃lɑ̃d] *nf* **la F.** Finland

finnois, -e [finwa, -az] **1** *adj* Finnish
2 *nm (langue)* Finnish

fiole [fjɔl] *nf (flacon)* phial

fioriture [fjɔrityr] *nf (dessin)* flourish

fioul [fjul] *nm* fuel oil

firmament [firmamɑ̃] *nm Litt* firmament

firme [firm] *nf* firm

FIS [fis] *nm (abrév* **Front islamique du salut)** **le F.** the Islamic Salvation Front

fisc [fisk] *nm Br* ≃ Inland Revenue, *Am* ≃ Internal Revenue

fiscal, -e, -aux, -ales [fiskal, -o] *adj* tax

fiscaliser [fiskalize] *vt* to tax

fiscalité [fiskalite] *nf* tax system

fissure [fisyr] *nf aussi Fig* crack

fissurer [fisyre] **1** *vt* to crack; *Fig* to split
2 **se fissurer** *vpr* to crack; *Fig* to split

fiston [fistɔ̃] *nm Fam* son, lad

FIV [ɛfive] *nf (abrév* **fécondation in vitro)** IVF

FIVETE, fivete [fivɛt] *nf (abrév* **fécondation in vitro et transfert embryonnaire)** GIFT; **une F.** a test-tube baby

fixateur, -trice [fiksatœr, -tris] *Phot* **1** *adj* fixing
2 *nm* fixer

fixatif [fiksatif] *nm* fixative

fixation [fiksasjɔ̃] *nf* (**a**) *(action)* fixing (**b**) *(de skis)* (ski) binding (**c**) *(obsession)* fixation; **faire une f. sur qn/qch** to become fixated on sb/sth

fixe [fiks] **1** *adj* (**a**) *(immobile)* (étagère, planche, regard) fixed (**b**) *(arrêté)* (prix, frais) fixed (**c**) *Tél (ligne)* fixed; *(poste)* landline
2 *nm* (**a**) *(salaire)* fixed salary (**b**) *Tél (poste fixe)* fixed *or* landline phone

fixement [fiksəmɑ̃] *adv* fixedly; **regarder f. qn/qch** to stare at sb/sth

fixer [fikse] **1** *vt* (**a**) *(immobiliser)* to fix; **f. son attention/son regard sur qch** to focus one's attention/one's gaze on sth; **f. qn (du regard)** to stare at sb (**b**) *(déterminer)* (date, heure, rendez-vous) to fix; *(prix, salaire)* to fix, to set (**à** at); **f. son choix sur qch** to decide on sth (**c**) *(informer)* **mainte-**

nant, tu es fixé now you know
2 se fixer *vpr* (**a**) *(s'installer)* to settle down (**b**) **son choix s'est fixé sur celui-ci** he/she decided on this one (**c**) **se f. un objectif** to set oneself a target
fixité [fiksite] *nf (du regard)* fixedness
fjord [fjɔrd] *nm* fjord
flacon [flakɔ̃] *nm* (small) bottle
flagada [flagada] *adj inv Fam* washed-out
flageller [flaʒele] *vt* to flog, to whip
flageoler [flaʒɔle] *vi (jambes)* to shake, to tremble
flageolet [flaʒɔlɛ] *nm (haricot)* flageolet (bean)
flagornerie [flagɔrnəri] *nf Péj* fawning, toadying
flagrant, -e [flagrɑ̃, -ɑ̃t] *adj* flagrant, blatant; **en f. délit** red-handed; **être pris en f. délit d'adultère** to be caught in flagrante
flair [flɛr] *nm* sense of smell; **avoir du f.** to have a good sense of smell; *Fig* to have good intuition
flairer [flɛre] *vt aussi Fig* to smell
flamand, -e [flamɑ̃, -ɑ̃d] **1** *adj* Flemish
2 *nm,f* **F.** Fleming
3 *nm (langue)* Flemish
flamant [flamɑ̃] *nm* **f. rose** flamingo
flambant [flɑ̃bɑ̃] *adv* (**a**) *(location)* **f. neuf** brand new (**b**) *Can Fam (complètement)* totally; **f. nu** stark naked, *Br* starkers
flambeau, -x [flɑ̃bo] *nm (torche)* torch; *Fig* **passer le f. à qn** to pass the torch on to sb
flambée [flɑ̃be] *nf* (**a**) *(feu)* blaze (**b**) *(de violence)* flare-up; *(des prix)* upsurge
flamber [flɑ̃be] **1** *vi* (**a**) *(brûler)* to blaze (**b**) *Fam (parier)* to gamble for big money
2 *vt* (**a**) *(volaille)* to singe (**b**) *(crêpes)* to flambé
flambeur, -euse [flɑ̃bœr, -øz] *nm,f Fam* big-time gambler
flamboyant, -e [flɑ̃bwajɑ̃, -ɑ̃t] *adj* (**a**) *(regard)* blazing; **d'un rouge f.** flaming red (**b**) *Archit* flamboyant
flamboyer [flɑ̃bwaje] *vi* to blaze
flamme [flam] *nf* (**a**) *(feu)* flame; **en flammes** on fire, ablaze; *Fig* **descendre qn/qch en flammes** to shoot sb/sth down in flames (**b**) *Fig (enthousiasme)* fire (**c**) *Litt (amour)* passion
flammèche [flamɛʃ] *nf* spark
flan [flɑ̃] *nm (dessert)* baked custard
flanc [flɑ̃] *nm* side; *(d'une armée)* flank; **être sur le f.** *(malade)* to be laid up; *(épuisé)* to be worn out; *Fam* **tirer au f.** to shirk, *Br* to skive
flancher [flɑ̃ʃe] *vi Fam* to give in
Flandre [flɑ̃dr] *nf* **la F., les Flandres** Flanders
flanelle [flanɛl] *nf* flannel
flâner [flɑne, flane] *vi* (**a**) *(se promener)* to stroll, to saunter (**b**) *(perdre son temps)* to hang about
flânerie [flɑnri, flanri] *nf (promenade)* stroll
flâneur, -euse [flɑnœr, flanœr, -øz] *nm,f (promeneur)* stroller
flanquer¹ [flɑ̃ke] *vt* (**a**) *(être à coté de)* to flank (**b**) *(accompagner)* **flanqué de** flanked by
flanquer² *Fam* **1** *vt* (**a**) *(jeter)* to chuck; **f. qn à la porte** *ou* **dehors** to kick sb out; *(licencier)* to fire sb, *Br* to sack sb; **f. qch par terre** to fling sth on the ground; *Fig* to mess sth up (**b**) **f. qch à qn** *(coup de pied, gifle)* to give sb sth; **f. la trouille** *ou* **les jetons à qn** to put the wind up sb
2 se flanquer *vpr* **se f. par terre** to go sprawling
flapi, -e [flapi] *adj Fam* dead beat
flaque [flak] *nf (d'huile, de sang)* pool; **f. (d'eau)** puddle

flash [flaʃ] *nm* (**a**) *(sur un appareil photo)* flash (**b**) *(à la radio, à la télévision)* flash; **f. d'information** newsflash; **f. publicitaire** commercial
flash-back [flaʃbak] *nm inv* flashback
flasher [flaʃe] *vi Fam* **f. sur qn/qch** to fall for sb/sth in a big way
flasque¹ [flask] *adj (chair)* flabby
flasque² *nf* flask
flatter [flate] **1** *vt* (**a**) *(complimenter)* to flatter (**b**) *(avantager)* to flatter (**c**) *(caresser)* *(animal)* to stroke
2 se flatter *vpr* to flatter oneself; **se f. de faire qch** to pride oneself on doing sth; **je ne m'en flatterais pas** it's not something I'd be proud of
flatterie [flatri] *nf* flattery
flatteur, -euse [flatœr, -øz] **1** *adj (remarque, portrait, couleur)* flattering; *(personne)* full of flattery
2 *nm,f* flatterer
flatulence [flatylɑ̃s] *nf* flatulence
FLE [flə] *nm (abrév* **français langue étrangère**) French as a foreign language
fléau, -x [fleo] *nm* (**a**) *(calamité)* scourge; *Fig (chose pénible)* pain (**b**) *(à céréales)* flail (**c**) *(d'une balance à plateaux)* beam
fléchage [fleʃaʒ] *nm* signposting
flèche [flɛʃ] *nf* (**a**) *(projectile, signe)* arrow; **partir comme une f.** to shoot off; **monter en f.** *(avion, prix)* to shoot up (**b**) *(attaque verbale)* jibe (**c**) *(d'une église)* spire (**d**) *Ordinat* **f. de défilement** scroll arrow; **flèches verticales** up and down arrow keys
flécher [34] [fleʃe] *vt (route, direction)* to arrow; **itinéraire fléché** signposted route
fléchette [fleʃɛt] *nf* dart; **jouer aux fléchettes** to play darts
fléchir [fleʃir] **1** *vt* (**a**) *(bras, jambe, genou)* to bend (**b**) *(faire céder)* to sway
2 *vi* (**a**) *(ployer) (branche)* to bend; *(jambes)* to give way; *(poutre)* to sag (**b**) *(faiblir)* to weaken (**c**) *(baisser) (prix, devises)* to fall
fléchissement [fleʃismɑ̃] *nm* (**a**) *(du genou)* bending; *(d'une poutre)* sagging (**b**) *(de prix, de devises, de résultats)* drop (**de in**)
flegmatique [flɛgmatik] *adj* phlegmatic
flegme [flɛgm] *nm* phlegm
flemmard, -e [flɛmar, -ard] *Fam* **1** *adj* lazy
2 *nm,f* lazybones
flemmarder [flemarde] *vi Fam* to laze about
flemmardise [flemardiz] *nf Fam* laziness
flemme [flɛm] *nf Fam* laziness; **j'ai la f. (de le faire)** I can't be bothered (to do it)
flétan [fletɑ̃] *nm* halibut
flétri, -e [fletri] *adj* withered
flétrir [fletrir] **1** *vt (peau, plantes)* to wither
2 se flétrir *vpr (visage, plantes)* to wither
fleur [flœr] *nf* (**a**) *(plante)* flower; **à fleurs** *(tissu)* floral; **en fleurs** *(arbre)* in flower; **être f. bleue** to be a romantic; *Fam* **faire une f. à qn** to do sb a favour; **fleurs des champs** wild flowers (**b**) *Can (farine)* flour (**c**) *(locutions)* **dans la f. de l'âge** in the prime of life; **la fine f. de qch** the cream of sth; **à f. d'eau** just above the surface of the water; **avoir les nerfs à f. de peau** to be all on edge
fleurdelisé [flœrdəlize] *nm Can (drapeau du Québec)* flag of Quebec
fleurer [flœre] **1** *vt Litt* to smell of
2 *vi* **f. bon** to smell nice
fleuret [flœrɛ] *nm (épée)* foil

fleurette [flœrɛt] *nf Vieilli* **conter f. à qn** to whisper sweet nothings to sb

fleuri, -e [flœri] *adj* (**a**) *(couvert de fleurs) (arbre)* in flower (**b**) *(orné de fleurs) (tissu, robe)* floral; *(vaisselle)* flower-patterned (**c**) *(style)* flowery (**d**) *(teint)* florid

fleurir [flœrir] **1** *vi* (**a**) *(plantes)* to flower (**b**) *(art, commerce)* to flourish
2 *vt (table)* to decorate with flowers; *(tombe)* to lay flowers on

fleuriste [flœrist] *nmf (commerçant)* florist

fleuron [flœrɔ̃] *nm (d'une collection)* jewel

fleuve [flœv] *nm* river; **le f. Jaune** the Yellow River

flexibilité [flɛksibilite] *nf aussi Fig* flexibility

flexible [flɛksibl] **1** *adj aussi Fig* flexible
2 *nm (tuyau)* hose(pipe)

flexion [flɛksjɔ̃] *nf (fléchissement)* bending; **être en f.** *(muscle, membre)* to be flexed

flibustier [flibystje] *nm* buccaneer

flic [flik] *nm Fam* cop

flingue [flɛ̃g] *nm Fam* shooter

flinguer [flɛ̃ge] *Fam* **1** *vt* (**a**) *(tuer)* to blow away (**b**) *Fig (critiquer sévèrement)* to shoot down
2 se flinguer *vpr* to blow one's brains out

flippant, -e [flipɑ̃, -ɑ̃t] *adj Fam (déprimant)* grim; *(effrayant)* creepy

flipper¹ [flipœr] *nm (appareil)* pinball machine; *(jeu)* pinball; **jouer au f.** to play pinball

flipper² [flipe] *vi Fam* (**a**) *(déprimer)* to feel down (**b**) *(paniquer)* to freak out; **ca me fait f.** it freaks me out

flirt [flœrt] *nm* (**a**) *(amourette)* flirtation (**b**) *(personne)* boyfriend, *f* girlfriend

flirter [flœrte] *vi aussi Fig* to flirt (**avec** with)

FLN [ɛfɛlɛn] *nm (abrév* **Front de libération nationale**) National Liberation Front *(in Algeria)*

FLNC [ɛfɛlɛnse] *nm (abrév* **Front de libération nationale de la Corse**) Corsican liberation front

FLNKS [ɛfɛlɛnkaɛs] *nm (abrév* **Front de libération nationale kanak et socialiste**) Kanak national liberation front *(in New Caledonia)*

flocon [flɔkɔ̃] *nm* flake; **flocons d'avoine** oat flakes; **f. de neige** snowflake

floconneux, -euse [flɔkɔnø, -øz] *adj* fluffy

flonflons [flɔ̃flɔ̃] *nmpl* tiddly-om-pom-pom

flop [flɔp] *nm Fam* flop; **faire un f.** to flop

flopée [flɔpe] *nf Fam* **une f. ou des flopées de** loads of, masses of

floraison [flɔrɛzɔ̃] *nf* flowering

floral, -e, -aux, -ales [flɔral, -o] *adj* floral

floralies [flɔrali] *nfpl* flower show

flore [flɔr] *nf* flora; **f. intestinale** intestinal flora

Floride [flɔrid] *nf* **la F.** Florida

florilège [flɔrilɛʒ] *nm* anthology

florin [flɔrɛ̃] *nm* florin

florissant, -e [flɔrisɑ̃, -ɑ̃t] *adj (affaire)* flourishing; *(santé)* blooming

flot [flo] *nm* (**a**) *(marée)* flood (tide) (**b**) *(quantité importante)* stream (**de** of) (**c**) *Litt* **les flots** *(la mer)* the waves (**d**) *(locutions)* **couler à flots** to flow freely; **être à f.** *(bateau)* to be afloat; *Fig (personne)* to have one's head above water; **remettre à f.** *(personne, entreprise)* to get back on an even keel

flottaison [flɔtɛzɔ̃] *nf* floating

flotte [flɔt] *nf* (**a**) *(bateaux)* fleet (**b**) *Fam (eau)* water; *(pluie)* rain

flottement [flɔtmɑ̃] *nm* (**a**) *(d'un drapeau)* fluttering (**b**) *(d'une monnaie)* fluctuation (**c**) *(hésitation)* wavering

flotter [flɔte] **1** *vi* (**a**) *(embarcation)* to float; *Fig* **il flotte dans sa veste** his jacket is far too big for him (**b**) *(drapeau)* to flutter; **f. au** *ou* **dans le vent** *(cheveux)* to stream in the wind
2 *v impersonnel Fam* **il flotte** it's raining

flotteur [flɔtœr] *nm* float

flottille [flɔtij] *nf (de bateaux)* flotilla

flou, -e [flu] **1** *adj* (**a**) *(contour, photographie)* blurred, fuzzy (**b**) *(idée, réponse)* vague
2 *nm (d'un contour, d'une photographie)* fuzziness; *(d'une idée, d'une réponse)* vagueness; **f. artistique** *(en photographie)* soft-focus effect; *Fig* deliberate vagueness

flouer [flue] *vt Fam* to swindle

flouse, flouze [fluz] *nm Fam (argent)* bread, dough

fluctuant, -e [flyktɥɑ̃, -ɑ̃t] *adj* fluctuating

fluctuation [flyktɥasjɔ̃] *nf* fluctuation

fluctuer [flyktɥe] *vi* to fluctuate

fluet, -ette [flyɛ, -ɛt] *adj* thin

fluide [flɥid] **1** *adj (liquide)* fluid; *(circulation)* flowing freely; *(style, pensée)* flowing
2 *nm* (**a**) *(substance)* fluid (**b**) *(pouvoir surnaturel)* occult power

fluidifier [66] [flɥidifje] *vt (sang)* to thin

fluidité [flɥidite] *nf (d'un corps)* fluidity; *(de la circulation)* free flow

fluo [flyo] *adj inv Fam* fluorescent

fluor [flyɔr] *nm* fluorine; **dentifrice au f.** fluoride toothpaste

fluorescent, -e [flyɔresɑ̃, -ɑ̃t] *adj* fluorescent

flûte [flyt] **1** *nf* (**a**) *(instrument)* flute; **f. à bec** recorder; **f. de Pan** panpipes; **f. traversière** concert flute (**b**) *(pain)* small French loaf (**c**) *(verre)* **f. à champagne** champagne flute
2 *exclam Fam* drat!, *Am* darn!

flûtiste [flytist] *nmf Br* flautist, *Am* flutist

fluvial, -e, -aux, -ales [flyvjal, -o] *adj* river; *(alluvions)* fluvial

flux [fly] *nm* (**a**) *(de paroles)* flow (**b**) *(de liquide)* flow; **le f. et le reflux** the ebb and flow; **f. migratoire** flow of migrants (**c**) *(électrique, magnétique)* flux

fluxion [flyksjɔ̃] *nf* inflammation; **f. de poitrine** pneumonia

FM [ɛfɛm] *nf (abrév* **frequency modulation**) FM

FME [ɛfɛmə] *nm (abrév* **fonds monétaire européen**) EMF

FMI [ɛfɛmi] *nm (abrév* **Fonds monétaire international**) IMF

FN [ɛfɛn] *nm (abrév* **Front national**) = far-right French political party

FNSEA [ɛfɛnɛsəa] *nf (abrév* **Fédération nationale des syndicats d'exploitants agricoles**) = French farmers' union

FO [ɛfo] *nf (abrév* **Force ouvrière**) = French trade union

foc [fɔk] *nm* jib

focal, -e, -aux, -ales [fɔkal, -o] *adj* focal

focaliser [fɔkalize] **1** *vt* to focus (**sur** on)
2 se focaliser *vpr* to focus (**sur** on)

fœtal, -e, -aux, -ales [fetal, -o] *adj* foetal

fœtus [fetys] *nm* foetus

fofolle [fɔfɔl] *adj voir* foufou

foi [fwa] *nf* (**a**) *(confiance)* faith, trust; **avoir f. en qn/qch** to have faith in sb/sth; **les candidatures devront nous parvenir le 1er mars dernier délai, le cachet de la poste faisant f.** applications should be postmarked no later than 1 March (**b**) *(croyance religieuse)* faith; **avoir/perdre la f.** to have/lose faith (**c**) *(locutions)* **bonne f.** sincerity; **mauvaise f.** insincerity; **être de bonne/mauvaise f.** to be sincere/insincere; **ma f., oui!** yes indeed!

foie [fwa] *nm* liver; *très Fam* **avoir les foies** to be scared shitless; **f. gras** foie gras; **f. de veau/volaille** calf's/chicken liver

foin [fwɛ̃] *nm (fourrage)* hay; **faire les foins** to make hay; *Fam* **faire du f.** *(causer un scandale)* to kick up a fuss; *(faire du bruit)* to make a din; *Can Fam* **avoir du f.** to be loaded

foire [fwar] *nf* (**a**) *(fête foraine)* funfair; *Fam* **faire la f.** to muck about; *Fam* **c'est la f., ici** it's bedlam in here; **f. d'empoigne** free-for-all (**b**) *(salon international, professionnel)* (trade) fair

foirer [fware] *vi très Fam* to be a cock-up; **il a tout fait f.** he *Br* ballsed *or Am* balled everything up

foireux, -euse [fwarø, -øz] *adj très Fam (projet, affaire)* hopeless

fois [fwa] *nf* time; **une f.** once; **il était une f. un roi** once upon a time there was a king; **deux f.** twice; **deux f. par jour/mois** twice a day/month; **ça coûte trois f. rien** it costs next to nothing; **trois f. quatre font douze** three times four is twelve; **trois f. plus grand** three times as big; **neuf f. sur dix** nine times out of ten; **combien de f.?** how many times?, how often?; **toutes les f. *ou* chaque f. que** every time (that), whenever; **encore une f.** once more, once again; **une (bonne) f. pour toutes** once and for all; **une f. que** once, as soon as; **pour cette f.** this once; **pour une f.** for once; **pour une f. que j'étais à l'heure, personne n'était là** for once I was on time, and no one was there; **à la f.** utile et pas cher both useful and inexpensive; **une chose à la f.** one thing at a time; **l'autre f.** *(il y a peu)* the other day; *Fam* **des f.** *(parfois)* sometimes; *Fam* **des f. qu'il viendrait** in case he comes; *Fam* **non, mais des f.!** really now!

foison [fwazɔ̃] *nf* **à f.** in abundance

foisonnement [fwazɔnmɑ̃] *nm (abondance)* abundance

foisonner [fwazɔne] *vi* to abound (**de** *ou* **en** in); **f. d'idées** *(personne)* to have plenty of ideas

fol [fɔl] *voir* **fou**

folâtre [fɔlɑtr] *adj (personne)* playful

folâtrer [fɔlɑtre] *vi (personne)* to romp, to frolic

foldingue [fɔldɛ̃g] *adj Fam* nutty

folichon, -onne [fɔliʃɔ̃, -ɔn] *adj Fam* **ce n'est pas f.** it's not much fun

folie [fɔli] *nf* madness; **aimer qn à la f.** to be madly in love with sb; **aimer qch à la f.** to adore sth; **faire des folies** *(faire des achats extravagants)* to go mad; **c'est de la f.!** it's madness!; **c'est de la f. douce** it's sheer madness; **la f. des grandeurs** delusions of grandeur

folio [fɔljo] *nm* folio

folk [fɔlk] *adj & nm* folk

folklo [fɔlklo] *adj inv Fam (personne)* eccentric; *(endroit, soirée)* bizarre

folklore [fɔlklɔr] *nm* folklore

folklorique [fɔlklɔrik] *adj* (**a**) *(costume)* traditional; *(danse)* folk (**b**) *Fam (personne)* eccentric; *(endroit, soirée)* bizarre

folle [fɔl] *adj voir* **fou**

follement [fɔlmɑ̃] *adv* madly

follet [fɔlɛ] *adj m voir* **feu¹**

fomenter [fɔmɑ̃te] *vt* to foment

foncé, -e [fɔ̃se] *adj* dark

foncer [16] [fɔ̃se] **1** *vt* to darken
2 *vi* (**a**) *(s'assombrir)* to darken (**b**) *(se hâter)* to get a

move on; **f. sur qn/qch** *(se précipiter sur)* to swoop on sb/sth (**c**) *Fam (s'y mettre)* to get one's head down

fonceur, -euse [fɔ̃sœr, -øz] *Fam* **1** *adj* go-getting **2** *nm,f* go-getter

foncier, -ère [fɔ̃sje, -ɛr] *adj* (**a**) *(impôt, crédit)* land (**b**) *(fondamental)* fundamental, basic

foncièrement [fɔ̃sjɛrmɑ̃] *adv* fundamentally, basically

fonction [fɔ̃ksjɔ̃] *nf* (**a**) *(poste)* office; **entrer en fonctions, prendre ses fonctions** to take up one's duties; **être en f.** to be in office; **de f.** *(voiture, appartement)* company; **la f. publique** the civil service (**b**) *(rôle)* function; **faire f. de qch** to act as sth (**c**) *Ordinat* **f. de comptage de mots** word count facility; **f. d'éditeur de texte** text editing feature; **f. multimédia** multimedia facility; **f. recherche et remplacement** search and replace function; **f. de sauvegarde** save function (**d**) **en f. de** according to

fonctionnaire [fɔ̃ksjɔnɛr] *nmf* ≃ civil servant; **haut f.** ≃ senior civil servant

Fonctionnaire

This term covers a broader range of public service employees than the term "civil servant", from high-ranking members of the state administration to public-sector teachers and post office workers. "Fonctionnaires", of whom there are more than four and a half million in France, are normally recruited through competitive state examination *(see box at* **concours***)* and enjoy greater job security and other privileges to which private sector employees are not automatically entitled.

fonctionnariat [fɔ̃ksjɔnarja] *nm* employment by the state

fonctionnel, -elle [fɔ̃ksjɔnɛl] *adj* functional

fonctionnement [fɔ̃ksjɔnmɑ̃] *nm (d'une machine)* working, functioning; **en état de f.** in (good) working order; *Ordinat* **f. en réseau** networking

fonctionner [fɔ̃ksjɔne] *vi (machine, mécanisme)* to work, to function; *Ordinat* to run; **faire f. qch** to operate sth

fond [fɔ̃] *nm* (**a**) *(d'un récipient, de la mer, de l'océan)* bottom; *(d'un espace clos, de la gorge)* back; **être assis au f. de la classe** to be sitting at the back of the class; **c'est au f. du couloir/de la salle** it's at the (far) end of the corridor/hall; **la pièce du f.** the room at the end, the far room; **au fin f. de qch** in the depths of sth; **il n'en reste qu'un f.** there's only a drop left; **du f. du cœur** from the bottom of one's heart; **tu connais le f. de ma pensée** you know what my feelings really are; **à f.** *(à bloc)* all the way; *(complètement)* thoroughly; *(totalement)* totally; **à f. de train** at full tilt; *Fam* **à f. la caisse** *(très vite)* hell for leather; **au f., dans le f.** when it comes down to it; **de f. en comble** from top to bottom; **f. d'artichaut** artichoke heart; **f. de bouteille** *(contenu)* dregs; **f. de teint** foundation (cream) (**b**) *(substance essentielle)* **le f. du problème** the heart of the problem; **avoir un bon/mauvais f.** to be basically a good/bad person; **le f. et la forme** form and content (**c**) *(arrière-plan)* background; **f. sonore** background music; **il y avait du jazz en f. sonore** there was jazz playing in the background

fondamental, -e, -aux, -ales [fɔ̃damɑ̃tal, -o] *adj* basic, fundamental

fondamentalement [fɔ̃damɑ̃talmɑ̃] *adv* fundamentally, basically

fondamentalisme [fɔ̃damɑ̃talism] *nm* fundamentalism

fondamentaliste [fɔ̃damɑ̃talist] *nmf* fundamentalist

fondant, -e [fɔ̃dɑ̃, -ɑ̃t] **1** *adj* (**a**) *(neige)* melting (**b**) *(poire)* that melts in the mouth; *(viande)* very tender **2** *nm (bonbon)* fondant

fondateur, -trice [fɔ̃datœr, -tris] **1** *adj (mythe)* underlying; **membre f.** founder member **2** *nm,f* founder

fondation [fɔ̃dasjɔ̃] *nf* (**a**) *(d'une ville, d'un hôpital)* founding (**b**) *(établissement)* foundation (**c**) **fondations** *(d'une construction)* foundations

fondé, -e [fɔ̃de] **1** *adj (reproches, doutes)* well-founded, justified; **être f. à faire qch** to have good reason to do sth **2** *nm,f* **f. de pouvoir** agent *(holding power of attorney)*; *(mandant)* proxy

fondement [fɔ̃dmɑ̃] *nm* foundation

fonder [fɔ̃de] **1** *vt* (**a**) *(créer) (ville, hôpital)* to found; *(société, journal)* to start, to set up; **f. un foyer** to start a family (**b**) *(baser)* **f. qch sur qch** to base sth on sth; **f. de grands espoirs sur qn** to pin one's hopes on sb **2** *se fonder vpr* **se f. sur qch** *(sujet: remarque, théorie)* to be based on sth; **sur quoi se fonde-t-il pour le nier?** what are his grounds for denying it?; **pour son livre, elle s'est fondée sur plusieurs articles** she based her book on several articles

fonderie [fɔ̃dri] *nf (usine)* foundry

fondre [fɔ̃dr] **1** *vt* (**a**) *(rendre liquide) (métal)* to melt down; *(sucre, sel)* to dissolve; *(neige, cire)* to melt (**b**) *(fabriquer) (cloche, arme)* to cast (**c**) *(combiner) (couleurs)* to blend; *(sociétés)* to merge **2** *vi* (**a**) *(se liquéfier)* to melt; *(sucre)* to dissolve; **faire f. qch** to melt sth; *(sucre)* to dissolve sth; **f. dans la bouche** to melt in the mouth; **f. en larmes** to dissolve into tears; *Fig* **je fonds** my heart melts (**b**) *Fig (diminuer)* to melt away (**c**) *Fam (maigrir)* to lose weight, to shed the pounds **3 fondre sur** *vt ind* to swoop on **4 se fondre** *vpr* **se f. dans** to merge into

fonds [fɔ̃] **1** *nm* (**a**) *(capital)* funds; *(organisme)* fund; **prêter son argent à f. perdu** to lend one's money without security; **f. commun de placement** mutual fund; **F. européen de développement** European Development Fund; **F. européen de développement régional** European Regional Development Fund; **F. monétaire européen** European Monetary Fund; **F. monétaire international** International Monetary Fund; **f. de roulement** working capital (**b**) *(d'un musée, d'une bibliothèque)* collection; *(ressources)* resource (**c**) **f. de commerce** business **2** *nmpl (ressources financières)* funds; **être en f.** to be in funds; **f. publics** government funds; *(valeurs)* government stocks

fondu, -e¹ [fɔ̃dy] **1** *adj Fam (fou)* round the bend, out to lunch **2** *nm,f Fam* **un f. d'informatique/de skateboard** a computer/skateboard freak **3** *nm* (**a**) *(de couleurs)* blending (**b**) *Cin* fade-out; **f. enchaîné** dissolve

fondue² [fɔ̃dy] *nf* **f. (savoyarde)** (cheese) fondue; **f. bourguignonne** fondue bourguignonne, = fondue consisting of cubes of raw beef cooked in hot oil

fongicide [fɔ̃ʒisid] **1** *adj* fungicidal **2** *nm* fungicide

font *voir* faire

fontaine [fɔ̃tɛn] *nf (source naturelle)* spring; *(construction publique)* fountain

fonte [fɔ̃t] *nf* (**a**) *(de métaux)* melting down; **la f. des neiges** the thaw (**b**) *(alliage)* cast iron; **poêle en f.** cast-iron stove (**c**) *Typ* font

fonts [fɔ̃] *nmpl* **f. baptismaux** font

foot [fut] *nm Fam Br* football, footie, *Am* soccer

football [futbol] *nm Br* football, *Am* soccer

footballeur, -euse [futbolœr, -øz] *nm,f Br* footballer, *Am* soccer player

footing [futiŋ] *nm* jogging; **faire du f.** to go jogging

for [fɔr] *nm* **dans** *ou* **en son f. intérieur** in one's heart of hearts, deep (down) inside

forage [fɔraʒ] *nm* drilling, boring

forain, -e [fɔrɛ̃, -ɛn] **1** *adj voir* **fête, marchand 2** *nm* fairground stallholder

forçat [fɔrsa] *nm (prisonnier)* convict; **travailler comme un f.** to work like a slave

force [fɔrs] *nf* (**a**) *(vigueur)* strength; **ne pas se sentir/ne pas être de f. à faire qch** not to feel/not to be up to doing sth; **de f. égale, de même f.** equally matched; **dans f. de l'âge** in the prime of life; **être à bout de forces** to have no strength left; **c'est au-dessus de ses forces** it's too much for him/her; **de toutes ses forces** *(pousser, frapper)* with all one's strength; *(vouloir)* with all one's heart; **f. de caractère** strength of character; **c'est une f. de la nature** *(personne)* he's/she's a force to be reckoned with; **les forces vives du pays** the country's resources (**b**) *(violence)* force; **faire qch de** *ou* **par la f.** to do sth by force; **par la f. des choses** through force of circumstance (**c**) *(puissance)* **f. centrifuge/centripète** centrifugal/centripetal force; *aussi Fig* **f. d'inertie** inertia; **f. motrice** motive power; *Fig* driving force (**d**) *(organisation)* **les forces armées** the armed forces; **les forces aériennes** the airforce; **f. de dissuasion** deterrent; **f. de frappe** strike force; **les forces de police** *ou* **de l'ordre** the police (force) (**e**) *(locutions)* **à f.** in the end; **à f. de volonté** through sheer willpower; **à f. d'insister, tu vas finir par m'agacer** if you keep going on about it, I'm going to get annoyed; **en f.** in force

forcé, -e [fɔrse] *adj* forced; *Fam* **c'est f.!** it's inevitable!

forcément [fɔrsemɑ̃] *adv* inevitably; **elle sera f. déçue** she's bound to be disappointed; **pas f.** not necessarily

forcené, -e [fɔrsəne] **1** *adj (partisan, individualiste)* fanatical; *(haine, lutte)* frenzied **2** *nm,f* maniac

forceps [fɔrsɛps] *nm* forceps

forcer [16] [fɔrse] **1** *vt* (**a**) *(obliger)* to force; **f. qn à faire qch** to force sb to do sth; **f. la main à qn** to force sb's hand; **f. le respect/l'admiration** to command respect/admiration (**b**) *(faire céder) (porte)* to force (open) (**c**) *(voix)* to strain; *Fig* **f. la dose** to overdo it **2** *vi (appuyer, tirer)* to force it; *(se surmener)* to overdo it; *Fam* **f. sur qch** to overdo sth **3** *se forcer vpr (s'obliger)* to force oneself (**à faire qch** to do sth)

forcing [fɔrsiŋ] *nm Sport* sustained pressure; **faire le f.** to put the pressure on; *Fam Fig* **faire du f.** to put on a lot of pressure

forcir [fɔrsir] *vi* (**a**) *(vent, tempête)* to get stronger (**b**) *(personne)* to get bigger

forer [fɔre] *vt* to drill, to bore

forestier, -ère [fɔrɛstje, -ɛr] **1** adj (zone, chemin) forest; **exploitation forestière** (activité) forestry **2** nm forester
forêt [fɔrɛ] nf forest; **F.-noire** (gâteau) Black Forest gateau; **f. pluviale** rainforest; **f. vierge** virgin forest
foreuse [fɔrøz] nf drill
forfait¹ [fɔrfɛ] nm (crime) heinous crime
forfait² nm (**a**) (contrat) fixed-price contract; **travailler au f.** to work for a flat fee (**b**) **être au f.** (fiscalement) to pay an estimated amount of tax (**c**) (prix global) all-in price; **f. week-end** weekend package (**d**) (de ski) pass
forfait³ nm voir **déclarer**
forfaitaire [fɔrfɛtɛr] adj (indemnités) basic; (prix) all-in
forfanterie [fɔrfɑ̃tri] nf bragging
forge [fɔrʒ] nf forge
forger [45] [fɔrʒe] **1** vt (**a**) (métal) to forge; Fig (caractère) to form; Prov **c'est en forgeant qu'on devient forgeron** practice makes perfect (**b**) (inventer) (histoire, excuse) to make up
2 se forger vpr **se f. une réputation** to carve out a reputation for oneself
forgeron [fɔrʒərɔ̃] nm (black)smith
formaliser [fɔrmalize] **1** vt to formalize
2 se formaliser vpr to take offence (**de** at)
formalisme [fɔrmalism] nm formalism
formalité [fɔrmalite] nf formality; **les formalités d'usage** the usual formalities
format [fɔrma] nm format; Ordinat **f. d'écran** screen format; Ordinat **f. de fichier** file format; Ordinat **f. d'impression** print format; **f. de papier** paper format; **f. de poche** pocket format
formatage [fɔrmataʒ] nm Ordinat formatting
formater [fɔrmate] vt Ordinat to format
formateur, -trice [fɔrmatœr, -tris] **1** adj formative **2** nm,f trainer
formation [fɔrmasjɔ̃] nf (**a**) (de roches, d'un mot) formation; (du caractère) forming (**b**) (éducation) training; **f. continue** ou **permanente** continuing education; **f. professionnelle** vocational training; **être en f.** to be undergoing training (**c**) (groupe) group
forme [fɔrm] nf (**a**) (configuration) shape, form; **formes** (d'une femme) curves; **en f. de qch** in the shape of sth; **en f. de L** L-shaped; **sous f. de qch** in the form of sth; **sous toutes ses formes** in all its forms; **sans f.** shapeless; **prendre f.** to take shape (**b**) (manière) form; **en bonne et due f.** in due form; **sans autre f. de procès** without further ado (**c**) (convention) **de pure f.** purely formal; **pour la f.** as a matter of form; **dans les formes** in the accepted way; **respecter les formes** to observe the proprieties (**d**) (bonne santé physique) form; **être en (pleine) f.** to be on (top) form
formel, -elle [fɔrmɛl] adj (**a**) (personne) positive; (ordre) express; (démenti, refus) flat; (interdiction) strict (**b**) (apparent) formal (**c**) (soutenu) formal
formellement [fɔrmɛlmɑ̃] adv (**a**) (interdire) strictly; (affirmer) categorically; (identifier) positively (**b**) (du point de vue de la forme) formally
former [fɔrme] **1** vt (**a**) (créer) (gouvernement, projet) to form (**b**) (constituer) to form; **ils forment une bonne équipe/un beau couple** they make a good team/a lovely couple (**c**) (tracer) (lettre) to form (**d**) (entraîner) to train (**e**) (développer) (caractère) to develop; (esprit, goût, jugement) to develop

2 se former vpr (**a**) (apparaître) to form; (association, liens) to be formed (**b**) (mûrir) (goût) to develop (**c**) (apprendre son métier) to train oneself
Formica® [fɔrmika] nm Formica®; **en F.** Formica®
formidable [fɔrmidabl] adj (**a**) (fantastique) great, fantastic (**b**) (gigantesque) tremendous
formol [fɔrmɔl] nm formalin
formulaire [fɔrmylɛr] nm form; **remplir un f.** to fill in or out a form; Ordinat **f. de saisie** input form
formulation [fɔrmylasjɔ̃] nf formulation, wording
formule [fɔrmyl] nf (**a**) (expression) expression, phrase; **selon la f. consacrée** as the expression goes; **f. magique** magic formula; **f. de politesse** polite phrase; (au début d'une lettre) standard opening; (à la fin d'une lettre) standard ending (**b**) (solution) method; **nouvelle f.** (menu, abonnement) new-style (**c**) (en mathématique, en chimie) formula (**d**) (automobile) **f. 1/2** Formula 1/2
formuler [fɔrmyle] vt to formulate
forniquer [fɔrnike] vi to fornicate
FORPRONU [fɔrprɔny] nf (abrév **Force de protection des Nations unies**) **la F.** UNPROFOR
forsythia [fɔrsisja] nm forsythia
fort, -e [fɔr, fɔrt] **1** adj (**a**) (vigoureux) strong; **f. comme un Turc** ou **un bœuf** as strong as an ox; **c'est une forte tête** he's/she's very strong-minded; **c'est plus f. que moi!** I can't help it!; Fam **c'est que... the best of it is,...; trop f.!** cool!, Br wicked!, Am awesome! (**b**) (doué) **être f. en qch** to be good at sth (**c**) (boisson, odeur, vent, lumière, accent) strong; (mer) heavy; (voix) loud (**d**) (robuste) (personne) large (**e**) (considérable) (somme d'argent) large; (pente) steep; **il y a de fortes chances (pour) que ça réussisse** there's a good chance it will work
2 adv (**a**) (parler, crier, chanter) loud, loudly; (frapper, tirer) hard; (sentir) strong; Fam **y aller f.** to overdo it; Fam **faire (très) f.** to do (really) brilliantly (**b**) (très) very (**c**) (beaucoup) very much; **avoir f. à faire (avec qn/qch)** to have one's work cut out (with sb/sth)
3 nm (**a**) (spécialité) strong point (**b**) (citadelle) fort (**c**) **au plus f. de qch** (hiver) in the depths of sth; (été, épidémie, tempête) at the height of sth
fortement [fɔrtəmɑ̃] adv (**a**) (tirer, pousser) hard (**b**) (désirer, souhaiter, influencer) strongly; (impressionner, irriter) greatly; (insister) firmly (**c**) (très) (épicé) highly; (conseillé) strongly
forteresse [fɔrtərɛs] nf fortress
fortifiant, -e [fɔrtifjɑ̃, -ɑ̃t] **1** adj (nourriture, boisson) fortifying
2 nm tonic
fortification [fɔrtifikasjɔ̃] nf fortification
fortifier [66] [fɔrtifje] vt (ville, mur) to fortify; (muscles, corps, sentiment) to strengthen
fortuit, -e [fɔrtɥi, -it] adj chance, fortuitous
fortune [fɔrtyn] nf (**a**) (richesse) fortune; **faire f.** to make one's fortune (**b**) (hasard) fortune, chance; **de f.** (moyens, installation) makeshift; **faire contre mauvaise f. bon cœur** to make the best of it
fortuné, -e [fɔrtyne] adj (riche) wealthy
forum [fɔrɔm] nm forum; Ordinat **f. de discussion** newsgroup, discussion forum
fosse [fos] nf (**a**) (creux) pit; **f. d'aisances** cesspool; **f. aux lions** lions' den; **f. d'orchestre** orchestra pit; **f.**

septique septic tank (**b**) *(tombe)* grave; **f. commune** mass grave

fossé [fose] *nm (le long de la route)* ditch; *(autour d'un château)* moat; *Fig (entre personnes)* gulf

fossette [fosɛt] *nf* dimple

fossile [fosil] **1** *adj* fossil
2 *nm aussi Fam Fig* fossil

fossoyeur [foswajœr] *nm* gravedigger; *Fig* destroyer

fou, folle [fu, fɔl]

> **fol** is used before masculine singular nouns beginning with a vowel or h mute.

1 *adj* (**a**) *(dément)* mad, insane; **f. de joie** beside oneself with joy; **f. à lier** raving mad; **être f. (amoureux) de qn/qch** to be mad about sb/sth (**b**) *(énorme)* tremendous; *(prix)* exorbitant (**c**) *(incroyable)* incredible (**d**) *(train)* runaway; *(boussole, aiguille)* crazy; **f. rire** uncontrollable giggling; **avoir un** *ou* **le f. rire** to have the giggles
2 *nm,f* madman, *f* madwoman; *Fam* **comme un f.** like mad; **entrer/sortir comme un f.** to storm in/out; **faire le f.** to play *or* act the fool; **un f. furieux** a maniac; **un f. du volant** a reckless driver; *Prov* **plus on est de fous, plus on rit** the more the merrier
3 *nm* (**a**) *(aux échecs)* bishop (**b**) *(bouffon)* jester (**c**) **f. de Bassan** gannet

foudre [fudr] **1** *nf* lightning; *Litt* **s'attirer les foudres de qn** to bring down sb's wrath on one
2 *nm* (**a**) *(tonneau)* tun (**b**) **un f. de guerre** a great warrior; *Fig* **ce n'est pas un f. de guerre** he's no bright spark

foudroyant, -e [fudrwajã, -ãt] *adj (maladie)* violent; *(crise cardiaque)* massive; *(révélation, nouvelle)* devastating; *(succès)* stunning; *(vitesse, progrès)* lightning; *(regard)* withering

foudroyer [32] [fudrwaje] *vt* to strike; **être foudroyé** to be struck by lightning; **f. qn du regard** to give sb a withering look

fouet [fwɛ] *nm (pour punir)* whip; *(de cuisine)* whisk; **de plein f.** head-on

fouetter [fwete] **1** *vt* (**a**) *(punir)* to whip; *Fam* **il n'y a pas de quoi f. un chat** it's nothing to make a fuss about; *Fam* **avoir d'autres chats à f.** to have other fish to fry (**b**) *(cingler)* to lash (against) (**c**) *(battre) (œufs)* to beat, to whisk; *(crème)* to whip
2 *vi Fam (puer)* to stink

foufou, fofolle [fufu, fɔfɔl] *adj Fam* crazy

fougasse [fugas] *nf* = type of flat bread often made with olives, herbs, bacon etc

fougère [fuʒɛr] *nf* fern

fougue [fug] *nf* fire, spirit

fougueusement [fugøzmã] *adv (s'élancer)* impetuously; *(s'embrasser)* passionately

fougueux, -euse [fugø, -øz] *adj (personne, tempérament)* fiery, ardent; *(cheval)* spirited

fouille [fuj] *nf* (**a**) *(d'une maison, d'une personne)* search; **faire une f.** to make a search; **f. corporelle** *(rapide)* frisking; *(approfondie)* body search (**b**) **fouilles** *(archéologiques)* excavations, dig (**c**) *Fam (poche)* pocket

fouillé, -e [fuje] *adj (approfondi)* detailed

fouiller [fuje] **1** *vt* (**a**) *(maison, personne)* to search (**b**) *(problème)* to go thoroughly into
2 *vi* to search (**dans** in)

fouillis [fuji] *nm* jumble, muddle

fouine [fwin] *nf* stone marten

fouiner [fwine] *vi* to nose about (**dans** in)

foulard [fular] *nm* scarf; **le F. islamique** the Muslim headscarf

Le Foulard islamique

The principle of secularism is a cornerstone of the French educational system, and the issue of the wearing of the Muslim headscarf in state schools and other establishments has long caused controversy in France. Traditionally, however, it was left to school heads to decide whether female Muslim pupils may wear the headscarf at school. But the growing number of girls being banned from school for insisting on wearing the headscarf, and refusing to take part in certain activities on religious grounds, led the government to pass a law in 2004 prohibiting the display of ANY obvious religious signs in state schools, as well as in state jobs that involve contact with the public. This measure was described as an attempt to safeguard the principle of secularism and to keep issues of ethnicity and religion from being a divisive factor among children.

foule [ful] *nf (de gens)* crowd; **il ne supporte pas la f.** he can't stand crowds; *Fig* **une f. de qch** lots of sth

foulée [fule] *nf (d'un coureur)* stride; *Fig* **dans la f., j'ai vérifié les comptes** while I was at it, I checked the accounts

fouler [fule] **1** *vt (sol)* to tread; *(raisins)* to press; *Fig* **f. qch aux pieds** to trample sth underfoot
2 **se fouler** *vpr* (**a**) **se f. la cheville** to sprain one's ankle (**b**) *Fam (se fatiguer)* to strain oneself

foulure [fulyr] *nf* sprain; **se faire une f. à la cheville** to sprain one's ankle

four [fur] *nm* (**a**) *(de cuisine)* oven; **f. à gaz/électrique/à micro-ondes** gas/electric/microwave oven; **cuit au f.** *(pain)* baked; *(viande)* roasted; **il fait noir comme dans un f.** it's pitch black; **on ne peut être à la fois au f. et au moulin** you can't be in two places at once (**b**) **petits fours** *(gâteaux)* petits fours (**c**) *(industriel)* kiln; *Hist* **les fours crématoires** the gas ovens (**d**) *Fam (fiasco)* flop; **faire un f.** to flop

fourbe [furb] **1** *adj* deceitful
2 *nmf* cheat

fourbi [furbi] *nm Fam* (**a**) *(désordre)* mess (**b**) *(truc)* thingy

fourbu, -e [furby] *adj* exhausted

fourche [furʃ] *nf* (**a**) *(outil)* fork (**b**) *(de bicyclette, sur une route)* fork; *(des cheveux)* split end; **faire une f.** to fork (**c**) *Belg Scol* break, gap *(in one's timetable)*

fourcher [furʃe] *vi* **sa langue a fourché** he/she made a slip of the tongue

fourchette [furʃɛt] *nf* (**a**) *(ustensile)* fork; *Fam* **avoir un joli** *ou* **bon coup de f.** to have a hearty appetite (**b**) *(écart)* bracket; **f. de prix** price bracket

fourchu, -e [furʃy] *adj (tronc, route)* forked; **aux pieds fourchus** cloven-hoofed; **avoir les cheveux fourchus** to have split ends

fourgon [furgɔ̃] *nm* (**a**) *(véhicule)* van; **f. cellulaire** *Br* police van, *Am* patrol wagon; **f. funèbre** *ou* **funéraire** hearse (**b**) *(d'un train)* **f. à bétail** cattle truck

fourgonnette [furgɔnɛt] *nf* small van

fourguer [furge] *vt Fam* **f. qch à qn** to unload sth onto sb

fourmi [furmi] *nf (a)* ant; *Fig (personne travailleuse)* busy bee; **avoir des fourmis (dans les jambes)** to have pins and needles (in one's legs); **travail de f.** painstaking work

fourmilière [furmiljɛr] *nf* anthill; *Fig* hive of activity

fourmillement [furmijmɑ̃] *nm* (**a**) *(sensation)* pins and needles (**b**) *(agitation)* swarming

fourmiller [furmije] **1** *vi ind* to swarm, to teem
2 fourmiller de *vt ind* to swarm with, to teem with

fournaise [furnɛz] *nf* (**a**) *(endroit surchauffé)* **c'est une vraie f. ici!** this place is like a furnace! (**b**) *Litt (feu)* blaze (**c**) *Can (poêle à bois)* (wood-burning) stove; *(poêle au charbon)* (coal-burning) stove; *(chaudière de chauffage central) Br* boiler, *Am* (central heating) furnace

fourneau, -x [furno] *nm* (**a**) *(de cuisine)* stove; **être aux fourneaux** to be cooking (**b**) *(de verrier, de fondeur)* furnace (**c**) *(d'une pipe)* bowl

fournée [furne] *nf aussi Fig* batch

fourni, -e [furni] *adj* (**a**) *(magasin)* **bien/mal f.** well/poorly stocked (**b**) *(barbe, sourcils)* bushy; **peu f.** sparse

fournil [furni] *nm* bakehouse

fournir [furnir] **1** *vt* (**a**) *(approvisionner)* to supply (**en** with) (**b**) *(procurer)* **f. qch à qn** to provide sb with sth (**c**) *(présenter)* *(preuve, alibi)* to provide; *(documents)* to provide; **pièces à f.** required documents (**d**) *(effort)* to make
2 se fournir *vpr* **se f. en qch** to get in supplies of sth; **se f. chez qn** to get one's supplies from sb

fournisseur, -euse [furnisœr, -øz] *nm,f* supplier; *Ordinat* **f. d'accès** access provider

fournitures [furnityr] *nfpl* **f. de bureau** office supplies; **f. scolaires** educational stationery

fourrage [furaʒ] *nm* fodder

fourrager¹ [45] [furaʒe] *vi Fam (fouiller)* to rummage (**dans** in)

fourrager², -ère [furaʒe, -ɛr] *adj (plante)* fodder

fourre [fur] *nf Suisse (d'un oreiller)* pillowcase; *(pour un édredon)* quilt cover; *(d'un disque)* sleeve; *(d'un livre)* jacket

fourreau, -x [furo] *nm* (**a**) *(d'épée)* sheath, scabbard; *(de parapluie)* cover (**b**) **(robe) f.** sheath dress; **jupe f.** pencil skirt

fourrer [fure] **1** *vt* (**a**) *(gâteau, bonbon)* to fill (**à** with); **bonbon fourré** *Br* soft-centred sweet, *Am* soft-centered candy (**b**) *Fam (mettre)* to stick
2 se fourrer *vpr Fam* **où est-il allé se f.?** where's he got to?; **ne pas savoir où se f.** not to know where to put oneself; **se f. dans une sale affaire** to get involved in a nasty business

fourre-tout [furtu] **1** *adj inv (placard)* junk; **un texte/une loi f.** a ragbag of a text/a law
2 *nm inv* (**a**) *(pièce)* junk room; *(placard)* junk cupboard (**b**) *(sac) Br* holdall, *Am* carryall

fourreur [furœr] *nm* furrier

fourrière [furjɛr] *nf* pound; **mettre en f.** *ou* **à la f.** *(voiture)* to impound; *(chien)* to put in the pound

fourrure [furyr] *nf* fur; **de** *ou* **en f.** fur

fourvoyer [32] [furvwaje] **se fourvoyer** *vpr Litt* to lose one's way; *Fig* to go astray

foutage [futaʒ] *nm très Fam* **c'est du f. de gueule!** you've/he's/*etc* gotta be kidding!, *Br* that's just taking the piss!

foutaise [futɛz] *nf Fam* crap, *Am* bull

foutoir [futwar] *nm Fam* dump

foutre [futr] *très Fam* **1** *vt* (**a**) *(mettre)* to stick; **f. qch par terre** to chuck sth on the ground; **f. qn à la porte** to kick sb out; **f. qch en l'air** *(le faire échouer)* to screw

sth up (**b**) *(faire)* to do; **ne rien f.** to do damn all; **je n'en ai rien à f.!** I don't give *Br* a toss *or Am* a rat's ass!; **qu'est-ce que ça peut f.?** what the hell does it matter? (**c**) *(donner)* *(correction, gifle)* to give; **f. la trouille à qn** to put the wind up sb (**d**) *(locutions)* **f. le camp** to piss off; **fous(-moi) le camp!** piss off!; **je t'en foutrais, du champagne!** champagne, you wish!; *Vulg* **va te faire f.!** fuck off!
2 se foutre *vpr* (**a**) *(se mettre)* **se f. un coup** to bang oneself; **se f. par terre** to go sprawling; **se f. dedans** to screw up (**b**) **se f. de (la gueule de) qn** *(se moquer de)* to take the piss out of sb; **se f. du monde** to take the piss (**c**) **se f. de qn/qch** *(être indifférent à)* not to give a damn about sb/sth; **je m'en fous** I don't give a damn

foutu, -e [futy] *adj Fam* (**a**) *(maudit)* damn (**b**) *(en mauvais état, perdu)* **être f.** to have had it; **c'est f.!** forget it! (**c**) **être bien/mal f.** *(bien/mal bâti)* to have/not to have a nice body; *(bien/mal conçu)* to be well/badly designed; **être mal f.** *(malade)* to be under the weather (**d**) *(capable)* **être f. de faire qch** to be quite likely to do sth; **elle n'est même pas foutue d'être à l'heure** she can't even be bothered to turn up on time

fox [fɔks], **fox-terrier** *(pl* **fox-terriers)** [fɔkstɛrje] *nm* fox terrier

foyer [fwaje] *nm* (**a**) *(domicile)* home; **le f. conjugal** the marital home (**b**) *(famille)* family (**c**) *(résidence)* *(d'étudiants)* residence; *(de travailleurs, de délinquants)* hostel (**d**) *(de chaleur, d'infection)* source; *(d'incendie, de conflits)* seat (**e**) *(âtre)* hearth (**f**) *(de lunettes)* focus

fracas [fraka] *nm* crash

fracassant, -e [frakasɑ̃, -ɑ̃t] *adj (bruit)* deafening; *(nouvelle, révélation)* shattering; *(succès)* resounding

fracasser [frakase] **1** *vt* to smash
2 se fracasser *vpr* to smash

fraction [fraksjɔ̃] *nf* (**a**) *(partie)* part, fraction; **pendant une f. de seconde** for a fraction of a second (**b**) *Math* fraction

fractionnement [fraksjɔnmɑ̃] *nm* splitting up

fractionner [fraksjɔne] **1** *vt* to split up (**en** into)
2 se fractionner *vpr* to split up (**en** into)

fracture [fraktyr] *nf* fracture; **f. du crâne** fractured skull; *Fig* **la f. sociale** the gap between the haves and the have-nots in society

fracturer [fraktyre] **1** *vt* (**a**) *(serrure, porte)* to break open (**b**) *(os)* to fracture
2 se fracturer *vpr* **se f. le tibia** to fracture one's tibia

fragile [fraʒil] *adj (matériau, objet)* fragile; *(santé, estomac, équilibre)* delicate; *(personne) (physiquement)* frail, *(mentalement)* sensitive; *(bonheur)* precarious; *(hypothèse)* shaky

fragiliser [fraʒilize] *vt* to weaken

fragilité [fraʒilite] *nf (d'un matériau, d'un objet)* fragility; *(d'une personne) (physique)* frailty; *(mentale)* sensitivity; *(du bonheur)* precariousness; *(d'une hypothèse)* shakiness; *(de la santé, de l'estomac, d'un équilibre)* delicacy

fragment [fragmɑ̃] *nm (d'un objet, de conversation)* fragment; *(d'un livre)* extract; *(de vérité)* shred

fragmentaire [fragmɑ̃tɛr] *adj* fragmentary

fragmenter [fragmɑ̃te] *vt* to fragment

fraîche [frɛʃ] *adj voir* **frais¹**

fraîchement [frɛʃmɑ̃] *adv* (**a**) *(recevoir, accueillir)* coolly (**b**) *(récemment)* newly

fraîcheur [frɛʃœr] *nf (de la température, d'un accueil)* coolness; *(d'aliments, du teint)* freshness

fraîchir [freʃir] *vi (temps)* to freshen

frais¹, fraîche [frɛ, frɛʃ] **1** *adj* (**a**) *(vent, air, accueil)* cool (**b**) *(aliments, fleurs, teint)* fresh; **f. et dispos** hale and hearty (**c**) *(souvenir, nouvelles)* recent; *(encre, peinture)* wet **2** *adv* **servir/boire f.** *(sur étiquette)* serve/drink chilled **3** *nm* **prendre le f.** to get a breath of fresh air; **mettre/conserver qch au f.** to put/keep sth in a cool place; **il fait f.** it's cool; *Can Fam Péj* **faire le f.** to show off **4** *nf* **à la fraîche** in the cool part of the day; *Can* **prendre la fraîche** *(sortir prendre l'air)* to go for a stroll; *(prendre froid)* to catch a chill

frais² *nmpl* expenses, costs; **faire de gros f.** to go to great expense; **tous f. payés** all expenses paid; **rentrer dans ses f.** to cover one's expenses; *Fig* **faire les f. de qch** *(être victime de)* to pay the price for sth; **faire les f. de la conversation** to keep the conversation going; **faire qch à ses f.** to do sth at one's own expense; **aux f. de la société** at the company's expense; **aux f. de la princesse** at the firm's/government's/*etc* expense; **à grands/peu de f.** at great/little cost; **se mettre en f.** to go to great expense; **en être pour ses f.** to have been wasting one's time; **f. de déplacement** travelling expenses; **f. généraux** overheads; **f. d'inscription** membership fee; **f. de port** postage and packing; **f. de scolarité** school fees; *Can Tél* **appeler qn a f. virés** *Br* to make a reverse-charge call to sb, *Am* to call sb collect; **faux f.** incidental expenses

fraise¹ [frɛz] *nf (fruit)* strawberry; **glace à la f.** strawberry(-flavoured) ice-cream; **f. des bois** wild strawberry

fraise² *nf (de dentiste)* drill

fraise³ *nf (collerette)* ruff

fraisier [frɛzje] *nm* (**a**) *(plante)* strawberry plant (**b**) *(gâteau)* strawberry cream cake

framboise [frãbwaz] *nf* raspberry

framboisier [frãbwazje] *nm* raspberry bush

franc¹ [frã] *nm* franc; *Anciennement* **f. français/belge** French/Belgian franc; **f. suisse** Swiss franc; **f. CFA** CFA franc; **ancien/nouveau f.** old/new franc; **f. symbolique** nominal sum

Le franc

On 17 February 2002, the French franc was officially replaced by the euro. Some shops continued to give prices in francs as well as in euros (for reference only), as many people found it difficult to think in terms of euros, especially where large amounts were concerned. When referring to the value of very expensive things, such as property, it is therefore common for people still to talk in francs. The situation is further complicated by the fact that some older people still think in terms of "anciens francs" (old francs), which were replaced by the "nouveau franc" (new franc) in 1960.

franc², franche [frã, frãʃ] **1** *adj* (**a**) *(sincère)* frank (**b**) *(zone, ville, port)* free (**c**) *(net) (couleur)* pure; *(rupture)* clean **2** *adv (parler)* frankly

français, -e [frãsɛ, -ɛz] **1** *adj* French **2** *nm,f* **F.** Frenchman, *f* Frenchwoman; **les F.** the French **3** *nm (langue)* French; **parler f.** to speak French;

(correctement) to speak properly; *Fam* **tu ne comprends pas le f.?** ≃ don't you understand plain English?

France [frãs] *nf* **la F.** France; *TV* **F. 2/3** = second/third French state-owned TV channel; **F. Télécom** = state-owned telecommunications company

Francfort [frãkfɔr] *n* Frankfurt

franche [frãʃ] *adj voir* **franc²**

franchement [frãʃmã] *adv* (**a**) *(sincèrement)* frankly (**b**) *(tout à fait, vraiment)* really (**c**) *(carrément)* **y aller f.** to get on with it

franchir [frãʃir] *vt (obstacle, difficulté)* to get over; *(porte)* to go through; *(fossé)* to jump (over); *(ligne d'arrivée, rivière, frontière)* to cross; *Fig (cap, seuil, niveau)* to pass

franchise [frãʃiz] *nf* (**a**) *(sincérité)* frankness; **en toute f.** quite frankly (**b**) *(exonération)* exemption; **f. postale** ≃ postage paid (**c**) *(d'assurance) Br* excess, *Am* deductible (**d**) *Com* franchise

franchouillard, -e [frãʃujar, -ard] *adj Fam* typically French

francilien, -enne [frãsiljɛ̃, -ɛn] **1** *adj* of the Île-de-France **2** *nm,f* **F.** person from the Île-de-France

franciscain, -e [frãsiskɛ̃, -ɛn] *adj & nm,f* Franciscan

franciser [frãsize] *vt* to gallicize

franc-maçon, -onne (*pl* **francs-maçons, franc-maçonnes**) [frãmasɔ̃, -ɔn] *nm,f* freemason

franc-maçonnerie [frãmasɔnri] *nf* freemasonry

franco [frãko] *adv* (**a**) *Fam (franchement)* **y aller f.** to get on with it (**b**) *Com* **f. (de port)** postage paid; **f. à bord** free on board

francophile [frãkɔfil] *adj & nmf* Francophile

francophobe [frãkɔfɔb] *adj & nmf* Francophobe

francophone [frãkɔfɔn] **1** *adj* French-speaking **2** *nmf* French speaker

francophonie [frãkɔfɔni] *nf* French-speaking world

franc-parler [frãparle] *nm* outspokenness; **avoir son f.** to speak one's mind

franc-tireur (*pl* **francs-tireurs**) [frãtirœr] *nm (combattant)* irregular (soldier); *Fig* maverick

frange [frãʒ] *nf* (**a**) *(décoratif) & Fig* fringe (**b**) *(de cheveux) Br* fringe, *Am* bangs

frangin, -e [frãʒɛ̃, -in] *nm,f Fam* brother, *f* sister

frangipane [frãʒipan] *nf* = almond-flavoured confectioner's custard

franglais [frãglɛ] *nm* Franglais

franquette [frãkɛt] *nf* **à la bonne f.** without ceremony

frappant, -e [frapã, -ãt] *adj* striking

frappe [frap] *nf* (**a**) *(sur un clavier d'ordinateur)* keying; *(sur une machine à écrire)* typing (**b**) *(de monnaie)* minting (**c**) *(au base-ball)* hit; *(au football)* kick; *(en boxe)* punch (**d**) *Fam (voyou)* hoodlum, *Br* yob (**e**) *Mil* strike; **f. aérienne** airstrike

frappé, -e [frape] *adj* (**a**) *(champagne)* chilled; *(café)* iced (**b**) *Fam (fou)* crazy

frapper [frape] **1** *vt* (**a**) *(donner un ou des coups à)* to hit, to strike; *Fig (faire une forte impression sur)* to strike (**b**) *(monnaie)* to mint (**c**) *(champagne)* to put on ice (**d**) *Can (entrer en collision avec)* to hit **2** *vi* (**a**) *(donner un coup)* to strike, to hit; **f. du poing sur la table** to bang (on) the table; **f. des mains** *ou* **dans ses mains** to clap (one's hands); **f. à la porte** to knock on *or* at the door; *Fig* **tu frappes à la bonne/mauvaise porte** you've come to the right/wrong place; **entrez sans f.** *(sur écriteau)* go straight in (**b**)

Fam (agir) to strike
3 se frapper *vpr* (**a**) *Fam (se faire du souci)* to get oneself worked up (**b**) *Can (entrer en collision)* to collide
frasques [frask] *nfpl* carryings-on
fraternel, -elle [fratɛrnɛl] *adj* fraternal, brotherly
fraterniser [fratɛrnize] *vi* to fraternize
fraternité [fratɛrnite] *nf* fraternity, brotherhood
fratricide [fratrisid] **1** *adj* fratricidal
2 *nmf (personne)* fratricide
3 *nm (crime)* fratricide
fraude [frod] *nf* fraud; **passer qch en f.** to smuggle sth in; **f. électorale** electoral fraud; **f. fiscale** tax evasion
frauder [frode] **1** *vt (douane)* to defraud; **f. le fisc** to evade tax
2 *vi* to cheat (**sur** on)
fraudeur, -euse [frodœr, -øz] *nm,f* defrauder
frauduleux, -euse [frodylø, -øz] *adj* fraudulent
frayer [53] [freje] **1** *vi (poisson)* to spawn; *Fig* **f. avec qn** to mix with sb
2 se frayer *vpr* **se f. un chemin** to clear a way (for oneself)
frayeur [frɛjœr] *nf* fright; **faire une f. à qn** to give sb a fright
fredaines [frədɛn] *nfpl* pranks, escapades
fredonner [frədɔne] *vt & vi* to hum
free-lance [frilɑ̃s] **1** *adj inv* freelance
2 *nm (travail)* freelance work; **travailler en f.** to work freelance
3 *nmf (pl* **free-lances)** freelance, freelancer
freezer [frizœr] *nm* freezer compartment
frégate [fregat] *nf* (**a**) *(oiseau)* frigate bird (**b**) *(navire)* frigate
frein [frɛ̃] *nm* (**a**) *(de voiture)* brake; **donner un coup de f.** to put on the brakes; *Fig* **mettre un f. à qch** to curb sth; **freins à disque** disc brakes; **f. à main** *Br* handbrake, *Am* parking brake; **f. moteur** engine brake (**b**) *(mors)* bit
freinage [frɛnaʒ] *nm* braking
freiner [frɛne] **1** *vt* (**a**) *(véhicule, processus)* to slow down; *(chute)* to break; *(inflation, production)* to curb (**b**) *(personne)* to restrain
2 *vi* to brake
3 se freiner *vpr* to restrain oneself
frelaté, -e [frəlate] *adj (vin)* adulterated
frelater [frəlate] *vt* to adulterate
frêle [frɛl] *adj* frail
frelon [frəlɔ̃] *nm* hornet
freluquet [frəlykɛ] *nm Fam* whippersnapper
frémir [fremir] *vi* (**a**) *(personne)* to tremble (**de** with) (**b**) *(eau chaude)* to simmer; *(feuillage)* to rustle
frémissant, -e [fremisɑ̃, -ɑ̃t] *adj (eau)* simmering; *(voix)* trembling; *(feuillage)* rustling
frémissement [fremismɑ̃] *nm* (**a**) *(de peur)* shudder; *(de plaisir, de joie)* thrill; *(de colère, d'impatience)* quiver (**b**) *(de l'eau)* simmering; *(des feuilles)* rustle
french cancan *(pl* **french cancans)** [frɛnʃkɑ̃kɑ̃] *nm* cancan
frêne [frɛn] *nm* ash
frénésie [frenezi] *nf* frenzy
frénétique [frenetik] *adj* frenzied
frénétiquement [frenetikmɑ̃] *adv* frenziedly
fréquemment [frekamɑ̃] *adv* frequently
fréquence [frekɑ̃s] *nf* frequency; **basse/haute f.** low/high frequency
fréquent, -e [frekɑ̃, -ɑ̃t] *adj* frequent

fréquentable [frekɑ̃tabl] *adj* **des gens peu fréquentables** people you wouldn't want to associate with
fréquentation [frekɑ̃tasjɔ̃] *nf* (**a**) *(d'un lieu)* frequenting; **la f. de qn** seeing sb regularly (**b**) **fréquentations** *(relations)* company; **avoir de mauvaises fréquentations** to keep bad company
fréquenté, -e [frekɑ̃te] *adj* **très f.** very busy; **bien/mal f.** of good/ill repute
fréquenter [frekɑ̃te] **1** *vt* (**a**) *(lieu)* to frequent (**b**) *(personne)* (voir régulièrement) to see regularly; *(sortir avec)* to go out with
2 se fréquenter *vpr (se voir régulièrement)* to see each other regularly; *(sortir ensemble)* to go out with each other
frère [frɛr] **1** *adj (pays, peuple)* fellow
2 *nm* brother; **faux f.** false friend; **frères d'armes** brothers-in-arms
frérot [frero] *nm Fam* kid brother
fresque [frɛsk] *nf* fresco
fret [frɛ, frɛt] *nm* freight
frétillant, -e [fretijɑ̃, -ɑ̃t] *adj (poisson)* wriggling; *(personne) (de joie)* quivering (**de** with)
frétiller [fretije] *vi (poisson, personne)* to wriggle; **f. de joie** to quiver with joy
fretin [frətɛ̃] *nm aussi Fig* **menu f.** small fry
freudien, -enne [frødjɛ̃, -ɛn] *adj* Freudian
freux [frø] *nm* rook
FRF *Anciennement (abrév* **franc(s) français)** FF
friable [frijabl] *adj* crumbly
friand, -e [frijɑ̃, -ɑ̃d] **1** *adj* **être f. de qch** to be fond of sth
2 *nm (salé)* = small savoury pastry; *(sucré)* = small almond cake
friandise [frijɑ̃diz] *nf* titbit, delicacy
fric [frik] *nm Fam* cash, dough
fricassée [frikase] *nf (ragoût)* fricassee; *Belg* fried egg and bacon
friche [friʃ] *nf* fallow land; **en f.** fallow; **f. industrielle** industrial wasteland
frichti [friʃti] *nm Fam* grub
fricot [friko] *nm Fam* grub; **faire le f.** to do the cooking
fricoter [frikɔte] *Fam* **1** *vt* (**a**) *(manigancer)* to cook up (**b**) *(plat)* to cook
2 *vi (avoir des activités suspectes)* to be on the fiddle
friction [friksjɔ̃] *nf* (**a**) *(massage)* rubdown; *(du cuir chevelu)* scalp massage (**b**) *(heurt)* friction
frictionner [friksjɔne] **1** *vt (partie du corps)* to rub; *(personne)* to rub down
2 se frictionner *vpr* to rub oneself
Frigidaire® [friʒidɛr] *nm* fridge
frigide [friʒid] *adj* frigid
frigidité [friʒidite] *nf* frigidity
frigo [frigo] *nm Fam* fridge
frigorifié, -e [frigɔrifje] *adj Fam (personne)* frozen stiff
frigorifier [66] [frigɔrifje] *vt (aliment)* to refrigerate
frigorifique [frigɔrifik] *adj voir* **camion**
frileux, -euse [frilø, -øz] *adj (personne)* sensitive to the cold; *(attitude, réponse)* timid
frime [frim] *nf Fam* show
frimer [frime] *vi Fam* to show off
frimeur, -euse [frimœr, -øz] *nm,f Fam* show-off
frimousse [frimus] *nf* (**a**) *Fam* sweet little face (**b**) *Ordinat (smiley)* smiley
fringale [frɛ̃gal] *nf Fam (faim)* hunger; *Fig (envie)* craving (**de** for); **avoir la f.** to be starving
fringant, -e [frɛ̃gɑ̃, -ɑ̃t] *adj (personne)* dashing

fringuer [frɛ̃ge] *Fam* **1** *vt* to dress
  2 se fringuer *vpr (se vêtir)* to get dressed; *(choisir ses vêtements)* to dress; **il se fringue super bien** he dresses really well, he's a really natty *or* snappy dresser

fringues [frɛ̃g] *nfpl Fam* gear, threads

fripé, -e [fripe] *adj* crumpled

friper [fripe] **1** *vt* to crumple
  2 se friper *vpr* to get crumpled

friperie [fripri] *nf* second-hand clothes shop

fripes [frip] *nfpl* second-hand clothes

fripier, -ère [fripje, -ɛr] *nm,f* second-hand clothes dealer

fripon, -onne [fripɔ̃, -ɔn] *Fam* **1** *adj* mischievous
  2 *nm,f* rascal

fripouille [fripuj] *nf Fam* rogue

friqué, -e [frike] *adj Fam* loaded

frire [19a] [frir] **1** *vt* to fry
  2 *vi* to fry; **faire f. qch** to fry sth

Frisbee® [frizbi] *nm* Frisbee®

frise [friz] *nf* frieze

frisé, -e [frize] **1** *adj (cheveux)* curly; *(personne)* curly-haired
  2 *nf* **frisée** *(salade)* curly endive

friser [frize] **1** *vt* (**a**) *(cheveux)* to curl (**b**) *(approcher)* **f. la catastrophe** to come within an inch of disaster; **elle doit f. la quarantaine** she must be getting on for forty; **cela frise le ridicule** it's verging on the ridiculous
  2 *vi (cheveux)* to curl; *(personne)* to have curly hair

frisette [frizɛt] *nf (de cheveux)* small curl

frisotter [frizɔte] **1** *vt (cheveux)* to frizz
  2 *vi* to be frizzy

frisquet, -ette [friskɛ, -ɛt] *adj Fam* chilly; **il fait f.** it's chilly

frisson [frisɔ̃] *nm (de froid, de peur)* shiver; *(de plaisir)* thrill; **avoir des frissons** to shiver; **donner des frissons** *ou* **le f. à qn** *(de peur)* to give sb the shivers

frissonner [frisɔne] *vi* (**a**) *(personne) (de froid, de peur)* to shiver (**b**) *Litt (feuillage)* to quiver; *(eau)* to ripple

frit, -e [fri, frit] **1** *adj* fried
  2 *nf* **frite** (**a**) *(de pomme de terre) Br* chip, *Am* (French) fry (**b**) *Fam* **avoir la frite** to be on form

friteuse [fritøz] *nf* deep frier, *Br* chip pan; **f. électrique** electric frier

friture [frityr] *nf* (**a**) *(mode de cuisson)* frying (**b**) *(corps gras)* frying fat (**c**) *(aliments)* fried food; **f. (de poissons)** fried fish (**d**) *Rad & Tél* crackling, static (**e**) *Belg (friterie) Br* chip stall, *Am* French fry vendor

frivole [frivɔl] *adj* frivolous

frivolité [frivɔlite] *nf* frivolity

froc [frɔk] *nm* (**a**) *Fam (pantalon) Br* trousers, *Am* pants (**b**) *(habit religieux)* habit

froid, -e [frwa, frwad] **1** *adj aussi Fig* cold
  2 *adv* **boire/manger qch f.** to drink/eat sth cold
  3 *nm* cold; **les grands froids** the coldest part of the winter; **il fait f.** it's cold; *Fam* **il fait un f. de canard** it's freezing (cold); *Fig* **ça fait f. dans le dos** it sends a shiver down your spine; **avoir f.** to be cold; **j'ai f. aux mains** my hands are cold, I've got cold hands; *Fig* **ne pas avoir f. aux yeux** to have plenty of nerve; **à f.** *(répondre)* off the top of one's head; *(humour)* deadpan; **être en f. (avec qn)** to be on bad terms (with sb); **prendre f.** to catch cold

froidement [frwadmã] *adv (accueillir, recevoir)* coldly; *(abattre)* cold-bloodedly; *(répondre)* coolly

froideur [frwadœr] *nf* coldness; **avec f.** coldly

froissement [frwasmã] *nm* (**a**) *(bruit)* rustle (**b**) *(de muscle)* straining

froisser [frwase] **1** *vt* (**a**) *(tissu, papier)* to crumple, to crease (**b**) *Fig (sentiment, personne)* to offend
  2 se froisser *vpr* (**a**) *(tissu)* to crease, to crumple (**b**) **se f. un muscle** to strain a muscle (**c**) *Fig (personne)* to take offence (**de** at)

frôlement [frolmã] *nm (contact)* brushing (**contre** against); *(son)* rustle

frôler [frole] **1** *vt* (**a**) *(effleurer)* to brush (against), to touch lightly (**b**) *Fig (la mort, la catastrophe)* to come close to; *(le ridicule)* to border on
  2 se frôler *vpr* to brush (against) each other

fromage [frɔmaʒ] *nm* (**a**) *(produit laitier)* cheese; *Fam Fig* **faire tout un f. de qch** to make a great fuss about sth; **f. blanc** fromage frais; **f. de brebis** sheep's *or* ewe's milk cheese; **f. de chèvre** goat's cheese; **f. frais** soft cheese; **f. à pâte molle/dure** soft/hard cheese; **f. à tartiner** cheese spread (**b**) **f. de tête** *Br* brawn, *Am* headcheese

fromager, -ère [frɔmaʒe, -ɛr] **1** *adj* cheese
  2 *nm,f (commerçant)* cheese seller; *(fabricant)* cheesemaker

fromagerie [frɔmaʒri] *nf (lieu de fabrication)* cheese dairy; *(magasin)* cheese shop

froment [frɔmã] *nm* wheat

fronce [frɔ̃s] *nf* gather

froncement [frɔ̃smã] *nm* **f. de(s) sourcils** frown

froncer [16] [frɔ̃se] *vt* (**a**) *(nez, front)* to wrinkle; **f. les sourcils** to frown (**b**) *(tissu)* to gather

fronde [frɔ̃d] *nf* (**a**) *(arme)* sling; *(jouet) Br* catapult, *Am* slingshot (**b**) *(révolte)* rebellion

frondeur, -euse [frɔ̃dœr, -øz] **1** *adj* rebellious
  2 *nm,f* rebel

front [frɔ̃] *nm* (**a**) *(partie du visage)* forehead (**b**) *(avant)* front; **faire f.** to face up to things; **faire f. à qn/qch** to face up to sb/sth; **de f.** *(marcher, avancer)* side by side; *(heurter, aborder un problème)* head-on; **mener plusieurs choses de f.** to have several things on the go at once; **f. de mer** seafront (**c**) *(audace)* **avoir le f. de faire qch** to have the nerve to do sth (**d**) *Mil & Météo* front

frontal, -e, -aux, -ales [frɔ̃tal, -o] *adj* (**a**) *(attaque, choc)* head-on; **machine à laver à chargement f.** front-loading washing machine (**b**) *Ordinat* front-end; **ordinateur f.** front end (**c**) *(os)* frontal

frontalier, -ère [frɔ̃talje, -ɛr] **1** *adj (région)* border, frontier
  2 *nm,f (habitant)* person living near the border; *(travailleur)* cross-border commuter

frontière [frɔ̃tjɛr] **1** *adj (ville, poste)* border, frontier
  2 *nf (entre pays)* border, frontier; *Fig (des langues)* boundary; *(de la connaissance)* frontier

frontispice [frɔ̃tispis] *nm* frontispiece

fronton [frɔ̃tɔ̃] *nm* (**a**) *(sur monument)* pediment (**b**) *(de pelote basque)* fronton

frottement [frɔtmã] *nm* (**a**) *(d'une chose contre une autre)* rubbing; *Tech* friction (**b**) *(heurt)* friction

frotter [frɔte] **1** *vt* to rub; *(allumette)* to strike; *(parquet)* to scrub; *Belg Fam* **f. la manche à qn** to soft-soap sb
  2 *vi* to rub (**contre** against)
  3 se frotter *vpr* to rub oneself; *aussi Fig* **se f. les mains** to rub one's hands; *Fig* **se f. à qn/qch** to be in contact with sb/sth; *Fig* **se f. à qn** *(l'attaquer)* to meddle with sb

frottis [frɔti] *nm Méd* smear; **f. vaginal** cervical smear
froufrou [frufru] *nm* (**a**) *(bruit)* rustling (**b**) **frou-frous** *(vêtements)* frills; **robe à froufrous** frilly dress
froufrouter [frufrute] *vi* to rustle
froussard, -e [frusar, -ard] *adj & nm,f Fam* chicken
frousse [frus] *nf Fam* fear; **avoir la f.** to be scared; **flanquer la f. à qn** to put the wind up sb
fructifier [66] [fryktifje] *vi (arbres, idée)* to bear fruit; *(terre)* to be productive; *(placements, capital)* to yield a profit; **faire f. qch** *(idée, projet)* to bring sth to fruition
fructose [fryktoz] *nm* fructose
fructueux, -euse [fryktɥø, -øz] *adj* fruitful, profitable
frugal, -e, -aux, -ales [frygal, -o] *adj* frugal
frugalité [frygalite] *nf* frugality
fruit [frɥi] *nm aussi Fig* fruit; **des fruits** (some) fruit; **un f.** some fruit, a piece of fruit; **fruits confits** crystallized fruit; *Fig* **le f. défendu** the forbidden fruit; **fruits de mer** seafood; **f. de la passion** passion fruit; **fruits rouges** red berries and currants; **fruits secs** dried fruit; *Suisse* **petits fruits** fruits of the forest; *Fig* **porter ses fruits** *(action, investissement)* to bear fruit
fruité, -e [frɥite] *adj* fruity
fruitier, -ère [frɥitje, -ɛr] **1** *adj voir* **arbre**
  2 *nm,f* fruit seller; *Br* fruiterer
frusques [frysk] *nfpl Fam* gear, threads
fruste [fryst] *adj (style, personne)* rough
frustrant, -e [frystrã, -ãt] *adj* frustrating
frustration [frystrasjɔ̃] *nf* frustration
frustré, -e [frystre] **1** *adj* frustrated
  2 *nm,f* frustrated person
frustrer [frystre] *vt* (**a**) *(décevoir)* to frustrate (**b**) *(priver)* **f. qn de qch** to deprive sb of sth
FTP [ɛftepe] **1** *nm Ordinat (abrév* **File Transfer Protocol**) FTP
  2 *nmpl Hist (abrév* **Francs-tireurs et partisans**) = Communist resistance during World War II
fuchsia [fyʃja] **1** *adj inv* (**rose**) **f.** fuchsia
  2 *nm (fleur, couleur)* fuchsia
fuel [fjul] *nm* fuel oil
fugace [fygas] *adj* fleeting
fugitif, -ive [fyʒitif, -iv] **1** *adj (fugace)* fleeting
  2 *nm,f* fugitive, runaway
fugue [fyg] *nf* (**a**) *(composition musicale)* fugue (**b**) *(d'un enfant)* **faire une f.** to run away
fuguer [fyge] *vi* to run away
fugueur, -euse [fygœr, -øz] **1** *adj* who runs away a lot
  2 *nm,f* runaway
fui *voir* **fuir**
fuir [38] [fɥir] **1** *vt (pays)* to flee; *(personne)* to run away from; *(guerre)* to escape; *(responsabilités)* to shirk
  2 *vi* (**a**) *(s'échapper)* to run away, to flee (**devant** from); **f. de son pays** to flee one's country (**b**) *(robinet, gaz, eau)* to leak (**c**) *(s'écouler rapidement)* to fly by
fuis, fuit *voir* **fuir**
fuite [fɥit] *nf* (**a**) *(escapade)* flight (**devant** from); *Fig (devant des difficultés, des problèmes)* avoidance (**devant** of); **prendre la f.** to take flight; **être en f.** to be on the run; **mettre qn en f.** to put sb to flight; **la f. des capitaux** the flight of capital; **la f. des cerveaux** the brain drain (**b**) *(de liquide, de gaz, d'informations)* leak

fulgurant, -e [fylgyrã, -ãt] *adj* (**a**) *(attaque, changement, rapidité)* lightning; *(succès)* spectacular (**b**) *(douleur)* searing
fulminer [fylmine] *vi* to fulminate (**contre** against)
fumant, -e [fymã, -ãt] *adj* (**a**) *(âtre, cendres)* smoking; *(potage)* steaming (**b**) *Fam (remarquable)* **faire un coup f.** to pull off a masterstroke
fumé, -e¹ [fyme] *adj* (**a**) *(poisson, viande)* smoked (**b**) *(verres)* tinted
fume-cigare [fymsigar] *nm inv* cigar holder
fumée² [fyme] *nf (de feu, de cigarette)* smoke; *(d'un liquide chaud)* steam; *Prov* **il n'y a pas de f. sans feu** there's no smoke without fire
fumer [fyme] **1** *vt (poisson, viande)* to smoke (**b**) *(tabac, cigarette)* to smoke; **f. la pipe** to smoke a pipe
  2 *vi* (**a**) *(feu, moteur)* to smoke; *(liquide, plat)* to steam (**b**) *(fumeur)* to smoke; **f. comme un pompier** *ou* **un sapeur** to smoke like a chimney
fumet [fymɛ] *nm (d'un mets)* aroma
fumeur, -euse¹ [fymœr, -øz] *nm,f* smoker; **fumeurs** *(sur panneau)* smoking
fumeux, -euse² [fymø, -øz] *adj (idées, explications, projets)* hazy
fumier [fymje] *nm* (**a**) *(engrais)* manure, dung (**b**) *très Fam (injure)* bastard
fumigation [fymigasjɔ̃] *nf* fumigation; *Méd* inhalation; **faire des fumigations de désinfectant** to fumigate with disinfectant
fumiste [fymist] **1** *nmf Fam (sur qui on ne peut compter)* joker
  2 *nm (technicien)* heating engineer
  3 *adj Fam* unreliable
fumisterie [fymistəri] *nf* (**a**) *(métier)* heating engineering (**b**) *Fam (farce)* con
fumoir [fymwar] *nm* smoking room
funambule [fynãbyl] *nmf* tightrope walker
funboard [fœnbɔrd] *nm* funboard
funèbre [fynɛbr] *adj* (**a**) *(cérémonie, marche)* funeral; **hymne** *ou* **chant f.** dirge (**b**) *(lugubre)* funereal
funérailles [fyneraj] *nfpl* funeral; **f. nationales** state funeral
funéraire [fynerɛr] *adj (dépenses, urne)* funeral; **pierre f.** tombstone, gravestone
funeste [fynɛst] *adj* (**a**) *(erreur, conséquences, influence)* disastrous (**b**) *Litt (accident)* fatal
funiculaire [fynikylɛr] *nm* funicular (railway)
funk [fœnk] *nm Mus* funk
funky [fœnki] *adj inv Fam* funky
fur [fyr] *nm* **au f. et à mesure** as one goes along, bit by bit; **au f. et à mesure de leurs recherches** as they progressed with their research
furax [fyraks] *adj inv Fam* livid
furet [fyrɛ] *nm* ferret
fureter [6] [fyrte] *vi (chercher)* to ferret about
fureur [fyrœr] *nf* (**a**) *(colère)* fury, rage (**b**) *(passion)* passion; **faire f.** to be all the rage
furibard, -e [fyribar, -ard] *adj Fam* livid
furibond, -e [fyribɔ̃, -ɔ̃d] *adj* furious
furie [fyri] *nf* (**a**) *(rage)* fury; **en f.** infuriated; **la f. du jeu** a passion for gambling (**b**) *Fig (femme)* shrew; **comme une f.** like a wild thing
furieux, -euse [fyrjø, -øz] **1** *adj* (**a**) *(en colère)* furious (**contre** with); *Fig (tempête)* raging; *(combat)* violent (**b**) *Fam (intense) (envie)* overwhelming, tremendous
furoncle [fyrɔ̃kl] *nm* boil
furtif, -ive [fyrtif, -iv] *adj* furtive, stealthy

furtivement [fyrtivmɑ̃] *adv* furtively, stealthily; **entrer f.** to sneak in

fusain [fyzɛ̃] *nm (crayon, dessin)* charcoal

fuseau, -x [fyzo] *nm* (**a**) *(pantalon)* ski pants (**b**) *(pour filer la laine)* spindle; *(pour faire de la dentelle)* bobbin (**c**) **f. horaire** time zone

fusée [fyze] *nf* (**a**) *(projectile)* rocket; **il est parti comme une f.** he shot off like a rocket; **f. éclairante** flare (**b**) *(d'axe)* spindle; *Aut* stub axle

fuselage [fyzlaʒ] *nm (d'un avion)* fuselage

fuselé, -e [fyzle] *adj (colonne, doigts)* tapering; *(voiture)* streamlined

fuser [fyze] *vi* **des rires/cris fusèrent de toutes parts** laughter was/cries were suddenly heard from all sides

fusible [fyzibl] *nm* fuse

fusil [fyzi] *nm* (**a**) *(arme)* gun, rifle; **f. à air comprimé** air gun; **f. d'assaut** assault rifle; **f. de chasse** shotgun; **f. à lunette** rifle with telescopic sight; *Fig* **changer son f. d'épaule** to change tack; **coup de f.** gunshot; *Fam* **c'est le coup de f. dans ce restaurant** the prices in this restaurant are extortionate; *Can* **partir/entrer en coup de f.** to storm in/out (**b**) *(personne)* shot (**c**) *(pour aiguiser)* steel

fusilier [fyzilje] *nm* fusilier; **f. marin** marine

fusillade [fyzijad] *nf (tir)* gunfire

fusiller [fyzije] *vt* (**a**) *(par un peloton d'exécution)* to shoot; *Fig* **f. qn du regard** to look daggers at sb (**b**) *Fam (abîmer)* to wreck

fusil-mitrailleur *(pl* **fusils-mitrailleurs)** [fyzimitrajœr] *nm* light machine-gun

fusion [fyzjɔ̃] *nf* (**a**) *(par la chaleur)* melting, *Spéc* fusion; *(en métallurgie)* smelting; **point de f.** melting point; **métal/roche en f.** molten metal/rock (**b**) *(de sociétés)* merger; **fusions et acquisitions** mergers and acquisitions; *Ordinat* **f. de fichiers** file merge

fusionner [fyzjɔne] *vi & vt aussi Ordinat* to merge

fustiger [45] [fystiʒe] *vt (critiquer)* to castigate

fût [fy] *nm* (**a**) *(tonneau)* cask, barrel (**b**) *(d'arbre)* bole (**c**) *(de colonne)* shaft (**d**) *(de fusil)* stock

futaie [fytɛ] *nf* forest *(producing timber from full-grown trees)*

futal [fytal] *nm,* **fute** [fyt] *nm Fam Br* trousers, *Am* pants

futé, -e [fyte] **1** *adj* crafty; **il n'est pas très f.** he's not very bright; *aussi Ironique* **ça, c'est f.!** that was clever!
2 *nm* crafty one

futile [fytil] *adj (argument, occupation, prétexte)* trivial, trifling; *(personne)* frivolous

futilement [fytilmɑ̃] *adv* frivolously

futilité [fytilite] *nf* triviality

futon [fytɔ̃] *nm* futon

futur, -e [fytyr] **1** *adj* future; **un f. artiste** a budding artist; **mon f. emploi** my next job; **mon f. mari** my husband-to-be
2 *nm,f Hum* **mon f./ma future** my intended
3 *nm* (**a**) *(avenir)* future (**b**) *Gram* future (tense); **au f. in the future (tense); **f. antérieur** future perfect

futurisme [fytyrism] *nm* futurism

futuriste [fytyrist] **1** *adj* futuristic
2 *nmf* futurist

fuyant, -e [fɥijɑ̃, -ɑ̃t] *adj* (**a**) *(ligne, menton)* receding; *Art* **lignes fuyantes** perspective lines (**b**) *(personne, attitude)* evasive; *(yeux)* shifty

fuyard, -e [fɥijar, -ard] *nm,f* fugitive, runaway

fuyez *etc voir* **fuir**

G¹, g [ʒe] *nm inv* G, g; **le G8** the G8
G² [ʒe] *nm Belg Fam (abrév* **GSM**) mobile (phone)
g. (**a**) *(abrév* **gauche**) L (**b**) *(abrév* **gramme(s)**) g
gabardine [gabardin] *nf* gabardine
gabarit [gabari] *nm* (**a**) *(dimension)* size (**b**) *Fam (corpulence)* **un grand/petit g.** a huge/tiny man, *f* a huge/tiny woman (**c**) *(valeur)* calibre (**d**) *(instrument)* gauge (**e**) *Ordinat* template
Gabon [gabɔ̃] *nm* **le G.** Gabon
gabonais, -e [gabɔnɛ, -ɛz] **1** *adj* Gabonese
2 *nm,f* **G.** Gabonese
gâcher [gɑʃe] *vt* (**a**) *(gaspiller)* to waste (**b**) *(gâter)* *(plaisir, soirée)* to spoil (**c**) *(mélanger)* *(mortier, plâtre)* to mix
gâchette [gɑʃɛt, gaʃɛt] *nf* trigger; *Fam* **avoir la g. facile** to be trigger-happy; **appuyer sur la g.** to pull the trigger
gâchis [gɑʃi] *nm* waste
gadelle [gadɛl] *nf Can Bot* currant; **g. rouge** redcurrant
gadget [gadʒɛt] *nm* gadget
gadoue [gadu] *nf* mud
gaélique [gaelik] *adj & nm* Gaelic
gaffe [gaf] *nf* (**a**) *Fam (maladresse)* blunder; **faire une g.** to put one's foot in it (**b**) *(perche)* boathook (**c**) *Fam* **faire g.** to be careful, to watch out
gaffer [gafe] **1** *vt (objet flottant)* to hook; *(poisson)* to gaff
2 *vi Fam* to put one's foot in it
gaffeur, -euse [gafœr, -øz] *nm,f Fam* blunderer
gag [gag] *nm* gag
gaga [gaga] *adj Fam* gaga
gage [gaʒ] *nm* (**a**) *(chez le prêteur sur gages)* pledge; *Fig (garantie)* guarantee; **laisser qch en g.** to leave sth as security; **mettre qch en g.** to pawn sth (**b**) *(preuve)* token; **en g. de notre amitié** as a token of our friendship (**c**) *(dans un jeu)* forfeit (**d**) *Vieilli (salaire)* **gages** wages
gager [45] [gaʒe] *vt Litt* **que...** to wager that...
gageure [gaʒyr] *nf* (**a**) *(action difficile)* challenge (**b**) *Litt (pari)* wager
gagnant, -e [gaɲɑ̃, -ɑ̃t] **1** *adj* winning
2 *nm,f* winner; **partir g.** to have a strong chance of winning
gagne-pain [gaɲpɛ̃] *nm inv* livelihood
gagne-petit [gaɲpəti] *nmf inv* low wage earner
gagner [gaɲe] **1** *vt* (**a**) *(remporter) (course, prix, guerre)* to win; **rien n'est encore gagné!** it's not in the bag yet! (**b**) *(comme rémunération)* to earn; **g. sa vie** to earn one's living (**c**) *(obtenir)* to gain; **g. du temps** *(aller plus vite)* to save time; *(temporiser)* to

gain time; **g. de l'espace** to save space; **chercher à g. du temps** to play for time; **c'est toujours ça de gagné** that's something, anyway; **tu as tout à g.** you've got everything to gain; **et moi, qu'est-ce que j'y gagne?** and what do I get out of it? (**d**) *(se concilier)* **g. qn à une cause** to win sb over to a cause; **g. la confiance/ l'estime de qn** to win or gain sb's confidence/respect (**e**) *(atteindre) (ville, sortie, porte)* to reach, to get to; *(sujet: maladie, infection)* to spread to; *(sujet: sentiment, sommeil)* to overcome; **le rire gagna l'assemblée tout entière** laughter spread through the whole audience (**f**) *(s'étendre à) (sujet: feu, épidémie)* to spread to; **g. du terrain** to gain ground (**g**) *(battre)* **g. qn de vitesse** to outstrip sb
2 *vi* (**a**) *(être vainqueur)* to win; **g. haut la main** to win hands down (**b**) *(profiter)* **g. à qch/à faire qch** to benefit from sth/from doing sth; **g. à être connu** to improve with acquaintance; **j'ai gagné au change** I got the best of the deal (**c**) *(croître)* to increase; **g. en intensité/en vigueur** to increase in intensity/in strength
gagneur, -euse [gaɲœr, -øz] *nm,f* winner
gai, -e [gɛ] *adj* (**a**) *(personne, voix, décor, musique)* cheerful; **g. comme un pinson** happy as a lark; *Fam* **être un peu g.** *(ivre)* to be tipsy; *Ironique* **ça va être g.!** that'll be fun! (**b**) *Belg (agréable)* nice, pleasant (**c**) *(homosexuel)* = gay
gaiement [gɛmɑ̃] *adv* cheerfully; *Ironique* **allons-y g.!** let's get on with it!
gaieté [gete] *nf* cheerfulness, gaiety; **je ne le fais pas de g. de cœur** I don't enjoy doing it
gaillard, -e [gajar, -ard] **1** *adj* (**a**) *(vigoureux) (personne)* strong; *(vieillard)* sprightly (**b**) *(jovial) (humeur)* merry; *(grivois) (histoire, commentaire)* bawdy
2 *nm* (**a**) *(homme)* hearty type; **un grand et solide g.** a great strapping man; **toi mon g., tu ne perds rien pour attendre!** just you wait, pal! (**b**) *Naut* **g. d'avant** forecastle; **g. d'arrière** poop
gaîment [gɛmɑ̃] = **gaiement**
gain [gɛ̃] *nm* (**a**) *(succès)* winning; **avoir** ou **obtenir g. de cause** to win one's case; **donner g. de cause à qn** to decide in favour of sb (**b**) *(profit)* gain, profit; **l'appât du g.** the lure of money (**c**) *(économie)* **ça fait un sacré g. de temps/de place** that saves an awful lot of time/space (**d**) **gains** *(au jeu)* winnings; *(à la Bourse)* profit (**e**) *Suisse* **par g. de paix** as a conciliatory gesture
gaine [gɛn] *nf* (**a**) *(étui)* sheath (**b**) *Anat & Bot* sheath (**c**) *(sous-vêtement)* girdle
gainer [gene] *vt* to sheathe (**de** in)
Gal *Mil (abrév* **Général**) Gen

gala [gala] *nm* gala; **en habit** *ou* **tenue de g.** in gala dress; *Fig* in one's best clothes

galamment [galamɑ̃] *adv* gallantly

galant, -e [galɑ̃, -ɑ̃t] **1** *adj (homme)* gallant; **rendez-vous g.** romantic rendezvous
  2 *nm Vieilli & Litt* gallant

galanterie [galɑ̃tri] *nf* gallantry; **dire des galanteries à qn** to pay sb compliments

Galapagos [galapagos] *nfpl* **les (îles) G.** the Galapagos (Islands)

galaxie [galaksi] *nf* galaxy

galbe [galb] *nm* curve

galbé, -e [galbe] *adj* shapely

gale [gal] *nf* (**a**) *Méd* scabies; *Fig* **je n'ai pas la g.!** I haven't got the plague! (**b**) *(de chien, de chat)* mange (**c**) *Bot* scab

galère [galɛr] *nf* (**a**) *(navire)* galley (**b**) *Fam (situation pénible)* hassle; **je me suis mis dans une g. pas possible** I got myself into a terrible mess; **être dans la même g.** to be in the same boat

galérer [34] [galere] *vi Fam* to have a hard time

galerie [galri] *nf* (**a**) *(passage, salle)* gallery; *Can (véranda)* porch; **g. d'art/de portraits** art/portrait gallery; **g. marchande** shopping arcade, *Am* mall (**b**) *(dans une mine)* gallery; *(de taupe)* tunnel (**c**) *(de voiture)* roof rack (**d**) *(de théâtre)* balcony; *Fig* **c'est pour (épater) la g.** it's just showing off

galérien [galerjɛ̃] *nm* galley slave

galet [galɛ] *nm* (**a**) *(caillou)* pebble; **plage de galets** shingle beach (**b**) *Tech* roller

galette [galɛt] *nf* (**a**) *(crêpe de blé noir)* buckwheat pancake; **g. des Rois** Twelfth Night cake (**b**) *(biscuit rond sablé)* butter biscuit (**c**) *Belg (gaufrette)* wafer (**d**) *Fam (argent)* cash, dough

galeux, -euse [galø, -øz] *adj (chien)* mangy; *(mur)* peeling

Galice [galis] *nf* **la G.** Galicia

galicien, -enne [galisjɛ̃, -ɛn] **1** *adj* Galician
  2 *nm,f* **G.** Galician

Galilée¹ [galile] *nf (région)* **la G.** Galilee

Galilée² *npr* Galileo

galimatias [galimatja] *nm* gibberish

galion [galjɔ̃] *nm* galleon

galipette [galipɛt] *nf Fam* somersault; **faire des galipettes** to do somersaults; *(ébats amoureux)* to have a romp

galipote [galipɔt] *nf Can* **courir la g.** to chase women

Galles [gal] *voir* **pays**

gallicisme [galisism] *nm Ling* Gallicism

gallois, -e [galwa, -az] **1** *adj* Welsh
  2 *nm,f* **G.** Welshman, *f* Welshwoman; **les G.** the Welsh
  3 *nm (langue)* Welsh

gallon [galɔ̃] *nm* gallon

gallo-romain, -e *(mpl* **gallo-romains,** *fpl* **gallo-romaines)** [galorɔmɛ̃, -ɛn] *adj* Gallo-Roman

galoche [galɔʃ] *nf* clog *(with leather upper)*

galon [galɔ̃] *nm* (**a**) *(en couture)* braid (**b**) *(de militaire)* stripe; *Fam* **prendre du g.** to get promoted (**c**) *Can* **g. (à mesurer)** measuring tape

galop [galo] *nm* gallop; **au g.** at a gallop; *Fig* **allez, au travail et au g.!** come on, to work, and be quick about it!; **g. d'essai** trial run

galopade [galɔpad] *nf* (**a**) *(de cheval)* gallop (**b**) *(de personnes)* stampede

galopant, -e [galɔpɑ̃, -ɑ̃t] *adj (inflation)* galloping; **phtisie galopante** galloping consumption

galoper [galɔpe] *vi (cheval)* to gallop; *(enfant)* to charge

galopin [galɔpɛ̃] *nm Fam* urchin; **espèce de petit g.!** you little rascal!

galure [galyr] *nm*, **galurin** [galyrɛ̃] *nm Fam* hat

galvaniser [galvanize] *vt* to galvanize

galvauder [galvode] **1** *vt (nom, réputation)* to bring into disrepute; *(talents, dons)* to prostitute; *(mot)* to overuse
  2 *se galvauder vpr* to damage one's reputation

gambade [gɑ̃bad] *nf* leap

gambader [gɑ̃bade] *vi* to leap *or* frisk about

gambas [gɑ̃bas] *nfpl* large prawns

gamberger [45] [gɑ̃berʒe] *vi Fam* to think hard

gambette [gɑ̃bɛt] *nf Fam (jambe)* leg, *Br* pin

Gambie [gɑ̃bi] *nf* **la G.** the Gambia

gamelle [gamɛl] *nf (de soldat)* mess tin; *(d'ouvrier)* billy(can); *(d'animal)* bowl; *Hum (assiette)* plate; *Fam* **aussi** *Fig* **(se) ramasser** *ou* **(se) prendre une g.** to fall flat on one's face, *Br* to come a cropper

gamète [gamɛt] *nm* gamete

gamin, -e [gamɛ̃, -in] **1** *nm,f (enfant)* kid; **une gamine de dix ans** a girl of ten
  2 *adj* (**a**) *(jeune)* **elle était encore toute gamine** she was still just a child (**b**) *(puéril)* childish

gaminerie [gaminri] *nf (acte)* childish prank; *(comportement)* childishness

gamme [gam] *nf* (**a**) *(de couleurs, de prix, d'articles)* range; **produit bas/haut de g.** bottom-of-the-range/top-of-the-range product (**b**) *Mus* scale

gammée [game] *adj f voir* **croix**

ganache [ganaʃ] *nf* (**a**) *Fam (imbécile)* **vieille g.** old fool (**b**) *(d'un cheval)* lower jaw

Gand [gɑ̃] *n* Ghent

gang [gɑ̃g] *nm* gang

Gange [gɑ̃ʒ] *nm* **le G.** the Ganges

ganglion [gɑ̃glijɔ̃] *nm* ganglion; **j'ai des ganglions** I've got swollen glands

gangrène [gɑ̃grɛn] *nf* (**a**) *Méd* gangrene (**b**) *Fig* canker

gangrener [46] [gɑ̃grəne] **1** *vt* (**a**) *Méd* to turn gangrenous (**b**) *Fig* to corrupt
  2 *se gangrener vpr* (**a**) *Méd* to go gangrenous (**b**) *Fig* to become corrupt

gangster [gɑ̃gstɛr] *nm* gangster

gangstérisme [gɑ̃gsterism] *nm* gangsterism

gangue [gɑ̃g] *nf (de minerai)* gangue; *(couche) (de boue, de glace)* layer; *Fig (carcan)* straitjacket

gant [gɑ̃] *nm* glove; **g. de boxe** boxing glove; **gants de caoutchouc** rubber gloves; **g. de toilette** facecloth; *Fig* **cela vous va comme un g.** it fits you like a glove; **prendre** *ou* **mettre des gants avec qn** to handle sb with kid gloves; **jeter le g. à qn** to throw down the gauntlet to sb; **relever le g.** to take up the gauntlet

ganté, -e [gɑ̃te] *adj (personne)* wearing gloves; *(main)* gloved

gantelet [gɑ̃tlɛ] *nm* gauntlet

garage [garaʒ] *nm (pour se garer, pour les réparations)* garage; **g. de** *ou* **à bicyclettes** bicycle shed; **g. d'autobus** bus depot; *Can* **vente de g.** garage sale

garagiste [garaʒist] *nmf (propriétaire)* garage owner; *(mécanicien)* garage mechanic

garant, -e [garɑ̃, -ɑ̃t] *nm,f* guarantor; **se porter g. de qn** *(à la banque)* to stand guarantor for sb; **se porter g. de qch** to vouch for sth

garantie [garɑ̃ti] *nf* (**a**) *(précaution)* guarantee, safeguard (**contre** against) (**b**) *(de produit)* guarantee;

être sous g. to be under guarantee (**c**) *(certitude)* guarantee

garantir [garɑ̃tir] *vt* (**a**) *(promettre)* to guarantee; **g. à qn que** to give sb a guarantee that; **je te le garantis** I can vouch for it (**b**) *Fin (émission d'actions)* to underwrite; *(emprunt)* to secure (**c**) *(protéger)* to protect (**de** from)

garce [gars] *nf très Fam* bitch

garçon [garsɔ̃] *nm* (**a**) *(enfant mâle, fils)* boy; *(jeune homme)* young man; **un mauvais g.** a bad sort; **vieux g.** confirmed bachelor; **g. manqué** tomboy (**b**) *(serveur)* waiter; **g. d'ascenseur** *Br* lift attendant, *Am* elevator operator; **g. de café** waiter; **g. d'honneur** best man

garçonne [garsɔn] *nf* **être coiffée à la g.** to have an Eton crop

garçonnet [garsɔnɛ] *nm* little boy

garçonnière [garsɔnjɛr] *nf* bachelor *Br* flat *or Am* apartment

garde¹ [gard] *nf* (**a**) *(protection)* care; *Jur* **g. des enfants** *(après un divorce)* custody of the children (**b**) *(surveillance)* guarding; **être de g.** to be on duty; **monter la g.** to mount guard; **médecin de g.** duty doctor; **pharmacie de g.** emergency chemist (**c**) *(méfiance)* **mettre qn en g. contre qn/qch** to warn sb against sb/sth; **être** *ou* **se tenir sur ses gardes** to be on one's guard; **prendre g. à qn/qch** to watch out for sb/sth; **prendre g. que... (ne)** + *subjunctive* to be careful that...; **prendre g. de ne pas faire qch** to be careful not to do sth (**d**) *(groupe de soldats)* **la g.** the guard; **g. d'honneur** guard of honour; **la G. républicaine** the Republican Guard *(of Paris)* (**e**) *Jur* **g. à vue** police custody; **il a été mis/est resté en g. à vue** he was put/was held in police custody (**f**) *(en boxe, en escrime)* guard; **se mettre en g.** to take one's guard; **en g.!** on guard! (**g**) *Aut* **g. au sol** ground clearance (**h**) *(d'une épée)* hilt

garde² **1** *nm* (**a**) *(soldat) (sentinelle)* guard; *(dans une garde)* guardsman; **g. mobile** = member of the security police (**b**) *(dans un domaine particulier)* **g. champêtre** rural policeman; **g. du corps** bodyguard; **g. forestier** *Br* forest warden, *Am* ranger (**c**) **le g. des Sceaux** the (French) Minister of Justice
  2 *nmf* **g. de nuit** *(pour un malade)* night nurse *(privately employed)*; **g. d'enfants** childminder

garde-à-vous [gardavu] *nm inv Mil* (position of) attention; **se mettre/être au g.** to stand to attention; **g.!** attention!

garde-barrière *(pl* **gardes-barrière(s)**) [gardəbarjɛr] *nmf Br* level-crossing *or Am* grade-crossing keeper

garde-boue [gardəbu] *nm inv* mudguard

garde-chasse *(pl* **gardes-chasse(s)**) [gardəʃas] *nm* gamekeeper

garde-chiourme *(pl* **gardes-chiourme(s)**) [gardəʃjurm] *nm (personne autoritaire et brutale)* martinet

garde-côte *(pl* **garde-côtes**) [gardəkot] *nm (bateau)* coastguard vessel

garde-feu [gardəfø] *nm inv* (**a**) *(grille)* fireguard (**b**) *Can (personne)* forest warden

garde-fou *(pl* **garde-fous**) [gardəfu] *nm (mur)* parapet; *(rambarde)* railing; *Fig* safeguard

garde-malade *(pl* **gardes-malade(s)**) [gardəmalad] *nmf* nurse

garde-manger [gardəmɑ̃ʒe] *nm inv* larder

garde-meuble *(pl* **garde-meubles**) [gardəmœbl] *nm* furniture repository; **mettre une table au g.** to put a table into storage

gardénia [gardenja] *nm* gardenia

garder [garde] **1** *vt* (**a**) *(conserver)* to keep; **g. qn à dîner** to get sb to stay for dinner; **g. la chambre** to keep to *or* stay in one's room; **devoir g. le lit** to be confined to bed; **g. la tête froide** to keep a cool head (**b**) *(surveiller) (maison, sac, enfants)* to look after, to mind; *Jur* **g. qn à vue** to hold sb in custody (**c**) *(protéger)* to protect (**de** from); **que Dieu nous garde!** God protect us!
  2 se garder *vpr* (**a**) *(se méfier)* **se g. de qn/qch** to beware of sb/sth (**b**) *(s'abstenir)* **se g. de faire qch** to be careful not to do sth (**c**) *Fam (conserver)* **tes réflexions, tu peux te les g.!** you can keep your thoughts to yourself! (**d**) *(se conserver)* to keep

garderie [gardəri] *nf Br* day nursery, *Am* daycare center; *(dans un magasin, une université) Br* crèche, *Am* baby-sitting service; *(le soir, après l'école)* childminding service

garde-robe *(pl* **garde-robes**) [gardərɔb] *nf (armoire, vêtements)* wardrobe

gardien, -enne [gardjɛ̃, -ɛn] **1** *nm,f (concierge)* caretaker, *Am* janitor; *(de musée, de parking)* attendant; *Fig (de libertés, traditions)* guardian; **g. de but** goalkeeper; **g. de nuit** night watchman; **g. de la paix** policeman; **g. de prison** prison *Br* warder *or Am* guard
  2 gardienne *nf* (**a**) *(personne)* **gardienne d'enfants** childminder (**b**) *Belg (école)* nursery school, kindergarten

gardiennage [gardjɛnaʒ] *nm (d'un bâtiment)* caretaking; *(de locaux)* guarding; **société de g.** security firm

gardon [gardɔ̃] *nm* roach; *Fig* **frais comme un g.** fresh as a daisy

gare¹ [gar] *nf* station; **g. maritime** harbour station; **g. de marchandises** goods station; **g. routière** bus station; **g. de triage** marshalling yard

gare² [gar] *exclam* (**a**) *(menace)* **g. à toi si on l'apprend** woe betide you if anyone finds out; *Fam* **si je te reprends à voler du gâteau, g. à tes fesses!** if I catch you stealing cake again, you've had it! (**b**) *(attention)* **g. aux orties!** mind the nettles!; **sans crier g.** without warning

garer [gare] **1** *vt (voiture)* to park
  2 se garer *vpr* (**a**) *(automobiliste)* to park (**b**) **se g. de qn/qch** to steer clear of sb/sth; *Fam* **garez-vous!** get out of the way!

gargariser [gargarize] **se gargariser** *vpr* to gargle; *Fam Péj* **se g. de qch** to revel in sth

gargarisme [gargarism] *nm (produit)* mouthwash; *(action)* gargling; **faire des gargarismes** to gargle

gargote [gargɔt] *nf Péj* cheap restaurant

gargouillement [gargujmɑ̃] *nm* gurgling; *(d'estomac)* rumbling

gargouiller [garguje] *vi* (**a**) *(eau)* to gurgle (**b**) *(estomac)* to rumble

gargouillis [garguji] = **gargouillement**

garnement [garnəmɑ̃] *nm* scamp, rascal

garni, -e [garni] *adj* (**a**) **bien g.** *(bourse)* well-lined (**b**) *(plat, viande)* with vegetables

garnir [garnir] *vt* (**a**) *(munir)* to fit out (**de** with); *(commode, tiroir)* to line; *(siège) (rembourrer)* to stuff; *(couvrir)* to cover (**b**) *(embellir) (robe, chapeau)* to trim (**de** with) (**c**) *Culin (plat)* to garnish (**d**) *(remplir)* to fill (**de** with); *(cave)* to stock (**de** with)

garnison [garnizɔ̃] *nf* garrison; **ville de g.** garrison town; **être en g. à** to be garrisoned at

garniture [garnityr] *nf* (**a**) *(ornement) (d'un chapeau, d'une robe)* trimming; **g. de lit** bedding; **g. de cheminée** mantelpiece ornaments (**b**) *(d'un plat)* garnish; *(légumes)* vegetables; *(d'un vol-au-vent)* filling (**c**) *Aut* **g. d'embrayage** clutch lining; **g. de frein** brake lining; *(de disque de frein)* brake pad

Garonne [garɔn] *nf* **la G.** the Garonne

garrigue [garig] *nf* scrubland *(typical of southern France)*

garrocher [garɔʃe] *vt Can Fam* to throw

garrot¹ [garo] *nm* (**a**) *Méd* tourniquet (**b**) *(supplice)* garrotte

garrot² *nm (de quadrupède)* withers; **mesurer 1,20 m au g.** to be 12 hands high

garrotter [garɔte] *vt (prisonnier)* to tie up; *Fig (opposants)* to muzzle

gars [gɑ] *nm Fam (jeune homme)* lad; *(homme)* guy

Gascogne [gaskɔɲ] *nf* **la G.** Gascony

gas-oil, gasoil [gazɔjl, gazwal] *nm* diesel oil

gaspillage [gaspijaʒ] *nm (d'argent, de nourriture, de temps)* wasting; **c'est du g.** it's a waste; **quel g.!** what a waste!

gaspiller [gaspije] *vt* to waste

gastéropode [gasterɔpɔd] *nm Zool* gastropod

gastrique [gastrik] *adj* gastric; **embarras g.** upset stomach

gastrite [gastrit] *nf Méd* gastritis

gastro-entérite *(pl* **gastro-entérites)** [gastroãterit] *nf Méd* gastroenteritis

gastro-entérologue *(pl* **gastro-entérologues)** [gastroãterɔlɔg] *nmf Méd* gastroenterologist

gastro-intestinal, -e, -aux, -ales [gastroɛ̃testinal, -o] *adj Méd* gastrointestinal

gastronome [gastrɔnɔm] *nmf* gastronome, gourmet

gastronomie [gastrɔnɔmi] *nf* gastronomy

gastronomique [gastrɔnɔmik] *adj* gastronomic

gastropode [gastrɔpɔd] *nm Zool* gastropod

gâté, -e [gɑte] *adj* (**a**) *(pourri) (fruit, dents)* bad (**b**) *Fig (enfant)* spoilt

gâteau, -x [gɑto] *nm* cake; *Suisse (tarte)* tart; **faire un g.** to make *or* bake a cake; *Fam Fig* **c'est du g.** it's a piece of cake; *Fam* **ce n'est pas du g.** it's not easy; *Fam* **se partager le g.** to share out the cake; **g. d'anniversaire** birthday cake; **g. de riz** rice pudding; **g. sec** *Br* biscuit, *Am* cookie

gâter [gɑte] **1** *vt* (**a**) *(gâcher)* to spoil (**b**) *(choyer) (personne)* to spoil; **on n'est pas gâtés!** just our luck!
2 se gâter *vpr (affaires, temps)* to take a turn for the worse; *(aliment)* to go bad

gâterie [gɑtri] *nf (petit cadeau, friandise)* treat

gâteux, -euse [gɑto, -øz] *Fam* **1** *nm,f* old dodderer
2 *adj (sénile)* senile, gaga; **avec leurs petits-enfants, ils sont complètement g.** they're totally besotted with their grandchildren

gâtisme [gɑtism] *nm* senility

GATT [gat] *nm Écon (abrév* **General Agreement on Tariffs and Trade) le G.** GATT

gauche [goʃ] **1** *adj* (**a**) *(par opposition à droite)* left (**b**) *(maladroit) (personne, attitude, démarche, style)* awkward, clumsy (**c**) *Tech (déformé)* warped
2 *nf* (**a**) *(côté)* left; **à ma g.** on my left; **le tiroir de g.** the left-hand drawer; **à g. (de)** on the left (of); **tournez à g.** turn left; **conduire à g.** to drive on the left; *Fam* **mettre de l'argent à g.** to put some money away (**b**) *Pol* **la g.** the left; **politique/gouvernement de g.** left-wing politics/government; **voter à g.** to vote for the left; *Fam* **la g. caviar** champagne socialism; **la g. plurielle** = the rainbow coalition of socialists, communists and environmentalists in the government of Lionel Jospin *(elected in 1997)*
3 *nm (en boxe)* left; **un crochet du g.** a left hook; **un direct du g.** a straight left

gaucher, -ère [goʃe, -ɛr] **1** *adj* left-handed
2 *nm,f* left-hander

gauchisant, -e [goʃizã, -ãt] *adj* leftish

gauchisme [goʃism] *nm* leftism

gauchiste [goʃist] *adj & nmf* leftist

gaufre [gofr] *nf* waffle

gaufrette [gofrɛt] *nf* wafer (biscuit)

gaufrier [gofrije] *nm* waffle iron

Gaule [gol] *nf* **la G.** Gaul

gaule [gol] *nf* pole; *(pour pêcher)* fishing rod

gauler [gole] *vt* (**a**) *(arbre fruitier, noyer)* to beat; *(fruits, noix)* to bring down *(using a pole)* (**b**) *Fam (attraper) Br* to nab, *Am* to bust; **se faire g.** to get *Br* nabbed *or Am* busted

gaullisme [golism] *nm* Gaullism

Gaullisme

The political ideology inspired by the ideas of General de Gaulle includes nationalism, independence from foreign powers, and a strong executive. Gaullists are strongly committed to the defence of France's prestige on the international scene.

gaulliste [golist] *adj & nmf* Gaullist

gaulois, -e [golwa, -az] **1** *adj* Gallic; **esprit g.** bawdy humour
2 *nm,f* **les G.** the Gauls
3 *nf* **Gauloise®** Gauloise® *(popular brand of cigarette)*

gauloiserie [golwazri] *nf (plaisanterie)* bawdy joke; *(caractère)* bawdiness

gausser [gose] **se gausser** *vpr Litt* **se g. de qn** to mock sb; **vous vous gaussez!** you jest!

gaver [gave] **1** *vt (engraisser) (volaille)* to force-feed; *(personne) (de nourriture)* to stuff (**de** with); *Fig* **g. qn de qch** to force-feed sb sth
2 se gaver *vpr Fam* to stuff oneself (**de** with); *Fig* **se g. de romans policiers/jeux vidéo** to read detective novels/play video games till they're coming out of one's ears

gay [gɛ] *adj & nmf* gay *(homosexual)*; **il/elle est g.** he's/she's gay

gaz [gaz] *nm* gas; *Fam* **il y a de l'eau dans le g.** things aren't going too well; *Fam* **mettre les g.** *Br* to put one's foot down, *Am* to step on the gas; *Aviat* to open up the throttle; **avoir des g.** to have wind; **g. carbonique** carbon dioxide; **g. de combat** poison gas; **g. d'échappement** exhaust fumes; **g. à effet de serre** greenhouse gas; **g. hilarant** laughing gas; **g. lacrymogène** tear gas; **g. naturel** natural gas; **g. de ville** town gas; **avoir le g. de ville** to be connected to the gas supply

Gaza [gaza] *n* **la bande de G.** the Gaza Strip

gaze [gaz] *nf* gauze

gazé, -e [gaze] **1** *adj* gassed
2 *nm,f (poison)* gas victim

gazéifier [66] [gazeifje] *vt* to gasify; *(boissons)* to carbonate

gazelle [gazɛl] *nf* gazelle; **avoir des yeux de g.** to be doe-eyed

gazer [gaze] **1** *vt (asphyxier)* to gas
2 *vi Fam* **ça gaze!** everything's cool!; **ça gaze?** how's things?
gazette [gazɛt] *nf (journal)* newspaper
gazeux, -euse [gazø, -øz] *adj* (**a**) *(eau, boisson)* fizzy (**b**) *Chim* gaseous
gazinière [gazinjɛr] *nf* gas cooker
gazoduc [gazɔdyk] *nm* gas pipeline
gazole [gazɔl] *nm* diesel oil
gazomètre [gazɔmɛtr] *nm* gasometer
gazon [gazõ] *nm* (**a**) *(herbe)* grass, turf (**b**) *(surface)* lawn
gazonner [gazɔne] *vt* to turf
gazouillement [gazujmã] *nm (des oiseaux)* twittering, chirping; *(d'un bébé)* gurgling; *(d'un ruisseau)* babbling
gazouiller [gazuje] *vi (oiseau)* to twitter, to chirp; *(bébé)* to gurgle; *(eau)* to babble
gazouillis [gazuji] = **gazouillement**
GDF [ʒedeɛf] *nm (abrév* **Gaz de France)** = French gas company
geai [ʒɛ] *nm* jay
géant, -e [ʒeã, -ãt] **1** *adj* (**a**) *(arbre, écran)* giant, gigantic; *(paquet)* giant(-size) (**b**) *Fam (formidable)* **c'est g.!** it's fantastic!
2 *nm,f* giant; *Fig* **les géants de la littérature classique** the giants *or* great names of classical literature; *Fig* **avancer** *ou* **aller à pas de g.** to make great strides
geignard, -e [ʒɛɲar, -ard] *Fam* **1** *adj* whiny
2 *nm,f* whiner
geindre [54] [ʒɛ̃dr] *vi* (**a**) *(gémir)* to moan, to groan (**de** with) (**b**) *Fam (se plaindre constamment)* to whine
gel [ʒɛl] *nm* (**a**) *(verglas)* frost; *Fig* **g. des négociations** suspension of negotiations; **g. des prix/salaires** price/wage freeze (**b**) *(produit cosmétique)* gel; **g. coiffant** hair gel; **g. douche** shower gel
gélatine [ʒelatin] *nf* gelatine
gélatineux, -euse [ʒelatinø, -øz] *adj* gelatinous
gelé, -e¹ [ʒəle] *adj* (**a**) *(lac, rivière)* frozen; *(plante)* frost-nipped (**b**) *Méd (orteil, doigt)* frostbitten (**c**) *(très froid)* frozen; **j'ai les pieds gelés/les mains gelées** my feet/hands are frozen (**d**) *(bloqué) (fonds)* frozen; *(négociations)* suspended
gelée² [ʒəle] *nf* (**a**) *(gel)* frost; **g. blanche** hoarfrost (**b**) *Culin* jelly; **g. royale** royal jelly
geler [39] [ʒəle] **1** *vt* (**a**) *(lac, rivière, liquide)* to freeze; **fleurs/salades gelées par le froid** flowers/lettuces nipped by the frost (**b**) *Fin (bloquer) (crédits, capital)* to freeze
2 *vi (lac, rivière)* to freeze (over); **on gèle dans cette salle** it's freezing in this room
3 *v impersonnel* **il gèle** it's freezing; **il gèle à pierre fendre** it's freezing hard; **il a gelé blanc cette nuit** there was a frost last night
4 **se geler** *vpr Fam* to freeze; *très Fam* **on se les gèle ici!** it's *Br* bloody *or Am* goddamn freezing here!
gélifiant [ʒelifjã] *nm* gelling agent
gélule [ʒelyl] *nf* capsule
gelure [ʒəlyr] *nf* frostbite
Gémeaux [ʒemo] *nmpl Astron & Astrol* Gemini; **être G.** to be (a) Gemini
gémir [ʒemir] *vi (personne)* to groan, to moan (**de** with); *(vent)* to moan
gémissant, -e [ʒemisã, -ãt] *adj (personne)* groaning; *(voix)* wailing
gémissement [ʒemismã] *nm (d'une personne)* groan, moan; *(de vent)* moaning

gemme [ʒɛm] *nf* (**a**) *(pierre)* gem(stone) (**b**) *(résine)* pine resin
gênant, -e [ʒɛnã, -ãt] *adj* (**a**) *(témoin, situation, silence)* awkward; *(bruit, lumière)* irritating (**b**) *(encombrant) (objet)* cumbersome
gencive [ʒãsiv] *nf* gum
gendarme [ʒãdarm] *nm* gendarme, policeman; **jouer aux gendarmes et aux voleurs** to play cops and robbers; *Fam* **faire le g.** to lay down the law; **g. couché** sleeping policeman; **g. mobile** = member of the flying squad
gendarmerie [ʒãdarməri] *nf* (**a**) *(corps) (en France)* gendarmerie, police force; **g. mobile** = flying squad; **g. nationale** national police force; **la G. royale du Canada** the Royal Canadian Mounted Police (**b**) *(lieu)* gendarmes' headquarters
gendre [ʒãdr] *nm* son-in-law
gène [ʒɛn] *nm* gene
gêne [ʒɛn] *nf* (**a**) *(confusion)* embarrassment; **ressentir de la g.** to feel embarrassed; **où (il) y a de la g., (il n')y a pas de plaisir** we don't need to stand on ceremony (**b**) *(dérangement)* inconvenience (**c**) *(difficulté physique)* discomfort; **g. respiratoire** difficulty in breathing (**d**) *(manque d'argent)* **être dans la g.** to be in financial difficulties
gêné, -e [ʒene] *adj* (**a**) *(embarrassé)* embarrassed; *Fam* **il n'est pas g., lui!** he's got a nerve! (**b**) *(serré)* **être g. dans un vêtement** to be uncomfortable in a garment (**c**) *(qui manque d'argent)* in financial difficulties
généalogie [ʒenealɔʒi] *nf* genealogy
généalogique [ʒenealɔʒik] *adj* genealogical; **arbre g.** family tree
gêner [ʒene] **1** *vt* (**a**) *(perturber) (sujet: bruit, fumée, chaleur)* to bother; *(opérations, déroulement)* to hamper; **g. la circulation** to hold up the traffic; **le passage** to be in the way; **pousse-toi, tu me gênes!** move over, you're in my way!; **ça te gêne si je fume?** do you mind if I smoke?; **cela ne te gênerait pas de me prêter ta voiture?** would you mind lending me your car?; **ce qui me gêne, c'est que...** what bothers me is that...; **sa présence me gêne** I feel awkward in his/her presence (**b**) *(être source d'inconfort)* **cette ceinture/ce col me gêne** this belt/this collar is uncomfortable (**c**) *(embarrasser)* to embarrass; **ça me gênerait de le rencontrer** I'd feel uncomfortable meeting him; *Fam* **et alors, ça te gêne?** what's it to you?
2 **se gêner** *vpr* (**a**) **je ne me suis pas gêné pour le lui dire** I didn't hesitate to tell him/her so; **elle aurait tort de se g.** she shouldn't feel bad about it; *aussi Ironique* **ne vous gênez pas pour moi!** don't mind me! (**b**) *(dans un lieu)* to be in each other's way (**c**) *Suisse (être intimidé)* to be shy
général, -e, -aux, -ales [ʒeneral, -o] **1** *adj* general; **assemblée/amnistie générale** general assembly/amnesty; **l'intérêt g.** the general interest; **à la surprise générale** to everyone's surprise; **à la demande générale** by popular request; **d'une façon générale** generally speaking; **en g.** *(globalement)* in general; *(habituellement)* as a rule, generally
2 *nm* (**a**) *Mil* general (**b**) *(ce qui est universel)* **passer du g. au particulier** to go from the general to the particular
3 *nf* **générale** (**a**) *Théât* dress rehearsal (**b**) *(femme de général)* general's wife
généralement [ʒeneralmã] *adv* generally

généralisation [ʒeneralizasjɔ̃] *nf* generalization
généraliser [ʒeneralize] **1** *vt* to generalize; *Méd* **un cancer généralisé** a generalized cancer
2 *vi* to generalize
3 se généraliser *vpr (utilisation, usage, phénomène)* to become widespread; *(conflit, grève)* to spread
généraliste [ʒeneralist] *adj & nmf* **(médecin) g.** general practitioner, GP
généralité [ʒeneralite] *nf* (**a**) *(notion générale)* generality; **s'en tenir à des généralités** to confine oneself to generalities (**b**) *(majorité)* **la g. de** the majority of
générateur, -trice [ʒeneratœr, -tris] **1** *adj (machine)* generating; *(organe)* generative; **être g. de** to generate
2 *nm* generator; *Ordinat* **g. de caractères** character generator; **g. d'effets numériques** digital effects generator; **g. d'effets spéciaux** (special) effects generator; **g. graphique** graphics generator
3 *nf* **génératrice** generator
génération [ʒenerasjɔ̃] *nf* (**a**) *(classe d'âge, degrés de filiation)* generation; **G. X / Y** Generation X/Y (**b**) *(action de produire)* generation; *Biol* **g. spontanée** spontaneous generation
générer [34] [ʒenere] *vt* to generate
généreusement [ʒenerøzmɑ̃] *adv* generously
généreux, -euse [ʒenerø, -øz] *adj* generous; **une terre généreuse** a fertile soil; **elle a des formes généreuses** she has generous curves
générique [ʒenerik] **1** *adj* generic
2 *nm Cin & TV* credits; **g. de fin** closing credits
générosité [ʒenerozite] *nf* generosity; **avec g.** generously
Gênes [ʒɛn] *n* Genoa
genèse [ʒənɛz] *nf* genesis; **la G.** Genesis
genêt [ʒənɛ] *nm* broom
généticien, -enne [ʒenetisjɛ̃, -ɛn] *nm,f* geneticist
génétique [ʒenetik] **1** *adj* genetic
2 *nf* genetics *(singulier)*
génétiquement [ʒenetikmɑ̃] *adv* genetically; **g. modifié** genetically modified
gêneur, -euse [ʒɛnœr, -øz] *nm,f* nuisance
Genève [ʒənɛv] *n* Geneva
genevois, -e [ʒənvwa, -az] **1** *adj* Genevan
2 *nm,f* **G.** Genevan
genévrier [ʒənevrije] *nm* juniper
génial, -e, -aux, -ales [ʒenjal, -o] *adj* (**a**) *(invention, œuvre, artiste)* brilliant (**b**) *Fam (extraordinaire)* fantastic, great
génialement [ʒenjalmɑ̃] *adv* brilliantly
génie¹ [ʒeni] *nm* (**a**) *(qualité, personne)* genius; **avoir du g.** to be a genius; **une idée/invention de g.** a brilliant idea/invention; **un trait de g.** a stroke of genius; **avoir le g. de qch/pour faire qch** to have a genius for sth/for doing sth (**b**) *(être mythique)* genie; **son bon/mauvais g.** his good/evil genius
génie² *nm Mil* **le (corps du) g.** ≃ the Engineers; **g. civil** civil engineering; *(corps)* civil engineers; **g. génétique** genetic engineering
genièvre [ʒənjɛvr] *nm (fruit)* juniper berry; *(arbre)* juniper (tree)
génique [ʒenik] *adj Méd* **thérapie g.** gene therapy
génisse [ʒenis] *nf* heifer
génital, -e, -aux, -ales [ʒenital, -o] *adj (glandes, hormones)* genital
géniteur, -trice [ʒenitœr, -tris] *nm,f Hum* parent
génocide [ʒenɔsid] *nm* genocide
génoise [ʒenwaz] *nf (gâteau)* sponge cake

génome [ʒenom] *nm Biol* genome
génothérapie [ʒenɔterapi] *nf Biol* genotherapy, gene therapy
génotype [ʒenɔtip] *nm Biol* genotype
genou, -x [ʒənu] *nm* knee; **enfoncé jusqu'aux genoux dans la boue** knee-deep in mud; **avoir les genoux en dedans** to be knock-kneed; **être à genoux** to be kneeling (down), to be on one's knees; **se mettre à genoux** to kneel (down); *Fig* **être à genoux devant qn** to worship sb; *Fig* **demander qch à genoux** to ask for sth on bended knee; *Fig* **être sur les genoux** to be on one's last legs; **tenir un enfant sur ses genoux** to hold a child on one's knee *or* one's lap
genouillère [ʒənujɛr] *nf (protection du genou)* kneepad; *Méd* knee bandage
genre [ʒɑ̃r] *nm* (**a**) *(sorte)* kind, sort; **en tout g., en tous genres** of all kinds; **très bon dans son g.** very good in its own way; **c'est ce qu'on fait de mieux dans le g.** it's the best of its kind; **c'est tout à fait son g. d'arriver en retard** it's just like him/her to be late; **ce n'est pas le g. (de femme) à se plaindre** she's not the sort (of woman) to complain; **tu vois le g.** you know the sort; **un vin blanc g. sauternes** a white wine similar to Sauternes (**b**) *(artistique, littéraire)* genre; **le g. comique** comedy (**c**) *(race)* **le g. humain** the human race (**d**) *(goût)* **ça fait bon/mauvais g.** it's in good/bad taste (**e**) *Gram* gender
gens [ʒɑ̃] *nmpl (individus)* people; **les g. du pays** *ou* **du coin** the local people; **jeunes g.** *(garçons et filles)* young people; *(jeunes hommes)* young men; **g. de lettres** men and women of letters; **g. du voyage** travelling people
gent [ʒɑ̃] *nf Vieilli ou Hum* **la g. féminine/masculine** the fair/male sex
gentiane [ʒɑ̃sjan] *nf (plante)* gentian
gentil, -ille [ʒɑ̃ti, -ij] *adj* (**a**) *(aimable)* kind, nice (**avec** to); *(sage)* good; **sois g., ferme la fenêtre** do me a favour and close the window (**b**) *(considérable)* **une gentille somme** a nice little sum
gentilhomme [ʒɑ̃tijɔm] *(pl* **gentilshommes** [ʒɑ̃tizɔm]*) nm* gentleman
gentillesse [ʒɑ̃tijɛs] *nf (bonté)* kindness; **auriez-vous la g. de...?** would you be so kind as to...?; **elle a eu la g. de venir elle-même** she was kind enough to come herself; **dire des gentillesses à qn** to say kind things to sb
gentillet, -ette [ʒɑ̃tijɛ, -ɛt] *adj Péj (roman, film)* pleasant enough
gentiment [ʒɑ̃timɑ̃] *adv (aimablement)* kindly; *(sagement)* nicely
génuflexion [ʒenyflɛksjɔ̃] *nf* genuflexion; **faire une g.** to genuflect
géo [ʒeo] *nf Fam Scol* geog
géographe [ʒeɔgraf] *nmf* geographer
géographie [ʒeɔgrafi] *nf* geography; **g. humaine/physique** human/physical geography
géographique [ʒeɔgrafik] *adj* geographic(al)
geôle [ʒol] *nf Litt* jail, *Br* gaol
geôlier, -ère [ʒolje, -ɛr] *nm,f Litt* jailer, *Br* gaoler
géologie [ʒeɔlɔʒi] *nf* geology
géologique [ʒeɔlɔʒik] *adj* geological
géologue [ʒeɔlɔg] *nmf* geologist
géomètre [ʒeɔmɛtr] *nm* **(arpenteur) g.** (land) surveyor
géométrie [ʒeɔmetri] *nf* geometry; **g. dans l'espace** solid geometry; *Fig* that varies according to circumstances
géométrique [ʒeɔmetrik] *adj* geometric(al)

géophysicien, -enne [ʒeofizisjɛ̃, -ɛn] *nm,f* geophysicist

géophysique [ʒeofizik] **1** *adj* geophysical **2** *nf* geophysics *(singulier)*

géopolitique [ʒeopɔlitik] **1** *adj* geopolitical **2** *nf* geopolitics *(singulier)*

Géorgie [ʒeɔrʒi] *nf* **la G.** *(aux États-Unis, dans le Caucase)* Georgia

géorgien, -enne [ʒeɔrʒjɛ̃, -ɛn] **1** *adj* Georgian **2** *nm,f* **G.** Georgian

géostationnaire [ʒeostasjɔnɛr] *adj voir* **satellite**

géothermie [ʒeotɛrmi] *nf* geothermics *(singulier)*

géothermique [ʒeotɛrmik] *adj* geothermal

gérance [ʒerɑ̃s] *nf* management; **prendre un commerce en g.** to take over the management of a business

géranium [ʒeranjɔm] *nm* geranium

gérant, -e [ʒerɑ̃, -ɑ̃t] *nm,f* manager

gerbe [ʒɛrb] *nf (de blé)* sheaf; *(d'étincelles)* shower; *(d'eau)* spray; **g. (de fleurs)** spray of flowers

gerber [ʒɛrbe] *vi Vulg (vomir)* to puke, to barf; *Fig* **ça me fait g.** it makes me want to throw up *or* puke

gercé, -e [ʒɛrse] *adj* chapped

gercer [16] [ʒɛrse] **1** *vt & vi* to chap **2 se gercer** *vpr* to chap

gerçure [ʒɛrsyr] *nf* **avoir des gerçures (aux mains/ lèvres)** to have chapped hands/lips

gérer [34] [ʒere] *vt* to manage

gériatrie [ʒerjatri] *nf Méd* geriatrics *(singulier)*

gériatrique [ʒerjatrik] *adj Méd* geriatric

germain, -e [ʒɛrmɛ̃, -ɛn] *adj voir* **cousin**

germanique [ʒɛrmanik] *adj* **(a)** *Hist (relatif aux Germains)* Germanic **(b)** *(allemand)* German **(c)** *(langue)* Germanic

germanophone [ʒɛrmanɔfɔn] **1** *adj* German-speaking **2** *nmf* German speaker

germe [ʒɛrm] *nm (embryon, virus)* germ; *(de pomme de terre)* eye; *Fig* **les germes de** *(origine)* the seeds of; **germes de soja** bean sprouts

germer [ʒɛrme] *vi (plante, idée)* to germinate; *(pommes de terre)* to sprout

germination [ʒɛrminasjɔ̃] *nf Biol* germination

gérondif [ʒerɔ̃dif] *nm Gram* gerund; *(cas latin)* gerundive

gérontologie [ʒerɔ̃tɔlɔʒi] *nf Méd* gerontology

gérontologue [ʒerɔ̃tɔlɔg] *nmf Méd* gerontologist

gésier [ʒezje] *nm* gizzard

gésir [40] [ʒezir] *vi Litt* to lie; **ci-gît...** *(sur une tombe)* here lies...

gestation [ʒɛstasjɔ̃] *nf Biol* gestation; *Fig* **en g.** in preparation

geste [ʒɛst] *nm* **(a)** *(mouvement)* gesture; **faire un g.** to make a gesture; **pas un g. ou je tire!** one move and I'll shoot!; **il lui montra la porte d'un g.** he motioned him/her towards the door; **d'un g. de la main** with a wave of the hand; **écarter qn d'un g.** to wave sb aside; **joindre le g. à la parole** to suit the action to the word **(b)** *(action)* gesture; **un beau g.** a fine gesture; **faire un g.** to make a gesture

gesticuler [ʒɛstikyle] *vi* to gesticulate

gestion [ʒɛstjɔ̃] *nf* management; **g. de bases de données** database management; *Ordinat* **g. des couleurs** colour management; **g. d'entreprise** business management; *Ordinat* **g. de fichiers** file management; *Ordinat* **g. de mémoire** memory management; *Ordinat*

g. sonore sound handling, sound management; **g. des stocks** stock control

gestionnaire [ʒɛstjɔnɛr] **1** *nmf (dirigeant)* administrator **2** *nm Ordinat* manager, driver; **g. de fichiers** file manager; **g. de périphérique** device driver; **g. de projets** project management package; **g. de réseau** network manager

gestuel, -elle [ʒɛstɥɛl] **1** *adj* gestural **2** *nf* **gestuelle** body language

geyser [ʒezɛr] *nm* geyser

Ghana [gana] *nm* **le G.** Ghana

ghanéen, -enne [ganeɛ̃, -ɛn] **1** *adj* Ghanaian **2** *nm,f* **G.** Ghanaian

ghetto [gɛto] *nm* ghetto

GIA [ʒeia] *nm (abrév* **Groupes islamiques armés)** GIA

gibecière [ʒibsjɛr] *nf (de chasseur)* game bag

gibelotte [ʒiblɔt] *nf Culin* **g. (de lapin)** = fricassee of rabbit cooked in white wine

gibet [ʒibɛ] *nm* gibbet, gallows *(singulier)*

gibier [ʒibje] *nm* game; *aussi Fig* **gros g.** big game; **g. à plumes** game birds; **g. à poil** game animals; *Fig* **g. de potence** gallows bird

giboulée [ʒibule] *nf* sudden shower; **giboulées de mars** ≃ April showers

Gibraltar [ʒibraltar] *n* Gibraltar

giclée [ʒikle] *nf* **(a)** *(d'eau, de sang)* spurt **(b)** *Suisse (petite quantité)* spot, smidgen **(c)** *Suisse (averse)* (rain) shower

gicler [ʒikle] *vi* **(a)** *(eau, sang)* to spurt out; *(boue)* to splash up **(b)** *Suisse (pleuvoir)* to rain

gicleur [ʒiklœr] *nm Aut* jet

GIE [ʒeiə] *nm (abrév* **groupement d'intérêt économique)** economic interest group

gifle [ʒifl] *nf aussi Fig* slap in the face; **donner une g. à qn** to give sb a slap in the face

gifler [ʒifle] *vt (sujet: personne)* to slap in the face; *(su-jet: vent)* to lash

gigahertz [ʒigaɛrts] *nm Phys* gigahertz

gigantesque [ʒigɑ̃tɛsk] *adj* gigantic

gigaoctet [ʒigaɔktɛ] *nm Ordinat* gigabyte

GIGN [ʒeiʒeɛn] *nm (abrév* **Groupe d'intervention de la gendarmerie nationale)** = special crack force of the gendarmerie, *Br* ≃ SAS, *Am* ≃ SWAT

gigogne [ʒigɔɲ] *adj* **tables gigognes** nest of tables; **lits gigognes** beds that fit one underneath the other; **poupées gigognes** nest of (Russian) dolls

gigolo [ʒigɔlo] *nm Fam* gigolo

gigot [ʒigo] *nm (d'agneau, de mouton)* leg

gigoter [ʒigɔte] *vi* to wriggle, to fidget

gigue¹ [ʒig] *nf (danse)* jig

gigue² *nf Fam* **une grande g.** *(fille)* a beanpole (of a girl)

gilet [ʒilɛ] *nm (sans manches) Br* waistcoat, *Am* vest; *(veste en laine)* cardigan; **g. pare-balles** bulletproof vest; **g. de sauvetage** life jacket, life vest

gin [dʒin] *nm* gin; **g. tonic** gin and tonic

gingembre [ʒɛ̃ʒɑ̃br] *nm* ginger

gingivite [ʒɛ̃ʒivit] *nf Méd* gingivitis

ginseng [ʒɛ̃sɑ̃, ʒinsɑ̃g] *nm* ginseng

girafe [ʒiraf] *nf* giraffe; *Fig (personne)* beanpole

giratoire [ʒiratwar] **1** *adj (mouvement)* gyratory **2** *nm Suisse (rond-point) Br* roundabout, *Am* traffic circle

girofle [ʒirɔfl] *nm voir* **clou**

giroflée [ʒirɔfle] *nf* stock

girolle [ʒirɔl] *nf* chanterelle (mushroom)

giron [ʒirɔ̃] *nm (partie du corps)* lap; *Fig* bosom
gironde [ʒirɔ̃d] *adj f Fam* curvy; *Péj* on the plump side
girondin, -e [ʒirɔ̃dɛ̃, -in] **1** *adj* of the Gironde
2 *nm,f* **G.** person from the Gironde
girouette [ʒirwɛt] *nf aussi Fig* weathercock
gisais *etc voir* **gésir**
gisement [ʒizmɑ̃] *nm (de minerai)* deposit; **g. de pétrole** oilfield
gît *voir* **gésir**
gitan, -e [ʒitɑ̃, -an] **1** *adj* gypsy
2 *nm,f* gypsy
3 *nf* Gitane® Gitane® *(popular brand of cigarette)*
gîte¹ [ʒit] *nm* (**a**) *(logement)* lodging; **offrir le g.** et le couvert à qn to offer sb board and lodging (**b**) *(en montagne, à la campagne)* **g. d'étape** = transit accommodation for hikers, cyclists etc; **g. rural** gîte, = self-catering holiday cottage or apartment (**c**) *(du lièvre)* form (**d**) *Culin* shank
gîte² *nf Naut* list; **donner de la g.** to list
gîter [ʒite] *vi Naut* to list
givre [ʒivr] *nm* frost
givré, -e [ʒivre] *adj* (**a**) *(couvert de givre)* covered with frost (**b**) *Fam (fou)* crazy
glabre [ɡlabr] *adj (rasé)* clean-shaven; *(imberbe) (personne)* smooth-chinned; *(visage)* hairless
glaçage [ɡlasaʒ] *nm (d'un gâteau) Br* icing, *Am* frosting
glaçant, -e [ɡlasɑ̃, -ɑ̃t] *adj (manières, accueil)* frosty
glace [ɡlas] *nf* (**a**) *(eau à l'état solide)* ice; **glaces** *(du pôle)* ice fields; *(en mer)* ice floes; **le navire est pris dans les glaces** the ship is icebound; *Fig* **rester de g.** to remain impassive; *Fig* **rompre la g.** to break the ice; **g. pilée** crushed ice (**b**) *(de voiture)* window (**c**) *(miroir)* mirror; **g. sans tain** two-way mirror (**d**) *(crème glacée)* ice cream; *(sucette) Br* ice lolly, *Am* Popsicle®; **g. à la vanille/à la fraise** vanilla/strawberry ice cream; **g. à l'eau** *Br* water ice, *Am* sherbet; **g. à l'italienne** soft ice cream
glacé, -e [ɡlase] *adj* (**a**) *(rivière, lac)* frozen (**b**) *(très froid) (pièce, eau, personne)* freezing (cold); *(avec des glaçons) (café)* iced; **j'ai les pieds glacés** my feet are freezing (**c**) *Fig (accueil, politesse, regard)* frosty (**d**) *(papier)* glossy (**e**) *Culin (fruits)* glacé
glacer [16] [ɡlase] **1** *vt* (**a**) *(refroidir, intimider)* to chill; *Fig* **à vous g. le sang** spine-chilling (**b**) *(gâteau)* to ice
2 se glacer *vpr (sang)* to run cold
glaciaire [ɡlasjɛr] *adj Géol (vallée)* glacial; **période g.** Ice Age
glacial, -e, -als *ou* **-aux, -ales** [ɡlasjal, -o] *adj (température, froid, air, vent)* freezing, icy; *Fig (ton, accueil, sourire)* frosty; *(personne)* cold
glacier¹ [ɡlasje] *nm (étendue de glace)* glacier
glacier² *nm (vendeur)* ice-cream seller; *(fabricant)* ice-cream maker
glacière [ɡlasjɛr] *nf (de pique-nique)* cool box; **cette chambre est une vraie g.!** this room's like an icebox!
glaçon [ɡlasɔ̃] *nm (pour rafraîchir une boisson)* ice cube; *(pendant)* icicle; *Fig (personne)* cold fish; **glaçons** *(sur une rivière)* drift ice; **avec ou sans glaçons?** with or without ice?; **un whisky avec des glaçons** a whisky on the rocks; **j'ai les pieds comme des glaçons** my feet are like blocks of ice
gladiateur [ɡladjatœr] *nm* gladiator
glaïeul [ɡlajœl] *nm* gladiolus; **des glaïeuls** gladioli
glaire [ɡlɛr] *nf (crachat)* phlegm; **g. cervicale** cervical mucus
glaise [ɡlɛz] *nf* **(terre) g.** clay

glaive [ɡlɛv] *nm (épée)* broadsword; *Fig (symbole)* sword
gland [ɡlɑ̃] *nm* (**a**) *(de chêne)* acorn (**b**) *(de passementerie)* tassel (**c**) *Anat* glans (**d**) *très Fam (personne) Br* prat, *Am* jerk
glande [ɡlɑ̃d] *nf (organe)* gland; *très Fam* **foutre les glandes à qn** *(énerver)* to piss sb off; *(mettre mal à l'aise)* to put the wind up sb; **glandes lacrymales** tear glands; **glandes sudoripares** sweat glands
glander [ɡlɑ̃de] *vi très Fam (ne rien faire)* to loaf around; *(attendre)* to hang around; **mais qu'est-ce qu'il glande?** *(que fait-il?)* what the hell's he up to?; **j'en ai rien à g.** I don't give a shit
glandeur, -euse [ɡlɑ̃dœr, -øz] *nm,f très Fam* layabout
glandouiller [ɡlɑ̃duje] *vi très Fam (ne rien faire)* to loaf around; *(attendre)* to hang around
glandulaire [ɡlɑ̃dylɛr], **glanduleux, -euse** [ɡlɑ̃dylø, -øz] *adj* glandular
glaner [ɡlane] *vt aussi Fig* to glean
glapir [ɡlapir] *vi (chien)* to yap; *(renard)* to bark; *(personne, radio)* to shriek
glapissements [ɡlapismɑ̃] *nmpl (d'un chien)* yapping; *(d'un renard)* barking; *(d'une personne, de la radio)* shrieking
glas [ɡlɑ] *nm* knell; **sonner le g.** to toll the knell; *Fig* **sonner le g. de qch** to sound the death knell for sth
glaucome [ɡlokom] *nm Méd* glaucoma
glauque [ɡlok] *adj (eau)* murky; *(ambiance, personne)* creepy
glissade [ɡlisad] *nf* sliding; *(de patineur)* gliding; *(pas de danse)* glissade; **faire une g./des glissades** to slide
glissant, -e [ɡlisɑ̃, -ɑ̃t] *adj* slippery; *Fig* **être sur un terrain g.** to be on dangerous ground
glisse [ɡlis] *nf* **sports de g.** = sports involving sliding motion, eg skiing, snowboarding, surfing
glissement [ɡlismɑ̃] *nm (action)* sliding; *(variation électorale)* swing (à to); **g. de sens** shift in meaning; **g. de terrain** landslide; *(moins important)* landslip
glisser¹ [ɡlise] **1** *vi* (**a**) *(par accident)* to slip; *(roue)* to skid; **le couteau lui a glissé des mains** the knife slipped out of his/her hands; *Aviat* **g. sur l'aile** to sideslip (**b**) *(volontairement)* to slide; **se laisser g. le long d'une corde** to slide down a rope; *Ordinat* **faire g.** *(pointeur)* to drag (**c**) *(avancer régulièrement)* to glide; *Fig (dans le sommeil, ne le désespoir)* to slip (**d**) **g. sur** *(sujet)* to skip over (**e**) *(avoir une surface glissante)* to be slippery
2 *(introduire)* to slip; **g. un mot à l'oreille de qn** to drop a word in sb's ear
3 se glisser *vpr* to slip (**dans** into)
glisser² *nm Ordinat* **g. d'icônes** icon drag
glissière [ɡlisjɛr] *nf* (**a**) *Tech* runner, slide; **à g.** sliding (**b**) **g. de sécurité** crash barrier (**c**) *Ind (pour le chariot)* chute
global, -e, -aux, -ales [ɡlɔbal, -o] *adj (somme)* total; *(paiement)* lump; *(vision)* overall; *Scol* **méthode globale** word recognition method
globalement [ɡlɔbalmɑ̃] *adv* overall
globalité [ɡlɔbalite] *nf* **prendre un problème dans sa g.** to tackle a problem as a whole
globe [ɡlɔb] *nm* (**a**) *(sphère)* globe; **g. oculaire** eyeball (**b**) *(terre)* globe; **faire le tour du g.** to go round the world; **g. terrestre** *(terre)* earth; *(mappemonde)* globe (**c**) *(en verre) (d'une pendule)* glass dome

globe-trotter (*pl* globe-trotters) [glɔbtrɔtœr] *nmf* globetrotter

globulaire [glɔbylɛr] *adj Méd* **numération g.** blood count

globule [glɔbyl] *nm (du sang)* corpuscle; **globules blancs/rouges** white/red corpuscles

globuleux, -euse [glɔbylø, -øz] *adj (yeux)* protruding

gloire [glwar] *nf* (**a**) *(renom)* glory; **tirer g. de qch** to glory in sth (**b**) *(personne célèbre)* celebrity; **il est la g.** de notre école he is the pride of our school (**c**) *(manifestation de respect)* **rendre g. à** to glorify; **g. à...! glory to...!; à la g. de qn** in praise of sb

glorieux, -euse [glɔrjø, -øz] *adj* glorious; **être promis à un avenir g.** to have a glorious future ahead of one; *Fam* **ce n'est pas très g.** *(pas très bon)* it's not exactly brilliant

glorifier [66] [glɔrifje] **1** *vt* to glorify
2 se glorifier *vpr* **se g. de (faire) qch** to glory in (doing) sth

gloriole [glɔrjɔl] *nf Fam* **faire qch par g.** to do sth in order to show off

glose [gloz] *nf (explication)* gloss

gloser [gloze] **gloser sur** *vt ind (discourir sur)* to ramble on about

gloss [glɔs] *nm (pour les lèvres)* lip gloss

glossaire [glɔsɛr] *nm (ouvrage)* glossary

glotte [glɔt] *nf Anat* glottis

glouglou [gluglu] *nm* (**a**) *(bruit d'un liquide)* gurgle; **faire g.** to gurgle (**b**) *(cri de la dinde)* gobble

gloussements [glusmã] *nmpl (d'une poule)* clucking; *(d'une dinde)* gobbling; *(d'une personne)* chuckling

glousser [gluse] *vi (poule)* to cluck; *(dinde)* to gobble; *(personne)* to chuckle

glouton, -onne [glutɔ̃, -ɔn] **1** *adj* greedy, gluttonous
2 *nm,f* glutton
3 *nm (animal)* wolverine

gloutonnement [glutɔnmã] *adv* greedily

gloutonnerie [glutɔnri] *nf* gluttony, greed

glu [gly] *nf (colle)* glue

gluant, -e [glyã, -ãt] *adj* slimy

glucide [glysid] *nm* carbohydrate

glucose [glykoz] *nm* glucose

gluten [glytɛn] *nm* gluten

glycémie [glisemi] *nf Méd* glycaemia

glycérine [gliserin] *nf* glycerine

glycine [glisin] *nf (plante)* wisteria

gnangnan [ɲãɲã] *adj inv Fam Péj (personne)* drippy; *(livre, film)* soppy

gnognot(t)e [ɲɔɲɔt] *nf Fam (mauvaise qualité)* **c'est de la g.** it's a load of rubbish; **c'est pas de la g., cette voiture** that car's quite something

gnole, gnôle [ɲɔl] *nf Fam* hooch

gnome [gnom] *nm* gnome; *Fig & Péj (homme)* midget

gnon [ɲɔ̃] *nm Fam (coup de poing)* thump; **se prendre un g.** to get thumped

GO 1 *Rad (abrév* **grandes ondes***)* LW
2 [ʒeo] *nm (abrév* **gentil organisateur***)* activity organizer *(at Club Méditerranée holiday villages)*

Go *Ordinat (abrév* **gigaoctet(s)***)* GB

go [go] **1** *nm inv* **(le jeu de) go** go
2 tout de go *adv* straight away

goal [gol] *nm* goalkeeper

gobelet [gɔblɛ] *nm (en argent, en étain)* tumbler; **g. en plastique/carton** plastic/paper cup

gober [gɔbe] *vt (nourriture)* to gulp down; *Fig (croire)* to swallow

goberger [45] [gɔbɛrʒe] **se goberger** *vpr Fam* (**a**) *(se prélasser)* to laze around (**b**) *(faire bonne chère)* to treat oneself

Gobi [gɔbi] *n voir* **désert**

godasse [gɔdas] *nf Fam* shoe

godelureau, -x [gɔdlyro] *nm Péj & Vieilli* popinjay

godet [gɔdɛ] *nm* (**a**) *(récipient)* pot; *Fam* **boire un g.** to have a jar (**b**) *(d'une noria)* scoop; *(d'un excavateur, d'une roue à eau)* bucket (**c**) *(d'une jupe)* **à godets** flared

godiche [gɔdiʃ] *Fam* **1** *adj* clumsy
2 *nf* clumsy oaf

godille [gɔdij] *nf* (**a**) *Naut* scull; **avancer à la g.** to scull (**b**) *(en ski)* wedeln; **faire de la g.** to wedeln

godiller [gɔdije] *vi* (**a**) *Naut* to scull (**b**) *(en ski)* to wedeln

godillot [gɔdijo] *nm Mil* boot; *Fam (gros soulier)* clodhopper

goéland [gɔelã] *nm* gull

goélette [gɔelɛt] *nf (navire)* schooner

goémon [gɔemɔ̃] *nm* wrack

gogo¹ [gogo] **à gogo** *adv Fam* galore

gogo² *nm Fam* sucker, mug

goguenard, -e [gɔgnar, -ard] *adj* mocking

goguette [gɔgɛt] *nf Fam* **être en g.** *(faire la noce)* to be out for a good time

goinfre [gwɛ̃fr] *Fam* **1** *nmf* pig
2 *adj* piggish

goinfrer [gwɛ̃fre] **se goinfrer** *vpr Fam* to pig out (**de** on)

goinfrerie [gwɛ̃frəri] *nf* piggishness

goitre [gwatr] *nm Méd* goitre

golden [gɔldɛn] *nf* Golden Delicious (apple)

golf [gɔlf] *nm* golf; **(terrain de) g.** golf course; **g. miniature** miniature golf

golfe [gɔlf] *nm* gulf, bay; **le G.** the Gulf; **le g. Persique** the Persian Gulf; **les États** *ou* **les pays du G.** the Gulf States; **le g. du Bengale** the Bay of Bengal; **le g. de Gascogne** the Bay of Biscay; **le g. du Mexique** the Gulf of Mexico

golfeur, -euse [gɔlfœr, -øz] *nm,f* golfer

Gomina® [gɔmina] *nf* hair cream

gominé, -e [gɔmine] *adj (cheveux)* plastered-down

gommage [gɔmaʒ] *nm* (**a**) *(pour effacer)* rubbing out, erasing (**b**) *(nettoyage de la peau)* face scrub; **se faire un g.** to give oneself a face scrub

gomme [gɔm] *nf* (**a**) *(pour effacer)* eraser, *Br* rubber (**b**) *(substance)* gum; **g. à mâcher** chewing gum (**c**) *Fam (locutions)* **mettre (toute) la g.** to get a move on; *(en voiture)* to step on it; **à la g.** useless

gommé, -e [gɔme] *adj (papier, enveloppe)* gummed

gommer [gɔme] *vt (effacer)* to rub out, to erase; *Fig (souvenir)* to erase

gond [gɔ̃] *nm (de porte)* hinge; **sortir de ses gonds** *(porte)* to come off its hinges; *Fig* to fly off the handle

gondole [gɔ̃dɔl] *nf (barque, présentoir)* gondola

gondoler [gɔ̃dɔle] **1** *vi (bois, disque)* to warp; *(papier)* to crinkle
2 se gondoler *vpr* (**a**) *(bois, disque)* to warp; *(papier)* to crinkle (**b**) *Fam (rire)* to fall about laughing

gondolier [gɔ̃dɔlje] *nm* gondolier

gonflable [gɔ̃flabl] *adj* inflatable

gonflage [gɔ̃flaʒ] *nm* **g. (des pneus)** tyre pressure

gonflant, -e [gɔ̃flã, -ãt] *adj* (**a**) *(coiffure)* bouffant (**b**) *très Fam (énervant)* maddening

gonflé, -e [gɔ̃fle] *adj* (**a**) *(boursouflé)* swollen (**b**) *Fam* **être g.** *(personne)* to have a lot of nerve; **c'est**

g., ce qu'il a fait là what he did took some nerve; **g. à bloc** *(sûr de soi)* raring to go
gonflement [gɔ̃fləmɑ̃] *nm (d'une partie du corps)* swelling
gonfler [gɔ̃fle] **1** *vt* (**a**) *(pneu, ballon, matelas pneumatique)* to blow up, to inflate; *(ses joues)* to puff out; *(sujet: vent) (voiles)* to fill (**b**) *(faire augmenter de volume)* to swell (**c**) *Fig (grossir) (résultats, conséquences)* to exaggerate; *Fam (moteur)* to soup up (**d**) *très Fam (énerver)* **g. qn** to get up sb's nose *or Br* on sb's tits
2 *vi* to swell; *(gâteau, pâte)* to rise
3 se gonfler *vpr (voiles, poumons)* to fill; *Fig* **se g. de joie** *(cœur)* to fill with joy
gonflette [gɔ̃flɛt] *nf Fam Péj* pumping iron; **faire de la g.** to pump iron
gong [gɔ̃g] *nm* (**a**) *(percussion)* gong (**b**) *(en boxe)* bell; *Fig* **sauvé par le g.** saved by the bell
gonzesse [gɔ̃zɛs] *nf très Fam* chick, *Br* bird
goret [gɔrɛ] *nm* piglet; *Fam (enfant malpropre)* little pig
gorge [gɔrʒ] *nf* (**a**) *(gosier, cou)* throat; **avoir mal à la g.** to have a sore throat; **avoir la g. serrée** to have a lump in one's throat; *Fig* **cela m'est resté en travers de la g.** it stuck in my throat; **trancher la g. à qn** to cut sb's throat; *Fig* **rire à la g.** to be in a stranglehold; **faire des gorges chaudes de qch** to laugh sth to scorn; **rire à g. déployée** to roar with laughter (**b**) *Litt (poitrine)* bosom (**c**) *(vallée)* gorge (**d**) *(d'une poulie)* groove
gorgé, -e¹ [gɔrʒe] *adj* **une éponge gorgée d'eau** a sponge full of water; **sol g. d'eau** waterlogged earth
gorgée² *nf* mouthful; **boire qch à petites gorgées** to sip sth; **avaler qch d'une g.** to swallow sth in one gulp
gorger [45] [gɔrʒe] **se gorger** *vpr* to gorge oneself (**de** on *or* with); **se g. d'eau** *(sol)* to get waterlogged
gorgonzola [gɔrgɔ̃zɔla] *nm* Gorgonzola
gorille [gɔrij] *nm (animal)* gorilla; *Fam (garde du corps)* minder
gosier [gozje] *nm* throat; *Fam* **avoir le g. sec** to be parched
gosse [gɔs] *nmf* (**a**) *Fam (enfant)* kid; **g. de riches** rich kid (**b**) *Fam* **être beau g.** to be good-looking (**c**) *Can Fam* **gosses** *(testicules)* balls
gosser [gɔse] *vt Can Fam* to whittle
gotha [gɔta] *nm* **le g. du show-business/de la finance** the show-business/financial elite
gothique [gɔtik] **1** *adj* Gothic; **écriture g.** Gothic script
2 *nm (style)* Gothic
gouache [gwaʃ] *nf* gouache
gouailleur, -euse [gwajœr, -øz] *adj (ton)* bantering
gouda [guda] *nm* Gouda
goudron [gudrɔ̃] *nm* tar; **goudrons** *(dans les cigarettes)* tar
goudronner [gudrɔne] *vt* to tar
gouffre [gufr] *nm* abyss; *Géol* sinkhole, *Br* swallow hole; *Fig* **être au bord du g.** to be on the edge of the abyss; *Fig* **un g. les sépare** there is a gulf between them; *Fig* **cette voiture est un g.** this car just swallows up money
gougère [guʒɛr] *nf Culin* gougère *(choux pastry with cheese)*
gouine [gwin] *nf très Fam* dyke, = offensive term used to refer to a lesbian
goujat [guʒa] *nm* boor
goujon [guʒɔ̃] *nm (poisson)* gudgeon
goulache, goulasch [gulaʃ] *nm* goulash

goulafre [gulafr] *adj Belg* greedy
goulée [gule] *nf (de liquide)* gulp; *(d'air)* lungful
goulet [gulɛ] *nm (défilé)* gully; **g. d'étranglement** bottleneck
gouleyant, -e [gulɛjɑ̃, -ɑ̃t] *adj (vin)* easy-drinking
goulot [gulo] *nm (d'une bouteille)* neck; **boire au g.** to drink straight from the bottle
goulu, -e [guly] **1** *adj* greedy, gluttonous
2 *nm,f* glutton
goulûment [gulymɑ̃] *adv* greedily
goupille [gupij] *nf (d'une grenade)* pin
goupiller [gupije] *Fam* **1** *vt (arranger)* to fix (up)
2 se goupiller *vpr* **bien se g.** to work out well; **ça s'est mal goupillé** it didn't work out
goupillon [gupijɔ̃] *nm* (**a**) *(pour eau bénite)* sprinkler (**b**) *(pour biberons, bouteilles)* bottle brush
gourd, -e¹ [gur, gurd] *adj* numb (with cold)
gourde² **1** *nf* (**a**) *(récipient)* flask (**b**) *Fam (personne)* dope
2 *adj Fam* dopey
gourdin [gurdɛ̃] *nm* club, cudgel
gourer [gure] **se gourer** *vpr Fam Br* to boob, *Am* to goof; **se g. d'adresse/de jour** to get the wrong address/day
gourgane [gurgan] *nf Can* broad bean
gourmand, -e [gurmɑ̃, -ɑ̃d] **1** *adj (personne)* who likes his/her food; *(à l'excès)* greedy; *Fig (intéressé) (regard)* greedy; **cet enfant est très g.** *(de sucreries)* that child has a sweet tooth
2 *nm,f* person who likes his/her food; **quel g.!** he certainly likes his food!
gourmandise [gurmɑ̃diz] *nf* (**a**) *(d'une personne)* love of food; *Fig* **avec g.** greedily (**b**) **gourmandises** *(sucreries)* delicacies
gourmet [gurmɛ] *nm* gourmet; **un fin g.** a great gourmet
gourmette [gurmɛt] *nf (bracelet)* chain (bracelet)
gourou [guru] *nm aussi Fig* guru
gousse [gus] *nf (de haricot, de petit pois)* pod; **g. d'ail** clove of garlic; **g. de vanille** vanilla pod
gousset [gusɛ] *nm (poche)* fob (pocket)
goût [gu] *nm* (**a**) *(saveur)* taste; **avoir un g. de banane/d'alcool** to taste of banana/alcohol; **manquer de g., ne pas avoir de g.** to be tasteless (**b**) *(sens)* taste (**c**) *(préférence, convenance)* taste; **avoir des goûts de luxe** to have expensive tastes; **trouver qn/qch à son g.** to find sb/sth to one's taste; **avoir du g. pour** *ou* **le g. de qch** to have a taste for sth; **elle n'a plus (de) g. à rien** she doesn't want to do anything any more; **faire qch par g.** to do sth because one likes to; **prendre g. à qch** to acquire a taste for sth; **chacun ses goûts** each to his own; **des goûts et des couleurs on ne discute pas, tous les goûts sont dans la nature** there's no accounting for taste (**d**) *(discernement, jugement)* taste; **s'habiller avec g.** to have good dress sense; **de bon g.** tasteful; **d'un g. douteux** in doubtful taste; **de mauvais g.** in bad taste (**e**) *(style)* **quelque chose dans ce g.-là** something of that sort
goûter¹ [gute] *nm (afternoon)* tea; **l'heure du g.** tea-time
goûter² **1** *vt* (**a**) *(essayer) (nourriture, boisson)* to taste, to try (**b**) *(apprécier)* to enjoy, to appreciate (**c**) *Belg & Can (avoir un goût de)* to taste of; **ce fruit goûte le pourri** this fruit tastes rotten
2 *vi (à quatre heures)* to have tea
3 goûter à *vt ind (aliment)* to taste, to try; *Fig* to have a taste of

goûteur, -euse [gutœr, -øz] *nm,f* taster
goutte [gut] **1** *nf* (**a**) *(de liquide)* drop; **couler g. à g.** to
drip; **il suait à grosses gouttes** the sweat was pouring off him; **gouttes** *(pour les yeux, les oreilles)* drops;
Fig **c'est la g.** **d'eau qui fait déborder le vase** it's the
straw that breaks/broke the camel's back; *Fam* **avoir
la g. au nez** to have a runny nose; **se ressembler
comme deux gouttes d'eau** to be as like as two peas
in a pod (**b**) *(petite quantité)* drop; **encore une g. de
café?** a drop more coffee?; *Fam* **boire la g.** to have a
nip (**c**) *Méd (maladie)* gout; **avoir la g.** to have gout
2 *adv Vieilli* **je n'y vois/entends g.** I can't see/understand anything
goutte-à-goutte [gutagut] *nm inv Méd* drip; **on lui a
mis un g.** he/she was put on a drip
gouttelette [gutlɛt] *nf* droplet
goutter [gute] *vi* to drip
gouttière [gutjɛr] *nf* (**a**) *(le long du toit)* gutter (**b**) *(le
long du mur)* drainpipe
gouvernail [guvɛrnaj] *nm Naut* rudder; **tenir le g.** to
be at the helm
gouvernant, -e[1] [guvɛrnɑ̃, -ɑ̃t] **1** *adj (classe, parti)*
governing, ruling
2 *nm* **les gouvernants** those in power
gouvernante[2] *nf (d'enfants)* governess; *(d'une personne, d'un hôtel)* housekeeper
gouverne [guvɛrn] *nf* (**a**) *Aviat* **gouvernes** control
surfaces (**b**) **pour votre g.** for your guidance
gouvernement [guvɛrnəmɑ̃] *nm* government; **sous
le g.** **Giscard** during Giscard's term of office
gouvernemental, -e, -aux, -ales [guvɛrnəmɑ̃tal,
-o] *adj* government; *(parti)* governing
gouverner [guvɛrne] **1** *vt* (**a**) *(diriger) (pays)* to govern, to rule; **un parti qui gouverne depuis des années** a party which has been in power for years (**b**)
(bateau) to steer
2 se gouverner *vpr* **le droit des peuples à se g. eux-
mêmes** the right of peoples to self-government
gouverneur [guvɛrnœr] *nm* governor; *Can* **G. Général** governor-general; *Can* **Lieutenant-G.** lieutenant-
governor
goyave [gɔjav] *nf* guava
GR® [ʒeɛr] *nm (abrév* **(sentier de) grande randonnée**)
= long-distance hiking path
grabat [graba] *nm* pallet
grabataire [grabatɛr] **1** *adj* bedridden
2 *nmf* bedridden invalid
grabuge [grabyʒ] *nm Fam* rumpus; **il va y avoir du g.**
there'll be trouble *or* a rumpus
grâce [grɑs] *nf* (**a**) *(charme)* grace; **avec g.** gracefully
(**b**) **g. à qn/qch** *(avec l'aide de)* thanks to sb/sth (**c**)
Litt (bienveillance, faveur) favour; **faites-moi la g.
d'oublier cette histoire** do me the favour of forgetting
this matter; **trouver g. aux yeux de qn** to find favour
in sb's eyes; **de g.!** for pity's sake! (**d**) *(volonté)* de
bonne g. willingly, readily; **de mauvaise g.** unwillingly, grudgingly (**e**) *(acquittement)* pardon; **demander ou crier g.** to beg for mercy; **faire g. à qn de qch**
(dette, tâche) to let sb off sth; **je vous fais g. des détails** I'll spare you the details; **g. présidentielle** presidential pardon (**f**) *(remerciements)* **rendre g. à** to give
thanks to (**g**) *Rel* grace
gracier [66] [grasje] *vt* to pardon
gracieusement [grasjøzmɑ̃] *adv* (**a**) *(avec grâce)*
gracefully (**b**) *(aimablement)* graciously (**c**) *(gratuitement)* free of charge

gracieux, -euse [grasjø, -øz] *adj* (**a**) *(qui a du
charme)* graceful (**b**) *(aimable)* gracious (**c**) *(gratuit)*
à titre g. free of charge
gracile [grasil] *adj* slender
gradation [gradasjɔ̃] *nf* gradation
grade [grad] *nm* (**a**) *(dans l'armée, dans l'administration)* rank; **monter en g.** to be promoted; *Fam* **en
prendre pour son g.** to be hauled over the coals (**b**)
Belg Scol & Univ (mention) distinction
gradé, -e [grade] *nm,f Mil* non-commissioned officer,
NCO
gradin [gradɛ̃] *nm (d'amphithéâtre, de stade)* row of
seats; **les gradins** *(d'un stade)* *Br* the terraces, *Am*
the bleachers
graduation [gradɥasjɔ̃] *nf* graduation
gradué, -e [gradɥe] *adj* (**a**) *(qui porte une graduation)*
graduated (**b**) *(progressif)* *(exercices, problèmes)*
graded
graduel, -elle [gradɥɛl] *adj* gradual
graduellement [gradɥɛlmɑ̃] *adv* gradually
graduer [gradɥe] *vt* (**a**) *(diviser en degrés)* to graduate
(**b**) *(augmenter)* to increase gradually
graffiti [grafiti] *nm* piece of graffiti; **des graffitis** graffiti
graillé, -e [graje] *adj Can (pour faire quelque chose)*
well-equipped; *Fam (bien monté)* well-hung
grailler [graje] *vi très Fam (manger)* to eat
graillon [grajɔ̃] *nm* **sentir le g.** to smell of burnt fat
grain[1] [grɛ̃] *nm* (**a**) *(graine, fruit, céréales)* grain; **g. de
café** coffee bean; **g. de poivre** peppercorn; **g. de raisin** grape (**b**) *(de sable, de poudre)* grain; *(de poussière)* speck; *(de chapelet)* bead; *Fig* **un g. de qch** *(un
peu de)* a hint of sth; **pas un g. de bon sens/de vérité**
not a grain of common sense/of truth; *Fam* **il a un g.**
he's not quite right in the head; **mettre son g. de sel** to
stick one's oar in; **g. de beauté** mole (**c**) *(d'un tissu,
d'une photographie)* grain; *(de la peau)* rough side
grain[2] *nm Naut* squall; *Fig* **veiller au g.** to keep a
weather eye open
graine [grɛn] *nf* seed; **monter en g.** to run to seed; *Fig
(personne)* to shoot up; **regarde un peu ce qu'a fait
ton cousin et prends-en de la g.!** just look at what
your cousin's done and take a leaf out of his book!;
c'est de la mauvaise g. he's/she's a bad lot; **g. de
voyou/voleur** little lout/thief
graissage [grɛsaʒ] *nm (d'une machine, d'un engrenage)* greasing
graisse [grɛs] *nf (d'animal, de personne)* fat; *(lubrifiant)* grease; **graisses animales/végétales** animal/
vegetable fat
graisser [grese] *vt (machine, engrenage)* to grease;
(bottes) to oil, *Br* to dubbin; **g. la patte à qn** to grease
sb's palm
graisseux, -euse [grɛsø, -øz] *adj* (**a**) *(taché de
graisse)* greasy (**b**) *(tumeur, tissu)* fatty
grammaire [gramɛr] *nf* (**a**) *(science, règles)* grammar; **faute/règle de g.** grammatical error/rule (**b**)
(livre) grammar (book)
grammairien, -enne [gramɛrjɛ̃, -ɛn] *nm,f* grammarian
grammatical, -e, -aux, -ales [gramatikal, -o] *adj*
grammatical
gramme [gram] *nm* gram; *aussi Fig* **pas un g. de** not
an ounce of
grand, -e [grɑ̃, grɑ̃d] **1** *adj* (**a**) *(en taille)* big; *(en
hauteur)* tall; *(en longueur)* long; *Phot* **g. angle** wide-
angle lens (**b**) *(principal)* chief, main; **grandes lignes**

(de train) main lines (**c**) *(adulte, plus âgé)* big; **tu es g.
maintenant** you're a big boy now (**d**) *(en quantité, en
intensité) (bruit)* loud; *(coup)* heavy; *(froid)* severe;
(différence, catastrophe) big; **le g. amour** true love;
un acteur sans g. talent a rather untalented actor; **il
fait g. jour** it's broad daylight; **c'est un g. buveur** he's
a big drinker; **les grands blessés** the seriously
wounded (**e**) *(puissant, prestigieux)* great; **une
grande dame de la littérature** a great literary lady
(**f**) *(dans un titre, un grade)* grand; **g. prêtre** high
priest; **g. reporter** chief reporter
  2 *adv* **ouvrir g. la bouche/la fenêtre** to open one's
mouth/the window wide; **g. ouvert** wide open
  3 *nm,f* **les grands** *(enfants)* the older ones; **grands et
petits** old and young, grown-ups and children; **les
grands de ce monde** those in high places; **les grands
du pétrole** the oil giants; **mon g.** mate, pal; **ma
grande** dear
grand-chose [grɑ̃ʃoz] **1** *pron indéfini* **pas g.** not
much; **ce ne sont que quelques fleurs, ce n'est pas
g.** it's just a few flowers, nothing much
  2 *nmf inv Fam (personne)* **un pas g.** a dead loss
grand-duc (*pl* **grands-ducs**) [grɑ̃dyk] *nm (noble)*
grand duke; *Fam* **faire la tournée des grands-ducs**
to go out on the town
grand-duché (*pl* **grands-duchés**) [grɑ̃dyʃe] *nm*
grand duchy
Grande-Bretagne [grɑ̃dbrətaɲ] *nf* **la G.** Great Britain
grande-duchesse (*pl* **grandes-duchesses**) [grɑ̃d-
dyʃɛs] *nf* grand duchess
grandement [grɑ̃dmɑ̃] *adv (beaucoup)* greatly; **se
tromper g.** to be greatly mistaken; **avoir g. le temps**
to have ample time; **avoir g. de quoi vivre** to have
plenty to live on
grandeur [grɑ̃dœr] *nf* (**a**) *(taille)* size; *(d'un arbre)*
height, size; **g. nature** life-size (**b**) *(importance)* importance (**c**) *Math* magnitude (**d**) *(gloire)* greatness,
grandeur; **g. et décadence d'un empire** rise and fall
of an empire (**e**) *(des sentiments)* nobility; **g. d'âme**
magnanimity (**f**) *Can* **à la g. de** throughout
grand-guignol [grɑ̃giɲɔl] *nm Péj* **c'est du g.** it's all
blood and gore
grandiloquence [grɑ̃dilɔkɑ̃s] *nf* grandiloquence
grandiloquent, -e [grɑ̃dilɔkɑ̃, -ɑ̃t] *adj* grandiloquent
grandiose [grɑ̃djoz] *adj* imposing
grandir [grɑ̃dir] **1** *vi (en taille)* to grow; *(en âge)* to
grow up; *(en importance)* to increase, to grow
  2 *vt* **g. qn** *(sujet: talons)* to make sb look taller; *Fig
(sujet: expérience, épreuve)* to improve sb's standing
  3 **se grandir** *vpr (en taille)* to make oneself taller
grandissant, -e [grɑ̃disɑ̃, -ɑ̃t] *adj* growing
grand-maman (*pl* **grand-mamans** *ou* **grands-ma-
mans**) [grɑ̃mamɑ̃] *Suisse & Can (en langage enfantin)*
granny, grandma
grand-mère (*pl* **grand-mères** *ou* **grands-mères**)
[grɑ̃mɛr] *nf* grandmother; *Fam (vieille femme)* old
granny
grand-oncle [grɑ̃tɔ̃kl] (*pl* **grands-oncles** [grɑ̃zɔ̃kl])
nm great-uncle
grand-papa (*pl* **grands-papas**) [grɑ̃papa] *Suisse &
Can (en langage enfantin)* grandpa, grandad
grand-peine [grɑ̃pɛn] **à grand-peine** *adv* with great
difficulty
grand-père (*pl* **grands-pères**) [grɑ̃pɛr] *nm* grandfather; *Fam (vieil homme)* grandpa, granddad

grand-route (*pl* **grand-routes**) [grɑ̃rut] *nf* main road
grand-rue (*pl* **grand-rues**) [grɑ̃ry] *nf* high street,
main street
grands-parents [grɑ̃parɑ̃] *nmpl* grandparents
grand-tante (*pl* **grand-tantes** *ou* **grands-tantes**)
[grɑ̃tɑ̃t] *nf* great-aunt
grand-voile (*pl* **grand-voiles** *ou* **grands-voiles**)
[grɑ̃vwal] *nf* mainsail
grange [grɑ̃ʒ] *nf* barn
granit(e) [granit] *nm* granite
granule [granyl] *nm* granule
granulé [granyle] *nm* granule
granuleux, -euse [granylø, -øz] *adj* granular
graphe [graf] *nm* graph
graphie [grafi] *nf Ling* written form
graphique [grafik] **1** *adj* graphic
  2 *nm* diagram; *(sur un axe)* graph; *Ordinat* graphic;
Ordinat **g. de gestion** management chart; **g. à** *ou* **en
barres** bar chart
graphisme [grafism] *nm* (**a**) *(écriture)* handwriting
(**b**) *Art (style)* style of drawing
graphiste [grafist] *nmf* graphic designer
graphite [grafit] *nm* graphite
graphologie [grafolɔʒi] *nf* graphology
graphologue [grafolɔg] *nmf* graphologist
grappe [grap] *nf (de raisin)* bunch; *(de fleurs, de gens)*
cluster; *Vulg* **lâche-moi la g.!** piss off!
grappiller [grapije] *vt (renseignements)* to glean; *(argent)* to make on the side
grappin [grapɛ̃] *nm Naut* grappling hook *or* iron; *Fam
Fig* **mettre le g. sur qn/qch** to get one's paws on sb/
sth
gras, grasse [grɑ, grɑs] **1** *adj* (**a**) *(nourriture, tissu)*
fatty (**b**) *(gros) (personne, animal)* fat; *(poulet)* plump
(**c**) *(graisseux) (chiffon, cheveux, peau)* greasy (**d**)
(épais) (terre) heavy, clayey; *(crayon)* soft lead; *(toux)*
loose; *(rire)* throaty (**e**) *Typ* bold; **caractères g.** bold
type (**f**) *Fig (bénéfices, récompense)* handsome; **faire
la grasse matinée** to have a lie-in (**g**) *(graveleux)*
(histoire) dirty, smutty
  2 *adv* **manger g.** to eat fatty food
  3 *nm* (**a**) *(de la jambe, du bras)* fleshy part (**b**) *(du
jambon, de la viande)* fat (**c**) *Typ* bold; **en g.** in bold
gras-double (*pl* **gras-doubles**) [grɑdubl] *nm* tripe
grassement [grɑsmɑ̃] *adv (récompenser, payer)*
handsomely
grasseyer [graseje] *vi* to pronounce one's r's at the
back of the throat
grassouillet, -ette [grɑsujɛ, -ɛt] *adj* plump, chubby
gratifiant, -e [gratifjɑ̃, -ɑ̃t] *adj* rewarding, gratifying
gratification [gratifikasjɔ̃] *nf* (**a**) *(prime)* bonus (**b**)
(satisfaction) gratification
gratifier [66] [gratifje] *vt* (**a**) **g. qn de qch** *(récompense)* to present sb with sth; *Ironique (sourire)* to bestow sth on sb (**b**) *(valoriser)* to gratify
gratin [gratɛ̃] *nm* (**a**) *(plat)* gratin *(baked dish with a
topping of grated cheese and sometimes breadcrumbs)*;
au g. au gratin; **chou-fleur au g.** cauliflower cheese;
g. dauphinois = sliced potatoes baked with cream
and browned on top (**b**) *Fam Fig* **le g.** *(le beau monde)*
the upper crust
gratiné, -e [gratine] **1** *adj* (**a**) *(au gratin)* au gratin
*(topped with grated cheese and sometimes bread-
crumbs)* (**b**) *Fam Fig (addition)* huge; *(examen, problème)* tough
  2 *nf* **gratinée** *Culin* onion soup au gratin

gratiner [gratine] **1** *vt* to brown
  2 *vi* **faire g. qch** to brown sth
gratis [gratis] **1** *adv* free (of charge)
  2 *adj* free
gratitude [gratityd] *nf* gratitude
gratos [gratos] *adj Fam* free (of charge)
gratouiller [gratuje] *vt Fam (démanger)* **ça (me) gratouille** it makes me itch
gratte [grat] *nf Can* snowplough
gratte-ciel [gratsjɛl] *nm inv* skyscraper
gratte-papier [gratpapje] *nm inv Péj* pen-pusher
gratter [grate] **1** *vt (avec les ongles)* to scratch; *(avec un objet)* to scrape; *(effacer) (mot, inscription)* to scratch out; *(tache)* to scrape off; *Fam* **ça me gratte** it makes me itch; **pull qui gratte** scratchy jumper; *Fig* **g. les fonds de tiroir** to scrape around for money
  2 *vi* **g. à la porte** to tap lightly at the door
  3 se gratter *vpr* to scratch oneself; **se g. jusqu'au sang** to scratch oneself raw; **se g. la tête/l'oreille** to scratch one's head/ear; *très Fam* **tu peux toujours te g.!** you can take a running jump!
gratteux, -euse [gratø, -øz] *Can* **1** *adj* stingy, mean
  2 *nm,f* miser
grattoir [gratwar] *nm* scraper; *(de boîte d'allumettes)* striking surface
grattouiller [gratuje] = **gratouiller**
gratuit, -e [gratɥi, -it] *adj* **(a)** *(billet, entrée, échantillon)* free; **à titre g.** free of charge **(b)** *(acte, violence)* gratuitous
gratuité [gratɥite] *nf* **(a)** *(fait de ne pas payer)* **la g. de l'enseignement/des soins hospitaliers** free education/hospital care **(b)** *(d'un acte, de la violence)* gratuitousness
gratuitement [gratɥitmã] *adv* **(a)** *(sans payer)* free (of charge) **(b)** *(sans motif)* gratuitously
gravats [grava] *nmpl* rubble
grave [grav] **1** *adj* **(a)** *(sérieux, dramatique)* serious; **ce n'est pas g.** *(ça n'a pas d'importance)* it doesn't matter; **un accident qui a fait deux blessés graves** an accident in which two people were seriously injured **(b)** *(solennel) (visage, ton, expression)* grave, solemn **(c)** *(note, voix)* low, deep **(d)** *Fam (dérangé)* off one's rocker
  2 *nm* **le g., les graves** *(notes)* the low notes; **les graves** *(sur une chaîne stéréo)* the bass
  3 *adv Fam* in a bad way; **il me prend la tête g.** he really bugs me
graveleux, -euse [gravlø, -øz] *adj* **(a)** *(histoire, chanson)* smutty, dirty **(b)** *(terre)* gravelly
gravement [gravmã] *adv* **(a)** *(malade, blessé)* seriously **(b)** *(avec dignité)* gravely, solemnly
graver [grave] *vt (matériau, motif)* to engrave; *(sur bois)* to carve; *(disque)* to make; *Fig* **rester gravé dans la mémoire de qn** to be engraved on sb's memory
graveur, -euse [gravœr, -øz] **1** *nm,f* engraver; **g. sur bois** woodcarver
  2 *nm Ordinat (de CD-ROM)* writer, burner; **g. de CD** CD writer *or* burner
gravier [gravje] *nm* gravel
gravillon [gravijɔ̃] *nm (caillou)* piece of gravel; **du g., des gravillons** gravel; **gravillons** *(sur panneau)* loose chippings
gravir [gravir] *vt* to climb; *Fig* **g. les échelons** to climb the ladder
gravissime [gravisim] *adj* extremely serious
gravitation [gravitasjɔ̃] *nf* gravitation

gravité [gravite] *nf* **(a)** *Phys* gravity **(b)** *(solennité)* gravity **(c)** *(importance)* seriousness; **sans g.** *(blessure, problème)* minor
graviter [gravite] *vi* **g. autour de qch** to orbit sth; *Fig* **g. autour de qn** to hover around sb
gravure [gravyr] *nf* **(a)** *(action)* engraving; **g. sur bois** woodcarving **(b)** *(ouvrage)* engraving; **g. sur bois** woodcut; *Fig* **c'est une vraie g. de mode** she dresses like a fashion model
gré [gre] *nm* **(a)** *(goût)* **à mon/son g.** for my/his/her liking **(b)** *(volonté)* **contre son g.** against one's will; **de son propre g., de son plein g.** of one's own free will; **de bon g.** willingly, gladly; **bon g. mal g.** whether we/you/*etc* like it or not; **faites-le venir de g. ou de force** make him come whether he wants to or not; **au g. des flots** at the mercy of the waves; **au g. des événements/des circonstances** *(agir, changer d'avis)* according to how events turn out/to the circumstances **(c)** *Sout (gratitude)* **nous vous saurions g. de bien vouloir...** we would be grateful if you would kindly...
grec, grecque [grɛk] **1** *adj* Greek
  2 *nm,f* **G.** Greek
  3 *nm (langue)* Greek; **g. ancien/moderne** ancient/modern Greek
  4 *nf* **grecque (a)** *Culin* **à la grecque** *(légumes)* marinated in olive oil, lemon juice and herbs and served cold **(b)** *(motif)* Greek key pattern
Grèce [grɛs] *nf* **la G.** Greece
gredin, -e [grədɛ̃, -in] *nm,f Fam Vieilli* rascal
gréement [gremã] *nm* **(a)** *Naut* rigging **(b)** *Can (ustensiles)* gear, equipment
greffe¹ [grɛf] *nf* **(a)** *(de peau, de tissu)* graft; *(d'organe)* transplant; **g. du cœur/du rein** heart/kidney transplant **(b)** *Bot (action)* grafting; *(bouture)* graft
greffe² *nm Jur* clerk of the court's office
greffé, -e [grɛfe] *nm,f Méd* **g. cardiaque** *ou* **du cœur** heart transplant patient
greffer [grefe] *vt (peau, tissu, bouture)* to graft; *(organe)* to transplant
greffier, -ère [grefje, -ɛr] *nm Jur* clerk (of the court)
greffon [grɛfɔ̃] *nm (de tissu, de peau)* graft; *(d'organe)* transplant; *(bouture)* graft
grégaire [gregɛr] *adj* gregarious; **l'instinct g.** the herd instinct
grège [grɛʒ] *adj (beige)* whitish-beige
grégorien, -enne [gregɔrjɛ̃, -ɛn] *adj* Gregorian
grêle¹ [grɛl] *adj (jambes, mains)* skinny; *(tige, silhouette)* slender; *(voix, son)* shrill
grêle² *nf aussi Fig* hail
grêlé, -e [grele] *adj (peau)* pockmarked
grêler [grele] *v impersonnel* to hail
grêlon [grɛlɔ̃] *nm* hailstone
grelot [grəlo] *nm* (small) bell
grelotter [grəlɔte] *vi* to shiver **(de** with)
Grenade [grənad] *nf (aux Antilles)* **la G.** Grenada
grenade [grənad] *nf* **(a)** *(projectile)* grenade; **g. lacrymogène** tear-gas grenade **(b)** *(fruit)* pomegranate
grenadine [grənadin] *nf* grenadine
grenaille [grənɑj] *nf* **(a)** *(plombs)* shot **(b)** *Belg (revêtement)* grit, fine gravel; **grenailles errantes** *(sur panneau)* loose chippings
grenat [grəna] **1** *nm* garnet
  2 *adj inv* dark red
grenier [grənje] *nm* **(a)** *(sous les combles)* attic **(b)** *(pour grain, fourrage)* granary; **g. à blé** wheat loft; **g. à foin** hayloft

grenouille [grənuj] *nf (animal)* frog; *Fig & Péj* **g. de bénitier** Bible basher
grenouillère [grənujɛr] *nf (pour bébé)* Babygro®
grès [grɛ] *nm* (**a**) *(pierre)* sandstone (**b**) *(céramique)* stoneware; **cruche en g.** stoneware jug
grésil [grezil, grezi] *nm* fine hail
grésillement [grezijmã] *nm (du feu, d'une radio)* crackling; *(de l'huile)* sizzling
grésiller [grezije] *vi (feu, radio)* to crackle; *(huile)* to sizzle
gressin [gresɛ̃] *nm* bread stick
grève[1] [grɛv] *nf (arrêt du travail)* strike; **se mettre en g.** to go out on strike, to strike; **être en g., faire g.** to be on strike; **g. des Postes** postal strike; **g. de la faim** hunger strike; **g. générale** general strike; **g. sauvage** wildcat strike; **g. sur le tas** sit-down strike; **g. tournante** staggered strike; **g. du zèle** work-to-rule, go-slow
grève[2] *nf (le long de la mer)* shore; *(d'un fleuve)* bank
grever [46] [grəve] *vt (pouvoir d'achat)* to restrict; *(budget)* to put a strain on
gréviste [grevist] *nmf* striker; **g. de la faim** hunger striker
gribouillage [gribujaʒ] *nm (écriture)* scribble, scrawl; *(dessin)* doodle
gribouille [gribuj] *nm Can (dispute)* quarrel, fight
gribouiller [gribuje] *vt & vi (écrire)* to scrawl, to scribble; *(dessiner)* to doodle
gribouillis [gribuji] = **gribouillage**
grief [grijɛf] *nm* grievance, ground for complaint; **faire** *ou* **tenir g. à qn de qch** to hold sth against sb
grièvement [grijɛvmã] *adv* seriously, badly
griffe [grif] *nf* (**a**) *(d'animal)* claw; **faire ses griffes** *(chat)* to sharpen its claws; *Fig* **montrer les griffes** to show one's claws; **arracher qn des griffes de qn** to snatch sb out of sb's clutches (**b**) *(sur un bijou)* claw (**c**) *(sur vêtements)* label; *Fig (style)* stamp (**d**) *Belg (rayure)* scratch
griffé, -e [grife] *adj (vêtement)* designer
griffer [grife] *vt* to scratch
griffon [grifɔ̃] *nm* (**a**) *(chien)* griffon (**b**) *(créature mythique)* griffin
griffonner [grifɔne] *vt & vi (écrire)* to scrawl, to scribble; *(dessiner)* to sketch quickly
griffure [grifyr] *nf* scratch
grignoter [griɲɔte] **1** *vt* to nibble; *Fig (libertés)* to erode; *(capital, économies)* to eat into
2 *vi* to nibble
gril [gril] *nm (de cuisine) Br* grill, *Am* broiler; **faire cuire qch sur le g.** to grill sth; *Fig* **être sur le g.** to be on tenterhooks
grillade [grijad] *nf (viande)* piece of grilled meat; *(poisson)* piece of grilled fish; **faire des grillades** to have a barbecue
grillage [grijaʒ] *nm (de fenêtre, de porte)* wire mesh; *(clôture)* wire netting
grillagé, -e [grijaʒe] *adj (fenêtre)* covered with wire mesh; *(jardin)* surrounded by wire netting
grille [grij] *nf* (**a**) *(à l'entrée d'un parc, d'un jardin)* gate; *(clôture basse)* railings (**b**) *(d'une cage, d'une fenêtre)* screen, netting; *Aut* **g. de radiateur** radiator grille (**c**) *(d'un évier, d'un égout)* grating, grate (**d**) *(tableau) (de mots croisés)* grid; **une g. de Loto** Loto card, *Br* ≃ a National Lottery ticket; *Rad & TV* **g. des programmes** programme schedule; **g. des salaires** salary scale
grille-pain [grijpɛ̃] *nm inv* toaster

griller [grije] **1** *vt* (**a**) *(rôtir) (viande)* to grill; *(pain)* to toast; *(café, marrons)* to roast (**b**) *(brûler)* to scorch, to burn; *(ampoule, fusible)* to blow; *Fam (cigarette)* to smoke (**c**) *Fam (dépasser)* **g. un concurrent** to leave a competitor standing; **g. un feu rouge** to jump the lights (**d**) *Fam (discréditer)* **il est grillé** his game's up
2 *vi* (**a**) *(viande)* to grill; *(pain)* to toast; *(marrons)* to roast; *Fig* **g. d'impatience** to be burning with impatience (**b**) *(ampoule, fusible)* to blow
3 se griller *vpr* **se g. au soleil** to roast in the sun; *Fam* **se g. auprès de qn** to blot one's copybook with sb
grillon [grijɔ̃] *nm* cricket
grimaçant, -e [grimasã, -ãt] *adj* grimacing
grimace [grimas] *nf* grimace; **faire une g. (à qn)** to make *or* pull a face (at sb); **faire la g.** to make *or* pull a face; **faire une g. de douleur** to wince with pain
grimacer [16] [grimase] *vi* to make *or* pull a face; **g. de douleur** to wince with pain
grimer [grime] **1** *vt* to make up
2 se grimer *vpr* to put one's make-up on
grimpant, -e [grɛ̃pã, -ãt] *adj (plante)* climbing
grimpe [grɛ̃p] *nf Fam* rock-climbing; **faire de la g.** to go rock-climbing
grimpée [grɛ̃pe] *nf (stiff)* climb
grimper [grɛ̃pe] **1** *vi aussi Fig* to climb; **g. aux arbres** to climb trees; **ça grimpe** it's steep
2 *vt (montagne, escalier)* to climb; *Fig* **g. les échelons** to climb the ladder
grimpeur, -euse [grɛ̃pœr, -øz] *nm,f* climber
grinçant, -e [grɛ̃sã, -ãt] *adj (qui grince)* creaking; *Fig (caustique)* caustic
grincement [grɛ̃smã] *nm (d'une porte, de roues)* creaking; **grincements de dents** grinding of teeth; *Fig* gnashing of teeth
grincer [16] [grɛ̃se] *vi (porte, roues)* to creak; **g. des dents** to grind one's teeth
grincheux, -euse [grɛ̃ʃø, -øz] **1** *adj* grumpy
2 *nm,f* grumpy person
gringalet [grɛ̃galɛ] **1** *nm* weakling
2 *adj m* puny
griotte [grijɔt] *nf* morello (cherry)
grippal, -e, -aux, -ales [gripal, -o] *adj* **soulage les états grippaux** *(sur médicament)* relieves flu symptoms
grippe [grip] *nf* (**a**) *(maladie)* flu; **avoir la g.** to have (the) flu; **g. aviaire** bird flu, *Spéc* avian flu; **g. intestinale** gastric flu (**b**) **prendre qn/qch en g.** to take a dislike to sb/sth
grippé, -e [gripe] *adj* (**a**) *(malade)* **être g.** to have (the) flu (**b**) *(moteur, mécanisme)* seized-up
grippe-sou *(pl* **grippe-sous** *ou* **grippe-sou)** [gripsu] *nm* skinflint, miser
gris, -e [gri, griz] **1** *adj* (**a**) *(couleur, temps)* grey; **il fait g. ce matin** it's a grey *or* dull morning; **g. ardoise** slate grey; **g. perle** pearl grey (**b**) *(ivre)* tipsy
2 *nm* (**a**) *(couleur)* grey; **s'habiller en g.** to wear grey; *Ordinat* **tons de g.** shades of grey (**b**) *(tabac)* shag
grisaille [grizaj] *nf (caractère morne)* dreariness
grisant, -e [grizã, -ãt] *adj (succès, atmosphère)* intoxicating; *(aventure, soirée)* exhilarating
grisâtre [grizɑtr] *adj* greyish
grisé [grize] *nm Ordinat* grey tone
griser [grize] **1** *vt* (**a**) *(enivrer)* to make tipsy; *Fig* to intoxicate (**b**) *Ordinat* to shade
2 se griser *vpr* **se g. de qch** *(air pur)* to get drunk on sth; *(paroles)* to get carried away by sth

grisonnant, -e [grizɔnɑ̃, -ɑ̃t] *adj (cheveux, personne)* greying; **avoir les tempes grisonnantes** to be greying at the temples
grisonner [grizɔne] *vi (cheveux, personne)* to go grey
grisou [grizu] *nm* firedamp; **coup de g.** firedamp explosion
grive [griv] *nf* thrush
grivois, -e [grivwa, -az] *adj* bawdy
grivoiserie [grivwazri] *nf (plaisanterie)* bawdy joke; *(histoire)* bawdy story; *(acte)* rude gesture
grizzli, grizzly [grizli] *nm* grizzly (bear)
Groenland [grɔɛnlɑ̃d] *nm* **le G.** Greenland
grog [grɔg] *nm* hot toddy
groggy [grɔgi] *adj inv Fam* groggy
grogne [grɔɲ] *nf Fam* discontent
grognement [grɔɲmɑ̃] *nm (d'un cochon)* grunt; *(d'un chien, d'une personne)* growl; **pousser des grognements** to grunt/to growl
grogner [grɔɲe] *vi* (**a**) *(gronder) (cochon)* to grunt; *(chien, personne)* to growl (**b**) *(protester)* to grumble
grognon [grɔɲɔ̃] *adj* grumpy
groin [grwɛ̃] *nm* snout
grol(l)e [grɔl] *nf très Fam* shoe
grommeler [9] [grɔmle] *vt & vi* to mutter
grommellements [grɔmɛlmɑ̃] *nmpl* muttering
grondement [grɔ̃dmɑ̃] *nm* (**a**) *(d'un chien)* growl (**b**) *(du tonnerre)* rumble; *(d'un torrent, des vagues, d'un moteur)* roar; *(des canons)* booming
gronder [grɔ̃de] **1** *vi* (**a**) *(chien)* to growl (**b**) *(tonnerre)* to rumble; *(torrent, vagues, moteur)* to roar; *(canons)* to boom; **la révolte/le mécontentement gronde** there are rumblings of rebellion/discontent
2 *vt (réprimander)* to scold, to tell off; **se faire g.** to get told off
groom [grum] *nm Br* page, *Am* bellhop
gros, grosse [gro, gros] **1** *adj* (**a**) *(corpulent)* big, fat (**b**) *(important, abondant)* big; *(rhume)* bad; *(dépenses, averse, mer)* heavy; *(somme)* large; *(faute)* serious; **g. buveur/mangeur** big drinker/eater; **avoir un g. chagrin** to be very upset; **la plus grosse partie de qch** the majority of sth; **un mensonge g. comme une maison** a whopper of a lie; *très Fam* **g. lard** big fat slob; *Fam* **g. nigaud** *ou* **bêta!** you great fool!; *Fam* **g. bonnet, grosse légume** big shot, bigwig (**c**) *(épais) (morceau, caractères)* big, large; *(toile)* coarse; *(pull, chaussettes, corde)* thick; *(chaussures)* strong, stout (**d**) *(peu subtil) (voix)* gruff; *(rire)* coarse; **c'est un peu g.!** that's a bit much!; **g. mot** swearword (**e**) *Mus* **grosse caisse** bass drum
2 *adv (beaucoup) (gagner, rapporter, risquer)* a lot; **je donnerais g. pour savoir qui a fait ça** I'd give a lot to know who did that
3 *nm,f* fat man, *f* fat woman
4 *nm* (**a**) *(partie la plus importante)* bulk; **le g. de** the majority of; **le plus g. est fait** the bulk of the work has been done (**b**) *Com* wholesale (trade); **faire du g.** to sell wholesale; **de g.** *(commerce, boucher)* wholesale (**c**) **en g.** *(en grosses lettres)* in big *or* large letters; *(approximativement)* roughly; *Com* wholesale
groseille [grozɛj] *nf* **g. (rouge)** redcurrant; **g. à maquereau** gooseberry
groseillier [grozeje] *nm* redcurrant bush; **g. à maquereau** gooseberry bush
grosse [gros] *voir* **gros**
grossesse [grosɛs] *nf* pregnancy; **g. extra-utérine** ectopic pregnancy; **g. nerveuse** phantom pregnancy; **g. à risque** high-risk pregnancy

grosseur [grosœr] *nf* (**a**) *(taille, volume)* size; **de la g. d'un œuf** the size of an egg (**b**) *Méd* lump
grossier, -ère [grosje, -ɛr] *adj* (**a**) *(impoli) (personne)* rude (**envers** to); *(langage, plaisanterie)* crude; **un g. personnage** an uncouth individual (**b**) *(peu raffiné) (nourriture, tissu)* coarse, rough; *(dessin)* crude, rough; *(goûts, traits du visage)* coarse; (**c**) *(important) (erreur)* gross
grossièrement [grosjɛrmɑ̃] *adv* (**a**) *(de façon impolie)* rudely (**b**) *(sans raffinement)* crudely (**c**) *(approximativement)* roughly
grossièreté [grosjɛrte] *nf* (**a**) *(incorrection)* coarseness (**b**) *(parole grossière)* coarse remark; *(obscénité)* rude joke; **dire des grossièretés** to swear; **il aime raconter des grossièretés** he likes telling rude jokes (**c**) *(caractère rudimentaire) (d'un dessin)* crudeness; *(d'un tissu, des goûts)* coarseness
grossir [grosir] **1** *vi (personne, animal)* to put on weight, to get fatter; *(mer)* to get rough; *(rivière)* to swell; **g. de 2 kilos** *(personne)* to put on 2 kilos
2 *vt (sujet: loupe, microscope)* to magnify; *Fig (exagérer)* to exaggerate; **g. qn** *(sujet: vêtement)* to make sb look fat; **g. les rangs de qch** to swell the ranks of sth
grossissant, -e [grosisɑ̃, -ɑ̃t] *adj* **miroir g.** distorting mirror
grossissement [grosismɑ̃] *nm* (**a**) *(augmentation de taille)* increase in size (**b**) *(pouvoir grossissant)* magnification
grossiste [grosist] *nmf* wholesaler
grosso modo [grosomɔdo] *adv* roughly; **g. c'est une comédie** broadly speaking it's a comedy
grotesque [grotɛsk] *adj* ludicrous, ridiculous
grotte [grɔt] *nf* cave; **g. artificielle** grotto
grouillant, -e [grujɑ̃, -ɑ̃t] *adj* swarming (**de** with)
grouiller [gruje] **1** *vi (se presser)* to swarm around; **g. de** to swarm with
2 se grouiller *vpr Fam* to get a move on
groupe [grup] *nm* (**a**) *(de gens, de choses)* group; *(de musiciens)* group, band; **en g.** in a group; **se mettre par groupes de trois** to get into *or* form groups of three; *Pol* **le G. des 8** the Group of Eight; **g. d'âge** age group; *Ordinat* **g. de discussion** discussion group; *Scol* **g. de niveau** stream; *Pol* **g. de pression** pressure group (**b**) *(industriel, de presse)* group; *(hospitalier, scolaire)* complex (**c**) *Gram* **g. verbal/nominal** verbal/nominal group (**d**) *Mil* **g. de combat** unit (**e**) *Méd* **g. sanguin** blood group (**f**) *Élec* **g. électrogène** generator
groupement [grupmɑ̃] *nm (association)* group; **g. d'achat** purchasing co-operative; **g. de consommateurs** consumer group
grouper [grupe] **1** *vt* to group (together); *(moyens, ressources)* to pool
2 se grouper *vpr (dans une association)* to form a group; *(dans un lieu)* to gather; **rester groupés** keep together
groupie [grupi] *nf Fam* groupie
groupuscule [grupyskyl] *nm* small group
gruau [gryo] *nm* (**a**) **g. (d'avoine)** groats; **(farine de) g. (fine)** wheat flour (**b**) *Can Culin* porridge
grue [gry] *nf* (**a**) *(oiseau)* crane; **faire le pied de g.** to hang about (**b**) *(machine)* crane; *TV & Cin* cherry picker (**c**) *très Fam Vieilli (prostituée)* tart
gruger [45] [gryʒe] *vt (rouler)* to swindle
grumeau, -x [grymo] *nm (dans une sauce, une pâte)* lump
grumeleux, -euse [grymlø, -øz] *adj (sauce, pâte)* lumpy
gruyère [gryjɛr] *nm* Gruyère (cheese)

GSM [ʒeɛsɛm] *nm* *Tél* (*abrév* **global system for mobile communications**) (**a**) (*système*) GSM; **réseau G.** GSM network (**b**) *Belg* (*téléphone portable*) *Br* mobile phone, *Am* cellphone

Guadeloupe [gwadlup] *nf* **la G.** Guadeloupe

guadeloupéen, -enne [gwadlupeɛ̃, -ɛn] **1** *adj* of Guadeloupe

2 *nm,f* **G.** person from Guadeloupe

Guatemala [gwatemala] *nm* **le G.** Guatemala

guatémaltèque [gwatemaltɛk] **1** *adj* Guatemalan

2 *nmf* **G.** Guatemalan

gué [ge] *nm* ford; **passer une rivière à g.** to ford a river

guéguerre [gegɛr] *nf Fam* squabble

guenilles [gənij] *nfpl* (old) rags; **en g.** in rags

guenon [gənɔ̃] *nf* female monkey

guépard [gepar] *nm* cheetah

guêpe [gɛp] *nf* wasp; *Fam* **pas folle, la g.!** she's nobody's fool!

guêpier [gepje] *nm* wasps' nest; *Fig* (*situation*) sticky situation; **se fourrer dans un g.** to get oneself into a sticky situation

guêpière [gɛpjɛr] *nf* basque

guère [gɛr] *adv* **ne... g.** (*pas beaucoup*) not much; (*pas longtemps*) hardly, scarcely; **il n'a g. d'argent/d'amis** he hasn't got much money/many friends; **il n'y a g. qu'elle qui soit au courant** she's about the only one who knows what's going on; **il ne mange g. que du pain** he eats hardly anything but bread; **il n'y a g. plus de six ans** just over six years ago; **et celui-là, comment le trouvez-vous? – g. mieux!** and what do you think of that one? – not much better!

guéri, -e [geri] *adj aussi Fig* cured (**de** of)

guéridon [geridɔ̃] *nm* pedestal table

guérilla [gerija] *nf* guerrilla warfare

guérillero [gerijero] *nm* guerrilla

guérir [gerir] **1** *vt* (*personne, maladie*) to cure; *Fig* **g. qn de qch** (*timidité, habitude*) to cure sb of sth

2 *vi* (*personne*) to get better, to recover; (*blessure*) to heal

3 **se guérir** *vpr* (*soi-même*) to cure oneself; *Fig* **se g. de qch** (*timidité, habitude*) to cure oneself of sth

guérison [gerizɔ̃] *nf* (*rétablissement*) recovery

guérissable [gerisabl] *adj* curable

guérisseur, -euse [gerisœr, -øz] **1** *nm,f* healer

2 *nm* (*d'une tribu*) medicine man

guérite [gerit] *nf Mil* sentry box

guerre [gɛr] *nf* (**a**) (*conflit*) war; (*technique*) warfare; **en temps de g.** in wartime; **être en g.** (**contre**) to be at war (with); **faire la g.** (*soldat*) to fight; **la drôle de g.** the phoney war; **la Grande G.** the Great War; **la Première/la Seconde G. mondiale** the First/Second World War, World War One/Two; **la g. de 14** the 1914–18 War; **la g. de 70** the Franco-Prussian War; **la g. d'Algérie** the Algerian War of Independence; **la g. de Cent Ans** the Hundred Years' War; **g. civile** civil war; **la g. de Corée** the Korean War; **g. éclair** blitzkrieg; **la g. d'Espagne** the Spanish Civil War; **la g. froide** the cold war; **la g. du Golfe** the Gulf War; **la g. d'Indochine** the first Indo-Chinese War (*1946–1954*); **g. sainte** holy war; **la g. de Sécession** the American Civil War; **la g. du Viêt Nam** the Vietnam War (**b**) (*locutions*) **elle fait la g. à son fils pour qu'il ne fume pas** she's fighting a running battle with her son about smoking; **faire la g. à qch** to wage war on sth; **partir en g. contre qch** to declare war on sth; **il est en g. ouverte contre sa hiérarchie** there's open war between him and his superiors; **à la g. comme à la g.** we'll/you'll/*etc* have

to do the best we/you/*etc* can; **c'est de bonne g.** that's fair enough; **de g. lasse** for the sake of peace and quiet

La guerre d'Algérie

This was the most bitter of France's post-colonial struggles, lasting from 1954 to 1962. In a country dominated by a million white settlers, the "**pieds noirs**" (*see box at this entry*), the French government's attempts to crush the revolt of the "Front de libération nationale" (**FLN**, *see entry*), and to put an end to their struggle for independence with massive military intervention, came to nothing. The return to power of General de Gaulle in 1958, and the Accords d'Évian in 1962, led to Algerian independence and the resettlement of the "pieds noirs" in France.

La guerre d'Indochine

French military operations in Indochina from 1940 to 1954 were first directed against Japan and Thailand, and then against the Vietminh revolutionary movement. After the defeat of the French forces at Dien Bien Phu in 1954, those countries with interests in the region held a conference in Geneva, which ended the war by dividing Vietnam into two independent northern and southern states. This war, together with the Algerian war, was a landmark in the French decolonization process.

guerrier, -ère [gɛrje, -ɛr] **1** *adj* warlike; (*chant*) war

2 *nm,f* warrior

guerroyer [32] [gɛrwaje] *vi Litt* to wage war (**contre** on)

guet [gɛ] *nm* **poste de g.** lookout post; **faire le g.** to be on the lookout

guet-apens (*pl* **guets-apens**) [gɛtapɑ̃] *nm* (*piège*) ambush; *Fig* trap; **tomber dans un g.** to be ambushed; *Fig* to fall into a trap

guêtre [gɛtr] *nf* gaiter; *Belg Fig* **il a la police à ses guêtres** the police are on his tail *or* hot on his heels

guetter [gete] *vt* (*occasion*) to watch out for; (*proie*) to lie in wait for; **il guette le facteur** he's on the lookout for the postman; **la dépression le guette** he's on the verge of a nervous breakdown

gueulante [gœlɑ̃t] *nf très Fam* **pousser une g.** to kick up a stink

gueulard, -e [gœlar, -ard] *très Fam* **1** *adj* (*personne*) loudmouthed; *Br* gobby; (*bébé*) screaming; (*couleur*) garish

2 *nm,f* (*personne*) loudmouth; (*bébé*) screaming kid

gueule [gœl] *nf* (**a**) (*d'un animal*) mouth; *Fig* **se jeter dans la g. du loup** to put one's head in the lion's mouth (**b**) *très Fam* (*bouche*) mouth; **ça emporte** *ou* **arrache la g!**. it blows your head off!; **une grande g.** (*personne*) a loudmouth; (*ferme*) **ta g.!** shut your mouth *or* face!, shut it!; **avoir la g. de bois** to have a hangover (**c**) *très Fam* (*visage*) mug, face; **avoir une sale g.** (*mine patibulaire*) to look shady; (*mauvaise mine*) to look rotten; **faire la g.** to sulk; **faire la g. à qn** to be in a huff with sb; **faire une g. d'enterrement** to look really pissed off; **se foutre de** *ou* **se payer la g. de qn** to take the piss out of sb; (**s')en prendre plein la g.** to get a right mouthful (of abuse) (**d**) *Fam* (*allure*) **avoir une drôle de g.** to look odd; **cette g. tableau a de la g.** that's some picture

gueuler [gœle] *très Fam* **1** *vi* to yell, to bawl; *(radio, télévision)* to blare; *(protester)* to kick up a fuss; **si je suis en retard, ça va g. à la maison** if I'm late, I'll get bawled out when I get home **2** *vt* to bawl out, to yell out

gueuleton [gœltɔ̃] *nm Fam* blowout; **faire un g.** to have a blowout

gueux, gueuse¹ [gø, gøz] *nm,f Vieilli (mendiant)* beggar

gueuse², gueuze [gøz] *nf* = type of strong double-fermented Belgian beer

gugusse [gygys] *nm Fam* twit; **faire le g.** to act the fool

gui [gi] *nm* mistletoe

guibol(l)e [gibɔl] *nf Fam (jambe)* leg, pin

guichet [giʃɛ] *nm* (**a**) *(de gare, de poste, de banque)* window; *(de théâtre)* box office; **on joue à guichets fermés** the performance is sold out; **g. automatique** *(de banque)* cash dispenser (**b**) *(de porte de prison)* hatch; *(de confessionnal)* grille (**c**) *(au cricket)* wicket

guichetier, -ère [giʃtje, -ɛr] *nm,f (de gare)* ticket clerk; *(de poste, de banque)* counter clerk

guide [gid] **1** *nm* (**a**) *(personne)* guide; **g. de haute montagne** mountain guide; **g.-interprète** bilingual tour guide (**b**) *(manuel)* guide (book); **g. de conversation** phrase book; **g. gastronomique** restaurant guide; **g. touristique** tourist guide (**c**) *Belg (indicateur de chemin de fer)* railway timetable; *(annuaire)* telephone directory **2** *nf (scout) Br* (Girl) Guide, *Am* Girl Scout

guider [gide] *vt* to guide; **se laisser g. par son intuition** to be guided by one's intuition

guidon [gidɔ̃] *nm* handlebars

guigne¹ [giɲ] *nf (cerise)* sweet cherry; *Fam* **se soucier de qn/qch comme d'une g.** not to give a fig about sb/sth

guigne² *nf Fam (malchance)* bad luck; **avoir la g.** to be out of luck

guigner [giɲe] *vt Fam (avoir des vues sur)* to have one's eye on

guignol [giɲɔl] *nm* (**a**) **G.** *(personnage)* ≃ Punch (**b**) *Péj (personne)* clown, joker; **faire le g.** to clown around (**c**) *(spectacle)* ≃ Punch and Judy show

Guillaume [gijom] *npr* **G. le Conquérant** William the Conqueror

guillemets [gijmɛ] *nmpl* inverted commas, quotation marks; **entre g.** in inverted commas, in quotation marks

guilleret, -ette [gijrɛ, -ɛt] *adj* jaunty, lively

guillotine [gijɔtin] *nf* guillotine

guillotiner [gijɔtine] *vt* to guillotine

guimauve [gimov] *nf (confiserie)* marshmallow; *Fig & Péj* **c'est de la g.** it's pure schmaltz

guimbarde [gɛ̃bard] *nf* (**a**) *Fam (vieille voiture) Br* old banger, *Am* jalopy (**b**) *(instrument de musique)* Jew's harp

guindé, -e [gɛ̃de] *adj (personne, air)* stiff; *(atmosphère)* strained; *(style)* stilted; *(réception)* swanky, *Br* posh

Guinée [gine] *nf* **la G.** Guinea; **la G. équatoriale** Equatorial Guinea

Guinée-Bissau [ginebiso] *nf* **la G.** Guinea-Bissau

guinéen, -enne [gineɛ̃, -ɛn] **1** *adj* Guinean **2** *nm,f* **G.** Guinean

guingois [gɛ̃gwa] **de guingois** *adv* askew, lopsided

guinguette [gɛ̃gɛt] *nf* riverside café

guirlande [girlɑ̃d] *nf (de fleurs)* garland; **g. lumineuse** string of lights; **g. de Noël** piece of tinsel; **g. de papier** paper chain

guise [giz] *nf* **faire qch à sa g.** to do sth as one likes; **n'en faire qu'à sa g.** to do just as one likes; **en g. de** by way of

guitare [gitar] *nf* guitar; **g. basse** bass guitar; **g. électrique** electric guitar; **g. sèche** acoustic guitar

guitariste [gitarist] *nmf* guitarist

gus [gys] *nm Fam* guy

gustatif, -ive [gystatif, -iv] *adj* **papilles gustatives** taste buds

guttural, -e, -aux, -ales [gytyral, -o] *adj* guttural

Guyana [gɥijana] *nm* **le G.** Guyana

guyanais, -e [gɥijanɛ, -ɛz] **1** *adj* Guianese **2** *nm,f* **G.** Guianese

Guyane [gɥijan] *nf* **la G.** Guiana; **la G. française** French Guiana

gym [ʒim] *nf Fam* gym; **faire de la g.** to do exercises

gymkhana [ʒimkana] *nm* rally

gymnase [ʒimnɑz] *nm* (**a**) *(salle)* gymnasium (**b**) *Suisse (lycée) Br* ≃ secondary school, *Am* ≃ high school

gymnaste [ʒimnast] *nmf* gymnast

gymnastique [ʒimnastik] *nf* gymnastics *(singulier)*; *Fig* **il faut faire toute une g. pour sortir de cette auto** you have to be a contortionist to get out of this car; **g. respiratoire** breathing exercises; **g. rythmique** eurhythmics *(singulier)*

gynécologie [ʒinekɔlɔʒi] *nf* gynaecology

gynécologique [ʒinekɔlɔʒik] *adj* gynaecological

gynécologue [ʒinekɔlɔg] *nmf* gynaecologist

gypse [ʒips] *nm* gypsum

gyrophare [ʒirofar] *nm* flashing light

H

H, h [aʃ] *nm inv* H, h; **h. aspiré** aspirate h; **h muet** mute h

***ha** [ɑ] *exclam* ah!; **ha, ha!** *(rire)* ha-ha!

habile [abil] *adj* (**a**) *(personne)* skilful; *(manœuvre, film, roman)* clever; **être h. de ses mains** to be good with one's hands; **être h. en affaires** to be a good businessman/businesswoman (**b**) *Jur* **h. à faire qch** able to do sth

habilement [abilmɑ̃] *adv* skilfully

habileté [abilte] *nf* skill

habiliter [abilite] *vt Jur* **h. qn à faire qch** to enable sb to do sth; **être habilité à faire qch** to be authorized to do sth

habillage [abijaʒ] *nm* (**a**) *(d'une personne)* dressing (**b**) **h. intérieur** *(d'une voiture)* trim (**c**) *TV & Rad* station identification

habillé, -e [abije] *adj* (**a**) *(vêtu)* dressed; **h. en femme/cosmonaute** dressed (up) as a woman/spaceman; **s'endormir tout h.** to go to sleep with one's clothes on (**b**) *(élégant) (personne, tenue)* smart; **soirée habillée** formal occasion

habillement [abijmɑ̃] *nm* (**a**) *(vêtements)* clothes (**b**) *(industrie)* clothing industry

habiller [abije] **1** *vt* (**a**) *(vêtir)* to dress; **h. qn en soldat/cow-boy** to dress sb up as a soldier/cowboy (**b**) *(fournir en vêtements)* to clothe (**c**) *(garnir)* to cover (**d**) *(aller à)* **un rien t'habille** you look good in anything

2 s'habiller *vpr* (**a**) *(se vêtir)* to get dressed, to dress; **elle s'habille n'importe comment** she wears any old thing; **comment vous habillez-vous pour la soirée?** what are you wearing to the party?; **s'h. en femme/cosmonaute** to dress up as a woman/spaceman (**b**) *(se fournir)* **elle s'habille chez Dior** she buys her clothes from Dior (**c**) *(élégamment)* to dress up

habilleur, -euse [abijœr, -øz] *nm,f* dresser

habit [abi] **1** *nm* (**a**) *(vêtement)* habits clothes; **habits du dimanche** Sunday best (**b**) *(tenue)* **h. (de soirée)** evening dress, tails; **l'h. vert** = the green coat worn by a member of the Académie française (**c**) *(d'un religieux)* habit; *Prov* **l'h. ne fait pas le moine** appearances can be deceptive

2 *nm ou nf Can (costume)* suit; **h. de neige** snowsuit

habitable [abitabl] *adj* (in)habitable

habitacle [abitakl] *nm (d'un avion)* cockpit; *(d'une voiture)* passenger compartment

habitant, -e [abitɑ̃, -ɑ̃t] **1** *nm,f* (**a**) *(d'une ville)* inhabitant, resident; *(d'une maison)* occupant; **loger chez l'h.** *(en voyage)* to stay with local people (**b**) *Can (fermier)* small-scale farmer

2 *adj Can (nourriture, objets)* rustic; *Péj* **il est un peu h.** he's a bit of a country bumpkin

habitat [abita] *nm (d'un animal, d'une plante)* habitat; *(de personnes) (mode de peuplement)* settlement; *(conditions de logement)* housing conditions

habitation [abitasjɔ̃] *nf* (**a**) *(fait de résider)* living; **locaux à usage d'h.** premises for residential use (**b**) *(lieu)* dwelling; **h. à loyer modéré** *Br* ≃ council flat/house, *Am* ≃ public housing unit

habiter [abite] **1** *vt (maison, lieu)* to live in; *Fig (âme, personne)* to possess; **la région n'est pas habitée** the area is uninhabited

2 *vi* to live (**à/en** in)

habitude [abityd] *nf* (**a**) *(comportement répété)* habit; **avoir l'h.** *ou* **avoir pour h. de faire qch** to be in the habit of doing sth; **ça ne la gênera pas, elle a l'h.** that won't bother her, she's used to it; **avoir l'h. de qch** to be used to sth; **prendre l'h. de faire qch** to get into the habit of doing sth; **faire qch par h.** to do sth out of habit; **ce n'est pas dans mes habitudes** I don't make a habit of it; **d'h.** usually; **meilleur/plus tôt que d'h.** better/earlier than usual; **comme d'h.** as usual (**b**) **habitudes** *(coutumes)* customs

habitué, -e [abitɥe] *nm,f (d'une maison)* regular visitor; *(d'un restaurant, d'un magasin)* regular (customer)

habituel, -elle [abitɥɛl] *adj* usual, customary

habituellement [abitɥɛlmɑ̃] *adv* usually

habituer [abitɥe] **1** *vt* **h. qn à qch/à faire qch** to get sb used to sth/to doing sth; **être habitué à qn/à qch/à faire qch** to be used *or* accustomed to sb/to sth/to doing sth

2 s'habituer *vpr* **s'h. à qn/à qch/à faire qch** to get used *or* accustomed to sb/to sth/to doing sth; **tu finiras par t'h.** you'll get used to it in the end

***hâbleur, -euse** [ablœr, -øz] *adj* boastful

***hache** [aʃ] *nf* axe; *Fig* **enterrer la h. de guerre** to bury the hatchet

***haché, -e** [aʃe] **1** *adj* (**a**) *(viande) Br* minced, *Am* ground; *(légumes, herbes)* chopped (**b**) *(style, phrases)* jerky

2 *nm Br* mince, *Am* ground meat

***hacher** [aʃe] *vt* to chop (up); *(viande) (dans un hachoir) Br* to mince, *Am* to grind; **h. menu qch** to chop sth (up) finely; *Fig* **h. qn menu (comme chair à pâté)** to make mincemeat of sb; *Fig* **se faire h.** *(se faire battre)* to be massacred

***hachette** [aʃɛt] *nf* hatchet

***hachis** [aʃi] *nm* **h. d'herbes** chopped herbs; **h. Parmentier** ≃ cottage pie; **h. de viande** *Br* mince, *Am* ground meat

---

The symbol * indicates that the initial **h** is aspirate and that hence there is no liaison, eg **les haricots** [leariko] and not [lezariko], or contraction in spelling, eg **la haine** and not **l'haine**.

*hachisch [aʃiʃ] *nm* hashish
*hachoir [aʃwar] *nm* (**a**) *(couteau)* chopper (**b**) *(machine) Br* mincer, *Am* grinder
*hachurer [aʃyre] *vt* to hatch
*hachures [aʃyr] *nfpl* hatching
*hagard, -e [agar, -ard] *adj (visage)* haggard; *(expression, regard, yeux)* wild
*haie [ɛ] *nf* (**a**) *(clôture)* hedge; **h. vive** quickset hedge (**b**) *(en athlétisme)* hurdle; *(en équitation)* fence; **400 mètres haies** 400-metre hurdles (**c**) *(d'arbres, de pieux, de curieux)* line, row; **h. d'honneur** guard of honour; **faire une h. d'honneur** to form a guard of honour
*haillons [ajɔ̃] *nmpl (vêtements)* rags; **en h.** in rags (and tatters)
*haine [ɛn] *nf* hate, hatred; **sa h. de/pour** his/her hatred of/for; *très Fam* **avoir la h.** *(être révolté)* to be full of rage; *(être furieux)* to be bloody furious
*haineux, -euse [ɛnø, -øz] *adj* full of hatred
*haïr [41] [air] *vt* to hate
    2 se haïr *upr (soi-même)* to hate oneself; *(l'un l'autre)* to hate each other
*hais *voir* haïr
*haïssable [aisabl] *adj* hateful
*hait *voir* haïr
Haïti [aiti] *n* Haiti
haïtien, -enne [aisjɛ̃, -ɛn] **1** *adj* Haitian
    2 *nm,f* **H.** Haitian
*halage [alaʒ] *nm* towing; **chemin de h.** towpath
*hâle [ɑl] *nm* (sun)tan
*hâlé, -e [ɑle] *adj* (sun)tanned
haleine [alɛn] *nf* breath; **avoir mauvaise h.** to have bad breath; **courir à perdre h.** to run until one is out of breath; **reprendre h.** to get one's breath (back); **tenir qn en h.** to keep sb in suspense; **hors d'h.** out of breath, breathless; **travail de longue h.** long job
*haler [ale] *vt* to tow
*haletant, -e [alətɑ̃, -ɑ̃t] *adj (coureur, malade, voix)* panting, gasping; *Fig (suspense)* unbearable; **respiration haletante** panting, gasping
*halètement [alɛtmɑ̃] *nm (d'un coureur, d'un malade)* panting, gasping
*haleter [6] [aləte] *vi (coureur, malade)* to pant, to gasp
*hall [ol] *nm (d'une maison)* entrance hall; *(d'un hôtel)* foyer, lobby; *(d'un aéroport)* lounge; **h. d'accueil** reception hall; **h. d'entrée** entrance hall; **h. de gare** station concourse; *Péj* **littérature/roman de h. de gare** trashy literature/novel
*halle [al] *nf* (**a**) *(marché)* (covered) market; **h. au poisson** fish market (**b**) *Suisse (bâtiment)* hall; **h. de fête** community centre

Les Halles

"Les Halles" refers to the central Paris wholesale food markets, dating from the Second Empire, and historically comparable to the markets at Covent Garden in London. Once a tourist attraction and also a source of traffic congestion, they were moved to the outskirts, mainly to Rungis, near Orly, in the 1960s. After much delay and controversy, the site (infamously known as the "trou des Halles") was redeveloped in the late 1970s with a Metro station and a modern shopping centre, the "Forum des Halles".

*hallebarde [albard] *nf* halberd; *Fam* **il pleut** *ou* **tombe des hallebardes** it's raining cats and dogs
hallucinant, -e [alysinɑ̃, -ɑ̃t] *adj (extraordinaire)* striking; *(incroyable)* incredible
hallucination [alysinasjɔ̃] *nf* hallucination; **avoir des hallucinations** *(malade, ivrogne)* to have hallucinations; *Fig (se tromper)* to see things
halluciner [alysine] *vi (avoir des hallucinations)* to hallucinate; *Fam Fig* **j'hallucine!** I don't believe it!
hallucinogène [alysinɔʒɛn] **1** *adj* hallucinogenic
    2 *nm* hallucinogen
*halo [alo] *nm aussi Fig* halo
halogène [alɔʒɛn] *nm Chim* halogen; **(lampe à) h.** halogen lamp
*halte [alt] *nf* (**a**) *(arrêt)* stop; **faire h.** to stop; **h.(-là)!** stop!; *Fig* **h.-là, je ne suis pas d'accord!** hold on, I don't agree!; **h. à l'armement!** stop the arms build-up! (**b**) *(lieu)* stopping place; *Rail* halt; *Can (point de vue)* viewing point, *Am* scenic overlook; *(aire de repos routière) Br* service area, *Am* rest area
*halte-garderie (*pl* **haltes-garderies**) [altəgardəri] *nf* crèche
haltère [altɛr] *nm* dumbbell; **faire des haltères** to do weightlifting
haltérophile [alterɔfil] *nmf* weightlifter
haltérophilie [alterɔfili] *nf* weightlifting
*hamac [amak] *nm* hammock
*Hambourg [ɑ̃bur] *n* Hamburg
*hamburger [ɑ̃burgœr] *nm* burger
*hameau, -x [amo] *nm* hamlet
hameçon [amsɔ̃] *nm* (fish-)hook; *Fig* **mordre à l'h.** to swallow the bait
*hammam [amam] *nm* Turkish baths
*hampe [ɑ̃p] *nf (d'un drapeau)* pole
*hamster [amstɛr] *nm* hamster
*hanche [ɑ̃ʃ] *nf* hip
*hand [ɑ̃d] *nm Fam* handball
*handball [ɑ̃dbal] *nm* handball
*handballeur, -euse [ɑ̃dbalœr, -øz] *nm,f* handball player
*handicap [ɑ̃dikap] *nm (physique, mental)* disability; *Sport & Fig* handicap; *Fig* **partir avec un h.** to start at a disadvantage
*handicapé, -e [ɑ̃dikape] **1** *adj* disabled
    2 *nm,f* disabled person; **les handicapés** the disabled; **h. mental** mentally handicapped person; **h. moteur** person with motor impairment
*handicaper [ɑ̃dikape] *vt (physiquement, mentalement)* to disable; *Fig* to handicap
*hangar [ɑ̃gar] *nm* shed; *(pour les trains, les bus)* depot; *(pour les avions)* hangar; **h. à bateaux** boathouse
*hanneton [anətɔ̃] *nm* cockchafer; *Fam* **pas piqué des hannetons** *(difficile)* tough; *(bon, beau)* incredible
Hanoi [anɔj] *n* Hanoi
*Hanovre [anɔvr] *n* Hanover
*hanté, -e [ɑ̃te] *adj* haunted
*hanter [ɑ̃te] *vt (sujet: fantôme, pensée)* to haunt; *Fig (bars, musées)* to hang round
*hantise [ɑ̃tiz] *nf* obsession; **avoir la h. de qch** to really dread sth
*happer [ape] *vt (dans sa gueule, son bec)* to snap up; *(sujet: véhicule)* to hit
*hara-kiri [arakiri] *nm* hara-kiri; **(se) faire h.** to commit hara-kiri
*harangue [arɑ̃g] *nf* harangue

---

*haranguer [arɑ̃ge] *vt* to harangue
*haras [ara] *nm* stud farm
*harassant, -e [arasɑ̃, -ɑ̃t] *adj* exhausting
*harassé, -e [arase] *adj* exhausted
*harasser [arase] *vt* to exhaust
*harcèlement [arsɛlmɑ̃] *nm* harassment; **h. sexuel** sexual harassment
*harceler [39] [arsəle] *vt (importuner)* to harass; *(insister auprès de)* to pester; **h. qn de questions** to pester sb with questions; **être harcelé de remords/regrets** to be plagued by remorse/regrets
*harceleur, -euse [arsəlœr, -øz] *nm,f* pest; **h. téléphonique** phone pest
*harde [ard] *nf (de cerfs)* herd
*hardes [ard] *nfpl (haillons)* rags
*hardi, -e [ardi] *adj (audacieux, original)* bold; *(osé)* brazen
*hardiesse [ardjɛs] *nf (audace, originalité)* boldness; *(caractère osé)* brazenness
*hardiment [ardimɑ̃] *adv (avec audace)* boldly
*hard-rock [ardrɔk] *nm* hard rock
*harem [arɛm] *nm* harem
*hareng [arɑ̃] *nm* herring; **h. saur** smoked herring
*harfang [arfɑ̃] *nm Can* snowy owl
*hargne [arɲ] *nf* bad temper; **avec h.** bad-temperedly
*hargneux, -euse [arɲø, -øz] *adj (personne)* bad-tempered; **d'un ton h.** bad-temperedly
*haricot [ariko] *nm* (**a**) *(légume)* bean; **haricots en grains** dried beans; *Fam* **c'est la fin des haricots** we've/they've/*etc* had it now; *Fam* **courir sur le h. à qn** to get up sb's nose; **h. beurre** butter bean; **h. blanc** haricot bean; **h. rouge** red kidney bean; **h. vert** green bean (**b**) *Culin* **h. de mouton** mutton stew
*harissa [arisa] *nf Culin* harissa *(hot pepper purée)*
*harki [arki] *nm* harki *(Algerian soldier who fought on the French side during the Franco-Algerian War)*
harmonica [armɔnika] *nm* harmonica, mouth organ
harmonie [armɔni] *nf* (**a**) *(accord)* & *Mus* harmony; **être en h. avec qch** to be in harmony with sth; **vivre en h.** to live in harmony (**b**) *(fanfare)* brass band
harmonieux, -euse [armɔnjø, -øz] *adj* harmonious
harmonique [armɔnik] *adj Mus* harmonic
harmonisation [armɔnizasjɔ̃] *nf* harmonization
harmoniser [armɔnize] **1** *vt* to harmonize (**avec** with)
2 s'harmoniser *vpr* to go well together
harmonium [armɔnjɔm] *nm* harmonium
*harnachement [arnaʃmɑ̃] *nm* (**a**) *(action)* harnessing (**b**) *(harnais)* harness; *Fig (vêtements)* get-up
*harnacher [arnaʃe] *vt (cheval)* to harness; *Fig* **il fallait voir comment elle était harnachée** you should have seen the get-up she was wearing
*harnais [arnɛ] *nm* (**a**) *(de cheval)* harness (**b**) **h. de sécurité** *(d'alpiniste, d'élagueur)* safety harness
*haro [aro] *nm* **crier h. sur** to rail against; **crier h. sur le baudet** to scream for blood
*harpe [arp] *nf* harp
*harpie [arpi] *nf aussi Fig* harpy
*harpiste [arpist] *nmf* harpist
*harpon [arpɔ̃] *nm* harpoon; **pêche au h.** harpoon fishing
*harponner [arpɔne] *vt* (**a**) *(poisson)* to harpoon (**b**) *Fam (sujet: police)* to nab; *(sujet: importun)* to corner
*hasard [azar] *nm* (**a**) *(sort)* chance, luck; **le h. a voulu que je sois à l'étranger** as it happened I was abroad; **coup de h.** stroke of luck; **par un heureux h.** by a happy coincidence; **ne rien laisser au h.** to leave nothing to chance; **le h. fait bien les choses!** what a stroke of luck!; **au h.** *(choisir, répondre)* at random; *(marcher)* aimlessly; **au h. de ses voyages/lectures** in the course of his/her travels/reading; **à tout h.** *(par précaution)* just in case; *(pour voir)* on the off chance; **par h.** by accident, by chance; **si par h. vous le voyez** if you (should) happen to see him; **comme par h.** as if by chance (**b**) **hasards** *(dangers)* hazards
*hasarder [azarde] **1** *vt (opinion, remarque)* to venture
2 se hasarder *vpr (dans l'obscurité, dans la jungle)* to venture; **se h. à faire qch** to risk doing sth
*hasardeux, -euse [azardø, -øz] *adj* risky, hazardous
*hasch [aʃ] *nm Fam* hash, pot
*haschisch [aʃiʃ] *nm* hashish
*hâte [ɑt] *nf* haste; **avoir h. de faire qch** *(avoir envie)* to be eager to do sth; **à la h.** hastily; **en h.** in a hurry, hurriedly
*hâter [ate] **1** *vt (accélérer)* to hasten; *(avancer)* to bring forward
2 se hâter *vpr* to hurry; **se h. de faire qch** to hurry to do sth
*hâtif, -ive [atif, -iv] *adj (trop rapide)* hasty
*hâtivement [ativmɑ̃] *adv* hastily
*hauban [obɑ̃] *nm* (**a**) *Naut* shroud (**b**) *(d'un pont)* stay
*hausse [os] *nf* rise, increase (**de** in); **être en h.** to be rising; **être à la h.** *(marché)* to be rising; **jouer à la h.** *(en Bourse)* to speculate on a rising market
*haussement [osmɑ̃] *nm* **h. d'épaules** shrug; **avec un h. de sourcils** with raised eyebrows
*hausser [ose] **1** *vt* to raise; **h. la voix/les sourcils** to raise one's voice/eyebrows; **h. les épaules** to shrug (one's shoulders)
2 se hausser *vpr* to raise oneself (up); **se h. sur la pointe des pieds** to stand on tiptoe
*haussier [osje] *adj m voir* marché
*haut, -e [o, ot] **1** *adj* (**a**) *(dans l'espace, en quantité, en intensité)* high; **une femme de haute taille** a tall woman; **un mur h. de 3 mètres** a 3-metre-high wall (**b**) *(dans une hiérarchie)* high; **la haute couture** high fashion; **les hauts salaires** the highly paid; **un athlète de h. niveau** a top-ranking athlete; **une montre de haute précision** a high-precision timepiece; **de hauts faits** daring deeds (**c**) *(note)* high (**d**) *(dans le temps)* early; **le h. Moyen Âge** the early Middle Ages (**e**) **h. en couleur** *(récit, personnage)* colourful
2 *adv* (**a**) *(dans l'espace)* high; **comme il est dit plus h.** as mentioned above; **h. les mains!** hands up!; **gagner h. la main** to win hands down; **h. les cœurs!** cheer up! (**b**) *(dans une hiérarchie)* highly (**c**) *(dans la gamme)* high (**d**) *(fort)* **dire qch tout h.** to say sth out loud; **dire tout h. ce que tout le monde pense tout bas** to say what everyone is thinking (but is too afraid to say) (**e**) **en h.** at the top; *(à l'étage supérieur)* upstairs; **les gens d'en h.** the people above *or* upstairs; **en h. de** at the top of
3 *nm* (**a**) *(hauteur)* **le mur fait 3 mètres de h.** the wall is 3 metres high (**b**) *(partie supérieure)* top; *Can (d'un immeuble)* top floor; **l'étagère du h.** the top shelf; **regarder qn de h. en bas** to look sb up and down; **connaître des hauts et des bas** to have one's ups and downs (**c**) *(corsage)* top
4 *nf Fam* **haute** upper crust
*hautain, -e [otɛ̃, -ɛn] *adj* haughty
*hautbois [obwa] *nm* oboe

---

*haut-commissaire (*pl* hauts-commissaires) [okɔ-misɛr] *nm* high commissioner
*haut-commissariat (*pl* hauts-commissariats) [okɔmisarja] *nm* high commission
*haut-de-chausses (*pl* hauts-de-chausses) [odə-ʃos] *nm* breeches
*haut-de-forme (*pl* hauts-de-forme) [odəfɔrm] *nm* top hat
*haute-contre (*pl* hautes-contre) [otkɔ̃tr] *nm* counter-tenor
*haute-fidélité (*pl* haute-fildélités) [otfidelite] *nf* hifi; **chaîne h.** hi-fi (system)
*hautement [otmɑ̃] *adv* (*très*) highly
*hauteur [otœr] *nf* (**a**) (*dimension*) height (**b**) (*altitude*) altitude; **prendre de la h.** to climb, to gain height; **à la h.** de qch (*dans l'espace*) level with sth; **à la h.** du Mans near Le Mans; *Fig* **être** *ou* **se montrer à la h.** de qch to be equal to *or* up to sth; **être à la h.** to be up to it; **à h. des yeux** at eye level; **l'eau nous arrivait à h. des épaules** the water came up to our shoulders; **contribuer à h. de deux millions** to contribute two million (**c**) (*colline*) hill; **hauteurs** heights; **il y a de la neige sur les hauteurs** there's snow on the higher slopes (**d**) (*d'une note de musique*) pitch
*haut-fond (*pl* hauts-fonds) [ofɔ̃] *nm* shallow
*haut-fourneau (*pl* hauts-fourneaux) [ofurno] *nm* blast furnace
*haut-le-cœur [oləkœr] *nm inv* **avoir un h.** to retch; **cette vision me donna un h.** the sight of it made me feel sick
*haut-parleur (*pl* haut-parleurs) [oparlœr] *nm* (loud)speaker
*Havane [avan] *n* **La Havane** Havana
*havane *nm* Havana (cigar)
*hâve [ɑv] *adj* (*visage*) gaunt; (*joues*) sunken
*havre [avr] *nm Litt* haven
Hawaii [awai] *n* Hawaii
hawaiien, -enne [awajɛ̃, -ɛn] **1** *adj* Hawaiian
  2 *nm,f* **H.** Hawaiian
*Haye [ɛ] *n* **La H.** The Hague
*hayon [ajɔ̃] *nm* (*d'une voiture*) hatchback
HCR [aʃseɛr] *nm* (*abrév* **Haut-Commissariat des Nations unies pour les réfugiés**) UNHCR
*hé [e] *exclam* (*pour interpeller*) hey!
hebdo [ɛbdo] *nm Fam* weekly; **h. télé** TV magazine programme
hebdomadaire [ɛbdɔmadɛr] *adj & nm* weekly
hébergement [ebɛrʒəmɑ̃] *nm* (*d'un ami*) putting up; (*d'un sans-abri, d'un réfugié*) taking in; (*d'un fugitif*) harbouring
héberger [45] [ebɛrʒe] *vt* (**a**) (*ami*) to put up; (*sans-abri, réfugié*) to take in; (*fugitif*) to harbour (**b**) *Ordinat* (*site Web*) to host
hébergeur [ebɛrʒœr] *nm Ordinat* (*de site Web*) host
hébété, -e [ebete] *adj* dazed
hébreu, -x [ebrø] **1** *adj m* Hebrew
  2 *nm* (*langue*) Hebrew; *Fam* **c'est de l'h. pour moi** it's all Greek to me
  3 *nmpl* **les Hébreux** the Hebrews
Hébrides [ebrid] *nfpl* **les H.** the Hebrides
HEC [aʃøe] *nf* (*abrév* **Hautes études commerciales**) = prestigious business school in Paris
hécatombe [ekatɔ̃b] *nf* (*tuerie*) slaughter, massacre; *Fig* **ça a été une h. cette année à l'examen!** the exam results were disastrous this year!
hectare [ɛktar] *nm* hectare
hectogramme [ɛktɔgram] *nm* hectogram

hectolitre [ɛktɔlitr] *nm* hectolitre
hectomètre [ɛktɔmɛtr] *nm* hectometre
hédonisme [edɔnism] *nm* hedonism
hédoniste [edɔnist] **1** *adj* hedonistic
  2 *nmf* hedonist
hégémonie [eʒemɔni] *nf* hegemony
*hein [ɛ̃] *exclam Fam* (**a**) (*pour faire répéter*) eh?, what? (**b**) (*pour insister*) **il fait beau aujourd'hui, h.?** it's a nice day, isn't it?; **ce n'est pas très bon, h.?** it's not very good, is it?; **ne refais jamais ça, h.!** don't ever do that again, OK?; **h. qu'il fait bien la cuisine!** he's a good cook, isn't he?
*hélas [elas] *exclam* unfortunately
*héler [34] [ele] *vt* to hail
hélice [elis] *nf* (**a**) (*d'un hélicoptère, d'un bateau*) propeller (**b**) *Math & Biol* helix
hélico [eliko] *nm Fam* chopper
hélicoïdal, -e, -aux, -ales [elikɔidal, -o] *adj* helical
hélicoptère [elikɔptɛr] *nm* helicopter
héliomarin, -e [eljɔmarɛ̃, -in] *adj Méd* **cure héliomarine** = course of treatment based on sun and sea air; **centre h.** = seaside convalescent home where heliotherapy is used
héliothérapie [eljɔterapi] *nf Méd* heliotherapy
héliport [elipɔr] *nm* heliport
héliporté, -e [elipɔrte] *adj* (*matériel*) transported by helicopter; (*troupes*) airborne
hélium [eljɔm] *nm* helium
*Helsinki [ɛlsinki] *n* Helsinki
helvétique [ɛlvetik] *adj* Swiss
hématie [emasi] *nf Biol* red blood corpuscle
hématologie [ematɔlɔʒi] *nf Méd* haematology
hématome [ematom] *nm* bruise, *Spéc* haematoma; **se faire un h.** to bruise oneself
hémicycle [emisikl] *nm* **l'h.** (*de l'Assemblée nationale*) the chamber
hémiplégie [emipleʒi] *nf Méd* hemiplegia
hémiplégique [emipleʒik] *adj & nmf Méd* hemiplegic
hémisphère [emisfɛr] *nm* hemisphere; **l'h. Nord/Sud** the Northern/Southern hemisphere
hémisphérique [emisferik] *adj* hemispheric(al)
hémistiche [emistiʃ] *nm* hemistich
hémoglobine [emɔglɔbin] *nf* haemoglobin; *Fig* (*dans un film*) blood and gore
hémophile [emɔfil] *Méd* **1** *adj* haemophilic
  2 *nm* haemophiliac
hémophilie [emɔfili] *nf Méd* haemophilia
hémorragie [emɔraʒi] *nf* haemorrhage, bleeding; *Fig* (*des capitaux*) drain; **h. interne** internal bleeding
hémorroïdes [emɔrɔid] *nfpl* haemorrhoids, piles
*henné [ene] *nm* henna; **se faire un h.** to henna one's hair
*hennir [enir] *vi* to neigh, to whinny; *Fig* (*personne*) to bray
*hennissement [enismɑ̃] *nm* neigh, whinny; *Fig* (*d'une personne*) braying; **hennissements** neighing, whinnying; *Fig* (*d'une personne*) braying
*hep [ɛp] *exclam* hey!
hépatique [epatik] *adj Méd* hepatic
hépatite [epatit] *nf* hepatitis; **h. A/B/C** hepatitis A/B/C
heptathlon [ɛptatlɔ̃] *nm* heptathlon
héraldique [eraldik] **1** *adj* heraldic
  2 *nf* heraldry
herbage [ɛrbaʒ] *nm* pasture
herbe [ɛrb] *nf* (**a**) (*de gazon*) grass; *Fig* **couper l'h. sous le pied à qn** to cut the ground from under sb's

feet; **en h.** *(céréale)* green; *Fig (débutant)* budding (**b**) *(plante)* herb; **fines herbes** mixed herbs; **omelette/ fromage aux fines herbes** omelette/cheese with herbs; **mauvaise h.** weed; **herbes folles** wild grass; *Can* **h. à la puce** poison ivy (**c**) *Fam (drogue)* grass, weed

herbeux, -euse [ɛrbø, -øz] *adj* grassy

herbicide [ɛrbisid] *adj & nm* (**produit**) **h.** weedkiller

herbier [ɛrbje] *nm (collection)* herbarium

herbivore [ɛrbivɔr] *Zool* **1** *adj* herbivorous
 2 *nm* herbivore

herboriser [ɛrbɔrize] *vi* to collect plants

herboriste [ɛrbɔrist] *nmf* herbalist

herboristerie [ɛrbɔristəri] *nf (boutique)* herbalist's (shop); *(commerce)* herb trade

herbu, -e [ɛrby] *adj* grassy

herculéen, -enne [ɛrkyleɛ̃, -ɛn] *adj* Herculean

***père** [ɛr] *nm* **pauvre h.** poor creature

héréditaire [ereditɛr] *adj (maladie, titre)* hereditary; **c'est h.!** it runs in the family!

hérédité [eredite] *nf Biol* heredity; **avoir une lourde h.** to come from a family with a history of mental/ physical illness

hérésie [erezi] *nf* heresy; *Fig* **c'est une h.** *ou* **de l'h.!** that's sacrilege!

hérétique [eretik] **1** *adj* heretical
 2 *nmf* heretic

***hérissé, -e** [erise] *adj* (**a**) *(cheveux)* spiky; *(moustache)* bristly (**b**) *(garni)* **h. de** bristling with

***hérisser** [erise] **1** *vt* (**a**) *(ses plumes)* to ruffle up; **h. ses poils** to bristle (**b**) *Fig (mettre en colère)* **h. qn** to get sb's back up
 2 se hérisser *vpr (animal)* to bristle; *(poils, cheveux)* to stand on end; *Fig (personne)* to bristle

***hérisson** [erisɔ̃] *nm* hedgehog

héritage [eritaʒ] *nm* inheritance; *Fig (spirituel, intellectuel)* heritage; **faire un h.** to come into an inheritance

hériter [erite] **1** *vt* to inherit (**de** from)
 2 hériter de *vt ind (fortune, objet, qualité)* to inherit; **h. de qn** to receive an inheritance from sb; *Fig* **h. de qn/qch** *(se retrouver avec)* to be landed with sb/sth

héritier, -ère [eritje, -ɛr] *nm,f* heir, *f* heiress (**de** to)

hermaphrodite [ɛrmafrɔdit] *nm & adj* hermaphrodite

hermétique [ɛrmetik] *adj* (**a**) *(récipient)* hermetically sealed; *(joint) (à l'air)* airtight; *(à l'eau)* watertight (**b**) *Fig (abscons)* abstruse; *(visage)* impenetrable; **être h. à qch** to be impervious to sth

hermétiquement [ɛrmetikmã] *adv* hermetically

hermine [ɛrmin] *nf (animal)* stoat; *(fourrure)* ermine

***hernie** [ɛrni] *nf* hernia; **h. discale** slipped disc

héroïne¹ [erɔin] *nf (personnage)* heroine

héroïne² *nf (drogue)* heroin

héroïnomane [erɔinɔman] *nmf* heroin addict

héroïque [erɔik] *adj* heroic

héroïquement [erɔikmã] *adv* heroically

héroïsme [erɔism] *nm* heroism

***héron** [erɔ̃] *nm* heron; **h. cendré** grey heron

***héros** [ero] *nm* hero; **mourir en h.** to die a hero's death

herpès [ɛrpɛs] *nm Méd* herpes; *(buccal)* cold sore

***herse** [ɛrs] *nf* (**a**) *(pour labourer)* harrow (**b**) *(de forteresse)* portcullis

hertz [ɛrts] *nm* hertz

hertzien, -enne [ɛrtsjɛ̃, -ɛn] *adj* Hertzian; *Rad* **réseau h.** radio relay system; *TV* **diffusion hertzienne** terrestrial broadcasting

hésitant, -e [ezitã, -ãt] *adj* hesitant

hésitation [ezitasjɔ̃] *nf* hesitation; **avoir une h.** to hesitate; **avec h.** hesitatingly; **sans h.** without hesitation

hésiter [ezite] *vi* to hesitate (**sur/entre** over/between); **je ne sais pas, j'hésite** I don't know, I can't make up my mind; **h. à faire qch** to hesitate to do sth

hétéro [etero] *adj & nmf Fam* straight

hétéroclite [eterɔklit] *adj* motley

hétérogène [eterɔʒɛn] *adj* mixed

hétérogénéité [eterɔʒeneite] *nf* heterogeneity

hétérosexualité [eterɔsɛksɥalite] *nf* heterosexuality

hétérosexuel, -elle [eterɔsɛksɥɛl] *adj & nm,f* heterosexual

***hêtre** [ɛtr] *nm* beech

***heu** [ø] *exclam* er

heure [œr] *nf* (**a**) *(soixante minutes)* hour; **8 euros l'h.** *ou* **de l'h.** 8 euros an hour; *Scol* **h. de cours** period; **heures supplémentaires** overtime; **faire des heures supplémentaires** to do overtime (**b**) *(de la journée)* time; **à h. fixe** at regular intervals; **à toute h.** at any time; **à toute h. du jour ou de la nuit** at any hour of the day or night; **quelle h. est-il?** what time is it?, what's the time?; **quelle h. avez-vous?** what time do you make it?; **il est deux heures** it's two o'clock; **cinq heures moins dix** ten to five; **trois heures vingt** twenty past three; **vingt heures quarante** eight forty pm; **à quelle h....?** what time...?; **ils devraient être arrivés à l'h.** qu'il est they ought to have arrived by now; **être à l'h.** *(personne)* to be on time; *(montre)* to be right; **mettre sa montre à l'h.** to set one's watch; **à la bonne h.!** marvellous!; **de bonne h.** early; **heures d'affluence** peak hours; **heures de bureau** office hours; **h. d'été** *Br* summer time, *Am* daylight-saving time; **heures d'ouverture** opening hours; **heures de pointe** rush hour (**c**) *(moment précis)* time; **l'h. du dîner/déjeuner** dinner/lunch time; **il est** *ou* **c'est l'h. (de faire qch)** it's time (to do sth); **son h. est venue** his/her time has come; **avoir son h. de gloire** to have one's moment of glory; **l'h. H** zero hour (**d**) *(moment présent)* **l'h. est grave** these are difficult times; **à l'h. actuelle** currently; **pour l'h.** for the present, for the time being; *Litt* **sur l'h.** at once

heureusement [œrøzmã] *adv* (**a**) *(par bonheur)* fortunately, luckily; **h. que j'étais là** it's a good thing I was there (**b**) *(avec succès)* successfully

heureux, -euse [œrø, -øz] **1** *adj* (**a**) *(satisfait)* happy (**de qch** with sth); **être h. en ménage** to be happily married; **vivre h.** to live happily; **être h. de faire qch** to be happy to do sth; **h. anniversaire!** happy birthday! (**b**) *(favorable) (dénouement)* successful; *(juste) (formule, style)* apt; *(choix)* happy (**c**) *(favorisé)* lucky; **par un h. concours de circonstances** by a lucky or fortunate coincidence; **h. au jeu/en amour** lucky at cards/in love; **s'estimer h. (de faire qch)** to consider oneself lucky (to do sth) (**d**) *(situation)* **c'est h. que vous soyez libre** it's a good thing you're free; *Fam* **encore h. (qu'il ait gardé le ticket de caisse)!** it's just as well (he held on to the receipt)!
 2 *nm,f* **si tu le lui donnes, tu vas faire un h.** if you give it to him, you'll make him a happy man; **faire des h.** to make some people happy

***heurt** [œr] *nm (choc)* collision; *Fig (conflit)* clash; **sans heurts** smoothly, without a hitch

---

The symbol * indicates that the initial **h** is aspirate and that hence there is no liaison, eg **les haricots** [leariko] and not [lezariko], or contraction in spelling, eg **la haine** and not **l'haine**.

*heurter [œrte] **1** *vt* (**a**) *(cogner)* to hit; *(entrer en collision avec)* to collide with (**b**) *(choquer)* to offend **2** *vi* (**a**) **h. contre qch** to hit sth (**b**) *Suisse* to knock; **h. à la porte** to knock at the door **3 se heurter** *vpr* (**a**) *(se cogner)* to collide (**à** *ou* **contre** with); *Fig* **se h. à qch** to meet with sth (**b**) *(couleurs, intérêts, personnes)* to clash

*heurtoir [œrtwar] *nm* (door) knocker

hévéa [evea] *nm* rubber tree

hexagonal, -e, -aux, -ales [ɛgzagɔnal, -o] *adj* hexagonal; *Fig* French

hexagone [ɛgzagɔn] *nm* hexagon; *Fig* **l'H.** France

hiatus [jatys] *nm* (**a**) *Ling & Anat* hiatus (**b**) *(décalage)* gap

hibernation [ibɛrnasjɔ̃] *nf* hibernation; *Méd* **h. artificielle** induced hypothermia

hiberner [ibɛrne] *vi* to hibernate

*hibou, -x [ibu] *nm* owl

*hic [ik] *nm inv Fam* **voilà le h.!** that's the snag!; **le h., c'est que...** the snag is...

*hideusement [idøzmɑ̃] *adv* hideously

*hideux, -euse [idø, -øz] *adj* hideous

hier [jɛr] *adv* yesterday; **h. matin/soir** yesterday morning/evening; **je m'en souviens comme si c'était h.** I remember it as if it were yesterday; **le journal d'h.** yesterday's paper; **cela ne date pas d'h.** that's nothing new; **je ne suis pas né d'h.** I wasn't born yesterday

*hiérarchie [jerarʃi] *nf* hierarchy

*hiérarchique [jerarʃik] *adj* hierarchical; **c'est mon supérieur h.** he's immediately above me in rank; **par la voie h.** through the official channels

*hiérarchisé, -e [jerarʃize] *adj* hierarchical

*hiéroglyphe [jerɔglif] *nm* hieroglyph

*hi-fi [ifi] *adj inv & nf inv* hi-fi

*hi-han [iɑ̃] *exclam* hee-haw!

hilarant, -e [ilarɑ̃, -ɑ̃t] *adj* hilarious

hilare [ilar] *adj* grinning

hilarité [ilarite] *nf* hilarity, mirth; **provoquer l'h. générale** to be the source of much hilarity

Himalaya [imalaja] *nm* **l'H.** the Himalayas

*hindi [indi] *nm* Hindi

hindou, -e [ɛ̃du] **1** *adj* Hindu
· **2** *nm,f* **H.** Hindu

hindouisme [ɛ̃duism] *nm* Hinduism

*hippie [ipi] *adj & nmf* hippy

hippie [ipik] *adj* **concours h.** horse show; **sport h.** equestrianism

hippisme [ipism] *nm* horse riding; *(courses)* horse racing

hippocampe [ipɔkɑ̃p] *nm* sea horse

hippodrome [ipɔdrom] *nm Br* racecourse, *Am* racetrack

hippopotame [ipɔpɔtam] *nm* hippopotamus

*hippy [ipi] = **hippie**

hirondelle [irɔ̃dɛl] *nf* swallow; *Prov* **une h. ne fait pas le printemps** one swallow doesn't make a summer; **h. de mer** tern

hirsute [irsyt] *adj (personne)* hairy; *(barbe)* shaggy; *(cheveux)* unkempt

hispanique [ispanik] *adj* Hispanic

hispano-américain, -e *(mpl* **hispano-américains,** *fpl* **hispano-américaines)** [ispanɔamerikɛ̃, -ɛn] **1** *adj* Spanish-American
2 *nm,f* **H. A.** Spanish-American, Hispanic

hispanophone [ispanɔfɔn] **1** *adj* Spanish-speaking
2 *nmf* Spanish speaker

*hisser [ise] **1** *vt* to hoist (up); **ho! hisse!** heave-ho!
2 se hisser *vpr* to heave oneself up; **se h. sur la pointe des pieds** to stand on tiptoe; *Fig* **se h. jusqu'au pouvoir** to rise to power

histogramme [istɔgram] *nm* bar chart, histogram

histoire [istwar] *nf* (**a**) *(discipline)* history; **l'h. de France** French history; **h. de l'art** history of art; **sachez, pour la petite h., que...** let me tell you in passing that...; *Fig* **c'est de l'h. ancienne** that's all ancient history (**b**) *(récit)* story; *Fam (mensonge)* fib, story; **raconter des histoires** *(mentir)* to tell fibs; **c'est toujours la même h.** it's always the same old story; **c'est une autre h.** it's quite a different matter; **une h. drôle** a joke, a funny story; **il m'est arrivé une drôle d'h.** a funny thing happened to me; **elle l'a dit, h. de dire quelque chose** she said it just for the sake of saying something; **c'est toute une h.** *(à raconter)* it's a long story; **c'est une h. de fous!** it's crazy! (**c**) *(problème)* fuss; **c'est toute une h. pour lui faire prendre son bain** it's quite a business getting him/her to have a bath; *Fam* **en voilà une h.!** what a fuss!, what a song and dance!; **faire des histoires** to make a fuss; **s'attirer des histoires** to get oneself into trouble; **faire des histoires à qn** to make trouble for sb; **au lit, et pas d'histoires!** off to bed now, and no fuss!

histologie [istɔlɔʒi] *nf* histology

historien, -enne [istɔrjɛ̃, -ɛn] *nm,f* historian

historique [istɔrik] **1** *adj (qui concerne l'histoire)* historical; *(important)* historic
2 *nm* historical account; *Ordinat (de document)* log; **faire l'h. des événements** to give a chronological account of events

historiquement [istɔrikmɑ̃] *adv* historically

*hit-parade *(pl* **hit-parades)** [itparad] *nm* charts

HIV [aʃive] *nm* HIV

hiver [ivɛr] *nm* winter; **en h.** in winter; **une soirée d'h.** a winter's night; **h. nucléaire** nuclear winter

hivernal, -e, -aux, -ales [ivɛrnal, -o] *adj* winter; *(temps)* wintry

hiverner [ivɛrne] *vi* to overwinter

*HLM [aʃɛlɛm] *nm ou nf (abrév* **habitation à loyer modéré)** *Br* ≃ block of council flats, *Am* ≃ low-rent apartment building

*hochement [ɔʃmɑ̃] *nm* **h. de tête** *(négatif)* shake of the head; *(affirmatif)* nod

*hocher [ɔʃe] *vt* **h. la tête** *(pour dire non)* to shake one's head; *(pour dire oui)* to nod

*hochet [ɔʃɛ] *nm* (child's) rattle

*hockey [ɔkɛ] *nm* (**a**) *(sport)* hockey; **h. sur gazon** *Br* hockey, *Am* field hockey; **h. sur glace** ice hockey, *Am* hockey (**b**) *Can (crosse)* ice-hockey stick

*holà [ɔla] **1** *exclam (pour appeler)* stop!, hold on!; **h., on se calme, hein!** hey, cool it, OK?
2 *nm* **mettre le h. à qch** to put a stop to sth

*holding [ɔldin] *nm* holding company

*hold-up [ɔldœp] *nm inv Fam* hold-up

*hollandais, -e [ɔlɑ̃dɛ, -ɛz] **1** *adj* Dutch
2 *nm,f* **H.** Dutchman, *f* Dutchwoman; **les H.** the Dutch
3 *nm (langue)* Dutch

*Hollande [ɔlɑ̃d] *nf* **la H.** Holland

holocauste [ɔlɔkost] *nm* holocaust

hologramme [ɔlɔgram] *nm* hologram

holographie [ɔlɔgrafi] *nf* holography

*homard [ɔmar] *nm* lobster

homélie [ɔmeli] *nf* homily

homéopathe [ɔmeɔpat] *nmf* homoeopath

---

homéopathie [ɔmeɔpati] *nf* homoeopathy
homéopathique [ɔmeɔpatik] *adj* homoeopathic;
Fig **à dose h.** in small doses
Homère [ɔmɛr] *npr* Homer
homicide [ɔmisid] **1** *adj* homicidal
  2 *nm* homicide; **h. involontaire** *ou* **par imprudence**
  manslaughter *(through negligence)*
hommage [ɔmaʒ] *nm* homage; **rendre h. à qn** to pay
  homage to sb; **hommages** respects; **mes hommages!**
  how do you do!
hommasse [ɔmas] *adj Péj* mannish
homme [ɔm] *nm* (**a**) *(adulte)* man; **rayon hommes**
  men's department; **parler à qn d'h. à h.** to have a
  man-to-man talk with sb; **il n'est pas h. à laisser pas-**
  ser cela he's not the sort of man to let something like
  that happen; **comme un seul h.** in unison; *Fam* **mon**
  h. my man; **jeune h.** young man; **h. d'affaires** businessman; **h. de barre** helmsman; **h. de confiance**
  right-hand man; **h. d'église** man of the church; **h.**
  d'équipage crewman; **h. d'État** statesman; **h. à**
  femmes ladies' man; *Suisse* **h. du feu** *Br* fireman,
  Am fire fighter; **c'est l'h. fort du parti** he's the kingpin
  of the party; **h. de loi** lawyer; **h. de main** henchman;
  h. du monde gentleman; **h. de paille** figurehead; **h.**
  de peine labourer; **h. politique** politician; **h. à tout**
  faire handyman; **h. de troupe** private (**b**) *(genre hu-*
  main) **l'h.** man, mankind; **de mémoire d'h.** within living memory; **les premiers hommes** early man
homme-grenouille   (*pl*   **hommes-grenouilles**)
  [ɔmgrənuj] *nm* frogman
homme-orchestre (*pl* **hommes-orchestres**) [ɔmɔ-
  rkɛstr] *nm* one-man band
homme-sandwich (*pl* **hommes-sandwichs**) [ɔm-
  sãdwitʃ] *nm* sandwich man
homo [ɔmo] *adj & nmf* gay
homogène [ɔmɔʒɛn] *adj* homogeneous
homogénéisation [ɔmɔʒeneizasjɔ̃] *nf* homogeniza-
  tion
homogénéiser [ɔmɔʒeneize] *vt* to homogenize
homogénéité [ɔmɔʒeneite] *nf* homogeneity
homologue [ɔmɔlɔg] *nmf* counterpart, opposite
  number
homologuer [ɔmɔlɔge] *vt (accord, décision, record)* to
  ratify; *(testament)* to prove
homonyme [ɔmɔnim] **1** *nm (mot)* homonym
  2 *nmf (personne)* namesake
homoparental, -e, -aux, -ales [ɔmɔparãtal, -o] *adj*
  relating to gay parenting; **famille homoparentale** family with gay parents
homoparentalité [ɔmɔparãtalite] *nf* gay parenting
homophobe [ɔmɔfɔb] **1** *adj* homophobic
  2 *nmf* homophobe
homophobie [ɔmɔfɔbi] *nf* homophobia
homosexualité [ɔmɔsɛksɥalite] *nf* homosexuality
homosexuel, -elle [ɔmɔsɛksɥɛl] *adj & nm,f* homosexual
*Honduras [ɔ̃dyras] *nm* **le H.** Honduras
*hondurien, -enne [ɔ̃dyrjɛ̃, -ɛn] **1** *adj* Honduran
  2 *nm,f* **H.** Honduran
*Hongrie [ɔ̃gri] *nf* **la H.** Hungary
*hongrois, -e [ɔ̃grwa, -az] **1** *adj* Hungarian
  2 *nm,f* **H.** Hungarian
  3 *nm (langue)* Hungarian
honnête [ɔnɛt] *adj* (**a**) *(intègre) (personne, conduite)*
  honest; **peu h.** dishonest; **être h. avec soi-même** to
  be honest with oneself (**b**) *(décent) (vie, gens)* decent;
  (intentions) honourable (**c**) *(acceptable) (prix, note,*

résultat) fair; **un repas/livre h., sans plus** an OK
meal/book, but nothing to write home about
honnêtement [ɔnɛtmã] *adv* (**a**) *(avec intégrité) (agir,*
  se comporter) honestly (**b**) *(franchement)* to be honest; **h., qu'est-ce que tu en penses?** be honest, what
  do you think? (**c**) *(raisonnablement)* decently
honnêteté [ɔnɛtte] *nf* (**a**) *(intégrité)* honesty (**b**) *(dé-*
  cence) decency
honneur [ɔnœr] *nm* honour; **mettre un point d'h. à**
  faire qch to make it a point of honour to do sth; **dé-**
  clarer/jurer sur l'h. que... to state/swear on one's
  honour that...; **sauver l'h.** to save one's honour; **en**
  tout bien tout h. with no ulterior motive; **en l'h. de**
  qn in sb's honour; **à qui ai-je l'h.?** to whom have I the
  honour (of speaking)?; *Fam* **en quel h. devrais-je t'ai-**
  der? give me one good reason why I should help you!;
  à vous l'h. after you; **être à l'h.** to have pride of place;
  c'est tout à ton h. it's to your credit; **faire h. à qn/qch**
  to be a credit to sb/sth; **faire h. à un repas** to do justice to a meal; **rechercher les honneurs** to court fame
*honnir [ɔnir] *vt* to disgrace
honorable [ɔnɔrabl] *adj* (**a**) *(profession, personne, in-*
  tentions) honourable (**b**) *(performance, résultat)*
  creditable, respectable
honorablement [ɔnɔrabləmã] *adv* (**a**) *(de façon re-*
  spectable) honourably (**b**) *(correctement)* **il s'en est**
  h. tiré he did quite creditably; **gagner h. sa vie** to
  earn a good living
honoraire [ɔnɔrɛr] **1** *adj (fonction, membre)* honorary
  2 *nmpl* **honoraires** fee, fees
honorer [ɔnɔre] **1** *vt* (**a**) *(rendre hommage à)* to honour; **h. qn de sa confiance** to put one's trust in sb (**b**)
  (facture, dette, engagements) to honour (**c**) *(valoir de*
  l'estime à) (personne, chose) to be a credit to (**d**) *Hum*
  (sexuellement) to service
  2 s'honorer *vpr* **s'h. de qch/d'avoir fait qch** to pride
  oneself on sth/on having done sth
honorifique [ɔnɔrifik] *adj* honorary
*honoris causa [ɔnɔriskoza] *adj* honoris causa; **doc-**
  teur h. doctor honoris causa, honorary doctor
*honte [ɔ̃t] *nf* (**a**) *(sentiment)* shame; **à ma grande h.**
  to my shame; **sans h.** shamelessly; **avoir h. (de)** to be
  ashamed (of); **avoir h. pour qn** to feel embarrassed
  for sb; **faire h. à qn** to make sb ashamed (**b**) *(chose*
  scandaleuse) disgrace; **c'est une h.!** it's a disgrace!
*honteux, -euse [ɔ̃tø, øz] *adj* (**a**) *(personne, air)*
  ashamed (**b**) *(conduite, acte)* shameful, disgraceful;
  c'est h.! it's a disgrace!
*hop [ɔp] *exclam* **allez h., saute!** go on, jump!; **allez h.,**
  tout le monde dehors! come on, everybody out!;
  h.-là! oops(-a-daisy)!
hôpital, -aux [ɔpital, -o] *nm* hospital; *Prov* **c'est l'h.**
  qui se moque de la charité it's the pot calling the kettle black; **h. de campagne** field hospital; **h. de jour**
  day hospital; **h. militaire** military hospital; **h. psy-**
  chiatrique psychiatric hospital
*hoquet [ɔkɛ] *nm* hiccup; **avoir le h.** to have (the) hiccups
*hoqueter [42] [ɔkəte] *vi* to hiccup
horaire [ɔrɛr] **1** *adj* hourly
  2 *nm* (**a**) *(des services de transport)* timetable, schedule; **être en retard sur l'h.** to be running late (**b**)
  (emploi du temps) timetable, schedule; **h. variable** *ou*
  flexible flexible hours, flexitime; **horaires de travail**
  working hours
*horde [ɔrd] *nf* horde

The symbol * indicates that the initial **h** is aspirate and that hence there is no liaison, eg **les haricots** [leariko] and not
[lezariko], or contraction in spelling, eg **la haine** and not **l'haine**.

horizon [ɔrizɔ̃] *nm aussi Fig* horizon; **ouvrir de nouveaux horizons à qn** to open up new horizons *or* prospects for sb; **à l'h.** on the horizon; **à l'h. 2020** in the year 2020; **h. intellectuel** intellectual horizons
horizontal, -e, -aux, -ales [ɔrizɔ̃tal, -o] **1** *adj* horizontal **2** *nf* **horizontale** horizontal line; **à l'horizontale** horizontal
horizontalement [ɔrizɔ̃talmɑ̃] *adv* horizontally; *(dans les mots croisés)* across
horloge [ɔrlɔʒ] *nf* clock; **réglé comme une h.** as regular as clockwork; **h. biologique** biological clock; **l'h. parlante** the speaking clock; *Ordinat* **h. du système** system clock; *Ordinat* **h. en temps réel** real-time clock
horloger, -ère [ɔrlɔʒe, -ɛr] **1** *adj* **l'industrie horlogère** the watchmaking industry **2** *nm,f* watchmaker
horloger-bijoutier *(pl* **horlogers-bijoutiers)** [ɔrlɔʒebiʒutje] *nm* jeweller and watchmaker
horlogerie [ɔrlɔʒri] *nf (industrie)* watchmaking; *(magasin)* watchmaker's (shop); **l'h.** *(ouvrages)* clocks and watches
***hormis** [ɔrmi] *prép Litt* except, save
hormonal, -e, -aux, -ales [ɔrmɔnal, -o] *adj* hormonal
hormone [ɔrmɔn] *nf* hormone
hormonothérapie [ɔrmɔnoterapi] *nf* hormone therapy
horodateur [ɔrɔdatœr] *nm* time-and-date stamping machine; *(de stationnement)* pay-and-display machine
horoscope [ɔrɔskɔp] *nm* horoscope
horreur [ɔrœr] *nf* (**a**) *(effroi)* horror (**b**) *(répugnance)* disgust; **avoir h. de qn/qch** to hate sb/sth; **avoir h. de faire qch** to hate doing sth; **avoir qn/qch en h.** to loathe sb/sth; **faire h. à qn** to disgust sb; *Fam* **c'est l'h.** it's the pits, it sucks (**c**) *(caractère horrible)* horror; **quelle h.!** how horrible!, how awful! (**d**) *(chose ou personne exécrable)* **être une h.** to be a nightmare (**e**) **horreurs** *(atrocités)* horrors; *(calomnies)* horrible things
horrible [ɔribl] *adj* (**a**) *(effrayant)* horrible (**b**) *(très laid)* hideous
horriblement [ɔribləmɑ̃] *adv (brûlé, défiguré)* horribly; *(cher, froid)* terribly
horrifiant, -e [ɔrifjɑ̃, -ɑ̃t] *adj* horrifying
horrifier [66] [ɔrifje] *vt* to horrify
horripilant, -e [ɔripilɑ̃, -ɑ̃t] *adj* exasperating
horripiler [ɔripile] *vt* to exasperate
***hors** [ɔr] *prép* (**a**) *(dehors)* **h.** outside; **h. d'ici!** get out (of here)!; **ça l'a mise la. d'elle** that infuriated her; **être h. de soi** to be beside oneself (**b**) *Litt (sauf)* except, save (**c**) *(en conjonction avec un nom)* **h. antenne** off-air; **h. d'atteinte** out of reach; **h. de combat** out of action; **h. jeu** offside; **mettre qn/qch h. la loi** to outlaw sb/sth; **h. pair** unrivalled; **h. piste** off piste; **h. de prix** extortionate; **h. de question** out of the question; **h. saison** off-season; **numéro h. série** special issue; **h. service** out of order; **h. sujet** not relevant; **h. taxe** net of tax; *(exempt de taxe)* tax-free; **boutique h. taxe** duty-free shop; **h. d'usage** *(vêtement)* worn out; *(machine)* beyond repair
***hors-bord** [ɔrbɔr] *nm inv* speedboat; **moteur h.** outboard motor
***hors-d'œuvre** [ɔrdœvr] *nm inv* (**a**) *(plat)* hors d'œuvre, starter (**b**) *Fig* starter, taster

***hors-jeu** [ɔrʒø] *nm inv* offside
***hors-la-loi** [ɔrlalwa] *nm inv* outlaw
***hors-piste** [ɔrpist] *nm inv (en ski)* off-piste skiing; **faire du h.** to ski off piste
hortensia [ɔrtɑ̃sja] *nm* hydrangea
horticole [ɔrtikɔl] *adj* horticultural; **exposition h.** flower show
horticulteur [ɔrtikyltœr] *nm* nurseryman
horticulture [ɔrtikyltyr] *nf* horticulture
hospice [ɔspis] *nm* (**a**) *(asile)* home (**b**) *(monastère)* hospice
hospitalier¹, -ère [ɔspitalje, -ɛr] *adj (accueillant)* hospitable
hospitalier², -ère *adj (relatif aux hôpitaux)* hospital; **en milieu h.** in a hospital environment; **personnel h.** hospital staff
hospitalisation [ɔspitalizasjɔ̃] *nf* hospitalization; **h. à domicile** home care
hospitaliser [ɔspitalize] *vt* to hospitalize; **faire h. qn** to have sb hospitalized
hospitalité [ɔspitalite] *nf* hospitality
hospitalo-universitaire *(pl* **hospitalo-universitaires)** [ɔspitaloynivɛrsitɛr] *adj* **centre h.** teaching hospital
hostie [ɔsti] *nf Rel* host
hostile [ɔstil] *adj* hostile (**à** towards)
hostilité [ɔstilite] *nf* hostility (**contre** *ou* **envers** towards); **hostilités** hostilities; **reprendre les hostilités** to reopen *or* resume hostilities
hosto [ɔsto] *nm Fam* hospital
hôte [ot] *nm* (**a**) *(personne qui invite)* host (**b**) *(invité)* guest, visitor; **h. payant** paying guest (**c**) *Biol* host
hôtel [otɛl] *nm* (**a**) *(pour l'hébergement)* hotel; **h. de passe** = hotel used as a brothel (**b**) *(bâtiment)* **h. des impôts** tax office; **l'h. de la Monnaie** = the French Mint; **h. (particulier)** mansion, town house; **h. des ventes** saleroom; **h. de ville** town hall
hôtelier, -ère [otəlje, -ɛr] **1** *adj* **l'industrie hôtelière** the hotel industry **2** *nm,f* hotel keeper, hotelier
hôtellerie [otɛlri] *nf* (**a**) *(hôtel)* inn (**b**) *(secteur)* **l'h.** the hotel industry
hôtel-restaurant *(pl* **hôtels-restaurants)** [otɛlrɛstɔrɑ̃] *nm* hotel and restaurant
hôtesse [otɛs] *nf* (**a**) *(personne qui reçoit)* hostess (**b**) *(dans un avion)* hostess, stewardess; **h. d'accueil** receptionist; **h. de l'air** air hostess
***hotte** [ɔt] *nf* (**a**) *(panier)* basket; **la h. du Père Noël** Santa (Claus)'s sack (**b**) *(pour la ventilation)* hood; **h. aspirante** extractor hood
***hou** [u] *exclam* boo!; **h.! la vilaine!** tut-tut, you naughty girl!
***houblon** [ublɔ̃] *nm* hops
***houe** [u] *nf* hoe
***houille** [uj] *nf* coal; **h. blanche** hydroelectric power
***houiller, -ère** [uje, -ɛr] **1** *adj (terrain)* rich in coal; **bassin h.** coalfield; **production houillère** coal output **2** *nf* **houillère** coalmine, colliery
***houle** [ul] *nf* swell
***houlette** [ulɛt] *nf* (**a**) *(de berger)* crook; *Fig* **sous la h. de** under the leadership of (**b**) *(petite bêche)* trowel
***houleux, -euse** [ulø, -øz] *adj (mer)* choppy; *Fig (réunion)* stormy
houmous [umus] *nm Culin* houmous, hummus
***houppette** [upɛt] *nf (de plumes)* small tuft; *(de cheveux)* quiff; *(à poudre)* powder puff

---

The symbol * indicates that the initial **h** is aspirate and that hence there is no liaison, eg **les haricots** [leariko] and not [lezariko], or contraction in spelling, eg **la haine** and not **l'haine**.

*hourra [ura] **1** *exclam* hurrah!; **hip, hip, hip, h.!** hip, hip, hooray!
2 *nm* hurrah; **pousser des hourras** to cheer
*houspiller [uspije] *vt* to tell off
*housse [us] *nf* cover; *(contre la poussière)* dust sheet; *(dans une voiture)* seat cover
*houx [u] *nm* holly
hovercraft [ɔvɛrkraft] *nm* hovercraft
*HS [aʃɛs] *adj Fam (abrév* **hors service)** *(appareil)* out of order, *Br* on the blink; *(personne) Br* knackered, *Am* bushed
HT (**a**) *(abrév* **haute tension)** HT (**b**) *(abrév* **hors taxe)** exclusive of tax
*HTML [aʃteɛmɛl] *nm Ordinat (abrév* **HyperText Markup Language)** HTML
*hublot [yblo] *nm (de bateau)* porthole; *(dans un avion, une machine à laver)* window
*huche [yʃ] *nf* chest; **h. à pain** bread bin
*hue [y, hy] *exclam (à un cheval)* gee up!; **tirer à h. et à dia** to pull in opposite directions
*huées [ɥe] *nfpl* booing; **quitter la scène sous les h.** to be booed off stage
*huer [ɥe] **1** *vt* to boo
2 *vi (hibou, chouette)* to hoot
huile [ɥil] *nf* (**a**) *(liquide)* oil; *Fig* **jeter de l'h. sur le feu** to add fuel to the fire; **une mer d'h.** a glassy sea; **h. d'amandes douces** almond oil; **h. d'arachide** groundnut oil; *Can* **h. de chauffage** heating oil; *Fig* **h. de coude** elbow grease; **h. essentielle** essential oil; **h. de foie de morue** cod liver oil; **h. de moteur** engine oil; **h. d'olive** olive oil; **h. de ricin** castor oil; **h. solaire** suntan oil; **h. de tournesol** sunflower oil; **h. végétale** vegetable oil; **h. de vidange** sump oil (**b**) *(peinture)* oil painting (**c**) *Fam (personne importante)* big shot
huiler [ɥile] *vt* to oil; *Fig* **une mécanique bien huilée** a well-oiled machine
huileux, -euse [ɥilø, -øz] *adj* oily
huis [ɥi] *nm* **à h. clos** behind closed doors; *Jur* **in camera**
huissier [ɥisje] *nm* (**a**) *Jur* bailiff (**b**) *(portier)* usher
*huit [ɥit] *adj & nm inv* eight; **h. jours** a week; **aujourd'hui/demain en h.** a week today/tomorrow; **donner ses h. jours à qn** to give sb a week's notice; *voir aussi* **trois**
*huitaine [ɥitɛn] *nf* (**a**) *(environ huit)* (about) eight (**b**) *(semaine)* week; **sous h.** within a week; **dans une h. de jours** in a week or so
*huitante [ɥitɑ̃t] *adj inv Suisse* eighty
*huitième [ɥitjɛm] *adj, nm & nmf* eighth; *voir aussi* **cinquième**
huître [ɥitr] *nf* oyster; **h. perlière** pearl oyster
*hulotte [ylɔt] *nf* tawny owl
*hululement [ylylmɑ̃] *nm* hoot; **des hululements** hooting
*hululer [ylyle] *vi* to hoot
*hum [œm] *exclam* hm!
humain, -e [ymɛ̃, -ɛn] **1** *adj* (**a**) *(relatif à l'homme)* human; **c'est h.** it's only human; **des pertes humaines énormes** a huge loss of life (**b**) *(compatissant)* humane
2 *nm* human (being)
humainement [ymɛnmɑ̃] *adv* (**a**) *(relatif à l'homme)* in human terms; **h. possible** humanly possible (**b**) *(avec bonté)* humanely
humaniser [ymanize] *vt* to make more human
humanisme [ymanism] *nm* humanism
humaniste [ymanist] *adj & nmf* humanist

humanitaire [ymanitɛr] **1** *adj* humanitarian; **organisation h.** relief *or* aid organization
2 *nmf (personne)* humanitarian (aid) worker
3 *nm* **l'h.** the humanitarian sector
humanité [ymanite] *nf* (**a**) *(genre humain)* humanity, mankind (**b**) *(bonté)* humanity; **avec h.** humanely
humanoïde [ymanɔid] *nm* humanoid
humble [œ̃bl] *adj* humble; **à mon h. avis** in my humble opinion
humblement [œ̃bləmɑ̃] *adv* humbly
humecter [ymɛkte] *vt* to moisten
*humer [yme] *vt (air)* to breathe in; *(parfum)* to smell
humérus [ymerys] *nm* humerus
humeur [ymœr] *nf* (**a**) *(disposition)* mood; **être de bonne/mauvaise h.** to be in a good/bad mood; **mettre qn de bonne/mauvaise h.** to put sb in a good/bad mood; **être d'une h. massacrante** to be in a foul mood; **plein de bonne h.** good-humoured; **être/ne pas être d'h. à faire qch** to be/not be in the mood to do sth (**b**) *(caractère)* temper, temperament; **d'h.** **égale** even-tempered; **d'h. inégale** *ou* **changeante** temperamental (**c**) *Litt (mauvaise humeur)* bad mood; **geste d'h.** ill-tempered gesture; **avec h.** irritably (**d**) *Anat* **h. aqueuse** aqueous humour; **h. vitrée** vitreous humour
humide [ymid] *adj (maison, linge)* damp, wet; *(climat)* humid; **les yeux humides (de larmes)** eyes moist with tears
humidificateur [ymidifikatœr] *nm* humidifier
humidifier [66] [ymidifje] *vt* to dampen; *(air)* to humidify
humidité [ymidite] *nf (d'une maison)* dampness; *(du climat, d'une région)* humidity; **il faut beaucoup d'h. à cette plante** this plant needs a lot of moisture; **craint l'h.** *(sur un paquet)* store in a dry place
humiliant, -e [ymiljɑ̃, -ɑ̃t] *adj* humiliating
humiliation [ymiljasjɔ̃] *nf* humiliation
humilier [66] [ymilje] **1** *vt* to humiliate
2 **s'humilier** *vpr* to humiliate oneself
humilité [ymilite] *nf* humility
humoriste [ymɔrist] *nmf* humorist
humoristique [ymɔristik] *adj* humorous; **dessin h.** cartoon
humour [ymur] *nm* humour; **avoir (le sens) de l'h.** to have a (good) sense of humour; **h. noir** black humour
*huppe¹ [yp] *nf (oiseau)* hoopoe
*huppe² *nf (d'un oiseau)* crest
*huppé, -e [ype] *adj* (**a**) *Fam (gens, endroit, quartier)* smart (**b**) *(oiseau)* crested
*hurlement [yrləmɑ̃] *nm (d'un loup, d'un chien)* howl; *(d'une personne)* scream; *(du vent)* roaring; *(d'une sirène)* wail
*hurler [yrle] **1** *vi (loup, chien)* to howl; *(personne)* to howl, to scream; *(vent, tempête)* to roar; *(sirène)* to wail; *(radio)* to blare; **j'ai dû h. pour qu'il m'entende** I had to shout for him to hear me; **h. de douleur/rage** to howl with pain/rage; **c'est à h. de rire** it's screamingly funny; **h. à la lune** to bay at the moon; **il faut h. avec les loups** if you can't beat them, join them
2 *vt (insultes, instructions)* to yell
hurluberlu [yrlybɛrly] *nm* oddball
*Huron [yrɔ̃] *n voir* **lac**
*husky (*pl* **huskies**) [œski] *nm* husky
*hussard [ysar] *nm* hussar
*hussarde [ysard] *nf* **à la h.** roughly
*hutte [yt] *nf* hut
hybride [ibrid] *adj & nm* hybrid

hydratant, -e [idratã, -ãt] *adj* moisturizing
hydratation [idratasjɔ̃] *nf (de la peau)* moisturizing
hydrate [idrat] *nm* hydrate; **h. de carbone** carbohydrate
hydrater [idrate] **1** *vt (peau)* to moisturize; *(organisme)* to hydrate **2 s'hydrater** *vpr* to take in water
hydraulique [idrolik] **1** *adj* hydraulic **2** *nf (science)* hydraulics *(singulier)*
hydravion [idravjɔ̃] *nm* seaplane
hydre [idr] *nf* hydra
hydrocarbure [idrɔkarbyr] *nm* hydrocarbon
hydrocution [idrɔkysjɔ̃] *nf* = loss of consciousness caused by immersion in cold water
hydroélectricité [idrɔelɛktrisite] *nf* hydroelectricity
hydroélectrique [idrɔelɛktrik] *adj* hydroelectric
hydrogène [idrɔʒɛn] *nm* hydrogen
hydroglisseur [idrɔglisœr] *nm* jetfoil
hydrographie [idrɔgrafi] *nf* hydrography
hydrolyse [idrɔliz] *nf* hydrolysis
hydromel [idrɔmɛl] *nm* mead
hydrophile [idrɔfil] *adj (coton)* absorbent
hydrothérapie [idrɔterapi] *nf* hydrotherapy
hydroxyde [idrɔksid] *nm* hydroxide
hyène [jɛn] *nf* hyena
Hygiaphone® [iʒjafɔn] *nm (au guichet)* grille; **parlez dans l'H.** speak into the grille
hygiène [iʒjɛn] *nf* hygiene; **par mesure d'h.** for hygiene reasons; **h. alimentaire** diet; **h. corporelle** personal hygiene; **h. mentale** mental health; **avoir une bonne h. de vie** to live healthily
hygiénique [iʒjenik] *adj (a) (propre)* hygienic; **peu h.** unhygienic *(b) (bon pour la santé)* healthy; **une promenade h.** a bracing walk
hymne [imn] *nm* hymn; **h. national** national anthem
hyper [ipɛr] *nm Fam (abrév* **hypermarché)** hypermarket, superstore
hyper- [ipɛr] *préf Fam* very, really
hyperactif, -ive [iperaktif, -iv] *adj* hyperactive
hyperbole [iperbɔl] *nf (a) (figure de style)* hyperbole **(b)** *Math* hyperbola
hyperbolique [iperbɔlik] *adj* hyperbolic
hyperglycémie [iperglisemi] *nf* hyperglycemia
hyperlien [iperljɛ̃] *nm Ordinat* hyperlink
hypermarché [ipermarʃe] *nm* hypermarket, superstore
hypermétrope [ipermetrɔp] *adj* long-sighted
hypernerveux, -euse [ipernɛrvø, -øz] **1** *adj* highly-strung **2** *nm,f* highly-strung person
hyperréaliste [iperealist] *adj* hyperrealistic
hypersensibilité [ipersãsibilite] *nf* hypersensitivity

hypersensible [ipersãsibl] *adj* hypersensitive
hypertendu, -e [ipertãdy] *adj* **être h.** to have high blood pressure
hypertension [ipertãsjɔ̃] *nf* high blood pressure, *Spéc* hypertension
hypertexte [ipertɛkst] *nm Ordinat* hypertext
hypertrophie [ipertrɔfi] *nf* enlargement, *Spéc* hypertrophy
hypertrophié, -e [ipertrɔfje] *adj* enlarged, *Spéc* hypertrophied
hypnose [ipnoz] *nf* hypnosis; **sous h.** under hypnosis; **être en état d'h.** to be under hypnosis
hypnotique [ipnɔtik] *adj* hypnotic
hypnotiser [ipnɔtize] *vt* to hypnotize
hypnotisme [ipnɔtism] *nm* hypnotism
hypoallergénique [ipɔalɛrʒenik] *adj* hypoallergenic
hypocalorique [ipɔkalɔrik] *adj (régime, aliment)* low-calorie
hypocondriaque [ipɔkɔ̃drijak] *adj & nmf* hypochondriac
hypocrisie [ipɔkrizi] *nf* hypocrisy
hypocrite [ipɔkrit] **1** *adj* hypocritical **2** *nmf* hypocrite
hypocritement [ipɔkritmã] *adv* hypocritically
hypodermique [ipɔdɛrmik] *adj* hypodermic
hypoglycémie [ipɔglisemi] *nf* hypoglycemia
hypokhâgne [ipɔkaɲ] *nf* = first-year arts class preparing students for the entrance examination for the "École normale supérieure"
hypophyse [ipɔfiz] *nf* pituitary gland
hypotendu, -e [ipɔtãdy] *adj* **être h.** to have low blood pressure
hypotension [ipɔtãsjɔ̃] *nf* low blood pressure, *Spéc* hypotension
hypoténuse [ipɔtenyz] *nf* hypotenuse
hypothalamus [ipɔtalamys] *nm* hypothalamus
hypothécaire [ipɔtekɛr] *adj* **contrat h.** mortgage deed; **prêt h.** mortgage (loan)
hypothèque [ipɔtɛk] *nf* mortgage
hypothéquer [34] [ipɔteke] *vt (propriété)* to mortgage; *Fig* **h. son avenir** to sign away one's future
hypothermie [ipɔtɛrmi] *nf* hypothermia
hypothèse [ipɔtɛz] *nf* hypothesis; **dans l'h. où nous échouerions** should we fail; **ils ont écarté l'h. du suicide** they have ruled out the possibility of suicide
hypothétique [ipɔtetik] *adj* hypothetical
hystérectomie [isterɛktɔmi] *nf* hysterectomy
hystérie [isteri] *nf* hysteria; **h. collective** mass hysteria
hystérique [isterik] **1** *adj* hysterical **2** *nmf* hysterical person

I, i [i] *nm inv* I, i
ibère [ibɛr] **1** *adj* Iberian
 2 *nmf* I. Iberian
ibérique [iberik] *adj* Iberian
ibis [ibis] *nm* ibis
iceberg [ajsbɛrg, isbɛrg] *nm* iceberg; *Fig* **la partie cachée de l'i.** the hidden aspects of the problem; *Fig* **la partie visible de l'i.** the tip of the iceberg
ichtyologie [iktjɔlɔʒi] *nf* ichthyology
ici [isi] *adv* (**a**) *(dans l'espace)* here; **i. et là** here and there; **i. même** on this very spot; **les gens d'i.** the people from round here, the locals; **c'est i.** this is the place; **c'est i. que ça s'est passé** this is where it happened; *Fig* **je reprends i. ses propres paroles** and here I'm using his/her own words; **i. Thomas** *(au téléphone)* this is Thomas (**b**) *(dans le temps)* **jusqu'i.** until now, up to now; **d'i. lundi/demain** by Monday/tomorrow; **d'i. là** by that time, by then; **d'i. peu** before long; **d'i. à ce que vous ayez fini, je serai parti** by the time you've finished, I'll have gone; **d'i. à ce qu'il la quitte, il n'y a pas loin** he will have left her before long
icône [ikon] *nf Rel & Ordinat* icon; *Ordinat* **i. de la corbeille** wastebasket icon, *Am* trash icon
iconoclaste [ikɔnɔklast] **1** *adj* iconoclastic
 2 *nmf* iconoclast
iconographie [ikɔnɔgrafi] *nf* (**a**) *(dans un domaine particulier)* iconography (**b**) *(dans l'édition)* illustrations, art work
iconographique [ikɔnɔgrafik] *adj* iconographic
idéal, -e, -als *ou* **-aux, -ales** [ideal, -o] **1** *adj* ideal
 2 *nm* ideal; **l'i.** *(solution parfaite)* the ideal thing; **dans l'i.** ideally; **l'i. serait que tu y ailles tout seul** it would be best if you went alone
idéalement [idealmã] *adv* ideally
idéalisation [idealizasjɔ̃] *nf* idealization
idéaliser [idealize] *vt* to idealize
idéalisme [idealism] *nm* idealism
idéaliste [idealist] **1** *adj* idealistic
 2 *nmf* idealist
idée [ide] *nf* (**a**) *(inspiration)* idea; **i. de génie, i. lumineuse** brilliant idea; **avoir la bonne i. de faire qch** to have the bright idea of doing sth; **avoir une i. derrière la tête** to be up to something; **donner des idées à qn** to put ideas into sb's head; **quelle drôle d'i.!, en voilà une i.!** the very idea!; **se faire des idées** to imagine things; **i. fixe** obsession; **idées noires** black thoughts; **i.** generally accepted idea (**b**) *(notion)* idea; **pour vous donner une i.** to give you an idea; **as-tu une i. du prix que ça coûte?** have you any idea how much it costs?; **je n'en ai pas la moindre i.** I haven't

got the faintest idea; *Fam* **on n'a pas i. de faire des choses pareilles!** whoever heard of such a thing! (**c**) *(opinion)* view, opinion; **avoir une haute i. de qn/qch** to have a high opinion of sb/sth; **se faire une i. de qn/qch** to get an idea of sb/sth; **avoir sa petite i. sur qch** to have one's pet theory about sth; **avoir les idées larges** to be broad-minded; **fais à ton i.** do as you like; **changer d'i.** to change one's mind (**d**) *(esprit)* **ça ne m'est jamais venu à l'i.** it's never occurred to me; **je ne peux pas lui ôter cela de l'i.** I can't get him/her to change his/her mind about it; **se mettre dans l'i. que/de faire qch** to get it into one's head that/to do sth; **cela m'était sorti de l'i.** it had slipped my mind
idem [idɛm] *adv* ditto
identifiant [idɑ̃tifjɑ̃] *nm Ordinat* identifier; **i. biométrique** biometric identifier
identification [idɑ̃tifikasjɔ̃] *nf* identification (**avec** *ou* **à** with); *Tél* **i. d'appel** caller identification, *Fam* caller ID; *Ordinat* **i. de l'utilisateur** user identification
identifier [66] [idɑ̃tifje] **1** *vt* to identify
 2 s'identifier *vpr* **s'i. à** *ou* **avec** to identify with
identique [idɑ̃tik] *adj* identical (**à** to)
identitaire [idɑ̃titɛr] *adj* **les revendications identitaires des minorités ethniques** ethnic minorities' demands for recognition; **obsession i.** obsession with issues of identity
identité [idɑ̃tite] *nf* identity; **papiers** *ou* **pièces d'i.** identity papers
idéogramme [ideɔgram] *nm* ideogram
idéologie [ideɔlɔʒi] *nf* ideology
idéologique [ideɔlɔʒik] *adj* ideological
idiomatique [idjɔmatik] *adj* idiomatic; **expression i.** idiom
idiome [idjom] *nm* idiom
idiot, -e [idjo, -ɔt] **1** *adj* *(stupide)* idiotic, stupid; *(regrettable)* stupid, silly; **ce système n'est pas i.** this system is pretty smart
 2 *nm,f* idiot; *Fam* **l'i. du village** the village idiot; **faire l'i.** *(faire des bêtises)* to act the fool; *(feindre de ne pas comprendre)* to act dumb
idiotie [idjɔsi] *nf* *(chose, parole idiote)* stupid thing; *(caractère stupide)* stupidity; **ne dites pas d'idioties!** don't talk nonsense!
idolâtrer [idɔlatre] *vt* to idolize
idolâtrie [idɔlatri] *nf* idolatry
idole [idɔl] *nf* idol; **i. des jeunes** teen idol
idylle [idil] *nf* (**a**) *(aventure)* romance (**b**) *(poème)* idyll
idyllique [idilik] *adj* idyllic

IEP [iɔpe] *nm* (*abrév* **Institut d'études politiques**) = higher education establishment for political science students

if [if] *nm* yew

IFOP [ifɔp] *nm* (*abrév* **Institut français d'opinion publique**) = French market research institute

IGF [iʒɛef] *nm inv Anciennement* (*abrév* **impôt sur les grandes fortunes**) wealth tax

igloo, iglou [iglu] *nm* igloo

IGN [iʒɛɛn] *nm* (*abrév* **Institut géographique national**) *Br* ≃ Ordnance Survey, *Am* ≃ United States Geological Survey

IGN

Created in 1940, this state agency is responsible for the official map of France and for keeping a geographical database. It is organized into regional offices and sponsors a school which trains 200 students a year.

ignare [iɲar] **1** *adj* ignorant
2 *nmf* ignoramus

ignifuge [iɲifyʒ] **1** *adj* fireproof
2 *nm* fireproofing material

ignifugé, -e [iɲifyʒe] *adj* fireproofed

ignoble [iɲɔbl] *adj* (**a**) (*personne, conduite*) vile (**b**) (*habitation, quartier*) filthy; (*nourriture*) disgusting

ignominie [iɲɔmini] *nf* (**a**) (*caractère*) ignominy; **se couvrir d'i.** to bring shame upon oneself (**b**) (*action*) shameful thing; **c'est une i.!** it's a disgrace!

ignorance [iɲɔrãs] *nf* ignorance; **être/tenir qn dans l'i.** to be/keep sb in the dark

ignorant, -e [iɲɔrã, -ãt] **1** *adj* ignorant (**de** of)
2 *nm,f* ignoramus; **faire l'i.** to play dumb

ignoré, -e [iɲɔre] *adj* unknown; (*négligé*) ignored; **vivre i.** to live in obscurity

ignorer [iɲɔre] **1** *vt* (**a**) (*ne pas savoir*) not to know (about); **j'ignorais qu'il était malade** I was unaware that he was ill; **il ignore tout de cela** he knows nothing about it; **ne rien i. de qch** to know all about sth; **personne n'ignore que...** everybody knows that...; **i. la peur/la jalousie** to feel no fear/jealousy (**b**) (*mépriser*) (*personne, conseil, interdiction*) to ignore
2 **s'ignorer** *vpr* (**a**) (*se mépriser l'un l'autre*) to ignore each other (**b**) (*se méconnaître*) **c'est un artiste qui s'ignore** he's an artist but he doesn't know it

iguane [igwan] *nm* iguana

il [il] *pron personnel* (**a**) (*personne*) he; (*chose, animal*) it; **ton père est-il toujours à l'hôpital?** is your father still in hospital? (**b**) (*impersonnel*) it; **il est six heures** it's six o'clock; **il pleut** it's raining; **il existe de nombreuses possibilités** there are many possibilities

île [il] *nf* island; **dans une î.** on an island; **î. déserte** desert island; **les îles Anglo-Normandes** the Channel Islands; *Culin* **î. flottante** floating island (*beaten egg whites served on custard*); **les îles Salomon** the Solomon Islands; **les îles de la Société** the Society Islands; **les îles Sous-le-Vent** the Leeward Islands

Île-de-France [ildəfrãs] *nf* **l'Î.** = administrative region including Paris

iliaque [iljak] *adj Anat* iliac; **os i.** ilium

illégal, -e, -aux, -ales [ilegal, -o] *adj* illegal

illégalement [ilegalmã] *adv* illegally

illégalité [ilegalite] *nf* illegality; **vivre dans l'i.** to live outside the law; **être dans l'i.** to break the law

illégitime [ileʒitim] *adj* (*enfant*) illegitimate; (*union*) unlawful; (*demande*) unwarranted

illettré, -e [iletre] *adj & nm,f* illiterate

illettrisme [iletrism] *nm* illiteracy

illicite [ilisit] *adj* illicit, unlawful

illico [iliko] *adv Fam* **i. (presto)** pronto

illimité, -e [ilimite] *adj* (*pouvoirs, moyens, crédit*) unlimited; (*confiance*) boundless

illisible [ilizibl] *adj* (**a**) (*indéchiffrable*) illegible; *Ordinat* (*fichier, disquette*) unreadable (**b**) (*incompréhensible*) unreadable

illogique [ilɔʒik] *adj* illogical

illumination [ilyminasjɔ̃] *nf* (**a**) (*action d'illuminer*) illumination; (*par projecteurs*) floodlighting (**b**) (*lumière*) **illuminations** illuminations (**c**) (*inspiration*) flash of inspiration

illuminé, -e [ilymine] **1** *adj* (*éclairé*) lit up, illuminated; (*par projecteurs*) floodlit
2 *nm,f Péj* fanatic

illuminer [ilymine] **1** *vt* (*éclairer*) to light up, to illuminate; (*par projecteurs*) to floodlight; *Fig* (*visage, yeux*) to light up
2 **s'illuminer** *vpr aussi Fig* to light up (**de** with)

illusion [ilyzjɔ̃] *nf* illusion; **se faire des illusions** to delude oneself; **je ne me fais aucune i. sur ses intentions** I have no illusions about his/her intentions; **perdre ses illusions** to become disillusioned; **enlever** *ou* **faire perdre ses illusions à qn** to disillusion sb; **faire i.** to take people in; **i. d'optique** optical illusion

illusionner [ilyzjɔne] **s'illusionner** *vpr* to delude oneself (**sur** about)

illusionniste [ilyzjɔnist] *nmf* conjurer

illusoire [ilyzwar] *adj* illusory

illustrateur, -trice [ilystratœr, -tris] *nm,f* illustrator

illustration [ilystrasjɔ̃] *nf* illustration

illustre [ilystr] *adj* illustrious; *Hum* **un i. inconnu** a famous person no one has ever heard of

illustré, -e [ilystre] **1** *adj* illustrated
2 *nm Vieilli* (*pour enfants*) comic

illustrer [ilystre] **1** *vt* (*livre, récit*) to illustrate (**de** with)
2 **s'illustrer** *vpr* to distinguish oneself (**par** by)

îlot [ilo] *nm* (*île*) small island; (*groupe d'immeubles*) block; *Fig* **î. de verdure** island of greenery

îlotage [ilotaʒ] *nm* community policing

ils [il] *pron personnel* they; **les magasins sont-i. ouverts le dimanche?** are the shops open on Sunday?

image [imaʒ] *nf* (**a**) (*dans un miroir*) reflection, image; (*à la télévision*) picture; **vingt-quatre images par seconde** twenty-four frames a second; **être à l'i.** to be on camera; **nous n'avons plus d'i.** the picture's gone; **i. d'archives** library picture; *Cin & TV* stock shot; *Ordinat* **i. bitmap** bitmap image; **images de synthèse** computer-generated images; *Ordinat* **i. vectorielle** outline image (**b**) *Fig* image; **soigner son i.** to cultivate one's image; **donner une bonne/mauvaise i. de** to present a good/bad image of; **i. de marque** (*d'un produit*) brand image; (*d'un homme politique, d'une entreprise*) public image (**c**) (*dessin*) picture; (*récompense scolaire*) ≃ gold star

imagé, -e [imaʒe] *adj* vivid

imagerie [imaʒri] *nf* imagery; *Méd* **i. médicale** medical imaging; *Méd* **i. par résonance magnétique** magnetic resonance imaging

imaginable [imaʒinabl] *adj* imaginable

imaginaire [imaʒinɛr] **1** *adj (personnage, pays, animal)* imaginary
2 *nm* **l'i.** the imagination

imaginatif, -ive [imaʒinatif, -iv] *adj* imaginative

imagination [imaʒinasjɔ̃] *nf* imagination; **avoir de l'i.** to be imaginative

imaginer [imaʒine] **1** *vt* (**a**) *(inventer)* to devise (**b**) *(se figurer)* to imagine; **tu l'imagines avec des enfants!** just imagine him/her with children!; **j'imagine qu'elle viendra vers neuf heures** she'll come about nine o'clock, I should imagine
2 **s'imaginer** *vpr* (**a**) *(croire)* **s'i. que** to think that; **il s'imagine tout savoir** he thinks he knows it all (**b**) *(se figurer)* to imagine; *(soi-même)* to picture oneself; **tu t'imagines la tête qu'elle va faire** you can imagine how she'll take it; **je me l'imaginais bien plus grand** I imagined him much taller

imam [imam] *nm* imam

imbattable [ɛ̃batabl] *adj* unbeatable

imbécile [ɛ̃besil] **1** *adj* idiotic, stupid
2 *nmf* idiot, fool; **c'est un i. heureux** he's living in blissful ignorance; **faire l'i.** *(faire des bêtises)* to play *or* act the fool; *(feindre de ne pas comprendre)* to play dumb

imbécillité [ɛ̃besilite] *nf* (**a**) *(caractère stupide)* idiocy, stupidity (**b**) *(parole, chose stupide)* idiotic thing; **dire des imbécillités** to talk nonsense

imberbe [ɛ̃bɛrb] *adj* beardless

imbiber [ɛ̃bibe] **1** *vt* **i. qch de qch** to soak sth in sth; **imbibé d'eau** *(coton, éponge)* saturated (with water); *(terrain)* waterlogged
2 **s'imbiber** *vpr* **s'i. de qch** to become soaked with sth

imbrication [ɛ̃brikasjɔ̃] *nf* overlapping; *Fig (ensemble complexe)* web; *Ordinat* embedding; *(de commandes)* nesting

imbriquer [ɛ̃brike] **1** *vt* to overlap; *Ordinat* to embed; *(commandes)* to nest
2 **s'imbriquer** *vpr (s'emboîter)* to overlap; *Fig (problèmes, situations)* to be interwoven

imbroglio [ɛ̃brɔljo] *nm* imbroglio

imbu, -e [ɛ̃by] *adj* **i. de sa personne** *ou* **de soi-même** full of oneself

imbuvable [ɛ̃byvabl] *adj* undrinkable; *Fig (personne)* insufferable

imitateur, -trice [imitatœr, -tris] *nm,f (amateur)* mimic; *(professionnel)* impersonator, impressionist

imitation [imitasjɔ̃] *nf* (**a**) *(d'une personne)* impersonation, impression; *(d'un produit, d'un style)* imitation; *(d'une signature, d'un billet)* forgery (**b**) *(copie)* imitation; **bijoux en i. argent** imitation silver jewellery

imiter [imite] *vt (personne) (singer)* to imitate; *(faire une imitation de)* to impersonate; *(produit, style)* to imitate; *(signature)* to forge; *(billet, pièce de monnaie)* to counterfeit; **il leva son verre et tout le monde l'imita** he raised his glass and everyone did the same

immaculé, -e [imakyle] *adj (draps, linge, réputation)* spotless; **d'un blanc i.** spotlessly white; *Rel* **l'Immaculée Conception** the Immaculate Conception

immangeable [ɛ̃mɑ̃ʒabl] *adj* inedible

immanquablement [ɛ̃mɑ̃kabləmɑ̃] *adv* inevitably

immatériel, -elle [imaterjɛl] *adj Phil* immaterial; *Fin (actif)* intangible; *Litt (pâleur, minceur)* ethereal

immatriculation [imatrikylasjɔ̃] *nf* registration (**à** with); **(numéro d')i.** *Br* registration number, *Am* license number

Immatriculation

The last two numbers on French number plates refer to the "**département**" *(see box at this entry)* where the vehicle was registered. Vehicles from the Val-de-Marne, for example, bear the number 94.

immatriculer [imatrikyle] *vt* to register (**à** with); **la voiture est immatriculée en Dordogne** the car has a Dordogne *Br* number plate *or Am* license plate

immature [imatyr] *adj* immature

immaturité [imatyrite] *nf* immaturity

immédiat, -e [imedja, -at] **1** *adj* immediate; *(contact)* direct; *(mort)* instantaneous
2 *nm* **dans l'i.** for the time being

immédiatement [imedjatmɑ̃] *adv* immediately

immémorial, -e, -aux, -ales [imemɔrjal, -o] *adj Litt* age-old; **en des temps immémoriaux** in ancient times

immense [imɑ̃s] *adj* immense

immensément [imɑ̃semɑ̃] *adv* immensely

immensité [imɑ̃site] *nf* immensity

immerger [45] [imɛrʒe] *vt* to immerse (**dans** in)

immérité, -e [imerite] *adj* unmerited, undeserved

immersion [imɛrsjɔ̃] *nf* immersion (**dans** in)

immettable [ɛ̃mɛtabl] *adj* unwearable

immeuble [imœbl] **1** *nm (bâtiment)* building; *(d'appartements) Br* block of flats, *Am* apartment block
2 *adj voir* **bien**

immigrant, -e [imigrɑ̃, -ɑ̃t] *adj & nm,f* immigrant

immigration [imigrasjɔ̃] *nf* immigration

immigré, -e [imigre] *adj & nm,f* immigrant

immigrer [imigre] *vi* to immigrate

imminence [iminɑ̃s] *nf* imminence

imminent, -e [iminɑ̃, -ɑ̃t] *adj* imminent

immiscer [16] [imise] **s'immiscer** *vpr* to interfere (**dans** in)

immobile [imɔbil] *adj* motionless, still; *Fig (figé)* unchanging

immobilier, -ère [imɔbilje, -ɛr] **1** *adj Br* property, *Am* real-estate
2 *nm* **l'i.** *Br* property, *Am* real estate

immobilisation [imɔbilizasjɔ̃] *nf* (**a**) *(fait de ne plus bouger)* immobilization (**b**) *Fin* **immobilisations** fixed assets

immobiliser [imɔbilize] **1** *vt* (**a**) *(blessé)* to immobilize; *(train)* to bring to a standstill; *(véhicule) (avec un sabot)* to clamp (**b**) *(capital)* to tie up
2 **s'immobiliser** *vpr* to come to a stop

immobilisme [imɔbilism] *nm* opposition to change

immobilité [imɔbilite] *nf* stillness; *(d'un visage)* immobility

immodéré, -e [imɔdere] *adj* immoderate

immodérément [imɔderemɑ̃] *adv* immoderately

immoler [imɔle] *Litt* **1** *vt aussi Fig* to sacrifice (**à** to)
2 **s'immoler** *vpr* to sacrifice oneself; **s'i. par le feu** to die by setting fire to oneself

immonde [imɔ̃d] *adj (sale)* foul; *(ignoble, laid)* vile

immondices [imɔ̃dis] *nfpl* refuse

immoral, -e, -aux, -ales [imɔral, -o] *adj* immoral

immoralité [imɔralite] *nf* immorality

immortaliser [imɔrtalize] *vt* to immortalize

immortalité [imɔrtalite] *nf* immortality

immortel, -elle [imɔrtɛl] **1** *adj (dieu, être)* immortal; *(amour)* everlasting
2 *nm,f* **I.** *(membre de l'Académie française)* member of the Académie Française
3 *nf* **immortelle** *(plante)* everlasting flower
immuable [imɥabl] *adj (vérité)* unchanging, immutable; *(opinion, sourire)* fixed
immunisation [imynizasjɔ̃] *nf* immunization (**contre** against)
immuniser [imynize] *vt* to immunize (**contre** against)
immunitaire [imynitɛr] *adj (système, réactions, défenses)* immune
immunité [imynite] *nf* immunity; **i.** parlementaire/diplomatique parliamentary/diplomatic immunity
immunodéficitaire [imynɔdefisitɛr] *adj Méd* immunodeficient
immunodépresseur [imynɔdeprɛsœr] *adj m & nm Méd* immunosuppressive
immunologie [imynɔlɔʒi] *nf* immunology
immunologique [imynɔlɔʒik] *adj* immunological
immunosuppresseur [imynɔsyprɛsœr] *adj m & nm Méd* immunosuppressive
impact [ɛ̃pakt] *nm* impact; **avoir un i. sur qch** to have an impact on sth
impair, -e [ɛ̃pɛr] **1** *adj (nombre, jours)* odd; *(côté d'une rue)* odd-numbered
2 *nm* (**a**) *(à la roulette)* odd numbers (**b**) *(maladresse)* blunder; **faire** *ou* **commettre un i.** to make a blunder
impalpable [ɛ̃palpabl] *adj* impalpable
imparable [ɛ̃parabl] *adj (coup)* unstoppable; *Fig (argument, logique)* irrefutable
impardonnable [ɛ̃pardɔnabl] *adj* unforgivable; **j'ai encore pris votre parapluie, je suis i.!** I've taken your umbrella again, how unforgivable of me!
imparfait, -e [ɛ̃parfɛ, -ɛt] **1** *adj* (**a**) *(qui a des défauts)* imperfect (**b**) *(inachevé)* unfinished
2 *nm Gram* imperfect (tense); **à l'i.** in the imperfect (tense)
impartial, -e, -aux, -ales [ɛ̃parsjal, -o] *adj* impartial, unbiased
impartialité [ɛ̃parsjalite] *nf* impartiality
impartir [ɛ̃partir] *vt Litt* **i. qch à qn** *(droit)* to grant sth to sb; *(tâche)* to assign sth to sb; **dans le délai imparti** within the time allowed; **le temps qui vous est imparti** the time allotted to you
impasse [ɛ̃pas] *nf* (**a**) *(cul-de-sac)* dead end, cul-de-sac; *Fig* impasse, deadlock; *Fig* **être dans une i.** to be deadlocked; *Fig* **sortir de l'i.** to break the deadlock (**b**) **faire une i.** *(en révisant)* = to miss out part of a subject when revising
impassibilité [ɛ̃pasibilite] *nf* impassiveness
impassible [ɛ̃pasibl] *adj* impassive
impatiemment [ɛ̃pasjamɑ̃] *adv* impatiently
impatience [ɛ̃pasjɑ̃s] *nf* impatience; **avec i.** impatiently
impatient, -e [ɛ̃pasjɑ̃, -ɑ̃t] **1** *adj* impatient; **d'un air i.** impatiently; **être i. de faire qch** to be impatient to do sth
2 *nf* **impatiente** *(plante)* Busy Lizzie
impatienter [ɛ̃pasjɑ̃te] **1** *vt* to annoy, to irritate
2 s'impatienter *vpr* to get impatient (**de/contre** at/with)
impavide [ɛ̃pavid] *adj Litt* impassive
impayable [ɛ̃pɛjabl] *adj Fam (histoire, personne)* priceless
impayé, -e [ɛ̃peje] **1** *adj* unpaid
2 *nm* outstanding payment

impec [ɛ̃pɛk] *adj Fam* spotless; **i.!** *(parfait)* great!
impeccable [ɛ̃pɛkabl] *adj* impeccable; **d'une propreté i.** impeccably clean; *Fam* **i.!** *(parfait)* great!
impeccablement [ɛ̃pɛkabləmɑ̃] *adv* impeccably
impénétrable [ɛ̃penetrabl] *adj* (**a**) *(forêt, citadelle)* impenetrable (**b**) *(visage, caractère, air)* inscrutable; *(mystère, texte)* impenetrable; **les voies du Seigneur sont impénétrables** God works in mysterious ways
impénitent, -e [ɛ̃penitɑ̃, -ɑ̃t] *adj* unrepentant
impensable [ɛ̃pɑ̃sabl] *adj* unthinkable; **il est i. que vous ne soyez pas remplacé** it's unthinkable that they're not going to replace you
imper [ɛ̃pɛr] *nm Fam* raincoat, *Br* mac
impératif, -ive [ɛ̃peratif, -iv] **1** *adj* (**a**) *(ton, geste)* imperious (**b**) *(nécessité, besoin)* imperative; **il est i. de connaître l'anglais** it is imperative to know English
2 *nm* (**a**) *(exigence)* requirement; **savoir nager est un i.** it is essential to be able to swim; **les impératifs de la mode** the dictates of fashion (**b**) *Gram* imperative (mood); **à l'i.** in the imperative (mood)
impérativement [ɛ̃perativmɑ̃] *adv* **il faut i. que je la voie** it is imperative that I see her
impératrice [ɛ̃peratris] *nf* empress
imperceptible [ɛ̃pɛrsɛptibl] *adj* imperceptible (**à** to)
imperceptiblement [ɛ̃pɛrsɛptibləmɑ̃] *adv* imperceptibly
imperdable [ɛ̃pɛrdabl] *adj* **le match/le procès est i.** the match/the case can't be lost
imperfectible [ɛ̃pɛrfɛktibl] *adj* imperfectible
imperfection [ɛ̃pɛrfɛksjɔ̃] *nf* imperfection
impérial, -e, -aux, -ales [ɛ̃perjal, -o] **1** *adj aussi Fig* imperial
2 *nf* **impériale** *(d'un bus)* top deck
impérialisme [ɛ̃perjalism] *nm* imperialism
impérialiste [ɛ̃perjalist] *adj & nmf* imperialist
impérieux, -euse [ɛ̃perjø, -øz] *adj* (**a**) *(autoritaire)* imperious (**b**) *(nécessité, désir, besoin)* urgent, pressing
impérissable [ɛ̃perisabl] *adj (œuvre, souvenir)* enduring; **ça ne m'a pas laissé un souvenir i.** it didn't make a lasting impression on me
imperméabilisant, -e [ɛ̃pɛrmeabilizɑ̃, -ɑ̃t] **1** *adj* waterproofing
2 *nm* waterproofing agent
imperméabiliser [ɛ̃pɛrmeabilize] *vt* to waterproof
imperméable [ɛ̃pɛrmeabl] **1** *adj* impermeable; *(à l'eau)* waterproof; *Fig* **être i. à qch** to be impervious to sth
2 *nm* raincoat, *Br* mackintosh
impersonnel, -elle [ɛ̃pɛrsɔnɛl] *adj* impersonal
impertinemment [ɛ̃pɛrtinamɑ̃] *adv* impertinently
impertinence [ɛ̃pɛrtinɑ̃s] *nf* impertinence; **avec i.** impertinently
impertinent, -e [ɛ̃pɛrtinɑ̃, -ɑ̃t] **1** *adj* impertinent
2 *nm,f* impertinent person; **un petit i.** an impertinent little boy
imperturbable [ɛ̃pɛrtyrbabl] *adj (personne)* imperturbable; *(optimisme)* unshakeable
imperturbablement [ɛ̃pɛrtyrbabləmɑ̃] *adv* imperturbably
impétigo [ɛ̃petigo] *nm* impetigo
impétueusement [ɛ̃petɥøzmɑ̃] *adv* impetuously

impétueux, -euse [ɛ̃petɥø, -øz] *adj* (**a**) *(personne)* impetuous; *(tempérament)* fiery (**b**) *Litt (torrent)* raging

impétuosité [ɛ̃petɥozite] *nf (fougue)* impetuosity

impie [ɛ̃pi] *Litt* **1** *adj* impious

2 *nmf* impious person

impitoyable [ɛ̃pitwajabl] *adj* merciless

impitoyablement [ɛ̃pitwajabləmɑ̃] *adv* mercilessly

implacable [ɛ̃plakabl] *adj (personne, vengeance, logique)* implacable; *(avancée)* relentless

implant [ɛ̃plɑ̃] *nm* implant; **i. mammaire** breast implant; **implants (capillaires)** hair graft

implantation [ɛ̃plɑ̃tasjɔ̃] *nf* (**a**) *(installation)* establishment (**b**) *(des cheveux)* line; *(des dents)* arch

implanter [ɛ̃plɑ̃te] **1** *vt* (**a**) *(installer)* to establish (**b**) *(chirurgicalement)* to implant

2 s'implanter *vpr* to become established

implication [ɛ̃plikasjɔ̃] *nf* (**a**) *(engagement)* involvement (**b**) **implications** *(conséquences)* implications

implicite [ɛ̃plisit] *adj* implicit

implicitement [ɛ̃plisitmɑ̃] *adv* implicitly

impliquer [ɛ̃plike] **1** *vt* (**a**) *(compromettre)* to implicate (**dans** in) (**b**) *(supposer)* to imply; **i. que** to imply that

2 s'impliquer *vpr* to get involved (**dans** in)

implorer [ɛ̃plɔre] *vt* to implore, to beseech; **i. le pardon de qn** to beg sb's forgiveness; **i. qn de faire qch** to implore *or* beseech sb to do sth

imploser [ɛ̃ploze] *vi* to implode

implosion [ɛ̃plozjɔ̃] *nf* implosion

impoli, -e [ɛ̃pɔli] *adj* impolite, rude

impoliment [ɛ̃pɔlimɑ̃] *adv* impolitely, rudely

impolitesse [ɛ̃pɔlitɛs] *nf* (**a**) *(d'une personne, d'une remarque)* impoliteness, rudeness (**b**) *(acte)* impolite act; *(remarque)* rude remark

impondérable [ɛ̃pɔ̃derabl] *adj & nm* imponderable

impopulaire [ɛ̃pɔpylɛr] *adj* unpopular

import [ɛ̃pɔr] *nm* (**a**) *Com* import; *Ordinat* **i. de données** data import (**b**) *Belg (montant)* amount; **une facture d'un i. de 2000 euros** a bill for 2,000 euros

importable [ɛ̃pɔrtabl] *adj (vêtement)* unwearable

importance [ɛ̃pɔrtɑ̃s] *nf* (**a**) *(d'un événement, d'un acte, d'une personne)* importance; **avoir de l'i. (pour)** to be important (to); **sans i.** unimportant; **cela n'a aucune i.** it's of no importance; **c'est d'une i. capitale** it's extremely important; **de la première** *ou* **de la plus haute i.** extremely important; **attacher** *ou* **donner de l'i. à qch** to attach importance to sth; **et alors, quelle i.?** well, so what? (**b**) *(d'une ville, d'une somme, d'un projet)* size; *(de dégâts, d'une catastrophe)* extent; **prendre de l'i.** *(société)* to expand; *(mouvement, parti)* to gain ground

important, -e [ɛ̃pɔrtɑ̃, -ɑ̃t] **1** *adj* (**a**) *(événement, acte, personne)* important (**pour** to); **il est i. que vous le sachiez** it's important for you to know; **peu i.** unimportant; **se donner des airs importants** to give oneself airs (**b**) *(ville, projet)* large; *(somme d'argent, dégâts, retard)* considerable; *(chiffre)* high

2 *nm,f Péj* **faire l'i.** to act important

3 *nm* **l'i., c'est que tu sois satisfait** the important thing is that you're satisfied

importateur, -trice [ɛ̃pɔrtatœr, -tris] **1** *nm,f* importer

2 *adj* importing; **les pays importateurs de pétrole** oil-importing countries

importation [ɛ̃pɔrtasjɔ̃] *nf* (**a**) *(de marchandises)* importing; **articles** *ou* **produits d'i.** imports; **licence d'i.** import licence (**b**) *(produit)* import

importer¹ [ɛ̃pɔrte] *vt (marchandises) & Ordinat* to import

importer² **1** *vi (compter)* to matter (**à** to); **ce qui importe, c'est que tu viennes** the important thing is that you come

2 *v impersonnel* (**a**) *(être important)* **il importe que vous y soyez** it's important that you're there; **peu importe** it doesn't matter; **peu m'importe** I don't mind; **qu'importe?** what does it matter? (**b**) **faire qch n'importe où/quand/comment** to do sth anywhere/any time/anyhow; *Fam* **n'importe comment, c'est trop tard** anyway, it's too late; **n'importe** never mind; **n'importe quel gamin** any child; **n'importe qui** anyone, anybody; **n'importe qui d'autre** anyone else; **n'importe quoi** anything; *Péj* **dire/écrire n'importe quoi** to talk/write nonsense; *Fam* **n'importe quoi!** rubbish!

import-export [ɛ̃pɔrɛkspɔr] *nm* import-export business

importun, -e [ɛ̃pɔrtœ̃, -yn] **1** *adj (personne, visiteur, question)* importunate; *(arrivée, remarque)* ill-timed

2 *nm,f (personne)* nuisance

importuner [ɛ̃pɔrtyne] *vt Sout* to bother

imposable [ɛ̃pozabl] *adj* taxable

imposant, -e [ɛ̃pozɑ̃, -ɑ̃t] *adj* imposing

imposé, -e [ɛ̃poze] *adj (taxé)* taxed; **être i. à la source** to be taxed at source

imposer [ɛ̃poze] **1** *vt* (**a**) *(une condition)* to impose (**à** on); **i. une tâche à qn** to set sb a task; **i. le respect** to command respect; **i. sa loi** to lay down the law; **i. le silence à qn** to make sb be quiet; **i. sa présence à qn** to impose on sb (**b**) *(soumettre à l'impôt)* to tax

2 *vi* **en i.** to be impressive; **en i. à qn** to impress sb

3 s'imposer *vpr* (**a**) *(faire reconnaître sa valeur)* to assert oneself; *(gagner)* to win (**b**) *(déranger)* **je ne voulais pas m'i.** I didn't want to impose (**c**) *(être nécessaire)* to be essential; **prendre les mesures qui s'imposent** to take the necessary steps (**d**) *(se contraindre)* **s'i. un sacrifice** to force oneself to make a sacrifice; **s'i. de faire qch** to make it a rule to do sth

imposition [ɛ̃pozisjɔ̃] *nf (taxation)* taxation

impossibilité [ɛ̃posibilite] *nf* impossibility; **être** *ou* **se trouver dans l'i. de faire qch** to find it impossible to do sth

impossible [ɛ̃posibl] **1** *adj* impossible; **i. à lire** impossible to read; **il est i. qu'il revienne avant lundi** he can't possibly be back before Monday; **il m'est i. de le faire** it's impossible for me to do it; **i. n'est pas français** there's no such word as can't; **rendre la vie i. à qn** to make life impossible for sb; **tu es i.!** you're impossible!

2 *nm* **tenter/demander l'i.** to attempt/ask the impossible; **faire l'i. pour faire qch** to do everything possible to do sth

imposteur [ɛ̃postœr] *nm* impostor

imposture [ɛ̃postyr] *nf* deception

impôt [ɛ̃po] *nm* tax; **payer 1000 euros d'impôts** to pay 1,000 euros in tax; *Fam* **les impôts m'ont envoyé une lettre** the tax man has sent me a letter; **i. direct/indirect** direct/indirect tax; **i. foncier** land tax; **i. sur les grandes fortunes** wealth tax; **impôts locaux**

local taxes; **i. sur le revenu** income tax; **i. sur les sociétés** corporation tax

Impôts locaux

These are taxes levied to finance local, departmental or regional government. The best-known are the "taxe d'habitation" (paid by rent-paying tenants), the "taxe foncière" (paid by home owners) and the "taxe professionnelle" (paid by the self-employed). The rate of each tax is decided at local level.

impotence [ɛpɔtɑ̃s] *nf (infirmité)* disability; *(due à la vieillesse)* infirmity

impotent, -e [ɛpɔtɑ̃, -ɑ̃t] **1** *adj (infirme)* disabled; *(à cause de la vieillesse)* infirm

  2 *nm,f (infirme)* disabled person; *(vieillard)* infirm person

impraticable [ɛpratikabl] *adj* (**a**) *(où l'on ne peut pas passer)* impassable (**b**) *(terrain de sport)* unfit for play (**c**) *(irréalisable)* impracticable

imprécation [ɛprekasjɔ̃] *nf Litt* imprecation

imprécis, -e [ɛpresi, -iz] *adj* imprecise

imprécision [ɛpresizjɔ̃] *nf* imprecision

imprégner [34] [ɛprɛɲe] **1** *vt* (**a**) *(sujet: eau, odeur)* to impregnate (**b**) *Fig (influencer)* **être imprégné de qch** to be full of sth

  2 s'imprégner *vpr* (**a**) *(s'imbiber)* to become impregnated (**de** with); **s'i. d'eau** to become soaked with water (**b**) *Fig* **s'i. d'un auteur** to immerse oneself in an author

imprenable [ɛprənabl] *adj* (**a**) *(forteresse, ville)* impregnable (**b**) *(vue)* unobstructed

imprésario [ɛpresarjo] *nm* manager

imprescriptible [ɛprɛskriptibl] *adj Jur* imprescriptible

impression [ɛpresjɔ̃] *nf* (**a**) *(sensation)* impression; **donner à qn l'i. que** to give sb the impression that; **faire bonne/mauvaise/forte i. (à qn)** to make a good/bad/strong impression (on sb); **ça m'a fait une drôle d'i.** it gave me a funny feeling; **j'ai l'i. de l'avoir déjà vue** I've a feeling that I've seen her before; **j'ai l'i. qu'elle est timide** I have the impression that she's shy (**b**) *(action d'imprimer)* printing; *(copie)* printout; *Ordinat* **i. écran** screen dump; **i. laser** laser printing; *(copie)* laser printout (**c**) *(motif)* **tissu à impressions florales** material with a floral pattern

impressionnable [ɛpresjɔnabl] *adj (personne)* impressionable

impressionnant, -e [ɛpresjɔnɑ̃, -ɑ̃t] *adj (imposant)* impressive; *(bouleversant)* upsetting

impressionner [ɛpresjɔne] *vt* (**a**) *(frapper)* to impress; *(bouleverser)* to upset; **se laisser i.** to let oneself be overawed (**b**) *Phot (pellicule)* to expose

impressionnisme [ɛpresjɔnism] *nm* impressionism

impressionniste [ɛpresjɔnist] *adj & nmf* impressionist

imprévisible [ɛprevizibl] *adj (temps, réaction, personne)* unpredictable; *(événement)* unforeseeable

imprévoyance [ɛprevwajɑ̃s] *nf* lack of foresight

imprévoyant, -e [ɛprevwajɑ̃, -ɑ̃t] *adj* lacking in foresight

imprévu, -e [ɛprevy] **1** *adj* unexpected, unforeseen

  2 *nm* (**a**) *(surprise)* **aimer l'i.** to like the unexpected; **un voyage plein d'i.** a journey full of surprises (**b**) *(incident)* unexpected *or* unforeseen event; **sauf i.,**

à moins d'un i. unless something unexpected happens

imprimable [ɛprimabl] *adj* printable

imprimante [ɛprimɑ̃t] *nf* printer; **i. à aiguilles** 24-pin printer; **i. à bulles (d'encre)** bubble-jet printer; **i. feuille à feuille** sheet-fed printer; **i. graphique** graphics printer; **i. à jet d'encre** ink-jet printer; **i. (à) laser** laser printer

imprimé, -e [ɛprime] **1** *adj* printed

  2 *nm* (**a**) *(formulaire)* form; **imprimés** *(journaux, prospectus)* printed matter (**b**) *(sur un tissu)* print; **un i. à fleurs/à motifs géométriques** a floral/geometric print

imprimer [ɛprime] *vt* (**a**) *(livre)* to print; *Ordinat* to print (out); *Ordinat* **i. un écran** to do a print screen (**b**) *(motif, empreinte, tissu)* to print (**c**) *(mouvement)* to impart (**à** to)

imprimerie [ɛprimri] *nf* (**a**) *(technique)* printing (**b**) *(atelier, usine)* printing works; **l'I. nationale** = French government printing office, *Br* ≃ Her Majesty's Stationery Office

imprimeur [ɛprimœr] *nm* printer

improbable [ɛprɔbabl] *adj* improbable, unlikely

improductif, -ive [ɛprɔdyktif, -iv] *adj* unproductive

impromptu, -e [ɛprɔ̃pty] *adj & nm* impromptu

imprononçable [ɛprɔnɔ̃sabl] *adj* unpronounceable

impropre [ɛprɔpr] *adj* (**a**) *(incorrect)* incorrect (**b**) *(inadapté)* **i. à qch** unfit for sth; **i. à la consommation** unfit for human consumption

improprement [ɛprɔprəmɑ̃] *adv* incorrectly

improvisation [ɛprɔvizasjɔ̃] *nf* improvisation; **faire une i.** to improvise

improvisé, -e [ɛprɔvize] *adj* improvised

improviser [ɛprɔvize] **1** *vt & vi* to improvise

  2 s'improviser *vpr* **un départ en vacances, ça ne s'improvise pas** going on holiday isn't something you can just like that

improviste [ɛprɔvist] **à l'improviste** *adv* unexpectedly

imprudemment [ɛprydamɑ̃] *adv (parler, agir)* rashly; *(conduire)* recklessly

imprudence [ɛprydɑ̃s] *nf (d'un acte, d'une personne)* rashness (**b**) *(acte)* **commettre une i.** to act rashly

imprudent, -e [ɛprydɑ̃, -ɑ̃t] **1** *adj* rash; *(conducteur)* reckless

  2 *nm,f* rash person

impubliable [ɛpyblijabl] *adj* unpublishable

impudence [ɛpydɑ̃s] *nf* impudence

impudent, -e [ɛpydɑ̃, -ɑ̃t] *adj* impudent

impudeur [ɛpydœr] *nf* shamelessness

impudique [ɛpydik] *adj* shameless

impuissance [ɛpɥisɑ̃s] *nf* (**a**) *(incapacité)* powerlessness (**à faire qch** to do sth) (**b**) *(sexuelle)* impotence

impuissant, -e [ɛpɥisɑ̃, -ɑ̃t] **1** *adj* (**a**) *(désarmé)* powerless (**b**) *(sexuellement)* impotent

  2 *nm* impotent man

impulsif, -ive [ɛpylsif, -iv] **1** *adj* impulsive

  2 *nm,f* impulsive person

impulsion [ɛpylsjɔ̃] *nf* (**a**) *Tech* impulse (**b**) *Fig (élan)* impulse; **faire qch sous l'i. de la colère** to do sth in a fit of anger (**c**) *(essor)* impetus

impulsivité [ɛpylsivite] *nf* impulsiveness

impunément [ɛpynemɑ̃] *adv* with impunity

impuni, -e [ɛpyni] *adj* unpunished

impunité [ɛpynite] *nf* impunity; **agir en toute i.** to act with impunity

impur, -e [ɛ̃pyr] *adj* impure
imputable [ɛ̃pytabl] *adj* (**a**) *(erreur)* attributable (**à** to) (**b**) *Fin* chargeable (**sur** to)
imputer [ɛ̃pyte] *vt* (**a**) *(crime, erreur)* **i. qch à qn** to attribute sth to sb (**b**) *Fin* **i. des frais sur un compte** to charge expenses to an account
inabordable [inabɔrdabl] *adj (endroit)* inaccessible; *(prix, marchandises)* unaffordable; *(personne)* unapproachable
inacceptable [inaksɛptabl] *adj* unacceptable
inaccessible [inaksesibl] *adj* (**a**) *(lieu)* inaccessible; *(objectif)* unattainable (**b**) *(personne)* unapproachable (**c**) *(insensible)* **i. à la pitié** incapable of pity; **i. à la flatterie** impervious to flattery
inachevé, -e [inaʃəve] *adj* unfinished
inactif, -ive [inaktif, -iv] **1** *adj* (**a**) *(personne)* inactive; *Écon* **la population inactive** the non-working population (**b**) *(remède)* ineffective
  2 *nm,f* **un i.** a person without paid employment; **les inactifs** the non-working population
inaction [inaksjɔ̃] *nf* inaction
inactivité [inaktivite] *nf* inactivity
inadapté, -e [inadapte] **1** *adj (personne) (socialement)* maladjusted; *(physiquement, mentalement)* handicapped; *(matériel)* unsuitable (**à** for)
  2 *nm,f (socialement)* maladjusted person; *(physiquement, mentalement)* handicapped person; **les inadaptés** the maladjusted/handicapped
inadéquation [inadekwasjɔ̃] *nf* inadequacy
inadmissible [inadmisibl] *adj* inadmissible
inadvertance [inadvɛrtɑ̃s] **par inadvertance** *adv* inadvertently
inaliénable [inaljenabl] *adj Jur (droit)* inalienable
inaltérable [inalterabl] *adj* (**a**) *(métal, revêtement)* stable (**b**) *Fig (constant)* unwavering
inamical, -e, -aux, -ales [inamikal, -o] *adj* unfriendly
inamovible [inamɔvibl] *adj* (**a**) *(four, autoradio)* built-in (**b**) *(juge, magistrat)* permanent
inanimé, -e [inanime] *adj* (**a**) *(mort)* lifeless; *(inconscient)* unconscious; **tomber i.** to fall down in a faint (**b**) *(objet)* inanimate
inanité [inanite] *nf (d'un effort)* futility; *(d'une conversation)* inanity
inanition [inanisjɔ̃] *nf* starvation; **mourir d'i.** to die of starvation
inaperçu, -e [inapɛrsy] *adj* **passer i.** to go unnoticed
inapplicable [inaplikabl] *adj (réforme, loi)* unenforceable; *(théorie)* inapplicable
inappréciable [inapresjabl] *adj (précieux)* invaluable
inapte [inapt] *adj (pour raisons médicales)* unfit; *(intellectuellement)* unsuited; **être i. à qch/à faire qch** *(pour raisons médicales)* to be unfit for sth/to do sth; *(intellectuellement)* to be unsuited for sth/to do sth; **être i. (au service)** *(appelé)* to be unfit (for service)
inaptitude [inaptityd] *nf (intellectuelle)* inaptitude; *(médicale, militaire)* unfitness (**à** for)
inarticulé, -e [inartikyle] *adj (son, cris)* inarticulate
inassouvi, -e [inasuvi] *adj (faim, désir, vengeance)* unsatisfied; *(soif)* unquenched
inattaquable [inatakabl] *adj* unassailable
inattendu, -e [inatɑ̃dy] *adj* unexpected
inattentif, -ive [inatɑ̃tif, -iv] *adj (distrait)* inattentive; **i. à qch** *(indifférent)* heedless of sth
inattention [inatɑ̃sjɔ̃] *nf* lack of attention; **un moment d'i.** a lapse of concentration

inaudible [inodibl] *adj* inaudible
inaugural, -e, -aux, -ales [inogyral, -o] *adj (discours, séance)* inaugural
inauguration [inogyrasjɔ̃] *nf (d'un bâtiment, d'une route)* (official) opening, inauguration; *(d'une statue, d'un monument)* unveiling; *Fig (d'une politique, d'une méthode)* implementation
inaugurer [inogyre] *vt (bâtiment, route)* to officially open, to inaugurate; *(statue, monument)* to unveil; *Fig (politique, méthode)* to implement; *(époque)* to usher in
inavouable [inavwabl] *adj* shameful
inavoué, -e [inavwe] *adj* unconfessed
INC [iɛnse] *nm (abrév* **Institut national de la consommation)** = national institute for consumer advice, *Br* ≃ National Consumer Council
inca [ɛ̃ka] **1** *adj* Inca
  2 *nmf* **I.** Inca
incalculable [ɛ̃kalkylabl] *adj* incalculable; **un nombre i. de fois** countless times
incandescence [ɛ̃kɑ̃desɑ̃s] *nf* incandescence
incandescent, -e [ɛ̃kɑ̃desɑ̃, -ɑ̃t] *adj* incandescent
incantation [ɛ̃kɑ̃tasjɔ̃] *nf* incantation
incantatoire [ɛ̃kɑ̃tatwar] *adj* incantatory
incapable [ɛ̃kapabl] **1** *adj* (**a**) *(incompétent)* incapable, incompetent; *Jur* incompetent (**b**) **être i. de faire qch** to be incapable of doing sth; **i. de lâcheté** incapable of cowardice
  2 *nmf* (**a**) *(incompétent)* incompetent; **espèce d'i.!** you useless idiot! (**b**) *Jur* incompetent person
incapacité [ɛ̃kapasite] *nf* (**a**) *(impossibilité)* **i. à faire qch** inability to do sth; **être dans l'i. de faire qch** to be unable to do sth (**b**) *(incompétence)* incompetence (**c**) *(invalidité)* disability; **i. de travail** unfitness for work (**d**) *Jur* incompetence
incarcération [ɛ̃karserasjɔ̃] *nf* incarceration
incarcérer [34] [ɛ̃karsere] *vt* to incarcerate
incarnation [ɛ̃karnasjɔ̃] *nf aussi Fig* incarnation
incarné, -e [ɛ̃karne] *adj* (**a**) *Rel & Fig* incarnate (**b**) *(ongle)* ingrowing
incarner [ɛ̃karne] **1** *vt* (**a**) *(représenter)* to embody (**b**) *Théât & Cin* **i. (le rôle de) qn** to play (the part of) sb
  2 **s'incarner** *vpr* (**a**) *Rel* to become incarnate (**b**) *(ongle)* to become ingrown
incartade [ɛ̃kartad] *nf* indiscretion
incassable [ɛ̃kasabl] *adj* unbreakable
incendiaire [ɛ̃sɑ̃djɛr] **1** *adj (bombe)* incendiary; *Fig (discours)* inflammatory
  2 *nmf (personne)* arsonist
incendie [ɛ̃sɑ̃di] *nm* fire; **i. de forêt** forest fire; **un i. criminel** arson
incendier [66] [ɛ̃sɑ̃dje] *vt* (**a**) *(mettre le feu à)* to set on fire (**b**) *Fam (accabler de reproches)* **i. qn** to haul sb over the coals; **se faire i.** to get hauled over the coals
incertain, -e [ɛ̃sɛrtɛ̃, -ɛn] *adj (fait, donnée, résultat)* uncertain; *(temps)* unsettled; *(mémoire)* unreliable; *(personne)* indecisive; *(démarche, pas)* unsteady; *(couleur)* vague
incertitude [ɛ̃sɛrtityd] *nf* uncertainty; **être dans l'i. (quant à)** to be uncertain (about)
incessamment [ɛ̃sesamɑ̃] *adv* very soon; **il doit arriver i.** he'll be here any minute now; *Hum* **i. sous peu** very soon
incessant, -e [ɛ̃sesɑ̃, -ɑ̃t] *adj* incessant, constant
incessible [ɛ̃sesibl] *adj (pension, titre de propriété)* non-transferable; *(droit)* inalienable

inceste [ɛ̃sɛst] *nm* incest

incestueux, -euse [ɛ̃sɛstɥø, -øz] *adj* incestuous; **enfant i.** child of an incestuous relationship

inchangé, -e [ɛ̃ʃɑ̃ʒe] *adj* unchanged

incidemment [ɛ̃sidamɑ̃] *adv* in passing

incidence [ɛ̃sidɑ̃s] *nf* (**a**) *(répercussion)* impact (**sur** on) (**b**) *Méd & Phys* incidence

incident, -e [ɛ̃sidɑ̃, -ɑ̃t] **1** *nm* (**a**) *(événement sans conséquence)* hitch; **se dérouler sans i.** to go off without incident; **i. de parcours** minor setback; **i. technique** technical hitch (**b**) *(événement plus grave)* incident; **i. diplomatique** diplomatic incident **2** *adj (question, remarque)* incidental

incinérateur [ɛ̃sineratœr] *nm* incinerator

incinération [ɛ̃sinerasjɔ̃] *nf (de déchets)* incineration; *(d'une personne)* cremation

incinérer [34] [ɛ̃sinere] *vt (déchets)* to incinerate; *(personne)* to cremate

inciser [ɛ̃size] *vt (peau)* to make an incision in; *(abcès)* to lance

incisif, -ive [ɛ̃sizif, -iv] **1** *adj (remarque, personne, style)* incisive **2** *nf* **incisive** *(dent)* incisor

incision [ɛ̃sizjɔ̃] *nf* incision; **pratiquer une i. dans** to make an incision in

incitation [ɛ̃sitasjɔ̃] *nf (à la violence, l'émeute)* incitement; *(encouragement)* incentive; **i. fiscale** tax incentive; **i. à l'achat** incentive to buy; **i. de mineurs à la débauche** corruption of minors

inciter [ɛ̃site] *vt* **i. qn à faire qch** to encourage sb to do sth; **i. qn à la prudence/la clémence** *(sujet: événement)* to incline sb to be cautious/merciful

inclassable [ɛ̃klasabl] *adj* unclassifiable; **un film/peintre i.** a film/painter that cannot be pigeonholed

inclinable [ɛ̃klinabl] *adj (siège, dossier)* reclining

inclinaison [ɛ̃klinɛzɔ̃] *nf (d'un toit)* slope; *(d'une pente)* incline; *(de la tête, d'un chapeau)* tilt

inclination [ɛ̃klinazjɔ̃] *nf* (**a**) **i. de la tête** *(pour saluer)* nod (**b**) *(tendance)* inclination (**pour** for)

incliné, -e [ɛ̃kline] *adj (mât, toit)* sloping; *(table à dessin, dossier)* tilted

incliner [ɛ̃kline] **1** *vt* (**a**) *(pencher)* to tilt; **i. la tête** *(en avant)* to bow one's head; *(en signe de salut)* to nod; *(sur le côté)* to tilt one's head to one side (**b**) *(pousser)* **i. qn à faire qch** to incline sb to do sth; **i. qn à la prudence/la clémence** to incline sb to be cautious/merciful **2** *vi* **j'incline à penser qu'elle a tort** I'm inclined to think she's wrong **3** **s'incliner** *vpr* (**a**) *(terrain)* to slant, to slope; *(bateau)* to heel *or* keel over; *(avion)* to bank (**b**) *(se pencher)* *(en avant)* to lean forward; *(sur le côté)* to lean to one side; *(pour saluer)* to bow; *Fig* **s'i. devant qch** to bow to sth (**c**) *(se soumettre)* to give in (**devant** to) (**d**) *(être battu)* to lose (**devant** to)

inclure [17b] [ɛ̃klyr] *vt* (**a**) *(dans un courrier)* to enclose (**dans** with) (**b**) *(englober, insérer) & Math* to include

inclus, -e [ɛ̃kly, -yz] *adj* (**a**) *(compris)* **jusqu'à la page 5 incluse** up to and including page 5; **jusqu'au mardi i.** *Br* up to and including Tuesday, *Am* through Tuesday; **du 7 au 18 i.** from the 7th to the 18th inclusive; **ils seront trente-cinq, professeurs i.** there will be thirty-five of them, including the teachers (**b**) *(dent)* impacted

inclusion [ɛ̃klyzjɔ̃] *nf* (**a**) *(dans un courrier)* enclosure (**dans** with) (**b**) *(insertion)* insertion (**c**) *(objet dé-*

coratif) = flower, shell etc set into plastic and used as a paperweight, an ornament, jewellery etc (**d**) *(d'une dent)* impacting (**e**) *Ordinat (de fichier)* insertion

incognito [ɛ̃kɔɲito] **1** *adv* incognito **2** *nm* **garder l'i.** to remain incognito

incohérence [ɛ̃kɔerɑ̃s] *nf (d'une personne, dans un film, une histoire)* inconsistency; *(d'un discours, d'idées)* incoherence

incohérent, -e [ɛ̃kɔerɑ̃, -ɑ̃t] *adj (personne, histoire, attitude)* inconsistent; *(idées, argumentation, discours)* incoherent; **tenir des propos incohérents** to talk incoherently

incollable [ɛ̃kɔlabl] *adj* (**a**) *(riz)* non-stick (**b**) *Fam (personne)* **elle est i. sur la question/en histoire** you can't catch her out on the subject/on history

incolore [ɛ̃kɔlɔr] *adj* colourless

incomber [ɛ̃kɔ̃be] **incomber à** *vt ind (responsabilité)* to lie with; *(devoirs)* to fall to; **il m'incombe/il lui incombe de...** it falls to me/to him/her to...

incombustible [ɛ̃kɔ̃bystibl] *adj* incombustible

incommensurable [ɛ̃kɔmɑ̃syrabl] *adj (richesse)* immeasurable; *(espace)* boundless; *Hum* **être d'une bêtise i.** to be incredibly stupid

incommodant, -e [ɛ̃kɔmɔdɑ̃, -ɑ̃t] *adj* discomforting

incommode [ɛ̃kɔmɔd] *adj (horaire, arrangement)* inconvenient; *(situation)* awkward

incommoder [ɛ̃kɔmɔde] *vt* to bother

incomparable [ɛ̃kɔ̃parabl] *adj (sans pareil)* beyond compare, matchless

incomparablement [ɛ̃kɔ̃parabləmɑ̃] *adv* incomparably

incompatibilité [ɛ̃kɔ̃patibilite] *nf* incompatibility; **i. d'humeur** *ou* **de caractère** mutual incompatibility

incompatible [ɛ̃kɔ̃patibl] *adj* incompatible (**avec** with)

incompétence [ɛ̃kɔ̃petɑ̃s] *nf* incompetence

incompétent, -e [ɛ̃kɔ̃petɑ̃, -ɑ̃t] *adj* incompetent

incomplet, -ète [ɛ̃kɔ̃plɛ, -ɛt] *adj* incomplete

incompréhensible [ɛ̃kɔ̃preɑ̃sibl] *adj* incomprehensible

incompréhension [ɛ̃kɔ̃preɑ̃sjɔ̃] *nf* incomprehension

incompressible [ɛ̃kɔ̃prɛsibl] *adj* (**a**) *(matériau)* incompressible (**b**) *Jur (peine)* to be served in full (**c**) *(dépenses)* which cannot be reduced

incompris, -e [ɛ̃kɔ̃pri, -iz] **1** *adj* misunderstood **2** *nm,f* **être un i.** to be misunderstood

inconcevable [ɛ̃kɔ̃səvabl] *adj* inconceivable

inconciliable [ɛ̃kɔ̃siljabl] *adj (théorie)* irreconcilable (**avec** with); *(mode de vie, activité)* incompatible (**avec** with)

inconditionnel, -elle [ɛ̃kɔ̃disjɔnɛl] **1** *adj (soutien, retrait)* unconditional; *(obéissance)* unquestioning, unconditional; *(supporter)* staunch **2** *nm,f* fan; **c'est un i. de la pêche/du hard rock** he's absolutely mad about fishing/hard rock

inconfort [ɛ̃kɔ̃fɔr] *nm (matériel)* discomfort; *(moral)* awkwardness

inconfortable [ɛ̃kɔ̃fɔrtabl] *adj aussi Fig* uncomfortable

incongru, -e [ɛ̃kɔ̃gry] *adj* inappropriate; *(bruit)* rude

incongruité [ɛ̃kɔ̃grɥite] *nf* (**a**) *(manque d'à-propos)* inappropriateness (**b**) *(remarque déplacée)* inappropriate remark

inconnu, -e [ɛ̃kɔny] **1** *adj (auteur, civilisation, destination)* unknown (**de** to); *(lieu, visage)* strange; **il m'est i.** I've never heard of him/it; **né de père i.** *(sur document administratif)* father unknown; **i. à cette adresse** not known at this address; *Fam* **Durand? i. au bataillon!** Durand? never heard of him!
2 *nm,f (étranger)* stranger; *(personne non célèbre)* unknown
3 *nm* **la peur de l'i.** fear of the unknown
4 *nf* **inconnue** *Math & Fig* unknown (quantity)
inconsciemment [ɛ̃kɔ̃sjamɑ̃] *adv* (**a**) *(sans réfléchir)* without thinking (**b**) *(dans l'inconscient)* subconsciously
inconscience [ɛ̃kɔ̃sjɑ̃s] *nf* (**a**) *(perte de connaissance)* unconsciousness; **sombrer** *ou* **tomber dans l'i.** to lose consciousness (**b**) *(manque de jugement)* recklessness; **c'est de l'i.!** it's sheer madness!
inconscient, -e [ɛ̃kɔ̃sjɑ̃, -ɑ̃t] **1** *adj* (**a**) *(évanoui)* unconscious (**b**) *(acte)* unconscious; **i. du danger** oblivious to the danger (**c**) *(irréfléchi) (personne)* reckless
2 *nm* **l'i.** the unconscious, the subconscious; **l'i. collectif** the collective unconscious
inconséquence [ɛ̃kɔ̃sekɑ̃s] *nf (caractère)* recklessness; *(acte)* reckless act
inconséquent, -e [ɛ̃kɔ̃sekɑ̃, -ɑ̃t] *adj* (**a**) *(irréfléchi)* reckless (**b**) *(illogique)* inconsistent
inconsidéré, -e [ɛ̃kɔ̃sidere] *adj (acte, remarque)* ill-considered; *(dépenses)* reckless
inconsistance [ɛ̃kɔ̃sistɑ̃s] *nf* (**a**) *(d'une pâte, d'une soupe)* thinness (**b**) *(d'une personne, d'une conduite)* inconsistency (**c**) *(d'une intrigue, d'un film, d'un roman)* flimsiness
inconsistant, -e [ɛ̃kɔ̃sistɑ̃, -ɑ̃t] *adj* (**a**) *(pâte, crème, soupe)* thin (**b**) *(conduite, personne)* inconsistent (**c**) *(intrigue, film, roman)* flimsy
inconsolable [ɛ̃kɔ̃sɔlabl] *adj* inconsolable
inconstance [ɛ̃kɔ̃stɑ̃s] *nf (instabilité)* changeable nature; *(infidélité)* fickleness
inconstant, -e [ɛ̃kɔ̃stɑ̃, -ɑ̃t] *adj (instable)* changeable; *(infidèle)* fickle
inconstitutionnel, -elle [ɛ̃kɔ̃stitysjɔnɛl] *adj* unconstitutional
incontestable [ɛ̃kɔ̃tɛstabl] *adj* indisputable
incontestablement [ɛ̃kɔ̃tɛstabləmɑ̃] *adv* indisputably
incontesté, -e [ɛ̃kɔ̃tɛste] *adj* undisputed
incontinence [ɛ̃kɔ̃tinɑ̃s] *nf Méd* incontinence; *Fig* **i. verbale** verbal diarrhoea
incontinent, -e [ɛ̃kɔ̃tinɑ̃, -ɑ̃t] *adj Méd* incontinent
incontournable [ɛ̃kɔ̃turnabl] *adj (problème)* that cannot be ignored; **son argument était i.** there was no getting away from his/her argument; **son dernier film est absolument i.** his/her latest film is an absolute must *or* is not to be missed
incontrôlable [ɛ̃kɔ̃trolabl] *adj* (**a**) *(incendie, bâillements)* uncontrollable; **des éléments incontrôlables** rowdy elements (**b**) *(affirmation)* unverifiable
incontrôlé, -e [ɛ̃kɔ̃trole] *adj (éléments, bande)* uncontrolled
inconvenance [ɛ̃kɔ̃vənɑ̃s] *nf (indécence)* impropriety; **dire/commettre une i.** to say/do something improper
inconvenant, -e [ɛ̃kɔ̃vənɑ̃, -ɑ̃t] *adj (propos, remarque, acte)* improper
inconvénient [ɛ̃kɔ̃venjɑ̃] *nm* drawback, disadvantage; **je n'y vois pas d'i.** I have no objection

inconvertible [ɛ̃kɔ̃vɛrtibl] *adj (monnaie)* non-convertible
incorporation [ɛ̃kɔrpɔrasjɔ̃] *nf* (**a**) *(mélange)* blending, mixing (**de qch dans qch** of sth into sth) (**b**) *Mil* conscription
incorporé, -e [ɛ̃kɔrpɔre] *adj (flash, micro)* built-in
incorporer [ɛ̃kɔrpɔre] **1** *vt* (**a**) *(mélanger)* **i. qch à qch** to blend *or* mix sth into sth (**b**) *(insérer)* to insert (**à** in) (**c**) *(troupes)* to draft
2 s'incorporer *vpr* **s'i. dans un groupe** to join a group
incorrect, -e [ɛ̃kɔrɛkt] *adj* (**a**) *(erroné)* incorrect, wrong (**b**) *(personne)* impolite; *(attitude)* improper (**c**) *(tenue) (déplacée)* unsuitable; *(indécente)* improper
incorrectement [ɛ̃kɔrɛktəmɑ̃] *adv* (**a**) *(en faisant des erreurs)* incorrectly, wrongly (**b**) *(impoliment)* impolitely (**c**) *(habillé) (de façon déplacée)* unsuitably; *(de façon indécente)* improperly
incorrection [ɛ̃kɔrɛksjɔ̃] *nf* (**a**) *(impolitesse)* impoliteness (**b**) *(action)* impolite action; *(propos)* impolite remark (**c**) *(grammaticale)* mistake
incorrigible [ɛ̃kɔriʒibl] *adj* incorrigible
incorruptible [ɛ̃kɔryptibl] **1** *adj* incorruptible
2 *nmf* incorruptible person
incrédule [ɛ̃kredyl] *adj (sceptique)* incredulous; **d'un air i.** with a look of disbelief
incrédulité [ɛ̃kredylite] *nf* incredulity
increvable [ɛ̃krəvabl] *adj* (**a**) *(pneu)* puncture-proof (**b**) *Fam (personne)* tireless; *(voiture, moteur)* indestructible
incriminer [ɛ̃krimine] *vt (personne)* to accuse; *(sujet, événement)* to condemn; *(comportement, décision)* to condemn
incrochetable [ɛ̃krɔʃtabl] *adj* unpickable
incroyable [ɛ̃krwajabl] *adj* incredible; **c'est i., ça!** don't believe it!; **d'une bêtise i.** incredibly stupid
incroyablement [ɛ̃krwajabləmɑ̃] *adv* incredibly
incroyance [ɛ̃krwajɑ̃s] *nf* unbelief
incroyant, -e [ɛ̃krwajɑ̃, -ɑ̃t] **1** *adj* unbelieving
2 *nm,f* unbeliever
incrustation [ɛ̃krystasjɔ̃] *nf* (**a**) *(ornement)* inlay (**b**) *(dépôt calcaire)* fur, scale (**c**) *TV (image)* inset
incruste [ɛ̃kryst] *nf Fam* **si on l'invite, il va encore taper l'i.** if we invite him, we'll never get rid of him; **elle a tapé l'i. à ma soirée** she gatecrashed my party
incruster [ɛ̃kryste] **1** *vt* (**a**) *(bois, métal)* to inlay (**de** with) (**b**) *(entartrer)* to scale, to fur up
2 s'incruster *vpr* (**a**) *(adhérer)* to become encrusted (**b**) *(chaudière, bouilloire)* to fur up (**c**) *Fam (s'imposer)* **quand on l'invite, il s'incruste** once you invite him you can't get rid of him
incubateur [ɛ̃kybatœr] *nm* incubator
incubation [ɛ̃kybasjɔ̃] *nf* incubation; **période d'i.** incubation period
incuber [ɛ̃kybe] *vt* to incubate, to hatch
inculpation [ɛ̃kylpasjɔ̃] *nf* indictment; **sous l'i. d'assassinat** charged with murder
inculpé, -e [ɛ̃kylpe] *nm,f* **l'i.** the accused
inculper [ɛ̃kylpe] *vt* to indict, to charge (**de** with)
inculquer [ɛ̃kylke] *vt* to instil (**à qn** in sb)
inculte [ɛ̃kylt] *adj (terre, personne)* uncultivated
incultivable [ɛ̃kyltivabl] *adj* untillable
inculture [ɛ̃kyltyr] *nf* lack of culture
incurable [ɛ̃kyrabl] **1** *adj* incurable; **d'une paresse i.** incurably lazy
2 *nmf* person with an incurable disease

incurie [ɛ̃kyri] *nf Sout* negligence

incursion [ɛ̃kyrsjɔ̃] *nf* (**a**) *(invasion)* raid, incursion (**b**) *Fig (entrée soudaine)* intrusion; **faire une i. dans une pièce/une réunion** to burst into a room/a meeting

incurvé, -e [ɛ̃kyrve] *adj* bent, curved

indatable [ɛ̃databl] *adj* that cannot be dated

Inde [ɛ̃d] *nf* **l'l.** India

indé, -e [ɛ̃de] *adj Fam (abrév* **indépendant**) indie; **le rock i.** indie (rock)

indéboulonnable [ɛ̃debulɔnabl] *adj* **il est i.!** they'll never be able to sack him!

indécence [ɛ̃desɑ̃s] *nf* indecency

indécent, -e [ɛ̃desɑ̃, -ɑ̃t] *adj* indecent

indéchiffrable [ɛ̃deʃifrabl] *adj* (**a**) *(illisible)* indecipherable (**b**) *(incompréhensible)* impenetrable

indéchirable [ɛ̃deʃirabl] *adj* tearproof

indécis, -e [ɛ̃desi, -iz] **1** *adj* (**a**) *(personne) (de caractère)* indecisive; *(ponctuellement)* undecided; **je suis encore i.** I haven't made my mind up yet (**b**) *(peu net) (victoire, bataille)* inconclusive; *(contour)* vague
2 *nm,f* indecisive person; *Pol* **les i.** the floating voters

indécision [ɛ̃desizjɔ̃] *nf (de caractère)* indecisiveness; *(ponctuelle)* indecision

indécrottable [ɛ̃dekrɔtabl] *adj Fam (incorrigible)* hopeless; **être d'une bêtise i.** to be hopelessly stupid

indéfendable [ɛ̃defɑ̃dabl] *adj* indefensible

indéfini, -e [ɛ̃defini] *adj* (**a**) *(illimité)* indefinite (**b**) *(imprécis) (tristesse, malaise)* vague, undefined (**c**) *Gram (pronom, article)* indefinite

indéfiniment [ɛ̃definimɑ̃] *adv* indefinitely

indéfinissable [ɛ̃definisabl] *adj* indefinable

indéformable [ɛ̃defɔrmabl] *adj* that keeps its shape

indélébile [ɛ̃delebil] *adj* indelible

indélicat, -e [ɛ̃delika, -at] *adj* (**a**) *(sans tact)* tactless, insensitive (**b**) *(malhonnête)* dishonest

indélicatesse [ɛ̃delikatɛs] *nf* (**a**) *(manque de tact)* tactlessness (**b**) *(malhonnêteté)* dishonesty; *(acte malhonnête)* dishonest act; **commettre une i.** to behave dishonestly

indemne [ɛ̃dɛmn] *adj* (**a**) *(physiquement)* unhurt, unharmed; **elle est sortie i. de la collision** she was unhurt in the collision (**b**) *(moralement)* unscathed; **il est sorti i. du scandale** he emerged unscathed from the scandal

indemnisation [ɛ̃dɛmnizasjɔ̃] *nf* compensation

indemniser [ɛ̃dɛmnize] *vt* to compensate (**de** for)

indemnité [ɛ̃dɛmnite] *nf* (**a**) *(pour perte encourue)* compensation; *(pour délai, non-livraison)* penalty (**b**) *(allocation)* allowance; **i. journalière** daily allowance; **i. de licenciement** severance pay, redundancy payment; **i. parlementaire** = salary paid to member of French parliament; **i. de transport** travel allowance

indémodable [ɛ̃demɔdabl] *adj* perennially fashionable

indémontrable [ɛ̃demɔ̃trabl] *adj* unprovable

indéniable [ɛ̃denjabl] *adj* undeniable

indéniablement [ɛ̃denjabləmɑ̃] *adv* undeniably

indenter [ɛ̃dɑ̃te] *vt Typ* to indent

indépendamment [ɛ̃depɑ̃damɑ̃] *adv* independently; **i. de** apart from

indépendance [ɛ̃depɑ̃dɑ̃s] *nf* independence; **accéder à l'i.** to gain independence

indépendant, -e [ɛ̃depɑ̃dɑ̃, -ɑ̃t] **1** *adj* (**a**) *(personne, pays, vie)* independent (**de** of); *(travailleur)* self-em-

ployed, freelance; *(appartement)* self-contained; **i. de ma volonté** beyond my control (**b**) *Gram* **proposition indépendante** main clause
2 *nm,f (travailleur)* self-employed person, freelancer; **travailler en i.** to work on a freelance basis

indépendantisme [ɛ̃depɑ̃datism] *nm* independence movement

indépendantiste [ɛ̃depɑ̃datist] *nmf Pol (partisan de l'indépendance)* supporter of independence; *(activiste)* freedom fighter

indéracinable [ɛ̃derasinabl] *adj (préjugés)* deep-rooted

indescriptible [ɛ̃dɛskriptibl] *adj* indescribable

indésirable [ɛ̃dezirabl] *adj & nmf* undesirable

indestructible [ɛ̃dɛstryktibl] *adj* indestructible

indétectable [ɛ̃detɛktabl] *adj* undetectable

indéterminé, -e [ɛ̃detɛrmine] *adj* (**a**) *(date, heure)* unspecified; *(raison)* unknown (**b**) *(personne)* undecided

index [ɛ̃dɛks] *nm* (**a**) *(doigt)* forefinger, index finger (**b**) *(de livre)* index; *Fig* **mettre qn/qch à l'i.** to blacklist sb/sth (**c**) *Ordinat* index (**d**) *Méd* **i. glycémique** glycaemic index

indexation [ɛ̃dɛksasjɔ̃] *nf* (**a**) *Écon* index-linking (**sur** to) (**b**) *Ordinat* indexing

indexer [ɛ̃dɛkse] *vt* (**a**) *Écon* to index-link (**sur** to) (**b**) *aussi Ordinat (ajouter un index à)* to index

indic [ɛ̃dik] *nm Fam* squealer, *Br* grass

indicateur, -trice [ɛ̃dikatœr, -tris] **1** *adj voir* **panneau, poteau**
2 *nm* (**a**) *(livre)* **i. des rues de Paris** Paris street finder; **i. des chemins de fer** railway timetable (**b**) *(instrument)* indicator, gauge; *Aviat* **i. d'altitude** altimeter; **i. de niveau de carburant** fuel gauge (**c**) *(informateur)* informer (**d**) *Écon* indicator

indicatif, -ive [ɛ̃dikatœr, -iv] **1** *adj* indicative (**de** of); **à titre i.** as a guide
2 *nm* (**a**) *Gram* indicative (mood); **à l'i.** in the indicative (**b**) *Tél Br* dialling code, *Am* dial code; *TV & Rad* theme tune

indication [ɛ̃dikasjɔ̃] *nf* (**a**) *(action)* indication (**b**) *(renseignement)* (piece of) information (**c**) *(directive)* instruction, direction; **sauf i. contraire** unless otherwise specified; *Théât* **indications scéniques** stage directions (**d**) *(sur notice pharmaceutique)* **indications:...** suitable for...

indice [ɛ̃dis] *nm* (**a**) *(signe)* sign, indication (**de** of); *(dans une enquête)* clue (**de** to) (**b**) *(chiffre indicateur) & Math* index; *Typ* subscript; *Méd* **i. de masse corporelle** body mass index; *Aut* **i. d'octane** octane rating; **i. des prix** price index; **i. de protection** *(d'une crème solaire)* protection factor

indicible [ɛ̃disibl] *adj Litt* indescribable

indien, -enne [ɛ̃djɛ̃, -ɛn] **1** *adj (de l'Inde)* Indian; *(d'Amérique)* American Indian, Native American
2 *nm,f* **I.** *(de l'Inde)* Indian; *(d'Amérique)* American Indian, Native American

indifféremment [ɛ̃diferamɑ̃] *adv (sans distinction)* equally

indifférence [ɛ̃diferɑ̃s] *nf* indifference

indifférencié, -e [ɛ̃diferɑ̃sje] *adj* undifferentiated

indifférent, -e [ɛ̃diferɑ̃, -ɑ̃t] *adj* (**a**) *(peu ou pas intéressé)* indifferent (**à** to); **laisser qn i.** to leave sb cold; **il m'est i.** I'm indifferent to him (**b**) *(sans importance)* irrelevant; **cela m'est i.** it makes no difference to me; **parler de choses indifférentes** to chat about nothing in particular

indifférer [34] [ɛ̃difere] *vt* **cela m'indiffère** it's a matter of complete indifference to me

indigence [ɛ̃diʒɑ̃s] *nf* destitution

indigène [ɛ̃diʒɛn] **1** *adj* native; *Bot & Zool* native, indigenous (**de** to)
  2 *nmf* (**a**) *(autochtone) & Bot & Zool* native (**b**) *Suisse (citoyen)* citizen

indigent, -e [ɛ̃diʒɑ̃, -ɑ̃t] **1** *adj* destitute
  2 *nm,f* pauper; **les indigents** the poor

indigeste [ɛ̃diʒɛst] *adj aussi Fig* indigestible

indigestion [ɛ̃diʒɛstjɔ̃] *nf* **avoir une i.** to have a stomach upset; **faire une i. de chocolat** to make oneself sick from eating chocolate; *Fig* **j'en ai une i.** I'm fed up with it

indignation [ɛ̃diɲasjɔ̃] *nf* indignation

indigne [ɛ̃diɲ] *adj (personne)* unworthy (**de** of); *(action, conduite)* shameful

indigner [ɛ̃diɲe] **1** *vt* to outrage
  2 s'indigner *vpr* to be indignant (**de** at)

indignité [ɛ̃diɲite] *nf* (**a**) *(d'une personne)* unworthiness; *(d'une action)* shamefulness (**b**) *(action)* shameful act

indigo [ɛ̃digo] *nm & adj inv* indigo

indiqué, -e [ɛ̃dike] *adj (recommandé)* advisable; **il est tout à fait i. pour ce poste** he's the right person for the job

indiquer [ɛ̃dike] *vt* (**a**) *(montrer) (sujet: personne)* to point out; **i. qch du doigt** to point to *or* at sth; **i. le chemin à qn** to tell sb the way, to direct sb (**b**) *(marquer) (sujet: panneau, étiquette, carte)* to show, to indicate; *(sujet: compteur)* to show, to read (**c**) *(donner) (date, adresse)* to give; **à l'heure indiquée** at the agreed time; **pourriez-vous m'i. le prix de ce vase?** could you tell me how much this vase costs? (**d**) *(recommander)* to recommend; **elle m'a indiqué un excellent dentiste/hôtel** she recommended an excellent dentist/hotel to me (**e**) *(dénoter)* to point to, to indicate

indirect, -e [ɛ̃dirɛkt] *adj aussi Gram* indirect

indirectement [ɛ̃dirɛktəmɑ̃] *adv* indirectly

indiscipline [ɛ̃disiplin] *nf* indiscipline

indiscipliné, -e [ɛ̃disipline] *adj* undisciplined; *(cheveux)* unmanageable

indiscret, -ète [ɛ̃diskrɛ, -ɛt] **1** *adj* (**a**) *(qui parle trop)* indiscreet (**b**) *(curieux)* inquisitive; **à l'abri des regards indiscrets** safe from prying eyes
  2 *nm,f* (**a**) *(qui parle trop)* indiscreet person (**b**) *(curieux)* inquisitive person

indiscrétion [ɛ̃diskresjɔ̃] *nf* (**a**) *(manque de discrétion)* indiscretion (**b**) *(curiosité)* inquisitiveness; **sans i., combien l'avez-vous payé?** if you don't mind me asking, how much did you pay for it? (**c**) *(remarque)* indiscreet remark; **commettre une i.** to say something one shouldn't

indiscutable [ɛ̃diskytabl] *adj* indisputable

indiscutablement [ɛ̃diskytabləmɑ̃] *adv* indisputably

indispensable [ɛ̃dispɑ̃sabl] **1** *adj* indispensable, essential (**à qch** for sth); **i. à qn** indispensable to sb; **il est i. que tu y ailles** it is essential that you go
  2 *nm* **l'i.** the essentials

indisponibilité [ɛ̃disponibilite] *nf* unavailability

indisponible [ɛ̃disponibl] *adj* unavailable

indisposé, -e [ɛ̃dispoze] *adj* indisposed, unwell; *Euph* **elle est indisposée** it's her time of the month

indisposer [ɛ̃dispoze] *vt* (**a**) *(rendre malade)* **i. qn** *(odeur, climat)* to make sb feel ill; *(nourriture)* to disagree with sb (**b**) *(contrarier)* to annoy

indisposition [ɛ̃dispozisjɔ̃] *nf* indisposition, slight illness

indissociable [ɛ̃disɔsjabl] *adj* indissociable (**de** from)

indissoluble [ɛ̃disɔlybl] *adj* indissoluble

indistinct, -e [ɛ̃distɛ̃, -ɛ̃kt] *adj* indistinct

indistinctement [ɛ̃distɛ̃ktəmɑ̃] *adv* (**a**) *(voir, parler)* indistinctly (**b**) *(indifféremment)* equally

individu [ɛ̃dividy] *nm* (**a**) *(être humain)* individual (**b**) *Péj (homme)* individual, character; **un drôle d'i.** a strange individual *or* character

individualiser [ɛ̃dividɥalize] *vt* (**a**) *(différencier)* to make individual (**b**) *(adapter)* to adapt to individual circumstances

individualisme [ɛ̃dividɥalism] *nm* individualism

individualiste [ɛ̃dividɥalist] **1** *adj* individualistic
  2 *nmf* individualist

individualité [ɛ̃dividɥalite] *nf* individuality

individuel, -elle [ɛ̃dividɥɛl] *adj* individual; *(liberté, responsabilité)* personal; *(maison)* detached; *(chambre)* single

individuellement [ɛ̃dividɥɛlmɑ̃] *adv* individually

indivisible [ɛ̃divizibl] *adj* indivisible

Indochine [ɛ̃dɔʃin] *nf* **l'I.** Indochina

indocile [ɛ̃dɔsil] *adj* disobedient

indo-européen, -enne (*mpl* **indo-européens**, *fpl* **indo-européennes**) [ɛ̃dɔørɔpeɛ̃, -ɛn] **1** *adj* Indo-European
  2 *nm,f* **I.-E.** Indo-European

indolence [ɛ̃dɔlɑ̃s] *nf* laziness

indolent, -e [ɛ̃dɔlɑ̃, -ɑ̃t] *adj* lazy

indolore [ɛ̃dɔlɔr] *adj* painless

indomptable [ɛ̃dɔ̃tabl] *adj* (**a**) *(animal)* untamable (**b**) *Fig (orgueil, caractère)* indomitable; *(passion)* uncontrollable

indompté, -e [ɛ̃dɔ̃te] *adj* (**a**) *(animal)* untamed (**b**) *Fig (passion, orgueil)* uncontrolled

Indonésie [ɛ̃dɔnezi] *nf* **l'I.** Indonesia

indonésien, -enne [ɛ̃dɔnezjɛ̃, -ɛn] **1** *adj* Indonesian
  2 *nm,f* **I.** Indonesian

indu, -e [ɛ̃dy] *adj* **à une heure indue** at an ungodly hour; **il rentre à des heures indues** he comes home at all hours

indubitable [ɛ̃dybitabl] *adj* indisputable, indubitable; **c'est i.** there's no doubt about it

indubitablement [ɛ̃dybitabləmɑ̃] *adv* undoubtedly

induire [18] [ɛ̃dɥir] *vt* (**a**) *(entraîner)* **i. qn à faire qch** to induce sb to do sth; **i. qn en erreur** to mislead sb (**b**) *(conclure)* to infer (**de** from)

indulgence [ɛ̃dylʒɑ̃s] *nf* (**a**) *(bienveillance)* indulgence, leniency; **faire preuve d'i. envers qn** to be indulgent towards sb; **rires sans i.** merciless laughter; **faire de qn un portrait sans i.** to describe sb warts and all (**b**) *Rel* indulgence

indulgent, -e [ɛ̃dylʒɑ̃, -ɑ̃t] *adj* indulgent

indûment [ɛ̃dymɑ̃] *adv* unduly

industrialisation [ɛ̃dystrijalizasjɔ̃] *nf* industrialization

industrialiser [ɛ̃dystrijalize] **1** *vt* to industrialize
  2 s'industrialiser *vpr* to become industrialized

industrie [ɛ̃dystri] *nf* industry; **travailler dans l'i.** to work in industry; **l'i. alimentaire** the food industry; **l'i. automobile** the car industry; **l'i. lourde** heavy industry; **l'i. pharmaceutique** the pharmaceutical industry

industriel, -elle [ɛ̃dystrijɛl] **1** adj industrial; Fam **des magazines en quantité industrielle** vast quantities of magazines **2** nm manufacturer, industrialist

industriellement [ɛ̃dystrijɛlmɑ̃] adv industrially

industrieux, -euse [ɛ̃dystrijø, -øz] adj Litt (habile) skilful, ingenious; (travailleur) industrious

inébranlable [inebrɑ̃labl] adj (mur, rocher) immovable; Fig unshakeable

inédit, -e [inedi, -it] **1** adj (a) (livre) previously unpublished; (disque) previously unreleased (b) (spectacle, projet, idée) new, original **2** nm (texte) previously unpublished work; (disque) previously unreleased record

ineffable [inefabl] adj ineffable, unutterable

ineffaçable [inefasabl] adj aussi Fig indelible

inefficace [inefikas] adj (personne) inefficient; (remède, méthode, loi) ineffective

inefficacité [inefikasite] nf (de personne) inefficiency; (d'un remède, d'une méthode, d'une loi) ineffectiveness

inégal, -e, -aux, -ales [inegal, -o] adj (a) (non égal) (parts, partage, force, lutte) unequal (b) (irrégulier) (sol) uneven; (pouls) irregular; Fig (travail, écrivain, style, qualité) inconsistent; (humeur) changeable

inégalable [inegalabl] adj incomparable, matchless

inégalé, -e [inegale] adj (qualité, personne) unequalled; (record) unbeaten

inégalement [inegalmɑ̃] adv (a) (injustement) unequally (b) (irrégulièrement) unevenly

inégalitaire [inegalitɛr] adj unequal

inégalité [inegalite] nf (a) (injustice) inequality (entre between) (b) (différence) disparity (de in) (c) (du sol) unevenness; Fig **i. d'humeur** moodiness

inélégant, -e [inelegɑ̃, -ɑ̃t] adj Litt (mal habillé) inelegant; (discourtois) discourteous

inéligible [ineliʒibl] adj ineligible

inéluctable [inelyktabl] adj inescapable

inemployable [inɑ̃plwajabl] adj unusable

inemployé, -e [inɑ̃plwaje] adj (objet, machine, talent) unused; (ressources) untapped; (forces) unchannelled

inénarrable [inenarabl] adj comical

inepte [inɛpt] adj (remarque, réponse, histoire) inane; (personne) inept

ineptie [inɛpsi] nf (a) (d'un comportement, d'un film) inanity (b) (action) stupid thing; (remarque) stupid comment; **dire des inepties** to talk nonsense

inépuisable [inepɥizabl] adj (réserves, sujet, curiosité) inexhaustible; (imagination) limitless; **sur ce sujet-là, elle est i.** you can never get her off the subject

inerte [inɛrt] adj (a) Phys inert (b) (personne) (inanimé) lifeless; (passif) apathetic

inertie [inɛrsi] nf (a) Phys inertia (b) (manque de réaction) apathy

inespéré, -e [inɛspere] adj unexpected, unhoped-for

inesthétique [inɛstetik] adj unaesthetic

inestimable [inɛstimabl] adj (dégâts, coût, richesse) incalculable; (aide, chance) invaluable; (œuvre d'art) priceless; **d'une valeur i.** priceless

inévitable [inevitabl] adj inevitable, unavoidable

inévitablement [inevitabləmɑ̃] adv inevitably, unavoidably

inexact, -e [inɛgzakt] adj (a) (incorrect) (réponse, description, détail) inaccurate; (somme, calcul) wrong, incorrect (b) (manquant de ponctualité) unpunctual

inexactitude [inɛgzaktityd] nf (a) (caractère erroné, erreur) inaccuracy (b) (manque de ponctualité) unpunctuality

inexcusable [inɛkskyzabl] adj inexcusable, unforgivable

inexhaustible [inɛgzostibl] adj Litt inexhaustible

inexistant, -e [inɛgzistɑ̃, -ɑ̃t] adj non-existent; Hum **il est totalement i.** he's a complete nonentity

inexistence [inɛgzistɑ̃s] nf non-existence

inexorable [inɛgzɔrabl] adj (destin) inexorable; (juge) pitiless; (volonté) inflexible

inexorablement [inɛgzɔrabləmɑ̃] adv inexorably

inexpérience [inɛksperjɑ̃s] nf inexperience

inexpérimenté, -e [inɛksperimɑ̃te] adj inexperienced

inexplicable [inɛksplikabl] adj inexplicable

inexpliqué, -e [inɛksplike] adj unexplained

inexploité, -e [inɛksplwate] adj (mine) unworked; (terre) undeveloped; (ressources) untapped

inexploré, -e [inɛksplɔre] adj unexplored

inexpressif, -ive [inɛkspresif, -iv] adj inexpressive, expressionless

inexprimable [inɛksprimabl] adj inexpressible

inexprimé, -e [inɛksprime] adj unexpressed

in extenso [inɛkstɛ̃so] adv in full

in extremis [inɛkstremis] adv at the last minute

inextricable [inɛkstrikabl] adj inextricable

inextricablement [inɛkstrikabləmɑ̃] adv inextricably

infaillibilité [ɛ̃fajibilite] nf infallibility

infaillible [ɛ̃fajibl] adj infallible

infailliblement [ɛ̃fajibləmɑ̃] adv infallibly

infaisable [ɛ̃fəzabl] adj not feasible, impossible

infamant, -e [ɛ̃famɑ̃, -ɑ̃t] adj (a) (déclaration, accusation) defamatory, slanderous (b) Jur (peine) involving loss of civil rights

infâme [ɛ̃fam] adj (mensonge, personne) despicable; (acte, crime) unspeakable; (taudis) squalid; (odeur, nourriture) revolting

infamie [ɛ̃fami] nf (a) (caractère infâme) infamy (b) (action) unspeakable act; (remarque) slanderous remark

infant, -e [ɛ̃fɑ̃, -ɑ̃t] nm,f infante, f infanta

infanterie [ɛ̃fɑ̃tri] nf infantry; **i. de marine** marine corps, marines

infanticide [ɛ̃fɑ̃tisid] **1** adj infanticidal **2** nmf (personne) child-killer, infanticide **3** nm (crime) infanticide

infantile [ɛ̃fɑ̃til] adj (a) (maladie) childhood (b) Péj (comportement, personne) childish, infantile

infantiliser [ɛ̃fɑ̃tilize] vt Péj **la télévision infantilise les gens** television makes people behave like children

infarctus [ɛ̃farktys] nm heart attack; **i. du myocarde** myocardial infarction, coronary thrombosis

infatigable [ɛ̃fatigabl] adj tireless

infatué, -e [ɛ̃fatɥe] adj Litt conceited; **i. de soi-même** full of oneself

infécond, -e [ɛ̃fekɔ̃, -ɔ̃d] adj infertile

infect, -e [ɛ̃fɛkt] adj foul

infecter [ɛ̃fɛkte] **1** vt (**a**) (plaie, blessure) to infect (**b**) (atmosphère, eau, sol) to contaminate
2 s'infecter vpr to become infected, to go septic
infectieux, -euse [ɛ̃fɛksjø, -øz] adj infectious
infection [ɛ̃fɛksjɔ̃] nf (**a**) Méd & Ordinat infection; **i. sexuellement transmissible** sexually transmitted infection (**b**) (puanteur) stench, stink; **quelle i. dans cette pièce!** this room stinks!
inférieur, -e [ɛ̃ferjœr] **1** adj (**a**) (qui est en bas) (étagère, niveau) bottom; (étages, lèvre, paupière, membres, mâchoire) lower; **partie inférieure** bottom (part); **allez voir à l'étage i.** go and look on the floor below (**b**) (dans une hiérarchie) (qualité, marchandises, intelligence) inferior; **d'un rang i.** of a lower rank; **être rétrogradé à l'échelon i.** to be demoted to the grade below (**c**) (dans une comparaison) **i. à** (qualité) inferior to; (quantité) less than; **i. ou égal à** less than or equal to; **note inférieure à douze** mark below twelve; **i. en nombre** fewer in number; **i. à la moyenne** below average
2 nm,f inferior
infériorité [ɛ̃ferjɔrite] nf inferiority
infernal, -e, -aux, -ales [ɛ̃fɛrnal, -o] adj (**a**) (de l'enfer) infernal; Fig (cruauté, méchanceté) diabolical (**b**) Fam (insupportable) (chaleur, bruit) infernal; **à une vitesse infernale** at breakneck speed; **des cadences infernales** an impossible rate of work; **cet enfant est i.** that child's a little devil
infertile [ɛ̃fɛrtil] adj infertile
infertilité [ɛ̃fɛrtilite] nf infertility
infester [ɛ̃fɛste] vt (sujet: vermine) to infest; Fig (sujet: personnes) to overrun; **infesté de** infested/overrun with
infidèle [ɛ̃fidɛl] **1** adj (**a**) (déloyal) unfaithful (**à** to) (**b**) (inexact) (traduction, rapport) inaccurate (**c**) Rel infidel
2 nmf Rel infidel
infidélité [ɛ̃fidelite] nf (**a**) (déloyauté) unfaithfulness (**à** to); **faire des infidélités à** to be unfaithful to (**b**) (manque d'exactitude) (dans une traduction, un compte rendu) inaccuracy
infiltration [ɛ̃filtrasjɔ̃] nf (**a**) (d'un liquide) infiltration; **il y a des infiltrations dans le plafond** there are some leaks in the ceiling (**b**) (d'espions) infiltration (**c**) (piqûre) **faire des infiltrations à qn** to give sb injections
infiltrer [ɛ̃filtre] **1** vt (noyauter) (parti, pays) to infiltrate
2 s'infiltrer vpr (**a**) (fluide) to infiltrate; **s'i. dans** seep into (**b**) (espion) **s'i. dans** to infiltrate
infime [ɛ̃fim] adj tiny
infini, -e [ɛ̃fini] **1** adj infinite; **ça prend un temps i.** it takes an eternity
2 nm l'i. infinity; **à l'i.** (s'étendre, se refléter) to infinity; (discutailler) ad infinitum
infiniment [ɛ̃finimɑ̃] adv (énormément) infinitely; **i. petit** infinitesimal; **i. reconnaissant** extremely grateful; **je regrette i.** I'm terribly sorry
infinité [ɛ̃finite] nf infinity; **une i. de** an infinite number of
infinitésimal, -e, -aux, -ales [ɛ̃finitezimal, -o] adj infinitesimal
infinitif, -ive [ɛ̃finitif, -iv] **1** adj infinitive
2 nm infinitive; **à l'i.** in the infinitive
infirmation [ɛ̃firmasjɔ̃] nf Jur invalidation
infirme [ɛ̃firm] **1** adj disabled
2 nmf disabled person; **les infirmes** the disabled

infirmer [ɛ̃firme] vt to invalidate
infirmerie [ɛ̃firmɔri] nf (d'une prison, d'une caserne) infirmary; (à l'école, dans un bateau) sick bay
infirmier, -ière [ɛ̃firmje, -ɛr] nf nurse; **i. de jour/nuit** day/night nurse
infirmité [ɛ̃firmite] nf disability
inflammable [ɛ̃flamabl] adj inflammable, flammable
inflammation [ɛ̃flamasjɔ̃] nf Méd inflammation; **j'ai une i. au genou** my knee is inflamed
inflation [ɛ̃flasjɔ̃] nf inflation
inflationniste [ɛ̃flɑsjɔnist] adj inflationary
infléchir [ɛ̃fleʃir] **1** vt (**a**) (rayon) to bend (**b**) (politique) to change the direction of; **i. le cours des événements** to change the course of events
2 s'infléchir vpr (**a**) (dévier) (route, ligne) to bend (**b**) (changer) (politique) to change direction
inflexibilité [ɛ̃flɛksibilite] nf inflexibility
inflexible [ɛ̃flɛksibl] adj inflexible
inflexion [ɛ̃flɛksjɔ̃] nf (**a**) (mouvement) **i. du corps** bend of the body; (pour saluer) bow; **i. de (la) tête** tilt of the head; (pour saluer, acquiescer) nod (**b**) (de la voix) inflection (**c**) (de courbe, rayon) inflection
infliger [45] [ɛ̃fliʒe] vt **i. qch à qn** (punition) to inflict sth on sb; (peine, amende) to impose sth on sb
influençable [ɛ̃flyɑ̃sabl] adj easily influenced
influence [ɛ̃flyɑ̃s] nf influence (**sur** on); **trafic d'i.** corruption (involving a public official)
influencer [16] [ɛ̃flyɑ̃se] vt to influence; **il ne faut pas te laisser i.** you mustn't let yourself be influenced; **il se laisse facilement i.** he's easily influenced
influent, -e [ɛ̃flyɑ̃, -ɑ̃t] adj influential
influer [ɛ̃flye] vi **i. sur** to influence
influx [ɛ̃fly] nm **i. nerveux** nerve impulse
info [ɛ̃fo] nf Fam (nouvelle) news item; **les infos** the news (singulier)
Infographie® [ɛ̃fɔgrafi] nf computer graphics
informateur, -trice [ɛ̃fɔrmatœr, -tris] nm,f informant; (de police) informer
informaticien, -enne [ɛ̃fɔrmatisjɛ̃, -ɛn] **1** nm,f computer scientist
2 adj **ingénieur i.** computer engineer
information [ɛ̃fɔrmasjɔ̃] nf (**a**) (renseignement) (piece of) information; **informations** information; **pour votre i.** for your information; **à titre d'i.** for information; **assurer l'i. du public en matière de santé** to ensure that the public is kept informed about health matters; **le droit à l'i.** freedom of information (**b**) (nouvelle) news item; **une i. de dernière minute** some late news; **les informations** the news (singulier) (**c**) (médias) l'i. the media (**d**) Ordinat data, information; **les sciences de l'i.** information sciences, informatics; **traitement de l'i.** data processing; **théorie de l'i.** information theory (**e**) Jur (enquête) inquiry; (instruction préparatoire) preliminary investigation; **ouvrir une i.** to begin legal proceedings
informatique [ɛ̃fɔrmatik] nf (traitement de l'information) data processing; (science) computer science, IT; **travailler dans l'i.** to work in computers or IT; **société/magazine/cours d'i.** computer company/magazine/course
informatisation [ɛ̃fɔrmatizasjɔ̃] nf computerization
informatiser [ɛ̃fɔrmatize] **1** vt to computerize
2 s'informatiser vpr to become computerized; **depuis que je me suis informatisé** since I got a computer

informe [ɛ̃fɔrm] *adj (masse, objet, vêtement)* shapeless; *(monstre, être)* misshapen
informé, -e [ɛ̃fɔrme] **1** *adj* informed; **bien i.** well-informed; **mal i.** ill-informed; **dans les milieux informés** in informed circles
2 *nm Jur* inquiry; **jusqu'à plus ample i.** until we have further information
informel, -elle [ɛ̃fɔrmɛl] *adj* informal
informer [ɛ̃fɔrme] **1** *vt* to inform (**de** of); **i. qn que...** to inform sb that...; **nous informons les voyageurs que...** we would like to inform passengers that...
2 s'informer *vpr (se renseigner)* to inquire, to ask (**de/au sujet de** about); *(se tenir au courant)* to keep oneself informed
inforoute [ɛ̃fɔrut] *nf Can Ordinat* information superhighway, infohighway
infortune [ɛ̃fɔrtyn] *nf* misfortune; **compagnons d'i.** companions in adversity
infortuné, -e [ɛ̃fɔrtyne] **1** *adj* unfortunate
2 *nm,f* unfortunate wretch
infoutu, -e [ɛ̃futy] *adj Fam* **être i. de faire qch** to be downright incapable of doing sth
infraction [ɛ̃fraksjɔ̃] *nf (à un règlement, à la loi)* infringement (**à** of); *(délit)* offence; **être en i.** to be committing an offence
infranchissable [ɛ̃frɑ̃ʃisabl] *adj (rivière, col, gouffre)* impassable; *(obstacle, difficulté)* insurmountable
infrarouge [ɛ̃fraruʒ] *adj & nm* infrared
infrastructure [ɛ̃frastryktyr] *nf* (**a**) *Constr* substructure (**b**) *(d'équipements)* infrastructure; **i. routière/touristique** road/tourist infrastructure
infructueux, -euse [ɛ̃fryktɥø, -øz] *adj* fruitless
infumable [ɛ̃fymabl] *adj* unsmokable
infuse [ɛ̃fyz] *adj f voir* **science**
infuser [ɛ̃fyze] **1** *vi (thé)* to brew; *(tisane)* to infuse; **faire i. qch** to brew sth
2 *vt* (**a**) *(faire pénétrer)* to instil (**dans** into) (**b**) *(herbes)* to infuse; *(thé)* to brew
infusion [ɛ̃fyzjɔ̃] *nf* (**a**) *(boisson)* herb tea; **une i. de camomille** some camomile tea (**b**) *(processus)* infusion; *(de thé)* brewing
ingénier [66] [ɛ̃ʒenje] **s'ingénier** *vpr* **s'i. à faire qch** to strive to do sth; **il s'ingénie à me contredire** he goes out of his way to contradict me
ingénierie [ɛ̃ʒeniri] *nf* engineering
ingénieur [ɛ̃ʒenjœr] *nm* engineer; **i. agronome** agricultural engineer; **i. électronicien** electronics engineer; **i. mécanicien** mechanical engineer; **i. des mines** mining engineer; **i. des ponts et chaussées** civil engineer; **i. du son** sound engineer; **i. des travaux publics** civil engineer
ingénieur-conseil *(pl* **ingénieurs-conseils)** [ɛ̃ʒenjœrkɔ̃sɛj] *nm* consultant engineer
ingénieusement [ɛ̃ʒenjøzmɑ̃] *adv* ingeniously
ingénieux, -euse [ɛ̃ʒenjø, -øz] *adj* ingenious
ingéniosité [ɛ̃ʒenjozite] *nf* ingenuity
ingénu, -e [ɛ̃ʒeny] **1** *adj* ingenuous
2 *nm,f* ingenuous person
ingénuité [ɛ̃ʒenɥite] *nf* ingenuousness
ingérence [ɛ̃ʒerɑ̃s] *nf* interference (**dans** in)
ingérer [34] [ɛ̃ʒere] *vt* to ingest
ingestion [ɛ̃ʒɛstjɔ̃] *nf* ingestion
ingrat, -e [ɛ̃gra, -at] **1** *adj (personne)* ungrateful (**envers** to); *(sol, terre)* barren; *(tâche)* thankless; *(travail, sujet)* unrewarding; *(physique, visage)* unattractive
2 *nm,f* ungrateful person
ingratitude [ɛ̃gratityd] *nf* ingratitude

ingrédient [ɛ̃gredjɑ̃] *nm* ingredient
inguérissable [ɛ̃gerisabl] *adj* incurable
ingurgiter [ɛ̃gyrʒite] *vt (aliment, boisson)* to gulp down; *Fam Fig (connaissances)* to cram into one's head
inhabitable [inabitabl] *adj* uninhabitable
inhabité, -e [inabite] *adj* uninhabited
inhabituel, -elle [inabitɥɛl] *adj* unusual
inhalation [inalasjɔ̃] *nf* (**a**) *(respiration)* breathing in, inhalation (**b**) *Méd* (steam) inhalation; **le mieux pour les rhumes, c'est de faire des inhalations** inhaling steam is the best thing for a cold
inhaler [inale] *vt* to inhale
inhérent, -e [inerɑ̃, -ɑ̃t] *adj* inherent (**à** in)
inhiber [inibe] *vt* to inhibit
inhibition [inibisjɔ̃] *nf* inhibition
inhospitalier, -ère [inɔspitalje, -ɛr] *adj* inhospitable
inhumain, -e [inymɛ̃, -ɛn] *adj* inhuman
inhumanité [inymanite] *nf* inhumanity
inhumation [inymasjɔ̃] *nf* burial
inhumer [inyme] *vt* to bury
inimaginable [inimaʒinabl] *adj* unimaginable
inimitable [inimitabl] *adj* inimitable
inimitié [inimitje] *nf* enmity
ininflammable [inɛ̃flamabl] *adj* non-flammable
inintelligent, -e [inɛ̃teliʒɑ̃, -ɑ̃t] *adj* unintelligent
inintelligible [inɛ̃teliʒibl] *adj* unintelligible
inintéressant, -e [inɛ̃terɛsɑ̃, -ɑ̃t] *adj* uninteresting
ininterrompu, -e [inɛ̃terɔ̃py] *adj* continuous
inique [inik] *adj* iniquitous
iniquité [inikite] *nf* iniquity
initial, -e, -aux, -ales [inisjal, -o] **1** *adj* initial
2 *nf* **initiale** initial
initialement [inisjalmɑ̃] *adv* initially
initialisation [inisjalizasjɔ̃] *nf Ordinat* initialization
initialiser [inisjalize] *vt Ordinat (disque)* to initialize; *(ordinateur)* to boot (up)
initiateur, -trice [inisjatœr, -tris] **1** *nm,f (d'un projet, d'une réforme)* initiator
2 *adj* initiatory
initiation [inisjasjɔ̃] *nf* (**a**) *(formation)* introduction (**à** to) (**b**) *(rituels)* initiation (**à** into)
initiatique [inisjatik] *adj* initiatory
initiative [inisjativ] *nf* initiative; **à l'i. de qn** on sb's initiative; **prendre l'i. de faire qch** to take the initiative in doing sth; **faire qch de sa propre i.** to do sth on one's own initiative; **il n'a aucune i.** he's got no initiative
initié, -e [inisje] *nm,f* initiate
initier [66] [inisje] **1** *vt* (**a**) *(former)* to introduce (**à** to) (**b**) *(rituellement)* to initiate (**à** into)
2 s'initier *vpr* **s'i. à qch** to start learning sth
injectable [ɛ̃ʒɛktabl] *adj* injectable
injecté, -e [ɛ̃ʒɛkte] *adj* **yeux injectés de sang** bloodshot eyes
injecter [ɛ̃ʒɛkte] *vt (substance, capitaux)* to inject (**dans** into)
injection [ɛ̃ʒɛksjɔ̃] *nf (de substance, de capital)* injection; **moteur à i.** fuel-injection engine
injonction [ɛ̃ʒɔ̃ksjɔ̃] *nf* injunction; **i. de payer** order to pay; **recevoir l'i. de faire qch** to get the order to do sth
injure [ɛ̃ʒyr] *nf* insult; **injures** abuse, insults; **faire i. à qn** to insult sb
injurier [66] [ɛ̃ʒyrje] *vt* to insult, to abuse
injurieux, -euse [ɛ̃ʒyrjø, -øz] *adj* insulting, abusive

injuste [ɛ̃ʒyst] *adj* unfair (**envers** *ou* **avec** to *or* towards)

injustement [ɛ̃ʒystəmɑ̃] *adv* unjustly, unfairly

injustice [ɛ̃ʒystis] *nf* (**a**) *(iniquité)* injustice, unfairness (**envers** towards); **i. sociale** social injustice (**b**) *(acte, parole)* injustice

injustifiable [ɛ̃ʒystifjabl] *adj* unjustifiable

injustifié, -e [ɛ̃ʒystifje] *adj* unjustified

inlassable [ɛ̃lasabl] *adj* untiring

inlassablement [ɛ̃lasabləmɑ̃] *adv* untiringly; *(répéter)* ceaselessly

inné, -e [ine] *adj* innate, inborn

innocemment [inɔsamɑ̃] *adv* innocently

innocence [inɔsɑ̃s] *nf* innocence; **en toute i.** in all innocence

innocent, -e [inɔsɑ̃, -ɑ̃t] **1** *adj* innocent (**de** of) **2** *nm,f (non coupable)* innocent person; *(idiot)* simpleton; **ne fais pas l'i.!** don't act the innocent!; *Prov* **aux innocents les mains pleines** fortune favours fools

innocenter [inɔsɑ̃te] *vt* to clear (**de** of)

innocuité [inɔkɥite] *nf* harmlessness

innombrable [inɔ̃brabl] *adj* innumerable, countless; *(foule)* huge

innommable [inɔmabl] *adj Péj (conduite, actes)* unspeakable; *(nourriture, odeur)* vile

innovateur, -trice [inɔvatœr, -tris] **1** *adj* innovative **2** *nm,f* innovator

innovation [inɔvasjɔ̃] *nf* innovation

innover [inɔve] *vi* to innovate

inoccupé, -e [inɔkype] *adj* unoccupied

inoculation [inɔkylasjɔ̃] *nf Méd* inoculation

inoculer [inɔkyle] *vt* (**a**) **i. un virus/un vaccin à qn** to inoculate sb with a virus/a vaccine; **i. une maladie à qn** to infect sb with a disease; *Fig* **elle nous a inoculé sa gaieté** she infected us with her cheerfulness (**b**) **i. qn (contre une maladie)** to inoculate sb (against a disease)

inodore [inɔdɔr] *adj* odourless

inoffensif, -ive [inɔfɑ̃sif, -iv] *adj* harmless

inondation [inɔ̃dasjɔ̃] *nf* flood; *(action)* flooding

inondé, -e [inɔ̃de] *adj (lieu)* flooded; **populations inondées** flood victims; **visage i. de larmes** face streaming with tears; **i. de lumière** flooded with light

inonder [inɔ̃de] *vt (lieu)* to flood; *Fig (marché)* to flood, to inundate (**de** with); **être inondé de réclamations** to be inundated with complaints

inopérable [inɔperabl] *adj* inoperable

inopérant, -e [inɔperɑ̃, -ɑ̃t] *adj* ineffective

inopiné, -e [inɔpine] *adj* unexpected

inopportun, -e [inɔpɔrtœ̃, -yn] *adj* inopportune

inoubliable [inublijabl] *adj* unforgettable

inouï, -e [inwi] *adj* (**a**) *(ahurissant)* incredible; **il leur est arrivé une histoire inouïe** something incredible happened to them; **c'est/vous êtes i.!** it's/you're incredible! (**b**) *(nouveau)* unheard-of

Inox® [inɔks] *nm* stainless steel

inoxydable [inɔksidabl] *adj (métal)* rustproof; **acier i.** stainless steel

inqualifiable [ɛ̃kalifjabl] *adj* unspeakable

inquiet, -ète [ɛ̃kjɛ, -ɛt] **1** *adj (anxieux) (personne, air, voix)* worried, anxious (**au sujet de** about); *(attente)* anxious **2** *nm,f* worrier

inquiétant, -e [ɛ̃kjetɑ̃, -ɑ̃t] *adj* (**a**) *(alarmant)* worrying (**b**) *(qui effraie) (air, sourire)* frightening

inquiéter [34] [ɛ̃kjete] *vt* to worry; **être inquiété par la police** to be bothered by the police **2 s'inquiéter** *vpr* (**a**) *(se faire du souci)* to worry; **il n'y a pas de quoi s'i.** there's nothing to worry about; **s'i. pour qn** to be worried about sb; **ne t'inquiète pas pour elle!** don't (you) worry about her! (**b**) **s'i. de** *(se faire du souci pour)* to bother about; *(s'informer de)* to inquire about; **sans s'i. de rien** without a care in the world

inquiétude [ɛ̃kjetyd] *nf* anxiety, worry; **sujet d'i.** cause for anxiety; **éprouver quelques inquiétudes** to feel a bit worried; **soyez sans i.** rest easy

inquisiteur, -trice [ɛ̃kizitœr, -tris] **1** *adj (regard)* inquisitive **2** *nm* inquisitor; **le Grand I.** the Inquisitor General

inquisition [ɛ̃kizisjɔ̃] *nf* inquisition; **l'I.** the Inquisition

inratable [ɛ̃ratabl] *adj* unmissable, not to be missed

insaisissable [ɛ̃sezisabl] *adj* (**a**) *(personne)* elusive (**b**) *(son, différence, nuance)* imperceptible

insalubre [ɛ̃salybr] *adj (climat, habitation, pays)* insalubrious; *(occupation)* unhealthy

insanité [ɛ̃sanite] *nf (de raisonnement, de propos)* insanity; **des insanités** complete nonsense

insatiable [ɛ̃sasjabl] *adj* insatiable

insatisfait, -e [ɛ̃satisfɛ, -ɛt] **1** *adj (personne)* dissatisfied; *(désir)* unsatisfied **2** *nm,f* **c'est un éternel i.** he's never satisfied

inscription [ɛ̃skripsjɔ̃] *nf* (**a**) *(action) (dans un journal, un registre)* entering; *(immatriculation)* registration (**b**) *(sur une tombe, un mur)* inscription; *(dans un livre de comptes)* entry

inscrire [30] [ɛ̃skrir] **1** *vt* (**a**) *(renseignements, date)* to write down; *(dans un journal, dans un registre)* to enter (**b**) *(pour participer)* **i. qn à un club/à une activité** to enrol sb in a club/for an activity; **i. un enfant dans une école** to enrol a child at a school (**c**) *(dans la pierre)* to inscribe **2 s'inscrire** *vpr (à l'université) Br* to matriculate, *Am* to register (**à** at); *(à un tournoi, à un concours)* to enter (**à** for); *(à une activité)* to enrol (**à** for); *(dans une école)* to enrol (**dans** at); **s'i. dans un club/à un parti** to join a club/party; **s'i. sur les listes électorales** to register to vote; **s'i. en faux contre qch** to deny sth; **s'i. dans le cadre de** to come within the framework of

inscrit, -e [ɛ̃skri, -it] **1** *adj (électeur, candidat)* registered **2** *nm,f (à l'université)* registered student; *(à un concours)* registered entrant; *(électeur)* registered voter

insécable [ɛ̃sekabl] *adj* indivisible

insecte [ɛ̃sɛkt] *nm* insect

insecticide [ɛ̃sɛktisid] **1** *adj* insecticidal **2** *nm* insecticide

insectivore [ɛ̃sɛktivɔr] **1** *adj* insectivorous **2** *nm* insectivore

insécurité [ɛ̃sekyrite] *nf* insecurity

INSEE [inse] *nm (abrév* **Institut national de la statistique et des études économiques)** = French national institute of statistics and information about the economy

insémination [ɛ̃seminasjɔ̃] *nf* insemination; **i. artificielle** artificial insemination

inséminer [ɛ̃semine] *vt* to inseminate

insensé, -e [ɛ̃sɑ̃se] **1** *adj (projet, idée)* crazy; *(action, espoir, dépenses)* wild; **c'est i.!** it's crazy! **2** *nm,f* madman, *f* madwoman

insensibilité [ɛ̃sɑ̃sibilite] *nf* insensitivity (**à** to)

insensible [ɛ̃sɑ̃sibl] *adj (à la douleur, au froid)* insensitive (**à** to); **i. à la critique** impervious to criticism; **elle demeura i. à leurs larmes** she remained unmoved by their tears

insensiblement [ɛ̃sɑ̃sibləmɑ̃] *adv* imperceptibly

inséparable [ɛ̃separabl] *adj* inseparable

insérer [34] [ɛ̃sere] **1** *vt* to insert (**dans** in); **i. une annonce dans un journal** to put an advertisement in a newspaper
2 s'insérer *vpr* (**a**) *(s'attacher)* to be attached (**sur** to) (**b**) *(s'intégrer)* **s'i. dans** *(réformes, politique)* to fit into

insertion [ɛ̃sɛrsjɔ̃] *nf* insertion; **i. sociale** (social) integration; **i. professionnelle** integration into the job market; *Ordinat* **mode d'i.** insert mode; *Ordinat* **i. de ligne** line insert; **i. publicitaire** advertisement

insidieusement [ɛ̃sidjøzmɑ̃] *adv* insidiously

insidieux, -euse [ɛ̃sidjø, -øz] *adj* insidious

insigne¹ [ɛ̃siɲ] *nm* badge; **insignes de la royauté** insignia of royalty

insigne² *adj* (**a**) *Formal (remarquable)* signal (**b**) *Hum (indiscrétion, maladresse)* remarkable

insignifiant, -e [ɛ̃siɲifjɑ̃, -ɑ̃t] *adj* insignificant

insinuation [ɛ̃sinɥasjɔ̃] *nf* insinuation

insinuer [ɛ̃sinɥe] **1** *vt* to insinuate; **que voulez-vous i.?** what are you insinuating?
2 s'insinuer *vpr* **s'i. dans** *(froid, odeur)* to creep into; *(personne)* to worm one's way into; **le doute/l'idée qui s'insinue dans mon esprit** the doubt/the idea that is creeping into my mind; **s'i. dans les bonnes grâces de qn** to insinuate oneself into sb's favour

insipide [ɛ̃sipid] *adj* insipid

insistance [ɛ̃sistɑ̃s] *nf* insistence; **avec i.** insistently

insistant, -e [ɛ̃sistɑ̃, -ɑ̃t] *adj* insistent

insister [ɛ̃siste] *vi* (**a**) *(persévérer)* to insist; **elle a beaucoup insisté** she was very insistent; **i. pour faire qch** to insist on doing sth; **elle a essayé la planche à voile mais elle n'a pas insisté** she tried windsurfing but soon gave it up; **j'ai dit non, n'insistez pas** *ou* **inutile d'i.!** I said no, don't go on about it!; **ça ne répond pas – insiste encore un peu** there's no answer – hang on a bit (**b**) *(mettre l'accent sur)* **i. sur qch** to stress sth; **nous insistons particulièrement sur la ponctualité** we lay particular stress on punctuality

insolation [ɛ̃sɔlasjɔ̃] *nf* (**a**) *Méd* sunstroke; **attraper une i.** to get sunstroke (**b**) *(ensoleillement)* sunshine

insolence [ɛ̃sɔlɑ̃s] *nf* (**a**) *(impertinence)* insolence (**b**) *(remarque, action)* impertinence

insolent, -e [ɛ̃sɔlɑ̃, -ɑ̃t] **1** *adj* (**a**) *(impertinent)* insolent (**envers** *ou* **avec** to) (**b**) *(dans la victoire)* haughty (**c**) *(succès)* outrageous; *(luxe)* unashamed
2 *nm,f* insolent person

insolite [ɛ̃sɔlit] **1** *adj* unusual, strange
2 *nm* **l'i.** the unusual

insoluble [ɛ̃sɔlybl] *adj* insoluble

insolvable [ɛ̃sɔlvabl] *adj* insolvent

insomniaque [ɛ̃sɔmnjak] *adj & nmf* insomniac

insomnie [ɛ̃sɔmni] *nf* insomnia; **avoir des insomnies** to have insomnia; **j'ai eu une i. la nuit dernière** I couldn't sleep last night

insondable [ɛ̃sɔ̃dabl] *adj (océan, gouffre, mystère)* unfathomable; *(bêtise)* immense

insonorisation [ɛ̃sɔnɔrizasjɔ̃] *nf* soundproofing

insonoriser [ɛ̃sɔnɔrize] *vt* to soundproof

insouciance [ɛ̃susjɑ̃s] *nf* carefree attitude; **vivre dans l'i.** to live a carefree life

insouciant, -e [ɛ̃susjɑ̃, -ɑ̃t] *adj* carefree; **i. de son avenir** unconcerned about his future

insoumis, -e [ɛ̃sumi, -iz] **1** *adj* (**a**) *(peuple, tribus)* unsubdued (**b**) *(personne)* rebellious (**c**) *Mil (soldat)* absentee
2 *nm Mil* absentee

insoupçonnable [ɛ̃supsɔnabl] *adj (personne)* beyond suspicion

insoupçonné, -e [ɛ̃supsɔne] *adj* unsuspected (**de** by)

insoutenable [ɛ̃sutnabl] *adj* (**a**) *(spectacle, odeur)* unbearable (**b**) *(opinion, position)* untenable

inspecter [ɛ̃spɛkte] *vt* to inspect

inspecteur, -trice [ɛ̃spɛktœr, -tris] *nm,f* inspector; **i. d'Académie** school inspector; **i. de police** police inspector; **i. du travail** factory inspector; *Hum* **i. des travaux finis** *Br* skiver *(who arrives after the work has been done)*

inspection [ɛ̃spɛksjɔ̃] *nf* (**a**) *(examen)* inspection; **faire l'i. de** to inspect (**b**) *(service)* inspectorate; **i. académique** school inspectorate; **i. du travail** factory inspectorate

inspiration [ɛ̃spirasjɔ̃] *nf* (**a**) *(créatrice)* inspiration; **avoir de l'i.** to be inspired; **un poème d'i. romantique** a poem in the romantic style (**b**) *(idée)* inspiration (**c**) *(d'air)* breathing in

inspiré, -e [ɛ̃spire] *adj (style, poète, artiste, air)* inspired (**de** by); **être bien/mal i. de faire qch** to do the right/wrong thing in doing sth

inspirer [ɛ̃spire] **1** *vt* (**a**) *(donner de l'inspiration à)* to inspire; **ça m'a inspiré une chanson** it inspired me to write a song; *Hum* **ça ne m'inspire pas** it doesn't exactly inspire me (**b**) *(susciter)* **i. confiance à qn** to inspire confidence in sb; **ça m'inspire la plus grande inquiétude** it gives me great cause for concern (**c**) *(air)* to breathe in
2 *vi* to breathe in
3 s'inspirer *vpr* **s'i. de** to be inspired by; **une toile inspirée de Renoir** a painting inspired by Renoir

instabilité [ɛ̃stabilite] *nf* instability; *(du temps)* changeability

instable [ɛ̃stabl] *adj* unstable; *(temps)* changeable

installateur, -trice [ɛ̃stalatœr, -tris] *nm,f* fitter

installation [ɛ̃stalasjɔ̃] *nf* (**a**) *(fait d'installer) (d'une machine, du chauffage, d'un ascenseur)* installation; *(d'une cuisine)* fitting out; *(de rideaux)* putting up (**b**) *(emménagement)* move; **prévoir son i.** dans une région to plan to settle in an area (**c**) *(d'un ecclésiastique, d'un magistrat)* installation (**d**) *Ordinat* **programme d'i.** installation program; **i. en réseau** network installation (**e**) *(équipements)* installations *(d'une maison, d'un atelier)* fittings; **l'i. électrique** the wiring; **installations sanitaires** sanitary fittings; **installations touristiques** tourist facilities

installer [ɛ̃stale] **1** *vt* (**a**) *(mettre en place) (machine, chauffage, ascenseur)* to install, to put in; *(cuisine)* to fit out; *(rideaux)* to put up (**b**) *(placer)* **i. qn dans un fauteuil/devant la télévision** to settle sb down in an armchair/in front of the television; **je les ai installés dans la chambre bleue** I've put them in the blue room (**c**) *(aménager)* **les nouveaux bureaux sont très bien installés** the new offices are very well fitted out; **il a installé son bureau au grenier** he set up his office in the attic (**d**) *(dans une fonction) (ecclésiastique, magistrat)* to install
2 s'installer *vpr (supermarché, cirque)* to be set up; *(personne) (dans un fauteuil)* to settle down; *(dans un bureau)* to install oneself; **confortablement installé dans un fauteuil** comfortably installed in an arm-

chair; **s'i. à la campagne** to settle in the country; **des bourgeois bien installés** comfortably off middle-class people; **s'i. comme médecin** to set up as a doctor; **un climat d'insécurité s'est installé dans le pays** a climate of insecurity has taken hold of the country

instamment [ɛ̃stamɑ̃] *adv* earnestly

instance [ɛ̃stɑ̃s] *nf* (**a**) *Litt (insistance)* plea, entreaty; **demander à qn de faire qch avec i.** to plead with sb to do sth (**b**) *Jur* proceedings; **en seconde i.** on appeal (**c**) *(autorité)* authority; **les instances internationales** the international authorities; **l'i. compétente** the relevant authority (**d**) *(cours)* **être en i. de divorce** to be waiting for a divorce; **courrier en i.** mail waiting to go out; **être en i.** *(affaire)* to be pending

instant [ɛ̃stɑ̃] *nm* moment, instant; **à chaque** *ou* **tout i.** all the time; **pendant un i.** for a moment; **un i.!** one moment!; **sans perdre un i.** without wasting a second; **d'un i. à l'autre** at any moment; **à l'i.** (just) a moment ago; **à l'i. même où** at the very moment that; **j'en reviens à l'i.** I've just come back from there; **pour l'i.** for the moment; **dans un i.** in a moment; **en un i.** in no time at all

instantané, -e [ɛ̃stɑ̃tane] **1** *adj (mort, riposte)* instantaneous; *(café, soupe)* instant
2 *nm (photo)* snap

instantanément [ɛ̃stɑ̃tanemɑ̃] *adv* instantaneously

instar [ɛ̃star] **à l'instar de** *prép* following the example of; **à l'i. de ses parents, il sera enseignant** like his parents, he's going to be a teacher

instauration [ɛ̃storasjɔ̃] *nf* establishment

instaurer [ɛ̃store] **1** *vt* to establish
2 s'instaurer *vpr* to be established

instigateur, -trice [ɛ̃stigatœr, -tris] *nm,f* instigator

instigation [ɛ̃stigasjɔ̃] *nf* instigation; **à l'i. de qn** at sb's instigation

instinct [ɛ̃stɛ̃] *nm* instinct; **faire qch d'i.** to do sth by instinct

instinctif, -ive [ɛ̃stɛ̃ktif, -iv] *adj* instinctive

instinctivement [ɛ̃stɛ̃ktivmɑ̃] *adv* instinctively

instit [ɛ̃stit] *nmf Fam* (primary school) teacher

instituer [ɛ̃stitɥe] *vt* to establish

institut [ɛ̃stity] *nm* institute; **i. de beauté** beauty salon; **i. médico-légal** institute of forensic medicine

instituteur, -trice [ɛ̃stitytœr, -tris] *nm,f* (primary school) teacher

institution [ɛ̃stitysjɔ̃] *nf* (**a**) *(création)* establishment (**b**) *(école)* private school (**c**) *(coutume)* institution (**d**) *Pol* **institutions** institutions

institutionnaliser [ɛ̃stitysjɔnalize] *vt* to institutionalize

institutionnel, -elle [ɛ̃stitysjɔnɛl] *adj* institutional

instructeur [ɛ̃stryktœr] **1** *nm* instructor
2 *adj m Jur* **juge i.** examining magistrate

instructif, -ive [ɛ̃stryktif, -iv] *adj* instructive

instruction [ɛ̃stryksjɔ̃] *nf* (**a**) *(éducation)* education; *Mil* training; **avoir de l'i.** to be well educated; **sans i.** uneducated; **i. civique** civics *(singulier)*; **i. musicale** musical training; **i. religieuse** religious instruction (**b**) *Ordinat* instruction (**c**) *(circulaire)* memo (**d**) *Jur (d'une affaire)* preliminary investigation (**e**) **instructions** *(directives)* instructions

instruire [18] [ɛ̃strɥir] **1** *vt* (**a**) *(enseigner à)* to teach, to educate; **i. par le jeu** to teach through play (**b**) *(soldats)* to train (**c**) *(informer)* **i. qn de qch** to inform sb of sth (**d**) *Jur (affaire)* to investigate
2 s'instruire *vpr* to educate oneself; **s'i. de** to find out about

instruit, -e [ɛ̃strɥi, -it] *adj* educated

instrument [ɛ̃strymɑ̃] *nm* (**a**) *(outil)* instrument; **i. de mesure/de précision** measuring/precision instrument; *Fig* **il n'a été qu'un i.** he was merely a tool (**b**) **i. (de musique)** (musical) instrument; **i. à vent/cordes** wind/string instrument

instrumental, -e, -aux, -ales [ɛ̃strymɑ̃tal, -o] *adj* instrumental

instrumentiste [ɛ̃strymɑ̃tist] *nmf* instrumentalist

insu [ɛ̃sy] **à l'insu de** *prép* without the knowledge of; **à leur i.** without their knowing; **je l'ai fait à mon i.** I did it without realizing

insubmersible [ɛ̃sybmɛrsibl] *adj* unsinkable

insubordination [ɛ̃sybɔrdinasjɔ̃] *nf* insubordination

insuccès [ɛ̃syksɛ] *nm* failure

insuffisamment [ɛ̃syfizamɑ̃] *adv* insufficiently, inadequately

insuffisance [ɛ̃syfizɑ̃s] *nf* (**a**) *(manque)* insufficiency; *(de personnel, de réserves)* shortage; *(de moyens)* inadequacy (**b**) *Méd (d'un organe)* insufficiency; **i. cardiaque** cardiac insufficiency; **i. respiratoire** respiratory failure *or* insufficiency (**c**) **insuffisances** *(faiblesses)* shortcomings

insuffisant, -e [ɛ̃syfizɑ̃, -ɑ̃t] *adj (quantité)* insufficient; *(moyens, mesures)* inadequate; **tes résultats sont insuffisants** your results are not good enough

insuffler [ɛ̃syfle] *vt Méd* to insufflate *(dans into)*; **ce succès a insufflé un nouvel élan à l'entreprise** this success breathed new life into the company

insulaire [ɛ̃sylɛr] **1** *adj* island; *Péj (mentalité)* insular
2 *nmf* islander

insuline [ɛ̃sylin] *nf* insulin

insulte [ɛ̃sylt] *nf* insult; **il nous a fait l'i. de refuser** he insulted us by refusing

insulter [ɛ̃sylte] *vt* to insult

insupportable [ɛ̃sypɔrtabl] *adj* unbearable

insurgé, -e [ɛ̃syrʒe] *adj & nm,f* insurgent

insurger [45] [ɛ̃syrʒe] **s'insurger** *vpr* to rise up (**contre** against)

insurmontable [ɛ̃syrmɔ̃tabl] *adj (difficulté, obstacle)* insurmountable; *(aversion, dégoût)* unconquerable

insurrection [ɛ̃syrɛksjɔ̃] *nf* uprising, rebellion; **en état d'i.** in a state of rebellion

insurrectionnel, -elle [ɛ̃syrɛksjɔnɛl] *adj* insurrectionary

intact, -e [ɛ̃takt] *adj* intact

intangible [ɛ̃tɑ̃ʒibl] *adj (loi, institution)* sacred

intarissable [ɛ̃tarisabl] *adj* inexhaustible

intégral, -e, -aux, -ales [ɛ̃tegral, -o] **1** *adj* (**a**) *(paiement, remboursement)* full; *(texte)* unabridged; *Fam* **un fumiste/crétin/menteur i.** a complete clown/idiot/liar (**b**) *Math* **calcul i.** integral calculus
2 *nf* **intégrale** (**a**) *Math* integral (**b**) *(totalité)* **l'intégrale des symphonies de Beethoven/des œuvres de Shakespeare** the complete Beethoven symphonies/works of Shakespeare

intégralement [ɛ̃tegralmɑ̃] *adv (citer, rembourser)* fully, in full

intégralité [ɛ̃tegralite] *nf* **l'i.** the whole (**de** of); **dans son i.** in its entirety

intégrante [ɛ̃tegrɑ̃t] *adj f* **une partie i. de** an integral part of; **faire partie i. de** to be an integral part of

intégration [ɛ̃tegrasjɔ̃] *nf (au sein d'un groupe) & Math* integration; *(dans une grande école)* admission; *Écon* **i. horizontale/verticale** horizontal/vertical integration

intègre [ɛ̃tɛgr] *adj* upright, honest

intégrer [34] [ɛ̃tegre] **1** *vt (incorporer)* to integrate (**à/ dans** into)
2 **s'intégrer** *vpr* to become integrated (**à/dans** into); **cette sculpture s'intègre bien au paysage** this sculpture blends in well with the countryside
intégrisme [ɛ̃tegrism] *nm* fundamentalism
intégriste [ɛ̃tegrist] *adj & nmf* fundamentalist
intégrité [ɛ̃tegrite] *nf* integrity; *Ordinat* **i. des données** data integrity
intellect [ɛ̃telɛkt] *nm* intellect
intellectuel, -elle [ɛ̃telɛktɥɛl] **1** *adj* intellectual; *(fatigue)* mental; *(travail)* non-manual
2 *nm,f* intellectual
intelligemment [ɛ̃teliʒamɑ̃] *adv* intelligently
intelligence [ɛ̃teliʒɑ̃s] *nf* (**a**) *(intellect)* intelligence; **avoir l'i. de faire qch** to have the intelligence to do sth; **i. artificielle** artificial intelligence (**b**) *(compréhension)* understanding (**c**) *(entente)* **vivre en bonne/mauvaise i. avec qn** to be on good/bad terms with sb (**d**) *(connivence)* **un regard/sourire d'i.** a knowing look/smile; **faire des signes d'i. à qn** to signal to sb
intelligent, -e [ɛ̃teliʒɑ̃, -ɑ̃t] *adj* intelligent, clever; *Ordinat* smart, intelligent
intelligentsia [intelidʒɛnsja] *nf* **l'i.** the intelligentsia
intelligible [ɛ̃teliʒibl] *adj (compréhensible)* intelligible; *(clair)* clear; **à haute et i. voix** in a loud, clear voice
intello [ɛ̃telo] *nmf Fam souvent Péj* intellectual, highbrow
intempéries [ɛ̃tɑ̃peri] *nfpl* bad weather; **exposé aux i.** exposed to the elements
intempestif, -ive [ɛ̃tɑ̃pɛstif, -iv] *adj* untimely, illtimed
intemporel, -elle [ɛ̃tɑ̃pɔrɛl] *adj (hors du temps)* timeless
intenable [ɛ̃tənabl] *adj (chaleur, situation)* intolerable, unbearable; *(position)* untenable; *Fam (enfant)* uncontrollable
intendance [ɛ̃tɑ̃dɑ̃s] *nf* (**a**) *Scol* bursary; *(bureau)* bursar's office (**b**) *Mil* commissariat (**c**) *(d'un domaine)* stewardship (**d**) *Fig (questions matérielles)* practical matters
intendant [ɛ̃tɑ̃dɑ̃] *nm* (**a**) *Scol* bursar (**b**) *Mil* quartermaster (**c**) *(d'un domaine)* steward
intendante [ɛ̃tɑ̃dɑ̃t] *nf* (**a**) *Scol* (woman) bursar (**b**) *(d'une maison)* housekeeper
intense [ɛ̃tɑ̃s] *adj* intense
intensément [ɛ̃tɑ̃semɑ̃] *adv* intensely
intensif, -ive [ɛ̃tɑ̃sif, -iv] *adj* intensive
intensification [ɛ̃tɑ̃sifikasjɔ̃] *nf* intensification
intensifier [66] [ɛ̃tɑ̃sifje] **1** *vt* to intensify
2 **s'intensifier** *vpr* to intensify
intensité [ɛ̃tɑ̃site] *nf* intensity
intenter [ɛ̃tɑ̃te] *vt Jur* **i. une action contre qn** to bring an action against sb; **i. un procès à** *ou* **contre qn** to institute proceedings against sb
intention [ɛ̃tɑ̃sjɔ̃] *nf (projet)* intention; *Jur* intent; **avoir l'i. de faire qch** to intend to do sth; **dans l'i. de faire qch** with a view to *or* with the intention of doing sth; **elle a de bonnes intentions** she means well; **c'est l'i. qui compte** it's the thought that counts; **à l'i. de...** *(pour)* for...; *(en l'honneur de)* in honour of...; *(sur une lettre)* for the attention of...
intentionné, -e [ɛ̃tɑ̃sjɔne] *adj* **bien/mal i.** well-/ill-intentioned; **bien/mal i. envers qn** well-/ill-disposed towards sb

intentionnel, -elle [ɛ̃tɑ̃sjɔnɛl] *adj* intentional, deliberate
intentionnellement [ɛ̃tɑ̃sjɔnɛlmɑ̃] *adv* intentionally, deliberately
interactif, -ive [ɛ̃tɛraktif, -iv] *adj Ordinat* interactive
interaction [ɛ̃tɛraksjɔ̃] *nf* interaction
interallié, -e [ɛ̃tɛralje] *adj* allied
interbancaire [ɛ̃tɛrbɑ̃kɛr] *adj* interbank
intercalaire [ɛ̃tɛrkalɛr] **1** *adj (jour)* intercalary; **feuillet i.**
2 *nm (feuillet)* insert; *(dans un classeur)* divider
intercaler [ɛ̃tɛrkale] **1** *vt (dans un texte, un film)* to insert, to include; *(dans un programme, entre deux événements)* to slot in
2 **s'intercaler** *vpr* to come in between
intercéder [34] [ɛ̃tɛrsede] *vi* to intercede (**en faveur de/auprès de** on behalf of/with)
intercepter [ɛ̃tɛrsɛpte] *vt (lettre, avion, ballon, personne)* to intercept; *(bruit, lumière)* to shut out
interchangeable [ɛ̃tɛrʃɑ̃ʒabl] *adj* interchangeable
interclasse [ɛ̃tɛrklas] *nm* = short break between classes
intercontinental, -e, -aux, -ales [ɛ̃tɛrkɔ̃tinɑ̃tal, -o] *adj* intercontinental
intercours [ɛ̃tɛrkur] *nm Belg Scol* = short break between classes
interdépartemental, -e, -aux, -ales [ɛ̃tɛrdepartəmɑ̃tal, -o] *adj* = shared by several French "départements"
interdépendant, -e [ɛ̃tɛrdepɑ̃dɑ̃, -ɑ̃t] *adj* interdependent
interdiction [ɛ̃tɛrdiksjɔ̃] *nf* (**a**) *(défense)* ban, banning; **i. de fumer/stationner** *(sur panneau)* no smoking/parking (**b**) *(suspension)* banning; **i. de séjour** = order banning former prisoner from certain areas
interdire [27b] [ɛ̃tɛrdir] **1** *vt* (**a**) *(défendre) (stationnement, port d'armes)* to ban; **i. qch à qn** to forbid sb sth; **le centre-ville est interdit aux camions** lorries are not allowed in the town centre; **i. à qn de faire qch** *(personne)* to forbid sb to do sth; *(règlement)* to prohibit sb from doing sth; **il nous est interdit de révéler...** we are not allowed to reveal... (**b**) *(empêcher)* to prevent, to stop (**de faire qch** from doing sth)
2 **s'interdire** *vpr* **s'i. l'alcool** to abstain from drinking; **il s'interdit d'y penser** he doesn't let himself think about it
interdit, -e [ɛ̃tɛrdi, -it] **1** *adj* (**a**) *(défendu)* forbidden; **il est i. de fumer** smoking is not allowed; **i. au public** *(sur un écriteau)* no unauthorized entry; **un film i. aux moins de 18 ans** *Br* an "18" film, *Am* an adults-only movie; **i. de séjour** = banned from living in certain areas; **être i. de chéquier** to have (had) one's chequebook facilities withdrawn; *Ordinat* **i. d'écriture** *(disquette)* write-protected (**b**) *(déconcerté)* disconcerted, taken aback
2 *nm,f Jur* **i. de séjour** = former prisoner banned from certain areas
3 *nm (social)* taboo; *(religieux)* interdict; **frapper qn/qch d'i.** to impose a ban on sb/sth
intéressant, -e [ɛ̃tɛresɑ̃, -ɑ̃t] **1** *adj* (**a**) *(attirant)* interesting (**b**) *(avantageux)* worthwhile; *(prix)* attractive; *(lucratif)* profitable
2 *nm,f Fam* **faire l'i.** to show off
intéressé, -e [ɛ̃terese] **1** *adj* (**a**) *(concerné)* **les parties intéressées** the interested parties, the persons concerned (**b**) *(égoïste) (personne)* self-seeking, *(sentiment)* self-interested; *(conseil)* biased; **agir dans un**

but i. to have an axe to grind
2 *nm,f* **l'i.** the person concerned
intéresser [ɛ̃terese] **1** *vt* (**a**) *(captiver)* to interest; **l'art m'intéresse beaucoup** I'm very interested in art; **est-ce que ça t'intéresse d'aller au cinéma?** would you like to go to the cinema? (**b**) *Ind & Com* **i. les employés (aux bénéfices)** to operate a profit-sharing scheme; **être intéressé dans une affaire** to have a financial interest in a business (**c**) *(concerner)* to concern, to affect
2 s'intéresser *vpr* **s'i. à qn/qch** to take an interest in sb/sth, to be interested in sb/sth
intérêt [ɛ̃terɛ] *nm* (**a**) *(avantage)* interest; **c'est dans mon i.** de le faire it's in my interest to do it; **elle a tout i. à se taire** she'd be well-advised to remain silent; **on a i. à réserver si on veut avoir des places** we'd better book if we want seats; *Fam* **tu n'as pas i. à recommencer!** you'd better not do it again!; **agir dans/contre l'i. de qn** to act in/against sb's interest(s); **agir par i. personnel** to act out of self-interest; **faire un mariage d'i.** to marry for money; **l'i. des vacances en groupe, c'est de faire des rencontres** the advantage of a group holiday is that you meet people; *Fam* **tu viens à la réunion du syndicat? – y a i.!** are you coming to the union meeting? – you bet (I am)! (**b**) *(attrait)* interest; **sans i.** uninteresting (**c**) *(curiosité)* interest (**pour** in); **éprouver de l'i. pour qch** to be interested *or* to take an interest in sth (**d**) *Fin* interest; **i. fixe** fixed interest; **i. variable** variable-rate interest
interface [ɛ̃tɛrfas] *nf Ordinat* interface; **i. graphique** graphic interface; **i. d'imprimante** printer interface; **i. numérique** digital interface; **i. parallèle** parallel interface; **i. utilisateur** user interface; **i. vidéo numérique** digital video interface
interférence [ɛ̃tɛrferɑ̃s] *nf (d'ondes)* interference; *Fig (d'événements)* combination
interférer [34] [ɛ̃tɛrfere] *vi aussi Fig* to interfere
intergouvernemental, -e, -aux, -ales [ɛ̃tɛrguvɛrnəmɑ̃tal, -o] *adj* intergovernmental
intérieur, -e [ɛ̃terjœr] **1** *adj* (**a**) *(dans l'espace) (escalier)* interior, inside; *(cour)* inner; *(poche)* inside; *(partie)* inside, internal; *(mer)* inland (**b**) *(national)* domestic (**c**) *(vie, sentiments, force)* inner
2 *nm* (**a**) *(dedans)* inside, interior; **à l'i.** inside; **à l'i. de la gare** inside the station; **fermé de l'i.** locked from the inside; **tourné en i.** *(film)* shot indoors (**b**) *(d'un pays)* interior; **dans l'i. du pays** inland (**c**) *(maison)* home; **femme d'i.** houseproud housewife
intérieurement [ɛ̃terjœrmɑ̃] *adv* inwardly
intérim [ɛ̃terim] *nm (travail intérimaire)* temporary work, temping; **faire de l'i.** to temp; **par i., Belg ad i.** acting; **assurer l'i. (de qn)** to stand in (for sb)
intérimaire [ɛ̃terimɛr] **1** *adj (fonction, employé)* temporary; *(directeur, ministre)* acting; *(cabinet, gouvernement)* caretaker
2 *nmf (travailleur)* temporary worker; *(secrétaire)* temp
intérioriser [ɛ̃terjɔrize] *vt* to internalize
interjection [ɛ̃tɛrʒɛksjɔ̃] *nf* interjection
interligne [ɛ̃tɛrliɲ] *nm* line spacing; **dans l'i.** in the space between the lines; **simple/double i.** single/double spacing
interlocuteur, -trice [ɛ̃tɛrlɔkytœr, -tris] *nm,f* (**a**) *(dans une conversation)* speaker; **mon i.** the person I was/am speaking to (**b**) *(dans une négociation)* discussion partner
interloqué, -e [ɛ̃tɛrlɔke] *adj* taken aback

interlude [ɛ̃tɛrlyd] *nm* interlude
intermède [ɛ̃tɛrmɛd] *nm aussi Fig* interlude
intermédiaire [ɛ̃tɛrmedjɛr] **1** *adj* intermediate; **i. entre** halfway between; **trouver une solution i.** to find a compromise solution; **pointure i.** size in-between
2 *nmf (personne)* intermediary, go-between; *Com* middleman; **sans i.** directly
3 *nm* **par l'i. de** through; **sans l'i. de** without
interminable [ɛ̃tɛrminabl] *adj* interminable
interministériel, -elle [ɛ̃tɛrministerjɛl] *adj* interministerial
intermittence [ɛ̃tɛrmitɑ̃s] *nf* **par i.** intermittently, on and off
intermittent, -e [ɛ̃tɛrmitɑ̃, -ɑ̃t] **1** *adj (lumière, bruit, tir)* intermittent, sporadic; *(travail)* casual
2 *nm,f* casual worker
internat [ɛ̃tɛrna] *nm* (**a**) *Scol (système)* boarding; *(pensionnat)* boarding school (**b**) *Méd (concours)* entrance examination for *Br* a housemanship *or Am* an internship; *(formation) Br* clinicals, *Am* internship
international, -e, -aux, -ales [ɛ̃tɛrnasjɔnal, -o] **1** *adj & nm,f* international
2 *nf* **l'Internationale** *(groupement)* the International; *(chant)* the Internationale
internationalisation [ɛ̃tɛrnasjɔnalizasjɔ̃] *nf* internationalization
internationaliser [ɛ̃tɛrnasjɔnalize] **1** *vt* to internationalize
2 s'internationaliser *vpr* to become international
internaute [ɛ̃tɛrnot] *nmf* Internet surfer
interne [ɛ̃tɛrn] **1** *adj (structure, paroi, hémorragie)* internal; *(côté)* inner; *(de l'entreprise)* in-house
2 *nmf (élève)* boarder; **i. (des hôpitaux)** *Br* house doctor, *Am* intern
internement [ɛ̃tɛrnəmɑ̃] *nm (emprisonnement)* internment; *(hospitalisation)* confinement
interner [ɛ̃tɛrne] *vt (emprisonner)* to intern; *(hospitaliser)* to commit
Internet [ɛ̃tɛrnɛt] *nm* **l'I.** the Internet; **sur I.** on the Internet
interparlementaire [ɛ̃tɛrparləmɑ̃tɛr] *adj (réunion)* interparliamentary; *(commission)* joint
interpellation [ɛ̃tɛrpelasjɔ̃] *nf (appel)* calling out; *(au Parlement)* question; **la police a procédé à plusieurs interpellations** the police took several people in for questioning
interpeller [ɛ̃tɛrpəle] **1** *vt* (**a**) *(appeler)* to call (out) to; *(sujet: police)* to take in for questioning; *(ministre)* to question; *(à une réunion, un spectacle)* to heckle; *(sujet: sentinelle)* to challenge (**b**) *(toucher)* **ce roman m'a interpellé** I can really relate to this novel
2 s'interpeller *vpr (s'appeler)* to call (out) to each other; *(s'insulter)* to shout insults at each other
Interphone® [ɛ̃tɛrfɔn] *nm (de bureau)* intercom; *(d'immeuble)* Entryphone®; **à l'I.** on the intercom/Entryphone®
interplanétaire [ɛ̃tɛrplanetɛr] *adj* interplanetary
interpolation [ɛ̃tɛrpolasjɔ̃] *nf* interpolation
interpoler [ɛ̃tɛrpole] *vt* to interpolate
interposé, -e [ɛ̃tɛrpoze] *adj* **par personne interposée** through an intermediary
interposer [ɛ̃tɛrpoze] **1** *vt* to interpose (**entre** between)
2 s'interposer *vpr (intervenir)* to intervene
interprétariat [ɛ̃tɛrpretarja] *nm* interpreting

interprétation [ɛ̃tɛrpretasjɔ̃] *nf* (**a**) *(d'un texte, d'un rêve, d'un rôle)* interpretation (**b**) *(traduction)* interpreting
interprète [ɛ̃tɛrprɛt] *nmf (dans une autre langue)* interpreter; *(d'un rôle, d'une œuvre musicale)* performer; *(porte-parole)* spokesman, *f* spokeswoman; **i. de conférence** conference interpreter
interpréter [34] [ɛ̃tɛrprete] *vt* (**a**) *(rôle, œuvre musicale)* to perform, to interpret (**b**) *(texte, paroles, geste, rêve)* to interpret; **mal i. les paroles de qn** to misinterpret sb's words
interro [ɛ̃tɛro] *nf Fam Scol (abrév* **interrogation**) test
interrogateur, -trice [ɛ̃tɛrɔgatœr, -tris] **1** *adj* questioning
	2 *nm,f (examinateur)* (oral) examiner
interrogatif, -ive [ɛ̃tɛrɔgatif, -iv] **1** *adj* (**a**) *(air, ton)* inquiring, questioning (**b**) *Gram (pronom, phrase)* interrogative
	2 *nm Gram* interrogative
	3 *nf Gram* **interrogative** interrogative (clause)
interrogation [ɛ̃tɛrɔgasjɔ̃] *nf* (**a**) *(question)* question; **i. directe/indirecte** direct/indirect question (**b**) *Scol* test; **i. écrite/orale** written/oral test (**c**) *(d'un prisonnier, d'un suspect)* questioning, interrogation (**d**) *Ordinat (d'une base de données) (question)* inquiry, query; *(activité)* interrogation; **i. à distance** remote interrogation
interrogatoire [ɛ̃tɛrɔgatwar] *nm* questioning
interroger [45] [ɛ̃tɛrɔʒe] **1** *vt* (**a**) *(personne)* to question; *(candidat, élève)* to test; **i. qn du regard** to look at sb questioningly (**b**) *Ordinat (base de données)* to query, to interrogate
	2 s'interroger *vpr* to ask oneself, to wonder (**sur** about)
interrompre [ɛ̃tɛrɔ̃pr] **1** *vt* to interrupt; *(trafic)* to hold up; *(grossesse)* to terminate
	2 s'interrompre *vpr* to break off
interrupteur [ɛ̃tɛryptœr] *nm* switch; **i. à bascule** toggle switch
interruption [ɛ̃tɛrypsjɔ̃] *nf (arrêt)* interruption; *(de négociations)* breaking off; **sans i.** non-stop, continuously; *Ordinat* **fonction d'i.** interrupt function; *Méd* **i. volontaire de grossesse** termination (of pregnancy)
intersection [ɛ̃tɛrsɛksjɔ̃] *nf* intersection, junction; **à l'i. des deux routes** where the two roads intersect *or* meet
intersidéral, -e, -aux, -ales [ɛ̃tɛrsideral, -o] *adj* interstellar
interstice [ɛ̃tɛrstis] *nm* chink, crack
intersyndical, -e, -aux, -ales [ɛ̃tɛrsɛ̃dikal, -o] **1** *adj* interunion
	2 *nf* **intersyndicale** *(association)* interunion group
intertitre [ɛ̃tɛrtitr] *nmJourn* subheading; *Cin* subtitle
interurbain, -e [ɛ̃tɛryrbɛ̃, -ɛn] **1** *adj* interurban; *Vieilli Tél* **appel i.** trunk call
	2 *nm Vieilli Tél* long-distance service
intervalle [ɛ̃tɛrval] *nm* (**a**) *(dans le temps, en musique)* interval; **un i. d'une heure** a one-hour interval; **à deux mois d'i.** two months apart; **par intervalles** at intervals, now and then; **dans l'i.** in the meantime, meanwhile (**b**) *(dans l'espace)* gap, space; **à 2 mètres d'i.** 2 metres apart (**c**) *Math* interval
intervenant, -e [ɛ̃tɛrvənɑ̃, -ɑ̃t] *nm,f (dans une conférence, un débat)* speaker, contributor
intervenir [70] [ɛ̃tɛrvənir] *vi* (**a**) *(agir, prendre la parole)* to intervene (**dans** in); **i. pour faire qch** to intervene *or* step in to do sth; **i. en faveur de qn** to

intervene on sb's behalf; **i. auprès de qn** to intercede with sb; **faire i. qn** to bring sb in (**b**) *(arriver) (événement, changement)* to occur; *(accord)* to be reached (**c**) *(jouer un rôle)* to play a part (**dans** in)
intervention [ɛ̃tɛrvɑ̃sjɔ̃] *nf* (**a**) *(intercession, ingérence)* intervention (**en faveur de/auprès de** on behalf of/with) (**b**) *(prise de parole)* intervention; *(discours)* speech (**c**) *(opération)* **i. (chirurgicale)** operation
interventionniste [ɛ̃tɛrvɑ̃sjɔnist] *adj & nmf* interventionist
interversion [ɛ̃tɛrvɛrsjɔ̃] *nf* inversion, reversal
intervertir [ɛ̃tɛrvɛrtir] *vt (l'ordre de qch)* to invert, to reverse; *(objets, éléments)* to switch (round); *(rôles)* to reverse
intervienne *voir* **intervenir**
interview [ɛ̃tɛrvju] *nm ou nf* interview
interviewer [ɛ̃tɛrvjuve] *vt* to interview
intervieweur, -euse [ɛ̃tɛrvjuvœr, -øz] *nm,f* interviewer
intestin¹, -e [ɛ̃tɛstɛ̃, -in] *adj Litt* internal
intestin² *nm* intestine; **intestins** intestines, bowels; **gros i.** large intestine; **i. grêle** small intestine
intestinal, -e, -aux, -ales [ɛ̃tɛstinal, -o] *adj* intestinal
intime [ɛ̃tim] **1** *adj* intimate; *(hygiène, toilette)* personal; **être i. avec qn** to be close to sb; **avoir l'i. conviction que...** to be thoroughly convinced that...
	2 *nmf* close friend; **pour les intimes** to my/her/etc friends
intimement [ɛ̃timmɑ̃] *adv* intimately; **i. liés** *(amis)* very close; *(phénomènes)* closely linked; **être i. persuadé que...** to be thoroughly convinced that...
intimer [ɛ̃time] *vt* (**a**) *(ordonner)* **i. à qn l'ordre de faire qch** to order sb to do sth (**b**) *Jur* to summon before the Court of Appeal
intimidant, -e [ɛ̃timidɑ̃, -ɑ̃t] *adj* intimidating
intimidation [ɛ̃timidasjɔ̃] *nf* intimidation
intimider [ɛ̃timide] *vt* to intimidate; **ne te laisse pas i. par eux!** don't let them intimidate you!
intimité [ɛ̃timite] *nf (vie privée)* privacy; *(familiarité)* intimacy, closeness; **dans l'i.** in private; **le mariage a eu lieu dans la plus stricte i.** only close family and friends attended the wedding
intitulé [ɛ̃tityle] *nm (de livre)* title; *(de chapitre)* heading, title
intituler [ɛ̃tityle] **1** *vt (livre, chanson)* to give a title to; **un livre intitulé...** a book entitled *or* called...
	2 s'intituler *vpr (livre, chanson)* to be entitled, to be called; *(personne)* to call oneself
intolérable [ɛ̃tɔlerabl] *adj* intolerable
intolérance [ɛ̃tɔlerɑ̃s] *nf* intolerance; *Méd* **i. à qch** intolerance to sth
intolérant, -e [ɛ̃tɔlerɑ̃, -ɑ̃t] *adj* intolerant
intonation [ɛ̃tɔnasjɔ̃] *nf* intonation
intouchable [ɛ̃tuʃabl] *adj & nmf* untouchable
intox [ɛ̃tɔks] *nf Fam* brainwashing
intoxication [ɛ̃tɔksikasjɔ̃] *nf (empoisonnement)* poisoning; *Fig* brainwashing; **i. alimentaire** food poisoning
intoxiquer [ɛ̃tɔksike] **1** *vt (empoisonner)* to poison; *Fig* to brainwash
	2 s'intoxiquer *vpr* to poison oneself
intradermique [ɛ̃tradɛrmik] *Méd* **1** *adj* intradermal
	2 *nf* intradermal injection
intraduisible [ɛ̃tradɥizibl] *adj* untranslatable

intraitable [ɛ̃trɛtabl] *adj* uncompromising, inflexible (**sur** about)

intra-muros [ɛ̃tramyros] **1** *adj inv* **Londres/Paris i.** inner London/Paris **2** *adv* within the city

intramusculaire [ɛ̃tramyskylɛr] **1** *adj* intramuscular **2** *nf* intramuscular injection

Intranet [ɛ̃tranɛt] *nm Ordinat* Intranet

intransigeance [ɛ̃trɑ̃ziʒɑ̃s] *nf* intransigence

intransigeant, -e [ɛ̃trɑ̃ziʒɑ̃, -ɑ̃t] *adj (personne)* intransigent, uncompromising (**envers/sur** with/about); *(morale)* uncompromising

intransitif, -ive [ɛ̃trɑ̃zitif, -iv] *adj & nm Gram* intransitive

intransmissible [ɛ̃trɑ̃smisibl] *adj* (**a**) *Biol* intransmissible (**b**) *Jur* untransferable

intransportable [ɛ̃trɑ̃spɔrtabl] *adj (objet)* untransportable; *(blessé)* unfit to travel

intraveineux, -euse [ɛ̃travɛnø, -øz] **1** *adj* intravenous **2** *nf* **intraveineuse** intravenous injection

intrépide [ɛ̃trepid] *adj* intrepid, fearless

intrépidité [ɛ̃trepidite] *nf* fearlessness

intrigant, -e [ɛ̃trigɑ̃, -ɑ̃t] **1** *adj* scheming, plotting **2** *nm,f* schemer

intrigue [ɛ̃trig] *nf (machination)* intrigue; *(liaison amoureuse)* (love) affair; *(d'un roman, d'un film)* plot

intriguer [ɛ̃trige] **1** *vt* to intrigue **2** *vi* to scheme, to intrigue

intrinsèque [ɛ̃trɛ̃sɛk] *adj* intrinsic

intrinsèquement [ɛ̃trɛ̃sɛkmɑ̃] *adv* intrinsically

intro [ɛ̃tro] *nf Fam* intro; *(musicale)* theme tune

introductif, -ive [ɛ̃trɔdyktif, -iv] *adj* (**a**) *(discours, exposé)* introductory, opening (**b**) *Jur* introductory

introduction [ɛ̃trɔdyksjɔ̃] *nf* introduction; *(insertion)* insertion, introduction (**dans** into); *(au rugby)* put-in; **i. en Bourse** listing on the stock market

introduire [18] [ɛ̃trɔdɥir] **1** *vt (dans une serrure, dans un trou)* to insert (**dans** into); *(marchandises)* to bring in; *(coutume, réforme, mesures, mode)* to introduce; *(étranger, visiteur)* to show in; **i. qn auprès de qn** *(faire entrer)* to show sb in to see sb; *(présenter)* to introduce sb to sb; **i. en Bourse** to list on the stock market; **i. sur le marché** to launch onto the market **2** **s'introduire** *vpr* **s'i. dans une maison** to get into a house; **l'eau s'introduit partout** there's water coming in in everywhere

intronisation [ɛ̃trɔnizasjɔ̃] *nf* enthronement; *Fig* establishment

introniser [ɛ̃trɔnize] *vt* to enthrone; *Fig* to establish

introspection [ɛ̃trɔspɛksjɔ̃] *nf* introspection

introuvable [ɛ̃truvabl] *adj (produit, denrées)* unobtainable; *(personne)* nowhere to be found

introversion [ɛ̃trɔvɛrsjɔ̃] *nf* introversion

introverti, -e [ɛ̃trɔvɛrti] **1** *adj* introverted **2** *nm,f* introvert

intrus, -e [ɛ̃try, -yz] *nm,f* intruder, *Ordinat* intruder, hacker

intrusion [ɛ̃tryzjɔ̃] *nf* intrusion (**dans** into)

intuitif, -ive [ɛ̃tɥitif, -iv] **1** *adj* intuitive **2** *nm,f* **c'est un i.** he's very intuitive

intuition [ɛ̃tɥisjɔ̃] *nf* intuition; **avoir l'i. de qch/que** to sense sth/that

intuitivement [ɛ̃tɥitivmɑ̃] *adv* intuitively

inuit [inɥit] **1** *adj inv* Inuit **2** *nmf inv* **les I.** the Inuit *or* Inuits

inusable [inyzabl] *adj aussi Fig* hard-wearing

inusité, -e [inyzite] *adj (mot)* uncommon

inutile [inytil] *adj (qui ne sert à rien)* useless; *(effort)* vain, pointless; *(précautions, démarche, bagages)* unnecessary; **c'est i.!** *(ça ne sert à rien)* it's pointless!; *(ce n'est pas nécessaire)* you/he/etc needn't bother!; **i. de dire que...** needless to say,...; **c'est i. d'attendre** there's no point in waiting; **i. d'insister, je ne viens pas** don't go on about it, I'm not coming

inutilement [inytilmɑ̃] *adv* needlessly, unnecessarily

inutilisable [inytilizabl] *adj* unusable

inutilisé, -e [inytilize] *adj* unused

inutilité [inytilite] *nf (d'un objet)* uselessness; *(d'un effort, d'un argument)* pointlessness

invaincu, -e [ɛ̃vɛ̃ky] *adj* undefeated

invalidant, -e [ɛ̃validɑ̃, -ɑ̃t] *adj* disabling

invalidation [ɛ̃validasjɔ̃] *nf Jur* invalidation

invalide [ɛ̃valid] **1** *adj* disabled **2** *nmf* disabled person, invalid; **i. de guerre** disabled ex-serviceman/ex-servicewoman

invalider [ɛ̃valide] *vt Jur* to invalidate

invalidité [ɛ̃validite] *nf* disability

invariable [ɛ̃varjabl] *adj* invariable

invariablement [ɛ̃varjabləmɑ̃] *adv* invariably

invasif, -ive [ɛ̃vazif, -iv] *adj Méd (traitement, chirurgie)* invasive

invasion [ɛ̃vazjɔ̃] *nf aussi Fig* invasion

invective [ɛ̃vɛktiv] *nf* invective; **invectives** abuse

invectiver [ɛ̃vɛktive] **1** *vt* to hurl abuse at **2** **s'invectiver** *vpr* to hurl abuse at each other

invendable [ɛ̃vɑ̃dabl] *adj* unsellable

invendu, -e [ɛ̃vɑ̃dy] **1** *adj* unsold **2** *nm* **invendus** unsold goods; *(journaux, livres)* unsold copies; *(revendus moins cher)* remainders

inventaire [ɛ̃vɑ̃tɛr] *nm* (**a**) *(liste)* inventory (**b**) *(de marchandises)* stocklist; **faire** *ou* **dresser l'i. (des stocks)** to stocktake; **fermé pour cause d'i.** *(sur un écriteau)* closed for stocktaking (**c**) *Fig (de peintures, de richesses artistiques)* survey

inventer [ɛ̃vɑ̃te] **1** *vt (machine)* to invent; *(concept, moyen)* to think up; *(histoire, excuse)* to make up; *(expression)* to coin; **qu'est-ce qu'il va encore i.?** what's he going to come out with next?; *Fam* **il n'a pas inventé la poudre** *ou* **le fil à couper le beurre** he'll never set the world alight **2** **s'inventer** *vpr* **ça ne s'invente pas** you can't make something like that up; **s'i. un passé** to invent a past for oneself

inventeur, -trice [ɛ̃vɑ̃tœr, -tris] *nm,f* (**a**) *(d'une machine, d'un procédé)* inventor (**b**) *Jur (d'un trésor)* finder

inventif, -ive [ɛ̃vɑ̃tif, -iv] *adj* inventive

invention [ɛ̃vɑ̃sjɔ̃] *nf* (**a**) *(action)* invention; *(faculté)* inventiveness (**b**) *(chose découverte, mensonge)* invention (**c**) *Jur (d'un trésor)* finding

inventorier [66] [ɛ̃vɑ̃tɔrje] *vt* to inventory; *(marchandises)* to make a stocklist of

invérifiable [ɛ̃verifjabl] *adj* unverifiable

inverse [ɛ̃vɛrs] **1** *adj aussi Math* inverse; **en sens i. (de)** in the opposite direction (to); **dans l'ordre i.** in reverse order; **dans le sens i. des aiguilles d'une montre** *Br* anticlockwise, *Am* counterclockwise **2** *nm* **l'i.** the opposite, the reverse; **faire l'i. (de)** to do the opposite (of); **à l'i. de** contrary to

inversement [ɛ̃vɛrsəmɑ̃] *adv* et **i.** and vice versa; **i.,
on peut dire que...** conversely, one can say that...; **i.
proportionnel (à)** inversely proportional (to)
inverser [ɛ̃vɛrse] *vt (ordre, tendance)* to reverse; *(deux
mots)* to invert
inversion [ɛ̃vɛrsjɔ̃] *nf (d'ordre, de mots)* inversion
invertébré, -e [ɛ̃vɛrtebre] *adj & nm* invertebrate
inverti, -e [ɛ̃vɛrti] **1** *adj (sucre)* invert
  2 *nm,f Vieilli (homosexuel)* homosexual, invert
investigateur, -trice [ɛ̃vɛstigatœr, -tris] **1** *adj (regard)* searching
  2 *nm,f* investigator
investigation [ɛ̃vɛstigasjɔ̃] *nf* investigation
investir [ɛ̃vɛstir] **1** *vt* (**a**) *(argent, temps, énergie)* to
invest (**dans** in) (**b**) *(ville, édifice)* to besiege (**c**)
(charger) **i. qn d'une mission** to entrust sb with a mission
  2 *vi* to invest (**dans** in)
  3 **s'investir** *vpr* **s'i. dans qch** to put a lot into sth
investissement [ɛ̃vɛstismɑ̃] *nm* investment; **i. à
court/long terme** short-/long-term investment
investisseur [ɛ̃vɛstisœr] *nm* investor; **les investis-
seurs institutionnels** institutional investors
investiture [ɛ̃vɛstityr] *nf (d'un candidat)* nomination;
(d'un gouvernement) voting in; *(d'un évêque)* investiture
invétéré, -e [ɛ̃vetere] *adj* inveterate
invincible [ɛ̃vɛ̃sibl] *adj (armée, adversaire)* invincible;
(peur) unconquerable
inviolabilité [ɛ̃vjɔlabilite] *nf Jur* inviolability; *(d'un
parlementaire)* immunity; **i. diplomatique** diplomatic
immunity
inviolable [ɛ̃vjɔlabl] *adj (coffre)* burglarproof; *(droit,
asile)* inviolable; *(parlementaire)* immune
invisibilité [ɛ̃vizibilite] *nf* invisibility
invisible [ɛ̃vizibl] *adj* invisible
invit' [ɛ̃vit] *nf Fam (abrév* **invitation***)* invite
invitation [ɛ̃vitasjɔ̃] *nf* invitation; **venir à ou sur l'i. de
qn** to come at sb's invitation; **sur i.** by invitation
invite [ɛ̃vit] *nf Ordinat* prompt; **i. du DOS** DOS prompt;
i. du système system prompt
invité, -e [ɛ̃vite] *nm,f* guest
inviter [ɛ̃vite] **1** *vt* (**a**) *(convier)* to invite; **i. qn à dîner**
to invite *or* ask sb to dinner (**b**) **i. qn à faire qch** *(inciter)* to urge sb to do sth; *(prier)* to request sb to do
sth; **je vous invite à me suivre** would you be so kind
as to follow me
  2 *vi (payer)* **ce soir, c'est moi qui invite!** it's my treat
tonight!
  3 **s'inviter** *vpr* to invite oneself
in vitro [invitro] *adj inv & adv* in vitro
invivable [ɛ̃vivabl] *adj* unbearable
in vivo [invivo] *adj inv & adv* in vivo
invocation [ɛ̃vɔkasjɔ̃] *nf* invocation
involontaire [ɛ̃vɔlɔ̃tɛr] *adj (mouvement, geste)* involuntary; *(erreur, réaction)* unintentional; *(témoin)* unwilling
involontairement [ɛ̃vɔlɔ̃tɛrmɑ̃] *adv* involuntarily,
unintentionally
invoquer [ɛ̃vɔke] *vt* (**a**) *(raison, argument)* to put forward; *(prétexte, excuse)* to plead; *(loi, texte)* to refer to
(**b**) *(Dieu, divinité, esprit)* to invoke; **i. l'aide de qn** to
call upon sb's help
invraisemblable [ɛ̃vrɛsɑ̃blabl] *adj* (**a**) *(hypothèse)*
unlikely (**b**) *(excuses, alibi)* implausible (**c**) *(extra
ordinaire)* incredible

invraisemblance [ɛ̃vrɛsɑ̃blɑ̃s] *nf (improbabilité)* un-
likelihood; *(d'un récit, d'une excuse)* implausibility;
des invraisemblances implausibilities
invulnérabilité [ɛ̃vylnerabilite] *nf* invulnerability
invulnérable [ɛ̃vylnerabl] *adj* invulnerable
iode [jɔd] *nm* iodine
iodé, -e [jɔde] *adj (eau, air)* iodized
ion [jɔ̃] *nm* ion
iota [jɔta] *nm inv* iota; **ça n'a pas changé d'un i.** it
hasn't changed one iota; **ne pas bouger d'un i.** not
to budge an inch
ipso facto [ipsofakto] *adv* ipso facto
Ipsos [ipsos] *nm* = French market research institute
ira, irai *etc voir* aller
Irak [irak] *nm* **l'I.** Iraq
irakien, -enne [irakjɛ̃, -ɛn] **1** *adj* Iraqi
  2 *nm,f* **I.** Iraqi
Iran [irɑ̃] *nm* **l'I.** Iran
iranien, -enne [iranjɛ̃, -ɛn] **1** *adj* Iranian
  2 *nm,f* **I.** Iranian
  3 *nm (langue)* Iranian
Iraq [irak] = **Irak**
iraquien, -enne [irakjɛ̃, -ɛn] = **irakien**
irascible [irasibl] *adj Litt* irascible
iriez, irions *voir* aller
iris [iris] *nm* (**a**) *(de l'œil)* iris (**b**) *(fleur)* iris
irisé, -e [irize] *adj* iridescent
irlandais, -e [irlɑ̃dɛ, -ɛz] **1** *adj* Irish
  2 *nm,f* **I.** Irishman, *f* Irishwoman; **I. du Nord** person
from Northern Ireland; **les I.** the Irish
  3 *nm (langue)* Irish
Irlande [irlɑ̃d] *nf* **l'I.** Ireland, Eire; **l'I. du Nord** Northern Ireland, Ulster
IRM [iɛrɛm] *nf Méd (abrév* **imagerie par résonance
magnétique***)* MRI
ironie [irɔni] *nf* irony; **l'i. du sort a voulu que...** as fate
would have it,...
ironique [irɔnik] *adj* ironic(al)
ironiquement [irɔnikmɑ̃] *adv* ironically
ironiser [irɔnize] *vi* to be ironical (**sur** about)
irradiation [iradjasjɔ̃] *nf Phys & Méd* irradiation
irradier [66] [iradje] **1** *vi (rayons)* to radiate; *(douleur)*
to spread
  2 *vt* to irradiate
irraisonné, -e [irɛzɔne] *adj* irrational
irrationnel, -elle [irasjɔnɛl] *adj* irrational
irrattrapable [iratrapabl] *adj (retard)* that cannot be
made up; *(erreur)* irredeemable
irréalisable [irealizabl] *adj (rêve)* unrealizable; *(projet)* impracticable
irréaliste [irealist] *adj* unrealistic
irréalité [irealite] *nf* unreality
irrecevable [irəsəvabl] *adj (inacceptable)* unacceptable; *Jur (preuve, demande)* inadmissible
irrécupérable [irekyperabl] *adj (argent)* irrecover-
able; *(personne)* irredeemable; *(appareil, voiture)* beyond repair
irrécusable [irekyzabl] *adj* (**a**) *(indéniable) (preuve,
signe)* indisputable (**b**) *Jur (témoignage, juge)* unim-
peachable
irréductible [iredyktibl] **1** *adj* (**a**) *(volonté, optimisme)* indomitable, invincible; *(attachement, fidélité)* unshakeable; *(opposition, ennemi)* implacable
(**b**) *Math (fracture, fraction)* irreducible
  2 *nmf* die-hard

irréel, -elle [ireɛl] **1** *adj* unreal
  2 *nm* **l'i.** the unreal; *Gram* **l'i.** du présent/passé the hypothetical present/passé
irréfléchi, -e [irefleʃi] *adj* rash
irréfutable [irefytabl] *adj* irrefutable
irrégularité [iregylarite] *nf* (**a**) *(du sol, d'un terrain)* unevenness; *(du pouls, de traits, d'horaires)* irregularity (**b**) *(acte)* irregularity
irrégulier, -ère [iregylje, -ɛr] *adj* (**a**) *(sol, terrain)* uneven; *(rythme, respiration, traits, verbe)* irregular; *(résultats, athlète)* inconsistent (**b**) *(malhonnête) (procédure, situation)* irregular; **être en situation irrégulière** *(étranger)* not to have one's residence papers in order; *(voyageur)* not to hold a valid ticket
irrégulièrement [iregyljɛrmɑ̃] *adv* irregularly
irréligieux, -euse [ireliʒjø, -øz] *adj* irreligious
irrémédiable [iremedjabl] *adj* (*préjudice, perte, problème*) irreparable; *(désastre)* irreversible
irrémissible [iremisibl] *adj Litt* (**a**) *(impardonnable)* unpardonable (**b**) *(irrémédiable)* irreversible
irremplaçable [irɑ̃plasabl] *adj* irreplaceable
irréparable [ireparabl] **1** *adj (tort, perte, erreur)* irreparable; *(affront)* unpardonable; *(vêtement, voiture, télévision)* beyond repair
  2 *nm* **commettre l'i.** to go beyond the point of no return
irrépressible [irepresibl] *adj* irrepressible
irréprochable [ireprɔʃabl] *adj (personne, conduite)* irreproachable; *(tenue, travail)* impeccable; **d'une propreté i.** impeccably clean
irrésistible [irezistibl] *adj (personne, charme)* irresistible; *(envie, besoin)* compelling
irrésolu, -e [irezɔly] *adj* (**a**) *(personne)* indecisive; *(pas)* uncertain (**b**) *(problème)* unresolved
irrespect [irɛspɛ] *nm* disrespect (**envers** towards)
irrespectueux, -euse [irɛspɛktɥø, -øz] *adj* disrespectful (**envers** towards)
irrespirable [irɛspirabl] *adj (air)* unbreathable; *Fig (atmosphère)* unbearable
irresponsable [irɛspɔ̃sabl] **1** *adj* irresponsible
  2 *nmf* irresponsible person
irrévérence [ireverɑ̃s] *nf* irreverence
irrévérencieux, -euse [ireverɑ̃sjø, -øz] *adj* irreverent
irréversible [irevɛrsibl] *adj* irreversible
irrévocabilité [irevɔkabilite] *nf* irrevocability
irrévocable [irevɔkabl] *adj* irrevocable
irrévocablement [irevɔkabləmɑ̃] *adv* irrevocably
irrigation [irigasjɔ̃] *nf* irrigation; **l'i. du cerveau** the blood supply to the brain
irriguer [irige] *vt* to irrigate; **le cerveau n'est plus irrigué** the brain is no longer being supplied with blood
irritable [iritabl] *adj* irritable
irritant, -e [iritɑ̃, -ɑ̃t] *adj* (**a**) *(personne, comportement)* irritating (**b**) *(substance)* irritant (**pour** to)
irritation [iritasjɔ̃] *nf aussi Méd* irritation
irrité, -e [irite] *adj* (**a**) *(énervé)* irritated (**contre** with) (**b**) *(enflammé)* irritated, inflamed
irriter [irite] **1** *vt (énerver, enflammer)* to irritate
  2 **s'irriter** *vpr* (**a**) *(s'énerver)* **s'i. contre qn/de qch** to get irritated with sb/at sth (**b**) *(s'enflammer)* to become irritated *or* inflamed
irruption [irypsjɔ̃] *nf* (**a**) *(entrée)* irruption; **faire i. dans** to burst into (**b**) *(invasion)* invasion (**c**) *(émergence)* upsurge
islam [islam] *nm* **l'i.** Islam
islamique [islamik] *adj* Islamic

islamiste [islamist] *nmf* Islamic fundamentalist
islamophobe [islamɔfɔb] *adj* Islamophobic
islamophobie [islamɔfɔbi] *nf* Islamophobia
islandais, -e [islɑ̃dɛ, -ɛz] **1** *adj* Icelandic
  2 *nm,f* **I.** Icelander
  3 *nm (langue)* Icelandic
Islande [islɑ̃d] *nf* **l'I.** Iceland
isobare [izɔbar] **1** *adj* isobaric
  2 *nf* isobar
isocèle [izɔsɛl] *adj* isosceles
isolant, -e [izɔlɑ̃, -ɑ̃t] **1** *adj (contre le froid, en électricité)* insulating; *(contre le bruit)* soundproofing
  2 *nm (contre le froid, en électricité)* insulating material; *(contre le bruit)* soundproofing (material)
isolation [izɔlasjɔ̃] *nf (électrique)* insulation; **i. acoustique** *ou* **phonique** soundproofing; **i. thermique** (thermal) insulation
isolationniste [izɔlasjɔnist] *adj & nmf* isolationist
isolé, -e [izɔle] *adj* (**a**) *(personne, cas, endroit, maison)* isolated (**b**) *(protégé) (en électricité, du froid)* insulated; *(du bruit)* soundproofed
isolement [izɔlmɑ̃] *nm* (**a**) *(d'une personne, d'une maison)* isolation (**b**) *(isolation)* insulation
isolément [izɔlemɑ̃] *adv (agir)* in isolation; *(interroger des gens)* individually
isoler [izɔle] **1** *vt* (**a**) *(séparer)* to isolate (**de** from) (**b**) *(protéger) (du froid, d'un courant électrique)* to insulate; *(du bruit)* to soundproof
  2 **s'isoler** *vpr* to isolate oneself
isoloir [izɔlwar] *nm* polling booth
isotherme [izɔtɛrm] **1** *adj* maintained at a constant temperature; **boîte/sac i.** cool box/bag; **bouteille i.** vacuum flask
  2 *nf* isotherm
Israël [israɛl] *n* Israel
israélien, -enne [israeljɛ̃, -ɛn] **1** *adj* Israeli
  2 *nm,f* **I.** Israeli
israélite [israelit] **1** *adj* (**a**) *(juif)* Jewish (**b**) *(dans la Bible)* Israelite
  2 *nmf* (**a**) *(juif)* Jew (**b**) *(dans la Bible)* Israelite
issu, -e [isy] *adj* **être i. de** *(être originaire de)* to come from; *(résulter de)* to stem from
issue [isy] *nf* (**a**) *(sortie)* exit; *Fig (solution)* way out; **i. de secours** emergency exit (**b**) *(fin)* outcome; **à l'i. de** at the end of
IST [iɛste] *nf Méd (abrév* **infection sexuellement transmissible**)) STI
Istanbul [istɑ̃bul] *n* Istanbul
isthme [ism] *nm* isthmus
Italie [itali] *nf* **l'I.** Italy
italien, -enne [italjɛ̃, -ɛn] **1** *adj* Italian
  2 *nm,f* **I.** Italian
  3 *nm (langue)* Italian
  4 *nf* **italienne** *Ordinat* **imprimer à l'italienne** to print landscape
italique [italik] **1** *adj* italic
  2 *nm* **en italique(s)** in italics
Ithaque [itak] *nf* Ithaca
itinéraire [itinerɛr] *nm* route, itinerary; **i. bis** = alternative route recommended when roads are highly congested, especially at peak holiday times; **i. touristique** tourist route; **i. vert** nature trail
itinérance [itinerɑ̃s] *nf Tél* roaming
itinérant, -e [itinerɑ̃, -ɑ̃t] *adj (comédiens, exposition)* travelling; *(ambassadeur)* roving
itou [itu] *adv Fam Vieilli* likewise, ditto; **et moi i.!** me too!

IUFM [iyɛfɛm] *nm* (*abrév* **Institut universitaire de formation des maîtres**) ≃ teacher training college

IUT [iyte] *nm* (*abrév* **Institut universitaire de technologie**) = vocational higher education college

IVG [iveʒe] *nf* (*abrév* **interruption volontaire de grossesse**) termination (of pregnancy)

ivoire [ivwar] *nm* ivory

ivoirien, -enne [ivwarjɛ̃, -ɛn] **1** *adj* of the Ivory Coast **2** *nm, f* **I.** person from the Ivory Coast

ivre [ivr] *adj* drunk; **i. mort** blind drunk; **i. de joie** beside oneself with joy

ivresse [ivrɛs] *nf (ébriété)* drunkenness; *(extase)* exhilaration; **conduite en état d'i.** *Br* drink-driving, *Am* drunk-driving

ivrogne [ivrɔɲ] *nmf* drunkard

ivrognerie [ivrɔɲri] *nf* drunkenness

ixième [iksjɛm] *adj* **pour la i. fois** for the umpteenth time

J, j [ʒi] *nm inv* J, j
j' [ʒ] *voir* je
jabot [ʒabo] *nm* (**a**) *(d'oiseau)* crop (**b**) *(de chemise)* frill, ruffle
jacassements [ʒakasmã] *nmpl (d'une pie, d'une personne)* chattering
jacasser [ʒakase] *vi (pie, personne)* to chatter
jachère [ʒaʃɛr] *nf* leaving land fallow; **laisser en j.** *(champ)* to leave fallow; *Fig (talent)* to leave undeveloped
jacinthe [ʒasɛ̃t] *nf* hyacinth
jacquard [ʒakar] *adj (pull)* argyle
jacquet [ʒakɛ] *nm* backgammon
jacter [ʒakte] *vi Fam* to gab
Jacuzzi® [ʒakuzi] *nm* Jacuzzi®
jade [ʒad] *nm* (**a**) *(pierre)* jade; **un collier en j.** a jade necklace (**b**) *(objet)* jade object
jadis [ʒadis] *Litt* **1** *adv* in times past, formerly; **les chevaliers de j.** the knights of old **2** *adj* **au temps j.** in the olden days
jaguar [ʒagwar] *nm* jaguar
jaillir [ʒajir] *vi* (**a**) *(source, liquide)* to gush out; *(étincelles, flammes, foule)* to shoot out; *(lumière)* to flash (**b**) *(rires, cris)* to burst out
jais [ʒɛ] *nm* jet; **(d'un noir) de j.** jet-black
Jakarta [dʒakarta] *n* Jakarta
jalon [ʒalɔ̃] *nm* ranging pole; *Fig (référence)* milestone, landmark; *Fig* **poser des jalons** to pave the way, to prepare the ground
jalonner [ʒalɔne] *vt (marquer) (parcelle, piste d'atterrissage)* to mark out; *(ponctuer) (route, côte)* to line (**de** with); *Fig* to punctuate
jalousement [ʒaluzmã] *adv* jealously
jalouser [ʒaluze] *vt* to be jealous of
jalousie [ʒaluzi] *nf* (**a**) *(sentiment)* jealousy; **éprouver de la j. envers qn** to feel jealous of sb; **être malade de j.** to be green with envy (**b**) *(store)* Venetian blind
jaloux, -ouse [ʒalu, -uz] **1** *adj* jealous (**de** of); **j. comme un tigre** wildly jealous **2** *nm,f* **c'est un j.** he's a jealous man; **faire des j.** to make people jealous
jamaïcain, -e, jamaïquain, -e [ʒamaikɛ̃, -ɛn] **1** *adj* Jamaican **2** *nm,f* **J.** Jamaican
Jamaïque [ʒamaik] *nf* **la J.** Jamaica
jamais [ʒamɛ] *adv* (**a**) *(positif)* ever; **plus que j.** more than ever; **à (tout) j.** for good, for ever; **si j. elle revenait** if she ever came back; **le film le plus drôle que j'aie j. vu** the funniest film I've ever seen (**b**) *(négatif)* never; **je ne l'ai j. vu** I've never seen him; **il a passé toute sa vie sans j. boire un verre d'alcool**

he's gone all his life without ever touching a drop of alcohol; **j. plus** never again; **j., au grand j., je ne le dirai** I shall never ever tell; **elle n'a j. que dix minutes de retard** she's only ten minutes late; *Fam* **j. de la vie!** not on your life!; *Prov* **j. deux sans trois** things come in threes
jambe [ʒãb] *nf* leg; **jambes nues** bare-legged; **traîner la j.** *(de fatigue)* to drag one's feet; *(en boitant)* to drag one foot behind one; **à toutes jambes** as fast as one can; **prendre ses jambes à son cou** to take to one's heels; **être dans les jambes de qn** to be under sb's feet; **traiter qn par-dessous** *ou* **par-dessus la j.** to treat sb in an offhand manner; *Fam* **ça me fait une belle j.!** a fat lot of good that does me!; *Fam* **tenir la j. à qn** to bend sb's ear; **j. de bois** wooden leg
jambière [ʒãbjɛr] *nf* (**a**) *(de sport)* (shin) pad (**b**) *(pour tenir chaud)* legwarmer
jambon [ʒãbɔ̃] *nm* ham; **j. blanc** boiled ham; **j. cru** raw ham; **j. fumé** smoked ham; **j. de Parme** Parma ham; **j. d'York** boiled ham on the bone
jambonneau, -x [ʒãbɔno] *nm* knuckle of ham
jante [ʒãt] *nf* rim
janvier [ʒãvje] *nm* January; **en j., au mois de j.** in January; **nous sommes le 7 j.** it's the 7th of January, it's January the 7th; **j'y vais le 7 j.** I'm going on the 7th of January *or* January the 7th
Japon [ʒapɔ̃] *nm* **le J.** Japan
japonais, -e [ʒapɔnɛ, -ɛz] **1** *adj* Japanese **2** *nm,f* **J.** Japanese; **les J.** the Japanese **3** *nm (langue)* Japanese
jappement [ʒapmã] *nm* yap, yelp; **jappements** yapping, yelping
japper [ʒape] *vi* to yap, to yelp
jaquette [ʒakɛt] *nf* (**a**) *(d'homme)* morning coat; *(de femme)* jacket; *Can (chemise de nuit)* nightdress (**b**) *(de livre)* (dust) jacket, (dust) cover
jardin [ʒardɛ̃] *nm (public)* garden; *(privé) Br* garden, *Am* yard; *Fig* **c'est mon j. secret** I keep it very much to myself; **j. botanique** botanical garden(s); **j. d'enfants** kindergarten; **j. potager** vegetable garden; **j. public** gardens; **j. zoologique** zoological gardens
jardinage [ʒardinaʒ] *nm* gardening
jardiner [ʒardine] *vi* to do some gardening
jardinet [ʒardinɛ] *nm* small garden
jardinier, -ère [ʒardinje, -ɛr] **1** *nm,f* gardener **2** *nf* **jardinière** (**a**) *(pour balcon)* window box; *(intérieure)* jardinière (**b**) *Culin* **jardinière (de légumes)** mixed vegetables
jargon [ʒargɔ̃] *nm* (**a**) *(argot, de métier)* jargon (**b**) *(langage incompréhensible)* gibberish

jarre [ʒar] *nf* (**a**) *(vase)* (earthenware) jar (**b**) *Can (bocal)* preserving jar

jarret [ʒarɛ] *nm* (**a**) *(de personne)* back of the knee; *(de cheval)* hock (**b**) *(morceau de viande) (de veau)* knuckle; *(de bœuf)* shin

jarretelle [ʒartɛl] *nf Br* suspender, *Am* garter

jarretière [ʒartjɛr] *nf* garter

jars [ʒar] *nm* (**a**) *Zool* gander (**b**) *Can* **faire le j.** to show off

jaser [ʒaze] *vi* (**a**) *(médire)* to gossip; **cela va faire j.** that'll set tongues wagging (**b**) *Can (bavarder)* to chatter (**de** about)

jasmin [ʒasmɛ̃] *nm* jasmine

jatte [ʒat] *nf* (**a**) *(petite)* bowl; *(grande)* basin (**b**) *Belg (récipient)* coffee cup; *(contenu)* cup of coffee

jauge [ʒoʒ] *nf* (**a**) *(instrument de mesure)* gauge; **j. d'essence** *Br* petrol *or Am* gas gauge; **j. de niveau d'huile** oil-level indicator; *(manuelle)* dipstick (**b**) *(de navire)* tonnage

jauger [45] [ʒoʒe] **1** *vt* (**a**) *(mesurer) (tonneau, réservoir)* to measure the capacity of; *(navire)* to measure the tonnage of (**b**) *Fig (personne, situation)* to size up **2** *vi* **j. 300 tonneaux** to have a tonnage of 300 tons

jaunâtre [ʒonɑtr] *adj* yellowish

jaune [ʒon] **1** *adj (couleur, objet)* yellow; *(teint)* sallow; **j. canari** canary yellow; **j. citron** lemon yellow; **j. moutarde** mustard yellow; **j. d'or** golden yellow; **j. paille** straw-coloured **2** *nm* (**a**) *(couleur)* yellow (**b**) **j. d'œuf** (egg) yolk **3** *nmf Péj* (**a**) *(non gréviste)* strikebreaker (**b**) *Can (lâche)* yellowbelly **4** *adv* **rire j.** to give a forced laugh

jauni, -e [ʒoni] *adj* yellowed

jaunir [ʒonir] *vt & vi* to turn yellow

jaunisse [ʒonis] *nf* jaundice; *Fam Fig* **en faire une j.** to get into a state about it

Java® [ʒava] *nm Ordinat* Java®

java [ʒava] *nf* (**a**) *(danse)* = type of popular waltz (**b**) *Fam (fête)* **faire la j.** to live it up

Javel [ʒavɛl] *n voir* **eau**

javelot [ʒavlo] *nm* javelin

jazz [dʒaz] *nm* jazz

J.-C. *(abrév* **Jésus-Christ)** JC; **av. J.-C.** BC; **ap. J.-C.** AD

je [ʒə]

> **j'** is used before a word beginning with a vowel or h mute.

pron personnel I

jean [dʒin] *nm (pantalon)* jeans; *(tissu)* denim; **un j.** (a pair of) jeans; **veste en j.** denim jacket

Jeanne [ʒan] *npr* **J. d'Arc** Joan of Arc

Jeep® [dʒip] *nf* Jeep®

Jéhovah [ʒeova] *npr* Jehovah

je-m'en-foutisme [ʒmɑ̃futism] *nm très Fam* couldn't-care-less attitude

je-m'en-foutiste *(pl* **je-m'en-foutistes)** [ʒmɑ̃futist] *nmf très Fam* couldn't-care-less type

je-ne-sais-quoi [ʒənsɛkwa] *nm inv* **un j.** a certain something

jérémiades [ʒeremjad] *nfpl* whining

jerrican(e), jerrycan [dʒerikan, ʒerikan] *nm* jerry can

Jérusalem [ʒeryzalɛm] *n* Jerusalem

jésuite [ʒezɥit] **1** *adj* Jesuit; *Fig & Péj* jesuitical **2** *nm* Jesuit

Jésus(-Christ) [ʒezy(kri)] *npr* Jesus (Christ)

jet¹ [ʒɛ] *nm* (**a**) *(lancer) (de pierre)* throwing; *Fig* **faire qch d'un seul j.** to do sth in one go (**b**) *(de liquide, de vapeur)* jet; **premier j.** *(d'un roman)* first draft; **j. d'eau** *(fontaine)* fountain

jet² [dʒɛt] *nm (avion)* jet

jetable [ʒətablə] *adj* disposable

jeté, -e¹ [ʒəte] **1** *nm (en danse)* jeté (**b**) **j. de lit** bedspread **2** *adj très Fam* crazy

jetée² *nf* jetty, pier

jeter [42] [ʒəte] **1** *vt* (**a**) *(lancer)* to throw; *(plus fort)* to fling, to hurl; *(filets)* to cast; **j. qch à qn** to throw sb sth, to throw sth to sb; **j. qn à terre** to throw sb to the ground; **j. qch à terre** *ou* **par terre** to throw sth on the ground; **j. qn en prison** to throw sb in prison; **j. les bras autour de qn** to throw one's arms around sb; **j. quelques idées sur le papier** to jot down a few ideas; **j. le trouble dans l'esprit de qn** to trouble sb; **ça a jeté un froid** it cast a chill (**b**) *(se défaire de)* to throw away *or* out; **j. son argent par les fenêtres** to throw one's money down the drain; *Fam* **se faire j. (de)** to get chucked out (of) (**c**) *(émettre) (cri)* to utter; **j. un regard à qn** to glance at sb; **j. un coup d'œil (sur qch)** to have a quick glance (at sth) (**d**) *(établir)* **j. les fondements de qch** to lay the foundations for sth (**e**) *Fam* **ça (en) jette!** it's really something! **2** **se jeter** *vpr* (**a**) *(fleuve, rivière)* **se j. dans** to flow into (**b**) *(personne)* to throw oneself; **se j. dans le vide** *(suicidaire)* to jump; *Fig* to pounce on sb; **se j. sur** *(nourriture)* to pounce on; *(occasion)* to jump at; **se j. sur qn** to throw oneself at sb; **se j. à l'eau** to plunge into the water; *Fig* to take the plunge; **se j. par la fenêtre** to throw oneself out of the window; **se j. aux pieds de qn** to throw oneself at sb's feet; *Fig* **se j. à la tête de qn** *(le draguer)* to throw oneself at sb

jeton [ʒətɔ̃] *nm* (**a**) *(au jeu)* chip; *(pour téléphone, machine)* token; **j. de présence** *(objet)* token *(issued as voucher for attendance at meeting); (honoraires)* director's fees (**b**) *Fam* **avoir les jetons** to have the jitters

jeu, -x [ʒø] *nm* (**a**) *(amusement)* play; **faire qch par j.** to do sth for fun; *Fig* **entrer en j.** to come into play; *Fig* **c'est un j. d'enfant** it's child's play; *Prov* **jeux de mains, jeux de vilains** all this fooling around is going to end in tears; **j. de mots** play on words, pun; **j. de rôles** role-playing

(**b**) *(activité)* game; **mettre la balle en j.** to bring the ball into play; *Fig* **jouer le j.** to play the game; *Fig* **jouer franc j. (avec qn)** to play fair (with sb); *Fig* **se prendre au j.** to get caught up in it; *Fig* **faire le j. de qn** to play into sb's hands; **on aurait beau j. de répondre** it would be quite easy to answer; **j. d'adresse** game of skill; **j. de cartes** card game; **j. électronique** computer game; **le j. de l'oie** = board game similar to snakes and ladders; **les jeux Olympiques** the Olympic Games, the Olympics; **jeux de société** *(charades, devinettes)* parlour games; *(petits chevaux, jeu de l'oie)* board games; **j. télévisé** (television) game show; *(avec questions)* (television) quiz show; **j. vidéo** video game

(**c**) *(au casino)* **le j.** gambling; **se ruiner au j.** to bankrupt oneself gambling; **mettre qch en j.** *(argent, voiture, carrière)* to stake sth; *Fig* **être en j.** to be at stake; **les jeux sont faits** *(à la roulette)* les jeux sont faits; **faites vos jeux!** place your bets!; **jeux de hasard** games of chance

(**d**) *(cartes en main)* hand; **avoir du j.** to have a good hand; **cacher son j.** to hide one's hand; *Fig* to keep one's cards close to one's chest; *Fig* **sortir le grand j.** to pull out all the stops

(**e**) *(au tennis)* game; **j., set et match** game, set and match; **j. Mauresmo** game (to) Mauresmo; **j. blanc** love game

(**f**) *(d'un acteur)* acting; *(d'un musicien)* playing; **j. de jambes** *(d'un boxeur, d'un tennisman)* footwork

(**g**) *(d'outils, de clefs)* set; **j. de boules/quilles** set of bowls/skittles; **j. de cartes** *Br* pack *or Am* deck of cards; **j. d'échecs** chess set

(**h**) **il y a du j.** *(ça bouge)* there's a bit of play; **le vis a** *ou* **prend du j.** the screw is loose

(**i**) *(mécanisme)* **le j. de l'offre et de la demande** the system of supply and demand

jeu-concours *(pl* **jeux-concours**) [ʒøkɔ̃kur] *nm* competition

jeudi [ʒødi] *nm* Thursday; **le j. saint** MaundyThursday; *Fam* **la semaine des quatre jeudis,** *Can* **dans la semaine des trois jeudis** when pigs fly; *voir aussi* **samedi**

jeun [ʒœ̃] **à jeun 1** *adj* **être à j.** *(sans avoir mangé ni bu)* not to have eaten or drunk anything; *(pas ivre)* to be sober

2 *adv* **prendre qch à j.** to take sth on an empty stomach

jeune [ʒœn] **1** *adj (personne, vin, pays)* young; *(apparence, allure)* youthful; *(coiffure, vêtement)* that makes one look young; **être j. d'esprit** to have a youthful outlook; **faire plus j. que son âge** to look younger than one's age; **elle n'est plus toute j.** she's not as young as she was

2 *nmf* **un j.** a youngster; **une j.** a girl; *Fam* **un petit j.** a young guy; **les jeunes** young people

3 *adv* **s'habiller j.** to dress in a youthful style; **ça fait j.** it makes you/her/etc look young

jeûne [ʒøn] *nm* (**a**) *(période)* fast; **rompre le j.** to break one's fast (**b**) *(pratique)* fasting

jeûner [ʒøne] *vi* to fast

jeunesse [ʒœnɛs] *nf* (**a**) *(période)* youth (**b**) *(d'apparence, d'esprit)* youthfulness (**c**) *(jeunes gens)* young people

jeunot, -otte [ʒœno, -ɔt] *Fam* **1** *adj* youngish

2 *nm,f Péj* youngster; **un petit j.** a young kid

JF (**a**) *(abrév* **jeune fille**) girl (**b**) *(abrév* **jeune femme**) young woman

JH *(abrév* **jeune homme**) young man

jingle [dʒingəl] *nm* jingle

JO [ʒio] **1** *nm (abrév* **Journal officiel**) = French government publication, *Br* ≃ Hansard, *Am* ≃ Federal Register

2 *nmpl (abrév* **jeux Olympiques**) Olympic Games

joaillerie [ʒɔajri] *nf* (**a**) *(magasin)* jeweller's shop (**b**) *(bijoux)* jewellery

joaillier, -ère [ʒɔaje, -ɛr] *nm,f* jeweller

job [dʒɔb] *nm Fam* job

jockey [ʒɔkɛ] *nm* jockey

Joconde [ʒɔkɔ̃d] *nf* **la J.** the Mona Lisa

joggeur, -euse [dʒɔgœr, -øz] *nm,f* jogger

jogging [dʒɔgiŋ] *nm* (**a**) *(vêtement)* track suit (**b**) *(activité)* jogging; *(course)* run; **faire du j.** to go jogging, to jog

Johannesburg [ʒɔanɛsbur] *n* Johannesburg

joie [ʒwa] *nf* joy, delight; **avec j.** *(volontiers)* with pleasure, gladly; *Fam* **c'est pas la j.!** it's no fun!; **faire la j. de qn** to make sb happy; **se faire une j. de faire qch** *(envisager)* to look forward to doing sth; *(faire avec*

plaisir) to be delighted to do sth; **faire une fausse j. à qn** to falsely raise sb's hopes; **j. de vivre** joie de vivre

joignable [ʒwaɲabl] *adj* contactable

joignais *etc voir* **joindre**

joindre [43] [ʒwɛ̃dr] **1** *vt* (**a**) *(réunir)* to join; **j. les mains** to put one's hands together; *Fam Fig* **j. les deux bouts** to make ends meet (**b**) *(ajouter)* to add (**à** to); *(dans une lettre, un colis)* to enclose (**à** with); **j. le geste à la parole** to suit the action to the word; **j. l'utile à l'agréable** to combine business with pleasure (**c**) *(contacter)* to contact

2 se joindre *vpr* **se j. à qn** to join sb; **se j. à qch** to join in sth

joint, -e [ʒwɛ̃, -ɛt] **1** *pp de* **joindre**

2 *adj* **sauter à pieds joints** to jump from a standing position; **les mains jointes** with hands together; **pièces jointes** *(dans une lettre)* enclosures

3 *nm* (**a**) *(d'étanchéité)* seal; *(articulation)* joint; **j. de culasse** cylinder head gasket; **j. de dilatation** expansion joint (**b**) *Fam (à fumer)* joint

jointure [ʒwɛ̃tyr] *nf (articulation)* joint

jojo [ʒɔʒo] *Fam* **1** *nm voir* **affreux**

2 *adj inv* **ne pas être j.** *(physiquement)* not to look very nice; *(moralement)* not to be very nice

jojoba [ʒɔʒoba] *nm* jojoba

joker [ʒɔkɛr] *nm (aux cartes)* joker; *Ordinat* wild-card

joli, -e [ʒɔli] **1** *adj* (**a**) *(personne, ville, voix)* pretty, attractive; **il est j. garçon** he's a good-looking lad; **j. comme un cœur** pretty as a picture; **faire le j. cœur** to flirt (**b**) *(situation, somme)* nice; **c'est bien j. tout ça mais...** that's all well and good but...; *Fam* **c'est pas j. j.** *(blâmable)* that's not very nice; *(laid)* it's not a pretty sight

2 *nm Ironique* **c'est du j.!** marvellous!

joliment [ʒɔlimã] *adv* (**a**) *(bien)* nicely; **c'est j. dit** that's nicely put; *Ironique* **te voilà j. arrangé!** you're in a right mess! (**b**) *Fam (extrêmement)* really; **elle s'est j. fait engueuler** she got a good telling-off

jonc [ʒɔ̃] *nm (plante)* rush

joncher [ʒɔ̃ʃe] *vt* to strew (**de** with)

jonction [ʒɔ̃ksjɔ̃] *nf* junction

jongler [ʒɔ̃gle] *vi* (**a**) *(avec des balles)* & *Fig* to juggle (**avec** with) (**b**) *Can (rêvasser)* to daydream

jonglerie [ʒɔ̃gləri] *nf (avec des balles)* & *Fig* to juggle

jongleur, -euse [ʒɔ̃glœr, -øz] *nm,f* juggler

jonquille [ʒɔ̃kij] *nf* daffodil

Jordanie [ʒɔrdani] *nf* **la J.** Jordan

jordanien, -enne [ʒɔrdanjɛ̃, -ɛn] **1** *adj* Jordanian

2 *nm,f* **J.** Jordanian

jos-connaissant *(pl* **jos-connaissants**) [djokɔnɛsɑ̃] *nm Can Fam Péj* know-all

jouable [ʒwabl] *adj* playable

joual, -e [ʒwal] *Can* **1** *nm* joual *(French-Canadian dialect)*

2 *adj* **langue jouale** joual

joue [ʒu] *nf (de personne, d'animal)* cheek; **j. contre j.** cheek to cheek; **mettre qn en j.** to take aim at sb; **tenir qn en j.** to keep sb in one's sights; **en j.!** take aim!

jouer [ʒwe] **1** *vt* (**a**) *(parier)* to stake (**sur** on); *(cheval)* to back, to bet on (**b**) *(participer à)* **j. la finale** to play in the final (**c**) *(carte)* to play; *(pion, pièce)* to move (**d**) *(rôle)* to act, to play; **j. la surprise** to pretend to be surprised; **j. les héros** to play the hero; *Hum* **j. la fille de l'air** to vanish into thin air (**e**) *(air)* to play; **j. du Bach** to play (some) Bach

2 *vi* (**a**) *(s'amuser)* to play; *Fig* **j. sur les mots** to play with words; *Fig* **j. avec les sentiments de qn** to play with sb's feelings; *Fig* **j. avec son avenir** to risk one's future; *Fig* **j. avec le feu** to play with fire; **c'est à qui de j.?** whose turn is it?; *(aux échecs, aux dames)* whose move is it?; *Fig* **maintenant à vous de j.** now it's your turn (**b**) *(acteur)* to act; *(troupe)* to perform; **il joue très mal** he's a very bad actor (**c**) *(parier)* to gamble; **j. en Bourse** to speculate on the stock market (**d**) *(fonctionner)* **j. en faveur/défaveur de qn** to work in sb's favour/against sb; **faire j. un ressort** to release a spring; *Fig* **faire j. ses relations pour obtenir qch** to pull a few strings to get sth (**e**) *(bois)* to warp; *(pièce)* to work loose (**f**) *Suisse (convenir)* to be alright; **avec un peu de chance ça pouvait j.** with a bit of luck it could work out

3 jouer à *vt ind* (**a**) *(pratiquer)* to play; **j. au tennis/ aux cartes** to play tennis/cards; **j. aux gendarmes et aux voleurs** to play cops and robbers; **j. à la marchande** to play at shops; *Fig* **j. au plus fin** to try to outwit each other (**b**) *(parier sur)* **j. aux courses** to bet on *or* back horses

4 jouer de *vt ind* **j. du piano/de la harpe** to play the piano/the harp; *Fig* **j. des coudes** to elbow one's way through

5 se jouer *vpr* (**a**) *(match)* to be played (**b**) *(se décider)* **son sort est en train de se j.** his fate is hanging in the balance (**c**) **se j. de qn** to trifle with sb; **se j. des lois** to make a mockery of the law; **se j. des difficultés** to make light of difficulties (**d**) *(pièce de théâtre, film)* to be on

jouet [ʒwɛ] *nm* toy; *Fig* **être le j. des dieux** to be the plaything of the gods

joueur, -euse [ʒwœr, -øz] **1** *nm,f* (**a**) *(d'un jeu, d'un sport, d'un instrument de musique)* player; **j. de tennis/cartes** tennis/card player; **être beau/mauvais j.** to be a good/bad loser (**b**) *(au casino)* gambler **2** *adj (enfant, chien)* playful

joufflu, -e [ʒufly] *adj (bébé, angelot)* chubby-cheeked; *(visage)* chubby

joug [ʒu] *nm aussi Fig* yoke

jouir [ʒwir] *vi* (**a**) *(profiter)* **j. de qch** to enjoy sth (**b**) *(sexuellement)* to come (**c**) *(être en possession)* **j. d'une bonne réputation** to have a good reputation; **j. d'une bonne santé** to enjoy good health

jouissance [ʒwisɑ̃s] *nf* (**a**) *(plaisir)* enjoyment; *(sexuel)* orgasm (**b**) *Jur (usage)* use

jouisseur, -euse [ʒwisœr, -øz] *nm,f* sensualist

jouissif, -ive [ʒwisif, -iv] *adj très Fam* orgasmic

joujou, -x [ʒuʒu] *nm (langage enfantin)* toy; **faire j.** to play

joule [ʒul] *nm* joule

jour [ʒur] *nm* (**a**) *(clarté)* daylight; **au petit j.** at daybreak; **en plein j.** in broad daylight; *Fig* **au grand j.** publicly; **travailler le** *ou* **de j.** to work days; **j. et nuit** day and night; *Fig* **elle et son mari, c'est le j. et la nuit** she and her husband are like chalk and cheese; **elle est belle comme le j.** she's a real beauty; **il fait j.** it's light

(**b**) *(journée)* day; **huit jours** a week; **quinze jours** two weeks, *Br* a fortnight; **un j. ou l'autre** one day; **de j. en j.** day by day; **du j. au lendemain** overnight; **nous l'attendons d'un j. à l'autre** we're expecting him/her any day (now); **un de ces jours** one of these days; **un beau j.**, **elle décida de...** one day, she decided to...; **vivre au j. le j.** *(sans faire de projets)* to live from day to day; *(financièrement)* to live from hand to mouth; **mettre qch à j.** to update sth, to bring sth up to date; **tenir qch à j.** to keep sth up to date;

décidément, ce n'est pas mon j.! it just isn't my day today!; **il y a les jours avec et les jours sans** there are good days and bad days; **le j. de l'an** New Year's Day; **j. de congé** day off; **j. férié** public holiday, *Br* bank holiday; **le jour J** D-day; **le j. de Noël** Christmas Day; **j. ouvrable** working day; **j. de repos** day off (**c**) *(date)* day; **quel j. sommes-nous?** what's the date (today)?; **le j. de mes vingt ans** my twentieth birthday; **il y a six ans j. pour j.** six years ago to the day; **à ce j.**, **nous n'avons toujours pas reçu votre lettre** to date we still have not received your letter (**d**) *(époque)* **passer des jours heureux** to have a good time; **de nos jours** these days, nowadays; **les beaux jours** the fine days of summer; **pour mes vieux jours** for my old age

(**e**) *(vie)* **donner le j. à un enfant** to give birth to a child; **mettre fin à ses jours** to put an end to one's life; **ses jours ne sont plus en danger** we no longer fear for his/her life; **il vit le j. à Paris** he was born in Paris; **jusqu'à mon dernier j.** to my dying day

(**f**) *(éclairage)* light; *Fig* **voir qch sous un j. nouveau/ sous un vrai j.** to see sth in a new light/in its true light; *Fig* **présenter qch sous un j. favorable** to present sth in a favourable light

(**g**) *(ouverture)* gap

Jourdain [ʒurdɛ̃] *nm* **le J.** the River Jordan

journal, -aux [ʒurnal, -o] *nm* (**a**) *(publication)* paper, newspaper; **j. (télévisé)** (television) news (**b**) *(récit d'événements, d'expériences)* journal; *Ordinat* log; **tenir un j.** to keep a journal; **j. de bord** log (book); **j. intime** *Br* diary, *Am* journal; **J. officiel** = French government publication, *Br* ≃ Hansard, *Am* ≃ Federal Register

Journal officiel

This bulletin prints information about new laws and summaries of parliamentary debates, and informs the public of any important government business. When new companies are established, they are obliged by law to publish an announcement in the "Journal officiel".

journalier, -ère [ʒurnalje, -ɛr] **1** *adj* daily **2** *nm,f (ouvrier agricole)* day labourer

journalisme [ʒurnalism] *nm* journalism; **j. d'investigation** investigative journalism

journaliste [ʒurnalist] *nmf* journalist; **elle est j. au Monde** she's a journalist with Le Monde; **j. sportif** sports journalist

journalistique [ʒurnalistik] *adj* journalistic

journée [ʒurne] *nf* (**a**) *(par opposition à nuit)* day(-time); **pendant la j.** in the daytime, during the day; **dans la j.** in the course of the day; **toute la j.** all day (**b**) *(unité de temps)* day; **j. de travail** *(jour non chômé)* working day; *(quantité de travail)* day's work; **faire la j. continue** *(personne)* to work through lunch; **j. d'appel de préparation à la défense** = day during which young people are introduced to issues connected with national security; **j. portes ouvertes** *Br* open day, *Am* open house

journellement [ʒurnɛlmɑ̃] *adv* daily

joute [ʒut] *nf (combat médiéval)* joust; *Fig* **joutes oratoires** verbal jousting

jouvence [ʒuvɑ̃s] *nf Litt* **cela a été un bain** *ou* **une cure de j.** it has rejuvenated me

jouvenceau, -x [ʒuvɑ̃so] *nm Hum* stripling

jouvencelle [ʒuvɑ̃sɛl] *nf Hum* maiden

jouxter [ʒukste] *vt* to adjoin
jovial, -e, -als *ou* **-aux, -ales** [ʒɔvjal, -o] *adj* jovial, jolly
jovialité [ʒɔvjalite] *nf* joviality, jolliness
joyau, -x [ʒwajo] *nm aussi Fig* jewel
joyeusement [ʒwajøzmɑ̃] *adv* joyfully
joyeux, -euse [ʒwajø, -øz] *adj* joyful; **j. anniversaire!** happy birthday!; **j. Noël!** Happy *or* Merry Christmas!
JT [ʒite] *nm (abrév* **journal télévisé***)* TV news
jubilation [ʒybilasjɔ̃] *nf* jubilation
jubilé [ʒybile] *nm* jubilee
jubiler [ʒybile] *vi* to be jubilant; *(méchamment)* to gloat
jucher [ʒyʃe] **1** *vt* to perch (**sur** on)
 2 se jucher *vpr* to perch (**sur** on)
judaïque [ʒydaik] *adj* Jewish; *(loi)* Judaic
judaïsme [ʒydaism] *nm* Judaism
judas [ʒyda] *nm (ouverture)* peephole
judéo-chrétien, -enne *(mpl* **judéo-chrétiens,** *fpl* **judéo-chrétiennes)** [ʒydeɔkretjɛ̃, -ɛn] *adj* Judaeo-Christian
judiciaire [ʒydisjɛr] *adj (pouvoir, enquête, acte)* judicial; *(aide, autorité)* legal
judicieusement [ʒydisjøzmɑ̃] *adv* judiciously
judicieux, -euse [ʒydisjø, -øz] *adj* judicious; **peu j.** injudicious
judo [ʒydo] *nm* judo
judoka [ʒydɔka] *nmf Sport* judoka
juge [ʒyʒ] *nm* judge; **Monsieur le J.** Your Honour; **les juges** the bench; **je vous laisse j.** I'll let you be the judge; *Fig* **être à la fois j. et partie** to sit in judgment on oneself; **j. d'instruction** examining magistrate; **j. de ligne** line judge; **j. de touche** *(au football)* assistant referee, linesman; *(au rugby)* touch judge
jugé [ʒyʒe] **au jugé** *adv (tirer)* blind; *(calculer)* roughly
jugement [ʒyʒmɑ̃] *nm* (**a**) *Jur (d'une affaire)* trial; **passer en j.** to stand trial (**b**) *Jur (décision)* decision; *(dans des affaires criminelles)* sentence (**c**) *(opinion)* judgment; **porter un j. sur qch** to pass judgment on sth; **j. de valeur** value judgment (**d**) *(discernement)* judgment
jugeote [ʒyʒɔt] *nf Fam* common sense
juger¹ [45] [ʒyʒe] **1** *vt* (**a**) *(affaire, prévenu)* to try; *(demande, litige)* to adjudicate (**b**) *(évaluer, condamner)* to judge (**sur** by); **à toi de j.** it's for you to judge (**c**) *(croire)* **j. que** to consider that; **on le jugeait fou** people considered him mad; **j. superflu de faire qch** to consider it superfluous to do sth
 2 juger de *vt ind* to judge; **jugez de ma surprise!** imagine my surprise!; **à en j. par...** judging by...
juger² = **jugé**
jugulaire [ʒygylɛr] *nf* (**a**) *(veine)* jugular (vein) (**b**) *(de casque)* chin strap
juguler [ʒygyle] *vt (rébellion)* to quell; *(inflation, épidémie)* to check
juif, -ive [ʒyif, -iv] **1** *adj* Jewish
 2 *nm,f* **J.** Jew
juillet [ʒɥijɛ] *nm* July; **le 14 j.** Bastille Day *(day of national celebration in France)*; *voir aussi* **janvier**

La fête du 14 juillet

The celebrations to mark the anniversary of the storming of the Bastille begin on 13 July with outdoor public dances ("les bals du 14 Juillet") and firework displays, and continue on the 14th with a military parade in the morning. Firework displays are also held in the evening of Bastille Day.

juin [ʒɥɛ̃] *nm* June; *voir aussi* **janvier**
juke-box [dʒykbɔks, ʒykbɔks] *nm inv* jukebox
Jules [ʒyl] *npr* **J. César** Julius Caesar
jules [ʒyl] *nm Fam (mari, petit ami)* **mon/son j.** my/her man *or Br* bloke
julienne [ʒyljɛn] *nf* **j. de légumes** julienne of vegetables *(cut into thin strips)*
jumbo [dʒœmbo], **jumbo-jet** *(pl* **jumbo-jets)** [dʒœmbodʒɛt] *nm* jumbo (jet)
jumeau, -elle, -x, -elles [ʒymo, -ɛl] **1** *adj (frère, sœur)* twin
 2 *nm,f* twin; *(sosie)* double; **vrais/faux jumeaux** identical/fraternal twins
jumelage [ʒymlaʒ] *nm (de villes)* twinning
jumelé, -e [ʒymle] *adj (maisons)* semi-detached; **villes jumelées** *Br* twin towns, *Am* sister cities
jumeler [ʒymle] *vt (villes) Br* to twin, *Am* to make sister cities
jumelles [ʒymɛl] *nfpl* **(paire de) j.** (pair of) binoculars; **j. de théâtre** opera glasses
jument [ʒymɑ̃] *nf* mare
jungle [ʒœ̃gl] *nf aussi Fig* jungle
junior [ʒynjɔr] **1** *adj (mode, taille)* junior
 2 *nmf Sport* junior *(19 to 20 years old)*
junte [ʒœ̃t] *nf* junta
jupe [ʒyp] *nf* skirt; *Fam* **être dans les** *ou* **pendu aux jupes de sa mère** to be clinging to one's mother's skirts; **j. droite** straight skirt; **j. plissée** pleated skirt
jupe-culotte *(pl* **jupes-culottes)** [ʒypkylɔt] *nf* culottes
jupette [ʒypɛt] *nf* skirt
Jupiter [ʒypitɛr] *npr (dieu, planète)* Jupiter
jupon [ʒypɔ̃] *nm* underskirt, petticoat
Jura [ʒyra] *nm* **le J.** the Jura (Mountains)
jurassique [ʒyrasik] *Géol* **1** *adj* Jurassic
 2 *nm* **le J.** the Jurassic period
juré, -e [ʒyre] **1** *adj* **ennemi j.** sworn enemy
 2 *nm,f* juror; **les jurés** the jury
jurer [ʒyre] **1** *vt* to swear; **je le jure** I swear; **je te jure que c'est vrai!** I swear it's true!; **j. qch sur la tête de qn** to swear sth on sb's grave; **j'aurais juré qu'il était là** I could have sworn it was there; **j. de faire qch** to swear to do sth; **ne j. que par** to swear by; *Prov* **il ne faut j. de rien** you never can tell
 2 *vi* (**a**) *(dire des gros mots)* to swear (**b**) *(couleurs, vêtements)* to clash (**avec** with)
 3 se jurer *vpr* (**a**) *(l'un à l'autre)* **se j. fidélité** to swear to be faithful to each other (**b**) *(à soi-même)* **se j. que** to swear (to oneself) that; **se j. de faire qch** to swear to do sth
juridiction [ʒyridiksjɔ̃] *nf (compétence)* jurisdiction; *(tribunaux)* courts
juridique [ʒyridik] *adj* legal
jurisprudence [ʒyrisprydɑ̃s] *nf* case law; **faire j.** to set a (legal) precedent
juriste [ʒyrist] *nmf* legal expert; **j. d'entreprise** company lawyer
juron [ʒyrɔ̃] *nm* swearword
jury [ʒyri] *nm* (**a**) *(d'un tribunal)* jury (**b**) *(pour l'attribution d'un prix)* (panel of) judges; *(d'examen)* board of examiners
jus [ʒy] *nm* (**a**) *(de fruits, de légumes)* juice; *(de viande)* juices; **j. d'orange/de fruit** orange/fruit juice; *Can Fam* **j. de bras** elbow grease; *Fam Hum* **j. de chaussettes** *(café)* dishwater (**b**) *Fam (courant électrique)* juice; **prendre le j.** to get an electric shock
jusant [ʒyzɑ̃] *nm* ebb tide

jusque [ʒysk, ʒyskə] *prép* (**a**) **jusqu'à** *(délimite un espace)* as far as; *(délimite une mesure)* up to; **jusqu'ici** as far as here; **j.-là** as far as there; *Fam* **s'en mettre j.-là** to stuff oneself; **jusqu'où?** how far?; **avoir de l'eau jusqu'à la taille** to have water right up to one's waist; **compter jusqu'à dix** to count (up) to ten; **jusqu'au bout (de la rue)** to the end (of the street); **j. dans les campagnes** right into the countryside; *Fig* **aller jusqu'au bout d'un raisonnement** to follow an argument through; **aller jusqu'à faire qch** to go so far as to do sth (**b**) *(indique le temps)* until, till; **jusqu'ici, jusqu'à maintenant, jusqu'à présent** until now, up to now; **j.-là, jusqu'alors** until then, up to then; **jusqu'à ce que** + *subjunctive* until, till; **jusqu'à (l'âge de) quinze ans** up to the age of fifteen; **jusqu'à nouvel ordre** until further notice; **jusqu'au jour** *ou* **moment où…** until the time when…; **si nous remontons jusqu'en** *ou* **jusqu'à 1800** if we go right back to 1800 (**c**) *(également)* **jusqu'à** even

justaucorps [ʒystokɔr] *nm (de sport)* leotard

juste [ʒyst] **1** *adj* (**a**) *(équitable)* fair (**avec** *ou* **envers** to); **à j. titre** rightly (**b**) *(exact) (calcul, réponse)* right, correct; *(raisonnement)* sound; *(note)* right; **arriver à l'heure j.** to arrive right on time; **avez-vous l'heure j.?** do you have the right time? (**c**) *(trop petit) (chaussures, vêtement)* tight; **une bouteille pour six, c'est un peu j.** one bottle isn't quite enough for six people (**d**) *Fam (financièrement)* **être (un peu) j.** to be (a bit) strapped for cash

    2 *adv* (**a**) *(avec exactitude) (viser, parler)* accurately; *(chanter)* in tune; *Fam* **tomber j.** to guess right; **tout j.!** that's right! (**b**) *(précisément)* just; **à dix heures j.** on the stroke of ten; **j. au coin/en face/à côté** just *or* right on the corner/opposite/next door; **arriver j. à temps** to arrive just in time; **ça fait 10 euros tout j.** that's 10 euros exactly (**c**) *(à peine)* just; **c'est tout j. s'il sait lire** he can barely read; **avoir j. le temps (de**

faire qch) to have just enough time (to do sth); **ils ont tout j. fini de manger** they've only just finished eating (**d**) *(trop peu)* **calculer trop j. (pour)** not to allow enough (for) (**e**) **au j.** *(exactement)* exactly

justement [ʒystəmɑ̃] *adv* (**a**) *(précisément)* exactly; **j'allais j. t'appeler** I was just going to ring you (**b**) *(avec justesse)* rightly (**c**) *(avec justice)* justly

justesse [ʒystɛs] *nf* (**a**) *(précision) (d'une expression, d'une remarque)* aptness (**b**) **de j.** (only) just; **j'ai eu mon train de j.** I (only) just caught my train

justice [ʒystis] *nf* (**a**) *(équité)* justice; **faire** *ou* **rendre j. à qn** to do justice to sb; **se faire j.** *(se venger)* to take the law into one's own hands; *(se tuer)* to take one's own life (**b**) *Jur* **la j.** the law; **aller en j.** to go to court; **passer en j.** to stand trial, to appear in court

justicier, -ère [ʒystisje, -ɛr] *nm,f* righter of wrongs

justifiable [ʒystifjabl] *adj* justifiable

justificatif, -ive [ʒystifikatif, -iv] **1** *adj* justificatory; **pièces justificatives** *(d'un dossier)* supporting documents

    2 *nm* written proof

justification [ʒystifikasjɔ̃] *nf* (**a**) *(explication)* justification (**de** for *or* of) (**b**) *(preuve)* proof (**c**) *Typ & Ordinat* justification

justifié, -e [ʒystifje] *adj* (**a**) *(légitime)* justified; **peu j.** unjustified (**b**) *Typ & Ordinat* justified; **j. à droite/à gauche** right-/left-justified

justifier [ʒystifje] **1** *vt* (**a**) *(légitimer, démontrer)* to justify (**b**) *Typ & Ordinat* to justify; **j. à droite/gauche** to right-/left-justify

    2 se justifier *vpr* to justify oneself

jute [ʒyt] *nm* jute; **(toile de) j.** hessian

juter [ʒyte] *vi* to be juicy

juteux, -euse [ʒytø, -øz] *adj aussi Fam Fig* juicy

juvénile [ʒyvenil] *adj* youthful

juxtaposer [ʒykstapoze] *vt* to juxtapose

juxtaposition [ʒykstapozisjɔ̃] *nf* juxtaposition

K, k¹ [ka] *nm inv* K, k
k² *(abrév* **kilo(s)**) k
K7 [kaset] *nf (abrév* **cassette**) tape
Kaboul [kabul] *n* Kabul
kaki¹ [kaki] *adj inv & nm inv (couleur)* khaki
kaki² *nm (arbre, fruit)* persimmon
kaléidoscope [kaleidɔskɔp] *nm aussi Fig* kaleidoscope
kamikaze [kamikaz] *nm* kamikaze; *Fig* **être k.** to have
a death wish
kanak, -e [kanak] = **canaque**
kangourou [kãguru] *nm* kangaroo
kapok [kapɔk] *nm* kapok
karaoké [karaɔke] *nm* karaoke
karaté [karate] *nm* karate
karatéka [karateka] *nmf* karate expert
karma [karma] *nm* karma
kart [kart] *nm* (go-)kart
karting [kartiŋ] *nm* karting, go-kart racing; **faire du
k.** to go karting
kasher [kaʃɛr] *adj inv Rel* kosher
Katmandou [katmãdu] *n* Katmandu
kayak [kajak] *nm* (**a**) *(embarcation de sport)* canoe,
kayak; **faire du k.** to go canoeing (**b**) *(esquimau)*
kayak
kayakiste [kajakist] *nmf* canoeist
kazakh, -e [kazak] **1** *adj* Kazakh
   2 *nm,f* **K.** Kazakh
Kazakhstan [kazakstã] *nm* **le K.** Kazakhstan
keffieh [kefje] *nm* kaffiyeh
kendo [kɛndo] *nm* kendo
Kenya [kenja] *nm* **le K.** Kenya
kenyan, -e [kenjã, -an] **1** *adj* Kenyan
   2 *nm,f* **K.** Kenyan
képi [kepi] *nm* kepi
kératine [keratin] *nf* keratin
kermesse [kɛrmɛs] *nf* (**a**) *(dans les Flandres)* village
fair (**b**) *(fête de bienfaisance)* (charity) fête
kern [kɛrn] *nm Belg Pol* inner cabinet
kérosène [kerozɛn] *nm* kerosene
ketchup [kɛtʃœp] *nm* (tomato) ketchup
keuf [kœf] *nm très Fam* cop
kg *(abrév* **kilogramme(s)**) kg
KGB [kaʒebe] *nm* **le K.** the KGB
khâgne [kaɲ] *nf* = second-year arts class preparing
students for the entrance examination for the "École
normale supérieure"
khâgneux, -euse [kaɲø, -øz] *nm,f* = student in the
"khâgne"
Khartoum [kartum] *n* Khartoum

khmer, -ère [kmɛr] **1** *adj* Khmer
   2 *nm,f* **K.** Khmer; **les Khmers rouges** the Khmer
Rouge
khôl [kol] *nm* kohl
kibboutz [kibuts] *nm inv* kibbutz
kidnapper [kidnape] *vt* to kidnap
kidnappeur, -euse [kidnapœr, -øz] *nm,f* kidnapper
kidnapping [kidnapiŋ] *nm* kidnapping
kif-kif [kifkif] *adj inv Fam* **c'est k. (bourricot)** it's six of
one and half a dozen of the other
kiki [kiki] *nm Fam* (**a**) *(cou)* **serrer le k. à qn** to wring
sb's neck (**b**) *(langage enfantin) (pénis) Br* willy, *Am*
peter (**c**) **c'est parti mon k.!** here we go!
kilo [kilo] *nm* kilo
kilobaud [kilobo] *nm Ordinat* kilobaud
kilocalorie [kilɔkalɔri] *nf* kilocalorie
kilogramme [kilɔgram] *nm* kilogram(me)
kilohertz [kilɔɛrts] *nm* kilohertz
kilojoule [kilɔʒul] *nm* kilojoule
kilométrage [kilɔmetraʒ] *nm (distance)* ≃ mileage; **k.
illimité** *(de voiture de location)* unlimited mileage
kilomètre [kilɔmɛtr] *nm* kilometre; **100 kilomètres à
l'heure, 100 kilomètres-heure** 100 kilometres per *or*
an hour; **taper du texte au k.** to type text straight in
(and leave the formatting etc until later); **k. zéro** =
point near Notre-Dame from which distances from
Paris are measured
kilométrique [kilɔmetrik] *adj voir* **borne**
kilo-octet *(pl* **kilo-octets**) [kilɔɔktɛ] *nm Ordinat*
kilobyte
kilovolt [kilɔvɔlt] *nm* kilovolt
kilowatt [kilɔwat] *nm* kilowatt
kilowattheure [kilɔwatœr] *nm Phys* kilowatt-hour
kilt [kilt] *nm* kilt
kimono [kimɔno] *nm* kimono
kiné [kine] *Fam* **1** *nmf (médecin)* physio
   2 *nf (discipline)* physio
kinésiste [kinezist] *nmf Belg Br* physiotherapist, *Am*
physical therapist
kinésithérapeute [kineziterapøt] *nmf Br* physiotherapist, *Am* physical therapist
kinésithérapie [kineziterapi] *nf Br* physiotherapy,
Am physical therapy
Kinshasa [kinʃasa] *n* Kinshasa
kiosque [kjɔsk] *nm* (**a**) *(pavillon)* pavilion; *(point de
vente)* kiosk; **k. à journaux** newspaper kiosk, newsstand; **k. à musique** bandstand (**b**) *(sur Minitel®)*
K.® = service accessible on the Minitel® information
network
kippa [kipa] *nf* kippa

kir [kir] *nm* kir *(white wine with blackcurrant liqueur)*; **k. royal** kir royal *(champagne with blackcurrant liqueur)*

kirghiz, -e [kirgiz] **1** *adj* Kirg(h)iz
  2 *nm,f* **K.** Kirg(h)iz
  3 *nm (langue)* Kirg(h)iz

Kirghizistan [kirgizistã] *nm* **le K.** Kirg(h)izia, Kirg(h)izstan

kirsch [kirʃ] *nm* kirsch

kit [kit] *nm* (self-assembly) kit; **en k.** in kit form; *Ordinat* **k. d'extension** *ou* **d'évolution** upgrade kit

kitch [kitʃ] = **kitsch**

kitchenette [kitʃənɛt] *nf* kitchenette

kitsch [kitʃ] *adj inv & nm inv* kitsch

kiwi [kiwi] *nm* (**a**) *(fruit)* kiwi fruit (**b**) *(oiseau)* kiwi

Klaxon® [klaksɔn] *nm* horn; **donner un coup de K.** to sound one's horn

klaxonner [klaksɔne] **1** *vi* to sound one's horn
  2 *vt* to sound one's horn at

klebs [klɛps] = **clebs**

Kleenex® [klinɛks] *nm inv* tissue, Kleenex®; *Fig* **emploi k.** job with no security; **salarié k.** disposable employee

kleptomane [klɛptɔman] *adj & nmf* kleptomaniac

kleptomanie [klɛptɔmani] *nf* kleptomania

klondike [klɔndajk] *nm Can Fam* plum job, high-paying job

km *(abrév* **kilomètre(s))** km

km/h *(abrév* **kilomètres à l'heure, kilomètres-heure)** kph

Ko *nm (abrév* **kilo-octet(s))** K, KB

K-O [kao] **1** *nm inv* knockout
  2 *adj inv* (**a**) *(assommé)* knocked out; **mettre qn K-O** to knock sb out (**b**) *Fam (fatigué) Br* shattered, *Am* bushed

koala [kɔala] *nm* koala (bear)

kop [kɔp] *nm Belg Sport (club de supporters)* fan club; *(groupement de supporters)* fans

kopeck [kɔpɛk] *nm* kopeck; *Fam* **ça ne vaut pas un k.** it's not worth a bean

koter [kɔte] *vi Belg Fam* to rent a room

kouglof [kuglɔf] *nm* kugelhopf

Koweït [kɔwɛjt, kɔwɛt] *nm* **le K.** Kuwait

koweïtien, -enne [kɔwɛjtjɛ̃, kɔwɛtjɛ̃, -ɛn] **1** *adj* Kuwaiti
  2 *nm,f* **K.** Kuwaiti

krach [krak] *nm* **k. (boursier)** (stock market) crash

kraft [kraft] *nm voir* **papier**

Kremlin [krɛmlɛ̃] *nm* **le K.** the Kremlin

kumquat [kɔmkwat, kumkwat] *nm (fruit)* kumquat

kung-fu [kuŋfu] *nm inv* kung fu

kurde [kyrd] **1** *adj* Kurdish
  2 *nmf* **K.** Kurd
  3 *nm (langue)* Kurdish

Kurdistan [kyrdistã] *nm* **le K.** Kurdistan

kW *(abrév* **kilowatt(s))** kW

K-way® [kawɛ] *nm inv* cagoule

kWh *(abrév* **kilowattheure(s))** kWh

kyrielle [kirjɛl] *nf (de mots, de fautes)* string; *(d'insultes)* stream; *(d'enfants)* crowd; **elle a toute une k. d'amis** she has masses of friends

kyste [kist] *nm* cyst

L, l¹ [εl] *nm inv* L, l
l² *(abrév* **litre(s)**) l
l' [l] **1** *art défini voir* **le¹**
 2 *pron personnel voir* **la², le²**
la¹ [la] *art défini voir* **le¹**
la²

> **l'** is used before a word beginning with a vowel or h mute.

pron personnel (femme, fille) her; *(chose, idée)* it; *(animal)* it, her; **je la connais bien** I know her well; **il te la rendra demain** he'll give it back to you tomorrow; **et ta cousine, tu l'as vue?** have you seen your cousin?; **la voilà** here she/it is
la³ *nm inv (note)* A; *(chantée)* la
là [la] **1** *adv* (**a**) *(là-bas)* there; *(ici)* here; **il est là** *(présent)* he's in; *(près d'ici)* he's here; *(là-bas)* he's there; **est-ce que Paul est là?** *(au téléphone)* is Paul there?; **je suis là pour ça** that's what I'm here for; **à quelques mètres de là** a few metres away; **de là à Paris, il n'y a que quelques kilomètres** it's only a few kilometres (away) from Paris; **là en bas/haut** down/up there; **qui va là?** who goes there? (**b**) *(à ce point)* **restons-en là** let's leave it at that; **la question n'est pas là** that's not the point; **c'est bien là le problème** that's the problem; **je sais bien qu'il est bizarre mais de là à dire qu'il est fou...** I know he's strange, but to say he's mad...; **je ne vois là aucune raison de s'inquiéter** I can't see any cause for concern; **de là sa réaction** hence his/her reaction (**c**) **c'est là que j'habite** that's where I live; **c'est là que j'ai compris** that's when I understood (**d**) **ce vin-là** that wine; **ces vins-là** those wines
 2 *exclam* **oh là là!** my goodness!; **alors là, je n'aurais jamais cru!** I'd never have expected THAT!
là-bas [laba] *adv* over there; *(dans cette région, dans ce pays)* there
label [labεl] *nm Com* quality label
labeur [labœr] *nm Litt* labour
labo [labo] *nm Fam* lab; **l. photo** darkroom
laborantin, -e [labɔrãtɛ̃, -in] *nm,f* laboratory assistant
laboratoire [labɔratwar] *nm* laboratory; **l. d'analyses (médicales)** pathology laboratory
laborieusement [labɔrjøzmɑ̃] *adv* laboriously
laborieux, -euse [labɔrjø, -øz] *adj* (**a**) *(difficile)* laborious; *Péj (style)* laboured; *Fam* **il n'a pas encore fini? c'est l.!** hasn't he finished yet? he's making heavy weather of it! (**b**) *Litt* **les masses laborieuses** the toiling masses

labour [labur] *nm* (**a**) *(labourage)* ploughing (**b**) **labours** *(champs)* ploughed land
labourage [laburaʒ] *nm* ploughing
labourer [labure] *vt* (**a**) *(terre)* to plough (**b**) *Fig (griffer)* to claw; **visage labouré de rides** face furrowed with wrinkles
laboureur [laburœr] *nm* ploughman
labrador [labradɔr] *nm* labrador
labyrinthe [labirɛ̃t] *nm* maze, labyrinth
lac [lak] *nm* lake; **les Grands Lacs** the Great Lakes; **le l. Baïkal** Lake Baikal; **le l. Érié** Lake Erie; **le l. Huron** Lake Huron; **le l. Léman** *ou* **de Genève** Lake Geneva; **le l. Michigan** Lake Michigan; **le l. Ontario** Lake Ontario; **le l. Supérieur** Lake Superior
lacer [16] [lase] **1** *vt (chaussures)* to tie (up); *(corset)* to lace up
 2 se lacer *vpr (chaussures)* to tie (up); *(corset)* to lace up
lacérer [34] [lasere] *vt (déchirer)* to tear to shreds; *(blesser)* to lacerate
lacet [lase] *nm* (**a**) *(de chaussure, de corset)* lace; **faire ses lacets** to tie one's laces (**b**) *(tournant)* sharp bend; **faire des lacets** to twist and turn (**c**) *(collet)* snare
lâche [laʃ] **1** *adj* (**a**) *(ressort, nœud)* loose; *(vêtement)* loose-fitting; *(discipline)* lax (**b**) *Péj (personne, acte, attitude)* cowardly
 2 *nmf* coward
lâchement [laʃmɑ̃] *adv (sans courage)* in a cowardly way
lâcher [laʃe] **1** *vt* (**a**) *(desserrer) (corde, ceinture)* to loosen (**b**) *(ne plus tenir)* to let go of; *(laisser tomber)* to drop; *Fam Fig (cesser d'importuner)* to leave alone; **l. prise** to let go; *Fam* **il ne m'a pas lâché d'une semelle** he stuck to me like a leech; *Fam* **lâche-moi les baskets** *ou* **la grappe!** get off my back!; *Can Fam* **l. son fou** to let one's hair down (**c**) *Fam (abandonner) (associé)* to walk out on; *(ami)* to let down; *(amant)* to dump; *(emploi)* to chuck in; **la voiture nous a lâchés** the car died on us (**d**) *(distancer) (poursuivant)* to shake off; *(dans une course)* to leave behind (**e**) *(libérer)* to release; **l. un chien sur qn** to set a dog on sb (**f**) *(laisser échapper) (juron, cri, pet)* to let out; *(sottise, plaisanterie)* to come out with; *Fam* **l. le morceau** to spill the beans
 2 *vi (corde, câble)* to break; *(mécanisme, pièce)* to go; *(moteur)* to die; *(freins)* to fail; *Fig* **ses nerfs ont lâché** he/she broke down
 3 *nm (de colombes, de ballons)* release
lâcheté [laʃte] *nf* cowardice

lâcheur, -euse [lɑʃœr, -øz] *nm,f Fam* unreliable person

lacis [lasi] *nm (de nerfs, de fils)* network; *(de ruelles)* maze

laconique [lakɔnik] *adj* laconic

laconiquement [lakɔnikmɑ̃] *adv* laconically

lacrymal, -e, -aux, -ales [lakrimal, -o] *adj* tear, *Spéc* lachrymal

lacrymogène [lakrimɔʒɛn] *adj voir* gaz, grenade

lacté, -e [lakte] *adj (produit)* which contains milk; *(régime)* milk

lactique [laktik] *adj Chim* lactic

lactose [laktoz] *nm Chim* lactose

lacune [lakyn] *nf (dans une liste, ses connaissances, ses souvenirs)* gap; **avoir des lacunes en qch** to have a patchy knowledge of sth

lacustre [lakystr] *adj* lakeside

lad [lad] *nm* stable lad

là-dedans [ladədɑ̃] *adv* inside, in there; **il y a l. quelque chose que je ne comprends pas** there's something here I don't understand; **elle n'a rien à voir l.!** she's got nothing to do with it!; *Fam* **il y en a l.!** he's/she's got a lot up top!

là-dessous [latsu] *adv* underneath, under there; *Fig* **il y a quelque chose l.** there's something behind it

là-dessus [latsy] *adv* on there; *(sur ces mots)* with that; **tout le monde est d'accord l.** everybody agrees about it; **c'est l. que tu dois te concentrer** that's what you have to concentrate on

lagon [lagɔ̃] *nm* lagoon

lagopède [lagɔpɛd] *nm* **l. d'Écosse** grouse

lagune [lagyn] *nf* lagoon

là-haut [lao] *adv* up there; *(à un étage supérieur)* upstairs

laïc [laik] = **laïque**

laïciser [laisize] *vt* to secularize

laïcité [laisite] *nf (des écoles)* secularity; *Pol* secularism

laid, -e [lɛ, lɛd] *adj* **(a)** *(personne, visage, bâtiment)* ugly; **l. comme un pou** *ou* **à faire peur** as ugly as sin **(b)** *(langage enfantin) (méprisable)* not nice

laideron [lɛdrɔ̃] *nm Péj (fille)* ugly girl; *(femme)* ugly woman

laideur [lɛdœr] *nf* **(a)** *(d'une personne, d'un visage, d'un bâtiment)* ugliness **(b)** *(bassesse)* meanness

laie [lɛ] *nf (animal)* wild sow

lainage [lɛnaʒ] *nm* **(a)** *(étoffe)* woollen fabric **(b)** *(vêtement en laine)* sweater; **lainages** woollens

laine [lɛn] *nf* **(a)** *(tissu)* wool; **en l.** woollen; **l. d'agneau** lambswool; **l. vierge** new wool; **(en) pure l.** pure wool **(b)** *(vêtement)* **(petite) l.** sweater, *Br* woolly **(c)** **l. de verre** glass wool

laineux, -euse [lɛnø, -øz] *adj (tissu)* fleecy; *(mouton, cheveux)* woolly

lainier, -ère [lɛnje, -ɛr] *adj* wool

laïque [laik] **1** *adj (État)* secular; *(école, enseignement)* non-religious
2 *nmf* layman, *f* laywoman

laisse [lɛs] *nf (pour chien)* lead, leash; **tenir un chien en l.** to keep a dog on a lead

laissé-pour-compte, laissée-pour-compte *(mpl* **laissés-pour-compte,** *fpl* **laissées-pour-compte)** [lesepurkɔ̃t] *nm,f* reject

laisser [lese] **1** *vt* **(a)** *(permettre à)* **l. qn faire qch** to let sb do sth; **laissez-le faire!** leave him alone!; **le toit laissait passer la pluie** the roof let the rain in; **l. sécher la peinture** to let the paint dry; *Fig* **laissez-moi**

rire! don't make me laugh!; *aussi Fig* **l. tomber qn/qch** to drop sb/sth; *Fam* **l. courir** to leave things alone; **l. dire** to let people talk; **laisse faire!** never mind! **(b)** *(quitter) (mari, femme)* to leave; **l. qn tout seul** to leave sb all on their own; **bon, je vous laisse!** well, I'll be off!; **il a laissé une veuve et trois enfants** he left a widow and three children **(c)** *(ne pas prendre)* to leave; **l. qch à qn** *(le lui réserver)* to leave sth for sb **(d)** *(maintenir)* **l. qch ouvert/fermé** to leave sth open/closed **(e)** *(oublier)* to leave **(f)** *(traces, impression, souvenir)* to leave **(g)** *(ne pas s'occuper de) (personne)* to leave; **laisse, je m'en occupe** don't bother about that, I'll see to it **(h)** *(donner)* **l. qch à qn** *(en héritage)* to leave sb sth; *(pour qu'il s'en occupe)* to leave sth to sb; **l. le choix à qn** to give sb a choice; **cela nous laisse le temps de...** that leaves us time to...; **ils ont laissé les enfants à la grand-mère** they left the children with their grandmother; **je vous le laisse pour 100 euros** I'll let you have it for 100 euros **(i)** *(perdre) (fortune, vie, membre)* to lose **(j)** *Sout* **cela n'a pas laissé de le surprendre** it could not fail to surprise him
2 se laisser *vpr* **se l. décourager/embrasser** to let oneself be discouraged/kissed; **ne te laisse pas faire!** don't let him/her walk all over you!; **se l. aller** to let oneself go; **se l. aller au découragement** to let oneself get discouraged; **ce vin se laisse boire** this wine is very drinkable; **je me suis laissé dire que...** I hear that...; **se l. vivre** to take life as it comes

laisser-aller [leseale] *nm inv (relâchement)* carelessness; **il y a du l. dans cette maison!** things are a bit too easy-going *or* slack in this house!

laissez-passer [lesepase] *nm inv* pass

lait [lɛ] *nm* **(a)** *(aliment)* milk; **petit l.** whey; *Fig* **boire du petit l.** to lap it up; **l. de brebis/de chèvre/de vache** sheep's/goat's/cow's milk; *Belg* **l. battu** buttermilk; **l. caillé** curd; **l. condensé** condensed milk; **l. cru** unpasteurized milk; **l. demi-écrémé** semi-skimmed milk; **l. écrémé** skimmed milk; **l. entier** whole milk; **l. longue conservation** long-life milk; **l. maternel** mother's milk; **l. maternisé** baby formula milk; **l. en poudre** powdered milk; **l. de soja** soya milk **(b)** *(cosmétique)* **l. après-soleil** after-sun (lotion); **l. bronzant** suntan lotion; **l. démaquillant** *ou* **de toilette** cleansing lotion

laitage [lɛtaʒ] *nm* dairy product

laitance [lɛtɑ̃s] *nf (de poisson)* milt; *Culin* soft roe

laiterie [lɛtri] *nf* dairy

laiteux, -euse [lɛtø, -øz] *adj (teint)* creamy; *(couleur, lumière)* milky

laitier¹, -ère [letje, -ɛr] **1** *adj* dairy
2 *nm,f (livreur)* milkman, *f* milkwoman
3 *nf* **laitière** *(vache)* dairy cow

laitier² *nm Ind* slag

laiton [lɛtɔ̃] *nm* brass

laitue [lɛty] *nf* lettuce

laïus [lajys] *nm (discours)* speech

lama¹ [lama] *nm Rel* lama; **le Grand l.** the Dalai Lama

lama² *nm (animal)* llama

lambda [lɑ̃bda] *adj inv (moyen)* average

lambeau, -x [lɑ̃bo] *nm (de tissu, de papier, de viande)* scrap; **vêtements en lambeaux** clothes in tatters; **tomber en lambeaux** to fall to pieces

lambin, -e [lɑ̃bɛ̃, -in] *Fam* **1** *adj* slow
2 *nm,f Br* slowcoach, *Am* slowpoke

lambiner [lɑ̃bine] *vi Fam* to dawdle

lambris [lɑ̃bri] *nm (en bois)* panelling; *(en marbre, en stuc)* lining

lambrissé, -e [lɑ̃brise] *adj (de bois)* panelled; *(de marbre, de stuc)* lined

lambswool [lɑ̃bswul] *nm* lambswool; **en l.** lambswool

lame [lam] *nf* (**a**) *(d'épée, de couteau)* blade; *(épée)* sword; *Fig* **une fine l.** a fine swordsman; **visage en l. de couteau** hatchet face; **l. de rasoir** razor blade (**b**) *(bande) (de métal, de verre, de parquet)* strip; *(de store)* slat (**c**) *(vague)* wave; **l. de fond** groundswell

lamé, -e [lame] **1** *adj* lamé; **l. or** gold lamé **2** *nm* lamé; **en l.** lamé

lamelle [lamɛl] *nf* (**a**) *(de métal, de verre)* thin strip; *Bot (de champignon)* gill; *Culin* **couper en (fines) lamelles** to cut into (wafer-)thin slices (**b**) *(de microscope)* cover slip

lamentable [lamɑ̃tabl] *adj* appalling, awful; *(personne)* hopeless, pathetic

lamentablement [lamɑ̃tabləmɑ̃] *adv (échouer)* miserably

lamentations [lamɑ̃tasjɔ̃] *nfpl* (**a**) *(cris, pleurs)* wailing (**b**) *Péj (plaintes)* moaning, complaining

lamenter [lamɑ̃te] **se lamenter** *vpr* to moan; **se l. sur qch** to bemoan sth

laminage [laminaʒ] *nm (du métal)* rolling; **l. à chaud/à froid** hot-/cold-rolling

laminer [lamine] *vt* (**a**) *(métal)* to roll (**b**) *Fig (revenus)* to erode; *(parti politique)* to annihilate

laminoir [laminwar] *nm Ind* rolling mill

lampadaire [lɑ̃padɛr] *nm* (**a**) *(d'intérieur) Br* standard lamp, *Am* floor lamp (**b**) *(réverbère)* lamppost

lampe [lɑ̃p] *nf* (**a**) *(appareil d'éclairage)* lamp; **l. à alcool** spirit lamp; **l. de bureau** desk lamp; **l. de chevet** bedside lamp; **l. à pétrole** oil lamp; **l. de poche** *Br* torch, *Am* flashlight (**b**) *Fam* **s'en mettre plein la l.** to have a good blowout

lampée [lɑ̃pe] *nf Fam* gulp

lampe-tempête *(pl* **lampes-tempête)** [lɑ̃ptɑ̃pɛt] *nf* hurricane lamp

lampion [lɑ̃pjɔ̃] *nm* paper lantern

lampiste [lɑ̃pist] *nm (subalterne)* underling

lamproie [lɑ̃prwa] *nf* lamprey

lance [lɑ̃s] *nf* (**a**) *(pique)* spear (**b**) *(tuyau)* **l. d'incendie** fire hose

lancée [lɑ̃se] *nf* **continuer sur sa l.** to keep going; **j'ai fait les exercices 5 et 6, et sur ma l. j'ai aussi fait le 7** I did exercises 5 and 6, and while I was at it I did 7 as well

lance-flammes [lɑ̃sflam] *nm inv* flamethrower

lancement [lɑ̃smɑ̃] *nm* (**a**) *(d'une fusée, d'un projet, d'un produit)* launch(ing) (**b**) *Ordinat (d'impression)* start; *(de programme)* running, starting (up)

lance-missiles [lɑ̃smisil] *nm inv* missile launcher

lance-pierre *(pl* **lance-pierres)** [lɑ̃spjɛr] *nm Br* catapult, *Am* slingshot; *Fam Fig* **manger avec un l.** to wolf one's food down; *Fam Fig* **être payé avec un l.** to be paid peanuts

lancer [16] [lɑ̃se] **1** *vt* (**a**) *(projeter)* to throw (à to); *(flèche)* to shoot; *(fusée)* to launch; *(bombe)* to drop; *(étincelles)* to shoot out; *Fig (idée, proposition)* to throw out; *(remarque)* to come out with; *(plaisanterie)* to crack; *(juron)* to let out; **l. un coup d'œil à qn** to dart or shoot a glance at sb; **l. le poids** to put the shot (**b**) *(envoyer) (signaux de détresse, SOS)* to send out (**c**) *(projet, produit, artiste)* to launch; *(mode)* to start; *Fin* **l. un emprunt** to issue a bond (**d**) *(faire démarrer)*

(moteur) to start (up); **être lancé** *(dans une course, dans un travail)* to have got going; **l. qn sur un sujet** to start sb (off) on a subject (**e**) *Ordinat (impression)* to start; *(programme)* to run, to start (up)
2 *nm* (**a**) **(pêche au) l.** rod-and-reel fishing (**b**) *Sport* **l. du javelot/du disque/du marteau** throwing the javelin/the discus/the hammer; **l. du poids** putting the shot; **l. franc** *(au basket)* free throw
3 se lancer *vpr* (**a**) *(se jeter)* **se l. dans le vide** to throw oneself off; **se l. en avant** to rush forward; **se l. à la poursuite de qn** to rush off in pursuit of sb (**b**) *(s'engager)* **se l. dans** *(affaire, discussion, aventure)* to embark on; *(dépenses)* to get involved in; *(domaine)* to launch out into (**c**) *(se faire connaître)* to make a name for oneself

lance-roquettes [lɑ̃srɔkɛt] *nm inv* rocket launcher

lance-torpilles [lɑ̃storpij] *nm inv* torpedo tube

lanceur, -euse [lɑ̃sœr, -øz] *nm,f (au cricket)* bowler; *(au base-ball)* pitcher; **l. de javelot/disque/marteau** javelin/discus/hammer thrower; **l. de poids** shot putter

lancinant, -e [lɑ̃sinɑ̃, -ɑ̃t] *adj (douleur)* shooting; *(souvenir, air, musique)* haunting; *(regret)* nagging

landau [lɑ̃do] *nm (voiture d'enfant) Br* pram, *Am* baby carriage

lande [lɑ̃d] *nf* moor, heath

langage [lɑ̃gaʒ] *nm* (**a**) *(langue, vocabulaire)* language; *Fig* **changer de l.** to change one's tune; **l. chiffré** cipher, code (**b**) *Ordinat* language; **l. de description de page** page description language; **l. d'imprimante par pages** page printer language; **l. d'interrogation** query language; **l. machine** machine language; **l. naturel** natural language; **l. à objets** object-oriented language; **l. de programmation** programming language; **l. utilisateur** user language

lange [lɑ̃ʒ] *nm (couche) Br* nappy, *Am* diaper; *Vieilli* **langes** swaddling clothes

langer [45] [lɑ̃ʒe] *vt (mettre une couche à)* to put a *Br* nappy or *Am* diaper on; *Vieilli* to wrap in swaddling clothes

langoureusement [lɑ̃gurøzmɑ̃] *adv* languorously

langoureux, -euse [lɑ̃gurø, -øz] *adj* languorous

langouste [lɑ̃gust] *nf* crayfish

langoustine [lɑ̃gustin] *nf* Dublin Bay prawn

langue [lɑ̃g] *nf* (**a**) *(organe)* tongue; **tirer la l. à qn** to stick one's tongue out at sb; *Fig* **j'ai tiré la l.** *(peiné)* it was hard going; **avoir la l. bien pendue** to have the gift of the gab; **ne pas avoir la l. dans sa poche** never to be at a loss for words; **donner sa l. au chat** to give up; **tu as avalé ou perdu ta l.?** has the cat got your tongue?; *Culin* **l. de bœuf** ox tongue (**b**) *(langage, style, jargon)* language; **peuples/pays de l. anglaise** English-speaking people/countries; **parler la l. de bois** to come out with clichés; **l. étrangère** foreign language; **l. maternelle** native language, mother tongue; **l. morte** dead language; **l. d'oc** = medieval French dialect spoken in Southern France; **l. d'oïl** = medieval French dialect spoken in Northern France; **langues vivantes** *(matière)* modern languages (**c**) *(personne)* **une mauvaise l.** a backbiter; **une l. de vipère** a spiteful gossip (**d**) *(bande)* **l. de terre** strip of land

langue-de-chat *(pl* **langues-de-chat)** [lɑ̃gdəʃa] *nf* finger biscuit

languedocien, -enne [lɑ̃gdɔsjɛ̃, -ɛn] **1** *adj* of the Languedoc **2** *nm,f* **L.** person from the Languedoc

languette [lɑ̃gɛt] *nf (de bois, de métal, de chaussure)* tongue
langueur [lɑ̃gœr] *nf* (**a**) *(apathie)* listlessness (**b**) *(mélancolie, rêverie)* languor
languir [lɑ̃gir] *vi* (**a**) *Litt ou Hum (dépérir)* to languish (**b**) *(attendre avec impatience)* **ne nous faites pas l.** don't keep us in suspense; *Litt* **l. de faire qch** to long to do sth (**c**) *(conversation)* to be flagging
lanière [lanjɛr] *nf (de sac, de sandale)* strap; *(de fouet)* lash; **découper qch en lanières** to cut sth into strips
lanoline [lanɔlin] *nf* lanolin
lanterne [lɑ̃tɛrn] *nf* (**a**) *(lampe)* lantern; *Fig* **éclairer la l. de qn** to enlighten sb; **l. chinoise** Chinese lantern (**b**) *(de véhicule) Br* sidelight, *Am* parking light
lanterner [lɑ̃tɛrne] *vi Fam* to dawdle; **faire l. qn** to keep sb hanging about
Laos [laɔs] *nm* **le L.** Laos
laotien, -enne [laɔsjɛ̃, -ɛn] **1** *adj* Laotian **2** *nm,f* **L.** Laotian
lapalissade [lapalisad] *nf* statement of the obvious
laper [lape] *vt* to lap up
lapidaire [lapidɛr] *adj (style, formule)* concise, succinct
lapidation [lapidasjɔ̃] *nf* stoning
lapider [lapide] *vt (mettre à mort)* to stone (to death); *Fig (critiquer)* to lambast
lapin [lapɛ̃] *nm* rabbit; **manteau en (peau de) l.** rabbitskin coat; **poser un l. à qn** to stand sb up; **mon petit l.** sweetheart; **l. de garenne** wild rabbit; *Fam* **un chaud l.** a horny *or Br* randy devil; *Can Fam* **en criant l.** in a flash
lapine [lapin] *nf* doe (rabbit)
lapis [lapis], **lapis-lazuli** [lapislazyli] *nm inv* lapis lazuli
lapon, -one *ou* **-onne** [lapɔ̃, -ɔn] **1** *adj* Lapp **2** *nm,f* **L.** Lapp, Laplander
Laponie [lapɔni] *nf* **la L.** Lapland
laps [laps] *nm* **un l. de temps** a period of time; **un l. de temps de trois heures** a period of three hours
lapsus [lapsys] *nm (oral)* slip of the tongue; *(écrit)* slip of the pen; **faire un l.** to make a slip (of the tongue/pen); **un l. révélateur** a Freudian slip
laquais [lakɛ] *nm* footman; *Fig & Péj* lackey
laque [lak] **1** *nf* (**a**) *(vernis)* lacquer (**b**) *(pour les cheveux)* hair spray, lacquer (**c**) *(peinture)* gloss (paint) **2** *nm (objet)* piece of lacquerwork; **des laques** lacquerware, lacquerwork
laquelle [lakɛl] *voir* **lequel**
laquer [lake] *vt* (**a**) *(vernir)* to lacquer (**b**) *(cheveux)* to lacquer (**c**) *(peindre)* to paint with gloss
larbin [larbɛ̃] *nm Fam* flunkey
larcin [larsɛ̃] *nm (vol)* petty theft
lard [lar] *nm* (**a**) *(du porc) (viande)* bacon; *(gras)* fat; *Fig* **se demander si c'est du l. ou du cochon** to wonder what to make of it; **l. fumé** smoked bacon; **l. maigre** streaky bacon (**b**) *Fam (graisse)* **faire du l.** to sit around and get fat; **rentrer dans le l. à qn** to lay into sb
larder [larde] *vt Culin* to lard; *Fig* **l. qn de coups de couteau** to hack at sb with a knife; **l. un texte de citations** to pepper a text with quotations
lardon [lardɔ̃] *nm* (**a**) *Culin* piece of chopped bacon (**b**) *très Fam (enfant)* kid
large [larʒ] **1** *adj* (**a**) *(route, porte, chaussures)* wide; *(vêtement)* loose-fitting; *(visage, nez, geste)* broad; **l. d'épaules** broad-shouldered; **l. de 10 mètres** 10 metres wide; **terme employé dans son sens l.** term

used in its broad sense; **avoir l'esprit l.**, **être l. d'esprit** to be broad-minded (**b**) *(considérable)* large; *(ressources)* ample; **dans une l. mesure** to a large extent (**c**) *(généreux)* generous
2 *nm* (**a**) *(espace)* **être au l.** to have plenty of room (**b**) *(haute mer)* open sea; **au l. de off**; **prendre le l.** to take to the open sea; *Fig (s'enfuir)* to beat it (**c**) *(largeur)* **faire 10 mètres de l.** to be 10 metres wide
3 *adv* **compter l.** to allow for more
largement [larʒəmɑ̃] *adv* (**a**) *(répandu, critiqué)* widely (**b**) *(abondamment) (récompenser, payer, servir)* generously; *(dépasser)* by a long way; **avoir l. de quoi vivre** to have easily enough to live on; **avoir l. le temps** to have plenty of time; **c'est l. suffisant, ça suffit l.** it's more than enough
largesse [larʒɛs] *nf* (**a**) *(générosité)* generosity (**envers** towards) (**b**) **largesses** *(dons)* generous gifts
largeur [larʒœr] *nf* (**a**) *(dimension)* width, breadth; *(de voie ferrée)* gauge; **en l., dans la l.** widthwise; **les policiers barraient la rue sur toute sa l.** the policemen blocked off the whole width of the street; *Rad* **l. de bande** bandwidth; *Ordinat* **l. de papier** paper width (**b**) *Fig* **l. d'esprit** *ou* **de vues** broadmindedness
largué, -e [large] *adj Fam (qui ne comprend plus)* lost
larguer [large] *vt* (**a**) *(amarres)* to cast off; *(cordage)* to loose; *(voile)* to unfurl (**b**) *(par avion) (parachutiste, vivres, bombe)* to drop (**c**) *Fam (abandonner) (personne)* to chuck; **il a tout largué pour partir vivre aux Caraïbes** he chucked everything in and went to live in the Caribbean
larme [larm] *nf* (**a**) *(pleur)* tear; **larmes de joie** tears of joy; **avoir facilement la l. à l'œil** to be easily moved to tears; **avoir les larmes aux yeux** to have tears in one's eyes; **en larmes** in tears; **larmes de crocodile** crocodile tears (**b**) *(petite quantité)* drop
larmoyant, -e [larmwajɑ̃, -ɑ̃t] *adj* (**a**) *(pleurnicheur) (voix, ton)* tearful (**b**) *Péj (histoire, film, sentimentalité)* mawkish
larmoyer [32] [larmwaje] *vi* (**a**) *(yeux)* to water (**b**) *Péj (personne)* to snivel
larron [larɔ̃] *nm* **s'entendre comme larrons en foire** to be as thick as thieves
larve [larv] *nf* (**a**) *(de batracien, de poisson)* larva; *(d'insecte)* grub (**b**) *Fam (personne apathique)* wimp
larvé, -e [larve] *adj (guerre, conflit)* latent
laryngite [larɛ̃ʒit] *nf Méd* laryngitis
laryngologie [larɛ̃gɔlɔʒi] *nf Méd* laryngology
laryngologiste [larɛ̃gɔlɔʒist], **laryngologue** [larɛ̃gɔlɔg] *nmf Méd* throat specialist, *Spéc* laryngologist
larynx [larɛ̃ks] *nm Anat* larynx
las, lasse [lɑ, lɑs] *adj Litt* weary; **être l. de qch/de faire qch** to be weary of sth/of doing sth
lasagnes [lazaɲ] *nfpl* lasagne
lascar [laskar] *nm Fam* hooligan, *Br* yob, chav
lascif, -ive [lasif, -iv] *adj* lascivious
lascivement [lasivmɑ̃] *adv* lasciviously
laser [lazɛr] *nm* laser
lassant, -e [lasɑ̃, -ɑ̃t] *adj* tiresome
lasser [lase] **1** *vt* to tire **2 se lasser** *vpr* **se l. (de qch/de faire qch)** to get tired (of sth/of doing sth)
lassitude [lasityd] *nf* weariness
lasso [laso] *nm* lasso; **prendre un animal au l.** to lasso an animal
latent, -e [latɑ̃, -ɑ̃t] *adj* latent; **à l'état l.** latent

latéral, -e, -aux, -ales [lateral, -o] *adj (entrée, rue, vent, choc)* side
latéralement [lateralmã] *adv (se déplacer)* sideways; *(être situé)* at the side
latex [latɛks] *nm* latex
latin, -e [latɛ̃, -in] **1** *adj* Latin; *(langue)* Romance
2 *nm* Latin; **l. de cuisine** dog Latin; *Fig* **j'y perds mon l.** I can't make head nor tail of it
latiniste [latinist] *nmf (spécialiste)* Latinist; *(étudiant)* Latin student
latino [latino] *nmf Fam* Latino
latino-américain, -e *(mpl* **latino-américains,** *fpl* **latino-américaines)** [latinoamerikɛ̃, -ɛn] **1** *adj* Latin-American
2 *nm,f* **L.-A.** Latin-American
latitude [latityd] *nf* (**a**) *Géog* latitude; **à 30° de l. nord** at latitude 30° north; **sous ces latitudes** in these latitudes (**b**) *(liberté)* latitude, scope; **avoir/donner à qn toute l. pour agir** to have/to give sb total freedom of action
latrines [latrin] *nfpl* latrines
latte [lat] *nf* lath; *Fam* **donner un coup de l. à qn** to give sb a kick
lattis [lati] *nm* lathing
laudanum [lodanɔm] *nm* laudanum
lauréat, -e [lɔrea, -at] **1** *adj* (prize)winning
2 *nm,f* (prize)winner
laurier [lɔrje] *nm* (**a**) *(plante)* laurel; *Culin* bay leaves (**b**) *Fig (gloire)* **lauriers** laurels; **se reposer** *ou* **s'endormir sur ses lauriers** to rest on one's laurels; **être couvert de lauriers** to be covered with glory
laurier-rose *(pl* **lauriers-roses)** [lɔrjeroz] *nm* oleander
lavable [lavabl] *adj* washable; **l. en machine/à la main** machine-/hand-washable
lavabo [lavabo] *nm* (**a**) *(cuvette)* washbasin (**b**) **lavabos** *(toilettes)* toilets
lavage [lavaʒ] *nm* washing; **l. de cerveau** brainwashing; **faire subir un l. de cerveau à qn** to brainwash sb; **faire un l. d'estomac à qn** to pump sb's stomach
lavande [lavãd] **1** *nf (fleur)* lavender; **(eau de) l.** lavender water
2 *adj inv* **(bleu) l.** lavender blue
lavandière [lavãdjɛr] *nf* (**a**) *(blanchisseuse)* washerwoman (**b**) *(oiseau)* wagtail
lave [lav] *nf* lava
lave-autos [lavoto] *nm inv Can* carwash
lave-glace *(pl* **lave-glaces)** [lavglas] *nm Br* windscreen *or Am* windshield washer
lave-linge [lavlɛ̃ʒ] *nm inv* washing machine
lave-mains [lavmɛ̃] *nm inv* handbasin
lavement [lavmã] *nm* enema
laver [lave] **1** *vt* (**a**) *(nettoyer)* to wash; *(plaie)* to bathe; **l. qch à l'eau froide** to wash sth in cold water; **il faut l. son linge sale en famille** don't wash your dirty linen in public (**b**) *(disculper)* **l. qn d'une accusation/de tout soupçon** to clear sb of an accusation/of all suspicion (**c**) *(venger)* **l'affront a été lavé dans le sang** the insult was paid for in blood
2 se laver *vpr* (**a**) *(se nettoyer)* to wash (oneself), to have a wash; **se l. les dents** to clean *or* brush one's teeth; **se l. les cheveux/les mains** to wash one's hair/one's hands; *Fig* **je m'en lave les mains** I wash my hands of it (**b**) *(pouvoir être lavé)* **se l. à la main/à la machine** to be hand-/machine-washable
laverie [lavri] *nf* **l. automatique** *Br* launderette, *Am* Laundromat®

lavette [lavɛt] *nf* (**a**) *(de vaisselle)* dishcloth (**b**) *Belg & Suisse (gant de toilette) Br* face cloth, *Am* washcloth (**c**) *Fam Fig (homme)* drip
laveur, -euse [lavœr, -øz] *nm,f* washer; **l. de vitres** window cleaner
lave-vaisselle [lavvɛsɛl] *nm inv* dishwasher
lave-vitre *(pl* **lave-vitres)** [lavvitr] *nm Br* windscreen *or Am* windshield washer
lavis [lavi] *nm* (**a**) *(procédé)* washing (**b**) *(dessin)* wash drawing
lavoir [lavwar] *nm* (**a**) *(établissement)* **l. (public)** (public) washhouse (**b**) *(bassin)* washtub (**c**) *Belg (blanchisserie)* **l. (automatique)** self-service laundry
lavomatic [lavomatik] *nm Br* launderette, *Am* Laundromat®
laxatif, -ive [laksatif, -iv] *adj & nm* laxative
laxisme [laksism] *nm* laxness
laxiste [laksist] **1** *adj* lax
2 *nmf* lax person
layette [lɛjɛt] *nf* baby clothes
le¹, la, les [lə, la, le]

> **l'** is used instead of **le** or **la** before a word beginning with a vowel or h mute.

article défini (**a**) *(pour définir les noms)* the; **le soleil** the sun; **la lune** the moon; **l'étoile** the star; **les planètes** the planets; **le pull que je me suis acheté** the sweater I bought myself; **le Paris de 1900** Paris in 1900, the Paris of 1900; **oh, la jolie robe!** what a lovely dress!; **debout, les enfants!** get up, children! (**b**) *(avec des notions ou des généralités)* **le français** French; **la biologie** biology; **l'amour** love; **l'homme et la femme** man and woman; **the chien est l'ami de l'homme** a dog is a man's best friend; **aider les pauvres** to help the poor; **fumer la pipe** to smoke a pipe (**c**) *(avec les noms de lieux)* **la France** France; **les États-Unis** the United States; **le mont Blanc** Mont Blanc; **les Alpes** the Alps; **la Seine** the Seine (**d**) *(avec les noms de personnes)* **la reine d'Angleterre** the Queen of England; **le roi Henri IV** King Henry IV; **le Docteur Goron** Doctor Goron (**e**) *(avec les parties du corps)* **avoir les yeux verts** to have green eyes; **avoir mal à la gorge** to have a sore throat; **hausser les épaules** to shrug one's shoulders; **se laver les pieds** to wash one's feet (**f**) *(avec un adjectif)* **je préfère le rouge** I prefer the red one (**g**) *(distributif)* **8 euros le mètre** 8 euros a metre; **15 euros de l'heure** 15 euros an hour (**h**) *(dans un complément de temps)* **le dimanche, il ne travaille pas** he doesn't work on Sundays; **il va à l'école le matin** he goes to school in the mornings; **il y fait vraiment froid l'hiver** it's really cold there in the winter; **je n'ai rien mangé de la journée** I haven't eaten all day; **Londres, le 9 novembre 2007** *(dans une lettre)* 9 November 2007; **je suis arrivé le 10** I arrived on the 10th
le²

> **l'** is used before a word beginning with a vowel or h mute.

pron personnel (**a**) *(homme, garçon)* him; *(chose, idée)* it; *(animal)* it, him; **elle l'admire** she admires him; **je te le rendrai demain** I'll give it back to you tomorrow; **et lui, tu le connais?** do you know him?; **le voici** here it/he is (**b**) *(remplace une proposition)* **elle me l'a dit** she told me; **il me l'a confirmé** he confirmed it (**c**) *(remplace un adjectif, un nom)* **est-ce qu'elle est disponible? – oui, je crois qu'elle l'est** is she available? – yes, I think she is; **jaloux, il l'est sans**

aucun doute he's undoubtedly jealous; **son frère est médecin, il voudrait l'être aussi** his brother is a doctor and he'd like to be one too
leader [lidœr] *nm* leader
leasing [liziŋ] *nm* leasing; **acheter une auto en l.** to buy a car on a leasing basis
lèche [lɛʃ] *nf très Fam* bootlicking; **faire de la l.** to be a bootlicker
lèche-bottes [lɛʃbɔt] *Fam* **1** *adj inv* **elle est l.** she's a bootlicker
2 *nmf inv* bootlicker
lèche-cul [lɛʃky] *nm inv Vulg Br* arse-licker, *Am* brown-nose
lécher [34] [leʃe] **1** *vt* (**a**) *(avec la langue)* to lick; *Fam* **l. les bottes à qn** to lick sb's boots (**b**) *(fignoler) (travail, style)* to polish (**c**) *(effleurer) (sujet: vagues)* to lap against; *(sujet: flammes)* to lick
2 se lécher *vpr* **se l. les doigts** to lick one's fingers
lèche-vitrines [lɛʃvitrin] *nm Fam* window-shopping; **faire du l.** to go window-shopping
leçon [ləsɔ̃] *nf* (**a**) *(cours, contenu)* lesson; **leçons de chant** singing lessons; **l. de choses** general science *(in primary school)*; **l. particulière** private lesson; **le bricolage en dix leçons** DIY in ten easy lessons (**b**) *(conseil)* **faire la l. à qn** to give sb a lecture; **donner une l. à qn** to teach sb a lesson; **je n'ai pas de l. à recevoir de toi** I don't need your advice; **que cela te serve de l.!** let that be a lesson to you!
lecteur, -trice [lɛktœr, -tris] **1** *nm,f* (**a**) *(personne qui lit)* reader (**b**) *(dans l'édition)* (publisher's) reader (**c**) *Univ* foreign language assistant
2 *nm* (**a**) *(dispositif)* **l. de cassettes** cassette player; **l. de CD** CD player; **l. de DVD** DVD player; **l. MP3** MP3 player; **l. optique** optical reader (**b**) *Ordinat* **l. (de disquettes)** (disk) drive, floppy (disk) drive; **l. de CD-ROM** *ou* **de disque optique** CD-ROM drive; **l. de disque dur** hard disk drive; **l. Zip®** Zip® drive
lecteur-encodeur *(pl lecteurs-encodeurs)* [lɛktœrãkɔdœr] *nm Ordinat* reader-encoder
lectorat [lɛktɔra] *nm* (**a**) *Univ* assistantship (**b**) *(lecteurs)* readership
lecture [lɛktyr] *nf* (**a**) *(action de lire)* reading; **faire la l. à qn** to read aloud to sb; *Pol* **en deuxième l.** at the second reading (**b**) *(ce qu'on lit)* reading; **elle m'a apporté de la l.** she brought me something to read; **avoir de mauvaises lectures** to read the wrong things; **livre de l.** reading book (**c**) *(interprétation)* reading (**d**) *Ordinat* read(ing); **l. optique** optical reading; **l. au scanneur** scan; **en l. seule** in read-only mode; **l. sur disque** reading to disk
ledit, ladite [lədi, ladit] *(mpl* **lesdits** [ledi], *fpl* **lesdites** [ledit]) *adj* the aforementioned
légal, -e, -aux, -ales [legal, -o] *adj* legal
légalement [legalmã] *adv* legally
légalisation [legalizasjɔ̃] *nf* legalization; *(de signature)* authentication
légaliser [legalize] *vt (rendre légal)* to legalize; *(authentifier)* to authenticate
légalité [legalite] *nf* (**a**) *(de mesure, décision)* legality (**b**) *(situation légale)* **la l.** the law; **agir en toute l.** to act within the law
légataire [legatɛr] *nmf* legatee; **l. universel** sole legatee
légendaire [leʒãdɛr] *adj* legendary
légende [leʒãd] *nf* (**a**) *(histoire, fable)* legend; *Fig (mensonge)* fairy tale; **entrer dans la l.** to become a

legend; **de l.** *(personnage, pays)* fairy-tale (**b**) *(d'un dessin, d'une photo)* caption; *(d'une carte)* key
léger, -ère [leʒe, -ɛr] **1** *adj* (**a**) *(de peu de poids)* light; **l. comme une plume** as light as a feather; **avoir le cœur l.** to be light-hearted (**b**) *(blessure, amélioration, nuance)* slight; *(brise, vin, parfum)* light; *(tabac)* mild; *(thé, café)* weak; **il y a eu quelques blessés légers** some people were slightly injured (**c**) *(insuffisant)* *(preuves, arguments)* lightweight; *Fam* **ses résultats sont un peu légers** his/her marks are a bit on the low side (**d**) *(désinvolte) (personne)* thoughtless; *(en amour)* fickle; **femme légère** *ou* **de mœurs légères** loose woman
2 *nf* **à la légère** *(agir, parler)* thoughtlessly; **prendre qch à la légère** to make light of sth
3 *adv* **je vais manger l.** I'll have a light meal; **s'habiller l.** to wear light clothes
légèrement [leʒɛrmã] *adv* (**a**) *(habillé)* lightly (**b**) *(un peu)* slightly; **ça sent l. le moisi** there's a slight smell of mildew; **pourrais-tu l. baisser le volume?** could you turn the volume down a bit *or* slightly? (**c**) *(avec désinvolture) (agir)* thoughtlessly
légèreté [leʒɛrte] *nf* (**a**) *(d'un objet, d'un danseur, d'une démarche)* lightness (**b**) *(faiblesse) (d'une blessure, d'une nuance)* slightness; *(d'un vin)* lightness (**c**) *(désinvolture)* thoughtlessness; **avec l.** *(agir, parler)* thoughtlessly (**d**) *(en amour)* fickleness; *(des mœurs)* looseness
légiférer [34] [leʒifere] *vi* to legislate (**sur** on)
légion [leʒjɔ̃] *nf* legion; *Fig (multitude)* huge number; **ils sont l.** they are legion; **la L. (étrangère)** the Foreign Legion; **la L. d'honneur** the Legion of Honour

Légion d'honneur

Intended to reward not only acts of military bravery but also outstanding civilian achievements, the Legion of Honour is the highest distinction that can be conferred by the French state. It can be awarded regardless of the nationality of its recipients. It is divided into five ranks ("chevalier", "officier", "commandeur", "grand officier" and "grand-croix"). The order of the Legion of Honour is currently made up of one-third civilians and two-thirds soldiers. Some relatively recent recipients of this award are the twenty-two players of the victorious French football team in the 1998 World Cup.

légionnaire [leʒjɔnɛr] *nm* (**a**) *Hist* legionary (**b**) *(à la Légion étrangère)* legionnaire
législateur, -trice [leʒislatœr, -tris] *Jur* **1** *nm,f* legislator
2 *nm (corps législatif)* legislature
3 *adj* legislative
législatif, -ive [leʒislatif, -iv] **1** *adj* legislative; **le pouvoir l.** the legislature
2 *nm* **le l.** legislative power
3 *nfpl* **les législatives** the parliamentary elections
législation [leʒislasjɔ̃] *nf* legislation
législature [leʒislatyr] *nf* (**a**) *(durée)* term of office (**b**) *(corps)* legislature
légiste [leʒist] *nm* jurist
légitime [leʒitim] *adj* (**a**) *(légal) (pouvoir, enfant)* legitimate; *(action)* lawful; *(propriétaire)* legal; *(héritier)* rightful (**b**) *(juste) (récompense, motif, désir)* legitimate (**c**) *(justifié) (colère, action)* justified; **l. défense** self-defence; **elle était en état de l. défense** she was acting in self-defence

légitimement [leʒitimmɑ̃] adv legitimately; Jur lawfully

légitimer [leʒitime] vt (a) (enfant, union) to legitimize (b) (action, demande) to justify (c) (titre, pouvoir) to recognize

légitimité [leʒitimite] nf legitimacy

legs [lɛg] nm (a) Jur legacy, bequest; **faire un l. à qn** to leave sb a legacy (b) Fig (héritage) legacy

léguer [34] [lege] vt (a) Jur to bequeath (à to) (b) (tradition, qualité) to pass on (à to)

légume [legym] **1** nm (a) (aliment) vegetable; **légumes verts** green vegetables, greens; **légumes secs** pulses (b) Fam Fig (personne végétative) vegetable **2** nf Fam **grosse l.** bigwig

leitmotiv [lajtmɔtif, lɛtmɔtif] nm leitmotiv

Léman [lemɑ̃] nm **le lac L.** Lake Geneva

lendemain [lɑ̃dmɛ̃] nm (a) (jour suivant) **le l.** the next day; **le l. matin/soir** the next morning/evening; **le l. de la bataille** the day after the battle (b) (avenir) **penser au l.** to think of the future; **des lendemains prometteurs** a promising future; **sans l.** (succès, aventures) short-lived (c) (période qui suit) **au l. de la guerre/de ce scandale** soon after the war/this scandal

lent, -e [lɑ̃, lɑ̃t] adj slow; **être l. à comprendre** to be slow to understand; **avoir l'esprit l.** to be slow-witted

lente [lɑ̃t] nf nit

lentement [lɑ̃tmɑ̃] adv slowly; **l. mais sûrement** slowly but surely

lenteur [lɑ̃tœr] nf slowness; **avec l.** slowly; **les lenteurs de la justice** the slowness of the courts

lentille [lɑ̃tij] nf (a) (plante) lentil; **l. d'eau** duckweed (b) (en optique) lens; **lentilles de contact** contact lenses

léopard [leɔpar] nm (animal) leopard; (fourrure) leopard skin

LEP [ɛləpe, lɛp] nm Anciennement (abrév lycée d'enseignement professionnel) ≃ technical college

lèpre [lɛpr] nf leprosy

lépreux, -euse [leprø, -øz] **1** adj leprous **2** nm,f leper

lequel, laquelle [ləkɛl, lakɛl] (mpl lesquels [lekɛl], fpl lesquelles [lekɛl])

> lequel and lesquel(le)s contract with **à** to form **auquel** and **auxquel(le)s**, and with **de** to form **duquel** and **desquel(le)s**.

1 pron relatif (personne) who; (après une préposition) whom; (chose) which; **il était avec sa sœur, laquelle m'a reconnu** he was with his sister, who recognized me; **l'actrice à laquelle je pense** the actress (that) I'm thinking of or of whom I'm thinking; **le stylo avec l. j'écris** the pen I'm writing with or with which I'm writing **2** adj relatif **j'ai vu son adversaire, l. adversaire est impressionnant** I've seen his/her opponent, he's impressive; **auquel cas** in which case **3** pron interrogatif which (one)

les¹ [le] voir **le¹**

les² pron personnel them; **l. voilà** here they are

lesbien, -nne [lɛsbjɛ̃, -ɛn] **1** adj lesbian **2** nf **lesbienne** lesbian

lèse-majesté [lɛzmaʒɛste] nf inv **crime de l.** high treason, crime of lese-majesty

léser [34] [leze] vt (a) (désavantager) (personne) to wrong; (intérêts) to harm; **la partie lésée** the injured party (b) Méd to injure

lésiner [lezine] vi to skimp (**sur** on); **ne pas l. sur les moyens** not to spare any expense

lésion [lezjɔ̃] nf lesion

lesquels, lesquelles [lekɛl] voir **lequel**

lessivable [lesivabl] adj washable

lessivage [lesivaʒ] nm washing

lessive [lesiv] nf (a) (produit) (en poudre) washing powder; (liquide) liquid detergent (b) (action de laver) wash(ing); **faire la l.** to do the washing; **j'ai fait trois lessives ce matin** I've done three washes this morning (c) (linge propre) washing

lessivé, -e [lesive] adj Fam washed out

lessiver [lesive] vt (a) (nettoyer) to wash (b) Fam (fatiguer) to wear out

lessiveuse [lesivøz] nf (a) Anciennement boiler (for clothes) (b) Belg (machine à laver) washing machine

lest [lɛst] nm (de bateau, ballon) ballast; **lâcher du l.** to discharge ballast; Fig (faire des concessions) to make concessions

leste [lɛst] adj (a) (agile) nimble (b) (grivois) risqué

lestement [lɛstəmɑ̃] adv (avec agilité) nimbly

lester [lɛste] vt (a) (bateau, ballon) to ballast (b) Fam (poche, portefeuille) to stuff

letchi [lɛtʃi] nm lychee

léthargie [letarʒi] nf lethargy

léthargique [letarʒik] adj lethargic

letton, -onne ou **-one** [lɛtɔ̃, -ɔn] **1** adj Latvian **2** nm,f **L.** Latvian **3** nm (langue) Latvian

Lettonie [lɛtɔni] nf **la L.** Latvia

lettre [lɛtr] nf (a) (de l'alphabet) letter; **l. majuscule/minuscule** capital/small letter; **écrire qch en toutes lettres** to write sth out in full; **au pied de la l.** literally; **à la l.** (suivre, exécuter) to the letter; **il fut surréaliste avant la l.** he was a surrealist before the word had been invented; **rester l. morte** to remain a dead letter; **gagner ses lettres de noblesse** to prove one's/its worth (b) (missive) letter; **l. d'accompagnement** Br covering letter, Am cover letter; **l. de change** bill of exchange; **l. de motivation** Br covering letter, Am cover letter (sent with job application); **l. ouverte (à)** open letter (to); **l. recommandée** Br registered letter, Am certified letter; Fam **ça s'est passé comme une l. à la poste** it went off without a hitch; Fam **la nouvelle est passée comme une l. à la poste** the news was received without any fuss (c) **lettres** (littérature) literature; (à l'université) arts subjects; **homme/femme de lettres** man/woman of letters; **avoir des lettres** to be well-read; **faculté de lettres** faculty of arts; **lettres classiques** classics; **lettres modernes** (à l'université) French

lettré, -e [letre] **1** adj (a) (cultivé) well-read (b) Belg (sachant lire et écrire) **il est l.** he can read and write **2** nm,f (a) (personne cultivée) well-read person (b) Belg (personne sachant lire et écrire) = person who can read and write

leu [lø] **à la queue leu leu** adv in single file

leucémie [løsemi] nf leukaemia; **avoir une l.** to have leukaemia

leucocyte [løkɔsit] nm leucocyte

leur, leurs [lœr] **1** adj possessif their; **l. chien** (il y a un chien) their dog; (chacun a son chien) their dogs; **leurs enfants** their children; **l. père et l. mère** their father and mother; **un de leurs amis** one of their friends, a friend of theirs; Fam **ils ont eu l. vendredi** they got Friday off **2** pron possessif (a) **le l., la l., les leurs** theirs; (en

insistant) their own; **ils te prêtent le l.** you can borrow theirs; **ils n'en ont pas besoin, ils ont le l.** they don't need it, they've got their own (**b**) to them; **donne-l. ta carte de visite** give them your business card; **je le l. ai montré** I showed it to them
  3 *nm* **il faut qu'ils y mettent du l.** they have to do their share
  4 *nmpl* **les leurs** *(leur famille)* their family; **nous serons des leurs ce soir** we'll be joining them tonight

leurre [lœr] *nm* (**a**) *(à la chasse)* decoy (**b**) *(illusion)* illusion

leurrer [lœre] **1** *vt (tromper)* to delude
  2 se leurrer *vpr* to delude oneself (**sur** about)

levage [ləvaʒ] *nm* lifting; **appareil de l.** lifting apparatus

levain [ləvɛ̃] *nm* leaven; **pain au/sans l.** leavened/unleavened bread

levant [ləvɑ̃] **1** *adj m* **soleil l.** rising sun; **au soleil l.** at sunrise
  2 *nm* (**a**) *Litt* **le l.** the east (**b**) **le L.** the Levant (**c**) *Belg Fam* **bien/mal l.** in a good/bad mood

levé, -e[1] [ləve] **1** *adj* (**a**) *(en l'air) (main, poing)* raised (**b**) *(personne, soleil)* up
  2 *nm (de terrain)* survey

levée[2] *nf* (**a**) *(d'une interdiction, de sanctions)* lifting; *(d'une séance)* close; *(d'un siège)* raising; *(de scellés)* breaking (**b**) *(de troupes)* levying (**c**) *(de lettres)* collection (**d**) *(aux cartes)* trick; **faire une l.** to take a trick (**e**) *(remblai)* levee (**f**) *Fig* **l. de boucliers** general outcry; **l. du corps** = removal of the coffin; **l. d'écrou** release from prison

lever[1] [46] [ləve] *vt* (**a**) *(objet)* to lift, to raise; **l. son verre (à qn/qch)** to raise one's glass (to sb/sth) (**b**) *(bras, main, jambe)* to raise, to lift; **l. la tête** to look up; **l. les yeux au ciel** to raise one's eyes to heaven; **l. les bras au ciel** to throw up one's hands; **l. la main sur qn** to raise one's hand to sb; **l. le doigt** to put one's hand up; **il n'a pas levé le petit doigt** he didn't lift a finger; *Fam* **l. le pied** *(ralentir)* to slow down (**c**) *(faire cesser) (embargo, peine, interdiction)* to lift; *(difficulté, doute, ambiguïté)* to remove; *(siège)* to raise; *(séance)* to close (**d**) *(à la chasse) (oiseau)* to flush; *très Fam (séduire) Br* to pull, *Am* to hook up with; **l. un lièvre** to start a hare; *Fig* to open a can of worms (**e**) *(faire sortir du lit) (enfant, malade)* to get up (**f**) *(collecter) (courrier, impôts)* to collect (**g**) *(enrôler) (troupes, armée)* to raise, to levy (**h**) *(plan)* to draw
  2 *vi* (**a**) *(blé, grain)* to shoot (**b**) *(pâte)* to rise
  3 se lever *vpr* (**a**) *(se mettre debout)* to stand up, to get up; **se l. de sa chaise** to get up from one's chair; **se l. de table** to leave the table (**b**) *(quitter le lit)* to get up; *Fam* **se l. du pied gauche** to get out of bed on the wrong side (**c**) *(apparaître) (soleil, lune)* to rise; *(vent)* to get up; *(jour)* to break (**d**) *(s'éclaircir) (brouillard, brume)* to lift, to clear (**e**) *(monter) (rideau de théâtre)* to go up, to rise

lever[2] *nm* (**a**) *(du lit)* getting up; **demain, l. six heures trente** tomorrow, get up six thirty; **au l., buvez un jus d'orange** first thing in the morning, have a drink of orange juice (**b**) *(apparition)* **le l. du jour** daybreak; **le l. du soleil** sunrise (**c**) **l. de rideau** *(début du spectacle)* curtain up; *(première partie)* curtain raiser (**d**) *(de terrain)* survey

lève-tard [lɛvtar] *nmf inv Fam* late riser

lève-tôt [lɛvto] *nmf inv Fam* early riser

lève-vitre *(pl* **lève-vitres**) [lɛvvitr] *nm* window winder

levier [ləvje] *nm aussi Fig* lever; **faire l.** to act as a lever; **l. de commande** control lever; *Fig* **être aux leviers de commande** to be in control; **l. (de changement) de vitesse** *Br* gear lever, *Am* gearshift

lévitation [levitasjɔ̃] *nf* levitation; **être en l.** to be levitating

lèvre [lɛvr] *nf* (**a**) *(de la bouche)* lip; **un cigare aux lèvres** with a cigar in his/her mouth; **le sourire aux lèvres** with a smile on his/her lips; **manger du bout des lèvres** to pick at one's food; **rire du bout des lèvres** to force a laugh; **accepter du bout des lèvres** to accept grudgingly; *Fig* **nous étions tous suspendus à ses lèvres** we were all hanging on his/her every word (**b**) *(de la vulve)* **lèvres** labia; **les grandes/petites lèvres** the labia majora/minora (**c**) *(bord) (de plaie)* lip; *(de cratère)* rim

levrette [ləvrɛt] *nf* greyhound bitch

lévrier [levrije] *nm* greyhound; **l. afghan** Afghan hound

levure [ləvyr] *nf* yeast; **l. de boulanger** fresh *or* baker's yeast; **l. chimique** baking powder

lexical, -e, -aux, -ales [lɛksikal, -o] *adj* lexical

lexicographe [lɛksikɔgraf] *nmf* lexicographer

lexicographie [lɛksikɔgrafi] *nf* lexicography

lexique [lɛksik] *nm* (**a**) *(dictionnaire)* lexicon; *(glossaire)* glossary (**b**) *(mots d'un auteur)* vocabulary

lézard [lezar] *nm (animal)* lizard; *(cuir)* lizard skin

lézarde [lezard] *nf* crack

lézarder [lezarde] **1** *vt* to crack
  2 *vi Fam* to lounge in the sun
  3 se lézarder *vpr* to crack

liaison [ljɛzɔ̃] *nf* (**a**) *(dans les transports)* **l. aérienne/maritime/ferroviaire/routière** air/sea/rail/road link; **toutes les liaisons Paris-Téhéran sont suspendues** all services between Paris and Teheran have been suspended (**b**) *Tél* link; **l. radio/téléphonique** radio/telephone link; **l. par satellite** satellite link; **établir une l. radio** to establish radio contact; *Ordinat* **l. par modem** modem link; *Ordinat* **l. spécialisée** dedicated line (**c**) *(entre des personnes)* contact; **assurer la l. entre deux personnes/services** to liaise between two people/departments; **être en l. avec qn** to be in contact with sb; **travailler en l. (étroite) avec qn** to work (closely) with sb (**d**) *(relation amoureuse)* (love) affair (**e**) *(enchaînement logique)* connection (**f**) *Ling* liaison *(sounding of final consonant before initial vowel sound)*; **faire la l.** to make the liaison

liane [ljan] *nf* creeper

liant, -e [ljɑ̃, -ɑ̃t] **1** *adj* sociable
  2 *nm Tech* binder

liasse [ljas] *nf (de lettres, de papiers)* bundle; *(de billets)* wad

Liban [libɑ̃] *nm* **le L.** (the) Lebanon

libanais, -e [libanɛ, -ɛz] **1** *adj* Lebanese
  2 *nm,f* **L.** Lebanese; **les L.** the Lebanese

libations [libasjɔ̃] *nfpl* libations; **faire des l.** *(boire)* to drink copious amounts (of alcohol)

libellé [libele] *nm* wording

libeller [libele] *vt (document, acte, contrat)* to word; **l. un chèque à l'ordre de** to make out a cheque to

libellule [libɛlyl] *nf* dragonfly

libéral, -e, -aux, -ales [liberal, -o] **1** *adj* (**a**) *Pol & (aux idées larges)* liberal (**b**) *Écon* free-market
  2 *nm,f Pol* Liberal

libéralisation [liberalizasjɔ̃] *nf* (**a**) *(d'un régime, des mœurs)* liberalization (**b**) *Écon* deregulation

libéraliser [liberalize] **1** *vt* (**a**) *(régime, mœurs)* to liberalize (**b**) *Écon* to deregulate
   2 se libéraliser *vpr (régime)* to become more liberal; *(mœurs)* to become freer
libéralisme [liberalism] *nm* (**a**) *Pol* liberalism (**b**) *Écon* free-market economics
libéralité [liberalite] *nf* (**a**) *(générosité)* generosity (**b**) *(cadeau)* generous gift; **vivre des libéralités de ses amis** to live off the generosity of one's friends
libérateur, -trice [liberatœr, -tris] **1** *adj* liberating
   2 *nm,f* liberator
libération [liberasjɔ̃] *nf* (**a**) *(mise en liberté) (d'un prisonnier)* release; *(d'un soldat)* discharge; **l. conditionnelle** (release on) parole (**b**) *(affranchissement)* liberation (**c**) *(fin de l'Occupation)* **la L.** the Liberation *(from the Germans in 1944–45)* (**d**) *(d'énergie, d'une substance)* release
libéré, -e [libere] **1** *adj* liberated; **jeune homme l. des obligations militaires** young man who has carried out his national service duties
   2 *nm,f* released prisoner
libérer [34] [libere] **1** *vt* (**a**) *(rendre sa liberté à) (otage, prisonnier)* to free, to release; *(pays, peuple)* to liberate (**b**) *(laisser partir) (élèves, étudiants)* to let go; *(soldat)* to discharge (**c**) *(soulager)* **l. qn d'un souci** *ou* **d'un poids** to take a weight off sb's mind (**d**) *(rendre disponible) (appartement, chambre d'hôtel)* to vacate (**e**) *(débloquer) (prix)* to free; *(cran de sûreté)* to release; *(instincts, passions)* to unleash; **l. le passage** to clear the way (**f**) *(décharger)* **l. qn de qch** *(dette)* to free sb from sth; *(engagement)* to release sb from sth (**g**) *(émettre) (substance, énergie)* to release
   2 se libérer *vpr* (**a**) *(s'affranchir)* to free oneself (**de** from) (**b**) *(se rendre disponible)* **je tâcherai de me l. ce jour-là** I'll try and be free that day; **je n'ai pas pu me l. plus tôt** I couldn't get away any earlier; **il y a un poste qui vient de se l.** a job vacancy has just come up
Liberia [liberja] *nm* **le L.** Liberia
libérien, -enne [liberjɛ̃, -ɛn] **1** *adj* Liberian
   2 *nm,f* **L.** Liberian
libertaire [libɛrtɛr] *adj & nmf* libertarian
liberté [libɛrte] *nf* (**a**) *(condition)* freedom, liberty; **en l.** *(fugitif)* at large; *(animal)* in the wild; **rendre sa l. à qn/un animal** to let sb/an animal go; **reprendre sa l.** to regain one's freedom; **mettre qn en l.** to set sb free; **(mise en) l. provisoire** *ou* **sous caution** (release on) bail; **l. conditionnelle** parole; **l. surveillée** probation; **mettre qn en l. provisoire/conditionnelle/surveillée** to release sb on bail/parole/probation (**b**) *(droit de l'individu)* freedom, liberty; **l., égalité, fraternité** liberty, equality, fraternity; **l. d'expression** freedom of expression *or* speech; **l. d'opinion** freedom of opinion; **l. de la presse** freedom of the press (**c**) *(absence de contrainte)* freedom; **l. d'entreprise** free enterprise; **avoir toute l. d'action** to have complete freedom of action; **avoir toute l. pour faire qch** to have complete freedom to do sth; **en toute l.** *(s'exprimer, agir)* freely; **prendre la l. de faire qch** to take the liberty of doing sth (**d**) *(familiarités)* **prendre** *ou* **se permettre des libertés avec** to take liberties with
libertin, -e [libɛrtɛ̃, -in] **1** *adj (personne)* dissolute; *(livre, propos)* licentious
   2 *nm,f* libertine
libertinage [libɛrtinaʒ] *nm* licentiousness
libidineux, -euse [libidinø, -øz] *adj* lustful
libido [libido] *nf* libido
libraire [librɛr] *nmf* bookseller

librairie [librɛri] *nf (magasin)* bookshop; *(activité)* bookselling
librairie-papeterie *(pl* **librairies-papeteries)** [librɛripapɛtri] *nf* bookshop and stationer's
libre [libr] *adj* (**a**) *(non soumis) (personne, pays)* free; **être l. de faire qch** to be free to do sth; **l. à vous de le faire** you're quite at liberty to do it; **donner l. cours à son enthousiasme/son imagination** to give one's enthusiasm/imagination free rein; **l. de** *(souci, contrainte, préjugé)* free from; **l. arbitre** free will; **l. pensée** free thinking; **l. penseur** free thinker (**b**) *(disponible) (personne, siège)* free; *(appartement, chambre)* available; *(toilettes)* vacant; **je n'ai pas eu une minute de l. aujourd'hui** I haven't had a spare minute today; **être l. comme l'air** to be as free as a bird; **avoir les mains libres** to have one's hands free; *Fig* to have a free hand; **l. de suite** *(dans une annonce)* available immediately; **la ligne n'est pas l.** the line's *Br* engaged *or Am* busy (**c**) *(non bloqué) (route)* clear; *Fig* **la voie est l.** the coast is clear (**d**) *(privé)* **enseignement / école l.** independent Catholic education/school; **radio l.** independent radio (**e**) *(non réglementé) (prix)* free; *(honoraires)* unrestricted; **la l. entreprise** free enterprise; **il pratique les honoraires libres** there are no restrictions on his fees
libre-échange [librəʃɑ̃ʒ] *nm* free trade
librement [librəmɑ̃] *adv* freely
libre-service *(pl* **libres-services)** [librəsɛrvis] *nm* (**a**) *(principe)* self-service; **station-service en l.** self-service *Br* petrol *or Am* gas station (**b**) *(magasin)* self-service shop; *(restaurant)* self-service restaurant
Libreville [librəvil] *n* Libreville
Libye [libi] *nf* **la L.** Libya
libyen, -enne [libjɛ̃, -ɛn] **1** *adj* Libyan
   2 *nm,f* **L.** Libyan
lice [lis] *nf* **entrer en l.** to enter the fray
licence [lisɑ̃s] *nf* (**a**) *Univ* (bachelor's) degree; **l. ès de lettres/ès** *ou* **de sciences/en droit** arts/science/law degree; **faire une l.** to do a degree (**b**) *(dans le commerce)* licence (**c**) *Sport* permit *(giving right of entry into competition)* (**d**) *(liberté)* licence; **l. poétique** poetic licence (**e**) *(dérèglement)* licentiousness
licencié, -e [lisɑ̃sje] *nm,f* (**a**) *Univ* **l. ès lettres/ès** *ou* **en sciences/en droit** arts/science/law graduate (**b**) *Sport* permit holder
licenciement [lisɑ̃simɑ̃] *nm (pour raisons économiques)* layoff, *Br* redundancy; *(pour faute professionnelle)* dismissal; **l. collectif** mass layoffs *or Br* redundancies; **l. économique** layoff, *Br* redundancy
licencier [66] [lisɑ̃sje] *vt (pour raisons économiques)* to lay off, *Br* make redundant; *(pour faute professionnelle)* to dismiss; **se faire l.** to be laid off *Br* made redundant
lichen [likɛn] *nm* lichen
lichette [liʃɛt] *nf Fam (de pain, fromage)* tiny bit
licol [likɔl] *nm* halter
licorne [likɔrn] *nf* unicorn
licou [liku] *nm* halter
LICRA [likra] *nf (abrév* **Ligue internationale contre le racisme et l'antisémitisme)** = anti-racist movement
lie [li] *nf* dregs; *Litt* **boire la coupe** *ou* **le calice jusqu'à la l.** to drink one's cup of sorrow to the dregs; *Fig* **la l. de la société** the dregs of society
lié, -e [lje] *adj* (**a**) *(attaché)* bound; **avoir les mains liées** to have one's hands tied; *Fig* **j'ai les mains liées** my hands are tied; *Fig* **être pieds et poings liés** to be

bound hand and foot (**b**) *(en relation étroite)* **être** (**très**) **l. avec qn** to be (great) friends with sb

liège [ljɛʒ] *nm* cork; **bouchon de l.** cork

liégeois, -e [ljeʒwa, -az] **1** *adj* (**a**) *(de Liège)* of Liège (**b**) *Culin* **café/chocolat l.** coffee/chocolate ice cream topped with whipped cream **2** *nm,f* **L.** person from Liège

lien [ljɛ̃] *nm* (**a**) *(attache)* bond; *aussi Fig* **se libérer de ses liens** to free oneself from one's bonds (**b**) *(relation)* link, connection; **l. de parenté** *ou* **de famille** family relationship; **il y a un l. de parenté entre ces deux familles** the two families are related; **les liens du mariage** the bonds of marriage; **l. d'amitié** bond of friendship; **l. social** social *or* civic bond; **la crise du l. social** the breakdown of a sense of community in society (**c**) *Ordinat* **l. hypertexte** hypertext link

lier [66] [lje] **1** *vt* (**a**) *(attacher)* (*sujet: contrat, serment*) to be binding on (**b**) *(unir) (personnes)* to bind together (**c**) *(établir un rapport entre) (événements, paragraphes)* to connect, to link; **tout est lié** everything's connected (**d**) *Culin (sauce)* to thicken (**e**) **l. amitié/conversation avec qn** to strike up a friendship/conversation with sb **2 se lier** *vpr* **se l. (d'amitié) avec qn** to strike up a friendship with sb

lierre [ljɛr] *nm* ivy

liesse [ljɛs] *nf* jubilation; **en l.** jubilant

lieu¹, -x [ljø] *nm* (**a**) *(endroit)* place; **en l. sûr** in a safe place; **un l. de passage** a busy place; **les lieux** *(local)* the premises; *(d'un accident, d'un crime)* the scene; **quitter les lieux** to vacate the premises; **un haut l. de** a mecca for; **en haut l.** in high places; **l. de naissance** place of birth; **l. de perdition** den of vice; **l. public** public place; **l. de rendez-vous** meeting place; **l. saint** holy place (**b**) *(pour indiquer un ordre)* **en premier l.** in the first place; **en dernier l.** last(ly) (**c**) **l. commun** commonplace (**d**) *(locutions)* **avoir l.** to take place; **il y a l. de supposer que...** there is reason to suppose that...; **il n'y a pas l. de s'inquiéter** there's no need to worry; **s'il y a l.** if necessary; **donner l. à qch** to give rise to sth; **tenir l. de qch** to take the place of sth; **au l. de** instead of; **au l. de te plaindre** instead of complaining; **au l. de cela** instead

lieu² *(pl lieus) (poisson)* **l. jaune** pollack; **l. noir** coalfish

lieu-dit *(pl lieux-dits)* [ljødi] *nm* locality

lieue [ljø] *nf* league; *Naut* **l. marine** league; **j'étais à cent** *ou* **mille lieues de penser que...** I never dreamt for a single moment that...

lieutenant [ljøtnɑ̃] *nm (dans l'armée de terre)* lieutenant; *(dans l'armée de l'air) Br* flying officer, *Am* first lieutenant; *(dans la marine marchande)* mate

lieutenant-colonel *(pl lieutenants-colonels)* [ljøtnãkɔlɔnɛl] *nm (dans l'armée de terre)* lieutenant-colonel; *(dans l'armée de l'air) Br* wing commander, *Am* lieutenant-colonel

lièvre [ljɛvr] *nm* hare; **courir deux lièvres à la fois** to try to do two things at once

lifter [lifte] *vt* (**a**) *Sport (balle)* to put topspin on (**b**) *(faire un lifting à)* to perform a face lift on; *Fig (rénover)* to give a face lift to

liftier, -ère [liftje, -ɛr] *nm,f Br* lift attendant, *Am* elevator operator

lifting [liftiŋ] *nm* face lift; **se faire faire un l.** to have a face lift

ligament [ligamã] *nm* ligament

ligature [ligatyr] *nf Méd* ligature; **l. des trompes** tying of tubes

ligaturer [ligatyre] *vt Méd* to ligature

ligne [liɲ] *nf* (**a**) *(trait)* line; **l. droite** straight line; **avancer en l. droite** to advance in a straight line; **lire les lignes de la main à qn** to read sb's palm; **l. d'arrivée** finishing line; **l. blanche** *(sur la route) Br* white line, *Am* yellow line; **l. continue** *(sur la route)* continuous line; **l. de démarcation** demarcation line; **l. de départ** starting line; **l. discontinue** *(sur la route)* broken line; **l. de flottaison** waterline; **l. d'horizon** horizon; **l. jaune** *(sur la route) Br* white line, *Am* yellow line; **l. de mire** line of sight; *Fig* **avoir qn dans sa l. de mire** to have sb in one's sights; **l. de touche** touchline

(**b**) *(d'écriture)* line; **lire entre les lignes** to read between the lines; **aller à la l.** to begin a new paragraph; **à la l.** *(en dictant)* new paragraph; *Fig* **entrer en l. de compte** to be taken into consideration

(**c**) *(contour, silhouette) (de voiture, d'objet)* line; *(de personne)* figure; **avoir la l.** to have a good figure

(**d**) *(rangée)* line; **se mettre en l.** to line up; *Mil & Fig* **en première l.** in the front line; *Mil* **les lignes ennemies** the enemy lines; *Fig* **sur toute la l.** completely

(**e**) *(orientation)* line; **l. d'action/de conduite** line of action/conduct; **la l. du parti** the party line; **l. directrice** guideline

(**f**) *(dans les transports)* **l. de chemin de fer** *Br* railway *or Am* railroad line; **grandes lignes** main lines; **l. maritime/aérienne** shipping/air route; **l. d'autobus** bus service; *(parcours)* bus route; **lignes de banlieue** suburban lines; **l. de métro** *Br* underground *or Am* subway line

(**g**) *Élec* **l. électrique** power line; **l. à haute tension** high tension line

(**h**) *Tél* **l. (téléphonique)** (telephone) line; **rappelez plus tard, elle est en l.** call back later, her line's *Br* engaged *or Am* busy; **vous êtes en l.** you're through; **l. directe** direct line; **l. extérieure** outside line

(**i**) *(fil)* line; *(de pêche)* (fishing) line

(**j**) *(de produits)* line, range

(**k**) *(filiation)* **descendre en l. directe** *ou* **en droite l. de...** to be directly descended from...

(**l**) *Ordinat* line; **en l.** online; **hors l.** offline

(**m**) *Belg (raie des cheveux) Br* parting, *Am* part

lignée [liɲe] *nf* descendants; *Fig* **dans la l. de** in the tradition of

lignite [liɲit] *nm* lignite

ligoter [ligɔte] *vt* to tie up (**à** to)

ligue [lig] *nf* league

liguer [lige] **1** *vt* **être ligués contre** to be lined up against **2 se liguer** *vpr (États)* to form a league (**avec/contre** with/against); *(personnes)* to gang up (**avec/contre** with/against)

lilas [lila] *nm & adj inv* lilac

lilliputien, -enne [lilipysjɛ̃, -ɛn] *adj (minuscule)* Lilliputian

Lima [lima] *n* Lima

limace [limas] *nf* slug; *Fam (personne lente) Br* slowcoach, *Am* slowpoke

limaille [limaj] *nf* filings

limande [limãd] *nf* dab; **l.-sole** lemon sole

lime [lim] *nf (outil)* file; **l. à ongles** nail file

limer [lime] **1** *vt* to file; *(barreaux de cellule)* to file through **2 se limer** *vpr* **se l. les ongles** to file one's nails

limier [limje] *nm (chien)* bloodhound; *Fig* sleuth; **un fin l.** a supersleuth
limitatif, -ive [limitatif, -iv] *adj* restrictive
limitation [limitasjɔ̃] *nf* limitation; **l. des naissances** birth control; **l. de vitesse** speed limit
limite [limit] **1** *nf* (**a**) *(frontière)* boundary (**b**) *(maximum)* limit; **ma patience a des limites!** there are limits to my patience!; **mettre une l./des limites à qch** to set a limit/limits to sth; **c'est à la l. de la vulgarité/du supportable** it's bordering on vulgarity/the unacceptable; **dans la l. des stocks disponibles** while stocks last; **à la l., on pourrait changer d'hôtel** if it came to it, we could change hotels; **sans limites** unbounded, limitless
2 *adj* **cas l.** borderline case; **vitesse l.** maximum speed; **je ne lui ai pas mis une claque, mais c'était l.** I didn't slap him/her, but it was a close call; *Fam* **je suis un peu l. financièrement** I'm a bit short of cash
limité, -e [limite] *adj (réduit)* limited; *Fam Péj (obtus)* thick
limiter [limite] **1** *vt* (**a**) *(délimiter) (pays, territoire)* to bound (**b**) *(restreindre)* to limit, to restrict (**à** to); *Fam* **l. les dégâts** to limit the damage
2 se limiter *vpr (personne)* to limit oneself; **se l. à qch/à faire qch** *(personne)* to limit or restrict oneself to sth/to doing sth; **son œuvre se limite à quelques essais** his works amount to no more than a few essays
limitrophe [limitrɔf] *adj* neighbouring; **être l. de** *(pays)* to border on; *(région)* to adjoin
limogeage [limɔʒaʒ] *nm* dismissal
limoger [45] [limɔʒe] *vt* to dismiss; **se faire l.** to be dismissed
limon [limɔ̃] *nm (alluvions)* silt
limonade [limɔnad] *nf (boisson gazeuse)* lemonade
limousine [limuzin] *nf* limousine
limpide [lɛ̃pid] *adj (eau, diamant, regard)* limpid; *(explication)* lucid
limpidité [lɛ̃pidite] *nf (de l'eau, d'un diamant, d'un regard)* limpidity; *(d'une explication)* lucidity
lin [lɛ̃] *nm* (**a**) *(tissu)* linen (**b**) *(plante)* flax
linceul [lɛ̃sœl] *nm* shroud
linéaire [lineɛr] **1** *adj* (**a**) *(récit) & Math* linear (**b**) *(dessin)* line
2 *nm (dans un magasin)* shelf space
linge [lɛ̃ʒ] *nm* (**a**) *(draps, serviettes, nappes)* linen; **l. de maison** household linen; **l. de table** table linen (**b**) *(lessive)* washing (**c**) *(dessous)* **l. (de corps)** underwear; *Fam Fig* **du beau l.** top-drawer people (**d**) *(morceau de tissu)* cloth (**e**) *Suisse (serviette)* towel
lingerie [lɛ̃ʒri] *nf* (**a**) *(dessous)* underwear, lingerie (**b**) *(pièce)* linen room
lingot [lɛ̃go] *nm (de métal)* ingot; **l. (d'or)** gold bar or ingot
linguiste [lɛ̃gɥist] *nmf* linguist
linguistique [lɛ̃gɥistik] **1** *adj* linguistic
2 *nf* linguistics *(singulier)*
lino [lino] *nm Fam* lino
linoléum [linɔleɔm] *nm* linoleum
linotte [linɔt] *nf voir* tête
linteau, -x [lɛ̃to] *nm Constr* lintel
lion [ljɔ̃] *nm* (**a**) *(animal)* lion; **tourner comme un l. en cage** to prowl around (**b**) *Astron & Astrol* **le L.** Leo; **être L.** to be (a) Leo
lionceau, -x [ljɔ̃so] *nm* lion cub
lionne [ljɔn] *nf* lioness
lipide [lipid] *nm* lipid

liposome [lipozom] *nm Chim* liposome
liposuccion [liposysjɔ̃] *nf* liposuction
liquéfaction [likefaksjɔ̃] *nf* liquefaction
liquéfier [66] [likefje] **1** *vt* to liquefy
2 se liquéfier *vpr* to liquefy
liquette [likɛt] *nf* grandad shirt
liqueur [likœr] *nf* (**a**) *(spiritueux)* liqueur (**b**) *Can* **l. (douce)** soft drink
liquidation [likidasjɔ̃] *nf* (**a**) *Jur* liquidation; **être en l.** to have gone into liquidation; **l. judiciaire** official receivership (**b**) *(d'une dette, en Bourse)* settlement (**c**) *Com (de stocks)* selling off; **l. totale** *(sur une vitrine)* stock clearance (**d**) *Fam (meurtre)* liquidation
liquide [likid] **1** *adj (non solide)* liquid; *(trop fluide)* thin
2 *nm* (**a**) *(substance)* liquid, fluid; **l. correcteur** correction fluid; **l. de frein** brake fluid; **l. vaisselle** washing-up liquid (**b**) *(espèces)* cash; **payer en l.** to pay cash
liquider [likide] *vt* (**a**) *Jur (affaire)* to liquidate (**b**) *Fin (dette)* to settle (**c**) *Fam (tuer)* to liquidate (**d**) *Fam (travail, restes, bouteille)* to polish off (**e**) *(stocks)* to sell off; **on liquide** *(sur une vitrine)* stock clearance
liquidités [likidite] *nfpl Fin* liquid assets
liquoreux, -euse [likɔrø, -øz] *adj (vin)* syrupy
lire¹ [44] [lir] **1** *vt* (**a**) *(déchiffrer, interpréter)* to read; **l. qch à qn** to read sth to sb; **lu et approuvé** read and approved; **l. dans les pensées de qn** to read sb's thoughts (**b**) *Fig (deviner) (sur un visage, dans un regard)* to read
2 se lire *vpr (se deviner)* to show
lire² *nf (monnaie)* lira
lis [lis] *nm* lily; **l. blanc** white lily
lisais *etc voir* lire¹
Lisbonne [lizbɔn] *n* Lisbon
lise *etc voir* lire¹
liseré [lizre], **liséré** [lizere] *nm* border, edging
liseron [lizrɔ̃] *nm* bindweed, convolvulus
lisibilité [lizibilite] *nf (d'une écriture)* legibility; *(d'un roman, d'un fichier informatique)* readability
lisible [lizibl] *adj (écriture)* legible; *(roman, fichier informatique)* readable
lisiblement [lizibləmɑ̃] *adv* legibly
lisière [lizjɛr] *nf (d'un champ, d'une forêt)* edge
lisiez *etc voir* lire¹
lisse [lis] *adj (surface, peau, eau)* smooth; *(pneu)* bald; *(cheveux)* sleek
lisser [lise] *vt (cheveux)* to smooth down; *(vêtement)* to smooth out; *(sujet: oiseau) (plumes)* to preen
liste [list] *nf* list; **l. d'attente** waiting list; *Ordinat* **l. de diffusion** distribution or mailing list; **l. électorale** electoral roll; *Ordinat* **l. de fichiers à imprimer** print list, print queue; **l. de mariage** wedding list; **l. noire** blacklist; **être sur (la) l. rouge** *(du téléphone) Br* to be ex-directory, *Am* to be unlisted
listing [listiŋ] *nm Ordinat* listing, printout
lit [li] *nm* (**a**) *(meuble)* bed; **être au l.** to be in bed; **aller au l.** to go to bed; **mettre qn au lit** to put sb to bed; **au l., les enfants!** bedtime, children!; **faire son l.** to make one's bed; **faire l. à part** to sleep in separate beds; **enfant d'un premier l.** child from a first marriage; **l. à baldaquin** four-poster (bed); **l. de camp** *Br* camp bed, *Am* cot; **l. conjugal** marital bed; **grand l.** double bed; **l. d'enfant** *Br* cot, *Am* crib; **lits jumeaux** twin beds; **être sur son l. de mort** to be on one's death bed; **l. une place/deux places** single/double bed; **lits superposés** bunk beds (**b**) *(couche) (d'argile, de*

pierres) bed, layer; *Culin* bed (**c**) *(de rivière)* bed; **sortir de son l.** to burst its banks

litanie [litani] *nf aussi Fig* litany

litchi [litʃi] *nm* lychee

literie [litri] *nf* bedding

lithium [litjɔm] *nm Chim* lithium; **piles au l.** lithium batteries

lithographie [litografi] *nf* (**a**) *(technique)* lithography (**b**) *(œuvre)* lithograph

litière [litjɛr] *nf* (**a**) *(pour cheval, pour chat)* litter (**b**) *(palanquin)* litter

litige [litiʒ] *nm (conflit)* dispute; *(procès)* lawsuit

litigieux, -euse [litiʒjø, -øz] *adj (question, cas)* contentious

litote [litɔt] *nf* understatement, *Spéc* litotes

litre [litr] *nm* litre

litron [litrɔ̃] *nm Fam* bottle of wine

littéraire [literɛr] **1** *adj* literary
  2 *nmf* (**a**) *(doué pour la littérature)* literary person (**b**) *(étudiant)* student of literature

littéral, -e, -aux, -ales [literal, -o] *adj (traduction, sens)* literal

littéralement [literalmã] *adv* literally

littérature [literatyr] *nf (œuvres, documentation)* literature; *(métier)* writing

littoral, -e, -aux, -ales [litɔral, -o] **1** *adj* coastal
  2 *nm* coast(line)

Lituanie [lituani] *nf* **la L.** Lithuania

lituanien, -enne [lituanjɛ̃, -ɛn] **1** *adj* Lithuanian
  2 *nm,f* **L.** Lithuanian
  3 *nm (langue)* Lithuanian

liturgie [lityrʒi] *nf* liturgy

liturgique [lityrʒik] *adj* liturgical

livide [livid] *adj (pâle)* pallid

living [liviŋ], **living-room** (*pl* **living-rooms**) [liviŋrum] *nm Vieilli* living room

livraison [livrɛzɔ̃] *nf* (**a**) *(de marchandises)* delivery; **payable à la l.** payable on delivery; **faire la l. de pain/journaux** to deliver the bread/the newspapers; **prendre l. de qch** to take delivery of sth; **l. à domicile** home delivery (**b**) *(d'ouvrage publié en fascicules)* part

livre¹ [livr] *nm* (**a**) *(ouvrage, partie d'un ouvrage)* book; **l. d'histoire/d'anglais** history/English book; **l. de chevet** bedside book; **l. de classe** *ou* **scolaire** schoolbook; **l. de cuisine** *ou* **de recettes** cookery book, cookbook; **l. pour enfants** children's book; **l. d'images** picture book; **l. de poche** paperback; **l. de prières** prayer book (**b**) *(édition)* **l'industrie du l., le l.** the book trade (**c**) *(registre)* **l. de bord** *Naut* log(-book); *Scol* (teacher's) record book; **l. de comptes** account book; **l. d'or** visitors' book; **grand l.** ledger

livre² *nf* (**a**) *(unité de poids)* half kilo, ≃ pound; *Can* pound (**b**) *(monnaie)* **l. (sterling)** pound (sterling); **l. irlandaise** Irish pound, punt

livre-cassette (*pl* **livres-cassettes**) [livrəkasɛt] *nm* audio book

livrée [livre] *nf (de domestique)* livery

livrer [livre] **1** *vt* (**a**) *(marchandises)* to deliver; **nous livrons à domicile** we deliver; **vous serez livré dès demain** you'll receive delivery tomorrow (**b**) *(abandonner)* **l. un village au pillage/un pays à l'anarchie** to abandon a village to pillage/a country to anarchy; **livré à soi-même** left to oneself (**c**) *(remettre)* **l. qn à qn** *(coupable, complice)* to hand sb over to sb; **l. un secret à qn** to reveal a secret to sb (**d**) *(locutions)* **l. bataille** to join battle; **l. passage à qn** to let sb pass

2 se livrer *vpr* (**a**) *(se rendre)* to give oneself up (**à** to) (**b**) *(se confier)* to open up; **se l. à qn** to confide in sb (**c**) *(s'abandonner)* **se l. à qch** *(vice, spéculations)* to indulge in sth; *(désespoir)* to give way to sth (**d**) *(s'occuper)* **se l. à qch** *(occupations, recherches)* to be engaged in sth; *(étude, lecture)* to devote oneself to sth

livret [livrɛ] *nm* (**a**) *(petit livre)* booklet; **l. (de caisse) d'épargne** bankbook, passbook; **l. de famille** family record book *(for registration of births and deaths)*; **l. militaire** service record; **l. scolaire** (school) report book (**b**) *Mus (d'opéra)* libretto (**c**) *Suisse* multiplication table

livreur, -euse [livrœr, -øz] *nm,f* delivery man, *f* delivery woman

lob [lɔb] *nm* lob; **faire un l.** to hit a lob

lobe [lɔb] *nm* (**a**) *Anat & Bot* lobe (**b**) *Archit* foil

lober [lɔbe] *vt & vi* to lob

lobotomie [lɔbɔtɔmi] *nf Méd* lobotomy

local, -e, -aux, -ales [lɔkal, -o] **1** *adj aussi Méd* local; *(averses)* scattered
  2 *nm* (**a**) *(lieu) (de société, d'organisation)* premises; *(sans usage précis)* place; **locaux commerciaux** business premises (**b**) *Can Tél* extension

localement [lɔkalmã] *adv* locally

localisation [lɔkalizasjɔ̃] *nf* (**a**) *(repérage)* location; *(d'un appel téléphonique)* tracing (**b**) *Ordinat* **l. de logiciel** software localization

localisé, -e [lɔkalize] *adj (circonscrit)* localized

localiser [lɔkalize] *vt (repérer) (bruit, gène, personne)* to locate; *(appel téléphonique)* to trace

localité [lɔkalite] *nf (ville)* town; *(village)* village

locataire [lɔkatɛr] *nmf* tenant; *(chez le propriétaire)* lodger

locatif, -ive [lɔkatif, -iv] *adj voir* **charge**

location [lɔkasjɔ̃] *nf* (**a**) *(de voiture, d'équipement, de costume) (par le locataire)* renting, *Br* hiring; *(par le propriétaire)* renting out, *Br* hiring out; **prendre qch en l.** to rent sth, *Br* to hire sth; **donner qch en l.** to rent sth out, *Br* to hire sth out; **l. de voitures** car rental, *Br* car hire (**b**) *(de logement) (par le locataire)* renting; *(par le propriétaire)* renting out, *Br* letting (out) (**c**) *(appartement, maison)* rented accommodation (**d**) *(de places de spectacle)* booking

location-vente (*pl* **locations-ventes**) [lɔkasjɔ̃vãt] *nf Br* hire purchase, *Am* installment plan; **acheter qch en l.** to buy sth on *Br* hire purchase *or Am* on the installment plan

loche [lɔʃ] *nf (poisson)* loach

locomoteur, -trice [lɔkɔmɔtœr, -tris] *adj* locomotor

locomotion [lɔkɔmɔsjɔ̃] *nf* locomotion; **moyen de l.** means of transport

locomotive [lɔkɔmɔtiv] *nf* (**a**) *(de train)* locomotive, engine; **l. à vapeur** steam engine (**b**) *Fig (leader)* pacemaker; *(entreprise, secteur)* powerhouse

locuteur, -trice [lɔkytœr, -tris] *nm,f Ling* speaker

locution [lɔkysjɔ̃] *nf* expression, phrase

loft [lɔft] *nm* converted loft

logarithme [lɔgaritm] *nm* logarithm

loge [lɔʒ] *nf* (**a**) *(d'artiste)* dressing room (**b**) *(sièges)* box; *Fig* **être aux premières loges** to have a ringside seat (**c**) *(maçonnique, de concierge)* lodge (**d**) *Belg* **l. foraine** stall

logement [lɔʒmã] *nm* (**a**) *(habitation)* accommodation; *(maison)* house; *(appartement) Br* flat, *Am* apartment; **l. de fonction** accommodation that goes with the job; **logements sociaux** *Br* ≃ council flats, *Am* ≃

low-rent housing (**b**) *(action)* housing; **la crise du l.** the housing shortage

loger [45] [lɔʒe] **1** *vi (en permanence)* to live; *(temporairement)* to stay; **l. chez l'habitant** *(en vacances)* to stay in a private house

2 *vt* (**a**) *(héberger)* to put up; **être logé et nourri** to have board and lodging (**b**) *(contenir) (sujet: hôtel, maison)* to accommodate (**c**) *(placer)* to put

3 se loger *vpr* (**a**) **(trouver à) se l.** *(en permanence)* to find somewhere to live; *(temporairement)* to find accommodation (**b**) *(se placer)* to lodge itself

logeur, -euse [lɔʒœr, -øz] *nm,f* landlord, *f* landlady *(of furnished apartments)*

loggia [lɔdʒja] *nf Archit* loggia

logiciel [lɔʒisjɛl] *nm Ordinat* software; **un l.** a (software) package; **l. d'application** application software; **l. bureautique** business software (package); **l. de communication** communications package *or* software; **l. de compression de données** data compression software; **l. de comptabilité** accounts package *or* software; **l. de décompression** decompression software, decompressor; **l. de dessin** art package, drawing program; **l. espion** spyware; **l. d'exploitation** operating system software; **l. grapheur** graphics package *or* software; **l. de jeu** games software; **l. de mise en page** desktop publishing package; **l. de navigation** browser; **l. public** freeware; **l. de reconnaissance de caractères** OCR software, character recognition software; **l. de reconnaissance vocale** voice recognition software; **l. de réseau** network software; **l. de SGBD** DBMS software; **l. de télémaintenance** remote access software; **logiciels de traitement de texte** word-processing software

logique [lɔʒik] **1** *adj* logical

2 *nf* logic; **en toute l.,...** logically,...; *Ordinat* **l. câblée** wired logic; **l. floue** fuzzy logic

logiquement [lɔʒikmã] *adv* (**a**) *(avec cohérence)* logically (**b**) *(normalement)* **l., il devrait bientôt être là** if all goes well, he should soon be here

logis [lɔʒi] *nm Litt (maison)* dwelling, abode

logistique [lɔʒistik] **1** *adj* logistic

2 *nf* logistics *(singulier)*

logo [logo] *nm* logo

logopède [logopɛd] *nmf Belg & Suisse* speech therapist

logotisé, -e [lɔgɔtize] *adj Com* **produits logotisés** branded goods

loi [lwa] *nf* law; **nul n'est censé ignorer la l.** ignorance of the law is no excuse; **faire la** *ou* **sa l.** to lay down the law; *Pol* **l. de finances** Finance Act; **la l. de la jungle** the law of the jungle; **l. martiale** martial law; **la l. de l'offre et de la demande** the law of supply and demand; **la l. du plus fort** the law of the strongest; **la l. du talion** an eye for an eye

loi-cadre (*pl* **lois-cadres**) [lwakadr] *nf* outline law

loin [lwɛ̃] **1** *adv* (**a**) *(dans l'espace)* far (**de** from); **la poste est l.** the post office is a long way away; **c'est encore l., le théâtre/Annecy?** is it far to the theatre/Annecy?; **il y a l. d'ici à Paris** it's a long way to Paris; **plus l.** further (on); **voir plus l.** *(dans un texte)* see below; **de l.** *(reconnaître, admirer)* from a distance; *Prov* **l. des yeux, l. du cœur** out of sight, out of mind (**b**) *(dans le temps)* far away (**de** from); **comme c'est l., tout ça!** that all happened such a long time ago!; **ce jour est encore l.** that day is still a long way off; **d'aussi l.** *ou* **du plus l. qu'elle se souvienne** for as long as she can remember (**c**) *Fig* **de là à l'accuser de men-**

songe il n'y a pas l. it's practically calling him/her a liar; **aller l.** *(réussir)* to go far; **aller trop l.** *(exagérer)* to go too far; **nous étions l. de penser que...** we never thought for a moment that...; **elle est l. d'être bête** she's far from stupid; **je ne suis pas fâché, l. de là!** I'm not angry, far from it!; **l. de moi l'idée d'insinuer que...** far be it from me to insinuate that...; **l. de moi cette idée!** I wouldn't dream of it!, perish the thought!; **pas l. de** *(presque)* not far off; **de l.** *(de beaucoup)* by far; **de l. en l.** *(de temps en temps)* every now and then (**d**) *Suisse (absent)* **il est l.** he's not here

2 *nm* **au l.** in the distance

lointain, -e [lwɛ̃tɛ̃, -ɛn] **1** *adj (dans l'espace, dans le temps)* distant; *(ressemblance)* vague; *(air, regard)* faraway; **dans un avenir l.** in the distant future

2 *nm* **dans le l., au l.** in the distance

loir [lwar] *nm* dormouse

Loire [lwar] *nf* **la L.** the Loire

loisir [lwazir] *nm* (**a**) *(temps libre)* leisure; **activités de l.** leisure *or* spare-time activities; **loisirs** spare time; **avoir des loisirs** to have some spare time (**b**) *(activité)* pastime; **les loisirs** leisure *or* spare-time activities (**c**) *Sout (possibilité, temps nécessaire)* **avoir le l. de faire qch** to have time to do sth; **donner** *ou* **laisser à qn le l. de faire qch** to give sb the opportunity to do sth; *Litt* **à** one's leisure

lolo [lolo] *nm Fam* (**a**) *(langage enfantin) (lait)* milk (**b**) *(sein)* boob

lombaire [lɔ̃bɛr] *Anat* **1** *adj* lumbar

2 *nf* lumbar vertebra

lombalgie [lɔ̃balʒi] *nf Méd* lumbago

lombric [lɔ̃brik] *nm* earthworm

Lomé [lɔme] *n* Lomé

londonien, -enne [lɔ̃dɔnjɛ̃, -ɛn] **1** *adj* London

2 *nm,f* **L.** Londoner

Londres [lɔ̃dr] *n* London

long, longue [lɔ̃, lɔ̃g] **1** *adj* (**a**) *(dans l'espace)* long; *(personne)* long; **l. de 5 mètres** 5 metres long (**b**) *(dans le temps)* long; **dix jours, c'est l.** ten days is a long time; **ce ne sera pas l.** it won't take long; **pendant de longues années** for many years; **longue durée** *(pile)* long-life; **de longue durée** *(chômage, chômeur)* long-term (**c**) *(lent)* slow; **être l. à faire qch** to be slow to do sth

2 *nm* (**a**) *(dans l'espace)* **faire 2 mètres de l.** to be 2 metres long; **(tout) le l. de** *(all)* along; **de tout son l.** *(être étendu)* at full length; *(tomber)* flat on one's face; **de l. en large** up and down, to and fro; **en l.** *(couper, fendre)* lengthwise; *Fam* **expliquer qch en l. et en large** *ou* **en l., en large et en travers** to explain sth in great detail (**b**) *(dans le temps)* **tout au l. de** throughout

3 *adv* (**a**) *(beaucoup)* **en dire l.** *(être révélateur)* to speak volumes; **en savoir l. (sur)** to know a lot (about) (**b**) **s'habiller l.** to wear long clothes

long-courrier (*pl* **long-courriers**) [lɔ̃kurje] **1** *adj (navire)* ocean-going; *(avion)* long-haul

2 *nm (navire)* ocean-going ship; *(avion)* long-haul aircraft

longe¹ [lɔ̃ʒ] *nf (pour guider)* leading rein; *(pour attacher)* tether

longe² *nf Culin (de veau, de porc)* loin

longer [45] [lɔ̃ʒe] *vt* (**a**) *(sujet: personne, voiture) (route, rivière)* to go along; *(mur, côte)* to hug (**b**) *(sujet: sentier, canal, voie ferrée)* to run alongside

longévité [lɔ̃ʒevite] *nf (longue vie)* longevity; *(espérance de vie)* life expectancy

longiligne [lɔ̃ʒiliɲ] *adj* willowy

longitude [lɔ̃ʒityd] *nf Géog* longitude; **à 10° de l.** ouest at longitude 10° west

longitudinal, -e, -aux, -ales [lɔ̃ʒitydinal, -o] *adj* longitudinal, lengthwise

longtemps [lɔ̃tɑ̃] *adv* (**a**) *(attendre, rester)* (for) a long time; **ça ne durera pas l.** it won't last (for) long; *Fig* **tu peux attendre l.** you'll have a long wait (**b**) *(avec une préposition, avec "il y a")* **avant l.** before long; **pas avant l.** not for a long time; **cela existe depuis l.** it has existed for a long time; **pendant l.** for a long time; **je n'en ai pas pour l.** I won't be long; **il n'en a plus pour l.** *(il va bientôt mourir)* he doesn't have long left; **il y a l.** a long time ago; **il y a l. qu'il est mort** he's been dead for a long time; **il y a l. que je ne l'ai pas vue** it's a long time since I saw her; **l. avant/après** long before/after

longue [lɔ̃g] **1** *adj voir* **long**
   2 à la longue *adv* in the end

longuement [lɔ̃gmɑ̃] *adv (attendre, réfléchir, s'attarder)* for a long time; *(parler, expliquer)* at length; **il a l. insisté pour que je vienne** he kept on insisting I should come

longuet, -ette [lɔ̃gɛ, -ɛt] *adj Fam* longish

longueur [lɔ̃gœr] *nf* (**a**) *(dimension, durée) & Sport* length; **jardin de 100 mètres de l.** *ou* **d'une l. de 100 mètres** garden 100 metres long; **en l., dans le sens de la l.** *(couper, fendre)* lengthwise; **avoir une l. d'avance sur** *Sport* to be one length ahead of; *Fig* to have a clear lead over; **à l. de journée/de semaine/d'année** all day/week/year long (**b**) *Péj (développement trop long)* **longueurs** drawn-out passages; **il y a des longueurs dans le film** the film is a little tedious in parts (**c**) *Rad* **l. d'ondes** wavelength; *Fig* **être sur la même l. d'ondes** to be on the same wavelength

longue-vue (*pl* **longues-vues**) [lɔ̃gvy] *nf* telescope

look [luk] *nm Fam* (**a**) *(style)* look; **le l. des années 60** the 60s look; **avoir un l. d'enfer** to look out of this world (**b**) *(présentation)* image; **soigner son l.** to cultivate one's image

looké, -e [luke] *adj Fam* **être l.** punk/grunge to have a punky/grungy look *or* image

looping [lupiŋ] *nm Aviat* loop; **faire un l./des loopings** to loop the loop

lopin [lɔpɛ̃] *nm* **l. de terre** patch *or* plot of land

loquace [lɔkas] *adj* talkative

loque [lɔk] *nf* (**a**) *(vêtement)* rag; **être en loques** to be in rags; **tomber en loques** to fall to pieces (**b**) *Belg (serpillière)* mop (**c**) *Fig (personne)* wreck

loquet [lɔkɛ] *nm* latch

lordose [lɔrdoz] *nf Méd* hollow-back, *Spéc* lordosis

lorgner [lɔrɲe] *vt* (**a**) *(regarder indiscrètement)* to eye; *(avec concupiscence)* to eye up (**b**) *(convoiter)* to have one's eye on

lorgnette [lɔrɲɛt] *nf* opera glasses; *Fig* **regarder** *ou* **voir les choses par le petit bout de la l.** to take a narrow-minded view of things

lorgnon [lɔrɲɔ̃] *nm (avec tige)* lorgnette; *(avec ressort)* pince-nez

lorrain, -e [lɔrɛ̃, -ɛn] **1** *adj* of Lorraine
   2 *nm,f* **L.** person from Lorraine

lors [lɔr] *adv* **l. de** *(pendant)* during; *(au moment de)* at the time of; *Litt* **depuis l.** from that time

lorsque [lɔrsk] *conj* when

losange [lɔzɑ̃ʒ] *nm (forme)* diamond; *(en géométrie)* rhombus

Los Angeles [lɔsɑ̃dʒələs] *n* Los Angeles

lot [lo] *nm* (**a**) *(dans une loterie)* prize; **gros l.** jackpot; *Fam Fig* **tirer le gros l.** to hit the jackpot; **l. de consolation** consolation prize (**b**) *Com (de marchandises)* batch; *(de serviettes, de casseroles)* set; *(de chaussettes, de savonnettes)* pack; *Fig* **dans le l., il y en aura bien un de bon** *(choses, personnes)* at least one out of this lot should be some good; **se détacher** *ou* **être au-dessus du l.** to stand out from the crowd (**c**) *(de terrain)* plot (**d**) *Litt (sort)* lot (**e**) *Ordinat* **traitement par lots** batch processing

loterie [lɔtri] *nf* lottery; **gagner à la l.** to win on the lottery; **l. nationale** national lottery

loti, -e [lɔti] *adj* **être bien/mal l.** to be well/badly off

lotion [losjɔ̃] *nf* lotion; **l. après-rasage** aftershave (lotion); **l. capillaire** hair lotion; **l. tonique** toner

lotissement [lɔtismɑ̃] *nm (ensemble résidentiel)* housing estate

loto [lɔto] *nm* (**a**) *(jeu de hasard)* lotto (**b**) *(jeu national)* national lottery; **jouer au l.** to play *or* do the lottery

Loto

"Loto" is a popular game of chance with large cash prizes. Printed grids ("bulletins") are available at tobacconists' or special kiosks. Players mark six numbers on the grid and pay a fee. The twice-weekly prize draw is broadcast on television. "Loto Sportif" is a version of "Loto" in which players bet on the football results.

lotte [lɔt] *nf (de rivière)* burbot; *(de mer)* monkfish

lotus [lɔtys] *nm* lotus; **fleur de l.** lotus; **position du l.** lotus position

louable [lwabl] *adj (admirable)* praiseworthy, laudable

louage [lwaʒ] *nm* **contrat de l.** rental agreement; **voiture de l.** hired carriage

louange [lwɑ̃ʒ] *nf* praise; **digne de louange(s)** praiseworthy; **chanter les louanges de qn** to sing sb's praises

loubard [lubar] *nm Fam* hooligan

louche¹ [luʃ] *adj* shady, *Br* dodgy

louche² *nf* ladle

loucher [luʃe] *vi (volontairement)* to squint; *(être atteint de strabisme)* to have a squint; **l. de l'œil gauche** to have a squint in one's left eye; *Fig* **l. sur qch** *(regarder)* to eye sth; *(convoiter)* to have one's eye on sth

louer¹ [lwe] *vt* (**a**) *(donner en location) (logement)* to rent out, *Br* to let (out) (à to); *(équipement, véhicule, costume)* to rent out, *Br* to hire out (à to); **maison à l.** house *Br* to let *or Am* for rent (**b**) *(prendre en location) (logement)* to rent (à from); *(équipement, véhicule, costume)* to hire (à from); *(place de spectacle)* to book

louer² **1** *vt (exalter)* to praise; **l. qn de** *ou* **pour qch** to praise sb for sth; **louons le Seigneur!** praise the Lord!
   2 se louer *upr* **se l. de qch** to be very satisfied with sth; **je n'ai qu'à me l. de lui/de ses services** I have nothing but praise for him/for his work; **se l. d'avoir fait qch** to congratulate oneself on having done sth

loufdingue [lufdɛ̃g], **loufoque** [lufɔk] *adj Fam* crazy

louis [lwi] *nm* **l. (d'or)** louis(-d'or)

Louisiane [lwizjan] *nf* **la L.** Louisiana

loukoum [lukum] *nm* piece of Turkish delight; **des loukoums** Turkish delight

loup [lu] *nm* (**a**) *(mammifère)* wolf; *Fig* **il est connu comme le l. blanc** everybody knows him; **quand on parle du l. on en voit la queue** talk of the devil; *Fig* **jeune l.** young go-getter; *(en politique)* Young Turk; *Fam* **mon petit l., mon gros l.** darling, pet (**b**) *(poisson)* bass (**c**) *(demi-masque)* eye mask (**d**) **(vieux) l. de mer** *(marin)* old salt, sea dog

loupe [lup] *nf* (**a**) *(instrument d'optique)* magnifying glass; **regarder qch à la l.** to look at sth through a magnifying glass; *Fig* to put sth under the microscope (**b**) *Bot* knur; **l. d'érable/de noyer** *(en ébénisterie)* burr maple/walnut

louper [lupe] *Fam* **1** *vt* (**a**) *(ne pas réussir) (travail, plat)* to botch, to bungle; *(examen)* to flunk; **l. son entrée** *(au théâtre)* to fluff one's entrance; **loupé!** missed!; **la soirée est loupée** the party's a flop (**b**) *(ne pas prendre) (son tour, occasion, train)* to miss; **il n'en loupe pas une!** *(en actions)* it's one stupid thing after another!; *(en paroles)* he's always opening his big mouth!; **je ne vais pas le l.!** I won't let him get away with it!

2 *vi* **je lui ai dit qu'il attraperait froid et ça n'a pas loupé** I told him he'd catch cold and sure enough he did

3 **se louper** *vpr* (**a**) *(ne pas se rencontrer)* to miss each other (**b**) *(manquer son suicide)* to bungle it; *Ironique* **il ne s'est pas loupé!** he made a proper job of it!

loup-garou *(pl* **loups-garous**) [lugaru] *nm* werewolf; *(pour faire peur aux enfants)* bogeyman

loupiote [lupjɔt] *nf Fam (lampe)* small light

loup-marin [lumarɛ̃] *nm Can* seal

lourd, -e [lur, lurd] **1** *adj* (**a**) *(pesant)* heavy; **j'ai la tête lourde** I've got a thick head; **avoir l'estomac l.** to feel bloated; **yeux lourds de fatigue** eyes heavy with tiredness (**b**) *(à l'aspect pesant) (personne)* heavily built; *(tentures)* heavy (**c**) *(peu subtil) (personne, plaisanterie)* unsubtle; *(mouvement, style)* heavy (**d**) *(perte, dépenses, responsabilité)* heavy (**e**) *(temps)* close; *(parfum)* heavy (**f**) *(plein)* **l. de conséquences** fraught with consequences; **l. de menaces** ominous **2** *adv* **peser l.** to weigh a lot, to be heavy; *Fam* **pas l.** not much

lourdaud, -e [lurdo, -od] **1** *adj* oafish **2** *nm,f* oaf

lourdement [lurdəmɑ̃] *adv* heavily; **se tromper l.** to be greatly mistaken; **insister l.** to keep on insisting

lourder [lurde] *vt Fam* **l. qn** to give sb the boot; **se faire l. (par qn)** to get the boot (from sb)

lourdeur [lurdœr] *nf (poids, manque de subtilité)* heaviness; *(de la bureaucratie)* unwieldiness; *(d'une responsabilité, d'une tâche)* weight; *(du temps)* closeness; **l. d'esprit** slow-wittedness; **j'ai des lourdeurs d'estomac** I feel bloated

lourdingue [lurdɛ̃g] *adj Fam (style)* heavy; *(personne, plaisanterie)* unsubtle

loustic [lustik] *nm Fam* **un drôle de l.** *(louche)* a shady or *Br* dodgy character

loutre [lutr] *nf* otter; *(fourrure)* otter skin

louve [luv] *nf* she-wolf

louveteau, -x [luvto] *nm* (**a**) *(animal)* wolf cub (**b**) *(jeune scout)* Cub (Scout)

louvoyer [32] [luvwaje] *vi Naut* to tack; *Fig* to hedge

Louvre [luvr] *nm* **le (palais du) L.** the Louvre

---

lover [lɔve] **se lover** *vpr (serpent)* to coil up; *(personne)* to curl up

low-cost [lokɔst] **1** *adj (compagnie aérienne)* low-cost, no-frills **2** *nm ou nf* low-cost *or* no-frills airline

loyal, -e, -aux, -ales [lwajal, -o] **1** *adj* (**a**) *(honnête)* fair (**b**) *(fidèle) (serviteur, ami)* loyal; **après vingt-cinq ans de bons et loyaux services** after twenty-five years of good and faithful service **2** *nf loyal Fam* **se battre à la loyale** to fight cleanly

loyalement [lwajalmɑ̃] *adv* (**a**) *(honnêtement)* fairly (**b**) *(fidèlement)* loyally

loyaliste [lwajalist] *adj & nmf Pol* loyalist

loyauté [lwajote] *nf* (**a**) *(honnêteté)* fairness (**b**) *(fidélité)* loyalty (**envers** to)

loyer [lwaje] *nm* rent; **j'ai trois loyers de retard** I'm three months behind with the rent; *Can* **être a l.** to be in rented accommodation

LP [ɛlpe] *nm (abrév* **lycée professionnel**) vocational secondary school

LSD [ɛlɛsde] *nm* LSD

lu, -e *voir* **lire¹**

lubie [lybi] *nf* whim, fad

lubrifiant, -e [lybrifjɑ̃, -ɑ̃t] **1** *adj* lubricating **2** *nm* lubricant

lubrifier [66] [lybrifje] *vt* to lubricate

lubrique [lybrik] *adj* lustful, lecherous

lucarne [lykarn] *nf* (**a**) *(dans un toit)* skylight; *(en saillie)* dormer (window) (**b**) *(au football)* top corner

lucide [lysid] *adj* lucid

lucidement [lysidmɑ̃] *adv* lucidly

lucidité [lysidite] *nf* lucidity

Lucifer [lysifɛr] *npr* Lucifer

luciole [lysjɔl] *nf* firefly

lucratif, -ive [lykratif, -iv] *adj* lucrative; **à but l.** profit-making; **sans but l.** *Br* non-profit-making, *Am* not-for-profit

lucre [lykr] *nm Litt* lucre

ludique [lydik] *adj* play(ful), *Spéc* ludic

ludothèque [lydotɛk] *nf* toy and game library

luette [lɥɛt] *nf* (**a**) *Anat* uvula (**b**) *Can Fam (locution)* **se mouiller** *ou* **se rincer la l.** *(prendre un verre)* to wet one's whistle; *(se soûler)* to get sloshed *or* drunk

lueur [lɥœr] *nf* (**a**) *(lumière faible)* glow; **à la l. d'une bougie/des étoiles** by candlelight/starlight; **à la l. des derniers événements** in the light of recent events (**b**) *Fig (de lucidité, de colère)* flash; *(d'intelligence, d'espoir)* glimmer

luge [lyʒ] *nf* toboggan, *Br* sledge, *Am* sled; **faire de la l.** to go tobogganing *or Br* sledging *or Am* sledding

luger [45] [lyʒe] *vi* (**a**) *(descendre en luge)* to toboggan, *Br* to sledge, *Am* to sled (**b**) *Suisse (déraper)* to skid

lugubre [lygybr] *adj* gloomy; *(son, cri)* mournful

lui [lɥi] *pron personnel* (**a**) *(sujet) (personne)* he; *(chose, animal)* it; **l., il aurait fait un effort** HE would have made an effort; **mon frère, l., n'est pas venu**

as for my brother, he didn't come; **si j'étais l.**, **je me méfierais** if I were him I'd be careful (**b**) *(objet direct)* *(personne)* him; *(chose, animal)* it; **et l., tu le connais?** and what about him, do you know him? (**c**) *(objet indirect)* *(homme)* to him; *(femme)* to her; *(chose, animal)* to it; **donnez-le-l.** give it to him/her/it, give him/her/it it; **je l. ai serré la main** I shook his/her hand; **il l. jeta une pierre** he threw a stone at him/her/it (**d**) *(avec préposition)* *(personne)* him; *(chose, animal)* it; **elle pense encore à l.** she still thinks about him; **dis-le-lui, à l.** tell HIM; **ce livre est à l.** this book is his (**e**) *(réfléchi)* *(personne)* himself; *(chose, animal)* itself; **il ne pense qu'à l.** he thinks only of himself; **il a un appartement à l.** he's got his own flat; **un ami à l.** a friend of his (**f**) *(dans les comparaisons)* him; **elle gagne plus que l.** she earns more than him *or* than he does

lui-même [lɥimɛm] *pron personnel (personne)* himself; *(chose, animal)* itself

luire [18] [lɥir] *vi (métal, astre, yeux)* to shine; *(surface de l'eau, trottoir mouillé)* to glisten; *(flamme, braises)* to glow

luisais *etc voir* **luire**

luisant, -e [lɥizã, -ãt] **1** *adj (étoile, métal, yeux)* shining; *(surface, pelage, peau)* shiny; *(braise)* glowing; **front l. de sueur** forehead glistening with sweat **2** *nm* sheen

lumbago [lɔbago] *nm* lumbago

lumière [lymjɛr] *nf* (**a**) *(clarté)* light; **à la l. de la lune** by moonlight; **il y a de la l. chez lui** there's a light on/ there are lights on at his place; *Fig* **j'ai besoin de tes lumières** I need the benefit of your knowledge; **l. d'ambiance** subdued lighting (**b**) *(locutions)* **à la l. de son exposé,...** in the light of his/her account,...; **faire (toute) la l. sur qch** to get (right) to the bottom of sth; **mettre qch en l.** to bring sth out; *Fam* **ce n'est pas une l.** she's not very bright

lumignon [lymiɲɔ̃] *nm* small light

luminaire [lyminɛr] *nm* **magasin de luminaires** lighting shop

luminescent, -e [lyminɛsã, -ãt] *adj* luminescent

lumineux, -euse [lyminø, -øz] *adj* (**a**) *(corps, cadran)* luminous; *(pièce, ciel)* bright (**b**) *(radieux)* *(regard)* radiant; *(teint)* glowing (**c**) *(explication, propos)* lucid; *(idée)* brilliant

luminosité [lyminozite] *nf* (**a**) *(du ciel)* brightness; *(d'un regard, du teint)* radiance; *Phot* **la l.** the amount of light available (**b**) *(d'un écran)* brightness

lump [lœp] *nm* **œufs de l.** lumpfish roe

lunaire [lynɛr] *adj* lunar; *Fig* **un visage l.** a moon face

lunatique [lynatik] *adj* quirky

lunch [*pl* lunchs *ou* lunches] [lœntʃ] *nm* buffet lunch

lundi [lœdi] *nm* Monday; **le l. de Pâques/de la Pentecôte** Easter/Whit Monday; *voir aussi* **samedi**

lune [lyn] *nf* (**a**) *(astre)* moon; *Fig* **je ne te demande pas la l.** I'm not asking for the moon; **être dans la l.** to be miles away; **la nouvelle/pleine l.** the new/full moon; **l. de miel** honeymoon (**b**) *Fam (derrière)* butt, *Br* bum

luné, -e [lyne] *adj Fam* **être bien/mal l.** to be in a good/bad mood

lunette [lynɛt] *nf* (**a**) *(pour la vue)* **lunettes** glasses, spectacles; **lunettes noires** dark glasses; **lunettes de soleil,** *Belg* **lunettes solaires** sunglasses; **lunettes de vue** corrective glasses (**b**) *(instrument d'optique)* **l.** telescope (**c**) *(siège des W.-C.)* seat (**d**) *(de voiture)* **l. arrière** rear window

lupin [lypɛ̃] *nm* lupin

lurette [lyrɛt] *nf* **il y a belle l.** ages ago; **il y a belle l. que je ne l'ai pas vu** I haven't seen him for ages

luron [lyrɔ̃] *nm* **c'est un gai** *ou* **joyeux l.** he's a bit of a lad

lusophone [lyzɔfɔn] **1** *adj* Portuguese-speaking **2** *nmf* Portuguese speaker

lustre¹ [lystr] *nm* (**a**) *(lampe)* chandelier (**b**) *(brillant)* lustre (**c**) *(prestige)* lustre

lustre² *nm* **ça dure depuis des lustres** it's been going on for ages

lustrer [lystre] *vt (glace, meuble, voiture)* to polish; **lustré par l'usure** shiny with wear

lustrine [lystrin] *nf* cotton lustre

luth [lyt] *nm* lute

luthier [lytje] *nm* stringed-instrument maker

lutin [lytɛ̃] *nm* imp, sprite

lutrin [lytrɛ̃] *nm* (**a**) *(à la messe)* lectern; *(pour soutenir un livre, des feuilles)* reading stand (**b**) *Belg, Can & Suisse (pupitre à musique)* music stand

lutte [lyt] *nf* (**a**) *(combat)* fight, struggle; *(antagonisme)* conflict; *(contre une maladie, contre la pollution)* fight; **entrer/être en l. contre qn** to enter into/ to be in conflict with sb; **gagner de haute l.** to win after a hard struggle; **l. armée** armed struggle; **la l. des classes** the class struggle (**b**) *Sport* wrestling; **faire de la l.** to wrestle

lutter [lyte] *vi* (**a**) *(se battre)* to struggle, to fight; **l. contre** *(adversaire, oppresseur)* to fight against; *(maladie, incendie, tentation)* to fight; *(sommeil)* to fight off (**b**) *(rivaliser)* lustre (**c**) *(prestige)* lustre **l. de vitesse avec qn** to race sb (**c**) *Sport* to wrestle (**avec** *ou* **contre** with)

lutteur, -euse [lytœr, -øz] *nm,f Sport* wrestler

luxation [lyksasjɔ̃] *nf Méd* dislocation

luxe [lyks] *nm* (**a**) *(abondance, richesse)* luxury; *(d'une maison, de l'ameublement)* luxuriousness (**b**) *(qualité)* **de l.** *(produits)* luxury; *(voiture, édition)* de luxe; **boutique de l.** luxury goods shop (**c**) *(bien superflu)* luxury; *Fig* **s'offrir** *ou* **se payer le l. de faire qch** to give oneself the luxury of doing sth; **je vais faire nettoyer ce vieil imperméable, ce ne sera pas du l.** I'm going to have this old raincoat cleaned, and not before time (**d**) *(profusion)* **un l. de précautions/de détails** a wealth of precautions/details

Luxembourg [lyksãbur] **1** *n (ville)* Luxembourg **2** *nm* **le L.** Luxembourg

luxembourgeois, -e [lyksãburʒwa, -az] **1** *adj* of Luxembourg **2** *nm,f* **L.** Luxembourger **3** *nm (langue)* Luxembourgish

luxer [lykse] **se luxer** *vpr* **le l. l'épaule/le poignet** to dislocate one's shoulder/one's wrist

luxueux, -euse [lyksɥø, -øz] *adj* luxurious

luxure [lyksyr] *nf Litt* lust

luxuriant, -e [lyksyrjã, -ãt] *adj (végétation, forêt, chevelure)* luxuriant; *(imagination)* fertile

luzerne [lyzɛrn] *nf Br* lucerne, *Am* alfalfa

lycée [lise] *nm Br* ≃ secondary school, *Am* ≃ high school *(for pupils aged fifteen to eighteen)*; **l. professionnel** vocational secondary school; **l. technique** technical school

lycéen, -enne [liseɛ̃, -ɛn] *nm,f Br* ≃ secondary school pupil, *Am* ≃ high school pupil

Lycra® [likra] *nm* Lycra®

lymphatique [lɛ̃fatik] *adj* (**a**) *Biol* lymphatic (**b**) *(personne)* lethargic

lymphe [lɛ̃f] *nf* lymph

lymphocyte [lɛ̃fɔsit] *nm Biol* lymphocyte
lyncher [lɛ̃ʃe] *vt* to lynch
lynx [lɛ̃ks] *nm* lynx; *Fig* **avoir des yeux de l.** to have eyes like a hawk
Lyon [ljɔ̃] *n* Lyons
lyonnais, -e [ljɔnɛ, -ɛz] **1** *adj* of Lyons **2** *nm,f* **L.** person from Lyons

lyophilisé, -e [ljɔfilize] *adj* freeze-dried
lyre [lir] *nf* lyre
lyrique [lirik] *adj* (**a**) *(poème, poète)* lyric (**b**) *(passionné)* lyrical
lyrisme [lirism] *nm* lyricism; **parler de qch avec l.** to wax lyrical about sth
lys [lis] = **lis**

M, m¹ [ɛm] *nm inv* M, m
m² (**a**) *(abrév* **mètre(s)**) m; **1 m 50** 1.5 m (**b**) *Gram* *(abrév* **masculin**) m
M. *(abrév* **Monsieur**) Mr
m' [m] *voir* **me**
ma [ma] *voir* **mon**
MA [ɛma] *nm (abrév* **maître auxiliaire**) *Br* supply *orAm* substitute teacher
maboule, -e [mabul] *Fam* **1** *adj (fou)* crazy, nuts **2** *nm,f* nutcase
mac [mak] *nm très Fam (maquereau)* pimp
macabre [makabr] *adj (découverte, histoire)* macabre, gruesome; *(humour)* macabre
macadam [makadam] *nm* (**a**) *(revêtement)* macadam; **m. goudronné** tarmac(adam) (**b**) *(route)* road
macaque [makak] *nm* (**a**) *(singe)* macaque; **m. rhésus** rhesus monkey (**b**) *Fam (personne laide)* pig
macareux [makarø] *nm* puffin
macaron [makarɔ̃] *nm* (**a**) *Culin* macaroon (**b**) **macarons** *(coiffure)* coils *(over the ears)* (**c**) *(badge)* badge; *(décoration)* rosette; *(autocollant)* sticker; *Journ* **m. de presse** press badge
macaroni [makarɔni] *nm* (**a**) *(pâte)* piece of macaroni; **des macaronis** macaroni (**b**) *(Italien)* Eyetie, = racist term used to refer to an Italian
MacDo [makdo] *nm Fam* McDonalds®
Macédoine [masedwan] *nf* **la M.** Macedonia
macédoine [masedwan] *nf* **m. de fruits** fruit salad; **m. de légumes** mixed vegetables
macédonien, -enne [masedɔnjɛ̃, -ɛn] **1** *adj* Macedonian **2** *nm,f* **M.** Macedonian
macération [maserasjɔ̃] *nf* steeping
macérer [34] [masere] **1** *vt* to steep **2** *vi* to steep; **faire m. qch** to steep sth; *Fig* **laisser m. qn** to leave sb to stew
mâche [maʃ] *nf* lamb's lettuce
mâcher [maʃe] *vt (nourriture)* to chew; **ne pas m. ses mots** not to mince one's words
machette [maʃɛt] *nf* machete
machiavélique [makjavelik] *adj* Machiavellian
machin [maʃɛ̃] *nm Fam* (**a**) *(objet)* thingy, thingummy (**b**) *(personne)* what's-his-name, *f* what's-her-name; **monsieur M.** Mr What's-his-name; **madame M.** Mrs What's-her-name
machinal, -e, -aux, -ales [maʃinal, -o] *adj (action, geste, travail)* mechanical; *(réaction)* automatic
machinalement [maʃinalmɑ̃] *adv (agir)* mechanically; *(réagir, répondre)* automatically
machination [maʃinasjɔ̃] *nf* conspiracy

machine [maʃin] *nf* (**a**) *(appareil)* machine; **m. à café** coffee machine; **m. à calculer** calculator; *(plus grande)* calculating machine; **m. à coudre** sewing machine; **m. à écrire** typewriter; **écrire qch à la m.** to type sth; **m. à laver**, *Belg* **m. à lessiver** washing machine; **m. à sous** slot machine, *Br* fruit machine; **m. à tricoter** knitting machine (**b**) *(dans un bateau)* **stopper les machines** to stop engines; **faire m. arrière** to reverse engines; *Fig* to backtrack (**c**) *(locomotive)* engine; *Fam (moto)* machine (**d**) *(organisation)* machinery
machine-outil (*pl* **machines-outils**) [maʃinuti] *nf* machine tool
machiner [maʃine] *vt* to plot
machinisme [maʃinism] *nm* mechanization
machiniste [maʃinist] *nmf* (**a**) *(dans un théâtre)* sceneshifter, stagehand; *(au cinéma, à la télévision)* grip (**b**) *(conducteur d'autobus)* driver
machisme [matʃism, maʃism] *nm* machismo
macho [matʃo] *adj & nm Fam* macho
mâchoire [maʃwar] *nf* (**a**) *(d'une personne, d'un animal)* jaw (**b**) *(d'une poulie)* flange (**c**) *mâchoires (d'un étau, d'une tenaille)* jaws; *(de frein)* shoes
mâchonner [maʃɔne] *vt (mâcher)* to chew (**b**) *(marmonner)* to mutter
mâchouiller [maʃuje] *vt Fam* to chew away at
maçon [masɔ̃] *nm* (**a**) *(d'ouvrage en briques)* bricklayer; *(d'ouvrage en pierre)* (stone)mason (**b**) *(franc-maçon)* mason
maçonnerie [masɔnri] *nf* (**a**) *(de briques)* brickwork; *(de pierres)* masonry, stonework (**b**) *(franc-maçonnerie)* masonry
maçonnique [masɔnik] *adj* masonic
macramé [makrame] *nm* macramé
macrobiotique [makrobjɔtik] **1** *adj* macrobiotic **2** *nf* macrobiotics *(singulier)*
macro-commande (*pl* **macro-commandes**) [makrokɔmɑ̃d] *nf Ordinat* macro(-command)
macroéconomie [makroekɔnɔmi] *nf* macro-economics *(singulier)*
macrolangage [makrolɑ̃gaʒ] *nm Ordinat* macro-language
maculer [makyle] *vt* to stain (**de** with)
Madagascar [madagaskar] *n* Madagascar
madame [madam] (*pl* **mesdames** [medam]) *nf* (**a**) *(titre)* Mrs; **M. Martin** Mrs Martin; **M. le Ministre** the Minister (**b**) *(en apostrophe)* madam; *(à l'école)* Miss; **M. le Ministre** Madam Minister; **au revoir, m.** goodbye; **M.,** *(dans une lettre)* Dear Madam,; *Fam* **et en plus, M. exige des excuses!** so Her Ladyship wants an apology as well, does she?; **par ici, mesdames** this

way, ladies; **mesdames, messieurs** ladies and gentlemen

madeleine [madlɛn] *nf (gâteau)* madeleine

mademoiselle [madmwazɛl] *(pl* **mesdemoiselles** [medmwazɛl]) *nf* (**a**) *(suivi d'un nom)* Miss; **M. Martin** Miss Martin; **Mesdemoiselles Martin et Durand** the Misses Martin and Durand (**b**) *(en apostrophe)* Miss, Madam; *(à l'école)* Miss; **merci m.** thank you; *Fam* **et en plus, M. se plaint!** so, Her Ladyship is complaining as well, is she?; **mesdemoiselles, un peu de silence je vous prie!** *(dans une classe)* let's have some quiet, girls, please! (**c**) *(dans une lettre)* **M.** Dear Madam (**d**) *(utilisé seul)* **M. se plaint que... *(dans un magasin)* this young lady is complaining that...

Madère [madɛr] *n* Madeira

madère [madɛr] *nm* Madeira (wine)

madone [madɔn] *nf* Madonna

madras [madrɑs] *nm (tissu)* madras (cotton)

Madrid [madrid] *n* Madrid

madrier [madrije] *nm* beam

madrilène [madrilɛn] **1** *adj* of Madrid **2** *nmf* **M.** person from Madrid

maestria [maɛstrija] *nf* mastery

maf(f)ia [mafja] *nf* Mafia; **la M.** the Mafia

maf(f)ieux, -euse [mafjø, -øz] **1** *adj* Mafia **2** *nm,f* Mafioso

maf(f)ioso [mafjozo] *(pl* **maf(f)iosi** [mafjozi]) *nm* Mafioso

maganer [magane] *vt Can (chose)* to spoil, to waste; *(personne)* to manhandle

magasin [magazɛ̃] *nm* (**a**) *(boutique)* Br shop, Am store; **avoir qch en m.** to have sth in stock; **courir** *ou* **faire les magasins** to go shopping; **grand m.** department store; *Can* **m. général** general store (**b**) *(entrepôt)* warehouse (**c**) *(d'un appareil photo, d'une arme)* magazine

magasinage [magazinaʒ] *nm* (**a**) *(mise en dépôt)* warehousing (**b**) *(droits)* warehouse charges (**c**) *Can* **faire du m.** to go shopping

magasiner [magazine] *vi Can* to go shopping

magasinier [magazinje] *nm* warehouseman

magazine [magazin] *nm* (**a**) *(journal)* magazine (**b**) *(émission à la radio ou à la télévision)* magazine programme

mage [maʒ] *nm* magus

Maghreb [magrɛb] *nm* **le M.** the Maghreb

maghrébin, -e [magrebɛ̃, -in] **1** *adj* of the Maghreb **2** *nm,f* **M.** person from the Maghreb

Maghrébin

This term usually refers to people from Algeria, Morocco and Tunisia, although it can also refer to Libyans and Mauritanians. It has a particular resonance in contemporary France, where immigrants from these countries constitute the largest ethnic minority.

magicien, -enne [maʒisjɛ̃, -ɛn] *nm,f* magician

magie [maʒi] *nf* magic; **m. blanche/noire** white/black magic

magique [maʒik] *adj* (**a**) *(surnaturel)* magic (**b**) *(extraordinaire)* magical

magiquement [maʒikmɑ̃] *adv* magically

magistère [maʒistɛr] *nm (diplôme)* = post-graduate vocational qualification (**b**) *(autorité)* authority

magistral, -e, -aux, -ales [maʒistral, -o] *adj* (**a**) *(admirable) (interprétation, démonstration)* masterly;

(réussite) brilliant (**b**) *(énorme) (correction, dispute)* proper; *(erreur)* colossal (**c**) *(docte) (ton)* magisterial

magistralement [maʒistralmɑ̃] *adv* authoritatively

magistrat [maʒistra] *nm (qui rend la justice)* judge; *(qui applique la loi)* Br public prosecutor, Am prosecuting attorney

magistrature [maʒistratyr] *nf* **la m.** the judicial authorities; **la m. assise** the Bench *or* judges; **la m. debout** the (body of) Br public prosecutors *or Am* prosecuting attorneys

magma [magma] *nm* (**a**) *Géol* magma (**b**) *(ensemble confus)* jumble

magnanime [maɲanim] *adj* magnanimous

magnanimité [maɲanimite] *nf* magnanimity

magnat [magna] *nm* magnate, tycoon; **m. de la presse** press baron

magner [maɲe] **se magner** *vpr Fam* to get a move on

magnésium [maɲezjɔm] *nm* magnesium

magnétique [maɲetik] *adj* magnetic

magnétiser [maɲetize] *vt* (**a**) *(matériau, corps)* to magnetize (**b**) *(personne, foule)* to hypnotize

magnétisme [maɲetism] *nm (d'un matériau, de la terre, d'une personne)* magnetism

magnéto [maɲeto] *nm Fam* tape recorder

magnétophone [maɲetɔfɔn] *nm* tape recorder

magnétoscope [maɲetɔskɔp] *nm* video(recorder)

magnificence [maɲifisɑ̃s] *nf* magnificence

magnifier [66] [maɲifje] *vt* to magnify, to glorify

magnifique [maɲifik] *adj* magnificent

magnifiquement [maɲifikmɑ̃] *adv* magnificently

magnitude [maɲityd] *nf* magnitude

magnolia [maɲɔlja] *nm* magnolia (tree)

magnum [magnɔm] *nm* magnum

magot [mago] *nm Fam* hoard

magouille [maguj] *nf Fam* scheming; **faire des magouilles** to scheme

magouiller [maguje] *vt & vi Fam* to scheme

magouilleur, -euse [magujœr, -øz] *nm,f Fam* schemer

magret [magrɛ] *nm (de canard)* fillet

Mahomet [maɔmɛ] *npr* Mohammed

mai [mɛ] *nm* May; **le premier m.** *(fête)* May Day; **le huit m.** *(fête)* VE day; *voir aussi* janvier

Mai 68

The events of May 1968 came about when student protests, coupled with widespread industrial unrest, culminated in a general strike and rioting. De Gaulle's government survived the crisis, but the issues raised made the events a turning point in French social history.

maigre [mɛgr] **1** *adj* (**a**) *(très mince) (personne, partie du corps)* thin (**b**) *(sans gras) (viande)* lean; *(fromage, yaourt)* low-fat (**c**) *(peu abondant) (filet d'eau)* thin; *(repas, salaire)* meagre; *(végétation, barbe)* sparse (**d**) *(peu conséquent) (conclusions, explication)* thin; *(succès)* very limited **2** *nm (de viande)* lean part **3** *nmf* thin person **4** *adv* **faire m.** not to eat meat

maigrelet, -ette [mɛgrəlɛ, -ɛt] *adj* skinny

maigreur [mɛgrœr] *nf (d'une personne)* thinness

maigrichon, -onne [mɛgriʃ5, -ɔn] *adj* skinny

maigrir [mɛgrir] *vi* to get thinner

mailing [mɛliŋ] *nm* mailshot

maillage [majaʒ] *nm* networking

maille [maj] *nf* (**a**) *(de tricot)* stitch; **m. à l'endroit/à l'envers** plain/purl stitch (**b**) *(de filet)* mesh; *Fig* **passer entre les mailles du filet** to slip through the net (**c**) *(tissu)* knitted fabric (**d**) *(de chaîne)* link (**e**) **avoir m. à partir avec qn** to have a set-to with sb

maillet [majɛ] *nm* mallet

maillon [majɔ̃] *nm* link

maillot [majo] *nm* *(de footballeur, de coureur cycliste)* shirt, jersey; **m. de bain** *(pour femmes)* swimsuit; *(pour hommes)* (swimming) trunks; **m. de corps** *Br* vest, *Am* undershirt; **m. jaune** yellow jersey *(in the Tour de France)*

main [mɛ̃] **1** *nf* hand; **haut les mains!, les mains en l'air!** hands up!; **les mains bien propres** empty-handed; *Fig* **les mains dans les poches** unprepared; **avoir qch en m.** *(situation)* to have sth in hand; *(voiture)* to have the feel of sth; **avoir la m. heureuse** to be lucky; **avoir la m. leste** to be quick to raise one's hand; **avoir la m. lourde** *(être brutal)* to be heavy-handed; **il a eu la m. lourde avec le sel** he was a bit heavy-handed with the salt; **donner la m. à qn** to hold sb's hand; **faire m. basse sur qch** to get one's hands on sth; **mettre la m. sur qch** *(trouver ce que l'on cherchait)* to lay one's hands on sth; **mettre la m. à la pâte** *ou* **à l'ouvrage** to lend a hand; **mettre la dernière m. à qch** to put the finishing touches to sth; **en mettre sa m. au feu** *ou* **à couper** to stake one's life on it; **ne pas y aller de m. morte** *(en frappant, en insultant)* not to pull one's punches; *(forcer une description, une action)* to overdo it; **prendre qn par la m.** to take sb's hand; *Fig* **se prendre par la m.** to take oneself in hand; **prendre qn/qch en m.** to take sb/sth in hand; **prendre qn la m. dans le sac** to catch sb red-handed; **sous la m.** handy; **à la m.** *(faire, fabriquer)* by hand; *(tenir, avoir)* in one's hand; **écrit à la m.** handwritten; **fait à la m.** *(pull, poterie)* handmade; **à deux mains** in both hands; **à quatre mains** *(morceau)* for four hands; *(jouer)* four-handed; **à m. armée** *(vol, attaque)* armed; **à main(s) nue(s)** with bare hands; **à pleines mains** by the handful; **de m. en m.** from hand to hand; **de la m. à la m.** cash in hand; **de m. de maître** with a master's hand; **de première m.** firsthand; **de seconde m.** secondhand; *Tél* **mains libres** hands-free; **en mains propres** in person; **m. courante** handrail **2** *adv* **tricoté/fait/cousu m.** hand-knitted/-made/-sewn

main-d'œuvre [mɛ̃dœvr] *nf* labour

main-forte [mɛ̃fɔrt] *voir* **prêter**

mainmise [mɛ̃miz] *nf* seizure (**sur** of)

maint, -e [mɛ̃, mɛ̃t] *adj indéfini Litt* many a; **maintes et maintes fois, en maintes et maintes occasions** time and (time) again

maintenance [mɛ̃tnɑ̃s] *nf* maintenance

maintenant [mɛ̃tnɑ̃] *adv* now

maintenir [70] [mɛ̃tnir] **1** *vt* (**a**) *(soutenir)* to hold in position (**b**) *(empêcher d'avancer)* *(foule)* to hold back; **m. qn à distance** to keep sb at a distance (**c**) *(conserver)* *(tradition, paix)* to maintain, to keep; *(décision)* to abide by; **m. qn en vie** to keep sb alive (**d**) *(affirmer)* to maintain (**que** that) **2 se maintenir** *upr* to hold up

maintien [mɛ̃tjɛ̃] *nm* (**a**) *(conservation)* maintenance; *(de la loi)* upholding; **m. de l'ordre** maintenance of law and order (**b**) *(allure, posture)* bearing

maintiendrai *etc voir* **maintenir**

maire [mɛr] *nm* mayor

Maire

In France, the mayor has obligations not only to the community but also to national government. He or she is responsible for promulgating national law as well as supervising the local police and officiating at civic occasions. Mayors are elected by the "conseil municipal" (and thus indirectly by the town's residents).

mairie [mɛri] *nf* *(lieu)* *Br* town hall, *Am* city hall; *(administration)* *Br* town council, *Am* city hall

Mairie

Also called the "hôtel de ville", this is the centre of municipal government. The "mairie" serves as a vital information source for town residents. People go there to ask about taxes, to get married in a civil ceremony, to enrol in certain community-sponsored classes etc.

mais [mɛ] **1** *conj* (**a**) *(marque l'opposition ou la transition)* but; **non seulement..., m. aussi** *ou* **encore...** not only... but also...; **m. qu'est-ce qui t'arrive?** whatever's the matter with you?; **m. j'y pense, je ne l'ai pas encore appelée!** I've just thought, I haven't rung her yet! (**b**) *(emphatique)* **m. oui!** of course!; **m. non!** of course not!; **m. enfin** well really; **elle ne fait rien, m. vraiment rien** she does nothing all day, and I mean nothing; **j'ai faim, m. faim!** I'm so hungry! **2** *nm* **il y a un m.** there's a but

maïs [mais] *nm* *Br* maize, *Am* corn

maison [mɛzɔ̃] **1** *nf* (**a**) *(habitation)* house; **m. de campagne** *(résidence secondaire)* house in the country; **m. individuelle** detached house; **m. de poupée** *Br* doll's house, *Am* dollhouse (**b**) *(foyer)* home; **à la m.** at home; **toute la m. dort** the whole house is asleep (**c**) *(entreprise)* company; **m. de couture** fashion house; **m. d'édition** publishing house; **m. mère** parent company (**d**) *(lignée)* house (**e**) *(institution)* **m. d'arrêt** remand centre; **m. close** *ou* **de passe** brothel; **m. de correction** *ou* **de redressement** detention centre; **m. de la culture** arts centre; **m. des jeunes et de la culture** = youth club and arts centre; **m. de repos** rest *or* convalescent home; **m. de retraite** old people's home **2** *adj inv* (**a**) *(artisanal)* home-made (**b**) *(au sein de l'entreprise)* in-house (**c**) *Fam (en intensif)* almighty

Maison-Blanche [mɛzɔ̃blɑ̃ʃ] *nf* **la M.** the White House

maisonnée [mɛzɔne] *nf* household

maisonnette [mɛzɔnɛt] *nf* small house

maître [mɛtr] **1** *nm* (**a**) *(de situation, de chien)* master; **m. de maison** host; **en m.** authoritatively; **être m. de son destin** to be master of one's own destiny; **être m. de soi** to have self-control; **il n'était plus m. de ses actes** he didn't know what he was doing (**b**) *(dans des fonctions)* **m. (d'école)** *(Br* primary school *or Am* elementary school)* teacher; **m. auxiliaire** *Br* supply *or Am* substitute teacher; **m. de conférence** *Br* (senior) lecturer, *Am* assistant professor; **m. d'hôtel** *(dans une maison)* butler; *(dans un restaurant)* head waiter; **m. nageur** swimming instructor; **m. d'œuvre** project manager (**c**) *(titre octroyé à un peintre, à un musicien)* maestro; **les grands maîtres** the great masters; **être passé m. dans l'art de qch/de faire qch** to be a past master at sth/at doing sth (**d**) *(titre donné à* *un avocat)* = form of address for lawyer (**e**) **m. chanteur** blackmailer

2 *adj* **m. mot** key word

maîtresse [mɛtrɛs] **1** *nf* mistress; **être m. de son destin** to be mistress of one's own destiny; **être m. de soi** to have self-control; **m. (d'école)** (*Br* primary school *or Am* elementary school) teacher; **m. de maison** hostess

2 *adj* main, principal; **m. femme** capable woman

maîtrise [metriz] *nf* (**a**) *(diplôme universitaire)* ≃ master's degree (**de** in) (**b**) *(contrôle) (de ses passions)* mastery; **m. de soi** self-control (**c**) *(connaissance)* mastery (**d**) *(école de chant)* choir school

maîtriser [metrize] **1** *vt* (**a**) *(soumettre) (agresseur)* to overpower; *(élèves, animal)* to control; *(flammes, opposition)* to subdue; *(incendie, épidémie)* to control (**b**) *(contrôler) (passion)* to control; *(peur)* to overcome (**c**) *(connaître parfaitement) (sujet, langue)* to master; **il ne maîtrise pas la langue** he hasn't mastered the language (**d**) *(rester maître de) (véhicule)* to have under control

2 se maîtriser *vpr* to control oneself

Maïzena® [maizena] *nf Br* cornflour, *Am* cornstarch

majesté [maʒɛste] *nf* (**a**) *(noblesse)* majesty (**b**) **Sa M. (le Roi)** His Majesty (the King); **Sa M. (la Reine)** Her Majesty (the Queen) (**c**) *Art* **Christ en m.** Christ in majesty

majestueux, -euse [maʒɛstɥø, -øz] *adj* majestic

majeur, -e [maʒœr] **1** *adj* (**a**) *(principal)* major (**b**) *(personne)* of age (**c**) *Mus (mode, intervalle)* major

2 *nm (doigt)* middle finger

major [maʒɔr] *nm* (**a**) *(d'une promotion)* top student (**b**) *Mil (officier)* regimental adjutant *(with administrative duties); Belg, Can & Suisse* ≃ major

majoration [maʒɔrasjɔ̃] *nf (d'une facture)* surcharge (**de** on); *(d'un prix)* increase (**de** in)

majordome [maʒɔrdɔm] *nm* butler

majorer [maʒɔre] *vt (facture)* to put a surcharge on; *(prix)* to increase

majorette [maʒɔrɛt] *nf* (drum) majorette

majoritaire [maʒɔritɛr] *adj* majority; **être m.** to be in the majority

majorité [maʒɔrite] *nf* (**a**) *(supériorité en nombre)* majority; **en m.** for the most part; **avoir la m.** to be in the majority (**b**) *(dans des élections)* majority; **m. relative/absolue** relative/absolute majority (**c**) *(parti politique)* majority party (**d**) **m. civile** majority, coming of age

Majorque [maʒɔrk] *n* Majorca

majorquin, -e [maʒɔrkɛ̃, -in] **1** *adj* Majorcan

2 *nm,f* **M.** Majorcan

majuscule [maʒyskyl] **1** *adj (lettre)* capital

2 *nf* capital letter

mal¹, maux [mal, mo] *nm* (**a**) *(douleur)* pain, ache; **avoir m. à l'estomac/à la tête/au dos** to have stomach ache/a headache/backache; **avoir m. à la gorge** to have a sore throat; **j'ai m. au bras** my arm hurts, I have a sore arm; **avoir m. aux dents** to have toothache; **avoir des maux d'estomac/de tête** to get stomach ache/headaches; **où avez-vous m.?** where does it hurt?; **faire m. à qn** to hurt sb; **mon genou/œil me fait m.** my knee/eye hurts; **se faire m.** to hurt oneself; *Fam* **attraper du m.** to catch cold; **ça fait m. au cœur de voir ça!** it's sickening to see things like that!; *Fam* **ça me ferait m.!** I'm not having it!; **être en m. de qch** to crave sth; **être en m. d'enfants** to be broody; **m. de cœur** sickness; **m. de dents** tooth-

ache; **m. de gorge** sore throat; **m. de mer** seasickness; **avoir le m. de mer** to be seasick; **m. du pays** homesickness; **avoir le m. du pays** to be homesick; *Litt* **m. du siècle** world-weariness; **m. de tête** headache; **m. des transports** travel-sickness; *Prov* **aux grands maux les grands remèdes** desperate times call for desperate measures

(**b**) *(préjudice)* harm; **faire du m. à qn** to harm sb; **n'a jamais fait de m. à personne!** it never did anyone any harm!; **vouloir du m. à qn** to mean to harm sb; **cela fera plus de m. que de bien** it will do more harm than good; **le m. est fait** the damage has been done; **un m. nécessaire** a necessary evil; **il n'y a pas de m. à cela** there's no harm in that; *Fam* **il n'y a pas de m.** there's no harm done; **dire du m. de qn** to speak ill of sb; **ne pas penser à m.** to mean well

(**c**) *(contraire du bien)* wrong; **le bien et le m.** right and wrong, good and evil; **voir le m. partout** to always see the bad side

(**d**) *(difficulté)* **avoir du m. à faire qch** to have difficulty *or* trouble doing sth; *Fam* **avoir un m. de chien à faire qch** to have a hell of a job doing sth; **non sans m.** not without difficulty; **se donner du m. pour faire qch** to take pains to do sth; **donner du m. à qn** to give sb trouble

mal² **1** *adv* (**a**) *(médiocrement)* badly; *(incorrectement)* wrongly; **elle chante m.** she's a bad singer; **la porte est m. fermée** the door isn't closed properly; **il travaille m. à l'école** he's a poor student; **cette lampe éclaire m.** this lamp doesn't give much light; **m. comprendre** to misunderstand; **m. interpréter** to misinterpret; **m. choisir** to make the wrong choice; **ça va m. finir** it'll end in tears; **on y mange m.** the food's not very good there; **on dort m. dans ce canapé-lit** this sofa bed isn't very comfortable; **je ne pensais pas m. faire** I didn't think I was doing anything wrong; **aller de m. en pis** to go from bad to worse; **on voit m. d'ici** you can't see very well from here; *Fam* **se mettre m. avec qn** to fall out with sb; *Fam* **être m. avec qn** to be on bad terms with sb; **vous ne feriez pas m. de...** you would be wise to... (**b**) *(en mauvaise santé)* **se sentir m.** to feel ill; **se trouver m.** to faint; **aller m.** to be ill; **être au plus m.** to be at death's door; **être m. en point** to be in a bad way (**c**) *(une certaine quantité)* **pas m. de** quite a lot of; **il y en a pas m.** there is/are quite a lot; **cela m'a pris pas m. de temps** it took me quite a while

2 *adj inv* (**a**) *(immoral)* bad, wrong; **c'est très m. de faire ça** it's very naughty to do that (**b**) *(peu satisfaisant)* *Fam* **c'est pas m.** it's not bad, it's quite good; *Fam* **elle n'est pas m.** she's not bad-looking; **on n'est pas m. ici** we've found a nice place here

malabar [malabar] *nm Fam* hulk

malade [malad] **1** *adj* (**a**) *(souffrant)* ill, sick; *(nauséeux)* sick; **tomber m.** to fall *or* be taken ill; **je suis m. en bateau/voiture/avion** I suffer from seasickness/carsickness/airsickness; **être m. du cœur/du foie** to have heart/liver trouble; **être m. d'inquiétude/de jalousie** to be sick with worry/jealousy (**b**) *(qui fonctionne mal) (organe, dent)* bad; *Fig (industrie)* ailing (**c**) *(dérangé intellectuellement)* mad

2 *nmf* sick person; *(dans un hôpital)* patient; **un m. mental** a mentally ill person; *(dans un hôpital)* a mental patient; **un m. imaginaire** a hypochondriac

maladie [maladi] *nf* illness, disease; *Fig* **en faire une m.** to make a song and dance about it; **la m. d'Alzheimer** Alzheimer's disease; **m. bleue** cyanosis; **la m. de**

Parkinson Parkinson's disease; **m. sexuellement transmissible** sexually transmitted disease; **m. de la vache folle** mad cow disease

maladif, -ive [maladif, -iv] *adj* (**a**) *(personne, teint)* sickly (**b**) *(curiosité, pensées)* morbid (**c**) *(susceptibilité, jalousie)* pathological

maladresse [maladrɛs] *nf* (**a**) *(manque d'habileté physique)* clumsiness, awkwardness (**b**) *(manque de tact)* tactlessness; *(bévue)* blunder

maladroit, -e [maladrwa, -at] **1** *adj* (**a**) *(inhabile)* clumsy, awkward (**b**) *(manquant de tact)* tactless
  2 *nm,f* (**a**) *(personne inhabile)* clumsy *or* awkward person (**b**) *(personne sans tact)* tactless person

maladroitement [maladrwatmɑ̃] *adv* (**a**) *(de façon gauche)* clumsily (**b**) *(sans tact)* tactlessly

malais, -e [malɛ, -ɛz] **1** *adj* Malaysian
  2 *nm,f* **M.** Malaysian
  3 *nm (langue)* Malay

malaise [malɛz] *nm* (**a**) *(trouble physique)* feeling of sickness; *(étourdissement)* dizzy spell; **avoir un m.** to feel faint (**b**) *(inconfort moral)* uneasiness (**c**) *(état de crise)* unrest

malaisé, -e [malɛze] *adj* difficult

Malaisie [malɛzi] *nf* **la M.** Malaysia

malaria [malarja] *nf* malaria; **avoir la m.** to have malaria

malavisé, -e [malavize] *adj Litt* unwise (**de faire qch** to do sth)

Malawi [malawi] *nm* **le M.** Malawi

malaxer [malakse] *vt* to knead

malchance [malʃɑ̃s] *nf* bad luck; **par m.** as bad luck would have it

malchanceux, -euse [malʃɑ̃sø, -øz] **1** *adj* unlucky
  2 *nm,f* unlucky person

malcommode [malkɔmɔd] *adj* (**a**) *(appareil)* impractical; *(vêtement)* unsuitable (**b**) *Can (personne) (indiscipliné)* unruly; *(hargneux)* cantankerous

Maldives [maldiv] *nfpl* **les (îles) M.** the Maldives

maldonne [maldɔn] *nf* misdeal; *Fig* **il y a m.** something's gone wrong somewhere

mâle [mɑl] **1** *adj* (**a**) *(du sexe masculin)* male (**b**) *(viril) (courage, assurance)* manly; *(style)* virile (**c**) **prise m.** plug
  2 *nm* male

malédiction [malediksjɔ̃] *nf* curse

maléfice [malefis] *nm* evil spell

maléfique [malefik] *adj* evil

malencontreusement [malɑ̃kɔ̃trøzmɑ̃] *adv* unfortunately

malencontreux, -euse [malɑ̃kɔ̃trø, -øz] *adj* unfortunate

malentendant, -e [malɑ̃tɑ̃dɑ̃, -ɑ̃t] **1** *adj* hard of hearing
  2 *nm,f* person who is hard of hearing

malentendu [malɑ̃tɑ̃dy] *nm* misunderstanding

mal-en-train [malɑ̃trɛ̃] *adj Can* unwell, *Br* poorly; **avoir l'air m.** to look peaky *or* out-of-sorts

malfaçon [malfasɔ̃] *nf* defect

malfaisant, -e [malfəzɑ̃, -ɑ̃t] *adj* harmful

malfaiteur [malfɛtœr] *nm* criminal

malfamé, -e [malfame] *adj* disreputable

malformation [malfɔrmasjɔ̃] *nf* malformation

malfrat [malfra] *nm Fam* crook

malgache [malgaʃ] **1** *adj* Madagascan
  2 *nmf* **M.** Madagascan
  3 *nm (langue)* Malagasy

malgré [malgre] *prép (en dépit de)* in spite of, despite; **m. tout** *(en dépit de tout)* in spite of *or* despite everything; *(pourtant)* all the same

malhabile [malabil] *adj* clumsy, awkward

malheur [malœr] **1** *nm* (**a**) *(drame, catastrophe)* misfortune; **le m., c'est que...** the unfortunate thing is that...; **faire un m.** to be a big hit; **un m. n'arrive jamais seul** it never rains but it pours (**b**) *(chagrin, infortune)* misfortune; **faire le m. de qn** to cause sb a lot of unhappiness (**c**) *(malchance)* bad luck; **par m.** unfortunately; **porter m. à qn** to bring sb bad luck; **avoir le m. de faire qch** to make the big mistake of doing sth
  2 *exclam* hell!

malheureusement [malørøzmɑ̃] *adv* unfortunately; **m. pour toi, il ne reste plus de petites tailles** you're out of luck, there are no small sizes left

malheureux, -euse [malørø, -øz] **1** *adj* (**a**) *(triste)* unhappy, miserable (**b**) *(malchanceux) (personne)* unlucky; *(candidat, tentative)* unsuccessful; *(amour)* unrequited; **m. au jeu/en amour** unlucky at gambling/in love (**c**) *(regrettable)* unfortunate (**d**) *(négligeable)* miserable, wretched
  2 *nm,f* (**a**) *(personne infortunée)* poor wretch (**b**) *(indigent)* poor *or* needy person; **les m.** the poor, the needy

malhonnête [malɔnɛt] *adj* (**a**) *(personne, pratique)* dishonest (**b**) *(indécent) (proposition)* indecent

malhonnêteté [malɔnɛtte] *nf* dishonesty

Mali [mali] *nm* **le M.** Mali

malice [malis] *nf* (**a**) *(espièglerie)* mischief (**b**) *(méchanceté)* malice; **sans m.** without malice

malicieusement [malisjøzmɑ̃] *adv* mischievously

malicieux, -euse [malisjø, -øz] *adj (espiègle)* mischievous

malien, -enne [maljɛ̃, -ɛn] **1** *adj* Malian
  2 *nm,f* **M.** Malian

malignité [maliɲite] *nf* (**a**) *(méchanceté)* malice (**b**) *(d'une tumeur)* malignancy

malin, -igne [malɛ̃, -iɲ] **1** *adj* (**a**) *(rusé) (personne)* crafty; *(regard)* knowing; *Ironique* **c'est m.!** that's clever! (**b**) *(méchant) (plaisir)* perverse, malicious; **prendre un m. plaisir à faire qch** to take a perverse *or* malicious pleasure in doing sth (**c**) *(tumeur)* malignant
  2 *nm,f* crafty person; **faire le m.** to show off

malingre [malɛ̃gr] *adj* puny

malintentionné, -e [malɛ̃tɑ̃sjɔne] *adj* ill-intentioned

malle [mal] *nf* (**a**) *(valise)* trunk; *Fam* **se faire la m.** to clear off (**b**) *(de voiture) Br* boot, *Am* trunk (**c**) *Can* **mettre une lettre à la m.** to mail *or Br* post a letter

malléable [maleabl] *adj* malleable

mallette [malɛt] *nf (porte-documents)* briefcase

malmener [46] [malməne] *vt* (**a**) *(brutaliser) (personne)* to manhandle, to treat roughly; *(verbalement)* to attack; *(matériel, véhicule)* to mistreat (**b**) *(dominer)* **m. qn** to give sb a hard time

malnutrition [malnytrisjɔ̃] *nf* malnutrition

malodorant, -e [malɔdɔrɑ̃, -ɑ̃t] *adj* smelly

malotru, -e [malɔtry] *nm,f* lout

Malouines [malwin] *nfpl* **les (îles) M.** the Falkland Islands, the Falklands

malpoli, -e [malpɔli] *Fam* **1** *adj* rude
  2 *nm,f* rude person

malpropre [malprɔpr] *adj* (**a**) *(sale) (mains)* dirty; *(apparence, travail)* slovenly (**b**) *(inconvenant)* smutty (**c**) *(malhonnête)* despicable

malsain, -e [malsɛ̃, -ɛn] *adj* (**a**) *(dangereux pour la santé)* unhealthy (**b**) *(pernicieux)* unhealthy; *(personne)* unwholesome

malséant, -e [malseɑ̃, -ɑ̃t] *adj Litt* unseemly

malt [malt] *nm* malt

maltais, -e [maltɛ, -ɛz] **1** *adj* Maltese
  2 *nm,f* **M.** Maltese; **les M.** the Maltese
  3 *nm (langue)* Maltese

Malte [malt] *n* Malta

maltraitance [maltrɛtɑ̃s] *nf* ill-treatment

maltraitant, -e [maltrɛtɑ̃, -ɑ̃t] *adj* abusive

maltraiter [maltrɛte] *vt* (**a**) *(brutaliser)* to ill-treat (**b**) *(verbalement)* to attack

malus [malys] *nm* partial loss of no-claims bonus *(due to insurance claim)*

malveillance [malvɛjɑ̃s] *nf* spite

malveillant, -e [malvɛjɑ̃, -ɑ̃t] *adj* spiteful

malvenu, -e [malvəny] *adj* out of place, inappropriate

malversation [malvɛrsasjɔ̃] *nf* embezzlement

maman [mamɑ̃] *nf Br* mum, *Am* mom; *(langage enfantin) Br* mummy, *Am* mommy

mamelle [mamɛl] *nf (de vache)* udder; *(de chienne, de truie)* teat

mamelon [mamlɔ̃] *nm* (**a**) *(du sein)* nipple (**b**) *(colline)* hillock

mamie [mami] *nf* grandma, gran(ny)

mammaire [mamɛr] *adj* mammary

mammifère [mamifɛr] **1** *adj* mammalian
  2 *nm* mammal

mammographie [mamɔgrafi] *nf* mammography

mammouth [mamut] *nm* mammoth

mamours [mamur] *nmpl Fam* kissing and cuddling; **faire des m. à qn** to kiss and cuddle sb

manager¹ [manadʒɛr] *nm* manager

manager² [45] [manadʒe] *vt* to manage

manant [manɑ̃] *nm* (**a**) *Hist (villageois)* villager; *(paysan)* peasant (**b**) *Litt (mufle)* churl, boor

Manche [mɑ̃ʃ] *nf* **la M.** the (English) Channel

manche¹ [mɑ̃ʃ] *nf* (**a**) *(de vêtement)* sleeve; **en manches de chemise** in one's shirtsleeves; **manches longues/courtes** long/short sleeves; **manches ballon/kimono/raglan** puff/kimono/raglan sleeves (**b**) *(de jeu, de compétition)* round; *(au tennis)* set (**c**) *Fam* **faire la m.** to beg

manche² *nm* (**a**) *(d'outil)* handle; **m. à balai** broomstick; *(d'avion)* joystick (**b**) *(de guitare)* neck (**c**) *Fam* **s'y prendre comme un m.** to make a real mess of things

manchette [mɑ̃ʃɛt] *nf* (**a**) *(extrémité de la manche)* cuff (**b**) *(de journal)* headline (**c**) *(au catch)* forearm smash; *(au volley-ball)* dig

manchon [mɑ̃ʃɔ̃] *nm* (**a**) *(vêtement)* muff (**b**) *Tech* sleeve

manchot¹, -e [mɑ̃ʃo, -ɔt] **1** *adj (privé d'un bras)* one-armed; *Fam* **il n'est pas m.** *(adroit)* he's clever with his hands; *(il peut le faire lui-même)* he's got hands, hasn't he?
  2 *nm,f* one-armed person

manchot² *nm (oiseau)* penguin

mandale [mɑ̃dal] *nf très Fam* clout, slap

mandarin [mɑ̃darɛ̃] *nm* (**a**) *(de Chine)* mandarin (**b**) *Fig & Péj (personnage influent)* mandarin (**c**) *(langue)* Mandarin (Chinese)

mandarine [mɑ̃darin] *nf (fruit)* mandarin (orange)

mandat [mɑ̃da] *nm* (**a**) *(mission) (de député)* mandate; *(de président)* term of office (**b**) *(ordre)* warrant;

m. d'amener = summons; **m. d'arrêt** arrest warrant; **m. de dépôt** committal order; **m. de perquisition** search warrant (**c**) *(mode de paiement)* order; **m. postal** *Br* postal order, *Am* money order (**d**) *(autorité)* mandate (**e**) *(procuration)* power of attorney

mandataire [mɑ̃datɛr] *nmf (d'électeurs)* representative; *(dans une réunion)* proxy

mandat-carte *(pl* **mandats-cartes**) [mɑ̃dakart] *nm Br* postal order, *Am* money order *(in postcard form)*

mandater [mɑ̃date] *vt* (**a**) *(représentant)* to commission; *(membre parlementaire)* to give a mandate to (**b**) *(frais)* to pay by order

mandat-lettre *(pl* **mandats-lettres**) [mɑ̃dalɛtr] *nm Br* postal order, *Am* money order *(in letter-card form)*

mandibule [mɑ̃dibyl] *nf* mandible

mandoline [mɑ̃dɔlin] *nf* mandolin

mandrin [mɑ̃drɛ̃] *nm (pour percer)* punch; *(pour élargir un trou)* drift

manège [manɛʒ] *nm* (**a**) *(attraction foraine) Br* roundabout, merry-go-round, *Am* carousel (**b**) *(en équitation)* riding school (**c**) *(manigances)* game

manette [manɛt] *nf* lever; **m. de jeux** joystick; *Fam* **à fond les manettes** at full speed

manga [mɑ̃ga] *nm* manga

manganèse [mɑ̃ganɛz] *nm* manganese

mangeable [mɑ̃ʒabl] *adj* (**a**) *(comestible)* edible (**b**) *(médiocre)* eatable

mangeoire [mɑ̃ʒwar] *nf* manger

manger [45] [mɑ̃ʒe] **1** *vt* (**a**) *(aliments)* to eat; **m. qn/qch des yeux** to look at sb/sth longingly; **m. ses mots** to mumble; **ça ne mange pas de pain** it doesn't cost anything; **je ne mange pas de ce pain-là** I don't go in for that sort of thing (**b**) *(attaquer)* to eat away (**c**) *(consommer)* to get through (**d**) *(dépenser)* to get through
  2 *vi* to eat; **donner à m. à qn** to give sb something to eat; **m. comme quatre** *ou* **comme un ogre** to eat like a horse; **m. comme un oiseau** to eat like a sparrow; **m. à sa faim** to eat one's fill
  3 **se manger** *vpr* to be eaten

mange-tout [mɑ̃ʒtu] *nm inv (pois) Br* mangetout, *Am* snow pea; *(haricot) Br* runner bean, *Am* string bean

mangeur, -euse [mɑ̃ʒœr, -øz] *nm,f* **gros m.** big eater; **tigre/requin m. d'hommes** man-eating tiger/shark; *Can Fam Péj* **m. de balustrades** sanctimonious man, *f* sanctimonious woman

mangue [mɑ̃g] *nf* mango

maniable [manjabl] *adj (outil)* handy; *(véhicule)* easy to handle

maniaque [manjak] **1** *adj* (**a**) *(pointilleux)* fussy (**b**) *(fou)* manic
  2 *nmf* (**a**) *(pointilleux) Br* fusspot, *Am* fussbudget; **être un m. de qch** to be fanatical about *or* obsessed with sth (**b**) *(fou)* maniac

manichéen, -enne [manikeɛ̃, -ɛn] *adj* Manichean

manichéisme [manikeism] *nm* Manicheism

manie [mani] *nf* (**a**) *(habitude)* odd habit (**b**) *(idée fixe)* mania, obsession (**c**) *Méd* mania

maniement [manimɑ̃] *nm* handling

manier [66] [manje] *vt* (**a**) *(manipuler) (objet)* to handle (**b**) *(utiliser) (véhicule)* to handle; *(outil, ironie)* to use

manière [manjɛr] *nf* (**a**) *(façon)* way, manner; **faire qch à sa m.** to do sth one's (own) way; **de m. à faire**

qch so as to do sth; **de m. que** + *subjunctive* so that, in such a way that; **d'une** *ou* **de m. générale** generally speaking; **en aucune m.** under no circumstances; **de toute m.** in any case; **d'une certaine m.** in a manner of speaking, in a sense; **c'est sa m. d'être** that's the way he/she is; **la m. forte** strong-arm tactics (**b**) *(conduite)* **manières** manners; **faire des manières** *(agir de façon pompeuse)* to put on airs and graces; *(se faire prier)* to make a fuss (**c**) *(d'une œuvre)* **à la m. de** in the style of

maniéré, -e [manjeʁe] *adj* affected

maniérisme [manjeʁism] *nm* mannerism

manif [manif] *nf Fam* demo

manifestant, -e [manifɛstɑ̃, -ɑ̃t] *nm,f* demonstrator

manifestation [manifɛstasjɔ̃] *nf* (**a**) *(de sentiments)* display (**b**) *(rassemblement politique)* demonstration (**c**) *(événement organisé)* event

manifeste[1] [manifɛst] *adj* obvious, manifest

manifeste[2] *nm* manifesto

manifestement [manifɛstəmɑ̃] *adv* obviously, manifestly

manifester [manifɛste] **1** *vt (exprimer)* to show
   2 *vi* to demonstrate
   3 se manifester *vpr* (**a**) *(personne)* to make oneself known (**b**) *(maladie)* to show *or* manifest itself (*par in*)

manigancer [16] [manigɑ̃se] *vt* to scheme

manigances [manigɑ̃s] *nfpl* scheming

Manille [manij] *n* Manila

manioc [manjɔk] *nm* manioc, cassava

manipulateur, -trice [manipylatœr, -tris] **1** *nm,f* (**a**) *(de machines)* operator; **m. de laboratoire** laboratory technician; **m. radio(graphe)** X-ray technician (**b**) *Péj (de personnes)* manipulator
   2 *nm (appareil de transmission)* (sending) key

manipulation [manipylasjɔ̃] *nf* (**a**) *(d'appareils, de produits)* handling; **m. génétique** genetic engineering (**b**) *(en science)* experiments, practical work (**c**) *Péj (de personnes)* manipulation (**d**) *Ordinat* **m. de documents** document handling; **m. de données** data manipulation

manipuler [manipyle] *vt* (**a**) *(appareils, produits)* to handle (**b**) *Péj (personnes)* to manipulate (**c**) *(statistiques)* to massage

manivelle [manivɛl] *nf* crank

manne [man] *nf (dans la Bible)* manna; *Fig (don inespéré)* godsend

mannequin [mankɛ̃] *nm* (**a**) *(personne)* model (**b**) *(de magasin, de couturier)* dummy

mannequinat [mankina] *nm (carrière)* modelling

manœuvre[1] [manœvr] *nf (a)* *(conduite, direction)* *(de machines)* operation; *(de véhicules)* manoeuvring; **faire une m.** to (do a) manoeuvre; **faire une fausse m.** *(en voiture)* to manoeuvre badly; *Fig* to get it wrong (**b**) *(intrigue)* manoeuvre; **manœuvres** manoeuvring (**c**) *Mil (dans une bataille)* manoeuvre; **être en manœuvres** to be on manoeuvres (**d**) *(d'un bateau)* manoeuvre

manœuvre[2] *nm (ouvrier)* unskilled worker

manœuvrer [manœvre] **1** *vt* (**a**) *(faire fonctionner)* *(machine)* to operate; *(véhicule)* to manoeuvre (**b**) *(influencer)* to influence
   2 *vi aussi Fig* to manoeuvre

manoir [manwar] *nm* manor house

manomètre [manɔmɛtr] *nm* pressure gauge, manometer

manquant, -e [mɑ̃kɑ̃, -ɑ̃t] *adj* missing

manque [mɑ̃k] **1** *nm* (**a**) *(insuffisance)* lack; **par m. de** through lack of; **m. de chance!** bad luck!; **m. à gagner** loss of earnings (**b**) *(lacune)* gap (**c**) *(d'un drogué)* withdrawal symptoms; **être en (état de) m.** to have withdrawal symptoms
   2 *nf Fam* **à la m.** useless, pathetic

manqué, -e [mɑ̃ke] **1** *adj* (**a**) *(occasion, rendez-vous)* missed (**b**) *(tentative, expérience)* unsuccessful (**c**) *(personne)* **c'est un poète/un médecin m.** he should have been a poet/doctor
   2 *nm (gâteau)* = sponge cake with almond-flavoured or fruit-flavoured icing

manquement [mɑ̃kmɑ̃] *nm* breach (**à** of)

manquer [mɑ̃ke] **1** *vt* (**a**) *(cible, train, occasion)* to miss (**b**) *(échouer à)* to fail
   2 *vi* (**a**) *(faire défaut)* to be lacking; **le temps/la place me manque** I don't have enough time/room; **elle me manque** I miss her (**b**) *(échouer)* to fail; **ça n'a pas manqué, il est arrivé en retard** sure enough, he was late (**c**) *(être absent)* to be missing (**à** from)
   3 *v impersonnel* **il ne manque personne** there's no one missing; **il manque quelques pages** there are a few pages missing; **il manque un bouton à la veste** there's a button missing from your jacket; **il me manque 10 euros** I'm 10 euros short; **il ne manquait plus que cela!** that's all I/he/*etc* needed!
   4 manquer à *vt ind (devoir, honneur)* to fail in; *(parole, promesses)* to break
   5 manquer de *vt ind* (**a**) *(argent, main-d'œuvre)* to be short of, to lack; *(temps)* to be short of; *(courage, bon sens, charme)* to lack; **ne m. de rien** to have all that one needs; **m. de respect à qn** to show a lack of respect towards sb; **on manque d'air ici** there isn't enough air in here (**b**) *(faillir)* **m. (de) faire qch** to almost do sth (**c**) *(à la forme négative)* **ne pas m. de faire qch** to be sure to do sth; **je n'y manquerai pas** I certainly will
   6 se manquer *vpr* to miss each other *(by not being in the same place at the same time)*

mansarde [mɑ̃sard] *nf* attic

mansardé, -e [mɑ̃sarde] *adj (chambre)* attic

mante [mɑ̃t] *nf* mantis; **m. religieuse** praying mantis

manteau, -x [mɑ̃to] *nm* coat; **m. de fourrure** fur coat; *Fig* **sous le m.** secretly

mantille [mɑ̃tij] *nf* mantilla

manucure [manykyr] **1** *nmf (personne)* manicurist
   2 *nf (soin)* manicure; **se faire faire une m.** to have a manicure

manuel[1]**, -elle** [manɥɛl] **1** *adj (travail, activité)* manual; **être m.** *(personne)* to be good with one's hands
   2 *nm,f* (**a**) *(travailleur)* manual worker (**b**) *(personne adroite de ses mains)* **c'est un m.** he's good with his hands

manuel[2] *nm (d'utilisation, d'entretien)* manual, handbook; *(scolaire)* textbook

manuellement [manɥɛlmɑ̃] *adv* manually

manufacture [manyfaktyr] *nf (usine)* factory

manufacturer [manyfaktyre] *vt* to manufacture

manu militari [manymilitari] *adv* by force

manuscrit, -e [manyskri, -it] **1** *adj* handwritten
   2 *nm* manuscript

manutention [manytɑ̃sjɔ̃] *nf* handling

manutentionnaire [manytɑ̃sjɔnɛr] *nmf* warehouseman, *f* warehousewoman

maous, -ousse [maus] *adj Fam* enormous, massive

mappemonde [mapmɔ̃d] *nf* (**a**) *(carte)* map of the world *(in two hemispheres)* (**b**) *(globe)* globe
maquereau¹, -x¹ [makro] *nm (poisson)* mackerel
maquereau², -x² *nm très Fam (souteneur)* pimp
maquerelle [makrɛl] *nf très Fam* madam
maquette [makɛt] *nf* (**a**) *(de livre)* dummy (**b**) *(d'une construction architecturale)* (scale) model; *(de mise en page)* paste-up (**c**) *(jouet)* model; **m. d'avion/de bateau** model plane/boat
maquettiste [makɛtist] *nmf* (**a**) *(dans une entreprise)* model maker (**b**) *(graphiste)* graphic designer
maquignon [makiɲɔ̃] *nm* (**a**) *(marchand de chevaux)* horse dealer (**b**) *Fig (entremetteur malhonnête)* crooked dealer
maquillage [makijaʒ] *nm* (**a**) *(de visage)* *(action)* making up; *(produits)* make-up (**b**) *(de documents)* forging; *(de photos)* faking; *(de comptes)* falsification
maquiller [makije] **1** *vt* (**a**) *(personne, visage)* to make up (**b**) *(documents)* to forge; *(photos)* to fake; *(comptes)* to falsify; **m. un meurtre en suicide** to make a murder look like a suicide
  2 se maquiller *vpr* to put one's make-up on
maquilleur, -euse [makijœr, -øz] *nm,f* make-up artist
maquis [maki] *nm* (**a**) *(végétation)* maquis (**b**) *Fig (d'une procédure, de l'administration)* jungle (**c**) *Hist* maquis *(Resistance movement in World War II)*; **prendre le m.** to take to the hills
maquisard [makizar] *nm Hist* member of the maquis, Resistance fighter *(in World War II)*
marabout [marabu] *nm* (**a**) *(sorcier)* witchdoctor (**b**) *(oiseau)* marabou (**c**) *Can (personne acariâtre)* bad-tempered person
maracas [marakas] *nfpl* maracas
maraîcher, -ère [mareʃe, -ɛr] **1** *adj* **culture maraîchère** *Br* market gardening, *Am* truck farming; **produits maraîchers** *Br* market garden produce, *Am* truck
  2 *nm,f Br* market gardener, *Am* truck farmer
marais [marɛ] *nm* marsh; **m. salant** saltern
marasme [marasm] *nm* (**a**) *(ralentissement)* stagnation (**b**) *(découragement)* depression
marathon [maratɔ̃] *nm* marathon
marathonien, -enne [maratɔnjɛ̃, -ɛn] *nm,f* marathon runner
marâtre [maratr] *nf* (**a**) *(belle-mère)* stepmother (**b**) *(mère cruelle)* cruel mother
maraude [marod] *nf* (**a**) *(vol)* pilfering (**b**) **un taxi en m.** a cruising taxi
marauder [marode] *vi* (**a**) *(voler)* to pilfer (**b**) *(taxi)* to cruise for fares (**c**) *(rôdeur)* to prowl around
maraudeur, -euse [marodœr, -øz] *nm,f* pilferer
marbre [marbr] *nm* (**a**) *(roche)* marble; **en** *ou* **de m.** marble; *Fig* **rester de m.** to remain impassive (**b**) *(statue)* marble (statue) (**c**) *(de presse)* bed
marbré, -e [marbre] *adj* (**a**) *(surface, couverture de livre)* marbled; *(pierre)* veined (**b**) *(peau)* blotchy (**c**) **gâteau m.** marble cake
marbrier [marbrije] *nm* monumental mason
marbrière [marbrijɛr] *nf* marble quarry
marbrure [marbryr] *nf* (**a**) *(sur un livre)* marbling (**b**) *(sur la peau)* mottling
marc [mar] *nm* (**a**) *(de raisins, d'olives)* marc (**b**) *(eau-de-vie)* marc (brandy) (**c**) *(de café)* grounds
marcassin [markasɛ̃] *nm* young wild boar

marchand, -e [marʃɑ̃, -ɑ̃d] **1** *adj (prix)* trade
  2 *nm,f (dans un magasin) Br* shopkeeper, *Am* storekeeper; *(de vin)* merchant; *(de meubles, de chevaux)* dealer; **m. ambulant** street vendor; **m. forain** travelling stallholder; **m. de glaces** ice cream seller; **m. de journaux** *Br* newsagent, *Am* newsdealer; **m. de légumes** greengrocer; **m. de tableaux** art dealer; **m. de tapis** carpet dealer
marchandage [marʃɑ̃daʒ] *nm* haggling
marchander [marʃɑ̃de] **1** *vt* to haggle over
  2 *vi* to haggle
marchandisage [marʃɑ̃dizaʒ] *nm* merchandizing
marchandise [marʃɑ̃diz] *nf* commodity; **marchandises** goods, merchandise
marche [marʃ] *nf* (**a**) *(d'escalier)* step, stair (**b**) *(action de marcher)* walking; *(promenade)* walk; *(allure)* pace; **faire de la m.** to go walking; **faire une m.** to go for a walk; **à deux heures de m.** two hours' walk away; **m. à pied** walking (**c**) *(défilé, manifestation)* march; **ouvrir la m.** to lead the way; **fermer la m.** to bring up the rear (**d**) *(morceau de musique)* march; **m. funèbre** funeral march (**e**) *(déplacement)* **être en m.** *(véhicule)* to be moving; *(mouvement, progrès)* to be on the march; **se mettre en m.** *(véhicule)* to move off; *(personne)* to set off *or* out; **dans le sens de la m.** *(en voyage)* facing forward; **dans le sens contraire de la m.** facing backwards; **m. avant/arrière** *(vitesse)* forward/reverse gear; **faire m. arrière** *(véhicule)* to reverse; *Fig* to backtrack (**f**) *(fonctionnement)* running, working; **mettre qch en m.** to start sth; **mettre en m.** to start (**g**) *(des événements, de l'histoire)* course; *(du temps)* march; **m. à suivre** procedure
marché [marʃe] *nm* (**a**) *(accord)* deal, bargain; *(plus officiel)* contract; **m. conclu!** (it's a) deal!; **par-dessus le m.** into the bargain; **bon m.** cheap (**b**) *(lieu public de vente)* market; **faire son m.** to go shopping; **M. commun** Common Market; **m. noir** black market; **m. aux puces** flea market; **M. unique (européen)** Single (European) Market (**c**) *(débouché économique)* market (**d**) *Fin* market; **m. des changes** foreign exchange market; **m. haussier/baissier** bull/bear market; **m. à terme** futures market
marchepied [marʃəpje] *nm* (**a**) *(de train)* step (**b**) *(escabeau)* steps (**c**) *Fig* stepping-stone
marcher [marʃe] *vi* (**a**) *(se déplacer à pied)* to walk; *(mettre le pied)* to step (**dans/sur** in/on); *aussi Fig* **m. sur les pieds de qn** to tread on sb's toes; *Fig* **m. droit** to keep on the straight and narrow (**b**) *(fonctionner)* *(machine)* to work, to run; *(plans)* to work; **faire m. qch** to work *or* operate sth; **comment ça marche?** how does it work?; *Fig* **les affaires marchent (bien)** business is doing well; **ça marche!** *(d'accord)* sure! (**c**) *(avancer)* to march (**vers/sur** towards/on) (**d**) *Fam (croire sans réserve)* to fall for it; **faire m. qn** to pull sb's leg (**e**) *Fam (accepter)* to go along with it
marchette [marʃɛt] *nf Can (chariot d'enfant)* baby-walker; *(support de marche)* walking frame
marcheur, -euse [marʃœr, -øz] *nm,f* walker
mardi [mardi] *nm* Tuesday; **M. gras** Shrove Tuesday; *voir aussi* **samedi**

Mardi gras

This is a very popular festival, falling on the eve of Ash Wednesday, at the end of the carnival. People celebrate by eating crêpes, and children dress up at school.

mare [mar] *nf* (**a**) *(étendue d'eau)* pond (**b**) *(grande quantité)* pool

marécage [mareka3] *nm* marsh, bog

marécageux, -euse [mareka3œ, -øz] *adj* (**a**) *(terrain)* marshy, boggy (**b**) *(plante)* marsh

maréchal, -aux [mareʃal, -o] *nm* **m.** (**de France**) *(officier général)* field marshal; *(d'un roi)* marshal; **m. des logis** sergeant

maréchal-ferrant [mareʃalfɛrɑ̃] *(pl* **maréchaux-ferrants** [mareʃoferɑ̃]*) nm* blacksmith

marée [mare] *nf* (**a**) *(de la mer)* tide; **à m. haute/basse** at high/low tide; **à la m. montante/descendante** when the tide comes in/goes out; **m. noire** oil slick (**b**) *Fig (de personnes)* surging mass (**c**) *(fruits de la pêche)* fresh seafood

marelle [marɛl] *nf* hopscotch

marémoteur, -trice [maremɔtœr, -tris] *adj (énergie)* tidal; **usine marémotrice** tidal power station

mareyeur, -euse [marɛjœr, -øz] *nm,f* fish wholesaler

margarine [margarin] *nf* margarine

marge [mar3] *nf* (**a**) *(de page)* margin; **en m. de** on the fringes of; **vivre en m.** (**de la société**) to live on the fringes of society (**b**) *(liberté d'action)* leeway; **avoir de la m.** to have some leeway; *(temps)* to have time to spare; **m. d'erreur** margin of error; **m. de négociation/manœuvre** room for negotiation/manoeuvre; **m. de sécurité** safety margin (**c**) *(commerciale)* **m.** (**bénéficiaire**) profit margin

margelle [mar3ɛl] *nf (de puits)* coping, curb

marger [45] [mar3e] *vt (page)* to feed in; *Ordinat* to set the margins for

marginal, -e, -aux, -ales [mar3inal, -o] **1** *adj* (**a**) *(personne, mode de vie)* on the fringes of society (**b**) *(secondaire) (occupations, importance)* marginal

2 *nm,f* dropout

marginalisation [mar3inalizasjɔ̃] *nf* marginalization

marginaliser [mar3inalize] **1** *vt* to marginalize

2 se marginaliser *vpr* to become marginalized

marguerite [margorit] *nf* (**a**) *(fleur)* daisy (**b**) *(de machine à écrire)* daisy wheel

mari [mari] *nm* husband

mariage [marja3] *nm* (**a**) *(cérémonie)* wedding; *(union)* marriage; **m. d'amour** love match; **m. blanc** marriage in name only *(primarily in order to acquire nationality)*; **m. civil** ≃ registry office wedding; **m. homosexuel** gay marriage; *Can* **m. obligé** shotgun wedding; **m. de raison** marriage of convenience (**b**) *(de choses)* combination, marriage; *(de couleurs)* blend(ing)

Mariage

In France, a civil ceremony (which takes place at the "mairie") is required of all couples wishing to marry, though some choose to have a church wedding as well. The traditional wedding involves a long and sumptuous meal at which the wedding cake, a "pièce montée" is served.

Marianne [marjan] *nf* = young woman symbolizing the French Republic

marié, -e [marje] **1** *adj* married; **non m.** unmarried, single

2 *nm,f* groom; *f* bride; **les mariés** the bride and groom; **les jeunes mariés** the newly-weds

marie-jeanne [mari3an] *nf inv Fam (cannabis)* Mary-Jane, pot

marier [66] [marje] **1** *vt* (**a**) *(sujet: prêtre)* to marry; *(sujet: père)* to marry off (**b**) *(qualités)* to combine; *(sociétés)* to merge; *(couleurs)* to blend; *(styles)* to harmonize

2 se marier *vpr* (**a**) *(personnes)* to get married, to marry; **se m. avec qn** to marry sb (**b**) *(couleurs)* to blend (**avec** with); *(styles)* to go together (**avec** with)

marieur, -euse [marjœr, -øz] *nm,f Fam* matchmaker

marihuana [marirwana], **marijuana** [mari3yana] *nf* marijuana

marin, -e¹ [marɛ̃, -in] **1** *adj* (**a**) *(air, brise)* sea; *(plante, animal)* marine (**b**) *(carte)* sea; *(mille)* nautical

2 *nm* seaman, sailor; **m. pêcheur** (deep-sea) fisherman; **m. d'eau douce** landlubber

marina [marina] *nf* marina

marinade [marinad] *nf (mélange aromatique)* marinade; **m. de poissons/de gibier** marinated fish/game

marine² [marin] **1** *nf* (**a**) *(flotte)* navy; **la m. de guerre** the navy; **la m. marchande** the merchant navy; **la M. nationale** the French navy (**b**) *(navigation)* seamanship (**c**) *(tableau)* seascape

2 *adj inv* navy (blue)

3 *nm (fusilier) Br* (Royal) Marine, *Am* marine

mariner [marine] **1** *vt* to marinate

2 *vi* (**a**) *(aliment)* to marinate; **faire m. qch** to marinate sth; **harengs marinés** pickled herrings (**b**) *Fam Fig (personne)* to hang around; **faire** *ou* **laisser m. qn** *(dans un lieu)* to keep sb hanging around; *(dans une situation)* to leave sb to stew

maringouin [marɛ̃gwɛ̃] *nm Can* mosquito

marinier [marinje] *nm Br* bargee, *Am* bargeman

marinière [marinjɛr] *nf* blouse

mariole [marjɔl] *nm Fam* sly devil; **faire le m.** to try to be clever

marionnette [marjɔnɛt] *nf* puppet

marionnettiste [marjɔnetist] *nmf* puppeteer

marital, -e, -aux, -ales [marital, -o] *adj* marital

maritalement [maritalmɑ̃] *adv* **vivre m.** to cohabit

maritime [maritim] *adj* (**a**) *(navigation, plante, trafic)* maritime; *(ville)* seaside (**b**) *Can* **les Maritimes** the Maritimes

marivaudage [marivoda3] *nm Litt* light-hearted banter

marjolaine [mar3ɔlɛn] *nf* marjoram

mark [mark] *nm Anciennement* (German) mark

marketing [marketiŋ] *nm* marketing

marmaille [marmɑj] *nf Fam* brood, kids

marmelade [marməlad] *nf* compote; **m.** (**d'oranges**) (orange) marmalade; *Fig* **en m.** reduced to a pulp

marmite [marmit] *nf (cooking)* pot; *Fig* **faire bouillir la m.** to bring home the bacon

marmonner [marmɔne] *vt & vi* to mumble, to mutter

marmot [marmo] *nm Fam* kid

marmotte [marmɔt] *nf* marmot

marmotter [marmɔte] *vt* to mumble, to mutter

marner [marne] *vi Fam* to slog

Maroc [marɔk] *nm* **le M.** Morocco

marocain, -e [marɔkɛ̃, -ɛn] **1** *adj* Moroccan

2 *nm,f* **M.** Moroccan

maronite [marɔnit] *adj & nmf* Maronite

maroquin [marɔkɛ̃] *nm* morocco (leather)

maroquinerie [marɔkinri] *nf* (**a**) *(fabrication)* leather tanning (**b**) *(magasin)* leather goods shop (**c**) *(articles)* leather goods

maroquinier [marɔkinje] *nm* (**a**) *(fabricant)* leather worker (**b**) *(commerçant)* leather goods dealer

marotte [marɔt] *nf (idée fixe)* craze

marquant, -e [markã, -ãt] *adj (incident, personne, journée)* remarkable; *(épisode)* significant

marque [mark] *nf* (**a**) *(signe, trace)* mark (**b**) *(de produits, d'appareils)* brand; *(de voiture)* make; **de m.** *(produits)* branded; *(vêtements)* designer; **m. déposée** registered trademark (**c**) *(preuve) (d'amitié)* token; *(de confiance)* sign (**d**) *(cachet)* stamp; **porter la m. du génie** to bear the stamp of genius (**e**) *Ordinat* marker; **m. d'insertion** insertion marker (**f**) **de m.** *(important)* distinguished, prominent (**g**) **marques** *(repères)* marks; **à vos marques! prêts? partez!** on your marks! get set! go!

marqué, -e [marke] *adj* (**a**) *(visage)* lined; **il est très m.** his face is very lined (**b**) *(différence, penchant)* marked

marque-page *(pl* **marque-pages)** [markpaʒ] *nm* bookmark

marquer [marke] **1** *vt* (**a**) *(faire un signe sur)* to mark (**b**) *(écrire)* to write (**c**) *(délimiter)* to mark (**d**) *Sport (adversaire)* to mark; *(but, essai)* to score (**e**) *(indiquer)* to show (**f**) *(accentuer)* to mark; **m. le pas** to mark time; *Fig* **m. le coup** to mark the occasion (**g**) *(impressionner)* to make an impression on (**h**) *Ordinat* to mark
2 *vi (laisser une trace)* to leave a mark

marqueterie [markətri] *nf* marquetry

marqueur [markœr] *nm* (**a**) *(stylo)* (felt-tip) marker (**b**) *(biologique, génétique)* marker

marquis [marki] *nm* marquis

marquise [markiz] *nf* (**a**) *(auvent)* canopy (**b**) *(canapé)* (two-seater) sofa (**c**) *(personne)* marchioness

Marquises [markiz] *nfpl* **les (îles) M.** the Marquesas Islands

marraine [marɛn] *nf* (**a**) *(d'un enfant)* godmother (**b**) *(d'un bateau)* = woman who launches a new boat

Marrakech [marakɛʃ] *n* Marrakesh

marrant, -e [marã, -ãt] *adj Fam* funny

marre [mar] *adv Fam* **en avoir m. (de qn/qch)** to be fed up (with sb/sth); **en avoir m. de faire qch** to be fed up with doing sth

marrer [mare] **se marrer** *vpr Fam* to have a good laugh

marron¹ [marɔ̃] **1** *adj inv (couleur)* brown
2 *nm* (**a**) *(fruit)* chestnut; **marrons chauds** roast chestnuts; **marrons glacés** marrons glacés; **m. d'Inde** horse chestnut (**b**) *(couleur)* brown (**c**) *Fam (coup de poing)* thump; **flanquer un m. à qn** to wallop sb

marron², -onne [marɔ̃, -ɔn] *adj (médecin, homme de loi)* quack

marronnier [marɔnje] *nm* horse chestnut (tree); **m. d'Inde** horse chestnut (tree)

Mars [mars] *npr (dieu, planète)* Mars

mars [mars] *nm* March; *voir aussi* **janvier**

marseillais, -e [marsejɛ, -ɛz] **1** *adj* of Marseilles
2 *nm,f* **M.** person from Marseilles
3 *nf* **la Marseillaise** the Marseillaise

Marseille [marsɛj] *n* Marseilles

marsouin [marswɛ̃] *nm* (**a**) *Zool* porpoise (**b**) *Can Fam (malin)* rascal

marsupial, -e, -aux, -ales [marsypjal, -o] *adj & nm* marsupial

marteau, -x [marto] **1** *adj Fam* crazy
2 *nm* (**a**) *(outil)* hammer; **m. piqueur** pneumatic drill; *Fig* **être entre le m. et l'enclume** to be between

the devil and the deep blue sea (**b**) *(de porte)* (door) knocker (**c**) *(de piano)* hammer

martel [martɛl] *nm* **se mettre m. en tête** to worry oneself sick

martèlement [martɛlmã] *nm* hammering

marteler [39] [martəle] *vt* (**a**) *(métal, pieu)* to hammer; **m. la table à coups de poing** to hammer on the table (**b**) *(mot, phrase)* to hammer out

martial, -e, -aux, -ales [marsjal, -o] *adj* martial

martien, -enne [marsjɛ̃, -ɛn] *adj & nm,f* Martian

martinet¹ [martinɛ] *nm (fouet)* strap

martinet² *nm (oiseau)* swift

martingale [martɛ̃gal] *nf (sur un vêtement)* half belt

martiniquais, -e [martinikɛ, ɛz] **1** *adj* Martinican
2 *nm,f* **M.** Martinican

Martinique [martinik] *nf* **la M.** Martinique

martin-pêcheur *(pl* **martins-pêcheurs)** [martɛ̃pɛʃœr] *nm* kingfisher

martyr, -e [martir] **1** *adj (enfant)* battered; *(peuple)* martyred
2 *nm,f* martyr

martyre [martir] *nm* martyrdom

martyriser [martirize] *vt (maltraiter)* to batter; *(harceler)* to bully

marxisme [marksism] *nm* Marxism

marxisme-léninisme [marksismleninism] *nm* Marxism-Leninism

marxiste [marksist] *adj & nmf* Marxist

marxiste-léniniste *(pl* **marxistes-léninistes)** [marksistleninist] *adj & nmf* Marxist-Leninist

mas [mɑ, mɑs] *nm (en Provence) (ferme)* farm; *(maison)* farmhouse

mascara [maskara] *nm* mascara

mascarade [maskarad] *nf* masquerade; *Fig* sham

mascotte [maskɔt] *nf* mascot

masculin, -e [maskylɛ̃, -in] **1** *adj* (**a**) *(sexe, mode, métier)* male; *(trait de caractère, femme)* masculine (**b**) *(nom, genre)* masculine (**c**) *(rime)* masculine
2 *nm* masculine; **au m.** in the masculine

masculinité [maskylinite] *nf* masculinity

maskinongé [maskinɔ̃ʒe] *nm Can* muskellunge

maso [mazo] *Fam* **1** *adj* masochistic
2 *nmf* masochist

masochisme [mazɔʃism] *nm* masochism

masochiste [mazɔʃist] **1** *adj* masochistic
2 *nmf* masochist

masquage [maskaʒ] *nm Ordinat* masking

masque [mask] *nm* (**a**) *(déguisement)* mask; **m. à gaz/oxygène** gas/oxygen mask; **m. de plongée** diving mask (**b**) *(apparence)* façade; **lever le m.** to remove one's mask (**c**) *(soin cosmétique)* **m. (de beauté)** face pack (**d**) *Ordinat* mask; **m. d'entrée, m. de saisie** input mask

masqué, -e [maske] *adj (personne)* masked

masquer [maske] *vt* to mask

massacrante [masakrãt] *adj f voir* **humeur**

massacre [masakr] *nm* (**a**) *(tuerie)* massacre (**b**) *Fig (travail mal fait)* mess; **faire un m.** *(travailler mal)* to make a complete mess; *(remporter un grand succès)* to be a runaway success

massacrer [masakre] *vt* (**a**) *(tuer, exterminer)* to massacre (**b**) *Fam (abîmer) (travail)* to botch; *(mal interpréter) (morceau de musique, texte)* to murder

massage [masaʒ] *nm* massage; **faire un m. à qn** to give sb a massage

masse¹ [mas] *nf* (**a**) *(volume)* mass; **m. d'air** air mass; **taillé/sculpté dans la m.** carved/sculpted from the block; **tomber comme une m.** to fall in a heap (**b**) *(grande quantité)* mass; **de m.** *(culture, communication)* mass; **en m.** en masse; **une m. de** masses of; *Fam* **pas des masses** not much; *(nombre)* not many; **m. monétaire** money supply; **m. salariale** wage bill (**c**) **les masses** *(le peuple)* the masses; **masses laborieuses** toiling masses (**d**) *Phys* mass (**e**) *Élec Br* earth, *Am* ground; **mettre qch à la m.** *Br* to earth sth, *Am* to ground sth; *Fam Fig* **être à la m.** to be off one's head

masse² *nf (marteau)* siedgehammer

massepain [maspɛ̃] *nm* marzipan

masser¹ [mase] **1** *vt (rassembler)* to assemble; *(troupes)* to mass

  2 se masser *vpr* to assemble

masser² **1** *vt (faire un massage à)* to massage; **se faire m.** to have a massage

  2 se masser *vpr* to massage oneself; **se m. le pied** to massage one's foot

masseur, -euse [masœr, -øz] *nm,f* masseur, *f* masseuse

massicot [masiko] *nm* guillotine

massif, -ive [masif, -iv] **1** *adj* (**a**) *(formes, meuble, porte)* massive; *(personne)* heavily built (**b**) *(argent, or, bois)* solid (**c**) *(dose)* massive

  2 *nm* (**a**) *(de plantes, d'arbres)* clump; **m. de fleurs** flower bed (**b**) *(ensemble de montagnes)* massif; **le M. central** the Massif Central *(mountains in central France)*

massivement [masivmã] *adv (répondre, voter)* en masse

mass media, mass-média(s) [masmedja] *nmpl* mass media

massue [masy] **1** *adj inv (argument)* sledgehammer

  2 *nf* club

mastectomie [mastɛktɔmi] *nf* mastectomy

master, mastère [mastɛr] *nm (diplôme)* master's (degree)

mastic [mastik] *nm (pour fenêtres)* putty; *(pour bois)* mastic

mastication [mastikasjɔ̃] *nf* chewing

mastiquer¹ [mastike] *vt (mâcher)* to chew

mastiquer² *vt (fissures)* to fill (in); *(vitre)* to put putty round

mastoc [mastɔk] *adj inv Fam (personne)* hulking; *(construction)* clumsy

mastodonte [mastɔdɔ̃t] *nm* (**a**) *Fam (personne)* hulk; *(objet)* hulking great thing (**b**) *(animal)* mastodon

masturbation [mastyrbasjɔ̃] *nf* masturbation

masturber [mastyrbe] **1** *vt* to masturbate

  2 se masturber *vpr* to masturbate

m'as-tu-vu [matyvy] *nmf inv Fam* show-off

masure [mazyr] *nf* hovel

mat¹, -e [mat] *adj (métal, couleur)* matt; *(teint)* darkish; *(son)* dull

mat² **1** *adj inv (aux échecs)* checkmated

  2 *nm* checkmate

mat' [mat] *nm Fam* **deux/trois heures du m.** two/three a.m. *or* in the morning

mât [mɑ] *nm* (**a**) *(d'un voilier)* mast (**b**) *(poteau)* pole; **m. de cocagne** greasy pole

matador [matadɔr] *nm* matador

match *(pl* **matchs** *ou* **matches)** [matʃ] *nm Br* match, *Am* game; **m. aller/retour** first/return leg; **un m. amical** a friendly; **m. nul** draw; **faire m. nul** to draw

matelas [matlɑ] *nm* mattress; **m. pneumatique** air bed

matelassé, -e [matlase] *adj (tissu, blouson)* quilted; *(enveloppe)* padded

matelot [matlo] *nm* sailor

mater¹ [mate] *vt (se rendre maître de) (personne)* to bring to heel; *(rébellion)* to put down

mater² *vt Fam (regarder)* to ogle

matérialisation [materjalizasjɔ̃] *nf* materialization

matérialiser [materjalize] **se matérialiser** *vpr* to materialize

matérialisme [materjalism] *nm* materialism

matérialiste [materjalist] **1** *adj* materialistic

  2 *nmf* materialist

matériau, -x [materjo] *nm* (**a**) *(substance)* material (**b**) **matériaux** *(de construction)* material(s); *(documents)* material

matériel¹, -elle [materjɛl] *adj (confort, besoins, dégâts)* material; *(organisation, problème)* practical

matériel² *nm* (**a**) *(pour une activité, un sport)* equipment; **m. de bureau** office equipment; **m. pédagogique** teaching material; **m. agricole** farm equipment (**b**) *(d'une entreprise)* plant; **m. d'exploitation** working plant (**c**) *Ordinat* **m. (informatique)** (computer) hardware

matériellement [materjɛlmã] *adv* (**a**) *(sur le plan matériel)* materially (**b**) **c'est m. impossible** it's physically impossible

maternel, -elle [matɛrnɛl] *adj* (**a**) *(personne, attitude, gestes)* maternal (**b**) *(langue)* native

maternelle [matɛrnɛl] *nf* nursery (school)

Maternelle

Nursery education for children from two to six years old is provided by the state and is available to all families in France. Although it is not compulsory, a vast majority of children attend nursery schools and are thus well-prepared for entry into primary school.

materner [matɛrne] *vt* to mother

maternisé, -e [matɛrnize] *adj* **lait m.** milk suitable for infants

maternité [matɛrnite] *nf* (**a**) *(fait d'être mère)* motherhood (**b**) *(hôpital)* maternity hospital (**c**) *(tableau)* Madonna and Child

mathématicien, -enne [matematisjɛ̃, -ɛn] *nm,f* mathematician

mathématique [matematik] **1** *adj* (**a**) *(science)* mathematical (**b**) *(esprit)* logical; *(rigueur)* mathematical (**c**) *Fig (inévitable)* inevitable

  2 *nfpl* **les mathématiques** mathematics *(singulier)*

mathématiquement [matematikmã] *adv* mathematically

matheux, -euse [matø, -øz] *nm,f Fam Br* maths *or Am* math whizz

maths [mat] *nfpl Fam Br* maths, *Am* math; **M. Sup/Spé** = first/second year of classes preparing students for entrance to science-oriented "grandes écoles"

matière [matjɛr] *nf* (**a**) *(substance)* material; **matières grasses** fat; **m. grise** grey matter; *Fam* **faire fonctionner sa m. grise** to exercise one's grey matter; **m. plastique** plastic; **matières premières** raw materials (**b**) *(sujet) (scolaire)* subject; *(pour en faire un film, un livre, une étude)* material; **il n'y a pas m. à rire** it's no laughing matter; **donner m. à qch** to give cause for sth; **en m. de** as regards (**c**) *(d'un corps physique)* matter

Matignon [matiɲɔ̃] *n* (**l'hôtel**) **M.** = French Prime Minister's offices

Matignon
The name of the Prime Minister's offices is often used to refer to the Prime Minister and his or her administrative staff, for example "L'Élysée et Matignon ont fini par se mettre d'accord".

matin [matɛ̃] *nm* morning; **ce m.**, *Can* **à m.** this morning; **quatre heures du m.** four o'clock in the morning, 4 am; **le jeudi 2 au m.** on the morning of Thursday the 2nd; **faire qch le m.** to do sth in the morning; **être du m.** to be a morning person; **tous les lundis m.** every Monday morning; **de grand** *ou* **bon m.** early in the morning, in the early morning; **au petit m.** in the small *or* early hours; **du m. au soir** from morning till night

matinal, -e, -aux, -ales [matinal, -o] *adj* (**a**) (*heure*) early; (*excursion, activité*) morning (**b**) (*personne*) **être m.** to be an early riser

mâtiné, -e [matine] *adj* crossbred; **m. de** crossed with; *Fig* mixed with

matinée [matine] *nf* (**a**) (*matin*) morning; **dans la m.** in (the course of) the morning; **en fin de m.** towards the end of the morning (**b**) (*au théâtre, cinéma*) matinée

maton, -onne [matɔ̃, -ɔn] *nm,f Fam* screw (*prison warder*)

matos [matos] *nm Fam* stuff, gear

matou [matu] *nm* tom (cat)

matraquage [matrakaʒ] *nm* (**a**) (*avec une matraque*) bludgeoning (**b**) (*insistance*) **m. publicitaire** hype

matraque [matrak] *nf* bludgeon; (*d'agent de police*) *Br* truncheon, *Am* nightstick

matraquer [matrake] *vt* (**a**) (*frapper*) to club (**b**) *Fig* (*harceler*) to bombard (**c**) *Fam* (*faire payer très cher*) to rip off, to fleece

matriarcal, -e, -aux, -ales [matrijarkal, -o] *adj* matriarchal

matrice [matris] *nf* (**a**) (*moule*) matrix, die; (*de disque*) matrix (**b**) *Math & Ordinat* matrix; *Ordinat* **m. d'aiguilles** dot matrix

matricide [matrisid] *nm* matricide

matriciel, -elle [matrisjɛl] *Ordinat* **1** *adj* **imprimante matricielle** dot matrix printer
2 *nf* **matricelle** dot matrix

matricule [matrikyl] **1** *nm* (*numéro*) number
2 *nf* (*registre*) register

matrimonial, -e, -aux, -ales [matrimɔnjal, -o] *adj* matrimonial

matrone [matrɔn] *nf* (**a**) *Péj* (*femme corpulente*) stout woman (**b**) *Can* (*gardienne de prison*) prison wardress

mature [matyr] *adj* mature

mâture [mɑtyr] *nf* masts

maturité [matyrite] *nf* (**a**) (*de personne*) maturity; (*de fruit*) ripeness; **manquer de m.** to be immature; **arriver** *ou* **venir à m.** (*fromage, vin*) to mature; (*fruit*) to ripen (**b**) *Suisse* (*baccalauréat*) school-leaving diploma (*from a "gymnase", granting admission to university*)

maudire [modir] *vt* to curse

maudit, -e [modi, -it] *adj* (**a**) (*damné*) cursed (**b**) (*avant le nom*) (*insupportable*) damn(ed)

maugréer [24] [mogree] *vi* to grumble (**contre** about *or* at)

maure [mɔr] **1** *adj* Moorish
2 *nm* **M.** Moor

mauresque [mɔrɛsk] **1** *adj* Moorish
2 *nf* **M.** Moorish woman

Maurice [mɔris] *n* **l'île M.** Mauritius

mauricien, -enne [mɔrisjɛ̃, -ɛn] **1** *adj* Mauritian
2 *nm,f* **M.** Mauritian

Mauritanie [mɔritani] *nf* **la M.** Mauritania

mauritanien, -enne [mɔritanjɛ̃, -ɛn] **1** *adj* Mauritanian
2 *nm,f* **M.** Mauritanian

mausolée [mozɔle] *nm* mausoleum

maussade [mosad] *adj* (**a**) (*de mauvaise humeur*) sullen (**b**) (*temps, paysage*) gloomy

mauvais, -e [mɔvɛ, -ɛz] **1** *adj* (**a**) (*défectueux*) (*santé, vue, excuse*) poor (**b**) (*incompétent*) (*élève, professeur, mère*) bad (**en** at) (**c**) (*nuisible*) bad (**pour** for) (**d**) (*inapproprié*) (*clef, numéro, moment*) wrong (**e**) (*méchant*) (*personne*) bad, nasty; (*chien*) vicious (**f**) (*mer*) rough (**g**) *Fam* **la trouver** *ou* **l'avoir mauvaise** to be hacked off *or* bummed
2 *adv* (**a**) **sentir m.** to smell (bad) (**b**) **il fait m.** the weather's bad

mauve [mov] **1** *adj* mauve
2 *nm* (*couleur*) mauve

mauviette [movjɛt] *nf Fam* wimp

max [maks] *nm Fam* **un m. de gens** (*le plus possible*) as many people as possible; (*énormément*) loads of people

max. (*abrév* **maximum**) max.

maxi [maksi] *adv Fam* max, tops; **on sera vingt m.** there'll be twenty of us max *or* tops

maxillaire [maksilɛr] *nm* jawbone, *Spéc* maxilla

maxima [maksima] *voir* **maximum**

maximal, -e, -aux, -ales [maksimal, -o] *adj* maximum

maxime [maksim] *nf* maxim

maximiser [maksimize] *vt* to maximize

maximum (*pl* **maximums** *ou* **maxima** [maksima]) [maksimɔm] **1** *adj* maximum
2 *nm* maximum; **faire le m. (pour faire qch)** to do one's very best (to do sth); **au m.** at the most; *Fam* **un m.** (*beaucoup*) loads; *Fam* **un m. de gens** (*le plus possible*) as many people as possible; (*énormément*) loads of people

maya [maja] **1** *adj* Maya, Mayan
2 *nmf* **M.** Maya, Mayan
3 *nm* (*langue*) Mayan

mayonnaise [majɔnɛz] *nf* mayonnaise

mazout [mazut] *nm* (*fuel*) oil

mazouté, -e [mazute] *adj* (*plage*) oil-polluted; (*oiseau*) covered in oil

Mbps *Ordinat* (*abrév* **mégabits par seconde**) mbps

MDR *Ordinat & Tél* (*abrév* **mort de rire**) LOL

me [mə]

> **m'** is used before a word beginning with a vowel or h mute.

pron personnel (**a**) (*objet direct*) me; **il est venu me chercher** he came to fetch me; **me voici** here I am (**b**) (*objet indirect*) to me; **il m'a écrit** he wrote to me; **elle m'a serré la main** she shook my hand; **ils m'ont lancé des cailloux** they threw stones at me (**c**) (*dans les réfléchis*) myself; **je vais me doucher** I'm going to have a shower (**d**) (*dans les pronominaux*) **je me suis trompé** I made a mistake

mea culpa [meakylpa] *nm inv* **faire son m.** to own up

méandre [meɑ̃dr] *nm (de rivière)* meander; *(de route)* bend; *Fig* **méandres** *(d'un raisonnement)* intricacies

mec [mɛk] *nm Fam (homme, amoureux)* guy, *Br* bloke

mécanicien, -enne [mekanisjɛ̃, -ɛn] *nm,f* (**a**) *(garage or motor)* mechanic (**b**) *(conducteur de train) Br* train driver, *Am* engineer

mécanique [mekanik] **1** *adj* mechanical
2 *nf* (**a**) *(science du mouvement)* mechanics *(singulier)* (**b**) *(des moteurs, des machines)* mechanical engineering (**c**) *(mécanisme)* mechanism

mécaniquement [mekanikmɑ̃] *adv* mechanically

mécanisation [mekanizasjɔ̃] *nf* mechanization

mécanisme [mekanism] *nm* (**a**) *(d'une machine, d'une montre, d'un moteur)* mechanism (**b**) *(de la pensée, de la parole)* mechanics

mécénat [mesena] *nm* sponsorship; **m. d'entreprise** corporate sponsorship

mécène [mesɛn] *nm* sponsor

méchamment [meʃamɑ̃] *adv* (**a**) *(avec méchanceté)* nastily (**b**) *Fam (en intensif)* **être m. déçu/embêté** to be terribly disappointed/annoyed

méchanceté [meʃɑ̃ste] *nf* (**a**) *(d'une personne, d'une remarque)* nastiness; *(d'un enfant)* naughtiness (**b**) *(action)* nasty action; *(parole)* nasty remark

méchant, -e [meʃɑ̃, -ɑ̃t] **1** *adj* (**a**) *(personne, remarque)* nasty; *(enfant)* naughty; *(animal)* vicious; **(attention) chien m.** *(sur panneau)* beware of the dog (**b**) *(désagréable) (affaire)* unpleasant; *(blessure, grippe)* nasty; *(humeur)* foul
2 *nm,f Fam* baddie, baddy

mèche¹ [mɛʃ] *nf* (**a**) *(de bougie, de lampe)* wick; *(de charge explosive)* fuse (**b**) *(de perceuse)* bit (**c**) *(de cheveux)* strand; *(boucle)* lock; **se faire des mèches** to get highlights (in one's hair)

mèche² *nf* **être de m. avec qn** to be in cahoots with sb

méchoui [meʃwi] *nm* spit-roasted lamb

méconduite [mekɔ̃dɥit] *nf Belg* misbehaviour

méconnaissable [mekɔnɛsabl] *adj* unrecognizable

méconnaître [20] [mekɔnɛtr] *vt* (**a**) *(faits)* to fail to take account of (**b**) *(talent, artiste)* to fail to recognize

méconnu, -e [mekɔny] *adj (talent, artiste)* unrecognized

mécontent, -e [mekɔ̃tɑ̃, -ɑ̃t] **1** *adj (insatisfait)* displeased (**de** with); *(contrarié)* annoyed
2 *nm,f* grumbler; *(électeur)* malcontent

mécontentement [mekɔ̃tɑ̃tmɑ̃] *nm (insatisfaction)* displeasure; *(contrariété)* annoyance

mécontenter [mekɔ̃tɑ̃te] *vt (ne pas satisfaire)* to displease; *(contrarier)* to annoy

Mecque [mɛk] *n* **La M.** Mecca

médaille [medaj] *nf* (**a**) *(prix, décoration)* medal; **la m. d'or/d'argent/de bronze** the gold/silver/bronze medal (**b**) *(bijou) (avec le nom)* pendant *(with name engraved on it)*; *(à l'effigie d'un saint)* medal (**c**) *(de chat, de chien)* identity disc

médaillé, -e [medaje] **1** *adj (sportif)* holding a medal; *(soldat)* decorated
2 *nm,f (sportif)* medallist; *(soldat)* medal-holder

médaillon [medajɔ̃] *nm* (**a**) *(bijou)* locket (**b**) *(de poisson, de viande)* medallion

médecin [medsɛ̃] *nm* doctor; **m. généraliste** general practitioner, GP; **m. légiste** *Br* forensic scientist, *Am* medical examiner; **m. traitant** consulting physician; **m. du travail** = doctor who carries out the annual

medical examination, required by law, of a company's employees

médecine [medsin] *nf* medicine; **exercer la m.** to practise medicine; **m. douce** *ou* **parallèle** alternative medicine; **m. générale** general medicine; **m. du travail** industrial medicine

média [medja] *nm* medium; **les médias** the media; **médias électroniques** electronic media

médian, -e [medjɑ̃, -an] **1** *adj* median
2 *nf* **médiane** median

médiateur, -trice [medjatœr, -tris] **1** *adj* mediating
2 *nm,f* mediator
3 *nm* **le M. (de la République)** ≃ Ombudsman, Parliamentary Commissioner for Administration

médiathèque [medjatɛk] *nf* media library

médiation [medjasjɔ̃] *nf* mediation

médiatique [medjatik] *adj (événement, campagne)* media; **il est très m.** *(il passe bien a la télévision)* he comes over well on television

médiatisation [medjatizasjɔ̃] *nf* media coverage

médiatiser [medjatize] *vt* to give media coverage to

médiator [medjatɔr] *nm Mus* plectrum

médiatrice [medjatris] *nf* median

médical, -e, -aux, -ales [medikal, -o] *adj* medical

médicalisé, -e [medikalize] *adj* **logement m.** nursing home

médicaliser [medikalize] *vt* (**a**) *(région, pays, population)* to make medical care available to (**b**) *(grossesse)* to treat as a medical matter

médicament [medikamɑ̃] *nm* medicine; **m. de confort** = pharmaceutical product not considered to be essential and not fully reimbursed by the French social security system; **m. homéopathique** homeopathic drug

médicinal, -e, -aux, -ales [medisinal, -o] *adj* medicinal

médico-légal, -e *(mpl* **médico-légaux,** *fpl* **médico-légales)** [medikolegal, -o] *adj* forensic

médico-social, -e *(mpl* **médico-sociaux,** *fpl* **médico-sociales)** [medikosɔsjal, -o] *adj* **centre m.** health centre

médiéval, -e, -aux, -ales [medjeval, -o] *adj* medieval

médiocre [medjɔkr] *adj* mediocre

médiocrement [medjɔkrəmɑ̃] *adv* indifferently

médiocrité [medjɔkrite] *nf* mediocrity

médire [27b] [medir] **médire de** *vt ind* to speak ill of

médisance [medizɑ̃s] *nf* (**a**) *(action)* scandalmongering, gossiping (**b**) *(propos)* piece of scandal *or* gossip; **médisances** scandal, gossip

médisant, -e [medizɑ̃, -ɑ̃t] *adj (paroles)* slanderous; *(personne)* scandalmongering

méditation [meditasjɔ̃] *nf* meditation

méditer [medite] **1** *vt* (**a**) *(considérer par une profonde réflexion)* to contemplate (**b**) *(préparer)* to mull over
2 *vi* to meditate
3 **méditer sur** *vt ind* to meditate on

Méditerranée [mediterane] *nf* **la (mer) M.** the Mediterranean (Sea)

méditerranéen, -enne [mediteraneɛ̃, -ɛn] **1** *adj* Mediterranean
2 *nm,f* **M.** person from a Mediterranean country

médium [medjɔm] *nmf (voyant)* medium

médius [medjys] *nm* middle finger

méduse [medyz] *nf* jellyfish

méduser [medyze] *vt* to dumbfound

meeting [mitiŋ] *nm* meeting; **m. aérien** air show

méfait [mefɛ] *nm* misdemeanour; **les méfaits du tabac** the damage caused by smoking

méfiance [mefjɑ̃s] *nf (manque de confiance)* distrust; *(suspicion)* mistrust, suspicion; **m.!** be careful!

méfiant, -e [mefjɑ̃, -ɑ̃t] *adj (n'ayant pas confiance)* distrustful; *(suspicieux)* suspicious (**à l'égard de** *ou* **avec** of)

méfier [66] [mefje] **se méfier** *vpr* to be careful; **se m. de qn** not to trust sb; **se m. de qch** *(faire attention à)* to watch out for sth; *(douter de)* to be wary of sth

méga¹ [mega] *nm Ordinat* megabyte, meg

méga² *adj inv Fam* mega

mégabit [megabit] *nm Ordinat* megabit

mégalo [megalo] *adj & nmf Fam* megalomaniac

mégalomane [megaloman] *adj & nmf* megalomaniac

mégalomanie [megalomani] *nf* megalomania

mégalopole [megalopol] *nf* megalopolis

mégaoctet [megaɔktɛ] *nm Ordinat* megabyte

mégaphone [megafɔn] *nm Br* megaphone, *Am* bullhorn

mégarde [megard] **par mégarde** *adv* inadvertently, accidentally

mégère [meʒɛr] *nf (femme)* shrew

mégot [mego] *nm Br* fag butt *or* end, *Am* dog-end

mégoter [megote] *vi Fam* to skimp (**sur** on)

meilleur, -e [mɛjœr] **1** *adj* (**a**) *(comparatif de* **bon**) better (**que** than) (**b**) *(superlatif de* **bon**) **le m. élève** *(de la classe)* the best pupil; *(parmi deux élèves)* the better pupil

   2 *nm,f (personne)* **le m.** *(de tous)* the best; *(des deux)* the better; *Fam* **alors ça, c'est la meilleure!** that's just great!

   3 *nm (ce qu'il y a de mieux)* **le m.** the best; **pour le m. et pour le pire** for better and for worse

   4 *adv* **il fait m.** it's warmer

méjuger [45] [meʒyʒe] **1** *vt Litt (mal juger)* to misjudge; *(sous-estimer)* to underestimate

   2 méjuger de *vt ind (mal juger)* to misjudge; *(sous-estimer)* to underestimate

mél [mel] *nm (courrier électronique)* e-mail; *(adresse électronique)* e-mail address

mélancolie [melɑ̃kɔli] *nf* melancholy

mélancolique [melɑ̃kɔlik] *adj* melancholy

Mélanésie [melanezi] *nf* **la M.** Melanesia

mélanésien, -enne [melanezjɛ̃, -ɛn] **1** *adj* Melanesian

   2 *nm,f* **M.** Melanesian

   3 *nm (langue)* Melanesian

mélange [melɑ̃ʒ] *nm* (**a**) *(action)* mixing (**b**) *(résultat)* mixture; **je ne fais jamais de mélanges** I never mix my drinks

mélanger [45] [melɑ̃ʒe] **1** *vt* (**a**) *(mettre ensemble)* to mix (**b**) *(confondre, déranger)* to mix up; **je mélange tout en français** I get everything in French mixed up (**c**) *(cartes)* to shuffle

   2 se mélanger *vpr* (**a**) *(s'incorporer)* to mix (**b**) *(se confondre)* to get mixed up (**c**) *Fam* **se m. les pédales** *ou* **les pinceaux** to get into a muddle

mélangeur [melɑ̃ʒœr] *nm* **(robinet) m.** *Br* mixer tap, *Am* mixing faucet

mélanome [melanom] *nm Méd* melanoma

mêlant [mɛlɑ̃] *adj m Can* **c'est pas m.** there's no doubt about it

mélasse [melas] *nf Br* (black) treacle, *Am* molasses *(singulier)*; *Fam* **être dans la m.** to be in a mess

Melba [mɛlba] *adj inv* **pêche M.** peach Melba

mêlé, -e¹ [mele] *adj* (**a**) *(mélangé)* mixed (**de** with) (**b**) *Can (embrouillé)* mixed-up; *(désorienté)* disoriented; **être m. dans ses papiers** to be confused

mêlée² *nf* (**a**) *(conflit)* fray, mêlée (**b**) *(au rugby)* scrum, scrummage

mêler [mele] **1** *vt* (**a**) *(mettre ensemble)* to mix (**à** *ou* **avec** with) (**b**) *(impliquer)* **m. qn à qch** *(affaire, conversation)* to involve sb in sth

   2 se mêler *vpr* (**a**) *(substances)* to combine (**b**) *(se joindre)* **se m. à qch** *(foule)* to mingle with sth; *(cortège)* to join sth; *(conversation)* to join in sth (**c**) *(s'occuper)* **se m. de qch** to get involved in sth; **mêle-toi de tes affaires!** mind your own business!

mélèze [melɛz] *nm* larch (tree)

méli-mélo *(pl* **mélis-mélos)** [melimelo] *nm Fam* jumble

mélo [melo] *Fam* **1** *adj (qui tient du mélodrame)* melodramatic; *(qui donne dans la sensiblerie)* sentimental

   2 *nm* melodrama

mélodie [melɔdi] *nf* (**a**) *(composition musicale)* melody, tune (**b**) *(de vers, d'une langue)* melodiousness, tunefulness

mélodieusement [melɔdjøzmɑ̃] *adv* melodiously, tunefully

mélodieux, -euse [melɔdjø, -øz] *adj* melodious, tuneful

mélodique [melɔdik] *adj* melodic

mélodiste [melɔdist] *nmf* melody writer

mélodramatique [melɔdramatik] *adj* melodramatic

mélodrame [melɔdram] *nm* melodrama

mélomane [melɔman] **1** *adj* music-loving

   2 *nmf* music lover

melon [məlɔ̃] *nm* (**a**) *(fruit)* melon (**b**) *(chapeau) Br* bowler (hat), *Am* derby

membrane [mɑ̃bran] *nf* membrane

membre [mɑ̃br] **1** *adj (État, pays)* member

   2 *nm* (**a**) *(partie du corps)* limb; **m. supérieur/inférieur** upper/lower limb; **m. viril** male member (**b**) *(d'une association, d'un groupe)* member

mémé [meme] *nf (grand-mère)* gran(ny), grandma; *Fam (vieille femme)* old dear

même [mɛm] **1** *adj indéfini* (**a**) *(avant le nom) (identique)* same; **j'ai la m. voiture que toi** I have the same car as you (do) (**b**) *(après le nom, pour insister)* **je l'ai fait le jour m.** I did it that (very) same day; **c'est cela m.** that's exactly; **c'est la gentillesse m.** she's kindness itself *or* personified

   2 *pron indéfini* **le/la m.** the same (one); **j'ai les mêmes que lui** I have the same (ones) as him; **cela revient au m.** it comes *or* amounts to the same thing

   3 *adv (pour insister)* even; **il n'est m. pas beau** he's not even good-looking; **m. moi, je le sais!** even I know that!; **m. si je l'avais, je ne te le donnerais pas** even if I had it, I wouldn't give it to you; **elle habite ici m.** she lives in this very place; **aujourd'hui m.** this very day; **je pense m. qu'il sera d'accord** I think he'll actually agree (**b**) **être à m. de faire qch** to be able *or* in a position to do sth; **dormir à m. le sol** to sleep on the bare ground; **porter un pull-over à m. la peau** to wear a jumper next to one's bare skin; **de m.** likewise; **Joyeux Noël – vous de m.** Merry Christmas – same to you; **il en est de m. des autres** the same goes for the others; **faire de m.** to follow suit; **de m. que qn**

just like sb; **de m. que qch** just like sth; *(aussi bien que qch)* as well as sth; **tout de m.**, *Fam* **quand m.** all the same; *Fam* **enfin, quand m.!** honestly!; *Fam* **m. que je te l'avais déjà dit!** but I already TOLD you!

mémento [memɛ̃to] *nm* (**a**) *(pour réviser)* revision notes; **m. de chimie** chemistry revision notes (**b**) *(carnet)* diary

mémère [memɛr] *nf Fam Péj* old dear; **une grosse m.** a fat old bag

mémo [memo] *nm* memo

mémoire¹ [memwar] *nf* (**a**) *(faculté)* memory; **avoir de la m.** to have a good memory; **avoir la m. des noms/dates** to have a good memory for names/dates; **avoir la m. courte** to have a short memory; **se rafraîchir la m.** to refresh one's memory; **à la m. de qn** *(monument)* in memory of sb; **de m.** *(citer)* from memory; **de m. d'homme** within living memory; **pour m.** for the record; **si j'ai bonne m.** if I remember correctly; **avoir une m. d'éléphant** to have a memory like an elephant; **la m. collective** collective memory (**b**) *Ordinat* memory; **mettre un dossier en m.** to write a file to memory; **carte d'extension de m.** memory expansion card; **m. cache** cache memory; **m. centrale** main memory; **m. à disque** disk memory, RAM disc; **m. étendue** extended memory; **m. expansée** expanded memory; **m. haute** high memory; **m. de masse** mass storage; **m. morte** read-only memory; **m. non effaçable** non-erasable memory; **m. paginée** expanded memory; **m. permanente** permanent memory; **m. tampon** buffer (store *or* memory); **m. vidéo** video memory; **m. vive** random access memory, RAM; **m. vive dynamique** DRAM, dynamic random access memory; **m. vive statique** static RAM, static random access memory

mémoire² *nm* (**a**) *(thèse)* thesis, dissertation (**b**) *(rapport)* report (**c**) **Mémoires** *(chronique)* memoirs

mémorable [memɔrabl] *adj* memorable

mémorandum [memɔrɑ̃dɔm] *nm* (**a**) *(note)* memorandum (**b**) *(carnet)* notebook

mémorial, -aux [memɔrjal, -o] *nm (monument)* memorial

mémoriser [memɔrize] *vt* to memorize

menaçant, -e [mənasɑ̃, -ɑ̃t] *adj* threatening, menacing

menace [mənas] *nf* threat (**de** of); **menaces de mort** death threats

menacer [16] [mənase] **1** *vt* to threaten (**de** with); **m. qn du poing** to shake one's fist at sb; **m. de faire qch** to threaten to do sth
  2 *vi (tempête, orage, révolution)* to be brewing; **la pluie menace** it's threatening to rain

ménage [menaʒ] *nm* (**a**) *(nettoyage)* **faire le m.** *(à la maison)* to do the housework; *Fig* to have a shake-up; **faire des ménages** to do cleaning for people (**b**) *(couple)* couple; **se mettre en m.** to move in together; **se mettre en m. avec qn** to move in with sb; **faire bon/mauvais m. (avec qn)** to get on well/badly (with sb); **m. à trois** ménage à trois (**c**) *Écon* household

ménagement [menaʒmɑ̃] *nm* care, caution; *(tact)* consideration; **sans m.** *(annoncer)* bluntly

ménager¹, -ère [menaʒe, -ɛr] **1** *adj* (**a**) *(de la maison)* *(équipement, appareils)* household (**b**) *Can (économe)* thrifty, careful (with money)
  2 *nf* **ménagère** *(femme)* housewife

ménager² [45] **1** *vt* (**a**) *(utiliser avec parcimonie) (argent)* to use sparingly; *(forces)* to conserve, to save; *(santé)* to take care of; **ne pas m. sa peine** to put in a lot of effort (**b**) *(traiter avec soin)* to treat carefully; *Fig* **m. la chèvre et le chou** to keep everyone happy (**c**) *(arranger) (entrevue, réunion)* to arrange, to organize; *(sortie)* to provide; *(réconciliation)* to bring about
  2 se ménager *vpr* (**a**) *(prendre soin de soi)* to take care of oneself, to look after oneself (**b**) *(se réserver)* to set aside

ménagerie [menaʒri] *nf* menagerie

mendiant, -e [mɑ̃djɑ̃, -ɑ̃t] **1** *adj (moine, ordre)* mendicant
  2 *nm,f* beggar

mendicité [mɑ̃disite] *nf* begging

mendier [66] [mɑ̃dje] **1** *vt* to beg for
  2 *vi* to beg

mener [46] [məne] **1** *vt* (**a**) *(accompagner)* to take (**à** to) (**b**) *(cortège, course)* to lead; **m. qch à bien** to bring sth to a successful conclusion; *Fig* **m. la danse** to call the tune (**c**) *(vie)* to lead; **m. la vie dure à qn** to give sb a hard time (**d**) *(débat, enquête)* to lead (**e**) *(contrôler) (personne)* **m. qn à la baguette** to have sb under one's thumb; **m. qn par le bout du nez** to lead sb by the nose
  2 *vi* (**a**) *(dans un match, une compétition)* to lead; **m. par 2 buts à 1** to lead by 2 goals to 1 (**b**) **m. à un lieu** to lead to a place; *Fig* **cela ne mène à rien** this is getting us nowhere (**c**) *Fam* **elle n'en menait pas large** her heart was in her mouth

meneur, -euse [mənœr, -øz] **1** *nm,f (de parti politique)* leader; *(agitateur)* ringleader; **m. d'hommes** born leader; **m. de jeu** question master, quiz master; *Sport* play maker
  2 *nf* **meneuse de revue** principal chorus girl; *Can* **meneuse de claques** cheerleader

menhir [menir] *nm* menhir

méninges [menɛ̃ʒ] *nfpl Fam* brains

méningite [menɛ̃ʒit] *nf* meningitis; **avoir une m.** to have meningitis

ménisque [menisk] *nm* meniscus

ménopause [menɔpoz] *nf* menopause

menotte [mənɔt] *nf* (**a**) *Fam (petite main)* little hand (**b**) **menottes** *(bracelets métalliques)* handcuffs; **mettre** *ou* **passer les menottes à qn** to handcuff sb, to put handcuffs on sb

mensonge [mɑ̃sɔ̃ʒ] *nm* (**a**) *(propos)* lie; **petit m., pieux m.** white lie (**b**) *(acte)* lying

mensonger, -ère [mɑ̃sɔ̃ʒe, -ɛr] *adj (propos)* untrue; *(publicité)* misleading

menstruation [mɑ̃stryasjɔ̃] *nf* menstruation

menstruel, -elle [mɑ̃stryɛl] *adj* menstrual

mensualiser [mɑ̃syalize] *vt* to pay monthly; **être mensualisé** *(pour les impôts)* = to pay one's income tax in advance monthly instalments, the amount paid being an estimation based on previous years

mensualité [mɑ̃syalite] *nf* monthly payment

mensuel, -elle [mɑ̃syɛl] **1** *adj* monthly
  2 *nm (publication)* monthly (magazine)

mensuellement [mɑ̃syɛlmɑ̃] *adv* monthly, every month

mensuration [mɑ̃syrasjɔ̃] *nf* (**a**) *(action)* measurement, measuring (**b**) **mensurations** *(dimensions)* measurements

mental, -e, -aux, -ales [mɑ̃tal, -o] **1** *adj* mental
  2 *nm* mental attitude

mentalement [mɑ̃talmɑ̃] *adv* mentally

mentalité [mɑ̃talite] *nf* mentality; **les mentalités ont changé** (people's) attitudes have changed; *Ironique* **jolie m.!** that's a nice way of thinking!

menteur, -euse [mɑ̃tœr, -øz] **1** *adj (personne)* untruthful, lying
2 *nm,f* liar

menthe [mɑ̃t] *nf (plante)* mint; **dentifrice a la m.** mint *or* mint-flavoured toothpaste; **m. à l'eau** peppermint cordial

menthol [mɑ̃tɔl] *nm* menthol

mentholé, -e [mɑ̃tɔle] *adj* menthol, mentholated

mention [mɑ̃sjɔ̃] *nf* (**a**) *(fait de citer)* mention; **faire m. de qn/qch** to mention sb/sth (**b**) **rayer la m. inutile** *(sur formulaire)* delete where inapplicable (**c**) *(à un examen)* **m. passable** ≃ C; **m. assez bien** ≃ B; **m. bien/très bien** ≃ A

mentionner [mɑ̃sjɔne] *vt* to mention

mentir [64b] [mɑ̃tir] *vi* to lie (**à** to); **sans m.** honestly

menton [mɑ̃tɔ̃] *nm* chin; **m. en galoche** protruding chin; **m. fuyant** receding chin; **double m.** double chin

mentor [mɑ̃tɔr] *nm* mentor

menu¹, -e [məny] **1** *adj* (**a**) *(détail, monnaie)* small (**b**) *(taille)* slim; *(personne)* petite
2 *adv* small, fine

menu² *nm* (**a**) *(au restaurant)* set menu, fixed-price menu (**b**) *Ordinat* menu; **contrôlé par m.** menu-driven; **m. d'aide** help menu; **m. déroulant** pull-down menu; **m. fichier** file menu; **m. local** pop-up menu; **m. primaire/secondaire/principal** primary/secondary/main menu

menuet [mənɥɛ] *nm* minuet

menuiserie [mənɥizri] *nf* (**a**) *(atelier)* (joiner's) workshop (**b**) *(travail du bois, résultat)* joinery, woodwork

menuisier [mənɥizje] *nm* joiner, carpenter

méprendre [58] [meprɑ̃dr] **se méprendre** *vpr* to be mistaken (**sur** about); **elle te ressemble à s'y m.** she looks exactly like you

mépris¹, -e¹ *voir* **méprendre**

mépris² [mepri] *nm* contempt, scorn; **avec m.** scornfully, contemptuously; **avoir du m. pour qn** to despise sb; **au m. de qch** regardless of sth

méprisable [meprizabl] *adj* contemptible, despicable

méprisant, -e [meprizɑ̃, -ɑ̃t] *adj* scornful, contemptuous

méprise² [mepriz] *nf* mistake

mépriser [meprize] *vt* (**a**) *(dédaigner) (personne, argent)* to despise (**b**) *(ignorer) (conseil, offre, danger)* to disregard

mer [mɛr] *nf* (**a**) *(étendue d'eau)* sea; **en haute** *ou* **pleine m.** (out) at sea; **au bord de la m.** at the seaside; **aller à la m.** to go to the seaside; **prendre la m.** to set sail, to put (out) to sea; *Fam* **ce n'est pas la m. à boire** it's no big deal; **une m. d'huile** a sea as calm as a millpond; **la m. Adriatique** the Adriatic Sea; **la m. d'Aral** the Aral Sea; **la m. Caspienne** the Caspian Sea; **la m. de Chine** the China Sea; **la m. de Corail** the Coral Sea; **la m. Égée** the Aegean Sea; **la m. d'Irlande** the Irish Sea; **la m. Morte** the Dead Sea; **la m. Noire** the Black Sea; **la m. du Nord** the North Sea; **la m. Rouge** the Red Sea; **la m. des Sargasses** the Sargasso Sea (**b**) *(marée)* tide

mercantile [mɛrkɑ̃til] *adj* mercenary

mercatique [mɛrkatik] *nf* marketing

mercenaire [mɛrsənɛr] *adj & nm* mercenary

mercerie [mɛrsəri] *nf* (**a**) *(magasin) Br* haberdasher's (shop), *Am* notions store (**b**) *(articles) Br* haberdashery, *Am* notions

merchandising [mɛrʃɑ̃dajziŋ] *nm* merchandising

merci [mɛrsi] **1** *exclam* thank you, thanks (**de** *ou* **pour** for); (**non) m.** no thank you, no thanks; **dire m. (à qn)** to say thank you *or* thanks (to sb); **m. bien, m. beaucoup** thank you *or* thanks very much
2 *nm* thank you
3 *nf* **être à la m. de qn/qch** to be at the mercy of sb/sth; **sans m.** merciless

mercier, -ère [mɛrsje, -ɛr] *nm,f Br* haberdasher, *Am* notions dealer

mercredi [mɛrkrədi] *nm* Wednesday; **le m. des Cendres** Ash Wednesday; *voir aussi* **samedi**

Mercure [mɛrkyr] *npr (dieu, planète)* Mercury

mercure [mɛrkyr] *nm* mercury

Mercurochrome® [mɛrkyrɔkrom] *nm* Mercurochrome®

merde [mɛrd] *Vulg* **1** *nf* shit; *Fig* **être dans la m.** to be in the shit; **ne pas se prendre pour de la m.** to think the sun shines out of one's arse; **c'est de la m.** *(c'est de la mauvaise qualité)* it's shit; **de m.** *(voiture, idée)* shitty
2 *exclam* shit!; *Fig* **dire m. à qn** *(l'envoyer au diable)* to tell sb to bugger off; **je te dis m.!** *(bonne chance)* break a leg!; **m. alors!** oh shit!

merder [mɛrde] *vi très Fam (ne pas fonctionner) (projet)* to get screwed up; **ça merde entre eux** things between them are really screwed up; **j'ai merdé à l'examen** I really screwed up in the exam

merdeux, -euse [mɛrdø, -øz] *très Fam* **1** *adj* **se sentir m.** to feel shitty
2 *nm,f (enfant)* **un petit m.** a little shit

merdier [mɛrdje] *nm Vulg* **être dans le m.** to be in the shit

merdique [mɛrdik] *adj très Fam* shitty

mère [mɛr] **1** *adj voir* **maison**
2 *nf* (**a**) *(parent)* mother; **elle est m. de trois enfants** she is a mother of three; **m. célibataire** single mother; **être m. de famille** to be a wife and mother; **m. nourricière** foster mother; **m. patrie** mother country, motherland; **m. porteuse** surrogate mother; **poule** mother hen (**b**) *Fam (femme)* **la m. Martin** old Mrs Martin

merguez [mɛrgɛz] *nf* merguez *(spicy North African sausage)*

méridien, -enne [meridjɛ̃, -ɛn] **1** *adj (ligne)* meridian, meridional
2 *nm Géog* meridian
3 *nf* **méridienne** *(canapé)* day bed

méridional, -e, -aux, -ales [meridjɔnal, -o] **1** *adj (du Sud)* southern; *(du sud de la France)* from the South of France
2 *nm,f (du Sud)* southerner; *(du sud de la France)* person from the South of France

meringue [mərɛ̃g] *nf* meringue

mérinos [merinos] *nm* (**a**) *Zool* merino (**b**) *Tex* **(laine) m.** merino wool

merisier [mərizje] *nm (arbre)* wild cherry (tree); *(bois)* cherry(wood)

méritant, -e [meritɑ̃, -ɑ̃t] *adj* deserving

mérite [merit] *nm* merit; *(honneur)* credit; **avoir du m. (à faire qch)** to deserve credit (for doing sth); **au moins, son livre a le m. de la clarté** at least his/her

book has the merit of being clearly written; **tout le m.**
lui revient he/she deserves all the credit
mériter [merite] *vt* (**a**) *(après une action)* to deserve;
m. d'être puni/récompensé to deserve to be pun-
ished/rewarded; **elle mérite qu'on le lui dise** she deserves to be told (**b**) *(demander)* to be worth; **m.**
réflexion to be worth thinking about; **ce livre mérite**
d'être lu this book is worth reading
méritoire [meritwar] *adj* commendable, praiseworthy
merlan [mɛrlɑ̃] *nm* (**a**) *(poisson)* whiting (**b**) *très Fam*
(coiffeur) hairdresser, *Br* crimper
merle [mɛrl] *nm* blackbird
merlu [mɛrly] *nm* hake
mérou [meru] *nm* grouper
mérovingien, -enne [merɔvɛ̃jɛ̃, -ɛn] **1** *adj* Mero-
vingian
  2 *nmpl* **les Mérovingiens** the Merovingians
merveille [mɛrvɛj] *nf* (**a**) *(chose remarquable)* marvel, wonder; **à m.** wonderfully (well); **se porter à m.**
to be in the best of health; *Fig* **faire des merveilles**
to work wonders; **les Sept Merveilles du monde**
the Seven Wonders of the World (**b**) *(gâteau)* = sweet
fritter
merveilleusement [mɛrvɛjøzmɑ̃] *adv* marvellously,
wonderfully
merveilleux, -euse [mɛrvɛjø, -øz] **1** *adj* marvellous,
wonderful
  2 *nm* **le m.** the supernatural
mes [me] *voir* **mon**
mésalliance [mezaljɑ̃s] *nf* unsuitable marriage; **faire**
une m. to marry beneath oneself
mésallier [66] [mezalje] **se mésallier** *vpr* to marry beneath oneself
mésange [mezɑ̃ʒ] *nf* tit; **m. bleue** blue tit; **m. charbon-**
nière coal tit
mésaventure [mezavɑ̃tyr] *nf* misadventure
mesdames [medam] *nfpl voir* **madame**
mesdemoiselles [medmwazɛl] *nfpl voir* **mademoi-**
selle
mésentente [mezɑ̃tɑ̃t] *nf* disagreement
mésestimer [mezɛstime] *vt* to underestimate
mésothérapie [mezoterapi] *nf* = treatment consisting of injecting minute quantities of medication into
the affected area
mesquin, -e [mɛskɛ̃, -in] *adj* mean, petty
mesquinement [mɛskinmɑ̃] *adv* meanly
mesquinerie [mɛskinri] *nf* (**a**) *(d'un caractère, d'un*
procédé) meanness, pettiness (**b**) *(action)* mean or
petty thing (to do)
mess [mɛs] *nm Mil* mess
message [mesaʒ] *nm* message; *Ordinat* **m. d'accueil**
welcome message; *Ordinat* **m. d'alerte** warning message, alert box; *Ordinat* **m. électronique** e-mail; **en-**
voyer un m. électronique à qn to e-mail sb; **m.**
enregistré recorded message; *Ordinat* **m. d'erreur**
error message; *Ordinat* **m. instantané** instant message; *Ordinat* **m. d'invite** *(du système)* prompt; **m.**
publicitaire advertisement; **m. texte** text message;
m. vocal voicemail (message), voice message
messager, -ère [mesaʒe, -ɛr] *nm,f* messenger
messagerie [mesaʒri] *nf* (**a**) *(service de transports)*
courier company; **messageries aériennes** air freight
company (**b**) *(service télématique)* **m. électronique**
electronic mail service, e-mail; **m. instantanée** instant messaging; **m. vocale** voice mail (service) (**c**)

(entreprise de routage) **m. de presse** newspaper dis-
tributing service
messe [mɛs] *nf (office religieux, composition musi-*
cale) mass; **aller à la m.** to go to mass; *Fig* **faire des**
messes basses to whisper; **m. de minuit** midnight
mass
messeigneurs [mesɛɲœr] *nmpl voir* **monseigneur**
Messie [mesi] *nm* **le M.** the Messiah
messieurs [mesjø] *nmpl voir* **monsieur**
mesurable [məzyrabl] *adj* measurable
mesure [məzyr] *nf* (**a**) *(dimension)* measurement;
(action) measurement, measuring; **prendre les me-**
sures de qn/qch to measure sb/sth; *Fig* **prendre la**
m. de qn/qch to size sb/sth up; **sur m.** *(costume)*
made to measure; *(rôle, emploi)* ideal; **donner toute**
sa m. to show what one is capable of; **être à la m. de**
qn/qch to measure up to sb/sth; **être sans commune**
m. avec qch to be out of proportion to sth; **elle a**
trouvé quelqu'un/un homme à sa m. she met her
match (**b**) *(moyen)* measure; **prendre des mesures**
to take measures; **m. de sécurité** safety measure or
precaution; **par m. d'économie** as a way to save
money (**c**) *(quantité, unité)* measure; **sans commune**
m. unrivalled (**d**) *(modération)* moderation; **sans m.**
(ambition, jalousie) limitless (**e**) *Mus (temps)* time;
(division) bar; **m. à quatre temps** four-four time,
common time; **battre la m.** to beat time; **en m.** in time
(**f**) *(locutions)* **à m. que** as; **(au fur et) à m.** as one
goes along; **dans une certaine m.** to some or a certain extent; **dans une large m.** to a large extent; **dans**
la m. où in so far as; **dans la m. du possible** as far as is
possible; **être en m. de faire qch** to be in a position to
do sth
mesuré, -e [məzyre] *adj (pas)* measured; *(langage,*
personne) restrained
mesurer [məzyre] **1** *vt* (**a**) *(dimensions, taille)* to measure; *(tissu)* to measure off (**b**) *(déterminer)* to assess
(**c**) *(limiter)* to limit; **m. l'argent à qn** to ration out
money to sb (**d**) **m. ses paroles** to moderate one's
language
  2 *vi* to measure; **m. 2 mètres** *(personne)* to be 2
metres tall; *(tour, colonne)* to be 2 metres high
  3 **se mesurer** *vpr* **se m. avec** *ou* **à qn** to pit oneself
against sb
met *voir* **mettre**
métabolique [metabɔlik] *adj* metabolic
métabolisme [metabɔlism] *nm* metabolism
métairie [metɛri] *nf* small farm *(worked by share-*
cropper)
métal, -aux [metal, -o] *nm* metal
métallique [metalik] *adj* metallic
métallisé, -e [metalize] *adj (peinture, couleur)*
metallic
métallo [metalo] *nm Fam* metalworker
métallurgie [metalyrʒi] *nf* (**a**) *(industrie)* metallurgical industry (**b**) *(procédé)* metallurgy
métallurgique [metalyrʒik] *adj* metallurgical
métallurgiste [metalyrʒist] *nm* (**a**) *(ouvrier)* metalworker (**b**) *(chef d'entreprise)* metallurgist
métamorphose [metamɔrfoz] *nf aussi Fig* metamorphosis
métamorphoser [metamɔrfoze] **1** *vt* to transform
(**en** into)
  2 **se métamorphoser** *vpr Biol* to metamorphose; *Fig*
to be transformed (**en** into)
métaphore [metafɔr] *nf* metaphor
métaphorique [metafɔrik] *adj* metaphorical

métaphoriquement [metafɔrikmɑ̃] *adv* meta-phorically

métaphysique [metafizik] **1** *adj* metaphysical **2** *nf* metaphysics *(singulier)*

métastase [metastɑz] *nf* metastasis

métayer, -ère [metɛje, -ɛr] *nm,f* sharecropper

météo [meteo] *Fam* **1** *adj* weather **2** *nf (bulletin)* weather forecast; *(organisme)* Br weather centre, *Am* weather bureau; **Monsieur M.** the weatherman

météore [meteɔr] *nm* meteor

météorite [meteɔrit] *nf* meteorite

météorologie [meteɔrɔlɔʒi] *nf* meteorology

météorologique [meteɔrɔlɔʒik] *adj (bulletin, prévisions)* weather

météorologiste [meteɔrɔlɔʒist], **météorologue** [meteɔrɔlɔg] *nmf* meteorologist

météque [metɛk] *nm* = racist term used to refer to any dark-skinned foreigner living in France, especially one from the Mediterranean

méthadone [metadɔn] *nf* methadone

méthane [metan] *nm* methane

méthanol [metanɔl] *nm* methanol

méthode [metɔd] *nf* (**a**) *(démarche)* method; **m. pour faire qch** method of doing sth (**b**) *(ordre)* method; **avec m.** methodically (**c**) *(livre)* **m. d'anglais** English course book; **m. de piano** piano tutor

méthodique [metɔdik] *adj* methodical

méthodiquement [metɔdikmɑ̃] *adv* methodically

méthodiste [metɔdist] *adj & nmf* Methodist

méthodologie [metɔdɔlɔʒi] *nf* methodology

méthodologique [metɔdɔlɔʒik] *adj* methodological

méthylène [metilɛn] *nm* methylene

méticuleusement [metikyløzmɑ̃] *adv* meticulously

méticuleux, -euse [metikylø, -øz] *adj* meticulous

méticulosité [metikylozite] *nf* meticulousness

métier [metje] *nm* (**a**) *(manuel, commercial)* trade; *(intellectuel)* profession; **exercer un m.** to have a job; **j'exerce le m. de journaliste** I'm a journalist by profession; **quel m. veux-tu faire plus tard?** what do you want to be when you grow up?; **il n'est pas** *ou* **il n'y a pas de sot m.** a job's a job; **être du m.** to be in the business; **connaître son m.** to know what one is doing; **parler m.** to talk shop (**b**) *(savoir-faire, expérience)* experience; **avoir du m.** to have experience; **elle a plusieurs années de m.** she has several years' experience (**c**) *(machine)* **m. à tisser** loom

métis, -isse [metis] **1** *adj (personne)* half-caste **2** *nm,f (personne)* half-caste **3** *nm (tissu)* linen and cotton mixture

métissage [metisaʒ] *nm* crossbreeding

métisser [metise] *vt* to cross(breed); **une population très métissée** a highly intermixed population; **musique métissée** crossover *or* fusion music

métrage [metraʒ] *nm* (**a**) *(action)* measuring (**b**) *(coupon de tissu)* length (**c**) *(longueur d'un film)* footage, length; **long/moyen/court m.** feature/medium-length/short film

mètre¹ [mɛtr] *nm* (**a**) *(unité de longueur)* metre; **m. carré/cube** square/cubic metre (**b**) *(pour mesurer)* tape measure; *(en bois, en métal)* rule; **m. à ruban** tape measure

mètre² *nm (en poésie)* metre

métreur [metrœr] *nm* quantity surveyor

métrique¹ [metrik] *adj (système)* metric

métrique² **1** *adj (en poésie)* metrical **2** *nf* metrics *(singulier)*

métro [metro] *nm* Br underground, *Am* subway; **le premier/dernier m.** the first/last train; **m. aerien** elevated *or* overhead railway

métronome [metrɔnɔm] *nm* metronome

métropole [metrɔpɔl] *nf* (**a**) *(grande ville)* metropolis (**b**) *(pays)* mother country

métropolitain, -e [metrɔpɔlitɛ̃, -ɛn] **1** *adj (non insulaire)* metropolitan **2** *nm Vieilli (métro)* Br underground, *Am* subway

métrosexuel, -elle [metrɔsɛksɥɛl] **1** *adj* metrosexual **2** *nm* metrosexual

mets¹ *voir* mettre

mets² [mɛ] *nm* dish

mettable [mɛtabl] *adj* wearable

mette *etc voir* mettre

metteur [mɛtœr] *nm* **m. en scène** director

mettre [47] [mɛtr] **1** *vt* (**a**) *(placer)* to put; **m. qch sur/dans qch** to put sth on/in sth; **m. qn à mal** *(verbalement)* to berate sb; *(physiquement)* to beat sb up (**b**) *(vêtement, chaussures, lunettes, pansement)* to put on (**c**) *(moquette)* to lay; *(papier peint, étagères)* to put up (**d**) *(allumer)* to put on, to switch on; **m. qch en marche** to turn sth on; **m. qch plus fort** to turn sth up; **m. de la musique** to put some music on; **m. le réveil (à cinq heures)** to set the alarm (for five o'clock); **faire m. le téléphone** to get the phone put in (**e**) **elle y a mis beaucoup d'argent** she's spent a lot of money on it (**f**) **elle a mis du temps/deux ans à le faire** it took her a while/two years to do it; **combien de temps met-on pour y aller?** how long does it take to get there? (**g**) **ça va prendre, mettons, trois mois** it will take, (let's) say, three months; **mettons que je n'ai rien dit** pretend I didn't say anything (**h**) *(écrire)* to put (**i**) *Fam* **qu'est-ce qu'on leur a mis!** we really thrashed them!; **m. les bouts** *ou* **les voiles** to make a move; *Vulg* **va te faire m.!** go fuck yourself!

2 *vi* **m. bas** to give birth

3 se mettre *vpr* (**a**) *(se placer)* **mets-toi là!** *(va là-bas)* stand there!; *(assieds-toi là-bas)* sit there!; **se m. au soleil** *(s'asseoir)* to sit in the sun; *(s'allonger)* to lie in the sun; **se m. au lit** to get into bed; **se m. sur le dos/ventre** to lie on one's back/stomach; *(en se tournant)* to turn (over) onto one's back/stomach; *Belg* **mettez-vous!** take a seat!, sit down!; *Fig* **se m. en avant** to push oneself forward; *Fig* **je ne savais plus où me m.** I didn't know where to put myself (**b**) *(maquillage, vêtement)* to put on; **je n'ai plus rien à me m.** I haven't got a thing to wear (**c**) *(commencer)* **se m. à qch** *(activité)* to take sth up; **se m. au travail** to get (down) to work; **se m. à faire qch** to begin *or* to start doing sth; **le temps s'est mis à la pluie** it turned to rain; *Fam* **si tu t'y mets aussi!** don't YOU start! (**d**) **il a fallu se m. à trois pour le déplacer** it took three of us to move it (**e**) *Fam* **qu'est-ce qu'ils se sont mis!** they really laid into each other!

meuble [mœbl] **1** adj (**a**) (sol, terre, roche) soft (**b**) (biens) movable **2** nm piece of furniture; **meubles** furniture; **être dans ses meubles** to have a place of one's own; Fam **faire partie des meubles** to be part of the furniture

meublé, -e [mœble] **1** adj furnished; **non m.** unfurnished **2** nm (chambre) furnished room; (appartement) furnished Br flat or Am apartment

meubler [mœble] **1** vt (**a**) (pièce, maison) to furnish (**de** with) (**b**) (remplir) to fill (**de** with); **m. la conversation** to make conversation **2 se meubler** vpr to furnish one's home

meuf [mœf] nf très Fam Br bird, Am chick

meuglement [mœgləmɑ̃] nm moo; **des meuglements** mooing

meugler [mœgle] vi to moo

meule [møl] nf (**a**) (d'herbe, de céréales) stack; **m. de foin** haystack (**b**) (de moulin) millstone (**c**) (de fromage) round

meunier, -ère [mønje, -ɛr] **1** adj (**a**) (industrie) flour-milling (**b**) (à la) **meunière** (poisson) = coated with flour and fried in butter **2** nm,f miller **3** nf **meunière** (épouse) miller's wife

meurs, meurt voir **mourir**

meurtre [mœrtr] nm murder

meurtri, -e [mœrtri] adj bruised

meurtrier, -ère [mœrtrije, -ɛr] **1** adj (guerre, attentat, colère) murderous; (arme, épidémie) deadly **2** nm,f murderer **3** nf **meurtrière** Archit loophole

meurtrir [mœrtrir] vt to bruise

meurtrissure [mœrtrisyr] nf bruise

meute [møt] nf aussi Fig pack

MEV [mɛv] nf Ordinat (abrév **mémoire vive**) RAM

mexicain, -e [mɛksikɛ̃, -ɛn] **1** adj Mexican **2** nm,f **M.** Mexican

Mexico [mɛksiko] n Mexico City

Mexique [mɛksik] nm **le M.** Mexico

mézigue [mezig] pron personnel Fam yours truly

mezzanine [mɛdzanin] nf (**a**) (entre deux étages) mezzanine (floor) (**b**) (au théâtre) Br dress circle, Am mezzanine

mezzo-soprano (pl **mezzo-sopranos**) [mɛdzo-soprano] **1** nm (voix) mezzo-soprano **2** nf (cantatrice) mezzo-soprano

MF [ɛmɛf] nf Rad (abrév **modulation de fréquence**) FM

mg (abrév **milligramme(s)**) mg

Mgr Rel (abrév **Monseigneur**) Mgr

mi [mi] nm inv (note) E; (chantée) mi

mi- [mi] adv **la mi-avril** mid-April; **à mi-hauteur** (en montant) halfway up; (en descendant) halfway down; **elle avait de l'eau jusqu'à mi-jambe** the water was halfway up her legs; **mi-amusé, mi-intrigué** half-amused, half-puzzled; **mi-figue, mi-raisin** (sourire) half-hearted; (plaisanterie) half-serious

miam-miam [mjammjam] exclam yum yum!

miaou [mjau] exclam miaow!

miasme [mjasm] nm miasma

miaulement [mjolmɑ̃] nm miaowing

miauler [mjole] vi to miaow

mi-bas [miba] nm inv (en laine) knee sock; (en voile) popsock

mica [mika] nm mica

mi-carême (pl **mi-carêmes**) [mikarɛm] nf = third Thursday in Lent

miche [miʃ] nf (**a**) (pain) round loaf (**b**) Fam **miches** (fesses) Br bum, Am butt

Michel-Ange [mikɛlɑ̃ʒ] npr Michelangelo

micheline [miʃlin] nf railcar

mi-chemin [miʃmɛ̃] **à mi-chemin** adv halfway

Michigan [miʃigɑ̃] n voir **lac**

mi-clos, -e (mpl **mi-clos**, fpl **mi-closes**) [miklo, mikloz] adj half-closed

micmac [mikmak] nm Fam (**a**) (complications) muddle (**b**) Can (désordre) mess

mi-côte [mikot] **à mi-côte** adv halfway up the hill

mi-course [mikurs] **à mi-course** adv at the halfway mark

micro [mikro] **1** nm (**a**) (microphone) mike (**b**) Ordinat micro(computer) **2** nf Ordinat microcomputing

microbe [mikrɔb] nm (**a**) (germe) microbe, germ (**b**) Fam (personne chétive) little squirt

microbien, -enne [mikrɔbjɛ̃, -ɛn] adj microbial

microbiologie [mikrɔbjɔlɔʒi] nf microbiology

microchirurgie [mikroʃiryrʒi] nf microsurgery

microcircuit [mikrosirkɥi] nm Ordinat microcircuit; **microcircuits** microcircuitry

microclimat [mikroklima] nm microclimate

microcosme [mikrokɔsm] nm microcosm

microéconomie [mikroekonomi] nf microeconomics (singulier)

microéconomique [mikroekonomik] adj microeconomic

microédition [mikroediʒɔ̃] nf Ordinat desktop publishing, DTP

microfiche [mikrofiʃ] nf microfiche

microfilm [mikrofilm] nm microfilm

micro-informatique [mikroɛ̃fɔrmatik] nf Ordinat microcomputing

micron [mikrɔ̃] nm micron

Micronésie [mikronezi] nf **la M.** Micronesia

micro-ondes [mikroɔ̃d] nm inv microwave

micro-ordinateur (pl **micro-ordinateurs**) [mikro-ɔrdinatœr] nm Ordinat microcomputer

micro-organisme (pl **micro-organismes**) [mikro-ɔrganism] nm micro-organism

microphone [mikrofɔn] nm microphone

micropilule [mikropilyl] nf mini pill

microprocesseur [mikroprɔsɛsœr] nm Ordinat microprocessor

microscope [mikroskɔp] nm microscope; **au m.** under a microscope; **m. électronique** electron microscope

microscopique [mikroskɔpik] adj microscopic

microsillon [mikrosijɔ̃] nm (de disque) groove

microsite [mikrosit] nm Ordinat microsite

micro-trottoir (pl **micros-trottoirs**) [mikrotrɔtwar] nm street interview, Br vox pop

midi [midi] nm (**a**) (heure) twelve o'clock, midday; **m. et demie** half past twelve; **entre m. et deux** at lunchtime (**b**) (moment du déjeuner) lunchtime (**c**) (partie sud) south; **le M. (de la France)** the South of France

midinette [midinɛt] nf silly young girl

mi-distance [midistɑ̃s] **à mi-distance** adv halfway (**de** in)

mie [mi] nf (de pain) soft part

miel [mjɛl] nm honey

mielleusement [mjɛləzmɑ̃] *adv (parler)* in honeyed tones

mielleux, -euse [mjɛlø, -øz] *adj (discours, sourire)* sugary; *(personne)* smooth

mien, mienne *(mpl* miens, *fpl* miennes) [mjɛ̃, mjɛn] **1** *pron possessif* le m., la mienne, les miens, les miennes mine; *(en insistant)* my own; je te prête le m. you can borrow mine; je n'en ai pas besoin, j'ai le m. I don't need it, I've got my own **2** *nm* j'y ai mis du m. I did my share **3** *nmpl* les miens *(ma famille)* my family

miette [mjɛt] *nf (de pain, de gâteau)* crumb; *Fig* en miettes in pieces; mettre qch en miettes *(briser)* to smash sth to pieces; ne pas perdre une m. de qch *(conversation)* not to miss a word of sth; après le partage, je n'ai eu que des miettes I had to make do with what little was left over after the inheritance was shared out

mieux [mjø] **1** *adv* (**a**) *(comparatif)* better; m. que better than; il vaut m. les surveiller it's best to watch them; vous feriez m. de m'écouter you'd do better to listen to me; elle va m. she's (feeling) better; c'est on ne peut m. it couldn't be better; j'espérais m. de votre part I expected better of you; plus on se voit et m. on s'apprécie the more we see each other, the more we like each other; de m. en m. better and better; faire qch à qui m. m. to try to outdo each other in doing sth (**b**) *(superlatif)* c'est elle qui s'exprime le m. she expresses herself (the) best; le plus tôt sera le m. the sooner the better; le m. serait de... the best thing would be to...; ils s'entendent le m. du monde they get on extremely well; être au m. avec qn to be on the best of terms with sb; un service des m. organisés an extremely well-organized department **2** *adj* better; *(plus beau)* better-looking; si tu n'as rien de m. à faire if you've nothing better to do; c'est le m. (de tous) *(le plus beau)* he's the best-looking (of all) **3** *nm* espérer m. to hope for better things; il y a un m. *ou* du m. there's been a change for the better; faire *ou* agir pour le m. to act for the best; faire de son m. to do one's best; fais du m. que tu peux do the best you can

mièvre [mjɛvr] *adj* insipid

mièvrerie [mjɛvrəri] *nf* insipidness

mignon, -onne [miɲɔ̃, -ɔn] **1** *adj* (**a**) *(joli, charmant)* cute (**b**) *(gentil)* nice **2** *nm (favori)* minion **3** *nm,f* mon m. darling

migraine [migrɛn] *nf (douleur violente)* migraine; *(mal de tête)* headache; avoir des migraines to get migraines/headaches

migraineux, -euse [migrɛnø, -øz] *nm,f* migraine sufferer

migrant, -e [migrɑ̃, -ɑ̃t] *adj & nm,f* migrant

migrateur, -trice [migratœr, -tris] *adj (animaux)* migratory

migration [migrasjɔ̃] *nf* migration

migratoire [migratwar] *adj* migratory

migrer [migre] *vi aussi Ordinat* to migrate (vers to)

mijaurée [miʒɔre] *nf (jeune fille)* affected girl; faire la *ou* sa m. to give oneself airs

mijoter [miʒɔte] **1** *vt* (**a**) *(faire cuire)* to simmer; *(préparer avec soin)* to cook up (**b**) *(tramer)* to cook up **2** *vi* to simmer; faire m. to simmer

mikado [mikado] *nm (jeu)* jack-straws, spillikins

mil¹ [mil] *adj inv* l'an m. the year one thousand

mil² [mij, mil] *nm (céréale)* millet

Milan [milɑ̃] *n* Milan

mildiou [mildju] *nm (des céréales)* mildew; *(de la vigne)* brown rot

mile [majl] *nm* mile

milice [milis] *nf* militia

milicien, -enne [milisjɛ̃, -ɛn] *nm,f* militiaman, *f* militiawoman

milieu, -x [miljø] *nm* (**a**) *(centre)* middle; au m. de in the middle of; en plein *ou* au beau m. de qch right in the middle of sth; la table du m. the middle table (**b**) *(environnement)* environment; *(social)* background; *Phys* medium; le m. familial the home environment; dans les milieux autorisés in official circles (**c**) *(position intermédiaire)* middle course; le juste m. the happy medium (**d**) *(pègre)* le m. the underworld

militaire [militɛr] **1** *adj* military; *(port)* naval **2** *nm* serviceman; m. de carrière professional soldier

militant, -e [militɑ̃, -ɑ̃t] *adj & nm,f* militant

militantisme [militɑ̃tism] *nm* militancy

militarisation [militarizasjɔ̃] *nf* militarization

militariser [militarize] *vt* to militarize

militariste [militarist] **1** *adj* militaristic **2** *nmf* militarist

militer [milite] *vi* to campaign (pour *ou* en faveur de/ contre for/against)

milk-shake *(pl* milk-shakes) [milkʃɛk] *nm* milk shake

mille¹ [mil] **1** *adj inv* (**a**) *(cardinal)* a *or* one thousand; deux m. two thousand; l'an m. the year one thousand (**b**) *Fig (nombreux) (exemples, occasions)* countless; je vous l'ai dit m. fois I've told you a thousand times; vous avez m. fois raison you're absolutely right; c'est m. fois trop grand it's far too big **2** *nm inv* (**a**) *(nombre)* a *or* one thousand; plusieurs centaines de m. several hundred thousand; cinq pour m. five per thousand (**b**) *(locutions)* mettre (en plein) dans le m. to hit the bull's-eye; gagner des m. et des cents to make a mint; *voir aussi* trois

mille² *nm* m. (marin *ou* nautique) nautical mile

mille-feuille *(pl* mille-feuilles) [milfœj] *nm Br* ≃ vanilla slice, millefeuille, *Am* ≃ napoleon

millénaire [milenɛr] **1** *adj* thousand-year-old **2** *nm* millennium

mille-pattes [milpat] *nm inv* centipede, millipede

millepertuis [milpɛrtɥi] *nm* St John's wort

millésime [milezim] *nm (de vin, de voiture)* year; *(sur pièce de monnaie)* date

millésimé, -e [milezime] *adj (vin)* vintage; *(pièce de monnaie)* dated

millet [mijɛ] *nm* millet

milliard [miljar] *nm* billion

milliardaire [miljardɛr] **1** *adj* billionaire; être m. to be a billionaire; être plusieurs fois m. to be worth billions **2** *nmf* billionaire

millibar [milibar] *nm* millibar

millième [miljɛm] *nmf, nm & adj* thousandth; *voir aussi* cinquième

millier [milje] *nm* thousand; un m. de personnes a thousand people; des milliers de personnes thousands of people; par milliers in thousands

milligramme [miligram] *nm* milligram(me)

millilitre [mililitr] *nm* millilitre

millimètre [milimɛtr] *nm* millimetre
millimétré, -e [milimetre], **millimétrique** [milimetrik] *adj voir* papier
million [miljɔ̃] *nm* million; **un m. d'euros** a million euros; **quatre millions d'hommes** four million men; **par millions** in millions
millionnaire [miljɔnɛr] **1** *adj* millionaire; **être m.** to be a millionaire
 2 *nmf* millionaire
millivolt [milivɔlt] *nm* millivolt
mime [mim] **1** *nm (art)* mime
 2 *nmf (artiste)* mime (artist)
mimer [mime] *vt* (**a**) *(exprimer)* to mime (**b**) *(imiter)* to mimic
mimétisme [mimetism] *nm* mimicry
mimi [mimi] **1** *nm (langage enfantin)* kiss; **faire un m. à qn** to give sb a kiss
 2 *adj inv Fam (mignon)* sweet
mimique [mimik] *nf* expression
mimolette [mimɔlɛt] *nf* = type of Dutch hard cheese
mimosa [mimoza] *nm* mimosa
min *(abrév* **minute(s)**) min
min. *(abrév* **minimum**) min
minable [minabl] **1** *adj* (**a**) *(mesquin, pauvre)* shabby (**b**) *(incompétent, insuffisant)* pathetic
 2 *nmf* failure, loser
minaret [minarɛ] *nm* minaret
minauder [minode] *vi* to simper
minauderie [minodri] *nf* simpering; **faire des minauderies** to simper
mince [mɛ̃s] **1** *adj* (**a**) *(fin) (tranche, mur)* thin; *(taille, personne)* slim (**b**) *(insuffisant)* slight; **c'est un peu m., comme excuse!** it's a bit of a poor excuse!
 2 *exclam Fam* **m. (alors)!** *(surprise)* well, blow me!; *(déception)* blast!
minceur [mɛ̃sœr] *nf* (**a**) *(d'une tranche, d'un tissu)* thinness; *(de la taille, d'une personne)* slimness (**b**) *(insuffisance)* slightness
mincir [mɛ̃sir] *vi* to get slimmer
mine¹ [min] *nf* (**a**) *(gisement)* mine; *Fig* **une m. de renseignements** a mine of information; **m. de charbon** coalmine; *aussi Fig* **m. d'or** goldmine (**b**) *(de crayon)* lead (**c**) *(explosif)* mine (**d**) **les Mines** = government department responsible for supervising all construction projects involving tunnelling; **École des Mines,** *Fam* **les Mines** = university-level institute for geological engineers
mine² *nf* (**a**) *(expression)* look; **avoir bonne/mauvaise m.** to look well/ill; **avoir une m. de papier mâché** *ou* **de déterré** to look like death warmed up; **faire** *ou* **avoir triste m.** to look down in the dumps; **faire grise m.** not to look pleased; **faire m. de faire qch** to make as if to do sth (**b**) *(allure)* appearance; **juger les gens sur la m.** to judge people by appearances; *Fam* **ne pas payer de m.** not to be much to look at; *Fam* **m. de rien, il n'est pas bête** you wouldn't think it to look at him, but he's not stupid (**c**) *Péj* **mines** *(simagrées)* faces; **faire des mines** to make faces
miner¹ [mine] *vt* (**a**) *(creuser)* to eat away (**b**) *(ruiner moralement)* to wear down
miner² *vt (poser des explosifs dans)* to mine
minerai [minrɛ] *nm* ore; **m. de fer** iron ore
minéral, -e, -aux, -ales [mineral, -o] *adj & nm* mineral
minéralogique [mineralɔʒik] *adj* (**a**) **plaque m.** *Br* number *or Am* license plate (**b**) *Géol* mineralogical

minerve [minɛrv] *nf* (surgical) collar
minestrone [minɛstron] *nm* minestrone
minet, -ette [minɛ, -ɛt] *nm,f Fam* (**a**) *(chat)* pussy cat (**b**) *(personne coquette)* trendy
mineur¹ [minœr] *nm (ouvrier)* miner; **m. de fond** underground worker
mineur², -e 1 *adj* (**a**) *(secondaire)* minor (**b**) *(qui n'a pas la majorité légale)* underage (**c**) *Mus* minor
 2 *nm,f* minor
mini [mini] *Fam* **1** *adj inv (jupe, robe)* mini
 2 *nm* (**a**) *(mode)* **le m.** miniskirts (**b**) *(mini-ordinateur)* mini
miniature [minjatyr] **1** *nf* miniature; **en m.** in miniature
 2 *adj* miniature
miniaturiser [minjatyrize] *vt* to miniaturize
minibus [minibys] *nm* minibus
minichaîne [miniʃɛn] *nf* mini-hifi
MiniDisc® [minidisk] *nm* MiniDisc®
mini-écouteur (*pl* **mini-écouteurs**) [miniekutør] *nm* earbud, in-ear headphone
minier, -ère [minje, -ɛr] *adj* mining
minigolf [minigɔlf] *nm* crazy golf
minijupe [miniʒyp] *nf* miniskirt
minima [minima] *voir* **minimum**
minimal, -e, -aux, -ales [minimal, -o] *adj* minimum; *(art)* minimal
minimaliste [minimalist] *adj & nmf* minimalist
minime [minim] **1** *adj* minimal
 2 *nmf Sport* junior *(13 to 15 years old)*
mini-message [minimesaʒ] *nm* text message
minimiser [minimize] *vt* to minimize
minimum [minimɔm] *(pl* **minimums** *ou* **minima** [minima]) **1** *adj* minimum
 2 *nm* minimum; **avec un m. d'efforts** with a minimum of effort; **en un m. de temps** in as short a time as possible; **réduire qch au m.** to minimize sth; **faire le m. (pour faire qch)** to do the bare minimum (to do sth); **c'est vraiment le m. que tu puisses faire pour elle** it's the very least you can do for her; **au m.** at the very least; **le m. vital** a minimum to live on; **le strict m.** the absolute minimum; **m. vieillesse** basic state pension
mini-ordinateur (*pl* **mini-ordinateurs**) [miniɔrdinatœr] *nm* minicomputer
minipilule [minipilyl] *nf* mini pill
mini-slip (*pl* **mini-slips**) [minislip] *nm* thong
ministère [ministɛr] *nm* (**a**) *(département)* government department, *Br* ministry; **m. des Affaires étrangères** *Br* ≃ Foreign Office, *Am* ≃ State Department; **m. de la Défense (nationale)** *Br* ≃ Ministry of Defence, *Am* ≃ Department of Defense; **m. de l'Éducation nationale** Department of Education (**b**) *(gouvernement)* government (**c**) *Jur* **le m. public** ≃ the Crown Prosecution Service (**d**) *Rel* ministry
ministériel, -elle [ministerjɛl] *adj (arrêté, décret, entourage)* ministerial; *(crise, remaniement)* cabinet
ministre [ministr] *nm* (**a**) minister, *Br* minister; **m. des Affaires étrangères** *Br* ≃ Foreign Secretary, *Am* ≃ Secretary of State; **m. de la Défense (nationale)** ≃ Secretary of State for Defence; **m. de l'Éducation nationale** ≃ Secretary of State for Education; **m. d'État** ≃ secretary of state, *Br* ≃ cabinet minister; **m. de la Justice** *Br* ≃ Lord (High) Chancellor, *Am* ≃ Attorney General; **Premier m.** Prime Minister; *Can (d'une province)* Premier (**b**) *(pasteur)* minister; **m. du culte** minister

Minitel® [minitɛl] *nm* = consumer information network accessible via home computer terminal; **le M. rose** = dating and erotic entertainment service available on Minitel®

Minitel®

The domestic viewdata service run by France Télécom has become a familiar part of French life. The basic monitor and keyboard are given free of charge, and the subscriber is charged for the services used on his or her ordinary telephone bill. The subscriber dials a four-figure number (typically 3615); a code word then gives access to the particular service required. Some Minitel® services are purely informative (the weather, road conditions, news etc); others are interactive (enabling users to carry out bank transactions, book tickets for travel, register for and obtain the results of nationwide examinations, for example). The Minitel® also serves as an electronic telephone directory. Nowadays the services offered by Minitel® are increasingly available on the Internet.

minitéliste [minitelist] *nmf* Minitel® user
minois [minwa] *nm* pretty face
minorer [minɔre] *vt* (**a**) *(minimiser)* to downplay (**b**) *(faire baisser)* to reduce
minoritaire [minɔritɛr] *adj* minority; **être m.** to be in the minority
minorité [minɔrite] *nf* (**a**) *(de choses, de personnes)* minority; **être en m.** to be in the minority; **m. ethnique** ethnic minority (**b**) *(avant la majorité légale)* minority
Minorque [minɔrk] *n* Minorca
minorquin, -e [minɔrkɛ̃, -in] **1** *adj* Minorcan
 2 *nm,f* **M.** Minorcan
minoterie [minɔtri] *nf* (*moulin*) flour mill; *(activité)* flour-milling
minou [minu] *nm* (**a**) *Fam (chat)* pussy cat (**b**) *Can (boule de poussière)* dust bunny
Minsk [minsk] *n* Minsk
minuit [minɥi] *nm* midnight, twelve o'clock
minuscule [minyskyl] **1** *adj* (**a**) *(très petit)* tiny, minute (**b**) *(lettre)* small
 2 *nf* small letter
minute [minyt] **1** *nf* (**a**) *(unité de temps)* minute; **une m. de silence** a minute's silence; **de dernière m.** last-minute; **faire qch à la m.** to do sth this very minute; **d'une m. à l'autre** any minute (**b**) *(court moment)* minute, moment; **la m. de vérité** the moment of truth; **m.!** hold on a minute! (**c**) *(de contrat)* minute; *(d'acte notarié, de jugement)* record
 2 *adj (sur panneau)* **nettoyage m.** dry-cleaning while you wait; **talons m.** heel bar
minuter [minyte] *vt* to time
minuterie [minytri] *nf (pour l'éclairage)* time switch; *(d'un four)* timer
minuteur [minytœr] *nm* timer
minutie [minysi] *nf* meticulousness; **avec m.** meticulously
minutieusement [minysjøzmɑ̃] *adv* meticulously
minutieux, -euse [minysjø, -øz] *adj* meticulous
mioche [mjɔʃ] *nmf Fam* kid
MIPS [mips] *nm Ordinat (abrév* **million d'instructions par seconde)** MIPS
mirabelle [mirabɛl] *nf* mirabelle plum

miracle [mirakl] **1** *nm* miracle; **faire un m.** to perform a miracle; *Fig* **faire des miracles** to work miracles; **par m.** by a miracle, miraculously
 2 *adj inv* miracle
miraculé, -e [mirakyle] **1** *adj (malade)* miraculously cured; *(rescapé)* miraculously saved
 2 *nm,f (malade)* miraculously cured person; *(rescapé)* miraculous survivor
miraculeusement [mirakyløzmɑ̃] *adv* miraculously
miraculeux, -euse [mirakylø, -øz] *adj* miraculous
mirador [miradɔr] *nm* watchtower
mirage [miraʒ] *nm* mirage
mire [mir] *nf* test card
mirer [mire] **se mirer** *vpr Litt* (**a**) *(se regarder)* to gaze at oneself (**b**) *(se refléter)* to be reflected
mirettes [mirɛt] *nfpl Fam* eyes, *Br* peepers
mirifique [mirifik] *adj* wonderful
miro [miro] *adj Fam* short-sighted
mirobolant, -e [mirɔbɔlɑ̃, -ɑ̃t] *adj* fabulous
miroir [mirwar] *nm* mirror; *Fig* **m. aux alouettes** lure; **m. de courtoisie** vanity mirror; **m. grossissant** magnifying mirror; **m. de poche** pocket mirror
miroiter [mirwate] *vi* to shimmer; *Fig* **faire m. qch à qn** to lure sb with the prospect of sth
miroton [mirɔtɔ̃] *nm* = beef boiled in sauce with onions
mis, -e¹ *pp de* mettre
misanthrope [mizɑ̃trɔp] **1** *adj* misanthropic
 2 *nmf* misanthropist, misanthrope
mise² [miz] *nf* (**a**) *(placement)* putting; **m. en accusation** committal (for trial); **m. en application** implementation; **m. en demeure** formal demand; **m. en disponibilité** leave of absence; *Can* layoff; **m. en examen** indictment; **m. à feu** *(d'une fusée)* launch; **m. de fonds** investment; **m. en garde** warning; **m. à jour** updating; **m. en liberté provisoire** release on bail; **m. à mort** killing; **m. en page(s)** page make-up; **m. à pied** *(disciplinaire)* suspension; *Can* layoff; **m. en place** putting into place; **m. en plis** set *(hairstyle)*; **m. au point** *(d'un objectif)* focusing; *(d'une technique)* perfecting; *(d'un moteur)* tuning; *(d'un document, d'un rapport)* finalization; *Fig* **faire une m. au point** to make things clear; **m. en route** start-up; **m. en scène** *(d'une pièce de théâtre)* production; *(d'un film)* direction; **m. en service** *(d'une machine)* commissioning; **m. en vigueur** implementation (**b**) *(habillement)* attire (**c**) *(au jeu)* stake; *(à une vente aux enchères)* bid; *Fig* **sauver la m. à qn** to get sb out of a tight spot (**d**) **être de m.** to be appropriate (**e**) *Ordinat* **m. en attente des fichiers à imprimer** printer spooling; **m. en forme** formatting; **m. en mémoire** saving; **m. en relation** *(avec un service)* log-on; **m. en réseau** networking; **m. hors tension** power-down; **m. sous tension** power-up (**f**) *Suisse (vente)* auction (sale)
miser [mize] *vt* to stake (**sur** on); **m. sur qn/qch** *(parier)* to bet on sb/sth; *(compter sur)* to count on sb/sth; **m. sur tous les tableaux** to hedge one's bets
misérabilisme [mizerabilism] *nm* sordid realism
misérabiliste [mizerabilist] *adj* sordidly realistic
misérable [mizerabl] **1** *adj* (**a**) *(indigent) (personne)* poor; *(condition, existence)* wretched (**b**) *(pitoyable, insignifiant)* miserable
 2 *nmf* (**a**) *(personne indigente)* poor wretch (**b**) *(coquin, fripouille)* scoundrel
misérablement [mizerabləmɑ̃] *adv* (**a**) *(pauvrement)* wretchedly (**b**) *(pitoyablement)* miserably

misère [mizɛr] *nf* (**a**) *(indigence)* extreme poverty; **être dans la m.** to be poverty-stricken; **être dans une m. noire** to be destitute; **salaire de m.** starvation wage (**b**) *(ennui)* trouble; **faire des misères à qn** to give sb trouble (**c**) *(vétille)* **payer qch une m.** to pay next to nothing for sth

miséreux, -euse [mizerø, -øz] *adj* poverty-stricken

miséricorde [mizerikɔrd] **1** *nf* mercy
2 *exclam Vieilli* mercy!

miséricordieux, -euse [mizerikɔrdjø, -øz] *adj* merciful (**envers** to)

misogyne [mizɔʒin] **1** *adj* misogynous
2 *nmf* misogynist

misogynie [mizɔʒini] *nf* misogyny

miss (*pl* **miss** *ou* **misses**) [mis] *nf* *(reine de beauté)* beauty queen; **M. Monde/France** Miss World/France

missel [misɛl] *nm* missal

missile [misil] *nm* missile; **m. guidé** guided missile, smart missile

mission [misjɔ̃] *nf* (**a**) *(tâche)* mission; *(d'un employé)* task; **partir en m.** *(cadre)* to go away on business; *(diplomate)* to go off on a mission (**b**) *(groupe)* delegation; **m. scientifique** scientific expedition (**c**) *Rel (vocation, organisation)* mission; *(bâtiment)* mission (station)

missionnaire [misjɔnɛr] *adj & nmf* missionary

Mississippi [misisipi] *nm (fleuve)* **le M.** the Mississippi

missive [misiv] *nf Litt* missive

mistral [mistral] *nm* mistral

mitaine [mitɛn] *nf* fingerless glove; *Can & Suisse (moufle)* mitten

mite [mit] *nf* moth; **rongé aux mites** moth-eaten

mité, -e [mite] *adj* moth-eaten

mi-temps [mitɑ̃] **1** *nf inv (moitié)* half; *(pause)* half-time
2 *nm inv* part-time job; **travailler** *ou* **être à m.** to work part-time

miteux, -euse [mitø, -øz] *adj* shabby

mitigé, -e [mitiʒe] *adj (enthousiasme, accueil)* lukewarm; *(sentiments, impressions)* mixed

mitigeur [mitiʒœr] *nm* mixer *Br* tap *or Am* faucet

mitonner [mitɔne] **1** *vt* (**a**) *(cuire à feu doux)* to simmer (**b**) *Fig (projet)* to concoct
2 *vi* to simmer

mitoyen, -enne [mitwajɛ̃, -ɛn] *adj (mur)* party; **maisons mitoyennes** *(deux)* semi-detached houses; *(rangée)* terraced houses

mitrailler [mitraje] *vt* to machine-gun; *Fig* **m. qn de questions** to bombard sb with questions

mitraillette [mitrajɛt] *nf* submachine gun

mitrailleuse [mitrajøz] *nf* machine gun

mitre [mitr] *nf* (**a**) *(d'évêque)* mitre (**b**) *(de cheminée)* cowl

mi-voix [mivwa] **à mi-voix** *adv* in a low voice

mixage [miksaʒ] *nm* mixing

mixer¹ [mikse] *vt* (**a**) *(film)* to mix (**b**) *(ingrédients) (mélanger)* to mix; *(réduire à l'état liquide)* to blend

mixer², mixeur [miksœr] *nm (pour mélanger)* mixer; *(pour réduire à l'état liquide)* blender

mixité [miksite] *nf* coeducation

mixte [mikst] *adj* (**a**) *(des deux sexes)* mixed; **double m.** *(au tennis)* mixed doubles (**b**) *(combiné) (commission)* joint; *(mariage)* mixed; *(cuisinière)* gas-and-electric

mixture [mikstyr] *nf* (**a**) *(pharmaceutique)* mixture (**b**) *Fig* concoction

MJC [ɛmʒise] *nf* (*abrév* **maison des jeunes et de la culture**) community centre

ml (*abrév* **millilitre(s)**) ml

MLF [ɛmɛlɛf] *nm* (*abrév* **Mouvement de libération des femmes**) ≃ Women's Liberation Movement

Mlle (*abrév* **Mademoiselle**) Miss

Mlles (*abrév* **Mesdemoiselles**) **M. Armand et Duchêne** Miss Armand and Miss Duchêne

MM (*abrév* **Messieurs**) Messrs

mm (*abrév* **millimètre(s)**) mm

Mme (*abrév* **Madame**) Mrs

Mmes (*abrév* **Mesdames**) **M. Binoche et Huppert** Mrs Binoche and Mrs Huppert

MMS [ɛmɛmɛs] *nm Tél* (*abrév* **multimedia message service**) MMS

Mo *nm Ordinat* (*abrév* **méga-octet(s)**) Mb

mobile [mɔbil] **1** *adj* (**a**) *(cloison)* movable; *(feuillets)* loose; *(cible)* moving (**b**) *(expression, regard)* shifting; *(visage)* lively (**c**) *(personne âgée, main d'œuvre, population)* mobile
2 *nm* (**a**) *(motif)* motive (**de** for) (**b**) *(objet décoratif)* mobile (**c**) *(objet en mouvement)* moving body (**d**) *(téléphone portable) Br* mobile (phone), *Am* cell(phone)

mobile home (*pl* **mobile homes**) [mɔbilom] *nm Br* mobile home, *Am* RV

mobilier, -ère [mɔbilje, -ɛr] **1** *adj Jur* movable
2 *nm* furniture

mobilisation [mɔbilizasjɔ̃] *nf* mobilization; **m. générale** general mobilization

mobiliser [mɔbilize] **1** *vt* to mobilize; *Fig (énergie, courage)* to summon up
2 se mobiliser *vpr* to mobilize (**contre/en faveur de** against/in support of)

mobilité [mɔbilite] *nf* mobility

Mobylette® [mɔbilɛt] *nf* moped

mocassin [mɔkasɛ̃] *nm* moccasin

moche [mɔʃ] *adj Fam* (**a**) *(laid)* ugly (**b**) *(moralement)* rotten

modal, -e, -aux, -ales [mɔdal, -o] *adj* modal

modalité [mɔdalite] *nf* (**a**) *(manière)* mode; **modalités de paiement** conditions of payment (**b**) *(d'un acte juridique)* clause

mode¹ [mɔd] **1** *adj inv* **c'est très m.** it's very fashionable
2 *nf* (**a**) *(vestimentaire, de consommation)* fashion; **à la m.** fashionable; **revenir à la m.** to come back into fashion (**b**) *(manière)* **à la m. de Lyon/Provence** Lyons/Provence style

mode² *nm* (**a**) *(manière)* **m. de** means of; **m. de cuisson** cooking instructions; **m. d'emploi** instructions; **m. de paiement** means of payment; **m. de transport** mode of transport; **m. de vie** way of life (**b**) *Gram* mood (**c**) *Mus* mode (**d**) *Ordinat* mode; **m. paysage/portrait** landscape/portrait mode

modèle [mɔdɛl] **1** *adj (parfait)* model; *(appartement, maison)* show
2 *nm* (**a**) *(exemple)* model; **prendre qn pour m.** to take sb as one's model; **m. de lettre** standard letter (**b**) *(personne)* **m. de générosité/fidélité** model of generosity/fidelity; **m. de vertu** paragon of virtue (**c**) *(exemplaire) (de voiture, d'appareil)* model; *(de robe)* style; *(de tricot)* pattern; **vous n'auriez pas un plus grand m.?** do you have it in a larger size?; **m. déposé** registered design (**d**) *(d'un peintre, d'un sculpteur)* model (**e**) *(maquette)* **m. réduit** small-scale model

modeler [39] [mɔdle] **1** *vt (argile, pot)* to model; *Fig (relief, caractère, destinée)* to shape; **m. sa personnalité sur celle de qn** to model oneself on sb
2 se modeler *vpr* **se m. sur qn** to model oneself on sb
modélisme [mɔdelism] *nm* model-making
modem [mɔdɛm] *nm Ordinat* modem; **carte m.** modem card; **m. fax** fax modem
modem-câble (*pl* **modems-câbles**) [mɔdɛmkɑbl] *nm Ordinat* cable modem
modérateur, -trice [mɔderatœr, -tris] **1** *adj* moderating
2 *nm,f (personne)* moderator
3 *nm (de moteur)* regulator
modération [mɔderasjɔ̃] *nf* (**a**) *(retenue)* moderation; **avec m.** in moderation; **à consommer avec m.** *(dans les publicités)* drink in moderation *(health warning on all products advertising alcoholic drinks)* (**b**) *(réduction)* reduction
modéré, -e [mɔdere] *adj & nm,f* moderate
modérément [mɔderemɑ̃] *adv* moderately; *Euph* **j'ai m.** **apprécié sa remarque** I didn't much appreciate his/her remark
modérer [34] [mɔdere] **1** *vt* (**a**) *(passions, désirs, envies)* to moderate, to restrain; *Hum* **modère tes ardeurs!** control yourself!; **je te prie de m. ton langage!** please mind your language! (**b**) *(prix, vitesse)* to reduce
2 se modérer *vpr (personne)* to calm down
moderne [mɔdɛrn] **1** *adj* modern
2 *nm* **le m.** the modern style
modernisation [mɔdɛrnizasjɔ̃] *nf* modernization
moderniser [mɔdɛrnize] **1** *vt* to modernize
2 se moderniser *vpr* to modernize
modernisme [mɔdɛrnism] *nm* modernism
moderniste [mɔdɛrnist] *adj & nmf* modernist
modernité [mɔdɛrnite] *nf* modernity
modeste [mɔdɛst] **1** *adj* modest
2 *nmf* **faire le m.** to be modest
modestement [mɔdɛstəmɑ̃] *adv* modestly; **être m. logé** to live in modest surroundings
modestie [mɔdɛsti] *nf* modesty; **fausse m.** false modesty
modeux, -euse [mɔdø, -øz] *nm,f Fam* fashionista
modicité [mɔdisite] *nf* lowness
modifiable [mɔdifjabl] *adj* modifiable
modification [mɔdifikasjɔ̃] *nf* alteration, modification; **apporter** *ou* **faire une m. à qch** to make an alteration to sth
modifier [66] [mɔdifje] **1** *vt* to alter, to modify; *Gram* to modify
2 se modifier *vpr* to alter
modique [mɔdik] *adj* modest
modiste [mɔdist] *nmf* milliner
modulable [mɔdylabl] *adj (horaires)* flexible; *(éclairage, chauffage)* adjustable
modulaire [mɔdylɛr] *adj* modular
modulation [mɔdylasjɔ̃] *nf* (**a**) *(des sons, de la voix)* modulation (**b**) *(adaptation)* adjustment (**en fonction de** in relation to) (**c**) *Rad* modulation; **m. de fréquence** frequency modulation
module [mɔdyl] *nm* (**a**) *(élément d'un tout)* unit; **m. (d'enseignement)** module (**b**) *(d'un vaisseau spatial)* module; **m. lunaire/de commande** lunar/command module (**c**) *Ordinat* **m. d'extension** plug-in

moduler [mɔdyle] **1** *vt* (**a**) *(sons, amplitude, voix)* to modulate (**b**) *(adapter)* to adjust (**en fonction de** in relation to)
2 *vi* to modulate
modus vivendi [mɔdysvivɛ̃di] *nm inv* modus vivendi
moelle [mwal] *nf* marrow; *Fig* **jusqu'à la m.** to the core; **m. épinière** spinal cord; **m. osseuse** bone marrow
moelleusement [mwaløzmɑ̃] *adv* snugly
moelleux, -euse [mwalø, -øz] *adj* (**a**) *(au toucher)* soft (**b**) *(fromage, vin)* smooth; *(gâteau)* spongy
moellon [mwalɔ̃] *nm* quarry stone
mœurs [mœr, mœrs] *nfpl* (**a**) *(coutumes)* customs; **entrer** *ou* **passer dans les m.** to become part of everyday life (**b**) *(d'animaux)* habits (**c**) *(sens moral)* morals; **bonnes m.** morality; **contraire aux bonnes m.** contrary to accepted standards of behaviour; **femme de m. légères** *ou* **faciles** woman of easy virtue
mohair [mɔɛr] *nm* mohair; **un pull en m.** a mohair sweater
moi [mwa] **1** *pron personnel* (**a**) *(sujet)* I; **qui vient avec nous? – m.** who's coming with us? – I am *or* me; **m., quand je serai grand...** when I grow up,...; **m., je n'aurais pas fait comme ça** I wouldn't have done it like that (**b**) *(objet direct)* me; **et m., tu m'oublies?** and what about me, have you forgotten me? (**c**) *(avec préposition)* me; **fais-m. voir, à m.** show ME; **ce livre est à m.** this book is mine; **j'ai mes petits secrets à m.** I've got my own little secrets; *Fam* **un ami à m.** a friend of mine; **à m.!** help!; **je ne le fais pas que pour m.** I'm not doing it just for myself (**d**) *(dans les comparaisons)* me; **elle boit plus que m.** she drinks more than me *or* than I do
2 *nm* ego, self
moignon [mwaɲɔ̃] *nm* stump
moi-même [mwamɛm] *pron personnel* myself
moindre [mwɛ̃dr] *adj* (**a**) *(comparatif)* lesser; *(prix)* lower; *(quantité)* smaller; *(vitesse)* slower; **c'est un m. mal** it's not as bad as it might have been (**b**) *(superlatif)* **le/la m.** the least; **pas la m. chance/idée** not the slightest chance/idea; **au m. reproche** at the slightest reproach; **dans les moindres détails** in the smallest detail; **c'est la m. des choses** it's the least I/he/*etc* can do; **on a fait venir un expert, et non des moindres** we called in an expert, and not just any old one
moine [mwan] *nm* monk
moineau, -x [mwano] *nm* sparrow
moins [mwɛ̃] **1** *adv* (**a**) *(comparatif)* less; **je gagne m. que vous** I earn less than you (do); **elle est m. intelligente que sa sœur** she's not as intelligent as her sister; **il n'est pas m. nerveux que toi** he's no less nervous than you (are); **m. de** *(argent, patience)* less; *(hommes, occasions)* fewer; *(avec un nombre)* less than; **elle a m. de vingt ans** she's under twenty; **tu feras d'exercice, plus tu grossiras** the less exercise you do, the fatter you'll get; **de m. en m.** less and less; **celui-ci coûte 10 euros de m. que l'autre** this one costs 10 euros less than the other one; **il y a eu 20% de visiteurs de m.** *ou* **en m.** there have been 20% fewer visitors; **il n'en est pas m. vrai que...** the fact remains that... (**b**) *(superlatif)* **le m.** the least; **c'est celui qui me plaît le m.** that's the one I like (the) least; **les élèves les m. appliqués** the least industrious pupils; **pas le m. du monde** not in the least *or* slightest (**c**) *(locutions)* **à m. d'un imprévu/d'un**

miracle barring unforeseen circumstances/a miracle; **à m.** de partir tout de suite unless I/you/*etc* leave at once; **à m. que...** + *subjunctive* unless...; **au m.** at least; *Fam* **tu as fait ton travail, au m.?** you've done your work, I hope?; **du m.** at least; **c'est pour le m.** surprenant it's surprising, to say the least; *Fam* **un m. que rien** a nobody **2** *prép (dans les calculs, les températures)* minus; **une heure m.** cinq five (minutes) to one; **il est m.** vingt it's twenty to; *Fam* **il était m.** une it was a close shave *or* a near thing **3** *nm (signe)* minus (sign)
moins-value (*pl* **moins-values**) [mwɛ̃valy] *nf Fin* depreciation; *(après une vente)* capital loss
moire [mwar] *nf* moire
moiré, -e [mware] *adj* (**a**) *(tissu)* watered, moiré (**b**) *(aux reflets changeants)* shimmering
mois [mwa] *nm* (**a**) *(période)* month; **au m. d'août** in August; **un m. de vacances/salaire** a month's holiday/wages (**b**) *(paie mensuelle)* monthly salary; **treizième m.** extra month's salary *(paid as an annual bonus)*
Moïse [mɔiz] *npr* Moses
moisi, -e [mwazi] **1** *adj (aliment)* mouldy; *(mur, livre)* mildewed **2** *nm (sur un aliment)* mould; *(sur un mur, un tissu)* mildew
moisir [mwazir] *vi* (**a**) *(aliment)* to go mouldy; *(mur, livre)* to go mildewed (**b**) *(personne) (stagner)* to moulder away; *(attendre longtemps)* to hang about; **m. en prison** to rot in prison
moisissure [mwazisyr] *nf* mould
moisson [mwasɔ̃] *nf* (**a**) *(récolte, époque)* harvest; **faire la m.** *ou* **les moissons** to harvest (**b**) *Fig (de documents, d'idées)* wealth
moissonner [mwasɔne] *vt* (**a**) *(céréales)* to harvest; *(champ)* to reap (**b**) *Fig (informations, idées)* to collect, to gather
moissonneur, -euse [mwasɔnœr, -øz] **1** *nm,f* harvester **2** *nf* **moissonneuse** *(machine)* harvester
moissonneuse-batteuse (*pl* **moissonneuses-batteuses**) [mwasɔnøzbatøz] *nf* combine harvester
moite [mwat] *adj (mains, front, chaleur)* sticky; *(atmosphère, air)* muggy
moiteur [mwatœr] *nf (des mains, du front)* stickiness; *(d'atmosphère, d'air)* mugginess
moitié [mwatje] *nf* (**a**) *(d'un tout)* half; **la m. des livres/de la journée** half (of) the books/the day; **m. anglais, m. écossais** half English, half Scottish; **c'est m. moins cher** it's half the price; *Fam* **m.-m.** fifty-fifty; **faire m.-m.** to go halves; **à m. plein/vide** half-full/-empty; **à m. mort** half-dead; **vendre qch à m. prix** to sell sth (at) half-price; **ne pas faire les choses à m.** not to do things by halves (**b**) *Fam (époux, épouse)* **ma m.** my other *or* better half
mojito [mɔito] *nm (cocktail)* mojito
moka [mɔka] *nm* (**a**) *(café)* mocha (**b**) *(gâteau)* coffee cake
molaire [mɔlɛr] *nf* molar
moldave [mɔldav] **1** *adj* Moldavian **2** *nmf* **M.** Moldavian
Moldavie [mɔldavi] *nf* **la M.** Moldavia
mole [mɔl] *nf Phys* mole
moléculaire [mɔlekylɛr] *adj* molecular
molécule [mɔlekyl] *nf* molecule
moleskine [mɔlɛskin] *nf* imitation leather

molester [mɔlɛste] *vt* to manhandle
molette [mɔlɛt] *nf* (**a**) *(de briquet, de clé)* wheel; *(de jumelles)* focus wheel (**b**) *(pour couper le verre)* cutting wheel
Molières [mɔljɛr] *nmpl* **les M.** *(cérémonie)* = French theatre awards ceremony
mollard [mɔlar] *nm très Fam* gob of spit
mollasson, -onne [mɔlasɔ̃, -ɔn] *Fam* **1** *adj (personne)* lethargic **2** *nm,f* lazy lump
molle [mɔl] *voir* **mou¹**
mollement [mɔlmã] *adv* (**a**) *(avec abandon)* languidly; *(avec lenteur)* gently (**b**) *(sans énergie)* feebly
mollesse [mɔlɛs] *nf* (**a**) *(d'un coussin, d'un matelas)* softness; *(de tissus, de muscles)* flabbiness (**b**) *(d'une personne)* lethargy; *(d'un gouvernement)* laxness; *(du style)* limpness
mollet¹ [mɔlɛ] *adj m (œuf)* soft-boiled
mollet² *nm* calf; **avoir des mollets de coq** to have spindly legs
molleton [mɔltɔ̃] *nm* (**a**) *(tissu) (en coton)* flannelette; *(en laine)* flannel (**b**) *(sous-nappe)* table felt
molletonné, -e [mɔltɔne] *adj* fleece-lined
mollir [mɔlir] *vi* (**a**) *(faiblir) (vent)* to die down; *(courage, enthousiasme)* to flag; **sentir ses jambes m.** to feel one's legs give way (**b**) *(devenir moins ferme) (matière)* to soften; *(sol)* to give way (**sous** beneath)
mollo [mɔlo] *adv Fam* **y aller m.** to take it easy
mollusque [mɔlysk] *nm* (**a**) *(animal)* mollusc (**b**) *Fam (personne)* lazy lump
molosse [mɔlɔs] *nm* big dog
môme [mom] *nmf Fam (enfant)* kid
moment [mɔmã] *nm* (**a**) *(point précis dans le temps)* moment; **arriver au bon m.** to arrive at just the right time; **le m. venu** *(dans le passé)* when the time came; *(dans l'avenir)* when the time comes; **c'est le m. ou jamais** it's now or never; **c'est le m. ou jamais de le faire** now's the time to do it; **au m. de qch** at the time of sth; **au m. où j'allais me coucher, le téléphone a sonné** just as I was going to bed, the phone rang; **à quel m. de sa vie?** at what point in his/her life?; **à un m. donné** at one point; **dans ces moments-là** at times like that; **d'un m. à l'autre** (at) any moment; **en ce m.** at the moment, just now; **jusqu'au m. où... until...;** **par moments** at times, now and again; **pour le m.** for the moment, for the time being; **sur le m.** at the time; **à tout m., à tous moments** *(sans cesse)* constantly; *(n'importe quand)* (at) any moment; **à un m.-là** then; *(dans ces conditions)* in that case (**b**) *(durée)* moment; **un m.!** just a moment!; **je suis à vous dans un m.** I'll be with you in a moment; **passer un bon m.** to have a good time; **passer un mauvais m.** to have a bad time of it; **à passer** it'll soon be over with; **j'en ai pour un m.** I'll be a while; **ne pas avoir un m. à soi** not to have a moment to oneself; **dans un m. de bonté** in a moment of kindness (**c**) *(temps présent)* **du m.** *(disque, star)* of the moment (**d**) *(locutions)* **du m. que...** seeing that...
momentané, -e [mɔmãtane] *adj (bref)* brief; *(temporaire)* temporary
momentanément [mɔmãtanemã] *adv (brièvement)* briefly; *(temporairement)* temporarily
momie [mɔmi] *nf (mort)* mummy
momifier [66] [mɔmifje] **1** *vt* to mummify **2** **se momifier** *vpr* to become fossilized

mon, ma, mes [mɔ̃, ma, me]

ma becomes **mon** before a word beginning with a vowel or mute h.

adj possessif (**a**) *(marquant la possession)* my; **m. chien** my dog; **ma voiture** my car; **m. ami/amie** my friend; **mes enfants** my children; **mon père et ma mère** my father and mother; **un de mes amis** one of my friends, a friend of mine; *Fam* **j'ai eu m. vendredi** I got Friday off (**b**) *(en s'adressant à quelqu'un)* **non, m. général** no, General
monacal, -e, -aux, -ales [mɔnakal, -o] *adj* monastic
Monaco [mɔnako] *nm* Monaco
monarchie [mɔnarʃi] *nf* monarchy
monarchique [mɔnarʃik] *adj* monarchical
monarchiste [mɔnarʃist] *adj & nmf* monarchist
monarque [mɔnark] *nm* monarch
monastère [mɔnastɛr] *nm (d'hommes)* monastery; *(de femmes)* convent
monastique [mɔnastik] *adj* monastic
monceau, -x [mɔ̃so] *nm* heap, pile
mondain, -e [mɔ̃dɛ̃, -ɛn] **1** *adj* (**a**) *(soirée, journaliste)* society (**b**) *Péj (personne)* **être très m.** to be a great socialite
  2 *nm,f* socialite
  3 *nf Fam Vieilli* **la mondaine** the vice squad
mondanités [mɔ̃danite] *nfpl* (**a**) *(événements)* society life (**b**) *(politesses)* social niceties; *(conversations superficielles)* social chitchat
monde [mɔ̃d] *nm* (**a**) *(univers, humanité)* world; **l'autre m.** the next world; **dans le m. entier** *(connu, en vente)* worldwide, all over the world; **personne au m.** no one in the world; **pour rien au m.** not for anything in the world; **mettre un enfant au m.** to bring a child into the world; **venir au m.** to come into the world; *Litt* **il n'est plus de ce m.** he is no longer of this world; **les meilleurs amis du m.** the best friends in the world; **en ce bas m.** here on earth; *Fam* **c'est (quand même) un m.!** that's a bit much!; *Fam* **se faire un m. de qch** to get worked up about sth; **comme le m. est petit!** it's a small world!; **c'est le m. à l'envers** the world's gone mad (**b**) *(milieu)* world; **être du même m.** to belong to the same crowd; **le (beau) m.** (fashionable) society (**c**) *(gens)* people; **tout le m.** everyone, everybody; **il y a du m.** *(beaucoup de gens)* there are a lot of people; **peu de m., pas grand m.** not many people; **avoir du m. à dîner** to have people to dinner; **comment va tout votre petit m.?** how are all the family?; *Can* **le grand m.** the grown-ups, the adults (**d**) *(vie séculière)* world
mondial, -e, -aux, -ales [mɔ̃djal, -o] *adj* world, global; **guerre mondiale** world war
mondialement [mɔ̃djalmɑ̃] *adv* throughout the world
mondialisation [mɔ̃djalizasjɔ̃] *nf* globalization
mondialiser [mɔ̃djalize] **1** *vt* to globalize
  2 se mondialiser *vpr* to become globalized
monégasque [mɔnegask] **1** *adj* Monegasque
  2 *nmf* **M.** Monegasque
monétaire [mɔnetɛr] *adj (unité, système, questions)* monetary; *(marché)* money
monétarisme [mɔnetarism] *nm* monetarism
monétariste [mɔnetarist] *adj & nmf* monetarist
Monétique® [mɔnetik] *nf* electronic banking, e-banking

mongol, -e [mɔ̃gɔl] **1** *adj* Mongolian
  2 *nm,f* **M.** Mongolian
  3 *nm (langue)* Mongolian
Mongolie [mɔ̃gɔli] *nf* **la M.** Mongolia
mongolien, -enne [mɔ̃gɔljɛ̃, -ɛn] **1** *adj* **être m.** to have Down's syndrome
  2 *nm,f (bébé)* Down's syndrome baby; *(personne)* person with Down's syndrome
mongolisme [mɔ̃gɔlism] *nm* Down's syndrome
moniteur, -trice [mɔnitœr, -tris] **1** *nm,f* (**a**) *(d'activités sportives, d'auto-école)* instructor (**b**) *(dans une colonie de vacances)* Br assistant, Am (camp) counselor
  2 *nm aussi Ordinat* monitor; **m. cardiaque** heart monitor
monitoring [mɔnitɔriŋ] *nm* monitoring
monnaie [mɔnɛ] *nf* (**a**) *(argent)* money; *(d'un pays)* currency; **m. électronique** electronic money; *UE* **m. unique** single currency; **fausse m.** counterfeit money; **m. courante** legal currency; *Fig* **c'est m. courante dans ce milieu** it's common in these circles; **m. légale** legal tender; *Fam* **m. de singe** Monopoly money; *Fig* **payer qn en m. de singe** to fob sb off (**b**) *(pièces)* change; **avoir la m. de 50 euros** to have change for 50 euros; **faire (de) la m.** to get some change; **faire la m. de 50 euros** to get change for 50 euros; **petite** *ou* **menue m.** small change
monnayable [mɔnɛjabl] *adj* convertible into cash; *Fig* **être m.** *(expérience, information)* to be worth money
monnayer [53] [mɔneje] **1** *vt* (**a**) *(terrains, biens)* to convert into cash (**b**) *(expérience, information)* to cash in on
  2 se monnayer *vpr* **ici tout se monnaye** money can buy you anything here
monnayeur [mɔnɛjœr] *nm (appareil)* change machine
monochrome [mɔnokrom] *adj* monochrome
monocle [mɔnɔkl] *nm* monocle
monocoque [mɔnɔkɔk] *nm* monohull
monocorde [mɔnokɔrd] *adj* monotonous
monoculture [mɔnokyltyr] *nf* monoculture
monogame [mɔnɔgam] *adj* monogamous
monogamie [mɔnɔgami] *nf* monogamy
monogramme [mɔnɔgram] *nm* monogram
monoï [mɔnɔj] *nm inv* scented coconut oil
monokini [mɔnokini] *nm* monokini; **faire du m.** to go topless
monolingue [mɔnolɛ̃g] *adj* monolingual
monolithe [mɔnɔlit] *nm* monolith
monolithique [mɔnɔlitik] *adj aussi Fig* monolithic
monologue [mɔnolɔg] *nm* monologue; **m. intérieur** interior monologue
monologuer [mɔnologe] *vi* (**a**) *(monopoliser la parole)* to carry on a monologue (**b**) *(au théâtre)* to soliloquize
monôme [mɔnom] *nm Math* monomial
mononucléose [mɔnonykleoz] *nf* **m. (infectieuse)** glandular fever
monoparental, -e, -aux, -ales [mɔnoparɑ̃tal, -o] *adj (famille)* single-parent, one-parent
monoparentalité [mɔnoparɑ̃talite] *nf* single parenthood
monoplace [mɔnoplas] *adj & nm* single-seater
monopole [mɔnopɔl] *nm* monopoly; **avoir le m. de qch** to have a monopoly on sth; **m. d'État** state monopoly

monopoliser [mɔnɔpɔlize] *vt* to monopolize
monoposte [mɔnɔpɔst] *nm Ordinat* stand-alone
monoski [mɔnoski] *nm* monoski; **faire du m.** to monoski
monospace [mɔnospas] *nm* people carrier, people mover
monosyllabe [mɔnosilab] **1** *adj* monosyllabic **2** *nm* monosyllable
monosyllabique [mɔnosilabik] *adj* monosyllabic
mono-tâche [mɔnotɑʃ] *adj inv Ordinat* single-tasking
monothéisme [mɔnoteism] *nm* monotheism
monotone [mɔnɔtɔn] *adj* monotonous
monotonie [mɔnɔtɔni] *nf* monotony
monoxyde [mɔnɔksid] *nm* **m. de carbone** carbon monoxide
monseigneur [mɔ̃sɛɲœr] (*pl* **messeigneurs** [mesɛɲœr]) *nm* (**a**) *(titre) (d'un prince)* His Royal Highness; *(d'un cardinal)* His Eminence; *(d'un évêque)* His Lordship (**b**) *(en s'adressant au prince)* Your Royal Highness; *(au cardinal)* Your Eminence; *(à l'évêque)* Your Lordship
monsieur [mɔsjø] (*pl* **messieurs** [mesjø]) *nm* (**a**) *(titre)* **M. Robert Marceau** Mr Robert Marceau; **M. le Ministre** the Minister; *Fam* **m. je-sais-tout** Mr Know-it-all; **m. tout-le-monde** the man in the street (**b**) *(en apostrophe)* sir; **M. le Ministre** Minister; **au revoir, m.** goodbye; **M.,...**(*dans une lettre*) Dear Sir,...; *Fam* **et en plus, M. exige des excuses!** His Lordship wants an apology as well, does he?; **que prendront ces messieurs?** what will you have, gentlemen?; **bonsoir, messieurs-dames!** good evening everybody! (**c**) *(homme quelconque)* gentleman
monstre [mɔ̃str] **1** *adj Fam* huge; **j'ai un boulot m.** I've got loads *or* tons *or* piles of work to do **2** *nm* monster; **m. d'ingratitude/d'égoïsme** ungrateful/selfish monster; **petit m.!** you little monster!; **m. sacré** giant
monstrueusement [mɔ̃stryøzmɑ̃] *adv* monstrously
monstrueux, -euse [mɔ̃stryø, -øz] *adj* (**a**) *(malformé)* monstrous (**b**) *(énorme)* huge; **être d'un égoïsme m.** to be extremely selfish (**c**) *(scandaleux)* monstrous
monstruosité [mɔ̃stryozite] *nf* monstrosity
mont [mɔ̃] *nm* mountain; *Fig* **être toujours par monts et par vaux** to be always on the move; **le m. Blanc** Mont Blanc
montage [mɔ̃taʒ] *nm* (**a**) *(pose) (de bijou)* mounting; *(d'appareils)* assembling (**b**) *(d'un film)* editing; *(image truquée)* montage; **m. vidéo** video(tape) editing (**c**) *Écon* **m. financier** financial arrangement (**d**) *(d'installation électrique)* wiring (up)
montagnard, -e [mɔ̃taɲar, -ard] **1** *adj* mountain **2** *nm,f* mountain dweller
montagne [mɔ̃taɲ] *nf* (**a**) *(élévation)* mountain; *(région)* mountains; **à la m.** in the mountains; *Fig* **se faire une m. de qch** to make a great song and dance about sth; **en haute m.** high in the mountains (**b**) **faire de la m.** *(alpinisme)* to go mountain climbing; *(randonnée)* to go hill walking (**c**) *Fig (grande quantité)* **une m. de** a mountain of (**d**) **montagnes russes** *(attraction foraine)* big dipper, roller-coaster
montagneux, -euse [mɔ̃taɲø, -øz] *adj* mountainous
montant [mɔ̃tɑ̃] *nm* (**a**) *(somme)* amount; **versement d'un m. de 500 euros** payment of 500 euros; **montants**

compensatoires subsidies (**b**) *(d'échelle)* upright; *(de lit)* post; *(de fenêtre)* jamb
mont-de-piété (*pl* **monts-de-piété**) [mɔ̃dpjete] *nm* pawnshop
monté, -e [mɔ̃te] *adj (équipé)* **être bien m. (en qch)** to be well stocked (with sth); *Fam Fig* **être bien m.** to be well-hung
monte-charge (*pl* **monte-charges**) [mɔ̃tʃarʒ] *nm* goods *Br* lift *or Am* elevator
montée [mɔ̃te] *nf* (**a**) *(côte)* slope, hill (**b**) *(d'une côte)* climb; *(d'un avion)* ascent; **la m. des eaux** the rise in the water level (**c**) *(des prix)* rise (**de** in) (**d**) *(apparition) (du nationalisme, du fascisme)* rise, growth
monte-plats [mɔ̃tpla] *nm inv* dumb waiter
monter [mɔ̃te] **1** *vt* (*aux* **avoir**) (**a**) *(colline, escalier) (en s'éloignant)* to go up, to climb (up); *(en s'approchant)* to come up, to climb (up); **m. la rue en courant** to run up the street (**b**) *(porter en haut) (en s'éloignant)* to take up; *(en s'approchant)* to bring up (**c**) *(son, chauffage)* to turn up (**d**) *(assembler) (meuble)* to assemble; *(tente)* to put up; *(bijou, photo)* to mount (**e**) *(pièce de théâtre)* to put on, to stage (**f**) *(film)* to edit (**g**) *(créer) (entreprise, magasin)* to set up; *(complot)* to hatch; **m. un coup** to plan a job (**h**) *(trousseau)* to put together (**i**) *(en tricot)* **m. les mailles** to cast on (**j**) *(cheval)* to ride (**k**) *(locutions)* **m. la garde** to mount guard; **m. (la tête à) qn contre qn** to set sb against sb
2 *vi* (*aux* **être**) (**a**) *(aller vers le haut)* to go up; *(venir vers le haut)* to come up; *(oiseau)* to fly up; *(avion)* to climb; **m. se coucher** to go (up) to bed; **faire m. qn** to show sb up; **m. sur qch** to climb onto sth; **m. à qch** to climb (up) sth; **m. à Paris** *(y déménager)* to move up to Paris; *(en visite)* to go up to Paris; **m. à la tête à qn** *(sang)* to rush to sb's head; *Fig* to go to sb's head; **les larmes lui sont montées aux yeux** his/her eyes filled with tears (**b**) *(prendre place)* **m. dans qch** *(voiture, barque)* to get in sth; *(train, autobus, avion)* to get on sth; **m. sur qch** to get on sth; **m. à bord** to go on board; **m. à bicyclette** to ride a bicycle; **m. à cheval** to ride, to go riding; **m. en voiture** to get into a car (**c**) *(route)* to climb (**d**) *(prix, baromètre, marée)* to rise; **m. en flèche** *(prix)* to soar; **faire m. les prix** to put up prices; **m. à** *(s'élever à)* to amount to, to come to
3 se monter *vpr* (**a**) *(s'élever)* **se m. à** to come to, to amount to (**b**) *(s'équiper)* **se m. en qch** to provide oneself with sth (**c**) *Fam* **se m. la tête** *(s'exalter)* to get carried away with oneself
monteur, -euse [mɔ̃tœr, -øz] *nm,f Cin* editor
Montevideo [mɔ̃tevideo] *n* Montevideo
montgolfière [mɔ̃gɔlfjɛr] *nf* hot-air balloon
monticule [mɔ̃tikyl] *nm* hillock, mound
montre [mɔ̃tr] *nf* (**a**) *(instrument)* watch; **à ma m. il est midi** by my watch it's twelve o'clock; **m. en main** exactly; **m. de plongée** diver's watch; **m. à quartz** quartz watch (**b**) *(preuve)* **faire m. de qch** to show sth
Montréal [mɔ̃real] *n* Montreal
montréalais, -e [mɔ̃realɛ, -ɛz] **1** *adj* of Montreal **2** *nm,f* **M.** Montrealer
montre-bracelet (*pl* **montres-bracelets**) [mɔ̃trə-braslɛ] *nf* wristwatch
montrer [mɔ̃tre] **1** *vt* (**a**) *(révéler)* to show (**à** to); **tu devrais m. ça au médecin** you should let the doctor take a look at it; **m. le chemin à qn** to show sb the way; **m. les dents** to show *or* bare one's teeth (**b**) *(désigner)*

to point out; **m. qn/qch du doigt** to point at sb/sth; *Fig* to point the finger at sb/sth (**c**) *(faire preuve de)* to show
2 se montrer *vpr* (**a**) *(se présenter) (personne)* to show oneself (**b**) *(s'avérer)* **se m. gentil/courageux** to be kind/courageous
montreur, -euse [mɔ̃trœr, -øz] *nm,f* **m. d'ours** bear leader
monture [mɔ̃tyr] *nf* (**a**) *(de lunettes)* frame; *(de bijou)* setting (**b**) *(cheval)* mount
monument [mɔnymɑ̃] *nm* (**a**) *(statue)* monument; **m. funéraire** monument *(over a tomb)*; **m. aux morts** war memorial (**b**) *(édifice public)* monument; **m. classé** listed building; **être classé m. historique** to be a listed building (**c**) *Fig (livre, film)* masterpiece
monumental, -e, -aux, -ales [mɔnymɑ̃tal, -o] *adj* monumental
moquer [mɔke] **se moquer** *vpr* (**a**) *(rire)* **se m. de qn/qch** to make fun of sb/sth; *Fig* **il se moque du monde** who does he think he is? (**b**) *(ignorer)* **se m. de qch** not to care about sth; *Fam* **se m. de qch comme de l'an quarante** *ou* **comme de sa première chemise** not to give two hoots about sth
moquerie [mɔkri] *nf* mockery
moquette [mɔkɛt] *nf* (fitted) carpet; **poser de la m.** to fit a carpet
moqueur, -euse [mɔkœr, -øz] **1** *adj (remarque, rires)* mocking; *(personne)* given to mockery
2 *nm* **les moqueurs** mocking people
moraine [mɔrɛn] *nf* moraine
moral, -e, -aux, -ales [mɔral, -o] **1** *adj* moral
2 *nm* morale; **avoir le m.** to be in good spirits; **avoir le m. au beau fixe** to be in fine spirits; **avoir un m. d'acier** to be very resilient; *Fam* **avoir le m. à zéro** to feel really down; **remonter le m. à qn** to cheer sb up
morale [mɔral] *nf* (**a**) *(bien)* morals; **contraire à la m.** immoral (**b**) *(règles)* morality; **faire une leçon de m. à qn, faire la m. à qn** to lecture sb (**c**) *(d'une histoire)* moral
moralement [mɔralmɑ̃] *adv* morally
moralisateur, -trice [mɔralizatœr, -tris] **1** *adj (discours, personne)* moralizing
2 *nm,f* moralizer
moraliste [mɔralist] **1** *adj* moralistic
2 *nmf* moralist
moralité [mɔralite] *nf* (**a**) *(conduite, attitude)* morality; **être d'une m. irréprochable** to have impeccable moral standards (**b**) *(d'une histoire)* moral; **m.: quand on veut, on peut** the moral of the story is, you can do anything if you put your mind to it
moratoire [mɔratwar] *nm Jur* moratorium
morbide [mɔrbid] *adj* morbid
morbidité [mɔrbidite] *nf* morbidness
morceau, -x [mɔrso] *nm* (**a**) *(de nourriture)* piece, bit; *Fam* **le gros m.** *(le plus difficile)* the big one; *Fam* **manger un m.** to have a bite to eat; *Fam Fig* **lâcher** *ou* **cracher le m.** to spill the beans; **m. de choix** choice morsel; **bas morceaux** *(de viande)* cheap cuts (**b**) *(de savon, de tissu, de papier)* piece, bit; *(de sucre)* lump; *(de terre)* piece; **en morceaux** in pieces; **mettre qch en morceaux** to tear sth to pieces; **tomber en morceaux** to fall to pieces (**c**) *(de musique)* piece (**d**) *(extrait)* **m. d'anthologie** anthology piece; **m. de bravoure** purple passage; **morceaux choisis** selected passages *or* extracts

morceler [9] [mɔrsəle] *vt* to divide up
morcellement [mɔrsɛlmɑ̃] *nm* dividing up
mordant, -e [mɔrdɑ̃, -ɑ̃t] **1** *adj* (**a**) *(esprit, remarque, ton)* biting, caustic (**b**) *(froid)* biting
2 *nm (causticité)* bite
mordicus [mɔrdikys] *adv Fam* stubbornly
mordiller [mɔrdije] *vt* to nibble
mordoré, -e [mɔrdɔre] *adj (couleur)* bronze
mordre [mɔrdr] **1** *vt* (**a**) *(sujet: personne, animal)* to bite; **m. qn au bras** to bite sb's arm, to bite sb on the arm; **se faire m. par un chien** to be bitten by a dog (**b**) *(entamer) (sujet: lime)* to bite into; *(sujet: acide)* to eat into
2 *vi (personne, chien)* to bite; **m. dans une pomme** to bite into an apple; **ça mord?** *(poissons)* are the fish biting?
3 mordre à *vt ind* (**a**) *(poisson) & Fig* **m. à l'appât** *ou* **à l'hameçon** to rise to the bait (**b**) *Fam (prendre goût à)* to take to
4 mordre sur *vt ind (déborder)* **m. sur qch** to encroach (up)on sth; **m. sur la ligne** *(sportif)* to have one's foot over the line
5 se mordre *vpr* **se m. la langue** to bite one's tongue; *Fig* **se m. les doigts d'avoir fait qch** to kick oneself for doing sth; **vous vous en mordrez les doigts** you'll be sorry
mordu, -e [mɔrdy] *Fam* **1** *adj* (**a**) *(amoureux)* madly in love (**b**) *(passionné)* **être m. de qch** to be mad on sth
2 *nm,f* fanatic; **un m. de bridge/cinéma** a bridge/movie fanatic
morfal, -e, -als, -ales [mɔrfal] *nm,f Fam* greedyguts
morfler [mɔrfle] *vi Fam* (**a**) *(être abîmé)* to get smashed up; *(être blessé)* to get injured (**b**) *(être puni, pâtir)* to catch it
morfondre [mɔrfɔ̃dr] **se morfondre** *vpr* (**a**) *(languir)* to mope (**b**) *Can (s'épuiser)* to wear oneself out
morgue¹ [mɔrg] *nf (arrogance)* haughtiness; **plein de m.** haughty
morgue² *nf (dans un hôpital)* mortuary; *(pour les corps non identifiés)* morgue
moribond, -e [mɔribɔ̃, -ɔ̃d] **1** *adj* dying
2 *nm,f* dying man, f dying woman
morille [mɔrij] *nf* morel
mormon, -e [mɔrmɔ̃, -ɔn] *adj & nm,f* Mormon
morne [mɔrn] *adj (personne, regard)* glum; *(silence)* gloomy; *(temps)* dismal, dreary
morose [mɔroz] *adj (personne, humeur)* morose; *(temps)* miserable
morosité [mɔrozite] *nf (d'une personne, de l'humeur)* moroseness; *(du temps)* miserable nature
morphine [mɔrfin] *nf* morphine
morphologie [mɔrfɔlɔʒi] *nf* morphology
morphologique [mɔrfɔlɔʒik] *adj* morphological
morpion [mɔrpjɔ̃] *nm* (**a**) *très Fam (pou)* crab (**b**) *Fam (enfant)* kid (**c**) *(jeu) Br* noughts and crosses, *Am* tick-tack-toe
mors [mɔr] *nm* bit; *Fig* **prendre le m. aux dents** to take the bit between one's teeth
morse¹ [mɔrs] *nm (animal)* walrus
morse² *nm (code)* Morse (code)
morsure [mɔrsyr] *nf* bite
mort¹, -e [mɔr, mɔrt] **1** *pp de* **mourir**
2 *adj* (**a**) *(personne, feuille, langue)* dead; **plus m. que vif** more dead than alive; **m. de peur/d'inquiétude/de froid** frightened/worried/frozen to death;

Fam **être m. de rire** to fall about laughing; *Fam* **être m. (de fatigue)** to be dead tired (**b**) *(hors d'usage)* *(pile)* dead; *Fam* **être m.** *(voiture, chaussures)* to have had it

3 *nm,f* dead man, *f* dead woman; **les morts** the dead; *Rel* **le jour** *ou* **la fête des morts** All Souls' Day; **faire le m.** to pretend to be dead; *Fig* to lie low; **l'accident a fait trois morts** three people were killed in the accident

4 *nm (aux cartes)* dummy

mort² *nf* death; **trouver la m. dans un accident** to die in an accident; **se donner la m.** to take one's own life; **mettre qn à m.** to put sb to death; **en vouloir à qn à m.** to have a huge grudge against sb; **la m. dans l'âme** with a heavy heart; *Fam* **c'est pas la m.!** it won't kill you/him/*etc*!; **m. subite du nourrisson** *Br* cot death, *Am* crib death

mortadelle [mɔrtadɛl] *nf* mortadella

mortaise [mɔrtɛz] *nf* mortise

mortalité [mɔrtalite] *nf* mortality, death rate; **m. infantile** infant mortality

mort-aux-rats [mɔrora] *nf inv* rat poison

mortel, -elle [mɔrtɛl] **1** *adj* (**a**) *(éphémère)* mortal (**b**) *(fatal) (maladie, accident)* fatal; *(dose) (champignon, poison)* deadly (**c**) *(péché, ennemi)* deadly; *(silence)* deathly; **d'une pâleur mortelle** deathly pale (**d**) *Fam (excellent)* cool, *Br* wicked, *Am* awesome; *(mauvais)* crap, lousy; *(ennuyeux)* deadly boring

2 *nm,f* mortal

3 *adv Fam* **on s'est éclatés m.!** we had a blast!; *très Fam* **on s'est fait chier m.** we were bored shitless

mortellement [mɔrtɛlmã] *adv (blessé)* fatally; *(ennuyeux)* deadly

morte-saison *(pl* mortes-saisons*)* [mɔrtsɛzɔ̃] *nf* off-season; **à la m.** in the off-season

mortier [mɔrtje] *nm* mortar; **tirs de m.** mortar fire

mortifiant, -e [mɔrtifjã, -ãt] *adj* mortifying

mortification [mɔrtifikasjɔ̃] *nf* mortification

mortifié, -e [mɔrtifje] *adj* mortified

mortifier [66] [mɔrtifje] **1** *vt* to mortify

2 se mortifier *vpr* to mortify oneself

mort-né, -e *(mpl* mort-nés, *fpl* mort-nées*)* [mɔrne] **1** *adj aussi Fig* stillborn

2 *nm,f* stillborn child

mortuaire [mɔrtɥɛr] *adj* death

mort-vivant, morte-vivante *(mpl* morts-vivants, *fpl* mortes-vivantes*)* [mɔrvivã, -ãt] *nm,f* member of the living dead; **les morts-vivants** the living dead

morue [mɔry] *nf* (**a**) *(poisson)* cod (**b**) *très Fam (prostituée)* tart

morve [mɔrv] *nf* snot

morveux, -euse [mɔrvø, -øz] **1** *adj (enfant)* snotty-nosed; *(nez)* runny

2 *nm,f Fam Péj (gamin)* brat; *(jeune prétentieux)* upstart

mosaïque [mɔzaik] *nf* (**a**) *(en décoration)* mosaic (**b**) *Fig (de couleurs)* kaleidoscope; *(de populations)* medley

Moscou [mɔsku] *n* Moscow

moscovite [mɔskɔvit] **1** *adj* Muscovite

2 *nmf* **M.** Muscovite

mosquée [mɔske] *nf* mosque

mot [mo] *nm* (**a**) *(parole)* word; **avoir son m. à dire** to have one's say; **avoir toujours le m. pour rire** to be always ready with a joke; **avoir des mots avec qn** to have words with sb; **avoir le dernier m.** to have the

last word; **je n'ai pas dit mon dernier m.** I'm not finished yet; **dire un m.** *ou* **deux mots à qn** to have a word with sb; **se donner le m.** to pass the word around; **prendre qn au m.** to take sb at his/her word; **traduire m. à m., faire du m. à m.** to translate word for word; **répéter qch m. pour m.** to repeat sth word for word; **sans m. dire** without (saying) a word; **sur ces mots** and with these words; **en un m.** in a word; **au bas m.** at least; **à mots couverts** in veiled terms; **mots doux, mots d'amour** sweet nothings; **mots croisés** crossword; **faire des mots croisés** to do crosswords; **m. d'ordre** watchword, slogan; **m. de passe** password; **bon m.** witty remark; **gros m.** swear word; **dire des gros mots** to swear (**b**) *(message écrit)* note; **envoyer un m. à qn** to drop sb a line; **m. d'excuse** note *(explaining absence)* (**c**) *Ordinat* **m. de 6 bits** 6-bit byte; **m. binaire** binary word

motard, -e [mɔtar, -ard] **1** *nm,f Fam (conducteur de moto)* biker

2 *nm (policier)* motorcycle policeman

mot-clef *(pl* mots-clefs*)* [mokle] *nm* keyword

motel [mɔtɛl] *nm* motel

moteur, -trice [mɔtœr, -tris] **1** *adj* (**a**) *(force, roue)* driving; **à deux/quatre roues motrices** two-/four-wheel drive (**b**) *(nerf, trouble)* motor

2 *nm* engine; *(électrique)* motor; *Fig* driving force; *Cin* **m.!** camera!; **à m.** motor(-driven); **m. à deux/quatre temps** two-/four-stroke engine; **m. à explosion** internal combustion engine; **m. à injection** fuel-injected engine; **m. à réaction** jet engine; *Ordinat* **m. de recherche** search engine

3 *nf Rail* **motrice** engine

motif [mɔtif] *nm* (**a**) *(raison)* reason (de for); **elle n'a aucun m. de mécontentement** she has no reason to be unhappy (**b**) *(dessin)* pattern, motif (**c**) *(dans un morceau de musique)* motif

motion [mosjɔ̃] *nf* motion; **m. de censure** motion of censure

motivant, -e [mɔtivã, -ãt] *adj (travail)* motivating; *(salaire, rémunération)* attractive

motivation [mɔtivasjɔ̃] *nf* motivation

motivé, -e [mɔtive] *adj* (**a**) *(personne)* motivated (**b**) *(action)* justified

motiver [mɔtive] *vt* (**a**) *(provoquer, stimuler)* to motivate (**b**) *(justifier)* to justify

moto [moto] *nf* motorbike; **faire de la m.** to ride a motorbike; **m. tout terrain** trial bike

motocross [motokrɔs] *nm* motocross

motocrotte [mɔtokrɔt] *nf Fam* = motorized scooter with an attachment for cleaning up dog dirt in the street

motoculteur [motokyltœr] *nm* motor cultivator

motocyclette [motosiklɛt] *nf* motorcycle

motocycliste [motosiklist] *nmf* motorcyclist; *Mil* dispatch rider

motomarine [motomarin] *nf Can* jet ski

motoneige [motonɛʒ] *nf Can* snowmobile

motorisé, -e [mɔtorize] *adj* motorized; **être m.** *(personne)* to have transport

motrice [mɔtris] *voir* **moteur**

motricité [mɔtrisite] *nf* motor function

motte [mɔt] *nf* (**a**) *(de terre)* clod, clump (**b**) *(de beurre)* block

motus [mɔtys] *exclam* **m. (et bouche cousue)!** mum's the word!

mou¹, molle [mu, mɔl] **1** *adj* (**a**) *(matelas, substance)* soft; *(chair, ventre)* flabby; **j'ai les jambes molles** my

legs are like jelly (**b**) *(personne, gouvernement)* spineless; *(protestation)* feeble; *(poignée de main)* limp
  2 *nm,f Fam* wimp
  3 *nm (d'un cordage, d'un câble)* slack
mou² *nm (abats)* lights, lungs
mouais [mwɛ] *exclam Fam* well, yeah; **alors, t'as aimé le film? – m., j'ai vu pire** did you like the movie, then? – well, yeah, I've seen worse; **m., ce n'est pas mal** it's OK, I guess
mouchard, -e [muʃar, -ard] *Fam* **1** *nm,f (informateur) Br* grass, *Am* fink; *(à l'école) Br* sneak, *Am* snitch
  2 *nm (de camion)* tachograph; *(d'avion)* black box
moucharder [muʃarde] *Fam* **1** *vt (personne)* to squeal *or Br* grass on; *(élève)* to *Br* sneak *or Am* snitch on
  2 *vi (élève)* to *Br* sneak *or Am* snitch on people
mouche [muʃ] *nf* (**a**) *(insecte)* fly; **prendre** *ou Suisse* **piquer la m.** to fly off the handle; **elle ne ferait pas de mal à une m.** she wouldn't hurt a fly; **quelle m. te pique?** what's got into you?; **m. tsé-tsé** tsetse fly; **fine m.** sharp customer (**b**) *(de cible)* bull's-eye; **faire m.** to hit the bull's-eye; *Fig* to hit home (**c**) *(accessoire cosmétique)* beauty spot
moucher [muʃe] *vt* (**a**) *(nez)* to blow; **m. un enfant** to blow a child's nose (**b**) *Fig* **m. qn** to put sb in his/her place (**c**) *(chandelle)* to snuff out
  2 se moucher *vpr* to blow one's nose; *Fam* **ne pas se m. du coude** *ou* **du pied** to think one is the bee's knees
moucheron [muʃrɔ̃] *nm* midge
moucheté, -e [muʃte] *adj (cheval)* dappled; *(tissu)* speckled
mouchoir [muʃwar] *nm* handkerchief; **arriver dans un m.** to come in neck and neck; **grand comme un m. de poche** no bigger than a pocket handkerchief; **m. en papier** tissue; **m. en tissu** handkerchief
moudre [48] [mudr] *vt* to grind
moue [mu] *nf* pout; **faire la m.** to pout
mouette [mwɛt] *nf* (sea)gull
moufle [mufl] *nf* mitten, mitt
mouflet, -ette [muflɛ, -ɛt] *nm,f Fam* kid
mouflon [muflɔ̃] *nm* moufflon
mouillage [mujaʒ] *nm* (**a**) *(de bateau) (manœuvre)* anchoring; *(emplacement)* anchorage; **être au m.** to be riding at anchor (**b**) *(du vin)* watering down
mouillé, -e [muje] *adj (vêtement, personne, pieds)* wet; **tout m.** soaking wet
mouiller [muje] **1** *vt* (**a**) *(rendre humide)* to wet; **se faire m.** to get wet; *Fig* **m. sa chemise** to work up a sweat (**b**) *(vin, lait)* to water down (**c**) *(ancre)* to drop (**d**) *Fam (compromettre)* to involve (**e**) *Can Fam (fêter)* **il va falloir m. ça!** this calls for a celebration!
  2 *vi (bateau)* to anchor
  3 se mouiller *vpr* (**a**) *(personne)* to get wet; **se m. les pieds** to get one's feet wet (**b**) *Fam (prendre position)* to stick one's neck out
mouillette [mujɛt] *nf* finger *(of bread)*
mouise [mwiz] *nf très Fam* **être dans la m.** to be hard-up
moulage [mulaʒ] *nm* (**a**) *(action)* casting (**b**) *(objet)* plaster cast
moule¹ [mul] *nm aussi Fig* mould; *Fig* **être coulé dans le même m.** to be cast in the same mould; **m. à gâteaux** *Br* cake tin, *Am* cake pan; **m. à gaufres** waffle iron; **m. à tarte** flan dish

moule² *nf* mussel; **moules frites** mussels and *Br* chips *or Am* French fries *(speciality of Belgium and the North of France)*; **moules marinières** moules marinières, = mussels in white wine; *Belg* **moules parquées** = mussels served raw
mouler [mule] *vt* (**a**) *(statue)* to mould (**b**) *(sujet: vêtement)* to fit closely
moulin [mulɛ̃] *nm* (**a**) *(bâtiment)* mill; **on y entre comme dans un m.** anyone can just walk in; **m. à eau** watermill; *Can* **m. à scie** sawmill; **m. à vent** windmill (**b**) *(appareil)* **m. à café** coffee grinder; **m. à légumes** vegetable mill *or* grinder; *Fig* **m. à paroles** chatterbox; **m. à poivre** pepper mill
mouliner [muline] *vt (aliment)* to pass through a food mill
moulinet [mulinɛ] *nm* (**a**) *(de canne à pêche)* reel (**b**) *(rotation)* **faire des moulinets (avec les bras)** to circle one's arms
Moulinette® [mulinɛt] *nf* food mill
moult [mult] *adv Hum ou Vieilli* many
moulu, -e [muly] **1** *pp de* **moudre**
  2 *adj* (**a**) *(café, poivre)* ground (**b**) *Fig* **être m. (de fatigue)** to be *Br* shattered *or Am* beat
moulure [mulyr] *nf* (ornamental) moulding
moumoute [mumut] *nf Fam* (**a**) *(perruque)* rug, wig (**b**) *(veste)* sheepskin jacket
mourant, -e [murɑ̃, -ɑ̃t] **1** *adj* dying
  2 *nm,f* dying man, f dying woman
mourir [49] [murir] *(aux* **être**) **1** *vi* (**a**) *(personne, animal, plante)* to die; **m. de sa belle mort** *ou* **de mort naturelle** to die a natural death; **m. de vieillesse** to die of old age; **m. assassiné** to be murdered; **m. d'inquiétude/de peur** to be worried/frightened to death; **m. de faim** to starve to death; *Fam (avoir très faim)* to be starving; **m. de soif/d'ennui** to die of thirst/boredom; **s'ennuyer à m.** to be bored to death; **aimer qn à en m.** to be desperately in love with sb; **à m. d'ennui** deadly boring; **à m. de rire** hilarious, hysterical; **m. d'envie de faire qch** to be dying to do sth; *Fig* **tu ne vas pas en m.!** it won't kill you! (**b**) *(coutume, industrie, civilisation)* to die out; *(feu, région)* to die
  2 *v impersonnel* **il meurt des milliers d'enfants chaque jour** thousands of children die every day
  3 se mourir *vpr Litt (personne)* to be dying
mouroir [murwar] *nm Fam Péj* old folks' home
mouron [murɔ̃] *nm Fam* **se faire du m.** to worry
mousquetaire [muskətɛr] *nm* musketeer
mousqueton [muskətɔ̃] *nm* (**a**) *(anneau)* snap clasp; *(d'alpiniste)* karabiner (**b**) *(arme)* carbine
moussaka [musaka] *nf* moussaka
moussant, -e [musɑ̃, ɑ̃t] *adj* **être peu m.** not to produce a lot of lather; **bain m.** bubble bath
mousse¹ [mus] *nf* (**a**) *(végétation)* moss (**b**) *(écume)* foam; *(sur un verre de bière)* head; *(de savon)* lather; *Fam* **une m.** *(bière)* a beer; **m. à raser** shaving foam (**c**) *(plat, dessert)* mousse; **m. au chocolat/de saumon** chocolate/salmon mousse (**d**) *(matériau synthétique)* **m.** foam rubber
mousse² *nm* ship's boy
mousseline [muslin] *nf (tissu)* muslin; **m. de soie** chiffon
mousser [muse] *vi (bière)* to froth; *(savon, lessive)* to lather; *(vin, eau gazeuse)* to fizz; *Fam Fig* **se faire m.** to show off
mousseux, -euse [musø, -øz] **1** *adj* (**a**) *(vin, cidre)* sparkling (**b**) *(lait, bière)* frothy
  2 *nm* sparkling wine

mousson [musɔ̃] *nf* monsoon
moussu, -e [musy] *adj* mossy
moustache [mustaʃ] *nf* (**a**) *(d'un homme)* moustache; **porter la m.** to have a moustache (**b**) *(de chat, de rongeur)* whiskers
moustachu, -e [mustaʃy] **1** *adj* with a moustache; **être m.** to have a moustache
2 *nm* man with a moustache
moustiquaire [mustikɛr] *nf* mosquito net
moustique [mustik] *nm* (**a**) *(insecte)* mosquito (**b**) *Fam (gamin)* kid, mite
moût [mu] *nm (de raisins)* must; *(de bière)* wort
moutard [mutar] *nm Fam* kid
moutarde [mutard] **1** *adj inv* **(jaune) m.** mustard (yellow)
2 *nf* mustard; *Fig* **la m. me monte au nez** I'm beginning to lose my temper; **m. forte/de Dijon** strong/Dijon mustard
moutardier [mutardje] *nm (pot)* mustard pot
mouton [mutɔ̃] *nm* (**a**) *(animal)* sheep; **(peau de) m.** sheepskin; **être frisé comme un m.** to have curly hair; *Fig* **revenons à nos moutons** let's get back to the subject; **compter les moutons** *(pour s'endormir)* to count sheep; *Fig* **m. à cinq pattes** rare bird (**b**) *(viande)* mutton (**c**) **moutons** *(écume)* white horses; *(poussière)* fluff (**d**) *Can* **m. noir** *(nuage)* rain cloud
moutonner [mutɔne] *vi (mer)* to be flecked with foam
moutonneux, -euse [mutɔnø, -øz] *adj* (**a**) *(mer)* foam-flecked (**b**) *(ciel)* dotted with fleecy clouds
mouture [mutyr] *nf* (**a**) *(action de moudre)* grinding (**b**) *(d'un ouvrage, d'un livre)* version
mouv' [muv] *nm Fam (abrév* **mouvement**) **c'est dans le m.** it's totally cool
mouvance [muvɑ̃s] *nf* **il faisait partie de la m. surréaliste** he moved in surrealist circles
mouvant, -e [muvɑ̃, ɑ̃t] *adj (terrain)* unstable; *(cible)* moving; *Fig (situation)* uncertain
mouvement [muvmɑ̃] *nm* (**a**) *(déplacement)* movement, motion; *(des marchandises, des capitaux)* movement; *(geste)* gesture; **faire un m.** to make a movement; **faire un faux m.** *(se faire mal)* to move the wrong way; **en m.** in motion; **ralentir le m.** to slow down; **suivre le m.** to go with the flow; **il y eut un m. de foule** a ripple ran through the crowd; **m. de tête** *(pour acquiescer)* nod; *(pour nier)* shake of the head (**b**) *(de gymnastique)* exercise (**c**) *(élan)* impulse; **m. d'humeur** outburst (of temper); **m. de colère** fit of anger (**d**) *(politique, artistique)* movement; **m. de grève** strike action; **mouvements sociaux** industrial action (**e**) *(d'un concerto, d'une symphonie)* movement
mouvementé, -e [muvmɑ̃te] *adj (discussion, débat)* animated, lively; *(journée, voyage, vie)* eventful
mouvoir [31b] [muvwar] **1** *vt Litt* (**a**) *(machine)* to drive; *(bateau)* to propel; **mû par la vapeur** steam-driven (**b**) *(pousser)* **mû par l'intérêt** prompted by self-interest
2 se mouvoir *upr* to move
moyen¹, -enne [mwajɛ̃, -ɛn] *adj* (**a**) *(du milieu)* middle; **trouver un m. terme** to find a happy medium (**b**) *(coût, taille, vitesse)* average; **de taille moyenne** medium-sized; *(personne)* of average height (**c**) *(quelconque, médiocre)* average; **le Français m.** the average Frenchman

moyen² *nm* (**a**) *(façon, possibilité)* means, way; *aussi Hum* **trouver le m. de faire qch** to manage to do sth; **se donner les moyens de faire qch** to provide oneself with the means to do sth; **faire qch par ses propres moyens** to do sth on one's own; **employer les grands moyens** to take extreme measures; **au m. de qch** by means of sth; **par tous les moyens** any way I/you/*etc* can; **il n'y a pas m. de le lui faire comprendre** it's impossible to make him/her understand; **faire avec les moyens du bord** to make do with what one has; **moyens de communication/production/transport** means of communication/production/transport (**b**) **avoir des moyens** *(capacité mentale)* to be bright; **perdre tous ses moyens** to go to pieces (**c**) **moyens** *(financiers)* means; **j'en ai/je n'en ai pas les moyens** I can/can't afford it
Moyen Âge [mwajɛnɑʒ] *nm* **le M.** the Middle Ages
moyenâgeux, -euse [mwajɛnɑʒø, -øz] *adj* medieval
moyen-courrier *(pl* **moyen-courriers**) [mwajɛ̃kurje] *nm* **(avion) m.** medium-haul aircraft
moyennant [mwajɛnɑ̃] *prép* (in return) for; **faire qch m. finance** to do sth in return for payment; **m. quoi** in return for which
moyenne [mwajɛn] **1** *adj voir* **moyen¹**
2 *nf* (**a**) *(niveau le plus courant)* average; **en m.** on average (**b**) *(à un examen)* pass mark; *(sur une période)* average (mark); **avoir 10 sur 20 de m.** to average 10 out of 20
moyennement [mwajɛnmɑ̃] *adv* moderately, fairly
Moyen-Orient [mwajɛnɔrjɑ̃] *nm* **le M.** the Middle East
moyeu [mwajø] *nm* hub
mozambicain, -e [mɔzɑ̃bikɛ̃, -ɛn] **1** *adj* Mozambican
2 *nm,f* **M.** Mozambican
Mozambique [mɔzɑ̃bik] *nm* **le M.** Mozambique
mozzarella [mɔdzarɛla], **mozzarelle** [mɔdzarɛl] *nf* mozzarella
MP3 [ɛmpetrwa] *nm inv Ordinat* MP3
MRAP [mrap] *nm (abrév* **Mouvement contre le racisme, l'antisémitisme et pour la paix)** = French anti-racist pacifist movement
MRG [ɛmɛrʒe] *nm (abrév* **Mouvement des radicaux de gauche)** = French left-wing political party
MST¹ [ɛmɛste] *nf (abrév* **maladie sexuellement transmissible)** STD
MST² *nf (abrév* **maîtrise de sciences et techniques)** = master's degree in science and technology
mû *pp de* **mouvoir**
mucoviscidose [mykovisidoz] *nf* cystic fibrosis
mucus [mykys] *nm* mucus
mue [my] **1** *pp de* **mouvoir**
2 *nf* (**a**) *(d'oiseaux, de mammifères)* moulting; *(de reptiles)* sloughing (**b**) *(à la puberté)* breaking of the voice
muer [mɥe] **1** *vi* (**a**) *(mammifère)* to moult; *(serpent)* to slough (**b**) *(voix)* to break; **il commence à m.** his voice is breaking
2 se muer *upr* **se m. en** to change into
muesli [mysli] *nm* muesli
muet, -ette [mɥɛ, -ɛt] **1** *adj* (**a**) *(personne)* dumb; *Fig (silencieux)* silent; **m. d'étonnement/de colère** speechless with astonishment/anger; **m. comme la tombe** silent as the grave; **il est resté m. comme une carpe** he didn't open his mouth (**b**) *(film,*

réprobation) silent; *(rôle)* non-speaking (**c**) *Ling* silent
2 *nm,f* mute
3 *nm Cin* **le m.** silent movies *or Br* films
muezzin [mцɛdzin] *nm* muezzin
mufle [myfl] *nm* (**a**) *Fam (homme)* lout (**b**) *(du bœuf, du bison)* muffle; *(du lion, du taureau)* muzzle
muge [myʒ] *nm* mullet
mugir [myʒir] *vi* (**a**) *(vache)* to moo; *(taureau)* to bellow (**b**) *(vent)* to howl
mugissement [myʒismɑ̃] *nm* (**a**) *(de vache)* moo; *(de taureau)* bellow; **des mugissements** *(de vache)* mooing; *(de taureau)* bellowing (**b**) *(du vent)* howling
muguet [mygɛ] *nm (plante)* lily of the valley

Muguet
On May Day in France, bunches of lily of the valley are sold in the streets and given as presents. The flowers are supposed to bring good luck.

mulâtre [mylɑtr] *adj & nm* mulatto
mulâtresse [mylɑtrɛs] *nf* mulatto
mule¹ [myl] *nf (animal)* mule; *Fam (personne entêtée)* mule
mule² *nf (chaussure)* mule
mulet¹ [mylɛ] *nm (équidé)* mule
mulet² *nm (poisson)* grey mullet
muletier, -ère [myltje, -ɛr] **1** *adj* **chemin** *ou* **sentier m.** mule track
2 *nm,f* mule driver
mulot [mylo] *nm* field mouse
multicarte [myltikart] *adj (représentant)* for several companies
multicolore [myltikɔlɔr] *adj* multicoloured
multicoque [myltikɔk] *nm* multihull
multicritère [myltikritɛr] *nm Ordinat* multicriterion
multiculturel, -elle [myltikyltyrɛl] *adj* multicultural
multidisciplinaire [myltidisiplinɛr] *adj* multidisciplinary
multi-écran *(pl* **multi-écrans)** [myltiekrɑ̃] *nm* split screen
multifonctions [myltifɔ̃ksjɔ̃] *adj* multi-functional
multiforme [myltifɔrm] *adj* multifaceted
multijoueur [myltiʒwœr] *adj* multiplayer
multilatéral, -e, -aux, -ales [myltilateral, -o] *adj* multilateral
multilingue [myltilɛ̃g] *adj* multilingual
multimédia [myltimedja] *adj & nm* multimedia
multimilliardaire [myltimiljardɛr] *adj & nmf* multimillionaire
multimillionnaire [myltimiljɔnɛr] *adj & nmf* multimillionaire
multinational, -e, -aux, -ales [myltinasjɔnal, -o] **1** *adj* multinational
2 *nf* **multinationale** multinational (company)
multiple [myltipl] **1** *adj* (**a**) *(nombreux)* many, numerous; **à usages multiples** multipurpose; **à de multiples reprises** repeatedly; *Ordinat* **à accès m.** multi-access (**b**) *(divers)* many, multiple
2 *nm Math* multiple; **le plus petit commun m.** the lowest common multiple
multiplex [myltiplɛks] *adj inv & nm inv* multiplex
multiplexe [myltiplɛks] *nm* multiplex *(Br* cinema *or Am* movie theatre)

multiplicateur, -trice [myltiplikatœr, -tris] **1** *adj* multiplying
2 *nm* multiplier
multiplication [myltiplikasjɔ̃] *nf* (**a**) *(calcul)* multiplication (**b**) *(augmentation)* increase (**de** in)
multiplicité [myltiplisite] *nf* multiplicity
multiplier [66] [myltiplije] **1** *vt* (**a**) *(somme, chiffre)* to multiply (**par** by) (**b**) *(répéter)* **m. les mises en garde** to issue repeated warnings; **m. les erreurs** to make mistake after mistake
2 se multiplier *vpr* (**a**) *(augmenter)* to increase (**b**) *(se reproduire)* to multiply
multiposte [myltipɔst] *adj Ordinat* multi-station
multiprocesseur [myltiprɔsesœr] *nm Ordinat* multiprocessor
multiprogrammation [myltiprɔgramasjɔ̃] *nf Ordinat* multiprogramming
multipropriété [myltiprɔprijete] *nf* time-share; **acheter une maison en m.** to buy a time-share house
multiracial, -e, -aux, -ales [myltirasjal, -o] *adj* multiracial
multirisque [myltirisk] *adj* comprehensive
multisalles [myltisal] *adj* complexe **m.** multiplex *(Br* cinema *or Am* movie theatre)
multitâche [myltitaʃ] *adj Ordinat* multitasking
multithérapie [myltiterapi] *nf Méd* combination therapy
multitraitement [myltitrɛtmɑ̃] *nm Ordinat* multiprocessing
multitude [myltityd] *nf* multitude (**de** of)
multi-utilisateurs [myltiytilizatœr] *adj inv Ordinat* multiuser
municipal, -e, -aux, -ales [mynisipal, -o] **1** *adj* municipal
2 *nfpl* **les municipales** municipal *or* local (government) elections

Municipales
These are the elections where residents choose the town councils. Electors vote for a list of council members whose leader or "tête de liste" will become the mayor, a ceremonial and political post.

municipalité [mynisipalite] *nf* (**a**) *(commune)* municipality (**b**) *(maire et conseillers)* (local) council
munir [mynir] **1** *vt (personne)* to supply, to provide (**de** with); *(voiture, chambre)* to fit, to equip (**de** with)
2 se munir *vpr* **se m. de qch** to take sth
munitions [mynisjɔ̃] *nfpl* ammunition, munitions
munster [mœ̃stɛr] *nm* Munster (cheese)
muqueuse [mykøz] *nf* mucous membrane
mur [myr] *nm* (**a**) *(construction)* wall; **l'ennemi est dans nos murs** the enemy is within the gates; **le m. de Berlin** the Berlin Wall; **le M. des lamentations** the Wailing Wall; **m. porteur** load-bearing wall; **m. du son** sound barrier; **franchir le m. du son** to break the sound barrier; **m. de soutènement** retaining wall (**b**) *Fig (résistance)* brick wall
mûr, -e¹ [myr] *adj* (**a**) *(fruit)* ripe; *Fig* **être m. pour qch** to be ripe for sth (**b**) *(personne, esprit)* mature (**c**) *(intense)* **après mûre réflexion** after careful consideration
muraille [myrɑj] *nf* wall; **la Grande M. de Chine** the Great Wall of China
mural, -e, -aux, -ales [myral, -o] *adj* wall
mûre² [myr] *nf* mulberry; *(fruit de la ronce)* blackberry

mûrement [myrmɑ̃] *adv* **après avoir m. réfléchi** after careful consideration; **un projet m. réfléchi** a carefully thought-out plan

murène [myrɛn] *nf* moray (eel)

murer [myre] **1** *vt* (**a**) *(ville, jardin)* to wall in (**b**) *(porte, fenêtre, personne)* to wall up
  2 se murer *vpr* to shut oneself away; **se m. dans le silence/la solitude** to retreat into silence/solitude

muret [myrɛ] *nm (mur bas)* low wall; *(de pierres sèches)* dry-stone wall

murette [myrɛt] *nf* = **muret**

mûrier [myrje] *nm* (**a**) *(arbre)* mulberry tree (**b**) *(roncier)* blackberry bush

mûrir [myrir] *vi* (**a**) *(fruit)* to ripen (**b**) *(projet, sentiment)* to evolve, to develop (**c**) *(personne)* to mature

murmure [myrmyr] *nm* murmur

murmurer [myrmyre] *vt & vi* to murmur

musaraigne [myzarɛɲ] *nf* shrew

musarder [myzarde] *vi (flâner)* to wander around; *(fainéanter)* to lounge around

musc [mysk] *nm* musk

muscade [myskad] *nf* **m., noix (de) m.** nutmeg

muscat [myska] *nm* (**a**) *(raisin)* muscat grape (**b**) *(vin)* muscatel (wine)

muscle [myskl] *nm* muscle; **être tout en m.** to be all muscle

musclé, -e [myskle] *adj* (**a**) *(personne, bras, jambes)* muscular (**b**) *Fig (campagne électorale, discours)* punchy; *(intervention)* forceful; *(politique, mesure)* tough

muscler [myskle] **1** *vt* to develop the muscles of
  2 se muscler *vpr* to develop one's muscles

muscu [mysky] *Fam* = **musculation**

musculaire [myskylɛr] *adj (système, tissu, force)* muscular; *(fibre)* muscle

musculation [myskylasjɔ̃] *nf* body-building; **faire de la m.** to do body-building

musculature [myskylatyr] *nf* musculature

muse [myz] *nf* muse

museau, -x [myzo] *nm* (**a**) *(d'animal)* muzzle, snout (**b**) *Fam (visage)* face

musée [myze] *nm* museum; **m. (de peinture)** art gallery; **m. des horreurs** chamber of horrors

museler [9] [myzle] *vt aussi Fig* to muzzle

muselière [myzəljɛr] *nf* muzzle

musette [myzɛt] **1** *nf* (**a**) *(instrument de musique)* musette (**b**) *(sac)* bag; *(de soldat)* haversack; *(d'écolier)* satchel
  2 *nm Fam* **le m.** accordion music

muséum [myzeɔm] *nm* natural history museum

musical, -e, -aux, -ales [myzikal, -o] *adj* musical

musicalement [myzikalmɑ̃] *adv* musically

music-hall *(pl music-halls)* [myzikol] *nm (genre, salle)* music hall

musicien, -enne [myzisjɛ̃, -ɛn] **1** *adj* musical
  2 *nm,f* musician

musicologie [myzikɔlɔʒi] *nf* musicology

musicologue [myzikɔlɔɡ] *nmf* musicologist

musique [myzik] *nf* (**a**) *(art, notation ou science)* music; **mettre qch en m.** to set sth to music; **faire de la m.** to make music; *Fig* **connaître la m.** to have heard it all before; *Can* **faire face à la m.** to face the music; **m. d'ambiance** *ou* **de fond** background music; **m. de chambre** chamber music; **m. classique** classical music; **m. folklorique** folk music; **m. religieuse** religious music; **m. sacrée** sacred music (**b**) *Belg, Suisse & Can* **m. à bouche** harmonica, mouth organ

musqué, -e [myske] *adj (odeur)* musky

must [mœst] *nm Fam* **c'est un m.** it's a must

mustang [mystɑ̃g] *nm* mustang

musulman, -e [myzylmɑ̃, -an] *adj & nm,f* Moslem, Muslim

mutant, -e [mytɑ̃, ɑ̃t] *adj & nm,f* mutant

mutation [mytasjɔ̃] *nf* (**a**) *(de personnel)* transfer (**b**) *(changement)* change, alteration

muter [myte] *vt* to transfer

mutilation [mytilasjɔ̃] *nf* mutilation

mutilé, -e [mytile] *nm,f* **mutilés de guerre** disabled ex-servicemen

mutiler [mytile] **1** *vt (personne)* to mutilate, to maim; *(partie du corps)* to badly injure; *(paysage)* to disfigure
  2 se mutiler *vpr* to mutilate oneself

mutin¹ [mytɛ̃] *nm* mutineer

mutin², -e [mytɛ̃, -in] *adj (espiègle)* mischievous

mutiner [mytine] **se mutiner** *vpr* to mutiny (**contre** against)

mutinerie [mytinri] *nf* mutiny

mutisme [mytism] *nm* silence; **observer un m. absolu** to maintain total silence

mutualité [mytɥalite] *nf* mutual insurance

mutuel, -elle [mytɥɛl] **1** *adj* mutual
  2 *nf* **mutuelle** mutual insurance company

Mutuelle
A "mutuelle" is a non-profit-making health insurance company which provides insurance complementary to that of the "**Sécurité sociale**" *(see box at that entry)*. Often these companies are set up for a particular profession: there is a "mutuelle" for students, one for teachers etc.

mutuellement [mytɥɛlmɑ̃] *adv* each other, one another

Myanmar [mjanmar] *nm* **le M.** Myanmar

mycose [mikoz] *nf* fungal infection, *Spéc* mycosis

mygale [migal] *nf* trapdoor spider

myocarde [mjɔkard] *nm* myocardium

myopathe [mjɔpat] *nmf* person with muscular dystrophy

myopathie [mjɔpati] *nf* muscular dystrophy

myope [mjɔp] **1** *adj* shortsighted, *Spéc* myopic; *Fig* **m. comme une taupe** as blind as a bat
  2 *nmf* shortsighted person

myopie [mjɔpi] *nf* shortsightedness, *Spéc* myopia

myosotis [mjɔzɔtis] *nm* forget-me-not

myriade [mirjad] *nf* myriad (**de** of)

myrrhe [mir] *nf* myrrh

myrtille [mirtij] *nf Br* bilberry, *Am* blueberry

mystère [mistɛr] *nm* (**a**) *(énigme)* mystery; **faire des mystères** to be mysterious; **faire m. de qch** to make a secret of sth; **il n'y a pas de m.** it's quite simple; *Fam* **m. et boule de gomme!** search me! (**b**) *(pièce de théâtre)* mystery (play) (**c**) **Mystère®** *(dessert glacé)* = vanilla ice cream filled with meringue and coated with chopped nuts

mystérieusement [misterjøzmɑ̃] *adv* mysteriously

mystérieux, -euse [misterjø, -øz] *adj* mysterious; *(secret)* secret

mysticisme [mistisism] *nm* mysticism

mystification [mistifikasjɔ̃] *nf* hoax

mystifier [66] [mistifje] *vt* to take in

mystique [mistik] **1** *adj* mystical
  2 *nmf* mystic

mythe [mit] *nm* myth; **elle fait un m. vivant** she was a legend in her own lifetime

mythique [mitik] *adj* mythical

mythologie [mitɔlɔʒi] *nf* mythology

mythologique [mitɔlɔʒik] *adj* mythological

mythomane [mitɔman] **1** *adj* **être m.** to be a pathological liar

  2 *nmf* pathological liar, *Spéc* mythomaniac

mythomanie [mitɔmani] *nf* mythomania

myxomatose [miksɔmatoz] *nf* myxomatosis

N¹, n [ɛn] *nm inv* N, n
N² 1 (*abrév* **Nord**) N
   2 *nf* (*abrév* **route nationale**) = designation of major road
nabot, -e [nabo, -ɔt] *nm,f Péj* midget
nacelle [nasɛl] *nf* (**a**) (*de montgolfière*) basket; (*de dirigeable*) gondola (**b**) (*de landau*) (*détachable*) carrycot; (*fixe*) carriage
nacre [nakr] *nf* mother-of-pearl; **un collier de** *ou* **en n.** a mother-of-pearl necklace
nacré, -e [nakre] *adj* pearly
nage [naʒ] *nf* (**a**) (*activité*) swimming; (*manière*) stroke; **traverser une rivière à la n.** to swim across a river; **le 100 mètres quatre nages** the 4 x 100 metres relay; **n. indienne** sidestroke; **n. libre** freestyle (**b**) **être en n.** to be bathed in perspiration
nageoire [naʒwar] *nf* (*de poisson*) fin; (*de dauphin, de cétacé*) flipper
nager [45] [naʒe] **1** *vi* to swim; **aller n.** to go for a swim; **n. vers la côte** to swim for the shore; *Fig* **n. entre deux eaux** to sit on the fence; *Fig* **n. dans son sang** to be bathed in blood; *Fig* **n. dans le bonheur** to be on cloud nine; *Fam* **il nage dans ses vêtements** his clothes are far too baggy on him; *Fam* **je nage complètement!** I'm totally at sea!
   2 *vt* (**a**) (*la brasse, le crawl*) to do, to swim (**b**) (*disputer*) **n. le 100 mètres** to swim (in) the 100 metres
nageur, -euse [naʒœr, -øz] *nm,f* swimmer
naguère [nagɛr] *adv Litt* not long ago; (*autrefois*) formerly
naïf, -ïve [naif, -iv] **1** *adj* naive
   2 *nm,f* (**a**) (*personne*) fool (**b**) (*peintre*) naive painter
nain, -e [nɛ̃, nɛn] **1** *adj* (*animal*) dwarf
   2 *nm,f* dwarf
   3 *nm* **n. de jardin** garden gnome
Nairobi [nerobi] *n* Nairobi
naissance [nɛsɑ̃s] *nf* (**a**) *aussi Fig* birth; **sourd/aveugle de n.** deaf/blind from birth, born deaf/blind; **français de n.** French by birth; **donner n. à un enfant** to give birth to a child; **donner n. à une rumeur** to give rise to a rumour; **il était blond à la n.** his hair was blond when he was born (**b**) (*d'ongle*) root; (*du cou*) base; **prendre n.** to originate; (*rivière*) to rise
naissant, -e [nɛsɑ̃, -ɑ̃t] *adj* (*jour*) dawning; (*beauté*) nascent; **une barbe naissante** stubble
naître [50a] [nɛtr] *vi* (*aux* **être**) (**a**) (*personne, animal*) to be born; **enfant à n.** unborn child; **il naît plus de filles que de garçons** more girls are born than boys; **elle est née en 1880** she was born in 1880; *Fam* **je ne suis pas né d'hier** I wasn't born yesterday (**b**) (*espoir*) to arise; (*projet, idée*) to originate (**de** in); **faire n.**

(*espoir, doute, soupçons*) to give rise to; (*sourire*) to raise
naïvement [naivmɑ̃] *adv* naively
naïveté [naivte] *nf* naivety; **avoir la n. de croire qch** to be naive enough to believe sth
Namibie [namibi] *nf* **la N.** Namibia
namibien, -enne [namibjɛ̃, -ɛn] **1** *adj* Namibian
   2 *nm,f* **N.** Namibian
nana [nana] *nf Fam Br* bird, *Am* chick
nanisme [nanism] *nm* dwarfism
nano- [nano] *préf* nano-
nanti, -e [nɑ̃ti] **1** *adj* well-to-do
   2 *nm,f* well-to-do person; **les nantis** the well-to-do
nantir [nɑ̃tir] *vt* **n. qn de qch** to provide sb with sth
napalm [napalm] *nm* napalm
naphtaline [naftalin] *nf* naphthalene; **boules de n.** mothballs; *Can Fig* **sortir qch de la n.** to take sth out of mothballs
Napoléon [napɔleɔ̃] **1** *npr* Napoleon
   2 *nm Anciennement* **n.** (*pièce*) 20-franc piece (*bearing the likeness of Napoleon*)
nappage [napaʒ] *nm* coating
nappe [nap] *nf* (**a**) (*de table*) tablecloth; **mettre la n.** to put the tablecloth on; **ôter la n.** to take the tablecloth off (**b**) *Fig* **n. de brouillard** fog patch; **n. d'eau** expanse of water; **n. de pétrole** (*souterraine*) layer of oil; (*de marée noire*) oil slick; **n. phréatique** water table
napper [nape] *vt* to coat (**de** with)
napperon [naprɔ̃] *nm* mat
narcisse [narsis] *nm* (**a**) (*fleur*) narcissus (**b**) (*personne*) narcissist
narcissique [narsisik] *adj* narcissistic
narcissisme [narsisism] *nm* narcissism
narcodollars [narkodɔlar] *nmpl* drug money
narcotique [narkɔtik] *adj & nm* narcotic
narcotrafic [narkɔtrafik] *nm* drug trafficking
narcotrafiquant, -e [narkɔtrafikɑ̃, -ɑ̃t] *nm,f* drug trafficker
narguer [narge] *vt* to taunt
narine [narin] *nf* nostril
narquois, -e [narkwa, -az] *adj* taunting
narquoisement [narkwazmɑ̃] *adv* tauntingly
narrateur, -trice [naratœr, -tris] *nm,f* narrator
narratif, -ive [naratif, -iv] *adj* narrative
narration [narasjɔ̃] *nf* (**a**) (*genre*) narration (**b**) (*récit*) narrative
narrer [nare] *vt Litt* to narrate
narval, -als [narval] *nm* narwhal
nasal, -e, -aux, -ales [nazal, -o] *adj* nasal

nase [naz] *Fam* **1** *adj* (**a**) *(épuisé) Br* knackered, *Am* beat (**b**) *(stupide)* dense, *Am* dumb (**c**) *(hors d'usage)* kaput, *Br* clapped-out (**d**) *(de mauvaise qualité)* crap, lousy
2 *nmf (personne stupide)* idiot, *Am* jerk
naseau, -x [nazo] *nm* nostril
nasillard, -e [nazijar, -ard] *adj* nasal; *(vieux disque)* tinny
nasse [nas] *nf* lobster pot
natal, -e, -als, -ales [natal] *adj* native; **sa maison natale** the house where he/she was born
nataliste [natalist] *adj* **politique n.** pro-birth policy
natalité [natalite] *nf* **(taux de) n.** birth rate
natation [natasjɔ̃] *nf* swimming; **faire de la n.** to swim; **n. synchronisée** synchronized swimming
natif, -ive [natif, -iv] **1** *adj* native; **être n. de** to be a native of
2 *nm,f* native
nation [nasjɔ̃] *nf* nation; **les Nations unies** the United Nations
national, -e, -aux, -ales [nasjɔnal, -o] **1** *adj* national
2 *nmpl* **nationaux** nationals
3 *nf* **nationale** *(route) Br* ≃ A road, *Am* ≃ highway
nationalisation [nasjɔnalizasjɔ̃] *nf* nationalization
nationaliser [nasjɔnalize] *vt* to nationalize
nationalisme [nasjɔnalism] *nm* nationalism
nationaliste [nasjɔnalist] *adj & nmf* nationalist
nationalité [nasjɔnalite] *nf* nationality; **être de n. française** to be a French national
national-socialisme [nasjɔnalsɔsjalism] *nm Hist* National Socialism
nativité [nativite] *nf (Noël, peinture)* Nativity
natte [nat] *nf* (**a**) *(de cheveux) Br* plait, *Am* braid (**b**) *(de paille)* mat
natter [nate] *vt (cheveux, paille) Br* to plait, *Am* to braid
naturalisation [natyralizasjɔ̃] *nf* naturalization
naturaliser [natyralize] *vt* to naturalize; **se faire n.** to become naturalized; **il s'est fait n. français** he was granted French citizenship
naturalisme [natyralism] *nm* naturalism
nature [natyr] **1** *nf* (**a**) *(univers)* nature; **contre n.** unnatural; **plus grand que n.** larger than life; **laisser faire la n.** to let nature take its course; *Fam* **elle n'est pas gâtée par la n.** nature hasn't been kind to her (**b**) *(campagne)* country; **en pleine n.** in the middle of the country; *Fig* **disparaître dans la n.** to vanish into thin air (**c**) *(caractère)* nature; **être timide de ou par n.** to be shy by nature; **être de n. à faire qch** to be likely to do sth; **chez elle, c'est une seconde n.** it's second nature to her; *Fam* **c'est une petite n.** he's a bit fragile (**d**) **payer en n.** to pay in kind (**e**) **n. morte** still life
2 *adj inv* (**a**) *(omelette)* plain; *(yaourt)* natural; **thé n.** tea without milk (**b**) *Fam (personne)* natural
naturel, -elle [natyrɛl] **1** *adj* natural; *(besoin)* bodily; **mort naturelle** death from natural causes; **mais c'est tout n.** don't mention it
2 *nm* (**a**) *(caractère)* nature; **être d'un n. peureux** to be timid by nature; *Prov* **chassez le n., il revient au galop** what's bred in the bone will come out in the flesh (**b**) *(simplicité)* naturalness; **avec (beaucoup de) n.** (very) naturally (**c**) **thon au n.** tuna in brine
naturellement [natyrɛlmɑ̃] *adv* naturally
naturisme [natyrism] *nm* naturism
naturiste [natyrist] *adj & nmf* naturist

naufrage [nofraʒ] *nm* (ship)wreck; *Fig (d'entreprise)* failure; **faire n.** *(bateau)* to be wrecked; *(marin)* to be shipwrecked; *Fig (entreprise)* to founder
naufragé, -e [nofraʒe] **1** *adj (bateau)* wrecked; *(marin)* shipwrecked
2 *nm,f* shipwrecked person
nauséabond, -e [nozeabɔ̃, -ɔ̃d] *adj (odeur)* nauseating; *(personne, pièce)* foul-smelling; *Fig (thèses)* sickening
nausée [noze] *nf* (**a**) *(envie de vomir)* nausea, sickness; **avoir la n., avoir des nausées** to feel sick (**b**) *Fig* disgust; **ça me donne la n.** it makes me sick
nauséeux, -euse [nozeø, -øz] *adj* **se sentir n.** to feel sick *or* nauseous
nautique [notik] *adj* nautical
nautisme [notism] *nm* water sports
naval, -e, -als, -ales [naval] *adj* naval
navet [navɛ] *nm* turnip; *Fam* **c'est un n.** *(film, pièce)* it's a load of rubbish, *Am* it's a turkey
navette [navɛt] *nf* (**a**) *(véhicule)* shuttle; **faire la n. entre deux endroits/services** to shuttle back and forth between two places/departments; **n. gratuite** courtesy bus (**b**) *(fusée)* **n. (spatiale)** (space) shuttle
navetteur, -euse [navɛtœr, -øz] *nm,f Belg* commuter
navigable [navigabl] *adj* navigable
navigant, -e [navigɑ̃, -ɑ̃t] *adj voir* **personnel**
navigateur, -trice [navigatœr, -tris] **1** *nm,f (marin)* navigator; **n. solitaire** lone yachtsman
2 *nm Ordinat* browser
navigation [navigasjɔ̃] *nf* navigation; **après un mois de n.** after a month at sea; *Ordinat* **n. sur l'Internet** browsing the Internet, Internet surfing; **n. par satellite** satellite navigation, *Fam* sat nav
naviguer [navige] *vi* to sail (**vers** to); **n. sur l'Internet** to surf the Net, to browse the Web
navire [navir] *nm* ship; **n.-école** training ship; **n. de guerre** warship
navrant, -e [navrɑ̃, -ɑ̃t] *adj* appalling; **un film n. de bêtise** an appallingly stupid film
navré, -e [navre] *adj (personne, expression, ton)* distressed; **être n. (de qch)** to be terribly sorry (about sth)
navrer [navre] *vt* to appal
naze [naz] = **nase**
nazi, -e [nazi] *adj & nm,f Hist* Nazi
nazisme [nazism] *nm Hist* Nazism
NB *(abrév nota bene)* NB
NDLR *(abrév note de la rédaction)* Ed
NdT *(abrév note du traducteur)* translator's note
ne [nə] *adv* (**a**) *voir* **aucun, guère, jamais, pas², personne, plus, que⁴, rien** (**b**) *(utilisé seul)* **je n'ai que faire de vos conseils** I have no need of your advice; **elle est plus vigoureuse qu'elle n'y paraît** she's stronger than she looks; **qui ne connaît cette œuvre?** who doesn't know this work?
né, -e [ne] **1** *pp de* **naître**
2 *adj* born; **Mme Martin, née Dupont** Mrs Martin, née Dupont; **né de parents anglais/inconnus** of English/unknown parentage; **être bien né** to be of noble birth; *Fig* **être né coiffé** to be born with a silver spoon in one's mouth; **c'est un conteur né** he's a born storyteller
néanmoins [neɑ̃mwɛ̃] *adv* nevertheless
néant [neɑ̃] *nm* (**a**) *(ce qui n'existe pas)* nothingness; **réduire qch à n.** to reduce sth to nothing (**b**) *(sur formulaire)* none

nébuleux, -euse [nebylø, -øz] **1** *adj aussi Fig* hazy **2** *nf* **nébuleuse***Astron* nebula

nécessaire [nesesɛr] **1** *adj* necessary (à for); **n. pour faire qch** necessary to do sth; **il est n. que vous y alliez** you must go; **elles n'ont pas jugé n. de me le dire** they didn't think it necessary to tell me **2** *nm* **le n.** the necessities; **n'emportez que le strict n.** just take the basic essentials; **faire le n.** to do what's necessary; **n. à chaussures** shoe-cleaning kit; **n. de couture** sewing kit; **n. de toilette** toilet bag; **n. de voyage** overnight bag

nécessairement [nesesɛrmɑ̃] *adv* necessarily

nécessité [nesesite] *nf* necessity; **être dans la n. de faire qch** to have no choice but to do sth; **quelle n. y avait-il de le faire?** what need was there to do it?; **faire de n. vertu** to make a virtue out of necessity; **produits de première n.** basic essentials; *Prov* **n. fait loi** needs must

nécessiter [nesesite] *vt* to require, to necessitate

nécessiteux, -euse [nesesitø, -øz] **1** *adj* needy **2** *nm,f* person in need; **les n.** the needy

nec plus ultra [nɛkplyzyltra] *nm inv* **le n.** the best there is

nécrologie [nekrɔlɔʒi] *nf (notice)* obituary; *(liste)* obituary column

nécrologique [nekrɔlɔʒik] *adj voir* **rubrique**

nécropole [nekrɔpɔl] *nf* necropolis

nécrose [nekroz] *nf* necrosis

nécroser [nekroze] **1** *vt* to necrose **2 se nécroser** *vpr* to necrose

nectar [nɛktar] *nm* nectar

nectarine [nɛktarin] *nf* nectarine

néerlandais, -e [neɛrlɑ̃dɛ, -ɛz] **1** *adj* Dutch **2** *nm,f* **N.** Dutchman; *f* Dutchwoman; **les N.** the Dutch **3** *nm (langue)* Dutch

nef [nɛf] *nf (d'église)* **n. (centrale)** nave; **n. latérale** aisle

néfaste [nefast] *adj* harmful

nèfle [nɛfl] *nf* medlar; *Fam* **des nèfles!** no way!

négatif, -ive [negatif, -iv] **1** *adj* negative **2** *nm Phot* negative **3 négative** *nf* **dans la negative** if not; **répondre par la n.** to give a negative answer, to answer in the negative

négation [negasjɔ̃] *nf* (**a**) *(fait de nier)* negation (**b**) *Gram* negative

négationnisme [negasjɔnism] *nm* revisionism

négationniste [negasjɔnist] *adj & nmf* revisionist

négativement [negativmɑ̃] *adv (réagir)* negatively; *(répondre)* in the negative

négligé, -e [negliʒe] **1** *adj* (**a**) *(peu soigné)* slovenly (**b**) *(délaissé)* neglected **2** *nm (vêtement)* negligée, negligee

négligeable [negliʒabl] *adj* negligible; **un avantage non n.** a not inconsiderable advantage; **une quantité non n. de** a significant quantity of

négligemment [negliʒamɑ̃] *adv* (**a**) *(habillé)* carelessly (**b**) *(répondre, lire)* casually

négligence [negliʒɑ̃s] *nf* (**a**) *(manque de soin)* carelessness, negligence; *(abandon)* neglect; **avec n.** carelessly (**b**) *(acte négligent)* act of carelessness; *(oubli)* oversight; **par n.** through carelessness

négligent, -e [negliʒɑ̃, -ɑ̃t] *adj* careless, negligent

négliger [45] [negliʒe] **1** *vt* (**a**) *(délaisser)* to neglect (**b**) *(omettre)* to disregard; **n. de faire qch** to neglect to do sth **2 se négliger** *vpr* to neglect oneself

négoce [negɔs] *nm* trade

négociable [negɔsjabl] *adj* negotiable

négociant, -e [negɔsjɑ̃, -ɑ̃t] *nm,f* merchant, dealer

négociation [negɔsjasjɔ̃] *nf* negotiation; **entamer des négociations sur qch** to enter into negotiations on sth; **être en n. avec qn** to be in negotiation with sb

négocier [66] [negɔsje] **1** *vt* (**a**) *(prêt, salaire, paix)* to negotiate; **prix à n.** price negotiable (**b**) *(virage)* to negotiate **2** *vi (discuter)* to negotiate (**avec** with)

nègre [nɛgr] **1** *nm* (**a**) Negro (**b**) *Fig (écrivain)* ghost writer; **être le n. de qn** to ghost for sb **2** *adj* (**a**) **l'art n.** Negro art (**b**) *(personne)* Negro

négresse [negrɛs] *nf* Negress

neige [nɛʒ] *nf* (**a**) *(flocons)* snow; *Can* **banc de n.** snow bank; **être bloqué par la n.** to be snowbound; **aller à la n.** to go on a skiing *Br* holiday *or Am* vacation; **fondre comme n. au soleil** to melt away; **être blanc comme n.** to be as white as snow; *Fig* to be as pure as the driven snow; **n. artificielle** *ou Can* **fabriquée** artificial snow; **n. carbonique** dry ice; **neiges éternelles** perpetual snow; **n. fondue** *(qui tombe)* sleet; *(par terre)* slush (**b**) *très Fam (cocaïne)* snow

neiger [45] [neʒe] *v impersonnel* to snow

neigeux, -euse [neʒø, -øz] *adj (temps, blanc)* snowy; *(pic, pente)* snow-covered

nem [nɛm] *nm* spring roll

néné [nene] *nm Fam* tit, boob

nénette [nenɛt] *nf Fam* (**a**) *(jeune fille) Br* bird, *Am* chick (**b**) *(petite amie)* girl (**c**) *(tête)* **se casser la n.** to rack one's brains

nénuphar [nenyfar] *nm* water lily

néo- [neo] *préf* neo-

néo-calédonien, -enne *(mpl* **néo-calédoniens,** *fpl* **néo-calédoniennes)** [neokaledɔnjɛ̃, -ɛn] **1** *adj* New Caledonian **2** *nm,f* **N.-C.** New Caledonian

néoclassique [neoklasik] *adj* neoclassical

néocolonialisme [neokɔlɔnjalism] *nm* neocolonialism

néolithique [neolitik] *Géol* **1** *adj* Neolithic **2** *nm* **le N.** the Neolithic period

néologisme [neɔlɔʒism] *nm* neologism

néon [neɔ̃] *nm (gaz)* neon; *(tube)* neon tube; *(enseigne)* neon sign

néonazi, -e [neonazi] *adj & nm,f* neo-Nazi

néonazisme [neonazism] *nm* neo-Nazism

néophyte [neofit] *nmf (nouvel adepte)* novice

néo-zélandais, -e *(mpl* **néo-zélandais,** *fpl* **néo-zélandaises)** [neozelɑ̃dɛ, -ɛz] **1** *adj* New Zealand **2** *nm,f* **N.-Z.** New Zealander

Népal [nepal] *nm* **le N.** Nepal

népalais, -e [nepalɛ, -ɛz] **1** *adj* Nepalese **2** *nm,f* **N.** Nepalese; **les N.** the Nepalese **3** *nm (langue)* Nepali

néphrétique [nefretik] *adj voir* **colique**

népotisme [nepotism] *nm* nepotism

Neptune [nɛptyn] *npr (dieu, planète)* Neptune

nerf [nɛr] *nm* (**a**) *(optique, spinal)* nerve; **viande pleine de nerfs** meat full of gristle; **avoir les nerfs solides** to have strong nerves; **être malade des nerfs** to suffer from nerves; **être sur les nerfs** to live on one's nerves; **être à bout de nerfs** to be at the end of one's tether; **passer ses nerfs sur qn/qch** to take it out on sb/sth; *Fam* **avoir les nerfs en pelote** *ou* **en boule** to be all on edge; *Fam* **porter** *ou* **taper** *ou Can* **tomber sur les nerfs à qn** to get on sb's nerves; *Fam* **c'est un**

paquet *ou* **une boule de nerfs** he's a bag of nerves (**b**) *(force)* **un peu de n.!, du n.!** get stuck in!; **l'argent est le n. de la guerre** money is the sinews of war
nerveusement [nɛrvøzmɑ̃] *adv* nervously
nerveux, -euse [nɛrvø, -øz] **1** *adj* (**a**) *(système, maladie)* nervous (**b**) *(émotif) (personne, rire, toux)* nervous (**c**) *(dynamique) (personne, style)* dynamic; **une conduite nerveuse** a jerky way of driving (**d**) *(corps, main)* sinewy; *(viande)* stringy
 2 *nm,f* nervous person
nervosité [nɛrvozite] *nf (excitation)* nervousness; *(irritabilité)* irritability
nervure [nɛrvyr] *nf* (**a**) *(de feuille, d'aile d'insecte)* vein (**b**) *(de voûte)* rib
n'est-ce pas [nɛspɑ] *adv* **tu viendras, n.?** you'll come, won't you?; **tu l'as, n.?** you've got it, haven't you?; **n. qu'elle est mignonne?** she's cute, isn't she?; **le problème, n., c'est qu'il est déjà tard** the problem is that it's already late, don't you think?
Net [nɛt] *nm Ordinat* **le N.** the Net
net, nette [nɛt] **1** *adj* (**a**) *(propre)* clean; *Fig (conscience)* clear; **faire place nette** to clear everything out (**b**) *(précis) (contour)* sharp; *(différence, souvenir)* clear; *(écriture)* neat; *(cassure)* clean; **il fait plus froid, c'est très n.** it's noticeably colder (**c**) *(prix, salaire, profit)* net; **n. d'impôt** net of tax (**d**) *Fam* **il n'est pas n.** *(fou)* he's not all there; *(louche)* he's a bit of a shady *or Br* dodgy character
 2 *adv* (**a**) *(brutalement)* **refuser (tout) n.** to refuse point-blank; **s'arrêter n.** to stop dead; **se casser n.** to break clean through; **tué n.** killed outright (**b**) *Com* **100 euros n.** 100 euros net; **n. à payer** net payable
netiquette [nɛtikɛt] *nf Ordinat* netiquette
nettement [nɛtmɑ̃] *adv* (**a**) *(avec précision)* clearly (**b**) *(incontestablement)* distinctly (**c**) *(beaucoup)* much; **il va n. mieux** he's much better; **il est n. moins bon qu'elle** he's not nearly as good as her
netteté [nɛtte] *nf* (**a**) *(propreté)* cleanness (**b**) *(précision) (de cassure)* cleanness (**c**) *(clarté) (de vision, d'objet)* distinctness; *(d'image)* sharpness; *(de refus)* flatness
nettoiement [nɛtwamɑ̃] *nm* cleaning; **service du n.** refuse collection service
nettoyage [nɛtwajaʒ] *nm* cleaning; **faire du n.** to do the cleaning; **faire le n. par le vide** to throw everything out; **grand n. de printemps** spring cleaning; **n. à sec** dry-cleaning
nettoyant, -e [nɛtwajɑ̃, -ɑ̃t] **1** *adj* cleaning
 2 *nm* cleaning product
nettoyer [32] [nɛtwaje] **1** *vt* (**a**) *(rendre propre)* to clean; **n. à sec** to dry-clean (**b**) *Fam (sujet: cambrioleur) (maison)* to clean out; **se faire n. au jeu** to be cleaned out gambling
 2 **se nettoyer** *vpr* (**a**) **se n. les oreilles/les mains** to clean one's ears/hands (**b**) **le four se nettoie automatiquement** the oven is self-cleaning
neuf¹ [nœf] *adj & nm inv* nine; *voir aussi* **trois**
neuf², neuve [nœf, nœv] **1** *adj* new; **tout n.** brand new; **comme n.** as good as new; **quoi de n.?** what's new?
 2 *nm* **habillé de n.** wearing new clothes; **acheter du n.** *(dans l'immobilier)* to buy new; **remettre qch à n.** to make sth as good as new; *(machine)* to recondition sth
neurasthénie [nørasteni] *nf* depression
neurasthénique [nørastenik] *adj & nmf* depressive
neurochirurgie [nøroʃiryrʒi] *nf* neurosurgery

neurochirurgien, -enne [nøroʃiryrʒjɛ̃, -ɛn] *nm,f* neurosurgeon
neuroleptique [nørolɛptik] *adj & nm* neuroleptic
neurologie [nørolɔʒi] *nf* neurology
neurologue [nørolɔg] *nmf* neurologist
neurone [nørɔn, nøron] *nm* neuron
neutraliser [nøtralize] **1** *vt* to neutralize
 2 **se neutraliser** *vpr* to neutralize each other
neutralité [nøtralite] *nf* neutrality; **sortir de sa n.** to abandon one's neutral position
neutre [nøtr] **1** *adj* (**a**) *(ni masculin ni féminin)* neuter (**b**) *(impartial)* neutral (**c**) *(ton de voix, couleur)* neutral (**d**) *Chim & Élec* neutral
 2 *nm* (**a**) *Gram* neuter (**b**) *Can Aut* neutral; **se mettre sur le n.** to go into neutral
neutron [nøtrɔ̃] *nm* neutron
neuvième [nœvjɛm] *nmf, nm & adj* ninth; *voir aussi* **cinquième**
névé [neve] *nm* névé, firn
neveu, -x [nəvø] *nm* nephew; *Fam* **un peu, mon n.!** you bet!, sure thing!
névralgie [nevralʒi] *nf* neuralgia; **avoir des névralgies** to suffer from neuralgia
névralgique [nevralʒik] *adj* neuralgic
névrose [nevroz] *nf* neurosis; **n. post-traumatique** post-traumatic stress disorder
névrosé, -e [nevroze] *adj & nm,f* neurotic
New York [nujɔrk] *n* New York
new-yorkais, -e (*mpl* **new-yorkais**, *fpl* **new-yorkaises**) [njujɔrkɛ, -ɛz] **1** *adj* of New York
 2 *nm,f* **N.-Y.** NewYorker
nez [ne] *nm* (**a**) *(organe)* nose; **n. en trompette** turned-up nose; **parler du n.** to speak through one's nose; **sentir qch à plein n.** to smell strongly of sth; **rire au n. de qn** to laugh in sb's face; **faire qch au n. et à la barbe de qn** to do sth right under sb's nose; **fermer ou claquer la porte au n. de qn** to shut the door in sb's face; **se trouver n. à n. avec qn** to find oneself face to face with sb; **avoir le n. dans son journal** to have one's nose in one's newspaper; **avoir le n. en l'air** to be looking up in the air; *Fig (rêvasser)* to have one's head in the clouds; *Fig* **mener qn par le bout du n.** to lead sb by the nose; *Fam* **fourrer** *ou* **mettre son n. dans les affaires de qn** to poke one's nose into sb's affairs; *Fam* **avoir un verre** *ou* **un coup dans le n.** to have had one too many; **je n'ai pas mis le n. dehors de toute la journée** I didn't set foot outside all day; **tu ne vois pas plus loin que le bout de ton n.** you can't see past the end of your nose; *Fam* **elle nous a dans le n.** she can't stand us; **ça lui pend au n.** he's/she's got it coming to him/her; **ça se voit comme le n. au milieu de la figure** it's as plain as the nose on your face; **où est-il? – il est sous ton n.** *ou* **tu as le n. dessus** where is it? – it's right under your nose (**b**) *(odorat)* sense of smell; **avoir le n. fin** to have a good nose; *Fig* **avoir du n.** to be shrewd (**c**) *(de bateau, d'avion)* nose (**d**) *(parfumeur)* nose
ni [ni] *conj* **ni... ni...** neither... nor...; **ni Pierre ni Paul ne sont venus** neither Pierre nor Paul came; **sans argent ni bagages** without money or luggage; **il est parti sans manger ni boire** he left without eating or drinking; **ni l'un ni l'autre** neither (of them); **ni plus ni moins** neither more nor less
niais, -e [njɛ, njɛz] **1** *adj* silly
 2 *nm,f* fool
niaisage [njɛzaʒ] *nm Can* idleness
niaisement [njɛzmɑ̃] *adv* foolishly

niaiser [njɛze] *Can* **1** *vt* **n. qn** *(faire tourner en bourrique)* to drive sb crazy; *(se moquer de)* to laugh at sb; *(raconter des histoires à)* to pull sb's leg
2 *vi (ne rien faire)* to hang around doing nothing

niaiserie [njɛzri] *nf* (**a**) *(caractère stupide)* silliness (**b**) *(acte, remarque)* silly thing

niaiseux, -euse [njɛzø, -øz] *Can Fam* **1** *adj* silly
2 *nm,f* fool

Nicaragua [nikaragwa] *nm* **le N.** Nicaragua

nicaraguayen, -enne [nikaragwajɛ̃, -ɛn] **1** *adj* Nicaraguan
2 *nm,f* **N.** Nicaraguan

niche [niʃ] *nf* (**a**) *(renfoncement)* niche, recess (**b**) *(de chien)* kennel

nichée [niʃe] *nf (d'oisillons)* brood; *(de souris, de chiots)* litter

nicher [niʃe] **1** *vi (oiseau)* to nest (**dans** in)
2 *vt* **n. sa tête au creux de l'épaule de qn** to nestle one's head against sb's shoulder
3 se nicher *vpr* (**a**) *(oiseau)* to nest (**b**) *Fam (se cacher)* **où est-elle allée se n.?** where's she hiding (herself)?

nichon [niʃɔ̃] *nm Fam* boob, tit

nickel [nikɛl] **1** *nm* nickel
2 *adj inv Fam (propre)* spotlessly clean

nicotine [nikɔtin] *nf* nicotine

nid [ni] *nm aussi Fig* nest; *Fig* **n. à poussière** dust trap; *Prov* **petit à petit, l'oiseau fait son n.** slow and steady wins the race

nid-de-poule *(pl* **nids-de-poule**) [nidpul] *nm* pothole

nièce [njɛs] *nf* niece

nier [66] [nje] **1** *vt* to deny; **je nie l'avoir vue** I deny having seen her; **on ne peut pas n. que...** there's no denying that...; **n. l'évidence** to deny the obvious
2 *vi (accusé)* to deny the charge

niet [njɛt] *exclam Fam* no way!, not a chance!

nigaud, -e [nigo, -od] *nm,f* ninny; **gros n.!** you big ninny!

Niger [niʒɛr] *nm* **le N.** *(pays)* Niger; *(fleuve)* the Niger

Nigeria [niʒerja] *nm* **le N.** Nigeria

nigérian, -e [niʒerjɑ̃, -an] **1** *adj* Nigerian
2 *nm,f* **N.** Nigerian

nigérien, -enne [niʒerjɛ̃, -ɛn] **1** *adj* Nigerien
2 *nm,f* **N.** Nigerien

nihilisme [niilism] *nm* nihilism

nihiliste [niilist] **1** *adj* nihilistic
2 *nmf* nihilist

Nil [nil] *nm* **le N.** the Nile

n'importe [nɛ̃pɔrt] *voir* **importer²**

NIP [nip] *nm Can Fin (abrév* **numéro d'identification personnelle**) ≃ PIN (number)

nipper [nipe] *Fam* **1** *vt* to dress; **bien nippé** dolled up
2 se nipper *vpr* to dress; **il sait pas se n.** he's got no dress sense

nippes [nip] *nfpl Fam (vêtements)* gear, threads

nippon, -onne *ou* **-one** [nipɔ̃, -ɔn] **1** *adj* Japanese
2 *nm,f* **N.** Japanese; **les Nippons** the Japanese

nique [nik] *nf Fam* **faire la n. à qn** to thumb one's nose at sb

niquer [nike] *vt* (**a**) *très Fam (abîmer)* to knacker (**b**) *Vulg (sexuellement)* to screw, *Br* to shag (**c**) *très Fam (escroquer)* **se faire n.** to get screwed

nitrate [nitrat] *nm* nitrate

nitreux, -euse [nitrø, -øz] *adj* nitrous

nitrique [nitrik] *adj* nitric

nitroglycérine [nitrogliserin] *nf* nitroglycerine

niveau, -x [nivo] *nm* (**a**) *(hauteur, étage)* level; **n. de l'eau/de la mer** water/sea level; **au n. de la mer** at sea level; **au n. du carrefour, vous tournez à droite** when you come to the crossroads, turn right; **au n. régional/local** at regional/local level; *Fam* **au n. sentimental** as far as one's love life is concerned; *aussi Fig* **se mettre au n. de qn** to put oneself on sb's level; **l'eau nous arrivait au n. de la taille** the water came up to our waists (**b**) *(degré)* level; *Scol* standard; **avoir le n. (requis), être au n.** to be up to standard; **ne pas avoir le n. pour passer un concours** not to be of a high enough standard to take an examination; **elle a un très bon n. en physique** her physics is of a very high standard; **ils sont d'un n. social différent** they are from different social backgrounds; *Ordinat* **n. d'accès** *(dans un réseau)* access level; *Ordinat* **n. de gris** grey scale; **n. de langue** register; **n. de vie** standard of living

niveler [9] [nivle] *vt* (**a**) *(sol)* to level (**b**) *(fortunes)* to even out

nivellement [nivɛlmɑ̃] *nm (de terrain, des classes sociales)* levelling; **n. par le bas** levelling down

nobéliser *vt (décerner un prix Nobel à)* to award the Nobel prize to

nobiliaire [nɔbiljɛr] *adj* **titre n.** title; **particule n.** nobiliary particle

noble [nɔbl] **1** *adj* noble; **le n. art** *(boxe)* the noble art
2 *nmf* nobleman, *f* noblewoman; **les nobles** the nobility

noblement [nɔbləmɑ̃] *adv* nobly

noblesse [nɔblɛs] *nf* nobility; **la haute et la petite n.** the nobility and the gentry; **n. oblige** noblesse oblige

noce [nɔs] *nf* (**a**) *(cérémonie du mariage)* wedding; *(ensemble des invités)* wedding party; **noces d'argent/ d'or/de diamant** silver/golden/diamond wedding; **il l'a épousée en secondes noces** she's his second wife (**b**) *Fam* **faire la n.** to live it up (**c**) *Fam* **je n'étais pas à la n.** it was no picnic

noceur, -euse [nɔsœr, -øz] *nm,f Fam* party animal

nocif, -ive [nɔsif, -iv] *adj* harmful

nocivité [nɔsivite] *nf* harmfulness

noctambule [nɔktɑ̃byl] *nmf* night owl

nocturne [nɔktyrn] **1** *adj (animal)* nocturnal; *(attaque, visite)* night; **évasion n.** escape by night
2 *nm (musique)* nocturne
3 *nf* (**a**) *(de magasin)* late-night opening (**b**) **match (disputé) en n.** evening game

nodal, -e, -aux, -ales [nɔdal, -o] *adj* nodal

nodule [nɔdyl] *nm Géol & Méd* nodule

Noé [nɔe] *n* Noah

Noël [nɔɛl] *nm* (**a**) *(fête)* Christmas; **à N.** at Christmas (time); **le jour de N.** Christmas Day; **arbre** *ou* **sapin de N.** Christmas tree; **joyeux N.!** Happy *or* Merry Christmas! (**b**) *(chanson)* **n.** (Christmas) carol (**c**) *(cadeau)* **(petit) n.** Christmas present

nœud [nø] *nm* (**a**) *(entrecroisement)* knot; **faire un n. (à qch)** to make *or* tie a knot (in sth); **n. coulant** *(pour serrer)* slipknot; *(pour étrangler)* noose; **n. de vipères** nest of vipers (**b**) *(ornement)* bow; **n. de cravate** tie knot; **faire un n. de cravate** to knot a tie; **n. papillon,** *Fam* **n. pap** bow tie (**c**) *(de courbe)* & *Ordinat* node (**d**) *(sur bois)* knot (**e**) *Naut (vitesse)* knot; **filer** *ou* **faire 20 nœuds** to do *or* make 20 knots (**f**) *Vulg (pénis)* cock

noie *etc voir* **noyer²**

noir, -e [nwar] **1** *adj* (**a**) *(couleur)* black; **la place était noire de monde** the square was swarming with people (**b**) *(très sombre)* dark; **il fait tout n.** it's pitch-black (**c**) *(sale)* black (**d**) *Fig (pensées, dessein, regard)* black; **être d'une humeur noire** to be in a black mood

2 *nm,f* **N.** Black (man), *f* Black (woman)

3 *nm* (**a**) *(couleur)* black; **en n. et blanc** *(film, photo)* black and white; **être en n.** to be dressed in black; **c'était écrit n. sur blanc** it was there in black and white (**b**) *(obscurité)* dark; **avoir peur du n.** to be afraid of the dark (**c**) *(salissure)* **avoir du n. sur le visage** to have a black mark on one's face (**d**) *(d'une cible)* bull's-eye (**e**) *(café)* **un (petit) n.** a (small) black coffee (**f**) *Fig* **voir tout en n.** to look on the black side of everything (**g**) *Fam* **le travail au n.** moonlighting; **travailler au n.** to moonlight

4 *nf* **noire** *(note de musique) Br* crotchet, *Am* quarter note

noirâtre [nwaratr] *adj* blackish

noirceur [nwarsœr] *nf* (**a**) *(couleur)* blackness; *Litt (d'un crime)* heinousness (**b**) *Can (obscurité)* dark, darkness; **dans la n.** in the dark *or* darkness; **avoir peur dans la n.** to be afraid of the dark

noircir [nwarsir] **1** *vt* to blacken; **n. du papier** to write pages and pages; *Fig* **n. (la réputation de)** qn to blacken sb's reputation; *Fig* **n. le tableau** *ou* **la situation** to paint things blacker than they are

2 *vi* to turn or go black

3 **se noircir** *vpr* (**a**) *(ciel)* to darken (**b**) **se n. le visage** to black one's face; *Théât* to black up

noise [nwaz] *nf* **chercher n.** *ou* **des noises à qn** to try to pick a quarrel with sb

noisetier [nwaztje] *nm (arbre)* hazel tree; *(bois)* hazel (wood)

noisette [nwazet] **1** *nf* (**a**) *(fruit)* hazelnut (**b**) *(petite quantité) (de beurre)* small knob; *(de gel)* small amount

2 *adj inv* **yeux n.** hazel eyes

noix [nwa] *nf* (**a**) *(fruit)* walnut; **n. de cajou** cashew nut; **n. de coco** coconut; **n. de pécan** pecan (**b**) *(petite quantité) (de beurre)* knob (**c**) **n. de veau** cushion of veal (**d**) *Fam* **à la n.** lousy

nom [nɔ̃] *nm* (**a**) *(de personne, de chose)* name; **un homme du n. de Pierre** a man by the name of Pierre; **n.... prénom...** *(sur formulaire)* surname... first name...; **vos n., prénoms et adresse** your full name and address; **porter le n. de sa mère** to be named after one's mother; **sous le n. de Leduc** under the name of Leduc; **se faire un n.** to make a name for oneself; **appeler les choses par leur n.** to call a spade a spade; **traiter qn de tous les noms** to call sb everything under the sun; **quelqu'un dont je tairai le n.** someone who shall remain nameless; **une impolitesse sans n.** unspeakable rudeness; **un grand n. de la musique** one of the great names in music; **faire une proposition au n. de qn** to make a proposal for sb *or* on behalf of sb; **au n. de la loi/de l'amitié** in the name of the law/of friendship; *Fam* **avoir un n. à coucher dehors** to have a totally unpronounceable name; **n. de baptême** Christian name; *Ordinat* **n. de champ** field name; *Ordinat* **n. de domaine** domain name; **n. d'emprunt** assumed name; **n. de famille** surname; *Ordinat* **n. de fichier** file name; **n. de jeune fille** maiden name; **n. à particule** aristocratic name *(with a nobiliary particle)*; **n. de plume** nom de plume, pen name; *Fam* **n. à rallonges** *ou* **à tiroirs** long aristocratic name, *Br* ≃ double-barrelled name; **n. de scène** *ou* **de théâtre** stage name; **n.**

commun common noun; **n. composé** compound (noun); **n. propre** proper noun (**c**) *Fam* **n. d'une pipe!, n. d'un chien!** hell!

nomade [nɔmad] **1** *adj* nomadic

2 *nmf* nomad

nomadisme [nɔmadism] *nm* nomadism

nombre [nɔ̃br] *nm aussi Gram* number; **un grand/petit n. d'entre nous** many/a few of us; **le plus grand n.** the majority; **(bon) n. de** a good many; **supérieur en n.** superior in number(s); **nous sommes en n. suffisant** there are enough of us; **venir en n.** to come in large numbers; **ils sont au n. de huit** there are eight of them; **être au n.** *ou* **du n. de** to be among; **faire n.** to make up the numbers; *Phys* **n. atomique** atomic number; *Math* **n. décimal** decimal (number); *Math* **n. entier** whole number, integer; *Math* **n. premier** prime number

nombreux, -euse [nɔ̃brø, -øz] *adj (membres, objets)* numerous, many; *(famille, armée, groupe)* large; **nous sommes peu n.** there aren't many of us; **venir (très) n.** to come in (very) large numbers

nombril [nɔ̃bri, nɔ̃bril] *nm* navel; **une chemise ouverte jusqu'au n.** a shirt open to the waist; **il se prend pour le n. du monde** he thinks the whole world revolves around him; *Fig* **se regarder le n.** to contemplate one's navel; *Can* **ne pas avoir le n. sec** to be (still) wet behind the ears

nombrilisme [nɔ̃brilism] *nm* navel-gazing

nombriliste [nɔ̃brilist] *adj* self-absorbed

nomenclature [nɔmɑ̃klatyr] *nf (de termes techniques)* nomenclature; *(d'un dictionnaire)* word list

nominal, -e, -aux, -ales [nɔminal, -o] *adj* (**a**) *(prix, autorité) & Fin* nominal (**b**) *(par noms de famille)* **appel n.** roll call; **liste nominale** list of names (**c**) *Gram* noun

nominalement [nɔminalmɑ̃] *adv* (**a**) *(de nom seulement)* in name only (**b**) *Gram (employé)* as a noun

nominatif, -ive [nɔminatif, -iv] *adj (carte d'adhérent, billet)* nontransferable; *Fin (titre)* registered

nomination [nɔminasjɔ̃] *nf* (**a**) *(à un poste)* appointment (à to) (**b**) *(pour une remise de récompense)* nomination (à for)

nominativement [nɔminativmɑ̃] *adv* by name

nominé, -e [nɔmine] *adj* nominated (à for)

nommé, -e [nɔme] **1** *adj (personne, objet)* named

2 *nm,f* **un n. Bertrand a appelé** someone called Bertrand rang

nommément [nɔmemɑ̃] *adv* (**a**) *(par son nom)* by name (**b**) *(spécialement)* especially, in particular

nommer [nɔme] **1** *vt* (**a**) *(donner un prénom à)* to name, to call (**b**) *(donner un nom à)* **on nomme aumôniers les prêtres attachés à un régiment** priests attached to a regiment are called chaplains (**c**) *(désigner)* to name; *Hum* **M. Boivin, pour ne pas le nommer** without mentioning any names, Mr Boivin (**d**) *(à un poste)* to appoint (à to); **être nommé à Lille** to be posted to Lille

2 **se nommer** *vpr* (**a**) *(avoir pour nom)* to be called (**b**) *(s'identifier)* to give one's name

non [nɔ̃] **1** *adv* (**a**) *(en réponse, exprime la surprise, l'indignation)* no; **je pense que n.** I don't think so; **faire signe que n.** *(de la tête)* to shake one's head; **n. mais!** honestly! (**b**) *(n'est-ce pas?)* **c'est dégoûtant, n.?** it's disgusting, isn't it?; **il est pas mal, n.?** he's not bad-looking, is he? (**c**) *(pas)* not; **n. loin** not far; **qu'elle vienne ou n.** whether she comes or not; **elle veut déménager, lui n.** she wants to move house but

he doesn't; *Litt* **n. (pas) que je le craigne** not that I fear him
2 *nm inv* no
nonagénaire [nɔnaʒenɛr] *adj & nmf* nonagenarian
non-agression [nɔnagresjɔ̃] *nf voir* **pacte**
non-alcoolisé, -e [nɔnalkɔlize] *adj* non-alcoholic
non-aligné, -e [nɔnaliɲe] *adj Pol* non-aligned
nonante [nɔnɑ̃t] *adj & nm inv Belg & Suisse* ninety; *voir aussi* **trois**
non-assistance [nɔnasistɑ̃s] *nf Jur* **n. à personne en danger** = failure to assist a person in danger, for example at the scene of an accident
non-autorisé, -e [nɔnotɔrize] *adj Ordinat (nom de fichier)* illegal
non-belligérant, -e [nɔ̃beliʒerɑ̃, -ɑ̃t] *adj* non-belligerent
nonchalamment [nɔ̃ʃalamɑ̃] *adv* nonchalantly
nonchalance [nɔ̃ʃalɑ̃s] *nf* nonchalance; **avec n.** nonchalantly
nonchalant, -e [nɔ̃ʃalɑ̃, -ɑ̃t] *adj* nonchalant
non-conformisme [nɔ̃kɔ̃fɔrmism] *nm* non-conformism
non-conformiste [nɔ̃kɔ̃fɔrmist] *adj & nmf* non-conformist
non-conformité [nɔ̃kɔ̃fɔrmite] *nf* nonconformity
non-connecté, -e [nɔ̃kɔnɛkte] *adj Ordinat* off-line
non-dit [nɔ̃di] *nm* **le n.** what is unspoken; **un film riche en non-dits** a movie *or Br* film full of meaningful silences
non-formaté, -e [nɔ̃fɔrmate] *adj Ordinat* unformatted
non-fumeur, -euse [nɔ̃fymœr, -øz] **1** *adj* non-smoking
2 *nm,f* non-smoker
non-ingérence [nɔnɛ̃ʒerɑ̃s] *nf* noninterference
non-initialisé, -e [nɔninisjalize] *adj Ordinat* uninitialized
non-initié, -e [nɔninisje] *nm,f* uninitiated person; **les non-initiés** the uninitiated
non-inscrit, -e [nɔnɛ̃skri, -it] *nm,f Pol* independent
non-intervention [nɔnɛ̃tɛrvɑ̃sjɔ̃] *nf* non-intervention
non-interventionniste [nɔnɛ̃tɛrvɑ̃sjɔnist] *adj* non-interventionist
non-lieu, -x [nɔ̃ljø] *nm Jur* **bénéficier d'un n.** to be discharged through lack of evidence
nonne [nɔn] *nf* nun
nono, -ote [nɔno, -ɔt] *nm,f Can Fam* idiot
non-paiement [nɔ̃pɛmɑ̃] *nm* non-payment
non-polluant, -e [nɔ̃pɔlɥɑ̃, -ɑ̃t] *adj* environmentally friendly
non-prolifération [nɔ̃prɔliferajɔ̃] *nf* nonproliferation
non-remboursable [nɔ̃rɑ̃bursabl] *adj* non-refundable
non-respect [nɔ̃rɛspɛ] *nm (d'une loi)* non-observance
non-retour [nɔ̃rɔtur] *nm* **point de n.** point of no return
non-salarié, -e [nɔ̃salarje] *nm,f* self-employed person
non-sens [nɔ̃sɑ̃s] *nm inv* **(a)** *(dans une traduction)* meaningless phrase **(b)** *(absurdité)* **un n.** a nonsense
non-stop [nɔnstɔp] *adj inv & adv Fam* non-stop
non-syndiqué, -e [nɔ̃sɛ̃dike] **1** *adj* non-union
2 *nm,f* non-union worker
non-violence [nɔ̃vjɔlɑ̃s] *nf* non-violence
non-violent, -e [nɔ̃vjɔlɑ̃, -ɑ̃t] *adj* non-violent

non-voyant, -e *(mpl* **non-voyants,** *fpl* **non-voyantes)** [nɔ̃vwajɑ̃, -ɑ̃t] *nm,f* unsighted person; **les non-voyants** the unsighted
nord [nɔr] **1** *nm* north; **un vent du n.** a northerly *or* north wind; **le vent du n.** the north wind; **au n.** in the north; **au n. de** (to the) north of; *Fig* **il ne perd pas le n.** he's keeping a cool head; **le grand N.** the Frozen North
2 *adj inv (côte, face)* north; *(régions)* northern
nord-africain, -e *(mpl* **nord-africains,** *fpl* **nord-africaines)** [nɔrafrikɛ̃, -ɛn] **1** *adj* North African
2 *nm,f* **N.-A.** North African
nord-américain, -e *(mpl* **nord-américains,** *fpl* **nord-américaines)** [nɔramerikɛ̃, -ɛn] **1** *adj* North American
2 *nm,f* **N.-A.** North American
nord-coréen, -enne *(mpl* **nord-coréens,** *fpl* **nord-coréennes)** [nɔrkɔreɛ̃, -ɛn] **1** *adj* North Korean
2 *nm,f* **N.-C.** North Korean
nord-est [nɔrɛst] *nm & adj inv* northeast
nordique [nɔrdik] **1** *adj* Nordic, Scandinavian
2 *nmf* **N.** Scandinavian
nordiste [nɔrdist] *adj & nmf* Unionist
nord-nord-est [nɔrnɔrɛst] *nm & adj inv* north-north-east
nord-nord-ouest [nɔrnɔrwɛst] *nm & adj inv* north-north-west
nord-ouest [nɔrwɛst] *nm & adj inv* northwest
nord-vietnamien, -enne *(mpl* **nord-vietnamiens,** *fpl* **nord-vietnamiennes)** [nɔrvjɛtnamjɛ̃, -ɛn] **1** *adj* North Vietnamese
2 *nm,f* **N.-V.** North Vietnamese
noria [nɔrja] *nf* noria
normal, -e, -aux, -ales [nɔrmal, -o] **1** *adj* **(a)** *(dans la norme, naturel)* normal; **c'est tout à fait n. que la jeunesse se rebelle** it's quite normal for young people to rebel; **ce n'est pas n.** **(** que + *subjunctive)* it's not right (that); **en temps n.** in normal circumstances **(b)** *(moyen) (poids, taille)* standard
2 *nf* normale **(a) la normale** normal, the norm; **au-dessus/au-dessous de la normale** above/below average; **température au-dessous des normales saisonnières** temperature below the seasonal average **(b)** *Fam Univ* **Normale Sup'** = university-level college preparing students for senior posts in teaching
normalement [nɔrmalmɑ̃] *adv* normally
normalien, -enne [nɔrmaljɛ̃, -ɛn] *nm,f Univ* = student or former student of the "École normale supérieure"
normalisation [nɔrmalizasjɔ̃] *nf* **(a)** *(des relations diplomatiques)* normalization **(b)** *Ind* standardization
normaliser [nɔrmalize] *vt* **(a)** *(relations diplomatiques)* to normalize **(b)** *Ind* to standardize
normalité [nɔrmalite] *nf* normality
normand, -e [nɔrmɑ̃, -ɑ̃d] *aussi Hist* **1** *adj* Norman
2 *nm,f* **N.** Norman
Normandie [nɔrmɑ̃di] *nf* **la N.** Normandy
norme [nɔrm] *nf* **(a)** *(règle)* norm; **dans la n.** within the norm **(b)** *Ind & Com* standard
noroît [nɔrwa] *nm* north-wester
Norvège [nɔrvɛʒ] *nf* **la N.** Norway
norvégien, -enne [nɔrveʒjɛ̃, -ɛn] **1** *adj* Norwegian
2 *nm,f* **N.** Norwegian
3 *nm (langue)* Norwegian
nos [no] *voir* **notre**

nostalgie [nɔstalʒi] *nf* nostalgia; *(mal du pays)* homesickness; **avoir la n. de qch** to feel nostalgic for sth; **avoir la n. du pays** to be homesick

nostalgique [nɔstalʒik] *adj* nostalgic

nota bene [nɔtabene] *nm inv* nota bene

notable [nɔtabl] *adj & nm* notable

notablement [nɔtabləmɑ̃] *adv* notably

notaire [nɔtɛr] *nm* notary (public)

notamment [nɔtamɑ̃] *adv* notably

notarié, -e [nɔtarje] *adj Jur* **acte n.** notarized deed

notation [nɔtasjɔ̃] *nf* (**a**) *(d'un travail scolaire)* marking (**b**) *(par des symboles)* notation

note [nɔt] *nf* (**a**) *(annotation, communication écrite)* note; **prendre des notes** to take (down) notes; **prendre bonne n. de qch** to take due note of sth; *Typ & Ordinat* **n. de** *ou* **en bas de page** footnote; **n. de service** memo (**b**) *(appréciation)* Br mark, Am grade (**c**) *Mus* note (**d**) *(facture)* bill; *(dans un hôtel)* Br bill, Am check; **n. de frais** expenses; **n. de téléphone** phone bill (**e**) *(nuance)* touch, note

notebook [nɔtbuk] *nm Ordinat* notebook

noter [nɔte] *vt* (**a**) *(mettre par écrit)* to note down, to make a note of (**b**) *(remarquer)* to note; **note bien que…** mind you,…; *Fig* **c'est noté, je note** got it (**c**) *(travail scolaire, élève)* Br to mark, Am to grade

notice [nɔtis] *nf (mode d'emploi)* instructions; *(d'un médicament)* directions

notification [nɔtifikasjɔ̃] *nf Jur* notification

notifier [66] [nɔtifje] *vt* **n. qch à qn** to notify sb of sth

notion [nɔsjɔ̃] *nf* (**a**) *(concept)* notion, concept; **perdre la n. du temps/de la réalité** to lose track of time/all sense of reality (**b**) **notions** *(connaissances sommaires)* basics; **avoir des notions de qch** to know the basics of sth

notoire [nɔtwar] *adj (fait)* well-known; *(criminel, mesquinerie)* notorious

notoriété [nɔtɔrjete] *nf (d'une personne)* fame; **il est de n. publique que…** it's common knowledge that…

notre, nos [nɔtr, no] *adj possessif* our; **n. chien** *(il y a un chien)* our dog; *(chacun a son chien)* our dogs; **nos enfants** our children; **n. père et n. mère** our mother and father; **un de nos amis** one of our friends, a friend of ours; *Fam* **nous avons n. vendredi** we've got Friday off

nôtre [nɔtr] **1** *pron possessif* **le n., la n., les nôtres** ours; *(en insistant)* our own; **nous te prêtons le n.** you can borrow ours; **nous n'en avons pas besoin, nous avons le n.** we don't need it, we've got our own; *Fam* **à la n.!** here's to us!

2 *nm* **il faut y mettre du n.** we have to do our share

3 *nmpl* **les nôtres** *(notre famille)* our family; **serez-vous des nôtres ce soir?** will you be joining us this evening?

nouba [nuba] *nf Fam* party; **faire la n.** to party

noué, -e [nwe] *adj* **avoir l'estomac n.** to have a knot in one's stomach; **avoir la gorge nouée** to have a lump in one's throat

nouer [nwe] **1** *vt* (**a**) *(ficelle, ruban, lacets)* to tie; *(cheveux)* to tie up; *(cravate)* to knot (**b**) *(relations)* to establish (**avec** with)

2 **se nouer** *vpr* (**a**) *(amitié)* to be formed (**b**) *(intrigue)* to take shape

noueux, -euse [nwø, -øz] *adj (bois)* knotty; *(tronc d'arbre, mains, doigts)* gnarled

nougat [nuga] *nm* nougat

nougatine [nugatin] *nf* nougatine

nouille [nuj] **1** *nf* (**a**) *Culin* **nouilles** noodles; *(pâtes en général)* pasta (**b**) *Fam (personne) (molle)* drip; *(niaise)* dimwit

2 *adj Fam (niais)* dumb, dopey

nounou [nunu] *nf (langage enfantin)* nanny

nounours [nunurs] *nm (langage enfantin)* teddy (bear)

nourri, -e [nuri] *adj (applaudissements)* prolonged; *(feu)* heavy

nourrice [nuris] *nf* (**a**) *(assistante maternelle)* child minder; **n. agréée** registered child minder (**b**) *Vieilli (qui allaite)* wet nurse

nourricier, -ère [nurisje, -ɛr] *adj Litt (terre)* nourishing

nourrir [nurir] **1** *vt* (**a**) *(personnes, animaux)* to feed (**de** with); **le lait nourrit** milk is nourishing (**b**) *(peau, visage, cuir)* to nourish; *(feu)* to feed (**c**) *Litt (entretenir) (idées de vengeance, illusion)* to harbour; *(espoir)* to cherish; *(projet)* to nurse

2 **se nourrir** *vpr (manger)* to eat; **se n. de qch** to live on sth; *Fig & Litt* to feed on sth

nourrissant, -e [nurisɑ̃, -ɑ̃t] *adj* nourishing

nourrisson [nurisɔ̃] *nm* infant

nourriture [nurityr] *nf* food

nous [nu] **1** *pron personnel* (**a**) *(sujet)* we; **n. deux/tous** both/all of us; **n. autres Français** we French; **n., n. n'aurions pas fait comme ça** WE wouldn't have done it like that (**b**) *(objet direct)* us; **et n., tu n. oublies?** and what about us, have you forgotten us? (**c**) *(objet indirect)* to us; **lisez-le-n.** read it to us; **il n. a serré la main** he shook our hands; **les enfants n. ont jeté des pierres** the children threw stones at us (**d**) *(avec préposition)* us; **n. ne pensons pas qu'à n.** we're not just thinking of ourselves; **tu n. le montres, à n.?** can you show US?; **ce livre est à n.** this book is ours; **n. avons nos règles à n.** we have our own rules; *Fam* **un ami à n.** a friend of ours; **à n. deux** *(sur un ton menaçant)* I want a word with you; *Hum* I'm all yours (**e**) *(dans les réfléchis)* ourselves; **n. n. sommes habillés** we got dressed (**f**) *(dans les pronominaux)* **n. n. déciderons demain** we'll decide tomorrow (**g**) *(réciproque)* each other (**h**) *(dans les comparaisons)* us; **vous buvez plus que n.** you drink more than us *or* than we do

2 *nm* **le n. de majesté** the royal we

nous-mêmes [numɛm] *pron personnel* ourselves

nouveau, -elle, -x, -elles [nuvo, -ɛl] **1** *adj*

> **nouvel** is used before masculine singular nouns beginning with a vowel or h mute.

(**a**) *(récent, moderne, autre)* new; *(mode)* latest; **les nouveaux pères** modern fathers; *Fam* **tout n. tout beau** it's all new and exciting; **le nouvel an** the New Year; **nouvelle cuisine** nouvelle cuisine; *Péj* **n. riche** nouveau riche (**b**) *(avec une fonction adverbiale)* **les nouveaux arrivants** the newcomers; **les nouveaux élus** those newly elected; **n. pays industrialisé** newly industrialized country (**c**) **à n., de n.** again

2 *nm* **il y a du n.** there's been a new development; **rien de n. depuis la dernière fois** nothing new since last time

3 *nm,f (personne)* new person; *(à l'école)* new pupil

Nouveau-Brunswick [nuvobrœzvik] *nm* **le N.** New Brunswick

Nouveau-Mexique [nuvomɛksik] *nm* **le N.** New Mexico

nouveau-né, -e *(mpl* **nouveau-nés**, *fpl* **nouveau-nées)** [nuvone] **1** *adj* newborn

2 *nm,f* newborn (baby)

nouveauté [nuvote] *nf* (**a**) *(caractère nouveau)* novelty (**b**) *(produit récent) (livre)* new publication; *(disque)* new release; *Fam* **ce n'est pas une n.!** that's nothing new!

nouvel [nuvɛl] *voir* nouveau

nouvelle [nuvɛl] **1** *adj voir* nouveau
  2 *nf* (**a**) *(annonce d'un événement)* **une n.** a piece of news; **je viens d'apprendre la n.** I've just heard the news; *Fam* **première n.!** that's news to me! (**b**) *(information)* **avoir des nouvelles de qn** *(directement)* to have heard from sb; *(indirectement)* to have had news about sb; *Fig* **vous aurez de mes nouvelles!** you'll be hearing from me!; **demander** *ou* **prendre des nouvelles de qn** to inquire *or* ask about sb; **être sans nouvelles de qn** to have no news from sb; **aux dernières nouvelles,...** the last I/we/*etc* heard,...; **les nouvelles vont vite!** (good) news travels fast!; **goûtez cela, vous m'en direz des nouvelles** taste this, you'll love it; **pas de nouvelles, bonnes nouvelles** no news is good news (**c**) *Journ* news item; **les nouvelles** the news (**d**) *(roman court)* short story

Nouvelle-Angleterre [nuvɛlãglətɛr] *nf* **la N.** New England

Nouvelle-Calédonie [nuvɛlkaledɔni] *nf* **la N.** New Caledonia

Nouvelle-Écosse [nuvɛlekɔs] *nf* **la N.** Nova Scotia

nouvellement [nuvɛlmã] *adv* newly, recently

Nouvelle-Orléans [nuvɛlɔrleã] *n* **La N.** New Orleans

Nouvelles-Hébrides [nuvɛlzebrid] *nfpl* **les N.** the New Hebrides

Nouvelle-Zélande [nuvɛlzelãd] *nf* **la N.** New Zealand

novateur, -trice [nɔvatœr, -tris] **1** *adj* innovative
  2 *nm,f* innovator

novembre [nɔvãbr] *nm* November; **le onze n.** *(fête) Br* Armistice Day, *Am* Veterans Day; *voir aussi* **janvier**

novice [nɔvis] *nmf aussi Rel* novice

noyade [nwajad] *nf* drowning

noyau, -x [nwajo] *nm* (**a**) *(de fruit)* stone, *Am* pit (**b**) *(centre) (d'atome, de cellule)* nucleus; *(de la terre)* core (**c**) *(petit groupe)* small group; **le n. dur** the hard core (**d**) *Ordinat* node

noyauter [nwajote] *vt* to infiltrate

noyé, -e [nwaje] **1** *adj* (**a**) *(dans l'eau)* **mourir n.** to die by drowning; *Fig* **être n.** *(perdu)* to be out of one's depth (**b**) *(plein)* **yeux noyés de larmes** eyes brimming with tears (**c**) *(perdu)* **le village était n. dans la brume** the village was shrouded in mist; **les points essentiels sont noyés dans le détail** the essential points are buried in too many details
  2 *nm,f* drowned person

noyer¹ [nwaje] *nm* (*arbre*) walnut (tree); *(bois)* walnut

noyer² [32] **1** *vt* (**a**) *(personne, animal)* to drown; *(terres, champs)* to swamp; *Fig* **n. une rébellion dans le sang** to bloodily quash a rebellion; **n. son chagrin (dans l'alcool)** to drown one's sorrows (in drink); **n. le poisson** to confuse the issue deliberately (**b**) *(moteur)* to flood (**c**) *(diluer) (vin)* to drown
  2 se noyer *vpr (accidentellement)* to drown; *(volontairement)* to drown oneself; *Fig* **se n. dans les détails** to get bogged down in details; **se n. dans un verre d'eau** to make a mountain out of a molehill

NPI [ɛnpei] *nm (abrév* **nouveau pays industrialisé)** NIC

nu, -e¹ [ny] **1** *adj* (**a**) *(dévêtu) (personne)* naked; *(partie du corps)* bare; *Art* nude; **être tout nu** to be naked *or* in the nude; **se baigner tout nu** to go swimming in the nude; **nu comme un ver** stark naked; **aller pieds nus** to go barefoot; **se battre à mains nues** to fight with bare fists (**b**) *Fig (paysage, arbre, pièce)* bare; *(style)* plain
  2 *nm Art* nude; **mettre qch à nu** *(surface)* to expose sth; *(fil électrique)* to strip sth

nuage [nɥaʒ] *nm* (**a**) *(dans le ciel)* cloud; **sans nuages** *(ciel)* cloudless; *Fig (vie, avenir)* unclouded; *(bonheur)* perfect; *Fig* **être dans les nuages** to have one's head in the clouds; **n. radioactif** cloud of radioactive dust (**b**) *(de lait)* drop (**c**) *Can (foulard)* scarf

nuageux, -euse [nɥaʒø, -øz] *adj* cloudy

nuance [nɥãs] *nf* (**a**) *(de couleur)* shade (**b**) *(légère trace)* touch, hint (**c**) *(subtilité)* nuance; *(légère différence)* slight difference; **tout en nuances** full of nuances; **j'ai dit peut-être, pas oui, n.!** I said perhaps, not yes, there's a slight difference!; **être sans nuances** *(personne)* to see everything in black and white

nuancé, -e [nɥãse] *adj* full of nuances

nuancer [16] [nɥãse] *vt* to qualify

nucléaire [nykleɛr] **1** *adj* nuclear
  2 *nm* **le n.** nuclear power

nucléon [nykleɔ̃] *nm Phys* nucleon

nudisme [nydism] *nm* nudism

nudiste [nydist] *nmf* nudist

nudité [nydite] *nf (d'une personne)* nudity, nakedness; *(d'un mur, d'un paysage)* bareness; *(d'un style)* plainness

nue² [ny] *nf* **porter qn/qch aux nues** to praise sb/sth to the skies; **tomber des nues** to be taken aback

nuée [nɥe] *nf* (**a**) *(d'insectes, de criquets)* cloud, swarm; *(de personnes)* horde (**b**) *Litt (dans le ciel)* cloud

nui *voir* **nuire**

nuire [18] [nɥir] **1 nuire à** *vt ind* to harm; **nuit gravement à la santé** *(sur paquet de cigarettes)* tobacco seriously damages health; **mettre qn hors d'état de n.** *(en lieu sûr)* to put sb out of harm's way
  2 se nuire *vpr* **se n. (à soi-même)** to do oneself harm

nuisais *etc voir* **nuire**

nuisance [nɥizãs] *nf* nuisance; **nuisances acoustiques** noise pollution

nuise *voir* **nuire**

nuisette [nɥizɛt] *nf* baby doll nightie

nuisible [nɥizibl] *adj* harmful (**à** to); **animaux nuisibles** vermin, pests

nuit [nɥi] *nf* night; **cette n.** *(ce soir)* tonight; *(passée)* last night; **bonne n.!** good night!; **le train/bateau de n.** the night train/boat; **voyager de n.** to travel by *or* at night; **il commence à faire n.** it's getting dark; **il fait n.** it's dark; **il fait n. noire** it's pitch-black; **à la n. tombante** at nightfall; *Fig* **perdu dans la n. des temps** lost in the mists of time; *Prov* **la n. porte conseil** it would be best to sleep on it; *Prov* **la n., tous les chats sont gris** all cats are grey in the dark; **passer une n. blanche** *(avoir une insomnie)* to have a sleepless night; *(volontairement)* to stay up all night; **n. de noces** wedding night

nuitée [nɥite] *nf* overnight stay

nul, nulle [nyl] **1** *adj* (**a**) *(inexistant) (différence, risques, écart)* nil (**b**) *(non valable) (bulletin de vote)* spoilt; *Jur* **n. et non avenu** null and void (**c**) *Fam (qui ne vaut rien) (réponse, personne)* useless; *(film, livre, chanson, blague)* rubbish; **être n. en qch** to be useless at sth; *Vulg* **c'est n. à chier!** it's a load of crap!
  2 *nm,f Fam* useless idiot
  3 *adj indéfini Litt* no
  4 *pron indéfini Litt* no one, nobody

nullard, -e [nylar, -ard] *nm,f très Fam* useless idiot
nullement [nylmɑ̃] *adv* not at all
nulle part [nylpar] *adv* nowhere; **je ne les vois n.** I can't see them anywhere; **n. ailleurs** nowhere else
nullité [nylite] *nf (d'un contrat, d'un mariage)* nullity, invalidity
numéraire [nymerɛr] *nm* cash
numéral, -e, -aux, -ales [nymeral, -o] *adj & nm* numeral
numérateur [nymeratœr] *nm Math* numerator
numération [nymerasjɔ̃] *nf Math* numeration; *Méd* **n. globulaire** blood count
numérique [nymerik] **1** *adj* (**a**) *(valeur, supériorité)* numerical (**b**) *Ordinat (ordinateur, données)* digital; **balance à affichage n.** digital scales
   2 *nm Ordinat* **le n.** digital technology; *TV* **n. hertzienne, n. terrestre** digital terrestrial (broadcasting)
numérisation [nymerizasjɔ̃] *nf Ordinat* digitization
numériser [nymerize] *vt Ordinat* to digitize
numériseur [nymerizœr] *nm Ordinat* digitizer; **n. d'image** image digitizer
numéro [nymero] *nm* (**a**) *(chiffre)* number; *Fig* **tirer le bon n.** to strike (it) lucky; **n. azur** = special telephone number for which users are charged at local rate irrespective of distance; **n. de compte** account number; **n. de fax** fax number; **n. d'immatriculation** *(de véhicule) Br* registration number, *Am* license number; *Belg Vieilli & Suisse* **n. postal** *Br* postcode, *Am* zip code; **n. de téléphone** telephone number; **n. vert** *Br* Freefone® number, *Am* toll-free number; **n. de vol**

flight number (**b**) *(de périodique)* issue, number; **la suite au prochain n.** (to be) continued in the next issue; *Fig* watch this space; **n. spécial** special issue (**c**) *(spectacle)* act, number; *Fam Fig* **faire son petit n.** to do one's little act (**d**) *Fam (personne)* character
numérotation [nymerɔtasjɔ̃] *nf* (**a**) *(attribution d'un numéro)* numbering (**b**) *Tél* dialling; **n. abrégée** speed dial
numéroter [nymerɔte] **1** *vt* to number
   2 *vi Tél* to dial
numismate [nymismat] *nmf* numismatist
numismatique [nymismatik] **1** *adj* numismatic
   2 *nf* numismatics *(singulier)*
nunuche [nynyʃ] *adj Fam* twee
nu-pieds [nypje] **1** *nm inv* sandal
   2 *adv* barefoot
nuptial, -e, -aux, -ales [nypsjal, -o] *adj (anneau, marche)* wedding; *(chambre, cortège)* bridal
nuque [nyk] *nf* nape, back of the neck
nurse [nœrs] *nf Vieilli* nanny
nu-tête [nytɛt] *adv* bareheaded
nutritif, -ive [nytritif, -iv] *adj* nutritious
nutrition [nytrisjɔ̃] *nf* nutrition
nutritionniste [nytrisjɔnist] *nmf* nutritionist
Nylon® [nilɔ̃] *nm* nylon
nymphe [nɛ̃f] *nf (déesse)* nymph
nymphette [nɛ̃fɛt] *nf* nymphet
nymphomane [nɛ̃fɔman] *adj & nf* nymphomaniac
nymphomanie [nɛ̃fɔmani] *nf* nymphomania

O¹, o [o] *nm inv* O, o

O² *(abrév* **ouest)** W

ô [o] *exclam Litt* O!

OAS [oaɛs] *nf (abrév* **Organisation de l'armée secrète)** OAS *(terrorist group opposed to Algerian independence)*

oasis [ɑazis] *nf* oasis; *Fig* haven

obédience [ɔbedjɑ̃s] *nf* **d'o. communiste/musulmane** of the Communist/Muslim persuasion

obéir [ɔbeir] *vi* (**a**) *(personne)* to obey; **o. à qn/qch** to obey sb/sth; **o. à une impulsion** to act on an impulse; **o. à qn au doigt et à l'œil** to be at sb's beck and call; **se faire o.** to command obedience (**b**) *(freins, mécanisme)* to respond (**à** to)

obéissance [ɔbeisɑ̃s] *nf* obedience (**à** to); **jurer o. à qn** to swear allegiance to sb

obéissant, -e [ɔbeisɑ̃, -ɑ̃t] *adj* obedient

obélisque [ɔbelisk] *nm* obelisk

obèse [ɔbɛz] **1** *adj* obese
2 *nmf* obese person

obésité [ɔbezite] *nf* obesity

objecter [ɔbʒɛkte] *vt* (**a**) *(rétorquer)* **n'avoir rien à o. à qch** to have no objection to sth; **o. que...** to object that... (**b**) *(invoquer)* **on lui objecta sa jeunesse** his/her youth was held against him/her

objecteur [ɔbʒɛktœr] *nm* **o. de conscience** conscientious objector

objectif, -ive [ɔbʒɛktif, -iv] **1** *adj* objective
2 *nm* (**a**) *(but, cible)* objective (**b**) *(d'un appareil photo)* lens; *(d'un microscope)* objective; *Fig* **devant l'o.** in front of the camera

objection [ɔbʒɛksjɔ̃] *nf aussi Jur* objection; **je ne vois pas d'o. à continuer le débat/à ce que vous partiez** I have no objection to our continuing the debate/to your leaving

objectivement [ɔbʒɛktivmɑ̃] *adv* objectively

objectivité [ɔbʒɛktivite] *nf* objectivity; **en toute o.** quite objectively

objet [ɔbʒɛ] *nm* (**a**) *(chose)* object; **(bureau des) objets trouvés** *Br* lost-property office, *Am* lost and found; **femme-o.** sex object; **o. d'art** objet d'art; **objets de valeur** valuables; **o. volant non identifié** unidentified flying object (**b**) *Gram* object; **o. direct/indirect** direct/indirect object (**c**) *(sujet)* *(d'une dispute, d'une conversation)* subject; **être** *ou* **faire l'o. de qch** to be the object of sth; *Hum* **l'o. de ses désirs** the object of his/her desires (**d**) *(but)* object, aim; **ma visite a pour o. de...** the object of my visit is to...; **sans o.** *(remarque, réclamation)* unjustified (**e**) *Ordinat* object

obligataire [ɔbligatɛr] *Fin* **1** *nmf* bondholder, debenture holder
2 *adj (emprunt, marché)* debenture

obligation [ɔbligasjɔ̃] *nf* (**a**) *(contrainte)* obligation; **tu viens si tu veux, mais ce n'est pas une o.** you can come if you want, but you're not obliged to; **avoir l'o. de faire qch** to be under an obligation to do sth; **être** *ou* **se voir dans l'o. de faire qch** to be obliged to do sth; **sans o. d'achat** no purchase necessary; **être dégagé des obligations militaires** to have done one's military service (**b**) *Fin* bond, debenture; **o. au porteur** bearer bond

obligatoire [ɔbligatwar] *adj* obligatory, compulsory; *Fam (inévitable)* inevitable

obligatoirement [ɔbligatwarmɑ̃] *adv* **vous devez o. montrer votre passeport** you are required to show your passport; **pas o.** not necessarily

obligé, -e [ɔbliʒe] *adj* (**a**) *Fam (inévitable)* inevitable (**b**) *Sout (reconnaissant)* **être o. à qn de qch** to be obliged to sb for sth

obligeance [ɔbliʒɑ̃s] *nf Sout* **avoir l'o. de faire qch** to be so kind as to do sth

obligeant, -e [ɔbliʒɑ̃, -ɑ̃t] *adj* obliging, kind

obliger [45] [ɔbliʒe] **1** *vt* (**a**) *(contraindre)* **o. qn à faire qch** to force sb to do sth; **son état de santé l'oblige au repos** the state of his/her health means he/she has to rest; **être obligé de faire qch** to be obliged to do sth; **ne te crois pas obligé de tout manger** don't feel you have to eat everything; **tu y es allé? – bien obligé!** did you go? – I had to! (**b**) *Sout (rendre service à)* **vous m'obligeriez en fermant la porte** I'd be obliged if you would close the door
2 s'obliger *vpr* **s'o. à faire qch** to force oneself to do sth

oblique [ɔblik] **1** *adj (ligne)* oblique; *(regard)* sidelong
2 *nf* oblique (line)

obliquement [ɔblikmɑ̃] *adv* obliquely

obliquer [ɔblike] *vi* **o. à gauche/à droite** to bear left/right

oblitérer [34] [ɔblitere] *vt* (**a**) *(timbre)* to cancel (**b**) *Litt (souvenirs, passé)* to obliterate

oblong, -ongue [ɔblɔ̃, -ɔ̃g] *adj* oblong

obnubiler [ɔbnybile] *vt* to obsess

obole [ɔbɔl] *nf* small contribution; **apporter** *ou* **verser son o. à qch** to make a small contribution to sth

obscène [ɔpsɛn] *adj* obscene

obscénité [ɔpsenite] *nf* obscenity; **dire des obscénités** to utter obscenities

obscur, -e [ɔpskyr] *adj* (**a**) *(sombre)* dark (**b**) *(difficile à comprendre)* obscure (**c**) *(pressentiment, impression)* vague (**d**) *(écrivain, peintre)* obscure
obscurantisme [ɔpskyrɑ̃tism] *nm* obscurantism
obscurcir [ɔpskyrsir] **1** *vt* (**a**) *(assombrir)* to darken (**b**) *(rendre confus) (faits, sens)* to obscure; *(jugement)* to cloud
   2 s'obscurcir *vpr (pièce, ciel)* to darken, to grow dark; *(esprit, vue)* to grow dim
obscurément [ɔpskyremɑ̃] *adv* vaguely
obscurité [ɔpskyrite] *nf* (**a**) *(noirceur)* darkness; **dans l'o.** in the dark (**b**) *(anonymat)* obscurity
obsédant, -e [ɔpsedɑ̃, -ɑ̃t] *adj (souvenir, musique)* haunting; *(pensée)* obsessive
obsédé, -e [ɔpsede] *nm,f* fanatic; **o. (sexuel)** sex maniac; **un o. du cinéma/du rangement** a movie *or Br* film/tidiness fanatic
obséder [34] [ɔpsede] *vt* to obsess; **être obsédé par qch** to be obsessed by *or* with sth
obsèques [ɔpsɛk] *nfpl* funeral; **o. nationales** state funeral
obséquieux, -euse [ɔpsekjø, -øz] *adj* obsequious
observateur, -trice [ɔpsɛrvatœr, -tris] **1** *adj* observant
   2 *nm,f* observer
observation [ɔpsɛrvasjɔ̃] *nf* (**a**) *(étude, surveillance)* observation; **être en o.** *(à l'hôpital)* to be under observation; **avoir l'esprit d'o.** to be very observant (**b**) *(remarque)* observation; *(critique)* remark (**c**) *(respect)* observance
observatoire [ɔpsɛrvatwar] *nm (astronomique, météorologique)* observatory; *Mil* observation post
observer [ɔpsɛrve] **1** *vt* (**a**) *(regarder)* to watch, to observe; **se sentir observé** to feel one is being watched (**b**) *(remarquer)* to notice; **faire o. qch à qn** to point sth out to sb; **faire o. qn que...** to point out to sb that... (**c**) *(étudier)* to observe (**d**) *(respecter)* to observe; **o. une minute de silence** to observe a minute's silence
   2 s'observer *vpr* (**a**) *(l'un l'autre)* to watch *or* observe each other (**b**) *(phénomène, attitude)* to be seen
obsession [ɔpsesjɔ̃] *nf* obsession; **mais c'est une o. ou de l'o.!** you're/he's/*etc* obsessed!
obsessionnel, -elle [ɔpsesjɔnɛl] *adj Psy* obsessional
obsidienne [ɔpsidjɛn] *nf* obsidian
obsolète [ɔpsɔlɛt] *adj* obsolete
obstacle [ɔpstakl] *nm aussi Fig* obstacle; *(aux courses)* fence, jump; **faire o. à qch** to stand in the way of sth
obstétricien, -enne [ɔpstetrisjɛ̃, -ɛn] *nm,f* obstetrician
obstétrique [ɔpstetrik] *nf* obstetrics *(singulier)*
obstination [ɔpstinasjɔ̃] *nf* obstinacy, stubbornness
obstiné, -e [ɔpstine] *adj (personne, caractère)* obstinate, stubborn; *(résistance, efforts)* dogged; *(refus)* stubborn
obstinément [ɔpstinemɑ̃] *adv (travailler, avancer)* doggedly; *(refuser)* stubbornly
obstiner [ɔpstine] s'obstiner *vpr* to persist; **s'o. à faire qch** *(continuer)* to persist in doing sth; *(vouloir)* to be set on doing sth; **s'o. dans ses convictions** to cling stubbornly to one's convictions
obstruction [ɔpstryksjɔ̃] *nf* obstruction; **faire de l'o.** *Pol* to be obstructive; *Sport* to obstruct
obstructionnisme [ɔpstryksjɔnism] *nm Pol* obstructionism
obstruer [ɔpstrye] *vt* to obstruct

obtempérer [34] [ɔptɑ̃pere] **obtempérer à** *vt ind* to comply with; *Jur* **refus d'o.** obstruction
obtenir [70] [ɔptənir] *vt* to get, to obtain; **o. qch de qn** to get sth from sb; **faire o. qch à qn** to get sth for sb; **o. de faire qch** to get permission to do sth; **j'ai obtenu qu'elle revienne** I got her to come back
obtention [ɔptɑ̃sjɔ̃] *nf* obtaining; **depuis l'o. de son diplôme** since obtaining his/her diploma
obtenu, -e *voir* obtenir
obtiendrai *etc voir* obtenir
obtienne *voir* obtenir
obturateur [ɔptyratœr] *nm Phot* shutter
obtus, -e [ɔpty, -yz] *adj (angle, personne)* obtuse
obus [ɔby] *nm* shell
OC *nfpl Rad (abrév* **ondes courtes**) SW
oc [ɔk] *voir* langue
ocarina [ɔkarina] *nm* ocarina
occase [ɔkaz] *nf Fam* (**a**) *(affaire)* bargain (**b**) *(article de seconde main)* second-hand item; **d'o.** second-hand
occasion [ɔkazjɔ̃] *nf* (**a**) *(circonstance favorable)* opportunity, chance; **avoir l'o. de faire qch** to have the opportunity *or* chance to do sth; *Hum* **tu as encore perdu l'o. de te taire** why can't you keep your big mouth shut?; **c'est l'o. ou jamais** it's now or never; **c'est l'o. ou jamais d'essayer** now's the time to try; **venez boire un coup à l'o.** come for a drink when you get the chance; **à la première o.** at the first opportunity; *Prov* **l'o. fait le larron** opportunity makes the thief (**b**) *(moment)* occasion; **à plusieurs occasions** on several occasions; **à l'o. de** *(pour fêter)* on the occasion of; **à l'o. d'une visite de routine** during a routine visit; **dans/pour les grandes occasions** on/for special occasions; **être l'o. de qch** to be the occasion of sth (**c**) *(affaire)* bargain (**d**) *(article de seconde main)* second-hand item; **le marché de l'o.** the second-hand market; **d'o.** second-hand
occasionnel, -elle [ɔkazjɔnɛl] *adj* occasional; *(rencontre)* chance; *(aide)* casual
occasionnellement [ɔkazjɔnɛlmɑ̃] *adv* occasionally
occasionner [ɔkazjɔne] *vt* to cause
occident [ɔksidɑ̃] *nm* west; *Pol* **l'O.** the West
occidental, -e, -aux, -ales [ɔksidɑ̃tal, -o] **1** *adj* western; **l'Europe occidentale** Western Europe
   2 *nm,f* **O.** Westerner
occidentaliser [ɔksidɑ̃talize] **1** *vt* to westernize
   2 s'occidentaliser *vpr* to become westernized
occiput [ɔksipyt] *nm* back of the head
occire [ɔksir] *vt* to slay
occitan, -e [ɔksitɑ̃, -an] **1** *adj* of the langue d'oc
   2 *nm (langue)* = language spoken in some parts of southern France
occlusion [ɔklyzjɔ̃] *nf* occlusion; **o. intestinale** intestinal obstruction
occulte [ɔkylt] *adj (surnaturel)* occult; *(secret)* secret; *(cause)* hidden; *(rôle)* clandestine
occulter [ɔkylte] *vt Astron* to occult; *(signal lumineux)* to block out; *Fig (informations, intentions)* to conceal
occupant, -e [ɔkypɑ̃, -ɑ̃t] **1** *adj (armée)* occupying
   2 *nm,f (d'une maison)* occupier, occupant; *Mil* **l'o.** the occupying forces
occupation [ɔkypasjɔ̃] *nf* (**a**) *(d'un lieu)* & *Mil* occupation; *Hist* **l'O.** the Occupation; **grève avec o. des locaux** sit-down strike (**b**) *(activité)* occupation; **vaquer à ses occupations** to go about one's business

occupé, -e [ɔkype] *adj (personne)* busy; *(place)* taken; *(ligne téléphonique) Br* engaged, *Am* busy; *(toilettes)* engaged; **en territoire o.** in occupied territory

occuper [ɔkype] **1** *vt* (**a**) *(maison, lieu)* to occupy; *(place)* to take up, to occupy; **le magasin occupe le rez-de-chaussée** the shop takes up *or* occupies the ground floor (**b**) *(par la force)* to occupy (**c**) *(temps)* to fill, to occupy (**d**) *(poste, fonction)* to have, to hold (**e**) **o. qn** *(employer)* to employ sb; *(donner une activité à)* to keep sb busy, to occupy sb
 2 s'occuper *vpr* (**a**) *(avoir une activité)* to keep oneself busy *or* occupied, to occupy oneself; **s'o. en lisant** to spend one's time reading; **on a toujours de quoi s'o.** there's always something to keep you busy (**b**) **s'o. de** *(s'intéresser à)* to be interested in; *(se charger de)* to take care of; **s'o. de faire qch** to see about doing sth; **je m'en occuperai** I'll see to it; *Fam* **occupe-toi de ce qui te regarde** *ou* **de tes affaires** *ou* **de tes oignons!** mind your own business!; *Fam* **t'occupe (pas)!** keep your nose out!; *Ironique* **je vais m'o. de lui** I'll take care of him; **est-ce qu'on s'occupe de vous?** *(dans un magasin)* are you being served?

occurrence [ɔkyrɑ̃s] *nf* (**a**) *(circonstance)* **en l'o.** in this case (**b**) *Ling* occurrence

OCDE [osedeə] *nf (abrév* **Organisation de coopération et de développement économiques)** OECD

océan [ɔseɑ̃] *nm* ocean; **l'O.** *(l'Atlantique)* the Atlantic; **l'o. Atlantique/Pacifique/Indien** the Atlantic/Pacific/Indian Ocean; **l'o. (Glacial) Arctique** the Arctic Ocean; *Fig* **un o. de fleurs/couleurs** a sea of flowers/colour

Océanie [ɔseani] *nf* **l'O.** Oceania

océanique [ɔseanik] *adj* oceanic

océanographie [ɔseanɔgrafi] *nf* oceanography

ocelot [ɔslo] *nm* ocelot

ocre [ɔkr] *nm & adj inv* ochre

octane [ɔktan] *nm* octane

octante [ɔktɑ̃t] *adj & nm inv Belg & Suisse* eighty; *voir aussi* **trois**

octave [ɔktav] *nf* octave

octet [ɔktɛ] *nm Ordinat* byte; **milliard d'octets** gigabyte

octobre [ɔktɔbr] *nm* October; *voir aussi* **janvier**

octogénaire [ɔktɔʒenɛr] *adj & nmf* octogenarian

octogonal, -e, -aux, -ales [ɔktɔgɔnal, -o] *adj* octagonal

octogone [ɔktɔgɔn] *nm* octagon

octroyer [32] [ɔktrwaje] **1** *vt* **o. qch à qn** to grant sb sth
 2 s'octroyer *vpr* **s'o. qch** to grant oneself sth

oculaire [ɔkylɛr] **1** *adj* **hygiène o.** eye care; **témoin o.** eyewitness
 2 *nm* eyepiece

oculiste [ɔkylist] *nmf* eye specialist

ode [ɔd] *nf* ode

odeur [ɔdœr] *nf* smell; **une o. de brûlé** a smell of burning; **sans o.** odourless; **bonne/mauvaise o.** pleasant/unpleasant smell; *Fig* **ne pas être en o. de sainteté auprès de qn** to be in sb's bad books; *Prov* **l'argent n'a pas d'o.** money has no smell

odieux, -euse [ɔdjø, -øz] *adj (comportement)* odious; *(crime)* heinous; **être o. avec qn** to be horrible to sb

odorant, -e [ɔdɔrɑ̃, -ɑ̃t] *adj (agréable)* sweet-smelling, fragrant; *(désagréable)* strong-smelling

odorat [ɔdɔra] *nm* (sense of) smell

odyssée [ɔdise] *nf* odyssey; **l'O.** the Odyssey

œcuménique [ekymenik, økymenik] *adj* ecumenical

œdème [edɛm, ødɛm] *nm* oedema; **avoir un o. aux poumons** to have pulmonary oedema

œil [œj] *(pl* **yeux** [jø]) *nm* (**a**) *(organe)* eye; **avoir les yeux bleus** to have blue eyes; **o. de verre** glass eye; **un o. au beurre noir, un o. poché** a black eye; **j'ai le soleil dans les yeux** *ou* **dans l'o.** the sun's in my eyes; **visible à l'o. nu** visible to the naked eye; **voir qch de ses (propres) yeux** to see sth with one's own eyes; **je n'ai pas fermé l'o. de la nuit** I didn't sleep a wink all night; **faire qch les yeux fermés** to do sth with one's eyes closed; **ouvrir de grands yeux** to look surprised; **faire les gros yeux (à qn)** to glare (at sb); *Fam* **avoir de petits yeux** to look tired; **ouvrir des yeux ronds** to gape in amazement; *Fam* **entre quat'z'yeux** in private; **les yeux dans les yeux** gazing into each other's eyes; **o. pour o., dent pour dent** an eye for an eye, a tooth for a tooth; **je ne le fais pas pour ses beaux yeux** I'm not doing it just to please him/her; **tu as les yeux plus gros** *ou* **grands que le ventre** your eyes are bigger than your belly; **n'avoir plus que les** *ou* **ses yeux pour pleurer** to have nothing left but the clothes on one's back; *Fam* **mon o.!** my foot!; *Fam* **à l'o.** free; **faire les yeux doux à qn** to make eyes at sb; *Fam* **faire de l'o. à qn** to give sb the eye; **le mauvais o.** the evil eye; **sous mes/leurs yeux** right before my/their eyes; **avoir qch sous les yeux** to have sth right in front of one; *Can Fam* **tomber dans l'o. à qn** to catch sb's eye
 (**b**) *(vue)* **yeux** (eye)sight, eyes; **avoir de bons/mauvais yeux** to have good/bad (eye)sight; **avoir des yeux de lynx** to be eagle-eyed
 (**c**) *(attention)* **avoir l'o. sur qch** to keep an eye on sth; **avoir qn à l'o.** to keep an eye on sb; **avoir l'o. à tout** to keep an eye on everything; *Fam* **ouvrir l'o. (et le bon)** to keep one's eyes open *or* peeled; **ne pas avoir les yeux en face des trous** to be half-asleep; *Fam* **ne pas avoir les yeux dans sa poche** to have sharp eyes; **fermer les yeux sur qch** to turn a blind eye to sth; **coup d'o.** glance; **au** *ou* **du premier coup d'o.** at a glance; **jeter un coup d'o. sur qch** to have a glance at sth; **avoir le coup d'o., avoir l'o.** to have a good eye; **ça vaut** *ou* **ça mérite le coup d'o.** it's worth a look
 (**d**) *(point de vue)* **voir qch d'un autre o.** to look at sth differently; **voir qch d'un bon/mauvais o.** to look favourably/unfavourably on sth; **aux yeux de la loi** in the eyes of the law; **à mes yeux** in my eyes
 (**e**) *(dans la soupe)* speck of fat
 (**f**) *(d'un cyclone)* eye

œil-de-bœuf *(pl* **œils-de-bœuf**) [œjdəbœf] *nm* bull's-eye (window)

œillade [œjad] *nf* wink; **lancer une o. à qn** to wink at sb

œillère [œjɛr] *nf Br* blinker, *Am* blinder; *Fig* **avoir des œillères** to wear *Br* blinkers *or Am* blinders

œillet [œjɛ] *nm* (**a**) *(fleur)* carnation (**b**) *(trou) (de vêtement, de chaussure)* eyelet (**c**) *(en papeterie)* reinforcement ring

œnologie [enɔlɔʒi, ønɔlɔʒi] *nf* oenology

œnologue [enɔlɔg, ønɔlɔg] *nmf* oenologist

œsophage [ezɔfaʒ, øzɔfaʒ] *nm* oesophagus

œstrogène [ɛstrɔʒɛn, østrɔʒɛn] *adj & nm* oestrogen

œuf [œf, *pl* ø] *nm* egg; **œufs (de poisson)** spawn, hard roe; *Fig* **mettre tous ses œufs dans le même panier** to put all one's eggs in one basket; *Fam Fig* **marcher sur des œufs** *(avancer)* to walk carefully; *(être prudent)* to be walking on eggs; *Fam* **va te faire cuire un**

o.! take a running jump!; **étouffer** *ou* **tuer qch dans l'o.** to nip sth in the bud; **œufs brouillés** scrambled eggs; **o. en chocolat** chocolate egg; **o. à la coque** boiled egg; **o. dur** hard-boiled egg; **o. mollet** soft-boiled egg; **œufs à la neige** floating islands *(beaten egg whites served on custard)*; **œufs en neige** beaten egg whites; **o. de Pâques** Easter egg; **o. au plat** *ou* **sur le plat** fried egg; **o. poché** poached egg; **o. à repriser** darning egg

œuvre [œvr] **1** *nf* (**a**) *(travail)* work; **être à l'o.** to be at work; **se mettre à l'o.** to get down to work; **mettre qch en o.** *(traité, loi, système)* to implement sth; **mettre tout en o.** to do everything possible; **les bonnes œuvres** charitable work (**b**) *(création)* work; *(ensemble de créations)* works; **o. d'art** work of art; **œuvres complètes/choisies** complete/selected works **2** *nm* Constr **gros o.** fabric; **à pied d'o.** on site; *Fig* ready to start work

œuvrer [œvre] *vi* to work (**pour** for)
offensant, -e [ɔfɑ̃sɑ̃, -ɑ̃t] *adj* offensive
offense [ɔfɑ̃s] *nf* (**a**) *(affront)* insult (**b**) *Rel* transgression
offenser [ɔfɑ̃se] **1** *vt* (**a**) *(insulter)* to offend; **sans vouloir vous o....** with all due respect... (**b**) *Litt (bon goût, délicatesse)* to offend against **2 s'offenser** *vpr* to take offence (**de** at)
offensif, -ive [ɔfɑ̃sif, -iv] **1** *adj* offensive **2** *nf* offensive offensive; **passer à l'offensive** to go on the offensive; **offensive de charme** charm offensive
offert, -e *voir* offrir
office [ɔfis] *nm* (**a**) *(charge)* office; **faire o. de secrétaire/témoin** to act as secretary/witness; **d'o.** without having any say in the matter; **être commis d'o.** to be appointed by the court (**b**) *(assistance)* **recourir aux bons offices de qn** to turn to sb for assistance (**c**) *Rel* service (**d**) *(pièce)* pantry (**e**) *(agence)* **o. du tourisme** tourist information centre; *Suisse* **o. de poste** post office
officialiser [ɔfisjalize] *vt* to make official
officiel, -elle [ɔfisjɛl] *adj & nm* official
officiellement [ɔfisjɛlmɑ̃] *adv* officially
officier¹ [ɔfisje] *nm* officer; **o. de réserve** reserve officer
officier² [66] *vi* to officiate
officieusement [ɔfisjøzmɑ̃] *adv* unofficially; *(en confidence)* off-the-record
officieux, -euse [ɔfisjø, -øz] *adj* unofficial; *(confidentiel)* off-the-record
off-line [ɔflajn] *adj* Ordinat off-line
offrande [ɔfrɑ̃d] *nf* offering; **en o.** as an offering
offrant [ɔfrɑ̃] *nm* **vendre au plus o.** to sell to the highest bidder
offre [ɔfr] *nf* offer; *(dans un appel d'offres)* tender; *(dans une vente aux enchères)* bid; **o. d'emploi** job offer; **o. spéciale** special offer; **o. publique d'achat** takeover bid; **faire** *ou* **lancer une o. publique d'achat (sur)** to make a takeover bid (for); **l'o. et la demande** supply and demand
offrir [52] [ɔfrir] **1** *vt* (**a**) *(cadeau)* to give (**à** to); **c'est pour o.** it's a gift; **je t'offre un verre** I'll buy you a drink; **o. la main de sa fille à qn** to offer one's daughter's hand in marriage to sb (**b**) *(proposer)* to offer; **o. de faire qch** to offer to do sth; **combien t'en a-t-elle offert?** how much did she offer you for it? (**c**) *(présenter) (avantage, garantie)* to offer; **o. une résistance acharnée** to put up stiff resistance

2 s'offrir *vpr* (**a**) *(se proposer) (sexuellement)* to offer oneself; **s'o. pour faire qch** to offer to do sth; **s'o. aux regards** *(spectacle, vue)* to meet our/your/etc eyes (**b**) *(se présenter) (occasion, possibilité)* to present itself (**c**) *(s'acheter)* **s'o. un bon cigare/une nouvelle robe** to treat oneself to a good cigar/a new dress; **je ne peux pas m'o. de vacances** I can't afford a *Br* holiday *or Am* vacation
offset [ɔfsɛt] *nm inv* offset
offusquer [ɔfyske] **1** *vt* to offend **2 s'offusquer** *vpr* to take offence (**de** at)
ogive [ɔʒiv] *nf* (**a**) *Archit* (diagonal) rib (**b**) *Mil (d'un obus)* head; *(d'une roquette)* nose cone; **o. nucléaire** nuclear warhead
OGM [ɔʒeɛm] *nm (abrév* **organisme génétiquement modifié**) genetically modified organism, GMO
ogre [ɔgr] *nm* ogre
ogresse [ɔgrɛs] *nf* ogress
oh [o] *exclam* oh!; *(pour interpeller)* hey!; **oh! hisse!** heave-ho!
ohé [ɔe] *exclam* hey!
ohm [om] *nm* ohm
oie [wa] *nf* goose; **o. sauvage** wild goose; *Fig* **une o. blanche** an innocent young thing
oignon [ɔɲɔ̃] *nm* (**a**) *(légume)* onion; **oignons blancs** *(pour les salades)* spring onions; **petits oignons** *(au vinaigre)* pickling onions; *Fam Fig* **aux petits oignons** first-rate; *Fam* **mêle-toi de tes oignons** mind your own business; *Fam* **ce ne sont pas tes oignons** it's none of your business (**b**) *Bot* bulb (**c**) *Méd* bunion
oindre [43] [wɛ̃dr] *vt* (**a**) *(enduire)* to oil (**b**) *Rel* to anoint
oiseau, -x [wazo] *nm* bird; *Fam Fig* **c'est un drôle d'o.** he's an odd character; **o. de malheur, o. de mauvais augure** bird of ill omen; **o. marin** sea bird; **o. nocturne** nocturnal bird; *Fig* **o. de nuit** night owl; **o. de proie** bird of prey; **l'o. rare** the ideal person
oiseau-lyre *(pl* **oiseaux-lyres**) [wazolir] *nm* lyrebird
oiseau-mouche *(pl* **oiseaux-mouches**) [wazomuʃ] *nm* hummingbird
oiseleur [wazlœr] *nm* bird catcher
oiseux, -euse [wazø, -øz] *adj (conversation)* idle; *(débat)* pointless; *(explication)* unsatisfactory
oisif, -ive [wazif, -iv] **1** *adj* idle **2** *nm,f* person of leisure
oisillon [wazijɔ̃] *nm* fledgling
oisiveté [wazivte] *nf* idleness; *Prov* **l'o. est (la) mère de tous les vices** the Devil finds work for idle hands
OIT [oite] *nf (abrév* **Organisation internationale du travail**) ILO
okapi [ɔkapi] *nm* okapi
oléagineux, -euse [ɔleaʒinø, -øz] **1** *adj* oil-yielding **2** *nmpl* oil-yielding plants
oléoduc [ɔleɔdyk] *nm* pipeline
olé olé [ɔleɔle] *adj inv Fam (propos, spectacle)* risqué; *(gens)* wild
olfactif, -ive [ɔlfaktif, -iv] *adj* olfactory
olibrius [ɔlibrijys] *nm Fam* oddball
oligarchie [ɔligarʃi] *nf* oligarchy
oligarchique [ɔligarʃik] *adj* oligarchic
oligoélément [ɔligoelemɑ̃] *nm* trace element
olivâtre [ɔlivatr] *adj* olive-greenish; *(teint)* sallow
olive [ɔliv] **1** *adj inv* olive (green) **2** *nf* olive
oliveraie [ɔlivrɛ] *nf* olive grove
olivier [ɔlivje] *nm (arbre)* olive tree; *(bois)* olive (wood)

OLP [ɔɛlpe] *nf* (*abrév* **Organisation de libération de la Palestine**) PLO
olympiade [ɔlɛ̃pjad] *nf* Olympiad
olympique [ɔlɛ̃pik] *adj* Olympic
ombilical, -e, -aux, -ales [ɔ̃bilikal, -o] *adj* umbilical
ombrage [ɔ̃braʒ] *nm* shade; **prendre o. de qch** to take umbrage at sth; **porter o. à qn** to give offence to sb
ombragé, -e [ɔ̃braʒe] *adj* shady
ombrageux, -euse [ɔ̃braʒø, -øz] *adj* (*personne*) touchy
ombre¹ [ɔ̃br] *nf* (**a**) (*forme*) shadow; **ombres chinoises** shadow play; *Fig* **jeter une o. sur qch** to cast a shadow over sth (**b**) (*zone sombre*) shade; **40 degrés à l'o.** 40 degrees in the shade; **faire de l'o. à qn** to be in sb's light; *Fig* to put sb in the shade; *Fig* **il y a une o. au tableau** there's a fly in the ointment (**c**) (*obscurité*) darkness; *Fig* (*anonymat*) obscurity; *Fig* **rester dans/sortir de l'o.** to remain in/emerge from obscurity; *Fig* **laisser qch dans l'o.** to keep sth dark; *Fig* **travailler dans l'o.** to work behind the scenes; *Fam* **mettre qn à l'o.** to put sb inside (**d**) *Litt* (*fantôme*) shade; *Fig* **n'être plus que l'o. de soi-même** to be a mere shadow of one's former self (**e**) (*trace*) hint; **vous n'avez pas l'o. d'une chance** you haven't the ghost of a chance; **il n'y a pas l'o. d'un doute** there isn't the shadow of a doubt; **pas l'o. d'un** not a single one (**f**) **o. à paupières** eye shadow
ombre² *nm* (*poisson*) char; **o. de rivière** grayling
ombré [ɔ̃bre] *nm Ordinat* shading
ombrelle [ɔ̃brɛl] *nf* sunshade, parasol
OMC [ɔɛmse] *nf* (*abrév* **Organisation mondiale du commerce**) WTO
omelette [ɔmlɛt] *nf* omelette; *Fig* **on ne fait pas d'o. sans casser des œufs** you can't make an omelette without breaking eggs; **o. norvégienne** baked Alaska
omettre [47] [ɔmɛtr] *vt* to omit; **o. de faire qch** to omit to do sth
omis, -e *voir* omettre
omission [ɔmisjɔ̃] *nf* (*d'un mot, d'un détail*) omission; (*oubli*) oversight
omnibus [ɔmnibys] *nm* slow train
omnipotence [ɔmnipɔtɑ̃s] *nf* omnipotence
omnipotent, -e [ɔmnipɔtɑ̃, -ɑ̃t] *adj* omnipotent
omniprésence [ɔmniprezɑ̃s] *nf* omnipresence
omniprésent, -e [ɔmniprezɑ̃, -ɑ̃t] *adj* omnipresent
omniscience [ɔmnisjɑ̃s] *nf* omniscience
omniscient, -e [ɔmnisjɑ̃, -ɑ̃t] *adj* omniscient
omnisports [ɔmnispɔr] *adj inv* **stade/centre o.** sports stadium/centre
omnivore [ɔmnivɔr] **1** *adj* omnivorous **2** *nm* omnivore
omoplate [ɔmɔplat] *nf* shoulder blade, *Spéc* scapula
OMS [ɔɛmɛs] *nf* (*abrév* **Organisation mondiale de la santé**) WHO
on [ɔ̃] *pron indéfini* (**a**) (*indéterminé*) you, people; (*quelqu'un*) somebody, someone; **on ne sait jamais** you never know; **on nous prend parfois pour deux sœurs** people sometimes take us for sisters; **on dit qu'il est malade, on le dit malade** they say he's ill; **on sonne** there's somebody at the door; **dans tous les pays où l'on parle français** in every country where French is spoken; **on m'a volé mon sac** my bag's been stolen, someone's stolen my bag (**b**) *Fam* (*nous*) we; **on ne s'est plus jamais quittés** we've been together ever since

onanisme [ɔnanism] *nm* onanism
once [ɔ̃s] *nf aussi Fig* ounce
oncle [ɔ̃kl] *nm* uncle; **o. d'Amérique** rich uncle
onctueux, -euse [ɔ̃ktɥø, -øz] *adj aussi Fig & Péj* smooth
onctuosité [ɔ̃ktɥozite] *nf* smoothness
onde [ɔ̃d] *nf* (**a**) *Phys* wave; *Rad* **grandes ondes** long wave; *Rad* **ondes courtes/moyennes** short/medium wave; **o. de choc** shock wave; **sur les ondes** on the radio; **passer sur les ondes** to be on the radio; **o. sonore** sound wave (**b**) *Litt* (*eau*) waters; **l'o. limpide du ruisseau** the clear waters of the stream
ondée [ɔ̃de] *nf* sudden downpour
on-dit [ɔdi] *nm inv* rumour, hearsay; **ce ne sont que des o.** it's only hearsay
ondoyant, -e [ɔ̃dwajɑ̃, -ɑ̃t] *adj Litt* undulating
ondoyer [32] [ɔ̃dwaje] *vi* (*blés*) to sway; (*drapeau*) to wave; (*surface de l'eau*) to ripple; (*flamme*) to flicker
ondulant, -e [ɔ̃dylɑ̃, -ɑ̃t] *adj* (*plaine*) rolling, undulating; (*vagues*) rippling; (*chevelure*) wavy; (*démarche*) swaying
ondulation [ɔ̃dylasjɔ̃] *nf* (*des vagues*) ripple; **les ondulations de la plaine** the rolling *or* undulating plain; **les ondulations de sa chevelure** his/her wavy hair
ondulé, -e [ɔ̃dyle] *adj* (*sol*) undulating; (*cheveux*) wavy; (*tôle, carton*) corrugated
onduler [ɔ̃dyle] *vi* to undulate; (*cheveux*) to be wavy; **o. des hanches** to sway one's hips
onduleur [ɔ̃dylœr] *nm Ordinat* uninterruptible power supply, UPS
onéreux, -euse [ɔnerø, -øz] *adj* costly
ONF [ɔɛnɛf] *nm* (*abrév* **Office national des forêts**) *Br* ≃ Forestry Commission, *Am* ≃ National Forestry Service
ONG [ɔɛnʒe] *nf* (*abrév* **organisation non gouvernementale**) NGO
ongle [ɔ̃gl] *nm* (finger)nail; (*des orteils*) (toe)nail; (*d'un animal*) claw; (*d'un oiseau de proie*) talon; **se faire les ongles** to do one's nails; **o. incarné** ingrowing nail; *Fig* **jusqu'au bout des ongles** to one's fingertips
onglée [ɔ̃gle] *nf* **j'ai l'o.** my fingers are numb with cold
onglet [ɔ̃glɛ] *nm* (**a**) (*d'un répertoire*) tab; (*d'un canif*) thumbnail groove; **dictionnaire à onglets** thumb-indexed dictionary (**b**) *Culin* flank of beef
onguent [ɔ̃gɑ̃] *nm Litt* ointment
onirique [ɔnirik] *adj* dreamlike
onomatopée [ɔnɔmatɔpe] *nf* onomatopoeia
ont *voir* avoir¹
Ontario [ɔ̃tarjo] *n voir* lac
ONU [ɔny, ɔɛny] *nf* (*abrév* **Organisation des Nations unies**) UN
onyx [ɔniks] *nm* onyx
onze [ɔ̃z] *adj & nm inv* eleven; *voir aussi* **trois**
onzième [ɔ̃zjɛm] *nmf, nm & adj* eleventh; *voir aussi* **cinquième**
OPA [ɔpea] *nf* (*abrév* **offre publique d'achat**) takeover bid; **lancer une O. (sur)** to make a takeover bid (for)
opacité [ɔpasite] *nf* opacity
opale [ɔpal] *nf* opal
opaque [ɔpak] *adj aussi Fig* opaque
OPEP [ɔpɛp] *nf* (*abrév* **Organisation des pays exportateurs de pétrole**) OPEC
opéra [ɔpera] *nm* (**a**) (*genre, œuvre*) opera (**b**) (*lieu*) opera house; **aller à l'o.** to go to the opera; **l'O. (de Paris)** the Paris Opera House; **o. bouffe** comic opera
opérable [ɔperabl] *adj* operable

opérateur, -trice [ɔperatœr, -tris] **1** *nm,f (personne)* operator; *Cin* cameraman; **o. de saisie** keyboarder **2** *nm* (**a**) *Math* operator (**b**) *Ordinat* **o. logique** logical operator

opération [ɔperasjɔ̃] *nf* (**a**) **o. (chirurgicale)** operation; **o. à cœur ouvert** open-heart surgery (**b**) *Math* operation; **faire des opérations** to do some calculations (**c**) *(transaction)* deal, transaction; **o. financière** financial transaction (**d**) *(action)* operation; **o. de police** police operation

opérationnel, -elle [ɔperasjɔnɛl] *adj* operational

opératoire [ɔperatwar] *adj (procédure)* operating

opérer [34] [ɔpere] **1** *vt* (**a**) *(réforme, restructuration)* to carry out; *(changement, distinction)* to make (**b**) *(patient)* to operate on; **se faire o.** to have an operation; **se faire o. des amygdales** to have one's tonsils (taken) out; **se faire o. du cœur/de la hanche** to have a heart/hip operation; **se faire o. d'une tumeur** to have an operation to remove a tumour **2** *vi* (**a**) *(être efficace)* to work (**b**) *(procéder)* to operate **3** *s'opérer vpr (changement, transformation)* to take place

opérette [ɔperɛt] *nf* operetta

ophtalmo [ɔftalmo] *nmf Fam* ophthalmologist

ophtalmologie [ɔftalmɔlɔʒi] *nf Méd* ophthalmology

ophtalmologiste [ɔftalmɔlɔʒist], **ophtalmologue** [ɔftalmɔlɔg] *nmf Méd* ophthalmologist

opiner [ɔpine] *vi* **o. du chef** *ou* **du bonnet** to nod one's assent

opiniâtre [ɔpinjatr] *adj* stubborn

opinion [ɔpinjɔ̃] *nf* opinion (**de/sur** of/about); **se faire une o. sur qch** to make up one's mind about sth, to form an opinion about sth; **changer d'o.** to change one's mind; **sans o.** *(dans un sondage)* don't know; **avoir une bonne/mauvaise o. de qn/qch** to have a good/bad opinion of sb/sth; **o. publique** public opinion

opiomane [ɔpjɔman] *nmf* opium addict

opium [ɔpjɔm] *nm* opium

opossum [ɔpɔsɔm] *nm* opossum

opportun, -e [ɔpɔrtœ̃, -yn] *adj (arrivée)* timely, opportune; *(moment, jour)* right

opportunément [ɔpɔrtynemã] *adv* opportunely

opportunisme [ɔpɔrtynism] *nm* opportunism

opportuniste [ɔpɔrtynist] *adj & nmf* opportunist

opportunité [ɔpɔrtynite] *nf (d'une arrivée)* timeliness; *(d'un projet, d'une décision)* advisability

opposant, -e [ɔpozɑ̃, -ɑ̃t] **1** *adj* opposing **2** *nm,f* opponent (**à** of)

opposé, -e [ɔpoze] **1** *adj* (**a**) *(en contradiction) (armées, caractères, équipe)* opposing; *(intérêts)* conflicting (**b**) *(dans l'espace) (côtés, rivage, direction)* opposite (**c**) *(contre)* **être o. à qch** to be opposed to sth **2** *nm (contraire)* **l'o.** the opposite; **à l'o.** *(côté)* on the opposite side; *(direction)* in the opposite direction; *Fig* on the other hand; **à l'o. de** *(côté)* on the opposite side to; *(contrairement à)* unlike; **à l'o. de sa mère, elle n'aimait pas la peinture** unlike her mother, she didn't like painting; **son deuxième livre est à l'o. du premier** his/her second book is the complete opposite of his/her first

opposer [ɔpoze] **1** *vt* (**a**) *(mettre en conflit) (armées, pays)* to bring into conflict (with each other); *(équipes)* to pit against each other; **o. à** *(armée, pays)* to bring into conflict with; *(équipe)* to pit against (**b**)

(objecter) (argument) to put forward (**à** against); **o. une résistance vigoureuse** to put up stiff resistance (**c**) *(mettre en contraste) (théories, styles, conceptions)* to contrast **2** *s'opposer vpr* (**a**) *(théories, styles, conceptions)* to contrast; *(équipes, adversaires)* to confront each other (**b**) **s'o. à qch** to be opposed to sth; **je m'oppose à ce qu'elle revienne** I'm against *or* opposed to her coming back

opposition [ɔpozisjɔ̃] *nf* (**a**) *(résistance)* opposition; *Pol* **l'o.** the Opposition; **faire o. à un chèque** to stop a cheque (**b**) *(contraste)* contrast; **tout cela est en o. totale avec ce que je pense** all that is the complete opposite of what I think; **par o. à qch** as opposed to sth

oppressant, -e [ɔprɛsɑ̃, -ɑ̃t] *adj* oppressive

oppresser [ɔprɛse] *vt* (**a**) *(sujet: situation, atmosphère)* to oppress (**b**) *Litt (peuple, nation)* to oppress

oppresseur [ɔprɛsœr] **1** *nm* oppressor **2** *adj* oppressive

oppression [ɔprɛsjɔ̃] *nf* (**a**) *(asservissement)* oppression (**b**) *Méd* tightness of the chest

opprimé, -e [ɔprime] **1** *adj* oppressed **2** *nm,f* **les opprimés** the oppressed

opprimer [ɔprime] *vt (peuple, nation)* to oppress

opprobre [ɔprɔbr] *nm Litt* opprobrium; **jeter l'o. sur qn** to cast opprobrium on sb

opter [ɔpte] *vi* **o. pour qch** to opt for sth; **o. entre deux choses** to choose between two things

opticien, -enne [ɔptisjɛ̃, -ɛn] *nm,f* optician

optimal, -e, -aux, -ales [ɔptimal, -o] *adj* optimum, optimal

optimiser [ɔptimize] *vt* to optimize

optimisme [ɔptimism] *nm* optimism; **avec o.** optimistically

optimiste [ɔptimist] **1** *adj* optimistic **2** *nmf* optimist

option [ɔpsjɔ̃] *nf* (**a**) *(choix)* option (**b**) *(chose facultative)* optional extra; *Scol (matière)* option; **le flash est en o.** the flash is an optional extra; *Scol* **matières à o.** optional subjects (**c**) *(d'achat)* **prendre une o. sur qch** to take (out) an option on sth (**d**) *Ordinat* **o. d'impression** print option; **o. de menu** menu option

optionnel, -elle [ɔpsjɔnɛl] *adj* optional

optique [ɔptik] **1** *adj (nerf)* optic; *(verre)* optical **2** *nf* (**a**) *(science)* optics *(singulier)*; **instruments d'o.** optical instruments (**b**) *(perspective)* perspective; **dans cette o.** from this perspective (**c**) *(d'un projecteur)* optical system

opulence [ɔpylɑ̃s] *nf* (**a**) *(richesse)* opulence (**b**) *(des formes)* fullness

opulent, -e [ɔpylɑ̃, -ɑ̃t] *adj (pays, personne)* opulent; *(pâturage)* abundant; *(poitrine)* full

opuscule [ɔpyskyl] *nm* opuscule

or[1] [ɔr] *nm* (**a**) *(métal)* gold; **montre/dent en or** gold watch/tooth; *Fam* **j'ai une femme en or** my wife is worth her weight in gold; **pour tout l'or du monde** for all the money in the world; *Fig* **c'est de l'or en barre** it's a safe investment; **le silence est d'or** silence is golden; **or fin** fine gold; **or massif** solid gold; **or noir** black gold; **or pur** pure gold; **l'or vert** agricultural earnings (**b**) *(couleur)* gold; **cheveux d'or** golden hair

or[2] *conj (pour introduire une précision)* now; *(pour introduire une opposition)* well

oracle [ɔrakl] *nm* oracle

orage [ɔraʒ] *nm* (thunder)storm; *aussi Fig* **il y a de l'o. dans l'air** there's a storm brewing

orageux, -euse [ɔraʒø, -øz] *adj aussi Fig* stormy

oraison [ɔrɛzɔ̃] *nf* prayer; **o. funèbre** funeral oration

oral, -e, -aux, -ales [ɔral, -o] **1** *adj* oral; **par voie orale** orally
2 *nm (examen)* oral; **il n'est pas très bon à l'o.** his oral work isn't very good

oralement [ɔralmã] *adv* orally

orange [ɔrãʒ] **1** *nf* orange; **o. givrée** = orange sorbet served inside the skin of a whole orange; **o. pressée** = freshly-squeezed orange juice served with water and sugar; **o. sanguine** blood orange
2 *nm (couleur)* orange; **passer à l'o.** *(automobiliste)* to go through (the lights) on amber
3 *adj inv* orange

orangé, -e [ɔrãʒe] *adj* orange-coloured

orangeade [ɔrãʒad] *nf* Br orange squash, *Am* orangeade

oranger [ɔrãʒe] *nm* orange tree

orangeraie [ɔrãʒrɛ] *nf* orange grove

orangerie [ɔrãʒri] *nf* orangery

orang-outan *(pl* orangs-outans), **orang-outang** *(pl* **orangs-outangs)** [ɔrãutã] *nm* orang-outang, orang-utan

orateur, -trice [ɔratœr, -tris] *nm,f (personne éloquente)* orator; *(personne qui prend la parole)* speaker

oratoire¹ [ɔratwar] *adj* oratorical

oratoire² *nm (chapelle)* oratory

oratorio [ɔratɔrjo] *nm* oratorio

orbite [ɔrbit] *nf* (**a**) *(Astron & Fig)* orbit; **être en** *ou* **sur o.** to be in orbit; **mettre** *ou* **placer un satellite en** *ou* **sur o.** to put a satellite into orbit (**b**) *(de l'œil)* socket

Orcades [ɔrkad] *nfpl* **les (îles) O.** the Orkneys, the Orkney Islands

orchestral, -e, -aux, -ales [ɔrkɛstral, -o] *adj* orchestral

orchestration [ɔrkɛstrasjɔ̃] *nf aussi Fig* orchestration

orchestre [ɔrkɛstr] *nm* (**a**) *(de musiciens)* orchestra; **o. de chambre** chamber orchestra; **o. de jazz** jazz band (**b**) *(partie de la salle)* Br stalls, *Am* orchestra

orchestrer [ɔrkɛstre] *vt aussi Fig* to orchestrate

orchidée [ɔrkide] *nf* orchid

ordi [ɔrdi] *nm Fam* computer, *Br* puter

ordinaire [ɔrdinɛr] **1** *adj* (**a**) *(habituel)* ordinary, usual; **peu** *ou* **pas o.** unusual (**b**) *(commun)* ordinary
2 *nm* (**a**) *(habitude)* **d'o.** usually; **comme à l'o.** as usual; **moins/plus que d'o.** less/more than usual (**b**) *(moyenne)* **ça sort de l'o.** it's out of the ordinary (**c**) *(régime habituel)* standard fare; *Mil* (company) mess (**d**) *(essence)* Br two-star, *Am* regular

ordinal, -e, -aux, -ales [ɔrdinal, -o] *adj* ordinal

ordinariat [ɔrdinarja] *nm Belg Univ* tenured *Br* lectureship *or Am* professorship

ordinateur [ɔrdinatœr] *nm* computer; **o. autonome** stand-alone (computer); **o. bloc-notes** notebook (computer); **o. de bureau** desktop computer; **o. central** mainframe (computer); **o. domestique** home computer; **o. individuel** personal computer; **o. de poche** palmtop (computer); **o. portable** laptop (computer)

ordination [ɔrdinasjɔ̃] *nf* ordination

ordonnance [ɔrdɔnãs] *nf* (**a**) *(document)* prescription; **délivré seulement sur o.** available only on prescription (**b**) *(disposition)* arrangement (**c**) *Jur* order, ruling (**d**) *Mil* orderly

ordonné, -e [ɔrdɔne] **1** *adj* (**a**) *(vie)* orderly (**b**) *(personne, armoire, bureau)* tidy

2 *nf* **ordonnée** *Math* ordinate; **axe des ordonnées** Y-axis

ordonner [ɔrdɔne] *vt* (**a**) *(mettre de l'ordre dans)* to organize (**b**) *(commander)* to order; **o. à qn de faire qch** to order sb to do sth (**c**) *Rel* to ordain

ordre [ɔrdr] *nm* (**a**) *(organisation)* order; **par o. alphabétique/chronologique** in alphabetical/chronological order; **procéder par o.** to do things in order; **par o. d'apparition à l'écran** in order of appearance; *Fig* **c'est dans l'o. des choses** it's in the nature of things (**b**) *(de pièce, de personne)* tidiness; **en o.** *(bureau, maison)* tidy; *(comptes)* in order; **mettre de l'o.** to tidy up (**c**) *(discipline)* order; **maintenir/rétablir l'o.** to maintain/restore order; **tout est rentré dans l'o.** everything has returned to normal; **l'o. établi** the established order; **l'o. public** law and order; **troubler l'o. public** to cause a breach of the peace (**d**) *(catégorie)* order; **de premier/second/troisième o.** first-/second-/third-rate; **renseignements/idées d'o. général** general information/ideas; **d'o. privé/pratique** of a private/practical nature; **du même o.** of the same order; **de l'o. de** in the order of (**e**) *(communauté)* order; **o. religieux** religious order; **entrer dans les ordres** to take holy orders; **l'o. des médecins** *Br* ≃ the British Medical Association, *Am* ≃ the American Medical Association (**f**) *(commandement)* order; **donner l'o. à qn de faire qch** to give sb the order to do sth; **je ne suis pas à tes ordres!** I don't take orders from you!; **à vos ordres, mon général!** yes sir!; **sur l'o. de qn** on the order of sb; **jusqu'à nouvel o.** until further notice (**g**) *Fin* order; **à l'o. de...** payable to (the order of)... (**h**) **o. du jour** *(d'un comité)* agenda; *Mil* order of the day

ordure [ɔrdyr] *nf* (**a**) *(saleté)* dirt, filth (**b**) **ordures** *(déchets)* Br rubbish, *Am* garbage; **ordures ménagères** household *Br* rubbish *or Am* garbage; **jeter** *ou* **mettre qch aux ordures** to throw sth in the *Br* dustbin *or Am* garbage can (**c**) *Fam (personne méprisable)* bastard

ordurier, -ère [ɔrdyrje, -ɛr] *adj* filthy

orée [ɔre] *nf* **à l'o. de la forêt/du bois** on the edge of the forest/wood

oreille [ɔrɛj] *nf* (**a**) *(d'une personne, d'un animal)* ear; **o. externe/interne** outer/inner ear; *Fam* **avoir les oreilles en feuilles de chou** to have big sticky-out ears; **il partit l'o. basse** he went off with his tail between his legs; **tirer les oreilles à qn** to pull sb's ears; *Fig* to give sb a telling off; **n'écouter que d'une o.**, **écouter d'une o. distraite** to listen with half an ear; **dire qch à l'o. de qn** to whisper sth in sb's ear; **dresser** *ou* **tendre l'o.** to prick up one's ears; **je n'en crois pas mes oreilles** I can't believe my ears; **les oreilles ont dû lui siffler** his/her ears must have been burning; **faire la sourde o.** to turn a deaf ear; **ce n'est pas tombé dans l'o. d'un sourd** it didn't fall on deaf ears; *Fig* **elle ne l'entend pas de cette o.** she won't hear of it; **être dur d'o.** to be hard of hearing; **avoir de l'o.** to have a good ear (**b**) *(d'un fauteuil)* wing; *(d'un plat, d'un vase)* handle; *(d'une casquette)* ear flap; **écrou à oreilles** wing nut

oreiller [ɔreje] *nm* pillow; **sur l'o.** in bed; **confidences sur l'o.** pillow talk

oreillette [ɔrejɛt] *nf* (**a**) *(du cœur)* auricle (**b**) *(d'une casquette)* ear flap

oreillons [ɔrejɔ̃] *nmpl* mumps; **avoir les o.** to have mumps

Orénoque [ɔrenɔk] *nm* **l'O.** the Orinoco

ores [ɔr] **d'ores et déjà** *adv* already
orfèvre [ɔrfɛvr] *nm (d'or)* goldsmith; *(d'argent)* silversmith; *Fig* **être o. en la matière** to be an expert in the matter
orfèvrerie [ɔrfɛvrəri] *nf (travail de l'or)* goldsmith's trade; *(travail de l'argent)* silversmith's trade; *(objets)* plate
organe [ɔrgan] *nm* (**a**) *Anat* organ; **organes génitaux** genitals (**b**) *(d'une machine)* part; **organes de transmission** transmission system (**c**) *Fig (instrument)* organ; **o. de publicité** advertising agency; **l'o. officiel du parti** the official organ of the party (**d**) *Hum (voix)* voice
organigramme [ɔrganigram] *nm* organization chart; *Ordinat* (data) flow chart
organique [ɔrganik] *adj* organic
organisateur, -trice [ɔrganizatœr, -tris] **1** *adj* organizing
 2 *nm,f* organizer; **o. de conférences/de congrès** conference organizer; **o. d'événements** event *or* events organizer; **o. de mariages** wedding planner; **o. de voyages** tour operator
organisation [ɔrganizasjɔ̃] *nf* (**a**) *(action, résultat)* organization (**b**) *(groupement)* organization; **o. à but non lucratif** *Br* non-profit-making *or Am* not-for-profit organization; **o. politique/syndicale** political/trade-union organization; **O. mondiale de la santé** World Health Organization; **O. des Nations unies** United Nations Organization; **O. du Traité de l'Atlantique Nord** North Atlantic Treaty Organization
organisé, -e [ɔrganize] *adj* organized
organiser [ɔrganize] **1** *vt* to organize
 2 s'organiser *vpr* to get organized
organisme [ɔrganism] *nm* (**a**) *Biol & Zool* organism; *Anat* system (**b**) *(organisation)* organization, body; **o. de crédit** credit institution; **o. international** international organization
organiste [ɔrganist] *nmf* organist
orgasme [ɔrgasm] *nm* orgasm
orge [ɔrʒ] *nf* barley
orgeat [ɔrʒa] *nm* **sirop d'o.** barley water
orgelet [ɔrʒəlɛ] *nm* sty
orgie [ɔrʒi] *nf* orgy
orgue [ɔrg] **1** *nm* organ; **o. de Barbarie** barrel organ
 2 *nfpl* **orgues** (**a**) *Mus* organ; **les grandes orgues de la cathédrale** the great organ of the cathedral (**b**) *Géol* **orgues de basalte** basalt columns
orgueil [ɔrgœj] *nm* pride
orgueilleux, -euse [ɔrgœjø, -øz] *Péj* **1** *adj* proud
 2 *nm,f* proud person
orient [ɔrjɑ̃] *nm* east; **l'O.** the East, the Orient; **en O.** in the East
orientable [ɔrjɑ̃tabl] *adj (grue)* swivelling; *(lampe, antenne)* adjustable
oriental, -e, -aux, -ales [ɔrjɑ̃tal, -o] **1** *adj (région, côte)* eastern; *(langue)* oriental
 2 *nm,f* **O.** Oriental
orientateur, -trice [ɔrjɑ̃tatœr, -tris] = **orienteur, -euse**
orientation [ɔrjɑ̃tasjɔ̃] *nf* (**a**) *(détermination de position)* orientation; **avoir le sens de l'o.** to have a good sense of direction (**b**) *Scol* careers guidance; **choisir une o.** to choose a course of study (**c**) *(d'une grue, d'une antenne)* positioning (**d**) *(d'une maison)* aspect (**e**) *(d'une politique, de recherches)* direction
orienté, -e [ɔrjɑ̃te] *adj* (**a**) *(disposé)* **maison/pièce orientée au sud** house/room facing south (**b**) *(peu*

objectif) biased (**c**) *Ordinat* **o. ligne** line-orientated; **o. objet** object-orientated
orienter [ɔrjɑ̃te] **1** *vt* (**a**) *(bâtiment)* to orientate; *(canon, fusil, télescope)* to point (**vers** *ou* **sur** at) (**b**) *(voyageur)* to direct, to guide; *Scol* **on l'a bien/mal orientée** she was given good/bad careers advice; **o. la conversation sur** to steer the conversation to; **o. ses recherches vers** to direct one's research towards
 2 s'orienter *vpr* (**a**) *(trouver sa route)* to get one's bearings (**b**) *Fig* **s'o. vers** *(sujet: étudiant)* to specialize in; *(sujet: recherches)* to be directed towards
orienteur, -euse [ɔrjɑ̃tœr, -øz] *nm,f Scol Br* careers adviser, *Am* career counselor
orifice [ɔrifis] *nm* opening; *(du corps)* orifice; *Tech* port
oriflamme [ɔriflam] *nf* (**a**) *Hist* oriflamme (**b**) *(bannière)* banner
origan [ɔrigɑ̃] *nm* oregano
originaire [ɔriʒinɛr] *adj* **être o. de** *(sujet: personne)* to be a native of; *(sujet: coutume, plat)* to originate from
original, -e, -aux, -ales [ɔriʒinal, -o] **1** *adj* (**a**) *(premier, nouveau)* original (**b**) *(excentrique)* eccentric
 2 *nm,f (excentrique)* eccentric
 3 *nm (œuvre, document)* original; *(d'un fichier, d'une disquette)* master copy
originalité [ɔriʒinalite] *nf* (**a**) *(nouveauté)* originality (**b**) *(excentricité)* eccentricity (**c**) *(trait original)* original feature
origine [ɔriʒin] *nf* origin; **des origines à nos jours** from the earliest times to the present day; **à l'o.** originally; **être à l'o. de qch** to be at the origin of sth; **être d'o. modeste** to be of humble origin; **être d'o. anglaise, être anglais d'o.** to be of English origin
originel, -elle [ɔriʒinɛl] *adj* original
orignal, -aux [ɔriɲal, -o] *nm* moose
oripeaux [ɔripo] *nmpl* rags, tatters
ORL [ɔɛrɛl] *nmf Méd (abrév* **oto-rhino-laryngologiste)** ENT specialist
orme [ɔrm] *nm* elm
ormeau, -x [ɔrmo] *nm* (**a**) *(arbre)* young elm (**b**) *(mollusque)* abalone
ornement [ɔrnəmɑ̃] *nm aussi Mus* ornament
ornemental, -e, -aux, -ales [ɔrnəmɑ̃tal, -o] *adj* ornamental
orner [ɔrne] *vt* to decorate (**de** with); *(vêtement)* to trim (**de** with)
ornière [ɔrnjɛr] *nf* rut; *Fig* **sortir de l'o.** to get out of trouble
ornithologie [ɔrnitɔlɔʒi] *nf* ornithology
ornithologiste [ɔrnitɔlɔʒist], **ornithologue** [ɔrnitɔlɔg] *nmf* ornithologist
oronge [ɔrɔ̃ʒ] *nf* agaric
orphelin, -e [ɔrfəlɛ̃, -in] **1** *adj* orphan(ed); **o. de père** fatherless; **o. de mère** motherless
 2 *nm,f* orphan
orphelinat [ɔrfəlina] *nm* orphanage
orque [ɔrk] *nf* killer whale
Orsay [ɔrsɛ] *n voir* **quai**
ORSEC [ɔrsɛk] *(abrév* **organisation des secours) le plan O.** = disaster contingency plan

Le plan ORSEC
This scheme is set in motion whenever there is a major disaster in France, such as flooding or forest fires. Under the provisions of the scheme, the "préfet", or chief of police, is empowered to mobilize both public and private resources to deal with a civil emergency.

orteil [ɔrtɛj] *nm* toe; **gros/petit o.** big/little toe
orthodontiste [ɔrtodɔ̃tist] *nmf* orthodontist
orthodoxe [ɔrtɔdɔks] **1** *adj aussi Rel* orthodox; **peu o.** unorthodox **2** *nmf Rel (de stricte obédience)* person of orthodox beliefs; *(de l'Église orthodoxe)* member of the Orthodox Church
orthodoxie [ɔrtɔdɔksi] *nf* orthodoxy
orthogonal, -e, -aux, -ales [ɔrtɔgɔnal, -o] *adj* orthogonal
orthographe [ɔrtɔgraf] *nf* spelling; **avoir une bonne o.** to be good at spelling
orthographier [66] [ɔrtɔgrafje] *vt* to spell; **mal o. un mot** to misspell a word
orthographique [ɔrtɔgrafik] *adj* orthographic
orthopédie [ɔrtɔpedi] *nf* orthopaedics *(singulier)*
orthopédique [ɔrtɔpedik] *adj* orthopaedic
orthopédiste [ɔrtɔpedist] *nmf* (**a**) *(médecin)* orthopaedist (**b**) *(fabricant)* maker of orthopaedic apparatus
orthophonie [ɔrtɔfɔni] *nf* speech therapy
orthophoniste [ɔrtɔfɔnist] *nmf* speech therapist
ortie [ɔrti] *nf* nettle
ortolan [ɔrtɔlɑ̃] *nm* ortolan (bunting)
OS [oɛs] *nm (abrév* **ouvrier spécialisé)** semi-skilled worker
os [ɔs, *pl* o] *nm* bone; *Fam Fig (obstacle)* snag; **mouillé ou trempé jusqu'aux os** soaked to the skin; **il ne fera pas de vieux os** he won't make old bones; *Fam* **tomber sur un os** to hit a snag; *très Fam* **je l'ai dans l'os** I've had it; **os à moelle,** *Belg* **os à la moelle** marrowbone
oscar [ɔskar] *nm Cin (récompense)* Oscar
oscarisé, -e [ɔskarize] *adj Cin* Oscar-winning; **l'acteur o. pour "Gladiator"** the actor who won an Oscar for "Gladiator"
oscariser [ɔskarize] *vt Cin* to award an Oscar to
oscillateur [ɔsilatœr] *nm Phys* oscillator
oscillation [ɔsilasjɔ̃] *nf* (**a**) *(d'un pendule)* swing; *(d'une aiguille)* flickering; *(d'un bateau)* rocking; *Phys* oscillation (**b**) *Fig (du marché, de l'opinion)* fluctuation
osciller [ɔsile] *vi* (**a**) *(pendule)* to swing; *(aiguille)* to flicker; *(bateau)* to rock; *Phys* to oscillate (**b**) *(hésiter)* **o. entre** to waver between
osé, -e [oze] *adj* daring
oseille [ozɛj] *nf* (**a**) *(plante)* sorrel (**b**) *Fam (argent)* cash, dough
oser [oze] *vt* **o. faire qch** to dare (to) do sth; **j'ose croire que...** I dare say that...; **si j'ose dire** if I may say so; **comment osez-vous!** how dare you!
osier [ozje] *nm* (**a**) *(arbre)* osier (**b**) *(en vannerie)* wicker
Oslo [ɔslo] *n* Oslo
osmose [ɔsmoz] *nf aussi Fig* osmosis
ossature [ɔsatyr] *nf* (**a**) *(d'un homme, d'un animal)* frame (**b**) *Fig (d'un bâtiment, d'un texte)* framework
osselets [ɔslɛ] *nmpl* **jouer aux o.** to play at knucklebones
ossements [ɔsmɑ̃] *nmpl* bones
osseux, -euse [ɔsø, -øz] *adj (visage, main)* bony; *(tissu, greffe)* bone
ossuaire [ɔsɥɛr] *nm* ossuary
ostensible [ɔstɑ̃sibl] *adj* open
ostensiblement [ɔstɑ̃sibləmɑ̃] *adv* openly
ostensoir [ɔstɑ̃swar] *nm Rel* monstrance

ostentation [ɔstɑ̃tasjɔ̃] *nf* ostentation; **sans o.** unostentatiously
ostéopathe [ɔsteopat] *nmf* osteopath
ostéopathie [ɔsteopati] *nf* osteopathy
ostéoporose [ɔsteopɔroz] *nf Méd* osteoporosis
ostracisme [ɔstrasism] *nm* ostracism
ostréiculteur, -trice [ɔstreikyltœr, -tris] *nm,f* oyster farmer
ostréiculture [ɔstreikyltyr] *nf* oyster farming
otage [ɔtaʒ] *nm* hostage; **prendre qn en o.** to take sb hostage
otalgie [ɔtalʒi] *nf Méd* earache, *Spéc* otalgia
OTAN [ɔtɑ̃] *nf (abrév* **Organisation du traité de l'Atlantique Nord)** l'O. NATO
otarie [ɔtari] *nf* sea lion
OTASE [ɔtaz] *nf (abrév* **Organisation du traité de l'Asie du Sud-Est)** l'O. SEATO
ôter [ote] **1** *vt* (**a**) *(enlever)* to take away, to remove; *(vêtement)* to take off; *(tache)* to remove; *(assiettes)* to clear away; **ô. qch à qn** to take sth away from sb; *(illusions)* to rid sb of sth; **cela lui a ôté l'appétit** it took away his/her appetite; **je vais t'ô. l'envie de recommencer!** I'll teach you not to start that again!; **tu ne m'ôteras pas de l'idée que...** I'm quite convinced that... (**b**) *Math* **10 ôté de 30 égale 20** 10 from 30 leaves 20 **2 s'ôter** *vpr* **ôtez-vous de là!** move yourself!; **s'ô. une idée de la tête** to get an idea out of one's head
otite [ɔtit] *nf Méd* ear infection, *Spéc* otitis
oto-rhino *(pl* oto-rhinos) [ɔtorino] *nmf Fam* ENT specialist
oto-rhino-laryngologiste *(pl* oto-rhino-laryngologistes) [ɔtorinolarɛ̃gɔlɔʒist] *nmf* ear, nose and throat specialist
Ottawa [ɔtawa] *n* Ottawa
ou [u] *conj* or; **ou... ou (bien)...** either... or (else)...
où [u] **1** *adv* (**a**) *(interrogatif, relatif)* where; **d'où vient ce mot?** where does this word come from?; **par où est-il passé?** which way did he go?; **je ne sais pas où aller** I don't know where to go (**b**) *(indéfini)* **où que vous soyez** wherever you may be (**c**) *(exprime la conséquence)* **d'où sa tristesse** hence his/her sadness **2** *pron relatif* (**a**) *(dans l'espace)* where; **là où** where; **partout où** wherever (**b**) *(dans le temps)* when (**c**) *(dans lequel, auquel)* **dans l'état où elle est** in the state she's in; **au prix où est le champagne** with champagne the price it is
OUA [oya] *nf (abrév* **Organisation de l'unité africaine)** l'O. the OAU
ouache [waʃ] *nf Can* bear's den
ouah [wa] *exclam* (**a**) *(aboiement)* woof! (**b**) *(exprime l'admiration)* wow!
ouailles [waj] *nfpl Litt ou Hum* flock
ouais [wɛ] *exclam Fam* yeah!
ouananiche [wananiʃ] *nf Can* freshwater salmon
ouaouaron [wawarɔ̃] *nm Can* bullfrog
ouate [wat] *nf* (**a**) *(pour soins)* Br cotton wool, Am absorbent cotton (**b**) *(pour rembourrage)* padding
ouatine [watin] *nf* quilting (material)
ouatiné, -e [watine] *adj* quilted
oubli [ubli] *nm* (**a**) *(trou de mémoire)* oversight; *(lacune)* omission (**b**) *(général)* oblivion; **tomber dans l'o.** to sink into oblivion (**c**) *(acte d'oublier)* forgetting
oublier [66] [ublije] **1** *vt* to forget; *(omettre)* to leave out; **o. de faire qch** to forget to do sth; *Hum* **il a oublié d'être bête** he's not lacking in brains **2 s'oublier** *vpr* (**a**) *(se relâcher)* to forget oneself;

Euph (chien) to make a mess (**b**) *(sortir de la mémoire)* to be forgotten; **c'est comme le vélo, ça ne s'oublie pas** it's like riding a bike, once you learn you never forget

oubliettes [ublijɛt] *nfpl* dungeon; *Fig* **mettre qch aux o.** to shelve sth

ouèbe [wɛb] *nm Ordinat* **l'o.** the Web

ouest [wɛst] **1** *nm* west; **un vent d'o.** a westerly wind; **le vent d'o.** the west wind; **à l'o.** in the west; **à l'o. de** (to the) west of; *Géog & Pol* **l'O.** the West
2 *adj inv (côte, face)* west; *(régions)* western

ouf [uf] *exclam* phew!; *Fam* **elle n'a pas eu le temps de dire o.** she didn't even have time to catch her breath

Ouganda [ugɑ̃da] *nm* **l'O.** Uganda

ougandais, -e [ugɑ̃dɛ, -ɛz] **1** *adj* Ugandan
2 *nm,f* **O.** Ugandan

oui [wi] **1** *adv* yes; **répondre par o. ou par non** to answer yes or no; **je crois que o.** I think so; **faire signe que o.** to nod (one's head); **ah, o.?** really?; *Fam* **tu viens, o.?** are you coming?; *Fam* **tu viens, o. ou non?** are you coming or aren't you?
2 *nm inv Pol* aye; *Fam* **se quereller/pleurer pour un o., pour un non** to quarrel/cry over the slightest thing

ouï-dire [widir] *nm* hearsay; **par o.** by hearsay

ouïe [wi] *nf* (**a**) *(sens)* hearing; **avoir l'o. fine** to have sharp ears; *Hum* **être tout o.** to be all ears (**b**) *(de poisson)* **ouïes** gills (**c**) *Mus* **ouïes** sound holes

ouille [uj] *exclam* ouch!, ow!

ouïr [51] [wir] *vt* (**a**) *Littéraire ou Hum* to hear (tell); **j'ai ouï dire que...** I heard tell that...; **j'ai souvent ouï dire que...** I have often heard it said that... (**b**) *Jur* **o. des témoins** to hear witnesses

ouistiti [wistiti] *nm* marmoset; *Fam Fig* **un drôle de o.** an odd character

ouragan [uragɑ̃] *nm* hurricane; *Fig (de protestations)* storm; **entrer comme un o. dans une pièce** to burst into a room

Oural [ural] *nm* **l'O.** *(montagnes)* the Urals

ourler [urle] *vt* (**a**) *(faire un ourlet à)* to hem (**b**) *(border)* to edge (**de** with)

ourlet [urlɛ] *nm* (**a**) *(d'un vêtement)* hem; **faire un o. à** to put a hem on (**b**) *(de l'oreille)* rim

ours [urs] *nm aussi Fig* bear; *Prov* **il ne faut pas vendre la peau de l'o. avant de l'avoir tué** don't count your chickens before they're hatched; **o. blanc** polar bear; **o. brun** brown bear; *Fig* **o. mal léché** boor; **o. en peluche** teddy bear; **o. polaire** polar bear

ourse [urs] *nf* she-bear; *Astron* **la Grande O.** the Great Bear; **la Petite O.** the Little Bear

oursin [ursɛ̃] *nm* sea urchin

ourson [ursɔ̃] *nm* bear cub

oust(e) [ust] *exclam (pour presser)* get a move on!; *(pour chasser)* scram!

outarde [utard] *nf Can* Canada goose

outer [awte] *vt Fam (révéler l'homosexualité de)* to out

outil [uti] *nm aussi Fig* tool; **outils pédagogiques** teaching aids; **o. de production** production tool; **o. de travail** tool

outillage [utijaʒ] *nm* (**a**) *(ensemble d'outils)* (set of) tools (**b**) *(industriel, agricole)* equipment

outiller [utije] **1** *vt* to equip
2 **s'outiller** *vpr (bricoleur)* to equip oneself; *(usine)* to equip itself

outrage [utraʒ] *nm (au bon goût, au bon sens)* insult (**à** to); *Euph & Litt* **faire subir les derniers outrages à une femme** to violate a woman; *Jur* **o. aux bonnes mœurs** affront to public decency; **o. à magistrat** contempt of court; **o. à la pudeur** public indecency

outrageant, -e [utraʒɑ̃, -ɑ̃t] *adj (proposition, refus)* insulting; *(plaisanterie, propos)* offensive; *(accusation)* outrageous

outrageusement [utraʒøzmɑ̃] *adv (excessivement)* outrageously

outrance [utrɑ̃s] *nf (d'une tenue, d'une attitude, de propos)* extravagance; **à o.** excessively

outre¹ [utr] *nf* wine skin

outre² [utr] **1** *prép* (**a**) *(en plus de)* besides (**b**) **o. mesure** unduly
2 *adv* **en o.** besides; **passer o.** *(malgré une interdiction)* to carry on regardless; **passer o. à qch** to disregard sth
3 *conj* **o. (le fait) que...** apart from the fact that...

outré, -e [utre] *adj* (**a**) *(indigné)* outraged (**de** *ou* **par** by) (**b**) *(excessif)* overdone

outre-Atlantique [utratlɑ̃tik] *adv* across the Atlantic

outrecuidance [utrəkɥidɑ̃s] *nf Litt* (**a**) *(insolence)* impertinence; **avoir l'o. de faire qch** to have the impertinence to do sth (**b**) *(orgueil)* presumptuousness

outrecuidant, -e [utrəkɥidɑ̃, -ɑ̃t] *adj* (**a**) *(insolent)* impertinent (**b**) *(orgueilleux)* presumptuous

outre-Manche [utrəmɑ̃ʃ] *adv* across the Channel

outre-mer [utrəmɛr] *adv* overseas; **la France d'o.** France's overseas territories and departments

outrepasser [utrəpase] *vt* to exceed, to go beyond

outre-Rhin [utrərɛ̃] *adv* across the Rhine

outre-tombe [utrətɔ̃b] **d'outre-tombe** *adj (voix)* sepulchral

ouvert, -e [uvɛr, -ɛrt] **1** *pp de* **ouvrir**
2 *adj* (**a**) *(porte, yeux, plaie, vêtement, magasin)* open; **grand o.** wide open; **être o. à qn** *(lieu, concours)* to be open to sb (**b**) *(gaz, robinet)* on (**c**) *Fig (franc, sans préjugés)* open; **avoir l'esprit o.** to be open-minded; **être o. à toute proposition** to be open to suggestions

ouvertement [uvɛrtəmɑ̃] *adv* openly

ouverture [uvɛrtyr] *nf* (**a**) *(d'une porte, d'une séance, d'un compte)* opening; *(des hostilités)* outbreak; **l'o. de la chasse/de la pêche** the start of the hunting season/fishing season; **à l'o.** *(de la Bourse)* at the start of trading; *Fig* **o. d'esprit** open-mindedness; *Ordinat* **o. de session** log-on (**b**) *(orifice)* opening (**c**) **ouvertures** *(avances)* overtures; **faire des ouvertures à qn** to make overtures to sb (**d**) *Mus* overture (**e**) *Phot* aperture (**f**) *Pol* **politique d'o.** policy of conciliation (**g**) *(aux échecs, aux cartes)* opening

ouvrable [uvrabl] *adj voir* **jour**

ouvrage [uvraʒ] *nm* (**a**) *(travail)* work; **se mettre à l'o.** to get down to work (**b**) *Constr* work; **ouvrages d'art** civil engineering works (**c**) *(livre)* work; **o. de référence** reference work (**d**) *(résultat d'un travail)* piece of work; *(tricot, broderie)* work
2 *nf Fam* **c'est de la belle o.** that's a nice piece of work

ouvragé, -e [uvraʒe] *adj* elaborate

ouvrant, -e [uvrɑ̃, -ɑ̃t] *adj voir* **toit**

ouvre-boîtes [uvrəbwat] *nm inv* can opener

ouvre-bouteilles [uvrəbutɛj] *nm inv* bottle opener

ouvreur, -euse [uvrœr, -øz] *nm,f* usher, *f* usherette

ouvrier, -ère [uvrije, -ɛr] **1** *adj (quartier, tradition)* working-class; *(agitation)* industrial
2 *nm,f* worker; **une famille d'ouvriers** a working-class family; **o. agricole** farm worker; **o. qualifié**

skilled worker; **o. spécialisé** semi-skilled worker
3 *nm (dans les travaux publics, le bâtiment)* workman
4 *nf* **ouvrière** *(abeille, fourmi)* worker
ouvrir [52] [uvrir] **1** *vt* (**a**) *(porte, boîte, bouteille, rideaux)* to open; *(verrou)* to draw; *(avec une clef)* to unlock; *(robinet, gaz)* to turn on; *(électricité)* to switch on; **o. à qn** to let sb in; **ouvre, c'est moi** open the door, it's me (**b**) *Méd (abcès)* to lance; *(pour opérer)* to open up (**c**) *(lancer) (boutique, compte, débat)* to open; **o. la marche** to lead the way; *Ordinat* **o. une session** to log in *or* on (**d**) *Fig* **cela ouvre l'appétit** it whets the appetite; **o. son cœur à qn** to open one's heart to sb; **o. l'esprit à qn** to broaden sb's mind; **o. qch à qn** *(domaine, profession, perspectives)* to open up sth to sb
2 *vi (magasin, porte)* to open
3 s'ouvrir *vpr* (**a**) *(porte, yeux, séance, fleur)* to open; *Fig* **s'o. à qn** *(perspectives, domaine)* to open up for sb (**b**) *(se couper)* **s'o. la main/le menton** to cut open one's hand/chin; **s'o. les veines** to slash one's wrists (**c**) *(s'épancher)* to open up; **s'o. à qn de qch** to open one's heart to sb about sth, to confide in sb about sth
ouzbek [uzbɛk] **1** *adj* Uzbek
2 *nmf* **O.** Uzbek
Ouzbékistan [uzbekistɑ̃] *nm* **l'O.** Uzbekistan
ovaire [ɔvɛr] *nm* ovary
ovale [ɔval] *adj & nm* oval
ovariectomie [ɔvarjɛktɔmi] *nf Méd* ovariectomy
ovarien, -enne [ɔvarjɛ̃, -ɛn] *adj* ovarian
ovation [ɔvasjɔ̃] *nf* ovation; **faire une o. à qn** to give sb an ovation
ovationner [ɔvasjɔne] *vt* **o. qn** to give sb an ovation

overbooké, -e [ɔvœrbuke] *adj Fam (personne)* booked-up, busy
overdose [ɔvœrdoz] *nf aussi Fig* overdose; **faire une o. (de qch)** *(drogue)* to take an overdose (of sth); *Fig* to overdose (on sth)
ovin, -e [ɔvɛ̃, -in] *Zool* **1** *adj* ovine
2 *nm* sheep
OVNI, Ovni [ɔvni] *nm (abrév* **objet volant non identifié)** UFO; *Fig* **faire figure d'O.** to stand out, to break the mould
ovulation [ɔvylasjɔ̃] *nf* ovulation
ovule [ɔvyl] *nm* ovum
ovuler [ɔvyle] *vi* to ovulate
oxhydrique [ɔksidrik] *adj* oxyhydrogen
oxydant, -e [ɔksidɑ̃, -ɑ̃t] **1** *adj* oxidizing
2 *nm* oxidizer
oxydation [ɔksidasjɔ̃] *nf* oxidization
oxyde [ɔksid] *nm Chim* oxide; **o. de carbone** carbon monoxide
oxyder [ɔkside] **1** *vt* to oxidize
2 s'oxyder *vpr* to oxidize
oxygéné, -e [ɔksiʒene] *adj Chim* oxygenated; *(cheveux)* peroxide blonde, bleached
oxygène [ɔksiʒɛn] *nm* oxygen; *Fig* **j'ai besoin d'o.** I need some fresh air
oxygéner [34] [ɔksiʒene] **1** *vt* (**a**) *Chim (liquide, tissu vivant)* to oxygenate; *(élément, produit chimique)* to oxidize (**b**) *(cheveux)* to bleach, to peroxide
2 s'oxygéner *vpr (respirer)* to get some fresh air
oyat [ɔja] *nm* marram grass
ozone [ɔzon] *nm* ozone

P, p [pe] *nm inv* P, p
PAC [pak] *nf (abrév* **politique agricole commune**) CAP
PACA [paka] *nf (abrév* **Provence-Alpes-Côte d'Azur**) = region of south-eastern France
pacage [pakaʒ] *nm (champ)* pasture
pacemaker [pɛsmɛkœr] *nm* pacemaker
pacha [paʃa] *nm* pasha; *Fig* **mener une vie de p.** to live like a lord
pachyderme [paʃidɛrm] *nm* pachyderm; *Fig (personne)* lumbering oaf
pacification [pasifikasjɔ̃] *nf* pacification
pacifier [66] [pasifje] *vt* to pacify
pacifique [pasifik] **1** *adj (sans violence, calme)* peaceful; *(qui aime la paix)* peace-loving
  2 *nm* **le P.** *(océan)* the Pacific; **le P. sud** the South Pacific
pacifisme [pasifism] *nm* pacifism
pacifiste [pasifist] *adj & nmf* pacifist
pack [pak] *nm (lot) & Sport* pack; **vendu en p.** sold in packs
pacotille [pakɔtij] *nf* junk; **de p.** *(marchandise)* shoddy; *(bijoux)* paste; *Fig* third-rate
PACS [paks] *nm inv (abrév* **Pacte civil de solidarité**) civil solidarity pact *(law introduced in France in 1999 extending the legal rights of married couples to unmarried couples, particularly with regard to inheritance and taxation)*

PACS

The "Pacte civil de solidarité", more commonly known by its acronym "PACS", is a contract which offers legal recognition to adult cohabiting couples, including homosexuals. The law allows same-sex or heterosexual couples to register their union formally in a magistrates' court. Controversial when first proposed, the "PACS" became law in 1999, after more than 120 hours of parliamentary debate.

pacser [pakse] *Fam* **1** *vi* = to sign a "PACS" contract, to enter into a civil solidarity pact
  2 se pacser *vpr* = to sign a "PACS" contract, to enter into a civil solidarity pact
pacson [paksɔ̃] *nm Fam (argent)* packet
pacte [pakt] *nm* pact; **p. de non-agression** non-aggression pact; *UE* **P. de stabilité et de croissance** Stability and Growth Pact; **le p. de Varsovie** the Warsaw Pact
pactiser [paktize] *vi* **p. avec l'ennemi** to make a pact with the enemy

pactole [paktɔl] *nm Fam (au loto)* jackpot; **un joli p.** a nice little sum
paddock [padɔk] *nm* paddock; *Fam* bed
paella [paɛla] *nf* paella
PAF [paf] *nm Rad & TV (abrév* **paysage audiovisuel français**) = French broadcasting
paf [paf] **1** *exclam (chute)* bang!; *(claque)* slap!; *(coup de poing)* wham!
  2 *adj inv Fam* **(a)** *(saoul)* plastered **(b)** *Belg* **être/rester p.** to be flabbergasted
pagaie [pagɛ] *nf* paddle
pagaïe, pagaille [pagaj] *nf Fam* **(a)** *(désordre)* mess; **en p.** in a mess; **arrête de mettre la p. dans mes affaires** stop messing up my things **(b)** *(confusion)* chaos; **semer la p.** to cause chaos **(c)** **des cadeaux/des jouets en p.** loads of presents/toys
pagayer [53] [pageje] *vi* to paddle
page¹ [paʒ] *nf* **(a)** *(d'un livre, d'un cahier, sur l'Internet)* page; *Fig (extrait)* passage; *(de l'histoire, d'une vie)* chapter; **en première p. (des journaux)** on the front page (of the newspapers); *Typ* **mettre qch en page(s)** to make sth up; **perdre la p.** to lose one's place; *Fig* **tourner la p.** to make a fresh start; *Ordinat* **p. d'accueil** home page; **p. centrale** *(d'un magazine)* centre pages; **p. de garde** *(d'un livre)* flyleaf; *(d'un fax)* cover sheet; *Ordinat* splash page; **les pages jaunes** *(de l'annuaire)* the Yellow Pages®; *Ordinat* **p. perso, p. personnelle** personal home page; *Ordinat* **p. précédente** page up; *Rad & TV* **p. de publicité** commercial break; *Ordinat* **p. de résultats** results page; *Ordinat* **p. suivante** page down; *Ordinat* **p. web** Web page **(b)** **être à la p.** *(à la mode)* to be up to date
page² *nm* page(boy)
pager, pageur [paʒœr] *nm Ordinat* pager
pagination [paʒinasjɔ̃] *nf* pagination
paginer [paʒine] *vt* to paginate
pagne [paɲ] *nm* loincloth; *(en paille)* grass skirt
pagode [pagɔd] *nf* pagoda
paie [pɛ] **1** *voir* **payer**
  2 *nf* **(a)** *(salaire)* pay, wages **(b)** *Fam* **ça fait une p.** it's ages ago; **ça fait une p. que je ne l'ai pas vue** I haven't seen her for ages
paiement [pɛmɑ̃] *nm* payment; *aussi Fig* **en p. de qch** as payment for sth; **p. à la commande** cash with order; **p. à la livraison** cash on delivery; *Ordinat* **p. sécurisé** secure (electronic) transaction
païen, -enne [pajɛ̃, -ɛn] *adj & nm,f* pagan, heathen
paiera *etc voir* **payer**
paillard, -e [pajar, -ard] *adj* bawdy
paillasse [pajas] *nf* **(a)** *(matelas)* straw mattress **(b)** *(de l'évier)* draining board; *(de laboratoire)* bench

paillasson [pɑjasɔ̃] *nm aussi Fig* doormat
paille [pɑj] **1** *nf* (**a**) *(de céréales)* straw; *Fig* **être sur la p.** to be down and out; **tirer à la courte p.** to draw lots; **p. de fer** steel wool (**b**) *(pour boire)* straw; **boire avec une p.** to drink through a straw
2 *adj inv (jaune)* straw-coloured
paillé, -e [pɑje] *adj (chaise)* straw-bottomed
pailleté, -e [pɑjte] *adj* sequined
paillette [pɑjɛt] *nf* (**a**) *(sur vêtement)* sequin; **paillettes** *(pour se maquiller)* glitter; **à paillettes** sequined (**b**) *(d'or)* speck; *(de savon)* flake
paillote [pɑjɔt] *nf* straw hut
pain [pɛ̃] *nm* (**a**) *(aliment)* bread; *(miche)* loaf; *Fig* **avoir du p. sur la planche** to have a lot on one's plate; **gagner son p.** to earn one's living; **je ne mange pas de ce p.-là** I'm having nothing to do with that; **ça ne mange pas de p.** it won't cost you/him/*etc* anything; **ôter le p. de la bouche à qn** to take the bread out of sb's mouth; **petit p.** (bread) roll; *Fig* **partir** *ou* **se vendre comme des petits pains** to sell like hot cakes; **p. azyme** unleavened bread; **p. bénit** consecrated bread; **p. bis** brown bread; **p. de campagne** farmhouse bread; **p. au chocolat** chocolate-filled pastry; **p. complet** wholemeal bread; **p. d'épices** ≃ gingerbread; **p. grillé** toast; *Can* **p. d'habitant** *ou* **de famille** *ou* **du pays** homemade bread; **p. au lait** sweet roll; **p. de mie** sliced white bread; **p. perdu** French toast; **p. aux raisins** currant bun; **p. de seigle** rye bread; **p. au** *ou* **de son** bran bread; **p. de sucre** sugarloaf (**b**) *(de savon)* bar (**c**) *Fam (coup de poing)* punch
paintball [pɛjntbol] *nm* paintball; **faire du p.** to go paintballing
pair, -e[1] [pɛr] **1** *adj (nombre, jours)* even
2 *nm* (**a**) *(égal)* **être jugé par ses pairs** to be judged by one's peers; **aller de p. avec qch** to go hand in hand with sth (**b**) *(noble)* peer (**c**) **jeune fille au p.** au pair; **être** *ou* **travailler au p.** to work as an au pair (**d**) *(au jeu)* even numbers
paire[2] [pɛr] *nf* pair; *(de gibier à plumes, de pistolets)* brace; **il a reçu une p. de claques** he got his face slapped; *Fam Fig* **ça, c'est une autre p. de manches** that's a different kettle of fish
paisible [pɛzibl] *adj* peaceful; *(personne)* quiet
paisiblement [pɛziblǝmɑ̃] *adv* peacefully
paître [50b] [pɛtr] **1** *vt (herbe)* to crop; *(feuilles)* to feed on
2 *vi* to feed; *(manger de l'herbe)* to graze; *(manger des feuilles)* to browse; *Fam Fig* **envoyer p. qn** to send sb packing
paix [pɛ] *nf* (**a**) *(entre États)* peace; **faire la p. (avec qn)** to make peace (with sb); *Fig* to make it up (with sb); **vivre en p. avec sa conscience** to have a clear conscience (**b**) *Rel* **à son âme** may his/her soul rest in peace; **allez en p.** go in peace (**c**) *(tranquillité)* peace; **avoir la p.** to have some peace (and quiet); **faire qch en p.** to do sth in peace (and quiet); **laisser qn en p.** to leave sb in peace; *Fam* **fiche-moi** *ou très Fam* **fous-moi la p.!** get off my back!; *Fam* **la p.!** quiet!
Pakistan [pakistɑ̃] *nm* **le P.** Pakistan
pakistanais, -e [pakistanɛ, -ɛz] **1** *adj* Pakistani
2 *nm,f* **P.** Pakistani
Pal [pal] *adj inv TV (abrév* **phase alternation line***)* PAL
palabrer [palabre] *vi Péj* to talk endlessly
palabres [palabr] *nfpl Péj* endless discussion
palace [palas] *nm* luxury hotel
palais[1] [palɛ] *nm* (**a**) *(d'un roi, d'un noble)* palace; **le p. Bourbon** = home of the French parliament; **p. des**

congrès conference centre; **le p. de l'Élysée** the Élysée (Palace) *(official residence of the French President)*; **le p. Garnier** = the Paris Opera House; **le p. du Luxembourg** = home of the French Senate; **p. des sports** sports centre (**b**) *(tribunal)* **le P. (de justice)** the law courts
palais[2] *nm (partie de la bouche, goût)* palate; **avoir le p. fin** to have a refined palate
palan [palɑ̃] *nm* hoist
pale [pal] *nf* blade
pâle [pal] *adj* (**a**) pale; **p. comme un linge** as white as a sheet; **p. comme la mort** deathly pale; *Fam Mil* **se faire porter p.** to report sick (**b**) *Fig (sourire)* faint; *(style)* colourless; **une p. imitation de qch** a pale imitation of sth
palefrenier [palfrǝnje] *nm* groom
paléolithique [paleolitik] *Géol* **1** *adj* Palaeolithic
2 *nm* **le P.** the Palaeolithic period
paléontologie [paleɔ̃tɔlɔʒi] *nf* palaeontology
paléontologiste [paleɔ̃tɔlɔʒist], **paléontologue** [paleɔ̃tɔlɔg] *nmf* palaeontologist
Palerme [palɛrm] *n* Palermo
Palestine [palɛstin] *nf* **la P.** Palestine
palestinien, -enne [palɛstinjɛ̃, -ɛn] **1** *adj* Palestinian
2 *nm,f* **P.** Palestinian
palet [palɛ] *nm* (**a**) *(pour hockey)* puck (**b**) *(gâteau sec)* = round *Br* butter biscuit *or Am* butter cookie
paletot [palto] *nm (short)* overcoat; *Fam Fig* **tomber sur le p. à qn** *(l'attaquer)* to jump on sb; *(pour lui parler)* to buttonhole sb; *Belg Fig* **vieux paletots** old guard
palette [palɛt] *nf* (**a**) *(de peintre)* palette; *Fig (éventail)* range; *Ordinat* **p. graphique** graphics palette; *Ordinat* **p. d'outils** tool palette (**b**) *(pour la manutention)* pallet (**c**) *Culin (de mouton, de porc)* shoulder
palétuvier [paletyvje] *nm* mangrove
pâleur [palœr] *nf (d'une personne)* pallor; *(d'une couleur, de la lumière)* paleness; *(du style)* colourlessness; **d'une p. mortelle** deathly pale
pâlichon, -onne [paliʃɔ̃, -ɔn] *adj Fam* a bit pale
palier [palje] *nm* (**a**) *(d'escalier)* landing (**b**) *(dans une évolution)* plateau; **par paliers** in stages
palindrome [palɛ̃drom] *nm Ling* palindrome
pâlir [palir] *vi (personne)* to turn or go pale; *(lumière, couleur, souvenir)* to fade; **p. de rage** to turn white with anger; *Fig* **faire p. qn de jalousie** to make sb green with envy
palissade [palisad] *nf* fence
palliatif, -ive [paljatif, -iv] **1** *adj* palliative
2 *nm Méd* palliative; *Fig* stopgap measure
pallier [66] [palje] **1** *vt (manque)* to compensate for; *(erreur, problème)* to lessen the impact of
2 pallier à *vt ind (manque)* to compensate for; *(erreur, problème)* to lessen the impact of
palmarès [palmarɛs] *nm (à un concours)* list of prizewinners; *(d'une compétition sportive)* list of winners; **le p. (de la chanson)** the charts; **être** *ou* **figurer au p.** *(d'un concours, d'une compétition)* to be among the (prize-)winners; *(de la chanson)* to be in the charts; **avoir** *ou* **compter cinquante victoires à son p.** to have fifty wins to one's credit
palme [palm] *nf* (**a**) *(de palmier)* palm (branch) (**b**) *(récompense)* **les palmes académiques** = decoration awarded to teachers; **la P. d'or** *(du festival de Cannes)* the Palme d'or (**c**) *(pour nager)* flipper

palmé, -e [palme] *adj* (**a**) *(feuille)* palmate (**b**) *(pattes)* webbed

palmeraie [palmərɛ] *nf* palm grove

palmier [palmje] *nm* (**a**) *(arbre)* palm (tree); **p. dattier** date palm (**b**) *(gâteau sec)* = heart-shaped pastry

palmipède [palmipɛd] *nm Zool* web-footed bird, *Spéc* palmiped

palombe [palɔ̃b] *nf* wood pigeon

pâlot, -otte [palo, -ɔt] *adj Fam* a bit pale

palourde [palurd] *nf* clam

palpable [palpabl] *adj* palpable

palpation [palpasjɔ̃] *nf Méd* palpation

palper [palpe] *vt* (**a**) *(objet)* to feel (with one's hands); *Méd* to palpate (**b**) *Fam (somme)* to be paid, to get

palpitant, -e [palpitɑ̃, -ɑ̃t] **1** *adj* (**a**) *(cœur, pouls)* fluttering; *(plus fort)* throbbing; *(personne) (d'émotion)* quivering (**b**) *(passionnant)* thrilling
  2 *nm Fam (cœur)* heart, *Br* ticker

palpitations [palpitasjɔ̃] *nfpl* palpitations

palpiter [palpite] *vi (cœur, pouls)* to flutter; *(plus fort)* to throb

paludisme [palydism] *nm* malaria

pâmer [pame] **se pâmer** *vpr Vieilli* to swoon; *Fig & Hum* **se p. d'aise** to be blissfully happy; *Fig & Hum* **se p. (devant)** to swoon (over)

pamphlet [pɑ̃flɛ] *nm* satirical tract

pamplemousse [pɑ̃pləmus] *nm* grapefruit

pan¹ [pɑ̃] *nm* (**a**) *(de chemise, de manteau)* tail; *(de jupe)* panel (**b**) *(morceau)* section, piece; *Fig (d'une époque)* part; **p. de mur** section of wall

pan² *exclam (coup de feu)* bang!; *(gifle)* whack!; **et p., la voilà qui entre!** and lo and behold, in she walks!

panacée [panase] *nf* panacea

panachage [panaʃaʒ] *nm* mixing; *(de liste électorale)* = voting for candidates from more than one list

panache [panaʃ] *nm* (**a**) *(plume)* plume (**b**) *(brio, éclat)* panache

panaché, -e [panaʃe] **1** *adj* multicoloured; **p. de blanc** streaked with white, with white streaks; **un demi p.** a shandy
  2 *nm (boisson)* shandy

panacher [panaʃe] *vt* to mix

panade [panad] *nf Fam* **être dans la p.** *(avoir des ennuis)* to be in a bit of a mess; *(manquer d'argent)* to be strapped for cash

panafricain, -e [panafrikɛ̃, -ɛn] *adj* Pan-African

panais [panɛ] *nm* parsnip

Panama [panama] *nm* **le P.** Panama

panama [panama] *nm (chapeau)* panama hat

Paname [panam] *n Fam* Paris

panaméen, -enne [panameɛ̃, -ɛn] **1** *adj* Panamanian
  2 *nm,f* **P.** Panamanian

panaméricain, -e [panamerikɛ̃, -ɛn] *adj* Pan-American

panard [panar] *nm Fam* (**a**) *(pied)* foot (**b**) *(plaisir intense)* **quel p.!** great!, terrific!; **ce n'est pas le p.** it's not exactly a load of laughs or a barrel of fun

panaris [panari] *nm* whitlow

pan-bagnat *(pl* **pans-bagnats)** [pɑ̃baɲa] *nm* = large bread roll filled with salade niçoise

pancarte [pɑ̃kart] *nf (affiche)* sign, notice; *(pour manifestation)* placard

pancréas [pɑ̃kreas] *nm* pancreas

panda [pɑ̃da] *nm* panda

pané, -e [pane] *adj* coated with breadcrumbs, breaded

panégyrique [paneʒirik] *nm* eulogy; **faire le p. de qn** to eulogize sb

panel [panɛl] *nm (groupe)* panel; *(échantillon)* sample (group)

paneuropéen, -enne [panørɔpeɛ̃, -ɛn] *adj* Pan-European

panier [panje] *nm* (**a**) *(corbeille)* basket; **mettre** *ou* **jeter qch au p.** to throw sth in the wastepaper basket; *Fig* **le dessus du p.** the pick of the bunch; *Fig* **c'est un p. de crabes** they're always at each other's throats; *Fam* **mettre la main au p. à qn** to goose sb; **p. à linge** linen basket; *Fam* **p. percé** *(personne dépensière)* spendthrift; *Can (personne indiscrète)* blabbermouth; **p. à provisions** shopping basket; **p. à salade** salad shaker; *Fam (convoi cellulaire) Br* black Maria, *Am* paddy wagon (**b**) *(au basket-ball)* basket (**c**) *(pour diapositives)* slide magazine (**d**) *(de robe)* hoop

panier-repas *(pl* **paniers-repas)** [panjerəpa] *nm* packed lunch

panique [panik] **1** *nf* panic; **être pris de p.** to panic; **ne pas céder à la p.** not to panic; **il y a eu un début de p.** people started to panic; **il y a eu un mouvement de p.** people panicked
  2 *adj* **peur p.** panic

paniqué, -e [panike] *adj Fam* in a panic

paniquer [panike] *vt & vi Fam* to panic

panislamisme [panislamism] *nm* Pan-Islamism

panne [pan] *nf* breakdown; *Ordinat* failure, crash; **être en p.** *(machine)* to be out of order; *(automobiliste)* to have broken down; **tomber en p.** to break down; **tomber en p. d'essence, tomber en p. sèche** to run out of *Br* petrol *or Am* gas; *Fam* **il m'a fait le coup de la p.** he tried to pull the old "the car won't start" trick on me; **p. (de courant** *ou* **d'électricité)** power failure *or* cut; **p. de moteur** engine failure; **p. de secteur** power failure

panneau, -x [pano] *nm* (**a**) *(pour afficher)* board; **p. d'affichage** *Br* notice board, *Am* bulletin board; **p. publicitaire** *Br* hoarding, *Am* billboard (**b**) *(sur la route)* **p. (indicateur** *ou* **de signalisation routière)** road sign (**c**) *(élément plan)* panel (**d**) *Fig* **tomber** *ou* **donner dans le p.** to fall into the trap

panonceau, -x [panɔ̃so] *nm* (**a**) *(de notaire)* plaque (**b**) *(pancarte)* sign

panoplie [panɔpli] *nf* (**a**) *(habit)* outfit; **une p. de Zorro/d'infirmière** a Zorro/nurse's outfit (**b**) *(assortiment)* set

panorama [panɔrama] *nm* panorama; *Fig* overview

panoramique [panɔramik] *adj (vue)* panoramic; *(restaurant)* with panoramic views; *(écran)* wide

panouille [panuj] *nf Fam* (**a**) *(personne stupide)* idiot, fool (**b**) *(petit rôle)* bit-part

panse [pɑ̃s] *nf* (**a**) *(de ruminant)* rumen (**b**) *Fam (ventre)* belly; **s'en mettre plein la p.** to stuff oneself

pansement [pɑ̃smɑ̃] *nm* dressing; **p. (adhésif)** *Br* (sticking) plaster, *Am* Band-aid®; **faire un p. (à qn)** to put a dressing on (sb); **refaire un p. à qn** to change sb's dressing

panser [pɑ̃se] *vt* (**a**) *(blessure)* to dress; *(membre)* to bandage; **p. qn** to dress sb's wounds; *Fig* **p. ses blessures** to lick one's wounds (**b**) *(cheval)* to groom

pantagruélique [pɑ̃tagryelik] *adj* gigantic

pantalon [pɑ̃talɔ̃] *nm Br* trousers, *Am* pants; **un p.** a pair of *Br* trousers *or Am* pants; **p. de golf** plus-fours; **p. à pattes d'éléphant** flares; **p. à pinces** pleated *Br* trousers *or Am* pants; **p. de pyjama** *Br* pyjama trousers, *Am* pajama pants

pantalonnade [pɑ̃talɔnad] *nf (spectacle)* burlesque farce

pantelant, -e [pɑ̃tlɑ̃, -ɑ̃t] *adj Litt (à bout de souffle)* panting

panthère [pɑ̃tɛr] *nf* leopard; **p. noire** panther

pantin [pɑ̃tɛ̃] *nm (jouet)* jumping-jack; *Péj (fantoche)* puppet

pantois, -e [pɑ̃twa, -az] *adj* speechless; **en rester p.** to be speechless

pantomime [pɑ̃tɔmim] *nf (art)* mime; *(spectacle)* mime show

pantouflard, -e [pɑ̃tuflar, -ard] *adj & nm,f Fam* stay-at-home

pantoufle [pɑ̃tufl] *nf* slipper

pantoufler [pɑ̃tufle] *vi Fam* to join the private sector

PAO [peao] *nf Ordinat (abrév* **publication assistée par ordinateur)** DTP

paon [pɑ̃] *nm* peacock

papa [papa] *nm* dad; *(langage enfantin)* daddy; **p. gâteau** indulgent father; **p. poule** doting father; *Fam Péj* **de p.** old-fashioned; **jouer au p. et à la maman** to play mummies and daddies

papal, -e, -aux, -ales [papal, -o] *adj* papal

paparazzi [paparadzi] *nmpl* paparazzi

papauté [papote] *nf* papacy

papaye [papaj] *nf* papaya

pape [pap] *nm* pope; *Fam* **sérieux comme un p.** solemn as a judge

papelard [paplar] *nm Fam* piece of paper

paperasse [papras] *nf Péj* papers, *Br* bumf

paperasserie [paprasri] *nf Péj* **(a)** *(documents)* papers, *Br* bumf; **faire de la p.** to do paperwork **(b)** *(d'un système bureaucratique)* red tape

papeterie [papɛtri] *nf (usine)* paper mill; *(magasin)* stationer's; *(articles)* stationery

papetier, -ère [papətje, -ɛr] *nm,f* **(a)** *(industriel)* paper manufacturer **(b)** *(commerçant)* stationer

papi [papi] *nm* grandpa, granddad

papier [papje] *nm* **(a)** *(pour écrire)* paper; **un p.** a piece of paper; *Fam* **être dans les petits papiers de qn** to be in sb's good books; *Fam* **p. alu** *Br* tinfoil, *Am* aluminum foil; **p. avion** airmail paper; *Ordinat* **p. à bandes perforées** perforated paper; **p. de bonbon** sweet wrapper; **p. cadeau** gift wrap, wrapping paper; *Ordinat* **p. continu** continuous paper *or* stationery; *Ordinat* **p. continu plié en accordéon** fanfold paper; **p. crépon** crêpe paper; *très Fam* **p. cul** toilet paper, *Br* bog roll; **p. à dessin** drawing paper; **p. d'emballage** brown paper; **p. à en-tête** headed notepaper; **p. glacé** glazed paper; **papiers gras** litter; **p. hygiénique** toilet paper; **p. journal** newspaper; **p. kraft** brown paper; **p. à lettres** writing paper; *Ordinat* **p. listing** listing paper; **p. mâché** papier-mâché; **p. machine** typing paper; **p. millimétré** *ou* **millimétrique** graph paper; **p. à musique** manuscript paper; *Fig* **être réglé comme du p. à musique** *(événement)* to be as regular as clockwork; **elle est réglée comme du p. à musique** you can set your watch by her; **p. peint** wallpaper; **p. recyclé** recycled paper; **p. de soie** tissue paper; **p. toilette** toilet paper; **p. de verre** sandpaper; **passer qch au p. de verre** to sandpaper sth **(b)** *(documents officiels)* papers; **papiers (d'identité)** (identity) papers; *(d'un automobiliste) Br* driving licence, *Am* driver's license **(c)** *Fam (article de journal)* article

Papiers

papilles [papij] *nfpl* **p. gustatives** taste buds

papillon [papijɔ̃] *nm* **(a)** *(insecte)* butterfly; **p. de nuit** moth; *Fam* **minute p.!** hold on a minute! **(b)** *(écrou)* wing nut **(c)** *(sur document)* flag **(d)** *Fam (contravention)* (parking) ticket **(e)** *(nage)* butterfly

papillonner [papijɔne] *vi* **(a)** *(paupières)* to flutter **(b)** *(d'une personne à une autre)* to flit about

papillote [papijɔt] *nf* **(a)** *(en papier alu)* **cailles en papillotes** quails in papillotes *(cooked in foil)* **(b)** *(de gigot)* frill **(c)** *(bigoudi)* curlpaper; *Fam* **tu peux en faire des papillotes** you can chuck it away

papilloter [papijɔte] *vi (yeux)* to blink; *(lumière)* to flicker

papoter [papɔte] *vi Fam* to chat

papou, -e [papu] **1** *adj* Papuan
  2 *nm,f* **P.** Papuan

Papouasie-Nouvelle-Guinée [papwazinuvɛlgine] *nf* **la P.** Papua New Guinea

papouille [papuj] *nf Fam* **faire des papouilles à qn** to tickle sb

paprika [paprika] *nm* paprika

papyrus [papirys] *nm* papyrus

paqson [paksɔ̃]* = pacson

Pâque [pɑk] *nf* **P., la P. juive** Passover

paquebot [pakbo] *nm* liner

pâquerette [pɑkrɛt] *nf* daisy

pâques [pɑk] **1** *nfpl* **joyeuses p.!** Happy Easter!
  2 *nm* **P.** Easter; *Fam* **à P. ou à la Trinité!** never in a month of Sundays!

Pâques

paquet [pakɛ] *nm* **(a)** *(sac)* packet; *(de sucre)* bag; *(de cigarettes)* packet, *Am* pack; *(postal)* parcel, package **(b)** *Fam (grande quantité)* **un p. de** a pile *or* stack of; **toucher un joli p.** to make a packet; **mettre le p.** to pull out all the stops; *Fam* **c'est un p. de nerfs** she's a bundle *or* a bag of nerves; **p.-cadeau** gift-wrapped parcel; **je vous fais un p.-cadeau?** would you like it gift-wrapped? **(c)** **p. de mer** big wave **(d)** *Ordinat* packet

paquetage [paktaʒ] *nm* (soldier's) pack; **faire son p.** to get one's kit ready

par [par] *prép* **(a)** *(à travers)* through; **p. la porte/le trou de la serrure** through the door/the keyhole; **regarder p. la fenêtre** *(de l'intérieur)* to look out (of) the window; *(de l'extérieur)* to look through the window; **passer p. Calais** to go via Calais; **p. ici/là**

this/that way; **p. où est-il passé?** which way did he go?

(**b**) *(position)* **p. ici** round about here; **p. là** over there; **p. 200 mètres de fond** at a depth of 200 metres; **p. endroits** in places

(**c**) *(pendant)* **p. une belle journée d'automne** on a beautiful autumn day; **p. cette chaleur** in this heat; **p. le passé** in the past; *Litt* **p. deux fois** twice

(**d**) *(introduit le complément d'agent)* by; **c'est p. eux que je l'ai appris** I found out from them; **faire faire qch p. qn** to have sth done by sb

(**e**) *(indique la cause)* out of; **faire qch p. amitié/pitié** to do sth out of friendship/pity; **p. hasard/erreur** by chance/mistake; **p. malheur** unfortunately, as bad luck would have it; **p. pitié!** for pity's sake!

(**f**) *(au moyen de)* with, by; **retenu p. une corde** held by a rope; **fermé p. un cadenas** padlocked; **p. train/avion/voiture/bateau** by train/plane/car/boat; **conduire/prendre qn p. la main** to lead/take sb by the hand; **tenir qn p. la taille** to hold sb round the waist; **pendu p. les pieds** hanging by the feet; **envoyer qch p. la poste** to send sth by post; **répondre p. oui ou p. non** to answer yes or no; **se terminer p. un divorce/une dispute** to end in divorce/an argument; **p. tous les moyens** by every possible means; **il est monté p. l'escalier** he took the stairs up; **obtenir qch p. la force** to obtain sth by force; **appeler qn p. son nom** to call sb by his/her name

(**g**) *(selon)* according to; **p. ordre de grandeur** according to size

(**h**) *(distributif)* per, a; **deux p. deux** two by two; **p. groupes de six** in groups of six; **deux jours p. semaine** two days a week; **20 000 euros p. an** 20,000 euros a year; **un siège p. personne** one seat per person

(**i**) **de p.** *(à cause de)* due to; **de p. le monde** the world over

para [para] *nm Fam* para

parabole [parabɔl] *nf* (**a**) *(allégorie)* parable (**b**) *(courbe)* parabola (**c**) *(antenne)* (satellite) dish

parabolique [parabɔlik] *adj* parabolic

paracétamol [parasetamɔl] *nm* paracetamol

parachever [46] [paraʃəve] *vt* to complete, to finish off

parachutage [paraʃytaʒ] *nm* parachuting

parachute [paraʃyt] *nm* parachute; **faire du p.** to go parachuting; **p. ascensionnel** parascending

parachuter [paraʃyte] *vt* *(vivres, soldats)* to parachute in; *Fam (nommer)* to draft in

parachutisme [paraʃytism] *nm* parachuting; **faire du p.** to go parachuting

parachutiste [paraʃytist] *nmf* (**a**) *(sportif)* parachutist (**b**) *(soldat)* paratrooper

parade¹ [parad] *nf* (**a**) *(exhibition)* show, ostentation; **faire p. de qch** to show sth off (**b**) *(défilé)* parade

parade² *nf* (**a**) *(en escrime, boxe)* parry (**b**) *(réplique)* riposte; *Fig* **je n'ai pas encore trouvé la p.** I haven't come up with a way of handling him/it/*etc* yet

parader [parade] *vi* to show off

paradis [paradi] *nm* heaven; *Fig* paradise; **le p. terrestre** the Garden of Eden; *Fig* heaven on earth; **aller au p.** to go to heaven; **un p. fiscal** a tax haven; *Fam* **le p.** *(d'un théâtre)* the gods; *Fam* **il ne l'emportera pas au p.** he won't get away with it, he'll be sorry

paradisiaque [paradizjak] *adj* heavenly

paradoxal, -e, -aux, -ales [paradɔksal, -o] *adj* paradoxical

paradoxalement [paradɔksalmã] *adv* paradoxically

paradoxe [paradɔks] *nm* paradox

parafe [paraf] = **paraphe**

parafer [parafe] = **parapher**

paraffine [parafin] *nf* paraffin

parafiscalité [parafiskalite] *nf* = taxes paid to the state and used for administration purposes

parages [paraʒ] *nmpl* (**a**) *Naut* waters (**b**) *(alentours)* **dans les p. de...** in the vicinity of...; *Fam* **est-ce qu'elle est dans les p.?** is she around?

paragraphe [paragraf] *nm* (**a**) paragraph (**b**) *Typ* paragraph (sign)

Paraguay [paragwɛ] *nm* **le P.** Paraguay

paraguayen, -enne [paragwɛjẽ, -ɛn] **1** *adj* Paraguayan

2 *nm,f* **P.** Paraguayan

paraître [20] [parɛtr] **1** *vi* (**a**) *(apparaître)* to appear; *(étoile, lune)* to appear, to come out; **laisser p. sa déception** to let one's disappointment show; **un faible sourire parut sur ses lèvres** he/she smiled weakly; **elle ne pense qu'à p.** all she thinks about is showing off (**b**) *(livre)* to come out, to be published (**c**) *(sembler)* to seem, to appear; **cette décision me paraît bizarre** it seems a strange decision to me; **elle paraissait furieuse** *(à la voir)* she looked furious; *(à l'entendre)* she sounded furious

2 *v impersonnel* (**a**) *(sembler)* **il me paraît utile de...** I think it would be useful to...; **demain, il n'y paraîtra plus** there'll be no trace of it tomorrow; **sans qu'il y paraisse** without it being apparent (**b**) **il paraît que...** *(on dit)* it seems *or* appears that...; **il paraît qu'elle s'en va, elle s'en va, paraît-il** it seems *or* appears that she's leaving, apparently she's leaving; **il paraît que ça fait maigrir** apparently it helps you lose weight; **il paraît que oui** so it would appear, apparently (so); **il paraît que non** it would appear not, apparently not; **à ce qu'il paraît** apparently

3 *nm* **le p.** appearance

parallèle [paralɛl] **1** *adj* parallel (**à** to *or* with); *(police, marché)* unofficial; **mener une vie p.** to lead a secret life; *Ordinat* **imprimante/interface p.** parallel printer/interface

2 *nf* parallel (line)

3 *nm* parallel; **mettre qch en p. avec qch, établir un p. entre qch et qch** to draw a parallel between sth and sth

parallèlement [paralɛlmã] *adv* parallel (**à** to *or* with); *(simultanément)* at the same time (**à** as)

parallélépipède [paralelepipɛd] *nm* parallelepiped

parallélisme [paralelism] *nm* parallelism; **p. (des roues)** (wheel) alignment

parallélogramme [paralelɔgram] *nm* parallelogram

paralysant, -e [paralizã, -ãt] *adj* paralysing

paralysé, -e [paralize] *adj aussi Fig* paralysed

paralyser [paralize] *vt aussi Fig* to paralyse; **le froid lui paralyse les mains** his hands are numb with cold

paralysie [paralizi] *nf aussi Fig* paralysis; **p. générale** creeping paralysis

paralytique [paralitik] *adj & nmf* paralytic

paramédical, -e, -aux, -ales [paramedikal, -o] **1** *adj* paramedical

2 *nm* **les emplois du p.** paramedical jobs

paramétrable [parametrabl] *adj Ordinat* configurable; **p. par l'utilisateur** user-definable

paramétrage [parametraʒ] *nm Ordinat* configuration

paramètre [paramɛtr] *nm Math & Fig* parameter; *Ordinat* **paramètres** settings

paramétrer [34] [parametre] *vt Ordinat* to configure
paramilitaire [paramilitɛr] *adj* paramilitary
parano [parano] *Fam* **1** *adj* paranoid
  2 *nf* **faire de la p.** to be paranoid
paranoïa [paranɔja] *nf* paranoia
paranoïaque [paranɔjak] *adj & nmf* paranoiac
paranormal, -e, -aux, -ales [paranɔrmal, -o] *adj* paranormal
parapente [parapɑ̃t] *nm (activité)* paragliding; *(parachute)* paraglider; **faire du p.** to go paragliding
parapet [parapɛ] *nm* parapet
paraphe [paraf] *nm* initials
parapher [parafe] *vt* to initial
paraphrase [parafraz] *nf* paraphrase
paraphraser [parafraze] *vt* to paraphrase
paraplégie [parapleʒi] *nf* paraplegia
paraplégique [parapleʒik] *adj & nmf* paraplegic
parapluie [paraplɥi] *nm* umbrella
parapsychologie [parapsikɔlɔʒi] *nf* parapsychology
parascolaire [paraskɔlɛr] *adj* extra-curricular
parasite [parazit] **1** *nm aussi Fig* parasite; **parasites** *(à la radio)* interference
  2 *adj (insecte, plante)* parasitic
parasol [parasɔl] *nm* parasol, sunshade; *(de plage)* beach umbrella
parastatal, -e, -aux, -ales [parastatal, -o] *adj Belg* semi-public
paratonnerre [paratɔnɛr] *nm* lightning conductor
paravent [paravɑ̃] *nm aussi Fig* screen; *Fig* **servir de p. à qch** to be a screen for sth
parbleu [parblø] *exclam Vieilli* good Lord!; *(évidemment)* good Lord, yes!
parc [park] *nm* **(a)** *(jardin)* park; *(d'un château)* grounds; **p. aquatique** water park; **p. d'attractions** theme park; **p. naturel** nature reserve; **p. à thème** theme park; **p. zoologique** zoo **(b)** *(enclos) (pour enfant)* playpen; **p. des expositions** exhibition centre; **p. à huîtres** oyster bed; **p. de stationnement** *Br* car park, *Am* parking lot **(c)** *(ensemble)* **le p. automobile français** the number of cars in France
parcelle [parsɛl] *nf* small piece; **p. de terrain** plot; *Fig* **pas la moindre p. d'intelligence** not an ounce of intelligence
parce que [parskə] *conj* because; **ce n'est pas parce qu'il fait froid qu'on doit rester à la maison** just because it's cold doesn't mean we have to stay in; **pourquoi ne viens-tu pas? – p.** why aren't you coming? – (just) because
parchemin [parʃəmɛ̃] *nm* parchment
parcimonie [parsimɔni] *nf* thrift; **avec p.** sparingly
parcimonieux, -euse [parsimɔnjø, -øz] *adj* thrifty
parcmètre [parkmɛtr] *nm* (parking) meter
parcourir [22] [parkurir] *vt* **(a)** *(lieu)* to walk round; *(pays)* to travel through; *(rues)* to walk through; *(mer)* to sail; **p. un lieu à la recherche de qn** to scour a place for sb; **p. la terre entière pour retrouver qn** to travel the world to find sb; **p. une distance de plusieurs kilomètres** to cover a distance of several kilometres; **il reste 2 kilomètres à p.** there are 2 kilometres to go; *Fig* **un frisson me parcourut l'échine** *ou* **le dos** a shiver ran down my spine; *Fig* **un murmure a parcouru la foule** a murmur ran through the crowd **(b)** *(regarder) (texte, journal)* to skim through; *Ordinat* to scroll through; **p. qch des yeux** *ou* **du regard** to glance at sth
parcours [parkur] *nm (de défilé, de bus)* route; *(circuit automobile)* circuit; *(d'équitation, de golf, d'un fleuve)* course; *(évolution personnelle)* career, path; **p. du combattant** *Mil* assault course; *Fig* obstacle course; **faire un p. sans faute** *(cheval)* to have a clear round; *Fig (dans une carrière)* to follow a textbook career path; **refaire le p. pour retrouver qch** to retrace one's steps to find sth; **elle fait plusieurs fois le p. dans la journée** she does the journey several times a day
par-delà [pardəla] *prép & adv* beyond
par-derrière [pardɛrjɛr] **1** *prép* behind
  2 *adv (attaquer)* from behind; *(se boutonner)* at the back; **passer p.** to go in the back door; *Fig* **dire des choses de qn p.** to talk about sb behind his/her back
par-dessous [pardəsu] **1** *prép* under, underneath
  2 *adv* underneath
pardessus [pardəsy] *nm* overcoat
par-dessus [pardəsy] **1** *prép* over; **p. tout** above all
  2 *adv* over; **j'ai mis un T-shirt avec une chemise p.** I wore a T-shirt with a shirt on top *or* over it
par-devant [pardəvɑ̃] *prép Jur* **acte signé p. notaire** deed signed in the presence of a lawyer
  2 *adv (attaquer)* from the front; *(se boutonner)* at the front
pardi [pardi] *exclam Fam* of course!
pardon [pardɔ̃] *nm* **(a)** *(grâce)* forgiveness; **accorder son p. à qn** to forgive sb; **demander p. à qn** to apologize to sb; **(je vous demande) p.!** *(pour passer)* excuse me!; *(pour s'excuser)* (I'm) sorry!; **(je vous demande) p.?** *(je n'ai pas entendu)* pardon?; *(je suis indigné)* I beg your pardon!; *Fam* **elle est intelligente, mais sa fille, p.!** she's pretty clever but you should see her daughter! **(b)** *Rel* **le Grand P.** the Day of Atonement, Yom Kippur
pardonnable [pardɔnabl] *adj* forgivable, excusable
pardonner [pardɔne] **1** *vt* to forgive; **p. qch à qn** to forgive sb sth; **elle m'a pardonné d'avoir oublié** she forgave me for forgetting; **pour me/te/etc faire p. to** make it up; **tu es tout pardonné** I'll let you off
  2 *vi* **(a)** *(oublier une faute)* to forgive **(b)** **ça ne pardonne pas** it's fatal
  3 **se pardonner** *vpr* **je ne me le pardonnerai jamais** I'll never forgive myself
paré, -e [pare] *adj* **(a)** *(prêt)* prepared (**contre** for) **(b)** *(revêtu)* adorned (**de** with)
pare-avalanches [paravalɑ̃ʃ] *nm inv* avalanche barrier
pare-balles [parbal] *adj inv* bullet-proof
pare-boue [parbu] *nm inv* mudflap
pare-brise [parbriz] *nm inv Br* windscreen, *Am* windshield
pare-chocs [parʃɔk] *nm inv* bumper
pare-feu [parfø] *nm inv* **(a)** *(dans la forêt)* fire-break **(b)** *(de cheminée)* fireguard **(c)** *Ordinat* firewall
pareil, -eille [parɛj] **1** *adj* **(a)** *(identique)* the same; **elles sont presque pareilles** they're almost the same; **ce n'est pas p.** it's not the same (thing); *Litt* **à nul autre p.** unparalleled; **p. que** *ou* **à** the same as, just like; *Fam* **si ça ne te plaît pas, c'est p.** if you don't like it, too bad **(b)** *(tel)* such; **en p. cas** in such cases; **dans des moments pareils** at times like these; **mais je n'ai jamais dit une chose pareille!** but I never said any such thing!
  2 *nm,f* **elle n'a pas sa pareille** she's second to none; **sans p.** unparalleled; **mes pareils** my equals
  3 *nf* **rendre la pareille à qn** *(se venger de quelqu'un)* to get one's own back on sb, to pay sb back; *(rendre un service à quelqu'un)* to repay sb
  4 *nm Fam* **c'est du p. au même** it's six of one and half

a dozen of the other
5 *adv Fam* the same; **faire p.** to do the same (thing)
pareillement [parɛjmɑ̃] *adv* (**a**) *(de la même manière)* in a similar manner, in the same way (**b**) *(aussi)* likewise
parement [parmɑ̃] *nm (de manche, de col)* facing
parent, -e [parɑ̃, -ɑ̃t] **1** *adj* related
 2 *nm,f (tante, oncle, cousin)* relative, relation; **parents** *(père et mère)* parents; **parents adoptifs** adoptive parents; **parents biologiques** biological parents
parental, -e, -aux, -ales [parɑ̃tal, -o] *adj* parental
parenté [parɑ̃te] *nf* relationship; **avoir un lien de p. avec qn** to be related to sb
parenthèse [parɑ̃tɛz] *nf* bracket, parenthesis; *Fig (dans un discours)* digression; **entre parenthèses** in brackets; *Fig (à propos)* incidentally, by the way
paréo [pareo] *nm* sarong
parer¹ [pare] **1** *vt* (**a**) *aussi Fig (éviter)* to parry (**b**) *(protéger)* to protect (**contre** against)
 2 parer à *vt ind (accident)* to prevent; *(problème)* to avoid; **p. au plus pressé** to attend to the most urgent things first
parer² *Litt* **1** *vt (vêtir)* to adorn (**de** with); *Fig* **p. qn de toutes les vertus** to endow sb with every virtue
 2 se parer *vpr* (**a**) *(s'habiller avec élégance)* to get dressed up (**de** in) (**b**) *Can (se préparer)* to get ready
pare-soleil [parsɔlɛj] *nm inv (de voiture)* sun visor
paresse [parɛs] *nf* (**a**) *(indolence)* laziness; **d'une p. incroyable** incredibly lazy (**b**) *(lenteur)* **p. intellectuelle** laziness of mind; **p. intestinale** sluggishness of the bowels
paresser [parɛse] *vi* to laze about *or* around
paresseux, -euse [parɛsø, -øz] **1** *adj* (**a**) *(nonchalant)* lazy (**b**) *(intestin)* sluggish
 2 *nm,f* lazy person
 3 *nm (animal)* sloth
parfaire [36] [parfɛr] *vt (travail)* to finish off, to complete; *(technique)* to perfect
parfait, -e [parfɛ, -ɛt] **1** *adj* (**a**) *(sans fautes)* perfect (**b**) *(complet) (bonheur)* perfect, complete; *(ressemblance)* exact; *Fam* **un p. imbécile** an utter fool
 2 *nm* parfait; **p. au café** coffee parfait
parfaitement [parfɛtmɑ̃] *adv* (**a**) *(sans fautes)* perfectly; **parler p. l'anglais** to speak perfect English (**b**) *(complètement)* completely, thoroughly; *(compréhensible, clair, heureux)* perfectly; **ça m'est p. égal** it makes absolutely no difference to me; **j'ai p. conscience de...** I'm perfectly aware of... (**c**) *(tout à fait)* **vous affirmez que vous l'avez vu? - p.!** you say you saw it? – I certainly did!
parfois [parfwa] *adv* sometimes
parfum [parfœ̃] *nm* (**a**) *(essences)* perfume (**b**) *(senteur) (d'une fleur)* fragrance, scent; *(d'un vin)* bouquet; *Fig* **un p. de scandale** a whiff of scandal (**c**) *(de glace, de yaourt)* flavour (**d**) *Fam* **être au p.** to be in the know; **mettre qn au p.** to fill sb in
parfumer [parfyme] **1** *vt* (**a**) *(embaumer)* to scent (**b**) *(gâteau, glace)* to flavour (**à** with) (**c**) *(mouchoir)* to scent; **je vous parfume?** *(à une cliente)* would you like to try some perfume?
 2 se parfumer *vpr* to put perfume on
parfumerie [parfymri] *nf (magasin)* perfumery; *(rayon)* perfume counter; *(produits)* perfumes; *(industrie)* perfume industry
parfumeur, -euse [parfymœr, -øz] *nm,f* perfumer
pari [pari] *nm* bet; **faire un p. avec qn** to make a bet with sb; **p. mutuel** *Br* ≃ tote, *Am* ≃ pari-mutuel

paria [parja] *nm Fig* pariah, (social) outcast
parier [66] [parje] **1** *vt* to bet; **il y a fort** *ou* **gros à p. que...** the odds are that...; **je te parie qu'elle viendra I** bet you she'll come; **je l'aurais parié** I thought as much
 2 *vi* to bet; **p. avec qn/sur qch** to bet with sb/on sth; **je te dis qu'elle viendra – on parie?** she'll come, I tell you – (do you) want to bet?
parieur, -euse [parjœr, -øz] *nm,f* better
parigot, -e [parigo, -ɔt] *Fam* **1** *adj* Parisian
 2 *nm,f* **P.** Parisian
Paris [pari] *n* Paris
parisien, -enne [parizjɛ̃, -ɛn] **1** *adj* Parisian
 2 *nm,f* **P.** Parisian
parité [parite] *nf aussi Ordinat* parity; **nous devons arriver à une p. hommes-femmes au parlement** we must ensure that there are an equal number of men and women in parliament
parjure [parʒyr] **1** *nm (action)* perjury
 2 *nmf (personne)* perjurer
 3 *adj* treacherous
parjurer [parʒyre] **se parjurer** *vpr* to perjure oneself
parka [parka] *nm ou nf* parka
parking [parkiŋ] *nm Br* car park, *Am* parking lot; **p. couvert** underground *Br* car park *or Am* parling lot **p. payant** *Br* ≃ pay-and-display car park
parlant, -e [parlɑ̃, -ɑ̃t] *adj (geste)* eloquent, meaningful; *(description)* vivid
parlé, -e [parle] *adj* **le français p.** spoken French; **journal p.** news (programme)
parlement [parləmɑ̃] *nm* **le P.** Parliament; **le P. européen** the European Parliament
parlementaire [parləmɑ̃tɛr] **1** *adj* parliamentary
 2 *nmf* member of parliament, *Am* Congressman, *f* Congresswoman
parlementarisme [parləmɑ̃tarism] *nm* parliamentary government
parlementer [parləmɑ̃te] *vi* to negotiate (**avec** with)
parler¹ [parle] **1** *vi* (**a**) *(s'exprimer)* to speak, to talk; *(avouer)* to talk; **elle parle bien** *(oratrice)* she's a good speaker; **p. par signes** to use sign language; **parlez-vous sérieusement?** are you serious?; **les résultats/faits parlent d'eux-mêmes** the results/facts speak for themselves; **p. pour ne rien dire** to talk for the sake of talking; **c'est comme si je parlais à un mur** it's like talking to a brick wall; **p. de qn/qch (à qn)** to talk (to sb) about sb/sth; **p. de** *(sujet: livre, film)* to be about; **on m'a beaucoup parlé de vous** I've heard a lot about you; **n'en parlons plus** let's drop the subject; **faire p. de soi** to be talked about; **p. de faire qch** to talk about doing sth (**b**) *(locutions)* **je sais de quoi je parle** I know what I'm talking about; *Fam* **tu peux p.!** YOU can talk!; *Fam* **parle pour toi!** speak for yourself!; *Fam* **tu parles!** you bet!; *Fam* **tu parles d'une occasion/d'un idiot!** talk about an opportunity/an idiot!; *Fam* **sa timidité? parlons-en!** his/her shyness? that's a good one! *or* you've got to be joking!; *Fam* **ne m'en parlez pas!** you're telling me!; **sans p. de...** not to mention...; **trouver à qui p.** to get more than one bargains for
 2 *vt (langue)* to speak; **p. (le) français** to speak French; **ici on parle anglais** *(dans un magasin)* English spoken; **p. chiffons/cuisine** to talk about clothes/cooking; **p. affaires/politique** to talk business/politics
 3 se parler *vpr* (**a**) *(langue)* to be spoken (**b**) *(l'un à l'autre)* to talk to each other

parler² *nm* speech; *(régional)* dialect; **il a un p. très rude** he has a very abrupt way of speaking

parleur, -euse [parlœr, -øz] *nm,f Péj* **beau p.** smooth talker

parloir [parlwar] *nm* (**a**) *(d'une prison)* visiting room (**b**) *Belg (salon)* parlour

parlot(t)e [parlɔt] *nf Fam* chat; **faire la p. (avec qn)** to chat (with sb), to have a chat (with sb)

Parme [parm] *n* Parma

parmesan [parmøzɑ̃] *nm* Parmesan (cheese)

parmi [parmi] *prép* among; **choisir p. plusieurs possibilités** to choose from several possibilities; **nous espérons vous revoir p. nous** we hope to see you back with us

parodie [parɔdi] *nf* parody

parodier [66] [parɔdje] *vt* to parody

parodique [parɔdik] *adj* parodic

paroi [parwa] *nf* (**a**) *(d'une falaise, d'une montagne)* face (**b**) *(d'une pièce, d'une caverne)* wall; *(d'un tunnel, de l'estomac)* lining

paroisse [parwas] *nf* parish

paroissial, -e, -aux, -ales [parwasjal, -o] *adj* parish

paroissien, -enne [parwasjɛ̃, -ɛn] *nm,f* parishioner

parole [parɔl] *nf* (**a**) *(mot)* word; **paroles** *(de chanson)* lyrics, words; **histoire sans paroles** short silent movie *or Br* film; **une p. blessante** a hurtful remark; *Ironique* **de belles paroles** fine words; **ce ne sont que des paroles en l'air** they're just empty threats (**b**) *Fig (engagement)* promise, word; **tenir p.** to keep one's promise *or* word; **manquer à sa p.** to break one's promise *or* word; **il n'a qu'une p.** he's a man of his word; **donner sa p. (d'honneur) à qn que...** to give sb one's word that...; **(ma) p. d'honneur!** I give you my word!; **je te crois sur p.** I'll take your word for it (**c**) **la p.** *(faculté de parler)* speech; *(diction)* delivery; **adresser la p. à qn** to speak to sb; **couper la p. à qn** to interrupt sb; **prendre la p.** to speak; **laisser la p. à qn** to let sb speak; **la p. est à M. Renant, M. Renant a la p.** Mr Renant has the floor; **la p. est d'argent mais le silence est d'or** speech is silver, silence is golden (**d**) *(aux cartes)* **p.!** pass!; *(au bridge)* no bid!

parolier, -ère [parɔlje, -ɛr] *nm,f* lyricist

paroxysme [parɔksism] *nm* **atteindre son p.** to reach its peak *or* climax; **être au p. de la joie** to be ecstatically happy

parpaing [parpɛ̃] *nm* breeze block

parquer [parke] *vt (bétail)* to pen in; *(prisonniers)* to confine

parquet [parkɛ] *nm* (**a**) *(sol)* wooden floor; *(avec des motifs)* parquet floor (**b**) *Jur* public prosecutor's office

parrain [parɛ̃] *nm (pour un baptême, d'une organisation criminelle)* godfather; *(d'un sportif, d'un membre d'un club)* sponsor

parrainer [parene] *vt (sportif, nouveau membre)* to sponsor

parricide [parisid] **1** *adj* parricidal **2** *nmf & nm* parricide

pars *voir* **partir**

parsemer [46] [parsøme] *vt* to scatter (**de** with)

part¹ *voir* **partir**

part² [par] *nf* (**a**) *(partie d'un tout)* part; *(d'un marché, d'un héritage, de travail)* share; *(d'un gâteau, d'une pizza)* slice; **diviser qch en parts égales** to divide sth into equal parts; **ils viennent pour une bonne p. des environs de Lille** a good many of them come from the Lille area; **à p. entière** fully-fledged; **pour ma p.** personally, as for me; **faire la p. du feu** to cut one's losses; **la p. du lion** the lion's share (**b**) *(participation)* share, part; **prendre p. à qch** to take part in sth; *(joie, douleur)* to share sth; **faire p. de qch à qn** to inform sb of sth, to tell sb about sth; **faire la p. des choses** to get things into perspective (**c**) *(côté)* **de p. et d'autre** on both sides; **de p. en p.** right through; **d'une p...., d'autre p....** on the one hand..., on the other hand...; **de toutes parts** on all sides (**d**) **de la p. de qn** *(en provenance de)* from sb; *(à la place de)* on sb's behalf; **c'est de la p. de qui?** *(au téléphone)* who's calling?; **ce serait bien aimable de votre p.** that would be very kind of you; **cela m'étonne de sa p.** that surprises me, coming from him/her (**e**) *(locutions)* **prendre qn à p.** to take sb aside; **à p. lui/quelques erreurs** apart from him/a few mistakes; **c'est un cas à p.** he's/she's a special case; *Fam* **à p. que...** apart from the fact that...

partage [parta3] *nm* (**a**) *(action)* *(d'une fortune, d'un domaine)* dividing up; *(de tâches, de responsabilités)* sharing out; **faire le p. de qch** to divide sth up; **sans p.** *(amour)* total; *Ordinat* **p. d'imprimantes** printer sharing (**b**) *(lot)* **recevoir qch en p.** to be left sth *(in a will)*

partagé, -e [parta3e] *adj* (**a**) *(entre plusieurs personnes)* shared; *(amour)* mutual; *Ordinat* **travail en temps p.** timesharing (**b**) *(indécis)* **être p.** to be torn; **les avis sont partagés** opinions are divided

partager [45] [parta3e] **1** *vt* (**a**) *(répartir)* to divide (up); **p. son temps entre** to divide one's time between; **p. qch en deux** to divide sth in two (**b**) *(avoir en commun)* to share (**avec** with); **p. l'avis de qn** to share sb's opinion; **p. la joie de qn** to share (in) sb's joy **2** *vi* to share **3** **se partager** *vpr* (**a**) *(se répartir)* **ils se le sont partagé** they shared it between them (**b**) *(partager son temps)* to divide one's time (**entre** between)

partageur, -euse [parta3œr, -øz] *adj* willing to share

partance [partɑ̃s] *nf* **en p.** *(train, bus)* about to depart; **en p. pour Bordeaux** for Bordeaux

partant¹ [partɑ̃] *conj Litt* consequently, therefore

partant², -e [partɑ̃, -ɑ̃t] **1** *adj Fam* **je suis p.!** count me in! **2** *nm,f (coureur, cheval)* starter

partenaire [partønɛr] *nmf* partner; **les partenaires sociaux** workers and management

partenariat [partønarja] *nm* partnership; **p. public-privé** public-private partnership

parterre [partɛr] *nm* (**a**) *(de fleurs)* flower bed; *(plate-bande)* border (**b**) *(au théâtre)* *Br* stalls, *Am* orchestra (**c**) *Fam (sol)* floor

parti¹ [parti] *nm* (**a**) *(camp)* side; **prendre le p. de qn** to take sb's side; **prendre p. pour qn** to side with sb; **prendre qn contre qn** to take sides against sb (**b**) **p. (politique)** *(political)* party; **le P. (communiste)** the Communist Party (**c**) *(personne)* **un beau p.** a good match (**d**) *(choix)* **prendre le p. de faire qch** to make up one's mind to do sth; **en prendre son p.** to resign oneself to the fact (**e**) *(profit)* **tirer p. de qch** to make good use of sth (**f**) **p. pris** bias; **avoir un p. pris contre** to be biased against; **être de p. pris** to be biased; **être sans p. pris** to be unbiased

parti², -e *adj Fam (ivre)* far gone; *(drogué)* high

partial, -e, -aux, -ales [parsjal, -o] *adj* biased

partialement [parsjalmɑ̃] *adv* in a biased way

partialité [parsjalite] *nf* bias (**envers/contre** in favour of/against)

participant, -e [partisipã, -ãt] **1** *adj* participating **2** *nm,f (personne présente)* participant (**à** in); *(sportif)* competitor

participation [partisipasjɔ̃] *nf* (**a**) *(collaboration, en classe)* participation (**à** in); *(argent)* contribution (**à** towards); *(nombre de votants)* turnout (**à** at); **avec la p. de Jean Martin (dans le rôle de...)** with Jean Martin (as...); **p. aux frais** contribution towards costs; **p. aux bénéfices** profit-sharing (**b**) *Fin* interest (**à** in)

participe [partisip] *nm Gram* participle; **p. présent/passé** present/past participle

participer [partisipe] **participer à** *vt ind* (**a**) *(assister à)* to take part in, to participate in; *(spectacle)* to appear in; **p. activement à qch** to take an active part in sth (**b**) *(financièrement)* to contribute to (**c**) **p. aux bénéfices** to share in the profits

particulariser [partikylarize] *vt* to particularize

particularisme [partikylarism] *nm* particularism

particularité [partikylarite] *nf* distinctive feature

particule [partikyl] *nf* particle; **p. élémentaire** elementary *or* fundamental particle

particulier, -ère [partikylje, -εr] **1** *adj* (**a**) *(propre)* characteristic (**à** of) (**b**) *(remarquable)* unusual, exceptional; *(soin, intérêt)* particular (**c**) *Péj (bizarre)* peculiar (**d**) *(privé) (maison, voiture)* private; *(salle de bain)* en suite (**e**) **en p.** *(spécialement)* in particular; *(en privé)* in private **2** *nm (individu)* private individual; **un simple p.** an ordinary person; **vente de p. à p.** private sale

particulièrement [partikyljεrmã] *adv* particularly; **j'attire tout p. votre attention sur...** I would particularly like to draw your attention to...

partie [parti] *nf* (**a**) *(morceau)* part; **la plus grande p. de qch** the greatest part of sth; **en p.** partly, in part; **en grande** *ou* **majeure p.** for the most part; **être en p. remboursé** to be partially refunded; **faire p. de qch** to be part of sth; *Fam* **faire p. des meubles** to be part of the furniture; **les parties communes** the communal areas; *Fam* **les parties** the private parts; **les parties génitales** the genitals (**b**) *(domaine)* field, subject; **je ne suis pas de la p.** that's not my field (**c**) *(d'un chanteur, d'un instrument)* part (**d**) *(fête)* party; **ce n'est pas une p. de plaisir!** it's not my idea of fun!; **p. de campagne** day in the country; **p. de chasse** shooting party; *Fam* **p. de jambes en l'air** roll in the hay; *Can* **p. de sucre** sugaring-off party (**e**) *(jeu)* game; **faire une p. de cartes** to have a game of cards; *Fig* **ce n'est que p. remise** we'll do it another time (**f**) *Jur* party; **la p. adverse** the other side; **être p. prenante** to be an interested party; **p. civile** plaintiff; **se constituer** *ou* **se porter p. civile** to institute proceedings *(in a civil case)* (**g**) *(locutions)* **avoir affaire à forte p.** to have a tough opponent on one's hands; **prendre qn à p.** to take sb to task; **avoir p. liée avec qn** to be hand in glove with sb

partiel, -elle [parsjεl] **1** *adj* partial; **élection partielle** by-election; **travailler à temps p.** to work part-time **2** *nm Univ* end-of-term exam **3** *nf* **partielle** by-election

partiellement [parsjεlmã] *adv* partially

partir [64a] [partir] *vi (aux* **être***)* (**a**) *(s'en aller)* to go, to leave; *(commencer un voyage)* to set off; *(sans destination particulière)* to go off; *(bateau, avion)* to leave; *(moteur)* to start; *(fusil, pétard)* to go off; *Euph (mourir)* to pass away; **p. en vacances** to go (away) on *Br* holi-

day *or Am* vacation; **p. en promenade** to go for a stroll; **p. faire ses courses** to go out shopping; **p. en courant** to run off; **p. de rien** to start from nothing; **p. d'un éclat de rire** to burst out laughing; **être bien/mal parti** to have got off to a good/bad start; **faire p.** *(fusil)* to fire; *(feux d'artifice)* to let off; *(moteur)* to start; *Fam* **c'est parti, mon kiki!** here we go! (**b**) *(disparaître) (douleur, bleu)* to go, to disappear; *(tache)* to come out; *(peinture, vernis)* to come off; **faire p. une tache** to get a stain out (**c**) *(sortir)* **p. de** *(sujet: route, chemin)* to start from; **en partant du principe que...** assuming that...; **ça partait d'un bon sentiment** the thought was there; **et, partant de là,...** on that assumption,... (**d**) **à p. du village** from the village; **à p. d'aujourd'hui** from today (onwards); **à p. de maintenant** from now on; **à p. de 50 euros** from 50 euros (upwards)

partisan, -e [partizã, -an] **1** *nm* (**a**) *(fidèle)* supporter (**b**) *(combattant)* partisan **2** *adj (esprit)* partisan; **querelles partisanes** sectarian quarrels; **être p. de qch/de faire qch** to be in favour of sth/of doing sth

partitif, -ive [partitif, -iv] *adj & nm Gram* partitive

partition [partisjɔ̃] *nf (musique)* score

partout [partu] *adv* (**a**) *(en tous lieux)* everywhere; **p. où je vais** everywhere I go; **un peu p.** all over the place; **j'ai mal p.** I'm aching all over (**b**) **3 buts p.** *(au football)* 3 all; **15/30 p.** *(au tennis)* 15/30 all; **40 p.** *(au tennis)* deuce

partouze [partuz] *nf Fam* orgy

paru, -e *pp de* **paraître**

parure [paryr] *nf (ensemble)* set; **p. de lit** set of bed linen

parution [parysjɔ̃] *nf* appearance, publication

parvenir [70] [parvənir] **parvenir à** *vt ind (aux* **être***)* (**a**) *(atteindre) (endroit, personne)* to reach; **p. à ses fins** to achieve one's ends; **faire p. qch à qn** to send sth to sb (**b**) *(réussir)* **p. à faire qch** to manage to do sth

parvenu, -e [parvəny] *nm,f Péj* upstart

parvis [parvi] *nm* square *(in front of a church or a public building)*

pas¹ [pɑ] *nm* (**a**) *(enjambée, de danse)* step; *(allure)* pace; **p. à p.** step by step; **à p. de loup** stealthily; **marcher à grands p.** to stride along; **marcher à petits p.** to toddle along; **marcher d'un p. hésitant** to walk hesitantly; **faire un faux p.** to trip; *Fig* to make a faux pas; **faire un p. (vers)** to take a step (towards); **faire un p. en avant/en arrière** to take a) step forward/back; **faire les cent p.** to pace up and down; *Fig* **faire le premier p.** to take the first step; **marcher au p.** *(soldat)* to march in step; **rouler au p.** *(en voiture)* to crawl along; **ils habitent à deux p. d'ici** they live a few yards away; **j'y vais de ce p.** I'll do it right away; **p. de deux** pas de deux; **p. de course** *ou* **gymnastique** jog trot (**b**) *(trace)* footprint; **revenir** *ou* **retourner sur ses p.** to retrace one's steps (**c**) *(seuil)* **p. de la porte** doorstep (**d**) *(passage)* **le p. de Calais** the Straits of Dover (**e**) *(de vis, d'hélice)* pitch (**f**) *(locutions)* **prendre le p. sur qch** to take precedence over sth; **tirer qn d'un mauvais p.** to get sb out of a tight spot

pas² *adv* not; **je ne sais p.** I don't know; **je ne l'ai p. vue** I haven't seen her; **il est difficile de ne p. le lui dire** it's difficult to tell him; **qu'elle vienne ou p.** whether she comes or not; **viendra? viendra p.?** will he/she come or won't he/she?; **p. mal** not bad; **une explication p. claire** an unclear explanation; **p. un n'a réagi**

not one of them reacted; **p. de sucre/lecteurs** no sugar/readers; **p. du tout** not at all

pascal¹, -e, -als *ou* **-aux, -ales** [paskal, -o] *adj* Easter; *(agneau)* paschal

pascal², -als *nm* (**a**) *Phys* pascal (**b**) *Anciennement Fam (billet)* 500-franc note

passable [pasabl] *adj* passable, fair

passablement [pasabləmã] *adv* fairly

passade [pasad] *nf* passing fancy

passage [pasaʒ] *nm* (**a**) *(d'une route, d'une rivière)* crossing; *(d'un lieu)* passing; **on sourit sur son p.** people smile as he/she goes by; **les soldats ont tout détruit sur leur p.** the soldiers destroyed everything in their path; **être de p. dans une ville** to be passing through a town; *Fig* **et au p., je te ferai remarquer que...** and incidentally, let me draw your attention to the fact that...; *Fam* **p. à tabac** beating up (**b**) *(chemin)* passage; *(ruelle)* alley(way); *(galerie commerciale)* (shopping) arcade; **p. clouté** *Br* pedestrian crossing, *Am* crosswalk; **p. à niveau** *Br* level crossing, *Am* grade crossing; **p. pour piétons** *Br* pedestrian crossing, *Am* crosswalk; *(souterrain)* subway, *Br* underpass; **p. souterrain** subway, *Br* underpass (**c**) *(extrait)* passage (**d**) *(changement)* change, transition; **le p. de l'autocratie à la démocratie** the changeover *or* transition from autocracy to democracy (**e**) *(moment)* **p. nuageux/pluvieux** cloudy/rainy spell; *Fam* **avoir un p. à vide** to go through a bad patch (**f**) *Psy* **p. à l'acte** acting out

passager, -ère [pasaʒe, -ɛr] **1** *adj* momentary; **des pluies passagères** occasional showers; **ils ont eu une petite brouille passagère** they fell out for a while **2** *nm,f* passenger; **p. clandestin** stowaway

passant¹ [pasã] *nm (de ceinture)* loop

passant², -e [pasã, -ãt] **1** *adj (rue)* busy **2** *nm,f* passer-by

passation [pasasjɔ̃] *nf (d'un accord)* signing; **p. de pouvoirs** transfer of power

passe¹ [pas] *nf* (**a**) *(au football)* pass; **p. en avant/en retrait** forward/back pass (**b**) *(d'une prostituée)* trick; **hôtel de p.** = hotel used by prostitutes and their clients; **maison de p.** brothel (**c**) *(à la roulette)* passe *(any number above 18)* (**d**) *Fig* **être en p. de faire qch** to be on the way to doing sth; **être dans une mauvaise p.** to be going through a bad patch

passe² *nm Fam (clef)* master key

passé, -e [pase] **1** *adj* (**a**) *(écoulé) (temps)* past; **la semaine passée** last week; **il est quatre heures passées** it's gone *or* after four; **elle a quarante ans passés** she's over forty (**b**) *(terminé)* over; **penser à son enfance passée** to think about one's childhood (**c**) *(décoloré)* faded (**d**) **p. de mode** out of fashion **2** *nm* (**a**) *(période)* **le p.** the past; **par le p.** in the past; **tout ça, c'est du p.** that's all in the past (**b**) *Gram* past (tense); **p. antérieur** past anterior; **p. composé** perfect (tense); **p. simple** preterite, past historic; **au p.** in the past (tense) **3** *prép* after

passe-droit *(pl* **passe-droits**) [pasdrwa] *nm* privilege

passéiste [paseist] *Péj* **1** *adj* living in the past **2** *nmf* person who lives in the past

passe-montagne *(pl* **passe-montagnes**) [pasmɔtaɲ] *nm* balaclava (helmet)

passe-partout [paspartu] **1** *adj inv* all-purpose **2** *nm inv* master key

passe-plat *(pl* **passe-plats**) [paspla] *nm* serving hatch

passeport [paspɔr] *nm aussi Fig* passport; **p. biométrique** biometric passport

passer [pase] **1** *vi (aux* **être**) (**a**) *(se déplacer)* to go past; **p. devant qn/qch** to go past sb/sth; **laisser p. qn** to let sb past; *(dans une queue)* to let sb in; **je ne peux pas p.** I can't get by *or* past; **p. sur les détails** to skip the details; **elle nous a fait p. dans son bureau** she showed us into her office; **mais où est-il passé?** where's he got to?; **dire qch en passant** to mention sth in passing; **soit dit en passant** incidentally (**b**) *(évoluer)* **p. de qch à qch** to go from sth to sth; **p. dans la classe supérieure** to move up a class; **p. en première/seconde** *(en voiture)* to change into first/second; **p. capitaine** to be promoted to captain (**c**) *(traverser)* **p. par le village/Paris** to go through the village/Paris; **par où est-il passé?** which way did he go?; **laisser p. qch** *(lumière, air)* to let sth in (**d**) *(apparaître)* **p. à la radio/télévision** to be on the radio/television; **p. au cinéma** to be on at the *Br* cinema *or Am* movies (**e**) *(aller)* **je suis passé chez elle/à la boucherie** I went round to her house/to the butcher's; **le facteur est déjà passé** the postman's already been; **je ne fais que p.** I'm not staying (**f**) *(disparaître)* to go; **laisser p. qch** *(occasion)* to pass up sth; *(erreur)* to miss sth; **le plus dur est passé** the worst is over; **j'avais mal à la tête mais ça m'a passé** I had a headache but it's gone away; **il était amoureux d'elle mais ça lui a passé** he was in love with her but he's got over it (**g**) *(année, temps)* to pass, to go by (**h**) *(être considéré)* **p. pour un génie** to be considered a genius; **faire p. qn pour** to pass sb off as (**i**) *(être adopté) (loi, proposition)* to be passed, to go through (**j**) **passe!** *(aux cartes)* pass! (**k**) *Fam* **il a bien failli y p.** *(mourir)* he nearly didn't make it; **toute sa fortune y est passée** he/she spent his/her entire fortune on it **2** *vt (aux* **avoir**) (**a**) *(pont, rivière, frontière)* to go over; *(porte, douane)* to go through; **il a passé la soixantaine** he's in his sixties (**b**) *(donner) (ballon, témoin)* to pass; **p. qch à qn** to pass *or* give sth to sb; *Fam* **p. son rhume à qn** to give sb one's cold; **p. la parole à qn** to hand over to sb; **pourriez-vous me la p.?** *(au téléphone)* could you put me through to her? (**c**) *(mettre) (vêtement)* to slip on; **p. un coup d'éponge sur qch** to give sth a sponge; **p. la tête par la fenêtre** to lean one's head out of the window; **p. le doigt sur qch** to run one's finger over sth; **p. la seconde/troisième** *(en voiture)* to change into second/third; *Fam* **qu'est-ce qu'il va nous p.!** he's going to make us wish we'd never been born! (**d**) *(film)* to show; *(disque)* to play; *(vidéo)* to put on (**e**) *(temps, vacances)* to spend; **p. son temps à faire qch** to spend one's time doing sth; **pour p. le temps** to pass the time (**f**) *(pardonner)* **elle lui passe tout** she lets him/her get away with everything (**g**) *(omettre)* to leave out; **p. son tour** to miss a turn; **j'en passe et des meilleures** and that's not the half of it (**h**) *(examen)* to take *or* sit; *(visite médicale)* to have; **faire p. un examen à qn** to take sb for an exam (**i**) *(accord, contrat)* to enter into, to sign; *(commande)* to place (**à** with) (**j**) *(liquide)* to strain; *(café)* to filter

3 se passer *vpr* (**a**) *(se produire)* to happen; **que se passe-t-il?, qu'est-ce qui se passe?** what's happening?; **ça s'est bien passé** it went well; **l'histoire se passe en 1900/en Normandie** the story takes place in 1900/in Normandy; *Fam* **ça ne se passera pas comme ça!** I'm not having it!
(**b**) *(mettre)* **se p. la main dans les cheveux** to run one's fingers through one's hair; **se p. de l'eau sur la figure** to splash one's face with water; **se p. de la crème sur les mains** to put some cream on one's hands
4 se passer de *vt ind (se priver de)* to do without; **il ne peut pas se p. de télévision** he can't live without TV

passereau, -x [pasro] *nm* passerine
passerelle [pasrɛl] *nf* (**a**) *(au-dessus d'une rue, d'un ruisseau)* footbridge (**b**) *(de navire)* bridge; **p. de débarquement** *ou* **d'embarquement** *(de navire)* gangway; *(d'avion) (amovible)* steps (**c**) *Fig (intermédiaire)* link (**d**) *Ordinat* **p. (de connexion) (avec)** gateway (to)
passe-temps [pastã] *nm inv* pastime
passe-thé [paste] *nm inv* tea-strainer
passeur, -euse [pasœr, -øz] *nm,f* (**a**) *(de bac)* ferryman, *f* ferrywoman (**b**) *(d'immigrants clandestins)* smuggler; **il trouva un p. qui l'aida à gagner les États-Unis** he found someone to get him over the border into the United States
passible [pasibl] *adj* liable (**de** to)
passif, -ive [pasif, -iv] **1** *adj* passive
2 *nm* (**a**) *Gram* passive; **au p.** in the passive (**b**) *Fin* liabilities
passif-agressif, passive-agressive *(mpl* **passifs-agressifs,** *fpl* **passives-agressives)** [pasifagrɛsif, pasifagrɛsiv] *adj Psy* passive-aggressive
passion [pasjɔ̃] *nf* (**a**) *(sentiment dévorant)* passion; **avoir une p. pour qn/qch** to have a passion for sb/sth; **avoir la p. de qch** to have a passion for sth; **vivre une p.** to have a passionate love affair; **avec p.** passionately (**b**) *Rel* **la P. selon saint Jean** the St John Passion
passionnant, -e [pasjɔnã, -ãt] *adj* fascinating
passionné, -e [pasjɔne] **1** *adj* passionate; **p. de qch** extremely keen on sth
2 *nm,f* enthusiast; **un p. de football** a football enthusiast
passionnel, -elle [pasjɔnɛl] *adj (relation)* passionate
passionnément [pasjɔnemã] *adv* passionately
passionner [pasjɔne] **1** *vt (sujet: livre, film)* to fascinate; **son métier la passionne** she finds her job fascinating
2 se passionner *vpr* **se p. pour qch** to have a passion for sth
passivement [pasivmã] *adv* passively
passivité [pasivite] *nf* passivity, passiveness
passoire [paswar] *nf (avec un grillage)* sieve; *(avec de petits trous)* colander; *Fam* **ce gardien de but est une vraie p.!** this goalkeeper lets everything in!
pastel [pastɛl] *nm & adj inv* pastel
pastèque [pastɛk] *nf* watermelon; *Fam* **j'ai la tête comme une p.** my head's throbbing
pasteur [pastœr] *nm* (**a**) *Litt (berger)* shepherd (**b**) *(religieux)* pastor, minister
pasteurisation [pastœrizasjɔ̃] *nf* pasteurization
pasteuriser [pastœrize] *vt* to pasteurize
pastiche [pastiʃ] *nm* pastiche

pastille [pastij] *nf (bonbon mou)* pastille; *(médicament)* lozenge; **p. contre la toux** cough sweet *or* lozenge; **p. de menthe** mint; **p. verte** = green label on a low-emission vehicle indicating that it may be driven on days when restrictions are placed on traffic due to high levels of atmospheric pollution
pastis [pastis] *nm* (**a**) *(boisson)* pastis (**b**) *Fam* **être dans le p.** to be in a fix
pastoral, -e, -aux, -ales [pastɔral, -o] **1** *adj* pastoral
2 *nf* **pastorale** *(musique)* pastorale
patachon [pataʃɔ̃] *nm Fam* **mener une vie de p.** to lead a wild life
Patagonie [patagɔni] *nf* **la P.** Patagonia
patapouf [patapuf] **1** *exclam* flop!
2 *nm (langage enfantin)* **gros p.** fatty
pataquès [patakɛs] *nm (faute de langage)* malapropism
patate [patat] *nf Fam (pomme de terre)* spud; *Fig (imbécile)* clot; *Can* **patates frites** French fries, *Br* chips; *Fig* **en avoir gros sur la p.** to be down in the mouth
patati [patati] *exclam Fam* **et p. et patata** and so on and so forth
patatras [patatra] *exclam Fam* crash!
pataud, -e [pato, -od] *adj Fam* clumsy
Pataugas® [patogas] *nm* canvas walking boot
pataugeoire [patoʒwar] *nf* paddling pool
patauger [45] [patoʒe] *vi (s'embourber)* to squelch (**dans** in); *(barboter)* to splash about (**dans** in); *Fam (s'embrouiller)* to flounder (**dans** in)
patch [patʃ] *nm Méd* patch
pâte [pat] *nf* (**a**) *(pour une tarte)* pastry; *(pour le pain)* dough; *(pour un gâteau)* mixture; **p. brisée** shortcrust pastry; **p. à choux** choux pastry; **p. à crêpes** pancake batter; **p. feuilletée** puff *or* flaky pastry; **p. à frire** batter; **p. à pain** bread dough; **p. sablée** rich shortcrust pastry; **p. à tarte** pastry; **p. à tartiner** chocolate spread (**b**) *(mixture)* **p. d'amandes** marzipan; **p. de fruits** fruit jelly; **p. à modeler** modelling clay; **p. à papier** pulp
pâté [pate] *nm* (**a**) *(terrine)* pâté; **p. de campagne** pâté de campagne *(coarse pâté made with pork); Can* **p. chinois** shepherd's pie; **p. en croûte** ≃ pork pie; **p. de foie** liver pâté (**b**) *Belg (gâteau)* cake (**c**) **p. (de sable)** sandpie (**d**) **p. de maisons** block of houses (**e**) *(tache d'encre)* blot; **faire un p. sur qch** to get a blot on sth
pâtée [pate] *nf* (**a**) *(de chat)* cat food; *(de chien)* dog food (**b**) *Fam (défaite)* **prendre la p.** to get thrashed; **mettre la p. à qn** to thrash sb
patelin¹ [patlɛ̃] *nm Fam* village
patelin², -e [patlɛ̃, -in] *adj Litt & Péj* unctuous
patent, -e [patã, -ãt] *adj* (**a**) *(évident)* patent (**b**) **lettres patentes** letters patent
patente [patãt] *nf (impôt)* tax *(paid by self-employed people)*
patenté, -e [patãte] *adj* licensed
patère [patɛr] *nf (coat)* peg
paternaliste [patɛrnalist] *adj* paternalistic
paternel, -elle [patɛrnɛl] **1** *adj* paternal; *(ton)* fatherly; **du côté p.** on the father's side; **ma grand-mère paternelle** my grandmother on my father's side
2 *nm Fam* **le p.** the old man
paternité [patɛrnite] *nf* paternity, fatherhood; **recherche de p.** establishment of paternity
pâtes [pat] *nfpl* pasta; **p. fraîches** fresh pasta

pâteux, -euse [pɑtø, -øz] *adj* (**a**) *(nourriture)* doughy; **avoir la langue pâteuse** to have a furry tongue (**b**) *(sauce)* thick

pathétique [patetik] *adj* pathetic, moving

pathogène [patɔʒɛn] *adj* pathogenic

pathologique [patɔlɔʒik] *adj aussi Fam Fig* pathological

patibulaire [patibylɛr] *adj* **avoir une mine p.** to have a sinister look

patiemment [pasjamɑ̃] *adv* patiently

patience [pasjɑ̃s] *nf* (**a**) *(qualité)* patience; **avoir de la p. (avec qn)** to be patient (with sb); **avoir une p. d'ange** to have the patience of a saint; **prendre son mal en p.** to suffer in silence; **perdre p.** to lose patience; **p., j'ai presque fini!** hold on *or* just a minute, I've almost finished!; *Prov* **p. et longueur de temps font plus que force ni que rage** all things take their time (**b**) *(jeu de cartes) Br* patience, *Am* solitaire

patient, -e [pasjɑ̃, -ɑ̃t] **1** *adj* patient
2 *nm,f (malade)* patient

patienter [pasjɑ̃te] *vi* to wait; **faire p. qn** to ask sb to wait

patin [patɛ̃] *nm* (**a**) *(de patineur)* skate; **patins à glace/à roulettes** ice/roller skates; **faire du p. à glace/à roulettes** to go ice-/roller-skating; *Can Fam Fig* **être vite sur ses patins** to be quick off the mark (**b**) *(pour parquet)* cloth pad (**c**) *Tech* shoe; **p. de frein** brake shoe

patinage [patinaʒ] *nm (sport)* skating; **p. artistique** figure skating; **p. de vitesse** speed skating

patine [patin] *nf* patina

patiner¹ [patine] *vi* (**a**) *(faire du patinage)* to skate (**b**) *(glisser) (voiture)* to skid; *(embrayage)* to slip; **ça patine!** it's like an ice rink!

patiner² *vt* to give a patina to

patinette [patinɛt] *nf* scooter

patineur, -euse [patinœr, -øz] *nm,f* skater

patinoire [patinwar] *nf* skating *or* ice rink; **ce trottoir est une vraie p.** this pavement is like an ice rink

pâtir [pɑtir] *vi* to suffer (**de** because of)

pâtisserie [pɑtisri] *nf* (**a**) *(magasin)* cake shop; **p.-confiserie** confectioner's (**b**) *(gâteau)* pastry, cake (**c**) *(confection)* pastry-making; **faire de la p.** to make cakes

pâtissier, -ère [pɑtisje, -ɛr] **1** *nm,f (artisan)* pastry cook; *(commerçant)* confectioner
2 *adj voir* **crème**

patois [patwa] *nm* patois

patraque [patrak] *adj Fam* out of sorts

patriarcal, -e, -aux, -ales [patriarkal, -o] *adj* patriarchal

patriarche [patrijarʃ] *nm* patriarch

patrie [patri] *nf* homeland; **ma seconde p.** my second home; *Fig* **la p. des arts** the cradle of the arts

patrimoine [patrimwan] *nm* heritage; *(biens)* property; **p. culturel** cultural heritage; *Biol* **p. génétique** genotype

patriote [patrijɔt] **1** *adj* patriotic
2 *nmf* patriot

patriotique [patrijɔtik] *adj* patriotic

patriotisme [patrijɔtism] *nm* patriotism

patron, -onne [patrɔ̃, -ɔn] **1** *nm,f* (**a**) *(dirigeant)* boss; *(propriétaire)* owner (**b**) *Rel* patron saint (**de** of)
2 *nm* (**a**) *(médecin)* senior consultant (**b**) *(pour la couture)* pattern

patronage [patrɔnaʒ] *nm* (**a**) *(parrainage)* patronage; **placé sous le p. de...** sponsored by... (**b**) *(organisation)* youth club

patronal, -e, -aux, -ales [patrɔnal, -o] *adj* employers'

patronat [patrɔna] *nm* employers

patronnesse [patrɔnɛs] *adj f* **dame p.** lady bountiful

patronyme [patrɔnim] *nm* patronymic

patrouille [patruj] *nf* patrol

patrouiller [patruje] *vi* to patrol

patte [pat] *nf* (**a**) *(jambe)* leg; *(pied) (de chien, de chat)* paw; *(d'oiseau)* foot; **pattes de devant** forelegs; *(pieds)* front paws; **pattes de derrière** hind legs; *(pieds)* back paws; **court/haut sur pattes** short-/long-legged; **marcher/se mettre à quatre pattes** to walk/get down on all fours; *Fig* **tirer dans les pattes à qn** to give sb a hard time; *Fig* **retomber sur ses pattes** to land on one's feet; *Fig* **montrer p. blanche** to show one's credentials; *Fam* **bas les pattes!** hands off!; *Fam* **pattes de mouche(s)** cramped handwriting (**b**) *(de cartable, de sac)* tab (**c**) *(de poche)* flap; *(d'épaule)* epaulette (**d**) *Suisse (torchon)* cloth (**e**) **pattes** *(favoris)* sideburns

patte-d'oie *(pl* **pattes-d'oie)** [patdwa] *nf* (**a**) *(carrefour)* crossroads *(singulier)* (**b**) *(ride)* crow's foot

pattemouille [patmuj] *nf* damp cloth *(for ironing clothes)*

pâturage [pɑtyraʒ] *nm (endroit)* pasture; **pâturages** pasture land

paume [pom] *nf* palm

paumé, -e [pome] *Fam* **1** *adj (perdu)* lost; *(isolé)* godforsaken
2 *nm,f* loser

paumer [pome] *Fam* **1** *vt* to lose
2 se paumer *vpr* to get lost

paupérisation [poperizasjɔ̃] *nf* impoverishment

paupière [popjɛr] *nf* eyelid

paupiette [popjɛt] *nf* (meat) olive; **paupiettes de veau** veal olives

pause [poz] *nf* (**a**) *(dans une activité)* break; *(en parlant)* pause; **faire une p.** to have a break; *(en parlant)* to pause; **p. de midi** lunch break; **p.-café** coffee break (**b**) *Mus Br* semibreve rest, *Am* whole rest

pauvre [povr] **1** *adj* (**a**) *(personne, sol)* poor; **p. en vitamine C** with a low vitamin C content; **p. de moi!** poor old me! (**b**) *(misérable) (robe, meubles)* shabby; *(sourire)* weak; *(excuse)* poor (**c**) *Péj* pathetic, *Br* sad; *Fam* **p. mec!** you loser!, *Br* you saddo!
2 *nmf* poor man, *f* poor woman; **les pauvres** the poor; *Fig* **p. d'esprit** half-wit

pauvrement [povrəmɑ̃] *adv* poorly

pauvresse [povrɛs] *nf (fille)* poor girl; *(femme)* poor woman

pauvreté [povrəte] *nf aussi Fig* poverty

pavane [pavan] *nf Mus* pavane

pavaner [pavane] **se pavaner** *vpr* to strut about

pavé [pave] *nm* (**a**) *(morceau de grès)* paving stone; *Fam Péj (livre)* massive tome; *Fig* **un p. dans la mare** a bombshell (**b**) *(revêtement)* paving; *Fig* **tenir le haut du p.** to be at the top; *Fig* **battre le p.** to hang about the streets; *Fig* **être sur le p.** to be on the street (**c**) *Ordinat* keypad; **p. numérique** numeric keypad

paver [pave] *vt* to pave *(with small stones)*; *Fig* **l'enfer est pavé de bonnes intentions** the road to hell is paved with good intentions

pavillon [pavijɔ̃] *nm* (**a**) *(petite maison)* detached house; **p. de chasse** hunting lodge (**b**) *(d'hôpital)* wing (**c**) *(partie évasée) (d'un haut-parleur)* horn; *(d'une trompette)* bell; *(d'un entonnoir)* mouth; **p. de l'oreille** external ear (**d**) *(drapeau)* flag; **p. de complaisance** flag of convenience

pavillonnaire [pavijɔnɛr] *adj* **banlieue p.** suburb *(consisting of houses as opposed to high-rise apartment buildings)*

pavoiser [pavwaze] *vi Fam* to gloat

pavot [pavo] *nm* poppy

payable [pɛjabl] *adj* payable; **p. comptant** payable in cash; **p. à la livraison** payable on delivery; **p. à vue** payable at sight

payant, -e [pɛjɑ̃, -ɑ̃t] *adj (qui paie) (hôte, élève)* paying; *(où il faut payer)* with a charge for admission; **l'entrée est payante** there is a charge for admission; *Fig* **ça s'est avéré p.** it turned out to be worth it

paye [pɛj] = **paie**

payement [pɛjmɑ̃] = **paiement**

payer [53] [peje] **1** *vt* (**a**) *(somme, dette, loyer, personne)* to pay; *(objet, service)* to pay for; **faire p. qch** *(service)* to charge for sth; *(somme)* to charge sth; **se faire p.** to get or be paid; **je le lui ai payé 50 euros** I paid him/her 50 euros for it; *Fam* **p. qch à qn** *(le lui offrir)* to buy sth for sb; *Fig* **p. les pots cassés** to carry the can (**b**) *Fig (expier)* to pay for; **il l'a payé de sa vie** he paid for it with his life; **tu me le paieras!** you'll pay for it!; *Fam* **je suis payé pour le savoir** I've learnt it the hard way

2 *vi* (**a**) *(verser de l'argent)* to pay; **p. en liquide/par carte (de crédit)/par chèque** to pay (in) cash/by credit card/by cheque; **p. de sa poche** to pay out of one's own pocket (**b**) *Fig* **p. de sa personne** to put oneself out; **il ne paie pas de mine, mais il est doué** he doesn't look it, but he's very clever (**c**) *(rapporter)* to pay

3 se payer *vpr Fam* **se p. qch** *(s'offrir)* to treat oneself to sth; *(être chargé de)* to be landed or saddled with sth; **se p. du bon temps** to have a fantastic time; **se p. un arbre** to crash into a tree; **je me suis payé un 2 à l'oral** I got a 2 in the oral; **se p. la tête de qn** to take the mickey out of sb; **se p. le culot de faire qch** to have the nerve to do sth

payeur, -euse [pɛjœr, -øz] *nm,f* payer; **mauvais p.** bad debtor, defaulter

pays [pei] *nm* (**a**) *(nation)* country; **p. de cocagne** land of plenty; **p. en voie de développement** developing country; **les p. de l'Est** Eastern European countries (**b**) *(région)* region; **voir du p.** to travel around; **revenir au p.** to go back home; **p. de chasse/pêche** hunting/fishing country (**c**) **le P. basque** the Basque country; **le p. de Galles** Wales

paysage [peizaʒ] *nm* (**a**) *(site)* landscape; *(vue)* scenery; *Fig (ensemble)* scene; **le p. audiovisuel français** French broadcasting (**b**) *(peinture)* landscape (painting) (**c**) *Ordinat* **mode p.** landscape mode

paysager, -ère [peizaʒe, -ɛr] *adj (jardin)* landscaped; *(bureau)* open-plan

paysagiste [peizaʒist] *nmf* (**a**) *(peintre)* landscape painter (**b**) **(jardinier) p.** landscape gardener

paysan, -anne [peizɑ̃, -an] **1** *adj* country; *Péj* peasant; **syndicat p.** farmers' union

2 *nm,f* farmer; *Péj* peasant

paysannerie [peizanri] *nf* **la p.** the peasantry

Pays-Bas [peiba] *nmpl* **les P.** the Netherlands

PC [pese] *nm* (**a**) *(abrév* **parti communiste)** CP (**b**) *Ordinat (abrév* **personal computer)** PC

PCF [peseɛf] *nm (abrév* **parti communiste français)** French Communist Party

PCV [peseve] *nm* **(appel en) P.** *Br* reverse-charge call, *Am* collect call; **appeler en P.** *Br* to reverse the charges, *Am* to call collect

P-DG [pedeʒe] *nm inv (abrév* **président-directeur général)** *Br* chairman and managing director, *Am* CEO

péage [peaʒ] *nm* (**a**) *(droit)* toll; **pont à p.** toll bridge (**b**) *(installation)* tollbooth (**c**) **chaîne (de télévision) à p.** pay channel

peau, -x [po] *nf* (**a**) *(derme)* skin; **avoir la p. grasse** to have greasy skin; **avoir la p. blanche/noire** to be white/black; **avoir une p. de pêche** to have velvety skin; *Fig* **faire p. neuve** *(personne)* to turn over a new leaf; *(entreprise, parti)* to get a new image; **entrer dans la p. d'un personnage** to get right inside a character; **n'avoir que la p. et les os** to be nothing but skin and bone; **diminuer comme une p. de chagrin** to dwindle away; *Fam* **être bien/mal dans sa p.** to feel/not to feel good about oneself; *Fam* **avoir qch dans la p.** to have sth in one's blood; *Fam* **avoir qn dans la p.** to be crazy about sb; *Fam* **tenir à sa p.** to value one's life; *Fam* **risquer sa p.** to risk one's neck; *Fam* **sauver sa p.** to save one's skin; *Fam* **avoir la p. de qn** to have sb's hide; *Fam* **prendre douze balles dans la p.** to be shot by a firing squad; *Fam* **p. de vache** *(homme)* bastard; *(femme)* bitch (**b**) *(dépouille) (d'un animal)* skin; *(d'un animal à fourrure)* pelt (**c**) *(cuir)* hide, leather; *(d'un tambour)* skin; **p. de chamois** chamois (leather); **p. de mouton** sheepskin; **p. de serpent** snakeskin (**d**) *(de fruit, de légume)* skin; *(d'agrume, de pomme)* peel; **p. de banane** banana skin; **p. d'orange** orange peel; *Fig* orange-peel skin (**e**) *(du lait)* skin (**f**) *(des ongles)* hangnail

peaufiner [pofine] *vt* to polish *(with a chamois leather)*; *Fam Fig (fignoler)* to add the finishing touches to

Peau-Rouge *(pl* **Peaux-Rouges)** [poruʒ] *nmf* Red Indian, Redskin

peausserie [posri] *nf* (**a**) *(commerce)* skin trade (**b**) *(marchandise)* leatherwear

pécari [pekari] *nm* peccary

peccadille [pekadij] *nf* peccadillo

péché [peʃe] *nm* sin; **les sept péchés capitaux** the seven deadly sins; **p. de jeunesse** youthful indiscretion; **p. mignon** weakness; **le p. originel** original sin

pêche¹ [pɛʃ] **1** *nf* (**a**) *(fruit)* peach; **p. blanche** white peach; **p. jaune** yellow peach (**b**) *Fam (coup)* clout (**c**) *Fam (forme)* **avoir la p.** to be on form

2 *adj inv* peach(-coloured)

pêche² *nf* (**a**) *(activité)* fishing; **aller à la p.** to go fishing; **p. à la ligne** angling; **p. à la mouche** fly fishing; *Can* **p. sous la glace** ice fishing (**b**) *(produits pêchés)* catch; **faire une bonne p.** to get a good catch

pécher [34] [peʃe] *vi* to sin; **il pèche par excès de timidité** he's painfully shy; **cette enquête pèche sur un point** the inquiry falls down on one point; **p. par omission** to sin by omission

pêcher¹ [peʃe] *nm* peach tree

pêcher² **1** *vt* (**a**) *(chercher à prendre)* to fish for; *(prendre)* to catch; **p. la baleine** to go whaling (**b**) *Fam (trouver)* **où avez-vous pêché cela?** where did you pick that up?

2 *vi* to fish; **p. à la ligne** to go angling; *Fig* **p. en eau trouble** to fish in troubled waters

pécheresse [peʃrɛs] *voir* **pécheur**

pêcherie [pɛʃri] *nf* fishery, fishing ground

pécheur, -eresse [peʃœr, peʃrɛs] *nm,f* sinner
pêcheur, -euse [pɛʃœr, -øz] *nm,f* fisherman, *f* fisherwoman; **p. à la ligne** angler; **p. de baleines** whaler; **p. de corail** coral fisher
pécore [pekɔr] *nmf Fam Péj* yokel, *Am* hick
pectoral, -e, -aux, -ales [pɛktɔral, -o] **1** *adj* pectoral
2 *nm* pectoral muscle
pécule [pekyl] *nm* savings, nest egg
pécuniaire [pekynjɛr] *adj* financial
pédagogie [pedagɔʒi] *nf* (**a**) *(discipline)* pedagogy (**b**) *(qualité du pédagogue)* teaching skills
pédagogique [pedagɔʒik] *adj* *(voyage, sortie)* educational; *(méthode)* teaching
pédagogue [pedagɔg] **1** *adj* **elle est très p.** she's a very good teacher
2 *nmf* (**a**) *(spécialiste)* educationalist (**b**) *(personne qui sait enseigner)* teacher
pédale [pedal] *nf* (**a**) *(de vélo, de voiture, de piano)* pedal; **p. d'accélérateur** accelerator pedal; **p. d'embrayage** clutch pedal; *Fam Fig* **mettre la p. douce** to go easy; *Fam Fig* **perdre les pédales** *(s'affoler)* to lose one's head (**b**) *Fam Péj (homosexuel) Br* queer, *Am* fag, = offensive term used to refer to a male homosexual
pédaler [pedale] *vi* to pedal; *Fam* **p. dans la choucroute** *ou* **la semoule** to be all at sea
pédalier [pedalje] *nm* (**a**) *(de vélo)* crank gear (**b**) *(clavier d'orgue)* pedal board
Pédalo® [pedalo] *nm* pedal boat, pedalo; **faire du P.** to go out on a Pedalo
pédant, -e [pedɑ̃, -ɑ̃t] **1** *adj* pedantic
2 *nm,f* pedant
pédé [pede] *nm très Fam Br* queer, *Am* fag, = offensive term used to refer to a male homosexual
pédéraste [pederast] *nm* (**a**) *(homosexuel)* homosexual (**b**) *(pédophile)* pederast
pédestre [pedɛstr] *adj (voyage)* on foot; **chemin** *m* **p.** footpath; **randonnée** *f* **p.** hike
pédiatre [pedjatr] *nmf* paediatrician
pédiatrie [pedjatri] *nf* paediatrics *(singulier)*
pédicure [pedikyr] *nmf* chiropodist
pedigree [pedigre] *nm* pedigree
pédomètre [pedɔmɛtr] *nm* pedometer
pédoncule [pedɔkyl] *nm* peduncle
pédophile [pedɔfil] *adj & nmf* paedophile
pédophilie [pedɔfili] *nf* paedophilia
pègre [pɛgr] *nf* underworld
peignais, peigne *etc voir* **peindre**
peigne [pɛɲ] *nm* (**a**) *(pour les cheveux)* comb; **se donner un coup de p.** to give one's hair a comb; **p. fin** fine-tooth comb; *Fig* **passer qch au p. fin** to go through sth with a fine-tooth comb (**b**) *(pour la laine)* card
peigne-cul *(pl* peigne-culs*)* [pɛɲky] *nm très Fam Péj* creep
peignée [pɛɲe] *nf Fam* thrashing; **flanquer une p. à qn** to give sb a thrashing
peigner [pɛɲe] **1** *vt* (**a**) *(cheveux)* to comb; **p. un enfant** to comb a child's hair; *Fam* **p. la girafe** to waste one's time (**b**) *(laine)* to card
2 **se peigner** *vpr* to comb one's hair
peignoir [pɛɲwar] *nm* (**a**) *(vêtement d'intérieur)* housecoat; *(robe de chambre)* dressing gown; **p. (de bain)** bathrobe (**b**) *(chez le coiffeur)* cape
peinard, -e [pɛnar, -ard] *adj Fam (poste)* cushy; *(personne)* nice and comfy

peindre [54] [pɛ̃dr] **1** *vt* (**a**) *(avec de la peinture)* to paint; **p. qch en vert** to paint sth green (**b**) *(décrire)* to depict
2 *vi* to paint
3 **se peindre** *vpr* **l'émotion/la consternation se peignit sur son visage** emotion/dismay was written on his/her face
peine [pɛn] *nf* (**a**) *(sanction)* punishment; **p. capitale** capital punishment; **p. de mort** death penalty; **p. de prison** prison sentence; **défense d'entrer sous p. d'amende** *(sur panneau)* trespassers will be prosecuted; **pour la** *ou* **ta p., tu vas descendre la poubelle** just for that, you can take the bin down (**b**) *(chagrin)* sorrow, sadness; **avoir de la p.** to be upset; **faire de la p. à qn** to upset sb; **elle fait p. à voir** she's a pitiful sight; **p. de cœur** heartache (**c**) *(effort)* trouble; **se donner de la p. pour faire qch** to go to a lot of trouble to do sth; **donnez-vous** *ou* **prenez la p. d'entrer** please come in; **c'est p. perdue** it's a waste of time; **elle n'est pas au bout de ses peines** her troubles aren't over yet; **en être pour sa p.** to have nothing to show for one's trouble; **ça vaut la p. d'essayer** it's worth a try; **ça ne vaut pas la p.** it's not worth it; **ce n'est pas la p. de débarrasser la table** there's no point (in) clearing the table; **est-ce que ça vaut la p. que je vienne?** do I need to come?; *Ironique* **c'était bien la p. de se donner tout ce mal!** it was really worth going to all that trouble! (**d**) *(difficulté)* difficulty; **avoir de la p. à faire qch** to have difficulty doing sth; **j'ai (de la) p. à croire que...** I find it hard to believe that...; **elle serait bien en p. de t'expliquer comment ça marche** she'd be hard put to explain to you how it works; **cela n'a pas été sans p.** it was no easy matter (**e**) **à p.** hardly, scarcely; **c'est à p. si je le connais** I hardly know him; **il est à p. trois heures** it's only just three o'clock; **à p. étions-nous sortis que...** we'd only just gone out when...; **j'arrive à p.** I've only just arrived; **à p. arrivée, elle alluma une cigarette** no sooner had she arrived than she lit a cigarette
peiner [pene] **1** *vt* to upset, to sadden; **d'un ton peiné** in a sad voice
2 *vi* to labour
peint, -e *pp de* **peindre**
peintre [pɛ̃tr] *nm* (**a**) *(artisan, artiste)* painter; **p. en bâtiment** painter and decorator (**b**) *Fig* portrayer
peinture [pɛ̃tyr] *nf* (**a**) *(art, action)* painting; **faire de la p.** to paint; **p. à l'eau** watercolour (painting); **p. à l'huile** oil painting; **p. sur soie** silk painting (**b**) *(tableau)* painting, picture; *Fig (description)* depiction; *Fig* **je ne peux pas le voir en p.** I can't stand the sight of him; **p. murale** mural (**c**) *(matière)* paint; **p. fraîche** *(sur écriteau)* wet paint (**d**) *(surface peinte)* paintwork; **il faudra refaire les peintures** the paintwork will have to be done
peinturer [pɛ̃tyre] *vt Can* to paint
peinturlurer [pɛ̃tyrlyre] *vt Fam* to daub with paint; **se p. le visage** to plaster make-up on one's face
péjoratif, -ive [peʒɔratif, -iv] *adj* pejorative
Pékin [pekɛ̃] *n* Peking, Beijing
pékinois, -e [pekinwa, -az] **1** *adj* of Peking, of Beijing
2 *nm,f* person from Peking *or* Beijing
3 *nm* *(chien)* pekin(g)ese (**b**) *(langue)* Pekingese
PEL [peɔɛl] *nm Fin (abrév* plan d'épargne-logement*)* = savings plan entitling savers to low mortgages, *Br* ≃ building society account, *Am* ≃ savings and loan association account

pelade [pəlad] *nf* alopecia

pelage [pəlaʒ] *nm* coat, fur

pelé, -e [pəle] **1** *adj (personne, fourrure)* bald; *Fig (paysage)* bare; *(tissu)* threadbare
2 *nm Fam* **il y avait trois pelés et un tondu** there was hardly a soul there

pêle-mêle [pɛlmɛl] **1** *adv* higgledy-piggledy
2 *nm inv (cadre)* multiple (photo) frame

peler [39] [pəle] **1** *vt* to peel
2 *vi (peau)* to peel; **j'ai le nez qui pèle** my nose is peeling; *Fam Fig* **je pèle (de froid)** I'm freezing (cold)
3 se peler *vpr Fam* **on se pèle (de froid)** it's freezing (cold)

pèlerin [pɛlrɛ̃] *nm* pilgrim

pèlerinage [pɛlrinaʒ] *nm* pilgrimage; **faire un p., aller en p.** to go on a pilgrimage

pèlerine [pɛlrin] *nf* cape

pélican [pelikɑ̃] *nm* pelican

pelisse [pəlis] *nf* pelisse

pelle [pɛl] *nf* shovel; *(d'enfant)* spade; *Fig* **à la p.** by the bucketful; *Fam* **ramasser** *ou* **se prendre une p.** to fall flat on one's face; **p. mécanique** mechanical shovel; **p. à ordures** dustpan; **p. à tarte** cake slice

pelletée [pɛlte] *nf* shovelful

pelleteuse [pɛltøz] *nf* mechanical shovel

pellicule [pelikyl] *nf* (**a**) *(de glace, de peinture)* thin layer; *(sur un liquide)* film (**b**) *Cin & Phot* film (**c**) *(dans les cheveux)* **pellicules** dandruff; **avoir des pellicules** to have dandruff

pelote [pəlɔt] *nf* (**a**) *(de laine, de ficelle)* ball; *Can* **p. de neige** snowball; *Fig* **avoir les nerfs en p.** to be on edge (**b**) *(sport)* **p. (basque)** pelota (**c**) **p. (à épingles)** pincushion

peloter [pəlɔte] *vt Fam* to grope

peloton [pəlɔtɔ̃] *nm* (**a**) *(en cyclisme)* pack; *aussi Fig* **le p. de tête** the leaders (**b**) *Mil* platoon; **p. d'exécution** firing squad (**c**) *(petite pelote)* small ball

pelotonner [pəlɔtɔne] **se pelotonner** *vpr* to curl up; *(pour avoir chaud)* to snuggle up

pelouse [pəluz] *nf* lawn; **p. interdite** *(sur panneau)* keep off the grass

peluche [pəlyʃ] *nf* (**a**) *(tissu)* plush; **jouet en p.** soft *or* cuddly toy (**b**) *(jouet)* soft *or* cuddly toy (**c**) *(bout d'étoffe)* piece of fluff

pelucheux, -euse [pəlyʃø, -øz] *adj* fluffy

pelure [pəlyr] *nf* (**a**) *(peau) (de fruit)* peel; *(de légumes)* peelings; **p. d'oignon** onion skin (**b**) *Fam (vêtement)* coat

pelvis [pɛlvis] *nm* pelvis

pénal, -e, -aux, -ales [penal, -o] *adj* penal

pénaliser [penalize] *vt* to penalize

pénalité [penalite] *nf* penalty

penalty [penalti] *nm* penalty

pénates [penat] *nmpl Fam* **regagner ses p.** to return home

penaud, -e [pəno, -od] *adj* sheepish; **d'un air p.** sheepishly

penchant [pɑ̃ʃɑ̃] *nm (tendance)* propensity (**pour** for); *(préférence)* penchant (**pour** for)

penché, -e [pɑ̃ʃe] *adj* leaning; *(écriture)* sloping

pencher [pɑ̃ʃe] **1** *vt (récipient, meuble)* to tilt; **p. la tête en avant/en arrière** to lean forward/backwards; **p. la tête à droite** to lean one's head to the right
2 *vi (s'écarter de la position verticale)* to lean over; *(bateau)* to list; **p. vers la droite** to lean to the right; *Fig* **p. pour qch** to incline towards sth
3 se pencher *vpr* to lean over; **se p. en avant/en ar-**

rière/sur le côté to lean forward/backwards/to the side; **se p. par la fenêtre** to lean out of the window; *Fig* **se p. sur un problème** to look into a problem

pendaison [pɑ̃dɛzɔ̃] *nf* hanging; **p. de crémaillère** housewarming (party)

pendant¹, -e [pɑ̃dɑ̃, -ɑ̃t] **1** *adj* (**a**) *(qui pend)* hanging; *(jambes)* dangling; **le chien avait la langue pendante** the dog's tongue was hanging out (**b**) *(en attente)* pending
2 *nm* (**a**) **p. (d'oreille)** drop earring (**b**) *(d'un tableau, d'un bibelot)* matching piece (**de** to); **se faire p.** to go together

pendant² **1** *prép* (**a**) *(au cours de)* during; **p. mon séjour** during my stay (**b**) *(pour une durée de)* **p. dix minutes/deux mois** for ten minutes/two months; **p. tout le trajet** throughout the journey, for the whole journey; **p. ce temps(-là)** in the meantime
2 *conj* **p. que** while; **p. que vous y êtes** while you're at it

pendentif [pɑ̃dɑ̃tif] *nm (bijou)* pendant

penderie [pɑ̃dri] *nf Br* wardrobe, *Am* closet

pendouiller [pɑ̃duje] *vi Fam* to dangle

pendre [pɑ̃dr] **1** *vt* (**a**) *(accrocher)* to hang (up) (**b**) *(mettre à mort)* to hang; **p. qn haut et court** to string sb up; *Fam Fig* **qu'il aille se faire p. ailleurs** let him go hang; *Fig* **je veux bien être pendu si...** I'll be hanged if...
2 *vi* to hang; *(cheveux)* to hang down; *(langue d'un animal)* to hang out; *(bras, jambes)* to dangle; **ton pan de chemise pend** your shirt's hanging out; *Fam* **ça lui pend au nez** he's/she's got it coming to him/her
3 se pendre *vpr* (**a**) *(se suicider)* to hang oneself (**b**) *(s'accrocher)* **se p. à qch** to hang from sth; **se p. au cou de qn** to throw one's arms round sb's neck

pendu, -e [pɑ̃dy] **1** *adj* (**a**) *(mort)* hanged (**b**) *(accroché)* hanging up; **p. à** hanging from; **p. aux jupes de sa mère** clinging to one's mother's skirts; *Fig* **avoir la langue bien pendue** to be a great talker; **elle est toujours pendue au téléphone** she's never off the phone
2 *nm,f* hanged man, *f* hanged woman; **le p.** *(jeu)* hangman

pendule [pɑ̃dyl] **1** *nf* clock; *Fig* **remettre les pendules à l'heure** to get things straight
2 *nm* pendulum

pendulette [pɑ̃dylɛt] *nf* small clock

pêne [pɛn] *nm* bolt

pénétrant, -e [penetrɑ̃, -ɑ̃t] *adj (vent, froid)* piercing; *(pluie)* soaking; *(odeur, regard, esprit)* penetrating

pénétration [penetrasjɔ̃] *nf* penetration

pénétré, -e [penetre] *adj (air, ton)* earnest; **p. d'un sentiment/d'une idée** imbued with a feeling/an idea; **il est p. de son importance** he's full of his own importance

pénétrer [34] [penetre] **1** *vi* to penetrate; **p. dans une maison** to get into a house
2 *vt* (**a**) *(sujet: balle)* to penetrate; *(sujet: liquide)* to soak into; *Fig (pensée, intentions)* to fathom; *(marché)* to penetrate (**b**) *(sexuellement)* to penetrate
3 se pénétrer *vpr* **se p. d'une idée** to become convinced of an idea

pénible [penibl] *adj* (**a**) *(tâche, voyage, vie)* hard; *(hiver, froid)* severe (**b**) *(spectacle, nouvelles)* painful (**c**) *Fam (personne)* **ce qu'il est p.!** he's such a pain!

péniblement [peniblǝmɑ̃] *adv* with difficulty; **avancer** *ou* **marcher p.** to struggle along

péniche [peniʃ] *nf* barge

pénicilline [penisilin] *nf* penicillin

péninsule [penɛ̃syl] *nf* peninsula; **la p. Ibérique** the Iberian Peninsula

pénis [penis] *nm* penis

pénitence [penitɑ̃s] *nf* (**a**) *Rel (repentir)* penitence; *(peine)* penance; **faire p.** to repent (**b**) *(punition)* punishment; **mettre un enfant en p.** to punish a child

pénitencier [penitɑ̃sje] *nm* prison, *Am* penitentiary

pénitent, -e [penitɑ̃, -ɑ̃t] *adj & nm,f* penitent

pénitentiaire [penitɑ̃sjɛr] *adj* prison

penne [pɛn] *nmpl (pâtes)* penne

Pennsylvanie [pɛnsilvani] *nf* **la P.** Pennsylvania

pénombre [penɔ̃br] *nf* half-light

pensable [pɑ̃sabl] *adj* **ce n'est pas p.** it's unthinkable

pensant, -e [pɑ̃sɑ̃, -ɑ̃t] *adj* thinking; **mal p.** unorthodox

pense-bête *(pl* pense-bêtes) [pɑ̃sbɛt] *nm* reminder

pensée¹ [pɑ̃se] *nf (fleur)* pansy

pensée² *nf (idée)* thought; *(activité)* thinking; **perdu dans ses pensées** lost in thought; **deviner les pensées de qn** to guess what sb is thinking; **dire le fond de sa p.** to say what one really thinks; **à la p. des vacances,...** at the thought of the *Br* holidays *or Am* vacation,...; **la seule p. de ce repas me met l'eau à la bouche** just thinking about this meal makes my mouth water; **la p. marxiste/bouddhiste** Marxist/Buddhist thought *or* thinking; **je suis avec vous en p. ou par la p.** you're in my thoughts; **avoir une p. pour qn** to think of sb

penser [pɑ̃se] **1** *vi* (**a**) *(songer, réfléchir)* to think; **p. à qn/qch** to think of *or* about sb/sth; **pensez-vous!** what an idea!; **vous n'y pensez pas!** you're not serious!; **n'y pensons plus** let's forget (about) it; **ce n'est même pas la peine d'y p.** it's not even worth thinking about; **ah, j'y pense!** by the way!; **rien que d'y p., ça me donne des frissons** just thinking about it gives me the shivers; **elle l'a fait sans p. à mal** she didn't mean any harm by it (**b**) *(se souvenir)* **p. à faire qch** to remember to do sth; **fais-moi p. à vérifier que...** remind me to check that...; **elle me fait p. à ma sœur** she reminds me of my sister

2 *vt* (**a**) *(estimer)* to think; **c'est bien ce que je pensais** I thought as much; **je pense que oui/non** I think/ don't think so; *Fam* **pensez si j'étais furieux** you can imagine how angry I was; **p. du bien/du mal de qn** to think a lot/not to think much of sb (**b**) **p. faire qch** *(espérer)* to hope to do sth; *(avoir l'intention)* to be thinking of doing sth (**c**) *(croire à)* to mean; **elle ne pense pas ce qu'elle dit** she doesn't mean what she says (**d**) *(concevoir)* **c'est bien/mal pensé** it's well/ badly thought out

penseur, -euse [pɑ̃sœr, -øz] *nm,f* thinker

pensif, -ive [pɑ̃sif, -iv] *adj* pensive, thoughtful; **d'un air p.** thoughtfully

pension [pɑ̃sjɔ̃] *nf* (**a**) *(allocation)* pension; **p. alimentaire** maintenance, alimony; **p. de retraite** (retirement *or* old age) pension (**b**) *(pensionnat)* boarding school; **mettre un enfant en p.** to send a child to boarding school (**c**) *(hôtel)* **p. (de famille)** boarding house; **être en p. chez qn** to board with sb; **prendre qn en p.** to take sb in as a lodger; **p. complète** *Br* full board, *Am* American plan (**d**) *Belg (cessation d'activité)* retirement; **l'âge de la p.** retirement age

pensionnaire [pɑ̃sjɔnɛr] *nmf (dans une pension de famille, à l'école)* boarder; *(dans une maison privée)* lodger; *Fam (d'une prison)* inmate

pensionnat [pɑ̃sjɔna] *nm* boarding school

pensionné, -e [pɑ̃sjɔne] *nm,f* pensioner

pensionner [pɑ̃sjɔne] **1** *vt* to pension **2** *vi Can (être en pension)* to be a boarder

pensivement [pɑ̃sivmɑ̃] *adv* thoughtfully, pensively

pensum [pɛ̃sɔm] *nm* (**a**) *(travail ennuyeux)* chore (**b**) *Vieilli Scol* imposition

pentagone [pɛ̃tagɔn] *nm* (**a**) *(figure)* pentagon (**b**) **le P.** *(aux États-Unis)* the Pentagon

pente [pɑ̃t] *nf* slope; **en p.** sloping; *Fig* **être sur une mauvaise p.** to be going downhill; *Fig* **remonter la p.** to get back on one's feet

Pentecôte [pɑ̃tkot] *nf Rel* Pentecost; *(jours fériés)* Whit(sun)

pentu, -e [pɑ̃ty] *adj* sloping

pénultième [penyltjɛm] *adj & nf* penultimate

pénurie [penyri] *nf* shortage, scarcity

people [pipɔl] *Fam* **1** *adj inv* **la presse p.** the celebrity press **2** *nmpl* **les p.** celebrities, celebs

PEP [pɛp] *nm Fin (abrév* **plan d'épargne populaire)** = personal pension plan

pépé [pepe] *nm (grand-père)* grandpa, grandad; *Fam (vieux monsieur)* grandad

pépée [pepe] *nf Fam Br* bird, *Am* chick

pépère [pepɛr] *Fam* **1** *adj (endroit)* quiet; *(travail)* cushy; **un petit coin p.** a nice quiet little spot; **être p.** *(dans une situation confortable)* to have it easy **2** *nm* (**a**) **c'est un gros p.** *(enfant)* he's a chubby little fellow (**b**) *(grand-père)* grandad

pépie [pepi] *nf Fam* **avoir la p.** to be parched

pépiement [pepimɑ̃] *nm* cheeping, chirping

pépier [66] [pepje] *vi* to cheep, to chirp

pépin [pepɛ̃] *nm* (**a**) *(de fruit)* seed, *Br* pip; **sans pépins** seedless (**b**) *Fam (ennui)* hitch; **avoir un p.** to have a problem (**c**) *Fam (parapluie)* umbrella, *Br* brolly

pépinière [pepinjɛr] *nf* (**a**) *(d'arbustes)* nursery (**b**) *Fig* training ground (**de** for)

pépite [pepit] *nf (d'or)* nugget; **pépites de chocolat** chocolate chips

peps [pɛps] *nm Fam* energy, get-up-and-go; **avoir du p.** to have plenty of get-up-and-go, to be full of life

péquenaud, -e [pekno, -od] *nm,f Fam* yokel, *Am* hick

péquiste [pekist] **1** *adj* of the Parti Québécois **2** *nmf (membre)* member of the Parti Québécois; *(partisan)* supporter of the Parti Québécois

percale [pɛrkal] *nf* percale

perçant, -e [pɛrsɑ̃, -ɑ̃t] *adj (regard, cri)* piercing; *(voix)* penetrating; *(vue)* sharp

percée [pɛrse] *nf* (**a**) *(ouverture)* opening (**b**) *Mil, Sport & Fig* breakthrough

percement [pɛrsəmɑ̃] *nm (d'un trou, d'un passage, d'un tunnel)* boring; *(d'une avenue)* opening; *(d'un canal)* cutting

perce-neige [pɛrsənɛʒ] *nm ou nf inv* snowdrop

perce-oreille *(pl* perce-oreilles) [pɛrsɔrɛj] *nm* earwig

percepteur [pɛrsɛptœr] *nm* (**a**) *(receveur des impôts)* tax collector (**b**) *Belg (receveur des postes)* postmaster, *f* postmistress

perceptible [pɛrsɛptibl] *adj* (**a**) *(que l'on peut percevoir)* perceptible (**b**) *(impôt)* collectable

perception [pɛrsɛpsjɔ̃] *nf* (**a**) *(par les sens)* perception (**b**) *(d'impôts, de droits, de loyer)* collection (**c**) *(bureau)* tax office
percer [16] [pɛrse] **1** *vt* (**a**) *(transpercer) (corps, surface, armure)* to pierce; *(abcès)* to lance; **le soleil perce les nuages** the sun's breaking through the clouds (**b**) *(découvrir) (complot, secret)* to uncover; *(mystère, énigme)* to solve; **p. qch à jour** to see through sth (**c**) *(trouer)* to make a hole in; *(trou)* to make; *(avec une perceuse)* to drill, to bore; *(tunnel)* to bore; *(avenue)* to open; *(canal)* to cut; *(coffre-fort)* to crack; **se faire p. les oreilles** to have one's ears pierced
2 *vi* (**a**) *(apparaître) (soleil)* to break through; *(dents)* to come through (**b**) *(être révélé)* to get out; **rien n'a percé de leur entretien** nothing's got out about their meeting (**c**) *(devenir célèbre)* to make a name for oneself
perceuse [pɛrsøz] *nf* drill
percevable [pɛrsəvabl] *adj (impôt)* collectable
percevoir [60] [pɛrsəvwar] *vt* (**a**) *(par les sens, l'intellect)* to perceive; *(bruit)* to hear; **être bien/mal perçu** to be well/badly received (**b**) *(impôts, loyers)* to collect; *(intérêts, allocation, commission)* to receive
perchaude [pɛrʃod] *nf Can* yellow perch
perche¹ [pɛrʃ] *nf (tige)* pole; *(pour micro)* boom; *Fam Fig* **une grande p.** *(personne)* a beanpole; *Fig* **tendre la p. à qn** to throw sb a line
perche² *nf (poisson)* perch
percher [pɛrʃe] **1** *vi* (**a**) *(oiseaux)* to perch; *(poules)* to roost (**b**) *Fam (personne)* to live
2 *vt Fam (mettre)* to perch
3 se percher *vpr* to perch
percheron [pɛrʃərɔ̃] *nm* percheron
perchiste [pɛrʃist] *nmf* (**a**) *Sport* pole vaulter (**b**) *Cin & TV* boom operator
perchman [pɛrʃman] *nm* (**a**) *(au ski)* ski-lift attendant (**b**) *Cin & TV* boom operator
perchoir [pɛrʃwar] *nm aussi Fig* perch; *(pour les volailles)* roost
perclus, -e [pɛrkly, -yz] *adj* **p. de rhumatismes** crippled with rheumatism
percolateur [pɛrkɔlatœr] *nm* percolator
perçu, -e *pp de* **percevoir**
percussion [pɛrkysjɔ̃] *nf* percussion
percussionniste [pɛrkysjɔnist] *nmf* percussionist
percutant, -e [pɛrkytɑ̃, -ɑ̃t] *adj* forceful
percuter [pɛrkyte] **1** *vt* to crash into
2 *vi* (**a**) **p. contre qch** to crash into sth (**b**) *Fam (comprendre)* to catch on, to get it
3 se percuter *vpr* to crash into each other
percuteur [pɛrkytœr] *nm* firing pin
perdant, -e [pɛrdɑ̃, -ɑ̃t] **1** *adj* losing; **partir p.** to start out with low hopes
2 *nm,f* loser; **être bon/mauvais p.** to be a good/bad loser
perdition [pɛrdisjɔ̃] *nf* (**a**) *Rel* perdition; **lieu de p.** den of iniquity (**b**) *Naut* **navire en p.** ship in distress; *Fig* **entreprise en p.** company in difficulties
perdre [pɛrdr] **1** *vt* (**a**) *(égarer)* to lose; *(habitude)* to get out of; *(occasion)* to miss; *aussi Fig* **p. qn/qch de vue** to lose sight of sb/sth; **p. de son assurance/sa souplesse** to lose some of one's confidence/suppleness; **il perd son pantalon** his *Br* trousers *or Am* pants keep slipping down; **tu ne perds rien pour attendre!** just you wait!; **p. son temps** to waste one's time; **il n'y a pas de temps à p.** there's no time to lose; **tu n'as**

rien perdu en ne venant pas you didn't miss anything by not coming; **y p.** *(dans un échange)* to lose out; *(dans une vente)* to make a loss; **p. au change** to lose out on the deal (**b**) *(ruiner)* **ta générosité/ton ambition te perdra** your generosity/ambition will be the ruin of you
2 se perdre *vpr* (**a**) *(s'égarer)* to get lost; *Fig* **se p. de vue** to lose touch with each other; **se p. en conjectures/dans les détails** to get lost in conjecture/details; *Fam* **je m'y perds** I'm lost (**b**) *(être gâché) (nourriture, récolte)* to go to waste; **il y a des claques qui se perdent** you/they/*etc* need a good slap (**c**) *(disparaître) (usage, tradition)* to die out
perdreau, -x [pɛrdro] *nm* young partridge
perdrix [pɛrdri] *nf* partridge; **p. des neiges** ptarmigan
perdu, -e [pɛrdy] *adj (égaré)* lost; *(vêtement, récolte)* ruined; *(endroit)* out-of-the-way; *(emballage)* non-returnable; **p. dans ses pensées** lost in thought; **il est p.** *(d'un malade)* there's no hope for him; **à mes moments perdus, à mes heures perdues** in my spare time; **un de p., dix de retrouvés** there are plenty more fish in the sea
perdurer [pɛrdyre] *vi Litt* to continue
père [pɛr] *nm* (**a**) *(géniteur)* father; **p. de famille** father; **de p. en fils** from father to son; *Prov* **tel p., tel fils** like father, like son; **nos pères** our forefathers, our ancestors; *Fig* **le p. du cubisme** the father of cubism; *Fam* **(mon) petit p.** *Br* old chap, *Am* old buddy; **le p. Paul** old Paul; **le p. Noël** Father Christmas, Santa Claus; *aussi Fam Fig* **croire au p. Noël** to believe in Father Christmas (**b**) *Rel* father; **le (révérend) p. Martin** Father Martin; **mon p.** father
pérégrinations [peregrinasjɔ̃] *nfpl* peregrinations
péremption [perɑ̃psjɔ̃] *nf* **date de p.** use-by date
péremptoire [perɑ̃ptwar] *adj* peremptory
pérennité [perenite] *nf* permanence
péréquation [perekwasjɔ̃] *nf* equalization
perestroïka [perɛstrɔika] *nf* perestroika
perfectif, -ive [pɛrfɛktif, -iv] *adj & nm* perfective
perfection [pɛrfɛksjɔ̃] *nf* perfection; **à la p.** to perfection
perfectionné, -e [pɛrfɛksjɔne] *adj* sophisticated
perfectionnement [pɛrfɛksjɔnmɑ̃] *nm* (**a**) *(action)* perfecting, improving; *(formation)* further training; **cours de p.** proficiency course (**b**) *(résultat)* improvement; **apporter des perfectionnements à qch** to improve sth
perfectionner [pɛrfɛksjɔne] **1** *vt* to perfect, to improve
2 se perfectionner *vpr* to improve; **se p. en allemand** to improve one's German
perfectionnisme [pɛrfɛksjɔnism] *nm* perfectionism
perfectionniste [pɛrfɛksjɔnist] **1** *adj* **être p.** to be a perfectionist
2 *nmf* perfectionist
perfide [pɛrfid] *adj* perfidious; **la p. Albion** perfidious Albion
perfidie [pɛrfidi] *nf Litt* (**a**) *(déloyauté)* perfidiousness (**b**) *(action)* perfidy
perforation [pɛrfɔrasjɔ̃] *nf* (**a**) *(action)* perforation; *Ordinat* punching (**b**) *(trou) & Méd* perforation; *Ordinat* punch (hole)
perforatrice [pɛrfɔratris] *nf (pour papier)* (hole) punch
perforer [pɛrfɔre] *vt* (**a**) *(papier, organe)* to perforate; *(cuir)* to punch; *(sujet: missile)* to pierce (**b**) *Ordinat*

(carte, bande) to punch; **bande perforée** punched tape; **carte perforée** punch card
perforeuse [pɛrfɔrøz] nf hole punch
performance [pɛrfɔrmɑ̃s] nf (en sport) performance; Fig (exploit) feat, achievement; **performances** (d'une voiture, d'un ordinateur) performance
performant, -e [pɛrfɔrmɑ̃, -ɑ̃t] adj (machine) high-performance; (personne) highly efficient
perfusion [pɛrfyzjɔ̃] nf Méd drip; **être sous p.** to be on a drip
péricliter [periklite] vi to collapse
péridurale [peridyral] nf Méd epidural; **accoucher sous p.** to give birth under an epidural
Périgord [perigɔr] nm **le P.** Périgord
périgourdin, -e [perigurdɛ̃, -in] **1** adj of Périgord
2 nm,f **P.** person from Périgord
péril [peril] nm peril, danger; **au p. de sa vie** at the risk of one's life; **en p.** in peril; **mettre qch en p.** to imperil or endanger sth; **à ses risques et périls** at one's own risk; **il n'y a pas p. en la demeure** it's not a matter of urgency
périlleux, -euse [perijø, -øz] adj perilous, dangerous
périmé, -e [perime] adj (billet, passeport, coupon) out of date; (nourriture, article) past its sell-by date; (idée, conception) outdated
périmètre [perimɛtr] nm perimeter; **dans un p. de 50 km** within a 50-km radius
périnée [perine] nm perineum
période [perjɔd] nf period; **p. bleue/blanche/rouge** (de trains) = off-peak/peak/high-peak periods of rail schedules during which ticket prices vary accordingly; **p. d'essai** trial period
périodique [perjɔdik] **1** adj (**a**) (cyclique) periodic (**b**) (hygiénique) **serviette p.** sanitary Br towel or Am napkin
2 nm periodical
périodiquement [perjɔdikmɑ̃] adv periodically
péripétie [peripesi] nf Litt event
périph [perif] nm Fam Br ring road, Am beltway
périphérie [periferi] nf periphery; (banlieue) outskirts; **à la p. des grandes villes** on the outskirts of cities
périphérique [periferik] **1** adj aussi Ordinat peripheral; **boulevard p.** Br ring road, Am beltway; **radio ou station p.** = private radio station broadcasting from outside national territory
2 nm (**a**) (route) Br ring road, Am beltway (**b**) Ordinat peripheral; **p. d'impression** printer peripheral; **p. de sortie** output device
périphrase [perifraz] nf circumlocution, Spéc periphrasis
périple [peripl] nm (voyage) tour, journey; (par mer) voyage
périr [perir] vi to perish
périscolaire [periskɔlɛr] adj extracurricular
périscope [periskɔp] nm periscope
périssable [perisabl] adj (denrées, produits) perishable; Fig (sentiment) transient
péristyle [peristil] nm peristyle
péritonite [peritɔnit] nf peritonitis
perle [pɛrl] nf (**a**) (naturelle) pearl; (de verre, de métal) & Fig (de sueur) bead; **p. fine/de culture** real/cultured pearl; Fig **jeter des perles aux pourceaux** to cast pearls before swine; Fam Fig **enfiler des perles** to waste one's time on trivia (**b**) (personne) gem, treasure; **c'est la p. des sœurs** she's the best sister in

the world; **ma bonne est une p. rare** my maid is a real gem (**c**) Hum (erreur) howler (**d**) Can (prunelle) pupil (of the eye)
perlé, -e [pɛrle] adj (orné de perles) set with pearls; (de perles de verre) beaded; **grève perlée** Br go-slow, Am slowdown
perler [pɛrle] vi (larmes, sueur) to form in beads
perlimpinpin [pɛrlɛ̃pɛ̃pɛ̃] nm **poudre de p.** magic powder
perm [pɛrm] nf Fam (**a**) Mil leave; **en p.** on leave (**b**) Scol study room; **avoir deux heures de p.** to have two hours' private study
permanence [pɛrmanɑ̃s] nf (**a**) (continuité) permanence; **en p.** permanently (**b**) (lieu) duty office; **la p. est assurée le dimanche** there's someone on duty on Sundays; **être de p.** to be on duty (**c**) Scol study room, Am study hall; **avoir deux heures de p.** to have two hours' private study or Am study hall
permanent, -e [pɛrmanɑ̃, -ɑ̃t] **1** adj (commission) standing; (spectacle) continuous; (tribunal) permanent; **cinéma p.** Br cinema or Am movie theatre with continuous showings
2 nm,f Pol official
3 nf permanente perm; **se faire faire une permanente** to have a perm, to have one's hair permed
perméable [pɛrmeabl] adj permeable (**à** to); Fig susceptible (**à** to)
permettre [47] [pɛrmɛtr] **1** vt (**a**) (autoriser) to allow, to permit; **p. à qn de faire qch** to allow or permit sb to do sth; **p. qch à qn** to allow sb sth; **permettez-moi de...** allow me to...; **permettez!** excuse me!; **vous permettez?** may I?; **il se croit tout permis** he thinks he can do whatever he likes; Fam **il est égoïste comme ce n'est pas permis!** he's incredibly selfish! (**b**) (rendre possible) to allow; **p. à qn de faire qch** to allow sb to do sth; **mes moyens ne me le permettent pas** I can't afford it; **si le temps le permet** weather permitting; **si mon emploi du temps le permet** if my schedule allows it
2 se permettre vpr se **p. qch** to allow oneself sth; **se p. de faire qch** to take the liberty of doing sth; **je me permets d'attirer votre attention sur...** may I draw your attention to...
permis, -e [pɛrmi, -iz] **1** pp de **permettre**
2 adj allowed, permitted
3 nm permit, licence; **p. de chasse** hunting permit; **p. de conduire** driving licence, Am driver's license; (examen) driving test; **p. de construire** planning permission; **p. de séjour** residence permit; **p. de travail** work permit
permissif, -ive [pɛrmisif, -iv] adj permissive
permission [pɛrmisjɔ̃] nf (**a**) (autorisation) permission; **demander/donner la p. à qn de faire qch** to ask/give sb permission to do sth (**b**) Mil (congé) leave; (certificat) pass; **en p.** on leave
permissionnaire [pɛrmisjɔnɛr] nmf person on leave
permutation [pɛrmytasjɔ̃] nf (**a**) (échange) exchange of posts; Mil transfer (**b**) (de lettres, de chiffres) transposition; Math permutation
permuter [pɛrmyte] **1** vt (lettres, chiffres) to transpose; Math to permute
2 vi to exchange posts
pernicieux, -euse [pɛrnisjø, -øz] adj pernicious
péroné [perone] nm fibula
péroraison [perɔrɛzɔ̃] nf peroration
pérorer [perɔre] vi Péj to hold forth

Pérou [peru] *nm* **le P.** Peru; *Fig* **ce n'est pas le P.** *(pas extraordinaire)* it's no great shakes; *(peu d'argent)* it's not a fortune

peroxyde [pɛrɔksid] *nm* peroxide

perpendiculaire [pɛrpãdikylɛr] *adj & nf* perpendicular (**à** to)

perpète [pɛrpɛt] *nf Fam* (**a**) *(perpétuité)* **condamné à p.** sentenced to life; **prendre p.** to get life; **jusqu'à p.** for ever (**b**) *(distance)* **à p.** miles away

perpétrer [34] [pɛrpetre] *vt* to perpetrate

perpette [pɛrpɛt] = **perpète**

perpétuel, -elle [pɛrpetɥɛl] *adj* perpetual; *(secrétaire, membre)* permanent

perpétuellement [pɛrpetɥɛlmã] *adv* perpetually

perpétuer [pɛrpetɥe] **1** *vt* to perpetuate
2 se perpétuer *vpr* to be perpetuated

perpétuité [pɛrpetɥite] *nf* perpetuity; **à p.** *(concession)* in perpetuity; *(emprisonnement)* for life; **être condamné (à la réclusion) à p.** to be sentenced to life (imprisonment)

perplexe [pɛrplɛks] *adj* perplexed, puzzled; **laisser qn p.** to perplex *or* puzzle sb

perplexité [pɛrplɛksite] *nf* perplexity

perquisition [pɛrkizisjɔ̃] *nf* search; **faire une p.** to make a search

perquisitionner [pɛrkizisjɔne] **1** *vi* to make a search
2 *vt* to search

perron [perɔ̃] *nm* steps *(leading to a building)*

perroquet [pɛrɔkɛ] *nm* (**a**) *(oiseau)* parrot; **p. de mer** puffin (**b**) *(voile)* topgallant

perruche [peryʃ] *nf* budgerigar

perruque [peryk] *nf* wig

perruquier, -ère [perykje, -ɛr] *nm,f* wig maker

pers [pɛr] *adj m Litt* blue-green

persan, -e [pɛrsã, -an] **1** *adj* Persian
2 *nm,f* **P.** Persian
3 *nm (langue)* Persian

perse [pɛrs] **1** *adj* Persian
2 *nmf* **P.** Persian
3 *nm (langue)* Persian
4 *nf* **la P.** Persia

persécuter [pɛrsekyte] *vt* to persecute

persécution [pɛrsekysjɔ̃] *nf* persecution; **manie** *ou* **délire de p.** persecution mania

persévérance [pɛrseverãs] *nf* perseverance

persévérant, -e [pɛrseverã, -ãt] *adj* persevering

persévérer [34] [pɛrsevere] *vi* to persevere (**dans** in)

persienne [pɛrsjɛn] *nf* shutter

persiflage [pɛrsiflaʒ] *nm (propos)* taunts, scoffs

persifler [pɛrsifle] *vt* to mock, to ridicule

persil [pɛrsi] *nm* parsley

persillé, -e [pɛrsije] *adj (viande)* marbled; *(assaisonné de persil)* sprinkled with chopped parsley; *(fromage)* veined

Persique [pɛrsik] *adj voir* **golfe**

persistance [pɛrsistãs] *nf* persistence (**à faire qch** in doing sth); **avec p.** persistently; **p. dans le mensonge** persistent lying

persistant, -e [pɛrsistã, -ãt] *adj* persistent; **à feuillage p.** evergreen

persister [pɛrsiste] *vi* (**a**) *(persévérer)* to persist (**dans** in); **p. à faire qch** to persist in doing sth (**b**) *(continuer)* to persist; **il persiste un doute** there remains a doubt

perso [pɛrso] *adj Fam (abrév* **personnel**) personal, private

personnage [pɛrsɔnaʒ] *nm* (**a**) *(de fiction)* character; *aussi Fig* **jouer un p.** to play a part *or* a role (**b**) *(individu)* character (**c**) *(image publique)* image, persona (**d**) *(personnalité)* important person; **p. célèbre** celebrity; **p. officiel** VIP; **un grand p. de l'État** a state dignitary

personnalisation [pɛrsɔnalizasjɔ̃] *nf* personalization

personnalisé, -e [pɛrsɔnalize] *adj* personalized; *(voiture, crédit)* customized

personnaliser [pɛrsɔnalize] *vt* to personalize; *(voiture)* to customize

personnalité [pɛrsɔnalite] *nf* (**a**) *(caractère)* personality; **avoir de la p.** to have lots of personality; **manquer de p.** to have no personality (**b**) *(personnage important)* personality (**c**) *Jur* **p. juridique** legal personality

personne [pɛrsɔn] **1** *nf* (**a**) *(individu)* person; **deux personnes** two people; **les personnes intéressées** those interested; **les personnes âgées** the elderly, elderly people; **une grande p.** a grown-up; **une jeune p.** a young lady (**b**) *(soi-même)* **en p.** in person, personally; **être bien de sa p.** to be good-looking; **être satisfait de sa petite p.** to be pleased with oneself (**c**) *Jur* **p. morale** legal entity; **p. physique** natural person (**d**) *Gram* person
2 *pron indéfini* (**a**) *(quiconque)* anyone, anybody; **elle le sait mieux que p.** she knows better than anyone (**b**) *(aucune personne)* no one, nobody; **p. n'est venu** no one has come; **il n'y a p. de blessé** no one has been injured; **p. d'autre** no one else, nobody else; **je n'y suis pour p.** I'm not at home to anyone; **ne connaissez-vous p. qui puisse nous aider?** don't you know anyone who could help us?; *Fam* **dès qu'il s'agit de travailler, il n'y a plus p.** as soon as there's work to be done, you can't see anyone for dust

personnel, -elle [pɛrsɔnɛl] **1** *adj* (**a**) *(à soi)* personal (**b**) *(égoïste)* selfish; *(intérêt)* vested
2 *nm (d'une firme, d'une école)* staff; *(d'une usine)* workforce; *(dans l'armée)* personnel; **faire partie du p. de...** to be on the staff of...; **manquer de p.** to be understaffed; **un membre du p.** a member of staff; **p. de bureau** office *or* clerical staff; **p. navigant** flight personnel; **p. au sol** ground personnel

personnellement [pɛrsɔnɛlmã] *adv* personally

personnifier [66] [pɛrsɔnifje] *vt* to personify; **il est la bêtise personnifiée** he's stupidity personified

perspective [pɛrspɛktiv] *nf* (**a**) *(de dessin)* perspective (**b**) *(idée)* prospect; **à la p. de faire qch** at the prospect of doing sth; **en p.** in prospect; **des perspectives de reprise** outlook for recovery; **des perspectives d'avenir** future prospects (**c**) *(point de vue)* viewpoint, point of view

perspicace [pɛrspikas] *adj* shrewd

perspicacité [pɛrspikasite] *nf* shrewdness

persuader [pɛrsɥade] **1** *vt* **p. qn (de qch)** to persuade *or* convince sb (of sth); **p. qn de faire qch** to persuade sb to do sth; **être persuadé de qch/que...** to be convinced of sth/that...
2 se persuader *vpr* **se p. de qch/que...** to convince oneself of sth/that...

persuasif, -ive [pɛrsɥazif, -iv] *adj* persuasive

persuasion [pɛrsɥazjɔ̃] *nf* persuasion

perte [pɛrt] *nf* (**a**) *(d'un objet, d'une personne, d'un procès)* loss; **de lourdes pertes en hommes et en matériel** heavy losses of men and equipment; **à p. de vue** as far as the eye can see; **vendre qch à p.** to sell sth at a loss; *aussi Fig* **passer qch par pertes et profits** to write sth off; **p. sèche** dead loss; **ce n'est pas une grosse p.** it's no great loss (**b**) *(gaspillage)* **une p. de temps** a waste of time; **en pure p.** to no purpose (**c**) *(déperdition)* loss; **être en p.** de vitesse to be losing speed; *Fig* to be running out of steam; **pertes blanches** vaginal discharge; **p. de chaleur** heat loss; **p. de connaissance** loss of consciousness; *Ordinat* **p. de données irréparable** irretrievable data loss (**d**) *(destruction)* ruin; **jurer la p. de qn** to swear to ruin sb; **courir à sa p.** to be heading for disaster

pertinemment [pɛrtinamɑ̃] *adv* **savoir qch p.** to know sth for a fact

pertinence [pɛrtinɑ̃s] *nf* pertinence, relevance

pertinent, -e [pɛrtinɑ̃, -ɑ̃t] *adj* pertinent, relevant

perturbant, -e [pɛrtyrbɑ̃, -ɑ̃t] *adj* disturbing, upsetting

perturbateur, -trice [pɛrtyrbatœr, -tris] **1** *adj* disruptive
  2 *nm,f* troublemaker

perturbation [pɛrtyrbasjɔ̃] *nf* disruption; **p. (atmosphérique)** (atmospheric) disturbance

perturber [pɛrtyrbe] *vt (services publics, circulation)* to disrupt; *(personne)* to perturb, to upset

péruvien, -enne [peryvjɛ̃, -ɛn] **1** *adj* Peruvian
  2 *nm,f* **P.** Peruvian

pervenche [pɛrvɑ̃ʃ] *nf* (**a**) *(plante)* periwinkle; **(bleu) p.** periwinkle blue (**b**) *Fam (contractuelle) Br* (female) traffic warden, *Am* meter maid

pervers, -e [pɛrvɛr, -ɛrs] **1** *adj* perverse
  2 *nm,f* pervert

perversion [pɛrvɛrsjɔ̃] *nf* perversion

perversité [pɛrvɛrsite] *nf* perversity

perverti, -e [pɛrvɛrti] **1** *adj* perverted
  2 *nm,f* pervert

pervertir [pɛrvɛrtir] **1** *vt* to pervert
  2 se pervertir *vpr* to become perverted

pesamment [pəzamɑ̃] *adv* heavily

pesant, -e [pəzɑ̃, -ɑ̃t] **1** *adj* heavy; *(sommeil)* deep; *(ambiance)* oppressive; **marcher à pas pesants** to walk heavily
  2 *nm* **valoir son p. d'or** to be worth one's/its weight in gold

pesanteur [pəzɑ̃tœr] *nf* (**a**) *(attraction terrestre)* gravity (**b**) *(lourdeur)* heaviness

pesée [pəze] *nf* (**a**) *(pour connaître le poids)* weighing; *(de boxeur, de chevaux)* weigh-in (**b**) *(pression)* force

pèse-lettre (*pl* pèse-lettres) [pɛzlɛtr] *nm* letter scales

pèse-personne (*pl* pèse-personnes) [pɛzpɛrsɔn] *nm* (bathroom) scales

peser [46] [pəze] **1** *vt* to weigh; *Fig* **p. le pour et le contre** to weigh up the pros and cons; *Fig* **p. ses mots** to weigh one's words; *Fig* **tout bien pesé** all things considered
  2 *vi (être lourd)* to be heavy; **p. 2 kilos** to weigh 2 kilos; **p. sur qch** to press on sth; *Fig* **p. sur la conscience** to lie heavy on one's conscience; *Fig* **p. sur l'estomac** to lie heavy on the stomach; *Fig* **p. sur** *ou* **dans une décision** to carry weight in a decision; **la solitude me pèse** the solitude is getting me down
  3 se peser *vpr* to weigh oneself

peseta [pezeta] *nf* peseta

peso [pɛzo] *nm* peso

pessimisme [pesimism] *nm* pessimism

pessimiste [pesimist] **1** *adj* pessimistic
  2 *nmf* pessimist

peste [pɛst] *nf* (**a**) *(maladie)* plague; *Fig* **je me méfie de lui comme de la p.** I don't trust him as far as I could throw him; **la p. bubonique** the bubonic plague; *Hist* **la p. noire** the Black Death (**b**) *Fig & Péj (personne)* pest

pester [pɛste] *vi* **p. contre qn/qch** to curse sb/sth

pesticide [pɛstisid] **1** *adj* pesticidal
  2 *nm* pesticide

pestiféré, -e [pɛstifere] **1** *adj* plague-stricken
  2 *nm,f* plague victim; **traiter qn comme un p.** to treat sb like a pariah *or* a leper

pestilentiel, -elle [pɛstilɑ̃sjɛl] *adj* stinking

pet [pɛ] *nm Fam (gaz)* fart; **lâcher un p.** to fart; **ça ne vaut pas un p. (de lapin)** it isn't worth a monkey's fart; **il a toujours un p. de travers** there's always something up with him

pétale [petal] *nm* petal

pétanque [petɑ̃k] *nf* ≃ bowls *(played in the South of France)*

Pétanque

Originally invented in the South of France, where it has become a local institution, this bowling game is equally popular with tourists. The game, which requires two teams and is played up to a score of thirteen points, is played outdoors on a flat sandy or earth surface. Each team consists of two to three players, each of whom has three steel "boules". Each player tosses or rolls their "boule" so that it ends up as near as possible to the "cochonnet" (a small wooden ball thrown from a distance of 6 to 10 metres), at the same time trying to hit the other team's "boules" so as to scatter them. Players take turns, and whoever ends up closest to the "cochonnet" when all balls are played, wins.

pétant, -e [petɑ̃, -ɑ̃t] *adj Fam* **à une heure pétante** at one o'clock on the dot

Pétaouchnock [petauʃnɔk] *n Fam* **ils l'ont envoyé à P.** they sent him to some place in the back of beyond *or* to Timbuktu

pétarade [petarad] *nf* (**a**) *(de feux d'artifice, d'armes à feu)* crackling (**b**) *(de véhicule)* backfiring

pétarader [petarade] *vi* (**a**) *(feux d'artifice, armes à feu)* to crackle (**b**) *(véhicule)* to backfire

pétard [petar] *nm* (**a**) *(feu d'artifice)* (fire)cracker, *Br* banger (**b**) *Fam (pistolet)* shooter (**c**) *Fam (cigarette de cannabis)* joint (**d**) *Fam (postérieur)* butt, *Br* bum (**e**) *Fam* **être en p. (contre)** to be raging (at)

pétasse [petas] *nf Vulg* slut

pétaudière [petodjɛr] *nf Fam* bedlam

pété, -e [pete] *adj Fam (ivre) Br* pissed, *Am* wasted

péter [34] [pete] *Fam* **1** *vi* (**a**) *(bois qui brûle)* to crackle; *(bouchon)* to pop; *(personne)* to fart; *Vulg* **il pète plus haut que son cul** he thinks he's God's gift to humanity (**b**) *(exploser)* to blow up; *Fig* **je veux que ça pète!** get your finger out! (**c**) *(casser)* to bust
  2 *vt* (**a**) **p. le feu** *ou* **la forme** to be full of beans; **p. les plombs** to blow one's top (**b**) *(casser)* to bust
  3 se péter *vpr (se casser)* to bust; **se p. la gueule** to get wasted; *Can* **se p. les bretelles** to be full of oneself

pète-sec [pɛtsɛk] *adj inv Fam* curt

péteux, -euse [petø, -øz] *Fam Péj* **1** *adj (honteux)* sheepish
  2 *nm,f* (**a**) *(lâche)* chicken (**b**) *(prétentieux)* upstart

pétillant, -e [petijɑ̃, -ɑ̃t] *adj (vin, yeux)* sparkling; *(eau)* fizzy

pétillement [petijmɑ̃] *nm (du vin, des yeux)* sparkling
pétiller [petije] *vi (vin, yeux)* to sparkle; **p. d'intelligence** *(yeux)* to sparkle with intelligence
petit, -e [pəti, -it] **1** *adj* (**a**) *(de taille réduite)* small, little; *(distance, séjour)* short; *(somme)* small; **tout p.** tiny; **un p. moment** a little while; **une petite demi-heure** barely half an hour; *Fig* **se faire tout p.** to make oneself as inconspicuous as possible; **petites et moyennes entreprises** small and medium-sized businesses; *Can* **p. suisse** chipmunk (**b**) *(peu grave) (problème, erreur)* small; *(accident)* minor; *(rhume)* slight (**c**) *(jeune)* little, young; **mon p. frère** my little brother; **p. cousin** first cousin once removed; **un p. Anglais** an English boy (**d**) *(faible) (voix)* small; *(bruit)* little; **avoir une petite santé** to be delicate (**e**) *(de niveau inférieur) Scol* **les petites classes** the lower classes; **petite route** minor road; **p. commerçant/artisan** small trader/craftsman (**f**) *(pour insister)* little; **p. crétin/con!** little idiot/bastard!; **mon p. ange** my little angel; **je fumerais bien une petite cigarette** I'd love a cigarette; *Fam* **p. nom** first name (**g**) *(mesquin)* petty
2 *nm,f* (**a**) *(enfant)* (little) boy, *f* (little) girl; **les petits** the little ones; *Fam* **mon p.** my dear; **pauvre p.!** poor little thing! (**b**) *(en taille)* **les petits devant, les grands derrière** small people in front and the tall ones behind
3 *nm (d'un chien)* puppy; *(d'un chat)* kitten; **faire** *ou* **avoir des petits** to have puppies/kittens/*etc*; *Fam* **faire des petits** *(argent)* to multiply
4 *adv (écrire)* small; **p. à p.** little by little
petit-beurre *(pl* **petits-beurre**) [pətibœr] *nm* butter *Br* biscuit *or Am* cookie
petit-bourgeois, petite-bourgeoise *(mpl* **petits-bourgeois**, *fpl* **petites-bourgeoises**) [pətiburʒwa, pətitburʒwaz] *aussi Péj* **1** *adj* lower middle class
2 *nm,f* member of the lower middle class
petite-fille *(pl* **petites-filles**) [pətitfij] *nf* granddaughter
petitesse [pətitɛs] *nf (d'un objet)* smallness; *Péj (mesquinerie)* pettiness
petit-fils *(pl* **petits-fils**) [pətifis] *nm* grandson
pétition [petisjɔ̃] *nf* petition
petit-lait *(pl* **petits-laits**) [pətilɛ] *nm* whey; *Fam* **se boire comme du p.** to go down a treat; *Fig* **boire du p.** to lap it up
petit-nègre [pətinɛgr] *nm Fam (mauvais français)* pidgin French; **c'est du p.** *(mal écrit)* it's gibberish
petits-enfants [pətizɑ̃fɑ̃] *nmpl* grandchildren
petit-suisse *(pl* **petits-suisses**) [pətisɥis] *nm* = small dessert of thick fromage frais
pétoche [petɔʃ] *nf Fam* jitters; **avoir la p.** to have the jitters; **flanquer la p. à qn** to give sb the jitters
pétoire [petwar] *nf Fam (fusil)* popgun
pétri, -e [petri] *adj* **p. de qch** *(orgueil)* puffed up with sth; *(contradictions)* riddled with sth
pétrifier [66] [petrifje] *vt aussi Fig* to petrify
pétrin [petrɛ̃] *nm* kneading trough; *Fam* **être dans le p.** to be in a mess
pétrir [petrir] *vt (pâte à pain, argile)* to knead
pétrochimique [petroʃimik] *adj* petrochemical
pétrodollar [petrodɔlar] *nm Fin* petrodollar
pétrole [petrɔl] *nm* oil, petroleum
pétrolette [petrɔlɛt] *nf Fam* moped
pétrolier, -ère [petrɔlje, -ɛr] **1** *adj* **l'industrie pétrolière** the oil industry
2 *nm* (oil) tanker

pétrolifère [petrɔlifɛr] *adj* oil-bearing; **gisement p.** oilfield
pétulant, -e [petylɑ̃, -ɑ̃t] *adj* exuberant
pétunia [petynja] *nm* petunia
peu [pø] **1** *adv* (**a**) *(avec un verbe)* not much; **elle mange/parle p.** she doesn't eat/talk much (**b**) *(avec un adjectif ou un adverbe)* not very; **il a agi p. honorablement** he didn't behave very honourably; **très/trop p.** very/too little (**c**) *(avec un nom)* **p. de** *(temps, courage, vin)* little, not much; *(amis, lettres, illusions)* few, not many; **ne te fâche pas pour si p.** don't get angry over such a small thing; **c'est p. de chose** it's nothing; *Fam* **très p. pour moi!** not for me! (**d**) *(un petit nombre)* few; **p. ont compris** few (people) understood (**e**) *(indique la durée)* **sous p., avant p., d'ici p.** soon, shortly; **p. après** shortly afterwards; **depuis p.** lately, recently; **c'est ouvert depuis p.** it hasn't been open long; **j'ai manqué le train de p.** I (only) just missed the train; **il y a p.** not very long ago, recently; **p. à p.** little by little, gradually (**f**) **pour p. que** + *subjunctive* if by chance; **pour p. qu'il ait oublié la clé,...** if by chance he's forgotten the key,...
2 *nm* (**a**) *(petite quantité)* **le p. que je sais d'elle** the little I know about her; **le p. d'argent qu'il me reste** what little money I have left; **son p. d'instruction** what little education he/she has had (**b**) **un p.** a little *or* a bit; **un peu grand/ennuyeux** a little *or* a bit big/boring; **un p. de temps/sucre** a bit of *or* a little time/sugar; **je le connais un p.** I know him slightly *or* a little; **un p. plus/moins** a little *or* a bit more/less; **un tout petit p.** a tiny bit; **il est un p. artiste** he's a bit of an artist; **un p. plus et elle tombait** she very nearly fell; **pour un p. je l'aurais jeté dehors** I all but *or* I very nearly threw him out; **écoutez un p.** just listen; **viens un p. ici** come here a minute; *Fam* **tu ferais ça? – un p.!** you'd do that? – you bet! (**c**) *(de temps)* **un p.** a bit, a little while; **restez encore un p.** stay a bit longer, stay a little (while) longer
peuchère [pøʃɛr] *exclam* heavens!
peuh [pø] *exclam* bah!
peuplade [pœplad] *nf* tribe
peuple [pœpl] *nm* (**a**) *(nation)* people; **le p. français** the French people (**b**) *(citoyens)* people; **les gens du p.** ordinary people (**c**) *Fam (foule)* crowd
peuplé, -e [pœple] *adj* inhabited *(de* by); **très/peu p.** densely/sparsely populated
peuplement [pœpləmɑ̃] *nm (d'une région)* populating
peupler [pœple] **1** *vt* (**a**) *(installer une population dans)* to populate (**b**) *(habiter)* to inhabit; *Fig* **peuplé de qch** full of sth
2 **se peupler** *upr* to become populated
peuplier [pœplije] *nm* poplar
peur [pœr] *nf* fear; *(subite)* fright; **avoir p. (de)** to be afraid *or* frightened (of); *Fam* **avoir une p. bleue de qn/qch** to be scared stiff *or* to death of sb/sth; **faire p. à qn** to frighten *or* scare sb; **par p. de qch** through fear of sth; **de p. de faire qch** for fear of doing sth; **de p. qu'il ne le fasse** for fear that he would do it; **j'ai bien p. qu'il (ne) soit en retard** I'm very much afraid he's going to be late
peureux, -euse [pœrø, -øz] **1** *adj* fearful
2 *nm,f* fearful person
peut *voir* **pouvoir**²
peut-être [pøtɛtr] *adv* perhaps, maybe; **p. que oui, p. que non** perhaps, perhaps not; **p. (bien) qu'elle viendra, p. viendra-t-elle** perhaps she'll come; **je ne suis**

p. pas riche, mais... I may not be rich, but...; *Ironique* **tu le sais mieux que moi, p.?** you think you know better, do you?

peux *voir* **pouvoir²**
pèze [pɛz] *nm très Fam (argent)* cash, dough
pH [peaʃ] *nm Chim* pH
phacochère [fakɔʃɛr] *nm* warthog
phagocyter [fagɔsite] *vt Biol* to phagocytose; *Fig* to swallow up
phalange [falɑ̃ʒ] *nf (du doigt)* phalanx
phallique [falik] *adj* phallic
phallocrate [falɔkrat] *nm Péj* male chauvinist
phalloïde [falɔid] *adj voir* **amanite**
phallus [falys] *nm* phallus
phantasme [fɑ̃tasm] = **fantasme**
pharamineux, -euse [faraminø, -øz] = **faramineux**
pharaon [faraɔ̃] *nm* Pharaoh
phare [far] **1** *nm* (**a**) *(pour navires)* lighthouse; *(pour avions)* beacon (**b**) *(de voiture)* headlight; **faire un appel de phares** *Br* to flash one's headlights; **se mettre en phares** *Br* to dip *or Am* to dim one's headlights; **p. antibrouillard** foglight
  2 *adj* **film-p.** seminal movie *or Br* film; **épreuve-p.** star event
pharmaceutique [farmasøtik] *adj* pharmaceutical
pharmacie [farmasi] *nf* (**a**) *(science)* pharmacy (**b**) *(magasin) Br* chemist's, *Am* drugstore (**c**) *(médicaments)* pharmaceuticals; **(armoire à) p.** medicine cabinet; **p. de voyage** travelling first-aid kit
pharmacien, -enne [farmasjɛ̃, -ɛn] *nm,f (vendeur) Br* chemist, *Am* druggist; *(chercheur)* pharmacist, *Br* chemist
pharmacologie [farmakɔlɔʒi] *nf* pharmacology
pharyngite [farɛ̃ʒit] *nf Méd* pharyngitis
pharynx [farɛ̃ks] *nm Anat* pharynx
phase [faz] *nf* phase; **cancer en p. terminale** terminal cancer; *Phys* **être en p.** to be in phase; *Fam* **être en p. (avec qn)** to be on the same wavelength (as sb)
phénicien, -enne [fenisjɛ̃, -ɛn] *Hist* **1** *adj* Phoenician
  2 *nm,f* **P.** Phoenician
phénix [feniks] *nm (animal mythologique)* phoenix; *Fig & Litt* paragon
phénoménal, -e, -aux, -ales [fenɔmenal, -o] *adj Fam* phenomenal
phénomène [fenɔmɛn] *nm* phenomenon; *Fam (personne)* character; **un p. de foire** a freak
Philadelphie [filadɛlfi] *n* Philadelphia
philanthrope [filɑ̃trɔp] *nmf* philanthropist
philanthropique [filɑ̃trɔpik] *adj* philanthropic
philatélie [filateli] *nf* philately, stamp collecting
philatéliste [filatelist] *nmf* philatelist, stamp collector
philharmonique [filarmɔnik] *adj* philharmonic
philippin, -e [filipɛ̃, -in] **1** *adj* Filipino
  2 *nm,f* **P.** Filipino
Philippines [filipin] *nfpl* **les P.** the Philippines
philosophale [filɔzɔfal] *adj f voir* **pierre**
philosophe [filɔzɔf] **1** *nmf* philosopher
  2 *adj* philosophical
philosopher [filɔzɔfe] *vi* to philosophize
philosophie [filɔzɔfi] *nf* philosophy; *Fig* **avec p.** philosophically
philosophique [filɔzɔfik] *adj* philosophical
philtre [filtr] *nm* philtre; **p. d'amour** love potion
phlébite [flebit] *nf Méd* phlebitis
phlébologue [flebɔlɔg] *nmf Méd* vein specialist, *Spéc* phlebologist

Phnom Penh [pnɔmpɛn] *n* Phnom Penh
phobie [fɔbi] *nf* phobia; **avoir la p. de qch** to have a phobia about sth
phonème [fɔnɛm] *nm* phoneme
phonétique [fɔnetik] **1** *adj* phonetic
  2 *nf* phonetics *(singulier)*
phonographe [fɔnɔgraf] *nm Vieilli Br* gramophone, *Am* phonograph
phoque [fɔk] *nm* (**a**) *(animal)* seal; *très Fam* **il est pédé comme un p.** he's a screaming queen (**b**) *(fourrure)* sealskin
phosphate [fɔsfat] *nm* phosphate; **sans phosphates** phosphate-free
phosphore [fɔsfɔr] *nm* phosphorus
phosphorescent, -e [fɔsfɔresɑ̃, -ɑ̃t] *adj* phosphorescent
photo [foto] **1** *nf* (**a**) *(cliché)* photo; **prendre qn/qch en p.** to take a photo of sb/sth; *Fam* **tu veux ma p.?** who do you think you're staring at?; **p. d'identité** passport-sized photograph; **p. de mode** fashion photo; **p. souvenir** souvenir photo (**b**) *(activité)* **faire de la p.** *(en amateur)* to take photographs; *(en professionnel)* to be a photographer
  2 *adj inv voir* **appareil**
photocomposition [fotokɔ̃pozisjɔ̃] *nf* photosetting
photocopie [fotokɔpi] *nf* photocopy
photocopier [66] [fotokɔpje] *vt* to photocopy
photocopieur [fotokɔpjœr] *nm, nf* photocopier
photocopieuse [fotokɔpjøz] *nf* photocopier
photoélectrique [fotoelɛktrik] *adj* photoelectric
photo-finish *(pl* **photos-finish)** [fotofiniʃ] *nf* photo finish; *(appareil)* photo-finish camera
photogénique [fotoʒenik] *adj* photogenic
photographe [fotograf] *nmf* (**a**) *(professionnel)* photographer; **p. de mode** fashion photographer; **p. de presse** press photographer (**b**) *(commerçant)* **chez le p.** at the photo shop
photographie [fotografi] *nf* (**a**) *(technique)* photography; **faire de la p.** to take photographs (**b**) *(cliché)* photograph; **prendre une p. de** to take a photograph of; **p. aérienne** aerial photograph
photographier [66] [fotografje] *vt* to photograph; **se faire p.** to have one's photograph taken
photographique [fotografik] *adj* photographic
photogravure [fotogravyr] *nf* photogravure
Photomaton® [fotomatɔ̃] *nm* photo booth
photomontage [fotomɔ̃taʒ] *nm* photomontage
photon [fotɔ̃] *nm Phys* photon
photoreportage [fotorəpɔrtaʒ] *nm* photo report
photosensible [fotosɑ̃sibl] *adj* photosensitive
photostyle [fotostil] *nm Ordinat* light pen
photosynthèse [fotosɛ̃tɛz] *nf Biol* photosynthesis
phrase [fraz] *nf* sentence; *(musicale)* phrase; *Fig* **faire de grandes phrases** to use flowery language
phrasé [fraze] *nm Mus* phrasing
phraséologie [frazeɔlɔʒi] *nf* phraseology; *Péj* flowery language
phréatique [freatik] *adj voir* **nappe**
phrygien, -enne [friʒjɛ̃, -ɛn] *adj Hist* **bonnet p.** Phrygian cap *(in French Revolution)*
phtisie [ftizi] *nf Vieilli* consumption
phylloxéra, phylloxera [filɔksera] *nm* phylloxera
physicien, -enne [fizisjɛ̃, -ɛn] *nm,f* physicist
physiologie [fizjɔlɔʒi] *nf* physiology
physiologique [fizjɔlɔʒik] *adj* physiological

physionomie [fizjɔnɔmi] *nf* (**a**) *(traits du visage)* features; **juger les gens à leur p.** to judge people by appearances (**b**) *(aspect)* face
physionomiste [fizjɔnɔmist] *adj* **être p.** to have a good memory for faces
physiothérapie [fizjɔterapi] *nf* natural medicine
physique [fizik] **1** *adj* physical; *Fam* **je ne le supporte pas, c'est p.** he absolutely repulses me
  2 *nf (science)* physics *(singulier)*; **p. nucléaire** nuclear physics
  3 *nm (d'une personne)* physique; **avoir un p. avantageux** to have a good physique; **avoir le p. de l'emploi** to look the part
physiquement [fizikmɑ̃] *adv* physically
phytoplancton [fitoplɑ̃ktɔ̃] *nm* phytoplankton
phytothérapie [fitoterapi] *nf* herbal medicine
piaf [pjaf] *nm Fam* sparrow
piaffer [pjafe] *vi (cheval)* to paw the ground; *Fig* **p. d'impatience** to fidget impatiently
piaillement [pjajmɑ̃] *nm (d'un oiseau)* cheeping; *Fam (d'un enfant)* squealing
piailler [pjaje] *vi (oiseau)* to cheep; *Fam (enfant)* to squeal
pianiste [pjanist] *nmf* pianist
piano¹ [pjano] *nm* piano; **jouer** *ou* **faire du p.** to play the piano; **p. demi-queue** baby grand; **p. droit** upright piano; **p. à queue** grand piano
piano² *adv Mus* piano; *Fig* gently
pianoter [pjanɔte] *vi (mal jouer)* to tinkle away (**a**) *(tapoter)* **p. sur la table** to drum one's fingers on the table; *Fam* **p. sur son clavier** to tap away at one's keyboard
piastre [pjastr] *nf* piastre; *Can Fam (dollar)* buck
piaule [pjol] *nf Fam* pad
piauler [pjole] *vi (poussins)* to cheep
PIB [peibe] *nm Écon (abrév* **produit intérieur brut)** GDP
pic [pik] *nm* (**a**) *(pioche)* pick(axe); **p. à glace** ice pick (**b**) *(sommet)* peak; **couler à p.** to sink like a stone; **tomber à p.** *(falaise)* to go straight down; *Fam* to come at just the right moment
picard, -e [pikar, -ard] **1** *adj* of Picardy
  2 *nm,f* **P.** person from Picardy
Picardie [pikardi] *nf* **la P.** Picardy
picaresque [pikaresk] *adj* picaresque
pichenette [piʃnɛt] *nf* flick
pichet [piʃɛ] *nm Br* jug, *Am* pitcher
pickpocket [pikpɔkɛt] *nm* pickpocket
pick-up [pikœp] *nm inv* (**a**) *Vieilli (électrophone)* record player (**b**) *(véhicule)* pick-up (truck)
picoler [pikɔle] *vi Fam* to booze
picoleur, -euse [pikɔlœr, -øz] *nm,f Fam (buveur)* boozer
picorer [pikɔre] **1** *vt (sujet: oiseau)* to peck (at); *(sujet: personne)* to nibble
  2 *vi (oiseau)* to pick about; *(personne)* to pick at one's food
picotement [pikɔtmɑ̃] *nm (dans la gorge, dans le nez)* tickling; *(dans les yeux)* stinging; *(sur la peau)* prickling
picoter [pikɔte] *vt* **j'ai la gorge qui (me) picote** I've got a tickle in my throat; **la fumée me picotait les yeux** the smoke made my eyes sting; **j'ai la peau qui (me) picote** my skin's prickling
Pictes [pikt] *nmpl* **les P.** the Picts
pictogramme [piktɔgram] *nm* pictogram
pictural, -e, -aux, -ales [piktyral, -o] *adj* pictorial

pic-vert (*pl* **pics-verts**) [pivɛr] = **pivert**
pie [pi] **1** *nf* magpie; *Fam (personne)* chatterbox; *Fam* **être bavard comme une p.** to be a real chatterbox
  2 *adj inv (cheval)* piebald; *(vache)* black-and-white
pièce [pjɛs] *nf* (**a**) *(salle)* room (**b**) *(élément)* piece; *(d'un mécanisme)* part; **un service complet de trente-six pièces** a complete thirty-six piece service; **coûter 10 euros p.** to cost 10 euros each; **travailler à la p.** to do piecework; *Fig* **être tout d'une p.** to be straightforward; *Fig* **une histoire fabriquée de toutes pièces** a completely made-up story; **mettre qch en pièces** to tear sth to pieces; **p. de bœuf** cut *ou* piece of beef; **p. de collection** collector's item; **p. d'eau** ornamental lake; *(plus petite)* ornamental pond; **p. montée** = large tiered cake served at weddings, christenings etc; **p. de musée** museum piece; **pièces de rechange, pièces détachées** spare parts, spares; **p. de résistance** main dish; *Fig* pièce de résistance (**c**) *(argent)* **p. (de monnaie)** coin; **p. de 2 euros** 2-euro coin *ou* piece (**d**) **p. (de théâtre)** play (**e**) *(raccord)* patch; **mettre une p. à qch** to put a patch on sth (**f**) *(document)* document; **juger sur pièces** to judge on the evidence; **p. à conviction** exhibit *(in criminal case)*; **p. d'identité** proof of identity; **p. jointe** *(à une lettre)* enclosure (**g**) *(aux échecs)* piece; *(aux dames) Br* draught, *Am* checker

Pièce

Flats in France are referred to in terms of the total number of rooms they have (excluding the kitchen and bathroom). "Un deux-pièces" is a flat with a living room and one bedroom; "un cinq-pièces" is a flat with five rooms.

piécette [pjesɛt] *nf* small coin
pied [pje] *nm* (**a**) *(d'une personne)* foot; **avoir les pieds plats** to have flat feet; **avoir un p. bot** to have a club foot; **se prendre les pieds dans qch** to get one's feet caught in sth; **avoir p.** to be within one's depth; **perdre p.** to get out of one's depth; **mettre p. à terre** *(de cheval, de vélo)* to dismount; **de p. en cap** from head to toe
  (**b**) *(de cheval)* hoof; *Culin* **p. de porc** pig's trotter
  (**c**) *(de vigne)* stock; *(de céleri, de salade)* head
  (**d**) *(de chaise, de table)* leg; *(de verre)* stem; *(d'appareil photo, de lampadaire)* stand
  (**e**) *(base)* foot
  (**f**) **à p.** on foot; **j'y suis allé à p.** I walked there, I went there on foot; **faire 2 kilomètres à p.** to walk 2 kilometres; **tu en as pour dix minutes à p.** it'll take you ten minutes to walk (there)
  (**g**) *(mesure)* foot; *Fig* **six pieds sous terre** six feet under
  (**h**) *(locutions)* **mettre qch sur p.** to set sth up; **être sur p.** *(personne)* to be up and about; **être à p. d'œuvre** to be ready to get on with the job; **être sur un p. d'égalité avec qn** to be on an equal footing with sb; *Fig* **être sur le p. de guerre** to be ready for action; **avoir bon p. bon œil** to be hale and hearty; **avoir un p. dans la tombe** to have one foot in the grave; **avoir le p. marin** to be a good sailor; **mettre qn au p. du mur** to get sb with his/her back to the wall; **attendre qn de p. ferme** to be ready and waiting for sb; **se lever du p. gauche** to get out of bed on the wrong side; **faire qch au p. levé** to do sth at a moment's notice; **faire un p. de nez à qn** to cock a snook at sb; *Fam* **il chante/conduit comme un p.** he can't sing/drive to save his

life; *Fam* **s'y prendre comme un p.** to make a real mess of it; *Fam* **mettre les pieds dans le plat** to put one's foot in it; *Fam* **je ne remettrai jamais les pieds chez lui** I'll never set foot in his house again; *Fam* **faire des pieds et des mains pour obtenir qch** to move heaven and earth to get sth; *Fam* **faire du p. à qn** to play footsie with sb; *Fam* **ça lui fera les pieds!** that'll teach him/her a lesson!; *Fam* **prendre son p.** to get one's kicks; *Fam* **c'est le p.!** it's fantastic!

pied-à-terre [pjetatɛr] *nm inv* pied-à-terre
pied-bot (*pl* **pieds-bots**) [pjebo] *nm* club-footed person
pied-de-biche (*pl* **pieds-de-biche**) [pjedbiʃ] *nm (outil)* nail claw
pied-de-poule (*pl* **pieds-de-poule**) [pjedpul] *adj inv* & *nm* hound's-tooth
piédestal, -aux [pjedɛstal, -o] *nm* pedestal; *Fig* **mettre** *ou* **placer qn sur un p.** to put *or* to set sb on a pedestal
pied-noir (*pl* **pieds-noirs**) [pjenwar] *nmf Fam* = French settler in North Africa

Pied noir
This is the name given to the French settlers who settled in North Africa (notably in Algeria) during the period of French colonial expansion. Most of them resettled in France (mainly on the south coast) after the colonies regained their independence. The largest wave of these settlers to arrive in France was in 1962, following the "**guerre d'Algérie**" (*see box at this entry*).

piège [pjɛʒ] *nm aussi Fig* trap; **tendre un p. (à)** to set a trap (for); **prendre un animal au p.** to catch an animal in a trap; **tomber dans un p.** to fall into a trap; *très Fam* **p. à cons** con
piéger [59] [pjeʒe] *vt* (**a**) *aussi Fig (attraper)* to trap; **se faire p.** to be trapped; **se laisser p.** to fall into a trap (**b**) *(placer une bombe dans)* to booby-trap; **colis piégé** parcel bomb; **lettre piégée** letter bomb; **voiture piégée** car bomb
Piémont [pjemɔ̃] *nm* **le P.** Piedmont
piémontais, -e [pjemɔ̃tɛ, -ɛz] **1** *adj* Piedmontese
2 *nm,f* **P.** Piedmontese
3 *nm (langue)* Piedmontese
piercing [pirsiŋ] *nm* body piercing
pierraille [pjɛraj] *nf* loose stones
pierre [pjɛr] *nf* (**a**) *(matière, caillou)* stone; *(rocher)* rock; **mur de p.** stone wall; **maison en p.** stone(-built) house; **investir dans la p.** to invest in bricks and mortar; **poser la première p. de qch** to lay the foundation stone for sth; *Fig* **jeter la p. à qn** to reproach sb; *Fig* **faire d'une p. deux coups** to kill two birds with one stone; *Fig* **être malheureux comme les pierres** to be extremely unhappy; *Prov* **p. qui roule n'amasse pas mousse** a rolling stone gathers no moss; **p. d'achoppement** stumbling block; *aussi Fig* **p. angulaire** cornerstone; **p. à briquet** flint *(for lighter)*; **p. philosophale** philosopher's stone; **p. ponce** pumice stone; **p. de taille** dressed stone; **p. tombale** tombstone; *aussi Fig* **p. de touche** touchstone (**b**) *(en bijouterie)* stone; **p. précieuse** precious stone, gem; **p. fine** *ou* **semi-précieuse** semi-precious stone
pierreries [pjɛrəri] *nfpl* precious stones, gems
pierreux, -euse [pjɛrø, -øz] *adj (sol, route)* stony; *(lit de rivière)* gravelly
piétaille [pjetaj] *nf Péj* rank and file

piété [pjete] *nf* (**a**) *(ferveur religieuse)* piety (**b**) *(affection)* **p. filiale** filial devotion
piétinement [pjetinmɑ̃] *nm (bruit)* stamping; *(marche sur place)* standing around; *Fig (stagnation)* lack of progress
piétiner [pjetine] **1** *vt* **p. qch** *(en trépignant)* to stamp on sth; *(en marchant)* to trample on sth; *(écraser)* to trample sth underfoot; **ils sont morts piétinés par la foule** they were trampled to death by the crowd
2 *vi* (**a**) **p. d'impatience** to stamp (one's feet) impatiently (**b**) *(faire du surplace)* to stand around; *Fig* to make no progress
piéton, -onne [pjetɔ̃, -ɔn] **1** *nm,f* pedestrian
2 **rue piétonne** pedestrianized street; **zone piétonne** pedestrian precinct
piétonnier, -ère [pjetɔnje, -ɛr] *adj* pedestrian; **rue piétonnière** pedestrianized street; **zone piétonnière** pedestrian precinct
piètre [pjɛtr] *adj Litt (compagnon)* wretched; *(excuse)* paltry; *(consolation)* small
pieu¹, -x¹ [pjø] *nm (piquet)* stake
pieu², -x² *nm Fam (lit)* bed; **se mettre au p., aller au p.** *Br* to hit the sack, *Am* to hit the hay
pieuter [pjøte] **se pieuter** *vpr Fam Br* to hit the sack, *Am* to hit the hay
pieuvre [pjœvr] *nf* octopus
pieux³, -euse [pjø, -øz] *adj* pious, devout
pif [pif] *nm Fam (nez)* conk, *Br* hooter; *Fig* **faire qch au p.** to do sth by guesswork; **répondre au p.** to hazard a guess; **au p., je dirais...** at a rough guess, I'd say...
pif(f)er [pife] *vt Fam* **je ne peux pas le p.** I can't stomach him
pifomètre [pifɔmɛtr] *nm Fam* **faire qch au p.** to do sth by guesswork; **répondre au p.** to hazard a guess; **au p., je dirais...** at a rough guess, I'd say...
pige [piʒ] *nf* (**a**) *(article)* freelance contribution; **faire des piges** to do freelance work (**b**) *Fam (année)* **elle a quarante-cinq piges** she's forty-five; **à soixante piges** at sixty
pigeon [piʒɔ̃] *nm* (**a**) *(oiseau)* pigeon; **p. d'argile** clay pigeon; **p. ramier** wood pigeon; **p. vole** = children's game with forfeits; ≃ Simon says; **p. voyageur** carrier pigeon, homing pigeon (**b**) *Fam Péj (personne)* sucker
pigeonnant, -e [piʒɔnɑ̃, -ɑ̃t] *adj Fam* **poitrine pigeonnante** high bust; **soutien-gorge p.** uplift bra
pigeonnier [piʒɔnje] *nm* dovecot
piger [45] [piʒe] *Fam* **1** *vt* to get; **ne rien p. à qch** *(maths, anglais)* not to have a clue about sth; **je n'ai rien pigé à ce qu'il a dit** I didn't get any of what he said
2 *vi* to get it
pigiste [piʒist] *nmf* freelance journalist
pigment [pigmɑ̃] *nm* pigment
pigmentation [pigmɑ̃tasjɔ̃] *nf* pigmentation
pignon¹ [piɲɔ̃] *nm (de mur)* gable; **avoir p. sur rue** to be of some standing
pignon² *nm (petite roue)* pinion
pignon³ *nm (graine)* pine nut
pilage [pilaʒ] *nm* crushing
pile¹ [pil] *nf* (**a**) *(tas)* pile; **en p.** in a pile (**b**) **p. (électrique)** battery; **marcher avec des piles** to run on batteries, to be battery-operated; **p. atomique** atomic pile
pile² **1** *nf (d'une pièce)* reverse; **p. ou face?** heads or tails?; **tirer à p. ou face** to toss for it
2 *adv Fam* **s'arrêter p.** to stop dead; **tomber p.** to

come at just the right time; **à six heures p.** at six on the dot; **nous étions p. dix à table** there were exactly ten of us at the table; **elle est arrivée p. le même jour que moi** she arrived on exactly the same day as I did

piler [pile] **1** *vt* (**a**) *(broyer)* to crush; *(amandes)* to grind (**b**) *Fam (battre)* to thrash
2 *vi Fam* to slam on the brakes

pileux, -euse [pilø, -øz] *adj* hair; **système p.** body hair

pilier [pilje] *nm* (**a**) *(colonne)* pillar (**b**) *(au rugby)* prop (forward) (**c**) *Fig (défenseur)* pillar; *Fam Péj* **c'est un p. de bar** he's always propping up the bar

pillage [pijaʒ] *nm* pillaging, looting; *(lors d'une émeute)* looting

pillard, -e [pijar, -ard] **1** *adj* pillaging, looting; *(lors d'une émeute)* looting
2 *nm,f* pillager; *(lors d'une émeute)* looter

piller [pije] *vt* to pillage, to loot; *(lors d'une émeute)* to loot

pilleur, -euse [pijœr, -øz] *nm,f* pillager; *(lors d'une émeute)* looter; **p. d'épaves** looter of wrecks

pilon [pilɔ̃] *nm* (**a**) *(de pharmacien)* pestle; *Fig* **mettre un livre au p.** to pulp a book (**b**) *(de poulet)* drumstick (**c**) *(jambe de bois)* wooden leg

pilonnage [pilɔnaʒ] *nm (bombardement)* bombardment

pilonner [pilɔne] *vt (bombarder)* to bombard

pilori [pilɔri] *nm* pillory; *aussi Fig* **mettre qn au p.** to pillory sb

pilosité [pilozite] *nf* hairiness

pilotage [pilɔtaʒ] *nm* (**a**) *(d'un navire, d'un avion)* piloting; **p. automatique** automatic piloting (**b**) *Ordinat* control

pilote [pilɔt] **1** *nm* (**a**) *(de navire, d'avion)* pilot; *(de voiture de course)* driver; *(de moto de course)* rider; *Fig* **servir de p. à qn** to show sb round; **p. automatique** automatic pilot, autopilot; **p. de chasse** fighter pilot; **p. d'essai** test pilot; **p. de ligne** airline pilot (**b**) *Ordinat* driver; **p. d'affichage** display driver; **p. d'imprimante** printer driver
2 *adj* **installation(-)p.** pilot plant; **université(-)p.** experimental university

piloter [pilɔte] *vt* (**a**) *(navire)* to pilot; *(avion)* to pilot, to fly; *(voiture)* to drive; *(moto)* to ride; *Fig (projet)* to be in charge of; *(touriste)* to show round (**b**) *Ordinat* to drive; **piloté par menu** menu-driven

pilotis [pilɔti] *nmpl* stilts

pilule [pilyl] *nf (pill, tablet;* **la p.** *(contraceptif)* the pill; **prendre la p.** to be on the pill; **p. abortive** abortion pill; **p. du lendemain** morning-after pill

pimbêche [pɛ̃bɛʃ] **1** *adj* stuck-up
2 *nf (fille)* stuck-up girl; *(femme)* stuck-up woman

piment [pimɑ̃] *nm* (**a**) *(piquant)* chilli; **p. doux** (sweet) pepper (**b**) *Fig* spice

pimenter [pimɑ̃te] *vt aussi Fig* to spice up

pimpant, -e [pɛ̃pɑ̃, ɑ̃t] *adj* smart

pin [pɛ̃] *nm* pine; **p. maritime** maritime pine; **p. parasol** umbrella pine; **p. sylvestre** Scots pine

pinacle [pinakl] *nm* **être au p.** to be at the top; **porter qn au p.** to praise sb to the skies

pinailler [pinaje] *vi Fam* to nitpick (**sur** over)

pinailleur, -euse [pinajœr, -øz] *Fam* **1** *adj* nitpicking
2 *nm,f* nitpicker

pinard [pinar] *nm Fam* wine, *Br* plonk

pince [pɛ̃s] *nf* (**a**) *(outil)* (pair of) pliers; *(de forgeron)* (pair of) tongs; **p. à cheveux** *Br* hair clip, *Am* barrette; **p. crocodile** crocodile clip; **p. à épiler** tweezers; **p. à**

linge clothes peg; **p. à sucre** sugar tongs; **p. à vélo** bicycle clip (**b**) *(des crustacés)* pincer, claw (**c**) *(sur un vêtement)* dart (**d**) *Fam* **serrer la p. à qn** to shake hands with sb (**e**) *Fam* **à pinces** on foot

pincé, -e [pɛ̃se] *adj (air)* stiff, starchy; *(sourire)* tight-lipped; *(lèvres)* pursed

pinceau, -x [pɛ̃so] *nm (brosse)* brush, paintbrush; **avoir un bon coup de p.** to be a good painter

pincée [pɛ̃se] *nf* pinch

pincement [pɛ̃smɑ̃] *nm* (**a**) **avoir un p. au cœur** *(être ému)* to feel a pang of sadness (**b**) *(fait de pincer)* pinching; *(des cordes d'un instrument)* plucking

pince-monseigneur [pl **pinces-monseigneur**] [pɛ̃smɔ̃sɛɲœr] *nf* jemmy

pince-nez [pɛ̃sne] *nm inv* pince-nez

pincer [16] [pɛ̃se] **1** *vt* (**a**) *(serrer)* to pinch, to nip; *(lèvres)* to purse; *(cordes d'un instrument)* to pluck (**b**) *Fam (attraper) Br* to nab, *Am* to bust; **se faire p.** to get *Br* nabbed *or Am* busted (**c**) *Fam* **en p. pour qn** to be crazy about sb (**d**) *Fam* **ça pince** it's freezing
2 se pincer *vpr* **se p. le doigt** to catch one's finger; **se p. le nez** to hold one's nose

pince-sans-rire [pɛ̃ssɑ̃rir] **1** *adj inv* dry, deadpan
2 *nmf inv* person with a dry sense of humour

pincette [pɛ̃sɛt] *nf* (**a**) *(petite pince)* tweezers; **pincettes** *(à feu)* (fire) tongs; *Fig* **il n'est pas à prendre avec des pincettes** he's like a bear with a sore head (**b**) *Suisse (pince à linge)* clothes peg

pinçon [pɛ̃sɔ̃] *nm* pinch mark

pinède [pinɛd] *nf* pine wood

pingouin [pɛ̃gwɛ̃] *nm* auk; *(manchot)* penguin

ping-pong [piŋpɔ̃g] *nm* table tennis, ping-pong

pingre [pɛ̃gr] *adj* stingy

pingrerie [pɛ̃grəri] *nf* stinginess

pin's [pinz] *nm inv* badge

pinson [pɛ̃sɔ̃] *nm* chaffinch

pintade [pɛ̃tad] *nf* guinea fowl

pinte [pɛ̃t] *nf (ancienne mesure)* pint *(0.93 litres)*; *(au Royaume-Uni, aux États-Unis)* pint; *Can* quart

pinter [pɛ̃te] *Fam* **1** *vi* to booze
2 se pinter *vpr* to get smashed

pinteur, -euse [pɛ̃tœr, -øz] *nm,f Belg & Suisse Fam* boozer

pin-up [pinœp] *nf inv* pin-up

pioche [pjɔʃ] *nf* (**a**) *(outil)* pick, pickaxe (**b**) *(aux cartes, aux dominos)* stock, pile

piocher [pjɔʃe] **1** *vt (creuser)* to dig *(with a pick)*
2 *vi (aux cartes, aux dominos)* to pick up; *Fig* **p. dans qch** *(tas)* to plunge one's hand into sth; *(économies, réserves)* to dip into sth

piolet [pjɔlɛ] *nm* ice axe

pion¹ [pjɔ̃] *nm (de jeu de société)* piece; *(aux échecs)* pawn; *(aux dames) Br* draught, *Am* checker; *Fig* **n'être qu'un p. (sur l'échiquier)** to be only a pawn in the game

pion², -onne [pjɔ̃, pjɔn] *nm,f Fam (surveillant)* supervisor *(paid to supervise pupils outside class hours)*

Pion

In French lycées, the "pions" (officially called "surveillants") are responsible for supervising pupils outside class hours; they are often university students who do the job to make a little extra money.

pioncer [16] [pjɔ̃se] *vi Fam* to sleep

pionnier, -ère [pjɔnje, -ɛr] *nm,f aussi Fig* pioneer

pipe [pip] *nf* (**a**) *(de fumeur)* pipe; *Fam Fig* **casser sa p.** to kick the bucket (**b**) *Vulg* **faire** *ou* **tailler une p. à qn** to give sb a blowjob

pipeau, -x [pipo] *nm Mus* (reed) pipe; *Fam* **c'est du p.** it's all claptrap

pipelette [piplɛt] *nf Fam* gossip

pipeline, pipe-line (*pl* **pipe-lines**) [piplin, pajplajn] *nm* pipeline

piper [pipe] *vt* (**a**) *(dés)* to load; *(cartes)* to mark; *Fig* **les dés sont pipés** the dice are loaded (**b**) **ne pas p.** (**mot**) to keep mum

pipette [pipɛt] *nf* pipette; *Suisse* **ça ne vaut pas p.** it's not worth a bean *or* a red cent

pipi [pipi] *nm Fam* pee; **faire p.** to pee; **faire p. au lit** to wet the bed; *Fam Péj* **c'est du p. de chat** *(boisson)* it's dishwater

pipole [pipɔl] *nmf Fam* celebrity, celeb; **les pipoles** celebs

piquant, -e [pikɑ̃, ɑ̃t] **1** *adj* (**a**) *(au goût)* spicy, hot; *(moutarde)* hot (**b**) *(plante)* prickly, thorny; *(barbe)* prickly; *(vent)* biting (**c**) *Fig (détail, style, situation)* piquant; *(histoire)* spicy; **une petite brune piquante** a striking little brunette

2 *nm* (**a**) *(d'une plante)* thorn; *(d'un porc-épic, d'un hérisson)* spine; *(de barbelé)* spike, barb (**b**) *(d'un style, d'une situation)* piquancy; *(d'une histoire)* spice; **avoir du p.** *(femme)* to be striking

pique¹ [pik] **1** *nf (arme)* pike; *(d'un picador)* lance
2 *nm (carte)* spade; *(couleur)* spades

pique² *nf (méchanceté)* spiteful remark; **envoyer** *ou* **lancer des piques à qn** to have a go at sb

piqué, -e [pike] **1** *adj* (**a**) *(bois)* wormeaten; *(livre)* foxed; *(miroir)* tarnished; *(métal)* pitted; *Fam* **une histoire/angine pas piquée des hannetons** *ou* **des vers** one heck of a story/sore throat (**b**) *(vin)* sour (**c**) *Fam (fou)* nuts (**d**) *Mus (note)* staccato
2 *nm* (**a**) *Aviat* **descente en p.** nose dive (**b**) *(tissu)* piqué

pique-assiette (*pl* **pique-assiettes**) [pikasjɛt] *nmf Fam* scrounger, sponger

pique-feu [pikfø] *nm inv* poker

pique-nique (*pl* **pique-niques**) [piknik] *nm* picnic; **faire un p.** to have a picnic

pique-niquer [piknike] *vi* to have a picnic, to picnic

piquer [pike] **1** *vt* (**a**) *(avec une pointe)* to prick; *(sujet: guêpe)* to sting; *(sujet: puce, moustique)* to bite; *(cheval)* to spur on; *(bœuf)* to goad; **la fumée me pique les yeux** the smoke is making my eyes sting; **ça me pique la gorge/le nez** it tickles my throat/nose (**b**) *Fam (faire une piqûre à)* **p. qn** to give sb *Br* a jab *or Am* a shot; **p. un chien** to put a dog down, to put a dog to sleep (**c**) *Fam (voler)* to pinch, *Br* to nick (**à** from); **je me suis fait p. mon stylo** my pen got pinched *or Br* nicked (**d**) *(coudre)* to stitch (**e**) *(enfoncer)* to stick (**dans** into) (**f**) *Fam* **p. un cent mètres** to sprint off; **p. une crise** to throw a fit; **p. une tête** to dive (**g**) *(vexer)* **p. qn au vif** to cut sb to the quick (**h**) *(exciter)* **p. la curiosité de qn** to arouse *or* excite sb's curiosity (**i**) *(sujet: acide, vers)* to eat into; *(sujet: humidité)* to spot, to mark (**j**) *Culin* **p. qch d'ail** to stick garlic into sth

2 *vi* (**a**) *Aviat* **p. (du nez)** to nosedive; *Fig* **p. du nez** *(s'assoupir)* to nod off; *(baisser les yeux)* to look down (**b**) *(plat)* to be spicy *or* hot; *(vin)* to be sour (**c**) *(guêpe)* to sting; *(puce, moustique)* to bite; *(plante)* to be prickly; **tu piques!** *(à un homme mal rasé)* you're all bristly!

3 se piquer *vpr* (**a**) *(se blesser)* to prick oneself; **se p. le doigt** to prick one's finger (**b**) *(se faire une piqûre)* to give oneself an injection; *Fam (se droguer)* to shoot up; **se p. à l'héroïne** to shoot heroin (**c**) *(se vexer)* to take offence (**d**) *(vin)* to (turn) sour (**e**) *(locutions)* **se p. au jeu** to get into it; *Litt* **se p. de faire qch** to pride oneself on doing sth

piquet [pikɛ] *nm* (**a**) *(pieu)* stake, post; *(de tente)* peg (**b**) *Vieilli Scol* **mettre** *ou* **envoyer qn au p.** to send sb to stand in the corner (**c**) **p. de grève** picket

piquette [pikɛt] *nf* (**a**) *Péj (vin)* cheap wine, *Br* plonk (**b**) *Fam (défaite)* **prendre une** *ou* **la p.** to get thrashed

piqûre [pikyr] *nf* (**a**) *(de guêpe)* sting; *(de puce, de moustique)* bite; **p. d'épingle** pinprick (**b**) *Méd* injection, shot; **faire une p. à qn** to give sb an injection (**c**) *(d'un tissu, de cuir)* stitching (**d**) *(de rouille, de moisi)* spot, speck

piranha [pirana] *nm* piranha

piratage [pirataʒ] *nm* pirating; **p. informatique** hacking

pirate [pirat] **1** *nm* (**a**) *(des mers)* pirate; *Fig (escroc)* crook; **p. de l'air** hijacker (**b**) *(de logiciels, de DVD)* pirate; **p. informatique** hacker
2 *adj (logiciel, DVD, radio)* pirate

pirater [pirate] *vt (logiciel, DVD)* to pirate; *Ordinat* to hack

piraterie [piratri] *nf* (**a**) *(sur les mers)* piracy (**b**) *Fig (escroquerie)* swindling; *(plagiat)* piracy; **p. informatique** hacking

pire [pir] **1** *adj* (**a**) *(comparatif)* worse; **c'est de p. en p.** it's getting worse and worse; *Can Fam* **p. que p.** dire, as bad as it can get (**b**) *(superlatif)* worst
2 *nm* **le p., c'est que...** the worst thing about it is...; **craindre le/s'attendre au p.** to fear/to expect the worst; **au p....** if the worst comes to the worst...

pirogue [pirɔg] *nf* dugout (canoe)

pirouette [pirwɛt] *nf* (**a**) *(tour sur soi-même)* pirouette; *(saut périlleux)* somersault; **faire un p.** to pirouette (**b**) *Fig (dérobade)* flippant answer; **s'en tirer par une p.** to answer flippantly

pis¹ [pi] *nm (mamelle)* udder

pis² **1** *adv* **aller de mal en p.** to go from bad to worse
2 *adj Litt* worse
3 *nm* (**a**) *Litt (comparatif)* worse; **il y a p.** there is/are worse (**b**) *Litt (superlatif)* worst; **au p.** if the worst comes to the worst; **au p. aller** at the very worst (**c**) **dire p. que pendre de qn** to call sb every name under the sun

pis-aller [pizale] *nm inv* stopgap (solution)

pisciculture [pisikyltyr] *nf* fish farming

piscine [pisin] *nf* (swimming) pool; **p. couverte/en plein air** indoor/outdoor pool

Pise [piz] *n* Pisa

pisse [pis] *nf très Fam* piss, pee

pisse-froid [pisfrwa] **1** *adj inv* **il est très p.** he's a bit of a cold fish
2 *nm inv Fam* cold fish

pissenlit [pisɑ̃li] *nm* dandelion; *Fam* **manger les pis-senlits par la racine** to be pushing up the daisies

pisser [pise] **1** *vi* (**a**) *très Fam (uriner)* to piss; **c'est comme si je pissais dans un violon** it's like pissing in the wind; **laisse p.!** forget it!; **c'était à p. de rire** we were pissing ourselves (laughing) (**b**) *Fam (fuir)* to leak
2 *vt* (**a**) *très Fam* **p. du sang** to piss blood (**b**) *Fam* **son bras pissait le sang** blood was pouring from *or* gushing out of his/her arm

pisseux, -euse [pisø, -øz] *adj Fam (couleur)* washed out

pissotière [pisɔtjɛr] *nf Fam* (public) urinal

pistache [pistaʃ] **1** *nf (graine)* pistachio (nut); **glace à la p.** pistachio ice cream
2 *adj inv (couleur)* pistachio (green)

piste [pist] *nf* (**a**) *(trace)* track, trail; *(indices)* lead; **être sur la p. de qn** to be on sb's track; **suivre une fausse p.** to be on the wrong track (**b**) *Sport* track; *(de courses de chevaux) Br* racecourse, *Am* racetrack; *(de course automobile)* racetrack; *(de ski)* run, piste; *(de cirque)* ring; **p. artificielle** *(de ski)* artificial *or* dry ski slope; **p. de danse** dance floor (**c**) *Aviat* runway; **p. d'atterrissage** landing strip; *(dans la brousse, dans la forêt)* airstrip (**d**) *(chemin)* track, trail; **p. cyclable** cycle path (**e**) *(de magnétophone, de disque)* track; *Ordinat* **p. magnétique** magnetic strip

pister [piste] *vt (animal)* to track; *(personne)* to tail

pistil [pistil] *nm Bot* pistil

pistolet [pistɔlɛ] *nm* (**a**) *(arme à feu)* pistol, gun; **p. à air comprimé** air pistol; **p. à eau** water pistol (**b**) *(à peinture)* paint gun

pistolet-mitrailleur *(pl* pistolets-mitrailleurs) [pistɔlɛmitrajœr] *nm* submachine-gun

piston [pistɔ̃] *nm* (**a**) *Tech* piston (**b**) *Fam Fig (recommandation)* string-pulling; **il a eu la place par p.** someone pulled some strings to get him the job (**c**) *(d'instrument à vent)* valve

pistonner [pistɔne] *vt Fam* to pull strings for; **elle s'est fait p.** she got someone to pull strings for her

pistou [pistu] *nm (sauce)* pesto; *(soupe)* vegetable soup with pesto

pita [pita] *nf* pitta bread

pitance [pitɑ̃s] *nf Vieilli (nourriture)* sustenance

pit-bull *(pl* pit-bulls) [pitbul] *nm* pit bull (terrier)

piteux, -euse [pitø, -øz] *adj* (**a**) *(mauvais) (résultat)* poor, pitiful; **en p. état** in a sorry state (**b**) *(honteux)* shamefaced

pithiviers [pitivje] *nm Culin* = cake made of puff pastry containing rum and almond-flavoured cream

pitié [pitje] *nf* (**a**) *(compassion)* pity; **avoir p. de qn** to pity sb; **il me faisait p.** I felt sorry for him; **faire p. (à voir)** to be a pitiful sight; **être sans p.** to be ruthless; **(par) p.!** *(pour demander grâce)* (have) mercy!; *(exprime l'agacement)* for pity's sake! (**b**) *(tristesse)* **quelle p.!** what a terrible shame!

piton [pitɔ̃] *nm* (**a**) *Tech* eye bolt; *(d'alpiniste)* piton (**b**) *(sommet)* **p. (rocheux)** (rocky) peak

pitoyable [pitwajabl] *adj* (**a**) *(digne de pitié)* pitiful (**b**) *Péj (excuse, plaisanterie)* pathetic

pitre [pitr] *nm* clown; **faire le p.** to clown around

pitrerie [pitrəri] *nf* piece of clowning; **pitreries** clowning

pittoresque [pitɔrɛsk] *adj (lieu)* picturesque; *(description, style)* vivid

pivert [pivɛr] *nm* green woodpecker

pivoine [pivwan] *nf* peony

pivot [pivo] *nm* (**a**) *(axe)* pivot; *(de levier)* fulcrum; *(de compas, de boussole)* centre pin; *(en dentisterie)* post (**b**) *Fig (d'un drame, d'une argumentation)* pivot (**c**) *(au basket)* pivot, post

pivotant, -e [pivɔtɑ̃, ɑ̃t] *adj (grue, lampe)* swivelling; *(présentoir)* revolving

pivoter [pivɔte] *vi* to pivot, to swivel (**sur** on); **faire p. qch** to swivel sth round

pixel [piksɛl] *nm Ordinat* pixel

pixélisé, -e [pikselize] *adj Ordinat* bit-mapped

pizza [pidza] *nf* pizza

pizzeria [pidzerja] *nf* pizzeria

PJ [peʒi] *nf Fam (abrév* **police judiciaire)** *Br* ≃ CID, *Am* ≃ FBI

placage [plakaʒ] *nm* (**a**) *(bois)* veneer; *(métal)* plating (**b**) *(au rugby)* tackle

placard [plakar] *nm* (**a**) *(armoire) Br* cupboard, *Am* closet; *Fam Fig* **mettre qn au p.** to sideline sb; *Fam Fig* **mettre qch au p.** to put sth on ice, to shelve sth (**b**) *(affiche)* poster (**c**) *Fam (prison)* slammer, clink

placarder [plakarde] *vt (affiche)* to stick up, to put up; **p. un mur d'affiches** to cover a wall with posters

place [plas] *nf* (**a**) *(endroit, rôle)* place; **changer qch de p.** to move sth; *Fig* **se mettre à la p. de qn** to put oneself in sb's position; **mettre qch en p.** to put sth in place; **être en p.** *(objet)* to be in place; *(au pouvoir)* to be in office; **les gens en p.** people in high places; *Fig* **remettre qn à sa p.** to put sb in his/her place; **il ne tient pas en p.** he can't keep still; **à la p. de qn** *(au lieu de)* instead of sb; **à votre p....** if I were you...; **sur p.** on the spot; **faire p. nette** to have a clearout; **p. de parking** parking place *or* space (**b**) *(espace)* room, space; **prendre beaucoup de p.** to take up a lot of room *or* space; **faire de la p. à qn** to make room for sb; *Fig* **faire p. à qn/qch** to make way for sb/sth (**c**) *(siège)* seat; **(voiture à) deux/quatre places** two-/four-seater (car); **prendre p.** to take a seat; **p. assise** seat; **p. debout** *(billet)* standing ticket; **la p. du mort** the passenger seat (**d**) *(poste)* job, post; *Suisse* **p. de travail** job (**e**) *(lieu public)* square; **p. du marché** market place (**f**) *(rang)* place (**g**) *Mil* **p. forte** fortified town (**h**) *Com & Fin* market; **sur la p. de Paris** on the Paris market; **p. financière** financial market (**i**) *Belg (pièce d'habitation)* room

placé, -e [plase] *adj* **être bien/mal p. pour faire qch** to be well/badly placed to do sth

placebo [plasebo] *nm* placebo

placement [plasmɑ̃] *nm* (**a**) *(d'argent)* investment; **faire des placements** to invest (money) (**b**) *(à un emploi)* placement, placing

placenta [plasɛ̃ta] *nm* placenta

placer [16] [plase] **1** *vt* (**a**) *(mettre à sa place)* to place, to put; *(faire asseoir)* to seat (**b**) *(procurer un emploi à)* to find a job for, to place; **p. qn comme apprenti chez qn** to apprentice sb to sb (**c**) *(vendre)* to sell (**d**) *(dans la conversation)* to get in; *Fam* **avec elle, on ne peut pas en p. une!** you can't get a word in edgeways with her! (**e**) *(argent)* to invest
2 se placer *vpr* (**a**) *(debout)* to stand; *(assis)* to sit (**b**) **se p. sous la protection de qn** to place oneself under sb's protection; **il faut se p. dans son optique** you have to look at things from his/her point of view (**c**) *(trouver un emploi)* to find a job

placide [plasid] *adj* placid, calm

placoter [plakɔte] *vi Can Fam* to chat

plafond [plafɔ̃] *nm aussi Fig* ceiling; **être haut/bas de p.** to have a high/low ceiling; **prix/vitesse p.** maximum price/speed

plafonner [plafɔne] *vi (quantité, salaire)* to have reached a ceiling (**à** of)

plafonnier [plafɔnje] *nm* ceiling light

plage [plaʒ] *nf* (**a**) *(grève)* beach; **aller en vacances à la p.** *Br* to go on holiday to the seaside, *Am* to go to the beach on vacation; **p. de sable/de galets** sandy/pebble beach (**b**) *(surface)* area (**c**) *(dans un emploi du temps, à la télé, à la radio)* slot; **p. horaire** time slot

(**d**) *(d'un disque)* track (**e**) **p. arrière** *(d'une voiture)* back shelf
plagiaire [plaʒjɛr] *nmf* plagiarist
plagiat [plaʒja] *nm* plagiarism
plagier [66] [plaʒje] *vt* to plagiarize
plaid [plɛd] *nm* travelling rug
plaider [plede] **1** *vt* to plead; **p. coupable/non coupable** to plead guilty/not guilty; **p. la cause de qn** *Jur* to plead sb's case; *Fig* to plead sb's cause
2 *vi (avocat)* to plead; **p. pour/contre qn** to defend/prosecute sb; *Fig* **p. en faveur de qn/qch** to speak for sb/sth, to defend sb/sth
plaideur, -euse [plɛdœr, -øz] *nm,f* litigant
plaidoirie [plɛdwari] *nf Jur* speech for the defence
plaidoyer [plɛdwaje] *nm Jur* speech for the defence; *Fig* plea
plaie [plɛ] *nf* (**a**) *aussi Fig* wound (**b**) *(fléau)* affliction, scourge; *(personne, chose)* pest, nuisance
plaignant, -e [plɛɲɑ̃, -ɑ̃t] *nm,f Jur* plaintiff
plaindre [23] [plɛ̃dr] **1** *vt* to pity, to feel sorry for; **je vous plains de voyager dans ces conditions** I feel sorry for you having to travel in these conditions; **elle n'est pas à p.** she's got nothing to worry about
2 se plaindre *vpr* (**a**) *(protester)* to complain; **se p. de** to complain about; *(douleur)* to complain of (**b**) *(gémir)* to moan
plaine [plɛn] *nf* plain
plain-pied [plɛ̃pje] **de plain-pied** *adv (pièce)* on the same level (**avec** as); *(maison)* single-storey
plainte [plɛ̃t] *nf* (**a**) *(protestation)* complaint (**b**) *(gémissement)* moan (**c**) *Jur* complaint; **porter p. contre qn (auprès de)** to lodge a complaint against sb (with); **p. contre X** complaint against person or persons unknown
plaintif, -ive [plɛ̃tif, -iv] *adj* plaintive
plaire [55a] [plɛr] **1** *vi* (**a**) *(être apprécié)* **il me plaît** I like him; **ce livre/film m'a plu** I liked *or* enjoyed the book/film; **cette offre devrait lui p.** the offer should appeal to him; **ça plaît beaucoup** it's very popular; **je fais ce qui me plaît** I do whatever I want; **que cela te plaise ou non** whether you like it or not (**b**) *(se rendre agréable)* to please; **rien à faire, elle ne plaît pas** *(physiquement)* no matter what she does, no one finds her attractive
2 *v impersonnel* **s'il te/vous plaît** please; **s'il vous plaît!** *(dit par un client)* excuse me!; *Belg (dit par un serveur)* here you are!; **et pas n'importe qui, s'il vous plaît** and not just anybody, if you please; **comme il vous plaira** just as you like
3 se plaire *vpr* (**a**) *(soi-même)* **elle se plaît dans cette robe** she likes herself in that dress (**b**) *(l'un l'autre)* to like each other (**c**) *(se trouver bien)* **je me plais beaucoup à Paris** I'm very happy in Paris; **se p. à faire qch** to enjoy *or* like doing sth
plaisance [plɛzɑ̃s] *nf* **la (navigation de) p.** boating
plaisancier, -ère [plɛzɑ̃sje, -ɛr] *nm,f* (amateur) yachtsman, *f* yachtswoman
plaisant, -e [plɛzɑ̃, -ɑ̃t] **1** *adj* (**a**) *(agréable)* pleasant, agreeable (**b**) *(drôle)* funny, amusing
2 *nm* **mauvais p.** malicious joker
plaisanter [plɛzɑ̃te] **1** *vi* to joke; **dire qch en plaisantant** to say sth as a joke; **vous plaisantez!** you're joking!; **on ne plaisante pas avec la santé** you shouldn't take any chances with your health
2 *vt* to tease, to poke fun at (**sur** about)
plaisanterie [plɛzɑ̃tri] *nf (acte, propos)* joke; **elle ne comprend pas la p.** she can't take a joke; **par p.** for a joke; **tourner qch en p.** to make a joke out of sth; **les plaisanteries les plus courtes sont les meilleures** brevity is the soul of wit
plaisantin [plɛzɑ̃tɛ̃] *nm* joker
plaise *etc voir* **plaire**
plaisir [plɛzir] *nm* (**a**) *(sensation agréable)* pleasure; **j'ai le p. de vous apprendre que...** I'm pleased to be able to tell you that...; **faire qch pour le p.** to do sth for fun; *Ironique* **je vous souhaite bien du p.!** the best of luck!; **ça m'a fait p. de te revoir** I was pleased to see you again; **ça me ferait p. que tu viennes** I'd be pleased if you came; **fais-moi p., viens danser** do me a favour, come and dance; **si cela peut te faire p.** if it makes you happy; **il va se faire un p. de te téléphoner demain** he'll be only too pleased to phone you tomorrow; **cela fait p. à voir** it's good to see; **prendre p. à qch/à faire qch** to enjoy sth/doing sth; **les plaisirs de la table** fine food and wine (**b**) *(distraction)* pleasure; **c'est son plus grand p.** it's his/her greatest pleasure
plan¹, -e [plɑ̃, plan] **1** *adj (terrain, surface)* flat; *Math* plane
2 *nm* (**a**) *Math* plane (**b**) *(surface)* **p. de cuisson** hob; **p. d'eau** lake; **p. incliné** inclined plane; **p. de travail** *(d'une cuisine)* worktop (**c**) *Cin, Phot & Fig* **au premier p.** in the foreground; **au second p.** in the background; **un artiste de premier p.** a leading artist; **sur le même p. (que)** on the same level (as); **sur le p. politique/économique** from a political/an economic point of view; **gros p.** close-up; **en gros p.** in close-up
plan² *nm* (**a**) *(relevé)* plan; *(carte) (de ville)* map; **p. d'occupation des sols** land-use map (**b**) *(projet)* plan; *Fam* **j'ai un bon p. pour les vacances** I've got a great idea for the *Br* holidays *or Am* vacation; **p. de carrière** career strategy; **p. social** = corporate restructuring plan, usually involving job losses (**c**) *(d'un roman, d'un devoir)* plan, framework (**d**) *Fin* **p. d'épargne** savings plan; **p. d'épargne en actions** personal equity plan, PEP; **p. d'épargne-logement** = savings plan entitling savers to low mortgages, *Br* ≃ building society account, *Am* ≃ savings and loan association account; **p. d'épargne-retraite** personal pension plan
plan³ *nm Fam* **laisser qn en p.** to leave sb in the lurch; **tout laisser en p.** to drop everything
planant, -e [planɑ̃, ɑ̃t] *adj Fam* mind-blowing
planche [plɑ̃ʃ] *nf* (**a**) *(pièce de bois)* plank; *(plus large)* board; **faire la p.** *(flotter)* to float on one's back; *Fam* **c'est une vraie p. à pain** she's as flat as a pancake; **p. à découper** chopping board; **p. à dessin** drawing board; **p. à repasser** ironing board; **p. de salut** last hope (**b**) *Théât* **monter sur les planches** to go on the stage, to tread the boards (**c**) *(d'imprimerie, de gravure)* plate, block (**d**) *Sport* **p. (de surf)** surfboard; *Can* **p. à neige** snowboard; **p. à roulettes** skateboard; **faire de la p. à roulettes** to skateboard; **p. (à voile)** windsurfer *(board)*; **faire de la p. à voile** to go windsurfing
plancher¹ [plɑ̃ʃe] *nm* (**a**) *(sol)* floor; *(pour le jardin)* decking; *Fam* **le p. des vaches** dry land, terra firma; *Fig* **mettre le pied au p.** to put one's foot down (**b**) *Fig (minimum)* minimum; **prix p.** bottom price
plancher² **1** *vi Fam Scol* to have an exam
2 plancher sur *vt ind* **p. sur un problème** to work on a problem
plancton [plɑ̃ktɔ̃] *nm* plankton
plané [plane] *adj m voir* **vol¹**

planer [plane] vi (**a**) (oiseau, planeur) to glide; (brume, fumée) to hang; Fig **p. sur qn/qch** (danger) to hang over sb/sth (**b**) Fam (se sentir bien) to be floating on air, to be on a high; (après s'être drogué) to be high; (rêver) to dream

planétaire [planetɛr] adj (**a**) Astron planetary (**b**) (expansion, action) worldwide

planétarium [planetarjɔm] nm planetarium

planète [planɛt] nf planet

planeur [planœr] nm (avion) glider

planification [planifikasjɔ̃] nf Écon planning

planifier [66] [planifje] vt to plan

planisphère [planisfɛr] nm planisphere

planning [planiŋ] nm schedule; **p. familial** family planning; (lieu) family planning clinic

planque [plɑ̃k] nf Fam (**a**) (d'un gangster) hideout; (pour un butin) hiding place (**b**) (travail facile) cushy job

planqué, -e [plɑ̃ke] nm,f Fam person with a cushy job; Mil draft dodger

planquer [plɑ̃ke] Fam **1** vt to hide
2 se planquer vpr to hide

plant [plɑ̃] nm (d'arbre) sapling; (de plante) seedling

plantaire [plɑ̃tɛr] adj Anat plantar

plantation [plɑ̃tasjɔ̃] nf (exploitation agricole) plantation

plante¹ [plɑ̃t] nf **p. du pied** sole of the foot

plante² nf (végétal) plant; Fam Fig **une belle p.** (femme) a curvy woman; **p. d'appartement** house plant; **p. grasse** succulent (plant); **p. potagère** plant grown for food; **p. verte** house plant

planté, -e [plɑ̃te] adj (**a**) (debout) standing; Fam **rester p. (comme un piquet)** (immobile) to stand there doing nothing, Br to stand there like a lemon (**b**) **bien p.** (robuste) sturdy

planter [plɑ̃te] vt (**a**) (graines, fleurs, arbre) to plant; **une colline plantée d'arbres** a hill planted with trees (**b**) (clou) to hammer in; (tente) to put up, to pitch; **p. un clou dans qch** to hammer a nail into sth; Fig **p. un baiser sur la joue à qn** to plant a kiss on sb's cheek (**c**) Fam **p. là qn** to dump sb; **il veut tout p. là** he wants to pack it all in (**d**) Fam (tuer) to knife to death
2 vi Fam Ordinat to go down, to crash
3 se planter vpr (**a**) (se tenir immobile) to stand (**b**) Fam (se tromper) to get it wrong (**c**) Fam (tomber) Br to come a cropper, Am to take a spill (**d**) Fam (en voiture) to crash

planteur [plɑ̃tœr] nm (**a**) (exploitant) planter (**b**) (cocktail) planter's punch

plantigrade [plɑ̃tigrad] nm Zool plantigrade

planton [plɑ̃tɔ̃] nm Mil orderly

plantureux, -euse [plɑ̃tyrø, -øz] adj (femme) buxom; (poitrine) ample

plaquage [plakaʒ] = **placage (b)**

plaque [plak] nf (**a**) (de métal) plate, sheet; (de marbre) slab; (de chocolat) bar; (de beurre) pack; (de verglas) sheet; **p. chauffante** hotplate; **p. d'égout** manhole cover; Fig **p. tournante** hub, centre (**b**) (sur une porte) nameplate; (commémorative) plaque; **p. d'immatriculation** ou **minéralogique** Br number plate, Am license plate; **p. de rue** street sign (**c**) (sur la peau) patch; **p. (dentaire)** (dental) plaque (**d**) Fam **être à côté de la p.** to be wide of the mark

plaqué, -e [plake] **1** adj **p. or/argent** gold-/silver-plated
2 nm (**a**) **p. or/argent** gold/silver plate; **montre en p. or** gold-plated watch (**b**) (bois) veneered wood

plaquer [plake] **1** vt (**a**) (cheveux) to plaster down; **p. qn contre un mur** to pin sb against a wall (**b**) Fam (petit ami) to dump, to chuck; **tout p.** to chuck it all in (**c**) (au rugby) to tackle (**d**) Mus (accord) to play (**e**) (bois) to veneer; (métal) to plate
2 se plaquer vpr **se p. au sol** to lie flat on the ground; **se p. contre un mur** to flatten oneself against a wall

plaquette [plakɛt] nf (**a**) (de métal) (small) plate; (portant une inscription) (small) plaque; Ordinat circuit board; Aut **p. de frein** brake pad (**b**) (de chocolat) bar; (de beurre) pack (**c**) (petit livre) booklet (**d**) Méd **plaquettes** (blood) platelets

plasma [plasma] nm Biol & Phys plasma

plastic [plastik] nm plastic explosive

plasticage [plastikaʒ] nm bombing (**de** of)

plastifier [66] [plastifje] vt to laminate

plastiquage [plastikaʒ] = **plasticage**

plastique [plastik] **1** adj & nm plastic
2 nf (**a**) (art) art of modelling (**b**) (du corps) figure

plastiquer [plastike] vt to bomb

plastron [plastrɔ̃] nm (**a**) (de chemise) shirt front (**b**) (d'escrimeur) plastron

plat, -e [pla, plat] **1** adj (**a**) (sans relief) flat, level; (chaussure) flat; (mer) smooth; (eau) still; Fam **plate comme une limande** (femme) as flat as a pancake (**b**) Fig (ennuyeux) flat, dull (**c**) **à p.** (pneu, batterie) flat; Fam **être à p.** (épuisé) to be run down; **mettre qch à p.** to lay sth (down) flat; Fig **tomber à p.** (proposition, plaisanterie) to fall flat; **se mettre à p. ventre** to lie face down; Fig **se mettre à p. ventre devant qn** to grovel to sb
2 nm (**a**) (assiette) dish; Fig **mettre les petits plats dans les grands** to put on a marvellous spread (**b**) (mets) dish; (partie du menu) course; Fam **en faire tout un p.** to make a song and dance about it; **p. cuisiné** ready meal; **p. du jour** today's special, dish of the day; Fam Fig **p. de nouilles** Br prat, Am jerk; **p. principal** ou **de résistance** main course (**c**) (de la main, d'une épée) flat (**d**) (en cyclisme, en hippisme) **sur le p.** on the flat (**e**) **faire un p.** (en plongeant) to do a bellyflop (**f**) Fam **faire du p. à qn** Br to chat sb up, Am to hit on sb

platane [platan] nm plane tree

plateau, -x [plato] nm (**a**) (plat) tray; **p. à fromages** cheeseboard; **p. de fruits de mer** seafood platter (**b**) (d'une balance) pan; (d'une platine, d'un four micro-ondes) turntable (**c**) Géog plateau; **haut p.** high plateau (**d**) TV & Cin set (**e**) (de vélo) chain wheel

plateau-repas (pl **plateaux-repas**) [platorəpa] nm meal on a tray

plate-bande (pl **plates-bandes**) [platbɑ̃d] nf flower bed; Fam **marcher sur les plates-bandes de qn** to tread on sb's toes

plate-forme (pl **plates-formes**) [platfɔrm] nf (**a**) (surface plane) platform; **p. pétrolière** ou **de forage** oil rig (**b**) Géog **p. continentale** continental shelf (**c**) Ordinat platform

platement [platmɑ̃] adv (**a**) (s'exprimer, écrire) dully (**b**) (s'excuser) humbly

platine¹ [platin] nf (tourne-disque) turntable; **platines** decks; **p. cassettes** cassette or tape deck; **p. laser** CD player

platine² **1** nm platinum
2 adj inv **cheveux (blonds) p.** platinum blond hair

platiné, -e [platine] adj (**a**) (recouvert de platine) platinum-plated (**b**) (cheveux) platinum blond; **une blonde platinée** a platinum blonde

platitude [platityd] *nf* (**a**) *(manque d'intérêt)* dullness (**b**) *(propos)* platitude; **débiter des platitudes** to talk in platitudes
Platon [platɔ̃] *npr* Plato
platonique [platɔnik] *adj (amour)* platonic
plâtras [platra] *nmpl* (plaster) rubble
plâtre [platr] *nm* plaster; *(sculpture)* plaster cast; *(pour jambe cassée)* plaster (cast); **avoir la jambe dans le p.** to have one's leg in plaster; *Fig* **essuyer les plâtres** to have to put up with the teething problems
plâtrer [platre] *vt* (**a**) *(mur, plafond)* to plaster; *(trou, fissure)* to plaster over (**b**) *(jambe, bras)* to put in plaster
plâtreux, -euse [platrø, -øz] *adj (fromage)* chalky
plâtrier [platrije] *nm* plasterer
plausible [plozibl] *adj* plausible
play-back [plɛbak] *nm inv* miming; **chanter en p.** to mime
play-boy *(pl* **play-boys)** [plɛbɔj] *nm* playboy
plèbe [plɛb] *nf* **la p.** the plebs
plébéien, -enne [plebejɛ̃, -ɛn] *adj & nm,f* plebeian
plébiscite [plebisit] *nm* plebiscite
plébisciter [plebisite] *vt* (**a**) *(élire)* **p. qn/qch** to vote for sb/sth by plebiscite (**b**) *Fig* to endorse
pléiade [plejad] *nf* **une p. de** a host of
plein, -e [plɛ̃, plɛn] **1** *adj* (**a**) *(rempli)* full (**de** of); **il a les doigts pleins d'encre** his fingers are covered with ink; **p. à craquer** full to bursting; **p. comme un œuf** chock-full (**b**) *(complet) (accord, pouvoirs)* full; **pleine lune** full moon; **pleine mer** high tide; **p. tarif** full price; *(de transports)* full fare; **travailler à p. temps** to work full-time (**c**) *(solide)* solid (**d**) *(en intensif)* **une pleine bouteille** a whole bottle; **p. sud** due south; **en p. (milieu du) désert/village** right in the middle of the desert/village; **en p. dans/devant/sur** right in/in front of/on; **en pleine figure/poitrine** right in the face/chest; **être en p. travail** to be hard at work; **en p. hiver** in the depths of winter; **en p. soleil** in the full heat of the sun (**e**) *(animal)* pregnant (**f**) *Fam (soûl)* plastered
2 *adv* **il avait des larmes p. les yeux** his eyes were full of tears; **elle avait de la colle p. les mains** her hands were covered with glue; **à p.** *(fonctionner)* at full capacity; *Fam* **gentil tout p.** really kind; *Fam* **p. de** *(beaucoup de)* lots *or* loads of
3 *nm* (**a**) *(d'essence)* **faire le p. (d'essence)** to fill up (with *Br* petrol *or Am* gas); **le p., s'il vous plaît** fill her up, please; *Fig* **faire le p. d'air pur/de soleil** to get a good dose of fresh air/of sunshine (**b**) *(trait)* downstroke (**c**) **battre son p.** to be in full swing
pleinement [plɛnmã] *adv* fully; **profiter p. de qch** to take full advantage of sth
plein-emploi [plɛnãplwa] *nm* full employment
plénier, -ère [plenje, -ɛr] *adj* plenary
plénipotentiaire [plenipɔtãsjɛr] *adj & nm* plenipotentiary
plénitude [plenityd] *nf* fullness
pléonasme [pleɔnasm] *nm* pleonasm
pléthore [pletɔr] *nf* plethora (**de** of)
pleurer [plœre] **1** *vi* (**a**) *(verser des larmes)* to cry, to weep (**sur/pour** over/for); **p. sur son sort** to bewail one's fate; **p. de joie** to weep for joy; **p. de rage** to cry with rage; **p. à chaudes larmes**, *Fam* **p. comme une madeleine** *ou* **comme un veau** to cry one's eyes out; **bête/triste à p.** terribly stupid/sad; **j'ai les yeux qui pleurent** my eyes are watering (**b**) *Fig & Péj (réclamer plaintivement)* to beg; **aller p. auprès de qn** to go begging to sb

2 *vt* (**a**) *(regretter) (personne disparue)* to mourn (for) (**b**) **p. toutes les larmes de son corps** to cry one's eyes out
pleurésie [plœrezi] *nf* pleurisy
pleureur [plœrœr] *adj m voir* **saule**
pleureuse [plœrøz] *nf* (hired) mourner
pleurnichard, -e [plœrniʃar, -ard] = **pleurnicheur**
pleurnicher [plœrniʃe] *vi Fam* to whine
pleurnicheur, -euse [plœrniʃœr, -øz] *Fam* **1** *nm,f* whiner
2 *adj* whiny
pleurote [plœrɔt] *nm* oyster mushroom
pleurs [plœr] *nmpl* tears; **en p.** in tears
pleut *voir* **pleuvoir**
pleutre [pløtr] *adj & nm Litt* craven
pleuvoir [56] [pløvwar] **1** *v impersonnel* to rain; **il pleut** it's raining; **il pleut à verse** it's pouring (down); *Fam* **il pleut des cordes** it's bucketing down *or Br* chucking it down; *Fam* **il pleut comme vache qui pisse** it's pissing down; **des cadeaux comme s'il en pleuvait** presents galore
2 *vi (obus, coups, insultes)* to rain down (**sur** on)
plèvre [plɛvr] *nf* pleura
Plexiglas® [plɛksiglas] *nm Br* Perspex®, *Am* Plexiglass®
plexus [plɛksys] *nm* plexus; **p. solaire** solar plexus
pli [pli] *nm* (**a**) *(de rideaux, de tissu, de papier)* fold; *(en couture)* pleat; **(faux) p.** crease; *Fig* **ça ne fait pas un p.** there's no doubt about it; *Fig* **prendre le p. (de faire qch)** to get into the habit (of doing sth); *Fig* **prendre un mauvais p.** to get into a bad habit (**b**) *(de la peau) (du ventre, du cou, du menton)* fold; *(de la bouche, des yeux)* wrinkle; *(du front)* line (**c**) *(enveloppe)* envelope; *(lettre)* letter; **sous p. séparé** under separate cover; **p. cacheté** sealed envelope; **envoyer qch sous p. cacheté** to send sth in a sealed envelope (**d**) *(aux cartes)* trick; **faire un p.** to take a trick (**e**) *Géol* fold
pliage [plijaʒ] *nm* folding
pliant, -e [plijã, -ãt] **1** *adj (chaise, table)* folding
2 *nm* folding stool
plie [pli] *nf* plaice
plier [66] [plije] **1** *vt* (**a**) *(draps, vêtements)* to fold; *(page)* to turn down; *(voile)* to furl; *(parapluie, pliant)* to fold up; *Fig* **p. bagage** to pack one's bags (**b**) *(courber) (branche, genou)* to bend; *Fam Fig* **être plié de rire/de douleur** to be doubled up with laughter/with pain; **être plié en deux** *(de rire, de douleur)* to be doubled up *or* bent double; **être plié en quatre** *(de rire)* to be doubled up *or* bent double; **p. qn à une discipline/une règle** to impose discipline/a rule on sb
2 *vi* (**a**) *(se courber)* to bend (over); **p. sous le poids de qch** *(poutre, branches)* to bend under the weight of sth (**b**) *(se soumettre)* to submit, to yield; *(armée, troupes)* to give way
3 se plier *vpr* (**a**) *(pouvoir être plié) (parapluie, chaise)* to fold up (**b**) *(se soumettre)* **se p. à la discipline** to submit to discipline; **se p. aux lois** to obey the law; **se p. aux caprices/volontés de qn** to give in to sb's whims/wishes
plinthe [plɛ̃t] *nf* (**a**) *(de mur) Br* skirting (board), *Am* baseboard (**b**) *(de colonne)* plinth
plissé, -e [plise] **1** *adj* (**a**) *(visage, front)* wrinkled (**b**) **jupe plissée** pleated skirt
2 *nm* pleats

plissement [plismã] *nm* (**a**) *(des yeux)* screwing up (**b**) *Géol* fold

plisser [plise] **1** *vt* (**a**) *(front)* to wrinkle; *(lèvres)* to pucker; *(yeux)* to screw up (**b**) *(tissu, jupe)* to pleat
 2 *vi (vêtement)* to crease
 3 se plisser *vpr (étoffe)* to crease; *(bouche)* to pucker; *(yeux)* to wrinkle up; **son front se plissa** he/she frowned

pliure [plijyr] *nf (d'un tissu)* fold; *(de papier)* folding; *(du genou)* bend

plomb [plɔ̃] *nm* (**a**) *(métal)* lead; **ciel de p.** leaden sky; **soleil de p.** blazing sun; *Fig* **n'avoir pas de p. dans la tête** to be scatterbrained; **cela lui mettra un peu de p. dans la tête** *ou* **dans la cervelle** that'll knock some sense into him/her (**b**) *(de chasse)* shot; *Fam Fig* **avoir du p. dans l'aile** to be in a bad way (**c**) *Élec (fusible)* fuse; **faire sauter les plombs** to blow the fuses; *très Fam* **j'ai pété les plombs** I blew my top (**d**) *(pour la pêche)* sinker (**e**) *(sceau)* lead seal

plombage [plɔ̃baʒ] *nm* (**a**) *(fait de mettre des plombs)* weighting with lead (**b**) *(d'une dent)* filling

plombe [plɔ̃b] *nf Fam* hour

plombé, -e [plɔ̃be] *adj (toit)* lead(-covered); *Fig (teint)* livid; *(ciel)* leaden

plomber [plɔ̃be] **1** *vt* (**a**) *(couvrir de plomb)* to cover with lead (**b**) *(mettre des plombs à)* to weight with lead (**c**) *(dent)* to fill
 2 se plomber *vpr (ciel)* to become leaden

plomberie [plɔ̃bri] *nf (installations, métier)* plumbing

plombier [plɔ̃bje] *nm* plumber

plonge [plɔ̃ʒ] *nf Fam* dishwashing, *Br* washing up; **faire la p.** *(dans un restaurant)* to wash dishes

plongeant, -e [plɔ̃ʒã, -ãt] *adj (tir, décolleté)* plunging; **vue plongeante (sur)** bird's-eye view (of)

plongée [plɔ̃ʒe] *nf* (**a**) *(discipline)* diving; **faire de la p.** to dive; **p. sous-marine** scuba diving (**b**) *(de sous-marin)* dive (**c**) *Cin & TV* elevated shot; *(verticale)* bird's-eye view

plongeoir [plɔ̃ʒwar] *nm* diving board

plongeon [plɔ̃ʒɔ̃] *nm* (**a**) *(fait de plonger)* dive; **faire un p.** *(nageur, gardien de but)* to dive; *Fam Fig* **faire le p.** to hit the rocks (**b**) *(oiseau) Br* diver, *Am* loon

plonger [45] [plɔ̃ʒe] **1** *vi* (**a**) *(nageur, sous-marin)* to dive (**dans** into) (**b**) *(avion, oiseau)* to dive (**sur** onto)
 2 *vt aussi Fig* to plunge (**dans** into); **plongé dans ses pensées** lost *or* deep in thought; **la pièce fut plongée dans l'obscurité** the room was plunged into darkness
 3 se plonger *vpr* **se p. dans l'étude** to immerse oneself in one's studies

plongeur, -euse [plɔ̃ʒœr, -øz] **1** *nm,f* (**a**) *(dans l'eau)* diver; **p. sous-marin** scuba diver (**b**) *Fam (dans un restaurant)* dishwasher *(person)*, *Br* washer-up
 2 *nm (oiseau)* diver

plot [plo] *nm* (**a**) *Élec* contact (**b**) **p. de départ** starting block

plouc [pluk] *Péj* **1** *nm* yokel, *Am* hick
 2 *adj Fam* uncool, *Br* naff; **ça fait p.!** that's so uncool!

plouf [pluf] *exclam* plop!; *(objet plus lourd)* splash!

ploutocratie [plutokrasi] *nf* plutocracy

ployer [32] [plwaje] **1** *vi (courber)* to bend; *(plancher, poutre)* to sag; *(sous un joug, un fardeau)* to bend
 2 *vt* to bend

plu *pp de* **plaire, pleuvoir**

pluie [plɥi] *nf* (**a**) *(précipitations)* rain; **pluies acides** acid rain; **p. battante** driving rain; **p. fine** drizzle; **temps de p.** rainy *or* wet weather; **sous la p.** in the rain; **parler de la p. et du beau temps** to talk of this

and that; **il n'est pas tombé** *ou* **né de la dernière p.** he wasn't born yesterday; *Fam* **faire la p. et le beau temps** to rule the roost; *Prov* **après la p., le beau temps** = things will turn out all right in the end (**b**) *Fig (de coups, de projectiles)* hail, shower; *(d'injures, de compliments)* stream

plumage [plymaʒ] *nm* plumage

plumard [plymar] *nm Fam* bed

plume [plym] *nf* (**a**) *(d'oiseau)* feather; *Fam Fig* **il y a laissé des plumes** he didn't come out of it unscathed; *Fam Fig* **on lui a volé dans les plumes** they laid into him; **léger comme une p.** as light as a feather; *Hum* **perdre ses plumes** to go thin on top (**b**) *(de stylo)* nib; **p. (d'oie)** quill (pen); **écrire au fil de la p.** to write just what comes into one's head; **dessin à la p.** pen (and ink) drawing; **prendre la p.** to put pen to paper; **vivre de sa p.** to live by one's pen; **avoir la p. facile** to have a gift for writing

plumeau, -x [plymo] *nm* feather duster

plumer [plyme] *vt (volaille)* to pluck; *Fam (personne)* to fleece

plumier [plymje] *nm* pencil box

plupart [plypar] *nf* **la p.** most; **la p. des gens/des cas** most people/cases; **la p. d'entre eux** most of them; **la p. du temps** most of the time; *(en général)* in most cases; **pour la p.** for the most part, mostly

pluralisme [plyralism] *nm* pluralism

pluridisciplinaire [plyridisiplinɛr] *adj* multi-disciplinary

pluriel, -elle [plyrjɛl] **1** *adj* plural
 2 *nm* plural; **au p.** in the plural

plurilingue [plyrilɛ̃g] *adj* multilingual

plus **1** *adv* [ply] (**a**) *(comparatif)* more; **je gagne p. que vous** I earn more than you (do); **il est p. grand que moi** he's taller than I am *or* than me; **elle est p. jolie que belle** she is pretty rather than beautiful; **p. de** *(temps, hommes)* more; *(avec un nombre)* more than; **il a p. de vingt ans** he's over twenty; **p.... p....** the more... the more...; **p.... moins...** the more... the less...; **p. on va vers le sud, p. les jours allongent** the further south you go, the longer the days get; **de p. en p.** more and more; **de p. en p. froid** colder and colder; **celui-ci coûte 10 euros de p. que l'autre** this one costs 10 euros more than the other one; **cette année, il y a trois élèves de** *ou* **en p.** this year there are three more *or* extra pupils; **le vin est en p.** the wine is extra; **de p.** *(aussi)* furthermore; **en p.** *(aussi)* what's more; **en p. de** besides; **sans p. attendre** without further ado (**b**) *(superlatif)* **le p.** the most; **la p. longue rue** *ou* **la rue la p. longue de la ville** the longest street in the town; **c'est tout ce qu'il y a de p. simple** nothing could be simpler; **une soirée des p. réussies** a most successful evening; **qui peut le p. peut le moins** you've/he's/etc done more difficult things than that before (**c**) *(indique la négation)* **ne... p.** no more, no longer; **je ne les vois p.** I don't see them any more, I no longer see them; **je ne le ferai p.** I won't do it again; **il n'y a p. rien** there's nothing left; **p. que dix minutes!** only ten minutes left!; **non p.** neither; **je ne suis jamais allé en Afrique – moi non p.** I've never been to Africa – neither *or* nor have I (**d**) *(locutions)* **p. ou moins** more or less; **ni p. ni moins** no more no less; **sans p.** but no more than that
 2 *conj* [plys] *(dans les calculs, dans les températures)* plus
 3 *nm* [plys] (**a**) *(signe)* plus (sign) (**b**) *Fig (atout)* plus

plusieurs [plyzjœr] *adj indéfini & pron indéfini* several

plus-que-parfait (*pl* **plus-que-parfaits**) [plyskə-parfɛ] *nm* pluperfect, past perfect

plus-value (*pl* **plus-values**) [plyvaly] *nf* (*bénéfice*) profit; (*augmentation de la valeur*) appreciation; (*excédent*) (*d'impôts*) surplus; **impôt sur les plus-values** capital gains tax

Pluton [plytɔ̃] *npr* (*dieu, planète*) Pluto

plutonium [plytɔnjɔm] *nm* plutonium

plutôt [plyto] *adv* rather; (*à la place*) instead; **p. mourir!** I'd rather die!; **n'y va pas en voiture, prends p. le train** don't go by car, take the train instead; **p. que de faire qch** rather than doing sth

pluvial, -e, -aux, -ales [plyvjal, -o] *adj* pluvial; **eau pluviale** rainwater

pluvieux, -euse [plyvjø, -øz] *adj* rainy, wet

PME [peɛmə] *nf* (*abrév* **petite et moyenne entreprise**) small business

PMI [peɛmi] *nf* (*abrév* **petite et moyenne industrie**) small industrial firm

PMU [peɛmy] *nm* (*abrév* **Pari mutuel urbain**) = state-run betting system

PNB [peɛnbe] *nm* (*abrév* **produit national brut**) GNP

pneu [pnø] *nm* (**a**) (*de véhicule*) tyre; **avoir un p. à plat/crevé** to have a flat/a puncture; **p. à clous, p. clouté** studded tyre; *Can* **p. d'hiver** winter tyre; **p. neige** snow tyre; **p. pluie** wet-weather tyre; *Can* **p. quatre-saisons** all-season tyre (**b**) (*lettre*) express letter (*sent through a pneumatic dispatch system*)

pneumatique [pnømatik] **1** *adj* (*qui fonctionne à l'air*) pneumatic; (*gonflable*) inflatable
  2 *nm* = **pneu**

pneumonie [pnømɔni] *nf* pneumonia

pneumothorax [pnømotɔraks] *nm* pneumothorax

poche [pɔʃ] *nf* (**a**) (*de vêtement*) pocket; **p. revolver** hip pocket; *Fam* **faire les poches à qn** to go through sb's pockets; **de p.** pocket; **en être de sa p.** to be out of pocket; **payer de sa p.** to pay out of one's own pocket; *Fig* **connaître un endroit comme sa p.** to know a place like the back of one's hand; *Fam Fig* **se remplir les poches, s'en mettre plein les poches** to make a packet; **sans un sou en p.** without a penny in one's pocket; *Fam* **c'est dans la p.** it's in the bag (**b**) (*sac*) bag; **p. de glace** ice pack (**c**) (*amas de substance*) pocket; **p. de pétrole/gaz** pocket of oil/gas (**d**) (*déformation*) **poches sous les yeux** bags under the eyes; **son pantalon fait des poches aux genoux** his *Br* trousers *or Am* pants are baggy at the knees (**e**) (*de kangourou*) pouch (**f**) (*zone*) **p. de résistance/pauvreté** pocket of resistance/deprivation

pocher [pɔʃe] *vt* (*œuf, poisson*) to poach (**b**) *Fam* **p. l'œil à qn** to give sb a black eye

pochette [pɔʃɛt] *nf* (**a**) (*petit sac*) (small) bag; (*d'un disque*) sleeve; (*de photos*) wallet; **p. d'allumettes** book of matches (**b**) (*mouchoir*) pocket handkerchief

pochette-surprise (*pl* **pochettes-surprises**) [pɔʃɛt-syrpriz] *nf* lucky bag; *Fam* **il a eu son permis dans une p.** it's a wonder he passed his driving test

pochoir [pɔʃwar] *nm* stencil

podcast [pɔdkast] *nm Ordinat* podcast

podiatre [pɔdiatr] *nmf Can Br* chiropodist, *Am* podiatrist

podium [pɔdjɔm] *nm* podium; **monter sur le p.** to mount the podium

podomètre [pɔdɔmɛtr] *nm* pedometer

poêle¹ [pwal] *nf* frying pan; **passer qch à la p.** to fry sth

poêle² *nm* (*appareil de chauffage*) stove; **p. à mazout** oil stove

poêlon [pwalɔ̃] *nm* casserole (dish)

poème [pɔɛm] *nm* poem; *Fam* **ta fille, c'est (tout) un p.!** your daughter's really something else!

poésie [pɔezi] *nf* (**a**) (*art*) poetry (**b**) (*poème*) poem

poète [pɔɛt] *nm aussi Fig* poet

poétesse [pɔetɛs] *nf* poetess

poétique [pɔetik] *adj* poetic

poétiquement [pɔetikmɑ̃] *adv* poetically

pogne [pɔɲ] *nf Fam* paw

pognon [pɔɲɔ̃] *nm Fam* cash, dough

pogrom(e) [pɔgrɔm] *nm* pogrom

poids [pwa] *nm* (**a**) (*masse*) weight; **de tout son p.** with all one's weight; **perdre/prendre du p.** to lose/gain weight; **vendre au p.** to sell by weight; *Fam* **il ne fait pas le p.** he's not up to scratch; **p. net/brut** net/gross weight; **p. léger** (*en boxe*) lightweight; **p. lourd** (*camion*) *Br* lorry, *Am* truck; (*en boxe*) heavyweight; **p. mouche** flyweight; **p. plume** (*en boxe*) featherweight; *Fig* lightweight (**b**) *Fig* (*charge pénible*) burden; *Litt* **le p. des ans** the weight of the years; **le p. des impôts** the burden of taxation (**c**) *Fig* (*importance*) weight; **donner du p. à qch** to give weight to sth; **avoir du p.** to carry weight; **faire deux poids deux mesures** to apply double standards (**d**) (*sport*) shot; **lancer le p.** to put the shot

poignant, -e [pwaɲɑ̃, -ɑ̃t] *adj* poignant

poignard [pwaɲar] *nm* dagger

poignarder [pwaɲarde] *vt* to stab; **se faire p.** to be stabbed

poigne [pwaɲ] *nf* grip; **avoir de la p.** to have a strong grip; *Fig* to be firm

poignée [pwaɲe] *nf* (**a**) (*quantité, petit nombre*) handful (**b**) (*de porte, de sac*) handle; (*d'épée*) hilt (**c**) **p. de main** handshake

poignet [pwaɲɛ] *nm* (**a**) (*du bras*) wrist; *Fig* **faire qch à la force du p.** to do sth by sheer hard work (**b**) (*de chemise*) cuff

poil [pwal] *nm* (**a**) (*d'un animal, d'une personne, d'une plante*) hair; (*pelage*) coat; (*d'une brosse, d'un pinceau*) bristle; **à p. long/ras** long-/short-haired; *Fam* **caresser qn dans le sens du p.** to rub sb up the right way; *Fam* **tomber sur le p. à qn** to lay into sb; *Fam* **à p.** stark naked; *Fam* **se mettre à p.** to strip off; *Fam* **avoir un p. dans la main** to be bone idle; *Fam* **reprendre du p. de la bête** to pick up again; *Fam Fig* **de tous poils** of all sorts; *Fam* **être de bon/mauvais p.** to be in a good/bad mood; *Fam* **au quart de p.** perfectly; *Fam* **à un p. près** very nearly; *Fam* **un p. plus haut/moins vite** a touch higher/slower; *Fam* **au p.** great; *Fam* **tomber au p.** to arrive at just the right moment (**b**) **p. à gratter** itching powder

poiler [pwale] **se poiler** *vpr Fam* to kill oneself laughing

poilu, -e [pwaly] **1** *adj* hairy
  2 *nm Fam* poilu (*French soldier in the 1914–1918 war*)

poinçon [pwɛ̃sɔ̃] *nm* (*de graveur*) style; (*de cordonnier*) awl; (*marque*) hallmark

poinçonner [pwɛ̃sɔne] *vt* (*perforer*) to punch; (*or, argent*) to hallmark

poinçonneur, -euse [pwɛ̃sɔnœr, -øz] **1** *nm,f* (*personne*) ticket puncher
  2 *nf* **poinçonneuse** punching machine

poindre [43] [pwɛ̃dr] *vi* (*jour*) to dawn, to break; (*plantes, étoiles*) to appear

poing [pwɛ̃] *nm* fist; **sabre/revolver au p.** sword/revolver in hand; **les poings sur les hanches** hands on hips; **dormir à poings fermés** to sleep like a log

point¹ [pwɛ̃] *nm* (**a**) *(endroit)* point, spot; *(en géométrie)* point; **les quatre points cardinaux** the (four) points of the compass; **p. chaud** *(zone de conflits)* hot spot, trouble spot; *Ordinat (pour accès WiFi)* hotspot; **p. de côté** *(douleur)* stitch; *aussi Fig* **p. de départ** starting point; **p. d'eau** *(dans le désert)* waterhole; **p. de mire** target; *Fig* focus; *Aut* **p. mort** neutral; *Fig* **être au p. mort** to be at a standstill; **p. noir** *(comédon)* blackhead; *(embouteillage)* blackspot; **p. de rencontre** meeting point; **p. de vente** *(magasin)* point of sale, sales outlet; **p. de vue** *(panorama)* viewpoint; *(opinion)* point of view; **du p. de vue international/économique** from an international/economic point of view

(**b**) *(marque)* dot; *(en fin de ligne) Br* full stop, *Am* period; *Fig* **mettre les points sur les i (à qn)** to make oneself perfectly clear (to sb); *Typ & Ordinat* **points par pouce** dots per inch; **p. d'exclamation** exclamation *Br* mark or *Am* point; **p. final** *Br* full stop, *Am* period; *Fam* **un p., c'est tout!, p. final!** and that's that!; *aussi Fig* **p. d'interrogation** question mark; **points de suspension** suspension points; *Ordinat* **p. de tabulation** tab marker

(**c**) *(aspect, question)* point; **en tous points** in every way, in all respects; **p. faible/fort** weak/strong point

(**d**) *(de couture, de tricot)* stitch; **p. de croix** cross-stitch; **p. mousse** garter stitch

(**e**) *(phase, degré)* point, stage; **traiter un problème en trois points** to deal with a problem in three stages; **(cuit) à p.** done to a turn; *(steak)* medium-rare; **jusqu'à un certain p.** to a certain extent, up to a (certain) point; **au p. où j'en suis...** at the stage I've reached...; **à tel p. que..., au p. que...** to such an extent that..., so much so that...; **vous n'êtes pas malade à ce p.-là** you're not as ill as all that; **au plus haut p.** extremely

(**f**) *(dans le temps)* point; **être sur le p. de faire qch** to be about to do sth, to be on the point of doing sth; **arriver à p. nommé** to arrive just at the right moment

(**g**) *(dans un score, dans un pourcentage)* point; *(dans une notation)* mark; **bon p.** *Scol* ≃ gold star; *Fig* brownie point

(**h**) **mettre au p.** *(objectif)* to focus; *(moteur)* to tune; *(technique)* to perfect; *(stratégie)* to finalize; **être au p.** to be up to scratch

(**i**) *Naut & Av* **faire le p.** to take one's bearings; *Fig* to take stock; *Fig* **faire le p. sur qch** to take stock of sth

point² *adv Vieilli* = **pas²**

pointage [pwɛ̃taʒ] *nm* (**a**) *(contrôle) (de noms sur une liste)* ticking off; *(de votes)* counting; *(au travail) (à l'arrivée)* clocking in; *(au départ)* clocking out (**b**) *(d'un télescope)* pointing; *(de fusil)* aiming

pointe [pwɛ̃t] *nf* (**a**) *(extrémité) (d'aiguille, de couteau)* point; *(de flèche)* tip; *(de balle)* nose; *(de chaussure)* toe; *(de sein)* nipple; **p. d'asperge** asparagus tip; **en p.** pointed; **sur la p. des pieds** on tiptoe; **entrer sur la p. des pieds** to tiptoe in; **faire des pointes** *(en danse)* to go up on points (**b**) *(maximum)* peak; **p. de vitesse** burst of speed; **faire une p. de vitesse** to put on a burst of speed; **vitesse de p.** top speed (**c**) *(summum)* **être à la p. de la technique/de la recherche** to be in the forefront of technology/of research; **de p.** *(secteur, industrie, technique)* state-of-the-art (**d**) *(petite quantité) (d'accent, d'ironie)* hint;

(d'ail, de vanille) dash (**e**) *(raillerie)* dig; **lancer des pointes à qn** to make digs at sb (**f**) *(clou)* nail; *(pour tapis)* tack; *(sur une chaussure de sport)* spike; **chaussures à pointes** spiked shoes

pointer¹ [pwɛte] **1** *vt* (**a**) *(vérifier) (noms sur une liste)* to tick off; *(votes)* to count (**b**) *(dresser)* **p. les oreilles** *(sujet: animal)* to prick up its ears (**c**) *(diriger) (télescope)* to point (**sur** at); *(fusil)* to aim (**sur** at); *Ordinat (curseur)* to position (**sur** on); **j'ai pointé le doigt vers lui** I pointed (my finger) at him

2 *vi* (**a**) *(au travail) (à l'arrivée)* to clock in; *(à la sortie)* to clock out; **p. à l'ANPE** *ou* **au chômage** to register as unemployed, *Br* to sign on (**b**) *(apparaître) (plante)* to come up; *(jour)* to dawn (**c**) *(se dresser) (clocher, tour, arbre)* to rise (**d**) *(au jeu de boules)* to get one's ball nearest to the jack

3 se pointer *vpr Fam* to show up

pointer² [pwɛtɛr] *nm (chien)* pointer

pointeur, -euse [pwɛtœr, -øz] **1** *nm,f (contrôleur)* timekeeper; *(en sport)* scorer

2 *nm Ordinat* pointer

3 *nf* **pointeuse** *(machine)* timeclock

pointillé [pwɛtije] *nm* (**a**) *(trait)* dotted line; *(sur une feuille détachable)* perforations; **découper suivant les pointillés** cut along the dotted line; **les frontières sont en p. sur la carte** the frontiers are drawn as dotted lines on the map (**b**) *(technique de dessin)* stippling

pointilleux, -euse [pwɛtijø, -øz] *adj* particular, fussy (**sur** about)

pointu, -e [pwɛty] **1** *adj* (**a**) *(en forme de pointe)* pointed; *(voix)* shrill (**b**) *Fig (susceptible) (ton de la voix, humeur)* touchy (**c**) *(accent)* Parisian (**d**) *Fig (spécialisé)* specialized

2 *adv* **parler p.** to speak with a Parisian accent

pointure [pwɛtyr] *nf* size; *Fam Fig* **une (grosse) p. du cinéma français** a big name in French cinema

point-virgule *(pl* **points-virgules***)* [pwɛ̃virgyl] *nm* semicolon

poire [pwar] *nf* (**a**) *(fruit)* pear; *Fig* **couper la p. en deux** to meet each other halfway; *(faire la moyenne entre deux quantités)* to split the difference (**b**) *(objet en forme de poire) (d'un appareil photo)* bulb; *(interrupteur)* switch (**c**) *Fam (tête)* mug; **en pleine p.** right in the face (**d**) *Fam (idiot)* sucker, mug; **et moi, bonne p., j'ai accepté** and like the sucker *or* mug I am, I accepted

poireau, -x [pwaro] *nm* leek; *Fam* **faire le p.** to hang around

poireauter [pwarote] *vi Fam* to hang around

poirier [pwarje] *nm* (**a**) *(arbre)* pear tree; **faire le p.** to do a headstand, to stand on one's head (**b**) *(bois)* pear-tree wood

pois [pwa] *nm* (**a**) *(plante)* pea; **petit p.** (garden) pea; **p. cassés** split peas; **p. chiche** chickpea; **p. de senteur** sweet pea (**b**) *(rond)* (polka) dot; **à p.** polka-dot

poison [pwazɔ̃] **1** *nm* poison

2 *nmf Fam (personne)* pest

poisse [pwas] *nf Fam* bad luck

poisseux, -euse [pwasø, -øz] *adj* sticky

poisson [pwasɔ̃] *nm* (**a**) *(animal)* fish; **p. d'eau douce/de mer** freshwater/saltwater fish; *Prov* **petit p. deviendra grand** great oaks from little acorns grow; **p. d'argent** silverfish; **p. d'avril** April fool; **p. rouge** goldfish; **p. volant** flying fish (**b**) *Astron & Astrol* **les Poissons** Pisces; **être Poissons** to be (a) Pisces

Poisson d'avril

In France and in French-speaking countries, on the first of April, children cut fish shapes out of paper and stick them on their unsuspecting classmates' backs, and people play practical jokes on one another before crying out "Poisson d'avril!" ("April fool!"). This custom is referred to in Quebec as "courir le poisson d'avril".

poisson-chat (*pl* **poissons-chats**) [pwasɔ̃ʃa] *nm* catfish

poissonnerie [pwasɔnri] *nf* fish shop, *Br* fishmonger's

poissonneux, -euse [pwasɔnø, -øz] *adj* full of fish

poissonnier, -ère [pwasɔnje, -ɛr] *nm,f Br* fishmonger, *Am* fish merchant

poitevin, -e [pwatvɛ̃, -in] *adj (de Poitiers)* of Poitiers; *(du Poitou)* of Poitou

poitrail [pwatraj] *nm (d'animal)* breast; *Fam (poitrine)* chest

poitrinaire [pwatrinɛr] *adj & nmf Vieilli* consumptive

poitrine [pwatrin] *nf* (**a**) *(thorax)* chest; *(seins)* bust; **serrer qn contre sa p.** to hold sb to one's breast; **ne pas avoir beaucoup de p.** to have a small bust (**b**) *Culin (de veau)* breast; *(de bœuf)* brisket; *(de porc)* belly

poivre [pwavr] *nm* pepper; **p. en grains** peppercorns; **p. et sel** *(cheveux, barbe)* pepper-and-salt

poivré, -e [pwavre] *adj* (**a**) *(nourriture, odeur)* peppery (**b**) *Fig (histoire)* spicy

poivrer [pwavre] **1** *vt* to put pepper on/in
2 se poivrer *vpr Fam* to get plastered

poivrier [pwavrije] *nm* (**a**) *(plante)* pepper plant (**b**) *(petit pot)* pepper pot; *(moulin)* pepper mill

poivron [pwavrɔ̃] *nm* pepper, *Am* bell pepper

poivrot, -e [pwavro, -ɔt] *nm,f Fam* drunk

poix [pwa] *nf* pitch

poker [pɔkɛr] *nm* poker

polaire [pɔlɛr] *adj* (**a**) *(faune, expédition)* polar; *(froid)* Arctic (**b**) *Tex* **laine p.** fleece, fleecy material; **fourrure p.** fleecy jacket

polar [pɔlar] *nm Fam* whodunnit

polarisation [pɔlarizasjɔ̃] *nf* (**a**) *Phys* polarization (**b**) *Fig (focalisation)* focusing

polariser [pɔlarize] **1** *vt Phys* to polarize; *Fig (attention)* to focus
2 se polariser *vpr* **se p. sur** to focus on

Polaroid® [pɔlarɔid] *nm* Polaroid® (camera)

pôle [pol] *nm* (**a**) *Géog* pole; **p. Nord/Sud** North/South Pole (**b**) *Fig* **p. d'intérêt** focus of interest; **p. d'attraction** centre of attention

polémique [pɔlemik] **1** *adj* polemical
2 *nf* controversy; **une vive p. s'ensuivit** a heated debate ensued

polémiquer [pɔlemike] *vi* to debate

poli¹, -e¹ [pɔli] *adj (lisse)* polished

poli², -e² *adj (courtois)* polite (**avec** to)

police¹ [pɔlis] *nf* (**a**) *(maintien de l'ordre)* policing; **faire la p.** to keep order (**b**) *(institution)* **la p.** the police; **la p. est prévenue** the police have been called; **appeler p. secours** to call the police *(in an emergency)*; **être de** *ou* **dans la p.** to be in the police; **p. de l'air et des frontières** airport and border police; **p. judiciaire** police investigation department; **p. mondaine** *ou* **des mœurs** vice squad; **p. montée**

mounted police; **p. municipale** local police; **la p. nationale** the national police force; **p. secrète** secret police

Police nationale

The "Police nationale" operates under the authority of the Ministry of the Interior, unlike the "Gendarmerie", which is an army corps.

police² *nf* (**a**) *(d'assurance)* policy; **p. d'assurance** insurance policy (**b**) *Ordinat* **p. (de caractères)** font; **p. bitmap** *ou* **pixélisée** bitmap font; **p. de taille variable** scalable font; **p. vectorielle** outline font

polichinelle [pɔliʃinɛl] *nm* (**a**) *(marionnette)* Punch (**b**) *Fig & Péj* buffoon

policier, -ère [pɔlisje, -ɛr] **1** *adj (enquête, État, régime)* police; *(roman, film)* detective
2 *nm* (**a**) *(personne)* policeman, police officer; **femme p.** policewoman, woman police officer (**b**) *(roman)* detective novel; *(film)* detective movie *or Br* film

policlinique [pɔliklinik] *nf* outpatients' clinic

poliment [pɔlimɑ̃] *adv* politely

polio [pɔljo] **1** *nf* polio; **avoir la p.** to have polio
2 *nmf* polio victim

poliomyélite [pɔljɔmjelit] *nf* poliomyelitis

polir [pɔlir] *vt* to polish

polisson, -onne [pɔlisɔ̃, -ɔn] **1** *nm,f (enfant espiègle)* rascal
2 *adj* (**a**) *(espiègle)* mischievous (**b**) *(grivois)* saucy

politesse [pɔlitɛs] *nf* politeness; **par p.** out of politeness; **ce serait la moindre des politesses de le prévenir** it's only polite to warn him; **rendre la p. à qn** to return sb's favour

politicien, -enne [pɔlitisjɛ̃, -ɛn] **1** *nm,f* politician
2 *adj Péj* **politique politicienne** politicking

politique [pɔlitik] **1** *adj* political; **homme/femme p.** politician
2 *nf* (**a**) *(de gouvernement, d'entreprise)* policy; **p. intérieure/extérieure** domestic/foreign policy; **la p. du pire** is the policy of presenting one's situation in the worst possible light in order to achieve one's objectives; **la p. agricole commune** the Common Agricultural Policy (**b**) *(affaires publiques)* politics; **faire de la p.** *(en tant que politicien)* to be in politics; *(en tant que militant)* to be involved in politics
3 *nmf (personne)* politician

politiquement [pɔlitikmɑ̃] *adv* politically

politisation [pɔlitizasjɔ̃] *nf* politicization

politiser [pɔlitize] *vt* to politicize

politologue [pɔlitɔlɔg] *nmf* political scientist

polka [pɔlka] *nf* polka

pollen [pɔlɛn] *nm* pollen

polluant, -e [pɔlɥɑ̃, -ɑ̃t] **1** *adj* polluting; **produit p.** pollutant
2 *nm* pollutant

pollué, -e [pɔlɥe] *adj* polluted

polluer [pɔlɥe] *vt* to pollute

pollueur, -euse [pɔlɥœr, -øz] **1** *adj* polluting
2 *nm,f* polluter

pollution [pɔlysjɔ̃] *nf* pollution

polo [pɔlo] *nm* (**a**) *(sport)* polo (**b**) *(chemise)* polo shirt

polochon [pɔlɔʃɔ̃] *nm Fam* bolster; **bataille de polochons** pillow fight

Pologne [pɔlɔɲ] *nf* **la P.** Poland

polonais, -e [pɔlɔnɛ, -ɛz] **1** *adj* Polish
 2 *nm,f* P. Pole
 3 *nm (langue)* Polish
 4 *nf* **polonaise** *(danse)* polonaise
poltron, -onne [pɔltrɔ̃, -ɔn] **1** *adj* cowardly
 2 *nm,f* coward
polyamide [pɔliamid] *nm* polyamide
polychrome [pɔlikrom] *adj* polychrome
polyclinique [pɔliklinik] *nf* polyclinic
polycopie [pɔlikɔpi] *nf (procédé)* duplication; *(document)* duplicate
polycopié, -e [pɔlikɔpje] **1** *adj* duplicated
 2 *nm* duplicate; *Scol & Univ* duplicated course notes
polycopier [66] [pɔlikɔpje] *vt* to duplicate
polyculture [pɔlikyltyr] *nf* mixed farming
polyester [pɔliɛstɛr] *nm* polyester
polygame [pɔligam] **1** *adj* polygamous
 2 *nm* polygamist
polygamie [pɔligami] *nf* polygamy
polyglotte [pɔliglɔt] *adj & nmf* polyglot
polygone [pɔligɔn, pɔligon] *nm* (**a**) *(figure)* polygon
 (**b**) *Mil* **p. de tir** shooting range
polymère [pɔlimɛr] **1** *adj* polymeric
 2 *nm* polymer
Polynésie [pɔlinezi] *nf* **la P.** Polynesia; **la P. française** French Polynesia
polynésien, -enne [pɔlinezjɛ̃, -ɛn] **1** *adj* Polynesian
 2 *nm,f* **P.** Polynesian
polype [pɔlip] *nm* polyp
polyphonie [pɔlifɔni] *nf* polyphony
polysémique [pɔlisemik] *adj* polysemous
polystyrène [pɔlistirɛn] *nm* polystyrene
polytechnicien, -enne [pɔlitɛknisjɛ̃, -ɛn] *nm,f* graduate of the "École polytechnique"
Polytechnique [pɔlitɛknik] *nf* **(l'École) p., P.** = "grande école" specializing in technology

École polytechnique

Founded in 1794, this prestigious engineering college has close connections with the Ministry of Defence. Formerly situated in the heart of the 5th arrondissement, the college moved to Palaiseau, near Paris, in the 1970s. It is popularly known as "l'X". Students are effectively enlisted in the army and must repay their education through government service.

polythéisme [pɔliteism] *nm* polytheism
polyvalence [pɔlivalɑ̃s] *nf (en chimie)* polyvalency; *Fig (d'une personne)* versatility
polyvalent, -e [pɔlivalɑ̃, -ɑ̃t] **1** *adj* (**a**) *(en chimie)* polyvalent (**b**) *(salle)* multi-purpose; *(outil, personne)* versatile
 2 *nm,f* tax inspector
pomélo [pɔmelo] *nm* pomelo
pommade [pɔmad] *nf* ointment; *Fam* **passer de la p. à qn** to butter sb up
pomme [pɔm] *nf* (**a**) *(fruit)* apple; *Fam* **haut comme trois pommes** knee-high to a grasshopper; *Fam* **tomber dans les pommes** to pass out; *Fam* **être dans les pommes** to be out for the count; **p. d'Adam** Adam's apple; **p. de discorde** bone of contention; **p. de pin** pine cone; *(de sapin)* fir cone (**b**) *(partie arrondie) (de bois de lit, de canne)* knob; *(d'arrosoir)* rose; **p. de douche** shower head (**c**) *(pomme de terre)* **pommes allumettes** matchstick *Br* chips *or Am* potatoes; **pommes chips** (potato) *Br* crisps *or Am* chips;

pommes dauphine dauphine potatoes; **p. de terre** potato; **pommes (de terre) à l'eau** boiled potatoes; **pommes (de terre) frites** *Br* chips, *Am* (French) fries; **pommes (de terre) sautées** sauté potatoes; **pommes vapeur** steamed potatoes (**d**) *Fam (personne)* **ma p.** yours truly; **ta p.** you; **sa p.** him/her (**e**) *Fam (idiot)* mug; **être bonne p.** to be a mug
pommeau, -x [pɔmo] *nm (d'un sabre, d'une selle)* pommel; *(d'une canne, d'un levier de vitesse)* knob
pommelé, -e [pɔmle] *adj* dappled; **gris p.** *(cheval)* dapple-grey; **ciel p.** mackerel sky
pommer [pɔme] *vi (chou, salade)* to form a heart
pommeraie [pɔmrɛ] *nf* apple orchard
pommette [pɔmɛt] *nf* cheekbone
pommier [pɔmje] *nm* apple tree; **p. sauvage** crab-apple tree
pompage [pɔ̃paʒ] *nm* pumping
pompe¹ [pɔ̃p] *nf (cérémonie)* pomp, ceremony; **en grande p.** with great (pomp and) ceremony
pompe² *nf* (**a**) *(machine)* pump; **p. à essence** *(distributeur)* *Br* petrol *or Am* gas pump; *(station-service)* *Br* petrol *or Am* gas station; **p. à incendie** water pump *(on a fire engine)*; **p. à vélo** bicycle pump; *Fam* **à toute p.** like lightning; *Fam* **faire des pompes** to do *Br* press-ups *or Am* push-ups (**b**) *Fam* **pompes** *(chaussures)* shoes; *Fig* **il est à côté de ses pompes** he's not with it (**c**) **pompes funèbres** undertaker's
pomper [pɔ̃pe] **1** *vt* (**a**) *(puiser) (eau, air)* to pump; *(faire monter)* to pump up; *(évacuer)* to pump out; *Fam Fig* **p. qn** *(épuiser)* to do sb in; *Fam* **être pompé** to be done in; *Fam* **tu me pompes l'air** you're getting on my nerves (**b**) *Fam (boisson)* to knock back (**c**) *Fam Scol* to crib (**sur** from)
 2 *vi* (**a**) *(faire marcher une pompe)* to pump (**b**) *Fam Scol* to crib (**sur** from)
pompette [pɔ̃pɛt] *adj Fam* tipsy
pompeux, -euse [pɔ̃pø, -øz] *adj Péj* pompous
pompier¹ [pɔ̃pje] *nm* fireman; **appeler les pompiers** to call the fire *Br* brigade *or Am* department
pompier², -ère [pɔ̃pje, -ɛr] *adj Art* pompier; *Péj (style)* pompous
pompiste [pɔ̃pist] *nmf* pump attendant
pom-pom girl [pɔmpɔmgœrl] *nf* cheerleader
pompon [pɔ̃pɔ̃] *nm* pompom, bobble; **bonnet à p.** bobble hat; *Fam* **c'est le p.!** that's the limit!
pomponner [pɔ̃pɔne] **se pomponner** *vpr Fam* to get dolled up
ponce [pɔ̃s] *adj voir* **pierre**
poncer [16] [pɔ̃se] *vt* (**a**) *(au papier de verre, avec une ponceuse)* to sand (down) (**b**) *(passer à la pierre ponce)* to pumice
ponceuse [pɔ̃søz] *nf* sander
poncho [pɔ̃tʃo] *nm* poncho
poncif [pɔ̃sif] *nm* cliché, commonplace
ponction [pɔ̃ksjɔ̃] *nf Méd* puncture; *(de poumon)* tapping; **p. lombaire** lumbar puncture; *Fig* **faire des ponctions dans ses économies** to draw on one's savings; **p. fiscale** taxation
ponctualité [pɔ̃ktɥalite] *nf* punctuality
ponctuation [pɔ̃ktɥasjɔ̃] *nf* punctuation
ponctuel, -elle [pɔ̃ktɥɛl] *adj* (**a**) *(à l'heure)* punctual (**b**) *(unique)* *Br* one-off, *Am* one-of-a-kind; *(isolé)* selective
ponctuellement [pɔ̃ktɥɛlmɑ̃] *adv (de façon limitée)* on an ad hoc basis
ponctuer [pɔ̃ktɥe] *vt aussi Fig* to punctuate (**de** with)
pondaison [pɔ̃dɛzɔ̃] *nf* egg-laying time

pondérale [põderal] *adj f voir* **surcharge**
pondération [põderasjõ] *nf* (**a**) *(modération)* level-headedness (**b**) *Écon* weighting
pondéré, -e [põdere] *adj* (**a**) *(personne)* level-headed (**b**) *Écon* weighted
pondeuse [põdøz] *adj f & nf* (**poule**) **p.** layer
pondre [põdr] *vt* (**a**) *(œuf)* to lay (**b**) *Fam (produire)* to turn out
poney [põnɛ] *nm* pony
pont [põ] *nm* (**a**) *(sur un cours d'eau)* bridge; **les Ponts et Chaussées** the Highways Department; *Fig* **faire un p. d'or à qn** to give sb a golden hello; **p. suspendu** suspension bridge (**b**) *Fig (congés)* long weekend; **le p. du premier mai** the May Day long weekend; **faire le p.** to make a long weekend of it (**c**) *(d'un navire)* deck; **sur le p.** on deck (**d**) *(lien)* **couper les ponts (avec qn)** to break off all relations (with sb); **p. aérien** airlift; *Ordinat* **p. routeur** routing node (**e**) *Ind* **p. roulant** travelling crane
pontage [põtaʒ] *nm Méd* bypass (operation)
ponte¹ [põt] *nf (action)* (egg) laying; *(œufs)* eggs (laid)
ponte² *nm Fam* (**grand**) **p.** *(personnage important)* big shot
pontife [põtif] *nm Rel* pontiff; **le souverain p.** the Supreme Pontiff
pontifiant, -e [põtifjã, -ãt] *adj Péj* pontificating
pontifical, -e, -aux, -ales [põtifikal, -o] *adj* papal
pontifier [66] [põtifje] *vi* to pontificate
pont-l'évêque [põlevɛk] *nm inv* Pont-l'Évêque (cheese)
pont-levis (*pl* ponts-levis) [põləvi] *nm* drawbridge
ponton [põtõ] *nm* pontoon
pop [pɔp] *adj inv & nf* pop
pop-corn [pɔpkɔrn] *nm inv* popcorn
pope [pɔp] *nm Rel* (Orthodox) priest
popeline [pɔplin] *nf* poplin
popote [pɔpɔt] **1** *nf*(**a**) *Fam (cuisine)* cooking; **faire la p.** to do the cooking (**b**) *Mil* officers' mess
2 *adj inv Fam* stay-at-home
popotin [pɔpɔtɛ̃] *nm Fam Br* bum, *Am* butt
populace [pɔpylas] *nf* rabble, mob
populaire [pɔpylɛr] *adj* (**a**) *(du peuple, qui plaît)* popular (**b**) *(langue, expression)* vernacular (**c**) *(ouvrier)* working-class; **les classes populaires** the working classes
populariser [pɔpylarize] *vt* to popularize
popularité [pɔpylarite] *nf* popularity
population [pɔpylasjõ] *nf* population; **p. active** working population
populeux, -euse [pɔpylø, -øz] *adj* crowded
populisme [pɔpylism] *nm* populism
populo [pɔpylo] *nm Fam (foule)* crowd (of people)
pop-up (*pl* pop-ups) [pɔpœp] *nm ou nf Ordinat* pop-up (ad)
porc [pɔr] *nm* (**a**) *(animal)* pig, *Am* hog; *Fam Fig (homme)* pig (**b**) *(viande)* pork (**c**) *(cuir)* pigskin
porcelaine [pɔrsəlɛn] *nf (matière)* porcelain, china; *(objet)* piece of porcelain; **une tasse de** *ou* **en p.** a porcelain *or* china cup
porcelet [pɔrsəlɛ] *nm* piglet
porc-épic (*pl* porcs-épics) [pɔrkepik] *nm* porcupine
porche [pɔrʃ] *nm* porch
porcherie [pɔrʃəri] *nf aussi Fig Br* pigsty, *Am* pigpen
porcin, -e [pɔrsɛ̃, -in] **1** *adj* pig; *Péj (visage, yeux)* piggy
2 *nm* porcins pigs, *Am* hogs
pore [pɔr] *nm* pore; **elle sue la suffisance par tous les pores** she exudes *or* oozes self-importance

poreux, -euse [pɔrø, -øz] *adj* porous
porno [pɔrno] *adj & nm Fam* porn
pornographie [pɔrnɔgrafi] *nf* pornography
pornographique [pɔrnɔgrafik] *adj* pornographic
port¹ [pɔr] *nm* (**a**) *(pour bateaux)* harbour; *(plus important)* port; *Fig* **arriver à bon p.** to arrive safe and sound; **p. d'attache** home port; *Fig* home base; **p. de commerce** commercial port; **p. de pêche** fishing port; **p. de plaisance** marina (**b**) *Ordinat* port; **p. de communication** comms port, communications port; **p. d'entrée/sortie** input/output port; **p. d'E/S** I/O port; **p. d'extension** expansion port; **p. modem** modem port; **p. parallèle** parallel port; **p. série** serial port; **p. souris** mouse port
port² *nm* (**a**) *(fait de transporter)* carrying; **p. d'armes** carrying of firearms (**b**) *(fait de revêtir)* wearing; **le p. du casque est obligatoire** *(sur panneau)* safety helmets must be worn (**c**) *(de marchandises)* carriage; *(de paquets, de lettres, de télégrammes)* delivery; **p. et emballage** postage and packing; **p. franc** *(de marchandises)* carriage paid; **p. payé** *(de magazine)* postage paid (**d**) *(allure)* bearing; **un gracieux p. de tête** a graceful manner of holding one's head
portabilité [pɔrtabilite] *nf Ordinat* portability
portable [pɔrtabl] **1** *adj* (**a**) *(ordinateur, machine à écrire)* portable; **téléphone p.** *Br* mobile (phone), *Am* cellphone (**b**) *(vêtement)* wearable
2 *nm (ordinateur)* laptop; *(téléphone)* *Br* mobile (phone), *Am* cell(phone)
portage [pɔrtaʒ] *nm Can* portage
portager [45] [pɔrtaʒe] *vi Can* to portage
portail [pɔrtaj] *nm aussi Ordinat* portal
portant, -e [pɔrtã, -ãt] *adj* **être bien/mal p.** to be in good/poor health
portatif, -ive [pɔrtatif, -iv] *adj* portable
Port-au-Prince [pɔrɔprɛ̃s] *n* Port-au-Prince
porte [pɔrt] *nf* (**a**) *(de maison, de placard, de véhicule)* door; **à ma p.** on my doorstep; **de p. à p.** door to door; *Fig* **entre deux portes** briefly; **mettre qn à la p.** to throw sb out; *(d'un emploi)* to fire sb; **trouver p. close** to find nobody in; *Fam* **ce n'est pas la p. à côté** it's hardly just around the corner; **c'est la p. ouverte à...** it's leaving the door wide open to...; **(voiture) deux/quatre/cinq portes** two-/four-/five-door car; **p. cochère** carriage entrance; **p. de derrière** back door; **p. d'entrée**, *Belg* **p. de rue** front door; **p. tournante, p. à tambour** revolving door; **p. vitrée** glass door (**b**) *(d'une ville)* gate; **aux portes du désert** at the gateway to the desert; **p. (d'embarquement)** *(dans un aéroport)* (boarding) gate (**c**) *(en ski)* gate
porté, -e [pɔrte] *adj (enclin)* **être p. à faire qch** to be inclined to do sth; *Fam* **être p. sur la bouteille** to be fond of the bottle; *Fam* **être p. sur la chose** to have a one-track mind
porte-à-faux [pɔrtafo] **en porte-à-faux** *adv* overhanging; *Fig* **être en p.** to be awkwardly placed
porte-à-porte [pɔrtapɔrt] *nm* door-to-door selling; **faire du p.** *(pour vendre)* to sell from door to door; *(faire des enquêtes)* to go from door to door
porte-avions [pɔrtavjõ] *nm inv* aircraft carrier
porte-bagages [pɔrtbagaʒ] *nm inv (de bicyclette)* carrier; *(de train)* luggage rack
porte-bébé (*pl* porte-bébés) [pɔrtbebe] *nm* baby carrier
porte-bonheur [pɔrtbɔnœr] *nm inv* (lucky) charm
porte-bouteilles [pɔrtbutɛj] *nm inv (pour stocker)* wine rack; *(pour porter)* bottle-carrier

porte-cartes [pɔrtəkart] *nm inv (portefeuille)* card-holder

porte-cigarettes [pɔrtsigarɛt] *nm inv* cigarette case

porte-clefs, porte-clés [pɔrtəkle] *nm inv* key ring

porte-documents [pɔrtdɔkymɑ̃] *nm inv* briefcase

porte-drapeau *(pl* **porte-drapeaux** *ou* **porte-drapeau)** [pɔrtdrapo] *nm aussi Fig* standard bearer

portée [pɔrte] *nf* (**a**) *(petits)* litter; *(d'une truie)* farrow (**b**) *(amplitude) (d'un fusil, d'un émetteur, de la voix)* range; *Fig (d'un traité)* scope; **à p. de (la) main** within reach, to hand; **à p. de (la) voix** within earshot; **à la p. de toutes les bourses** within everyone's means; **c'est à ma p.** *(objet)* it's within my reach; *Fig (livre)* I can understand it; **hors de ma p.** *(objet)* beyond my reach; *Fig (livre)* beyond me; **hors de p.** out of reach (**c**) *Fig (impact) (de paroles, d'une décision)* significance (**d**) *Mus* stave

portefaix [pɔrtəfɛ] *nm* porter

porte-fenêtre *(pl* **portes-fenêtres)** [pɔrtfənɛtr] *nf* French window

portefeuille [pɔrtəfœj] *nm* (**a**) *(pour l'argent)* wallet, *Am* billfold; **faire un lit en p.** to make an apple-pie bed; **jupe p.** wrapover skirt (**b**) *Fin & Pol* portfolio; **p. d'actions/de titres** share/securities portfolio

porte-jarretelles [pɔrtʒartɛl] *nm inv Br* suspender *or Am* garter belt

porte-malheur [pɔrtmalœr] *nm inv* jinx

portemanteau, -x [pɔrtmɑ̃to] *nm (au mur)* coat rack; *(sur pied)* coat stand

portemine [pɔrtəmin] *nm* propelling pencil

porte-monnaie [pɔrtmɔnɛ] *nm inv* purse; **p. électronique** electronic purse

porte-parapluies [pɔrtparaplɥi] *nm inv* umbrella stand

porte-parole [pɔrtparɔl] *nm inv* spokesperson, spokesman, *f* spokeswoman

porte-plume [pɔrtəplym] *nm inv* penholder

porter [pɔrte] **1** *vt* (**a**) *(soutenir)* to carry; **mes jambes ne me portent plus** my legs won't carry me any further; **je ne le porte pas dans mon cœur** he's not exactly my favourite person
(**b**) *(emporter)* to take; *(amener)* to bring
(**c**) *(vêtement, chapeau, lunettes)* to wear; *(signature, date)* to bear; *(prénom, nom)* to have; **p. une moustache/la barbe** to have a moustache/a beard; **p. les cheveux courts/longs** to wear one's hair short/long, to have short/long hair; **p. le nom de qn** to be named after sb; **p. le titre de...** *(livre, film)* to be entitled...
(**d**) *(produire) (fruits)* to bear
(**e**) *(diriger)* **p. un coup à qn** to strike sb; **p. la main à son front** to hold one's hand to one's forehead; **p. son attention sur qch** to turn one's attention to sth, to give sth one's attention; **p. une affaire devant les tribunaux** to bring a matter to court; **p. qch à la connaissance de qn** to bring sth to sb's attention
(**f**) *(inscrire)* to enter; **se faire p. malade** to report sick
(**g**) *(inciter)* **tout (me) porte à croire que...** everything leads me to believe that...
(**h**) *(à un niveau plus élevé)* **p. la température à 100°** to raise the temperature to 100°; **portez le liquide à ébullition** bring the liquid to the boil; **cela portera à 30 euros le prix du billet** that will bring the price of the ticket up to 30 euros

2 *vi* (**a**) *(cogner)* **p. sur/contre qch** to hit sth (**b**) *(atteindre son objectif) (coup)* to strike home, to hit its target; *(voix)* to carry

3 **porter sur** *vt ind* (**a**) *(avoir pour sujet)* to be about (**b**) *Fam* **p. sur les nerfs à qn** to get on sb's nerves

4 **se porter** *vpr* (**a**) *(physiquement)* **se p. bien** to be well; **je ne m'en porte pas plus mal** I'm none the worse for it; *Hum* **moins je le vois, mieux je me porte** the less I see him, the better I feel
(**b**) *(devoir être porté)* to be worn; *(être à la mode)* to be fashionable
(**c**) *(se présenter comme)* **se p. acquéreur de qch** to offer to buy sth; **se p. candidat** to *Br* stand *or Am* run as a candidate; **se p. caution** to stand surety
(**d**) *(aller)* **se p. au secours de qn** to go to sb's assistance
(**e**) **se p. sur** *(sujet: regard, choix)* to fall on

porte-savon *(pl* **porte-savons** *ou* **porte-savon)** [pɔrtsavɔ̃] *nm* soapdish

porte-serviettes [pɔrtsɛrvjɛt] *nm inv* towel rail

porteur, -euse [pɔrtœr, -øz] **1** *nm,f* (**a**) *(d'un message, de nouvelles)* bearer; **par p.** by messenger (**b**) *(de gare, d'aéroport)* porter; **p. d'eau** water carrier (**c**) *Méd* carrier; **p. sain** = carrier who doesn't have the symptoms of the disease (**d**) *(détenteur)* holder; *(d'un chèque)* bearer; **payable au p.** payable to bearer

2 *adj* (**a**) *Élec* **fréquence/onde porteuse** carrier frequency/wave (**b**) *(marché, créneau)* growth

porte-voix [pɔrtəvwa] *nm inv* megaphone; *(électrique) Br* loudhailer, *Am* bullhorn; **mettre ses mains en p.** to cup one's hands round one's mouth

portier [pɔrtje] *nm* porter, doorkeeper; *(dans un hôtel)* commissionaire; **p. de nuit** night porter

portière [pɔrtjɛr] *nf (d'une voiture, d'un train)* door

portillon [pɔrtijɔ̃] *nm* gate; *(d'un passage à niveau)* side gate; **p. (automatique)** *(de gare, de métro)* ticket barrier

portion [pɔrsjɔ̃] *nf* portion; **être réduit à la p. congrue** to get the smallest share

portique [pɔrtik] *nm* (**a**) *(colonnes)* portico (**b**) *(pour agrès)* (cross)beam

Porto [pɔrto] *n* Oporto

porto [pɔrto] *nm* port

portoricain, -e [pɔrtɔrikɛ̃, -ɛn] **1** *adj* Puerto Rican **2** *nm,f* **P.** Puerto Rican

Porto Rico [pɔrtoriko] *n* Puerto Rico

portrait [pɔrtrɛ] *nm* (**a**) *(peinture, dessin, photo)* portrait; **le p.** *(genre)* portrait painting, portraiture; **faire le p. de qn** to do a portrait of sb; *Fig* **c'est le p. vivant de son père, c'est tout le p. de son père** he's the spitting image of his father; *Fam* **il s'est fait abîmer** *ou* **arranger le p.** he got his face rearranged; *Fam* **se faire tirer le p.** to have one's photo taken (**b**) *(description)* description; **faire le p. de qn/qch** to paint a picture of sb/sth (**c**) *Ordinat* **mode p.** portrait mode

portraitiste [pɔrtretist] *nmf* portrait painter, portraitist

portrait-robot *(pl* **portraits-robots)** [pɔrtrɛrɔbo] *nm* Photofit® (picture), Identikit® picture; *Fig* profile

portuaire [pɔrtɥɛr] *adj* port, harbour

portugais, -e [pɔrtygɛ, -ɛz] **1** *adj* Portuguese **2** *nm,f* **P.** Portuguese **3** *nm (langue)* Portuguese **4** *nf* **portugaise** (**a**) *(huître)* Portuguese oyster (**b**) *Fam (oreille)* ear; **avoir les portugaises ensablées** to be as deaf as a post

Portugal [pɔrtygal] *nm* **le P.** Portugal

pose [poz] *nf* (**a**) *(de rideaux, de papier peint)* putting up, hanging; *(d'une vitre)* putting in; *(de moquette, de câbles)* laying; *(d'appareils)* installation; *(d'une* *bombe)* planting; *Méd (d'un stérilet)* putting in; *(de ventouses)* application (**b**) *(pour photo, portrait)* pose; **prendre la p.** to pose; **garder la p.** to hold the pose; *Péj* **prendre des poses** to pose (**c**) *Phot* exposure; **pellicule de 24 poses** 24-exposure film

posé, -e [poze] *adj (réfléchi)* composed, calm

posément [pozemã] *adv* calmly

poser [poze] **1** *vt* (**a**) *(mettre)* to put down; **p. qch sur/sous qch** to put sth on/under sth; *Fig* **p. son regard sur qn/qch** to look at sb/sth (**b**) *(formuler) (question)* to ask; *(hypothèse)* to put forward; *(principe)* to lay down; **p. une question à qn** to ask sb a question; **p. un problème à qn** to pose a problem for sb; **p. sa candidature** *(aux élections)* to put oneself forward (as a candidate), *Br* to stand (as a candidate); *(à un poste)* to apply (**c**) *(rideaux, papier peint)* to put up, to hang; *(vitre)* to put in; *(moquette, câble)* to lay; *(appareil)* to install; *(bombe)* to plant; *Méd* **p. qch à qn** *(stérilet)* to put sth in sb; *(ventouses)* to apply sth to sb (**d**) *Math (opération, équation)* to set out; **je pose deux et je retiens un** put down two and carry one (**e**) *Can (photographier)* to photograph, to take a photograph of
2 *vi (pour une photo, pour un tableau)* to pose; *Péj* **p. pour la galerie** to play to the gallery
3 se poser *vpr* (**a**) *(oiseau, avion)* to land; *Fig* **se p. sur** *(sujet: regard)* to rest on (**b**) *(question, problème)* to arise, to come up (**c**) *(à soi-même)* **se p. des questions** to ask oneself questions; *(avoir des doutes)* to have one's doubts (**d**) *Fam* **comme bricoleur/cuisinier, il se pose un peu là!** some handyman/cook, I don't think!; **comme enquiquineur, il se pose là!** he's a real pain in the neck! (**e**) *(se prétendre)* **se p. en réformateur/redresseur de torts** to set oneself up as a reformer/a righter of wrongs

poseur, -euse [pozœr, -øz] *nm,f* (**a**) *(de câbles, de carrelage)* layer; **p. d'affiches** billsticker, billposter; **la police recherche les poseurs de bombes** the police are hunting the people who planted the bombs (**b**) *Péj (pédant)* show-off, poseur

positif, -ive [pozitif, -iv] *adj* positive; **il est p.** *(à l'Alcotest, au contrôle antidopage)* he tested positive

position [pozisjõ] *nf* (**a**) *(emplacement)* position; **être en première/deuxième p.** *(dans une course)* to be in first/second place; *(sur une liste)* to be first/second; **arriver en première/deuxième p.** to come first/second (**b**) *(attitude, en danse)* position; **être/se mettre en p.** to be in/get into position; **en p. debout/assise** in a standing/sitting position (**c**) *(opinion)* position (**sur** on); **prendre p.** to take a stand; **rester sur ses positions** to stand one's ground (**d**) *(situation)* position; **être en p. de faire qch** to be in a position to do sth; **p. sociale** social position

positionner [pozisjone] **1** *vt* to position
2 se positionner *vpr* to position oneself

positivement [pozitivmã] *adv* positively

positiver [pozitive] *vi* to think positive *or* positively

posologie [pozolɔʒi] *nf Méd* dosage

possédé, -e [posede] **1** *adj (du démon)* possessed
2 *nm,f* person possessed; **hurler comme un p.** to scream like one possessed

posséder [34] [posede] *vt* (**a**) *(biens matériels)* to possess, to own; *(talent, qualité)* to possess, to have (**b**) *(sujet)* to have a thorough knowledge of; *(langue, technique)* to have mastered (**c**) *(sujet: démon, passion)* to possess (**d**) *Fam (tromper)* to take in; **se faire p.** to be taken in (**e**) *Litt (femme)* to possess

possesseur [posesœr] *nm* owner; *(d'un titre)* holder

possessif, -ive [posesif, -iv] *adj & nm* possessive

possession [posesjõ] *nf* (**a**) *(fait d'avoir)* ownership, possession; *(d'un titre)* holding; **avoir qch en sa p.** to have sth in one's possession; **être en p. de qch** to be in possession of sth; **prendre p. de qch** to take possession of sth (**b**) *(bien, territoire)* possession (**c**) *(par le démon)* possession (**d**) *(maîtrise)* **être en p. de toutes ses facultés** to be in full possession of one's faculties; **être en pleine p. de ses moyens** to be at the peak of one's powers

possibilité [posibilite] *nf* (**a**) *(éventualité)* possibility (**b**) *(moyen, occasion)* opportunity, chance; **avoir la p. de faire qch** to have the opportunity *or* the chance of doing sth (**c**) **possibilités** *(intellectuelles)* potential; *(financières)* means (**d**) *Ordinat* **possibilités d'extension** upgradeability

possible [posibl] **1** *adj* (**a**) *(faisable, vraisemblable)* possible; **il leur est p. de vous héberger** it's possible for them to put you up; **il est p. qu'il soit mort** it's possible that he's dead, he might be dead; **aussitôt que p., dès que p.** as soon as possible; *Fam* **pas p.!** I don't believe it!; **si p.** if possible (**b**) *(comme superlatif)* **elle nous en parle le moins/plus p.** she talks to us about it as little/much as possible; **le moins/plus souvent p.** as infrequently/frequently as possible; **le moins/plus de détails p.** as few/many details as possible; **la boîte la plus grande p.** the largest box possible; **tous les détails possibles (et imaginables)** every possible detail (**c**) *Fam (supportable)* **pas p.** *(personne, situation)* impossible; **ça n'est plus p.!** I've had enough!
2 *nm* **faire tout son p. (pour faire qch)** to do everything one possibly can (to do sth)

postal, -e, -aux, -ales [postal, -o] *adj (tarif, services)* postal; *(train, wagon)* mail

postdater [postdate] *vt* to postdate

post-doctoral, -e, -aux, -ales [postdoktɔral, -o] *adj Univ* post-doctoral, post-doctorate

post-doctorat *(pl* **post-doctorats)** [postdoktɔra] *nm Univ* post-doctorate

poste¹ [post] *nf* (**a**) *(service)* mail, *Br* post; **la P.** the postal service; **mettre qch à la p.** to mail *or Br* post sth; **par la p.** by mail, *Br* by post; **p. aérienne** airmail (**b**) *(lieu)* **(bureau de) p.** post office; **p. restante** *Br* poste restante, *Am* general delivery

poste² *nm* (**a**) *(fonction)* position, post; **p. à pourvoir** vacancy (**b**) *(appareil)* **p. (de radio/télévision)** radio/television (set); *Rad* **p. émetteur** *(équipement)* transmitter; *Ordinat* **p. de travail** work station (**c**) *(local)* **p. (de police)** (police) station; **p. d'aiguillage** signal box; **p. d'essence** *Br* petrol *or Am* gas station; (**d**) *(d'un soldat)* post; **être à son p.** to be at one's post; **p. de pilotage** cockpit (**e**) *(d'un standard)* extension (**f**) *(comptable)* entry, item

poster¹ [poste] **1** *vt (sentinelle, hommes, troupes)* to post, to station
2 se poster *vpr* to take up a position, to station oneself

poster² *vt (courrier)* to mail, *Br* to post

poster³ [postɛr] *nm* poster

postérieur, -e [posterjœr] **1** *adj* (**a**) *(dans le temps)* later, subsequent; **p. à** after (**b**) *(de derrière) (pattes)* back, hind; *Anat* posterior
2 *nm Hum (derrière)* posterior

postérieurement [posterjœrmã] *adv* later, subsequently; **p. à** after

postérité [pɔsterite] *nf* posterity; **passer à la p.** *(personne)* to go down in history; *(œuvre, mot)* to be handed down to posterity
postface [pɔstfas] *nf* postscript
posthume [pɔstym] *adj* posthumous
postiche [pɔstiʃ] **1** *adj* false
  2 *nm* hairpiece
postier, -ère [pɔstje, -ɛr] *nm,f* postal worker
postillon [pɔstijɔ̃] *nm* (**a**) *Hist (cocher)* postilion (**b**) **postillons** *(salive)* shower of spit; **envoyer des postillons** to splutter
postillonner [pɔstijɔne] *vi* to splutter
postindustriel, -elle [pɔstɛ̃dystrijɛl] *adj* post-industrial
postmoderne [pɔstmɔdɛrn] *adj* post-modernist
postopératoire [pɔstɔperatwar] *adj* *Méd* post-operative
post-scriptum [pɔstskriptɔm] *nm inv* postscript
postsynchroniser [pɔstsɛ̃krɔnize] *vt* *Cin* to dub
postulant, -e [pɔstylɑ̃, -ɑ̃t] *nm,f* *(à un emploi)* applicant, candidate (**à** for)
postulat [pɔstyla] *nm* postulate
postuler [pɔstyle] *vi* **p. à** *ou* **pour un emploi** to apply for a job
posture [pɔstyr] *nf* (**a**) *(attitude)* posture (**b**) *(situation)* **être en fâcheuse p.** to be in an awkward situation
pot [po] *nm* (**a**) *(récipient, contenu)* pot; *(en verre)* jar; **p. à eau/à lait** water/milk jug; *Fam* **le p.** *(pour enfant)* the potty; **mettre en p.** *(plante)* to pot; *Fam* **quel p. de colle!** he sticks to you like glue!; **découvrir le p. aux roses** to find out what's been going on; **petit p.** *(pour bébé)* jar of baby food; **p. de chambre** chamber pot; **p. de fleurs** *(récipient)* flowerpot; *(plante)* pot of flowers; *Fam* **c'est un vrai p. de peinture!** *(femme)* she puts her make-up on with a trowel! (**b**) *Fam (chance)* **avoir du p.** to be lucky; **manque de p.,...** unfortunately,... (**c**) *(tuyau)* **p. (d'échappement)** *Br* exhaust (pipe), *Am* tail pipe; **p. catalytique** catalytic converter (**d**) *Fam (boisson)* drink; **viens, je t'offre un p.** come on, I'll buy you a drink; **ils font un p. pour son départ à la retraite** they're having a little get-together for his/her retirement (**e**) *Fam* **plein p.** *(à toute vitesse) Br* like the clappers, *Am* like sixty
potable [pɔtabl] *adj* (**a**) *(que l'on peut boire)* drinkable; **eau p./non p.** drinking/non-drinking water (**b**) *Fam (correct)* passable
potache [pɔtaʃ] *nm* *Fam* schoolboy
potage [pɔtaʒ] *nm* soup; **p. aux légumes** vegetable soup
potager, -ère [pɔtaʒe, -ɛr] **1** *adj voir* **jardin, plante²**
  2 *nm* vegetable *or* kitchen garden
potasser [pɔtase] *vt Fam (matière)* to bone up on, *Br* to swot up; *(examen)* to bone up for, *Br* to swot up for
potassium [pɔtasjɔm] *nm* *Chim* potassium
pot-au-feu [pɔtofø] *nm inv* = boiled beef with vegetables
pot-de-vin *(pl* **pots-de-vin)** [pɔdvɛ̃] *nm* bribe
pote [pɔt] *nm* *Fam* pal
poteau, -x [pɔto] *nm* (**a**) *(piquet)* post; *(de but)* (goal)-post; *Fam* **poteaux** *(jambes)* legs like tree-trunks; **p. (d'exécution)** execution stake; *Belg* **p. d'éclairage** street lamp; **p. électrique** electricity pylon; **p. indicateur** signpost; **p. télégraphique** telegraph pole (**b**) *Fam (ami)* pal
potée [pɔte] *nf* = boiled beef or pork with vegetables
potelé, -e [pɔtle] *adj* chubby, plump

potence [pɔtɑ̃s] *nf* (**a**) *(gibet)* gallows *(singulier)* (**b**) *(pièce de charpente)* bracket
potentiel, -elle [pɔtɑ̃sjɛl] *adj & nm* potential
potentiellement [pɔtɑ̃sjɛlmɑ̃] *adv* potentially
poterie [pɔtri] *nf* (**a**) *(art)* pottery; **faire de la p.** to make pottery (**b**) *(objet)* piece of pottery; *(objets)* pottery
potiche [pɔtiʃ] *nf* (**a**) *(vase)* oriental vase (**b**) *Fig* figurehead
potier, -ère [pɔtje, -ɛr] *nm,f* potter
potin [pɔtɛ̃] *nm* *Fam* (**a**) **potins** *(ragots)* gossip (**b**) *(bruit)* row; **faire du p.** to kick up a row
potion [posjɔ̃] *nf* potion
potiron [pɔtirɔ̃] *nm* pumpkin
pot-pourri *(pl* **pots-pourris)** [popuri] *nm (fleurs séchées)* potpourri; *(chanson)* medley
pou, -x [pu] *nm* louse; *Fam* **chercher des poux dans la tête à qn** to try and pick a quarrel with sb
poubelle [pubɛl] *nf* (**a**) *(récipient) Br* (dust)bin, *Am* garbage can; **jeter** *ou* **mettre qch à la p.** to throw sth out; **faire les poubelles** to scrounge in *Br* dustbins *or* *Am* garbage cans (**b**) *Ordinat* wastebasket, *Am* trash (**c**) *Fam (voiture) Br* old banger, *Am* jalopy
pouce [pus] *nm* (**a**) *(doigt)* thumb; *(gros orteil)* big toe; *Fam* **se tourner les pouces** to twiddle one's thumbs; *Suisse* **tenir les pouces à qn** to keep one's fingers crossed for sb; **p.!** *(dans un jeu)* truce!; *Fig* **manger sur le p.** to grab something to eat on the go (**b**) *(mesure)* inch; **ne pas bouger d'un p.** not to move an inch (**c**) *Can* **faire du p.** *(faire du stop)* to hitch(hike)
Poucet [pusɛ] *npr* **le Petit P.** TomThumb
poudre [pudr] *nf* (**a**) *(poussière)* powder; **réduire qch en p.** to reduce sth to powder; *Fig* **jeter de la p. aux yeux à qn** to try and dazzle sb; **p. compacte/libre** *(maquillage)* pressed/loose powder; **p. à éternuer** sneezing powder; **p. à laver**, *Belg* **p. à lessiver** washing powder; **p. à récurer** scouring powder; *Vieilli* **p. de riz** face powder (**b**) *(explosif)* (gun)powder (**c**) *Fam (héroïne)* smack, skag; *(cocaïne)* coke, charlie
poudrer [pudre] **1** *vt* to powder; **une femme poudrée** a woman with a powdered face
  2 **se poudrer** *vpr* to powder one's face
poudrerie [pudrəri] *nf* (**a**) *(fabrique de poudre)* (gun)powder factory (**b**) *Can (neige)* drifting snow
poudreux, -euse [pudrø, -øz] **1** *adj* powdery; **neige poudreuse** powder snow
  2 *nf* **poudreuse** powder snow
poudrier [pudrije] *nm* (powder) compact
poudrière [pudrijɛr] *nf* *(entrepôt)* powder magazine; *Fig* powder keg
pouf [puf] **1** *exclam (chute)* thud!
  2 *nm* (**a**) *(meuble)* pouf (**b**) *Belg* **à p.** *(à crédit)* on tick; **taper à p.** *(deviner)* to make a wild guess
pouffer [pufe] *vi* **p. (de rire)** to burst out laughing
pouffiasse [pufjas] *nf Vulg* bitch, *Br* cow
pouilleux, -euse [pujø, -øz] **1** *adj (personne)* filthy; *(quartier, maison)* squalid
  2 *nm,f* down-and-out
poulailler [pulaje] *nm* (**a**) *(basse-cour)* hen house (**b**) *(au théâtre)* **le p.** the gods
poulain [pulɛ̃] *nm* foal; *Fig* protégé
poulamon [pulamɔ̃] *nm* *Can* tomcod
poularde [pulard] *nf* fattened pullet
poulbot [pulbo] *nm* *Vieilli* = street urchin of Montmartre
poule¹ [pul] *nf* (**a**) *(animal)* hen; *Culin* (boiling) fowl; *Fig* **la p. aux œufs d'or** the goose that lays the golden

eggs; **quand les poules auront des dents** when pigs fly; **p. d'eau** moorhen; **p. faisane** hen pheasant; *Péj* **p. mouillée** wimp; **p. au pot** boiled chicken (**b**) *(terme d'affection)* **ma (petite) p.** darling (**c**) *Fam Péj (femme légère)* floozie; *(maîtresse)* mistress

poule² *nf (compétition)* tournament; *(groupe)* group

poulet [pulɛ] *nm* (**a**) *(animal)* chicken; **p. d'élevage** battery-reared chicken; **p. fermier** free-range chicken; **p. de grain** corn-fed chicken; **p. rôti** roast chicken (**b**) *(terme d'affection)* **mon (petit) p.** darling (**c**) *Fam (policier)* cop

poulette [pulɛt] *nf* (**a**) *(jeune poule)* pullet (**b**) *(terme d'affection)* **ma p.** darling

pouliche [puliʃ] *nf* filly

poulie [puli] *nf* pulley

poulpe [pulp] *nm* octopus

pouls [pu] *nm* pulse; **tâter le p. à qn** to feel sb's pulse; **prendre le p. à qn** to take sb's pulse

poumon [pumɔ̃] *nm* lung; **p. d'acier** iron lung; **respirer à pleins poumons** to breathe deeply

poupe [pup] *nf Naut* stern, poop

poupée [pupe] *nf* (**a**) *(jouet)* doll; **jouer à la p.** to play with dolls; **p. mannequin** Barbie® doll; **poupées russes** Russian dolls (**b**) *Fam (jolie fille)* doll (**c**) *(pansement)* finger bandage

poupin, -e [pupɛ̃, -in] *adj (personne)* chubby-cheeked; **visage p.** baby face

poupon [pupɔ̃] *nm* (**a**) *(bébé)* tiny baby (**b**) *(jouet)* baby doll

pouponner [pupɔne] *vi* to play the doting mother/father

pour [pur] **1** *prép* (**a**) *(indique le but, la destination)* for; **tiens, c'est p. toi** look, it's for you; **livres p. enfants** children's books; **p. faire qch** (in order) to do sth; **p. ne pas être en retard** so as not to be late; **p. bien faire** to do things properly; **p. que** + *subjunctive* so that, in order that; **j'épargne p. quand je serai vieux** I'm saving for when I'm old; **p. affaires** on business; **je viens p. la machine à laver** I've come about the washing machine; **c'est p. cela qu'il est venu** that's why he came, that's the reason he came; **p. quoi faire?** what for?; **tout ça p. rien!** all that for nothing!; *Fam* **c'est fait p.** that's what it's there for

(**b**) *(indique la direction)* for; **partir p. l'Espagne** to leave for Spain; **le train p. Paris** the Paris train, the train to *or* for Paris

(**c**) *(dans le temps)* for; **j'en ai p. une heure** it'll take me an hour, I'll be an hour; **il sera ici p. midi** he'll be here by midday

(**d**) *(contre)* for; **il me l'a vendu p. trois fois rien** he sold it to me for next to nothing; **donnez-moi p. 40 euros d'essence** give me 40 euros' worth of petrol

(**e**) *(en faveur de)* for, in favour of; **je suis p.** I'm (all) for it, I'm in favour of it

(**f**) *(à la place de)* for

(**g**) *(comme)* for; **j'avais p. ambition de...** my ambition was to...; **laisser qn p. mort** to leave sb for dead

(**h**) *(quant à, par rapport à)* for; **il est grand p. son âge** he's tall for his age; **p. ce qui est de...** as regards..., with regard to...; **p. moi, c'est absurde** in my opinion it's ridiculous, I think it's ridiculous

(**i**) *(indique le résultat)* **être trop faible p. marcher** to be too weak to walk; **cette situation n'était pas p. lui déplaire** the situation was rather to his/her liking

(**j**) *(à cause de)* for; **on l'apprécie p. sa gentillesse** people like him/her because he's/she's so kind; **puni**

p. avoir désobéi punished for having disobeyed *or* for disobeying

(**k**) *Litt (indique la concession)* **p. être célèbre, il n'en est pas moins modeste** although famous, he's nonetheless modest

(**l**) *(locutions)* **être p. beaucoup dans qch** to have a lot to do with sth; **je n'y suis p. rien!** it's got nothing to do with me!; *Fam* **être p. faire qch** *(être sur le point de)* to be about to do sth; *Fam* **p. une surprise, c'est une surprise!** that's a surprise and a half!; **perdre p. perdre, autant que tu...** if you're going to lose anyway, you might as well...

2 *nm inv* **le p. et le contre** the pros and cons

pourboire [purbwar] *nm* tip; **5 euros/10 pourcent de p.** a 5-euro/10 per cent tip; **être payé au p.** to be paid in tips

pourceau, -x [purso] *nm Litt* swine

pourcentage [pursɑ̃taʒ] *nm* percentage; **être payé au p.** to be paid on a commission basis

pourchasser [purʃase] *vt* to pursue

pourfendre [purfɑ̃dr] *vt Hum (injustices, hypocrisie)* to combat

pourlécher [34] [purleʃe] **se pourlécher** *vpr* **se p. (les babines)** to lick one's lips

pourparlers [purparle] *nmpl* talks, negotiations; **entrer/être en p. (avec)** to enter into/be having talks (with); **p. de paix** peace talks *or* negotiations

pourpre [purpr] **1** *adj & nm* crimson
2 *nf (teinte naturelle)* purple (dye)

pourquoi [purkwa] **1** *adv & conj* why; **c'est p....** that's why...; **p. pas?** why not?
2 *nm inv (raison)* **le p. de** the reason for; **le p. et le comment** the whys and wherefores

pourrais *etc voir* **pouvoir²**

pourri, -e [puri] **1** *adj* (**a**) *(bois, dent)* rotten; *(chair)* putrid; *(fruit, œufs)* bad (**b**) *Fam (corrompu)* corrupt (**c**) *Fam (déplaisant)* rotten (**d**) *Fam* **être p. de fric** to be stinking rich
2 *nm* (**a**) *(d'un fruit)* bad part; **sentir le p.** to smell rotten (**b**) *très Fam (homme)* bastard, *(femme)* bitch

pourriel [purjɛl] *nm Ordinat* spam e-mail; **pourriels** spam

pourrir [purir] **1** *vi (bois, dent)* to rot; *(corps)* to putrefy; *(aliments)* to go bad; *Fig* **p. en prison** to rot in prison
2 *vt* (**a**) *(gâter)* to rot (**b**) *Fam (enfant)* to spoil

pourriture [purityr] *nf* (**a**) *(décomposition)* rot (**b**) *Fam (corruption)* corruption (**c**) *très Fam (homme)* bastard; *(femme)* bitch

poursuite [pursɥit] *nf* (**a**) *(chasse)* pursuit; **se lancer à la p. de qn** to set off in pursuit of sb; **être à la p. de qch** *(bonheur, paix)* to be in pursuit of sth (**b**) *(continuation)* continuation (**c**) *Jur* **poursuites (judiciaires)** (legal) proceedings; *(en droit pénal)* prosecution; **engager des poursuites contre qn** to start proceedings against sb; *(en droit pénal)* to prosecute sb (**d**) *(course cycliste)* pursuit

poursuivant, -e [pursɥivɑ̃, -ɑ̃t] *nm,f* pursuer

poursuivre [65] [pursɥivr] **1** *vt* (**a**) *(pourchasser)* to pursue; *(sujet: idée, crainte)* to haunt; *(sujet: malchance)* to dog (**b**) *(idéal, rêve, but)* to pursue (**c**) *(harceler)* to pester (**de** with); *(sujet: créancier)* to hound; **p. qn de ses assiduités** to force one's attentions on sb (**d**) *Jur* **p. qn (en justice)** to bring proceedings against sb; *(en droit pénal)* to prosecute sb (**e**) *(continuer)* to continue, to go on with; **poursuivez** *(à quelqu'un qui parle)* go on
2 se poursuivre *vpr (continuer)* to continue, to go on

pourtant [purtã] *adv* yet; **tout avait p. bien commencé** yet it all started so well; **je ne peux p. pas l'empêcher de venir** still, I can't stop him/her from coming; **ça n'est p. pas compliqué!** it's hardly complicated!

pourtour [purtur] *nm* circumference, perimeter

pourvoi [purvwa] *nmJur* appeal; **p. en cassation** appeal to a higher court

pourvoir [73b] [purvwar] **1** *vt* **p. qn de qch** to provide sb with sth; **p. qch de qch** to equip *or* fit sth with sth **2 pourvoir à** *vt ind (besoins)* to provide *or* cater for **3 se pourvoir** *vpr* (**a**) *(se munir)* **se p. de qch** to provide oneself with sth (**b**) *Jur* **se p. en cassation** to take one's case to the Court of Appeal

pourvoyeur, -euse [purvwajœr, -øz] *nm,f* supplier

pourvu¹ [purvy] **pourvu que** *conj* (**a**) *(condition)* **p. que tu y sois** provided (that) *or* so long as you're there (**b**) *(souhait)* **p. qu'il le fasse!** let's just hope he does it!

pourvu², -e *voir* pourvoir

pousse [pus] *nf* (**a**) *(des feuilles, des cheveux)* growth (**b**) *(bourgeon)* shoot; **p. de bambou** bamboo shoot; *Fig* **jeune p.** *(société)* start-up

poussé, -e [puse] *adj (en profondeur)* thorough

pousse-café [puskafe] *nm inv* (glass of) liqueur *(after coffee)*

poussée [puse] *nf* (**a**) *(pression)* pressure; *(d'un liquide)* upthrust; **la p. de la foule** the pushing and shoving of the crowd (**b**) *(croissance)* growth; *(de boutons, d'herpès)* eruption; **p. de fièvre** sudden rise in temperature; **p. démographique** population boom; **faire une p. de croissance** to shoot up (**c**) *Fig (des prix)* upsurge (**de** in)

pousse-pousse [puspus] *nm inv* rickshaw

pousser [puse] **1** *vt* (**a**) *(soumettre à une force)* to push; *(sujet: vent) (embarcation)* to drive; **p. qn du coude** to nudge sb with one's elbow; *Fam* **faut pas p. Mémé** *ou* **Mémère dans les orties!** don't push your luck! (**b**) *(inciter)* **p. qn à faire qch** *(sujet: faim, jalousie)* to drive sb to do sth; *(sujet: personne)* to urge sb to do sth; **p. qn à qch** to drive sb to sth; **poussé par la curiosité** prompted by curiosity (**c**) *(continuer)* **p. trop loin une plaisanterie** to take a joke too far; **il a poussé la générosité jusqu'à l'héberger** he was so generous that he even put him/her up (**d**) *(émettre)* **p. un cri** to shout, to give a shout; **p. des cris** to shout; **p. un soupir** to sigh, to heave a sigh; **p. un gémissement** to groan; *Fam* **p. la chansonnette** to sing a song **2** *vi* (**a**) *(exercer une pression)* to push; *(aux toilettes)* to strain; *(en accouchant)* to push; *Fam* **faut pas p.!** don't push your luck! (**b**) *(continuer)* **p. jusqu'au bois** to push on as far as the wood (**c**) *(plante, cheveux, ongles)* to grow; *(bourgeon)* to sprout; *(dents)* to come through; *Fam (enfant)* to shoot up; **se laisser p. la barbe** to grow a beard **3 se pousser** *vpr (pour faire de la place)* to move over *or* up

poussette [puset] *nf (pour enfants) Br* pushchair, *Am* stroller

poussière [pusjɛr] *nf* dust; **une p.** a speck of dust; *Fam* **faire la p.** *ou* **les poussières** to do the dusting, to dust; *Fig* **tomber en p.** to crumble to dust; *Fig* **mordre la p.** to bite the dust; *Fam* **10 euros et des poussières** 10-and-a-bit euros

poussiéreux, -euse [pusjerø, -øz] *adj* dusty; *Fig* stuffy

poussif, -ive [pusif, -iv] *adj (moteur, personne)* wheezy

poussin, -e [pusɛ̃, -in] **1** *nm* chick; *Fam* **mon p.** pet, sweetie **2** *nm,f Sport* junior *(9 years old)*

poutre [putr] *nf (en bois)* beam; *(en métal)* girder; **p. apparente** exposed beam; **p. maîtresse** main beam/girder

poutrelle [putrɛl] *nf* girder

pouvoir¹ [puvwar] *nm* (**a**) *(puissance)* power; **avoir du p. sur qn** to have power *or* influence over sb; **prendre le p.** to assume power; **être au p.** to be in power; **p. absolu** absolute power; **p. exécutif** executive power; **p. judiciaire** judicial power; **p. législatif** legislative power; **les pouvoirs publics** the authorities (**b**) *(attributions)* power; **il n'est pas en mon p. de...** it is not within my power to... (**c**) **p. d'achat** purchasing power

pouvoir² [57] **1** *vt* (**a**) *(être capable de)* can, to be able; **p. faire qch** can *or* to be able to do sth; **si je peux** if I can, if I'm able to; **je ne peux pas** I can't, I'm unable to; **comment a-t-il pu dire cela?** how could he say that?; **on n'y peut rien** it can't be helped, there's nothing that can be done about it; **on ne peut plus/moins aimable** extremely friendly/unfriendly; **il n'en peut plus** *(de fatigue)* he's exhausted; *(d'exaspération, d'impatience)* he can't take any more; **dès que je pourrai** as soon as I can; **où peut-il bien être?** where can he be?; **nous ne pouvons rien pour vous** we can't do anything for you (**b**) *(avoir le droit, la permission de)* can, to be allowed; **vous pouvez partir** you can go; **puis-je entrer?** can I come in?; **si je puis m'exprimer ainsi** if I may use the phrase (**c**) *(être possible)* **la porte a pu se fermer toute seule** the door might have *or* could have closed on its own; **tout le monde peut se tromper** anyone can make a mistake; **elle peut bien s'excuser, je ne lui pardonnerai pas** she can apologize all she likes, but I won't forgive her; *Fam* **qu'est-ce que ça peut te faire?** what's that got to do with you? **2** *v impersonnel* **cela se peut/se pourrait (bien)** it's quite possible; **il se peut qu'il vienne** he may *or* might come

PQ [peky] *nm* (**a**) *Can Pol (abrév* **Parti Québécois**) PQ (**b**) *Fam (papier hygiénique)* toilet paper, *Br* bog roll

pragmatique [pragmatik] *adj* pragmatic

pragois, -e [pragwa, -az] **1** *adj* of Prague **2** *nm,f* **P.** person from Prague

Prague [prag] *n* Prague

praire [prɛr] *nf* clam

prairie [preri] *nf* meadow; *Géog* **la P.** the Prairies

praline [pralin] *nf* praline

praliné, -e [praline] *adj (chocolat)* praline-filled; *(glace)* praline-flavoured

praticable [pratikabl] *adj* (**a**) *(route)* passable, negotiable; *(terrain)* playable (**b**) *(réalisable)* practicable

praticien, -enne [pratisjɛ̃, -ɛn] *nm,f (médecin)* (medical) practitioner

pratiquant, -e [pratikã, -ãt] **1** *adj* practising; **je ne suis pas p.** I'm not religious **2** *nm,f* practising Christian/Jew/Muslim/*etc*

pratique [pratik] **1** *adj (méthode, personne)* practical; *(outil)* handy; *(date, heure, jour)* convenient; **avoir l'esprit p.** to be practically-minded **2** *nf* (**a**) *(application)* practice; **mettre qch en p.** to put sth into practice; **dans la p.** in practice (**b**) *(expérience)* (practical) experience; **avoir une longue**

p. de qch to have had a lot of (practical) experience of sth (**c**) *(d'un sport)* playing; **la p. du yoga** doing yoga (**d**) *(procédé, coutume)* practice

pratiquement [pratikmã] *adv* (**a**) *(concrètement)* in practice (**b**) *(presque)* practically

pratiquer [pratike] **1** *vt* (**a**) *(religion)* to practise; *(activité)* to take part in; *(langue)* to use; *(sport)* to play; **p. la natation** to swim; **les prix pratiqués ici** the prices being asked here (**b**) *(faire) (ouverture)* to make; *(opération chirurgicale)* to carry out
2 *vi* (**a**) *(médecin, avocat)* to practise (**b**) *(être religieux)* to practise one's religion; **il est catholique mais il ne pratique pas** he's a Catholic but he doesn't go to church
3 se pratiquer *upr (sport)* to be played; *(coutume)* to be practised

pré [pre] *nm* meadow

préadolescent, -e [preadɔlɛsɑ̃, -ɑ̃t] *nm,f* preadolescent, preteen

préalable [prealabl] **1** *adj* previous, prior (**à** to); *(accord)* prior; *(formalités)* preliminary
2 *nm (condition)* prerequisite, precondition; **au p.** first, beforehand

préalablement [prealabləmɑ̃] *adv* first, beforehand; **p. à...** prior to...

préambule [preɑ̃byl] *nm* preamble (**de** to); **sans p., elle annonça...** without any warning, she announced...

PréAO [preao] *nf Ordinat (abrév* **présentation assistée par ordinateur)** computer-assisted presentation

préau, -x [preo] *nm (de cour d'école)* covered area; *(salle)* hall

préavis [preavi] *nm* (advance) notice; **un p. de trois mois** three months' notice; **p. de grève** strike notice; **déposer un p. de grève** to give notice of strike action; **p. de licenciement** notice (of dismissal)

précaire [prekɛr] *adj (position)* precarious; *(santé)* delicate; **être en équilibre p.** to be precariously balanced; **il a un emploi p.** he's got no job security

précambrien, -enne [prekɑ̃brijɛ̃, -ɛn] *Géol* **1** *adj* Precambrian
2 *nm* **le P.** the Precambrian period

précarité [prekarite] *nf* precariousness; **la p. de l'emploi** the lack of job security

précaution [prekosjɔ̃] *nf* (**a**) *(mesure)* precaution; **par (mesure de) p.** as a precaution; **prendre des ou ses précautions** to take precautions; *Prov* **deux précautions valent mieux qu'une** better safe than sorry (**b**) *(prudence)* caution, care; **pour plus de p.** to be on the safe side

précautionneux, -euse [prekosjɔnø, -øz] *adj* careful

précédemment [presedamɑ̃] *adv* previously, before

précédent, -e [presedɑ̃, -ɑ̃t] **1** *adj* previous
2 *nm* precedent; **sans p.** unprecedented, without precedent

précéder [34] [presede] **1** *vt* to precede; **je l'ai précédé de dix minutes** I got there ten minutes before he did
2 *vi* **la page qui précède** the preceding *or* previous page; **dans les jours qui précèdent** in the preceding days; **ce qui précède** the foregoing

précepte [presɛpt] *nm* precept

précepteur, -trice [presɛptœr, -tris] *nm,f* (private) tutor

préchauffage [preʃofaʒ] *nm* preheating

préchauffer [preʃofe] *vt* to preheat

prêcher [preʃe] **1** *vt* (**a**) *(enseigner)* to preach (**à** to) (**b**) *(prôner)* to advocate; *Hum* **p. la bonne parole** to spread the good word
2 *vi (prononcer un sermon)* to preach; *Fig* **p. dans le désert** to be a voice crying in the wilderness; *Fig* **p. pour sa paroisse** to look after one's own interests

prêchi-prêcha [preʃipreʃa] *nm inv Fam Péj* preachifying

précieusement [presjøzmɑ̃] *adv* **garder** *ou* **conserver qch p.** to keep sth safe

précieux, -euse [presjø, -øz] *adj* (**a**) *(coûteux)* precious (**b**) *(conseil, temps)* valuable (**à** to) (**c**) *(style, personne)* precious, affected

préciosité [presjozite] *nf Litt* affectation, preciosity

précipice [presipis] *nm* chasm, abyss; *(d'une falaise, d'un ravin)* precipice; *Fig* abyss; *Fig* **être au bord du p.** to be on the edge of an abyss

précipitamment [presipitamɑ̃] *adv* hurriedly, hastily; **entrer/sortir p.** to rush *or* dash in/out

précipitation [presipitasjɔ̃] *nf* (**a**) *(hâte)* haste; **dans ma p., j'ai oublié les clés** I was in such a hurry, I forgot the keys (**b**) *Chim* precipitation (**c**) **précipitations** *(pluies)* precipitation

précipité, -e [presipite] **1** *adj* hasty, hurried
2 *nm Chim* precipitate

précipiter [presipite] **1** *vt* (**a**) *(entraîner)* to throw down, to hurl down; *Fig* to plunge; **p. qn dans le vide** to hurl sb over the edge (**b**) *(hâter)* to speed up; *(événements)* to precipitate; *(la mort de quelqu'un)* to hasten; **il ne faut rien p.** we mustn't rush things (**c**) *Chim* to precipitate
2 *vi Chim* to precipitate
3 se précipiter *upr* (**a**) *(se hâter)* to rush, to hurry (**b**) *(s'accélérer)* **les événements se sont précipités** things started happening quickly (**c**) *(se jeter)* to rush (**sur/vers** at/towards)

précis, -e [presi, -iz] **1** *adj* precise, exact; **à deux heures précises** at two o'clock precisely *or* exactly; **penser à quelque chose de p.** to have something specific in mind
2 *nm* précis, summary; *(livre)* handbook; **p. d'histoire de France** short history of France

précisément [presizemɑ̃] *adv* precisely, exactly

préciser [presize] **1** *vt* (**a**) *(déterminer) (date)* to specify (**b**) *(clarifier) (pensée)* to clarify; **je tiens à p. que...** I wish to make it clear that...; **pourriez-vous p.?** could you be more specific?
2 se préciser *upr* to become clear(er); *(idée)* to take shape

précision [presizjɔ̃] *nf* (**a**) *(d'une information, d'une description)* accuracy; *(de mouvements)* preciseness, precision; **avec p.** precisely (**b**) *(détail)* **une p.** a precise detail; **donner** *ou* **apporter des précisions sur qch** to give precise details about sth; **demander des précisions sur qch** to ask for further information about sth

précoce [prekɔs] *adj (enfant)* precocious; *(fruit, été)* early; *(sénilité, calvitie)* premature

précocité [prekɔsite] *nf* precociousness; *(d'un fruit, d'une saison)* earliness

précolombien, -enne [prekɔlɔ̃bjɛ̃, -ɛn] *adj* pre-Columbian

préconçu, -e [prekɔ̃sy] *adj* preconceived

préconiser [prekɔnize] *vt* to advocate; *(remède)* to recommend

précuit, -e [prekɥi, -it] *adj* precooked

précurseur [prekyrsœr] **1** *nm* precursor, forerunner
2 *adj m* **signe p.** forewarning
prédateur [predatœr] *nm* predator
prédécesseur [predesesœr] *nm* predecessor
prédécoupé, -e [predekupe] *adj* precut
prédestination [predɛstinasjɔ̃] *nf* predestination
prédestiné, -e [predɛstine] *adj* predestined (**à qch/à faire qch** for sth/to do sth)
prédestiner [predɛstine] *vt* to predestine (**à qch/à faire qch** for sth/to do sth)
prédicat [predika] *nm Gram* predicate
prédicateur, -trice [predikatœr, -tris] *nm,f* preacher
prédiction [prediksjɔ̃] *nf* prediction
prédilection [predilɛksjɔ̃] *nf* predilection, partiality; **de p.** favourite; **avoir une p. pour qch** to be partial to sth, *Formal* to have a predilection for sth
prédire [27b] [predir] *vt* to predict; **p. qch à qn** to predict sth for sb; **elle m'a prédit que je voyagerais** she predicted that I would travel
prédisposer [predispoze] *vt* to predispose (**à** to)
prédisposition [predispozisjɔ̃] *nf* predisposition (**à** to)
prédominant, -e [predɔminɑ̃, -ɑ̃t] *adj* predominant
prédominer [predɔmine] *vi* to predominate
préélectoral, -e, -aux, -ales [preelɛktɔral, -o] *adj* pre-electoral, pre-election
préemballé, -e [preɑ̃bale] *adj* prepacked
prééminence [preeminɑ̃s] *nf* pre-eminence
prééminent, -e [preeminɑ̃, -ɑ̃t] *adj* pre-eminent
préempter [preɑ̃pte] *vt Jur* to pre-empt
préemption [preɑ̃psjɔ̃] *nf Jur* pre-emption
préenregistré, -e [preɑ̃rɔʒistre] *adj* prerecorded
préétablir [preetablir] *vt* to pre-establish
préexistant, -e [preɛgzistɑ̃, -ɑ̃t] *adj* pre-existing
préexister [preɛgziste] *vi* to pre-exist; **p. à qch** to pre-exist sth
préfabrication [prefabrikasjɔ̃] *nf* prefabrication
préfabriqué, -e [prefabrike] **1** *adj* prefabricated **2** *nm* prefabricated material; **c'est du p.** it's prefabricated
préface [prefas] *nf* preface, foreword (**à** *ou* **de** to)
préfacer [16] [prefase] *vt* to preface
préfectoral, -e, -aux, -ales [prefɛktɔral, -o] *adj* = relating to a "préfecture" or "préfet"
préfecture [prefɛktyr] *nf* prefecture; *(ville)* = administrative centre of a "département"; **la P. de police** police headquarters

Préfecture
This refers to the main administrative office of each "département". The word has also come to refer to the town where the office is located. One goes to the "préfecture" to obtain a driving licence or a "carte de séjour", for example.

préférable [preferabl] *adj* preferable (**à** to); **il serait p. de le revoir** *ou* **que nous le revoyions** it would be preferable to see him again
préféré, -e [prefere] *adj & nm,f* favourite
préférence [preferɑ̃s] *nf* preference; **de p.** preferably; **de p. à** in preference to
préférentiel, -elle [preferɑ̃sjɛl] *adj* preferential
préférer [34] [prefere] *vt* to prefer (**à** to); **je préférerais du thé** I'd prefer tea, I'd rather have tea; **je préférerais que vous veniez** I'd prefer it if you came, I'd rather you came; **p. faire qch** to prefer to do sth

préfet [prefɛ] *nm* (**a**) *(fonctionnaire)* prefect *(administrative head of a "département")*; **p. de police** = chief commissioner of police (**b**) *Belg Scol Br* head teacher, *Am & Ir* principal

Préfet
In France a "préfet" is a high-ranking official, one of a body of civil servants created by Napoleon in 1800. The "préfet" is the general administrator of the "département", the chief executive officer and the executive chief of police.

préfigurer [prefigyre] *vt* to prefigure, to foreshadow
préfixe [prefiks] *nm* prefix
pré-formaté, -e *(mpl* **pré-formatés**, *fpl* **pré-formatées)** [preformate] *adj Ordinat* pre-formatted
préhension [preɑ̃sjɔ̃] *nf* gripping
préhistoire [preistwar] *nf* prehistory
préhistorique [preistɔrik] *adj* prehistoric
pré-impression [preɛ̃presjɔ̃] *nf Typ* pre-press
préindustriel, -elle [preɛ̃dystrijɛl] *adj* pre-industrial
préinscription [preɛ̃skripsjɔ̃] *nf* pre-check-in
préjudice [preʒydis] *nm (à une cause)* prejudice, detriment; *(à une personne)* harm, wrong; *Jur* tort; **subir un p. matériel** to sustain damage; **subir un p. moral** to suffer mental distress; **porter p. à qn** to do sb harm; **au p. de qch** to the detriment of sth
préjugé [preʒyʒe] *nm* prejudice, bias (**contre** against); **avoir un p. contre qn/qch** to be prejudiced *or* biased against sb/sth; **n'avoir aucun p.** to be totally unprejudiced *or* unbiased
prélasser [prelase] **se prélasser** *vpr* to lounge
prélat [prela] *nm* prelate
prélavage [prelavaʒ] *nm* pre-wash
prélèvement [prelɛvmɑ̃] *nm* (**a**) *(en argent)* deduction (**sur** from); **faire un p. sur un compte** to debit an account; **p. automatique** direct debit; **prélèvements obligatoires** = tax and social security contributions (**b**) *(extraction) (d'un organe)* removal; *(de sécrétions)* taking a sample; *(d'un échantillon)* taking; **faire un p. de sang** *ou* **sanguin à qn** to take a blood sample from sb (**c**) *(partie prélevée) (de sécrétions)* swab; *(de sang)* sample
prélever [46] [prelve] *vt* (**a**) *(argent)* to deduct (**sur** from); *(impôt)* to levy (**b**) *(organe)* to remove; *(sécrétions, échantillon)* to take; **p. du sang à qn** to take a blood sample from sb
préliminaire [preliminɛr] **1** *adj* preliminary **2** *nm* **préliminaires** preliminaries
prélude [prelyd] *nm Mus & Fig* prelude (**de** *ou* **à** to)
prématuré, -e [prematyre] **1** *adj* premature; **être p. de six semaines** to be six weeks premature **2** *nm,f* premature baby
prématurément [prematyremɑ̃] *adv* prematurely
préméditation [premeditasjɔ̃] *nf* premeditation; **meurtre avec p.** premeditated murder
préméditer [premedite] *vt* to premeditate
prémenstruel, -elle [premɑ̃stryɛl] *adj* premenstrual
premier, -ère [prəmje, -ɛr] **1** *adj* (**a**) *(initial, dominant)* first; **les trois premières années** the first three years; **la première marche** the bottom stair; **le p. rang** the front row; **prendre la première place** *(dans une course)* to take the lead; **le p. venu** the first person who comes along; **les premiers arrivés** the first to arrive; **je suis le p. concerné** I'm the one most affected; **en p.** in the first place, firstly (**b**) *(original)* primary, original

2 *nm,f* (**a**) *(dans un classement)* first; **arriver le p.** *ou* **en p.** to arrive first; **être le p. de sa classe** to be top of one's class; **être le p. à faire qch** to be (the) first to do sth; *voir aussi* **cinquième** (**b**) *(acteur)* **jeune p.** (young) romantic lead; *Fig* **avoir des airs de jeune p.** to look like a movie star **3** *nm (date)* **le p. janvier** the first of January, January the first; **le p. de l'an** NewYear's Day **4** *nf* **première** (**a**) *(d'une pièce)* first *or* opening night; *(d'un film)* première (**b**) *(classe) Br* ≃ lower sixth, *Am* ≃ eleventh grade (**c**) *(de train, d'avion)* first class; **voyager en première** to travel first-class (**d**) *(vitesse)* first (gear) (**e**) *(de chaussure)* insole (**f**) *Fam* **de première** *(de très bonne qualité)* first-rate, first-class

premièrement [prəmjɛrmã] *adv* first, in the first place

prémisse [premis] *nf* premise

prémix [premiks] *nm (boisson)* ready-mixed alcoholic drink

prémolaire [premɔlɛr] *nf* premolar

prémonition [premɔnisjɔ̃] *nf* premonition

prémonitoire [premɔnitwar] *adj* premonitory

prémunir [premynir] **se prémunir** *vpr* **se p. contre qch** to be on one's guard against sth

prenant, -e [prənã, -ãt] *adj (livre, spectacle)* fascinating; *(travail)* time-consuming

prénatal, -e, -als, -ales [prenatal] *adj* antenatal, prenatal

prendre [58] [prãdr] **1** *vt* (**a**) *(saisir)* to take; **p. qch dans un tiroir** to take sth out of a drawer; **prends-le par la poignée** take hold of it by the handle; **c'est à p. ou à laisser** take it or leave it; *Fam* **il faut savoir le p.** you have to know how to handle him; *Fam* **c'est toujours ça de pris** that's something at least; *Fam* **qu'est-ce qu'on va p.!** we're in for it!

(**b**) *(enlever)* to take (away); **p. qch à qn** to take sth (away) from sb; **cela m'a pris du temps/deux heures** it took me a while/two hours; **p. 20 euros de l'heure** to take 20 euros an hour

(**c**) *(s'emparer de) (personne, gibier)* to catch; *(ville, région)* to take, to capture; **se laisser p.** to let oneself be *or* get caught; *Fig* to let oneself be taken in; *Prov* **tel est pris qui croyait p.** it's a case of the biter bit

(**d**) *(aller chercher)* to collect, to pick up; **attends, je vais p. mon parapluie** wait till I get my umbrella

(**e**) *(acheter)* to get; *(chambre, studio)* to take; **cette robe me plaît, je la prends** I like this dress, I'll take it

(**f**) *(accepter) (bonne, assistant)* to take on; *(pensionnaire)* to take in; *(travail)* to take; **être pris** *(élève, candidat)* to be accepted; *(acteur)* to get the part

(**g**) *(repas, boisson, bain)* to have; *(médicament)* to take

(**h**) *(moyen de transport)* to take

(**i**) *(apparence)* to take on, to assume; *(attitude)* to take; *(accent)* to pick up

(**j**) **p. l'eau** *(bateau)* to be leaking, to be letting in water

(**k**) *(personne)* **p. qn comme exemple** to take sb as an example; **p. qn/qch pour** to take sb/sth for

(**l**) *Fam (arriver)* **qu'est-ce qui lui prend?** what's come over him?; **ça te prend souvent?** do you get like that often?

2 *vi* (**a**) *(ciment, flan)* to set

(**b**) *(plante)* to take (root)

(**c**) *(feu)* to catch

(**d**) *(réussir) (vaccin)* to take effect; *(mode)* to catch

on; *Fam* **avec moi, ça ne prend pas!** you can't fool me!

(**e**) *(tourner)* **p. à gauche/droite** to go left/right

(**f**) **p. sur soi** to restrain *or* contain oneself

3 se prendre *vpr* (**a**) *(s'accrocher)* **se p. dans une porte/à un clou** to get caught in the door/on a nail

(**b**) *(se considérer)* **se p. pour un héros** to consider oneself a hero; **pour qui vous prenez-vous?** who do you think you are?

(**c**) *(locutions)* **s'en p. à qn/qch** to take it out on sb/sth; **ne t'en prends qu'à toi-même** you've only got yourself to blame; **s'y p. bien avec qn** to know how to handle sb; **s'y p. mal avec qn** not to handle sb the right way; **vous vous y prenez mal** you're going about it the wrong way; **s'y p. à deux fois pour faire qch** to take two attempts to do sth

preneur, -euse [prənœr, -øz] *nm,f* (**a**) *(acheteur)* buyer, purchaser; **trouver p.** to find a buyer; **je suis p.!** I'm interested! (**b**) **p. d'otages** hostage taker; **p. de son** sound engineer

prenne *etc voir* **prendre**

prénom [prenɔ̃] *nm Br* first *or* Christian name, *Am* given name

prénommé, -e [prenɔme] *adj* **le p. Victor** the man/boy called *or* named Victor

prénommer [prenɔme] **1** *vt* to call, to name

2 se prénommer *vpr* **il se prénomme Adam** his *Br* first *or* Christian *or Am* given name is Adam

prénuptial, -e, -aux, -ales [prenypsjal, -o] *adj* premarital; **examen p.** premarital medical check-up

préoccupant, -e [preɔkypã, -ãt] *adj* worrying

préoccupation [preɔkypasjɔ̃] *nf* concern, preoccupation; **j'ai d'autres préoccupations** I have other things to worry about

préoccupé, -e [preɔkype] *adj* worried

préoccuper [preɔkype] **1** *vt* to worry; **être préoccupé par qch** to be worried about sth; **sa santé me préoccupe** I'm worried about his/her health

2 se préoccuper *vpr* **se p. de qn/qch** to concern oneself with sb/sth

prépa [prepa] *nf Fam Scol* preparatory class *(for the entrance exam to the "grandes écoles")*; **faire une p., être en p.** to be studying for the entrance exam to the "grandes écoles"

préparateur, -trice [preparatœr, -tris] *nm,f* laboratory assistant; **p. en pharmacie** pharmacist's *or Br* chemist's assistant

préparatifs [preparatif] *nmpl* preparations (**de** for)

préparation [preparasjɔ̃] *nf* preparation (**à** for); **faire une p. militaire** = to do an officer training course in preparation for military service; **faire une p. aux grandes écoles** to prepare for the entrance exam to the "grandes écoles"

préparatoire [preparatwar] *adj* preparatory

préparer [prepare] **1** *vt* (**a**) *(discours, repas, plat)* to prepare; *(réunion, soirée, vacances)* to make preparations for, to arrange; *(ordonnance)* to make up; **plats tout préparés** ready meals; *Fig* **je suis sûr qu'il nous prépare quelque chose** I'm sure he's up to something

(**b**) *(personne)* **p. qn à qch** to prepare sb for sth; *(entraîner)* to train sb for sth (**c**) *(examen)* to prepare for, to study for

2 se préparer *vpr* (**a**) *(être imminent)* to be in the offing (**b**) *(s'apprêter)* to get ready; **se p. à qch/à faire qch** to prepare *or* get ready for sth/to do sth (**c**) *(se faire)* **se p. qch** *(boisson, plat)* to make *or Am* fix oneself sth; **tu te prépares bien des désillusions** you're in for a big disappointment

prépayé, -e [prepeje] *adj* prepaid
prépondérant, -e [prepɔ̃derã, -ãt] *adj* predominant
préposé, -e [prepoze] *nm,f (employé)* employee; *(dans un vestiaire)* attendant; **p. (des postes)** *Br* postman, *f* postwoman, *Am* mailman, *f* mailwoman
préposer [prepoze] *vt* **p. qn à qch** to appoint sb to sth
préposition [prepozisjɔ̃] *nf Gram* preposition
prépuce [prepys] *nm Anat* foreskin, *Spéc* prepuce
préraphaélite [prerafaelit] *adj & nm* Pre-Raphaelite
préretraite [preratrɛt] *nf* early retirement; *(pension)* early retirement pension; **partir en p.** to take early retirement
prérogative [prerɔgativ] *nf* prerogative
près [prɛ] *adv* (**a**) *(dans l'espace)* near, close; *(dans le temps)* close; **de p.** closely; **voir qch de p.** to see sth close up; **à quelques détails p.** except for a few details; **la longueur, à 5 centimètres p.** the length, to within 5 centimetres; **à deux minutes p., je ratais le train** two minutes later and I would have missed the train; **je n'en suis pas à 5 euros p.** 5 euros more or less doesn't matter; **à peu de chose(s) p.** more or less (**b**) **p. de** *(dans l'espace)* near (to), close to; *(dans le temps)* close to; *(environ)* nearly, almost; **p. de là** nearby, close by; **p. de chez eux** near (to) *or* close to where they live; *Fam* **être p. de ses sous** to be tight-fisted; *Hum* **nous ne sommes pas p. de le revoir** we won't see him again in a hurry (**c**) **à peu p.** *(pas tout à fait)* nearly, almost; *(approximativement)* about, approximately; **il est à peu p. certain que...** it is fairly certain that...
présage [prezaʒ] *nm* omen, sign; **mauvais p.** bad omen
présager [45] [prezaʒe] *vt* (**a**) *(annoncer)* to presage; **cela ne présage rien de bon** it doesn't bode well (**b**) *(prévoir)* to predict; **ces gros nuages noirs laissent p. un orage** those big black clouds are a sure sign of a storm
pré-salé *(pl prés-salés)* [presale] *nm (mouton)* salt-meadow sheep; *(viande)* salt-meadow lamb
presbyte [prɛsbit] *adj* long-sighted
presbytère [prɛsbitɛr] *nm* presbytery
presbytérien, -enne [prɛsbiterjɛ̃, -ɛn] *adj & nm,f* Presbyterian
presbytie [prɛsbisi] *nf* long-sightedness
préscolaire [preskɔlɛr] *adj* preschool
prescription [prɛskripsjɔ̃] *nf* (**a**) *Jur* **après cinquante ans, il y a p.** the statute of limitations expires after fifty years (**b**) *(ordonnance)* prescription (**c**) *(instruction)* rule, regulation
prescrire [30] [prɛskrir] *vt (médicament)* to prescribe; **à la date prescrite** on the date specified
préséance [preseãs] *nf* precedence, priority (**sur** over)
présélection [preselɛksjɔ̃] *nf* preselection; *(de candidats)* short-listing
présélectionner [preselɛksjone] *vt* to preselect; *(candidats)* to short-list
présence [prezãs] *nf* (**a**) *(dans un lieu)* presence; *(à l'école)* attendance; **il ignore votre p.** he doesn't know you're here; **avoir de la p.** *(acteur)* to have great presence; **les parties en p.** the parties present; **en p. de toute la famille** in front of the whole family; **en p. du virus** when the virus is present (**b**) **avoir la p. d'esprit de faire qch** to have the presence of mind to do sth
présent¹, -e [prezã, -ãt] **1** *adj* (**a**) *(physiquement)* present; **les personnes présentes** those present;

Jacques Martelin, ici p., vous le dira Jacques Martelin, who is here with us, will tell you; **Tardieu? – p.!** Tardieu? – here! *or* present! (**b**) *(situation, moment)* present; **vivre dans l'instant p.** to live in the present **2** *nm* (**a**) *Gram* present (tense); **le p. du subjonctif/de l'indicatif** the present subjunctive/indicative; **au p.** in the present (**b**) *(moment présent)* present; **vivre dans le p.** to live in the present (**c**) **à p.** at present, (just) now; **jusqu'à p.** up to now, until now; **jusqu'à p., je n'ai pas reçu de nouvelles** I've not received any news as yet; **dès à p.** from now on; **à p. que...** now that... **3** *nf* **par la présente** *(par cette lettre)* hereby
présent² *nm Litt (cadeau)* present, gift; **faire p. de qch à qn** to present sth to sb
présentable [prezãtabl] *adj* presentable
présentateur, -trice [prezãtatœr, -tris] *nm,f* presenter; *(d'un spectacle télévisé)* compère; **p. de journal télévisé** newscaster, newsreader
présentation [prezãtasjɔ̃] *nf* (**a**) *(de faits, d'un billet)* presentation; **10% de réduction sur p. de la carte** 10% discount on presentation of this card (**b**) *(apparence) (d'une personne)* appearance; *(d'un document)* presentation, layout; **recherche hôtesses, excellente p.** *(petite annonce)* hostesses required, must have smart appearance; *Ordinat* **p. assistée par ordinateur** computer-aided presentation (**c**) *(dans un groupe)* introduction (**à** to); **faire les présentations** to make the introductions (**d**) *(d'un film)* showing, presentation; **p. de mode** fashion show
présenter [prezãte] **1** *vt* (**a**) *(montrer)* to show, to present; *(symptôme)* to present; *(facture)* to submit (**b**) *(par écrit)* to present (**c**) *(oralement) (arguments)* to present, to set out; *(spectacle)* to present, to host; **p. ses condoléances à qn** to offer sb one's condolences (**d**) *(projet de loi)* to bring in, to introduce; **p. sa candidature à un poste** to apply for a job (**e**) *(personne)* **p. qn à qn** to introduce sb to sb; **je vous présente Marie** this is Marie **2** *vi Fam* **bien/mal p.** to look/not to look good **3 se présenter** *vpr* (**a**) *(occasion, cas)* to arise, to present itself; **ça se présente bien** things are looking promising (**b**) *(à un poste)* to apply (**à** for); **se p. à un examen** to take *or Br* sit an examination; **se p. aux élections** to be a candidate at *or Br* stand at the elections (**c**) *(arriver)* to turn up; **présentez-vous au commissariat à huit heures** be at the police station at eight o'clock; **se p. chez qn** to call on sb (**d**) *(dire son nom)* to introduce oneself (**à** to) (**e**) **le bébé se présente par la tête/le siège** the baby is presenting normally/in a breech position
présentoir [prezãtwar] *nm* display unit
préservatif [prezɛrvatif] *nm* condom; **p. féminin** female condom
préservation [prezɛrvasjɔ̃] *nf* preservation, protection
préserver [prezɛrve] **1** *vt* to preserve, to protect (**de** from); **le ciel m'en préserve!** heaven forbid! **2 se préserver** *vpr* to protect oneself (**de** from)
présidence [prezidãs] *nf* (**a**) *(d'un état)* presidency (**b**) *(d'un club)* chairmanship
président, -e [prezidã, -ãt] *nm,f* (**a**) *(d'un état)* president; **le p. de la République** the President of the Republic (**b**) *(d'une assemblée, d'un club)* chairman, *f* chairwoman; **p. du conseil d'administration** Chairman of the Board; **p.-directeur général** *Br* chairman and managing director, *Am* chief executive officer

(**c**) *(magistrat)* presiding judge; **p. du jury** foreman of the jury

présidentiel, -elle [prezidɑ̃sjɛl] **1** *adj* presidential **2** *nfpl* **présidentielles** presidential elections

Présidentielles

Since 1873, the French president has traditionally been elected for a renewable seven-year term ("le septennat"). However, as a result of a referendum held in September 2000 the French parliament ruled that the seven-year term of office was to be replaced in 2002 by a five-year term ("le quinquennat"). Candidates are usually nominated by the main political parties, but anyone who collects the requisite number of sponsors can run. If no candidate wins an outright majority in the first round of voting, a runoff between the two frontrunners is held two weeks later.

présider [prezide] **1** *vt* (**a**) *(conseil)* to preside over; *(réunion)* to chair (**b**) *(banquet)* to be the guest of honour at **2** **présider à** *vt ind Litt* **p. aux destinées de...** to preside over the destinies of...

présomption [prezɔ̃psjɔ̃] *nf* presumption; **p. d'innocence** presumption of innocence

présomptueux, -euse [prezɔ̃ptɥø, -øz] *adj* presumptuous

presque [prɛsk] *adv* (**a**) *(à peu près)* almost, nearly; **p. jamais/rien** scarcely *or* hardly ever/anything; **je ne dors p. pas** I hardly *or* scarcely get any sleep; **rien ou p.** scarcely anything (**b**) *(devant un nom)* **la p. totalité de son œuvre** nearly *or* almost all of his/her work

presqu'île [prɛskil] *nf* peninsula

pressant, -e [prɛsɑ̃, -ɑ̃t] *adj* (*personne*) in a hurry *or* rush; **p. de faire qch** in a hurry to do sth; *(demande, vendeur)* insistent; *Fam Euph* **avoir un besoin p.** to be desperate (for the toilet)

presse [prɛs] *nf* (**a**) *(ensemble des journaux)* press; **travailler dans la p.** to work in journalism; **je l'ai lu dans la p.** I read it in the papers; *Fig* **avoir bonne/mauvaise p. (auprès de)** to be well/badly thought of (by); **la p. écrite** the print media, the press; **la p. à scandale, la p. à sensation** the popular press, *Br* the tabloids (**b**) *Tech* press (**c**) *(pour imprimer)* (printing) press; **mettre qch sous p.** to send sth to press

pressé, -e [prɛse] *adj* (**a**) *(personne)* in a hurry *or* rush; **p. de faire qch** in a hurry to do sth; **être p. par le temps** to be pushed for time; **d'un pas p.** hurriedly; **on n'est pas p.** there's no rush (**b**) *(urgent)* urgent; **aller** *ou* **parer au plus p.** to deal with the most urgent thing(s) first

presse-agrumes [prɛsagrym] *nm inv* juice extractor, juicer

presse-ail [prɛsaj] *nm inv* garlic press

presse-citron [prɛssitrɔ̃] *nm inv* lemon squeezer

pressentiment [presɑ̃timɑ̃] *nm* presentiment; *(d'un malheur)* foreboding; **j'ai le p. que...** I've got a (funny) feeling that...

pressentir [64a] [presɑ̃tir] *vt* (**a**) *(deviner)* to have a premonition of, to sense; *(malheur)* to have a foreboding of (**b**) **p. qn (pour qch)** to sound sb out (about sth)

presse-papiers [prɛspapje] *nm inv* paperweight; *Ordinat* clipboard

presse-purée [prɛspyre] *nm inv* potato masher

presser [prɛse] **1** *vt* (**a**) *(agrume, éponge)* to squeeze; *(raisin, pommes)* to press; **p. qn contre son cœur** to clasp sb in one's arms, to hug sb (**b**) *(sonnette, bouton)* to press, to push (**c**) *(harceler)* **p. qn de questions** to ply *or* bombard sb with questions; **p. qn de faire qch** to urge sb to do sth (**d**) *(faire se hâter)* *(personne)* to hurry (up); *(travail, mouvement)* to speed up; **p. le pas** *ou* **l'allure** to speed up, to quicken one's pace **2** *vi* **le temps presse** there isn't much time (left); **rien ne presse** there's no hurry *or* rush; **allons, pressons!** come on, let's get a move on! **3** **se presser** *vpr* (**a**) *(se dépêcher)* to hurry (up); **se p. de faire qch** to hurry to do sth; **faire qch sans se p.** to take one's time doing sth (**b**) *(se serrer)* **se p. contre** to press (oneself) against; **se p. autour de** to crowd *or* cluster around

pressing [presiŋ] *nm* dry cleaner's

pression [presjɔ̃] *nf* (**a**) *Tech* pressure; **mettre qch sous p.** to pressurize sth; **sous p.** *(récipient)* pressurized; *Fig* **être sous p.** to be under pressure; *Méd* **p. artérielle** blood pressure; *Météo* **p. atmosphérique** atmospheric pressure; **zone de hautes/basses pressions** area of high/low pressure (**b**) *(action de presser)* pressure; **d'une simple p. du doigt** at the touch of a button (**c**) *Fig (influence)* pressure; **faire p. sur qn** to put pressure on sb, to pressurize sb; **subir des pressions** to be under pressure; *Fam* **mettre la p. à qn** to pressurize sb, to put pressure on sb (**d**) *(bouton)* *Br* press stud, *Am* snap fastener (**e**) **bière (à la) p.** draught beer; **une p., s'il vous plaît** *Br* ≃ half a lager *or* a half pint of lager, please, *Am* ≃ a beer, please

pressoir [preswar] *nm* (**a**) *(instrument)* press (**b**) *(lieu)* press house, press room

pressurer [presyre] *vt* *(exploiter)* to squeeze

pressurisation [presyrizasjɔ̃] *nf* pressurization

prestance [prestɑ̃s] *nf* presence; **avoir de la p.** to have (great) presence

prestataire [prestatɛr] **1** *nmf* (**a**) *(bénéficiaire)* person receiving benefits (**b**) *(fournisseur)* **p. de service** service provider **2** *nm Ordinat* **p. d'accès** access provider

prestation [prestasjɔ̃] *nf* (**a**) *(allocation)* benefit; **prestations familiales** family benefits; **prestations sociales** social security benefits (**b**) **prestations** *(services fournis)* services (**c**) *(fait de fournir)* provision; **p. de service** provision of a service (**d**) *(d'un comédien)* performance (**e**) **p. de serment** taking the oath

preste [prest] *adj* nimble

prestement [prestəmɑ̃] *adv* promptly

prestidigitateur, -trice [prestidiʒitatœr, -tris] *nm,f* conjurer, magician

prestidigitation [prestidiʒitasjɔ̃] *nf* conjuring, magic

prestige [prestiʒ] *nm* prestige; **de p.** *(voiture, hôtel)* luxury; *(réalisation)* prestige; **le p. de l'uniforme** the glamour of a uniform

prestigieux, -euse [prestiʒjø, -øz] *adj* prestigious

présumer [prezyme] **1** *vt* *(supposer)* to presume, to assume; **p. qn innocent** to presume sb (to be) innocent **2** **présumer de** *vt ind* **trop p. de soi** to be overconfident; **p. de ses forces** to overestimate one's strength

présupposer [presypoze] *vt* to presuppose

présure [prezyr] *nf* rennet

prêt¹, -e [prɛ, prɛt] *adj* ready; **être p. à tout** to be prepared to do anything; **être p. à faire qch** to be ready to do sth

prêt² *nm (action)* lending; *(somme)* loan; **p. bancaire** bank loan; **p. immobilier** home loan, ≃ mortgage

prêt-à-porter [prɛtapɔrte] *nm* (**a**) *(vêtements)* ready-to-wear clothes (**b**) *(secteur)* ready-to-wear (clothing business)

prétendant, -e [pretɑ̃dɑ̃, -ɑ̃t] **1** *nm,f (à un poste)* applicant, candidate (**à** for); *(à un bien, à un titre)* claimant (**à** to); *(au trône)* pretender (**à** to)
2 *nm (d'une femme)* suitor

prétendre [pretɑ̃dr] **1** *vt (déclarer)* to maintain, to claim; **on prétend que...** people say that..., it is said that...; **à ce qu'il prétend** according to him; **il ne prétend pas être artiste** he doesn't claim *or* pretend to be an artist; **on le prétend fou** they say he's mad
2 prétendre à *vt ind* to lay claim to; **p. à la victoire** to aim to win
3 se prétendre *vpr* to claim to be

prétendu, -e [pretɑ̃dy] *adj (coupable, voleur)* alleged; *(progrès, égalité, héros)* so-called

prétendument [pretɑ̃dymɑ̃] *adv* supposedly

prête-nom *(pl* **prête-noms)** [prɛtnɔ̃] *nm Fig* figurehead

prétentieux, -euse [pretɑ̃sjø, -øz] **1** *adj* pretentious
2 *nm,f* pretentious person

prétention [pretɑ̃sjɔ̃] *nf* (**a**) *(vanité)* pretentiousness, pretension; **sans p.** *(repas, maison, personne)* unpretentious (**b**) *(revendication, ambition)* pretension, claim (**à** to); **avoir la p. de faire qch** to claim *or* pretend to be able to do sth; **quelles sont vos prétentions?** *(salaire demandé)* what are your salary expectations?

prêter [prɛte] **1** *vt* (**a**) *(temporairement)* to lend, *Am* to loan; **p. qch à qn** to lend sth to sb, to lend sb sth; **p. sur gages** to lend against security; *Prov* **on ne prête qu'aux riches** people don't lend money to those who really need it; *Fig* people are judged according to their reputation (**b**) *(donner)* **p. son appui** *ou* **son concours à qn** to give sb one's support; **p. assistance** *ou* **secours à qn** to lend *or* give assistance to sb; **p. main-forte à qn** to lend *or* give sb a hand; **p. l'oreille (à)** to listen *or* lend an ear (to); **p. attention à qch** to pay attention to sth; **p. serment** to take an oath; **p. le flanc à la critique** to lay oneself open to criticism (**c**) *(attribuer)* **p. qch à qn** *(propos, intentions)* to attribute *or* ascribe sth to sb
2 prêter à *vt ind* **p. à confusion** to give rise to confusion; **cela prête à rire** that's laughable
3 se prêter *vpr* (**a**) *(consentir)* **se p. à** to lend oneself to (**b**) *(convenir)* **se p. à** to lend itself to; **la situation ne s'y prête pas** the situation isn't ideal

prétérit [preterit] *nm* preterite (tense); **au p.** in the preterite

prêteur, -euse [prɛtœr, -øz] **1** *adj* ready *or* willing to lend things; **je ne suis pas p.** I don't like lending things
2 *nm,f* lender; **p. sur gages** pawnbroker

prétexte [pretɛkst] *nm* pretext, excuse; **pour toi, tout est p. à rire** you find cause for laughter in everything; **sous p. de faire qch** on the pretext of doing sth; **sous p. que...** on the pretext that...; **sous aucun p.** on no account, under no circumstances

prétexter [pretɛkste] *vt* to give as a pretext *or* an excuse; **il a prétexté qu'il était malade** he gave the excuse that he was ill; **p. la fatigue** to plead tiredness

Pretoria [pretɔrja] *n* Pretoria

prêtre [prɛtr] *nm* priest

prêtresse [prɛtrɛs] *nf* priestess

prêtrise [prɛtriz] *nf* priesthood

preuve [prœv] *nf* (**a**) *(pour démontrer)* piece of evidence; **il nous faut des preuves** we need proof *or* evidence; **faire la p. de qch** to prove sth; **avoir la p. que/de...** to have proof that/of...; **faire p. d'intelligence/de courage** to show intelligence/courage; **faire ses preuves** *(personne)* to prove oneself, to show one's ability; *(technique)* to be tried and tested; **jusqu'à p. du contraire** until there's proof to the contrary; *Fam* **elle ne m'aime pas: la p., elle ne m'écrit jamais** I know she doesn't like me because she never writes to me; **j'en veux pour p....** the proof of it is...; **p. d'achat** proof of purchase (**b**) *Jur* evidence (**c**) *(témoignage)* **une p. d'amour/d'amitié** a token of love/friendship (**d**) *Math* **faire la p. d'une opération** to prove *or* test the validity of a mathematical operation; **faire la p. par neuf** to cast out nines

prévaloir [69b] [prevalwar] **1** *vi* to prevail (**sur** over); **faire p. son opinion** to win acceptance for one's opinion
2 se prévaloir *vpr* **se p. de qch** *(profiter de)* to take advantage of sth; *(s'enorgueillir)* to pride oneself on sth

prévenant, -e [prevnɑ̃, -ɑ̃t] *adj (personne)* kind (**envers** *ou* **avec** to), considerate (**envers** *ou* **avec** towards); *(geste)* thoughtful (**envers** *ou* **avec** towards)

prévenir [70] [prevnir] *vt* (**a**) *(informer)* to inform, to let know (**de** about *or* of); *(mettre en garde)* to warn; **tu es prévenu!** you've been warned!; **partir sans p.** to leave without telling anyone *or* without warning (**b**) *(empêcher)* *(maladie)* to prevent, to guard against; *(danger, accident)* to avert; *Prov* **mieux vaut p. que guérir** prevention is better than cure (**c**) *(devancer)* *(désir)* to anticipate; *(objection)* to forestall

préventif, -ive [prevɑ̃tif, -iv] *adj* preventive; *Jur* **détention préventive** custody; **être en détention préventive** to be remanded in custody

prévention [prevɑ̃sjɔ̃] *nf* (**a**) *(pour empêcher)* prevention; **p. routière** road safety (**b**) *Jur* custody; **mettre qn en p.** to remand sb in custody

prévenu, -e [prevny] *nm,f Jur* defendant, accused

prévisible [previzibl] *adj* foreseeable

prévision [previzjɔ̃] *nf* forecast; *(activité)* forecasting; **en p. de qch** in expectation *or* anticipation of sth; **prévisions budgétaires** budget projections *or* forecasts; **prévisions météorologiques** weather forecast

prévisionnel, -elle [previzjɔnɛl] *adj (coûts)* estimated; *(budget)* projected; *(analyse)* preliminary

prévoir [73c] [prevwar] *vt* (**a**) *(météo)* to forecast; *(action, difficultés, retards)* to expect, to anticipate; **on ne peut pas tout p.** you can't think of everything (**b**) *(programmer)* *(sortie, vacances)* to plan; **la réunion est prévue pour demain** the meeting is scheduled for tomorrow; **il faudra p. des vêtements de pluie** we'll have to take waterproof clothes; **qu'est-ce que tu as prévu pour le dessert?** what are you planning to have for dessert?; **comme prévu** as planned; **cela s'est passé comme prévu** it went according to plan; **plus tôt/tard que prévu** sooner/later than expected; **cela n'était pas prévu au programme** that wasn't on the agenda

prévoyance [prevwajɑ̃s] *nf* foresight, forethought

prévoyant, -e [prevwajɑ̃, -ɑ̃t] *adj* far-sighted

prie-Dieu [pridjø] *nm inv* prie-dieu, prayer stool

prier [66] [prije] **1** *vi* to pray (**pour** for)
2 *vt* (**a**) *(dieu)* to pray to (**b**) *(supplier)* to beg; **il ne s'est pas fait p. pour venir** he didn't need much persuading to come; **allez, viens, arrête de te faire p.!**

come on, stop being so difficult!; **sans se faire p.**
without hesitation (**c**) *(demander à)* **p. qn de faire
qch** to ask sb to do sth; **je te prie de te dépêcher!**
please hurry up!; **taisez-vous, je vous prie!** please
be quiet!; **je te prie de croire qu'elle a été surprise!**
she was surprised, believe you me!; **je vous en prie!**
(faites-le) please do!, of course!; *(taisez-vous)* stop it!;
(il n'y a pas de quoi) you're welcome!

prière [prijɛr] *nf* (**a**) *Rel* prayer; **faire** *ou* **dire sa p.** to
say one's prayers (**b**) *(demande)* request; **p. de ne pas
fumer** *(sur écriteau)* no smoking; **p. de fermer la
porte** *(sur écriteau)* please close the door

prieuré [prijœre] *nm* priory

primaire [primɛr] **1** *adj* (**a**) *(école, couleur, secteur,
ère)* primary (**b**) *Péj (personne)* simple-minded; *(réaction, racisme)* narrow-minded
2 *nm* (**a**) *Scol* primary education; **être en p.** to be at
primary school (**b**) *Géol* Primary era (**c**) *Écon* primary sector

primate [primat] *nm Zool* primate

primauté [primote] *nf* primacy

prime¹ [prim] *adj* (**a**) **de p. abord** at first sight; *Litt* **dès
sa p. jeunesse** since his/her early youth (**b**) *Math* **B p.**
B prime

prime² *nf (d'assurance)* premium; *(allocation)* grant;
(sur salaire) bonus; **et vous aurez droit à un stylo
en p.** and you will receive a free pen; *Fig* **en p.** into
the bargain; **p. d'ancienneté** long-service award; **p.
d'assurance** insurance premium; **p. de départ** severance pay, golden handshake; **p. de licenciement** severance allowance; **p. de transport** transport
allowance

primer¹ [prime] **1** *vt (avoir la priorité sur)* to take precedence over
2 *vi* to come first; **p. sur** to take precedence over

primer² *vt (attribuer un prix à)* to award a prize to; **
primé** *(taureau)* prize(winning); *(roman, film)* prize-
winning, award-winning

primeur [primœr] *nf* (**a**) **primeurs** *(fruits et légumes)*
(early) fruit and vegetables; **marchand de primeurs**
greengrocer *(selling early produce)* (**b**) *(exclusivité)*
avoir la p. d'une nouvelle to be the first to hear a
piece of news

primevère [primvɛr] *nf* primrose

primitif, -ive [primitif, -iv] **1** *adj* primitive; *(originel)*
original
2 *nm,f (artiste)* primitive

primo [primo] *adv* first(ly), in the first place

primordial, -e, -aux, -ales [primɔrdjal, -o] *adj* essential, primordial

prince [prɛ̃s] *nm* prince; **comme un p.** *(traité, élevé,
habillé)* like a prince; **être** *ou* **se montrer bon p.** to
be very decent; **le p. charmant** Prince Charming

prince-de-galles [prɛ̃sdəgal] *adj inv* Prince of Wales
check

princesse [prɛ̃sɛs] *nf* princess

princier, -ère [prɛ̃sje, -ɛr] *adj* princely

principal, -e, -aux, -ales [prɛ̃sipal, -o] **1** *adj aussi
Gram* main; *(question, raison, but)* main, principal;
(rôle, acteur) leading
2 *nm* (**a**) *(ce qui compte le plus)* **le p.** the main thing,
the most important thing (**b**) *(d'une école) Br* headmaster, *f* headmistress, *Am* principal

principalement [prɛ̃sipalmɑ̃] *adv* mainly, principally

principauté [prɛ̃sipote] *nf* principality

principe [prɛ̃sip] *nm* principle; **un accord de p.** an
agreement in principle; **partir du p. que...** to assume
that...; **c'est une question de p.** it's a matter of principle; **avoir pour p. de...** to make it a matter of principle
to...; **avoir des principes** to have (high) principles; **en
p.** in principle, theoretically; **par p.** on principle

printanier, -ère [prɛ̃tanje, -ɛr] *adj* spring

printemps [prɛ̃tɑ̃] *nm* spring; **au p.** in (the) spring(-
time); **une journée de p.** a spring day; *Fig* **ses vingt-
six p.** her twenty-six summers

prion [priɔ̃] *nm Biol* prion

prioritaire [prijɔritɛr] *adj* (that has) priority; **être p.** to
have priority; *(en voiture)* to have the right of way

priorité [prijɔrite] *nf* (**a**) *(précédence)* priority; **donner
la p. à qn/qch** to give sb/sth priority; **leur dossier
sera traité en p.** their file will get priority treatment;
avoir la p. sur to have priority over (**b**) *Aut* right of
way, priority; **avoir la p.** to have the right of way; **accorder** *ou* **laisser la p. à une voiture** *Br* to give way or
Am to yield to a car; **refuser la p.** to refuse to *Br* give
way *orAm* yield; **p. à droite** *(sur panneau)* = give way
to vehicles coming from the right

pris, -e [pri, priz] **1** *pp de* **prendre**
2 *adj* (**a**) *(siège)* occupied, taken; **avoir les mains
prises** to have one's hands full (**b**) *(personne)* busy;
je suis déjà p. ce jour-là I've already got something
on that day (**c**) *(saisi)* **p. de peur** seized with fear; **p.
de panique** panic-stricken; **p. de remords** racked
with guilt (**d**) *(gelé)* frozen (over) (**e**) *(encombré)*
avoir le nez p. to have a blocked nose; **avoir la gorge
prise** to have a sore throat (**f**) **avoir la taille bien prise**
to have a trim waist

prise [priz] *nf* (**a**) *(d'une ville, de prisonniers)* taking,
capture; *(à la pêche)* catch; *(de drogue)* seize (**b**) *(de
médicaments)* taking (**c**) *Élec* **p. (de courant** *ou* **électrique)** *(femelle) Br* socket, *Am* outlet; *(mâle)* plug; **p.
multiple** adaptor; *Ordinat* **p. Péritel**® Scart connec-
tor; **p. de terre** *Br* earth *orAm* ground (connection)
(**d**) *Cin, Phot & TV* **p. de son** sound recording; **p. de
vue** *(cliché)* shot; *(de tournage)* take; *(action)* shooting
(**e**) *Tech* **en p.** in gear, engaged; *Fig* **en p. (directe)
sur** *ou* **avec qch** in touch with sth (**f**) *(de judo, de lutte)*
hold; *(pour se retenir)* hold; *(plus ferme)* grasp, grip;
(pour le pied) foothold; *Fig* **avoir p. sur qn** to have a
hold on or over sb; **lâcher p.** to lose one's grip; *Fig* to
give up; **donner p. aux reproches/critiques** to lay
oneself open to reproach/criticism; **être aux prises
avec des difficultés** to be grappling with difficulties;
être aux prises avec qn to be at odds with sb (**g**) *(locutions) Fam* **p. de bec** row, squabble; **p. en charge**
(par un taxi) (d'un passager) picking up; *(somme)*
minimum charge; *(par la Sécurité sociale)* (guaranteed) reimbursement; **p. de conscience** awareness,
realization; **p. de contact** initial contact *or* meeting;
p. de notes note-taking; **p. d'otages** hostage-taking;
p. de position stance; **p. de pouvoir** (political) takeover; **faire une p. de sang à qn** to take a blood sample from sb

priser¹ [prize] **1** *vt* **p. du tabac** to take snuff
2 *vi* to take snuff

priser² *vt Litt (estimer)* to prize, to value

prisme [prism] *nm* prism

prison [prizɔ̃] *nf* (**a**) *(lieu de détention)* prison, jail;
mettre qn en prison to put sb in prison; **faire de la
p.** to serve a prison sentence (**b**) *(peine)* imprisonment; **cinq ans de p.** five years' imprisonment

prisonnier, -ère [prizɔnje, -ɛr] **1** *nm,f* prisoner; **faire qn p.** to take sb prisoner; **p. de droit commun** common criminal; **p. de guerre** prisoner of war, POW; **p. d'opinion** prisoner of conscience; **p. politique** political prisoner
2 *adj* imprisoned, in prison; **ils sont encore prisonniers sous les décombres** they are still trapped in the rubble; **être p. de** to be a prisoner of; *Fig* to be a slave to

privation [privasjɔ̃] *nf* (**a**) *(action de priver)* deprivation (**b**) **privations** *(manque)* hardship, privation; **s'imposer des privations** to deprive oneself, to go without

privatisation [privatizasjɔ̃] *nf* privatization

privatiser [privatize] *vt* to privatize

privautés [privote] *nfpl* (undue) familiarity; **prendre** *ou* **se permettre des p. avec qn** to be over-familiar with sb

privé, -e [prive] **1** *adj* private; **à titre p.** in a private capacity
2 *nm* (**a**) *(secteur)* **le p.** the private sector; *Scol* the private education system; **mes enfants sont dans le p.** my children go to a private school (**b**) *(intimité)* **dans le p.** privately; **connaître qn dans le p.** to know sb personally; **en p.** in private (**c**) *Fam (détective)* private eye

priver [prive] *vt* **p. qn de qch** to deprive sb of sth; **p. qn de sorties** not to allow sb to go out; **être privé de dessert** to go without pudding; **privé d'eau/d'air/de sommeil** deprived of water/air/sleep; **ça ne le prive pas du tout de ne plus fumer** he doesn't find it a hardship not to smoke any more
2 se priver *vpr* to do *or* go without; **se p. de** to do *or* go without; *(plaisir)* to deprive oneself of, to deny oneself; **ne pas se p. de faire qch** not to hesitate to do sth

privilège [privilɛʒ] *nm* privilege

privilégié, -e [privileʒje] **1** *adj (personne, site)* privileged; *(conditions)* privileged, favourable; *(relations)* special
2 *nm,f* privileged person; **les privilégiés** the privileged

privilégier [66] [privileʒje] *vt (personne, groupe)* to privilege; *(facteur, aspect)* to prioritize

prix [pri] *nm* (**a**) *(coût)* price; **à tout p.** at all costs, at any price; **à aucun p.** not at any price, on no account; **se vendre à p. d'or** to fetch huge prices; **acheter qch à p. d'or** to pay a (small) fortune for sth; **payer qch au p. fort** to pay a high price for sth; **faire un p. à qn** to give sb a good deal; **je vous fais un p.** d'ami I'll let you have it cheap; **y mettre le p.** to pay a high price; **la santé/le bonheur, ça n'a pas de p.** you can't put a price on health/happiness; **mettre à p. la tête de qn** to put a price on sb's head; **c'est mon dernier p.** that's my final offer; **votre p. sera le mien** name your price; **au p. coûtant** at cost price; **p. de revient** cost price; **p. de vente** selling price (**b**) *(importance)* **attacher beaucoup de p.** *ou* **un grand p. à qch** to set great store by sth (**c**) *(récompense)* prize; **p. de consolation** consolation prize; **le p. Goncourt** = prestigious French literary prize; **p. Nobel** *(récompense)* Nobel Prize; *(personne)* Nobel Br prizewinner *or* Am laureate; **le p. Nobel de la Paix** *(récompense)* the Nobel Peace Prize

pro [pro] *nmf Fam* pro

probabilité [prɔbabilite] *nf* probability, likelihood; **selon toute p.** in all probability *or* likelihood; *Math* **calcul des probabilités** theory of probability

probable [prɔbabl] *adj* probable, likely; **il est p. qu'elle viendra** she'll probably come; **peu p.** improbable, unlikely; **il est peu p. qu'elle vienne** she's not likely *or* she's unlikely to come

probablement [prɔbabləmɑ̃] *adv* probably

probant, -e [prɔbɑ̃, -ɑ̃t] *adj* convincing, conclusive

probité [prɔbite] *nf* probity, integrity

problématique [prɔblematik] **1** *adj* problematic(al)
2 *nf* set of problems

problème [prɔblɛm] *nm* problem; **c'est tout un p.!** it's such a problem!; **peau/cheveux à problèmes** problem skin/hair; **avoir des problèmes familiaux/d'argent** to have family/money problems

procédé [prɔsede] *nm* (**a**) *(façon de faire)* method; **échange de bons procédés** exchange of friendly services (**b**) *(technique)* process; **p. de fabrication** manufacturing process; *Péj* **ça sent le p.** it seems rather artificial

procéder [34] [prɔsede] **1** *vi* (**a**) *(agir)* to proceed, to act; **p. par ordre** to do things in order; **p. avec méthode** to proceed methodically; **p. par élimination** to follow a process of elimination (**b**) *Sout* **p. de** *(venir de)* to arise out of, to originate in
2 procéder à *vt ind (recherches, arrestation, vérification)* to carry out; *(élections)* to hold

procédure [prɔsedyr] *nf* (**a**) *(méthode)* procedure (**b**) *Jur* proceedings; **engager une p.** to take proceedings (**c**) *Ordinat* procedure; **p. de chargement** loading procedure

procédurier, -ère [prɔsedyrje, -ɛr] *adj* quibbling

procès [prɔsɛ] *nm Jur* (legal) proceedings; *(civil)* lawsuit; *(criminel)* (criminal) trial; **engager un p.** to take legal action; **faire** *ou* **intenter un p. à qn** to take proceedings against sb; **être en p. avec qn** to be involved in legal proceedings with sb; **gagner/perdre son p.** to win/lose one's case; **faire un p. d'intention à qn** to accuse sb on the basis of assumptions not facts; **faire le p. de qn/qch** *(critiquer)* to attack sb/sth; *Fig* **sans autre forme de p.** without (any) further ceremony, without further ado

processeur [prɔsesœr] *nm Ordinat* processor; **p. central** central processing unit, CPU; **p. de données** data processor

procession [prɔsesjɔ̃] *nf* procession

processus [prɔsesys] *nm* process

procès-verbal [prɔsɛvɛrbal] *(pl* **procès-verbaux** [prɔsɛvɛrbo]) *nm* (**a**) *Jur* policeman's report *(about an offence)*; *(amende)* fine (**b**) *(rapport)* (official) report; *(d'une réunion)* minutes; *(d'un témoignage)* record

prochain, -e [prɔʃɛ̃, -ɛn] **1** *adj* (**a**) *(qui suit)* next; **il sera pour une prochaine fois** Br another time, perhaps, Am I'll take a rain check; **à la prochaine (fois)!** see you (soon)!; *Fam* **je descends à la prochaine** I'm getting off at the next stop (**b**) *(imminent)* imminent; **dans un avenir p.** in the near *or* not too distant future; **un jour p.** one day soon
2 *nm (semblable)* **aimer son p.** to love one's neighbour

prochainement [prɔʃɛnmɑ̃] *adv* shortly, soon; **p. sur vos écrans** coming soon to a Br cinema *or* Am movie theater near you

proche [prɔʃ] **1** *adj* (**a**) *(dans l'espace)* near, close; **p. de qch** close to *or* near sth (**b**) *(dans l'avenir)* near, imminent; **dans un avenir p.** in the near *or* not too distant future; **la fin est p.** the end is nigh (**c**) *(récent)* recent (**d**) *(semblable, intime)* close (**de** to); **ils sont**

proches parents they are closely related (**e**) **de p. en p.** gradually, step by step
2 *nm* close relative *or* relation
Proche-Orient [prɔʃɔrjɑ̃] *nm* **le P.** the Middle East
proclamation [prɔklamasjɔ̃] *nf* proclamation
proclamer [prɔklame] *vt* to proclaim; *(résultats de scrutin)* to declare
procréation [prɔkreasjɔ̃] *nf* procreation
procréer [24] [prɔkree] *vi* to procreate
procuration [prɔkyrasjɔ̃] *nf* proxy, power of attorney; **par p.** by proxy, *Spéc* per pro(curationem); *Fig* **vivre par p.** to live vicariously *or* by proxy
procurer [prɔkyre] **1** *vi* **p. qch à qn** *(sujet: personne)* to get sth for sb; *(sujet: chose)* to bring sb sth
2 se procurer *vpr* to get (hold of), to obtain
procureur [prɔkyrœr] *nm Jur* procurator, proxy; **p. général/de la République** *(système anglais)* ≃ public prosecutor; *(système écossais)* ≃ procurator fiscal; *(système américain)* ≃ district attorney
prodigalité [prɔdigalite] *nf* extravagance, prodigality
prodige [prɔdiʒ] **1** *nm* wonder, marvel; *(personne)* prodigy; **faire des prodiges** to work wonders; **tenir du p.** to be extraordinary, to be something of a miracle
2 *adj* **enfant p.** child prodigy
prodigieusement [prɔdiʒjøzmɑ̃] *adv* prodigiously
prodigieux, -euse [prɔdiʒjø, -øz] *adj* prodigious, extraordinary
prodigue [prɔdig] *adj (dépensier)* wasteful, spendthrift; *(généreux)* lavish, unsparing (**de** in *or* with)
prodiguer [prɔdige] *vt* **p. qch à qn** to lavish sth on sb; **p. des conseils à qn** to pour out advice to sb
producteur, -trice [prɔdyktœr, -tris] **1** *adj* **pays p. de blé/pétrole** wheat-growing/oil-producing country
2 *nm,f* producer
productif, -ive [prɔdyktif, -iv] *adj* productive
production [prɔdyksjɔ̃] *nf* (**a**) *Ind & Cin* production; *(d'électricité)* production, generation (**b**) *(produit)* product; *Cin* production; *(d'une usine)* output; **p. littéraire** literary output
productivité [prɔdyktivite] *nf* productivity
produire [18] [prɔdɥir] **1** *vt* (**a**) *(marchandise, émission, gaz)* to produce; *(chaleur, électricité, odeur)* to generate, to produce (**b**) *(résultat, effet)* to produce, to bring about; *(irritation, sensation)* to cause
2 se produire *vpr* (**a**) *(événement)* to happen (**b**) *(acteur)* to appear
produit [prɔdɥi] *nm* (**a**) *(marchandise)* product; **produits agricoles** agricultural *or* farm produce; **p. de beauté** beauty product; **produits blancs** white goods; **p. chimique** chemical; **p. de consommation** consumer product; **p. d'entretien** (household) cleaning product; **p. fini** finished product; **p. intérieur brut** gross domestic product; **p. de luxe** luxury product; **p. manufacturé** manufactured product; **produits ménagers** (household) cleaning products; **p. national brut** gross national product (**b**) *(profit)* yield; **p. d'une vente** proceeds of a sale; **le p. de dix années de travail** the result of ten years' work; **vivre du p. de la terre** to live off the land (**c**) *Math (d'une multiplication)* product (**d**) *(création)* **c'est le p. de son imagination** it's the product of his/her imagination
proéminent, -e [prɔeminɑ̃, -ɑ̃t] *adj* prominent
prof [prɔf] *nmf Fam* teacher

profanateur, -trice [prɔfanatœr, -tris] *nm,f (de tombes)* desecrator
profanation [prɔfanasjɔ̃] *nf* desecration, violation
profane [prɔfan] **1** *adj* non-religious, secular; *Fig* **être p. en la matière** to know nothing about the subject
2 *nmf (non-initié)* layman, *f* laywoman
profaner [prɔfane] *vt (église)* to desecrate; *(tombe)* to desecrate, to violate; *(souvenir, mémoire)* to defile
proférer [34] [prɔfere] *vt* to utter
professer [prɔfese] *vt* to profess
professeur [prɔfesœr] *nm* teacher; *(à l'université)* professor; **p. des écoles** primary school teacher; **p. principal** *Br* class *or* form teacher, *Am* homeroom teacher
profession [prɔfesjɔ̃] *nf* (**a**) *(métier)* profession, occupation; *(d'artisans)* trade; **de p.** *(musicien)* professional; *(menuisier)* by trade; **p. libérale** profession; **sans p.** *(dans un questionnaire)* not working; **je suis sans p.** I don't work (**b**) *(déclaration)* **faire p. de qch** to profess sth; **p. de foi** profession of faith
professionnalisation [prɔfesjɔnalizasjɔ̃] *nf* professionalization
professionnalisme [prɔfesjɔnalism] *nm* professionalism
professionnel, -elle [prɔfesjɔnɛl] **1** *adj (attitude, sportif)* professional; *(enseignement)* vocational; *(maladie)* occupational
2 *nm,f* professional
professionnellement [prɔfesjɔnɛlmɑ̃] *adv* professionally
professoral, -e, -aux, -ales [prɔfesɔral, -o] *adj* (**a**) *(de professeur)* professorial (**b**) *(pédant)* patronizing, lecturing
professorat [prɔfesɔra] *nm* teaching profession *(especially in higher education)*
profil [prɔfil] *nm aussi Fig* profile; **dessiner qn de p.** to draw sb in profile; **se mettre de p.** to turn one's face *(so it is in profile)*; *Fig* **adopter un p. bas** to adopt a low profile; **p. de poste** job description; **avoir le p. de l'emploi** to fit the job description
profilé, -e [prɔfile] **1** *adj (carrosserie)* streamlined
2 *nm* section
profiler [prɔfile] **se profiler** *vpr* to stand out (in profile), to be outlined (**sur** *ou* **contre** against); *(problèmes)* to emerge, to loom; *(solution)* to emerge; *(événement)* to be in the offing
profit [prɔfi] *nm* (**a**) *(avantage)* profit, benefit; **mettre qch à p.** to put sth to good use; **tirer p. de qch** to take advantage of sth; **ce manteau m'a fait du p.** this coat has served me well; **au p. des pauvres** in aid of the poor; **concert donné au p. des orphelins** benefit concert for orphans; **perdre des voix au p. de qn** to lose votes to sb (**b**) *(gain)* profit; **il n'y a pas de petits profits** every little helps
profitable [prɔfitabl] *adj* profitable
profiter [prɔfite] **1 profiter de** *vt ind* to take advantage of; **je profite d'un moment de calme pour vous dire que...** I'm using these few moments of peace and quiet to tell you that...; **p. de la vie/de sa jeunesse** to make the most of life/one's youth
2 profiter à *vt ind* to be of benefit to, to benefit; **ses vacances lui ont bien profité** his/her holiday has done him/her a lot of good
3 *vi Fam (enfant, plante)* to thrive
profiteur, -euse [prɔfitœr, -øz] *nm,f Péj* profiteer
profond, -e [prɔfɔ̃, -ɔ̃d] **1** *adj* (**a**) *(trou, lac, voix)* deep; *(décolleté)* plunging; *(forêt)* dense, thick; *(som-*

meil) deep, sound (**b**) *(cause)* underlying (**c**) *(paroles)* profound; *(haine, silence, dégoût)* profound, deep; *(soupir)* heavy
2 *adv* deep
3 *nm* **au plus p. de mon cœur** in my heart of hearts, deep down; **au plus p. de la nuit** at dead of night
profondément [prɔfɔ̃demɑ̃] *adv (choqué, déçu, ému)* deeply, profoundly; *(aimer, mépriser)* deeply; *(dormir)* soundly; *(creuser)* deep; **p. endormi** sound *or* fast asleep; **j'en suis p. convaincu** I'm quite convinced of it
profondeur [prɔfɔ̃dœr] *nf* (**a**) *(de l'eau, d'un trou)* depth; **faire 10 mètres de p.** to be 10 metres deep; **en p.** *(étude, analyse)* in-depth; *Phot* **p. de champ** depth of field (**b**) *(d'un sentiment)* depth; *(d'un texte)* profoundness, profundity
profusion [prɔfyzjɔ̃] *nf* profusion, abundance; **à p.** in profusion
progéniture [prɔʒenityr] *nf* progeny, offspring
progiciel [prɔʒisjɛl] *nm Ordinat* software package; **p. de communication** comms package
prognathe [prɔgnat] *adj (visage)* undershot, underhung, *Spéc* prognathous
programmable [prɔgramabl] *adj* programmable
programmateur, -trice [prɔgramatœr, -tris] **1** *nm,f* (**a**) *Rad & TV* programme planner (**b**) *Ordinat* programmer
2 *nm Tech* automatic control (device)
programmation [prɔgramasjɔ̃] *nf* (**a**) *TV & Rad* programme planning (**b**) *Ordinat* programming
programme [prɔgram] *nm* (**a**) *(émissions, œuvres)* programme; *(brochure) (de télévision)* TV guide; *(de cinéma) Br* cinema *or Am* movie guide; *(au concert, au théâtre)* programme (**b**) *(d'activités)* programme (**c**) *Scol (en général)* curriculum; *(d'un cours)* syllabus; **les auteurs au** *ou* **du p.** the set books (**d**) *(d'un parti politique)* manifesto; **p. électoral** (election) platform; *Fig* **c'est tout un p.!** that'll be interesting! (**e**) *Ordinat* program; **p. d'amorçage** boot program; **p. d'arrière-plan** background program; **p. d'auto-test** self-test program; **p. de configuration** configuration program; **p. de conversion** conversion program; **p. détecteur de virus** virus detection program; **p. éditeur de liens** link program; **p. d'évaluation de performance** benchmark program; **p. de formatage** formatter
programmer [prɔgrame] *vt* (**a**) *Ordinat* to program (**b**) *TV & Rad* to schedule (**c**) *(vacances, changements)* to plan
programmeur, -euse [prɔgramœr, -øz] *nm,f Ordinat* programmer
progrès [prɔgrɛ] *nm* progress; **faire des p.** to make progress; **être en p.** to be making progress; *Fam* **il y a du** *ou* **un p.** there's been an improvement
progresser [prɔgrɛse] *vi* (**a**) *(avancer) (armée)* to advance, to progress; *(marcheur)* to make progress (**b**) *(épidémie, incendie)* to spread; *(chômage, délinquance)* to rise, to increase (**c**) *(faire des progrès)* to make progress
progressif, -ive [prɔgrɛsif, -iv] *adj* progressive; *(changement)* gradual
progression [prɔgrɛsjɔ̃] *nf* (**a**) *(avance) (d'une armée)* advance, progress; *(de marcheurs)* progress (**b**) *(d'un incendie, d'une épidémie)* spread; *(de la délinquance, du chômage)* rise, increase; **être en p.** *(secteur économique)* to be growing *or* expanding; *(maladie)* to be spreading; *(chômage, criminalité)* to be rising, to be on the increase

progressiste [prɔgrɛsist] *adj & nmf* progressive
progressivement [prɔgrɛsivmɑ̃] *adv* progressively
prohiber [prɔibe] *vt* to prohibit, to forbid
prohibitif, -ive [prɔibitif, -iv] *adj* prohibitive
prohibition [prɔibisjɔ̃] *nf* prohibition; *Hist* **la P.** Prohibition
proie [prwa] *nf* prey; **être la p. de qn** to fall prey *or* victim to sb; **être en p. à** *(remords, doute)* to be racked *or* tormented by; *(hallucinations)* to suffer from; **lâcher la p. pour l'ombre** to go chasing after rainbows
projecteur [prɔʒɛktœr] *nm* (**a**) *Cin & Phot* projector (**b**) *(dans un stade, sur un monument)* floodlight; *Théât* spotlight; *Fig* **sous les projecteurs de l'actualité** in the limelight
projectile [prɔʒɛktil] *nm* missile
projection [prɔʒɛksjɔ̃] *nf* (**a**) *(lancer)* projection; *(d'un liquide, de boue)* splashing; *(de graisse)* spattering; *(de cendres, de roches)* spewing out; **des projections de boue** splashes of mud (**b**) *Cin* projection; *(séance)* screening, showing; **p. de diapositives** slide show; **p. privée** private screening (**c**) *Math, Géom & (prévision)* projection
projectionniste [prɔʒɛksjɔnist] *nmf* projectionist
projet [prɔʒɛ] *nm* *(intention)* plan; *(étude)* project; **faire des projets** to make plans; **p. de loi** bill; **en p.** at the planning stage; **c'est resté à l'état de p.** it never got off the ground
projeter [42] [prɔʒte] **1** *vt* (**a**) *(lancer)* to project; *(graisse)* to spatter; *(liquide, boue)* to splash; *(cendres, roches)* to spew out; **être projeté au sol** to be hurled to the ground (**b**) *(prévoir)* to plan; **p. de faire qch** to plan to do sth (**c**) *(film)* to show, to screen (**d**) *(faire apparaître) (ombre)* to cast, to throw; *(image)* to project (**e**) *Psy* to project (**sur** onto)
2 se projeter *vpr (ombre)* to be cast
prolétaire [prɔletɛr] *adj & nmf* proletarian
prolétariat [prɔletarja] *nm* proletariat
prolétarien, -enne [prɔletarjɛ̃, -ɛn] *adj* proletarian
prolifération [prɔliferasjɔ̃] *nf* proliferation
proliférer [34] [prɔlifere] *vi* to proliferate
prolifique [prɔlifik] *adj* prolific
prolixe [prɔliks] *adj* wordy, verbose
prolo [prɔlo] *Fam* **1** *adj* plebby
2 *nmf* pleb, prole
prologue [prɔlɔg] *nm* prologue (**de** to)
prolongation [prɔlɔ̃gasjɔ̃] *nf (de discussions)* prolongation; *(d'un congé, d'une pause)* extension; **jouer les prolongations** *(au football)* to play extra time *or Am* overtime
prolongé, -e [prɔlɔ̃ʒe] *adj (absence, séjour)* prolonged, lengthy; *(effort)* prolonged, sustained; *(week-end)* long; **pas d'utilisation prolongée sans avis médical** *(sur un médicament)* ≃ if symptoms persist, consult your doctor
prolongement [prɔlɔ̃ʒmɑ̃] *nm* (**a**) *(d'une rue)* continuation; *(d'un mur, d'une voie de chemin de fer)* extension; **être dans le p. de qch** *(meuble)* to be flush with sth; *(rue)* to be a continuation of sth (**b**) **prolongements** *(d'une action)* repercussions
prolonger [45] [prɔlɔ̃ʒe] **1** *vt (vie, débat, repas)* to prolong; *(séjour, absence)* to prolong, to extend; *(mur, route, voie ferrée)* to extend
2 se prolonger *vpr (séjour, absence)* to be prolonged *or* extended; *(réunion)* to go on; *(rue)* to continue, to extend

promenade [prɔmnad] *nf* (**a**) *(marche)* walk; *(courte)* stroll; **faire une p.** to go for a walk/stroll; **faire une p. en voiture** to go for a drive; **faire une p. à bicyclette** to go for a bike ride; **faire une p. à cheval** to go *Br* (horse)riding *or Am* (horseback) riding; **l'heure de la p.** *(d'un détenu)* exercise time (**b**) *(avenue)* promenade

promener [46] [prɔmne] **1** *vt* (**a**) *(personne, chien)* to take for a walk; *Fig* **p. qn de musée en musée** to take sb from museum to museum; *Fam* **cela te promènera un peu** it'll get you out a bit (**b**) *(passer)* **p. sa main/ son regard sur qch** to run one's hand/one's eyes over sth
  2 se promener *vpr* (**a**) *(à pied)* to go for a walk; **aller se p.** to go for a walk (**b**) *(mains, regard)* **se p. sur** to wander over; *Ordinat* **se p. dans** *(texte)* to scroll through

promeneur, -euse [prɔmnœr, -øz] *nm,f* walker

promesse [prɔmɛs] *nf* promise; **faire une p. à qn** to make sb a promise; **tenir sa p.** to keep one's promise; **p. de Gascon** empty promise; **p. d'achat/de vente** undertaking to buy/to sell

prometteur, -euse [prɔmɛtœr, -øz] *adj* promising

promettre [47] [prɔmɛtr] **1** *vt* (**a**) *(s'engager à)* to promise; **p. qch à qn** to promise sb sth; **je ne peux rien te p.** I can't promise (you) anything; **tu me le promets?** (do you) promise?; **je te promets de le faire** I promise you I'll do it; **je le ferai, c'est promis** I'll do it, I promise; **p. monts et merveilles à qn** to promise sb the earth *or* the moon (**b**) *(être prometteur)* **la soirée promet d'être amusante** it promises to be an amusing evening; *Fam* **ça ne promet rien de bon** it doesn't look good
  2 *vi (projet, enfant)* to be promising; *Fam Ironique* **ça promet!** that's promising!
  3 se promettre *vpr* **se p. qch** *(à soi-même)* to promise oneself sth; *(l'un l'autre)* to promise each other sth; **se p. de faire qch** *(à soi-même)* to resolve to do sth; **ils se sont promis de ne jamais se quitter** they promised each other they'd never part

promis, -e [prɔmi, -iz] **1** *adj* promised
  2 *nm,f Vieilli* betrothed

promiscuité [prɔmiskɥite] *nf* overcrowding; **vivre dans la p.** to live in crowded accommodation

promo [prɔmo] *nf Fam* promo; **en p.** on special offer

promontoire [prɔmɔ̃twar] *nm* promontory, headland

promoteur, -trice [prɔmɔtœr, -tris] *nm,f* (**a**) **p. (immobilier)** property developer (**b**) *(créateur)* originator (**de** of)

promotion [prɔmosjɔ̃] *nf* (**a**) *(avancement)* promotion; **p. à l'ancienneté** promotion by seniority; **p. interne** internal promotion; **p. sociale** upward mobility (**b**) *(d'une école) Br* year, *Am* class; **premier de sa p.** first in one's *Br* year *or Am* class (**c**) *(dans le commerce)* promotion; **faire la p. de qch** to promote sth; **la p. de la semaine** this week's special offer; **en p.** on special offer

promotionnel, -elle [prɔmosjɔnɛl] *adj (article)* promotional; *(tarif)* special; **vente promotionnelle** special offer

promouvoir [31a] [prɔmuvwar] *vt aussi Fig* to promote; **être promu chef du personnel** to be promoted to personnel manager

prompt, -e [prɔ̃, prɔ̃t] *adj (réaction)* prompt; **p. à faire qch** quick to do sth; **p. à la riposte** quick with a riposte

promptement [prɔ̃tmɑ̃, prɔ̃ptəmɑ̃] *adv Litt* promptly

promptitude [prɔ̃tityd] *nf Litt (d'une réaction)* promptness

promu, -e *voir* **promouvoir**

promulgation [prɔmylgasjɔ̃] *nf* promulgation

promulguer [prɔmylge] *vt* to promulgate

prôner [prone] *vt* to advocate

pronom [prɔnɔ̃] *nm Gram* pronoun; **p. personnel/ indéfini/interrogatif** personal/indefinite/interrogative pronoun

pronominal, -e, -aux, -ales [prɔnɔminal, -o] *adj Gram* pronominal

prononcé, -e [prɔnɔ̃se] **1** *adj* pronounced, strong
  2 *nm Jur* **le p. du jugement** the verdict

prononcer [16] [prɔnɔ̃se] **1** *vt* (**a**) *(articuler)* to pronounce; **mal p. un mot** to mispronounce a word (**b**) *(dire) (mot)* to utter; *(discours)* to deliver; *(sentence, divorce)* to pronounce
  2 se prononcer *vpr* (**a**) *(être articulé)* to be pronounced; **ça s'écrit comme ça se prononce** it's written as it's pronounced (**b**) *(s'exprimer)* to give one's opinion; *(juge)* to give a verdict; **se p. pour** *ou* **en faveur de qn/qch** to express one's support for sb/sth; **se p. contre qn/qch** to express one's opposition to sb/sth; **50 pour cent ne se prononcent pas** *(dans un sondage)* 50 per cent are undecided

prononciation [prɔnɔ̃sjasjɔ̃] *nf* pronunciation; **elle a une bonne/mauvaise p.** her pronunciation is good/ bad

pronostic [prɔnɔstik] *nm* forecast; *(d'un médecin)* prognosis

propagande [prɔpagɑ̃d] *nf* propaganda; **faire de la p. pour qn/qch** to put out propaganda for sb/sth; *(pour une élection)* to campaign for sb/sth

propagation [prɔpagasjɔ̃] *nf* spreading

propager [45] [prɔpaʒe] **1** *vt* to spread
  2 se propager *vpr* (**a**) *(épidémie, nouvelle, idée)* to spread (**b**) *(lumière, son)* to be propagated

propane [prɔpan] *nm Chim* propane

propension [prɔpɑ̃sjɔ̃] *nf* propensity (**à** for); **p. à faire qch** propensity to do sth

prophète [prɔfɛt] *nm* prophet; **p. de malheur** prophet of doom; *Prov* **nul n'est p. en son pays** no man is a prophet in his own country

prophétie [prɔfesi] *nf* prophecy

prophétique [prɔfetik] *adj* prophetic

prophylactique [prɔfilaktik] *adj* prophylactic

propice [prɔpis] *adj* **le moment p.** the right moment; **p. à qch** good for sth; **un endroit p. au repos** a restful spot; **un endroit p. aux rencontres** a good place to meet people

proportion [prɔpɔrsjɔ̃] *nf* proportion; **respecter les proportions** to get the proportions right; **en p. de qch** in proportion to sth; **hors de (toute) p. avec** out of (all) proportion to; **toutes proportions gardées** relatively speaking

proportionné, -e [prɔpɔrsjɔne] *adj* (**a**) *(bâti)* **bien/ mal p.** well-/badly-proportioned (**b**) *(lié)* **être p. à** to be proportionate to

proportionnel, -elle [prɔpɔrsjɔnɛl] **1** *adj* proportional (**à** to); **inversement p. à qch** inversely proportional to sth
  2 *nf* **proportionnelle** *Pol* proportional representation; **être élu à la proportionelle** to be elected by proportional representation

proportionnellement [prɔpɔrsjɔnɛlmɑ̃] *adv* proportionally (**à** to)

propos [prɔpo] *nm* (**a**) *(sujet)* à p. de qn/qch about sb/sth; à ce p.,... talking of which...; à tout p. constantly; à p., avez-vous lu ce livre? by the way, have you read this book?; c'est à quel p.? what's it about?; arriver fort à p. to arrive at just the right moment; juger à p. de faire qch to think it right to do sth; hors de p. *(remarque)* inappropriate (**b**) *(intention)* purpose, intention; de p. délibéré deliberately, on purpose (**c**) *(parole)* des p. talk, words; tenir des p. étonnants to say some surprising things

proposer [prɔpoze] **1** *vt (suggérer)* to suggest, to propose; *(offrir)* to offer; *(amendement, loi)* to table; p. qch à qn to suggest *or* propose sth to sb; *(argent, travail)* to offer sth to sb; je vous en propose 200 euros/un bon prix I'll give you 200 euros/a good price for it; voilà ce que je vous propose this is what I suggest; le cinéma Le César vous propose cette semaine... Le César will be showing the following films this week...; je leur ai proposé de venir avec moi I suggested (to them) that they should come with me; elle m'a proposé de m'aider she offered to help me; je propose qu'on y aille demain I suggest going tomorrow

2 se proposer *upr* (**a**) *(être volontaire)* to offer one's services; se p. pour faire qch to offer to do sth (**b**) se p. de faire qch *(en avoir l'intention)* to propose to do sth

proposition [prɔpozisjɔ̃] *nf* (**a**) *(suggestion)* suggestion, proposal; *(offre)* offer; faire une p. (à qn) to make a suggestion *or* proposal (to sb); faire des propositions à une femme to proposition a woman; sur la p. de qn at sb's suggestion; p. de loi bill (**b**) *Phil & Math* proposition (**c**) *Gram* clause; p. principale main clause

propre [prɔpr] **1** *adj* (**a**) *(impeccable) (personne, linge, maison)* clean; *(bébé)* potty-trained; *(chien)* Br house-trained, Am house-broken; *(copie d'élève)* neat; n'utilise pas la serviette des autres, ce n'est pas p.! don't use other people's towels, it's not hygienic!; p. comme un sou neuf spick and span; Fam nous voilà propres! now we're in a mess! (**b**) *(à soi)* own; voir qch de ses propres yeux to see sth with one's own eyes; ce sont là ses propres paroles those are his/her very words (**c**) *(particulier)* être p. à qn/qch to be characteristic of or peculiar to sb/sth (**d**) *(adapté)* être p. à qch to be suitable for sth (**e**) *(littéral)* au sens p. in the literal sense, literally

2 *nm* (**a**) *(caractéristique)* characteristic feature (**b**) appartenir en p. à qn to be sb's sole property (**c**) *(sens propre)* au p. literally (**d**) recopier qch au p. to make a clean copy of sth (**e**) *(propreté)* sentir le p. to smell clean; *Belg* faire du p. to spring-clean (**f**) *Fam* c'est du p.! that's a fine way to carry on!

propre-à-rien *(pl* propres-à-rien) [prɔprarjɛ̃] *nmf* good-for-nothing

proprement [prɔprəmɑ̃] *adv* (**a**) *(avec propreté)* cleanly; *(vêtu)* tidily; manger p. to eat without making a mess (**b**) *(strictement)* strictly; c'est un problème p. urbain it's strictly an inner-city problem; à p. parler strictly speaking; voilà la bibliothèque p. dite there's the actual library (**c**) *Fam (vraiment)* c'est p. scandaleux! it's an absolute disgrace!

propreté [prɔprəte] *nf (hygiène)* cleanliness; *(des vêtements, de la vaisselle, d'une maison)* cleanness; *(d'un travail)* neatness

propriétaire [prɔprijetɛr] *nmf* (**a**) *(d'une voiture, d'une propriété, d'un hôtel)* owner; devenir *ou* se rendre

p. de qch to become the owner of sth; être p. to be a landowner; *(de maison)* to be a home owner; p. foncier landowner (**b**) *(d'une location)* landlord, *f* landlady

propriété [prɔprijete] *nf* (**a**) *(fait de posséder)* ownership; p. littéraire copyright; p. property ownership; *Jur* p. intellectuelle intellectual property (**b**) *(chose ou terre possédée)* property; p. privée private property (**c**) *(caractéristique)* property

proprio [prɔprijo] *nmf Fam* landlord, *f* landlady

propulser [prɔpylse] **1** *vt* to propel

2 se propulser *upr Fam* se p. en tête du peloton to shoot to the front of the pack

propulsion [prɔpylsjɔ̃] *nf* propulsion; sous-marin à p. nucléaire nuclear-powered submarine

prorata [prɔrata] *nm inv* proportion; au p. de qch in proportion to sth

prorogation [prɔrɔgasjɔ̃] *nf (de contrat, de bail)* extension

proroger [45] [prɔrɔʒe] *vt (contrat, bail)* to extend; *(échéance)* to defer

prosaïque [prozaik] *adj* prosaic

proscrire [30] [prɔskrir] *vt* to ban, to proscribe

proscrit, -e [prɔskri, -it] **1** *adj* banned, proscribed

2 *nm,f Litt (banni)* exile

prose [proz] *nf* prose; en p. *(écrire)* in prose; *(texte, poème)* prose

prosélytisme [prɔzelitism] *nm* proselytism; faire du p. to proselytize

prosodie [prɔzɔdi] *nf* prosody

prospecter [prɔspɛkte] *vt* (**a**) *(terrain)* to prospect (**b**) *(client)* to canvass; *(marché)* to explore

prospecteur, -trice [prɔspɛktœr, -tris] *nm,f* (**a**) *(de terrain)* prospector (**b**) *(de clients)* canvasser

prospection [prɔspɛksjɔ̃] *nf* (**a**) *(de terrain)* prospecting; faire de la p. to prospect; p. minière/pétrolière mining/oil exploration (**b**) *(de clients)* canvassing; faire de la p. to explore the market; p. téléphonique telephone canvassing

prospectus [prɔspɛktys] *nm* (**a**) *(brochure)* leaflet (**b**) *Fin* prospectus

prospère [prɔspɛr] *adj* prosperous; *(santé)* glowing

prospérer [34] [prɔspere] *vi* to prosper

prospérité [prɔsperite] *nf* prosperity; en période de p. in times of prosperity

prostate [prɔstat] *nf Anat* prostate (gland)

prosterner [prɔstɛrne] se prosterner *vpr (saluer)* to prostrate oneself (devant before); *Fig (s'abaisser)* to grovel, to kowtow (devant to)

prostitué, -e [prɔstitɥe] *nm,f (homme)* male prostitute; *(femme)* prostitute

prostituer [prɔstitɥe] **1** *vt* to prostitute

2 se prostituer *vpr* to prostitute oneself

prostitution [prɔstitysjɔ̃] *nf* prostitution

prostré, -e [prɔstre] *adj* prostrate

protagoniste [prɔtagɔnist] *nmf* protagonist

protecteur, -trice [prɔtɛktœr, -tris] **1** *adj (qui protège)* protective (avec towards); *Péj (ton)* patronizing

2 *nm,f* (**a**) *(d'une personne)* protector; *(d'une prostituée)* pimp (**b**) *(des arts)* patron

protection [prɔtɛksjɔ̃] *nf* (**a**) *(défense)* protection (contre from *or* against); de p. *(écran, visière, vernis)* protective; sous la p. de la police under police protection; p. de l'environnement protection of the environment; p. sociale social welfare system; *Ordinat* p. contre l'écriture write-protection; p. contre la copie copy protection; p. de fichiers file protection; p.

par mot de passe password protection (**b**) *(serviette hygiénique)* **p. (féminine)** sanitary *Br* towel *or Am* napkin

protectionnisme [prɔtɛksjɔnism] *nm Écon* protectionism

protectionniste [prɔtɛksjɔnist] *adj & nmf* protectionist

protectorat [prɔtɛktɔra] *nm* protectorate

protégé, -e [prɔteʒe] **1** *adj* protected; *Ordinat* **p. contre la copie** copy-protected; **p. contre l'écriture** *ou* **en écriture** write-protected
2 *nm,f* protégé, *f* protégée

protège-cahier *(pl* **protège-cahiers**) [prɔtɛʒkaje] *nm* exercise book cover

protège-dents [prɔtɛʒdɑ̃] *nm inv* gum shield

protéger [59] [prɔteʒe] **1** *vt* to protect (**contre/de** against/from); **ça protège bien** it gives good protection; **que Dieu vous protège!** God keep you!; *Ordinat* **p. contre l'écriture** *ou* **en écriture** to write-protect
2 se protéger *vpr* to protect oneself (**contre/de** against/from)

protège-slip *(pl* **protège-slips**) [prɔtɛʒslip] *nm* panty-liner

protéine [prɔtein] *nf* protein

protestant, -e [prɔtɛstɑ̃, -ɑ̃t] *adj & nm,f* Protestant

protestantisme [prɔtɛstɑ̃tism] *nm* Protestantism

protestataire [prɔtɛstatɛr] *nmf* protester

protestation [prɔtɛstasjɔ̃] *nf* (**a**) *(plainte)* protest; **émettre des protestations** to voice one's protest; **en signe de p.** as a protest (**b**) **des protestations d'amitié** protestations of friendship

protester [prɔtɛste] **1** *vi* to protest (**contre** against); **p. auprès de qn** to protest to sb
2 protester de *vt ind* (*innocence, bonne foi*) to protest

prothèse [prɔtɛz] *nf* prosthesis; **p. auditive** hearing aid; **p. dentaire** (*complète*) false teeth, dentures; *(partielle)* bridge

protocole [prɔtɔkɔl] *nm* (**a**) *(usages)* protocol, etiquette (**b**) *Jur & Pol* **p. d'accord** protocol of agreement; **le P. de Kyoto** the Kyoto Protocol (**c**) *Ordinat* protocol; **p. de téléchargement** download protocol; **p. de transmission** transmission protocol

proton [prɔtɔ̃] *nm* proton

prototype [prɔtɔtip] *nm* prototype

protozoaire [prɔtɔzɔɛr] *nm* protozoan; **les protozoaires** the Protozoa

protubérance [prɔtyberɑ̃s] *nf* protuberance

protubérant, -e [prɔtyberɑ̃, -ɑ̃t] *adj* protuberant

proue [pru] *nf* bows, prow

prouesse [pruɛs] *nf* feat; **faire des prouesses pour obtenir qch** to work wonders to get sth

prouver [pruve] **1** *vt* (**a**) *(établir comme vrai)* to prove; **p. qch à qn** to prove sth to sb; **p. qch par A plus B** to prove sth in a logical fashion; **cela reste à p.** it still has to be proved (**b**) *(être la preuve de)* to prove, to show (**que** that)
2 se prouver *vpr* **se p. qch** *(à soi-même)* to prove sth to oneself

provenance [prɔvnɑ̃s] *nf* origin; **marchandises de p. italienne** goods of Italian origin; **en p. de Bordeaux** *(train, bus)* from Bordeaux

provençal, -e, -aux, -ales [prɔvɑ̃sal, -o] **1** *adj* Provençal
2 *nm,f* **P.** person from Provence
3 *nm* (*langue*) Provençal

Provence [prɔvɑ̃s] *nf* **la P.** Provence

provenir [70] [prɔvnir] *vi* **p. de** to come from; *(difficultés)* to arise from

proverbe [prɔvɛrb] *nm* proverb; **comme dit le p.** as the proverb goes

proverbial, -e, -aux, -ales [prɔvɛrbjal, -o] *adj* proverbial

providence [prɔvidɑ̃s] *nf* (**a**) *(sort)* providence; **cette auberge est la p. des marcheurs** this inn is a haven for walkers (**b**) **la P.** Providence

providentiel, -elle [prɔvidɑ̃sjɛl] *adj* providential

province [prɔvɛ̃s] **1** *nf* (**a**) *(région)* province; *Can* **les Provinces Maritimes** the Maritime Provinces (**b**) **la p.** the provinces; **de p.** provincial; **en p.** in the provinces; **arriver de sa p.** to be new in town
2 *adj inv Fam Péj* provincial

provincial, -e, -aux, -ales [prɔvɛ̃sjal, -o] *adj & nm,f* provincial

proviseur [prɔvizœr] *nm* (**a**) *(directeur) Br* headmaster, *f* headmistress, *Am* principal (**b**) *Belg (adjoint)* deputy head

provision [prɔvizjɔ̃] *nf* (**a**) *(réserve)* stock, supply; **provisions** *(nourriture)* shopping; **faire des provisions** *ou* **faire p. de qch** to stock up on sth (**b**) *(de compte bancaire)* credit; *(acompte)* deposit

provisionnel, -elle [prɔvizjɔnɛl] *adj voir* **tiers**

provisoire [prɔvizwar] *adj* temporary; **à titre p.** temporarily

provisoirement [prɔvizwarmɑ̃] *adv* temporarily, provisionally

provocant, -e [prɔvɔkɑ̃, -ɑ̃t] *adj* provocative

provocateur, -trice [prɔvɔkatœr, -tris] **1** *adj* provocative; **agent p.** agent provocateur
2 *nm,f* troublemaker

provocation [prɔvɔkasjɔ̃] *nf* provocation; **il l'a dit par p.** he said it to be provocative

provoquer [prɔvɔke] *vt* (**a**) *(personne)* to provoke (**b**) *(réaction)* to provoke; *(incendie, mort, malaise)* to cause; *(jalousie, colère)* to arouse; **p. l'accouchement** to induce labour

proxénète [prɔksenɛt] *nmf* pimp

proxénétisme [prɔksenetism] *nm* pimping

proximité [prɔksimite] *nf* closeness, proximity; **à p.** close by; **à p. de qch** close to sth; **commerces de p.** local shops; **emplois de p.** = employment in the community *(as a way of reducing unemployment)*

Prozac® [prɔzak] *nm Pharm* Prozac®

prude [pryd] *Péj* **1** *adj* prudish
2 *nf* prude

prudemment [prydamɑ̃] *adv* carefully, cautiously

prudence [prydɑ̃s] *nf* care, caution; **par (mesure de) p.** as a precaution; *Prov* **p. est mère de sûreté** discretion is the better part of valour

prudent, -e [prydɑ̃, -ɑ̃t] *adj* (*personne*) careful, cautious; *(décision)* wise, sensible

prud'homme [prydɔm] *nm Jur* member of an industrial tribunal; **conseil des prud'hommes** industrial tribunal

prune [pryn] **1** *nf* (*fruit*) plum; *(liqueur)* plum brandy; *Fam* **pour des prunes** for nothing
2 *adj inv* plum-coloured

pruneau, -x [pryno] *nm* (**a**) *(fruit)* prune (**b**) *Fam (balle)* slug

prunelle [prynɛl] *nf* (*pupille*) pupil; *Fig* **j'y tiens comme à la p. de mes yeux** it's the apple of my eye

prunier [prynje] *nm* plum tree; *Fam* **secouer qn comme un p.** to shake sb like a rag doll

prurit [pryrit] *nm Méd* pruritus

Prusse [prys] *nf* **La P.** Prussia; *voir aussi* **bleu**
prussien, -enne [prysjɛ̃, -ɛn] **1** *adj* Prussian
 2 *nm,f* **P.** Prussian
PS [pɛɛs] *nm* (**a**) (*abrév* **Parti socialiste**) Socialist Party
 (**b**) (*abrév* **post-scriptum**) PS
psalmodier [66] [psalmɔdje] **1** *vt* to chant; *Fig* to
 drone out
 2 *vi* to chant; *Fig* to drone on
psaume [psom] *nm* psalm
pseudo- [psødo] *préf* pseudo-; **un p.-intellectuel** a
 pseudo-intellectual
pseudonyme [psødɔnim] *nm* (*pour un écrivain*) pen
 name, pseudonym; (*pour la scène*) stage name
psy [psi] *nmf Fam* (*médecin*) shrink
psychanalyse [psikanaliz] *nf* psychoanalysis; **faire
 une p.** to be in psychoanalysis
psychanalyser [psikanalize] *vt* to psychoanalyse; **se
 faire p.** to be psychoanalysed
psychanalyste [psikanalist] *nmf* psychoanalyst
psyché [psiʃe] *nf* (*miroir*) cheval glass
psychédélique [psikedelik] *adj* psychedelic
psychiatre [psikjatr] *nmf* psychiatrist
psychiatrie [psikjatri] *nf* psychiatry
psychiatrique [psikjatrik] *adj* psychiatric
psychique [psiʃik] *adj* psychic
psychisme [psiʃism] *nm* psyche
psychodrame [psikodram] *nm* role-playing, *Spéc*
 psychodrama
psychologie [psikɔlɔʒi] *nf* (**a**) (*étude, mentalité*) psychology; **comprendre la p. de qn** to understand the
 way sb's mind works (**b**) (*intuition*) perception; **faire
 preuve de p.** to be very perceptive; **tu manques de p.**
 you're not very perceptive
psychologique [psikɔlɔʒik] *adj* psychological
psychologiquement [psikɔlɔʒikmã] *adv* psychologically
psychologue [psikɔlɔg] **1** *nmf* psychologist; *Fig* **être
 fin p.** to be a good psychologist
 2 *adj* **être p.** to be a good psychologist
psychopathe [psikɔpat] *nmf* psychopath
psychose [psikoz] *nf* psychosis; **p. maniaco-dépres-
 sive** manic depression; *Fig* **la p. de la maladie** an obsessive fear of illness
psychosomatique [psikosɔmatik] *adj* psychosomatic
psychothérapeute [psikoterapøt] *nmf* psychotherapist
psychothérapie [psikoterapi] *nf* psychotherapy; **p.
 de groupe** group therapy
psychotique [psikɔtik] *adj & nmf* psychotic
PTT [petete] *nfpl* (*abrév* **Postes, Télécommunications
 et Télédiffusion**) *Anciennement* ≃ Post Office and
 Telecommunications Service
pu *pp de* **pouvoir²**
puant, -e [pɥã, -ãt] *adj* stinking; *Fig* cocky
puanteur [pɥãtœr] *nf* stink, stench
pub [pyb] *nf Fam* (**a**) (*secteur*) advertising (**b**) (*message*) ad
pubère [pybɛr] *adj* pubescent
puberté [pybɛrte] *nf* puberty
pubis [pybis] *nm Anat* pubis; (*os*) pubic bone
public, -ique [pyblik] **1** *adj* public
 2 *nm* (*d'un spectacle*) audience; **en p.** in public;
 (*émission*) before a live audience; **le grand p.** the general public

publication [pyblikasjɔ̃] *nf* (**a**) (*d'un ouvrage, d'une
 nouvelle*) publication; **p. assistée par ordinateur**
 desktop publishing (**b**) (*ouvrage*) publication
publiciel [pyblisjɛl] *nm Can Ordinat* public domain
 software
publiciste [pyblisist] *nmf Fam* advertising executive
publicitaire [pyblisitɛr] **1** *adj* advertising
 2 *nmf* advertising executive
publicité [pyblisite] *nf* (**a**) (*secteur*) advertising; **être
 dans la p.** to be in advertising; **faire de la p. pour
 qch** to advertise sth; *Fig* **faire de la p. à qn** to be publicity for sb; **p. comparative** comparative advertising;
 p. mensongère misleading advertising (**b**) (*message*) advertisement, advert; **une pleine page de p.**
 a full page advertisement
publier [66] [pyblije] *vt* to publish; (*communiqué*) to
 issue
Publiphone® [pyblifɔn] *nm* card phone
publiquement [pyblikmã] *adv* publicly
puce [pys] *nf* (**a**) (*insecte*) flea; **le marché aux puces,
 les puces** the flea market; *Fig* **mettre la p. à l'oreille à
 qn** to make sb suspicious; *Fam* **secouer les puces à
 qn** to give sb a good telling-off; *Fam* **être excité
 comme une p.** to be jumping up and down with
 excitement (**b**) *Ordinat* (*électronique*) (micro)chip;
 p. mémoire memory chip; **p. de reconnaissance
 vocale** voice recognition chip (**c**) *Ordinat & Typ*
 (*symbole*) bullet point (**d**) (*terme affectueux*) **ma p.**
 sweetie
puceau, -x [pyso] *nm & adj m Fam* virgin
pucelle [pysɛl] *nf & adj f* virgin; **la P. d'Orléans, Jeanne
 la P.** the Maid of Orléans, Joan of Arc
puceron [pysrɔ̃] *nm* greenfly
pudeur [pydœr] *nf* modesty; **avec p.** modestly; **sans p.**
 boldly; **par p.** out of a sense of decency; **avoir la p. de
 faire qch** to have the decency to do sth
pudibond, -e [pydibɔ̃, -ɔ̃d] *adj* prudish
pudique [pydik] *adj* modest
puer [pɥe] **1** *vi* to stink; **il pue des pieds** his feet
 stink
 2 *vt* to stink of; *Fig* **p. la méchanceté/l'hypocrisie** to
 be oozing spitefulness/hypocrisy
puériculteur, -trice [pɥerikyltœr, -tris] *nf* nursery
 nurse
puériculture [pɥerikyltyr] *nf* child care
puéril, -e [pɥeril] *adj* childish, puerile
pugilat [pyʒila] *nm* brawl
pugnace [pygnas] *adj Litt* pugnacious
puis¹ [pɥi] *adv* then; **et p.** (*ensuite*) and then; (*d'ailleurs*) and besides; **et p. c'est tout!** and that's all there
 is to it!; **et p. après?** (*et ensuite?*) then what?; *Fam* (*et
 alors?*) so what?
puis² *voir* **pouvoir²**
puisatier [pɥizatje] *nm* well digger
puiser [pɥize] *vt* (*eau, carte*) to draw (**à** from); *Fig* (*inspiration, idées*) to draw (**dans/chez** from); **p. dans
 ses réserves** to draw on one's reserves; **p. dans la
 caisse** to have one's hand in the till
puisque [pɥiskə] *conj* since, as; **p. c'est comme ça** if
 that's the way it is; **p. je te dis que je l'ai vu!** I'm telling
 you I saw him!; **tu en es bien sûr? – mais p. je te le
 dis!** are you really sure? – I've said I am, haven't I?
puissamment [pɥisamã] *adv* powerfully
puissance [pɥisãs] *nf* power; **p. de feu** fire power; **les
 grandes puissances** the great powers; *Math* **élever
 un nombre à la p. trois/quatre** to raise a number to

the third/fourth power; **dix (à la) p. quatre** ten to the power of four; **en p.** *(meurtrier)* potential

puissant, -e [pɥisɑ̃, -ɑ̃t] *adj* powerful

puisse *etc voir* **pouvoir²**

puits [pɥi] *nm* (**a**) *(pour l'eau)* well; **p. de pétrole** oil well; *Fig* **c'est un p. de science** she's a fount of knowledge (**b**) *(de mine)* shaft, pit

pull [pyl] *nm Fam* sweater, *Br* jumper

pull-over *(pl* **pull-overs**) [pylɔvœr] *nm* sweater, *Br* jumper

pulluler [pylyle] *vi* (**a**) *(se reproduire)* to proliferate (**b**) *(exister en profusion)* to abound

pulmonaire [pylmɔnɛr] *adj* pulmonary

pulpe [pylp] *nf* (**a**) *(de fruit)* pulp; **yaourt à la p. de fruits** yoghurt with real fruit (**b**) *(des doigts, des orteils)* pad; *(des dents)* pulp

pulpeux, -euse [pylpø, -øz] *adj* fleshy; *(femme)* curvaceous

pulsar [pylsar] *nm Astron* pulsar

pulsation [pylsasjɔ̃] *nf (de cœur)* & *Mus* beat; **pulsations cardiaques** heartbeats

pulsion [pylsjɔ̃] *nf* impulse; **pulsions sexuelles** sexual urges; **p. de mort** death wish

pulvérisateur [pylverizatœr] *nm* spray

pulvérisation [pylverizasjɔ̃] *nf (de liquides)* spraying

pulvériser [pylverize] *vt* (**a**) *(réduire en poudre)* to pulverize; *Fam (voiture)* to smash up (**b**) *(vaporiser)* to spray (**c**) *Fam (record)* to smash

puma [pyma] *nm* puma

punaise [pynɛz] *nf* (**a**) *(insecte)* bug; *Fam* **oh, p.!** oh, sugar! (**b**) *(pour accrocher) Br* drawing pin, *Am* thumbtack

punaiser [pynɛze] *vt Fam* to pin up; **p. qch à qch** to pin sth to sth

punch¹ [pɔ̃ʃ] *nm (boisson)* punch

punch² [pœnʃ] *nm* punch; *Fig (de personne)* drive

punching-ball *(pl* **punching-balls**) [pœnʃiŋbol] *nm* punchball

punir [pynir] *vt (personne, crime)* to punish; **p. qn de mort** to punish sb with death; **p. qn d'un crime** to punish sb for a crime; **me voilà puni de ma gourmandise!** (it) serves me right for being greedy!

punitif, -ive [pynitif, -iv] *adj* punitive

punition [pynisjɔ̃] *nf* punishment; **p. corporelle** corporal punishment

punk [pœnk] *adj inv* & *nmf* punk

pupille¹ [pypij] *nmf (orphelin)* ward; **pupilles de la Nation** war orphans

pupille² *nf (de l'œil)* pupil

pupitre [pypitr] *nm* (**a**) *(d'écolier)* desk; *(d'orateur)* lectern; *(de musicien)* music stand (**b**) *Ordinat* **p. (de commande)** console (desk); **p. de visualisation** visual display unit

pupitreur, -euse [pypitrœr, -øz] *nm,f Ordinat* console operator; *(clavitse)* keyboard operator

pur, -e [pyr] *adj* (**a**) *(or, air)* pure; *(ciel)* clear; *(whisky, gin)* straight, neat; **pure laine** pure wool; **biscuits p. beurre** all-butter *Br* biscuits or *Am* cookies (**b**) *(recherche, mathématique, théorie)* pure; **un communiste p. et dur** a hard-line Communist; **la vérité pure et simple** the plain and simple truth; **du vol p. et simple** sheer robbery; **c'est de la folie pure** it's sheer madness (**c**) *(lignes)* clean; *(visage)* clean-cut

purée [pyre] **1** *nf* purée; **réduire qch en p.** to purée sth; *Fig* to smash sth to a pulp; **p. (de pommes de terre)** mashed potatoes; *Fam Fig* **p. de pois** *(brouillard)* peasouper

2 *exclam Fam (colère)* hell!; *(surprise)* wow!

purement [pyrmɑ̃] *adv* purely; **p. et simplement** purely and simply

pureté [pyrte] *nf* purity; *(du ciel)* clearness; *(de lignes)* cleanness

purgatoire [pyrgatwar] *nm* purgatory

purge [pyrʒ] *nf* (**a**) *(pour raisons médicales)* purge (**b**) *(à des fins politiques)* purge (**c**) *(de freins, de radiateur)* bleeding

purger [45] [pyrʒe] *vt* (**a**) *(patient)* to purge (**b**) *(freins, radiateur)* to bleed (**c**) *(peine)* to serve

purifiant, -e [pyrifjɑ̃, -ɑ̃t] *adj* purifying

purificateur, -trice [pyrifikatœr, -tris] *adj* purifying

purification [pyrifikasjɔ̃] *nf* purification; **p. ethnique** ethnic cleansing

purifier [66] [pyrifje] **1** *vt aussi Fig* to purify; *(sang, teint)* to cleanse

2 se purifier *vpr* to be purified

purin [pyrɛ̃] *nm* liquid manure

puriste [pyrist] *nmf* purist

puritain, -e [pyritɛ̃, -ɛn] **1** *nm,f* puritan; *Hist* Puritan

2 *adj* puritanical; *Hist* Puritan

puritanisme [pyritanism] *nm* puritanism; *Hist* Puritanism

pur-sang [pyrsɑ̃] *nm inv* thoroughbred

purulent, -e [pyrylɑ̃, -ɑ̃t] *adj* suppurating

pus [py] *nm* pus

pusillanime [pyzilanim] *adj Litt* pusillanimous

pustule [pystyl] *nf* pustule

putain [pytɛ̃] *Vulg* **1** *nf* (**a**) *(prostituée)* whore (**b**) **p. de machine/cravate!** (this) fucking machine/tie!

2 *exclam* fuck!

pute [pyt] *nf Vulg* whore; **fils de p.** son of a bitch

putois [pytwa] *nm* polecat; *Fam* **crier comme un p.** to scream blue murder

putréfaction [pytrefaksjɔ̃] *nf* putrefaction; **matière en p.** putrefying matter

putréfier [66] [pytrefje] **1** *vt* to putrefy

2 se putréfier *vpr* to putrefy

putrescent, -e [pytresɑ̃, -ɑ̃t] *adj* putrescent

putride [pytrid] *adj* putrid

putsch [putʃ] *nm* putsch

putschiste [putʃist] **1** *adj* putsch

2 *nmf* putschist

puzzle [pœzl] *nm* jigsaw (puzzle); *Fig* puzzle

P.-V. [peve] *nm Fam (abrév* **procès-verbal)** (parking) ticket

PVC [pevese] *nm (abrév* **polychlorure de vinyle)** PVC; **siège en P.** PVC seat

PVD [pevede] *nm (abrév* **pays en voie de développement)** developing country

pygmée [pigme] *nmf* pygmy

pyjama [piʒama] *nm* pyjamas; **un p.** a pair of pyjamas

pylône [pilon] *nm* pylon; *(pour fils télégraphiques)* mast

pyramidal, -e, -aux, -ales [piramidal, -o] *adj* pyramid-shaped

pyramide [piramid] *nf* pyramid; **p. des âges** population pyramid; **structure en p.** pyramid-like structure

pyrénéen, -enne [pireneɛ̃, -ɛn] **1** *adj* Pyrenean

2 *nm,f* **P.** Pyrenean

3 *nm (chien)* Pyrenean mountain dog

Pyrénées [pirene] *nfpl* **les P.** the Pyrenees

Pyrex® [pirɛks] *nm* Pyrex®; **plat en P.** Pyrex® dish

pyrogravure [pirogravyr] *nf* poker work, pyrography; *(gravure)* pyrograph

pyrolyse [piroliz] *nf* pyrolysis; **four à p.** self-cleaning oven

pyromane [piroman] *nmf* arsonist; *Psy* pyromaniac

pyromanie [piromani] *nf* pyromania

pyrotechnique [piroteknik] *adj* pyrotechnic

python [pitɔ̃] *nm* python

Q, q [ky] *nm inv* Q, q
Qatar [katar] *nm* **le Q.** Qatar
QCM [kysɛɛm] *nm inv* (*abrév* **questionnaire à choix multiple**) multiple-choice questionnaire
QG [kyʒe] *nm inv* (*abrév* **quartier général**) HQ
QI [kyi] *nm inv* (*abrév* **quotient intellectuel**) IQ
quad [kwad] *nm Sport* quad bike; **faire du q.** to go quad biking
quadra [kwadra] *nmf Fam* fortysomething
quadragénaire [kwadraʒenɛr] **1** *adj* **être q.** to be in one's forties
2 *nmf* person in his/her forties
quadrangulaire [kwadrãgylɛr] *adj* quadrangular
quadrature [kwadratyr] *nf* quadrature; **c'est la q. du cercle** it's like trying to square the circle
quadriceps [kwadrisɛps] *nm* quadriceps
quadrilatère [kwadrilatɛr, kadrilatɛr] *nm* quadrilateral
quadrillage [kadrijaʒ] *nm* (**a**) (*par la police*) tight surveillance (**b**) (*d'un tissu*) check pattern; (*sur une carte*) grid
quadrille [kadrij] *nm* quadrille
quadrillé, -e [kadrije] *adj* (*papier*) squared
quadriller [kadrije] *vt* (**a**) (*quartier, ville, région*) to put under tight surveillance (**b**) (*papier*) to mark into squares
quadrimoteur [kwadrimɔtœr, kadrimɔtœr] **1** *adj* four-engined
2 *nm* four-engined plane
quadriparti, -e [kwadriparti], **quadripartite** [kwadripartit] *adj* (*traité*) quadripartite; (*conférence, commission*) (*entre partis*) four-party; (*entre pays*) four-power
quadriphonie [kwadrifoni] *nf* quadraphony
quadrupède [kwadrypɛd, kadrypɛd] *adj & nm* quadruped
quadruple [kwadrypl, kadrypl] **1** *adj* quadruple, fourfold; *Mus* **q. croche** *Br* hemidemisemiquaver, *Am* sixty-fourth note
2 *nm* **le q. (de)** (*quantité, prix*) four times as much (as); (*nombre*) four times as many (as); **douze est le q. de trois** twelve is four times three
quadrupler [kwadryple, kadryple] *vt & vi* to quadruple, to increase fourfold
quadruplés, -ées [kwadryple, kadryple] *nmpl, nfpl* quadruplets
quai [kɛ] *nm* (**a**) (*de gare, de métro*) platform (**b**) (*d'un port*) quay; **se mettre à q.** to berth (**c**) (*d'une rivière, d'un fleuve*) embankment; **le Q. des Orfèvres** Police Headquarters (*in Paris*); **le Q. d'Orsay** the French Foreign Office

qualificatif, -ive [kalifikatif, -iv] *Gram* **1** *adj* (*adjectif*) qualifying
2 *nm* term
qualification [kalifikasjɔ̃] *nf* (**a**) (*formation*) qualification (**b**) (*d'une équipe, d'un sportif*) qualification (**c**) (*désignation*) description
qualifié, -e [kalifje] *adj* (**a**) (*compétent*) qualified (**pour faire qch** to do sth) (**b**) (*délit, vol*) aggravated
qualifier [66] [kalifje] **1** *vt* (**a**) (*appeler*) to describe (**de** as) (**b**) (*autoriser*) **q. qn pour qch/pour faire qch** to qualify sb for sth/to do sth
2 se qualifier *vpr* (*sportif, équipe*) to qualify (**pour** for)
qualitatif, -ive [kalitatif, -iv] *adj* qualitative
qualité [kalite] *nf* (**a**) (*d'un produit*) quality; **de q.** quality; **de bonne/mauvaise q.** of good/poor quality; *Ordinat* **q. brouillon, q. liste rapide, q. listing** draft quality; *Ordinat* **q. courrier** (near) letter quality; **q. de la vie** quality of life (**b**) (*d'une personne*) quality; **elle n'a pas que des qualités** she isn't all good (**c**) (*occupation*) occupation; (*fonction*) capacity; **en q. de** in my/her/*etc* capacity as
quand [kã] **1** *conj* (**a**) (*lorsque*) when; **je lui en parlerai q. je le verrai** I'll mention it to him when I see him; *Fam* **q. je pense que le voyage devait être annulé!** when I think that they were going to cancel the trip!; **q. bien même** even if (**b**) (*alors que*) when
2 *adv* when; **q. viendra-t-il?** when will he come?; **demande-lui q. il va partir** ask him when he's going to leave; **à q. le mariage?** when's the wedding?; **de q. est ce journal?** what's the date of this paper?; **pour q. est la réunion?** when is the meeting?
quant [kã] **quant à** *prép* as for
quant-à-soi [kãtaswa] *nm inv* **rester sur** *ou* **se tenir sur son q.** to keep oneself to oneself
quantième [kãtjɛm] *nm* day of the month
quantifiable [kãtifjabl] *adj* quantifiable
quantifier [66] [kãtifje] *vt* to quantify
quantitatif, -ive [kãtitatif, -iv] *adj* quantitative
quantitativement [kãtitativmã] *adv* quantitatively
quantité [kãtite] *nf* quantity; **en grande/petite q.** in large/small quantities; **en q.** in abundance; **q. de gens/réponses** a great many people/replies
quarantaine [karãtɛn] *nf* (**a**) (*environ quarante*) **une q. (de)** about forty, forty or so (**b**) (*âge*) **avoir la q.** to be about forty; **approcher de la q.** to be getting on for forty (**c**) (*isolement*) quarantine; **mettre qn en q.** to put sb in quarantine; *Fig* to send sb to Coventry

quarante [karɑ̃t] *adj & nm inv* forty; *Fam* **se ficher de qch comme de l'an q.** not to give two hoots about sth; *Can* **vieux comme l'an q.** ancient, as old as the hills; *voir aussi* **trois**

quarante-cinq tours [karɑ̃tsɛ̃tur] *nm inv* single, 45

quarantième [karɑ̃tjɛm] *nmf, nm & adj* fortieth; *voir aussi* **cinquième**

quart¹ [kar] *adj* **le q. monde** *(dans les pays riches)* the underclass

quart² *nm* (**a**) *(fraction)* quarter; **un q. de siècle/de beurre** a quarter (of a) century/kilo of butter; **un q. d'heure** a quarter of an hour; *Fam* **passer un mauvais q. d'heure** to have a bad time of it; **deux heures et q.** (a) quarter past *or Am* after two; **deux heures moins le q.** (a) quarter to *or Am* of two; **il est moins le q.** it's (a) quarter to; **démarrer** *ou* **partir au q. de tour** *(voiture)* to start first time; *(personne)* to fly off the handle; **q. de cercle** quadrant; **q. de finale** quarter final; *Mus* **q. de soupir** *Br* semiquaver *or Am* sixteenth rest (**b**) *(bouteille, pichet)* quarter litre (**c**) *(veille sur un bateau)* watch; **être de q.** to be on watch

quart-arrière [kararjɛr] *nm Can* quarterback

quarte [kart] *nf Mus* fourth

quarté [karte] *nm* = bet in which the punter predicts the first four horses to finish a race

quartette [kwartɛt] *nm* jazz quartet

quartier [kartje] *nm* (**a**) *(d'une ville)* district, area; **les beaux quartiers** the fashionable districts; **les quartiers nord de la ville** the north side of the town; **de q., du q.** (**b**) *(morceau) (d'une orange)* segment; *(d'une pomme)* piece (**c**) *(de la lune)* quarter (**d**) *(de viande)* quarter (**e**) *(en héraldique)* quarter; **avoir quatre quartiers de noblesse** to belong to the established nobility (**f**) *(locutions)* **avoir q. libre** to be off duty; **ne pas faire de q.** to give no quarter

quartz [kwarts] *nm* quartz; **horloge/montre à q.** quartz clock/watch

quasi [kazi] *adv* almost, nearly

quasi- [kazi] *préf* **la q.-totalité des membres** almost all the members

quasiment [kazimɑ̃] *adv* almost, nearly; **je n'ai q. rien senti** I hardly felt a thing

quaternaire [kwatɛrnɛr] *Géol* **1** *adj* Quaternary **2** *nm* Quaternary era

quatorze [katɔrz] *adj & nm inv* fourteen; *voir aussi* **trois**

quatorzième [katɔrzjɛm] *nmf, nm & adj* fourteenth; *voir aussi* **cinquième**

quatrain [katrɛ̃] *nm* quatrain

quatre [katr] *adj & nm inv* four; **aux q. coins du monde** throughout the world; **monter l'escalier q. à q.** to rush up the stairs; *Fig* **se mettre en q. pour qn/ pour faire qch** to bend over backwards for sb/to do sth; *voir aussi* **trois**

quatre-quarts [katkar, katrəkar] *nm inv* ≃ pound cake

quatre-quatre [katkatr] *nm inv ou nf inv* four-wheel drive

quatre-saisons [katsɛzɔ̃, katrəsɛzɔ̃] *nfpl* **marchand des q.** fruit-and-vegetable merchant *(with outdoor stall)*

quatre-vingt [katrəvɛ̃] *voir* **quatre-vingts**

quatre-vingt-dix [katrəvɛ̃dis] *adj & nm inv* ninety; *voir aussi* **trois**

quatre-vingt-dixième [katrəvɛ̃dizjɛm] *adj, nmf & nm* ninetieth; *voir aussi* **cinquième**

quatre-vingtième [katrəvɛ̃tjɛm] *adj, nmf & nm* eightieth; *voir aussi* **cinquième**

quatre-vingts [katrəvɛ̃] *adj & nm inv* eighty; **q. personnes** eighty people; **quatre-vingt-deux** eighty-two; **page quatre-vingt** page eighty; *voir aussi* **trois**

quatrième [katrijɛm] **1** *adj* fourth; **le q. âge** extreme old age; *Fam* **en q. vitesse** in a hurry, at breakneck speed **2** *nmf* fourth **3** *nf* (**a**) *(classe) Br* ≃ third form, *Am* ≃ ninth grade (**b**) *(vitesse)* fourth (gear); *voir aussi* **cinquième**

quatrièmement [katrijɛmmɑ̃] *adv* fourthly

quatuor [kwatɥɔr] *nm* quartet; **q. à cordes** string quartet

que¹ [k(ə)]

En anglais, le pronom relatif objet (voir (**a**)) peut être omis.

pron relatif (**a**) *(objet) (personne)* that, whom; *(chose)* that, which; **l'homme q. vous voyez** the man (that) you see; **la tarte q. j'ai fait cuire** the tart (that) I baked; **c'est le meilleur q. nous ayons** it is the best (that) we have (**b**) *(attribut)* **il mourut en brave soldat qu'il était** he died like the brave soldier he was (**c**) *(dans le temps)* **il y a trois mois q. j'habite Paris** I've been living in Paris for three months; **un jour q. j'étais de service** one day when I was on duty

que² *pron interrogatif* what; **q. voulez-vous?** what do you want?; **il ne savait q. penser** he didn't know what to think

que³ *adv exclamatif* **qu'elle est intelligente!** she's so intelligent!; **q. de monde!** what a lot of people!

que⁴

La conjonction "that" peut être omise après les verbes d'opinion, ainsi que "say", "know", etc: **je sais que c'est possible** I know (that) it's possible.

conj (**a**) *(complétif)* that; **je pense qu'il a raison** I think (that) he's right; **je veux qu'il vienne** I want him to come; **c'est q. je ne le savais pas** I just didn't know (**b**) *(exprime le souhait)* **qu'elle entre!** let her come in! (**c**) *(exprime l'hypothèse)* **q. la machine chauffe, et il y aura un accident** let the machine get hot and there will be an accident; **qu'il essaie encore une fois!** just let him try again! (**d**) *(dans une alternative)* **q. tu le veuilles ou non** whether you like it or not (**e**) *(relie deux conditionnels)* **il me le dirait lui-même q. je ne le croirais pas** he could tell me himself and I still wouldn't believe it (**f**) *(afin que, pour que)* **approchez qu'on vous entende** come closer so (that) we can hear you (**g**) *(pour ne pas répéter une autre conjonction)* **quand tu iras mieux et q. tu voudras sortir** when you're better and you want to go out; **si ça te plaît et que tu veux l'acheter...** if you like it and you want to buy it... (**h**) *(dans les comparaisons)* **plus/ moins grand q. moi** bigger/smaller than me; **aussi grand q. moi** as big as me (**i**) **ne... q.** only; **il n'a qu'une jambe** he's only got one leg; **il ne me reste plus q. 5 euros** I've only got 5 euros left (**j**) *Fam* **ah! q. non!** surely not!; **il va au cercle – qu'il dit!** he's going to the club – so he says!

Québec [kebɛk] **1** *nm (province)* **le Q.** Quebec **2** *n (ville)* Quebec

québécisme [kebesism] *nm* = word or expression peculiar to Quebec French

québécois, -e [kebekwa, -az] **1** *adj* of Quebec
2 *nm,f* **Q.** Quebecker
3 *nm (langue)* Quebec French
quel, quelle [kɛl] **1** *adj interrogatif (personne)* which; *(chose)* which, what; **q. homme?** which man?; **quelle heure est-il?** what time is it?, what's the time?; **q. genre d'homme est-ce?** what sort of a man is he?; **si tu savais à q. point il y tient** if you knew how fond he is of it; **à q. film faites-vous référence?** which *or* what film are you referring to?; **quelles sont ses raisons?** what are his/her reasons?; *Litt* **q. est cet homme?** who is this man?
2 *adj exclamatif* **q. homme!** what a man!; **quelle surprise!** what a surprise!; **quelle bêtise de sa part!** how stupid of him!
3 *adj relatif* **q. que soit le coupable** whoever the culprit may be; **q. que soit le résultat** whatever the result may be; **q. que soit l'endroit où...** no matter where...
4 *pron interrogatif* which (one)
quelconque [kɛlkɔ̃k] **1** *adj indéfini* **donne-moi un livre q.** give me any book; **sous un prétexte q.** on some pretext or other
2 *adj (insignifiant)* ordinary
quelle [kɛl] *voir* **quel**
quelque [kɛlk] **1** *adj indéfini* some; **quelques** some, a few; **il y a quelques jours** a few days ago; **et quelque(s)** or so; **cent et quelques mètres** a hundred metres plus; **q.... que** + *subjunctive* whatever; **sous q. prétexte que ce soit** on whatever pretext; **de q. côté que vous regardiez** whichever way you look
2 *adv* some, about; **q. dix ans** some *or* about ten years; **les q. 100 euros qu'il m'a prêtés** the 100 euros or so that he lent me
quelque chose [kɛlkəʃoz] *pron indéfini* something; **avez-vous q. à dire?** do you have anything *or* something to say?; **est-ce que je peux te dire q.?** can I tell you something?; **q. d'autre/de neuf** something else/new; **cela m'a fait q.** it touched me; **ça te ferait vraiment q. si je m'en allais?** would it really matter to you if I went away?; *Fam* **ah, mais c'est q., ça!** that's a bit much!; *Fam* **un petit q.** *(cadeau)* a little something
quelquefois [kɛlkəfwa] *adv* sometimes
quelque part [kɛlkəpar] *adv* somewhere; *(dans les questions, les hypothèses)* anywhere; **q. où tu n'es jamais allé** somewhere you've never been before; *Fam* **je lui ai donné un coup de pied q.** I kicked him where it hurts
quelques-uns, quelques-unes [kɛlkəzœ̃, -yn] *pron indéfini* some, a few (**de** of)
quelqu'un [kɛlkœ̃] *pron indéfini* (**a**) *(une personne)* someone, somebody; *(dans les questions, les hypothèses)* anyone, anybody; **q. de trop** one too many; **q. d'important** someone important; **c'est q. de bien** he's a decent person (**b**) *(personne importante)* somebody
quémander [kemɑ̃de] *vt* to beg for (**à** from)
qu'en-dira-t-on [kɑ̃diratɔ̃] *nm* **le q.** gossip
quenelle [kənɛl] *nf Culin* quenelle
quenotte [kənɔt] *nf Fam* tooth
quenouille [kənuj] *nf (pour filer)* distaff; *Fig* **tomber en q.** to go to rack and ruin
quéquette [keket] *nf Fam Br* willy, *Am* peter
querelle [kərɛl] *nf* quarrel; **chercher q. à qn** to try to pick a quarrel with sb; **q. de clocher** petty dispute

quereller [kərele] **se quereller** *vpr* to quarrel (**avec** with)
querelleur, -euse [kərɛlœr, -øz] *adj* quarrelsome
quérir [kerir] *vt Litt* **aller q. qn/qch** to go and fetch sb/sth
qu'est-ce que [kɛskə] **1** *pron interrogatif* what; **q. vous voulez?** what do you want?; **q. c'est que ça?** what's that?; *Fam* **q. tu avais besoin d'aller lui dire ça?** what did you have to go and tell him/her that for?
2 *pron exclamatif* **qu'est-ce qu'il fait beau!** what lovely weather!; **qu'est-ce qu'il fait chaud!** it's so hot!; **qu'est-ce qu'on a rigolé!** we had such a good laugh!; **q. tu as changé!** how you've changed!; **q. j'ai mangé!** I've eaten so much!
qu'est-ce qui [kɛski] *pron interrogatif* what
question [kɛstjɔ̃] *nf* (**a**) *(interrogation)* question (**sur** about); **q. de confiance** vote of confidence; **q. piège** trick question; **q. subsidiaire** tie-break (**b**) *(affaire)* question, matter; **le dossier en q.** the file in question; **remettre qch en q.** to call sth into question; **une q. d'argent/de temps/d'habitude** a question *or* matter of money/of time/of habit; **c'est une q. de vie ou de mort** it's a matter of life or death; **il est q. qu'ils déménagent** there's some talk of them moving; **il n'en est pas q.** it's out of the question; **là n'est pas la q.** that's not the point; *Fam* **pas q.!** no way!, no chance!; *Fam* **q. argent, ça va** moneywise *or* as far as money goes, things are OK
questionnaire [kɛstjɔnɛr] *nm* questionnaire; **q. à choix multiple** multiple-choice questionnaire
questionner [kɛstjɔne] *vt* to question (**sur** about)
quête [kɛt] *nf* (**a**) *(recherche)* quest, search (**de** for); **se mettre en q. de qn/qch** to go in search of sb/sth (**b**) *(collecte)* collection; **faire la q.** *(à l'église)* to take the collection
quêter [kete] **1** *vt* to seek
2 *vi* to collect money (**pour** for)
quêteux, -euse [kɛtø, -øz] *nm,f Can* beggar
quetsche [kwɛtʃ] *nf* (**a**) *(prune)* dark-red plum (**b**) *(eau-de-vie)* plum brandy
queue [kø] *nf* (**a**) *(d'animal)* tail; **n'avoir ni q. ni tête** to have neither rhyme nor reason; **une histoire sans q. ni tête** a shaggy-dog story; **faire une q. de poisson à qn** to cut (in) in front of sb; **finir en q. de poisson** *(pièce de théâtre, projet)* to end up in the air (**b**) *(d'une casserole)* handle; *(d'une comète, d'un cerf-volant)* tail; *(d'un fruit, d'une fleur)* stalk; *(d'une note de musique)* stem (**c**) *(d'une procession)* rear; **de q.** *(voiture, wagon)* rear; **être en q. de peloton** to be at the back of the bunch; **être en q. de classement** to be bottom of the table (**d**) *(file) Br* queue, *Am* line; **à la q. leu leu** in single file; **faire la q.** *Br* to queue (up), *Am* to wait in line (**e**) *(pour le billard)* cue (**f**) *Vulg (pénis)* cock
queue-de-cheval (*pl* queues-de-cheval) [kødʃəval] *nf* ponytail
queue-de-pie (*pl* queues-de-pie) [kødpi] *nf Fam* tails
qui¹ [ki]

En anglais, le pronom relatif objet peut être omis lorsque la préposition qui l'introduit est rejetée en fin de phrase: **l'amie avec qui j'ai passé mes vacances** the friend (who) I spent my holidays with.

pron relatif (**a**) *(personne)* who, that; *(animal, chose)* which, that; **vous q. êtes du pays, pourriez-vous**

me dire si... you being from the country, could you tell me if...; **je le vois q. vient** I can see him coming

(**b**) *(ce qui)* **q. plus est** what's more; **voilà q. me plaît** that's what I like

(**c**) *(après une préposition)* who, whom; **voilà l'homme à q. je pensais** there's the man (who) I was thinking about; **il cherche quelqu'un avec q. jouer** he's looking for someone to play with; **c'est à q. finira le premier** everyone's trying to be the first to finish

(**d**) *(n'importe qui)* whoever; **emmenez q. vous voulez** take whoever you like with you; **q. que vous soyez** whoever you are; **je défie q. que ce soit de le prouver** I challenge anyone to prove it

qui² *pron interrogatif* who; *(complément d'objet ou après une préposition)* who, whom; **q. a dit cela?** who said that?; **savez-vous q. a dit cela?** do you know who said that?; **à q. est-ce?** whose is it?; **de q. parlez-vous?** who are you talking about?; **de q. êtes-vous le fils?** whose son are you?; **q. d'autre?** who else?; *Fam* **q. ça?** who's that?; *Fam* **il est là – q. donc?** he's here – who?

quiche [kiʃ] *nf* quiche; **q. lorraine** quiche lorraine

quiconque [kikɔ̃k] *pron indéfini (sujet)* whoever, anyone who; *(complément)* anyone, anybody; **q. désobéira sera puni** anyone who disobeys will be punished; **sans l'aide de q.** without anyone's help

quidam [kidam] *nm* fellow

quiétude [kjetyd] *nf Litt* peace; **en toute q.** *(sans être dérangé)* without being disturbed; *(sans souci)* with an easy mind

quignon [kiɲɔ̃] *nm* hunk

quille¹ [kij] *nf* (**a**) **quilles** *(jeu)* skittles (**b**) *Fam* **la q.** *(fin du service militaire)* discharge, *Br* demob (**c**) *Fam* **quilles** *(jambes)* legs, *Br* pins

quille² *nf (d'un bateau)* keel

quilleur, -euse [kijœr, -øz] *nm,f Can* skittle player

quincaillerie [kɛ̃kajri] *nf* (**a**) *(magasin)* hardware shop, *Br* ironmonger's (**b**) *(ustensiles)* hardware (**c**) *Fam (bijoux voyants)* cheap jewellery

quincaillier, -ère [kɛ̃kaje, -ɛr] *nm,f* hardware dealer, *Br* ironmonger

quinconce [kɛ̃kɔ̃s] **en quinconce** *adv* in staggered rows

quinine [kinin] *nf* quinine

quinquagénaire [kɛ̃kaʒenɛr] **1** *adj* **être q.** to be in one's fifties

2 *nmf* person in his/her fifties

quinquennal, -e, -aux, -ales [kɛ̃kenal, -o] *adj (plan)* five-year; *(exposition, élection)* five-yearly

quinquennat [kɛ̃kena] *nm* five-year term

quintal, -aux [kɛ̃tal, -o] *nm* quintal *(= 100 kg)*

quinte [kɛ̃t] *nf* (**a**) *(accès)* **q. de toux** coughing fit (**b**) *Mus* fifth

quinté [kɛ̃te] *nm* = bet in which the punter predicts the first five horses to finish a race

quintessence [kɛ̃tesɑ̃s] *nf* quintessence

quintet [kɛ̃tɛt] *nm* (jazz) quintet

quintette [kɛ̃tɛt, kɥɛ̃tɛt] *nm* quintet; **q. à cordes** string quintet

quintuple [kɛ̃typl] **1** *adj* quintuple, fivefold

2 *nm* **le q. (de)** *(quantité, prix)* five times as much (as); *(nombre)* five times as many (as); **quinze est le q. de trois** fifteen is five times three

quintupler [kɛ̃typle] *vt & vi* to quintuple, to increase fivefold

quintuplés, -ées [kɛ̃typle] *nmpl, nfpl* quintuplets

quinzaine [kɛ̃zɛn] *nf* (**a**) *(environ quinze)* **une q. (de)** about fifteen, fifteen or so (**b**) *(deux semaines)* two weeks, *Br* fortnight; *Com* = sale lasting two weeks

quinze [kɛ̃z] **1** *adj inv* fifteen; **q. jours** two weeks, *Br* a fortnight

2 *nm inv* fifteen; **demain en q.** two weeks *or Br* a fortnight tomorrow; *Anciennement* **les Quinze** *(de l'Europe)* the 15 member countries of the EU; *voir aussi* **trois**

quinzième [kɛ̃zjɛm] *nmf, nm & adj* fifteenth; *voir aussi* **cinquième**

quiproquo [kiprɔko] *nm* mix-up

quittance [kitɑ̃s] *nf* receipt; **q. de loyer** rent receipt

quitte [kit] *adj* (**a**) *(libéré)* **nous sommes quittes** we're quits (**b**) *(locutions)* **en être q. pour qch** to get off with sth; *Belg* **être q. de qch** to be deprived of sth; **q. ou double** double or quits; **q. à faire qch** even if it means doing sth

quitter [kite] **1** *vt* (**a**) *(personne, lieu)* to leave; *(chambre d'hôtel)* to vacate; **q. la route** *(par accident)* to go off the road; *(délibérément)* to turn off the road; **un ami très cher vient de nous q.** we have just lost a very dear friend; *Ordinat* **q. le système** to quit (the system) (**b**) *(fonctions, poste)* to leave (**c**) *(vêtement)* to take off (**d**) *(au téléphone)* **ne quittez pas** hold the line (**e**) **ne pas q. qn/qch des yeux** to keep one's eye on sb/sth

2 se quitter *vpr* to part; **ils ne se quittent plus** they are inseparable

qui-vive [kiviv] *nm* **être** *ou* **se tenir sur le q.** to be on the alert

quoi¹ [kwa] *pron relatif* (**a**) what; **ce à q. je m'oppose** what I object to; **après q.** after which; **sur q.** whereupon; **avoir de q. vivre** to have enough to live on; **avez-vous de q. écrire?** do you have something to write with?; **il n'y a pas de q. être fier** that's nothing to be proud of; **il y a de q. se mettre en colère** it's enough to make you really angry!; **je suis en colère – il y a de q.** I'm angry – you've every right to be; **il n'y a pas de q.** *(après des remerciements)* don't mention it, not at all

(**b**) **q. que tu dises** whatever you say; **q. qu'il advienne** whatever happens; **q. qu'il en soit** be that as it may

quoi² *pron interrogatif* what; **q. d'autre?** what else?; **de neuf?** what's new?; **q. de plus simple?** what could be simpler?; **je ne sais q. penser** I don't know what to think; **à q. pensez-vous?** what are you thinking about?; **de q. parlez-vous?** what are you talking about?; **à q. bon?** what's the use?; *Fam* **tu es sourd ou q.?** are you deaf or what?; *Fam* **q.?** *(pardon?)* what?

quoi³ *exclam* what!; **et q. encore!** whatever next!; *Fam* **enfin, c'était nul, q.!** it was crap, basically!; **décide-toi, q.!** well make up your mind!

quoique [kwak] *conj* (al)though; **q. je le sache déjà** (al)though I already know

quolibet [kɔlibɛ] *nm* gibe, jeer

quorum [kwɔrɔm] *nm* quorum; **atteindre le q.** to have a quorum

quota [kɔta] *nm* quota; *Can Fig* **avoir son q.** to be fed up

quote-part *(pl* **quotes-parts)** [kɔtpar] *nf* share

quotidien, -enne [kɔtidjɛ̃, -ɛn] **1** *adj (de chaque jour)* *(promenade, repas, entraînement)* daily;

(préoccupations) everyday; **leurs disputes étaient devenues presque quotidiennes** they'd got to the stage where they were arguing almost every day

2 *nm* (**a**) *(journal)* daily (paper); **grand q.** national daily (paper) (**b**) *(routine)* daily life; **au q.** on a day-to-day basis

quotidiennement [kɔtidjɛnmɑ̃] *adv* daily

quotient [kɔsjɑ̃] *nm* quotient; **q. intellectuel** intelligence quotient

R

R, r [ɛr] *nm inv* R, r
rab [rab] *nm Fam (nourriture)* extra; **faire du r.** *(au travail)* to put in a bit of overtime; **en r.** left over
rabâchage [rabɑʃaʒ] *nm* tedious repetition
rabâcher [rabɑʃe] **1** *vt (conseils, recommandations)* to keep on repeating; *(leçon)* to repeat parrot-fashion
2 *vi* to say the same thing over and over again
rabais [rabɛ] *nm* discount, reduction; **faire un r. à qn (sur qch)** to give sb a discount (on sth); *Fig* **au r.** *(travail)* badly paid
rabaisser [rabese] **1** *vt* (**a**) *(prétentions)* to moderate (**b**) *(personne, valeur, talents)* to belittle
2 se rabaisser *vpr* to belittle oneself
Rabat [raba] *n* Rabat
rabat [raba] *nm* (**a**) *(de sac à main, d'enveloppe)* flap (**b**) *(de costume officiel)* bands
rabat-joie [rabaʒwa] **1** *adj inv* **être r.** to be a killjoy
2 *nm inv* killjoy
rabattable [rabatabl] *adj (siège, dossier)* fold-down
rabatteur, -euse [rabatœr, -øz] *nm,f* (**a**) *(à la chasse)* beater (**b**) *Fig* tout
rabattre [11] [rabatr] **1** *vt* (**a**) *(col)* to turn down (**b**) *(couvercle)* to close; *(strapontin) (en se levant)* to fold up; *(pour s'asseoir)* to fold down (**c**) *(gibier, foule)* to drive (**vers** towards) (**d**) *(somme)* to deduct (**de** from) (**e**) *(prétentions)* to moderate
2 se rabattre *vpr* (**a**) *(strapontin)* to fold down (**b**) *(véhicule)* to pull back in (**c**) *(foule)* **se r. vers qch** to veer off towards sth (**d**) *(avoir recours)* **se r. sur qn/qch** to fall back on sb/sth
rabbin [rabɛ̃] *nm* rabbi; **grand r.** chief rabbi
rabibocher [rabiboʃe] *Fam* **1** *vt* to patch things up between
2 se rabibocher *vpr* to patch things up (**avec** with)
rabiot [rabjo] = rab
râble [rabl] *nm (de lièvre, lapin)* back; **r. de lièvre** *(plat)* saddle of hare
râblé, -e [rable] *adj* stocky
rabot [rabo] *nm* plane
raboter [rabɔte] *vt* to plane
raboteuse [rabɔtøz] *nf* planing machine
raboteux, -euse [rabɔtø, -øz] *adj* uneven
rabougri, -e [rabugri] *adj (plante, personne)* stunted
rabougrir [rabugrir] **se rabougrir** *vpr* to shrivel up
rabrouer [rabrue] *vt* to snub
racaille [rakaj] *nf* (**a**) **la r.** *(voyous)* trash, scum, *Br* yobs; *Vieilli (populace)* rabble, riff-raff (**b**) **une r.** a hooligan, *Br* a yob, a chav
raccommodage [rakɔmɔdaʒ] *nm (de vêtements)* mending; *(de bas, de chaussettes)* darning; **faire du r.** to do some mending/darning

raccommoder [rakɔmɔde] **1** *vt* (**a**) *(vêtement)* to mend; *(bas, chaussette)* to darn (**b**) *Fam (personnes)* to patch things up between
2 se raccommoder *vpr Fam* to patch things up (**avec** with)
raccompagner [rakɔ̃paɲe] *vt* to take back
raccord [rakɔr] *nm* (**a**) *(de papier peint)* join; *(de peinture)* touch-up (**b**) *(pièce d'assemblage)* connection (**c**) *Cin* continuity; *(plan)* link
raccordement [rakɔrdəmɑ̃] *nm* (**a**) *(lien)* link, connection (**b**) *Ordinat* link
raccorder [rakɔrde] **1** *vt* (**a**) *(relier) (canalisations, bâtiments, routes)* to link up, to connect (**à** to); *Ordinat* to connect (**b**) *(bande magnétique)* to splice
2 se raccorder *vpr* to link up; *Ordinat* **se r. à** to link up to
raccourci [rakursi] *nm* short cut; **en r.** *(en bref)* in brief; *(en miniature)* in miniature; *Ordinat* **r. clavier** keyboard shortcut
raccourcir [rakursir] **1** *vt* to shorten (**de** by)
2 *vi* to get shorter
raccrocher [rakrɔʃe] **1** *vt* to hang up again; **r. l'appareil** *ou* **le téléphone** to hang up
2 *vi* (**a**) *(au téléphone)* to hang up, to put the phone down; **r. au nez de qn** to hang up on sb, to put the phone down on sb (**b**) *Fam (sportif)* to retire
3 se raccrocher *vpr* **se r. à qch** to catch hold of sth; *Fig (espérance)* to cling to sth
race [ras] *nf* (**a**) *(ethnie)* race; **la r. blanche/noire** the white/black race; **la r. humaine** the human race (**b**) *(animale)* breed; **de r.** *(chien)* pedigree; *(cheval)* thoroughbred
racé, -e [rase] *adj (animal)* pure-bred; *(cheval, voiture)* thoroughbred; *(personne)* noble-looking
rachat [raʃa] *nm* (**a**) *(d'une voiture, d'un appartement)* repurchase, buying back (**b**) *(d'une société)* buy-out (**c**) *(d'un péché)* atonement
racheter [6] [raʃte] **1** *vt* (**a**) *(acheter davantage de)* to buy some more (**b**) *(remplacer)* to buy another (**à** for) (**c**) *(compagnie)* to buy out (**d**) *(après une vente)* to buy back (**à** from) (**e**) *(otage, prisonnier)* to pay a ransom for (**f**) *(faute, faiblesse)* to make up for; *(péché)* to atone for; *(honneur, réputation)* to retrieve
2 se racheter *vpr* to make amends, to redeem oneself
rachitique [raʃitik] *adj (malade)* suffering from rickets; *(très maigre)* scrawny
rachitisme [raʃitism] *nm* rickets *(singulier)*
racial, -e, -aux, -ales [rasjal, -o] *adj* racial
racine [rasin] *nf* root; **prendre r.** *(plante, personne)* to take root; **r. carrée/cubique** square/cube root

racisme [rasism] *nm* racism
raciste [rasist] *adj & nmf* racist
racket [rakɛt] *nm Fam* racket
racketter [rakɛte] *vt Fam (personne)* to extort money from; **se faire r.** to pay protection money
raclage [raklaʒ] *nm* scraping
raclée [rakle] *nf Fam* thrashing; **mettre une r. à qn** *(battre)* to give sb a good thrashing; *(vaincre)* to thrash sb; **prendre une r.** to get a thrashing
raclement [rakləmɑ̃] *nm* scraping (noise)
racler [rakle] **1** *vt* to scrape; *(peinture, boue)* to scrape off; *Fig* **r. les fonds de tiroirs** to scrape some money together; *Fam* **r. la gorge** *ou* **le gosier** *(vin)* to be rough on the throat
  2 se racler *vpr* **se r. la gorge** to clear one's throat
raclette [raklɛt] *nf* **(a)** *(plat)* raclette *(Swiss dish consisting of potatoes covered in melted cheese)* **(b)** *(outil)* scraper
racloir [raklwar] *nm* scraper
racolage [rakɔlaʒ] *nm (d'une prostituée)* soliciting; *(d'un publicitaire)* touting for business; **faire du r.** *(prostituée)* to solicit; *(publicitaire)* to tout for business
racoler [rakɔle] **1** *vt (sujet: prostituée)* to solicit; *(sujet: commerçant)* to tout for
  2 *vi (prostituée)* to solicit; *(commerçant)* to tout for business
racoleur, -euse [rakɔlœr, -øz] **1** *adj (publicité, affiche)* eye-catching
  2 *nm,f (politicien)* = canvasser who attempts to recruit party members using unscrupulous means; *(commerçant)* tout
  3 *nf* **racoleuse** streetwalker
racontable [rakɔ̃tabl] *adj* relatable; **ce n'est pas r. devant les enfants** it's not something to be spoken about in front of the children
racontar [rakɔ̃tar] *nm* piece of gossip; **racontars** gossip
raconter [rakɔ̃te] **1** *vt* **(a)** *(histoire, mensonge)* to tell; *(événement)* to tell about; **r. qch à qn** *(histoire)* to tell sb sth; *(événement)* to tell sb about sth **(b)** *(dire)* to say; **qu'est-ce qu'il raconte?** what's he talking about?; **alors, qu'est-ce que tu racontes (de beau** *ou* **de neuf)?** so, what's new?
  2 se raconter *vpr* **(a)** *(parler de soi)* to talk about oneself **(b)** *(être raconté)* to be talked about
racornir [rakɔrnir] **1** *vt* **(a)** *(durcir)* to harden **(b)** *(ratatiner)* to shrivel
  2 se racornir *vpr* **(a)** *(durcir)* to harden **(b)** *(se ratatiner)* to shrivel
radar [radar] *nm* radar; *Fam* **être** *ou* **avancer au r.** to be on autopilot
rade [rad] *nf* harbour; **en r. de Toulon** off Toulon; *Fam* **laisser en r.** *(personne)* to leave in the lurch; *(projet)* to jettison; *Fam* **être en r.** *(personne)* to be stranded
radeau, -x [rado] *nm* raft; **r. pneumatique** inflatable raft; **r. de sauvetage** life raft
radial, -e, -aux, -ales [radjal, -o] *adj voir* carcasse
radiateur [radjatœr] *nm* radiator; **r. électrique** electric heater
radiation¹ [radjasjɔ̃] *nf (sur une liste)* striking off
radiation² *nf (d'une onde)* radiation
radical, -e, -aux, -ales [radikal, -o] **1** *adj* radical; **c'est r. (contre)** *(médicament, méthode)* it works like magic (on)
  2 *nm (d'un mot)* stem

radicalement [radikalmɑ̃] *adv* radically
radicaliser [radikalize] **1** *vt* to radicalize
  2 se radicaliser *vpr* to become more radical
radier [66] [radje] *vt* to strike off (**de** from)
radiesthésiste [radjɛstezist] *nmf* diviner
radieux, -euse [radjø, -øz] *adj (soleil, personne)* radiant; *(temps)* glorious
radin, -e [radɛ̃, -in] *Fam* **1** *adj* stingy, *Br* tight
  2 *nm,f* skinflint, tightwad
radiner [radine] **se radiner** *vpr Fam* to roll up; **tu te radines?** are you coming or not?
radio [radjo] **1** *nf* **(a)** *(poste)* radio; *(station)* radio station; **à la r.** on the radio; **faire de la r.** to be *or* work as a radio presenter; **r. libre** independent radio station; **r. locale** local radio station **(b)** *(radiotéléphonie)* radio **(c)** *Méd* X-ray; **passer une r.** to have an X-ray
  2 *nm (opérateur)* radio operator
  3 *adj inv* radio
radioactif, -ive [radjoaktif, -iv] *adj* radioactive
radioactivité [radjoaktivite] *nf* radioactivity
radioamateur [radjoamatœr] *nm* radio amateur
radiocassette [radjokasɛt] *nf* radio cassette player
radiodiffuser [radjodifyze] *vt* to broadcast
radiodiffusion [radjodifyzjɔ̃] *nf* broadcasting
radiographie [radjɔgrafi] *nf* **(a)** *(technique)* radiography **(b)** *(cliché)* X-ray
radiographier [66] [radjɔgrafje] *vt* to X-ray
radioguidé, -e [radjogide] *adj* radio-controlled; *(missile)* guided
radiologie [radjɔlɔʒi] *nf* radiology
radiologique [radjɔlɔʒik] *adj* radiological
radiologue [radjɔlɔg], **radiologiste** [radjɔlɔʒist] *nmf (médecin)* radiologist; *(technicien)* radiographer
radiophonique [radjofonik] *adj (de radio)* radio; *(bon pour la radio)* good for radio
radioreportage [radjorǝpɔrtaʒ] *nm (activité)* radio reporting; *(émission)* radio report
radioreporter [radjorǝpɔrtɛr] *nmf* radio reporter
radio-réveil *(pl* **radios-réveils)** [radjorevɛj] *nm* radio-alarm (clock)
radioscopie [radjoskɔpi] *nf* radioscopy
radioscopique [radjoskɔpik] *adj (examen)* X-ray
radio-taxi *(pl* **radio-taxis)** [radjotaksi] *nm* radio taxi
radiotélescope [radjoteleskɔp] *nm* radio telescope
radiotélévisé, -e [radjotelevize] *adj* broadcast on both radio and television
radiothérapie [radjoterapi] *nf* radiotherapy
radis [radi] *nm* radish; *Fam* **ne plus avoir un r.** not to have a bean; **r. noir** black radish
radium [radjom] *nm* radium
radius [radjys] *nm* radius
radon [radɔ̃] *nm Chim* radon
radotage [radɔtaʒ] *nm (rabâchage)* going on and on; *(divagations)* rambling
radoter [radɔte] **1** *vi (rabâcher)* to go on and on; *(divaguer)* to ramble on
  2 *vt Fam* **qu'est-ce que tu radotes?** what are you drivelling on about?
radoteur, -euse [radɔtœr, -øz] *nm,f* rambling old fool
radoub [radu] *nm* **bassin de r.** dry dock
radoucir [radusir] **1** *vt* **(a)** *(temps)* to make milder **(b)** *(personne)* to calm down; *(caractère)* to soften
  2 se radoucir *vpr* **(a)** *(temps)* to become milder **(b)** *(personne)* to calm down

radoucissement [radusismã] *nm* (**a**) *(de la température)* milder spell (**b**) *(d'une personne)* calming down

rafale [rafal] *nf* (**a**) *(de vent, de pluie)* gust; **par** *ou* **en rafales** in gusts (**b**) *(de coups de feu)* burst

raffermir [rafɛrmir] **1** *vt* (**a**) *(peau, muscles)* to firm up (**b**) *(autorité, courage)* to strengthen
2 se raffermir *vpr* (**a**) *(muscles, peau)* to firm up (**b**) *(gouvernement) (devenir plus intransigeant)* to take a stronger line; *(devenir plus fort)* to become stronger; *(autorité)* to strengthen

raffermissement [rafɛrmismã] *nm* (**a**) *(des muscles, de la peau)* firming up (**b**) *(de l'autorité, du pouvoir)* strengthening

raffinage [rafinaʒ] *nm* refining

raffiné, -e [rafine] *adj* refined

raffinement [rafinmã] *nm* refinement

raffiner [rafine] **1** *vt* to refine
2 raffiner sur *vt ind* to be overparticular about

raffinerie [rafinri] *nf* refinery; **r. de pétrole/sucre** oil/sugar refinery

raffoler [rafole] **raffoler de** *vt ind* **Fam r. de qch** to be mad about sth

raffut [rafy] *nm Fam (bruit)* din, racket; **faire du r.** *(bruit)* to make a racket; *(scandale)* to set tongues wagging; *(pour protester)* to kick up a fuss

rafiot [rafjo] *nm Péj* old tub

rafistolage [rafistolaʒ] *nm Fam* patching up

rafistoler [rafistole] *vt Fam* to patch up

rafle [rafl] *nf* raid; **la police a fait une r. dans le club** the police raided the club

rafler [rafle] *vt Fam* to swipe

rafraîchir [rafreʃir] **1** *vt* (**a**) *(rendre frais) (aliment, boisson)* to chill; *(pièce)* to air; *(atmosphère)* to cool (**b**) *(raviver) (couleur, maquillage, peintures)* to freshen up; *(appartement)* to brighten up; *Fam* **r. la mémoire à qn** to refresh sb's memory
2 *vi* to cool down
3 se rafraîchir *vpr* (**a**) *(temps)* to turn cooler (**b**) *(se mouiller le visage)* to freshen up (**c**) *Fam (boire)* to have a cold drink

rafraîchissant, -e [rafreʃisã, -ãt] *adj* refreshing

rafraîchissement [rafreʃismã] *nm* (**a**) *(de la température, d'une boisson)* cooling (**b**) *(boisson)* cold drink; **rafraîchissements** refreshments (**c**) *Ordinat* refresh

rafting [raftiŋ] *nm* rafting

ragaillardir [ragajardir] *Fam* **1** *vt* to buck up
2 se ragaillardir *vpr* to buck up

rage [raʒ] *nf* (**a**) *(maladie)* rabies (**b**) *(colère)* rage; **faire r.** *(tempête)* to rage; **avoir la r. au cœur** to be seething with rage; **ivre** *ou* **fou de r.** furious; **mettre qn en r.** to enrage sb; **r. de l'air** air rage; **r. de dents** raging toothache; **r. au volant** road rage (**c**) *(passion)* passion (**de qch** for sth); **avoir la r. du jeu** to have a passion for gambling

rageant, -e [raʒã, -ãt] *adj Fam* infuriating

rager [45] [raʒe] *vi Fam* to fume; **faire r. qn** to make sb mad

rageur, -euse [raʒœr, -øz] *adj (ton, voix)* furious

rageusement [raʒøzmã] *adv* furiously

raglan [raglã] *nm* raglan coat

ragot [rago] *nm Fam* piece of gossip; **ragots** gossip

ragoût [ragu] *nm* stew; **en r.** stewed

ragoûtant, -e [ragutã, -ãt] *adj* **peu** *ou* **pas r.** *(plat)* unappetizing; *(personne)* unsavoury

rai [rɛ] *nm (de lumière)* ray

raï [raj] *nm inv* rai,= North African popular music influenced by rock music

raid [rɛd] *nm* raid; **r. aérien** air raid

raide [rɛd] **1** *adj* (**a**) *(membre, articulation)* stiff; *(cheveux)* straight; *(câble)* taut (**b**) *(escalier, pente)* steep (**c**) *(personne, démarche)* stiff; **r. comme un piquet** as stiff as a ramrod (**d**) *(caractère)* inflexible; *(manières)* stiff (**e**) *Fam (difficile à croire)* far-fetched (**f**) *Fam (osé)* risqué (**g**) *Fam (fort) (alcool)* rough
2 *adv* (**a**) *(de façon abrupte)* steeply (**b**) *(brutalement)* **tomber r.** to fall to the ground; **tomber r. mort** to drop dead

raideur [rɛdœr] *nf* (**a**) *(d'un membre, d'une articulation, d'un mouvement)* stiffness; **avoir une r. dans le cou/à l'épaule** to have a stiff neck/shoulder (**b**) *(d'une personne)* stiffness (**c**) *(de caractère)* inflexibility (**d**) *(d'une pente)* steepness

raidillon [rɛdijõ] *nm (chemin)* steep path; *(partie de route)* steep rise

raidir [rɛdir] **1** *vt (bras, jambes)* to brace; *(corde, câble)* to tauten; *(tissu)* to stiffen
2 se raidir *vpr* (**a**) *(membres, articulations)* to stiffen; *(câble)* to tauten (**b**) *(personne)* to tense up

raidissement [rɛdismã] *nm* (**a**) *(d'une matière, des muscles)* stiffening; *(d'une corde)* tautening (**b**) *(montée de la tension)* **r. des rapports internationaux** increase of tension in international relations; **le r. des ouvriers face à la direction** the tougher line taken by the workers with the management

raie¹ [rɛ] *nf* (**a**) *(motif)* stripe (**b**) *(dans les cheveux)* *Br* parting, *Am* part (**c**) *(des fesses)* cleft

raie² *nf (poisson)* skate

raifort [rɛfor] *nm* horseradish

rail [raj] *nm* (**a**) *(sur une voie de chemin de fer)* rail; *Fig* **remettre qn sur les rails** to get sb back on the rails (**b**) **le r.** *(les chemins de fer)* rail (**c**) **r. de sécurité** crash barrier (**d**) *(couloir) (aérien, maritime)* lane

railler [raje] *vt* to mock

raillerie [rajri] *nf* gibe

railleur, -euse [rajœr, -øz] **1** *adj* mocking
2 *nm,f* scoffer

rainette [rɛnɛt] *nf* (**a**) *(grenouille)* tree frog (**b**) *(pomme)* pippin

rainure [rɛnyr] *nf* groove

raisin [rɛzɛ̃] *nm* grapes; **raisins de Corinthe** currants; **raisins secs** raisins; **raisins de Smyrne** sultanas

raisinet [rezinɛ] *nm Suisse* redcurrant

raison [rɛzõ] *nf* (**a**) *(motif)* reason (**de** for); **en r. de qch** because of sth; **être absent pour r. de santé** to be absent for health reasons; **à plus forte r.** all the more so; **r. de plus (pour faire qch)** all the more reason (to do sth); **la r. pour laquelle il est venu** the reason (why) he came; **la r. d'État** reasons of State; **d'être** raison d'être; **r. de vivre** reason for living (**b**) *(entendement)* reason; **recouvrer la r.** to come to one's senses; **perdre la r.** to take leave of one's senses; **entendre r.** to listen to reason; **l'âge de r.** the age of reason; **mariage de r.** marriage of convenience (**c**) *(satisfaction)* satisfaction; **avoir r. de qn/qch** to get the better of sb/sth (**d**) *(proportion)* **à r. de** at the rate of (**e**) *(désignation)* **r. sociale** company name (**f**) *(locutions)* **avoir r. (de faire qch)** to be right (to do sth); **donner r. à qn** *(personne)* to admit that sb is right; *(événement)* to prove sb right; **se faire une r.** to accept the inevitable, to resign oneself; **comme de r.** as one might expect; **plus que de r.** more than is reasonable

raisonnable [rɛzɔnabl] *adj* reasonable
raisonnablement [rɛzɔnabləmɑ̃] *adv* (**a**) *(avec bon sens)* reasonably (**b**) *(modérément)* in moderation
raisonné, -e [rɛzɔne] *adj (argumentation, choix)* reasoned
raisonnement [rɛzɔnmɑ̃] *nm (argumentation)* argument; *(faculté)* reasoning; **tenir un r.** to use an argument; **r. par l'absurde** reductio ad absurdum
raisonner [rɛzɔne] **1** *vt (personne)* to reason with
2 *vi* (**a**) *(penser)* to reason (**sur** about); *Fam* **r. comme une pantoufle** to talk through one's hat (**b**) *(discuter)* to argue (**avec** with)
3 se raisonner *vpr (personne)* to see reason
raisonneur, -euse [rɛzɔnœr, -øz] **1** *adj* reasoning; *Péj* argumentative
2 *nm,f Péj* arguer
rajeunir [raʒœnir] **1** *vt* (**a**) **r. qn** *(faire paraître plus jeune)* to make sb look younger; *(faire se sentir plus jeune)* to make sb feel younger (**b**) *(donner un âge moins élevé à)* **r. qn** to underestimate how old sb is; **r. qn de trois ans** to take three years off sb's age (**c**) *(robe, veste)* to update (**d**) *(organisation, bureau)* to modernize; *(équipe)* to bring new blood into
2 *vi (physiquement)* to look younger; *(moralement)* to seem younger; **il a rajeuni de dix ans** he looks ten years younger; **ça ne nous rajeunit pas!** we're showing our age!
3 se rajeunir *vpr (se prétendre plus jeune)* to make oneself out to be younger than one is
rajeunissant, -e [raʒœnisɑ̃, -ɑ̃t] *adj* rejuvenating
rajeunissement [raʒœnismɑ̃] *nm* (**a**) *(après un traitement)* rejuvenation (**b**) *(de la population, d'un secteur professionnel)* decrease in age
rajout [raʒu] *nm* (**a**) addition (**b**) **rajouts** *(pour les cheveux)* extensions
rajouter [raʒute] *vt* to add; *Fam* **en r.** to exaggerate
rajuster [raʒyste] **1** *vt (vêtement)* to adjust, to straighten
2 se rajuster *vpr* to tidy oneself up
râle [ral] *nm (bruit aux poumons)* rale; *(d'un agonisant)* death rattle
ralenti, -e [ralɑ̃ti] **1** *adj* slow
2 *nm* (**a**) *(régime du moteur)* idling speed; **au r.** *(vivre, fonctionner)* at a slower pace; **tourner au r.** *(moteur, usine) Br* to tick over, *Am* to turn over (**b**) *Cin* slow motion; **au r.** in slow motion
ralentir [ralɑ̃tir] *vt & vi* to slow down
ralentissement [ralɑ̃tismɑ̃] *nm* slowing down; *(embouteillage)* hold-up
ralentisseur [ralɑ̃tisœr] *nm (dos d'âne)* speed bump
râler [rale] *vi* (**a**) *Fam (protester)* to moan (**b**) *(mourant)* to give a death rattle
râleur, -euse [ralœr, -øz] *Fam* **1** *adj* bad-tempered, grumpy
2 *nm,f* grouch
ralliement [ralimɑ̃] *nm* rallying; **cri de r.** rallying cry
rallier [66] [ralje] **1** *vt* (**a**) *(regagner) (lieu)* to return to (**b**) *(gagner à sa cause)* to win over (**à** to) (**c**) *(réunir) (adhérents)* to rally; **r. tous les suffrages** to win general approval (**d**) *(regrouper) (troupes)* to rally
2 se rallier *vpr* **se r. à** *(avis)* to come round to; *(parti)* to join; *(cause)* to rally to
rallonge [ralɔ̃ʒ] *nf* (**a**) *(de table)* extension (**b**) *(électrique)* extension (lead) (**c**) *Fam (d'argent)* extra money; *(de temps)* extra time

rallonger [45] [ralɔ̃ʒe] **1** *vt (vêtement)* to lengthen; *(période, route)* to extend (**de** by)
2 *vi* to get longer
rallumer [ralyme] **1** *vt* (**a**) *(appareil électrique, lumière)* to switch on again (**b**) *(feu, cigarette)* to light again; *(querelle, colère, espoir)* to rekindle
2 se rallumer *vpr* (**a**) *(lumière, appareil électrique)* to come back on (**b**) *(feu, guerre, dispute)* to flare up again; *(espoir)* to rekindle
rallye [rali] *nm* (**a**) *(épreuve sportive)* (car) rally (**b**) *(soirée)* = dance attended by young people from rich families looking for a marriage partner
RAM [ram] *nf Ordinat* RAM
ramadan [ramadɑ̃] *nm* Ramadan; **faire le r.** to observe Ramadan
ramage [ramaʒ] *nm* (**a**) *(chant des oiseaux)* song (**b**) **ramages** *(motif)* leafy design
ramassage [ramasaʒ] *nm* (**a**) *(de fruits, de noix)* gathering (**b**) *(d'ordures, de vêtements, de vieux journaux)* collection; **car de r.** *scolaire* school bus
ramassé, -e [ramase] *adj* (**a**) *(trapu) (personne)* stocky (**b**) *(style)* compact
ramasse-miettes [ramasmjɛt] *nm inv* table tidy *(small brush and pan for clearing crumbs off the table)*
ramasser [ramase] **1** *vt* (**a**) *(prendre par terre) (objet, personne)* to pick up; *(fruits, noix, coquillages)* to gather; *(champignons)* to pick; *(pommes de terre)* to dig up; *Fam* **se faire r. par la police** to get picked up by the police (**b**) *(cartes)* to pick up; *r. ses forces* to gather one's strength (**c**) *(enfants, ouvriers, courrier)* to pick up, to collect (**d**) *Fam (gifle)* to get; *(procès-verbal)* to pick up; *(maladie)* to catch
2 se ramasser *vpr* (**a**) *(après une chute)* to pick oneself up (**b**) *(se pelotonner)* to curl up (**c**) *Fam (tomber)* to fall flat on one's face; *(échouer)* to come a cropper (**d**) *(gifle)* to get; *(procès-verbal)* to pick up
ramassette [ramasɛt] *nf Belg* dustpan
ramasseur, -euse [ramasœr, -øz] *nm,f* (**a**) *(de champignons)* picker; *(de fruits)* gatherer (**b**) *(au tennis)* **r. de balles** ball boy, *f* ball girl
ramassis [ramasi] *nm Péj (de choses)* jumble; *(de gens)* bunch; *(d'idées)* hotchpotch; **un r. de mensonges** a tissue of lies
rambarde [rɑ̃bard] *nf* (guard)rail
ramdam [ramdam] *nm Fam* racket; **faire du r.** to make a heck of a racket
rame¹ [ram] *nf (pour plantes grimpantes)* stick
rame² *nf (aviron)* oar
rame³ *nf* (**a**) *(de papier)* ream (**b**) *(de wagons)* train; **r. (de métro)** *(Br* underground *orAm* subway) train
rameau, -x [ramo] *nm* (**a**) *(d'arbre)* branch (**b**) **les Rameaux** Palm Sunday
ramener [46] [ramne] **1** *vt* (**a**) *(amener)* to bring back; *(raccompagner)* to take back; **r. qn en voiture** to give sb a lift back; **r. qn à la vie** to bring sb back to life; **r. qn à la raison** to bring sb back to his/her senses (**b**) *Fam (rapporter, revenir avec)* to bring back; **r. tout à soi** to bring everything back to oneself (**c**) *(remettre) (couverture, châle)* to pull up *(sur* over) (**d**) *(rétablir) (ordre, paix)* to restore (**e**) *(réduire)* **r. qch à qch** to reduce sth to sth (**f**) *Fam* **r. sa fraise, la r.** to show off
2 se ramener *vpr* (**a**) *(se réduire)* **se r. à** to boil down to (**b**) *Fam (arriver)* to roll up
ramequin [ramkɛ̃] *nm* ramekin
ramer [rame] *vi* (**a**) *(pagayer)* to row (**b**) *Fam (peiner)* to sweat blood

rameur, -euse [ramœr, -øz] *nm,f* rower
ramier [ramje] *adj m voir* **pigeon**
ramification [ramifikasjɔ̃] *nf (d'une plante)* ramification; *(d'une famille, d'une science)* branch; **ramifications** *(d'une société, d'une affaire)* ramifications
ramifier [66] [ramifje] **se ramifier** *vpr* to branch out (en into)
ramolli, -e [ramɔli] *adj Fam (mentalement)* softheaded
ramollir [ramɔlir] **1** *vt (substance)* to soften; *Fam* **r. qn** *(intellectuellement)* to make sb soft in the head
 2 se ramollir *vpr (substance)* to soften; *Fam Fig (personne)* to become unfit
ramollissement [ramɔlismɑ̃] *nm* softening; **r. cérébral** softening of the brain
ramon [ramɔ̃] *nm Belg* broom
ramonage [ramɔnaʒ] *nm* chimney sweeping
ramoner [ramɔne] *vt (cheminée)* to sweep
ramoneur [ramɔnœr] *nm* (chimney) sweep
rampant, -e [rɑ̃pɑ̃, -ɑ̃t] *adj* **(a)** *(plante)* creeping; *(animal)* crawling; *Péj (personne, caractère)* grovelling **(b) personnel r.** *(de l'aviation)* ground crew **(c)** *(inflation)* rampant
rampe [rɑ̃p] *nf* **(a)** *(d'escalier)* banister, handrail **(b)** *(plan incliné)* slope, incline; **r. d'accès** *(d'un pont)* access ramp; *(d'une autoroute) Br* slip road, *Am* ramp; **r. de lancement** launching ramp **(c)** *(rebord d'une scène de théâtre)* footlights
ramper [rɑ̃pe] *vi (animal, enfant, soldat)* to crawl; *Péj* **r. devant qn** to grovel to sb
ramure [ramyr] *nf* **(a)** *(d'un arbre)* branches **(b)** *(d'un cerf)* antlers
rancard [rɑ̃kar] *nm Fam (rendez-vous)* meeting; *(amoureux)* date
rancarder [rɑ̃karde] *très Fam* **1** *vt* **r. qn sur qch** to tip sb off about sth
 2 se rancarder *vpr* to find out (**sur** about)
rancart [rɑ̃kar] *nm Fam* **mettre qch au r.** to chuck sth out; **mettre qn au r.** to put sb on the rubbish heap
rance [rɑ̃s] **1** *adj* rancid
 2 *nm* **goût de r.** rancid taste
ranch [rɑ̃tʃ] *nm* ranch
rancir [rɑ̃sir] *vi* to go rancid
rancœur [rɑ̃kœr] *nf* resentment, rancour; **avoir de la r. pour** *ou* **contre qn** to feel resentment towards sb
rançon [rɑ̃sɔ̃] *nf* ransom; *Fig* **la r. de la gloire** the price of fame
rançonner [rɑ̃sɔne] *vt* **r. qn** to hold sb to ransom
rancune [rɑ̃kyn] *nf* spite; **garder r. à qn, avoir de la r. contre qn** to have a grudge against sb, to bear sb a grudge; **sans r.!** no hard feelings!
rancunier, -ère [rɑ̃kynje, -ɛr] **1** *adj* spiteful
 2 *nm,f* spiteful person
randonnée [rɑ̃dɔne] *nf* **(a)** *(marche à pied)* **r. (pédestre)** hike; *(activité)* hiking, rambling; *(en montagne)* hill-walking; **faire une r.** to go for a hike; **faire de la r.** to go hiking *or* rambling; *(en montagne)* to go hill-walking **(b)** *(en voiture)* drive; **(c)** *(excursion à ski)* ski-mountaineering
randonneur, -euse [rɑ̃dɔnœr, -øz] *nm,f (à pied)* hiker, rambler
rang [rɑ̃] *nm* **(a)** *(d'arbres, de sièges)* row; **se mettre en r. (par deux/trois)** to line up (in twos/threes); *Hum* **en r. d'oignons** in a neat row; **en rangs serrés** in serried ranks; *Fig* **se mettre sur les rangs** to put oneself in the running **(b)** *(position sociale)* station; *(de militaire)* rank; **de haut r.** high-ranking **(c)** *(classement)*

rank; **par r. de taille** in order of size **(d)** *Can (chemin)* concession road
rangé, -e¹ [rɑ̃ʒe] *adj* **(a)** *(maison, chambre)* tidy **(b)** *(personne)* steady; *(vie)* settled
rangée² *nf* row
rangement [rɑ̃ʒmɑ̃] *nm* **(a)** *(action)* tidying up; **faire du r.** to do some tidying up; **faire du r. dans ses affaires** to tidy up one's things **(b)** *(placard)* **rangements** storage space **(c)** *Ordinat* storage
ranger [45] [rɑ̃ʒe] **1** *vt* **(a)** *(pièce, maison)* to tidy (up) **(b)** *(affaires, vêtements)* to put away **(c)** *(mettre)* to put **(d)** *(classer)* to rank (**parmi** among); **r. par** *(ordre alphabétique, taille)* to arrange by **(e)** *(véhicule, vélo)* to park **(f)** *(soldats, élèves)* to line up **(g)** *Ordinat* **r. en mémoire** to store
 2 se ranger *vpr* **(a)** *(se disposer)* to line up **(b)** *(s'écarter)* *(piéton)* to stand aside; *(véhicule)* to pull over **(c)** *(prendre position pour)* **se r. du côté de qn** to side with sb, to take sb's side; **se r. à l'opinion de qn** to come round to sb's opinion **(d)** *(se mettre)* to go **(e)** *Fam (s'assagir)* to settle down; **se r. des voitures** to settle down
ranimer [ranime] **1** *vt* **(a)** *(personne)* *(après un évanouissement)* to bring round; *(après un arrêt cardiaque)* to resuscitate **(b)** *(feu)* to rekindle **(c)** *(sentiment, souvenir, espoir)* to reawaken; *(débat)* to revive
 2 se ranimer *vpr* **(a)** *(personne)* to come round **(b)** *(feu)* to flicker into life
rap [rap] *nm* **le r.** *(musique)* rap
rapace [rapas] **1** *nm* bird of prey
 2 *adj* **(a)** *(oiseau)* predatory **(b)** *(personne)* grasping
rapacité [rapasite] *nf* rapaciousness
rapatrié, -e [rapatrije] **1** *adj* repatriated
 2 *nm,f* repatriate
rapatriement [rapatrimɑ̃] *nm* repatriation
rapatrier [66] [rapatrije] *vt* to repatriate
râpe [rap] *nf* **(a)** *(de cuisine)* grater; **r. à fromage** cheese grater **(b)** *(lime)* rasp **(c)** *Suisse Fam Péj (avare)* miser
râpé, -e [rape] **1** *adj* **(a)** *(fromage, carotte)* grated **(b)** *(vêtement)* threadbare **(c)** *Fam (raté)* **c'est r.!** we've had it!
 2 *nm (fromage)* grated cheese
râper [rape] *vt* **(a)** *(carotte, fromage)* to grate **(b)** *(racler)* **ce vin râpe la gorge** this wine's rough on the throat **(c)** *(limer)* to rasp
rapetasser [raptase] *vt Fam (vêtement)* to patch up
rapetisser [raptise] **1** *vt* **(a)** *(rendre plus petit)* to make smaller **(b)** *(dévaluer)* to belittle **(c)** *(faire paraître plus petit)* to make look smaller
 2 *vi (vêtement, personne)* to shrink
râpeux, -euse [rapø, -øz] *adj (langue)* rough; *(vin)* harsh
raphia [rafja] *nm* raffia
rapiat, -e [rapja, -at] *Fam* **1** *adj (avare)* stingy, *Br* tight
 2 *nm,f* skinflint, tightwad
rapide [rapid] **1** *adj* **(a)** *(coureur, voiture, itinéraire)* fast; *(pouls, progrès)* rapid; **r. comme l'éclair** as quick as lightning; **r. comme une flèche** as swift as an arrow **(b)** *(courant)* swift-flowing **(c)** *(prompt)* *(personne, esprit, intelligence)* quick **(d)** *(fait en peu de temps)* *(lecture, décision)* quick **(e)** *(pente)* steep
 2 *nm* **(a)** *(train)* express (train) **(b)** *(dans un fleuve)* rapid
rapidement [rapidmɑ̃] *adv* quickly, rapidly

rapidité [rapidite] *nf* (**a**) *(d'actions, d'une décision, d'une réponse)* speed; **r. d'esprit** quickness of mind (**b**) *Ordinat* **r. d'impression** print speed; **r. de traitement** processing speed

rapiécer [16/34] [rapjese] *vt* to patch

rapine [rapin] *nf Litt* pillage

raplapla [raplapla] *adj inv Fam* (**a**) *(pneu, coussin)* flat as a pancake (**b**) *(personne)* washed out

rappel [rapɛl] *nm* (**a**) *(d'un événement, d'une promesse)* reminder; **r. de couleurs** repeat of colours; **r. à l'ordre** *(à un membre d'une assemblée)* call to order; *(d'un employé)* warning; **le r. des titres (de l'actualité)** the headlines; **dernier r.** *(de facture)* final demand (**b**) *(d'un ambassadeur, de réservistes)* recall (**c**) *(d'un salaire)* back pay (**d**) *(de vaccin)* booster; **faire un r.** to have a booster (**e**) *(au théâtre)* curtain call; *(à un concert)* encore (**f**) *(en alpinisme)* abseiling; **faire une descente** *ou* **descendre en r., faire du r.** to abseil down (**g**) *Ordinat (de texte)* restore

rappeler [9] [rapəle, raple] **1** *vt* (**a**) *(appeler) (personne)* to call back; *(chien)* to call off (**b**) *(au téléphone) (sujet: personne appelée)* to call back; *(sujet: personne qui appelle)* to call again; **r. dix fois** to call ten times (**c**) *(faire revenir) (personne)* to call back; *(ambassadeur)* to recall; **r. qn à l'ordre** *(membre d'une association)* to call sb to order; *(employé)* to warn sb (**d**) *(acteur, chanteur)* to call back (**e**) *(faire penser à)* **r. qn/qch à qn** to remind sb of sb/sth; **cela ne me rappelle rien** it doesn't ring a bell (**f**) *(remettre en mémoire)* **r. qch à qn** to remind sb of sth; **rappelez-moi votre nom** what was your name again?; **r. qn au bon souvenir de qn** to remember sb to sb
2 se rappeler *vpr* (**a**) **se r. qn/qch** *(se souvenir de)* to remember sb/sth; **rappelle-toi que...** don't forget that... (**b**) *Fam (au téléphone)* **on se rappelle la semaine prochaine** we'll talk again next week

rappeur, -euse [rapœr, -øz] *nm,f* rapper

rappliquer [raplike] *vi Fam* to roll up

rapport [rapɔr] *nm* (**a**) *(relation)* **rapports** relations, relationship; **avoir de bons/mauvais rapports avec qn** to be on good/bad terms with sb; **entretenir des rapports amicaux avec qn** to stay on friendly terms with sb; **mettre qn en r. avec qn** to put sb in touch with sb; **être en r. avec qn** to be in touch with sb; **r. de forces** battle of wills (**b**) *(lien)* connection, link (**avec** with); **avoir un r. avec qch** to have something to do with sth; **n'avoir aucun r. avec qch** to have nothing to do with sth; **faire le r.** to make the connection; **être sans r. avec qch** to be unconnected with sth; **en r.** *(lié à)* in keeping with; **par r. à qch** *(en comparaison)* compared with sth (**c**) *(aspect)* **sous ce r.** in this respect; **bien sous tous rapports** nice in every respect (**d**) *(proportion)* ratio, proportion; **en r. avec** in proportion to; **d'un bon r. qualité-prix** good value for money (**e**) *(compte rendu)* report; **faire** *ou* **rédiger un r. sur qch** to draw up a report on sth; **r. annuel** annual report; **r. commercial** market report (**f**) *(profit)* return, yield; **d'un bon r.** profitable; **d'un mauvais r.** unprofitable (**g**) **rapports** *(relations sexuelles)* (sexual) intercourse; **avoir des rapports avec qn** to have sex with sb

rapporter [rapɔrte] **1** *vt* (**a**) *(apporter avec soi)* to bring back; **r. qch à qn** to bring sb sth back (**b**) *(rendre)* to bring back (**à** to); *(remporter)* to take back (**à** to) (**c**) *(ajouter) (poche, pièce)* to sew on (**d**) *(raconter)* to report; **on rapporte que...** it is reported that... (**e**) *(produire) (bénéfice, intérêt)* to yield; **r. (de**

l'argent) to be profitable; **r. qch à qn** *(financièrement)* to bring sb in sth; *Fig (moralement)* to bring sb sth (**f**) *Péj (répéter)* to report (**à** to) (**g**) *(sujet: chien)* to retrieve; **rapporte! rapporte!** fetch!
2 se rapporter *vpr* (**a**) **se r. à qch** *(concerner)* to relate to sth (**b**) *(se remettre)* **s'en r. à qn/qch** to rely on sb/sth

rapporteur, -euse [rapɔrtœr, -øz] **1** *adj Péj* sneaky
2 *nm,f Péj* telltale, sneak
3 *nm* (**a**) *(d'une commission)* reporter (**b**) *(instrument)* protractor

rapproché, -e [raprɔʃe] *adj (dans l'espace, dans le temps)* close; *(yeux)* close-set; **des maisons très rapprochées** houses very close together; **des rendez-vous très rapprochés (dans le temps)** appointments very close to each other

rapprochement [raprɔʃmɑ̃] *nm* (**a**) *(rapport) (de faits, d'idées)* connection; **faire le r. (entre deux choses)** to make a connection (between two things) (**b**) *(de deux objets)* bringing together (**c**) *(réconciliation) (entre personnes)* reconciliation; *(entre pays)* rapprochement

rapprocher [raprɔʃe] **1** *vt* (**a**) *(mettre plus près) (deux ou plusieurs objets)* to move closer together; *(un objet)* to move closer (**de** to); **ça te rapprochera (de chez toi)** that'll get you a bit closer (to home) (**b**) *(réunir) (deux objets)* to join (**c**) *(séances)* to group closer together (**d**) *(unir) (personnes)* to bring together (**e**) *(lier) (idées, textes)* to compare (**de** with)
2 se rapprocher *vpr* (**a**) *(aller plus près)* to get closer (**de** to); **se r. de la vérité** to get close to the truth (**b**) *(devenir proche)* to get closer (**de** to); *(après une brouille)* to become reconciled (**de** with) (**c**) **se r. de qn/qch** *(ressembler à)* to be similar to sb/sth

rapsodie [rapsɔdi] *nf* rhapsody

rapt [rapt] *nm* abduction

raquer [rake] *très Fam* **1** *vt* to fork out
2 *vi* to pay up, to cough up

raquette [rakɛt] *nf* (**a**) *(de tennis, de badminton, de squash)* racket; *(de ping-pong)* bat (**b**) *(pour marcher dans la neige)* snowshoe

rare [rar] *adj* (**a**) *(peu commun, peu fréquent)* rare; **c'est r. qu'il pleuve ici** it rarely rains here; **cela n'a rien de r.** it's quite common (**b**) *(peu nombreux, peu abondant)* **être r.** to be scarce; **c'est une des rares personnes que je connaisse à s'y opposer** he's one of the few people I know who's against it (**c**) *(exceptionnel)* rare (**d**) *(clairsemé) (végétation)* sparse; **avoir le cheveu r.** to have thinning hair (**e**) **tu te fais r.** we've hardly seen you lately

raréfaction [rarefaksjɔ̃] *nf* (**a**) *(d'une denrée, de l'argent)* growing scarcity (**b**) *(de l'air)* rarefaction

raréfier [66] [rarefje] **se raréfier** *vpr* (**a**) *(denrée, argent)* to become scarce (**b**) *(air)* to become rarefied

rarement [rarmɑ̃] *adv* rarely, seldom

rareté [rarte] *nf* (**a**) *(de denrées, de main-d'œuvre)* scarcity; *(de visites)* infrequency; *(d'un phénomène, d'un mot, d'une maladie)* rareness (**b**) *(objet rare)* rarity

RAS [ɛraɛs] *Fam (abrév rien à signaler)* everything OK

ras, -e [rɑ, rɑz] **1** *adj* (**a**) *(cheveux)* close-cropped; *(barbe)* short; *(tapis)* short-pile (**b**) *(entier) (mesure)* full; **deux cuillerées rases** two level spoonfuls (**c**) *(locutions)* **à r. bord** to the brim; **en rase campagne** in the open country
2 *nm* (**a**) *(bord)* **à** *ou* **au r. de** level with; **voler au r. du sol/de l'eau** to fly close to the ground/water; *Fam*

Fig **au r. des pâquerettes** lowbrow (**b**) **r. du cou** *(pull-over)* crew-neck sweater

3 *adv* short; *Fam* **en avoir r. le bol (de qch)** to have had it up to here *or* be fed up to the back teeth (with sth)

rasade [razad] *nf* glassful

rasage [raza3] *nm* shaving

rasant, -e [razɑ̃, -ɑ̃t] *adj* (**a**) *Fam (personne, discours, film)* boring (**b**) *(lumière)* low-angled; *(tir)* grazing

rascasse [raskas] *nf* scorpion fish

rasé, -e [raze] *adj* shaven; **r. de près** close-shaven

rase-mottes [razmɔt] *nm inv Fam* **faire du** *ou* **voler en r.** to hedgehop

raser [raze] **1** *vt* (**a**) *(visage, personne)* to shave; *(moustache, barbe, cheveux)* to shave off (**b**) *(passer très près de) (sol, eau)* to skim; *(filet, trottoir)* to graze; **r. les murs** to hug the walls (**c**) *(détruire) (bâtiment, ville)* to raze to the ground (**d**) *Fam (ennuyer)* to bore

2 se raser *vpr* (**a**) *(se couper la barbe)* to shave, to have a shave; **se r. les jambes** to shave one's legs (**b**) *Fam (s'ennuyer)* to be bored

raseur, -euse [razœr, -øz] *nm,f Fam* bore

rasibus [razibys] *adv Fam* **la balle est passée r.** the bullet whizzed past really close

ras-le-bol [ralbɔl] *Fam* **1** *nm inv* discontent

2 *exclam* enough's enough!

rasoir [razwar] **1** *nm* razor; **r. électrique** electric razor *or* shaver

2 *adj inv Fam* boring

rassasier [66] [rasazje] **1** *vt (faim, curiosité)* to satisfy; **r. qn** to satisfy sb's hunger

2 se rassasier *vpr* **se r. de qch** to get one's fill of sth

rassemblement [rasɑ̃bləmɑ̃] *nm* (**a**) *(attroupement)* gathering (**b**) *(de documents, d'objets)* collecting, gathering (**c**) *(union politique)* union (**d**) *Mil* fall in, parade; **sonner le r.** to sound the assembly

rassembler [rasɑ̃ble] **1** *vt* (**a**) *(personnes, choses, documents)* to gather (together) (**b**) *(courage, forces)* to muster, to summon up; **r. ses idées** to collect one's thoughts; **r. ses esprits** to collect oneself

2 se rassembler *vpr (manifestants)* to gather, to assemble; *(famille)* to get together

rasseoir [10a] [raswar] **se rasseoir** *vpr* to sit down again

rasséréner [34] [raserene] **1** *vt* **r. qn** to put sb's mind at rest

2 se rasséréner *vpr* to calm down

rassir [rasir] *vi* to go stale

rassis, -e [rasi, -iz] *adj* (**a**) *(pain)* stale (**b**) *Litt (personne, esprit)* calm

rassurant, -e [rasyrɑ̃, -ɑ̃t] *adj* reassuring

rassuré, -e [rasyre] *adj* at ease; **me voilà r.!** that's a relief!

rassurer [rasyre] **1** *vt* to reassure; **ah, tu me rassures!** well, that's a relief!

2 se rassurer *vpr* to reassure oneself; **rassurez-vous** rest assured

rasta [rasta] *adj inv* & *nmf* Rasta

rat [ra] *nm* (**a**) *(animal)* rat; **r. d'égout** sewer rat; *Fam* **être fait comme un r.** to be caught like a rat in a trap; **petit r. (de l'Opéra)** ballet pupil (at the Paris Opéra); **mon petit r.** darling; *Fam* **r. de bibliothèque** bookworm; **r. d'hôtel** hotel thief (**b**) *Can (sournois)* tricky customer

2 *adj Fam* (**a**) *(avare)* stingy, *Br* tight (**b**) *Can (sournois)* wily, sly

ratage [rata3] *nm Fam* botch-up

ratatiné, -e [ratatine] *adj* (**a**) *(fruit)* shrivelled (**b**) *Fam (vieillard)* wizened (**c**) *Fam (véhicule)* smashed-up

ratatiner [ratatine] *Fam* **1** *vt* (**a**) *(voiture)* to smash up (**b**) *(équipe)* to thrash

2 se ratatiner *vpr* (**a**) *(fruit)* to shrivel up (**b**) *(vieillard)* to become wizened

ratatouille [ratatuj] *nf* ratatouille

rate¹ [rat] *nf (organe)* spleen

rate² *nf (animal)* female rat

raté, -e [rate] **1** *nm,f Fam* loser

2 *nm* misfiring; *Fig* hitch; **avoir des ratés** to misfire

râteau, -x [rɑto] *nm* (**a**) *(de jardin)* rake (**b**) *Suisse Fam Péj (avare)* skinflint, tightwad

râtelier [rɑtəlje] *nm* (**a**) *(pour le fourrage)* rack; *Fig* **manger à tous les râteliers** to have a finger in every pie (**b**) *(à outils, à armes)* rack (**c**) *Fam (dentier)* (set of) false teeth

rater [rate] **1** *vt* (**a**) *(examen)* to fail; *(vie, plat)* to make a mess of; **c'est raté** it hasn't worked; *Fig* **r. son coup** to make a mess of things (**b**) *(train, avion, personne, occasion)* to miss; **tu n'as pas raté grand-chose** you didn't miss much (**c**) *Fam (locutions)* **ne pas r. qn** to let sb have it; **elle n'en rate pas une** she's always putting her foot in it

2 *vi* to fail; **faire r. qch** to ruin sth; **j'étais sûr qu'elle allait oublier, et ça n'a pas raté** I was sure she was going to forget, and sure enough she did

3 se rater *vpr Fam* (**a**) *(ne pas se rencontrer)* to miss each other (**b**) *(personne suicidaire)* to bungle one's suicide attempt

ratiboiser [ratibwaze] *vt Fam* (**a**) *(ruiner)* to clean out; **se faire r.** to be cleaned out (**b**) *(cheveux)* **se faire r.** to get scalped

ratier [ratje] *nm (chien)* ratter

ratière [ratjɛr] *nf* rat trap

ratification [ratifikasjɔ̃] *nf* ratification

ratifier [66] [ratifje] *vt (traité, acte)* to ratify; *(décision)* to confirm

ratio [rasjo] *nm* ratio

ration [rasjɔ̃] *nf (de pain, de nourriture)* ration; *Fig (de critiques, de difficultés)* share; **r. alimentaire** food ration

rationaliser [rasjɔnalize] *vt* to rationalize

rationnel, -elle [rasjɔnɛl] *adj* rational

rationnellement [rasjɔnɛlmɑ̃] *adv* rationally

rationnement [rasjɔnmɑ̃] *nm* rationing

rationner [rasjɔne] **1** *vt* to ration

2 se rationner *vpr* to ration oneself

ratissage [ratisa3] *nm* (**a**) *(allée, sol)* raking (**b**) *Fam (par la police)* combing

ratisser [ratise] **1** *vt* (**a**) *(allée, sol)* to rake; *(feuilles)* to rake up (**b**) *Fam (quartier)* to comb (**c**) *Fam (personne)* to clean out; **se faire r.** *(au jeu)* to be cleaned out

2 *vi* **r. large** to cast one's net wide

raton [ratɔ̃] *nm* (**a**) *(animal)* young rat; **r. laveur** raccoon (**b**) *Fam (Maghrébin)* = racist term used to refer to a North African Arab

ratonnade [ratɔnad] *nf* = racist attack on North African Arabs

ratoureux, -euse [raturø, -øz] *Can* **1** *adj* wily, devious

2 *nm,f* shady customer

RATP [ɛratepe] *nf (abrév* **Régie autonome des transports parisiens**) = Parisian transport authority

rattachement [rataʃmɑ̃] *nm (d'une région)* uniting (**à** with)

rattacher [rataʃe] **1** *vt* (**a**) *(attacher de nouveau) (lacets, chien, objet)* to tie up again (**à** to); *(cheveux)* to put up again; **r. qch sur qch** to tie sth onto sth again (**b**) *(région)* to unite (**à** with) (**c**) **être rattaché à** *(faire partie de)* to be attached to (**d**) *(lier)* **c'était la seule chose qui nous rattachait l'un à l'autre** it was the only thing that bound us together; **c'est tout ce qui le rattache à la vie** it's the only thing keeping him alive
2 se rattacher *vpr* **se r. à qch** to be linked to sth

rattrapage [ratrapaʒ] *nm* **être admis au r., être admis à passer les épreuves de r.** = to be allowed to sit further oral examinations to gain a pass mark in the baccalauréat; **cours de r.** remedial class

rattraper [ratrape] **1** *vt* (**a**) *(prisonnier, chien)* to recapture; **se faire r. par la police** to get caught by the police (**b**) *(objet ou personne qui tombe)* to catch (**c**) *(rejoindre) (personne, voiture)* to catch up with (**d**) *(regagner)* **r. le temps perdu** to make up for lost time; **r. son retard** to catch up; **avoir du sommeil à r.** to have to catch up on some sleep (**e**) *(rétablir) (erreur)* to correct; *(situation)* to salvage
2 se rattraper *vpr* (**a**) *(se retenir)* to catch oneself in time; **se r. à qch** to catch hold of sth (**b**) *(se reprendre)* to stop oneself (**c**) *(se faire pardonner)* to make up for it (**d**) *(compenser son retard)* to catch up

rature [ratyr] *nf* crossing-out, deletion; **faire une r.** to make a deletion

raturer [ratyre] *vt (mot)* to cross out, to delete; **les devoirs raturés ne seront pas corrigés** homework with too many crossings-out will not be marked

rauque [rok] *adj (cri)* raucous; *(voix) (enrouée)* hoarse; *(voilée)* husky

ravagé, -e [ravaʒe] *adj* (**a**) *(visage)* ravaged, haggard (**b**) *Fam (fou)* crazy, nuts

ravager [45] [ravaʒe] *vt* to ravage, to devastate

ravages [ravaʒ] *nmpl (du feu, de la tempête)* devastation; *(d'une guerre, d'une maladie)* ravages; **faire des r.** to wreak havoc; *Fig (mode)* to be all the rage; *(personne séduisante)* to break hearts

ravageur, -euse [ravaʒœr, -øz] *adj* devastating

ravalement [ravalmɑ̃] *nm* cleaning

ravaler [ravale] **1** *vt* (**a**) *(façade)* to clean; **se faire r. la façade** to have a facelift (**b**) *(avaler de nouveau) (salive)* to swallow; *Fig* **faire r. ses paroles à qn** to make sb eat his/her words (**c**) *(cacher) (sanglot, larmes)* to choke back; *(colère, indignation, reproches)* to stifle (**d**) *(abaisser)* **r. qn à** to lower sb to
2 se ravaler *vpr* to lower oneself; *Fam* **se r. la façade** to put on the warpaint

ravaudage [ravodaʒ] *nm Vieilli (de vêtements)* mending, repairing

ravauder [ravode] *vt* (**a**) *Vieilli (vêtements)* to mend, to repair (**b**) *Can (errer)* to wander about; *(faire l'idiot)* to fool around (**c**) *Can (faire du bruit)* to make a racket

rave¹ [rav] *nf (radis)* radish; *(navet)* turnip

rave² [rɛv] *nf (soirée)* rave

ravi, -e [ravi] *adj* delighted (**de** with); **je suis r. de vous voir** I'm delighted to see you; **je suis r. que ça te plaise** I'm delighted you like it; **r. de vous connaître** pleased to meet you

ravier [ravje] *nm* hors d'oeuvres dish

ravigotant, -e [ravigɔtɑ̃, -ɑ̃t] *adj Fam* invigorating

ravigote [ravigɔt] *nf* = highly seasoned oil-and-vinegar dressing with herbs and capers

ravigoter [ravigɔte] *vt Fam* **r. qn** to put new life into sb

ravin [ravɛ̃] *nm* ravine

ravine [ravin] *nf* gully

raviné, -e [ravine] *adj (visage)* deeply lined

ravinement [ravinmɑ̃] *nm* gullying

raviner [ravine] *vt* to gully

ravioli [ravjɔli] *nm* piece of ravioli; **des raviolis** ravioli

ravir [ravir] *vt* (**a**) *(plaire)* to delight; **à r.** *(jouer, chanter)* delightfully; **belle à r.** ravishingly beautiful; **aller à r. à qn** to suit sb beautifully (**b**) *Litt* **r. qch à qn** to rob sb of sth

raviser [ravize] **se raviser** *vpr* to change one's mind

ravissant, -e [ravisɑ̃, -ɑ̃t] *adj* delightful

ravissement [ravismɑ̃] *nm* (**a**) *(enchantement)* rapture, ecstasy; **avec r.** *(écouter, contempler)* with great delight (**b**) *Litt (d'une femme)* ravishing

ravisseur, -euse [ravisœr, -øz] *nm,f* abductor

ravitaillement [ravitajmɑ̃] *nm (action)* supplying (**en** with); *(marchandises)* supplies; **r. (en carburant)** refuelling

ravitailler [ravitaje] **1** *vt (personne, groupe)* to supply; *(véhicule)* to refuel
2 se ravitailler *vpr* to get in supplies; **se r. (en carburant)** to refuel

raviver [ravive] *vt* (**a**) *(feu)* to rekindle (**b**) *(couleur)* to brighten up (**c**) *(colère, souvenir, querelle)* to rekindle; *(douleur)* to revive

ravoir [ravwar] **1** *vt* (**a**) *(avoir de nouveau)* to have back (**b**) *Fam (nettoyer)* to get clean
2 se ravoir *vpr Belg (reprendre haleine)* to get one's breath back; *(retrouver ses esprits)* to come to one's senses

rayé, -e [rɛje] *adj* (**a**) *(tissu)* striped (**b**) *(disque, parquet, carrosserie de voiture)* scratched (**c**) *(canon de fusil)* rifled

rayer [53] [rɛje] *vt* (**a**) *(verre, carrosserie de voiture, disque)* to scratch (**b**) *(mention, mot)* to cross out; **r. qn du barreau** to strike sb off; **r. qn/le nom de qn d'une liste** to cross sb/sb's name off a list

rayon¹ [rɛjɔ̃] *nm* (**a**) *(faisceau) (de lumière)* ray, beam; **r. laser** laser beam; **r. de soleil** sunbeam; *Fig* **être le r. de soleil de qn** to be sb's ray of sunshine; **rayons X** X-rays (**b**) *(d'un cercle)* radius; **dans un r. de 2 kilomètres (autour de)** within a radius of 2 kilometres (of); **r. d'action** range (**c**) *(de roue)* spoke

rayon² *nm* (**a**) *(dans un magasin)* department; *Fig* **c'est mon r.** that's my department (**b**) *(d'une étagère)* shelf; *Fam Fig* **en connaître un r. (sur qch)** to be well clued up (about sth) (**c**) **r. de miel** honeycomb

rayonnage [rɛjɔnaʒ] *nm* shelving, shelves

rayonnant, -e [rɛjɔnɑ̃, -ɑ̃t] *adj (chaleur, lumière)* radiant; *Fig (visage)* beaming; **r. de bonheur** radiant with happiness; **r. de santé** glowing with health

rayonne [rɛjɔn] *nf* rayon

rayonnement [rɛjɔnmɑ̃] *nm* (**a**) *(du soleil)* radiance (**b**) *(influence)* influence

rayonner [rɛjɔne] *vi* (**a**) *(soleil, visage)* to beam; **r. de joie** to beam with joy (**b**) *(voyager)* to travel around *(from a central base)* (**c**) *(se propager)* to spread its influence (**d**) *(avenues, douleur)* to radiate

rayure [rɛjyr] *nf* (**a**) *(motif)* stripe; **tissu à rayures** striped *or* stripy material (**b**) *(sur miroir, sur carrosserie)* scratch (**c**) *(d'un canon de fusil)* groove

raz de marée [radmare] *nm inv* tidal wave; *Fig* **r. électoral** landslide

razzia [razja] *nf* raid; *Fam* **faire une r. sur qch** to raid sth

RD [ɛrde] *nf* (*abrév* **route départementale**) = designation of secondary road, *Br* ≃ B-road

RDA [ɛrda] *nf Anciennement* (*abrév* **République démocratique allemande**) GDR

rdc (*abrév* **rez-de-chaussée**) *Br* ground *orAm* first floor

RDS [ɛrdeɛs] *nm* (*abrév* **Remboursement de la Dette Sociale**) = contribution paid by every taxpayer in France towards the social security deficit

ré [re] *nm inv* (*note*) D; (*chantée*) re

réabonnement [reabɔnmã] *nm* subscription renewal

réabonner [reabɔne] **1** *vt* **r. qn** to renew sb's subscription (**à** to)
 2 se réabonner *vpr* to renew one's subscription (**à** to)

réac [reak] *adj & nmf Fam Péj* reactionary

réaccoutumer [reakutyme] **1** *vt* to reaccustom (**à** to)
 2 se réaccoutumer *vpr* **se r. à qch** to become reaccustomed to sth

réacteur [reaktœr] *nm* (**a**) (*moteur*) jet engine (**b**) **r. nucléaire** nuclear reactor

réaction [reaksjɔ̃] *nf* (**a**) (*attitude*) reaction; **n'avoir aucune r.** not to react; **il eut une r. de peur/de colère** his reaction was one of fear/anger; **faire qch par r.** to do sth as a reaction; **en r. à qch** in reaction to sth; **rester sans r.** not to react; **r. en chaîne** chain reaction (**b**) (*d'un organe, du corps*) reaction; **r. cutanée** skin reaction

réactionnaire [reaksjɔnɛr] *adj & nmf Péj* reactionary

réactiver [reaktive] *vt* (*feu, négociations, sentiments*) to revive

réactualisation [reaktɥalizasjɔ̃] *nf* updating

réactualiser [reaktɥalize] *vt* to update

réadaptation [readaptasjɔ̃] *nf* rehabilitation

réadapter [readapte] **1** *vt* to rehabilitate
 2 se réadapter *vpr* to readjust

réaffirmer [reafirme] *vt* to reaffirm

réagir [reaʒir] *vi* to react (**à/contre** to/against); **r. sur qch** to affect sth

réajuster [reaʒyste] = **rajuster**

réalisable [realizabl] *adj* (**a**) (*projet, proposition*) feasible; (*rêve*) attainable (**b**) (*avoirs*) realizable

réalisateur, -trice [realizatœr, -tris] *nm,f* (*d'un film, d'un feuilleton*) director; (*d'une émission de radio ou de télévision*) producer

réalisation [realizasjɔ̃] *nf* (**a**) (*d'un projet*) realization; (*d'un rêve*) fulfilment (**b**) (*d'un film, d'un feuilleton*) direction; (*d'une émission de radio ou de télévision*) production (**c**) (*d'une œuvre d'art*) creation

réaliser [realize] **1** *vt* (**a**) (*comprendre*) to realize (**que** that) (**b**) (*ambition, projet*) to realize; (*rêve*) to fulfil (**c**) (*œuvre d'art*) to create (**d**) (*film, feuilleton*) to direct; (*émission de radio ou de télévision*) to produce (**e**) (*bénéfices*) to make; **r. un chiffre d'affaires de 10 millions d'euros** to have a turnover of 10 million euros
 2 se réaliser *vpr* (**a**) (*prédiction, rêve*) to come true (**b**) (*personne*) to fulfil oneself

réalisme [realism] *nm* realism; **faire preuve de r.** to be realistic; **avec r.** realistically

réaliste [realist] **1** *adj* (*personne, description, portrait*) realistic; (*écrivain, peintre*) realist
 2 nmf realist

réalité [realite] *nf* reality; **c'est une r.** it's a reality; **en r.** in reality; *Ordinat* **r. virtuelle** virtual reality

réamorcer [16] [reamɔrse] *Ordinat* **1** *vt* to reboot
 2 se réamorcer *vpr* to reboot

réanimation [reanimasjɔ̃] *nf* resuscitation; **service de r.** intensive care unit; **en r.** in intensive care

réanimer [reanime] *vt* to resuscitate

réapparaître [20] [reaparɛtr] *vi* to reappear; (*douleur*) to come back, to recur

réapparition [reaparisjɔ̃] *nf* reappearance; (*d'une douleur*) recurrence

réapprovisionner [reaprɔvizjɔne] **1** *vt* (*magasin*) to restock (**en** with); (*personne*) to resupply (**en** with)
 2 se réapprovisionner *vpr* to stock up again (**en** with)

réargenter [rearʒɑ̃te] *vt* to resilver

réarmement [rearməmɑ̃] *nm* rearmament

réarmer [rearme] **1** *vt* (**a**) (*région, pays*) to rearm (**b**) (*arme à feu*) to recock; (*appareil photo*) to reset
 2 *vi* (*pays, région*) to rearm

réassortir [reasɔrtir] **1** *vt* (*magasin*) to restock
 2 se réassortir *vpr* to restock

rebaptiser [rəbatize] *vt* (*rue*) to rename

rébarbatif, -ive [rebarbatif, -iv] *adj* (**a**) (*sujet, tâche*) daunting; (*style*) off-putting (**b**) (*visage, mine*) forbidding

rebâtir [rəbatir] *vt* to rebuild

rebattre [11] [rəbatr] *vt* **r. les oreilles à qn de qch** to go on to sb about sth

rebattu, -e [rəbaty] *adj* (*histoire, sujet*) hackneyed

rebelle [rəbɛl] **1** *adj* (**a**) (*personne, esprit*) rebellious; (*camp, armée, troupes*) rebel; **r. à toute discipline** unamenable to discipline (**b**) (*mèches, boucle*) unruly (**c**) (*fièvre*) stubborn; **r. aux antibiotiques** resistant to antibiotics
 2 nmf rebel

rebeller [rəbɛle] **se rebeller** *vpr* to rebel (**contre** against)

rébellion [rebɛljɔ̃] *nf* rebellion

rebelote [rəbəlɔt] *exclam Fam* here we go again!

rebiffer [rəbife] **se rebiffer** *vpr Fam* to hit back (**contre** at)

rebiquer [rəbike] *vi Fam* (*mèche*) to stick up

reblochon [rəblɔʃɔ̃] *nm* Reblochon (*type of cheese from Savoie*)

reboisement [rəbwazmã] *nm* reafforestation

reboiser [rəbwaze] *vt* to reafforest

rebond [rəbɔ̃] *nm* (*d'un ballon*) bounce

rebondi, -e [rəbɔ̃di] *adj* (*joues, personne*) chubby

rebondir [rəbɔ̃dir] *vi* (**a**) (*ballon*) to bounce; **r. contre** *ou* **sur qch** to bounce off sth (**b**) *Fig* (*affaire, crise*) to be revived; **faire r. la discussion** to get the discussion going again (**c**) *Can* (*chèque*) to bounce

rebondissement [rəbɔ̃dismã] *nm* (**a**) (*d'un ballon*) bounce (**b**) *Fig* (*d'une affaire*) revival

rebord [rəbɔr] *nm* (*d'une table, d'un puits*) edge; (*de fenêtre*) sill

reboucher [rəbuʃe] *vt* (**a**) (*bouteille*) to recork; (*tube*) to put the top back on (**b**) (*trou*) to fill in again

rebours [rəbur] **à rebours** *adv* (*à l'envers*) (*compter, lire*) backwards; (*dans le mauvais sens*) the wrong way; *Fig* the wrong way round

rebouteux, -euse [rəbutø, -øz] *nm,f Fam* bonesetter

reboutonner [rəbutɔne] **1** *vt* to button up again
 2 se reboutonner *vpr* to do oneself up again

rebrousse-poil [rəbruspwal] **à rebrousse-poil** *adv* the wrong way; **prendre qn à r.** to rub sb up the wrong way

rebrousser [rəbruse] *vt* **r. chemin** to turn back

rebuffade [rəbyfad] *nf* rebuff; **essuyer une r.** to meet with a rebuff

rébus [rebys] *nm* rebus

rebut [rǝby] *nm* (**article de**) **r.** reject; **mettre qch au r.** to throw sth out

rebutant, -e [rǝbytã, -ãt] *adj (tâche, manières, personne) (décourageant)* off-putting; *(repoussant)* repulsive

rebuter [rǝbyte] *vt* (**a**) *(décourager)* to put off (**b**) *(déplaire)* to disgust

récalcitrant, -e [rekalsitrã, -ãt] *adj & nm,f* recalcitrant

recaler [rǝkale] *vt Fam* to fail; **être recalé, se faire r.** to fail

récapitulatif, -ive [rekapitylatif, -iv] **1** *adj* recapitulatory

2 *nm* recapitulation

récapitulation [rekapitylasjɔ̃] *nf* recapitulation; **faire la r. de qch** to recapitulate sth

récapituler [rekapityle] *vt & vi* to recapitulate

recaser [rǝkaze] *Fam* **1** *vt* (**a**) *(retrouver un emploi à)* to find a new job for (**b**) *(retrouver un logement à)* to rehouse

2 se recaser *vpr* (**a**) *(retrouver un emploi)* to find a new job (**b**) *(se remarier)* to get hitched again

recel [rǝsɛl] *nm* receiving stolen goods; **r. de malfaiteur** harbouring a (known) criminal

receler [rǝsǝle] *vt* (**a**) *(biens volés)* to receive; *(criminel)* to harbour (**b**) *Litt (renfermer) (secret, trésor)* to conceal

receleur, -euse [rǝsǝlœr, -øz] *nm,f* receiver

récemment [resamã] *adv* recently

recensement [rǝsãsmã] *nm (d'objets)* inventory; *(de la population)* census

recenser [rǝsãse] *vt (objets)* to make an inventory of; *(habitants)* to take a census of

récent, -e [resã, -ãt] *adj* recent

recentrer [rǝsãtre] *vt* (**a**) *(parti politique)* to reorientate (**b**) *(balle)* to centre again

récépissé [resepise] *nm* receipt

réceptacle [reseptakl] *nm* (**a**) *(d'objets)* receptacle; *(de personnes)* gathering place (**b**) *Ordinat* **r. pour extension** extension slot

récepteur, -trice [reseptœr, -tris] **1** *adj* receiving

2 *nm* (**a**) *(de téléphone)* receiver (**b**) *Rad & TV* set, receiver (**c**) *Ordinat* **r. de données** data receiver

réceptif, -ive [reseptif, -iv] *adj* receptive (**à** to)

réception [resepsjɔ̃] *nf* (**a**) *(accueil)* reception; **faire une bonne/mauvaise r. à qn** to give sb a good/poor reception (**b**) *(d'une lettre, d'une commande, de biens)* receipt; **à payer à la r.** cash on delivery; **r. des travaux** acceptance of work (**c**) *(soirée)* reception (**d**) *(dans un hôtel)* reception (desk) (**e**) *(d'une radio)* reception (**f**) *(d'un gymnaste)* landing; *(d'un joueur de football)* control

réceptionner [resepsjɔne] **1** *vt* (**a**) *(marchandises livrées)* to take delivery of (**b**) *(ballon)* to take

2 se réceptionner *vpr* to land

réceptionniste [resepsjɔnist] *nmf* receptionist

récessif, -ive [resesif, -iv] *adj* recessive

récession [resesjɔ̃] *nf* recession

recette [rǝsɛt] *nf* (**a**) *(pour plat) & Fig* recipe (**de** for) (**b**) *(bureau)* tax office (**c**) *(gain)* **recettes** takings; **recettes fiscales** tax revenue; **faire r.** to be a success

recevable [rǝsǝvabl] *adj (excuse, témoignage)* admissible

recevant, -e [rǝsǝvã, -ãt] *adj Can (personne)* hospitable, who likes entertaining

receveur, -euse [rǝsǝvœr, -øz] *nm,f* (**a**) *(fonctionnaire)* **r. des contributions** tax collector; **r. des Postes** postmaster, *f* postmistress (**b**) *(de bus)* (bus) conductor, *f* (bus) conductress

recevoir [60] [rǝsǝvwar] **1** *vt* (**a**) *(lettre, coup de téléphone, fleurs)* to receive, to get (**de** from); **r. la visite de qn** to have a visit from sb; **r. des nouvelles de qn** to hear from sb; **je n'ai de conseils à r. de personne!** I don't need advice from anybody!; **nous avons bien reçu votre lettre** we are in receipt of your letter (**b**) *(blâme, gifle, coup, balle)* to get; *Fam* **qu'est-ce que j'ai reçu!** I really got it! (**c**) *(amis, invités)* to receive, to welcome; **être mal/bien reçu** to get a poor/good reception; **r. qn à dîner** to have sb (round) to dinner; **aimer r.** to enjoy entertaining; **savoir r.** to be a good host/hostess; **ils reçoivent très peu** they don't do much entertaining (**d**) *(clients)* to see; **le docteur ne reçoit que sur rendez-vous** the doctor will see patients by appointment only (**e**) *(proposition, projet)* to receive (**f**) *(élève, candidat)* to admit; **être reçu à l'Académie française** to be admitted to the Académie française; **être reçu à un examen** to pass an exam (**g**) *(pluie, soleil, lumière)* to get; **r. des radiations** to be exposed to radiation, to receive a dose of radiation (**h**) *(chaîne)* to get; *(station de radio)* to pick up, to receive (**i**) *(communion, absolution)* to receive

2 se recevoir *vpr (gymnaste)* to land

rechange [rǝʃãʒ] **de rechange** *adj* spare; *Fig* alternative

rechaper [rǝʃape] *vt (pneu)* to retread; **pneu rechapé** retread

réchapper [reʃape] *vi* **r. de qch** to survive sth

recharge [rǝʃarʒ] *nf* (**a**) *(de stylo, de briquet)* refill; **r. d'encre** ink refill (**b**) *(action) (d'une batterie)* recharging

rechargeable [rǝʃarʒabl] *adj (briquet, vaporisateur)* refillable; *(pile)* rechargeable

recharger [45] [rǝʃarʒe] **1** *vt* (**a**) *(batterie, pile)* to recharge; *Fam* **r. ses batteries** *ou* **ses accus** to recharge one's batteries; **r. un téléphone portable** *(recharger la batterie)* to charge (up) *or* recharge a *Br* mobile phone *or Am* cellphone; *(ajouter des unités)* to credit *or Br* top up a mobile phone, *Am* to refill a cellphone (**b**) *(camion, arme, appareil photo)* to reload (**c**) *(stylo, briquet, vaporisateur)* to refill

2 se recharger *vpr Ordinat* to reload

réchaud [reʃo] *nm (portable)* stove; **r. à gaz** gas ring

réchauffé, -e [reʃofe] **1** *adj* (**a**) *(plat)* reheated, warmed-up (**b**) *(plaisanterie)* stale

2 *nm* **c'est du r.** *(plaisanterie)* that's a stale joke; *(nouvelles, politique)* that's old hat

réchauffement [reʃofmã] *nm* warming up; **le r. de la planète** *ou* **de l'atmosphère** global warming

réchauffer [reʃofe] **1** *vt* (**a**) *(plat)* to reheat, to warm up (**b**) *(personne)* to warm up (**c**) *Fig (émotions)* to rekindle; *(cœur)* to warm

2 se réchauffer *vpr* (**a**) *(temps)* to get warmer (**b**) *(personne)* to get warm; **se r. les pieds/les mains** to warm one's feet/one's hands

rechausser [rǝʃose] **se rechausser** *vpr* to put one's shoes on again

rêche [rɛʃ] *adj* rough

recherche [rǝʃɛrʃ] *nf* (**a**) *(prospection, quête)* search (**de** for); *(de la célébrité, du pouvoir)* quest (**de** for), pursuit (**de** of); **être à la r. de** to be in search of (**b**) **recherches** *(par la police) (pour retrouver une personne disparue)* search, hunt; **faire des recherches**

to make inquiries (**c**) *(scientifique)* research (**sur** into); **faire de la r.** to do research; **faire des recherches sur qch** to do research into sth (**d**) *(raffinement)* elegance; **avec r.** elegantly; **sans r.** *(style)* straightforward (**e**) *Ordinat* find, search; **r. et remplacement** search and replace; **r. et remplacement global** global search and replace

recherché, -e [rəʃɛrʃe] *adj* (**a**) *(demandé) (objet)* sought-after (**b**) *(apprécié) (personne)* in demand (**c**) *(raffiné)* elegant; *(plat)* exquisite (**d**) *(criminel)* wanted

rechercher [rəʃɛrʃe] *vt* (**a**) *(chercher) (personne, objet, solution)* to look for, to search for; *(emploi)* to look for; *(sens, mot)* to look up; *(faveurs, honneurs)* to seek (**b**) *Ordinat* **r. qch** to search *or* do a search for sth; **r. et remplacer** to search and replace; **r. vers le bas/haut** to search down/up

rechigner [rəʃiɲe] *vi* **r. à qch** to balk at sth; **r. à faire qch** to be reluctant to do sth; **faire qch en rechignant** to do sth with bad grace; **faire qch sans r.** to do sth without (making) a fuss

rechute [rəʃyt] *nf* relapse; **faire une r.** to have a relapse

rechuter [rəʃyte] *vi* to have a relapse

récidive [residiv] *nf* (**a**) *(d'un délinquant)* repeat offence (**b**) *(d'une maladie)* recurrence

récidiver [residive] *vi* (**a**) *(délinquant)* to reoffend; *Fig* to do it again (**b**) *(maladie)* to recur

récidiviste [residivist] *nmf* repeat offender

récif [resif] *nm* reef; **r. de corail** *ou* **corallien** coral reef

récipient [resipjã] *nm* container

réciproque [resiprɔk] **1** *adj (sentiments)* mutual; *(bénéfices, accord, concessions)* reciprocal; **elle ne veut plus me voir, et c'est r.** she doesn't want to see me again, and the feeling's mutual
2 *nf* **la r.** the reverse

réciproquement [resiprɔkmã] *adv* mutually; **et r.** and vice versa

récit [resi] *nm* story; **faire le r. de qch** to give an account of sth

récital, -als [resital] *nm* recital

récitant, -e [resitã, -ãt] *nm,f* narrator

récitation [resitasjã] *nf* recitation

réciter [resite] *vt* to recite

réclamation [reklamasjã] *nf* complaint; **faire une r.** to make a complaint; **le service des réclamations, les réclamations** the complaints department

réclame [reklam] *nf* (**a**) *(publicité)* advertising; **faire de la r. pour qch** to advertise sth (**b**) *(annonce)* advertisement (**c**) *(promotion)* **en r.** on special offer

réclamer [reklame] **1** *vt* (**a**) *(demander)* to ask for; *(droit, allocation)* to claim; **la fillette réclame ses parents** the little girl is calling for her parents (**b**) *(exiger)* to demand; **r. des dommages et intérêts** to claim damages (**c**) *(nécessiter)* to require
2 se réclamer *vpr* **se r. de qn** *(se recommander)* to mention sb's name; **se r. de qch** *(d'un parti, d'une idéologie)* to identify with sth

reclasser [rəklase] *vt* (**a**) *(fichiers)* to reclassify (**b**) *(chômeur)* to find a new job for (**c**) *(personnel, salaires)* to regrade

reclus, -e [rəkly, -yz] **1** *adj* cloistered
2 *nm,f* recluse

réclusion [reklyzjã] *nf (peine)* imprisonment; **r. à perpétuité** life imprisonment

recoiffer [rəkwafe] **se recoiffer** *vpr* (**a**) *(arranger ses cheveux)* to redo one's hair (**b**) *(remettre son chapeau)* to put one's hat back on

recoin [rəkwɛ̃] *nm (d'un lieu)* nook; *(de la mémoire)* recess

reçois, reçoit, reçoive *etc voir* **recevoir**

recoller [rəkɔle] *vt (objet cassé)* to stick back together; *(timbre)* to stick back on; *(enveloppe)* to stick back down; *Fam* **r. les morceaux** to patch things up

récoltant, -e [rekɔltã, -ãt] **1** *adj* **apiculteur r.** honey producer; **viticulteur r.** = winegrower who harvests his own grapes
2 *nm,f* **mis en bouteille chez le r.** estate-bottled

récolte [rekɔlt] *nf* (**a**) *(action)* harvesting; **faire la r.** to harvest the crops (**b**) *(résultat)* harvest (**c**) *(d'informations)* crop

récolter [rekɔlte] *vt (cultures)* to harvest; *Fig (renseignements, documents)* to collect; *Fam (ennuis, maladie)* to get

recommandable [rəkɔmãdabl] *adj (personne, lieu)* reputable; **peu r.** *(personne, lieu)* disreputable

recommandation [rəkɔmãdasjã] *nf (appui, conseil)* recommendation

recommandé, -e [rəkɔmãde] **1** *adj* (**a**) *(lettre)* registered (**b**) *(conseillé)* recommended; **ce n'est pas très r.** it's not very advisable
2 *nm* **en r.** *(lettre)* registered

recommander [rəkɔmãde] **1** *vt* (**a**) *(lieu, produit, personne)* to recommend (**à** to) (**b**) *(conseiller)* to advise; **r. à qn de faire qch** to advise sb to do sth; **r. la prudence à qn** to advise sb to be cautious (**c**) *(lettre, paquet)* to register
2 se recommander *vpr (demander de l'aide)* **se r. à qn** to commend oneself to sb (**b**) **se r. de qn** *(pour un emploi)* to give sb's name as a reference (**c**) *Suisse (insister)* **se r. auprès de qn que...** to point out to sb that...

recommencement [rəkɔmãsmã] *nm* renewal; **la vie est un éternel** *ou* **perpétuel r.** life is a constant succession of new beginnings

recommencer [16] [rəkɔmãse] **1** *vt* to start *or* begin again
2 *vi* to start *or* begin again; **ne recommencez pas!** don't do it again!
3 recommencer à *vt ind* **r. à faire qch** to start *or* begin to do sth again

récompense [rekɔ̃pãs] *nf* reward; *(prix)* award; **1000 euros de r.** 1,000 euros reward; **en r. (de)** as a reward (for)

récompenser [rekɔ̃pãse] *vt* to reward (**de** for); **ce film a été récompensé à Cannes** this film won an award at Cannes

recomposer [rəkɔ̃poze] *vt (numéro de téléphone)* to redial

recompter [rəkɔ̃te] *vt* to count again

réconciliation [rekɔ̃siljasjã] *nf* reconciliation

réconcilier [66] [rekɔ̃silje] **1** *vt* to reconcile (**avec** with); **r. qn avec la vie** to renew sb's appetite for life
2 se réconcilier *vpr* to make it up (**avec** with)

reconductible [rəkɔ̃dyktibl] *adj (contrat, bail)* renewable

reconduction [rəkɔ̃dyksjã] *nf* (**a**) *(d'un bail, d'un contrat)* renewal; **r. tacite** *(d'un accord)* tacit renewal (**b**) *(d'un budget, d'une politique, d'une grève)* continuation

reconduire [18] [rəkɔ̃dɥir] *vt* (**a**) *(personne)* to take sb back; **r. qn (à la porte)** to show sb out; **r. qn à la**

frontière to escort sb back to the border (**b**) *(bail, contrat)* to renew (**c**) *(budget, politique, grève)* to continue

réconfort [rekɔ̃fɔr] *nm* comfort

réconfortant, -e [rekɔ̃fɔrtɑ̃, -ɑ̃t] *adj* comforting

réconforter [rekɔ̃fɔrte] *vt* to comfort; **cela me réconforte de le savoir** I'm glad to know it

reconnaissable [rəkɔnɛsabl] *adj* recognizable (**à** by or from); **r. entre tous** unmistakable

reconnaissance [rəkɔnɛsɑ̃s] *nf* (**a**) *(action de reconnaître)* recognition; **en r. de qch** in recognition of sth (**b**) *(d'un droit, d'un gouvernement)* recognition; **r. de dette** IOU (**c**) *(gratitude)* gratitude (**pour** for); **avec r.** gratefully (**d**) *Mil* reconnaissance; **partir en r.** to go off on reconnaissance; *Fam Fig* to go and reconnoitre (**e**) *Ordinat* **r. de l'écriture manuscrite** handwriting recognition; **r. optique des caractères** optical character recognition, OCR; **r. de la parole, r. vocale** speech recognition

reconnaissant, -e [rəkɔnɛsɑ̃, -ɑ̃t] *adj* grateful; **être r. à qn de qch** to be grateful to sb for sth; **je vous serais r. de ne plus en parler** I'd be grateful if you didn't mention it again

reconnaître [20] [rəkɔnɛtr] **1** *vt* (**a**) *(identifier)* to recognize (**à** by or from); **je te reconnais bien là!** that's just like you! (**b**) *(admettre)* *(vérité, droit, gouvernement)* to recognize; *(enfant)* to acknowledge; **r. qn pour chef** to recognize sb as leader (**c**) *(avouer)* *(erreur, faute)* to acknowledge; **je reconnais que j'ai eu tort** I admit I was wrong (**d**) *(accorder)* **je lui reconnais des qualités** I recognize his/her qualities (**e**) *(position, terrain)* to reconnoitre
2 se reconnaître *vpr* (**a**) *(soi-même)* to recognize oneself (**b**) *(l'un l'autre)* to recognize each other (**c**) *(s'avouer)* **se r. vaincu/coupable** to acknowledge defeat/one's guilt (**d**) *(se retrouver)* to find one's way around; **je ne me reconnais plus** I can't find my way around any more (**e**) *(être identifiable)* **le mâle se reconnaît à...** the male can be recognized by...

reconnu, -e [rəkɔny] *adj* recognized

reconquérir [7] [rəkɔ̃kerir] *vt (estime, amitié)* to win back; *(territoire)* to reconquer

reconquête [rəkɔ̃kɛt] *nf* reconquest

reconsidérer [34] [rəkɔ̃sidere] *vt* to reconsider

reconstituant, -e [rəkɔ̃stituɑ̃, -ɑ̃t] *adj & nm* tonic

reconstituer [rəkɔ̃stitɥe] *vt* (**a**) *(reformer)* *(armée, gouvernement)* to reconstitute; *(société, parti)* to revive; *(fortune, forces)* to build up again (**b**) *(rétablir)* *(objet archéologique, faits)* to piece together; *(bâtiment, quartier)* to restore (**c**) *(avec simulation)* *(crime)* to reconstruct

reconstitution [rəkɔ̃stitysjɔ̃] *nf (d'un crime, d'une bataille)* reconstruction; **r. historique** historical reconstruction

reconstruction [rəkɔ̃stryksjɔ̃] *nf* reconstruction, rebuilding

reconstruire [18] [rəkɔ̃strɥir] *vt* to reconstruct, to rebuild

reconversion [rəkɔ̃vɛrsjɔ̃] *nf* (**a**) *(d'une usine)* conversion; **r. économique** economic restructuring (**b**) *(d'une personne)* retraining

reconvertir [rəkɔ̃vɛrtir] **1** *vt* (**a**) *(entreprise)* to convert (**b**) *(personne)* to retrain
2 se reconvertir *vpr (entreprise)* to convert (**dans** to); *(personne)* to retrain; **se r. dans qch** to retrain for a new career in sth

recopier [66] [rəkɔpje] *vt* (**a**) *(faire un double de)* to recopy (**b**) *(mettre au propre)* to copy out

record [rəkɔr] **1** *adj inv (chiffre, vitesse)* record
2 *nm* record; **détenir le r. (de qch)** to hold the record (for sth); **battre le r. (de qch)** to break the record (for sth)

recordman [rəkɔrdman] *(pl* **recordmen** [rəkɔrdmɛn]*) nm* (men's) record holder

recordwoman [rəkɔrdwuman] *(pl* **recordwomen** [rəkɔrdwumɛn]*) nf* (women's) record holder

recoucher [rəkuʃe] **1** *vt (personne)* to put to bed again
2 se recoucher *vpr* to go back to bed

recoudre [21] [rəkudr] *vt (bouton)* to sew back on; *(déchirure, plaie)* to sew or stitch up; *Fam (personne)* to stitch up

recoupement [rəkupmɑ̃] *nm* crosscheck; **faire le r.** to crosscheck; **par r.** by crosschecking

recouper [rəkupe] **1** *vt* (**a**) *(couper à nouveau)* *(vêtement)* to recut; **r. du pain** to cut some more bread; **r. une tranche de gâteau** to cut another slice of cake (**b**) *(faire coïncider)* to confirm; **r. des témoignages** to crosscheck testimony
2 se recouper *vpr (témoignages)* to tally

recourbé, -e [rəkurbe] *adj (bec)* curved; *(nez)* hooked

recourber [rəkurbe] **1** *vt* to bend
2 se recourber *vpr* to bend

recourir [22] [rəkurir] **1** *vt (épreuve sportive)* to run again
2 *vi (courir de nouveau)* to run again
3 recourir à *vt ind* (**a**) *(personne)* to turn to (**b**) *(moyen, violence)* to resort to

recours [rəkur] *nm* (**a**) *(personne, chose)* recourse; **en dernier r.** as a last resort; **avoir r. à qn** to turn to sb; **avoir r. à qch** to resort to sth (**b**) *Jur* **r. en cassation** appeal; *Can* **r. collectif** class action; **r. en grâce** petition for reprieve

recouvrement [rəkuvrəmɑ̃] *nm (de dettes, d'une facture)* recovery; *(de l'impôt)* collection

recouvrer [rəkuvre] *vt* (**a**) *(biens, argent, santé)* to recover; *(forces, liberté, vue)* to regain; *(courage, enthousiasme)* to get back (**b**) *(percevoir)* *(dettes)* to recover; *(impôts)* to collect

recouvrir [52] [rəkuvrir] *vt* (**a**) *(couvrir de nouveau)* *(cahier, toit)* to re-cover; *(enfant)* to cover up again (**b**) *(couvrir complètement)* to cover (**de** with) (**c**) *(tapisser)* to cover (**de** with) (**d**) *(inclure)* to cover

recracher [rəkraʃe] *vt* to spit out

récré [rekre] *nf Fam Br* break, *Am* recess; *(pour les plus jeunes)* playtime

récréatif, -ive [rekreatif, -iv] *adj (activité)* entertaining; *(lecture)* light

récréation [rekreasjɔ̃] *nf* (**a**) *(à l'école) Br* break, *Am* recess; *(pour les plus jeunes)* playtime (**b**) *(détente)* recreation

recréer [24] [rəkree] *vt* to re-create

récrier [66] [rekrije] **se récrier** *vpr (mécontents)* to protest (**contre** about)

récrimination [rekriminasjɔ̃] *nf* recrimination

récriminer [rekrimine] *vi* to make recriminations (**contre** against)

récrire [30] [rekrir] = **réécrire**

récriture [rekrityr] = **réécriture**

recroquevillé, -e [rəkrɔkvije] *adj* huddled up

recroqueviller [rəkrɔkvije] **se recroqueviller** *vpr (personne)* to huddle up; *(papier, feuille morte)* to shrivel up

recru, -e¹ [rəkry] *adj Litt* **r. (de fatigue)** exhausted

recrudescence [rəkrydesɑ̃s] *nf* renewed outbreak

recrue² [rəkry] *nf* recruit; **faire une nouvelle r.** to gain a new recruit

recrutement [rəkrytmɑ̃] *nm* recruitment

recruter [rəkryte] **1** *vt* to recruit; **r. par concours** to recruit by competition

2 se recruter *vpr* to be recruited (**parmi** from)

rectal, -e, -aux, -ales [rɛktal, -o] *adj* rectal

rectangle [rɛktɑ̃gl] *nm* rectangle

rectangulaire [rɛktɑ̃gylɛr] *adj* rectangular

recteur [rɛktœr] *nm (d'une académie) Br* director *or Am* commissioner of education

rectificatif, -ive [rɛktifikatif, -iv] **1** *adj (lettre)* of amendment; *(texte, facture)* amended

2 *nm* correction

rectification [rɛktifikasjɔ̃] *nf (d'un texte, d'un calcul, d'une erreur)* correction; *(d'un compte, d'une courbe)* adjustment; *(d'un alignement)* straightening; **faire** *ou* **apporter une r.** to make a correction

rectifier [66] [rɛktifje] *vt* (**a**) *(texte, calcul, erreur)* correct; *(prix, compte, courbe)* to adjust; *(alignement)* to straighten; **r. le tir** to adjust the range; *Fig* to take a slightly different tack (**b**) *Fam (tuer)* to bump off

rectiligne [rɛktilin] *adj (mouvement, figure)* rectilinear; *(avenue)* straight

rectitude [rɛktityd] *nf (d'un jugement, d'un raisonnement)* soundness

recto [rɛkto] *nm* front, *Spéc* recto; **r. verso** on both sides

rectorat [rɛktɔra] *nm* ≃ *Br* local education authority, *Am* board of education

rectum [rɛktɔm] *nm* rectum

reçu¹, -e¹ *pp de* **recevoir**

reçu², -e² [rəsy] **1** *nm* receipt

2 *nm,f (à un examen)* successful candidate

recueil [rəkœj] *nm (de poèmes, de chansons, de recettes)* collection; *(de lois)* body; **r. de morceaux choisis** anthology

recueillement [rəkœjmɑ̃] *nm* meditation; **avec r.** meditatively

recueilli, -e [rəkœji] *adj* meditative

recueillir [5] [rəkœjir] **1** *vt* (**a**) *(argent, renseignements)* to collect (**b**) *(votes)* to win; *Fig* **r. le fruit de qch** to reap the fruit of sth (**c**) *(personne, animal)* to take in (**d**) *(miel)* to gather (**e**) *Jur* **r. un héritage** to inherit

2 se recueillir *vpr* to meditate; **se r. pour prier** to gather one's thoughts before praying

recuire [18] [rəkɥir] *vt (plat)* to cook longer

recul [rəkyl] *nm* (**a**) *(mouvement) (d'un glacier, d'une armée)* retreat; *(d'un canon)* recoil; **avoir un mouvement de r.** to recoil (**b**) *(déclin)* decline (**c**) *(baisse)* decline (**de** in) (**d**) *(espace nécessaire)* room to move back (**e**) *Fig (distance)* **considérer qch avec du r.** to consider sth with detachment; **manquer de r.** to be too closely involved; **prendre du r.** to stand back from things

reculade [rəkylad] *nf (d'une armée)* retreat; *Fig & Péj* climbdown

reculé, -e [rəkyle] *adj (endroit, époque)* remote

reculer [rəkyle] **1** *vi* (**a**) *(aller en arrière) (personne)* to move back; *(automobiliste, voiture)* to reverse; *(troupes)* to retreat; *(glacier, eaux)* to recede; **faire r. la foule** to move the crowd back (**b**) *(régresser) (épidémie)* to lose ground; *(chômage)* to decline; *Fig* **faire r. la maladie** to bring the disease under control (**c**) *(renoncer)* to retreat (**devant** in the face of); **il ne re-**

cule devant rien nothing daunts him; **faire r. qn** to put sb off; **il est trop tard pour r.** it's too late to pull out; **c'est r. pour mieux sauter** it's just putting off the evil day

2 *vt* (**a**) *(meuble)* to move back; *(voiture)* to reverse (**b**) *(paiement, décision)* to postpone

reculons [rəkylɔ̃] **à reculons** *adv* backwards; *Fig (avec réticence)* unwillingly, under protest

récupérable [rekyperabl] *adj (déchets)* salvageable; **les heures supplémentaires sont récupérables** additional time off may be taken in lieu

récupération [rekyperasjɔ̃] *nf* (**a**) *(d'une somme d'argent, d'un objet)* recovery; **la r. des heures supplémentaires** time off in lieu; **temps de r.** *(d'un sportif)* recovery time (**b**) *(de déchets)* salvage (**c**) *(d'un parti, d'une pensée)* exploitation

récupérer [34] [rekypere] *vt* (**a**) *(objet prêté ou perdu)* to get back, to recover (**b**) *(passer prendre) (personne, affaires, objet)* to collect; *(bagages)* to retrieve, to reclaim (**c**) *(retrouver) (forces)* to recover (**d**) *(recycler)* to salvage (**e**) *(détourner à son profit) (mouvement, idée)* to exploit (**f**) **r. des heures supplémentaires** to take time off in lieu

récurer [rekyre] *vt* to scour; **poudre/tampon à r.** scouring powder/pad

récurrent, -e [rekyrɑ̃, -ɑ̃t] *adj* recurring; *Ordinat* **processus r.** recursive process

récusable [rekyzabl] *adj (témoignage)* impugnable

récuser [rekyze] **1** *vt* to challenge

2 se récuser *vpr* to decline to give an opinion

recyclable [rəsiklabl] *adj* recyclable

recyclage [rəsiklaʒ] *nm* (**a**) *(de matériaux)* recycling (**b**) *(d'une personne)* retraining

recycler [rəsikle] **1** *vt* (**a**) *(matériaux)* to recycle (**b**) *(personne)* to retrain

2 se recycler *vpr (personne)* to retrain

rédacteur, -trice [redaktœr, -tris] *nm,f (d'un journal, d'un dictionnaire)* editor; **r. en chef** editor in chief

rédaction [redaksjɔ̃] *nf* (**a**) *(d'un texte)* writing (**b**) *(poste)* editorship; *(personnel)* editorial staff; *(département)* editorial department; **(salle de) r.** editorial office (**c**) *Scol* essay, composition

rédactionnel, -elle [redaksjɔnɛl] *adj* editorial

reddition [redisjɔ̃] *nf* surrender

redécouvrir [52] [rədekuvrir] *vt (auteur, œuvre)* to rediscover

redéfinir [rədefinir] *vt Ordinat (touche)* to redefine

redemander [rədəmɑ̃de] *vt* (**a**) *(en reposant une question)* to ask again; **r. de l'aide à qn** to ask sb again for help (**b**) *(pour en avoir plus)* **r. du pain/des timbres** to ask for more bread/stamps; **r. un litre/un kilo de qch** to ask for another litre/kilo of sth; **des gens comme ça, on en redemande** there aren't enough people like that in the world; *Ironique* **il en redemande** he's still asking for it (**c**) *(pour récupérer)* **r. qch** to ask for sth back

redémarrer [rədemare] *vi (voiture)* to start again; *(économie, ventes)* to take off again; *Ordinat* to reboot; **faire r. une voiture** to start a car again

rédemption [redɑ̃psjɔ̃] *nf* redemption

redéploiement [rədeplwamɑ̃] *nm* redeployment

redescendre [rədesɑ̃dr, rədɛsɑ̃dr] **1** *vi (en s'approchant)* to come back down; *(en s'éloignant)* to go back down; **r. de voiture** to get back out of the car

2 *vt* (**a**) *(apporter)* to bring back down; *(emporter)* to take back down (**b**) *(escalier, rivière)* to go/come back down

redevable [rədəvabl] *adj* **être r. de qch à qn** to be indebted to sb for sth; **je vous suis r. de 50 euros** I owe you 50 euros

redevance [rədəvãs] *nf (pour la télévision)* licence fee

redevenir [70] [rədəvənir] *vi* to become again; **r. silencieux** to fall silent again; **r. normal** to get back to normal

rédhibitoire [redibitwar] *adj (prix)* prohibitive; *(conditions, salaire)* unacceptable

rediffuser [rədifyze] *vt (émission)* to repeat, to rebroadcast; *(film)* to show again

rediffusion [rədifyzjõ] *nf (d'une émission)* repeat, rebroadcasting; *(d'un film)* rerun

rédiger [45] [rediʒe] *vt (contrat)* to draw up; *(article, lettre)* to write; *(ordonnance)* to write out; **savoir r.** to write well; **être bien/mal rédigé** to be well/badly written

redingote [rədɛ̃gɔt] *nf* (**a**) *(manteau cintré)* fitted coat (**b**) *(manteau à basques)* frock coat

redire [27a] [rədir] **1** *vt* (**a**) *(répéter)* to say again, to repeat; **pourrais-tu lui r. que...?** could you tell him/her again that...?; **on ne le redira jamais assez** it can never be said often enough (**b**) *(révéler)* to repeat (**à** to)

2 redire à *vt ind* **avoir** *ou* **trouver à r. à qch** to find fault with sth; **il n'y a rien à r. à cela** there's nothing wrong with that

redite [rədit] *nf* (useless) repetition

redondance [rədõdãs] *nf aussi Ordinat* redundancy; **redondances** redundancy

redondant, -e [rədõdã, -ãt] *adj* redundant

redonner [rədɔne] *vt* (**a**) *(donner davantage de)* **redonne-lui de la soupe** give him/her some more soup (**b**) *(rendre)* to give back; **r. de l'appétit/du courage à qn** to restore sb's appetite/courage; **r. envie à qn de faire qch** to make sb want to do sth again; **r. des forces à qn** to give sb back his/her strength (**c**) *(donner de nouveau)* to give again

redorer [rədɔre] *vt* to regild; *Fig* **r. son blason** to restore one's reputation

redoublant, -e [rədublɑ̃, -ɑ̃t] *nm,f (élève)* pupil repeating a year

redoublé, -e [rəduble] *adj* **frapper à coups redoublés** to knock harder

redoublement [rədubləmɑ̃] *nm* (**a**) *(de douleur, de joie, de prudence)* increase (**b**) *(d'une syllabe)* reduplication (**c**) *Scol* = repeating of a year; **le professeur principal décidera des redoublements** the head teacher will decide who will have to repeat the year

redoubler [rəduble] **1** *vt* (**a**) *(douleur, joie, prudence)* to increase; *(efforts)* to redouble (**b**) *Scol* **r. une classe** to repeat a year

2 *vi* (**a**) *Scol* to repeat a year (**b**) *(sentiment)* to intensify (**c**) *(orage)* to intensify, to become more severe; *(vent)* to grow stronger

3 redoubler de *vt ind* **r. de violence** *(orage, vent)* to become more and more severe; **r. d'efforts** to redouble one's efforts; **r. de prudence/d'attention/de douceur** to be twice as cautious/attentive/gentle

redoutable [rədutabl] *adj (adversaire, arme)* formidable; *(maladie)* dreadful

redouter [rədute] *vt* to dread; **r. de faire qch** to dread doing sth; **je redoute qu'il ne soit déjà trop tard** I'm afraid it's already too late

redoux [rədu] *nm* milder weather

redressement [rədrɛsmɑ̃] *nm* (**a**) *(économique, financier)* recovery (**b**) *(correction)* **r. fiscal** tax adjustment (**c**) *Jur* **r. judiciaire** receivership; **être mis en r. judiciaire** to go into receivership

redresser [rədrese] **1** *vt* (**a**) *(objet penché)* to put up straight; **r. la tête** to hold up one's head; *(la lever)* to raise one's head (**b**) *(rectifier) (erreur, situation)* to rectify; *(économie, entreprise)* to put back on its feet (**c**) *(bois courbé, tôle cabossée)* to straighten (out)

2 *vi (automobiliste)* to straighten up

3 se redresser *vpr* (**a**) *(personne)* to straighten up (**b**) *(économie, pays, ventes)* to recover

redresseur [rədrɛsœr] *nm* **r. de torts** righter of wrongs

réducteur, -trice [redyktœr, -tris] *adj (simpliste)* simplistic

réduction [redyksjõ] *nf* (**a**) *(des prix, des dépenses, de la production)* reduction (**de** in) (**b**) *(rabais)* reduction; **faire une r. de 25 euros (à qn)** to give (sb) a reduction of 25 euros (**c**) *(reproduction)* small reproduction (**d**) *(d'une fracture)* setting

réduire [18] [redɥir] **1** *vt* (**a**) *(diminuer)* to reduce (**de** by); *(texte)* to shorten, to cut; **réduit de moitié** half the size (**b**) *(transformer)* **r. qch en qch** to reduce sth to sth (**c**) *(contraindre)* **r. qn à qch** *(misère, désespoir)* to reduce sb to sth; **en être réduit à faire qch** to be reduced to doing sth (**d**) *(fracture)* to set (**e**) *(photographie, dessin)* to reduce

2 *vi (sauce)* to reduce; **faire r. qch** to reduce sth

3 se réduire *vpr* (**a**) **se r. à** *(se ramener à)* to come down to (**b**) **se r. en** *(se transformer en)* to be reduced to

réduit [redɥi] *nm (pièce)* small room

rééchelonnement [reeʃəlɔnmɑ̃] *nm* rescheduling

rééchelonner [reeʃəlɔne] *vt* to reschedule

réécrire [30] [reekrir] *vt* to rewrite

réécriture [reekrityr] *nf* rewriting

rééditer [reedite] *vt* (**a**) *(ouvrage)* to reissue (**b**) *(fait)* to repeat

réédition [reedisjõ] *nf* (**a**) *(d'un ouvrage)* reissue (**b**) *(d'un fait)* repeat

rééducation [reedykasjõ] *nf* (**a**) *(d'une partie du corps)* re-education; *(d'un handicapé, d'un accidenté)* rehabilitation; **faire de la r.** *(chez un kinésithérapeute)* to have physiotherapy (**b**) *(de délinquants)* rehabilitation

rééduquer [reedyke] *vt (handicapé, accidenté, délinquant)* to rehabilitate; *(partie du corps)* to re-educate

réel, -elle [reɛl] **1** *adj* real

2 *nm* (**a**) *(nombre)* real number (**b**) **le r.** *(la réalité)* reality

réélection [reelɛksjõ] *nf* re-election

réélire [44] [reelir] *vt* to re-elect

réellement [reɛlmɑ̃] *adv* really

réembaucher [reãboʃe] *vt* to take on again

réenregistrable [reãrʒistrabl] *adj* rerecordable

rééquilibrage [reekilibraʒ] *nm (de pneus)* balancing; *Fig* **le r. du budget** balancing the budget again

rééquilibrer [reekilibre] *vt (pneus)* to balance; *Fig (budget)* to balance again

réessayer [53] [reeseje] **1** *vt* to try again; *(vêtement)* to try on again

2 *vi* to try again

réévaluer [reevalɥe] *vt (monnaie)* to revalue; *(prix)* to reassess

réexamen [reɛgzamɛ̃] *nm* re-examination; *(d'une décision)* reconsideration

réexaminer [reɛgzamine] *vt* to re-examine; *(décision)* to reconsider

réexpédier [66] [reɛkspedje] *vt* (**a**) *(à une autre adresse)* to send on, to forward (**b**) *(à l'expéditeur)* to send back, to return

réexpédition [reɛkspedisjɔ̃] *nf* (**a**) *(à une autre adresse)* forwarding (**b**) *(à l'expéditeur)* return

refaire [36] [rəfɛr] **1** *vt* (**a**) *(faire à nouveau) (travail)* to do again, to redo; *(voyage)* to make again; **r. du riz** to make some more rice; **r. ses lacets** to tie one's laces again; *Hum* **ton éducation est à r.** where were you brought up?; **et si c'était à r.?** and if you had to do it again?; **r. le monde** to put the world to rights; **r. sa vie** to make a new life for oneself (**b**) *(remettre en état) (pièce, appartement)* to do up; **r. la peinture de qch** to repaint sth; **r. la moquette de qch** to recarpet sth; **r. qch à neuf** *(moteur)* to recondition sth; *(appartement)* to renovate sth completely (**c**) *Fam (duper)* to take in; **je me suis fait r. de 20 euros** I was done out of 20 euros

2 se refaire *vpr* (**a**) *(se changer)* to change the way one is; **on ne se refait pas** you can't change the way you are (**b**) *(se rétablir)* **se r. une santé** to recover (**c**) *Fam (financièrement)* to recoup one's losses (**d**) *(s'habituer)* **se r. à qch** to get used to sth again

réfection [refɛksjɔ̃] *nf* repair

réfectoire [refɛktwar] *nm* refectory, dining hall

référence [referɑ̃s] *nf* (**a**) *(renvoi)* reference (**à** to); **faire r. à qch** to refer to sth; **en r.** à with reference to (**b**) *(sur une lettre, sur un document)* reference; **r. à rappeler** please quote reference (**c**) *(d'employeur)* **références** references

référencer [16] [referɑ̃se] *vt Ordinat* to reference

référendum [referɛ̃dɔm] *nm* referendum; **faire un r.** to hold a referendum

référer [34] [refere] **1 référer à** *vt ind* **en r. à qn** to refer the matter to sb

2 se référer *vpr* **se r. à qch** to refer to sth; **se r. à un auteur** to refer to an author

refermer [rəfɛrme] **1** *vt* to shut *or* close again

2 se refermer *vpr (porte)* to close *or* shut again; *(fleur, blessure)* to close up

refiler [rəfile] *vt Fam* **r. qch à qn** *(pour s'en débarrasser)* to palm sth off on sb; *(maladie)* to give sb sth

réfléchi, -e [refleʃi] *adj* (**a**) *(personne)* thoughtful (**b**) *(action, opinion)* considered; **c'est tout r.** I've made up my mind; **tout bien r.** all things considered (**c**) *(verbe, pronom)* reflexive

réfléchir [refleʃir] **1** *vt* (**a**) *(image, lumière, son)* to reflect (**b**) **r. que** to realize that

2 *vi* to think (**à** *ou* **sur** about); **je réfléchis** I'm thinking; *(avant de décider)* I'm thinking about it; **sans r.** without thinking

3 se réfléchir *vpr* to be reflected

réfléchissant, -e [refleʃisɑ̃, -ɑ̃t] *adj* reflective

réflecteur, -trice [reflɛktœr, -tris] *adj* reflecting

reflet [rəflɛ] *nm* (**a**) *(dans un miroir, dans l'eau)* reflection; *(d'un tissu)* sheen; *(de la lune)* glint; **reflets** *(de cheveux)* highlights (**b**) *Fig (image)* reflection; **être le r. de qn** to be exactly like sb; **être le r. d'une époque** to symbolize an era

refléter [34] [rəflete] **1** *vt aussi Fig* to reflect

2 se refléter *vpr aussi Fig* to be reflected

refleurir [rəflœrir] **1** *vi* to flower again; *Fig* to flourish again

2 *vt (tombe)* to put fresh flowers on

réflexe [reflɛks] **1** *adj* reflex

2 *nm* reflex; **avoir de bons réflexes** to have good reflexes; **devenir un r.** to become automatic; **avoir le r. de faire qch** to do sth instinctively; **r. conditionné** conditioned reflex

réflexion [reflɛksjɔ̃] *nf* (**a**) *(d'une image, de la lumière, du son)* reflection (**b**) *(pensée)* reflection, thought; **r. faite, à la r.** on reflection, on second thoughts (**c**) *(remarque)* remark; **faire une r. à qn** to make a remark to sb

réflexologie [reflɛksɔləʒi] *nf* reflexology

réflexologiste [reflɛksɔləʒist] *nmf* reflexologist

refluer [rəflye] *vi (liquide)* to flow back; *(marée)* to ebb; *(foule)* to surge back

reflux [rəfly] *nm (de la marée)* ebb; *(d'une foule)* backward surge

refondre [rəfɔ̃dr] *vt (ouvrage)* to revise

refonte [rəfɔ̃t] *nf (d'un ouvrage)* revision

reformater [rəfɔrmate] *vt Ordinat (page, disque)* to reformat

réformateur, -trice [reformatœr, -tris] **1** *adj* reforming

2 *nm,f* reformer

réforme [refɔrm] *nf* reform; *Hist* **la R.** the Reformation

réformé, -e [reforme] **1** *adj (protestant)* Protestant

2 *nm,f (recrue)* recruit rejected as unfit; *(soldat)* soldier discharged as unfit

reformer [rəfɔrme] **1** *vt* to re-form; **r. les rangs** to fall into line again

2 se reformer *vpr* to re-form

réformer [reforme] *vt* (**a**) *(abus, loi)* to reform (**b**) *(recrue)* to reject as unfit; *(soldat)* to discharge as unfit

réformisme [reformism] *nm* reformism

réformiste [reformist] *adj & nmf* reformist

reformuler [rəfɔrmyle] *vt* to reformulate

refoulé, -e [rəfule] *adj* repressed

refouler [rəfule] **1** *vt* (**a**) *(faire reculer) (foule)* to drive or force back; *(étranger)* to turn away (**b**) *(sentiments, colère, souvenir)* to repress; *(larmes)* to hold back

2 *vi* **l'évier refoule** the water's coming up through the plughole in the sink

réfractaire [refraktɛr] *adj* (**a**) *(rebelle)* insubordinate; **r. à** *(loi, conseils, proposition)* unwilling to accept (**b**) *(brique, argile)* fireproof (**c**) *(prêtre)* non-juring

réfraction [refraksjɔ̃] *nf* refraction

refrain [rəfrɛ̃] *nm (d'une chanson)* chorus, refrain; *Fam* **c'est toujours le même r.** it's always the same old story

refréner [rəfrene], **réfréner** [refrene] [34] *vt* to curb

réfrigérant, -e [refriʒerɑ̃, -ɑ̃t] *adj* (**a**) *(appareil, produit)* refrigerating (**b**) *Fam (accueil, personne)* frosty

réfrigérateur [refriʒeratœr] *nm* refrigerator

réfrigération [refriʒerasjɔ̃] *nf* refrigeration

réfrigéré, -e [refriʒere] *adj (wagon)* refrigerated (**b**) *Fam (personne)* frozen

réfrigérer [34] [refriʒere] *vt (aliment, boisson)* to refrigerate

refroidir [rəfrwadir] **1** *vt* (**a**) *(eau)* to cool (down) (**b**) *Fig (amitié)* to cool; *(enthousiasme)* to dampen; *Fam* **sa réaction m'a refroidi** his/her reaction dampened my enthusiasm (**c**) *très Fam (tuer)* to bump off

2 *vi* (**a**) *(devenir froid)* to get cold; *(devenir moins chaud)* to cool down; **laisser r. qch** *(volontairement)* to let sth cool down; *(par négligence)* to let sth get cold (**b**) *(temps)* to get colder

3 se refroidir *vpr* (**a**) *(temps)* to get colder (**b**) *Fig*

(amitié, relations) to cool (**c**) *(prendre froid)* to catch a chill

refroidissement [rǝfrwadismɑ̃] *nm* (**a**) *(de la température)* drop in temperature; *(de l'eau)* cooling (**b**) *(indisposition)* chill (**c**) *Fig (dans une amitié, dans des relations)* cooling off

refuge [rǝfyʒ] **1** *nm* (**a**) *(lieu)* & *Fig* refuge; **trouver/ chercher r. (auprès de qn)** to find/seek refuge (with sb) (**b**) *(en montagne)* (mountain) hut (**c**) *(sur la route)* traffic island
  2 *adj* **valeur r.** safe investment

réfugié, -e [refyʒje] *nm,f* refugee

réfugier [66] [refyʒje] **se réfugier** *vpr* to take refuge (**dans** in)

refus [rǝfy] *nm (d'une invitation, d'une offre)* refusal; *(d'une proposition, d'un candidat, d'un manuscrit)* rejection; **essuyer un r.** to meet with a refusal; **opposer un r. à qn/qch** to turn sb/sth down; *Fam* **ce n'est pas de r.** I won't say no; **r. de priorité** *(infraction)* failure to *Br* give way or *Am* yield

refuser [rǝfyze] **1** *vt* (**a**) *(offre, invitation, demande)* to refuse, to turn down; *(proposition, marchandises, manuscrit)* to reject; **r. qch à qn** to refuse sb sth (**b**) *(clients, spectateurs)* to turn away (**c**) *(candidat)* **être refusé** to fail
  2 *vi* to refuse; **r. de faire qch** to refuse to do sth
  3 se refuser *vpr* (**a**) *(être rejeté)* **une offre pareille, ça ne se refuse pas** you can't refuse an offer like that (**b**) **se r. qch** *(se priver de)* to deny oneself sth; **ne rien se r.** not to stint oneself (**c**) *(résister)* **se r. à l'évidence** to shut one's eyes to the facts; **se r. à tout commentaire** to refuse to comment; **se r. à faire qch** to refuse to do sth

réfuter [refyte] *vt* to refute

regagner [rǝgaɲe] *vt* (**a**) *(confiance, affection, estime)* to regain, to get back (**b**) *(argent perdu)* to win back; **r. le temps perdu** to make up for lost time (**c**) **r. du terrain** *(reprendre l'avantage)* to make up lost ground (**d**) *(endroit)* to get back to; **r. son foyer** to get back home

regain [rǝgɛ̃] *nm (d'intérêt, d'activité)* renewal; **un r. d'espoir** renewed hope

régal, -als [regal] *nm* treat

régalade [regalad] *nf* **boire à la r.** to drink without letting the bottle touch one's lips

régaler [regale] **1** *vt* **r. qn** to give sb a delicious meal
  2 *vi Fam* **c'est moi qui régale** (it's) my treat
  3 se régaler *vpr* **je me régale** *(en mangeant)* I'm really enjoying it; *(je m'amuse)* I'm having a great time

regard [rǝgar] *nm* (**a**) *(coup d'œil)* look; **porter son r. sur qn/qch** to look at sb/sth; **jeter** *ou* **lancer un r. à qn** to glance at sb; **jeter un r. à** *ou* **sur qch** to glance at sth; **lancer un r. furieux à qn** to glare at sb; **chercher qn/qch du r.** to look round for sb/sth; **interroger qn du r.** to give sb a questioning look; **soustraire qn/qch aux regards (de qn)** to keep sb/sth hidden (from sb); **attirer le r.** to attract attention; **sous les regards de la foule** while the crowd looked on; *Fig* **porter un nouveau r./un r. critique sur qch** to take a fresh look/a critical look at sth (**b**) *(expression)* look (**c**) *(ouverture)* *(d'une porte)* peephole; *(d'un égout)* manhole (**d**) *(locutions)* **au r. de la loi** in the eyes of the law; **en r.** *(en face)* opposite

regardant, -e [rǝgardɑ̃, -ɑ̃t] *adj* (**a**) *Fam (avare)* careful with money (**b**) *(exigeant)* particular (**sur** about)

regarder [rǝgarde] **1** *vt* (**a**) *(personne, objet)* to look at; *(émission, film)* to watch; **r. qn droit dans les yeux**

to look sb in the eye; **r. qn fixement** to stare at sb; **r. qn faire qch** to watch sb do sth; **regarde où tu marches!** watch where you're going!; *Fam* **non, mais tu ne m'as pas regardé!** what do you take me for? (**b**) *(considérer)* to regard, to consider (**comme** as); **r. qch en face** to face up to sth; **r. les choses telles qu'elles sont** to see things as they are (**c**) *(concerner)* to concern; **cela ne regarde que moi** that's nobody's business but mine; **cela ne vous regarde pas** that's none of your business
  2 *vi* (**a**) *(observer)* to look; **r. autour de soi/en bas/ en arrière** to look round/down/back; **r. par** *ou* **à la fenêtre** *(du dedans)* to look out of the window; *(du dehors)* to look in through the window (**b**) *(être orienté)* **r. sur** *ou* **vers** *(jardin, rue)* to look onto
  3 regarder à *vt ind* (**a**) *(apparence, détail)* to pay attention to; **r. à la dépense** to be careful with money; **y r. à deux fois avant de faire qch** to think twice before doing sth; **y r. de près** to look at it closely (**b**) *Belg (veiller sur)* to look after
  4 se regarder *vpr* (**a**) *(soi-même)* to look at oneself; *Fam* **elle ne s'est pas regardée!** she can talk! (**b**) *(l'un l'autre)* to look at each other; **se r. dans les yeux** to look into each other's eyes (**c**) *(se faire face)* to face each other

regarnir [rǝgarnir] *vt (garde-manger, étagères)* to restock

régate [regat] *nf* regatta

régence [reʒɑ̃s] **1** *adj inv* **style R.** Regency style
  2 *nf* regency; *Hist* **la R.** the Regency

régénération [reʒenerasjɔ̃] *nf* (**a**) *(d'une cellule, de la peau)* regeneration (**b**) *Ordinat* **r. de l'écran** screen refresh

régénérer [34] [reʒenere] **1** *vt* to regenerate
  2 se régénérer *vpr* to regenerate

régent, -e [reʒɑ̃, -ɑ̃t] *nm,f* (**a**) *(chef du gouvernement)* regent (**b**) *Belg Scol* (secondary) schoolteacher

régenter [reʒɑ̃te] *vt* **vouloir tout r.** to want to run the whole show

reggae [rege] **1** *adj inv* reggae
  2 *nm* **le r.** reggae

régie [reʒi] *nf* (**a**) *(entreprise publique)* state-controlled company (**b**) *Cin & TV (organisation)* production management (**c**) *TV (lieu)* control room

regimber [rǝʒɛ̃be] *vi (personne)* to balk (**contre** at); **il est inutile de r.** it's no use protesting

régime [reʒim] *nm* (**a**) **r. (alimentaire)** diet; **être au r.** to be on a diet; **faire** *ou* **suivre un r.** to diet; **se mettre au r.** to go on a diet; **r. amincissant** slimming diet; *Fam* **être au r. sec** to be off the booze, *Br* to be on the wagon (**b**) *(forme de gouvernement)* government, regime (**c**) *(pénitentiaire, hospitalier)* system; *(de retraite)* scheme; **r. matrimonial** marriage settlement; **r. de Sécurité sociale** = division of social security system applying to some professional groups (**d**) *(d'un moteur)* speed; **r. de croisière** cruising speed; *Fig* **à ce r.** at this rate (**e**) *(d'une rivière, d'un fleuve)* rate of flow (**f**) *(de bananes, de dattes)* bunch

régiment [reʒimɑ̃] *nm (unité militaire)* regiment; *Fig (d'admirateurs, de créanciers)* host; *Fam* **il y en a pour un r.** there's enough for a whole army

région [reʒjɔ̃] *nf* area, region; **la r. parisienne** the Paris area *or* region; **la R.** = administrative area comprising several "départements"; **en r.** *(en province)* in the provinces

régional, -e, -aux, -ales [reʒjɔnal, -o] *adj* regional

régionalisme [reʒjɔnalism] *nm* regionalism

régionaliste [reʒjɔnalist] **1** *adj* regionalist **2** *nmf* regionalist; *(écrivain)* regional writer

régir [reʒir] *vt* (**a**) *(déterminer)* to govern (**b**) *(domaine)* to manage

régisseur [reʒisœr] *nm* (**a**) *(d'un domaine)* manager (**b**) *Cin & TV* assistant production manager; *Théât* stage manager

registre [rəʒistr] *nm* (**a**) *(livre)* register; *(de comptabilité)* account book; **r. du commerce** trade register; **r. de l'état civil** register of births, marriages and deaths (**b**) *(d'une voix, d'un instrument)* register (**c**) *Ordinat* register; **r. d'accès mémoire** memory access register (**d**) *(d'une œuvre)* style

réglable [reglabl] *adj* adjustable

réglage [reglaʒ] *nm* (**a**) *(d'un siège, d'un appareil)* adjustment; **r. automatique** automatic control (**b**) *(d'une radio, d'une télévision)* tuning; **r. du contraste** contrast control

règle [rɛgl] *nf* (**a**) *(de conduite, de grammaire)* rule; *Fig* **la r. du jeu** the rules of the game; **en r.** *(passeport, papiers)* in order; **en r. générale** as a general rule; **dans** *ou* **selon les règles de l'art** according to the book; **r. d'or** golden rule; *Math* **r. de trois** rule of three (**b**) *(pour tracer des lignes)* ruler (**c**) *Ordinat (sur écran)* ruler line (**d**) **règles** *(menstruation)* period; **avoir ses règles** to have one's period

réglé, -e [regle] *adj* (**a**) *(papier)* ruled (**b**) *(organisé)* well-ordered (**c**) *(résolu)* **c'est r.** it's settled (**d**) *(jeune fille)* who has started having periods

règlement [rɛgləmɑ̃] *nm* (**a**) *(résolution)* settlement; **en cours de r.** being settled; **r. à l'amiable** amicable settlement; **r. de comptes** settling of scores (**b**) *(paiement)* payment; **pour r. de tout compte** in full settlement (**c**) *(règle)* regulations; **r. intérieur** *(d'une école)* school rules; *(d'un bureau)* company rules; **c'est le r.** that's the rule

réglementaire [rɛgləmɑ̃tɛr] *adj (tenue)* regulation; **faire qch dans le temps r.** to do sth in the time allowed

réglementation [rɛgləmɑ̃tasjɔ̃] *nf* (**a**) *(action)* regulation (**b**) *(ensemble de lois)* regulations; **la r. du travail** labour legislation

réglementer [rɛgləmɑ̃te] *vt* to regulate

régler [34] [regle] **1** *vt* (**a**) *(mécanisme, appareil, image)* to adjust; *(radio, moteur)* to tune (**b**) *(journée, emploi du temps)* to plan (**c**) **r. qch sur qch** *(conduite)* to model sth on sth; *(pas)* to adjust sth to sth (**d**) *(résoudre) (question, dispute)* to settle; **r. ses affaires** to put one's affairs in order; **r. qch à l'amiable** to settle sth out of court (**e**) *(payer) (facture)* to settle, to pay; *(employé, commerçant, loyer)* to pay; *(achats)* to pay for
2 *vi* to pay
3 **se régler** *vpr* (**a**) **se r. sur qn** to model oneself on sb (**b**) *(se conclure)* to be settled

réglette [reglɛt] *nf* small ruler

réglisse [reglis] *nf* liquorice

réglo [reglo] *adj inv Fam (personne)* on the level; *(activités)* legit, kosher; **des affaires pas très r.** a shady business

régnant, -e [reɲɑ̃, -ɑ̃t] *adj (prince, famille)* reigning; *(idéologie, opinion)* prevailing

règne [rɛɲ] *nm* (**a**) *(d'un souverain)* reign; *Fig (de l'argent, de la technologie)* rule (**b**) *(végétal, animal)* kingdom

régner [34] [reɲe] *vi* (**a**) *(souverain)* to reign, to rule (**sur** over); **r. en maître sur qch** to reign supreme over

sth (**b**) *(exister) (idée)* to prevail; *(silence, atmosphère)* to reign; **faire r. la paix/l'ordre** to keep the peace/law and order; *Ironique* **la confiance règne!** there's confidence for you!

regonfler [rəgɔ̃fle] *vt (ballon, pneu)* to blow up again, to reinflate

regorger [45] [rəgɔrʒe] *vi* **r. de qch** to be overflowing with sth; **r. de monde** to be packed with people

régresser [regrese] *vi* (**a**) *(criminalité, idéologie, production)* to decline (**b**) *(personne)* to regress

régression [regresjɔ̃] *nf* (**a**) *(de la criminalité, d'une idéologie, de la production)* decline; **être en r.** to be on the decline (**b**) *(d'une personne)* regression; **être en r.** to be regressing

regret [rəgrɛ] *nm* regret (**de** for); **avoir des regrets** to have regrets; **à r.** with regret; **j'ai le r.** *ou* **je suis au r. de vous annoncer que...** I regret to tell you that...; **à mon (grand) r.** (much) to my regret

regrettable [rəgrɛtabl] *adj* regrettable

regretter [rəgrɛte] *vt* (**a**) *(avoir des remords sur)* to regret; **je ne regrette rien** I have no regrets; **il me ferait presque r. ma gentillesse** I'm almost sorry I was so kind to him; **r. de faire qch** to regret to do sth; **r. d'avoir fait qch** to regret having done sth; **r. que +** *subjunctive* to be sorry that; **il est à r. que...** it is to be regretted that...; **je regrette!** I'm sorry! (**b**) *(personne, endroit)* to miss; **r. sa jeunesse/son enfance** to wish one was young/a child again

regroupement [rəgrupmɑ̃] *nm* (**a**) *(action)* grouping; *(d'animaux, d'enfants)* round-up; *(de sociétés)* amalgamation; *Mil* regrouping; **le r. familial** = policy of authorizing the families of immigrant workers in possession of long-term work permits to join their relatives in France (**b**) *(groupe)* grouping

regrouper [rəgrupe] **1** *vt* (**a**) *(personnes, objets)* to gather together; *(animaux, enfants)* to round up (**b**) *(sociétés)* to amalgamate
2 **se regrouper** *vpr* (**a**) *(personnes)* to gather together (**b**) *(sociétés)* to amalgamate

régularisation [regylarizasjɔ̃] *nf* (**a**) *(d'une situation)* regularization; *(d'un compte)* adjustment (**b**) *(d'un fleuve, d'un fonctionnement, de la circulation)* regulation

régulariser [regylarize] *vt* (**a**) *(situation)* to regularize; *(compte)* to adjust; **ils ont régularisé la situation** *(ils se sont mariés)* they made it official (**b**) *(fleuve, fonctionnement, circulation)* to regulate

régularité [regylarite] *nf* (**a**) *(exactitude)* regularity (**b**) *(constance)* steadiness (**c**) *(d'une décision, d'une situation)* legality

régulateur, -trice [regylatœr, -tris] **1** *adj* regulating **2** *nm* regulator

régulation [regylasjɔ̃] *nf* control; **r. des naissances** birth control

régulier, -ère [regylje, -ɛr] **1** *adj* (**a**) *(à intervalles fixes)* regular (**b**) *(constant)* steady; *(travail, résultats)* consistent (**c**) *(écriture, ligne, couche)* even; *(traits du visage)* regular (**d**) *(légal) (situation)* legitimate; **être en situation régulière** to have one's papers in order (**e**) *Gram* regular (**f**) *Fam (honnête)* on the level (**g**) *(clergé)* regular
2 *nf* **régulière** *Fam Hum (femme)* steady

régulièrement [regyljɛrmɑ̃] *adv* (**a**) *(à intervalles fixes)* regularly (**b**) *(avec constance)* steadily (**c**) *(réparti, étalé)* evenly (**d**) *(selon la loi)* legitimately

régurgiter [regyrʒite] *vt (nourriture)* to regurgitate

réhabilitation [reabilitasjɔ̃] *nf* (**a**) *(de délinquant)* rehabilitation (**b**) *(de bâtiment, de quartier)* renovation
réhabiliter [reabilite] **1** *vt* (**a**) *(délinquant)* to rehabilitate (**b**) *(personne accusée)* to clear (**c**) *(bâtiment, quartier)* to renovate
  2 se réhabiliter *vpr* to rehabilitate oneself
réhabituer [reabitɥe] **1** *vt* r. qn à qch/à faire qch to get sb used to sth/to doing sth again
  2 se réhabituer *vpr* se r. à qch/à faire qch to get used to sth/to doing sth again
rehausser [rəose] *vt* (**a**) *(mur, bâtiment)* to make higher (**b**) *(couleur, teint)* to set off; *(détail)* to accentuate
réimplanter [reɛ̃plɑ̃te] **1** *vt* to relocate
  2 se réimplanter *vpr* to relocate
réimpression [reɛ̃presjɔ̃] *nf* reprinting; **en cours de r.** *(ouvrage)* being reprinted
réimprimer [reɛ̃prime] *vt* to reprint
rein [rɛ̃] *nm* (**a**) *(organe)* kidney; **r. artificiel** kidney *or* dialysis machine (**b**) **reins** *(bas du dos)* lower back; **la chute** *ou* **le creux des reins** the small of the back; **avoir mal aux reins** to have a pain in the small of one's back; *Fig* **avoir les reins solides** to be tough; *(financièrement)* to have money behind one
réincarnation [reɛ̃karnasjɔ̃] *nf* reincarnation
réincarner [reɛ̃karne] **se réincarner** *vpr* to be reincarnated (**en** as)
reine [rɛn] *nf* (**a**) *(souveraine, épouse d'un roi)* queen; **un port** *ou* **un maintien de r.** a queenly bearing; **la r. Anne** Queen Anne; **la r. mère** the Queen Mother (**b**) *(femme)* **r. de beauté** beauty queen; **la r. du bal** the belle of the ball (**c**) *(abeille)* queen (bee) (**d**) **la petite r.** *(cyclisme)* cycling
reine-claude (*pl* **reines-claudes**) [rɛnklod] *nf* greengage
reinette [rɛnɛt] *nf* pippin; **r. grise** russet
réinitialiser [reinisjalize] *vt Ordinat* to reset; *(mémoire)* to reinitialize
réinscription [reɛ̃skripsjɔ̃] *nf* reregistration
réinscrire [30] [reɛ̃skrir] **1** *vt* to reregister (**à** for)
  2 se réinscrire *vpr* to reregister (**à** for)
réinsérer [34] [reɛ̃sere] **1** *vt* (**a**) *(personne)* to reintegrate (**dans** into) (**b**) *Ordinat (bloc)* to reinsert
  2 se réinsérer *vpr* to reintegrate (**dans** into)
réinsertion [reɛ̃sɛrsjɔ̃] *nf* reintegration; **r. sociale** rehabilitation
réintégrer [34] [reɛ̃tegre] *vt* (**a**) *(fonctionnaire)* **r. qn (dans ses fonctions)** to reinstate sb (**b**) *(lieu)* **r. son domicile** to return to one's home
réintroduire [18] [reɛ̃trɔdɥir] *vt* to reintroduce
réitérer [34] [reitere] *vt (demande, promesse, question)* to repeat, to reiterate; *(démarche)* to repeat
rejaillir [rəʒajir] *vi* to spurt out; *Fig* **r. sur qn** *(scandale)* to reflect on sb
rejet [rəʒɛ] *nm* (**a**) *(de produits chimiques)* discharge (**b**) *(d'une proposition, d'une personne, d'une greffe)* rejection (**c**) *(en poésie)* enjambment
rejeter [42] [rəʒte] *vt* (**a**) *(relancer)* to throw back (**b**) *(candidature, offre, greffe)* to reject; *(témoignage)* to disallow; *(réclamation, accusation)* to dismiss; *(projet de loi)* to throw out (**c**) *(personne)* to reject (**d**) *(repousser)* **r. ses cheveux en arrière** to toss one's hair back; **r. la tête en arrière** to throw one's head back; **r. un mot en fin de phrase** to put a word at the end of a sentence (**e**) *(déchets, gaz toxiques)* to discharge; *(nourriture)* to regurgitate; *(épaves)* to cast up (**f**) *(blâme, responsabilité)* to shift (**sur** on)

rejeton [rəʒtɔ̃] *nm Fam Hum (enfant)* kid
rejoindre [43] [rəʒwɛ̃dr] **1** *vt* (**a**) *(personne) (pour un rendez-vous)* to meet; *(rattraper)* to catch up (with) (**b**) *(aboutir sur) (rue, rivière)* to join (up with) (**c**) *(atteindre) (lieu)* to reach; *(régiment, poste)* to return to (**d**) *(concorder avec)* to coincide with
  2 se rejoindre *vpr* (**a**) *(amis)* to meet up (**b**) *(rivières, routes, lignes)* to join up (**c**) *(propos, idées)* to coincide
rejouer [rəʒwe] *vt (match, point)* to replay; *(morceau de musique)* to play again; *(pièce de théâtre)* to do again
réjoui, -e [reʒwi] *adj* joyful
réjouir [reʒwir] **1** *vt (personne)* to delight
  2 se réjouir *vpr* to be delighted (**de** at); **se r. que** + *subjunctive* to be delighted that; **se r. de faire qch** to be delighted to be doing sth; *Suisse* **se r. de qch/de faire qch** to look forward to sth/to doing sth
réjouissance [reʒwisɑ̃s] *nf* rejoicing; **en signe de r.** to mark the occasion; **réjouissances** festivities
réjouissant, -e [reʒwisɑ̃, -ɑ̃t] *adj* delightful
relâche [rəlɑʃ] *nf* (**a**) *(arrêt)* **sans r.** without a break (**b**) *(au théâtre)* **il y a r. ce soir** there is no performance this evening; **faire r.** to be closed; **r.** *(sur panneau)* closed
relâché, -e [rəlɑʃe] *adj (mœurs, conduite)* lax
relâchement [rəlɑʃmɑ̃] *nm* (**a**) *(des muscles)* relaxing; *(d'une corde)* slackening (**b**) *(de la discipline)* relaxation; *(des mœurs)* laxness; *(des efforts)* let-up; *(de l'attention)* wavering; **il y a du r. dans votre travail** you're letting your work slide
relâcher [rəlɑʃe] **1** *vt* (**a**) *(muscles)* to relax; *(corde, étreinte)* to loosen (**b**) *(discipline)* to relax; *(efforts)* to let up; **r. son attention** to let one's attention waver (**c**) *(prisonnier)* to release, to let go
  2 se relâcher *vpr* (**a**) *(muscles)* to relax; *(corde)* to slacken; *(étreinte)* to loosen (**b**) *(discipline, mœurs)* to become lax; *(élève, employé)* to slack off; *(attention)* to waver
relais [rəlɛ] *nm* (**a**) *(épreuve sportive)* **(course de) r.** relay (race); **r. 4 x 100 mètres** 4 x 100-metre relay (**b**) *(relève)* **passer le r. à qn** to hand over to sb; **prendre le r. (de)** to take over (from) (**c**) *(intermédiaire)* intermediary (**d**) *(auberge)* coaching inn; **r. gastronomique** gourmet restaurant (**e**) *(dispositif émetteur)* relay
relance [rəlɑ̃s] *nf* (**a**) *(de l'économie, de la production)* revival (**b**) *(au jeu)* raise
relancer [16] [rəlɑ̃se] *vt* (**a**) *(lancer de nouveau)* to throw again; *(rendre)* to throw back (**b**) *(économie, ventes, production)* to boost (**c**) *(moteur)* to restart; *Ordinat (programme)* to rerun; *(logiciel)* to restart (**d**) *(client)* to follow up
relater [rəlate] *vt Litt (raconter)* to relate
relatif, -ive [rəlatif, -iv] **1** *adj* relative; **r. à** relating to; **tout est r.** it's all relative
  2 *nm (pronom)* relative pronoun
  3 *nf* **relative** *(proposition)* relative clause
relation [rəlasjɔ̃] *nf* (**a**) *(rapports entre personnes)* relationship; **être en r. avec qn** to be in touch with sb; **mettre qn en r. (avec qn)** to put sb in touch (with sb); **avoir de bonnes/mauvaises relations avec qn** to be on good/bad terms with sb; **r. (amoureuse)** (love) affair; **relations extérieures** foreign affairs; **relations publiques** public relations; **relations sexuelles** (sexual) intercourse (**b**) *(lien) (entre des phénomènes, des faits)* relationship, connection; **être sans r. avec qch** to bear no relation to sth; **en r. avec...** in relation to...;

r. de cause à effet cause-and-effect relationship; **relations spatiales** spatial relations (**c**) *(connaissance)* acquaintance; **avoir des relations** to have contacts; **une r. de travail** a colleague (**d**) *(récit)* account

relationnel, -elle [rəlasjɔnɛl] *adj* relational; *Ordinat* **base de données relationnelles** relational database

relativement [rəlativmɑ̃] *adv* (**a**) *(assez)* relatively (**b**) **r. à** *(par rapport à)* compared to

relativiser [rəlativize] *vt* to put into perspective; **il faut r.** you have to put things into perspective

relativisme [rəlativism] *nm* relativism

relativité [rəlativite] *nf* relativity

relax [rəlaks] *adj Fam* laid-back

relaxant, -e [rəlaksɑ̃, -ɑ̃t] *adj* relaxing

relaxation [rəlaksasjɔ̃] *nf* relaxation; **faire de la r.** to do relaxation exercises

relaxer [rəlakse] **1** *vt* (**a**) *(détendre)* to relax (**b**) *(prisonnier)* to release
    2 se relaxer *upr* to relax

relayer [rəleje] **1** *vt (personne)* to take over from
    2 se relayer *upr* (**a**) *(se remplacer)* to take turns; **se r. pour faire qch** to take turns doing sth; **on se relaie toutes les trois heures** we change over every three hours (**b**) *(coureurs)* to take over from each other

relecture [rəlɛktyr] *nf* (**a**) *(d'épreuves)* proofreading (**b**) *(d'un livre, d'un texte)* rereading

reléguer [34] [rəlege] *vt* to relegate (**à/en** to); *Fig* **r. qch au second plan** to push sth into the background

relent [rəlɑ̃] *nm* (**a**) *(odeur)* stench (**b**) *(de scandale)* whiff

relevable [rəlvabl] *adj (dossier, appuie-tête)* adjustable; *(accoudoir)* folding

relevé, -e [rəlve] **1** *adj* (**a**) *(style)* lofty (**b**) *(sauce, plat)* spicy, highly seasoned
    2 *nm (d'un compteur)* reading; **r. de compte** bank statement; **r. d'identité bancaire** = document giving details of one's bank account

Relevé d'identité bancaire

An "RIB" is a small slip of paper with all of a person's bank details. Employers, utility companies and other financial institutions may ask for one to effect standing orders.

relève [rəlɛv] *nf* relief; **assurer** *ou* **prendre la r. (de qn)** to take over (from sb)

relèvement [rəlɛvmɑ̃] *nm* (**a**) *(d'une économie, d'un pays)* recovery (**b**) *(des salaires, des tarifs, d'un impôt)* raising

relever [46] [rəlve] **1** *vt* (**a**) *(objet renversé)* to pick up; *(personne)* to help back up; **r. la tête** to look up; *Fig* to stand up for oneself (**b**) *(économie, pays)* to revive (**c**) *(col)* to turn up; *(manches, bas de pantalon)* to roll up, to turn up; *(voilette, jupe)* to lift (up); *(cheveux)* to put up (**d**) *(augmenter)* to raise (**e**) *(contradiction, erreur)* to pick out; *(traces, empreinte)* to find (**f**) *(prêter attention à)* **r. l'allusion** to pick up on the hint; **je n'ai pas relevé** I let it go (**g**) *(adresse, coordonnées)* to take down; *(compteur)* to read; *(copies)* to collect; **r. le gaz** to read the gas meter (**h**) *(défi)* to accept (**i**) *(sauce, plat)* to spice up (**j**) *(remplacer)* *(troupes, sentinelle)* to relieve (**k**) *(libérer)* **r. qn de ses fonctions** to relieve sb of his/her duties
    2 relever de *vt ind* (**a**) *(dépendre de)* *(personne, autorité)* to be answerable to; **r. de l'article 7** to come under article 7; **cette affaire relève de la justice** this is a matter for the courts; **son cas relève de la folie**

he's well and truly insane (**b**) *(se remettre de)* to be recovering from
    3 se relever *upr* (**a**) *(après une chute)* to get up (**b**) *(accoudoir, siège)* to lift up (**c**) *(se remettre)* **se r. de qch** to get over sth, to recover from sth

relief [rəljɛf] *nm* (**a**) *(d'un paysage, d'une médaille)* relief; **en r.** in relief; *Fig* **mettre qch en r.** *(idées, qualité)* to bring sth out; *(beauté)* to set sth off; *(avantage)* to highlight sth; **sans r.** *(paysage, style)* flat (**b**) *Litt* **reliefs** *(d'un repas)* remains; *Fig (de la gloire)* shreds (**c**) *Ordinat* highlight; **mettre qch en r.** to highlight sth

relier [66] [rəlje] **1** *vt* (**a**) *(mettre en contact)* to connect, to link (**à** to) (**b**) *(idées, faits)* to link together (**c**) *(livre)* to bind
    2 se relier *upr Ordinat* to link up

relieur, -euse [rəljœr, -øz] *nm,f* (book)binder

religieusement [rəliʒjøzmɑ̃] *adv* (**a**) *(selon la religion)* religiously; **se marier r.** to get married in church (**b**) *(avec révérence)* reverently (**c**) *(scrupuleusement)* religiously

religieux, -euse [rəliʒjø, -øz] **1** *adj* religious; *(mariage)* church; *Fig (silence)* respectful
    2 *nm (moine)* monk
    3 *nf* **religieuse** (**a**) *(sœur)* nun (**b**) *(gâteau)* cream puff

religion [rəliʒjɔ̃] *nf* religion; **entrer en r.** to join a religious order

reliquaire [rəlikɛr] *nm* reliquary

reliquat [rəlika] *nm (d'argent)* remainder; **r. de caisse** cash balance; **r. de compte** account balance

relique [rəlik] *nf* relic

relire [44] [rəlir] **1** *vt* (**a**) *(livre, auteur, notes)* to reread (**b**) *(épreuves)* to proofread
    2 se relire *upr* to read (over) what one has written

reliure [rəljyr] *nf* (**a**) *(activité, art)* bookbinding (**b**) *(couverture)* binding

reloger [45] [rələʒe] *vt* to rehouse

relookage [rəlukaʒ] *nm Fam* revamping, makeover

relooker [rəluke] *Fam* **1** *vt* to revamp, to give a makeover to
    2 se relooker *upr* to give oneself a makeover

relooking [rəlukiŋ] = relookage

reluire [18] [rəlɥir] *vi (parquet, meuble, métal)* to shine, to gleam; **faire r. qch** to polish sth (up)

reluisant, -e [rəlɥizɑ̃, -ɑ̃t] *adj* (**a**) *(parquet, meuble, métal)* shining, gleaming (**b**) *Fig* **ce qu'il a fait n'est pas très r.** what he did doesn't reflect very well on him

reluquer [rəlyke] *vt Fam* to eye up

remâcher [rəmɑʃe] *vt (colère, échec)* to brood over

remake [rimɛk] *nm* remake

remaniement [rəmanimɑ̃] *nm* (**a**) *(d'un texte)* revision (**b**) **r. ministériel** cabinet reshuffle

remanier [66] [rəmanje] *vt* (**a**) *(texte)* to revise (**b**) *(ministère)* to reshuffle

remariage [rəmarjaʒ] *nm* remarriage

remarier [66] [rəmarje] **se remarier** *upr* to remarry; **se r. avec qn** to remarry sb

remarquable [rəmarkabl] *adj* remarkable (**par** for)

remarquablement [rəmarkabləmɑ̃] *adv* remarkably

remarque [rəmark] *nf* (**a**) *(orale)* remark; **faire une r.** to make a remark; **faire une r. à qn sur qch** to pass a remark to sb about sth (**b**) *(écrite)* comment

remarqué, -e [rəmarke] *adj (entrée, absence)* conspicuous; *(intervention)* that attracted attention

remarquer [rəmarke] **1** *vt* (**a**) *(observer)* to notice; **faire r. qch à qn** to point sth out to sb; **je vous ferai**

r. que... I'd like to point out that...; **se faire r.** to attract attention; *Fam* **remarque, il n'est pas le seul** he's not the only one, mind you (**b**) *(dire)* to remark, to observe **2 se remarquer** *vpr (tache, cicatrice)* to show

remballer [rɑ̃bale] *vt (marchandises)* to repack; *Fig (compliment)* to keep to oneself

rembarrer [rɑ̃bare] *vt Fam* to snub; **se faire r.** to be snubbed *or* rebuffed

remblai [rɑ̃blɛ] *nm* embankment

remblayer [53] [rɑ̃bleje] *vt (route, voie ferrée)* to bank (up)

rembobiner [rɑ̃bɔbine] **1** *vt* to rewind **2 se rembobiner** *vpr* to rewind

rembourrage [rɑ̃buraʒ] *nm (action, matériau)* stuffing

rembourrer [rɑ̃bure] *vt* to stuff

remboursable [rɑ̃bursabl] *adj (emprunt)* repayable; *(frais)* refundable

remboursement [rɑ̃bursəmɑ̃] *nm (d'un emprunt)* repayment; *(de frais)* refund

rembourser [rɑ̃burse] *vt* (**a**) *(frais, achat)* to refund; *(emprunt, dettes)* to pay back; **ce médicament est remboursé à 70%** 70% of the cost of this medicine will be refunded (**b**) *(personne)* to pay back; **r. qn de qch** to reimburse sb for sth; **se faire r.** to get a refund; *Fam* **remboursez!** *(au théâtre)* give us our money back!

rembrunir [rɑ̃brynir] **se rembrunir** *vpr (visage, personne)* to become sullen

remède [rəmɛd] *nm* remedy, cure (**contre** for); **r. de bonne femme** old wives' remedy; **r. de cheval** kill-or-cure remedy

remédier [66] [rəmedje] **remédier à** *vt ind (erreur, situation)* to remedy; *(inconvénient)* to make up for

remembrement [rəmɑ̃brəmɑ̃] *nm (de terres)* grouping of land

remémorer [rəmemɔre] **se remémorer** *vpr* to remember

remerciement [rəmɛrsimɑ̃] *nm* **lettre de r.** thank-you letter; **remerciements** thanks; *(dans un livre)* acknowledgements

remercier [66] [rəmɛrsje] *vt* (**a**) *(dire merci à)* to thank (**de** *ou* **pour** for); **r. qn d'avoir fait qch** to thank sb for doing sth; **(non,) je vous remercie** no, thank you (**b**) *Euph (congédier)* to ask to leave

remettre [47] [rəmɛtr] **1** *vt* (**a**) **r. qch à qn** *(lettre, télégramme, colis)* to deliver sth to sb; *(rapport)* to submit sth to sb; *(démission)* to hand sth in to sb; *(rançon)* to hand sth over to sb; **r. qn à la justice** to turn sb over to the police; **r. son sort entre les mains de qn** to put one's fate in sb's hands

(**b**) *(retarder)* to postpone (**à** to *or* till); **r. qch à plus tard** to put sth off till later

(**c**) *(replacer)* to put back; **r. qch à sa place** *ou* **en place** to put sth back in its place; **r. qch en cause** *ou* **en question** to call sth into question; **r. qn en liberté** to set sb free

(**d**) *(reconnaître)* **je ne vous remets pas** I can't place you

(**e**) *(dans un état antérieur)* **r. une montre à l'heure** to set a watch to the right time; **r. qch à zéro** to reset sth to zero; **r. qch en marche** *(moteur, machine)* to restart sth; **r. qch en ordre** *(dossiers, maison)* to tidy sth (up)

(**f**) *(rétablir la santé de)* to make better

(**g**) *(manteau, chapeau)* to put back on

(**h**) *(chauffage, télévision)* to turn on again; *(disque, chanson)* to put on again

(**i**) *(ajouter) (sel, eau)* to add (**dans** to)

(**j**) *Fam (recommencer)* **on remet ça?** how about another (one)?; **tu ne vas pas r. ça!** you're not going to start that again, are you?; *Belg* **r. le couvert** to start again

(**k**) *Belg & Suisse (céder)* to sell

2 se remettre *vpr* (**a**) *(dans un endroit, dans un état)* **se r. debout** to get up again; **se r. au lit** to go back to bed; **se r. en cause** *ou* **en question** to question oneself; **le temps s'est remis au beau** the weather has brightened up again

(**b**) *(recommencer)* **se r. à qch/à faire qch** to start sth/doing sth again; **se r. au français/au tennis** to take up French/tennis again

(**c**) *(après une maladie, un choc)* to recover (**de** from); *Fig* **voyons, remettez-vous!** come on, pull yourself together!

(**d**) *(faire confiance)* **je m'en remets à vous** I'll leave it to you, it's up to you

(**e**) *(se placer)* **se r. entre les mains de qn** to place oneself in sb's hands

(**f**) *Fam (renouer)* **se r. ensemble** to get back together

réminiscence [reminisɑ̃s] *nf (souvenir imprécis)* vague recollection

remise [rəmiz] *nf* (**a**) *(dans son lieu ou son état d'origine)* **r. en état** *(d'une maison)* restoration; **r. à neuf** *(d'une machine)* reconditioning; **r. en question** *ou* **cause** questioning (**b**) *(d'une lettre)* delivery (**à** to); *(d'une rançon)* handing over (**à** to); **r. des prix** prize-giving (**c**) *(réduction)* **r. de peine** reduction of sentence (**d**) *(rabais)* discount; **faire une r. à qn** to give sb a discount (**e**) *(appentis)* shed (**f**) *Ordinat* **r. à blanc** *(d'une disquette)* reformatting; **r. en forme** *(de texte)* reformatting

remiser [rəmize] *vt* to put away

rémission [remisjɔ̃] *nf* (**a**) *(d'un péché)* remission; *Fig* **sans r.** *(travailler)* unremittingly; *(punir)* mercilessly (**b**) *(d'une maladie)* remission; **être en r.** to be in remission

remix [rəmiks] *nm Mus* remix

remixer [rəmikse] *vt Mus* to remix

remmener [46] [rɑ̃mne] *vt* to take back; **r. qn en voiture** to drive sb back

remodeler [39] [rəmɔdle] *vt* (**a**) *(refaçonner)* to remodel (**b**) *(réorganiser)* to restructure

remontant [rəmɔ̃tɑ̃] *nm* tonic

remontée [rəmɔ̃te] *nf* (**a**) *(d'une pente)* ascent (**b**) *(dans un classement sportif)* recovery (**c**) *(des eaux)* rising (**d**) *(pour skieurs)* **r. mécanique** ski lift

remonte-pente *(pl* **remonte-pentes)** [rəmɔ̃tpɑ̃t] *nm* ski-tow

remonter [rəmɔ̃te] **1** *vt* (**a**) *(pente, escalier) (en s'éloignant)* to go up again, to climb back up; *(en s'approchant)* to come up again, to climb back up; **r. la rue** to go/come up the street; **r. la rivière** to go upstream (**b**) *(hausser) (étagère, poster)* to move up; *(pantalon, jupe)* to hitch up; *(manche, chaussettes)* to pull up; *(fermeture éclair)* to do up; *(vitre de voiture)* to wind up (**c**) *(porter en haut)* to take/bring up (**d**) *(horloge, montre)* to wind (up) (**e**) *(revigorer) (personne)* to cheer up (**f**) *(pièces d'une machine)* to reassemble

2 *vi* (**a**) *(dans l'espace) (personne)* to go/come back up; *(marée)* to flow; *(baromètre)* to rise again; *(route, ruelle)* to climb again; *(jupe)* to ride up; **r. en voiture** to get back in one's car; *Fig* **r. dans les sondages** to improve one's position in the polls (**b**) *(dans le temps)* to go back (**à** to); **ça remonte à loin** *(tradition)* it goes back a long way; *(épisode)* it was a long time ago (**c**) *(actions, monnaie, température)* to go up again, to rise again

3 se remonter *vpr (moralement)* to cheer up; *(physiquement)* to recover one's strength

remontoir [rəmɔ̃twar] *nm* winder

remontrance [rəmɔ̃trɑ̃s] *nf* remonstrance; **faire des remontrances à qn** to remonstrate with sb

remontrer [rəmɔ̃tre] **1** *vt* **en r. à qn** to show one knows better than sb

2 se remontrer *vpr* to show oneself again

remords [rəmɔr] *nm* remorse; **avoir du** *ou* **des r.** to feel remorse; **je n'ai aucun r.!** I'm not the slightest bit sorry!

remorque [rəmɔrk] *nf* (**a**) *(véhicule)* trailer (**b**) **prendre qch en r.** to take sth in tow; *Fig* **être à la r.** to lag behind

remorquer [rəmɔrke] *vt (voiture, bateau)* to tow; *(train)* to pull

remorqueur [rəmɔrkœr] *nm* tug(boat)

rémoulade [remulad] *nf Culin* (**sauce**) **r.** remoulade (sauce) *(mayonnaise sauce with mustard and herbs)*

rémouleur [remulœr] *nm* knife grinder

remous [rəmu] *nm (d'une rivière)* eddy; *(d'un bateau)* wash; *Fig (de la foule)* ripple; *Fig* **provoquer** *ou* **faire des r.** to cause a stir

rempailler [rɑ̃paje] *vt* to reseat

rempart [rɑ̃par] *nm* rampart; **remparts** walls; **faire un r. de son corps à qn** to shield sb with one's body

rempiler [rɑ̃pile] *vi Fam Hum* to sign up again

remplaçable [rɑ̃plasabl] *adj* replaceable

remplaçant, -e [rɑ̃plasɑ̃, -ɑ̃t] *nm,f (personne)* replacement; *(d'un médecin)* locum (tenens); *(d'un enseignant) Br* supply teacher, *Am & Ir* substitute teacher

remplacement [rɑ̃plasmɑ̃] *nm* replacement; **en r. de qn/qch** in place of sb/sth; **faire des remplacements** *(professeur)* to work as *Br* a supply teacher *or Am & Ir* a substitute teacher

remplacer [16] [rɑ̃plase] *vt* (**a**) *(être à la place de)* to take the place of, to replace; *(professionnellement)* to stand in for; **se faire r.** to get somebody to stand in *or* cover for one (**b**) *(substituer)* to replace (**par** with)

remplir [rɑ̃plir] **1** *vt* (**a**) *(récipient)* to fill (**de** with); *(espace, trou)* to fill (in); *Fig (journée, vie)* to take up; **r. qn de joie/colère** to fill sb with joy/anger (**b**) *(formulaire)* to fill in *or* out; *(chèque)* to write, to make out; *(page)* to fill (**c**) *(promesse, rôle, contrat)* to fulfil; *(devoirs, tâche)* to carry out

2 se remplir *vpr* to fill up (**de** with); *Fig* **se r. les poches** to line one's pockets

remplissage [rɑ̃plisaʒ] *nm* (**a**) *(d'un tonneau, d'un réservoir)* filling (up); *(d'un trou, d'un espace)* filling (in) (**b**) *Péj* **faire du r.** *(dans un texte)* to pad

remplumer [rɑ̃plyme] **se remplumer** *vpr Fam* (**a**) *(financièrement)* to be in funds again (**b**) *(grossir)* to put some weight back on

rempocher [rɑ̃pɔʃe] *vt* to put back in one's pocket

remporter [rɑ̃pɔrte] *vt* (**a**) *(reprendre)* to take back *or* away (**b**) *(gagner) (prix, victoire)* to win; *(succès)* to achieve; *Fig* **r. tous les suffrages** to meet with universal approval

rempoter [rɑ̃pɔte] *vt* to repot

remuant, -e [rəmɥɑ̃, -ɑ̃t] *adj* hyperactive

remue-ménage [rəmymenaʒ] *nm inv* commotion; **faire du r.** to cause a commotion *or* stir

remuer [rəmɥe] **1** *vt* (**a**) *(partie du corps)* to move around; *(lèvres)* to move; **r. la queue** *(chien)* to wag its tail; **r. les oreilles** *(chien)* to waggle its ears (**b**) *(mobilier, objets)* to move, to shift (**c**) *(sauce, café)* to stir; *(salade)* to toss; *(terre)* to turn over; *Fig (vieux souvenirs, passé)* to rake up; **r. ciel et terre pour faire qch** to move heaven and earth to do sth (**d**) *(émouvoir)* to move

2 *vi (personne)* to move; *(queue)* to wag; **arrête de r.!** don't fidget!, keep still!

3 se remuer *vpr* (**a**) *(bouger)* to move (**b**) *Fam (être actif)* to have plenty of get-up-and-go; **remue-toi un peu!** get up off your backside!

rémunérateur, -trice [remyneratœr, -tris] *adj (travail)* remunerative; *(placement)* interest-bearing

rémunération [remynerasjɔ̃] *nf* remuneration (**de** for); *(salaire)* pay

rémunérer [34] [remynere] *vt (personne)* to pay; *(travail, services)* to pay for; **travail bien/mal rémunéré** well-paid/badly-paid job

renâcler [rənakle] *vi (personne)* to balk (**à faire** at doing); **il a accepté en renâclant** he accepted grudgingly

renaissance [rənɛsɑ̃s] *nf* (**a**) *(d'une personne)* rebirth (**b**) *(des lettres, des arts)* renaissance; **la R.** the Renaissance

renaître [50a] [rənɛtr] *vi* (**a**) *(personne)* to be born again; **r. de ses cendres** to rise again from its ashes (**b**) *(industrie, arts, espoir)* to revive; *Litt (printemps, plantes)* to return; *(nature)* to reawaken; **faire r. la confiance** to restore confidence

rénal, -e, -aux, -ales [renal, -o] *adj* renal

renard [rənar] *nm* (**a**) *(animal)* fox; *Fig* **c'est un vieux r.** he's a sly old fox (**b**) *(fourrure)* fox (fur)

renardeau, -x [rənardo] *nm* fox cub

rencard, rencart [rɑ̃kar] = rancard

renchérir [rɑ̃ʃerir] *vi* (**a**) *(prix, loyers, marchandises)* to go up (**b**) *(dire ou faire plus)* to go one better (**sur** than)

rencontre [rɑ̃kɔ̃tr] *nf* (**a**) *(de personnes)* meeting; *(de routes, de cours d'eau)* junction; **faire la r. de qn** to meet sb; **faire de mauvaises rencontres** to meet the wrong kind of people; **aller à la r. de qn** to go to meet sb (**b**) *(d'athlétisme)* meeting; *(match)* game, *Br* match

rencontrer [rɑ̃kɔ̃tre] **1** *vt* (**a**) *(personne)* to meet; **r. qn par hasard** to bump into *or* run into sb (**b**) *(trouver)* to come across; *(opposition, difficulté)* to encounter, to come up against

2 se rencontrer *vpr* (**a**) *(gens, rivières)* to meet (**b**) *Hum (être d'accord)* **les grands esprits se rencontrent** great minds think alike

rendement [rɑ̃dmɑ̃] *nm* (**a**) *(d'une terre, d'un impôt)* yield; *(d'un investissement)* return, yield (**b**) *(de travailleurs, d'une usine, d'une machine)* output; *(d'un ordinateur)* throughput; **travailler à plein r.** *(usine)* to work at full capacity

rendez-vous [rɑ̃devu] *nm inv* (**a**) *(rencontre)* appointment; *(amoureux)* date; **avoir r. chez le médecin** to have an appointment with the doctor; **donner r. à qn** to arrange to meet sb; **prendre r. avec qn/chez le médecin** to make an appointment with sb/with the doctor (**b**) *(endroit)* meeting place

rendormir [29] [rɑ̃dɔrmir] **se rendormir** *vpr* to fall asleep again

rendre [rɑ̃dr] **1** *vt* (**a**) *(objet emprunté)* to give back, to return (**à** to); *(achat)* to take back (**à** to); *(copies,* *cadeau*) to give back (**à** to); *(otages)* to hand back (**à** to); **r. sa liberté à qn** to set sb free (**b**) *(rembourser)* to pay back (**c**) *(en retour)* **je lui ai rendu son compliment/son invitation** I returned his/her compliment/his/her invitation; **r. la monnaie à qn** to give sb his/her change; *Fig* **r. à qn la monnaie de sa pièce** to get even with sb; **r. les armes** *(soldats)* to surrender; *Fig* to give up; *Fig* **elle l'aime, mais il ne le lui rend pas** she loves him, but the feeling isn't mutual (**d**) *(vomir)* to bring up (**e**) *(son)* to make; *(jus, eau)* to release (**f**) *Jur (jugement, verdict)* to deliver; **r. la justice** to dispense justice (**g**) *(sens, nuance)* to render, to express (**h**) *(faire devenir)* to make; **r. qn triste** to make sb sad; **r. qn fou** to drive sb mad; **r. qn aveugle/sourd** to make sb go blind/deaf; *Fig* **l'amour l'a rendu aveugle** he was blinded by love

2 *vi* (**a**) *(terre)* to be productive; *(placement)* to yield (**b**) *(vomir)* to vomit

3 se rendre *vpr* (**a**) *(aller)* **se r. à** to go to; **se r. chez qn** to call on sb (**b**) *(se soumettre)* to give oneself up (**c**) *(devenir)* **se r. malade/utile** to make oneself ill/useful (**d**) *(locutions)* **se r. compte de qch/que...** to realize sth/that...; *Fam* **tu te rends compte!** who'd have believed it!; **se r. à la raison** to see reason

rendu, -e [rãdy] *adj* (**a**) *(arrivé)* **être r.** to have arrived (**b**) *Vieilli (fatigué)* tired out

rêne [rɛn] *nf* rein; *Fig* **c'est lui qui tient les rênes** he's the one who's really in charge

renégat, -e [renega, -at] *nm,f* renegade

renfermé, -e [rãfɛrme] **1** *adj (personne)* withdrawn
    2 *nm* **odeur de r.** musty smell; **sentir le r.** to smell musty

renfermer [rãfɛrme] **1** *vt (contenir)* to contain
    2 se renfermer *vpr* to withdraw into oneself

renflé, -e [rãfle] *adj* bulging

renflement [rãfləmã] *nm* bulge

renflouer [rãflue] *vt* (**a**) *(bateau échoué)* to refloat (**b**) *(entreprise, personne)* to bail out

renfoncement [rãfõsmã] *nm* recess

renforcement [rãfɔrsəmã] *nm (d'une poutre, d'une armée, d'une équipe)* strengthening, reinforcement; *(de la sécurité)* tightening up

renforcer [16] [rãfɔrse] **1** *vt* (**a**) *(poutre, armée, équipe)* to strengthen, to reinforce; *(sécurité)* to tighten up (**b**) *(couleur, éclairage)* to intensify (**c**) *(crainte)* to heighten; *(impression, convictions)* to strengthen; **r. qn dans une opinion** to confirm sb in an opinion
    2 se renforcer *vpr (tendance, impression, convictions)* to grow

renfort [rãfɔr] *nm* **renforts** reinforcements; *Fig* **demander du r.** to ask for help; **à grand r. de qch** with the help of lots of sth

renfrogné, -e [rãfrɔɲe] *adj* scowling

renfrogner [rãfrɔɲe] **se renfrogner** *vpr* to scowl

rengager [45] [rãgaʒe] **1** *vt (personnel)* to take on again; *(combat)* to renew; *(conversation, partie, débat)* to pick up again
    2 se rengager *vpr Mil* to re-enlist

rengaine [rãgɛn] *nf* tune; *Fam Fig* **c'est toujours la même r.** it's (always) the same old story

rengainer [rãgɛne] *vt (épée)* to sheathe; *Fig (compliment)* to keep to oneself

rengorger [45] [rãgɔrʒe] **se rengorger** *vpr* to strut

reniement [rənimã] *nm (d'une foi)* denial; *(d'idées, d'une action)* repudiation

renier [66] [rənje] **1** *vt (fils, racines)* to disown; *(foi)* to deny; *(action, idées)* to repudiate
    2 se renier *vpr* to repudiate one's opinions

reniflement [rənifləmã] *nm* (**a**) *(action)* sniffing (**b**) *(bruit)* sniff

renifler [rənifle] **1** *vi* to sniff
    2 *vt (fleur)* to sniff (at); *(tabac à priser)* to sniff (up); *Fig (bonne affaire, embrouille)* to sniff out

renipper [rənipe] *Can* **1** *vt (rénover) (maison, pièce)* to renovate, to do up
    2 se renipper *vpr* to smarten oneself up

renne [rɛn] *nm* reindeer

renom [rənõ] *nm* renown; **de r.** famous, renowned; **de grand r.** extremely famous

renommé, -e [rənɔme] *adj* renowned, famous (**pour** for)

renommée [rənɔme] *nf* fame, renown; **un musicien de r. internationale** a world-famous musician, a musician of international repute *or* renown

renommer [rənɔme] *vt Ordinat (fichier)* to rename

renoncement [rənõsmã] *nm* renunciation (**à** of)

renoncer [16] [rənõse] **renoncer à** *vt ind (droit, projet, activité)* to give up, to abandon; *(vacances, voyage)* to sacrifice, to forego; **r. à faire qch** to give up doing sth; *(avant d'avoir commencé)* to give up the idea of doing sth; **je renonce!** I give up!

renonciation [rənõsjasjõ] *nf* renunciation (**à** of)

renoncule [rənõkyl] *nf* buttercup

renouer [rənwe] **1** *vt* (**a**) *(ruban, lacet)* to tie (up) again; *(cravate)* to do up again (**b**) *(conversation, relations)* to resume; *(amitié)* to renew
    2 renouer avec *vt ind* **r. avec qn** to take up with sb again; **r. avec qch** *(tradition)* to revive sth; *(habitude)* to go back to sth

renouveau, -x [rənuvo] *nm* revival

renouvelable [rənuvlabl] *adj (contrat, énergie)* renewable; *(expérience)* repeatable

renouveler [9] [rənuvle] **1** *vt* (**a**) *(stock, équipement)* to renew, to replace; *(eau)* to change (**b**) *(passeport, abonnement, demande)* to renew; *(expérience)* to repeat (**c**) *(style)* to change
    2 se renouveler *vpr* (**a**) *(cellule)* to be renewed (**b**) *(se produire de nouveau)* to recur, to happen again (**c**) *(changer)* to change; **un artiste/auteur qui ne se renouvelle pas** an artist/author whose style never changes

renouvellement [rənuvɛlmã] *nm* (**a**) *(de stock, d'équipement)* replacement, renewal (**b**) *(d'un style)* change (**c**) *(d'un traité, d'un contrat)* renewal

rénovateur, -trice [renovatœr, -tris] **1** *adj* reforming
    2 *nm,f* reformer

rénovation [renovasjõ] *nf* (**a**) *(d'un bâtiment, du mobilier)* renovation; **en (cours de) r.** undergoing renovation (**b**) *(d'une institution)* updating, reform

rénover [renove] *vt* (**a**) *(bâtiment, mobilier)* to renovate (**b**) *(institution)* to update, to reform

renseigné, -e [rãsɛɲe] *adj* **bien/mal r.** well-/ill-informed

renseignement [rãsɛɲəmã] *nm* (**a**) *(précision)* piece of information; **renseignements** information; **pour tout r....** for information...; **prendre des renseignements sur qn/qch** to make enquiries about sb/sth; **aller aux renseignements** to go and make enquiries (**b**) *Tél* **les renseignements (téléphoniques)** *Br* directory enquiries, *Am* information (**c**) **les renseignements généraux** = secret intelligence branch of the French police, *Br* ≃ the Special Branch, *Am* ≃ the FBI

renseigner [rɑ̃seɲe] **1** vt r. qn (sur qch) to give sb some information (about sth), to inform sb (about sth); **on vous a mal renseigné** you have been misinformed

2 se renseigner vpr to make enquiries; *(sur un point précis)* to find out (**sur** about)

rentabiliser [rɑ̃tabilize] vt to make profitable

rentabilité [rɑ̃tabilite] nf profitability

rentable [rɑ̃tabl] adj profitable

rente [rɑ̃t] nf (**a**) *(revenu)* **rentes** private income (**b**) *(pension)* annuity, pension; **r. viagère** life annuity (**c**) *(emprunt d'État)* loan

rentier, -ère [rɑ̃tje, -ɛr] nm,f person of private means

rentré, -e[1] [rɑ̃tre] adj (**a**) *(yeux)* sunken (**b**) *(colère)* suppressed

rentre-dedans [rɑ̃tdədɑ̃] nm inv Fam **faire du r. à qn** to come on to sb

rentrée[2] [rɑ̃tre] nf (**a**) *(retour)* return; **la r. (des classes)** the start of the new school year; **r. parlementaire** reopening of Parliament; **la r. sociale** the return to work (**b**) *(d'argent)* **attendre une r. d'argent** to expect some money

La rentrée

The time of the year when children go back to school – in September – has considerable cultural significance in France. Coming after the long summer break or "grandes vacances", it is the time when academic, political, social and commercial activity begins again in earnest.

rentrer [rɑ̃tre] **1** vi *(aux* **être)** (**a**) *(entrer de nouveau)* *(en s'éloignant)* to go in again; *(en s'approchant)* to come in again; *(entrer)* to go/come in, to enter; **rentre!** come in! (**b**) *(à la maison)* to go/come back home, to return home; **r. de vacances/de Paris** to come back from Br holiday or Am vacation/from Paris; **r. en France/à Paris** to return to France/to Paris; **r. dans son pays** to go back to one's own country; **r. tard/tôt** to come or get home late/early; **en rentrant chez moi** on my way home; **en rentrant de l'école** on my/his/etc way home from school (**c**) *(reprendre ses occupations)* *(école)* to re-open; *(élève, professeur)* to go back (**d**) *(tenir)* *(objets)* to go in, to fit (in); **je ne rentre plus dans ce jean!** I can't get into these jeans any more! (**e**) *(pénétrer)* to get in; **r. dans qch** to get into sth (**f**) *(être inclus)* **r. dans une catégorie** to fall into a category (**g**) *(argent)* to come in (**h**) *(recouvrer)* **r. dans ses frais** to recover one's expenses (**i**) **r. dans** *(sujet: voiture)* to crash into; *(sujet: piéton)* to bang into; Fam Fig **elle m'est rentrée dedans** ou **dans le chou** she laid into me

2 vt *(aux* **avoir)** (**a**) *(linge, troupeau)* *(en venant)* to bring in; *(en allant)* to take in (**b**) *(introduire, mettre)* to put in; **r. qch dans qch** to put sth into sth (**c**) *(train d'atterrissage)* to retract, to raise; **r. ses griffes** *(chat)* to retract its claws; Fig to draw in one's claws; **r. le ventre** to pull one's stomach in (**d**) *(colère, larmes)* to stifle

renversant, -e [rɑ̃vɛrsɑ̃, -ɑ̃t] adj Fam astounding

renverse [rɑ̃vɛrs] **à la renverse** adv **partir** ou **tomber à la r.** to fall backwards; Fig **j'ai failli tomber à la r.** you could have knocked me over with a feather

renversé, e [rɑ̃vɛrse] adj (**a**) *(à l'envers)* *(image)* reversed (**b**) *(tombé)* overturned (**c**) Fam *(stupéfait)* staggered

renversement [rɑ̃vɛrsəmɑ̃] nm (**a**) *(d'une tendance, des rôles)* reversal; *(d'opinions)* (dramatic) shift; **r. de situation** reversal of the situation (**b**) *(d'un gouvernement)* overthrow

renverser [rɑ̃vɛrse] **1** vt (**a**) *(tendance, rôles)* to reverse; *(ordre)* to invert; Fig **r. la vapeur** to do a U-turn; **r. la situation** to reverse the situation (**b**) *(pencher en arrière)* **r. la tête** to tilt one's head back (**c**) *(faire tomber)* to knock over; *(liquide)* to spill; **se faire r. par une voiture** to get knocked down by a car (**d**) *(gouvernement)* to overthrow (**e**) Fam *(stupéfier)* to stagger

2 se renverser vpr (**a**) *(récipient)* to fall over; *(véhicule)* to overturn (**b**) *(personne)* **se r. en arrière** to lean back

renvoi [rɑ̃vwa] nm (**a**) *(de lettres, de marchandises, de colis)* return, sending back (**b**) *(d'employés)* dismissal, Br sacking; *(d'un élève)* expulsion (**c**) *(ajournement)* postponement; Jur adjournment (**d**) *(dans un texte)* cross-reference (**e**) Jur *(devant une autre juridiction)* transfer (**devant** to) (**f**) *(éructation)* burp, belch; **avoir des renvois** to burp, to belch

renvoyer [33] [rɑ̃vwaje] **1** vt (**a**) *(au point de départ)* *(personne)* to send back; *(cadeau, lettre)* to send back, to return; *(ballon)* to throw back; *(balle de tennis)* to return (**b**) *(employé)* to dismiss, Br to sack; *(élève)* to expel; *(visiteur)* to send away (**c**) *(son)* to echo; *(chaleur, lumière)* to reflect (**d**) *(ajourner)* to postpone; Jur to adjourn (**e**) *(lecteur)* to refer (**à** to); Ordinat to cross-refer (**f**) Jur *(devant une autre juridiction)* to transfer (**devant** to)

2 vi Can to vomit

réorganisation [reɔrganizasjɔ̃] nf reorganization

réorganiser [reɔrganize] **1** vt to reorganize

2 se réorganiser vpr to get reorganized

réorienter [reɔrjɑ̃te] vt to reorientate; Univ to put on a different course

réouverture [reuvɛrtyr] nf reopening

repaire [rəpɛr] nm *(d'animaux)* den, lair; *(de malfrats)* haunt

repaître [50c] [rəpɛtr] Litt **1** vt **r. ses yeux de qch** to feast one's eyes on sth

2 se repaître vpr (**a**) *(manger à satiété)* to eat one's fill (**b**) Fig **se r. de qch** to revel in sth

répandre [repɑ̃dr] **1** vt (**a**) *(renverser)* *(accidentellement)* to spill; *(volontairement)* to spread (**b**) *(émettre)* *(lumière)* to shed; *(odeur, chaleur)* to give off (**c**) *(larmes, sang)* to shed (**d**) *(rumeur, terreur, doctrine)* to spread

2 se répandre vpr (**a**) *(liquide)* to spill (**b**) *(odeur, chaleur)* to spread (**c**) *(rumeur, opinion, pratique)* to become widespread (**d**) *(foule, touristes)* to spill (**dans** into) (**e**) **se r. en excuses** to apologize profusely

répandu, -e [repɑ̃dy] adj *(commun)* widespread

réparable [reparabl] adj (**a**) *(chaussure, machine)* repairable (**b**) *(erreur)* which can be put right; *(perte financière)* which can be made up

reparaître [20] [rəparɛtr] vi to reappear

réparateur, -trice [reparatœr, -tris] **1** adj *(sommeil)* refreshing

2 nm,f repairman, f repairwoman

réparation [reparasjɔ̃] nf (**a**) *(action)* repairing, mending; *(résultat)* repair; **faire des réparations** to do repairs (**b**) *(dédommagement)* reparation; **demander r. (de qch)** to seek redress (for sth)

réparer [repare] *vt* (**a**) *(toit, appareil, chaussures)* to repair, to mend; *(déchirure, accroc)* to mend (**b**) *(faute)* to make amends for; *(erreur)* to put right, to rectify; *(dommage)* to make good

reparler [rəparle] *vi* to speak again; **r. à qn** to speak to sb again; **elle ne lui a pas reparlé depuis** she hasn't spoken to him/her since; **r. de qch** to speak about sth again; **on en reparlera** we'll talk about it later

repartie [rəparti], **répartie** [reparti] *nf* retort; **avoir l'esprit de r., avoir de la r.** to be good at repartee

repartir [64a] [rəpartir] *vi* *(voyageur, train)* to set off again (**pour** to); *(machine)* to start (up) again; *Fam* **c'est reparti, ils ont encore mis la musique à fond!** they're at it again, they've put their music on full blast!; *Fam* **c'est reparti comme en quarante!** here we go again!

répartir [repartir] **1** *vt* (**a**) *(tâches, argent, vivres)* to divide (**entre** between); *(responsabilités)* to allocate (**entre** between); *(frais)* to share (**entre** between) (**b**) *(dans le temps)* to spread (out) (**sur** over) (**c**) *(classifier)* to divide (**en** into) (**d**) *(poids, charge)* to distribute
2 se répartir *vpr* (**a**) *(se diviser)* to split up (**en** into) (**b**) *(se classer)* to be divided (**en** into) (**c**) **se r. qch** to divide sth up

répartition [repartisjɔ̃] *nf* (**a**) *(de la population, du poids)* distribution (**b**) *(des tâches, d'argent, de vivres)* distribution (**entre** between); *(des dépenses, des responsabilités)* allocation (**entre** to) (**c**) *(dans le temps)* spreading (**sur** over)

repas [rəpɑ] *nm* meal; **prendre un r.** to have a meal; **r. d'affaires** business lunch/dinner; **r. chaud/froid** hot/cold meal; **r. de noce** wedding breakfast

repassage [rəpasaʒ] *nm* ironing; **faire du r.** to do some ironing

repasser [rəpase] **1** *vi* (**a**) *(passer à nouveau)* *(aller)* to go by again, to pass by again; *(venir)* to come by again, to pass by again; *(retourner)* to go/come back; **r. chez qn** to drop in on sb again (**b**) *(film)* to be on again
2 *vt* (**a**) *(vêtement)* to iron (**b**) *(montagne, frontière)* to go across again (**c**) *(cassette, disque)* to play again; *(film)* to show again (**d**) *(leçon)* to go over; **r. qch dans son esprit** to go over sth in one's mind (**e**) *(examen)* to resit (**f**) **r. qch à qn** *(donner à nouveau)* to give sb sth again (**g**) *(au téléphone)* **je vous le repasse** I'll put you back on to him

repêchage [rəpeʃaʒ] *nm* (**a**) *(d'un véhicule, d'un noyé)* fishing out (**b**) *(d'un candidat)* **épreuve de r.** resit; **être reçu au r.** to pass on the resit

repêcher [rəpeʃe] *vt* (**a**) *(retirer de l'eau)* to fish out (**b**) *(candidat)* to let through

repeindre [54] [rəpɛ̃dr] *vt* to repaint

repenser [rəpɑ̃se] **1** *vt* *(concept)* to rethink
2 repenser à *vt ind* to think again about; **quand j'y repense** when I think back

repenti, -e [rəpɑ̃ti] *adj* repentant, penitent

repentir¹ [rəpɑ̃tir] *nm (remords)* regret

repentir² [64a] **se repentir** *vpr* to repent; **se r. de qch/d'avoir fait qch** to repent of sth/doing sth; *Fig* to regret sth/doing sth

repérage [rəperaʒ] *nm* (**a**) *Ordinat* marking, flagging (**b**) *(d'un lieu de tournage)* recce

répercussion [reperkysjɔ̃] *nf* (**a**) *(du son)* reverberation (**b**) *(conséquence)* repercussion (**sur** on)

répercuter [reperkyte] **1** *vt* (**a**) *(son, lumière)* to reflect (**b**) *(ordre, augmentation)* to pass (**sur** on to)

2 se répercuter *vpr* (**a**) *(son, lumière)* to be reflected (**b**) *(avoir des conséquences)* **se r. sur** to have repercussions on

repère [rəpɛr] *nm* (**a**) *(point de référence)* mark; *(pour s'orienter)* landmark; *aussi Fig* **point de r.** reference point (**b**) *(dans le temps)* reference point (**c**) *Ordinat* marker, flag

repérer [34] [rəpere] **1** *vt* (**a**) *(marquer)* *(terrain)* to mark out (**b**) *(trouver)* *(défaut, endroit)* to locate; *(lieu de tournage)* to recce (**c**) *Fam (apercevoir)* to spot; **se faire r.** to attract attention
2 se repérer *vpr* to get one's bearings, to find one's way about

répertoire [repɛrtwar] *nm* (**a**) *(liste)* index, list (**b**) *(carnet)* notebook with alphabetical index; **r. à onglets** thumb index (**c**) *Ordinat* directory; **r. central** *ou* **principal** main directory; **r. racine** root directory (**d**) *(d'un théâtre, d'un artiste)* repertoire

répertorier [66] [repɛrtɔrje] *vt* to list

répéter [34] [repete] **1** *vt* (**a**) *(redire, refaire)* to repeat (**b**) *(pièce de théâtre, rôle)* to rehearse
2 *vi (acteur)* to rehearse
3 se répéter *vpr (personne)* to repeat oneself; *(événement)* to recur, to happen again; **l'histoire se répète** history repeats itself

répétitif, -ive [repetitif, -iv] *adj* repetitive

répétition [repetisjɔ̃] *nf* (**a**) *(d'un mot, d'une action, d'un événement)* repetition; **fusil à r.** repeating rifle; **avoir des rhumes à r.** to have one cold after another (**b**) *(d'une pièce de théâtre)* rehearsal; **r. générale** dress rehearsal (**c**) *Ordinat* **fonction de r.** repeat function

repeuplement [rəpœpləmɑ̃] *nm (d'un pays)* repopulation; *(d'un étang)* restocking; *(d'une forêt)* replanting

repeupler [rəpœple] **1** *vt (pays)* to repopulate; *(étang)* to restock; *(forêt)* to replant
2 se repeupler *vpr (pays)* to be repopulated; *(étang)* to be restocked; *(forêt)* to be replanted

repiquage [rəpikaʒ] *nm* (**a**) *(de plants)* pricking out, planting out (**b**) *(d'un disque, d'une cassette)* recording

repiquer [rəpike] **1** *vt* (**a**) *(plants)* to prick out, to plant out (**b**) *(disque, cassette)* to record (**c**) *Fam (reprendre)* to catch again
2 *vi Fam* **il y a repiqué** he's been at it again

répit [repi] *nm* respite, breathing space; **sans r.** *(travailler)* without a break, continuously

replacer [16] [rəplase] **1** *vt* (**a**) *(remettre à sa place)* to put back; **r. les évènements dans leur contexte** to put events into their context (**b**) *Can (reconnaître)* to recognize
2 se replacer *vpr (trouver un emploi)* to find (oneself) a new job

replanter [rəplɑ̃te] *vt* to replant

replâtrer [rəplɑtre] *vt* (**a**) *(mur)* to replaster (**b**) *Péj* to patch up

replet, -ète [rəplɛ, -ɛt] *adj (personne)* podgy; *(visage)* chubby

repli [rəpli] *nm* (**a**) *(d'une armée)* retreat, withdrawal (**b**) *(de la monnaie, des prix)* fall (**c**) *(d'un vêtement, de la peau, d'un terrain)* fold; *(d'une rivière)* bend

replier [66] [rəplije] **1** *vt* (**a**) *(objet)* to fold up; *(lame de couteau)* to fold away; *(jambes)* to tuck up; *(ailes)* to fold (**b**) *(troupes)* to withdraw
2 se replier *vpr* (**a**) *(objet)* to fold up; *Fig* **se r. sur**

soi-même to withdraw into oneself (**b**) *(troupes)* to retreat, to withdraw

réplique [replik] *nf* (**a**) *(réponse)* retort, rejoinder; **sans r.** unanswerable (**b**) *(d'un acteur)* line(s); **donner la r. à qn** to play opposite sb (**c**) *(copie)* replica; *(sosie)* double

répliquer [replike] **1** *vt* **r. que** to reply that; **je lui ai répliqué que...** I replied that...
   2 *vi* to reply; *(avec impertinence)* to answer back; **r. à qn** to answer sb back

replonger [45] [rəplɔ̃ʒe] **1** *vt aussi Fig* to plunge back (**dans** into)
   2 *vi* (**a**) *(plonger à nouveau)* to dive in again; *Fig* **r. dans l'alcoolisme/la délinquance** to relapse into alcoholism/delinquency (**b**) *Fam (délinquant)* to reoffend
   3 se replonger *vpr* **se r. dans qch** to immerse oneself in sth again

répondant [repɔ̃dɑ̃] *nm Fam* **avoir du r.** to have plenty of money stashed away

répondeur [repɔ̃dœr] *nm* **r. (automatique** *ou* **téléphonique)** (telephone) answering machine, answerphone

répondre [repɔ̃dr] **1** *vt* to answer, to reply; **je n'ai rien répondu** I made no reply
   2 répondre à *vt ind* (**a**) *(personne, lettre, question)* to answer, to reply to; *(salut)* to return; *(accusation)* to answer; **elle n'a pas encore répondu** she hasn't answered yet; **r. par un sourire** to answer with a smile; *Mil* **r. à l'appel** to answer the roll (**b**) *(téléphone, porte)* to answer; **laisse, je vais r.!** leave it, I'll get it!; **ça ne répond pas** there's no answer (**c**) *(amour)* to return (**d**) *(besoin, critères)* to meet; **ne pas r. à l'attente de qn** to fall short of sb's expectations (**e**) **les freins ne répondent plus** the brakes aren't responding any more
   3 répondre de *vt ind* to answer for; **j'en réponds** I guarantee it; **je ne réponds de rien** I'm promising nothing
   4 se répondre *vpr (personnes)* to answer each other

réponse [repɔ̃s] *nf* (**a**) *(à une question, à une lettre)* answer, reply (**à** to); *(à une offre d'emploi)* reply (**à** to); *Fig (solution)* answer (**à** to); **r. à tout** to have an answer for everything (**b**) *(réaction)* response (**c**) *Ordinat* answering; **r. automatique** unattended answering; **temps de r.** response time

report [rəpɔr] *nm* (**a**) *(de notes, de corrections)* transfer (**sur** to) (**b**) *(d'un rendez-vous)* postponement (**c**) *(en comptabilité)* carrying forward (**d**) *(dans une élection)* **r. de voix (sur)** transfer (to)

reportage [rəpɔrtaʒ] *nm* (**a**) *(article, émission)* report (**b**) *(activité)* reporting

reporter[1] [rəpɔrtɛr] *nm* reporter; **r.-cameraman** film reporter; **r.-photographe** photojournalist

reporter[2] [rəpɔrte] **1** *vt* (**a**) *(objet)* to take back, to return (**b**) *(affection)* to transfer (**sur** to) (**c**) *(différer)* **r. qch à plus tard** to postpone sth *or* put sth off until later (**d**) *(en comptabilité)* to carry forward (**e**) *(notes, corrections)* to transfer (**sur** to) (**f**) *(dans une élection)* **r. sa voix sur qn** to transfer one's vote to sb
   2 se reporter *vpr* (**a**) *(se référer)* **se r. à** *(document)* to refer to (**b**) **se r. sur** *(sujet: colère, affection)* to be transferred to

repos [rəpo] *nm* (**a**) *(détente)* rest; **un mois de r.** a month's rest; **prendre du r.** to rest; **le r. éternel** eternal rest (**b**) *(tranquillité)* peace; **ce n'est pas de tout r.!** it's not exactly restful! (**c**) *Mil* **r.!** (stand) at ease!

reposant, -e [rəpozɑ̃, -ɑ̃t] *adj* restful, relaxing

reposé, -e [rəpoze] *adj* rested, refreshed

repose-pied [rəpozpje] *nm inv* footrest

reposer [rəpoze] **1** *vt* (**a**) *(remettre)* to put back (down), to replace (**b**) *(appuyer)* **r. sa tête contre** *ou* **sur qch** to lean one's head against *or* on sth (**c**) *(détendre)* *(jambes, esprit)* to rest; **ça le reposera** it'll be a rest for him; **une couleur qui repose les yeux** a colour that is restful to the eyes (**d**) *(question)* to ask again; *(problème)* to bring up again; **r. une question à qn** to ask sb a question again (**e**) *Mil* **reposez arme!** order arms!
   2 *vi* (**a**) *(s'appuyer)* **r. sur** to rest on; *Fig (être basé sur)* to be based on; *(dépendre de)* to depend on (**b**) *(liquide)* to settle; *(pâte à tarte)* to rest (**c**) *(personne décédée)* to lie; **qu'il repose en paix** may he rest in peace
   3 se reposer *vpr* (**a**) *(se relaxer)* to rest; **se r. les yeux/les jambes** to rest one's eyes/legs (**b**) *(question, problème)* to crop up again (**c**) **se r. sur qn/qch** *(s'en remettre à)* to rely on sb/sth

repose-tête [rəpoztɛt] *nm inv* headrest

repoussant, -e [rəpusɑ̃, -ɑ̃t] *adj* repulsive

repousser [rəpuse] **1** *vt* (**a**) *(écarter)* to push aside *or* away; *(en arrière)* to push back (**b**) *(ennemi, attaque, avances)* to repel; *(offre, idée)* to reject, to turn down; *(prétendant)* to rebuff (**c**) *(rendez-vous, réunion)* to postpone, to put off (**à** until)
   2 *vi* (**a**) *(arbre, plante)* to shoot up again; *(cheveux, herbe, feuilles)* to grow again

repoussoir [rəpuswar] *nm (femme)* ugly woman; **servir de r. à qn** to serve as a foil to sb

répréhensible [repreɑ̃sibl] *adj* reprehensible

reprendre [58] [rəprɑ̃dr] **1** *vt* (**a**) *(ville, territoire, fugitif)* to recapture (**à** from) (**b**) *(se resservir de)* **r. du pain/vin** to take *or* have some more bread/wine; **vous reprendrez bien un peu de thé?** would you like some more tea? (**c**) *(rechercher)* *(personne)* to pick up (again) (**d**) *(récupérer)* *(objet)* to take back; **r. sa place** *(s'asseoir)* to return to one's seat; *Com* **les articles en solde ne sont ni repris ni échangés** ≃ sale goods are not returnable (**e**) *(surprendre)* **r. qn à faire qch** to catch sb doing sth again; **on ne m'y reprendra plus!** I won't be caught again!; **que je ne t'y reprenne plus!** don't let me catch you at it again! (**f**) *(conversation, fonctions, lutte)* to resume, to take up again; *(négociations, relations)* to re-open, to resume; **r. le travail** to return *or* go back to work; **r. connaissance** to regain consciousness; **r. la parole** to speak again; **"oui, mais...", reprit-il** "yes, but...," he continued; *Fam* **ça le reprend!** he's off again! (**g**) *(répéter)* to repeat; *(refrain)* to take up (**h**) *(retoucher)* *(vêtement)* to alter (**i**) *(corriger)* to correct
   2 *vi* (**a**) *(recommencer)* *(cours)* to start again; *(pourparlers, hostilités)* to resume, to re-open (**b**) *(prendre de la vigueur)* *(affaires)* to recover, to pick up; *(plante)* to pick up
   3 se reprendre *vpr* (**a**) *(se ressaisir)* to pull oneself together (**b**) *(se corriger)* to correct oneself (**c**) *(recommencer)* **s'y r. à plusieurs fois pour faire qch** to make several attempts at doing sth

repreneur [rəprənœr] *nm* purchaser, buyer

représailles [rəprezaj] *nfpl* reprisals, retaliation; **user de r. contre** to take retaliatory measures *or* to retaliate against; **en r.** in retaliation, as a reprisal

représentant, -e [rəprezɑ̃tɑ̃, -ɑ̃t] *nm,f* representative; **r. de commerce** sales representative

représentatif, -ive [rəprezãtatif, -iv] *adj* representative (**de** of)

représentation [rəprezãtasjɔ̃] *nf* (**a**) *(de la réalité, d'un concept)* representation (**b**) *(spectacle)* performance (**c**) *(métier)* commercial travelling (**d**) *Pol* **r. proportionnelle** proportional representation

représentativité [rəprezãtativite] *nf* representativeness

représenter [rəprezãte] **1** *vt* (**a**) *(candidat, papiers)* to present again (**b**) *(figurer)* to represent, to depict; **r. qn sous les traits de** to depict sb as (**c**) *(être le porte-parole de)* to represent (**d**) *(constituer, équivaloir à)* to represent; **r. qch pour qn** to represent sth for sb **2 se représenter** *vpr* (**a**) *(occasion)* to arise again (**b**) *(s'imaginer)* to imagine (**c**) **se r. à** *(examen)* to retake *or Br* resit; *(poste)* to apply for again; **se r. aux élections** *Br* to stand *or Am* to run for election again

répressif, -ive [represif, -iv] *adj* repressive

répression [represjɔ̃] *nf* repression; *(d'une émeute, d'un abus)* suppression

réprimande [reprimãd] *nf* reprimand, rebuke; **faire des réprimandes à qn** to reprimand *or* rebuke sb

réprimander [reprimãde] *vt* to reprimand, to rebuke

réprimer [reprime] *vt* (**a**) *(retenir)* to repress, to suppress (**b**) *(crime, révolte)* to suppress

repris [rəpri] *nm* **r. de justice** ex-prisoner

reprise [rəpriz] *nf* (**a**) *(d'un débat, des hostilités)* resumption; *(des négociations)* re-opening, resumption (**b**) *(des affaires)* recovery; **les grévistes ont voté la r. du travail** the strikers have voted to go back to work; **r. économique** economic recovery (**c**) *(d'une émission télévisée)* repeat (**d**) *(d'un moteur)* pick-up, acceleration (**e**) **à plusieurs/trois reprises** several/three times (**f**) *(raccommodage)* **faire une r. à qch** to mend sth (**g**) *(somme payée à un locataire)* = money paid for fixtures and fittings *(paid to outgoing tenant)*; *(rachat d'un objet d'occasion)* part exchange, trade-in

repriser [rəprize] *vt* to mend

réprobateur, -trice [reprobatœr, -tris] *adj* reproving

réprobation [reprobasjɔ̃] *nf* reproof

reproche [rəprɔʃ] *nm* (**a**) *(remontrance)* reproach; **faire des reproches à qn (sur qch)** to reproach sb (for sth); **sans r.** *(vie, personne)* beyond reproach, blameless (**b**) *(critique)* criticism

reprocher [rəprɔʃe] **1** *vt* **r. qch à qn** to blame *or* reproach sb for sth; **r. à qn de faire qch** to blame *or* reproach sb for doing sth; **je ne vous reproche rien** I'm not blaming you for anything; **qu'est-ce que vous reprochez à ce livre?** what have you got against the book? **2 se reprocher** *vpr* **se r. qch** to blame *or* reproach oneself for sth; **tu n'as rien à te r.** you've nothing to blame yourself for; **se r. d'avoir fait qch** to blame oneself for doing sth

reproducteur, -trice [rəprɔdyktœr, -tris] *adj* reproductive

reproduction [rəprɔdyksjɔ̃] *nf* (**a**) *(sexuelle)* reproduction (**b**) *(d'un document, d'une image, du son)* reproduction, reproducing; *(copie)* reproduction

reproduire [18] [rəprɔdɥir] **1** *vt* (**a**) *(son, image, document)* to reproduce; **nous reproduisons ici l'article du Monde** we reprint here the article from Le Monde (**b**) *(acte)* to repeat **2 se reproduire** *vpr* (**a**) *(sexuellement)* to reproduce (**b**) *(événement)* to recur, to happen again

reprogrammable [rəprɔgramabl] *adj* Ordinat *(touche)* reprogrammable

reprogrammer [rəprɔgrame] *vt* Ordinat to reprogram

réprouver [repruve] *vt* to condemn

reptation [reptasjɔ̃] *nf* crawling

reptile [reptil] *nm* reptile

repu, -e [rəpy] **1** *pp de* **repaître 2** *adj* pleasantly full

républicain, -e [repyblikɛ̃, -ɛn] *adj & nm,f* republican

république [repyblik] *nf* republic; **r. bananière** banana republic; **la R. centrafricaine** the Central African Republic; *Anciennement* **la R. démocratique allemande** the German Democratic Republic; **la R. démocratique du Congo** the Democratic Republic of the Congo; **la R. dominicaine** the Dominican Republic; *Anciennement* **la R. fédérale d'Allemagne** the Federal Republic of Germany; **la R. Tchèque** the Czech Republic

République

The French political system has been based on the concept of the "République" since the French Revolution. The proclamation of the First Republic (1792–1804) was marked by the dissolution of the monarchy. The Second Republic (1848–52) was established after the revolution of 1848. The Third Republic (1870–1940) was created after the Franco-Prussian War, but was replaced by the Vichy regime in 1940 when France was occupied by Germany. The Fourth Republic (1946–58) was plagued by instability, leading de Gaulle to call a referendum in October 1958. This resulted in the creation of the current Fifth Republic in January 1959, whose constitution provides for a much stronger executive government.

répudiation [repydjasjɔ̃] *nf* repudiation

répudier [66] [repydje] *vt* to repudiate

répugnance [repynãs] *nf* (**a**) *(aversion)* repugnance, loathing (**pour** for); **avoir de la r. pour qn/qch** to loathe sb/sth (**b**) *(appréhension)* reluctance (**à faire qch** to do sth)

répugnant, -e [repynã, -ãt] *adj* repulsive

répugner [repyne] *vi* (**a**) *(être répugnant)* **r. à qn** to be repugnant to sb, to repel sb (**b**) *(appréhender)* **r. à faire qch** to be reluctant to do sth

répulsion [repylsjɔ̃] *nf* repulsion

réputation [repytasjɔ̃] *nf* reputation; **avoir (une) bonne/mauvaise r.** to have a good/bad reputation; **sa r. de chirurgien** his reputation as a surgeon; **connaître qn de r.** to know sb by reputation; **avoir la r. d'être franc** to have a reputation for being frank

réputé, -e [repyte] *adj* well-known, renowned (**pour** for); **être r. intelligent** to be reputed to be intelligent

requérir [7] [rəkerir] *vt* (**a**) *(solliciter)* *(faveur)* to ask for, to seek; *(présence, aide)* to request (**b**) *(nécessiter)* *(explication, soin, patience)* to require, to call for (**c**) *Jur (sentence)* to demand, to call for

requête [rəkɛt] *nf* (**a**) *(demande)* request; Ordinat query; **adresser une r. à qn** to make a request to sb (**b**) *Jur* petition

requiem [rekɥijɛm] *nm inv* requiem

requiers, requiert *voir* requérir

requin [rəkɛ̃] *nm* shark

requinquer [rəkɛ̃ke] *Fam* **1** *vt* to perk up **2 se requinquer** *vpr* to perk up

requis, -e [rəki, -iz] **1** *pp de* **requérir**
  2 *adj* requisite, required; **les conditions requises** the requirements

réquisition [rekizisjɔ̃] *nf* (**a**) *(de vivres, de véhicules)* requisitioning, commandeering (**b**) *Jur (plaidoirie)* prosecution address

réquisitionner [rekizisjɔne] *vt* to requisition, to commandeer

réquisitoire [rekizitwar] *nm Jur* prosecution address; *Fig* indictment (**contre** of)

RER [ɛrəɛr] *nm* (*abrév* **Réseau express régional**) = express rail network serving Paris and its suburbs

RESA [reza] *nf* (*abrév* **réservation**) = TGV seat reservation ticket

rescapé, -e [rɛskape] **1** *adj* surviving
  2 *nm,f* survivor

rescousse [rɛskus] *nf* **aller/venir à la r. de qn** to go/come to sb's rescue; **appeler qn à la r.** to call on sb for help

réseau, -x [rezo] *nm* (**a**) *(de routes, de voies ferrées, de rivières)* network, system; **r. autoroutier** *Br* motorway *or Am* freeway network; **r. ferroviaire** rail network (**b**) *Fig (de relations)* network, circle (**c**) *Ordinat* network; **mise en r.** networking; **r. de télématique** *ou* **de communication de données** datacomms network; **r. de données** data network; **r. local** local area network, LAN; **grand r.** wide area network, WAN; **r. numérique à intégration de services** integrated services digital network

réseauter [rezote] *vi* to network

réséda [rezeda] *nm* reseda

réservation [rezɛrvasjɔ̃] *nf* reservation, booking; **faire une r.** to make a reservation

réserve [rezɛrv] *nf* (**a**) *(restriction)* reservation; **émettre des réserves (sur qch)** to voice reservations (about sth); **sous r. de qch** subject to sth; **sans r.** *(éloges, admiration)* unqualified (**b**) *(discrétion)* reserve; **sortir de sa r.** to come out of one's shell (**c**) *(de vivres, d'équipement, d'argent)* reserve; **en r.** in reserve (**d**) *Mil* reserve (**e**) *(de chasse, de pêche)* reserve; *Can* **r. faunique** wildlife reserve; **r. indienne** (Native American) reservation; **r. naturelle** nature reserve (**f**) *(de magasin)* storeroom; *(de bibliothèque, de musée)* reserve collection

réservé, -e [rezɛrve] *adj* (**a**) *(chambre, siège)* reserved, booked (**b**) *(consacré)* **être r. à qn/qch** to be reserved for sb/sth (**c**) *(personne, attitude)* reserved

réserver [rezɛrve] **1** *vt* (**a**) *(chambre, place)* to reserve, to book; **vous avez réservé?** do you have a reservation? (**b**) *(mettre de côté)* to set aside, to put by (**à/pour** for); **r. le meilleur pour la fin** to save the best till last (**c**) *Fig* **r. son jugement** to reserve judgement; **r. une surprise à qn** to have a surprise in store for sb; **r. un bon accueil à qn** to welcome sb with open arms; **ce que le sort nous réserve** what fate has in store for us
  2 se réserver *vpr* (**a**) *(garder pour soi)* **se r. qch** to keep sth for oneself; **se r. le droit de faire qch** to reserve the right to do sth (**b**) **se r. pour qch** to save oneself for sth

réserviste [rezɛrvist] *nm Mil* reservist

réservoir [rezɛrvwar] *nm* (**a**) *(bassin)* reservoir (**b**) *(cuve)* tank; **r. d'essence** *Br* petrol *or Am* gas tank

résidence [rezidɑ̃s] *nf* (**a**) *(demeure)* residence; **r. principale** main residence; **r. secondaire** second home (**b**) *(habitations de standing) Br* block of luxury flats, *Am* luxury apartment building (**c**) *Jur* **en r. surveillée** under house arrest (**d**) *(séjour)* residence

résident, -e [rezidɑ̃, -ɑ̃t] **1** *adj* (**a**) *(personne)* resident (**b**) *Ordinat* **r. en mémoire** memory-resident
  2 *nm,f* (**a**) *(habitant)* resident (**b**) *(étranger)* foreign resident; **les résidents français en Grande-Bretagne** French nationals resident in Great Britain (**c**) *Belg* **second r.** weekender, *Br* holiday *or Am* vacation resident

résidentiel, -elle [rezidɑ̃sjɛl] *adj* residential

résider [rezide] *vi* (**a**) *(personne)* to reside (**b**) *(consister)* to lie (**dans** in)

résidu [rezidy] *nm* *(reste)* residue; **résidus** *(déchets)* waste

résiduel, -elle [rezidɥɛl] *adj* residual

résignation [reziɲasjɔ̃] *nf* resignation

résigné, -e [reziɲe] *adj* resigned (**à** to)

résigner [reziɲe] **se résigner** *vpr* to resign oneself (**à** to); **se r. à faire qch** to resign oneself to doing sth

résiliable [reziljabl] *adj* *(contrat)* which may be terminated

résiliation [reziljasjɔ̃] *nf* *(d'un contrat)* termination

résilier [66] [rezilje] *vt* *(accord, contrat)* to terminate

résille [rezij] *nf* hairnet

résine [rezin] *nf* resin

résiné [rezine] *adj m & nm* (vin) **r.** retsina

résineux, -euse [rezinø, -øz] **1** *adj* (**a**) *(bois, odeur)* resinous (**b**) *(arbre, forêt)* coniferous
  2 *nm* conifer

résistance [rezistɑ̃s] *nf* (**a**) *(action)* resistance (**à** to); **n'offrir aucune r.** to put up *or* offer no resistance; **opposer une r. à qn/qch** to resist sb/sth; **r. passive** passive resistance (**b**) *Hist* **la R.** the Resistance (**c**) *(endurance)* stamina (**d**) *Élec* resistance (**e**) *(conducteur) (d'un appareil)* element (**f**) *(d'un matériau)* resistance

résistant, -e [rezistɑ̃, -ɑ̃t] **1** *adj* *(matériau)* tough; *(plante)* hardy; **c'est quelqu'un de très r.** he has a lot of stamina
  2 *nm,f* *(combattant)* freedom fighter; *(pendant la Résistance)* member of the Resistance

résister [reziste] **résister à** *vt ind* (**a**) *(attaque, agresseur)* to resist (**b**) *(tentation, influence, personne)* to resist; **je n'ai pas pu r., je les ai achetées** I couldn't resist, I bought them (**c**) *(supporter) (douleur, pression, froid)* to withstand; *(mauvais traitement)* to stand up to; *(maladie, épidémie, fatigue)* to overcome (**d**) *(s'opposer à)* to stand up to

résolu, -e [rezɔly] **1** *pp de* **résoudre**
  2 *adj* *(personne)* determined, resolute; **être r. à faire qch** to be determined to do sth

résolument [rezɔlymɑ̃] *adv* resolutely

résolution [rezɔlysjɔ̃] *nf* (**a**) *(décision)* resolution; **prendre la r. de faire qch** to make a resolution to do sth; **prendre des résolutions** to make resolutions (**b**) *(d'un problème)* solving (**c**) *(détermination)* determination, resolve (**d**) *(d'un écran)* resolution

résolvais *etc voir* **résoudre**

résonance [rezɔnɑ̃s] *nf aussi Tech* resonance; *Fig (écho)* echo

résonner [rezɔne] *vi* (**a**) *(retentir)* to resound (**b**) *(faire un écho)* to echo

résorber [rezɔrbe] **1** *vt* (**a**) *(surplus, déficit)* to absorb; *(chômage)* to bring down; *(dettes)* to clear (**b**) *(sang, pus)* to resorb
  2 se résorber *vpr* (**a**) *(surplus, déficit)* to be absorbed;

(chômage) to be brought down (**b**) *(sang, pus)* to be resorbed

résorption [rezɔrpsjɔ̃] *nf (d'un surplus, d'un déficit)* absorption; *(du chômage)* bringing down

résoudre [3b] [rezudr] **1** *vt* (**a**) *(difficulté, conflit, crise)* to resolve; *(équation, énigme, problème)* to solve (**b**) *(décider)* **r. de faire qch** to resolve to do sth (**c**) *(décomposer)* **r. qch en qch** to resolve sth into sth **2 se résoudre** *vpr* **se r. à faire qch** to resolve to do sth; **je ne peux pas me r. à la quitter** I can't bring myself to leave her

respect [rɛspɛ] *nm* respect (**pour** for); **élevé dans le r. des traditions** brought up to respect traditions; **avoir du r. pour qn** to have respect for sb; **manquer de r. envers qn** to show sb a lack of respect; **tenir qn en r.** to keep sb at a distance; **sauf le r. que je vous dois, sauf votre r.** with all due respect; **respects** *(hommages)* respects

respectabilité [rɛspɛktabilite] *nf* respectability

respectable [rɛspɛktabl] *adj* respectable

respecter [rɛspɛkte] **1** *vt* to respect; **faire r. la loi** to enforce the law; **se faire r.** to command respect; **r. la priorité** *(en voiture) Br* to give way, *Am* to yield **2 se respecter** *vpr* (**a**) *(soi-même)* to respect oneself; **comme tout homme qui se respecte** like any self-respecting man (**b**) *(l'un l'autre)* to respect each other

respectif, -ive [rɛspɛktif, -iv] *adj* respective

respectivement [rɛspɛktivmã] *adv* respectively

respectueusement [rɛspɛktɥøzmã] *adv* respectfully

respectueux, -euse [rɛspɛktɥø, -øz] *adj* respectful (**de/envers** of/to)

respirable [rɛspirabl] *adj* breathable; *Fig* **l'atmosphère n'était plus r.** the atmosphere had become unbearable

respirateur [rɛspiratœr] *nm* respirator

respiration [rɛspirasjɔ̃] *nf* breathing; **reprendre sa r.** to pause for breath; **retenir sa r.** to hold one's breath; **r. artificielle** artificial respiration

respiratoire [rɛspiratwar] *adj (organe)* respiratory; *(appareil, exercice, problème)* breathing

respirer [rɛspire] **1** *vi* (**a**) *(personne, plante)* to breathe (**b**) *Fig (être soulagé)* **je respire!** I can breathe again! (**c**) *Fig (se reposer)* to have a break **2** *vt* (**a**) *(inhaler)* to breathe (in) (**b**) *(exprimer)* **r. la santé** to be glowing with health; **il ne respire pas l'intelligence** he doesn't exactly radiate intelligence

resplendir [rɛsplãdir] *vi* (**a**) *(briller)* to shine (**b**) *(personne)* to be radiant; **r. de joie/santé** to radiate joy/health

resplendissant, -e [rɛsplãdisã, -ãt] *adj (personne, beauté)* radiant; **r. de joie/santé** radiant with joy/health; **il a une mine resplendissante** he looks wonderfully well

responsabiliser [rɛspɔ̃sabilize] *vt* **r. qn** to give sb a sense of responsibility

responsabilité [rɛspɔ̃sabilite] *nf (morale)* responsibility; *(légale)* liability (**de** for); **accepter une r.** to take on *or* accept a responsibility; **avoir la r. de qn/qch** to be responsible for sb/sth; **décliner toute r.** to accept no liability; **avoir un poste à responsabilités** to have a responsible job; **r. civile** public liability; **r. limitée** limited liability; **r. au tiers** third-party liability

responsable [rɛspɔ̃sabl] **1** *adj* (**a**) *(moralement)* responsible (**de** for); *(légalement)* liable (**de** for) (**b**) *(mûr)* responsible

2 *nmf* (**a**) *(auteur, coupable)* person responsible (**de** for); **qui est le r. de cette plaisanterie?** who's (the person) responsible for this prank? (**b**) *(personne qui a la responsabilité)* person in charge (**c**) *(dirigeant élu)* official

resquiller [rɛskije] *vi Fam (au théâtre, au concert)* to sneak in without paying; *(dans un bus, dans le métro)* to dodge paying one's fare

resquilleur, -euse [rɛskijœr, -øz] *nm,f Fam (au théâtre, au cinéma)* = person who sneaks in without paying; *(dans un bus, dans le métro) Br* fare-dodger, *Am* farebeater

ressac [rəsak] *nm* undertow

ressaisir [rəsezir] **se ressaisir** *vpr* to pull oneself together

ressasser [rəsase] *vt* (**a**) *(mentalement)* to brood over (**b**) *(répéter)* to keep coming out with

ressemblance [rəsãblãs] *nf (entre personnes)* resemblance, likeness; *(entre choses)* similarity

ressemblant, -e [rəsãblã, -ãt] *adj (portrait)* lifelike

ressembler [rəsãble] **1 ressembler à** *vt ind* (**a**) *(personne)* to resemble, to be like; **à quoi ressemble-t-elle?** what does she look like? (**b**) *Fig (chose)* **cela ne ressemble à rien** it doesn't look like anything; **cela ne lui ressemble pas** that's not like him/her **2 se ressembler** *vpr* to be alike, to resemble each other; **ils se ressemblent comme des frères** you'd take them for brothers; **se r. comme deux gouttes d'eau** to be as like as two peas in a pod; **les jours se suivent et ne se ressemblent pas** day follows day and you never know what to expect; *Prov* **qui se ressemble s'assemble** birds of a feather flock together

ressemeler [9] [rəsəmle] *vt* to resole

ressentiment [rəsãtimã] *nm* resentment (**de/contre** at/against)

ressentir [64a] [rəsãtir] **1** *vt* to feel **2 se ressentir** *vpr* **se r. de qch** *(personne, pays)* to feel the effects of sth; *(travail)* to show the effects of sth

resserrement [rəsɛrmã] *nm (d'une amitié, de liens)* strengthening

resserrer [rəsere] **1** *vt* (**a**) *(nœud, ceinture, écrou)* to tighten (**b**) *Fig (amitié, liens)* to strengthen **2 se resserrer** *vpr* (**a**) *(vallée, route)* to narrow (**b**) *(nœud)* to tighten (**c**) *Fig (liens)* to strengthen

resservir [63] [rəsɛrvir] **1** *vt (plat)* to serve up again; **r. qn** to give sb another helping **2** *vi* to be used again (**à** for) **3 se resservir** *vpr* **se r. de qch** *(plat)* to take another helping of sth; *(objet)* to use sth again

ressort [rəsɔr] *nm* (**a**) *(pièce)* spring (**b**) *(force morale)* resilience; **avoir du r.** to be resilient (**c**) *(motivation)* motive (**d**) **être du r. de qn** to be sb's responsibility (**e**) **en dernier r.** *Jur* without appeal; *Fig* as a last resort

ressortir¹ [64a] [rəsɔrtir] **1** *vi (aux être)* (**a**) *(personne)* *(en s'éloignant)* to go back out; *(en s'approchant)* to come back out (**b**) *(se détacher)* to stand out; **faire r.** *(couleur)* to bring out; *(regard, yeux, fait)* to highlight **2** *vt (aux avoir)* (**a**) *(parapluie, vêtements)* to get out again (**b**) *Fig (histoire)* to trot out again **3** *v impersonnel (aux être)* **il ressort de ceci que...** it emerges from this that...

ressortir² ressortir à *vt ind* (**a**) *(être de la compétence de)* to come under the jurisdiction of (**b**) *Litt (dépendre de)* to come within the province of

ressortissant, -e [rəsɔrtisã, -ãt] *nm,f* national

ressouder [rəsude] **1** *vt* to resolder; *Fig* to re-establish
 2 se ressouder *vpr (os, fracture)* to knit
ressource [rəsurs] *nf* (**a**) *(moyen)* possibility; **je n'ai d'autre r. que de...** the only course of action open to me is to...; **avoir de la r.** to be resourceful; **en dernière r.** as a last resort (**b**) **ressources** *(argent, moyens d'action)* resources; **être sans ressources** to have no means of support; **ressources humaines** human resources (**c**) *(d'une nation)* **ressources** resources
ressourcer [16] [rəsurse] **se ressourcer** *vpr Fam* to get back in touch with one's inner self
ressusciter [resysite] **1** *vt* (**a**) *(un mort)* to raise from the dead; *Fig* **ça ne va pas le r.** it won't bring him back (**b**) *(querelle, mode)* to revive
 2 *vi* to rise from the dead; **j'ai l'impression de r.** I feel like a new person
restant, -e [rɛstɑ̃, -ɑ̃t] **1** *adj* remaining
 2 *nm* remainder, rest; *Can* **restants** *(d'un repas)* leftovers
restaurant [rɛstɔrɑ̃] *nm* restaurant; **aller au r.** to eat out; **r. d'entreprise** staff canteen; **r. universitaire** university canteen *or* refectory
restaurateur, -trice [rɛstɔratœr, -tris] *nm,f* (**a**) *(de tableaux)* restorer (**b**) *(de restaurant)* restaurateur, restaurant owner
restauration [rɛstɔrasjɔ̃] *nf* (**a**) *(de tableaux, de bâtiments)* restoration (**b**) *(métier)* catering; **r. rapide** fast food (**c**) *Hist* **la R.** the Restoration *(return to power of the Bourbon dynasty 1814–1830)* (**d**) *Ordinat* restore (**e**) *Suisse (restaurant)* restaurant
restaurer [rɛstɔre] *vt* (**a**) *(rétablir, réparer)* to restore (**b**) *Ordinat* to restore (**c**) *Litt (faire manger)* **r. qn** to give sb something to eat
 2 se restaurer *vpr* to have something to eat
reste [rɛst] *nm* (**a**) *(de travail, d'argent, de vin)* rest, remainder; **le r. du temps** the rest of the time; **le r. (des gens)** the rest; **il y avait un r. de beurre/lait** there was a bit of butter/milk left (over) (**b**) **restes** *(d'un repas)* leftovers (**c**) *(ossements)* **restes** remains (**d**) *(locutions)* **du** *ou* **au r.** besides; **pour le r.** as for the rest; **avoir qch de r.** to have sth to spare; **pour ne pas être en r.** *(pour ne pas avoir de dette)* so as not to be indebted; *(pour ne pas être surpassé)* so as not to be outdone; **partir sans demander son r.** to leave without further ado; *Fam* **avoir de beaux restes** to still have one's looks
rester [rɛste] *(aux être)* **1** *vi* (**a**) *(subsister)* to remain, to be left; **les 5 euros qui restent** the remaining 5 euros, the 5 euros left; **c'est tout ce qui me reste** that's all I have left; **le nom lui est resté** the name stayed with him/her
 (**b**) *(demeurer)* to stay, to remain; **restez où vous êtes** stay where you are; **r. assis** to stay seated; **r. au lit** to stay in bed; **r. (à) dîner** to stay to dinner; **r. sur place** to stay put; *Fam* **j'y suis, j'y reste** here I am and here I stay; *Fam* **y r.** *(mourir)* to kick the bucket; **que cela reste entre nous** this is strictly between ourselves; **r. sur une impression** to be left with an impression; **cela m'est resté sur l'estomac** *(plat)* it's lying heavy on my stomach; *Fig* it still rankles with me; **en r. là** to stop there; **r. dans les mémoires** to live on in people's memories; **le plus dur reste à faire** the hardest part is still to be done
 2 *v impersonnel* **il me reste 5 euros** I've got 5 euros left; **il ne me reste qu'à vous remercier** it only remains for me to thank you; **il reste beaucoup de choses à faire** there still are a lot of things to be done;

il reste que... the fact remains that...; **il n'en reste pas moins que...** it is nevertheless the case that...; **(il) reste à savoir si c'est vrai** it remains to be seen whether it's true
restituer [rɛstitɥe] *vt* (**a**) *(reconstituer) (inscription, texte)* to restore; *(passé, ambiance)* to recreate (**b**) *(rendre) (objets volés)* to restore, to return; *(argent, prêt)* to repay, to pay back (**c**) *(son)* to reproduce
restitution [rɛstitysjɔ̃] *nf* (**a**) *(reconstitution) (d'un texte)* restoration; *(d'une ambiance, du passé)* recreation (**b**) *(d'objets volés)* return; *(d'argent, d'un prêt)* repayment (**c**) *(du son)* reproduction
Restoroute® [rɛstorut] *nm Br* motorway *or Am* freeway restaurant
restreindre [54] [rɛstrɛ̃dr] **1** *vt* to restrict (**à** to)
 2 se restreindre *vpr* (**a**) *(réduire ses dépenses)* to cut down (**b**) *(domaine, recherche)* to become more restricted
restreint, -e [rɛstrɛ̃, -ɛ̃t] *adj (production, vocabulaire)* restricted (**à** to); *(espace, service)* limited
restrictif, -ive [rɛstriktif, -iv] *adj* restrictive
restriction [rɛstriksjɔ̃] *nf* (**a**) *(diminution)* restriction (**b**) *(réserve)* reservation; **faire des restrictions** to express some reservations; **sans r.** *(accord)* unconditional; *(approuver)* unreservedly (**c**) *Ordinat* **r. d'accès** access restriction (**d**) **restrictions** *(mesures de rationnement)* restrictions
restructuration [rəstryktyrasjɔ̃] *nf* restructuring
restructurer [rəstryktyre] *vt* to restructure
résultant, -e [rezyltɑ̃, -ɑ̃t] **1** *adj* resulting
 2 *nf* **résultante** consequence, result
résultat [rezylta] *nm* result; **sans r.** to no effect; *Fam* **r.: il a été licencié** the upshot was he was sacked; **donner des résultats** to produce results; **résultats d'exercice** *ou* **d'exploitation** trading results
résulter [rezylte] **1** *vi* **r. de qch** to result from sth
 2 *v impersonnel* **il en résulte que...** the result of this is that...
résumé [rezyme] *nm* (**a**) *(d'un texte)* summary, résumé; **faire le r. de qch** *(d'un texte)* to give a summary of sth; *(d'une histoire, d'une situation)* to sum sth up; **en r.** *(en bref)* in short (**b**) *(livre)* study guide
résumer [rezyme] **1** *vt (article, idées)* to summarize; *(situation, histoire)* to sum up
 2 se résumer *vpr* (**a**) *(personne)* to sum up (**b**) *(se réduire)* **se r. à qch** to come down to sth
résurgence [rezyrʒɑ̃s] *nf* resurgence
resurgir [rəsyrʒir] *vi* to reappear suddenly
résurrection [rezyrɛksjɔ̃] *nf aussi Fig* resurrection
rétabli, -e [retabli] *adj (après une maladie)* recovered
rétablir [retablir] **1** *vt* (**a**) *(téléphone, eau, gaz)* to restore (**b**) *(guérir)* to restore to health (**c**) *(faits, vérité)* to re-establish (**d**) *(ordre, relations, réputation)* to restore (**e**) *(réhabiliter)* **r. qn** *(dans ses fonctions)* to reinstate sb; **r. qn dans ses droits** to restore sb's rights
 2 se rétablir *vpr* (**a**) *(malade)* to recover (**b**) *(silence, calme)* to return; *(situation)* to return to normal
rétablissement [retablismɑ̃] *nm* (**a**) *(de l'ordre, de la paix, d'une dynastie)* restoration (**b**) *(des communications, des relations)* restoration (**c**) *(d'un employé)* reinstatement (**d**) *(d'un malade)* recovery
rétamé, -e [retame] *adj Fam (fatigué) Br* knackered, *Am* bushed; *(hors d'usage)* kaput, *Br* clapped-out
rétamer [retame] *vt* (**a**) *(casserole)* to retin (**b**) *(miroir)* to resilver (**c**) *Fam (au jeu)* to clean out; **se faire r.** *(se faire battre)* to get hammered

retaper [rətape] **1** *vt* (**a**) *Fam (vieille maison, voiture)* to do up (**b**) *Fam (lit)* to straighten (**c**) *Fam* **r. qn** to buck sb up
2 se retaper *vpr Fam (convalescent)* to get back on one's feet

retard [rətar] *nm* (**a**) *(dans le temps)* delay; *(d'une personne attendue)* lateness; **je vous prie d'excuser mon r.** please excuse me for being late; **être en r.** to be late; *(sur un programme)* to be behind; **sans r.** without delay; **avoir du r.** to be late; **avoir une heure de r.** to be an hour late; **prendre du r.** *(personne)* to fall behind; *(train)* to be running late; **r. de paiement** late payment (**b**) *(dans un développement)* backwardness; **pays en r.** country lagging behind the others; **être en r. pour son âge** to be backward for one's age; **en r. sur son temps** behind the times; **r. mental** backwardness (**c**) *(d'un véhicule)* **r. à l'allumage** retarded ignition

retardataire [rətardatɛr] **1** *nmf* latecomer
2 *adj* **un élève r.** a pupil who arrives late

retardé, -e [rətarde] *adj* (**a**) *(départ, arrivée)* late (**b**) *(mentalement) (enfant)* backward

retardement [rətardəmɑ̃] *nm* **à r.** *(bombe)* time; *(longtemps après)* belatedly

retarder [rətarde] **1** *vt* (**a**) *(faire arriver en retard)* to delay; **r. qn dans ses études** to hold sb back in his/her studies (**b**) *(différer)* to delay; **r. qch d'une heure/d'une semaine** to put sth back an hour/a week (**c**) *(montre, horloge)* to put back (**de** by)
2 *vi* (**a**) *(horloge)* to be slow; **ma montre retarde/je retarde de dix minutes** my watch is/I'm ten minutes slow (**b**) **r. sur son temps** *ou* **son époque** to be behind the times (**c**) *Fam (ne pas être au courant)* to be behind the times

retendre [rətɑ̃dr] *vt (cordes)* to retighten

retenir [70] [rətənir] **1** *vt* (**a**) *(faire rester) (personne)* to keep, to detain; **r. qn prisonnier/en otage** to keep *or* hold sb prisoner/hostage; **je ne vous retiens pas** I won't keep you; **r. qn à dîner** to have sb stay for dinner; **r. qn par le bras** to hold sb back by the arm; **r. l'attention de qn** *(candidature, proposition)* to catch sb's attention (**b**) *(conserver) (eau, chaleur)* to retain (**c**) *(retirer) (argent)* to withhold; *(cotisation, impôt)* to deduct (**sur** from); **retenu à la source** deducted at source (**d**) *(se souvenir de) (leçon, nom)* to remember; **je le retiens, ton ami!** I won't forget your friend in a hurry! (**e**) *(réserver) (place, chambre, table)* to reserve, to book (**f**) *(accepter) (projet, suggestion)* to adopt; **votre candidature n'a pas été retenue** your application was unsuccessful (**g**) *(contenir) (colère)* to contain; *(larmes)* to hold back; *(cri)* to stifle; *(respiration, souffle)* to hold (**h**) *(garder en arrière) (personne, foule, chien)* to hold back, to restrain (**i**) *(empêcher)* **r. qn de faire qch** to restrain sb from doing sth, to hold sb back from doing sth; **qu'est-ce qui te retient de le lui dire?** what's stopping you telling him/her?; **qu'est-ce qui vous retient?** what's holding you back?
2 se retenir *vpr* (**a**) *(s'accrocher)* to hold on (**à** to) (**b**) *(se contenir)* to restrain oneself; **se r. de faire qch** to stop oneself (from) doing sth

rétention [retɑ̃sjɔ̃] *nf* retention; **faire de la r. d'information** to withhold information

retentir [rətɑ̃tir] *vi* (**a**) *(Klaxon, alarme)* to sound; *(tonnerre, canon)* to rumble; *(coup de feu, cri)* to ring out; **l'explosion retentit dans toute la ville** the explosion was heard right across the city (**b**) *(lieu)* **r.**

de to resound *or* echo with (**c**) *Fig* **r. sur** to have an impact on

retentissant, -e [rətɑ̃tisɑ̃, -ɑ̃t] *adj* (**a**) *(voix)* ringing (**b**) *Fig (succès, échec)* resounding; *(scandale)* sensational

retentissement [rətɑ̃tismɑ̃] *nm (d'un événement)* impact; **avoir un r. sur qch** to have an impact on sth

retenue [rətəny] *nf* (**a**) *(d'une somme)* deduction; **r. sur salaire** wage deduction; *(mensuel)* salary deduction (**b**) *(dans un calcul)* carry over; **n'oublie pas la r.** don't forget to carry over (**c**) *Scol* detention (**d**) *(discrétion)* restraint (**e**) *(barrage)* dam

réticence [retisɑ̃s] *nf* hesitation, unwillingness; **sans r.** unhesitatingly

réticent, -e [retisɑ̃, -ɑ̃t] *adj (hésitant)* hesitant, unwilling

rétif, -ive [retif, -iv] *adj (cheval)* stubborn; *(personne)* recalcitrant

rétine [retin] *nf* retina

retiré, -e [rətire] *adj* (**a**) *(lieu, vie)* secluded; **vivre r. du monde** to lead a secluded life (**b**) **être r. des affaires** to be retired from business

retirer [rətire] **1** *vt* (**a**) *(faire sortir) (objet coincé)* to get out; *(bouchon, épine)* to pull out (**de** of); **r. un enfant d'une école** to remove a child from a school; **r. qch de la circulation** to withdraw sth from circulation; **r. qch du marché** to take sth off the market; **r. les mains de ses poches** to take one's hands out of one's pockets (**b**) *(argent)* to withdraw (**de** from), to take out (**de** of); *(bagages, billet)* to collect (**de** from), to pick up (**de** from) (**c**) *(obtenir)* **r. un profit de qch** to make a profit out of sth; **r. du plaisir de qch** to get pleasure from sth (**d**) *(ôter) (gants, lunettes, vêtement)* to take off, to remove (**e**) *(confisquer)* to take away (**à** from); **r. son permis de conduire à qn** to ban sb from driving (**f**) *(ramener en arrière) (main)* to remove (**g**) *(ne pas maintenir) (offre, plainte, candidature)* to withdraw; **je retire ce que j'ai dit** I take back what I said
2 se retirer *vpr* (**a**) *(s'en aller) (personne)* to withdraw; *(foule)* to move back; **vous pouvez vous r.** you may go (**b**) *(eaux, mer)* to recede; *(marée)* to ebb (**c**) **se r. d'une association/élection** to withdraw from a partnership/an election; **se r. des affaires** to retire from business

retombées [rətɔ̃be] *nfpl* (**a**) *(répercussions)* repercussions; **avoir des retombées sur qch** to have repercussions on sth (**b**) *(déchets)* **retombées radioactives** radioactive fallout

retomber [rətɔ̃be] *vi (aux être)* (**a**) *(tomber de nouveau)* to fall again; **r. dans son fauteuil** to fall back into one's armchair; **laisser r. ses bras** to drop one's arms (**b**) *(après un saut, après avoir été en l'air) (personne, ballon)* to land; **r. sur ses pattes** *(chat)* to land on its feet; *Fig* **r. sur ses pieds** *ou Fam* **ses pattes** to land on one's feet (**c**) *(retourner)* **r. dans l'oubli** to sink back into obscurity; **r. dans le désespoir/le chaos** to fall back into despair/chaos; **r. en enfance** to lapse into one's second childhood (**d**) *(redevenir)* **r. malade** to fall ill again (**e**) *(rencontrer)* **r. sur qch** to come across sth again; *Fam* **r. sur qn** to bump into sb again (**f**) *(se répercuter)* **r. sur qn** *(blâme, responsabilité)* to fall on sb; *Fam* **ça va me r. dessus** I'm going to take the rap for it (**g**) *(baisser) (enthousiasme, intérêt, attention)* to fall off (**h**) *(cheveux, rideaux)* to hang (down) (**sur** over)

rétorquer [retorke] *vt* to retort

retors, -e [rətɔr, -ɔrs] *adj (personne)* crafty, wily

rétorsion [rətɔrsjɔ̃] *nf* retaliation

retouche [rətuʃ] *nf* (**a**) *(sur photo)* touching up; *TV, Cin & Ordinat* **r. d'image(s)** image retouching (**b**) *(d'un texte, d'un vêtement)* alteration

retoucher [rətuʃe] *vt* (**a**) *(photo)* to touch up (**b**) *(texte, vêtement)* to alter

retour [rətur] **1** *nm* (**a**) *(d'une personne, d'une saison)* return (**à** to); **être de r. (de)** to be back (again) (from); **de r. chez moi** back home; **à mon r.** on my return; **en r. (de)** in return (for); **payer qn de r.** to repay sb in kind; **par r. (du courrier)** by return (of post); **par un juste r.** des choses as is/was only right and proper; *Fam* **être sur le r.** to be past one's prime; **r. à l'envoyeur** return to sender; **r. de manivelle** backfire kick; *Fig* **il y a eu un r. de manivelle** it backfired (**b**) *(trajet)* return journey (**c**) *(changement) (de fortune)* reversal; **r. d'âge** change of life (**d**) *Ordinat* **r. d'information** feedback; **r. ligne** line feed; **r. chariot obligatoire** hard carriage return (**e**) *(sur clavier)* return; **r. arrière** backspace; **r. de chariot** carriage return

2 *adj inv (match, touche)* return

retournement [rəturnəmã] *nm (de situation)* turnaround (**de** in), reversal (**de** of)

retourner [rəturne] **1** *vt (aux avoir)* (**a**) *(gant, vêtement)* to turn inside out; *(poche)* to turn out; *Fam* **r. sa veste** to change sides; *Fig* **r. le couteau dans la plaie** to twist the knife, to rub it in (**b**) *(terre, matelas, crêpe)* to turn (over); *(carte)* to turn over *or* up; *Fig (idée, projet)* to turn over (**c**) *Fam (bouleverser) (personne)* to shake (**d**) *(renverser) (situation)* to reverse (**e**) *(rendre) (livre, lettre, compliment)* to return (**à** to) (**f**) *Fig (utiliser)* **r. un argument contre qn** to turn an argument against sb

2 *vi (aux être)* to go back, to return (**à** to)

3 *v impersonnel Fam* **voilà de quoi il retourne** that's what it's all about

4 se retourner *vpr* (**a**) *(dormeur, voiture)* to turn over; **il doit se r. dans sa tombe** he must be turning in his grave (**b**) *Fig (s'organiser)* to sort things out (**c**) *(tourner la tête)* to turn round; **partir sans se r.** to leave without looking back (**d**) **se r. contre qn** *(personne)* to turn against sb; *(action, ambition)* to backfire on sb (**e**) *(aller)* **s'en r. quelque part** to return somewhere

retracer [16] [rətrase] *vt (événement, vie)* to recount

rétractation [retraktasjɔ̃] *nf* retraction

rétracter¹ [retrakte] **1** *vt (griffes, antennes)* to retract

2 se rétracter *vpr (muscle)* to retract

rétracter² **1** *vt (paroles)* to retract, to withdraw

2 se rétracter *vpr (se dédire)* to retract

rétraction [retraksjɔ̃] *nf* retraction

retrait [rətrɛ] *nm* (**a**) *(d'un permis)* withdrawal; **r. du permis de conduire** driving ban (**b**) *(d'une candidature)* withdrawal (**c**) *(fait de récupérer)* **r. des bagages** baggage reclaim (**d**) *(d'argent)* withdrawal; **r. d'espèces** cash withdrawal (**e**) *(des eaux)* receding (**f**) *(en typographie)* indent; **mettre qch en r.** to indent sth (**g**) **en r.** *(étagère)* recessed; *(maison)* set back; *Fig* **être/rester en r.** *(personne)* to be/stay in the background

retraite [rətrɛt] *nf* (**a**) *(de la vie active)* retirement; **être à la r.** to be retired; **prendre sa r.** to retire; **être mis à la r.** to be retired; **r. anticipée** early retirement (**b**) *(pension)* (retirement) pension; **r. complémentaire** supplementary pension (**c**) *(procession)* **r. aux flambeaux** torchlight procession (**d**) *(refuge)* retreat;

(de voleurs) hideout (**e**) *(expérience religieuse)* retreat; **faire une r.** to go into retreat (**f**) *Mil* retreat

retraité, -e [rətrɛte] **1** *adj* retired

2 *nm,f* pensioner

retraitement [rətrɛtmã] *nm* reprocessing

retraiter [rətrɛte] *vt* to reprocess

retranchement [rətrãʃmã] *nm* entrenchment; *Fig* **forcer qn dans ses (derniers) retranchements** to drive sb to the wall

retrancher [rətrãʃe] **1** *vt* (**a**) *(soustraire) (chiffre)* to take away (**de** from); **r. qch sur une somme** to deduct sth from a sum of money (**b**) *(ôter) (passage, nom)* to remove (**de** from)

2 se retrancher *vpr (troupes)* to dig in; *Fig* **se r. dans le silence** to take refuge in silence; **se r. derrière qn/ qch** to hide behind sb/sth

retransmettre [47] [rətrãsmɛtr] *vt Rad & TV* to broadcast

retransmission [rətrãsmisjɔ̃] *nf Rad & TV* broadcast

retravailler [rətravaje] **1** *vt (discours, texte, pas de danse)* to work on again

2 *vi* (**a**) *(reprendre le travail)* to go back to work (**b**) *(retrouver du travail)* to work again

rétréci, -e [retresi] *adj* (**a**) **un pull r.** a pullover that has shrunk (**b**) *(route)* narrow

rétrécir [retresir] **1** *vt (vêtement)* to take in

2 *vi (vêtement, tissu)* to shrink

3 se rétrécir *vpr (route)* to narrow

rétrécissement [retresismã] *nm* (**a**) *(action) (de route)* narrowing; *(de vêtement, de tissu)* shrinking (**b**) *(partie étroite) (de tuyau, de route)* narrowing

rétribuer [retribɥe] *vt (employé)* to pay; *(travail)* to pay for

rétribution [retribysjɔ̃] *nf* payment, remuneration

rétro [retro] **1** *adj inv* retro

2 *adv* **s'habiller r.** to wear retro clothes; **meublé r.** furnished in retro style

3 *nm* (**a**) *(style)* retro (**b**) *Fam (rétroviseur)* rear-view mirror

rétroactes [retroakt] *nmpl Belg* antecedents; **j'ignore tout des r. de cette affaire** I know nothing of the events which gave rise to this situation

rétroactif, -ive [retroaktif, -iv] *adj* retroactive; **avec effet r. au 1er janvier** backdated to 1 January

rétroactivement [retroaktivmã] *adv* retroactively, with retrospective *or* retroactive effect

rétroactivité [retroaktivite] *nf* retroactivity

rétrocéder [34] [retrosede] *vt (revendre)* to resell

rétrograde [retrograd] *adj (idée, mesure, politique)* reactionary

rétrograder [retrograde] **1** *vt (fonctionnaire)* to demote

2 *vi (conducteur)* to change down; **r. de troisième en seconde** to change down from third to second

rétroprojecteur [retroprɔʒɛktœr] *nm* overhead projector

rétrospectif, -ive [retrɔspɛktif, -iv] **1** *adj* retrospective

2 *nf* **rétrospective** retrospective; *Cin* retrospective, season; **une retrospective Roman Polanski** a Roman Polanski season

rétrospectivement [retrɔspɛktivmã] *adv* retrospectively, in retrospect

retroussé, -e [rətruse] *adj (manches)* rolled-up; *(nez)* snub, turned-up

retrousser [rətruse] *vt* (**a**) *(manches, pantalon)* to roll up; *(babines)* to curl up (**b**) *(jupe)* to tuck up

retrouvailles [rətruvaj] *nfpl* reunion

retrouver [rətruve] **1** *vt* (**a**) *(personne disparue, objet perdu)* to find again; *(adresse, nom)* to find; **r. son chemin** to find one's way again; **nous avons retrouvé notre petite maison** here we are back in our little house again; **je ne retrouverai jamais une occasion pareille** I'll never have another opportunity like it (**b**) *(recouvrer) (santé, forces, enthousiasme)* to recover; *(voix, appétit)* to get back; **r. la forme** to get fit again, to be back on form (**c**) *(reconnaître)* **r. qch chez qn** to recognize sth in sb; **r. qn dans qch** to recognize sb in sth (**d**) *(rencontrer) (thème, image, motif)* to come across (**dans** in) (**e**) *(rejoindre) (amis, parents)* to meet, to see; *(lieu)* to get back to

  2 se retrouver *vpr* (**a**) *(être)* to find oneself; **se r. à la rue/sans un sou** to find oneself homeless/penniless (**b**) *(trouver son chemin)* to find one's way (**dans** round); *Fig* **je ne m'y retrouve plus!** I'm completely lost! (**c**) *Fam (financièrement)* **s'y r.** to get one's money back (**d**) *(se rencontrer)* to meet; *Fig* **on se retrouvera!** I'll get even with you!; **comme on se retrouve!** fancy meeting you! (**e**) *(soi-même)* to find oneself again (**f**) *(se reconnaître)* **se r. en qn** to recognize oneself in sb

rétroviseur [retrovizœr] *nm* rear-view mirror; **r. extérieur** *Br* wing mirror, *Am* side mirror

réunification [reynifikasjɔ̃] *nf* reunification

réunifier [66] [reynifje] *vt* to reunify

Réunion [reynjɔ̃] *nf* **la R.** Réunion

réunion [reynjɔ̃] *nf* (**a**) *(de faits)* gathering (together); *(d'ensembles mathématiques, de pays)* union; *(d'entreprises)* merging (**b**) *(assemblée)* meeting; **être en r.** to be in a meeting; **r. de comité** committee meeting; **r. de famille** family gathering; **r. du personnel** staff meeting

réunionnais, -e [reynjɔnɛ, -ɛz] **1** *adj* of Réunion

  2 *nm,f* **R.** = person from Réunion

réunir [reynir] **1** *vt* (**a**) *(rassembler) (objets)* to put together; *(faits, documents)* to gather together; *(fonds)* to get together, to raise (**b**) *(amis, famille)* to get together; *(après une rupture, une séparation)* to reunite (**c**) *(qualités, avantages)* to have, to possess (**d**) **r. qch à qch** to join sth to sth

  2 se réunir *vpr* (**a**) *(personnes)* to meet, to get together; **se r. autour de qn/qch** to gather round sb/sth (**b**) *(routes)* to meet (**c**) *(entreprises)* to merge; *(États)* to unite

réussi, -e [reysi] *adj* successful; *Ironique* **c'est r.!** well done!

réussir [reysir] **1** *vt* (**a**) *(bien faire)* to make a success of; *(au rugby) (essai)* to score; **son soufflé était très réussi** his/her soufflé was a great success (**b**) *(examen)* to pass

  2 *vi* (**a**) *(démarche, projet)* to be successful (**b**) *(personne)* to do well, to be successful

  3 réussir à *vt ind* (**a**) **r. à un examen** to pass an exam; **r. à faire qch** to manage to do sth (**b**) **r. à qn** *(climat, plat)* to agree with sb; **tout lui réussit** he's/she's successful in everything he/she does; **les réunions de famille ne me réussissent pas** family gatherings aren't my scene *or* aren't for me

réussite [reysit] *nf* (**a**) *(succès)* success; **fêter sa r. à un examen** to celebrate passing an exam; **la r. sociale** social success (**b**) *(aux cartes) Br* patience, *Am* solitaire; **faire une r.** to play *Br* patience *or* *Am* solitaire

réutiliser [reytilize] *vt* to reuse

revaloir [69a] [rəvalwar] *vt* **je te revaudrai ça** *(je me vengerai)* I'll get you back for this!; *(je te rendrai service)* I'll do the same for you some time

revalorisation [rəvalɔrizasjɔ̃] *nf* *(d'une monnaie)* revaluation; *(des salaires, des retraites)* upgrading (**b**) *(d'une image, d'une profession)* upgrading

revaloriser [rəvalɔrize] *vt* (**a**) *(monnaie)* to revalue; *(salaire, retraite)* to upgrade (**b**) *(image, profession)* to upgrade

revanchard, -e [rəvɑ̃ʃar, -ard] *adj* & *nm,f Péj* revanchist

revanche [rəvɑ̃ʃ] *nf* (**a**) *(vengeance)* revenge; **prendre sa r. (sur qn)** to get one's revenge (on sb) (**b**) *(d'un match, d'un jeu)* return game (**c**) *(locutions)* **en r.** on the other hand; **à charge de r.** on condition that I do the same for you

rêvasser [rɛvase] *vi* to daydream

rêve [rɛv] *nm* (**a**) *(de dormeur)* dream; **faire un r.** to (have a) dream; **faites de beaux rêves!** sweet dreams! (**b**) *(idéal)* dream; **de r.** *(voiture, maison)* dream; *(silhouette)* gorgeous

rêvé, -e [rɛve] *adj* perfect, ideal

revêche [rəvɛʃ] *adj* bad-tempered

réveil [revɛj] *nm* (**a**) *(d'une personne)* waking, awakening; **à mon r., au r.** on waking (**b**) *(d'un volcan)* renewed rumblings; *(de la nature, des nationalismes)* reawakening (**c**) *(pendule)* alarm (clock)

réveille-matin [revɛjmatɛ̃] *nm inv* alarm clock

réveiller [reveje] **1** *vt* (**a**) *(personne endormie)* to wake (up), to awaken; *Fig* **r. les consciences** to stir people's consciences (**b**) *(raviver) (douleur)* to revive

  2 se réveiller *vpr* (**a**) *(personne endormie)* to wake (up), to awake; *(personne dans le coma)* to regain consciousness; *Fig (peuple)* to wake up (**b**) *(douleur)* to come back (**c**) *(nature)* to reawaken

réveillon [revɛjɔ̃] *nm* *(repas)* midnight supper; *(soirée)* midnight party *(after midnight mass on Christmas Eve or New Year's Eve)*

Réveillons

Christmas is traditionally a family celebration. In Catholic families, the "crèche" or miniature nativity scene is decorated and everyone goes to midnight mass on Christmas Eve, after which the long and copious Christmas dinner is served: this includes oysters and, for dessert, the traditional "bûche de Noël" or yule log. The presents under the Christmas tree are opened either on Christmas Eve or on Christmas Day morning. The "réveillon de la Saint-Sylvestre" on New Year's Eve is usually celebrated among friends, either at home or in a restaurant. Champagne is drunk at midnight and everybody embraces and wishes each other a happy New Year. New Year greeting cards can, in theory, be sent up until the end of January.

réveillonner [revɛjɔne] *vi* to see in Christmas/the New Year *(with a midnight supper and party)*

révélateur, -trice [revelatœr, -tris] **1** *adj (signe, attitude, remarque)* revealing

  2 *nm* (**a**) *(indice)* sign (**b**) *Phot* developer

révélation [revelasjɔ̃] *nf* (**a**) *(action) (d'un secret, d'intentions)* revelation, disclosure; **faire des révélations** to disclose important information (**b**) *(découverte fondamentale)* revelation (**c**) *(personne)* discovery (**d**) *(divine)* revelation

révéler [34] [revele] **1** *vt* (**a**) *(dévoiler)* to reveal (**b**) *(témoigner de)* to show

2 se révéler *vpr* (**a**) *(personne)* to reveal oneself *or* one's character; *(talent, génie)* to be revealed, to reveal itself (**b**) **se r. intelligent/exact** to turn out to be intelligent/correct; **il s'est révélé un bon ami** he proved to be a good friend

revenant, -e [rəvnɑ̃, -ɑ̃t] *nm,f* (**a**) *(fantôme)* ghost (**b**) *Fam* **tiens, un r.!** hello, stranger!

revendeur, -euse [rəvɑ̃dœr, -øz] *nm,f* retailer; *(d'articles d'occasion)* secondhand dealer

revendicatif, -ive [rəvɑ̃dikatif, -iv] *adj (mouvement)* protest

revendication [rəvɑ̃dikasjɔ̃] *nf* demand, claim

revendiquer [rəvɑ̃dike] *vt* (**a**) *(demander)* to claim, to demand; *(droits)* to assert; *(territoire, succession)* to lay claim to; **r. le droit de faire qch** to claim the right to do sth (**b**) *(assumer) (responsabilité)* to claim; *(attentat)* to claim responsibility for

revendre [rəvɑ̃dr] *vt* (**a**) *(après achat)* to resell; *Fig* **avoir du temps/de l'énergie à r.** to have time/energy to spare (**b**) *(vendre de nouveau)* to sell again

revenez-y [rəvnezi] *nm inv Fam* **avoir un goût de r.** to be very moreish

revenir [70] [rəvənir, rəvnir] *(aux être)* **1** *vi* (**a**) *(retourner, rentrer)* to come back, to return; **r. à Paris/en France** to come back to Paris/France; **r. de Paris** to come back from Paris; *Fig* **r. de loin** *(avoir failli mourir)* to have been at death's door; *(avoir eu de graves ennuis)* to have had a close shave; **je reviens tout de suite** I'll be back in a minute; **quand l'été reviendra** when it's summer again (**b**) **r. dans qch** *(refrain, image)* to crop up in sth (**c**) **ses propos me sont revenus** what he/she said got back to me (**d**) **r. à la mémoire à qn** to come back to sb; **ça me revient maintenant!** it's come back to me!; **les forces me sont revenues** I got my strength back (**e**) *Fam* **j'en suis revenu, de l'informatique!** I'm finished with computers!; **je n'en reviens pas!** I can't get over it! (**f**) *Fam* **il a une tête qui ne me revient pas** I don't like the look of him (**g**) *Culin* **faire r. qch** to brown sth (**h**) **r. cher** to work out expensive

2 revenir à *vt ind* (**a**) *(coûter)* **r. à 100 euros par personne** to work out at 100 euros each; **ça me revient à 200 euros par mois** it costs me 200 euros a month (**b**) *(équivaloir à)* **cela revient à dire que...** that amounts to saying that...

3 revenir sur *vt ind* (**a**) *(sujet)* to get back to (**b**) *(aveux)* to retract; *(promesse, décision)* to go back on

4 *v impersonnel* **il me revient encore 100 euros** I still have 100 euros owing to me; **il lui revient de le faire** it's up to him/her to do it

5 s'en revenir *vpr Litt* to return, to make one's way back

revente [rəvɑ̃t] *nf* resale

revenu, -e [rəvəny, rəvny] **1** *pp de* **revenir**
2 *nm (d'une personne)* income; *(de l'État)* revenue

rêver [rɛve] **1** *vt* to dream of; **r. que...** to dream (that)...
2 *vi* (**a**) *(dormeur)* to dream; *Fig* **on croit r.!** we must be dreaming! (**b**) *(rêvasser)* to daydream
3 rêver à *vt ind* to dream of
4 rêver de *vt ind* (**a**) *(voir en rêve)* to dream of; *Fig* **j'en rêve la nuit** I dream about it at night (**b**) *(souhaiter)* to dream of; **r. de faire qch** to dream of doing sth

réverbération [reverberasjɔ̃] *nf (de la lumière, de la chaleur)* reflection; *(du son)* reverberation, echo

réverbère [reverbɛr] *nm* street lamp

réverbérer [34] [reverbere] *vt (chaleur, lumière)* to reflect, to throw back; *(son)* to reverberate

reverdir [rəverdir] *vi* to grow green again

révérence [reverɑ̃s] *nf* (**a**) *(salut) (d'une femme)* curtsey; **faire la r. à qn** to curtsey to sb; *Fig* **tirer sa r.** to leave (**b**) *(respect)* reverence (**envers** *ou* **pour** for)

révérend, -e [reverɑ̃, -ɑ̃d] **1** *adj* reverend
2 *nm* reverend

révérer [34] [revere] *vt* to revere

rêverie [rɛvri] *nf (activité, moment)* daydream, reverie

revers [rəvɛr] *nm* (**a**) *(de pièce)* reverse side, back; *(de la main)* back; **prendre l'ennemi à r.** *(par l'arrière)* to attack the enemy from the rear; *(par le côté)* to attack the enemy from the side; *Fig* **c'est le r. de la médaille** that's the other side of the coin (**b**) *(de veste)* lapel; *(de pantalon) Br* turn-up, *Am* cuff (**c**) *(échec)* **r. de fortune** reversal of fortune, setback (**d**) *(au tennis)* backhand (stroke)

reverser [rəvɛrse] *vt* (**a**) *(somme)* to transfer (**à** *ou* **sur** to) (**b**) *(liquide)* to pour out again

réversible [reversibl] *adj* reversible

revêtement [rəvɛtmɑ̃] *nm (enduit)* coating; *(de sol, d'un mur intérieur)* covering; *(d'un mur extérieur)* facing; *(pour canalisation, pour câble)* sheathing; *(de la chaussée)* surface (material)

revêtir [71] [rəvɛtir] *vt* (**a**) *(habiller)* **r. qn de qch** to dress sb in sth (**b**) *(endosser) (vêtement)* to don (**c**) *(enduire)* to coat; *(sol)* to cover; *(mur extérieur)* to face; *(chaussée)* to surface (**d**) *Fig (caractère, aspect, forme)* to assume, to take on (**e**) **pièce revêtue d'une signature** document bearing a signature

rêveur, -euse [rɛvœr, -øz] **1** *adj* dreamy; **laisser qn r.** to leave sb baffled
2 *nm,f* dreamer

rêveusement [rɛvøzmɑ̃] *adv* dreamily

revient [rəvjɛ̃] *nm voir* **prix**

revigorant, -e [rəvigɔrɑ̃, -ɑ̃t] *adj (vent, douche)* invigorating; *(boisson)* reviving

revigorer [rəvigɔre] *vt (vent, douche)* to invigorate; *(boisson)* to revive

revirement [rəvirmɑ̃] *nm (de sentiments, d'opinion)* complete change, about-turn

réviser [revize] *vt* (**a**) *(texte, loi)* to revise; *(contrat, procès, politique)* to review (**b**) *(leçon, programme) Br* to revise, *Am* to review (**c**) *(voiture, moteur)* to service (**d**) *Ordinat (texte, document)* to edit

révision [revizjɔ̃] *nf* (**a**) *(d'un texte, d'une loi)* revision; *(d'un contrat, d'un procès, d'une politique)* review; **r. des salaires** salary review (**b**) *(d'une leçon, d'un programme) Br* revision, *Am* review; **faire des révisions** to revise (**c**) *(d'une voiture, d'un moteur)* service (**d**) *Ordinat* edit

révisionnisme [revizjɔnism] *nm* revisionism

revisiter [rəvizite] *vt* (**a**) *(visiter à nouveau)* to revisit (**b**) *(voir sous un jour nouveau)* to reinterpret

revisser [rəvise] *vt* to screw back again

revitalisant, -e [rəvitalizɑ̃, -ɑ̃t] *adj* revitalizing

revitaliser [rəvitalize] *vt* to revitalize

revivre [72] [rəvivr] **1** *vt (passé, expérience)* to relive
2 *vi* (**a**) *(recouvrer son énergie)* to come alive again; **se sentir r.** to feel alive again; **faire r. qn** to bring sb back to life (**b**) **r. dans qn/qch** to live on in sb/sth; **faire r. qch** *(coutume, tradition)* to revive sth; *(village)* to bring sth back to life

révocable [revɔkabl] *adj (fonctionnaire)* removable; *(testament)* revocable

révocation [revɔkasjɔ̃] *nf (d'un fonctionnaire)* removal; *(d'un testament)* revocation
revoici [rəvwasi] *prép Fam* me r.! here I am again!; le r. au travail he's back at work
revoilà [rəvwala] = **revoici**
revoir¹ [rəvwar] au revoir 1 *exclam* goodbye
 2 *nm inv* goodbye
revoir² [73a] 1 *vt* (**a**) *(rencontrer) (personne)* to see *or* meet again (**b**) *(leçon) Br* to revise, *Am* to review; *(comptes, texte)* to go over again (**c**) *(se représenter mentalement)* to see again
 2 se revoir *vpr* (**a**) *(se rencontrer)* to see each other again, to meet again (**b**) *(soi-même)* to see oneself again
revoler [rəvɔle] *vi* (**a**) *(voler de nouveau)* to fly again (**b**) *Can (être projeté dans toutes les directions) (objets, personnes)* to fly in every direction; *(jaillir) (liquide, sang)* to splatter; les fenêtres ont revolé en miettes the windows were smashed to smithereens
révoltant, -e [revɔltã, -ãt] *adj* appalling, revolting
révolte [revɔlt] *nf* revolt; en r. (contre) in revolt (against)
révolté, -e [revɔlte] *adj* (**a**) *(indigné)* outraged, appalled (de by) (**b**) *(en révolte)* rebellious
révolter [revɔlte] 1 *vt* to outrage, to appal; ça me révolte d'entendre ça! I'm appalled to hear that!
 2 se révolter *vpr* to revolt, to rebel (contre *ou* devant against)
révolu, -e [revɔly] *adj (jours, époque)* past, bygone; avoir quarante ans révolus to be over forty years of age
révolution [revɔlysjɔ̃] *nf* revolution; faire la r. to cause a revolution; *Fig* être en r. to be up in arms; *Hist* la R. the French Revolution
révolutionnaire [revɔlysjɔnɛr] *adj & nmf* revolutionary
révolutionner [revɔlysjɔne] *vt* (**a**) *(transformer) (industrie, théorie)* to revolutionize (**b**) *Fam (mettre en émoi) (village)* to cause a stir in
revolver [revɔlvɛr] *nm* revolver
révoquer [revɔke] *vt* (**a**) *(fonctionnaire)* to remove from office (**b**) *(décret, contrat, testament)* to revoke
revue [rəvy] *nf* (**a**) *(examen)* review; passer qch en r. *(problèmes, possibilités)* to review sth; r. de presse *(de l'actualité)* review of the papers; *(sur un sujet particulier)* press review (**b**) *(magazine)* magazine; *(scientifique, littéraire)* review, journal (**c**) *(spectacle)* revue
révulsé, -e [revylse] *adj (yeux)* rolled back; *(personne)* disgusted
révulser [revylse] 1 *vt (dégoûter)* to disgust
 2 se révulser *vpr (yeux)* to roll back
Reykjavik [rekjavik] *n* Reykjavik
rez-de-chaussée [redʃose] *nm inv Br* ground floor, *Am* first floor; au r. on the *Br* ground *or Am* first floor
rez-de-jardin [redʒardɛ̃] *nm inv* garden level
RF [ɛrɛf] *nf (abrév* **République française**) = written abbreviation seen on official documents, government buildings etc
RFA [ɛrɛfa] *nf Anciennement (abrév* **République fédérale d'Allemagne**) FRG
RG *nmpl (abrév* **Renseignements généraux**) = secret intelligence branch of the French police, *Br* ≃ the Special Branch, *Am* ≃ the FBI
rhabiller [rabije] 1 *vt (personne)* to dress sb again
 2 se rhabiller *vpr (mettre ses vêtements)* to get dressed again; *Fam* il peut aller se r. he might as well give up and go home

rhapsodie [rapsɔdi] *nf* rhapsody
Rhénanie [renani] *nf* la R. the Rhineland
Rhésus [rezys] *nm* Rhesus factor; R. positif/négatif Rhesus positive/negative
rhétorique [retɔrik] 1 *adj (effet)* rhetorical
 2 *nf* rhetoric
Rhin [rɛ̃] *nm* le R. the Rhine
rhinocéros [rinɔserɔs] *nm* rhinoceros
rhino-pharyngite (*pl* rhino-pharyngites) [rinofarɛ̃ʒit] *nf* inflammation of the nose and throat, *Spéc* rhinopharyngitis
Rhodes [rɔd] *n* Rhodes
rhododendron [rɔdɔdɛ̃drɔ̃] *nm* rhododendron
Rhône [ron] *nm* le R. the Rhone
rhubarbe [rybarb] *nf* rhubarb
rhum [rɔm] *nm* rum
rhumatisant, -e [rymatizã, -ãt] *adj & nm,f* rheumatic
rhumatismal, -e, -aux, -ales [rymatismal, -o] *adj* rheumatic
rhumatisme [rymatism] *nm* rheumatism; avoir des rhumatismes to have rheumatism; r. articulaire rheumatoid arthritis; r. articulaire aigu rheumatic fever
rhumatologie [rymatɔlɔʒi] *nf* rheumatology
rhumatologue [rymatɔlɔg] *nmf* rheumatologist
rhume [rym] *nm* cold; attraper un r. to catch a cold; r. de cerveau head cold; r. des foins hay fever
riant, -e [rijã, -ãt] *adj* (**a**) *(visage)* smiling, cheerful; *(yeux)* laughing, merry (**b**) *(paysage, campagne)* cheerful, sunny
RIB [rib] *nm (abrév* **relevé d'identité bancaire**) = document showing details of one's bank account; *see box at* relevé
ribambelle [ribãbɛl] *nf (de personnes)* string, crowd
ricanement [rikanmã] *nm* sneer, snigger
ricaner [rikane] *vi* to sneer, to snigger
richard, -e [riʃar, -ard] *nm,f Péj* moneybags
riche [riʃ] 1 *adj* (**a**) *(personne, pays)* rich, wealthy (**b**) *(cuisine, aliment)* rich (**c**) *(vocabulaire)* extensive; *(style)* elaborate; *(description)* detailed (**d**) *(luxueux) (demeure)* luxurious; *(étoffe)* rich; *(vêtement)* sumptuous (**e**) *Fam* c'est une r. idée that's a fabulous idea (**f**) r. en qch rich in sth; la journée a été r. en événements it's been an action-packed day (**g**) r. de *(espérances)* full of; livre/expérience r. d'enseignements very instructive book/experience
 2 *nmf* rich person; les riches the rich
richement [riʃmã] *adv* richly
richesse [riʃɛs] *nf* (**a**) *(d'une personne, d'un pays)* wealth; c'est le tableau qui fait la r. de notre musée this painting is the prize item in our museum's collection; richesses *(biens)* riches, wealth; *Fam* voilà toutes mes richesses these are all my worldly goods (**b**) *(luxe) (d'une demeure)* luxuriousness; *(de vêtements)* sumptuousness (**c**) richesses *(ressources)* resources (**d**) *(du sol, d'un gisement)* richness; *(de la végétation)* lushness (**e**) *(de l'imagination)* vividness, liveliness; *(d'un style)* elaborateness; *(du vocabulaire)* richness; *(d'une description)* detailed nature
richissime [riʃisim] *adj Fam* extremely wealthy, loaded
ricin [risɛ̃] *nm voir* huile
ricocher [rikɔʃe] *vi (projectile)* to ricochet (sur off); *(sur l'eau)* to bounce (sur off)

ricochet [rikɔʃɛ] *nm (projectile)* ricochet; *(sur l'eau)* bounce; **faire des ricochets** *(pour s'amuser)* to skim pebbles; *Fig* **par r.** indirectly

ric-rac [rikrak] *adv Fam* (**a**) *(de justesse)* **réussir un examen r.** to scrape through an exam (**b**) **être r.** *(financièrement)* to be a bit strapped for cash

rictus [riktys] *nm* grimace

ride [rid] *nf* (**a**) *(sur le visage)* wrinkle, line; *Fam* **ne pas prendre une r.** not to age at all (**b**) *(sur l'eau)* ripple

ridé, -e [ride] *adj* wrinkled

rideau, -x [rido] *nm* (**a**) *(dans une pièce)* Br curtain, Am drape; **r. de fer** *(de boutique)* metal shutter; *Hist (en Europe)* Iron Curtain (**b**) *(de théâtre)* curtain (**c**) *(écran) (d'arbres)* screen, curtain; *(de feu, de fumée)* wall; *(de pluie)* curtain

rider [ride] **1** *vt* (**a**) *(front)* to wrinkle, to line; *(peau)* to wrinkle, to shrivel (**b**) *(eau, sable)* to ripple
2 se rider *vpr* (**a**) *(front, peau)* to become wrinkled *or* lined (**b**) *(eau)* to ripple

ridicule [ridikyl] **1** *adj* ridiculous, ludicrous; *(prix)* ridiculously low; **se rendre r.** to make a fool of oneself
2 *nm* (**a**) *(absurdité)* ridiculousness (**b**) *(dérision)* ridicule; **tourner qn/qch en r.** to ridicule sb/sth; **se couvrir de r.** to make a complete fool of oneself

ridiculement [ridikylmɑ̃] *adv* ridiculously, ludicrously

ridiculiser [ridikylize] **1** *vt* to ridicule, to make fun of
2 se ridiculiser *vpr* to make oneself look ridiculous, to make a fool of oneself

rien [rjɛ̃] **1** *pron indéfini* (**a**) *(avec ne)* nothing; **r. ne l'affecte** nothing affects him; **r. de ce que j'ai proposé ne leur a plu** they didn't like anything I suggested; **r. ne va plus!** *(au casino)* no more bets!; **ne... r.** nothing, not anything; **je n'ai r. à faire** I've got nothing to do; **il n'a r. mangé du tout** he hasn't eaten a thing; **personne n'osa r. dire** nobody dared say anything; **il n'y a r. de nouveau** there's nothing new, there isn't anything new; **ce n'est r.** it's nothing; **comme si de r. n'était** as if nothing had happened; **elle ne ressemble en r. à sa sœur** she's nothing like her sister; *Litt* **il n'en est r.** such is not the case; **il n'a r. d'un don Juan** he's no Casanova; *Fam* **r. de r.** nothing at all (**b**) *(sans ne)* **qu'avez-vous fait? – r. /presque r.** what did you do? – nothing/hardly anything; **de r.** *(je vous en prie)* you're welcome, don't mention it; **pour r.** *(gratuitement)* for nothing; **pourquoi demandez-vous cela? – pour r.** why do you ask? – no reason; **un petit problème de r. du tout** a trivial little problem; **quinze à r.** *(au tennis)* fifteen love (**c**) *(quelque chose)* anything; **y a-t-il r. de plus triste?** is there anything more depressing?; **sans r. faire** without doing anything; **sans nous gêner en r.** without troubling us at all *or* in the slightest (**d**) *(locutions)* **r. que** just, only; **je frémis r. que d'y songer** just thinking about it makes me shudder; **r. que la vérité** nothing but the truth; **élever quatre enfants, ce n'est pas r.!** raising four children is quite an achievement!
2 *nm* (**a**) *(bagatelle)* **un r. l'habille** he/she looks good in anything; **s'énerver pour un r.** to get annoyed over nothing; **il court un kilomètre comme un r.** he can run a kilometre just like that (**b**) **un r. long/bête** *(un peu)* a bit long/stupid; **un r. de...** *(un petit peu de)* a little...; **en un r. de temps** in no time at all

rieur, -euse [rijœr, -øz] *adj (air, visage)* cheerful, bright; *(yeux)* laughing, merry

Riga [riga] *n* Riga

rigide [riʒid] *adj* (**a**) *(matériau)* rigid; *(couverture de livre)* hard (**b**) *Fig (personne, règlement, système)* rigid, inflexible

rigidité [riʒidite] *nf* (**a**) *(d'un matériau)* rigidity (**b**) *Fig (d'une personne, d'un règlement, d'un système)* rigidity, inflexibility; **r. cadavérique** rigor mortis

rigolade [rigɔlad] *nf Fam* (**a**) *(amusement)* fun (**b**) **c'était de la r.** *(c'était facile)* it was a walkover; **ça n'est pas de la r.** *(c'est sérieux)* it's no joke; **prendre qch à la r.** to treat sth as a joke

rigolard, -e [rigɔlar, -ard] *adj Fam (air)* grinning

rigole [rigɔl] *nf (petit fossé)* channel; *(filet d'eau)* rivulet

rigoler [rigɔle] *vi Fam* (**a**) *(rire)* to laugh (**b**) *(s'amuser)* to have a laugh (**c**) *(plaisanter)* to joke (**avec** about); *Fig* **il ne faut pas r. avec le fisc** you shouldn't mess about with the tax man

rigolo, -ote [rigɔlo, -ɔt] *Fam* **1** *adj* funny
2 *nm,f (plaisantin)* scream, hoot; *Péj (fumiste)* clown

rigorisme [rigɔrism] *nm* strictness

rigoriste [rigɔrist] **1** *adj* strict, rigorous
2 *nmf* strict moralist

rigoureusement [rigurøzmɑ̃] *adv* (**a**) *(strictement) (interdit)* strictly; *(exact)* absolutely; *(rigoureusement)* (**b**) *(scrupuleusement)* **suivre r. les consignes** to follow the instructions to the letter (**c**) *(sévèrement)* severely

rigoureux, -euse [riguro, -øz] *adj* (**a**) *(dur) (punition, mesures, conditions)* severe, harsh; *(hiver)* hard; *(climat)* harsh (**b**) *(strict) (neutralité)* strict; *(analyse)* rigorous; **être r. dans qch** *(personne)* to be rigorous in sth

rigueur [rigœr] *nf* (**a**) *(dureté)* harshness, severity; *(de la loi)* rigour (**b**) *(austérité)* austerity (**c**) *(exactitude) (d'une analyse)* rigour; **manquer de r.** *(style, personne)* to be sloppy (**d**) *(locutions)* **à la r.** *(si nécessaire)* if need be; **être de r.** to be compulsory; **tenir r. à qn de qch** to hold sth against sb

rillettes [rijɛt] *nfpl* potted meat *(made from pork, rabbit, goose etc)*

rime [rim] *nf* rhyme; **sans r. ni raison** without rhyme or reason

rimer [rime] *vi* (**a**) *(mot)* to rhyme (**avec** with) (**b**) *Fig* **ne r. à rien** not to make any sense

Rimmel® [rimɛl] *nm* mascara

rinçage [rɛ̃saʒ] *nm* (**a**) *(action)* rinsing (**b**) *(pour les cheveux)* tint, rinse

rince-doigts [rɛ̃sdwa] *nm inv* finger bowl

rincée [rɛ̃se] *nf Fam* (**a**) *(averse)* downpour (**b**) *(volée de coups)* thrashing

rincer [16] [rɛ̃se] **1** *vt (vêtements, vaisselle, cheveux)* to rinse; *(verre, tasse)* to rinse (out)
2 se rincer *vpr (à l'eau douce)* to rinse oneself; **se r. la bouche** to rinse out one's mouth; *Fam* **se r. l'œil** to get an eyeful

ring [riŋ] *nm* (**a**) *(de boxe)* ring; **le r.** *(la boxe)* boxing (**b**) *Belg (rocade)* ring road

ringard, -e [rɛ̃gar, -ard] *Fam* **1** *adj (vêtements)* uncool, Br naff; *(décor)* tacky, Br naff; *(chanson)* corny, Br cheesy
2 *nm,f* geek, square

ringardise [rɛ̃gardiz] *nf Fam* tackiness, Br naffness

ringardissime [rɛ̃gardisim] *adj Fam* incredibly tacky *or* Br naff

Rio de Janeiro [rijodədʒaneRo] *n* Rio de Janeiro

ripaille [ripaj] *nf Fam* **faire r.** to have a blow-out

riposte [ripɔst] *nf* (**a**) *(en boxe, en escrime)* riposte (**b**) *(réponse)* riposte, retort (**c**) *(représailles)* counterattack

riposter [ripɔste] **1** *vt* **il m'a riposté que...** he retorted that...
2 *vi* (**a**) *(en boxe, en escrime)* to riposte (**b**) *(user de représailles)* to counterattack
3 riposter à *vt ind (attaque, injures)* to counter

ripou *(pl* **ripoux** *ou* **ripous)** [ripu] *Fam* **1** *adj (policier)* bent
2 *nm* bent cop

riquiqui [rikiki] *adj inv (tout petit)* teeny-weeny; *(portion, cadeau)* stingy, mean; *(maillot de bain)* skimpy

rire¹ [rir] *nm* laughter, laughing

rire² [61] **1** *vi* (**a**) *(personne)* to laugh; **r. comme un bossu** *or Fam* **comme une baleine** to laugh like a drain; **r. jaune** to give a forced laugh; **r. aux éclats** to roar with laughter; **r. aux larmes** to cry with laughter; **r. tout bas** to laugh to oneself (**b**) *(s'amuser)* to have fun, to have a laugh; **pour r.** for a joke; **vous voulez r.!** you're joking!; **laissez-moi r.!** don't make me laugh!
2 rire de *vt ind (se moquer de) (personne, remarques, situation)* to laugh at; *Litt* **je ris de leurs insultes** I'm impervious to their insults; **il vaut mieux en r.** you have to laugh
3 se rire *vpr Litt* **se r. de** *(se moquer de)* to laugh at; *(se jouer de)* to make light of

ris¹ [ri] *nm (sur une voile)* reef

ris² *nm* **r. de veau** calf's sweetbread

risée [rize] *nf* (**a**) *(moquerie)* mockery, derision; **s'exposer à la r. publique** to expose oneself to public scorn (**b**) **être la r. de** to be the laughing stock of

risette [rizɛt] *nf Fam* little smile; **fais des risettes à ton papa!** smile for daddy!, give daddy a smile!

risible [rizibl] *adj* laughable, ridiculous

risque [risk] *nm* risk; **prendre un r./des risques** to take a risk/risks; **courir le r. de faire qch** to risk doing sth; **c'est un r. à courir** it's a risk I/we/*etc* have to take; **avoir le goût du r.** to like taking risks; **les risques du métier** occupational hazards; **faire qch à ses risques et périls** to do sth at one's own risk; **au r. de sa vie** at the risk of his/her life; **au r. de faire qch** at the risk of doing sth

risqué, -e [riske] *adj* (**a**) *(dangereux)* risky (**b**) *(osé)* risqué

risquer [riske] **1** *vt* (**a**) *(mettre en danger) (vie, réputation)* to risk; **qu'est-ce que tu risques?** what have you got to lose?; **r. sa tête** to put one's head on the block; **r. le tout pour le tout** to go for broke (**b**) **r. un œil** to peep out; **r. une question** to venture a question
2 risquer de *vt ind* **il risque de se faire renvoyer** he's in danger of being sacked; **ça risque de durer longtemps** that may well last for a long time; *Fam* **il risque de gagner** he stands a good chance of winning; *Fam* **il ne risque pas de te le dire** fat chance of him telling you
3 se risquer *vpr* to take risks/a risk; **se r. à faire qch** to venture to do sth; **je ne m'y risquerais pas** I wouldn't risk it

risque-tout [riskətu] *nmf inv* daredevil

rissoler [risɔle] *vt & vi* to brown

ristourne [risturn] *nf* discount; **faire une r. à qn** to give sb a discount

rital, -e, -als, -ales [rital] *nm,f Fam (Italien)* wop, *Br* Eyetie, = racist term used to refer to an Italian

rite [rit] *nm* (**a**) *(religieux)* rite; **r. de passage** *ou* **initiatique** rite of passage (**b**) *Fig (cérémonie, habitude)* ritual

ritournelle [riturnɛl] *nf (phrase musicale)* ritornello; *Fam* **c'est toujours la même r.** it's always the same old story

rituel, -elle [ritɥɛl] **1** *adj* ritual
2 *nm* ritual; **r. d'initiation** initiation rites

rituellement [ritɥɛlmɑ̃] *adv* invariably

rivage [rivaʒ] *nm* shore

rival, -e, -aux, -ales [rival, -o] **1** *adj* rival
2 *nm,f* rival; **sans r.** unrivalled

rivaliser [rivalize] *vi* **r. avec qn** to compete with sb; **r. de qch avec qn** to try to outdo sb in sth

rivalité [rivalite] *nf* rivalry

rive [riv] *nf* (**a**) *(de rivière)* bank; *(de lac, de mer)* shore (**b**) **la r. gauche/droite** *(à Paris)* the Left/Right Bank

Rive droite, rive gauche

The Right (north) Bank of the Seine is traditionally associated with business and trade, and has a reputation for being more conservative than the Left Bank. The Left (south) Bank includes districts traditionally favoured by artists, students and intellectuals, and has a reputation for being Bohemian and unconventional.

river [rive] *vt* (**a**) *(fixer)* to rivet; *Fig* **être rivé à qch** to be glued to sth; **avoir les yeux rivés sur qn/qch** not to be able to take one's eyes off sb/sth (**b**) *(goupille, clou)* to clinch; *Fam* **r. son clou à qn** to shut sb up

riverain, -e [rivrɛ̃, -ɛn] **1** *adj (propriété) (le long d'une rivière)* riverside, waterside; *(autour d'un lac)* lakeside, waterside
2 *nm,f* (**a**) *(près d'une rivière)* owner of a riverside property; *(près d'un lac)* owner of a lakeside property (**b**) *(d'une rue)* resident; **interdit sauf aux riverains** *(sur panneau)* ≃ no entry except for access

rivet [rivɛ] *nm* rivet

rivetage [rivtaʒ] *nm* riveting

riveter [42] [rivte] *vt* to rivet

riveteuse [rivtøz] *nf* riveting machine

rivière [rivjɛr] *nf* (**a**) *(cours d'eau)* river (**b**) *(de lave, de boue)* river (**c**) **r. de diamants** diamond necklace, *Spéc* diamond rivière

rixe [riks] *nf* brawl

riz [ri] *nm* rice; **r. basmati** basmati rice; **r. cantonais** Cantonese rice; **r. créole** boiled rice; **r. au lait** rice pudding; **r. pilaf** pilaf *or* pilau rice

riziculture [rizikyltyr] *nf* rice growing

rizière [rizjɛr] *nf* rice field, paddy field

RMI [ɛrɛmi] *nm (abrév* **revenu minimum d'insertion**) *Br* ≃ income support, *Am* ≃ Welfare

RMiste [ɛrɛmist] *nmf* ≃ person on *Br* income support *or Am* Welfare

RN [ɛrɛn] *nf (abrév* **route nationale**) = designation of major road, *Br* ≃ A-road, *Am* ≃ state highway

RNIS [ɛrɛnies] *nm Ordinat (abrév* **réseau numérique à intégration de services**) ISDN

robe [rɔb] *nf* (**a**) *(de femme)* dress; **r. de grossesse** maternity dress; **r. d'intérieur** housecoat; **r. de mariée** wedding dress; **r. du soir** evening gown (**b**) **r. de chambre** *Br* dressing gown, *Am* robe; **pommes de terre en r. de chambre** *ou* **des champs** jacket potatoes (**c**) *(d'avocat, de juge)* robe, gown (**d**) *(habit religieux)* robe (**e**) *(pelage) (de cheval)* coat (**f**) *(du vin)* colour

robinet [ʀɔbinɛ] *nm Br* tap, *Am* faucet
robinetterie [ʀɔbinɛtri] *nf* plumbing
robineux [ʀɔbinø] *nm Can Fam Br* tramp, *Am* hobo
robot [ʀɔbo] *nm* robot; **r. ménager** food processor
robotique [ʀɔbɔtik] **1** *adj* robotic
  2 *nf* robotics *(singulier)*
robotisation [ʀɔbɔtizasjɔ̃] *nf* automation, robotization
robotiser [ʀɔbɔtize] *vt* to automate, to robotize
robuste [ʀɔbyst] *adj (personne)* robust; *(bras, jambe)* sturdy; *(appétit)* healthy; *(plante)* hardy; **être d'une santé r.** to have a sound constitution
robustesse [ʀɔbystɛs] *nf (d'une personne)* robustness; *(d'une plante)* hardiness; *(d'un véhicule)* sturdiness
roc [ʀɔk] *nm* rock
rocade [ʀɔkad] *nf (route)* bypass
rocaille [ʀɔkaj] **1** *nf* **(a)** *(terrain)* stony ground **(b)** *(jardin)* rockery
  2 *adj inv (style)* rocaille
rocailleux, -euse [ʀɔkajø, -øz] *adj* **(a)** *(pierreux)* stony, rocky **(b)** *Fig (voix)* harsh, rough
rocambolesque [ʀɔkɑ̃bɔlɛsk] *adj* fantastic, incredible
roche [ʀɔʃ] *nf* rock
rocher [ʀɔʃe] *nm* **(a)** *(masse de pierre)* rock; *(escarpé)* crag; **le R.** = Monaco; **le r. de Gibraltar** the Rock of Gibraltar **(b)** *(paroi)* rock face **(c)** **r. (au chocolat)** chocolate *(containing nuts)*
rocheux, -euse [ʀɔʃø, -øz] *adj (paysage, région)* rocky; **la paroi rocheuse** the rock face; **les (montagnes) Rocheuses** the Rocky Mountains
rock [ʀɔk] **1** *adj inv (concert, groupe, chanteur)* rock
  2 *nm inv* **le r.** rock; **danser le r.** to jive
rocker [ʀɔkœr] *nm*, **rockeur, -euse** [ʀɔkœr, -øz] *nm,f (musicien)* rock musician; *(fan)* rock fan
rocking-chair *(pl* **rocking-chairs)** [ʀɔkiɳtʃɛr] *nm* rocking chair
rock'n roll [ʀɔkɛnʀɔl] *nm* **le r.** rock and roll
rococo [ʀɔkoko] **1** *adj inv* **(a)** *(meuble, style)* rococo **(b)** *(démodé)* old-fashioned
  2 *nm* rococo
rodage [ʀɔdaʒ] *nm (d'une voiture)* running in; **en r.** *(sur panneau)* running in
rodéo [ʀɔdeo] *nm (avec des chevaux)* rodeo; *Fig (bagarre)* free-for-all
roder [ʀɔde] *vt (moteur, voiture)* to run in; *Fig (entreprise, spectacle)* to get into its stride; *(équipe, structure)* to break in; **être rodé** *(entreprise, spectacle)* to be into its stride; *(employé)* to have got the hang of things
rôder [ʀode] *vi* to be on the prowl
rôdeur, -euse [ʀodœr, -øz] *nm,f* prowler
rogne [ʀɔɲ] *nf Fam* bad temper; **être en r. (contre)** *Br* to be cross (with), *Am* to be mad (at); **mettre qn en r.** to make sb *Br* cross *or Am* mad; **se mettre** *ou très Fam* **se ficher en r.** to get *Br* cross *or Am* mad
rogner [ʀɔɲe] **1** *vt* **(a)** *(griffes, ongles)* to clip, to trim; *Fig (économies)* to eat away at; *Fig* **r. les ailes à qn** to clip sb's wings **(b)** *(retrancher)* **r. qch à qn** to gradually take sth away from sb **(c)** *Ordinat (image)* to crop
  2 rogner sur *vt ind* **r. sur qch** to cut down on sth
rognon [ʀɔɲɔ̃] *nm Culin* kidney
rognures [ʀɔɲyr] *nfpl (de cuir, de métal)* trimmings, parings
rogue [ʀɔg] *adj* arrogant, haughty
roi [ʀwa] **1** *nm* **(a)** *(souverain)* king; **tirer les rois** = to celebrate Twelfth Night; **les Rois mages** the Three

Wise Men; **le R.-Soleil** the Sun King **(b)** *Fig (le plus grand) (des animaux)* king; **c'est le r. des imbéciles** he's a prize idiot; *très Fam* **c'est le r. des cons** he's a complete *Br* arsehole *or Am* asshole **(c)** *(aux cartes, aux échecs)* king
  2 *adj inv* **bleu r.** royal blue

Tirer les rois

The French traditionally celebrate Epiphany with a round, almond-flavoured pastry ("la galette des Rois") containing a small porcelain figurine ("la fève" – originally a dried bean). The pastry is shared out and the person who finds the "fève" is appointed "king" or "queen" and given a cardboard crown to wear. This tradition is called "tirer les Rois".

roitelet [ʀwatlɛ] *nm (oiseau)* wren
rôle [ʀol] *nm* **(a)** *(d'une pièce de théâtre)* part, role; *Fig* **avoir le beau r.** to have the easy job; **premier r.** leading role; **r.-titre** title role **(b)** *(fonction) (du médecin, d'un organe, d'une activité)* role, function **(dans** in); **jouer un r. de premier plan** to play a key role; **jouer un r. secondaire** to play second fiddle
roller [ʀɔlœr] *nm* **(a)** *(activité)* rollerblading; **faire du r.** to go rollerblading **(b)** **rollers** rollerblades
rolleur, -euse [ʀɔlœr, -øz] **1** *nm,f* rollerblader
  2 *nm* = roller
ROM [ʀɔm] *nf Ordinat* ROM
romain, -e¹ [ʀɔmɛ̃, -ɛn] **1** *adj* Roman
  2 *nm,f* **R.** Roman
  3 *nm (caractère d'imprimerie)* roman
romaine² [ʀɔmɛn] *nf (salade) Br* cos lettuce, *Am* romaine; *Fig* **être bon comme la r.** to be extremely kind
roman¹ [ʀɔmɑ̃] *nm* **(a)** *(en prose)* novel; **le nouveau r.** the anti-novel, the nouveau roman; **r. d'amour** love story, romance; *Fam* **r. à l'eau de rose** soppy love story *or* romance; **r. noir** thriller; **r. policier** detective novel **(b)** *(poème)* romance **(c)** *Fig* **c'est du r.** *(c'est invraisemblable)* it's just a fairy tale; *Fig* **c'est tout un r.** *(c'est incroyable)* it's quite a tale
roman², -e [ʀɔmɑ̃, -an] **1** *adj* **(a)** *(langue)* Romance **(b)** *Archit* Romanesque
  2 *nm* **(a)** *(langue)* Romance **(b)** *Archit* Romanesque style
romance [ʀɔmɑ̃s] *nf (chanson)* sentimental song *or* ballad
romancer [16] [ʀɔmɑ̃se] *vt (événement, histoire)* to romanticize; *(biographie)* to fictionalize
romanche [ʀɔmɑ̃ʃ] *adj & nm* Romansch
romancier, -ère [ʀɔmɑ̃sje, -ɛr] *nm,f* novelist
romand, -e [ʀɔmɑ̃, -ɑ̃d] **1** *adj (Suisse)* French-speaking
  2 *nm,f* **R.** French-speaking Swiss person
romanesque [ʀɔmanɛsk] *adj* **(a)** *(personne, aventure)* romantic **(b)** *(technique)* novelistic
roman-feuilleton *(pl* **romans-feuilletons)** [ʀɔmɑ̃fœjtɔ̃] *nm* serial
roman-fleuve *(pl* **romans-fleuves)** [ʀɔmɑ̃flœv] *nm* saga
romanichel, -elle [ʀɔmaniʃɛl] *nm,f (Tzigane)* gypsy
roman-photo *(pl* **romans-photos)** [ʀɔmɑ̃foto] *nm* photo-story
romantique [ʀɔmɑ̃tik] **1** *adj* **(a)** *(peinture, littérature, artiste)* Romantic **(b)** *(personne, idées, film)* romantic
  2 *nmf* **(a)** *(artiste, auteur)* Romantic, Romanticist **(b)** *(personne)* romantic

romantisme [rɔmɑ̃tism] *nm* (**a**) *(courant artistique)* Romanticism (**b**) *(attitude, sensibilité)* romanticism

romarin [rɔmarɛ̃] *nm* rosemary

rombière [rɔbjɛr] *nf Fam* old dear

Rome [rɔm] *n* Rome

rompre [rɔ̃pr] **1** *vt* (**a**) *(casser)* to break; **r. ses digues** *(fleuve)* to burst its banks (**b**) *(négociations, fiançailles, relations)* to break off; *(contrat, charme, monotonie)* to break; *(équilibre)* to upset (**c**) *(locutions)* **applaudir à tout r.** to applaud wildly; **r. les rangs** to fall out
2 *vi* (**a**) *(casser)* to break (**b**) *(se séparer)* to split up (avec with); **r. avec sa famille** to break off relations with one's family (**c**) **r. avec la tradition** to break with tradition
3 se rompre *vpr (se casser)* to break; **son cœur battait à se r.** his/her heart was pounding; *Fig* **se r. le cou** to break one's neck

rompu, -e [rɔ̃py] *adj* (**a**) *(exténué)* **être r. (de fatigue)** to be worn out (**b**) *(expérimenté)* **r. à qch** used to sth

romsteck [rɔmstɛk] *nm* rump steak

ronce [rɔ̃s] *nf* (**a**) *(arbuste)* bramble (bush), blackberry bush (**b**) *(dans le bois)* **r. de noyer** burr walnut

ronchon, -onne [rɔ̃ʃɔ̃, -ɔn] *Fam* **1** *adj* grouchy, grumpy
2 *nm,f* grouch

ronchonnement [rɔ̃ʃɔnmɑ̃] *nm Fam* grumbling

ronchonner [rɔ̃ʃɔne] *vi Fam* to grumble

roncier [rɔ̃sje] *nm*, **roncière** [rɔ̃sjɛr] *nf* thick bramble bush

rond, -e [rɔ̃, rɔ̃d] **1** *adj* (**a**) *(balle, table, nappe)* round; *(ventre)* rounded; *(poitrine)* full; *(personne, joues, silhouette)* plump; **avoir le dos r.** to be round-shouldered (**b**) *(plein)* *(voix)* full (**c**) *(chiffre, compte)* round (**d**) **être r. en affaires** to be straightforward where business is concerned (**e**) *Fam (ivre)* plastered; **r. comme une queue de pelle** *Br* rat-arsed, *Am* stewed to the gills
2 *adv* **tout r.** *(exactement)* exactly
3 *nm* (**a**) *(figure)* circle; **en r.** in a circle; *Fam* **faire des ronds de jambe** to bow and scrape; *Fam* **en rester comme deux ronds de flan** to be absolutely staggered; **r. de serviette** napkin ring (**b**) *Fam (sou)* **il n'a pas un r.** he's *Br* stony broke *or Am* flat broke

rond-de-cuir (*pl* **ronds-de-cuir**) [rɔ̃dkɥir] *nm Fam Péj* pen-pusher

ronde [rɔ̃d] *nf* (**a**) *(danse)* round (dance); *(chanson)* round, roundelay (**b**) *(de gardien, de vigile)* round(s); *(de policier)* beat; **faire une/sa r.** *(gardien, vigile)* to patrol; *(policier)* to be on the beat (**c**) *Mus (note)* Br semibreve, *Am* whole note (**d**) **à la r.** *(autour)* **à 10 kilomètres à la r.** within a radius of 10 kilometres

rondeau, -x [rɔ̃do] *nm* rondo

rondelet, -ette [rɔ̃dlɛ, -ɛt] *adj* (**a**) *(personne)* plump, chubby (**b**) *(somme)* tidy

rondelle [rɔ̃dɛl] *nf* (**a**) *(de citron, de saucisson)* slice; **couper qch en rondelles** to slice sth (**b**) *Can* **r. (de hockey)** puck (**c**) *(d'écrou)* washer

rondement [rɔ̃dmɑ̃] *adv* (**a**) *(avec entrain)* briskly, promptly; **mener qch r.** to make short work of sth (**b**) *(franchement)* bluntly, frankly

rondeur [rɔ̃dœr] *nf* (**a**) *(d'un corps)* roundness; *(des joues)* plumpness (**b**) **rondeurs** *(d'une femme)* curves (**c**) *(amabilité)* **avec r.** bluntly, frankly

rondin [rɔ̃dɛ̃] *nm* log

rondo [rɔ̃do] *nm Mus* rondo

rondouillard, -e [rɔ̃dujar, -ard] *adj Fam (personne)* plump, chubby

rond-point (*pl* **ronds-points**) [rɔ̃pwɛ̃] *nm (sens giratoire)* Br roundabout, *Am* traffic circle

ronéotyper [rɔneɔtipe] *vt* to roneo

ronflant, -e [rɔ̃flɑ̃, -ɑ̃t] *adj Péj* high-flown, bombastic

ronflement [rɔ̃fləmɑ̃] *nm* (**a**) *(d'un dormeur)* snoring (**b**) *(d'un moteur, d'une machine)* whirring, purring

ronfler [rɔ̃fle] *vi* (**a**) *(dormeur)* to snore (**b**) *(moteur, machine)* to whir, to purr

ronfleur, -euse [rɔ̃flœr, -øz] *nm,f (personne)* snorer

ronger [45] [rɔ̃ʒe] **1** *vt* (**a**) *(bois)* to gnaw (at), to nibble (at); *(os)* to gnaw (on); **rongé par les vers** worm-eaten (**b**) *(acide, rouille)* to eat away or into; *(falaise)* to erode (**c**) *(tourmenter)* **être rongé de chagrin** to be tormented with grief; **être rongé de remords/par la jalousie/par l'anxiété** to be eaten up with remorse/jealousy/anxiety; **être rongé par la maladie** to be wasted by illness (**d**) *Fig* **r. son frein** to champ at the bit
2 se ronger *vpr* **se r. les ongles** to bite one's nails

rongeur, -euse [rɔ̃ʒœr, -øz] **1** *adj (mammifère)* rodent-like
2 *nm* rodent

ronron [rɔ̃rɔ̃], **ronronnement** [rɔ̃rɔnmɑ̃] *nm* (**a**) *(d'un chat)* purr (**b**) *(d'un moteur)* purr, whirr; *(d'un avion, d'une voix)* drone; *(d'une machine)* whirr (**c**) *(routine)* humdrum routine

ronronner [rɔ̃rɔne] *vi* (**a**) *(chat)* to purr (**b**) *(moteur)* to purr, to whirr; *(avion)* to drone; *(machine)* to whirr

roquefort [rɔkfɔr] *nm* Roquefort

roquet [rɔkɛ] *nm Péj (chien)* yappy little dog

roquette¹ [rɔkɛt] *nf (salade)* rocket

roquette² *nf (projectile)* rocket; **r. antichar** anti-tank rocket

rorqual, -als [rɔrkwal] *nm* rorqual, finback whale

rosace [rozas] *nf* (**a**) *(vitrail)* rose window (**b**) *(au plafond)* ceiling rose (**c**) *(de guitare)* rosette

rosaire [rozɛr] *nm* rosary; **dire** *ou* **réciter son r.** to say the rosary

rosâtre [rozatr] *adj* pinkish

rosbif [rɔzbif] *nm* (**a**) *(viande) (rôtie)* roast beef; *(à rôtir)* roasting beef (**b**) *Fam (Britannique)* Brit, = pejorative or humorous term used to refer to a British person

rose [roz] **1** *adj* pink; *Fig* **tout n'est pas r.** it's not all rosy; **r. bonbon** candy pink; **r. thé** tea rose; **vieux r.** old rose
2 *nf* (**a**) *(fleur)* rose; **frais comme une r.** fresh as a daisy; *Fam* **ne pas sentir la r.** to be a bit whiffy; **r. trémière** hollyhock (**b**) **r. des sables** desert rose; **r. des vents** compass card
3 *nm* pink; **voir la vie** *ou* **tout en r.** to see everything through rose-tinted *Br* spectacles *or Am* glasses

rosé, -e [roze] **1** *adj* pinkish
2 *nm (vin)* rosé

roseau, -x [rozo] *nm* reed

rosée [roze] *nf* dew

roseraie [rozrɛ] *nf* rose garden

rosette [rozɛt] *nf* (**a**) *(nœud)* bow; *(ornement)* rosette (**b**) *(insigne)* rosette *(especially of the Legion of Honour)*

rosier [rozje] *nm* rose-tree, rosebush

rosière [rozjɛr] *nf Vieilli* = village maiden awarded a wreath of roses for her virtuous conduct

rosir [rozir] **1** *vt* to turn pink
2 *vi* to go *or* turn pink

rosse [rɔs] *Péj* **1** *adj Fam (personne, conduite, remarque)* rotten
2 *nf* (**a**) *(cheval)* hack (**b**) *Fam (homme)* swine; *(femme)* bitch
rossée [rɔse] *nf Fam* thrashing
rosser [rɔse] *vt Fam* **r. qn** to beat sb up, to give sb a good hiding; **se faire r.** to get a hiding
rossignol [rɔsiɲɔl] *nm* (**a**) *(oiseau)* nightingale (**b**) *Fam (objet)* white elephant
rot [ro] *nm Fam* belch, burp; *(de bébé)* burp; **faire un r.** *(adulte)* to belch, to burp; *(bébé)* to burp
rotatif, -ive [rɔtatif, -iv] **1** *adj (pompe, moteur)* rotary
2 *nf* rotative rotary press
rotation [rɔtasjɔ̃] *nf* rotation; *(du stock, de fonds)* turnover
roter [rɔte] *vi Fam* to belch, to burp
rôti, -e [roti] **1** *adj* roast
2 *nm (viande)* joint, roast; **r. de porc** *(cuit)* roast pork; *(non cuit)* joint of pork
rotin¹ [rɔtɛ̃] *nm* rattan; **chaise en r.** cane *or* rattan chair
rotin² *nm Fam Vieilli (sou)* **il n'a plus un r.** he's *Br* stony broke *or Am* flat broke
rôtir [rotir] **1** *vt (viande)* to roast
2 *vi* (**a**) *(viande)* to roast (**b**) **r. au soleil** to bask in the sun
3 **se rôtir** *vpr* **se r. au soleil** to bask in the sun
rôtisserie [rotisri] *nf* (**a**) *(boutique du rôtisseur)* = shop selling roast meat (**b**) *(restaurant)* grillroom, steakhouse
rôtissoire [rotiswar] *nf* (rotating) spit, rotisserie
rotonde [rɔtɔ̃d] *nf* rotunda
rotor [rɔtɔr] *nm* rotor
rotule [rɔtyl] *nf* kneecap; *Fam* **être sur les rotules** to be dead beat
roturier, -ère [rɔtyrje, -ɛr] **1** *adj* common
2 *nm,f* commoner
rouage [rwaʒ] *nm* (**a**) *(d'un mécanisme)* works (**b**) *Fig (d'une administration, d'une organisation)* workings
roublard, -e [rublar, -ard] *Fam* **1** *adj (personne, air)* wily, cunning
2 *nm,f* wily *or* cunning devil
roublardise [rublardiz] *nf Fam* (**a**) *(caractère)* cunning, wiliness (**b**) *(acte)* crafty *or* cunning trick
rouble [rubl] *nm* rouble
roucoulade [rukulad] *nf (de pigeons)* cooing; *Fam* **roucoulades** *(d'amoureux)* billing and cooing
roucoulement [rukulmɑ̃] *nm (d'un pigeon)* cooing; *Fig (d'amoureux)* billing and cooing
roucouler [rukule] **1** *vi (pigeon)* to coo; *Fig (amoureux)* to bill and coo
2 *vt (mots doux, promesses)* to coo
roue [ru] *nf* (**a**) *(d'un véhicule)* wheel; **être la cinquième r. du carrosse** *Br* to be a spare part, *Am* to be the fifth wheel; **faire la r.** *(oiseau)* to spread its tail; *Fig & Péj* to strut, to swagger; **un deux roues** a two-wheeled vehicle; **r. libre** freewheel; **descendre en r. libre** to freewheel downhill; **r. de secours** spare wheel (**b**) *(figure de gymnastique)* cartwheel
roué, -e [rwe] *Litt* **1** *adj* cunning, sly
2 *nm,f* cunning person
rouer [rwe] *vt* **r. qn de coups** to beat sb black and blue
rouerie [ruri] *nf (acte)* cunning *or* sly trick (**envers** played on)
rouet [rwɛ] *nm* spinning wheel
rouge [ruʒ] **1** *adj* (**a**) *(tissu, objet, joue, vin)* red; **r. cerise** cherry-red; **r. sang** blood-red (**b**) *(personne)* **r.**

de colère/d'émotion red in the face with anger/emotion; **être r. de honte** to blush with shame; **être r. comme une écrevisse** to be as red as a lobster; **être r. comme une tomate** *ou* **une pivoine** to be as red as a *Br* beetroot *or Am* beet (**c**) *(chauffé) (fer)* red-hot
2 *adv* **se fâcher tout r.** to lose one's temper completely; **voir r.** to see red
3 *nm* (**a**) *(couleur)* red; **peindre/teindre qch en r.** to paint/dye sth red; **le r. lui monte aux joues** he's/she's going red in the face (**b**) *(chaleur extrême)* **porter** *ou* **chauffer qch au r.** to heat sth until it is red-hot (**c**) *(cosmétique)* **r. à lèvres** lipstick; **se mettre du r.** to put some *or* one's lipstick on (**d**) *Fam* **passer au r.** *(signal d'arrêt)* to turn *or* go red (**e**) *(vin)* red wine; *Fam* **gros r.** plonk (**f**) *Fam Fig* **être dans le r.** *(financièrement)* to be in the red
4 *nmf (communiste)* Red
rougeâtre [ruʒatr] *adj* reddish
rougeaud, -e [ruʒo, -od] **1** *adj* red-faced
2 *nm,f* red-faced person
rouge-gorge *(pl* **rouges-gorges)** [ruʒgɔrʒ] *nm* robin
rougeoiement [ruʒwamɑ̃] *nm* red glow
rougeole [ruʒɔl] *nf* measles *(singulier);* **avoir la r.** to have measles
rougeoyant, -e [ruʒwajɑ̃, -ɑ̃t] *adj* glowing (red)
rougeoyer [32] [ruʒwaje] *vi* to turn red
rouget [ruʒɛ] *nm* red mullet
rougeur [ruʒœr] *nf* (**a**) *(due à la chaleur, à l'émotion)* flush; *(due à la honte, à la gêne)* blush (**b**) *(tache)* blotch (**c**) *(couleur)* redness
rougir [ruʒir] **1** *vt* (**a**) *(ciel, feuilles)* to turn red (**b**) *(visage)* to redden
2 *vi* (**a**) *(ciel, feuilles)* to turn red (**b**) *(personne)* to turn red; *(de honte, de gêne)* to blush, to go red; *Fig (avoir honte)* to be ashamed; **r. jusqu'aux oreilles** to blush to the roots of one's hair; **r. de colère/d'émotion** to flush with anger/emotion
rougissant, -e [ruʒisɑ̃, -ɑ̃t] *adj (personne, visage)* blushing
rouille [ruj] **1** *adj inv* rust(-coloured)
2 *nf* (**a**) *(sur le fer)* rust (**b**) *(sauce)* = spicy sauce made with garlic and chillis, traditionally served with fish soup
rouillé, -e [ruje] *adj* (**a**) *(métal, clef)* rusty, rusted (**b**) *Fig (personne)* rusty
rouiller [ruje] **1** *vt (métal, clef)* to rust, to make rusty
2 *vi (métal, clef)* to rust, to go rusty
3 **se rouiller** *vpr* (**a**) *(métal, clef)* to rust, to get rusty (**b**) *Fig (personne) (physiquement)* to get stiff; *(intellectuellement) (langue, connaissances)* to get rusty
roulade [rulad] *nf* (**a**) *(en gymnastique)* **r. avant/arrière** forward/backward roll; **faire des roulades** to do rolls (**b**) *(vocalise)* roulade (**c**) *(charcuterie)* rolled and stuffed meat
roulage [rulaʒ] *nm Belg (circulation)* traffic; **accident de r.** traffic accident
roulant, -e [rulɑ̃, -ɑ̃t] *adj* (**a**) *(porte)* sliding; *(pont)* travelling (**b**) *(capital)* working (**c**) *Fam (drôle) (personne, blague, histoire)* comical
roulé, -e [rule] **1** *adj* (**a**) *(journal, carte, tapis)* rolled(-up); *(charcuterie)* rolled (**b**) *Fam (femme)* **être bien roulée** to be curvy
2 *nm (gâteau)* Swiss roll
rouleau, -x [rulo] *nm* (**a**) *(bande) (de papier, de Scotch®, de pellicule)* roll; *Fam* **être au bout du r.** to

be at the end of one's tether (**b**) *(objet circulaire) (pour peindre)* roller; **r. compresseur** steamroller; **r. à pâtisserie,** *Can & Suisse* **r. à pâte** rolling pin; **r. de printemps** spring roll (**c**) *(vague)* billow, roller (**d**) *(bigoudi)* roller (**e**) *(saut en hauteur)* **r. dorsal** Fosbury flop; **r. ventral** western roll

roulé-boulé (*pl* **roulés-boulés**) [rulebule] *nm (culbute)* roll *(executed tucked up in a ball)*

roulement [rulmɑ̃] *nm* (**a**) *(d'une balle)* rolling (**b**) *(bruit)* **un r. de tonnerre** a roll *or* rumble of thunder; **des roulements de tambour** drum rolls (**c**) *(alternance)* rotation; **par r.** in rotation (**d**) *(pièce)* bearing; **r. à billes** ball bearing (**e**) *Fin (de fonds)* circulation; *(de capitaux)* turnover

rouler [rule] **1** *vt* (**a**) *(pierre, tonneau)* to roll (along) (**b**) *(tapis, papier, manches)* to roll up; *(cigarette)* to roll (**c**) *(yeux)* to roll (**d**) *(balancer)* **r. les épaules** to roll one's shoulders; **r. les hanches** to swing one's hips (**e**) *Fam (duper)* to do (**de** out of); **se faire r.** to be done *or* had (**f**) *(locutions)* **r. les r** to roll one's r's; *très Fam* **r. une pelle** *ou* **un palot** *ou* **un patin à qn** to French-kiss *or Br* snog sb

2 *vi* (**a**) *(balle)* to roll; **faire r. qch sur le sol** to roll sth along the ground (**b**) *(dégringoler) (personne)* to roll, to tumble (**c**) *(dans une voiture, dans un train)* to go, to travel; **on a beaucoup roulé** we drove for a long time; **ça roule bien ce matin** there are no traffic problems this morning; **à quelle vitesse rouliez-vous?** what speed were you doing? (**d**) *Fam* **ça roule** everything's fine (**e**) *Fig* **r. sur l'or** to be rolling in money (**f**) *(conversation)* **r. sur qch** to be about sth (**g**) *(tonnerre)* to roll, to rumble; *(tambour)* to roll (**h**) *(navire)* to roll

3 se rouler *vpr* (**a**) *(sur soi-même)* **se r. par terre** to roll about on the floor; *(dehors)* to roll about on the ground (**b**) **se r. une cigarette** to roll a cigarette; *Fam* **se r. les pouces, se les r.** to twiddle one's thumbs

roulette [rulɛt] *nf* (**a**) *(de meuble)* castor; **à roulettes** *(meuble)* on castors; *Fam* **marcher** *ou* **aller comme sur des roulettes** to go like clockwork (**b**) *Fam (de dentiste)* drill (**c**) *(au jeu)* roulette; **r. russe** Russian roulette

rouli-roulant (*pl* **rouli-roulants**) [rulirulɑ̃] *nm Can* skateboard

roulis [ruli] *nm (d'un navire)* roll

roulotte [rulɔt] *nf (de bohémiens)* caravan

roulure [rulyr] *nf très Fam* whore

roumain, -e [rumɛ̃, -ɛn] **1** *adj* Romanian
2 *nm,f* **R.** Romanian
3 *nm (langue)* Romanian

Roumanie [rumani] *nf* **la R.** Romania

round [rawnd, rund] *nm (de boxe, d'un débat)* round

roupie [rupi] *nf* rupee

roupiller [rupije] *vi Fam* to sleep, *Br* to kip

roupillon [rupijɔ̃] *nm Fam* snooze, *Br* kip; **piquer un r.** to have a snooze *or Br* a kip

rouquin, -e [rukɛ̃, -in] *Fam* **1** *adj (personne)* red-haired
2 *nm,f* redhead

rouspéter [34] [ruspete] *vi Fam* to moan and groan, to grumble (**contre** about)

rouspéteur, -euse [ruspetœr, -øz] *Fam* **1** *adj* grumpy, grouchy
2 *nm,f* grouch

rousse [rus] *voir* **roux**

roussette [rusɛt] *nf* (**a**) *(poisson)* spotted dogfish (**b**) *(chauve-souris)* flying fox (**c**) *(grenouille)* common frog

rousseur [rusœr] *nf (couleur)* redness

roussi [rusi] *nm* **ça sent le r.** there's a smell of burning; *Fig* there's trouble brewing

roussir [rusir] **1** *vt* (**a**) *(rendre roux)* to turn brown (**b**) *(brûler)* to scorch, to singe
2 *vi (feuilles, arbres)* to turn brown

rouste [rust] *nf Fam* thrashing, hammering; **flanquer une r. à qn** to give sb a thrashing *or* a hammering

routage [ruta ʒ] *nm (d'imprimés)* sorting and mailing

routard, -e [rutar, -ard] *nm,f Fam* backpacker

route [rut] *nf* (**a**) *(voie)* road; **prendre la r. de Paris** to take the Paris road; **r. à double voie** *ou* **à deux voies** *Br* dual carriageway, *Am* divided highway; **par la r.** by road; **r. départementale** secondary road, *Br* B-road; **r. nationale** main road, *Br* ≃ A-road, *Am* ≃ state highway (**b**) *(itinéraire)* route, way; **montrer la r. à qn** to show sb the way; **c'est sur ma r.** it's on my way; **r. des vins** wine trail (**c**) *(trajet)* **après trois heures de r.** after three hours on the road; **se mettre en r.** *(personne)* to set off; **en r.!** let's be off!; *Fam Hum* **en r., mauvaise troupe!** come on, you lot!; **bonne r.!** have a good trip! (**d**) *Fig (chemin)* path (**e**) *(marche)* **mettre qch en r.** *(moteur)* to start sth up; *(projet, travaux)* to get sth under way; **avoir qch en r.** to be working on sth; *Fam* **ils ont un bébé en r.** they've got a baby on the way

routeur [rutœr] *nm Ordinat* router

routier, -ère [rutje, -ɛr] **1** *adj* road
2 *nm* (**a**) *(conducteur)* *Br* long-distance lorry driver, *Am* truck driver (**b**) *(restaurant)* *Br* transport cafe, *Am* truck stop

routine [rutin] *nf* routine; **s'enliser dans/sortir de la r.** to get into/out of a rut

routinier, -ère [rutinje, -ɛr] *adj (tâches, travail)* routine; **être r.** to be set in one's ways

rouvrir [52] [ruvrir] **1** *vt* to reopen
2 se rouvrir *vpr* to reopen, to open again

roux, rousse [ru, rus] **1** *adj (feuilles)* russet, reddish-brown; *(cheveux)* red; *(personne)* red-haired; *(sucre)* brown
2 *nm,f (personne)* red-haired person, redhead
3 *nm* (**a**) *(couleur)* russet, reddish-brown (**b**) *(préparation culinaire)* roux

royal, -e, -aux, -ales [rwajal, -o] *adj* (**a**) *(palais, visite)* royal (**b**) *(cadeau)* magnificent; *(pourboire)* huge (**c**) *(indifférence)* utter; *Fam* **ficher une paix royale à qn** to leave sb in complete peace

royalement [rwajalmɑ̃] *adv* (**a**) *(payé)* royally (**b**) *Fam* **je m'en fiche** *ou* **moque r.** I couldn't care less

royalisme [rwajalism] *nm* royalism

royaliste [rwajalist] **1** *adj* royalist; *Fig* **être plus r. que le roi** to overdo it
2 *nmf* royalist

royalties [rwajalti] *nfpl* royalties

royaume [rwajom] *nm* kingdom; *Fig* realm

Royaume-Uni [rwajomyni] *nm* **le R.** the United Kingdom

royauté [rwajote] *nf (monarchie)* monarchy; *(dignité)* kingship

RPR [ɛrpeɛr] *nm Pol (abrév* **Rassemblement pour la République)** = right-wing French political party

RSVP *(abrév* **répondez s'il vous plaît)** RSVP

ruade [rɥad] *nf (d'un cheval)* lashing out, kick

Ruanda [rwɑ̃da] = Rwanda
ruandais, -e [rwɑ̃dɛ, -ɛz] = rwandais
ruban [rybɑ̃] *nm* ribbon; **r. adhésif** adhesive *or* sticky tape; **r. encreur** *(de machine à écrire)* typewriter ribbon; *Ordinat* **r. perforé** punchtape
rubéole [rybeɔl] *nf* German measles *(singulier)*, rubella
rubicond, -e [rybikɔ̃, -ɔ̃d] *adj (teint)* florid, rubicund
rubis [rybi] *nm* (**a**) *(pierre précieuse)* ruby; *Fig* **payer r. sur l'ongle** to pay cash on the nail (**b**) *(de montre, d'horloge)* jewel
rubrique [rybrik] *nf* (**a**) *(article)* column (**b**) *(catégorie)* section; **r. nécrologique** obituary section
ruche [ryʃ] *nf* (**a**) *(abri)* beehive (**b**) *(essaim)* hive; *Fig (ville, école)* hive of activity
rucher [ryʃe] *nm* apiary
rude [ryd] *adj* (**a**) *(fruste)* rough, uncouth (**b**) *(sévère) (personne, voix)* harsh (**c**) *(peau, tissu)* rough (**d**) *(hiver, climat)* severe, harsh (**e**) *(tâche, métier)* tough
rudement [rydmɑ̃] *adv* (**a**) *(répondre)* harshly; **être r. éprouvé** to be severely tested (**b**) *(frapper, heurter)* hard (**c**) *Fam (très)* really
rudesse [rydɛs] *nf* harshness; **avec r.** harshly
rudimentaire [rydimɑ̃tɛr] *adj* rudimentary
rudiments [rydimɑ̃] *nmpl (d'une matière)* rudiments; **avoir des r. de chinois** to speak basic Chinese
rudoyer [32] [rydwaje] *vt* to treat harshly
rue [ry] *nf* street; **être/se retrouver à la r.** to be/find oneself out on the street; **mettre/jeter qn à la r.** to put/throw sb out on the street; **r. piétonnière** *ou* **piétonne** pedestrian precinct; **r. principale** main street; **la grande r.** the main street
ruée [rɥe] *nf* rush; **la r. vers l'or** the gold rush
ruelle [rɥɛl] *nf* lane, alley(way)
ruer [rɥe] **1** *vi (cheval)* to kick; *Fig* **r. dans les brancards** to rebel
2 se ruer *vpr* **se r. sur qn** to rush at sb; **se r. sur qch** to make a rush for sth; **les invités se sont rués sur le buffet** the guests made a dash for the buffet
rugby [rygbi] *nm* rugby; **r. à treize/quinze** Rugby League/Union
rugbyman [rygbiman] *(pl* **rugbymen** [rygbimɛn]*)* *nm* rugby player
rugir [ryʒir] **1** *vi* (**a**) *(fauve)* to roar (**b**) *(personne)* to roar (**de** with) (**c**) *(vent, tempête)* to howl
2 *vt* to roar
rugissement [ryʒismɑ̃] *nm* (**a**) *(d'un fauve)* roar; **des rugissements** roaring (**b**) *(d'une personne)* roar; **pousser des rugissements de colère** to roar with anger (**c**) *(du vent, d'une tempête)* howling
rugosité [rygozite] *nf* roughness; **rugosités** rough patches
rugueux, -euse [rygø, -øz] *adj* rough
ruine [rɥin] *nf* (**a**) *(écroulement) (d'un édifice)* **en r.** in ruins, ruined; **tomber en ruine(s)** to go to ruin (**b**) **ruines** *(décombres)* ruins (**c**) *Fig (d'une personne, d'une société)* ruin, downfall; **aller** *ou* **courir à la r.** to be on the road to ruin (**d**) *(vieille maison)* ruin (**e**) *Fam* **c'est la r.!** *(c'est coûteux)* it's outrageously expensive!
ruiner [rɥine] **1** *vt* to ruin; *(espoirs)* to ruin, to dash
2 se ruiner *vpr (perdre son argent)* to ruin *or* bankrupt oneself; *(dépenser beaucoup d'argent)* to spend a fortune
ruineux, -euse [rɥinø, -øz] *adj* ruinously expensive; **ce n'est pas r.** it won't ruin you/us/*etc*

ruisseau, -x [rɥiso] *nm* (**a**) *(cours d'eau)* brook, stream (**b**) *Fig (de sang, de lave)* stream; *(de larmes)* flood (**c**) *(caniveau)* gutter
ruisselant, -e [rɥislɑ̃, -ɑ̃t] *adj* dripping (**de** with)
ruisseler [9] [rɥisle] *vi* (**a**) *(liquide)* to stream, to run (**b**) *(surface)* to drip, to stream (**de** with); **le front ruisselant de sueur** with one's forehead dripping with sweat; **ses joues ruisselaient de larmes** tears were streaming down his/her cheeks
ruissellement [rɥisɛlmɑ̃] *nm* streaming, running
rumba [rumba] *nf* rumba
rumeur [rymœr] *nf* (**a**) *(bruit confus)* distant murmur; *(de la circulation, d'une ville)* hum; *(de voix)* murmur (**b**) *(nouvelle)* rumour
ruminant [ryminɑ̃] *nm* ruminant
rumination [ryminasjɔ̃] *nf* rumination, ruminating
ruminer [rymine] **1** *vt (herbe)* to chew; *Fig (idée, projet)* to mull over
2 *vi* to ruminate, to chew the cud; *Fig* to brood
rumsteck [rɔmstɛk] *nm* rump steak
rupestre [rypɛstr] *adj* (**a**) **peinture r.** rock painting; *(dans une caverne)* cave painting (**b**) *(plante)* rock
rupin, -e [rypɛ̃, -in] *Fam* **1** *adj (riche) (personne)* loaded; *(quartier)* plush, *Br* posh
2 *nm,f* **c'est un r.** he's loaded; **les rupins** the rich
rupture [ryptyr] *nf* (**a**) *(d'une corde, d'une poutre)* breaking; *(d'un barrage)* bursting; *(d'un tendon)* rupture (**b**) *(interruption) (de négociations)* breaking off (**de** of), breakdown (**de** in); **être en r. avec qn/qch** to be at odds with sb/sth; **en r. avec la tradition** in a break with tradition; **être en r. de stock** to be out of stock (**c**) *(annulation) (de fiançailles)* breaking off; *(de contrat)* breach (**d**) *(entre amoureux)* break-up; **être au bord de la r.** to be on the verge of breaking up
rural, -e, -aux, -ales [ryral, -o] **1** *adj (région, vie)* rural; *(chemin)* country
2 *nm,f* country person
ruse [ryz] *nf* (**a**) *(procédé)* ruse, trick; **r. de guerre** stratagem (of war); *Fig* dodge (**b**) *(calcul)* **faire qch par la r.** to do sth by trickery
rusé, -e [ryze] *adj* cunning, crafty
ruser [ryze] *vi* to use trickery *or* cunning
russe [rys] **1** *adj* Russian
2 *nmf* **R.** Russian
3 *nm (langue)* Russian
Russie [rysi] *nf* **la R.** Russia
rustaud, -e [rysto, -od] **1** *adj* uncouth
2 *nm,f Br* country bumpkin, *Am* hick
Rustine® [rystin] *nf* repair patch *(for mending inner tube of bicycle)*
rustique [rystik] *adj* (**a**) *(manières, vie)* rustic; *(meuble)* rustic-style (**b**) *(plante)* hardy
rustre [rystr] **1** *nm* uncouth
2 *nm* boor, lout
rut [ryt] *nm (de mâle)* rut(ting); *(de femelle)* heat; **en r.** *(mâle)* rutting; *(femelle) Br* on *or Am & Ir* in heat
rutabaga [rytabaga] *nm Br* swede, *Am* rutabaga
rutilant, -e [rytilɑ̃, -ɑ̃t] *adj* gleaming
rutiler [rytile] *vi* to gleam
Rwanda [rwɑ̃da] *nm* **le R.** Rwanda
rwandais, -e [rwɑ̃dɛ, -ɛz] **1** *adj* Rwandan
2 *nm,f* **R.** Rwandan
rythme [ritm] *nm* (**a**) *(succession)* rhythm; *(allure)* pace; **manquer de r.** *(film)* to be a bit slow; **au r. de** at the rate of; **r. cardiaque/respiratoire** heart/breathing rate; **les rythmes scolaires** the way in which the school year is organized (**b**) *(en musique)* rhythm;

en r. in time; **marquer le r.** to beat time; **suivre le r.** to follow the beat; *Fig* to keep up; **avoir le sens du r.** to have a sense of rhythm; **avoir le r. dans la peau** to have rhythm in one's blood (**c**) *(d'une phrase)* rhythm

rythmé, -e [ritme] *adj* rhythmic(al)
rythmer [ritme] *vt* to give rhythm to
rythmique [ritmik] **1** *adj* rhythmic(al)
    2 *nf (en poésie)* rhythmics *(singulier)*

S¹, s [ɛs] *nm inv* S, s; **faire des s** to zigzag; **en S** *(crochet)* S-shaped; *(route)* zigzagging

S² (**a**) *(abrév* **sud**) S (**b**) *(abrév* **seconde(s)**) sec

s' [s] *voir* **se**

SA [ɛsa] *nf (abrév* **société anonyme**) *Br* ≃ plc, *Am* ≃ Corp.

sa [sa] *voir* **son¹**

sabbat [saba] *nm* Sabbath

sabbatique [sabatik] *adj (repos, année, congé)* sabbatical; **prendre un an de congé s.** to take a year's sabbatical

sable [sabl] **1** *nm* sand; *Fam* **être sur le s.** *(sans travail)* to be out of work; *(sans argent)* to be down and out; *Fam* **mettre qn sur le s.** to ruin sb; **sables mouvants** quicksands
  2 *adj inv* sand-coloured

sablé, -e [sable] **1** *adj voir* **pâte**
  2 *nm* shortbread *Br* biscuit *or Am* cookie

sabler [sable] *vt* (**a**) *(chemin)* to sand; *(route)* to grit (**b**) *(bâtiment)* to sandblast (**c**) **s. le champagne** to crack open a bottle of champagne

sableuse [sabløz] *nf* sandblaster

sableux, -euse [sablø, -øz] *adj* sandy

sablier [sablije] *nm* hourglass

sablonneux, -euse [sablɔnø, -øz] *adj* sandy

sabord [sabɔr] *nm* = type of square porthole; *Fam Vieilli* **mille sabords!** ≃ shiver me timbers!

saborder [sabɔrde] **1** *vt (navire)* to scuttle; *Fig (entreprise)* to scupper
  2 se saborder *vpr* to scuttle one's ship

sabot [sabo] *nm* (**a**) *(de cheval)* hoof; *Fam* **ça ne se trouve pas sous le s. d'un cheval** it doesn't grow on trees (**b**) *(chaussure)* clog; *Fam* **je te vois venir avec tes gros sabots** I can see what you're after (**c**) **s. de Denver** *Br* wheel clamp, *Am* Denver boot; **mettre un s. de Denver à une voiture** *Br* to (wheel-)clamp a car; *Am* to put a Denver boot on a car

sabotage [sabotaʒ] *nm* sabotage; *(acte)* act of sabotage

saboter [sabɔte] *vt (voiture, entreprise, plan de paix)* to sabotage; *(travail)* to make a mess of

saboteur, -euse [sabɔtœr, -øz] *nm,f* saboteur

sabre [sabr] *nm* sabre; **s. au clair** with drawn sword

sabrer [sabre] *vt* (**a**) **une cicatrice lui sabrait la joue** there was the gash of a scar on his/her cheek (**b**) *Fam (raccourcir)* to slash (**c**) *Fam (critiquer)* to slate (**d**) *Fam* **se faire s.** *(étudiant) Br* to fail, *Am* to flunk; **il s'est fait s. par le prof** the teacher *Br* failed *or Am* flunked him (**e**) **s. le champagne** to crack open a bottle of champagne

sac¹ [sak] *nm* (**a**) *(contenant, contenu)* bag (**de** of); *(grand et en toile)* sack (**de** of); **s. de sable** sandbag; *Fam* **un s. de nœuds** a hornets' nest; **partir s. au dos** to set off with one's rucksack on one's back; *Fam* **vider son s.** to get it off one's chest; *Fam* **je les mets dans le même s.** they're as bad as each other; *Fam* **l'affaire est dans le s.** it's in the bag; **s. de couchage** sleeping bag; **s. à dos** rucksack, backpack; **s. à main** handbag; *Fam* **s. d'os** bag of bones; **s. à ouvrage** work bag; **s. poubelle** *Br* bin liner, *Am* garbage bag; **s. à provisions** shopping bag; *Fam* **s. à vin** drunk; **s. de voyage** travel *or* overnight bag (**b**) *Anciennement très Fam (somme)* 10 francs; **10 sacs** 100 francs

sac² *nm (pillage)* sacking; **mettre une ville à s.** to sack a town

saccade [sakad] *nf* jerk, jolt; **par saccades** in fits and starts

saccadé, -e [sakade] *adj* jerky

saccage [sakaʒ] *nm* havoc; **se livrer à un s. de** to wreak havoc in

saccager [45] [sakaʒe] *vt* (**a**) *(piller) (ville)* to sack; *(maison)* to ransack (**b**) *(dévaster) (ville, maison)* to wreak havoc in; **la récolte fut saccagée par l'orage** the crops were devastated by the storm

saccharose [sakaroz] *nm Chim* saccharose

sacerdoce [saserdɔs] *nm* priesthood; *Fig* vocation

sacerdotal, -e, -aux, -ales [saserdɔtal, -o] *adj* priestly

sachant, sache *etc voir* **savoir²**

sachet [saʃɛ] *nm* sachet; **s. de thé** teabag; **thé en sachets** teabags; **en s.-cuisson** boil-in-the-bag

sacoche [sakɔʃ] *nf* (**a**) *(de vélo)* saddlebag (**b**) *(besace)* bag (**c**) *Belg & Can* handbag, *Am* purse

sacquer [sake] *Fam* **1** *vt* (**a**) *(renvoyer)* to fire, *Br* to sack; **se faire s.** to get fired, *Br* to get the sack (**b**) *(noter sévèrement)* to give a bad *Br* mark *or Am* grade to; **se faire s. par un prof** to get a bad *Br* mark *or Am* grade from a teacher (**c**) *(supporter)* **je ne peux pas le s.** I can't stand him
  2 *vi (professeur)* to be a tough *Br* marker *or Am* grader

sacrant, -e [sakrɑ̃, -ɑ̃t] *adj Can Fam (fâcheux)* bothersome

sacre [sakr] *nm* (**a**) *(d'un roi)* coronation; *(d'un évêque)* consecration; *Fig* rite (**b**) *Can (juron)* swear word, expletive

sacré, -e [sakre] **1** *adj* (**a**) *Rel & Fig* sacred (**b**) *Fam (maudit)* damn, *Br* bloody; **s. Paul, qu'est-ce qu'on ferait sans lui!** good old Paul, what would we do without him?
  2 *nm* **le s.** the sacred

sacrement [sakrəmã] *nm* sacrament; **le saint S.** the Blessed Sacrament; **recevoir les derniers sacrements** to receive the last rites

sacrément [sakremã] *adv Fam* damn, *Br* bloody

sacrer [sakre] **1** *vt (roi)* to crown; *(évêque)* to consecrate; **s. qn roi** to crown sb king; *Fig* **il a été sacré champion de France en 1995** he won the French championship in 1995

2 *vi Can* to swear

sacrifice [sakrifis] *nm* sacrifice; **offrir qn/qch en s.** to offer sb/sth up as a sacrifice; **faire le s. de sa vie** to sacrifice one's life; *Fig* **faire des sacrifices (pour)** to make sacrifices (for)

sacrifier [66] [sakrifje] **1** *vt aussi Fig* to sacrifice (**à** to); **sacrifié** *(prix)* rock-bottom; *(article)* at a rock-bottom price

2 *vi* **s. à la mode** to be a slave to fashion

3 **se sacrifier** *vpr* to sacrifice oneself (**pour** for); *Fam* **allez, je me sacrifie, je vais les chercher à la gare!** right, I'll be the martyr and pick them up from the station!

sacrilège [sakrilɛʒ] **1** *adj* sacrilegious

2 *nmf (personne)* sacrilegious person

3 *nm (acte)* sacrilege

sacristie [sakristi] *nf* sacristy, vestry

sacro-saint, -e *(mpl* sacro-saints, *fpl* sacro-saintes) [sakrɔsɛ̃, -ɛ̃t] *adj aussi Ironique* sacrosanct

sadique [sadik] **1** *adj* sadistic

2 *nmf* sadist

sadisme [sadism] *nm* sadism

sadomaso [sadɔmazɔ] *adj inv Fam* SM, S & M

sadomasochisme [sadɔmazɔʃism] *nm* sadomasochism

sadomasochiste [sadɔmazɔʃist] **1** *adj* sadomasochistic

2 *nmf* sadomasochist

safari [safari] *nm* safari; **en s.** on safari; **s.-photo** photographic safari

safran [safrã] **1** *nm (plante, épice)* saffron

2 *adj inv* **(jaune) s.** saffron (yellow)

saga [saga] *nf aussi Fig* saga

sagace [sagas] *adj* shrewd, astute

sagacité [sagasite] *nf* shrewdness, astuteness; **avec s.** shrewdly, astutely

sage [saʒ] **1** *adj* (**a**) *(avisé) (personne, décision)* wise, sensible (**b**) *(calme) (enfant, animal)* good, well-behaved; **s. comme une image** as good as gold (**c**) *(chaste) (personne)* good; *(tenue, robe)* sober

2 *nm* wise man; **un vieux s.** a wise old man

sage-femme *(pl* sages-femmes) [saʒfam] *nf* midwife

sagement [saʒmã] *adv* (**a**) *(raisonnablement)* wisely, sensibly (**b**) *(tranquillement)* quietly

sagesse [saʒɛs] *nf* (**a**) *(intelligence)* wisdom, good sense; **avoir la s. de faire qch** to be wise *or* sensible enough to do sth; **plein de s.** very sensible; *Fig* **la voix de la s.** the voice of reason (**b**) *(calme)* good behaviour

Sagittaire [saʒitɛr] *nm Astron & Astrol* **le S.** Sagittarius; **être S.** to be (a) Sagittarius

sagouin [sagwɛ̃] *nm Fam (personne)* slob

Sahara [saara] *nm* **le S.** the Sahara (Desert)

saharienne [saarjɛn] *nf* safari jacket

Sahel [saɛl] *nm* **le S.** the Sahel

saignant, -e [sɛɲã, -ãt] *adj* (**a**) *(blessure)* bleeding (**b**) *(viande)* rare

saignée [sɛɲe] *nf* blood-letting; *Fig* drain; **faire une s. à qn** to bleed sb

saignement [sɛɲəmã] *nm* bleeding; **s. de nez** nosebleed

saigner [sɛɲe] **1** *vi (personne, blessure)* to bleed; **je saigne du nez** my nose is bleeding, I've got a nosebleed; *Fig & Litt* **mon cœur saigne** my heart bleeds; *Fam* **ça va s.** there's going to be trouble

2 *vt (poulet, personne)* to bleed; *Fig* **s. qn à blanc** to bleed sb dry

3 **se saigner** *vpr Fig* **se s. aux quatre veines** to bleed oneself dry

saillant, -e [sajã, -ãt] *adj (qui dépasse)* projecting; *(pommettes)* prominent; *(muscles)* bulging; *Fig (trait)* salient

saillie [saji] *nf* (**a**) *(partie en avant)* projection; **faire s.** to project, to jut out (**b**) *(par un mâle)* covering

saillir [67] [sajir] **1** *vt (femelle)* to cover

2 *vi (s'avancer)* to project, to jut out (**sur** over)

sain, -e [sɛ̃, sɛn] *adj* healthy; *(fruit, gestion)* sound; *(lectures)* wholesome; **s. de corps et d'esprit** sound in body and mind; **s. et sauf** safe and sound

sainement [sɛnmã] *adv* (**a**) *(vivre)* healthily (**b**) *(juger)* sensibly

saint, -e [sɛ̃, sɛ̃t] **1** *adj (lieu)* holy; *(personne, vie)* saintly; **s. patron** patron saint; **s. Pierre** St Peter; **sainte Catherine** St Catherine; *Fam* **avoir une sainte horreur de qch** to have a holy horror of sth; *Fam* **ne rien faire de toute la sainte journée** to do nothing the whole blessed day

2 *nm,f aussi Fig* saint; **ne savoir plus à quel s. se vouer** not to know which way to turn; *Hum* **il vaut mieux s'adresser à Dieu qu'à ses saints** it's best to go right to the top

3 *nm* **le S. des Saints** the Holy of Holies

saint-bernard [sɛ̃bɛrnar] *nm inv (chien)* St Bernard

Saint-Cyr [sɛ̃sir] *n* Saint-Cyr military academy

Sainte-Lucie [sɛ̃tlysi] *nf* St Lucia

sainte-nitouche *(pl* saintes-nitouches) [sɛ̃tnituʃ] *nf* little hypocrite; **avec ses airs de s.** looking as if butter wouldn't melt in her mouth

Saint-Esprit [sɛ̃tɛspri] *nm* **le S.** the Holy Ghost *or* Spirit; *Hum* **par l'opération du S.** by magic

sainteté [sɛ̃təte] *nf (d'une personne)* saintliness; *(de la loi, d'un serment)* sanctity; *(d'un lieu)* holiness; **sa S.** **(le pape)** His Holiness (the Pope)

saint-frusquin [sɛ̃fryskɛ̃] *nm Fam* **tout le s.** the whole caboodle; **il s'est pointé avec tout son s.** he turned up with all his gear

saint-glinglin [sɛ̃glɛ̃glɛ̃] **à la saint-glinglin** *adv Fam* **on sera payés à la s.** we'll be paid when pigs fly; **repoussé à la s.** postponed till whenever

saint-honoré [sɛ̃tɔnɔre] *nm inv* Saint-Honoré *(choux pastry ring filled with confectioner's custard)*

Saint-Jean [sɛ̃ʒã] *nf* (**a**) **la S.** Midsummer Day (**b**) *Can* **la Saint-Jean-Baptiste** Saint-Jean-Baptiste Day *(24 July)*

Saint-Laurent [sɛ̃lɔrã] *nm* **le S.** the St Lawrence (River); **la Voie maritime du S.** the St Lawrence Seaway

Saint-Marin [sɛ̃marɛ̃] *nm* San Marino

saint-nectaire [sɛ̃nɛktɛr] *nm inv* = type of firm cheese

Saint-Père [sɛ̃pɛr] *nm* **le S.** the Holy Father

Saint-Pétersbourg [sɛ̃petɛrsbur] *n* St Petersburg

Saint-Pierre-et-Miquelon [sɛ̃pjɛrəmiklɔ̃] *nm* St Pierre and Miquelon

Saint-Siège [sɛ̃sjɛʒ] *nm* **le S.** the Holy See

Saint-Sylvestre [sɛ̃silvɛstr] *nf* **la S.** New Year's Eve

sais *voir* savoir²

saisie [sezi] *nf (de biens)* seizure; *Ordinat* **s. de données** data capture, keyboarding; *Ordinat* **s. automatique/manuelle** automatic/manual input

saisine [sezin] *nf Jur* referral to a court

saisir [sezir] **1** *vt* (**a**) *(attraper) (personne, objet)* to take hold of; *(brusquement)* to grab; **s. l'occasion (de faire qch)** to seize *or* grasp the opportunity (to do sth); **j'ai été saisi par le froid** the cold really hit me (**b**) *(comprendre) (signification, nuance)* to grasp, to get; *(nom)* to catch, to get (**c**) *Ordinat (données)* to key, to enter (**d**) *Jur (biens)* to seize (**e**) *Jur* **s. un tribunal d'une affaire** to refer a matter to a court (**f**) *(viande)* to seal
2 *vi (comprendre)* to get it
3 se saisir *vpr* **se s. de qn/qch** to take hold of sb/sth; *(brusquement)* to grab sb/sth

saisissant, -e [sezisɑ̃, -ɑ̃t] *adj (froid)* biting; *(ressemblance)* striking; *(scène)* gripping

saisissement [sezismɑ̃] *nm* (**a**) *(sensation de froid)* sudden chill (**b**) *(émotion)* shock

saison [sɛzɔ̃] *nf* season; **en cette s.** at this time of year; **en toute s.** all (the) year round; **faire une bonne/mauvaise s.** *(équipe)* to have a good/bad season; **être de s.** *(fruits)* to be in season; **des fraises? mais ce n'est pas la s.!** strawberries? but it isn't the season for them!; **un temps de s.** seasonal weather; **la belle s.** the summer months; **la haute/basse s.** the high/low season; **la morte s.** the off season; **la s. touristique** the tourist season; **la s. des amours** the mating season; **la s. des pluies** the rainy season

saisonnier, -ère [sezɔnje, -ɛr] **1** *adj* seasonal
2 *nm,f* seasonal worker

sait *voir* **savoir²**

saké [sake] *nm* sake

salade [salad] *nf* (**a**) *(plante)* lettuce (**b**) *(plat)* salad; **s. composée** mixed salad; **s. de fruits** fruit salad; **s. grecque** Greek salad; **s. mixte** mixed salad; **s. niçoise** salade niçoise; **s. de tomates/de riz** tomato/rice salad; **s. verte** green salad; **haricots verts en s.** green bean salad (**c**) *Fam (désordre)* mess (**d**) *Fam* **vendre sa s.** to make a pitch (**e**) *Fam* **salades** *(mensonges)* tall stories, fibs

saladier [saladje] *nm* salad bowl

salaire [salɛr] *nm* (**a**) *(mensuel)* salary; *(hebdomadaire, journalier)* wages; *Prov* **toute peine mérite s.** the labourer is worthy of his hire; **s. de départ** starting salary; **s. minimum interprofessionnel de croissance** guaranteed minimum wage (**b**) *(récompense)* reward (**de** for); **le s. de la peur** the wages of fear

salaison [salezɔ̃] *nf (action)* salting; **des salaisons** salted meats

salamalecs [salamalɛk] *nmpl Fam* bowing and scraping

salamandre [salamɑ̃dr] *nf* salamander

salami [salami] *nm* salami

salant [salɑ̃] *adj m voir* **marais**

salarial, -e, -aux, -ales [salarjal, -o] *adj* wage/ *(mensuel)* salary

salarié, -e [salarje] **1** *adj* (**a**) *(travailleur) (payé mensuellement)* salaried; *(payé hebdomadairement)* wage-earning (**b**) *(travail)* paid
2 *nm,f (payé mensuellement)* salaried employee; *(payé hebdomadairement)* wage-earner; **salariés** *(d'une société)* employees

salarier [66] [salarje] *vt* to put on one's salaried staff

salaud [salo] *Vulg* **1** *nm* bastard
2 *adj* **c'était vraiment s. de faire ça** that was a really

shitty thing to do; **t'as vraiment été s.!** you were a real shit!

sale [sal] **1** *adj* (**a**) *(peu soigné)* dirty (**b**) *Fam (grave) (maladie, situation)* nasty; *(affaire)* dirty; **avoir une s. tête** *ou* **gueule** *(antipathique)* to look really nasty; *(malade)* to look awful; **faire un s. coup à qn** to play a dirty trick on sb; **s. bête** horrible beast; **s. boulot** rotten job; **faire le s. boulot** to do the dirty work; **s. gosse** little brat; **s. temps** filthy weather; **s. type** nasty character
2 *nm Fam* **mettre une chemise au s.** to put a dirty shirt in the wash

salé, -e [sale] **1** *adj* (**a**) *(conservé au sel)* salt; *(additionné de sel)* salted; *(au goût)* salty (**b**) *Fig (histoire, plaisanterie)* spicy (**c**) *Fam (condamnation)* stiff; *(addition)* steep
2 *nm* **le s.** savoury food; **petit s.** salt pork

salement [salmɑ̃] *adv* (**a**) *(manger, boire)* in a disgusting manner (**b**) *Fam (blessé, touché)* really badly; **je suis s. emmerdé** I'm in a real mess

saler [sale] *vt* to salt

saleté [salte] *nf* (**a**) *(manque de soin)* dirtiness; *(crasse)* dirt; **faire des saletés** to make a mess (**b**) *(objet)* trash, junk; **manger des saletés** to eat junk food (**c**) *(acte ou remarque obscène)* obscenity (**d**) *Fam (homme)* bastard; *(femme)* bitch

salière [saljɛr] *nf* salt cellar

saligaud [saligo] *nm Fam (ignoble individu)* bastard

salin, -e [salɛ̃, -in] **1** *adj* saline
2 *nm (marais salant)* salt marsh

salir [salir] **1** *vt* to make dirty, to dirty; *Fig* **s. le nom/la mémoire de qn** to sully sb's name/memory
2 se salir *vpr* to get dirty; *Fig* **se s. les mains** to get one's hands dirty

salissant, -e [salisɑ̃, -ɑ̃t] *adj* (**a**) *(travail)* dirty, messy (**b**) *(tissu, vêtement)* easily soiled; *(couleur)* that shows the dirt

salissure [salisyr] *nf* dirty mark

salivaire [salivɛr] *adj (glande)* salivary

salive [saliv] *nf* saliva

saliver [salive] *vi* to salivate; *Fig* **s. devant qch** to drool at the sight of sth

salle [sal] *nf* (**a**) *(pièce)* room; **s. d'armes** *(pour l'escrime)* fencing hall; *(pour les armes)* armoury; **s. d'attente** waiting room; **s. de bain(s)** bathroom; **s. des coffres** vaults; **s. commune** common room; **s. d'embarquement** *(d'un aéroport)* departure lounge; **s. d'exposition** showroom; *(pour une foire)* exhibition hall; **s. des fêtes** community hall; *(d'un village)* village hall; **s. de garde** *(d'hôpital)* staff room; *(de caserne)* guardroom; **s. de jeu** *(d'une maison)* Br playroom, Am rumpus room; *(d'un casino)* gaming room; **s. des machines** *(d'un navire)* engine-room; **s. à manger** dining room; *(meubles)* dining-room suite; **s. d'opération** operating theatre *or* Am room; **s. des pas perdus** *(dans une gare)* concourse; **s. des professeurs** staff room; **s. de réunion** meeting room; **s. du trône** throneroom; **s. des urgences** Br emergency ward, Am emergency room; **s. des ventes** saleroom (**b**) *(pour le cinéma, pour le théâtre)* **s. (de spectacle)** auditorium; **toute la s. applaudit** the whole audience applauded; **les salles obscures** Br the cinema, Am the movies

salmonelle [salmɔnɛl] *nf* salmonella

salmonellose [salmɔneloz] *nf* salmonella poisoning

Salomon [salɔmɔ̃] *voir* **île**

salon [salɔ̃] *nm* (**a**) *(pièce)* living room, *Br* lounge; *(dans un bateau)* saloon; *(dans un train)* saloon car; *Can* **s. de barbier** barber's; **s. de coiffure** hairdressing salon; **s. classe affaires** *(dans un aéroport)* business lounge; **s. d'essayage** fitting room; **s. de thé** tea room (**b**) *(meubles)* suite (**c**) *(exposition)* exhibition; **le S. des Arts ménagers** ≃ the Ideal Home Exhibition; **le S. de l'Automobile** *ou* **de l'Auto** the Motor Show; **le S. du Livre** the Book Fair; **le S. nautique** the Boat Show (**d**) *(littéraire)* salon; **tenir s.** to hold a salon

salon-lavoir *(pl* **salons-lavoirs**) [salɔ̃lavwar] *nm Belg & Suisse (lavomatique) Br* launderette, *Am* Laundromat®

salopard [salɔpar] *nm Vulg* bastard

salope [salɔp] *nf Vulg (femme méprisable)* bitch; *(homme méprisable)* bastard

saloper [salɔpe] *vt très Fam* (**a**) *(salir)* to dirty, to mess up (**b**) *(mal faire)* to make a dog's breakfast of

saloperie [salɔpri] *nf très Fam* (**a**) *(camelote)* trash, junk (**b**) *(coup bas)* dirty trick (**c**) **dire des saloperies sur qn** to bitch about sb

salopette [salɔpɛt] *nf Br* dungarees, *Am* overalls

salpêtre [salpɛtr] *nm* saltpetre

salsa [salsa] *nf* salsa

salsifis [salsifi] *nm* salsify

saltimbanque [saltɛ̃bɑ̃k] *nm* travelling acrobat

salto [salto] *nm* somersault

salubre [salybr] *adj* healthy

salubrité [salybrite] *nf* healthiness; **la s. publique** public health

saluer [salɥe] **1** *vt (en arrivant)* to greet; *(en partant)* to take one's leave of; *(s'incliner devant)* to bow to; *(sujet: soldat)* to salute; **s. qn d'une inclination de la tête** to nod to sb; **il est passé sans me s.** he walked past me without saying hello; **saluez-le de ma part** give him my regards; *Rel* **je vous salue, Marie** hail Mary

2 se saluer *vpr (en arrivant)* to greet each other; *(en partant)* to take leave of each other

salut [saly] **1** *nm* (**a**) *(salutation)* greeting; **faire un s. à qn** *(en se découvrant)* to raise one's hat to sb; *(en inclinant la tête)* to nod to sb (**b**) *(de soldat)* salute; **faire le s. militaire** to give a salute (**c**) *(sauvegarde)* rescue; *Rel* salvation

2 *exclam Fam* **s.!** *(en arrivant)* hi!; *(en partant)* bye!

salutaire [salytɛr] *adj (décision, mesure)* salutary; *(remède)* beneficial; **être s. à qn** to do sb good

salutation [salytasjɔ̃] *nf* greeting

Salvador [salvadɔr] *nm* **le S.** El Salvador

salvadorien, -enne [salvadɔrjɛ̃, -ɛn] **1** *adj* Salvadorean

2 *nm,f* **S.** Salvadorean

salve [salv] *nf* salvo, volley

Samaritain [samaritɛ̃] *nm* **le bon S.** the good Samaritan

samba [sɑ̃ba] *nf* samba

samedi [samdi] *nm* Saturday; **le S. saint** Easter Saturday; **s. prochain/dernier** next/last Saturday; **s. matin** Saturday morning; **s. soir** Saturday night *or* evening; **dans la nuit de s. à dimanche** on Saturday night; **s. 11 mai 2007** Saturday 11 May 2007; **nous sommes s. aujourd'hui** today's Saturday; **je commence s.** I'm starting on Saturday; **il vient le s./tous les samedis** he comes on Saturdays/every Saturday; **un s. sur deux** every second *or* other Saturday; **s. en huit/quinze** a week/fortnight on Saturday; **passer tout son s. à**

faire qch to spend one's whole Saturday doing sth; *Belg & Suisse* **faire le** *ou* **son s.** to do the weekly clean

Samoa [samɔa] *nfpl* **les S. occidentales** Western Samoa

samouraï [samuraj] *nm* samurai

samovar [samɔvar] *nm* samovar

sampler¹ [sɑ̃plœr] *nm Mus* sampler

sampler² [sɑ̃ple] *vt Mus* to sample

SAMU [samy] *nm (abrév* **Service d'aide médicale d'urgence)** = ambulance service; **appeler le S.** to call an ambulance; **le S. social** = mobile medical and support service for homeless people

sanatorium [sanatɔrjɔm] *nm* sanatorium

sanctifier [66] [sɑ̃ktifje] *vt* (**a**) *(rendre saint)* to sanctify (**b**) *(révérer)* **que Ton nom soit sanctifié** hallowed be Thy name

sanction [sɑ̃ksjɔ̃] *nf (punition)* sanction; *Fig (désavantage)* price; **prendre une s. contre qn** to take action against sb; **s. pénale** penalty; **sanctions économiques** economic sanctions

sanctionner [sɑ̃ksjɔne] *vt* (**a**) *(punir)* to punish (**b**) *(approuver)* to sanction; **sanctionné par l'usage** sanctioned by custom

sanctuaire [sɑ̃ktɥɛr] *nm aussi Fig* sanctuary

sandale [sɑ̃dal] *nf* sandal

sandalette [sɑ̃dalɛt] *nf* (light) sandal

sandre [sɑ̃dr] *nm* pikeperch

sandwich *(pl* **s.** *ou* **sandwiches**) [sɑ̃dwitʃ] *nm* sandwich; **s. au jambon/au fromage** ham/cheese sandwich; **s. grec** *Br* kebab, *Am* gyro; *Fam* **pris en s. (entre)** sandwiched (between)

San Francisco [sɑ̃frɑ̃sisko] *n* San Francisco

sang [sɑ̃] *nm* blood; **animaux à s. chaud/froid** warm-/cold-blooded animals; **être en s.** to be covered in blood; *Fig* **avoir le s. bleu** to have blue blood; *Fig* **avoir le s. chaud** to be hot-blooded; *Fig* **avoir qch dans le s.** to have sth in one's blood; *Fam* **avoir du s. de navet** to be spineless; *Fam* **se faire du mauvais s.** to get all worked up; *Fam* **se ronger les sangs, se faire un s. d'encre** to worry oneself sick; **le s. lui monta au visage** the blood rushed to his/her face; **mon s. n'a fait qu'un tour** *(de peur)* my heart missed a beat; *(de colère)* I saw red; *très Fam* **bon s. (de bonsoir)!**, **bon s. de bon Dieu!** damn and blast it!

sang-froid [sɑ̃frwa] *nm inv* composure, calm; **garder son s.** to keep calm, to keep one's head; **perdre son s.** to lose one's head, to lose one's composure; **tuer qn de s.** to kill sb in cold blood

sanglant, -e [sɑ̃glɑ̃, -ɑ̃t] *adj* bloody; *Fig (offensant)* scathing

sangle [sɑ̃gl] *nf* strap; *(de selle)* girth

sangler [sɑ̃gle] *vt* to put straps on; *(cheval)* to girth

sanglier [sɑ̃glije] *nm* (wild) boar

sanglot [sɑ̃glo] *nm* sob

sangloter [sɑ̃glote] *vi* to sob

sangria [sɑ̃grija] *nf* sangria

sangsue [sɑ̃sy] *nf (animal, personne)* leech

sanguin, -e [sɑ̃gɛ̃, -in] *adj (tempérament)* fiery; *(teint, visage)* ruddy

sanguinaire [sɑ̃ginɛr] *adj* (**a**) *(homme)* bloodthirsty (**b**) *(combat)* bloody

Sanisette® [sanizɛt] *nf* superloo

sanitaire [sanitɛr] **1** *adj* (**a**) *(personnel)* medical; *(mesures)* health (**b**) *(installation)* sanitary

2 *nmpl* **les sanitaires** *(toilettes)* the toilet; *(salle de bains et W.-C.)* the bathroom and toilet

sans [sɑ̃] **1** *prép* (**a**) *(indique l'absence, la privation, l'exclusion)* without; **s. parler** without speaking; **non s. difficulté** not without difficulty (**b**) *(indique la condition)* but for; **s. vous, je ne l'aurais jamais fait** but for you, I'd never have done it; **s. cela, s. quoi** otherwise; *Fam* **sois sage, s. ça tu seras puni!** be good or else you'll be punished!
2 *adv Fam* without it/them; **faire s.** to do without
3 *conj* **s. que nous le sachions** without our knowing
sans-abri [sɑ̃zabri] *nmf inv* homeless person; **les s.** the homeless
San Salvador [sɑ̃salvadɔr] *n* San Salvador
sans-cœur [sɑ̃kœr] *nmf inv Fam* heartless person
sans-culotte (*pl* **sans-culottes**) [sɑ̃kylɔt] *nm Hist* sansculotte *(person with extreme republican sympathies during the French Revolution)*
sans-emploi [sɑ̃zɑ̃plwa] *nmf inv* unemployed person; **les s.** the unemployed
sans-faute [sɑ̃fot] *nm inv* (de compétition hippique) clear round; **faire un s.** *(cheval)* to have a clear round; *Fig (personne)* not to put a foot wrong
sans-fil [sɑ̃fil] *nm inv* cordless telephone
sans-gêne [sɑ̃ʒɛn] **1** *adj inv* ill-mannered
2 *nm* lack of manners
sans-le-sou [sɑ̃ləsu] *nmf inv Fam* penniless person
sans-logis [sɑ̃lɔʒi] *nmf* homeless person; **les s.** the homeless
sans-papiers [sɑ̃papje] *nmf* illegal immigrant
sans-patrie [sɑ̃patri] *nmf inv* stateless person
santé [sɑ̃te] *nf* health; **être en bonne s.** to be in good health; **avoir une bonne/mauvaise s.** to be healthy/unhealthy; **être en parfaite s.** to be perfectly healthy; **avoir une petite s.** to be delicate; **c'est bon/mauvais pour la s.** it's good/bad for your health; **boire à la s. de qn** to drink sb's health; **(à votre) s.!** cheers!, good health!; *Suisse Fam* **s.!** *(quand on éternue)* bless you!; **la s. publique** public health
santiag [sɑ̃tjag] *nf Fam* cowboy boot
santon [sɑ̃tɔ̃] *nm* Christmas crib figure
São Tomé et Príncipe [saɔtomeeprɛ̃sip] *nm* São Tomé e Príncipe
saoudien, -enne [saudjɛ̃, -ɛn] **1** *adj* Saudi (Arabian)
2 *nm,f* **S.** Saudi (Arabian)
saoul, saouler *etc* = **soûl, soûler**
sape [sap] *nf* (**a**) *(tranchée)* sap; *Fig* **travail de s.** undermining (**b**) *Fam* **sapes** *(vêtements)* gear, threads
saper [sape] **1** *vt* (**a**) *aussi Fig* to undermine; **s. le moral à qn** to sap sb's morale (**b**) *Fam (habiller)* to dress; **être bien sapé** to be all dolled up
2 se saper *vpr Fam* to dress; **elle sait pas se s.** she's got no dress sense
sapeur-pompier (*pl* **sapeurs-pompiers**) [sapœrpɔ̃pje] *nm* fireman; **les sapeurs-pompiers** *(service)* the fire *Br* brigade *or Am* department
saphir [safir] *nm* sapphire
sapin [sapɛ̃] *nm* (**a**) *(arbre)* fir (tree) (**b**) *Fam* **ça sent le s.** that sounds as if you're heading for an early grave; **il sent le s.** he's done for (**c**) *Can* **se faire passer un s.** *(se faire avoir)* to be taken for a ride
sapristi [sapristi] *exclam Fam Vieilli ou Hum* good heavens!
saquer [sake] = **sacquer**
sarabande [sarabɑ̃d] *nf (danse, air)* saraband; *Fam (tapage)* racket, din
Sarajevo [sarajevo] *n* Sarajevo
sarbacane [sarbakan] *nf* blowpipe; *(jouet)* peashooter

sarcasme [sarkasm] *nm* sarcasm; *(remarque)* sarcastic remark
sarcastique [sarkastik] *adj* sarcastic
sarcler [sarkle] *vt (jardin)* to weed; *(sol)* to hoe; *(champ)* to clean
sarclette [sarklɛt] *nf* hoe
sarcloir [sarklwar] *nm* hoe
sarcome [sarkom] *nm Méd* sarcoma; **s. de Kaposi** Kaposi's sarcoma
sarcophage [sarkɔfaʒ] *nm* sarcophagus
Sardaigne [sardɛɲ] *nf* **la S.** Sardinia
sarde [sard] **1** *adj* Sardinian
2 *nmf* **S.** Sardinian
3 *nm (langue)* Sardinian
sardine [sardin] *nf* sardine; **sardines à l'huile/à la tomate** sardines in oil/in tomato sauce; *Fam* **serrés comme des sardines** packed together like sardines
sardonique [sardɔnik] *adj* sardonic
Sargasses [sargas] *voir* **mer**
SARL [ɛsaɛrɛl] *nf (abrév* **société à responsabilité limitée)** limited (liability) company; **Balacor S.** *Br* ≃ Balacor Ltd, *Am* ≃ Balacor Inc
sarment [sarmɑ̃] *nm (tige)* bine; *(de vigne)* vine shoot
saroual, -als [sarwal], **sarouel** [sarwɛl] *nm* = baggy trousers worn by North Africans
sarrasin, -e [sarazɛ̃, -in] **1** *adj Hist* Saracen
2 *nm,f Hist* **S.** Saracen
3 *nm (plante)* buckwheat
sarriette [sarjɛt] *nf* savory
sas [sas] *nm (pièce étanche)* airlock
Satan [satɑ̃] *npr* Satan
satané, -e [satane] *adj Fam* confounded
satanique [satanik] *adj* satanic; *Fig (cruauté, sourire)* fiendish
satellitaire [satelitɛr] *adj* satellite
satellite [satelit] **1** *nm* (**a**) *(corps céleste, engin)* satellite; **émission retransmise par s.** satellite broadcast; **télévision par s.** satellite television; **s.-espion** spy satellite; **s. géostationnaire** geostationary satellite; **s. de télécommunications** telecommunications satellite; **s. de télédiffusion** broadcast satellite (**b**) *Pol* satellite
2 *adj* **pays s.** satellite state
satiété [sasjete] *nf* **manger/boire à s.** to eat/drink one's fill
satin [satɛ̃] *nm* satin
satiné, -e [satine] **1** *adj (tissu)* satiny; *(papier)* glazed; *(peau)* satin-smooth; **peinture satinée** silk-finish paint
2 *nm* satin finish; *(de la peau)* satin smoothness
satire [satir] *nf* satire; **faire la s. de qch** to satirize sth
satirique [satirik] *adj* satirical
satiriser [satirize] *vt* to satirize
satiriste [satirist] *nmf* satirist
satisfaction [satisfaksjɔ̃] *nf* satisfaction; **à la s. générale** to everyone's satisfaction; **donner (entière) s. à qn** *(personne)* to give sb (complete) satisfaction; *(travail)* to fulfil sb (completely); **obtenir s.** to obtain satisfaction
satisfaire [36] [satisfɛr] **1** *vt* to satisfy
2 satisfaire à *vt ind (demande, condition, besoins)* to satisfy; *(règlement, normes de sécurité)* to comply with; *(obligation)* to fulfil
3 se satisfaire *vpr* **se s. de qch** to be satisfied with sth; **se s. de peu** to be content with very little; *Péj* to be easily satisfied

satisfaisant, -e [satisfəzɑ̃, -ɑ̃t] *adj (acceptable)* satisfactory; *(qui contente)* satisfying

satisfait, -e [satisfɛ, -ɛt] *adj* (**a**) *(heureux)* satisfied (**de** with); *Ironique* **vous voilà s.!** well, you asked for it!; **s. ou remboursé** *(dans une publicité)* satisfaction or your money back (**b**) *(suffisant)* satisfied

satisfecit [satisfesit] *nm inv Litt* **décerner un s. à qn** to congratulate sb on a job well done

saturation [satyrasjɔ̃] *nf aussi Fig* saturation; *(du réseau routier)* gridlock; *aussi Fig* **arriver à s.** to reach saturation point; *Ordinat (disquette)* to become full

saturer [satyre] **1** *vt* to saturate (**de** with); **les appels ont saturé le standard** the calls have jammed the switchboard
2 *vi Fam* **je sature** I've had it up to here

Saturne [satyrn] *npr (dieu, planète)* Saturn

satyre [satir] *nm* (**a**) *(demi-dieu)* satyr (**b**) *Fam (obsédé sexuel)* sex maniac

sauce [sos] *nf* (**a**) *(accompagnement)* sauce; **s. aux champignons** mushroom sauce; **s. de soja** soy sauce; **s. tomate** tomato sauce; *Fam Fig* **allonger la s.** to pad it out; *Fam* **mettre qch à toutes les sauces** to use sth in every way imaginable; *Fam* **à quelle s. sera-t-il mangé?** what's in store for him? (**b**) *Fam (pluie)* **prendre la s.** to get soaked

saucée [sose] *nf Fam (pluie)* downpour; **recevoir une s.** to get soaked

saucer [16] [sose] *vt* (**a**) *(assiette)* to mop up the sauce from (**b**) *Fam* **se faire s.** to get soaked

saucier [sosje] *nm* sauce cook

saucière [sosjɛr] *nf* sauce boat

sauciflard [sosiflar] *nm Fam* (slicing) sausage

saucisse [sosis] *nf* sausage; **s. de Francfort** frankfurter; **s. sèche** = thin salami-type sausage; **s. de Strasbourg/Toulouse** = type of beef/pork sausage

saucisson [sosisɔ̃] *nm* (slicing) sausage; **s. à l'ail** garlic sausage; *Hum* **s. à pattes** sausage dog; **s. pur porc** 100% pork sausage

saucissonné, -e [sosisɔne] *adj Fam* trussed up

saucissonner [sosisɔne] *vt Fam* (**a**) *(attacher)* to tie up (**b**) *(diviser)* **le film a été saucissonné** the film was divided up into episodes; **un film saucissonné par des publicités** a film with frequent commercial breaks

sauf¹, sauve [sof, sov] *adj (personne)* safe, unharmed; **avoir la vie sauve** to escape with one's life; **laisser la vie sauve à qn** to spare sb's life; **l'honneur est s.** honour is saved

sauf² *prép* except (for), apart from; **s. imprévu** unless anything unforeseen happens; **s. erreur de ma part** if I'm not mistaken; **s. votre respect** with all due respect; **s. s'il pleut** unless it rains; *Fam* **s. que...** except that...

sauf-conduit (*pl* **sauf-conduits**) [sofkɔ̃dɥi] *nm* safe conduct

sauge [soʒ] *nf* sage

saugrenu, -e [sogrəny] *adj* preposterous

saule [sol] *nm* willow; **s. pleureur** weeping willow

saumâtre [somatr] *adj (goût, eau)* brackish; *Fig* bitter

saumon [somɔ̃] **1** *nm* salmon; **s. fumé** smoked salmon, *Am* lox
2 *adj inv* **(rose) s.** salmon-pink

saumoné, -e [somɔne] *adj voir* **truite**

saumure [somyr] *nf* brine

sauna [sona] *nm* sauna

saupoudrer [sopudre] *vt* to sprinkle (**de** with)

saupoudreuse [sopudrøz] *nf* dredger

saur [sɔr] *adj m voir* **hareng**

saurai, saurais *etc voir* **savoir²**

saurien [sɔrjɛ̃] *nm* saurian

saut [so] *nm (bond)* jump, leap; **faire un s.** to jump, to leap; *Fig* **faire un s. à Paris/chez le boulanger/en ville** to pop *or Br* nip over to Paris/round to the baker's/into town; *Fig* **faire un s. de plusieurs années** to skip several years; **au s. du lit** first thing in the morning; **s. de l'ange** *Br* swallow dive, *Am* swan dive; **s. à l'élastique** bungee jumping; **s. en hauteur** high jump; **s. en longueur** long jump; **s. en parachute** parachute jump; *(activité)* parachute jumping; **faire du s. en parachute** to go parachute jumping; **s. à la perche** pole vault; *(activité)* pole vaulting; **s. périlleux** somersault; **s. en** *ou* **à skis** ski jump; *(activité)* ski jumping; **faire du s. à skis** to go ski jumping; *Ordinat* **s. de page** page break

saute [sot] *nf* **sautes de température** sudden changes in temperature; **sautes d'humeur** mood swings

sauté, -e [sote] **1** *adj* sautéed, sauté
2 *nm* **s. de lapin** sauté of rabbit

saute-mouton [sotmutɔ̃] *nm inv* leapfrog; **jouer à s.** to play leapfrog

sauter [sote] **1** *vt* (**a**) *(fossé, barrière)* to jump (over), to leap over; *Fig* **s. le pas** to take the plunge (**b**) *(omettre) (page, ligne, repas)* to skip; *(maille)* to drop; **s. une classe** to skip a year (**c**) *Vulg (coucher avec)* to screw, *Br* to shag; **se faire s. par qn** to screw *or Br* shag sb
2 *vi* (**a**) *(bondir)* to jump, to leap; **s. sur un pied** to hop; **s. à pieds joints** to jump with one's feet together; **s. à la perche** to pole-vault; **s. à la corde** *Br* to skip, *Am* to jump rope; **s. en parachute** to do a parachute jump; **s. à la gorge de qn** to go for sb; *(chien)* to fly at sb's throat; **s. au cou de qn** to fling one's arms round sb's neck; **s. aux yeux** to be obvious; **s. au plafond** *(bouchon)* to hit the ceiling; *Fig (de surprise)* to jump out of one's skin; *(d'indignation)* to hit the roof; **s. de joie** to jump for joy; *aussi Fam Fig* **s. sur qn** to pounce on sb; **faire s. un enfant sur ses genoux** to bounce a child on one's knees; **s. sur l'occasion** to jump at the opportunity; *Fig* **s. du coq à l'âne** to jump from one subject to another; **nous allons s. directement à la page 5** we're going to jump straight to page 5; *Fam* **et que ça saute!** and make it snappy! (**b**) *(exploser)* to blow up; *(bouton)* to come off; *(fusible)* to blow; *Fig (gouvernement)* to fall; **faire s.** *(rocher)* to blast; *(pont, mine)* to blow up; *(serrure)* to force; *Fig (gouvernement)* to bring down; *(personne)* to fire, *Br* to sack; *Fam* **faire s. la banque** to break the bank (**c**) *Culin* **faire s.** to sauté

sauterelle [sotrɛl] *nf* grasshopper; *(nuisible)* locust

sauterie [sotri] *nf Vieilli ou Hum* hop

sauteur, -euse [sotœr, -øz] **1** *adj* jumping
2 *nm,f* jumper; **s. en hauteur** high-jumper; **s. en longueur** long-jumper; **s. à la perche** pole-vaulter

sautillement [sotijmɑ̃] *nm* hopping about

sautiller [sotije] *vi* to hop about; **s. d'un pied sur l'autre** to hop from one foot to the other; **avancer en sautillant** to hop along

sautoir [sotwar] *nm* (**a**) *(collier)* chain; **s. de perles** string of pearls (**b**) *(de stade)* jumping area

sauvage [sovaʒ] **1** *adj* (**a**) *(plante, animal)* wild; **redevenir s.** *(animal apprivoisé)* to go back to the wild; **à l'état s.** wild (**b**) *(peuple, tribu)* savage, primitive (**c**) *(violent) (personne, agression)* savage (**d**) *(peu sociable)* unsociable (**e**) *(non autorisé)* unauthorized; **immigration s.** illegal immigration

2 *nmf* (**a**) *Vieilli (indigène)* savage; *Fam Hum* **on n'est pas des sauvages!** we're not savages!; *Fam Hum* **bande de sauvages!** you bunch of savages! (**b**) *(brute)* savage (**c**) *(solitaire)* recluse

sauvagement [sovaʒmɑ̃] *adv* savagely

sauvageon, -onne [sovaʒɔ̃, -ɔn] *nm,f (enfant)* little savage

sauvagerie [sovaʒri] *nf* (**a**) *(cruauté)* savagery (**b**) *(insociabilité)* unsociability

sauvegarde [sovgard] *nf* (**a**) *(protection)* safeguard (**contre** against); **s. des ressources naturelles** conservation of natural resources (**b**) *Ordinat* saving, backup; **faire la s. d'un fichier** to save a file; **s. automatique** autosave, automatic backup; **s. externe** off-line backup; **s. en ligne** on-line backup; **copie de s.** backup (copy)

sauvegarder [sovgarde] *vt* (**a**) *(protéger)* to safeguard (**contre** against) (**b**) *Ordinat (fichier)* to save, to back up; **s. un fichier sur disque** to save a file to disk

sauver [sove] **1** *vt* (**a**) *(personne)* to save, to rescue (**de** from); *(âme)* to save; **la vie à qn** to save sb's life; **le malade est sauvé** the patient is out of danger (**b**) *(navire, marchandises)* to salvage; **s. les apparences** to keep up appearances; *Fam Fig* **s. les meubles** to salvage something from the wreckage

2 *vi* **sauve qui peut!** every man for himself!

3 se sauver *vpr* (**a**) *(s'échapper)* to escape (**de** from) (**b**) *(s'enfuir)* to run away; *Fam* **sauve-toi, tu vas être en retard** be off, you'll be late (**c**) *(lait)* to boil over

sauvetage [sovtaʒ] *nm* (**a**) *(d'un accidenté)* rescue (**b**) *(d'un navire, de marchandises)* salvage; *(d'une entreprise)* rescue

sauveteur [sovtœr] *nm* rescuer

sauvette [sovɛt] **à la sauvette** *adv (pour ne pas être vu)* on the sly; *(à la hâte)* in a hurry; **vendre qch à la s.** *(illégalement)* to peddle sth illegally on the streets; **marchand à la s.** illegal street vendor

sauveur [sovœr] *nm* saviour

savamment [savamɑ̃] *adv* (**a**) *(avec érudition)* learnedly (**b**) *(habilement)* cleverly, skilfully

savane [savan] *nf* (**a**) *(dans les pays chauds)* savanna (**b**) *Can (marécage)* swamp

savant, -e [savɑ̃, -ɑ̃t] **1** *adj* (**a**) *(érudit)* learned (**b**) *(habile)* clever, skilful (**c**) *(animal)* performing

2 *nm (scientifique)* scientist; *(érudit)* scholar

savate [savat] *nf* (**a**) *Fam (pantoufle)* slipper; **traîner la s.** *(être pauvre)* to be *Br* down at heel *or Am* down at the heels (**b**) *Fam* **comme une s.** atrociously (**c**) *Sport* kick boxing

saveur [savœr] *nf* (**a**) *(d'un vin, d'un aliment)* flavour (**b**) *Fig (d'une remarque, d'un récit)* savour

Savoie [savwa] *nf* **la S.** Savoy

savoir[1] [savwar] *nm* knowledge, learning

savoir[2] [62] **1** *vt* (**a**) *(avoir connaissance de)* to know; **s. qch par cœur** to know sth by heart; **je n'en sais rien** I don't know; **je n'en sais trop rien** I'm not too sure; **en s. trop** to know too much; **qu'est-ce j'en sais?** what do I know?; **va s.!** who knows?; **je ne veux pas le s.** I don't want to know; **il n'a rien voulu s.** he didn't want to know; **reste à s. si...** it remains to be seen whether...; **je crois s. qu'il est ici** I understand he's here; **faire s. qch à qn** to tell sb sth, to let sb know about sth; **je le sais par ma sœur** I heard about it from my sister; **à s.** that is (to say), namely; **pas que je sache** not that I know of; **à ce que je sache, pour autant que je sache** as far as I know; **on ne sait jamais** you never know

(**b**) *(être conscient de)* to know; **sans le s.** without realizing; **sachez que...** be advised that..., please note that... (**c**) *(connaître)* **qui tu sais** you know who; **je ne le savais pas si jaloux** I didn't know he was so jealous (**d**) *(être capable de)* **s. faire qch** to be able to do sth, to know how to do sth; **savez-vous nager/conduire?** can you swim/drive?; **je ne saurais vous le dire** I really couldn't tell you (**e**) *Belg (pouvoir)* **je ne sais pas l'attraper** I can't reach it

2 se savoir *vpr* (**a**) *(se répandre)* **ça se saura vite** it'll soon get out (**b**) *(avoir conscience d'être)* **il se savait perdu/surveillé** he knew he was doomed/being watched

savoir-faire [savwarfɛr] *nm* expertise, know-how

savoir-vivre [savwarvivr] *nm* good manners; **manquer de s.** to have no manners

savon [savɔ̃] *nm* soap; **s. à barbe** shaving soap; **s. de Marseille** household soap; *Fam* **passer un s. à qn** to give sb a telling-off

savonner [savɔne] **1** *vt (mains, vêtement)* to soap; *(en faisant mousser)* to lather

2 se savonner *vpr* to soap oneself; **se s. les mains** to soap one's hands

savonnette [savɔnɛt] *nf* bar of soap

savonneux, -euse [savɔnø, -øz] *adj* soapy

savourer [savure] *vt aussi Fig* to savour

savoureux, -euse [savurø, -øz] *adj (plat)* tasty; *(vin)* full-flavoured; *Fig (récit, détails)* spicy

savoyard, -e [savwajar, -ard] **1** *adj* Savoyard

2 *nm,f* **S.** Savoyard

saxo [sakso] *nm Fam (instrument)* sax; *(musicien)* sax player

saxon, -onne [saksɔ̃, -ɔn] **1** *adj* Saxon

2 *nm,f* **S.** Saxon

saxophone [saksɔfɔn] *nm* saxophone

saxophoniste [saksɔfɔnist] *nmf* saxophonist

saynète [sɛnɛt] *nf (petite pièce)* sketch

sbire [sbir] *nm Péj* henchman

scabreux, -euse [skabrø, -øz] *adj* obscene

scalp [skalp] *nm (chevelure)* scalp

scalpel [skalpɛl] *nm* scalpel

scalper [skalpe] *vt* to scalp

scandale [skɑ̃dal] *nm* scandal; **faire s.** *(affaire)* to cause a scandal; **faire un s.** *(personne)* to make a scene; **au grand s. de** much to the indignation of; **c'est un s.!** it's a scandal!

scandaleux, -euse [skɑ̃dalø, -øz] *adj* scandalous, outrageous

scandaliser [skɑ̃dalize] **1** *vt* to scandalize, to shock

2 se scandaliser *vpr* to be scandalized *or* shocked (**de** by); **elle ne se scandalise de rien** nothing shocks her

scander [skɑ̃de] *vt (slogan)* to chant; *(vers)* to scan

scandinave [skɑ̃dinav] **1** *adj* Scandinavian

2 *nmf* **S.** Scandinavian

Scandinavie [skɑ̃dinavi] *nf* **la S.** Scandinavia

scanner[1] [skanɛr] *nm* (**a**) *Ordinat & TV* scanner; **s. à main** handheld scanner; **s. à plat** flatbed scanner; (**b**) *Méd* scanner; **on lui a fait un s.** he/she had a scan

scanner[2] [skane] *vt Ordinat* to scan

scanneur [skanœr] *nm* = **scanner**[1]

scaphandre [skafɑ̃dr] *nm* (**a**) *(de plongeur)* diving suit (**b**) *(d'astronaute)* space suit

scaphandrier [skafɑ̃drije] *nm* diver

scarabée [skarabe] *nm* beetle

scarlatine [skarlatin] *nf* scarlet fever; **avoir la s.** to have scarlet fever

scarole [skarɔl] *nf* endive
scatologique [skatɔlɔʒik] *adj* scatological
sceau, -x [so] *nm* seal; *Fig* **le s. du génie** the mark of genius; **sous le s. du secret** under the seal of secrecy
scélérat, -e [selera, -at] *Litt* **1** *adj* villainous
  2 *nm,f* villain
scellé, -e [sele] **1** *adj* sealed
  2 *nm* seal; **apposer/lever les scellés** to put on/remove the seals
sceller [sele] *vt* (**a**) *(apposer un sceau sur)* & *Fig* to seal (**b**) *Constr* to embed
scénario [senarjo] *nm* script, screenplay; *Fig* scenario
scénariste [senarist] *nmf* scriptwriter
scène [sɛn] *nf* (**a**) *(plateau)* stage; **la s.** *(le métier d'acteur)* the stage; **mettre en s.** *(pièce de théâtre)* to stage; *(film)* to direct; **entrer en s.** *(acteur)* to come on; *Fig* to appear on the scene; **sortir de s.** to go off; **quitter la s.** to retire from the stage; *Fig* **la s. politique/internationale** the political/international scene; *Fig* **occuper le devant de la s.** to be in the limelight, to hold centre stage (**b**) *(d'une pièce de théâtre, d'un film)* scene (**c**) *(action)* action; **la s. se passe au Moyen Âge** the action takes place in the Middle Ages (**d**) *(événement)* scene; **des scènes de panique** scenes of panic (**e**) *Fam (dispute)* scene; **il m'a fait une s.** he made a scene; **s. de ménage** domestic squabble (**f**) *(peinture)* **une s. de chasse** a hunting scene
scénique [senik] *adj* theatrical
scepticisme [sɛptisism] *nm* scepticism
sceptique [sɛptik] **1** *adj* sceptical
  2 *nmf* sceptic
sceptre [sɛptr] *nm* sceptre
schéma [ʃema] *nm* (**a**) *(dessin)* diagram (**b**) *(résumé)* outline (**c**) *Ordinat* **s. de clavier** keyboard map
schématique [ʃematik] *adj* schematic; *Péj* oversimplified
schématiquement [ʃematikmã] *adv (à l'aide d'un schéma)* schematically; *(en gros)* in outline
schématiser [ʃematize] *vt* to schematize; *Péj* to oversimplify
schisme [ʃism] *nm* schism
schiste [ʃist] *nm* schist, shale
schizophrène [skizɔfrɛn] *adj & nmf* schizophrenic
schizophrénie [skizɔfreni] *nf* schizophrenia
schlinguer [ʃlɛ̃ge] *vi très Fam* to stink
schnaps [ʃnaps] *nm* schnapps
schnock, schnoque [ʃnɔk] *nm Fam* **un vieux s.** *Br* an old codger, *Am* a geezer
schuss [ʃus] *nm* schuss; **descendre la piste en s.** *ou* **tout s.** to schuss down the slope
sciatique [sjatik] **1** *adj* sciatic
  2 *nf* sciatica
scie [si] *nf* (**a**) *(outil)* saw; **s. circulaire** circular saw; **s. mécanique** *ou* **à main** hand saw; **s. à métaux** hacksaw (**b**) **s. musicale** musical saw
sciemment [sjamã] *adv* knowingly
science [sjãs] *nf* (**a**) *(savoir)* science; *Fig* **je n'ai pas la s. infuse** I can't be expected to know everything (**b**) *(domaine spécifique)* science; **sciences économiques** economics; **sciences exactes** exact sciences; **sciences expérimentales** experimental science; **sciences humaines** ≃ social sciences; **sciences naturelles** natural science; **Sciences Po** = prestigious higher education establishment for students wishing to enter the Civil Service, the media etc

science-fiction [sjãsfiksjɔ̃] *nf* science fiction; *Fig & Hum* **c'est de la s.!** it's unreal!
scientifique [sjãtifik] **1** *adj* scientific
  2 *nmf* scientist
scientifiquement [sjãtifikmã] *adv* scientifically
scier [66] [sje] *vt* (**a**) *(bois, métal)* to saw; *(pour enlever)* *(branche)* to saw off (**b**) *Fam (étonner)* to dumbfound
scierie [siri] *nf* sawmill
scieur [sjœr] *nm* sawyer
scinder [sɛ̃de] **1** *vt* to split up (**en** into)
  2 se scinder *vpr* to split up (**en** into)
scintillement [sɛ̃tijmã] *nm (de bijou, de lumière, des yeux)* sparkling; *(d'étoile)* twinkling
scintiller [sɛ̃tije] *vi (bijou, lumière, yeux)* to sparkle; *(étoile)* to twinkle
scission [sisjɔ̃] *nf* split; **faire s.** to split away
sciure [sjyr] *nf* sawdust
sclérose [skleroz] *nf* sclerosis; *Fig* ossification; **s. en plaques** multiple sclerosis
scléroser [skleroze] **1** *vt Méd* to sclerose
  2 se scléroser *vpr Méd* to sclerose; *Fig* to become fossilized
scolaire [skɔlɛr] *adj* (**a**) *(résultats, réussite)* academic; *(réforme, organisation, vie)* school (**b**) *Péj (esprit, mentalité)* bookish
scolarisation [skɔlarizasjɔ̃] *nf* education
scolariser [skɔlarize] *vt* to send to school; **enfant scolarisé** child attending school
scolarité [skɔlarite] *nf* schooling; **prolonger la s.** to raise the school-leaving age
scoliose [skɔljoz] *nf* curvature of the spine
scoop [skup] *nm* scoop
scooter [skutɛr] *nm* (motor) scooter; **s. des mers** jet ski
scorbut [skɔrbyt] *nm* scurvy
score [skɔr] *nm* score; *(en politique)* result
scories [skɔri] *nfpl (dans l'industrie)* slag; *(d'éruption volcanique)* scoria
scorpion [skɔrpjɔ̃] *nm* (**a**) *(animal)* scorpion (**b**) *Astron & Astrol* **le S.** Scorpio; **être S.** to be (a) Scorpio
Scotch® [skɔtʃ] *nm (ruban adhésif)* *Br* Sellotape®, *Am* Scotch tape®
scotch [skɔtʃ] *nm (whisky)* scotch
scotché, -e [skɔtʃe] *adj* (**a**) *(collé)* taped, *Br* sellotaped, *Am* scotchtaped; *Fam Fig* **s. devant la télé** glued to the TV (**b**) *Fam (stupéfait)* **je suis resté s.** I was staggered *or Br* gobsmacked
scotcher [skɔtʃe] *vt Br* to sellotape, *Am* to scotch-tape; *Fam Fig* **il est toujours scotché devant la télé** he's always glued to the TV
scout [skut] *nm (garçon)* (Boy) Scout; *(fille)* *Br* (Girl) Guide, *Am* Girl Scout
scoutisme [skutism] *nm (activité)* scouting; *(mouvement)* *(pour garçons)* (Boy) Scout movement; *(pour filles)* *Br* (Girl) Guide *or Am* Girl Scout movement
scratcher [skratʃe] *vi Mus* to scratch
scribe [skrib] *nm* (**a**) *Péj* pen-pusher (**b**) *Hist* scribe
scribouillard, -e [skribujar, -ard] *nm,f Fam Péj* pen-pusher
script [skript] *nm* (**a**) *(écriture)* printing; **écrire en s.** to print (**b**) *Cin* (film) script
scripte [skript] *nmf Cin* continuity man, *f* continuity girl
scrupule [skrypyl] *nm* scruple; **sans scrupules** *(personne)* unscrupulous; *(agir)* unscrupulously
scrupuleusement [skrypyløzmã] *adv* scrupulously

scrupuleux, -euse [skrypylø, -øz] *adj* scrupulous; **peu s.** unscrupulous

scrutateur, -trice [skrytatœr, -tris] **1** *adj Litt (esprit, regard)* searching
2 *nm,f (d'un scrutin)* teller

scruter [skryte] *vt* to scrutinize; *(horizon, paysage)* to scan

scrutin [skrytɛ̃] *nm* (**a**) *(élection)* poll; **s. secret** secret vote (**b**) *(vote)* ballot (**c**) *(système)* voting system; **s. majoritaire** first-past-the-post system; **s. proportionnel** voting by proportional representation; **s. uninominal** voting for a single candidate

sculpter [skylte] *vt* to sculpt; *(dans du bois)* to carve (**dans** out of)

sculpteur [skyltœr] *nm* sculptor; **s. sur bois** woodcarver

sculptural, -e, -aux, -ales [skyltyral, -o] *adj (art)* sculptural; *(silhouette, beauté)* statuesque

sculpture [skyltyr] *nf (œuvre, art)* sculpture; **s. sur bois** woodcarving; **faire de la s.** to sculpt

SDF [ɛsdeɛf] *nmf inv (abrév* **sans domicile fixe)** person of no fixed abode; *(sans abri)* homeless person; **les S.** *(sans abri)* the homeless

SDN [ɛsdeɛn] *nf (abrév* **Société des Nations) la S.** the League of Nations

se [sə]

> **s'** is used before a word beginning with a vowel or h mute.

pron personnel (**a**) *(soi) (homme)* himself; *(femme)* herself; *(chose)* itself; *(indéfini)* oneself; *(pluriel)* themselves; **se flatter** to flatter oneself; **il se rase** he is shaving; *Fam* **on s'est blessés** we hurt ourselves (**b**) *(à soi) (homme)* to himself; *(femme)* to herself; *(chose)* to itself; *(indéfini)* to oneself; *(pluriel)* to themselves; **elle s'est coupé le doigt** she has cut her finger; *Fam* **on va s'acheter une voiture** we're going to buy (ourselves) a car (**c**) *(réciproque) (objet direct)* each other; *(objet indirect)* to each other; **se nuire (l'un à l'autre)** to hurt each other; **ils se sont quittés en bons termes** they parted on good terms (**d**) *(passif)* **ça se mange froid** you eat it cold; **les couteaux se rangent dans ce tiroir** the knives go in this drawer

séance [seɑ̃s] *nf* (**a**) *(réunion)* session, meeting; **tenir s.** to be in session (**b**) *(de travail, d'entraînement)* session; **s. de photo** photo session; **s. de pose** sitting (**c**) *Cin & Théât* performance; *Cin* **s. privée** private showing (**d**) *TV* **à la s.** *(film, programme)* pay-per-view (**e**) **s. tenante** straightaway, at once

séant, -e [seɑ̃, -ɑ̃t] **1** *adj Litt (convenable)* fitting
2 *nm Litt ou Hum* **se mettre sur son s.** to sit up

seau, -x [so] *nm* bucket; *(contenu)* bucket(ful); *Fam* **il pleut à seaux** it's pouring *or* bucketing down; **s. à champagne** champagne bucket; **s. à charbon** coal scuttle; **s. à glace** ice bucket

sébacé, -e [sebase] *adj* sebaceous

sébum [sebɔm] *nm* sebum

sec, sèche¹ [sɛk, sɛʃ] **1** *adj* (**a**) *(temps, saison, sol, peau, bois)* dry; *(morue, fruit)* dried; **à pied s.** without getting one's feet wet; **avoir la gorge sèche** *(avoir soif)* to be dry (**b**) *(vin, cidre)* dry (**c**) *(maigre) (personne)* lean; **être s. comme un coup de trique** to be wiry (**d**) *(austère) (personne)* hard; *(réponse, ton, voix)* sharp; **avoir le cœur s.** to be hard-hearted (**e**) *(non appuyé) (coup)* sharp (**f**) *(sans rien ajouter)* **boire qch s.** to drink sth neat
2 *adv* (**a**) *(beaucoup) (frapper, pleuvoir)* hard; *(boire)*

heavily; **démarrer s.** to shoot off (**b**) *Fam* **aussi s.** right away
3 *nm* (**a**) **tenir au s.** *(sur une étiquette)* keep in a dry place (**b**) **être à s.** *(source, puits, rivière)* to be dry; *Fam (sans argent)* to be broke

sécable [sekabl] *adj* divisible

sécateur [sekatœr] *nm* pruning shears, *Br* secateurs

sécession [sesesjɔ̃] *nf* secession; **faire s. (de)** to secede (from)

séchage [seʃaʒ] *nm* drying

sèche² [sɛʃ] **1** *adj voir* **sec**
2 *nf Fam Br* fag, *Am* cig

sèche-cheveux [sɛʃʃəvø] *nm inv* hairdryer

sèche-linge [sɛʃlɛ̃ʒ] *nm inv (appareil)* tumble-drier; *(armoire)* airing cupboard

sèche-mains [sɛʃmɛ̃] *nm inv* hand-drier

sèchement [sɛʃmɑ̃] *adv (parler, répondre)* curtly

sécher [34] [seʃe] **1** *vt* to dry; *Fam* **s. un cours** to skip a class
2 *vi* (**a**) *(vêtement, cheveux)* to dry; **mettre du linge à s.** to put clothes out to dry (**b**) *Fam (ne pouvoir répondre)* to be stumped
3 se sécher *vpr* to dry oneself; **se s. les cheveux/les mains** to dry one's hair/hands

sécheresse [sɛʃrɛs, seʃrɛs] *nf* (**a**) *(absence de pluie)* drought (**b**) *(de l'air, du sol, de la peau)* dryness (**c**) *(des manières, du ton)* curtness; *(du cœur)* hardness; *(du style)* dryness

séchoir [seʃwar] *nm* (**a**) *(appareil)* drier; **s. (à cheveux)** hairdryer (**b**) *(dispositif pliant)* **s. (à linge)** clothes-horse

second, -e¹ [səgɔ̃, -ɔ̃d] **1** *adj* second; *(rôle)* supporting, minor
2 *nm* (**a**) *(assistant)* assistant; *Mil* second-in-command; *Naut* first mate; *(de duelliste)* second (**b**) *(étage) Br* second *or Am* third floor
3 *nm,f* second; **je préfère le s.** I prefer the second one
4 *nf* **seconde** (**a**) *(vitesse)* second (gear) (**b**) *(dans les transports)* second class; **voyager en seconde** to travel second-class (**c**) *(classe) Br* ≃ fifth form, *Am* ≃ tenth grade (**d**) *Mus* second; *voir aussi* **cinquième**

secondaire [səgɔ̃dɛr] **1** *adj* (**a**) *Scol* secondary; **établissement d'enseignement s.** secondary school (**b**) *(pas essentiel)* secondary; *(personnage, rôle) Théât* minor; *Fig* secondary; **c'est s.** it's of secondary importance (**c**) *Écon & Géol* secondary
2 *nm Géol* secondary era; *Écon* secondary sector

seconde² [səgɔ̃d] *nf (unité de temps)* second; **(attendez) une s.!** just a second!; **pendant une fraction de s.** for a fraction of a second

seconder [səgɔ̃de] *vt* to assist

secouer [səkwe] **1** *vt* (**a**) *(arbre, tête, bouteille)* to shake; *(coussin, oreiller)* to plump up; *(vêtements, tapis)* to shake out; *(sujet: vent, vagues)* to buffet; **nous avons été secoués pendant la traversée** we were shaken about during the crossing; *Fam* **s. les puces à qn** *(réprimander)* to tell sb off (**b**) *(sujet: choc, maladie, nouvelles)* to shake (up) (**c**) *(se débarrasser de) (poussière, joug)* to shake off (**d**) *très Fam* **j'en ai rien à s.** I don't give a damn *or Br* a toss
2 *vi* **ça secoue** *(en avion, en train)* it's bumpy; *(en bateau)* it's rough
3 se secouer *vpr* (**a**) *(s'agiter)* to shake oneself (**b**) *(agir)* to snap out of it

secourable [səkurabl] *adj* helpful

secourir [22] [səkurir] *vt* to help, to assist

secourisme [səkurism] *nm* first aid

secouriste [səkurist] *nmf* first-aid worker

secours [səkur] *nm* (**a**) *(aide)* help; *(financier, matériel)* aid; *Mil (renforts)* relief; **appel au s.** call for help; **appeler au s.** to call out for help; **au s.!** help!; **premiers s.** first aid; **porter s. à qn** to give sb help; **demander du s.** to ask for help; **aller au s. de qn** to go to sb's assistance; **cela m'a été d'un grand s.** it's been a great help to me (**b**) **de s.** *(trousse, poste)* first-aid; *(sortie, éclairage)* emergency; *(roue)* spare; *Ordinat (copie, fichier)* backup

secousse [səkus] *nf* jolt, jerk; **par secousses** *(avancer)* jerkily; **s. (sismique** *ou* **tellurique)** (earth) tremor

secret¹, -ète [səkrɛ, -ɛt] *adj* (**a**) *(non divulgué)* secret (**b**) *(personne)* reticent

secret² *nm* (**a**) *(confidence, mystère)* secret; **garder un s.** to keep a secret; **mettre qn dans le s.** to let sb in on the secret; **être dans le s.** to be in on the secret; **ne pas avoir de secrets pour qn** *(discipline)* to hold no secrets for sb; **ce n'est un s. pour personne** it's no secret; **le s. du bonheur/de la réussite** the secret of happiness/of success; **secrets d'alcôve** pillow talk; **s. d'État** state secret; **s. de fabrication** trade secret; **s. de Polichinelle** open secret; **emporter un s. dans la tombe** to take a secret to the grave (**b**) *(discrétion)* secrecy; **dans le plus grand s.** in the strictest secrecy; **en s.** *(en cachette)* in secret; **s. bancaire** banking secrecy; **s. professionnel** professional secrecy (**c**) **mettre qn au s.** *(l'enfermer)* to put sb in solitary confinement

secrétaire [səkretɛr] **1** *nmf* secretary; **s. d'ambassade** secretary; **s. de direction** personal assistant; **s. d'État** Secretary of State; **s. général** secretary general; *Com* company secretary; **s. médicale** medical secretary; **s. particulier** private secretary; **s. de rédaction** sub-editor
2 *nm (meuble)* writing desk

secrétariat [səkretarja] *nm* (**a**) *(fonction)* secretaryship (**b**) *(bureau)* secretary's office; *(d'un organisme international)* secretariat (**c**) *(métier)* secretarial work (**d**) *Pol* **s. d'État** ministry

secrètement [səkrɛtmã] *adv* secretly

sécréter [34] [sekrete] *vt* to secrete; *Fig (ennui)* to exude

sécrétion [sekresjɔ̃] *nf* secretion

sectaire [sɛktɛr] *adj & nmf* sectarian

sectarisme [sɛktarism] *nm* sectarianism

secte [sɛkt] *nf* sect

secteur [sɛktœr] *nm* (**a**) *(zone)* area, district; *Fam* **changer de s.** to move somewhere else (**b**) *Élec* mains; **branché sur le s.** plugged into the mains (**c**) *Écon* sector; **le s. privé/public** the private/public sector; **s. primaire/secondaire/tertiaire** primary/secondary/tertiary sector; *Fam* **ce n'est pas mon s.** that's not my line (**d**) *Math & Ordinat* sector; *Ordinat* **s. d'initialisation** boot sector

section [sɛksjɔ̃] *nf* (**a**) *(division)* (d'un livre, d'un bâtiment, d'une autoroute) section; (d'une ligne d'autobus) stage; *(d'un parti politique, d'un syndicat)* branch (**b**) *(de l'infanterie)* platoon; *(de l'artillerie)* section (**c**) *(coupe)* section; **ça fait 5 centimètres de s.** the diameter of the section is 5 centimetres (**d**) *Scol* = one of the groups into which "baccalauréat" students are divided, depending on their chosen area of specialization

sectionner [sɛksjɔne] *vt* (**a**) *(couper)* to sever (**b**) *(fractionner)* (service, circonscription) to divide into sections

sectoriel, -elle [sɛktɔrjɛl] *adj* sectorial

sécu [seky] *nf Fam (abrév* **Sécurité sociale**) *Br* Social Security, *Am* Welfare

séculaire [sekylɛr] *adj* (**a**) *(très ancien)* centuries-old (**b**) *(qui existe depuis un siècle)* a hundred years old (**c**) *(qui a lieu tous les cent ans)* centennial

séculier, -ère [sekylje, -ɛr] *adj* secular

secundo [səgɔ̃do] *adv* secondly

sécurisant, -e [sekyrizã, -ãt] *adj* reassuring

sécuriser [sekyrize] *vt* to reassure; *Fin* **s. un paiement** *(sur Internet)* to guarantee the security of a transaction

sécuritaire [sekyritɛr] *adj (politique, idéologie)* law-and-order; **mesures sécuritaires** drastic security measures

sécurité [sekyrite] *nf* (**a**) *(ordre, stabilité)* security; **être/se sentir en s.** to be/feel secure; **s. de l'emploi** job security; **s. nationale/internationale** national/international security (**b**) *(absence de danger)* safety; **s. routière** road safety; **S. routière** = French road safety organization (**c**) *(dispositif)* safety catch; **porte munie d'une s.-enfants** door with a childproof lock (**d**) **S. sociale** *Br* Social Security, *Am* Welfare

Sécurité sociale

The "Sécu", as it is popularly known, was created in 1945 and provides services such as public health benefits, pensions and maternity benefit. These benefits are paid for by obligatory insurance contributions ("cotisations") made by employers ("cotisations patronales") and employees ("cotisations salariales"). Many French people have complementary health insurance provided by a "mutuelle" which guarantees payment of all or part of the expenses not covered by the "Sécurité sociale".

sédatif, -ive [sedatif, -iv] *adj & nm* sedative

sédentaire [sedãtɛr] *adj* (**a**) *(vie, travail, travailleur)* sedentary; *(population)* settled (**b**) *(casanier)* stay-at-home

sédentariser [sedãtarize] **1** *vt (population)* to settle
2 se sédentariser *vpr* to settle

sédiment [sedimã] *nm* sediment

sédimentaire [sedimãtɛr] *adj* sedimentary

sédimentation [sedimãtasjɔ̃] *nf* sedimentation

séditieux, -euse [sedisjø, -øz] **1** *adj* seditious
2 *nm,f* insurgent

sédition [sedisjɔ̃] *nf* sedition

séducteur, -trice [sedyktœr, -tris] **1** *nm,f* seducer, *f* seductress
2 *adj* seductive

séduction [sedyksjɔ̃] *nf* (**a**) *(physique)* seduction; *(par le charme)* charming (**b**) *(moyen de séduire)* attraction; **pouvoir de s.** power of attraction

séduire [18] [seduir] *vt* (**a**) *(charmer)* (sujet: personne) to charm; (sujet: projet, proposition) to appeal to (**b**) *(sexuellement)* to seduce

séduisant, -e [seduizã, -ãt] *adj* attractive

séfarade [sefarad] **1** *adj* Sephardic
2 *nmf* Sephardic Jew

segment [sɛgmã] *nm* segment

segmenter [sɛgmãte] *vt aussi Ordinat* to segment

ségrégation [segregasjɔ̃] *nf* segregation

ségrégationniste [segregasjɔnist] *adj & nmf* segregationist

seiche [sɛʃ] *nf* cuttlefish; **os de s.** cuttlebone

seigle [sɛgl] *nm* rye

seigneur [sɛɲœr] *nm* (**a**) *Hist* lord; **à tout s. tout honneur** honour where honour is due; **en grand s.** in grand style (**b**) *Rel* **le S.** the Lord

seigneurial, -e, -aux, -ales [sɛɲœrjal, -o] *adj* (*droits, domaine*) seigniorial

sein [sɛ̃] *nm* (*de femme*) breast; *Litt* (*poitrine*) bosom; **serrer** *ou* **presser qn sur son s.** to press sb to one's bosom; **donner le s. à un enfant, nourrir un enfant au s.** to breast-feed a child; **au s. de** within

Seine [sɛn] *nf* **la S.** the Seine

séisme [seism] *nm* earthquake; *Fig & Litt* upheaval

seize [sɛz] *adj & nm inv* sixteen; *voir aussi* **trois**

seizième [sɛzjɛm] *nmf, nm & adj* sixteenth; *voir aussi* **cinquième**

Seizième

This term often refers to the upper-class social background, lifestyle, way of dressing etc associated with the sixteenth arrondissement in Paris: "elle est très seizième".

séjour [seʒur] *nm* (**a**) (*période*) stay; **s. linguistique** language-learning trip (**b**) (*pièce*) (**salle de**) **s.** living room (**c**) *Litt* (*lieu*) abode

séjourner [seʒurne] *vi* to stay

sel [sɛl] *nm* (**a**) (*substance*) salt; **gros s.** coarse salt; **s. fin** fine salt; **sels** (*à respirer*) (smelling) salts; **sels de bain** bath salts (**b**) *Fig* (*esprit*) piquancy

sélect, -e [selɛkt] *adj Fam* (*soirée, clientèle*) select

sélectif, -ive [selɛktif, -iv] *adj* selective; *Ordinat* **en mode s.** in veto mode

sélection [selɛksjɔ̃] *nf* selection

sélectionné, -e [selɛksjɔne] **1** *adj* selected
2 *nm,f* (*sportif*) selected competitor; (*d'une équipe*) selected player

sélectionner [selɛksjɔne] *vt* to select; *Ordinat* (*texte*) to block, to select

sélectionneur, -euse [selɛksjɔnœr, -øz] *nm,f* selector

self [sɛlf] *nm Fam* self-service restaurant

self-service (*pl* **self-services**) [sɛlfsɛrvis] *nm* (*restaurant*) self-service restaurant; (*magasin*) self-service shop

selle [sɛl] *nf* (**a**) (*de cheval, de bicyclette, de moto*) saddle; **se mettre en s.** to mount; **monter sans s.** to ride bareback (**b**) **selles** (*matières fécales*) stools, *Br* motions; **aller à la s.** to have a bowel movement (**c**) *Culin* **s. de mouton/d'agneau** saddle of mutton/lamb

seller [sele] *vt* to saddle

sellette [sɛlɛt] *nf Fam* **mettre qn/être sur la s.** to put sb/to be in the hot seat

selon [səlɔ̃] *prép* (**a**) (*d'après*) according to; **s. moi** in my opinion (**b**) (*conformément à*) in accordance with; **s. toute vraisemblance** in all probability (**c**) (*en fonction de*) **varier s. les cas/les saisons** to vary from case to case/season to season; *Fam* **c'est s.** it all depends; **s. que...** depending on whether...

SEM [sɛm] *nf Écon* (*abrév* **société d'économie mixte**) = company financed by state and private capital

semailles [səmaj] *nfpl* (**a**) (*action*) sowing; (**temps des**) **s.** sowing time (**b**) (*graines*) seeds

semaine [səmɛn] *nf* (**a**) (*sept jours*) week; **vivre à la petite s.** to live from day to day; **jour de s.** weekday;

en s. during the week, on weekdays; **la s. de 35 heures** the 35-hour working week; **la s. sainte** Holy Week (**b**) (*salaire*) week's pay; (*argent de poche*) week's pocket money (**c**) *Mil* (*tour de service*) week's duty; **être de s.** to be on duty for the week; **officier de s.** duty officer for the week

semainier [səmenje] *nm* (*agenda*) desk diary

sémantique [semɑ̃tik] **1** *adj* semantic
2 *nf* semantics (*singulier*)

sémaphore [semafɔr] *nm Rail* semaphore signal; *Naut* signal station

semblable [sɑ̃blabl] **1** *adj* (**a**) (*pareil*) similar; **s. à qch** similar to sth, like sth; **je n'ai rien dit de s.** I said nothing of the sort (**b**) (*tel*) **de semblables projets/propos** such plans/remarks, plans/remarks like that
2 *nm* (*être humain*) fellow man; **vous et vos semblables** you and your kind

semblant [sɑ̃blɑ̃] *nm* (**a**) (*apparence*) **un s. de** a semblance of (**b**) **faire s.** to pretend; **faire s. de faire qch** to pretend to do sth; **en faisant s. de rien** without making it obvious

sembler [sɑ̃ble] **1** *vi* to seem
2 *v impersonnel* **il semble que...** it seems that...; **il me/leur semble que...** it seems to me/them that...; **me semble-t-il** it seems to me; **il me semble avoir entendu son nom** I've a feeling I've heard his/her name; **il me semble idiot d'attendre encore plus longtemps** it seems stupid to me to wait any longer; **faites comme bon vous semble** *ou* **semblera** do as you think best; **il le fera si bon lui semble** he'll do it if he thinks fit

semé, -e [səme] *adj* **s. de** strewn with; (*fleurs*) dotted with; (*étoiles*) studded with; (*citations*) sprinkled with; **s. d'embûches** full of traps

semelle [səmɛl] *nf* sole; **s. (intérieure)** insole; **s. de caoutchouc/de cuir** rubber/leather sole; **ne pas avancer d'une s.** to make no progress whatsoever; **il ne reculera pas d'une s.** he won't give an inch; **ne pas quitter qn d'une s.** to be always at sb's heels; **c'est de la s.!** it's as tough as old boots!

semence [səmɑ̃s] *nf* (*graine*) seed; (*sperme*) semen

semer [46] [səme] *vt* (**a**) (*graines*) to sow (**b**) (*discorde, confusion, panique, doute*) to sow, to spread; *Prov* **qui sème le vent récolte la tempête** he who sows the wind shall reap the whirlwind (**c**) *Fam* (*distancer*) to shake off (**d**) *Fam* (*perdre*) to lose

semestre [səmɛstr] *nm* half-year, six-month period; *Scol & Univ* term

semestriel, -elle [səmɛstrijɛl] *adj* half-yearly, six-monthly

semi-automatique [səmiɔtɔmatik] *adj* semi-automatic

semi-liberté [səmilibɛrte] *nf Jur* partial release

sémillant, -e [semijɑ̃, -ɑ̃t] *adj* (*personne*) spirited; (*regard*) bright

séminaire [seminɛr] *nm* (**a**) (*colloque*) seminar (**b**) *Rel* seminary

séminariste [seminarist] *nm Rel* seminarist

sémiologie [semjɔlɔʒi] *nf* semiology

sémiotique [semjɔtik] **1** *adj* semiotic
2 *nf* semiotics (*singulier*)

semi-précieux, -euse (*mpl* **semi-précieux**, *fpl* **semi-précieuses**) [səmipresjø, -øz] *adj* semi-precious

semi-remorque (*pl* **semi-remorques**) [səmirəmɔrk] *nm* (*poids lourd*) *Br* articulated lorry, *Am* trailer truck

semis [səmi] *nm* (**a**) (*action*) sowing (**b**) (*terrain*) seedbed (**c**) (*jeune plante*) seedling

sémite [semit] **1** *adj* Semitic
2 *nmf* **S.** Semite
sémitique [semitik] *adj* Semitic
semoir [səmwar] *nm* (**a**) *(sac)* seed bag (**b**) *(machine)* seeder
semonce [səmɔ̃s] *nf (remontrance)* reprimand; *aussi Fig* **coup de s.** warning shot
semoule [səmul] *nf* semolina
sempiternel, -elle [sɑ̃pitɛrnɛl] *adj* never-ending, endless
sénat [sena] *nm* senate

Sénat

This is the upper house of the French Parliament. Its members are elected for a nine-year mandate by the Deputies of the "Assemblée nationale" and certain other government officals. The President of the Senate may deputize for the President of the Republic in the case of incapacity or death. The powers of the "Sénat" are almost as extensive as those of the "Assemblée nationale", although the latter is empowered to override the decisions of the "Sénat" in cases where the two houses disagree.

sénateur [senatœr] *nm* senator
sénatorial, -e, -aux, -ales [senatɔrjal, -o] *adj* senatorial
Sénégal [senegal] *nm* **le S.** Senegal
sénégalais, -e [senegalɛ, -ɛz] **1** *adj* Senegalese
2 *nm,f* **S.** Senegalese; **les S.** the Senegalese
sénile [senil] *adj* senile
sénilité [senilite] *nf* senility
senior [senjɔr] *adj* & *nmf Sport* senior *(over the age of 20)*
sens¹ *voir* **sentir**
sens² [sɑ̃s] *nm* (**a**) *(de la perception)* sense; **les cinq s.** the five senses; **le sixième s.** the sixth sense (**b**) **les s.** *(sensualité)* the senses; **plaisir des s.** sensual pleasure (**c**) *(jugement)* sense; **avoir le s. de l'humour/du ridicule** to have a sense of humour/of the ridiculous; **avoir le s. des affaires/de l'orientation** to have good business sense/a good sense of direction; **s. commun** common sense; **s. moral** moral sense; **s. pratique** practical sense; **bon s.** common sense; **un homme de bon s.** a sensible man (**d**) *(avis)* **à mon s.** to my mind (**e**) *(signification) (d'un mot)* meaning, sense; **au s. propre/figuré** in the literal/figurative sense, literally/figuratively; **cela n'a aucun s.** it doesn't make (any) sense; **en ce s. que...** in the sense that... (**f**) *(direction)* direction; **tenir qch dans le mauvais s.** to hold sth the wrong way round; **en s. inverse** in the opposite direction; **dans le s. des aiguilles d'une montre** clockwise; **dans le s. inverse des aiguilles d'une montre** *Br* anticlockwise, *Am* counterclockwise; **dans le s. du courant** with the current; **dans le s. de la longueur** lengthwise, lengthways; **dans le s. de la largeur** widthwise, across; **s. dessus dessous** *(en désordre)* upside down; **s. devant derrière** back to front, the wrong way round; **dans les deux s.** both ways; *Fig* **ces mesures vont dans le bon s.** these measures are a step in the right direction; *Ordinat* **s. de déroulement** flow direction; **s. giratoire** *Br* roundabout, *Am* traffic circle; **s. interdit** *(sur panneau)* no entry; **s. unique** *(sur panneau)* one way
sensas(s) [sɑ̃sas] *adj Fam* fantastic, great
sensation [sɑ̃sasjɔ̃] *nf* (**a**) *(perception physique)* sensation (**b**) *(impression)* feeling; **avoir la s. que...** to

have a *or* the feeling that... (**c**) *(scandale)* **faire s.** to create a sensation
sensationnel, -elle [sɑ̃sasjɔnɛl] *adj* (**a**) *(à sensation)* sensational (**b**) *Fam (fantastique)* fantastic, great
sensé, -e [sɑ̃se] *adj* sensible
sensibilisation [sɑ̃sibilizasjɔ̃] *nf* (**a**) **s. de l'opinion (à qch)** increasing public awareness (of sth) (**b**) *Phot & Méd* sensitization
sensibiliser [sɑ̃sibilize] *vt* (**a**) *(rendre conscient)* **s. qn à qch** to increase sb's awareness of sth; **s. l'opinion (à qch)** to increase public awareness (of sth) (**b**) *Phot & Méd* to sensitize
sensibilité [sɑ̃sibilite] *nf* sensitivity; **avoir une s. à fleur de peau** to be hypersensitive
sensible [sɑ̃sibl] *adj* (**a**) *(émotif)* sensitive (**b**) *(réceptif)* **être s. à qch** to be sensitive to sth; *(influence)* to be susceptible to sth (**c**) *(douloureux)* sensitive (**d**) *(appréciable)* noticeable, appreciable; **de manière s.** noticeably (**e**) *(balance, thermomètre, plaque)* sensitive; **s. à la lumière** light-sensitive
sensiblement [sɑ̃sibləmɑ̃] *adv* (**a**) *(notablement)* noticeably, appreciably (**b**) *(à peu près)* roughly, more or less
sensiblerie [sɑ̃sibləri] *nf* sentimentality
sensoriel, -elle [sɑ̃sɔrjɛl] *adj* sensory
sensualité [sɑ̃sɥalite] *nf* sensuality
sensuel, -elle [sɑ̃sɥɛl] *adj* sensual
sent *voir* **sentir**
sentence [sɑ̃tɑ̃s] *nf* (**a**) *(jugement)* sentence (**b**) *(maxime)* maxim
sentencieux, -euse [sɑ̃tɑ̃sjø, -øz] *adj* sententious
senteur [sɑ̃tœr] *nf* scent; *(dans un parfum)* note
senti, -e [sɑ̃ti] *adj* **bien s.** appropriate
sentier [sɑ̃tje] *nm* path; *Fig* **sortir des sentiers battus** to go off the beaten track; **sur le s. de la guerre** on the warpath
sentiment [sɑ̃timɑ̃] *nm* feeling; **prendre qn par les sentiments** to appeal to sb's feelings; *Fam* **ça partait d'un bon s.** it was well meant; **en affaires, je ne fais pas de s.** I don't let sentiment interfere with business; **avoir le s. que...** to have a *or* the feeling that...; **j'avais le s. de m'être trompé** I had the feeling I'd made a mistake
sentimental, -e, -aux, -ales [sɑ̃timɑ̃tal, -o] **1** *adj (personne, chanson, valeur)* sentimental; **vie sentimentale** love life
2 *nm,f* **c'est un(e) grand(e) sentimental(e)** he's/she's a great romantic
sentimentalisme [sɑ̃timɑ̃talism] *nm* sentimentalism; **faire du s.** to be sentimental
sentinelle [sɑ̃tinɛl] *nf* sentry
sentir [64a] *(douleur, sensation tactile)* **1** *vt* (**a**) to feel; *Fam Fig* **je ne sens plus mes jambes/mes pieds** *(de froid)* I can't feel my legs/my feet; *(de fatigue)* my legs/my feet are killing me (**b**) *(être conscient de) (danger)* to sense; **s. que...** to have a *or* the feeling that...; **faire s. à qn que...** to make sb feel that...; **se faire s.** to make itself felt; *Fig* **on sent l'influence de Wagner** one can detect Wagner's influence; *Fam* **je l'ai sentie passer** *(claque, fracture)* I certainly knew about it (**c**) *(parfum, fleur)* to smell; **faire s. qch à qn** to let sb smell sth (**d**) *(avoir l'odeur de)* to smell of; **ça sent le brûlé** there's a smell of burning; **ça sent bon le pain frais** there's a delicious smell of fresh bread; *Fig & Péj* **ce livre sent l'effort** this book was very laboured; **s. le soufre** to smack of heresy (**e**) *Fam (supporter)* **je ne peux pas le s.** I can't stand him (**f**) *Fam (être*

convaincu par) **je ne le sens pas, ton projet** I'm not convinced by your plan; **je ne la sens pas pour le rôle** my feeling is that she's not right for the part **2** *vi* (**a**) *(avoir comme odeur)* **s. bon/mauvais** to smell good/bad; **s. fort** to have a strong smell (**b**) *Fam (puer)* to smell; **s. des pieds** to have smelly feet **3 se sentir** *vpr* (**a**) *(être perceptible)* **cela se sent** you can tell (**b**) *(suivi d'un adjectif ou d'un infinitif)* **se s. revivre** to feel oneself coming alive again; **se s. bien/fatigué** to feel well/tired; *Fam* **tu ne te sens pas bien, non?** have you taken leave of your senses?; **se s. capable de faire qch** to feel capable of doing sth (**c**) *(avoir)* **se s. le courage de faire qch** to feel up to doing sth (**d**) *Fam (se contrôler)* **il ne se sent plus!** he's too big for his boots! (**e**) *Fam (se supporter)* **ils ne peuvent pas se s.** they can't stand each other

seoir [10a] [swar] *Litt* **1** *vi* **s. à** to suit **2** *v impersonnel* **il lui sied mal de...** it ill becomes him/her to...

Séoul [seul] *n* Seoul

séparable [separabl] *adj* separable (**de** from)

séparation [separasjɔ̃] *nf* (**a**) *(de personnes, d'objets)* separation (**de** from); *Ordinat* **s. automatique des pages** automatic pagination (**b**) *(cloison)* partition, division (**c**) *Jur* **s. de biens** = marriage settlement under which husband and wife administer their separate properties

séparatisme [separatism] *nm* separatism

séparatiste [separatist] *adj & nmf* separatist

séparé, -e [separe] *adj* (**a**) *(notions, chambres)* separate (**b**) *(personnes)* separated (**de** from); **nous vivons séparés** we live apart

séparément [separemɑ̃] *adv* separately

séparer [separe] **1** *vt* (**a**) *(éloigner)* to separate (**de** from) (**b**) *(partager)* to divide (**en** into) (**c**) *(opposer)* to divide; **tout les sépare** they are poles apart **2 se séparer** *vpr* (**a**) *(époux)* to separate (**de** from), to split up (**de** with) (**b**) *(foule, assemblée)* to break up (**c**) *(se défaire)* **se s. de qch** to part with sth; **se s. de qn** *(employé)* to let sb go (**d**) *(rivière, route)* to divide (**en** into); **c'est ici que nos chemins se séparent** this is where we go our separate ways

sept [sɛt] *adj & nm inv* seven; *voir aussi* **trois**

septante [sɛptɑ̃t] *adj & nm inv Belg & Suisse* seventy; *voir aussi* **trois**

septembre [sɛptɑ̃br] *nm* September; *voir aussi* **janvier**

septennat [sɛptena] *nm* (seven-year) term

septentrional, -e, -aux, -ales [sɛptɑ̃trijɔnal, -o] *adj* northern

septicémie [sɛptisemi] *nf* blood poisoning, septicaemia

septième [sɛtjɛm] *nmf, nm & adj* seventh; *voir aussi* **cinquième**

septique [sɛptik] *adj* septic

septuagénaire [sɛptɥaʒenɛr] *adj & nmf* septuagenarian

sépulcre [sepylkr] *nm* sepulchre

sépulture [sepyltyr] *nf Litt* (**a**) *(inhumation)* burial (**b**) *(lieu)* burial place

séquelles [sekɛl] *nfpl* *(d'une maladie, d'un accident)* after-effects; *(d'une guerre, d'une catastrophe)* aftermath

séquençage [sekɑ̃saʒ] *nm Biol* sequencing

séquence [sekɑ̃s] *nf* (**a**) *(d'objets, de mots)* sequence; *Ordinat* **s. de caractères** character string, sequence of characters (**b**) *(de film)* sequence (**c**) *(de cartes)* run

séquestre [sekɛstr] *nm (action)* sequestration; **mettre qch sous s.** to sequester sth

séquestrer [sekɛstre] *vt* (**a**) *(personne)* **s. qn** to keep sb locked up (**b**) *(biens)* to sequester

séquoia [sekɔja] *nm* sequoia

sera, serai, serais *etc voir* **être²**

sérail [seraj] *nm* seraglio; *Fig* inner circle

serbe [sɛrb] **1** *adj* Serb, Serbian **2** *nmf* **S.** Serb, Serbian

Serbie [sɛrbi] *nf* la **S.** Serbia

serbo-croate (*pl* **serbo-croates**) [sɛrbɔkrɔat] **1** *adj* Serbo-Croat, Serbo-Croatian **2** *nm (langue)* Serbo-Croat

Sercq [sɛrk] *nf* Sark

serein, -e [sərɛ̃, -ɛn] *adj (personne, visage, esprit)* serene; *(ciel, nuit)* clear

sereinement [sərɛnmɑ̃] *adv* calmly

sérénade [serenad] *nf* (**a**) *Mus* serenade; **donner la s. à qn** to serenade sb (**b**) *Fam (tapage)* racket, din

sérénité [serenite] *nf* serenity; **avec s.** serenely

serf, serve [sɛrf, sɛrv] *nm,f Hist* serf

sergent [sɛrʒɑ̃] *nm* sergeant

sergent-chef (*pl* **sergents-chefs**) [sɛrʒɑ̃ʃɛf] *nm* staff sergeant

série [seri] *nf* (**a**) *(suite, collection)* series; *(d'échantillons)* range; *(de casseroles)* set; **des démissions en s.** a series of resignations (**b**) *Rad & TV* series (**c**) *Ind* **production en s.** mass production; **fabriquer qch en s.** to mass-produce sth; **voiture de s.** standard car; **s. limitée** limited run (**d**) *(catégorie)* group; *Sport* heat; **(film de) s.** B B-movie (**e**) *(locutions)* **s. noire** *(suite de catastrophes)* series *or* catalogue of disasters; **(roman de) s. noire** crime thriller

sérieusement [serjøzmɑ̃] *adv* seriously; **parlez-vous s.?** are you serious?

sérieux, -euse [serjø, -øz] **1** *adj* (**a**) *(personne, lecture)* serious; **d'un air s.** seriously; **ce n'est pas s.!** you're not serious!; *Fam* **s. comme un pape** as solemn as a judge (**b**) *(offre, acheteur)* serious, genuine; *(information, entreprise)* reliable; *(employé)* conscientious (**c**) *(important) (problèmes, ennuis)* serious; *(progrès)* good **2** *nm* (**a**) *(application)* conscientiousness; **avec s.** conscientiously (**b**) *(gravité)* **garder son s.** to keep a straight face; **prendre qn/qch au s.** to take sb/sth seriously; **se prendre au s.** to take oneself seriously

sérigraphie [serigrafi] *nf* silk-screen printing

serin [sərɛ̃] *nm (oiseau)* canary

seriner [sərine] *vt Fam* **s. qch à qn** to go on and on at sb about sth; **s. à qn que...** to keep telling sb that...

seringue [sərɛ̃g] *nf* syringe

serment [sɛrmɑ̃] *nm* (**a**) *(parole solennelle)* oath; **prêter s.** to take an oath; **sous s.** on oath (**b**) *(promesse)* pledge; *(d'amoureux)* vow; **faire le s. de faire qch** to swear *or* vow to do sth

sermon [sɛrmɔ̃] *nm* (**a**) *Rel* sermon (**b**) *Fam (remontrance)* lecture, sermon

sermonner [sɛrmɔne] *vt Fam* to lecture

séronégatif, -ive [serɔnegatif, -iv] **1** *adj* HIV negative **2** *nm,f* person who is HIV negative

séropositif, -ive [serɔpɔzitif, -iv] **1** *adj* HIV positive **2** *nm,f* person who is HIV positive

sérotonine [serɔtɔnin] *nf* serotonin

serpe [sɛrp] *nf* billhook

serpent [sɛrpɑ̃] *nm* (**a**) *(reptile)* snake; **s. à sonnette** rattlesnake (**b**) *Écon* **le s. monétaire européen** the European currency snake

serpenter [sɛrpɑ̃te] *vi* to wind

serpentin [sɛrpɑ̃tɛ̃] *nm (cotillon)* streamer

serpillière [sɛrpijɛr] *nf* floorcloth; **passer la s. dans la cuisine** to clean the kitchen floor

serpolet [sɛrpɔlɛ] *nm* wild thyme

serre [sɛr] *nf* (**a**) *(local)* greenhouse (**b**) **serres** *(d'oiseau de proie)* claws, talons

serré, -e [sɛre] **1** *adj* (**a**) *(chaussures, vêtement)* tight; *(personnes)* packed together; *(écriture)* cramped; *(rangs)* serried; *(dents)* clenched; *(lèvres)* pressed tightly together (**b**) *(emploi du temps, budget)* tight; *(surveillance, lutte, score)* close (**c**) *(café)* strong
   2 *adv* **écrire s.** to have cramped handwriting; *Fig* **jouer s.** to play a tight game

serre-livres [sɛrlivr] *nm inv* book-end

serrement [sɛrmɑ̃] *nm* **avoir un s. de cœur** to feel a pang

serrer [sɛre] **1** *vt* (**a**) *(tenir)* to grip; **s. la main à qn** to shake hands with sb, to shake sb's hand; **s. qn dans ses bras** to hug sb; **s. qn/qch contre soi** to hold sb/ sth tightly to one; *Fig* **le cœur à qn** to wring sb's heart (**b**) *(sujet: vêtement, chaussures)* to be too tight for (**c**) *(nœud, écrou, ceinture)* to tighten; *(joint)* to clamp; *(poings)* to clench; **s. les dents** to clench one's teeth; *Fig* to grit one's teeth; *Fam Fig* **s. les fesses** to be scared stiff (**d**) *(rapprocher)* to put close together; **s. les rangs** to close ranks (**e**) *(ranger)* to put away (**f**) *(raser) (trottoir)* to hug; **s. qn de près** to follow sb closely; **évite de s. la voiture de devant** don't drive too close to the car in front
   2 *vi* **serrez à droite/gauche** *(sur panneau)* keep to the right/left
   3 se serrer *vpr* (**a**) *(se rapprocher)* to squeeze up; **se s. contre qn** to snuggle up to sb (**b**) *Fig* **ma gorge se serra** I had a lump in my throat (**c**) *(pour se saluer)* **se s. la main** to shake hands

serre-tête [sɛrtɛt] *nm inv* headband

serriculture [serikyltyr] *nf* hothouse growing

serrure [seryr] *nf* lock

serrurerie [seryrri] *nf (métier)* locksmith's trade; *(magasin)* locksmith's (shop)

serrurier [seryrje] *nm* locksmith

sers, sert *etc voir* **servir**

sertir [sɛrtir] *vt (pierre précieuse)* to set

sérum [serɔm] *nm* serum; **s. physiologique** saline solution

servage [sɛrvaʒ] *nm* serfdom; *Fig* bondage

servante [sɛrvɑ̃t] *nf* (maid)servant

serve [sɛrv] *voir* **serf**

serveur, -euse [sɛrvœr, -øz] **1** *nm,f* (**a**) *(dans un bar)* barman, *f* barmaid; *(dans un restaurant)* waiter, *f* waitress (**b**) *(au tennis)* server
   2 *nm Ordinat* server; **s. de fichiers** file server; **s. de réseau** network server; **s. télématique** bulletin board (system); **s. Web** web server

serviable [sɛrvjabl] *adj* obliging, helpful

service [sɛrvis] *nm* (**a**) *(pour un client, pour un maître)* service; *Écon* **services** services; **faire le s.** *(à table)* to serve; **être au s. de qn** to be in sb's service; **à votre s.** at your service; **s. compris/non compris** service included/not included; **premier/deuxième s.** *(au restaurant)* first/second sitting; **s. après-vente** *(dépannage)* after-sales service; *Ordinat* **s. en ligne** on-line service (**b**) *Mil* **s. militaire** *ou* **national** mili-tary service; **faire son s.** to do one's military service; **bon pour le s.** fit for service (**c**) *(au tennis)* service; **au s., Martin** Martin to serve (**d**) *(travail)* duty; **être de s.** to be on duty; **prendre/quitter son s.** to go on/off duty; **reprendre du s.** to be employed for a supplementary period; *Fam* **le crétin de s.** the inevitable *or* obligatory idiot (**e**) *(département)* department; **s. d'ordre** *(surveillance)* crowd control; *(personnes)* crowd control staff; **s. du personnel** personnel department; **s. public** public utility; **s. de renseignements** military intelligence department; *Ordinat* **s. télématique** bulletin board service (**f**) *(d'une machine)* **en s.** in service; **mettre qch en s.** to bring sth into service (**g**) *(de transports en commun)* service; **assurer le s. entre** to provide a service between (**h**) *(aide)* favour; **rendre (un) s. à qn** *(personne)* to do sb a favour; *(objet)* to be of use to sb; **rendre un mauvais s. à qn** to do sb a bad turn (**i**) *(de vaisselle)* set

Service militaire

Military service (for a period of ten months) used to be compulsory for French men aged between 18 and 26 unless they were declared unfit for service ("réformé"). As an alternative to military service, some chose to do voluntary work overseas as part of a scheme known as "la coopération". However, a reform was introduced in order to gradually abolish military service and move towards an exclusively professional army. This process was completed in 2001, putting an end to compulsory military service in France.

serviette [sɛrvjɛt] *nf* (**a**) *(en tissu)* **s. (de table)** serviette, napkin; **s. (de toilette)** towel; **s. de plage** beach towel (**b**) *(sac)* briefcase (**c**) **s. hygiénique** sanitary *Br* towel *or Am* napkin

serviette-éponge (*pl* **serviettes-éponges**) [sɛrvjɛtepɔ̃ʒ] *nf* terry towel

servile [sɛrvil] *adj* servile; *(imitation, traduction)* slavish

servilement [sɛrvilmɑ̃] *adv* servilely; *(imiter, traduire)* slavishly

servir [63] [sɛrvir] **1** *vt* (**a**) *(client, convive, nourriture)* to serve; **tout le monde est servi?** *(à table)* has everybody been served?; **s. frais** *(sur étiquette)* serve chilled; **s. à boire à qn** to give sb a drink; *Ironique* **côté ennuis, je suis servi!** I've got more than my share of worries! (**b**) *(favoriser) (personne)* to serve; *(intérêts)* to further (**c**) *(au tennis)* to serve (**d**) *(aux cartes)* **à vous de s.** it's your deal
   2 *vi* (*dans une administration*) to serve (**sous** under)
   3 *servir à vt ind* (*être utile à*) to be of use to; **ça peut toujours s.** it might still come in useful (**b**) *(être utilisé pour)* **s. à qch/à faire qch** to be used for sth/for doing sth; **ne s. à rien** to be useless; **ne pas s. à grand-chose** not to be much use; **à quoi ça sert?** *(objet)* what's that used for?; *(démarche)* what's the use of that?
   4 *servir de vt ind* (*faire fonction de*) *(objet)* to serve as, to be used as; *(personne)* to act as; **ça me sert de porte-crayons** I use it as a pencil-holder
   5 *v impersonnel Litt* **il ne sert à rien de pleurer** there's no point in crying
   6 se servir *vpr* (**a**) *(prendre)* to help oneself; **je me suis déjà servie deux fois** I've already had two helpings; **se s. des pâtes/du poulet** to help oneself to pasta/to chicken (**b**) *(plat, vin)* to be served; **le**

champagne se sert frappé champagne should be served chilled (**c**) **se s. de qn/qch** *(utiliser)* to use sb/sth (**d**) *(s'approvisionner)* **se s. chez...** to shop at...
serviteur [sɛrvitœr] *nm* servant
servitude [sɛrvityd] *nf* (**a**) *(asservissement)* servitude (**b**) *(contrainte)* constraint
ses [se] *voir* **son¹**
sésame [sezam] *nm* (**a**) *(plante)* sesame (**b**) *Fig* **s., ouvre-toi!** open sesame!
session [sesjɔ̃] *nf* (**a**) *(d'une assemblée, d'un tribunal)* session, sitting (**b**) *(période d'examens)* (exam) session; **s. de rattrapage** repeat exams, *Br* resits
SET® [ɛsœte] *nf Ordinat (abrév* **secure electronic transaction)** SET®
set [sɛt] *nm* (**a**) *(au tennis)* set (**b**) **s. de table** *(napperon)* table mat
setter [setɛr] *nm* setter; **s. irlandais** Irish setter
seuil [sœj] *nm* (**a**) *(entrée)* doorway, threshold; **sur le s.** in the doorway (**b**) *Fig* threshold; *Litt* **au s. de...** on the threshold of...; **s. de rentabilité** break-even point
seul, -e [sœl] **1** *adj* (**a**) *(unique)* only; **une seule personne** *(et pas plus)* a single person; *(parmi d'autres)* only one person; **comme un s. homme** as one man; **il suffit d'une seule fois** once is enough; **la seule pensée de sa venue** the mere thought of him/her coming (**b**) *(isolé)* alone; **se sentir s.** to feel lonely *or* alone; **être s. au monde** to be alone in the world; **parler s. à s. à qn** to speak to sb in private; **faire qch tout s.** to do sth (by) oneself *or* on one's own; **parler tout s.** to talk to oneself; **cela va tout s.** it's plain sailing, it's straightforward; **ça descend tout s.** *(boisson)* it just slides down (**c**) *(seulement)* only, alone; **s. un miracle...** only a miracle...
2 *nm,f* **le s.** the only one; **un s.** *(personne, objet)* only one
seulement [sœlmɑ̃] *adv* only; **je te demande s. un peu de patience** I'm just asking you to be a bit patient; **non s.... mais en plus...** not only... but also...; *Fam* **essaie s.!** just you try!
sève [sɛv] *nf* (**a**) *(d'une plante)* sap (**b**) *Fig (de la jeunesse)* vitality
sévère [sevɛr] *adj* severe; *(principe, règle)* strict; **être s. envers** *ou* **avec qn** to be hard on sb
sévèrement [sevɛrmɑ̃] *adv* severely; *(de façon stricte)* strictly
sévérité [severite] *nf* severity; *(d'une discipline, d'une éducation)* strictness
sévices [sevis] *nmpl* ill-treatment; **s. sexuels** sexual abuse
Séville [sevij] *n* Seville
sévir [sevir] *vi* (**a**) *(agir avec rigueur)* to act ruthlessly; **s. contre qn/qch** to deal ruthlessly with sb/sth (**b**) *(épidémie, guerre)* to rage; *(malfaiteurs)* to operate; **la crise qui sévit actuellement** the present crisis
sevrage [səvraʒ] *nm* *(d'un enfant)* weaning; *(d'un drogué, d'un alcoolique)* withdrawal
sevrer [səvre] *vt* (**a**) *(enfant)* to wean; *(drogué)* to get off drugs; *(alcoolique)* to get off drink (**b**) *Litt (priver)* **s. qn de qch** to deprive sb of sth
sexagénaire [sɛgzaʒenɛr, sɛksaʒenɛr] *nmf* person in his/her sixties
sex-appeal [sɛksapil] *nm Fam* sex appeal
sexe [sɛks] *nm* (**a**) *(genre)* sex; *Hum* **le beau s.** the fair sex; **le s. faible** the weaker sex; **le s. fort** the stronger sex (**b**) *(organes sexuels)* genitals (**c**) *(sexualité)* sex
sexisme [sɛksism] *nm* sexism
sexiste [sɛksist] *adj & nmf* sexist

sexologue [sɛksɔlɔg] *nmf* sexologist
sex-shop *(pl* **sex-shops)** [sɛksʃɔp] *nm* sex shop
sextant [sɛkstɑ̃] *nm* sextant
sextuor [sɛkstɥɔr] *nm* sextet
sextuplé, -e [sɛkstyple] *nm,f* sextuplet
sexualité [sɛksɥalite] *nf* sexuality
sexué, -e [sɛksɥe] *adj (plante, animal)* sexed; *(reproduction)* sexual
sexuel, -elle [sɛksɥɛl] *adj (rapport)* sexual; *(vie, acte, organe)* sex
sexuellement [sɛksɥɛlmɑ̃] *adv* sexually
sexy [sɛksi] *adj inv Fam* sexy
seyant, -e [sejɑ̃, -ɑ̃t] *adj* becoming
Seychelles [seʃɛl] *nfpl* **les S.** the Seychelles
SF [ɛsɛf] *nf Fam (abrév* **science fiction)** sci-fi, SF
SFIO [ɛsɛfio] *nf (abrév* **Section française de l'Internationale ouvrière)** = French Socialist Party 1905–1969
shaker [ʃɛkœr] *nm* cocktail shaker
shakespearien, -enne [ʃɛkspirjɛ̃, -ɛn] *adj* Shakespearean
shampo(o)ing [ʃɑ̃pwɛ̃] *nm* shampoo; **faire un s. à qn** to shampoo sb's hair, to give sb a shampoo
shampouiner [ʃɑ̃pwine] *vt* to shampoo
shampouineur, -euse [ʃɑ̃pwinœr, -øz] **1** *nm,f* shampooer
2 *nf* **shampouineuse (à moquettes)** *(machine)* carpet shampooer
shérif [ʃerif] *nm* sheriff
shetland [ʃɛtlɑ̃d] **1** *nfpl* **les (îles) S.** the Shetland Islands, the Shetlands
2 *nm* (**a**) *(laine)* Shetland wool; *(pull)* Shetland jumper (**b**) *(poney)* Shetland pony
shiatsu [ʃiatsu] *nm* shiatsu, shiatzu
shinto [ʃinto], **shintoïsme** [ʃintɔism] *nm* Shinto, Shintoism
shit [ʃit] *nm très Fam* hash, weed
shoot [ʃut] *nm* shot
shooter [ʃute] **1** *vi (au football)* to shoot
2 se shooter *vpr Fam (se droguer)* to shoot up; **se s. à l'héroïne** to shoot (up) heroin
shopping [ʃɔpiŋ] *nm* shopping; **faire du s.** to go shopping
short [ʃɔrt] *nm* (pair of) shorts
show [ʃo] *nm* show
show-business [ʃobiznɛs] *nm* show business
si¹ [si] *adv* (**a**) *(tellement)* so; **un si bon dîner** such a good dinner; **il n'est pas si bête (que ça)** he's not that stupid; **il était si nerveux qu'il a tout oublié** he was so nervous (that) he forgot everything (**b**) *(indique la concession)* **si... que** + *subjunctive* however...; **si jeune qu'il soit** however young he may be; **si habile soit-il** however capable (he may be) (**c**) *(oui)* yes; **je crois que si** I think so; **mais si, je l'ai vue** I DID see her; **tu ne sais pas? – si, si** you don't know? – yes, I do (**d**) *(dans les questions indirectes)* if, whether; *Fam* **si je connais Paris?** do I know Paris?; *Fam* **si c'est pas malheureux**
si² **1** *conj* (**a**) *(exprime l'hypothèse, la condition)* if; **qui le fera si ce n'est moi?** who'll do it if I don't?; **un des plus grands, si ce n'est le plus grand** one of the biggest, if not the biggest; **si ce n'est que...** *(sauf que)* apart from the fact that...; **et si elle l'apprend?** and what if she finds out?; **si on faisait une partie de bridge?** what about a game of bridge?; **oui, si on veut** yes, if you like; **si seulement...** if only...; **si tant est que...** + *subjunctive* if... (**b**) *(combien)* how; **pensez si j'étais furieux!** imagine how angry I was! (**c**) *(dans les questions indirectes)* if, whether; *Fam* **si je connais Paris?** do I know Paris?; *Fam* **si c'est pas malheureux**

(de voir ça)! isn't it just dreadful (to see that)!

2 *nm inv* **tes si et tes mais** your ifs and buts

si³ *nm inv (note)* B; *(chantée)* ti

siamois, -e [sjamwa, -az] **1** *adj* **frères/sœurs s.** Siamese twins

2 *nm (chat)* Siamese (cat)

Sibérie [siberi] *nf* **la S.** Siberia

sibérien, -enne [siberjɛ̃, -ɛn] **1** *adj* Siberian

2 *nm,f* **S.** Siberian

sibyllin, -e [sibilɛ̃, -in] *adj (énigmatique)* cryptic, enigmatic

SICAV [sikav] *nf inv* Fin *(abrév* **société d'investissement à capital variable)** (**a**) *(organisme) Br* ≃ unit trust, *Am* ≃ mutual fund (**b**) *(titre)* share in a *Br* unit trust *orAm* mutual fund

Sicile [sisil] *nf* **la S.** Sicily

sicilien, -enne [sisiljɛ̃, -ɛn] **1** *adj* Sicilian

2 *nm,f* **S.** Sicilian

sida [sida] *nm (abrév* **syndrome immunodéficitaire acquis)** Aids; **avoir le s.** to have Aids

side-car *(pl* **side-cars**) [sajdkar, sidkar] *nm* sidecar

sidéen, -enne [sideɛ̃, -ɛn] **1** *adj* suffering from Aids

2 *nm,f* Aids sufferer

sidéral, -e, -aux, -ales [sideral, -o] *adj* sidereal

sidérant, -e [siderɑ̃, -ɑ̃t] *adj Fam* staggering

sidérer [34] [sidere] *vt Fam* to stagger

sidérurgie [sideryrʒi] *nf* (**a**) *(technique)* iron and steel metallurgy (**b**) *(industrie)* iron and steel industry

sidérurgique [sideryrʒik] *adj (industrie, usine)* iron and steel

sidérurgiste [sideryrʒist] *nmf* iron and steel worker

siècle [sjɛkl] *nm* (**a**) *(cent ans)* century; **au vingtième s.** in the twentieth century; **avoir un s.** to be a hundred years old; *Fam* **ça fait des siècles que j'attends** I've been waiting for ages (**b**) *(époque)* age; **le s. des Lumières** the Age of Enlightenment; **il est de son s.** he's a man of his times

sied *voir* **seoir**

siège [sjɛʒ] *nm* (**a**) *(meuble)* seat; **s. avant/arrière** front/back seat; **s. pliant** folding chair; **s. pour enfant** *(en voiture)* child seat (**b**) *(d'une société, d'un organisme)* headquarters; **s. administratif** administrative headquarters; **s. social** head office (**c**) *(lieu d'origine)* seat (**d**) *Mil* siege; **faire le s. de** to lay siege to; **lever le s.** to raise the siege; *Fam (partir)* to make tracks (**e**) *Pol* seat (**f**) *Méd* **accouchement par le s.** breech delivery; **se présenter par le s.** to be in the breech position

siéger [59] [sjeʒe] *vi* (**a**) *(tribunal, assemblée)* to sit (**b**) *(se trouver)* **c'est là que siège le mal** that's the root of the problem

sien, sienne *(mpl* **siens**, *fpl* **siennes**) [sjɛ̃, sjɛn] **1** *pron possessif* **le sien, la sienne, les siens, les siennes** *(possesseur masculin)* his; *(possesseur féminin)* hers; *(en insistant)* his/her own; **il te prête le s.** you can borrow his; **elle n'en a pas besoin, elle a le s.** she doesn't need it, she has her own; **on doit acheter la sienne** you must buy your own; **chacun doit apporter le s.** everyone must bring their own; **chaque pays a le s.** each country has its own

2 *nm* **il faut qu'il y mette du s.** he should do his share

3 *nmpl* **les siens** *(sa famille)* his/her/one's family

4 *nfpl Fam* **il a encore fait des siennes** he's been up to his old tricks again

Sierra Leone [sjeraleon] *nf* **la S.** Sierra Leone

sieste [sjɛst] *nf* siesta, nap; **faire la s.** to have a nap

sifflant, -e [siflɑ̃, -ɑ̃t] *adj (respiration, toux)* wheezing

sifflement [sifləmɑ̃] *nm (d'une personne, du vent)* whistling; *(d'un serpent, de la vapeur)* hissing; *(d'un asthmatique)* wheezing; **sifflements d'oreilles** ringing in the ears

siffler [sifle] **1** *vt* (**a**) *(air)* to whistle (**b**) *(chien, personne)* to whistle at (**c**) *(acteur, pièce)* to boo (**d**) *Fam (verre, bouteille)* to knock back

2 *vi* (**a**) *(personne, merle, bouilloire)* to whistle; *(serpent)* to hiss (**b**) *(avec un sifflet)* to blow one's whistle

sifflet [siflɛ] *nm* (**a**) *(instrument)* whistle; *Fam* **couper le s. à qn** to shut sb up (**b**) *(au théâtre)* **sifflets** booing, boos

siffleux [siflø] *nm Can* groundhog, woodchuck

siffloter [siflote] *vt & vi* to whistle to oneself

sigle [sigl] *nm (acronyme)* acronym; *(suite d'initiales)* abbreviation

siglé, -e [sigle] *adj (produit)* with a designer label

signal, -aux [siɲal, -o] *nm* (**a**) *(signe)* signal; **faire un s.** to signal; **envoyer** *ou* **lancer un s.** to send a signal; **au s., levez-vous** when the signal is given, stand up; *Ordinat* **s. horodateur** time and date signal; **s. lumineux** indicator light, warning light (**b**) *(panneau)* sign (**c**) *(dispositif sonore)* **s. d'alarme** alarm (signal); **s. d'alerte** warning (signal); *Tél* **s. d'appel** call(ing) signal; **s. de détresse** distress signal; **s. sonore** warning sound

signalement [siɲalmɑ̃] *nm* description, particulars

signaler [siɲale] **1** *vt* (**a**) *(faire remarquer)* to point out (à to); **s. à qn que...** to point out to sb that... (**b**) *(rapporter)* to report (à to); **rien à s.** nothing to report (**c**) *(par un panneau)* to signpost (**d**) *Ordinat (marquer)* to flag up

2 se signaler *vpr* to distinguish oneself (**par** by); **se s. à l'attention de qn** to catch sb's eye

signalétique [siɲaletik] *adj* **fiche s.** personal details card; **plaque s.** identification plate

signalisation [siɲalizasjɔ̃] *nf (signaux routiers)* signs and markings; *(signaux ferroviaires)* signals; *(de piste d'atterrissage)* lights and markings; **s. routière** road signs

signaliser [siɲalize] *vt (route)* to signpost and mark; *(voie ferrée)* to install signals on; *(piste d'atterrissage)* to install lights and markings on

signataire [siɲatɛr] *nmf* signatory

signature [siɲatyr] *nf* (**a**) *(griffe)* signature; **présenter qch à la s.** to present sth for signature; *Com & Ordinat* **s. électronique** *ou* **numérique** digital signature (**b**) *(acte)* signing

signe [siɲ] *nm* (**a**) *(indice)* sign; **il n'a pas donné s. de vie** there's been no sign of him; **il n'y a aucun s. de vie dans la maison** there's no sign of life at the house; **en s. de désapprobation/solidarité** as a sign of disapproval/solidarity; **s. avant-coureur** forerunner; **donner des signes d'usure** to show signs of wear (**b**) *(symbole)* sign, symbol; **s. moins/plus/égale** minus/plus/equals sign; **signes de ponctuation** punctuation marks (**c**) *Astrol* **s. du zodiaque** sign of the zodiac; **être né sous le s. du Capricorne** to be born under the sign of Capricorn; *Fig* **le sommet a eu lieu sous le s. de la réconciliation** the summit was held in a spirit of reconciliation (**d**) *(trait distinctif)* mark; **signes particuliers** distinguishing marks (**e**) *(geste)* sign, gesture; **faire un s. à qn** to gesture to sb; **parler par signes** to use sign language; **faire s. à qn** *(de la main)* to signal to sb; *(le contacter)* to get in touch with sb; **faire s. à qn de faire qch** to signal to sb to do sth;

faire s. que oui *(de la tête)* to nod (one's head); **faire s. que non** *(de la tête)* to shake one's head; *(du doigt)* to shake one's finger; **faire un s. de la main (à qn)** to wave (at sb); **faire un s. de tête (à qn)** to nod (to sb) (**f**) *Rel* **s. de croix** sign of the cross; **faire le s. de croix** to make the sign of the cross

signer [siɲe] **1** *vt (contrat, lettre, tableau)* to sign; *Fam Fig* **ça c'est signé!** no prizes for guessing who did that!
2 *vi* to sign; **s. de son nom** to sign one's name
3 se signer *vpr* to cross oneself

signet [siɲɛ] *nm (de livre, de page Web)* bookmark; *Ordinat* **créer un s. sur une page** to bookmark a page

significatif, -ive [siɲifikatif, -iv] *adj* significant; **s. de qch** indicative of sth

signification [siɲifikasjɔ̃] *nf* (**a**) *(d'un mot, d'un symbole)* meaning, sense; *(d'un fait)* significance (**b**) *Jur (d'un jugement)* notification

signifier [66] [siɲifje] *vt* (**a**) *(vouloir dire)* to mean; **qu'est-ce que ça signifie?** *(indignation)* what's the meaning of this? (**b**) *(notifier) (intentions)* to make known (**à** to); **s. son congé à qn** *(sujet: propriétaire, employeur)* to give sb notice; **s. qch à qn** to inform *or* notify sb of sth

signofil, signofile [siɲofil] *nm Suisse Aut Br* indicator, *Am* turn signal

silence [silɑ̃s] *nm* (**a**) *(absence de bruit)* silence; **un s. de mort** a deadly silence; **rompre le s.** to break the silence; **garder le s. (sur)** to keep silent (about); **faire qch en s.** to do sth in silence; **passer qch sous s.** not to mention sth (**b**) *Mus* rest

silencieusement [silɑ̃sjøzmɑ̃] *adv* silently

silencieux, -euse [silɑ̃sjø, -øz] **1** *adj* silent; *(qui ne fait pas beaucoup de bruit)* quiet
2 *nm (d'un véhicule) Br* silencer, *Am* muffler; *(d'une arme)* silencer

silex [silɛks] *nm* flint

silhouette [silwɛt] *nf* (**a**) *(du corps)* figure (**b**) *(d'un objet)* silhouette, outline

silice [silis] *nf* silica

silicium [silisjɔm] *nm Chim* silicon

silicone [silikɔn] *nf* silicone

sillage [sijaʒ] *nm (d'un navire)* wake; *Fig* **marcher dans le s. de qn** to follow in sb's wake

sillon [sijɔ̃] *nm* (**a**) *(d'un champ)* furrow (**b**) *(de disque)* groove

sillonner [sijɔne] *vt (parcourir)* to criss-cross

silo [silo] *nm* silo

simagrées [simagre] *nfpl* airs and graces; **faire des s.** to make a fuss

simiesque [simjɛsk] *adj* monkey-like, ape-like

similaire [similɛr] *adj* similar (**à** to)

similarité [similarite] *nf* similarity

simili [simili] *nm Fam (imitation)* imitation

similicuir [similikɥir] *nm* imitation leather

similitude [similityd] *nf* similarity

simple [sɛ̃pl] **1** *adj* (**a**) *(sans prétentions)* simple (**b**) *(facile)* simple, easy; **c'est s. comme bonjour** it's as easy as pie (**c**) *(crédule)* simple; **s. d'esprit** simple-minded (**d**) *(pur)* **c'est une s. question de temps** it's simply a matter of time (**e**) *(ordinaire)* ordinary; **s. soldat** private (soldier) (**f**) *(composé d'un élément) (nœud)* single; **cornet s.** *(de glace)* cone with one scoop; *Ordinat* **s. densité** single density
2 *nm* (**a**) *(au tennis)* singles (match) (**b**) *(somme, quantité)* **varier du s. au double** to vary by twice as much (**c**) *(personne)* **un s. d'esprit** a simpleton

simplement [sɛ̃pləmɑ̃] *adv* simply; **le plus s. du monde** as if it was the most natural thing in the world; **prendre les choses s.** to take things as they come

simplet, -ette [sɛ̃plɛ, -ɛt] *adj (personne)* simple; *(idée, explication)* simplistic

simplicité [sɛ̃plisite] *nf* simplicity; **recevoir qn en toute s.** to entertain sb very simply; **d'une s. enfantine** childishly simple

simplificateur, -trice [sɛ̃plifikatœr, -tris] *adj* simplifying

simplification [sɛ̃plifikasjɔ̃] *nf* simplification

simplifier [66] [sɛ̃plifje] *vt aussi Math* to simplify; **ça me simplifiera l'existence** it'll make my life easier

simplissime [sɛ̃plisim] *adj Fam* easy as pie

simpliste [sɛ̃plist] *adj Péj* simplistic

simulacre [simylakr] *nm* (**a**) *(représentation)* reconstruction (**b**) *(parodie)* **s. de combat/négociations** sham fight/negotiations; **ce fut un s. de procès** the trial was a farce

simulateur, -trice [simylatœr, -tris] **1** *nm,f (d'un sentiment)* pretender; *(d'une maladie)* malingerer
2 *nm Tech* simulator

simulation [simylasjɔ̃] *nf* (**a**) *(action)* feigning (**b**) *(d'un vol, d'un phénomène) & Ordinat* simulation

simulé, -e [simyle] *adj* (**a**) *(sentiment, maladie)* feigned; *(combat)* sham (**b**) *(vol, phénomène)* simulated

simuler [simyle] *vt* (**a**) *(sentiment, maladie, folie)* to feign (**b**) *(vol, phénomène)* to simulate

simultané, -e [simyltane] *adj* simultaneous

simultanéité [simyltaneite] *nf* simultaneousness, simultaneity

simultanément [simyltanemɑ̃] *adv* simultaneously

sincère [sɛ̃sɛr] *adj* sincere

sincèrement [sɛ̃sɛrmɑ̃] *adv* sincerely; **s., je trouve que...** frankly, I think...

sincérité [sɛ̃serite] *nf* sincerity; **en toute s.** in all sincerity

sinécure [sinekyr] *nf* sinecure; *Fam* **ce n'est pas une s.** it's not exactly a rest cure

sine die [sinedje] *adv* sine die

sine qua non [sinekwanɔn] *adj inv* **une condition s.** a prerequisite

Singapour [sɛ̃gapur] *n* Singapore

singapourien, -enne [sɛ̃gapurjɛ̃, -ɛn] **1** *adj* Singaporean
2 *nm,f* **S.** Singaporean

singe [sɛ̃ʒ] *nm* monkey; **grand s.** ape; **malin/adroit comme un s.** as crafty/clever as a monkey; **faire le s.** to clown around

singer [45] [sɛ̃ʒe] *vt (personne)* to ape, to mimic; *(sentiment)* to feign

singeries [sɛ̃ʒri] *nfpl (grimaces, gestes)* antics; **faire des singeries** to clown around

singulariser [sɛ̃gylarize] **1** *vt* **s. qn (de)** to set sb apart (from), to make sb stand out (from)
2 se singulariser *vpr* to draw attention to oneself; **il se singularise par sa façon de parler** the way he speaks makes him stand out

singularité [sɛ̃gylarite] *nf* peculiarity

singulier, -ère [sɛ̃gylje, -ɛr] **1** *adj* (**a**) *Gram* singular (**b**) *(combat)* single (**c**) *(remarquable)* remarkable; *(étrange)* peculiar, odd
2 *nm Gram* singular; **au s.** in the singular

singulièrement [sɛ̃gyljɛrmɑ̃] *adv* (**a**) *(étrangement)* oddly (**b**) *(en particulier)* especially, particularly (**c**) *(beaucoup)* remarkably, extremely

sinistre [sinistr] **1** adj (**a**) (effrayant) sinister; (à faire froid dans le dos) spooky (**b**) (déprimant) (paysage) bleak; (soirée, repas) dismal, grim (**c**) **un s. imbécile** a total idiot
2 nm (**a**) (catastrophe) disaster (**b**) Jur (dommage) damage
sinistré, -e [sinistr] **1** adj (population) stricken; (bâtiment) damaged; (région, zone) disaster
2 nm,f disaster victim
sinistrose [sinistroz] nf Fam pessimism, gloom
sinologue [sinɔlɔg] nmf sinologist
sinon [sinɔ̃] conj (**a**) (autrement) otherwise, or else (**b**) (excepté) except (**c**) (si ce n'est) if not
sinueux, -euse [sinɥø, -øz] adj (ligne) sinuous; (chemin, courant) winding, meandering; Fig (raisonnement) tortuous
sinuosité [sinɥozite] nf (d'un chemin, d'une rivière) bend; Fig **les sinuosités d'un raisonnement** the twists and turns of an argument
sinus¹ [sinys] nm Anat sinus
sinus² nm Math sine
sinusite [sinyzit] nf sinusitis
sionisme [sjɔnism] nm Zionism
sioniste [sjɔnist] adj & nmf Zionist
sioux [sju] **1** adj Sioux
2 nmf **S.** Sioux
siphon [sifɔ̃] nm (**a**) (tube) siphon (**b**) (bouteille) (soda) siphon (**c**) (d'un évier, d'une canalisation) U-bend, trap
siphonné, -e [sifɔne] adj Fam (fou) crazy, nuts
siphonner [sifɔne] vt to siphon
sire [sir] nm **S.** (à un souverain) Sire; Péj **un triste s.** an unsavoury character
sirène [sirɛn] nf (**a**) (personnage fantastique) mermaid, siren; Fig (femme) siren (**b**) (dispositif sonore) siren
sirop [siro] nm syrup; **s. de fraise/menthe** strawberry/mint cordial; **s. contre la toux** cough mixture or syrup
siroter [sirɔte] vt Fam to sip
sirupeux, -euse [sirypø, -øz] adj syrupy; (musique) slushy
sismique [sismik] adj seismic
sismographe [sismɔgraf] nm seismograph
sismologie [sismɔlɔʒi] nf seismology
sitar [sitar] nm sitar
sitcom [sitkɔm] nm ou nf sitcom
site [sit] nm (**a**) (emplacement) site (**b**) (pittoresque) beauty spot; **s. classé** conservation area; **s. historique/archéologique** historic/archaeological site; **s. touristique** place of interest, tourist attraction (**c**) Ordinat site; **s. miroir** mirror site; **s. sécurisé** secure website; **s. Web** website
sitôt [sito] adv **elle le fera s. ses devoirs finis** she'll do it as soon as she's finished her homework; **s. dit, s. fait** no sooner said than done; **s. que** as soon as; **s. après** immediately after; **on ne le reverra pas de s.** we won't see him again in a hurry
situation [sitɥasjɔ̃] nf (**a**) (d'une ville, d'un bâtiment) position, location (**b**) (circonstances) situation; **être en s. de faire qch** to be in a position to do sth; **mettre qn en s.** to give sb experience of a real-life situation; **l'homme de la s.** the right man for the job; **s. de famille** marital status (**c**) (emploi) job, position (**d**) Fin (de compte) balance
situé, -e [sitɥe] adj situated

situer [sitɥe] **1** vt (**a**) (placer) to situate (**b**) (trouver) to locate (**c**) (dans le temps) to set; **je situe l'action au milieu du XIXᵉ siècle** I'd say the action takes place in the middle of the 19th century (**d**) Fig (catégoriser) to categorize
2 se situer vpr (**a**) (être) to be; **se s. à droite** to be right-wing (**b**) (avoir lieu) to take place
six [sis] adj & nm inv six; voir aussi **trois**
sixième [sizjɛm] **1** adj, nmf & nm sixth; voir aussi **cinquième**
2 nf Scol (enseignement secondaire) Br ≃ first form, Am ≃ sixth grade
sixièmement [sizjɛmmɑ̃] adv in the sixth place, sixthly
six-quatre-deux [siskatdø] **à la six-quatre-deux** adv Fam in a slapdash way
sixte [sikst] nf Mus sixth
Skaï® [skaj] nm imitation leather
skate [skɛt], **skateboard** [skɛtbɔrd] nm skateboard; **faire du s.** to skateboard
skateboarder, -euse [skɛtbɔrdœr, -øz] nm,f skateboarder
skatepark [skɛtpark] nm skatepark
skateur, -euse [skɛtœr, -øz] nm,f skateboarder, skater
skeleton [skəlɛtɔn] nm (luge, sport) skeleton
sketch (pl sketches) [skɛtʃ] nm sketch
ski [ski] nm (**a**) (matériel) ski (**b**) (activité) skiing; **faire du s.** to ski; **s. alpin** downhill skiing; **s. artistique** freestyle skiing; **s. de fond** cross-country skiing; **s. nautique** water skiing
skiable [skjabl] adj voir **domaine**
skier [66] [skje] vi to ski
skieur, -euse [skjœr, -øz] nm,f skier
skin [skin], **skinhead** [skinɛd] nm skinhead
skipper [skipœr] nm skipper
skyscraper [skajskrɛpœr] nm Mktg skyscraper ad
slalom [slalɔm] nm slalom; Fig **faire du s. (entre)** to dodge in and out (between); **s. géant** giant slalom; **s. spécial** special slalom
slalomer [slalɔme] vi to slalom; Fig to dodge in and out (**entre** between)
slalomeur, -euse [slalɔmœr, -øz] nm,f slalom skier
slave [slav] **1** adj Slav, Slavonic
2 nmf **S.** Slav
3 nm (langue) Slavonic
slip [slip] nm (d'homme) (under)pants; (de femme) Br pants, knickers, Am panties; **s. de bain** (d'homme) swimming trunks; (de femme) bikini bottoms
slogan [slɔgɑ̃] nm slogan
slovaque [slɔvak] **1** adj Slovak
2 nmf **S.** Slovak
3 nm (langue) Slovak
Slovaquie [slɔvaki] nf **la S.** Slovakia
slovène [slɔvɛn] **1** adj Slovene
2 nmf **S.** Slovene
3 nm (langue) Slovene
Slovénie [slɔveni] nf **la S.** Slovenia
slow [slo] nm (chanson) slow song; (danse) slow dance
smala(h) [smala] nf Fam (famille) tribe
smash [smaʃ] nm smash; **faire un s.** to smash the ball
smasher [smaʃe] **1** vt to smash
2 vi to smash the ball
SME [ɛsəma] nm (abrév **Système monétaire européen**) EMS
SMIC [smik] nm (abrév **salaire minimum interprofessionnel de croissance**) guaranteed minimum wage

smicard, -e [smikar, -ard] *nm,f Fam* minimum wage earner

smoking [smɔkiŋ] *nm* dinner *or* evening suit

SMS [ɛsɛmɛs] *nm Tél* (*abrév* **short message service**) SMS; **envoyer un S. à qn** to text sb, to send sb a text

snack [snak], **snack-bar** (*pl* **snack-bars**) [snakbar] *nm* snack bar

SNCF [ɛsɛnseɛf] *nf* (*abrév* **Société nationale des chemins de fer français**) = French national railway company

sniffer [snife] *vt Fam* (*drogue*) to sniff, to snort

snob [snɔb] **1** *adj* snobbish
 2 *nmf* snob

snober [snɔbe] *vt* to snub

snobinard, -e [snɔbinar, -ard] *Fam Péj* **1** *adj* stuck-up, snobby
 2 *nm,f* stuck-up type, snob

snobisme [snɔbism] *nm* snobbery, snobbishness

sobre [sɔbr] *adj* (**a**) (*personne*) (*qui n'a pas bu*) sober; (*qui boit ou mange peu*) abstemious (**b**) (*repas, vie*) simple (**c**) (*style, lignes, discours*) sober

sobrement [sɔbrəmɑ̃] *adv* (*s'exprimer, s'habiller*) soberly

sobriété [sɔbrijete] *nf* (**a**) (*tempérance*) temperance, sobriety (**b**) (*d'un repas, d'une vie*) simplicity (**c**) (*d'un style, de lignes, d'un discours*) sobriety; **s'exprimer avec s.** to speak soberly

sobriquet [sɔbrikɛ] *nm* nickname

soccer [sɔkœr] *nm Can* soccer, *Br* football

sociabilité [sɔsjabilite] *nf* sociability

sociable [sɔsjabl] *adj* sociable

social, -e, -aux, -ales [sɔsjal, -o] **1** *adj* (*ordre, politique, réforme*) social
 2 *nm* **le s.** social issues

social-démocrate, sociale-démocrate (*mpl* **sociaux-démocrates**, *fpl* **sociales-démocrates**) [sɔsjaldemɔkrat, sɔsjodemɔkrat] *adj & nmf* social democrat

social-démocratie (*pl* **social-démocraties**) [sɔsjaldemɔkrasi] *nf* social democracy

socialement [sɔsjalmɑ̃] *adv* socially

socialisation [sɔsjalizasjɔ̃] *nf* socialization

socialiser [sɔsjalize] *vt* to socialize

socialisme [sɔsjalism] *nm* socialism

socialiste [sɔsjalist] *adj & nmf* socialist

sociétaire [sɔsjetɛr] *nmf* (**a**) (*membre*) member (**b**) (*actionnaire*) shareholder

société [sɔsjete] *nf* (**a**) (*communauté*) society; **en s.** in society; **s. de consommation** consumer society; **la haute s.** high society (**b**) (*association*) society, association; (*sportive*) club; *Hist* **la S. des Nations** the League of Nations; **la S. protectrice des animaux** *Br* ≃ the RSPCA, *Am* ≃ the ASPCA (**c**) (*compagnie*) company, firm; **s. par actions** *Br* joint-stock company, *Am* incorporated company; **s. anonyme** *Br* public limited company, *Am* corporation; **s. Internet** dotcom; **s. en participation** joint venture; **s. à responsabilité limitée** limited (liability) company (**d**) (*présence*) company

socioculturel, -elle [sɔsjokyltyrɛl] *adj* sociocultural

socio-économique (*pl* **socio-économiques**) [sɔsjoekɔnɔmik] *adj* socioeconomic

sociolinguistique [sɔsjɔlɛ̃gɥistik] **1** *adj* sociolinguistic
 2 *nf* sociolinguistics (*singulier*)

sociologie [sɔsjɔlɔʒi] *nf* sociology

sociologique [sɔsjɔlɔʒik] *adj* sociological

sociologiquement [sɔsjɔlɔʒikmɑ̃] *adv* sociologically

sociologue [sɔsjɔlɔg] *nmf* sociologist

socioprofessionnel, -elle [sɔsjɔprɔfɛsjɔnɛl] *adj* socioprofessional

socle [sɔkl] *nm* (*de statue, de colonne*) plinth, pedestal; (*de vase, de pendule, d'appareil*) base; *Ordinat* **s. orientable** *ou* **pivotant** (*d'un moniteur*) swivel base

socquette [sɔkɛt] *nf* ankle sock

Socrate [sɔkrat] *npr* Socrates

soda [sɔda] *nm Br* fizzy drink, *Am* soda (pop)

sodium [sɔdjɔm] *nm* sodium

sodomie [sɔdɔmi] *nf* sodomy, buggery

sodomiser [sɔdɔmize] *vt* to sodomize, to bugger

sœur [sœr] *nf* (**a**) (*parente*) sister; *Fam* **et ta s.!** get lost!; **s. de lait** foster sister (**b**) *Rel* nun, sister

sœurette [sœrɛt] *nf Fam* little sister

sofa [sɔfa] *nm* sofa, settee

Sofia [sɔfja] *n* Sofia

SOFRES [sɔfrɛs] *nf* (*abrév* **Société française d'enquêtes par sondage**) = French opinion poll company

software [sɔftwɛr] *nm Ordinat* software

soi [swa] *pron personnel* (**a**) (*personne indéfinie*) oneself; (*homme*) himself; (*femme*) herself; **chez s.** at home; **il faut regarder devant s.** you must keep looking in front of you; **revenir à soi** to come to, to come round (**b**) (*chose, concept*) **en s.** in itself, per se

soi-disant [swadizɑ̃] **1** *adv* supposedly
 2 *adj inv* so-called

soie [swa] *nf* (**a**) (*étoffe*) silk; **s. grège/naturelle** raw/natural silk (**b**) (*de sanglier, de porc*) bristle

soierie [swari] *nf* (**a**) (*tissu*) silk (**b**) (*commerce*) silk trade

soif [swaf] *nf aussi Fig* thirst; **avoir s.** to be thirsty; **donner s. à qn** to make sb thirsty; **boire jusqu'à plus s.** to drink one's fill; *Fig* **s. de qch/de faire qch** thirst for sth/to do sth

soignant, -e [swaɲɑ̃, -ɑ̃t] *adj* **personnel s.** nursing staff; **équipe soignante** team of nursing staff

soigné, -e [swaɲe] *adj* (**a**) (*travail*) careful; (*style*) polished (**b**) (*personne, apparence*) neat, tidy; (*mains, ongles, jardin*) well-kept (**c**) *Fam* (*addition*) extortionate

soigner [swaɲe] **1** *vt* (**a**) (*maladie*) to treat (**b**) (*malade*) (*sujet: médecin*) to treat; (*sujet: parent, infirmière*) to look after, to take care of; *Fam Fig* **il faut te faire s.!** you need your head examined! (**c**) (*apparence, invités, image*) to look after, to take care of; (*travail, présentation*) to take care over
 2 **se soigner** *vpr* (**a**) (*personne*) (*médicalement*) to treat oneself; (*faire attention à soi*) to take care of oneself, to look after oneself (**b**) (*maladie*) **ça se soigne très bien** it's easily treated; *Fam Hum* **ça se soigne, tu sais!** they have a cure for that these days, you know!

soigneur [swaɲœr] *nm* trainer; (*en boxe*) second

soigneusement [swaɲøzmɑ̃] *adv* carefully

soigneux, -euse [swaɲø, -øz] *adj* (**a**) (*attentif*) careful (**de** with) (**b**) (*méticuleux*) tidy, neat

soi-même [swamɛm] *pron personnel* oneself; *Prov* **on n'est jamais si bien servi que par s.** if you want something done, do it yourself

soin [swɛ̃] *nm* (**a**) (*attention*) care; **avec s.** carefully, with care; **sans s.** (*travail, exécution*) careless; (*travailler, exécuter*) carelessly; **aux bons soins de** (*sur une lettre*) care of..., c/o...; **avoir** *ou* **prendre s. de qn/qch** to look after *or* take care of sb/sth; **prendre s. de faire qch** to take care to do sth; **confier à qn le**

s. de faire qch to entrust sb with the task of doing sth; **laisser à qn le s. de faire qch** to leave it to sb to do sth; **les soins du ménage** housekeeping (**b**) *(traitement)* **soins** care, attention; **soins de beauté** beauty treatments; **être aux petits soins pour** *ou* **avec qn** to wait on sb hand and foot (**c**) *(traitement médical)* **premiers soins, soins d'urgence** first aid; **soins à domicile** home care *or* nursing; **soins intensifs** intensive care; **soins médicaux** medical care; **soins palliatifs** palliative care

soir [swar] *nm* evening; **ce s.** this evening, tonight; **à ce s.!** see you tonight!; **à dix heures du s.** at ten o'clock in the evening *or* at night; **le jeudi 2 au s.** on the evening of Thursday 2nd; **tous les lundis s.** every Monday evening; **faire qch le s.** to do sth in the evening; **être du s.** to be a night owl

soirée [sware] *nf* (**a**) *(soir)* evening; **dans la s.** in (the course of) the evening; **en fin de s.** towards the end of the evening (**b**) *(fête)* party; **s. dansante** dance (**c**) *Théât* evening performance; *Cin* evening showing; **le film passe en s.** there is an evening showing of the film

sois, soit¹ *etc voir* **être²**

soit² **1** *adv* [swat] all right
2 *conj* [swa] (**a**) *(supposons)* **s. un point P** given a point P (**b**) *(c'est-à-dire)* that is to say (**c**) **s.... s....** either... or...; **s. l'un, s. l'autre** (either) one or the other

soixantaine [swasɑ̃tɛn] *nf* (**a**) *(environ soixante)* **une s. (de)** about sixty, sixty or so (**b**) *(âge)* **avoir la s.** to be around sixty; **approcher de la s.** to be getting on for sixty

soixante [swasɑ̃t] *adj & nm inv* sixty; **s. et onze** seventy-one; *voir aussi* **trois**

soixante-dix [swasɑ̃tdis] *adj inv & nm* seventy; *voir aussi* **trois**

soixante-dixième [swasɑ̃tdizjɛm] *nmf, nm & adj* seventieth; *voir aussi* **cinquième**

soixante-huitard, -e *(mpl* **soixante-huitards,** *fpl* **soixante-huitardes)** [swasɑ̃tɥitar, -ard] *nm,f* = person involved in the events of May 1968

soixantième [swasɑ̃tjɛm] *nmf, nm & adj* sixtieth; *voir aussi* **cinquième**

soja [sɔʒa] *nm* soya

sol¹ [sɔl] *nm* (**a**) *(surface) (dehors)* ground; *(à l'intérieur)* floor; **au s.** at ground level (**b**) *(territoire)* soil (**c**) *(matière)* soil

sol² *nm inv (note)* G; *(chantée)* sol

sol-air [sɔlɛr] *adj inv (missile)* ground-to-air

solaire [sɔlɛr] *adj (système, chauffage, four)* solar; *(lotion, crème)* sun

solarium [sɔlarjɔm] *nm* (**a**) *(établissement)* solarium (**b**) *(terrasse)* sun terrace

soldat [sɔlda] *nm* (**a**) *(personne)* soldier; **s. de deuxième classe** private; **s. de première classe** *Br* lance-corporal, *Am* private first class; **s. Dubois!** private Dubois!; **le S. inconnu** the Unknown Soldier (**b**) *(jouet)* (toy) soldier; **s. de plomb** tin soldier

solde¹ [sɔld] *nf (rémunération)* pay; *Péj* **à la s. de qn** in sb's pay

solde² *nm* (**a**) *(de compte)* balance; **pour s. (de tout compte)** in (full *or* final) settlement (**b**) *(rabais)* **acheter qch en s.** to buy sth in the sale; **vendre qch en s.** to sell sth off; **c'était en s.** it was in the sale; **les soldes** *(articles)* sale goods; **faire les soldes** *(acheteur)* to go round the sales; **faire des soldes** *(magasin)* to have a sale

solder [sɔlde] **1** *vt* (**a**) *(compte)* to close (**b**) *(article)* to sell off, to clear
2 se solder *vpr* **se s. par qch** *Fin* to show sth; *Fig (résultat, échec)* to end in sth

soldeur, -euse [sɔldœr, -øz] *nm,f* discount trader

sole [sɔl] *nf (poisson)* sole

soleil [sɔlɛj] *nm* (**a**) *(astre)* sun; **s. de minuit** midnight sun (**b**) *(lumière, chaleur)* sun, sunshine; **il y a** *ou* **il fait du s.** the sun's shining, it's sunny; *Fig* **se faire une place au s.** to find a place in the sun; *Fig* **avoir des biens au s.** to own property

solennel, -elle [sɔlanɛl] *adj* (**a**) *(occasion, cérémonie)* formal; *(serment, déclaration)* solemn (**b**) *Péj* pompous

solennellement [sɔlanɛlmɑ̃] *adv (officiellement)* formally; *(gravement)* solemnly

solennité [sɔlanite] *nf* (**a**) *(d'une occasion, d'une cérémonie)* formality; *(d'un serment, d'une déclaration)* solemnity (**b**) *Péj* pomposity

Solex® [sɔlɛks] *nm* moped

solfège [sɔlfɛʒ] *nm* (**a**) *(théorie)* music theory (**b**) *(recueil)* music primer

solfier [66] [sɔlfje] *vt* to sol-fa

solidaire [sɔlidɛr] *adj* (**a**) *(personne)* **être s. de qn** to stand by sb, to support sb; **se sentir s. de qn** to feel a sense of solidarity with sb (**b**) *(pièces)* interdependent; **roue s. d'une autre** wheel integral with another

solidairement [sɔlidɛrmɑ̃] *adv* jointly

solidariser [sɔlidarize] **se solidariser** *vpr* to show solidarity (**avec** with)

solidarité [sɔlidarite] *nf (entre personnes)* solidarity; **par s. avec qn** out of fellow-feeling for sb, in order to show solidarity with sb

solide [sɔlid] **1** *adj* (**a**) *(résistant) (mur, meuble)* solid; *(tissu)* strong; *(personne)* sturdy; **s. sur ses jambes** steady on one's feet; **être s. comme un chêne** *ou* **un roc** to be hale and hearty (**b**) *(amitié, relation, liens)* strong (**c**) *(éducation, argumentation)* sound; *Fig* **ça ne repose sur rien de s.** there's no sound basis for that (**d**) *(repas)* solid; *(appétit)* healthy (**e**) *(position, affaire)* sound, strong (**f**) *(non liquide)* solid
2 *nm* (**a**) *(corps)* solid (**b**) *Fam* **c'est du s.!** *(meuble)* that's pretty solid!; *(vêtement)* it's indestructible!

solidement [sɔlidmɑ̃] *adv (construit)* solidly; *(attaché, implanté)* firmly

solidifier [66] [sɔlidifje] **1** *vt* to solidify
2 se solidifier *vpr* to solidify

solidité [sɔlidite] *nf* (**a**) *(d'un objet)* solidity; *(d'un matériau)* strength; **être d'une s. à toute épreuve** to be able to stand up to anything (**b**) *(d'un jugement)* soundness (**c**) *(d'une amitié)* strength

soliloque [sɔlilɔk] *nm* soliloquy

soliste [sɔlist] *nmf* soloist

solitaire [sɔlitɛr] **1** *adj* (**a**) *(personne) (par choix)* solitary; *(involontairement)* lonely; **passer des vacances solitaires** to spend one's *Br* holidays *or Am* vacation alone (**b**) *(arbre, maison)* solitary, lone
2 *nmf (personne)* loner; **en s.** *(vivre, travailler)* on one's own, alone; *(naviguer)* single-handed; *(course)* solo; *(navigation)* single-handed
3 *nm* (**a**) *(jeu)* solitaire (**b**) *(diamant)* solitaire

solitairement [sɔlitɛrmɑ̃] *adv* on one's own, alone

solitude [sɔlityd] *nf* (**a**) *(retraite)* solitude; *(involontaire)* loneliness; **aimer la s.** to like being alone (**b**) *(d'un lieu)* loneliness

solive [sɔliv] *nf Constr* joist

sollicitation [sɔlisitasjɔ̃] *nf* request

solliciter [sɔlisite] *vt* (**a**) *(entretien, audience)* to request; *(emploi)* to apply for (**b**) *(personne)* **s. qn (pour faire qch)** to appeal to sb (to do sth); **être sollicité de toutes parts** to be very much in demand (**c**) *(attention, regards)* to attract; *(curiosité)* to arouse

sollicitude [sɔlisityd] *nf* solicitude, concern (**pour** for)

solo [sɔlo] **1** *adj inv* solo
2 *nm* solo; **jouer en s.** to play solo

sol-sol [sɔlsɔl] *adj inv (missile)* ground-to-ground

solstice [sɔlstis] *nm* solstice; **s. d'été/d'hiver** summer/winter solstice

soluble [sɔlybl] *adj* (**a**) *(produit)* soluble; *(café)* instant (**b**) *(problème)* solvable

solution [sɔlysjɔ̃] *nf* (**a**) *(de problème, de situation, d'équation)* solution, answer (**de** to); **s. de facilité** easy way out (**b**) *(liquide)* solution

solutionner [sɔlysjɔne] *vt Fam* to solve

solvabilité [sɔlvabilite] *nf* solvency

solvable [sɔlvabl] *adj* solvent

solvant [sɔlvɑ̃] *nm* solvent

somali, -e [sɔmali] **1** *adj* Somali
2 *nm,f* **S.** Somali
3 *nm (langue)* Somali

Somalie [sɔmali] *nf* **la S.** Somalia

somalien, -enne [sɔmaljɛ̃, -ɛn] **1** *adj* Somalian
2 *nm,f* **S.** Somalian

somatique [sɔmatik] *adj* somatic

somatiser [sɔmatize] *vt* to react psychosomatically to

sombre [sɔ̃br] *adj* (**a**) *(couleur)* dark (**b**) *(forêt, pièce)* dark; *(ciel)* dull; **il fait s.** *(temps)* it's dull; *(dans une pièce)* it's dark (**c**) *(visage, pensées, caractère)* gloomy, sombre (**d**) *(sinistre)* **une s. histoire de...** a sordid tale of... (**e**) *Fam* **un s. imbécile** a total fool

sombrement [sɔ̃brəmɑ̃] *adv (tristement)* gloomily, sombrely

sombrer [sɔ̃bre] *vi* (**a**) *(navire)* to sink; *(empire)* to founder; *(affaire)* to fail (**b**) *(personne)* **s. dans la déprime/la misère** to sink into depression/destitution

sombrero [sɔ̃brero] *nm* sombrero

sommaire [sɔmɛr] **1** *adj* (**a**) *(récit)* brief (**b**) *(rudimentaire) (examen)* hasty; *(connaissances, repas, étude)* basic; *(jugement, exécution)* summary; **faire une toilette s.** to have a quick wash
2 *nm (table des matières)* contents; **et au s. de l'émission de ce soir...** coming up in tonight's programme...

sommairement [sɔmɛrmɑ̃] *adv* (**a**) *(expliquer, raconter)* briefly (**b**) *(de façon rudimentaire) (meublé)* basically; *(juger)* summarily

sommation [sɔmasjɔ̃] *nf* (**a**) *Jur (injonction)* demand (**b**) *Mil* warning

somme¹ [sɔm] *nf voir* **bête**

somme² *nf* (**a**) *(d'une addition)* sum, total; **faire la s. de** to add up (**b**) *(quantité) (d'objets)* number; *(de travail, d'efforts)* amount (**c**) *(argent)* **s. (d'argent)** sum (of money); **pour la s. de 500 euros** for 500 euros; **dépenser des sommes folles** to spend vast sums of money; **c'est une s.!** that's a lot of money! (**d**) *(locutions)* **en s.** *(tout compte fait)* on the whole; *(en bref)* in short; **s. toute** when all's said and done

somme³ *nm* nap, snooze; **faire un (petit) s.** to have or take a nap or a snooze

sommeil [sɔmɛj] *nm* (**a**) *(repos)* sleep; **avoir s.** to be or feel sleepy; **dormir d'un s. de plomb** to sleep like a log; **avoir le s. léger/profond** to be a light/heavy sleeper; **chercher le s.** to try to sleep; **tomber de s.** to be dead on one's feet; **je manque de s.** I haven't

been getting enough sleep; **j'en perds le s.** I'm losing sleep over it; *Fig* **le s. éternel** eternal rest; **s. paradoxal** REM sleep (**b**) **en s.** *(projet)* (lying) dormant; *Fig* **laisser qch en s.** to put sth on hold

sommeiller [sɔmeje] *vi* (**a**) *(personne)* to doze (**b**) *Fig* to lie dormant

sommelier [sɔməlje] *nm* wine waiter; *Suisse* waiter

sommer [sɔme] *vt* **s. qn de faire qch** to charge sb to do sth

sommes *voir* **être²**

sommet [sɔmɛ] *nm* (**a**) *(de montagne)* top, summit; *(d'arbre, de toit)* top; *(de vague)* crest; *(de la tête)* crown (**b**) *Fig (de hiérarchie)* top; *(du pouvoir, de la gloire)* height (**c**) *(rencontre politique)* summit; **conférence/rencontre au s.** summit conference/meeting (**d**) *(d'angle)* vertex

sommier [sɔmje] *nm* base; **s. à ressorts/lattes** sprung/slatted base

sommité [sɔmite] *nf* leading figure or light

somnambule [sɔmnɑ̃byl] **1** *adj* **être s.** to be a sleepwalker, to walk in one's sleep
2 *nmf* sleepwalker

somnambulisme [sɔmnɑ̃bylism] *nm* sleepwalking

somnifère [sɔmnifɛr] *nm (substance)* sedative; *(cachet)* sleeping pill

somnolence [sɔmnɔlɑ̃s] *nf* sleepiness, drowsiness; **peut provoquer un état de s.** *(sur notice)* may cause drowsiness

somnolent, -e [sɔmnɔlɑ̃, -ɑ̃t] *adj* sleepy, drowsy

somnoler [sɔmnɔle] *vi* to doze

somptuaire [sɔ̃ptɥɛr] *adj* extravagant

somptueusement [sɔ̃ptɥøzmɑ̃] *adv* sumptuously

somptueux, -euse [sɔ̃ptɥø, -øz] *adj* sumptuous

somptuosité [sɔ̃ptɥozite] *nf* sumptuousness

son¹, sa, ses [sɔ̃, sa, se]

> **sa** becomes **son** before a word beginning with a vowel or mute h.

adj possessif (possesseur masculin) his; *(possesseur féminin)* her; *(d'animal, de chose, de pays)* its; *(possesseur indéfini)* one's; **un de ses amis** one of his/her friends, a friend of his/hers; **chacun a pris s. sac** everyone took their bag; **perdre s. temps** to waste one's time; *Fam* **elle a eu s. vendredi** she got Friday off

son² *nm (de voix, d'instrument) & Cin* sound; *Fig* **n'entendre qu'un s. de cloche** to hear only one side of the story; *(spectacle)* **s. et lumière** son et lumière; **s. 3D** surround sound

son³ *nm (de grains)* bran

sonal, -als [sɔnal] *nm Offic* jingle

sonar [sɔnar] *nm* sonar

sonate [sɔnat] *nf* sonata; **s. pour violon** violin sonata

sondage [sɔ̃daʒ] *nm* (**a**) *(de population)* poll, survey; **faire un s.** to carry out a poll or a survey; **s. d'opinion** opinion poll; **s. par téléphone** telephone poll or survey (**b**) *(de terrain)* boring, drilling

sonde [sɔ̃d] *nf* (**a**) *(de bateau)* sounding line (**b**) *(de pompe, de puits)* sounding rod (**c**) *Météo & Av* **s. aérienne** sounding balloon; **s. spatiale** space probe (**d**) *Méd (pour examiner)* probe; *(pour intervenir)* tube (**e**) *(de terrain)* borer, drill

sondé, -e [sɔ̃de] *nm,f* respondent

sonder [sɔ̃de] *vt* (**a**) *(fond)* to sound; *Fig (mystère)* to fathom (**b**) *Météo (atmosphère)* to probe (**c**) *(terrain)* to bore, to drill; *Fig* **s. le terrain** to see how the land lies (**d**) *(personne, opinion, intentions)* to sound out (**e**) *Méd (blessure)* to probe; *(patient)* to sound

sondeur, -euse [sɔ̃dœr, -øz] **1** *nm (appareil)* sounder **2** *nm,f (d'opinions)* pollster
songe [sɔ̃ʒ] *nm Litt* dream; **en s.** in a dream; **faire un s.** to have a dream
songer [45] [sɔ̃ʒe] **1 songer à** *vt ind* (**a**) *(penser à, se souvenir de)* to think about (**b**) *(envisager)* to consider; **il ne faut pas y s.** that's quite out of the question; **s. à faire qch** to think of doing sth **2** *vt* **s. que** to think that
songerie [sɔ̃ʒri] *nf Litt* reverie
songeur, -euse [sɔ̃ʒœr, -øz] *adj* (**a**) *(rêveur)* dreamy (**b**) *(pensif)* pensive, thoughtful
sonnant, -e [sɔnɑ̃, -ɑ̃t] *adj* **arriver à dix heures sonnantes** to arrive on the stroke of ten *or* at ten o'clock sharp
sonné, -e [sɔne] *adj* (**a**) *(accompli)* **avoir quarante ans bien sonnés** to be well over forty (**b**) *Fam (étourdi)* groggy (**c**) *Fam (fou)* crazy, nuts
sonner [sɔne] **1** *vi* (**a**) *(horloge)* to strike; *(cloches, téléphone)* to ring; *(réveil)* to go off; **faire s. son réveil (à six heures)** to set one's alarm (for six o'clock); **s. creux** *(mur)* to sound hollow; *Fig* to ring hollow; *Fig* **s. faux** not to ring true; *Fig* **s. bien/mal** to sound good/bad (**b**) *(heure)* **six heures sonnèrent** the clock struck six; *Fig* **son heure** *ou* **sa dernière heure a sonné** his/her last hour has come (**c**) *(à la porte)* **on a sonné** that was the bell, there's someone at the door; **s. chez qn** to ring sb's bell; **s. avant d'entrer** *(sur panneau)* ring before entering (**d**) *(jouer)* **s. du clairon/de la trompette** to sound the bugle/the trumpet **2** *vt Fam* (**a**) *(cloche)* to ring; *Fam* **s. les cloches à qn** to tell sb off; **se faire s. les cloches** to get a good telling-off (**b**) *(heure)* to strike; *(messe, repas)* to ring the bell for (**c**) *(domestique, infirmière)* to ring for; *Fam* **on ne t'a pas sonné!** nobody asked you! (**d**) *Fam (assommer)* to knock out (**e**) *Belg (appeler)* to telephone, to call
sonnerie [sɔnri] *nf* (**a**) *(son) (de cloches, du téléphone)* ringing; *(de clairon, de trompette)* call (**b**) *(mélodie)* ringtone; **s. polyphonique** polyphonic ringtone (**c**) *(sonnette)* bell
sonnet [sɔnɛ] *nm* sonnet
sonnette [sɔnɛt] *nf* bell; **s. d'alarme** alarm bell; *aussi Fig* **tirer la s. d'alarme** to sound the alarm
sono [sɔno] *nf Fam* PA system
sonore [sɔnɔr] **1** *adj* (**a**) *(effet)* sound; *(pollution)* noise (**b**) *(voix)* ringing; *(rire)* resounding; *(salle)* echoing (**c**) *Ling (consonne)* voiced **2** *nf Ling* voiced consonant
sonorisation [sɔnɔrizasjɔ̃] *nf* (**a**) *(de film)* addition of the soundtrack (**de** to) (**b**) *(de salle)* fitting of a PA system (**de** to) (**c**) *(équipement)* PA system, public address system
sonoriser [sɔnɔrize] *vt* (**a**) *(film)* to add the soundtrack to (**b**) *(salle)* to fit with a PA system
sonorité [sɔnɔrite] *nf* tone
sont *voir* **être²**
Sopalin® [sɔpalɛ̃] *nm* kitchen paper
sophisme [sɔfism] *nm* sophism
sophistication [sɔfistikasjɔ̃] *nf* sophistication
sophistiqué, -e [sɔfistike] *adj* sophisticated
soporifique [sɔpɔrifik] *adj aussi Fig* soporific
soprano [sɔprano] **1** *adj (saxophone)* soprano **2** *nmf (personne)* soprano **3** *nm* soprano (voice)
sorbet [sɔrbɛ] *nm* sorbet
sorbetière [sɔrbətjɛr] *nf* ice-cream maker

sorbier [sɔrbje] *nm* sorb (tree), service (tree)
sorcellerie [sɔrsɛlri] *nf* witchcraft, sorcery
sorcier [sɔrsje] **1** *adj Fam* **ce n'est pas s.** it's simple enough **2** *nm* sorcerer, wizard
sorcière [sɔrsjɛr] *nf* sorceress, witch; *Fam Péj* **vieille s.** old witch
sordide [sɔrdid] *adj* (**a**) *(pièce, quartier)* squalid (**b**) *(crime, détails, avarice)* sordid
sorgho [sɔrgo] *nm* sorghum
Sorlingues [sɔrlɛ̃g] *nfpl* **les S.** the Scilly Isles
sornettes [sɔrnɛt] *nfpl* twaddle, rubbish
sors, sort¹ *etc voir* **sortir¹**
sort² [sɔr] *nm* (**a**) *(condition)* lot; *Fam* **faire un s. à qch** *(bouteille, plat)* to polish sth off (**b**) *(destin)* fate (**c**) *(hasard)* chance; **tirer au s.** to draw lots; **le s. en est jeté** the die is cast (**d**) *(magique)* spell; **jeter un s. à qn** to cast a spell on sb; **conjurer le mauvais s.** to ward off bad luck
sortable [sɔrtabl] *adj Fam* **tu n'es pas s.!** I can't take you anywhere!
sortant, -e [sɔrtɑ̃, -ɑ̃t] *adj (numéro de loterie)* winning; *(élu)* outgoing
sorte [sɔrt] *nf* (**a**) *(genre)* sort, kind; **toutes sortes de choses/gens, des choses/gens de toutes sortes** all sorts *or* kinds of things/people; **un homme de la s.** a man of that kind; **une s. de...** a sort *or* kind of...; **je n'ai rien dit/fait de la s.** I said/did no such thing, I said/did nothing of the sort (**b**) *(manière)* **de la s.** in that way; **en quelque s.** as it were, in a way; **de s. que je puisse...** so that I can...; **de s. qu'il est arrivé en retard** with the result that he arrived late; **de s. à faire qch** so as to do sth; **faire en s. que** + *subjunctive* to see to it that; **fais en s. d'être à l'heure** see to it that you're on time
sortie [sɔrti] *nf* (**a**) *(fait de sortir d'un lieu)* **c'était ma première s. depuis...** it was my first time out since...; **à sa s. de l'hôpital/de prison** when he/she came out of hospital/prison; **à la s. de l'école/du travail** after school/work; **à la s. des bureaux** when the offices come out (**b**) *(issue)* exit, way out; **à la s. de la gare** at the station exit; **s. d'autoroute** motorway exit; **s. de secours** emergency exit (**c**) *(d'un livre, d'un journal)* publication; *(d'un film, d'un disque)* release; *(d'un modèle)* launch; **à sa s. dans les salles parisiennes** when released in Parisian cinemas (**d**) *(de liquide, d'air)* outflow (**e**) *(dispositif)* outlet (**f**) *(de marchandises)* export (**g**) *(dépense)* **sorties** outgoings (**h**) *(excursion)* trip, outing; **priver qn de s.** to stop sb from going out, to ground sb; **s. en mer** short sea trip; **jour de s.** day out; **ce soir je suis de s.** I'm going out tonight; **désolé, mais elle est de s.** sorry, but she's out (**i**) *Mil* sortie (**j**) *Fam (emportement)* outburst (**k**) *Ordinat* exit; *(information)* output; **s. d'imprimante** printer output; **dispositif de s.** output device; **signal de s.** output signal; **s. écran** screen output; **s. imprimante** printout; **s. imprimée** printed output; **s. parallèle** parallel output; **s. série** serial output
sortie-de-bain *(pl* **sorties-de-bain)** [sɔrtidbɛ̃] *nf* bathrobe
sortilège [sɔrtilɛʒ] *nm* spell
sortir¹ [64a] [sɔrtir] **1** *vt (aux avoir)* (**a**) *(enfant, chien)* to take out; *(voiture)* to get out; **s. qn de** *(situation)* to get sb out of (**b**) *(objet)* to take out (**de** of); **et si tu sortais ton bon whisky?** how about getting out your good whisky? (**c**) *(mettre sur le marché) (livre, journal)* to bring out, to publish; *(film, disque)* to bring

out, to release (**d**) *Fam (dire)* to come out with (**e**) *Fam (expulser)* to throw out; *(vaincre)* to knock out **2** *vi (aux être)* (**a**) *(aller)* to go out (**de** of); *(venir)* to come out (**de** of); *(partir)* to leave; *(s'extraire, finir de travailler)* to get out (**de** of); **s. en courant/en boitant** to run/limp out; **est-ce que je peux s.?** *(en classe)* may I be excused?; **sortez (d'ici)!** get out (of here)!; **s. de table** to leave the table; **je sors d'une mauvaise grippe** I'm just getting over a bad dose of flu; **il est sorti discrédité de ce scandale** he came out of this scandal with his reputation in ruins; **cela ne doit pas s. d'ici** *(secret)* it mustn't go any further; *Fam* **d'où sors-tu?** *(d'où viens-tu?)* where did you spring from?; *(tu n'es pas au courant)* what planet have you been on?; **cela m'est sorti de la tête** it's gone right out of my head; **il ne sortira pas grand-chose de tout cela** nothing much will come of all this (**b**) *(pour s'amuser)* to go out; **s. avec qn** to go out with sb; *Fig* **il faut s. un peu!** *(pour être au courant)* what planet have you been on? (**c**) *(livre, journal)* to come out, to be published; *(film, disque)* to come out, to be released (**d**) *(être issu)* **s. de** *(famille, milieu)* to come from; **elle sort d'Harvard** she was at Harvard (**e**) *(numéro de loto, sujet d'examen)* to come up (**f**) *(apparaître) (fleur)* to come out; *(dent)* to come through; **les yeux lui sortaient de la tête** his/her eyes were popping out of his/her head (**g**) *Ordinat (d'un système)* to exit **3 se sortir** *vpr* **se s. de** *(situation)* to get out of; **s'en s.** *(d'un travail)* to manage; *(d'une difficulté)* to get through it; *(malade)* to pull through

sortir² *nm* **au s. du cinéma** on coming out of the cinema; **au s. de l'école** after school; **au s. de l'hiver** at the end of winter

SOS [ɛsoɛs] *nm* SOS; **lancer un S. (à)** to send (out) an SOS (to); **S. Amitié** = helpline for people in need of emotional support, ≃ the Samaritans; ; **S. femmes battues** = helpline for female victims of domestic violence; **S. médecins** = emergency medical service; **S.-Racisme** = anti-racist movement

sosie [sozi] *nm* lookalike, double; **c'est un s. de Brando** he's a Brando lookalike; **c'est le s. de mon frère** he's my brother's double

sot, sotte [so, sot] **1** *adj* stupid, foolish; **il n'y a pas de s. métier** there's no such thing as a worthless profession **2** *nm,f* fool

sottement [sotmã] *adv* stupidly, foolishly

sottise [sotiz] *nf* (**a**) *(stupidité)* stupidity, foolishness (**b**) *(action)* stupid act; **faire des sottises** to do stupid things; **faire une s.** to do something stupid (**c**) *(parole)* stupid remark; **dire des sottises** to say stupid things; **dire une s.** to say something stupid

sottisier [sotizje] *nm* collection of howlers

sou [su] *nm* (**a**) *(argent)* **être sans le s.** to be penniless; **il est toujours en train de compter ses sous** he's always counting every penny; **avoir des sous** to have money; **c'est une affaire de gros sous** there's big money involved; **être près de ses sous** to be a penny-pincher; *Fig* **n'avoir pas (pour) un s. de courage/bon sens** not to have an ounce of courage/common sense (**b**) *(pièce)* **un s. est un s.** every penny counts (**c**) *(ancienne monnaie)* sou (**d**) *Can (cent)* cent

soubassement [subasmã] *nm* (**a**) *(de construction)* base (**b**) *Can (sous-sol)* basement

soubresaut [subrəso] *nm* *(de véhicule)* jolt; *(de personne)* jerk

soubrette [subrɛt] *nf Théât* maid

souche [suʃ] *nf* (**a**) *(d'arbre)* stump; *Fam* **rester (planté) comme une s.** to be rooted to the spot; **dormir comme une s.** to sleep like a log (**b**) *(de famille)* founder; **faire s.** to found a line (**c**) *(de virus)* strain (**d**) *(de chèques, de tickets)* counterfoil, stub (**e**) *(de langue)* root

souci¹ [susi] *nm* (**a**) *(inquiétude)* worry, anxiety; **avoir des soucis** to have worries; **se faire du s. (pour)** to worry (about); **donner du s. à qn** to worry sb; **c'est le dernier** *ou* **le cadet de mes soucis** that's the least of my worries (**b**) *(soin)* concern (**de** for); **avoir le s. de plaire** to be anxious to please

souci² *nm (fleur)* marigold

soucier [66] [susje] **se soucier** *vpr* **se s. de** to worry about; **ne se s. de rien** not to worry about anything; *Fam* **se s. de qch comme de l'an quarante** *ou* **de sa première chemise** not to give a damn about sth

soucieux, -euse [susjø, -øz] *adj* (**a**) *(attentif)* anxious, concerned (**de** about); **être s. de faire qch** to be anxious to do sth; **peu s. de qch** unconcerned about sth (**b**) *(inquiet)* worried

soucoupe [sukup] *nf* saucer; **s. volante** flying saucer

soudain, -e [sudɛ̃, -ɛn] **1** *adv* suddenly, all of a sudden **2** *adj* sudden

soudainement [sudɛnmã] *adv* suddenly

soudaineté [sudɛnte] *nf* suddenness

Soudan [sudã] *nm* **le S.** the Sudan

soudanais, -e [sudanɛ, -ɛz] **1** *adj* Sudanese **2** *nm,f* **S.** Sudanese; **les S.** the Sudanese

soudard [sudar] *nm Fam* brutish soldier

soude [sud] *nf* soda; **s. caustique** caustic soda

souder [sude] **1** *vt* (**a**) *(par alliage)* to solder; *(par soudure autogène)* to weld (**b**) *(os fracturé)* to knit (**c**) *Fig (groupes, personnes)* to unite **2 se souder** *vpr* (**a**) *(os)* to knit (together) (**b**) *Fig (groupe)* to unite

soudeur, -euse [sudœr, -øz] *nm,f (avec soudure par alliage)* solderer; *(avec soudure autogène)* welder

soudoyer [32] [sudwaje] *vt* to bribe

soudure [sudyr] *nf* (**a**) *(opération) (par alliage)* soldering; *(autogène)* welding (**b**) *(résultat) (par alliage)* soldered joint; *(autogène)* weld (**c**) *(d'os)* knitting (**d**) *Fig* **faire la s.** to make ends meet

soufflage [suflaʒ] *nm (du verre)* blowing

souffle [sufl] *nm* (**a**) *(d'air, de vent)* breath, puff (**b**) *(respiration)* breathing; **avoir du s.** to have stamina; **retenir son s.** to hold one's breath; **manquer de s.** to be short-winded; **avoir le s. court** to be short of breath; **à bout de s.** out of breath; **jusqu'à mon dernier s.** as long as I live and breathe, to my dying day; *Fig* **couper le s. à qn** to take sb's breath away (**c**) *(d'une explosion)* blast (**d**) *(d'hélices)* slipstream, wash (**e**) *Méd* murmur; **s. au cœur** heart murmur (**f**) *(force créatrice)* inspiration (**g**) *(impulsion)* **donner un nouveau s. à qch** to give sth a new lease of life

soufflé, -e [sufle] **1** *adj* (**a**) *Culin* soufflé (**b**) *Fam (ahuri)* flabbergasted **2** *nm* soufflé; **s. au fromage/au chocolat** cheese/chocolate soufflé

souffler [sufle] **1** *vt* (**a**) *(fumée, poussière)* to blow; *(bougie)* to blow out (**b**) *(dire)* to whisper (**à** to); **s. une réplique à un acteur** to prompt an actor; **quelqu'un a dû lui s. l'idée** someone must have given him/her the idea; **ne pas s. mot (de qch)** not to breathe a word (about sth); **on ne souffle pas!** no prompting! (**c**) *Fam (prendre)* to pinch (**à** from); **se faire s. qch** to have sth pinched (**d**) *(détruire)* to blast (**e**) *Fam (ahurir)* to stagger (**f**) *(verre)* to blow

2 *vi* (**a**) *(expirer)* to blow; **s. dans ses doigts** to blow on one's fingers; **s. dans une trompette** to blow a trumpet; **inspirez! soufflez!** breathe in! breathe out! (**b**) *(se reposer)* **laisser s. qn** to give sb time to catch his/her breath (**c**) *(haleter)* to pant, to puff; *Fam* **s. comme un bœuf** to puff and pant (**d**) *(vent)* to blow; **le vent soufflait en rafales** there were gusts of wind; *Fig* **un vent de révolte soufflait sur le pays** there was a spirit of revolt in the country

soufflerie [suflǝri] *nf* (**a**) *(d'orgue, de forge)* bellows (**b**) *(de climatiseur)* blower

soufflet [sufle] *nm* (**a**) *(de forge)* bellows (**b**) *Rail (couloir)* concertina vestibule (**c**) *(en couture)* gusset (**d**) *(d'orgue)* swell (**e**) *Litt (gifle)* slap (in the face)

souffleter [42] [suflǝte] *vt Litt* **s. qn** to slap sb's face

souffleur, -euse [suflœr, -øz] **1** *nm* **s. de verre** glass blower

2 *nm,f (au théâtre)* prompter

3 *nf* **souffleuse** *Can* snowblower

souffrance [sufrɑ̃s] *nf* (**a**) *(douleur)* suffering (**b**) **en s.** *(travail)* pending

souffrant, -e [sufrɑ̃, -ɑ̃t] *adj (indisposé)* unwell, poorly

souffre-douleur [sufrǝdulœr] *nm inv* object of abuse

souffreteux, -euse [sufrǝtø, -øz] *adj* sickly

souffrir [52] [sufrir] **1** *vi* to suffer (**de** from); **faire s. qn** *(physiquement)* to hurt sb; *(moralement)* to make sb suffer; **je souffre de la voir malade** it upsets me to see her ill

2 *vt* (**a**) *(physiquement)* **s. le martyre** to go through agony; **faire s. le martyre à qn** to put sb through agony (**b**) *(supporter)* **je ne peux pas la s.** I can't stand her; **je ne peux pas s. qu'on vienne me déranger** I can't stand being disturbed; **il ne souffre pas la contradiction** he can't stand being contradicted; *Litt* **souffrez que je fasse une critique** permit me to make a criticism (**c**) *Litt (admettre)* **situation qui ne souffre aucun retard** situation that admits of no delay

3 se souffrir *vpr* **ils ne peuvent pas se s.** they can't stand each other

soufre [sufr] *nm* sulphur

souhait [swe] *nm* wish; **faire un s.** to make a wish; **à s.** *(à merveille)* perfectly; **doré/ensoleillé à s.** beautifully golden/sunny; **à vos souhaits!** bless you!

souhaitable [swetabl] *adj* desirable; **il serait s. que tu lui parles** it is desirable that you should talk to him/her

souhaiter [swete] *vt* to wish for; **s. qch à qn** to wish sb sth; **s. faire qch** to hope to do sth; **s. à qn de faire qch** to hope that sb does sth; **s. que** + *subjunctive* to hope that; **je vous souhaite une bonne année/un joyeux anniversaire** best wishes for a happy New Year/a happy birthday; *Ironique* **je te souhaite bien du plaisir!** have fun!

souiller [suje] *vt Litt* (**a**) *(vêtements)* to soil, to dirty (**de** with) (**b**) *(réputation, mémoire)* to tarnish

souillon [sujɔ̃] *nf Litt* slut, sloven

souillure [sujyr] *nf Litt* (**a**) *(sur un vêtement)* stain (**b**) *Fig (morale)* blot, blemish

souk [suk] *nm* (**a**) *(marché)* souk (**b**) *Fam (lieu en désordre)* shambles *(singulier)*

soul [sul] *adj inv & nf* soul

soûl, -e [su, sul] **1** *adj* drunk

2 *nm* **tout son s.** to one's heart's content

soulagement [sulaʒmɑ̃] *nm* relief (**pour** to)

soulager [45] [sulaʒe] **1** *vt (douleur)* to ease, to relieve; *(esprit, chagrin)* to soothe; *(personne)* to relieve; **ce médicament vous soulagera** this medicine will make you feel better; **donne-moi un de tes sacs, ça te soulagera** give me one of your bags, that will take some of the weight off you; *Fam* **s. qn de son portefeuille** to relieve sb of his/her wallet

2 se soulager *vpr* (**a**) *(en parlant)* to ease one's mind (**b**) *Fam (satisfaire un besoin naturel)* to relieve oneself

soûlant, -e [sulɑ̃, -ɑ̃t] *adj Fam* exhausting

soûlard, -e [sular, -ard], **soûlaud, -e** [sulo, -od] *nm,f Fam* drunk

soûler [sule] *Fam* **1** *vt* (**a**) *(enivrer)* **s. qn** to make sb drunk; *Fig (sujet: parfum, succès, idées)* to go to sb's head (**b**) *(ennuyer)* **arrête, tu me soûles!** stop, you're giving me a headache!

2 se soûler *vpr* to get drunk; *Fig* **se s. de paroles** to like the sound of one's own voice

soulèvement [sulɛvmɑ̃] *nm* (**a**) *(de terrain)* rising (**b**) *(révolte)* uprising

soulever [46] [sulve] **1** *vt* (**a**) *(charge, personne, couvercle)* to lift (up); *(rideau)* to raise (**b**) *(agiter) (poussière)* to raise, to throw up; *Fig* **s. le cœur à qn** to make sb feel sick (**c**) *(doutes, question, objection)* to raise (**d**) *(population)* to rouse, to stir up (**e**) *(passion, enthousiasme, indignation)* to excite, to arouse; **s. un tollé** to raise an outcry

2 se soulever *vpr* (**a**) *(s'élever)* to rise (**b**) *(se lever) (personne)* to raise oneself, to lift oneself up (**c**) *(se révolter)* to rise up

soulier [sulje] *nm* shoe; *Fam Fig* **être dans ses petits souliers** to feel awkward

souligner [suliɲe] *vt* (**a**) *(mot, passage)* to underline (**b**) *(yeux, taille)* to emphasize (**c**) *Fig (mettre en valeur)* to emphasize

soûlon [sulɔ̃] *nm Suisse & Can Fam* drunk

soumettre [47] [sumɛtr] **1** *vt* (**a**) *(population, pays, passions)* to subdue (**b**) *(rapport, demande, projet)* to submit (**à** to) (**c**) **s. qn à** *(examen)* to subject sb to; *(épreuve)* to put sb through; *(traitement)* to put sb on; **être soumis à des règles strictes** to be bound by strict rules; **s. les revenus à l'impôt** to make income liable to tax

2 se soumettre *vpr (obéir)* to submit; **se s. à** *(autorité)* to submit to; *(volonté)* to comply with; *(loi, décision)* to abide by

soumis, -e [sumi, -iz] *adj (docile)* submissive, obedient (**à** to)

soumission [sumisjɔ̃] *nf* (**a**) *(à une loi, à une autorité)* submission (**à** to) (**b**) *(docilité)* submissiveness, obedience (**à** to)

soupape [supap] *nf* valve; **s. de sécurité** safety valve

soupçon [supsɔ̃] *nm* (**a**) *(suspicion)* suspicion; **avoir des soupçons sur qn** to have (one's) suspicions about sb; **être au-dessus** *ou* **à l'abri de tout s.** to be above all suspicion; **éveiller les soupçons** to arouse suspicion; **de graves soupçons pèsent sur lui** grave suspicions hang over him (**b**) *(faible quantité) (de vinaigre, d'ail)* dash, hint; *(de fièvre, de fard, d'ironie)* touch; *(de vin)* drop

soupçonner [supsɔne] *vt* to suspect; **s. qn de qch/de faire qch** to suspect sb of sth/of doing sth; **je soupçonne qu'il le sait** I suspect that he knows

soupçonneux, -euse [supsɔnø, -øz] *adj* suspicious
soupe [sup] *nf* (**a**) *(plat)* soup; *Fam* **à la s.!** grub's up!; *Fam* **être s. au lait** to flare up easily (**b**) **s. populaire** soup kitchen
soupente [supɑ̃t] *nf (sous un toit)* loft; *(sous un escalier) Br* cupboard, *Am* closet
souper¹ [supe] *nm* (**a**) *(dîner)* dinner (**b**) *(après le spectacle)* supper
souper² *vi* (**a**) *(dîner)* to have dinner (**b**) *(après le spectacle)* to have supper (**c**) *Fam Fig (être excédé)* **avoir soupé de qn/qch** to be fed up with sb/sth
soupeser [46] [supǝze] *vt (objet)* to feel the weight of, to weigh in one's hand; *Fig (problème, argument)* to weigh up
soupière [supjɛr] *nf* soup tureen
soupir [supir] *nm* (**a**) *(souffle)* sigh; **pousser un s.** to let out *or* give a sigh; **rendre le dernier s.** to breathe one's last; **un gros s.** a heavy *or* deep sigh (**b**) *Mus Br* crotchet *or Am* quarter rest
soupirail, -aux [supiraj, -o] *nm* cellar window
soupirant [supirɑ̃] *nm Hum* suitor, admirer
soupirer [supire] **1** *vt* to sigh
 2 *vi* to sigh; **en soupirant** with a sigh
 3 **soupirer après** *vt ind Litt* to long for, to yearn for
souple [supl] *adj* (**a**) *(branche)* flexible; *(corps, danseur)* supple; *(reliure)* limp; *(cuir)* soft, supple (**b**) *Fig (système, loi, personne)* flexible; *(esprit)* adaptable
souplesse [suplɛs] *nf* (**a**) *(de branche)* flexibility; *(de corps, de danseur)* suppleness; **en s.** *(démarrer)* smoothly (**b**) *Fig (de système, de loi, de personne)* flexibility
source [surs] *nf* (**a**) *(d'eau)* spring; **s. d'eau minérale** mineral spring; **s. thermale** hot spring (**b**) *(de rivière)* source; **prendre sa s.** to rise (**c**) *(de chaleur, d'énergie)* source (**d**) *Fig (du mal, de richesse, d'informations)* source; **tenir qch de bonne s.** to have sth on good authority *or* from a reliable source; **apprendre qch de s. sûre** to learn sth from a reliable source; **s. de revenus** source of revenue (**e**) *Ordinat* **s. de données** data source; **code s.** source code
sourcier [sursje] *nm* water diviner
sourcil [sursil] *nm* eyebrow
sourciller [sursije] *vi* **ne pas s.** not to bat an eyelid *or* turn a hair; **sans s.** without batting an eyelid, without turning a hair
sourcilleux, -euse [sursijø, -øz] *adj* fussy, finicky
sourd, -e [sur, surd] **1** *adj* (**a**) *(personne)* deaf; **devenir s.** to go deaf; *Fig* **rester s. à qch** to turn a deaf ear to sth, to be deaf to sth; **s. de naissance** deaf from birth; **s. d'une oreille** deaf in one ear; *Fam* **s. comme un pot** deaf as a post (**b**) *(douleur, bruit)* dull; *(voix)* hollow; *(désir, lutte)* secret; *(hostilité)* veiled; *(consonne)* voiceless
 2 *nm,f (personne)* deaf person; **les sourds** the deaf, deaf people; **comme un s.** *(crier)* at the top of one's voice; *(frapper, taper)* wildly
 3 *nf* **sourde** *Ling* voiceless consonant
sourdine [surdin] *nf* mute; *(d'un piano)* practice pedal; **en s.** *(violons)* muted; *(en secret)* on the quiet; *Fam Fig* **mets-la en s.!** put a sock in it!
sourdingue [surdɛ̃g] *Fam* **1** *adj* cloth-eared
 2 *nmf* cloth-ears
sourd-muet, sourde-muette (*mpl* **sourds-muets**, *fpl* **sourdes-muettes**) [surmɥɛ, surdmɥɛt] **1** *adj* deaf-and-dumb
 2 *nm,f* deaf mute
souriant, -e [surjɑ̃, -ɑ̃t] *adj* smiling

souriceau, -x [suriso] *nm* young mouse
souricière [surisjɛr] *nf* mousetrap; *Fig* trap
sourire [61] [surir] **1** *vi* (**a**) *(personne)* to smile (**à** at); *Ironique* **ça fait s.** it makes you laugh (**b**) *(être favorable)* **la chance lui sourit** fortune smiles on him/her; **tout lui sourit** everything goes right for him/her
 2 *nm* smile; **le s. aux lèvres** with a smile on one's lips; **faire un s. à qn** to give sb a smile; **avoir le s.** to have a smile on one's face; **garder le s.** to keep smiling; **retrouver le s.** to be smiling again
souris [suri] *nf* (**a**) *(animal)* mouse; **s. blanche** white mouse (**b**) *Ordinat* mouse; **s. à trois boutons** three-button mouse; **s. à infrarouge** infrared mouse; **s. optique** optical mouse; **s. sans fil** cordless mouse; **s. tactile** touchpad mouse (**c**) *Fam (femme) Br* bird, *Am* chick (**d**) *(de gigot)* knuckle end
sournois, -e [surnwa, -az] **1** *adj* sly
 2 *nm,f* sly person
sournoisement [surnwazmɑ̃] *adv* slyly
sournoiserie [surnwazri] *nf* slyness
sous [su] *prép* (**a**) *(position)* under(neath); **s. terre** underground; **nager s. l'eau** to swim underwater; **lettre s. enveloppe** letter in an envelope; **s. la pluie** in the rain; **s. les tropiques** in the tropics; **s. les yeux de qn** before sb's eyes; **s. cet angle** from that angle; **chercher un mot s. la lettre S** to look up a word under the letter S (**b**) *(à l'époque de) (monarque, président)* under; **s. la IIIᵉ République** during the Third Republic (**c**) *(d'ici)* within; **s. huitaine** within a week; **s. peu** shortly, before long (**d**) *(locutions)* **connu s. le nom de...** known as...; **être s. antibiotiques** to be on antibiotics; **opérer s. anesthésie** to operate under anaesthetic; **s. le poids de qch** under the weight of sth; **travailler s. les ordres de qn** to work under sb; **s. certaines conditions** on certain conditions; **s. peine de mort** on *or* under pain of death
sous-alimentation [suzalimɑ̃tasjɔ̃] *nf* malnutrition, undernourishment
sous-alimenté, -e (*mpl* **sous-alimentés**, *fpl* **sous-alimentées**) [suzalimɑ̃te] *adj* malnourished, undernourished
sous-bois [subwa] *nm inv* undergrowth
sous-chef (*pl* **sous-chefs**) [suʃɛf] *nm* second-in-command
sous-continent (*pl* **sous-continents**) [sukɔ̃tinɑ̃] *nm* subcontinent
sous-couche (*pl* **sous-couches**) [sukuʃ] *nf* undercoat
souscripteur, -trice [suskriptœr, -tris] *nm,f (d'un emprunt)* subscriber (**de** to); *(d'une police d'assurance)* policy holder
souscription [suskripsjɔ̃] *nf (à un emprunt)* subscription (**à** to); **la s. d'une police d'assurance** taking out an insurance policy
souscrire [30] [suskrir] **1** *vt (police d'assurance)* to take out
 2 **souscrire à** *vt ind aussi Fig* to subscribe to
sous-culture (*pl* **sous-cultures**) [sukyltyr] *nf* subculture
sous-cutané, -e (*mpl* **sous-cutanés**, *fpl* **sous-cutanées**) [sukytane] *adj* subcutaneous
sous-développé, -e (*mpl* **sous-développés**, *fpl* **sous-développées**) [sudevlɔpe] *adj (pays)* underdeveloped
sous-développement [sudevlɔpmɑ̃] *nm* underdevelopment

sous-directeur, -trice *(mpl* **sous-directeurs,** *fpl* **sous-directrices)** [sudirɛktœr, -tris] *nm,f (dans une entreprise)* assistant manager, *f* assistant manageress

sous-division *nf* subdivision

sous-emploi [suzãplwa] *nm* underemployment

sous-employé, -e *(mpl* **sous-employés,** *fpl* **sous-employées)** [suzãplwaje] *adj* underemployed

sous-ensemble *(pl* **sous-ensembles)** [suzãsãbl] *nm* subset

sous-entendre [suzãtãdr] *vt* to imply

sous-entendu *(pl* **sous-entendus)** [suzãtãdy] *nm* insinuation

sous-équipé, -e *(mpl* **sous-équipés,** *fpl* **sous-équipées)** [suzekipe] *adj* underequipped

sous-estimer [suzɛstime] *vt* to underestimate

sous-évaluer [suzevalɥe] *vt* to undervalue

sous-exposer [suzɛkspoze] *vt* to underexpose

sous-fifre *(pl* **sous-fifres)** [sufifr] *nm Fam* underling

sous-homme *(pl* **sous-hommes)** [suzɔm] *nm* subhuman

sous-jacent, -e *(mpl* **sous-jacents,** *fpl* **sous-jacentes)** [suʒasã, -ãt] *adj* underlying

Sous-le-Vent [sulvã] *n* **les îles S.** the Leeward Islands

sous-lieutenant *(pl* **sous-lieutenants)** [suljøtnã] *nm* (**a**) *(dans l'armée de terre)* second lieutenant (**b**) *(dans la marine)* sub-lieutenant (**c**) *(dans l'armée de l'air) Br* pilot officer, *Am* second lieutenant

sous-locataire *(pl* **sous-locataires)** [sulɔkatɛr] *nmf* subtenant

sous-location *(pl* **sous-locations)** [sulɔkasjɔ̃] *nf* (**a**) *(par le locataire)* subletting (**b**) *(par le sous-locataire)* subrenting

sous-louer [sulwe] *vt* (**a**) *(sujet: locataire)* to sublet (**b**) *(sujet: sous-locataire)* to subrent

sous-main [sumɛ̃] *nm inv* desk blotter; *Fig* **en s.** secretly

sous-marin, -e *(mpl* **sous-marins,** *fpl* **sous-marines)** [sumarɛ̃, -in] **1** *adj* underwater
2 *nm* submarine; **s. nucléaire** nuclear(-powered) submarine

sous-marinier *(pl* **sous-mariniers)** [sumarinje] *nm* submariner

sous-multiple *(pl* **sous-multiples)** [sumyltipl] *nm Math* submultiple (**de** of)

sous-nappe *(pl* **sous-nappes)** [sunap] *nf* undercloth

sous-officier *(pl* **sous-officiers)** [suzɔfisje] *nm* non-commissioned officer

sous-payer [53] [supeje] *vt* to underpay

sous-peuplé, -e *(mpl* **sous-peuplés,** *fpl* **sous-peuplées)** [supœple] *adj* underpopulated

sous-plat *(pl* **sous-plats)** [supla] *nm Belg* table mat

sous-préfecture *(pl* **sous-préfectures)** [suprefɛktyr] *nf* subprefecture

sous-préfet *(pl* **sous-préfets)** [suprefɛ] *nm* subprefect

sous-production [suprɔdyksjɔ̃] *nf* under-production

sous-produit *(pl* **sous-produits)** [suprɔdɥi] *nm* by-product; *Fig* poor imitation

sous-prolétaire *(pl* **sous-prolétaires)** [suprɔletɛr] *nmf* member of the underclass

sous-prolétariat *(pl* **sous-prolétariats)** [suprɔletarja] *nm* underclass

sous-pull *(pl* **sous-pulls)** [supyl] *nm* thin sweater

sous-répertoire *(pl* **sous-répertoires)** [surepɛrtwar] *nm Ordinat* subdirectory

sous-secrétaire *(pl* **sous-secrétaires)** [susəkretɛr] *nmf* **s. d'État** Under-Secretary of State

soussigné, -e [susiɲe] *adj & nm,f* undersigned; **je, s. Éric Blanc, donne mon autorisation à...** I, the undersigned Éric Blanc, hereby authorize...

sous-sol *(pl* **sous-sols)** [susɔl] *nm* (**a**) *(d'une maison)* basement (**b**) *Géol* subsoil

sous-tasse *(pl* **sous-tasses)** [sutas] *nf* saucer

sous-tendre [sutãdr] *vt (théorie)* to underlie

sous-titrage *(pl* **sous-titrages)** [sutitraʒ] *nm Cin* subtitling

sous-titre *(pl* **sous-titres)** [sutitr] *nm (de livre, de film)* subtitle

sous-titrer [sutitre] *vt Cin* to subtitle; **film sous-titré en anglais** film with English subtitles

sous-total *(pl* **sous-totaux)** [sutɔtal, -o] *nm* subtotal

soustraction [sustraksjɔ̃] *nf* subtraction

soustraire [28] [sustrɛr] **1** *vt* (**a**) *(enlever)* **s. qch à qn** to take sth away *or* remove sth from sb; **s. qn au danger/à l'influence de qn** to protect *or* shield sb from danger/from sb's influence (**b**) *(chiffre, somme)* to subtract (**de** from)
2 se soustraire *vpr* **se s. à** *(influence, regard)* to avoid, to elude; *(obligation)* to shirk

sous-traitance [sutrɛtãs] *nf* subcontracting; **travaux effectués en s.** subcontracted work

sous-traitant, -e [sutrɛtã, -ãt] **1** *adj* subcontracting
2 *nm* subcontractor

sous-traiter [sutrete] *vt* to subcontract

sous-verre [suvɛr] *nm inv (cadre)* glass mount; *(photo, image)* = photograph or picture mounted under glass

sous-vêtement [suvɛtmã] *nm* undergarment; **sous-vêtements** underwear

soutane [sutan] *nf* cassock

soute [sut] *nf (de bateau)* store; *(d'avion)* hold; **s. à bagages** *(d'avion)* baggage hold

soutenable [sutnabl] *adj* (**a**) *(supportable)* bearable (**b**) *(défendable)* tenable

soutenance [sutnãs] *nf Univ* viva (voce)

soutènement [sutɛnmã] *nm voir* **mur**

souteneur [sutnœr] *nm* pimp

soutenir [70] [sutnir] **1** *vt* (**a**) *(maintenir)* to support, to hold up (**b**) *(aider)* to support (**c**) *(opinion, théorie)* to maintain, to uphold; **s. que...** to maintain that... (**d**) *Univ (thèse)* to defend (**e**) *(conversation, vitesse, rythme)* to keep up, to maintain (**f**) *(résister à) (regard)* to hold; **s. la comparaison** to bear comparison
2 se soutenir *vpr (personnes)* to support each other; **se s. moralement** to give each other moral support

soutenu, -e [sutny] *adj* (**a**) *(attention, effort, intérêt)* sustained; *(rythme)* steady (**b**) *(style, langage)* formal, elevated (**c**) *(couleur)* deep

souterrain, -e [sutɛrɛ̃, -ɛn] **1** *adj* (**a**) *(eau, explosion)* underground; *(économie)* black (**b**) *Fig (manœuvres)* secret
2 *nm* underground passage

soutien [sutjɛ̃] *nm (aide)* support; **apporter son s. à qn/qch** to give sb/sth one's support (**b**) *(personne, groupe)* support; **s. de famille** breadwinner

soutien-gorge *(pl* **soutiens-gorge)** [sutjɛ̃gɔrʒ] *nm* bra; **s. à armatures/d'allaitement** underwired/nursing bra; **s. de sport** sports bra

soutif [sutif] *nm Fam* bra

soutirer [sutire] *vt* (**a**) *(vin)* to rack, to decant (**b**) **s. qch à qn** *(argent, information)* to extract sth from sb

souvenance [suvnɑ̃s] *nf* avoir s. de qch to recollect sth

souvenir [70] [suvnir] **1** *nm* (**a**) *(réminiscence)* memory; **en s.** de in memory of; **en s. du passé** for old times' sake; **garder un bon/mauvais s.** de qch to have good/bad memories of sth; **souvenirs d'enfance** childhood memories (**b**) *(objet)* memento; *(touristique)* souvenir (**c**) *(dans une formule de politesse)* **mes meilleurs souvenirs à votre sœur** (my) kindest regards to your sister
  2 *v* impersonnel *Litt* **il me souvient que...** I recall that...
  3 se souvenir *vpr* **se s. de** to remember; **se s. que** to remember that; **je ne me souviens de rien** I can't remember anything

souvent [suvɑ̃] *adv* often; **le plus s.** usually, more often than not; **plus s. qu'à son tour** far too often

souverain, -e [suvrɛ̃, -ɛn] **1** *adj (puissance, état, remède)* sovereign; *(bonheur, mépris)* supreme
  2 *nm,f* sovereign

souverainement [suvrɛnmɑ̃] *adv (intelligent, doué)* supremely; *(agacer, déplaire)* intensely

souveraineté [suvrɛnte] *nf* sovereignty

soviétique [sɔvjetik] *Anciennement* **1** *adj* Soviet
  2 *nmf* S. Soviet (citizen)

soyeux, -euse [swajø, -øz] **1** *adj* silky
  2 *nm* silk merchant

soyez, soyons *etc voir* **être²**

SPA [ɛspea] *nf (abrév* **Société protectrice des animaux)** *Br* ≃ RSPCA, *Am* ≃ ASPCA

spa [spa] *nm* (**a**) *(bain à remous)* spa bath (**b**) *(centre d'hydrothérapie)* (health) spa

spacieusement [spasjøzmɑ̃] *adv* **être logé s.** to have spacious accommodation

spacieux, -euse [spasjø, -øz] *adj* spacious

spaghetti [spageti] *nm* piece of spaghetti; **des spaghettis** spaghetti

spam [spam] *nm Ordinat* spam e-mail

spammer [spamœr] *vt Ordinat* to spam

spammeur [spame] *nm Ordinat* spammer

spamming [spamiŋ] *nm Ordinat* spamming

sparadrap [sparadra] *nm Br* sticking plaster, *Am* adhesive tape

spartiate [sparsjat] **1** *adj* Spartan; *Fig* **à la s.** in a spartan way
  2 *nfpl* **spartiates** Roman sandals

spasme [spasm] *nm* spasm

spasmodique [spasmɔdik] *adj* spasmodic

spasmophilie [spasmɔfili] *nf* spasmophilia

spatial, -e, -aux, -ales [spasjal, -o] *adj* (**a**) *(de l'espace)* spatial (**b**) *(de l'espace interplanétaire)* space

spatio-temporel, -elle (*mpl* **spatio-temporels**, *fpl* **spatio-temporelles**) [spasjotɑ̃pɔrɛl] *adj* spatio-temporal

spatule [spatyl] *nf* (**a**) *(de cuisinier, de peintre)* spatula (**b**) *(de ski)* tip (**c**) *(oiseau)* spoonbill

speaker, speakerine [spikœr, spikrin] *nm,f* announcer

spécial, -e, -aux, -ales [spesjal, -o] *adj* (**a**) *(particulier, extraordinaire)* special (**b**) *(bizarre)* peculiar, odd

spécialement [spesjalmɑ̃] *adv (particulièrement)* especially, particularly; *(exprès)* specially

spécialisation [spesjalizasjɔ̃] *nf* specialization

spécialisé, -e [spesjalize] *adj (travail, enseignement)* specialized; *(ouvrier)* semi-skilled; *(école, hôpital)* special

spécialiser [spesjalize] **se spécialiser** *vpr* to specialize (**dans** *ou* **en** in)

spécialiste [spesjalist] *nmf* specialist (**de/en** in)

spécialité [spesjalite] *nf Br* speciality, *Am* specialty; **s. maison** speciality of the house

spécieux, -euse [spesjø, -øz] *adj Litt* specious

spécification [spesifikasjɔ̃] *nf* specification

spécificité [spesifisite] *nf* distinctiveness

spécifier [66] [spesifje] *vt* to specify

spécifique [spesifik] *adj* specific

spécifiquement [spesifikmɑ̃] *adv* specifically

spécimen [spesimɛn] *nm* (**a**) *(modèle)* specimen (**b**) *(livre, fascicule)* specimen copy

spectacle [spɛktakl] *nm* (**a**) *(représentation)* show; **le s.** *(industrie)* show business; **film à grand s.** epic (film); **s. de variétés** variety show (**b**) *(vue)* sight; **se donner en s.** to make an exhibition *or* a spectacle of oneself

spectaculaire [spɛktakylɛr] *adj* spectacular

spectateur, -trice [spɛktatœr, -tris] *nm,f* (**a**) *(d'un événement sportif)* spectator; *(d'un spectacle)* member of the audience; **spectateurs** *(au spectacle)* audience (**b**) *(témoin)* witness

spectre [spɛktr] *nm* (**a**) *(fantôme)* ghost, phantom; *Fig (de la guerre, de la misère)* spectre (**b**) *Phys* spectrum

spéculateur, trice [spekylatœr, -tris] *nm,f* speculator

spéculation [spekylasjɔ̃] *nf* speculation; **s. à la baisse** bear operations; **s. à la hausse** bull operations

spéculer [spekyle] *vi* (**a**) *(intellectuellement)* to speculate (**sur** on *or* about) (**b**) *(à la Bourse)* to speculate (**sur** on); *Fig* **s. sur qch** to count *or* bank on sth

spéculoos [spekylos] *nm Belg* ≃ ginger biscuit

speech (*pl* **speeches**) [spitʃ] *nm Fam* speech; **faire un s.** to make a speech; **faire un s. à qn sur qch** to give sb a speech about sth

speed [spid] *Fam* **1** *adj (nerveux)* hyper
  2 *nm (amphétamines)* speed

speedé, -e [spide] *adj Fam (hyperactif)* hyper

speeder [spide] *vi Fam* to get a move on

spéléologie [speleɔlɔʒi] *nf* (**a**) *(exploration) Br* potholing, *Am* spelunking (**b**) *(science)* speleology

spéléologue [speleɔlɔg] *nmf* (**a**) *(explorateur) Br* potholer, *Am* spelunker (**b**) *(spécialiste)* speleologist

spencer [spɛ̃sɛr] *nm* short jacket

spermatozoïde [spɛrmatozɔid] *nm* spermatozoon

sperme [spɛrm] *nm* sperm, semen

sphère [sfɛr] *nf* (**a**) *(boule)* sphere (**b**) *(d'activité, d'influence)* sphere; **les hautes sphères de la politique** the higher realms of politics

sphérique [sferik] *adj* spherical

sphinx [sfɛ̃ks] *nm* (**a**) *(monstre fabuleux)* sphinx (**b**) *(insecte)* hawk *or* sphinx moth

spirale [spiral] *nf* spiral; **en s.** *(s'élever)* in a spiral; *(escalier, coquillage)* spiral

spiritisme [spiritism] *nm* spiritualism

spiritualité [spiritɥalite] *nf* spirituality

spirituel, -elle [spiritɥɛl] *adj* (**a**) *(pouvoir, vie)* spiritual (**b**) *(fin)* witty; *Ironique* **que c'est s.!** very witty!

spirituellement [spiritɥɛlmɑ̃] *adv* (**a**) *(moralement)* spiritually (**b**) *(finement)* wittily

spiritueux [spiritɥø] *nm* spirit

spleen [splin] *nm Litt* spleen, melancholy; **avoir le s.** to be melancholic

splendeur [splɑ̃dœr] *nf* splendour; **c'est une s.** it's splendid

splendide [splãdid] *adj* splendid; *(soleil)* brilliant; *(œuvre d'art, personne)* magnificent

splendidement [splãdidmã] *adv* splendidly

spolier [66] [spɔlje] *vt* to despoil (**de** of)

spongieux, -euse [spɔ̃ʒjø, -øz] *adj* spongy

sponsor [spɔnsɔr] *nm* sponsor

sponsoriser [spɔnsɔrize] *vt* to sponsor

spontané, -e [spɔ̃tane] *adj* spontaneous

spontanéité [spɔ̃taneite] *nf* spontaneity

spontanément [spɔ̃tanemã] *adv* spontaneously

sporadique [spɔradik] *adj* sporadic

spore [spɔr] *nf* spore

sport [spɔr] **1** *nm* (**a**) *(activité)* sport; **de s.** *(chaussures, terrain, voiture)* sports; **faire du s.** to do sport; **s. d'équipe/individuel** team/individual sport; **s. de combat** combat sport; **sports extrêmes** extreme sports; **sports d'hiver** winter sports; **aller aux sports d'hiver** to go skiing/snowboarding; **sports nautiques** water sports (**b**) *Fam (locutions)* **il va y avoir du s.!** this is going to be fun!; **c'est du s.** it's a tough job
2 *adj inv (vêtement)* casual

sportif, -ive [spɔrtif, -iv] **1** *adj* (**a**) *(résultats, journal, club)* sports (**b**) *(fair-play)* sporting (**c**) *(dynamique)* sporty
2 *nm,f* sportsman, *f* sportswoman

sportivité [spɔrtivite] *nf* sportsmanship

spot [spɔt] *nm* (**a**) *(projecteur)* spot, spotlight (**b**) *TV & Rad* **s. publicitaire** commercial, advert

spoutnik [sputnik] *nm* sputnik

spray [sprɛ] *nm* spray, aerosol; **parfum en s.** spray-on perfume

sprint [sprint] *nm* *(accélération finale)* (final) sprint; *(course)* sprint; *Fam* **piquer un s.** to sprint

sprinter¹ [sprintœr] *nm* sprinter

sprinter² [sprinte] *vi* to sprint

squale [skwal] *nm* shark

square [skwar] *nm* public garden

squash [skwaʃ] *nm* squash

squat [skwat] *nm* squat

squatter¹ [skwatœr] *nm* squatter

squatter², squattériser [skwate], [skwaterize] *vt (bâtiment)* to squat in; *Fam Fig (monopoliser)* to take over, to hog

squatteur, -euse [skwatœr, -øz] *nm,f* squatter

squelette [skəlɛt] *nm* (**a**) *(d'être humain, d'animal)* skeleton; **c'est un vrai s.** he's/she's a bag of bones; **c'est un s. ambulant** he's/she's a walking skeleton (**b**) *Fig (de roman, de bâtiment)* skeleton, framework

squelettique [skəlɛtik] *adj* (**a**) *(personne, partie du corps)* skeleton-like (**b**) *(personnel, armée)* skeleton

SRAS [sras] *nm Méd (abrév* **syndrome respiratoire aigu sévère**) SARS

Sri Lanka [srilãka] *nm* **le S.** Sri Lanka

sri lankais, -e [srilãkɛ, -ɛz] **1** *adj* Sri Lankan
2 *nm,f* **S.** Sri Lankan

SRPJ [ɛsɛrpeʒi] *nm (abrév* **Service régional de la police judiciaire**) = regional crime unit

St *(abrév* **Saint**) St

stabilisateur, -trice [stabilizatœr, -tris] **1** *adj* stabilizing
2 *nm (de vélo)* stabilizer

stabilisation [stabilizasjɔ̃] *nf* stabilization

stabiliser [stabilize] **1** *vt* to stabilize
2 se stabiliser *vpr* to stabilize; *(personne)* to settle down

stabilité [stabilite] *nf* stability

stable [stabl] *adj* stable

stade [stad] *nm* (**a**) *(sportif)* stadium (**b**) *(étape)* stage; **en être au s. embryonnaire** to be at an embryonic stage

stage [staʒ] *nm (professionnel)* training course; **être en s.** to be on a training course; **s. en entreprise** *Br* work placement, *Am* internship; **s. de formation** training course, *Am* internship; **faire un s. de tennis/de voile** to have tennis/sailing lessons; *(vacances)* to go on a tennis/sailing *Br* holiday *or Am* vacation

stagiaire [staʒjɛr] *adj & nmf* trainee, *Am* intern

stagnant, -e [stagnã, -ãt] *adj* stagnant

stagnation [stagnasjɔ̃] *nf* stagnation

stagner [stagne] *vi* to stagnate

stalactite [stalaktit] *nf* stalactite

stalagmite [stalagmit] *nf* stalagmite

stalinien, -enne [stalinjɛ̃, -ɛn] *adj & nm,f* Stalinist

stalle [stal] *nf (dans une écurie, une église)* stall

stand [stãd] *nm* (**a**) *(d'exposition)* stand; *(de foire)* stall; **s. de tir** rifle range (**b**) *(de course automobile)* **s. (de ravitaillement)** pit

standard [stãdar] **1** *adj inv* standard
2 *nm* (**a**) *(norme)* standard (**b**) **s. (téléphonique)** switchboard

standardisation [stãdardizasjɔ̃] *nf* standardization

standardiser [stãdardize] *vt* to standardize

standardiste [stãdardist] *nmf* (switchboard) operator

standing [stãdiŋ] *nm* (social) standing; **de grand s.** *(appartement)* luxury; *(quartier)* select

staphylocoque [stafilɔkɔk] *nm* staphylococcus

star [star] *nf* star

starlette [starlɛt] *nf* starlet

starter [startɛr] *nm* (**a**) *(de voiture)* choke (**b**) *(dans une course)* starter

starting-block *(pl* **starting-blocks**) [startiŋblɔk] *nm* starting block

start-up *(pl* **start-ups**) [startœp] *nf* dot com (company)

station [stasjɔ̃] *nf* (**a**) *(de métro)* station; *(de train)* halt; *(de bus)* stop; **s. de taxis** *Br* taxi rank, *Am* taxi stand (**b**) *(ville, village)* **s. balnéaire** seaside resort; **s. de ski** ski resort; **s. de sports d'hiver** winter sports resort; **s. thermale** spa town (**c**) *(établissement)* station; **s. d'essence** *Br* petrol *or Am* gas station; **s. de lavage** car wash; **s. spatiale** space station (**d**) *(position)* **s. debout** standing position (**e**) **s. de radio** radio station (**f**) *Ordinat (d'un réseau)* station, node; **s. d'accueil** docking station; **s. individuelle** stand-alone workstation; **s. de travail** workstation

stationnaire [stasjɔnɛr] *adj (satellite)* stationary; *(baromètre)* steady; *(état d'un malade)* stable

stationnement [stasjɔnmã] *nm* (**a**) *(de voitures)* parking; **en s.** parked; **s. alterné semi-mensuel** = system in which parking is permitted on one side of the street only for alternating periods of two weeks; **s. interdit** *(sur panneau)* no parking; ≃ *(sur panneau)* restricted parking (**b**) *Can (parking)* car park, *Am* parking lot

stationner [stasjɔne] *vi* to park; **défense de s.** *(sur panneau)* no parking

station-service *(pl* **stations-service**) [stasjɔ̃sɛrvis] *nf* service station, *Br* petrol *or Am* gas station

statique [statik] **1** *adj* static
2 *nf* statics *(singulier)*

statisticien, -enne [statistisjɛ̃, -ɛn] *nm,f* statistician

statistique [statistik] **1** *adj* statistical
  2 *nf* (**a**) *(donnée)* statistic (**b**) *(science)* statistics *(singulier)*
statistiquement [statistikmã] *adv* statistically
statuaire [statɥɛr] *adj & nf* statuary
statue [staty] *nf* statue
statuer [statɥe] **statuer sur** *vt ind* to give a ruling on
statuette [statɥɛt] *nf* statuette
statu quo [statykwo] *nm* status quo
stature [statyr] *nf* stature
statut [staty] *nm* (**a**) *(position)* status; **s. juridique** *ou* **légal** legal status; **s. social** social status (**b**) **statuts** *(d'une société, d'une association)* statutes
statutaire [statytɛr] *adj* statutory
Ste *(abrév* **Sainte)** St
Sté *(abrév* **Société)** Co
steak [stɛk] *nm* steak; **s. frites** steak and chips; **un s. haché** a hamburger, *Br* a beefburger; **du s. haché** *Br* mince, *Am* ground beef; **s. au poivre** pepper steak; **s. tartare** steak tartare *(raw minced beef served with a raw egg)*
stèle [stɛl] *nf* stele
stellaire [stelɛr] *adj* stellar
stencil [stɛnsil] *nm* stencil
sténo [steno] **1** *nf (abrév* **sténographie)** shorthand; **prendre qch en s.** to take sth down in shorthand
  2 *nmf (abrév* **sténographe)** stenographer
sténodactylo [stenodaktilo] **1** *nf* shorthand typing
  2 *nmf* shorthand typist
sténodactylographie [stenodaktilɔgrafi] *nf* shorthand typing
sténographe [stenɔgraf] *nmf* stenographer
sténographie [stenɔgrafi] *nf* shorthand
sténographier [66] [stenɔgrafje] *vt* to take down in shorthand
sténographique [stenɔgrafik] *adj* shorthand
stentor [stɑ̃tɔr] *nm voir* **voix**
steppe [stɛp] *nf* steppe
stéréo [stereo] **1** *adj inv* stereo
  2 *nf* stereo; **en s.** in stereo
stéréophonie [stereɔfɔni] *nf* stereophony
stéréophonique [stereɔfɔnik] *adj* stereophonic
stéréotype [stereotip] *nm* stereotype
stéréotypé, -e [stereotipe] *adj* stereotyped
stérile [steril] *adj* (**a**) *(personne, animal)* sterile; *(mariage)* childless; *(terre)* barren (**b**) *(discussion, efforts)* futile (**c**) *(instrument, chambre)* sterile
stérilet [sterilɛ] *nm* coil, IUD
stérilisation [sterilizasjɔ̃] *nf* sterilization
stériliser [sterilize] *vt* to sterilize
stérilité [sterilite] *nf* (**a**) *(d'une personne, d'un animal)* sterility; *(de la terre)* barrenness (**b**) *(d'une discussion, d'efforts)* futility
sterling [stɛrliŋ] *adj inv voir* **livre²**
sterne [stɛrn] *nf* tern
sternum [stɛrnɔm] *nm* breastbone, *Spéc* sternum
stéthoscope [stetɔskɔp] *nm* stethoscope
steward [stjuwart, stiwart] *nm* steward
stick [stik] *nm (de colle, pour les lèvres)* stick; **déodorant en s.** stick deodorant
stigmate [stigmat] *nm* (**a**) *(trace)* mark (**b**) *Rel* **stigmates** stigmata
stigmatiser [stigmatize] *vt (dénoncer)* to condemn
stimulant, -e [stimylɑ̃, -ɑ̃t] **1** *adj* stimulating; *(résultats)* encouraging
  2 *nm* (**a**) *(remède)* stimulant (**b**) *Fig* stimulus, incentive

stimulateur [stimylatœr] *nm* **s. cardiaque** pacemaker
stimulation [stimylasjɔ̃] *nf* stimulation
stimuler [stimyle] *vt* to stimulate
stipuler [stipyle] *vt* to stipulate
stock [stɔk] *nm* stock; **en s.** in stock
stockage [stɔkaʒ] *nm* (**a**) *(de marchandises)* stocking (**b**) *Ordinat* storage; **s. en mémoire tampon** buffering
stock-car *(pl* **stock-cars)** [stɔkkar] *nm (voiture)* stock car; *(sport)* stock-car racing
stocker [stɔke] *vt* (**a**) *(marchandises)* to stock (**b**) *Ordinat* to store
Stockholm [stɔkɔlm] *n* Stockholm
stoïcisme [stɔisism] *nm* (**a**) *(attitude)* stoicism (**b**) *(doctrine philosophique)* Stoicism
stoïque [stɔik] *adj* stoical
stoïquement [stɔikmɑ̃] *adv* stoically
stomatologie [stɔmatɔlɔʒi] *nf* stomatology
stop [stɔp] **1** *exclam* stop!; *(dans un télégramme)* stop; **savoir dire s.** to know when to say stop
  2 *nm* (**a**) *(panneau)* stop sign (**b**) *(d'un véhicule)* brake light (**c**) *Fam (auto-stop)* hitching, hitchhiking; **faire du s.** to hitch, to hitchhike
stopper [stɔpe] *vt & vi (arrêter)* to stop
store [stɔr] *nm* (**a**) *(de fenêtre)* blind; **s. vénitien** Venetian blind (**b**) *(de magasin)* awning
strabisme [strabism] *nm* squint
stradivarius [stradivarjys] *nm* Stradivarius
strangulation [strɑ̃gylasjɔ̃] *nf* strangulation
strapontin [strapɔ̃tɛ̃] *nm (siège)* folding seat, tip-up seat
Strasbourg [strazbur] *n* Strasbourg
strasbourgeois, -e [strazburʒwa, -waz] **1** *adj* of Strasbourg
  2 *nm,f* **S.** person from Strasbourg
strass [stras] *nm* paste; **en s.** *(bijou)* paste
stratagème [strataʒɛm] *nm* stratagem
strate [strat] *nm* stratum
stratège [strateʒ] *nm* strategist
stratégie [strateʒi] *nf* strategy
stratégique [strateʒik] *adj* strategic
stratification [stratifikasjɔ̃] *nf* stratification
stratifié, -e [stratifje] *adj* (**a**) *(roche)* stratified (**b**) *(bois)* laminated
stratosphère [stratɔsfɛr] *nf* stratosphere
streptocoque [strɛptɔkɔk] *nm* streptococcus
stress [strɛs] *nm* stress
stressant, -e [strɛsɑ̃, -ɑ̃t] *adj* stressful
stresser [strɛse] **1** *vt* to put under stress; **être stressé** to be stressed
  2 *vi Fam* to get stressed
Stretch® [strɛtʃ] *nm* stretch material; **une jupe en S.** a stretch skirt
strict, -e [strikt] *adj* (**a**) *(obligation, principes)* strict; **au sens s.** in the strict sense of the word; **le s. minimum** the bare minimum; **le s. nécessaire** the bare essentials; **c'est la stricte vérité** that's the absolute truth; **c'est son droit le plus s.** it's his/her absolute right (**b**) *(personne)* strict *(sur* about) (**c**) *(costume, coupe de cheveux)* severe
strictement [striktəmã] *adv* (**a**) *(rigoureusement)* strictly; **je ne comprends s. rien** I don't understand a single thing (**b**) *(habillé)* severely
stricto sensu [striktosɛ̃sy] *adv* strictly speaking
strident, -e [stridã, -ãt] *adj* strident, shrill
strie [stri] *nf* groove

strié, -e [strije] *adj* grooved
string [striŋ] *nm* G-string
strip-tease (*pl* **strip-teases**) [striptiz] *nm* striptease
strip-teaseuse (*pl* **strip-teaseuses**) [striptizøz] *nf* stripper, striptease artist
stroboscope [strɔbɔskɔp] *nm* strobe, stroboscope
strophe [strɔf] *nf* stanza, verse
structural, -e, -aux, -ales [stryktyral, -o] *adj* structural
structuralement [stryktyralmã] *adv* structurally
structuralisme [stryktyralism] *nm* structuralism
structuraliste [stryktyralist] *adj & nmf* structuralist
structure [stryktyr] *nf* (**a**) (*disposition*) structure (**b**) (*organisation*) **s. d'accueil** reception facilities (**c**) *Or-dinat* **s. en anneau** ring structure; **s. en arbre** tree structure; **s. de bloc** block structure
structuré, -e [stryktyre] *adj* (*ensemble, langage*) structured
structurel, -elle [stryktyrɛl] *adj* structural
structurer [stryktyre] *vt* to structure
strychnine [striknin] *nf* strychnine
stuc [styk] *nm* stucco
studieusement [stydjøzmã] *adv* studiously
studieux, -euse [stydjø, -øz] *adj* (*personne*) studious; (*vacances*) study
studio [stydjo] *nm* (**a**) (*pour travailler*) studio; **s. de ci-néma** film studio; **tourné en s.** filmed in the studio; **s. d'enregistrement** recording studio (**b**) (*logement*) *Br* studio flat, *Am* studio apartment
stupéfaction [stypefaksjɔ̃] *nf* amazement, astonishment
stupéfait, -e [stypefɛ, -ɛt] *adj* amazed, astounded
stupéfiant, -e [stypefjã, -ãt] **1** *adj* amazing, astounding **2** *nm* drug, narcotic
stupéfier [66] [stypefje] *vt* to amaze, to astound
stupeur [stypœr] *nf* amazement, astonishment
stupide [stypid] *adj* stupid
stupidement [stypidmã] *adv* stupidly
stupidité [stypidite] *nf* (**a**) (*caractère*) stupidity (**b**) (*remarque*) stupid remark; **dire des stupidités** to say stupid things
style [stil] *nm* style; **de s.** (*meuble*) period; **s. Louis XIII/Régence** Louis XIII-/Regency-style; **avoir du s.** to have style, to be stylish; *Fam* **ça serait bien son s.!** that would be just his/her style!; **s. de vie** lifestyle; *Gram* **s. direct/indirect** direct/indirect speech
stylé, -e [stile] *adj* (*domestique*) trained
stylet [stilɛ] *nm* (**a**) (*poignard*) stiletto (**b**) *Ordinat* **s. lumineux** light pen
styliser [stilize] *vt* to stylize
stylisme [stilism] *nm* designing
styliste [stilist] *nmf* designer
stylistique [stilistik] **1** *adj* stylistic **2** *nf* stylistics (*singulier*)
stylo [stilo] *nm* pen; **s. à encre** *ou* **à plume** fountain pen; **s. (à) bille** ballpoint (pen), *Br* biro®; *Ordinat* **s. optique** light pen
stylo-feutre (*pl* **stylos-feutres**) [stiloføtr] *nm* felt-tip (pen)
su¹, -e *pp de* **savoir²**
su² [sy] *nm* **au vu et au su de tout le monde** quite openly
suave [sɥav] *adj* (**a**) (*parfum, mélodie*) sweet (**b**) (*ton, manières*) suave, smooth
suavité [sɥavite] *nf* (**a**) (*d'un parfum, d'une mélodie*) sweetness (**b**) (*des manières*) suavity

subalterne [sybaltɛrn] **1** *adj* (*officier, position*) subordinate, minor; (*employé*) junior **2** *nmf* subordinate
subconscient, -e [sybkɔ̃sjã, -ãt] *adj & nm* subconscious
subdiviser [sybdivize] **1** *vt* to subdivide (**en** into) **2 se subdiviser** *vpr* to be subdivided (**en** into)
subdivision [sybdivizjɔ̃] *nf* subdivision
subir [sybir] *vt* (**a**) (*violence, conséquences*) to suffer; (*défaite, pertes*) to suffer, to sustain; (*influence*) to be under; **faire s. qch à qn** to subject sb to sth (**b**) (*examen, opération, changement*) to undergo (**c**) *Fam* (*personne*) to put up with
subit, -e [sybi, -it] *adj* sudden
subitement [sybitmã] *adv* suddenly, all of a sudden
subjectif, -ive [sybʒɛktif, -iv] *adj* subjective
subjectivement [sybʒɛktivmã] *adv* subjectively
subjectivité [sybʒɛktivite] *nf* subjectivity
subjonctif, -ive [sybʒɔ̃ktif, -iv] *Gram* **1** *adj* subjunctive **2** *nm* subjunctive; **au s.** in the subjunctive
subjuguer [sybʒyge] *vt* (*séduire*) to captivate
sublimation [syblimasjɔ̃] *nf* sublimation
sublime [syblim] **1** *adj* sublime **2** *nm* **le s.** the sublime
sublimement [syblimmã] *adv* sublimely
sublimer [syblime] *vt* to sublimate
subliminal, -e, -aux, -ales [sybliminal, -o] *adj* subliminal
submerger [45] [sybmɛrʒe] *vt* to submerge; **submergé de travail** snowed under with work
submersible [sybmɛrsibl] **1** *adj* submersible **2** *nm* submarine
subodorer [sybɔdɔre] *vt* *Fam* (*danger, complot*) to scent
subordination [sybɔrdinasjɔ̃] *nf* subordination
subordonné, -e [sybɔrdɔne] **1** *adj* *Gram* (*proposition*) subordinate **2** *nm,f* (*personne*) subordinate **3** *nf* **subordonnée** *Gram* subordinate clause
subordonner [sybɔrdɔne] *vt* (**a**) (*dans une hiérarchie*) **être subordonné à qn** to be subordinate to sb (**b**) (*faire passer après*) **s. qch à qch** to accord less importance to sth than to sth (**c**) (*faire dépendre*) **être subordonné à qch** to be dependent on sth
subornation [sybɔrnasjɔ̃] *nf* *Jur* subornation
suborner [sybɔrne] *vt* (**a**) *Jur* (*témoin*) to suborn, to bribe (**b**) *Litt* (*séduire*) to seduce
subrepticement [sybrɛptismã] *adv* surreptitiously
subséquent, -e [sypsekã, -ãt] *adj* subsequent
subside [sybzid] *nm* subsidy, grant
subsidiaire [sybzidjɛr] *adj* subsidiary
subsidier [66] [sybzidje] *vt* *Belg* (*subventionner*) to subsidize
subsistance [sybzistãs] *nf* subsistence; **pourvoir à la s. de sa famille** to keep *or* support one's family
subsistant, -e [sybzistã, -ãt] *adj* remaining
subsister [sybziste] *vi* (**a**) (*chose*) to remain (**b**) (*personne*) to subsist
substance [sypstãs] *nf* substance; **en s.** in substance
substantiel, -elle [sypstãsjɛl] *adj* substantial
substantiellement [sypstãsjɛlmã] *adv* substantially
substantif, -ive [sypstãtif, -iv] *Gram* **1** *adj* substantive **2** *nm* noun, substantive
substantiver [sypstãtive] *vt* to use as a noun *or* substantively

substituer [sypstitɥe] **1** *vt* **s. qn/qch à** to substitute sb/sth for
2 se substituer *vpr* **se s. à** to substitute for, to take the place of
substitut [sypstity] *nm* (**a**) *Jur* deputy public prosecutor (**b**) *(remplacement)* substitute
substitution [sypstitysjɔ̃] *nf* substitution
substrat [sypstra] *nm Géol* substratum
subterfuge [sypterfyʒ] *nm* subterfuge; **user de subterfuges** to resort to subterfuge
subtil, -e [syptil] *adj* subtle
subtilement [syptilmã] *adv* subtly
subtiliser [syptilize] *vt* to make off with; **on lui a subtilisé son portefeuille** someone made off with his/her wallet
subtilité [syptilite] *nf* subtlety
subtropical, -e, -aux, -ales [syptrɔpikal, -o] *adj* subtropical
subvenir [70] [sybvənir] **subvenir à** *vt ind* to meet
subvention [sybvãsjɔ̃] *nf* subsidy, grant
subventionner [sybvãsjɔne] *vt* to subsidize
subversif, -ive [sybversif, -iv] *adj* subversive
subversion [sybversjɔ̃] *nf* subversion
suc [syk] *nm* (**a**) *(de fruit, de viande)* juice (**b**) *Fig & Litt* essence
succédané [syksedane] *nm* substitute (**de** for)
succéder [syksede] **1 succéder à** *vt ind* (**a**) *(personne)* to succeed, to take over from (**b**) *(phénomène)* **la résignation succéda à la colère** anger gave way to resignation
2 se succéder *vpr* to follow one another
succès [syksɛ] *nm* (**a**) *(réussite)* success; **avoir du s.** *(œuvre, artiste)* to be successful; *(suggestion)* to be very well-received; **il a beaucoup de s. auprès des jeunes** he's very popular with young people; **avoir un s. fou (auprès de qn)** to be a big hit (with sb); **faire le s. de qn** to make sb's name; **avec s.** successfully; **sans s.** unsuccessfully; **à s.** successful (**b**) *(pièce, chanson)* hit, success
successeur [syksesœr] *nm* successor (**de** to)
successif, -ive [syksesif, -iv] *adj* successive
succession [syksesjɔ̃] *nf* (**a**) *(suite)* succession (**b**) *(remplacement)* succession (**à** to); **prendre la s. de qn** to succeed sb, to take over from sb (**c**) *Jur (par héritage)* succession; *(biens)* inheritance
successivement [syksesivmã] *adv* successively
succinct, -e [syksɛ̃, -ɛ̃t] *adj* succinct
succinctement [syksɛ̃tmã] *adv* succinctly
succion [sysjɔ̃, syksjɔ̃] *nf* suction
succomber [sykɔ̃be] *vi* to succumb (**à** to); **s. sous le nombre** to yield to greater numbers
succulent, -e [sykylã, -ãt] *adj (nourriture)* succulent
succursale [sykyrsal] *nf* branch
sucer [16] [syse] *vt* to suck
sucette [sysɛt] *nf* (**a**) *(confiserie)* lollipop (**b**) *(tétine)* Br dummy, Am pacifier
suçon [sysɔ̃] *nm Fam Br* lovebite, Am hickey
suçoter [sysɔte] *vt* to suck (at)
sucre [sykr] *nm* (**a**) *(aliment, morceau)* sugar; *Fig* **être tout s. tout miel** to be all sweetness and light; **s. candi** candy sugar; **s. de canne** cane sugar; **s. cristallisé** granulated sugar; **s. glace** Br icing or Am confectioner's sugar; **s. en morceaux/en poudre** lump/caster sugar; **s. roux** brown sugar; **s. semoule** caster sugar (**b**) **s. d'orge** *(substance)* barley sugar; *(bâton)* stick of barley sugar

sucré, -e [sykre] *adj* (**a**) *(naturellement)* sweet; *(additionné de sucre)* sweetened (**b**) *Fig (paroles, sourire)* sugary
sucrer [sykre] **1** *vt* (**a**) *(boisson)* to sugar; *(mets)* to sweeten; *Fam Fig* **s. les fraises** *(trembler)* to shake; *(être gâteux)* to be an old dodderer (**b**) *Fam (supprimer) (passage, émission)* to cut; **on lui a sucré sa prime** he/she has been deprived of his/her bonus
2 *vi (miel, aspartame)* to sweeten
3 se sucrer *vpr Fam* (**a**) *(prendre du sucre)* to help oneself to sugar (**b**) *(s'enrichir)* to line one's pockets
sucrerie [sykrəri] *nf* (**a**) *(usine)* sugar refinery (**b**) *(friandise)* sucreries sweet things
Sucrette® [sykrɛt] *nf* (artificial) sweetener
sucrier, -ère [sykrije, -ɛr] **1** *adj* sugar
2 *nm* (**a**) *(récipient)* sugar bowl; *(verseur)* sugar shaker (**b**) *(fabricant)* sugar manufacturer
sud [syd] **1** *nm* south; **le vent du s.** the south wind; **dans le S. de l'Angleterre** in the South of England; **au s.** in the south; **au s. de** (to the) south of; **vers le s.** south, southward
2 *adj inv* southern
sud-africain, -e (*mpl* **sud-africains**, *fpl* **sud-africaines**) [sydafrikɛ̃, -ɛn] **1** *adj* South African
2 *nm,f* **S.-A.** South African
sud-américain, -e (*mpl* **sud-américains**, *fpl* **sud-américaines**) [sydamerikɛ̃, -ɛn] **1** *adj* South American
2 *nm,f* **S.-A.** South American
sud-coréen, -enne (*mpl* **sud-coréens**, *fpl* **sud-coréennes**) [sydkɔreɛ̃, -ɛn] **1** *adj* South Korean
2 *nm,f* **S.-C.** South Korean
sud-est [sydɛst] **1** *nm* south-east; **le S.-E. asiatique** South-east Asia
2 *adj inv* south-east
sudiste [sydist] *adj & nmf Hist* Confederate
sud-ouest [sydwɛst] *nm & adj inv* south-west
Suède [sɥɛd] *nf* **la S.** Sweden
suédine [sɥedin] *nf* suedette
suédois, -e [sɥedwa, -az] **1** *adj* Swedish
2 *nm,f* **S.** Swede
3 *nm (langue)* Swedish
suée [sɥe] *nf Fam* sweat; **prendre une s.** to work up a sweat
suer [sɥe] **1** *vi* (**a**) *(personne)* to sweat; **s. à grosses gouttes** to be pouring with sweat; *Fam* **faire s. qn** *(embêter)* to bug sb; *Fam* **se faire s.** to be bored stiff (**b**) *(mur)* to ooze (**c**) *Fig (travailler)* to labour, to sweat
2 *vt (ennui, hypocrisie)* to ooze; **s. sang et eau** to sweat blood and tears
sueur [sɥœr] *nf* sweat; **être en s.** to be sweating or in a sweat; **avoir des sueurs froides** to be in a cold sweat; **à la s. de son front** by the sweat of one's brow
suffire [19b] [syfir] **1** *vi* to be enough, to be sufficient (**à/pour** for); **ça suffit!** that's enough!, that'll do!
2 *v impersonnel* **il suffit d'appuyer sur le bouton** you just have to press the button; **il suffit que je sorte deux minutes pour que le téléphone sonne** I only have to go out for two minutes for the phone to start ringing; **il a suffi de quelques mots pour le persuader** a few words were enough to persuade him
3 se suffire *vpr* **se s. (à soi-même)** to be self-sufficient
suffisamment [syfizamã] *adv* sufficiently, enough; **s. de** sufficient, enough
suffisance [syfizãs] *nf (vanité)* self-importance

suffisant, -e [syfizɑ̃, -ɑ̃t] *adj* (**a**) *(satisfaisant)* sufficient, enough (**b**) *(vaniteux)* self-important, conceited

suffixe [syfiks] *nm Gram & Ordinat* suffix

suffocant, -e [syfɔkɑ̃, -ɑ̃t] *adj* (**a**) *(chaleur)* suffocating, stifling (**b**) *Fig (nouvelle, réponse)* staggering, astounding

suffocation [syfɔkasjɔ̃] *nf* suffocation

suffoquer [syfɔke] **1** *vt* (**a**) *(sujet: odeur, fumée, chaleur)* to suffocate (**b**) *Fig (sujet: nouvelles)* to stagger, to astound
2 *vi* to suffocate, to choke; *Fig* **s. de colère/d'indignation** to choke with anger/indignation

suffrage [syfraʒ] *nm (voix)* vote; *(système)* suffrage; **s. direct/indirect** direct/indirect suffrage; **s. universel** universal suffrage

suffragette [syfraʒɛt] *nf* suffragette

suggérer [34] [sygʒere] *vt* (**a**) *(proposer)* to suggest (**à** to); **s. de faire qch** to suggest doing sth; **s. à qn de faire qch** to suggest to sb that he/she should do sth (**b**) *(faire penser à)* to evoke

suggestif, -ive [sygʒɛstif, -iv] *adj* (**a**) *(ton, musique)* evocative (**b**) *(plaisanterie, geste)* suggestive

suggestion [sygʒɛstjɔ̃] *nf* suggestion

suicidaire [sɥisidɛr] **1** *adj* suicidal
2 *nmf* suicidal person

suicide [sɥisid] *nm* suicide; **s. assisté** assisted suicide

suicidé, -e [sɥiside] **1** *adj* who has committed suicide
2 *nm,f* suicide

suicider [sɥiside] **se suicider** *vpr* to commit suicide

suie [sɥi] *nf* soot

suif [sɥif] *nm* tallow

suintant, -e [sɥĩtɑ̃, -ɑ̃t] *adj (rocher, mur)* oozing, dripping; *(plaie)* weeping

suintement [sɥĩtmɑ̃] *nm (de rochers, de mur)* oozing, dripping; *(de plaie)* weeping

suinter [sɥĩte] *vi* (**a**) *(rocher, mur)* to ooze, to drip; *(plaie)* to weep (**b**) *(liquide)* to ooze

suis *voir* être²

Suisse [sɥis] *nf* **la S.** Switzerland; **la S. alémanique/romande** German-speaking/French-speaking Switzerland

suisse [sɥis] **1** *adj* Swiss
2 *nmf* **S.** Swiss (person); **les Suisses** the Swiss
3 *nm* (**a**) *(employé d'église)* verger (**b**) *Can* chipmunk (**c**) *Fam Fig* **manger/boire qch en s.** to eat/drink sth all to oneself

Suissesse [sɥisɛs] *nf* Swiss (woman)

suit *voir* suivre

suite [sɥit] *nf* (**a**) *(reste)* rest (**de** of); **faire s. à qch** to follow on from sth; **s. à votre lettre du 10 mars** further to your letter of 10th March; **donner s. à** *(demande, lettre)* to follow up; *(commande)* to deal with; *(décision)* to give effect to; **prendre la s. de** *(personne)* to take over from; *(affaires)* to take over; **à la s. (les uns des autres)** one after the other; **à la s. de cette discussion** following this discussion (**b**) *(de roman, de film)* sequel; *(nouvel épisode)* continuation; **s. à la page 30** continued on page 30; **s. et fin** concluded; **la s. au prochain numéro** continued in the next issue (**c**) *(cohérence)* coherence; **sans s.** *(paroles, pensées)* incoherent; *(parler)* incoherently; **avoir de la s. dans les idées** to be very single-minded (**d**) *(escorte)* *(d'un président)* suite; *(d'un monarque)* retinue (**e**) *(série)* series (**f**) *Math* series (**g**) *Mus* suite (**h**) *(conséquence)* consequence; **suites** *(de maladie)* aftereffects; **mourir des suites d'une blessure** to die as the result of an injury; **par s.** consequently; **par s. de qch** as a result of sth (**i**) *(appartement)* suite (**j**) *(locutions)* **de s.** in a row; **et ainsi de s.** and so on; **tout de s.**, *Fam* **de s.** right away, immediately; **par la s.** afterwards

suivant¹ [sɥivɑ̃] **1** *prép* (**a**) *(direction)* along (**b**) *(selon)* according to (**c**) *(conformément à)* **s. son habitude** as is/was his/her habit
2 *conj* **s. que** according to whether

suivant², -e [sɥivɑ̃, -ɑ̃t] **1** *adj* (**a**) *(page, jour)* next, following; **voir page 6 et suivantes** see page 6 and following; **notre méthode est la suivante** our method is as follows (**b**) *(personne)* next
2 *nm,f (prochain)* **le s., la suivante** the next (one); **au s.!** next!
3 *nf* **suivante** *(personnage de théâtre)* attendant

suiveur [sɥivœr] *nm* (**a**) *(personne sans initiative)* follower (**de** of) (**b**) *(dans une course cycliste)* **les suiveurs** = officials and back-up squads following a cycle race

suivi, -e [sɥivi] **1** *adj* (**a**) *(discours, raisonnement)* coherent (**b**) *(correspondance)* regular; *(travail, effort, qualité)* consistent (**c**) *(émission, feuilleton)* popular
2 *nm (d'un dossier)* follow-up; *(d'une procédure)* monitoring; **assurer le s. de qch** *(dossier)* to follow sth through; *(progrès, procédure)* to monitor

suivre [65] [sɥivr] **1** *vt* (**a**) *(aller derrière)* to follow; **nous sommes suivis** we're being followed; **partez, je vous suis** you go, I'll follow (on); **s. qn des yeux** *ou* **du regard** to follow sb with one's eyes (**b**) *(se placer après)* to follow, to come after (**c**) *(longer)* to go along, to follow (**d**) *(accompagner)* to go with, to accompany (**e**) *(ligne de conduite, conseil, intuition)* to follow; **s. son idée** to do things one's own way (**f**) *(comprendre)* to follow; **là je ne la suis plus** she's lost me there (**g**) *(faire attention à, observer)* *(propos, démonstration)* to follow; *(malade, élève)* to monitor the progress of; **suivez bien ce que je vais dire** pay attention to what I'm about to say; **c'est une affaire à s.** it's worth keeping an eye on (**h**) *(mode, traitement, régime)* to follow; **s. le mouvement** to follow the crowd; **s. l'exemple de qn** to follow sb's example; **voici la marche à s.** this is what you have to do (**i**) *(assister à)* *(série de concerts, de conférences)* to attend; *(cours)* to follow
2 *vi* (**a**) *(venir après)* to follow; **le reste du repas suit** the rest of the meal is coming; **les personnes dont les noms suivent** the following people; **faire s. une lettre** to forward a letter; **(prière de) faire s.** *(sur une enveloppe)* please forward; **faire s. ses bagages** to have one's luggage sent on; **à s.** *(à la fin d'un feuilleton)* to be continued (**b**) *(comprendre)* to follow; *(faire attention)* to pay attention (**c**) *(élève)* to keep up (**d**) *Fig (progresser au même rythme)* *(salaire)* to keep up
3 **se suivre** *vpr* to follow each other

sujet¹, -ette [syʒɛ, -ɛt] **1** *adj* **être s. à qch** *(maladie)* to be subject *or* prone to sth; **être s. à caution** to be unconfirmed; **être s. à faire qch** to be apt *or* liable to do sth
2 *nm,f (d'un monarque)* subject

sujet² *nm* (**a**) *(cause)* cause (**de** for); **s. de querelle** *ou* **dispute** cause for dispute; **avoir s. de se plaindre** to have cause for complaint (**b**) *(thème)* subject, topic; **changer de s.** to change the subject; **au s. de qn/qch** about sb/sth; **elle ne m'a rien dit à ce s.** she said nothing to me about it; **à ce s., je voulais vous dire que...** talking of which, I meant to tell you (that)... (**c**) *Gram & Ling* subject (**d**) *(individu)* individual; *Scol* **brillant s.** brilliant pupil (**e**) *(d'une expérience)* subject

sujétion [syʒesjɔ̃] *nf Litt* (**a**) *(servitude)* subjection (à to) (**b**) *(contrainte)* constraint
sulfate [sylfat] *nm* sulphate
sulfater [sylfate] *vt Agr & Ind* to sulphate
sulfure [sylfyr] *nm* sulphide
sulfureux, -euse [sylfyrø, -øz] *adj* (**a**) *(substance)* sulphurous; *(eau, source)* sulphur (**b**) *Fig (écrits, discours)* subversive; *(charme)* fiendish
sulfurique [sylfyrik] *adj* sulphuric
sulfurisé, -e [sylfyrize] *adj (papier)* greaseproof
sulky [sylki] *nm* sulky
sultan [syltɑ̃] *nm* sultan
sultanat [syltana] *nm* sultanate
sultane [syltan] *nf (épouse d'un sultan)* sultana, sultaness
summum [sɔmɔm] *nm* **le s. de** the height of
sumo [symo] *nm* sumo (wrestling)
sunnite [synit] *adj & nmf* Sunni
sup [syp] *adj inv Fam* **faire des heures s.** to do overtime
super [sypɛr] **1** *adj inv & exclam Fam* great, fantastic
2 *nm Br* four-star (petrol), *Am* premium gas; **s. sans plomb** *Br* four-star *or Am* premium unleaded
super- [sypɛr] *préf Fam* very, really
superbe [sypɛrb] **1** *adj* (**a**) *(lieu, temps, spectacle)* superb, magnificent (**b**) *(personne)* beautiful
2 *nf Litt* pride, haughtiness
superbement [sypɛrbəmɑ̃] *adv* superbly, magnificently
supercarburant [sypɛrkarbyrɑ̃] *nm Br* four-star petrol, *Am* premium gasoline
supercherie [sypɛrʃəri] *nf* deception, hoax
supérette [sypɛrɛt] *nf* mini-market, small supermarket
superfétatoire [sypɛrfetatwar] *adj Litt* superfluous
superficialité [sypɛrfisjalite] *nf* superficiality
superficie [sypɛrfisi] *nf* (**a**) *(étendue)* (surface) area (**b**) *(surface)* surface
superficiel, -elle [sypɛrfisjɛl] *adj* superficial
superficiellement [sypɛrfisjɛlmɑ̃] *adv* superficially
superflu, -e [sypɛrfly] **1** *adj* superfluous
2 *nm* **le s.** the superfluous
super-géant (*pl* **super-géants**) [sypɛrʒeɑ̃] *nm Sport* super-giant (slalom)
supergrand [sypɛrgrɑ̃] *nm* superpower
super-huit [sypɛrɥit] *adj inv & nm inv Cin* super-eight
supérieur, -e [sypɛrjœr] **1** *adj* (**a**) *(plus haut)* upper; **on a dû évacuer les étages supérieurs** the upper floors had to be evacuated; **elle est à l'étage s.** she's on the floor above (**b**) *(plus grand)* superior (à/en to/in); **s. à la moyenne** above average (**c**) *(intelligence, esprit)* superior (**d**) *(dans une hiérarchie)* (rang, grade) higher; *(cadre)* senior; **passer dans la classe supérieure** to go up into the class above (**e**) *(manières, ton)* superior, condescending
2 *nm,f aussi Rel* superior
supérieurement [sypɛrjœrmɑ̃] *adv* exceptionally
supériorité [sypɛrjɔrite] *nf* superiority
superlatif, -ive [sypɛrlatif, -iv] *adj & nm* superlative
supermarché [sypɛrmarʃe] *nm* supermarket
supernova [sypɛrnɔva] (*pl* **supernovae** [sypɛrnɔve]) *nf* supernova
superpétrolier [sypɛrpetrɔlje] *nm* supertanker
superposable [sypɛrpozabl] *adj (caisses)* stacking; *(images)* superimposable
superposé, -e [sypɛrpoze] *adj (images)* superimposed

superposer [sypɛrpoze] **1** *vt (caisses)* to stack; *(images)* to superimpose (à on); *Ordinat* **s. une écriture** to overwrite
2 se superposer *vpr (caisses, chaises)* to stack, to be stackable; *(images)* to be superimposed
superposition [sypɛrpozisjɔ̃] *nf (de caisses, de chaises)* stacking; *(d'images)* superimposition; *Ordinat* **mode de s. d'écriture** overwrite mode
superproduction [sypɛrprɔdyksjɔ̃] *nf* blockbuster
superpuissance [sypɛrpɥisɑ̃s] *nf* superpower
supersonique [sypɛrsɔnik] *adj* supersonic
superstar [sypɛrstar] *nf* superstar
superstitieux, -euse [sypɛrstisjø, -øz] *adj* superstitious
superstition [sypɛrstisjɔ̃] *nf* superstition
supertanker [sypɛrtɑ̃kœr] *nm* supertanker
superviser [sypɛrvize] *vt* to supervise; *Ordinat* to control
superviseur [sypɛrvizœr] *nm* supervisor; *Ordinat* **s. d'alimentation** power supply controller
supervision [sypɛrvizjɔ̃] *nf* supervision
supplanter [syplɑ̃te] *vt* to supplant, to supersede
suppléance [sypleɑ̃s] *nf Br* supply *or Am* substitute post
suppléant, -e [sypleɑ̃, -ɑ̃t] **1** *adj (fonctionnaire)* acting, temporary; *(juge)* surrogate
2 *nm,f* substitute, replacement (**de** for)
suppléer [24] [syplee] **1** *vt* (**a**) *(personne)* to stand in for, to replace; **se faire s.** to be replaced (**b**) *Litt (manque)* to supply, to make up (for)
2 suppléer à *vt ind* to make up for, to compensate for
supplément [syplemɑ̃] *nm* (**a**) *(surcroît)* **un s. de** *(information, travail)* additional, extra; **en s.** extra (**b**) *(de prix)* extra *or* additional charge; *(de billet de train)* supplement (**c**) *(livre, magazine)* supplement (**d**) *(de plat)* extra portion
supplémentaire [syplemɑ̃tɛr] *adj* additional, extra
suppliant, -e [syplijɑ̃, -ɑ̃t] *adj* imploring, pleading
supplication [syplikasjɔ̃] *nf* entreaty, plea
supplice [syplis] *nm* (**a**) *(torture)* torture (**b**) *(tourment, douleur)* torture, agony; **être au s.** to be in agony; **mettre qn au s.** to torture sb
supplicié, -e [syplisje] *nm,f* victim of torture
supplier [66] [syplije] *vt* **s. qn de faire qch** to implore *or* beg sb to do sth; **je vous en supplie!** I beg you!
supplique [syplik] *nf* petition
support [sypɔr] *nm* (**a**) *(étai)* support (**b**) *(d'outils, de lampe)* stand (**c**) *Fig (de communication)* medium; **s. audiovisuel** audio-visual aid; **s. publicitaire** publicity *or* advertising medium; **s. visuel** visual aid (**d**) *Ordinat* **s. d'affichage** billboard; **s. de sortie** output medium; **s. de souris** mouse support; **s. de stockage** storage medium
supportable [sypɔrtabl] *adj* (**a**) *(douleur)* bearable; *(comportement)* tolerable (**b**) *(acceptable)* reasonable
supporter¹ [sypɔrtɛr] *nm* supporter
supporter² [sypɔrte] **1** *vt* (**a**) *(résister à)* (*sujet: matériau, plante*) to withstand; **je supporte bien la chaleur** I can take the heat; **il ne supporterait pas le voyage** the journey would kill him; **je ne supporte pas l'aspirine/l'alcool** I can't take aspirin/alcohol (**b**) *(tolérer)* (*personne, situation*) to put up with; **je ne la supporte pas** I can't stand her; **il ne supporte pas qu'on le contredise** he can't stand *or* bear being contradicted (**c**) *(assumer)* (*conséquence, coût*) to bear (**d**) *(soutenir)* (*plafond, structure*) to support

2 se supporter *vpr (l'un l'autre)* to put up with each other; **ils ne se supportent plus** they can't stand each other any more

supposé, -e [sypoze] *adj (voleur)* alleged; *(auteur)* supposed

supposer [sypoze] *vt* (**a**) *(imaginer)* to suppose, to assume (**que** that); **à s. que...** + *subjunctive* suppose *or* supposing that...; **on suppose que...** it's thought that...; **être supposé faire qch** to be supposed to do sth (**b**) *(impliquer)* to imply (**que** that)

supposition [sypozisjɔ̃] *nf* supposition, assumption

suppositoire [sypozitwar] *nm* suppository

suppôt [sypo] *nm* henchman; **s. de Satan** fiend

suppression [sypresjɔ̃] *nf* (**a**) *(de loi, d'impôt)* abolition; *(de train)* cancellation; *(de crédits, d'emploi, de service)* axing (**b**) *(de mot, de phrase)* deletion (**c**) *Jur (de document)* suppression

supprimer [syprime] **1** *vt* (**a**) *(loi, impôt)* to abolish; *(autobus, train)* to cancel; *(financement, crédits)* to withdraw; *(emploi, service)* to axe (**b**) *(mot, phrase)* to delete (**c**) *Jur (document)* to suppress (**d**) *(sucre, sel)* to cut out (**de** from) (**e**) *(ôter)* **s. qch à qn** to take sth away from sb (**f**) *(tuer)* to do away with
2 se supprimer *vpr* to do away with oneself

suppurer [sypyre] *vi* to suppurate

supputation [sypytasjɔ̃] *nf* calculation

supputer [sypyte] *vt* to calculate

supranational, -e, -aux, -ales [sypranasjɔnal, -o] *adj* supranational

supranationalité [sypranasjɔnalite] *nf* supranationality

suprématie [sypremasi] *nf* supremacy

suprême [syprɛm] **1** *adj* (**a**) *(effort, bonheur)* supreme (**b**) *(dernier)* final, last
2 *nm Culin* **s. de volaille** chicken supreme

suprêmement [sypremmã] *adv* supremely

sur¹ [syr] *prép* (**a**) *(dessus)* on; *(avec mouvement)* on, onto; **s. la photo** in the picture; **regarder s. la carte** to look at the map; **la clef est s. la porte** the key's in the door; *aussi Fig* **les uns s. les autres** on top of each other (**b**) *(au-dessus de)* over, above; **un pont s. une rivière** a bridge over *or* across a river (**c**) *(vers)* towards; **fenêtre qui donne s. le jardin** window which looks onto the garden; **la police a tiré s. la foule** the police fired at the crowd; **s. la droite/gauche** on *or* to the right/left (**d**) *(à propos de)* on, about; **savoir qch s. qn** to know sth about sb (**e**) *(parmi)* out of; **7 s. 10** 7 out of 10; **une fois s. deux** every other time; **une femme s. deux** one in two women (**f**) *(mesure)* by; **10 mètres s. 2** 10 metres by 2; **virages s. 2 kilomètres** *(sur un panneau)* bends for 2 kilometres (**g**) *(avec)* **vivre s. ses économies** to live on *or* off one's savings; **s. des paroles de Prévert/une musique des Beatles** to words by Prévert/Beatles music; **ne me parle pas s. ce ton!** don't talk to me in that tone of voice!

sur², -e¹ [syr] *adj (fruit)* sour

sur- *préf* over-

sûr, -e² [syr] **1** *adj* (**a**) *(lieu)* safe; **peu s.** unsafe (**b**) *(digne de confiance) (personne, mémoire)* trustworthy, reliable; *(ami)* true; *(information, entreprise, goût)* reliable (**c**) *(certain)* sure, certain (**de** of); **je suis s. de te l'avoir dit** I'm sure I told you; **s. de soi** self-assured; **être s. et certain (de qch)** to be absolutely certain (of sth)
2 *nm* **le plus s. serait de...** the safest thing would be to...

surabondance [syrabɔ̃dãs] *nf* overabundance; **une s. de richesses/de détails** a wealth of riches/details

surabondant, -e [syrabɔ̃dã, -ãt] *adj* overabundant

surabonder [syrabɔ̃de] *vi* to be overabundant

suractivé, -e [syraktive] *adj* superactivated

surajouter [syraʒute] **1** *vt* to add (on)
2 se surajouter *vpr* to be added (on)

suralimentation [syralimãtasjɔ̃] *nf (de personne)* overfeeding; *(de malade)* feeding up

suralimenter [syralimãte] *vt (personne)* to overfeed; *(malade)* to feed up

suranné, -e [syrane] *adj* outdated, old-fashioned

surarmement [syrarməmã] *nm* excessive arms build-up

surbooker [syrbuke] *vt* to overbook

surbooking [syrbukiŋ] *nm* overbooking

surcapacité [syrkapasite] *nf* overcapacity

surcharge [syrʃarʒ] *nf* (**a**) *(poids) (de bagages)* excess weight; *(de véhicule)* excess load; **prendre des passagers en s.** to take on excess passengers; **rouler en s.** to drive an overloaded vehicle; *Méd* **s. pondérale** excess weight (**b**) *(action) (de véhicule)* overloading (**c**) *(d'accumulateur électrique)* overcharge (**d**) *Fig* **une s. de travail** excess work (**e**) *(à payer)* surcharge (**f**) *(correction)* correction

surcharger [45] [syrʃarʒe] *vt* (**a**) *(véhicule, cheval, estomac)* to overload; **s. qn de travail** to overload sb with work (**b**) *(accumulateur électrique)* to overcharge (**c**) *(épreuves, texte)* to write over with corrections

surchauffe [syrʃof] *nf* overheating

surchauffer [syrʃofe] *vt & vi* to overheat

surchoix [syrʃwa] *adj inv* top-quality

surclasser [syrklase] *vt* to outclass

surconsommation [syrkɔ̃sɔmasjɔ̃] *nf* overconsumption

surcroît [syrkrwa] *nm* **un s. de travail/dépenses** extra work/expenditure; **par s., de s.** in addition, moreover

surdéveloppé, -e [syrdevlɔpe] *adj* overdeveloped

surdéveloppement [syrdevlɔpmã] *nm* overdevelopment

surdimensionné, -e [syrdimãsjɔne] *adj* oversized

surdiplômé, -e [syrdiplome] *adj* overqualified

surdité [syrdite] *nf* deafness

surdose [syrdoz] *nf* overdose

surdoué, -e [syrdwe] **1** *adj* gifted
2 *nm,f* gifted child

sureau, -x [syro] *nm* elder (tree)

sureffectif [syrefɛktif] *nm* overmanning; **en s.** surplus

surélevé, -e [syrelve] *adj* (**a**) *(voie ferrée)* elevated (**b**) *(arche, rez-de-chaussée)* raised

surélever [46] [syrelve] *vt* to heighten, to raise

sûrement [syrmã] *adv* (**a**) *(probablement)* probably (**b**) *(absolument)* **s.!** certainly!; **s. pas!** certainly not! (**c**) *(sans risque)* safely

suremploi [syrãplwa] *nm* overemployment

surenchère [syrãʃɛr] *nf (dans une vente)* higher bid; *Fig* **faire de la s.** to try to outdo one's rivals

surenchérir [syrãʃerir] *vi* to bid higher; **s. sur qn** to outbid sb; *Fig* to go one further than sb

surencombré, -e [syrãkɔ̃bre] *adj* congested (**de** with)

surendetté, -e [syrãdɛte] *adj* overindebted

surendettement [syrãdɛtmã] *nm* overindebtedness

surentraîner [syrãtrɛne] *vt* to overtrain

suréquipement [syrekipmɑ̃] *nm* overequipment
suréquiper [syrekipe] *vt* to overequip
surestimer [syrɛstime] **1** *vt* (**a**) *(importance, capacité, personne)* to overestimate (**b**) *(œuvre d'art)* to overvalue
  2 se surestimer *vpr* to overestimate oneself
sûreté [syrte] *nf* (**a**) *(absence de danger)* safety; **être en s.** to be safe; **mettre qch en s.** to put sth in a safe place; **pour plus de s.** to be on the safe side; **de s.** *(rasoir, épingle)* safety (**b**) *(du goût, du jugement)* soundness (**c**) *(d'un pays)* security; **la s. de l'État** national security
surévaluation [syrevalɥasjɔ̃] *nf* overvaluation
surévaluer [syrevalɥe] *vt* (*objet, antiquité)* to overvalue; *(efficacité, capacités)* to overestimate
surexcitation [syrɛksitasjɔ̃] *nf* overexcitement
surexciter [syrɛksite] *vt* to overexcite
surexploiter [syrɛksplwate] *vt* to overexploit
surexposer [syrɛkspoze] *vt* to overexpose
surexposition [syrɛkspozisjɔ̃] *nf* overexposure
surf [sœrf] *nm* surfing; **faire du s.** to go surfing, to surf
surface [syrfas] *nf* (**a**) *(partie extérieure)* surface; **en s.** on the surface; *Fig* superficially; **remonter à la s.** to rise to the surface, to surface; **faire s.** *(remonter, se réveiller)* to surface (**b**) *(étendue)* (surface) area; **grande s.** hypermarket; **s. de réparation** *(au football)* penalty area; **s. au sol** floor area; **s. utile** floor space; **s. de vente** sales area (**c**) *Ordinat* **s. d'affichage** display area; **s. d'enregistrement** read-write surface
surfait, -e [syrfɛ, -ɛt] *adj* overrated
surfer [sœrfe] *vi* to surf; **s. sur l'Internet** to surf the Net *or* the Internet
surfeur, -euse [sœrfœr, -øz] *nm,f* surfer
surfiler [syrfile] *vt* *(vêtement)* to overcast, to oversew
surfin, -e [syrfɛ̃, -in] *adj* superfine
surgé [syrʒe] *nmf Fam* head supervisor *(person in charge of school discipline)*
surgelé, -e [syrʒəle] **1** *adj* frozen
  2 *nm* **surgelés** frozen foods
surgeler [39] [syrʒəle] *vt* to freeze
surgénérateur [syrʒeneratœr] *nm* breeder reactor
surgir [syrʒir] *vi* *(personne)* to appear suddenly; *(difficulté)* to crop up
surhomme [syrɔm] *nm* superman
surhumain, -e [syrymɛ̃, -ɛn] *adj* superhuman
surimposer [syrɛ̃poze] *vt* to overtax
surimposition [syrɛ̃pozisjɔ̃] *nf* overtaxation
surimpression [syrɛ̃presjɔ̃] *nf* (**a**) *(d'images)* superimposition; **en s.** superimposed (**b**) *Ordinat* overprinting, overstrike
Surinam(e) [syrinam] *nm* **le S.** Surinam
surinfection [syrɛ̃fɛksjɔ̃] *nf* secondary infection
surinformation [syrɛ̃fɔrmasjɔ̃] *nf* information overload
surinformé, -e [syrɛ̃fɔrme] *adj* overinformed
surinvestissement [syrɛ̃vɛstismɑ̃] *nm Fin & Psy* overinvestment
sur-le-champ [syrləʃɑ̃] *adv* at once, immediately
surlendemain [syrlɑ̃dmɛ̃] *nm* **le s.** two days later; **le s. de leur départ** two days after they left
surligner [syrliɲe] *vt* to highlight
surligneur [syrliɲœr] *nm* highlighter (pen)
surlouer [syrlwe] *vt* to overbook
surmédiatisation [syrmedjatizasjɔ̃] *nf* excessive media coverage
surmédiatiser [syrmedjatize] *vt* to give excessive media coverage to

surmenage [syrmənaʒ] *nm* overwork; **s. intellectuel** mental strain
surmené, -e [syrməne] *adj* overworked
surmener [46] [syrməne] **1** *vt* to overwork
  2 se surmener *vpr* to overdo it
surmonter [syrmɔ̃te] **1** *vt* (**a**) *(être placé sur)* to surmount (**b**) *Fig (obstacle, difficulté)* to overcome
  2 se surmonter *vpr* to control oneself
surnager [45] [syrnaʒe] *vi* to float (on the surface)
surnaturel, -elle [syrnatyrɛl] **1** *adj* supernatural
  2 *nm* **le s.** the supernatural
surnom [syrnɔ̃] *nm* nickname
surnombre [syrnɔ̃br] *nm* **il y avait trois passagers en s.** there were three passengers too many; **les exemplaires/passagers en s.** the excess copies/passengers
surnommer [syrnɔme] *vt* to nickname
surpasser [syrpase] **1** *vt (rival)* to surpass, to outdo
  2 se surpasser *vpr* to surpass *or* excel oneself
surpayer [53] [syrpeje] *vt (personne)* to overpay; *(activité)* to pay too much for
surpeuplé, -e [syrpœple] *adj (pays, région)* overpopulated; *(plage)* overcrowded
surpeuplement [syrpœpləmɑ̃] *nm (de pays, de région)* overpopulation; *(de plage)* overcrowding
surplace [syrplas] *nm* **faire du s.** *(cycliste)* to do a track stand; *Fig (automobiliste)* to crawl along; *(dans une carrière, dans des négociations)* to make no headway
surplomb [syrplɔ̃] *nm* overhang; **en s.** overhanging
surplomber [syrplɔ̃be] *vt* to overhang
surplus [syrply] *nm* surplus; **le s. de marchandises** the surplus goods, the goods that are left (over)
surpoids [syrpwa] *nm* excess weight; **être en s.** to be overweight
surpopulation [syrpɔpylasjɔ̃] *nf* overpopulation
surprenant, -e [syrprənɑ̃, -ɑ̃t] *adj* surprising; **et, chose surprenante...** and surprisingly...
surprendre [58] [syrprɑ̃dr] **1** *vt* (**a**) *(prendre par surprise)* to surprise; **s. qn en train de faire qch** to catch sb doing sth; **être surpris par la pluie** to be caught in the rain (**b**) *(découvrir) (conversation)* to overhear; *(regard)* to catch (**c**) *(étonner)* to surprise; **cela me surprendrait qu'il revienne** *ou* **s'il revenait** I'd be surprised if he came back
  2 se surprendre *vpr* **se s. à faire qch** to find oneself doing sth
surpris, -e [syrpri, -iz] *adj* surprised; **être s. de qch/de faire qch** to be surprised at sth/to do sth
surprise [syrpriz] *nf* surprise; **à sa grande s.** to his/her great surprise, much to his/her surprise; **à la s. générale** to everyone's surprise; **sans s.** *(expédition, voyage)* uneventful; **prendre qn par s.** to take sb by surprise
surprise-partie *(pl* **surprises-parties)** [syrprizparti] *nf Vieilli* party
surproduction [syrprɔdyksjɔ̃] *nf* overproduction
surqualifié, -e [syrkalifje] *adj* overqualified
surréalisme [syrrealism] *nm* surrealism
surréaliste [syrrealist] *adj & nmf* surrealist
sursaut [syrso] *nm* (**a**) *(mouvement)* start, jump; **en s.** with a start (**b**) *(regain) (d'énergie)* burst
sursauter [syrsote] *vi* to start, to jump; **faire s. qn** to make sb jump, to startle sb
surseoir [10b] [syrswar] **surseoir à** *vt ind (jugement)* to suspend; **s. à l'exécution d'un condamné** to reprieve a condemned man

sursis [syrsi] *nm* (**a**) *(d'exécution)* & *Fig* reprieve; **un an de prison avec s.** a one-year suspended sentence (**b**) *(de conscrit)* deferment of call-up

sursitaire [syrsitɛr] **1** *adj (conscrit)* provisionally exempted

2 *nm* provisionally exempted conscript

surtaxe [syrtaks] *nf (taxe supplémentaire)* surcharge; *(taxe excessive)* excessive tax

surtaxer [syrtakse] *vt (frapper d'une taxe supplémentaire)* to surcharge; *(frapper d'une taxe excessive)* to overcharge; *Tél* **numéro surtaxé** premium-rate number

surtout [syrtu] *adv* (**a**) *(particulièrement)* particularly, especially; *Fam* **s. que...** especially as... (**b**) *(avant tout)* above all; **s. pas!** certainly not!

surveillance [syrvejãs] *nf (de travail, d'élèves)* supervision; *(par la police, par un gardien)* surveillance, observation; *(de malade, de phénomène)* watch; **être sous s.** to be under surveillance; **s. médicale** medical supervision

surveillant, -e [syrvejã, -ãt] *nm,f* (**a**) *(d'une prison)* guard, *Br* warder (**b**) *(d'un hôpital)* supervisor (**c**) *Scol (pendant les examens)* invigilator; *(chargé de la discipline)* supervisor

surveiller [syrveje] **1** *vt* (**a**) *(contrôler) (travail, élèves)* to supervise; *(température, cuisson)* to keep a watch on; *(examen)* to invigilate (**b**) *(prendre soin de)* to watch (over) (**c**) *(situation)* to keep an eye on; **s. son langage** to watch *or* mind one's language; **s. sa ligne** to watch one's figure

2 se surveiller *vpr* to keep a watch on oneself

survenir [70] [syrvənir] *vi (événements)* to occur; *(crise, difficulté)* to arise

survêt [syrvɛt] *nm Fam* tracksuit, *Br* trackie

survêtement [syrvɛtmã] *nm* tracksuit

survie [syrvi] *nf* survival

survivance [syrvivãs] *nf (vestige)* survival, relic

survivant, -e [syrvivã, -ãt] **1** *adj* surviving

2 *nm,f* survivor

survivre [72] [syrvivr] **survivre à** *vt ind (personne)* to survive, to outlive; *(période, théorie)* to outlive; *(accident, maladie)* to survive

survol [syrvɔl] *nm* (**a**) **le s. d'un lieu** flying over a place (**b**) *Fig (de problème, de question)* cursory glance (**de** at)

survoler [syrvɔle] *vt* (**a**) *(lieu)* to fly over (**b**) *Fig (problème, question)* to skim over

survolté, -e [syrvɔlte] *adj Fam (personne)* overexcited; *(ambiance)* highly charged

sus [sys, sy] **1** *exclam* **s. à l'ennemi!** at them!

2 *adv* **en s.** in addition; **en s. de** in addition to, over and above

susceptibilité [syseptibilite] *nf* touchiness, sensitivity; **ménager la s. de qn** to tread carefully where sb is concerned

susceptible [syseptibl] *adj* (**a**) *(ombrageux)* touchy, sensitive (**b**) **s. de** *(interprétations, critiques)* open to; **être s. de faire qch** to be liable *or* likely to do sth

susciter [sysite] *vt (ennuis, problèmes)* to cause, to create; *(étonnement)* to cause; *(hostilité, intérêt)* to arouse; *(admiration, commentaires)* to attract

susdit, -e [sysdi, -it] *adj* aforesaid, above-mentioned

susmentionné, -e [sysmãsjɔne] *adj* above-mentioned, aforesaid

susnommé, -e [sysnɔme] *adj & nm,f* above-named

suspect, -e [syspɛ(kt), -ɛkt] **1** *adj (personne, action)* suspicious, suspect; *(idées, preuve, aliment)* suspect;

s. de qch suspected of sth

2 *nm,f* suspect

suspecter [syspɛkte] *vt (personne)* to suspect (**de** of); *(sincérité)* to suspect, to question

suspendre [syspãdr] **1** *vt* (**a**) *(vêtements, tableau, hamac)* to hang (up); **s. qch au mur/au plafond** to hang sth on the wall/from the ceiling (**b**) *(interrompre)* to suspend; *(séance)* to adjourn (**c**) *(démettre de ses fonctions)* to suspend

2 se suspendre *vpr* to hang (**à** from)

suspendu, -e [syspãdy] *adj* (**a**) *(pendu)* hanging; **s. au mur/au plafond** hanging on the wall/from the ceiling; *Fig* **être s. aux lèvres de qn** to be hanging on sb's every word (**b**) *(interrompu)* suspended; *(séance)* adjourned

suspens [syspã] **en suspens** *adv* (**a**) *(en l'air)* suspended (**b**) *(en attente)* outstanding

suspense [syspɛns] *nm* suspense

suspension [syspãsjõ] *nf* (**a**) *(de négociations, d'un travail)* suspension; *(d'une séance)* adjournment (**b**) *(retrait)* **s. du permis de conduire** driving ban (**c**) *(mise à pied)* suspension (**d**) *(de voiture)* suspension

suspicieux, -euse [syspisjø, -øz] *adj* suspicious

suspicion [syspisjõ] *nf* suspicion

sustenter [systãte] **se sustenter** *vpr Hum* to take sustenance

susurrer [sysyre] *vt & vi* to whisper, to murmur

suture [sytyr] *nf* suture; **point de s.** stitch

suzerain, -e [syzrɛ̃, -ɛn] *nm,f* suzerain

svastika [svastika] *nm* swastika

svelte [svɛlt] *adj* slender

sveltesse [svɛltɛs] *nf* slenderness

SVP [ɛsvepe] *(abrév* **s'il vous plaît)** please

swahili [swaili] **1** *adj* Swahili

2 *nm (langue)* Swahili

Swaziland [swazilãd] *nm* **le S.** Swaziland

sweat [swit] *nm Fam* sweatshirt; **s. à capuche** hoodie

sweat-shirt [swit∫œrt, swɛt∫œrt] *nm* sweatshirt; **s. à capuche** hooded top

swing [swiŋ] *nm* swing

swinguer [swiŋge] *vi* to swing

sycomore [sikɔmɔr] *nm* sycamore (tree)

syllabe [silab] *nf* syllable

syllabique [silabik] *adj* syllabic

sylphide [silfid] *nf* sylph

sylvestre [silvɛstr] *adj* woodland, sylvan

sylviculture [silvikyltyr] *nf* forestry

symbiose [sɛ̃bjoz] *nf* symbiosis; *Fig* **en s. avec qn/ qch** in harmony with sb/sth

symbole [sɛ̃bɔl] *nm* symbol

symbolique [sɛ̃bɔlik] **1** *adj* symbolic; *(paiement, geste)* token

2 *nf (système de symboles)* system of symbols

symboliquement [sɛ̃bɔlikmã] *adv* symbolically

symboliser [sɛ̃bɔlize] *vt* to symbolize

symbolisme [sɛ̃bɔlism] *nm* symbolism

symétrie [simetri] *nf* symmetry

symétrique [simetrik] *adj* symmetrical

symétriquement [simetrikmã] *adv* symmetrically

sympa [sɛ̃pa] *adj Fam* nice

sympathie [sɛ̃pati] *nf* (**a**) *(affinité)* liking; **avoir** *ou* **éprouver de la s. pour qn** to like sb; **inspirer la s.** to be likable (**b**) *(compassion, condoléances)* sympathy

sympathique [sɛ̃patik] *adj* (**a**) *(agréable)* nice (**b**) *Anat* sympathetic

sympathisant, -e [sɛ̃patizã, -ãt] *nm,f* sympathizer

sympathiser [sɛ̃patize] *vi* to get on well (**avec** with)

symphonie [sɛ̃fɔni] *nf* symphony
symphonique [sɛ̃fɔnik] *adj (forme, poème)* symphonic; *(orchestre)* symphony
symposium [sɛ̃pozjɔm] *nm* symposium
symptomatique [sɛ̃ptɔmatik] *adj* symptomatic (**de** of)
symptôme [sɛ̃ptom] *nm* symptom
synagogue [sinagɔg] *nf* synagogue
synchrone [sɛ̃kron] *adj* synchronous (**avec** with)
synchronisation [sɛ̃krɔnizasjɔ̃] *nf* synchronization
synchroniser [sɛ̃krɔnize] *vt* to synchronize (**avec** with)
synclinal, -e, -aux, -ales [sɛ̃klinal, -o] *adj* synclinal
syncope [sɛ̃kɔp] *nf* (**a**) *(perte de connaissance)* blackout; **tomber en s.** to black out, to pass out; *Fam* **elle a failli avoir une s.** she nearly passed out (**b**) *Mus* syncopation
syncopé, -e [sɛ̃kɔpe] *adj Mus* syncopated
syndic [sɛ̃dik] *nm* **s. (de copropriété)** property manager

Syndic

A "syndic" is an administrative body which represents the interests of the owners of all the flats in a building, collectively known as the "syndicat de copropriété". The role of the "syndic" is to ensure the upkeep of the building and to organize meetings during which a vote is taken on any repairs, improvements etc that are deemed necessary. The services of the "syndic" are paid for by the owners of the flats.

syndical, -e, -aux, -ales [sɛ̃dikal, -o] *adj (Br* trade *orAm* labor) union
syndicaliser [sɛ̃dikalize] = **syndiquer**
syndicalisme [sɛ̃dikalism] *nm* (**a**) *(mouvement)* Br trade *orAm* labor unionism (**b**) *(activité)* **faire du s.** to be involved in union activities
syndicaliste [sɛ̃dikalist] **1** *adj Br* (trade) union, *Am* (labor) union
  2 *nmf Br* trade *orAm* labor unionist
syndicat [sɛ̃dika] *nm* (**a**) *(de travailleurs) (Br* trade *or Am* labor) union (**b**) *(d'employeurs, de producteurs)* association; **s. patronal** employers' association (**c**) **s. d'initiative** tourist (information) office
syndiqué, -e [sɛ̃dike] **1** *adj* belonging to a (*Br* trade *or Am* labor) union; **être s.** to belong to a (*Br* trade *or Am* labor) union
  2 *nm,f (Br* trade *orAm* labor) union member

syndiquer [sɛ̃dike] **1** *vt* to unionize
  2 se syndiquer *vpr* (**a**) *(se constituer en syndicat)* to form a (*Br* trade *or Am* labor) union (**b**) *(adhérer à un syndicat)* to join a (*Br* trade *orAm* labor) union
syndrome [sɛ̃drom] *nm Méd* syndrome; **s. d'Asperger** Asperger's syndrome; **s. du choc toxique** toxic shock syndrome; **s. du côlon irritable** irritable bowel syndrome, IBS; **s. de Down** Down's syndrome; **s. de fatigue chronique** chronic fatigue syndrome; **s. prémenstruel** premenstrual syndrome
synergie [sinɛrʒi] *nf* synergy
synode [sinɔd] *nm* synod
synonyme [sinɔnim] **1** *adj* synonymous (**de** with)
  2 *nm* synonym
synopsis [sinɔpsis] *nm Cin* synopsis
synovial, -e, -aux, -ales [sinɔvjal, -o] *adj* synovial
syntagme [sɛ̃tagm] *nm* phrase
syntaxe [sɛ̃taks] *nf Gram & Ordinat* syntax
syntaxique [sɛ̃taksik] *adj* (**a**) *Gram* syntactic (**b**) *Ordinat* syntax
synthèse [sɛ̃tɛz] *nf* (**a**) *(exposé)* summary; **faire la s. (de qch)** to summarize (sth) (**b**) *(opération chimique)* synthesis; **de s.** synthetic
synthétique [sɛ̃tetik] **1** *adj* (**a**) *(présentation)* all-encompassing; *(bilan)* summary (**b**) *(tissu, fibres)* synthetic, man-made
  2 *nm* synthetic material
synthétiser [sɛ̃tetize] *vt* to synthesize
synthétiseur [sɛ̃tetizœr] *nm* synthesizer
syphilis [sifilis] *nf* syphilis
syphilitique [sifilitik] *adj & nmf* syphilitic
Syrie [siri] *nf* **la S.** Syria
syrien, -enne [sirjɛ̃, -ɛn] **1** *adj* Syrian
  2 *nm,f* **S.** Syrian
systématique [sistematik] **1** *adj (automatique, méthodique)* systematic; **il est toujours en retard, c'est s.** he's consistently late
systématiquement [sistematikmɑ̃] *adv* systematically
systématiser [sistematize] *vt* to systematize
système [sistɛm] *nm* system; *Fam* **il me tape** *ou* **porte sur le s.** he gets on my nerves; **s. D** resourcefulness; *Ordinat* **s. d'exploitation** operating system; *Ordinat* **s. de gestion de bases de données** database management system; **s. nerveux** nervous system; **s. solaire** solar system

T, t [te] *nm inv* T, t; **en T** T-shaped; **disposer qch en T** to arrange sth in a T-shape

t' [t] *voir* **te, tu**

ta [ta] *voir* **ton¹**

tabac¹ [taba] **1** *nm* (**a**) *(plante, produit)* tobacco; *Fam Fig* **du même t.** of the same ilk; **t. blond** Virginia tobacco; **t. brun** dark tobacco; **t. à chiquer** chewing tobacco; **t. à priser** snuff (**b**) *(boutique)* **(bureau de) t.** *Br* tobacconist's (shop), *Am* tobacco store *(which also sells stamps, phonecards and lottery tickets)*

2 *adj inv* buff

tabac² *nm* **coup de t.** *(tempête)* squall; *Fam* **passer qn à t.** to beat sb up; *Fam* **faire un t.** to be a smash hit

tabagie [taba3i] *nf* (**a**) *Fam* **c'est une vraie t. ici** you can't see a thing for the smoke in here (**b**) *Can (bureau de tabac) Br* tobacconist's (shop), *Am* tobacco store

tabagisme [taba3ism] *nm* smoking

tabasser [tabase] *vt Fam* **t. qn** to beat sb up; **se faire t.** to be *or* get beaten up

tabatière [tabatjɛr] *nf* (**a**) *(boîte)* snuffbox (**b**) *(lucarne)* skylight

tabelle [tabɛl] *nf Suisse* register, list

tabernacle [tabɛrnakl] *nm* tabernacle

tablar(d) [tablar] *nm Suisse* shelf

table [tabl] *nf* (**a**) *(meuble)* table; **mettre** *ou* **dresser la t.** to lay *or* set the table; **être à t.** to be at the table; **se mettre** *ou* **passer à t.** to sit down at the table; *Fam Fig* **se mettre à t.** *(avouer)* to spill the beans; **à t.!** food's ready!; *Fig* **faire t. rase de qch** to make a clean sweep of sth; **t. basse** coffee table; **t. de billard** billiard table; **t. de chevet** bedside table; **t. de cuisson** hob; **t. à dessin** drawing board; **faire t. d'hôte** = to provide a meal where all paying guests eat at the same table; **t. de jeu** card table; **t. à langer** changing table; **t. des négociations** negotiating table; **s'asseoir à la t. des négociations** to get round the negotiating table; **t. de nuit** bedside table; **t. d'opération** operating table; **t. d'orientation** orientation *or* panoramic table; **t. à repasser** ironing board; **t. ronde** *(conférence)* round table; **t. roulante** trolley (**b**) *(restaurant)* **les meilleures tables de Paris** the finest restaurants in Paris (**c**) *(écrit)* table; **Tables de la Loi** Tables of the Law; **t. des matières** (table of) contents; **t. de multiplication** multiplication table (**d**) *(console)* **mettre qn sur t. d'écoute** to tap sb's phone; **il est sur t. d'écoute** his phone is being tapped; **t. de mixage** mixing desk (**e**) *(d'un instrument à cordes)* **t. d'harmonie** sounding board (**f**) *Ordinat* **t. à digitaliser** digitizing pad; **t. des fichiers** file allocation table, FAT; **t. traçante** plotter

tableau, -x [tablo] *nm* (**a**) *(panneau, support)* board; **t. (noir)** (black)board; **t. d'affichage** *Br* notice *or Am* bulletin board; **t. de bord** *(d'une voiture)* dashboard; *(d'un avion)* instrument panel; *Ordinat* control panel; **t. interactif** interactive whiteboard (**b**) *(œuvre d'art)* painting, picture; **t. de maître** old master (**c**) *Fig & Hum (scène)* scene; **faire un joli/charmant t.** to make a pretty/charming sight *or* scene; *Fig* **pour compléter le t....** to crown it all... (**d**) *(au théâtre)* scene; **t. vivant** tableau (vivant) (**e**) *(liste)* list, table; *(graphique)* chart; **t. de chasse** *(de chasseur, d'aviateur)* bag; *Fig (conquêtes)* list of conquests (**f**) *Ordinat* **t. de connexions** plugboard (**g**) *(locutions)* **gagner sur les deux/sur tous les tableaux** to win on both/all counts

tablée [table] *nf (personnes à table)* table

tabler [table] **tabler sur** *vt ind* to count *or* bank on

tablette [tablɛt] *nf* (**a**) *(d'une étagère)* shelf; *(dans un avion)* table; **t. arrière** *(d'une voiture)* back shelf (**b**) *(de chocolat)* bar; *(de chewing-gum)* stick (**c**) *Ordinat* **t. graphique** graphics tablet

tableur [tablœr] *nm Ordinat* spreadsheet; **t. de graphiques** graphics spreadsheet

tablier [tablije] *nm* (**a**) *(vêtement)* apron; *(d'écolier)* smock; *Fig* **rendre son t.** to hand in one's notice (**b**) *(de cheminée)* hood (**c**) *(de pont)* roadway

tabloïd(e) [tablɔid] *adj & nm* tabloid

tabou, -e [tabu] *adj & nm* taboo

taboulé [tabule] *nm* tabbouleh

tabouret [taburɛ] *nm* stool; **t. de bar/de piano** bar/piano stool

tabulateur [tabylatœr] *nm* tab key, tabulator

tabulation [tabylasjɔ̃] *nf* tab

tac [tak] **du tac au tac** *adv* like a shot

tache [taʃ] *nf* (**a**) *(de boue, de sang, d'huile)* stain; *(de peinture, de couleur, de lumière)* splash; **tu as fait une t. à ta chemise** you've got a stain on your shirt; *Fig* **faire t.** to stick out like a sore thumb; **t. d'encre** inkstain; *Fig* **faire t. d'huile** to spread (**b**) *(sur la peau, sur un fruit)* mark; **t. de rousseur** freckle; **t. de vin** strawberry mark (**c**) *Fig (atteinte)* blot, stain; **sans t.** *(réputation)* spotless

taché, -e [taʃe] *adj* stained; **t. d'encre/de sang** ink-/blood-stained

tâche [taʃ] *nf* task, job; **être à la t.** to be on piecework; *Ordinat* **t. d'arrière-plan** *ou* **de fond** background task *or* job

tacher [taʃe] **1** *vt* (**a**) *(vêtement)* to stain (**b**) *(réputation)* to sully, to tarnish

2 *vi* to stain

3 se tacher *vpr (personne)* to stain one's clothes; *(tissu, vêtement)* to stain

tâcher [tɑʃe] **1** *vt* **tâchez que cela ne se reproduise plus** make sure it doesn't happen again **2 tâcher de** *vt ind* to try to

tâcheron [tɑʃrɔ̃] *nm Péj* drudge

tacheté, -e [taʃte] *adj* speckled (**de** with); **chat noir t. de blanc** black cat with white markings

tacheter [42] [taʃte] *vt* to spot, to speckle

tachycardie [takikardi] *nf* tachycardia

tachymètre [takimɛtr] *nm* tachometer; *Aut* speedometer

tacite [tasit] *adj* tacit

tacitement [tasitmɑ̃] *adv* tacitly

taciturne [tasityrn] *adj* taciturn

tacot [tako] *nm Fam Péj Br* old banger, *Am* jalopy

tact [takt] *nm* tact; **avoir du t.** to be tactful; **plein de t.** very tactful; **manquer de t.** to be tactless

tacticien, -enne [taktisjɛ̃, -ɛn] *nm,f* tactician

tactile [taktil] *adj* tactile

tactique [taktik] **1** *adj* tactical **2** *nf* tactics (*pluriel*)

tadjik [tadʒik] **1** *adj* Tadjik **2** *nm/*T. Tadjik

Tadjikistan [tadʒikistɑ̃] *nm* le T. Tadjikistan

taf [taf] *nm très Fam (travail)* work; *(emploi)* job; **j'ai du t.** *(travail)* I've got work to do; *(emploi)* I've got a job

taffe [taf] *nf très Fam (de cigarette)* drag

taffetas [tafta] *nm* taffeta

tag [tag] *nm* tag *(piece of graffiti)*

Tage [taʒ] *nm* le T. the Tagus

tagliatelle [taljatɛl] *nf* piece *or* strand of tagliatelle; **des tagliatelles** tagliatelle

taguer [tage] *vt* to cover in graffiti

tagueur, -euse [tagœr, -øz] *nm,f* tagger *(graffiti artist)*

Tahiti [taiti] *n* Tahiti

tahitien, -enne [taisjɛ̃, -ɛn] **1** *adj* Tahitian **2** *nm/*T. Tahitian **3** *nm (langue)* Tahitian

tai chi [taiʃi] *nm* tai chi

taie [tɛ] *nf* (**a**) *(enveloppe)* **t.** (**d'oreiller**) pillowcase, pillow slip (**b**) *(sur l'œil)* leucoma

taïga [taiga] *nf* taiga

taillader [tajade] *vt* to slash, to gash

taille [taj] *nf* (**a**) *(dimensions)* size; **une pêche de la t. d'un melon** a peach the size of a melon; **quelle t. faites-vous?** what size are you?, what size do you take?; **la t. en dessus/dessous** the next size up/down; **t. unique** one size (**b**) *(hauteur)* height; **de petite t.** short; *Fig* **être de t. à faire qch** to be capable of doing sth; *Fig* **trouver un adversaire à sa t.** to meet one's match (**c**) *(importance)* **de t.** *(erreur, mensonge)* big (**d**) *(partie du corps, sur un vêtement)* waist; **avoir la t. fine** to have a slim waist; **avoir une t. de guêpe** to be wasp-waisted; **un jean (à) t. basse** low-waisted *or* low-rise jeans (**e**) *(action) (de pierre)* cutting; *(d'un arbre)* pruning; *(haie, barbe)* trimming (**f**) *Ordinat* **t. de champ** field size; **t. de disque dur** hard disk size; **t. de mémoire** memory size (**g**) *Hist (impôt)* tallage

taillé, -e [taje] *adj* **être t. pour faire qch** to be cut out to do sth

taille-crayon (*pl* **taille-crayon** *ou* **taille-crayons**) [tajkrɛjɔ̃] *nm* pencil sharpener

tailler [taje] **1** *vt* (**a**) *(pierre, diamant)* to cut; *(arbre, vigne)* to prune; *(haie, barbe)* to trim; *(crayon)* to sharpen; **t. une armée en pièces** to cut an army to pieces (**b**) *(vêtement)* to cut out **2 se tailler** *vpr* (**a**) *(se couper)* **se t. la barbe** to trim one's beard (**b**) *(se faire)* **se t. un chemin à travers qch** to carve one's way through sth (**c**) *(s'attribuer)* **se t. un beau succès** to be very successful; **se t. un empire** to carve out an empire for oneself (**d**) *Fam (partir)* to beat it

tailleur [tajœr] *nm* (**a**) *(couturier)* tailor (**b**) *(ensemble pour femme)* suit (**c**) **s'asseoir en t.** to sit cross-legged

tailleur-pantalon (*pl* **tailleurs-pantalons**) [tajœrpɑ̃talɔ̃] *nm Br* trouser *or* Am pant suit

taillis [taji] *nm* copse, coppice

tain [tɛ̃] *nm* silvering; **glace** *ou* **miroir sans t.** two-way mirror

taire [55b] [tɛr] **1** *vt (affaire, secret)* to say nothing about, not to mention; *(vérité)* to hide; **une personne dont je tairai le nom** a person who shall remain nameless **2** *vi* **t. qn** to make sb be quiet; *(adversaire, critique)* to silence **3 se taire** *vpr* (**a**) *(être silencieux)* to be quiet *or* silent; *(cesser de parler)* to stop talking, to fall silent; *(décider de ne rien dire)* to keep quiet *or* silent; **tais-toi!** be quiet!; **tu as perdu une occasion de te t.** you should have kept your mouth shut (**b**) *(sujet: bruit)* to stop

taisais, taise *etc voir* **taire**

Taiwan [tajwan] *n* Taiwan

taiwanais, -e [tajwanɛ, -ɛz] **1** *adj* Taiwanese **2** *nm,f* T. Taiwanese

tajine [taʒin] *nm* tajine

talc [talk] *nm* talcum powder, talc

talé, -e [tale] *adj* bruised

talent [talɑ̃] *nm* (**a**) *(don)* talent; **son t. de pianiste** his/her talent as a pianist; **homme/musicien de t.** talented man/musician; **avoir du t.** to be talented (**b**) *(artiste)* **un jeune t.** a talented newcomer

talentueusement [talɑ̃tɥøzmɑ̃] *adv* with talent

talentueux, -euse [talɑ̃tɥø, -øz] *adj* talented

talion [taljɔ̃] *nm voir* **loi**

talisman [talismɑ̃] *nm* talisman

talkie-walkie (*pl* **talkies-walkies**) [tɔkiwɔki] *nm* walkie-talkie

Tallinn [talin] *n* Tallinn

Talmud [talmyd] *nm* le T. the Talmud

taloche [talɔʃ] *nf Fam (gifle)* clout, slap

talon [talɔ̃] *nm* (**a**) *(du pied, de chaussure, de bas)* heel; *Fig* **être sur les talons de qn** to be on sb's heels; **t. d'Achille** Achilles' heel; **talons aiguilles** stiletto heels; *(chaussures)* stilettos; **talons hauts** high heels; **talons plats** flat heels (**b**) *(de chèque)* stub, counterfoil (**c**) *(aux cartes)* stock

talonner [talɔne] **1** *vt* (**a**) *(suivre)* **t. qn** to follow on sb's heels (**b**) *(cheval)* to spur on **2** *vi (au rugby)* to heel

talonnette [talɔnɛt] *nf (dans une chaussure)* heel pad

talonneur [talɔnœr] *nm (au rugby)* hooker

talquer [talke] *vt* to put talcum powder on

talus [taly] *nm* (**a**) *(terrain en pente)* slope (**b**) *(d'une voie ferrée, d'un canal)* embankment

tamanoir [tamanwar] *nm* great anteater

tamaris [tamaris] *nm* tamarisk

tambouille [tɑ̃buj] *nf Fam* (**a**) *(cuisine)* cooking; **faire la t.** to do the cooking (**b**) *(nourriture)* grub

tambour [tɑ̃bur] *nm* (**a**) *(instrument de musique)* drum; **sans t. ni trompette** quietly, without any fuss; **faire qch t. battant** to do sth briskly (**b**) *(personne)* drummer (**c**) *(d'une machine à laver)* drum; **t. de frein** brake drum (**d**) *(à broder)* (embroidery) hoop, tambour

tambourin [tɑ̃burɛ̃] *nm (instrument plat)* tambourine; *(tambour)* tambourin
tambouriner [tɑ̃burine] **1** *vi* to drum
2 *vt* to drum out
tamis [tami] *nm (pour la farine)* sieve; *(pour le sable)* sifter; **passer au t.** *(farine)* to sieve; *(sable)* to sift
Tamise [tamiz] *nf* **la T.** the Thames
tamisé, -e [tamize] *adj (lumière)* subdued
tamiser [tamize] *vt (farine)* to sieve; *(sable)* to sift
tamoul, -e [tamul] **1** *adj* Tamil
2 *nm,f* **T.** Tamil
3 *nm (langue)* Tamil
tampon [tɑ̃pɔ̃] **1** *nm* (**a**) *(de coton)* pad; **t. hygiénique** *ou* **périodique** tampon (**b**) *(cachet, instrument)* stamp; *(de la poste)* postmark; **t. dateur** date stamp; **t. encreur** ink pad (**c**) *(pour nettoyer)* pad; **t. à récurer** scourer, scouring pad (**d**) *(bouchon)* plug, stopper (**e**) *(à l'extrémité des wagons) & Fig* buffer
2 *adj inv* **État/zone t.** buffer state/zone
tamponner [tɑ̃pɔne] **1** *vt* (**a**) *(document)* to stamp; *(lettre)* to postmark (**b**) *(plaie)* to dab (**c**) *(heurter)* to crash into
2 se tamponner *vpr* (**a**) *(se heurter)* to crash into each other (**b**) *(s'essuyer)* **se t. le front** to mop one's brow; **se t. les yeux** to dab one's eyes; *très Fam* **s'en t. (le coquillard)** not to give a damn
tamponneuse [tɑ̃pɔnøz] *adj f voir* **auto**
tam-tam (*pl* **tam-tams**) [tamtam] *nm (tambour africain)* tom-tom
tancer [16] [tɑ̃se] *vt Litt* to berate, to scold
tanche [tɑ̃ʃ] *nf* tench
tandem [tɑ̃dɛm] *nm* (**a**) *(bicyclette)* tandem (**b**) *(groupe de deux personnes)* duo; **travailler en t.** to work in tandem
tandis [tɑ̃di, tɑ̃dis] **tandis que** *conj* (**a**) *(marque l'opposition)* while, whereas (**b**) *(marque la simultanéité)* while
tanga [tɑ̃ga] *nm* thong, tanga
tangage [tɑ̃gaʒ] *nm (d'un bateau)* pitching
tangent, -e [tɑ̃ʒɑ̃, -ɑ̃t] **1** *adj Math* tangential (**à** to); *Fig* **c'était t.** it was touch and go, it was a near thing
2 *nf* **tangente** *Math* tangent (**à** to); *Fam* **prendre la tangente** *(partir)* to slip away
tangible [tɑ̃ʒibl] *adj* tangible
tango [tɑ̃go] *nm (danse, musique)* tango; **danser le t.** to tango, to dance the tango
tanguer [tɑ̃ge] *vi (bateau)* to pitch; **tout tanguait autour de moi** everything was spinning around me
tanière [tanjɛr] *nf* (**a**) *(d'animal)* den, lair (**b**) *(retraite)* retreat
tanin [tanɛ̃] *nm* tannin
tank [tɑ̃k] *nm* tank
tanker [tɑ̃kœr] *nm* tanker
tannant, -e [tɑ̃nɑ̃, -ɑ̃t] *adj Fam (ennuyeux)* annoying
tanné, -e [tane] *adj* (**a**) *(hâlé)* weather-beaten (**b**) *Can Fam* **être t.** *(en avoir assez)* to be fed up
tanner [tane] *vt* (**a**) *(peaux)* to tan (**b**) *Fam (harceler)* to pester
tannerie [tanri] *nf (établissement)* tannery; *(industrie)* tanning
tanneur [tanœr] *nm* tanner
tannin [tanɛ̃] = **tanin**
tant [tɑ̃] *adv* (**a**) *(tellement, à tel point)* so much; **t. de** *(quantité)* so much; *(nombre)* so many; **j'ai t. mangé que j'ai vomi** I ate so much I was sick; **pas t. que ça** *(quantité)* not that much; *(nombre)* not that many; **t. il est vrai que...** since it is the case that... (**b**) *(dans des*

comparaisons) **t. que** as much as; **t. pour vous que pour moi** for you as much as for me; **n'aimer rien t. que...** to like nothing more than... (**c**) *(substitué à un chiffre, à une date)* **t. pour cent** so much per cent; **votre lettre du t.** your letter of such and such a date (**d**) **t. que** *(aussi longtemps que)* as long as; *(pendant que)* while; **t. que vous y êtes** while you're at it (**e**) *(locutions)* **t. bien que mal** somehow or other; **t. et si bien que** so much so that; **t. s'en faut** far from it; **s'il était un t. soit peu intelligent** if he was at all intelligent; **t. qu'à faire, autant en acheter deux** you/we/*etc* might as well buy two; **en t. que** *(comme)* as; **t. mieux!** so much the better!; **t. mieux pour toi!** good for you!; **t. pis!** too bad!; **t. pis pour toi!** too bad (for you)!
tante [tɑ̃t] *nf* (**a**) *(parente)* aunt (**b**) *très Fam (homosexuel) Br* queer, *Am* fag, = offensive term used to refer to a male homosexual
tantine [tɑ̃tin] *nf Fam* auntie, aunty
tantinet [tɑ̃tinɛ] *nm Fam* **un t.** a tiny bit
tantôt [tɑ̃to] *adv* (**a**) *(parfois)* **t. triste, t. gai** sometimes sad, sometimes happy (**b**) *(cet après-midi)* this afternoon
Tanzanie [tɑ̃zani] *nf* **la T.** Tanzania
tanzanien, -enne [tɑ̃zanjɛ̃, -ɛn] **1** *adj* Tanzanian
2 *nm,f* **T.** Tanzanian
taoïsme [taoism] *nm* Taoism
taon [tɑ̃] *nm* gadfly, horsefly
tapage [tapaʒ] *nm* (**a**) *(bruit)* din, row; **faire du t.** to kick up a din *or* row; **t. nocturne** breach of the peace *(at night)* (**b**) *(publicité)* fuss; **faire du t. autour de qch** to make a fuss about sth
tapageur, -euse [tapaʒœr, -øz] *adj* (**a**) *(enfant)* rowdy (**b**) *(vêtements, couleur)* loud, flashy; *(publicité)* blatant (**c**) *(liaison)* scandalous
tapant, -e [tapɑ̃, -ɑ̃t] *adj* **à sept/dix heures t.** *ou* **tapantes** at seven/ten o'clock sharp
tape [tap] *nf (pour punir)* slap; *(affectueuse)* pat
tapé, -e [tape] *adj Fam (fou)* crazy
tape-à-l'œil [tapalœj] *Fam* **1** *adj inv* gaudy, flashy
2 *nm* **c'est du t.** it's just show
tapecul [tapky] *nm Fam (véhicule)* boneshaker
taper [tape] **1** *vt* (**a**) *(frapper)* to hit; *(affectueusement)* to pat; *(table)* to bang (**b**) *(dactylographier)* **t. qch (à la machine)** to type sth (**c**) *Ordinat* to key; **tapez entrée ou retour** press enter or return (**d**) *Fam (emprunter de l'argent à)* to cadge money off; **t. qn de 10 euros** to cadge 10 euros off sb
2 *vi* (**a**) *(frapper)* to knock; *(avec le poing)* to bang; **t. à la porte** to knock on the door; **t. du pied** to stamp one's foot; **t. du poing sur qch** to bang on sth; **t. dans un ballon** to kick a ball around; *Fam* **t. dans l'œil à qn** to take sb's fancy; **t. sur qn** to hit sb; *Fig (critiquer)* to knock sb (**b**) *(soleil)* to beat down; *Fam* **ça tape** it's scorching (**c**) *(dactylographier)* **t. (à la machine)** to type; **t. au toucher** to touch-type
3 se taper *vpr* (**a**) *(se cogner)* **se t. la tête/le coude** to bang one's head/elbow; *Fig* **c'est à se t. la tête contre les murs** it's enough to drive you up the wall (**b**) *Fam (repas, boisson)* to have; **je me taperais bien une bière** I could murder a beer (**c**) *Fam (corvée)* to get landed with; **on s'est tapé les embouteillages** we got stuck in traffic (**d**) *très Fam (coucher avec)* to screw (**e**) *Fam (se moquer)* **ses histoires de fesses, je m'en tape!** I couldn't care less about his/her sex life!
tapette [tapɛt] *nf* (**a**) *(pour tapis)* carpet beater; *(contre les mouches)* fly swatter (**b**) *(piège)* **t. (à souris)**

mousetrap (**c**) *(petite tape)* tap (**d**) *très Fam (homosexuel) Br* queer, *Am* fag, = offensive term used to refer to a male homosexual

tapeur, -euse [tapœr, -øz] *nm,f Fam* scrounger, sponger

tapin [tapɛ̃] *nm très Fam* **faire le t.** *Br* to be on the game, *Am* to work the streets

tapinois [tapinwa] **en tapinois** *adv* stealthily

tapioca [tapjɔka] *nm* tapioca

tapir¹ [tapir] *nm (animal)* tapir

tapir² **se tapir** *vpr (se blottir)* to crouch; *(se cacher)* to hide

tapis [tapi] *nm* (**a**) *(de sol)* carpet; *(de petite taille)* rug, mat; *Fig* **mettre qch sur le t.** to bring sth up for discussion; **t. roulant** *(de marchandises, pour bagages)* conveyor belt; *(pour piétons)* moving walkway, travelator; **t. de salle de bain** bath mat; **t. de sol** earth mat; *Ordinat* **t. de souris** mouse mat *or* pad; **t. de yoga** yoga mat (**b**) *(en boxe)* canvas; **aller au t.** to go down; **envoyer qn au t.** to floor sb

tapis-brosse (*pl* **tapis-brosses**) [tapibrɔs] *nm* doormat

tapisser [tapise] *vt* (**a**) *(pièce, appartement)* to paper, to wallpaper; *(fauteuil, canapé)* to upholster (**b**) *(couvrir)* **être tapissé de** *(sujet: mur)* to be covered with; *(sujet: sol)* to be carpeted with (**c**) *(paroi d'un organe)* to line

tapisserie [tapisri] *nf* (**a**) *(broderie)* tapestry work; **faire de la t.** to do tapestry work (**b**) *(tenture)* tapestry; *Fig* **faire t.** to be a wallflower (**c**) *(papier peint)* wallpaper

tapissier, -ère [tapisje, -ɛr] *nm,f* (**a**) *(tisseur)* tapestry maker (**b**) *(de meubles)* upholsterer (**c**) *(décorateur)* interior decorator

tapotement [tapɔtmɑ̃] *nm* tapping

tapoter [tapɔte] **1** *vt* to tap; *(joue, main)* to pat
2 *vi* **t. sur qch** to tap on sth

tapuscrit [tapyskri] *nm* typescript

taquet [takɛ] *nm* (**a**) *(de machine à écrire)* stop; *Ordinat* **t. de tabulation** tab stop (**b**) *(butée)* stop

taquin, -e [takɛ̃, -in] *adj* teasing

taquiner [takine] *vt (faire enrager)* to tease

taquinerie [takinri] *nf* **ce n'est qu'une t.** I'm/he's/*etc* only teasing; **j'en ai assez de ses taquineries** I've had enough of his/her teasing

tarabiscoté, -e [tarabiskɔte] *adj* over-elaborate

tarabuster [tarabyste] *vt* (**a**) *(harceler)* to pester (**b**) *(préoccuper)* to bother

tarama [tarama] *nm* taramasalata

taratata [taratata] *exclam Fam* rubbish!

tarauder [tarode] *vt* (**a**) *(acier)* to tap (**b**) *(obséder)* to gnaw at

tard [tar] **1** *adv* late; **plus t.** later (on); **au plus t.** at the latest; **t. dans la nuit** late at night; **pas plus t. qu'hier** only yesterday
2 *nm* **sur le t.** late in life

tarder [tarde] **1** *vi* to delay; **pourquoi tarde-t-elle?** why is she taking so long?; **il ne devrait pas t.** he shouldn't be long; **tu vas recevoir une gifle, cela ne va pas t.** you're going to get a slap before long; **sans t.** without delay; **t. à faire qch** to take a long time to do sth
2 *v impersonnel* **il me tarde de partir/qu'elle parte** I can't wait to leave/for her to leave

tardif, -ive [tardif, -iv] *adj (regrets, excuse)* belated; *(heure, récolte)* late

tardivement [tardivmɑ̃] *adv (prendre des mesures, s'excuser)* belatedly; *(rentrer, arriver)* late; *(se marier)* late in life

tare [tar] *nf* (**a**) *(défaut)* defect; *Hum* **ça n'est pas une t.!** it's not a crime! (**b**) *(pour calculer le poids net)* tare

taré, -e [tare] *adj* (**a**) *(anormal)* retarded (**b**) *Fam (fou)* crazy

tarentule [tarɑ̃tyl] *nf* tarantula

targette [tarʒɛt] *nf* bolt

targuer [targe] **se targuer** *vpr* **se t. de qch/de faire qch** to pride oneself on sth/on doing sth

tarif [tarif] *nm* (**a**) *(tableau des prix)* price list, *Br* tariff (**b**) *(prix)* rate; *(d'un billet d'avion, de train)* fare; **quels sont vos tarifs?** how much do you charge?; **payer plein t.** *(pour passagers)* to pay full fare; *(pour marchandises)* to pay the full rate; **faire un t. réduit pour les étudiants** to offer a student discount; **t. douanier** customs rate; **tarifs postaux** postal rates

tarifaire [tarifɛr] *adj (lois)* tariff

tarifer [tarife] *vt* to price

tarification [tarifikasjɔ̃] *nf* pricing

tarin [tarɛ̃] *nm Fam (nez) Br* hooter, *Am* schnozzle

tarir [tarir] **1** *vt (source, rivière)* to dry up; *(larmes)* to dry; *(créativité, inspiration)* to cause to dry up
2 *vi* (**a**) *(eau, source)* to dry up (**b**) *Fig (conversation, inspiration)* to dry up; **il ne tarit pas sur le sujet** he never stops talking *or* shuts up about it; **ne pas t. d'éloges sur qn/qch** to be be full of praise for sb/sth
3 **se tarir** *vpr* to dry up

tarissement [tarismɑ̃] *nm* drying up

tarot [taro] *nm* tarot; **jouer aux tarots** to play tarot

tartan [tartɑ̃] *nm* tartan

tartare [tartar] **1** *adj (sauce, steak)* tartare
2 *nmf* **T.** Tartar
3 *nm (steak)* steak tartare *(raw minced beef served with a raw egg)*

tarte [tart] **1** *nf* (**a**) *(salée ou sucrée) Br* tart, *Am* (open) pie; *Fam* **ce n'est pas de la t.** it's no picnic; **t. à la crème** *(au cinéma)* custard pie; *Fig* cliché; **t. aux pommes** apple *Br* tart *or Am* pie; **t. Tatin** tarte Tatin (**b**) *Fam (gifle)* slap
2 *adj Fam* (**a**) *(ridicule)* stupid-looking, *Br* naff (**b**) *(stupide)* thick, *Am* dumb

tartelette [tartəlɛt] *nf* tartlet

Tartempion [tartɑ̃pjɔ̃] *nm Fam* so-and-so

tartignole [tartiɲɔl] *adj Fam* ridiculous, *Br* naff

tartine [tartin] *nf* (**a**) *(tranche de pain)* slice of bread and butter; **t. de confiture** slice of bread and jam; **faire des tartines** to butter (some) bread (**b**) *Fam (texte)* screed; **en mettre des tartines** to write reams

tartiner [tartine] *vt* (**a**) *(beurre, pain)* to spread (**b**) *Fam (enduire en grande quantité)* **t. qn/qch de qch** to cover sb/sth in sth (**c**) *Fam (texte)* to churn out

tartre [tartr] *nm* (**a**) *(des dents, du vin)* tartar (**b**) *(dans une chaudière, dans une bouilloire)* fur, scale

tas [ta] *nm* (**a**) *(amas)* pile, heap; **mettre qch en t.** to pile sth up (**b**) *Fam (grand nombre)* **un t. de, des t. de** loads of, tons of (**c**) *(locutions)* **apprendre qch sur le t.** to learn sth on the job; *Fam* **dans le t. il y en aura bien un qui t'ira** you'll find one to suit you out of all that lot; *Fam* **tirer dans le t.** to fire at random

Tasmanie [tasmani] *nf* **la T.** Tasmania

tasse [tas] *nf* cup; **t. à café/thé** coffee/tea cup; **t. de café/thé** cup of coffee/tea; *Fam Fig* **boire la t.** *(en nageant)* to get a mouthful of water

tassé, -e [tase] *adj* (**a**) *(serré)* crammed, squashed (**b**) *Fam* **bien t.** *(fort) (café)* strong; *(alcool)* stiff; *(dans un grand verre)* large; **il a 50 ans bien tassés** he's 50 if he's a day

tasseau, -x [taso] *nm* batten

tassement [tasmɑ̃] *nm* (**a**) *(de terre, de neige)* packing down; **t. de vertèbres** spinal compression (**b**) *(de fondations)* settling (**c**) *(déclin)* slowdown (**de** in)

tasser [tase] **1** *vt* (**a**) *(objets, personnes)* to cram, to pack (**dans** into) (**b**) *(terre, neige)* to pack down

2 se tasser *vpr* (**a**) *(fondations)* to settle (**b**) *(personne)* to shrink (**c**) **se t. dans qch** *(se serrer dans)* to squeeze into sth (**d**) *Fam* **ça se tassera** *(ça s'arrangera)* things will settle down

taste-vin [tastəvɛ̃] *nm inv* wine taster

tata [tata] *nf Fam* auntie, aunty

tatami [tatami] *nm* tatami

tâter [tate] **1** *vt* (**a**) *(toucher)* to feel (**b**) *Fig* **t. le terrain** to see how the land lies

2 tâter de *vt ind (métier)* to try one's hand at; *(prison)* to have a taste of

3 se tâter *vpr (hésiter)* to be in two minds

tâte-vin [tatvɛ̃] = **taste-vin**

tatie [tati] *nf Fam* auntie, aunty

tatillon, -onne [tatijɔ̃, -ɔn] *adj* finicky

tâtonnements [tatɔnmɑ̃] *nmpl* (**a**) *(dans le noir)* groping (**b**) *Fig (essai)* trial and error; *(de la science, de la recherche)* tentative progress

tâtonner [tatɔne] *vi* (**a**) *(dans le noir)* to grope about (**b**) *Fig (chercher)* to proceed by trial and error

tâtons [tatɔ̃] **à tâtons** *adv* **entrer/sortir à t.** to feel one's way in/out

tatou [tatu] *nm* armadillo

tatouage [tatwaʒ] *nm (action)* tattooing; *(motif)* tattoo

tatouer [tatwe] *vt* to tattoo; **se faire t.** to get a tattoo

tatoueur [tatwœr] *nm* tattoo artist

taudis [todi] *nm* slum; *Fig* dump

taulard, -e [tolar, -ard] *nm,f Fam* jailbird

taule [tol] *nf Fam* clink, slammer; **faire de la t.** to do time

taulier, -ère [tolje, -ɛr] *nm,f Fam (propriétaire)* (hotel) owner; *(gérant)* (hotel) manager

taupe [top] *nf* (**a**) *(animal)* mole (**b**) *Fam (espion)* mole (**c**) *Fam Péj* **vieille t.** old hag

taupinière [topinjɛr] *nf* molehill

taureau, -x [tɔro] *nm* (**a**) *(animal)* bull; *Fam* **prendre le t. par les cornes** to take the bull by the horns (**b**) *Astron & Astrol* **T.** Taurus; **être T.** to be (a) Taurus

tauromachie [tɔrɔmaʃi] *nf* bullfighting

tautologie [totolɔʒi] *nf* tautology

tautologique [totolɔʒik] *adj* tautological

taux [to] *nm* (**a**) *(montant) (des salaires, des impôts)* rate (**b**) *(pourcentage)* rate; *(d'alcool, de cholestérol)* level; **t. fixe** fixed-rate; **t. de change** exchange rate; **t. de croissance** growth rate; **t. d'écoute** ratings; **t. d'épargne** savings rate; **t. d'inflation** rate of inflation; **t. d'intérêt** interest rate; **t. de pénétration** *(d'un marché)* penetration rate (**c**) *Ordinat* ratio, rate

tavelé, -e [tavle] *adj* marked

tavelure [tavlyr] *nf* mark

taverne [tavɛrn] *nf* (**a**) *(restaurant)* restaurant (**b**) *Can* beer parlour, tavern

tavernier, -ère [tavɛrnje, -ɛr] *nm,f* innkeeper

taxation [taksasjɔ̃] *nf* taxation

taxe [taks] *nf* tax; **toutes taxes comprises** inclusive of tax; **t. d'aéroport** airport tax; **t. d'apprentissage** =

tax paid by businesses to fund training programmes; **t. d'habitation** local tax; **t. professionnelle** = tax paid by companies and self-employed people; **t. sur la valeur ajoutée** value added tax

taxer [takse] *vt* (**a**) *(imposer)* to tax (**b**) *(accuser)* **t. qn de négligence** to accuse sb of negligence (**c**) *Fam (soutirer)* **t. qch à qn** to cadge sth off sb

taxi [taksi] *nm* (**a**) *(voiture)* taxi, cab; **prendre un t.** to take a taxi (**b**) *Fam (chauffeur)* taxi driver, cabby

taxidermiste [taksidɛrmist] *nmf* taxidermist

taximètre [taksimɛtr] *nm* meter

Taxiphone® [taksifɔn] *nm* pay phone

Tbilissi [tbilisi] *n* Tbilisi

Tchad [tʃad] *nm* **le T.** Chad

tchadien, -enne [tʃadjɛ̃, -ɛn] **1** *adj* Chadian

2 *nm,f* **T.** Chadian

tchador [tʃadɔr] *nm* chador

tchatche [tʃatʃ] *nf Fam* **avoir la t.** to have the gift of the gab

tchatcher [tʃatʃe] *vi Fam* to chat

tchatcheur, -euse [tʃatʃœr, -øz] *nm,f Fam* smooth talker

tchater [tʃate] *vi Fam* to chat online

tchécoslovaque [tʃekɔslɔvak] *Anciennement* **1** *adj* Czechoslovakian

2 *nmf* **T.** Czechoslovak

Tchécoslovaquie [tʃekɔslɔvaki] *nf Anciennement* **la T.** Czechoslovakia

tchèque [tʃɛk] **1** *adj* Czech

2 *nmf* **T.** Czech

3 *nm (langue)* Czech

tchétchène [tʃetʃɛn] **1** *adj* Chechen

2 *nmf* **T.** Chechen

Tchétchénie [tʃetʃeni] *nf* **la T.** Chechnya

tchin-tchin [tʃintʃin] *exclam Fam* cheers!

TD [tede] *nm (abrév* **travaux dirigés***) Univ* tutorial

te [tə]

> **t'** is used before a word beginning with a vowel or h mute.

pron personnel (**a**) *(objet direct)* you; **te voilà** there you are (**b**) *(objet indirect)* to you; **j'ai vu qu'elle t'a serré la main** I saw her shake your hand; **ils t'ont lancé des cailloux?** did they throw stones at you? (**c**) *(dans les réfléchis)* yourself; **va te doucher** go and have a shower (**d**) *(dans les pronominaux)* **tu t'es trompée** you made a mistake

té [te] *nm (règle)* T-square; **en té** T-shaped

technicien, -enne [tɛknisjɛ̃, -ɛn] *nm,f* technician

technicité [tɛknisite] *nf* technical nature

technico-commercial, -e, -aux, -ales [tɛknikokɔmɛrsjal, -jo] **1** *adj (service)* technical sales; **agent t.** sales engineer

2 *nm,f* sales engineer

technicolor® [tɛknikɔlɔr] *nm* Technicolor®

technique [tɛknik] **1** *adj* technical

2 *nf (d'un artiste, d'un spécialiste)* technique; **avec lui, j'ai ma t.** I have my own way of dealing with him; **t. de vente** sales technique

3 *nm* **le t.** *(enseignement)* technical training

techniquement [tɛknikmɑ̃] *adv* technically

techno [tɛknɔ] *adj inv & nf* techno

technocrate [tɛknɔkrat] *nmf* technocrat

technocratie [tɛknɔkrasi] *nf* technocracy

technologie [tɛknɔlɔʒi] *nf* technology; **de haute t.** high-tech

technologique [tɛknɔlɔʒik] *adj* technological

teck [tɛk] *nm* teak
teckel [tɛkɛl] *nm* dachshund
tectonique [tɛktɔnik] **1** *adj* tectonic
2 *nf* tectonics *(singulier)*; **t. des plaques** plate tectonics
Te Deum [tedeɔm] *nm inv* Te Deum
teenager [tinɛdʒœr] *nmf* teenager
tee-shirt *(pl* **tee-shirts)** [tiʃœrt] *nm* T-shirt, tee-shirt
Téflon® [teflɔ̃] *nm* Teflon®
tégument [tegymã] *nm* integument
Téhéran [teerã] *n* Tehran
teignais, teigne *etc voir* **teindre**
teigne [tɛɲ] *nf* (**a**) *(maladie)* ringworm (**b**) *Fam (homme)* rat; *(femme)* bitch
teigneux, -euse [tɛɲø, -øz] *adj Fam (personne)* nasty
teindre [54] [tɛ̃dr] **1** *vt (vêtement, cheveux)* to dye; **t. qch en rouge** to dye sth red
2 se teindre *vpr* (**a**) *(se colorer)* **se t. les cheveux (en blond)** to dye one's hair (blond) (**b**) *Litt* **se t. de** *(se mêler de)* to be tinged with
teint¹, -e¹ *pp de* **teindre**
teint² [tɛ̃] *nm* (**a**) *(du visage)* complexion; **t. de rose** rosy complexion (**b**) *(d'un tissu)* colour; **tissu bon** *ou* **grand t.** colourfast material; *Fig* **bon t.** *(catholique, communiste)* staunch, dyed-in-the-wool
teinte² [tɛ̃t] *nf* (**a**) *(couleur)* shade, tint (**b**) *Fig (nuance)* tinge
teinter [tɛ̃te] **1** *vt* (**a**) *(colorer)* to tint; *(bois, meuble)* to stain (**b**) *Fig (nuancer)* **teinté de** tinged with
2 se teinter *vpr* **se t. de** to become tinged with
teinture [tɛ̃tyr] *nf* (**a**) *(produit)* dye (**b**) *(action)* dyeing (**c**) *(préparation pharmaceutique)* tincture; **t. d'iode** tincture of iodine
teinturerie [tɛ̃tyrri] *nf (pressing)* dry cleaner's
teinturier, -ère [tɛ̃tyrje, -ɛr] *nm,f* dry cleaner
tek [tɛk] = **teck**
tel, telle [tɛl] **1** *adj* (**a**) *(semblable)* such; **un t. homme** such a man; **une telle conduite** such behaviour; **de telles choses** such things; **t. père, t. fils** like father like son; **rien de t. qu'un bon chocolat chaud** there's nothing like a nice cup of hot chocolate; **à t. ou t. endroit** in such and such a place; **il n'a rien dit de t.** he said nothing of the kind; **sa bonté est telle que...** he's/she's so kind that... (**b**) *(comme)* **t. que** such as, like; **voir les choses telles qu'elles sont** to see things as they are; **t. que je le connais, il ne sera pas d'accord** knowing him, he won't agree; *Litt* **t. une bête furieuse** like an enraged animal (**c**) *(locutions)* **à t. point que** to such an extent that; **de telle sorte que...** so that..., in such a way that...; **elle me l'a dit t. quel** *ou Fam* **t. que** she told me just like that
2 *pron indéfini* **t. ou t. vous dira que...** some people will tell you that...
3 *pron démonstratif* such; **t. est mon désir** such is my wish
4 *nm,f* **un t., une telle** so-and-so
télé [tele] *nf Fam* (**a**) *(appareil)* TV, *Br* telly (**b**) *(organisme)* **la t.** TV; **travailler à la t.** to work in TV
téléachat [teleaʃa] *nm (à la télévision)* teleshopping; *(par Internet)* on-line shopping
télécabine [telekabin] *nf* cable car
Télécarte® [telekart] *nf* phone card
téléchargement [teleʃarʒəmã] *nm Ordinat* downloading
télécharger [45] [teleʃarʒe] *vt Ordinat* to download; *(vers un gros ordinateur)* to upload
télécommande [telekɔmãd] *nf* remote control

télécommander [telekɔmãde] *vt* (**a**) *(appareil)* to operate by remote control (**b**) *Fig (complot, soulèvement)* to mastermind from a distance
télécommunications [telekɔmynikasjɔ̃] *nfpl* **les t.** telecommunications
téléconférence [telekɔ̃ferãs] *nf* teleconference
télécopie [telekɔpi] *nf* fax
télécopieur [telekɔpjœr] *nm* fax (machine)
télédiffuser [teledifyze] *vt* to televise
télédiffusion [teledifyzjɔ̃] *nf* televising
tel écran-tel écrit [telekrãtelekri] *adj Ordinat* WYSIWYG
télé-enseignement [teleãsɛɲmã] *nm* distance learning
téléfilm [telefilm] *nm* TV movie
télégénique [teleʒenik] *adj* telegenic
télégramme [telegram] *nm* telegram
télégraphe [telegraf] *nm* telegraph
télégraphier [66] [telegrafje] *vt* to cable, to wire
télégraphique [telegrafik] *adj (fil, poteau)* telegraph; **en style t.** in telegraphic style
télégraphiste [telegrafist] *nmf* (**a**) *(technicien)* telegraphist (**b**) *(porteur)* telegraph messenger
téléguidage [telegidaʒ] *nm* remote control
téléguidé, -e [telegide] *adj* remote-controlled
téléguider [telegide] *vt* (**a**) *(voiture, missile)* to operate by remote control (**b**) *Fig (complot, soulèvement)* to mastermind from a distance
télématique [telematik] **1** *adj* telematic
2 *nf* telematics *(singulier)*
télémessage [telemesaʒ] *nm Tél* text message
téléobjectif [teleɔbʒɛktif] *nm* telephoto lens
télépaiement [telepɛmã] *nm* telepayment
télépathe [telepat] **1** *adj* telepathic
2 *nmf* telepathist
télépathie [telepati] *nf* telepathy
télépathique [telepatik] *adj* telepathic
téléphérique [teleferik] *nm* cable car
téléphone [telefɔn] *nm* (**a**) *(appareil, système)* phone, telephone; **avoir le t.** to be on the phone, to have a phone; **être au t.** to be on the phone; **un coup de t.** a phone call; *Fam* **par le t. arabe** on the grapevine; **t. cellulaire** cellular phone; **t. mobile** mobile (phone); **t. portatif** portable phone; **t. public** public phone; *Pol* **t. rouge** hot line; **t. sans fil** cordless phone; **t. de voiture** car phone (**b**) *(numéro)* phone number
téléphoner [telefɔne] **1** *vt* (**a**) *(nouvelle)* to phone, to telephone (à to) (**b**) *Fam* **c'était téléphoné** you could see it coming
2 *vi* to phone, to telephone; **t. à qn** to phone sb
3 se téléphoner *vpr* to phone each other
téléphonie [telefɔni] *nf* telephony; **t. sans fil** wireless telephony; **la t. mobile** the mobile phone sector
téléphonique [telefɔnik] *adj* telephone
téléphoniste [telefɔnist] *nmf* (telephone) operator, *Br* telephonist
téléportation [telepɔrtasjɔ̃] *nf* teleportation
téléporter [telepɔrte] *vt* to teleport
télé-poubelle [telepubɛl] *nf Fam* trash television
téléprompteur [teleprɔ̃ptœr] *nm* Teleprompter®, *Br* Autocue®
téléprospecteur, -trice [teleprɔspɛktœr, -tris] *nm,f* telemarketer
téléprospection [teleprɔspɛksjɔ̃] *nf* telemarketing
télé-réalité [telerealite] *nf* reality TV
téléreportage [teler(ə)pɔrtaʒ] *nm (activité)* television reporting; *(document)* television report

téléroman [teleromã] *nm Can* television serial

télescopage [teleskopaʒ] *nm (de trains)* telescoping; **télescopages en série** *(de véhicules)* pile-up

télescope [teleskɔp] *nm* telescope

télescoper [teleskɔpe] **1** *vt (véhicules, trains)* to crash into
2 se télescoper *vpr* (**a**) *(véhicules, trains)* to concertina (**b**) *(souvenirs, images)* to intermingle

télescopique [teleskɔpik] *adj* telescopic

téléscripteur [teleskriptœr] *nm* teleprinter

télésiège [telesjeʒ] *nm* chair lift

téléski [teleski] *nm* ski tow

téléspectateur, -trice [telespɛktatœr, -tris] *nm,f* (television) viewer

télésurveillance [telesyrvɛjãs] *nf* electronic surveillance

Télétexte® [teletɛkst] *nm* teletext

télétravail [teletravaj] *nm* teleworking

télétravailleur, -euse [teletravajœr, -øz] *nm,f* teleworker

télé-vérité [televerite] *nf* reality TV

télévisé, -e [televize] *adj* televised

téléviseur [televizœr] *nm* television (set)

télévision [televizjɔ̃] *nf* (**a**) *(organisme, technique, émissions)* television; **à la t.** on television; **travailler à la t.** to work in television; **t. par câble** cable television; **t. à la carte** pay-per-view television; **t. en circuit fermé** closed-circuit television; **t. commerciale** commercial television; **t. haute définition** high-definition television; **t. numérique** digital television (**b**) *(poste)* television (set); **regarder la t.** to watch television; **t. en couleur, t. couleur** colour television

télévisuel, -elle [televizɥɛl] *adj* television

télex [telɛks] *nm* telex

télexer [telɛkse] *vt* to telex

tellement [tɛlmã] *adv* (**a**) *(si)* so; **c'était t. intéressant que...** it was so interesting that...; **ce n'est pas t. beau** it's not all that beautiful (**b**) *(tant)* so much; **t. de** *(nombre)* so many; *(quantité)* so much; **elle a t. grandi** she's grown so much; **je n'ai pas t. aimé** I didn't like it that much; **je n'ai plus t. envie d'y aller** I'm no longer that keen on going; **il a t. crié que...** he shouted so much that...; *Fam* **je vais craquer t. il m'énerve** he annoys me so much I'm going to crack up

tellurique [telyrik] *adj (courants)* telluric; **secousse t.** earth tremor

téméraire [temerɛr] *adj* reckless

témérité [temerite] *nf* recklessness

témoignage [temwaɲaʒ] *nm* (**a**) *Jur* evidence, testimony; **porter t. (en faveur de/contre qn)** to give evidence (on behalf of/against sb); **faux t.** perjury (**b**) *(compte rendu)* report, account (**c**) *(démonstration)* **en t. d'amitié** as a token of friendship

témoigner [temwaɲe] **1** *vt* (**a**) *(attester)* **t. que** to testify that (**b**) *(sentiments, gratitude)* to show (**à** to)
2 *vi* to testify, to give evidence (**en faveur de/contre** on behalf of/against)
3 **témoigner de** *vt ind* (**a**) *(montrer)* to show (**b**) *(se porter garant de)* to testify to

témoin [temwɛ̃] **1** *nm* (**a**) *(d'un événement, d'un mariage)* witness; **être t. de qch** to witness sth, to be a witness to sth; **prendre qn à t.** to call sb to witness; **Dieu m'est t. que...** as God is my witness...; **t. à charge** witness for the prosecution; **t. oculaire** eyewitness (**b**) *(dans un duel)* second (**c**) *(preuve)* **t. les coups que j'ai reçus** witness the blows I received (**d**)

(dans un relais) baton (**e**) *Rel* **T. de Jéhovah** Jehovah's Witness (**f**) *Can* **Ordinat** cookie
2 *adj inv (animal, plante)* control; **appartement t.** *Br* show flat, *Am* model apartment

tempe [tãp] *nf* temple

tempérament [tãperamã] *nm* (**a**) *(caractère)* disposition; *Fam* **avoir du t.** *(avoir du caractère)* to have character (**b**) **acheter qch à t.** to buy sth *Br* on hire purchase *or Am* on the installment plan

tempérance [tãperãs] *nf* moderation, temperance

température [tãperatyr] *nf* temperature; **avoir de la t.** to have a (high) temperature; *Fig* **prendre la t. de qch** to gauge the temperature of sth

tempéré, -e [tãpere] *adj (climat)* temperate

tempérer [34] [tãpere] *vt (enthousiasme, passion)* to moderate

tempête [tãpɛt] *nf* storm; *Fig* **une t. d'applaudissements** thunderous applause; *Fig* **une t. dans un verre d'eau** a storm in a *Br* teacup *or Am* teapot; **t. de neige** snowstorm, blizzard; **t. de sable** sandstorm

tempêter [tãpete] *vi* to storm, to rage

tempétueux, -euse [tãpetɥø, -øz] *adj Litt* stormy

temple [tãpl] *nm aussi Fig* temple; *(protestant)* church

tempo [tɛ̃po, tempo] *nm* tempo

temporaire [tãpɔrɛr] *adj* temporary

temporairement [tãpɔrɛrmã] *adv* temporarily

temporel, -elle [tãpɔrɛl] *adj* (**a**) *(qui concerne le temps)* temporal (**b**) *(terrestre)* temporal, worldly

temporellement [tãpɔrɛlmã] *adv* temporally

temporisateur, -trice [tãpɔrizatœr, -tris] *adj (stratégie)* delaying

temporiser [tãpɔrize] *vi* to play for time, to stall

temps [tã] *nm* (**a**) *(durée)* time; **avoir le t. de faire qch** to have (the) time to do sth; **avoir tout le t.** to have plenty of time; **prendre le t. de faire qch** to take the time to do sth; **prendre son t.** to take one's time; **ça prend du t.** it takes time; **ça a pris un certain t.** it took quite a while; **donner** *ou* **laisser le t. à qn de faire qch** to give sb the time to do sth; *Fig* **en deux t. trois mouvements** in two ticks; **avec le t.** in *or* with time, with time; **combien de t.** how long; **combien de t. faut-il pour y aller?** how long does it take to get there?; *Prov* **le t., c'est de l'argent** time is money; *Ordinat* **base de t.** time base; *Ordinat* **t. d'adressage** address speed
(**b**) *(moment)* time; **en t. de crise** in a crisis; **en t. de guerre/paix** in wartime/peacetime; **de t. en t., de t. à autre** from time to time; **en même t. (que)** at the same time (as); **pendant ce t.** meanwhile, in the meantime; **il y a peu de t.** not long ago, a little while ago; **peu de t. après** shortly after; **d'ici quelque t.** soon, shortly; **tout le t.** all the time; **les premiers t.** at the beginning; **ces t.-ci** these days; **ces derniers t.** this last while; **il y est resté quelque t.** he stayed there for a while; **ça n'a qu'un t.** it won't last forever; **les t. forts de l'actualité** the main points of the news; **t. libre** free time; **t. mort** lull; *(au basket-ball)* time out
(**c**) *(époque)* time, days; **de mon t.** in my day *or* time; **du t. de ma jeunesse** in my younger days; **de tout t.** from time immemorial; **dans le t.** in the old days; **en ce t.-là** at that time, then; **par les t. qui courent** these days; **être de son t., vivre avec son t.** to move with the times; **être en avance sur son t.** to be ahead of one's time; **le bon vieux t.** the good old days; **les t. sont durs** times are hard
(**d**) *(heure)* **faire qch à t.** to do sth in time; **en t. voulu** *ou* **utile** in due course; **il est t. qu'elle descende** it's time she came down; **il n'est plus t.** it's too late;

le paquet est enfin arrivé mais il était t.! the parcel's finally arrived and about time too!

(**e**) *(occasion)* il y a un t. pour tout there's a time for everything; **chaque chose en son t.** all in good time (**f**) *(météo)* weather; **par tous les t.** in all weathers; **quel t. fait-il?** what's the weather like?

(**g**) *Gram* tense (**h**) *Mus* beat (**i**) *(d'un athlète)* time

tenable [tənabl] *adj (situation)* bearable

tenace [tənas] *adj* (**a**) *(personne)* stubborn, tenacious (**b**) *(préjugé, volonté)* stubborn; *(odeur, douleur, souvenir)* lingering; *(habitude)* deep-rooted (**c**) *(colle)* strong

ténacité [tenasite] *nf* (**a**) *(d'une personne)* stubbornness, tenacity; **avec t.** stubbornly; *(travailler)* doggedly (**b**) *(d'un préjugé)* stubbornness; *(d'une odeur, d'une douleur, d'un souvenir)* lingering nature; *(d'une habitude)* deep-rootedness

tenailler [tənaje] *vt Litt* to torture; **tenaillé par la faim** ravenously hungry; **tenaillé par la douleur** gripped with pain

tenailles [tənaj] *nfpl* pincers

tenancier, -ère [tənɑ̃sje, -ɛr] *nm,f (d'un bar, d'une maison de jeu)* manager, *f* manageress

tenant, -e [tənɑ̃, -ɑ̃t] **1** *adj voir* **séance**
2 *nm* (**a**) *(partisan)* champion, defender (**b**) **le t. du titre** the title holder (**c**) *(locutions)* **d'un seul t.** in one piece; **les tenants et les aboutissants** *(d'une affaire)* the ins and outs

tendance [tɑ̃dɑ̃s] **1** *nf* (**a**) *(d'une personne)* tendency; **avoir t. à faire qch** to have a tendency to do sth; **avoir une t. à qch** to have a tendency to sth (**b**) *(de l'économie, du marché, d'une mode)* trend
2 *adj Fam (à la mode)* cool, trendy

tendanceur [tɑ̃dɑ̃sœr] *nm Mktg* trendspotter

tendancieusement [tɑ̃dɑ̃sjøzmɑ̃] *adv* tendentiously

tendancieux, -euse [tɑ̃dɑ̃sjø, -øz] *adj* tendentious

tendeur [tɑ̃dœr] *nm (pour bagages)* elastic strap

tendinite [tɑ̃dinit] *nf* tendinitis

tendon [tɑ̃dɔ̃] *nm* tendon; **t. d'Achille** Achilles tendon

tendre¹ [tɑ̃dr] **1** *adj* (**a**) *(bois, pierre, métal)* soft; *(viande, légume)* tender (**b**) *(couleur)* delicate, soft (**c**) *(personne, geste, cœur)* tender; **ne pas être t. (pour ou avec qn)** to be hard (on sb) (**d**) **l'âge t.** early childhood; **depuis ma plus t. enfance** since my earliest childhood
2 *nmf (personne)* softhearted person

tendre² **1** *vt* (**a**) *(corde)* to tighten; *(toile)* to stretch; *(muscle)* to tense; *(arc)* to bend (**b**) *(voile, filet)* to spread; *(papier peint, tapisserie)* to hang; **une pièce tendue de velours rouge** a room whose walls are covered in red velvet (**c**) *(piège)* to set (à for) (**d**) *(main, bras, jambe)* to stretch out, to hold out (à to); **les bras tendus** with outstretched arms; *Fig* **t. la main à qn** *(l'aider)* to offer sb a hand; *Fig* **t. l'oreille** to prick up one's ears
2 *vi* **t. vers zéro** to tend towards zero
3 **tendre à** *vt ind* (**a**) *(avoir pour but) (idéal)* to aim for (**b**) *(avoir tendance à)* **t. à faire qch** to tend to do sth (**c**) **t. à sa fin** to come to an end
4 **se tendre** *vpr (cordage)* to become taut; *Fig (relations, situation)* to become strained

tendrement [tɑ̃drəmɑ̃] *adv* tenderly, lovingly

tendresse [tɑ̃drɛs] *nf* (**a**) *(affection)* tenderness, affection; **avoir de la t. pour qn** to feel affection for sb; **avec t.** tenderly, affectionately (**b**) **tendresses** *(démonstrations)* expressions of affection

tendron [tɑ̃drɔ̃] *nm* (**a**) *(de veau)* flank (**b**) *Fam (jeune fille)* slip of a girl

tendu, -e [tɑ̃dy] *adj* (**a**) *(corde, toile)* taut, tight (**b**) *(main)* outstretched (**c**) *(relations, visage)* strained; *(personne, atmosphère, situation)* tense

ténèbres [tenɛbr] *nfpl* **les t.** the darkness

ténébreux, -euse [tenebrø, -øz] **1** *adj Litt* (**a**) *(obscur) (forêt)* dark, gloomy (**b**) *(mystérieux) (affaire)* murky; *(style)* obscure (**c**) *(personne)* melancholic
2 *nm* **beau t.** tall dark handsome man

teneur [tənœr] *nf* (**a**) *(d'un document, d'un discours)* content; *(d'un contrat)* terms (**b**) *(quantité)* content; **t. en eau/or** water/gold content

tenir [70] [tənir] **1** *vt* (**a**) *(à la main, sur ses genoux)* to hold; **t. qn par le cou/les épaules** to have one's arm round sb's neck/shoulders; *Fig* **je tiens mon homme/ la solution** I've got my man/the answer; *Fam* **t. un bon rhume** to have an awful *or Br* a stinking cold; *Fam* **qu'est-ce qu'il tient!** *(il est idiot)* what an idiot!; **tenez!** *(c'est pour vous)* here (you are)!; **tiens, voilà Paul!** oh, there's Paul!; *Prov* **un tiens vaut mieux que deux tu l'auras** a bird in the hand is worth two in the bush
(**b**) *(dans une position)* to hold; *(dans un état)* to keep; **t. sa droite** *(en voiture)* to keep to the right
(**c**) *(boutique, hôtel)* to run; *(caisse)* to be in charge of
(**d**) *(rôle)* to have
(**e**) *(parole, promesse)* to keep
(**f**) *(maîtriser)* *(enfants, cheval)* to control; **t. sa langue** to hold one's tongue
(**g**) *(résister à) Fam* **t. l'alcool** to hold one's drink; **t. la route** *(voiture)* to hold the road
(**h**) *(avoir)* **t. qch de qn** *(caractéristique)* to get sth from sb; **je tiens la nouvelle de ma mère** I got the news from my mother
(**i**) *(considérer)* **t. qn pour responsable** to hold sb responsible; **t. qch pour vrai** to consider sth to be true
2 *vi* (**a**) *(nœud, corde)* to hold; *(construction)* to stay up; *(autocollant, pansement)* to stay on; *(personne)* to last; *Fam* **il ne tient plus sur ses jambes** *ou* **debout** *(fatigué)* he's dead on his feet; *(ivre)* he can hardly stand; **t. debout** *(argument)* to stand up; **t. bon** *(personne)* to hold out; **je n'y tiens plus** I can't stand it any longer
(**b**) *(durer)* to last; **mon offre/le pari tient toujours** my offer/the bet still stands; **ça tient toujours pour dimanche?** is it still on for Sunday?
(**c**) *(être contenu)* to fit; **on tient à dix autour de cette table** this table seats ten; **ma conclusion tiendra en trois mots** my conclusion can be summed up in three words
3 *v impersonnel* **il ne tient qu'à vous que cela se fasse** it depends entirely on you whether it gets done; **s'il ne tenait qu'à moi...** if it was just up to me...; **qu'à cela ne tienne** that's not a problem
4 **tenir à** *vt ind* (**a**) *(liberté, amitié)* to value; *(ami)* to care about; *(objet)* to be attached to; **t. à faire qch** to be anxious *or* keen to do sth; **je tiens à ce que tout soit rangé** I want everything to be tidy; **si vous y tenez** if you insist
(**b**) *(provenir de)* to be the result of, to be due to
5 **tenir de** *vt ind (ressembler à) (personne)* to take after; *Fam* **entre son oncle et son père, il a de qui t.!** it's not surprising when you consider his uncle and his father!; **cela tient du miracle** it's something of a miracle
6 **se tenir** *vpr* (**a**) *(rester) (debout)* to stand; *(assis)* to

sit; **se t. debout** to be standing, to stand; **se t. tranquille** to keep quiet

(**b**) *(se comporter)* **bien se t.** to behave (oneself); *Fig* **il n'a qu'à bien se t.!** he'd better watch his step!; **se t. mal à table** to have no table manners

(**c**) *(s'accrocher)* to hold on (**à** to); **tenez-vous bien!** hold tight!; *Fig* **et alors, tiens-toi bien...!** and would you believe it...!; **se t. par la main** to hold hands; **ils se tenaient par la taille** they had their arms round each other's waist

(**d**) *(avoir lieu)* to be held, to take place

(**e**) *(être plausible)* to hang together

(**f**) **s'en t. à** *(généralités, sujet, budget)* to keep to; *(décision, consignes)* to abide by; **il ne s'en tint pas là** he didn't stop there; **je ne sais pas à quoi m'en t.** I don't know where I stand

(**g**) *(locutions)* **tiens-le-toi pour dit!** I'm telling you for the last time!

tennis [tenis] **1** *nm* (**a**) *(sport)* tennis; **t. de table** table tennis (**b**) *(court)* tennis court

2 *nm ou nf (chaussure)* tennis shoe

tennisman [tenisman] *(pl* **tennismen** [tenismɛn]) *nm* tennis player

ténor [tenɔr] **1** *adj (saxophone)* tenor

2 *nm* (**a**) *(voix, chanteur)* tenor (**b**) *Fig* **un t. de la politique** an influential figure in politics

tenseur [tɑ̃sœr] **1** *adj* **muscle t.** tensor

2 *nm* tensor

tension [tɑ̃sjɔ̃] *nf* (**a**) *(raideur, désaccord)* tension; **être sous t.** to be tense; **mettre qn sous t.** to put sb under stress; **t. nerveuse** nervous tension (**b**) **t.** (**artérielle**) blood pressure; **avoir de la t.** to have high blood pressure; **prendre la t. de qn** to take sb's blood pressure (**c**) *(électrique)* voltage, tension; **basse/haute t.** low/high voltage *or* tension

tentaculaire [tɑ̃takylɛr] *adj (ville)* sprawling; *(société, organisme)* octopus-like

tentacule [tɑ̃takyl] *nm* tentacle

tentant, -e [tɑ̃tɑ̃, -ɑ̃t] *adj* tempting

tentateur, -trice [tɑ̃tatœr, -tris] **1** *adj* tempting

2 *nm* tempter; *Rel* **le T.** the Tempter

3 *nf* **tentatrice** temptress

tentation [tɑ̃tasjɔ̃] *nf* temptation

tentative [tɑ̃tativ] *nf* attempt; **t. d'assassinat** attempted murder; **t. d'évasion** attempt to escape; **t. de suicide** suicide attempt

tente [tɑ̃t] *nf* (**a**) *(de camping)* tent; **coucher sous la t.** to sleep under canvas; **t. igloo** igloo tent (**b**) *Méd* **t. à oxygène** oxygen tent

tenter [tɑ̃te] *vt* (**a**) *(mettre à l'épreuve)* **t. sa chance** to try one's luck; *Fam* **t. le coup** to have a go; **t. le tout pour le tout** to go for broke (**b**) *(séduire)* to tempt; **être tenté de faire qch** to be tempted to do sth; **se laisser t.** to let oneself be tempted; **j'ai envie de me laisser t.** *(accepter)* I'm tempted to say yes; *(faire quelque chose)* I'm tempted to do it (**c**) *(essayer)* to try, to attempt; **t. de faire qch** to try *or* attempt to do sth

tenture [tɑ̃tyr] *nf (tapisserie)* hanging

tenu, -e¹ [təny] *adj* (**a**) **bien/mal t.** *(maison, jardin)* well/poorly kept (**b**) *(contraint)* **être t. de faire qch** to be obliged to do sth; **être t. à qch** to be bound by sth (**c**) *(note)* held

ténu, -e [teny] *adj* (**a**) *(fil)* fine; *(nuance)* subtle; *(lien)* tenuous; *(espoir)* slender (**b**) *(voix)* thin

tenue² [təny] *nf* (**a**) *(habillement)* outfit; *(militaire)* dress; **en t. légère** *(en vêtements d'été)* in light clothing; *Fam* **en petite t.** skimpily dressed; **t. de combat**

battledress; **t. de soirée** evening dress (**b**) *(bonne conduite)* good behaviour; **un peu de t.!** mind your manners!; **manquer de t.** to lack manners (**c**) *(maintien)* posture (**d**) *(niveau)* standard (**e**) *(d'une maison)* running (**f**) **t. de route** *(d'un véhicule)* road-holding

tequila [tekila] *nf* tequila

ter [tɛr] *adj* **5 t.** ≃ 5B

tercet [tɛrsɛ] *nm* tercet

térébenthine [terebɑ̃tin] *nf* turpentine

Tergal® [tɛrgal] *nm* *Br* Terylene®, *Am* Dacron®

tergiversations [tɛrʒiversasjɔ̃] *nfpl* equivocation

tergiverser [tɛrʒiverse] *vi* to equivocate

terme¹ [tɛrm] *nm* (**a**) *(fin)* end; **toucher à son t.** *(projet)* to be nearing completion; *(période)* to be drawing to a close; **mettre un t. à qch** to put an end to sth; **mener qch à son t.** to bring sth to a successful conclusion (**b**) *(date limite)* time (limit); **à court/long t.** *(projet, prévisions)* short-/long-term; **à court/long t....** in the short/long term... (**c**) *(d'une femme enceinte)* **être à t.** to have reached term; **avant t.** *(accoucher)* prematurely; *(accouchement)* premature (**d**) *(loyer)* rent; *(date de paiement du loyer)* rent day

terme² *nm* (**a**) *(mot)* term; **en d'autres termes** in other words (**b**) *(relations)* **être en bons/mauvais termes avec qn** to be on good/bad terms with sb (**c**) **termes** *(d'un contrat)* terms

terminaison [tɛrminɛzɔ̃] *nf* (**a**) *(d'un mot)* ending (**b**) *Anat* **t. nerveuse** nerve ending

terminal, -e, -aux, -ales [tɛrminal, -o] **1** *adj (de la fin)* final; *Méd (phase)* terminal; **être en phase terminale** *(malade)* to be terminally ill

2 *nm* (**a**) *(dans un aéroport)* terminal (**b**) *Ordinat* terminal, VDU

3 *nf Scol* **terminale** *Br* ≃ upper sixth, *Am* ≃ twelfth grade, senior year

terminer [tɛrmine] **1** *vt (discours, lettre, repas)* to end, to finish (**par** with); *(travail)* to finish, to complete; **en t. avec qch** to put an end to sth

2 se terminer *vpr (saison)* to come to a close; *(soirée, concert, vacances)* to end (**par** with); *(rue)* to end; **se t. en** *(mot)* to end in

terminologie [tɛrminɔlɔʒi] *nf* terminology

terminus [tɛrminys] *nm* terminus

termite [tɛrmit] *nm* termite

terne [tɛrn] *adj* dull

ternir [tɛrnir] **1** *vt (meuble)* to fade; *(miroir, métal, réputation)* to tarnish

2 se ternir *vpr (meuble)* to fade; *(miroir, métal, réputation)* to become tarnished

terrain [tɛrɛ̃] *nm* (**a**) *(parcelle)* piece *or* plot of land (**b**) *(espace au sol, relief)* ground; **tout t.** *(véhicule)* all-terrain (**c**) *(terre)* soil (**d**) *(destiné à une activité)* **t. d'atterrissage** landing strip; **t. d'aviation** airfield; **t. à bâtir** development site; **t. de camping** campsite; *Fig* **t. d'entente** common ground; **t. de jeu** *(pour les sports)* *Br* playing field, *Am* athletic field; *(pour les enfants)* playground; **t. de sport** sports ground; **t. vague** waste ground (**e**) *Méd* **présenter un t. favorable à qch** to be prone to sth (**f**) *(locutions)* **être sur son t.** to be on familiar ground; **sur le t.** *(apprendre)* in the field; **perdre/céder du t.** to lose/give ground; **préparer le t.** to pave the way

terrasse [tɛras] *nf* (**a**) *(d'un café, d'un restaurant)* *Br* pavement *or* *Am* sidewalk area; **en t.** outside; **prix des consommations en t.** price of drinks served outside (**b**) *(de maison, d'appartement)* terrace; **(toit en)**

t. terrace (roof) (**c**) *(levée de terre)* terrace; **en terrasses** *(jardin)* terraced; *(culture)* terrace
terrassement [tɛrasmɑ̃] *nm* (**a**) *(action)* excavation (**b**) *(remblai)* earthwork
terrasser [tɛrase] *vt (sujet: adversaire)* to floor; *(sujet: émotion, fatigue, nouvelle)* to overwhelm; *(sujet: maladie)* to lay low
terrassier [tɛrasje] *nm* labourer
terre [tɛr] *nf* (**a**) *(monde)* world; *Fig* **t. à t.** down-to-earth; *Fig* **revenir sur t.** to come down to earth; *Fig* **avoir les pieds sur t.** to have one's feet on the ground (**b**) *(planète)* **la T.** (the) Earth (**c**) *(sol)* ground; *(étendue)* land; **à t., par t.** on the ground; *Can Fam Fig* **être à t.** to be *or* feel down; **tomber par t.** to fall down; **faire tomber qch par t.** to drop sth; **sous t.** underground; **basses terres** lowlands; **hautes terres** highlands (**d**) *Élec Br* earth, *Am* ground; **relier** *ou* **raccorder à la t.** *Br* to earth, *Am* to ground (**e**) *(opposé à la mer)* land; **t. ferme** terra firma (**f**) *(matière)* soil, earth; **cultiver la t.** to cultivate the soil; **t. battue** mud; *(de court de tennis)* clay; **t. de Sienne** sienna (**g**) *(propriété)* **une t.** a piece of land; **terres** land (**h**) *(territoire)* land, country; **terres australes** southern lands; **la t. Adélie** Adélie Land; **la T. de Feu** Tierra del Fuego; **la T. promise** the Promised Land; **la T. sainte** the Holy Land (**i**) *(élément)* earth (**j**) *(argile)* clay; **cruche de** *ou* **en t.** earthenware jug; **t. cuite** terracotta; **une t. cuite** a piece of terracotta
terreau, -x [tɛro] *nm* compost
Terre-Neuve [tɛrnœv] *n* Newfoundland
terre-neuve [tɛrnœv] *nm inv* Newfoundland (dog)
terre-plein *(pl* **terre-pleins**) [tɛrplɛ̃] *nm (plate-forme)* platform; **t. central** *(sur route) Br* central reservation, *Am* median strip
terrer [tɛre] **se terrer** *vpr aussi Fig* to go to earth
terrestre [tɛrɛstr] *adj* (**a**) *(plante)* ground; *(animal)* land; *(transports)* surface (**b**) *(magnétisme, attraction)* of the earth (**c**) *(matériel)* worldly
terreur [tɛrœr] *nf* (**a**) *(effroi)* terror; **vivre dans la t.** to live in terror (**b**) *(emploi de la violence)* terror (**c**) *Fig (personne)* terror; **jouer les terreurs** to play the tough guy
terreux, -euse [tɛrø, -øz] *adj* (**a**) *(odeur)* earthy (**b**) *(mains)* muddy (**c**) *(teint, ciel, couleur)* muddy
terrible [tɛribl] *adj* (**a**) *(affreux, remarquable)* terrible (**b**) *Fam (formidable)* great, fantastic; **pas t.** nothing special
terriblement [tɛriblǝmɑ̃] *adv* terribly
terrien, -enne [tɛrjɛ̃, -ɛn] **1** *adj* (**a**) *(qui possède des terres)* landowning; **propriétaire t.** landowner (**b**) *(famille, vertu)* rural (**c**) *(de la Terre)* Earth
2 *nm,f (habitant de la Terre)* earthling
terrier¹ [tɛrje] *nm (d'un lapin)* burrow, hole; *(d'une taupe)* hole; *(d'un renard)* earth
terrier² *nm (chien)* terrier
terrifiant, -e [tɛrifjɑ̃, -ɑ̃t] *adj* terrifying
terrifier [66] [tɛrifje] *vt* to terrify
terril [tɛril] *nm* slag heap
terrine [tɛrin] *nf* terrine
territoire [tɛritwar] *nm* (**a**) *(d'un État, d'un animal)* territory; **t. d'outre-mer** overseas territory; *Can* **Territoires du Nord-Ouest** Northwest Territories (**b**) *(de juge, d'évêque)* jurisdiction; *(de commune, d'arrondissement)* area
territorial, -e, -aux, -ales [tɛritɔrjal, -o] *adj* territorial
territorialité [tɛritɔrjalite] *nf* territoriality

terroir [tɛrwar] *nm* soil; **du t.** *(produit, accent, expression)* local
terrorisant, -e [tɛrɔrizɑ̃, -ɑ̃t] *adj* terrifying
terroriser [tɛrɔrize] *vt (sujet: personne)* to terrorize; *(sujet: expérience, souvenir)* to terrify
terrorisme [tɛrɔrism] *nm* terrorism
terroriste [tɛrɔrist] *adj & nmf* terrorist
tertiaire [tɛrsjɛr] **1** *adj* tertiary
2 *nm* (**a**) *(secteur économique)* service sector (**b**) *Géol* Tertiary era
tertio [tɛrsjo] *adv* thirdly
tertre [tɛrtr] *nm* hillock, mound
tes [te] *voir* **ton¹**
tessiture [tesityr] *nf Mus* range
tesson [tesɔ̃] *nm* shard; **t. de bouteille** piece of broken bottle
test [tɛst] **1** *adj inv* test; *(période)* trial
2 *nm* test; **t. de grossesse** pregnancy test; **t. de recherche de paternité** paternity test
Testament [tɛstamɑ̃] *nm* **l'Ancien/le Nouveau T.** the Old/the New Testament
testament [tɛstamɑ̃] *nm (dernières volontés)* will; *Fig* legacy; **ceci est mon t.** this is my last will and testament
testamentaire [tɛstamɑ̃tɛr] *adj voir* **exécuteur**
tester [tɛste] *vt (élève, produit)* to test
testicule [tɛstikyl] *nm* testicle
testostérone [tɛstɔsterɔn] *nf* testosterone
tétanie [tetani] *nf* spasms, *Spéc* tetany; **avoir une crise de t.** to go into spasms
tétanique [tetanik] **1** *adj* tetanic
2 *nmf* tetanus sufferer
tétaniser [tetanize] *vt (muscle)* to cause spasms in; *Fig* **tétanisé de peur** paralysed with fear
tétanos [tetanos] *nm* tetanus
têtard [tɛtar] *nm* tadpole
tête [tɛt] *nf* (**a**) *(d'une personne, d'un animal)* head; **cent cinquante têtes de bétail** a hundred and fifty head of cattle; **j'ai la t. qui tourne** my head is spinning; **tenir t. à qn** to stand up to sb; *Fam* **j'en ai par-dessus la t.** I've had it up to here; *Fam* **avoir la t. près du bonnet** to have a short fuse; *Fam* **faire une grosse t.** *ou* **une t. au carré à qn** to smash sb's face in; *Fam* **tu es tombé sur la t. ou quoi?** are you out of your mind or what?; *Fig* **marcher la t. haute** to walk with one's head held high; **la t. la première** head first; *Fig* **foncer t. baissée** to jump in head first; **de la t. aux pieds** from head to foot; **la t. nue** bare-headed; *Fam* **50 euros par t. de pipe** 50 euros a head; **t. de mort** death's head
(**b**) *(visage)* face; **faire une drôle de t.** to look odd, to make an odd face; **avoir une drôle de t.** to look odd, to have an odd face; **faire la t.** to be in a huff
(**c**) *(personne)* **une t. rousse/blonde** a redhead/blonde; **nos chères têtes blondes** *(enfants)* our little ones; **t. brûlée** hothead; *Fam* **c'est une t. à claques** he/she has a face you just want to slap; *Fam* **t. de cochon** pig-headed person; *Fam* **c'est une t. de lard** *ou* **mule** he's/she's pig-headed; **t. de linotte** bird-brain; **t. de Turc** whipping boy; **forte t.** strong-minded person; *Fam* **grosse t.** highbrow; *Fam* **avoir la grosse t.** to have a big head, to be big-headed
(**d**) *(esprit)* mind; *(cerveau)* brains; **des idées plein la t.** full of ideas; **avoir qch en t.** to have sth in one's head; **ne pas avoir de t.** to be very forgetful; **avoir toute sa t.** to be all there; **perdre la t.** to lose it; **faire qch à t. reposée** to do sth at one's leisure; **où ai-je la**

t.! what am I thinking of!; **être t. en l'air** to have one's head in the clouds; **ne rien avoir dans la t.** to be empty-headed; **avoir la t. dure** to be pig-headed; **mettre qch dans la t. de qn** to put sth in sb's head; **se mettre en t. de faire qch** to get it into one's head to do sth; **se mettre dans la t. que...** to get it into one's head that...; **n'en faire qu'à sa t.** to do exactly as one pleases; **avoir une idée derrière la t.** to have an ulterior motive; **de t.** *(calculer, additionner)* in one's head (**e**) *(cheveux)* hair (**f**) *(d'une liste)* top; *(de chapitre)* heading; **t. d'affiche** top of the bill (**g**) *(d'ail)* head; *(d'un arbre)* top; *(du fémur)* head (**h**) *(d'une procession, d'un cortège)* head; *(d'un train)* front; **le wagon de t.** the front carriage; **prendre la t.** *(dans une course, un jeu)* to take the lead; **prendre la t. d'une entreprise** to take over as the head of a company; **être à la t. de qch** *(entreprise, fortune)* to be at the head of sth; *(protestation, révolte)* to be the leader of sth; **arriver en t.** to come in first; **être en t.** to be in the lead; **t. de lit** bed head; **t. de pont** bridgehead; **t. de série** *(au tennis)* seed (**i**) *(appareil)* **t. chercheuse** homing device; *Ordinat* **t. d'écriture** writing *or* write head; *Ordinat* **t. de lecture** read(ing) head; **t. à palpeur** sensor head
tête-à-queue [tɛtakø] *nm inv* spin; **faire un t.** to spin round
tête-à-tête [tɛtatɛt] *nm inv (rendez-vous)* tête-à-tête; **en t.** in private; **en t. avec** alone with
tête-bêche [tɛtbɛʃ] *adv (dormir)* head to foot
tête-de-nègre [tɛtdənɛgr] *adj inv & nm inv* dark brown
tétée [tete] *nf* feed; **donner la t. à un enfant** to feed a child
téter [34] [tete] *vt* (**a**) *(lait)* to suck; **t. sa mère** to feed (**b**) *(cigare, pipe, stylo)* to suck on
tétine [tetin] *nf* (**a**) *(d'un biberon)* teat (**b**) *(sucette) Br* dummy, *Am* pacifier
téton [tetɔ̃] *nm Fam (sein de femme)* tit, boob
tétraèdre [tetraɛdr] **1** *adj* tetrahedral **2** *nm* tetrahedron
tétralogie [tetralɔʒi] *nf* tetralogy
tétraplégie [tetrapleʒi] *nf* quadriplegia
tétraplégique [tetrapleʒik] *adj & nmf* quadriplegic
tétras [tetra] *nm* grouse
têtu, -e [tety] **1** *adj* stubborn, obstinate; *Fam* **t. comme une mule** as stubborn as a mule **2** *nm,f* stubborn *or* obstinate person
teuf [tœf] *nf Fam* party
teufer [tœfe] *vi Fam (faire la fête)* to party
teuf-teuf *(pl* teufs-teufs) [tœftœf] *Fam* **1** *nf (voiture) Br* old banger, *Am* jalopy **2** *nm (bruit)* chug-chug
teuton, -onne [tøtɔ̃, -ɔn] **1** *adj* Teutonic **2** *nm,f* **T.** Teuton
texan, -e [tɛksɑ̃, -an] **1** *adj* Texan **2** *nm,f* **T.** Texan
texte [tɛkst] *nm* (**a**) *(d'un livre, d'un dépliant)* text; **t. publicitaire** advertising copy; **lire un auteur dans le t.** to read an author in the original; **textes choisis (de)** selected passages (from) (**b**) *(d'un opéra)* libretto; *(d'une chanson)* words; *(d'un acteur)* lines; *(d'une pièce de théâtre)* script
textile [tɛkstil] **1** *adj* textile **2** *nm* (**a**) *(fibre)* textile (**b**) *(industrie)* **le t.** the textile industry, textiles

texto [tɛksto] *Fam* **1** *nm Tél* text (message); **envoyer un t. à qn** to text sb, to send sb a text (message) **2** *adv* word for word; **t.!** those were his/her/*etc* very words!
textuel, -elle [tɛkstɥɛl] *adj* (**a**) *(analyse)* textual (**b**) *(traduction)* word-for-word, literal; *Fam* **t.!** those were his/her/*etc* very words!
textuellement [tɛkstɥɛlmɑ̃] *adv* word for word, literally
texture [tɛkstyr] *nf (d'une substance, du sol)* texture
TF 1 [teɛfœ̃] *nf (abrév* **Télévision Française 1)** = French commercial television channel
TGB [teʒebe] *nf (abrév* **très grande bibliothèque)** = the new French national library in the Tolbiac area of Paris
TGV [teʒeve] *nm (abrév* **train à grande vitesse)** high-speed train
thaï, thaïe [taj] **1** *adj* Thai **2** *nm,f* **T.** Thai **3** *nm (langue)* Thai
thaïlandais, -e [tajlɑ̃dɛ, -ɛz] **1** *adj* Thai **2** *nm,f* **T.** Thai
Thaïlande [tajlɑ̃d] *nf* **la T.** Thailand
thalassothérapie [talasoterapi] *nf* thalassotherapy, seawater therapy
thé [te] *nm* (**a**) *(boisson)* tea; **t. au citron** tea with lemon; **t. glacé** iced tea; **t. à la menthe** mint tea; **t. nature/au lait** tea without milk/with milk; **t. en sachets** tea bags (**b**) *(goûter)* tea; **t. dansant** tea dance
théâtral, -e, -aux, -ales [teatral, -o] *adj* (**a**) *(œuvre, production)* theatrical; *(effet)* dramatic; *(représentation)* stage (**b**) *Péj (artificiel)* melodramatic
théâtre [teatr] *nm* (**a**) *(édifice, salle)* theatre; **t. de marionnettes** puppet theatre; **t. de verdure** open-air theatre (**b**) *(art, métier)* theatre; **c'est un homme de t.** he works in theatre; **faire du t.** *(professionnellement)* to be an actor/actress; *(en amateur)* to do some acting; **adapté pour le t.** adapted for the stage (**c**) *(œuvres) (d'un auteur)* plays; *(genre)* theatre; **t. de boulevard** light comedies (**d**) *Fig (attitude artificielle)* **c'est du t.** it's an act (**e**) *(d'un crime, d'un accident)* scene
théière [tejɛr] *nf* teapot
théine [tein] *nf* theine
thématique [tematik] **1** *adj* thematic **2** *nf* themes
thème [tɛm] *nm* (**a**) *(d'un discours, d'une œuvre, d'un morceau de musique)* theme (**b**) *(traduction)* prose (**c**) *(d'un verbe, d'un nom)* stem (**d**) *Astrol* **t. (astral)** birth chart
théocratie [teɔkrasi] *nf* theocracy
théocratique [teɔkratik] *adj* theocratic
théologie [teɔlɔʒi] *nf* theology
théologien, -enne [teɔlɔʒjɛ̃, -ɛn] *nm,f* theologian
théologique [teɔlɔʒik] *adj* theological
théorème [teɔrɛm] *nm* theorem
théoricien, -enne [teɔrisjɛ̃, -ɛn] *nm,f* theoretician, theorist
théorie [teɔri] *nf* theory; **en t.** in theory
théorique [teɔrik] *adj* theoretical
théoriquement [teɔrikmɑ̃] *adv* theoretically
thérapeute [terapøt] *nmf* therapist
thérapeutique [terapøtik] **1** *adj* therapeutic **2** *nf* (**a**) *(science)* therapeutics *(singulier)* (**b**) *(traitement)* therapy
thérapie [terapi] *nf* therapy; **t. de groupe** group therapy

thermal, -e, -aux, -ales [tɛrmal, -o] *adj* thermal

thermalisme [tɛrmalism] *nm* hydrotherapy

thermes [tɛrm] *nmpl* (**a**) *(établissement de soins)* thermal baths (**b**) *(chez les Anciens)* thermae, public baths

thermique [tɛrmik] *adj* thermal

thermoélectrique [tɛrmoelɛktrik] *adj* thermo-electric

thermomètre [tɛrmomɛtr] *nm* thermometer; *Fig (de l'opinion, d'une tendance)* barometer; **t. médical** clinical thermometer

thermonucléaire [tɛrmonykleɛr] *adj* thermonuclear

Thermos® [tɛrmos] *nm ou nf* (**bouteille**) **T.** Thermos® (*Br* flask *or Am* bottle)

thermostat [tɛrmɔsta] *nm* thermostat

thésard, -e [tezar, -ard] *nm,f* PhD student

thésaurisation [tezɔrizasjɔ̃] *nf* hoarding

thésauriser [tezɔrize] *vt & vi* to hoard

thésaurus [tezɔrys] *nm* thesaurus

thèse [tɛz] *nf* (**a**) *(proposition intellectuelle)* thesis; **roman/littérature à t.** novel/literature of ideas (**b**) *Univ* thesis *(submitted for doctorate)*

thon [tɔ̃] *nm* tuna; **t. blanc** longfin tuna ; **t. au naturel/ à l'huile** tuna in brine/in oil

thoracique [tɔrasik] *adj* thoracic

thorax [tɔraks] *nm* thorax

thriller [srilœr] *nm* thriller

thrombose [trɔ̃boz] *nf* thrombosis

thune [tyn] *nf* (**a**) *très Fam (argent)* cash, dough; **ne pas avoir une t.** to be totally broke *or Br* skint (**b**) *Suisse* = Swiss five-franc coin

thuya [tyja] *nm* thuja

thym [tɛ̃] *nm* thyme

thyroïde [tirɔid] *adj & nf* thyroid

thyroïdien, -enne [tirɔidjɛ̃, -ɛn] *adj* thyroid

tiaffe [tjaf] *nf Suisse Fam* (**a**) *(chaleur)* heatwave (**b**) *(neige fondante)* slush

tiare [tjar] *nf* tiara

Tibet [tibɛ] *nm* le **T.** Tibet

tibétain, -e [tibetɛ̃, -ɛn] **1** *adj* Tibetan

2 *nm,f* **T.** Tibetan

3 *nm (langue)* Tibetan

tibia [tibja] *nm* shinbone, *Spéc* tibia

Tibre [tibr] *nm* le **T.** the Tiber

tic [tik] *nm* (**a**) *(convulsion involontaire)* tic, twitch; **t. nerveux** nervous tic *or* twitch (**b**) *(manie)* habit, mannerism; **t. de langage** verbal mannerism

ticket [tikɛ] *nm* ticket; *Fam Fig* **avoir un** *ou* **le t. avec qn** to be in with sb; **t. de caisse** receipt; **t. modérateur** = portion of the cost of treatment paid by the patient; **t. de quai** platform ticket; **t. de rationnement** ration coupon

ticket-repas *(pl* **tickets-repas**) [tikɛrəpɑ] *nm Br* luncheon voucher, *Am* meal ticket

ticket-restaurant *(pl* **tickets-restaurant**) [tikɛrɛstɔrɑ̃] *nm Br* luncheon voucher, *Am* meal ticket

tic-tac [tiktak] *nm inv (d'une horloge)* tick-tock, ticking

tie-break *(pl* **tie-breaks**) [tajbrɛk] *nm* tie break

tiédasse [tjedas] *adj Péj* lukewarm, tepid

tiède [tjɛd] **1** *adv* **il fait t.** it's mild

2 *adj* (**a**) *(vent)* mild; *(bain, boisson)* tepid, lukewarm (**b**) *Péj (peu enthousiaste)* half-hearted

3 *nf Suisse* heatwave

tiédeur [tjedœr] *nf* (**a**) *(du vent)* mildness; *(de l'eau)* tepidness (**b**) *Péj (manque d'enthousiasme)* half-heartedness

tiédir [tjedir] **1** *vt (réchauffer)* to warm (up); *(refroidir)* to cool (down)

2 *vi* (**a**) *(devenir plus chaud)* to warm up; *(devenir moins chaud)* to cool down (**b**) *Fig (amitié, passion)* to cool off

tien, tienne *(mpl* **tiens**, *fpl* **tiennes**) [tjɛ̃, tjɛn] **1** *pron possessif* **le t., la tienne, les tiens, les tiennes** yours; *(en insistant)* your own; **tu me prêtes le t.?** can I borrow yours?; **tu n'en as pas besoin, tu as le t.** you don't need it, you've got your own; *Fam* **à la tienne!** cheers!

2 *nm* **il faut que tu y mettes du t.** you should really do your share

3 *nmpl* **les tiens** *(ta famille)* your family

4 *nfpl Fam* **tu as encore fait des tiennes!** you've been up to your old tricks again!

tiendrais, tienne, tiens *etc voir* **tenir**

tierce [tjɛrs] *adj voir* **tiers**

tiercé [tjɛrse] *nm* = bet in which the punter predicts the first three horses to finish a race; **jouer au t.** to bet on the horses; **le t. gagnant** the winning combination

tiers, tierce [tjɛr, tjɛrs] **1** *adj* third; **le t. état** the third estate; **une tierce personne** a third party

2 *nm* (**a**) *(fraction)* third; **t. payant** = system of direct payment for medical treatment by the insurer; **t. provisionnel** interim tax payment *(approximately one third of previous year's tax)* (**b**) *(personne)* third party

3 *nf* **tierce** (**a**) *Mus* third (**b**) *(aux cartes)* tierce

tiers-monde *(pl* **tiers-mondes**) [tjɛrmɔ̃d] *nm* **le t.** the Third World

tifs [tif] *nmpl Fam* hair

TIG [tiʒ] *nm (abrév* **travail d'intérêt général**) community service

tige [tiʒ] *nf* (**a**) *(d'une plante)* stem, stalk; **rosier sur t.** standard rose (**b**) *(d'une chaussure)* upper (**c**) *(en métal)* rod (**d**) *Fam (cigarette) Br* fag, *Am* smoke

tignasse [tiɲas] *nf Fam* mop (of hair)

Tigre [tigr] *nm* le **T.** the Tigris

tigre [tigr] *nm* tiger; **t. du Bengale** Bengal tiger

tigré, -e [tigre] *adj (rayé)* striped

tigresse [tigrɛs] *nf* tigress

tilde [tild] *nm* tilde

tilleul [tijœl] *nm* (**a**) *(arbre)* lime (tree) (**b**) *(infusion)* lime-blossom tea

tilt [tilt] *nm* **faire t.** *(au billard électrique)* to signal the end of the game; *Fig* **ça a fait t.** the penny dropped

timbale [tɛ̃bal] *nf* (**a**) *(gobelet)* (metal) drinking cup; *Fig* **décrocher la t.** to hit the jackpot (**b**) *(tambour)* kettledrum; **les timbales** *(dans un orchestre)* the timpani (**c**) *(moule, plat)* timbale

timbre [tɛ̃br] *nm* (**a**) *(vignette)* stamp; **t. de collection** collector's stamp; **t. fiscal** excise *or* tax stamp (**b**) *(instrument encreur, marque)* stamp; **t. dateur** date stamp (**c**) *(sonnette)* bell; **t. de bicyclette** bicycle bell (**d**) *(d'une voix, d'un instrument)* timbre, tone; **voix sans t.** toneless voice (**e**) *(pour traitement médical)* patch; **t. tuberculinique** TB patch

Timbre fiscal

These stamps are sold at most tobacconists and are used to pay fees due for obtaining official documents, such as identity papers, vehicle documents and legal certificates.

timbré, -e [tɛ̃bre] *adj* (**a**) *(document, enveloppe)* stamped (**b**) *Fam (fou)* crazy, nuts

timbre-poste *(pl* **timbres-poste**) [tɛ̃brəpɔst] *nm* (postage) stamp

timbrer [tɛ̃bre] **1** *vt* (**a**) *(lettre, paquet)* to put a stamp/stamps on (**b**) *(passeport, document)* to stamp
2 *vi Suisse (au chômage)* to sign on

timide [timid] **1** *adj* (**a**) *(personne, sourire, voix)* shy (**b**) *(critique, protestation, tentative)* timid
2 *nmf* shy person; **c'est un grand t.** he's very shy

timidement [timidmɑ̃] *adv* (**a**) *(sourire, parler)* shyly (**b**) *(critiquer, protester)* timidly

timidité [timidite] *nf* (**a**) *(d'une personne)* shyness (**b**) *(d'une critique, d'une protestation)* timidity

timing [tajmiŋ] *nm* timing

timoré, -e [timɔre] *adj* timorous, fearful

tintamarre [tɛ̃tamar] *nm Fam* din, racket; **faire du t.** to make a din *or* racket

tintement [tɛ̃təmɑ̃] *nm (de clochettes)* tinkling; *(de pièces de monnaie)* jingling; **t. d'oreilles** ringing in the ears

tinter [tɛ̃te] *vi* (**a**) *(clochettes)* to tinkle; *(pièces de monnaie)* to jingle (**b**) *(oreilles)* to ring

tintin [tɛ̃tɛ̃] *exclam Fam* no way José!; **faire t.** to go without

tintouin [tɛ̃twɛ̃] *nm Fam* (**a**) *(bruit)* din, racket (**b**) *(souci)* trouble

TIOP [tjɔp] *nm Fin (abrév* **taux interbancaire offert à Paris)** PIBOR

tipi [tipi] *nm* tepee

tique [tik] *nf* tick

tiquer [tike] *vi Fam (personne)* to wince; **il n'a pas tiqué** he didn't bat an eyelid

TIR [tir] *nm (abrév* **transports internationaux routiers)** TIR

tir [tir] *nm* (**a**) *(activité)* shooting; **t. à l'arc** archery; **faire du t. à l'arc** to do archery; **t. à la carabine** rifle shooting; **t. au pigeon** clay pigeon shooting (**b**) *(coup de feu)* shot (**c**) *(à la pétanque)* throw; **t. (au but)** *(au football)* shot (at goal) (**d**) *(stand)* rifle range; **t. (forain)** shooting gallery

tirade [tirad] *nf Théât* monologue; *Fig* tirade

tirage [tiraʒ] *nm* (**a**) *(impression)* printing (**b**) *(nombre d'exemplaires) (d'un journal)* circulation; *(d'un livre)* print run; **édition à t. limité** limited edition (**c**) *(d'une cheminée)* draught (**d**) *(de loterie)* draw (**de** for); **t. au sort** drawing lots; **procéder à un t. au sort** to draw lots

tiraillement [tirajmɑ̃] *nm* (**a**) *(crampe)* **tiraillements d'estomac** stomach cramps (**b**) *(conflit)* **tiraillements (entre)** conflict (between)

tirailler [tiraje] **1** *vt* (**a**) *(tirer sur)* to pull at, to tug at (**b**) *(écarteler)* **être tiraillé entre** to be torn between
2 *vi* (**a**) *(avec une arme)* to shoot wildly (**b**) *(peau)* **j'ai la peau qui tiraille** my skin feels tight

tirailleur [tirajœr] *nm (soldat éclaireur)* skirmisher

Tirana [tirana] *n* Tirana

tirant [tirɑ̃] *nm* (**a**) *(de botte)* boot strap (**b**) **t. d'eau** draught *(volume of water)*

tire [tir] *nf* (**a**) *Fam (voiture)* car (**b**) *Can (confiserie)* molasses toffee, *Am* molasses candy, taffy

tiré, -e [tire] **1** *adj* (**a**) *(traits)* drawn; **avoir les traits tirés** to look drawn (**b**) *(cheveux)* scraped back
2 *nf Fam* **tirée** *(trajet)* long haul

tire-au-flanc [tiroflɑ̃] *nm inv Fam* shirker, *Br* skiver

tire-bouchon *(pl* **tire-bouchons**) [tirbuʃɔ̃] *nm* corkscrew; **en t.** *(queue)* curly

tire-bouchonner [tirbuʃɔne] *vi (chaussettes)* to be at half-mast; *(pantalon)* to be crumpled

tire-d'aile [tirdɛl] **à tire-d'aile** *adv* **s'envoler à t.** to fly swiftly away; *Fig* **partir** *ou* **s'éloigner à t.** to fly off

tire-fesses [tirfɛs] *nm inv Fam* T-bar, drag lift

tire-jus [tirʒy] *nm inv très Fam* snot rag

tire-lait [tirlɛ] *nm inv* breast pump

tire-larigot [tirlarigo] **à tire-larigot** *adv Fam* to one's heart's content

tirelire [tirlir] *nf Br* moneybox, *Am* coin bank; *Fig* **casser sa t.** to break into one's piggy bank

tirer [tire] **1** *vt* (**a**) *(vers soi)* to pull; *(chaussettes)* to pull up; **t. qch vers le haut/bas** to pull sth up/down; **t. qn par la manche** to pull at sb's sleeve; **t. qn par le bras** to pull sb by the arm; **t. les cheveux à qn** to pull sb's hair
(**b**) *(rideaux)* to draw; *(store)* to pull down; *(verrou) (fermer)* to shoot; *(ouvrir)* to draw
(**c**) *(extraire)* **t. qch de qch** to pull sth out of sth; **t. de l'eau d'un puits** to draw water from a well; **une citation tirée d'un texte** a quotation taken from a text; **t. qn d'embarras** to get sb out of a tight spot; **t. qn de son lit** to drag sb out of bed; **t. son origine de qch** to have its origin in sth; **t. une conclusion de qch** to draw a conclusion from sth; **t. une leçon de qch** to learn a lesson from sth
(**d**) *(tendre) (tissu, fil)* to pull tight; *Fig* **t. les ficelles** to pull the strings
(**e**) *(carte)* to draw; **t. les cartes** *(cartomancienne)* to read the cards; **t. qch au sort** to draw lots for sth; **t. qn au sort** to draw lots to choose sb
(**f**) *(tracer) (trait)* to draw; *(plan)* to draw up
(**g**) *(imprimer)* to print; *Fam Hum* **se faire t. le portrait** to have one's photograph taken
(**h**) *(chèque)* to draw (**sur** on)
(**i**) *(coup de feu, balle)* to fire; *(flèche)* to shoot; *(feu d'artifice)* to let off; **t. un coup de revolver (sur)** to fire a gun (at)
(**j**) *(locutions) très Fam* **plus qu'un mois à t.!** just one more month to get through!; **je te tire mon chapeau!** I take my hat off to you!
2 *vi* (**a**) *(exercer une traction)* to pull; **t. sur qch** *(corde)* to pull on sth; *(pull)* to pull sth down; *(par tic)* to pull at sth
(**b**) *(personne armée, arme)* to shoot; **t. à la carabine** to shoot with a rifle; **t. sur qn/qch** to shoot sb/sth; **t. dans le dos à qn** to shoot sb in the back
(**c**) *(peau)* to feel tight
(**d**) *(être imprimé)* **t. à 100 000 exemplaires** to have a circulation of 100,000
(**e**) *(cheminée)* to draw
(**f**) *(à la pétanque)* to throw; *(au football)* to shoot
(**g**) *(aspirer)* **t. sur une cigarette/pipe** to puff on a cigarette/pipe
(**h**) *(locutions)* **ça ne tire pas à conséquence** it's of no consequence; **t. à sa fin** *(période, journée)* to be drawing to a close; *(réserves, économies)* to be running out; *Fam* **t. au flanc** to shirk, *Br* to skive
3 *tirer sur* *vt ind (se rapprocher de) (couleur)* to verge on
4 *se tirer* *vpr* (**a**) *(se sortir)* **se t. de qch** to get out of sth; **s'en t.** *(d'une maladie, d'un accident)* to pull through; *(financièrement)* to make it; **s'en t. avec qch** to get away with sth
(**b**) *Fam (partir)* to make tracks

tiret [tirɛ] *nm* dash

tirette [tirɛt] *nf* (**a**) *(d'un bureau)* pull-out shelf; *(d'une table)* leaf (**b**) *(de distributeur)* pull handle (**c**) *Belg (fermeture Éclair®) Br* zip, *Am* zipper

tireur, -euse [tirœr, -øz] **1** *nm,f* gunman; **t. d'élite** marksman, *f* markswoman; **c'est un bon t.** he's a good shot; **un t. embusqué** a sniper
2 *nf* **tireuse de cartes** fortune teller

tiroir [tirwar] *nm* drawer; *Fig* **à tiroirs** *(roman)* = containing individual episodes within the main story-line

tiroir-caisse *(pl* **tiroirs-caisses)** [tirwarkɛs] *nm* till, cash register

tisane [tizan] *nf* herbal tea

tison [tizɔ̃] *nm* (fire)brand

tisonner [tizɔne] *vt* to poke

tisonnier [tizɔnje] *nm* poker

tissage [tisaʒ] *nm* (**a**) *(activité)* weaving; **t. à la main/mécanique** hand-loom/power-loom weaving (**b**) *(établissement industriel)* cloth mill

tisser [tise] **1** *vt* (**a**) *(textile, liens, intrigue)* to weave (**b**) *(sujet: araignée)* to spin
2 se tisser *vpr (liens, intrigue)* to be woven

tisserand, -e [tisrɑ̃, -ɑ̃d] *nm,f* weaver

tissu [tisy] *nm* (**a**) *(étoffe)* material, cloth; *Fig (urbain, social)* fabric; **t. d'ameublement** furnishing fabric (**b**) *Fig (de mensonges, d'incohérences)* tissue (**c**) *Biol* tissue

tissu-éponge *(pl* **tissus-éponges)** [tisyepɔ̃ʒ] *nm* (terry) towelling

titan [titɑ̃] *nm* Titan; **travail de t.** Herculean task

titane [titan] *nm* titanium

titi [titi] *nm Fam* cheeky urchin

titiller [titije] *vt* to titillate

titrage [titraʒ] *nm* (**a**) *(de film)* titling (**b**) *(d'un alcool)* determination of the strength

titre [titr] *nm* (**a**) *(de livre, de chanson, de film)* title (**b**) *(de chapitre, de page)* heading; **les gros titres** the headlines; **faire les gros titres** to hit the headlines (**c**) *(d'une personne)* title; **en t.** *(titulaire)* permanent; *(attitré)* official (**d**) *(chanson, morceau)* track (**e**) *(qualité de champion)* title (**f**) *(diplôme)* qualification (**g**) *(certificat)* **t. de propriété** title deed; **t. de transport** ticket (**h**) *Fin* security (**i**) *(d'un alcool)* strength; *(de l'or, d'une monnaie)* fineness; *(d'un alliage)* grade (**j**) *(locutions)* **à ce t.** *(pour cette raison)* therefore; *(en cette qualité)* as such; **à quel t.?** *(de quel droit)* on what grounds?; **au même t. que** in the same way as; **à t. gratuit** free of charge; **à t. d'exemple** by way of example

titré, -e [titre] *adj (personne)* titled

titrer [titre] *vt* (**a**) *(livre, film)* to title (**b**) *(alcool)* to determine the strength of

tituber [titybe] *vi* to stagger (**de** with)

titulaire [titylɛr] **1** *adj* (**a**) *(dans l'administration)* with a permanent contract; *(professeur d'université)* with tenure (**b**) *(détenteur)* **être t. de qch** to be the holder of sth
2 *nmf (détenteur)* holder

titularisation [titylarizasjɔ̃] *nf* granting of permanent contract; *(à l'université)* granting of tenure

titulariser [titylarize] *vt* to give a permanent contract to; *(professeur d'université)* to give tenure to

T9 [tenœf] *nm Tél* predictive text (input), T9

TNT [teɛnte] **1** *nm Chim (abrév* **trinitrotoluène)** TNT
2 *nf TV (abrév* **télévision numérique terrestre)** digital television, DTT

toast [tost] *nm* (**a**) *(de pain)* piece *or* slice of toast; **t. beurré** piece *or* slice of buttered toast; **des toasts** toast (**b**) *(hommage)* toast; **porter un t. à qn** to drink a toast to sb

toboggan [tɔbɔgɑ̃] *nm* (**a**) *(de terrain de jeu)* slide; *(dans une piscine)* flume; **faire du t.** to play on the slide (**b**) *(pour marchandises)* chute (**c**) *(viaduc) Br* flyover, *Am* overpass (**d**) *Can (traîneau)* toboggan; **faire du t.** to go tobogganing

toc [tɔk] **1** *exclam* **t. t.!** knock knock!; *Fig* **et t.!** so there!
2 *adj inv Fam (faux)* fake; *(de mauvais goût)* tacky
3 *nm Fam* **bijoux en t.** fake jewellery; **c'est du t.** it's fake

toccata [tɔkata] *nf Mus* toccata

tocsin [tɔksɛ̃] *nm* alarm bell

toge [tɔʒ] *nf* (**a**) *(de magistrat, d'avocat)* gown (**b**) *(romaine)* toga

Togo [togo] *nm* **le T.** Togo

togolais, -e [tɔgɔlɛ, -ɛz] **1** *adj* Togolese
2 *nm,f* **T.** Togolese

tohu-bohu [tɔybɔy] *nm (désordre)* confusion; *(bruit)* hubbub

toi [twa] *pron personnel* (**a**) *(sujet)* you; **t., ne m'énerve pas!** don't annoy me!; **t., tu aurais certainement cédé** YOU would probably have given in (**b**) *(objet direct)* you; **et t., il t'a salué?** and what about you, did he say hello to you? (**c**) *(réfléchi)* yourself; **tais-t.!** be quiet! (**d**) *(avec préposition)* you; **je ne te le prêterai pas, à t.** I won't lend it to YOU; **c'est à t., tout ça?** is that all yours?; **tu auras ta chambre à t.** you'll have your own room; *Fam* **une copine à t.** a friend of yours; **tu ne penses qu'à t.** you think only of yourself (**e**) *(dans les comparaisons)* you; **je n'en sais pas plus que t.** I don't know any more about it than you (do)

toile [twal] *nf* (**a**) *(tissu)* cloth; **t. d'araignée** cobweb, spider's web; **t. cirée** oilcloth; **t. de fond** backdrop; *Fig* **en t. de fond** as a backdrop; **t. (de lin)** linen; **un pantalon en t.** linen *Br* trousers *or Am* pants; **t. à matelas** ticking; **t. de tente** canvas (**b**) *(tableau)* painting, canvas (**c**) *Fam (film)* **se faire une t.** to go to the *Br* pictures *or Am* movies (**d**) *Ordinat* **la T.** the Web

toilettage [twalɛtaʒ] *nm* (**a**) *(d'un chien)* grooming (**b**) *(d'un texte)* tidying up

toilette [twalɛt] *nf* (**a**) *(action de se laver)* washing; **faire sa t.** to have a wash (**b**) **toilettes** *(W.-C.) Br* toilet, *Am* rest room; *(publiques)* public convenience; **toilettes pour dames** ladies' *Br* toilet *or Am* room; **toilettes pour hommes** *Br* gents' toilet, *Am* men's room (**c**) *(vêtements)* outfit; **porter bien la t.** to look good in formal clothes

toiletter [twalete] **1** *vt* (**a**) *(chien)* to groom (**b**) *(texte)* to tidy up
2 se toiletter *vpr Can* to dress up (smartly)

toi-même [twamɛm] *pron personnel* yourself; *Fam* **menteur! – t.!** liar! – liar yourself!

toise [twaz] *nf* height gauge

toiser [twaze] **1** *vt* to look up and down
2 se toiser *vpr* to look each other up and down

toison [twazɔ̃] *nf* (**a**) *(de mouton)* fleece; **la T. d'or** the Golden Fleece (**b**) *(chevelure)* mane (of hair)

toit [twa] *nm* roof; *Fig* **être sans t.** not to have a roof over one's head; **accueillir qn sous son t.** to take sb in; **t. de chaume** thatched roof; **t. ouvrant** sun roof

toiture [twatyr] *nf* roofing, roof

Tokyo [tɔkjo] *n* Tokyo

tôle¹ [tol] *nf* (**a**) *(matériau)* sheet metal; **t. ondulée** corrugated iron (**b**) *(feuille)* metal sheet

tôle² = **taule**

tolérable [tɔlerabl] *adj* tolerable; **votre comportement n'est pas t.** your behaviour is intolerable

tolérance [tɔlerɑ̃s] *nf* tolerance; **t. zéro (vis-à-vis de qch)** zero tolerance (towards sth)

tolérant, -e [tɔlerɑ̃, -ɑ̃t] *adj* tolerant

tolérer [34] [tɔlere] **1** *vt* to tolerate; **je ne tolère pas qu'on me parle sur ce ton!** I won't tolerate being spoken to like that!

  2 se tolérer *vpr* to tolerate each other

tôlier [tolje] = **taulier**

tollé [tɔle] *nm* outcry; **t. général** public outcry

TOM [tɔm] *nm* (*abrév* **territoire d'outre-mer**) overseas territory

tomahawk [tɔmaok] *nm* tomahawk

tomate [tɔmat] *nf* tomato

tombal, -e, -als *ou* **-aux, -ales** [tɔ̃bal, -o] *adj voir* **pierre**

tombant, -e [tɔ̃bɑ̃, -ɑ̃t] *adj (épaules)* sloping; *(oreilles)* floppy

tombe [tɔ̃b] *nf* (**a**) *(sépulture)* grave; *(avec un monument)* tomb; **emporter un secret dans la t.** to take a secret to the grave; **suivre qn dans la t.** to follow sb to the grave (**b**) *(pierre tombale)* gravestone, tombstone

tombeau, -x [tɔ̃bo] *nm* tomb; *Fig* **à t. ouvert** at breakneck speed

tombée [tɔ̃be] *nf* **la t. du jour** *ou* **de la nuit** nightfall

tomber [tɔ̃be] **1** *vi* (*aux* **être**) (**a**) *(personne, objet)* to fall (down); *(précipitations, feuilles)* to fall; **t. de qch** *(chaise, échelle)* to fall off sth; *(arbre)* to fall out of sth; **t. dans un piège** to fall into a trap; **faire t. qn/qch** to knock sb/sth over; **laisser t.** *(objet)* to drop; *Fam* **laisser t. qn** to let sb down; *Fam* **laisse t., c'est inutile** forget it, it's pointless; **t. à l'eau** *(personne, objet)* to fall in (the water); *(projet)* to fall through; *Fig* **il faut être tombé bien bas** you have to have sunk pretty low; **t. de haut** to come back to earth with a bump (**b**) *(gouvernement, ville)* to fall (**c**) *(nouvelle)* to come through (**d**) *(mourir)* to fall; *Fam* **t. comme des mouches** to be dropping like flies (**e**) *(vent, prix, fièvre)* to drop; *(conversation)* to flag; *(enthousiasme)* to wane (**f**) *(nuit)* to fall (**g**) *(devenir brusquement)* **t. amoureux de qn,** *Can* **t. en amour avec qn** to fall in love with sb; *Fam* **t. enceinte** to get *ou* fall pregnant (**h**) *(date, événement)* to fall (**i**) *(pendre)* *(draperie, vêtement)* to hang; **ses cheveux lui tombent jusqu'aux reins** his/her hair hangs right down his/her back (**j**) *(locutions)* **t. bien** to come at just the right time; **t. mal** to come at the wrong time; **je suis bien/mal tombé** *(chanceux/malchanceux)* I was lucky/unlucky; **ça tombe sous le sens** it stands to reason; **t. sur qn** *(l'agresser)* to pitch into sb; *(le rencontrer par hasard)* to bump into sb; **t. sur qch** to come across sth; **il fallait que ça tombe sur moi!** it had to happen to me!

  2 *vt Fam* (*aux* **avoir**) (**a**) *(séduire)* *Br* to pull, *Am* to hook up with (**b**) *(enlever)* **t. la veste** to take off one's jacket

tombereau, -x [tɔ̃bro] *nm* (**a**) *(charrette)* tip-cart (**b**) *(contenu)* cartload

tombeur [tɔ̃bœr] *nm Fam* womanizer, ladykiller

tombola [tɔ̃bɔla] *nf* raffle

tome [tɔm] *nm (volume)* volume

tomme [tɔm] *nf* = cheese made in Savoie

ton¹, ta, tes [tɔ̃, ta, te]

> **ta** becomes **ton** before a word beginning with a vowel or mute h.

adj possessif your; **t. chien** your dog; **ta voiture** your car; **t. ami/amie** your friend; **tes enfants** your children; **t. père et ta mère** your mother and father; **un de tes amis** one of your friends, a friend of yours; *Fam* **tu as eu t. vendredi** you got Friday off

ton² *nm* (**a**) *(qualité de voix)* tone; **hausser/baisser le t.** to raise/lower one's voice; **sur le t. de la plaisanterie** in a joking tone of voice (**b**) *(goût)* **il est de bon t.** it's good form to do it (**c**) *(gamme)* key; *(intervalle musical)* tone; **donner le t.** to give the pitch; *Fig* to set the tone (**d**) *Ling* tone; **langue à tons** tonal language (**e**) *(teinte)* shade, tone; *Ordinat* **tons de gris** shades of grey

tonal, -e, -als, -ales [tɔnal] *adj Mus* tonal

tonalité [tɔnalite] *nf* (**a**) *(au téléphone)* *Br* dialling *or* *Am* dial tone (**b**) *(d'un morceau de musique)* key; *Fig (d'une œuvre)* tone

tondeuse [tɔ̃døz] *nf* (**a**) *(de jardin)* **t. (à gazon)** (lawn) mower (**b**) *(de coiffeur)* clippers

tondre [tɔ̃dr] *vt* (**a**) *(herbe)* to mow; *(mouton)* to shear; **se faire t.** *(très court)* to have one's hair cropped; *(complètement)* to have all one's hair shaved off (**b**) *Fam (dépouiller)* to fleece

toner [tɔnɛr] *nm (pour photocopieuse, imprimante)* toner

tong [tɔ̃g] *nf Br* flip-flop, *Am* thong

Tonga [tɔ̃ga] *nfpl* **les (îles) T.** Tonga

tonicité [tɔnisite] *nf* (**a**) *(des muscles)* tone (**b**) *(de l'air, du climat)* bracing effect

tonifiant, -e [tɔnifjɑ̃, -ɑ̃t] *adj (air, marche)* bracing

tonifier [66] [tɔnifje] *vt (peau, muscles)* to tone up; *(esprit)* to stimulate

tonique [tɔnik] **1** *adj* (**a**) *(climat, vent)* bracing, invigorating (**b**) *(boisson, remède)* tonic (**c**) *(personne)* energetic, dynamic (**d**) *(accent)* tonic; *(syllabe)* accented

  2 *nm* (**a**) *(remède)* tonic (**b**) *(lotion)* toner

  3 *nf Mus* tonic, keynote

tonitruant, -e [tɔnitryɑ̃, -ɑ̃t] *adj (voix, bruit)* thundering

tonnage [tɔnaʒ] *nm* tonnage

tonnant, -e [tɔnɑ̃, -ɑ̃t] *adj (voix)* thundering

tonne [tɔn] *nf* metric ton, tonne; *Fam Fig* **des tonnes de qch** tons of sth; *Fam* **en faire des tonnes** to go overboard

tonneau, -x [tɔno] *nm* (**a**) *(récipient)* barrel, cask; *Fig* **du même t.** of the same type (**b**) *(en voiture)* roll; **faire un t.** to roll over

tonnelier [tɔnəlje] *nm* cooper

tonnelle [tɔnɛl] *nf (charmille)* arbour, bower

tonner [tɔne] **1** *vi* (**a**) *(canons)* to thunder (**b**) *(fulminer)* to thunder (**contre** against)

  2 *v impersonnel* **il tonne** it's thundering

tonnerre [tɔnɛr] *nm* thunder; **un t. d'applaudissements** thunderous applause; *Fam Fig* **du t.** fantastic

tonsure [tɔ̃syr] *nf* tonsure

tonte [tɔ̃t] *nf (des moutons)* shearing; *(du gazon)* mowing

tonton [tɔ̃tɔ̃] *nm Fam* uncle

tonus [tɔnys] *nm* (**a**) *Fig (dynamisme)* energy, dynamism (**b**) *(d'un muscle)* tone

top [tɔp] **1** *nm* (**a**) *(signal sonore)* beep; **au quatrième t. il sera midi** at the fourth stroke it will be twelve o'clock (**b**) *(vêtement)* top (**c**) *Fam* **être au t. niveau** *(sportif)* to be at one's peak; **c'est le t.!** it's the business!

2 *adj Fam* great, *Br* fab, *Am* awesome

topaze [tɔpaz] *nf* topaz

toper [tɔpe] *vi Fam* **tope(-là)!** you're on!

topinambour [tɔpinɑ̃bur] *nm* Jerusalem artichoke

top model *(pl* **top models**) [tɔpmɔdɛl] *nm* supermodel, top model

topo [tɔpo] *nm Fam (discours)* lecture; *(exposé)* rundown; *Fig* **c'est toujours le même t.** it's always the same old story

topographie [tɔpɔgrafi] *nf* topography

topographique [tɔpɔgrafik] *adj* topographical

toponymie [tɔpɔnimi] *nf* toponymy

top secret [tɔpsəkrɛ] *adj inv* top secret

toquade [tɔkad] *nf Fam (pour une personne)* crush (**pour** on); *(pour un lieu, pour un objet)* craze (**pour** for)

toque [tɔk] *nf (de fourrure)* fur hat; *(de jockey)* cap; *(de cuisinier)* hat

toqué, -e [tɔke] *Fam* **1** *adj* crazy, nuts (**de** about)

2 *nm,f* nutcase

toquer [tɔke] **se toquer** *vpr Fam* **se t. de qn** to have a crush on sb; **se t. de qch** to go crazy for sth

Torah [tɔra] *nf* **la T.** the Torah

torche [tɔrʃ] *nf* torch; **t. électrique** *Br* (electric) torch, *Am* flashlight

torcher [tɔrʃe] *Fam* **1** *vt* (**a**) *(fesses, enfant)* to wipe (**b**) *(travail)* to botch (**c**) *(bouteille)* to polish off

2 se torcher *vpr* to wipe one's backside

torchis [tɔrʃi] *nm* cob *(for building)*

torchon [tɔrʃɔ̃] *nm* (**a**) *(de cuisine)* dish *or* tea towel; *Fam* **le t. brûle** they're at each other's throats; *Fig* **il ne faut pas mélanger les torchons et les serviettes** they're in a different league (**b**) *Fam (texte peu soigné)* mess (**c**) *Fam (journal)* rag (**d**) *Belg (serpillère)* floorcloth

tordant, -e [tɔrdɑ̃, -ɑ̃t] *adj Fam* hilarious

tord-boyaux [tɔrbwajo] *nm Fam* rotgut

tordre [tɔrdr] **1** *vt (barre de fer, métal)* to bend; *(fil de fer)* to twist; *(linge)* to wring; **t. le cou à qn** to wring sb's neck; **t. le bras à qn** to twist sb's arm

2 se tordre *vpr* **se t. les mains** to wring one's hands; **se t. la cheville** to twist one's ankle; **se t. de douleur** to writhe in pain; *Fam* **se t. (de rire)** to kill oneself (laughing)

tordu, -e [tɔrdy] **1** *adj* (**a**) *(objet)* twisted (**b**) *Fam (dérangé)* **être t.** to be a bit of a maniac *or Br* nutter; **avoir l'esprit t.** to have a warped mind

2 *nm,f Fam* maniac, *Br* nutter

toréador [tɔreadɔr] *nm* bullfighter, toreador

toréer [24] [tɔree] *vi* to fight *(in the bullring)*

torero [tɔrero] *nm* bullfighter

torgnole [tɔrɲɔl] *nf très Fam* clout, slap

tornade [tɔrnad] *nf* tornado; **comme une t.** like a whirlwind

Toronto [tɔrɔ̃to] *n* Toronto

torpeur [tɔrpœr] *nf* torpor

torpillage [tɔrpijaʒ] *nm* torpedoing

torpille [tɔrpij] *nf* (**a**) *(engin militaire)* torpedo (**b**) *(poisson)* torpedo, electric ray

torpiller [tɔrpije] *vt aussi Fig* to torpedo

torpilleur [tɔrpijœr] *nm* torpedo boat

torréfaction [tɔrefaksjɔ̃] *nf* roasting

torréfier [66] [tɔrefje] *vt* to roast

torrent [tɔrɑ̃] *nm (cours d'eau)* torrent; *Fig (de larmes, de lumière)* flood; *(d'injures)* torrent; *(de questions)* barrage; **pleuvoir à torrents** to pour down

torrentiel, -elle [tɔrɑ̃sjɛl] *adj* torrential

torride [tɔrid] *adj* torrid

tors, -e [tɔr, tɔrs] *adj* twisted

torsade [tɔrsad] *nf* (**a**) *(point de tricot)* cable; **pull à torsades** cable(-knit) sweater (**b**) *(de cheveux)* twist, coil

torsadé, -e [tɔrsade] *adj (pull)* cable(-knit)

torsader [tɔrsade] *vt* to twist

torse² [tɔrs] *nm* chest; **t. nu** stripped to the waist

torsion [tɔrsjɔ̃] *nf* twisting

tort [tɔr] *nm* (**a**) *(faute)* fault; **avoir tous les torts** to be entirely to blame; **c'est un t. de l'avoir fait** it was a mistake to do it; **avoir t. (de faire qch)** to be wrong (to do sth); **tu n'as pas t.** you're quite right; **donner t. à qn** *(personne)* to blame sb; *(résultat, preuve)* to prove sb wrong; **être en t.** *ou* **dans son t.** to be in the wrong (**b**) *(dommage)* wrong; **faire du t. à qn** to harm sb; *(désavantager)* to penalize sb (**c**) *(locutions)* **à t.** wrongly; **à t. ou à raison** rightly or wrongly; **à t. et à travers** *(dépenser)* recklessly; *(parler)* wildly

torticolis [tɔrtikɔli] *nm* stiff neck; **avoir le** *ou* **un t.** to have a stiff neck

tortillard [tɔrtijar] *nm Fam* slow local train

tortiller [tɔrtije] **1** *vt (papier, ruban, cheveux)* to twist; *(moustache)* to twirl

2 *vi Fam* **il n'y a pas à t.** there are no two ways about it

3 se tortiller *vpr (personne)* to wriggle

tortillon [tɔrtijɔ̃] *nm (de papier)* twist

tortionnaire [tɔrsjɔnɛr] *nmf* torturer

tortue [tɔrty] *nf* (**a**) *(reptile)* tortoise; **t. d'eau douce** terrapin; **t. de mer** turtle (**b**) *Fig (personne lente) Br* slowcoach, *Am* slowpoke

tortueusement [tɔrtɥøzmɑ̃] *adv (hypocritement)* deviously

tortueux, -euse [tɔrtɥø, -øz] *adj* (**a**) *(sinueux)* winding, tortuous (**b**) *(attitude, esprit)* devious; *(langage)* tortuous

torture [tɔrtyr] *nf aussi Fig* torture; *Fig* **mettre qn à la t.** to torture sb

torturer [tɔrtyre] **1** *vt aussi Fig* to torture

2 se torturer *vpr* to torture oneself; **se t. l'esprit** to rack one's brains

torve [tɔrv] *adj* menacing

toscan, -e [tɔskɑ̃, -an] **1** *adj* Tuscan

2 *nm,f* **T.** Tuscan

3 *nm (langue)* Tuscan

Toscane [tɔskan] *nf* **la T.** Tuscany

tôt [to] *adv* (**a**) *(bientôt, vite)* soon, early; **nous n'étions pas plus t. rentrés que...** no sooner had we returned than...; **au plus t.** at the earliest; *Fam* **ce n'est pas trop t.!** and about time too!; **elle a eu t. fait de changer d'avis** she soon changed her mind; **t. ou tard** sooner or later (**b**) *(de bonne heure)* early

total, -e, -aux, -ales [tɔtal, -o] **1** *adj* total

2 *nm* total; **faire le t.** to work out the total; **au t.** in all, in total; *(tout compte fait)* all in all; *Fam* **t., ils se sont fâchés** the upshot was that they fell out

3 *nf* **totale** *Fam* **on a eu droit à la totale: verglas, embouteillages, barrages routiers** black ice, traffic jams, lorry drivers' road blocks, you name it, we had it

totalement [tɔtalmɑ̃] *adv* totally

totaliser [tɔtalize] *vt* (**a**) *(additionner)* to total, to add up (**b**) *(avoir au total)* to have a total of

totalitaire [tɔtalitɛr] *adj* totalitarian
totalitarisme [tɔtalitarism] *nm* totalitarianism
totalité [tɔtalite] *nf* **la t. de** all of; **payer qch en t.** to pay sth in full
totem [tɔtɛm] *nm (mât)* totem pole
touareg [twarɛg] **1** *adj* Tuareg
  2 *nmf* **T.** Tuareg
  3 *nm (langue)* Tuareg
toubib [tubib] *nm Fam* doctor, doc
toucan [tukɑ̃] *nm* toucan
touchant, -e [tuʃɑ̃, -ɑ̃t] *adj* touching
touche [tuʃ] *nf* (**a**) *(d'un piano, d'un clavier)* key; *Ordinat* **t.** alt alt (key) (**b**) *(tache de couleur)* touch; **mettre la t. finale à qch** to put the finishing touches to sth (**c**) *(style)* touch (**d**) *(en escrime)* hit; *(à la pêche)* bite; *Fam* **avoir une t. avec qn** to be in with sb (**e**) *(remise en jeu)* throw-in; *(par les avants au rugby)* line-out; **sortir en t.** to go into touch; *aussi Fig* **rester sur la t.** to stay on the sidelines (**f**) *Fam (allure)* look; **avoir une drôle de t.** to look weird (**g**) *(de violon)* finger board; *(de guitare)* fret
touche-à-tout [tuʃatu] *nmf inv Fam* (**a**) *(enfant)* **c'est un t.** he's into everything (**b**) *(qui a plusieurs occupations)* dabbler
toucher¹ [tuʃe] *nm* (**a**) *(sens)* **le t.** touch; **au t.** to the touch (**b**) *(d'un pianiste)* touch
toucher² **1** *vt* (**a**) *(être en contact avec)* to touch; *(cible, adversaire)* to hit; **je touche du bois!** *Br* touch wood!, *Am* knock on wood!, *Fam* **pas touche!** hands off! (**b**) *(blesser)* to hit (**à** in) (**c**) *(émouvoir)* to touch, to move (**d**) *(concerner)* to concern, to affect (**e**) *(port)* to put in at; **t. le fond** *(navire)* to touch bottom; *Fig (moralement)* to hit rock bottom; **t. terre** *(bateau)* to reach dry land (**f**) *(argent, intérêt, paie)* to get; *(chèque)* to cash; **t. le tiercé** to win the "tiercé" (**g**) *(jouxter)* to adjoin (**h**) *(dire)* **t. un mot à qn (de qch)** to have a word with sb (about sth)
  2 toucher à *vt ind* (**a**) *(prendre, modifier)* to touch; *Fig* **avec son air de ne pas y t.** looking as if butter wouldn't melt in his/her mouth (**b**) *(problème, question)* to touch on (**c**) *(approcher de)* **t. au but** to be nearing one's goal; **t. à sa fin** to be nearing its end (**d**) *(concerner)* to concern
  3 se toucher *vpr (être en contact)* to touch; *(maisons)* to adjoin
touer [twe] *vt Can* to tow
touffe [tuf] *nf* tuft
touffu, -e [tufy] *adj* (**a**) *(bois, végétation)* dense; *(barbe, cheveux)* bushy (**b**) *Fig (livre)* dense
touiller [tuje] *vt Fam* to stir; *(salade)* to toss
toujours [tuʒur] *adv* (**a**) *(exprime la continuité, la répétition)* always; **t. plus nombreux** more and more numerous; **un ami de t.** a lifelong friend; **pour t.** for ever; **depuis t.** always (**b**) *(encore)* still; **cherchez t.** keep looking; **alors, il est rentré? – t. pas** he's back then? – not yet (**c**) *(quoi qu'il en soit)* **t. est-il que...** the fact remains that...; **elle peut t. attendre!** she'll have a long wait!; **c'est t. ça (de pris)** at least it's something
toulousain, -e [tuluzɛ̃, -ɛn] **1** *adj* of Toulouse
  2 *nm,f* **T.** person from Toulouse
Toulouse [tuluz] *n* Toulouse
toundra [tundra] *nf* tundra
toupet [tupɛ] *nm* (**a**) *Fam (audace)* cheek, nerve; **avoir du t., ne pas manquer de t.** to have a cheek *or* a nerve (**b**) *(de cheveux)* tuft of hair, *Br* quiff

toupie [tupi] *nf* (**a**) *(jouet)* (spinning) top (**b**) *Fam (femme)* old bag
toupin [tupɛ̃] *nm Suisse* cow bell
tour¹ [tur] *nf* (**a**) *(construction)* tower; **t. de contrôle** control tower; **la T. Eiffel** the Eiffel Tower (**b**) *(immeuble) Br* tower block, *Am* high-rise (**c**) *(aux échecs)* rook, castle (**d**) *Ordinat* tower

La Tour Eiffel

The Eiffel Tower is France's best known monument and has become a symbol for France itself. It was built in 1889 for the Universal Exhibition in Paris by engineer Gustave Eiffel (whose other achievements include designing the structural frame of the Statue of Liberty in 1886). At first the tower was supposed to be dismantled after the exhibition, but the decision was taken to keep it and it has since become the most distinctive feature of the Paris landscape. At 324 metres high, it was the world's tallest building until New York's Chrysler Building was built in 1930.

tour² *nm* (**a**) *(circonférence)* circumference; **t. de cou/de taille** collar/waist size *or* measurement; **avoir 75 cm de t. de taille** to have a waist measurement of 75 cm; **perdre 5 cm de t. de taille** to lose 5 cm round the waist; **t. de tête** hat size
  (**b**) *(mouvement circulaire)* **faire le t. (de qch)** to go round (sth); **faire faire à qn le t. du propriétaire** to show sb round *(a house)*; *Fig* **faire le t. de qch** *(situation, problème)* to review sth; *Fam* **faire le t. du cadran** to sleep for twelve hours; **faire un t. d'horizon** to review matters; **faire le t. du monde** to go round the world; **t. de piste** lap
  (**c**) *(de potier)* wheel
  (**d**) *(tournure) (d'une situation)* turn; **prendre un certain t.** to take a certain turn; **t. d'esprit** turn of mind; **t. de phrase** turn of phrase
  (**e**) *(rotation)* turn; **donner un t. de clé** to turn the key; **t. de bras** *(frapper)* with all one's might; *Fig (distribuer)* in huge quantities; **se faire un t. de reins** to strain one's back
  (**f**) *(promenade à pied)* stroll; *(à bicyclette, en voiture)* ride; **faire un t.** to go for a stroll/ride; **le T. de France** the Tour de France;
  (**g**) *(alternance)* turn; **à qui le t.?** whose turn is it?; **chacun (à) son t.** each in turn; **t. à t.** in turn; **à t. de rôle** in turn
  (**h**) *Pol* **t. (de scrutin)** ballot
  (**i**) *(mauvais coup)* trick; **jouer un t. à qn** to play a trick on sb; **jouer un t. de cochon à qn** to play a dirty trick on sb; **cela te jouera des tours** you'll live to regret it
  (**j**) *(de prestidigitateur)* trick; **t. de force** feat; *Fam* **en un t. de main** in no time at all; **t. de passe-passe** trick *(using sleight of hand)*

Tour de France

This world-famous annual cycle race starts in a different town each year, but the home stretch is always the Champs-Élysées in Paris. The widespread excitement caused by the race, along with the heroic status of many "coureurs cyclistes", reflects the continuing fondness of the French for cycling in general.

Touraine [turɛn] *nf* la T. Touraine
tourbe [turb] *nf* peat
tourbeux, -euse [turbø, -øz] *adj* peaty
tourbillon [turbijɔ̃] *nm* (**a**) *(de vent)* whirlwind; *(de poussière, de fumée)* swirl; *(de neige)* flurry (**b**) *(d'eau)* whirlpool (**c**) *Fig (de la vie, d'activité)* whirl
tourbillonnant, -e [turbijɔnɑ̃, -ɑ̃t] *adj* whirling
tourbillonner [turbijɔne] *vi aussi Fig* to whirl
tourelle [turɛl] *nf* turret
tourisme [turism] *nm* tourism; **faire du t.** *(dans un pays)* to go touring; *(dans une ville)* to go sightseeing; **t. écologique** eco tourism; **t. de masse** mass tourism; **t. organisé** package tourism; **t. sexuel** sex tourism; **t. spatial** space tourism
touriste [turist] **1** *adj (classe)* tourist
2 *nmf* tourist; *Fig & Péj* **faire qch en t.** to play at doing sth
touristique [turistik] *adj* tourist; *(route)* scenic
tourment [turmɑ̃] *nm Litt* torment
tourmente [turmɑ̃t] *nf* (**a**) *Litt (tempête)* storm (**b**) *(agitation politique)* upheaval
tourmenté, -e [turmɑ̃te] *adj* (**a**) *(paysage)* wild (**b**) *(mer, vie, période)* turbulent (**c**) *(visage, personne, âme)* tortured
tourmenter [turmɑ̃te] **1** *vt* to torment
2 se tourmenter *vpr* to worry
tournage [turnaʒ] *nm (d'un film)* shooting, filming; **sur le t.** on shoot
tournant, -e [turnɑ̃, -ɑ̃t] **1** *adj* (**a**) *(fauteuil, siège)* swivel; *(pont)* swing (**b**) *(grève)* rotating
2 *nm* (**a**) *(de route, de rivière)* bend (**b**) *Fig (changement)* turning point (**de** in)
tourné, -e [turne] *adj* (**a**) *(formulé)* **bien/mal t.** well/badly phrased (**b**) *(disposé)* **avoir l'esprit mal t.** to have a dirty mind (**c**) *Belg* **être bien/mal t.** to be in a good/bad mood
tournebouler [turnəbule] *vt Fam* to upset
tournebroche [turnəbrɔʃ] *nm* spit
tourne-disque *(pl* **tourne-disques)** [turnədisk] *nm* record player
tournedos [turnədo] *nm* tournedos, fillet steak
tournée [turne] *nf* (**a**) *(du facteur, d'un inspecteur)* round; **faire sa t.** to do one's rounds; **faire la t. de** *(magasins, musées)* to go round; **faire sa t. électorale** to go on one's election tour; **faire la t. des grands-ducs** to go out on the town
(**b**) *(théâtrale, musicale)* tour; **en t.** on tour
(**c**) *Fam (consommations)* round
tournemain [turnəmɛ̃] **en un tournemain** *adv Litt* in an instant
tourner [turne] **1** *vt* (**a**) *(clé, tête, yeux)* to turn; **t. et retourner qch entre ses mains** to turn sth over and over in one's hands; *Fig* **t. et retourner qch dans tous les sens)** to go over and over an idea (in one's mind); **t. le dos à qn/qch** *(action)* to turn one's back on sb/sth; *(position)* to have one's back to sb/sth; **t. les talons** *(partir)* to turn on one's heel; **t. la tête à qn** *(succès, vin)* to go to sb's head; *(personne)* to turn sb's head
(**b**) *(page)* to turn (over)
(**c**) *(remuer)* to stir; *(salade)* to toss
(**d**) *(film, documentaire, scène)* to shoot, to film
(**e**) *(attention, pensées)* to turn (**vers** to)
(**f**) *(changer)* **t. qn/qch en ridicule** to make fun of sb/sth
(**g**) *(contourner) (coin de la rue)* to turn, to go round; *(obstacle, difficulté, loi)* to get round

(**h**) *(confectionner) (pièce détachée)* to turn on a lathe; *(pot)* to throw; *Fig (phrase)* to turn; *(compliment)* to word
2 *vi* (**a**) *(clé, roue, aiguille, planète)* to turn; *(porte)* to swing; *(toupie)* to spin; **l'heure tourne** time is getting on; **t. de l'œil** to pass out
(**b**) *(se déplacer en rond)* to go round; *aussi Fig* **t. en rond** to go round in circles; *Fam* **il y a quelque chose qui ne tourne pas rond** there's something not right somewhere; *Fam* **il ne tourne pas rond en ce moment** he's not quite himself at the moment; *Fig* **t. autour de qch** *(avoir pour centre)* to centre on sth; *(par convoitise)* to hover round sth; *(valoir environ)* to be in the region of sth; *Fig* **t. autour du pot** to beat about the bush
(**c**) *(entreprise, moteur)* to run
(**d**) *(obliquer)* to turn; **tournez à gauche** turn left
(**e**) *(changer) (vent)* to shift (**à** to); *(chance)* to turn
(**f**) *(lait)* to turn, to go off
(**g**) *(avoir telle issue)* **t. court** to end abruptly; **bien/mal t.** *(personne)* to turn out well/badly; **ça va mal t.** it's going to go wrong; **t. à l'aigre** to turn sour
(**h**) *(dans un film)* to act
3 se tourner *vpr* to turn (**vers** towards); *Fig* **se t. vers qn/qch** to turn to sb/sth; *Fam* **se t. les pouces** to twiddle one's thumbs
tournesol [turnəsɔl] *nm* sunflower
tourneur, -euse [turnœr, -øz] *nm,f (ouvrier)* turner
tournevis [turnəvis] *nm* screwdriver; **t. cruciforme** Phillips® screwdriver
tournicoter [turnikɔte] *vi Fam* to wander round and round
tourniquet [turnikɛ] *nm* (**a**) *(barrière)* turnstile (**b**) *(porte à tambour)* revolving door (**c**) *(présentoir)* revolving stand (**d**) *(arroseur)* sprinkler (**e**) *Méd* tourniquet
tournis [turni] *nm Fam* **avoir le t.** to feel dizzy; **donner le t. à qn** to make sb dizzy
tournoi [turnwa] *nm* tournament
tournoiement [turnwamɑ̃] *nm (des oiseaux)* wheeling; *(des feuilles mortes)* swirl
tournoyer [32] [turnwaje] *vi (oiseaux)* to wheel; *(feuilles mortes)* to swirl (round); **faire t. qch** to twirl sth
tournure [turnyr] *nf* (**a**) *(des événements)* turn; **prendre une mauvaise t.** to take a turn for the worse (**b**) *(forme)* **prendre t.** to take shape; **t. d'esprit** turn of mind; **t. (de phrase)** turn of phrase
tournus [turnys] *nm Suisse* schedule, rota
tour-opérateur *(pl* **tour-opérateurs)** [turɔperatœr] *nm* tour operator
tourte [turt] *nf* pie
tourteau, -x [turto] *nm (crustacé)* edible crab
tourtereau, -x [turtəro] *nm* young turtledove; *Fig* **tourtereaux** *(amoureux)* lovebirds
tourterelle [turtərɛl] *nf* turtledove
tourtière [turtjɛr] *nf* (**a**) *(pour tourte)* pie dish (**b**) *Can* = (minced) pork pie
tous [tu, tus] *voir* **tout**
Toussaint [tusɛ̃] *nf* la T. All Saints' Day

Toussaint

All Saints' Day is a public holiday in France. It is the traditional occasion for a visit to the cemetery to lay flowers (usually chrysanthemums) on the graves of family and loved ones.

tousser [tuse] *vi* to cough; *Fig (moteur)* to splutter

toussotement [tusɔtmã] *nm* slight cough

toussoter [tusɔte] *vi (avoir une toux)* to have a slight cough; *(pour attirer l'attention)* to give a slight cough

tout, toute *(pl* **tous, toutes)** [tu, tut]

> When **tous** is a pronoun as in **3** (**b**), it is pronounced [tus].

1 *adj (entier)* **t. l'univers** the whole universe; **t. mon argent** all my money; **toute la journée** the whole day; **je ne l'ai pas vu de toute la journée** I haven't seen him all day; **le T.-Paris** anyone who's anyone in Paris

2 *adj indéfini* (**a**) *(n'importe quel)* any; **t. élève en retard sera puni** any pupil arriving late will be punished; **à t. moment** at any time; **t. autre que vous** anybody but you

(**b**) *(chaque)* every; **tous les élèves de la classe** every pupil *or* all the pupils in the class; **toutes nos chambres ont l'air conditionné** all our rooms have air-conditioning; **tous les deux jours** every second day, every other day; **ils se retournèrent t. deux** they both turned round

(**c**) *(emploi intensif)* **à la toute dernière minute** at the very last minute; **de toute beauté** magnificent; **donner toute satisfaction à qn** to give sb complete *or* full satisfaction; **pour toute réponse, il éclata en sanglots** his only answer was to burst into tears; **je suis t. à toi** I'm all yours

3 *pron indéfini* (**a**) *(au singulier)* everything; **elle a t. de son père** she's her father's daughter; **il a t. du fonctionnaire** he's the typical civil servant; **être t. pour qn** to mean everything to sb; **manger de t.** to eat everything *or* anything; **elle fera t. pour t'ennuyer** she'll do anything to annoy you; **t. ce qu'il y a d'intéressant dans ce film, c'est...** the only interesting thing in this film is...; **ce sera t.?** *(dans un magasin)* will that be all *or* everything?; **elle est jolie/gentille comme t.** she's really pretty/nice; **tu n'y vas pas et c'est t.!** you're not going and that's that!; *Fam* **...et t. et t.!** ...and all that sort of stuff

(**b**) *(au pluriel)* all; **ils sont tous partis** they all left

4 *adv* (**a**) *(très)* very; **t. près** very close

(**b**) *(complètement)* **être t. en blanc** to be (dressed) all in white; **être t. en sueur** to be pouring with sweat; **t. autrement** quite differently; **être t. à qch** to be engrossed in sth; **t. enfant, il...** as a very young child, he...

(**c**) *(suivi d'un gérondif)* **t. en conduisant/écrivant** while driving/writing

(**d**) **t. ignorant/secrétaire que je suis** *ou* **sois...** I may be ignorant/just a secretary, but...

(**e**) *(expressions)* **t. à fait** *(complètement)* quite, completely; *(exactement)* exactly; **pas du t.** not at all; **t. à coup** suddenly, all of a sudden; **t. à l'heure** *(dans le futur)* in a little while, shortly; *(dans le passé)* a little while ago; **à t. à l'heure!** see you later!; **t. de suite** right away, immediately; **à t. de suite** see you in a minute

5 *nm* **le t.** *(l'ensemble)* the whole; **le t., c'est de se concentrer** the most important thing is to concentrate

tout-à-l'égout [tutalegu] *nm inv* mains drainage

toutefois [tutfwa] *adv* however

toute-puissance [tutpɥisãs] *nf inv* absolute power

tout-fou *(pl* **tout-fous)** [tufu] *adj m Fam* nuts

toutou [tutu] *nm Fam* doggie

tout-petit *(pl* **tout-petits)** [tupəti] *nm* tot, toddler

tout-puissant, toute-puissante *(mpl* **tout-puissants,** *fpl* **toutes-puissantes)** [tupɥisã, -ãt] **1** *adj* all-powerful

2 *nm* **le T.** the Almighty

tout-terrain *(pl* **tout-terrains)** [tuterɛ̃] *adj (véhicule)* all-terrain, off-road; *(vélo)* mountain

tout-va [tuva] **à tout va** (**a**) *adv* like mad, like nobody's business (**b**) *adj* galore; **le magasin proposait des réductions à t.** the shop was offering discounts galore

tout-venant [tuvənã] *nm* **le t.** *(gens)* ordinary people; *(choses)* ordinary things

toux [tu] *nf* cough; **t. sèche/grasse** dry/loose cough

toxicité [tɔksisite] *nf* toxicity

toxico [tɔksiko] *nmf Fam* addict, junkie

toxicologie [tɔksikɔlɔʒi] *nf* toxicology

toxicomane [tɔksikɔman] **1** *adj* addicted to drugs

2 *nmf* drug addict

toxicomanie [tɔksikɔmani] *nf* drug addiction

toxine [tɔksin] *nf* toxin

toxique [tɔksik] *adj* toxic, poisonous; *(gaz)* poison

toxoplasmose [tɔksoplasmoz] *nf* toxoplasmosis

TP [tepe] *nmpl Scol & Univ (abrév* **travaux pratiques)** practical work

TPI [tepei] *nm (abrév* **Tribunal pénal international)** International Court of Justice

trac¹ [trak] *nm* nerves; *(au théâtre)* stage fright; **avoir le t.** to be nervous; *(acteur)* to have stage fright

trac² **tout à trac** *adv Vieilli* out of the blue

traçabilité [trasabilite] *nf* traceability

tracas [traka] *nm* worry, trouble

tracasser [trakase] **1** *vt* to worry, to bother

2 **se tracasser** *vpr* to worry (**pour** about)

tracasserie [trakasri] *nf* worry; **les tracasseries administratives** red tape

tracassier, -ère [trakasje, -ɛr] *adj* nitpicking

trace [tras] *nf* (**a**) *(d'animal, d'une personne, de pneus)* tracks; **être sur la t. de qn/qch** to be on the track of sb/sth; **disparaître sans laisser de t.** to disappear without trace; **perdre la t. de qn** to lose track of sb; *Fig* **marcher sur** *ou* **suivre les traces de qn** to follow in sb's footsteps; **t. directe** *(en ski)* direct descent (**b**) *(tache)* mark; **des traces de gras** greasy marks; **des traces de doigts** finger marks; **des traces de pas** footprints; *Fig* **laisser des traces chez qn** *(traumatisme)* to leave its mark on sb; *aussi Fig* **effacer toute t. de qch** to cover up all traces of sth (**c**) *(petite quantité, vestige)* trace

tracé [trase] *nm* (**a**) *(plan)* layout; **faire le t. de qch** to plan the layout of sth (**b**) *(d'une côte)* line

tracer [16] [trase] **1** *vt* (**a**) *(ligne, plan)* to draw; *Math (courbe, graphique)* to plot; *(lettre)* to write; *Fig* **t. les grandes lignes de qch** to give the general outline of sth (**b**) *(route, chemin)* to mark out; *Fig* **son chemin est tout tracé** his/her path is all mapped out for him/her

2 *vi* (**a**) *Fam (aller vite)* to bomb along (**b**) *Suisse* **t. après qn** *(le poursuivre)* to chase sb

traceur [trasœr] *nm Ordinat* **t. (de courbes)** plotter

trachée-artère *(pl* **trachées-artères)** [trafɛartɛr] *nf* windpipe; *Spéc* trachea

trachéite [trakeit] *nf* throat infection

tract [trakt] *nm* leaflet

tractations [traktasjɔ̃] *nfpl* dealings, negotiations

tracter [trakte] *vt* to tow

tracteur [traktœr] *nm* tractor

traction [traksjɔ̃] nf (**a**) (en gymnastique) (à la barre, aux anneaux) pull-up; (au sol) Br press-up, Am push-up (**b**) (véhicule) **t. avant/arrière** front-wheel/rear-wheel drive (**c**) (action) traction, pulling

tradition [tradisjɔ̃] nf tradition; **dans la plus pure t. française** in true French tradition

traditionalisme [tradisjɔnalism] nm traditionalism

traditionaliste [tradisjɔnalist] adj & nmf traditionalist

traditionnel, -elle [tradisjɔnɛl] adj (**a**) (fondé sur la tradition) traditional (**b**) (habituel) usual

traditionnellement [tradisjɔnɛlmɑ̃] adv traditionally

traducteur, -trice [tradyktœr, -tris] **1** nm,f translator **2** nm Ordinat translator

traduction [tradyksjɔ̃] nf (action, texte) translation (**de/en** from/into); **t. automatique/simultanée** machine/simultaneous translation; **t. assistée par ordinateur** computer-assisted translation

traduire [18] [tradɥir] **1** vt (**a**) (texte, terme) to translate (**de/en** from/into); Fig (sentiment) to express (**b**) **t. qn en justice** to bring sb before the courts **2** vi to translate (**de/en** from/into) **3** **se traduire** vpr (terme) to be translated; Fig **se t. par qch** (se manifester par) to be reflected in sth; (avoir pour résultat) to result in sth

traduisible [tradɥizibl] adj translatable

trafic [trafik] nm (**a**) (de véhicules) traffic; **t. aérien** air traffic (**b**) (de marchandises) traffic; **t. de drogue** drug trafficking

traficoter [trafikɔte] Fam **1** vi to be on the fiddle **2** vt (**a**) (vin) to doctor; (comptes) to fiddle (**b**) (manigancer) **je me demande ce qu'il traficote** I wonder what he's up to

trafiquant, -e [trafikɑ̃, -ɑ̃t] nm,f Péj trafficker; **t. d'armes** arms dealer; **t. de drogue** drug trafficker

trafiquer [trafike] vt Fam (**a**) (moteur) to tinker with; (freins, compteur) to tamper with; (vin) to doctor; (comptes) to fiddle (**b**) (manigancer) **qu'est-ce qu'il trafique?** what's he up to?

tragédie [traʒedi] nf tragedy; Fam Fig **ce n'est pas une t.!** it's not the end of the world!

tragédien, -enne [traʒedjɛ̃, -ɛn] nm,f tragic actor, f tragic actress

tragi-comédie (pl **tragi-comédies**) [traʒikɔmedi] nf tragi-comedy

tragi-comique (pl **tragi-comiques**) [traʒikɔmik] adj tragi-comic

tragique [traʒik] **1** adj tragic **2** nm (**a**) (d'un événement) tragedy; Fig **prendre qch au t.** to make a big thing out of sth (**b**) (genre) **le t.** tragedy (**c**) (auteur) tragic author

trahir [trair] **1** vt (**a**) (personne, pays) to betray (**b**) (secret) to betray, to give away (**c**) (gêne, ignorance) to betray (**d**) (sujet: jambes, forces) to fail **2** **se trahir** vpr to give oneself away

trahison [traizɔ̃] nf (d'une personne, d'un pays) betrayal; Jur treason; **haute t.** high treason

train [trɛ̃] nm (**a**) (moyen de transport, véhicule) train; **voyager en t.** ou **par le t.** to travel by train; **être dans un t.** to be on a train; Fig **prendre le t. en marche** to jump or climb on the bandwagon; **t. autocouchette(s)** car-sleeper train; **t. de banlieue** commuter train; **t. corail** express train; **t. électrique** electric train; **t. express** express train; **t. à grande vitesse** high-speed train; **t. de marchandises** Br goods or Am freight train (**b**) (de réformes) series (**c**) (derrière) (de chien) rump; Fam (d'une personne) backside, rear (**d**) (allure) pace; **au t.** où vont les choses at the rate things are going; **à ce t.-là** at this rate; **aller bon t.** to go at a good pace; **rouler à un t. d'enfer** to go hell for leather (**e**) **t. d'atterrissage** (d'un avion) landing gear, undercarriage (**f**) Can Fam (vacarme) noise, racket (**g**) (locutions) **en t.** (projet, affaire) under way; **mettre qch en t.** to get sth started; **être en t. de faire qch** to be doing sth; **mener grand t.** to live it up; **t. de vie** lifestyle

traînailler [trɛnaje] = **traînasser**

traînant, -e [trɛnɑ̃, -ɑ̃t] adj (**a**) (robe) trailing (**b**) (voix) drawling; (démarche, pas) dragging

traînard, -e [trɛnar, -ard] nm,f (promeneur) straggler; (travailleur) dawdler

traînasser [trɛnase] vi Fam (**a**) (errer) to hang around (**b**) (être lent) to dawdle

train-couchettes [trɛ̃kuʃɛt] nm inv sleeper

traîne [trɛn] nf (**a**) (d'une robe) train (**b**) (à la pêche) drag net (**c**) Can **t. sauvage** toboggan (**d**) Fam **être à la t.** to lag behind

traîneau, -x [trɛno] nm (tiré par des chevaux) sleigh; (tiré par des chiens) Br sledge, Am sled

traînée [trɛne] nf (**a**) (trace) trail; **se répandre comme une t. de poudre** to spread like wildfire (**b**) Fam Péj (femme) tart

traîne-misère [trɛnmizɛr] nmf inv Fam down-and-out

traîner [trɛne] **1** vt (**a**) (tirer) (objet, corps) to drag; (wagon) to pull (**b**) Fig **t. un rhume** to have a nagging cold (**c**) Péj (vieilles affaires) to drag around; **t. qn au théâtre** to drag sb along to the theatre (**d**) (locutions) **t. les pieds** to drag one's feet; Fam **t. ses guêtres** ou **bottes** to hang around **2** vi (**a**) **t. par terre** (jupe) to trail on the ground (**b**) (rester en arrière) to lag behind (**c**) (errer) to hang around (**d**) (virus) to go around (**e**) (affaires, livres, vêtements) to lie around; **laisser t. qch** to leave sth lying around (**f**) (être lent) (personne) to dawdle; (conversation, intrigue) to drag; **t. en longueur** to drag on; **ça ne traîne pas avec vous!** you don't hang about! **3** **se traîner** vpr (**a**) (sur le sol) to crawl; Fig (être fatigué) to feel like a wet rag; (aller à contrecœur) to drag oneself along (**b**) (journée, soirée) to drag on

training [trɛniŋ] nm (survêtement) tracksuit

train-train [trɛ̃trɛ̃] nm Fam routine; **le t. quotidien** the daily grind

traire [28] [trɛr] vt (**a**) (vache, chèvre) to milk (**b**) (lait) to draw

trait [trɛ] nm (**a**) (ligne) line; **d'un t. de plume** with a stroke of the pen; Fig **c'est sa sœur t. pour t.** she is her sister to a T; Fig **tirer un t. sur qch** to draw a line under sth; **t. d'union** hyphen; Fig link (**b**) (du visage) features; **des traits réguliers/fins** regular/fine features; **avoir les traits tirés** to look drawn (**c**) (caractéristique) feature, trait; **les grands traits de qch** the main features of sth; **t. de caractère** character trait (**d**) Fig **t. d'esprit** flash of wit; **t. de génie** stroke of genius (**e**) (de lumière) shaft (**f**) (locutions) **avoir t. à qch** to be connected with sth, to relate to sth; **boire qch à longs traits** to gulp sth down; **boire/lire qch d'un (seul) t.** to drink/read sth in one go

traitable [trɛtabl] adj (sujet) manageable

traitant, -e [trɛtɑ̃, -ɑ̃t] adj (shampooing, crème) medicated

traite [trɛt] nf (**a**) Fin draft, bill; **t. bancaire** bank draft (**b**) (des vaches) milking (**c**) (trafic) **la t. des Blanches**

the white slave trade; **la t. des Noirs** the slave trade (**d**) *(locutions)* **(tout) d'une t.**, **d'une seule t.** in one go

traité [trete] *nm* (**a**) *(ouvrage)* treatise (**de** *ou* **sur** on) (**b**) *(accord)* treaty

traitement [trɛtmɑ̃] *nm* (**a**) *(de personne, de maladie)* treatment; **t. de choc** shock treatment; **t. de faveur** preferential treatment (**b**) *(de matières premières)* processing; *(de l'eau)* treatment (**c**) *(rémunération)* salary (**d**) *Ordinat* processing; **données en t.**, **capacité** *ou* **débit de t.** throughput; **t. à distance** teleprocessing; **t. des données** data processing; **t. électronique de l'information** electronic data processing; **t. d'images** image processing; **t. de l'information** *ou* **des informations** data processing; **t. par lots** batch processing; **t. en temps réel** real time processing; **t. de texte** word processing, WP; *(logiciel)* word processor, word processing software

traiter [trete] **1** *vt* (**a**) *(se conduire envers)* to treat; **t. qn en ami/frère** to treat sb like a friend/a brother (**b**) *(qualifier)* **t. qn de lâche/de menteur** to call sb a coward/a liar (**c**) *(patient, maladie)* to treat (**d**) *(matières premières, minerai)* to process; *(eau, bois, cultures)* to treat (**e**) *Ordinat (informations)* to process; **données non traitées** raw data (**f**) *(marché)* to negotiate; *(affaire)* to handle; **t. avec qn** to deal with sb (**g**) *(sujet, question, demande)* to deal with
2 *traiter de vt ind (sujet, problème)* to deal with
3 se traiter *vpr* (**a**) *(l'un l'autre)* **se t. d'imbéciles/lâches** to call each other idiots/cowards (**b**) *(être guéri)* **cette maladie se traite très bien maintenant** this disease responds very well to treatment now

traiteur [trɛtœr] *nm* caterer; **chez le t.** at the deli

traître, -esse [trɛtr, trɛtrɛs] **1** *adj (personne, virage)* treacherous; *(soleil, vin)* deceptively strong; **pas un t. mot** not a single word
2 *nm,f* traitor, *f* traitress; **être t. à sa patrie** to be a traitor to one's country; **en t.** treacherously

traîtreusement [trɛtrøzmɑ̃] *adv* treacherously

traîtrise [trɛtriz] *nf* (**a**) *(caractère)* treachery (**b**) *(action)* act of treachery

trajectoire [traʒɛktwar] *nf* path, trajectory

trajet [traʒɛ] *nm* (**a**) *(voyage)* journey; **faire le t. en voiture** to do the journey by car; **deux heures de t.** a two-hour journey (**b**) *(distance)* distance (**c**) *(itinéraire)* route

tralala [tralala] *nm inv Fam* **faire des tralalas** to make a great fuss; **...et tout le t.** ...etcetera, etcetera

tram [tram] = **tramway**

trame [tram] *nf (d'un tissu)* weft; *Fig (d'un récit)* framework

tramer [trame] **1** *vt (complot)* to hatch; **t. quelque chose** to be plotting something
2 se tramer *vpr* **il se trame quelque chose** there's something afoot

tramontane [tramɔ̃tan] *nf* tramontana

trampoline [trɑ̃pɔlin] *nm* (**a**) *(appareil)* trampoline (**b**) *(sport)* trampolining; **faire du t.** to do trampolining

tramway [tramwɛ] *nm Br* tram, *Am* streetcar

tranchant, -e [trɑ̃ʃɑ̃, -ɑ̃t] **1** *adj* (**a**) *(outil, épée, bord)* sharp (**b**) *Fig (ton, personne)* curt
2 *nm (d'une lame)* cutting edge; *(de la main)* edge; *Fig* **à double t.** double-edged

tranche [trɑ̃ʃ] *nf* (**a**) *(de pain, de melon, de viande)* slice; **t. napolitaine** Neapolitan ice cream (**b**) *(d'un livre)* edge; **doré sur t.** gilt-edged (**c**) *(partie) (de*

paiement) instalment; *(de revenus)* group; *(d'imposition)* band, bracket; **t. d'âge** age bracket; **t. horaire** (time) slot; **t. de vie** slice of life (**d**) *Fam* **s'en payer une t.** to have the time of one's life

tranché, -e [trɑ̃ʃe] **1** *adj (opinion)* clear-cut
2 *nf* **tranchée** trench

trancher [trɑ̃ʃe] **1** *vt* (**a**) *(cordage, câble)* to cut; *(gorge)* to slit, to cut; **t. la tête à qn** to cut off sb's head; **la machine lui a tranché le doigt** the machine severed his/her finger (**b**) *(question, différend)* to settle
2 *vi* (**a**) *(décider)* to decide; *Fig* **t. dans le vif** to take drastic action (**b**) *(couleurs)* to contrast (**sur** with)

tranquille [trɑ̃kil] *adj* (**a**) *(paisible)* quiet; *(mer)* calm; *(sommeil)* peaceful; **laisser qn t.** to leave sb alone (**b**) *(rassuré)* **se sentir t.** to feel at peace; **vous pouvez dormir t.** you can rest easy; **soyez t.** don't worry; **je ne suis pas t.** I'm feeling uneasy; **avoir l'esprit t.** to have peace of mind

tranquillement [trɑ̃kilmɑ̃] *adv (calmement)* calmly; *(doucement)* quietly; *(dormir)* peacefully; *(partir)* with one's mind at rest

tranquillisant, -e [trɑ̃kilizɑ̃, -ɑ̃t] **1** *adj* (**a**) *(nouvelles, paroles)* reassuring; *(effet)* soothing (**b**) *(médicament)* tranquillizing
2 *nm* tranquillizer

tranquilliser [trɑ̃kilize] **1** *vt* to reassure
2 se tranquilliser *vpr* to set one's mind at rest

tranquillité [trɑ̃kilite] *nf (calme)* quietness; *(de la mer)* calmness; *(du sommeil)* peacefulness; **avoir besoin de t.** to need peace and quiet; **en toute t.** *(sans être dérangé)* without being disturbed; *(sans souci)* with an easy mind; **t. d'esprit** peace of mind

tranquillos [trɑ̃kilos] *adv Fam (tranquillement)* **ils étaient dans le canapé en train de siroter mon whisky, t.** they were on the sofa sipping away at my whisky, without a care in the world

transaction [trɑ̃zaksjɔ̃] *nf* (**a**) *(opération)* transaction (**b**) *Jur* compromise

transactionnel, -elle [trɑ̃zaksjɔnɛl] *adj* (**a**) *Jur (solution)* compromise (**b**) *Psy (analyse)* transactional

transalpin, -e [trɑ̃zalpɛ̃, -in] *adj* transalpine; *(italien)* Italian

transat [trɑ̃zat] **1** *nm Fam* deckchair
2 *nf* transatlantic race

transatlantique [trɑ̃zatlɑ̃tik] **1** *adj* transatlantic
2 *nm* (**a**) *(paquebot)* transatlantic liner (**b**) *(chaise longue)* deckchair

transbahuter [trɑ̃sbayte] *vt Fam* to cart, to lug

transbordement [trɑ̃sbɔrdəmɑ̃] *nm* transfer; *Naut* transhipment

transcendant, -e [trɑ̃sɑ̃dɑ̃, -ɑ̃t] *adj* transcendent; *Fam* **ce n'est pas t.** it's nothing special

transcendantal, -e, -aux, -ales [trɑ̃sɑ̃dɑ̃tal, -o] *adj* transcendental

transcender [trɑ̃sɑ̃de] **1** *vt* to transcend
2 se transcender *vpr* to surpass oneself

transcontinental, -e, -aux, -ales [trɑ̃skɔ̃tinɑ̃tal, -o] *adj* transcontinental

transcription [trɑ̃skripsjɔ̃] *nf* (**a**) *(action)* transcription; *(dans un autre alphabet)* transliteration; **t. phonétique** phonetic transcription; **t. génétique** genetic transcription (**b**) *(texte)* transcript

transcrire [30] [trɑ̃skrir] *vt* to transcribe; *(dans un autre alphabet)* to transliterate

transcutané, -e [trɑ̃skytane] *adj* transcutaneous

transdermique [trɑ̃sdɛrmik] *adj* transdermal

transe [trɑ̃s] *nf* trance; **être en t.** to be in a trance; *Fig* to be beside oneself

transept [trɑ̃sɛpt] *nm* transept

transférer [34] [trɑ̃sfere] *vt* to transfer

transfert [trɑ̃sfɛr] *nm* transfer; *Psy* transference; *Tél* **t. d'appels** call transfer; *Ordinat* **t. de données** data transfer; *Ordinat* **t. électronique de fonds** electronic funds transfer, EFT

transfigurer [trɑ̃sfigyre] *vt* to transfigure

transformable [trɑ̃sfɔrmabl] *adj* convertible

transformateur [trɑ̃sfɔrmatœr] *nm* transformer

transformation [trɑ̃sfɔrmasjɔ̃] *nf* (**a**) *(changement)* transformation; *(d'un local)* conversion (**b**) *(de matières premières)* processing (**c**) *(au rugby)* conversion; **faire une t.** to convert

transformer [trɑ̃sfɔrme] **1** *vt* (**a**) *(changer)* to transform; *(local, maison)* to convert; **t. qn/qch en qch** to turn sb/sth into sth (**b**) *(matières premières)* to process (**c**) *(au rugby)* (essai) to convert
2 se transformer *vpr* to change; **se t. en qch** to turn into sth

transfuge [trɑ̃sfyʒ] *nmf* defector

transfuser [trɑ̃sfyze] *vt (sang)* to transfuse; *Fam* **t. qn** to give sb a transfusion

transfusion [trɑ̃sfyzjɔ̃] *nf* **t. (sanguine)** (blood) transfusion; **faire une t. à qn** to give sb a transfusion

transgénique [trɑ̃sʒenik] *adj* transgenic

transgresser [trɑ̃sgrese] *vt (règlement, loi)* to infringe; *(ordres)* to disobey

transgression [trɑ̃sgresjɔ̃] *nf (du règlement, de la loi)* infringement; *(d'ordres)* disobeying

transhumance [trɑ̃zymɑ̃s] *nf* = the moving of livestock to different pastures according to the season

transhumer [trɑ̃zyme] *vt & vi* = to move to different pastures according to the season

transi, -e [trɑ̃zi] *adj* (**a**) *(paralysé)* **t. (de peur)** paralysed with fear; **t. (de froid)** chilled to the bone (**b**) *Fam (amoureux)* bashful

transiger [45] [trɑ̃ziʒe] **1** *vi* to compromise (**sur** on); **t. avec sa conscience** to compromise one's principles
2 *vt Can (contrat)* to negotiate

transistor [trɑ̃zistɔr] *nm* (**a**) *Élec (dispositif)* transistor (**b**) *(poste de radio)* transistor (radio)

transit [trɑ̃zit] *nm* (**a**) *(de passagers, de marchandises)* transit; **en t.** in transit (**b**) *(intestinal)* transit; **facilite le t. intestinal** *(sur paquet)* keeps you regular

transiter [trɑ̃zite] **1** *vt (marchandises)* to forward
2 *vi (marchandises, voyageurs)* to pass in transit (**par** through)

transitif, -ive [trɑ̃zitif, -iv] *adj Gram* transitive

transition [trɑ̃zisjɔ̃] *nf* transition; **assurer la t.** to ensure a smooth transition; **sans t.** abruptly

transitivement [trɑ̃zitivmɑ̃] *adv* transitively

transitivité [trɑ̃zitivite] *nf* transitivity

transitoire [trɑ̃zitwar] *adj* transitional

translation [trɑ̃slasjɔ̃] *nf Math* translation

translucide [trɑ̃slysid] *adj* translucent

transmanche [trɑ̃zmɑ̃ʃ] *adj inv* cross-Channel

transmetteur [trɑ̃smetœr] *nm Ordinat & Biol* transmitter

transmettre [47] [trɑ̃smɛtr] **1** *vt* (**a**) *(lumière, chaleur, énergie)* to transmit (**b**) *(maladie, virus)* to pass on, to transmit (**à** to) (**c**) *(recette, don)* to hand on (**à** to); *(tradition, objet)* to hand down (**à** to); *(pouvoir)* to hand over (**à** to) (**d**) *(message, ordre, amitiés)* to pass on (**à** to) (**e**) *Rad & TV (information)* to transmit; *(émission)* to broadcast (**f**) *Jur (propriété, droit)* to

transfer; *(actions)* to assign; **t. ses pouvoirs à qn** to hand over to sb
2 se transmettre *vpr* (**a**) *(maladie, virus)* to be passed on (**b**) *(recette, don)* to be handed on; *(tradition, objet)* to be handed down

transmissible [trɑ̃smisibl] *adj* (**a**) *(maladie)* transmissible; **maladie sexuellement t.** sexually transmitted disease (**b**) *(droit, fortune)* transferable

transmission [trɑ̃smisjɔ̃] *nf* (**a**) *(de la chaleur, de la lumière, d'une maladie, d'un virus)* transmission; *(d'un message, d'un ordre)* passing on; *(d'une tradition)* handing down; **t. de pensée** thought transference (**b**) *Rad & TV (d'une image, d'un message)* transmission; *(d'une émission)* broadcasting (**c**) *Ordinat* transmission; **t. de données** data transmission or transfer; **t. par modem** modem transmission; **t. de paquets** packet transmission (**d**) *Jur (d'une propriété, d'un droit)* transfer, transference; *(d'actions)* assignment (**e**) *Mil* **les transmissions** the signals

transocéanien, -enne [trɑ̃zɔseanjɛ̃, -ɛn], **transocéanique** [trɑ̃zɔseanik] *adj* transoceanic

transparaître [20] [trɑ̃sparɛtr] *vi* to show (through)

transparence [trɑ̃sparɑ̃s] *nf* (**a**) *(d'un tissu, d'une allusion, d'un parti politique)* transparency; **on peut le lire par t.** you can read it by holding it up to the light (**b**) *Cin* back projection

transparent, -e [trɑ̃sparɑ̃, -ɑ̃t] **1** *adj aussi Fig* transparent
2 *nm* transparency, OHP slide

transpercer [16] [trɑ̃spɛrse] *vt (sujet: lame, flèche, balle)* to pierce; *(sujet: froid, vent, pluie)* to go right through

transpiration [trɑ̃spirasjɔ̃] *nf* (**a**) *(sueur)* sweat, perspiration (**b**) *(action)* sweating, perspiration

transpirer [trɑ̃spire] *vi* (**a**) *(personne)* to sweat, to perspire; **t. des pieds/des aisselles** to have sweaty feet/armpits; **t. à grosses gouttes** to be dripping with sweat (**b**) *Fig (secret, nouvelles)* to leak out (**c**) *Fam* **t. sur** *(travailler à)* to sweat over

transplant [trɑ̃splɑ̃] *nm Méd* transplant

transplantation [trɑ̃splɑ̃tasjɔ̃] *nf* (**a**) *(d'arbres, de personnes)* transplantation (**b**) *(d'organes)* transplant; **t. cardiaque/rénale** heart/kidney transplant

transplanté, -e [trɑ̃splɑ̃te] *adj (organe)* transplanted; **malade t.** transplant patient

transplanter [trɑ̃splɑ̃te] *vt* to transplant

transport [trɑ̃spɔr] *nm* (**a**) *(de marchandises, de passagers)* transport; **les transports** transport; **les transports aériens** air transport; **les transports en commun** public transport; **t. fluvial** inland waterway transport; **les transports urbains** the urban transport system (**b**) *Jur (de biens, de droits)* transfer (**c**) *Litt (émotion)* rapture; *(de joie)* transport; *(de colère)* outburst

transportable [trɑ̃spɔrtabl] *adj (marchandises)* transportable; *(blessé)* able to be moved

transporter [trɑ̃spɔrte] *vt* (**a**) *(passagers, troupes, marchandises)* to transport, to carry; **t. qn à l'hôpital** to take sb to hospital (**b**) *(sujet: film, roman)* to transport (**c**) *Litt (ravir)* to transport; **t. qn de joie** to make sb rapturous

transporteur [trɑ̃spɔrtœr] *nm* carrier; **t. routier** road haulier

transposer [trɑ̃spoze] *vt* (**a**) *(mots, morceau de musique)* to transpose (**b**) **t. un roman à l'écran/à la scène** to adapt a novel for the screen/for the stage

transposition [trɑ̃spozisjɔ̃] *nf* (**a**) *(mot, morceau de musique)* transposition (**b**) **t. à l'écran/à la scène** screen/stage adaptation

transsexuel, -elle [trɑ̃ssɛksɥɛl] *adj & nmf* transsexual

Transsibérien [trɑ̃ssiberjɛ̃] *nm* **le T.** the Trans-Siberian Railway

transvaser [trɑ̃svɑze] *vt* to pour, to transfer; *(vin)* to decant

transversal, -e, -aux, -ales [trɑ̃svɛrsal, -o] *adj (vallée)* transverse; *(rue)* cross; **coupe transversale** cross-section

transversalement [trɑ̃svɛrsalmɑ̃] *adv* crosswise

trapèze [trapɛz] *nm* (**a**) *(forme géométrique) Br* trapezium, *Am* trapezoid (**b**) *(appareil de gymnastique)* trapeze; **faire du t.** to perform on the trapeze

trapéziste [trapezist] *nmf* trapeze artist

trappage [trapaʒ] *nm Can* trapping

trappe [trap] *nf* (**a**) *(dans le plancher)* trap door; **passer à la t.** to be whisked away (without trace) (**b**) *(piège)* trap

trappeur [trapœr] *nm* trapper

trapu, -e [trapy] *adj* (**a**) *(homme, cheval)* thickset, stocky; *(bâtiment)* squat (**b**) *Fam (élève, professeur)* brainy (**c**) *Fam (problème)* tough

traquenard [traknar] *nm* trap

traquer [trake] *vt (gibier, criminel)* to hunt; *(vedette)* to hound

traumatisant, -e [tromatizɑ̃, -ɑ̃t] *adj* traumatic

traumatiser [tromatize] *vt* to traumatize

traumatisme [tromatism] *nm* traumatism, trauma; **t. crânien** severe head injury

travail, -aux [travaj, -o] *nm* (**a**) *(activité)* work; *(de l'imagination, de la mémoire)* workings; **se mettre au t.** to get (down) to work; **allons, au t.!** come on, let's get (down) to work!; **cesser le t.** to stop work; **à t. égal, salaire égal** equal pay for equal work (**b**) *(emploi)* work, job; **chercher du t.** to look for work *or* a job; **être sans t.** not to have a job, to be out of work; **t. à mi-temps/à plein temps** part-time/full-time work; **t. de bureau** office work; **les travaux des champs** work in the fields; *Univ* **travaux dirigés** tutorial; **travaux forcés** hard labour; *Jur* **t. d'intérêt général** community service; *Scol* **travaux manuels** arts and crafts; **travaux ménagers** housework; **t. de nuit** night work; *Scol & Univ* **travaux pratiques** practical work (**c**) *(tâche)* (piece of) work, job; **un t. bien/mal fait** a good/bad piece of work; **faire de petits travaux** to do odd jobs; **c'est du beau t.** it's a fine piece of work; *Fam & Ironique* **c'est du beau t.!** that was clever! (**d**) *(lieu de travail)* work (**e**) *Ordinat* job; **t. multitâche** multitasking; **t. en réseau** networking (**f**) *(devoir)* work (**g**) **travaux** *(réparations)* work; **le magasin est en travaux** there's work being done on the shop; **attention travaux** *(sur panneau)* roadworks ahead (**h**) *(de l'accouchement)* labour (**i**) *(façonnage)* **le t. du bois** woodwork; **le t. du fer** ironworking; **le t. de l'ivoire/de pierres précieuses** the shaping of ivory/precious stones

travaillant, -e [travajɑ̃, -ɑ̃t] *Can* **1** *adj* hardworking **2** *nm,f* hard worker

travaillé, -e [travaje] *adj* (**a**) *(fer, bois, pierre)* worked (**b**) *(style)* elaborate (**c**) *(tourmenté)* **être t. par qch** to be tormented by sth

travailler [travaje] **1** *vt* (**a**) *(matière, pâte)* to work (**b**) *(sujet, rôle, style)* to work on; *(texte, auteur)* to study; *(morceau de musique, technique)* to practise (**c**) *(inquiéter)* to torment **2** *vi* (**a**) *(personne)* to work; **t. à la pièce** to do piece-work; **t. dans qch** to work in sth; **faire t. son argent** to make one's money work for one; **faire t. son imagination** to use one's imagination; *Fam* **t. du chapeau** to have a screw loose (**b**) *(s'entraîner) (sportif)* to train; *(musicien)* to practise (**c**) *(câble)* to strain; *(bois)* to warp; *(murs)* to crack; *(vin)* to ferment (**d**) *(agir)* **t. pour/contre qn** to be on sb's side/against sb **3** **travailler à** *vt ind (roman, documentaire)* to work on; **t. à la perte de qn** to try to ruin sb

travailleur, -euse [travajœr, -øz] **1** *adj* hard-working **2** *nm,f* worker; **t. manuel/intellectuel** manual/non-manual worker; **t. indépendant** self-employed worker

travailliste [travajist] *Pol* **1** *nmf* member of the Labour Party **2** *adj (parti)* Labour

travée [trave] *nf* (**a**) *(de sièges)* row (**b**) *Archit* bay

traveller's check, traveller's cheque [travlœr(s)-ʃɛk] *nm Br* traveller's cheque, *Am* traveler's check

travelling [travəliŋ] *nm Cin (déplacement)* tracking; *(plan)* tracking shot; **faire un t.** to do a tracking shot; **t. avant/arrière** track in/out

travelo [travlo] *nm Fam* transvestite

travers [travɛr] *nm* (**a**) *(défaut)* failing (**b**) *(largeur)* breadth; *Culin* **t. de porc** spare ribs (**c**) *(locutions)* **à t. qch, au t. de qch** through sth; **à t. les siècles** down the centuries; **à t. le monde** throughout the world; **voir à t. qch** to see through sth; **passer au t. de qch** to go through sth; **marcher de t.** not to walk in a straight line; *Fig* **aller de t.** to go wrong; **être de t.** *(chapeau, tableau)* to be crooked; **prendre qch de t.** to take sth the wrong way; **regarder qn de t.** to look sideways at sb; **comprendre qch de t.** to misunderstand sth; **en t.** crosswise; **en t. de qch** across sth; **se mettre en t. de qch** to get in the way of sth

traverse [travɛrs] *nf (sur une voie ferrée) Br* sleeper, *Am* tie

traversée [travɛrse] *nf (d'un cours d'eau)* crossing; *(d'une ville, d'une forêt)* going through; *Fig* **t. du désert** time in the wilderness

traverser [travɛrse] *vt* (**a**) *(rue, pont, cours d'eau)* to cross; *(ville, pays, forêt)* to go through; *Fig* **t. l'esprit à qn** *(idée, doute)* to cross sb's mind (**b**) *(tissu, mur)* to go (right) through (**c**) *(crise, période)* to go through; **t. les siècles** to come down through the ages

traversier, -ère [travɛrsje, -ɛr] **1** *adj voir* **flûte** **2** *nm Can (bac)* ferry

traversin [travɛrsɛ̃] *nm* bolster

travesti [travɛsti] *nm* transvestite

travestir [travɛstir] **1** *vt* (**a**) *(personne)* to dress up (**en** as) (**b**) *(vérité, faits, pensée)* to distort **2 se travestir** *upr* (**a**) *(se déguiser)* to put on fancy dress (**b**) *(s'habiller en femme)* to put on drag

traviole [travjɔl] **de traviole** *adv Fam* **marcher de t.** to be staggering all over the place; **être de t.** to be lopsided

trayeuse [trɛjøz] *nf* milking machine

trébucher [trebyʃe] *vi* to trip, to stumble (**sur/contre** over/against); **faire t. qn** to trip sb up

trèfle [trɛfl] *nm* (**a**) *(plante)* clover; **t. à quatre feuilles** four-leaf clover (**b**) *(carte)* club; *(couleur)* clubs (**c**) *(emblème irlandais)* shamrock

tréfonds [trefɔ̃] *nm Litt* **au t. de mon cœur** in my heart of hearts; **au t. de mon âme** in the depths of my soul

treillage [trɛjaʒ] *nm (clôture)* trellis fencing

treille [trɛj] *nf* (**a**) *(tonnelle)* vine arbour (**b**) *(vigne)* climbing vine

treillis [trɛji] *nm* (**a**) *(treillage)* trellis; **t. métallique** wire mesh (**b**) *(tissu)* canvas (**c**) *(uniforme militaire)* combat uniform; **pantalon de t.** *Br* combat trousers, *Am* combat pants, khakis

treize [trɛz] **1** *adj inv* thirteen; **il y en a t. à la douzaine** it's a baker's dozen; *Fig* **des informaticiens, il y en a t. à la douzaine** computer scientists are *Br* ten a penny *or Am* a dime a dozen
2 *nm inv* thirteen; *voir aussi* **trois**

treizième [trɛzjɛm] *adj, nmf & nm* thirteenth; *voir aussi* **cinquième**

trekking [trɛkiŋ] *nm* trek

tréma [trema] *nm* diaeresis; **e/i t.** e/i diaeresis

tremblant, -e [trɑ̃blɑ̃, -ɑ̃t] *adj* (**a**) *(genoux, main)* trembling, shaky; **être t. de peur** to be trembling *or* shaking with fear; **être t. de froid/fièvre** to be shivering with cold/fever (**b**) *(voix)* quavering

tremble [trɑ̃bl] *nm* aspen

tremblement [trɑ̃bləmɑ̃] *nm* (**a**) *(du corps, de la main)* trembling, shaking; *(de peur)* shudder; *(de fièvre)* shivering; **être pris de tremblements** to start to shake; **avec un t. dans la voix** with a tremor in his/her voice; *Fam* **et tout le t.** etcetera etcetera (**b**) *(de la voix)* quavering (**c**) **t. de terre** earthquake

trembler [trɑ̃ble] *vi* (**a**) *(main, genoux)* to shake, to tremble; *(lèvres)* to tremble; **t. de colère/peur** to tremble *or* shake with anger/fear; **t. de froid** to shiver with cold; **t. comme une feuille** to shake like a leaf; **t. de tout son corps** to be shaking all over (**b**) *(voix)* to quaver (**c**) *(terre, bâtiment)* to shake; *(feuilles)* to quiver; *(flamme)* to flicker; **faire t. les vitres** to make the windows shake *or* rattle; **faire t. un bâtiment** to rock *or* shake a building (**d**) *(avoir peur)* to tremble; **t. tout son corps** to tremble all over; **t. devant qn** to be terrified of sb; **t. pour qn** to tremble for sb

tremblotant, -e [trɑ̃blɔtɑ̃, -ɑ̃t] *adj (personne, corps)* trembling; *(voix)* tremulous; *(lumière)* flickering

tremblote [trɑ̃blɔt] *nf Fam* **avoir la t.** to be shaky; *(de peur)* to have the jitters; *(de froid)* to have the shivers

tremblotement [trɑ̃blɔtmɑ̃] *nm (des mains)* trembling, shaking; *(de la voix)* quavering; *(de la lumière)* flickering

trembloter [trɑ̃blɔte] *vi (personne, mains)* to tremble *or* shake slightly; *(voix)* to quaver; *(lumière)* to flicker

trémière [tremjɛr] *adj f voir* **rose**

trémolo [tremolo] *nm* tremolo; *Fig* **avec des trémolos dans la voix** with a tremor in one's voice

trémousser [tremuse] **se trémousser** *vpr* to jig about; **se t. sur sa chaise** to wriggle about on one's chair

trempage [trɑ̃paʒ] *nm* soaking

trempe [trɑ̃p] **1** *nf* (**a**) *(force de caractère)* calibre; **une femme de sa t.** a woman of her calibre (**b**) *Fam (volée de coups)* hiding
2 *adj Can & Suisse (personne, vêtements)* soaked, drenched; *(chaussures, jardin)* waterlogged

trempé, -e [trɑ̃pe] *adj* (**a**) *(personne, vêtements)* soaked; **t. de sueur** *(personne)* dripping with sweat; *(vêtement)* saturated with sweat (**b**) *(acier, verre)* hardened; *Fig* **bien t.** *(caractère)* sturdy

tremper [trɑ̃pe] **1** *vt* (**a**) *(mouiller)* to soak; **se faire t. (par la pluie)** to get soaked (**b**) *(plonger)* to dip (**dans**

in); **t. les lèvres** to take a small sip (**c**) *(acier)* to quench
2 *vi* (**a**) **faire t. qch, mettre qch à t.** *(linge)* to soak sth (**b**) *Fig (se compromettre)* **t. dans qch** to be mixed up in sth
3 **se tremper** *vpr (se baigner)* to have a quick dip; **se t. les pieds dans l'eau** to go for a paddle

trempette [trɑ̃pɛt] *nf Fam* **faire t.** to go for a paddle

tremplin [trɑ̃plɛ̃] *nm (pour sauteur, pour plongeur) & Fig* springboard; *(pour skieur)* ski jump

trench-coat *(pl* **trench-coats)** [trɛnʃkot] *nm* trench coat

trentaine [trɑ̃tɛn] *nf* (**a**) *(nombre)* **une t. (de)** about thirty (**b**) *(âge)* **avoir la t.** to be about thirty; **approcher de la t.** to be getting on for thirty

trente [trɑ̃t] **1** *adj inv* thirty; *(au tennis)* **t. à** thirty all
2 *nm inv* thirty; *Fig* **être sur son t. et un** to be dressed up to the nines; *voir aussi* **trois**

Les trente-cinq heures

In an attempt to create new jobs and reduce unemployment in France, the socialist government of Prime Minister Lionel Jospin (1997–2002) introduced a reduction of the average working week from 39 to 35 hours. There was considerable flexibility in the implementation of the law and many exemptions were allowed, especially for small and medium-sized businesses. Initially, employers were hostile to the idea but the fact that it reduced their national insurance contributions won over the majority. Overall, results have been mixed, with fewer jobs being created than expected. Some people have complained that they have to do the same amount of work in fewer hours, while others enjoy the extra leisure time. The centre-right government elected in 2002 has been moving towards introducing even more flexibility to the law.

trente-six [trɑ̃tsis] **1** *adj inv* thirty-six; *Fam (beaucoup)* umpteen; *Fig* **voir t. chandelles** *(après un coup sur la tête)* to see stars; *Fam* **il n'y a pas t. solutions** there are no two ways about it
2 *nm inv* thirty-six; *Fig* **tous les t. du mois** once in a blue moon; *Can Fam* **être sur son t.** to be dressed up to the nines; *voir aussi* **trois**

trente-sixième [trɑ̃tsizjɛm] *adj Fam Fig* **être au t. dessous** to be really down in the dumps; *voir aussi* **cinquième**

trente-trois tours [trɑ̃ttrwatur] *nm inv* LP

trentième [trɑ̃tjɛm] *nmf, nn & adj* thirtieth; *voir aussi* **cinquième**

trépanation [trepanasjɔ̃] *nf* trepanning

trépaner [trepane] *vt* to trepan

trépas [trepa] *nm Litt* death; **passer de vie à t.** to depart this life

trépasser [trepase] *vi Litt* to depart this life

trépidant, -e [trepidɑ̃, -ɑ̃t] *adj (vie, activité)* hectic

trépidation [trepidasjɔ̃] *nf (d'une machine, d'un moteur)* vibration

trépied [trepje] *nm* (**a**) *(d'appareil photo)* tripod (**b**) *(tabouret)* three-legged stool

trépignement [trepiɲəmɑ̃] *nm* stamping (of feet)

trépigner [trepiɲe] *vi* to stamp (one's feet); **t. de colère/d'impatience** to jump up and down with rage/impatience

très [trɛ] *adv* very; **avoir t. faim/chaud/froid** to be very hungry/hot/cold; **avoir t. envie de faire qch** to really want to do sth; **t. estimé** highly respected; **t. aimé** much liked; **t. peu utilisé** very rarely used

trésor [trezɔr] *nm* (**a**) *(objets précieux)* treasure; *Fam* **mon t.** darling; *Fig* **des trésors de patience/générosité** boundless patience/generosity; **t. de guerre** war chest (**b**) *(dans une église)* relics and ornaments (**c**) **leT. (public)** ≃ theTreasury

trésorerie [trezɔrri] *nf* (**a**) *(bureau)* accounts department (**b**) *(ressources)* funds, finances

trésorier, -ère [trezɔrje, -ɛr] *nm,f* treasurer

tressaillement [tresajmã] *nm (de surprise, de peur)* jump, start; *(de plaisir)* quiver; *(de douleur)* wince

tressaillir [67] [tresajir] *vi (de surprise, de peur)* to jump, to start; *(de plaisir)* to quiver; *(de douleur)* to wince

tressautement [tresotmã] *nm (secousse)* jolt

tressauter [tresote] *vi (être secoué)* to jolt about

tresse [trɛs] *nf* (**a**) *(de cheveux) Br* plait, *Am* braid; **se faire des tresses** to *Br* plait *orAm* braid one's hair (**b**) *(de fil)* braid (**c**) *Suisse (pain)* plaited loaf

tresser [trese] *vt (cheveux) Br* to plait, *Am* to braid; *(paille, osier)* to plait; *(panier, guirlande)* to weave; *Fig* **t. des couronnes à qn** to sing sb's praises

tréteau, -x [treto] *nm* trestle

treuil [trœj] *nm* winch, windlass

trêve [trɛv] *nf* (**a**) *(amnistie)* truce (**b**) *Fig (pause, arrêt)* respite, rest; *Fam* **t. de plaisanteries!** joking apart; **sans t.** unremittingly; *Fam* **t. des confiseurs** = truce over Christmas and New Year between opposing political parties

Trèves [trɛv] *n* Trier

tri [tri] *nm* (**a**) *(d'objets, d'idées)* sorting out; *(de lettres)* sorting; *(de candidats)* selection; **faire le t. dans qch** to sort sth out; **il va falloir faire le t.** we'll have to sort through them; **faire du t. dans ses vêtements/papiers** to sort through one's clothes/papers; **t. postal** mail sorting; **t. sélectif** sorting of *Br* rubbish *or Am* garbage *(for recycling purposes)* (**b**) *Ordinat* sort; **effectuer un t.** to do a sort; **t. alphabétique** alphabetic sort

triage [trijaʒ] *nm* sorting out; *(de lettres)* sorting

trial [trijal] *nm* motorbike trials

triangle [trijãgl] *nm* triangle; **t. des Bermudes** BermudaTriangle; **leT. d'or** the GoldenTriangle; **t. rectangle** right-angled triangle

triangulaire [trijãgylɛr] *adj* triangular

triathlon [triatlõ] *nm* triathlon

tribal, -e, -aux, -ales [tribal, -o] *adj* tribal

tribord [tribɔr] *nm* starboard; **à t.** on the starboard side

tribu [triby] *nf* tribe

tribulations [tribylasjõ] *nfpl* tribulations, troubles

tribun [tribœ̃] *nm* (**a**) *(magistrat romain)* tribune (**b**) *(orateur)* popular orator

tribunal, -aux [tribynal, -o] *nm (bâtiment) Br* court, *Am* courthouse; *(magistrats)* court; **porter une affaire devant les tribunaux** to take a case to court; **t. administratif** = court which deals with civil law; **t. de commerce** trade tribunal; **t. pour enfants** juvenile court; **t. de grande instance** ≃ Crown Court, *Scot* High Court; **t. d'instance** ≃ magistrates' court, *Scot* district court; **t. militaire** military tribunal

tribune [tribyn] *nf* (**a**) *(d'orateur)* rostrum, platform (**b**) *(débat)* forum; **t. libre** *(dans un journal)* opinion column (**c**) **les tribunes** *(dans un stade)* the stand; **t. d'honneur** grandstand; **t. de la presse** press gallery

tribut [triby] *nm* tribute; **le pays a payé un lourd t. à la guerre** the war cost the country dearly

tributaire [tribytɛr] *adj* (**a**) *(dépendant)* **être t. de** to be dependent on (**b**) *(cours d'eau)* tributary

tricentenaire [trisãtnɛr] **1** *adj* three hundred years old

2 *nm* tercentenary, tricentennial

triceps [trisɛps] *nm* triceps

triche [triʃ] *nf Fam* cheating

tricher [triʃe] *vi* to cheat; **t. sur qch** to lie about sth; **t. aux cartes/à un examen** to cheat at cards/in an exam

tricherie [triʃri] *nf* cheating

tricheur, -euse [triʃœr, -øz] *nm,f* cheat

trichloréthylène [triklɔretilɛn] *nm* trichlorethylene

tricolore [trikɔlɔr] **1** *adj* (**a**) *(à trois couleurs)* three-coloured (**b**) *(de la France)* French

2 *nmpl* **les tricolores** the French team

tricorne [trikɔrn] *nm* three-cornered hat, tricorn

tricot [triko] *nm* (**a**) *(activité)* knitting; **faire du t.** to do some knitting (**b**) *(ouvrage)* knitting (**c**) *(chandail)* sweater; **t. de corps** *Br* vest, *Am* undershirt (**d**) *(tissu)* knitted fabric

tricoter [trikɔte] **1** *vt* to knit; **tricoté (à la) main** hand-knitted

2 *vi* to knit; **t. à la main/à la machine** to hand-/machine-knit

tricycle [trisikl] *nm* tricycle; **faire du t.** to go tricycling

trident [tridã] *nm* (**a**) *(dans la mythologie)* trident (**b**) *(fourche)* three-pronged fork

tridimensionnel, -elle [tridimãsjɔnɛl] *adj* three-dimensional

triennal, -e, -aux, -ales [trienal, -o] *adj (élection, révision)* three-yearly, triennial; *(bail)* three-year

trier [66] [trije] *vt* (**a**) *(lettres)* to sort; *(vêtements, informations)* to sort *or* go through; *(fruits, lentilles)* to pick over; **t. qn/qch sur le volet** to hand-pick sb/sth (**b**) *Ordinat* to sort; **t. par ordre alphabétique** to sort in alphabetical order

trifouiller [trifuje] *vi Fam* **qu'est-ce que tu trifouilles?** what are you up to?; **t. dans qch** to rummage around in sth

triglycéride [trigliserid] *nf* triglyceride

trigonométrie [trigɔnɔmetri] *nf* trigonometry

trigonométrique [trigɔnɔmetrik] *adj* trigonometric

trilatéral, -e, -aux, -ales [trilateral, -o] *adj* trilateral

trilingue [trilɛ̃g] *adj* trilingual

trille [trij] *nm* trill

trilogie [trilɔʒi] *nf* trilogy

trimaran [trimarã] *nm* trimaran

trimbal(l)er [trɛ̃bale] *Fam* **1** *vt (paquets)* to lug *or* cart around; *(enfants)* to trail around

2 se trimbal(l)er *vpr* to trail about; **elle se trimbal(l)e partout avec sa marmaille** she trails her kids around with her everywhere she goes

trimer [trime] *vi Fam* to slave away; **faire t. qn** to keep sb hard at it

trimestre [trimɛstr] *nm* quarter; *Scol & Univ Br* term, *Am* trimester

trimestriel, -elle [trimɛstrijɛl] *adj* quarterly

tringle [trɛ̃gl] *nf* rod; **t. à rideau** curtain rod

trinité [trinite] *nf (groupe de trois éléments)* trinity; *Rel* **la (sainte) T.** the (Holy) Trinity; **la T.** *(fête)* Trinity Sunday

Trinité-et-Tobago [triniteetɔbago] *nf* Trinidad and Tobago

trinquer [trɛ̃ke] *vi* (**a**) *(porter un toast)* to clink glasses; **t. à qch** to drink to sth; **t. à la santé de qn** to drink a toast to sb (**b**) *Fam (souffrir)* to be the one who suffers

trio [trijo] *nm* (**a**) *(groupe de trois personnes)* threesome, trio (**b**) *(en musique)* trio

triolet [trijɔlɛ] *nm Mus* triplet

triomphal, -e, -aux, -ales [trijɔ̃fal, -o] *adj* triumphant

triomphalement [trijɔ̃falmɑ̃] *adv* triumphantly

triomphalisme [trijɔ̃falism] *nm* crowing; **sans faire de t....**while I don't want to crow...

triomphant, -e [trijɔ̃fɑ̃, -ɑ̃t] *adj* triumphant; **d'un ton t.** triumphantly

triomphe [trijɔ̃f] *nm* triumph (**sur** over); **faire un t. à qn** to give sb an ovation; **porter qn en t.** to carry sb one one's shoulders

triompher [trijɔ̃fe] **1** *vi* (**a**) *(gagner)* to triumph; *Fig (vérité)* to prevail (**b**) *(exulter)* to crow
2 triompher de *vt ind* to triumph over

trip [trip] *nm Fam (d'un drogué)* trip; **faire un t.** to trip; **être dans un t. écolo** to be on an environmental kick

triparti, -e [triparti], **tripartite** [tripartit] *adj* tripartite

tripatouillage [tripatujaʒ] *nm Fam (de textes, de comptes)* tampering with; *(de statistiques)* massaging

tripatouiller [tripatuje] *vt Fam* (**a**) *(textes, comptes)* to tamper with; *(statistiques)* to massage (**b**) *(cheveux)* to play or fiddle with; *(bouton)* to pick at

tripe [trip] *nf* (**a**) **tripes** *(d'un animal)* entrails; *Fam (d'une personne)* guts; *Fam* **prendre qn aux tripes** to get sb right there (**b**) **tripes** *(plat)* tripe (**c**) *Fam Fig* **avoir la t. républicaine** to be a republican through and through

triperie [tripri] *nf (boutique)* tripe shop

tripette [tripɛt] *nf Fam* **ça ne vaut pas t.** it's not worth a damn

triphasé, -e [trifaze] *adj Élec* three-phase

triphtongue [triftɔ̃g] *nf* triphthong

tripier, -ère [tripje, -ɛr] *nm,f* tripe butcher

triple [tripl] **1** *adj* (**a**) *(à trois éléments)* triple; **en t. exemplaire** in triplicate; *Mus* **t. croche** *Br* demisemiquaver, *Am* thirty-second note (**b**) *(trois fois plus grand)* triple, treble (**c**) *(emploi intensif) Fam* **t. buse** prize idiot; **au t. galop** at breakneck speed
2 *nm* **le t. (de)** *(quantité, prix)* three times as much (as); *(nombre)* three times as many (as); **douze est le t. de quatre** twelve is three times four

triplé, -e [triple] **1** *nm,f* triplet
2 *nm (triple succès)* triple victory; *(pari)* = bet on the first three horses in a race

triplement [triplǝmɑ̃] *adv* trebly, triply

tripler [triple] **1** *vt (somme, quantité)* to treble, to triple; **t. une classe** to repeat a year twice
2 *vi* to treble, to triple

Tripoli [tripɔli] *n* Tripoli

triporteur [tripɔrtœr] *nm* delivery tricycle

tripot [tripo] *nm* gambling den

tripotée [tripɔte] *nf Fam* (**a**) *(défaite)* hammering (**b**) *(grand nombre)* **une t. de** loads of, tons of

tripoter [tripɔte] *vt Fam* (**a**) *(objet, appareil, cheveux)* to play with, to fiddle with; *(boutons, plaie)* to pick at (**b**) *(personne)* to grope

triptyque [triptik] *nm* triptych

trique [trik] *nf* cudgel; *Fam* **mener qn à la t.** to rule sb with a rod of iron; *Vulg* **avoir la t.** to have a hard-on

trisomie [trizɔmi] *nf Méd* **t. 21** Down's syndrome

trisomique [trizɔmik] *adj Méd* with Down's syndrome; **être t.** to have Down's syndrome

triste [trist] *adj* (**a**) *(malheureux)* sad (**b**) *(sinistre)* dreary, depressing; *Fam* **c'était pas t.!** *(soirée)* it was a night and a half!; *Fam* **il est pas t., son frère!** his brother's quite a character! (**c**) *(pénible)* sad; *(époque)* grim; **dans un t. état** in a sorry state; **c'est la t. réalité** that's the sad or harsh reality (**d**) *Péj* sad

tristement [tristǝmɑ̃] *adv* sadly; **t. célèbre** notorious

tristesse [tristɛs] *nf* (**a**) *(d'une personne, d'un événement)* sadness; **c'est avec t. que je vous annonce...** I am sorry to have to tell you... (**b**) *(aspect sinistre)* dreariness

tristounet, -ette [tristunɛ, -ɛt] *adj Fam* gloomy

trithérapie [triterapi] *nf Méd* triple (combination) therapy

triton [tritɔ̃] *nm* (**a**) *(amphibien)* newt (**b**) *(mollusque)* triton, trumpet shell (**c**) *(personnage mythologique)* Triton

triturer [trityre] **1** *vt* (**a**) *(broyer)* to grind (**b**) *Fam (tripoter)* to fiddle with
2 se triturer *vpr Fam* **se t. la cervelle** ou **les méninges** to rack one's brains

triumvirat [trijɔmvira] *nm* triumvirate

trivial, -e, -aux, -ales [trivjal, -o] *adj* (**a**) *(vulgaire)* vulgar, coarse (**b**) *(commun)* banal

trivialité [trivjalite] *nf* (**a**) *(vulgarité)* vulgarity, coarseness (**b**) *(expression)* vulgar or coarse expression (**c**) *(banalité)* banality

troc [trɔk] *nm* (**a**) *(échange)* exchange (**b**) *(système économique)* barter; **faire du t.** to barter

troène [trɔɛn] *nm* privet

troglodyte [trɔglɔdit] *nm (personne)* cave dweller, *Spéc* troglodyte

trogne [trɔɲ] *nf Fam* face, mug

trognon [trɔɲ ɔ̃] **1** *nm (de pomme)* core
2 *adj inv Fam (mignon)* sweet

Troie [trwa] *n* Troy

troïka [trɔika] *nf* troika

trois [trwa] **1** *adj inv* three; **le t. août** *Br* (on) the third of August, *Am* (on) August third; **à t. heures** at three o'clock; **page t.** page three; **Henri T.** Henry the Third; **nous étions t.** there were three of us; **les t. quarts du temps** most of the time; **couper/partager qch en t.** to cut/divide sth into three; **t. par t.** three by three; **(hôtel) t. étoiles** three-star hotel; **en t. dimensions** in 3-D
2 *nm inv* three

trois-huit [trwaɥit] *nm inv* **faire les t.** = to work three alternating eight-hour shifts

troisième [trwazjɛm] **1** *adj, nmf & nm* third; **le t. âge** senior citizens
2 *nf* (**a**) *Scol Br* fourth year of secondary school, *Am* eighth grade (**b**) *(vitesse)* third (gear); *voir aussi* **cinquième**

troisièmement [trwazjɛmmɑ̃] *adv* thirdly

trois-mâts [trwama] *nm inv* three-master

trois-pièces [trwapjɛs] *nm inv* (**a**) *(appartement)* three-room *Br* flat or *Am* apartment; **t. cuisine** *Br* three-room flat with kitchen, *Am* three and a half (**b**) *(costume)* three-piece suit

trois-quarts [trwakar] *nm inv* (**a**) *(manteau)* three-quarter-length coat (**b**) *(au rugby)* three-quarter

trolley [trɔlɛ], **trolleybus** [trɔlɛbys] *nm* trolleybus

trombe [trɔ̃b] *nf* waterspout; **il pleut des trombes** it's pouring down; **sous des trombes d'eau** in the torrential rain; *Fam Fig* **passer/partir en t.** to tear past/off

trombine [trɔbin] *nf Fam* face, mug

trombone [trɔbɔn] *nm* (**a**) *(agrafe)* paper clip (**b**) *(instrument)* trombone; **t. à coulisse/à pistons** slide/valve trombone (**c**) *(instrumentiste)* trombone player, trombonist

trompe [trɔp] *nf* (**a**) *(d'éléphant)* trunk; *(d'insecte)* proboscis (**b**) *(instrument à vent)* horn (**c**) *Anat* **t. d'Eustache/de Fallope** Eustachian/Fallopian tube

trompe-l'œil [trɔplœj] *nm inv (décor)* trompe l'œil; **en t.** trompe l'œil

tromper [trɔpe] **1** *vt* (**a**) *(abuser)* to fool (**sur** about) (**b**) *(être infidèle à)* to be unfaithful to (**c**) *(vigilance, surveillance)* to elude, to escape (**d**) *Fig* **t. son ennui** to relieve the boredom; **t. sa faim** to stave off one's hunger
2 se tromper *vpr (faire une erreur)* to make a mistake; *(avoir tort)* to be mistaken; **se t. dans les dates/proportions** to get the dates/the proportions wrong; **se t. de numéro** *(au téléphone)* to dial the wrong number; **se t. d'heure/de jour** to get the time/day wrong

tromperie [trɔpri] *nf* deceit, deception

trompeter [42] [trɔpəte] *vt (nouvelles)* to shout from the rooftops

trompette [trɔpɛt] *nf* trumpet; *Fig* **avoir le nez en t.** to have a turned-up nose; **t. bouchée** muted trumpet

trompette-de-la-mort (*pl* **trompettes-de-la-mort**) [trɔpɛtdəlamɔr] *nf Bot* horn of plenty

trompettiste [trɔpɛtist] *nmf* trumpet player, trumpeter

trompeur, -euse [trɔpœr, -øz] *adj* (**a**) *(volontairement)* deceitful (**b**) *(symptôme, apparences)* deceptive; *(publicité)* misleading

tronc [trɔ̃] *nm* (**a**) *(d'un arbre, d'un corps)* trunk; *Fig* **t. commun** core syllabus; *Fam* **se casser le t.** to strain oneself (**b**) *(dans une église)* poor box

tronche [trɔ̃ʃ] *nf Fam (tête)* nut; *(visage)* face, mug; **faire la t.** to sulk

tronçon [trɔ̃sɔ̃] *nm* piece; *(de route)* section

tronçonner [trɔ̃sɔne] *vt* to cut into sections

tronçonneuse [trɔ̃sɔnøz] *nf* chain saw

trône [tron] *nm aussi Fam Fig* throne

trôner [trone] *vi* (**a**) *Hum (personne)* to sit on one's throne (**b**) *(objet)* to have pride of place

tronquer [trɔke] *vt (mot, scène)* to shorten

trop [tro] *adv* (**a**) *(avec un adjectif ou un adverbe)* too; **ça va? – pas t. mal** how are things? – not too bad; *Fam* **il est vraiment t.!** he's too much! (**b**) *(avec un verbe)* too much; **il n'y tient pas t.** he's not too bothered; **je ne sais pas t.** I'm not too sure; **ça te plaît? – pas t.** do you like it? – not much; **on ne saurait t. le répéter** it can't be repeated too often (**c**) *(quantité)* too much; *(nombre)* too many; **t. de** *(quantité)* too much; *(nombre)* too many; **nous sommes t.** there are too many of us; **il y a deux assiettes de** *ou* **en t.** there are two plates too many; **payer 50 euros de t.** *ou* **en t.** to pay 50 euros too much; **c'est une fois de t.** that's once too often; **se sentir de t.** to feel in the way; **t., c'est t.!** enough is enough!; **c'en est t.!** this really is too much!

trophée [trɔfe] *nm* trophy

tropical, -e, -aux, -ales [trɔpikal, -o] *adj* tropical

tropique [trɔpik] *nm* (**a**) *(parallèle)* tropic; **le T. du Cancer/du Capricorne** the tropic of Cancer/of Capricorn (**b**) **les tropiques** *(région)* the tropics; **sous les tropiques** in the tropics

trop-perçu (*pl* **trop-perçus**) [tropɛrsy] *nm* overpayment

trop-plein (*pl* **trop-pleins**) [troplɛ̃] *nm* (**a**) *(excédent)* overflow (**b**) *(dispositif d'évacuation)* overflow pipe

troquer [trɔke] *vt* **t. qch contre qch** to exchange sth for sth

troquet [trɔkɛ] *nm Fam* small café

trot [tro] *nm* trot; **aller au t.** to trot; *Fam Fig* **allez-y, et au t.!** go on, and be quick about it!; **t. attelé** harness race

trotskiste, trotskyste [trɔtskist] *adj* & *nmf* Trotskyist

trotte [trɔt] *nf Fam (distance)* **il y a une bonne t. d'ici à chez elle** it's a fair distance from here to her house

trotter [trɔte] *vi* (**a**) *(cheval)* to trot (**b**) *(personne)* to trot about (**c**) *Fig* **cet air me trotte dans la tête depuis hier** I haven't been able to get that tune out of my head since yesterday; **cette idée me trottait dans la tête** the idea was running through my head

trotteur [trɔtœr] *nm* (**a**) *(cheval)* trotter (**b**) *(chaussure)* flat shoe

trotteuse [trɔtøz] *nf (de montre)* second hand

trottiner [trɔtine] *vi (personne)* to trot about

trottinette [trɔtinɛt] *nf* scooter; **faire de la t.** to ride one's scooter

trottoir [trɔtwar] *nm Br* pavement, *Am* sidewalk; *Fam* **faire le t.** *Br* to be on the game, *Am* to work the streets; **t. roulant** moving walkway, travelator

trou [tru] *nm* (**a**) *(ouverture)* hole; *(d'aiguille)* eye; *Fam Fig* **faire son t.** to find one's niche; **t. d'air** air pocket; **le t. dans la couche d'ozone** the hole in the ozone layer; *Vulg aussi Fig* **t. du cul** *Br* arsehole, *Am* asshole; **t. noir** black hole; *Fig* **je suis tombé de l'échelle, et après c'est le t. noir** I fell off the ladder, and after that it's all a blank; **t. de serrure** keyhole; **t. de souris** mouse hole (**b**) *(dans un emploi du temps, dans ses connaissances)* gap; **j'ai un t. de cinq à sept** I'm free between five and seven; **avoir un t. (de mémoire)** to have a memory lapse (**c**) *(déficit)* hole, dent; *Fam* **le t. de la sécu** the Social Security deficit (**d**) *Fam Péj (lieu reculé)* hole; **il n'est jamais sorti de son t.** he has never been out of his own backyard (**e**) *Fam (prison)* clink, slammer (**f**) **faire le t. normand** = to drink a glass of Calvados between courses to aid digestion

troubadour [trubadur] *nm* troubadour

troublant, -e [trublɑ̃, -ɑ̃t] *adj* (**a**) *(déconcertant)* disconcerting (**b**) *(sensuel)* provocative

trouble¹ [trubl] **1** *adj* (**a**) *(liquide)* cloudy; *(lumière)* dim; *(image, photo)* blurred (**b**) *(comportement, affaire)* shady; *(période)* murky
2 *adv* **voir t.** to have blurred vision

trouble² *nm* (**a**) *(désordre)* confusion, disorder; **semer** *ou* **jeter le t. dans l'esprit de qn** to confuse sb (**b**) *(émoi)* agitation (**c**) **troubles** *(révolte)* unrest (**d**) **troubles** *(maladie)* disorder; **troubles de la vision/ respiratoires** eye/respiratory disorder; **troubles de la personnalité** personality disorder

trouble-fête [trubləfɛt] *nm inv Br* spoilsport, *Am* party-pooper; **jouer les t.** *Br* to be a spoilsport, *Am* to be a party-pooper

troubler [truble] **1** *vt* (**a**) *(eau)* to make cloudy; *Fig (esprit)* to cloud; **t. la vue à qn** to blur sb's eyes (**b**) *(sommeil, silence)* to disturb; *(bonheur)* to spoil; **t. l'ordre public** to disturb the peace (**c**) *(mettre en émoi)* to make flustered; *(rendre perplexe)* to confuse
2 se troubler *vpr* (**a**) *(liquide)* to get cloudy; *(vue)* to become blurred (**b**) *(se déconcerter)* to become flustered; **sans se t.** unperturbed

trouée [true] *nf (dans une haie, dans un mur)* gap, opening; **une t. de ciel bleu** a patch of blue sky

trouer [true] **1** *vt* to make a hole in

2 se trouer *vpr* **mes chaussures se sont trouées au bout d'une semaine** my shoes had holes in them after a week

troufion [trufjɔ̃] *nm Fam Br* soldier, *Am* grunt

trouillard, -e [trujar, -ard] *Fam adj & nm,f* chicken

trouille [truj] *nf Fam* fear; **avoir la t.** to be scared stiff

trouillomètre [trujɔmɛtr] *nm Fam* **avoir le t. à zéro** to be scared stiff

troupe [trup] *nf* (**a**) *(groupe)* troop, band; **t. de théâtre** company, troupe (**b**) *(de soldats)* troop; **troupes** *(armée)* troops, forces

troupeau, -x [trupo] *nm (de bétail, d'éléphants)* herd; *(de moutons)* flock; *(d'oies)* gaggle; *Péj (de gens)* herd

trousse [trus] *nf* (**a**) *(étui)* kit; **t. d'écolier** pencil case; **t. de secours** first-aid kit; **t. de toilette** toilet bag (**b**) *(locutions)* **être aux trousses de qn** to be hot on sb's heels; **avoir qn aux trousses** to have sb hot on one's heels

trousseau, -x [truso] *nm* (**a**) *(de clés)* bunch (**b**) *(de mariée)* trousseau (**c**) *(de pensionnaire)* clothes

trousser [truse] *vt* (**a**) *Culin (volaille)* to truss (**b**) **bien troussé** *(compliment)* well-written (**c**) *Vieilli (retrousser)* to turn up

trouvaille [truvaj] *nf* (**a**) *(chose trouvée)* find (**b**) *(bonne idée)* brainwave

trouver [truve] **1** *vt* (**a**) *(en cherchant)* to find; *(procédé, vaccin)* to discover; **je ne trouve pas mes clefs** I can't find my keys; **aller t. qn** to go and see sb; **t. quelque chose à redire** to be sure to have something to say; **t. le sommeil** to get to sleep; **exemple bien trouvé** well-chosen example; **je me demande où il est allé t. ça** I wonder where he got that idea from; *Ironique* **tu as trouvé ça tout seul?** did you think of that all on your own?

(**b**) *(par hasard)* to find, to come across; **t. porte close** to find nobody home; *Fig* **il va t. à qui parler!** he'll have me/him/*etc* to reckon with!; *Fig* **t. son maître** to meet one's match; **t. la mort** to meet one's death (**c**) *(juger)* to find; *(penser)* to think; **je trouve ça idiot** I think it's stupid; **qu'est-ce qu'elle lui trouve?** what does she see in him/her?; **je trouve que...** I think (that)...; **t. le temps long** to feel that time is dragging

2 se trouver *vpr* (**a**) *(dans une situation, dans un lieu)* to be; **où se trouve la gare?** where's the station?; **se t. dans l'impossibilité de faire qch** to be unable to do sth

(**b**) *(être disponible)* **ça se trouve dans les supermarchés** you can find or get it in supermarkets

(**c**) *(se sentir)* to feel; **je me trouve bien ici** I like it here; **se t. beau/gros** to think one is good-looking/fat; **se t. mal** to feel faint

(**d**) *(arriver)* **il se trouve que...** as it happens...; *Fam* **si ça se trouve** maybe

trouvère [truvɛr] *nm Hist* trouvère

truand [tryɑ̃] *nm Fam* crook

truander [tryɑ̃de] *Fam* **1** *vt* to rip off; **se faire t.** to get ripped off

2 *vi (à un examen)* to cheat (**à** in)

trublion [tryblijɔ̃] *nm* troublemaker

truc [tryk] *nm Fam* (**a**) *(chose)* thing; **j'ai un t. à faire/à te dire** I've got something to do/to tell you (**b**) *(astuce)* trick; **connaître les trucs du métier** to know the tricks of the trade (**c**) *(personne)* **T.** what's-his-name, *f* what's-her-name (**d**) *(domaine)* **c'est vraiment son t.** he's really into it; **ce n'est pas son t.** it's not his/her thing

trucage [tryka3] *nm* (**a**) *(dans un film)* special effect (**b**) *(d'une photographie)* faking; *(d'un match, d'une élection)* rigging; *(de comptes)* fiddling

truchement [tryʃmɑ̃] *nm* **par le t. de...** through...

trucider [tryside] *vt Fam Hum* to bump off

trucmuche [trykmyʃ] *nm Fam* (**a**) *(chose)* thingy (**b**) **T.** *(personne)* what's-his-name, *f* what's-her-name

truculence [trykylɑ̃s] *nf (d'un récit, d'un style)* colourfulness; *(d'une personne)* flamboyance

truculent, -e [trykylɑ̃, -ɑ̃t] *adj (récit, style)* colourful; *(personne)* flamboyant

truelle [tryɛl] *nf* trowel

truffe [tryf] *nf* (**a**) *(champignon, au chocolat)* truffle (**b**) *(de chien)* nose

truffer [tryfe] *vt* (**a**) *(plat)* to garnish with truffles (**b**) *Fig (remplir)* **être truffé de** *(citations, balles)* to be peppered with; *(fautes)* to be riddled with

truie [trɥi] *nf* sow

truite [trɥit] *nf* trout; **t. arc-en-ciel/saumonée** rainbow/salmon trout

truquage [tryka3] = **trucage**

truquer [tryke] *vt* (**a**) *(photographie)* to fake; *(match, élection)* to rig; *(comptes)* to fiddle; *(dés)* to load (**b**) *(scène)* to use special effects in

trust [trœst] *nm Fin* trust

truster [trœste] *vt aussi Fam* to monopolize

tsar [tsar, dzar] *nm* tsar, czar

tsé-tsé [tsetse] *nf inv voir* **mouche**

TSF [teɛsɛf] *nf (abrév* **télégraphie sans fil)** *Vieilli (procédé)* wireless telegraphy; *(poste)* wireless

t-shirt *(pl* **t-shirts**) [tiʃœrt] = **tee-shirt**

tsigane [tsigan] = **tzigane**

TSVP *(abrév* **tournez s'il vous plaît)** PTO

TTC [tetese] *(abrév* **toutes taxes comprises)** inclusive of tax

tu¹, -e *pp de* **taire**

tu² [ty] *pron personnel* you; **tu as raison** you're right; *Fam* **t'as déjà fini?** have you finished already?; **être à tu et à toi avec qn** to be on first-name terms with sb; **dire tu à qn** to address sb as "tu"

Tuamotu [twamotu] *nfpl* **les T.** the Tuamotu Archipelago

tuant, -e [tɥɑ̃, -ɑ̃t] *adj Fam* (**a**) *(fatigant)* exhausting (**b**) *(insupportable)* exasperating

tuba [tyba] *nm* (**a**) *(instrument de musique)* tuba (**b**) *(de plongée)* snorkel

tube [tyb] *nm* (**a**) *(tuyau)* tube; *Fam Fig* **à pleins tubes** at full blast; **t. digestif** digestive tract; **t. à essai** test tube (**b**) *(chanson)* hit (**c**) *(emballage)* tube; **t. de rouge à lèvres** lipstick

tubercule [tybɛrkyl] *nm (plante)* tuber

tuberculeux, -euse [tybɛrkylø, -øz] **1** *adj* with tuberculosis; **être t.** to have tuberculosis

2 *nm,f* person with tuberculosis

tuberculose [tybɛrkyloz] *nf* tuberculosis; **avoir la t.** to have tuberculosis

tubéreuse [tyberøz] *nf* tuberose

tubulaire [tybylɛr] *adj* tubular

TUC [tyk] *nm (abrév* **travaux d'utilité collective)** = community work project for unemployed young people

tuer [tɥe] **1** *vt* (**a**) *(être vivant)* to kill; **t. qn d'un coup de revolver/de couteau** to shoot/stab sb to death; **c'est le chagrin qui l'a tué** he died of grief; *Fig* **t. le**

temps to kill time (**b**) *Fam (épuiser)* **tous ces déplacements m'ont tué** all that travelling was a killer; **ces escaliers/ces enfants me tuent** these stairs/these children will be the death of me (**c**) *Fam (sidérer)* **ça me tue!** it kills me!
 2 se tuer *vpr* (**a**) *(se suicider)* to kill oneself (**b**) *(dans un accident)* to die, to be killed (**c**) *(l'un l'autre)* to kill one another (**d**) *Fig* **se t. au travail** *ou* **à la tâche** to work oneself to death; **se t. à faire qch** to wear oneself out doing sth

tuerie [tyri] *nf* slaughter

tue-tête [tytɛt] **à tue-tête** *adv* at the top of one's voice

tueur, -euse [tɥœr, -øz] **1** *adj* killer
 2 *nm,f* killer; **t. à gages** hired killer; **t. en série** serial killer

tuile [tɥil] *nf* (**a**) *(de toit)* tile (**b**) **t. aux amandes** = type of thin almond biscuit (**c**) *Fam (problème)* **il m'arrive une t.** I'm in a bit of a mess

tulipe [tylip] *nf (fleur)* tulip

tulle [tyl] *nm* (**a**) *(tissu)* tulle (**b**) *Méd* **t. gras** = dressing used for burns

tuméfié, -e [tymefje] *adj* swollen

tuméfier [tymefje] *vt* to cause to swell

tumeur [tymœr] *nf* tumour; **t. au cerveau** brain tumour

tumoral, -e, -aux, -ales [tymɔral, -o] *adj* tumorous, tumoral

tumulte [tymylt] *nm (de la foule)* commotion; *(des passions)* turmoil

tumultueux, -euse [tymyltɥø, -øz] *adj (réunion)* noisy, tumultuous; *(vie, période)* tumultuous; *(relation)* stormy

tuner [tynœr, tynɛr] *nm* tuner

tungstène [tœkstɛn] *nm* tungsten

tunique [tynik] *nf* tunic

Tunis [tynis] *n* Tunis

Tunisie [tynizi] *nf* la T. Tunisia

tunisien, -enne [tynizjɛ̃, -ɛn] **1** *adj* Tunisian
 2 *nm,f* T. Tunisian

tunisois, -e [tynizwa, -az] **1** *adj* of Tunis
 2 *nm,f* T. person from Tunis

tunnel [tynɛl] *nm* tunnel; **le t. sous la Manche** the Channel Tunnel

tuque [tyk] *nf Can* bobble hat

turban [tyrbɑ̃] *nm* turban

turbin [tyrbɛ̃] *nm Fam (travail)* grind; **aller au t.** to go off to the daily grind

turbine [tyrbin] *nf* turbine

turbiner [tyrbine] *vi Fam (travailler)* to slog (away)

turbo [tyrbo] **1** *adj* turbocharged
 2 *nm* turbo; *Fam* **mettre le t.** to get a move on

turboréacteur [tyrboreaktœr] *nm* turbojet (engine)

turbot [tyrbo] *nm* turbot

turbulence [tyrbylɑ̃s] *nf* (**a**) *turbulences (dans l'atmosphère)* turbulence (**b**) *(d'un enfant)* boisterousness

turbulent, -e [tyrbylɑ̃, -ɑ̃t] *adj (enfant, classe)* boisterous

turc, turque [tyrk] **1** *adj* Turkish
 2 *nm,f* T. Turk
 3 *nm (langue)* Turkish

turf [tœrf, tyrf] *nm (activité)* racing

turfiste [tœrfist, tyrfist] *nmf* racegoer

turkmène [tyrkmɛn] **1** *adj* Turkoman
 2 *nmf* T. Turkoman
 3 *nm (langue)* Turkmen

Turkménistan [tyrkmenistɑ̃] *nm* **le T.** Turkmenistan

turlupiner [tyrlypine] *vt Fam* to bother

turluter [tyrlyte] *vi Can Fam* to trill, to sing tra-la-la

turpitude [tyrpityd] *nf* (**a**) *(d'une conduite)* vileness, turpitude (**b**) *(action)* vile act

turque [tyrk] *voir* turc

Turquie [tyrki] *nf* la T. Turkey

turquoise [tyrkwaz] *nf, nm inv & adj inv* turquoise

tutelle [tytɛl] *nf* (**a**) *Jur* guardianship; *Pol* **territoires sous t.** trust territories (**b**) *(protection)* protection

tuteur, -trice [tytœr, -tris] **1** *nm,f* guardian; **t. légal** legal guardian
 2 *nm (pour plante)* support

tutoiement [tytwamɑ̃] *nm* = use of the familiar "tu" instead of the more formal "vous"; **le t. est de rigueur** everybody calls each other "tu"

Tutoiement et vouvoiement

Traditionally, non-native French speakers waited until they were addressed using the informal "tu" form before using it themselves, except when speaking to young children. However in the past twenty or thirty years people in France have become much more casual about using "tu", and it is now commonly used among colleagues in the workplace, while the "vous" form tends to be used when talking to people from an older generation or to hierarchical superiors (see also entries **tu** and **vous**).

tutoriel [tytɔrjɛl] *nm* tutorial

tutoyer [32] [tytwaje] **1** *vt* **t. qn** = to address sb as "tu"
 2 *se tutoyer* *vpr* = to address each other as "tu"

tutti quanti [tutikwãti] *adv* **et t.** etcetera, etcetera

tutu [tyty] *nm* tutu

tuyau, -x [tɥijo] *nm* (**a**) *(canalisation)* pipe; *(de cheminée)* flue; *(flexible)* tube; **t. d'arrosage** garden hose; **t. d'échappement** exhaust (pipe); **t. d'incendie** fire hose; **t. de poêle** stove pipe (**b**) *Fam (conseil)* tip; *(information)* tip-off

tuyauter [tɥijote] *vt Fam (conseiller)* to give a tip to (**sur** about); *(informer)* to tip off (**sur** about)

tuyauterie [tɥijotri] *nf* piping, pipes

TV [teve] *nf (abrév* **télévision***)* TV

TVA [tevea] *nf (abrév* **taxe à la valeur ajoutée***)* VAT

TVHD [teveaʃde] *nf TV (abrév* **télévision à haute définition***)* HDTV

tweed [twid] *nm* tweed

twin-set *(pl* **twin-sets***)* [twinsɛt] *nm* twinset

tympan [tɛ̃pɑ̃] *nm* (**a**) *Anat* eardrum (**b**) *Archit* tympanum

type [tip] **1** *adj* typical; **lettre t.** standard letter
 2 *nm* (**a**) *(genre)* type (**b**) *(personnification)* **le t. même de** the classic example of (**c**) *(apparence)* **avoir le t. latin/nordique** to have Latin/Nordic looks (**d**) *Fam (homme)* guy, *Br* bloke

typé, -e [tipe] *adj* **il est italien – oui, et il est très t.** he's Italian – yes, he looks typically Italian

typhoïde [tifɔid] **1** *adj (fièvre)* typhoid
 2 *nf* typhoid (fever)

typhon [tifɔ̃] *nm* typhoon

typhus [tifys] *nm* typhus (fever)

typique [tipik] *adj* typical

typiquement [tipikmɑ̃] *adv* typically

typographe [tipɔgraf] *nmf* typographer
typographie [tipɔgrafi] *nf* typography, letterpress
printing
typographique [tipɔgrafik] *adj* typographic
tyran [tirã] *nm* tyrant
tyrannie [tirani] *nf* tyranny

tyrannique [tiranik] *adj* tyrannical
tyranniser [tiranize] *vt (population)* to tyrannize; *(famille, collègue)* to bully
tzar [tsar, dzar] = **tsar**
tzigane [tsigan, dzigan] **1** *adj* gypsy
2 *nmf* T. gypsy

U, u [y] *nm inv* U, u; **en U** U-shaped; **tables disposées en U** tables arranged in a horseshoe (shape)
ubac [ybak] *nm* = shady side of an Alpine mountain, *Spéc* ubac
ubiquité [ybikµite] *nf* ubiquity; **avoir le don d'u.** to have the ability to be in several places at the same time
UDF [ydɛɛf] *nf Pol* (*abrév* **Union pour la démocratie française**) = right-of-centre French political party
UE [yə] *nf* (*abrév* **Union européenne**) EU
UEM [yəɛm] *nf Écon* (*abrév* **Union économique et monétaire**) EMU
UEO [yəo] *nf* (*abrév* **Union de l'Europe occidentale**) WEU
ufologie [yfɔlɔʒi] *nf* ufology
UFR [yɛfɛr] *nf* (*abrév* **unité de formation et de recherche**) = department (*in university*)
UHF [yaʃɛf] *Rad* (*abrév* **ultra-haute fréquence**) UHF
UHT [yaʃte] (*abrév* **ultra-haute température**) UHT
Ukraine [ykrɛn] *nf* **l'U.** the Ukraine
ukrainien, -enne [ykrɛnjɛ̃, -jɛn] **1** *adj* Ukrainian
　2 *nm,f* U. Ukrainian
　3 *nm* (*langue*) Ukrainian
ukulélé [jukulele] *nm* ukelele
ulcération [ylserasjɔ̃] *nf* ulceration
ulcère [ylsɛr] *nm* ulcer; **avoir un u. à l'estomac** to have a stomach ulcer
ulcéré, -e [ylsere] *adj* (**a**) *Méd* ulcerated (**b**) *Fig* (*en colère*) seething
ulcérer [34] [ylsere] **1** *vt* (**a**) *Méd* to ulcerate (**b**) *Fig* (*mettre en colère*) **u. qn** to make sb seethe
　2 **s'ulcérer** *vpr Méd* to ulcerate
ULM [yɛlɛm] *nm inv Aviat* (*abrév* **ultraléger motorisé**) microlight
ultérieur, -e [ylterjœr] *adj* later, subsequent (**à** to)
ultérieurement [ylterjœrmɑ̃] *adv* later (on), subsequently
ultimatum [yltimatɔm] *nm* ultimatum; **adresser un u. à qn** to give sb an ultimatum
ultime [yltim] *adj* last; (*préparatifs*) final
ultra- [yltra] *préf* ultra-
ultra-confidentiel, -elle [yltrakɔ̃fidɑ̃sjɛl] *adj* top-secret
ultra-conservateur, -trice [yltrakɔ̃sɛrvatœr] *adj Pol* ultra-conservative
ultramoderne [yltramɔdɛrn] *adj* high-tech
ultraportatif [yltraportatif] *nm* notebook computer
ultrarapide [yltrarapid] *adj* ultrafast
ultrasensible [yltrasɑ̃sibl] *adj* ultra-sensitive
ultrason [yltrasɔ̃] *nm Phys* ultrasound; **ultrasons** ultrasonic waves

ultraviolet, -ette [yltravjɔlɛ, -ɛt] *adj & nm* ultraviolet
ululer [ylyle] *vi* to ululate
Ulysse [ylis] *npr* Ulysses
UME [yɛmə] *nf* (*abrév* **union monétaire européenne**) EMU
un, une [œ̃, yn] **1** *adj* one; **il est une heure** it's one o'clock; **page un** page one; **un jour** one day; **un, deux, trois, partez!** one, two, three, go!
　2 *pron indéfini* one; **un de mes amis** one of my friends, a friend of mine; **un de ces jours** one of these days; **en voilà une qui sait ce qu'elle veut!** there's somebody who knows what she wants!; **il n'y en a pas un qui parle anglais** not one of them speaks English; *Fam* **être menteur/hypocrite comme pas un** to be a dreadful liar/hypocrite; **(l')un de nous, (l')un d'entre nous** one of us
　3 *art indéfini* (*pl* **des**) (**a**) (*en général*) a; (*devant une voyelle ou un h muet*) an; **un jour/une pomme/une heure** a day/an apple/an hour; **cela tombe un mardi** it falls on a Tuesday; **il y a des agrafes dans le tiroir** there are (some) staples in the drawer; **est-ce qu'il te reste des agrafes?** do you have any staples left?; **il y a des jours où...** there are days when..., some days... (**b**) (*intensif*) **il y a un de ces mondes en ville!** the town is so busy!; **il est d'une bêtise!** he's so stupid!; **il a fait une de ces têtes!** you should have seen his face!; **tu m'as fait une peur!** you gave me such a fright!
　4 *nm* (*chiffre*) one
　5 *nf* **une** (**a**) (*première page*) **la une** (*d'un journal*) the front page; **faire la une** (*d'un magazine*) to appear on the front cover; (*d'un journal*) to appear on the front page (**b**) **il n'a fait ni une ni deux** he didn't hesitate for a moment
unanime [ynanim] *adj* unanimous
unanimité [ynanimite] *nf* unanimity; **à l'u.** unanimously; **faire l'u.** to be accepted unanimously
underground [œndœrgrawnd] *adj inv & nm inv* underground
une [yn] *voir* **un**
UNEF [ynɛf] *nf* (*abrév* **Union nationale des étudiants de France**) = French union of students, ≃ *Br* NUS
Unesco [ynɛsko] *nf* (*abrév* **United Nations Educational Scientific and Cultural Organization**) Unesco
Unetelle *voir* **Untel**
uni, -e [yni] *adj* (**a**) (*famille, couple*) close (**b**) (*sans irrégularité*) (*sol, surface*) smooth, level (**c**) (*couleur*) plain; (*tissu, vêtement*) plain, *Br* self-coloured
Unicef [ynisɛf] *nf* (*abrév* **United Nations International Children's Emergency Fund**) **l'U.** Unicef
unicellulaire [yniselylɛr] *adj* unicellular

unidimensionnel, -elle [ynidimãsjɔnɛl] *adj* one-dimensional

unidirectionnel, -elle [ynidirɛksjɔnɛl] *adj* unidirectional

unidose [ynidoz] *adj* single-dose sachet

unifamilial, -e, -aux, -ales [ynifamiljal, -o] *Belg & Can* **1** *adj (logement)* for a single family
2 *nf* **unifamiliale** detached house *(for a single family)*

unificateur, -trice [ynifikatœr, -tris] *adj* unifying

unification [ynifikasjɔ̃] *nf* unification

unifier [66] [ynifje] *vt* (**a**) *(parti politique, pays)* to unify (**b**) *(tarifs, poids et mesures)* to standardize

uniforme [ynifɔrm] **1** *adj (opinions, expression)* uniform; *(vie)* unchanging; *(allure, surface)* even; *(mouvement)* regular
2 *nm* uniform

uniformément [ynifɔrmemɑ̃] *adv* uniformly, evenly

uniformisation [ynifɔrmizasjɔ̃] *nf* standardization

uniformiser [ynifɔrmize] *vt* to standardize

uniformité [ynifɔrmite] *nf* (**a**) *(monotonie)* monotony (**b**) *(de couleurs, de teintes)* uniformity

unijambiste [yniʒãbist] **1** *adj* one-legged
2 *nmf* one-legged person

unilatéral, -e, -aux, -ales [ynilateral, -o] *adj (décision, désarmement)* unilateral; *(contrat, accord)* one-sided

unilingue [ynilɛ̃g] *adj* unilingual, monolingual

uninominal, -aux [yninɔminal, -o] *adj m voir* **scrutin**

union [ynjɔ̃] *nf* (**a**) *(entre personnes)* closeness, unity; **vivre en parfaite u. avec qn** to live in perfect harmony with sb (**b**) *(association) (de partis, de consommateurs)* union, association; **u. douanière/économique/monétaire** customs/economic/monetary union; **l'U. européenne** the European Union; *Anciennement* **l'U. soviétique** the Soviet Union (**c**) *(mariage)* marriage; **u. libre** cohabitation; **vivre en u. libre** to cohabit

unique [ynik] *adj* (**a**) *(seul)* only; *(parti, prix)* single; *(occasion, cas)* unique; **être u. en son genre** to be one of a kind; **u. au monde** unlike anything else in the world; **c'est son seul et u. défaut** it's his/her one and only fault (**b**) *(incomparable)* unique (**c**) *Fam (très drôle)* priceless

uniquement [ynikmɑ̃] *adv* just, only

unir [ynir] **1** *vt* (**a**) *(relier) (personnes, territoires)* to unite; *(qualités)* to combine (**à** with) (**b**) *(réunir)* **l'amitié qui nous unit** the friendship that unites us (**c**) *(marier)* to join in marriage (**d**) *(sol, surface)* to smooth, to level
2 s'unir *vpr* (**a**) *(s'associer)* to join together, to unite; **s'u. à qn** to join forces with sb (**b**) *(se marier)* to become joined in marriage

unisexe [ynisɛks] *adj* unisex

unisson [ynisɔ̃] *nm* unison; **à l'u.** in unison

unitaire [yniter] *adj (système)* unitary; *(prix)* unit

unité [ynite] *nf* (**a**) *(pour mesurer)* unit; **u. de longueur/de poids** unit of measurement/weight (**b**) *(élément simple)* unit; **10 euros l'u.** 10 euros each; *Com* **prix à l'u.** unit price; **vendu à l'u.** sold singly; **chiffre des unités** units figure; **u. de production** production unit; *Univ* **u. de valeur** credit (**c**) *(cohésion) (d'une nation, d'une association)* unity; *(du style)* consistency (**d**) *Ordinat* unit; *(de disque)* drive; **u. centrale** central processing unit; **u. de disque/logique** disk/logical drive

univers [yniver] *nm* (**a**) *(espace)* universe (**b**) *Fig (milieu)* world

universaliser [yniversalize] *vt* to universalize

universalité [yniversalite] *nf* universality

universel, -elle [yniversɛl] *adj* universal; *(savoir)* all-embracing

universellement [yniversɛlmɑ̃] *adv* universally

universitaire [yniversiter] **1** *adj (ville, études)* university
2 *nmf* (**a**) *(enseignant)* academic (**b**) *Belg & Suisse (étudiant)* university student; *(diplômé)* graduate

université [yniversite] *nf* university; **aller à l'u.** to go to university; **u. d'été** summer school; *Pol* party conference *(for young members)*; **u. du troisième âge** = classes for senior citizens

Untel, Unetelle [ɛ̃tɛl, yntɛl] *nm,f* what's-his-name, f what's-her-name; **M./Mme U.** Mr/Mrs So-and-So

uppercut [ypɛrkyt] *nm* uppercut

uranium [yranjɔm] *nm* uranium; **u. appauvri/enrichi** depleted/enriched uranium

Uranus [yranys] *npr (dieu, planète)* Uranus

urbain, -e [yrbɛ̃, -ɛn] *adj* (**a**) *(développement, milieu, transport)* urban (**b**) *Litt (poli)* urbane

urbanisation [yrbanizasjɔ̃] *nf* urbanization

urbaniser [yrbanize] *vt* to urbanize

urbanisme [yrbanism] *nm* town planning, urban development

urbaniste [yrbanist] **1** *adj* urban
2 *nmf* town planner

urbanité [yrbanite] *nf Litt* urbanity

urbi et orbi [yrbietɔrbi] *adv* urbi et orbi; *Fig* far and wide

urée [yre] *nf* urea

urètre [yrɛtr] *nm* urethra

urgence [yrʒãs] *nf* (**a**) *(caractère pressé)* urgency; **en cas d'u.** in an emergency; **d'u.** urgently; **être opéré d'u.** to have an emergency operation; **il y a u.** it's a matter of urgency (**b**) *(à l'hôpital)* emergency; **les urgences** *(service)* Br casualty, accident and emergency, *Am* the emergency room

urgent, -e [yrʒã, -ãt] *adj* urgent; **il est u. de le faire** it must be done urgently

urgentiste [yrʒãtist] *Méd nmf* emergency doctor

urger [45] [yrʒe] *vi Fam* **ça urge** it's urgent

urinaire [yriner] *adj* urinary

urine [yrin] *nf* urine

uriner [yrine] *vi* to urinate

urinoir [yrinwar] *nm* (public) urinal

urique [yrik] *adj (acide)* uric

urne [yrn] *nf* (**a**) *(pour voter)* ballot box; **aller aux urnes** to go to the polls (**b**) *(vase)* urn

uro-génital, -e [uroʒenital, -o] *(mpl* **uro-génitaux,** *fpl* **uro-génitales)** [yroʒenital, -o] *adj* urogenital

urologie [yrɔlɔʒi] *nf* urology

urologue [yrɔlɔg] *nmf* urologist

URSS [yɛrɛsɛs, yrs] *nf Anciennement (abrév* **Union des républiques socialistes soviétiques)** **l'U.** the USSR

URSSAF [yrsaf] *nf (abrév* **Union de recouvrement des cotisations de Sécurité sociale et d'Allocations familiales)** = organization which collects social security and family allowance payments

urticaire [yrtiker] *nf* nettle rash, *Spéc* urticaria; **avoir une crise d'u.** to come out in nettle rash; *Fam* **donner de l'u. à qn** to set sb's teeth on edge

Uruguay [yrygwɛ] *nm* **l'U.** Uruguay

uruguayen, -enne [yrygwɛjɛ̃, -ɛn] **1** *adj* Uruguayan
2 *nm,f* **U.** Uruguayan

us [ys] *nmpl* **les us et coutumes** the habits and customs

usage [yzaʒ] *nm* (**a**) *(utilisation)* use; **faire u. de qch** to use sth; **faire bon u. de qch** to put sth to good use; **avoir l'u. de qch** to have the use of sth; **à u. externe/interne** *(médicament)* for external/internal use; **à l'u. des écoles/des étudiants** for use in schools/by students; **à usages multiples** multi-purpose; **hors d'u.** out of order; *Jur* **u. de faux** use of forged documents (**b**) *(d'un terme, d'une expression)* usage; **entrer dans l'u.** *(mot)* to come into common use; **le bon u.** correct usage (**c**) *(des vêtements)* **faire de l'u.** to wear well; **ce manteau vous fera de l'u.** you'll get a lot of wear out of this coat (**d**) *(coutume)* custom, practice; **c'est l'u.** it's the done thing; **comme il est d'u. en France** as is customary in France; **il est d'u. de** it's customary to

usagé, -e [yzaʒe] *adj* *(vêtement, livre)* worn; *(ticket)* used

usager [yzaʒe] *nm* user

usant, -e [yzɑ̃, -ɑ̃t] *adj Fam* (**a**) *(vie, travail)* exhausting, wearing (**b**) *(personne)* tiresome

usé, -e [yze] *adj* (**a**) *(vêtements)* worn, worn-out; **u. jusqu'à la corde** threadbare (**b**) *(eaux)* waste (**c**) *(sujet, plaisanterie)* tired, stale (**d**) *(épuisé)* worn-out

user [yze] **1** *vt* (**a**) *(consommer)* *(énergie, électricité)* to use (**b**) *(abîmer)* *(vêtements, chaussures)* to wear out; *Fig* *(résistance)* to break down; **u. qch jusqu'à la corde** to wear sth until it's threadbare (**c**) *(épuiser)* *(personne)* to wear down
    2 **user de** *vt ind* *(patience, violence, ruse)* to use; *(droit)* to exercise; **u. de douceur avec qn** to handle sb gently; **u. de son influence pour faire qch** to use one's influence to do sth
    3 **s'user** *vpr* (**a**) *(tissu, pneus, semelles)* to wear out; *(talons)* to wear down (**b**) *Fig* *(personne)* **s'u. à faire qch** to wear oneself out doing sth

usinage [yzinaʒ] *nm* machining

usine [yzin] *nf* factory, plant; **u. de fabrication** manufacturing plant; **u. à gaz** gasworks; *Fig* overly complicated system; **u. de montage** assembly plant; **u. de production** production plant

usiner [yzine] *vt* *(façonner)* to machine

usité, -e [yzite] *adj* *(mot)* in common use; **très u.** very common; **peu u.** little used

ustensile [ystɑ̃sil] *nm* implement, tool; **u. de cuisine** kitchen utensil

usuel, -elle [yzɥɛl] *adj* everyday; *(dénomination)* common

usufruit [yzyfrɥi] *nm Jur* usufruct

usuraire [yzyrɛr] *adj* usurious

usure¹ [yzyr] *nf* *(intérêt, délit)* usury

usure² *nf* *(de pneu)* wear; *(du sol, de roches)* wearing away; **résister à l'u.** to wear well; *Fam* **avoir qn à l'u.** to wear sb down; **guerre d'u.** war of attrition

usurier, -ère [yzyrje, -ɛr] *nm,f* usurer

usurpateur, -trice [yzyrpatœr, -tris] *nm,f* usurper

usurpation [yzyrpasjɔ̃] *nf* *(d'un titre, de droits, du pouvoir)* usurpation

usurper [yzyrpe] *vt* *(titre, droits)* to usurp (**sur** from)

ut [yt] *nm inv* *(note)* C

utérin, -e [yterɛ̃, -in] *adj* uterine

utérus [yterys] *nm* uterus, womb

utile [ytil] *adj* useful (**à** to); **en quoi puis-je vous être u.?** what can I do for you?; **vous nous avez été bien u.** you've been very helpful to us; **se rendre u.** to make oneself useful; **en temps u.** in due course

utilement [ytilmɑ̃] *adv* usefully; **il m'a u. renseigné** he gave me useful information

utilisable [ytilizabl] *adj* usable; **facilement u.** easy to use

utilisateur, -trice [ytilizatœr, -tris] *nm,f* user; **u. final** end-user

utilisation [ytilizasjɔ̃] *nf* use

utiliser [ytilize] *vt* (**a**) *(se servir de)* to use (**b**) *Péj* *(personne)* to use (**c**) *Ordinat* to run

utilitaire [ytilitɛr] **1** *adj* (**a**) utilitarian; *(véhicule)* commercial (**b**) *Ordinat* utility
    2 *nm Ordinat* utility; **u. de conversion** conversion utility

utilitarisme [ytilitarism] *nm* utilitarianism

utilité [ytilite] *nf* *(fonction)* usefulness; **être d'une grande u. (à qn)** to be very useful (to sb)

utopie [ytɔpi] *nf* utopia

utopique [ytɔpik] *adj* utopian

utopiste [ytɔpist] *nmf* Utopian

UV¹ [yve] *nf inv Univ* *(abrév* **unité de valeur**) credit

UV² *nm inv* *(abrév* **ultraviolet**) UV; **faire des UV** to go on a sunbed

V, v [ve] *nm inv* (**a**) *(lettre)* V, v; *Fam* **à la vitesse grand V** at a rate of knots (**b**) *(abrév* **voir**) see
va *voir* **aller**
vacance [vakɑ̃s] *nf* (**a**) *(d'un poste)* vacancy; **pendant la v. du pouvoir** while there is no one officially in power (**b**) **vacances** *(d'écoliers, de travailleurs) Br* holiday(s), *Am* vacation; **un jour de vacances** a day's *Br* holiday *or Am* vacation; **prendre des vacances** to take a *Br* holiday *or Am* vacation; **être en vacances** to be on *Br* holiday *or Am* vacation; **partir en vacances** to go away on *Br* holiday *or Am* vacation; *Fam* **faire des vacances à qn** to give sb a break; **vacances de neige** winter sports *Br* holiday *or Am* vacation; **vacances de Noël/Pâques** Christmas/Easter *Br* holidays *or Am* vacation; **vacances scolaires** *Br* school holidays *or Am* vacation; *Scol* **les grandes vacances** the summer *Br* holidays *or Am* vacation period
vacancier, -ère [vakɑ̃sje, -ɛr] *nm,f Br* holidaymaker, *Am* vacationer
vacant, -e [vakɑ̃, -ɑ̃t] *adj* vacant
vacarme [vakarm] *nm* uproar, din; **faire du v.** to make an uproar
vacataire [vakatɛr] *nmf* short-term worker
vacation [vakasjɔ̃] *nf* (**a**) *(de juge, d'expert)* sitting, session (**b**) *(rémunération)* fees
vaccin [vaksɛ̃] *nm* vaccine
vaccination [vaksinasjɔ̃] *nf* vaccination, inoculation
vacciner [vaksine] *vt* to vaccinate, to inoculate (**contre** against); **se faire v. (contre)** to get vaccinated (against); *Fam* **je suis vacciné!** I've learnt my lesson!; *Fam* **je suis majeur et vacciné!** I'm old enough to look after myself now!
vachard, -e [vaʃar, -ard] *adj Fam (coup)* rotten, nasty; *(question)* nasty
vache [vaʃ] **1** *nf* (**a**) *(animal)* cow; **v. à lait** dairy cow; *Fig* cash cow; **v. laitière** dairy cow; *Fam* **manger de la v. enragée** to have a hard time of it; *Fam* **parler français comme une v. espagnole** to speak rotten French; *Fam* **comme une v. qui regarde passer les trains** with a vacant look on one's face (**b**) *Fam (homme)* swine; *(femme)* bitch (**c**) *(cuir)* cowhide (**d**) *Fam (interjection)* **la v., qu'est-ce qu'il fait froid!** God, it's so cold!
2 *adj Fam* rotten, nasty; **être v. avec qn** to be rotten to sb
vachement [vaʃmɑ̃] *adv Fam (très)* really; *(beaucoup)* a hell of a lot
vacher, -ère [vaʃe, -ɛr] *nm,f* cowherd, *f* cowgirl
vacherie [vaʃri] *nf Fam (action)* dirty trick; *(remarque)* nasty remark

vacherin [vaʃrɛ̃] *nm* (**a**) *(fromage)* = type of soft cheese (**b**) *(dessert)* = meringue with cream, ice cream and fruit
vachette [vaʃɛt] *nf* (**a**) *(petite vache)* small cow; *(jeune vache)* calf (**b**) *(cuir)* calfskin
vacillant, -e [vasijɑ̃, -ɑ̃t] *adj* (**a**) *(flamme)* flickering; *(démarche)* staggering (**b**) *(santé, mémoire)* failing
vacillation [vasijasjɔ̃] *nf*, **vacillement** [vasijmɑ̃] *nm (d'une flamme)* flickering
vaciller [vasije] *vi* (**a**) *(chanceler)* to be unsteady, to sway; **v. sur ses jambes** to stagger; **tout vacillait autour de moi** everything was swimming around me (**b**) *(flamme)* to flicker (**c**) *(mémoire, raison)* to fail
va-comme-je-te-pousse [vakɔmʃtəpus] **à la va-comme-je-te-pousse** *adv Fam* any old how
vacuité [vakɥite] *nf* vacuity
vadrouille [vadruj] *nf* (**a**) *Fam (balade)* ramble, saunter; **partir** *ou* **aller en v.** to roam around; **il est rarement à son bureau, il est toujours en v.** he's rarely at his desk, he's always wandering around somewhere (**b**) *Can* mop
vadrouiller [vadruje] *vi Fam* to roam around
va-et-vient [vaevjɛ̃] *nm inv* (**a**) *(mouvement)* backward and forward movement; **faire le v. (entre)** *(personne)* to go back and forth (between) (**b**) *(circulation) (de personnes)* comings and goings (**c**) *(dispositif électrique)* two-way wiring (system)
vagabond, -e [vagabɔ̃, -ɔ̃d] **1** *adj* (**a**) *(vie)* wandering, roving (**b**) *Fig (pensées)* wandering, roaming; **avoir l'humeur vagabonde** to be in a restless mood
2 *nm,f* vagrant, tramp
vagabondage [vagabɔ̃daʒ] *nm* vagrancy
vagabonder [vagabɔ̃de] *vi (personne)* to wander, to roam; *Fig (pensées, imagination)* to wander, to stray
vagin [vaʒɛ̃] *nm* vagina
vaginal, -e, -aux, -ales [vaʒinal, -o] *adj* vaginal
vagir [vaʒir] *vi (nouveau-né)* to cry
vagissement [vaʒismɑ̃] *nm (de nouveau-né)* cry, wail
vague¹ [vag] *nf* (**a**) *(d'eau)* wave; *Fig* **faire des vagues** to make waves; **arriver par vagues** to come in waves; *aussi Fig* **v. de fond** ground swell (**b**) *(ondulations) (de chevelure, de dunes)* wave (**c**) *(courant artistique)* **nouvelle v.** new wave (**d**) *(d'enthousiasme, de tendresse)* wave, surge; **v. de chaleur** heat wave; **v. de froid** cold spell (**e**) *(afflux) (d'immigrants)* influx
vague² **1** *adj* (**a**) *(impression, geste, souvenir)* vague; *(forme)* indistinct; **regarder qn d'un air v.** to look vacantly at sb; **rester v. sur qch** to be vague about sth (**b**) *(avant le nom)* **quelque v. écrivain** some writer or other
2 *nm* (**a**) *(imprécision)* vagueness; **rester dans le v.**

to be vague; **avoir du v. à l'âme** to be melancholy (**b**) *(vide)* **regard perdu dans le v.** faraway look

vaguelette [vaglɛt] *nf* wavelet

vaguement [vagmɑ̃] *adv* vaguely

vahiné [vaine] *nf* Tahitian woman

vaillamment [vajamɑ̃] *adv* valiantly

vaillance [vajɑ̃s] *nf* valour, courage

vaillant, -e [vajɑ̃, -ɑ̃t] *adj* (**a**) *(courageux)* valiant, courageous; *(cœur)* stout (**b**) *(en forme)* **être v.** to be in good health

vaille, vailles *voir* **valoir**

vain, -e [vɛ̃, vɛn] *adj* (**a**) *(sans résultat) (démarche, entreprise)* futile; *(efforts)* vain; **en v.** in vain (**b**) *(vide de sens) (paroles, promesse)* empty; *(espoirs, regrets)* vain (**c**) *Litt (personne)* vain

vaincre [vɛ̃kr] *vt* (**a**) *(adversaire)* to defeat; *(en sport)* to beat (**b**) *Fig (maladie, difficulté)* to overcome

vaincu, -e [vɛ̃ky] **1** *adj* beaten, defeated; **s'avouer v.** to admit defeat
2 *nm,f* defeated man, *f* defeated woman

vainement [vɛnmɑ̃] *adv* in vain

vainqueur [vɛ̃kœr] **1** *nm* (**a**) *(dans une compétition sportive)* winner (**b**) *(d'une bataille, d'une lutte)* victor
2 *adj m (personne)* conquering, victorious

vairon¹ [vɛrɔ̃] *adj* **avoir les yeux vairons** to have different-coloured eyes

vairon² *nm (poisson)* minnow

vais *voir* **aller**

vaisseau, -x [vɛso] *nm* (**a**) **v. (sanguin)** blood vessel (**b**) **v. spatial** spaceship (**c**) *(d'une église)* nave (**d**) *Litt* ship, vessel; **v. de guerre** warship

vaisselier [vɛsəlje] *nm (meuble)* dresser

vaisselle [vɛsɛl] *nf* dishes, crockery; **faire** *ou* **laver la v.** to do the dishes *or Br* the washing-up

val [val] *nm* valley

valable [valabl] *adj* (**a**) *(ticket, raison, excuse)* valid; **ce qui est v. pour l'un est v. pour l'autre** what goes for one goes for the other (**b**) *(compétent) (interlocuteur)* authorized (**c**) *(de qualité) (roman)* good; *(idée)* valid

valdinguer [valdɛ̃ge] *vi Fam* **aller v. contre/sur qch** to go flying against/onto sth; **envoyer v. qch** to send sth flying

Valence [valɑ̃s] *n* (**a**) *(en Espagne)* Valencia (**b**) *(en France)* Valence

valériane [valerjan] *nf* valerian

valet [valɛ] *nm* (**a**) *(au jeu de cartes)* jack, knave (**b**) *(domestique)* **v. (de chambre)** valet; **v. de ferme** farmhand; **v. de pied** footman (**c**) *(meuble)* **v. de nuit** valet

valétudinaire [valetydinɛr] *adj & nmf* valetudinarian

valeur [valœr] *nf* (**a**) *(prix)* value, worth; **avoir de la v.** to be valuable; **de peu de v./de grande v.** of little/of great value; **d'une v. de 20 euros** worth 20 euros; **prendre de la v.** to increase in value; **v. d'achat** purchase value; **v. ajoutée** added value; **v. en Bourse** stock market value; **v. marchande** market value; **valeurs mobilières** stocks and shares; **v. nominale** nominal value (**b**) *(qualité, mérite)* value; **de v.** *(livre, œuvre)* of considerable merit; **homme de v.** *(de mérite)* man of merit; **avoir v. légale** to be legally binding; **attacher de la v. à qch** to value sth; **mettre en v.** to show to advantage; *(teint, yeux)* to bring out; *(mot)* to emphasize; **se mettre en v.** to show oneself off to advantage; **prendre toute sa v.** *(terme, expression)* to take on its full meaning (**c**) *Fin (titre)* security; **valeurs de tout repos** gilt-edged securities (**d**) *(d'une note)* time, length; *(d'une carte)* value (**e**) *(équi-*

valent) *(d'une mesure)* equivalent (**f**) *(morale)* **valeurs** values (**g**) *Litt (courage)* valour

valeureux, -euse [valørø, -øz] *adj Litt* gallant

validation [validasjɔ̃] *nf (d'un titre de transport)* validation; *(d'un document)* authentication

valide [valid] *adj* (**a**) *(contrat)* valid (**b**) *(personne) (en bonne santé)* fit; *(non blessé)* uninjured

valider [valide] *vt* (**a**) *(élection, mariage)* to validate; *(document)* to authenticate; **v. un titre de transport** *(dans une machine)* to stamp a ticket (**b**) *Ordinat (option)* to confirm; *(cellule, case)* to select

validité [validite] *nf (d'un contrat, d'un passeport)* validity

valise [valiz] *nf* (**a**) *(bagage)* suitcase; *aussi Fig* **faire ses valises** to pack one's bags (**b**) *(courrier)* **la v. diplomatique** the diplomatic *Br* bag *or Am* pouch (**c**) *Fam (sous les yeux)* bag

vallée [vale] *nf* valley; *Litt* **une v. de larmes** a vale of tears

vallon [valɔ̃] *nm* small valley

vallonné, -e [valɔne] *adj (région)* undulating, hilly

vallonnement [valɔnmɑ̃] *nm* undulation

valoche [valɔʃ] *nf Fam* case, bag

valoir [69a] [valwar] **1** *vi* (**a**) *(avoir comme valeur)* to be worth; **v. cher** *(objet en vente)* to be expensive; *(objet précieux)* to be worth a lot; *Fig* **ne pas v. cher** *(personne)* not to be up to much; **ne rien v.** *(objet)* to be worthless; *(idée)* to be useless; **ce climat ne vous vaut rien** this climate doesn't suit you; **il ne vaut pas mieux que son frère** he's no better than his brother; **ça vaut mieux comme ça** it's better that way (**b**) *(avoir un intérêt)* **et ça vaut pour tout le monde** and that goes for everyone; **faire v. qch** *(opinions, droits)* to assert sth
2 *vt* (**a**) *(équivaloir à)* to be equivalent to; **un euro vaut 1,5 livres** one euro is worth £1.50; **ça ne vaut pas ce qui m'est arrivé l'autre jour** that's nothing to what happened to me the other day; **rien ne vaut un bon petit déjeuner** there's nothing like a good breakfast (**b**) *(rapporter)* **v. qch à qn** *(punition)* to earn sb sth; *(soucis, ennuis)* to bring sb sth; **qu'est-ce qui me vaut cet honneur?** to what do I owe this honour?
3 *v impersonnel* **il vaut/vaudrait mieux faire qch** it's/it would be better to do sth; **il vaut mieux que vous restiez** you'd better stay, it would be better if you stayed; *Prov* **mieux vaut tard que jamais** better late than never
4 **se valoir** *upr* **tous les métiers se valent** one job is as good as another; **ils se valent** *(péjoratif)* they're as bad as each other; *(admiratif)* they're as good as each other

valorisant, -e [valɔrizɑ̃, -ɑ̃t] *adj* gratifying

valorisation [valɔrizasjɔ̃] *nf* (**a**) *(augmentation de la valeur)* increase in value (**b**) *(développement)* development

valoriser [valɔrize] *vt* (**a**) *(bien, monnaie)* to increase the value of (**b**) *(développer) (région)* to develop; *(personne)* to boost the self-esteem of

valse [vals] *nf* (**a**) *(morceau de musique, air de danse)* waltz (**b**) *Fam* **la v. des ministres** frequent cabinet reshuffles

valse-hésitation *(pl* **valses-hésitations**) [valsezitasjɔ̃] *nf Fam* pussyfooting, shilly-shallying

valser [valse] *vi* to waltz; **faire v. qn** to waltz with sb; *Fig* **faire v. les millions** to spend money like water; *Fam* **envoyer v. qn/qch** to send sb/sth flying

valseur, -euse [valsœr, -øz] *nm,f* waltzer

valu, -e *pp de* **valoir**

valve [valv] *nf* valve
vamp [vãp] *nf Fam* vamp
vampire [vãpir] *nm* (**a**) *(suceur de sang)* vampire (**b**) *Fig (parasite)* bloodsucker
vampiriser [vãpirize] *vt Fam* to dominate psychologically
van¹ [vã] *nm (fourgon à chevaux)* horse box
van² [van] *nm (camionnette)* van
Vancouver [vãkuvɛr] *n* Vancouver
vandale [vãdal] *nmf* vandal
vandaliser [vãdalize] *vt* to vandalize
vandalisme [vãdalism] *nm* vandalism
vanille [vanij] *nf* vanilla
vanillé, -e [vanije] *adj* vanilla-flavoured
vanité [vanite] *nf* (**a**) *(suffisance)* vanity; **tirer v. de qch** to pride oneself on sth (**b**) *Litt (insignifiance)* futility, emptiness
vaniteux, -euse [vanitø, -øz] **1** *adj* vain
   2 *nm,f* vain person
vanne¹ [van] *nf (de canalisation, d'écluse)* sluice gate, floodgate; **ouvrir/fermer les vannes** to open/close the floodgates
vanne² *nf Fam (remarque blessante)* dig, jibe; **envoyer une v. à qn** to have a dig at sb
vanné, -e [vane] *adj Fam* **être v.** to be dead beat
vanneau, -x [vano] *nm (oiseau)* lapwing, peewit
vanner [vane] *vt* (**a**) *Fam (fatiguer)* to wear out, to exhaust (**b**) *(grain)* to winnow
vannerie [vanri] *nf* (**a**) *(activité)* basket making, basketry (**b**) *(objets)* basketwork, wickerwork
vannier [vanje] *nm* basket worker *or* maker
vantard, -e [vãtar, -ard] **1** *adj* bragging, boastful
   2 *nm,f* braggart, boaster
vantardise [vãtardiz] *nf (caractère)* bragging, boastfulness; *(parole)* boast
vanter [vãte] **1** *vt* to praise, to speak highly of
   2 se vanter *vpr* to boast, to brag (**de** about)
Vanuatu [vanwatu] *n* Vanuatu
va-nu-pieds [vanypje] *nmf inv* tramp, beggar
vapes [vap] *nfpl Fam* **être dans les v.** to be all woozy; **tomber dans les v.** to pass out
vapeur¹ [vapœr] *nf* (**a**) *(d'eau bouillante)* **v. (d'eau)** steam; **cuire qch à la v.** to steam sth; **à toute v.** full steam ahead; *Fig* at full speed (**b**) *(gaz)* **vapeurs** *(d'alcool, d'essence)* fumes (**c**) *Méd* **avoir des vapeurs** to have a fit of the vapours
vapeur² *nm (bateau)* steamer, steamship
vaporeux, -euse [vaporø, -øz] *adj* (**a**) *(atmosphère)* steamy (**b**) *(robe)* flimsy
vaporisateur [vaporizatœr] *nm (de parfum)* spray, atomizer; *(pour plantes)* spray
vaporiser [vaporize] **1** *vt* (**a**) *(pulvériser)* to spray (**b**) *(transformer en vapeur)* to vaporize
   2 se vaporiser *vpr* to vaporize
vaquer [vake] **1** *vi (parlement, tribunal)* to be on vacation
   2 vaquer à *vt ind* **v. à qch** to attend to sth; **v. à ses affaires** *ou* **occupations** to go about one's business
varappe [varap] *nf* rock climbing; **faire de la v.** to go rock climbing
varapper [varape] *vi* to go rock climbing
varappeur, -euse [varapœr, -øz] *nm,f* rock climber
vareuse [varøz] *nf* (**a**) *(de marin)* pea jacket (**b**) *(d'uniforme)* tunic (**c**) *(veste large)* loose-fitting jacket
variable [varjabl] **1** *adj* (**a**) *(temps, humeur)* changeable; *(vitesse)* varying (**b**) *(différent)* varied; **être v.** to vary
   2 *nf* variable

variante [varjãt] *nf* variant, variation
variation [varjasjɔ̃] *nf* (**a**) *(écart)* change (**de** in); **les variations de la température** the variations in the temperature (**b**) *Mus* variation
varice [varis] *nf* varicose vein
varicelle [varisɛl] *nf* chickenpox, *Spéc* varicella; **avoir la v.** to have chickenpox
varié, -e [varje] *adj (alimentation, paysage, travail)* varied, *(vocabulaire)* wide
varier [66] [varje] **1** *vt (alimentation, occupations)* to vary; *Ironique* **pour v. les plaisirs** by way of a pleasant change
   2 *vi* to vary, to change; **les opinions varient sur ce point** opinions differ on this point; **il n'a jamais varié sur ce point** he's never changed his mind about it
variété [varjete] *nf* **1** *nf* variety
   2 *nfpl* **variétés** *TV* variety show; *(musique)* easy-listening; **chanteur de variétés** middle-of-the-road singer, **disque de v.** easy-listening record
variole [varjɔl] *nf* smallpox; **avoir la v.** to have smallpox
Varsovie [varsɔvi] *n* Warsaw
vas *voir* **aller**
vasculaire [vaskylɛr] *adj* vascular
vase¹ [vaz] *nm* vase; *Fig* **vivre en v. clos** to live in isolation; **vases communicants** communicating vessels
vase² *nf* mud, silt
vasectomie [vazɛktɔmi] *nf* vasectomy
vaseline [vazlin] *nf* Vaseline®, petroleum jelly
vaseux, -euse [vazø, -øz] *adj* (**a**) *Fam (mal en point)* off-colour (**b**) *(peu clair) (idée)* woolly; *(explication)* confused (**c**) *(plaisanterie)* unsavoury (**d**) *(rivière)* muddy, silty
vasistas [vazistɑs] *nm* fanlight
vasoconstricteur, -trice [vazokɔ̃striktœr, -tris] *adj & nm* vasoconstrictor
vasodilatateur, -trice [vazodilatatœr, -tris] *adj & nm* vasodilator
vasomoteur, -trice [vazomɔtœr, -tris] *adj (nerf)* vasomotor
vasouillard, -e [vazujar, -ard] *adj Fam (idée)* confused, muddled; **se sentir v.** to feel a bit under the weather
vasouiller [vazuje] *vi Fam* to flounder
vassal, -e, -aux, -ales [vasal, -o] *nm,f* vassal
vaste [vast] *adj* (**a**) vast, immense (**b**) *Fam (plaisanterie)* big, great; **c'est une v. fumisterie** it's a complete farce
Vatican [vatikã] *nm* **le V.** the Vatican; **la cité du V.** Vatican City
va-tout [vatu] *nm inv* **jouer son v.** to stake one's all
vaudeville [vodvil] *nm Théât* light farce; **tourner au v.** to become farcical
vaudou, -e [vodu] *adj & nm* voodoo
vaudrai, vaudras *etc voir* **valoir**
vau-l'eau [volo] **à vau-l'eau** *adv* **aller à v.** to fall through
vaurien, -enne [vorjɛ̃, -ɛn] *nm,f* (**a**) *(brigand)* good-for-nothing (**b**) *(enfant)* rascal
vaut *voir* **valoir**
vautour [votur] *nm* vulture
vautrer [votre] **se vautrer** *vpr* (**a**) *(cochon)* to wallow (**dans** in) (**b**) *(personne)* to sprawl (**dans** in); *Fig* **se v. dans la débauche** to wallow in vice
vauvert [vovɛr] *voir* **diable**
va-vite [vavit] **à la va-vite** *adv* in a rush
vaux *voir* **valoir**

VDQS [vedekɥɛs] *nm* (*abrév* **vin délimité de qualité supérieure**) = label certifying that wine is of good quality

veau, -x [vo] *nm* (**a**) (*animal*) calf (**b**) (*viande*) veal (**c**) (*cuir*) calfskin (**d**) *Fam* (*personne lente*) lump (**e**) *Fam* (*voiture*) car with poor acceleration

vecteur [vɛktœr] *nm* (**a**) *Math* vector (**b**) (*d'information, de progrès*) vehicle

vectoriel, -elle [vɛktɔrjɛl] *adj* vectorial; *Ordinat* **police vectorielle** outline font

vécu, -e [veky] **1** *pp de* vivre
2 *adj* (*expérience*) real-life
3 *nm* real-life experience

vedettariat [vədɛtarja] *nm* stardom

vedette [vədɛt] *nf* (**a**) (*acteur*) star; **v. de la chanson** singing star; **v. de cinéma** movie star; **avoir la v., être en v.** (*dans un spectacle*) to top the bill; (*dans un film*) to be the main star (**b**) *Fig* (*de la politique*) leading light (**c**) (*bateau à moteur*) (*de plaisancier*) launch; (*de police*) patrol boat

végétal, -e, -aux, -ales [veʒetal, -o] **1** *adj* (*huile*) vegetable
2 *nm* vegetable, plant

végétarien, -enne [veʒetarjɛ̃, -ɛn] *adj & nm,f* vegetarian

végétatif, -ive [veʒetatif, -iv] *adj* (*appareil*) vegetative; *Fig & Péj* (*existence*) vegetable-like

végétation [veʒetasjõ] *nf* (**a**) (*flore*) vegetation (**b**) *Méd* **végétations** (**adénoïdes**) adenoids

végéter [34] [veʒete] *vi Péj* (*personne*) to vegetate

véhémence [veemɑ̃s] *nf Litt* vehemence; **avec v.** vehemently

véhément, -e [veemɑ̃, -ɑ̃t] *adj Litt* vehement, violent

véhicule [veikyl] *nm* (**a**) (*moyen de transport*) vehicle; **v. utilitaire** commercial vehicle (**b**) (*support*) (*du son, de la lumière*) vehicle

véhiculer [veikyle] *vt* (**a**) (*transporter*) to transport, to convey (**b**) (*transmettre*) to convey

veille [vɛj] *nf* (**a**) (*jour qui précède*) **la v.** the previous day, the day before; **à la v. de la réunion** the day before the meeting; **la v. au soir** the previous evening, the evening before; **la v. de Noël** Christmas Eve; *Fig* **être à la v. de qch/de faire qch** to be on the verge of sth/of doing sth (**b**) (*éveil*) wakefulness; **entre la v. et le sommeil** between waking and sleeping; **après deux jours de v.** after staying up for two nights (**c**) (*garde*) (night) watch; **prendre la v.** to take one's turn on watch (**d**) *Ordinat* standby mode; **en v.** in standby mode

veillée [veje] *nf* (**a**) (*soirée*) evening; **v. au coin du feu** evening spent round the fire; **v. d'armes** knightly vigil (**b**) (*d'un mort*) watch, vigil (**c**) *Can* (*fête*) party

veiller [veje] **1** *vt* (*malade*) to sit up with; **v. un mort** to keep vigil over a dead body
2 *vi* to stay up
3 veiller à *vt ind* **v. à qch** to see to sth; **v. aux intérêts de qn** to look after sb's interests; **v. à ce que qn fasse qch** to make sure or see to it that sb does sth; *Fig* **v. au grain** to keep an eye open for trouble
4 veiller sur *vt ind* **v. sur qn** to take care of sb
5 se veiller *vpr Suisse Fam* to be careful, to watch out

veilleur [vɛjœr] *nm* **v. de nuit** night watchman

veilleuse [vɛjøz] *nf* (**a**) (*lampe*) night light; (*sur une télévision, sur un magnétoscope*) standby; *Fig* **mettre qch en v.** (*projet, problème*) to put sth on the back burner; *Fam* **la mettre en v.** to put a sock in it (**b**) (*d'un chauffe-eau, d'un réchaud*) pilot light (**c**) **veilleuses** (*d'une automobile*) sidelights

veinard, -e [vɛnar, -ard] *Fam* **1** *adj* lucky, *Br* jammy
2 *nm,f* lucky or *Br* jammy devil

veine [vɛn] *nf* (**a**) *Anat* vein; **v. cave** vena cava (**b**) *Fam* (*chance*) luck; **avoir de la v.** to be lucky; *Fam* **avoir une v. de cocu** to have the luck of the devil (**c**) (*dans le marbre, le bois*) vein (**d**) (*filon*) (*de minerai*) vein; (*de charbon*) seam (**e**) (*inspiration*) vein; **en v. de plaisanterie** in humorous vein; **être en v. de générosité** to be in a generous mood

veiné, -e [vene] *adj* (*marbre, bois*) grained

veineux, -euse [vɛnø, -øz] *adj* (*système, circulation*) venous

veinule [venyl] *nf* venule

Velcro® [vɛlkro] *nm* (*tissu*) Velcro®; (*fermeture*) Velcro® fastening

vêler [vɛle] *vi* to calve

vélin [velɛ̃] *nm* vellum

véliplanchiste [veliplɑ̃ʃist] *nmf* windsurfer (*person*)

velléitaire [veleitɛr] **1** *adj* indecisive
2 *nmf* indecisive person

velléités [veleite] *nfpl* vague desire; **avoir des v. de faire qch** to toy with the idea of doing sth

vélo [velo] *nm* bike; **aller au bureau en v.** to cycle to the office, to go to the office on one's bike; **faire du v.** (*comme activité*) to go cycling; **est-ce que tu sais faire du v.?** can you ride a bike?; **v. d'appartement** exercise bike; **v. de course** racing cycle; **v. tout-terrain** mountain bike

vélocité [velɔsite] *nf* speed, swiftness

vélodrome [velodrɔm] *nm* velodrome

vélomoteur [velomotœr] *nm* moped

velours [vəlur] *nm* (**a**) (*tissu*) velvet; **veste/rideaux en v.** velvet jacket/curtains; **v. côtelé** *ou* **à côtes** corduroy (**b**) *Fig* **faire des yeux de v. à qn** to make eyes at sb

velouté, -e [vəlute] **1** *adj* velvety
2 *nm* (**a**) (*texture*) velvetiness (**b**) (*soupe*) cream soup; **v. d'asperges** cream of asparagus soup

velouteux, -euse [vəlutø, -øz] *adj* velvety

Velpeau® [vɛlpo] *voir* **bande¹**

velu, -e [vəly] *adj* hairy

Vélux® [velyks] *nm* = window built into a sloping roof

venaison [vənɛzõ] *nf* venison

vénal, -e, -aux, -ales [venal, -o] *adj* (**a**) *Péj* (*intéressé*) venal, mercenary (**b**) (*valeur*) market

venant [vənɑ̃] *nm* **à tout v., à tous venants** to all comers, to all and sundry

vendable [vɑ̃dabl] *adj* saleable, sellable; **facilement/difficilement** easy/difficult to sell

vendange [vɑ̃dãʒ] *nf* (**a**) **vendanges** (*période*) grape-harvesting time (**b**) (*récolte*) grape harvest; **faire la v.** *ou* **les vendanges** to harvest or pick the grapes (**c**) (*raisin récolté*) grapes (harvested); **une bonne v.** a good vintage

vendanger [45] [vɑ̃dãʒe] **1** *vi* to harvest the grapes
2 *vt* (*vigne*) to pick the grapes from

vendangeur, -euse [vɑ̃dãʒœr, -øz] *nm,f* grape picker

vendetta [vɑ̃deta] *nf* vendetta

vendeur, -euse [vɑ̃dœr, -øz] **1** *adj* **être v.** to be willing to sell
2 *nm,f* (*dans un magasin*) *Br* (shop) assistant, *Am* (sales)clerk; (*non professionnel*) seller; **v. ambulant** travelling salesman, *f* travelling saleswoman; **v. à domicile** door-to-door salesman, *f* door-to-door

saleswoman; **v. de journaux** newspaper seller *or* vendor
vendre [vãdr] **1** *vt* (**a**) *(article, produit)* to sell; **v. qch 50 euros** to sell sth for 50 euros; **v. qch à qn** to sell sb sth, to sell sth to sb; **à v.** *(sur panneau)* for sale; *Fig* **v. son âme au diable** to sell one's soul to the devil (**b**) *(trahir) (personne)* to sell out; *(secret)* to sell; **v. la mèche** to spill the beans
2 se vendre *vpr* (**a**) *(produit, article)* to be sold; **cela se vend comme des petits pains** it's selling like hot cakes (**b**) *(soi-même)* to sell oneself
vendredi [vãdrədi] *nm* Friday; **le v. saint** Good Friday; *voir aussi* **samedi**
vendu, -e [vãdy] **1** *adj (corrompu)* bribed
2 *nm,f* traitor
vénéneux, -euse [venenø, -øz] *adj* poisonous
vénérable [venerabl] *adj* venerable
vénération [venerasjɔ̃] *nf* veneration; **avoir de la v. pour qn** to hold sb in veneration
vénère [venɛr] *Fam* **1** *adj (énervé) Br* wound up, *Am* ticked off
2 *vt (énervé)* **v. qn** to bug sb, *Br* to wind sb up
vénérer [34] [venere] *vt* to venerate
vénérien, -enne [venerjɛ̃, -ɛn] *adj* venereal
Venezuela [venezɥela] *nm* **le V.** Venezuela
vénézuélien, -enne [venezɥeljɛ̃, -ɛn] **1** *adj* Venezuelan
2 *nm,f* **V.** Venezuelan
vengeance [vãʒɑ̃s] *nf* revenge, vengeance; *Prov* **la v. est un plat qui se mange froid** revenge is a dish best eaten cold
venger [45] [vãʒe] **1** *vt* to avenge; **v. qn de qch** to avenge sb for sth
2 se venger *vpr* to get one's revenge; **se v. sur qn (de qch)** to get one's revenge on sb (for sth); *Fam* **pas la peine de te v. sur moi!** there's no point in taking it out on me!
vengeur, -eresse [vãʒœr, -ʒrɛs] *Litt* **1** *adj* vengeful
2 *nm,f* avenger
véniel, -elle [venjɛl] *adj (péché)* venial
venimeux, -euse [vənimø, -øz] *adj aussi Fig* venomous
venin [vənɛ̃] *nm aussi Fig* venom
venir [70] [vənir] *(aux* **être**) **1** *vi* (**a**) *(arriver)* to come (**de** from); **il vient passer quelques jours** he's coming to spend a few days; **viens me voir** come and see me; **d'où venez-vous?** where do you come from?; **je viens!** I'm coming!; **v. vers qn** to come up to sb; **vous y viendrez!** you'll come round to it, you'll change your mind; **dans les mois/années qui viennent** in the coming months/years; **le moment est venu de nous en aller** it's time we left; **le jour viendra où...** the day will come when...; **ton tour viendra** your turn will come, you'll get your turn; **l'eau leur venait aux genoux** the water came up to their knees (**b**) *(tirer son origine)* to come (**de** from); **la maison lui vient de sa mère** he/she inherited the house from his/her mother (**c**) **en v. à qch/à faire qch** to come to sth/to do sth; **j'en suis venu à me demander si...** I began to wonder whether...; **où voulez-vous en v.?** what are you getting at?; **en v. aux mains** to come to blows (**d**) **venir de faire qch** to have just done sth; **je viens de le lui dire** I've just told him/her; **je venais de terminer** I'd just finished
2 *v impersonnel* **s'il venait à pleuvoir** if it happened to rain; **il m'est venu une idée intéressante** an interesting idea occurred to me
3 s'en venir *vpr Litt* to come along

Venise [vəniz] *n* Venice
vénitien, -enne [venisjɛ̃, -ɛn] **1** *adj* Venetian
2 *nm,f* **V.** Venetian
vent [vã] *nm* (**a**) *(air)* wind; **les cheveux au v.** with one's hair streaming in the wind; **quel bon v. vous amène?** to what do I/we owe the pleasure?; *Fig* **avoir le v. en poupe** to have the wind in one's sails; *Fig* **avoir du v. dans les voiles** to be three sheets to the wind; **avoir v. de qch** to get wind of sth; **ce n'est que du v.** it's just hot air; *Fam* **être dans le v.** to be with it; **contre vents et marées** come hell or high water; *Ironique* **bon v.!** good riddance! (**b**) *(flatulence)* wind; **avoir des vents** to have wind
vente [vãt] *nf (transaction)* sale; *(activité)* selling; *Can (soldes)* sale; **en v.** *(par un particulier)* for sale; *(dans les magasins)* on sale; **en v. libre** available over the counter; **mettre qch en v.** to put sth up for sale; **v. de charité** charity sale; **v. par correspondance** mail order (selling); **v. à crédit** credit sale; **v. au détail** retailing; **v. aux enchères** (sale by) auction; **v. en gros** wholesaling; **v. en ligne** e-tail; **v. à température** *Br* hire purchase, *Am* installment plan
venter [vãte] *v impersonnel* **il vente** it's windy
venteux, -euse [vãtø, -øz] *adj* windy
ventilateur [vãtilatœr] *nm* (**a**) *(pour aérer)* fan (**b**) *Ordinat* **v. de refroidissement** cooling fan (**c**) *(d'une automobile)* blower
ventilation [vãtilasjɔ̃] *nf* (**a**) *(aération)* ventilation (**b**) *(des dépenses)* breakdown
ventiler [vãtile] *vt* (**a**) *(aérer)* to ventilate (**b**) *(dépenses)* to break down
ventouse [vãtuz] *nf* (**a**) *(pour fixer)* suction grip; *(pour déboucher)* plunger; **faire v.** to adhere by suction (**b**) *(en verre)* cupping glass; **poser des ventouses à qn** to cup sb
ventral, -e, -aux, -ales [vãtral, -o] *adj* ventral
ventre [vãtr] *nm* (**a**) *(estomac)* stomach; **avoir le v. plein/vide** to have a full/an empty stomach; **avoir du v.** to have a paunch; **v. à terre** at full speed, flat out; **avoir mal au v.** to have (a) stomach-ache; *Fig* **ça fait mal au v. de voir ça** it makes me sick to see that; *Fig* **ça me ferait mal au v.!** it would kill me!; **ne rien avoir dans le v.** to have no guts (**b**) *(utérus)* womb (**c**) *(d'une bouteille)* bulge
ventricule [vãtrikyl] *nm* ventricle
ventriloque [vãtrilɔk] *nmf* ventriloquist
ventru, -e [vãtry] *adj* (**a**) *(gros)* potbellied (**b**) *(colonne)* bulbous
venu, -e [vəny] **1** *adj* **bien v.** appropriate; **mal v.** inappropriate
2 *nm,f* **le premier v.** *(n'importe qui)* anybody; **un nouveau v.** a newcomer
3 *nf* **venue** *(d'une personne, du printemps)* coming; **dès sa venue au monde** since he/she came into the world
Vénus [venys] *npr (déesse, planète)* Venus
vêpres [vɛpr] *nfpl* vespers
ver [vɛr] *nm* (**a**) *(dans la terre)* & *Ordinat* worm; *(dans un fruit)* grub; *Fig* **tirer les vers du nez à qn** to drag it out of sb; **v. informatique** worm; **v. luisant** glowworm; **v. à soie** silkworm; **v. de terre** earthworm (**b**) *Méd* **v. solitaire** tapeworm; **avoir le v. solitaire** to have a tapeworm
véracité [verasite] *nf* truthfulness
véranda [verãda] *nf* veranda(h)
verbal, -e, -aux, -ales [vɛrbal, -o] *adj* verbal
verbalement [vɛrbalmã] *adv* verbally

verbaliser [vɛrbalize] **1** *vt (exprimer)* to verbalize **2** *vi (policier)* to record the details of an offence

verbe [vɛrb] *nm Gram* verb; **v. à particule** *(en anglais)* phrasal verb

verbeux, -euse [vɛrbø, -øz] *adj* verbose

verbiage [vɛrbjaʒ] *nm* verbiage

verdâtre [vɛrdɑtr] *adj* greenish

verdeur [vɛrdœr] *nf* (**a**) *(d'un fruit, d'un vin)* tartness (**b**) *(du langage)* crudeness (**c**) *(vitalité)* vigour, vitality

verdict [vɛrdikt] *nm* verdict; **prononcer** *ou* **rendre un v.** to return a verdict

verdir [vɛrdir] **1** *vt* to turn green **2** *vi* to turn green; *Fig* **v. de jalousie/de peur** to go *or* turn green with envy/white with fear

verdoyant, -e [vɛrdwajɑ̃, -ɑ̃t] *adj* green

verdoyer [32] [vɛrdwaje] *vi Litt* to be green

verdure [vɛrdyr] *nf* (**a**) *(couleur)* greenness (**b**) *(végétation)* greenery (**c**) *(légumes verts)* greens

véreux, -euse [verø, -øz] *adj* (**a**) *(fruit)* wormy, maggoty (**b**) *Péj (affaires, financier)* shady, dubious

verge [vɛrʒ] *nf* (**a**) *(pénis)* penis (**b**) *(baguette)* cane (**c**) *Can (mesure)* yard

verger [vɛrʒe] *nm* orchard

vergetures [vɛrʒətyr] *nfpl* stretch marks

verglacé, -e [vɛrglase] *adj* icy

verglas [vɛrgla] *nm Br* (black) ice, *Am* glare ice, glaze

vergogne [vɛrgɔɲ] **sans vergogne 1** *adj* shameless **2** *adv* shamelessly

véridique [veridik] *adj* truthful

vérifiable [verifjabl] *adj* verifiable

vérificateur, -trice [verifikatœr, -tris] **1** *nm,f (personne)* inspector, examiner; **v. de comptes** auditor **2** *nm Ordinat* **v. orthographique** spellchecker

vérification [verifikasjɔ̃] *nf* (**a**) *(d'un travail, des votes)* checking; **v. de comptes** *ou* **d'écritures** audit(ing) of accounts (**b**) *Ordinat* **v. antivirale** antiviral check; **v. orthographique** spellcheck

vérifier [66] [verifje] **1** *vt* to check; *(comptes)* to audit; **il doit être là, je vais v.** he must be there, I'll check **2** **se vérifier** *vpr* to prove correct

véritable [veritabl] *adj* (**a**) *(histoire, ami)* true; *(nom, or, cuir)* real (**b**) *(en intensif)* real

véritablement [veritabləmɑ̃] *adv* really

vérité [verite] *nf* (**a**) *(d'une déclaration)* truth; **dire la v.** to tell the truth; **c'est la v.** it's true, it's a fact; **à la v.** to tell the truth; **en v.** really, actually; **dire à qn ses quatre vérités** to tell sb a few home truths (**b**) *(d'un personnage, d'une description)* trueness to life (**c**) *(sincérité)* **un accent de v.** a ring of truth

verlan [vɛrlɑ̃] *nm* back slang

Verlan

This form of slang, mostly used among young French people and particularly in the impoverished areas of large cities, involves inverting the syllables of words and making any spelling changes necessary to facilitate pronunciation. The word "verlan" is itself the inverted form of "l'envers" meaning "the other way round". Some "verlan" terms are used or understood by a great many speakers, eg "laisse béton!" ("laisse tomber!" = "forget it!"), "ripou" ("pourri", used to refer to corrupt policemen), "meuf" ("femme") and "beur" ("arabe"). It is, however, an extremely generative form of slang and new words are constantly being made up.

vermeil, -eille [vɛrmɛj] **1** *adj* bright red **2** *nm* silver gilt

vermicelle [vɛrmisɛl] *nm* vermicelli

vermifuge [vɛrmifyʒ] *nm* vermifuge

vermillon [vɛrmijɔ̃] *adj inv & nm* vermilion

vermine [vɛrmin] *nf* (**a**) *(insectes)* vermin; **couvert** *ou* **grouillant de v.** crawling with vermin (**b**) *Péj (racaille)* **la v.** vermin

vermisseau, -x [vɛrmiso] *nm* small worm; *Fig (personne)* worm

vermoulu, -e [vɛrmuly] *adj* worm-eaten

vermouth [vɛrmut] *nm* vermouth

vernaculaire [vɛrnakylɛr] *adj* **langue v.** vernacular

verni, -e [vɛrni] *adj* (**a**) *(meuble, bois, parquet)* varnished; *(chaussures)* patent (leather); *(ongles)* varnished, painted (**b**) *Fam (chanceux)* lucky, *Br* jammy

vernir [vɛrnir] *vt* to varnish

vernis [vɛrni] *nm* (**a**) *(pour le bois)* varnish; **v. à ongles** nail varnish *or* polish; **se mettre du v. à ongles** to varnish *or* paint one's nails (**b**) *Fig* **un v. de culture** a smattering of knowledge

vernissage [vɛrnisaʒ] *nm* (**a**) *(du bois)* varnishing (**b**) *(d'une exposition)* opening, private viewing

vérole [verɔl] *nf Vieilli* syphilis; **la petite v.** smallpox

verra, verrai *etc voir* **voir**

verrat [vera] *nm* breeding boar

verre [vɛr] *nm* (**a**) *(matière)* glass; **sous v.** under glass; **gravure sous v.** glass-mounted engraving; **v. blanc** glass; **v. dépoli/feuilleté** frosted/laminated glass (**b**) *(récipient)* glass; **v. à dents** tooth glass; **v. doseur** *ou* **gradué** ≃ measuring jug; **v. à eau** large wine-glass; **v. à pied** stemmed glass; **v. à vin** wineglass; **v. à whisky** whisky glass (**c**) *(contenu)* glass(ful) (**d**) *(boisson)* drink; **boire** *ou* **prendre un v.** to have a drink (**e**) *(de lunettes)* lens; **verres de contact** contact lenses; **verres à double foyer** bifocals; **verres teintés** *ou* **fumés** tinted lenses

verrée [vɛre] *nf Suisse (tournée)* round (of drinks); *(soirée)* drinks party

verrerie [vɛrri] *nf* (**a**) *(fabrication)* glass-making (**b**) *(atelier)* glassworks (**c**) *(marchandise)* glassware

verrier [vɛrje] *nm (artisan)* glass-maker

verrière [vɛrjɛr] *nf* (**a**) *(toit)* glass roof; *(paroi)* glass wall (**b**) *(pièce)* conservatory

verroterie [vɛrɔtri] *nf* glass jewellery

verrou [veru] *nm* bolt; **mettre** *ou* **tirer le v.** to bolt the door; *Fig* **sous les verrous** behind bars, inside

verrouillage [vɛrujaʒ] *nm* (**a**) *(d'une porte)* bolting; *(à clé)* locking (**b**) *(d'un mécanisme)* locking; **v. central** central locking (**c**) *Ordinat (capitales)* locking; **v. des fichiers** file lock; **v. en lecture seule** read-only lock; **v. en majuscule(s)** caps lock

verrouiller [vɛruje] *vt* (**a**) *(porte)* to bolt; *(à clé)* to lock; *(prisonnier)* to lock up (**b**) *(quartier)* to close off, to seal off (**c**) *Ordinat (capitales)* to lock on; **verrouillé en majuscule(s)** *(clavier)* with caps lock on

verrue [vɛry] *nf* wart; **v. plantaire** verruca

vers¹ [vɛr] *nm (poétique)* line; **faire des v.** to write verse *or* poetry; **v. blancs** blank verse; **v. libres** free verse

vers² *prép* (**a**) *(dans la direction de)* towards (**b**) *(aux alentours de) (dans le temps)* about; *(dans l'espace)* near; **v. la fin** towards the end; *Fam* **v. les trois heures** about *or* around 3 o'clock

versant [vɛrsɑ̃] *nm* slope, side

versatile [vɛrsatil] *adj* changeable, fickle

versatilité [vɛrsatilite] *nf* changeability, fickleness
verse [vɛrs] **à verse** *adv* **il pleut à v.** it's pouring (down); **la pluie tombait à v.** the rain was coming down in torrents
versé, -e [vɛrse] *adj* **être v. dans qch** to be well-versed in sth
Verseau [vɛrso] *nm Astron & Astrol* **le V.** Aquarius; **être V.** to be (an) Aquarius *or* an Aquarian
versement [vɛrsəmɑ̃] *nm* payment
verser [vɛrse] **1** *vt* (**a**) *(liquide)* to pour (out) (**dans** into); **v. à boire à qn** to pour sb a drink, to pour a drink for sb (**b**) *(larmes, sang)* to shed (**c**) *(argent)* to pay; **v. de l'argent sur son compte** to pay *or* deposit money into one's account (**d**) *Jur (document)* to add (**à** to)
2 *vi (véhicule)* to overturn
3 **verser dans** *vt ind* to lapse into
verset [vɛrsɛ] *nm* verse
verseur, -euse [vɛrsœr, -øz] **1** *adj voir* **bec**
2 *nf* **verseuse** jug, pot *(for coffee machine)*
versification [vɛrsifikasjɔ̃] *nf* versification
version [vɛrsjɔ̃] *nf* (**a**) *(d'un événement, d'un texte)* version (**b**) *(traduction)* translation; *Scol & Univ* **v. anglaise/espagnole** translation from English/Spanish (**c**) *Cin* **en v. originale** in the original language; **en v. française** dubbed *(into French)* (**d**) *Ordinat* **v. alpha/bêta** alpha/beta version
verso [vɛrso] *nm* back; **voir au v.** see over(leaf)
vert, -e [vɛr, vɛrt] **1** *adj* (**a**) *(couleur)* green; *Fig* **v. de peur** white with fear; *Fig* **v. de jalousie** green with envy; *Fig* **avoir la main verte** to have *Br* green fingers *or Am* a green thumb (**b**) *(jeune) (bois)* green; *(fruit)* unripe; *(vin)* too young (**c**) *(écologique)* green (**d**) *(vieillard)* sprightly (**e**) *(histoire, propos)* spicy (**f**) *(réprimande)* sharp
2 *nm* (**a**) *(couleur)* green; **passer au v.** *(signal d'arrêt)* to go *or* turn green; **v. amande** almond green; **v. bouteille** bottle green; **v. d'eau** sea green; **v. émeraude** emerald green; **v. olive** olive green; **v. pomme** apple green (**b**) *Fam* **se mettre au v.** to go to the country (**c**) *Pol* **les Verts** ≃ The Green Party
3 *nf* **verte** *Fam* **en dire de vertes** to tell saucy tales; **il en a vu des vertes et des pas mûres** he's been through a lot
vert-de-gris [vɛrdəgri] **1** *nm inv* verdigris
2 *adj* grey-green
vertébral, -e, -aux, -ales [vɛrtebral, -o] *adj* vertebral
vertèbre [vɛrtɛbr] *nf* vertebra
vertébré, -e [vɛrtebre] *adj & nm* vertebrate
vertement [vɛrtəmɑ̃] *adv* sharply
vertical, -e, -aux, -ales [vɛrtikal, -o] **1** *adj* vertical; **en position verticale** *(objet)* in a vertical position, upright
2 *nf* **verticale** vertical; **à la verticale** vertically
verticalement [vɛrtikalmɑ̃] *adv* vertically; *(dans les mots croisés)* down
vertige [vɛrtiʒ] *nm* (**a**) *(au-dessus du vide)* vertigo; **avoir le v.** *(toujours)* to suffer from vertigo; *(ponctuellement)* to feel dizzy; **donner le v. à qn** *(vide)* to make sb dizzy; *Fig* to make sb's head spin (**b**) *(étourdissement)* dizziness, giddiness; **avoir des vertiges** to have dizzy spells
vertigineusement [vɛrtiʒinøzmɑ̃] *adv* **grimper v.** to rocket; **chuter v.** to plummet

vertigineux, -euse [vɛrtiʒinø, -øz] *adj (hauteur)* dizzy; *(vitesse)* breakneck; *(somme, hausse des prix)* staggering
vertu [vɛrty] *nf* (**a**) *(propriété)* property (**b**) *(qualité morale)* virtue (**c**) *Litt (chasteté)* virtue; **femme de petite v.** woman of easy virtue (**d**) **en v. de qch** *(principe, loi)* in accordance with sth; **en v. des pouvoirs qui me sont conférés** by virtue of the powers bestowed upon me; **en v. de quoi est-il intervenu?** what gave him the right to intervene?
vertueux, -euse [vɛrtɥø, -øz] *adj* virtuous; *(intention)* honourable
verve [vɛrv] *nf* verve; **être en v.** to be on top form
verveine [vɛrvɛn] *nf* (**a**) *(plante)* verbena (**b**) *(tisane)* verbena tea
vésicule [vezikyl] *nf* vesicle; **v. biliaire** gall bladder
vespasienne [vɛspazjɛn] *nf* street urinal
vespéral, -e, -aux, -ales [vɛsperal, -o] *adj Litt* evening
vessie [vesi] *nf* bladder; *Fig* **prendre des vessies pour des lanternes** to believe that the moon is made of green cheese; **il voudrait nous faire prendre des vessies pour des lanternes** he's trying to pull the wool over our eyes
veste [vɛst] *nf* jacket; **v. droite/croisée** single-/double-breasted jacket; *Fam Fig* **prendre une v.** *(échouer)* to come unstuck; *(être rejeté)* to get turned down
vestiaire [vɛstjɛr] *nm* (**a**) *(d'un théâtre)* cloakroom; *(d'un stade)* changing room, locker room; *Fig* **laisser sa fierté au v.** to forget one's pride (**b**) **récupérer son v.** to collect one's things from the cloakroom
vestibule [vɛstibyl] *nm* (entrance) hall
vestiges [vɛstiʒ] *nmpl* (**a**) *(ruines)* remains (**b**) *(traces)* relics
vestimentaire [vɛstimɑ̃tɛr] *adj (dépenses)* clothing
veston [vɛstɔ̃] *nm* jacket
Vésuve [vezyv] *nm* **le V.** Vesuvius
vêtement [vɛtmɑ̃] *nm* garment, article of clothing; **vêtements** clothes, clothing; **vêtements de travail** work clothes
vétéran [veterɑ̃] *nm* veteran
vétérinaire [veterinɛr] **1** *adj* veterinary
2 *nmf* vet; *(sur une plaque)* veterinary surgeon
vétille [vetij] *nf* trifle, triviality
vêtir [71] [vetir] *Litt* **1** *vt (personne)* to clothe, to dress (**de** in)
2 **se vêtir** *vpr* to dress (oneself) (**de** in)
vétiver [vetivɛr] *nm* vetiver
veto [veto] *nm* veto; **opposer son v. à qch** to veto sth; **droit de v.** right of veto
vêtu, -e [vety] *adj* dressed (**de** in)
vétuste [vetyst] *adj* dilapidated
vétusté [vetyste] *nf* dilapidation
veuf, veuve [vœf, vœv] **1** *adj* **être v.** to be a widower; **être veuve** to be a widow
2 *nm,f* widower, *f* widow
veuille *etc voir* **vouloir¹**
veule [vøl] *adj Litt (personne)* effete
veulerie [vølri] *nf Litt* effeteness
veut *voir* **vouloir¹**
veuvage [vœvaʒ] *nm (d'homme)* widowerhood; *(de femme)* widowhood
veux *voir* **vouloir¹**
vexant, -e [vɛksɑ̃, -ɑ̃t] *adj* (**a**) *(blessant)* hurtful (**b**) *(contrariant)* annoying
vexation [vɛksasjɔ̃] *nf* humiliation

vexatoire [vɛksatwar] *adj* humiliating
vexer [vɛkse] **1** *vt* to hurt, to upset; *Fam* être vexé comme un pou to be extremely upset
2 se vexer *vpr* to get upset (**de** at)
VF [veɛf] *nf* (*abrév* **version française**) en VF dubbed (into French)
via [vja] *prép* via
viabiliser [vjabilize] *vt* to service
viabilité¹ [vjabilite] *nf* (*d'un nouveau-né, d'un projet*) viability
viabilité² *nf* (*d'un chemin*) practicability
viable [vjabl] *adj* viable
viaduc [vjadyk] *nm* viaduct
viager, -ère [vjaʒe, -ɛr] **1** *adj* life
2 *nm* life annuity; **mettre qch en v.** to sell sth in return for a life annuity; **acheter une maison en v.** to buy a house so as to provide the seller with a life annuity
Viagra® [vjagra] *nm Pharm* Viagra®
viande [vjɑ̃d] *nf* meat; **v. blanche/rouge** white/red meat; **v. hachée** *Br* mince, *Am* ground meat
viander [vjɑ̃de] **se viander** *vpr très Fam* to get smashed up
vibrant, -e [vibrɑ̃, -ɑ̃t] *adj* (*discours, hommage*) rousing, stirring
vibraphone [vibrafɔn] *nm* vibraphone
vibration [vibrasjɔ̃] *nf* vibration
vibrato [vibrato] *nm* vibrato
vibrer [vibre] *vi* (**a**) (*objet*) to vibrate (**b**) (*personne*) to be stirred; **sa voix vibrait de colère** his/her voice was shaking with anger; **faire v. qn** to stir sb
vibromasseur [vibromasœr] *nm* vibrator
vicaire [vikɛr] *nm* (*dans la religion catholique*) assistant priest; (*dans la religion anglicane*) curate
vice [vis] *nm* (**a**) (*défaut moral*) vice (**b**) (*défectuosité*) defect; **v. caché** hidden *or* latent defect; **v. de fabrication** manufacturing defect; *Jur* **v. de forme** legal flaw (**c**) (*débauche*) vice; *Fig* **mais c'est du v.!** it's an obsession!
vice-amiral [visamiral] (*pl* **vice-amiraux** [visamiro]) *nm* vice admiral
vice-consul (*pl* **vice-consuls**) [viskɔ̃syl] *nm* vice consul
vice-présidence (*pl* **vice-présidences**) [visprezidɑ̃s] *nf* (*d'état, d'organisation*) vice-presidency; (*d'entreprise*) vice-chairmanship
vice-président, -e (*mpl* **vice-présidents**, *fpl* **vice-présidentes**) [visprezidɑ̃, -ɑ̃t] *nm,f* (*d'état, d'organisation*) vice-president; (*d'entreprise*) vice-chairman
vice versa [visvɛrsa] *adv* vice versa
vichy [viʃi] *nm* (*tissu*) gingham
vicié, -e [visje] *adj* (**a**) (*air*) polluted (**b**) *Jur* invalidated
vicieux, -euse [visjø, -øz] *adj* (**a**) (*pervers*) depraved (**b**) (*perfide*) underhand (**c**) (*chien*) vicious
vicissitudes [visisityd] *nfpl* vicissitudes
vicomte [vikɔ̃t] *nm* viscount
vicomtesse [vikɔ̃tɛs] *nf* viscountess
victime [viktim] *nf* victim; (*d'un accident*) casualty; **être v. d'un attentat/d'une agression** to be the victim of an assassination attempt/of an attack; **être la v. d'une illusion/d'un malentendu** to labour under an illusion/a misconception
victimisation [viktimizasjɔ̃] *nf* victimization
victimiser [viktimize] *vt* to victimize
victoire [viktwar] *nf* victory; (*en sport*) win, victory; **chanter** *ou* **crier v.** to claim victory

victorien, -enne [viktɔrjɛ̃, -ɛn] *adj* Victorian
victorieusement [viktɔrjøzmɑ̃] *adv* victoriously
victorieux, -euse [viktɔrjø, -øz] *adj* victorious; (*air, sourire*) triumphant
victuailles [viktɥaj] *nfpl* provisions
vidange [vidɑ̃ʒ] *nf* (**a**) (*d'un moteur*) oil change; **faire la v.** to change the oil (**b**) (*d'une fosse septique*) draining, emptying (**c**) *Belg* (*verre consigné*) returnable empties (**d**) *Can* **vidanges** (*ordures ménagères*) refuse, *Br* rubbish, *Am* garbage
vidanger [45] [vidɑ̃ʒe] *vt* (**a**) (*huile*) to change; (*moteur*) to change the oil in (**b**) (*fosse septique*) to drain, to empty
vide [vid] **1** *adj* empty; (*regard*) blank; **v. de sens** devoid of meaning, meaningless
2 *nm Phys* vacuum; (*espace*) empty space, gap; *Fig* (*dans un emploi du temps*) gap; **rouler à v.** (*bus*) to have no passengers; **emballé sous v.** vacuum-packed; **faire le v.** to create a vacuum; *Fig* (*se ressourcer*) to switch off; *Fig* **faire le v. dans son esprit** to clear one's mind; **regarder dans le v.** to stare into space; **c'est comme si je parlais dans le v.** it's like talking to a brick wall; **avoir peur du v.** to be afraid of *or* to have no head for heights; **il y a un v. juridique concernant cela** there's nothing in the law to cover that; **v. sanitaire** ventilation *or Am* crawl space
vidé, -e [vide] *adj Fam* (*épuisé*) dead beat
vidéo [video] **1** *adj inv* video
2 *nf* (*technique*) video; (*cassette*) video, videotape
vidéocassette [videokasɛt] *nf* video cassette, videotape
vidéo-clip [videoklip] *nm* video
vidéoconférence [videokɔ̃ferɑ̃s] *nf* videoconference; (*concept*) videoconferencing
vidéodisque [videodisk] *nm* videodisk
vide-ordures [vidordyr] *nm inv Br* rubbish *or Am* garbage chute
vidéothèque [videotɛk] *nf* video library
vide-poches [vidpɔʃ] *nm inv* (**a**) (*de voiture*) (*dans le tableau de bord*) storage tray; (*dans la porte*) door pocket (**b**) (*de maison*) tidy
vide-pomme (*pl* **vide-pommes**) [vidpɔm] *nm* apple corer
vidéoprojecteur [videoprɔʒɛktœr] *nm* video projector
vider [vide] **1** *vt* (**a**) (*enlever le contenu de*) to empty (**de** of); *Fam Fig* **v. son sac** to get sth off one's chest; *Fig* **v. son cœur** to pour out one's feelings (**b**) *Fam* (*épuiser*) to wear out (**c**) *Fam* (*expulser*) to chuck out; **se faire v.** to get chucked out (**d**) **v. les lieux** to vacate the premises (**e**) (*poisson*) to gut; (*volaille*) to draw (**f**) *Ordinat* **v. l'écran** to clear the screen; **v. la corbeille** to empty the wastebasket *or Am* the trash
2 se vider *vpr* to empty; **se v. de son sang** to bleed to death
videur, -euse [vidœr, -øz] *nm,f* bouncer
vie [vi] *nf* (**a**) (*d'êtres vivants*) life; **être en v.** to be alive; **être entre la v. et la mort** to be fighting for one's life; **donner la v. à un enfant** to give birth to a child; **avoir la v. dure** (*mauvaise herbe, parasite*) to be hard to kill off; (*superstitions, préjugés*) to die hard; **entre eux, c'est à la v., à la mort** they'd die for each other; **être plein de v.** to be full of life; **sans v.** lifeless (**b**) (*animation*) life; **donner de la v. à qch** to liven sth up (**c**) (*durée d'existence*) life, lifetime; **pour la v.** for life; **une (seule) fois dans la v.** once in a lifetime (**d**) (*biographie*) life story; *Fam* **raconter sa v. à qn** to tell sb one's

life story (**e**) *(façon de vivre)* life; **c'est la v. de châ-teau!** this is the life!; **v. active** professional life; **v. nocturne** nightlife; *Fam Vieilli* **faire la v.** to live it up (**f**) *(subsistance)* **la v. est très chère dans ces pays** the cost of living is very high in these countries

vieil [vjɛj] *voir* **vieux**

vieillard [vjɛjar] *nm* old man

vieille¹ *voir* **vieux**

vieille² [vjɛj] *nf (poisson)* wrasse

vieillerie [vjɛjri] *nf (objet)* old thing

vieillesse [vjɛjɛs] *nf* old age

vieilli, -e [vjeji] *adj* (**a**) *(mot, style)* old-fashioned, dated (**b**) *(personne)* aged

vieillir [vjejir] **1** *vi* (**a**) *(personne)* to get old, to age (**b**) *(mot, film, chanson)* to be dated (**c**) *(fromage, vin)* to mature
2 *vt (personne) (par l'apparence)* to age; **v. qn (de deux ans)** to make sb out to be (two years) older than he/she is
3 se vieillir *vpr* (**a**) *(par l'apparence)* to make oneself look older (**b**) *(se dire plus âgé)* to pretend to be older than one is

vieillissant, -e [vjejisã, -ãt] *adj (personne)* ageing; *(institution, style)* which is becoming outdated

vieillissement [vjejismã] *nm* (**a**) *(d'une personne, de la population)* ageing; **retarder le v. de la peau** to delay the ageing of the skin (**b**) *(d'un fromage, d'un vin)* maturing

vieillot, -otte [vjɛjo, -ɔt] *adj* old-fashioned

vielle [vjɛl] *nf* hurdy-gurdy

Vienne [vjɛn] *n* Vienna

vienne, viens *etc voir* **venir**

viennois, -e [vjɛnwa, -az] **1** *adj* Viennese; **un pain v.** a Vienna loaf
2 *nm,f* **V.** Viennese

viennoiserie [vjɛnwazri] *nf (gâteaux)* = pastries made with sweetened dough (croissants, brioche etc); *(magasin)* = shop selling pastries made with sweetened dough (croissants, brioche etc)

vierge [vjɛrʒ] **1** *adj* (**a**) *(personne)* **être v.** to be a virgin; **une fille v.** a virgin (**b**) *(sol, huile)* virgin (**c**) *(page, cassette)* blank; *(casier judiciaire)* clean (**d**) *Ordinat (ligne, espace)* blank; *(disquette)* blank, unformatted
2 *nf* (**a**) *(personne)* virgin; **la (Sainte) V.** the Blessed Virgin (Mary) (**b**) *Astron & Astrol* **la V.** Virgo; **être V.** to be (a) Virgo

Viêt Nam [vjɛtnam] *nm* **le V.** Vietnam

vietnamien, -enne [vjɛtnamjɛ̃, -ɛn] **1** *adj* Vietnamese
2 *nm,f* **V.** Vietnamese
3 *nm (langue)* Vietnamese

vieux, vieille¹ [vjø, vjɛj]

> **vieil** is used before masculine singular nouns beginning with a vowel or h mute.

1 *adj* old; **plus/moins v. que qn** older/younger than sb; **v. comme le monde** as old as the hills; **être v. jeu** to be old-fashioned
2 *nm,f* (**a**) *(personne)* old man, *f* old woman; **les v.** old people, the elderly; *Fam* **un v. de la vieille** one of the old brigade (**b**) *Fam* **il a pris un coup de v.** he's aged (**c**) *Fam (parent)* **mes v.** my folks; **mon v.** my old man; **ma vieille** my old woman (**d**) *Fam (ami)* **mon v.** mate, pal; **ma vieille** old girl

vif, vive¹ [vif, viv] **1** *adj* (**a**) *(plein de vie) (personne, discussion)* lively (**b**) *(brusque) (ton)* abrupt, sharp;

tu as été un peu trop v. avec elle you were a bit curt with her (**c**) *(imagination)* vivid; *(intelligence)* sharp; *(mouvement)* quick; *Euph* **il n'est pas très v.** he's not very bright (**d**) *(vent, douleur)* sharp (**e**) *(couleur)* bright (**f**) *(satisfaction, intérêt)* great; *(félicitations)* warm (**g**) **dire qch à qn de vive voix** to tell sb sth personally
2 *nm* (**a**) *Jur* living person (**b**) *(à la pêche)* live bait (**c**) *(locutions)* **à v.** *(plaie)* open; **avoir les nerfs à v.** to be on edge; **entrer dans le v. du sujet** to get to the heart of the matter; **une photo prise sur le v.** a natural *or* unposed photo

vif-argent [vifarʒã] *nm* quicksilver; *Fig (personne)* live wire

vigie [viʒi] *nf* (**a**) *(matelot)* lookout; **être de v.** to be on the lookout (**b**) *(poste) (sur un bateau)* lookout post; *(sur un train)* observation box

vigilance [viʒilɑ̃s] *nf* vigilance

vigilant, -e [viʒilɑ̃, -ɑ̃t] *adj* vigilant

vigile [viʒil] *nm* (night) watchman

vigne [viɲ] *nf* (**a**) *(petit arbre)* vine (**b**) *(vignoble)* vineyard (**c**) **v. vierge** Virginia creeper

vigneron, -onne [viɲərɔ̃, -ɔn] *nm,f* wine grower

vignette [viɲɛt] *nf* (**a**) *(pharmaceutique)* label *(showing details of medication and which has to be attached to the "feuille de maladie" in order to qualify for reimbursement by the Social Security)* (**b**) **la v. (automobile)** the (road) tax disc (**c**) *(motif)* vignette

vignoble [viɲɔbl] *nm* vineyard; **le v. français/californien** the French/Californian vineyards

vigoureusement [vigurøzmã] *adv* vigorously

vigoureux, -euse [vigurø, -øz] *adj (personne, animal)* vigorous; *(plante, arbre)* sturdy; *(résistance)* strong

vigueur [vigœr] *nf* (**a**) *(d'une personne, d'un animal, d'un style)* vigour; *(d'une plante, d'un arbre)* sturdiness (**b**) **en v.** *(décret)* in force; **entrer en v.** to come into force

VIH [veiaʃ] *nm (abrév* **virus de l'immunodéficience humaine)** HIV

viking [vikiŋ] **1** *adj* Viking
2 *nmf* **V.** Viking

vil, -e [vil] *adj* (**a**) *Litt (personne, motif)* vile (**b**) *(bas)* **à v. prix** at a very low price

vilain, -e [vilɛ̃, -ɛn] **1** *adj* (**a**) *(laid)* ugly (**b**) *(déplaisant)* nasty (**c**) *(pas sage)* naughty
2 *nm,f Fam* **oh, le v./la vilaine!** *(à un enfant)* you naughty boy/girl!
3 *nm* (**a**) *Fam* **il va y avoir du v.** there's going to be trouble (**b**) *Hist* villein

vilebrequin [vilbrəkɛ̃] *nm* (**a**) *(outil)* brace (**b**) *(dans un moteur)* crankshaft

vilenie [vileni] *nf Litt* (**a**) *(caractère)* vileness (**b**) *(action)* vile deed

villa [villa] *nf* villa

village [vilaʒ] *nm* village; **v. de pêcheurs** fishing village; **v. de vacances, v.-vacances** *Br* holiday *or* *Am* vacation village; **le v. mondial** *ou* **planétaire** the global village

villageois, -e [vilaʒwa, -az] *nm,f* villager

ville [vil] *nf* town; *(de grande taille)* city; **grande v.** city; **en v.** in (the) town; *(au centre ville)* *Br* in the town/city centre, *Am* downtown; **aller en v.** to go into town; **habiter à la v.** to live in a town *(as opposed to the country)*; **v. basse/haute** lower/upper part of town; **v. champignon** boom town; **v. d'eaux** spa (town); **v. nouvelle** new town

ville-dortoir (*pl* **villes-dortoirs**) [vildɔrtwar] *nf* dormitory town

villégiature [vileʒjatyr] *nf Br* holiday, *Am* vacation; **lieu de v.** *Br* holiday resort, *Am* resort

Vilnius [vilnjys] *n* Vilnius

vin [vɛ̃] *nm* (**a**) *(boisson)* wine; **avoir le v. gai/triste** to be/not to be a happy drunk; **grand v.** vintage wine; **v. d'appellation contrôlée** wine of guaranteed vintage; **v. blanc/rouge/rosé** white/red/rosé wine; **v. cuit** fortified wine; **v. mousseux** sparkling wine; **v. de pays** regional wine; **v. de table** *ou* **ordinaire** table wine (**b**) **v. d'honneur** reception *(where wine is served)*

vinaigre [vinɛgr] *nm* vinegar; *Fam* **tourner au v.** to turn sour; **v. blanc** distilled vinegar; **v. à l'estragon** tarragon vinegar

vinaigrette [vinɛgrɛt] *nf* vinaigrette, French dressing

vinasse [vinas] *nf Fam* cheap wine, *Br* plonk

vindicatif, -ive [vɛ̃dikatif, -iv] *adj* vindictive

vindicte [vɛ̃dikt] *nf* **désigner qn à la v. publique** to expose sb to public condemnation

vineux, -euse [vinø, -øz] *adj* (**a**) *(goût, odeur)* winy (**b**) *(couleur)* wine(-coloured)

vingt [vɛ̃] **1** *adj inv* twenty; **v.-quatre heures sur v.-quatre** round the clock, twenty-four hours a day **2** *nm inv* twenty; *voir aussi* **trois**

vingtaine [vɛ̃tɛn] *nf* **une v. (de)** about twenty, twenty or so

vingtième [vɛ̃tjɛm] *adj, nmf & nm* twentieth; *voir aussi* **cinquième**

vinicole [vinikɔl] *adj (région)* wine-growing

vintage [vintɛdʒ] **1** *adj inv (vêtements)* vintage **2** *nm (mode)* vintage

vinyle [vinil] *nm* vinyl

viol [vjɔl] *nm* (**a**) *(crime sexuel)* rape; **v. collectif** gang-rape (**b**) *(d'un sanctuaire)* violation

violacé, -e [vjɔlase] *adj* purplish-blue

violation [vjɔlasjɔ̃] *nf* (**a**) *(de la loi, de règles)* violation (**b**) *(d'une sépulture)* desecration; **v. de domicile** illegal entry

viole [vjɔl] *nf* viol

violemment [vjɔlamɑ̃] *adv* violently

violence [vjɔlɑ̃s] *nf (physique)* violence; *(verbale)* fierceness; *(d'un sentiment)* intensity; **se faire v.** to force oneself; **v. domestique** *ou* **familiale** domestic violence

violent, -e [vjɔlɑ̃, -ɑ̃t] *adj (personne, douleur, quartier)* violent; *(vent, paroles)* fierce; *(odeur)* pungent; *(effort)* strenuous; **mort violente** violent death

violenter [vjɔlɑ̃te] *vt (femme)* to assault

violer [vjɔle] *vt* (**a**) *(personne)* to rape (**b**) *(trêve, loi)* to violate, to break; *(traité, confiance)* to break; *(secret)* to divulge (**c**) *(sépulture)* to desecrate

violet, -ette [vjɔlɛ, -ɛt] **1** *adj* purple **2** *nm (couleur)* purple **3** *nf* **violette** *(fleur)* violet

violeur [vjɔlœr] *nm* rapist

violon [vjɔlɔ̃] *nm* (**a**) *(instrument)* violin; *Fam* **accordez vos violons** make up your minds; **v. d'Ingres** hobby (**b**) *(musicien)* violin (player); **premier v.** *(dans un orchestre)* first violin, *Br* leader, *Am* concertmaster (**c**) *Fam (prison)* **le v.** the cells, the lockup

violoncelle [vjɔlɔ̃sɛl] *nm* cello

violoncelliste [vjɔlɔ̃selist] *nmf* cellist

violoniste [vjɔlɔnist] *nmf* violinist, violin player

vipère [viper] *nf* adder, viper; *Fig (personne)* viper

virage [viraʒ] *nm* (**a**) *(mouvement)* turn (**b**) *(d'une route)* bend; **la route fait des virages** there are bends

in the road; **prendre un v.** to take a bend; **v. sans visibilité** blind corner (**c**) *Fig (changement)* change of direction

viral, -e, -aux, -ales [viral, -o] *adj* viral

virée [vire] *nf Fam (en voiture)* run, drive; *(dans les bars) Br* pub crawl, *Am* bar hop; **faire une v.** *(en voiture)* to go for a run or a drive; *(dans les bars) Br* to go on a pub crawl, *Am* to barhop

virement [virmɑ̃] *nm* (**a**) *(de banque)* transfer; **v. automatique** automatic transfer; **v. bancaire/interbancaire** bank/interbank transfer; **v. postal** post office transfer (**b**) *Naut* **v. de bord** tacking

virer [vire] **1** *vt* (**a**) *(somme)* to transfer (**sur** to) (**b**) *Fam (personne, objet)* to chuck out; *(employé)* to fire; **se faire v.** to get chucked out; *(employé)* to get fired **2** *vi* (**a**) *(véhicule)* to turn; **v. de bord** *(voilier)* to tack (**b**) *(couleur)* to change; **le parfum a viré** the perfume smells off **3** **virer à** *vt ind* **v. à l'orange/au vert** to turn orange/green **4** **se virer** *vpr Fam* **vire-toi de là!** shift (yourself)!

virevolte [virvɔlt] *nf* (**a**) *(d'un danseur)* spin (**b**) *(changement brusque)* U-turn, about-turn

virevolter [virvɔlte] *vi (danseur)* to spin round

virginal, -e, -aux, -ales [virʒinal, -o] *adj* virginal

Virginie [virʒini] *nf* **la V.** Virginia; **la V.-occidentale** West Virginia

virginité [virʒinite] *nf* virginity

virgule [virgyl] *nf* (**a**) *(signe de ponctuation)* comma; *Fig* **ne pas changer une v. à qch** not to make a single alteration to sth (**b**) *(entre deux chiffres)* decimal point; **trois v. cinq** three point five; *Ordinat* **v. fixe** fixed point; *Ordinat* **v. flottante** floating point

viril, -e [viril] *adj* (**a**) *(propre à l'homme)* male; *(sexuellement)* virile (**b**) *(énergique) (action)* manly; *(allure, démarche)* masculine

virilité [virilite] *nf* virility

virologie [virɔlɔʒi] *nf* virology

virtualité [virtyalite] *nf* potentiality

virtuel, -elle [virtɥɛl] *adj* potential; *(image)* virtual

virtuellement [virtɥɛlmɑ̃] *adv* virtually

virtuose [virtɥoz] *nmf* virtuoso

virtuosité [virtɥozite] *nf* virtuosity

virulence [virylɑ̃s] *nf* virulence

virulent, -e [virylɑ̃, -ɑ̃t] *adj* virulent

virus [virys] *nm Méd & Ordinat* virus

vis¹ *voir* **vivre, voir**

vis² [vis] *nf* screw; *Fig* **serrer la v. à qn** to crack down on sb

visa [viza] *nm* (**a**) *(pour passeport)* visa; **v. d'entrée/de sortie** entry/exit visa (**b**) *(d'un film)* **v. de censure** certificate; **v. d'exploitation** exploitation licence

visage [vizaʒ] *nm* face; **elle a changé de v.** her face *or* expression changed; **à deux visages** two-faced; **à v. découvert** openly; **sous un autre** *ou* **nouveau v.** in a new light; **v. pâle** paleface

visagiste [vizaʒist] *nmf* facialist; **coiffeur-v.** hair stylist

vis-à-vis [vizavi] **1** *prép* **v. de** *(en face de)* opposite *or* facing; *(envers)* towards; *(en comparaison de)* compared with, next to **2** *nm* (**a**) *(personne)* person opposite; **mon v.** the person opposite me; **il n'y a pas de v.** there's nothing opposite (**b**) *(meuble)* vis-à-vis

viscéral, -e, -aux, -ales [viseral, -o] *adj Anat* visceral; *Fig (haine)* deep-seated; *(peur)* gut-wrenching; *(réaction)* gut

viscères [visɛr] *nmpl* viscera, internal organs

viscose [viskoz] *nf* viscose

viscosité [viskozite] *nf (de liquide)* viscosity; *(de surface)* stickiness

visée [vize] *nf* (**a**) *(action)* aiming (**b**) *Fig* **visées** *(intentions)* aims; **avoir des visées sur qn/qch** to have designs on sb/sth

viser¹ [vize] **1** *vt* (**a**) *(cible)* to aim at; *Fig (poste)* to set one's sights on (**b**) *Fig* **ces paroles te visent** these remarks are aimed at you; **qui visais-tu par cette remarque?** who was your remark aimed at?; **je me suis senti visé** I felt the remark was aimed at me (**c**) *très Fam (regarder)* **vise un peu la fille!** check her out!

2 *vi* to aim, to take aim; *Fig* **v. haut** to aim high; **v. juste** to aim straight; *Fig* to hit the bull's-eye

3 viser à *vt ind* **v. à qch** to aim at sth; **v. à faire qch** to aim to do sth

viser² *vt (passeport)* to visa; *(document)* to stamp

viseur [vizœr] *nm (d'un appareil photo)* viewfinder; *(d'une arme)* sight

visibilité [vizibilite] *nf* visibility

visible [vizibl] *adj* (**a**) *(signe, changement)* visible (**b**) *(clair)* obvious; **il est v. que...** it's obvious that... (**c**) *Fam* **je ne suis pas v.** I'm not receiving visitors

visiblement [vizibləmɑ̃] *adv* visibly

visière [vizjɛr] *nf* (**a**) *(d'une casquette)* peak (**b**) *(d'un casque)* visor (**c**) *(pour protéger les yeux)* eyeshade

visioconférence [vizjokɔ̃ferɑ̃s] *nf* videoconference; *(concept)* videoconferencing

vision [vizjɔ̃] *nf* (**a**) *(sens)* sight (**b**) *(point de vue)* view (**c**) *(d'un créateur)* vision (**d**) *(hallucination)* vision; **avoir des visions** to have visions, to see things

visionnaire [vizjɔnɛr] *adj & nmf* visionary

visionner [vizjɔne] *vt (film)* to view

visionneuse [vizjɔnøz] *nf* viewer

visiophonie [vizjɔfɔni] *nf* video teleconferencing

visite [vizit] *nf* (**a**) *(à une personne, d'un lieu touristique)* visit; **faire une v. ou rendre v. à qn** to visit sb, to pay sb a visit; **recevoir la v. de qn** to have a visit from sb; **v. officielle** official visit (**b**) *Fam (personne)* visitor; **avoir de la v.** *(un visiteur)* to have a visitor; *(plusieurs visiteurs)* to have visitors (**c**) *(d'un médecin)* **visites (à domicile)** *(house)* calls (**d**) *(inspection)* *(d'un bâtiment, d'un navire)* inspection, examination (**e**) **v. médicale** medical examination

visiter [vizite] **1** *vt* (**a**) *(lieu touristique)* to visit; *(maison à vendre)* to view; **faire v. qch à qn** to show sb round sth (**b**) *(inspecter)* *(bâtiment)* to inspect, to examine (**c**) *(patient)* to visit; *(client)* to call on

2 se visiter *vpr* to be open to visitors; **le musée se visite en deux heures** it takes two hours to go round the museum

visiteur, -euse [vizitœr, -øz] *nm,f* (**a**) *(touriste, invité)* visitor (**b**) *(représentant)* **v. médical** medical representative (**c**) **v. de prison** prison visitor

vison [vizɔ̃] *nm* mink; *Fam (manteau)* mink coat

visqueux, -euse [viskø, -øz] *adj* (**a**) *(surface)* sticky (**b**) *(substance)* viscous (**c**) *Péj (personne, manière)* slimy

visser [vise] **1** *vt* (**a**) *(à quelque chose)* to screw down; *(ensemble)* to screw together; **être vissé à qch** to be screwed on to sth; **un chapeau vissé sur la tête** with a hat clamped on his/her head; *Fam* **être vissé sur sa chaise** to be glued to one's chair; *Fam* **être bien/mal vissé** to be in a good/foul mood (**b**) *(couvercle)* to screw on (**c**) *Fam (personne)* to crack down on, to

put the screws on; **il a toujours vissé ses gosses** he has always kept a tight rein on his kids

2 se visser *vpr (à quelque chose)* to screw on; *(ensemble)* to screw together

visualisation [vizɥalizasjɔ̃] *nf* visualization; *Ordinat* **console** *ou* **unité** *ou* **écran de v.** (visual) display unit; *Ordinat* **v. de la page à l'écran** page preview

visualiser [vizɥalize] *vt* (**a**) *(imaginer)* to visualize (**b**) *(rendre visible)* to make visible; *Ordinat* to display

visuel, -elle [vizɥɛl] **1** *adj* visual

2 *nm Ordinat* visual display unit, VDU

visuellement [vizɥɛlmɑ̃] *adv* visually

vit *voir* **vivre, vivant**

vital, -e, -aux, -ales [vital, -o] *adj* vital; **carte Vitale** = smart card on which information about a patient is recorded, used when making payments to a doctor or chemist for purposes of reclaiming medical expenses

vitalité [vitalite] *nf* vitality

vitamine [vitamin] *nf* vitamin; **la v. E** vitamin E

vitaminé, -e [vitamine] *adj* with added vitamins, vitamin-enriched

vite [vit] *adv* (**a**) *(rapidement)* quickly, fast; **v.!** quick!, quickly!; **plus v.!** faster!; **ça ne va pas v.** it's slow work; *Fam* **et plus v. que cela!** now then, get a move on!; **au plus v.** as quickly as possible; *Fig* **parler trop v.** to speak too soon; **c'est v. dit** it's easy to say; *Fam* **faire qch v. fait (bien fait)** to do sth in no time (**b**) *(sous peu)* soon; **avoir v. fait de faire qch** to be quick to do sth

vitesse [vitɛs] *nf* (**a**) *(rapidité)* speed; **prendre de la v.** to pick up *or* gather speed; *Fam* **prendre qn de v.** to beat sb to it; **à quelle v. allait-il?** how fast was he going?, what speed was he going at?; **une Europe à deux vitesses** a two-speed Europe; **à toute v.** at top speed; **à une v. folle** *(rouler)* at breakneck speed; *Fam* **en v.** quickly; **v. de croisière** cruising speed; *Fig* **trouver sa v. de croisière** to get into the swing of things; **v. de frappe** keying speed (**b**) *(d'un moteur)* gear; **changer de v.** to change gear; **passer en deuxième/troisième v.** to go into second/third (gear); *Fam Fig* **en quatrième v.** at top speed (**c**) *Ordinat* **v. d'affichage** display speed; **v. de calcul** processing *or* computing speed; **v. d'écriture** write speed; **v. d'exécution** execution speed; **v. d'impression** print speed; **v. du processeur** processor speed; **v. de traitement** processing speed

viticole [vitikɔl] *adj (région)* wine-growing

viticulteur, -trice [vitikyltœr, -tris] *nm,f* wine grower

viticulture [vitikyltyr] *nf* wine growing

vitrage [vitraʒ] *nm (vitres)* windows

vitrail, -aux [vitraj, -o] *nm* stained-glass window

vitre [vitr] *nf* window (pane); *(plaque de verre)* pane (of glass); *(de voiture, de train)* window; **faire les vitres** to clean the windows

vitré, -e [vitre] *adj (porte)* glazed

vitrer [vitre] *vt* to glaze

vitreux, -euse [vitrø, -øz] *adj (yeux, regard)* glazed, glassy

vitrier [vitrije] *nm* glazier

vitrification [vitrifikasjɔ̃] *nf* (**a**) *(du sable)* vitrification (**b**) *(du parquet)* varnishing, sealing

vitrifier [66] [vitrifje] *vt* (**a**) *(sable)* to vitrify (**b**) *(parquet)* to varnish, to seal

vitrine [vitrin] *nf* (**a**) *(de magasin)* (shop) window; *Fig* showcase; **mettre qch en v.** to display *or* put sth in the window (**b**) *(armoire)* display cabinet

vitriol [vitrijɔl] nm vitriol; Fig **au v.** vitriolic
vitupérer [34] [vitypere] **vitupérer contre** vt ind to protest about
vivable [vivabl] adj Fam (maison) livable in; (situation) tolerable; **il n'est pas v.** he's impossible to live with
vivace [vivas] adj (**a**) (plante) perennial (**b**) (croyance, tradition, sentiment) deep-rooted; (souvenir) vivid
vivacité [vivasite] nf (**a**) (d'une personne, d'une discussion) liveliness, vivacity; (d'une imagination) vividness; (d'une intelligence) sharpness; (d'un mouvement) quickness; **v. d'esprit** quick-wittedness (**b**) (de couleur) brightness (**c**) (de paroles) hastiness
vivant, -e [vivã, -ãt] **1** adj (**a**) (en vie) alive (**b**) (être, organisme) living (**c**) (rue, conversation, enfant) lively (**d**) Fig (souvenir) vivid; Hum **j'en suis la preuve vivante** I'm the living proof
2 nm (**a**) **les vivants** the living (**b**) **de son v.** in one's lifetime; **du v. de qn** in sb's lifetime
vivats [viva] nmpl cheers
vive[1] adj voir vif
vive[2] [viv] nf (poisson) weever
vive[3] exclam **v. le roi!** long live the King!; **v. la télévision!** God bless television!
vivement [vivmã] adv (**a**) (rapidement) quickly (**b**) (en colère) sharply (**c**) (éclairé, coloré) brightly (**d**) (remercier) warmly; (regretter) deeply; **s'intéresser v. à qch** to take a keen interest in sth; **être v. ému** to be deeply moved (**e**) (marque l'impatience) **v. le week-end!** roll on the weekend!; **v. qu'il parte!** I'll be glad when he's gone!
viveur [vivœr] nm fast liver
vivier [vivje] nm (à l'air libre) fish pond; (aquarium) fish tank; Fig breeding ground (**de** for)
vivifiant, -e [vivifjã, -ãt] adj (air, climat) invigorating, bracing
vivifier [66] [vivifje] vt to invigorate
vivipare [vivipar] adj viviparous
vivisection [viviseksjɔ̃] nf vivisection
vivoter [vivɔte] vi (**a**) (personne) to struggle to get by (**b**) (entreprise, usine) to struggle along
vivre [72] [vivr] **1** vi (**a**) (être en vie) to live, to be alive; **v. vieux** to live to a ripe old age; Prov **qui vivra verra** time will tell (**b**) (mener une certaine existence) to live; **avoir beaucoup vécu** to have seen life; **être facile/difficile à v.** to be easy/difficult to live with or to get on with; **se laisser v.** to take life as it comes; **il fait bon v. ici** life is pleasant here; Fam **je vais t'apprendre à v.!** I'll teach you some manners! (**c**) (économiquement) to live; **travailler pour v.** to work for a living; **faire v. sa famille** to support or keep one's family; **v. de qch** to live on sth; Fig **v. d'amour et d'eau fraîche** to live on fresh air
2 vt (**a**) **v. sa vie** to live one's own life (**b**) (événements, guerre) to live through; (moments difficiles, expérience) to go through
vivres [vivr] nmpl provisions, supplies; Fig **couper les v. à qn** to cut off sb's allowance
vivrier, -ère [vivrije, -ɛr] adj **cultures vivrières** food crops
vlan, v'lan [vlã] exclam bang!, wham!
vlimeux [vlimø] nm Can Fam (**a**) (chanceux) lucky or Br jammy devil (**b**) (intrigant) crafty devil
vMCJ [veemʒize] nm Méd (abrév **variant de la maladie de Creutzfeldt-Jakob**) vCJD
VO [veo] nf (abrév **version originale**) **en VO** in the original language

vocabulaire [vɔkabylɛr] nm (**a**) (d'une langue) vocabulary; (d'une science) glossary (**b**) (d'une personne) vocabulary
vocal, -e, -aux, -ales [vɔkal, -o] adj vocal
vocalise [vɔkaliz] nf voice exercise; **faire des vocalises** to do voice exercises
vocation [vɔkasjɔ̃] nf (**a**) (d'une personne) vocation, calling (**b**) (d'un pays, d'une institution) role, mission; **région à v. agricole/industrielle** agricultural/industrial region
vociférations [vɔsiferasjɔ̃] nfpl shouting
vociférer [34] [vɔsifere] **1** vt to shout (**contre** at)
2 vi to shout (**contre** about)
vodka [vɔdka] nf vodka
vœu, -x [vø] nm (**a**) (souhait) wish; **faire un v.** to make a wish; **faire le v. que** + subjunctive to pray that (**b**) (promesse) vow; **faire le v. de faire qch** to vow to do sth (**c**) Rel **faire v. de pauvreté/silence** to take a vow of poverty/silence; **prononcer ses vœux** to take one's vows (**d**) (au moment d'une fête) **tous mes/nos vœux, avec mes/nos meilleurs vœux** best wishes, with all good wishes; **tous mes vœux de bonheur** best wishes for your future happiness; **vœux de Bonne ou de Nouvelle Année** New Year's greetings
vogue [vɔg] nf fashion, vogue; **en v.** fashionable, in vogue
voguer [vɔge] vi Litt to sail
voici [vwasi] prép (**a**) (pour présenter, pour montrer) here is/are; **v. Paul** here's Paul; **v. mes neveux** (en les présentant) these are my nephews; (ils arrivent) these are my nephews; **nous v. à Paris/installés** here we are in Paris/all settled in; **la v. qui vient** here she comes; **la pendule que v.** this clock; **v. ce dont il s'agit** this is what it's all about; **v. ce qu'il m'a dit** this is what he told me; **v. pourquoi** this is why; **tu voulais des fruits, eh bien, en v.** you wanted some fruit, well here you are (**b**) (il y a) **v. trois ans** three years ago; **v. dix ans que je la connais** I've known her for ten years now
voie [vwa] nf (**a**) (route) road; **route à quatre voies** four-lane road; **les voies de communication** the road and rail links; **v. express** ou **rapide** Br motorway, Am expressway; **v. publique** public highway; **v. sans issue** dead end (**b**) **par la v. des airs** by air; **par v. de terre/de mer** by land/sea (**c**) (pour train) track; **v. ferrée** Br railway or Am railroad line; Fam **mettre qn sur une v. de garage** to put sb on the sidelines (**d**) Ordinat **v. d'accès** path; **v. d'entrée** input channel; **v. de transmission de données** data link (**e**) Fig (chemin) way; **mettre qn sur la v.** to put sb on the right track; **être sur la bonne v.** to be on the right track; **par la v. diplomatique/hiérarchique** through diplomatic/official channels; **la v. est libre** the coast's clear (**f**) **en v. d'achèvement** nearing completion; **en v. de construction** under construction; **un pays en v. de développement** a developing country; **être en v. de disparition** (animal) to be a dying breed or dying out; **être en v. de guérison** to be on the road to recovery (**g**) Jur **v. de fait** assault and battery (**h**) Anat passage, duct; **les voies digestives** the digestive tract; **par v. buccale** orally (**i**) **v. d'eau** leak (**j**) **la V. lactée** the Milky Way
voilà [vwala] prép (**a**) (pour présenter, pour montrer) there is/are; **v. Paul** there's Paul; **v. mes neveux** (en les présentant) these are my nephews; (ils arrivent) there are my nephews; **nous v. à Paris/installés** here we are in Paris/all settled in; **la v. qui vient** here she

comes; **la pendule que v.** that clock; **v. ce que j'avais à dire** that's what I wanted to say; **v. ce qu'il m'a dit** that's what he told me; **tu voulais des fruits, eh bien, en v.** you wanted some fruit, well there you go; **v. pourquoi** that's why; **en v. assez** that's enough; **en v. une idée!** what an idea!; **v. tout** that's all; **nous v. bien!** what are we going to do now?; **et v.!** there you go! (**b**) *(il y a)* **v. trois ans** three years ago; **v. dix ans que je le connais** I've known him for ten years

voilage [vwalaʒ] *nm (tissu)* net; **voilages** *(rideaux)* net curtains

voile[1] [vwal] *nf (de bateau)* sail; *(activité)* sailing; **faire de la v.** to sail; **toutes voiles dehors** in full sail; *Fam* **marcher à v. et à vapeur** to be AC/DC, to swing both ways

voile[2] *nm* (**a**) *(de femme)* veil; **prendre le v.** *(religieuse)* to take the veil (**b**) *(devant les yeux)* film, mist; **un v. de fumée/de brouillard** a veil of smoke/fog; *Fam* **jeter un v. sur qch** to draw a veil over sth; *Méd* **avoir un v. au poumon** to have a shadow on one's lung (**c**) *Anat* **v. du palais** soft palate, velum

voilé, -e [vwale] *adj* (**a**) *(femme)* veiled (**b**) *(lumière) (par le brouillard)* hazy; *(par les nuages)* dim; *(photo)* fogged; **le ciel est v.** it's hazy (**c**) *(voix)* husky; **des yeux voilés de larmes** eyes blurred with tears (**d**) *(allusion)* veiled; **en termes voilés** in veiled terms (**e**) *(roue, tige)* buckled

voiler [vwale] **1** *vt* (**a**) *(femme)* to veil; *(statue)* to cover; *Fig (trouble, émotion)* to hide, to conceal (**b**) *(lumière)* to dim; *(ciel, soleil)* to cover; *(photo)* to fog (**c**) *(roue, tige)* to buckle
2 se voiler *vpr* (**a**) *(personne)* to wear a veil; *Fig* **se v. la face** to hide *or* bury one's head in the sand (**b**) *(voix)* to become husky (**c**) *(ciel)* to cloud over; *(soleil)* to become hazy; *(yeux)* to mist over (**d**) *(roue, tige)* to buckle

voilette [vwalɛt] *nf (hat)* veil

voilier [vwalje] *nm (bateau à voiles)* sailing boat; *(bateau de plaisance)* yacht; **faire du v.** to go yachting

voilure [vwalyr] *nf* (**a**) *(d'un bateau)* sails (**b**) *(d'un avion)* wings

voir [73a] [vwar] **1** *vt* (**a**) *(distinguer)* to see; **v. page 23/ci-après** see page 23/below; **je l'ai vu de mes propres yeux, je l'ai vu comme je te vois** I saw it with my own eyes; **je le vois qui arrive** I can see him coming; **je l'ai vu tomber/courir** I saw him fall/running; **faire v. qch à qn** to show sth to sb, to show sb sth; **faites v.!** let me see (it)!, let's have a look!; **laisser v. son ignorance/émotion** to show one's ignorance/emotion (**b**) *(rendre visite à, fréquenter)* to visit; **aller/venir v. qn** to go/come and see sb (**c**) *(comprendre, constater)* to see; **à ce que je vois** from what I can see; **voyez vous-même!** see for yourself!; **on voit bien que...** you can see (that)...; **on verra bien** we'll see; **c'est ce que nous verrons!** we'll see about that!; *Fam* **vu?** understood?, OK? (**d**) *(considérer)* to see; **nous verrons demain** we'll see tomorrow (**e**) *(imaginer, envisager)* to see; **je ne le vois pas marié** I can't imagine him married; **elle voit en lui un père/un ami** she sees him as a father figure/a friend; **sa façon de v. les choses** his/her way of looking at things; **se faire bien/mal v. de qn** to get into sb's good/bad books; **être bien/mal vu** to be well-/badly thought of; **c'est plutôt mal vu dans ce milieu** it's rather frowned upon in these circles

(**f**) *Fam (pour renforcer)* **essayez v.** just try; *(menace)* just you try it; **voyons v.** let's see, let's have a look

(**g**) *(locutions) Fam* **on aura tout vu!** we've seen it all now!; *Fam* **c'est tout vu, tu n'y vas pas!** you're not going and that's that!; **il faut le v. pour le croire** you have to see it to believe it; **j'aimerais (bien) t'y v.!** I'd like to see you try!; *Fam* **en faire v. à qn** to give sb a hard time; **voyez-vous** *(pour insister)* you see; *Fam* **je ne peux pas le v.** I can't stand the sight of him; *Fam* **file, je t'ai assez vu!** off you go, I've had enough of you!; **il n'a rien à v. là-dedans** *ou* **à y v.** he's got nothing to do with it; **ça n'a rien à voir!** *(dans une discussion)* that's beside the point!, that's got nothing to do with it!; **voyons!** *(indique la désapprobation)* come on!; *Fam* **va v. là-bas si j'y suis!** get out of here!, *Br* on your bike!; *très Fam* **va te faire v.!** piss off!
2 *vi* to see; (**y**) **v. bien/mal** to have good/poor eyesight; **on n'y voit rien** you can't see a thing; *Fig* **v. grand** to think big
3 voir à *vt ind* **il va v. à nous loger** he'll see that we have somewhere to stay; *Fam* **il faudrait v. à vous dépêcher!** you'd better get a move on!
4 se voir *vpr* (**a**) *(objet, phénomène)* to be seen; **la cathédrale se voit de loin** you can see the cathedral from miles away; **cela ne se voit pas tous les jours** it's not something you see every day; **ça se voit que j'ai pleuré?** can you tell I've been crying?
(**b**) *(soi-même)* to see oneself; **elle ne se voit pas du tout avec des enfants** she just can't see herself with children
(**c**) *(avec un adjectif, un infinitif)* **se v. forcé de faire qch** to find oneself forced to do sth; **se v. refuser qch** to find oneself refused sth
(**d**) *(l'un l'autre) (se distinguer, se rencontrer)* to see each other

voire [vwar] *adv* indeed

voirie [vwari] *nf* = local council department responsible for road maintenance and refuse collection

voisin, -e [vwazɛ̃, -in] **1** *adj* (**a**) *(personne, pays, ville)* neighbouring; *(chambre)* next (**de** to); **les pays voisins de la France** the countries bordering on France; **deux maisons voisines** two houses next to each other (**b**) *(semblable)* similar (**de** to)
2 *nm,f* neighbour; **v. de palier** next-door neighbour; **mon v. de table** the person sitting next to me (at the table)

voisinage [vwazinaʒ] *nm* (**a**) *(proximité)* proximity, closeness (**b**) *(ensemble des voisins)* neighbourhood (**c**) *(alentours)* vicinity; **dans le v.** in the vicinity (**d**) **entretenir des relations de bon v. avec qn** to be on neighbourly terms with sb

voisiner [vwazine] *vi* **v. avec qch** to be side by side with sth

voiture [vwatyr] *nf* (**a**) *(automobile)* car; **en v.** by car; **v. de course** racing car; **v. de fonction** company car; **v. de location** rental *or Br* hired car; **v. d'occasion** used *or* second-hand car; **v. de sport** sports car; **v. de tourisme** private *or* touring car; **petite v.** *(jouet)* toy car (**b**) *(wagon) Br* coach, *Am* car; **en v.!** all aboard!; **v. fumeurs** smoker; **v. non-fumeurs** non-smoker (**c**) *(carriole) (pour passagers)* carriage; *(pour marchandises)* cart; **v. à bras** barrow, handcart (**d**) **v. d'enfant** *Br* pram, *Am* baby carriage

voix [vwa] *nf* (**a**) *(d'une personne)* voice; **à v. haute, à haute v.** aloud; **à v. basse** in a low voice; **élever la v.** to speak up; *(se mettre en colère)* to raise one's voice; **donner de la v.** *(chien)* to bay; *(personne)* to shout, to bawl; **donner de la v. contre qch** (*protester*) to protest vehemently against sth; **rester sans v.** to remain speechless; *Cin* **v. off** voice-over; **une v. de stentor** a booming voice (**b**) *Fig (de la raison)* voice; *(du sang)* call (**c**) *Mus (partie vocale)* voice; **chanter à trois v.** to sing in three parts; **être en v.** to be in good voice; **v. de basse/de ténor** bass/tenor voice; **v. de fausset** falsetto (voice); **v. de tête** head voice (**d**) *(d'électeur)* vote; **donner sa v. à qn** to vote for sb; **élu à la majorité des v.** elected by a majority; **mettre une question aux v.** to put a question to the vote (**e**) *Gram* voice; **à la v.** active/passive in the active/passive voice

vol¹ [vɔl] *nm* (**a**) *(d'un oiseau, d'un avion)* flight; **à trois heures de v. de Paris** three hours' flying time from Paris; **prendre son v.** to fly off; **en plein v.** mid-flight; **à v. d'oiseau** as the crow flies; **de haut v.** *(escroc)* big-time; *(discipline)* high-flying; **v. charter** charter flight; **v. habité** manned flight; **v. inaugural** maiden flight; **v. intérieur** domestic or internal flight; **v. de nuit** night flight; **v. plané** glide; *Fam Fig* **faire un v. plané** to go flying (**b**) *(nuée d'oiseaux)* flock, flight

vol² *nm (délit)* theft, stealing; *Fam* **c'est du v.!** it's a rip-off!, it's daylight robbery!; **v. avec effraction** breaking and entering; **v. à l'étalage** shoplifting; *Ordinat* **v. d'identité** identity theft; **v. à main armée** armed robbery; **v. à la portière** = act of theft whereby the thief opens the door of a vehicle waiting at traffic lights etc and steals any available valuable item before the driver has time to react; **v. à la tire** pickpocketing

volage [vɔlaʒ] *adj* fickle, flighty

volaille [vɔlaj] *nf (oiseau)* fowl; **la v.** poultry

volant, -e [vɔlɑ̃, -ɑ̃t] **1** *adj* (**a**) *(qui vole)* flying; **personnel v.** flight crew (**b**) **gardien de but v.** rush goalkeeper
2 *nm* (**a**) *(d'une automobile)* (steering) wheel; **prendre le v.** to take the wheel; **je te recommande la prudence au v.** drive carefully (**b**) *(de badminton)* shuttlecock (**c**) *(d'une robe)* flounce (**d**) *(de carnet)* tear-off portion

volatil, -e¹ [vɔlatil] *adj* volatile

volatile² [vɔlatil] *nm aussi Hum* winged creature

volatiliser [vɔlatilize] **se volatiliser** *vpr* to vanish into thin air

vol-au-vent [vɔlovɑ̃] *nm inv* vol-au-vent

volcan [vɔlkɑ̃] *nm* volcano; *Fig (personne)* spitfire; *Fig (situation)* volcano

volcanique [vɔlkanik] *adj (roche)* volcanic; *Fig (tempérament)* fiery

volcanologue [vɔlkanɔlɔg] *nmf* vulcanologist

volée [vɔle] *nf* (**a**) *(d'oiseaux)* flock, flight; *Fig (d'enfants)* swarm (**b**) *(au football, au tennis)* volley; **attraper une balle à la v.** to catch a ball in midair (**c**) *(de flèches)* flight; *Fam (de coups)* shower; *Fam* **recevoir une v.** to get a good thrashing (**d**) **sonner à toute v.** to ring out

voler¹ [vɔle] *vi (oiseau, avion)* to fly; **faire v. un cerf-volant** to fly a kite; *Fig* **v. de ses propres ailes** to stand on one's own two feet, to fend for oneself; *Fig* **v. au secours de qn** to fly to sb's assistance

voler² *vt* (**a**) *(objet, argent)* to steal (**à** from); **se faire v. qch** to have sth stolen; *Fig* **il ne l'a pas volé** *(il le mérite)* he's earned it; *(c'est bien fait pour lui)* it serves him right; *Prov* **qui vole un œuf vole un bœuf** there's no such thing as a petty thief (**b**) *(personne)* to rob; *(léser)* to swindle, to cheat

volet [vɔlɛ] *nm* (**a**) *(de fenêtre, de magasin)* shutter (**b**) *(d'un dépliant)* page; *(d'un formulaire)* section; *Fig (d'un plan)* stage

voleter [42] [vɔlte] *vi* to flutter

voleur, -euse [vɔlœr, -øz] **1** *nm,f* thief; **au v.!** stop thief!
2 *adj (personne)* thieving; **être v.** to be a thief

Volga [vɔlga] *nf* **la V.** the Volga

volière [vɔljɛr] *nf* aviary

volley [vɔlɛ] *nm Fam* volleyball

volley-ball [vɔlɛbɔl] *nm* volleyball; **v. de plage** beach volleyball

volleyeur, -euse [vɔlɛjœr, -øz] *nm,f* (**a**) *(joueur de volley-ball)* volleyball player (**b**) *(au tennis)* volleyer

volontaire [vɔlɔ̃tɛr] **1** *adj* (**a**) *(action, omission)* deliberate (**b**) *(enfant)* wilful; *(menton, front)* determined
2 *nmf* volunteer

volontairement [vɔlɔ̃tɛrmɑ̃] *adv* (**a**) *(spontanément)* voluntarily (**b**) *(délibérément)* deliberately

volontariat [vɔlɔ̃tarja] *nm* (**a**) *(travail bénévole)* voluntary work (**b**) *(dans l'armée)* = voluntary service in the armed forces

volontarisme [vɔlɔ̃tarism] *nm* voluntarism

volontariste [vɔlɔ̃tarist] *adj* voluntarist

volonté [vɔlɔ̃te] *nf* (**a**) *(faculté)* will; **la v. de vaincre/de puissance** the will to win/for power; **de sa propre v.** of one's own accord; **avec la meilleure v. du monde** with the best will in the world; **à v.** at will; **vin à v.** *(dans un restaurant)* unlimited wine (**b**) *(détermination)* willpower; **avoir de la v.** to have willpower (**c**) **bonne v.** willingness; **mauvaise v.** unwillingness; **mettre de la mauvaise v. à faire qch** to do sth with bad grace (**d**) *(souhait)* wish; **ses dernières volontés** his last wishes

volontiers [vɔlɔ̃tje] *adv* (**a**) *(avec plaisir)* willingly, gladly; **v.!** I'd be glad to! (**b**) **être v. pessimiste/bavard** to be naturally pessimistic/chatty

volt [vɔlt] *nm* volt

voltage [vɔltaʒ] *nm* voltage

volte-face [vɔltəfas] *nf inv Br* about-turn, *Am* about-face; *Fig* U-turn; **faire v.** to turn round; *Fig* to do a U-turn

voltige [vɔltiʒ] *nf* (**a**) *(sur un cheval)* acrobatics on horseback; *(sur un trapèze)* acrobatics; **haute v.** flying trapeze acrobatics (**b**) *(acrobatie aérienne)* aerobatics

voltiger [45] [vɔltiʒe] *vi* (**a**) *(sur un cheval)* to perform on horseback; *(sur un trapèze)* to perform on the trapeze (**b**) *(feuilles)* to flutter

volubile [vɔlybil] *adj* voluble

volubilité [vɔlybilite] *nf* volubility

volume [vɔlym] *nm* (**a**) *(livre)* volume (**b**) *(d'un solide, d'un fluide, des ventes)* volume (**c**) *(du son, de la voix)* volume; **baisser/monter le v.** to turn the volume down/up; **v. sonore** noise level

volumineux, -euse [vɔlyminø, -øz] *adj* voluminous, bulky

volupté [vɔlypte] *nf* sensual pleasure

voluptueusement [vɔlyptɥøzmɑ̃] *adv* voluptuously

voluptueux, -euse [vɔlyptɥø, -øz] *adj* voluptuous

volute [vɔlyt] *nf* (**a**) *(de fumée)* curl, wreath (**b**) *Archit* helix

vomi [vɔmi] *nm* vomit

vomir [vɔmir] **1** *vt* (**a**) *(aliment)* to vomit, to bring up (**b**) *(fumée, flammes)* to vomit, to belch forth; *Fig (injures)* to spew out (**c**) *Fig (détester)* to loathe
2 *vi* to be sick, to vomit; **avoir envie de v.** to feel sick

vomissement [vɔmismɑ̃] *nm (action)* vomiting; **avoir des vomissements** to vomit

vomitif, -ive [vɔmitif, -iv] *adj & nm* emetic

vont *voir* **aller**

vorace [vɔras] *adj* voracious

voracement [vɔrasmɑ̃] *adv* voraciously

voracité [vɔrasite] *nf* voracity

vortex [vɔrtɛks] *nm* vortex

vos [vo] *voir* **votre**

Vosges [voʒ] *nfpl* **les V.** the Vosges

votant, -e [vɔtɑ̃, -ɑ̃t] *nm,f* voter

votation [vɔtasjɔ̃] *nf Suisse* vote

vote [vɔt] *nm* (**a**) *(pour une élection)* vote; *(action)* voting; **le v. des femmes** the women's vote; **v. à bulletin secret** secret ballot; **v. à main levée** vote by a show of hands; **v. par procuration** proxy vote; **v. de protestation** protest vote (**b**) *(d'une loi)* passing; **v. de confiance** vote of confidence

voter [vɔte] **1** *vi* to vote (**pour/contre** for/against); **v. conservateur, v. pour les conservateurs** to vote conservative; **v. à bulletin secret** to vote in a secret ballot; **v. à main levée** to vote by a show of hands; **v. par procuration** to vote by proxy
2 *vt* (**a**) *(loi)* to pass (**b**) *(crédit)* to vote

votre [vɔtr] *(pl* **vos** [vo]*) adj possessif* your; **v. chien** your dog; **vos enfants** your children; **v. père et v. mère** *(à une personne)* your mother and father; *(à plusieurs personnes)* your mothers and fathers; **un de vos amis** one of your friends, a friend of yours; *Fam* **vous avez v. vendredi** you've got Friday off

vôtre [votr] **1** *pron possessif* **le v., la v., les vôtres** yours; *(en insistant)* your own; **vous me prêtez le v.?** can I borrow yours?; **vous n'en avez pas besoin, vous avez le v.** you don't need it, you've got your own; *Fam* **à la v.!** cheers!
2 *nm* (**a**) **il faut que vous y mettiez du v.** you should do your share (**b**) **les vôtres** *(votre famille)* your family; **je serai des vôtres ce soir** I'll be joining you tonight

voudra, voudrai *etc voir* **vouloir¹**

vouer [vwe] **1** *vt* (**a**) *(jurer)* to vow (**à** to) (**b**) *(consacrer)* to devote (**à** to) (**c**) **voué à l'échec** doomed to failure
2 **se vouer** *vpr* **se v. à qch** to devote oneself to sth

vouloir¹ [74] [vulwar] **1** *vt* (**a**) *(désirer)* to want; **rentrons, voulez-vous?** let's go in, shall we?; **si vous (le) voulez** if you like; **faites comme vous (le) voudrez** do what you like, do as you please; **que veux-tu que je fasse?** what do you want me to do?; **le mauvais sort voulut que...** as bad luck would have it...; **v. faire qch** to want to do sth; **quand j'ai voulu l'embrasser** when I tried to kiss him; **faire qch sans le v.** to do sth unintentionally; **le moteur ne veut pas démarrer** the engine won't start; **j'aurais tant voulu la voir** I would really have liked to see her; **que lui voulez-vous?** what do you want from him/her?; *(pourquoi le/la cherchez-vous?)* what do you want him/her for?; **ne pas v. de qn/qch** not to want sb/sth; **je ne veux pas de ça chez moi** I won't have that in my house; **en v.** *(être accrocheur)* to be very determined; **en v. à qn** *(de qch/d'avoir fait qch)* to bear sb a grudge (for sth/for doing sth); **ils en veulent à mon argent** they're after my money
(**b**) *(dans les formules de politesse)* **veuillez vous asseoir** please sit down; **voulez-vous faire moins de bruit!** will you please make less noise!
(**c**) *(exiger)* **la coutume veut que...+** *subjunctive*

custom dictates that...; **le règlement veut que...** + *subjunctive* the rules state that...
(**d**) *(locutions)* **je veux bien** *(volontiers)* with pleasure; *(j'admets)* granted, fair enough; **c'est comme ça, que veux-tu** that's the way it is, what can you do?; *Fam* **en veux-tu, en voilà** galore; **tu l'auras voulu!** if that's the way you want it!; **v. dire** to mean; *Fam* **je veux!** *(absolument)* absolutely!
2 **se vouloir** *vpr* (**a**) *(vouloir être)* **elle se veut différente** she likes to think she's different; **il se voulait rassurant** he was trying to be reassuring
(**b**) **s'en v. (de qch/de faire qch)** to be annoyed with oneself (about sth/for doing sth)

vouloir² *nm* will; **bon v.** goodwill; **mauvais v.** ill will

voulu, -e [vuly] **1** *pp de* **vouloir¹**
2 *adj* (**a**) *(requis)* required (**b**) *(délibéré)* deliberate, intentional

vous [vu] *pron personnel* (**a**) *(sujet)* you; **v. deux/tous** both/all of you; **v. autres les intellectuels** you intellectuals; **v., v. auriez certainement refusé** YOU would probably have refused (**b**) *(objet direct)* you; **et v., on v. a servis?** and what about you, have you been served? (**c**) *(objet indirect)* to you; **vous a-t-elle serré la main?** did she shake your hand?; **elle v. a jeté un regard furieux** she glared at you (**d**) *(réfléchi)* *(singulier)* yourself; *(pluriel)* yourselves; **taisez-v.!** be quiet! (**e**) *(réciproque)* each other (**f**) *(avec préposition)* **v. ne pensez qu'à v.** you think only of yourself; **je v. le montre, à v.?** shall I show it to YOU?; **cet argent n'est pas à v.** this money isn't yours; **v. aurez une chambre à v.** you'll have your own room; *Fam* **une connaissance à v.** an acquaintance of yours (**g**) *(dans les comparaisons)* you; **elle est aussi surprise que v.** she's as surprised as you (are) (**h**) *(remplace "on")* you

vous-même *(pl* **vous-mêmes**) [vumɛm] *pron personnel* yourself; **vous-mêmes** yourselves

voûte [vut] *nf* (**a**) *(arche)* arch; **la v. céleste** the vault or canopy of heaven; **v. d'ogive** vault (**b**) *Anat* **v. du palais** roof of the mouth; **v. plantaire** arch (of the foot)

voûté, -e [vute] *adj* bent; **avoir le dos v.** to have a stoop

voûter [vute] **se voûter** *vpr* to become bent, to begin to stoop

vouvoiement [vuvwamɑ̃] *nm* = use of the formal "vous" instead of the more familiar "tu"; **le v. est de rigueur** everybody calls each other "vous"; *voir aussi* l'encadré à **tutoiement**

vouvoyer [32] [vuvwaje] **1** *vt* **v. qn** = to address sb as "vous"
2 **se vouvoyer** *vpr* = to address each other as "vous"

voyage [vwajaʒ] *nm* trip, journey; **être en v.** to be away; **partir en v.** to go on a trip; **bon v.!** have a good trip!; **v. d'affaires** business trip; **v. d'agrément** pleasure trip; **v. de noces** honeymoon; **v. organisé** package tour

voyager [45] [vwajaʒe] *vi* to travel

voyageur, -euse [vwajaʒœr, -øz] *nm,f* traveller; *(passager)* passenger; **v. de commerce** commercial traveller, travelling salesman, *f* travelling saleswoman

voyagiste [vwajaʒist] *nmf* tour operator

voyais *etc voir* **voir**

voyance [vwajɑ̃s] *nf* clairvoyance

voyant, -e [vwajɑ̃, -ɑ̃t] **1** *adj (de mauvais goût)* loud, garish
2 *nm,f (extralucide)* clairvoyant

3 *nm* **v. (lumineux)** warning light; **v. d'huile/d'essence** oil/petrol indicator light

voyelle [vwajɛl] *nf* vowel

voyeur, -euse [vwajœr, -øz] *nm,f* voyeur, *f* voyeuse

voyeurisme [vwajœrism] *nm* voyeurism

voyez, voyons *etc voir* **voir**

voyou [vwaju] *nm* lout, hooligan

VPC [vepese] *nf* (*abrév* **vente par correspondance**) mail order (selling)

vrac [vrak] **en vrac** *adv* (**a**) *(sans emballage)* loose (**b**) *(en désordre)* higgledy-piggledy, in a jumble

vrai, -e [vrɛ] **1** *adj* (**a**) *(indéniable)* true; **c'est v.!** that's true!, that's right!; *Fam* **elle est gentille, pas v.?** she's nice, isn't she?; *Fam* **c'est pas v.!** you're joking! (**b**) *(véritable)* real; *(tableau, antiquité)* genuine; **il a été un v. père pour moi** he was like a father to me **2** *nm* **être dans le v.** to be right; **à v. dire, à dire v.** as a matter of fact, to tell the truth; *Fam* **pour de v.** for real

vraiment [vrɛmɑ̃] *adv* really

vraisemblable [vrɛsɑ̃blabl] *adj* probable, likely; *(crédible)* believable, credible; **il est v. qu'il sera là demain** he'll probably be there tomorrow

vraisemblablement [vrɛsɑ̃blabləmɑ̃] *adv* probably

vraisemblance [vrɛsɑ̃blɑ̃s] *nf* probability, likelihood; *(crédibilité)* credibility; **selon toute v.** in all probability

vrille [vrij] *nf* (**a**) *(de la vigne)* tendril (**b**) *(outil)* gimlet (**c**) *(en avion)* spin; **descendre en v.** to spin down

vrillé, -e [vrije] *adj* (*corde*) twisted

vriller [vrije] **1** *vt* to bore into **2** *vi* (**a**) *(avion)* to spin (**b**) *(corde)* to twist

vrombir [vrɔ̃bir] *vi* to hum

vrombissement [vrɔ̃bismɑ̃] *nm* hum, humming

VRP [veɛrpe] *nm* (*abrév* **voyageur représentant placier**) sales rep

VTT [vetete] *nm* (*abrév* **vélo tout terrain**) mountain bike

vu¹, -e¹ [vy] **1** *pp de* **voir** **2** *adj* **faire qch ni vu ni connu** to do sth without being seen

vu² *prép* in view of; **vu que** seeing that **2** *nm* **au vu et au su de tout le monde** openly

vue² [vy] *nf* (**a**) *(faculté de voir)* sight, eyesight; **perdre la v.** to lose one's sight; **avoir une bonne/mauvaise v.** to have good/bad eyesight (**b**) *(regard)* **connaître qn de v.** to know sb by sight; **hors de v.** out of sight; **hors de ma v.!** (get) out of my sight!; **une personnalité en v.** a prominent personality; **mettre qch en v.** to display sth prominently; **à v. d'œil** before one's eyes, visibly; *Fam* **à v. de nez** at a rough guess; *Fam* **en mettre plein la v. à qn** to dazzle sb (**c**) **seconde v.** second sight (**d**) *(opinion)* view; **c'est une v. de l'esprit** that's a very theoretical point of view (**e**) *(panorama)* view; **chambre avec v.** room with a view; *Fig* **v. d'ensemble** overall view (**f**) *Can Fam* **les vues** *Br* the movies, *Am* the movies; **aller aux (petites) vues** to go to the *Br* cinema *or Am* movies (**g**) *(locutions)* **à la v. de qn/qch** at the sight of sb/sth; **à première v.** at first sight; **à v.** *(tirer)* on sight; *(voler)* visually; **avoir qch en v.** to have sth in mind; **en v. de qch/de faire qch** with a view to sth/to doing sth; **avoir des vues sur qn/qch** to have designs on sb/sth

vulgaire [vylgɛr] *adj* (**a**) *(grossier)* vulgar (**b**) *(courant)* common (**c**) *(quelconque)* ordinary, common

vulgairement [vylgɛrmɑ̃] *adv* (**a**) *(grossièrement)* vulgarly (**b**) *(communément)* commonly

vulgarisation [vylgarizasjɔ̃] *nf* popularization

vulgariser [vylgarize] *vt* to popularize

vulgarité [vylgarite] *nf* vulgarity

vulnérabilité [vylnerabilite] *nf* vulnerability

vulnérable [vylnerabl] *adj* vulnerable

vulve [vylv] *nf* vulva

W, w [dublǝve] *nm inv* W, w

wagon [vagɔ̃] *nm* (**a**) *(de passagers) Br* carriage, *Am* car; *(de marchandises) Br* wagon, *Am* car; **w. à bagages** *Br* luggage van, *Am* baggage car; **w. à bestiaux** *Br* cattle truck, *Am* stock car; **w. frigorifique** refrigerated van; **w. de marchandises** *Br* goods wagon, *Am* freight car (**b**) *(contenu) Br* wagonload, *Am* carload (**de** of)

wagon-citerne (*pl* **wagons-citernes**) [vagɔ̃sitɛrn] *nm* tank *Br* wagon *or Am* car

wagon-lit (*pl* **wagons-lits**) [vagɔ̃li] *nm* sleeping car, sleeper

wagon-restaurant (*pl* **wagons-restaurants**) [vagɔ̃rɛstɔrɑ̃] *nm* dining *or* restaurant car

Walkman® [wɔkman] *nm* Walkman®

Wallis-et-Futuna [walisefutuna] *n* Wallis and Futuna Islands

wallon, -onne [walɔ̃, -ɔn] **1** *adj* Walloon

2 *nm,f* W. Walloon

3 *nm (langue)* Walloon

Wallonie [walɔni] *nf* la W. = the south and south-east regions of Belgium, where French and Walloon are spoken

WAP [wap] *nm Tél (abrév* **wireless application protocol**) WAP

wapiti [wapiti] *nm* wapiti, American elk

Washington [waʃintɔn, waʃiŋtɔn] *n* Washington

wassingue [wasɛ̃g] *nf* floorcloth

water-polo [watɛrpɔlo] *nm* water polo

watt [wat] *nm* watt

W.-C. [vese, dublǝvese] *nmpl* toilet

Web [wɛb] *nm inv Ordinat* **le W.** the Web

webcam [wɛbkam] *nf Ordinat* webcam

webcast [wɛbkast] *nm Ordinat* webcast

weblog [wɛblɔg] *nm Ordinat* weblog

webmarketing [wɛbmarketiŋ] *nm Ordinat* e-marketing

webmestre [wɛbmɛstr] *nm Ordinat* webmaster

week-end (*pl* **week-ends**) [wikɛnd] *nm* weekend; **partir en w.** to go away for the weekend

western [wɛstɛrn] *nm* western

whisky [wiski] *nm (écossais)* whisky; *(irlandais, américain)* whiskey

white-spirit [wajtspirit] *nm* white spirit

WiFi [wifi] *Ordinat (abrév* **wireless fidelity**) *adj & nm* WiFi

WWW [dublǝvedublǝvedublǝve] *nm Ordinat (abrév* **World Wide Web**) WWW

wysiwyg [wiziwig] *adj & nm Ordinat* WYSIWYG

X, x [iks] *nm inv* (**a**) *(lettre)* X, x (**b**) *(nombre ou personne inconnus)* X, x; **Monsieur X** Mr X; **x fois** umpteen times; **dans x années** in x number of years; **accoucher sous X** to give birth anonymously; **naître sous X** to be born to an unidentified mother (**c**) *Fam Univ* **l'X** = the "École Polytechnique", a "grande école" specializing in technology (**d**) *Cin* **film classé X** *Br* "18" film, *Am* adults-only movie (**e**) *Fam (ecstasy)* E

xénophobe [gsenɔfɔb] **1** *adj* xenophobic
  2 *nmf* xenophobe
xénophobie [gsenɔfɔbi] *nf* xenophobia
xérès [gzerɛs, kserɛs] *nm (vin)* sherry
xylophone [ksilɔfɔn, gzilɔfɔn] *nm* xylophone
xylophoniste [gzilɔfɔnist, gzilɔfɔnist] *nmf* xylophonist

Y, y¹ [igrɛk] *nm inv* Y, y

y² [i] **1** *adv* there; **n'y être pour personne** not to be in for anyone; **vous n'y êtes pas du tout** you're way off the mark; **pendant que tu y es, tu pourrais m'apporter...** while you're at it, you could bring me...
2 *pron* **j'y pense** I'm thinking about it; **il y croit** he believes in it/them; **elle s'y intéresse** she's interested in it/them; **elle y compte** she's counting on it; **je n'y suis pour rien** I've got nothing to do with it

yacht [jɔt] *nm* yacht

yachting [jɔtiŋ] *nm* yachting; **faire du y.** to go yachting

yaourt [jaurt] *nm* yoghurt; **y. bio** bio yoghurt; **y. maigre** low-fat yoghurt; **y. nature/aux fruits** plain *or* natural/fruit yoghurt

yaourtière [jaurtjɛr] *nf* yoghurt maker

Yémen [jemɛn] *nm* **le Y.** Yemen

yéménite [jemenit] **1** *adj* Yemeni
2 *nmf* **Y.** Yemeni

yen [jɛn] *nm* yen

yeux [jø] *voir* œil

yé-yé [jeje] *adj inv* Vieilli (chanteur, groupe) 60s style pop; (mode) 60s

yiddish [jidiʃ] *adj inv & nm* Yiddish

yoga [jɔga] *nm* yoga; **faire du y.** to do yoga

yogi [jɔgi] *nm* yogi

Yom Kippour [jɔmkipur] *nm* Yom Kippur

yorkshire [jɔrkʃœr], **yorkshire-terrier** (*pl* yorkshire-terriers) [jɔrkʃœrtɛrje] *nm* Yorkshire terrier

yougoslave [jugoslav] **1** *adj* Yugoslav, Yugoslavian
2 *nmf* **Y.** Yugoslav, Yugoslavian

Yougoslavie [jugoslavi] *nf* **la Y.** Yugoslavia; **l'ex-Y.** the former Yugoslavia

youpala [jupala] *nm* baby bouncer

youpi [jupi] *exclam* yippee!

youyou [juju] *nm* dinghy

Yo-Yo® [jojo] *nm inv* yo-yo

yuan [juan] *nm* yuan

yucca [juka] *nm* yucca

Yukon [jukɔ̃] *nm* **le Y.** the Yukon

Z, z [zɛd] *nm inv* Z, z
ZAC [zak] *nf (abrév* **zone d'aménagement concerté)** = area developed by the state and subsequently sold to the public or private sectors
ZAD [zad] *nf (abrév* **zone d'aménagement différé)** = area which the state has the priority to build on or sell
Zagreb [zagrɛb] *n* Zagreb
Zaïre [zair] *nm* **le Z.** Zaire
zaïrois, -e [zairwa, -az] **1** *adj* Zairean
  2 *nm,f* **Z.** Zairean
Zambie [zãbi] *nf* **la Z.** Zambia
zambien, -enne [zãbjɛ̃, -ɛn] **1** *adj* Zambian
  2 *nm,f* **Z.** Zambian
Zanzibar [zãzibar] *n* Zanzibar
zapper [zape] **1** *vi* to zap, to channel-hop
  2 *vt Fam* (**a**) *(supprimer)* to scrap, to scratch (**b**) *(oublier)* to forget; **j'ai complètement zappé** I completely forgot *or* it totally slipped my mind (**c**) *(négliger)* to neglect
zapping [zapiŋ] *nm* zapping, channel-hopping; **faire du z.** to zap, to channel-hop
zébré, -e [zebre] *adj* striped (**de** with)
zèbre [zɛbr] *nm* zebra; *Fam* **un drôle de z.** a strange character
zébrure [zebryr] *nf* streak; *(d'un zèbre, d'un tigre)* stripe; *Fig (cicatrice)* weal
zébu [zeby] *nm* zebu
zélateur, -trice [zelatœr, -tris] *nm,f* zealot
zélé, -e [zele] *adj* zealous
zèle [zɛl] *nm* zeal; **faire du z.** to be overzealous
zen [zɛn] **1** *adj inv* Zen; *Fam Fig* relaxed, laid-back; *Fam* **c'est très z. chez toi!** your place is very minimalist!
  2 *nm* Zen
zénith [zenit] *nm* zenith; *aussi Fig* **être à son z.** to be at one's zenith
ZEP [zɛp] *nf (abrév* **zone d'éducation prioritaire)** = area targeted for special help in education
zéphyr [zefir] *nm (vent)* zephyr
zéro [zero] **1** *nm* (**a**) *(chiffre)* zero, *Br* nought; *(dans un numéro de téléphone) Br* oh, *Am* zero (**b**) *(note)* zero (**c**) *Fam (personne)* loser (**d**) *(au football)* **trois à z.** three nil; *(au tennis)* **trois sets à z.** three sets to love (**e**) *(dans une graduation)* zero; **repartir à z.** to go back to square one; *Fam* **avoir le moral à z.** to be feeling really down; *très Fam* **les avoir à z.** to be scared stiff
  2 *adj* **z. degré Celsius** zero degrees Celsius; **z. faute** no mistakes; **z. heure** twelve (midnight)
zeste [zɛst] *nm* zest; **un z. de citron** a piece of lemon zest

zeugma [zøgma], **zeugme** [zøgm] *nm Ling* zeugma
zézaiement [zezɛmã] *nm* lisp
zézayer [53] [zezeje] *vi* to lisp
ZI [zɛdi] *nf (abrév* **zone industrielle)** *Br* industrial estate, *Am* industrial park
zibeline [ziblin] *nf* sable
zieuter [zjøte] = **zyeuter**
zigoto [zigɔto] *nm Fam* **c'est un drôle de z.** he's quite a character; **faire le z.** to clown around
zigouiller [ziguje] *vt Fam* to do in; **se faire z.** to get done in
zigzag [zigzag] *nm* zigzag; **en z.** *(chemin)* zigzag; *(éclair)* forked; **faire des zigzags** *(route)* to zigzag; *(personne ivre)* to zigzag along; **marcher en z.** to walk in a zigzag
zigzaguer [zigzage] *vi (route)* to zigzag; *(personne ivre)* to zigzag along
Zimbabwe [zimbabwe] *nm* **le Z.** Zimbabwe
zimbabwéen, -enne [zimbabweɛ̃, -ɛn] **1** *adj* Zimbabwean
  2 *nm,f* **Z.** Zimbabwean
zinc [zɛ̃g] *nm* (**a**) *(métal)* zinc (**b**) *Fam (comptoir)* counter, bar (**c**) *Fam (avion)* plane
zinzin [zɛ̃zɛ̃] *Fam* **1** *adj* off one's rocker
  2 *nm (truc)* thingummy, whatsit
Zip® [zip] *nm Br* zip, *Am* zipper
zippé, -e [zipe] *adj* with a *Br* zip *or Am* zipper, zip-up
zipper [zipe] *vt Ordinat* to zip
zizanie [zizani] *nf* discord; **semer la z.** to sow discord
zizi [zizi] *nm (langage enfantin) Br* willy, *Am* peter
zizique [zizik] *nf Fam* music
zloty [zlɔti] *nm* zloty
zodiaque [zɔdjak] *nm* **le z.** the zodiac
zombie [zɔ̃bi] *nm Fam* zombie
zona [zona] *nm* shingles *(singulier)*; **avoir un z.** to have shingles
zonard, -e [zonar, -ard] *nm,f Fam (marginal)* dropout
zone [zon] *nf* (**a**) *(espace)* zone; **z. artisanale** small industrial *Br* estate *or Am* park *(for craft-based businesses)*; **z. dangereuse** danger zone; *Météo* **z. de dépression, z. dépressionnaire** trough of low pressure; *UE* **z. euro** euro zone *or* area; **zone d'exclusion aérienne** no-fly zone; **z. fumeurs/non-fumeurs** smoking/no-smoking area; *Météo* **z. de haute pression** area of high pressure; **zone industrielle** industrial *Br* estate *or Am* park; **z. interdite** prohibited *or* restricted area; *Hist* **z. libre** unoccupied France; *Hist* **z. occupée** occupied France; **z. scientifique** science park; **z. tempérée** temperate zone; **z. verte** green belt (**b**) *Péj* **de seconde z.** second-rate (**c**) *Fam Péj* **la z.** *(bidonville)* the slums; *Fig* **c'est la z.!** it's a dump!

(**d**) *Ordinat* **z. de dialogue** dialogue box; **z. d'état** status box; **z. tampon** *(en mémoire)* (memory) buffer; **z. de travail** work area

Zone

The Paris area is divided into fare zones for public transport. Zones 1 and 2 cover metropolitan Paris and certain areas of the nearby suburbs. The remaining zones cover the outer suburbs: "j'habite en zone 3","une carte orange quatre zones". France is divided into three "zones" (A, B and C), the schools in the different zones taking their mid-term breaks and Easter holidays at different times to avoid swamping the public transport system and tourist infrastructure.

zoner [zone] *vi très Fam* to hang about
zoo [zo, zoo] *nm* zoo
zoologie [zɔɔlɔʒi] *nf* zoology
zoologique [zɔɔlɔʒik] *adj* zoological

zoologiste [zɔɔlɔʒist], **zoologue** [zɔɔlɔg] *nmf* zoologist
zoom [zum] *nm* (**a**) *(effet)* zoom (**b**) *(objectif)* zoom (lens)
zooplancton [zɔɔplãktɔ̃] *nm Zool* zooplankton
zou [zu] *exclam Fam* (**allez**) **z.!** off you go!
zouave [zwav] *nm (soldat)* Zouave; *Fam (pitre)* fool; *Fam* **faire le z.** to play the fool
zoulou, -e [zulu] **1** *adj* Zulu
  2 *nm,f* **Z.** Zulu
Zoulouland [zuzulãd] *nm* **le Z.** Zululand, Kwazulu
zozoter [zɔzɔte] *vi Fam* to lisp
ZUP [zyp] *nf (abrév* **zone à urbaniser en priorité**) priority development area
Zurich [zyrik] *n* Zurich
zut [zyt] *exclam Fam* blast!; **et puis z.!** what the heck!
zyeuter [zjøte] *vt Fam (regarder) (discrètement)* to have a look *or Br* a dekko at; *(avec insistance)* to eye up
zygomatique [zigɔmatik] *adj* zygomatic